Academic American Encyclopedia

Academic American Encyclopedia

Grolier Incorporated

Danbury, Connecticut

Library of Congress Cataloging-in-Publication Data

Academic American encyclopedia.

Includes bibliographies and index.
Summary: A twenty-one volume encyclopedia with 32,000 entries and more than 16,000 illustrations.
1. Encyclopedias and dictionaries. [1. Encyclopedias and dictionaries] I.
AE5.A23 1987 031 86–19416
ISBN 0-7172-2016–8 (set)

Printed and manufactured in the United States of America.

Index

Guide to the Use of This Encyclopedia

An index is the last volume of an encyclopedia to be compiled but the first to be consulted. Here the reader will find the key to the millions of facts contained in the encyclopedia. A few moments taken to read this introduction will enable you to get the most out of this set.

WHAT AN INDEX CAN DO FOR YOU

The index of this encyclopedia was constructed to provide quick, easy, direct access to the information in the text. An encyclopedia article on a given subject does not necessarily contain all the information on that subject found in the encyclopedia. For example, there is additional information on Charlemagne in articles on the Carolingians and the Franks, as well as in the articles on the history of France and of Germany. To locate all the relevant material in the most expeditious manner, it is necessary to consult this index, where you will find more than 15 references to information about Charlemagne.

This index also serves as a comprehensive guide to illustrations, maps, tables, and bibliographies. Moreover, not all subjects covered in the encyclopedia have individual articles. Learning in animals, for example, is not an article title in this encyclopedia; the set does, nevertheless, contain considerable information on that subject. If you turn to page 302 of this volume you will find references to 10 articles that contain information on learning in animals, including several illustrations. The index, then, can do much more for the reader than simply locate a specific fact—although that, of course, is its most important function.

Because of the manner in which this index was designed, it can also help the reader locate information related to the primary subject of interest, and it can provide an inventory of items in a particular category, such as lists of all the dogs recognized by the American Kennel Club. It can even suggest categories for investigation that the reader may not have thought of.

The reader interested in primitive religion, for example, might go directly to that article in the P volume. There will be found approximately 4 pages of text and illustrations and 25 cross-references for further investigation. In this index volume there are 30 references (some are the same) plus a subheading on religion among American Indian tribes that lists 13 articles on specific tribes and practices.

In summary, an index can locate a specific fact quickly, identify and locate related information not mentioned in the text of the article, and provide an analytical set of categories or a structured outline of a subject that will aid the reader in further research. The index also gathers under each main heading all encyclopedia references to substantive information on that heading.

INDEX ENTRIES

The index consists of index entries that have two parts: the *heading,* which identifies a topic on which there is information in the encyclopedia, and the *locator,* which tells where the information will be found. For example:

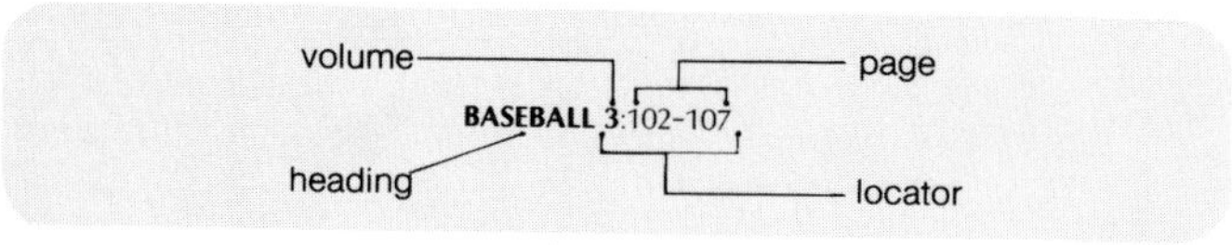
volume
page
BASEBALL 3:102–107
heading
locator

Note that locators for articles or information that appears on more than one page give both beginning and ending page numbers.

A main heading, such as the one above, may have subheadings that will lead you to information on the topic of the main heading in other articles in the encyclopedia. For example:

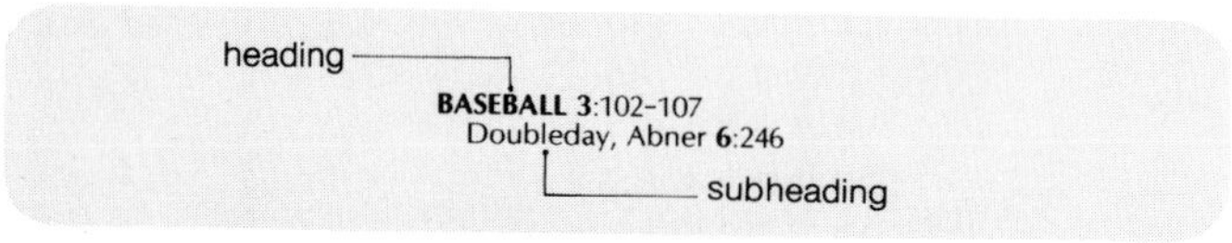
heading
BASEBALL 3:102–107
Doubleday, Abner **6**:246
subheading

This shows that there is information on baseball in the article on Abner Doubleday. In most cases, the subheadings in the index are article titles or article subheadings so that the user of the encyclopedia can easily find the place on the page where the desired information is printed.

Some of the main headings in the index are in **BOLDFACE CAPITAL LETTERS**, as in the example above. This indicates that there is an article with this title in the encyclopedia. Other main headings in the index are in ROMAN CAPITAL LETTERS. This indicates that information on this subject will be found in the encyclopedia, but that there is no article that deals with this subject only. For example, the entry

LENNON, JOHN
Beatles, The **3**:144–145 *illus.*

indicates that information about John Lennon, as well as an illustration, can be found in the article on The Beatles in volume 3.

Map locations are another type of entry. Roman capital letters indicate that although there is no article on that specific place, the reader can locate it on a map. The entry

HUMBOLDT (Arizona)
map (34° 30′N 112° 14′W) **2**:160

means that Humboldt is a town in Arizona and can be found on a map in volume 2, page 160, using the longitude and latitude coordinates provided.

In addition to the heading and the locator, main headings in the index often contain information about certain features of an article. For example, the index entry

ABSTRACT ART 1:63–65 *bibliog., illus.*

tells you that the article entitled ABSTRACT ART appears in volume 1, on pages 63-65, has a bibliography, and is illustrated. There are four notations that are used for this type of information:

bibliog.	this means that the article has a bibliography
illus.	this means that the article has illustration(s)
table(s)	this means that the article has table(s)
map(s)	this means that the article has map(s)

Other information sometimes appears in parentheses after a heading and is used to distinguish among identical main headings. For example:

BIG APPLE (dance)
BIG APPLE (New York City)

EHRLICH, PAUL (1854–1915)
EHRLICH, PAUL (1932–)

GONE WITH THE WIND (book)
GONE WITH THE WIND (film)

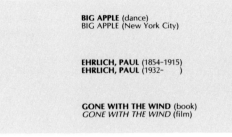

The index also has numerous cross-references of two types. *See* references lead the reader from one heading in the index to another. No locators are associated with *see* references because they are used primarily for synonyms, pseudonyms, alternative forms of headings, or alternative spellings. For example:

NUCLEAR-WASTE DISPOSAL *see*
NUCLEAR ENERGY

The second kind of cross-reference is the *see also* reference. These alert the reader to related main headings in the index. For example:

WOMEN IN SOCIETY
See also SUFFRAGE, WOMEN'S

The reason the reader is not sent directly to the article entitled SUFFRAGE, WOMEN'S in volume 18 is that not all the information on women's suffrage is found in that article; the reader, therefore, is directed to the index entry for a complete list of references.

ALPHABETIZATION OF INDEX HEADINGS

The headings in the index are arranged in alphabetical order by word, not by letter. This means that **BLACK FOREST, BLACK HAWK WAR,** and **BLACK HUMOR** precede **BLACKBERRY** and **BLACKBIRD.**

A comma has a special role in alphabetization; therefore **BLACK, HUGO L.** will come before **BLACK AMERICAN LITERATURE.**

The hyphen functions as a space in the alphabetization; thus **BLACK-EYED SUSAN** precedes **BLACKBEARD.**

Names beginning with *M', Mc,* or *Mac* are alphabetized as if all were spelled *Mac.*

Numerals are alphabetized as if they were spelled out. For example: **1st AMENDMENT** is alphabetized as if spelled **FIRST AMENDMENT.**

Mr., Mrs., and *Dr.* are alphabetized as if spelled *Mister, Mistress,* and *Doctor.*

Such words as *a, an, the, but, for, by,* and *of* are ignored in the alphabetization. Thus entries for the following organizations appear in the index in the order shown below:

AMERICAN ASSOCIATION OF COMMUNITY AND JUNIOR COLLEGES
AMERICAN ASSOCIATION FOR HIGHER EDUCATION
AMERICAN ASSOCIATION OF UNIVERSITY PROFESSORS

The reader should look up ***THE WAY OF ALL FLESH*** (book) under ***WAY OF ALL FLESH, THE*** (book).

HOW TO USE THE INDEX

When you are looking for information in the index, you should look under the most specific heading that will cover the information you want. For instance, if you want information on Norman architecture, look under **NORMAN ARCHITECTURE,** not under **ARCHITECTURE.** Under the main heading **ARCHITECTURE,** there is a subhead Norman architecture, which gives the locator for the article entitled NORMAN ARCHITECTURE. However, under the more specific main heading **NORMAN ARCHITECTURE,** in addition to the locator for this particular article, you will find subheadings and locators for other articles in the encyclopedia that contain information on that subject.

Likewise, if you want information on Presbyterianism, do not look under the main heading **RELIGION.** There you will find only a reference to the article PRESBYTERIANISM. Look under the main heading **PRESBYTERIANISM,** where you will find, in addition to the locator for the article PRESBYTERIANISM, locators for information on Presbyterianism that appears in other articles in the encyclopedia.

If you want general information on such topics as architecture, religion, weapons, or space exploration, however, look under the main heading for the topic. You will find locators there for general information on the topic, and you will also find locators for specific subdivisions of the topic. Once again, however, to gather all the information in the encyclopedia on a specific subdivision of a general topic, you should look in the index for the specific subdivision as a main heading.

SPECIAL FEATURES IN THE INDEX

The main headings for survey articles on the history of a particular country (for example: **FRANCE, HISTORY OF; GREAT BRITAIN, HISTORY OF; UNITED STATES, HISTORY OF THE**) are divided into chronological subdivisions. The entries under the chronological subdivisions will refer you to articles in the encyclopedia on important people or events in each particular period in the country's history. The main headings for countries that do not have separate history survey articles also contain references to articles on important people and events in the country's history.

In addition to an entry under the person's name, biographies of people of major importance in a given subject area are listed under the subject area: winners of Nobel Prizes, Pulitzer Prizes, and so on are listed as such under the field for which they received the prize.

Major organizations or institutions are listed under the field or activity for which they are noted and also appear as index entries under their own names.

In art, literature, and music most attention has been given to index entries under styles, genres, forms, periods, nationalities, names of individuals, and titles of works. In order to avoid long and clumsy lists, however, individuals are not listed under the general headings for art, literature, or music for the following national main headings: American, English, French, German, Italian, and Russian. Extensive cross-references make it possible to pull this material together. For other national groups, major figures in the arts are listed under their countries as well as under their names and the genres, styles, or forms with which they are associated.

BENTON (county in Washington)
map (46° 15′N 119° 35′W) **20**:35
BENTON (Wisconsin)
map (42° 34′N 90° 23′W) **20**:185
BENTON, THOMAS HART (painter)
3:205–206 *bibliog., illus.*
Jefferson City (Missouri) **11**:393
painting title
Threshing Wheat **3**:205 *illus.*
BENTON, THOMAS HART (political leader) **3**:206 *bibliog.*
BENTON CITY (Washington)
map (46° 16′N 119° 29′W) **20**:35
BENTON HARBOR (Michigan)
map (42° 6′N 86° 27′W) **13**:377
BENTONIA (Mississippi)
map (32° 38′N 90° 22′W) **13**:469
BENTONITE
clay minerals **5**:46–47
BENTONVILLE (Arkansas)
map (36° 22′N 94° 13′W) **2**:166
BENTWOOD ROCKING CHAIR **8**:379 *illus.*
BENUE RIVER
map (7° 48′N 6° 46′E) **14**:190
Nigeria **14**:189
BENZ (automobile) **2**:365 *illus.*
BENZ, KARL **3**:206 *bibliog.*
BENZALDEHYDE **3**:206
BENZALKONIUM CHLORIDE
antiseptic **2**:68
BENZEDRINE *see* AMPHETAMINE
main heading
BENZENE **3**:206 *bibliog., illus.*
aromatic compounds **2**:186
chemical bond **4**:314 *illus.*
derivatives: Baeyer, Adolf von **3**:20–21
Faraday, Michael **8**:21
MOLECULAR STRUCTURE
Kekulé structure, organic chemistry **14**:435 *illus.*
Kekulé von Stradonitz, Friedrich August **12**:37
phase equilibrium **15**:223 *illus.*
subhead
phenyl group **15**:226
pollutants, chemical **15**:410
BENZIE (county in Michigan)
map (44° 40′N 86° 0′W) **13**:377
BENZODIAZEPINES
Librium **12**:319
BENZOIC ACID **3**:207
BENZYLPENICILLIN *see* PENICILLIN
BEOGRAD *see* BELGRADE (Yugoslavia)
BEOWAWE (Nevada)
map (40° 35′N 116° 29′W) **14**:111
book title
BEOWULF (epic) **3**:207 *bibliog.*
Scandinavia, history of **17**:108
BEQUEST *see* TRUST; WILL (law)
BÉRAIN, JEAN **3**:207 *bibliog.*
BÉRANGER, PIERRE JEAN DE **3**:207
BERAT (Albania)
map (40° 42′N 19° 57′E) **1**:250
BERBER LANGUAGES
Afroasiatic languages **1**:179–180 *map*
BERBERA (Somalia)
map (10° 25′N 45° 2′E) **18**:60
BERBERATI (Central African Republic)
map (4° 16′N 15° 47′E) **4**:251
BERBERS **1**:145 *illus.*; **3**:207–208 *bibliog., illus.*
volume
Abd el-Krim **1**:54
Afroasiatic **1**:180
Almohads **1**:306
Almoravids **1**:307
Kabyle **12**:4
Libya **12**:321
Moorish art and architecture **13**:570
Moroccan history **13**:586
page
North Africa **14**:224
Tuareg **19**:325–326
BERBICK, TREVOR
Ali, Muhammad **1**:292
BERCEANU, GEORGHE **20**:287 *illus.*
BERCHEM, NICOLAES PIETERSZOON **3**:208 *bibliog.*
BERCHER, JEAN *see* DAUBERVAL, JEAN
BERCHTESGADEN (West Germany) **3**:208
BERCZY, WILLIAM
Canadian art and architecture **4**:89
BERDYAYEV, NIKOLAI **3**:208 *bibliog.*
BERGMAN, INGRID **3**:210 *bibliog.*;
locator
9:287 *illus.*
Bogart, Humphrey **3**:359
BERGMAN, SIR TORBERN **3**:210

BERING SEA **3**:212 *bibliog., map*
Bering Strait **3**:212
ISLANDS AND ISLAND GROUPS
Commander Islands (USSR) **5**:137
Pribilof Islands (Alaska) **15**:534
heading
map (60° 0′N 175° 0′W) **19**:388
shellfish **17**:255
BERING SEA CONTROVERSY **3**:212
BERING STRAIT **3**:212
Bering, Vitus Jonassen **3**:211
map (65° 30′N 169° 0′W) **1**:242
Northeast Passage **14**:253
BERINGIA *see* BERING LAND BRIDGE
cross reference
BERINGOVA
Commander Islands (USSR) **5**:137
BERIO, LUCIANO **3**:212 *bibliog.*
BERKELEY, BUSBY **3**:213 *bibliog., illus.*; **8**:85 *illus.*
BERKELEY, GEORGE **3**:213 *bibliog., illus.*
idealism **11**:30
philosophy **15**:245
Smibert, John **17**:366
bibliography
BERKELEY, JOHN, LORD
New Jersey **14**:133
BERKELEY, SIR WILLIAM **3**:213 *bibliog.*
United States, history of the **19**:437
BERKELEY HEIGHTS (New Jersey)
map (40° 41′N 74° 27′W) **14**:129
BERKELEY SPRINGS (West Virginia)
map (39° 38′N 78° 14′W) **20**:111
BERKELIUM **3**:213
actinide series **1**:88
element **7**:130 *table*
metal, metallic element **13**:328
Seaborg, Glenn T. **17**:171
transuranium elements **19**:286
BERKSHIRE HILLS **3**:214; **5**:195 *illus.*; **13**:208 *illus.*
illustration
map (42° 20′N 73° 10′W) **13**:206
BERKSHIRE MUSIC FESTIVAL **3**:214 *bibliog.*
Boston Symphony Orchestra **3**:410
BERLAGE, HENDRIK PETRUS **3**:214 *bibliog.*
BERLE, A. A. **3**:214 *bibliog.*
Liberal parties **12**:312
Roosevelt, Franklin Delano **16**:308
BERLE, MILTON **3**:214
BERLIN (Germany, East and West) **3**:214–217 *bibliog., illus., map*; **9**:142–143 *illus., table*
map
ARCHITECTURE
Schinkel, Karl Friedrich **17**:121
Berlin, Free University of **3**:217
Berlin Wall **3**:217
Brandenburg (East Germany) **3**:453
Brandenburg Gate **3**:453
economy **3**:215–216
Germany, East and West **9**:147
map (52° 31′N 13° 24′E) **9**:140
population **3**:214–215
subway **18**:318 *illus., table*
map locator
table
World War II **20**:275
BERLIN, CONFERENCE OF (1885)
colonialism **5**:112
Zaire **20**:352
BERLIN, CONGRESS OF (1878) **3**:217 *bibliog.*
Russo-Turkish Wars **16**:374
BERLIN, FREE UNIVERSITY OF **3**:217
BERLIN, IRVING **3**:217 *bibliog., illus.*
BERLIN, SIR ISAIAH **3**:217
BERLIN, TREATY OF (1878)
Berlin, Congress of **3**:217
Russo-Turkish Wars **16**:374
BERLIN AIRLIFT **3**:217 *bibliog.*; **5**:98 *illus.*; **19**:456 *illus.*
Clay, Lucius D. **5**:46
BERLIN PHILHARMONIC ORCHESTRA **3**:217
Nikisch, Arthur **14**:195
BERLIN WALL **3**:216 *map*; **3**:217 *bibliog.*; **5**:99 *illus.*
Kennedy, John F. **12**:43
BERLIN ZOO **3**:217
See also ZOOLOGICAL GARDEN
see also
BERLINER, EMILE **3**:218 *bibliog.*
phonograph **15**:253
BERLINER ENSEMBLE **3**:218 *bibliog., illus.*
Brecht, Bertolt **3**:471
Deutsches Theater **6**:136–137
Weigel, Helene **20**:92

INDEX PERSONNEL

Jill Schuler, *Chief Indexer*
Pauline M. Sholtys, *Indexer*

FIRST EDITION PERSONNEL

Index Supervisor
Barbara M. Preschel

Assistant Index Supervisor
Catherine Van Orman

Senior Index Editors
Phyllis Marchand
Joyce Post
Gwen Sloan
Dorothy Thomas

Index Editors
Margaret P. Roeske
Ronald B. Roth

Free-lance Indexers
Benedict Brooks
Joan C. D'Aoust
Judith B. Katz
Anne M. Pace
Bev Anne Ross
Karen Hegge Simmons
Mary F. Tomaselli
A. Cynthia Weber
Don Wigal

Index Assistants
Lisa K. Feldman
Chris Mank
Kathryn Adams Thompson

A

A (letter) **1**:49 *illus.*
A (vitamin) *see* VITAMIN A
AA *see* ALCOHOLICS ANONYMOUS
AAA *see* AGRICULTURAL ADJUSTMENT ADMINISTRATION
AAA *see* AMERICAN AUTOMOBILE ASSOCIATION
AAAS *see* AMERICAN ASSOCIATION FOR THE ADVANCEMENT OF SCIENCE
AACHEN (West Germany) **1**:49
Aix-la-Chapelle, Treaties of **1**:229
map (50° 47′N 6° 5′E) **9**:140
mosaic **13**:595
World War II **20**:273
AAKJAER, JEPPE **1**:49
AALBORG (Denmark) *see* ÅLBORG (Denmark)
AALST (Belgium)
map (50° 56′N 4° 2′E) **3**:177
AALTO, ALVAR **1**:49–50 *bibliog., illus.*
Finland **8**:97
AARAU (Switzerland)
map (47° 23′N 8° 3′E) **18**:394
AARDVARK **1**:50 *illus.*; **13**:104 *illus.*
Tubulidentata **19**:328
AARDWOLF **1**:50 *illus.*
AARE RIVER **1**:50
map (47° 37′N 8° 13′E) **18**:394
AARHUS (Denmark) *see* ARHUS (Denmark)
AARON **1**:50
Golden Calf **9**:231
Medina (Saudi Arabia) **13**:275
AARON, HENRY **1**:51 *bibliog., illus.*
AASEN, IVAN ANDREAS
Norway **14**:262
ABA (Nigeria)
map (5° 6′N 7° 21′E) **14**:190
ABA AL-BAWL HILL
map (24° 57′N 51° 13′E) **16**:4
ABACA (plant)
hemp **10**:120
ABACUS (architecture) **2**:131 *illus.*
ABACUS (arithmetic) **1**:51 *bibliog., illus.*
computer **5**:159
ABADAN (Iran) **1**:51
map (30° 20′N 48° 16′E) **11**:250
ABADIE, PAUL
Sacré-Coeur **17**:8
ABAJO PEAK
map (37° 51′N 109° 28′W) **19**:492
ABAKALIKI (Nigeria)
map (6° 21′N 8° 6′E) **14**:190
ABAKAN (USSR)
map (53° 43′N 91° 26′E) **19**:388
ABALONE **1**:51
ABANCAY (Peru)
map (13° 35′S 72° 55′W) **15**:193
ABANDONMENT **1**:51
ABAYA, LAKE
map (6° 20′N 37° 55′E) **7**:253
ABBADO, CLAUDIO **1**:51–52
ABBAS I **1**:52 *bibliog.*
Mashhad (Iran) **13**:196
Riza-i-Abbasi **16**:234
Valle, Pietro della **19**:507
ABBAS II
Qum (Iran) **16**:28
ABBASIDS **1**:52 *bibliog.*
Arabic literature **2**:101
caliphate **4**:39
Islam **11**:289
Merv **13**:313
Middle East, history of the **13**:403–404
Turks **19**:347
ABBE, ERNST **1**:52
ABBÉ, LAKE
map (11° 9′N 41° 47′E) **6**:208
ABBESS *see* ABBEY
ABBEVILLE (Alabama)
map (31° 34′N 85° 15′W) **1**:234
ABBEVILLE (Georgia)
map (31° 59′N 83° 18′W) **9**:114
ABBEVILLE (Louisiana)
map (29° 58′N 92° 8′W) **12**:430
ABBEVILLE (Mississippi)
map (34° 25′N 89° 37′W) **13**:469
ABBEVILLE (South Carolina)
map (34° 11′N 82° 23′W) **18**:98
ABBEVILLE (county in South Carolina)
map (34° 10′N 82° 30′W) **18**:98
ABBEVILLIAN **1**:52 *bibliog.*
ABBEY **1**:52
monastic art and architecture **13**:518 *illus.*
ABBEY, EDWIN AUSTIN **1**:52
ABBEY, HENRY E.
Metropolitan Opera **13**:348
ABBEY THEATRE **1**:52–53 *bibliog., illus.*
Gregory, Isabella Augusta, Lady **9**:355
Horniman, Annie Elizabeth Fredericka **10**:240
Irish Literary Renaissance **11**:267
O'Casey, Sean **14**:319–320
O'Connor, Frank **14**:347
Robinson, Lennox **16**:245
Synge, John Millington **18**:407
Yeats, William Butler **20**:321
ABBOT, FRANCIS ELLINGWOOD **1**:53 *bibliog.*
ABBOTSFORD (Wisconsin)
map (44° 57′N 90° 19′W) **20**:185
ABBOT *see* ABBEY
ABBOTT, BERENICE **1**:53
Atget, Eugène **2**:288
ABBOTT, BUD *see* ABBOTT AND COSTELLO
ABBOTT, GEORGE **1**:53
ABBOTT, GRACE **1**:53
ABBOTT, SIR JOHN JOSEPH CALDWELL **1**:53
ABBOTT, LYMAN **1**:53 *bibliog.*
ABBOTT AND COSTELLO **1**:53 *bibliog.*
ABC *see* AMERICAN BROADCASTING COMPANY
ABC ART *see* MINIMAL ART
ABD AL-HAMID II, SULTAN OF THE OTTOMAN EMPIRE **1**:53 *bibliog.*
Middle East, history of the **13**:406
Ottoman Empire **14**:465–466
Young Turks **20**:336
ABD AL-MALIK
Middle East, history of the **13**:403
ABD AL-RAHMAN I, EMIR OF CÓRDOBA **1**:53–54 *bibliog.*
Great Mosque (Córdoba) **18**:152 *illus.*
Spain, history of **18**:144
ABD AL-RAHMAN III, EMIR OF CÓRDOBA
Spain, history of **18**:144
ABD EL-KRIM **1**:54 *bibliog.*
ABDALLAH, AHMED
Comoros **5**:154
ABDOMEN **1**:54 *illus.*
hernia **10**:143–144
hysterectomy **10**:352
insect **11**:187
muscle **13**:654
peritonitis **15**:172
ABDU (Egypt) *see* ABYDOS (Egypt)
ABDUCTION *see* KIDNAPPING
ABDUH, MUHAMMAD
Egypt **7**:77
ABDUL-JABBAR, KAREEM **1**:54 *bibliog.*; **3**:111 *illus.*
ABDUL RAHMAN, TUNKU **1**:54 *bibliog.*
ABDULLAH **1**:54–55
ABDULLAH, HAJJ *see* PHILBY, H. ST. JOHN
ABE KOBO **1**:55 *bibliog.*
ABÉCHÉ (Chad)
map (13° 49′N 20° 49′E) **4**:266
ABEL **1**:55
ABEL, SIR FREDERICK AUGUSTUS **1**:55
ABEL, I. W. **1**:55
United Steelworkers of America **19**:465
ABEL, JOHN J. **1**:55
ABEL, NIELS HENRIK **1**:55 *bibliog.*
ABELARD, PETER **1**:55–56 *bibliog., illus.*
Bernard of Clairvaux, Saint **3**:220
ABELL, GEORGE O. **1**:56
ABELL, KJELD **1**:56 *bibliog.*
ABENGOUROU (Ivory Coast)
map (6° 44′N 3° 29′W) **11**:335
ÅBENRÅ (Denmark)
map (55° 2′N 9° 26′E) **6**:109
ABEOKUTA (Nigeria)
map (7° 10′N 3° 26′E) **14**:190
ABERCROMBIE, LASCELLES **1**:56 *bibliog.*
ABERDARE (Wales)
map (51° 43′N 3° 27′W) **19**:403
ABERDARE RANGE
map (0° 25′S 36° 38′E) **12**:53
ABERDEEN (Idaho)
map (42° 57′N 112° 50′W) **11**:26
ABERDEEN (Maryland)
map (39° 30′N 76° 10′W) **13**:188
ABERDEEN (Scotland) **1**:56
map (57° 10′N 2° 4′W) **19**:403
ABERDEEN (county in Scotland) **1**:56
ABERDEEN (South Dakota)
map (45° 28′N 98° 29′W) **18**:103
ABERDEEN (Washington)
map (46° 59′N 123° 50′W) **20**:35
ABERDEEN, GEORGE HAMILTON-GORDON, 4TH EARL OF **1**:56 *bibliog.*
ABERDEEN, UNIVERSITY OF **1**:56
ABERHART, WILLIAM **1**:56 *bibliog.*
Social Credit Party **18**:11
ABERNATHY (Texas)
map (33° 50′N 101° 51′W) **19**:129
ABERNATHY, RALPH DAVID **1**:56–57 *illus.*
ABERRATION, CHROMATIC **1**:57
ABERRATION, SPHERICAL **1**:57
ABERRATION, STELLAR **1**:57
Bradley, James **3**:437–438
ABERT, LAKE
map (42° 38′N 120° 13′W) **14**:427
ABERYSTWYTH (Wales) **1**:57
map (52° 25′N 4° 5′W) **19**:403
ABHIDHARMA
Buddhist sacred literature **3**:543
ABIDJAN (Ivory Coast) **1**:57; **11**:335 *illus., table*
map (5° 19′N 4° 2′W) **11**:335
ABILENE (Kansas) **1**:57
map (38° 55′N 97° 13′W) **12**:18
ABILENE (Texas) **1**:57
map (32° 27′N 99° 44′W) **19**:129
ABINGDON (Illinois)
map (40° 48′N 90° 24′W) **11**:42
ABINGDON (Virginia)
map (36° 43′N 81° 59′W) **19**:607
ABINGDON PRESS
Methodism **13**:344
ABINGTON (Massachusetts)
map (42° 7′N 70° 57′W) **13**:206
ABIQUIU (New Mexico)
map (36° 12′N 106° 19′W) **14**:136
ABITA SPRINGS (Louisiana)
map (30° 29′N 90° 2′W) **12**:430
ABITIBI, LAKE
map (48° 42′N 79° 45′W) **14**:393
ABITIBI RIVER
map (51° 3′N 80° 55′W) **14**:393
ABLATION
glaciers and glaciation **9**:194
ABM *see* ANTIBALLISTIC MISSILE
ABNAKI (American Indians) **1**:57 *bibliog.*
Micmac **13**:384
Narragansett **14**:21–22
Passamaquoddy **15**:104–105
Pennacook **15**:145
Penobscot **15**:153
Samoset **17**:47
ABNORMAL PSYCHOLOGY **1**:57–58 *bibliog.*
See also names of specific disorders, e.g., CATATONIA; PHOBIA; etc.
neurosis **14**:107
personality **15**:189–190
psychology **15**:594
psychopathology, treatment of **15**:599–601
psychopathy **15**:601
psychosis **15**:602
psychosomatic disorders **15**:602
ABNUB (Egypt)
map (27° 16′N 31° 9′E) **7**:76
ÅBO (Finland) *see* TURKU (Finland)
ABOISSO (Ivory Coast)
map (5° 28′N 3° 12′W) **11**:335
ABOLITIONISTS **1**:58 *bibliog., illus.*
Alcott, Louisa May **1**:267
Birney, James Gillespie **3**:293
black Americans **3**:307
Brown, John **3**:515
Child, Lydia Maria **4**:348
Civil War, U.S. **5**:16 *illus.*
Clay, Cassius Marcellus **5**:45
Douglass, Frederick **6**:248–249
Emigrant Aid Company **7**:156
Foster, Abigail **8**:248
Free-Soil Party **8**:295
Fugitive Slave Laws **8**:355
gag rules **9**:7
Garnet, Henry Highland **9**:49
Garrison, William Lloyd **9**:51
Grimké, Sarah Moore and Angelina Emily **9**:365
Grinnell, Josiah Bushnell **9**:366
Liberty party **12**:314
Lundy, Benjamin **12**:462
Mott, Lucretia Coffin **13**:616
Ohio **14**:362
Parker, Theodore **15**:91
Phillips, Wendell **15**:239
slavery **17**:355; **17**:357 *illus.*
Stevens, Thaddeus **18**:263
Sumner, Charles **18**:339–340
Tappan brothers **19**:34
Thoreau, Henry David **19**:178
Truth, Sojourner **19**:322
Tubman, Harriet **19**:327–328
Uncle Tom's Cabin **19**:382
Underground Railroad **19**:383
Walker, David **20**:12
Weld, Theodore Dwight **20**:96
Wilberforce, William **20**:147
Woolman, John **20**:215
Wright, Frances **20**:288
ABOMEY (Benin)
map (7° 11′N 1° 59′E) **3**:200
ABOMINABLE SNOWMAN **1**:59 *bibliog.*
ABORIGINES, AUSTRALIAN **1**:59–60 *bibliog., illus.*; **2**:335–336 *illus.*
Aranda **2**:109
Australia, history of **2**:339–340 *illus.*; **2**:342

ABORIGINES, AUSTRALIAN (cont.)
boomerang **3**:393
cannibalism **4**:109
dingo **6**:179
European contact, culture after **1**:59–60
hepatitis **10**:130
languages **12**:355 *map*
Oceanic languages **14**:339
sign language **17**:300
national parks **14**:44
primitive societies **15**:546
ritual and art **1**:59
bark painting **14**:338 *illus.*
creation accounts **5**:334–335
Oceanic art **14**:338–339 *illus.*
prehistoric art **15**:510–511 *illus.*
totem **19**:249
social organization and kinship **1**:59
yodel **20**:328
ABORTION 1:60 *bibliog.*
birth control **3**:293
brucellosis **3**:520
crime **5**:345
peritonitis **15**:172
pregnancy and birth **15**:502; **15**:504
starvation **18**:228
Supreme Court decisions **1**:60
Roe v. *Wade* and *Doe* v. *Bolton* **16**:267–268
syphilis **18**:410
ABRAHAM 1:61 *bibliog.*
Hagar **10**:9
Hebron **10**:103
Isaac **11**:285
Ishmael **11**:287
Islam **11**:288
Ur **19**:474
ABRAHAM, EDWARD PENLEY
antibiotics **2**:57
ABRAHAM, KARL
developmental psychology **6**:142
schizophrenia **17**:123
ABRAHAMS, PETER 1:61 *bibliog.*
ABRAHAMS BAY (Bahama Islands)
map (22° 21′N 72° 55′W) **3**:23
ABRAMOWITCH, SHOLEM YAKOB *see* MENDELE MOKHER SEFARIM
ABRAMS, CREIGHTON 1:61
ABRASIVE 1:61
carborundum **4**:139
emery **7**:155
pumice **15**:622
ABRAVANEL, ISAAC BEN JUDAH 1:61 *bibliog.*
ABRAVANEL, JUDAH 1:61 *bibliog.*
ABRUZZI (Italy) 1:61
ABRUZZI, LUIGI AMEDEO, DUCA DEGLI 1:62
Saint Elias, Mount **17**:18
ABRUZZI MOUNTAINS
map (42° 0′N 14° 0′E) **11**:321
ABRUZZO, BEN
aerial sports **1**:122
ABSALOM 1:62
ABSALOM, ABSALOM! (book) 1:62 *bibliog.*
Faulkner, William **8**:36
ABSAROKA RANGE
map (44° 45′N 109° 50′W) **20**:301
ABSAROKEE (Montana)
map (45° 31′N 109° 27′W) **13**:547
ABSCAM 1:62
entrapment **7**:209
Federal Bureau of Investigation **8**:41
ABSCESS 1:62
boil **3**:362
carbuncle **4**:141
ear disease **7**:7–8
skin diseases **17**:342
sty **18**:311
teeth **19**:71–72 *illus.*
ABSCISIC ACID 1:62
deciduous plant **6**:73
ABSECON (New Jersey)
map (39° 26′N 74° 30′W) **14**:129
ABSENTEE VOTING 1:62
ABSOLUTE (philosophy) 1:62
Bradley, Francis Herbert **3**:437
Hegel, Georg Wilhelm Friedrich **10**:105
idealism **11**:30
Schelling, Friedrich Wilhelm Joseph von **17**:119
ABSOLUTE MAGNITUDE
magnitude (astronomy) **13**:60–61
ABSOLUTE MUSIC 1:62
ABSOLUTE REALITY *see* REALITY, ABSOLUTE
ABSOLUTE TEMPERATURE SCALE *see* KELVIN SCALE
ABSOLUTE ZERO 1:62–63 *bibliog.*
cryogenics **5**:370–371
gas laws **9**:53
Kelvin, William Thomson, 1st Baron **12**:40
Kelvin scale **12**:40
temperature **19**:92–93
ABSOLUTISM 1:63 *bibliog.*
authoritarianism **2**:354–355
despotism **6**:132
dictatorship **6**:159
Europe, history of **7**:288–289
France, history of **8**:268–269
Germany, history of **9**:151–152
king **12**:80
Louis XIV, King of France **12**:427
monarchy **13**:517
Richelieu, Armand Jean du Plessis, Cardinal et Duc de **16**:213
totalitarianism **19**:248
ABSORAKA *see* CROW (American Indians)
ABSORPTION (physiology) 1:63
digestion, human **6**:171–172
digestive system **6**:174
drug **6**:275
gastrointestinal tract disease **9**:57
ABSORPTION, LIGHT 1:63 *bibliog.*
electromagnetic radiation **7**:118
greenhouse effect **9**:351–352 *illus.*
hygroscopicity **10**:345
laser **12**:210–211
photochemistry **15**:257–259
photosynthesis **15**:275
quantitative chemical analysis **16**:7
spectrophotometer **18**:168–169
spectrum **18**:172 *illus.*
ABSTRACT 1:63
ABSTRACT ART 1:63–65 *bibliog., illus.*
abstract expressionism **1**:65–66
Archipenko, Aleksandr **2**:129
Armory Show **2**:177
Balla, Giacomo **3**:40
Bauhaus **3**:129–130
Bonnard, Pierre **3**:381
Calder, Alexander **4**:25
constructivism **5**:224–225
cross **5**:361
cubism **5**:380–381
Delaunay, Robert **6**:87
Dove, Arthur **6**:250
Gabo, Naum **9**:3–4
Goncharova, Natalia Sergeyevna **9**:242
González, Julio **9**:245
Hélion, Jean **10**:112
Kandinsky, Wassily **12**:13–14
Kupka, František **12**:138
Larionov, Mikhail Fyodorovich **12**:207
Lissitzky, El **12**:366
Malevich, Kasimir **13**:88
minimal art **13**:446
Miró, Joan **13**:463–464
modern art **13**:493–496
Mondrian, Piet **13**:523
Newman, Barnett **14**:169
Olitski, Jules **14**:378
orphism **14**:448
painting **15**:23
Pereira, I. Rice **15**:163
Pevsner, Antoine **15**:216
photography, history and art of **15**:271 *illus.*
Picabia, Francis **15**:290
Rodchenko, Aleksandr Mikhailovich **16**:265
sculpture **17**:165
Stella, Frank **18**:250
suprematism **18**:354
synchromism **18**:406
Tatlin, Vladimir Yevgrafovich **19**:44
Vieira da Silva **19**:578
vorticism **19**:635
Whistler, James Abbott McNeill **20**:134
ABSTRACT EXPRESSIONISM 1:65–66 *bibliog., illus.*
Alechinsky, Pierre **1**:270
American art and architecture **1**:335
Appel, Karel **2**:87
Arp, Jean **2**:187
art criticism
Graham, John **1**:65–66
Greenberg, Clement **9**:349
Avery, Milton **2**:370
Baziotes, William **3**:135
Canadian art and architecture **4**:90
color-field painting **5**:114
de Kooning, Willem **6**:60
Diebenkorn, Richard **6**:161
expressionism (art) **7**:340
Francis, Sam **8**:274
Frankenthaler, Helen **8**:280
Gorky, Arshile **9**:252
Gottlieb, Adolph **9**:264
Hartigan, Grace **10**:62
Hartung, Hans **10**:64
Hofmann, Hans **10**:196
Johns, Jasper **11**:429–430
Kandinsky, Wassily **12**:13–14
Kline, Franz **12**:97–98
Krasner, Lee **12**:127
Marca-Relli, Conrad **13**:145
Mitchell, Joan **13**:483
modern art **13**:494
Motherwell, Robert **13**:607
Nakian, Reuben **14**:9
Newman, Barnett **14**:169
painting **15**:23
Pollock, Jackson **15**:409
Pousette-Dart, Richard **15**:476
Reinhardt, Ad **16**:132
Rosenberg, Harold **16**:315
Rothko, Mark **16**:322
sculpture **17**:166
Soulages, Pierre **18**:71
Stamos, Theodoros **18**:216
Still, Clyfford **18**:268
Tomlin, Bradley Walker **19**:232
Tworkov, Jack **19**:360–361
ABSTRACT SPACES (mathematics)
Fréchet, Maurice René **8**:289
topology **19**:237
ABSURD, THEATER OF THE *see* THEATER OF THE ABSURD
ABSURDISM (literature) 1:66 *bibliog.*
See also THEATER OF THE ABSURD
Camus, Albert **4**:68
ABU BAKR (caliph) 1:66 *bibliog.*
Middle East, history of the **13**:402
ABU DHABI (Abu Zabi) 1:66
map (24° 28′N 54° 22′E) **19**:401
United Arab Emirates **19**:400
ABU KAMAL (Syria)
map (34° 27′N 40° 55′E) **18**:412
ABU MADI, ILIYA 1:66
ABU NUWAS 1:66
ABU SHAHRAIN *see* ERIDU
ABU SIMBEL (Egypt) 1:66–67 *bibliog., illus.*; 7:81 *map*
temple **19**:95
ABU TIJ (Egypt)
map (27° 2′N 31° 19′E) **7**:76
ABUJA (Nigeria)
Nigeria **14**:192
ABUL-WAFA
mathematics, history of **13**:224
ABUNÃ (Brazil)
map (9° 42′S 65° 23′W) **3**:460
ABUNDANCE 1:67 *bibliog.*
ABYDOS (Egypt) 1:67 *bibliog.*; 7:81 *map*
temple **19**:94
ABYSSAL ZONE 1:67 *bibliog.*
benthonic zone **3**:205
ABYSSINIA *see* ETHIOPIA
ABYSSINIAN CAT 1:67 *illus.*; **4**:195 *illus.*
ABZUG, BELLA S. 1:67–68 *bibliog., illus.*
AC *see* ALTERNATING CURRENT
ACACIA 1:68 *illus.*
African savanna life **17**:98 *illus.*
mimosa **13**:436
ACADEMIA SECRETORUM NATURAE
scientific associations **17**:144
ACADEMIC FREEDOM 1:68–69 *bibliog.*
Lowell, Abbott Lawrence **12**:443
student movements **18**:307–308
ACADEMIC SOCIETY *see* HONORARY ACADEMIC SOCIETY
ACADÉMIE DES BEAUX-ARTS *see* ÉCOLE DES BEAUX-ARTS
ACADÉMIE DES INSCRIPTIONS ET BELLES-LETTRES
Institut de France **11**:195
ACADÉMIE DES SCIENCES 1:69 *bibliog.*
Institut de France **11**:195
scientific associations **17**:144–145
ACADÉMIE DES SCIENCES MORALES ET POLITIQUES
Institut de France **11**:195
ACADÉMIE FRANÇAISE 1:69
Chapelain, Jean **4**:284
Clair, René **5**:35
dictionary **6**:159
Institut de France **11**:195
Richelieu, Armand Jean du Plessis, Cardinal et Duc de **16**:213
Salon (art) **17**:36
Yourcenar, Marguerite **20**:337
ACADÉMIE ROYALE DE DANSE 1:69
ACADÉMIE ROYALE DE PEINTURE ET DE SCULPTURE
academies of art **1**:70
ACADEMIES OF ART 1:69–70 *bibliog., illus.*
art collectors and patrons **2**:204
Carracci (family) **4**:166–167
Düsseldorf Akademie **6**:308
Dutch art and architecture **6**:309
École des Beaux-Arts **7**:42
Hogarth, William **10**:198
painting **15**:21
ACADEMY 1:70–71 *illus.*
Plato's Academy
Carneades **4**:155
Euclidean geometry **7**:263
Plato **15**:360
skepticism **17**:337
secondary education **17**:179
ACADEMY, MILITARY *see* MILITARY ACADEMIES
ACADEMY AWARDS 1:71 *bibliog.*
acting
Andrews, Julie **1**:408
Astor, Mary **2**:269
Bancroft, Anne **3**:60
Barrymore (family) **3**:96
Beery, Wallace **3**:163
Bergman, Ingrid **3**:210
Bogart, Humphrey **3**:359
Brando, Marlon **3**:454
Brynner, Yul **3**:529–530
Burns, George **3**:579
Cagney, James **4**:16
Colbert, Claudette **5**:97
Colman, Ronald **5**:105
Cooper, Gary **5**:243
Crawford, Joan **5**:333
Crosby, Bing **5**:360
Davis, Bette **6**:50
De Havilland, Olivia **6**:60
De Niro, Robert **6**:62
Dressler, Marie **6**:271
Dunaway, Faye **6**:298
Ferrer, José **8**:59
Fonda, Henry **8**:205
Fonda, Jane **8**:205
Gordon, Ruth **9**:249
Guinness, Sir Alec **9**:400
Harrison, Rex **10**:60
Hayes, Helen **10**:82
Hepburn, Katharine **10**:130–131
Hoffman, Dustin **10**:195
Houseman, John **10**:274
Ives, Burl **11**:333
Jackson, Glenda **11**:342
Jannings, Emil **11**:359
Keaton, Diane **12**:35
Kelly, Grace **12**:39
Lancaster, Burt **12**:177
Laughton, Charles **12**:236–237
Loren, Sophia **12**:413
Mastroianni, Marcello **13**:217
Minnelli, Liza **13**:452
Muni, Paul **13**:641
Nicholson, Jack **14**:182
Niven, David **14**:204
Olivier, Laurence Kerr, Baron Olivier of Brighton **14**:379
Peck, Gregory **15**:130
Pickford, Mary **15**:293
Poitier, Sidney **15**:385
Redgrave, Vanessa **16**:115
Rogers, Ginger **16**:269
Scofield, Paul **17**:147
Scott, George C. **17**:153
Sinatra, Frank **17**:318–319
Steiger, Rod **18**:246
Stewart, James **18**:266
Streep, Meryl **18**:296
Streisand, Barbra **18**:297
Taylor, Elizabeth **19**:49
Tracy, Spencer **19**:262
Ustinov, Peter **19**:491
Wayne, John **20**:74
Welles, Orson **20**:99
Woodward, Joanne **20**:213
Young, Loretta **20**:334
art direction, color
Mielziner, Jo **13**:415
choreography
Robbins, Jerome **16**:240
cinematography
Howe, James Wong **10**:284
costume design
Beaton, Sir Cecil **3**:145
directing
Allen, Woody **1**:300
Beatty, Warren **3**:145
Capra, Frank **4**:128
Cukor, George **5**:383
Ford, John (film director) **8**:223
Forman, Milos **8**:234
Kazan, Elia **12**:33–34
Lean, David **12**:259
Nichols, Mike **14**:182
Reed, Sir Carol **16**:117–118
Wyler, William **20**:299
Zinnemann, Fred **20**:368–369
documentary, short
National Film Board of Canada **14**:32

film adaptations
  Chayefsky, Paddy 4:306
foreign films
  Buñuel, Luis 3:565
  Costa-Gavras, Henri 5:291
  Fellini, Federico 8:48
musical scores
  Arnold, Malcolm 2:185
  Chaplin, Charlie 4:285
  Fields, Dorothy 8:73
  Previn, André 15:534
screenwriting
  Chayefsky, Paddy 4:306
  Fuchs, Daniel 8:351
  Howard, Sidney Coe 10:283
  Sherwood, Robert E. 17:259
songs
  Bacharach, Burt 3:11
  Berlin, Irving 3:217
  Kern, Jerome 12:59
  Mercer, Johnny 13:304
  Styne, Jules 18:311
special awards
  Astaire, Fred 2:267
  Chaplin, Charlie 4:284–285
  Coward, Sir Noel 5:320
  Garland, Judy 9:48
  Griffith, D. W. 9:363
  Pickford, Mary 15:293
  Rooney, Mickey 16:306
  Sennett, Mack 17:204
  Zukor, Adolph 20:381
technical innovations
  Disney, Walt 6:197
ACADEMY OF MOTION PICTURE ARTS AND SCIENCES *see* ACADEMY AWARDS
ACADEMY OF SCIENCES OF THE GERMAN DEMOCRATIC REPUBLIC *see* AKADEMIE DER WISSENSCHAFTEN DER DDR
ACADEMY OF SCIENCES OF THE USSR 1:71 *bibliog.*
  Lysenko, Trofim Denisovich 12:480
  Special Astrophysical Observatory 18:166
ACADIA 1:71 *bibliog., map*
  Canada, history of 4:81
  Nova Scotia (Canada) 14:271
  people
    Cajuns 4:19
    Micmac 13:384
ACADIA (county in Louisiana)
  map (30° 18′N 92° 23′W) 12:430
ACADIA NATIONAL PARK 1:71; 13:72 *illus.*; 14:38 *map, table*
ACAJUTLA (El Salvador)
  map (13° 36′N 89° 50′W) 7:100
ACÁMBARO (Mexico)
  map (20° 2′N 100° 44′W) 13:357
ACANTHUS (architecture) 1:71–72 *bibliog., illus.*
ACANTHUS (plant) 1:72 *illus.*
ACAPONETA (Mexico)
  map (22° 30′N 105° 22′W) 13:357
ACAPULCO (Mexico) 1:72
  map (16° 51′N 99° 55′W) 13:357
ACARAI MOUNTAINS
  map (1° 50′N 57° 40′W) 9:410
ACARÍ (Peru)
  map (15° 26′S 74° 37′W) 15:193
ACARIGUA (Venezuela)
  map (9° 33′N 69° 12′W) 19:542
ACCADEMIA DEI LINCEI 1:72
  scientific associations 17:144
ACCADEMIA DEL CIMENTO 1:72 *bibliog.*
  scientific associations 17:144
ACCADEMIA DEL DISEGNO
  academies of art 1:70
ACCADEMIA DELLA CRUSA
  scientific associations 17:144
ACCADEMIA DI SAN LUCA
  academies of art 1:70
ACCADEMIA NAZIONALE DEI LINCEI *see* ACCADEMIA DEI LINCEI
ACCELERATION 1:72 *bibliog.*
  accelerometer 1:76
  free fall 8:294
  gravitation 9:304–305
  laws of motion 12:251
  measurement 13:255
  motion, planar 13:609
  velocity 19:538
ACCELERATOR, PARTICLE 1:72–76 *bibliog., illus.*; 2:311 *illus.*
  betatron 3:229
  bubble chamber 3:531
  cloud chamber 5:68
  Cockcroft, Sir John Douglas 5:86
  direct voltage accelerator 1:73
  electromagnetic induction 7:115
  fundamental particles 8:363
  fusion energy 8:382
  linear accelerator 1:73–74 *illus.*
  nuclear physics 14:285
  research institutions
    Argonne National Laboratory 2:152
    Brookhaven National Laboratory 3:510
    Desy Laboratory 6:133
    European Organization for Nuclear Research 7:301
    Fermi National Accelerator Laboratory 8:56
    Frascati National Laboratory 8:286
    Lawrence Berkeley and Lawrence Livermore laboratories 12:251
    Los Alamos National Scientific Laboratory 12:416
    Stanford Linear Accelerator Center 18:218
  synchrotron radiation 18:406
  Van de Graaff generator 19:512
ACCELERATOR, PLASMA
  magnetohydrodynamics 13:59
ACCELEROMETER 1:76
  guidance and control systems 9:394
  navigation 14:60–61
  space exploration 18:122
ACCENT 1:76
  versification 19:561–562
ACCENTOR 1:76
ACCESSORY 1:76
ACCIDENTS, AUTOMOBILE *see* SAFETY, AUTOMOTIVE
ACCOMAC (Virginia)
  map (37° 43′N 75° 40′W) 19:607
ACCOMACK (county in Virginia)
  map (37° 45′N 75° 40′W) 19:607
ACCOMPLICE 1:76
ACCORDION 1:76–77 *illus.*
  concertina 5:169
ACCOUNT EXECUTIVE (advertising) 1:112
ACCOUNTING 1:77–78 *bibliog.*
  See also BOOKKEEPING; NATIONAL ACCOUNTING
  amortization 1:376
  audit 2:318
  balance sheet 1:77 *illus.*
  careers 1:78
  earnings statement 1:77 *illus.*
  history 1:78
  specialties 1:77–78
ACCRA (Ghana) 1:79; 9:164 *table*; 9:165 *illus.*
  map (5° 33′N 0° 13′W) 9:164
ACCREDITATION OF SCHOOLS AND COLLEGES 1:79
  business education 3:588
  correspondence school 5:276
ACCULTURATION 1:79 *bibliog.*
  culture 5:385
  diffusion, cultural 6:170
  primitive societies 15:546
ACEGUÁ (Uruguay)
  map (31° 52′S 54° 12′W) 19:488
ACETABULARIA 1:79 *bibliog., illus.*
ACETALDEHYDE 1:79
ACETAMINOPHEN 1:79
  analgesic 1:388
ACETATE 1:80
  acetic acid 1:80
ACETIC ACID 1:80
  acetate 1:80
  Acetobacter 1:80
  caustic chemicals 4:219
ACETIC ALDEHYDE *see* ACETALDEHYDE
ACETOBACTER 1:80
ACETONE 1:80
  infrared spectrum 18:170 *illus.*
  ketone 12:61
  photodissociation 15:258
ACETOPHENETIDIN *see* PHENACETIN
ACETYL COENZYME A
  coenzyme 5:92
  pyruvic acid 15:639
ACETYL GROUP 1:80
  acetaldehyde 1:79
  acetic acid 1:80
  acetone 1:80
ACETYLCHOLINE 1:80
  Alzheimer's disease 1:320
  biopotential 3:276
  curare 5:391
  Dale, Sir Henry Hallett 6:11
  drug 6:277
  Katz, Sir Bernard 12:31
  muscle contraction 13:655
  myasthenia gravis 13:689
  neurophysiology 14:106
ACETYLENE 1:80
  alkyne 1:297
  petrochemicals 15:205
ACETYLSALICYLIC ACID *see* ASPIRIN
ACEVEDO (Argentina)
  map (33° 45′S 60° 27′W) 2:149
ACHAD HA-AM 1:80
ACHAEA 1:80 *bibliog.*
ACHAEAN LEAGUE
  Achaea 1:80
  Greece, ancient 9:333
  Messenia 13:323
  Sparta (Greece) 18:165
ACHAEMENIDS 1:80–81 *bibliog.*
  art and architecture 15:184–185 *illus.*
  Artaxerxes I, King of Persia 2:213
  Artaxerxes II, King of Persia 2:213
  Cyrus the Great, King of Persia 5:410
  Cyrus the Younger 5:410
  Darius I, King of Persia 6:38
  Darius III Codomannus, King of Persia 6:38
  inscription 11:185
  Persepolis 15:180
  Persia, ancient 15:181
  Persian Wars 15:187–188
  Ur 19:474
ACHEBE, CHINUA 1:81 *bibliog.*
ACHERON *see* HADES (mythology)
ACHESON, ARCHIBALD, 2D EARL OF GOSFORD *see* GOSFORD, ARCHIBALD ACHESON, 2D EARL OF
ACHESON, DEAN 1:81 *bibliog., illus.*
  Kennan, George F. 12:41
ACHEULEAN 1:81 *bibliog.*
  African prehistory 1:173
  Chellean 4:311
  Clactonian 5:35
  Combe Grenal (France) 5:130
  Homo erectus 10:216
  Olduvai Gorge (Tanzania) 14:377
  Olorgesailie (Kenya) 14:381
  Paleolithic Period 15:38–40 *illus.*
  points 15:38; 15:40
  prehistoric humans 15:513
  Ternifine man 19:118
  Terra Amata (France) 19:119
  Torralba and Ambrona (Spain) 19:243
ACHIEVEMENT MOTIVATION 1:81–82 *bibliog.*
ACHIEVEMENT TESTS *see* EDUCATIONAL MEASUREMENT
ACHILL ISLAND
  map (54° 0′N 10° 0′W) 11:258
ACHILLES 1:82 *illus.*
ACHINSK (USSR)
  map (56° 17′N 90° 30′E) 19:388
ACHONDRITE 1:82
ACID RAIN 1:82 *bibliog.*
  coal and coal mining 5:79
  pH 15:217
  pollution control 15:415
ACID ROCK
  rock music 16:249
ACIDOSIS 1:82
  diabetes 6:148
  metabolism 13:327
  stress, biological 18:297
ACIDS AND BASES 1:82–83 *bibliog.*
  alkali 1:295
  alkali metals 1:295
  alkaline earth metals 1:295–296
  amphoteric compounds 1:382
  anhydride 2:8
  Arrhenius, Svante August 2:188
  battery 3:125–126 *illus.*
  biological acids and bases
    abscisic acid 1:62
    alginic acid 1:290
    alkaloid 1:296
    amino acid 1:370–371
    ascorbic acid 2:228
    coenzyme 5:92–93
    fatty acid 8:35
    formic acid 8:234
    lactic acid 12:161
    maleic acid 13:87
    nucleic acid 14:288–291
    palmitic acid 15:51
    pyruvic acid 15:639
  Brønsted, Johannes Nicolaus 3:503
  buffer 3:547
  caustic chemicals 4:219–220
  chemical nomenclature 4:320
  electrolysis 7:114–115
  equivalent weight 7:227
  ester 7:246
  indicator (chemistry) 11:144 *table*
  inorganic acids 1:83
    aqua regia 2:92
    hydrochloric acid 10:331–332
    mineral acid 13:444
    sulfuric acid 18:336
  ion and ionization 11:239–240
  Lewis, Gilbert Newton 12:306
  neutralization 1:83; 14:108
  organic acids and bases 1:83
    acetic acid 1:80
    ammonia 1:372
    benzoic acid 3:207
    carboxylic acid 4:139–141
    citric acid 4:447
    nitric acid 14:202
    phenol 15:225
  pH 15:217–218
  qualitative chemical analysis 16:6–7
  reaction, chemical 16:98–100
  salt (chemistry) 17:37
  soap and detergent 18:6–8
  titration 19:215
  Wieland, Heinrich Otto 20:146
ACKERLY (Texas)
  map (32° 32′N 101° 43′W) 19:129
ACKERMAN (Mississippi)
  map (33° 19′N 89° 10′W) 13:469
ACKLEY (Iowa)
  map (42° 33′N 93° 3′W) 11:244
ACLU *see* AMERICAN CIVIL LIBERTIES UNION
ACMEISTS 1:83 *bibliog.*
  Akhmatova, Anna 1:230
  Gumilev, Nikolai Stepanovich 9:405
  Mandelstam, Osip Emilievich 13:111
ACNE 1:83
  skin 17:341
  skin diseases 17:342
ACOMA (American Indians) 1:83–84 *bibliog.*
ACOMAYO (Peru)
  map (13° 55′S 71° 41′W) 15:193
ACONCAGUA 1:84
  map (32° 39′S 70° 1′W) 2:149
ACORN
  oak 14:311–312 *illus.*
ACORN WORM
  hemichordate 10:117–118
ACOUSTICS *see* SOUND AND ACOUSTICS
ACQUIRED IMMUNE DEFICIENCY SYNDROME *see* AIDS
ACRE (Brazil) 1:84
  map (9° 0′S 70° 0′W) 3:460
ACRE (Israel) 1:84
  Crusades 5:368–369
  Hospitalers 10:259
  Jerusalem, Latin Kingdom of 11:401
  map (32° 55′N 35° 5′E) 11:302
ACRE (measurement)
  weights and measures 20:93 *table*
ACROBAT
  circus 4:444
ACROMEGALY
  endocrine system, diseases of the 7:170
ACROPHOBIA
  phobia 15:248–249
ACROPOLIS 1:84–85 *bibliog., illus.*; 2:192–193 *illus.*; 2:290 *map*
  Elgin, Thomas Bruce, 7th Earl of 7:137
  Elgin Marbles 7:137
  Greek architecture 9:337
  Greek art 9:340–341
  Mnesicles 13:486
  Parthenon 9:336 *illus.*; 19:96 *illus.*
ACROSS THE WIDE MISSOURI (book)
  De Voto, Bernard 6:64
ACROSTIC 1:85
ACRYLIC FIBERS
  synthetic fibers 18:409
ACRYLIC RESIN
  dentistry 6:116
  painting techniques 15:24
ACRYLONITRILE 1:85–86
ACS *see* AMERICAN CHEMICAL SOCIETY
ACT (literature)
  narrative and dramatic devices 14:22
ACT (psychology)
  Brentano, Franz 3:473
ACT OF GOD 1:86
ACT OF UNIFORMITY OF 1662 (British history)
  Clarendon Code 5:37
  Nonconformists 14:216
  Puritanism 15:630
ACTA DIURNA (journalism) 11:454
ACTAEON (mythology) 1:86
ACTH *see* ADRENOCORTICOTROPIC HORMONE
ACTIN
  biological locomotion 3:265
  muscle contraction 13:654–656
ACTING 1:86–88 *bibliog., illus.*
  labor union
    Actors' Equity Association 1:90
  schools

ACTING (cont.)
Actors Studio **1**:90
American Academy of Dramatic Art **1**:327
arts, education in the **2**:224–225
Baker, George Pierce **3**:27
Juilliard School, The **11**:465
Royal Academy of Dramatic Art **16**:329
theater, history of the **19**:147; **19**:150–151
theories **1**:86
Barrault, Jean Louis **3**:93
Delsarte, François **6**:95
eurhythmics **7**:265–266
Garrick, David **9**:50–51
Grotowski, Jerzy **9**:372–373
Living Theatre **12**:376
method acting **13**:343
Meyerhold, Vsevolod Emilievich **13**:369
Polish Laboratory Theater **15**:397
Stanislavsky, Konstantin **18**:218
Strasberg, Lee **18**:289
ACTINIDE SERIES **1**:88 *bibliog.*, *table*
actinium **1**:88
americium **1**:368
berkelium **3**:213
californium **4**:38–39
curium **5**:392
einsteinium **7**:94
fermium **8**:56
lawrencium **12**:251
mendelevium **13**:294
metal **13**:328
metallic elements **13**:328
neptunium **14**:89
nobelium **14**:211
physical properties **1**:88 *table*
plutonium **15**:373
protactinium **15**:574
Seaborg, Glenn T. **17**:171
thorium **19**:178
transuranium elements **19**:282
uranium **19**:477
ACTINIUM **1**:88
actinide series **1**:88
element **7**:130 *table*
Group IIIB periodic table **15**:167
Meitner, Lise **13**:283
metallic elements **13**:328
transition elements **19**:273
ACTINOMETER **1**:88–89
camera **4**:55–56
photography **15**:263
ACTINOMYCES **1**:89
ACTINOSPHAERIUM **1**:89 *bibliog.*
ACTION (federal agency) **1**:89 *bibliog.*
ACTION FRANÇAISE **1**:89 *bibliog.*
ACTION PAINTING *see* ABSTRACT EXPRESSIONISM
ACTIUM, BATTLE OF **1**:89
Antony, Mark **2**:71
Augustus, Roman emperor **2**:322
ACTIVE TRANSPORT **1**:89–90 *bibliog.*
albumin **1**:261
ACTIVITY (chemical) **1**:90 *bibliog.*
ACTON (Massachusetts)
map (42° 29′N 71° 26′W) **13**:206
ACTON, JOHN EMERICH EDWARD DALBERG ACTON, 1ST BARON **1**:90 *bibliog.*
ACTORS' EQUITY ASSOCIATION **1**:90
ACTORS STUDIO **1**:90 *bibliog.*
Crawford, Cheryl **5**:333
Kazan, Elia **12**:33–34
Strasberg, Lee **18**:289
ACTS OF THE APOSTLES **1**:90–91 *bibliog.*
Bible **3**:240
ACTUARY **1**:91
ACTUATOR
gyroscope **9**:416
ACUFF, ROY
Grand Ole Opry **9**:285
ACUPUNCTURE **1**:91 *bibliog.*, *illus.*
analgesic **1**:388
anesthetics **1**:410–411
Chinese medicine **4**:390–391 *illus.*
headache **10**:85
meridian points **1**:91 *illus.*; **13**:267 *illus.*
ACURACAY (Peru)
map (5° 35′S 74° 10′W) **15**:193
ACUSHNET (Massachusetts)
map (41° 41′N 70° 55′W) **13**:206
ACUTE MYOCARDIAL INFARCTION *see* HEART ATTACK
ACWORTH (Georgia)
map (34° 4′N 84° 41′W) **9**:114
ACYCLOVIR (drug)
genital herpes **10**:146
A/D CONVERTER *see* ANALOG-TO-DIGITAL CONVERTER
ADA *see* AMERICANS FOR DEMOCRATIC ACTION
ADA (computer language) **1**:91
computer language **5**:165
ADA (county in Idaho)
map (43° 30′N 116° 15′W) **11**:26
ADA (Minnesota)
map (47° 18′N 96° 31′W) **13**:453
ADA (Oklahoma)
map (34° 46′N 96° 41′W) **14**:368
ADA (Yugoslavia)
map (45° 48′N 20° 8′E) **20**:340
ADAIR (county in Iowa)
map (41° 17′N 94° 28′W) **11**:244
ADAIR (county in Kentucky)
map (37° 5′N 85° 15′W) **12**:47
ADAIR (county in Missouri)
map (40° 8′N 92° 22′W) **13**:476
ADAIR (county in Oklahoma)
map (35° 55′N 94° 40′W) **14**:368
ADAIRSVILLE (Georgia)
map (34° 22′N 84° 56′W) **9**:114
ADAK ISLAND
map (51° 45′N 176° 40′W) **1**:242
ADAM **1**:92
Eden, Garden of **7**:56
Eve **7**:315
Genesis, Book of **9**:78
Lilith **12**:341
original sin **14**:444
ADAM, ADOLPHE **1**:92
ADAM, ROBERT **1**:92 *bibliog.*, *illus.*
federal style **8**:42
Greek Revival **9**:345
Hepplewhite, George **10**:131
Osterley House **11**:213 *illus.*
Syon House **1**:92 *illus.*
ADAM BEDE (book) **1**:92
ADAM DE LA HALLE **1**:93
minstrels, minnesingers, and troubadours **13**:460
music, history of Western **13**:665
ADAM LE BOSSU *see* ADAM DE LA HALLE
ADAMAOUA MOUNTAINS
map (7° 0′N 12° 0′E) **4**:60
ADAMIC, LOUIS **1**:93 *bibliog.*
ADAMITE **13**:440 *illus.*
ADAMOV, ARTHUR **1**:93
ADAMS (county in Colorado)
map (39° 50′N 104° 30′W) **5**:116
ADAMS (county in Idaho)
map (44° 50′N 116° 25′W) **11**:26
ADAMS (county in Illinois)
map (39° 56′N 91° 23′W) **11**:42
ADAMS (county in Indiana)
map (40° 50′N 84° 56′W) **11**:111
ADAMS (county in Iowa)
map (41° 0′N 94° 42′W) **11**:244
ADAMS (Massachusetts)
map (42° 37′N 73° 7′W) **13**:206
ADAMS (county in Mississippi)
map (31° 30′N 91° 20′W) **13**:469
ADAMS (county in Nebraska)
map (40° 30′N 98° 30′W) **14**:70
ADAMS (New York)
map (43° 49′N 76° 1′W) **14**:149
ADAMS (North Dakota)
map (48° 25′N 98° 5′W) **14**:248
ADAMS (county in North Dakota)
map (46° 10′N 102° 40′W) **14**:248
ADAMS (county in Ohio)
map (38° 48′N 83° 32′W) **14**:357
ADAMS (county in Pennsylvania)
map (39° 48′N 77° 15′W) **15**:147
ADAMS (county in Washington)
map (47° 0′N 118° 30′W) **20**:35
ADAMS (Wisconsin)
map (43° 58′N 89° 49′W) **20**:185
ADAMS (county in Wisconsin)
map (43° 57′N 89° 47′W) **20**:185
ADAMS, ABIGAIL **1**:93 *bibliog.*, *illus.*
ADAMS, ANSEL **1**:93 *bibliog.*
Weston, Edward **20**:118
ADAMS, BROOKS **1**:93
ADAMS, CHARLES FRANCIS **1**:93 *bibliog.*
Civil War, U.S. **5**:32
ADAMS, CHARLES FRANCIS, JR. **1**:93–94 *bibliog.*
ADAMS, FRANKLIN PIERCE **1**:94
ADAMS, HARRIET S. *see* KEENE, CAROLYN
ADAMS, HENRY **1**:94 *bibliog.*
Education of Henry Adams, The **7**:64
ADAMS, HERBERT BAXTER **1**:94 *bibliog.*
ADAMS, JAMES TRUSLOW **1**:94 *bibliog.*
ADAMS, JOHN **1**:94–95 *bibliog.*, *illus.*
Adams, Abigail **1**:93
American Revolution **1**:353; **1**:357 *illus.*; **1**:365 *illus.*
Federalist party **8**:43
Jefferson, Thomas **11**:391
Marbury v. *Madison* **13**:144
Marshall, John **13**:172
Quincy (Massachusetts) **16**:27
XYZ Affair **20**:313
ADAMS, JOHN COUCH **1**:96
astronomy, history of **2**:279
ADAMS, JOHN QUINCY **1**:96–97 *bibliog.*, *illus.*
Amistad Case **1**:372
Clay, Henry **5**:46
gag rules **9**:7
Jackson, Andrew **11**:341
Monroe Doctrine **13**:543
Quincy (Massachusetts) **16**:27
Whig Party (United States) **20**:130
ADAMS, LÉONIE
Bogan, Louise **3**:359
ADAMS, MAUDE **1**:97 *bibliog.*, *illus.*
ADAMS, MOUNT (New Hampshire)
map (44° 18′N 71° 19′W) **14**:123
ADAMS, MOUNT (Washington)
map (46° 12′N 121° 28′W) **20**:35
ADAMS, ROBERT McCORMICK **1**:97
ADAMS, SAMUEL **1**:97–98 *bibliog.*, *illus.*
Hancock, John **10**:34
ADAMS, SAMUEL HOPKINS **1**:98
ADAMS, WALTER SYDNEY **1**:98
ADAM'S APPLE *see* LARYNX
ADAMS BRIDGE
map (9° 4′N 79° 37′E) **18**:206
ADAM'S NEEDLE
yucca **20**:338
ADAMS-ONÍS TREATY
Monroe, James **13**:542
United States, history of the **19**:444
West Florida Controversy **20**:108
ADAM'S PEAK **1**:98
map (6° 48′N 80° 30′E) **18**:206
ADAMSON, ROBERT *see* HILL, D. O., AND ADAMSON, ROBERT
ADAMSVILLE (Alabama)
map (33° 36′N 86° 57′W) **1**:234
ADAMSVILLE (Tennessee)
map (35° 14′N 88° 23′W) **19**:104
ADANA (Turkey) **1**:98
map (37° 1′N 35° 18′E) **19**:343
ADAPAZARI (Turkey)
map (40° 46′N 30° 24′E) **19**:343
ADAPTATION, BIOLOGICAL *see* ADAPTIVE RADIATION; EVOLUTION
ADAPTIVE RADIATION **1**:98
evolution **7**:320
grass **9**:295
perching birds **15**:161
ADARE, CAPE OF
map (71° 17′S 170° 14′E) **2**:40
ADDAMS, CHARLES **1**:98
ADDAMS, JANE **1**:98–99 *bibliog.*, *illus.*
Hull House **10**:296
ADDAX **1**:99 *illus.*
ADDER **1**:99 *bibliog.*, *illus.*
death adder **6**:68
puff adder **15**:384 *illus.*
ADDER'S-TONGUE (botany) **1**:99
ADDICTION *see* DRUG ABUSE
ADDING MACHINE **1**:99–100 *bibliog.*; **5**:159 *illus.*
abacus **1**:51
calculator, electronic **4**:23–24
Pascal, Blaise **15**:102
ADDIS ABABA (Ethiopia) **1**:100; **7**:253–254 *illus.*, *table*
map (9° 0′N 38° 50′E) **7**:253
ADDISON (Illinois)
map (41° 55′N 88° 0′W) **11**:42
ADDISON (county in Vermont)
map (44° 2′N 73° 7′W) **19**:554
ADDISON, JOSEPH **1**:100 *bibliog.*, *illus.*
Steele, Sir Richard **18**:243
ADDISON'S DISEASE **1**:101
endocrine system, diseases of the **7**:170
glucocorticoid **9**:211
hormone, animal **10**:237
ADDITION
arithmetic **2**:158
associative law **2**:266
commutative law **5**:153
distributive law **6**:201
ADDRESSOGRAPH MACHINE
business machines **3**:589
ADDU ATOLL
map (0° 38′S 73° 10′E) **13**:87
ADE, GEORGE **1**:101 *bibliog.*
ADEL (Georgia)
map (31° 8′N 83° 25′W) **9**:114
ADEL (Iowa)
map (41° 37′N 94° 1′W) **11**:244
ADELAIDE (Australia) **1**:101 *illus.*
education
Adelaide University **2**:345 *table*
Flinders University **2**:345 *table*
map (34° 55′S 138° 35′E) **2**:328
ADELAIDE (Bahama Islands)
map (25° 0′N 77° 31′W) **3**:23
ADELCRANTZ, CARL FREDRIK
Scandinavian art and architecture **17**:113
ADÉLIE COAST
French Southern and Antarctic Territories **8**:326
ADÉLIE PENGUIN **2**:42–43 *illus.*
ADEN (Yemen) **1**:101
map (12° 45′N 45° 12′E) **20**:324
Yemen (Aden) **20**:323–324 *illus.*
ADEN, GULF OF **1**:101
Bab el-Mandeb **3**:5
map (12° 30′N 48° 0′E) **2**:232
ADENA CULTURE
Mound Builders **13**:617
North American archaeology **14**:238–239
ADENAUER, KONRAD **1**:102 *bibliog.*, *illus.*
ADENINE
genetic code **9**:79–81 *illus.*
mutation **13**:686
nucleic acid **14**:289 *illus.*
protein synthesis **15**:575
ADENOIDS **1**:102
lymphatic system **12**:475–476 *illus.*
ADENOMA **1**:102
ADENOSINE DIPHOSPHATE *see* ADP
ADENOSINE MONOPHOSPHATE *see* AMP (biology)
ADENOSINE TRIPHOSPHATE *see* ATP
ADGER (Alabama)
map (33° 23′N 87° 6′W) **1**:234
ADH *see* ANTIDIURETIC HORMONE
ADHESION **1**:102 *bibliog.*
See also COHESION
capillarity **4**:123
ADHESIVE **1**:102
epoxy resins **7**:222
gum **9**:404–405
gum arabic **9**:405
mastic **13**:216
ADIABATIC PROCESS **1**:102–103 *bibliog.*
atmosphere **2**:300
cryogenics **5**:370
Joule-Thomson effect **11**:453
ADIGE RIVER **1**:103
ADIN (California)
map (41° 12′N 120° 57′W) **4**:31
ADIPOSE TISSUE *see* FAT
ADIRONDACK MOUNTAINS **1**:103
map (44° 0′N 74° 0′W) **14**:149
New York (state) **14**:148; **14**:150–151
Placid, Lake **15**:325
ADIVAR, HALIDE EDIB *see* HALIDE EDIB ADIVAR
ADJECTIVE
parts of speech **15**:101
ADKINS v. *CHILDREN'S HOSPITAL*
West Coast Hotel Company v. *Parrish* **20**:108
ADLER, ALFRED **1**:103 *bibliog.*, *illus.*
complex (psychology) **5**:156
Freud, Sigmund **8**:329
motivation **13**:610
psychoanalysis **15**:590
ADLER, CYRUS **1**:103–104 *bibliog.*
ADLER, DANKMAR **1**:104 *bibliog.*
Auditorium Building **2**:318
ADLER, FELIX **1**:104
Ethical Culture **7**:250
ADLER, JACOB, STELLA, AND LUTHER **1**:104 *bibliog.*
ADLER, KURT HERBERT
San Francisco Opera Association **17**:54
ADLER, LARRY
harmonica **10**:51
ADLER, LUTHER **1**:104
ADLER, MORTIMER J. **1**:104
Great Books Program **9**:309
ADLER, RENATA **1**:104
ADLER, STELLA **1**:104
ADMINISTRATIVE LAW **1**:104–105 *bibliog.*
bureaucracy **3**:568
law **12**:243
law, history of **12**:247
ADMINISTRATOR (law) **1**:105
ADMIRAL (Saskatchewan)
map (49° 43′N 108° 1′W) **17**:81
ADMIRAL'S MEN **1**:105 *bibliog.*
Fortune Theatre **8**:241–242
ADMIRALTY ISLAND (Alaska)
map (57° 50′N 134° 30′W) **1**:242
ADMIRALTY ISLANDS (Bismarck Archipelago) **1**:105
map (2° 10′S 147° 0′E) **15**:72
people **2**:54 *illus.*

ADMIRALTY LAW *see* MARITIME LAW
ADMIRALTY MOUNTAINS
map (71° 45′S 168° 30′E) **2**:40
ADO-EKITI (Nigeria)
map (7° 38′N 5° 12′E) **14**:190
ADOBE **1**:105–106
Anasazi **1**:393–394
Mesa Verde National Park (Colorado) **13**:313 *illus.*
ADOLESCENCE **1**:106–107 *bibliog.*
anorexia nervosa **2**:34
birth control **3**:294
bulimia **3**:557
child development **4**:348–350
cognitive development **1**:106
Erikson, Erik **7**:230
growth **9**:380
hyperactive children **10**:347
identity formation **1**:106
initiation passage rites **15**:103–104
menstruation **13**:300–302
middle schools and junior high schools **13**:412
parent-adolescent relations **1**:107
physiological change **1**:106
Piaget, Jean **15**:287–288
sex hormones **17**:226
sexual development **17**:230
young people **20**:335–336
ADOLFO (designer)
fashion design **8**:32
ADONAIS (poem) **1**:107
ADONIS **1**:107
fertility rites **8**:60
ADOPTION AND FOSTER CARE **1**:107 *bibliog.*
behavioral genetics **3**:170
kinship **12**:86
parent **15**:84
ADOPTIONISM **1**:107 *bibliog.*
monarchianism **13**:517
Paul of Samosata **15**:117–118
ADORNO, THEODOR W. **1**:108
authoritarian personality **2**:354
ADP
ATP **2**:312
metabolism **13**:326
muscle contraction **13**:656
photosynthesis **15**:277
Todd, Lord Alexander **19**:220
ADRANO (Italy)
map (37° 40′N 14° 50′E) **11**:321
ADRENAL GLAND **1**:108 *bibliog., illus.*
endocrine system **7**:169 *illus.*
endocrine system, diseases of the **7**:170
hormones
Addison's disease **1**:101
adrenaline **1**:108
aldosterone **1**:269
corticoid **5**:278
glucocorticoid **9**:211
noradrenaline **14**:218
sex hormones **17**:226
ADRENALINE **1**:108 *bibliog.*
See also ADRENAL GLAND
Abel, John J. **1**:55
emotion **7**:157
endocrine system **7**:169
ephedrine **7**:216
fear **8**:39
hormones **10**:236
metabolism **13**:327
noradrenaline **14**:218
shock, physiologic **17**:278
sleep **17**:360
ADRENOCORTICOTROPIC HORMONE **1**:109 *bibliog.*
endocrine system **7**:169
endocrine system, diseases of the **7**:170
hormone, animal **10**:236 *table*
pigment, skin **15**:300
pituitary gland **15**:322
ADRIAN (Georgia)
map (32° 32′N 82° 35′W) **9**:114
ADRIAN (Michigan)
map (41° 54′N 84° 2′W) **13**:377
ADRIAN (Minnesota)
map (43° 38′N 95° 56′W) **13**:453
ADRIAN (Missouri)
map (38° 24′N 94° 21′W) **13**:476
ADRIAN (Oregon)
map (43° 44′N 117° 4′W) **14**:427
ADRIAN (West Virginia)
map (38° 54′N 80° 17′W) **20**:111
ADRIAN, EDGAR DOUGLAS **1**:109 *bibliog.*
ADRIAN I, POPE **1**:109 *bibliog.*
ADRIAN IV, POPE **1**:109
ADRIAN VI, POPE **1**:109
ADRIANOPLE (Turkey) *see* EDIRNE (Turkey)
ADRIANOPLE, TREATY OF **1**:109
Russo-Turkish Wars **16**:374
ADRIATIC PLATE
plate tectonics **15**:351 *map*
ADRIATIC SEA **1**:109 *map*
map (42° 30′N 16° 0′E) **13**:277
ADSORPTION **1**:110 *bibliog.*
chromatography **4**:417–418
fuller's earth **8**:358
Langmuir, Irving **12**:196
water supply **20**:54
ADULT
children's rights **4**:354
sexual development **17**:230
ADULT EDUCATION **1**:110 *bibliog.*
agricultural extension service **1**:189
career education **4**:146
Chautauqua **4**:305
correspondence school **5**:276
lyceum **12**:474
New School for Social Research **14**:142
Smith-Lever Act of 1914 **17**:372
technical education **19**:59
Thomas Edison College **19**:174
vocational education **19**:624–625
ADULTERY **1**:110
courtly love **5**:317
divorce **6**:205–206
ADVANCED PLACEMENT PROGRAM **1**:110
ADVECTION **1**:110 *bibliog.*
ADVENT **1**:111
ADVENTISTS **1**:111 *bibliog.*
breakfast cereal **3**:468
Miller, William **13**:428
ADVENTURE (ship)
Cook, James **5**:236
ADVENTURES OF AUGIE MARCH, THE (book) **1**:111
Bellow, Saul **3**:190–191
ADVENTURES OF HUCKLEBERRY FINN, THE (book) *see* *HUCKLEBERRY FINN* (book)
ADVENTURES OF TOM SAWYER, THE (book) *see* *TOM SAWYER* (book)
ADVERB
parts of speech **15**:101
ADVERSARY PROCEDURE **1**:111
ADVERTISING **1**:111–114 *bibliog., illus.*
See also PUBLIC RELATIONS
advertising agencies **1**:112
cosmetics **5**:282 *illus.*
direct mail **6**:187
fashion photography **8**:33
mail-order business **13**:67
marketing **13**:159
mass communication **13**:201–203
media **1**:112–113; **1**:114
newspaper **14**:171–172
periodical **15**:170
propaganda **15**:568
pure food and drug laws **15**:628–629
radio and television **16**:54; **16**:56; **16**:60
regulation **1**:113
sales **17**:32
soap and detergent **18**:7 *illus.*
social impact **1**:113–114
subliminal perception **18**:313
ADVISE AND CONSENT (book)
Drury, Allen **6**:283
ADVOCATE **1**:114
ADVOCATE HARBOUR (Nova Scotia)
map (45° 20′N 64° 47′W) **14**:269
ADWA (Ethiopia)
map (14° 10′N 38° 55′E) **7**:253
ADY, ENDRE **1**:114 *bibliog.*
ADYGE
Circassians **4**:435
ADZ **1**:114 *illus.*
ADZOPÉ (Ivory Coast)
map (6° 6′N 3° 52′W) **11**:335
Æ (pseudonym) *see* RUSSELL, GEORGE W.
AEACUS **1**:114
AEF *see* AMERICAN EXPEDITIONARY FORCES
AEGEAN CIVILIZATION **1**:114–118 *bibliog., illus., map*
architecture **2**:131
Greek architecture **9**:334–337
house **10**:264
art
Cycladic art **5**:402–403
Greek art **9**:337–342
Minoan **13**:458–459
sculpture **17**:159–160
The Warrior Vase **9**:329 *illus.*
Bronze Age **3**:506
costume **5**:293 *illus.*
Crete **5**:342
decline **1**:117–118
Dorians **6**:242
early Aegean peoples **1**:115–116
Enkomi **7**:206
Evans, Sir Arthur **7**:312
fertility image **19**:119 *illus.*
Gla **9**:192
Greece, ancient **9**:329
Ionia **11**:241
Knossos **12**:101–102
Minoan civilization **1**:116
Mycenaean civilization **1**:116–117; **13**:689–690 *illus.*
Orchomenos **14**:420
Phaistos **15**:218
Pylos **15**:634
Samothrace **17**:47
Schliemann, Heinrich **17**:127
Sea Peoples **17**:170
temple **19**:95
Thera **19**:160
Tiryns **19**:209
tomb **19**:230
women in society **20**:201
writing systems
Linear B **12**:353–354
AEGEAN SEA **1**:118
islands and island groups
Cyclades (Greece) **5**:402
Delos (Greece) **6**:94–95
Dodecanese (Greece) **6**:212
Euboea (Greece) **7**:261
Lesbos (Greece) **12**:296
Melos (Greece) **13**:288
Naxos (Greece) **14**:66
Rhodes (Greece) **16**:201–202
Samos (Greece) **17**:47
map (38° 30′N 25° 0′E) **9**:325
Marmara, Sea of **13**:161
AEGINA (Greece) **1**:118
Greek art **9**:340
Temple of Aphaia **2**:131 *illus.*
AEGIRINE
pyroxene **15**:638
AEGIS **1**:118
AEGYPTOPITHECUS **1**:118
Dryopithecus **6**:285
prehistoric human origins **15**:512
ÆLFRIC **1**:118 *bibliog.*
AELIAN **1**:119 *bibliog.*
AENEAS **1**:119
Triton **19**:304
AENEID (epic) **1**:119 *bibliog.*
Aeneas **1**:119
Dido **6**:161
translations
Douglas, Gavin **6**:247
Vergil **19**:551
AEOLIAN HARP **1**:119 *bibliog.*
AEOLUS **1**:119
AEOSPUS, CLAUDIUS
theater, history of the **19**:145
AEPINUS, F. U. T.
physics, history of **15**:284
AERATION
water supply **20**:53
AERIAL EXPERIMENT ASSOCIATION
Bell, Alexander Graham **3**:185
AERIAL PHOTOGRAPHY **1**:119–120 *bibliog., illus.*; **9**:103 *illus.*
archaeology **2**:118–119 *illus.*
Fairchild, Sherman Mills **8**:9
hurricane and typhoon **10**:319 *illus.*
Landsat (artificial satellite) **12**:185
Mosquito (aircraft) **13**:602
Nadar **14**:4 *illus.*
remote sensing **16**:147–148
Steichen, Edward **18**:246
surveying **18**:369
AERIAL SPORTS **1**:121–122 *bibliog., illus.*
ballooning **1**:122 *illus.*; **3**:53
barnstorming **3**:86
gliding **1**:121–122 *illus.*
Elmira (New York State) **7**:149
glider **9**:208
hang gliding **1**:122 *illus.*
parachuting and skydiving **1**:122
Garnerin, André J. **9**:49
parachute **15**:75
AERIAL SURVEYS
aerial photography **1**:119–120
photography **15**:266
AERIAL TRAMWAY
cable car **4**:6
ÆRØ ISLAND
map (54° 53′N 10° 20′E) **6**:109
AEROBEE **1**:122
rockets and missiles **16**:254
sounding rocket **18**:77
AERODYNAMICS **1**:123–124 *bibliog., illus.*
Bernoulli's law **3**:223
drag
ballistics **3**:50–51
trucking industry **19**:315
glider **9**:207–208
hydrofoil **10**:335–336
Kármán, Theodore von **12**:28
Langley, Samuel Pierpont **12**:196
Leonardo da Vinci **12**:289–291
Reynolds, Osborne **16**:191
STOL **18**:278–279
supersonic transport **18**:353
wind tunnel **20**:171–172
AEROLITE
meteor and meteorite **13**:336–337 *illus.*
AERONAUTICS *see* AERODYNAMICS; AEROSPACE INDUSTRY; AIRCRAFT; AVIATION
AERONOMY
ionosphere **11**:241–243
AEROPHONES
musical instruments **13**:676–677 *illus.*
AEROSOL **1**:124–125 *bibliog., illus.*
aerosol can **1**:125 *illus.*
propellant
fluorine **8**:187–188
organic chemistry **14**:439
Q fever **16**:3
AEROSPACE INDUSTRY **1**:125–128 *bibliog., illus., table*
American Institute of Aeronautics and Astronautics **1**:341
aviation **2**:374
Houston (Texas) **10**:281
Huntsville (Alabama) **10**:315
International Association of Machinists and Aerospace Workers **11**:218
Messerschmitt, Willy **13**:323
National Aeronautics and Space Administration **14**:28
AEROSPACE LAW *see* SPACE LAW
AEROTHERMODYNAMIC DUCT *see* RAMJET
AÉROTRAIN
air-cushion vehicle **1**:205
AESCHINES **1**:128 *bibliog.*
AESCHYLUS **1**:128–129 *bibliog., illus.*
drama **6**:257
Oresteia **14**:432
theater, history of the **19**:144
AESIR (Norse deities)
mythology **13**:702
AESOP **1**:130 *bibliog., illus.*
fable **8**:4–5
AESTHETICISM **1**:130 *bibliog.*
art
Art Nouveau **2**:210
Pre-Raphaelites **15**:519
decadence **6**:72
literature
Baudelaire, Charles **3**:128–129
Dowson, Ernest **6**:252
Gautier, Théophile **9**:62
Parnassians **15**:96
Pater, Walter **15**:110–111
Ruskin, John **16**:348
Wilde, Oscar **20**:148–149
AESTHETICS **1**:130–131 *bibliog.*
art criticism **2**:207
Baumgarten, Alexander Gottlieb **3**:130
Benjamin, Walter **3**:202
Castelvetro, Lodovico **4**:187–188
Croce, Benedetto **5**:355
Fontana, Lucio **8**:206
golden section **9**:232
Gorgias **9**:251
Huysmans, J. K. **10**:326
Langer, Suzanne K. **12**:195
Schlegel, Friedrich von **17**:124
Sontag, Susan **18**:66
Villiers de L'Isle-Adam, Philippe **19**:598
ÆTHELBERT, KING OF KENT **1**:131
ÆTHELFLÆD **1**:131
Edward the Elder, King of Wessex **7**:67
ÆTHELRED, EALDORMAN OF MERCIA
Æthelflæd **1**:131
ÆTHELRED II, KING OF ENGLAND (Æthelred the Unready) **1**:131 *bibliog.*
Wessex **20**:106
AETIUS, FLAVIUS **1**:131
Valentinian III, Roman Emperor in the West **19**:505
AETOLIA **1**:131
Greece, ancient **9**:333
AFADJOTO
map (7° 5′N 0° 35′E) **9**:164
AFANASIEV, ALEKSANDR NIKOLAYEVICH **1**:132
AFARS AND THE ISSAS, FRENCH TERRITORY OF THE *see* DJIBOUTI (country)
AFFECT, ISOLATION OF
defense mechanisms **6**:83

AFFENPINSCHER **1**:132 *illus.*; **6**:217 *illus.*
AFFIDAVIT **1**:132
AFFILIATE BROADCASTING STATIONS *see* PUBLIC BROADCASTING SYSTEM; RADIO BROADCASTING
AFFINE GEOMETRY
  geometry **9**:107
AFFIRMATIVE ACTION **1**:132 *bibliog.*
  equal opportunity **7**:223
  equal protection of the laws **7**:224
  integration, racial **11**:203
  United Steelworkers of America v. *Weber* **19**:465
  University of California v. *Bakke* **19**:470
AFFLUENT SOCIETY, THE (book)
  Galbraith, John Kenneth **9**:13
AFGHAN HOUND **1**:132 *bibliog., illus.*; **6**:216 *illus.*
AFGHANISTAN **1**:132–135 *bibliog., illus., map, table*
  archaeology
    Bamian **3**:59
  cities
    Herat **10**:134
    Kabul **12**:4
    Kandahar **12**:13
  economic activity **1**:135
  education **1**:134
    South Asian universities **18**:95–96 *table*
  flag **1**:133 *illus.*
  government **1**:135
  history **1**:135
    Karmal, Babrak **12**:28
    Mahmud of Ghazni **13**:65–66
    refugee **16**:125
  land and resources **1**:132–133
  languages
    Dravidian languages **6**:263
    Indo-Iranian languages **11**:145–146
  map (33° 0′N 65° 0′E) **2**:232
  nomad **14**:215 *illus.*
  people **1**:133–134
    Baluch **3**:57
    Kafir **12**:5
    Pathan **15**:111
    Tadzhik **19**:7
    Turkmen **19**:347
    Uzbek **19**:499
  Persian art and architecture **15**:183–187
AFL-CIO *see* AMERICAN FEDERATION OF LABOR AND CONGRESS OF INDUSTRIAL ORGANIZATIONS
AFOGNAK ISLAND (Alaska)
  map (58° 15′N 152° 30′W) **1**:242
AFONSO *see* ALFONSO for Portuguese kings named AFONSO
AFRICA **1**:135–151 *bibliog., illus., map, table*
  See also names of specific countries, e.g., ETHIOPIA; TUNISIA; etc.
  aerial photograph **7**:11 *illus.*
  agriculture **1**:148–149
    food production **1**:197 *table*
  animal life **1**:142
    savanna life **17**:98 *illus.*
  archaeology *see* AFRICAN PREHISTORY
  art *see* AFRICAN ART
  climate **1**:140–141 *map*
    sirocco **17**:328
    weather variation and extremes **20**:80–81 *tables*
  colonialism **5**:112
  dance **6**:22 *illus.*
    Ailey, Alvin **1**:202–203
    Dunham, Katherine **6**:300
  demography **1**:148
  Du Bois, W. E. B. **6**:285–286
  economy **1**:148–151
  education **1**:147
    African universities **1**:175–178
    literacy and illiteracy **12**:368
  exploration *see* EXPLORATION—Africa
  forestry and fishing **1**:150
  geologic time
    Ordovician Period **14**:421 *map*
    Permian Period **15**:175 *map*
    Precambrian rock formations **15**:492 *map*
  geology **1**:140 *map*
    East African Rift System **7**:30–31
    plate tectonics **15**:351–354 *map*
  health **1**:148
    leishmaniasis **12**:279
    trachoma **19**:258
    trypanosomiasis (sleeping sickness) **19**:322
  history *see* AFRICA, HISTORY OF; AFRICAN PREHISTORY
  industry **1**:148
  land **1**:137–142 *illus., map*
  languages *see* AFRICAN LANGUAGES
  literature *see* AFRICAN LITERATURE
  marriage **13**:164
  money **13**:525 *illus.*
  national parks **14**:40–41 *map, table*
    Kenya **12**:55 *illus.*
  people **1**:144–148 *illus., map*
    Afrikaners **1**:177–178
    Akan **1**:229
    Arabs **2**:101–106
    Ashanti **2**:229
    Azande **2**:380
    Bamileke **3**:59
    Bantu **3**:71
    Bemba **3**:194
    Berbers **3**:207–208
    Chokwe **4**:403
    Dogon **6**:223
    Edo **7**:58–59
    Ewe **8**:325
    Fang **8**:20
    Fanti **8**:21
    Fon **8**:204
    Fulani **8**:356
    Galla **9**:16
    Ganda **9**:34–35
    Hausa **10**:69
    hunter-gatherers **10**:313
    Ibibio **11**:4
    Ibo **11**:6
    Ik **11**:39
    Kabyle **12**:4
    Kamba **12**:9
    Kanuri **12**:24
    Khoikhoi **12**:67
    Kikuyu **12**:76
    Kru **12**:131
    Luba **12**:446
    Lunda **12**:462
    Luo **12**:465
    Mande **13**:111
    Mangbetu **13**:115
    Masai **13**:194–195
    Mbundu **13**:251
    Mende **13**:293–294
    Mossi **13**:605
    Ndebele **14**:68
    Nguni **14**:176
    Nilotes **14**:197
    nomad **14**:214–215
    Nuba **14**:277
    Nuer **14**:291
    Nupe **14**:296–297
    Pygmy **15**:633
    race **16**:33–35 *illus., map*
    Sahara **17**:14 *illus.*
    San **17**:49–50
    Senufo **17**:205
    Serer **17**:208
    Shona **17**:281
    Sidamo **17**:294
    Somali **18**:59
    Songhai **18**:65
    Sotho **18**:70
    Sukuma **18**:332
    Swahili **18**:375
    Swazi **18**:379–380
    Temne **19**:91
    Thonga **19**:177
    Tuareg **19**:325–326
    Turkana **19**:342
    Tutsi **19**:355–356
    Wolof **20**:199
    Xhosa **20**:312
    Yao **20**:318–319
    Yoruba **20**:331
    Zulu **20**:381–382
  physical features
    Atlas Mountains **2**:297
    Elgon, Mount **7**:137
    Great Rift Valley **9**:321–322 *illus.*
    inselberg **11**:194
    Kalahari Desert **12**:7
    Kilimanjaro **12**:76
    Libyan Desert **12**:321–322
    mountains, highest **13**:620 *table*
    Namib Desert **14**:10
    Ruwenzori **16**:377
    Sahara **17**:13–14 *illus., map*
  regions
    East Africa **7**:30
    Maghrib **13**:49
    North Africa **14**:224
    Sahel **17**:14–15
    West Africa **20**:107
  religion **1**:147
  resources **1**:143–144; **1**:149 *map*
    electrical production **15**:485 *table*
    energy consumption and production **7**:174 *table*
    oil and gas reserves **15**:209 *table*
    petroleum industry **15**:210 *table*
    water resources **20**:51 *table*
  rivers, lakes, and waterways **1**:141–142
    Albert, Lake **1**:253
    Chad, Lake **4**:266
    Congo River **5**:183–184 *map*
    Edward, Lake **7**:67
    Gambia River **9**:26
    Kivu, Lake **12**:94
    Limpopo River **12**:347
    Niger River **14**:188 *map*
    Nile River **14**:196–197 *illus., map*
    Nyasa, Lake **14**:308
    Senegal River **17**:202–203
    Tanganyika, Lake **19**:22
    Ubangi River **19**:369–370
    Victoria, Lake **19**:573–574 *map*
    Victoria Falls **19**:575
    Zambezi River **20**:352
  secret societies **17**:181
  soils **1**:142
  sports
    soccer **18**:10
  Third World **19**:170
  trade **1**:150
  transportation and communication **1**:150
    railroad **16**:74–75 *illus.*
    truck and bus registration **19**:315 *table*
  vegetation **1**:142 *map*
    acacia **1**:68
    jungle and rain forest **11**:469
    savanna life **17**:98 *illus.*
AFRICA, HISTORY OF **1**:151–160 *bibliog., illus., maps*
  See also AFRICAN PREHISTORY; EGYPT, ANCIENT; the subheading history under names of specific countries, e.g., LIBYA; MOROCCO; etc.
  exploration *see* EXPLORATION—Africa
  socialism **18**:24
  Zulu **20**:381–382
  prior to 1600
    Aksum **1**:232
    ancient kingdoms **1**:151 *map*
    Benin, Kingdom of **3**:201
    Carthage **4**:173–174
    Cyrene **5**:409–410
    European exploration **1**:152–153; **1**:157 *map*
    Kongo, Kingdom of **12**:108
    Meroë **13**:311
    Nubia **14**:277–278
    Numidia **14**:295
    Songhai (empire) **18**:65
  1600-1884
    ancient kingdoms **1**:151 *map*
    Bambara kingdoms **3**:58
    British Empire **3**:496
    Islamic revolutions **1**:155–156
    Nalatale **14**:9
    slave trade **1**:154 *illus.*; **17**:353–356 *illus., maps*
    Zulu **1**:156 *illus.*
  1884–1950
    Fashoda Incident **8**:33
    French Equatorial Africa **8**:310
    French West Africa **8**:326
    German East Africa **9**:132
    Great Britain, history of **9**:317
    Lugard, Frederick John Dealtry Lugard, 1st Baron **12**:452
    partition **1**:156–159 *maps*
    Portugal, history of **15**:454
    World War II **20**:256; **20**:258; **20**:261–263 *illus., maps*
  1950-present **1**:151
    Congo crisis **5**:183
    Cuba **5**:380
    independence movements **1**:159–160
    Nkrumah, Kwame **14**:206–207
    Organization of African Unity **14**:440
    refugee **16**:125
    slavery **17**:357
    suffrage, women's **18**:326
AFRICAN ARCHAEOLOGY *see* AFRICAN PREHISTORY
AFRICAN ART **1**:160–164 *bibliog., illus.*
  See also the subheading Africa under ARCHITECTURE
  beads and beadwork **3**:138 *illus.*
  Chokwe **4**:403
  Edo **7**:59
  Ife **11**:32
  ivory and ivory carving **11**:337 *illus.*
  masks **13**:196–197 *illus.*
  Mossi **13**:605
  Ndebele **14**:68
  Nupe **14**:297
  prehistoric art **15**:510 *illus.*
  Senufo **17**:205
  wood carving **20**:209
  Yoruba **20**:331
AFRICAN EGG-EATING SNAKE **17**:380 *illus.*
AFRICAN ELEPHANT **7**:133–134 *illus.*
AFRICAN HUNTING DOG **1**:164–165 *illus.*
AFRICAN KILLER BEE *see* KILLER BEE
AFRICAN LANGUAGES **1**:165–167 *bibliog., map*; **12**:355 *map*
  Africa **1**:146
  Afroasiatic languages **1**:166; **1**:178–181
  Akan **1**:229
  Arabic language **2**:100
  Bantu **3**:71
  Berbers **3**:207–208
  classification **1**:166–167
    Greenberg, Joseph H. **9**:350
  grammatical characteristics **1**:166
  history **1**:165
  Khoisan languages **1**:167; **12**:355 *map*
  literary languages **1**:168
  Nguni **14**:176
  Niger-Congo languages **1**:166–167
  Niger-Kordofanian languages **1**:166–167; **12**:355 *map*
  Nilo-Saharan languages **1**:166; **12**:355 *map*
  phonetic characteristics **1**:165–166
  Saharan languages **1**:166
  Sotho **18**:70
  Swahili **18**:375
AFRICAN LITERATURE **1**:167–168 *bibliog.*
  authors
    Abrahams, Peter **1**:61
    Achebe, Chinua **1**:81
    Aluko, Timothy Mofolorunso **1**:314
    Amadi, Elechi **1**:320
    Awoonor, Kofi **2**:377
    Bebey, Francis **3**:150
    Beti, Mongo **3**:231
    Campbell, Roy **4**:66
    Césaire, Aimé **4**:262
    Clark, John Pepper **5**:38
    Cloete, Stuart **5**:64
    Damas, Léon Gontran **6**:18
    Diop, Birago Ismael **6**:185
    Diop, David **6**:185
    Ekwensi, Cyprian **7**:98
    Fugard, Athol **8**:355
    Gordimer, Nadine **9**:248
    Jonker, Ingrid **11**:445
    La Guma, Alex **11**:147
    Laye, Camara **12**:252
    Mofolo, Thomas **13**:500
    Ngugi wa Thiong'o **14**:176
    Nzekwu, Onuora **14**:310
    Okara, Gabriel **14**:365
    Okigbo, Christopher **14**:366
    Paton, Alan **15**:112
    Schreiner, Olive **17**:134–135
    Sembene, Ousmane **17**:195
    Senghor, Léopold Sédar **17**:203
    Soyinka, Wole **18**:115
    Tutuola, Amos **19**:356
  English-language literature **1**:168
  French-language literature **1**:168
  Mbundu **13**:251
  Portuguese-language literature **1**:168
  religious aspects **1**:167–168
AFRICAN METHODIST EPISCOPAL CHURCH
  Allen, Richard **1**:299–300
AFRICAN MUSIC **1**:168–171 *bibliog., illus.*
  function and performance **1**:170
  influence on Latin American music and dance **12**:231
  instruments **1**:168–170 *illus.*
    banjo **3**:67
    drum **6**:282
  musicians **1**:169–170 *illus.*
  stylistic traits **1**:170
AFRICAN NATIONAL CONGRESS **1**:171–172 *bibliog.*
  South Africa **18**:83
AFRICAN PARTY FOR THE INDEPENDENCE OF GUINEA AND CAPE VERDE (PAIGC)
  Guinea-Bissau **9**:399
AFRICAN PREHISTORY **1**:171–175 *bibliog., illus., map*
  animal husbandry **2**:23 *illus.*

Australopithecus 2:345–346 *illus.*
Bantu 3:71
Capsian 4:128
Clark, John Desmond 5:38
Engaruka 7:176
Homo erectus 10:215
Homo habilis 10:216
Iron Age 11:271–272
Laetolil 12:163
Leakey (family) 12:258–259
Makapansgat 13:77
Mapungubwe 13:142
Nalatale 14:9
Olduvai Gorge 14:376–377 *illus.*
Olorgesailie 14:381
Omo 14:388
Paleolithic Period 15:38–40
prehistoric humans 15:511–517
Proconsul 15:561
Skull 1470 17:346
Sterkfontein 18:260
Tassili n'Ajjer 19:43
Taung skull 19:45
Ternifine man 19:118
Zimbabwe Ruins 20:366–367 *illus.*
AFRICAN QUEEN, THE (book)
Forester, C. S. 8:230
AFRICAN REVIEW (periodical)
Mayfield, Julian 13:246
AFRICAN UNIVERSITIES 1:175–178 *bibliog., table*
AFRICAN VIOLET 1:177 *illus.*; 10:275 *illus.*
AFRICAN WILDCAT *see* KAFFIR CAT
AFRIKA CORPS
World War II 20:256
AFRIKANERS 1:145 *illus.*; 1:177–178 *bibliog., illus.*
Botha, Louis 3:415
commando 5:137
concentration camp 5:168
Great Trek 9:322–323
Hertzog, James Barry Munnik 10:149
Kruger, Paul 12:131
language
Germanic languages 9:135–137 *tables*
Malan, Daniel F. 13:79
Natal (province in South Africa) 14:26
Orange Free State (South Africa) 14:415
Pretorius, Andries 15:534
Pretorius, Marthinus Wessel 15:534
Smuts, Jan 17:374–375
South Africa 18:80; 18:81 *illus.*; 18:82
South African War 18:83–84 *map*
Xhosa 20:312
AFRO-AMERICAN CULTS 1:178
voodoo 19:634–635
AFRO-AMERICAN LITERATURE *see* BLACK AMERICAN LITERATURE
AFRO-AMERICANS *see* BLACK AMERICANS
AFROASIATIC LANGUAGES 1:178–181 *bibliog., map*; 12:355 *map*
African languages 1:166
Arabic language 2:100
Aramaic 1:179
alphabet 20:294 *table*
Middle East, history of the 13:401
Asian languages 2:244 *map*
Canaanite 1:179
Ebla 7:36
Hebrew language 10:101
characteristics 1:180–181
classification 1:178–180
Cushitic 1:180
Hamites 10:29
Hausa 10:69
Hebrew language 10:101
linguistic investigation 1:181
Nuba 14:277
Rosetta Stone 16:317
Semites 17:197–198
writing systems, evolution of 20:291–295 *illus.*
AFSCME *see* AMERICAN FEDERATION OF STATE, COUNTY, AND MUNICIPAL EMPLOYEES
AFSHAR (dynasty)
Nadir Shah 14:5
AFTERBIRTH *see* PLACENTA
AFTERIMAGES 1:181
AFTERNOON OF A FAUN, THE 1:181 *bibliog.*
Ballets Russes de Serge Diaghilev 3:48 *illus.*
Nijinsky, Vaslav 14:194
AFTON (New York)
map (42° 14'N 75° 32'W) 14:149
AFTON (Oklahoma)
map (36° 42'N 94° 58'W) 14:368
AFTON (Wyoming)
map (42° 44'N 110° 56'W) 20:301
AFYON (Turkey)
map (38° 45'N 30° 33'E) 19:343
AFZELIUS, ARVID AUGUST 1:181
AGA KHAN 1:181
AGADE
Kish 12:90
Lagash 12:165
AGADEZ (Niger) 14:187 *illus., table*
map (16° 58'N 7° 59'E) 14:187
AGADIR (Morocco) 1:181
AGALTA CORDILLERA MOUNTAINS
map (15° 0'N 85° 53'W) 10:218
AGAM, YAACOV 1:181
AGAMA 1:181–182 *bibliog.*; 17:98 *illus.*
AGAMEMNON (mythology) 1:181–182
Electra 7:105
Iliad 11:40
AGAMMAGLOBULINEMIA
immunodeficiency disease 11:59
AGANA (Guam) 1:182
AGANIPPE 1:182
AGAR 1:182 *bibliog.*
gel 9:69
gelatin 9:69
AGARTALA (India)
map (23° 49'N 91° 16'E) 11:80
AGASSIZ, LOUIS RODOLPHE 1:182 *bibliog., illus.*
Putnam, Frederic Ward 15:632
AGATE (Colorado)
map (39° 28'N 103° 56'W) 5:116
AGATE (mineral) 1:182–183 *illus.*; 9:74 *illus.*; 13:440 *illus.*
quartz 16:14
AGAVE 1:183
tequila 19:114
yucca 20:339
AGAWAM (Massachusetts)
map (42° 5'N 72° 37'W) 13:206
AGE *see* AGING; LIFE SPAN
AGE OF ANXIETY, THE (book)
Auden, W. H. 2:318
AGE OF CONSENT 1:183
AGE-DATING
dendrochronology 6:106–107
graptolite 9:294
radiometric age-dating 16:65–67
AGE OF REASON *see* AUGUSTAN AGE; ENLIGHTENMENT
AGEE, JAMES 1:183 *bibliog.*
Evans, Walker 7:313
AGEN (France)
map (44° 12'N 0° 37'E) 8:260
AGENA (rocket) 1:183 *illus.*
Gemini program 9:72–73
AGENCE FRANCE-PRESSE
press agencies and syndicates 15:533
AGENCE HAVAS
press agencies and syndicates 15:533
AGENCY (Iowa)
map (41° 0'N 92° 18'W) 11:244
AGENCY FOR INTERNATIONAL DEVELOPMENT 1:183 *bibliog.*
AGENT (law) 1:183–184
business law 3:588
AGENT ORANGE (2, 4, 5–T)
chemical and biological warfare 4:312
herbicide 10:135–136
pollutants, chemical 15:410
AGERATUM 1:184 *illus.*
AGESILAUS II, KING OF SPARTA 1:184 *bibliog.*
AGGREGATION 1:184
colloidal state 5:104–105
AGGRESSION 1:184–185 *bibliog.*
animal behavior 2:12 *illus.*; 2:17–18
animal communication 2:18–19
animal courtship and mating 2:21 *illus.*
conflict theory 5:178–179
frustration 8:350
hyperactive children 10:347
Lorenz, Konrad 12:414
sadism 17:10
Siamese fighting fish 17:290
social psychology 18:13
AGINCOURT, BATTLE OF 1:185 *bibliog.*
uniform 11:164 *illus.*
AGING 1:185–186 *bibliog.*
connective tissue 5:196
death and dying 6:68–69
degenerative diseases
Alzheimer's disease 1:320
atherosclerosis 2:291–292
eye diseases 7:351
osteoarthritis 14:457
osteoporosis 14:458
senility 17:203
geriatrics 9:122
life span 12:331
menopause 13:299
middle age 13:391
old age 14:373
Stanford-Binet test 18:217–218
AGLIPAY, GREGORIO 1:186
AGNATHA 1:186
AGNEW, SPIRO T. 1:186 *bibliog.*
Maryland 13:193
Nixon, Richard M. 14:206
Republican party 16:175
vice-president of the United States 19:570
AGNI (fire-god) 13:699 *illus.*
AGNON, S. Y. 1:187 *bibliog.*
AGNOSTICISM 1:187 *bibliog.*
AGORA 1:187
Greek architecture 9:334
ruins in ancient Athens 9:329 *illus.*
stoa 18:273
AGORAPHOBIA 1:187
AGOSTINO DI DUCCIO 1:187 *bibliog.*
AGOTY, JACOB FABIAN GAUTHIER D' *see* GAUTHIER D'AGOTY, JACOB FABIAN
AGOUTI 1:187 *bibliog., illus.*
AGRA (India) 1:187–188
map (27° 11'N 78° 1'E) 11:80
Mogul art and architecture 13:501
Taj Mahal 19:14–15
AGRANULOCYTOSIS 1:188
AGRARIANS AND FUGITIVES (literary group) *see* FUGITIVES AND AGRARIANS (literary group)
AGREEMENT OF THE PEOPLE
Levelers 12:302
AGRI DAGI *see* ARARAT, MOUNT
AGRIBUSINESS 1:188 *bibliog.*
See also AGRICULTURE AND THE FOOD SUPPLY; FOOD INDUSTRY
irrigation 11:280–283
AGRICOLA, GEORGIUS 1:188 *bibliog.*
De re metallica 6:62
dowsing 6:252
mineral 13:439
AGRICOLA, GNAEUS JULIUS 1:188 *bibliog.*
AGRICULTURAL ADJUSTMENT ADMINISTRATION 1:188 *bibliog.*
Roosevelt, Franklin Delano 16:308
United States v. *Butler* 19:464
AGRICULTURAL EDUCATION
agricultural extension service 1:189
agriculture and the food supply 1:198
farms and farming 8:27
land-grant colleges 12:178
Morrill Acts 13:588
AGRICULTURAL EXTENSION SERVICE 1:189
Smith-Lever Act of 1914 17:372
4-H program 8:253
AGRICULTURAL MARKETING ACT
Hoover, Herbert 10:229
AGRICULTURAL STABILIZATION AND CONSERVATION SERVICE, U.S.
Agriculture, U.S. Department of 1:193
AGRICULTURE, HISTORY OF 1:189–193 *bibliog., illus.*
Africa
Egypt, ancient 7:84 *illus.*
Engaruka 7:176
animal husbandry 2:22–25
Asia
Asia, history of 2:249; 2:251
China, history of 4:370
Indus civilization 11:153
Middle East, history of the 13:400–401
Canada 1:192
culture 5:385
draft horse 6:254
England
Townshend, Charles Townshend, 2d Viscount 19:255
Tull, Jethro 19:330–331
Europe 1:190–191
European prehistory 7:301–302
fertilizer 8:61–62
Indians, American 11:117; 11:118; 11:120; 11:130–134
Hohokam culture 10:199
Mississippian Mound Builders 13:617
North America c.1500 11:125 *map*
North American archaeology 14:238–240
South America c.1500 11:133 *map*
Industrial Revolution 11:158
irrigation 11:282–283
Mesoamerica 1:190
Chibcha 4:340
Chimu 4:359
Inca 11:72
Macneish, Richard S. 13:35
Maya 13:244
Middle Ages 1:190–191; 13:394
enclosure 7:163
manorialism 13:127
Neolithic Period 14:84
peasant 15:128–129
plow 15:369–370 *illus.*
pollen stratigraphy 15:407
prehistoric humans 15:516–517
Rome, ancient 1:190
Ceres (mythology) 4:260
Demeter (mythology) 6:96
rubber 16:333
slavery 17:351–357
technology, history of 19:61–66; 19:68
United States 1:192–193
Agricultural Adjustment Administration 1:188
Carver, George Washington 4:178–179
Deere, John 6:81
Dust Bowl 6:308
Hatch Acts 10:68
McCormick, Cyrus Hall 13:10
Smith-Lever Act of 1914 17:372
Watson, Elkanah 20:67
Whitney, Eli 20:141
AGRICULTURE, U.S. DEPARTMENT OF 1:193–194 *bibliog.*
agricultural extension service 1:189
flag 8:148 *illus.*
Food Stamp Program 8:212
4-H program 8:253
government regulation 9:271
National Forest System 14:32
public health 15:608
Secretary of Agriculture *see* articles on specific presidents, e.g., EISENHOWER, DWIGHT D.; ROOSEVELT, FRANKLIN DELANO; etc.
Washington, D.C. 20:41 *map*
AGRICULTURE AND THE FOOD SUPPLY 1:194–199 *bibliog., illus., map, tables*
See also FARMS AND FARMING; FOOD INDUSTRY; the subheading agriculture under names of countries
Africa 1:149 *map*
agribusiness 1:188
agricultural pests 1:196
aphid 2:77
cutworm 5:398
fruit fly 8:347
grasshopper 9:299
insect 11:193
Japanese beetle 11:379
June bug 11:467
locust 12:392
mite 13:484
mouse 13:626
parasitic diseases 15:82
pesticides 15:196–198
quelea 16:22
ricebird 16:209
snail 17:376
tayra 19:51
termite 19:116
thrips 19:182–183
treehopper 19:290
weevil 20:91
whitefly 20:139
agricultural wastes
waste disposal systems 20:46–47
animal husbandry 2:22–25
arable land 1:195–196
Asia 2:245; 2:247–248 *map*
beekeeping 3:161
cattle and cattle raising 4:214–217
climate 5:55
conservation 5:203
cooperative 5:244–245
dairying 6:7–10
diet, human 6:164
drought 6:273–274
egg production 7:72
employment and unemployment 7:159
women in society 20:204 *table*
energy use 1:196–197
Europe 7:278 *map*
European Economic Community 7:300
factory farming 8:6

AGRICULTURE AND THE FOOD SUPPLY (cont.)
fertilizer 8:61–62
Food and Agriculture Organization 8:208
food production 1:195–198 *map, table*
grain 9:281–282
grass 9:295
herbicide 10:135–136
manioc 13:118
meat and meat packing 13:257–258
migrant labor 13:417
milk 13:423
mushrooms 13:661
nitrogen cycle 14:203
North America 14:227–228; 14:231 *map*; 14:234–235 *illus.*
pig 15:298–299
plankton 15:332
plant 15:340–342
pollen stratigraphy 15:408
population 15:433
population genetics 15:440
poultry 15:473–475
prehistoric humans 15:516–517
remote sensing 16:147
Landsat (artificial satellite) 12:185
rice 16:207–208
sheep 17:248–249
slash-and-burn agriculture 17:350
soil 18:36–38
South America 18:90 *map*
soybean 18:115
subsistence agriculture 1:195
sugar production 18:328–330
technology
Borlaug, Norman Ernest 3:401
factory farming 8:6
food technology 8:213
gene bank 9:76
genetic engineering 9:84
green revolution 9:348
irrigation 11:280–283
plant breeding 15:342–343
technology, history of 19:61–66; 19:68
trucking industry 19:314; 19:315
vegetable 19:531–534
wheat 20:124–126
AGRIGENTO (Sicily) 1:199
map (37° 18′N 13° 35′E) 11:321
AGRIMONY 1:199
AGRINÍON (Greece)
map (38° 37′N 21° 24′E) 9:325
AGRIPPA, MARCUS VIPSANIUS 1:199 *bibliog.*
AGRIPPA I (Herod Agrippa)
Herod (dynasty) 10:144
AGRIPPA II (Herod Agrippa)
Herod (dynasty) 10:144
AGRIPPINA II 1:199
Nero, Roman Emperor 14:90
Rome, ancient 16:302
AGRONOMY
aerial photography 1:120
agriculture and the food supply 1:195–196 *illus.*
farms and farming 8:24–28
soil 18:36–38
AGSUMAL SABKHA
map (24° 21′N 12° 52′W) 13:585
AGT, ANDREAS VAN
Netherlands 14:103
AGU *see* AMERICAN GEOPHYSICAL UNION
AGUA CALIENTE (Mexico)
map (23° 20′N 105° 20′W) 13:357
AGUA CALIENTE, MOUNT
map (26° 27′N 106° 12′W) 13:357
AGUA VOLCANO
map (14° 28′N 90° 45′W) 9:389
AGUADA (Puerto Rico)
map (18° 23′N 67° 11′W) 15:614
AGUADA DE GUERRA (Argentina)
map (41° 4′S 68° 25′W) 2:149
AGUADA DE PASAJEROS (Cuba)
map (22° 23′N 80° 51′W) 5:377
AGUADILLA (Puerto Rico)
map (18° 26′N 67° 9′W) 15:614
AGUADULCE (Panama)
map (8° 15′N 80° 33′W) 15:55
AGUÁN RIVER
map (15° 57′N 85° 44′W) 10:218
AGUASCALIENTES (Mexico) 1:199
map (21° 53′N 102° 18′W) 13:357
AGUASCALIENTES (state in Mexico) 1:199
AGUILA (Arizona)
map (33° 56′N 113° 11′W) 2:160
AGUILAR (Colorado)
map (37° 24′N 104° 46′W) 5:116
AGUILERA, JAIME ROLDOS *see* ROLDOS AGUILERA, JAIME
AGUINALDO, EMILIO 1:199–200 *bibliog.*
Funston, Frederick 8:369
AGUIRRE, LOPE DE 1:200
Orinoco River 14:444
AGULHAS, CAPE 1:200
map (34° 52′S 20° 0′E) 18:79
AGULHAS CURRENT 1:200
ocean currents and wind systems, worldwide 14:322–323 *maps*
AGUSAN RIVER
map (9° 0′N 125° 31′E) 15:237
AGUSTÍN I, EMPEROR OF MEXICO *see* ITURBIDE, AGUSTÍN DE
AHAB, KING OF ISRAEL 1:200
Samaria 17:45
AHAD HA-AM *see* ACHAD HA-AM
AHAGGAR MOUNTAINS
map (23° 0′N 6° 30′E) 1:287
AHAGGAR PLATEAU
map (21° 0′N 6° 0′E) 1:287
AHAZ, KING OF JUDAH 1:200
AHIDJO, AHMADOU
Cameroon 4:61
AHITHOPHEL 1:200
AHLEN (Germany, East and West)
map (51° 46′N 7° 53′E) 9:140
AHLIN, LARS 1:200
AHMAD III *see* AHMED III, SULTAN OF THE OTTOMAN EMPIRE
AHMADABAD (India) 1:200
map (23° 2′N 72° 37′E) 11:80
AHMADU BIN HAMMADI BOUBOU
Africa, history of 1:155
AHMAR MOUNTAINS
map (9° 15′N 41° 0′E) 7:253
AHMED, FAKHRUDDIN ALI
India 11:88
AHMED, KHONDAKER MOSHTAQUE *see* MOSHTAQUE AHMED, KHONDAKER
AHMED III, SULTAN OF THE OTTOMAN EMPIRE 1:200 *bibliog.*
Levnî, Ressam 12:304
AHMED BEY ZOGU *see* ZOG I, KING OF ALBANIA
AHMET HAŞIM 1:200–201
AHMOSE I, KING OF EGYPT 1:201
AHMOSE II, KING OF EGYPT 1:201
AHO, JUHANI
Finnish literature 8:99
AHOSKIE (North Carolina)
map (36° 17′N 76° 59′W) 14:242
AHRENSBURGIAN INDUSTRY (archaeology)
Hamburgian 10:27
AHRIMAN
Zoroastrianism 20:380
AHUACATLÁN (Mexico)
map (21° 3′N 104° 29′W) 13:357
AHUACHAPÁN (El Salvador)
map (13° 55′N 89° 51′W) 7:100
AHURA MAZDA
Zoroastrianism 20:379–380 *illus.*
AHVAZ (Iran)
map (31° 19′N 48° 42′E) 11:250
AHVENANMAA ISLANDS
map (60° 15′N 20° 0′E) 8:95
AIA *see* AMERICAN INSTITUTE OF ARCHITECTS
AIAA *see* AMERICAN INSTITUTE OF AERONAUTICS AND ASTRONAUTICS
AIBS *see* AMERICAN INSTITUTE OF BIOLOGICAL SCIENCES
AID TO FAMILIES WITH DEPENDENT CHILDREN
social and welfare services 18:17–18
AÏDA (opera) 1:201
Mariette, Auguste 13:152
Verdi, Giuseppe 19:549–550
AIDS (disease) 1:201 *bibliog.*
AIEA (Hawaii)
map (21° 23′N 157° 56′W) 10:72
AIGRETTE
egret 7:74
AIGUÁ (Uruguay)
map (34° 12′S 54° 45′W) 19:488
AIJAL (India)
map (23° 44′N 92° 43′E) 11:80
AIKEN (South Carolina)
map (33° 34′N 81° 43′W) 18:98
AIKEN (county in South Carolina)
map (33° 30′N 81° 40′W) 18:98
AIKEN, CONRAD 1:201–202 *bibliog., illus.*
AIKEN, GEORGE DAVID 1:202 *bibliog.*
AIKEN, HOWARD HATHAWAY 1:202
computer 5:160
AIKEN, JOAN 1:202
AIKIDO
martial arts 13:177–178 *illus.*
AILANTHUS 1:202 *illus.*
AILEY, ALVIN 1:202–203 *bibliog., illus.*; 6:28 *illus.*
modern dance 13:497 *illus.*
AILLY, PIERRE D' 1:203 *bibliog.*
AIM *see* AMERICAN INDIAN MOVEMENT
AÏN HANECH (Tunisia) 1:203 *bibliog.*
AINSWORTH (Nebraska)
map (42° 33′N 99° 52′W) 14:70
AINU 1:203 *bibliog., illus.*; 16:34 *illus.*
Japan 11:363
passage rites 15:103
Ural-Altaic languages 19:476
AIP *see* AMERICAN INSTITUTE OF PHYSICS
AIR 1:203–204
See also ATMOSPHERE
advection 1:110
air pressure 1:203
compressor 5:157
humidifier 10:302
humidity 10:302
lapse rate 12:206
liquid, neon 14:85
microclimate 13:384–385
nitrogen 14:202
oxygen 14:476–478
refraction 16:124
wind 20:168–170
AIR BAG
safety, automotive 17:10–11
AIR BLADDER *see* SWIM BLADDER
AIR BRAKE
brake 3:451
Westinghouse, George 20:117
AIR CONDITIONING 1:204 *bibliog., illus.*
heat pump 10:98–99
Joule-Thomson effect 11:453
Legionnaires' disease 12:274
refrigeration 16:125
solar energy 18:41
thermostat 19:167 *illus.*
AIR-CUSHION VEHICLE 1:204–205 *bibliog., illus.*
naval vessels 14:57
AIR FORCE 1:206–209 *bibliog., illus.*
See also AIRCRAFT, MILITARY; LUFTWAFFE; ROYAL AIR FORCE; the subheading air force under names of specific countries, e.g., UNITED KINGDOM; UNITED STATES; etc.
aviation 2:370–372
defense, national 6:82 *table*
military academies 13:420
rockets and missiles 16:254–256 *illus.*
strategy and tactics, military 18:291
AIR LAW 1:209 *bibliog.*
See also SPACE LAW
airplane hijacking 1:222
AIR MASS 1:209
atmosphere 2:300
Rossby waves 16:318–319
AÏR MASSIF MOUNTAINS
map (18° 0′N 8° 30′E) 14:187
AIR NATIONAL GUARD
National Guard 14:34
AIR POLLUTION *see* POLLUTION, ENVIRONMENTAL
AIR RIGHTS 1:209
AIR SHOWS *see* BARNSTORMING
AIR SICKNESS
motion sickness 13:610
space medicine 18:133
AIR TAXI
aviation 2:372
AIR-TRAFFIC CONTROL *see* TRAFFIC CONTROL
AIR TRANSPORTATION *see* AIRCRAFT; AVIATION; TRANSPORTATION
AIR TRANSPORTATION DEREGULATION ACT OF 1978
airport 1:225
aviation 2:374
Civil Aeronautics Board 5:9
AIRBORNE TROOPS 1:210 *bibliog.*; 2:181 *illus.*
strategy and tactics, military 18:290
World War II 20:273 *illus.*
AIRBORNE WARNING AND CONTROL SYSTEM 1:210
military warning and detection systems 13:422
AIRBRUSH 1:210 *bibliog.*
AIRCRAFT 1:210–214 *bibliog., illus.*
See also AIRCRAFT, MILITARY; AIRPORT; AIRSHIP; AVIATION
aerodynamics 1:123–124 *illus.*
aerospace industry 1:125–128
Concorde 5:171
design 1:210–212
aviation 2:372; 2:374
titanium 19:211
engine
aviation 2:372
ramjet 16:80–81
Rolls-Royce 16:272
turbine 19:340
turbojet 11:406 *illus.*
flight 8:164
sound barrier 18:74
flight simulator 19:56 *illus.*
heavier-than-air aircraft
autogiro 2:356
glider 9:207–208
helicopter 10:111–112
history of 2:370–375 *illus.*
seaplane 17:174
STOL 18:278–279
supersonic transport 18:353
VTOL 19:639
labor union
United Auto Workers 19:401
lighter-than-air aircraft
airship 1:226–228
balloon 3:51–53
parts
guidance and control systems 9:393
jet propulsion 11:406–407
propeller 15:570
rudder 16:337–338
races *see* AERIAL SPORTS; BARNSTORMING
reconnaissance
aircraft, military 1:214
hurricane and typhoon 10:319
weather 13:343 *illus.*
tourism 19:252
United States
Boeing 747 2:372
Curtiss Jenny 5:395–396
DC-3 6:57
Ford Tri-motor 8:223–224
Piper Cub 15:312
Spirit of St. Louis 12:351
X-15 20:311
wind tunnel 20:171–172
AIRCRAFT, MILITARY 1:206 *illus.*; 1:214–220 *bibliog., illus., table*; 2:370–373 *illus.*
See also AIR FORCE; AVIATION
airborne troops 1:210
Airborne Warning and Control System 1:210 *illus.*
aircraft carrier 1:220–221 *illus.*
aircraft manufacture 2:374
bomb 3:373
defense, national 6:82 *table*
France 1:218–219 *table*
Mirage 13:462–463
SPAD 18:138
Germany 1:218–219 *table*
See also LUFTWAFFE
Dornier bomber 20:255 *illus.*
Fokker D-VII 8:194 *illus.*
Fokker E-III 2:370–371 *illus.*
Gotha (aircraft) 9:254
Messerschmitt Bf-109 13:323
Stuka 18:308 *illus.*
V-1 19:500
V-2 19:500
Great Britain 1:218–219 *table*
See also ROYAL AIR FORCE
Hurricane 10:317
Mosquito 13:602
Sopwith Camel 18:68
Spitfire 18:190
helicopter 10:112
VTOL 19:639
history 1:214–217; 2:370–373 *illus.*
Italy 1:218 *table*
Japan 1:219 *table*
Zero 20:361
machine gun 13:23
military warning and detection systems 13:421–422
naval vessels 14:56
night sights 14:193
parachute 15:75
ramjet 16:80–81
rockets and missiles 16:254–256 *illus.*
strategy and tactics, military 18:291
Union of Soviet Socialist Republics 1:218–219 *table*
MiG 13:416
Tupolev V-G "Backfire B" 1:216 *illus.*
United States 1:218–219 *table*
B-1 bomber 3:3–4
B-17 Flying Fortress 3:4
B-24 Liberator 3:4
B-29 Superfortress 3:4

B-52 Stratofortress **3**:4
Corsair **5**:277
DC-3, C-47 Skytrain **6**:57
F-15 Eagle **8**:3
F-16 Fighting Falcon **8**:3
F-86 Sabre **8**:3
Grumman, Leroy **9**:382
Grumman TBF-1 Avenger **9**:382
Mustang **13**:685
P-38 Lightning **15**:3
P-40 **15**:3
U-2 **19**:369
weapons **20**:75
World War I *see* WORLD WAR I
World War II *see* WORLD WAR II
AIRCRAFT CARRIER **1**:220–221 *bibliog., illus.*
naval vessels **14**:57 *illus.*
navy **14**:64–65
World War II **20**:265–266 *illus.*
AIRCRAFT INSTRUMENTATION
altimeter **1**:313
guidance and control systems **9**:393–394
radar **16**:38–40
AIREDALE TERRIER **1**:222 *illus.*; **6**:220 *illus.*
AIRFLOW PATTERN
aerodynamics **1**:123 *illus.*
AIRGLOW **1**:222 *bibliog.*
auroras **2**:325
OGO **14**:355
AIRLINER *see* AIRCRAFT
AIRLANGGA **1**:222
AIRMAIL **1**:222 *bibliog.*
aviation **2**:374
first regular service **15**:460 *illus.*
AIRPLANE *see* AIRCRAFT; AIRCRAFT, MILITARY; AIRPORT; AVIATION; SEAPLANE; names of specific aircraft, e.g., DC-3; SPITFIRE (aircraft); etc.
AIRPLANE HIJACKING **1**:222 *bibliog.*
air law **1**:209
Entebbe (Uganda) **7**:208
Mogadishu (Somalia) **13**:500
piracy **15**:312–313
AIRPORT **1**:223–225 *bibliog., illus., table*
airline deregulation **1**:225
aviation **2**:374–375
history **1**:223
Kennedy International Airport **17**:4 *illus.*
major airports worldwide **19**:281 *map*
Newark International Airport **14**:132 *illus.*
noise **1**:225
radar **16**:39–40
security **1**:225
traffic control **16**:38 *illus.*; **19**:264
types of airports **1**:223–224
AIRSHIP **1**:226–228 *bibliog., illus.*; **20**:57 *illus.*
aircraft **1**:212
Akron **1**:232
Graf Zeppelin **9**:278
Hindenburg **10**:168–169
Macon **1**:232
R-34 and *R-101* **16**:29
Shenandoah **17**:255
history **1**:227–228
Curtiss, Glenn Hammond **5**:395
Nobile, Umberto **14**:211
Santos-Dumont, Alberto **17**:70–71
Zeppelin, Ferdinand, Graf von **20**:360–361
military use **1**:227–228
World War I **20**:220; **20**:229; **20**:246–247
AIRY, SIR GEORGE BIDDELL **1**:228 *bibliog.*
Airy disk **1**:228
AIRY DISK **1**:228
AISHA **1**:228
Ali **1**:292
AISNE RIVER **1**:228
map (49° 26′N 2° 50′E) **8**:260
World War I **20**:225 *map*; **20**:241
AISSA, MOUNT
map (32° 51′N 0° 30′W) **1**:287
AITKEN, ROBERT GRANT **1**:228
AITKIN (Minnesota)
map (46° 32′N 93° 43′W) **13**:453
AITKIN (county in Minnesota)
map (46° 37′N 93° 20′W) **13**:453
AIX-EN-PROVENCE (France) **1**:228–229
AIX-LA-CHAPELLE (West Germany) *see* AACHEN (West Germany)
AIX-LA-CHAPELLE, TREATIES OF **1**:229
Devolution, War of **6**:143
French and Indian Wars **8**:313
lands acquired **8**:269 *map*
AIYINA (Greece) *see* AEGINA (Greece)
AJACCIO (Corsica) **1**:229
map (41° 55′N 8° 44′E) **8**:260
AJANTA (India) **1**:229 *bibliog.*
cave temples **19**:97 *illus.*
Mogul art and architecture **13**:501
wall painting **2**:251 *illus.*; **11**:95 *illus.*
AJANTA RANGE (mountain range)
map (20° 30′N 76° 0′E) **11**:80
AJAR, ÉMILE *see* GARY, ROMAIN
AJAX **1**:229
AJDABIYA (Libya)
map (30° 48′N 20° 14′E) **12**:320
AJMAN
United Arab Emirates **19**:400
AJO (Arizona)
map (32° 22′N 112° 52′W) **2**:160
AKADEMIE DER WISSENSCHAFTEN DER DDR **1**:229
AKAN **1**:229
AKBAR, MOGUL EMPEROR OF INDIA **1**:229–230 *bibliog., illus.*
Fatehpur Sikri **8**:34
India, history of **11**:91
Mogul art and architecture **13**:500–501
seige of Chitor **11**:90 *illus.*
AKC *see* AMERICAN KENNEL CLUB
AKEAKE **1**:230
AKELEY (Minnesota)
map (47° 0′N 94° 44′W) **13**:453
AKENSIDE, MARK **1**:230
AKERS (Louisiana)
map (30° 17′N 90° 24′W) **12**:430
AKETI (Zaire)
map (2° 44′N 23° 46′E) **20**:350
AKHAIA *see* ACHAEA
AKHENATEN **1**:230 *bibliog., illus.*; **7**:82 *illus.*
Amarna, Tell el- **1**:321–322
Egypt, ancient **7**:85
Nefertiti **14**:77
AKHIOK (Alaska)
map (56° 57′N 154° 10′W) **1**:242
AKHMATOVA, ANNA **1**:230 *bibliog.*
AKHMIM (Egypt)
map (26° 34′N 31° 44′E) **7**:76
AKIACHAK (Alaska)
map (60° 55′N 161° 27′W) **1**:242
AKIBA BEN JOSEPH (Rabbi Akiva) **1**:230 *bibliog.*; **11**:461 *illus.*
AKIHITO **1**:231 *bibliog.*
AKIMISKI ISLAND
map (53° 0′N 81° 20′W) **14**:393
AKITA (dog) **1**:231 *bibliog., illus.*; **6**:215 *illus.*
AKITA (Japan)
map (39° 43′N 140° 7′E) **11**:361
AKKAD **1**:231 *bibliog., map*; **3**:8 *map*
Asia, history of **2**:249
Ebla **7**:36
Gilgamesh, Epic of **9**:180
Mesopotamia **13**:316 *map*
Mesopotamian art and architecture **13**:319
Sargon, King **17**:78
Sumer **18**:339
Ur **19**:474
AKKADIAN LANGUAGE
languages, extinct **12**:198
writing systems, evolution of **20**:295
AKKO (Israel) *see* ACRE (Israel)
AKLAVIK (Northwest Territories)
map (68° 12′N 135° 0′W) **14**:258
AKMAK **1**:231 *bibliog.*
AKNATON *see* AKHENATEN
AKOBO RIVER
map (7° 48′N 33° 3′E) **7**:253
AKPATOK ISLAND
map (60° 25′N 68° 0′W) **16**:18
AKRAGAS (Sicily) *see* AGRIGENTO (Sicily)
AKRANES (Iceland)
map (64° 18′N 22° 2′W) **11**:17
AKRON (Colorado)
map (40° 10′N 103° 13′W) **5**:116
AKRON (Indiana)
map (41° 2′N 86° 1′W) **11**:111
AKRON (Ohio) **1**:231–232
map (41° 5′N 81° 31′W) **14**:357
Soap Box Derby **18**:6
AKRON* AND *MACON (airships) **1**:232
airship **1**:228
AKSAKOV, KONSTANTIN SERGEYEVICH **1**:232 *bibliog.*
AKSAKOV, SERGEI TIMOFEYEVICH **1**:232
AKSARAY (Turkey)
map (38° 23′N 34° 3′E) **19**:343
AKSEHIR (Turkey)
map (38° 21′N 31° 25′E) **19**:343
AKSENOV, VASILY PAVLOVICH **1**:232
AKSENOV, VLADIMIR **1**:232
AKSUM (Ethiopia) **1**:232
Africa, history of **1**:151
AKURE (Nigeria)
map (7° 15′N 5° 12′E) **14**:190
AKUREYRI (Iceland)
map (65° 44′N 18° 8′W) **11**:17
AKUTAGAWA RYUNOSUKE **1**:232
AKUTAN (Alaska)
map (54° 8′N 165° 46′W) **1**:242
AL- *see* under the second element of the name for Arabic names beginning with AL- not listed below
AL-AHMADI (Kuwait)
map (29° 5′N 48° 4′E) **12**:141
AL-AKHDAR MOUNTAINS
map (23° 15′N 57° 20′E) **14**:386
AL-AMARA (Iraq)
map (31° 50′N 47° 9′E) **11**:255
AL-AQABA (Jordan)
map (29° 31′N 35° 0′E) **11**:447
AL-ARAB RIVER
map (9° 2′N 29° 28′E) **18**:320
AL-ARD, CAPE
map (29° 21′N 48° 5′E) **12**:141
AL-ASSAD, LAKE
map (36° 5′N 38° 10′E) **18**:412
AL-BAB (Syria)
map (36° 22′N 37° 31′E) **18**:412
AL-BADARI (Egypt)
map (26° 59′N 31° 25′E) **7**:76
AL-BARR, CAPE
map (25° 47′N 50° 34′E) **3**:24
AL-BATRUN (Lebanon)
map (34° 15′N 35° 39′E) **12**:265
AL-BAYDA (Libya) *see* BEIDA (Libya)
AL-BIQA VALLEY
Lebanon **12**:264
AL-DAFRA (region in United Arab Emirates)
map (23° 25′N 53° 25′E) **19**:401
AL-DAHNA DESERT
map (24° 30′N 48° 10′E) **17**:94
AL-DAHY DESERT
map (22° 20′N 45° 35′E) **17**:94
AL-DAMMAN (Saudi Arabia)
map (26° 26′N 50° 7′E) **17**:94
AL-DAMUR (Lebanon)
map (33° 44′N 35° 27′E) **12**:265
AL-DIMANIYA (Iraq)
map (31° 59′N 44° 56′E) **11**:255
AL-DUKHAN, MOUNT
map (26° 2′N 50° 32′E) **3**:24
AL-FAIYUM (Egypt) **1**:232
map (29° 19′N 30° 50′E) **7**:76
AL-FALLUJA (Iraq)
map (33° 20′N 43° 46′E) **11**:255
AL-FASHIR (Sudan)
map (13° 38′N 25° 21′E) **18**:320
AL-FASHN (Egypt)
map (28° 49′N 30° 54′E) **7**:76
AL-FATAH
Palestine Liberation Organization **15**:46
AL-HADD (Bahrain)
map (26° 15′N 50° 39′E) **3**:24
AL-HADHR *see* HATRA (Iraq)
AL-HAITHAM
mathematics, history of **13**:224
AL-HAJAVA DESERT
map (30° 0′N 44° 0′E) **11**:255
AL-HAKIM
Druzes **6**:283
AL-HAMMAR, LAKE
map (30° 50′N 47° 10′E) **11**:255
AL-HASAKA (Syria)
map (36° 29′N 40° 45′E) **18**:412
AL-HASHA MOUNTAIN
map (13° 43′N 44° 31′E) **20**:325
AL-HIBA (Iraq) *see* LAGASH (Iraq)
AL-HIJAZ MOUNTAINS
map (19° 45′N 41° 55′E) **17**:94
AL-HILLA (Iraq)
map (32° 29′N 44° 25′E) **11**:255
AL-HUDAYDA (Yemen) (Sana)
map (14° 48′N 42° 57′E) **20**:325
AL-JABUL SABKHA
map (36° 3′N 37° 39′E) **18**:412
AL-JADIDA (Morocco)
map (33° 16′N 8° 30′W) **13**:585
AL-JAFR DEPRESSION
map (30° 17′N 36° 20′E) **11**:447
AL-JAWF (Libya)
map (24° 11′N 23° 19′E) **12**:320
AL-JUNAYNA (Sudan)
map (13° 27′N 22° 27′E) **18**:320
AL-KAIROUAN (Tunisia)
map (35° 41′N 10° 7′E) **19**:335
AL-KALB, CAPE
map (14° 2′N 48° 40′E) **20**:324
AL-KAZIMIYA (Iraq)
map (33° 22′N 44° 20′E) **11**:255
AL-KEF (Tunisia)
map (36° 11′N 8° 43′E) **19**:335
AL-KHABUR RIVER
map (35° 8′N 40° 26′E) **18**:412
AL-KHAWR (Qatar)
map (25° 41′N 51° 30′E) **16**:4
AL-KHUMS (Libya)
map (32° 39′N 14° 16′E) **12**:320
AL KHWARIZMI
mathematics, history of **13**:224
AL-KUFRA (Libya)
climate **1**:142 *table*; **12**:320 *table*
AL-KUT (Iraq)
map (32° 25′N 45° 49′E) **11**:255
AL-LAWZ, MOUNT
map (28° 40′N 35° 18′E) **17**:94
AL-LITANI RIVER
map (33° 20′N 35° 14′E) **12**:265
AL-MADINAH (Saudi Arabia) *see* MEDINA (Saudi Arabia)
AL-MAGHRIB *see* MAGHRIB
AL-MAHALLA AL-KUBRA (Egypt)
map (30° 58′N 31° 10′E) **7**:76
AL-MANSHA (Egypt)
map (26° 28′N 31° 48′E) **7**:76
AL-MANSURAH (Egypt)
map (31° 3′N 31° 23′E) **7**:76
AL-MARJ (Libya)
map (32° 30′N 20° 54′E) **12**:320
AL-MASIRA GULF
map (20° 10′N 58° 10′E) **14**:386
AL-MASIRA ISLAND
map (20° 25′N 58° 50′E) **14**:386
AL-MAWSIL (Iraq) *see* MOSUL (Iraq)
AL-METLAOUI (Tunisia)
map (34° 20′N 8° 24′E) **19**:335
AL-MILH, LAKE
map (32° 40′N 43° 35′E) **11**:255
AL-MINYA (Egypt) **1**:232
map (28° 6′N 30° 45′E) **7**:76
AL-MOKNINE (Tunisia)
map (35° 38′N 10° 54′E) **19**:335
AL-MUBARRAZ (Saudi Arabia)
map (25° 55′N 49° 36′E) **17**:94
AL-MUHARRAQ (Bahrain)
map (26° 16′N 50° 37′E) **3**:24
AL-MUKALLA
map (14° 32′N 49° 8′E) **20**:324
AL-NABK (Syria)
map (34° 1′N 36° 44′E) **18**:412
AL-NAJAF (Iraq)
map (31° 59′N 44° 20′E) **11**:255
AL-NASIRIYA (Iraq)
map (31° 2′N 46° 16′E) **11**:255
AL-QADARIF (Sudan)
map (14° 20′N 35° 24′E) **18**:320
AL-QAMISHLI (Syria)
map (37° 2′N 41° 14′E) **18**:412
AL-QATIF (Saudi Arabia)
map (26° 33′N 50° 0′E) **17**:94
AL-QUBAYYAT (Lebanon)
map (34° 34′N 36° 17′E) **12**:265
AL-QUNAYTIRA (Syria)
map (33° 7′N 35° 49′E) **18**:412
AL-RAMADI (Iraq)
map (33° 25′N 43° 17′E) **11**:255
AL-RAQQA (Syria)
map (35° 56′N 39° 1′E) **18**:412
AL-RIFA AL-GHARBI (Bahrain)
map (26° 7′N 50° 33′E) **3**:24
AL-SABIYA CHANNEL
map (29° 35′N 48° 10′E) **12**:141
AL-SABYA (Saudi Arabia)
map (17° 9′N 42° 37′E) **17**:94
AL-SALAMIYA (Syria)
map (35° 1′N 37° 3′E) **18**:412
AL-SALIMIYA (Kuwait)
map (29° 18′N 48° 3′E) **12**:141
AL-SAMAWA (Iraq)
map (31° 18′N 45° 17′E) **11**:255
AL-SAWDA PEAK
map (34° 18′N 36° 7′E) **12**:265
AL-SAWDA PLATEAU
map (28° 40′N 15° 30′E) **12**:320
AL-SAWWAN
map (30° 45′N 37° 15′E) **11**:447
AL-SHAM, MOUNT
map (23° 13′N 57° 16′E) **14**:386
AL-SULAYMANIYA (Iraq)
map (35° 33′N 45° 26′E) **11**:255
AL-SUWAYDA (Syria)
map (32° 42′N 36° 34′E) **18**:412
AL-TAIF (Saudi Arabia)
map (21° 16′N 40° 24′E) **17**:94
AL-UBAYYID (Sudan)
map (13° 11′N 30° 13′E) **18**:320
AL-UQSUR (Egypt)
map (25° 41′N 32° 39′E) **7**:76
AL-UWAYNAT, MOUNT
map (21° 54′N 24° 58′E) **12**:320
AL-ZARQA (Jordan)
map (32° 5′N 36° 6′E) **11**:447
AL-ZUBAYR (Iraq)
map (30° 23′N 47° 43′E) **11**:255
ALA *see* AMERICAN LIBRARY ASSOCIATION

ALA UD-DIN
Delhi Sultanate **6**:92
ALABAMA **1**:233–238 *bibliog., illus., map*
cities
Birmingham **3**:292
Gadsden **9**:7
Huntsville **10**:315
Mobile **13**:487
Montgomery **13**:556
Selma **17**:192
Tuscaloosa **19**:354
civil rights **1**:238
climate **1**:233
economy **1**:235–236
education **1**:235
Alabama, state universities of **1**:238
Talladega College **19**:16
Tuskegee Institute **19**:355
Washington, Booker T. **20**:39
flag **1**:233 *illus.*
government and politics **1**:236 *illus.*
history **1**:236–238
Alabama (American Indians) **1**:238
Wallace, George **20**:14
land and resources **1**:233
map (32° 50′N 87° 0′W) **19**:419
Marshall Space Flight Center **19**:633
people **1**:233–235
rivers, lakes, and waterways **1**:233
Alabama River **1**:239
Mobile River **13**:488
Tennessee River **19**:107
Tombigbee River **19**:231
seal, state **1**:233 *illus.*
ALABAMA (American Indians) **1**:238 *bibliog.*
ALABAMA (ship) **5**:32 *illus.*
Alabama Claims **1**:238
Semmes, Raphael **17**:198
ALABAMA, STATE UNIVERSITIES OF **1**:238
ALABAMA CLAIMS **1**:238 *bibliog.*
ALABAMA RIVER **1**:239
map (31° 8′N 87° 57′W) **1**:234
ALABASTER
gypsum **9**:415–416
ALABASTER (Alabama)
map (33° 15′N 86° 49′W) **1**:234
ALACA HÜYÜK (Turkey) **1**:239
Hittite art and architecture **10**:188
ALACHUA (Florida)
map (29° 47′N 82° 30′W) **8**:172
ALACHUA (county in Florida)
map (29° 45′N 82° 20′W) **8**:172
ALADDIN **1**:239
ALAGOAS (Brazil)
map (9° 0′S 36° 0′W) **3**:460
ALAGOINHAS (Brazil)
map (12° 7′S 38° 26′W) **3**:460
ALAIN-FOURNIER **1**:239
ALAJUELA (Costa Rica)
map (10° 1′N 84° 13′W) **5**:291
ALAKANUK (Alaska)
map (62° 41′N 164° 37′W) **1**:242
ALALAKEIKI CHANNEL
map (20° 35′N 156° 30′W) **10**:72
ALALAKH (Turkey) **1**:239 *bibliog.*
ALAMANCE (county in North Carolina)
map (36° 5′N 79° 25′W) **14**:242
ALAMANCE, BATTLE OF
Regulators **16**:129
ALAMANNI, LUIGI **1**:239
ALAMANNIA *see* SWABIA
ALAMANS
Germanic peoples **9**:138
Swabia **18**:375
ALAMEDA (California) **1**:239
map (37° 46′N 122° 16′W) **4**:31
ALAMEDA (county in California)
map (37° 35′N 121° 55′W) **4**:31
ALAMEDA (New Mexico)
map (35° 11′N 106° 37′W) **14**:136
ALAMEIN, EL **1**:239 *bibliog.*
strategy and tactics, military **18**:290
World War II **20**:258; **20**:262–263 *illus., map*
ALAMO (Georgia)
map (32° 9′N 82° 47′W) **9**:114
ALAMO (Nevada)
map (37° 22′N 115° 10′W) **14**:111
ALAMO (Tennessee)
map (35° 47′N 89° 7′W) **19**:104
ALAMO, THE **1**:239–240 *bibliog., illus.*
Bowie, James **3**:428
Santa Anna, Antonio López de **17**:66
Texas **19**:134–135 *illus.*
Travis, William B. **19**:285
ALAMOGORDO (New Mexico) **1**:240
map (32° 54′N 105° 57′W) **14**:136
ALAMOR (Ecuador)
map (4° 2′S 80° 2′W) **7**:52
ALAMOSA (Colorado)
map (37° 28′N 105° 52′W) **5**:116
ALAMOSA (county in Colorado)
map (37° 42′N 105° 40′W) **5**:116
ALANBROOKE, ALAN FRANCIS BROOKE, 1ST VISCOUNT **1**:240
ÅLAND ISLANDS
Bothnia, Gulf of **3**:415
ALAOTRA, LAKE
map (17° 30′S 48° 30′E) **13**:38
ALAPAHA (Georgia)
map (31° 23′N 83° 13′W) **9**:114
ALARCON, HERNANDO DE
Coronado, Francisco Vázquez de **5**:270
exploration of colonial America **19**:437 *map*
ALARCÓN, PEDRO ANTONIO DE **1**:240 *bibliog.*
ALARCON RESERVOIR
map (39° 36′N 2° 10′W) **18**:140
ALARCÓN Y MENDOZA, JUAN RUIZ DE *see* RUIZ DE ALARCÓN Y MENDOZA, JUAN
ALARIC I, KING OF THE VISIGOTHS **1**:240 *bibliog.*
Eleusis **7**:135
Goths **9**:263
ALARM SYSTEMS **1**:240 *bibliog.*
fire prevention and control **8**:103
smoke detector **17**:373
surveillance systems **18**:366
ALAS, LEOPOLDO **1**:240
Spanish literature **18**:159
ALASKA **1**:240–247 *bibliog., illus., map*
animal life **1**:243
archaeology **7**:239 *map*
Akmak **1**:231
Cape Denbigh **4**:120
Cape Krusenstern **4**:120
Eskimo **7**:241
Ipiutak **11**:248
Okvik **14**:372
auroras **2**:325 *illus.*
cities
Anchorage **1**:399
Barrow **3**:95
Fairbanks **8**:9
Juneau **11**:467
Nome **14**:215
Sitka **17**:330
Valdez **19**:503
climate **1**:241–243
earthquakes **7**:27 *illus.*
Richter scale **16**:215
economy **1**:245
education **1**:243
Alaska, University of **1**:247
fjord **8**:133
flag **1**:241 *illus.*
flower, state
forget-me-not **8**:234
glaciers and glaciation
Hubbard Glacier **9**:194
Malaspina Glacier **9**:194; **13**:80
government **1**:244–245
history **1**:245–247
Baranov, Aleksandr Andreyevich **3**:75
Bering, Vitus Jonassen **3**:211
Seward, William H. **17**:221
Shelekhov, Grigory Ivanovich **17**:250
Indians of North America, art of the **11**:138–139
land and resources **1**:241–243; **1**:247
map (65° 0′N 153° 0′W) **1**:242
money **13**:525 *illus.*
people **1**:243–244
Aleut **1**:272
Eskimo **7**:238–242
Haida **10**:12
Ingalik **11**:175–176
Tlingit **19**:216
Tsimshian **19**:323–324
physical features **1**:241
Aleutian Islands **1**:272 *map*
Alexander Archipelago **1**:273
Brooks Range **3**:511
Katmai, Mount **12**:30
Kodiak Island **12**:105
McKinley, Mount **13**:30
Malaspina Glacier **13**:80
Pribilof Islands **15**:534
Valley of Ten Thousand Smokes **19**:508
rivers, lakes, waterways, and bays **1**:241
Prudhoe Bay **15**:585
Yukon River **20**:344 *map*
seal, state **1**:241 *illus.*
tidal energy **19**:192
Trans-Alaska Pipeline **19**:266–267
vegetation **1**:243
tundra **19**:332
ALASKA, GULF OF **1**:247
Alaska Current **1**:248
Kodiak Island (Alaska) **12**:105
shellfish **17**:255
ALASKA, UNIVERSITY OF **1**:247
ALASKA BLACKFISH **1**:247–248; **8**:115 *illus.*
ALASKA CURRENT **1**:248
ocean currents and wind systems, worldwide **14**:322–323 *maps*
ALASKA HIGHWAY **1**:248
roads and highways **16**:238
ALASKA LANDS BILL
Alaska **1**:247
Arctic **2**:144
ALASKA PENINSULA
map (57° 0′N 158° 0′W) **1**:242
ALASKA RANGE **1**:243 *illus.*
map (62° 30′N 150° 0′W) **1**:242
ALASKAN MALAMUTE **1**:248 *bibliog., illus.*; **6**:214 *illus.*
ALAUNGPAYA (King of Burma)
Burma **3**:575
Rangoon (Burma) **16**:85
ALAUSÍ (Ecuador)
map (2° 12′S 78° 50′W) **7**:52
ALAVA, CAPE
map (48° 10′N 124° 43′W) **20**:35
ALAVI, BOZORG **1**:248
ALAWITES
Latakia (Syria) **12**:215
Morocco **13**:586
ALAYH (Lebanon)
map (33° 48′N 35° 36′E) **12**:265
ALBA, FERNANDO ÁLVAREZ DE TOLEDO Y PIMENTEL, DUQUE DE **1**:248 *bibliog.*
ALBA-IULIA (Romania)
map (46° 4′N 23° 35′E) **16**:288
ALBA LONGA **1**:248
ALBACETE (Spain)
map (38° 59′N 1° 51′W) **18**:140
ALBACORE
tuna **19**:332
ALBAN, SAINT **1**:248
Saint Albans (England) **17**:16
ALBANEL, CHARLES **1**:248
Canada, exploration of **4**:80 *map*
ALBANESE, LICIA **1**:248–249
ALBANIA **1**:249–251 *bibliog., illus., map, table*
cities
Durrës **6**:307
Shkodër **17**:278
Tiranë **19**:207
Vlorë **19**:624
climate **1**:249; **1**:251 *table*
economic activity **1**:250
education **1**:249
European universities **7**:307 *table*
flag **1**:249 *illus.*
government **1**:250
history **1**:250–251
Hoxha, Enver **10**:285–286
Illyria **11**:50
Skanderbeg **17**:332
Warsaw Treaty Organization **20**:32
Zog I, King **20**:371
land and resources **1**:249
map (41° 0′N 20° 0′E) **7**:268
people **1**:249–250
ALBANO, LAKE **1**:251
ALBANY (Georgia) **1**:251
map (31° 35′N 84° 10′W) **9**:114
ALBANY (Illinois)
map (41° 47′N 90° 13′W) **11**:42
ALBANY (Indiana)
map (40° 18′N 85° 14′W) **11**:111
ALBANY (Kentucky)
map (36° 42′N 85° 8′W) **12**:47
ALBANY (Minnesota)
map (45° 38′N 94° 34′W) **13**:453
ALBANY (Missouri)
map (40° 15′N 94° 20′W) **13**:476
ALBANY (New York) **1**:251; **14**:152 *illus.*
map (42° 39′N 73° 45′W) **14**:149
ALBANY (county in New York)
map (42° 39′N 73° 45′W) **14**:149
ALBANY (Ohio)
map (39° 14′N 82° 12′W) **14**:357
ALBANY (Oregon)
map (44° 38′N 123° 6′W) **14**:427
ALBANY (Texas)
map (32° 44′N 99° 18′W) **19**:129
ALBANY (Wisconsin)
map (42° 43′N 89° 26′W) **20**:185
ALBANY (county in Wyoming)
map (41° 45′N 105° 43′W) **20**:301
ALBANY CONGRESS **1**:251–252
Franklin, Benjamin **8**:283
ALBANY RIVER
map (52° 17′N 81° 31′W) **14**:393
ALBATEGNIUS *see* BATTANI, AL-
ALBATROSS **1**:252 *bibliog., illus.*; **3**:280–281 *illus.*
ALBEDO **1**:252 *bibliog.*
Saturn (astronomy) **17**:90–91
ALBEE, EDWARD (playwright) **1**:252–253 *bibliog., illus.*
Who's Afraid of Virginia Woolf? **20**:144
Zoo Story, The **20**:374
ALBEE, EDWARD FRANKLIN (vaudeville promoter)
music hall, vaudeville, and burlesque **13**:672
ALBEMARLE (North Carolina)
map (35° 21′N 80° 12′W) **14**:242
ALBEMARLE (county in Virginia)
map (38° 0′N 78° 35′W) **19**:607
ALBEMARLE, GEORGE MONCK, 1ST DUKE OF *see* MONCK, GEORGE, 1ST DUKE OF ALBEMARLE
ALBEMARLE SOUND
map (36° 3′N 76° 12′W) **14**:242
ALBÉNIZ, ISAAC **1**:253 *bibliog.*
ALBERDI, JUAN BAUTISTA **1**:253
ALBERS, JOSEF **1**:253 *bibliog., illus.*
Bauhaus **3**:129–130 *illus.*
Homage to the Square **1**:253 *illus.*
op art **14**:397
ALBERT, CARL **1**:253
ALBERT, EUGEN D' **1**:253 *bibliog.*
ALBERT, FIRST DUKE OF PRUSSIA **1**:254
Prussia **15**:585
Sigismund II, King of Poland **17**:299
ALBERT, LAKE **1**:253
map (1° 40′N 31° 0′E) **19**:372
ALBERT, PRINCE CONSORT OF ENGLAND **1**:254 *bibliog.*
Victoria, Queen of England, Scotland, and Ireland **19**:574
ALBERT I, KING OF THE BELGIANS **1**:254 *bibliog.*
World War I **20**:223
ALBERT I, KING OF GERMANY **1**:254
ALBERT I, MARGRAVE OF BRANDENBURG (Albert the Bear) **1**:254
ALBERT II, KING OF GERMANY **1**:254
ALBERT CANAL
map (50° 39′N 5° 37′E) **3**:177
ALBERT LEA (Minnesota)
map (43° 39′N 93° 22′W) **13**:453
ALBERT MEMORIAL (London) **9**:262 *illus.*
ALBERT NILE RIVER
map (3° 36′N 32° 2′E) **19**:372
ALBERTA (Alabama)
map (32° 14′N 87° 25′W) **1**:234
ALBERTA (Canada) **1**:254–258 *bibliog., illus., map*
cities
Banff **3**:62
Calgary **4**:28; **4**:76 *illus.*
Edmonton **7**:58
Lethbridge **12**:299
economic activity **1**:257
education
Alberta, University of **1**:259
Calgary, University of **4**:28–29; **4**:92 *table*
Edmonton, University of Alberta at **4**:92 *table*
Lethbridge, University of **4**:92 *table*
flag **1**:255 *illus.*
government **1**:257–258
history **1**:258
Aberhart, William **1**:56
land and resources **1**:254–257
landslide and avalanche **12**:193 *illus.*
map (54° 0′N 113° 0′W) **4**:70
people **1**:257
Assiniboin **2**:265
pipe and pipeline **15**:311
rivers, lakes, and waterways
Athabasca River **2**:288
Louise, Lake **12**:429
Peace River **15**:123
Saskatchewan River **17**:83
tar sands **19**:34
ALBERTA, MOUNT
map (52° 18′N 117° 28′W) **1**:256
ALBERTA, UNIVERSITY OF **1**:259
ALBERTI, LEON BATTISTA **1**:259 *bibliog.*
cathedrals and churches **4**:206
mathematics, history of **13**:224
Rimini (Italy) **16**:224
ALBERTI, RAFAEL **1**:259 *bibliog.*
ALBERTINA (museum) **1**:259 *bibliog.*

ALBERTO, CARLOS
  soccer **18**:11
ALBERTON (Prince Edward Island)
  map (46° 49′N 64° 4′W) **15**:548
ALBERTS v. *CALIFORNIA*
  Roth v. *United States* **16**:321
ALBERTUS MAGNUS, SAINT **1**:259–260 *bibliog., illus.*
ALBERTVILLE (Alabama)
  map (34° 16′N 86° 12′W) **1**:234
ALBIA (Iowa)
  map (41° 2′N 92° 48′W) **11**:244
ALBIGENSES (Cathari) **1**:260 *bibliog.*
  Bogomils **3**:360
  courtly love **5**:317
  Crusades **5**:369
  gnosticism **9**:214 *illus.*
  Languedoc (France) **12**:199
ALBIN (Wyoming)
  map (41° 25′N 104° 6′W) **20**:301
ALBINA (Suriname)
  map (5° 30′N 54° 3′W) **18**:364
ALBINISM **1**:260
  coloration, biological **5**:122
  Cuna Indians **5**:388
  deficiency disease, enzyme **7**:214
  genetic diseases **9**:82–84 *illus.*
ALBINONI, TOMMASO **1**:260 *bibliog.*
ALBION (California)
  map (39° 13′N 123° 46′W) **4**:31
ALBION (Illinois)
  map (38° 23′N 88° 4′W) **11**:42
ALBION (Indiana)
  map (41° 24′N 85° 25′W) **11**:111
ALBION (Iowa)
  map (42° 7′N 92° 59′W) **11**:244
ALBION (Michigan)
  map (42° 15′N 84° 45′W) **13**:377
ALBION (Nebraska)
  map (41° 42′N 98° 0′W) **14**:70
ALBION (New York)
  map (43° 15′N 78° 12′W) **14**:149
ALBION (Pennsylvania)
  map (41° 53′N 80° 22′W) **15**:147
ALBION (Washington)
  map (46° 48′N 117° 15′W) **20**:35
ALBITE
  feldspar **8**:46–47
ALBIZU CAMPOS, PEDRO **1**:261
ALBIZZIA
  mimosa **13**:436
ÅLBORG (Denmark) **1**:261; **6**:111 *illus.*
  map (57° 3′N 9° 56′E) **6**:109
ÅLBORG BAY
  map (56° 45′N 10° 30′E) **6**:109
ALBRECHTSBERGER, JOHANN GEORG **1**:261
ALBREDA (British Columbia)
  map (52° 38′N 119° 9′W) **3**:491
ALBRIGHT, IVAN LE LORRAINE **1**:261 *bibliog.*
ALBRIGHT, JACOB **1**:261 *bibliog.*
  Evangelical United Brethren Church **7**:312
ALBUMEN PRINT **1**:261 *bibliog.*
  Blanquart-Evrard, Louis Désirée **3**:327
ALBUMIN **1**:261
  egg **7**:72
  Sørensen, Søren Peter Lauritz **18**:69
ALBUQUERQUE (New Mexico) **1**:261; **14**:139 *illus.*
  map (35° 5′N 106° 40′W) **14**:136
ALBUQUERQUE, AFONSO DE **1**:261 *bibliog.*
ALBURG (Vermont)
  map (44° 59′N 73° 18′W) **19**:554
ALBURY (Australia)
  map (36° 5′S 146° 55′E) **2**:328
ALCAEUS **1**:262
ALCALÁ DE HENARES (Spain)
  map (40° 29′N 3° 22′W) **18**:140
ALCAMO (Italy)
  map (37° 59′N 12° 58′E) **11**:321
ALCÂNTARA, PEDRO DE *see* PEDRO II, EMPEROR OF BRAZIL
ALCÁNTARA BRIDGE (Spain) **3**:480 *illus.*
ALCÁNTARA RESERVOIR
  map (39° 45′N 6° 25′W) **15**:449
ALCATRAZ (California) **1**:262 *bibliog.*
ALCAYAGA, LUCILA GODOY *see* MISTRAL, GABRIELA (pseudonym)
ALCESTIS **1**:262
ALCHEMY **1**:262–263 *bibliog., illus.*
  aqua regia **2**:92
  arsenic **2**:189
  chemistry, history of **4**:324–325 *illus.*
  element **7**:129
  Geber **9**:66
  Paracelsus **15**:74
  transmutation of elements **19**:276–277
ALCIBIADES **1**:263 *bibliog.*
  Peloponnesian War **15**:139
ALCID *see* AUK
ALCINDOR, LEW *see* ABDUL-JABBAR, KAREEM
ALCIRA (Spain)
  map (39° 9′N 0° 26′W) **18**:140
ALCMAEON **1**:263
ALCMAN **1**:264
ALCOA (Tennessee)
  map (35° 48′N 83° 59′W) **19**:104
ALCOCK, SIR JOHN WILLIAM **1**:264
ALCOHOL **1**:264 *bibliog., table*
  aliphatic compounds **1**:295
  antiseptic **2**:68
    bacteria **3**:16
  denatured alcohol **6**:106
  ester **7**:246
  ethyl alcohol **7**:257
  fermentation **8**:55
  glycerol **9**:212
  glycol **9**:212
  hydroxyl group **10**:344
  methyl alcohol **13**:344
  monohydric alcohol **13**:536
  organic chemistry **14**:437
  phenol **15**:225
  physiological effects **1**:264
  polyhydric alcohol **15**:420
  properties **1**:264 *table*
  uses **1**:264
ALCOHOL CONSUMPTION **1**:264–266 *bibliog.*
  breath analyzer **3**:470
  delirium **6**:93
  denatured alchohol **6**:106
  ethyl alcohol **7**:257
  impotence **11**:62
  prohibition **15**:565
  psychotropic drugs **15**:603–604
  temperance movement **19**:92
  vertigo **19**:563
  young people **20**:336
ALCOHOLIC BEVERAGE
  ale **1**:270
  beer **3**:162–163
  bitters **3**:301
  brandy **3**:455
  champagne **4**:276
  cider **4**:429
  gin **9**:183
  mead **13**:251
  port (wine) **15**:442
  rum **16**:344
  sake **17**:28
  sherry **17**:259
  tequila **19**:114
  vermouth **19**:558–559
  vodka **19**:625
  whiskey **20**:132–133
  wine **20**:174–179
ALCOHOLICS ANONYMOUS **1**:266
  group therapy **9**:377
ALCOHOLISM **1**:265–266 *bibliog.*
  cirrhosis **4**:445
  Eskimo **7**:242
  jaundice **11**:385
  nervous system, diseases of the **14**:96
  thiamine deficiency **19**:619
  treatment
    disulfiram **6**:201–202
    hallucinogens **10**:24
ALCOLU (South Carolina)
  map (33° 45′N 80° 13′W) **18**:98
ALCONA (county in Michigan)
  map (44° 40′N 83° 30′W) **13**:377
ALCORN (county in Mississippi)
  map (34° 55′N 88° 35′W) **13**:469
ALCOTT, BRONSON **1**:266–267 *bibliog.*
  Peabody, Elizabeth **15**:122–123
ALCOTT, LOUISA MAY **1**:267 *bibliog., illus.*
ALCOY (Spain)
  map (38° 42′N 0° 28′W) **18**:140
ALCUIN **1**:267 *bibliog.*
ALDABRA ISLANDS
  map (9° 25′S 46° 22′E) **17**:232
ALDAMA, IGNACIO
  León (Mexico) **12**:289
ALDAN RIVER
  map (63° 28′N 129° 35′E) **19**:388
ALDANOV, M. A. **1**:267 *bibliog.*
ALDEBARAN (astronomy)
  Taurus **19**:45
ALDEBURGH FESTIVAL
  Britten, Benjamin **3**:498–499
ALDEHYDE **1**:267–268 *bibliog., illus.*
  acetaldehyde **1**:79
  benzaldehyde **3**:206
  carbonyl group **4**:139
  Claisen, Ludwig **5**:35
  formaldehyde **8**:234
ALDEN (Minnesota)
  map (43° 40′N 93° 34′W) **13**:453
ALDEN, JOHN **1**:268
  Mayflower **13**:247
ALDER **1**:268 *illus.*
ALDER, KURT **1**:268
ALDERFLY **1**:269
ALDERMAN **1**:269
ALDERNEY (Channel Islands) **4**:281 *map*
ALDERSON (West Virginia)
  map (37° 43′N 80° 39′W) **20**:111
ALDINE PRESS
  Manutius, Aldus **13**:134
ALDINGTON, RICHARD **1**:269
ALDISS, BRIAN W. **1**:269
ALDOSTERONE **1**:269 *bibliog.*
  Barton, Derek **3**:98
  corticoid **5**:278
  endocrine system **7**:169
  endocrine system, diseases of the **7**:170
  hormones **10**:236
  steroid **18**:261–262
ALDRICH, NELSON WILMARTH **1**:269 *bibliog.*
ALDRICH, ROBERT **1**:269
ALDRICH, THOMAS BAILEY **1**:269 *bibliog.*
ALDRIDGE, IRA **1**:269 *bibliog.*
ALDRIN, EDWIN E. **1**:269–270 *illus.*; **19**:458 *illus.*
  Apollo program **2**:80–82 *illus.*
  Gemini program **9**:73
ALDUS MANUTIUS *see* MANUTIUS, ALDUS
ALE **1**:270
  malt **13**:94
ALEA (Greece) *see* TEGEA (Greece)
ALEATORY MUSIC **1**:270 *bibliog.*
  composers
    Cage, John **4**:15–16
    Cowell, Henry **5**:321
    Jolas, Betsy **11**:441
    Lutosławski, Witold **12**:470
ALECHINSKY, PIERRE **1**:270 *bibliog.*
ALECSANDRI, VASILE **1**:270 *bibliog.*
ALEDO (Illinois)
  map (41° 12′N 90° 45′W) **11**:42
ALEGRÍA, CIRO **1**:270
ALEGROS MOUNTAIN
  map (34° 9′N 108° 11′W) **14**:136
ALEICHEM, SHOLEM **1**:270–271 *bibliog.*; **10**:102 *illus.*
ALEIJADINHO **1**:271 *bibliog.*
  The Prophet Daniel **12**:226 *illus.*
ALEIXANDRE, VICENTE **1**:271 *bibliog.*
ALEKNAGIK (Alaska)
  map (59° 17′N 158° 38′W) **1**:242
ALEKSANDROVSK (USSR) *see* ZAPOROZHYE (USSR)
ALEKSEYEVNA, SOPHIA *see* SOPHIA
ALEKSINAC (Yugoslavia)
  map (43° 32′N 21° 43′E) **20**:340
ALEMÁN, MATEO **1**:271 *bibliog.*
ALEMÁN VALDÉS, MIGUEL **1**:271
  Mexico, history of **13**:366
ALEMANIA (Argentina)
  map (25° 36′S 65° 38′W) **2**:149
ALEMBERT, JEAN LE ROND D' **1**:271
  astronomy, history of **2**:278
  encyclopedia **7**:164
ALENÇON (France)
  map (48° 26′N 0° 5′E) **8**:260
ALENUIHAHA CHANNEL
  map (20° 26′N 156° 0′W) **10**:72
ALEOTTI, GIOVANNI BATTISTA
  theater architecture and staging **19**:152
ALEPH
  A (letter) **1**:49
ALEPOUDELIS, ODYSSEUS *see* ELYTIS, ODYSSEUS
ALEPPO (Syria) **1**:271–272
  map (36° 12′N 37° 10′E) **18**:412
ALESSANDRI, ARTURO **1**:272
  Chile **4**:357
ALESSANDRIA (Italy) **1**:272
  map (44° 54′N 8° 37′E) **11**:321
ALESSI, GALEAZZO **1**:272 *bibliog.*
ÅLESUND (Norway)
  map (62° 28′N 6° 9′E) **14**:261
ALETHIANS *see* SHAKERS
ALETSCH GLACIER **1**:272
ALEUT **1**:272 *bibliog.*
  Eskimo **7**:240
  Indian schools, American **11**:106
ALEUT LANGUAGE *see* ESKIMO-ALEUT LANGUAGES
ALEUTIAN CURRENT **1**:272
  Alaska Current **1**:248
  ocean currents and wind systems, worldwide **14**:322–323 *maps*
ALEUTIAN ISLANDS **1**:272 *bibliog., map*
  map (52° 0′N 176° 0′W) **1**:242
  people
    Aleut **1**:272
    Eskimo **7**:238–242
  polar easterlies **15**:393
  Ring of Fire **16**:225
ALEUTIAN LOW
  cyclone and anticyclone **5**:405
ALEUTIAN RANGE
  map (59° 0′N 155° 0′W) **1**:242
ALEUTIAN TRENCH
  Pacific Ocean bottom **15**:6–7 *map*
  plate tectonics **15**:351 *map*
ALEWIFE **1**:273 *illus.*
ALEX (Oklahoma)
  map (34° 55′N 97° 47′W) **14**:368
ALEXANDER (botany) **1**:273
ALEXANDER (county in Illinois)
  map (37° 13′N 89° 20′W) **11**:42
ALEXANDER (county in North Carolina)
  map (35° 55′N 81° 10′W) **14**:242
ALEXANDER (North Dakota)
  map (47° 51′N 103° 39′W) **14**:248
ALEXANDER, GROVER CLEVELAND **1**:273
ALEXANDER, HAROLD GEORGE, 1ST EARL ALEXANDER OF TUNIS **1**:273 *bibliog.*
ALEXANDER, KING OF MOLOSSIA
  Epirus **7**:220
ALEXANDER, KING OF SERBIA **1**:276
ALEXANDER, KING OF YUGOSLAVIA **1**:276
  Yugoslavia **20**:343
ALEXANDER, LLOYD **1**:273
ALEXANDER, SAMUEL **1**:273
ALEXANDER I, EMPEROR OF RUSSIA **1**:275–276 *bibliog., illus.*
  Holy Alliance **10**:209
  Kutuzov, Mikhail Illarionovich **12**:140
  Paul I, Emperor of Russia **15**:118
  Romanov (dynasty) **16**:290
  Russia/Union of Soviet Socialist Republics, history of **16**:356
  Speransky, Mikhail Mikhailovich **18**:179
  Tilsit, Treaties of **19**:200
ALEXANDER II, EMPEROR OF RUSSIA **1**:276 *bibliog.*
  assassination of **16**:358 *illus.*
  narodniki **14**:21
  Romanov (dynasty) **16**:290
  Russia/Union of Soviet Socialist Republics, history of **16**:357–358
ALEXANDER III, EMPEROR OF RUSSIA **1**:276
  Russia/Union of Soviet Socialist Republics, history of **16**:358
ALEXANDER III, KING OF MACEDONIA *see* ALEXANDER THE GREAT, KING OF MACEDONIA
ALEXANDER III, KING OF SCOTLAND **1**:276 *bibliog.*
ALEXANDER III, POPE **1**:277 *bibliog.*; **9**:149 *illus.*; **15**:65 *illus.*
  Italy, history of **11**:329
ALEXANDER VI, POPE **1**:277 *bibliog.*
ALEXANDER ARCHIPELAGO **1**:273
  map (56° 30′N 134° 0′W) **1**:242
ALEXANDER CITY (Alabama)
  map (32° 56′N 85° 57′W) **1**:234
ALEXANDER THE GREAT, KING OF MACEDONIA **1**:273–275 *bibliog., illus.*
  Bucephalus **3**:532
  conquests **1**:274 *map*
  Demosthenes **6**:105
  depicted in a floor mosaic **9**:333 *illus.*
  Diadochi **6**:149
  Europe, history of **7**:280
  Gordion **9**:248
  Greece, ancient **9**:333
  Hellenistic Age **10**:114
  imperialism **11**:61
  India, history of **11**:89
  Multan (Pakistan) **13**:637
  mythical encounter with a talking tree **15**:182 *illus.*
  Olympias **14**:382
  Parmenion **15**:95
  Pella **15**:138
  Philip II, King of Macedonia **15**:233
  portraiture **15**:446
  Roxana **16**:328
  Thorvaldsen, Bertel **19**:180
  Tyre (Phoenicia) **19**:367
ALEXANDER OF HALES **1**:275
ALEXANDER* v. *HOLMES COUNTY (MISS.) BOARD OF EDUCATION **1**:275

ALEXANDER ISLAND
map (71° 0′S 70° 0′W) **2**:40
ALEXANDER NEVSKY **1**:275 *bibliog.*
Novgorod (USSR) **14**:276
Peipus, Lake **15**:134
ALEXANDRA OF DENMARK
Edward VII **7**:69 *illus.*
ALEXANDRA FYODOROVNA, EMPRESS OF RUSSIA **1**:277 *bibliog.*; **14**:181 *illus.*
Rasputin, Grigory Yefimovich **16**:91
Russian Revolutions of 1917 **16**:371 *illus.*
ALEXANDRESCU, GRIGORE **1**:277
ALEXANDRETTA, GULF OF
map (36° 30′N 35° 40′E) **19**:343
ALEXANDRIA (British Columbia)
map (52° 38′N 122° 27′W) **3**:491
ALEXANDRIA (Egypt) **1**:277 *bibliog.*
Cleopatra's Needles **5**:51
climate **7**:77 *table*
Egypt, ancient **7**:81 *map*
history **1**:277
map (31° 12′N 29° 54′E) **7**:76
mosaic **13**:593
Pharos of **17**:218 *illus.*
Ptolemy I, King **15**:607
ALEXANDRIA (Indiana)
map (40° 16′N 85° 41′W) **11**:111
ALEXANDRIA (Kentucky)
map (38° 58′N 84° 23′W) **12**:47
ALEXANDRIA (Louisiana) **1**:277–278
map (31° 18′N 92° 27′W) **12**:430
ALEXANDRIA (Minnesota)
map (45° 53′N 95° 22′W) **13**:453
ALEXANDRIA (South Dakota)
map (43° 39′N 97° 47′W) **18**:103
ALEXANDRIA (Tennessee)
map (36° 5′N 86° 2′W) **19**:104
ALEXANDRIA (Virginia) **1**:278
map (38° 48′N 77° 3′W) **19**:607
ALEXANDRIA BAY (New York)
map (44° 20′N 75° 55′W) **14**:149
ALEXANDRIA QUARTET, THE (literary series)
Durrell, Lawrence **6**:306–307
ALEXANDRINE **1**:278
ALEXANDRITE **9**:74 *illus.*
chrysoberyl **4**:420–421
ALEXEYEV, VASILY **1**:278; **14**:384 *illus.*
ALEXIS, TSAR OF RUSSIA **1**:278 *bibliog.*
Russia/Union of Soviet Socialist Republics, history of **16**:354
ALEXIUS I COMNENUS, BYZANTINE EMPEROR **1**:278 *bibliog.*
ALFALFA **1**:278–279 *illus.*
prairie alfalfa **9**:299 *illus.*
ALFALFA (county in Oklahoma)
map (36° 45′N 98° 20′W) **14**:368
ALFARO (Ecuador)
map (2° 12′S 79° 50′W) **7**:52
ALFARO, ELOY
Ecuador **7**:53
ALFIERI, VITTORIO **1**:279 *bibliog.*
tomb **19**:231 *illus.*
ALFONSÍN, RAÚL **1**:279
ALFONSO I, KING OF ASTURIAS
Spain, history of **18**:145
ALFONSO I, KING OF PORTUGAL **1**:279
Portugal, history of **15**:453
ALFONSO II, KING OF PORTUGAL **1**:279
Portugal, history of **15**:453
ALFONSO III, KING OF PORTUGAL **1**:279
Portugal, history of **15**:453
ALFONSO IV, KING OF PORTUGAL
Peter I, King of Portugal **15**:200
Portugal, history of **15**:453
ALFONSO V, KING OF ARAGON (Alfonso the Magnanimous) **1**:279
Naples, Kingdom of **14**:15
Two Sicilies, Kingdom of the **19**:360
ALFONSO VI, KING OF LEÓN AND CASTILE **1**:279
ALFONSO X, KING OF CASTILE (Alfonso the Wise) **1**:279
Spanish literature **18**:157
ALFONSO XII, KING OF SPAIN **1**:279
ALFONSO XIII, KING OF SPAIN **1**:280 *bibliog.*
Spain, history of **18**:148
ALFRED (Maine)
map (43° 29′N 70° 43′W) **13**:70
ALFRED (New York)
map (42° 15′N 77° 47′W) **14**:149
ALFRED, KING OF ENGLAND **1**:280 *bibliog.*
Great Britain, history of **9**:310
Wessex **20**:106
ALFVÉN, HANNES **1**:280 *bibliog.*
magnetohydrodynamics **13**:59
ALFVÉN WAVES
magnetohydrodynamics **13**:59
ALGAE **1**:280–283 *bibliog., illus.*
algal mat **1**:283
biological clock **3**:264
bloom, algal **3**:340
blue-green algae **3**:342–343
brown algae
Ectocarpus **7**:51
Fucus **8**:352
kelp **12**:40
classification, biological **5**:43
conjugation **5**:191
coral **5**:257–258
coral reef **5**:260
cryptomonad **5**:373
diatom **6**:154
dinoflagellate **6**:179
Euglena **7**:264
fossil record **8**:246 *illus.*
stromatolite **18**:302
green algae
Acetabularia **1**:79
Chlamydomonas **4**:400
Chlorella **4**:400
desmid **6**:132
Eudorina **7**:263
Gonium **9**:244
hornwort **10**:240
lichen **12**:322
Oedogonium **14**:352
Pleodorina **15**:367
Scenedesmus **17**:116
Spirogyra **18**:189
stentor **18**:253
stonewort **18**:283–284
Ulothrix **19**:377
Volvox **19**:633
hydra **10**:329–330
hyphochytrid **10**:349
intertidal life **11**:229 *illus.*
microbiology **13**:384
plankton **15**:331
plant **15**:333–335 *illus.*
poisonous plants and animals **15**:384
Protista **15**:577–578
red algae
agar **1**:182
dulse **6**:296
Irish moss **11**:268
Lithothamnion **12**:371
red tide **16**:114
reproduction **16**:162
seaweed **17**:177
soil organisms **18**:39 *illus.*
ALGAL MAT **1**:283 *bibliog.*
stromatolite **18**:302
ALGARDI, ALESSANDRO **1**:283 *bibliog.*
ALGEBRA **1**:283–285 *bibliog.*
algebraic geometry **1**:285
Betti, Enrico **3**:232
binomial theorem **3**:260
Boole, George **3**:392–393
Boolean algebra **3**:393
Cardano, Gerolamo **4**:143
determinant **6**:134
differential calculus **6**:167–168
Diophantus **6**:185
distributive law **6**:201
equation **7**:224–225
exponent **7**:339
exponential functions **7**:339–340
factor **8**:6
function **8**:359
Galois, Evariste **9**:21
group theory **1**:285; **9**:377
Harriot, Thomas **10**:57
Hermite, Charles **10**:143
history **1**:283
induction, mathematical **11**:151
Jordan, Camille **11**:450
linear algebra **12**:353
logarithm **12**:394
mathematics **13**:222
mathematics, education in **13**:222–223
mathematics, history of **13**:223; **13**:224
matrices **1**:283
Noether, Emmy **14**:212
polynomial **15**:421
progression **15**:563–564
quadratic function **16**:5
ring **16**:225
root (mathematics) **16**:311
square **18**:202
systems, isomorphism **11**:300
transformation **19**:270
Viète, François **19**:579–580
ALGEBRAIC GEOMETRY **1**:285 *bibliog.*
mathematics, history of **13**:226
ALGECIRAS (Spain) **1**:285
map (36° 8′N 5° 30′W) **18**:140
ALGECIRAS CONFERENCE **1**:285
Moroccan crises **13**:583
World War I **20**:220
ALGER (county in Michigan)
map (46° 20′N 86° 50′W) **13**:377
ALGER, HORATIO **1**:285–286 *bibliog.*
ALGERIA **1**:286–290 *bibliog., illus., map, table*
archaeology and historic sites
Iol **11**:239
Tassili n'Ajjer **19**:43
Timgad **19**:203
art
Moorish art and architecture **13**:570–571
prehistoric art **1**:174 *illus.*
cities
Algiers **1**:290
Constantine **5**:208
Oran **14**:414
climate **1**:286 *table*
economic activity **1**:288 *illus.*
education **1**:287
African universities **1**:176 *table*
flag **1**:286 *illus.*
government **1**:288
history **1**:288–290
Algerian War **1**:290
ben Bella, Ahmed **3**:194
Boumedienne, Houari **3**:422
Chadli Benjedid **4**:266–267
Fanon, Frantz **8**:20–21
Iranian hostage crisis **11**:254
World War II **20**:262 *map*
land and resources **1**:286–287
map (28° 0′N 3° 0′E) **1**:136
people **1**:287–288
Kabyle **12**:4
Tuareg **19**:325–326
ALGERIAN WAR **1**:290 *bibliog.*
Bidault, Georges **3**:246–247
Boumedienne, Houari **3**:422
de Gaulle, Charles **6**:59
ALGHERO (Italy)
map (40° 34′N 8° 19′E) **11**:321
ALGIERS (Algeria) **1**:290
climate **1**:286 *table*
map (36° 47′N 3° 3′E) **1**:287
ALGIN **1**:290
ALGINIC ACID
algin **1**:290
Fucus **8**:352
ALGOL (computer language) **1**:290–291
Pascal **15**:101
ALGOL (star) **1**:291
binary stars **3**:257
ALGOMA (Wisconsin)
map (44° 36′N 87° 27′W) **20**:185
ALGONA (Iowa)
map (43° 4′N 94° 14′W) **11**:244
ALGONAC (Michigan)
map (42° 37′N 82° 32′W) **13**:377
ALGONQUIN (Algonkin) (American Indians) **1**:291 *bibliog.*
Indians of North America, art of the **11**:141
Potawatomi **15**:466
village of Pomeioc **11**:130 *illus.*
ALGONQUIN HOTEL ROUND TABLE *see* ROUND TABLE (Algonquin Hotel)
ALGOOD (Tennessee)
map (36° 12′N 85° 27′W) **19**:104
ALGORITHM **1**:291
cybernetics **5**:401
flowchart **8**:178
programming, computer **15**:563
ALGORITHMIC LANGUAGE *see* ALGOL (computer language)
ALGREN, NELSON **1**:291 *bibliog.*
ALHAMBRA (buildings) **1**:291–292 *bibliog., illus.*; **18**:141 *illus.*
Islamic art and architecture **11**:295
Moorish art and architecture **13**:571 *illus.*
Spanish art and architecture **18**:152
ALHAMBRA (California)
map (34° 6′N 118° 8′W) **4**:31
ALHAZEN
mathematics, history of **13**:224
ALI (Caliph) **1**:292
Egypt **7**:80 *illus.*
Islam **11**:289
Middle East, history of the **13**:402
Shiites **17**:261
ALI, MUHAMMAD (boxer) **1**:292 *bibliog., illus.*; **3**:431 *illus.*
ALI, SABAHATTIN **1**:292
ALI BABA **1**:292
ALI PASHA, MUHAMMAD (Egyptian viceroy) *see* MUHAMMAD ALI PASHA
ALIA, RAMIZ
Albania **1**:251
ALIAS **1**:292
ALICANTE (Spain) **1**:292; **18**:139 *illus.*
climate **18**:141 *table*
map (38° 21′N 0° 29′W) **18**:140
ALICE (Texas)
map (27° 45′N 98° 4′W) **19**:129
ALICE SPRINGS (Australia) **1**:293; **2**:337 *illus.*
climate **2**:332 *table*
map (23° 42′S 133° 53′E) **2**:328
ALICE TOWN (Bahama Islands)
map (25° 44′N 79° 17′W) **3**:23
ALICE'S ADVENTURES IN WONDERLAND (book) **1**:293 *bibliog., illus.*; **4**:352 *illus.*
diseases, occupational **6**:193
Grandville **9**:286
pastoral literature **15**:109
Rackham, Arthur **16**:38 *illus.*
Tenniel, Sir John **19**:108 *illus.*
ALICEVILLE (Alabama)
map (33° 8′N 88° 9′W) **1**:234
ALICYCLIC COMPOUNDS **1**:293 *bibliog.*
chemical nomenclature **4**:321
cyclic compounds **5**:403
terpene **19**:118–119
ALIDADE **1**:293
ALIEN **1**:293
Alien and Sedition Acts **1**:293–294
deportation **6**:118
equal protection of the laws **7**:224
immigration **11**:54–56
migrant labor **13**:417
naturalization **14**:50–51
ALIEN, ILLEGAL
Hispanic Americans **10**:177–178; **10**:179
ALIEN REGISTRATION ACT *see* SMITH ACT
ALIEN AND SEDITION ACTS **1**:293–294 *bibliog.*
freedom of speech **8**:298
journalism **11**:454
Kentucky and Virginia Resolutions **12**:51–52
Madison, James **13**:42
nullification **14**:292
sedition **17**:186
ALIENATION **1**:294 *bibliog.*
concepts **1**:294
Marx, Karl **13**:182
Marxism **13**:183–184
socialism **18**:19
ALIENATION OF AFFECTIONS **1**:294
ALIGARH (India)
map (27° 53′N 78° 5′E) **11**:80
ALIGHIERI, DANTE *see* DANTE ALIGHIERI
ALIGNMENT CHART *see* NOMOGRAM
ALIMA RIVER
map (1° 36′S 16° 36′E) **5**:182
ALIMENTARY CANAL *see* DIGESTION, HUMAN; DIGESTIVE SYSTEM
ALIMONY **1**:294
desertion **6**:131
ALINARI BROTHERS
photography, history and art of **15**:269
ALINGSÅS (Sweden)
map (57° 56′N 12° 31′E) **18**:382
ALINSKY, SAUL **1**:295
ALIPHATIC COMPOUNDS **1**:295 *bibliog.*
alkane **1**:296
alkene **1**:296–297
alkyne **1**:297
organic chemistry **14**:436–437
ALIQUIPPA (Pennsylvania)
map (40° 37′N 80° 15′W) **15**:147
ALIX (Alberta)
map (52° 24′N 113° 11′W) **1**:256
ALIZARIN **1**:295
madder **13**:39
ALKADIENE *see* DIENE (chemistry)
ALKALI **1**:295
feldspar **8**:46–47
halide minerals **10**:21
production
chemical industry **4**:317–318
Gossage, William **9**:254
Mond (family) **13**:522
Solvay process **18**:58
soap and detergent **18**:6
sodium **18**:32
soil distribution, worldwide **18**:37 *illus.*
ALKALI METALS **1**:295
cesium **4**:262
francium **8**:277
ion and ionization **11**:240
lithium **12**:370–371
oxidation and reduction **14**:475

potassium 15:464–465
rubidium 16:336
sodium 18:32–33
ALKALINE EARTH METALS 1:295–296 *bibliog.*
barium 3:81–82
beryllium 3:227
calcium 4:22
Davy, Sir Humphry 6:53–54
halide minerals 10:21
magnesium 13:53–54
oxidation and reduction 14:475
radium 16:68
strontium 18:303
ALKALOID 1:296 *bibliog.*
caffeine 4:15
cancer 4:105 *illus.*
curare 5:390–391
ephedrine 7:216
hellebore 10:114
henbane 10:121
jimsonweed 11:419
mandrake 13:112
medicinal plants 13:266–267
morning glory 13:583
nightshade 14:194
occurrence 1:296
opium 14:406
Pelletier, Pierre Joseph 15:183
poppy 15:432
Robinson, Sir Robert 16:245
strophanthus 18:303
strychnine 18:304
uses 1:296
Willstätter, Richard 20:163
ALKALOSIS 1:296 *bibliog.*
ALKAN, CHARLES 1:296
ALKANE 1:296 *bibliog.*
butane 3:591
carbon 4:135
ethane 7:249
gasoline 9:55
homologous series 10:216
isomer 11:299
methane 13:343
organic chemistry 14:436–437
pentane 15:155
propane 15:569
ALKANET 1:296
ALKENE 1:296–297 *bibliog., illus.*
chlorohydrin 4:401
cis-trans isomerism 4:445
diene 6:162
ethylene 7:258
homologous series 10:216
methylene 13:345
organic chemistry 14:437
ALKMAAR (Netherlands) 1:297; 14:101 *illus.*
map (52° 37′N 4° 44′E) 14:99
ALKYD
polyester 15:418–419
ALKYL GROUP 1:297
chemical nomenclature 4:321
ethyl group 7:257
halide 10:20
methyl group 13:344–345
ALKYNE 1:297 *bibliog., illus.*
acetylene 1:80
isomer 11:299
organic chemistry 14:437
ALL-AMERICA FOOTBALL CONFERENCE
football 8:217
ALL HALLOWS' EVE *see* HALLOWEEN
"ALL IN THE FAMILY" (television series)
Lear, Norman 12:359
radio and television broadcasting 16:59
ALL-INDIA MUSLIM LEAGUE *see* MUSLIM LEAGUE
ALL THE KING'S MEN (book) 1:298
Warren, Robert Penn 20:31
ALL THE PRESIDENT'S MEN (book) 1:298
Bernstein, Carl, and Woodward, Bob 3:223
ALL QUIET ON THE WESTERN FRONT (book) 1:297
Remarque, Erich Maria 16:144
ALL QUIET ON THE WESTERN FRONT (film)
Milestone, Lewis 13:419
ALL SAINTS CHURCH (Brixworth, Northamptonshire) 7:181 *illus.*
ALL SAINTS CHURCH (London)
Butterfield, William 3:593
ALL SAINTS' DAY 1:297
ALL SOULS COLLEGE, (Oxford University) 14:474
ALL SOULS' DAY 1:297–298
ALL-TERRAIN VEHICLE (ATV) *see* JEEP
ALLAGASH RIVER
map (47° 5′N 69° 2′W) 13:70
ALLAH 1:298 *bibliog., illus.*
Islam 11:288
ALLAHABAD (India) 1:298
map (25° 27′N 81° 51′E) 11:80
ALLAKAKET (Alaska)
map (66° 34′N 152° 41′W) 1:242
ALLAN (Saskatchewan)
map (51° 53′N 106° 4′W) 17:81
ALLAN, SIR HUGH
Pacific Scandal 15:8
ALLANMYO (Burma)
map (19° 22′N 95° 13′E) 3:573
ALLANTOIS (embryology)
development 6:138 *illus.*; 6:140 *illus.*; 6:141 *illus.*
ALLATOONA LAKE
map (34° 8′N 84° 38′W) 9:114
ALLEGAN (Michigan)
map (42° 32′N 85° 51′W) 13:377
ALLEGAN (county in Michigan)
map (42° 35′N 85° 53′W) 13:377
ALLEGANY (county in Maryland)
map (39° 40′N 78° 40′W) 13:188
ALLEGANY (New York)
map (42° 6′N 78° 30′W) 14:149
ALLEGANY (county in New York)
map (42° 13′N 78° 2′W) 14:149
ALLEGHANY (county in North Carolina)
map (36° 30′N 81° 10′W) 14:242
ALLEGHANY (county in Virginia)
map (37° 50′N 80° 0′W) 19:607
ALLEGHENY (county in Pennsylvania)
map (40° 26′N 79° 59′W) 15:147
ALLEGHENY COLLEGE 1:298
ALLEGHENY FRONT (ridge)
map (39° 30′N 79° 0′W) 20:111
ALLEGHENY MOUNTAINS 1:298
map (38° 30′N 80° 0′W) 2:86
ALLEGHENY OBSERVATORY
Schlesinger, Frank 17:125
ALLEGHENY PLATEAU
map (41° 15′N 78° 45′W) 15:147
ALLEGHENY RESERVOIR
map (42° 0′N 78° 56′W) 15:147
ALLEGHENY RIVER 1:298
map (40° 27′N 80° 0′W) 15:147
ALLEGIANCE 1:298
pledge of allegiance 15:364
state (in political philosophy) 18:228
treason 19:285
ALLEGORY 1:298–299 *bibliog., illus.*
See also UTOPIAN LITERATURE
bestiary 3:229
Bunyan, John 3:565
Calderón de la Barca, Pedro 4:26
Death in Venice 6:70
Divine Comedy, The 6:203
Dryden, John 6:284–285
Everyman 7:316
fable 8:4–5
Faerie Queene, The 8:7
Faust 8:38
France, Anatole 8:273
Goethe, Johann Wolfgang von 9:223–224
Golding, William 9:234–235
Gulliver's Travels 9:404
iconography 11:21
Kafka, Franz 12:5–6
Keats, John 12:35–36
Lord of the Flies 12:413
"Masque of the Red Death, The" 13:200
medieval drama 13:273–274
Orwell, George 14:451
parable 15:73
Piers Plowman 15:297
Pilgrim's Progress 15:302
Republic, The 16:172
Roman de la Rose, Le 16:278
Shelley, Percy Bysshe 17:253
Swift, Jonathan 18:389
Tolkien, J. R. R. 19:226–227
Trial, The 19:292
ALLELE
evolution 7:319
genetic diseases 9:82
genetics 9:86–90
heredity 10:140 *illus.*
population genetics 15:439–440
ALLEN (county in Indiana)
map (41° 4′N 85° 9′W) 11:111
ALLEN (county in Kansas)
map (37° 50′N 95° 20′W) 12:18
ALLEN (county in Kentucky)
map (36° 45′N 86° 10′W) 12:47
ALLEN (county in Louisiana)
map (30° 40′N 92° 47′W) 12:430
ALLEN (county in Ohio)
map (40° 46′N 84° 6′W) 14:357
ALLEN (Oklahoma)
map (34° 53′N 96° 25′W) 14:368
ALLEN, BRYAN
flight, human-powered 8:164–165 *illus.*
ALLEN, EBENEZER
Rochester (New York) 16:247
ALLEN, EDGAR
Doisy, Edward 6:224
ALLEN, ETHAN 1:299 *bibliog.*
Green Mountain Boys 9:348
Ticonderoga 19:192
ALLEN, FRED 1:299
ALLEN, FREDERICK LEWIS 1:299 *bibliog.*
ALLEN, GRACIE *see* BURNS AND ALLEN
ALLEN, HERVEY 1:299
ALLEN, JAMES EDWARD, JR. 1:299
Right-to-Read Program 16:222
ALLEN, LAKE
map (54° 8′N 8° 8′W) 11:258
ALLEN, RICHARD 1:299–300 *bibliog.*
ALLEN, STEVE 1:300
ALLEN, VIOLA 1:300
ALLEN, WOODY 1:300 *bibliog., illus.*
ALLEN PARK (Michigan)
map (42° 15′N 83° 13′W) 13:377
ALLENBY, EDMUND HENRY HYNMAN, 1ST VISCOUNT ALLENBY OF MEGIDDO 1:300 *bibliog.*
World War I 20:239–240; 20:243–244
ALLENDALE (Illinois)
map (38° 32′N 87° 43′W) 11:42
ALLENDALE (South Carolina)
map (33° 6′N 81° 18′W) 18:98
ALLENDALE (county in South Carolina)
map (33° 0′N 81° 20′W) 18:98
ALLENDE, SALVADOR 1:300–301 *bibliog., illus.*; 12:222 *illus.*
Central Intelligence Agency 4:254
Chile 4:357
Pinochet Ugarte, Augusto 15:307
ALLENTOWN (Pennsylvania) 1:301
map (40° 36′N 75° 29′W) 15:147
ALLERGY 1:301–302 *bibliog.*
anaphylaxis 1:391
antibody 2:60
antihistamine 2:63
asthma 2:268
decongestant drugs 6:76
dermatitis 6:121–122
drug 6:277
eczema 7:54
gastrointestinal tract disease 9:57
glucocorticoid 9:211
goldenrod 9:233
headache 10:85
hives 10:190
immunity 11:57
immunology 11:60
inflammation 11:169
poisonous plants and animals 15:385
ragweed 16:70
respiratory system disorders 16:181
rhinitis 16:196
serum sickness 17:210
shock, physiologic 17:279
sinusitis 17:326
sneezeweed 18:3
sulfites 18:334
ALLERTON (Iowa)
map (40° 42′N 93° 22′W) 11:244
ALLEYN, EDWARD 1:302 *bibliog.*
ALLIANCE 1:302
See also names of specific alliances, e.g., NORTH ATLANTIC TREATY ORGANIZATION; QUADRUPLE ALLIANCE; TRIPLE ENTENTE; etc.
balance of power 3:32
congress system 5:187–188
foreign policy 8:225
World War I 20:219–222 *maps*
ALLIANCE (Nebraska)
map (42° 6′N 102° 52′W) 14:70
ALLIANCE (Ohio)
map (40° 55′N 81° 6′W) 14:357
ALLIANCE FOR PROGRESS 1:302 *bibliog.*
ALLIED POWERS
World War I 20:219–248 *maps*
World War II 20:248–281 *maps*
ALLIER RIVER
map (45° 5′N 3° 35′E) 8:260
ALLIGATOR 1:302–303 *bibliog., illus.*; 5:356 *illus.*
American alligator 18:377 *illus.*
anatomy 16:168 *illus.*
brain 3:443 *illus.*
jaw 13:99 *illus.*
ALLIGATOR PEAR *see* AVOCADO
ALLIGATOR POND (Jamaica)
map (17° 52′N 77° 34′W) 11:351
ALLIGATOR RIVER
map (35° 58′N 75° 58′W) 14:242
ALLINGHAM, MARGERY 1:303
ALLIS, EDWARD PHELPS 1:303
ALLISON (Iowa)
map (42° 45′N 92° 48′W) 11:244
ALLITERATION
figures of speech 8:76
ALLMAKEE (county in Iowa)
map (43° 15′N 91° 15′W) 11:244
ALLOSAURUS 1:303 *bibliog., illus.*; 6:180 *illus.*; 11:475 *illus.*
ALLOSTERIC REGULATION
enzyme 7:214
ALLOTROPE (chemistry) 1:303
antimony 2:63
arsenic 2:189
carbon 4:134
element 7:131
phosphorus 15:256
selenium 17:190
sulfur 18:335
tin 19:204
ALLOUEZ, CLAUDE JEAN 1:303
Oshkosh (Wisconsin) 14:454
ALLOWAY, LAWRENCE
pop art 15:429
ALLOY 1:303–304
aluminum 1:317–319
amalgam, metallic 1:320–321
antimony 2:64
babbitt metals 3:6
brass 3:457
bronze 3:505
cadmium 4:12
cerium 4:260
chromium 4:419
cobalt 5:82
copper 5:252–253
indium 11:144
iron 11:271
iron and steel industry 11:278
lanthanide series 12:200–201
magnesium 13:54
manganese 13:114
materials technology 13:219–221
metal 13:328
metallurgy 13:330
molybdenum 13:514
nickel 14:183
platinum 15:359
rhodium 16:203
ruthenium 16:375
stainless steel 18:213
tellurium 19:91
tin 19:204–205
titanium 19:211
zinc 20:367–368
zirconium 20:370
ALLPORT, GORDON W. 1:304
ALLSPICE 1:304 *illus.*
spicebush 18:181
ALLSTON, WASHINGTON 1:304–305 *bibliog., illus.*
ALLUSION
narrative and dramatic devices 14:22
ALLUVIAL FANS 1:305 *bibliog., illus.*
basin and range province 3:110
desert 6:128 *illus.*
floodplain 8:166
glaciers and glaciation 9:193 *illus.*
landform evolution 12:183
river delta 16:232–233
soil distribution, worldwide 18:37 *illus.*
ALLYSON, JUNE 1:305
ALMA (Arkansas)
map (35° 29′N 94° 13′W) 2:166
ALMA (Georgia)
map (31° 33′N 82° 28′W) 9:114
ALMA (Kansas)
map (39° 1′N 96° 17′W) 12:18
ALMA (Michigan)
map (43° 23′N 84° 39′W) 13:377
ALMA (Nebraska)
map (40° 6′N 99° 22′W) 14:70
ALMA (Quebec)
map (48° 33′N 71° 39′W) 16:18
ALMA (Wisconsin)
map (44° 20′N 91° 55′W) 20:185
ALMA-ATA (USSR) 1:305
map (43° 15′N 76° 57′E) 19:388
ALMA-TADEMA, SIR LAWRENCE 1:305 *bibliog.*
ALMAGEST 1:305–306 *bibliog.*; 13:224 *illus.*
astronomy, history of 2:277–278
mathematics, history of 13:224 *illus.*
Ptolemy 15:606
ALMAGRO, DIEGO DE 1:306 *bibliog.*
Pizarro, Francisco 15:324–325
ALMANAC 1:306 *bibliog.*
Banneker, Benjamin 3:70
Poor Richard's Almanack 15:429
Wallace, Irving 20:14

ALMANDINE
garnet 9:49
ALMEIDA, FRANCISCO DE 1:306
bibliog.
ALMEIRIM (Brazil)
map (1° 32′S 52° 34′W) 3:460
ALMELO (Netherlands)
map (52° 21′N 6° 39′E) 14:99
ALMENA (Kansas)
map (39° 54′N 99° 43′W) 12:18
ALMENDRA RESERVOIR
map (41° 15′N 6° 10′W) 15:449
ALMERÍA (Spain) 1:306
climate 18:141 *table*
map (36° 50′N 2° 27′W) 18:140
ALMIRA (Washington)
map (47° 43′N 118° 56′W) 20:35
ALMIRANTE (Panama)
map (9° 18′N 82° 24′W) 15:55
ALMO (Idaho)
map (42° 6′N 113° 38′W) 11:26
ALMOHADS 1:306
Moorish art and architecture 13:571
Spain, history of 18:145–146 *map*
ALMOND (tree) 1:306–307 *illus.*
benzaldehyde 3:206
laetrile 12:163
ALMOND (Wisconsin)
map (44° 16′N 89° 24′W) 20:185
ALMORAVIDS 1:307
Marrakech (Morocco) 13:163
Moorish art and architecture 13:570
Spain, history of 18:145
ALMQVIST, CARL JONAS LOVE 1:307
ALOE 1:307 *illus.*
ALONSO, ALICIA 1:307 *bibliog.*
Ballets Russes de Monte Carlo 3:48
ALONSO, DÁMASO 1:307–308
ALOPECIA *see* BALDNESS
ALOR SETAR (Malaysia)
map (6° 7′N 100° 22′E) 13:84
ALORESE 1:308 *bibliog.*
ALOUETTE (artificial satellite) 1:308
ionosphere 11:242
ALPACA 1:308 *illus.*
ALPENA (Arkansas)
map (36° 17′N 93° 18′W) 2:166
ALPENA (Michigan)
map (45° 4′N 83° 26′W) 13:377
ALPENA (county in Michigan)
map (45° 0′N 83° 35′W) 13:377
ALPHA
A (letter) 1:49
ALPHA CENTAURI
Centaurus 4:249
Proxima Centauri 15:584
star 18:225 *table*
ALPHA CORDILLERA
map (83° 0′N 178° 0′E) 2:139
ALPHA PARTICLE 1:308
atomic nucleus 2:309
periodic table 15:168
radioactivity 16:61–62 *illus.*
ALPHA WAVE
brain 3:447
ALPHABET *see* WRITING SYSTEMS, EVOLUTION OF; specific letters of the alphabet
ALPHARETTA (Georgia)
map (34° 4′N 84° 18′W) 9:114
ALPHER, R. A.
big bang theory 3:248
ALPHONSUS LIGUORI, SAINT 1:308
ALPHORN 1:308–309 *illus.*
ALPINE (county in California)
map (38° 41′N 119° 47′W) 4:31
ALPINE (New Jersey)
map (40° 56′N 73° 56′W) 14:129
ALPINE (Texas)
map (30° 22′N 103° 40′W) 19:129
ALPINE BUTTERFLY 3:595–596 *illus.*
ALPINE SKIING *see* SKIING
ALPINE TUNDRA
biome 3:273 *map*; 3:274
tundra 19:332–333
ALPORT'S SYNDROME
kidney disease 12:71
ALPS 1:309–310 *bibliog., illus., map*; 7:270 *illus.*
Austria 2:347
Brenner Pass 3:473
chalet 4:271 *illus.*
climate and drainage 1:310
geology
Bertrand, Marcel Alexandre 3:226
Lugeon, Maurice 12:452–453
Italy 11:320; 11:322
map (46° 25′N 10° 0′E) 1:309
Mer de Glace 13:303
ranges and peaks
Apennines 2:76
Blanc, Mont 3:326
Dinaric Alps 6:178
Dolomites 6:226
Jungfrau 11:468
Jura 11:474
Matterhorn 13:231
regional cultures 1:309
Saint Bernard Pass 17:16
Saint Gotthard Pass 17:18–19
Simplon Pass 17:316
Switzerland 18:394–396 *illus.*
topography 1:309–310
mountain 13:620
mudflow 13:631
tunnel 19:337 *table*
Saint Gotthard Tunnel 17:19
vegetation and animal life 1:310
mountain life 13:622–623
yodel 20:328
Yugoslavia 20:340–341 *illus.*
ALS ISLAND
map (54° 59′N 9° 55′E) 6:109
ALSACE-LORRAINE (France) 1:310
bibliog., map; 8:264 *illus.*
cities
Metz 13:350
Nancy 14:12
Europe, history of 7:293
Germany, history of 9:153 *map*
Lotharingia 12:419–420
Polish Succession, War of the 15:398
Vosges 19:635
wine 20:175
World War I 20:222
ALSASK (Saskatchewan)
map (51° 23′N 109° 59′W) 17:81
ALSATIAN (dog) *see* GERMAN SHEPHERD
ALSEN (North Dakota)
map (48° 38′N 98° 42′W) 14:248
ALSOP, JOSEPH AND STEWART 1:310
bibliog.
ALSTON, WALTER 1:310
ALTA (Iowa)
map (42° 40′N 95° 18′W) 11:244
ALTA GRACIA (Argentina)
map (31° 40′S 64° 26′W) 2:149
ALTADENA (California)
map (34° 12′N 118° 8′W) 4:31
ALTAGRACIA DE ORITUCO (Venezuela)
map (9° 52′N 66° 23′W) 19:542
ALTAI MOUNTAINS 1:311
map (48° 0′N 90° 0′E) 13:529
ALTAIC LANGUAGES *see* URAL-ALTAIC LANGUAGES
ALTAIC PEOPLES *see* TURKS
ALTAMAHA RIVER
map (31° 19′N 81° 17′W) 9:114
ALTAMIRA (Spain) 1:311 *bibliog., illus.*
cave painting 15:508 *illus.*
mural painting 13:646
Spanish art and architecture 18:151
ALTAMIRANO, IGNACIO MANUEL
1:311 *bibliog.*
ALTAMONT (Oregon)
map (42° 12′N 121° 44′W) 14:427
ALTAMONT (Tennessee)
map (35° 26′N 85° 43′W) 19:104
ALTAMURA (Italy)
map (40° 50′N 16° 33′E) 11:321
ALTAR 1:311 *bibliog.*
Ara Pacis *see* ARA PACIS
Greek architecture 9:334
Juni, Juan de 11:470
Pacher, Michael 15:4
pre-Columbian art and architecture 15:497
Roman art and architecture 16:276
ALTAR DESERT
map (31° 50′N 114° 15′W) 13:357
ALTAR OF PEACE *see* ARA PACIS
ALTATA (Mexico)
map (24° 38′N 107° 55′W) 13:357
ALTAVISTA (Virginia)
map (37° 6′N 79° 17′W) 19:607
ALTDORF (Switzerland)
map (46° 53′N 8° 39′E) 18:394
ALTDORFER, ALBRECHT 1:311–312
bibliog., illus.
Danube Landscape near Regensburg 1:312 *illus.*; 12:189 *illus.*
Danube school 6:36
ALTENBURG (Germany, East and West)
map (50° 59′N 12° 26′E) 9:140
ALTER, DAVID 1:312
element 7:130
ALTERATION, MINERAL 1:312
mineral 13:442
ore deposits 14:422
vein deposit 19:536
ALTERNATING CURRENT 1:312–313
bibliog., illus.
capacitor 4:119
circuit, electric 4:436–438
electromagnetic induction 7:115
impedance 11:61
Josephson effect 18:350
motor 13:611–612 *illus.*
rectifier 16:110–111
Stanley, William 18:219
Steinmetz, Charles Proteus 18:249
transformer 19:270–271
Westinghouse, George 20:117
ALTERNATION OF GENERATIONS 1:313
algae 1:280
bryophyte 3:530
fern 8:56–57
kelp 12:40
liverwort 12:376
moss 13:605
club moss 5:70–71
Irish moss 11:268
plant 15:339
pollen 15:406
reproduction 16:162
tracheophyte 19:258
ALTERNATIVE SCHOOLS 1:313
bibliog.
free schools 8:294–295
ALTERNATOR
generator 9:78
ALTGELD, JOHN PETER 1:313 *bibliog.*
ALTHAEA 1:313
ALTHING (parliament)
Iceland 11:18
ALTIMETER 1:313
ALTIPLANO 15:194 *illus.*
map (18° 0′S 68° 0′W) 3:366
ALTITUDE (astronomy) 1:313
ALTITUDE (height)
altimeter 1:313
biome 3:274
mountain life 13:623
ALTITUDE SICKNESS *see* HYPOXIA
ALTMAN, ROBERT B. 1:313–314
bibliog., illus.
ALTO *see* CONTRALTO
ALTO ARAGUAIA (Brazil)
map (17° 19′S 53° 12′W) 3:460
ALTON (Alabama)
map (33° 35′N 86° 38′W) 1:234
ALTON (Illinois)
map (38° 54′N 90° 10′W) 11:42
ALTON (Iowa)
map (42° 59′N 96° 1′W) 11:244
ALTON (Kansas)
map (39° 28′N 98° 57′W) 12:18
ALTON (Missouri)
map (36° 42′N 91° 24′W) 13:476
ALTON (New Hampshire)
map (43° 27′N 71° 13′W) 14:123
ALTONA (Manitoba)
map (49° 6′N 97° 33′W) 13:119
ALTOONA (Iowa)
map (41° 39′N 93° 28′W) 11:244
ALTOONA (Kansas)
map (37° 32′N 95° 40′W) 12:18
ALTOONA (Pennsylvania) 1:314
map (40° 30′N 78° 24′W) 15:147
ALTOONA (Wisconsin)
map (44° 48′N 91° 26′W) 20:185
ALTRICIAL ANIMAL 1:314
bird 3:287 *illus.*
ALTRUISM 1:314 *bibliog.*
animal behavior 2:17
social psychology 18:13
ALTURAS (California)
map (41° 29′N 120° 32′W) 4:31
ALTUS (Arkansas)
map (35° 27′N 93° 46′W) 2:166
ALTUS (Oklahoma)
map (34° 38′N 99° 20′W) 14:368
ALUKO, TIMOTHY MOFOLORUNSO
1:314
ALUM 1:314–315
double salt 6:246
ALUMINA
aluminum 1:317
new ceramics applications 4:258
refractory materials 16:124
ALUMINUM 1:315–319 *bibliog., illus., map, table*
abundance of aluminum 7:131 *table*
alloys 1:317
alum 1:314–315
aluminum industry 1:316
anodizing 2:34
bauxite 3:131
corrosion 5:276–277
corundum 5:279
cryolite 5:371
electrolysis 7:114
element 7:130 *table*
feldspar 8:46
future trends 1:318
Group IIIA periodic table 12:167
kyanite 12:143
laterite 12:215
metallurgy 13:330
ore deposits, worldwide 14:423 *map*
physical properties 1:315–316 *table*
processing 1:316–317 *illus.*
silicate minerals 17:304–305
superconductivity 18:350 *table*
uranium minerals 19:478
wavellite 20:71
ALUMINUM HYDROXIDE
antacid 2:38
ALUMINUM SULFATE *see* ALUM
ALVA (Oklahoma)
map (36° 48′N 98° 40′W) 14:368
ALVA, DUQUE DE *see* ALBA, FERNANDO ÁLVAREZ DE TOLEDO Y PIMENTEL, DUQUE DE
ALVARADO (Mexico)
map (18° 46′N 95° 46′W) 13:357
ALVARADO (Texas)
map (32° 24′N 97° 13′W) 19:129
ALVARADO, JUAN BAUTISTA 1:319
ALVARADO, JUAN VELASCO *see* VELASCO ALVARADO, JUAN
ALVARADO, PEDRO DE 1:319 *bibliog.*
Mexico, history of 13:362–363
ÁLVARES, LUIS ECHEVERRÍA *see* ECHVERRÍA ÁLVARES, LUIS
ÁLVARES PEREIRA, NUNO *see* PEREIRA, NUNO ÁLVARES
ALVAREZ, A. 1:319
ALVAREZ, GREGORIO
Uruguay 19:490
ALVAREZ, LUIS WALTER 1:319
ÁLVAREZ DE FARIA, MANUEL DE GODOY Y *see* GODOY, MANUEL DE
ÁLVAREZ QUINTERO, SERAFÍN AND JOAQUÍN 1:319–320 *bibliog.*
ALVARO, CORRADO 1:320
ALVEOLI
lungs 12:464 *illus.*
ALVIN (Texas)
map (29° 25′N 95° 15′W) 19:129
ALVIN AILEY AMERICAN DANCE THEATER
Ailey, Alvin 1:202–203
ALYSSUM 1:320 *illus.*
ALZETTE RIVER
map (49° 22′N 6° 9′E) 12:472
ALZHEIMER'S DISEASE 1:320 *bibliog.*
AM *see* AMPLITUDE MODULATION; AM RADIO
AM RADIO
FM radio 8:192
radio 16:46–47
wavelength and frequency, electromagnetic 7:117 *table*
AMA *see* AMERICAN MEDICAL ASSOCIATION
AMADEUS VIII, COUNT OF SAVOY
Savoy (dynasty) 17:102
AMADI, ELECHI 1:320
AMADO, JORGE 1:320
Brazilian literature 3:464
AMADOR (county in California)
map (38° 21′N 120° 46′W) 4:31
AMAGER ISLAND
map (55° 37′N 12° 37′E) 6:109
AMALEKITES 1:320
AMALFI (Italy) 1:320
AMALGAM, METALLIC 1:320–321
mercury 13:306
AMALGAMATED CLOTHING AND TEXTILE WORKERS UNION
1:321 *bibliog.*
clothing industry 5:66
Hillman, Sidney 10:165
AMALIENBURG PAVILION 1:321
bibliog.
rococo style 16:264 *illus.*
AMALTHEA (satellite)
Jupiter (planet) 11:473–474 *table*
AMAMI ISLANDS
map (28° 15′N 129° 20′E) 11:361
Ryukyu Islands 16:380
AMANA SOCIETY 1:321 *bibliog.*
Iowa 11:248
AMAPÁ (Brazil)
map (2° 3′N 50° 48′W) 3:460
AMAPÁ TERRITORY
map (1° 0′N 52° 0′W) 3:460
AMAPALA (Honduras)
map (13° 17′N 87° 40′W) 10:218
AMARANTH (botany) 1:321 *illus.*
AMARANTH (Manitoba)
map (50° 36′N 98° 43′W) 13:119
AMARAVATI (India) 1:321
AMARGOSA DESERT
map (36° 45′N 116° 45′W) 14:111
AMARGOSA RANGE
map (36° 30′N 116° 45′W) 4:31
AMARILLO (Texas) 1:321
map (35° 13′N 101° 49′W) 19:129

AMARNA, TELL EL- (Egypt) **1**:321–322; **7**:81 *map*; **7**:85 *illus.*
AMARNA STYLE
  Egyptian art and architecture **7**:88
AMARYLLIS **1**:322 *illus.*
  narcissus **14**:21
  snowdrop **18**:5
  Sternbergia **18**:261 *illus.*
AMASA (Michigan)
  map (46° 14′N 88° 27′W) **13**:377
AMASIS *see* AHMOSE I, KING OF EGYPT; AHMOSE II, KING OF EGYPT
AMATERASU (Japanese deity) **1**:322
AMATEUR ATHLETIC ASSOCIATION **1**:322
  track and field **19**:259
AMATEUR ATHLETIC CLUB *see* AMATEUR ATHLETIC ASSOCIATION
AMATEUR ATHLETIC UNION OF THE UNITED STATES **1**:322
  Brundage, Avery **3**:523
  Sullivan Award **18**:337
  track and field **19**:259
AMATEUR RADIO *see* HAM RADIO
AMATEUR SOFTBALL ASSOCIATION
  softball **18**:35
AMATI (family) **1**:322 *bibliog.*
AMATITLAN (Guatemala)
  map (14° 29′N 90° 37′W) **9**:389
AMAURY (Mauritius)
  map (20° 8′S 57° 40′E) **13**:237
AMAZING STORIES (periodical)
  science fiction **17**:144 *illus.*
AMAZON HIGHWAY *see* TRANS-AMAZONIAN HIGHWAY
AMAZON RIVER **1**:323–324 *bibliog.*, *illus.*, *map*
  Brazil **3**:459–460
  map (0° 5′S 50° 0′W) **1**:323
  Orellana, Francisco de **14**:432
  South America **18**:88
  tidal bore **19**:192
AMAZONAS (Brazil)
  map (4° 0′S 58° 0′W) **3**:460
AMAZONITE
  feldspar **8**:46 *illus.*
AMAZONS **1**:324
  Antiope **2**:64
  Hippolyte **10**:174
  Orellana, Francisco de **14**:432
  Sarmatians **17**:78
AMBARTSUMIAN, VIKTOR AMAZASPOVICH **1**:324 *bibliog.*
AMBASSADOR **1**:324
  See also names of specific ambassadors, e.g., KOLLANTAI, ALEKSANDRA; WOODCOCK, LEONARD; etc.
  foreign service **8**:226
AMBASSADORS, THE (book) **1**:324–325
AMBATO (Ecuador)
  map (1° 15′S 78° 37′W) **7**:52
ÁMBELOS, CAPE
  map (39° 56′N 23° 55′E) **9**:325
AMBER **1**:325 *illus.*
AMBERG (Germany, East and West)
  map (49° 27′N 11° 52′E) **9**:140
AMBERG (Wisconsin)
  map (45° 30′N 88° 0′W) **20**:185
AMBERGRIS **1**:325
  whale **20**:122
AMBLER (Alaska)
  map (67° 5′N 157° 52′W) **1**:242
AMBLER (Pennsylvania)
  map (40° 9′N 75° 13′W) **15**:147
AMBLER, ERIC **1**:325
AMBOISE, JACQUES D' *see* D'AMBOISE, JACQUES
AMBON (Indonesia)
  map (3° 43′S 128° 12′E) **11**:147
AMBONESE **1**:325 *bibliog.*
AMBOSITRA (Madagascar)
  map (20° 31′S 47° 15′E) **13**:38
AMBOY (Illinois)
  map (41° 44′N 89° 20′W) **11**:42
AMBOY (Minnesota)
  map (43° 59′N 94° 10′W) **13**:453
AMBRE, CAPE
  map (11° 57′S 49° 17′E) **13**:38
AMBRIDGE (Pennsylvania)
  map (40° 36′N 80° 14′W) **15**:147
AMBRONA (Spain) *see* TORRALBA AND AMBRONA (Spain)
AMBROSE, SAINT **1**:325 *bibliog.*
  Ambrosian Library **1**:325
  hymn **10**:346
  Italian music **11**:317
  Theodosius I, Roman Emperor (Theodosius the Great) **19**:156–157
AMBROSIAN LIBRARY **1**:325
AMBROTYPE **1**:325
AMBULANCE **1**:326 *bibliog.*
  paramedic **15**:80
AMCHITKA ISLAND
  map (51° 30′N 179° 0′E) **1**:242
AMEAGLE (West Virginia)
  map (37° 57′N 81° 25′W) **20**:111
AMEBIASIS **1**:326 *bibliog.*
  Entamoeba **7**:208
  protozoal diseases **15**:581
AMEBIC DYSENTERY *see* AMOEBIC DYSENTERY
AMELAND ISLAND
  map (53° 25′N 5° 45′E) **14**:99
AMELIA (county in Virginia)
  map (37° 20′N 78° 10′W) **19**:607
AMELIA COURT HOUSE (Virginia)
  map (37° 21′N 77° 59′W) **19**:607
AMELIA ISLAND
  map (30° 37′N 81° 27′W) **8**:172
AMELING, ELLY **1**:326
AMELUNG, JOHN FREDERICK
  glassware, decorative **5**:111 *illus.*; **9**:204
AMENEMHET I, KING OF EGYPT **1**:326 *bibliog.*
AMENHOTEP I, KING OF EGYPT **1**:326
AMENHOTEP II, KING OF EGYPT **1**:326
AMENHOTEP III, KING OF EGYPT **1**:326 *bibliog.*
  death mask **15**:447 *illus.*
AMENHOTEP IV *see* AKHENATEN
AMENOPHIS *see* AMENHOTEP
AMENORRHEA **1**:326
  endocrine system, diseases of the **7**:171
  menstruation **13**:301
AMENT (Egyptian goddess) **7**:88 *illus.*
AMERICA **1**:326
  See also CENTRAL AMERICA; LATIN AMERICA; NORTH AMERICA; SOUTH AMERICA; UNITED STATES
  Vespucci, Amerigo **19**:564
AMERICA THE BEAUTIFUL (song)
  Bates, Katharine Lee **3**:121
AMERICAN, THE (book) **1**:326–327
  James, Henry **11**:354
AMERICAN ACADEMY OF ARTS AND LETTERS **1**:327
AMERICAN ACADEMY OF ARTS AND SCIENCES **1**:327
  Daedalus **6**:5
  Mitchell, Maria **13**:483
  Rumford, Benjamin Thomson, Count **16**:344–345
AMERICAN ACADEMY OF DRAMATIC ART **1**:327
AMERICAN ANTI-SLAVERY SOCIETY
  abolitionists **1**:58
  Garrison, William Lloyd **9**:51
AMERICAN ANTIQUARIAN SOCIETY
  Thomas, Isaiah **19**:173
AMERICAN ART AND ARCHITECTURE **1**:327–336 *bibliog.*, *illus.*
  See also the subheading United States under names of specific art forms, movements, and historic periods, e.g., ARCHITECTURE; PAINTING; NEOCLASSICISM (art); PREHISTORIC ART; etc.; names of specific artists, e.g., CURRIER AND IVES; TIFFANY, LOUIS C OMFORT; etc.
  abstract expressionism **1**:335–336
  Armory Show **2**:177
  Art Deco **2**:207–208
  Art Nouveau **2**:212
  Ashcan School (art group) **2**:229–230
  book illustration **3**:388
  brownstone **3**:519
  calligraphy **4**:43
  Carrère and Hastings **4**:168
  cast-iron architecture **4**:185–186
  cathedrals and churches **4**:208
  Chicago school of architecture **4**:342–343
  colonial styles in North America **5**:109–111
  costume **5**:302–303 *illus.*
  craft **5**:326; **5**:327 *illus.*
  dome **6**:230
  earthworks **7**:28
  federal style **8**:42
  film, history of **8**:80–87
  folk art **8**:196–198 *illus.*
  furniture **8**:378–379
  graphic arts **9**:294
  Greek Revival **9**:346
  hard-edge painting **10**:45
  historic preservation **10**:181–182
  house (in Western architecture) **10**:270–271
  Hudson River school **10**:290
  Indians of North America, art of the **11**:138–141
  International Style (Bauhaus art) **11**:223
  landscape architecture **12**:188
    garden **9**:41
  limners **12**:345
  Luminism **12**:459
  magic realism **13**:51
  minimal art **13**:446
  modern art **13**:493–496
  photography, history and art of **15**:267–273
  photorealism **15**:274–275
  pop art **15**:429
  pottery and porcelain **15**:472
  rugs and carpets **16**:343
  skyscraper **17**:348–350
  social realism **18**:13
  Spanish missions **18**:160–161 *illus.*
  stained glass **18**:212
  surrealism (art) **18**:364–365
  synchromism **18**:406
  urban planning **19**:484
AMERICAN ASSOCIATION FOR THE ACCREDITATION OF LABORATORY ANIMAL CARE
  vivisection **19**:623
AMERICAN ASSOCIATION FOR THE ADVANCEMENT OF SCIENCE **1**:336
AMERICAN ASSOCIATION OF COMMUNITY AND JUNIOR COLLEGES **1**:336
AMERICAN ASSOCIATION FOR HIGHER EDUCATION **1**:336
AMERICAN ASSOCIATION OF PHYSICAL ANTHROPOLOGY
  Hrdlička, Aleš **10**:286
AMERICAN ASSOCIATION OF RETIRED PERSONS **1**:336–337
AMERICAN ASSOCIATION OF UNIVERSITY PROFESSORS **1**:337
  academic freedom **1**:68
AMERICAN ASSOCIATION OF UNIVERSITY WOMEN **1**:337
  Palmer, Alice Freeman **15**:50
AMERICAN ASTRONOMICAL SOCIETY **1**:337
AMERICAN AUTOMOBILE ASSOCIATION **1**:337
AMERICAN BALLET CARAVAN
  Carter, Elliott **4**:171
AMERICAN BALLET THEATRE **1**:337 *bibliog.*
  Alonso, Alicia **1**:307
  ballet **3**:44
  Baryshnikov, Mikhail **3**:99
  Bruhn, Erik **3**:523
  Chase, Lucia **4**:301
  Fracci, Carla **8**:257–258
  Gregory, Cynthia **9**:355
  Kirkland, Gelsey **12**:89
  Nagy, Ivan Akos **14**:7
  Smith, Oliver **17**:370
  Tcherkassky, Marianna **19**:52
  Tudor, Antony **19**:329
  van Hamel, Martine **19**:515
AMERICAN BANKERS ASSOCIATION **1**:337
AMERICAN BAR ASSOCIATION **1**:337
AMERICAN BOARD OF PROFESSIONAL PSYCHOLOGY
  psychopathology, treatment of **15**:600
AMERICAN BOARD OF PSYCHIATRY
  psychopathology, treatment of **15**:600
AMERICAN BOOK AWARDS
  National Book Awards **14**:30
AMERICAN BROADCASTING COMPANY
  radio and television broadcasting **16**:57; **16**:59
AMERICAN BULL TERRIER *see* BOSTON TERRIER
AMERICAN CANCER SOCIETY **1**:337
  fund raising **8**:360
AMERICAN CHEMICAL SOCIETY **1**:337
AMERICAN CHIROPRACTOR'S ASSOCIATION
  chiropractic **4**:397
AMERICAN CIVIL LIBERTIES UNION **1**:337–338 *bibliog.*
  Flynn, Elizabeth Gurley **8**:191
  Frankfurter, Felix **8**:281
AMERICAN COLLEGE TESTING PROGRAM
  scholarships, fellowships, and loans **17**:130
AMERICAN COLONIZATION SOCIETY **1**:338 *bibliog.*
  Finley, Robert **8**:98
  Liberia **12**:313–314
  Monrovia (Liberia) **13**:543
AMERICAN COMMISSION ON STRATIGRAPHIC NOMENCLATURE
  stratigraphy **18**:292
AMERICAN COPPER BUTTERFLY **3**:597 *illus.*
  butterflies and moths **3**:595
AMERICAN COUNCIL ON EDUCATION **1**:338
  Educational Testing Service **7**:66
AMERICAN COUNCIL OF LEARNED SOCIETIES **1**:338
AMERICAN DANCE FESTIVAL **1**:338 *bibliog.*
  Limón, José **12**:346
AMERICAN DANCE THEATER **6**:28 *illus.*
AMERICAN DENTAL ASSOCIATION **1**:338
AMERICAN DREAM, AN (book) **1**:338
  Mailer, Norman **13**:67
AMERICAN EAGLE (ship) **16**:200 *illus.*
AMERICAN EDUCATIONAL THEATRE ASSOCIATION **1**:338
AMERICAN ELK *see* WAPITI
AMERICAN ENGLISH *see* ENGLISH LANGUAGE
AMERICAN ETHNOLOGICAL SOCIETY
  Gallatin, Albert **9**:17
AMERICAN EXPEDITIONARY FORCES
  Pershing, John J. **15**:180–181
  World War I **20**:243
AMERICAN EXPRESS COMPANY
  Butterfield, John **3**:593
AMERICAN FALLS *see* NIAGARA FALLS
AMERICAN FALLS (Idaho)
  map (42° 47′N 112° 51′W) **11**:26
AMERICAN FALLS RESERVOIR
  map (43° 0′N 113° 0′W) **11**:26
AMERICAN FARM BUREAU FEDERATION **1**:338 *bibliog.*
AMERICAN FEDERATION OF GOVERNMENT EMPLOYEES
  American Federation of State, County, and Municipal Employees **1**:339
AMERICAN FEDERATION OF LABOR AND CONGRESS OF INDUSTRIAL ORGANIZATIONS **1**:338–339 *bibliog.*
  Actors' Equity Association **1**:90
  Amalgamated Clothing and Textile Workers Union **1**:321
  American Federation of Musicians **1**:339
  American Federation of State, County, and Municipal Employees **1**:339
  American Federation of Teachers **1**:339
  Carpenters and Joiners of America, United Brotherhood of **4**:164
  Dubinsky, David **6**:287
  Electrical, Radio and Machine Workers, International Union of **7**:106
  Electrical Workers, International Brotherhood of **7**:107
  Gompers, Samuel **9**:241
  Green, William **9**:347
  Hillman, Sidney **10**:165
  Hotel and Restaurant Employees and Bartenders International Union **10**:262
  industrial union **11**:160
  International Association of Machinists and Aerospace Workers **11**:218
  International Ladies' Garment Workers Union **11**:221
  International Longshoremen's Unions **11**:222
  International Typographical Union **11**:224–225
  Kirkland, Lane **12**:89
  labor union **12**:153; **12**:154; **12**:155
  Lewis, John L. **12**:306
  Meany, George **13**:253
  Newspaper Guild **14**:173
  Ohio **14**:362
  Reuther, Walter P. **16**:184
  Socialist party **18**:25
  Teamsters, Chauffeurs, Warehousemen, and Helpers of America, International Brotherhood of **19**:58
  union label **19**:387
  United Auto Workers **19**:401

AMERICAN FEDERATION OF LABOR AND CONGRESS OF INDUSTRIAL ORGANIZATIONS (cont.)
United Mine Workers of America **19**:411–412
AMERICAN FEDERATION OF MUSICIANS **1**:339 *bibliog.*
AMERICAN FEDERATION OF STATE, COUNTY, AND MUNICIPAL EMPLOYEES **1**:339
AMERICAN FEDERATION OF TEACHERS **1**:339
AMERICAN FILM INSTITUTE **1**:339
Kennedy Center for the Performing Arts **12**:44
Life Achievement Award
Davis, Bette **6**:50
Fonda, Henry **8**:205 *illus.*
Welles, Orson **20**:99
AMERICAN FOOTBALL LEAGUE
football **8**:217–218 *tables*
AMERICAN FORK (Utah)
map (40° 23′N 111° 48′W) **19**:492
AMERICAN FOXHOUND **1**:339–340 *bibliog., illus.*; **6**:216 *illus.*
AMERICAN FREEDOM TRAIN
Bicentennial, U.S. **3**:243
AMERICAN FRIENDS SERVICE COMMITTEE **1**:340 *bibliog.*
Jones, Rufus Matthew **11**:444
AMERICAN FUR COMPANY **1**:340 *bibliog.*
Astor, John Jacob **2**:268
mountain men **13**:623–624
AMERICAN GEOGRAPHICAL SOCIETY OF NEW YORK
geographical societies **9**:100
Greely, Adolphus Washington **9**:347
AMERICAN GEOPHYSICAL UNION **1**:340
AMERICAN G.I. FORUM
Chicano **4**:343
AMERICAN GOTHIC (Grant Wood) **20**:207 *illus.*
AMERICAN HEART ASSOCIATION **1**:340
AMERICAN HIGHLAND
map (72° 30′S 78° 0′E) **2**:40
AMERICAN HISTORICAL ASSOCIATION **1**:340
Adams, Herbert Baxter **1**:94
Dunning, William Archibald **6**:301
White, Andrew Dickson **20**:134
AMERICAN HISTORY *see* UNITED STATES, HISTORY OF THE
AMERICAN HOGCHOKER (fish)
sole **18**:53
AMERICAN HORSE SHOWS ASSOCIATION
horse show **10**:250
AMERICAN INDEPENDENT PARTY **1**:340 *bibliog.*
Wallace, George **20**:14
AMERICAN INDIAN LANGUAGES *see* INDIAN LANGUAGES, AMERICAN
AMERICAN INDIAN MOVEMENT **1**:340–341
Indian Affairs, Bureau of **11**:94
Indians, American **11**:130
National Congress of American Indians **14**:31
Wounded Knee **20**:285
AMERICAN INDIAN SCHOOLS *see* INDIAN SCHOOLS, AMERICAN
AMERICAN INDIANS *see* INDIANS, AMERICAN
AMERICAN INSTITUTE OF AERONAUTICS AND ASTRONAUTICS **1**:341
AMERICAN INSTITUTE OF ARCHITECTS **1**:341 *bibliog.*
Hunt, Richard Morris **10**:312
AMERICAN INSTITUTE OF BIOLOGICAL SCIENCES **1**:341
AMERICAN INSTITUTE OF CERTIFIED PUBLIC ACCOUNTANTS
audit **2**:318
AMERICAN INSTITUTE OF CHEMISTS **1**:341
AMERICAN INSTITUTE OF PHYSICS **1**:341
AMERICAN INSTITUTE FOR PSYCHOANALYSIS
Horney, Karen **10**:239
AMERICAN JEWISH CONGRESS
Wise, Stephen Samuel **20**:189
AMERICAN JOURNAL OF EDUCATION (periodical)
Barnard, Henry **3**:86
AMERICAN JOURNAL OF PHYSICAL ANTHROPOLOGY (periodical)
Hrdlička, Aleš **10**:286
AMERICAN JOURNAL OF SCIENCE AND ARTS (periodical)
Silliman, Benjamin **17**:309
AMERICAN KENNEL CLUB **1**:341
dog **6**:213
dog shows **6**:221
AMERICAN LABOR PARTY **1**:341
Liberal parties **12**:312
Marcantonio, Vito **13**:145
AMERICAN LADYBIRD **17**:252 *illus.*
AMERICAN LANGUAGE, THE (books)
Mencken, H. L. **13**:293
AMERICAN LARCH
tamarack **19**:18
AMERICAN LAVENDER
mint (botany) **13**:461
AMERICAN LEGION **1**:341
Legionnaires' disease **12**:274
AMERICAN LIBRARY ASSOCIATION **1**:341–342
Caldecott Medal **4**:25
Dewey, Melvil **6**:147
Newbery Medal **14**:164
AMERICAN LITERATURE **1**:342–348 *bibliog., illus.*
See also the subheading American literature under CRITICISM, LITERARY; DRAMA; NOVEL; POETRY; names of specific authors, e.g., FAULKNER, WILLIAM; HAWTHORNE, NATHANIEL; etc.; names of specific literary styles or periods, e.g., NATURALISM (literature); ROMANTICISM (literature); etc.; names of specific literary works, e.g., *AS I LAY DYING* (book); *GONE WITH THE WIND* (book); etc.
American Academy of Arts and Letters **1**:327
Colonial period **1**:342
Bay Psalm Book **3**:132
National Book Awards *see* NATIONAL BOOK AWARDS
19th century **1**:343–345
Pulitzer Prize *see* LITERATURE—Pulitzer Prize
Revolutionary period **1**:342–343
20th century **1**:345–348
beat generation **3**:144
AMERICAN MAGAZINE (periodical)
periodical **15**:169
Steffens, Lincoln **18**:245
AMERICAN MEDICAL ASSOCIATION **1**:348 *bibliog.*
chiropractic **4**:397
Journal of the American Medical Association **11**:453
AMERICAN MEN OF SCIENCE (book)
Cattell, James McKeen **4**:214
AMERICAN MERCURY, THE (periodical)
Mencken, H. L. **13**:293
Nathan, George Jean **14**:27
AMERICAN MOTORCYCLIST ASSOCIATION (AMA)
Grand National Champions **13**:614 *table*
motorcycling **13**:614–616
AMERICAN MOTORS CORPORATION
automotive industry **2**:366; **2**:368
jeep **11**:391
Nash, Charles William **14**:23
AMERICAN MUSEUM (New York City)
Barnum, P. T. **3**:86
AMERICAN MUSEUM OF NATURAL HISTORY **1**:348
Andrews, Roy Chapman **1**:408
Mead, Margaret **13**:252
New York (city) **14**:145 *map*
Putnam, Frederic Ward **15**:632
Simpson, George Gaylord **17**:317
AMERICAN MUSIC **1**:348–352 *bibliog., illus.*
See also FOLK MUSIC; names of specific composers, e.g., COPLAND, AARON; FOSTER, STEPHEN; etc.
American Academy of Arts and Letters **1**:327
bluegrass music **3**:345
blues **3**:345–346
colonial period **1**:348–349
Damrosch (family) **6**:20
finances **1**:351–352
fuging tune **8**:355
gospel music **9**:253–254
hymn **10**:346–347
jazz **11**:387–390
Kennedy Center for the Performing Arts **12**:44
Mason (family) **13**:198
music, history of Western **13**:667
music festivals **13**:670–671
19th century **1**:349–351 *illus.*
ragtime **16**:70
rhythm and blues **16**:204–205
rock music **16**:247–250
salsa **17**:36
song **18**:64
soul music **18**:71
spirituals **18**:189
Tin Pan Alley **19**:205
20th century **1**:351–352 *illus.*
vibraphone **19**:567
AMERICAN NATIONAL THEATER AND ACADEMY **1**:352
AMERICAN NATURALIST, THE (periodical)
Cope, Edward **5**:248
Putnam, Frederic Ward **15**:632
AMERICAN NAUTICAL ALMANAC OFFICE
Newcomb, Simon **14**:165
AMERICAN NEWSPAPER GUILD
Broun, Heywood **3**:512
AMERICAN NEWSPAPER PUBLISHERS ASSOCIATION **1**:352
AMERICAN ORGAN
reed organ **16**:118
AMERICAN OSTEOPATHIC ASSOCIATION
osteopathic medicine **14**:457
AMERICAN PARTY *see* KNOW-NOTHING PARTY
AMERICAN PHARMACEUTICAL ASSOCIATION
pharmacy **15**:221
AMERICAN PHILOSOPHICAL ASSOCIATION
Creighton, James Edwin **5**:337–338
AMERICAN PHILOSOPHICAL SOCIETY **1**:352
AMERICAN PHYSICAL SOCIETY **1**:352
AMERICAN PRIMROSE
cowslip (botany) **5**:322
AMERICAN PSYCHIATRIC ASSOCIATION
psychopathy **15**:601
AMERICAN PUBLIC HEALTH ASSOCIATION
sex education **17**:225
AMERICAN QUARTER HORSE *see* QUARTER HORSE
AMERICAN RADIO RELAY LEAGUE
ham radio **10**:26
AMERICAN RAILWAY EXPRESS COMPANY
Wells, Fargo and Company **20**:101
AMERICAN RAILWAY UNION
Debs, Eugene V. **6**:70
AMERICAN RED CROSS
Red Cross **16**:112
AMERICAN REVOLUTION **1**:353–365 *bibliog., illus., map*
abolitionists **1**:58
Albany Congress **1**:251–252
American advantages **1**:356
American military figures
Allen, Ethan **1**:299
Arnold, Benedict **2**:184–185
Attucks, Crispus **2**:316
Barry, John **3**:96
Clark, George Rogers **5**:38
Dearborn, Henry **6**:68
Gates, Horatio **9**:58
Greene, Nathanael **9**:350–351
Hale, Nathan **10**:18
Herkimer, Nicholas **10**:142
Hopkins, Esek **10**:231
Jones, John Paul **11**:443
Knox, Henry **12**:102
Lee, Charles **12**:269
Lincoln, Benjamin **12**:349–350
Marion, Francis **13**:157
Mifflin, Thomas **13**:416
Molly Pitcher **13**:512
Montgomery, Richard **13**:556
Morgan, Daniel **13**:578
Putnam, Israel **15**:632
Revere, Paul **16**:185–186
Schuyler, Philip John **17**:138
Shelby, Isaac **17**:250
Stark, John **18**:227
Sullivan, John **18**:336–337
Sumter, Thomas **18**:340
Warner, Seth **20**:30
Washington, George **20**:43
Wayne, Anthony **20**:73
Whipple, Abraham **20**:131
Wilkinson, James **20**:153
American political figures
Adams, John **1**:94–95
Adams, Samuel **1**:97–98
Boudinot, Elias **3**:420
Bowdoin, James **3**:427
Deane, Silas **6**:68
Dickinson, John **6**:158
Fitzsimons, Thomas **8**:132
Franklin, Benjamin **8**:283–284
Galloway, Joseph **9**:21
Hamilton, Alexander **10**:27–28
Hancock, John **10**:34
Henry, Patrick **10**:122–123
Jay, John **11**:387
Jefferson, Thomas **11**:391
Laurens, Henry **12**:238
Lynch, Charles **12**:476
Morris, Robert (merchant) **13**:588
Paine, Thomas **15**:16
Pendleton, Edmund **15**:142
Salomon, Haym **17**:36
Thomson, Charles **19**:175
Trumbull, Jonathan **19**:319
Warren, Joseph **20**:31
Wilson, James **20**:165
battles and campaigns **1**:359 *map*
Bennington (Vermont) **3**:204
Brandywine, Battle of the **3**:455
Bunker Hill, Battle of **3**:562
Concord (Massachusetts) **5**:170
Cowpens, Battle of **5**:322
Fort Moultrie **8**:237
Green Mountain Boys **9**:348
Lexington and Concord **12**:309
Long Island, Battle of **12**:406
Monmouth **13**:535–536
Morristown (New Jersey) **13**:590
New Brunswick (New Jersey) **14**:115
New Haven (Connecticut) **14**:126
New London (Connecticut) **14**:134
Northern war **1**:359 *map*
Petersburg (Virginia) **15**:202
Rome (New York) **16**:297
Saratoga **17**:75
Saratoga Springs (New York) **17**:75
Southern war **1**:359 *map*; **1**:363
Spartanburg (South Carolina) **18**:165
Ticonderoga **19**:192
Trenton, Battle of **19**:291
Valley Forge **19**:507
Vincennes (Indiana) **19**:599
Warner, Seth **20**:30
Western war **1**:362–363
Wilkes-Barre (Pennsylvania) **20**:152
Yorktown Campaign **20**:331
Bicentennial celebration **3**:243
British disadvantages **1**:356–358
British military and political figures
André, John **1**:406
Burgoyne, John **3**:570
Carleton, Guy, 1st Baron Dorchester **4**:151
Clinton, Sir Henry **5**:60
Cornwallis, Charles Cornwallis, 1st Marquess **5**:270
Gage, Thomas **9**:8
Germain, Lord George **9**:123
Girty, Simon **9**:190
Grenville, George **9**:359
Howe, Richard Howe, Earl **10**:284
Howe, William Howe, 5th Viscount **10**:284
North, Lord **14**:223–224
Rockingham, Charles Watson-Wentworth, 2d Marquess of **16**:260
St. Leger, Barry **17**:22
Simcoe, John Graves **17**:313
causes
Boston Massacre **3**:410
Boston Tea Party **3**:410–411
Gaspee **9**:56
Grenville, George **9**:359
Hutchinson, Thomas **10**:323
Intolerable Acts **11**:231–232
Molasses Act **13**:505
Stamp Act **18**:216
taxation without representation **1**:354–355
Townshend Acts **19**:255–256
Common Sense **5**:141
Connecticut **5**:196
Continental Congress **5**:228
Conway Cabal **5**:234
Daughters of the American Revolution, National Society of the **6**:45
effects **1**:364–365
foreign aid
Beaumarchais, Pierre Caron de **3**:146
Estaing, Jean Baptiste Charles Henri Hector, Comte d' **7**:246
French alliance **1**:360–361
Grasse, François Joseph Paul, Comte de **9**:298
Kalb, Johann **12**:7
Knyphausen, Wilhelm, Baron von **12**:103

Kościuszko, Tadeusz **12**:123
Lafayette, Marie Joseph Paul Yves Roch Gilbert du Motier, Marquis de **12**:163–164
Pułaski, Kasimierz **15**:618
Rochambeau, Jean Baptiste Donatien de Vimeur, Comte de **16**:246
Steuben, Friedrich Wilhelm, Baron von **18**:262
French alliance **1**:360–361
Georgia **9**:117
guerrillas **9**:391
Hessians **10**:153
Indian participation
Brant, Joseph **3**:455
Cornplanter **5**:269
Indian participation **11**:108 *illus.*
journalism **11**:454
literature
American literature **1**:342–343
Freneau, Philip **8**:326
Hopkinson, Francis **10**:232
Loyalists **12**:445
Maine **13**:74
Maryland **13**:192
Massachusetts **13**:211 *illus.*
minutemen **13**:462
naval activity
Bonhomme Richard batters Serapis **14**:62 *illus.*
Howe, Richard Howe, Earl **10**:284
navy **14**:63
Turtle **19**:352
New Hampshire **14**:126
New Jersey **14**:133
New York (state) **14**:153
North Carolina **14**:246
Paris, treaties of **15**:87
peace negotiations **1**:365 *illus.*
Pennsylvania **15**:150
recruitment poster **1**:356 *illus.*
Rhode Island **16**:201
Sons of Liberty **18**:66
South Carolina **18**:101
Tennessee **19**:106
toppling of statue of King George III in New York (1776) **9**:315 *illus.*
uniform **1**:358 *illus.*; **2**:182 *illus.*
United States, history of the **19**:439–441 *illus.*
Virginia **19**:611
AMERICAN RIVER
map (38° 36′N 121° 30′W) **4**:31
AMERICAN SADDLE HORSE **1**:366 *illus.*; **10**:243 *illus.*
saddle horse **17**:9
AMERICAN SAMOA (U.S.) **1**:366 *map*
cities
Pago Pago **15**:14
map (14° 20′S 170° 0′W) **14**:334
Samoa **17**:46 *map*
AMERICAN SCHOLAR (periodical) **1**:366
AMERICAN SCHOLAR, THE (speech) **1**:366
AMERICAN SCIENCE AND ENGINEERING COMPANY
X-ray astronomy **20**:306
AMERICAN SCIENTIST (periodical) **1**:366
AMERICAN SHAKESPEARE FESTIVAL COMPANY
Carnovsky, Morris **4**:159
AMERICAN SHORTHAIR CAT **1**:366–367 *illus.*; **4**:195 *illus.*
AMERICAN SIGN LANGUAGE
sign language **17**:300
AMERICAN SOCCER LEAGUE (ASL)
soccer **18**:11
AMERICAN SOCIETY OF CIVIL ENGINEERS
civil engineering **5**:11
AMERICAN SOCIETY OF INDUSTRIAL DESIGNERS
Dreyfuss, Henry **6**:272
AMERICAN SOCIETY OF MECHANICAL ENGINEERS
mechanical engineering **13**:260
AMERICAN SOCIETY OF NEWSPAPER EDITORS **1**:367
AMERICAN SOCIETY FOR THE PREVENTION OF CRUELTY TO ANIMALS
Society for the Prevention of Cruelty to Animals **18**:26
AMERICAN SOCIETY FOR TESTING AND MATERIALS
metallurgy **13**:331
sand **17**:59
AMERICAN SPEECH AND HEARING ASSOCIATION
speech therapy **18**:176
AMERICAN SPELLER (book)
primary education **15**:537
AMERICAN STAFFORDSHIRE TERRIER **1**:367 *illus.*; **6**:220 *illus.*
AMERICAN STOCK EXCHANGE
stock market **18**:274–275
AMERICAN SURETY BUILDING
skyscraper **17**:350
AMERICAN SYSTEM (national development program)
Clay, Henry **5**:46
AMERICAN TEACHERS ASSOCIATION
National Education Association **14**:32
AMERICAN TELEPHONE AND TELEGRAPH COMPANY
radio and television broadcasting **16**:54–55
telephone **19**:80
AMERICAN TEMPERANCE SOCIETY
temperance movement **19**:92
AMERICAN THEATRE ASSOCIATION
American Educational Theatre Association **1**:338
AMERICAN TRAGEDY, AN (book) **1**:367
Dreiser, Theodore **6**:269–270
AMERICAN TRUCKING ASSOCIATIONS
trucking industry **19**:314
AMERICAN TRUMPETER
waterfowl **20**:63
AMERICAN UNIVERSITY **1**:367
AMERICAN UNIVERSITY OF BEIRUT **1**:367
AMERICAN VOLUNTEER GROUP
Chennault, Claire L. **4**:330
P-40 **15**:3
World War II **20**:260 *illus.*
AMERICAN WATER SPANIEL **1**:367 *illus.*; **6**:219 *illus.*
AMERICAN WEEKLY MERCURY (periodical)
Pennsylvania **15**:149
AMERICAN WOMAN SUFFRAGE ASSOCIATION
Stone, Lucy **18**:281
suffrage, women's **18**:326
AMERICAN WOMEN'S EDUCATIONAL ASSOCIATION
Beecher, Catharine Esther **3**:161
AMERICAN YOUTH HOSTELS
youth hostel **20**:337
AMERICANS FOR DEMOCRATIC ACTION **1**:367–368 *bibliog.*
Niebuhr, Reinhold **14**:184
AMERICA'S CUP **1**:368 *bibliog., table*; **16**:200 *illus.*
Lipton, Sir Thomas **12**:364
AMERICIUM **1**:368
actinide series **1**:88
element **7**:130 *table*
Seaborg, Glenn T. **17**:171–172
transuranium elements **19**:286
AMERICUS (Georgia)
map (32° 4′N 84° 14′W) **9**:114
AMERICUS (Kansas)
map (38° 30′N 96° 16′W) **12**:18
AMERINDIAN LANGUAGES *see* INDIAN LANGUAGES, AMERICAN
AMERSFOORT (Netherlands)
map (52° 9′N 5° 24′E) **14**:99
AMERY (Manitoba)
map (56° 34′N 94° 3′W) **13**:119
AMERY (Wisconsin)
map (45° 19′N 92° 22′W) **20**:185
AMERY ICE SHELF
map (69° 30′S 72° 0′E) **2**:40
AMES (Iowa)
map (42° 2′N 93° 37′W) **11**:244
AMES (Nebraska)
map (41° 27′N 96° 37′W) **14**:70
AMES, OAKES
Crédit Mobilier of America **5**:336
AMES TEST
cancer **4**:104
AMESBURY (Massachusetts)
map (42° 51′N 70° 56′W) **13**:206
AMESLAN *see* AMERICAN SIGN LANGUAGE
AMETHYST **1**:368 *illus.*; **3**:296 *illus., table*; **9**:74 *illus.*; **13**:441 *illus.*
geode **9**:97 *illus.*
quartz **16**:13
AMHARA (Ethiopian people) **1**:368–369 *bibliog.*
Tigré **19**:197
AMHARA PLATEAU
map (9° 0′N 38° 0′E) **7**:253
AMHERST (Massachusetts) **1**:369
Amherst College **1**:369
map (42° 23′N 72° 31′W) **13**:206
AMHERST (New York)
map (42° 58′N 78° 48′W) **14**:149
AMHERST (Nova Scotia) **1**:369
map (45° 49′N 64° 14′W) **14**:269
AMHERST (Ohio)
map (41° 24′N 82° 14′W) **14**:357
AMHERST (Virginia)
map (37° 35′N 79° 3′W) **19**:607
AMHERST (county in Virginia)
map (37° 35′N 79° 10′W) **19**:607
AMHERST, JEFFREY, BARON AMHERST **1**:369
French and Indian Wars **8**:313–314 *map*
Pontiac's Rebellion **15**:427
Ticonderoga **19**:192
AMHERST COLLEGE **1**:369
Webster, Noah **20**:89
AMHERSTDALE (West Virginia)
map (37° 47′N 81° 49′W) **20**:111
AMICHAI, YEHUDA **1**:369
AMICUS CURIAE (law) **1**:369
brief **3**:485
AMIDA BUDDHA *see* AMITABHA BUDDHA
AMIDE **1**:369 *bibliog.*
organic chemistry **14**:437–438
AMIDON (North Dakota)
map (46° 29′N 103° 19′W) **14**:248
AMIENS (France) **1**:369
Amiens Cathedral **1**:370
map (49° 54′N 2° 18′E) **8**:260
AMIENS, TREATY OF **1**:369
Napoleonic Wars **14**:19
AMIENS CATHEDRAL **1**:370 *bibliog.*
architecture **2**:133; **2**:134 *illus.*
cathedrals and churches **4**:206
Gothic art and architecture **9**:257–260 *illus.*
wooden relief **20**:208 *illus.*
AMIN, HAFIZULLAH
Afghanistan **1**:135
AMIN DADA, IDI **1**:370
genocide **9**:93
Obote, Milton **14**:316
Uganda **19**:373
AMINDIVI
Laccadive Islands (India) **12**:158
AMINE **1**:370 *bibliog., table*
aliphatic compounds **1**:295
aniline **2**:8
hormone, animal **10**:234
organic chemistry **14**:437
physical properties **1**:370 *table*
AMINO ACID **1**:370–371 *bibliog., illus.*
cystinuria **5**:411
enzyme **7**:212–215
Fischer, Emil Hermann **8**:110
genetic code **9**:79–82 *illus.*
Hopkins, Sir Frederick Gowland **10**:231
hormone, animal **10**:234
life **12**:326–327
major amino acids **1**:371 *illus.*
Moore, Stanford **13**:570
mutation **13**:686
nucleic acid **14**:289–291
peptide **15**:157
protein **15**:574
protein synthesis **15**:575–576
Vauquelin, Louis Nicolas **19**:529
AMINOGLYCOSIDES
antibiotics **2**:57; **2**:58; **2**:59
AMIRANTE ISLANDS
map (6° 0′S 53° 10′E) **17**:232
AMIS, KINGSLEY **1**:372
AMISH
folk art **8**:197 *illus.*
Mennonites **13**:298–299
AMISK LAKE
map (54° 35′N 102° 13′W) **17**:81
AMISTAD CASE **1**:372 *bibliog.*
AMISTAD RESERVOIR
map (29° 34′N 101° 15′W) **19**:129
AMITABHA BUDDHA **3**:539 *illus.*
AMITE (Louisiana)
map (30° 44′N 90° 30′W) **12**:430
AMITE (county in Mississippi)
map (31° 10′N 90° 50′W) **13**:469
AMITE RIVER
map (30° 12′N 90° 35′W) **12**:430
AMITY (Arkansas)
map (34° 16′N 93° 28′W) **2**:166
AMMAN (Jordan) **1**:372; **11**:449 *illus., table*
map (31° 57′N 35° 56′E) **11**:447
AMMANATI, BARTOLOMMEO **1**:372
Pitti Palace **15**:321
AMMANN, OTHMAR HERMANN **1**:372
Verrazano-Narrows Bridge **19**:560
AMMENEMES *see* AMENEMHET I, KING OF EGYPT
AMMETER **1**:372
circuit, electric **4**:436
measurement **13**:256
AMMON (Idaho)
map (43° 30′N 111° 57′W) **11**:26
AMMONIA **1**:372
amine **1**:370
chemical industry **4**:318–319 *illus.*
excretory system **7**:328
Haber, Fritz **10**:4
nitrogen cycle **14**:203
origin of life **12**:327 *illus.*
refrigeration **16**:125
Saturn (astronomy) **17**:90
synthesis
hydrogen **10**:338
nitrogen **14**:202
AMMONITE **1**:372–373 *bibliog., illus.*
Earth, geological history of **7**:14
Mesozoic Era **13**:322
Triassic Period **19**:293 *illus.*
AMMONIUM
uranium minerals **19**:478
AMMONIUM CARBONATE
smelling salts **17**:365
AMMONOOSUC RIVER
map (44° 10′N 72° 2′W) **14**:123
AMMONS, A. R. **1**:373
AMMONS, ALBERT
boogie-woogie **3**:383
AMMUNITION **1**:373–375 *bibliog., illus.*
bomb **3**:373–374
dumdum bullet **6**:298
explosives **7**:339
firearms **8**:105–106
gunpowder **9**:405–406
lead **12**:256
mine (explosive) **13**:437–438
mortar **13**:591
phosphorus **15**:256
torpedo (projectile) **19**:242–243
weapons **20**:74–75
AMNESIA **1**:375
apraxia **2**:92
memory **13**:292
AMNESTY **1**:375
pardon **15**:83
AMNESTY INTERNATIONAL **1**:375
AMNIOCENTESIS **1**:375 *bibliog.*
birth defects **3**:295
genetic diseases **9**:83–84
Tay-Sachs disease **19**:48
AMNION (embryology)
development **6**:138 *illus.*; **6**:140 *illus.*; **6**:141 *illus.*
AMOBARBITOL
barbituate **3**:78
AMOEBA **1**:376 *bibliog., illus.*; **15**:579 *illus.*
amebiasis **1**:326
biological locomotion **3**:265; **15**:581 *illus.*
Entamoeba **7**:208
muscle contraction **13**:654
reproduction **15**:581 *illus.*
Rhizopoda **16**:196
slime mold **17**:362
AMOEBIC DYSENTERY **6**:320
amebiasis **1**:326
amoeba **1**:376
Entamoeba **7**:208
parasitic cycle 15:83 *illus.*
protozoal diseases **15**:581
AMOL (Iran)
map (36° 23′N 52° 20′E) **11**:250
AMON-RE (Egyptian god) **1**:376
temples of Amon-re at Thebes **12**:28; **19**:155 *illus.*
AMORC
Rosicrucians **16**:317
AMORITES **1**:376
Hammurabi, King of Babylonia **10**:32
Mesopotamia **13**:316
AMORTIZATION **1**:376
AMORY (Mississippi)
map (33° 59′N 88° 29′W) **13**:469
AMOS (Quebec)
map (48° 35′N 78° 7′W) **16**:18
AMOS, BOOK OF **1**:376 *bibliog.*
AMOS 'N' ANDY (radio comedy team) **1**:376 *bibliog.*
radio and television broadcasting **16**:56
AMOY (China) **1**:376
map (24° 28′N 118° 7′E) **4**:362
AMP (biology)
ATP **2**:312
cyclic AMP **5**:403
AMPERE **1**:377
circuit, electric **4**:436–438
coulomb **5**:308
electromagnetic units **7**:118
units, physical **19**:466 *tables*
AMPÈRE, ANDRÉ MARIE **1**:377 *bibliog.*
mathematics, history of **13**:226
AMPÈRE'S LAW
electromagnetic units **7**:118–119
Maxwell's equations **13**:242

AMPEROMETRY
electrochemistry 7:113
AMPHETAMINE 1:377
drug abuse 6:279
psychotropic drugs 15:604
stimulant 18:271
AMPHIBIANS 1:377–380 *bibliog., illus., table*
aging 1:186
anatomy 1:379–380
brain 3:443 *illus.*
classification, biological 1:377–379
coloration, biological 5:122
evolution 7:321–323
frog 8:336–337
gill 9:180–181
habitat 1:378
herpetology 10:146
history 1:377 *table*
life cycle 1:379–380 *illus.*
lungs 12:463–465
maximum life span 12:330 *table*
molting 13:513
Paleozoic Era 15:43
parthenogenesis 15:100
Permian Period 15:174 *illus.*
physiology 1:379–380
pigment, skin 15:301
regeneration 16:126–127
respiratory system 16:179–180 *illus.*
salamander and newt 17:29–30
teeth 19:71
toad 19:217
AMPHIBIOUS VEHICLE *see* AIR-CUSHION VEHICLE
AMPHIBIOUS WARFARE 1:380–381 *bibliog.*
landing at Normandy beaches 19:455 *illus.*
naval vessels 14:56
strategy and tactics, military 18:291
World War II 20:267–268 *illus.*; 20:272 *illus.*; 20:278–279 *illus.*
AMPHIBOLE 1:381 *bibliog., illus.*
diorite 6:185
granite 9:287
granodiorite 9:287
monoclinic system 13:536
monzonite 13:560
silicate minerals 17:305
AMPHIBOLITE
metamorphic rock 13:332 *table*
AMPHIDROMIC POINT 1:381 *bibliog.*
AMPHINEURA *see* CHITON (mollusk)
AMPHIOXUS 1:381 *illus.*
chordate 4:407
AMPHIPOD 1:382 *bibliog., illus.*
intertidal life 11:230
AMPHISBAENA *see* WORM LIZARD
AMPHITHEATER
Colosseum 5:122–123
Greece, ancient 17:293 *illus.*
stadium 18:208
AMPHITRYON 1:382
AMPHORA
Chinese archaeology 4:378 *illus*
AMPHOTERIC COMPOUNDS 1:382
zwitterion 20:384
AMPHOTERICIN
antibiotics 2:57
histoplasmosis 10:181
respiratory system disorders 16:181
AMPICILLIN
antibiotics 2:59
penicillin 15:143
AMPLIFIER 1:382–383 *bibliog.*
electron tube 7:122
feedback 8:44
heterodyne principle 10:153–154
integrated circuit 11:201–202
Black, Harold 3:303
operation 1:382
operational amplifier 14:402–403
oscillator 14:453
radio 16:45–47
radio astronomy 16:52
sound recording and reproduction 18:74–77
television 19:86
transistor 19:271–272
triode 19:301
tuner 19:333
types 1:382
AMPLITUDE 1:383
interference 11:209
resonance (physics) 16:178
waves and wave motion 20:72
AMPLITUDE MODULATION 1:383 *bibliog.*
ionosphere 11:242
modulation 13:500 *illus.*
radio 16:46–47
AMPUDIA, PEDRO DE
Mexican War 13:353
AMPUTATION 1:383
neuralgia 14:105
regeneration 16:126–127
AMRITSAR (India) 1:383
Golden Temple 17:302 *illus.*
map (31° 35′N 74° 53′E) 11:80
AMRUM ISLAND
map (54° 39′N 8° 21′E) 9:140
AMSBERG, CLAUS VON
Beatrice, Queen of the Netherlands 3:145
AMSTERDAM (Netherlands) 1:383–385 *bibliog., illus., map*; 7:278 *illus.*
art and architecture
Berlage, Hendrik Petrus 3:214
Campen, Jacob van 4:66
Keyser, Hendrik de 12:64
Quellinus, Artus 16:23
climate 14:98 *table*
harbor 10:43
jewelry 11:410
map (52° 22′N 4° 54′E) 14:99
AMSTERDAM (New York)
map (42° 57′N 74° 11′W) 14:149
AMSTERDAM ISLAND
French Southern and Antarctic Territories 8:326
AMSTERDAM-RHINE CANAL
map (51° 57′N 5° 20′E) 14:99
AMSTETTEN (Austria)
map (48° 7′N 14° 53′E) 2:348
AMTRAK 1:385 *bibliog.*
Metroliner 13:347
railroad 16:73
AMU DARYA (river) 1:385–386
map (43° 40′N 59° 1′E) 19:388
AMUBRI (Costa Rica)
map (9° 31′N 82° 56′W) 5:291
AMULET 1:385–386 *bibliog.*
evil eye 7:318
horseshoe 10:252
mana 13:107
staurolite 18:239
AMUN *see* AMON-RE
AMUNDSEN, ROALD 1:386 *bibliog., illus.*
Antarctica 2:44 *map*
Arctic 2:142 *map*
Ellsworth, Lincoln 7:149
exploration 7:336–337 *map*
Northwest Passage 14:256–257 *map*
Sverdrup, Harald Ulrik 18:375
AMUNDSEN GULF
map (71° 0′N 124° 0′W) 14:258
AMUNDSEN SEA
map (72° 30′S 112° 0′W) 2:40
AMUR RIVER 1:386
map (52° 56′N 141° 10′E) 19:388
AMUSEMENT PARK 1:386 *bibliog.*
Disneyland and Walt Disney World 6:197
Ferris wheel 8:59
AMVETS 1:386
AMYGDALIN
laetrile 12:163
AMYL NITRITE 1:386
aphrodisiac 2:78
AMYLOIDOSIS
kidney disease 12:71–72
AMYLOPECTIN
starch 18:226
AMYLOSE
starch 18:226
AMYOTROPHIC LATERAL SCLEROSIS 1:386–387 *bibliog.*
Gehrig, Lou 9:67
nervous system, diseases of the 14:96
AMYUN (Lebanon)
map (34° 18′N 35° 49′E) 12:265
AN *see* ANU (Mesopotamian deity)
AN LU-SHAN
China, history of 4:372
AN-SHAN (Anshan) (China) 1:387 *bibliog.*
map (41° 8′N 122° 59′E) 4:362
ANA MARIA ,GULF OF
map (21° 25′N 78° 40′W) 5:377
ANABAENA 1:387
blue-green algae 3:342 *illus.*
fern 8:56–57 *illus.*
ANABAPTISTS 1:387 *bibliog.*
Baptists 3:73–74
Hutterian Brethren 10:323
Menno Simons 13:298
Mennonites 13:298
Münzer, Thomas 13:644
Reformation 16:121 *map*; 16:123
ANABAR (Nauru)
map (0° 30′S 166° 57′E) 14:51
ANABASIS (book)
Xenophon 20:312
ANABATIC WIND *see* MOUNTAIN AND VALLEY WINDS
ANABOLISM *see* METABOLISM
ANACO (Venezuela)
map (9° 27′N 64° 28′W) 19:542
ANACOCO (Louisiana)
map (31° 15′N 93° 20′W) 12:430
ANACONDA (Montana) 1:387
map (46° 8′N 112° 57′W) 13:547
ANACONDA (snake) 1:387 *illus.*
ANACONDA COPPER MINING COMPANY
Daly, Marcus 6:15
ANACONDA RANGE
map (45° 55′N 113° 30′W) 13:547
ANACORTES (Washington)
map (48° 30′N 122° 37′W) 20:35
ANACOSTIA RIVER
map (38° 52′N 77° 1′W) 13:188
ANACREON 1:387
ANADARKO (Oklahoma)
map (35° 4′N 98° 15′W) 14:368
ANAEROBE 1:387
bacteria 3:16
fermentation 8:55
ANAEROBIC REACTIONS
metabolism 13:326
ANAGRAM 1:388 *bibliog.*
ANAHEIM (California) 1:388
Disneyland 6:197
map (33° 51′N 117° 57′W) 4:31
ANAHUAC (Texas)
map (29° 46′N 94° 41′W) 19:129
ANAI, MOUNT
map (10° 10′N 77° 4′E) 11:80
ANALCIME *see* ZEOLITE
ANALECTS (book)
Confucianism 5:179
ANALGESIC 1:388 *bibliog.*
acetaminophen 1:79
aspirin 2:262–263
codeine 5:90
Darvon 6:40
Demerol 6:96
drugs 1:388
headache 10:85
heroin 10:145
methadone 13:343
morphine 13:587
phenacetin 15:225
phenazocine 15:225
psychotropic drugs 15:603; 15:605
techniques 1:388
ANALOG DEVICES 1:388–389 *bibliog.*
computer 5:158–159
differential analyzer 6:166
hybrid computer 10:328–329
operational amplifier 14:402–403
process control 15:560
ANALOG-TO-DIGITAL CONVERTER 1:389
multiplexer 13:638
ANALYSIS (mathematics)
mathematics 13:222
mathematics, history of 13:225–226
ANALYSIS OF BEAUTY (book)
Hogarth, William 10:198
ANALYTIC GEOMETRY 1:390–391 *bibliog.*
axis 2:378
coordinate systems (mathematics) 5:246–247
Descartes, René 6:125–126
Fermat, Pierre de 8:55
history 1:390
hyperbola 10:347–348
line 12:352–353
mathematics, history of 13:225
Möbius, August Ferdinand 13:488
plane analytic geometry 1:390
slope 17:363
solid analytic geometry 1:391
translation (mathematics) 19:274
ANALYTIC AND LINGUISTIC PHILOSOPHY 1:389–390 *bibliog.*
Austin, John Langshaw 2:327
Ayer, Sir Alfred Jules 2:378
Black, Max 3:303
Carnap, Rudolf 4:154
epistemology 7:222
logical positivism 12:397
metaphysics 13:335
Moore, G. E. 13:567–568
Quine, Willard Van Orman 16:27
Russell, Bertrand 16:349
Ryle, Gilbert 16:380
Strawson, Peter Frederick 18:296
Wisdom, John 20:189
Wittgenstein, Ludwig 20:193–194
ANALYTICAL CHEMISTRY 1:391 *bibliog.*
applications 1:391
chemistry 4:323–324 *illus.*
history 4:330
instruments
balance 3:30–31 *illus.*
calorimeter 4:47
densitometer 6:113
indicator 11:144
pH meter 15:218
photometer 15:273–274
polarimeter 15:393
polariscope 15:394
polarographic analyzer 15:395
spectroscope 18:169–170 *illus.*
turbidimeter 19:339
methods
chromatography 4:417–419 *illus.*
electrochemistry 7:112–113
electrophoresis 7:126
filtration 8:91
fractionation 8:258
mass spectrometry 13:204
optical activity 14:408
polarized light 15:395
precipitation (chemistry) 15:493
radiochemistry 16:63
spectroscopy 18:170–172 *illus.*
stoichiometry 18:276–277
titration 19:215
X-ray diffraction 20:308–309 *illus.*
Pregl, Fritz 15:502
qualitative chemical analysis 16:6–7
quantitative chemical analysis 16:7
ANALYTICAL PSYCHOLOGY
Jung, Carl 11:467
ANAMA BAY (Manitoba)
map (51° 56′N 98° 5′W) 13:119
ANAMOOSE (North Dakota)
map (47° 53′N 100° 15′W) 14:248
ANAMORPHOSIS 1:391 *bibliog.*
Holbein, Hans, the Younger 10:201
ANAMOSA (Iowa)
map (42° 7′N 91° 17′W) 11:244
ANANDA TEMPLE (Pagan)
Pagan (Burma) 15:13
ANAPEST
versification 19:562
ANAPHASE *see* MEIOSIS; MITOSIS
ANAPHYLACTIC SHOCK *see* ANAPHYLAXIS; SHOCK, PHYSIOLOGIC
ANAPHYLAXIS 1:391–392 *bibliog.*
stress, biological 18:298
ANÁPOLIS (Brazil)
map (16° 20′S 48° 58′W) 3:460
ANARCHISM 1:392 *bibliog., illus.*
See also NIHILISM; SYNDICALISM
Bakunin, Mikhail Aleksandrovich 3:30
Godwin, William 9:221
Goldman, Emma 9:235
Haymarket Riot 10:83
Kropotkin, Pyotr Alekseyevich 12:131
Living Theatre 12:376–377
Proudhon, Pierre Joseph 15:582
socialism 18:20–21
ANASAZI (American Indians) 1:392–394 *bibliog., illus.*
Arizona 2:163
art
Indians of North America, art of the 11:140 *illus.*
pottery 14:240 *illus.*
Basket Makers 1:393
Canyon de Chelly National Monument 4:119
Chaco Canyon 4:264–265
cliff dwellings 5:55; 11:120 *illus.*
Hopi 10:231
Kiva 12:93
Mesa Verde National Park (Colorado) 13:313–314 *illus.*
North American archaeology 14:239–240
origins 1:329–393
Pueblo Indians 15:613
Pueblo people 1:393–394
Zuñi 20:382
ANASTASIA *see* ROMANOV, ANASTASIA
ANASTASIUS 17:161 *illus.*
ANATOLIA 1:394–395 *map*; 19:344 *illus.*
See also TURKEY (country)
archaeology
Alaca Hüyük 1:239
Alalakh 1:239
Boğazköy 3:359–360
Bronze Age 3:506
Çatal Hüyük 4:197–198
Chalcolithic Period 4:270
Ephesus 7:216
Garstang, John 9:52
Halicarnassus 10:20
Kültepe 12:136
Magnesia 13:53
Neolithic Period 14:84
Pergamum 15:164–165
Priene 15:536
Sardis 17:77

Troy **19**:312–313
Urartu **19**:479–480
Xanthus **20**:311
art
Hittite art and architecture **10**:188–189
Islamic art and architecture **11**:293–297
coin **14**:296 *illus.*
Galatia **9**:10
history
Armenia **2**:172
Bithynia **3**:300
Cappadocia **4**:127–128
Cilicia **4**:430
Cimmerians **4**:431
Hittites **10**:189–190
Ionia **11**:241
Lausanne, Treaty of **12**:239–240
Lycia **12**:474
Lydia **12**:474
Middle East, history of the **13**:401
Miletus **13**:419
Mithradates VI, King of Pontus **13**:484
Ottoman Empire **14**:464–466
Phrygia **15**:278
Pontus **15**:428
Turks **19**:348
languages, extinct **12**:198–199
people **2**:242 *illus.*
Celts **4**:241
Cimmerians **4**:431
Tatar **19**:43–44
ANATOMICAL PATHOLOGY *see* PATHOLOGY
ANATOMY **1**:395–398 *bibliog., illus.*
See also BIOLOGY; HISTOLOGY; PHYSIOLOGY
ancient civilizations **1**:395–396
cat family **4**:196
chest **4**:336
chordate **4**:407
circulatory system **4**:438–442
clam **5**:35 *illus.*
classification, biological **5**:43
coelenterate **5**:91
coelom **5**:92
comparative anatomy **5**:154
crab **5**:324 *illus.*
crustacean **5**:369–370
developmental anatomy
embryology **7**:153–154
history **1**:397–398
dog **6**:213 *illus.*
dog family **6**:221
Erasistratus **7**:227
eye **7**:348–349 *illus.*
fish **8**:112–114
Chondrichthyes **4**:404
swim bladder **18**:390
Galen **9**:13
Gray's Anatomy **9**:307
Hemiptera **10**:119
horse **10**:241
human body
abdomen **1**:54 *illus.*
brain **3**:444–447 *illus.*
digestive system **6**:173 *illus.*
ear **7**:6
embryo **15**:503 *illus.*
eye **7**:348–350
heart **10**:91–92 *illus.*
intestine **11**:230–231 *illus.*
kidneys **12**:72
larynx **12**:209 *illus.*
ligament **12**:333
liver **12**:374–375 *illus.*
lymphatic system **12**:475–476
nose **14**:266
pelvis **15**:140
peripheral nervous system **15**:171
reproductive system, human **16**:63–66 *illus.*
spleen **18**:191
stomach **18**:279–280 *illus.*
tongue **19**:234 *illus.*
lizard **12**:379–382 *illus.*
mammal **13**:97–98 *illus.*
medicine **13**:267–270
microscopic anatomy
cytology **5**:411
history **1**:396
Hooke, Robert **10**:226
Leeuwenhoek, Antoni van **12**:271–272
Malpighi, Marcello **13**:93
modern studies **1**:398
mole (animal) **13**:506
mollusk **13**:510–511
monkey **13**:532–535
mushrooms **13**:661 *illus.*
perissodactyl **15**:171
plant **15**:335–337 *illus.*
primate **15**:539
race **16**:33
shark **17**:242
snail **17**:375–376 *illus.*
snake **17**:376–379 *illus.*
spider **18**:182–183 *illus.*
sponge **18**:193–194
termite **19**:116–117
triggerfish **19**:297
trout **19**:311
turtle **19**:352–353
Vesalius, Andreas **19**:564
whale **20**:121
worm **20**:283
zoology **20**:376–377
ANATOMY OF MELANCHOLY, THE (book) **1**:398 *bibliog.*
Burton, Robert **3**:581
ANATOSAURUS **19**:258 *illus.*
ANAWRATHA **1**:398 *bibliog.*
Burma **3**:575
Pagan (Burma) **15**:13
ANAXAGORAS **1**:398 *bibliog.*
pre-Socratic philosophy **15**:533
ANAXIMANDER **1**:398 *bibliog.*
Milesian school **13**:419
ANAXIMENES **1**:398
Milesian school **13**:419
ANAYA, PEDRO MARÍA
Mexican War **13**:354
ANC *see* AFRICAN NATIONAL CONGRESS
ANCESTOR WORSHIP **1**:398–399 *bibliog.*
genealogy **9**:76
primitive religion **15**:545
totem **19**:249
ANCHIETA, JOSÉ DE **1**:399 *bibliog.*
ANCHISAURUS **1**:399 *bibliog.*
ANCHISES **1**:399
ANCHOR **1**:399 *illus.*
ANCHOR POINT (Alaska)
map (59° 46′N 151° 52′W) **1**:242
ANCHOR RING *see* TORUS
ANCHORAGE (Alaska) **1**:244 *illus.*; **1**:399
climate **14**:228 *table*; **19**:421 *table*
map (61° 13′N 149° 53′W) **1**:242
ANCHORMAN (television) **1**:399 *bibliog.*
Brinkley, David **3**:486–487
Chancellor, John **4**:278
Cronkite, Walter **5**:359
ANCHOVY **1**:399–400 *illus.*; **8**:117 *illus.*; **8**:124 *illus.*
South America **18**:94
upwelling, oceanic **19**:474
world fishing grounds **8**:125 *map*
ANCIENT MARINER see RIME OF THE ANCIENT MARINER, THE (poem)
ANCÓN, TREATY OF (1883)
Pacific, War of the **15**:5
Tacna-Arica Dispute **19**:6
ANCÓN DE SARDINAS BAY
map (1° 30′N 79° 0′W) **7**:52
ANCONA (Italy) **1**:400
map (43° 38′N 13° 30′E) **11**:321
ANCONE *see* RETABLE
ANCRE, CONCINO CONCINI, MARQUIS D'
Marie de Médicis **13**:152
ANCUD (Chile)
map (41° 52′S 73° 50′W) **4**:355
ANCUS MARCIUS
Rome, ancient **16**:297
ANCYCLOSTOMIASIS *see* HOOKWORM
AND ISLAND
map (69° 8′N 15° 54′E) **14**:261
AND QUIET FLOWS THE DON (book)
Sholokhov, Mikhail Aleksandrovich **17**:281
ANDALE (Kansas)
map (37° 48′N 97° 38′W) **12**:18
ANDALGALÁ (Argentina)
map (27° 36′S 66° 19′W) **2**:149
ANDALUCITE
orthorhombic system **14**:451
ANDALUS, AL- *see* ANDALUSIA (Spain)
ANDALUSIA (Alabama)
map (31° 19′N 86° 29′W) **1**:234
ANDALUSIA (Spain) **1**:400 *bibliog.*; **18**:141 *illus.*
cities
Algeciras **1**:285
Córdoba **5**:261
Spain, history of **18**:144–145
ANDALUSITE **1**:400
metamorphic rock **13**:332 *table*
sillimanite **17**:309
ANDAMAN ISLANDS (India) **1**:400
Andamanese **1**:400
map (12° 0′N 92° 45′E) **11**:80
Radcliffe-Brown, Sir Alfred R. **16**:41
ANDAMAN AND NICOBAR ISLANDS
map (10° 0′N 93° 0′E) **11**:80
ANDAMAN SEA **1**:400
map (10° 0′N 95° 0′E) **2**:232
ANDAMANESE **1**:400 *bibliog.*
ANDAMARCA (Bolivia)
map (18° 49′S 67° 31′W) **3**:366
ANDERLECHT (Belgium)
map (50° 50′N 4° 18′E) **3**:177
ANDERS, WILLIAM ALISON **1**:401
ANDERSEN, HANS CHRISTIAN **1**:401 *bibliog., illus.*
Little Mermaid **6**:110 *illus.*
Odense (Denmark) **14**:348
ANDERSEN-NEXØ, MARTIN *see* NEXØ, MARTIN ANDERSEN-
ANDERSON (Alabama)
map (34° 50′N 87° 16′W) **1**:234
ANDERSON (California)
map (40° 27′N 122° 18′W) **4**:31
ANDERSON (Indiana)
map (40° 10′N 85° 41′W) **11**:111
ANDERSON (county in Kansas)
map (38° 15′N 97° 40′W) **12**:18
ANDERSON (county in Kentucky)
map (38° 0′N 85° 0′W) **12**:47
ANDERSON (South Carolina)
map (34° 31′N 82° 39′W) **18**:98
ANDERSON (county in South Carolina)
map (34° 30′N 82° 45′W) **18**:98
ANDERSON (county in Tennessee)
map (36° 8′N 84° 15′W) **19**:104
ANDERSON (Texas)
map (30° 29′N 95° 59′W) **19**:129
ANDERSON (county in Texas)
map (31° 47′N 95° 40′W) **19**:129
ANDERSON, BRONCO BILLY
film, history of **8**:82
ANDERSON, CARL DAVID **1**:401
cloud chamber **5**:68
muon **13**:644
ANDERSON, CARL EMIL WILHELM *see* MILLES, CARL
ANDERSON, IAN
Jethro Tull **11**:408
ANDERSON, JACK **1**:401–402 *illus.*
Pearson, Drew **15**:128
ANDERSON, JOHN **1**:402
ANDERSON, DAME JUDITH **1**:401
ANDERSON, LINDSAY
documentary **6**:211
ANDERSON, MARGARET **1**:402
ANDERSON, MARIAN **1**:402 *bibliog., illus.*
ANDERSON, MAXIE
aerial sports **1**:122
ANDERSON, MAXWELL **1**:402 *bibliog.*
Weill, Kurt **20**:94
ANDERSON, PHILIP WARREN **1**:402
ANDERSON, MAJOR ROBERT
Fort Sumter **8**:237
ANDERSON, ROBERTA JOAN *see* MITCHELL, JONI
ANDERSON, SHERWOOD **1**:402–403 *bibliog.*
Winesburg, Ohio **20**:179
ANDERSON DAM (Idaho)
map (43° 30′N 115° 30′W) **11**:26
ANDERSON RANCH RESERVOIR
map (43° 25′N 115° 20′W) **11**:26
ANDERSONVILLE PRISON **1**:403
ANDERSSEN, ADOLF
chess **4**:336
ANDERSSON, DAN **1**:403
ANDERSSON, JOHAN GUNNAR **1**:403
ANDES **1**:403–404 *bibliog., illus., map*
art
Latin American art and architecture **12**:222
pre-Columbian art and architecture **15**:499–501
Bolivia **3**:366
Chile **4**:357 *illus.*
chinchilla **4**:377
climate, vegetation, and animal life **1**:404
economy **1**:404
Latin America, history of **12**:216–217
map (20° 0′S 68° 0′W) **1**:403
peaks
Aconcagua **1**:84
Chimborazo **4**:358
Cordillera Darwin **18**:92 *illus.*
Cotopaxi **5**:304
Huascarán **10**:287
Peru **15**:192; **15**:194 *illus.*
Ring of Fire **16**:225
skiing **18**:91 *illus.*
South America **18**:86
subduction zone **18**:312
Titicaca, Lake **19**:213
topography **1**:404
Trans-Andine Railroad **19**:267
volcano **19**:628
ANDESINE
feldspar **8**:47
ANDESITE **1**:404
igneous rock **11**:33
ANDESITE LINE
Pacific Ocean **15**:7–8
ANDHRA PRADESH (India) **1**:405
cities
Hyderabad **10**:329
map (16° 0′N 79° 0′E) **11**:80
ANDIZHAN (USSR)
map (40° 45′N 72° 22′E) **19**:388
ANDKHVOY (Afghanistan)
map (36° 56′N 65° 8′E) **1**:133
ANDO HIROSHIGE *see* HIROSHIGE
ANDOAS (Peru)
map (2° 50′S 76° 30′W) **15**:193
ANDORRA **1**:405–406 *bibliog., illus., map*
economy **1**:405
flag **1**:405 *illus.*
government **1**:405–406
history **1**:405–406
land and people **1**:405
map (42° 30′N 1° 30′E) **7**:268
map (42° 30′N 1° 31′E) **1**:405
ANDORRA VALLEY
map (42° 30′N 1° 30′E) **1**:405
ANDOVER (Maine)
map (44° 38′N 70° 45′W) **13**:70
ANDOVER (Massachusetts)
map (42° 39′N 71° 8′W) **13**:206
ANDOVER (New York)
map (42° 9′N 77° 48′W) **14**:149
ANDOVER (Ohio)
map (41° 36′N 80° 34′W) **14**:357
ANDOVER (South Dakota)
map (45° 25′N 97° 54′W) **18**:103
ANDOVER NEWTON THEOLOGICAL SCHOOL **1**:406
ANDRADA E SILVA, JOSÉ BONIFÁCIO DE **1**:406
ANDRADE, FRANCISCO D' **14**:400 *illus.*
ANDRADE, JORGE CARRERA *see* CARRERA ANDRADE, JORGE
ANDRADE, MÁRIO DE **1**:406
Brazilian literature **3**:464
ANDRADITE
garnet **9**:49
ANDRÁSSY, GYULA, COUNT **1**:406
ANDRE, CARL **1**:406 *bibliog.*
ANDRÉ, JOHN **1**:406; **2**:184 *illus.*
ANDREA DA FIRENZE
Saint Thomas Aquinas **2**:94 *illus.*
ANDREA DEL CASTAGNO **1**:406 *bibliog.*
ANDREA DEL SARTO **1**:407 *bibliog., illus.*
Louvre **12**:437
Madonna of the Harpies **1**:407 *illus.*
ANDREA DORIA (ship)
Doria, Andrea **6**:242
ANDREANOF ISLANDS
map (52° 0′N 176° 0′W) **1**:242
ANDREINI, ISABELLA
theater, history of the **19**:147
ANDRETTI, MARIO **1**:407 *bibliog.*
automobile racing **2**:360 *illus.*
ANDREW (county in Missouri)
map (40° 0′N 94° 50′W) **13**:476
ANDREW, SAINT **1**:407
cross **5**:360; **5**:361 *illus.*
Patras (Greece) **15**:113
ANDREW II, KING OF HUNGARY **1**:407
Golden Bull **9**:231
ANDREWES, LANCELOT **1**:407–408 *bibliog.*
ANDREWS (Indiana)
map (40° 52′N 85° 36′W) **11**:111
ANDREWS (North Carolina)
map (35° 12′N 83° 49′W) **14**:242
ANDREWS (South Carolina)
map (33° 27′N 79° 34′W) **18**:98
ANDREWS (Texas)
map (32° 19′N 102° 33′W) **19**:129
ANDREWS (county in Texas)
map (32° 22′N 102° 37′W) **19**:129
ANDREWS, CHARLES McLEAN **1**:408 *bibliog.*
ANDREWS, DAME CICILY ISABEL FAIRFIELD *see* WEST, REBECCA
ANDREWS, JULIE **1**:408
musical comedy **13**:673 *illus.*
ANDREWS, ROY CHAPMAN **1**:408 *bibliog.*
Gobi **9**:217
ANDREWS, THOMAS **1**:408
ANDREYEV, LEONID NIKOLAYEVICH **1**:408 *bibliog.*
ANDRIĆ, IVO **1**:408

ANDROCLES 1:408
ANDROGEN
sex hormones 17:226–227
steroid 18:261–262
ANDROGENIC HORMONE
hormone, animal 10:237 *table*
ANDROMACHE (Greek legend) 1:408
ANDROMACHE (play)
Racine, Jean 16:37
ANDROMEDA (constellation) 1:408
Andromeda galaxy 1:409
ANDROMEDA (mythology) 1:409; 3:576 *illus.*
ANDROMEDA GALAXY 1:409 *bibliog., illus.*
Andromeda (constellation) 1:408
Baade, Walter 3:4
extragalactic systems 7:342–343 *map*
Hubble, Edwin 10:288
Local Group of galaxies 12:385
ANDRONICUS, LIVIUS *see* LIVIUS ANDRONICUS
ANDROPOV, YURI V. 1:409 *illus.*
ÁNDROS (Greece)
Cyclades (Greece) 5:402
ANDROS, SIR EDMUND 1:409 *bibliog.*
Massachusetts 13:211
ANDROS ISLAND
Bahama Islands 3:23
map (24° 26′N 77° 57′W) 3:23
ÁNDROS ISLAND (Greece)
map (37° 45′N 24° 42′E) 9:325
ANDROS TOWN (Bahama Islands)
map (24° 43′N 77° 47′W) 3:23
ANDROSCOGGIN (county in Maine)
map (44° 8′N 70° 15′W) 13:70
ANDROSCOGGIN RIVER
map (43° 55′N 69° 55′W) 13:70
ANÉCHO (Togo)
map (6° 14′N 1° 36′E) 19:222
ANEGADA
Virgin Islands 19:605
ANEGADA ISLAND
map (18° 45′N 64° 20′W) 19:605
ANEGADA PASSAGE
map (18° 30′N 63° 40′W) 19:605
ANEGAM (Arizona)
map (32° 23′N 112° 2′W) 2:160
ANEMIA 1:409–410 *bibliog.*
aplasia 2:78
blood 3:337–338
Cooley's anemia 5:240
hemoglobin 10:119
methemoglobinemia 13:343
Minot, George 13:460
nutritional-deficiency diseases 14:307
pregnancy and birth 15:505
sickle-cell anemia 17:293
starvation 18:228
uremia 19:485
vitamins and minerals 19:620
Whipple, George Hoyt 20:131
ANEMOMETER 1:410
meteorology 13:342
ANEMONE (botany) 1:410 *illus.*; 8:170 *illus.*
Adonis 1:107
wood anemone 8:228 *illus.*
ANEMONE, SEA *see* SEA ANEMONE
ANEMONE FISH *see* DAMSELFISH
ANEMOPHILY
pollination 15:408–409
ANERIO, GIOVANNI FRANCESCO
oratorio 14:416
ANESTHETICS 1:410–411 *bibliog.*
acupuncture 1:91
analgesic 1:388
chloroform 4:401
cocaine 5:85
curare 5:390
dentistry 6:116
ether 7:249
henbane 10:121
history 1:410
Morton, William 13:593
Willstätter, Richard 20:163
hypnosis 1:411
lidocaine 12:323
nitrogen 14:202
procainamide 15:559
procaine 15:559
surgery 18:361
ANETA (North Dakota)
map (47° 41′N 97° 59′W) 14:248
ANETO PEAK
map (42° 38′N 0° 40′E) 18:140
ANEURYSM 1:411 *bibliog.*
cardiovascular diseases 4:144
DeBakey, Michael 6:70
Kawasaki disease 12:32
nervous system, diseases of the 14:95–96
stroke 18:302
ANFINSEN, CHRISTIAN BOEHMER 1:411
ANGARA RIVER 1:411
map (58° 6′N 93° 0′E) 19:388
ANGEL 1:411–412 *bibliog.*
Gabriel 9:6
ÁNGEL DE LA GUARDA ISLAND
map (29° 20′N 113° 25′W) 13:357
ANGEL DUST 1:412
ANGEL FALLS 1:412; 19:543 *illus.*
map (5° 57′N 62° 30′W) 19:542
ANGELES (Philippines)
map (15° 9′N 120° 35′E) 15:237
ANGELES, VICTORIA DE LOS *see* DE LOS ANGELES, VICTORIA
ANGELFISH 1:412 *bibliog., illus.*
ANGELIC DOCTOR *see* AQUINAS, SAINT THOMAS
ANGELICA TREE 1:413
Hercules' club 10:138
ANGELICO, FRA 1:413–414 *bibliog., illus.*
Annunciation 15:19 *illus.*
Lamentation over the Dead Christ 1:413 *illus.*
Sermon on the Mount 11:404 *illus.*
The Stoning of Saint Stephen 13:520 *illus.*
ANGELINA (county in Texas)
map (31° 15′N 94° 45′W) 19:129
ANGELL (family) 1:414 *bibliog.*
ANGELL, JAMES BURRILL
Angell (family) 1:414
ANGELL, JAMES ROWLAND
Angell (family) 1:414
ANGELOU, MAYA 1:414
ANGELUS, THE
Millet, Jean François 13:430
ANGER, KENNETH
film, history of 8:87
ANGERMAN RIVER
map (62° 48′N 17° 56′E) 18:382
ANGERS (France) 1:414
map (47° 28′N 0° 33′W) 8:260
ANGERSTEIN, J. J.
National Gallery, London 14:33
ANGEVINS (dynasties) 1:414
England
Edward I, King of England 7:67–68
Edward II, King of England 7:68
Edward III, King of England 7:68
Great Britain, history of 9:311
Henry II, King of England 9:310 *map*; 10:124–125
Henry III, King of England 10:125
Hundred Years' War 10:304–305
John, King of England 11:426–427
Richard I, King of England 16:209–210
Richard II, King of England 16:210
Hungary
Charles I, King of Hungary 4:296
Louis I, King of Hungary (Louis the Great) 12:428
Naples and Sicily
Charles I, King of Naples 4:296
Charles II, King of Naples 4:296
Charles III, King of Naples (Charles of Durazzo) 4:296
Joan I, Queen of Naples 11:420
René of Anjou, King of Naples 16:157
Normans 14:222
Sicilian Vespers 17:292
ANGIER (North Carolina)
map (35° 31′N 78° 44′W) 14:242
ANGINA *see* HEART DISEASES
ANGIOGENIN 1:414
ANGIOGRAPHY
See also CARDIAC CATHETERIZATION
radiology 16:64
ANGIOLINI, GASPERO
Kirov Ballet 12:89
ANGIOSPERM 1:414 *bibliog.*
flower 8:178–184
fossil record 8:245
Cenozoic Era 4:246
herbaceous plant 10:134
plant 15:334–337 *illus.*
reproduction 16:162
seed 17:186
spermatophyte 18:179
tracheophyte 19:258
tree 19:286–287 *illus.*
ANGIOTENSIN
endocrine system 7:169
hypertension 10:349
ANGKOR (Kampuchea) 1:414–415 *bibliog.*
Angkor Wat 2:253 *illus.*; 18:108 *illus.*
temple 19:98
Kampuchea (Cambodia) 12:12
Khmer Empire 12:67
Southeast Asian art and architecture 18:109
ANGLE 1:415 *illus.*
cosine 5:280
measurement 13:254
goniometer 9:244
surveying 18:366–369
theodolite 19:155–156
transit, surveying 19:273
radian 16:42
secant 17:178
sine 17:319
tangent 19:22
triangle (mathematics) 19:292
trigonometry 19:298–299
ANGLERFISH 1:415–416 *illus.*; 6:78 *illus.*
bioluminescence 3:272
ANGLESEY *see* GWYNEDD
ANGLESEY ISLAND
map (53° 15′N 4° 20′W) 19:403
ANGLESITE 1:416
ANGLETON (Texas)
map (29° 10′N 95° 26′W) 19:129
ANGLICAN COMMUNION 1:416 *bibliog.*
Australia, Church of England in 2:342
book of common prayer 3:386
catechism 4:202
Canada, Anglican Church of 4:87
canon law 4:114
Canterbury, archbishop of 4:116
cantor 4:118
England, Church of 7:181
Episcopal church 7:221
mass (musical setting) 13:201
New Zealand, Church of the Province of 14:161
Oxford movement 14:475
Thirty-nine Articles 19:170
ANGLO-AFGHAN WARS
Afghanistan 1:135
ANGLO-ARABIAN HORSE
saddle horse 17:9
ANGLO-AUSTRALIAN OBSERVATORY 1:416
ANGLO-CATHOLIC
catholic 4:211
ANGLO-DUTCH WARS 2:3 *bibliog.*
Charles II, King of England, Scotland, and Ireland 4:292
Cromwell, Oliver 5:358
Frederick William, Elector of Brandenburg (the Great Elector) 8:293
Great Britain, history of 9:314
Louis XIV, King of France 12:426
Nijmegen (Netherlands) 14:195
Ruyter, Michiel Adriaanszoon de 16:377
Tromp (family) 19:306
Vauban, Sébastien le Prestre de 19:528
Witt, Johan de 20:193
ANGLO-FRENCH WAR *see* OPIUM WARS
ANGLO-GERMAN NAVAL PACT
Hitler, Adolf 10:188
ANGLO-SAXON CHRONICLE, THE (book) 2:3 *bibliog.*
ANGLO-SAXON LANGUAGE *see* OLD ENGLISH
ANGLO-SAXONS 2:3 *bibliog., map*
art
English art and architecture 7:181
illuminated manuscripts 11:47–48
interior design 11:211 *illus.*
Great Britain, history of 9:309–310
invasion of Europe 7:282 *map*
kingdoms
East Anglia 7:31
England (8th century) 9:309 *map*
Mercia 13:304
Northumbria 14:256
Wessex 20:106
kings
Æthelbert, King of Kent 1:131
Æthelred II 1:131
Alfred, King of England 1:280
Athelstan, King of Wessex 2:289
Canute, King 4:118
Edward the Confessor, King of England 7:67
Edward the Elder, King of England 7:67
Egbert, King of Wessex 7:71–72
Harold II, King of England 10:53–54
Oswald, Saint 14:459
settlements in the United Kingdom 19:407
shoes 17:279
Sutton Hoo ship burial 18:374
ANGMAGSSALIK (Greenland)
map (65° 36′N 37° 41′W) 9:353
ANGOL (Chile)
map (37° 48′S 72° 43′W) 4:355
ANGOLA 2:3–6 *bibliog., illus., map, table*
Cabinda 4:5
cities
Benguela 3:199
Huambo 10:287
Luanda 12:446
climate 2:6 *table*
economic activity 2:4–6 *illus.*
education
African universities 1:176 *table*
flag 2:4 *illus.*
government 2:6
history 2:6
Africa, history of 1:160
Neto, Agostinho António 14:103
Thirty Years' War 19:171
land 2:3–4
map (12° 30′S 18° 30′E) 1:136
people 2:4
Chokwe 4:403
Herero 10:141
Luba 12:446
Lunda 12:462
Mbundu 13:251
Ovambo 14:469
San 17:49–50
ANGOLA (Indiana)
map (41° 38′N 85° 0′W) 11:111
ANGOLA (New York)
map (42° 38′N 79° 2′W) 14:149
ANGOLA BASIN
Atlantic Ocean bottom 2:295 *map*
ANGOON (Alaska)
map (57° 30′N 134° 35′W) 1:242
ANGORA (fiber) 2:6 *bibliog.*; 8:67 *illus.*
goat 9:215
ANGORA (Turkey) *see* ANKARA (Turkey)
ANGORA CAT 2:6 *illus.*; 4:195 *illus.*
longhaired cats 12:407–408
Maine coon cat 13:75 *illus.*
ANGOSTURA RESERVOIR
map (43° 18′N 103° 27′W) 18:103
ANGOULÊME (France) 2:6
cathedral 8:304 *illus.*
map (45° 39′N 0° 9′E) 8:260
ANGOUMOIS (France) 2:6
ANGRY YOUNG MEN 2:7 *bibliog.*
Amis, Kingsley 1:372
Osborne, John 14:452
Sillitoe, Alan 17:309
Waterhouse, Keith 20:64
Wilson, Colin 20:164
ANGSTROM 2:7
ÅNGSTRÖM, ANDERS JONAS 2:7
ANGUIER BROTHERS 2:7 *bibliog.*
ANGUILLA 2:7
map (18° 15′N 63° 5′W) 20:109
West Indies Associated States 20:109
ANGUILLA (Mississippi)
map (32° 58′N 90° 50′W) 13:469
ANGUISSOLA, SOFONISBA 2:7
ANGULAR FREQUENCY *see* MOTION, CIRCULAR
ANGULAR MOMENTUM 2:7 *bibliog.*
conservation, laws of 5:204
Coriolis effect 5:263
moment of inertia 13:515
nuclear physics 14:285
planetary systems 15:329
precession 15:493
quantum mechanics 16:11
torque 19:243
ANGULAR VELOCITY *see* MOTION, CIRCULAR
ANGUS (Scotland) 2:7–8
ANGUS, EARLS OF
Douglas (family) 6:246–247
ANGUS CATTLE 4:216 *illus.*
ANHINGA 2:8; 18:377 *illus.*
ANHWEI (Anhui) (China) 2:8
cities
Hofei (Hefei) 10:194
ANHYDRIDE 2:8 *illus.*
ANHYDRITE 2:8
ANI 2:8 *illus.*
ANIBARE (Nauru)
map (0° 32′S 166° 57′E) 14:51
ANIBARE BAY
map (0° 32′S 166° 57′E) 14:51
ANIE PEAK
map (42° 57′N 0° 43′W) 8:260
ANILINE 2:8
ANIMAL 2:8–11 *bibliog., illus.*

See also EXTINCT SPECIES; FOSSIL RECORD; MARINE BIOLOGY; PREHISTORIC ANIMALS; names of specific groups of animals, e.g., DINOSAUR; REPTILE; SONGBIRDS; ZOOPLANKTON; etc.; names of specific animals, e.g., CARIBOU; PARAMECIUM; etc.
altricial animal 1:314
animal experimentation 2:22
animal husbandry 2:22–25
animal rights 2:28
Arctic 2:140–142 *illus.*
body temperature 3:357 *table*
cell
cholesterol 4:403
protein synthesis 15:575
classification, biological 2:9–11 *illus.*; 5:43
Lamarck, Jean Baptiste 12:173–174
coloration, biological 5:121–122
comparative anatomy 5:154
deep-sea life 6:78–79
desert life 6:130–131
diet see NUTRITION, ANIMAL
diseases, animal 6:190–192
ecology 7:42–46
endangered species 7:165–168 *illus.*
evolution 7:318–325
forest 8:227–228
genetics 9:90
grasslands 9:299–301
growth 9:378–380
habitat 10:4–6
ice ages 11:10
infectious diseases 11:166
invertebrate 11:234–237
jungle and rain forest 11:469 *illus.*
lake (body of water) 12:168 *illus.*
metabolism 13:325; 13:327
nutrient cycles 14:304
poisonous plants and animals 15:383–385
precocial animal 15:495
Protozoa 15:579–581
radiation injury 16:42–43
reproduction 16:162–163
fertilization 8:60–61
gestation 9:160
viviparity 19:622
savanna life 17:97–99
Society for the Prevention of Cruelty to Animals 18:26
swamp, marsh, and bog 18:376–378
taxidermy 19:47–48
tundra 19:333
veterinary medicine 19:566–567
zoological gardens 20:374–375
zoology 20:375–378
zoophobia 20:378
ANIMAL BEHAVIOR 2:11–18 *bibliog., illus.*
aggression 1:184–185
altruism 1:314
animal communication 2:18–20
animal courtship and mating 2:20–22
animal migration 2:25–28
bird
birdsong 3:291–292
crow 5:363
duck 6:292
gull 9:404
hoatzin 10:191
imprinting 11:68–69
penguin 15:143
robin 3:286 *illus.*
woodpecker 20:212
comparative psychology 5:154
culture 5:384
emotion 7:157
ethology 7:257
evolution 2:15–17; 7:324
feral children 8:51
fish
cichlid 4:429
grunion 9:383–384
shark 17:242–244
stickleback 18:267
genetics 2:13–14
handedness 10:35
hibernation 10:156
Huxley, Sir Julian 10:325 *illus.*
insect 11:191–193
defenses 11:193
Fabre, Jean Henri 8:5
flight 11:193
Frisch, Karl von 8:334
termite 19:116–117
wasp 20:45–46
instinct 2:13; 11:194–195
invertebrate
crab 5:325
snail 17:375
lizard 12:379–382 *illus.*
Lorenz, Konrad 12:414
mammal 13:98–99; 13:101 *illus.*
ape 2:75
cat 4:196
chimpanzee 4:359
deer 6:80–81
Goodall, Jane 9:245
gorilla 9:251
Harlow, Harry F. 10:50–51
hippopotamus 10:175
kangaroo 12:15
mole 13:507
primate 15:539
siamang 17:299 *illus.*
whale 20:121
wolf 20:196
Morgan, Conway Lloyd 13:578
motivation 13:610
Nobel Prize 2:12
Pavlov, Ivan Petrovich 15:120
physiology 2:14–15
population biology 15:438
psychology 15:593
radar 16:40
sociobiology 18:27
territoriality 2:16 *illus.*; 3:286 *illus.*; 19:121–122 *illus.*
Tinbergen, Nikolaas 19:206
Watson, John B. 20:68
ANIMAL COLORATION see COLORATION, BIOLOGICAL
ANIMAL COMMUNICATION 2:18–20 *bibliog., illus.*
animal behavior 2:12–16
animal courtship and mating 2:20–22
bird
birdsong 2:13; 3:291–292
honey guide 10:220
hoopoe 10:228
parrot 15:98 *illus.*
songbirds 18:65
insect 11:188; 11:191–193
ant 2:36
bee 3:158 *illus.*; 3:159
cricket 5:344
katydid 12:31
instinct 11:194
krill 12:129–130
mammal
chimpanzee 4:359
dolphin 6:228
fox 8:255
primate 15:541
whale 20:121
wolf 20:196
pheromone 15:226
ANIMAL COURTSHIP AND MATING 2:20–22 *bibliog., illus.*
animal behavior 2:13–16
animal communication 2:19
bioluminescence 3:272
bird 3:284–287 *illus.*
birdsong 3:291
bowerbird 3:428
grebe 3:286 *illus.*
ostrich 14:458
peacock 15:124
pigeon 15:299
sand grouse 17:61
swift 18:389
waxbill 20:73
whooping crane 20:143
woodcock 20:210
earthworm 7:30
ethology 7:257
fertilization 8:60–61
fiddler crab 8:70 *illus.*
fish
anglerfish 6:78 *illus.*
cichlid 4:429
salmon 17:35
Siamese fighting fish 17:291
imprinting 11:69
insect 11:189; 11:193
instinct 11:194
mammal 13:98–99; 13:101 *illus.*
mule 13:636
primate 15:539
midwife toad 13:414–415
pheromone 15:226
population genetics 15:439–440
reproduction 16:162–163
sexual selection 17:231–232
snake 17:382
python 15:640
spider 18:183
territoriality 19:121
ANIMAL EXPERIMENTATION 2:22 *bibliog.*
animal rights 2:28
behavioral genetics 3:170
cancer 4:102–104
guinea pig 9:400
hamster 10:33
insect 11:193
mouse 13:626
pigeon 15:299–300
rat 16:92
rhesus monkey 16:193
rodent 16:265
shark 17:244
Skinner box 17:344
spider 18:183
vivisection 19:622–623
ANIMAL FARM (book) 2:22 *bibliog.*
Orwell, George 14:451
ANIMAL HUSBANDRY 2:22–25 *bibliog., illus.*
agriculture, history of 1:189–193
African prehistory 1:173–174
prehistoric humans 15:517
agriculture and the food supply 1:196 *map*
artificial insemination 2:220
cattle and cattle raising 4:214–217
chicken 4:345
factory farming 8:6
genetics 9:90
goat 9:215
hybrid 10:328
pig 15:298–299
reindeer 16:131
reproduction 16:162–163
sheep 17:248–249
transportation 19:278
ANIMAL INTELLIGENCE see INTELLIGENCE
ANIMAL LEARNING see LEARNING IN ANIMALS
ANIMAL LOCOMOTION see BIOLOGICAL LOCOMOTION
ANIMAL MIGRATION 2:25–28 *bibliog., illus.*
animal behavior 2:16–17
bat 3:121
bird 3:288–289 *map*
eel 7:71
instinct 11:194
lemming 12:280
plover 15:369
population genetics 15:440
salmon 17:35
stork 18:285
swallow 18:376 *illus.*
tern 19:117–118
whale 20:121
ANIMAL NUTRITION see NUTRITION, ANIMAL
ANIMAL PSYCHOLOGY see ANIMAL BEHAVIOR; ANIMAL COMMUNICATION
ANIMAL RIGHTS 2:28 *bibliog.*
animal experimentation 2:22
ANIMAL WELFARE ACT
animal experimentation 2:22
vivisection 19:623
ANIMAL WORSHIP
Egypt, Ancient
cat 4:193
Mesoamerica
quetzal 16:24 *illus.*
ANIMAS (New Mexico)
map (31° 57′N 108° 48′W) 14:136
ANIMAS MOUNTAIN
map (34° 46′S 55° 19′W) 19:488
ANIMAS PEAK
map (31° 35′N 108° 47′W) 14:136
ANIMAS RIVER
map (36° 53′N 107° 58′W) 5:116
ANIMAS VALLEY
map (32° 5′N 108° 50′W) 14:136
ANIMATION 2:28–29 *bibliog., illus.*
Disney, Walt 6:196–197
film, history of 8:87
Fischinger, Oskar 8:111
history 2:29
McLaren, Norman 13:31–32 *illus.*
Mickey Mouse 13:383
ANIMISM 2:29 *bibliog.*
medicine 13:270
primitive religion 15:543
Southeast Asian art and architecture 18:107–108
Tylor, Sir Edward B. 19:362
ANION 2:29
battery 3:125–126
cation 4:212
chemical nomenclature 4:320
salt (chemistry) 17:37
ANISE 2:29–30 *illus.*
ANISOTROPIC MINERALS
optical mineralogy 14:409
ANITA (Iowa)
map (41° 27′N 94° 46′W) 11:244
ANJOU (France) 2:30 *map*
Angevins (dynasties) 1:414
Louis XI, King of France 12:425
Philip II, King of France (Philip Augustus) 15:232
ANJOUAN ISLAND
Comoros 5:153–154 *map*
map (12° 15′S 44° 25′E) 5:153
ANKARA (Turkey) 2:30–31 *illus.*; 19:343–344 *illus., table*
map (39° 56′N 32° 52′E) 19:343
ANKARATRA MOUNTAINS
map (19° 25′S 47° 12′E) 13:38
ANKENY (Iowa)
map (41° 44′N 93° 36′W) 11:244
ANKH see CRUX ANSATA
ANKLE
clubfoot 5:71
ANKOLE CATTLE 4:216 *illus.*
ANN ARBOR (Michigan) 2:31
map (42° 18′N 83° 45′W) 13:377
ANNA (Illinois)
map (37° 28′N 89° 15′W) 11:42
ANNA (Nauru)
map (0° 30′S 166° 56′E) 14:51
ANNA, EMPRESS OF RUSSIA 2:31 *bibliog.*
ANNA COMNENA 2:31
ANNA KARENINA (book) 2:31 *bibliog.*
Tolstoi, Count Leo 19:228
ANNA AND THE KING OF SIAM (book)
Mongkut, King of Siam 13:528
ANNA POINT
map (0° 30′S 166° 56′E) 14:51
ANNABA (Algeria)
map (36° 54′N 7° 46′E) 1:287
ANNALES (journal)
history 10:185
ANNALS 2:31
ANNALY (Ireland) see LONGFORD (Ireland)
ANNAM 2:31
Asia, history of 2:255 *map*
Bao Dai, Emperor 3:72
Vietnam 19:583
ANNAMESE CORDILLERA
map (17° 0′N 106° 0′E) 12:203
ANNAMESE LANGUAGES
Asia 2:244 *map*
ANNAN, THOMAS
photojournalism 15:273
ANNAPOLIS (Maryland) 2:31–32 *illus.*; 13:190 *illus.*; 13:192 *illus.*
map (38° 59′N 76° 30′W) 13:188
United States Naval Academy 19:463–464
ANNAPOLIS CONVENTION 2:32
ANNAPOLIS ROYAL (Nova Scotia) 2:32
map (44° 45′N 65° 31′W) 14:269
ANNAPURNA (Nepal) 2:32
map (28° 34′N 83° 50′E) 14:86
ANNATTO TREE 2:32
ANNE, QUEEN OF ENGLAND, SCOTLAND, AND IRELAND 2:32 *bibliog.*
Harley, Robert, 1st Earl of Oxford 10:50
horse racing 10:247–248
Marlborough, Sarah Churchill, Duchess of 13:160
ANNE, SAINT 2:32
ANNE ARUNDEL (county in Maryland)
map (38° 59′N 76° 30′W) 13:188
ANNE OF AUSTRIA 2:32 *bibliog.*
Louis XIII, King of France 12:426
Mazarin, Jules 13:249–250
ANNE OF BRITTANY 2:32
ANNE OF CLEVES 2:32 *bibliog.*
Cromwell, Thomas, 1st Earl of Essex 5:358
Henry VIII, King of England 10:127
ANNE OF GREEN GABLES (book)
Montgomery, L. M. 13:556
ANNEALING 2:33 *bibliog.*
materials technology 13:221
ANNECY (France)
map (45° 54′N 6° 7′E) 8:260
ANNELID 2:33 *bibliog.*
earthworm 7:29–30
invertebrate 11:235
leech 12:271
lugworm 12:453
palolo worm 15:52
Peripatus 15:171
polychaete 15:418
rag worm 16:69
worm 20:283 *illus.*
ANNENBERG SCHOOL OF COMMUNICATIONS
Pennsylvania, University of 15:152
ANNEXATION 2:33
imperialism 11:61
municipal government 13:642–643
ANNIE ALLEN (book)
Brooks, Gwendolyn 3:511

ANNIHILATION **2**:33
gamma rays **9**:34
ANNISTON (Alabama)
map (33° 40′N 85° 50′W) **1**:234
ANNUAL (botany)
flower **8**:181
gardening **9**:43
ANNUITY **2**:33–34
de Moivre, Abraham **6**:62
life insurance **12**:329
ANNULMENT (law)
divorce **6**:205
ANNUNCIATION *see* MARY
ANNUNZIO, GABRIELE D′ *see* D′ANNUNZIO, GABRIELE
ANNVILLE (Kentucky)
map (37° 19′N 83° 58′W) **12**:47
ANNVILLE (Pennsylvania)
map (40° 19′N 76° 31′W) **15**:147
ANODIZING **2**:34 *bibliog.*
ANOINTING OF THE SICK **2**:34
ANOKA (Minnesota)
map (45° 11′N 93° 23′W) **13**:453
ANOKA (county in Minnesota)
map (45° 15′N 93° 15′W) **13**:453
ANOLE **12**:381 *illus.*
ANOMALON **2**:34
ANOMALOPIA
color blindness **5**:113–114
ANOMIE
alienation **1**:294
ANOPLURA **2**:34
louse **12**:436
ANOREXIA NERVOSA **2**:34 *bibliog.*
menstruation **13**:301
starvation **18**:228
ANOREXIC DRUGS
dieting **6**:165
ANORTHITE
feldspar **8**:46–47
ANORTHOSITE
igneous rock **11**:36
Moon **13**:563
ANOUILH, JEAN **2**:34–35 *bibliog.*
ANS (Belgium)
map (50° 39′N 5° 32′E) **3**:177
ANSARI **2**:35
ANSBACH (Germany, East and West)
map (49° 17′N 10° 34′E) **9**:140
ANSE-D′HAINAULT (Haiti)
map (18° 30′N 74° 27′W) **10**:15
ANSELM, SAINT **2**:35 *bibliog., illus.*
William II, King of England (William Rufus) **20**:156
ANSELMO (Nebraska)
map (41° 37′N 99° 52′W) **14**:70
ANSERMET, ERNEST **2**:35 *bibliog.*
ANSHAN (China) *see* AN-SHAN (China)
ANSINA (Uruguay)
map (31° 54′S 55° 28′W) **19**:488
ANSKY, SHLOIME **2**:35 *bibliog.*
ANSLEY (Nebraska)
map (41° 18′N 99° 23′W) **14**:70
ANSON (county in North Carolina)
map (35° 0′N 80° 5′W) **14**:242
ANSON (Texas)
map (32° 45′N 99° 54′W) **19**:129
ANSONIA (Connecticut)
map (41° 20′N 73° 5′W) **5**:193
ANSONVILLE (North Carolina)
map (35° 6′N 80° 7′W) **14**:242
ANSTED (West Virginia)
map (38° 8′N 81° 6′W) **20**:111
ANSWER (law)
legal procedure **12**:273
ANT **2**:35–38 *bibliog., illus.*; **11**:469 *illus.*
anatomy **2**:36 *illus.*
animal communication **2**:18 *illus.*
aphid **2**:77
army ants **2**:36–37
classification, biological **2**:38
colony **2**:37 *illus.*
fossil record **2**:38
leafcutting ants **11**:191 *illus.*
male **2**:36–37 *illus.*
nest **2**:36 *illus.*
parthenogenesis **15**:100
physiology **2**:36
queen **2**:36–37 *illus.*
soil organisms **18**:39 *illus.*
worker **2**:36–37 *illus.*
ANT BEAR *see* AARDVARK
ANT LION **2**:38 *illus.*
ANTA *see* AMERICAN NATIONAL THEATER AND ACADEMY
ANTABUSE *see* DISULFIRAM
ANTACID **2**:38
ANTAEUS **2**:38
ANTAGONIST
narrative and dramatic devices **14**:22
ANTAKYA (Turkey) *see* ANTIOCH (Turkey)
ANTALAHA (Madagascar)
map (14° 53′S 50° 16′E) **13**:38
ANTALYA (Turkey)
map (36° 53′N 30° 42′E) **19**:343
ANTALYA, GULF OF
map (36° 30′N 31° 0′E) **19**:343
ANTANANARIVO (Tananarive) (Madagascar) **2**:39; **13**:38 *illus*; **13**:39 *graph*
map (18° 55′S 47° 31′E) **13**:38
ANTANDROY (tribe)
Madagascar **13**:38
ANTARCTIC OCEAN
dimensions **14**:326 *table*
upwelling, oceanic **19**:474
Weddell Sea **20**:89
ANTARCTIC PENINSULA **2**:39
map (69° 30′S 65° 0′W) **2**:40
ANTARCTIC TREATY
Antarctica **2**:45
ANTARCTICA **2**:39–45 *bibliog., illus., map*
animal and plant life **2**:42–43 *illus.*
climate **2**:41; **2**:43
polar climate **15**:392
polar easterlies **15**:393
weather variation and extremes **20**:80–81 *tables*
exploration *see* EXPLORATION—Antarctica
geologic time
Ordovician Period **14**:421 *map*
Precambrian rock formations **15**:492 *map*
Tertiary Period **19**:123 *map*
geology **2**:41
glaciers and glaciation **9**:193
iceberg **11**:15
pack ice **15**:10–11
permafrost **15**:173–174
physical features
Antarctic Peninsula **2**:39
Erebus, Mount **7**:228
mountains, highest **13**:620 *table*
Ross Ice Shelf **16**:318
Vinson Massif **19**:601
plate tectonics
Antarctic plate **15**:351 *map*
continental drifting **15**:354 *map*
Pacific-Antarctic Ridge **15**:351 *map*
regions
British Antarctic Territory **3**:489
French Southern and Antarctic Territories **8**:326
Ross Dependency **16**:318
snowmobile **18**:5
topography **2**:39–40 *map*
tundra **19**:332
ANTARES
Scorpius **17**:149
ANTBIRD **2**:45
ANTE-BELLUM MANSION *see* PLANTATION
ANTEATER **2**:45 *illus.*; **11**:469 *illus.*; **13**:104 *illus.*
edentates **7**:56
numbat **14**:292
pangolin **15**:59
skin **17**:340 *illus.*
spiny anteater **18**:188
ANTELAMI, BENEDETTO **2**:45 *bibliog.*
Romanesque art and architecture **16**:285 *illus.*
ANTELOPE **2**:45–47 *bibliog., illus.*
addax **1**:99
blesbok **3**:331
bongo **3**:378
chiru **4**:398
duiker **6**:294
eland **7**:102
gazelle **9**:64–65
gemsbok **9**:75–76
horn (biology) **10**:238
impala **11**:60
kob **12**:104
mountain goat **13**:622
oryx **14**:451
pronghorn **15**:567–568
ruminant **16**:345
saiga **17**:15; **18**:257 *illus.*
springbok **18**:199–200
steppe life **18**:257 *illus.*
topi **17**:98 *illus.*
wildebeest **20**:149
ANTELOPE (county in Nebraska)
map (42° 10′N 98° 5′W) **14**:70
ANTENNA (biology) **2**:47 *bibliog., illus.*
emperor moth **15**:226 *illus.*
insect **11**:188–189 *illus.*
ANTENNA (electronics) **2**:47–48 *bibliog., illus.*
ground wave **9**:373
microwaves **13**:389
propagation of signals **2**:47
radar **16**:38–39 *illus.*
radio **16**:46
radio astronomy **16**:47–53 *illus.*
receiving antennas **2**:48
television **19**:86
transmitting antennas **2**:48
types **2**:47
ANTEQUERA (Spain)
map (37° 1′N 4° 33′W) **18**:140
ANTERO RESERVOIR
map (39° 0′N 105° 55′W) **5**:116
ANTHEIL, GEORGE **2**:48–49 *bibliog.*
ANTHELMINTIC DRUGS **2**:49
ANTHEM **2**:49 *bibliog.*
See also the subheading national anthem under names of specific countries, e.g., NORWAY; FRANCE; etc.
composers
Billings, William **3**:255–256
Byrd, William **3**:602
Purcell, Henry **15**:628
English music **7**:203
hymn **10**:347
ANTHEMIUS OF TRALLES **2**:49 *bibliog.*
Hagia Sophia **2**:133 *illus.*; **4**:204 *illus.*; **10**:10
ANTHER SAC
pollen **15**:406
pollen cone **15**:407
pollination **15**:408
ANTHESIN
hormone, animal **10**:237
ANTHOLOGY **2**:49
Palgrave, Francis **15**:47
ANTHON (Iowa)
map (42° 23′N 95° 52′W) **11**:244
ANTHONY (Florida)
map (29° 18′N 82° 7′W) **8**:172
ANTHONY (Kansas)
map (37° 9′N 98° 2′W) **12**:18
ANTHONY (New Mexico)
map (32° 0′N 106° 36′W) **14**:136
ANTHONY, SAINT **2**:49 *bibliog.*
ANTHONY, EARL **2**:49
ANTHONY, SUSAN B. **2**:49–50 *bibliog., illus.*
Rochester (New York) **16**:247
Stanton, Elizabeth Cady **18**:220
suffrage, women′s **18**:326 *illus.*
ANTHONY OF PADUA, SAINT **2**:50
ANTHRACENE
Dumas, Jean Baptiste André **6**:297
ANTHRACITE COAL
coal and coal mining **5**:76–77 *illus., map*
heat content **8**:353 *table*
ANTHRACNOSE *see* DISEASES, PLANT
ANTHRAX **2**:50
bacteria **3**:17 *illus.*
chemical and biological warfare **4**:313
deerfly **6**:81
diseases, animal **6**:190; **6**:192
Koch, Robert **12**:104
Pasteur, Louis **15**:108
ulcer **19**:376
ANTHROPOGEOGRAPHY
Ratzel, Friedrich **16**:94
ANTHROPOLOGICAL LINGUISTICS **2**:50–51 *bibliog.*
communication **5**:144
ANTHROPOLOGY **2**:51–55 *bibliog., illus.*
anthropologists
Benedict, Ruth **3**:197
Blumenbach, Johann Friedrich **3**:347
Boas, Franz **3**:349
Broca, Paul **3**:500
Clark, Sir W. E. Le Gros **5**:39
Coon, Carleton **5**:243
Evans-Pritchard, Sir Edward **7**:313
Firth, Sir Raymond **8**:109
Fortes, Meyer **8**:238
Frazer, Sir James **8**:289
Freyre, Gilberto **8**:330
Geertz, Clifford **9**:67
Goodall, Jane **9**:245
Goodenough, Ward **9**:246
Hrdlička, Aleš **10**:286
Kluckholn, Clyde **12**:98
Kroeber, Alfred L. **12**:130–131
Leach, Sir Edmund **12**:256
Leakey (family) **12**:258–259
Lévi-Strauss, Claude **12**:303–304
Malinowski, Bronislaw **13**:91
Mauss, Marcel **13**:238
Mead, Margaret **13**:251–252
Morgan, Lewis Henry **13**:578–579
Murdock, George Peter **13**:648
Oakley, Kenneth **14**:312
Putnam, Frederic Ward **15**:632
Radcliffe-Brown, Sir Alfred R. **16**:41
Redfield, Robert **16**:115
Sapir, Edward **17**:72
Sauer, Carl **17**:96
Schoolcraft, Henry Rowe **17**:134
Smith, Sir Elliot **17**:368
Tylor, Sir Edward B. **19**:362
Weidenreich, Franz **20**:91
Westermarck, Edward Alexander **20**:115
Wissler, Clark **20**:190
archaeology **2**:116–126
cultural anthropology **2**:52
See also names of specific peoples and tribes, e.g., ABORIGINES, AUSTRALIAN; BORORO (American Indians); MOJAVE (American Indians); etc.
acculturation **1**:79
amulet **1**:386
animism **2**:29
anthropological linguistics **2**:50–51
archaeology *see* ARCHAEOLOGY
body marking **3**:356–357
bride-price **3**:479
burial **3**:571
cannibalism **4**:109–110
cargo cults **4**:147
caste **4**:186–187
cemetery **4**:244–245
chief **4**:346
civilization **5**:34
clan **5**:36
concubinage **5**:171
culture **5**:384–385
culture area **5**:386
diffusion, cultural **6**:170
ethnography **7**:256–257
ethnohistory **7**:257
family **8**:15–18
fertility rites **8**:60
fetish **8**:63
folklore **8**:203
folkways **8**:204
funeral customs **8**:363–365
head-hunting **10**:85
human ecology **10**:297
Human Relations Area Files (G. P. Murdock) **13**:648
hunter-gatherers **10**:313
incest **11**:73–74
infanticide **11**:163
kinship **12**:85–86
magic **13**:49–50
marriage **13**:163–166
nomad **14**:214–215
passage rites **15**:103–104
primitive religion **15**:543–546
primitive societies **15**:546
shaman **17**:238–239
social anthropology **18**:11
social structure and organization **18**:16–17
sociology **18**:28
superstition **18**:353
taboo **19**:5
totem **19**:249
tribe **19**:295
urban anthropology **19**:480
women in society **20**:201
evolution, human *see* PREHISTORIC HUMANS
nature and scope **2**:51–52
paleoanthropology *see* PREHISTORIC HUMANS
physical anthropology **2**:52–55
See also ARCHAEOLOGY; PREHISTORIC HUMANS; names of specific fossil types, e.g., *AUSTRALOPITHECUS*; CRO-MAGNON MAN; *HOMO ERECTUS*; etc.
anthropometry **2**:55
cave dwellers **4**:224–225
cephalic index **4**:256
forensic science **8**:227
genetics **9**:90
population genetics **15**:439–440
primate **15**:539–542
race **16**:33–35
semantics (linguistics) **17**:193
ANTHROPOMETRY **2**:55 *bibliog.*
anthropology **2**:53
Bertillon system **3**:226
cephalic index **4**:256
Hrdlička, Aleš **10**:286
ANTHROPOSOPHY
Steiner, Rudolf **18**:249
theosophy **19**:160
ANTI ATLAS MOUNTAINS
map (30° 0′N 8° 30′W) **13**:585

ANTI-COMINTERN PACT
Hitler, Adolf **10**:188
ANTI-CORN LAW LEAGUE
Corn Laws **5**:267
ANTI-DEFAMATION LEAGUE
B'nai B'rith **3**:348
ANTI-FASCIST PEOPLE'S FREEDOM LEAGUE (Burma)
Aung San **2**:323
ANTI-FEDERALISTS **2**:61 *bibliog.*
Democratic party **6**:99
genesis of the Constitution **5**:213
ANTI-HERO **2**:62–63 *bibliog.*
ANTI-LEBANON MOUNTAINS
map (33° 35′N 36° 0′E) **12**:265
ANTI-MASONIC PARTY **2**:63
political convention **15**:399
ANTI-SALOON LEAGUE
temperance movement **19**:92
ANTI-SEMITISM **2**:68 *bibliog.*
Chamberlain, Houston Stewart **4**:273
Dreyfus Affair **6**:271–272
Germany, history of **9**:155
ghetto **9**:167
Hitler, Adolf **10**:187–188
Jewish Defense League **11**:412
Jews **11**:414–416
nazism **14**:67–68
pogrom **15**:380
Protocols of the Elders of Zion **15**:578
racism **16**:37–38
Torquemada, Tomás de **19**:243
ANTIAIRCRAFT SYSTEMS **2**:55–56 *bibliog., illus.*
artillery **2**:224
instrumentation **2**:55
ANTIANXIETY DRUG *see* TRANQUILIZER
ANTIBALLISTIC MISSILE **2**:56–57 *bibliog., illus.*
nuclear strategy **14**:288
rockets and missiles **16**:254–256
ANTIBIOTICS **2**:57–59 *bibliog., illus.*
antiseptic **2**:68
bacteria **3**:16
plasmid **15**:347
boil **3**:362
bubonic plague **3**:532
cancer **4**:105 *illus.*
candidiasis **4**:107
dentistry **6**:116
drug **6**:277; **6**:278
Dubos, Rene **6**:289
factory farming **8**:6
Fleming, Sir Alexander **8**:159
food processing **8**:212
fungi **8**:365
fungus diseases **8**:369
hexachlorophene **10**:154
infectious diseases **11**:165; **11**:168
penicillin **15**:143–144
propionates **15**:572
protein synthesis **15**:575
psittacosis **15**:588
Waksman, Selman Abraham **20**:8
ANTIBODY **2**:59–60 *bibliog., illus.*
allergy **1**:301
antigen **2**:61–62
antitoxin **2**:69
autoimmune diseases **2**:356
biopharmaceuticals **3**:275
blood **3**:336; **3**:337 *illus.*
breast-feeding **3**:469
drug **6**:277
genetic engineering **9**:84; **9**:85
globulin **9**:209
immunity **11**:57–58
immunodeficiency disease **11**:59
immunology **11**:60
infectious diseases **11**:165
inflammation **11**:169
radioimmunoassay **16**:63–64
ANTICHOLINERGIC DRUGS
drug **6**:277
ANTICHRIST **2**:60
eschatology **7**:237
millenarianism **13**:426–427
Second Coming of Christ **17**:178
ANTICLINE
fold **8**:194 *illus.*
syncline **18**:406
ANTICOAGULANT **2**:60
heparin **10**:130
ANTICONVULSANT
phenobarbital **15**:225
ANTICOSTI ISLAND
map (49° 30′N 63° 0′W) **16**:18
ANTIDEPRESSANTS **2**:60–61 *bibliog.*
headache **10**:85
psychotropic drugs **15**:604
ANTIDIURETIC HORMONE **2**:61 *bibliog.*
diabetes insipidus **6**:148
Du Vigneaud, Vincent **6**:287
endocrine system, diseases of the **7**:170
hormone, animal **10**:236 *table;* **10**:237
hunger and thirst **10**:310–311
pituitary gland **15**:322
urine **19**:487
ANTIETAM, BATTLE OF **2**:61 *bibliog., map;* **5**:25 *illus.*
ANTIETAM CREEK
map (39° 25′N 77° 45′W) **13**:188
ANTIFERROMAGNETIC MATERIALS
Néel, Louis Eugène Félix **14**:76
solid-state physics **18**:55
ANTIFREEZE **2**:61
ethyl alcohol **7**:257
genetic engineering **9**:85
glycol **9**:212
ANTIGEN **2**:61–62 *bibliog.*
allergy **1**:301
antibody **2**:60
antihistamine **2**:63
asthma **2**:268
Australia antigen
Blumberg, Baruch S. **3**:346
hepatitis **10**:130
blood **3**:336–337 *illus.*
drug **6**:277
genetic engineering **9**:85
immunity **11**:57
immunodeficiency disease **11**:59
immunology **11**:60
infectious diseases **11**:165
inflammation **11**:169
influenza **11**:171–172
lymphatic system **12**:475
parasitic diseases **15**:83
radioimmunoassay **16**:63–64
Rh factor **16**:192
ANTIGO (Wisconsin)
map (45° 9′N 89° 9′W) **20**:185
ANTIGONE (mythology) **2**:62 *bibliog.*
ANTIGONE (play)
Sophocles **18**:67
ANTIGONISH (Nova Scotia)
map (45° 35′N 61° 55′W) **14**:269
ANTIGONUS I MONOPHTHALMUS, MACEDONIAN KING **2**:62 *bibliog.*
Demetrius I Poliorcetes **6**:96–97
Seleucus I Nicator, Macedonian King **17**:191
ANTIGONUS II GONATAS, MACEDONIAN KING **2**:62 *bibliog.*
ANTIGONUS III DOSON, MACEDONIAN KING **2**:62
Greece, ancient **9**:333
ANTIGUA (Guatemala) **2**:62; **9**:388 *illus.*
map (14° 34′N 90° 44′W) **9**:389
San Carlos University (c.1763) **12**:225 *illus.*
ANTIGUA AND BARBUDA **2**:62 *illus.*
flag **8**:142 *illus.*
map (17° 3′N 61° 48′W) **20**:109
ANTIHISTAMINE **2**:63 *bibliog.*
allergy **1**:302
anaphylaxis **1**:392
Bovet, Daniele **3**:426
Dramamine **6**:262
hives **10**:190
inflammation **11**:169
sedative **17**:182
ANTIINFLAMMATORY DRUG
inflammation **11**:169
ANTILLES, GREATER AND LESSER **2**:63
Dominica **6**:232–233 *illus.*
French West Indies **8**:326
Guadeloupe **9**:385
history **4**:149
Leeward Islands **12**:272
map (15° 0′N 61° 0′W) (Lesser Antilles) **20**:109
map (20° 0′N 74° 0′W) (Greater Antilles) **20**:109
Montserrat (island) **13**:560
Netherlands Antilles **14**:103
Saint Lucia **17**:23
Saint Vincent and the Grenadines **17**:27
ANTILLES CURRENT
Gulf Stream **9**:403
ANTIMATTER **2**:63 *bibliog.*
fundamental particles **8**:362
ANTIMONY **2**:63–64 *bibliog.*
element **7**:130 *table*
Group VA periodic table **15**:167
stibnite **18**:266
sulfide minerals **18**:333
ANTIMONY (Utah)
map (38° 7′N 111° 55′W) **19**:492
ANTINEUTRINO
neutrino **14**:108
ANTINOMIANISM **2**:64 *bibliog.*
Hutchinson, Anne **10**:322
ANTIOCH (California)
map (38° 1′N 121° 49′W) **4**:31
ANTIOCH (Illinois)
map (42° 29′N 88° 6′W) **11**:42
ANTIOCH (Turkey) **2**:64
Bohemond I, Prince **3**:361
map (36° 14′N 36° 7′E) **19**:343
patriarch **15**:113
Seleucus I Nicator, Macedonian King **17**:191
ANTIOCH COLLEGE **2**:64
ANTIOCHUS III, SELEUCID KING (Antiochus the Great) **2**:64 *bibliog.*
Rome, ancient **16**:300
Seleucids (dynasty) **17**:190
ANTIOCHUS IV EPIPHANES, SELEUCID KING **2**:64 *bibliog.*
Seleucids (dynasty) **17**:190–191
ANTIOCHUS VII, SELEUCID KING
Seleucids (dynasty) **17**:191
ANTIOPE **2**:64
ANTIOXIDANTS **2**:64–65 *bibliog.*
ascorbic acid **2**:228
food preservation **8**:212
hydroquinone **10**:344
inhibitor **11**:178
ANTIPATER (Macedonian regent) **2**:65
ANTIPATER (procurator of Judea)
Herod (dynasty) **10**:144
ANTIPATER OF SIDON
Seven Wonders of the World **17**:216
ANTIPHON **2**:65 *bibliog.*
plainsong **15**:326
ANTIPODES ISLANDS **2**:65
map (49° 40′S 178° 47′E) **14**:334
ANTIPROTON
Chamberlain, Owen **4**:274
Segrè, Emilio **17**:188
ANTIPSYCHOTIC DRUG *see* TRANQUILIZER
ANTIPYRETIC DRUG
acetaminophen **1**:79
aspirin **2**:262–263
fever **8**:66
ANTIQUARIANS *see* ANTIQUE COLLECTING; ART COLLECTORS AND PATRONS
ANTIQUE COLLECTING **2**:65–68 *bibliog., illus.*
colonial styles in North America **5**:109–111
Gulbenkian, Calouste Sarkis **9**:402
netsuke **14**:104
ANTIQUITIES ACT OF 1906
historic preservation **10**:181
ANTIQUITIES OF ATHENS (book)
Stuart, James **18**:305
ANTIRENT WAR **2**:68
ANTISEPTIC **2**:68 *bibliog.*
bacteria **3**:16
bromine **3**:502
chlorine compounds **4**:400–401
gentian violet **9**:94
iodine **19**:621
Lister, Joseph **12**:366
phenol **15**:225
Semmelweis, Ignaz Philipp **17**:198
silver **17**:313
surgery **18**:361–362 *illus.*
ANTISOCIAL PERSONALITY DISORDER *see* PSYCHOPATHY
ANTISTHENES **2**:68–69 *bibliog.*
ANTITHESIS
figures of speech **8**:76
ANTITOXIN **2**:69 *bibliog.*
Behring, Emil Adolf von **3**:171
Wassermann, August von **20**:46
ANTITRUST LAWS **2**:69
cartoon (c.1890) **19**:451 *illus.*
Clayton Anti-Trust Act **5**:47
conglomerate (business) **5**:180–181
corporation **5**:273–274
government regulation **9**:270
merger **13**:310
monopoly and competition **13**:539–540
petroleum industry **15**:214
Robinson-Patman Act **16**:246
Sherman Anti-Trust Act **17**:258–259
ANTIWAR MOVEMENT *see* PACIFISM AND NONVIOLENT MOVEMENTS
ANTLER
deer **6**:79
ANTLERS (Oklahoma)
map (34° 14′N 95° 37′W) **14**:368
ANTOFAGASTA (Chile) **2**:69
map (23° 39′S 70° 24′W) **4**:355
ANTOFALLA VOLCANO
map (25° 34′S 67° 55′W) **2**:149
ANTOINE, ANDRÉ **2**:69 *bibliog.*
ANTON (Texas)
map (33° 49′N 102° 10′W) **19**:129
ANTON CHICO (New Mexico)
map (35° 12′N 105° 9′W) **14**:136
ANTONELLO DA MESSINA **2**:69–70 *bibliog., illus.*
Portrait of a Man **2**:69 *illus.*
Saint Jerome in his Study **11**:398 *illus.*
ANTONESCU, ION **2**:70
Iron Guard **11**:272
ANTONGIL, BAY OF
map (15° 45′S 49° 50′E) **13**:38
ANTONINE WALL **2**:70 *bibliog.*
Hadrian's Wall **10**:8
ANTONINES
Rome, ancient **16**:303
ANTONINUS, MARCUS AURELIUS *see* CARACALLA, ROMAN EMPEROR
ANTONINUS PIUS, ROMAN EMPEROR **2**:70 *bibliog.*
column frieze **16**:303 *illus.*
ANTÓNIO ENES (Mozambique)
map (16° 14′S 39° 58′E) **13**:627
ANTONIONI, MICHELANGELO **2**:70 *bibliog., illus.*
ANTONITO (Colorado)
map (37° 5′N 106° 0′W) **5**:116
ANTONIUS, MARCUS *see* ANTONY, MARK
ANTONY, MARK **2**:70–71 *bibliog.*
Actium, Battle of **1**:89
Augustus, Roman Emperor **2**:321–322
Cleopatra, Queen of Egypt **5**:50
Roman coin **16**:301 *illus.*
Rome, ancient **16**:302
Tarsus (Turkey) **19**:39–40
ANTONY AND CLEOPATRA (play) **2**:71 *bibliog.*
ANTRIM (county in Michigan)
map (45° 0′N 85° 10′W) **13**:377
ANTRIM (Northern Ireland) **2**:71
Belfast **3**:174
Dunluce Castle ruins **19**:405 *illus.*
Giant's Causeway **9**:171–172 *illus.*
ANTSIRABE (Madagascar)
map (19° 51′S 47° 2′E) **13**:38
ANTUM, AERT VAN
Spanish Armada **18**:151 *illus.*
ANTWERP (Belgium) **2**:71 *illus.*
harbor and port **10**:43
map (51° 13′N 4° 25′E) **3**:177
ANTWERP (Ohio)
map (41° 11′N 84° 45′W) **14**:357
ANTWREN *see* ANTBIRD
ANU (Mesopotamian deity) **2**:71
Uruk **19**:490
ANUBIS **2**:72; **7**:84 *illus.*; **13**:400 *illus.*
ANURA (Salientia)
amphibians **1**:378–379 *illus.*
ANURADHAPURA (Sri Lanka) **2**:72
map (8° 21′N 80° 23′E) **18**:206
ANUS
intestine **11**:230–231
skunk anal glands **17**:346
ANUSHIRVAN *see* KHOSRU I, KING OF PERSIA
ANUSZKIEWICZ, RICHARD **2**:72 *bibliog.*
op art **14**:397
ANVERS (Belgium) *see* ANTWERP (Belgium)
ANVIL (ear bone)
ear **7**:6 *illus.*
ANVIL (forging) **8**:232 *illus.*
ANXIETY **2**:72 *bibliog.*
breast-feeding **3**:469
fear **8**:39
meprobamate **13**:303
neurosis **14**:107
passage rites **15**:103–104
sedative **17**:181
symptoms **2**:72
theories **2**:72
tranquilizer **19**:266
vertigo **19**:563
ANYANG (China) **2**:72 *bibliog.*
Asia, history of **2**:251
Chinese archaeology **4**:378
oracle bones **4**:379 *illus.*; **14**:413
ANZA, JUAN BAUTISTA DE **2**:72–73 *bibliog.*
ANZAC (Australian and New Zealand Army Corps)
Gallipoli campaign **9**:20
ANZENGRUBER, LUDWIG
Austrian literature **2**:354
ANZIO (Italy) **2**:73
World War II **20**:271
ANZUS TREATY **2**:73
AO-MEN *see* MACAO

AOJI (Korea)
map (42° 31′N 130° 23′E) **12**:113
AOMORI (Japan)
map (40° 39′N 140° 45′E) **11**:361
AOPO (Western Samoa)
map (13° 29′S 172° 30′W) **20**:117
AORTA 2:73
cardiovascular diseases **4**:144
circulatory system **4**:440 *illus.*; **4**:442
heart **10**:91–92
AOSTA (Italy)
map (45° 44′N 7° 20′E) **11**:321
AOUKALÉ RIVER
map (9° 17′N 22° 42′E) **4**:251
AOUKÂR (region in Mauritania)
map (18° 0′N 9° 30′W) **13**:236
A & P *see* GREAT ATLANTIC AND PACIFIC TEA COMPANY
APACHE (American Indians) 2:73–74 *bibliog., illus.*
Indians, American **11**:131–133
Indians of North America, art of the **11**:140
Indians of North America, music and dance of the **11**:143
Jeffords, Thomas **11**:394
leaders
Cochise **5**:85–86
Geronimo **9**:157–158
Mangas Coloradas **13**:114–115
Victorio **19**:576
Navajo **14**:53
North American archaeology **14**:240
Pima **15**:303–304
Wichita (American Indians) **20**:144
wickiup **20**:145
APACHE (county in Arizona)
map (35° 0′N 109° 35′W) **2**:160
APACHE (Oklahoma)
map (34° 54′N 98° 22′W) **14**:368
APACHE WARS **11**:109 *map*
APALACHEE (American Indians) 2:74 *bibliog.*
APALACHEE BAY
map (30° 0′N 84° 13′W) **8**:172
APALACHICOLA (Florida)
map (29° 44′N 84° 59′W) **8**:172
APALACHICOLA BAY
map (29° 40′N 85° 0′W) **8**:172
APALACHICOLA RIVER
Chattahoochee River **4**:303
map (29° 44′N 84° 59′W) **8**:172
APAPORIS RIVER
map (1° 23′S 69° 25′W) **5**:107
APARTHEID 2:74 *bibliog.*
African National Congress **1**:171–172
Hertzog, James Barry Munnik **10**:149
integration, racial **11**:203
Johannesburg (South Africa) **11**:422
Malan, Daniel F. **13**:79
Paton, Alan **15**:112
Shona **17**:281
South Africa **18**:78; **18**:81; **18**:83
Verwoerd, Hendrik F. **19**:563
APARTMENT
condominium **5**:173
housing **10**:276; **10**:278; **10**:279
rent control **16**:159
APATITE 2:74 *illus.*
conodont **5**:197
new ceramics applications **4**:259
phosphate minerals **15**:255
phosphorite **15**:256
sediment, marine **17**:184
APATZINGÁN [DE LA CONSTITUCIÓN] (Mexico)
map (19° 5′N 102° 21′W) **13**:357
APAYAO
Igorot **11**:38
APC MIXTURES
phenacetin **15**:225
APE 2:74–76 *bibliog., illus.*
Aegyptopithecus **1**:118
behavior **2**:75
chimpanzee **4**:359
gibbon **9**:172
Gigantopithecus **9**:178
gorilla **9**:251
learning and intelligence **2**:76
orangutan **14**:415–416
primate **15**:539
Proconsul **15**:561
siamang **17**:290
APE MAN *see HOMO ERECTUS*
APELDOORN (Netherlands)
map (52° 13′N 5° 58′E) **14**:99
APELLES 2:76 *bibliog.*
Nichomachos **14**:183
APENNINES 2:76; 7:270 *illus.*
Italy **11**:322
map (43° 0′N 13° 0′E) **11**:321
APERTURE 2:76 *bibliog., illus.*
camera **4**:55
lens **12**:286
APERTURE CARD *see* MICROFILM
APERTURE SYNTHESIS 2:76
radio astronomy **16**:52
APGAR SCORING
pregnancy and birth **15**:506
APHAIA, TEMPLE OF (Aegina) **2**:131 *illus.*
APHAKIA
eye diseases **7**:351
APHASIA 2:76–77 *bibliog.*
nervous system, diseases of the **14**:95
speech **18**:175
speech therapy **18**:176
APHELANDRA 2:77 *illus.*
APHELION *see* ORBITAL ELEMENTS
APHERESIS
blood bank **3**:338
APHID 2:77 *bibliog., illus.*
lacewing **12**:160
APHORISM, MAXIM, AND PROVERB 2:77 *bibliog.*
folklore **8**:203
Franklin, Benjamin **8**:283
La Rochefoucauld, François, Duc de **12**:148
APHRODISIAC 2:78 *bibliog.*
amyl nitrite **1**:386–387
rhinoceros horn **10**:238
APHRODITE 2:78
Adonis **1**:107
fertility rites **8**:60
myrtle **13**:691
APHRODITE OF MELOS *see VENUS DE MILO*
APIA (Western Samoa) 2:78
map (13° 50′S 171° 44′W) **20**:117
APICULTURE *see* BEEKEEPING
APIS 2:78
APISHAPA RIVER
map (38° 8′N 103° 57′W) **5**:116
APL (computer language) 2:78
APLAHOUE (Benin)
map (6° 56′N 1° 41′E) **3**:200
APLASIA 2:78
APLASTIC ANEMIA **1**:410
aplasia **2**:78
APNEA 2:78 *bibliog.*
sleep **17**:360
APO, MOUNT
map (6° 59′N 125° 16′E) **15**:237
APOCALYPTIC LITERATURE 2:78–79 *bibliog.*
Commentary on the Apocalypse **16**:286 *illus.*
Daniel, Book of **6**:31–32
eschatology **7**:237
Four Horsemen of the Apocalypse, The **8**:253
Revelation, Book of **16**:185
Swedenborg, Emanuel von **18**:386
APOCRYPHA 2:79 *bibliog.*
Dead Sea Scrolls **6**:65
Ecclesiastes, Book of **7**:37
Esther, Book of **7**:246–247
Judith, Book of **11**:464
pseudepigrapha **15**:587
Septuagint **17**:206
APOCRYPHAL NEW TESTAMENT 2:79 *bibliog.*
APODA *see* GYMNOPHIONA (Apoda)
APODACA, JERRY
New Mexico **14**:138
APOLIMA STRAIT
map (14° 50′S 172° 10′W) **20**:117
APOLLINAIRE, GUILLAUME 2:79 *bibliog., illus.*
surrealism (art) **18**:364
APOLLINARIANISM 2:79
APOLLINOPOLIS MAGNA (Egypt) *see* EDFU (Egypt)
APOLLO (mythology) 2:80
caduceus **4**:12
Cassandra **4**:183
Delphi **6**:95
Greek music **9**:345
Italian art and architecture **11**:311 *illus.*
kithara (musical instrument) **12**:93
mythology **13**:701
Pythian Games **15**:640
APOLLO (Pennsylvania)
map (40° 35′N 79° 34′W) **15**:147
APOLLO BELVEDERE *see* BELVEDERE TORSO
APOLLO BUTTERFLY **3**:597 *illus.*
butterflies and moths **3**:595
APOLLO PROGRAM 2:80–84 *bibliog., illus., table*
Apollo-Soyuz Test Project **2**:84
astronauts **2**:274
Aldrin, Edwin E. **1**:269–270
Anders, William Alison **1**:401
Armstrong, Neil A. **2**:179–180
Bean, Alan **3**:140
Cernan, Eugene **4**:260
Chaffee, Roger **4**:267
Collins, Michael **5**:104
Conrad, Pete **5**:198
Cunningham, R. Walter **5**:390
Duke, Charles, Jr. **6**:295
Eisele, Donn F. **7**:94
Evans, Ronald **7**:313
Gordon, Richard F., Jr. **9**:249
Grissom, Virgil I. **9**:367
Haise, Fred W. **10**:15
Irwin, James **11**:285
Lovell, James **12**:438
McDivitt, James **13**:11–12
Mattingly, Thomas **13**:232
Mitchell, Edgar D. **13**:482–483
Roosa, Stuart A. **16**:307
Schirra, Walter M., Jr. **17**:122
Schmitt, Harrison H. **17**:128
Schweickart, Russell L. **17**:135
Scott, David R. **17**:153
Shepard, Alan B., Jr. **17**:256
Stafford, Thomas P. **18**:209
Swigert, John L., Jr. **18**:390
White, Edward H., II **20**:135
Worden, Alfred M. **20**:216
Young, John W. **20**:333
landing sites on the moon **13**:564 *map*
lunar surface experiments **2**:82–83 *illus.*
Moon **13**:562–564 *illus., map*
National Aeronautics and Space Administration **14**:28
photograph of earth from space **7**:11 *illus.*
preliminary programs
Gemini program **9**:71
Lunar Orbiter **12**:461
Ranger (space probe) **16**:84
Surveyor **18**:369–370
space centers
Johnson Space Center **11**:437
Kennedy Space Center **12**:44
space exploration **18**:127–129 *illus.*
space medicine **18**:133
spacecraft elements
Command and Service Module **2**:80 *illus.*
life-support systems **12**:331–333
Lunar Excursion Module **12**:460
Lunar Rover **12**:461–462 *illus.*
Saturn (rocket) **17**:91–92
SNAP **17**:383–384
space station **18**:136
APOLLO-SOYUZ TEST PROJECT 2:84 *bibliog., illus.*
Brand, Vance **3**:453
Bykovsky, Valery **3**:602
Dzhanibekov, Vladimir **6**:320
Filipchenko, Anatoly V. **8**:79
Kubasov, Valery N. **12**:134
Leonov, Aleksei **12**:292
Rukavishnikov, Nikolay **16**:344
Saturn (rocket) **17**:92
Slayton, D. K. **17**:359
space exploration **18**:129
Stafford, Thomas P. **18**:209
APOLLODORUS OF DAMASCUS 2:84 *bibliog.*
Basilica Ulpia **3**:110 *illus.*
APOLLONIUS OF PERGA 2:84 *bibliog.*
astronomy, history of **2**:277
APOLLONIUS OF RHODES 2:84–85 *bibliog.*
APOLO (Bolivia)
map (14° 43′S 68° 31′W) **3**:366
APOLOGIE FOR POETRIE, AN (essay)
Sidney, Sir Philip **17**:295
APOLOGY (book) 2:85 *bibliog.*
APOPKA, LAKE
map (28° 37′N 81° 38′W) **8**:172
APOPLEXY
stroke **18**:302
APOSTLE 2:85 *bibliog.*
Andrew, Saint **1**:407
Bartholomew, Saint **3**:97
James, Saint (James the Great) **11**:353
James, Saint (James the Lesser) **11**:353
John, Saint **11**:423
Judas Iscariot **11**:463
Luke, Saint **12**:454
Matthew, Saint **13**:231
Matthias, Saint **13**:231
ministry, Christian **13**:450
Peter, Saint **15**:199
Simon, Saint **17**:314
Thaddaeus, Saint **19**:138
Thomas, Saint **19**:172
APOSTLE-BIRD *see* AUSTRALIAN MUDNEST BUILDER
APOSTLE OF THE INDIES *see* LAS CASAS, BARTOLOMÉ DE
APOSTLE TO THE NEGROES *see* CLAVER, SAINT PETER
APOSTLES' CREED
creed **5**:337
heresy **10**:141
APOSTOLIC FATHERS 2:85 *bibliog.*
Clement I, Saint **5**:49
Didache **6**:160
Docetism **6**:210
Hermas **10**:142
Papias of Hierapolis **15**:71
patristic literature **15**:113–114
APOSTOLIC SUCCESSION 2:85 *bibliog.*
holy orders **10**:209
APOSTOLOS ANDREAS, CAPE OF
map (35° 42′N 34° 35′E) **5**:409
APOSTROPHE (literature)
figures of speech **8**:76
APOTHECARY 2:85
See also PHARMACY
American College of Apothecaries **2**:85
history **2**:85
Pharmaceutical Society of Great Britain **2**:85
APPALACHIA (Virginia)
map (36° 54′N 82° 47′W) **19**:607
APPALACHIAN MOUNTAINS 2:85–86 *bibliog., illus., map*; **19**:431 *illus.*
Allegheny Mountains **1**:298
Appalachian Trail **2**:86
Black Mountains **3**:317
Blue Ridge Mountains **3**:343
coal and coal mining **5**:76
employment and unemployment **7**:160
Cumberland Plateau **5**:387
Great Smoky Mountains **9**:322
Green Mountians **9**:348
Maine **13**:69; **13**:71
map (41° 0′N 77° 0′W) **2**:86
Maryland **13**:189
North America **14**:227
North Carolina **14**:241
Permian Period **15**:174
Quebec (province in Canada) **16**:16
APPALACHIAN TRAIL 2:86 *bibliog.*
APPALOOSA 2:86–87 *illus.*; **10**:243 *illus.*
Nez Percé **14**:175
saddle horse **17**:9
APPANOOSE (county in Iowa)
map (40° 45′N 92° 52′W) **11**:244
APPEAL (law) 2:87
criminal justice **5**:350
legal procedure **12**:273
APPEALS, COURT OF *see* COURT OF APPEALS
APPEL, KAREL 2:87 *illus.*
Dutch art and architecture **6**:313
Scream for Freedom **2**:87 *illus.*
APPELLATE COURT *see* COURT OF APPEALS
APPENDICITIS
enteritis **7**:208
gastrointestinal tract disease **9**:56 *illus.*
APPENDIX 2:87–88 *illus.*; **9**:56 *illus.*
intestine **11**:230
surgery **18**:361
APPERT, NICOLAS 2:88
APPETITE
hunger and thirst **10**:310
APPETITE SUPPRESSANT
amphetamine **18**:271
APPIA, ADOLPHE 2:88 *bibliog., illus.*
APPIAN WAY *see* ROMAN ROADS
APPLE 2:88–89 *bibliog., illus.*; **8**:348 *illus.*
Chapman, John **4**:285
cider **4**:429
plant reproduction **15**:338 *illus.*
varieties **2**:89 *illus.*
APPLE BRANDY *see* CIDER
APPLE MAGGOT
fruit fly **8**:347
APPLE ORCHARD MOUNTAIN
map (37° 31′N 79° 31′W) **19**:607
APPLE VALLEY (California)
map (34° 32′N 117° 14′W) **4**:31
APPLEJACK *see* CIDER
APPLESEED, JOHNNY *see* CHAPMAN, JOHN (Johnny Appleseed)
APPLETON (Minnesota)
map (45° 12′N 96° 1′W) **13**:453
APPLETON (Wisconsin) 2:89
map (44° 16′N 88° 25′W) **20**:185
APPLETON, SIR EDWARD VICTOR 2:89 *bibliog.*
APPLETON, NATHAN 2:89 *bibliog.*

APPLETON CITY (Missouri)
  map (38° 11'N 94° 2'W) 13:476
APPLICATIONS TECHNOLOGY SATELLITE 2:89–90 *table*
APPLIED ARTS *see* DECORATIVE ARTS
APPLIED BEHAVIOR ANALYSIS *see* BEHAVIOR MODIFICATION
APPLIED LINGUISTICS 2:90–91 *bibliog.*
  See also PSYCHOLINGUISTICS; SOCIOLINGUISTICS
  dyslexia 6:320
  language disability 2:90–91
  lexicography 2:90
  linguistics applied to teaching 2:90
  structuralism 18:303
APPLIED PSYCHOLOGY 15:595
  industrial psychology 11:157
  Thorndike, Edward L. 19:179
APPLING (Georgia)
  map (33° 33'N 82° 19'W) 9:114
APPLING (county in Georgia)
  map (31° 45'N 82° 15'W) 9:114
APPLIQUÉ 2:91 *bibliog.*
APPOMATTOX (Virginia)
  map (37° 21'N 78° 50'W) 19:607
APPOMATTOX (county in Virginia)
  map (37° 20'N 78° 50'W) 19:607
APPOMATTOX COURT HOUSE 2:91 *bibliog.*
  Lee's surrender 5:30 *illus.*
APPOMATTOX RIVER
  map (37° 18'N 77° 18'W) 19:607
APPORTIONMENT 2:91
  See also PROPORTIONAL REPRESENTATION
  Baker v. *Carr* 3:28
  equal protection of the laws 7:224
  gerrymander 9:158
  representation 16:160–161
  Reynolds v. *Sims* 16:191
APPRAISAL 2:91
APPRENTICESHIP 2:91 *bibliog.*
  career education 4:146
  guilds 9:395
  vocational education 19:624
APPROUAGUE RIVER
  map (4° 38'N 51° 58'W) 8:311
APRAXIA 2:91 *bibliog.*
APRICOT 2:91–92 *illus.*
  laetrile 12:163
APRIL
  birthstones 3:296 *illus., table*
  calendar 4:28
APRIL THESES
  Lenin, Vladimir Ilich 12:283
APS *see* AMERICAN PHYSICAL SOCIETY
APSE 2:92
  cathedrals and churches 4:204
  Romanesque art and architecture 16:282
APSIDES *see* ORBITAL ELEMENTS
APTERYX *see* KIWI (bird)
APTITUDE TESTS *see* EDUCATIONAL MEASUREMENT
APULEIUS 2:92 *bibliog.*
  Golden Ass, The 9:231
APULIA (Italy) 2:92
  cities
    Bari 3:81
    Foggia 8:193
    Taranto 19:35
APURE RIVER
  map (7° 37'N 66° 25'W) 19:542
APURIMAC RIVER
  map (11° 48'S 74° 3'W) 15:193
AQABA, GULF OF 2:92
  map (29° 0'N 34° 40'E) 7:76
AQUA APPIA
  aqueduct 2:94
AQUA MARCIA
  aqueduct 2:94
AQUA REGIA
  gold 9:226
AQUA TEPULA
  aqueduct 2:94
AQUACULTURE *see* FISH FARMING
AQUALUNG
  Cousteau, Jacques-Yves 5:317
  skin diving 17:342 *illus.*
AQUAMARINE 3:296 *illus., table*; 9:74 *illus.*
  beryl 3:227
AQUAPLANE *see* WATERSKIING
AQUARIUM 2:92–93 *bibliog., illus.*
  brine shrimp 3:486
  duckweed 6:292
  eelgrass 7:71
  fish
    cichlid 4:429 *illus.*
    goldfish 9:234
    guppy 9:406
    gymnotid 9:414
    loach 12:384
    minnow 13:458
    tetra 19:127
    tropical fish 19:307
AQUARIUS (constellation) 2:93 *bibliog.*
AQUATINT 2:93 *bibliog.*
  engraving 7:205–206
  etching 7:248–249
AQUEDUCT 2:93–94 *bibliog., illus.*
  ancient systems 2:94
  Eupalinus 7:265
  Frontius, Sextus Julius 8:345
  pipe and pipeline 15:310
  Pont du Gard 8:266 *illus.*
  technology, history of 19:63 *illus.*
  water supply 20:56 *illus.*
AQUEOUS HUMOR
  eye 7:348 *illus.*
AQUIDABÁN RIVER
  map (23° 11'S 57° 32'W) 15:77
AQUIDAUANA (Brazil)
  map (20° 28'S 55° 48'W) 3:460
AQUIDNECK ISLAND *see* RHODE ISLAND
AQUIFER 2:94
  artesian well 2:214
  Darcy, Henry Philibert Gaspard 6:37
  hydrologic cycle 10:342
  spring (water) 18:199
  water well 20:60
AQUILA 2:94
AQUIN (Haiti)
  map (18° 17'N 73° 24'W) 10:15
AQUINAS, SAINT THOMAS 2:94–95 *bibliog., illus.*; 15:241 *illus.*
  Cajetan 4:19
  Gilson, Étienne 9:183
  law 12:242
  Mercier, Désiré Joseph 13:304–305
  natural law 14:48
  predestination 15:501
  scholasticism 17:131–132 *illus.*
  state (in political philosophy) 18:230
  Summa Theologiae 18:339
AQUINO, BENIGNO S. 2:95 *illlus.*
AQUINO, CORAZON C. 2:95 *illus.*
AQUINO, IVA IKUKI TOGURI D'
  Tokyo Rose 19:226
AQUITAINE (France) 2:95–96 *map*
  Bordeaux 3:396
  Edward, the Black Prince 7:67
  Eleanor of Aquitaine 7:103
  Louis VII, King of France 12:424
ARA PACIS (altar) 7:281 *illus.*; 16:276 *illus.*; 16:302 *illus.*; 17:161 *illus.*
ARAB (Alabama)
  map (34° 19'N 86° 29'W) 1:234
ARAB-AMERICAN OIL COMPANY
  Saudi Arabia 17:95 *illus.*
ARAB-ISRAELI WARS 2:96–98 *bibliog., maps*
  Arafat, Yasir 2:107
  Bunche, Ralph 3:562
  Dayan, Moshe 6:56
  Egypt 7:80–81
  First Palestine War (1948–49) 2:96 *map*
  Gaza Strip 9:64
  Golan Heights 11:303 *illus.*
  Hussein I, King of Jordan 10:320–321
  Israel 11:306
  Lebanon 12:267
  Middle East, history of the 13:408–409
  Nasser, Gamal Abdel 14:25
  October War (1973) 2:97–98 *map*
  Palestine 15:45–46 *maps*
  Sadat, Anwar al- 17:8
  Sharm al-Sheikh 17:244
  Sinai 17:318
  Six-Day War (1967) 2:97 *map*
    Elat (Israel) 7:102
    Jerusalem (Israel) 11:399
    Jordan 11:449–450
    Red Sea 16:113
  Suez Canal 18:324
  Suez-Sinai War (1956) 2:96–97 *map*
  Syria 18:414
  United Nations 19:413–414
  West Bank 20:108
ARAB LEAGUE 2:98; 2:105 *map*
  Arabs 2:102–103
  boycott 3:433
  member countries 13:409 *map*
ARAB REPUBLIC OF EGYPT *see* EGYPT
ARAB SOCIALIST UNION (political party)
  Egypt 7:79
ARABELO (Venezuela)
  map (4° 55'N 64° 13'W) 19:542
ARABESQUE (art) 2:98
  Islamic art and architecture 11:294
ARABI (Louisiana)
  map (29° 57'N 90° 2'W) 12:430
ARABIA 2:98 *bibliog.*
  exploration 7:338
  herbs and spices 10:137
  history
    Lawrence, T. E. 12:250–251
    Middle East, history of the 13:402–410
    Philby, H. St. John 15:231
    Sheba 17:247–248
    World War I 20:234 *illus.*; 20:239 *map*
  Islamic art and architecture 11:293–297
  literature *see* ARABIC LITERATURE
  plate tectonics
    Arabian plate 15:351 *map*
ARABIAN BASIN
  Indian Ocean bottom 11:105 *map*
ARABIAN DESERT 2:98–99 *bibliog.*
  Egypt 7:74
  map (28° 0'N 32° 0'E) 7:76
ARABIAN HORSE 2:99 *illus.*; 10:243 *illus.*
  horse racing 10:246–247
  saddle horse 17:9
ARABIAN MUSIC 2:99–100 *bibliog., illus.*
ARABIAN NIGHTS (book) 2:100 *bibliog.*
  Aladdin 1:239
  Ali Baba 1:292
  Harun al-Rashid 10:64
  Scheherazade 17:118
ARABIAN ORYX *see* ANTELOPE
ARABIAN PENINSULA *see* ARABIA
ARABIAN SEA 2:100
  Laccadive Islands 12:158
  map (15° 0'N 65° 0'E) 2:232
  monsoon 13:543
  seas, gulfs, and bays
    Oman, Gulf of 14:387
    Persian Gulf 15:187 *map*
ARABIC LANGUAGE 2:100–101 *bibliog.*
  Afroasiatic languages 1:179
  creole 5:338
  Islamic art and architecture 11:294
ARABIC LITERATURE 2:101 *bibliog.*
  Arabian Nights 2:100
  Arabic language 2:100
  authors
    Abu Madi, Iliya 1:66
    Abu Nuwas 1:66
    Gibran, Kahlil 9:175
    Hakim, Tawfiq al- 10:17
    Ibn al-Muqaffa 11:5
    Imru' al-Qais 11:69
    Jahiz, Abu Uthman Amr al- 11:349
    Mahfuz, Najib 13:64
    Mutanabbi, al- 13:686
    Tabari, al- 19:3
    Taha Husayn 19:10
  courtly love 5:317
  Egypt 7:77
  Koran 12:110
ARABIC NUMERAL
  numeral 14:294
ARABS 2:101–106 *bibliog., illus., map*
  See also ISLAMIC ART AND ARCHITECTURE
  alchemy 1:263
  Arab League 2:98; 2:105 *map*
    Algeria 1:286–290
    Bahrain 3:24–25
    Djibouti 6:207–208
    Egypt 7:79–81
    Iraq 11:254–256
    Jordan 11:447–450
    Kuwait 12:140–142
    Lebanon 12:264–267
    Libya 12:319–321
    Mauritania 13:235–237
    Morocco 13:583–587
    Oman 14:385–387
    Palestine Liberation Organization 15:46
    Qatar 16:3–4
    Saudi Arabia 17:95
    Somalia 18:59–61
    Sudan 18:321–322
    Syria 18:411–414
    Tunisia 19:337
    United Arab Emirates 19:400–401
    Yemen (Aden) 20:323–324
    Yemen (Sana) 20:324–326
  Arabic language 2:100
  Baath party 3:5
  costume 2:106
  decimal 6:73
  geography 9:101
  Idrisi, al- 11:32
  historians *see* HISTORY—Arab historians
  history 2:101–103
    See also MIDDLE EAST, HISTORY OF THE
    Africa, history of 1:151–152; 1:157 *map*
    Asia, history of 2:254
    Europe, history of 7:283
    India, history of 11:90
    Israel 11:306
    Jerusalem (Israel) 11:399–401
    Jews 11:414
    Kenya 12:56
    Masudi, al- 13:218
    Nasser, Gamal Abdel 14:25
    Palestine 15:44–46
    Sassanians 17:84
    Sinai 17:318
    Syria 18:414
    Umayyads 19:380
    United Arab Republic 19:401
    West Bank 20:108
  knife 18:399 *illus.*
  Middle Eastern universities 13:410–412
  people 2:103–106 *illus.*
    Bedouin 3:154
    Berbers 3:207 *illus.*
    Jordanian 2:242 *illus.*
    Kurds 12:139
    Moor 13:567
    Semites 17:197–198
  religion 2:103–104
    hajj 2:101 *illus.*; 2:106
    Islam 11:290 *illus.*
    mosque 13:601
  ship 17:266
  women 2:104–106 *illus.*
    harem 10:49
ARACAJU (Brazil)
  map (10° 55'S 37° 4'W) 3:460
ARACHNE 2:106
ARACHNID 2:106–107 *bibliog., illus.*
  See also names of specific animals, e.g., DADDY LONGLEGS; MITE; SCORPION; etc.
  spider 18:181–183
  venom 19:546
ARACHOSIA
  Persia, ancient 15:182 *map*
ARAD (Israel)
  map (31° 15'N 35° 13'E) 11:302
ARAD (Romania)
  map (46° 11'N 21° 20'E) 16:288
ARAFAT, YASIR 2:107 *bibliog., illus.*
  Palestine Liberation Organization 15:46
ARAFURA SEA
  map (9° 0'S 133° 0'E) 11:147
  Torres Strait 19:244
ARAGO (France)
  Homo erectus 10:215
ARAGO, CAPE
  map (43° 18'N 124° 25'W) 14:427
ARAGO, DOMINIQUE
  optical activity 14:408
ARAGO, FRANÇOIS 2:107
ARAGON (Georgia)
  map (34° 3'N 85° 3'W) 9:114
ARAGON (Spain) 2:107 *bibliog.*
  cities
    Saragossa 17:74
  history
    Alfonso V, King 1:279
    Ferdinand II, King of Aragon 8:52
    James I, King (James the Conqueror) 11:355
    James II, King 11:355
    Peter III, King (Peter the Great) 15:200
    Sancho III, King of Navarre (Sancho the Great) 17:58
    Spain, history of 18:145–146 *maps*
ARAGON, LOUIS 2:107 *bibliog.*
ARAGONITE 2:107–108
  calcium carbonate 4:22–23
  carbonate minerals 4:137
ARAGUAIA RIVER 2:108
  map (5° 21'S 48° 41'W) 3:460
ARAK (Iran)
  map (34° 5'N 49° 41'E) 11:250
ARAL SEA 2:108
  map (45° 0'N 60° 0'E) 19:388
ARALES 2:108 *bibliog., illus.*
ARAMAEANS 2:108–109 *bibliog.*
  Semites 17:197
ARAMAIC LANGUAGE
  Afroasiatic languages 1:179
  alphabet 20:294 *table*
  Middle East, history of the 13:401

ARAMBOURG, CAMILLE
  Ternifine man **19**:118
ARAMCO *see* ARAB-AMERICAN OIL COMPANY
ARAMID FIBERS
  synthetic fibers **18**:409
ARAN ISLANDS
  map (53° 7′N 9° 43′W) **11**:258
ARANDA **2**:109 *bibliog.*
  creation accounts **5**:334
ARANGO, DOROTEO *see* VILLA, PANCHO
ARANJUEZ (Spain)
  map (40° 2′N 3° 36′W) **18**:140
ARANSAS (county in Texas)
  map (28° 5′N 97° 0′W) **19**:129
ARANSAS PASS (Texas)
  map (27° 54′N 97° 9′W) **19**:129
ARANY, JÁNOS **2**:109
ARAPAHO (American Indians) **2**:109 *bibliog.*
  ghost dance **9**:169
  Gros Ventres **9**:370
  Sand Creek Massacre **17**:59
  Sun dance **18**:346
ARAPAHO (Oklahoma)
  map (35° 34′N 98° 57′W) **14**:368
ARAPAHOE (county in Colorado)
  map (39° 40′N 104° 20′W) **5**:116
ARAPAHOE (Nebraska)
  map (40° 18′N 99° 54′W) **14**:70
ARAPAIMA **2**:109
ARAPESH **2**:109 *bibliog.*
ARAPEY (Uruguay)
  map (30° 58′S 57° 32′W) **19**:488
ARARAQUARA (Brazil)
  map (21° 47′S 48° 10′W) **3**:460
ARARAT *see* URARTU
ARARAT, MOUNT **2**:109
  map (39° 42′N 44° 18′E) **19**:343
ARATA, ISOZAKI *see* ISOZAKI ARATA
ARAUCA (Colombia)
  map (7° 5′N 70° 45′W) **5**:107
ARAUCA RIVER
  map (7° 24′N 66° 35′W) **19**:542
ARAUCANIANS (American Indians) **2**:109–110 *bibliog.*; **11**:135 *illus.*
  Chile **4**:357
  Concepción (Chile) **5**:169
  Lautaro **12**:240
  Valdivia, Pedro de **19**:503
ARAVALLI RANGE
  map (25° 0′N 73° 30′E) **11**:80
ARAWAK (American Indians) **2**:110 *bibliog.*
  Carib **4**:147
  Latin America, history of **12**:218
  San Salvador Island **17**:58
  tobacco **19**:218
ARBENZ GUZMÁN, JACOBO
  Guatemala **9**:388–389
ARBER, WERNER **2**:110
  Nathans, Daniel **14**:27
  Smith, Hamilton **17**:368
ARBITRAGE **2**:110 *bibliog.*
ARBITRATION (international law) **2**:110 *bibliog.*
  mediation **13**:264
  Root, Elihu **16**:311
ARBITRATION (labor-management and commercial) **2**:110 *bibliog.*
  grievance procedure **9**:362
  industrial relations **11**:158
  Kerr, Clark **12**:59–60
  mediation **13**:264
  National Mediation Board **14**:35
  Roosevelt, Theodore **16**:310
ARBON (Switzerland)
  map (47° 31′N 9° 26′E) **18**:394
ARBORETUM *see* BOTANICAL GARDEN
ARBORICULTURE **2**:110–111
ARBORVITAE **2**:111 *illus.*
ARBUCKLE (California)
  map (39° 1′N 122° 3′W) **4**:31
ARBUCKLE, FATTY **2**:111 *bibliog.*
ARBUCKLES, LAKE OF THE
  map (34° 25′N 97° 0′W) **14**:368
ARBUS, DIANE **2**:111 *bibliog.*, *illus.*
ARBUTUS **2**:111–112 *bibliog.*, *illus.*
ARC (geometry) **2**:112
ARC, ELECTRIC **2**:112 *bibliog.*
  Ayrton, Hertha and William Edward **2**:379
  discharge, electrical **6**:188
  electric furnace **7**:106
  lighthouse **12**:337
  lighting devices **12**:338
  new ceramics applications **4**:259
ARC DE TRIOMPHE DE L'ÉTOILE **2**:112
  Chalgrin, Jean François Thérèse **4**:271
  Rude, François **16**:338
  World War II **20**:254 *illus.*
ARC DE TRIOMPHE DU CARROUSEL
  Fontaine, Pierre François Léonard **8**:205
  Percier, Charles **15**:162
ARCACHON (France)
  map (44° 37′N 1° 12′W) **8**:260
ARCADE **2**:112
  Gothic art and architecture **9**:255
  Romanesque art and architecture **16**:282
ARCADE (New York)
  map (42° 32′N 78° 25′W) **14**:149
ARCADELT, JACOB
  madrigal **13**:45
  music, history of Western **13**:665
  Renaissance music **16**:156
ARCADIA (California)
  map (34° 8′N 118° 1′W) **4**:31
ARCADIA (Florida)
  map (27° 14′N 81° 52′W) **8**:172
ARCADIA (Greece) **2**:112
  Megalopolis **13**:280
  Messene **13**:322
  Tegea **19**:72
ARCADIA (Kansas)
  map (37° 38′N 94° 37′W) **12**:18
ARCADIA (Louisiana)
  map (32° 33′N 92° 55′W) **12**:430
ARCADIA (Michigan)
  map (44° 30′N 86° 14′W) **13**:377
ARCADIA (Nebraska)
  map (41° 25′N 99° 7′W) **14**:70
ARCADIA (Pennsylvania)
  map (40° 47′N 78° 51′W) **15**:147
ARCADIA (South Carolina)
  map (34° 57′N 82° 0′W) **18**:98
ARCADIA (Wisconsin)
  map (44° 15′N 91° 30′W) **20**:185
ARCADIA CONFERENCE
  World War II **20**:257–258
ARCADIUS, ROMAN EMPEROR IN THE EAST **2**:112
ARCANUM (Ohio)
  map (39° 59′N 84° 33′W) **14**:357
ARCARO, EDDIE **2**:112–113 *illus.*
ARCATA (California)
  map (40° 52′N 124° 5′W) **4**:31
ARCATAO (El Salvador)
  map (14° 5′N 88° 45′W) **7**:100
ARCE, MANUEL JOSÉ
  Morazán, Francisco **13**:575
ARCELLA **2**:113
  Rhizopoda **16**:197
ARCH AND VAULT **2**:113–114 *bibliog.*, *illus.*
  bridge (engineering) **3**:480 *illus.*; **3**:482
  buttress **3**:600–601
  Candela, Félix **4**:106
  dome **6**:229–230
  Gothic art and architecture **9**:255–262
  Italian art and architecture **11**:308–310
  Norman architecture **14**:220
  Persian art and architecture **15**:185
  Roman art and architecture **16**:273–274
  Romanesque art and architecture **16**:282–286
  squinch **18**:204
  technology, history of **19**:62–64 *illus.*
  triumphal arch **19**:304
ARCHAEMINIDS
  Susa **18**:370
ARCHAEOASTRONOMY **2**:114–115 *bibliog.*, *illus.*
  astronomy, history of **2**:277
  medicine wheel **2**:115 *illus.*
  megalith **13**:279
  Nazca earth drawings **14**:67 *illus.*
  stone alignments **18**:281–282 *illus.*
  Stonehenge **18**:283
ARCHAEOCYATHID **2**:115 *bibliog.*
  Cambrian Period **4**:52
ARCHAEOLOGICAL AND HISTORIC PRESERVATION ACT (1974)
  salvage archaeology **17**:40
ARCHAEOLOGY **2**:116–126 *bibliog.*, *illus.*
  See also names of ancient cultures and regions, e.g., MAYA; MESOPOTAMIA; etc.; names of specific monuments and sites, e.g., ROSETTA STONE; TROY (archaeological site); etc.; the subheading archaeology under modern names of countries and regions, e. g., FRANCE; IRAQ; etc.
  Abbevillian **1**:52
  Acheulean **1**:81
  Aegean civilization **1**:114–118
  aerial photography **2**:118 *illus.*
  African prehistory **1**:171–175
  animal domestication **2**:23 *illus.*
  archaeoastronomy **2**:114–115
  archaeologists
    Adams, Robert McCormick **1**:97
    Andersson, Johan Gunnar **1**:403
    Belzóni, Giovanni Battista **3**:194
    Binford, Lewis R. **3**:258
    Bordes, François **3**:398
    Botta, Paul Émile **3**:417
    Braidwood, Robert **3**:442
    Breasted, James Henry **3**:469–470
    Breuil, Henri **3**:475–476
    Carnarvon, George Edward, 5th Earl of **4**:154
    Carter, Howard **4**:171
    Caso, Alfonso **4**:182
    Catherwood, Frederick **4**:210
    Caton-Thompson, Gertrude **4**:213
    Champollion, Jean François **4**:278
    Childe, V. Gordon **4**:351
    Cunningham, Sir Alexander **5**:389
    Dörpfeld, Wilhelm **6**:243
    Douglass, Andrew Ellicott **6**:248
    Evans, Sir Arthur **7**:312
    Evans, Sir John **7**:312–313
    Foote, Robert Bruce **8**:219
    Garstang, John **9**:52
    Giddings, J. Louis **9**:176
    Grotefend, Georg Friedrich **9**:372
    Humboldt, Alexander von **10**:301
    Kidder, Alfred Vincent **12**:70–71
    Layard, Sir Austen **12**:252
    Leakey (family) **12**:258–259
    Lubbock, John, 1st Baron Avebury **12**:446
    Mallowan, Sir Max **13**:92–93
    Mariette, Auguste **13**:152
    Marshall, Sir John Hubert **13**:172–173
    Maspero, Sir Gaston **13**:199
    Petrie, Sir Flinders **15**:204
    Pitt-Rivers, Augustus Henry Lane-Fox **15**:321
    Rawlinson, Sir Henry Creswicke **16**:95–96
    Schliemann, Heinrich **17**:126–127
    Smith, George **17**:368
    Stein, Sir Aurel **18**:246
    Stephens, John Lloyd **18**:255
    Stukeley, William **18**:308
    Talbot, William Henry **19**:15
    Thompson, Edward Herbert **19**:175
    Thomsen, Christian Jürgensen **19**:175
    Uhle, Max **19**:374
    Valle, Pietro della **19**:507
    Wheeler, Sir Mortimer **20**:129
    Winckelmann, Johann **20**:168
    Winckler, Hugo **20**:168
    Woolley, Sir Leonard **20**:215
    Worsaae, Jens Jacob Asmussen **20**:284
  art conservation and restoration **2**:204–206 *illus.*
  Aurignacian **2**:324
  Azilian **2**:381
  barrow **3**:95
  biblical archaeology **3**:241–242
  Bronze Age **3**:505–506
  burial **3**:571
  cairn **4**:17
  Capsian **4**:128–129
  carbon-14 radiodating **10**:20
  cave dwellers **4**:224–225
  Chalcolithic Period **4**:270
  Châtelperronian **4**:303
  Chellean **4**:311
  chert and flint **4**:332–333
  Chinese archaeology **4**:377–379
  civilization **5**:34
  Clactonian **5**:35
  cliff dwellers **5**:54–55
  Creswellian **5**:339
  Cro-Magnon man **5**:353–354
  dating **2**:120–121 *illus.*
  dendrochronology **2**:120 *illus.*; **6**:106–107
  earthworks **7**:28
  Egyptology **7**:90
  European prehistory **7**:301–306
  excavation methods **2**:117–119 *illus.*; **2**:124 *illus.*
  Folsom culture **8**:204
  geologic time **9**:103–105 *table*
  Gravettian **9**:303
  Hamburgian **10**:27
  history of **2**:121–126
  Indus civilization **11**:153–154
  industrial archaeology **11**:154
  inscription **11**:185–186
  Iron Age **11**:271–272
  lake dwelling **12**:171
  Levalloisian **12**:301–302
  Magdalenian **13**:46
  magnetometer **2**:119
  megalith **13**:278–279
  Mesolithic Period **13**:314–315
  midden **13**:390
  Mound Builders **13**:617–618
  Mousterian **13**:626
  Neanderthalers **14**:68–69
  Neolithic Period **14**:83–84
  North American archaeology **14**:236–240
  Oldowan **14**:376
  Paleolithic Period **15**:38–41
  Perigordian **15**:166
  prehistoric art **15**:506–511
  prehistoric humans **15**:511–517
  prehistory **15**:517
  salvage archaeology **17**:40
  Solutrean **18**:58
  stone alignments **2**:118–119
  stratigraphy **2**:118 *illus.*; **2**:124 *illus.*
  tell **19**:90
  underwater archaeology **2**:119 *illus.*
ARCHAEOPTERYX **2**:127 *bibliog.*, *illus.*; **3**:278–279 *illus.*; **11**:476 *illus.*
  De Beer, Sir Gavin **6**:58
  Jurassic Period **11**:476
  Mesozoic Era **13**:322
ARCHANGEL
  angel **1**:412
ARCHANGEL (USSR) *see* ARKHANGELSK (USSR)
ARCHANGEL BLUE (cat) *see* RUSSIAN BLUE (cat)
ARCHBOLD (Ohio)
  map (41° 31′N 84° 18′W) **14**:357
ARCHDALE (North Carolina)
  map (35° 56′N 79° 57′W) **14**:242
ARCHEAN ERA
  paleobotany **15**:30–31
  Precambrian time **15**:491
ARCHELAUS, KING OF MACEDONIA
  Macedonia, Kingdom of **13**:15
  Pella **15**:138
ARCHEOZOIC ERA *see* ARCHEAN ERA
ARCHER (Florida)
  map (29° 32′N 82° 31′W) **8**:172
ARCHER (county in Texas)
  map (33° 38′N 98° 45′W) **19**:129
ARCHER, FREDERICK SCOTT **2**:127
  ambrotype **1**:325
ARCHER, THOMAS **2**:127 *bibliog.*
ARCHER CITY (Texas)
  map (33° 36′N 98° 38′W) **19**:129
ARCHERFISH **2**:127 *illus.*
ARCHERY **2**:127–128 *bibliog.*, *illus.*
  Ascham, Roger **2**:228
  bow and arrow **3**:426–427
ARCHES NATIONAL MONUMENT (Utah) **20**:82 *illus.*
ARCHETYPE
  narrative and dramatic devices **14**:22
ARCHIBALD THE GRIM
  Douglas (family) **6**:246–247
ARCHIBALD RUSSEL (sailing ship)
  ship **17**:271 *illus.*
ARCHIGRAM (architectural group)
  postmodern architecture **15**:464
ARCHILOCHUS **2**:128 *bibliog.*
  satire **17**:88
ARCHIMEDES **2**:128 *bibliog.*
  Diophantine equations **6**:185
  mathematics, history of **13**:223
  Pharos of Alexandria **17**:218
ARCHIMEDES' PRINCIPLE **2**:128 *bibliog.*
  buoyancy **2**:128
ARCHIMEDES' SCREW **2**:128–129 *illus.*
ARCHIPENKO, ALEKSANDR **2**:129 *bibliog.*
ARCHIPIÉLAGO DE COLÓN *see* GALÁPAGOS ISLANDS
ARCHITECTURE **2**:129–137 *bibliog.*, *illus.*
  See also MODERN ARCHITECTURE; POSTMODERN ARCHITECTURE; VISIONARY ARCHITECTURE
  Africa
    Nalatale **14**:9
    Zimbabwe Ruins **20**:366–367
  American architecture *see* ARCHITECTURE—United States
  apse **2**:92
  arcade **2**:112
  arch and vault **2**:113–114
  architrave **2**:137

ARCHITECTURE (cont.)
Argentina
Camanito Street (Buenos Aires) **18**:93 *illus.*
Art Deco **2**:207–208
Arts and Crafts movement **2**:225
attic **2**:314
Austria
Austrian art and architecture **2**:352–354
Fischer von Erlach, Johann Bernhard **8**:111
Hildebrandt, Johann Lucas von **10**:163
Hoffmann, Josef **10**:195
Hollein, Hans **10**:204
Kiesler, Frederick John **12**:75
Loos, Adolf **12**:411
Olbrich, Joseph Maria **14**:373
Pöppelmann, Matthäus Daniel **15**:432
Prandtauer, Jakob **15**:489
Schönbrunn Palace **17**:133
Thumb (family) **19**:184
Urban, Joseph **19**:480
Wagner, Otto **20**:4
baroque art and architecture **3**:88–91
Belgium
Flemish art and architecture **8**:162
Horta, Victor **10**:254
Van de Velde, Henry **19**:512
belvedere **3**:193
Brazil
Aleijadinho **1**:271
Costa, Lúcio **5**:290
Neimeyer, Oscar **14**:185
building construction **3**:548–552
buttress **3**:600–601
Byzantine
Anthemius of Tralles **2**:49
Byzantine art and architecture **3**:604–606
Hagia Sophia **10**:10
Isidorus of Miletus **11**:288
Canada
Canadian art and architecture **4**:91
cantilever **4**:117
caryatid **4**:179
cast-iron architecture **4**:185–186
castle **4**:189–191
cathedrals and churches **4**:204–208
cella **4**:236
China
Chinese art and architecture **4**:386–388
Great Wall of China **9**:323
pagoda **15**:14
civil engineering **5**:10–11
colonial styles in North America **5**:109–111
colonnade **5**:112
column **5**:129
Coptic art and architecture **5**:255
cornice **5**:269
Czechoslovakia
Dientzenhofer (family) **6**:162
Denmark
Bindesbøll, Michael Gottlieb Birkner **3**:257
Danish art and architecture **17**:111–114
Jacobsen, Arne **11**:346
dome **6**:229–230
Dutch architecture *see* ARCHITECTURE—Netherlands
Early Christian art and architecture **7**:9–10
Ecuador
San Guillermo (Quito, Ecuador) **12**:223 *illus.*
education **2**:129–130
Bauhaus **3**:129–130
École des Beaux-Arts **7**:42
Egypt
Egyptian art and architecture **7**:85–86
Imhotep **11**:54
obelisk **14**:314–315
pyramids **15**:634–636
Senmut **17**:203
sphinx **18**:180
entablature **7**:208
Ethiopia
Lalibela **12**:171
facade **8**:5
Finland
Aalto, Alvar **1**:49–50
Saarinen, Eliel **17**:4
Scandinavian art and architecture **17**:111–114
France
Amiens Cathedral **1**:370
Arc de Triomphe de l'Étoile **2**:112
Beaubourg **3**:145
Bélanger, François Joseph **3**:173
Blois, Château de **3**:335
Boullée, Étienne Louis **3**:422
Brosse, Salomon de **3**:512
Carolingian art and architecture **4**:160
Chalgrin, Jean François Thérèse **4**:271
Chartres Cathedral **4**:300–301
Chenonceaux, Château de **4**:330–331
Clérisseau, Charles Louis **5**:51
Cotte, Robert de **5**:304
Delorme, Philibert **6**:94
Eiffel Tower **7**:91
Flamboyant Gothic style **8**:150
Fontaine, Pierre François Léonard **8**:205
Fontainebleau, Château de **8**:205
French art and architecture **8**:303–308
Gabriel (family) **9**:6
Garnier, Jean Louis Charles **9**:49
Guimard, Hector **9**:396–397
Labrouste, Henri **12**:157
Le Corbusier **12**:253–254
Le Vau, Louis **12**:255
Ledoux, Claude Nicolas **12**:268
Lemercier, Jacques **12**:280
Lescot, Pierre **12**:296
Louis, Victor **12**:422
Luxembourg Palace **12**:472
Mansart, François **13**:127
Marot (family) **13**:162
Merovingian art and architecture **13**:311
Mont-Saint-Michel **13**:544
Norman architecture **14**:219–220
Notre Dame de Paris **14**:267
Perrault, Claude **15**:178
Perret, Auguste **15**:178
Petit Trianon **15**:203
Rayonnant style **16**:98
Reims Cathedral **16**:131
Robert, Hubert **16**:241
rose window **16**:314
Sacré-Coeur **17**:8
Saint-Denis (church) **17**:17
Sainte-Chapelle **17**:28
Soufflot, Jacques Germain **18**:70
Strasbourg Cathedral **18**:289
Versailles, Palace of **19**:561
Villard de Honnecourt **19**:598
visionary architecture **19**:617
frieze **8**:333
Germany
Amalienburg Pavilion **1**:321
Asam brothers **2**:226
Bauhaus **3**:129–130
Behrens, Peter **3**:171
Böhm, Gottfried **3**:361
Brandenburg Gate **3**:453
Cuvilliés, François **5**:399
Eiermann, Egon **7**:91
Fischer, Johann Michael **8**:110–111
Gärtner, Friedrich von **9**:52
German art and architecture **9**:123–128
Glyptothek **9**:212–213
Gropius, Walter **9**:369
International Style **11**:222–223
Klenze, Leo von **12**:97
Langhans, Carl Gotthard **12**:195
Louis II's Bavarian palaces **12**:423
Mendelsohn, Eric **13**:295
Mies van der Rohe, Ludwig **13**:415
Moholy-Nagy, László **13**:503
Neumann, Johann Balthasar **14**:104
Nymphenburg Palace **14**:309
Ottonian art and architecture **14**:467
Rayonnant style **16**:98
Sans Souci **17**:65
Scharoun, Hans **17**:117
Schinkel, Karl Friedrich **17**:121
Schlüter, Andreas **17**:127
Semper, Gottfried **17**:198
Zimmermann, Dominikus **20**:367
golden section **9**:232
Gothic art and architecture **9**:255–262
Gothic Revival **9**:262–263
Great Britain
Adam, Robert **1**:92
Archer, Thomas **2**:127
Barry, Sir Charles **3**:95
Blenheim Palace **3**:330
Buckingham Palace **3**:536
Burlington, Richard Boyle, 3d Earl of **3**:572
Butterfield, William **3**:593
Campbell, Colen **4**:65
Canterbury Cathedral **4**:116
cast-iron architecture **4**:185–186
Chambers, Sir William **4**:274–275
Cockerell, Charles Robert **5**:87
Coventry Cathedral **5**:319
Crystal Palace **5**:376
Dance, George **6**:28
Durham Cathedral **6**:306
Elizabethan style **7**:146
English art and architecture **7**:181–188
Fry, Edwin Maxwell **8**:350
Georgian style **9**:119
Gibbs, James **9**:174
Hampton Court **10**:33
Hawksmoor, Nicholas **10**:78
Holland, Henry **10**:203
Jacobean style **11**:345
Jones, Inigo **11**:442–443
Kent, William **12**:45
Lutyens, Sir Edwin Landseer **12**:471
Mackintosh, Charles Rennie **13**:31
Nash, John **14**:23–24
Perpendicular Gothic style **15**:177
Pugin, Augustus **15**:617
Queen Anne style **16**:21
Royal Pavilion at Brighton **16**:330–331
St. James's Palace **17**:19
Saint Paul's Cathedral **17**:25
Salisbury Cathedral **17**:34
Scott, Sir George Gilbert **17**:153
Shaw, Richard Norman **17**:246
Smirke, Sir Robert **17**:366
Smithson, Alison and Peter **17**:372
Soane, Sir John **18**:6
Spence, Sir Basil **18**:177
Stirling, James Frazer **18**:272
Tower of London **19**:254
Tudor style **19**:329
Vanbrugh, Sir John **19**:516–517
Victorian style **19**:575–576
Voysey, Charles Francis Annesley **19**:638
Westminster Abbey **20**:117–118
Westminster Palace **20**:118
Whitehall Palace **20**:139
Windsor Castle **20**:174
Wood (family) **20**:205
Wren, Sir Christopher **20**:286
Wyatt, James **20**:297
Greece *see* GREEK ARCHITECTURE
Greek Revival **9**:345–346
Guatemala
San Carlos University (Guatemala) **12**:225 *illus.*
handicapped persons, architectural barriers to **10**:36
historic preservation **10**:181–182
Hittite art and architecture **10**:188–189
Honduras
Copán **5**:248
house (in Western architecture) **10**:264–272
illusions **11**:48–49
India
Indian art and architecture **11**:96
Mogul art and architecture **13**:500–502
Qutb Minar **16**:28
stupa **18**:308
Taj Mahal **19**:14–15
Indians of North America
Chaco Canyon **4**:264–265
Pueblo cliff dwellers **5**:55
Indonesia
Borobudur **3**:402 *illus.*
interior design **11**:210–214
Iran *see* ARCHITECTURE—Persian architecture; ARCHITECTURE—Islamic architecture
Islamic architecture **11**:294
minaret **13**:437
Israel
Safdie, Moshe **17**:10
Italy
See also ARCHITECTURE—Rome, ancient
Alberti, Leon Battista **1**:259
Alessi, Galeazzo **1**:272
Ammanati, Bartolommeo **1**:372
Apollodorus of Damascus **2**:84
Arnolpho di Cambio **2**:186
Bernini, Giovanni Lorenzo **3**:222–223
Borromini, Francesco **3**:404–405
Bramante, Donato **3**:451–452
Briosco, Andrea **3**:487
Brunelleschi, Filippo **3**:524–525
campanile **4**:64–65
Castel Sant'Angelo **4**:187
Certosa di Pavia **4**:261
Codussi, Mauro **5**:90
Cortona, Pietro da **5**:279
Doge's Palace **6**:222
Farnese Palace **8**:28
Fontana, Carlo **8**:206
Fontana, Domenico **8**:206
Galli da Bibiena (family) **9**:18–19
Giulio Romano **9**:191–192
Guarini, Guarino **9**:387
Italian art and architecture **11**:308–310
Juvarra, Filippo **11**:479–480
Lombardo (family) **12**:399
Maderno, Carlo **13**:40
Maiano (family) **13**:66
Mannerism **13**:125
Michelangelo **13**:372–375
Michelozzo **13**:375
Mysteries, Villa of the **13**:692
Nervi, Pier Luigi **14**:91
Palladio, Andrea **15**:48
Peruzzi, Baldassare **15**:196
Piranesi, Giovanni Battista **15**:314–315
Pitti Palace **15**:321
Ponti, Gio **15**:427
Porta, Giacomo della **15**:443
Raphael **16**:89
Rossellino (family) **16**:319
Saint Mark's Basilica **17**:23–24
Saint Peter's Basilica **17**:25–26
San Carlo alle Quattro Fontane **17**:51
San Carlo Alle Quattro Fonte **11**:310 *illus.*
San Vitale **17**:58
Sangallo (family) **17**:64
Sanmicheli, Michele **17**:65
Sansovino, Jacopo **17**:66
Santa Costanza **17**:67
Sant'Ambrogio **17**:69
Sant'Elia, Antonio **17**:69
Scamozzi, Vincenzo **17**:107
Serlio, Sebastiano **17**:209
Tempietto **19**:93
Trevi Fountain **19**:291
Vanvitelli, Luigi **19**:521
Vasari, Giorgio **19**:525
Vignola, Giacomo Barozzida **19**:592
Zucalli, Enrico **20**:380
Japan
Isozaki, Arata **11**:301
Japanese art and architecture **11**:372–379
pagoda **15**:14
Tange, Kenzo **19**:22
Korea
Korean art **12**:117–118
labyrinth and maze **12**:157–158
Lamaist art and architecture **12**:172
landscape architecture **12**:185–188
Latin American art and architecture **12**:222–228
See also national subheadings under ARCHITECTURE
Mannerism **13**:125
mastaba **13**:214
Mesopotamian art and architecture **13**:318–322
Mexico
Barragán, Luis **3**:92
Candela, Félix **4**:106
Latin American art and architecture **12**:222–228
O'Gorman, Juan **14**:355
pyramids **15**:636
San Cayetano (Guanajuato, Mexico) **12**:225 *illus.*
minaret **13**:437
Mogul art and architecture **13**:500–501
monastic art and architecture **13**:517–521
Moorish art and architecture **13**:570–571
mosque **13**:601–602
music and concert halls **13**:669–670
neoclassicism (art) **14**:81–82
Netherlands
Berlage, Hendrik Petrus **3**:214
Campen, Jacob van **4**:66
Cuypers, Petrus **5**:399
de Stijl **6**:63–64
Dutch architecture **6**:311–313
Keyser, Hendrik de **12**:64
Oud, Jacobus Johannes Pieter **14**:467

ARCHITECTURE (cont.)
Rietveld, Gerrit Thomas **16**:219
new towns **14**:143
Norman architecture **14**:219–220
Norway
Scandinavian art and architecture **17**:111–114
opera houses **14**:401–402
Persian architecture **15**:183–187
Masjid-i-shah **15**:185 *illus.*
Portugal
Arruda (family) **2**:189
Ludovice, João Pedro Frederico **12**:452
Portuguese art and architecture **15**:455–456
post and lintel **15**:459
pre-Columbian art and architecture **15**:495–501
Pritzker Architecture Prize **15**:556
professional and educational organizations
American Institute of Architects **1**:341
pyramids **15**:634–636
Regency style **16**:126
Renaissance art and architecture **16**:149–155
rococo style **16**:263–265
Romanesque art and architecture **16**:282–286
romanticism **16**:291–292
Rome, ancient
aqueduct **2**:93–94
atrium **2**:312–313
bridge (engineering) **3**:480 *illus.*
Caracalla, Baths of **4**:129–130
Colosseum **5**:122
Column of Trajan **5**:129
Diocletian, Baths of **6**:182
Diocletian's Palace **6**:183
Hadrian's Villa **10**:8
Pantheon (Rome) **15**:62
Roman art and architecture **16**:273–275
triumphal arch **19**:304
Vitruvius **19**:621
rose window **16**:314
Russia
Cameron, Charles **4**:59
constructivism **5**:224
Kremlin **12**:128–129
Quarenghi, Giacomo **16**:12
Rastrelli, Bartolommeo Francesco **16**:91
Russian art and architecture **16**:361–364
Winter Palace **20**:181
Zakharov, Adrian **20**:352
Scandinavian art and architecture **17**:111–114
skyscraper **17**:348–350
solar energy **18**:42 *illus.*
Southeast Asian art and architecture **18**:107–110
Spain
Alhambra **1**:291–292 *illus.*
Buen Retiro Palace **3**:544
Churriguera (family) **4**:427
Egas, Enrique **7**:71
Escorial **7**:238
Figueroa (family) **8**:75
Gaudi, Antonio **9**:59
Giralda (tower) **9**:188
Herrera, Juan de **10**:146
Machuca, Pedro **13**:26
Sert, José Luis **17**:210
Siloe, Diego de **17**:310
Spanish art and architecture **18**:152–156
Villanueva, Juan de **19**:598
squinch **18**:204
stained glass **18**:211–213
Sweden
Asplund, Erik Gunnar **2**:263
Erskine, Ralph **7**:235
Markelius, Sven Gottfrid **13**:159
Scandinavian art and architecture **17**:111–114
Tessin (family) **19**:126
technology, history of **19**:62–64
temple **19**:94–99
terra-cotta **19**:120
theater architecture and staging **19**:151–153
transept **19**:269
triforium **19**:297
truss **19**:320
Turkey
See also ARCHITECTURE—Byzantine
Saint Savior in the Chora **17**:26
Sinan **17**:318
tympanum **19**:362
United States
Adler, Dankmar **1**:104
American art and architecture **1**:327–330
Barnes, Edward Larrabee **3**:86
Bel Geddes, Norman **3**:173
Belluschi, Pietro **3**:192
Benjamin, Asher **3**:201
Blake, Peter (architect) **3**:325
Bogardus, James **3**:359
Breuer, Marcel **3**:475
Bulfinch, Charles **3**:553
Bunshaft, Gordon **3**:564
Burnham, Daniel Hudson **3**:577
Capitol of the United States **4**:126
Carrère and Hastings **4**:168
Chicago school of architecture **4**:342–343
Cram, Ralph Adams **5**:328
Cranbrook Foundation **5**:329
Davis, Alexander Jackson **6**:50
Eisenman, Peter **7**:96
Ellwood, Craig **7**:149
Empire State Building **7**:158
Esherick, Joseph **7**:238
federal style **8**:42
Flagg, Ernest **8**:149
Flatiron Building **8**:156
Fuller, R. Buckminster **8**:357–358
Furness, Frank **8**:372–373
Geddes, Robert L. **9**:67
Gilbert, Cass **9**:178
Gill, Irving **9**:181–182
Giurgola, Romaldo **9**:192
Goff, Bruce Alonzo **9**:224
Goldberg, Bertrand **9**:231
Goldsmith, Myron **9**:236
Goodhue, Bertram Grosvenor **9**:246
Grand Central Terminal **9**:285
Graves, Michael **9**:302
Greene and Greene **9**:351
Griffin, Marion Mahony **9**:362
Griffin, Walter Burley **9**:362–363
Gruen, Victor **9**:382
Guggenheim Museum **9**:393
Gwathmey, Charles **9**:411
Harrison, Peter **10**:60
Harrison, Wallace K. **10**:60
Hejduk, John **10**:110
Hitchcock, Henry-Russell **10**:186
Hoban, James **10**:191
Holabird, William **10**:200
Hood, Raymond **10**:225
Hunt, Richard Morris **10**:312
Independence Hall **11**:78
Jefferson, Thomas **11**:391–393
Jenney, William LeBaron **11**:396
Johnson, Philip **11**:435
Kahn, Albert **12**:6
Kahn, Louis **12**:6
Latrobe, Benjamin Henry **12**:235
L'Enfant, Pierre Charles **12**:281–282
Lincoln Center for the Performing Arts **12**:350
McKim, Mead, and White **13**:29
Maybeck, Bernard **13**:246
Meier, Richard **13**:281
Mills, Robert **13**:430–431
Moholy-Nagy, László **13**:503
Monticello **13**:557
Moore, Charles Willard **13**:567
Mount Vernon (Washington's home) **13**:618
Neutra, Richard **14**:108
Nowicki, Matthew **14**:277
Pei, I. M. **15**:133–134
Pelli, Cesar Antonio **15**:138
Pope, John Russell **15**:430–431
Post, George Browne **15**:458–459
prairie school **15**:489
Renwick, James **16**:159
Richardson, Henry Hobson **16**:212
Robie House **16**:243
Roche, Kevin **16**:246–247
Root, John Wellborn **16**:311
Rudolph, Paul **16**:338–339
Saarinen, Eero **17**:4
Saint John the Divine, Cathedral of **17**:19
Saint Patrick's Cathedral **17**:24
Schindler, Rudolf M. **17**:121
Seagram Building **17**:173
Sears Tower **17**:175
Skidmore, Owings, and Merrill **17**:337
Soleri, Paolo **18**:53
Stern, Robert A. M. **18**:260
Stone, Edward Durell **18**:280
Strickland, William **18**:298
Stubbins, Hugh **18**:306
Sullivan, Louis **18**:337
Taliesin West **19**:16
Town, Ithiel **19**:254
Turnbull, William, Jr. **19**:349
Upjohn, Richard **19**:471
Vaux, Calvert **19**:529
Venturi, Robert **19**:546
Walter, Thomas U. **20**:19
Watts Towers **20**:69–70
White, Stanford **20**:136
White House **20**:137–138
Woolworth Building **20**:216
World Trade Center **20**:219
World's Columbian Exposition of 1893 **20**:281–282
Wright, Frank Lloyd **20**:288–289
Yamasaki, Minoru **20**:316
urban planning **19**:481–485
Venezuela
Latin American art and architecture **12**:222–228
Villanueva, Carlos Raúl **19**:597
window **20**:173
Yugoslavia
Diocletian's Palace **6**:183
ziggurat **20**:363
ARCHITECTURE PARLANTE *see* VISIONARY ARCHITECTURE
ARCHITRAVE **2**:131 *illus.*; **2**:137
ARCHIVES OF AMERICAN ART
National Collection of Fine Arts **14**:30
ARCHONS **2**:137 *bibliog.*
ARCHOSAUR
crocodile **5**:356
ARCHULETA (county in Colorado)
map (37° 15′N 107° 0′W) **5**:116
ARCHY AND MEHITABEL (book)
Marquis, Don **13**:163
ARCIMBOLDO, GIUSEPPE **2**:137 *illus.*
Summer **2**:137 *illus.*
ARCINIEGA, CLAUDIO DE
Latin American art and architecture **12**:223
ARCO (Idaho)
map (43° 38′N 113° 18′W) **11**:26
ARCOLA (Illinois)
map (39° 41′N 88° 19′W) **11**:42
ARCOLA (Mississippi)
map (33° 16′N 90° 53′W) **13**:469
ARCOSANTI *see* SOLERI, PAOLO
ARCTIC **2**:138–144 *bibliog.*, *illus.*, *map*
animals **2**:140–142 *illus.*
Bering Land Bridge **3**:212
climate **2**:139
mountain climates **13**:620–621
polar climate **15**:392
taiga climate **19**:11
dogsled **6**:223
exploration *see* EXPLORATION—Arctic
ice cover **2**:142 *map*
iceberg **11**:15
islands and island groups **2**:138–139 *map*
Baffin Island **3**:21
Fletcher's Ice Island **8**:163
Greenland **9**:352–353 *illus.*, *map*
Novaya Zemlya **14**:272
Svalbard (Norway) **18**:374
Wrangel Island (USSR) **20**:285
Lapland **12**:205
mineral resources **2**:139
Northwest Territories (Canada) **14**:257–259
pack ice **15**:10–11 *map*
people **2**:142–143
Eskimo **2**:138 *illus.*; **2**:143; **7**:238–242
Indians, American **11**:126
permafrost **15**:173–174 *map*
plants **2**:141
topography **2**:138–139 *map*
patterned ground **15**:115
tundra **19**:332
ARCTIC BAY (Northwest Territories)
climate **14**:228 *table*
map (73° 2′N 85° 11′W) **14**:258
ARCTIC FOX **2**:141 *illus.*
ARCTIC HARE **13**:104 *illus.*
ARCTIC OCEAN **2**:144 *bibliog.*
Nansen, Fridtjof **14**:13
ocean bottom
Lomonosov Ridge **12**:400
Mid-Arctic Ridge **15**:351 *map*
mid-oceanic ridge **13**:389
seas, gulfs, and bays
Baffin Bay **3**:21
Barents Sea **3**:80
Beaufort Sea **3**:146
Bering Strait **3**:212
Chukchi Sea **4**:422
Prudhoe Bay **15**:585
tributaries and ocean, dimensions **14**:326 *table*
ARCTIC SLED DOG
Eskimo dog **7**:242
ARCTIC SMALL TOOL TRADITION **7**:239 *map*
Eskimo **7**:241
Giddings, J. Louis **9**:176
ARCTIC VILLAGE (Alaska)
map (68° 8′N 145° 19′W) **1**:242
ARCTURUS
Boötes **3**:394
ARD *see* PLOW
ARDABIL (Iran)
map (38° 15′N 48° 18′E) **11**:250
ARDAGH CHALICE **9**:229 *illus.*
ARDASHIR I, KING OF PERSIA **2**:144
Persia, ancient **15**:183
Sassanians **17**:83
ARDENNES **2**:144
map (50° 10′N 5° 45′E) **3**:177
ARDENNES, BATTLE OF THE *see* BULGE, BATTLE OF THE
ARDILL (Saskatchewan)
map (49° 53′N 105° 49′W) **17**:81
ARDMORE (Alabama)
map (34° 59′N 86° 52′W) **1**:234
ARDMORE (Oklahoma)
map (34° 10′N 97° 8′W) **14**:368
ARDMORE (Pennsylvania)
map (40° 1′N 75° 18′W) **15**:147
ARDREY, ROBERT **2**:144 *bibliog.*
ARDUINO, GIOVANNI **2**:144–145 *bibliog.*
AREA (mathematics) **2**:145 *bibliog.*
circle **4**:435
cone **5**:175
cylinder **5**:406
integral calculus **11**:200
Kepler's laws **12**:58
measurement **13**:254
rectangle **16**:110
sphere **18**:180
square **18**:202
weights and measures **20**:93 *table*
ARECIBO (Puerto Rico)
map (18° 28′N 66° 43′W) **15**:614
ARECIBO OBSERVATORY **2**:145 *illus.*; **16**:51 *illus.*
radar astronomy **16**:40
AREF, ABDUL SALAM
Iraq **11**:256
ARENAC (county in Michigan)
map (44° 5′N 83° 55′W) **13**:377
ARENAL POINT
map (10° 3′N 61° 56′W) **19**:300
ARENDAL (Norway)
map (58° 27′N 8° 48′E) **14**:261
ARENDT, HANNAH **2**:145
ARENILLAS (Ecuador)
map (3° 33′S 80° 4′W) **7**:52
ARENSBERG, LOUISE AND WALTER
Philadelphia Museum of Art **15**:229
ARENSKY, ANTON STEPANOVICH **2**:145 *bibliog.*
AREOLA *see* BREAST
AREOPAGITICA (book) **2**:145
freedom of the press **8**:296
AREOPAGUS **2**:145–146
AREQUIPA (Peru)
map (16° 24′S 71° 33′W) **15**:193
AREQUITO (Argentina)
map (33° 9′S 61° 28′W) **2**:149
ARES **2**:146
ARÊTE (geology) **2**:146
glaciers and glaciation **9**:193 *illus.*
ARETÊ (philosophy) **2**:146 *bibliog.*
ARETHUSA **2**:146
depicted on a coin **18**:410 *illus.*
ARETINO, PIETRO **2**:146 *bibliog.*
Titian **19**:212
ARÉVALO, JUAN JOSÉ
Guatemala **9**:388
ARÉVALO, MARCO VINICIO CEREZO *see* CEREZO ARÉVALO, MARCO VINICIO
AREZZO (Italy)
map (43° 25′N 11° 53′E) **11**:321
AREZZO, GUIDO D' *see* GUIDO D'AREZZO
ARGALI (animal) **13**:624; **17**:248
ARGALL, SAMUEL
Pocahontas **15**:376
ARGAND, AIMÉ
lamp **12**:176
ARGAND DIAGRAM
complex number **5**:156–157
ARGAND LAMP
lamp **12**:175 *illus.*; **12**:176
lighthouse **12**:336
ARGELANDER, FRIEDRICH WILHELM AUGUST **2**:146
astronomy, history of **2**:280
Bonner Durchmusterung **3**:381
ARGENTA (Illinois)
map (39° 59′N 88° 49′W) **11**:42
ARGENTEUIL (France) **2**:146
ARGENTINA **2**:146–152 *bibliog.*, *illus.*, *map*, *table*

architecture *see* the subheading Argentina under ARCHITECTURE
cities
Bahía Blanca **3**:24
Buenos Aires **3**:544–546 *map*
Córdoba **5**:261
La Plata **12**:148
Mar del Plata **2**:150 *illus.*
Paraná **15**:80
Rosario **16**:312
Salta **18**:86 *table*
Tucumán **19**:328
Ushuaia **19**:490
climate **2**:147; **2**:148 *table*
economic activity **2**:148
education **2**:148
Latin American universities **12**:233 *table*
flag **2**:147 *illus.*; **8**:134
government **2**:148; **2**:150 *illus.*
defense, national **6**:82 *table*
history **2**:150–151
Alberdi, Juan Bautista **1**:253
Belgrano, Manuel **3**:182
Falkland Islands **8**:13
Frondizi, Arturo **8**:339
Galtieri, Leopoldo Fortunato **9**:22
Latin America, history of **12**:220–222
Mitre, Bartolomé **13**:485
Pérez Esquivel, Adolfo **15**:164
Perón, Eva **15**:176
Perón, Isabel **15**:176
Perón, Juan D. **15**:177
Quiroga, Juan Facundo **16**:28
Roca, Julio A. **16**:246
Rosas, Juan Manuel de **16**:312
San Martín, José de **17**:57
Sarmiento, Domingo Faustino **17**:78
Triple Alliance, War of the **19**:302
Urquiza, Justo José de **19**:487
Videla, Jorge Rafael **19**:577
land and resources **2**:146–147
language **2**:147
literature
Borges, Jorge Luis **3**:398–399
Cortázar, Julio **5**:278
Echeverría, Esteban **7**:37
Güiraldes, Ricardo **9**:400
Lugones, Leopoldo **12**:453
Lynch, Benito **12**:476
Mallea, Eduardo **13**:92
Puig, Manuel **15**:617
Sábato, Ernesto **17**:4
map (34° 0′S 64° 0′W) **18**:85
music and dance
Ginastera, Alberto **9**:183
tango **19**:23
newspaper **14**:172
people **2**:147–148
Araucanians **2**:109–110
Guaraní **9**:386
Indians **11**:132 *map*
Tehuelche **19**:73
physical features
Aconcagua **1**:84
Pampas **15**:53
polo (sport) **15**:417
railroad **16**:73
Trans-Andine Railroad **19**:267
religion **2**:147
rivers, lakes, and waterways **2**:147
Iguaçu Falls **11**:38
vegetation and animal life **2**:147
ARGENTINA, LA **2**:152 *bibliog.*
ARGENTINE (fish) **2**:152
ARGENTINE BASIN
Atlantic Ocean bottom **2**:295 *map*
ARGENTITE **2**:152
ARGENTO, DOMINICK **2**:152
ARGERSINGER* v. *HAMLIN **2**:152
legal aid **12**:272
ARGEŞ RIVER
map (44° 4′N 26° 37′E) **16**:288
ARGHANDAB RIVER
map (31° 27′N 64° 23′E) **1**:133
ARGO **2**:152
ARGON **2**:152
abundances of common elements **7**:131 *table*
element **7**:130 *table*
Group 0 periodic table **15**:167
inert gases **11**:161
laser **12**:213 *table*
radiometric age-dating **16**:66
Rayleigh, Lord **16**:97
Travers, Morris William, discoverer **19**:284
ARGONAUT (animal)
nautilus **14**:52
ARGONAUTICA (epic)
Apollonius of Rhodes **2**:84–85
ARGONAUTS (mythology)
Jason **11**:384
ARGONIA (Kansas)
map (37° 16′N 97° 46′W) **12**:18
ARGONNE (France) **2**:152
ARGONNE (Wisconsin)
map (45° 40′N 88° 53′W) **20**:185
ARGONNE NATIONAL LABORATORY **2**:152
ARGOS **2**:152–153
Nemea **14**:80
ARGOS (Indiana)
map (41° 14′N 86° 15′W) **11**:111
ARGOSY (periodical)
pulp magazines **15**:620
ARGUEDAS, ALCIDES **2**:153
ARGUIEN, MARIE CASIMIERE D′
John III, King of Poland (John Sobieski) **11**:427
ARGUS **2**:153
ARGYLE (Minnesota)
map (48° 20′N 96° 49′W) **13**:453
ARGYLE, LAKE
map (16° 15′S 128° 45′E) **2**:328
ARGYLL (Scotland) **2**:153
stone alignments **18**:281
ÅRHUS (Denmark) **2**:153
map (56° 9′N 10° 13′E) **6**:109
ARIA **2**:153 *bibliog.*
baroque music **3**:91–92
cantata **4**:115
Peking Opera **15**:136
ARIADNE (mythology) **2**:153
ARIANE **2**:153
European Space Agency **7**:306
ARIANISM **2**:153–154 *bibliog.*
Athanasius, Saint **2**:288
Constantine I, Roman Emperor **5**:209
Cyril of Jerusalem, Saint **5**:410
Damasus I, Pope **6**:19
Eunomius **7**:265
Eusebius of Nicomedia **7**:310
Hilary of Poitiers, Saint **10**:163
ARICA (CHILE) **2**:154
climate **4**:356 *table*; **18**:86 *table*
map (18° 29′S 70° 20′W) **4**:355
Tacna-Arica Dispute **19**:6
ARICA (Colombia)
map (2° 8′S 71° 47′W) **5**:107
ARICHAT (Nova Scotia)
map (45° 31′N 61° 1′W) **14**:269
ARID CLIMATE **2**:154 *bibliog.*
cacti and other succulents **4**:9–11 *illus.*
desert **6**:126–129
landform evolution **12**:183
paleoclimatology **15**:33
soil distribution, worldwide **18**:37 *map*
ARIDAL SABKHA
map (26° 12′N 14° 5′W) **13**:585
ARIEL (satellite)
Uranus (astronomy) **19**:478–479
ARIES **2**:154
ARIKAMEDU (India)
archaeology **2**:118 *illus.*
ARIKARA (American Indians) **2**:154 *bibliog.*
Hidatsa **10**:158
Omaha (American Indians) **14**:385
South Dakota **18**:105
ARIKAREE RIVER
map (40° 1′N 101° 56′W) **5**:116
ARIMA (Trinidad and Tobago)
map (10° 38′N 61° 17′W) **19**:300
ARION
Periander, Tyrant of Corinth **15**:165
ARIOSO
recitative **16**:107
ARIOSTO, LUDOVICO **2**:154 *bibliog.*
Orlando Furioso **14**:445
ARIPUANÃ (Brazil)
map (9° 10′S 60° 38′W) **3**:460
ARIPUANÃ RIVER
map (5° 7′S 60° 24′W) **3**:460
ARISTA, MARIANO **2**:154–155
Mexican War **13**:352 *map*
ARISTAEUS (mythology) **2**:155
ARISTARCHUS (moon crater) **13**:563 *illus.*
ARISTARCHUS OF SAMOS **2**:155 *bibliog.*
astronomy, history of **2**:279
heliocentric world system **10**:112
mathematics, history of **13**:224
On the Sizes and Distances of the Sun and Moon **2**:155
ARISTIDES **2**:155
ARISTIPPUS **2**:155
ARISTOCRACY **2**:155
class, social **5**:40
government **9**:267; **9**:269
Greece, ancient **9**:330–331
primogeniture **15**:547
titles of nobility and honor **19**:213–214
ARISTOCRATIC REVOLT (1788)
French Revolution **8**:322
ARISTODEMUS
Cumae **5**:386
ARISTOGITON
Harmodius **10**:51
ARISTOPHANES **2**:155–156 *bibliog., illus.*
Clouds, The **5**:68
comedy **5**:132
Lysistrata **12**:480
ARISTOTELIAN PHILOSOPHY
Albertus Magnus, Saint **1**:259–260
Aquinas, Saint Thomas **2**:95
Aristotle **2**:158
Avempace **2**:369
Averroës **2**:370
Avicenna **2**:376
Levi ben Gershon **12**:303
Maimonides **13**:68
ARISTOTLE **2**:156–158 *bibliog., illus.*
anatomy **1**:395–396
astronomy, history of **2**:277
biology **3**:268
causality **4**:219
chemistry, history of **4**:324
classification, biological **5**:42
criticism, literary **5**:351
ethics **7**:251
Europe, history of **7**:280
geocentric world system **9**:95
geography **9**:100–101
government **9**:267
law **12**:242
logic **12**:395–396
medicine **13**:268
narrative and dramatic devices **14**:22–23
oligarchy **14**:377
Peripatetics **15**:170–171
philosophy **15**:241 *illus.*; **15**:244
photosynthesis **15**:275
physics, history of **15**:282–283 *illus.*; **15**:285
Poetics **15**:378
poetry **15**:379
portrait **15**:446
rhetoric and oratory **16**:194
riddles **16**:216
scholasticism **17**:132
sensation **17**:204
slavery **17**:352
state (in political philosophy) **18**:229–230
substance **18**:317
syllogism **18**:401–402
teleology **19**:78
thought **2**:157–158
writings **2**:156
zoology **20**:377–378
ARITHMETIC **2**:158–159 *bibliog.*
associative law **2**:266
binary number **3**:256
commutative law **5**:153
decimal **6**:73
distributive law **6**:201
duodecimal system **6**:301–302
exponent **7**:339–340
history **2**:159
mathematics **13**:222
mathematics, education in **13**:222–223 *bibliog.*
mathematics, history of **13**:223
number **14**:292–293
number theory **14**:293
ARITHMETIC MEAN *see* MEAN
ARITHMETIC PROGRESSION
progression **15**:563–564
ARITOMO, YAMAGATA *see* YAMAGATA ARITOMO
ARITON (Alabama)
map (31° 36′N 85° 43′W) **1**:234
ARIUS
Arianism **2**:153
ARIZONA **2**:159–164 *bibliog., illus., map*
archaeology and historic sites **2**:162
Anasazi Ruins **1**:394
Canyon de Chelly National Monument **4**:119
Hohokam culture **10**:199
Montezuma Castle National Monument **13**:555
Oraibi **14**:413–414
Tombstone **19**:231–232
cities
Flagstaff **8**:150
Mesa **13**:313
Nogales **14**:212
Phoenix **15**:251 *illus.*
Prescott **15**:522
Tombstone **19**:231–232
Tucson **19**:328
Yuma **20**:346
climate **2**:161
economy **2**:163
education **2**:162
Arizona, state universities of **2**:164
flag **2**:159 *illus.*
flower, state
saguaro **4**:10 *illus.*
government and politics **2**:162–163
history **2**:163–164
Hayden, Carl **10**:80
Indians, American
Indians of North America, art of the **11**:140
land and resources **2**:159–161
map (34° 0′N 112° 0′W) **19**:419
people **2**:161–162
Apache **2**:73
Hopi **10**:231
Mojave **13**:504–505
Navajo **14**:53–54
Papago **15**:66
Pima **15**:303–304
Pueblo **15**:613
Yaqui **20**:319
Yuma **20**:346
physical features
Colorado Plateau **5**:120
Grand Canyon **9**:284–285 *illus.*
Meteor Crater **13**:337
Monument Valley **13**:560
Painted Desert **15**:17
Petrified Forest National Park **15**:204; **15**:205
prehistory
Anasazi **1**:392–394
North American archaeology **14**:239–240
rivers, lakes, and waterways **2**:161
Colorado River (Colorado) **2**:161
Gila River **9**:178
Glen Canyon Dam **2**:163 *illus.*
Mead, Lake **13**:251
seal, state **2**:159 *illus.*
vegetation and animal life **2**:161
ARIZONA (ship)
Pearl Harbor **15**:126
ARIZONA, STATE UNIVERSITIES OF **2**:164
ARK **2**:164
Noah **14**:207
ARK OF THE COVENANT **2**:164
tabernacle **19**:4
ARKABUTLA LAKE
map (34° 45′N 90° 6′W) **13**:469
ARKADELPHIA (Arkansas)
map (34° 7′N 93° 4′W) **2**:166
ARKANSAS **2**:164–170 *bibliog., illus., map*
cities
Fort Smith **8**:237
Hot Springs **10**:259
Little Rock **12**:373
Pine Bluff **15**:305
Texarkana **19**:128
climate **2**:165
cultural institutions **2**:167
economy **2**:167–168
education **2**:167
Arkansas, state universities and colleges of **2**:170
flag **2**:165 *illus.*
government and politics **2**:168 *illus.*
historic sites **2**:167
history **2**:168–170
land and resources **2**:164–167
map (34° 50′N 92° 30′W) **19**:419
Ozark Mountains **14**:480
people **2**:167
rivers, lakes, and waterways **2**:165
Arkansas River **2**:170
Buffalo River **2**:167 *illus.*
seal, state **2**:165 *illus.*
vegetation and animal life **2**:165
ARKANSAS (American Indians) *see* QUAPAW
ARKANSAS (county in Arkansas)
map (34° 20′N 91° 20′W) **2**:166
ARKANSAS, STATE UNIVERSITIES AND COLLEGES OF **2**:170
ARKANSAS CITY (Arkansas)
map (33° 36′N 91° 12′W) **2**:166
ARKANSAS CITY (Kansas)
map (37° 4′N 97° 2′W) **12**:18
ARKANSAS RIVER **2**:170
map (33° 48′N 91° 4′W) **13**:474
Royal Gorge **16**:330
ARKHAM HOUSE
Derleth, August **6**:121
ARKHANGELSK (USSR) **2**:170
climate **7**:272 *table*
map (64° 34′N 40° 32′E) **19**:388

ARKOSE 2:170
ARKTIKA (ship)
Arctic **2**:142 *map*
icebreaker **11**:16
ARKWRIGHT, SIR RICHARD 2:170 *bibliog.*
Bolton **3**:372
spinning **18**:186
spinning machine **19**:136 *illus.*
ARLECCHINO *see* HARLEQUIN
ARLEE (Montana)
map (47° 10′N 114° 5′W) **13**:547
ARLEN, HAROLD 2:170–171 *bibliog.*
ARLES, KINGDOM OF
Burgundy **3**:570
ARLINGTON (Georgia)
map (31° 27′N 84° 44′W) **9**:114
ARLINGTON (Iowa)
map (42° 45′N 91° 40′W) **11**:244
ARLINGTON (Kentucky)
map (36° 47′N 89° 1′W) **12**:47
ARLINGTON (Massachusetts)
map (42° 25′N 71° 9′W) **13**:206
ARLINGTON (Nebraska)
map (41° 27′N 96° 21′W) **14**:70
ARLINGTON (New York)
map (41° 42′N 73° 54′W) **14**:149
ARLINGTON (Ohio)
map (40° 54′N 83° 39′W) **14**:357
ARLINGTON (Oregon)
map (45° 16′N 120° 13′W) **14**:427
ARLINGTON (South Dakota)
map (44° 22′N 97° 8′W) **18**:103
ARLINGTON (Tennessee)
map (35° 18′N 89° 40′W) **19**:104
ARLINGTON (Texas) 2:171
map (32° 44′N 97° 7′W) **19**:129
ARLINGTON (Vermont)
map (43° 5′N 73° 9′W) **19**:554
ARLINGTON (Virginia)
map (38° 52′N 77° 5′W) **19**:607
Pentagon, The **15**:154
ARLINGTON (Washington)
map (48° 12′N 122° 8′W) **20**:35
ARLINGTON HEIGHTS (Illinois)
map (42° 5′N 87° 59′W) **11**:42
ARLINGTON NATIONAL CEMETERY 2:171; **4**:244 *illus.*
Washington, D.C. **20**:41 *map*
ARLISS, GEORGE 2:171
ARM
joint (in anatomy) **11**:439 *illus.*
muscle **13**:654
skeleton, human **17**:336
ARMADA, SPANISH *see* SPANISH ARMADA
ARMADILLO 2:171 *illus.*
edentates **7**:56
shell **17**:252 *illus.*
ARMADILLO LIZARD **9**:189 *illus.*
ARMAGEDDON 2:171
ARMAGH (Northern Ireland) 2:171
ARMAGNACS AND BURGUNDIANS 2:171
Orléans (family) **14**:446
ARMAMENTS *see* FIREARMS; WEAPONS
ARMAND-BOMBARDIER, JOSEPH
snowmobile **18**:5
ARMANT (Egypt)
map (25° 37′N 32° 32′E) **7**:76
ARMATURE 2:171
electromagnet **7**:115
generator **9**:78
motor **13**:611
stator **18**:238
ARMED FORCES *see* AIR FORCE; ARMY; DEFENSE, NATIONAL; MARINE CORPS, U.S.; NAVY; specific branches of the service under specific countries, e.g., JAPAN—navy; UNITED KINGDOM—army; etc.; names of specific military headings, e.g., MILITARY JUSTICE; MILITARY POLICE; etc.
ARMENIA 2:172 *bibliog., map*
Armenian Soviet Socialist Republic **2**:173
Tigranes I, King **19**:197
ARMENIA (Colombia)
map (4° 31′N 75° 41′W) **5**:107
ARMENIAN CHURCH 2:172–173 *bibliog.*
Monophysitism **13**:537
ARMENIAN LANGUAGE 2:173 *bibliog.*
languages, extinct **12**:198–199
ARMENIAN SOVIET SOCIALIST REPUBLIC (USSR) 2:173 *bibliog.*
Armenian church **2**:172–173
Yerevan **20**:326
ARMENIANS (people)
Armenia **2**:172
Armenian church **2**:172–173
Armenian Soviet Socialist Republic **2**:173
Turks **19**:348
ARMIDALE (Australia)
New England University **2**:345 *table*
ARMILLARY SPHERE 2:173
planetarium **15**:328–329
ARMINIANISM 2:173 *bibliog.*
Great Awakening **9**:308
Remonstrants **16**:146
ARMINIUS (chief of the German Cherusci tribe) 2:173
ARMINIUS, JACOBUS
Arminianism **2**:173
ARMISTICE DAY 2:173
ARMITAGE, KENNETH 2:173–174 *bibliog.*
ARMONICA *see* GLASS HARMONICA
ARMOR 2:174–175 *bibliog., illus.*
Aegean civilization **1**:117 *illus.*
cavalry **4**:221 *illus.*
cuirass **7**:190 *illus.*
Dean, Bashford **6**:67
heraldry **10**:134
knight **12**:100 *illus.*
naval vessels **14**:55–56
Norman horseman **14**:222 *illus.*
weapons **20**:74
ARMORED VEHICLE 2:175–177 *bibliog., illus.*
armored car **2**:175
defense, national **6**:82 *table*
Ericsson, John **7**:229
Guderian, Heinz **9**:390
recoilless rifle **16**:108
tanks **2**:175–177 *illus.*
World War I **20**:237 *illus.*; **20**:247 *illus.*
World War II **20**:268 *illus.*
ARMORY SHOW 2:177 *bibliog.*
abstract art **1**:63–65
American art and architecture **1**:331; **1**:335
Ashcan School **2**:229–230
Bellows, George **3**:191
Davies, Arthur B. **6**:49
Davis, Stuart **6**:52
Duchamp, Marcel **6**:290
Picabia, Francis **15**:290
Prendergast, Maurice **15**:518
Sloan, John **17**:362–363
Steiglitz, Alfred **18**:267
ARMOUR (South Dakota)
map (43° 19′N 98° 21′W) **18**:103
ARMOUR, PHILIP DANFORTH 2:177–178 *bibliog.*
ARMS, COAT OF *see* HERALDRY
ARMS CONTROL 2:178 *bibliog., illus.*
Carter, Jimmy **4**:172
chemical and biological warfare **4**:313
cold war **5**:99
defense, national **6**:81–82
détente **6**:134
Geneva conferences **9**:91
Hague conferences **10**:11
hydrogen bomb **10**:339–340
Myrdal, Alva **13**:691
neutron bomb **14**:109
Noel-Baker, Philip John, Baron Noel-Baker **14**:212
nuclear strategy **14**:288
plutonium
nuclear energy **14**:283
rockets and missiles **16**:255
United Nations **19**:414–415
weapons **20**:75
ARMS AND THE MAN (play) 2:179
Shaw, George Bernard **17**:245
ARMSTRONG (county in Pennsylvania)
map (40° 49′N 79° 32′W) **15**:147
ARMSTRONG (county in Texas)
map (34° 57′N 101° 20′W) **19**:129
ARMSTRONG, EDWIN 2:179 *bibliog.*
frequency modulation (FM) **8**:327
radio **16**:45 *illus.*
radio and television broadcasting **16**:56
ARMSTRONG, HELEN PORTER *see* MELBA, DAME NELLIE
ARMSTRONG, HENRY 2:179 *bibliog.*; **3**:432 *illus.*
ARMSTRONG, JOHN 2:179
ARMSTRONG, LOUIS 1:351 *illus.*; **2**:179 *bibliog., illus.*
jazz **11**:388 *illus.*
ARMSTRONG, NEIL A. 2:179–180 *illus.*
Apollo Program **2**:179–180
bootprint on the moon **13**:563 *illus.*
Gemini program **9**:72–73
ARMSTRONG, WILLIAM GEORGE, BARON ARMSTRONG OF CRAIGSIDE 2:180
ARMSTRONG-JONES, ANTONY, 1ST EARL OF SNOWDON *see* SNOWDON, ANTONY ARMSTRONG-JONES, 1ST EARL OF
ARMY 2:180–183 *bibliog., illus.*
See also WEAPONS; names of specific military headings, e.g., MILITARY JUSTICE; MILITARY POLICE; etc.; the subheading army under names of specific countries, e.g., FRANCE; UNION OF SOVIET SOCIALIST REPUBLICS; etc.
airborne troops **1**:210
ancient **2**:180
artillery **2**:222–224
battalion **3**:124
brigade **3**:486
cannon **4**:111–112
cavalry **4**:221–222
commando **5**:137
conscription **2**:181; **5**:201
defense, national **6**:82 *table*
division (military) **6**:205
general staff **9**:77
grenadier (military) **9**:358
guerrillas **9**:391–392
hoplite **10**:232
hussar **10**:320
infantry **11**:163–164
legion, Roman **12**:274
mechanized armies **2**:181–182
mercenaries **13**:304
military academies **13**:420
militia **13**:422–423
mutiny **13**:687
rangers **16**:85
rank, military **16**:85–86 *table*
regiment **16**:128
revolution **16**:188
rockets and missiles **16**:254–256
trench fever **19**:290
World War I **20**:220
ARMY ANT **2**:36–37
ARMY AND NAVY GAZETTE
Russell, Sir William Howard **16**:351
ARMY OF SOUTH VIETNAM (ARVN)
Vietnam War **19**:585–589
ARMY WAR COLLEGE *see* UNITED STATES ARMY WAR COLLEGE
ARNARSON, INGÓLFUR
Reykjavik (Iceland) **16**:190
ARNAUDVILLE (Louisiana)
map (30° 24′N 91° 56′W) **12**:430
ARNAULD, ANTOINE 2:183
Pascal, Blaise **15**:102
ARNAULD, JACQUELINE MARIE ANGÉLIQUE 2:183
ARNAUTI, CAPE OF
map (35° 6′N 32° 17′E) **5**:409
ARNAZ, DESI
Ball, Lucille **3**:40
"I Love Lucy" (television series) **16**:59 *illus.*
ARNE
Gla **9**:192
ARNE, THOMAS 2:183–184 *bibliog.*
ARNETT (Oklahoma)
map (36° 8′N 99° 46′W) **14**:368
ARNHEIM, RUDOLF
film, history of **8**:80
ARNHEM (Netherlands) 2:184
map (51° 59′N 5° 55′E) **14**:99
ARNHEM LAND (Australia) 2:184
Aborigines, Australian **1**:59 *illus.*
map (13° 10′S 134° 30′E) **2**:328
ARNIM, ACHIM AND BETTINA VON 2:184
ARNO, PETER 2:184
ARNO RIVER 2:184
ARNOLD (Missouri)
map (38° 26′N 90° 23′W) **13**:476
ARNOLD (Nebraska)
map (41° 26′N 100° 12′W) **14**:70
ARNOLD, BENEDICT 2:184–185 *bibliog., illus.*
American Revolution **1**:359 *map*
André, John **1**:406
ARNOLD, HENRY HARLEY 2:185 *bibliog.*
ARNOLD, MALCOLM 2:185
ARNOLD, MATTHEW 2:185 *bibliog., illus.*
Culture and Anarchy **5**:385
Dover Beach **6**:250–251
Rugby School **16**:340
ARNOLD, THOMAS 2:185
ARNOLD, THURMAN
legal realism **12**:243
ARNOLD OF BRESCIA 2:186 *bibliog.*
ARNOLFO DI CAMBIO 2:186 *bibliog.*
Florence Cathedral **16**:150
ARNPRIOR (Ontario)
map (45° 26′N 76° 21′W) **14**:393
ARNULF, FRANKISH EMPEROR 2:186
AROMATIC COMPOUNDS 2:186 *bibliog.*
alicyclic compounds **1**:293
aniline **2**:8
aryl group **2**:226
azo group **2**:381
benzene **3**:206
carbon **4**:135
carboxylic acid **4**:140–141
chemical nomenclature **4**:321 *illus.*
hydrocarbon **10**:331
hydroquinone **10**:344
Laurent, Auguste **12**:238–239
molecule **13**:508
naphthalene **14**:14
organic chemistry **14**:437; **14**:438
petrochemicals **15**:205
phenol **15**:225
phenyl group **15**:226
pollutants, chemical **15**:410
polyester **15**:418–419
resonance (chemistry) **16**:177–178
ARON, PIETRO
Renaissance music **16**:156
ARON, RAYMOND CLAUDE FERDINAND 2:186
ARONSON, BORIS 2:186–187
AROOSTOOK (county in Maine)
map (46° 45′N 68° 30′W) **13**:70
AROOSTOOK RIVER
map (46° 48′N 67° 45′W) **13**:70
AROOSTOOK WAR 2:187
Van Buren, Martin **19**:511
AROUET, FRANÇOIS MARIE *see* VOLTAIRE
ARP, BILL (pseudonym) *see* SMITH, CHARLES HENRY
ARP, JEAN 2:187 *bibliog., illus.*
Human Concretion **2**:187 *illus.*; **13**:494 *illus.*; **17**:165 *illus.*
ÁRPÁD FAMILY
Hungary **10**:309
ARPEGGIO 2:187
ARPINO, GERALD 2:187 *bibliog.*
ARRABAL, FERNANDO 2:187 *bibliog.*
ARRAIGNMENT 2:188
criminal justice **5**:349
ARRAIZ, ANTONIO
Venezuela **19**:543
ARRAN ISLAND
map (55° 35′N 5° 15′W) **19**:403
ARRAS (France) 2:188
map (50° 17′N 2° 47′E) **8**:260
tapestry **19**:32–33
ARRAU, CLAUDIO 2:188
ARREBO, ANDERS
Danish literature **3**:32
ARREST (law) 2:188 *bibliog.*
criminal justice **5**:349
tort **19**:245
warrant **20**:30
ARREY (New Mexico)
map (32° 51′N 107° 19′W) **14**:136
ARRHENIUS, SVANTE AUGUST 2:188
chemistry, history of **4**:327
dissociation **6**:198
enzyme **7**:213
ion and ionization **11**:239
life **12**:327
ARRHYTHMIA
heart diseases **10**:96
ARRIAN 2:188
ARRIBA (Colorado)
map (39° 17′N 103° 17′W) **5**:116
ARRIGHI, LUDOVICO DEGLI
calligraphy **4**:43 *illus.*
ARROW, KENNETH JOSEPH 2:188
ARROWHEAD (artifact) 2:188 *bibliog.*
ARROWHEAD (plant) 2:188
ARROWHEAD LAKE
map (47° 20′N 98° 50′W) **14**:248
ARROWROOT 2:188
ARROWSMITH (book) 2:188–189
de Kruif, Paul **6**:60
Lewis, Sinclair **11**:306–307
ARROWWOOD *see* VIBURNUM
ARROWWORM 2:189
invertebrate **11**:235
zooplankton **20**:378
ARROYO GRANDE (California)
map (35° 7′N 120° 34′W) **4**:31
ARROYO HONDO (New Mexico)
map (36° 32′N 105° 40′W) **14**:136
ARRUDA (family) 2:189 *bibliog.*
ARSACIDS 2:189 *bibliog.*
Ctesiphon **5**:377
Parthia **15**:100
Persia, ancient **15**:182
ARSENATE MINERALS 2:189 *illus.*
See also ARSENIC
mimetite **2**:189; **13**:434
mineral **13**:443 *table*
phosphate minerals **15**:255–256

structure **2**:189
uranium minerals **19**:478
ARSENIC **2**:189 *bibliog.*
abundances of common elements **7**:131 *table*
cobaltite **5**:83
element **7**:130 *table*
Group VA periodic table **15**:167
hepatitis **10**:130
history **2**:189
native elements **14**:47
ore deposits
arsenate minerals **2**:189
arsenopyrite **2**:189–190
poisoning **2**:189
pollutants, chemical **15**:410
properties **2**:189
transition elements **19**:273 *table*
uranium minerals **19**:478
ARSENIDE MINERALS
niccolite **14**:180
ARSENOPYRITE **2**:189–190
arsenic **2**:189
ARSON **2**:190
fire prevention and control **8**:103
ARSPHENAMINE *see* SALVARSAN
ART **2**:190–202 *bibliog., illus.*
See also ART EDUCATION; ART HISTORY; CRAFT; names of specific artists, e.g., CALDER, ALEXANDER; MICHELANGELO; etc.; names of specific types of art media, e.g., GOUACHE; TEMPERA; etc.; specific art terms, e.g., CHIAROSCURO; ILLUSIONISM; etc.
abstract art **1**:63–65
academies of art **1**:69–70
aesthetics **1**:130–131
African art **1**:160–164
American art and architecture **1**:327–336
antique collecting **2**:65–68
architecture **2**:129
art brut **2**:203
art collectors and patrons **2**:203–204
art conservation and restoration **2**:204–206
art criticism **2**:207
Art Deco **2**:207–208 *illus.*
Art Nouveau **2**:209–212
auction **2**:317
Austrian art and architecture **2**:352–354
baroque art and architecture **3**:88–91
basketry **3**:115–116
Bauhaus **3**:129–130
beads and beadwork **3**:137–138
black Americans **3**:311–312
book illustration **3**:386–388
Byzantine art and architecture **3**:604–606
calligraphy **4**:41–46
Canadian art and architecture **4**:88–91
Carolingian art and architecture **4**:160–161
Celtic art **4**:238–241
Chinese art and architecture **4**:379–388
collage **5**:102
comic strip **5**:135–136
conceptual art **5**:169
constructivism **5**:224
Coptic art and architecture **5**:255
cubism **5**:380–381
Cycladic art **5**:402–403
Dada **6**:4–5
decadence **6**:72
decorative arts **6**:76
drawing **6**:263–265
Dutch art and architecture **6**:309–313
Early Christian art and architecture **7**:9–11
eclecticism **7**:40
Egyptian art and architecture **7**:85–90 *illus.*
English art and architecture **7**:181–188
engraving **7**:205–206
environmental art **7**:209–210
etching **7**:248–249
Etruscan art *see* ETRUSCANS
expressionism (art) **7**:340
Fascist art **8**:30–31
fashion design **8**:31–33
Fauvism **8**:38–39
Flemish art and architecture **8**:159–162
folk art **8**:195–199
forgery in art **8**:233–234
French art and architecture **8**:303–308
futurism **8**:383–384
German art and architecture **9**:123–129
gold and silver work **9**:230
golden section **9**:232
Gothic art and architecture **9**:255–262
graffiti **9**:278
graphic arts **9**:291–294
Greek art **9**:337–342
history of western art **2**:192–202
Hittite art and architecture **10**:188
iconography **11**:21–24
illuminated manuscripts **11**:46–48
illusionism **11**:49–50
impressionism **11**:62–68
Indian art and architecture **11**:94–98
Indians of North America, art of the **11**:138–141
interior design **11**:210–214
International Style (Gothic art) **11**:223
Islamic art and architecture **11**:293–297
Italian art and architecture **11**:308–314
Japanese art and architecture **11**:372–379
jewelry **11**:408–411
kinetic art **12**:78
Korean art **12**:117–118
Kresge Foundation **12**:129
Lamaist art and architecture **12**:172–173
landscape painting **12**:188–192
language and literature **12**:196–197
Latin American art and architecture **12**:222–228
lithograph **12**:371
magic realism **13**:51
Mannerism **13**:124–125
mathematics as **13**:221
Maya **13**:243–245 *illus.*
Merovingian art and architecture **13**:311
Mesopotamian art and architecture **13**:317–322
minimal art **13**:446
Minoan art **13**:458–459
modern art **13**:493–496
Mogul art and architecture **13**:500–502
Moorish art and architecture **13**:570–571
mosaic **13**:593–596
mural painting **13**:645–647
museums, art **13**:657–659
Nazarenes **14**:66
needlework **14**:76
neoclassicism (art) **14**:81–82
neoexpressionism **14**:83
neoimpressionism **14**:83
Oceanic art **14**:336–339
op art **14**:397
orphism **14**:448
Ottonian art and architecture **14**:466–467
painting **15**:18–23
paper folding **15**:70–71
pastel **15**:106
Persian art and architecture **15**:183–187
Phoenician art **15**:250–251
photorealism **15**:274
pop art **15**:429
portraiture **15**:446–448
Portuguese art and architecture **15**:455–456
postimpressionism **15**:462–463
pottery and porcelain **15**:468–472
pre-Columbian art and architecture **15**:495–501
prehistoric art **15**:506–511
primitive art **15**:543
realism (art) **16**:103
Renaissance art and architecture **16**:149–155
rococo style **16**:263–265
Roman art and architecture **16**:273–277
Romanesque art and architecture **16**:282–286
romanticism (art) **16**:291–292
rugs and carpets **16**:340–343
Russian art and architecture **16**:361–364
Salon (art) **17**:36
Scandinavian art and architecture **17**:111–114
sculpture **17**:159–166
Secession movement **17**:178
silhouette **17**:304
social realism **18**:13
Southeast Asian art and architecture **18**:107–110
Spanish art and architecture **18**:151–156
stained glass **18**:211–213
steppe art **18**:255–256
surrealism (art) **18**:364–365
symbolism (art) **18**:402–403
synchromism **18**:406
tapestry **19**:31–33
vorticism **19**:635
wood carving **20**:207–209
woodcuts and wood engravings **20**:210–211
ART FOR ART'S SAKE *see* AESTHETICISM
ART BRUT **2**:203 *bibliog.*
ART COLLECTORS AND PATRONS **2**:203–204 *bibliog., illus.*
antique collecting **2**:65–68
Berenson, Bernard **3**:208
Caillebotte, Gustave **4**:16–17
Courtauld Institute of Art **5**:316
Covarrubias, Miguel **5**:318
Dresden State Art Collections **6**:270–271
du pont, henry francis
Winterthur Museum **20**:181
duke of berry
Limbourg brothers **12**:343
Dutch art and architecture **6**:309
Duveen, Joseph, Baron Duveen of Millbank **6**:316
Elgin, Thomas Bruce, 7th Earl of **7**:137
Fitzwilliam Museum **8**:132
Freer, Charles Lang **8**:300
Frick, Henry Clay **8**:330
Frick Collection **8**:330
Gardner Museum **9**:45
Getty, J. Paul **9**:160
Guggenheim (family) **9**:392
Guggenheim, Peggy **9**:392–393
Guggenheim Museum **9**:393
Gulbenkian, Calouste Sarkis **9**:402
Hirshhorn Museum and Sculpture Garden **10**:176
Islamic art and architecture **11**:294
Kress, Samuel H. **12**:129
Mellon, Andrew W. **13**:287
Mellon, Paul **13**:287
Metropolitan Museum of Art, The **13**:348
Morgan (family) **13**:577
National Gallery of Art **14**:33
Philadelphia Museum of Art **15**:229
portraiture **15**:446
Rockefeller (family)
Cloisters, The **5**:64
Stein, Gertrude **18**:247
Sung Hui-tsung (Song Huizong) **18**:348
Tate Gallery, The **19**:44
Vatican museums and galleries **19**:527–528
Vollard, Ambroise **19**:630
Wallace Collection, The **20**:15
Walters Art Gallery **20**:20
Watson (family) **20**:67
Whitney, Gertrude Vanderbilt **20**:141–142
ART CONSERVATION AND RESTORATION **2**:204–206 *bibliog., illus.*
chemistry **4**:324
forgery in art **8**:233–234
stained glass **18**:213
ART CRITICISM **2**:207 *bibliog.*
See also ART HISTORY
Apollinaire, Guillaume **2**:79
Berenson, Bernard **3**:208
Céspedes, Pablo de **4**:262
Clark, Kenneth M. **5**:39
Fenollosa, Ernest Francisco **8**:50–51
Greenberg, Clement **9**:349
Grigorovich, Dmitry Vasilievich **9**:364
Huxtable, Ada Louise **10**:325
Lessing, Gotthold **12**:298–299
Malraux, André **13**:93–94
O'Hara, Frank **14**:355
Pater, Walter **15**:110–111
Read, Sir Herbert **16**:100
Reynolds, Sir Joshua **16**:191
Rosenberg, Harold **16**:315
Ruskin, John **16**:348
Winckelmann, Johann **20**:168
Wölfflin, Heinrich **20**:198
ART DECO **2**:207–208 *bibliog., illus.*
Art Nouveau **2**:212
Arts and Crafts movement **2**:225
Chrysler Building **4**:420
Eleven Executioners **4**:4 *illus.*
fashion accessories **2**:208 *illus.*
furnishing accessories **2**:208 *illus.*
glassware, decorative **9**:204
gold and silver work **9**:230 *illus.*
industrial design **11**:155 *illus.*
interior design **11**:214
Lalique, René **12**:171–172
Radio City Music Hall **16**:53
ART EDUCATION
academies of art **1**:69–70
arts, education in the **2**:224–225
École des Beaux-Arts **7**:42
Hofmann, Hans **10**:196
Moholy-Nagy, László **13**:503
Moore College of Art **13**:570
National Gallery of Art **14**:33
National Portrait Gallery **14**:45
Parsons School of Design **15**:99
Pennsylvania Academy of the Fine Arts **15**:152
Pratt Institute **15**:490
Rhode Island School of Design **16**:201
Royal Ontario Museum **16**:330
Squarcione, Francesco **18**:202
Winterthur Museum **20**:181
ART FORGERY *see* FORGERY IN ART
ART HISTORY
See also AESTHETICS
Baldinucci, Filippo **3**:34
Barr, Alfred H., Jr. **3**:92
Berenson, Bernard **3**:208
Coomaraswamy, Ananda Kentish **5**:242–243
Fenollosa, Ernest Francisco **8**:50–51
Focillon, Henry **8**:192
Frankl, Paul **8**:282
Friedlaender, Walter **8**:331
Friedländer, Max J. **8**:331
Fuseli, Henry **8**:381
Giedion, Sigfried **9**:177
Giocondo, Fra Giovanni **9**:186
Gombrich, Sir Ernst H. **9**:241
Hamilton, George Heard **10**:29
Hartt, Frederick **10**:63
Hitchcock, Henry-Russell **10**:186
Janson, H. W. **11**:359
Mander, Carel van **13**:111
Panofsky, Erwin **15**:60
Pevsner, Sir Nikolaus **15**:216
Ruskin, John **16**:348
Schapiro, Meyer **17**:117
Taft, Lorado **19**:7
Vasari, Giorgio **19**:525
Wittkower, Rudolf **20**:194
ART MUSEUMS *see* MUSEUMS, ART
ART NOUVEAU **2**:209–212 *bibliog., illus.*
architectural motifs **2**:211 *illus.*
Art Deco **2**:207
Arts and Crafts movement **2**:225
Beardsley, Aubrey **3**:142–143
Flemish art and architecture **8**:162
Fulfillment (Gustav Klimt) **2**:353 *illus.*
furniture **2**:209 *illus.*
Gallé, Émile **9**:17
Gaudí, Antonio **9**:59
German art and architecture **9**:128
glass and ceramic designs **2**:211 *illus.*
glassware, decorative **9**:204
Guimard, Hector **9**:396–397
Hodler, Ferdinand **10**:194
Horta, Victor **10**:254
interior design **11**:214
jewelry **2**:210 *illus.*; **11**:411
Klimt, Gustav **12**:97
Mackintosh, Charles Rennie **13**:31
modern architecture **13**:493
Mucha, Alfons **13**:630
poster **15**:461 *illus.*
Rackham, Arthur **16**:38
Secession movement **17**:178
side table **8**:378 *illus.*
Spanish art and architecture **18**:154–156 *illus.*
stained glass **18**:212 *illus.*
Tiffany, Louis Comfort **19**:196
Toulouse-Lautrec, Henri de **19**:250–251
Van de Velde, Henry **19**:512
ART REPRODUCTION
gravure
printing **15**:552
ART RESTORATION *see* ART CONSERVATION AND RESTORATION
ART ROCK
rock music **16**:249 *illus.*
ART SONG *see* SONG
ARTABANUS
Xerxes I, King of Persia **20**:312
ARTAUD, ANTONIN **2**:212–213 *bibliog., illus.*

ARTAUD, ANTONIN (cont.)
improvisational and experimental theater **11**:69
Living Theatre **12**:376
ARTAXERXES I, KING OF PERSIA 2:213
ARTAXERXES II, KING OF PERSIA 2:213 *bibliog.*
Cyrus the Younger **5**:410
palace relief **15**:182 *illus.*
Tissaphernes, Persian Satrap **19**:209
ARTAXERXES III, KING OF PERSIA
Persia, ancient **15**:181
Philip II, King of Macedonia **15**:233
ARTEMIDORUS
mummy **13**:639 *illus.*
ARTEMIS 2:213
Ephesus **7**:216
temple at Ephesus **17**:217 *illus.*
ARTEMISA (Cuba)
map (22° 49′N 82° 46′W) **5**:377
ARTERIOSCLEROSIS 2:213 *bibliog.*
arteriolar sclerosis **2**:213
atherosclerosis **2**:291–292
Fothergill, John **8**:248
nervous system, diseases of the **14**:96
ARTERY 2:213–214 *bibliog., illus.*
aorta **2**:73
blood pressure **3**:339
cardiovascular diseases **4**:144
circulatory system **4**:440 *illus.*; **4**:442 *illus.*
coronary artery **5**:271
diseases and disorders
aneurysm **1**:411
arteriosclerosis **2**:213
atherosclerosis **2**:291–292 *illus.*
pulse (biology) **15**:621
ARTESIA (New Mexico)
map (32° 51′N 104° 24′W) **14**:136
ARTESIAN WELL 2:214
groundwater **9**:375 *illus.*
spring (water) **18**:199
ARTEVELDE (family) 2:214 *bibliog.*
ARTHRITIS 2:214–216 *bibliog., illus.*
collagen disease **5**:102
gout **9**:266–267
myasthenia gravis **13**:689
osteoarthritis **14**:457
rheumatic fever **16**:194
rheumatism **16**:194–195
spondylitis **18**:192
treatment **2**:216
aspirin **2**:262
colchicine **5**:97
uric acid **19**:486
ARTHRODIRE 2:216 *bibliog., illus.*
ARTHROPOD 2:216–218 *bibliog., illus.*
See also names of specific animals, e.g., GRASSHOPPER; LOBSTER; TICK; etc.
biological locomotion **3**:266 *illus.*
classes of arthropods
Arachnida **2**:106–107 *illus.*
Chilopoda (centipedes) **4**:250 *illus.*
Crustacea **5**:369–370 *illus.*
Diplopoda (millipedes) **13**:430 *illus.*
Insecta **11**:186–193 *illus.*
myriapod **13**:691
Onychophera (peripatus) **15**:171 *illus.*
eurypterid **7**:310
evolution **2**:216
invertebrate **11**:235
life cycle **2**:217
molting **13**:513
morphogenesis **2**:216–217
parasitic diseases **15**:82
physiology **2**:217–218
abdomen **1**:54
endocrine system **7**:168
sex **2**:217
skeletal system **2**:217–218
trilobite **19**:299
ARTHROSCOPE
joint (in anatomy) **11**:440
ARTHUR (Illinois)
map (39° 43′N 88° 28′W) **11**:42
ARTHUR (Nebraska)
map (41° 35′N 101° 41′W) **14**:70
ARTHUR (county in Nebraska)
map (41° 35′N 101° 40′W) **14**:70
ARTHUR (North Dakota)
map (47° 6′N 97° 13′W) **14**:248
ARTHUR, CHESTER ALAN 2:218–219 *bibliog., illus.*
Republican party **16**:173
ARTHUR AND ARTHURIAN LEGEND 2:219 *bibliog., illus.*
Breton literature **3**:475
Brut **3**:528
Camelot **4**:54
Chrétien de Troyes **4**:410
fata morgana **8**:34
Galahad, Sir **9**:9–10
Gawain, Sir **9**:63
Geoffrey of Monmouth **9**:98
German literature **9**:132
Grail, Holy **9**:281
Guinevere **9**:400
Hartmann von Aue **10**:63
Idylls of the King **11**:32
Lancelot, Sir **12**:178
Layamon **12**:252
Malory, Sir Thomas **13**:93
Merlin **13**:311
Morte Darthur **13**:591
Parsifal **15**:98
Sir Gawain and the Green Knight **17**:327
tapestry **19**:32 *illus.*
Tristan and Isolde **19**:303
Welsh literature **20**:101
ARTHUR KILL
map (40° 30′N 74° 15′W) **14**:129
ARTIBONITE RIVER
map (19° 15′N 72° 47′W) **10**:15
ARTICHOKE 2:219–220 *illus.*; **19**:532 *illus.*
ARTICLES OF CONFEDERATION 2:220 *bibliog.*
American Revolution **1**:365
Continental Congress **5**:228
genesis of the Constitution **5**:212–213
origins of the Civil War **5**:15
United States, history of the **19**:441
ARTICLES OF RELIGION 2:220
Thirty-nine Articles **19**:170
ARTICLES OF WAR *see* MILITARY JUSTICE
ARTIFICIAL INSEMINATION 2:220–221 *bibliog.*
cattle and cattle raising **4**:216–217
dairying **6**:9
eugenics **7**:264
human reproduction **2**:220–221
hybrid **10**:328
semen **17**:195
sperm **18**:179
ARTIFICIAL INTELLIGENCE 2:221–222 *bibliog.*
automata, theory of **2**:356–357
cognitive psychology **5**:95
cybernetics **5**:401
expert system **7**:334
programming, computer **15**:563
robot **16**:246
ARTIFICIAL LIMBS 2:222 *bibliog., illus.*
bionics **3**:274–275
prosthetics **15**:573
ARTIFICIAL ORGANS 2:222 *bibliog.*
heart, artificial **10**:94–95
kidney, artificial **12**:71
pacemaker, artificial **15**:4
prosthetics **15**:573
ARTIFICIAL RESPIRATION *see* CARDIOPULMONARY RESUSCITATION; FIRST AID
ARTIGAS (Uruguay)
map (30° 24′S 56° 28′W) **19**:488
ARTIGAS, JOSÉ GERVASIO 2:222 *bibliog.*
ARTILLERY 2:222–224 *bibliog., illus.*
See also FIREARMS
ammunition **1**:373–375 *illus.*
ballistics **3**:49–51
bazooka **3**:135
cannon **4**:111–112
catapult **4**:200
chemical and biological warfare **4**:313
howitzer **10**:285
mortar **13**:591
naval vessels **14**:55–56
stability, ballistics **3**:51
weapons **20**:75
World War I **20**:247 *illus.*
ARTILLERY PLANT (botany) 2:224
ARTIODACTYL 2:224 *bibliog.*
bovid **3**:426
mammal **13**:105–106 *illus.*
perissodactyl **15**:171
ARTOIS (France) 2:224
World War I **20**:229
ARTS, EDUCATION IN THE 2:224–225 *bibliog.*
Stuck, Franz von **18**:307
ARTS AND CRAFTS MOVEMENT 2:225 *bibliog., illus.*
Art Nouveau **2**:209
book **3**:385
Crane, Walter **5**:331
English art and architecture **7**:187
furniture **8**:378–379
gold and silver work **9**:230
jewelry **11**:411
Morris, William **13**:588–589
Tiffany, Louis Comfort **19**:196
Wiener Werkstätte **20**:146
ARUA (Uganda)
map (3° 1′N 30° 55′E) **19**:372
ARUBA 2:225–226 *bibliog.*
ARUGOLA *see* ROQUETTE
ARUM 2:226 *illus.*
Arales **2**:108
calla **4**:40
Dieffenbachia **6**:161
jack-in-the-pulpit **11**:341
monstera **13**:544
philodendron **15**:240
skunk cabbage **17**:346
taro **19**:37–38
ARUNACHAL PRADESH TERRITORY
map (28° 30′N 95° 0′E) **11**:80
ARUNDEL, 4th EARL OF (1346–1397)
Richard II, King of England **16**:210
ARUNTA *see* ARANDA
ARUNTA DESERT *see* SIMPSON DESERT
ARUSHA (Tanzania)
map (3° 22′S 36° 41′E) **19**:27
ARUSHA DECLARATION
Tanzania **19**:26
ARVADA (Colorado)
map (39° 50′N 105° 5′W) **5**:116
ARVIN (California)
map (35° 12′N 118° 50′W) **4**:31
ARX, WILLIAM S. VON *see* VON ARX, WILLIAM S.
ARYAN 2:226 *bibliog.*
Asia, history of **2**:250
India, history of **11**:88–89
Indus civilization **11**:154
racism **16**:37
slavery **17**:352
ARYAN LANGUAGES *see* INDO-IRANIAN LANGUAGES
ARYL GROUP 2:226
ARZHAK, NIKOLAY *see* DANIEL, YULI
AS I LAY DYING (book) 2:226
AS YOU LIKE IT (play) 2:226 *bibliog.*
ASADABAD (Afghanistan)
map (34° 52′N 71° 9′E) **1**:133
ASAHI, MOUNT
map (43° 40′N 142° 51′E) **11**:361
ASAHIKAWA (Japan)
map (43° 46′N 142° 22′E) **11**:361
ASAM BROTHERS 2:226–227 *bibliog.*
Moosbrugger, Caspar **13**:571
ASANSOL (India)
map (23° 41′N 86° 59′E) **11**:80
ASBESTOS 2:227 *bibliog.*
cancer **4**:103
dust, atmospheric **6**:308
pollutants, chemical **15**:410
serpentine **17**:210
ASBESTOS (Quebec)
map (45° 46′N 71° 57′W) **16**:18
ASBJØRNSEN, PETER CHRISTEN 2:227
ASBURY, FRANCIS 2:227 *bibliog.*
ASBURY PARK (New Jersey)
map (40° 13′N 74° 1′W) **14**:129
ASCANIAN FAMILY
Saxony **17**:105
ASCARIASIS 2:227
trichinosis **19**:296
worm **20**:283 *illus.*
ASCENSION (county in Louisiana)
map (30° 14′N 90° 53′W) **12**:430
ASCENSION OF CHRIST 2:227; **13**:450 *illus.*
ASCENSION DAY AT VENICE (Canaletto) **4**:98 *illus.*
ASCENSION ISLAND 2:227
ASCETICISM 2:228 *bibliog.*
celibacy **4**:231
fakir **8**:11
fasting **8**:33
Jainism **11**:349–350
monasticism **13**:521
Simeon Stylites, Saint **17**:314
ASCH, SHOLEM 2:228 *bibliog.*
ASCH, SOLOMON
conformity **5**:179
ASCHAFFENBURG (Germany, East and West)
map (49° 59′N 9° 9′E) **9**:140
ASCHAM, ROGER 2:228 *bibliog.*
ASCHELMINTHES *see* NEMATODE
ASCHERSLEBEN (Germany, East and West)
map (51° 45′N 11° 27′E) **9**:140
ASCHHEIM, S.
zoology **20**:377
ASCHHEIM-ZONDEK TEST *see* PREGNANCY TEST
ASCIDIAN *see* SEA SQUIRT
ASCLEPIUS (mythology) 2:228
Epidaurus **7**:218
Messene **13**:323
ASCOLI PICENO (Italy)
map (42° 51′N 13° 34′E) **11**:321
ASCON **18**:193 *illus.*
ASCORBIC ACID (Vitamin C) 2:228
cold, common **5**:97
Haworth, Sir Walter Norman **10**:78
jujube **11**:465
lind, james
medicine **13**:270
megavitamin therapy **13**:280
methemoglobinemia **13**:343
Pauling, Linus Carl **15**:119
scurvy **17**:167
speedwell **18**:176
Szent-Györgyi, Albert von **18**:416
vitamins and minerals **19**:620
Recommended Dietary Allowances **19**:618 *table*
ASEAN 2:228
Abdul Rahman, Tunku **1**:54
ASENOVGRAD (Bulgaria)
map (42° 1′N 24° 52′E) **3**:555
ASEPSIS
surgery **18**:361
ASEPTIC CONTAINERS
aluminum **1**:319
ASEXUAL REPRODUCTION *see* REPRODUCTION
ASGARD 2:228
ÁSGRIMSSON, EYSTEINN
Icelandic literature **11**:19
ASH
volcano **19**:627
ASH (botany) 2:228–229 *illus.*
See also PRICKLY ASH (botany)
lumber **12**:457 *illus.*
wood **20**:205 *illus.*
ASH FLAT (Arkansas)
map (36° 14′N 91° 37′W) **2**:166
ASH FORK (Arizona)
map (35° 13′N 112° 29′W) **2**:160
ASH WEDNESDAY 2:229
ASHANTI 2:229 *bibliog.*
African slave trade **1**:154
ancient kingdom **1**:151 *map*
Fanti **8**:21
ASHBEE, CHARLES ROBERT
gold and silver work **9**:230
ASHBERY, JOHN 2:229 *bibliog.*
ASHBURN (Georgia)
map (31° 43′N 83° 39′W) **9**:114
ASHBURTON (New Zealand)
map (43° 55′S 171° 45′E) **14**:158
ASHBURTON RIVER
map (21° 40′S 114° 56′E) **2**:328
ASHBURTON-WEBSTER TREATY *see* WEBSTER-ASHBURTON TREATY
ASHCAN SCHOOL (art group) 2:229–230 *bibliog., illus.*
American art and architecture **1**:335
Armory Show **2**:177
Bellows, George **3**:191–192
Bishop, Isabel **3**:297
Davies, Arthur B. **6**:49
Glackens, William **9**:195
Henri, Robert **10**:122
Luks, George **12**:454
Shinn, Everett **17**:262
Sloan, John **17**:362
ASHCROFT (British Columbia)
map (50° 43′N 121° 17′W) **3**:491
ASHCROFT, DAME PEGGY 2:230 *bibliog.*
ASHDOD (Israel)
map (31° 49′N 34° 40′E) **11**:302
ASHDOWN (Arkansas)
map (33° 41′N 94° 8′W) **2**:166
ASHE (county in North Carolina)
map (36° 30′N 81° 30′W) **14**:242
ASHE, ARTHUR 2:230 *bibliog., illus.*
ASHE, GORDON (pseudonym) *see* CREASEY, JOHN
ASHEBORO (North Carolina)
map (35° 42′N 79° 49′W) **14**:242
ASHER, JUDAH LOEB BEN *see* GORDON, JUDAH LEIB
ASHEVILLE (North Carolina) 2:230
map (35° 34′N 82° 33′W) **14**:242
ASHI 2:230
ASHIKAGA *see* MUROMACHI
ASHIKAGA TAKAUJI **11**:368 *illus.*
ASHIKAGA YOSHIAKI
Nobunaga **14**:211–212
ASHKELON (Ashqelon) (Israel)
map (31° 40′N 34° 35′E) **11**:302
ASHKENAZI, VLADIMIR 2:230
ASHKENAZIM 2:230–231 *bibliog.*
Hertz, Joseph Herman **10**:149
ASHKHABAD (USSR) 2:231
map (37° 57′N 58° 23′E) **19**:388
ASHLAND (Alabama)
map (33° 16′N 85° 50′W) **1**:234
ASHLAND (Illinois)
map (34° 53′N 90° 1′W) **11**:42

ASHLAND (Kansas)
map (37° 11′N 99° 46′W) **12**:18
ASHLAND (Kentucky)
map (38° 28′N 82° 38′W) **12**:47
ASHLAND (Massachusetts)
map (42° 16′N 71° 28′W) **3**:409
ASHLAND (Mississippi)
map (34° 50′N 89° 11′W) **13**:469
ASHLAND (Montana)
map (45° 35′N 106° 16′W) **13**:547
ASHLAND (Nebraska)
map (41° 3′N 96° 22′W) **14**:70
ASHLAND (New Hampshire)
map (43° 42′N 71° 38′W) **14**:123
ASHLAND (Ohio)
map (40° 52′N 82° 19′W) **14**:357
ASHLAND (county in Ohio)
map (40° 52′N 82° 19′W) **14**:357
ASHLAND (Oregon)
map (42° 12′N 122° 42′W) **14**:427
ASHLAND (Virginia)
map (37° 45′N 77° 29′W) **19**:607
ASHLAND (Wisconsin)
map (46° 35′N 90° 53′W) **20**:185
ASHLAND (county in Wisconsin)
map (46° 15′N 90° 43′W) **20**:185
ASHLAND, MOUNT
map (42° 5′N 122° 43′W) **14**:427
ASHLAND CITY (Tennessee)
map (36° 16′N 87° 4′W) **19**:104
ASHLAR
stonemasonry **18**:283
ASHLEY (county in Arkansas)
map (33° 10′N 91° 50′W) **2**:166
ASHLEY (Illinois)
map (38° 20′N 89° 11′W) **11**:42
ASHLEY (Michigan)
map (43° 11′N 84° 29′W) **13**:377
ASHLEY (North Dakota)
map (46° 2′N 99° 22′W) **14**:248
ASHLEY (Ohio)
map (40° 25′N 82° 57′W) **14**:357
ASHLEY, WILLIAM HENRY **2**:231 *bibliog.*
fur trade **8**:371
ASHLEY RIVER
map (32° 44′N 79° 57′W) **18**:98
ASHMOLEAN MUSEUM
Evans, Sir Arthur **7**:312
Oxford, University of **14**:474
ASHMORE REEF
map (12° 14′S 123° 5′E) **2**:328
ASHQELON (Ashkelon) (Israel)
map (31° 40′N 34° 35′E) **11**:302
ASHTABULA (Ohio)
map (41° 52′N 80° 48′W) **14**:357
ASHTABULA (county in Ohio)
map (41° 44′N 80° 46′W) **14**:357
ASHTABULA, LAKE
map (47° 11′N 97° 58′W) **14**:248
ASHTON (Idaho)
map (44° 4′N 111° 27′W) **11**:26
ASHTON (Illinois)
map (41° 52′N 89° 13′W) **11**:42
ASHTON (Iowa)
map (43° 19′N 95° 47′W) **11**:244
ASHTON, SIR FREDERICK **2**:231 *bibliog., illus.*
Fonteyn, Dame Margot **8**:207
Royal Ballet, The **16**:329
ASHTON-WARNER, SYLVIA **2**:231
ASHUANIPI LAKE
map (52° 35′N 66° 10′W) **14**:166
ASHUELOT RIVER
map (42° 46′N 72° 29′W) **14**:123
ASHURBANIPAL, KING OF ASSYRIA **2**:231–232 *bibliog.*; **13**:400 *illus.*
Nineveh **14**:199 *illus.*; **14**:200
ASHURNASIRPAL II, KING OF ASSYRIA **2**:232 *bibliog.*
Nimrud **14**:199
palace hunting relief **13**:320 *illus.*
ASHVILLE (Alabama)
map (33° 50′N 86° 15′W) **1**:234
ASHVILLE (Ohio)
map (39° 43′N 82° 57′W) **14**:357
ASIA **2**:232–248 *bibliog., illus., maps, table*
See also names of specific countries, e.g., BURMA; KOREA; etc.
agriculture **2**:245–247 *illus., map*; **2**:248
rice **16**:207
animal life **2**:239
art
See also art of specific countries, e.g., INDIAN ART AND ARCHITECTURE; JAPANESE ART AND ARCHITECTURE; etc.
Fenollosa, Ernest Francisco **8**:50–51
Freer, Charles Lang **8**:300
Lamaist art and architecture **12**:172–173
rugs and carpets **16**:342–343
San Francisco art museums **17**:54
Southeast Asian art and architecture **18**:107–110
climate **2**:236–238 *map, table*
monsoon **13**:543–544
weather variation and extremes **20**:80–81 *tables*
demography **2**:243–244 *map*; **2**:245 *map*; **2**:248
economic development **2**:244–248 *illus., map*
education **2**:242–243
literacy and illiteracy **12**:368
South Asian universities **18**:96 *table*
Southeast Asian universities **18**:111–112 *table*
exploration *see* EXPLORATION—Asia
food supply **2**:248
geologic time
Ordovician Period **14**:421 *map*
Permian Period **15**:175 *map*
Precambrian rock formations **15**:492 *map*
Silurian Period **17**:311
Tertiary Period **19**:123 *map*
geology **2**:236 *map*
health **2**:242–243
trachoma **19**:258
history *see* ASIA, HISTORY OF
languages **2**:242; **2**:244 *map*
Afroasiatic languages **1**:178–181
Arabic language **2**:100
Armenian language **2**:173
Baltic languages **3**:54–55
Caucasian language and literature **4**:218
Dravidian languages **6**:263
Indo-Iranian languages **11**:145–146
Japanese language **11**:379
Korean language **12**:118
Malayo-Polynesian languages **13**:82–84
Sino-Tibetan languages **17**:324–325
Slavic languages **17**:357–358
Southeast Asian languages **18**:110–111
Ural-Altaic languages **19**:474–476
manufacturing **2**:246–248 *illus.*
chemical industry **4**:319
silk **17**:307–308
migration to the United States **11**:55 *map*
music, non-Western **13**:667–668
national parks **14**:41–42 *map, table*
people **2**:240–244 *illus., map*; **2**:245 *map*
Ainu **1**:203
Alorese **1**:308
Ambonese **1**:325
Andamanese **1**:400
Aryan **2**:226
Badaga **3**:18
Bakhtiari **3**:28–29
Balinese **3**:37
Baluch **3**:57
Batak **3**:121
Bhil **3**:234
Bisayan **3**:297
Bugis **3**:548
Burmese **3**:575–576
Buryat **3**:583
Chukchi **4**:422
Dayak **6**:56
Doukhobors **6**:249
Garo **9**:50
Gond **9**:243
Gurkha **9**:406
Ho **10**:190
Hui **10**:295
Igorot **11**:38
Javanese **11**:386
Kafir **12**:5
Kalmyk **12**:8
Karakalpak **12**:26
Kazakh **12**:33
Khalkhas **12**:65
Khamseh **12**:65
Khants **12**:65
Khasi **12**:66
Khazars **12**:66
Khmer **12**:66–67
Khond **12**:68
Kirghiz **12**:87–88
Kurds **12**:139
Lao **12**:201–202
Lushai **12**:467
Malays **13**:84
Maratha **13**:143
Meo **13**:303
Minangkabau **13**:436–437
Mon **13**:515
Mongols **13**:530
Montagnards **13**:544
Mundari **13**:640
Naga (people) **14**:6
Nivkh **14**:204
Oraon **14**:416
Pahari **15**:14
Pathan **15**:111
Qashqai **16**:3
race **16**:33–35 *illus., map*
Rajput **16**:78
Santal **17**:68–69
Sherpa **17**:259
Sinhalese **17**:322–323
Tadzhik **19**:7
Tamil **19**:19
Tasaday **19**:41
Tatar **19**:43–44
Thai **19**:138
Tungus **19**:334
Turkmen **19**:347
Turks **19**:347–349
Tuvan **19**:356
Uighur **19**:374–375
Untouchables **19**:470–471
Uzbek **19**:499
women in society **20**:204 *table*
Yakut **20**:314
physical features
Altai Mountains **1**:311
Everest, Mount **7**:315
Gobi **9**:216–217 *illus., map*
Himalayas **10**:166–167 *illus., map*
Hindu Kush **10**:169
Karakoram Range **12**:27
Kunlun Mountains **12**:137
mountains, highest **13**:620 *table*
Pamirs **15**:53
Tien Shan **19**:195
topography **2**:233–236 *illus., map*
regions
Anatolia **1**:394–395 *map*
Bactria **3**:18
Central Asia **4**:253
Far East **8**:21
Southeast Asia **18**:107
Turkistan **19**:347
religions **2**:242
Buddhism **3**:539–543 *illus.*
Confucianism **5**:179–180 *illus.*
Hinduism **10**:169–173 *illus.*
Islam **11**:288–293 *illus.*
Shinto **17**:262–263 *illus.*
Taoism **19**:28–29 *illus.*
Zoroastrianism **20**:379–380 *illus.*
resources **2**:233–235
arable land resources **2**:239
electrical production **15**:485 *table*
energy consumption and production **7**:174 *table*
energy and power generation **2**:247
forest and fish resources **2**:239–240
gas reserves **15**:209 *table*
mineral resources and mining **2**:239; **2**:245; **2**:247 *map*
petroleum industry **15**:210 *table*
water resources **2**:239; **20**:51 *table*
rivers, lakes, and waterways **2**:238–239
Amur River **1**:386
Brahmaputra River **3**:440
Ganges River **9**:36–37 *map*
Indus **11**:152 *map*
Irrawaddy River **11**:280
Mekong River **13**:284 *map*
social unrest **2**:248
soils **2**:239
Third World **19**:170
trade **2**:248
transportation and communication **2**:247–248
truck and bus registration **19**:315 *table*
vegetation **2**:238 *map*; **2**:239
ASIA, HISTORY OF **2**:249–260 *bibliog., illus., maps*
See also CHINA, HISTORY OF; INDIA, HISTORY OF; JAPAN, HISTORY OF; KOREA, HISTORY OF; MIDDLE EAST, HISTORY OF THE; etc.; the subheading history under names of specific countries and areas, e.g., BURMA; PALESTINE; etc.
Annam **2**:31
British Empire **3**:495–496
Buddhism **3**:539–543
colonialism **5**:112
Confucianism **5**:179–180
French Empire **8**:309–310
Hinduism **10**:169–173
Islam **11**:288–293
refugee **16**:125
Shinto **17**:262–263
spice trade **18**:180–181
Taoism **19**:28–29
Tonkin (Vietnam) **19**:234
Turks **19**:347–348
Zoroastrianism **20**:379–380
prior to 300 AD **2**:249–254
See also CHINESE ARCHAEOLOGY; INDUS CIVILIZATION; MESOPOTAMIA; PERSIA, ANCIENT
Fertile Crescent **8**:60
Media **13**:263–264
300–1500 **2**:254–256
c. 1294 **2**:255 *map*
Champa **4**:276
c.8th century **2**:254 *map*
Khmer Empire **12**:67
Majapahit Empire **13**:76
Merv **13**:313
Mongols **13**:530 *map*
Srivijaya Empire **18**:207
1500–1900 **2**:257–259
Ottoman Empire **14**:464–466
1900-present **2**:259–260
c. 1900 **2**:257 *map*
Colombo Plan **5**:109
communism **5**:148–150
Indochina **11**:146
Korean War **12**:119–122
recent developments **2**:248
Russo-Japanese War **16**:373
Sino-Japanese Wars **17**:323
Vietnam War **19**:585–591
World War II **20**:248–281
ASIA MINOR *see* ANATOLIA
ASIAN AMERICANS *see* ORIENTAL AMERICANS
ASIAN ELEPHANT *see* INDIAN ELEPHANT
ASIDE (literature)
narrative and dramatic devices **14**:22
ASIMOV, ISAAC **2**:260 *bibliog., illus.*
ASINARA, GULF OF
map (41° 0′N 8° 30′E) **11**:321
ASIR (region in Saudi Arabia)
map (19° 0′N 42° 0′E) **17**:94
ASIR, CAPE **2**:261
map (11° 48′N 51° 22′E) **18**:60
ASITY **2**:261 *bibliog.*
ASL *see* AMERICAN SIGN LANGUAGE
ASMARA (Ethiopia) **2**:261
map (15° 20′N 38° 53′E) **7**:253
ASNEN LAKE
map (56° 38′N 14° 42′E) **18**:382
ASOKA, EMPEROR OF INDIA **2**:261 *bibliog.*
Asia, history of **2**:251
Buddhism **3**:540
India, history of **11**:89
Maurya (dynasty) **13**:238
Sanchi **17**:58
Sarnath **17**:78
temple **19**:97
ASOTIN (Washington)
map (46° 20′N 117° 3′W) **20**:35
ASOTIN (county in Washington)
map (46° 10′N 117° 12′W) **20**:35
ASP **2**:261 *bibliog.*
ASPARAGINE
Vauquelin, Louis Nicolas **19**:529
ASPARAGUS **2**:261 *illus.*; **19**:533 *illus.*
ASPARAGUS FERN **2**:261–262 *illus.*; **10**:275 *illus.*
ASPARTAME
sugar **18**:327
ASPCA *see* SOCIETY FOR THE PREVENTION OF CRUELTY TO ANIMALS
ASPDIN, JOSEPH
cement and concrete **4**:243
ASPEN (botany) **2**:262 *illus.*
poplar **15**:431
ASPEN (Colorado) **2**:262
map (39° 11′N 106° 49′W) **5**:116
ski slopes **5**:117 *illus.*
ASPEN BUTTE
map (42° 19′N 122° 5′W) **14**:427
ASPERGILLOSIS **2**:262
diseases, animal **6**:192
fungus diseases **8**:369
ASPERMONT (Texas)
map (33° 8′N 100° 14′W) **19**:129
ASPHALT *see* TAR, PITCH, AND ASPHALT

ASPHYXIA 2:262
suffocation **18**:325
ASPIDISTRA 2:262
ASPIRIN 2:262–263 *bibliog.*
acetaminophen **1**:79
analgesic **1**:388
deafness **6**:67
inflammation **11**:169
psychotropic drugs **15**:605
Reye's syndrome **16**:190
ASPIRING, MOUNT
map (44° 23′S 168° 44′E) **14**:158
ASPLUND, ERIK GUNNAR 2:263 *bibliog.*
ASQUITH, HERBERT HENRY, 1ST EARL OF OXFORD AND ASQUITH 2:263 *bibliog., illus.*
Liberal parties **12**:311
ASS 2:263 *bibliog., illus.*
donkey **6**:238
horse **10**:245
kiang **12**:69–70
mule **13**:636
perissodactyl **15**:171
steppe life **18**:257 *illus.*
ASSABET RIVER
map (42° 28′N 71° 21′W) **3**:409
ASSAD, HAFEZ AL- 2:264 *bibliog.*
Syria **18**:413; **18**:414
ASSAL, LAKE
map (11° 41′N 42° 25′E) **6**:208
ASSAM (India) 2:264
Garo **9**:50
Indo-Iranian languages **11**:145
map (26° 0′N 92° 0′E) **11**:80
ASSAM RUBBER
fig **8**:75
ASSASSIN BUG 2:264 *illus.*
ASSASSINS 2:264 *bibliog.*
Ismailis **11**:298
ASSAULT AND BATTERY 2:264
tort **19**:245
ASSAWOMPSET POND
map (41° 50′N 70° 55′W) **13**:206
ASSAY OF ORES 2:264 *bibliog.*
ore deposits **14**:422
ASSEMBLAGE (art)
See also COLLAGE
Cornell, Joseph **5**:268
Dine, Jim **6**:178
Kaprow, Allan **12**:25
Kienholz, Edward **12**:74–75
Marisol **13**:157
Nevelson, Louise **14**:115
Paolozzi, Eduardo **15**:62
Rauschenberg, Robert **16**:94
Samaras, Lucas **17**:45
surrealism **18**:365
ASSEMBLIES OF GOD
Pentecostalism **15**:155
ASSEMBLY LINE 2:264–265 *bibliog.*
automotive industry **2**:363–366 *illus.*; **13**:381; **19**:67 *illus.*; **19**:432 *illus.*
computerized robots **19**:68 *illus.*
clothing industry **5**:65
Ford (family) **8**:220–221
industrial management **11**:156
manufacturing **13**:133
mass production **13**:204
Model T **13**:490
ASSEN (Netherlands)
map (52° 59′N 6° 34′E) **14**:99
ASSER (Welsh monk)
Offa's Dyke **14**:353
ASSESSMENT (evaluation)
technology **19**:60–61
ASSESSMENT (tax) 2:265
ASSESSMENT, EDUCATIONAL *see* EDUCATIONAL MEASUREMENT
ASSETS *see* BOOKKEEPING
ASSIGNMENT 2:265
ASSINIBOIA (Saskatchewan)
map (49° 38′N 105° 59′W) **17**:81
ASSINIBOIN (American Indians) 2:265 *bibliog.*
ASSINIBOINE, MOUNT
map (50° 52′N 115° 38′W) **1**:256
ASSINIBOINE RIVER 2:265
map (49° 53′N 97° 8′W) **13**:119
ASSISI (Italy) 2:265
Cimabue **4**:430
Francis of Assisi, Saint **8**:274
Giotto di Bondone **9**:187
ASSIZE COURT
development of common law **5**:139
ASSOCIATED PRESS (AP)
press agencies and syndicates **15**:533
ASSOCIATED UNIVERSITIES, INC.
National Radio Astronomy Observatory **14**:45
ASSOCIATION, CHEMICAL
buffer **3**:547
chemical symbolism and notation **4**:322
ASSOCIATION OF AMERICAN GEOGRAPHERS
Davis, William Morris **6**:53
geographical societies **9**:100
ASSOCIATION CANADIENNE DES BIBLIOTHÈQUES *see* CANADIAN LIBRARY ASSOCIATION
ASSOCIATION FOOTBALL *see* SOCCER
ASSOCIATION OF SOUTHEAST ASIAN NATIONS *see* ASEAN
ASSOCIATION FOR THE ADVANCEMENT OF PSYCHOANALYSIS
Horney, Karen **10**:239
ASSOCIATION OF UNIVERSITIES FOR RESEARCH IN ASTRONOMY
Kitt Peak National Observatory **12**:93
ASSOCIATIONISM 2:265–266 *bibliog.*
Enlightenment **7**:207
Freud, Sigmund **8**:329
motivation **13**:610
psychology, history of **15**:596
ASSOCIATIVE LAW 2:266
algebra **1**:284
arithmetic **2**:158
group theory **9**:377
ASSONANCE
versification **19**:452
ASSUMPTION (Illinois)
map (39° 31′N 89° 3′W) **11**:42
ASSUMPTION (county in Louisiana)
map (29° 53′N 91° 5′W) **12**:430
ASSUMPTION OF MARY 2:266
Mary **13**:184–185
Pius XII, Pope **15**:324
ASSURBANIPAL *see* ASHURBANIPAL, KING OF ASSYRIA
ASSURNASIRPAL II *see* ASHURNASIRPAL II, KING OF ASSYRIA
ASSYRIA 2:266 *bibliog., map*; **3**:8 *map*
Asia, history of **2**:250
building construction **19**:63 *illus.*
cities
Khorsabad **12**:68
Kültepe **12**:136
Nimrud **14**:199
Nineveh **14**:199–200
Urartu **19**:479
cuneiform **5**:389 *illus.*
Cyaxares, King of Media **5**:400
Egypt, ancient **7**:83
Fertile Crescent **8**:60
kings
Ashurbanipal, King **2**:231–232
Ashurnasirpal II, King **2**:232
Esarhaddon, King **7**:236
Sargon II, King **17**:78
Sennacherib, King **17**:203
Shalmaneser III, King **17**:238
Tiglath-Pileser III, King **19**:197
Mesopotamia **13**:316
Mesopotamian art and architecture **13**:317–322 *illus.*
Mitanni **13**:482
Rawlinson, Sir Henry Creswicke **16**:95–96
Smith, George **17**:368
ASSYRIAN CHURCH *see* NESTORIAN CHURCH
ASTADHYAYI (Eight Books) *see* PANINI
ASTAIRE, FRED 2:267 *bibliog., illus.*; **8**:85 *illus.*
ASTARTE 2:267
See also ISHTAR
ASTATINE 2:267 *bibliog.*
element **7**:130 *table*
Group VIIA periodic table **15**:167
halogens **10**:25
ASTER 2:267–268 *bibliog., illus.*
ageratum **1**:184
ASTEROID 2:268
Baade, Walter **3**:4
Ceres (astronomy) **4**:260
Chiron (astronomy) **4**:397
dinosaur **6**:182
Eros (astronomy) **7**:232
Kowal, Charles T. **12**:126
libration **12**:319
meteor and meteorite **13**:337
Moon **13**:563
Olbers, Heinrich **14**:373
Pallas **2**:268
Phobos **15**:249
planets **15**:329
solar system **18**:50–57 *illus.*
Trojans **19**:305
Wolf, Max **20**:196
ASTHMA 2:268 *bibliog.*
allergy **2**:268
bronchodilators **3**:503
fungus diseases **8**:369
immunity **11**:57
jimsonweed **11**:419
types **2**:268
ASTI (Italy)
map (44° 54′N 8° 12′E) **11**:321
ASTIGMATISM
contact lens **5**:227
eye diseases **7**:350
ASTLEY, PHILIP 2:268
circus **4**:443–444
ASTON, FRANCIS WILLIAM 2:268
ASTOR (family) 2:268–269 *bibliog.*
American Fur Company **1**:340
Waldorf-Astoria (New York City) **10**:260 *illus.*
ASTOR, JOHN JACOB (1763–1848)
Astor (family) **2**:268–269
Michigan **13**:379 *illus.*
New York Public Library **14**:155
North West Company **14**:252
ASTOR, LADY 2:269 *bibliog., illus.*
ASTOR, MARY 2:269 *bibliog.*
ASTOR PLACE RIOT 2:269 *bibliog., illus.*
Buntline, Ned **3**:565
ASTORIA (Illinois)
map (40° 14′N 90° 21′W) **11**:42
ASTORIA (Oregon) 2:269
map (46° 11′N 123° 80′W) **14**:427
ASTOUNDING (periodical)
pulp magazines **15**:620
ASTRA (Argentina)
map (45° 44′S 67° 30′W) **2**:149
ASTRAKHAN (USSR) 2:269–270
climate **19**:390 *table*
map (46° 21′N 48° 3′E) **19**:388
ASTRINGENT 2:270
ASTROARCHAEOLOGY
archaeoastronomy **2**:114
ASTROBLEME
meteorite craters **13**:338–339
ASTROCHEMISTRY 2:270 *bibliog., table*
carbon cycle (astronomy) **4**:135–136
interstellar matter **11**:225–228
life, extraterrestrial **12**:328
proton-proton reaction **15**:578–579
ASTRODOME **18**:208–209 *illus.*
Houston (Texas) **10**:281 *map*
ASTRODYNAMICS
astronautics **2**:274
celestial mechanics **4**:230
ASTROGEOLOGY 2:270 *bibliog.*
Schmitt, Harrison H. **17**:128
ASTROLABE 2:270–271 *bibliog., illus.*
Danjon, André Louis **6**:33
navigation **14**:59
ASTROLABE, PRISMATIC 2:271
ASTROLOGY 2:271–273 *bibliog., illus.*
Aquarius **2**:93
Aries **2**:154
astrological chart **2**:272 *illus.*
astrology wheel **2**:271 *illus.*
astronomy, history of **2**:277
Cancer **4**:100
Capricornus **4**:128
constellation **5**:212
Gemini **9**:71
influence on alchemy **1**:263
Leo **12**:287
Libra **12**:314
Nostradamus **14**:266–267
Pisces **15**:317
Ptolemy **15**:606–607
Sagittarius **17**:12
Scorpius **17**:149
Taurus **19**:45
Virgo **19**:613
zodiac **20**:371
ASTROMETRY 2:273 *bibliog., illus.*
distance, astronomical **6**:198–200
Hubble's constant **10**:288
Hyades **10**:327
interferometer **11**:209–210
Kapteyn, Jacobus Cornelius **12**:26
radar astronomy **16**:40
research institutions
United States Naval Observatory **19**:464
Yerkes Observatory **20**:326–327
ASTRONAUT 2:274 *bibliog., illus.*
manned space program
Apollo program **2**:80–84
Apollo-Soyuz Test Project **2**:84
Gemini program **9**:71–73
Mercury program **13**:307–308
Skylab **17**:347–348
Spacelab **18**:138
Space Shuttle **18**:134–136
National Aeronautics and Space Administration **14**:28
space exploration **18**:119–132
space law **18**:132
space medicine **18**:132–134
life-support systems **12**:331–333
sensory deprivation **17**:205
space station **18**:136–137
training **18**:122 *illus.*
U.S. astronauts
Aldrin, Edwin E. **1**:269–270
Anders, William Alison **1**:401
Armstrong, Neil A. **2**:179–180
Bean, Alan **3**:140
Bluford, Guion S. **3**:346
Borman, Frank **3**:401
Brand, Vance **3**:453
Carpenter, Scott **4**:164
Carr, Gerald **4**:166
Cernan, Eugene **4**:260
Chaffee, Roger **4**:267
Collins, Michael **5**:104
Conrad, Pete **5**:198–199
Cooper, Leroy Gordon, Jr. **5**:244
Crippen, Robert **5**:350
Cunningham, R. Walter **5**:390
Duke, Charles, Jr. **6**:295
Eisele, Donn F. **7**:94
Evans, Ronald **7**:313
Garriot, Owen **9**:51
Gibson, Edward **9**:176
Glenn, John H., Jr. **9**:207
Gordon, Richard F., Jr. **9**:249
Grissom, Virgil I. **9**:367
Haise, Fred W. **10**:15
Irwin, James **11**:285
Jarvis, Gregory **11**:383
Kerwin, Joseph **12**:60
Lousma, Jack **12**:436
Lovell, James **12**:438
McAuliffe, Christa **13**:6
McDivitt, James **13**:11–12
McNair, Ronald E. **13**:35
Mattingly, Thomas **13**:232
Mitchell, Edgar D. **13**:482–483
Onizuka, Ellison **14**:391
Pogue, William Reid **15**:380
Resnik, Judith A. **16**:177
Ride, Sally **16**:216
Roosa, Stuart A. **16**:307
Schirra, Walter M., Jr. **17**:122
Schmitt, Harrison H. **17**:128
Schweickart, Russell L. **17**:139
Scobee, Francis R. **17**:147
Scott, David R. **17**:153
Shepard, Alan B., Jr. **17**:255–256
Slayton, D. K. **17**:359
Smith, Michael **17**:370
Stafford, Thomas P. **18**:209
Swigert, John L., Jr. **18**:390
Weitz, Paul J. **20**:96
White, Edward H., II **20**:135
Worden, Alfred M. **20**:216
Young, John W. **20**:333
ASTRONAUTICS 2:274–276 *bibliog., illus.*
astrodynamics **2**:274–275
escape velocity **7**:236–237
Goddard, Robert **9**:219–220
guidance and control systems **9**:393–394
Oberth, Hermann, founder **14**:315
orbital maneuvers **2**:274–275 *illus.*
professional and educational organizations
American Institute of Aeronautics and Astronautics **1**:341
satellite, artificial **17**:85
space exploration **18**:122
Tsiolkovsky, Konstantin **19**:324
ASTRONOMER ROYAL
Airy, Sir George Biddell **1**:228
Bradley, James **3**:437–438
Flamsteed, John **8**:151–152
Gill, Sir David **9**:181
Halley, Edmond **10**:22–23
Hamilton, Sir William Rowan **10**:29
Ryle, Sir Martin **16**:380
ASTRONOMICAL CATALOGS AND ATLASES 2:276 *bibliog.*
Astronomische Gesellschaft Katalog **2**:276
astronomy, history of **2**:280
astrophotography **2**:285
Cape Photographic Durchmusterung (Sir David Gill) **9**:181
Bonner Durchmusterung **3**:381
Cannon, Annie Jump **4**:112
carte du ciel
Paris Observatory **15**:88
Flamsteed, John **8**:151–152
Franklin-Adams Charts **2**:276
Gill, Sir David **9**:181
Gould, Benjamin Apthorp **9**:265
Grimaldi, Francesco Maria **9**:364

Henry Draper Catalogue **10**:123
Herschel, Sir John **10**:147
Herschel, Sir William **10**:147–148
Hipparchus **10**:173
infrared astronomy **11**:175
Janssen, Jules **11**:359
Lalande, Joseph Jérôme Le Français de **12**:171
Messier, Charles **13**:324
National Geographic Society—Palomar Observatory Sky Survey **2**:276
New General Catalogue of Nebulae and Clusters of Stars
Dreyer, J. L. E. **6**:271
Newcomb, Simon **14**:165
Piazzi, Giuseppe **15**:290
Schlesinger, Frank **17**:126
Struve, Friedrich Georg Wilhelm von **18**:304
Uhuru catalogs **19**:374
Yale Catalog of Bright Stars **2**:276
ASTRONOMICAL INSTRUMENTATION
aperture synthesis **2**:76
armillary sphere **2**:173
astrolabe **2**:270–271
astrolabe, prismatic **2**:271
astrometry **2**:273
binoculars **3**:259–260
blink microscope **3**:333
bolometer **3**:371
coelostat **5**:92
compass, navigational **5**:155
coronagraph **5**:270–271
equatorium **7**:226
gamma-ray astronomy **9**:34
Graham, George **9**:279
inclinometer **11**:74
interferometer **11**:209–210
Jacob's staff **11**:346
micrometer **13**:385
navigation **14**:60–61
OAO **14**:312–313
observatory, astronomical **14**:317–319
OGO **14**:355
OSO **14**:456
pbs detector
infrared astronomy **11**:175
photographic zenith tube **15**:260
photometer, meridian
Pickering, Edward Charles **15**:293
planetarium **15**:328–329
quadrant **16**:4–5
radio astronomy **16**:50–53 *illus.*
remote sensing **16**:147–148
sextant **17**:227–228
spectroheliograph **18**:168
telescope **19**:80–83
Cassegrainian telescope **4**:183–184
coudé telescope **5**:308
Schmidt telescope **17**:128
Space Telescope **18**:137
transit circle **19**:273
ultraviolet-blue-visual (UBV) system
photometry, astronomical **15**:274
Voyager **19**:638
ASTRONOMICAL OBSERVATORY *see* OBSERVATORY, ASTRONOMICAL
ASTRONOMICAL UNIT **2**:276
distance, astronomical **6**:199
light-year **12**:336
Titius-Bode law **19**:213
ASTRONOMY, HISTORY OF **2**:276–281 *bibliog.*, *illus.*
Abell, George O. **1**:56
Adams, John Couch **1**:96
Adams, Walter Sydney **1**:98
Airy, Sir George Biddell **1**:228
Aitken, Robert Grant **1**:228
Ambartsumian, Viktor Amazaspovich **1**:324
Arago, François **2**:107
Argelander, Friedrich Wilhelm August **2**:146
Aristarchus of Samos **2**:155
Baade, Walter **3**:4
Babcock, Horace Welcome **3**:6
Baily, Francis **3**:26
Barnard, Edward Emerson **3**:85
Battani, al- **3**:125
Bessel, Friedrich **3**:228
Bode, Johann Elert **3**:355
Bok, Bart Jan **3**:363
Bond, William Cranch **3**:376
Bondi, Hermann **3**:376
Bowen, Ira Sprague **3**:428
Bradley, James **3**:437–438
Brahe, Tycho **3**:439–440
Brouwer, Dirk **3**:513
Campbell, William Wallace **4**:66
Cannon, Annie Jump **4**:112
Cassini (family) **4**:184
Chandrasekhar, Subrahmanyan **4**:280
Clark, Alvan Graham **5**:37
Copernicus, Nicolaus **5**:250
Curtis, Heber Doust **5**:395
Danjon, André Louis **6**:33
Darwin, Sir George Howard **6**:42
development
astronomy history of **2**:276–281
astrophysics **2**:279–280
big bang theory **3**:248
Copernican theory **2**:278
observatory, astronomical **14**:317–319
radio astronomy **16**:47
space exploration **18**:118–121
Dicke, Robert **6**:156
Digges, Thomas **6**:174
Douglass, Andrew Ellicott **6**:248
Draper, Henry **6**:262–263
Dreyer, J. L. E. **6**:271
Eddington, Sir Arthur **7**:55
Encke, Johann Franz **7**:162
Europe, history of **7**:287
Fabricius, David **8**:5
Fitz, Henry **8**:130
Flammarion, Camille **8**:151
Flamsteed, John **8**:151–152
Friedman, Herbert **8**:331
Galileo Galilei **9**:15
Galle, Johann Gottfried **9**:17
Gamow, George **9**:34
Gauss, Carl Friedrich **9**:61–62
Gill, Sir David **9**:181
Gold, Thomas **9**:228
Gould, Benjamin Apthorp **9**:265
Graham, George **9**:279
Hale, George Ellery **10**:18
Halley, Edmond **10**:22–23
Harriot, Thomas **10**:57
Hawking, Stephen William **10**:77
Heracleides Ponticus **10**:131
Herschel, Sir John **10**:147
Herschel, Sir William **10**:147–148
Hertzsprung, Ejnar **10**:149
Hewish, Antony **10**:154
Hipparchus **10**:173
Hoyle, Sir Fred **10**:286
Hubble, Edwin **10**:288
Huggins, Sir William **10**:292
Hulst, Hendrik Christoffell van de **10**:296
Humason, Milton La Salle **10**:300
Humboldt, Alexander von **10**:301
Huygens, Christiaan **10**:325
Jansky, Karl **11**:359
Janssen, Jules **11**:359
Jeans, Sir James **11**:390
Jeffreys, Sir Harold **11**:394
Kapteyn, Jacobus Cornelius **12**:25–26
Kepler, Johannes **12**:57–58
Kowal, Charles T. **12**:126
Kuiper, Gerard **12**:135
Lacaille, Nicolas Louis de **12**:158
Lalande, Joseph Jérôme Le Français de **12**:171
Landau, Lev **12**:181
Langley, Samuel Pierpont **12**:196
Laplace, Pierre Simon **12**:205
Lassell, William **12**:214
Leavitt, Henrietta Swan **12**:263–264
Lemaître, Georges Édouard **12**:280
Leverrier, Urbain Jean Joseph **12**:303
Lockyer, Sir Joseph Norman **12**:388
Lovell, Sir Bernard **12**:438
Lowell, Percival **12**:444
Lundmark, Knut **12**:462
Lyot, Bernard Ferdinand **12**:479
Mayer, Johann Tobias **13**:246
Mayr, Simon **13**:249
Menzel, Donald Howard **13**:303
Messier, Charles **13**:324
Meton **13**:345
Milne, Edward Arthur **13**:431
Mitchell, Maria **13**:483
Newcomb, Simon **14**:165
Newton, Sir Isaac **14**:173–175
Nostradamus **14**:266–267
Olbers, Heinrich **14**:373
Oort, Jan Hendrik **14**:396
Payne-Gaposchkin, Cecilia **15**:122
Peurbach, Georg von **15**:216
Piazzi, Giuseppe **15**:290
Picard, Jean **15**:290
Pickering, Edward Charles **15**:293
Pickering, William Henry **15**:293
Ptolemy **15**:606–607
Pythagoras of Samos **15**:639–640
Quételet, Lambert Adolphe **16**:23
Reber, Grote **16**:106
Regiomontanus **16**:129
Rheticus **16**:194
Rittenhouse, David **16**:229
Rømer, Ole **16**:304–305
Russell, Henry Norris **16**:350
Ryle, Sir Martin **16**:380
Sacrobosco, Johannes **17**:8
Sagan, Carl Edward **17**:11
Saha, Meghnad N. **17**:12–13
Schiaparelli, Giovanni Virginio **17**:120
Schlesinger, Frank **17**:125–126
Schmidt, Maarten **17**:128
Schwabe, Samuel Heinrich **17**:138
Schwarzschild, Karl **17**:139
Schwarzschild, Martin **17**:139
Shapley, Harlow **17**:241
Shklovsky, Iosif Samuilovich **17**:278
Sigüenza y Góngora, Carlos de **17**:302
Sitter, Willem de **17**:330
Slipher, Vesto Melvin **17**:362
Spitzer, Lyman, Jr. **18**:190–191
Strömgren, Bengt Georg Daniel **18**:302
Struve, Friedrich Georg Wilhelm von **18**:304
Struve, Otto **18**:304
Tombaugh, Clyde William **19**:231
Trumpler, Robert Julius **19**:320
van de Kamp, Peter **19**:512
Velikovsky, Immanuel **19**:537–538
Von Däniken, Erich **19**:633
Whipple, Fred Lawrence **20**:131
Wilson, Robert W., and Penzias, Arno A. **20**:165
Wolf, Max **20**:196
Wolf-Rayet stars **20**:197
Zwicky, Fritz **20**:384
ASTRONOMY AND ASTROPHYSICS **2**:281–285 *bibliog.*, *illus.*
See also ASTRONOMICAL INSTRUMENTATION
asteroid **2**:268
astronomical catalogs and atlases **2**:276
Astronomical Journal
Gould, Benjamin Apthorp **9**:265
astronomical unit **2**:276
astronomy, history of **2**:276–281
Astronomy and Astrophysics (periodical)
Hale, George Ellery **10**:18
astrophotography **2**:285
Astrophysical Journal
Hale, George Ellery **10**:18
big bang theory **3**:248
BL Lacertae objects **3**:303
black hole **3**:315–316
branches
archaeoastronomy **2**:114–115
astrochemistry **2**:270
astrogeology **2**:270
astrology **2**:271–273
astrometry **2**:273
astronautics **2**:274–276
astrophysics **2**:281
celestial mechanics **4**:230
cosmogony **5**:284
cosmology (astronomy) **5**:284–289
faint object detection **8**:8
gamma-ray astronomy **9**:33–34
geophysics **9**:108
infrared astronomy **11**:175
photometry, astronomical **15**:274
radar astronomy **16**:40
radio astronomy **2**:281; **16**:47–53
systemic astronomy, Hipparchus **10**:173
ultraviolet astronomy **19**:378
X-ray astronomy **20**:305–308
brown dwarf **3**:516
carbon cycle (astronomy) **4**:135–136
celestial sphere **4**:230
cluster, star **5**:72
clusters of galaxies **5**:72
color index **5**:114
comet **5**:133–134
conjunction **5**:191
constellation **5**:210–212
coordinate systems **5**:245–246
corona **5**:270
cosmic rays **5**:283–284
distance, astronomical **6**:198–200
Doppler effect **6**:240–241
Earth, motions of **7**:18–19
Earth, size and shape of **7**:19
Earth sciences **7**:24
eclipse **7**:40–41
ecliptic **7**:41
elevation **7**:136
ephemeris **7**:216
equinox **7**:226
extinction **7**:341
extragalactic systems **7**:341–346
Fraunhofer lines **8**:288–289
Galaxy, The **9**:10–13
geocentric world system **9**:95
globule **9**:209
gravitational collapse **9**:305
gravitational lens **9**:305–306
gravitational waves **9**:306
halo **10**:24
Harvard classification of stars **10**:64
Hayashi evolutionary track **10**:80
Hertzsprung-Russell diagram **10**:149–150
hour angle **10**:264
Hubble's constant **10**:288
interstellar matter **11**:225–228
interstellar reddening **11**:229
Julian day **11**:466
Kepler's laws **12**:58
libration **12**:319
life, extraterrestrial **12**:327–329
magnetic storm **13**:55
magnetosphere **13**:59–60
magnitude **13**:60–61
Mayan religion **13**:245
meteor and meteorite **13**:336–337
meteorite craters **13**:337–339
nebula **14**:74–75
new techniques **2**:281
occultation **14**:320
Olbers's paradox **14**:373
parsec **15**:98
period-luminosity relation **15**:166
perturbation **15**:191
planetary systems **15**:329
planets **15**:329
professional and educational organizations
American Astronomical Society **1**:337
Royal Astronomical Society **16**:329
quasar **16**:14–15
radiation pressure **16**:43
radio galaxies **16**:53–54
red shift **16**:114
Regiomontanus **16**:129
relativity **16**:132–137
research institutions
Lunar and Planetary Laboratory **12**:135
observatory, astronomical **14**:317–319
satellite **17**:84–85
Seyfert galaxies **17**:232–233
sidereal time **17**:294
sky **17**:346
solar system **18**:44–53
space exploration **18**:118–132
star **18**:220–225
stellar evolution **18**:250–252
stellar spectrum **18**:252
Sun **18**:340–345
three-body problem **19**:181
time (physics) **19**:201
two-body problem **19**:360
year **20**:320
zodiacal light **20**:371
ASTROPHOTOGRAPHY **2**:285 *bibliog.*
asteroid
Wolf, Max **20**:196
astronomical catalogs and atlases **2**:285
Barnard, Edward Emerson **3**:85
Draper, Henry **6**:262–263
faint object detection **8**:8
globule **9**:209
infrared astronomy **11**:175
interstellar matter **11**:226
Janssen, Jules **11**:359
Kitt Peak National Observatory **12**:93
Lyot, Bernard Ferdinand **12**:479
nebula **11**:227 *illus.*
Phobos **15**:249
Pickering, William Henry **15**:293
Schwarzschild, Karl **17**:139
Space Telescope **18**:137
star **18**:221–222
surveys
Anglo-Australian Telescope **1**:416
ASTROPHYSICS *see* ASTRONOMY AND ASTROPHYSICS
ASTROPHYSICS, HISTORY OF *see* ASTRONOMY, HISTORY OF
ASTURIAS (Spain) **2**:285
Oviedo (Spain) **14**:471
Spain, history of **18**:145
ASTURIAS, MIGUEL ÁNGEL **2**:285–286 *bibliog.*
ASUNCIÓN (Paraguay) **2**:286; **15**:77 *illus.*, *table*
map (25° 16′S 57° 40′W) **15**:77
ASUNCION MITA (Guatemala)
map (14° 20′N 89° 43′W) **9**:389
ASWAN (Egypt) **2**:286
climate **7**:77 *table*

ASWAN (cont.)
map (24° 5′N 32° 53′E) 7:76
obelisk **14**:315
ASWAN HIGH DAM **2**:286 *bibliog.*
Abu Simbel **1**:66–67
Edfu **7**:56
Egypt **7**:75
Nasser, Gamal Abdel **14**:25
Nasser, Lake **14**:25
Philae **15**:229
salvage archaeology **17**:40
ASYLUM *see* RIGHT OF ASYLUM
ASYMMETRY *see* SYMMETRY (physics)
ASYMPTOTE **2**:286 *illus.*
ASYUT (Egypt) **2**:286
map (27° 11′N 31° 11′E) **7**:76
ATACAMA DESERT **2**:286–287; **18**:89 *illus.*
map (24° 30′S 69° 15′W) **4**:355
ATAHUALPA **2**:287 *bibliog.*; **11**:70–71 *illus.*
Huayna Capac **10**:288
Inca **11**:73
Pizarro, Francisco **15**:324
ATAKORA RANGE
map (10° 30′N 1° 20′E) **3**:200
ATAKPAMÉ (Togo)
map (7° 32′N 1° 8′E) **19**:222
ATALANTA **2**:287
ATALAYA (Peru)
map (10° 44′S 73° 45′W) **15**:193
ATANASOFF, JOHN V. **2**:287
ATAR (Mauritania)
map (20° 31′N 13° 3′W) **13**:236
ATARAX
tranquilizer **19**:266
ATASCADERO (California)
map (35° 29′N 120° 40′W) **4**:31
ATASCOSA (county in Texas)
map (28° 55′N 98° 50′W) **19**:129
ATATÜRK, KEMAL **2**:287 *bibliog., illus.*
Chanak Crisis **4**:278
Turkey **19**:346
World War I **20**:231
ATAXIA **2**:287
ATBARA (Sudan)
map (17° 42′N 33° 59′E) **18**:320
ATBARA RIVER
map (17° 40′N 33° 56′E) **18**:320
Nile River **14**:196–197
ATCHAFALAYA BAY
map (29° 25′N 91° 20′W) **12**:430
ATCHAFALAYA RIVER
map (29° 53′N 91° 28′W) **12**:430
ATCHANA, TELL *see* ALALAKH
ATCHISON (Kansas) **2**:288
map (39° 34′N 95° 7′W) **12**:18
ATCHISON (county in Kansas)
map (39° 30′N 95° 15′W) **12**:18
ATCHISON (county in Missouri)
map (40° 25′N 95° 25′W) **13**:476
ATCHISON, TOPEKA, AND SANTA FE (railroad) **19**:268 *map*
ATELECTASIS
hyaline membrane disease **10**:327
ATELIER 17
Hayter, Stanley William **10**:84
ATEMOYA *see* CUSTARD APPLE
ATGET, EUGÈNE **2**:288 *bibliog., illus.*
photography, history and art of **15**:270–271; **15**:272
ATHABASCA (Alberta)
map (54° 43′N 113° 17′W) **1**:256
tar sands **19**:34
ATHABASCA, LAKE **2**:288
map (59° 7′N 110° 0′W) **17**:81
ATHABASCA RIVER **1**:257 *illus.*; **2**:288
map (58° 40′N 110° 50′W) **1**:256
ATHANASIAN CREED
creed **5**:337
ATHANASIUS, SAINT **2**:288 *bibliog.*
ATHAPASKAN TRIBES
Carrier Indians **4**:168
ATHEISM **2**:288–289 *bibliog.*
ATHELING, WILLIAM, JR. *see* BLISH, JAMES
ATHELSTAN, KING OF WESSEX **2**:289
ATHENA **2**:289; **4**:257 *illus.*
Medusa **13**:278
temple **19**:96 *illus.*
ATHENA (Oregon)
map (45° 49′N 118° 30′W) **14**:427
ATHENA ALEA, TEMPLE OF
Tegea **19**:72
ATHENA NIKE, TEMPLE OF
Acropolis **1**:84–85
Callicrates **4**:41
ATHENAGORAS **2**:289
ATHENS (Alabama)
map (34° 48′N 86° 58′W) **1**:234
ATHENS (Georgia) **2**:289
map (33° 57′N 83° 23′W) **9**:114
ATHENS (Greece) **2**:289–291 *bibliog., illus., map*; **9**:327 *illus.*
architecture
Acropolis **1**:84–85
Erechtheum **1**:85
Parthenon **9**:336 *illus.*
stoa **18**:273
climate **9**:324 *table*
Eleusis **7**:135
Greek art **9**:339
history **2**:290–291
Aeschines **1**:128
agora **9**:329 *illus.*
Alcibiades **1**:263
archons **2**:137
Areopagus **2**:145–146
Aristides **2**:155
Callias **4**:41
Callistratus **4**:46
Cecrops **4**:228
Cimon **4**:431
Cleisthenes **5**:48
Cleon **5**:50
Delian League **6**:92–93
Demosthenes **6**:104–105
Draco **6**:254
Europe, history of **7**:280
Greece, ancient **9**:331–333 *map*
Harmodius and Aristogiton **10**:51
Lycurgus **12**:474
Miltiades **13**:432
Olynthus **14**:385
Peisistratus **15**:134
Peloponnesian War **9**:333 *map*; **15**:139
Pericles **15**:165
Persian Wars **15**:188
Philip II, King of Macedonia **15**:233
Phocion **15**:249
Piraeus **15**:314
Solon **18**:57
Themistocles **19**:155
Theramenes **19**:160
Theseus **19**:167–168
Thrasybulus **19**:181
in 5th century **9**:332 *map*
map (37° 58′N 23° 43′E) **9**:325
Olympic Games **14**:382 *illus.*
subway **18**:318 *table*
ATHENS (Illinois)
map (39° 58′N 89° 44′W) **11**:42
ATHENS (Maine)
map (44° 55′N 69° 41′W) **13**:70
ATHENS (New York)
map (42° 16′N 73° 49′W) **14**:149
ATHENS (Ohio)
map (39° 20′N 82° 6′W) **14**:357
ATHENS (county in Ohio)
map (39° 20′N 82° 3′W) **14**:357
ATHENS (Pennsylvania)
map (41° 57′N 76° 31′W) **15**:147
ATHENS (Tennessee)
map (35° 27′N 84° 36′W) **19**:104
ATHENS (Texas)
map (32° 12′N 95° 51′W) **19**:129
ATHENS (Wisconsin)
map (45° 2′N 90° 5′W) **20**:185
ATHEROSCLEROSIS **2**:291–292 *bibliog., illus.*
arteriosclerosis **2**:213
cholesterol **4**:404
gastrointestinal tract disease **9**:57
hypertension **10**:349
stroke **18**:302
ATHERTON, GERTRUDE FRANKLIN **2**:292
ATHLETE OF THE DECADE
Nicklaus, Jack **14**:183
ATHLETE'S FOOT
skin diseases **17**:342
ATHLETICS
See also EXERCISE; specific athletic activities, e.g., HANDBALL; RUNNING AND JOGGING; etc.
Amateur Athletic Association **1**:322
Amateur Athletic Union of the United States **1**:322
Highland Games **10**:162
National Collegiate Athletic Association **14**:30
scholarships, fellowships, and loans **17**:131
turnverein **19**:351
ATHLONE (Ireland)
map (53° 25′N 7° 56′W) **11**:258
ATHODYD *see* RAMJET
ATHOL (Massachusetts)
map (42° 36′N 72° 14′W) **13**:206
ATHOS, MOUNT **2**:292
ATICO (Peru)
map (16° 14′S 73° 39′W) **15**:193
ATIKOKAN (Ontario)
map (48° 45′N 91° 37′W) **14**:393
ATIKONAK LAKE
map (52° 40′N 64° 30′W) **14**:166
ATITLÁN, LAKE **9**:389 *illus.*
map (14° 42′N 91° 12′W) **9**:389
ATKA (Alaska)
map (52° 12′N 174° 12′W) **1**:242
ATKINS (Arkansas)
map (35° 14′N 92° 56′W) **2**:166
ATKINSON (county in Georgia)
map (31° 18′N 82° 50′W) **9**:114
ATKINSON (Illinois)
map (41° 25′N 90° 1′W) **11**:42
ATKINSON (Nebraska)
map (42° 32′N 98° 59′W) **14**:70
ATKINSON (North Carolina)
map (34° 28′N 78° 6′W) **14**:242
ATKINSON, BROOKS **2**:292
ATLANTA (Georgia) **2**:292–293 *bibliog., illus., map*; **9**:115 *illus.*
map (33° 45′N 84° 23′W) **9**:114
ATLANTA (Illinois)
map (40° 16′N 89° 14′W) **11**:42
ATLANTA (Michigan)
map (45° 0′N 84° 9′W) **13**:377
ATLANTA (Missouri)
map (39° 54′N 92° 29′W) **13**:476
ATLANTA (Texas)
map (33° 7′N 94° 10′W) **19**:129
ATLANTA CAMPAIGN **2**:293 *bibliog., map*; **5**:30–31 *illus.*
Hood, John B. **10**:225
Johnston, Joseph E. **11**:438
Sherman, William Tecumseh **17**:258
ATLANTIC (Iowa)
map (41° 24′N 95° 1′W) **11**:244
ATLANTIC (county in New Jersey)
map (39° 27′N 74° 44′W) **14**:129
ATLANTIC (North Carolina)
map (34° 54′N 76° 20′W) **14**:242
ATLANTIC & PACIFIC RAILROAD **19**:268 *map*
ATLANTIC CABLE **2**:294 *bibliog.*
Great Eastern **9**:319
Kelvin, William Thomson, 1st Baron **12**:40
ATLANTIC CHARTER **2**:294
Four Freedoms **8**:253
Roosevelt, Franklin Delano **16**:309
World War II **20**:257 *illus.*
ATLANTIC CITY (New Jersey) **2**:294
map (39° 22′N 74° 26′W) **14**:129
Monopoly **13**:537
Resorts International casino **14**:132 *illus.*
ATLANTIC DOGWINKLE **17**:251 *illus.*
ATLANTIC HIGHLANDS (New Jersey)
map (40° 25′N 74° 3′W) **14**:129
ATLANTIC-INDIAN BASIN
Atlantic Ocean bottom **2**:295 *map*
ATLANTIC MONTHLY (periodical) **2**:294 *bibliog.*
Howells, William Dean **10**:285
Lowell, James Russell **11**:444
ATLANTIC OCEAN **2**:294–296 *bibliog., map*
Atlantic-Indian basin **11**:105 *map*
Atlantic-Indian Ridge **15**:351 *map*
Bermuda Triangle **3**:219
climate **2**:296
Continental rise **2**:295 *map*
economy **2**:296
EXPLORATION *see* EXPLORATION
Grand Banks **9**:284 *map*
history **2**:296
World War II **20**:251–252; **20**:256; **20**:264–265 *illus., map*
intertidal life **11**:229–230
island arc **11**:297
islands and island groups
Ascension Island **2**:227
Azores **2**:381–382 *map*
Bahama Islands **3**:23–24 *illus., map*
Bermuda **3**:219 *map*
British Isles **3**:497
Canary Islands **4**:99 *map*
Cape Verde **4**:121–122 *map*
Devil's Island **6**:143
Faeroe Islands **8**:7
Falkland Islands **8**:13
Hebrides **10**:102–103
Iceland **11**:16–18 *illus., map, table*
Ireland **11**:257–261 *illus., map, table*
Madeira Islands **13**:40 *map*
Martha's Vineyard (Massachusetts) **13**:176
Sable Island (Nova Scotia) **17**:6
Saint Helena **17**:19
Saint Pierre and Miquelon (France) **17**:26
Scilly Islands **17**:146
Skye **17**:346
Tristan da Cunha Islands **19**:303
Mid-Atlantic Ridge **2**:295 *map*; **14**:328 *map*
fit of continents around **15**:353 *map*
Woods Hole Oceanographic Institution **20**:213
North Atlantic Ocean
tributaries and ocean, dimensions **14**:326 *table*
ocean bottom **2**:294–296 *map*
mid-oceanic ridge **13**:389–390
ocean currents
Brazil Current **3**:464
Canaries Current **4**:98
Gulf Stream **9**:403
ocean currents and wind systems, worldwide **14**:322–323 *maps*
oceanic basins **2**:295 *map*
oceanic ridge **2**:295 *map*
oceanic trenches **2**:295 *map*; **14**:342
seas, gulfs, and bays
Baltic Sea **3**:55 *map*
Biscay, Bay of **3**:297
Bristol Channel **3**:488
Buzzards Bay **3**:601
Caribbean Sea **4**:147–149 *map*
Chesapeake Bay **4**:333
Davis Strait **6**:53
Delaware Bay **6**:91
Drake Passage **6**:257
English Channel **7**:188–189
Florida, Straits of **8**:176
Fundy, Bay of **8**:363
Gibraltar, Strait of **9**:175
Guinea, Gulf of **9**:398
Intracoastal Waterway **11**:232
Irish Sea **11**:269
Long Island Sound **12**:406
Magellan, Strait of **13**:48
Mexico, Gulf of **13**:366
Narragansett Bay **14**:22
North Sea **14**:252
St. Lawrence, Gluf of **17**:20–21
Sargasso Sea **17**:77
Scotia Sea **17**:149
Weddell Sea **20**:89
ship crossings
See also OCEAN LINER
Savannah **17**:99
South Atlantic Ocean
tributaries and ocean, dimensions **14**:326 *table*
upwelling, oceanic **19**:474
water characteristics **2**:296
ATLANTIDA (Uruguay)
map (34° 46′S 55° 45′W) **19**:488
ATLANTIS **2**:296 *bibliog.*
Thera **19**:160
ATLAS (book of maps) **2**:297
See also ASTRONOMICAL CATALOGS AND ATLASES; MAPS AND MAPMAKING
linguistic atlases **9**:98
Ortelius, Abraham **14**:449
ATLAS (missile) **2**:297 *bibliog., illus.*
Centaur (rocket) **4**:249
Mecury program **13**:309
rockets and missiles **16**:255–256 *illus.*
ATLAS (mythology) **2**:297
Medusa **13**:278
ATLAS MOUNTAINS **2**:297
map (33° 0′N 2° 0′W) **1**:136
Medusa **13**:278
Morocco **13**:584; **13**:586 *illus.*
ATLIN (British Columbia)
map (59° 35′N 133° 42′W) **3**:491
ATLIN LAKE
map (59° 20′N 133° 45′W) **3**:491
ATMORE (Alabama)
map (31° 2′N 87° 29′W) **1**:234
ATMOSPHERE **2**:298–304 *bibliog., illus.*
advection **1**:110
Aerobee **1**:122
aerosol **1**:124–125
atmospheric sciences **2**:304
auroras **2**:325
circulation and winds **2**:300–302 *illus.*
Ferrel cell **8**:59
Hadley cell **10**:8
Rossby waves **16**:318–319
climate **5**:55–58
cloud **5**:66–68
composition and structure **2**:298–300
air **1**:203–204
continental climate **5**:227–228
cyclone and anticyclone **5**:405–406
desert **6**:126–129
dust, atmospheric **6**:308
Earth, structure and composition of **7**:23

Earth sciences 7:24
evapotranspiration 7:314–315
fallout 8:14
Flammarion, Camille 8:151
front 8:339–340
geochemistry 9:96
geophysics 9:108
ground temperature 9:373
high pressure
hyperbaric chamber 10:347
region 10:162
history of studies 2:298
humidity 10:302
hurricane and typhoon 10:317–319
hydrologic cycle 10:341
ice crystals
halo 10:24
impact of humans 2:303
insolation 11:194
instability
inversion 11:233–234
sandstorm and dust storm 17:63–64
inversion 11:233–234
jet stream 11:407–408
lapse rate 12:206
layers
chemosphere 4:329
exosphere 7:333
ionosphere 11:241
magnetosphere 13:59–60
mesosphere 13:322
ozone layer 14:480
stratification 2:299–300
stratosphere 18:293
thermosphere 19:167
tropopause 19:310
troposphere 19:310
lightning 12:339–340
low-pressure region 12:443
meteorology 13:341–343
microclimate 13:384–385
mirage 13:463
moist processes 2:300
mountain climates 13:620–621
nitrogen cycle 14:203
ocean-atmosphere interaction 14:321–322
origin 2:303–304
paleoclimatology 15:32–34
photochemistry 15:259
planets 15:329
Herzberg, Gerhard 10:150
Jupiter (planet) 11:472
Mars (planet) 13:167–168
Neptune (planet) 14:88
Venus (planet) 19:547
polar easterlies 15:393
pollution, environmental 15:411–415
Precambrian time 15:492
precipitation (weather) 15:493–495
radiation and energy transfer 2:300–301 *map*
red beds 16:112
Saint Elmo's fire 17:18
sky 17:346
solar radiation 18:44
static stability 2:299–300
stellar atmosphere
photosphere 15:275
thermal convection, atmospheric 2:300–302
thunderstorm 19:185
tornado 19:241–242
trade winds 19:263
upper atmosphere 2:298–304
vacuum 19:501–502
Van Allen radiation belts 19:510
weather disturbances 2:302–303
weather forecasting 20:76–79
weather modification 20:79–80
weather variation and extremes 20:80–82
whirlwind 20:132
whistler 20:134
ATMOSPHERIC EXPLOSION
shock wave 17:279
ATMOSPHERIC REFRACTION 2:304
rainbow 16:77 *illus.*
ATMOSPHERIC SCIENCES 2:304 *bibliog.*
atmospheric tide 2:304
Bjerknes, Vilhelm and Jacob 3:302
Buys Ballot, Christoph Hendrik Diederik 3:601
carbon cycle (atmosphere) 4:136
climate 5:55–58
meteorological instrumentation 2:298
cloud 5:66–68
cosmic rays 5:283–284
cumulonimbus clouds 5:388
cumulus clouds 5:388
cyclone and anticyclone 5:405–406
drought 6:273–274
exosphere 7:333
Geiger, Rudolf Oskar Robert Williams 9:68
geochemistry 9:95–97
geophysics 9:108
greenhouse effect 9:351–352
International Years of the Quiet Sun 11:225
ionosphere 11:241–243
jet stream 11:407–408
lightning 12:339–340
magnetic storm 13:55
mesosphere 13:322
meteorology 13:341–343
Milankovich theory 13:418–419
mirage 13:463
monsoon 13:543–544
National Oceanic and Atmospheric Administration 14:35
nitrogen cycle 14:203
ocean-atmosphere interaction 14:321
ozone layer 14:480
precipitation 15:493–495
radar meteorology 16:41
research institutions
National Center for Atmospheric Research 14:30
Rossby waves 16:318–319
Schaefer, Vincent Joseph 17:116
squall and squall line 18:201–202
stratus clouds 18:293
thunderstorm 19:185
tornado 19:239–240
tropical climate 19:307
twilight 19:360
weather forecasting 20:76–79
weather modification 20:79–80
weather variation and extremes 20:80–82
wind 20:168–170
World Meteorological Organization 20:219
World Weather Watch 20:281
ATMOSPHERIC TIDE 2:304 *bibliog.*
ATNA PEAK
map (53° 57′N 128° 3′W) 3:491
ATOKA (Oklahoma)
map (34° 23′N 96° 8′W) 14:368
ATOKA (county in Oklahoma)
map (34° 20′N 96° 5′W) 14:368
ATOLL 5:258 *illus.*
ATOM 2:304–306 *bibliog., illus.*
angstrom 2:7
anion 2:29
atomic nucleus 2:309–311
atomic number 2:311
atomic weight 2:311–312
chemical bond 4:313–315
chemical symbolism and notation 4:321–322
configuration 5:178
electron configuration 7:120
conversion electron 5:233
electrochemical equivalent 7:112
electron 7:120
electronegativity 7:124
exoelectron 7:333
free radical 8:294
fundamental particles 8:361–363
interstellar matter 11:226
ion and ionization 11:239–240
isotope 11:301
kinetic theory of matter 12:78–79
laser 12:210–211 *illus.*; 12:213
ligand 12:333
magnetic moment 13:55
magnetism 13:55–58 *illus.*
mass defect 13:203
mass number 13:203
matter 13:230
molecule 13:507–508
neutron 14:108–109
orbital 14:417
radical (chemistry) 16:43
radiometric age-dating 16:65 *table*
structure 2:305
Bohr, Niels 3:361–362
chemistry, history of 4:325; 4:327–328
electricity 7:110
element 7:131
exclusion principle 7:250
Lewis, Gilbert Newton 12:306
mineral 13:440
periodic table 15:167–168
Perrin, Jean Baptiste 15:178
physics 15:281
Prout, William 15:583
quantum mechanics 16:10
radioactivity 16:61
Rutherford, Sir Ernest 16:375–376
spectroscopy 18:170
Thomson, Sir Joseph John 19:176
theory 2:304–305
atomism 2:312
Dalton, John 6:14–15
element 7:129
orbital 14:416–417
transition elements 19:273
valence 19:503
ATOMIC BOMB 2:307–308 *bibliog., illus.*
aircraft, military 1:217
Bacher, Robert Fox 3:11
Bethe, Hans 3:230
Bohr, Niels 3:361–362
Chadwick, Sir James 4:267
civil defense 5:10
development 2:307
Einstein, Albert 7:94
fallout 8:14
fallout shelter 8:14–15
Fermi, Enrico 8:55–56
Hahn, Otto 10:11
Hiroshima (Japan) 10:176
Los Alamos (New Mexico) 12:416
Los Alamos National Scientific Laboratory 12:416
Manhattan Project 13:116
Nagasaki (Japan) 14:6
Oppenheimer, J. Robert 14:407–408
Szilard, Leo 18:416
Teller, Edward 19:90
terrorist bombs 3:374
tests
Bikini (Marshall Islands) 3:250
Eniwetok (Marshall Islands) 7:206
Lop Nor (China) 12:412
theory 2:307
Truman, Harry S. 19:317
types 2:307
hydrogen bomb 10:339–340
neutron bomb 14:109
plutonium bomb 2:307
United States, history of the 19:455
uranium 19:477
Dempster, Arthur Jeffrey 6:105
weapons 20:75
Wigner, Eugene Paul 20:147
World War II 20:279 *illus.*
ATOMIC CLOCK 2:308
cesium 4:262
day 6:54
laser 12:213
NAVSTAR 14:62
radio astronomy 16:53
time (physics) 19:201
ATOMIC CONSTANTS 2:308–309 *bibliog., table*
Avogadro's number 2:308
Boltzmann's constant 2:308–309
dielectric 6:161
electron mass 2:308–309
elementary unit of charge 2:308–309
gravitational constant 2:308–309
Millikan's oil-drop experiment 13:430
Planck's constant 15:327
proton mass 2:309
Rydberg's constant 2:309
values 2:309 *table*
velocity of light 2:308–309
ATOMIC ENERGY *see* NUCLEAR ENERGY
ATOMIC ENERGY COMMISSION *see* NUCLEAR REGULATORY COMMISSION
ATOMIC FISSION *see* FISSION, NUCLEAR
ATOMIC MASS *see* ATOMIC WEIGHT
ATOMIC NUCLEUS 2:309–311 *bibliog., illus.*
binding energy 3:257–258
Bohr, Aage Niels 3:361
composition 2:310–311
forces
fundamental interactions 8:361
nuclear force 2:311
Yukawa, Hideki 20:344
fundamental particles 8:361–363
mass defect 13:203
mass number 13:203
Mayer, Maria Goeppert 13:246
Mottelson, Ben Roy 13:616
neutron 2:310–311
nuclear physics 2:311; 14:285–287
nuclear transformations 2:310
proton 15:578
spectroscopy 18:170–172
stability, beta decay 3:229
structure
Jensen, Hans 11:396
Rainwater, James 16:78
symmetry (physics) 18:404
theory 2:309–310
Rutherford's model 2:309–310
Thomson's model 2:309
time reversal invariance 19:202
ATOMIC NUMBER 2:311
mass number 13:203
nuclear charge
Moseley, Henry Gwyn Jeffreys 13:599
periodic table 15:168
ATOMIC PHYSICS *see* NUCLEAR PHYSICS
ATOMIC PROPERTIES
metal 13:328
ATOMIC SPECTRA
spectrum 18:172
ATOMIC THEORY *see* ATOM; ATOMIC NUCLEUS
ATOMIC TIME
atomic clock 2:308
time 19:201
ATOMIC WEIGHT 2:311–312
Berzelius, Jöns Jakob 3:227
chemical combination, laws of 4:315
determination
Cannizzaro, Stanislao 4:111
Richards, Theodore William 16:211
Stas, Jean Servais 18:228
Dulong and Petit's law
Dulong, Pierre Louis 6:296
electrochemical equivalent 7:112
element 7:129; 7:131
Marignac, Jean Charles Galissard de 13:152
mass defect 13:203
mass number 13:203
Prout, William 15:583
specific heat and 4:326
ATOMISM 2:312
Democritus 6:103
determinism 6:134
Gassendi, Pierre 9:56
Leucippus 12:300
life, extraterrestrial 12:327
materialism 13:219
Xenocrates 20:312
ATOMS FOR PEACE AWARD
Bohr, Aage Niels 3:361
Szilard, Leo 18:416
Wigner, Eugene Paul 20:147
ATONALITY 2:312 *bibliog.*
harmony 10:52
jazz 11:389
ATONEMENT 2:312 *bibliog.*
Aulén, Gustav 2:323
ATONEMENT, DAY OF *see* YOM KIPPUR
ATOPIC DERMATITIS *see* ECZEMA
ATP 2:312
active transport 1:89–90
biological locomotion 3:265–266
blue-green algae 3:343
cell 4:233
fermentation 8:55
Krebs cycle 12:128
metabolism 13:326
muscle contraction 13:654–656
phosphorus 15:256
photosynthesis 15:275; 15:277
stress, biological 18:298
Todd, Lord Alexander 19:220
ATRAK RIVER
map (37° 28′N 53° 57′E) 11:250
ATRATO RIVER
map (8° 17′N 76° 58′W) 5:107
ATREUS
treasury of Atreus 19:230 *illus.*
Greece, ancient 9:329
Mycenae 13:690
ATREUS (mythology) 2:312
ATRIA (heart)
heart 10:91–94 *illus.*
ATRISCO (New Mexico)
map (34° 59′N 106° 41′W) 14:136
ATRIUM 2:312–313 *bibliog.*
Roman art and architecture 16:274
ATROPHY 2:313
muscle 13:653
skin diseases 17:341
ATROPINE 2:313
medicinal plants 13:266
ATSINA *see* GROS VENTRES (American Indians)
ATTACHMENT (law) 2:313
installment plan 11:194
ATTACHMENT (psychology) 2:313 *bibliog.*
importance 2:313
infancy 11:163
mother and child 2:313
social psychology 18:13
theories 2:313
ATTAINDER, BILL OF 2:313

ATTAINGNANT, PIERRE
Renaissance music **16**:156
ATTALA (county in Mississippi)
map (33° 5′N 89° 35′W) **13**:469
ATTALLA (Alabama)
map (34° 1′N 86° 5′W) **1**:234
ATTALUS I, KING OF PERGAMUM **2**:313–314 *bibliog.*
ATTALUS II, KING OF PERGAMUM
Demetrius I Soter, Seleucid King **6**:97
ATTAPEU (Laos)
map (14° 48′N 106° 50′E) **12**:203
ATTAPULGITE
clay minerals **5**:47
ATTAR, FARID AL-DIN ABU HAMID **2**:314
ATTAWAPISKAT (Ontario)
map (52° 55′N 82° 26′W) **14**:393
ATTENBOROUGH, RICHARD **2**:314
ATTENTION (psychology) **2**:314 *bibliog.*
cognitive psychology **5**:94–95
ATTENTIONAL DEFICIT DISORDER (ADD) *see* HYPERACTIVE CHILDREN
ATTIC **2**:314
ATTICA (Greece) **2**:314
ATTICA (Indiana)
map (40° 17′N 87° 15′W) **11**:111
ATTICA (Kansas)
map (37° 15′N 98° 13′W) **12**:18
ATTICA (New York)
map (42° 52′N 78° 17′W) **14**:149
ATTICA (Ohio)
map (41° 4′N 82° 53′W) **14**:357
ATTICA PRISON RIOT **2**:314 *bibliog.*
Kunstler, William **12**:137
Rockefeller, Nelson A. **16**:250
ATTILA THE HUN **2**:315 *bibliog.*
Aetius, Flavius **1**:131
Huns **10**:311
Udine (Italy) **19**:370–371
ATTITUDE AND ATTITUDE CHANGE **2**:315 *bibliog.*
existence of, explanation **2**:315
family **8**:17
folklore **8**:203
moral awareness **13**:572
propaganda **15**:568–569
ATTLEBORO (Massachusetts)
map (41° 56′N 71° 17′W) **13**:206
ATTLEE, CLEMENT, 1ST EARL ATTLEE **2**:315–316 *bibliog., illus.*
Labour party **12**:157
Potsdam Conference **20**:275–276 *illus.*
ATTORNEY **2**:316 *bibliog.*
advocate **1**:114
barrister **3**:95
common law **5**:140
defense counsel **6**:83
law **12**:243
legal procedure **12**:273
paralegal services **15**:78
prosecuting attorney **15**:572
ATTORNEY-CLIENT PRIVILEGE
evidence **7**:317
ATTORNEY GENERAL **2**:316
Justice, U.S. Department of **11**:478
ATTUCKS, CRISPUS **2**:316
ATUFU (Tokelau) **19**:223
ATUM (creator-god)
Heliopolis **10**:112–113
ATWATER (California)
map (37° 21′N 120° 36′W) **4**:31
ATWATER (Minnesota)
map (45° 8′N 94° 47′W) **13**:453
ATWATER (Saskatchewan)
map (50° 47′N 102° 10′W) **17**:81
ATWATER FACTORS
nutrition, human **14**:304
ATWOOD (Illinois)
map (39° 48′N 88° 28′W) **11**:42
ATWOOD (Kansas)
map (39° 48′N 101° 3′W) **12**:18
ATWOOD, MARGARET **2**:316
AU GRES (Michigan)
map (44° 3′N 83° 42′W) **13**:377
AU SABLE FORKS (New York)
map (44° 27′N 73° 41′W) **14**:149
AU SABLE RIVER
map (44° 25′N 83° 20′W) **13**:377
AUAU CHANNEL
map (20° 51′N 156° 45′W) **10**:72
AUBER, DANIEL FRANÇOIS ESPRIT **2**:316
AUBIGNAC, ABBÉ D' **2**:316
AUBIGNÉ, AGRIPPA D' **2**:316 *bibliog.*
AUBIGNÉ, FRANÇOISE D', MARQUISE DE MAINTENON *see* MAINTENON, FRANÇOISE D'AUBIGNÉ, MARQUISE DE
AUBREY, JAMES
radio and television broadcasting **16**:58
AUBREY, JOHN **2**:316 *bibliog.*
Stonehenge **18**:283
AUBREY HOLES
Stonehenge **18**:283
AUBURN (Alabama)
map (32° 36′N 85° 29′W) **1**:234
AUBURN (Illinois)
map (39° 36′N 89° 45′W) **11**:42
AUBURN (Indiana)
map (41° 22′N 85° 4′W) **11**:111
AUBURN (Kentucky)
map (36° 52′N 86° 43′W) **12**:47
AUBURN (Maine)
map (44° 6′N 70° 14′W) **13**:70
AUBURN (Massachusetts)
map (42° 12′N 71° 50′W) **13**:206
AUBURN (Nebraska)
map (40° 23′N 95° 51′W) **14**:70
AUBURN (New York)
map (42° 56′N 76° 34′W) **14**:149
AUBURN (Washington)
map (47° 18′N 122° 13′W) **20**:35
AUBURN SYSTEM
prison **15**:554
AUBUSSON (France) **2**:316 *bibliog.*
Lurçat, Jean **12**:466
rugs and carpets **16**:343
tapestry **19**:33
AUCHINCLOSS, LOUIS **2**:316–317
realism (literature) **16**:104
AUCKLAND (New Zealand) **2**:317 *illus.*
climate **14**:157 *table*
map (36° 52′S 174° 46′E) **14**:158
AUCKLAND ISLANDS **2**:317
map (50° 40′S 166° 30′E) **14**:334
AUCTION **2**:317 *bibliog.*
antique collecting **2**:65–68
livestock **12**:21 *illus.*
AUDEN, W. H. **2**:317–318 *bibliog., illus.*
Spender, Stephen **18**:177–178
AUDERGHEM (Belgium)
map (50° 49′N 4° 26′E) **3**:177
AUDIENCIA **2**:318 *bibliog.*
AUDIO FREQUENCY **2**:318
heterodyne principle **10**:153–154
AUDION TUBE *see* TRIODE
AUDIOVISUAL TEACHING AIDS *see* TEACHING AIDS, AUDIOVISUAL
AUDIT **2**:318
accounting **1**:78
American Institute of Certified Public Accountants **2**:318
AUDITORIUM BUILDING (Chicago) **2**:318 *bibliog.*
Adler, Dankmar **1**:104
Sullivan, Louis **18**:337
Weese, Harry **20**:90
AUDITORIUM CHURCH
Mills, Robert **13**:430–431
AUDITORY CANAL
ear **7**:6 *illus.*
AUDITORY NERVE **7**:6 *illus.*
ear **7**:7
AUDRAIN (county in Missouri)
map (39° 15′N 91° 55′W) **13**:476
AUDUBON (Iowa)
map (41° 43′N 94° 55′W) **11**:244
AUDUBON (county in Iowa)
map (41° 38′N 94° 52′W) **11**:244
AUDUBON (New Jersey)
map (39° 54′N 75° 4′W) **14**:129
AUDUBON, JOHN JAMES **2**:318–319 *bibliog., illus.*
The Wood Duck **2**:319 *illus.*
AUDUBON SOCIETY, NATIONAL **2**:319
bird-watching **3**:290
AUE (Germany, East and West)
map (50° 35′N 12° 42′E) **9**:140
AUE, HARTMANN VON *see* HARTMANN VON AUE
AUENBRUGGER, LEOPOLD
examination, medical **7**:326
medicine **13**:270
AUER, LEOPOLD **2**:319 *bibliog.*
AUERBACH, ARNOLD JACOB "RED" *see* AUERBACH, RED
AUERBACH, BERTHOLD **2**:319
AUERBACH, ERICH **2**:319
AUERBACH, RED **2**:319 *bibliog.*
AUGEAS (mythology) **2**:319
AUGERVILLE (Connecticut)
map (41° 22′N 72° 54′W) **5**:193
AUGIER, ÉMILE **2**:319 *bibliog.*
AUGITE
pyroxene **15**:638
AUGLAIZE (county in Ohio)
map (40° 34′N 84° 12′W) **14**:357
AUGLAIZE RIVER
map (41° 17′N 84° 21′W) **14**:357
AUGSBURG (West Germany) **2**:319–320
map (48° 23′N 10° 53′E) **9**:140
AUGSBURG, LEAGUE OF **2**:320
Grand Alliance, War of the **9**:284
AUGSBURG, PEACE OF **2**:320
Europe, history of **7**:287
Ferdinand I, Holy Roman Emperor **8**:52–53
Germany, history of **9**:151
Lutheranism **12**:470
AUGSBURG CONFESSION **2**:320 *bibliog.*
Luther, Martin **12**:469
Melanchthon, Philipp **13**:284
AUGURS, TOMB OF THE **7**:259 *illus.*
AUGUST
birthstones **3**:296 *illus., table*
calendar **4**:28
AUGUSTA (Arkansas)
map (35° 17′N 91° 22′W) **2**:166
AUGUSTA (Georgia) **2**:320
map (33° 29′N 81° 57′W) **9**:114
AUGUSTA (Illinois)
map (40° 14′N 90° 57′W) **11**:42
AUGUSTA (Italy)
map (37° 13′N 15° 13′E) **11**:321
AUGUSTA (Kansas)
map (37° 41′N 96° 58′W) **12**:18
AUGUSTA (Kentucky)
map (38° 46′N 84° 0′W) **12**:47
AUGUSTA (Maine) **2**:320
map (44° 19′N 69° 47′W) **13**:70
AUGUSTA (Montana)
map (47° 30′N 112° 24′W) **13**:547
AUGUSTA (county in Virginia)
map (38° 10′N 79° 10′W) **19**:607
AUGUSTA (Wisconsin)
map (44° 41′N 91° 7′W) **20**:185
AUGUSTAN AGE **2**:320
See also NEOCLASSICISM (literature)
authors
Addison, Joseph **1**:100
Chesterfield, Philip, 4th Earl of **4**:336
Dryden, John **6**:284–285
Gay, John **9**:63
Pope, Alexander **15**:430
Steele, Sir Richard **18**:243
English literature **7**:196–197
AUGUSTINE, SAINT **2**:320–321 *bibliog., illus.*
City of God, The **5**:8
Confessions of St. Augustine, The **5**:178
educational psychology **7**:66
innate ideas **11**:179
law **12**:242
Neoplatonism **14**:85
predestination **15**:502
scholasticism **17**:131–132
state (in political philosophy) **18**:230 *illus.*
AUGUSTINE OF CANTERBURY, SAINT **2**:321 *bibliog.*
AUGUSTINIANS **2**:321; **13**:396 *illus.*
AUGUSTUS, ROMAN EMPEROR **2**:321–322 *bibliog., illus.*
Actium, Battle of **1**:89
Antony, Mark **2**:70–71
Ara Pacis **7**:281 *illus.*; **16**:276 *illus.*
caesar **4**:13
Cleopatra, Queen of Egypt **5**:50
Gemma Augustea **16**:275 *illus.*
Lepidus, Marcus Aemilius **12**:295
Livia Drusilla **12**:376
Octavia **14**:347
Philippi **15**:235
Roman expansion under **16**:299 *map*
Roman law **16**:278
Rome, ancient **16**:302 *illus.*
Senate, Roman **17**:199
Tiberius, Roman Emperor **19**:189
Trier (West Germany) **19**:297
AUGUSTUS II, KING OF POLAND **2**:322
Northern War, Great **14**:256
AUGUSTUS III, KING OF POLAND **2**:322
Polish Succession, War of the **15**:398
AUGUSTYN, FRANK **3**:41 *illus.*; **14**:29 *illus.*
AUK **2**:322–323 *illus.*; **6**:204 *illus.*
guillemot **9**:396
AUKI (Solomon Islands)
map (8° 45′S 160° 42′E) **18**:56
AULACOGEN
rift
plate tectonics **15**:353
AULANDER (North Carolina)
map (36° 14′N 77° 6′W) **14**:242
AULARD, ALPHONSE **2**:323
AULÉN, GUSTAV **2**:323
AULOS **2**:323; **9**:345 *illus.*
AULT (Colorado)
map (40° 30′N 104° 45′W) **5**:116
AUMER, JEAN **2**:323 *bibliog.*
AUNG SAN **2**:323 *bibliog.*
Burma **3**:575
AUNIS (France) **2**:324
AUOB RIVER
map (26° 25′S 20° 35′E) **14**:11
AURA (organization) *see* ASSOCIATION OF UNIVERSITIES FOR RESEARCH IN ASTRONOMY
AURANGZEB, MOGUL EMPEROR OF INDIA **2**:324 *bibliog.*
AURELIA (Iowa)
map (42° 42′N 95° 28′W) **11**:244
AURELIAN, ROMAN EMPEROR **2**:324 *bibliog.*
Homs (Syria) **10**:217
AURELIUS, MARCUS *see* MARCUS AURELIUS, ROMAN EMPEROR
AURIC, GEORGES **2**:324
AURIGA **2**:324
AURIGNACIAN **2**:324 *bibliog.*
cave dwellers **4**:224 *illus.*
Grimaldi man **9**:364
Mousterian **13**:626
prehistoric art **15**:507
Venus of Willendorf **19**:548
AURILLAC (France)
map (44° 56′N 2° 26′E) **8**:260
AURIOL, VINCENT **2**:324
AUROBINDO, SRI **2**:324–325 *bibliog.*
AURORA *see* EOS
AURORA (Colorado)
map (39° 44′N 104° 52′W) **5**:116
AURORA (Illinois)
map (42° 46′N 88° 19′W) **11**:42
AURORA (Indiana)
map (39° 4′N 84° 54′W) **11**:111
AURORA (Minnesota)
map (47° 31′N 92° 14′W) **13**:453
AURORA (Missouri)
map (36° 58′N 93° 43′W) **13**:476
AURORA (Nebraska)
map (40° 52′N 98° 0′W) **14**:70
AURORA (New York)
map (42° 46′N 76° 42′W) **14**:149
AURORA (North Carolina)
map (35° 18′N 76° 47′W) **14**:242
AURORA (Ontario)
map (44° 0′N 79° 28′W) **14**:393
AURORA (county in South Dakota)
map (43° 45′N 98° 35′W) **18**:103
AURORAS (astronomy) **2**:325 *bibliog., illus.*
auroral substorm, magnetic storm **13**:55
Celsius, Anders **4**:238
ionosphere **11**:241
magnetosphere **13**:59–60
AUSANGATE MOUNTAIN
map (13° 48′S 71° 14′W) **15**:193
AUSCHWITZ **2**:325 *bibliog.*
concentration camp **5**:168
Krupp (family) **12**:132
map (50° 3′N 19° 12′E) **15**:388
AUSONIUS **2**:325
AUSTEN, JANE **2**:326 *bibliog., illus.*; **7**:199 *illus.*
Emma **7**:156
Pride and Prejudice **15**:536
Winchester (England) **20**:168
AUSTEN, JOHN
Emma Bovary **14**:274 *illus.*
AUSTERLITZ, BATTLE OF **2**:326
howitzer **10**:285 *illus.*
AUSTERLITZ, FREDERICK *see* ASTAIRE, FRED
AUSTIN (Indiana)
map (38° 45′N 85° 48′W) **11**:111
AUSTIN (Minnesota)
map (43° 40′N 92° 59′W) **13**:453
AUSTIN (Nevada)
map (39° 30′N 117° 4′W) **14**:111
AUSTIN (Pennsylvania)
map (41° 38′N 78° 5′W) **15**:147
AUSTIN (Texas) **2**:326–327
map (30° 16′N 97° 45′W) **19**:129
AUSTIN (county in Texas)
map (29° 53′N 96° 15′W) **19**:129
AUSTIN, ALFRED **2**:327
AUSTIN, JOHN **2**:327 *bibliog.*
law **12**:242
AUSTIN, JOHN LANGSHAW **2**:327 *bibliog.*
semantics (linguistics) **17**:194
AUSTIN, MARY HUNTER **2**:327
AUSTIN, RICHARD
Michigan **13**:382
AUSTIN, STEPHEN F. **2**:327 *bibliog., illus.*
Texas **19**:133–134

AUSTIN, TRACY 2:327 illus.
AUSTIN MOTOR COMPANY
automotive industry 2:366
AUSTRAL ISLANDS
French Polynesia 8:321–322
AUSTRALIA 2:328–339 bibliog., illus., maps, table
agriculture 2:335 illus., map; 2:338
sheep ranch 2:25 illus.
animal life 2:334–335
bird of paradise 3:290
bowerbird 3:428
desert life, habitat 10:5 illus.
dingo 6:178–179
flap-footed lizard 8:153
habitat 10:5 illus.
kangaroo 12:15
kelpie 12:40
koala 12:103–104
kookaburra 12:110
marsupial 13:174
megapode 13:280
art
Nolan, Sidney 14:213
Oceanic art 14:339
prehistoric art 15:510–511 illus.
cities
Adelaide 1:101 illus.
Alice Springs 1:293; 2:337 illus.
Brisbane 3:487 illus.
Broken Hill 3:501
Canberra 2:337 illus.; 4:99–100 map
Darwin 6:40–41
Hobart 10:192
Kalgoorlie 12:8
Melbourne 13:285–286 illus., map
Newcastle 14:164
Perth 15:191
Sydney 18:400–401 illus., map
Wollongong 20:199
civil service 5:14
climate 2:332–333 map, table
maritime climate 13:157
Mediterranean climate 13:276
weather variation and extremes 20:80–81 tables
crime 5:346 table
cultural activity 2:337–338
dance
Helpmann, Sir Robert 10:116
demography 2:336 map
economy 2:338
consumer price index 11:170 table
education 2:336–337
Australian universities 2:344–345 table
exploration see EXPLORATION—Australia
flag 2:329 illus.
forestry and fishing 2:338
geologic time
Australian plate 15:351 map
Ordovician Period 14:421 map
Permian Period 15:175 map
Precambrian rock formations 15:492 map
Silurian Period 17:310–311
Tertiary Period 19:123 map
geology 2:331 map
government and politics 2:338-339
defense, national 6:82 table
Liberal parties 12:311
medals and decorations 13:262 illus.
welfare spending 20:98 table
health 2:337
history see AUSTRALIA, HISTORY OF
land 2:331
Arnhem Land 2:184
meteorite craters 13:339
mountains, highest 13:620
regions 2:328 map; 2:331
language 2:336
Oceanic languages 14:339
literature see AUSTRALIAN LITERATURE
manufacturing and industry 2:338
map (25° 0′S 135° 0′E) 14:334
national parks 14:41–42 map, table
newspaper
Murdoch, Rupert 13:648
people 2:335–338
Aborigines, Australian 1:59–60
Aranda 2:109
race 16:33–34 illus., map
women in society 20:204 table
physical features 2:330 illus.
Ayers Rock 2:378–379 illus.
Cape York Peninsula 4:122
Flinders Range 8:165
Gibson Desert 9:176
Great Artesian Basin 9:308
Great Australian Bight 9:308
Great Barrier Reef 9:308 illus.
Great Dividing Range 9:319
Great Sandy Desert 9:322
Great Victoria Desert 9:323
Kosciusko, Mount 12:123
Macdonnell Ranges 13:13
Nullarbor Plain 14:292
Simpson Desert 17:317
Snowy Mountains 18:5
plate tectonics
continental drifting 15:354 map
religion 2:336
Aborigines, Australian 1:59
Australia, Church of England in 2:342
resources 2:331
electrical production 15:485 table
energy and power generation 2:338
mineral resources 2:334–335 illus., map
opal 14:397
petroleum 15:209; 15:210
sylvanite 18:402
water resources 20:51 table
rivers, lakes, and waterways 2:333–334 illus.
Bass Strait 3:117
Botany Bay 3:414
Darling River 6:39
Eyre, lake 7:352
Murray River 13:650
Murrumbidgee River 13:651
soils 2:334
sports
Goolagong, Evonne 9:246
states and territories
Australian Capital Territory 2:342
Australian External Territories 2:342
Christmas Island (Indian Ocean) 4:415
Cocos Islands 5:89
Heard Island and the McDonald Islands 10:89
New South Wales 14:142 map
Norfolk Island 14:218
Northern Territory 14:255–256 map
Queensland 16:22 map
South Australia 18:96 map
Tasmania 19:42 map
Victoria 19:573
Western Australia 20:115–116 map
trade 2:338
transportation 2:338
railroad 16:74
vegetation 2:333–334 illus., map
acacia 1:68
habitat 10:5 illus.
wine 20:176
AUSTRALIA, CHURCH OF ENGLAND IN 2:342
AUSTRALIA, HISTORY OF 2:339–342 bibliog., illus., map, table
exploration see EXPLORATION—Australia
1788–1901 colonization
British Empire 3:496
Burke, Robert O'Hara 3:571
bushrangers 3:586
Deakin, Alfred 6:67
Grey, Sir George 9:360
Parkes, Sir Henry 15:91
penal and free colonies 2:339–340 illus., map
Phillip, Arthur 15:239
squatter 18:203
Wentworth, William Charles 20:103–104
1901-present
after World War II 2:341–342
Anzus Treaty 2:73
Barton, Sir Edmund 3:98
Bruce, Stanley Melbourne, 1st Viscount of Melbourne 3:520
Chifley, Joseph Benedict 4:347
Curtin, John 5:394
federation 2:340–341
first Federal Parliament 2:341 illus.
Fraser, J. Malcolm 8:287
Gallipoli Campaign 9:20
Gilroy, Norman Thomas 9:183
Gorton, John Grey 9:253
Hawke, Robert 10:77
Holt, Harold 10:208
Hughes, William Morris 10:293–294
Kerr, Sir John Robert 12:60
Lyons, Joseph Aloysius 12:478
McEwen, Sir John 13:16
McMahon, William 13:33
Mawson, Sir Douglas 13:238
Menzies, Sir Robert Gordon 13:303
Papua New Guinea 15:73
prime ministers 2:342 table
White Australia policy 2:341
Whitlam, Gough 20:140
World War II see WORLD WAR II
AUSTRALIA DAY 2:339 illus.; 2:342
AUSTRALIAN CAPITAL TERRITORY 2:342
Canberra 4:99–100 map
map (35° 30′S 149° 0′E) 2:328
AUSTRALIAN CATTLE DOG 2:342 bibliog.
AUSTRALIAN COLONIES GOVERNMENT ACT OF 1850
Australia, history of 2:340
AUSTRALIAN ENGLISH see ENGLISH LANGUAGE
AUSTRALIAN EXTERNAL TERRITORIES 2:342
AUSTRALIAN FRILLED LIZARD 2:342–343 illus.; 10:5 illus.; 12:379 illus.
AUSTRALIAN LITERATURE 2:343–344 bibliog., illus.
authors
Browne, Thomas Alexander 3:517
Fitzgerald, Robert David 8:131
Franklin, Miles 8:285
Gilmore, Dame Mary 9:183
Gordon, Adam Lindsay 9:249
Lawson, Henry 12:251–252
Neilson, John Shaw 14:79
Paterson, A. B. 15:111
Richardson, Henry Handel 16:211–212
Slessor, Kenneth 17:360–361
Stead, Christina 18:239–240
Stewart, Douglas Alexander 18:265
West, Morris L. 20:107
White, Patrick 20:135–136
Wright, Judith Arundel 20:290
AUSTRALIAN MUDNEST BUILDER 2:344
AUSTRALIAN NATIONAL RADIO ASTRONOMY OBSERVATORY 2:344
AUSTRALIAN NATIVE CAT 13:104 illus.
AUSTRALIAN PINE see CASUARINA
AUSTRALIAN TERRIER 2:344 bibliog., illus.; 6:220 illus.
AUSTRALIAN TREE-CREEPER 2:344
AUSTRALIAN UNIVERSITIES 2:344–345 bibliog., table
AUSTRALIAN WALER (horse)
saddle horse 17:9
AUSTRALIAN WARBLER see WREN WARBLER
AUSTRALIAN WILD DOG see DINGO
AUSTRALIAN WREN see WREN WARBLER
AUSTRALOPITHECUS 2:53 illus.; 2:53 illus.; 2:345–346 bibliog., illus.
African prehistory 1:172
cave dwellers 4:224
Dart, Raymond 6:39
Homo erectus 10:215–216
Homo habilis 10:216
Java man 11:385
Laetolil 12:163
Leakey (family) 12:259
Makapansgat 13:77
Meganthropus 13:280
Oldowan 14:376
Olduvai Gorge 14:377
Omo 14:388
prehistoric human origins 15:512–513 illus.
sites 15:514 map
Skull 1470 17:346
Sterkfontein 18:260
Taung skull 19:45
AUSTRASIA 2:346
AUSTRIA 2:346–351 bibliog., illus., map, table
archaeology
Hallstatt 10:23
art see AUSTRIAN ART AND ARCHITECTURE
cities
Bregenz 3:472
Graz 9:307
Innsbruck 11:181
Linz 12:360
Salzburg 17:44 illus.
Vienna 19:578–579 illus.
climate 2:347
economic activity 2:349
education 2:348
European universities 7:307 table
flag 2:346 illus.
government 2:349
history 2:349–351
See also AUSTRIA-HUNGARY; HOLY ROMAN EMPIRE
annexed by Germany in 1938 9:156 map
Austrian Succession, War of the 2:354
Bavarian Succession, War of the 3:131
Charles I, Emperor of Austria-Hungary 4:291
Dollfuss, Engelbert 6:226
Europe, history of 7:290
Francis II, Holy Roman Emperor 8:276
Francis Joseph, Emperor of Austria 8:274–275
French Revolutionary Wars 8:325–326
Germany in 1648 9:151 map
Habsburg (dynasty) 10:6
Hitler, Adolf 10:188
Kreisky, Bruno 12:128
Metternich, Klemens, Fürst von 13:349–350
Napoleonic Wars 14:19–20
Poland, Partitions of 15:392 map
Revolutions of 1848 16:188–189
Schuschnigg, Kurt von 17:138
Schwarzenberg (family) 17:139
Seven Weeks' War 17:216
Seven Years' War 17:218 map
Taafe, Eduard, Graf von 19:3
World War II 20:250
land and resources 2:347–348 illus., map
literature see AUSTRIAN LITERATURE
map (47° 20′N 13° 20′E) 7:268
music see GERMAN AND AUSTRIAN MUSIC
nuclear energy 14:284
people 2:348–349
population 15:437
physical features
Brenner Pass 3:473
rivers, lakes, and waterways 2:347
provinces
Styria 18:312
Tyrol 19:367–368 map
theater
puppet 15:627
Salzburg Festival 17:44–45
Schikaneder, Emanuel 17:120
vegetation and animal life 2:347
AUSTRIA-HUNGARY 2:351–352 bibliog., map
Andrássy, Gyula 1:406
boundaries c.1815 7:291 map
boundaries 1914 7:294 map
Deák, Ferenc 6:67
Esterházy (family) 7:246
Eugene of Savoy 7:263
Europe, history of 7:292
Ferdinand I, Emperor of Austria 8:52
Francis Joseph, Emperor of Austria 8:274–275
Galicia 9:14
Habsburg (dynasty) 10:6
language groups 2:351 map
Triple Alliance 19:302
World War I 20:219–238
AUSTRIAN ART AND ARCHITECTURE 2:352–354 bibliog., illus.
See also the subheading Austria under specific art forms, e.g., ARCHITECTURE; PAINTING; SCULPTURE; etc.; the subheading Austria under BAROQUE ART AND ARCHITECTURE; PREHISTORIC ART; names of specific artists, e.g., KLIMT, GUSTAV; LOOS, ADOLF; etc.
Albertina 1:259
Biedermeier 3:247
museums, art 13:658
Salzburg 17:44
Secession movement 17:178
Vienna 19:578 illus.
AUSTRIAN LITERATURE 2:354 bibliog.
authors
Bachmann, Ingeborg 3:11
Bernhard, Thomas 3:221
Broch, Hermann 3:500
Brod, Max 3:501
Doderer, Heimito von 6:212
Grillparzer, Franz 9:364

AUSTRIAN LITERATURE (cont.)
Handke, Peter **10**:37
Hofmannsthal, Hugo von **10**:196–197
Johannes von Tepl **11**:422
Kafka, Franz **12**:5–6
Kraus, Karl **12**:127
Musil, Robert **13**:681
Nestroy, Johann **14**:97
Schnitzler, Arthur **17**:129
Stifter, Adalbert **18**:267–268
Suttner, Bertha von **18**:373
Trakl, Georg **19**:266
Werfel, Franz **20**:104
Zweig, Stefan **20**:383
Biedermeier **3**:247
AUSTRIAN MUSIC *see* GERMAN AND AUSTRIAN MUSIC
AUSTRIAN SUCCESSION, WAR OF THE **2**:354 *bibliog.*
Aix-la-Chapelle, Treaties of **1**:229
French and Indian Wars **8**:313
Germany, history of **9**:152
Maria Theresa, Austrian Archduchess, Queen of Hungary and Bohemia **13**:150
AUSTRIC LANGUAGES *see* OCEANIC LANGUAGES
AUSTRO-PRUSSIAN WAR *see* SEVEN WEEKS' WAR
AUSTRONESIAN LANGUAGES *see* MALAYO-POLYNESIAN LANGUAGES
AUTAUGA (county in Alabama)
map (32° 30′N 86° 35′W) **1**:234
AUTHORITARIAN PERSONALITY **2**:354
Adorno, Theodor W. **1**:108
Milgram, Stanley **13**:419
AUTHORITARIANISM (political) **2**:354–355 *bibliog.*
communism **5**:146–150
fascism **8**:30
newspaper **14**:172
AUTISTIC CHILDREN **2**:355 *bibliog.*
shock therapy **17**:279
sign language **17**:300
AUTLÁN DE NAVARRO (Mexico)
map (19° 46′N 104° 22′W) **13**:357
AUTO WORKERS, UNITED *see* UNITED AUTO WORKERS
AUTOBAHN **2**:355
roads and highways **16**:238
World War II **20**:276 *illus.*
AUTOBIOGRAPHY **2**:355–356 *bibliog.*
American literature **1**:342; **1**:344–345
Aiken, Conrad **1**:202
Education of Henry Adams, The **7**:64
Fisher, M. F. K. **8**:122
Haley, Alex **10**:19
Stein, Gertrude **18**:247
Up from Slavery **19**:471
confessional literature **5**:177
diary **6**:153
English literature
De Quincey, Thomas **6**:62
Harris, Frank **10**:57
Sitwell, Osbert **17**:330–331
erotic and pornographic literature **7**:234
French literature
Confessions, Les **5**:177
Saint-Simon, Louis de Rouvroy, Duc de **17**:27
Japanese literature
Dazai Osamu **6**:57
Latin literature
Confessions of St. Augustine, The **5**:178
AUTOBIOGRAPHY OF ALICE B. TOKLAS, THE (book) **2**:356
Stein, Gertrude **18**:247
AUTOBIOGRAPHY OF MALCOLM X, THE (book) **13**:86
AUTOEROTICISM *see* MASTURBATION
AUTOGIRO **2**:356 *bibliog., illus.*
Cierva, Juan de la **4**:429
AUTOIMMUNE DISEASES **2**:356 *bibliog.*
immunity **11**:58
lupus erythematosus **12**:466
multiple sclerosis **13**:638
myasthenia gravis **13**:689
rheumatic fever **16**:194
AUTOMATA, THEORY OF **2**:356–357 *bibliog.*
artificial intelligence **2**:221
automaton **2**:358
cybernetics **5**:401
information theory **11**:174–175
AUTOMATIC TRANSMISSION *see* TRANSMISSION, AUTOMOTIVE
AUTOMATIC WRITING **2**:357
Masson, André **13**:214
AUTOMATION **2**:357–358 *bibliog.*
artificial intelligence **2**:221
automata, theory of **2**:356
automobile assembly **19**:68 *illus.*
clothing industry **5**:66
cybernetics **5**:401
Evans, Oliver **7**:313
factory farming **8**:6
feedback **8**:44
history **2**:357
machine tools **13**:24–25 *illus.*
manufacturing **13**:133
principles **2**:357
process control **15**:560–561
robot **16**:246
industrial robot **2**:358
servomechanisms **2**:357–358
AUTOMATON **2**:358 *bibliog.*
See also AUTOMATA, THEORY OF; ROBOT
AUTOMOBILE **2**:358–359 *bibliog., illus.*
See also AUTOMOBILE RACING; AUTOMOTIVE INDUSTRY
aluminum **1**:319
American Automobile Association **1**:337
automotive instrumentation **2**:368
battery **3**:125–126 *illus.*
voltage regulator **19**:631
body design **2**:359
safety, automotive **17**:10–11
brake **3**:449–451
choke
inductor **11**:152
circuit, electric **4**:437 *illus.*
classic cars **2**:366 *illus.*
emission
catalytic converter **4**:199
engine **2**:358 *illus.*
antifreeze **2**:61
carburetor **4**:140–141
cooling system, engine **5**:241–242
diesel engine **2**:367
exhaust system **7**:331–332
ignition system **11**:36–38
internal-combustion engine **11**:215–216 *illus.*
lubrication **12**:447–448 *illus.*
Stirling engine **18**:272–273
valve **19**:509 *illus.*
fuel
fuel cell **8**:354
gasohol **9**:55
gasoline **9**:55
octane number **14**:347
generator **9**:78 *illus.*
headlights **13**:464 *illus.*
parabola **15**:74
heat exchanger **10**:97–98
insurance **11**:199
no-fault insurance **14**:207
machine **13**:21
makes and models **2**:365–367 *illus.*
mirror **13**:464 *illus.*
pollution control **15**:416
production
assembly line **2**:264–265
roads and highways **16**:239 *illus.*
steering system **2**:358–359 *illus.*; **18**:244–245 *illus.*
brake **3**:449–451
differential **6**:166 *illus.*
drive shaft **2**:359 *illus.*
suspension system **18**:371–372
theft **5**:346
tire **19**:207–208
tourism **19**:252
transmission, automotive **19**:275–276
clutch **13**:20 *illus.*
transportation **19**:279 *illus.*; **19**:282
types
electric car **7**:105
jeep **11**:390–391
Model T **13**:490 *illus.*
sports cars **2**:367 *illus.*
taxicab **19**:47
Volkswagen **19**:630
voltage regulator **19**:631
AUTOMOBILE ACCIDENT
whiplash **20**:131
AUTOMOBILE RACING **2**:360–363 *bibliog., illus., tables*
Andretti, Mario **1**:407
Bonneville Salt Flats **3**:381
Clark, Jim **5**:38
classic racing automobiles **2**:363 *illus.*
Daytona Beach (Florida) **6**:57
demolition derby **6**:104
drag racing **2**:362 *illus.*; **6**:254
Fangio, Juan Manuel **8**:20
Foyt, A. J. **8**:257
Grand Prix World Champions **2**:361 *table*
Gurney, Dan **9**:407
Guthrie, Janet **9**:409
history **2**:362
Indianapolis 500 Winners **2**:361 *table*
Lauda, Niki **12**:236
Le Mans (France) **12**:254
Moss, Stirling **13**:605
off-road racing **2**:362
official world speed records **2**:361 *table*; **2**:362
Oldfield, Barney **14**:376
Petty, Richard **15**:216
rallies **2**:362
Soap Box Derby **18**:6
Stewart, Jackie **18**:265
stock car racing **2**:361 *illus.*; **2**:362
types of races **2**:360–362
Unser, Al **19**:470
Unser, Bobby **19**:470
Yarborough, Cale **20**:319
AUTOMOTIVE INDUSTRY **2**:363–368 *bibliog., illus., table*
See also AUTOMOBILE; names of specific companies, e.g., AMERICAN MOTORS CORPORATION; FORD MOTOR COMPANY; etc.
bus **3**:583
Canada
Oshawa (Ontario) **14**:453
diesel engine **6**:163 *illus.*
electric car **7**:105
Europe **2**:363–368 *table*
fuel **2**:367
Great Britain **2**:364; **2**:366 *table*
Rolls-Royce **16**:272
history **2**:363–364
Bendix, Vincent **3**:196
Benz, Karl **3**:206
Bosch, Robert **3**:406–407
Chrysler, Walter Percy **4**:420
Couzens, James **5**:318
Daimler, Gottlieb **6**:7
Durant, William Crapo **6**:303
Duryea, Charles E. and J. Frank **6**:307
Ford (family) **8**:220–221
Iacocca, Lee **11**:3
Kettering, Charles Franklin **12**:61
Lenoir, Jean Joseph Étienne **12**:285
Maxim, Hiram Percy **13**:239
Maybach, Wilhelm **13**:246
Midgley, Thomas, Jr. **13**:413
Nash, Charles William **14**:23
Studebaker (family) **18**:307
technology, history of **19**:68 *illus.*
transportation **19**:280
Japan **2**:364; **2**:366 *table*; **11**:365 *illus.*
jeep **11**:390–391 *illus.*
labor union
International Association of Machinists and Aerospace Workers **11**:218
United Auto Workers **19**:401
multinational operations **2**:368
Nader, Ralph **14**:5 *illus.*
patents **2**:363
petrochemicals **15**:206
petroleum **15**:207
pollution control **2**:367
production **2**:364; **2**:366–367 *table*
assembly line **2**:264–265; **13**:381 *illus.*; **19**:432 *illus.*
mass production **2**:363–367 *illus.*
robot assembly **19**:68 *illus.*
tire **19**:207–208
trucking industry **19**:315–316
United States **2**:363–368 *table*
Detroit (Michigan) **6**:136
Flint (Michigan) **8**:165
Lansing (Michigan) **12**:200
Michigan **13**:382
Volkswagen **19**:630
AUTOMOTIVE INSTRUMENTATION **2**:368 *bibliog.*
accelerometer **1**:76
tachometer **19**:6
temperature indicators **5**:242
AUTONOMIC NERVOUS SYSTEM *see* NERVOUS SYSTEM
AUTOPSY **2**:368 *bibliog.*
death and dying **6**:69
examination, medical **7**:326
pathology **15**:112
AUTORADIOGRAPHY
radioactivity **16**:62
AUTOS-DA-FÉ **11**:183 *illus.*
inquisition **11**:184
AUTOSTRADA *see* ROADS AND HIGHWAYS
AUTOSUCCESSION *see* PLANT SUCCESSION
AUTUN (France)
cathedral of saint lazare **8**:304 *illus.*; **16**:284 *illus.*
Gislebertus **9**:191
AUTUNITE **13**:441 *illus.*
AUVERGNE (France) **2**:368–369
cities
Clermont-Ferrand **5**:52
house (in Western architecture) **10**:268 *illus.*
AUVERGNE, WILLIAM OF *see* WILLIAM OF AUVERGNE
AUWERS, GEORGE FRIEDRICH JULIUS ARTHUR VON
astronomy, history of **2**:280
AUXERRE (France)
map (47° 48′N 3° 34′E) **8**:260
AUXIN (plant hormone) **2**:369
tropism **19**:309
AUXVASSE (Missouri)
map (39° 1′N 91° 54′W) **13**:476
AUYÁN-TEPUÍ
map (5° 55′N 62° 32′W) **19**:542
AVA (Illinois)
map (37° 53′N 89° 30′W) **11**:42
AVA (Missouri)
map (36° 57′N 92° 40′W) **13**:476
AVAHI
indri **11**:150–151
AVALANCHE *see* LANDSLIDE AND AVALANCHE
AVALOKITESVARA **11**:373 *illus.*; **12**:172 *illus.*
AVALON (New Jersey)
map (39° 6′N 74° 43′W) **14**:129
AVALON PENINSULA
map (47° 30′N 53° 30′W) **14**:166
AVANT (Oklahoma)
map (36° 29′N 96° 4′W) **14**:368
AVANT-GARDE **2**:369 *bibliog.*
brutalism **3**:528
concrete poetry **5**:171
constructivism **5**:224
cubism **5**:380–381
Dada **6**:4–5
electronic music **7**:124–126
expressionism (art) **7**:340
futurism **8**:383–384
happenings **10**:41
literary modernism **12**:370
new novel **14**:140
orphism **14**:448
performance art **10**:41
suprematism **18**:354
surrealism (art) **18**:364–365
surrealism (film, literature, theater) **18**:366
theater of the absurd **19**:154
vorticism **19**:635
AVARS **2**:369
AVATAR **2**:369
AVE MARIA **2**:369
AVEBURY (England) **2**:369 *bibliog.*
megalith **13**:279 *illus.*
Stukeley, William **18**:308
AVEBURY, JOHN LUBBOCK, 1ST BARON *see* LUBBOCK, JOHN, 1ST BARON AVEBURY
AVEDON, RICHARD **2**:369
AVEIRO (Portugal)
map (40° 38′N 8° 39′W) **15**:449
AVELLANEDA (Argentina)
map (34° 39′S 58° 23′W) **2**:149
AVELLINO (Italy)
map (40° 54′N 14° 47′E) **11**:321
AVEMPACE **2**:369
AVENAL (California)
map (36° 0′N 120° 8′W) **4**:31
AVENEL (New Jersey)
map (40° 35′N 74° 17′W) **14**:129
AVENGER (aircraft) *see* GRUMMAN TBF-1 AVENGER
AVERAGE *see* MEAN
AVERCAMP, HENDRIK VAN **2**:369–370 *bibliog.*
AVERLINO FILARETE, ANTONIO *see* FILARETE, ANTONIO AVERLINO
AVERNUS, LAKE **2**:370
AVERROËS **2**:370 *bibliog.*
Aquinas, Saint Thomas **2**:94–95 *illus.*
Lull, Raymond **12**:454
Siger de Brabant **17**:299
AVERSIVE CONDITIONING *see* BEHAVIOR MODIFICATION
AVERY (Idaho)
map (47° 15′N 115° 49′W) **11**:26

AVERY (county in North Carolina)
map (36° 5′N 81° 55′W) **14**:242
AVERY, MILTON 2:370 *bibliog.*
AVERY, OSWALD T. 2:370 *bibliog.*
McCarty, Maclyn **13**:9
MacLeod, Colin M. **13**:32
nucleic acid **14**:289
AVERY FISHER HALL
Lincoln Center for the Performing Arts **12**:350
AVERY ISLAND (Louisiana)
map (29° 55′N 91° 55′W) **12**:430
AVES *see* BIRD
AVESTA (Sweden)
map (60° 9′N 16° 12′E) **18**:382
AVEZZANO (Italy)
map (42° 2′N 13° 25′E) **11**:321
AVIATION **2**:370–375 *bibliog.*, *illus.*
See also AIRCRAFT
aerial photography **1**:119–120 *illus.*
aerial sports **1**:121–122 *illus.*
aerodynamics **1**:123–124 *illus.*
aerospace industry **1**:125–128
air force **1**:206–209
air law **1**:209
air rights **1**:209
airborne troops **1**:210
airmail **1**:222
airplane hijacking **1**:222
airport **1**:223–225 *illus.*; **2**:374–375
balloon **3**:51–53
barnstorming **3**:86
commercial aviation **2**:372; **2**:374–375 *illus.*
Civil Aeronautics Board **5**:9
containerization **5**:227
helicopter **10**:112
National Mediation Board **14**:35
routes, worldwide **19**:281 *map*
communications
frequency allocation **8**:326–327
flight **8**:164
flight, human-powered **8**:164–165
fuel
kerosene **12**:59
general aviation **2**:372–374
Ford Tri-motor **8**:223–224
government regulation **2**:374
Civil Aeronautics Board **5**:9
Federal Aviation Administration **8**:40
International Civil Aviation Organization **11**:219
history 1500–1918 **1**:210
aviation **2**:370–371 *illus.*
Blériot, Louis **3**:330–331
Boeing, William Edward **3**:358
Chanute, Octave **4**:282
Garnerin, André J. **9**:49
Lilienthal, Otto **12**:341
Montgolfier brothers **13**:556
Pénaud, Alphonse **15**:141
Richthofen, Manfred, Freiherr von **16**:215
Santos-Dumont, Alberto **17**:70–71
Wright, Orville and Wilbur **20**:290
history 1919-present
Alcock, Sir John William **1**:264
Bendix, Vincent **3**:196
Bennett, Floyd **3**:202
Blériot, Louis **3**:330–331
Boeing, William Edward **3**:358
Cierva, Juan de la **4**:429
Cochran, Jacqueline **5**:86
Concorde **5**:171 *illus.*
Curtiss, Glenn Hammond **5**:395
DC-3 **6**:57
Doolittle, James **6**:240
Douglas, Donald Wills **6**:247
Earhart, Amelia **7**:8
Ellsworth, Lincoln **7**:149
F-86 Sabre **8**:3
Fairchild, Sherman Mills **8**:9
flight, human-powered **8**:164–165
Fokker, Anthony Hermann Gerard **8**:193
Ford Tri-motor **8**:223–224
Grumman, Leroy **9**:382
Hindenburg **10**:168–169
Hughes, Howard **10**:292
Lilienthal, Otto **12**:341
Lindbergh, Charles A. **12**:351
Messerschmitt, Willy **13**:323
Mitchell, Billy **13**:482–483
Northrop, John Howard **14**:256
Pénaud, Alphonse **15**:141
Richthofen, Manfred, Freiherr von **16**:215
Rickenbacker, Eddie **16**:215
Rolls-Royce **16**:272
Santos-Dumont, Alberto **17**:70–71
Sikorsky, Igor **17**:303
technology, history of **19**:68
transportation **19**:280–281
Turner, Roscoe **19**:351
Whittle, Sir Frank **20**:142
Wilkins, Sir George Hubert **20**:152
Wright, Orville and Wilbur **20**:290
military aviation **2**:370–373 *illus.*
air force **1**:206–209 *illus.*
aircraft, military **1**:214–220
motion sickness **13**:610
National Air and Space Museum **14**:28–29
navigation **14**:60
parachute **15**:74–75
radar **16**:38–40
space medicine **18**:132–134
hypoxia **10**:351
weightlessness **20**:92
traffic control **1**:224–225 *illus.*; **19**:264
AVICENNA **2**:376 *bibliog.*
anatomy **1**:395–396
medicine **13**:268
perfume **15**:164
AVIERO, JOÃO AFONSO DE
Benin, Kingdom of **3**:201
AVIGNON (France) **2**:376
map (43° 57′N 4° 49′E) **8**:260
Philip IV, King of France (Philip the Fair) **15**:232
ÁVILA (Spain)
map (40° 39′N 4° 42′W) **18**:140
ÁVILA CAMACHO, MANUEL **2**:376
Mexico, history of **13**:366
AVILÉS (Spain)
map (43° 33′N 5° 55′W) **18**:140
AVILÉS, PEDRO MENÉNDEZ DE *see* MENÉNDEZ DE AVILÉS, PEDRO
AVIS, HOUSE OF
Portugal, history of **15**:453
AVISON, MARGARET **2**:376
AVOCA (Iowa)
map (41° 29′N 95° 20′W) **11**:244
AVOCADO **2**:376 *illus.*
AVOCET **2**:376 *illus.*
shorebirds **17**:283
AVOGADRO, AMEDEO **2**:377 *bibliog.*
chemistry, history of **4**:326
organic chemistry **14**:435
AVOGADRO NUMBER **2**:377
atomic constants **2**:309
equivalent weight **7**:227
mole (unit of substance) **13**:507
AVOGADRO'S LAW **2**:377
Cannizzaro, Stanislao **4**:111
AVOIRDUPOIS
weights and measures **20**:93–94 *table*
AVOLA (British Columbia)
map (51° 47′N 119° 19′W) **3**:491
AVON (England) **2**:377
cities
Bath **3**:121–122
AVON (Massachusetts)
map (42° 8′N 71° 2′W) **3**:409
AVON (Minnesota)
map (45° 37′N 94° 27′W) **13**:453
AVON (New York)
map (42° 55′N 77° 45′W) **14**:149
AVON, ANTHONY EDEN, 1ST EARL OF *see* EDEN, SIR ANTHONY
AVON, RIVER **2**:377
map (52° 25′N 1° 31′W) **19**:403
AVON LAKE (Ohio)
map (41° 30′N 82° 1′W) **14**:357
AVON PARK (Florida)
map (27° 36′N 81° 31′W) **8**:172
AVON RIVER (Nova Scotia)
map (45° 10′N 64° 15′W) **14**:269
AVONDALE (Arizona)
map (33° 26′N 112° 21′W) **2**:160
AVONDALE (Colorado)
map (38° 14′N 104° 21′W) **5**:116
AVONMORE (Pennsylvania)
map (40° 32′N 79° 28′W) **15**:147
AVOYELLES (county in Louisiana)
map (31° 5′N 92° 0′W) **12**:430
AWACS *see* AIRBORNE WARNING AND CONTROL SYSTEM
AWALI (Bahrain)
map (26° 5′N 50° 33′E) **3**:24
AWAMI LEAGUE
Bangladesh **3**:66
Mujibur Rahman **13**:635
AWARDS *see* MEDALS AND DECORATIONS
AWASH RIVER **7**:254 *illus.*
map (11° 45′N 41° 5′E) **7**:253
AWKA (Nigeria)
map (6° 12′N 7° 5′E) **14**:190
AWOONOR, KOFI **2**:377
AX *see* HAND TOOLS
AXEL HEIBURG ISLAND
map (80° 30′N 92° 0′W) **14**:258
AXELROD, JULIUS **2**:377
Katz, Sir Bernard **12**:31
AXINITE
triclinic system **19**:296
AXIOM **2**:377–378 *bibliog.*
Euclidean geometry **7**:263
proof, mathematical **15**:568
AXIOS (VARDAR) RIVER
map (40° 31′N 22° 43′E) **20**:340
AXIS (mathematics) **2**:378
AXIS (rotation)
Earth, motions of **7**:18–19
Earth, size and shape of **7**:19
telescope **19**:83
AXIS (World War II) **2**:378
See also WORLD WAR II
Hitler, Adolf **10**:188
AXLE
wagon **20**:6
wheel **20**:127–129
AXOLOTL **2**:378 *illus.*
larva **12**:208
Mexican salamander **13**:351
neoteny **14**:86
AXON *see* NERVE CELL; NERVOUS SYSTEM
AXTELL (Nebraska)
map (40° 29′N 99° 8′W) **14**:70
AXUM *see* AKSUM (Ethiopia)
AYABACA (Peru)
map (4° 38′S 79° 43′W) **15**:193
AYACUCHO (Argentina)
map (37° 9′S 58° 29′W) **2**:149
AYACUCHO (Peru)
map (13° 7′S 74° 13′W) **15**:193
AYALA, FELIPE HUAMAN POMA DE
history of the Incan Empire **11**:71 *illus.*
AYALA, PLAN OF (1911)
Zapata, Emiliano **20**:356 *illus.*
AYALA, TURBAY
Colombia **5**:109
AYAPEL (Colombia)
map (8° 19′N 75° 9′W) **5**:107
AYAVIRI (Peru)
map (14° 52′S 70° 35′W) **15**:193
AYCKBOURN, ALAN **2**:378
AYDEN (North Carolina)
map (35° 25′N 77° 20′W) **14**:242
AYE-AYE **2**:378 *illus.*; **15**:540 *illus.*
AYER (Massachusetts)
map (42° 34′N 71° 35′W) **13**:206
AYER, SIR ALFRED JULES **2**:378
ethics **7**:250
logical positivism **12**:397
AYERS ROCK (Australia) **2**:378–379 *illus.*
AYIN
O (letter) **14**:310
AYLLÓN, LUCAS VÁSQUEZ DE **2**:379
exploration of colonial America **19**:437 *map*
AYMARA (American Indians) **2**:379 *bibliog.*
AYMÉ, MARCEL **2**:379
AYO AYO (Bolivia)
map (17° 5′S 68° 0′W) **3**:366
AYR (Scotland) **2**:379
map (55° 28′N 4° 38′W) **19**:403
AYRES, AGNES **8**:83 *illus.*
AYRSHIRE CATTLE **4**:216 *illus.*
AYRTON, HERTHA AND WILLIAM EDWARD **2**:379
AYUB KHAN, MUHAMMAD **2**:379 *bibliog.*
Pakistan **15**:29
AYUHWA (American Indians)
Iowa **11**:248
AYUTHIA (Thailand) **2**:379–380
AYUTLA DE LOS LIBRES (Mexico)
map (16° 54′N 99° 13′W) **13**:357
AYUTTHAYA (kingdom)
Thailand **19**:141
AYYUBIDS **2**:380 *bibliog.*
Egypt **7**:79–80
Middle East, history of the **13**:404
Saladin **17**:29
AZ-ZAHRAN (Saudi Arabia) *see* DHAHRAN (Saudi Arabia)
AZAD KASHMIR
flag **8**:144 *illus.*
Kashmir **12**:31
AZALEA **2**:380 *illus.*
rhododendron **16**:203
AZAÑA, MANUEL **2**:380
AZANDE **2**:380 *bibliog.*
magic **13**:49–50
passage rites **15**:103
AZAOUAD (region in Mali)
map (19° 0′N 3° 0′W) **13**:89
AZAZ (Syria)
map (36° 35′N 37° 3′E) **18**:412
AZCAPOTZALCO
Aztec **2**:382
AZEOTROPIC MIXTURE **2**:380
ethyl alcohol **7**:257
phase equilibrium **15**:223
AZERBAIJAN SOVIET SOCIALIST REPUBLIC (USSR) **2**:380–381
Baku **3**:29–30
AZIDE **2**:381 *bibliog.*
AZILIAN **2**:381 *bibliog.*
writing systems, evolution of **20**:292
AZIMUTH
coordinate systems (astronomy) **5**:245–246 *illus.*
AZNAVOUR, CHARLES **2**:381 *bibliog.*
AZNAVURJAN, CHARLES *see* AZNAVOUR, CHARLES
AZO GROUP **2**:381 *illus.*
AZOBENZENE **2**:381
AZOGUES (Ecuador)
map (2° 44′S 78° 50′W) **7**:52
AZORES (Portugal) **2**:381–382 *map*
cities
Ponta Delgada **15**:426
map (38° 30′N 28° 0′W) **15**:449
AZORES HIGH
Hadley cell **10**:8
high-pressure region **10**:162
AZORÍN (pseudonym) *see* RUIZ, JOSÉ MARTÍNEZ
AZOV, SEA OF **2**:382; **3**:318 *map*
map (46° 0′N 36° 0′E) **19**:388
Russo-Turkish Wars **16**:374
AZTEC **2**:382–384 *bibliog.*, *illus.*, *map*
agriculture, history of **1**:190
archaeological sites
México (state) **13**:366
Tehuacán Valley **19**:73
Tenochtitlán **19**:112
Teotihuacán **19**:113–114
art
Codex Borbonicus **12**:223 *illus.*
codex portraying Quetzalcóatl **16**:24 *illus.*
Latin American art and architecture **12**:222–223
mosaic **15**:498 *illus.*
pre-Columbian art and architecture **15**:498–499 *illus.*
calendar **15**:545 *illus.*
cannibalism **4**:109 *illus.*
Caso, Alfonso **4**:182
emperors
Cuauhtémoc **5**:377
Montezuma II **13**:555
history **2**:382–383
Cortés, Hernán **5**:278; **11**:134 *illus.*
Latin America, history of **12**:216–217 *illus.*; **12**:218–219
Mexico, history of **13**:362
Tlaxcala (state) **19**:216
Indians, American **11**:118
Mixtec, relations with **13**:486
mythology and religion **2**:384
Huitzilopochtli **10**:295
quetzal **16**:24
Quetzalcóatl **11**:122 *illus.*; **16**:24
Tezcatlipoca **19**:138
shield **11**:121 *illus.*
Tarascan, relations with **19**:35
Toltec **19**:228–229
writing systems, evolution of **20**:292
Zapotec, relations with **20**:356
AZTEC (New Mexico)
map (36° 49′N 107° 59′W) **14**:136
AZUA (Dominican Republic)
map (18° 27′N 70° 44′W) **6**:233
AZUCENA (Argentina)
map (37° 29′S 59° 18′W) **2**:149
AZUCHI (Japan)
castle **4**:190
Nobunaga **14**:212
AZUELA, MARIANO **2**:384
AZUERO PENINSULA
map (7° 40′N 80° 35′W) **15**:55
AZUL (Argentina)
map (36° 47′S 59° 51′W) **2**:149
AZURE COAST *see* CÔTE D'AZUR (France)
AZURITE **2**:384 *illus.*
AZZEL MATTI SABKHA
map (25° 55′N 0° 56′E) **1**:287

B

B (letter) **3**:3 *illus.*
B. EVERETT JORDAN LAKE
map (35° 45′N 79° 0′W) **14**:242
B_1 (vitamin) *see* THIAMINE

B_{12} (vitamin) *see* VITAMIN B_{12}
B-1 BOMBER 3:3–4 *illus.*
B-17 FLYING FORTRESS 1:216 *illus.*; 3:4 *illus.*; 20:266 *illus.*
B-24 LIBERATOR 3:4
B-25 BOMBER 20:266 *illus.*
B-29 SUPERFORTRESS 1:216 *illus.*; 3:4
B-52 STRATOFORTRESS 1:216 *illus.*; 3:4
X-15 20:311
BA JIN *see* PA CHIN (Ba Jin)
BA XIAN *see* PA HSIEN (Ba Xian)
BAADE, WALTER 3:4 *bibliog.*
Zwicky, Fritz 20:384
BAAL 3:5 *bibliog.*; 15:250 *illus.*
mythology 13:698–699 *illus.*
BAAL SHEM TOV 3:5 *bibliog.*
Hasidism 10:66
BAALBEK (Lebanon) 3:5; 12:267 *illus.*
map (34° 0′N 36° 12′E) 12:265
BAATH PARTY 3:5 *bibliog.*
Iraq 11:256
BAB EL-MANDEB 3:5
map (12° 40′N 43° 20′E) 6:208
Red Sea 16:113–114
BABA (Ecuador)
map (1° 47′S 79° 40′W) 7:52
BABAHOYO (Ecuador)
map (1° 49′S 79° 31′W) 7:52
BABAR *see* BABUR, MOGUL EMPEROR OF INDIA
BABBAGE, CHARLES 3:5 *bibliog.*
computer 5:160 *illus.*
mathematics, history of 13:226
BABBITT (book) 3:5 *bibliog.*
Lewis, Sinclair 11:306–307
BABBITT (Minnesota)
map (47° 43′N 91° 57′W) 13:453
BABBITT (Nevada)
map (38° 39′N 118° 37′W) 14:111
BABBITT, IRVING 3:5 *bibliog.*
BABBITT, MILTON 3:5–6 *bibliog.*
serial music 17:208
BABBITT METALS 3:6
bearing 3:143
BABBLER 3:6
rockfowl 16:260
wren-tit 20:286
BABCOCK, ALPHEUS
piano 15:288
BABCOCK, HAROLD D.
Babcock, Horace Welcome 3:6
BABCOCK, HORACE WELCOME 3:6
BABCOCK, JOSEPH P.
Mah-Jongg 13:63
BABCOCK, ORVILLE E.
Whiskey Ring 20:133
BABCOCK, STEPHEN MOULTON 3:6
BABDA (Lebanon)
map (33° 50′N 35° 32′E) 12:265
BABEL, ISAAK EMMANUILOVICH 3:6 *bibliog.*
BABEL, TOWER OF 3:6; 19:95 *illus.*
Mesopotamian art and architecture 13:321
BABER *see* BABUR, MOGUL EMPEROR OF INDIA
BABESIA 3:6
BABEUF, FRANÇOIS NOËL 3:6 *bibliog.*
socialism 18:19
BABINE LAKE
map (54° 45′N 126° 0′W) 3:491
BABINGTON PLOT *see* MARY, QUEEN OF SCOTS
BABIRUSA 3:6–7 *illus.*
BABISM 3:7 *bibliog.*
Bahaullah 3:24
BABITS, MIHÁLY
Hungarian literature 10:306
BABIUCH, EDWARD
Poland 15:390
BABOL (Iran)
map (36° 34′N 52° 42′E) 11:250
BABOON 3:7 *bibliog.*, *illus.*
social behavior 13:101 *illus.*
BABOQUIVARI PEAK
map (31° 46′N 111° 35′W) 2:160
BABUR, MOGUL EMPEROR OF INDIA 3:7 *bibliog.*
India, history of 11:91
Moguls (dynasty) 13:502
Timurids (dynasty) 19:204
BABUYAN ISLANDS
map (19° 10′N 121° 40′E) 15:237
BABY *see* INFANCY
BABY SNOOKS
Brice, Fanny 3:477
BABYLON 3:8 *bibliog.*, *illus.*, *map*
Etemenaki ziggurat 13:321 *illus.*; 19:95 *illus.*
fortification 8:238
Hanging Gardens 17:216–217 *illus.*
Ishtar Gate 13:321 *illus.*
Mesopotamian art and architecture 13:320–321 *illus.*
BABYLONIA 3:8–9 *bibliog.*, *map*
Akkad 1:231
Asia, history of 2:249–250
Assyria 2:266
astronomy, history of 2:277
Chaldea 4:270–271
cities
Babylon 3:8 *map*
Kish 12:90
Lagash 12:165
Sippar 17:327
Ur 19:474
cuneiform 5:389 *illus.*
Cyrus the Great, King of Persia 5:410
Enuma Elish 7:209
Fertile Crescent 8:60
Hammurabi, Code of 10:31
Hammurabi, King 10:32
Jews 11:414
Kassites 12:30
mathematics, history of 13:223
medicine 13:267 *illus.*
Mesopotamia 13:316
Mesopotamian art and architecture 13:317; 13:320–322
Nebuchadnezzar II, King 14:74
Sennacherib, King of Assyria 17:203
Tiglath-Pileser III, King of Assyria 19:197
BABYLONIAN CAPTIVITY (Jewish history) 3:9
Cyrus the Great, King of Persia 5:410
diaspora 6:153
Ezekiel, Book of 7:352
BABYLONIAN CAPTIVITY (papacy)
Clement V, Pope 5:49
Clement VI, Pope 5:50
Middle Ages 13:393
papacy 15:65
BABYLONIAN EMPIRE *see* BABYLONIA
BABYLONIAN MYTHOLOGY *see* NEAR EASTERN MYTHOLOGY
BABY'S BREATH (botany) 3:9
BAC LIEU (Vietnam)
map (9° 17′N 105° 44′E) 19:580
BAC NINH (Vietnam)
map location (21° 11′N 106° 3′E) 19:580
BACA (county in Colorado)
map (37° 20′N 102° 30′W) 5:116
BACALL, LAUREN 3:9 *bibliog.*
Bogart, Humphrey 3:359
BACĂU (Romania)
map (46° 34′N 26° 55′E) 16:288
BACCALONI, SALVATORE 3:9
BACCARAT (card game) 3:9 *bibliog.*
BACCARAT (glassware)
glassware, decorative 9:204
perfume flask 2:208 *illus.*
BACCHAE, THE (play) 3:9 *bibliog.*
BACCHANALIA 3:9
BACCHUS 3:9; 17:66 *illus.*
BACCHYLIDES 3:9–10 *bibliog.*
BACCIO DELLA PORTA *see* BARTOLOMMEO, FRA
BACH, CARL PHILIPP EMANUEL 3:10 *bibliog.*, *table*
BACH, JOHANN CHRISTIAN 3:10 *bibliog.*, *table*
BACH, JOHANN SEBASTIAN 3:10–11 *bibliog.*, *illus.*, *table*; 9:130 *illus.*
Albinoni, Tommaso 1:260
cantata 4:116
capriccio 4:128
fugue 8:355
Leipzig (East Germany) 12:278
music, history of Western 13:665 *illus.*
prelude 15:518
recitative 16:107
sons
Bach, Carl Philipp Emanuel 3:10
Bach, Johann Christian 3:10
Bach, Wilhelm Friedemann 3:11
toccata 19:220
BACH, WILHELM FRIEDEMANN 3:11 *bibliog.*, *table*
BACHARACH, BURT 3:11
BACHELIER, JEAN JACQUES
Sèvres ware 17:221
BACHELOR'S BUTTON (botany) 3:11
BACHER, ROBERT FOX 3:11
BACHERELLI, VINCENZO
Portuguese art and architecture 15:456
BACHMANN, INGEBORG 3:11
BACHMAN'S SNOUT BUTTERFLY 3:595–596 *illus.*
BACHOFEN, JOHANN JAKOB 3:12
women in society 20:201
BACICCIO *see* GAULLI, GIOVANNI BATISTA
BACILLARY DYSENTERY 6:320
BACILLUS
bacteria 3:15
spore 18:195
BACITRACIN
antibiotics 2:57
BACK
chiropractic 4:397
lumbago 12:454
muscle 13:654
sciatica 17:141
sports medicine 18:198
BACK CREEK
map (38° 2′N 79° 54′W) 13:188
BACK RIVER
map (67° 15′N 95° 15′W) 14:258
BAČKA PALANKA (Yugoslavia)
map (45° 15′N 19° 24′E) 20:340
BACKACHE
lumbago 12:454
BACKBONE *see* SPINE (backbone)
BACKBONE MOUNTAIN
map (39° 14′N 79° 29′W) 13:188
BACKFIRE (aircraft) *see* TUPOLEV V-G "BACKFIRE B" AIRCRAFT
BACKGAMMON 3:12 *bibliog.*, *illus.*
BACKGROUND RADIATION 3:12 *bibliog.*
big bang theory 3:248
cosmic rays 5:283–284
discovery 3:12
ether (physics) 7:250
radio astronomy 16:50
Wilson, Robert W., and Penzias, Arno A. 20:165
BACKHAUS, WILHELM 3:12–13
BACKHOE
earth-moving machinery 7:24
BACKPACKING *see* HIKING
BACKSTAFF 14:58 *illus.*
BACKSTROKE
swimming 18:390–391 *illus.*
BACKSWIMMER (insect) 3:13
See also WATER BUG
BACON 3:13 *bibliog.*
nitrite 14:202
BACON (county in Georgia)
map (31° 35′N 82° 25′W) 9:114
BACON, FRANCIS (painter) 3:13 *bibliog.*, *illus.*
Study of Velázquez's Portrait of Innocent X 3:13 *illus.*; 7:188 *illus.*
BACON, FRANCIS (philosopher) 3:13–14 *bibliog.*, *illus.*
James I, King of England 11:356
science, philosophy of 17:142
BACON, PEGGY 3:14 *bibliog.*
BACON, ROGER 3:14 *bibliog.*
alchemy 1:263
BACON'S REBELLION 3:14 *bibliog.*
medicinal plants 13:266
United States, history of the 19:437
BACONTON (Georgia)
map (31° 23′N 84° 10′W) 9:114
BACTERIA 3:14–18 *bibliog.*, *illus.*
See also EUBACTERIA; names of specific bacteria, e.g., PNEUMOCOCCUS; *STREPTOCOCCUS*; etc.
anaerobe 1:387
antibiotics 2:57–58
antibody 2:59–60
antigen 2:61
bacteriology, history of
Avery, Oswald T. 2:370
Bordet, Jules 3:398
Carroll, James 4:168
Cohn, Ferdinand J. 5:96
de Kruif, Paul 6:60
Delbrück, Max 6:91–92
Ehrlich, Paul (1854–1915) 7:90
Hershey, Alfred Day 10:148
Koch, Robert 12:104–105
Luria, Salvador 12:467
Roux, Pierre Paul Émile 16:327
biological locomotion 3:265
bioluminescence 3:272
cancer 4:104
chlorophyll 4:402
classification, biological 5:43
Cohn, Ferdinand J. 5:96
conjugation 5:191
Delbrück, Max 6:91–92
dentistry 6:114
destruction 3:16
digestive system 6:174
digestion, human 6:172
ruminant 16:345
diseases
abscess 1:62
blood, septicemia 17:206
diseases, animal 6:191–192
Dubos, Rene 6:289
endocarditis 7:168
gastrointestinal tract disease 9:56–57
infectious diseases 11:165
Legionnaires' disease 12:274
leprosy 12:295
leptospirosis 12:296
peritonitis 15:172
pneumonia 15:375–376
reproduction 16:162
respiratory system disorders 16:181
rickettsia 16:215
fermentation 8:55
genetic engineering 9:84–85
housefly 10:274
Lederberg, Joshua 12:268
life span 12:330
microbiology 13:384
myxobacteria 13:704
nitrogen cycle 14:203
pathogenic
poisonous plants and animals 15:383
photosynthesis 15:275
plant 15:333–335 *illus.*
plasmid 15:347
spirochete 18:189
spontaneous generation 18:194
spore 18:195
virus 19:614
water quality 20:51
BACTERIOLOGY *see* BACTERIA
BACTERIOPHAGE
Delbrück, Max 6:92
Luria, Salvador 12:467
parasite 15:82
virus 19:613–615 *illus.*
BACTRIA 3:18 *bibliog.*
Persia, ancient 15:182 *map*
BACTRIAN CAMEL
camel 4:53–54 *illus.*
BAD AXE (Michigan)
map (43° 48′N 83° 0′W) 13:377
BAD ISCHI (Austria)
map (47° 43′N 13° 37′E) 2:348
BAD KREUZNACH (Germany, East and West)
map (49° 52′N 7° 51′E) 9:140
BAD RIVER
map (44° 22′N 100° 22′W) 18:103
BADAGA 3:18 *bibliog.*
BADAJOZ (Spain) 3:18–19
map (38° 53′N 6° 58′W) 18:140
BADALONA (Spain) 3:19
BADDECK (Nova Scotia)
map (46° 7′N 60° 45′W) 14:269
BADEN (Pennsylvania)
map (40° 38′N 80° 14′W) 15:147
BADEN (Switzerland)
map (47° 29′N 8° 18′E) 18:394
BADEN (West Germany) 3:19 *bibliog.*
Black Forest 3:315
Germany in 1648 9:151 *map*
Germany 1815–1871 9:153 *map*
Swabia 18:375
BADEN-BADEN (West Germany) 3:19
map (48° 46′N 8° 14′E) 9:140
BADEN-POWELL, ROBERT STEPHENSON SMYTH, 1st BARON BADEN-POWELL OF GILWELL 3:19 *bibliog.*
Scouting 17:156
BADEN-WÜRTTEMBERG (West Germany)
See also BADEN (West Germany); WÜRTTEMBERG (West Germany)
cities
Baden-Baden 3:19
Freiburg im Breisgau 8:301
Heidelberg 10:107
Karlsruhe 12:28
Mannheim 13:125
Stuttgart 18:310
BADGER 3:19 *bibliog.*, *illus.*; 8:228 *illus.*
BADGER (Minnesota)
map (48° 47′N 96° 1′W) 13:453
BADGER (Newfoundland)
map (48° 59′N 56° 2′W) 14:166
BADGER, DANIEL
cast-iron architecture 4:186
BADGER DOG *see* DACHSHUND
BADGES *see* MEDALS AND DECORATIONS
BADILLO, HERMAN 10:178
BADINGS, HENK 3:19

BADLANDS 3:19–20; 14:250 *illus.*; 18:104 *illus.*; 19:424 *illus.*
map (43° 30′N 102° 20′W) 18:103
national parks 14:38 *map, table*
Painted Desert (Arizona) 15:17
BADMINTON 3:20 *bibliog., illus.*
BADOGLIO, PIETRO 3:20
Victor Emmanuel III, King of Italy 19:573
World War II 20:268
BADULLA (Sri Lanka)
map (6° 59′N 81° 3′E) 18:206
BAECK, LEO 3:20 *bibliog.*
BAEDEKER, KARL 3:20
BAEKELAND, LEO HENDRIK
plastics 15:348
BAER, KARL ERNST VON 3:20 *bibliog.*
biology 3:270
BÆRTLING, OLLE
Scandinavian art and architecture 17:114
BAEYER, ADOLF VON 3:20–21
indigo 11:144
pyrrole 15:639
BAEZ, JOAN 3:21; 8:202 *illus.*
BAEZA (Ecuador)
map (0° 27′S 77° 53′W) 7:52
BAFATÁ (Guinea-Bissau)
map (12° 10′N 14° 40′W) 9:399
BAFFIN, WILLIAM 3:21
BAFFIN BAY 3:21
Davis Strait 6:53
map (73° 0′N 66° 0′W) 4:70
BAFFIN ISLAND (Northwest Territories) 3:21
climate 4:74 *table*
map (68° 0′N 70° 0′W) 14:258
BAFING RIVER
map (13° 49′N 10° 50′W) 13:236
BAFRA (Turkey)
map (41° 34′N 35° 56′E) 19:343
BAGAZA, JEAN BAPTISTE
Burundi 3:583
BAGDAD (Arizona)
map (34° 34′N 113° 11′W) 2:160
BAGÉ (Brazil)
map (31° 20′S 54° 6′W) 3:460
BAGEHOT, WALTER 3:21 *bibliog.*
Social Darwinism 18:11–12
BAGGARA 3:21 *bibliog.*
BAGGS (Wyoming)
map (41° 2′N 107° 39′W) 20:301
BAGHDAD (Iraq) 3:21–22 *bibliog., illus.*; 11:255 *illus., table*
Mansur, al- 13:129
map (33° 21′N 44° 25′E) 11:255
BAGHDAD PACT *see* CENTRAL TREATY ORGANIZATION
BAGHLAN (Afghanistan)
map (36° 13′N 68° 46′E) 1:133
BAGLEY (Minnesota)
map (47° 31′N 95° 24′W) 13:453
BAGLEY, SARAH G. 3:22
BAGLEY, WILLIAM C.
middle schools and junior high schools 13:412
BAGNOLD, ENID 3:22
BAGOT, CHARLES
Rush, Richard 16:347
BAGPIPE 3:22–23 *bibliog., illus.*; 17:149 *illus.*
BAGRYANA, ELISAVETA
Bulgarian literature 3:557
BAGUIO (Philippines) 3:23
map (16° 25′N 120° 36′E) 15:237
BAHA' ALLAH *see* BAHAULLAH
BAHA'I 3:23 *bibliog.*
Bahaullah 3:24
BAHAIA, MOUNT
map (11° 13′N 49° 43′E) 18:60
BAHAMA ISLANDS 3:23–24 *bibliog., illus., map*
flag 3:23 *illus.*
history 3:23–24
map (24° 15′N 76° 0′W) 20:109
Nassau 3:24 *illus.*; 14:25
San Salvador Island 17:57–58
BAHAULLAH 3:24 *bibliog.*
BAHAWALNAGAR
map (29° 59′N 73° 16′E) 15:27
BAHAWALPUR
map (29° 24′N 71° 41′E) 15:27
BAHIA (Brazil)
map (11° 0′S 42° 0′W) 3:460
BAHÍA BLANCA (Argentina) 3:24
map (38° 43′S 62° 17′W) 2:149
BAHÍA DE CARÁQUEZ (Ecuador)
map (0° 36′S 80° 25′W) 7:52
BAHÍA LAURA (Argentina)
map (48° 24′S 66° 29′W) 2:149
BAHÍA NEGRA (Paraguay)
map (20° 15′S 58° 12′W) 15:77
BAHR AL-JEBEL
Nile River 14:196; 14:197
BAHRAIN 3:24–25 *bibliog., illus., map, table*
Dilmun 6:176
education
Middle Eastern universities 13:410–412 *table*
flag 3:24 *illus.*
history 3:25
Manama 13:108
map (26° 0′N 50° 30′E) 2:232
BAHRAIN, GULF OF
map (25° 45′N 50° 40′E) 3:24
BAHRAM CHOBIN, KING OF PERSIA
Persia, ancient 15:183
BAHRAM V, KING OF PERSIA
Persia, ancient 15:183
BAHUTU *see* HUTU
BAIA-MARE (Romania)
map (47° 40′N 23° 35′E) 16:288
BAIE-COMEAU (Quebec)
map (49° 13′N 68° 10′W) 16:18
BAIE-SAINT-PAUL (Quebec)
map (47° 27′N 70° 30′W) 16:18
BAIE VERTE (Newfoundland)
map (49° 56′N 56° 11′W) 14:166
BAIKAL, LAKE 3:25 *map*; 19:396 *illus.*
Buryat 3:583
map (53° 0′N 107° 40′E) 19:388
Trans-Siberian Railroad 19:267
BAIKONUR COSMODROME 3:26 *bibliog.*
Sputnik 18:201
BAIL 3:26
criminal justice 5:349–350
BAILEY (North Carolina)
map (35° 47′N 78° 7′W) 14:242
BAILEY (county in Texas)
map (34° 2′N 102° 48′W) 19:129
BAILEY, F. LEE 3:26 *bibliog.*
BAILEY, JAMES A. *see* BARNUM, P. T.
BAILEY, LIBERTY HYDE 3:26
BAILEY BRIDGE 3:26
BAILEY HORTORIUM
Bailey, Liberty Hyde 3:26
BAILEY* v. *DREXEL FURNITURE COMPANY 3:26
BAILLIE, BRUCE
film, history of 8:87
BAILLIES BACOLET (Grenada)
map (12° 2′N 61° 41′W) 9:358
BAILY, FRANCIS 3:26
BAILY'S BEADS
Baily, Francis 3:26
BAIN, ALEXANDER
associationism 2:265–266
BAINBRIDGE (Georgia)
map (30° 54′N 84° 34′W) 9:114
BAINBRIDGE (Ohio)
map (39° 14′N 83° 16′W) 14:357
BAINBRIDGE, WILLIAM 3:26–27 *bibliog.*
BAIRD (Texas)
map (32° 24′N 99° 24′W) 19:129
BAIRD, BIL AND CORA 3:27
BAIRD, JOHN L.
television 19:88 *illus.*
BAIRD, SPENCER F. 3:27 *bibliog.*
BAIRE, RENÉ 3:27
mathematics, history of 13:226
BAIROIL (Wyoming)
map (42° 15′N 107° 33′W) 20:301
BAJ, ENRICO 3:27 *bibliog.*
BAJA (Hungary)
map (46° 11′N 18° 57′E) 10:307
BAJA CALIFORNIA (Mexico) 3:27
cities
La Paz 12:148
Mexicali 13:350
Tijuana 19:198
Kino, Eusebio Francisco 12:84–85
map (28° 0′N 113° 30′W) 13:357
BAJADA *see* ALLUVIAL FANS
BAKAU (Gambia)
map (13° 29′N 16° 41′W) 9:25
BAKELITE 3:27
plastics 15:348
BAKER (California)
map (35° 16′N 116° 4′W) 4:31
BAKER (county in Florida)
map (30° 20′N 82° 15′W) 8:172
BAKER (county in Georgia)
map (31° 20′N 84° 30′W) 9:114
BAKER (Louisiana)
map (30° 35′N 91° 10′W) 12:430
BAKER (Montana)
map (46° 22′N 104° 17′W) 13:547
BAKER (Oregon)
map (44° 47′N 117° 50′W) 14:427
BAKER (county in Oregon)
map (44° 45′N 117° 40′W) 14:427
BAKER, SIR BENJAMIN 3:27
BAKER, GEORGE PIERCE 3:27 *bibliog.*
BAKER, HOWARD (political figure) 3:27
BAKER, HOWARD E. (scientist)
paleogeography 15:37
BAKER, JAMES A. 3:27
BAKER, JANET 3:28 *bibliog.*
BAKER, JOHN
dentistry 6:115
BAKER, JOSEPHINE 3:28 *bibliog.*
BAKER, MOUNT
map (48° 47′N 121° 49′W) 20:35
BAKER, NEWTON DIEHL 3:28 *bibliog.*
BAKER, NORMA JEAN *see* MONROE, MARILYN
BAKER, PHILIP JOHN NOEL-, BARON NOEL-BAKER *see* NOEL-BAKER, PHILIP JOHN, BARON NOEL-BAKER
BAKER, RAY STANNARD 3:28
BAKER, RUSSELL 3:28
BAKER, SIR SAMUEL WHITE 3:28 *bibliog.*
Africa 1:157 *map*
BAKER ISLAND
map (0° 15′N 176° 27′W) 14:334
United States outlying territories 19:464
BAKER LAKE (Northwest Territories)
map (64° 15′N 96° 0′W) 14:258
BAKER LAKE (Washington)
map (48° 43′N 121° 37′W) 20:35
BAKER* v. *CARR 3:28
apportionment 2:91
BAKERSFIELD (California) 3:28
map (35° 23′N 119° 1′W) 4:31
BAKERSVILLE (North Carolina)
map (36° 1′N 82° 9′W) 14:242
BAKHTIARI 3:28–29 *bibliog.*; 11:251 *illus.*
BAKING INDUSTRY 3:29 *bibliog.*
bread 3:465–467
cake and pastry 4:20–21
BAKING POWDER 3:29
BAKING SODA *see* SODIUM BICARBONATE
BAKKARA *see* BAGGARA
BAKKE CASE *see* *UNIVERSITY OF CALIFORNIA v. BAKKE*
BAKONY MOUNTAINS
map (46° 55′N 17° 40′E) 10:307
BAKR, AHMAD HASSAN AL-
Iraq 11:256
BAKST, LÉON 3:29 *bibliog.*
Art Deco 2:207
Ballets Russes de Serge Diaghilev 3:48
dance 6:25 *illus.*
set for *Schéhérazade* 16:363 *illus.*
BAKU (USSR) 3:29–30
map (40° 23′N 49° 51′E) 19:388
BAKUNIN, MIKHAIL ALEKSANDROVICH 3:30 *bibliog.*
anarchism 1:392
International, Socialist 11:218
Marx, Karl 13:182
socialism 18:20–21
BALABAC ISLAND
map (7° 57′N 117° 1′E) 15:237
BALABAC STRAIT
map (7° 35′N 117° 0′E) 15:237
BALAGUER, JOAQUÍN 3:30
Dominican Republic 6:234
BALAKIREV, MILY ALEKSEYEVICH 3:30 *bibliog.*
Five, The 8:132
BALAKLAVA, BATTLE OF 3:30 *bibliog.*
Crimean War 5:348
BALALAIKA 3:30 *bibliog., illus.*
BALANCE (weighing device) 3:30–31 *bibliog., illus.*
Fairbanks, Thaddeus 8:9
measurement 13:254–255 *illus.*
BALANCE, BIOLOGICAL *see* BIOLOGICAL EQUILIBRIUM
BALANCE OF PAYMENTS 3:31–32
balance of trade 3:32
International Monetary Fund 11:222
tariff 19:36
BALANCE OF POWER 3:32 *bibliog.*
Metternich, Klemens, Fürst von 13:349–350
Palmerston, Henry John Temple, 3d Viscount 15:51
Utrecht, Peace of 19:498
Vienna, Congress of 19:579
BALANCE SHEET 3:392 *illus.*
BALANCE OF TRADE *see* BALANCE OF PAYMENTS
BALANCHINE, GEORGE 3:32–33 *bibliog., illus.*; 13:667 *illus.*
ballet 3:44–45 *illus.*
Ballets Russes de Monte Carlo 3:48
Ballets Russes de Serge Diaghilev 3:48–49
choreography 4:409 *illus.*
Dance Theatre of Harlem 6:30
Farrell, Suzanne 8:30
Martins, Peter 13:181
New York City Ballet 14:154–155
Stravinsky, Igor 18:295
Tallchief, Maria 19:16
BALANTIDIASIS 3:33
Ciliata 4:430
BALAQUIRI, MOUNT
map (0° 55′N 13° 12′E) 9:5
BALARD, ANTOINE JÉRÔME 3:33
bromine 3:502
BALASSI, BÁLINT
Hungarian literature 10:305
BALATON (Minnesota)
map (44° 14′N 95° 52′W) 13:453
BALATON, LAKE 3:33; 10:310 *illus.*
map (46° 50′N 17° 45′E) 10:307
BALBO, ITALO 3:33
BALBOA, VASCO NÚÑEZ DE 3:33 *bibliog.*
exploration 7:335
Panama, Isthmus of 15:56
BALBULUS, NOTKER
sequence (music) 17:207
BALCARCE (Argentina)
map (37° 50′S 58° 15′W) 2:149
BALCH, EMILY GREENE 3:33
BALD CYPRESS 3:33 *illus.*
Eocene Epoch 19:124 *illus.*
BALD EAGLE *see* EAGLE
BALD KNOB (Arkansas)
map (35° 19′N 91° 34′W) 2:166
BALD KNOB MOUNTAIN (Virginia)
map (37° 56′N 79° 51′W) 19:607
BALD KNOB MOUNTAIN (West Virginia)
map (38° 26′N 79° 56′W) 20:111
BALD MOUNTAINS
map (35° 56′N 82° 23′W) 14:242
BALDACCINI, CÉSAR *see* CÉSAR
BALDER 3:33
mythology 13:702
BALDINUCCI, FILIPPO 3:34
BALDNESS 3:34
BALDOVINETTI, ALESSO 3:34 *bibliog.*
BALDUNG-GRIEN, HANS 3:34–35 *bibliog., illus.*
BALDUS, E. D.
photography, history and art of 15:268
BALDWIN (county in Alabama)
map (30° 50′N 87° 45′W) 1:234
BALDWIN (county in Georgia)
map (33° 5′N 83° 15′W) 9:114
BALDWIN (Michigan)
map (43° 54′N 85° 51′W) 13:377
BALDWIN (Pennsylvania)
map (40° 23′N 79° 58′W) 15:147
BALDWIN, JAMES 3:35 *bibliog., illus.*
Fire Next Time, The 8:103
BALDWIN, MATTHIAS W. 3:35
BALDWIN, ROBERT 3:35 *bibliog., illus.*
Lafontaine, Sir Louis Hippolyte 12:164
BALDWIN, STANLEY, 1ST EARL BALDWIN OF BEWDLEY 3:35–36 *bibliog., illus.*
BALDWIN CITY (Kansas)
map (38° 47′N 95° 11′W) 12:18
BALDWIN I, LATIN EMPEROR OF CONSTANTINOPLE
Constantinople, Latin Empire of 5:209
BALDWIN II, LATIN EMPEROR OF CONSTANTINOPLE
Constantinople, Latin Empire of 5:209–210
BALDWINSVILLE (New York)
map (43° 9′N 76° 20′W) 14:149
BALDWINVILLE (Massachusetts)
map (42° 36′N 72° 5′W) 13:206
BALDWYN (Mississippi)
map (34° 31′N 88° 38′W) 13:469
BALDY MOUNTAIN (Manitoba)
map (51° 28′N 100° 44′W) 13:119
BALDY PEAK
map (33° 55′N 109° 35′W) 2:160
BALE, JOHN 3:36
BALEARIC ISLANDS (Spain) 3:36 *map*
Ibiza 11:5
Majorca 13:77
map (39° 30′N 3° 0′E) 18:140
Minorca 13:459
Palma 15:49–50
BALEARIC SEA
map (40° 30′N 2° 0′E) 18:140
BALEEN WHALE 20:120 *illus.*
See also WHALE; WHALING
BALENCIAGA, CRISTÓBAL 3:36 *bibliog.*
fashion design 8:32
BALEWA, SIR ABUBAKAR TAFAWA 3:36

BALFE, MICHAEL WILLIAM 3:37 *bibliog.*
BALFOUR, ARTHUR, 1ST EARL OF BALFOUR 3:37 *bibliog.*
BALFOUR DECLARATION 3:37 *bibliog.*
  Gaster, Moses 9:56
  Jews 11:416
  Kook, Abraham Isaac 12:109
  Palestine 15:45
  Weizmann, Chaim 20:96
  Zionism 20:369–370
BALI (Indonesia) 3:37; 11:148–149 *illus.*
  Balinese 3:37
  caste 4:187
  cremation 8:364 *illus.*; 15:104 *illus.*
  map (8° 20′S 115° 0′E) 11:147
  music
    gamelan 9:29
    music, non-Western 13:668
  shadow play 17:234
    puppets 8:198 *illus.*
  Southeast Asian art and architecture 18:110
BALI CATTLE *see* BANTENG
BALIKESIR (Turkey)
  map (39° 39′N 27° 53′E) 19:343
BALIKPAPAN (Indonesia)
  map (1° 17′S 116° 50′E) 11:147
BALIN, MARTY
  Jefferson Airplane 11:393
BALINESE 3:37 *bibliog.*
  mask 13:197 *illus.*
BALINESE CAT 3:37–38 *illus.*; 4:195 *illus.*
  longhaired cats 12:408
BALIOL, EDWARD DE
  Baliol, John de 3:38
  David II, King of Scotland 6:49
BALIOL, JOHN DE 3:38
BALKAN LEAGUE
  Balkan Wars 3:38
BALKAN MOUNTAINS
  map (43° 15′N 25° 0′E) 3:555
BALKAN PENINSULA *see* BALKANS
BALKAN WARS 3:38 *bibliog.*
  World War I 20:222
BALKANS 3:38–40 *bibliog.*, *map*
  See also ALBANIA; BULGARIA; GREECE; ROMANIA; TURKEY; YUGOSLAVIA
  history 3:38–40 *map*
    Eastern Question 7:33–34
    Illyria 11:50
    Thrace 19:180–181
    World War I 20:227 *map*; 20:230–231; 20:234; 20:238–239; 20:243
    World War II 20:253 *map*; 20:255
  Islamic art and architecture 11:293–297
  land 3:38–39 *map*
  people 3:38
  religion 3:38
BALKH (Afghanistan)
  map (36° 46′N 66° 54′E) 1:133
BALKHASH, LAKE 3:40
  map (46° 0′N 74° 0′E) 19:388
BALL (Louisiana)
  map (31° 25′N 92° 25′W) 12:430
BALL (play object)
  toy 19:256
BALL, LUCILLE 3:40 *bibliog.*, *illus.*
  radio and television broadcasting 16:59 *illus.*
BALL, THOMAS 3:40 *bibliog.*
BALL BEARING 3:143–144 *illus.*
  roller-skating 16:272
BALL GAME, MESOAMERICAN
  El Tajín 7:101
BALL GROUND (Georgia)
  map (34° 21′N 84° 23′W) 9:114
BALL LIGHTNING 12:340
BALL-POINT PEN 15:140–141 *illus.*
BALL STATE UNIVERSITY
  Indiana, state universities of 11:115
BALLA, GIACOMO 3:40 *bibliog.*
BALLAD (poetic form) 3:40 *bibliog.*
  Bürger, Gottfried August 3:568
  Chinese literature 4:389
  folk music 8:202
  Paterson, A.B. 15:111
BALLAD OF THE SAD CAFÉ, THE (book)
  McCullers, Carson 13:11
BALLADE 3:40–41
  music, history of Western 13:665
  Villon, François 19:598–599
BALLARAT (Australia)
  map (37° 34′S 143° 52′E) 2:328
BALLARD (county in Kentucky)
  map (37° 5′N 89° 0′W) 12:47
BALLARD, J. G. 3:41 *bibliog.*
BALLATA
  music, history of Western 13:665
BALLET 3:41–47 *bibliog.*, *illus.*
  Afternoon of a Faun, The 1:181
  Canada 3:44
    National Ballet of Canada 14:29–30
  choreographers 4:408–409 *illus.*
    Ashton, Sir Frederick 2:231
    Balanchine, George 3:32–33
    Baryshnikov, Mikhail 3:99
    Béjart, Maurice 3:173
    Bournonville, August 3:425
    Butler, John 3:591
    Cranko, John 5:331
    Dantzig, Rudi Van 6:35
    Dauberval, Jean 6:45
    de Mille, Agnes 6:61
    Diaghilev, Serge Pavlovich 6:149
    Feld, Eliot 8:45–46
    Fokine, Mikhail 8:193
    Grigorovich, Yury Nikolayevich 9:364
    Helpmann, Sir Robert 10:116
    Ivanov, Lev Ivanovich 11:333
    Jooss, Kurt 11:446
    Lubovitch, Lar 12:447
    MacMillan, Kenneth 13:34
    Martins, Peter 13:181
    Massine, Leonid 13:213
    Neumeier, John 14:105
    Nijinska, Bronislava 14:194
    Noverre, Jean Georges 14:276
    Page, Ruth 15:13
    Perrot, Jules 15:178
    Petit, Roland 15:202
    Robbins, Jerome 16:240
    Saint-Léon, Arthur 17:22
    Taglioni (family) 19:9
    Tetley, Glen 19:127
    Tudor, Antony 19:328–329
    Viganò, Salvatore 19:591
  dance 6:24–26 *illus.*
  dancers
    Alonso, Alicia 1:307
    Baryshnikov, Mikhail 3:99
    Bruhn, Erik 3:523
    Bujones, Fernando 3:553
    Camargo, Marie 4:50
    Cerrito, Fanny 4:260
    Cragun, Richard Allan 5:328
    Danilova, Alexandra 6:32
    Dowell, Anthony 6:251
    Eglevsky, André 7:73
    Elssler, Fanny 7:150
    Farrell, Suzanne 8:30
    Fonteyn, Dame Margot 8:207
    Fracci, Carla 8:257–258
    Franklin, Frederic 8:284
    Godunov, Aleksandr 9:221
    Grahn, Lucile 9:281
    Gregory, Cynthia 9:355
    Grisi, Carlotta 9:367
    Haydée, Marcia 10:80
    Hayden, Melissa 10:81
    Helpmann, Sir Robert 10:116
    Karssvina, Tamara Platonovna 12:29
    Kirkland, Gelsey 12:89
    McBride, Patricia 13:7
    Madsen, Egon 13:45
    Makarova, Natalia 13:77–78
    Markova, Dame Alicia 13:160
    Martins, Peter 13:181
    Nijinsky, Vaslav 14:194–195
    Nureyev, Rudolf 14:297–298
    Pavlova, Anna 15:120–121
    Riabouchinska, Tatiana 16:205
    Rubinstein, Ida Lvovna 16:337
    Schaufuss, Peter 17:117
    Skeaping, Mary 17:333
    Skibine, George 17:337
    Spessivtseva, Olga Aleksandrovna 18:179
    Taglioni (family) 19:9
    Tallchief, Maria 19:16
    Tomasson, Helgi 19:229
    Verdy, Violette 19:550
    Vestris (family) 19:565
    Youskevitch, Igor 20:337
  Denmark
    Royal Danish Ballet 16:330
  England 3:43
    Ashton, Sir Frederick 2:231
    Dolin, Anton 6:224
    Rambert, Dame Marie 16:80
    Royal Ballet, The 16:329
    Valois, Dame Ninette de 19:508
  France 3:41–43 *illus.*
    Académie Royale de Danse 1:69
    Adam, Adolphe 1:92
    Aumer, Jean 2:323
    Ballets Russes de Monte Carlo 3:48
    Ballets Russes de Serge Diaghilev 3:49
    dance 6:24–25 *illus.*
    Delibes, Léo 6:93
    Petit, Roland 15:202
  Germany
    Stuttgart Ballet 18:310
  glossary of terms 3:45–47
  historians and scholars 3:41–43 *illus.*
    de Cuevas, Marquis George 6:58
    Kirstein, Lincoln 12:90
    Lifar, Serge 12:326
  Netherlands
    Dutch National Ballet 6:314
    Netherlands Dance Theater 14:103
  positions 3:44–47 *illus.*
  Russia 3:43 *illus.*
    Bolshoi Ballet 3:371–372
    dance 6:25–26 *illus.*
    Ivanov, Lev Ivanovich 11:333
    Karsavina, Tamara Platonovna 12:29
    Kirov Ballet 12:89–90
    Minkus, Ludwig 13:451
    Petipa, Marius 15:202
    Ulanova, Galina Sergeyevna 19:376
    Vaganova, Agrippina 19:502
  stage, set, and costume design
    Aronson, Boris 2:186–187
    Bakst, Léon 3:29
    Benois, Aleksandr Nikolayevich 3:204
    Karinska, Barbara 12:27
    Smith, Oliver 17:370
  Sweden
    Royal Swedish Ballet 16:331
  United States 3:44–45
    Ailey, Alvin 1:202–203
    Alonso, Alicia 1:307
    American Ballet Theatre 1:337
    dance 6:26
    Dance Theatre of Harlem 6:30
    Franklin, Frederic 8:284
    Harkness Ballet 10:49
    Joffrey Ballet 11:421–422
    Kirstein, Lincoln 12:90
    New York City Ballet 14:154–155
    Page, Ruth 15:13
    Robbins, Jerome 16:240
    Tamiris, Helen 19:19
    Villela, Edward 19:598
BALLET FOLKLÓRICA OF MEXICO 12:232 *illus.*
BALLET REVIEW (magazine)
  Croce, Arlene 5:355
BALLET SOCIETY *see* NEW YORK CITY BALLET
BALLET THEATRE *see* AMERICAN BALLET THEATRE
BALLETS JOOSS *see* JOOSS, KURT
BALLETS RUSSES DE MONTE CARLO 3:48 *bibliog.*, *illus.*
  Danilova, Alexandra 6:32
  Riabouchinska, Tatiana 16:205
BALLETS RUSSES DE SERGE DIAGHILEV 3:48–49 *bibliog.*, *illus.*
  Afternoon of a Faun, The 1:181
  Art Deco 2:207
  Bakst, Léon 3:29
  Balanchine, George 3:32–33
  ballet 3:43–44 *illus.*
  Benois, Aleksandr Nikolayevich 3:204
  dance 6:25–26 *illus.*
  Danilova, Alexandra 6:32
  Diaghilev, Serge Pavlovich 6:149
  Fokine, Mikhail 8:193
  Goncharova, Natalia Sergeyevna 9:242
  Jones, Robert Edmond 11:444
  Karsavina, Tamara Platonovna 12:29
  Larionov, Mikhail Fyodorovich 12:207
  Lifar, Serge 12:326
  Massine, Leonid 13:213
  Nijinsky, Vaslav 14:194–195
  Schéhérazade 16:363 *illus.*
  Stravinsky, Igor 18:295
BALLINGER (Texas)
  map (31° 44′N 99° 57′W) 19:129
BALLINGER, RICHARD A. 3:49 *bibliog.*
BALLIOL, JOHN DE *see* BALIOL, JOHN DE
BALLIOL COLLEGE (Oxford University) 14:474
BALLISTA 4:200 *illus.*; 8:239 *illus.*
  fortification 8:238
  weapons 20:74
BALLISTIC MISSILE 3:49 *bibliog.*
  antiaircraft systems 2:55–56
  antiballistic missile 2:56–57
  BMEWS 3:348
  hydrogen bomb 10:340
  land-launched
    Atlas, United States 2:297
    Jupiter (rocket) 11:474
    Minuteman missile 13:462
    MX missile 13:688
    Redstone 16:116–117
    Saturn (rocket) 17:91–92
    Thor (rocket) 19:177
    Titan (rocket) 19:210
  nuclear strategy 14:288
  nuclear submarine 18:315
  rockets and missiles 16:254–256
  submarine-launched
    Polaris (missile) 15:393
    Poseidon (missile) 15:458
    Trident 19:296–297
  surface-to-air missile 18:359
  Vandenberg Air Force Base 19:518
  von Braun, Wernher 19:633
BALLISTIC MISSILE EARLY WARNING SYSTEM *see* BMEWS
BALLISTICS 3:49–51 *bibliog.*
  See also AMMUNITION
  artillery 2:223
  Bernoulli, Jacques 3:223
  exterior 3:50–51
  interior 3:49–50
  Tartaglia, Niccolò 19:40
  terminal 3:51
  theory 3:49
  trajectory 3:50
    center of gravity and 4:250
  weapons 20:75
BALLOON 3:51–53 *bibliog.*, *illus.*
  aerial photography
    Nadar 14:4 *illus.*
  aviation 2:370
  ballooning 1:122 *illus.*; 3:53
  flight
    Blanchard, Jean 3:327
    Charles, Jacques 4:290
    Montgolfier brothers 13:556
    Piccard, Auguste 15:292
  helium 10:113
  meteorological use 3:53
    meteorology 13:341 *illus.*
  military use 3:52
    military warning and detection systems 13:421
  space exploration 18:118
  transcontinental crossing 3:51–53 *illus.*
BALLOONFISH
  porcupine fish 15:441 *illus.*
BALLOONFLOWER 3:53 *illus.*
BALLOONING *see* AERIAL SPORTS
BALLOT 3:53 *bibliog.*
  election 7:104
  voting machine 19:637
BALLOU, HOSEA 3:53
BALLROOM DANCING *see* DANCE, SOCIAL
BALLSTON SPA (New York)
  map (43° 0′N 73° 51′W) 14:149
BALLWIN (Missouri)
  map (38° 35′N 90° 33′W) 13:476
BALM 3:53
BALM OF GILEAD *see* BALM
BALMACEDA, JOSÉ 3:53 *bibliog.*
BALMAIN, PIERRE
  fashion design 8:32
BALMER, JOHANN JAKOB 3:53
  Balmer series, hydrogen spectrum 10:340 *table*
  chemistry, history of 4:327
BALMONT, KONSTANTIN DMITRIYEVICH 3:54 *bibliog.*
BALMORHEA (Texas)
  map (30° 59′N 103° 45′W) 19:129
BALOCH *see* BALUCH
BALSA 3:54 *illus.*
BALSAM 3:54
  fir 8:100
  jewelweed 11:411
  sweet gum 18:387
BALSAM FIR 3:54 *illus.*
BALSAM LAKE (Wisconsin)
  map (45° 27′N 92° 27′W) 20:185
BALSAS (Brazil)
  map (7° 31′S 46° 2′W) 3:460
BALSAS RIVER
  map (17° 55′N 102° 10′W) 13:357
BALSEMÃO, FRANCISCO PINTO *see* PINTO BALSEMÃO, FRANCISCO
BALTASAR BRUM (Uruguay)
  map (30° 44′S 57° 19′W) 19:488
BALTASAR CARLOS, PRINCE OF SPAIN 18:153 *illus.*
BALTHUS 3:54
BALTIC-BLACK-CASPIAN SEA LINK
  canal 4:97
BALTIC LANGUAGES 3:54–55 *bibliog.*

Curonian 3:55
Lapps 12:205–206
Lettish (Latvian) 3:55
Lithuanian 3:55
Prussian 3:55
BALTIC SEA 3:55
Ertebølle culture 7:235
gulfs and bays
Bothnia, Gulf of 3:415
Finland, Gulf of 8:98
Kattegat 12:31
islands and island groups
Bornholm 3:402
Gotland (Sweden) 9:263
map (57° 0′N 19° 0′E) 7:268
BALTIC STATES 3:55 *map*
Estonian Soviet Socialist Republic 7:247 *map*
history
Hanseatic League 10:40–41
Northern War, Great 14:256
Peter I, Emperor of Russia (Peter the Great) 15:200–201
Scandinavia, history of 17:108–109 *maps*
World War II 20:251
Latvian Soviet Socialist Republic 12:235–236 *map*
Lithuanian Soviet Socialist Republic 12:371–372 *map*
BALTICA (ancient landmass)
plate tectonics 15:354 *map*
BALTIMORE (Maryland) 3:55–56 *bibliog., map*; 13:192 *illus.*
art and architecture
Roman Catholic Cathedral 4:208; 12:235 *illus.*
Walters Art Gallery 20:20
economic activity
Maryland 13:191
Garrett, John Work 9:50
history
Know-Nothing party 12:102 *illus.*
map (39° 17′N 76° 37′W) 13:188
BALTIMORE (county in Maryland)
map (39° 24′N 76° 36′W) 13:188
BALTIMORE (Ohio)
map (39° 51′N 82° 36′W) 14:357
BALTIMORE, BARON *see* CALVERT (family)
BALTIMORE, DAVID 3:56
BALTIMORE & OHIO RAILROAD
locomotive 12:391
BALTIMORE CANYON *see* SUBMARINE CANYON
BALTIMORE CATECHISM
catechism 4:202
BALTIMORE CATHEDRAL 12:235 *illus.*
BALTIMORE COLLEGE OF SURGERY
dentistry 6:115
BALTIMORE HIGHLANDS (Maryland)
map (39° 14′N 76° 38′W) 13:188
BALTIMORE ORIOLE 14:444 *illus.*
BALTO-SLAVIC LANGUAGES
Baltic languages 3:54–55
BALUCH 3:57
BALUCHISTAN (Pakistan) 3:57
Indus civilization 11:153
BALUCHITHERIUM 3:57 *bibliog., illus.*
rhinoceros 16:196
BALZAC, HONORÉ DE 3:57–58 *bibliog., illus.*
Balzac (Rodin statue) 2:200–201 *illus.*
Comédie humaine, La 5:131–132
French literature 8:317–318 *illus.*
realism (literature) 16:104
BALZAR (Ecuador)
map (1° 22′S 79° 54′W) 7:52
BALZERS (Liechtenstein)
map (47° 4′N 9° 30′E) 12:325
BAMAKO (Mali) 3:58
climate 13:89 *table*
map (12° 39′N 8° 0′W) 13:89
BAMBARA KINGDOMS 3:58
African music 1:168–171
BAMBARI (Central African Republic)
map (5° 45′N 20° 40′E) 4:251
BAMBERG (Germany, East and West)
map (49° 53′N 10° 53′E) 9:140
BAMBERG (South Carolina)
map (33° 17′N 81° 2′W) 18:98
BAMBERG (county in South Carolina)
map (33° 10′N 81° 5′W) 18:98
BAMBERG RIDER 9:260 *illus.*
BAMBOCCIANTI 3:58 *bibliog.*
Laer, Pieter van 12:163
BAMBOCCIO *see* LAER, PIETER VAN
BAMBOO 3:58–59 *illus.*
panda 15:58
pipe and pipeline 15:310 *illus.*
BAMENDA (Cameroon)
map (5° 56′N 10° 10′E) 4:61
BAMIAN (Afghanistan) 3:59
map (34° 50′N 67° 50′E) 1:133
Yün-kang (Yungang) (China) 20:346
BAMILEKE 3:59
mask 13:197 *illus.*
BAMINGUI RIVER
map (8° 33′N 19° 5′E) 4:251
BAMPUR RIVER
map (27° 18′N 59° 6′E) 11:250
BAN CHIANG (Thailand) 3:59
BAÑA POINT
map (40° 34′N 0° 38′E) 18:140
BANABA
Kiribati 12:88
BANACH, STEFAN 3:59
BANAM (Kampuchea)
map (11° 19′N 105° 18′E) 12:11
BANANA 3:59–60 *bibliog., illus.*
Honduras 10:219
BANANA (Zaire)
map (6° 1′S 12° 24′E) 20:350
BANANA FISH *see* BONEFISH
BANANAQUIT 3:60
BANAS, CAPE OF
map (23° 54′N 35° 48′E) 7:76
BANCROFT (Idaho)
map (42° 43′N 111° 53′W) 11:26
BANCROFT (Ontario)
map (45° 3′N 77° 51′W) 14:393
BANCROFT, ANNE 3:60
BANCROFT, GEORGE 3:60 *bibliog.*
United States Naval Academy 19:463
BANCROFT, HUBERT HOWE 3:61 *bibliog.*
BANCROFT, SIR SQUIRE 3:61 *bibliog.*
BAND (music) 3:61 *bibliog.*
American music 1:350
cornet 5:268–269 *illus.*
Goldman, Edwin Franko 9:235
Indians of North America, music and dance of the 11:143
jazz 11:387–390 *illus.*
Jones, Spike 11:444
Sousa, John Philip 18:77–78
swing 18:392–393
tuba 19:326
BAND, SWING *see* SWING (music)
BANDA, H. KAMUZU 3:61 *bibliog.*
BANDA DEL RÍO SALÍ (Argentina)
map (26° 50′S 65° 10′W) 2:149
BANDA ORIENTAL *see* URUGUAY
BANDA SEA
map (5° 0′S 128° 0′E) 11:147
BANDAMA BLANC RIVER
map (6° 54′N 5° 31′W) 11:335
BANDAMA RIVER
map (5° 10′N 5° 0′W) 11:335
BANDAMA ROUGE RIVER
map (6° 54′N 5° 31′W) 11:335
BANDAR ABBAS (Iran)
map (27° 11′N 56° 17′E) 11:250
BANDAR-E PAHLAVI (Iran)
map (37° 28′N 49° 27′E) 11:250
BANDAR SERI BEGAWAN (Brunei)
map (4° 56′N 114° 55′E) 3:524
BANDARANAIKE, SIRIMAVO 3:61 *illus.*
Sri Lanka 18:207
BANDARANAIKE, SOLOMON W. R. D. 3:61
Sri Lanka 18:207
BANDED ANTEATER *see* NUMBAT
BANDEIRA PEAK
map (20° 26′S 41° 47′W) 3:460
BANDEIRANTE (Brazil)
map (13° 41′S 50° 48′W) 3:460
BANDELLO, MATTEO 3:62
BANDERA (Texas)
map (29° 44′N 99° 4′W) 19:129
BANDERA (county in Texas)
map (29° 45′N 99° 15′W) 19:129
BANDERA MOUNTAIN
map (18° 49′N 70° 37′W) 6:233
BANDICOOT 3:62 *bibliog., illus.*
rabbit-eared 10:5 *illus.*
BANDINELLI, BACCIO 3:62 *bibliog.*
BANDKERAMIK CULTURE *see* DANUBIAN CULTURE
BANDON (Oregon)
map (43° 7′N 124° 25′W) 14:427
BANDUNDU (Zaire)
map (3° 18′S 17° 20′E) 20:350
BANDUNG (Indonesia) 3:62
map (6° 54′S 107° 36′E) 11:147
BANEBERRY 3:62
BANES (Cuba)
map (20° 58′N 75° 43′W) 5:377
BANFF (Alberta) 3:62
map (51° 10′N 115° 34′W) 1:256
BANFF (Scotland) 3:62
BANFF NATIONAL PARK (Canada) 4:72 *illus.*
Louise, Lake 12:429
BANFFSHIRE (Scotland) *see* BANFF (Scotland)
BANG, HERMAN 3:62–63 *bibliog.*
BANGALORE (India) 3:63
map (12° 58′N 77° 36′E) 11:80
BANGASSOU (Central African Republic)
map (4° 50′N 23° 7′E) 4:251
BANGIL (Indonesia)
map (7° 36′S 112° 47′E) 11:147
BANGKA ISLAND
map (1° 48′N 125° 9′E) 11:147
BANGKOK (Thailand) 3:63 *bibliog., illus.*; 19:140–141 *illus., table*
map (13° 45′N 100° 31′E) 19:139
BANGLADESH 3:63–66 *bibliog., illus., map, table*
agriculture 3:66
Bengal 3:198–199
cities
Chittagong 4:399
Dacca 6:3–4 *illus.*
climate 3:64; 3:65 *table*
economic activity 3:65–66 *illus.*
education 3:65
South Asian universities 18:95 *table*
flag 3:64 *illus.*
government 3:66
history 3:66
Ershad, Hussain Muhammad 7:235
Mujibur Rahman 13:635
Pakistan 15:29
land and resources 3:63–64 *map*
languages
Indo-Iranian languages 11:145–146
map (24° 0′N 90° 0′E) 2:232
people 3:64–65
Garo 9:50
rivers, lakes, and waterways
Brahmaputra River 3:440
Ganges River 9:36–37 *map*
vegetation and animal life 3:64
BANGOR (Maine) 3:66
map (44° 49′N 68° 47′W) 13:70
BANGOR (Pennsylvania)
map (40° 52′N 75° 13′W) 15:147
BANGS (Texas)
map (31° 43′N 99° 8′W) 19:129
BANG'S DISEASE *see* BRUCELLOSIS
BANGUI (Central African Republic) 3:66; 4:252 *table*
map (4° 22′N 18° 35′E) 4:251
BANGWEULU, LAKE 3:66
map (11° 5′S 29° 45′E) 20:354
BANGWEULU SWAMP
map (11° 30′S 30° 15′E) 20:354
BANHA (Egypt)
map (30° 28′N 31° 11′E) 7:76
BANÍ (Dominican Republic)
map (18° 17′N 70° 20′W) 6:233
BANI MAZAR (Egypt)
map (28° 30′N 30° 48′E) 7:76
BANI RIVER
map (14° 30′N 4° 12′W) 13:89
BANI-SADR, ABOLHASSAN 3:66
Iran 11:253
Khomeini, Ayatollah Ruhollah 12:68
BANI SUWAYF (Egypt)
map (29° 5′N 31° 5′E) 7:76
BANISTER RIVER
map (36° 42′N 78° 48′W) 19:607
BANJA LUKA (Yugoslavia)
map (44° 46′N 17° 11′E) 20:340
BANJARMASIN (Indonesia) 3:67; 11:150 *illus.*
map (3° 20′S 114° 35′E) 11:147
BANJO 3:67 *illus.*; 13:677 *illus.*; 18:300–301 *illus.*
BANJUL (Gambia) 3:67
climate 9:25 *table*
map (13° 28′N 16° 39′W) 9:25
BANK
eye diseases 7:351
BANK OF CANADA 3:67
central bank 4:253
BANK DRAFT *see* BILL OF EXCHANGE
BANK OF ENGLAND 3:67
architecture
Soane, Sir John 18:6
banking systems 3:68
central bank 4:253
Halifax, Charles Montagu, 1st Earl of 10:21
BANK FOR INTERNATIONAL SETTLEMENTS 3:67
BANK OF MANHATTAN BUILDING
skyscraper 17:350
BANK OF NORTH AMERICA
Morris, Robert (merchant) 13:588
BANK OF THE UNITED STATES 3:67 *bibliog.*
banking systems 3:68–69 *illus.*
First 3:67
Hamilton, Alexander 10:28
United States, history of the 19:443
national bank 14:30
Second 3:67; 9:346 *illus.*
Biddle, Nicholas 3:247
Jackson, Andrew 11:342
United States, history of the 19:445; 19:446
BANKHEAD, TALLULAH 3:67–68 *bibliog.*
BANKHEAD LAKE
map (33° 30′N 87° 15′W) 1:234
BANKING SYSTEMS 3:68–69 *bibliog., illus.*
assets 3:69
bill of exchange 3:251
Canada 3:69
Bank of Canada 3:67
central bank 4:253–254
check 4:306
clearinghouse 5:47
computer 5:160f
demand deposit 6:96
deposits 3:68–69
discount rate 6:189
draft (banking) 6:254
electronic funds transfer 3:69
escrow 7:238
fractional reserve system 3:68
France 3:68
Law, John 12:247
Mississippi Scheme 13:474
future developments 3:69
Great Britain 3:68–69
Bank of England 3:67
history 3:68
Fugger (family) 8:355
Medici (family) 13:265
Rothschild (family) 16:322
interest 11:206–207
international banking 3:69
Bank for International Settlements 3:67
Eurodollar 7:267
Export-Import Bank 7:340
World Bank 20:218
letter of credit 12:299
loans 3:68–69
money 13:527
negotiable instrument 14:77–78
NOW (Negotiable Order of Withdrawal) accounts 3:69
panic, financial 15:59
regulation and control 3:68–69
savings bank 17:100
savings and loan association 17:100
traveler's check 19:284
trust 19:321
United States 3:68–69
American Bankers Association 1:337
Bank of the United States 3:67
Comptroller of the Currency, Office of the 5:159
Cooke, Jay 5:237
Federal Deposit Insurance Corporation 8:41
Federal Home Loan Bank Board 8:41
Federal Reserve System 8:41–42
Fitzsimons, Thomas 8:132
Giannini, Amadeo Peter 9:171
Girard, Stephen 9:188
Glass, Carter 9:201
Independent Treasury System 11:78
Jackson, Andrew 11:342
Lehman, Herbert H. 12:275–276
monetary policy 13:524
moratorium 13:574
Morgan (family) 13:577
national bank 14:30
Rockefeller (family) 16:250
Roosevelt, Franklin Delano 16:308
state banks 3:68
Warburg, Paul Moritz 20:28
BANKRUPTCY 3:70
business law 3:589
receiver (law) 16:106
BANKS (Alabama)
map (31° 44′N 85° 50′W) 1:234
BANKS (county in Georgia)
map (34° 25′N 83° 30′W) 9:114
BANKS, SIR JOSEPH 3:70 *bibliog.*
biology 3:269
Botany Bay 3:414
Brown, Robert 3:516
BANKS, NATHANIEL PRENTISS 3:70 *bibliog.*
Civil War, U.S. 5:23 *map*
BANKS ISLAND (Australia)
map (10° 12′S 142° 16′E) 2:328
BANKS ISLAND (British Columbia)
map (53° 25′N 130° 10′W) 3:491

BANKS ISLAND (Northwest Territories)
map (73° 15′N 121° 30′W) 14:258
BANKS LAKE
map (47° 45′N 119° 15′W) 20:35
BANKSIA 3:70 *illus.*
BANKY, VILMA 6:30 *illus.*
BANN RIVER
map (55° 10′N 6° 45′W) 11:258
BANNEKER, BENJAMIN 3:70 *bibliog.*
BANNER
Lamaist art and architecture 12:172–173
BANNER (county in Nebraska)
map (41° 30′N 103° 40′W) 14:70
BANNER ELK (North Carolina)
map (36° 12′N 81° 54′W) 14:242
BANNERMANN, SIR HENRY CAMPBELL- *see* CAMPBELL-BANNERMANN, SIR HENRY
BANNISTER, ROGER 3:71
BANNOCK (American Indians) 3:71 *bibliog.*
BANNOCK (county in Idaho)
map (42° 40′N 112° 15′W) 11:26
BANNOCK-PAIUTE UPRISING 11:109 *map*
BANNOCKBURN, BATTLE OF 3:71
Robert I, King of Scotland (Robert the Bruce) 16:241
BAÑOS (Ecuador)
map (1° 24′S 78° 25′W) 7:52
BANPOCUN *see* PAN-P'O-TS'UN (Banpocun) (China)
BANSHEE 3:71
BANSKÁ BYSTRICA (Czechoslovakia)
map (48° 44′N 19° 7′E) 5:413
BANTENAN, CAPE
map (8° 47′S 114° 33′E) 11:147
BANTENG 3:71 *illus.*
BANTING, SIR FREDERICK G. 3:71 *bibliog.*
Best, Charles 3:228
insulin 11:198
MacLeod, John James Rickard 13:33
BANTU 1:145 *map*; 3:71 *bibliog.*; 16:34 *illus.*
Cameroon 4:61
Kenya 12:54
languages
African languages 1:167
Sotho 18:70
Swahili 18:375
Namibia 14:11–12
Natal (province in South Africa) 14:26
peoples
Bemba 3:194
Chokwe 4:403
Ganda 9:34–35
Kamba 12:9
Luba 12:446
Lunda 12:462
Mbundu 13:251
Ovambo 14:469
Sukuma 18:332
Swahili 18:375
Tutsi 19:355–356
residences 18:80 *illus.*
South Africa 18:80–81; 18:82; 18:83
Tanzania 19:28
BANVILLE, THÉODORE DE 3:71–72
BANYAN 3:72 *illus.*
BANYUWANGI (Indonesia)
map (8° 12′S 114° 21′E) 11:147
BANZART (Tunisia) *see* BIZERTE (Tunisia)
BANZER SUÁREZ, HUGO 3:72
Bolivia 3:369
BAO DAI, EMPEROR OF ANNAM 3:72 *bibliog.*
Vietnam War 19:584–585
BAOBAB 3:72 *illus.*; 17:98 *illus.*
bottle tree 3:419
BAPTISM 3:72–73 *bibliog., illus.*
Anabaptists 1:387
font 8:205
BAPTISTERY 3:73 *bibliog., illus., map*
flat 8:205
Italian art and architecture 11:308
BAPTISTS 3:73–74 *bibliog.*
education
Mercer University 13:304
Morehouse College 13:577
Redlands, University of 16:115
Spelman College 18:177
Wake Forest University 20:8
gospel music 9:253–254
BAQQARAH *see* BAGGARA
BAQUBA (Iraq)
map (33° 45′N 44° 38′E) 11:255
BAR (submerged riverbank)
floodplain 8:165–166
BAR, OFFSHORE 3:74 *bibliog.*
river delta 16:232–233
BAR GRAPH *see* HISTOGRAM
BAR HARBOR (Maine) 3:74
map (44° 23′N 68° 13′W) 13:70
BAR KOCHBA 3:74 *bibliog.*
BAR MITZVAH 3:74 *bibliog.*
BAR SAUMA, RABBAN 3:74 *bibliog.*
BARA, THEDA 3:74 *bibliog., illus.*
BARABBAS 3:74
BARABOO (Wisconsin)
map (43° 28′N 89° 45′W) 20:185
BARACOA (Cuba)
map (20° 21′N 74° 30′W) 5:377
BARAGA (county in Michigan)
map (46° 50′N 88° 20′W) 13:377
BARAGA, FREDERICK 3:74–75 *bibliog.*
BARAKA, IMAMU AMIRI 3:75 *bibliog., illus.*
BARAKI BARAK (Afghanistan)
map (33° 56′N 68° 55′E) 1:133
BARANOF ISLAND
map (57° 0′N 135° 0′W) 1:242
BARANOV, SIR ALEKSANDR ANDREYEVICH 3:75 *bibliog.*
Russian-American Company 16:360
Sitka (Alaska) 17:330
Tlingit 19:216
BÁRÁNY, ROBERT 3:75
BARATARIA (Louisiana)
map (29° 44′N 90° 8′W) 12:430
BARATARIA BAY
map (29° 22′N 89° 57′W) 12:430
BARATOV, N. N.
World War I 20:234
BARB (fish)
tropical fish 19:308 *illus.*
BARBACENA (Brazil)
map (21° 14′S 43° 46′W) 3:460
BARBADOS 3:75–76 *bibliog., map*
Bridgetown 3:485
flag 3:75 *illus.*
map (13° 10′N 59° 32′W) 20:109
BARBADOS CHERRY 3:76
BARBARI, JACOPO DE' 3:76 *bibliog.*
BARBARIANS *see* GERMANIC PEOPLES
BARBAROSSA (pirate)
Barbary States 3:76
BARBAROSSA, FREDERICK *see* FREDERICK I, KING OF GERMANY AND HOLY ROMAN EMPEROR (Frederick Barbarossa)
BARBARY APE 3:76 *illus.*
BARBARY PIRATES *see* BARBARY STATES
BARBARY STATES 3:76 *bibliog.*
Charles V, Holy Roman Emperor 4:295
Decatur, Stephen 6:72–73
piracy 15:312–313; 19:303 *illus.*
Tripolitan War 19:302–303
BARBED WIRE 3:76–77 *bibliog.*
Glidden, Joseph Farwell 9:207
BARBEL 3:77
BARBELL (weight lifting) *see* WEIGHT LIFTING (sport)
BARBER 3:77 *bibliog.*
BARBER (county in Kansas)
map (37° 15′N 98° 4′W) 12:18
BARBER, JOHN
turbine 19:340
BARBER, SAMUEL 3:77 *bibliog., illus.*
BARBER OF SEVILLE, THE (opera) 3:77 *bibliog.*
BARBER OF SEVILLE, THE (play)
Beaumarchais, Pierre Caron de 3:146
BARBER-SURGEON COMPANY
dentistry 6:115
BARBERINI (family)
opera 14:399
BARBERINI FAUN 3:78 *bibliog.*
BARBERINI PALACE (Rome)
Cortona, Pietro da 5:279
BARBERRY 3:78
mandrake 13:112
BARBER'S ITCH *see* FOLLICULITIS
BARBERS POINT
map (21° 18′N 158° 7′W) 10:72
BARBERSHOP QUARTET 3:78
BARBERTON (Ohio)
map (41° 1′N 81° 36′W) 14:357
BARBERTON (South Africa)
map (25° 48′S 31° 3′E) 18:79
BARBET 3:78 *illus.*
BARBEY D'AUREVILLEY, JULES AMÉDÉE 3:78 *bibliog.*
BARBIERI, FRANCISCO ASENJO
Spanish music 18:162
zarzuela 20:356
BARBIERI, GIOVANNI FRANCESCO *see* GUERCINO
BARBIROLLI, SIR JOHN 3:78 *bibliog.*
BARBITURATE 3:78 *bibliog.*
anesthetics 1:410
drug 6:277
drug abuse 6:279
phenobarbital 15:225
psychotropic drugs 15:603–604
Seconal 17:178
sedative 17:182
sodium pentothal 18:33
suicide 18:331
BARBIZON SCHOOL (art group) 3:79 *bibliog., illus.*
Bonington, Richard Parkes 3:380
Daubigny, Charles François 6:45
Diaz de la Peña, Narcisse Virgile 6:155
Harpignies, Henri 10:55
landscape painting 12:192
Michel, Georges 13:372
Rousseau, Théodore 16:327
Troyon, Constant 19:313
Walker, Horatio 20:12
BARBOUR (county in Alabama)
map (31° 50′N 85° 20′W) 1:234
BARBOUR (county in West Virginia)
map (39° 8′N 80° 0′W) 20:111
BARBOUR, JOHN 3:79
BARBOURSVILLE (West Virginia)
map (38° 24′N 82° 18′W) 20:111
BARBOURVILLE (Kentucky)
map (36° 52′N 83° 53′W) 12:47
BARBUDA *see* ANTIGUA AND BARBUDA
BARBUSSE, HENRI 3:79
BARCA, HAMILCAR *see* HAMILCAR BARCA
BARCELONA (Spain) 3:79–80 *illus.*
architecture
Casa Milá 9:59 *illus.*; 18:155 *illus.*
Gaudí, Antonio 9:59
Catalonia 4:198
history 3:80
map (41° 23′N 2° 11′E) 18:140
Spain, history of 18:146 *map*
subway 18:318 *table*
BARCELONA (Venezuela)
map (10° 8′N 64° 42′W) 19:542
BARCELONA CHAIR 8:379 *illus.*
BARCLAY, ALEXANDER 3:80
BARCO VARGAS, VIRGILIO
Colombia 5:109
BARD 3:80
Eisteddfod (Welsh festival) 7:97
BARD COLLEGE 3:80
BARDEEN, JOHN 3:80
Shockley, William Bradford 17:279
superconductivity 18:350
transistor, inventor 19:271
BARDI, GIOVANNI
opera 14:399
BARDIYA
Darius I, King of Persia 6:38
BARDO THODOL (book) *see TIBETAN BOOK OF THE DEAD, THE*
BARDOT, BRIGITTE 3:80; 9:219 *illus.*
BARDSTOWN (Kentucky)
map (37° 49′N 85° 28′W) 12:47
BARDWELL (Kentucky)
map (36° 52′N 89° 1′W) 12:47
BAREBONE'S PARLIAMENT
Cromwell, Oliver 5:358
Long Parliament 12:407
BAREFOOT DOCTORS
China 4:366–367
BAREILLY (India)
map (28° 21′N 79° 25′E) 11:80
BARELLI, AGOSTINO
Nymphenburg Palace 14:309
BARENBOIM, DANIEL 3:80
BARENTS, WILLEM 3:80
Arctic 2:142 *map*
Northeast Passage 14:253
BARENTS SEA 3:80
Franz Josef Land 8:286
map (74° 0′N 36° 0′E) 19:388
White Sea 20:138
BARGAINING *see* GAME THEORY
BARGE 3:80–81 *illus.*; 4:95–96 *illus.*; 20:351 *illus.*
tugboat 19:329
BARGELLO (museum) 3:81 *bibliog.*
Florence (Italy) 8:168–169 *map*
BARGHOORN, E. S.
paleobotany 15:32
BARHAM, RICHARD HARRIS 3:81
BARI (Italy) 3:81
map (41° 7′N 16° 52′E) 11:321
BARINAS (Venezuela)
map (8° 38′N 70° 12′W) 19:542
BARING, EVELYN, 1ST EARL OF CROMER *see* CROMER, EVELYN BARING, 1ST EARL OF
BARISAL (Bangladesh)
map (22° 42′N 90° 22′E) 3:64
BARISAN MOUNTAINS
map (3° 0′S 102° 15′E) 11:147
BARITE 3:81 *illus.*
barium 3:81
oceanic mineral resources 14:340
orthorhombic system 14:451
BARITONE 3:81
BARIUM 3:81–82
abundances of common elements 7:131 *table*
alkaline earth metals 1:295
element 7:130 *table*
flame test
qualitative chemical analysis 16:6 *illus.*
Group IIA periodic table 15:167
Hahn, Otto 10:11
metal, metallic element 13:328
new ceramics applications 4:259
psilomelane 15:588
sulfate minerals 18:333
barite 3:81
uranium minerals 19:478
BARIUM CARBONATE 3:82
BARIUM OXIDE 3:82
BARK (botany) 3:82 *bibliog., illus.*
bark cloth 3:82–83
cinnamon 4:435
cork 5:264
tree 19:286–287 *illus.*
BARK BEETLE 3:82 *bibliog., illus.*
BARK CLOTH 3:82–83 *bibliog., illus.*
Oceanic art 14:336–339
BARKER, HARLEY GRANVILLE *see* GRANVILLE-BARKER, HARLEY
BARKER, ROBERT
panoramas 15:60
BARKERVILLE (British Columbia)
map (53° 4′N 121° 31′W) 3:491
BARKHAMSTED RESERVOIR
map (41° 57′N 72° 57′W) 5:193
BARKING DEER *see* MUNTJAC
BARKING FROG 3:83
BARKLA, CHARLES GLOVER 3:83
BARKLEY, ALBEN W. 3:83 *bibliog.*
BARKLEY, LAKE
map (36° 40′N 87° 55′W) 12:47
BARKLY TABLELAND
map (18° 0′S 136° 0′E) 2:328
BARKSDALE (Texas)
map (29° 44′N 100° 2′W) 19:129
BARLACH, ERNST 3:83–84 *bibliog., illus.*
Ecstasy 9:129 *illus.*; 20:208 *illus.*
BARLEE, LAKE
map (29° 10′S 119° 30′E) 2:328
BARLETTA (Italy)
map (41° 19′N 16° 17′E) 11:321
BARLEY 3:84 *bibliog., illus.*; 9:281 *illus.*
beer 3:162–163
whiskey 20:132–133
BARLING (Arkansas)
map (34° 20′N 94° 17′W) 2:166
BARLOW (Kentucky)
map (37° 3′N 89° 3′W) 12:47
BARLOW, JOEL 3:84–85 *bibliog.*
BARLOW, PETER
telescope 19:83
BARLOW, WILLIAM
mineral 13:439
BARMEN (West Germany) *see* WUPPERTAL (West Germany)
BARN 3:85 *bibliog.*
BARNABAS, SAINT 3:85
BARNACLE 3:85 *bibliog., illus.*
intertidal life 11:229
BARNARD, CHRISTIAAN 3:85 *bibliog.*
heart diseases 10:96
BARNARD, EDWARD EMERSON 3:85 *bibliog.*
Yerkes Observatory 20:327
BARNARD, FREDERICK AUGUSTUS PORTER 3:86
BARNARD, HENRY 3:86
BARNARD COLLEGE 3:86
Barnard, Frederick Augustus Porter 3:86
Seven Sisters Colleges 17:216
BARNARD'S STAR 3:86
Barnard, Edward Emerson 3:85
proper motion 15:570 *illus.*
BARNAUL (USSR)
map (53° 22′N 83° 45′E) 19:388
BARNBURNERS *see* HUNKERS AND BARNBURNERS
BARNEGAT (New Jersey)
lighthouse 14:128 *illus.*
map (39° 45′N 74° 13′W) 14:129
BARNEGAT BAY
map (39° 52′N 74° 7′W) 14:129
BARNES (county in North Dakota)
map (46° 30′N 98° 0′W) 14:248
BARNES, CLIVE 3:86
BARNES, DJUNA 3:86

BARNES, EDWARD LARRABEE 3:86
BARNESBORO (Pennsylvania)
map (40° 40′N 78° 47′W) **15**:147
BARNESVILLE (Georgia)
map (33° 4′N 84° 9′W) **9**:114
BARNESVILLE (Minnesota)
map (46° 39′N 96° 25′W) **13**:453
BARNESVILLE (Ohio)
map (39° 59′N 81° 11′W) **14**:357
BARNHART (Missouri)
map (38° 23′N 92° 40′W) **13**:476
BARNHART (Texas)
map (31° 8′N 101° 10′W) **19**:129
BARNSTABLE (Massachusetts)
map (41° 42′N 70° 18′W) **13**:206
BARNSTABLE (county in Massachusetts)
map (41° 42′N 70° 18′W) **13**:206
BARNSTAPLE (England)
map (51° 5′N 4° 4′W) **19**:403
BARNSTORMING 3:86 *bibliog.*
Curtiss Jenny **5**:396
BARNUM, P. T. 3:86–87 *bibliog., illus.*
American music **1**:349
Bridgeport **3**:484
Jumbo **11**:466
Lind, Jenny **12**:351
BARNUM & BAILEY SHOW *see* BARNUM, P. T.; CIRCUS; RINGLING (family)
BARNWELL (South Carolina)
map (33° 15′N 81° 23′W) **18**:98
BARNWELL (county in South Carolina)
map (33° 15′N 81° 25′W) **18**:98
BARO RIVER
map (8° 26′N 33° 13′E) **7**:253
BAROCCI, FEDERICO 3:87 *bibliog.*
BARODA (India) 3:87
map (22° 18′N 73° 12′E) **11**:80
BAROGRAPH **13**:339 *illus.*
BAROJA Y NESSI, PIO 3:87 *bibliog.*
BAROMETER 3:87–88 *bibliog., illus.*
aneroid barometer **3**:87–88 *illus.*
high-pressure region **10**:162
humidity **10**:302
mercury barometer **3**:87–88 *illus.*
meteorology **13**:341–343
Torricelli, Evangelista **19**:244
BAROMETRIC PRESSURE
measurement, barometer **3**:87–88
ocean currents and wind systems, worldwide **14**:322–323 *maps*
BARON (title)
titles of nobility and honor **19**:214
BARON, MICHEL
theater, history of the **19**:147
BARON, SALO WITTMAYER 3:88
BARONET (title)
titles of nobility and honor **19**:214
BARONIUS, CAESAR 3:88
BARONS' WAR 3:88 *bibliog.*
Edward I, King of England **7**:67
Henry III, King of England **10**:125
Montfort, Simon de, Earl of Leicester **13**:555–556
BAROQUE ART AND ARCHITECTURE **2**:197–198; **3**:88–91 *bibliog., illus.*
anamorphosis **1**:391
architecture **2**:135
art criticism **2**:207
Austria
Austrian art and architecture **2**:352–354
Donner, Georg Raphael **6**:239–240
Fischer von Erlach, Johann Bernhard **8**:111
Hildebrandt, Johann Lucas von **10**:163
Pöppelmann, Matthäus Daniel **15**:432
Prandtauer, Jakob **15**:489
Schönbrunn Palace **17**:133
Thumb (family) **19**:184
Belgium
Jordaens, Jacob **11**:447
cathedrals and churches **4**:207 *illus.*
characteristics **3**:90
costume **5**:297–298 *illus.*
France
Anguier brothers **2**:7
Boffrand, Germain **3**:358
Coypel (family) **5**:323
French art and architecture **8**:305
Hardouin-Mansart, Jules **10**:47
Lafosse, Charles de **12**:165
Largillière, Nicolas de **12**:207
Le Vau, Louis **12**:255
Mansart, François **13**:127
Pigalle, Jean Baptiste **15**:299
Poussin, Nicolas **15**:476–477
Puget, Pierre **15**:617
styles of Louis XIII-XVI **18**:311
Vaux-le-Vicomte, Château de **19**:529
Vouet, Simon **19**:637
furniture **8**:376
Germany
Asam brothers **2**:226–227
Dientzenhofer (family) **6**:162
Dresden (East Germany) **6**:270 *illus.*
Elsheimer, Adam **7**:150
German art and architecture **9**:127
Germany, history of **9**:152
Langhans, Carl Gotthard **12**:195
Mannheim (West Germany) **13**:125
Neumann, Johann Balthasar **14**:104
Nymphenburg Palace **14**:309
Permoser, Balthasar **15**:176
Schlüter, Andreas **17**:127
Würzburg Residenz **20**:297
Great Britain
Archer, Thomas **2**:127
Blenheim Palace **3**:330
English art and architecture **7**:184–186
Hawksmoor, Nicholas **10**:78
Lely, Sir Peter **12**:279
Saint Paul's Cathedral **17**:25
Thornhill, Sir James **19**:179
interior design **11**:212–213 *illus.*
Italy
Algardi, Alessandro **1**:283
Bernini, Giovanni Lorenzo **3**:222–223
Bologna, Giovanni da **3**:370–371
Borromini, Francesco **3**:404–405
Caravaggio, Michelangelo Merisi da **4**:131–132
Carracci (family) **4**:166–167
Correggio **5**:275–276
Cortona, Pietro da **5**:279
Domenichino **6**:230–231
Fontana, Carlo **8**:206
Galli da Bibiena (family) **9**:18–19
Gaulli, Giovanni Battista **9**:61
Giordano, Luca **9**:186
Guarini, Guarino **9**:387
Italian art and architecture **11**:310; **11**:311; **11**:313
Lanfranco, Giovanni **12**:194
Michelangelo **13**:372–375
Moderno, Stefano **13**:40
Rastrelli, Bartolommeo Francesco **16**:91
Reni, Guido **16**:157
Ricci (family) **16**:206
Rosa, Salvator **16**:312
Salvi, Nicola **17**:40
Strozzi, Bernardo **18**:303
Trevi Fountain **19**:291
Upper Belvedere, The (Lucas von Hildebrandt) **2**:352 *illus.*
Vanvitelli, Luigi **19**:521
Zucalli, Enrico **20**:380
Zuccarelli, Francesco **20**:381
lace **12**:159 *illus.*
Latin American art and architecture **12**:224–228 *illus.*
mural painting **13**:646
Netherlands
painting **15**:20–21
Ruysch, Rachel **16**:377
opera houses **14**:402
painting **15**:20–21
perspective **15**:191
Portuguese art and architecture **15**:456
Russia
Winter Palace **20**:181
Scandinavian art and architecture **17**:112–113
sculpture **17**:164 *illus.*
Spain
Buen Retiro Palace **3**:544
Churriguera (family) **4**:427
Fernández, Gregorio **8**:58
Herrera, Francisco de **10**:146
Murillo, Bartolomé Esteban **13**:648–649
Roldán (family) **16**:271
Spanish art and architecture **18**:153–154
Velázquez, Diego **19**:536–537
Zurbarán, Francisco de **20**:382–383
tomb **19**:231
BAROQUE LITERATURE 3:91 *bibliog.*
Crashaw, Richard **5**:332
Góngora y Argote, Luis de **9**:243–244
Marino, Giambattista **13**:156–157
Spanish literature **18**:157
Vondel, Joost van den **19**:634
BAROQUE MUSIC 3:91–92 *bibliog., illus.*
Bach, Johann Sebastian **3**:10–11
Bononcini (family) **3**:381
Charpentier, Marc Antoine **4**:299
choral music **4**:406
church music **4**:424 *illus.*
Corelli, Arcangelo **5**:262
Couperin (family) **5**:313–314
Deller, Alfred **6**:94
figured bass **8**:75
French music **8**:320–321
Frescobaldi, Girolamo **8**:328
Froberger, Johann Jacob **8**:335
fugue **8**:355
gavotte **9**:63
Geminiani, Francesco **9**:73
German and Austrian music **9**:129–130
Gluck, Christoph Willibald **9**:211
Graun, Karl Heinrich **9**:302
ground bass **9**:373
Handel, George Frideric **10**:36
harpsichord **10**:56
Italian music **11**:318–319
mass (musical setting) **13**:201
Monteverdi, Claudio **13**:554
motet **13**:606
music, history of Western **13**:666
oboe **14**:316 *illus.*
opera **14**:399–400
oratorio **14**:416
orchestra and orchestration **14**:417–418
Pachelbel, Johann **15**:4
passacaglia and chaconne **15**:103
Philidor (family) **15**:231
Praetorius, Michael **15**:487
Rameau, Jean Philippe **16**:80
scherzo **17**:119
Schütz, Heinrich **17**:138
sonata **18**:63
Te Deum laudamus **19**:53
Telemann, Georg Philipp **19**:78
Vivaldi, Antonio **19**:622
BAROUCHE
coach and carriage **5**:73
BAROZZI, GIACOMO *see* VIGNOLA, GIACOMO BAROZZI DA
BARQUISIMETO (Venezuela)
map (10° 4′N 69° 19′W) **19**:542
BARR, ALFRED H., JR. 3:92 *bibliog.*
abstract expressionism **1**:65
Museum of Modern Art **13**:657
BARRA DO CORDA (Brazil)
map (5° 30′S 45° 15′W) **3**:460
BARRACUDA 3:92 *bibliog., illus.*; **8**:116 *illus.*
BARRACUDINA 3:92 *illus.*
BARRAGÁN, LUIS 3:92–93 *bibliog.*
BARRANCA (Peru)
map (4° 50′S 76° 42′W) **15**:193
BARRANCABERMEJA (Colombia)
map (7° 3′N 73° 52′W) **5**:107
BARRANCAS (Venezuela)
map (8° 42′N 62° 11′W) **19**:542
BARRANQUERAS (Argentina)
map (27° 29′S 58° 56′W) **2**:149
BARRANQUILLA (Colombia) 3:93
map (10° 59′N 74° 48′W) **5**:107
BARRAQUÉ, JEAN 3:93 *bibliog.*
BARRAS, CHARLES M.
musical comedy **13**:674
BARRAS, PAUL FRANÇOIS JEAN NICOLAS, VICOMTE DE 3:93 *bibliog.*
American Revolution **1**:359 *map*
Napoleon I, Emperor of the French (Napoléon Bonaparte) **14**:15–16
BARRATRY 3:93
BARRAUD, FRANCIS
His Master's Voice **15**:253 *illus.*
BARRAULT, JEAN LOUIS 3:93
BARRE (Massachusetts)
map (42° 26′N 72° 6′W) **13**:206
BARRE (Vermont) 3:93; **19**:557 *illus.*
map (44° 12′N 72° 30′W) **19**:554
BARRE, ISAAC
Wilkes-Barre (Pennsylvania) **20**:152
BARRE, RAYMOND 3:93
BARRE DES ÉCRINS MOUNTAIN
map (44° 55′N 6° 22′E) **8**:260
BARREIRAS (Brazil)
map (12° 8′S 45° 0′W) **3**:460
BARREIRO (Portugal)
map (38° 40′N 9° 4′W) **15**:449
BARREIROS (Brazil)
map (8° 49′S 35° 12′W) **3**:460
BARREL 3:93–94 *bibliog., illus.*
BARREL CACTUS
cacti and other succulents **4**:10
BARREL ORGAN 3:94 *bibliog., illus.*
calliope **4**:46
BARREN (county in Kentucky)
map (37° 0′N 86° 0′W) **12**:47
BARREN LAKE
map (36° 45′N 86° 2′W) **12**:47
BARREN RIVER
map (37° 11′N 86° 37′W) **12**:47
BARRENO, MARIA ISABEL
Three Marias, The (Portuguese literary trio) **19**:182
BARRENS
Pine Barrens of New Jersey **18**:378
savanna life **17**:97–99
BARRÈS, MAURICE 3:94
BARRHEAD (Alberta)
map (54° 8′N 114° 24′W) **1**:256
BARRICADES, DAYS OF
Fronde **8**:339
BARRIE (Ontario)
map (44° 24′N 79° 40′W) **14**:393
BARRIE, SIR JAMES MATTHEW 3:94–95 *bibliog., illus.*
Peter Pan **15**:200
BARRIENTOS ORTUÑO, RENÉ
Bolivia **3**:369
BARRINGTON (Illinois)
map (42° 9′N 88° 8′W) **11**:42
BARRINGTON (Nova Scotia)
map (43° 34′N 65° 34′W) **14**:269
BARRINGTON (Rhode Island)
map (41° 44′N 71° 18′W) **16**:198
BARRIOS, EDUARDO 3:95 *bibliog.*
Chile **4**:355
BARRIOS, JUSTO RUFINO 3:95
Guatemala **9**:388
BARRISTER 3:95
law **12**:244
BARRITA VIEJA (Guatemala)
map (13° 55′N 90° 54′W) **9**:389
BARRON (Wisconsin)
map (45° 24′N 91° 51′W) **20**:185
BARRON (county in Wisconsin)
map (45° 25′N 91° 52′W) **20**:185
BARRON, CLARENCE WALKER 3:95
BARRON'S NATIONAL BUSINESS AND FINANCIAL WEEKLY
Barron, Clarence Walker **3**:95
BARROW (Alaska) 3:95
map (71° 17′N 156° 47′W) **1**:242
BARROW (archaeology) 3:95
Battle-Axe culture **3**:126
European prehistory **7**:302; **7**:305
Knowth **12**:102
megalith **13**:279 *illus.*
Wessex culture **20**:106
BARROW (county in Georgia)
map (34° 0′N 83° 45′W) **9**:114
BARROW, CLYDE 3:95 *bibliog.*
BARROW, ISAAC 3:95 *bibliog.*
mathematics, history of **13**:225
BARROW, JOE LOUIS *see* LOUIS, JOE
BARROW, SIR JOHN 3:95
BARROW-IN-FURNESS (England)
map (54° 7′N 3° 14′W) **19**:403
BARROWS (Manitoba)
map (52° 49′N 101° 27′W) **13**:119
BARRY (Illinois)
map (39° 42′N 91° 2′W) **11**:42
BARRY (county in Michigan)
map (42° 35′N 85° 18′W) **13**:377
BARRY (county in Missouri)
map (36° 45′N 93° 50′W) **13**:476
BARRY, SIR CHARLES 3:95–96 *bibliog.*
Houses of Parliament **2**:136 *illus.*
Westminster Palace **20**:118
BARRY, ELIZABETH
theater, history of the **19**:147
BARRY, JEANNE BÉCU, COMTESSE DU *see* DU BARRY, JEANNE BÉCU, COMTESSE
BARRY, JOHN 3:96 *bibliog.*
BARRY, MARION
District of Columbia **6**:201
BARRY, PHILIP 3:96
BARRYMORE (family) 3:96 *bibliog., illus.*
BARRYMORE, ETHEL *see* BARRYMORE (family)
BARRYMORE, JOHN
Barrymore (family) **3**:96
Flynn, Errol **8**:191
BARRYMORE, LIONEL *see* BARRYMORE (family)
BARRYMORE, MAURICE *see* BARRYMORE (family)
BARSTOW (California)
map (34° 54′N 117° 1′W) **4**:31
BARSTOW (Texas)
map (31° 28′N 103° 24′W) **19**:129
BART (subway) *see* BAY AREA RAPID TRANSIT (BART)
BART, LIONEL
musical comedy **13**:675
BARTER
money **13**:526–527
BARTH, HEINRICH 3:96

BARTH, HEINRICH (cont.)
Africa **1**:157 *map*
exploration **7**:337 *map*
BARTH, JOHN **3**:96–97 *bibliog.*
BARTH, KARL **3**:97 *bibliog.*
Brunner, Emil **3**:525
predestination **15**:502
BARTHELME, DONALD **3**:97 *bibliog.*
BARTHES, ROLAND **3**:97
BARTHOLDI, FRÉDÉRIC AUGUSTE **3**:97
Statue of Liberty **14**:146 *illus.*; **18**:238
BARTHOLOMEW (county in Indiana)
map (39° 13′N 85° 55′W) **11**:111
BARTHOLOMEW, SAINT **3**:97
BARTHOLOMEW BAYOU
map (33° 0′N 91° 45′W) **2**:166
BARTICA (Guyana)
map (6° 24′N 58° 37′W) **9**:410
BARTLESVILLE (Oklahoma)
map (36° 45′N 95° 59′W) **14**:368
BARTLETT (Nebraska)
map (41° 53′N 98° 33′W) **14**:70
BARTLETT (New Hampshire)
map (44° 5′N 71° 17′W) **14**:123
BARTLETT (Tennessee)
map (35° 12′N 89° 52′W) **19**:104
BARTLETT (Texas)
map (30° 48′N 97° 26′W) **19**:129
BARTLETT, JENNIFER **3**:97
BARTLETT, NEIL
chemistry, history of **4**:328
BARTLETT COVE (Alaska)
map (58° 27′N 135° 55′W) **1**:242
BARTLETT RESERVOIR
map (33° 52′N 111° 37′W) **2**:160
BARTLETTS HARBOUR (Newfoundland)
map (50° 57′N 57° 0′W) **14**:166
BARTÓK, BÉLA **3**:97–98 *bibliog., illus.*
Hungarian music **10**:306
BARTOLO, DOMENICO DI
fresco showing wounded man **13**:269 *illus.*
BARTOLOMEO, MICHELOZZO DI *see* MICHELOZZO
BARTOLOMMEO, FRA **3**:98 *bibliog.*
BARTOLOZZI, FRANCESCO **3**:98
BARTOLOZZI, LUCIA ELISABETTA *see* VESTRIS, MADAME
BARTON (county in Kansas)
map (38° 30′N 98° 45′W) **12**:18
BARTON (county in Missouri)
map (37° 30′N 94° 20′W) **13**:476
BARTON (Vermont)
map (44° 45′N 72° 11′W) **19**:554
BARTON, CLARA **3**:98 *bibliog.*
BARTON, DEREK **3**:98
BARTON, SIR EDMUND **3**:98 *bibliog.*
BARTOW (Florida)
map (27° 54′N 81° 50′W) **8**:172
BARTOW (county in Georgia)
map (34° 15′N 84° 50′W) **9**:114
BARTRAM, JOHN **3**:98 *bibliog.*
BARTSCH, ADAM VON **3**:98–99
BARUCH, BERNARD M. **3**:99 *bibliog.*
BARUCH, BOOK OF **3**:99
BARUCH COLLEGE *see* BERNARD M. BARUCH COLLEGE
BARWON RIVER
map (30° 0′S 148° 5′E) **2**:328
BARYCENTER
Earth, motions of **7**:19 *illus.*
BARYE, ANTOINE LOUIS **3**:99 *bibliog.*
bronzes **3**:508
BARYLAMBDA **3**:99
BARYON **3**:99
fermion **8**:56
fundamental particles **8**:362
hadron **10**:8
proton **15**:578
quark **16**:12
BARYSHNIKOV, MIKHAIL **3**:99 *bibliog., illus.*
American Ballet Theatre **1**:337
BARYSPHERE
lithosphere **12**:371
BARZUN, JACQUES **3**:99–100 *bibliog.*
BAS MITZVAH
bar mitzvah **3**:74
BAS-RELIEF **3**:100–101 *bibliog., illus.*
Egyptian **5**:51 *illus.*
Nineveh **14**:200
sculpture techniques **17**:166
Stone Mountain **18**:282
BASAL METABOLISM *see* METABOLISM
BASALT **3**:101 *bibliog., illus.*
Cenozoic Era **4**:245
eclogite **7**:41
gabbro **9**:3
igneous rock **11**:33
kimberlite **12**:77
lava **12**:240
magma **13**:51–52
mid-oceanic ridge **13**:390
mineral occurrence **13**:442
oceanic mineral resources **14**:340
Paleolithic Period **15**:38
plate tectonics **15**:355
pre-Columbian monuments **15**:496 *illus.*
pyroxene **15**:638
rock **16**:247
scoria **17**:148
Tertiary Period **19**:125
zeolite **20**:360
BASAWAN **3**:101 *bibliog.*
BASCOM, GEORGE
Cochise **5**:86
BASCULE BRIDGE **3**:480–481 *illus.*; **3**:483 *table*
BASE (chemistry) *see* ACIDS AND BASES
BASE (mathematics) **3**:102 *bibliog.*
binary number **3**:256
decimal **6**:73
duodecimal system **6**:301–302
e **7**:3
logarithm **12**:394
BASEBALL **3**:102–107 *bibliog., illus., tables*
baseball field **3**:104 *illus.*
batting area **3**:104 *illus.*
black baseball leagues
Gibson, Josh **9**:176
Paige, Satchel **15**:14
commissioners and executives
Frick, Ford **8**:330
Landis, Kenesaw Mountain **12**:184
Rickey, Branch **16**:216
Cooperstown (New York) **5**:245
Cy Young Award Winners **3**:105 *table*
Doubleday, Abner **6**:246
equipment **3**:104 *illus.*
history **3**:102–103 *illus.*; **18**:196 *illus.*
how to play the game **3**:103–107
Japanese baseball
Oh, Sadaharu **14**:355
Little League baseball **12**:373
Major League Pennant Winners **3**:105 *table*
managers
Alston, Walter **1**:310
Durocher, Leo **6**:306–307
McCarthy, Joe **13**:8
McGraw, John **13**:16
Mack, Connie **13**:26–27
Rickey, Branch **16**:216
Robinson, Frank **16**:244
Stengel, Casey **18**:253
Most Valuable Player Award **3**:106 *table*
pitching circle **3**:104 *illus.*
players and coaches
Aaron, Henry **1**:51
Alexander, Grover Cleveland **1**:273
Bench, Johnny **3**:196
Berra, Yogi **3**:224
Brock, Lou **3**:501
Campanella, Roy **4**:64
Carew, Rod **4**:146
Carlton, Steve **4**:152
Chandler, Happy **4**:279
Clemente, Roberto **5**:50
Cobb, Ty **5**:83
Collins, Eddie **5**:104
Dean, Dizzy **6**:67
Dickey, Bill **6**:157
DiMaggio, Joe **6**:177
Feller, Bob **8**:47–48
Ford, Whitey **8**:223
Foxx, Jimmie **8**:257
Gehrig, Lou **9**:67
Gibson, Bob **9**:175
Gibson, Josh **9**:176
Hornsby, Rogers **10**:240
Hubbell, Carl **10**:288
Jackson, Reggie **11**:343
Johnson, Walter Perry **11**:436
Koufax, Sandy **12**:125
Mantle, Mickey **13**:130–131
Maris, Roger **13**:157
Mathewson, Christy **13**:228
Mays, Willie **13**:249
Musial, Stan **13**:661
Paige, Satchel **15**:14
Parker, Dave **15**:90
Perry, Gaylord **15**:179
Robinson, Brooks **16**:243
Robinson, Frank **16**:244
Robinson, Jackie **16**:245
Rose, Pete **16**:314
Ruth, Babe **16**:375
Ryan, Nolan **16**:378
Seaver, Tom **17**:176
Sisler, George **17**:328
Spahn, Warren **18**:138
Speaker, Tris **18**:165
Thorpe, Jim **19**:180
Wagner, Honus **20**:4
Wilhelm, Hoyt **20**:151
Williams, Ted **20**:160
Yastrzemski, Carl **20**:320
Young, Cy **20**:333 *illus.*
softball **18**:35
stadium **18**:208–209
World Series champions **3**:105 *table*
BASEL (Switzerland) **3**:108
map (47° 33′N 7° 35′E) **18**:394
tapestry **19**:32 *illus.*
BASEL, COUNCIL OF **3**:108 *bibliog.*
Hussites **10**:321
BASELEVEL **3**:108
river and stream **16**:230
BASEMENT ROCK **3**:108
BASENJI **3**:108 *bibliog., illus.*; **6**:216 *illus.*
BASHAW (Alberta)
map (52° 35′N 112° 58′W) **1**:256
BASHO **3**:108 *bibliog.*
BASIC (computer language) **3**:108
computer, personal **5**:160i
computer languages **5**:160o; **5**:160p
computer programming **5**:163–164
BASIC EDUCATIONAL OPPORTUNITY GRANTS
scholarships, fellowships, and loans **17**:130
BASIC ENGLISH
languages, artificial **12**:197
Richards, I. A. **16**:211
BASIC VIOLET 3 *see* GENTIAN VIOLET
BASIE, COUNT **3**:109 *bibliog.*
BASIL (botany) **3**:109 *illus.*
BASIL THE GREAT, SAINT **3**:109
BASIL I, BYZANTINE EMPEROR (Basil the Macedonian) **3**:109
Byzantine Empire **3**:607–608
BASIL II, BYZANTINE EMPEROR (Basil Bulgaroktonus) **3**:109
BASIL III, GRAND DUKE OF MOSCOW *see* VASILY III, GRAND DUKE OF MOSCOW
BASIL IV SHUISKI, RUSSIAN TSAR *see* VASILY IV, RUSSIAN TSAR
BASILAN ISLAND
map (6° 34′N 122° 3′E) **15**:237
BASILE (Louisiana)
map (30° 29′N 92° 36′W) **12**:430
BASILE, GIOVANNI BATTISTA **3**:109
BASILICA **3**:109–110 *bibliog., illus.*; **3**:180 *illus.*
architecture **2**:133
atrium **2**:313
Byzantine art and architecture **3**:604
campanile **4**:64–65
cathedrals and churches **4**:204
Coptic art and architecture **5**:255
Early Christian art and architecture **7**:9
Merovingian art and architecture **13**:311
nave **14**:58
Norman architecture **14**:220
Roman art and architecture **16**:273
Romanesque art and architecture **16**:282
Saint Mark's **17**:23–24
Saint Peter's **17**:25–26
triumphal arch **19**:304
BASILICA (Imperial Laws)
Leo VI, Byzantine Emperor (Leo the Wise) **12**:288
BASILICA ULPIA (Rome)
floor plan **3**:110 *illus.*
BASILICATA (Italy) **3**:110
BASILIDES **3**:110
BASILISK **3**:110; **12**:381 *illus.*
BASIN (Montana)
map (46° 16′N 112° 16′W) **13**:547
BASIN (Wyoming)
map (44° 23′N 108° 2′W) **20**:301
BASIN AND RANGE PROVINCE **3**:110
horst and graben **10**:254
inselberg **11**:194
meander, river **13**:253
Oregon **14**:428
playa **15**:363
United States **19**:420
BASIN STREET **3**:110
BASKERVILLE, JOHN **3**:110 *bibliog.*
typeface **19**:364
BASKET MAKERS (American Indians) *see* ANASAZI (American Indians)
BASKETBALL **3**:111–115 *bibliog., illus., tables*
basketball court **3**:111 *illus.*
Gulick, Luther Halsey **9**:404
Hall of Fame
Springfield (Massachusetts) **18**:200
Harlem Globetrotters **3**:112; **10**:50
history **3**:111–112; **18**:197 *illus.*
Naismith, James **14**:8
NBA Most Valuable Player Award **3**:114 *table*
NBA Playoff Winners **3**:114 *table*
NBA Scoring Leaders **3**:114 *table*
NCAA Champions **3**:114 *table*
players and coaches
Abdul-Jabbar, Kareem **1**:54
Auerbach, Red **2**:319
Baylor, Elgin **3**:134
Bird, Larry **3**:290
Bradley, Bill **3**:437
Chamberlain, Wilt **4**:274
Cousy, Bob **5**:318
Erving, Julius **7**:235
Havlicek, John **10**:71
Knight, Bobby **12**:100
Luisetti, Hank **12**:453
Maravich, Pete **13**:144
Mikan, George **13**:417
Pettit, Bob **15**:216
Robertson, Oscar **16**:242
Rupp, Adolph **16**:347
Russell, Bill **16**:350
Walton, Bill **20**:20
West, Jerry **20**:107
Wooden, John **20**:211
professional basketball **3**:112–114
rules and equipment **3**:114–115
women's basketball **3**:112; **3**:113–114
BASKETRY **3**:115–116 *bibliog., illus.*
Anasazi **1**:394 *illus.*
Indians of North America, art of the **11**:139–140 *illus.*
North American archaeology **14**:239 *illus.*
Oceanic art **14**:338
Pomo **15**:423
rush **16**:347
weaving **20**:83–84
BASKIN, LEONARD **3**:116 *bibliog.*
BASLE (Switzerland) *see* BASEL (Switzerland)
BASOTHO *see* SOTHO
BASOV, NIKOLAI GENNADIYEVICH **3**:116
BASQUE LANGUAGE **3**:116 *bibliog.*
Europe **7**:274 *map*
BASQUES **3**:116 *bibliog.*
Basque language **3**:116
Biarritz (France) **3**:237
Bilbao (Spain) **3**:250
Nevada **14**:112 *illus.*
Spain **18**:142
Spain, history of **18**:149
BASRA (Iraq) **3**:116
map (30° 30′N 47° 47′E) **11**:255
BASS (fish) **3**:116–117 *bibliog., illus.*
grouper **9**:377–378
largemouth black bass **12**:168 *illus.*
sea bass **17**:168
BASS (music) **3**:117
BASS, ROBERT WILLIAM
Dickens' Dream **6**:157 *illus.*
BASS, SAM **3**:117 *bibliog.*
BASS DRUM **6**:282 *illus.*; **13**:675 *illus.*; **15**:162 *illus.*
BASS ISLANDS
map (41° 40′N 82° 50′W) **14**:357
BASS RIVER (Nova Scotia)
map (45° 25′N 63° 47′W) **14**:269
BASS STRAIT **3**:117
map (39° 20′S 145° 30′E) **2**:328
BASS VIOL *see* DOUBLE BASS
BASSANI, GIORGIO **3**:117
BASSANO (Alberta)
map (50° 47′N 112° 28′W) **1**:256
BASSANO (family) **3**:117–118 *bibliog., illus.*
BASSANO, JACOPO
The Adoration of the Shepherds **3**:117 *illus.*
Bassano (family) **3**:118
BASSARI (Togo)
map (9° 15′N 0° 47′E) **19**:222
BASSE SANTA SU (Gambia)
map (13° 19′N 14° 13′W) **9**:25
BASSE-TAILLE
enamel **7**:161–162
BASSE-TERRE (Guadeloupe) **3**:118
Guadeloupe **9**:385
BASSE TERRE (Trinidad and Tobago)
map (10° 8′N 61° 18′W) **19**:300
BASSEIN (Burma)
map (16° 47′N 94° 44′E) **3**:573
BASSET HOUND **3**:118 *bibliog., illus.*; **6**:217 *illus.*

BASSETT (Nebraska)
map (42° 35′N 99° 32′W) **14**:70
BASSETT (Virginia)
map (36° 46′N 79° 59′W) **19**:607
BASSIANUS, VARIUS AVITUS *see* HELIOGABALUS, ROMAN EMPEROR
BASSO CONTINUO
figured bass **8**:75
BASSO OSTINATO *see* GROUND BASS
BASSOON **3**:118–119 *bibliog., illus.*; **13**:676 *illus.*
wind instruments **20**:171 *illus.*
BASSORAH *see* BASRA (Iraq)
BASSWOOD *see* LINDEN
BASSWOOD LAKE
map (48° 6′N 91° 40′W) **13**:453
BAST
Bubastis **3**:530–531
BASTARD OF ORLÉANS *see* DUNOIS, JEAN, COMTE DE (the Bastard of Orléans)
BASTARD TOADFLAX **3**:119
See also TOADFLAX
BASTIA (France)
map (42° 42′N 9° 27′E) **8**:260
BASTIANINI, GIOVANNI
forgery in art **8**:233
BASTIDAS, RODRIGO DE
Panama **15**:56
Santa Marta (Colombia) **17**:68
BASTIEN-LEPAGE, JULES **3**:119
BASTILLE **3**:119; **16**:187 *illus.*
Paris **15**:87 *map*
BASTOGNE (Belgium)
World War II **20**:273 *illus.*
BASTROP (Louisiana)
map (32° 47′N 91° 55′W) **12**:430
BASTROP (Texas)
map (30° 7′N 97° 19′W) **19**:129
BASTROP (county in Texas)
map (33° 0′N 97° 18′W) **19**:129
BASUTO *see* SOTHO
BASUTOLAND *see* LESOTHO
BAT **3**:119–121 *bibliog., illus.*
anatomy **3**:120 *illus.*
bone **7**:323 *illus.*
cave **4**:222
echolocation **7**:39
feeding habits **3**:119
forelimb **5**:155 *illus.*; **13**:102 *illus.*
fruit bat **13**:104 *illus.*
leaf-nosed bat **13**:104 *illus.*
long-eared bat **13**:100 *illus.*
pollination **15**:409
sound frequencies produced **18**:73 *table*
BAT MITZVAH
bar mitzvah **3**:74
BATA (Equatorial Guinea)
map (1° 51′N 9° 45′E) **7**:226
BATAAN (Philippines) **3**:121
BATAAN DEATH MARCH
Bataan **3**:121
World War II **20**:260–261 *illus.*
BATABANÓ, GULF OF
map (22° 15′N 82° 30′W) **5**:377
BATAILLE, HENRY **3**:121
BATAK **3**:121 *bibliog.*
BATAN ISLANDS
map (20° 30′N 121° 50′E) **15**:237
BATAN-600 (telescope)
Special Astrophysical Observatory **18**:166
BATAVIA (Illinois)
map (41° 51′N 88° 19′W) **11**:42
BATAVIA (Indonesia) *see* JAKARTA (Indonesia)
BATAVIA (Iowa)
map (41° 0′N 92° 10′W) **11**:244
BATAVIA (New York)
map (43° 0′N 78° 11′W) **14**:149
BATAVIA (Ohio)
map (39° 5′N 84° 11′W) **14**:357
BATCH PROCESSING (computer term) **5**:160b
BATES (county in Missouri)
map (38° 15′N 94° 20′W) **13**:476
BATES, H. W.
mimicry **13**:435
BATES, KATHARINE LEE **3**:121
BATES COLLEGE **3**:121
BATESBURG (South Carolina)
map (33° 54′N 81° 33′W) **18**:98
BATESON, GREGORY **3**:121
BATESON, TIMOTHY **19**:154 *illus.*
BATESON, WILLIAM
zoology **20**:378
BATESVILLE (Arkansas)
map (35° 46′N 91° 39′W) **2**:166
BATESVILLE (Indiana)
map (39° 18′N 85° 13′W) **11**:111
BATESVILLE (Mississippi)
map (34° 18′N 90° 0′W) **13**:469
BATFISH **3**:121 *bibliog.*
anglerfish **1**:415
BATH (bathing) **3**:122 *bibliog., illus.*
Caracalla, Baths of **3**:122; **4**:129–130
Diocletian, Baths of **6**:182
Indus civilization **11**:154 *illus.*
Roman art and architecture **16**:274
spa, medicinal bath **3**:122
BATH (England) **3**:121–122
map (51° 23′N 2° 22′W) **19**:403
Roman bath **3**:122 *illus.*
Wood (family) **20**:205
BATH (county in Kentucky)
map (38° 10′N 83° 45′W) **12**:47
BATH (Maine) **3**:122
map (43° 55′N 69° 49′W) **13**:70
BATH (New York)
map (42° 20′N 77° 19′W) **14**:149
BATH (county in Virginia)
map (38° 5′N 79° 45′W) **19**:607
BATH YAM (Israel)
map (32° 0′N 34° 45′E) **11**:302
BATHGATE (North Dakota)
map (48° 53′N 97° 29′W) **14**:248
BATHOLITH **3**:122 *bibliog.*
granite **9**:287
granodiorite **9**:287
BÁTHORY (family) **3**:122–123
BATHSHEBA (Barbados)
map (13° 13′N 59° 31′W) **3**:75
BATHSHEBA (biblical queen) **3**:123
BATHURST (Gambia) *see* BANJUL (Gambia)
BATHURST (New Brunswick) **3**:123
map (47° 36′N 65° 39′W) **14**:117
BATHURST INLET (Northwest Territories)
map (66° 50′N 108° 1′W) **14**:258
BATHURST ISLAND (Australia)
map (11° 37′S 130° 27′E) **2**:328
BATHURST ISLAND (Northwest Territories)
map (76° 0′N 100° 30′W) **14**:258
BATHYAL ZONE **3**:123 *bibliog.*
benthonic zone **3**:205
fossil record **8**:247
BATHYLLUS
theater, history of the **19**:145
BATHYSCAPHE **3**:123 *illus.*
Cousteau, Jacques-Yves **5**:317
Marianas Trench **13**:151
oceanic trenches **14**:341
Piccard, Auguste, builder **15**:292
BATHYTHERMOGRAPHC **14**:343 *illus.*
BATIK **3**:123–124 *bibliog., illus.*
BATISTA, FULGENCIO **3**:124
Cuba **5**:380
Grau San Martín, Ramón **9**:301–302
BATLLE Y ORDÓÑEZ, JOSÉ **3**:124
Uruguay **19**:490
BATMAN **5**:136 *illus.*
BATNA (Algeria)
map (35° 34′N 6° 11′E) **1**:287
BATON **3**:124
BATON ROUGE (Louisiana) **3**:124
map (30° 23′N 91° 11′W) **12**:430
BATONI, POMPEO GIROLAMO **3**:124 *bibliog.*
BATSWANA *see* TSWANA
BATTALION **3**:124
BATTAMBANG (Kampuchea) **3**:124
map (13° 6′N 103° 12′E) **12**:11
BATTANI, AL- **3**:125
mathematics, history of **13**:224
BATTERED CHILD *see* CHILD ABUSE
BATTERING RAM **3**:125
fortification **8**:239 *illus.*
BATTERY **3**:125–126 *bibliog., illus.*
circuit, electric **4**:436–438
electric car **7**:105
electricity **7**:108 *illus.*
electrochemical battery
Bunsen, Robert Wilhelm **3**:564
electrochemistry **7**:112
electrode **7**:113
electromotive force **7**:119
lead-acid **3**:126
mercury **13**:306
nickel-cadmium **3**:126; **4**:12
nuclear-powered battery
promethium **15**:567
primary **3**:125–126
storage battery **3**:125–126
antimony **2**:64
electrolysis **7**:114
Volta, Alessandro, Count, inventor **19**:631
voltage regulator **19**:631
zinc-copper battery
Daniell, John Frederic **6**:32
BATTERY (law) *see* ASSAULT AND BATTERY
BATTERY FARMING *see* FACTORY FARMING
BATTICALOA (Sri Lanka)
map (7° 43′N 81° 42′E) **18**:206
BATTISTA, GIOVANNI *see* VICO, GIAMBATTISTA
BATTLE, TRIAL BY *see* TRIAL BY BATTLE
BATTLE-AXE CULTURE **3**:126 *bibliog.*
Beaker culture **3**:139
European prehistory **7**:302
Scandinavia, history of **17**:6
BATTLE CREEK (Michigan) **3**:126
map (42° 19′N 85° 11′W) **13**:377
BATTLE CREEK (Nebraska)
map (42° 0′N 97° 36′W) **14**:70
BATTLE GROUND (Indiana)
map (40° 31′N 86° 50′W) **11**:111
BATTLE HARBOUR (Newfoundland)
map (52° 16′N 55° 35′W) **14**:166
"BATTLE HYMN OF THE REPUBLIC, THE" (poem)
Howe, Julia Ward **10**:284
BATTLE LAKE (Minnesota)
map (46° 17′N 95° 43′W) **13**:453
BATTLE MOUNTAIN (Nevada)
map (40° 38′N 116° 56′W) **14**:111
BATTLE OF *see under the latter part of the name, e.g.*, BUNKER HILL, BATTLE OF; GETTYSBURG, BATTLE OF; *etc.*
BATTLE RIVER
map (52° 43′N 108° 15′W) **17**:81
BATTLE OF THE NATIONS
Leipzig (East Germany) **12**:278
BATTLEMENT MESA
map (39° 20′N 108° 0′W) **5**:116
BATTLESHIP **3**:126–128 *bibliog., illus.*
Dreadnought **6**:266 *illus.*
Ericsson, John **7**:229
galleon **9**:17–18 *illus.*
galley (ship) **9**:18 *illus.*
Mahan, Alfred Thayer **13**:64
naval vessels **14**:55–56 *illus.*
navy **14**:63–64
ship **17**:274
BATTUTA, IBN *see* IBN BATTUTA
BATU KHAN **3**:128 *bibliog.*
Golden Horde, Khanate of the **9**:232
BATU MOUNTAIN
map (6° 55′N 39° 46′E) **7**:253
BATU PAHAT (Malaysia)
map (1° 51′N 102° 56′E) **13**:85
BATUMI (USSR) **3**:128
map (41° 38′N 41° 38′E) **19**:388
Russo-Turkish Wars **16**:374
BATWA *see* TWA (people)
BATY, GASTON **3**:128
BAUCHI (Nigeria)
map (10° 19′N 9° 50′E) **14**:190
BAUD (computer term) **5**:160h
BAUDELAIRE, CHARLES **3**:128–129 *bibliog., illus.*; **8**:318 *illus.*
decadence **6**:72
Flowers of Evil, The **8**:184
realism (art) **16**:103
BAUDETTE (Minnesota)
map (48° 43′N 94° 36′W) **13**:453
BAUDOT, ÉMILE
multiplex system
telegraph **19**:77
BAUDOUIN I, KING OF THE BELGIANS **3**:129
BAUDRIER, YVES
Jolivet, André **11**:441
BAUER, GEORGE *see* AGRICOLA, GEORGIUS
BAUER, HAROLD **3**:129 *bibliog.*
BAUGH, SAMMY **3**:129
BAUHAUS **2**:136 *illus.*; **3**:129–130 *bibliog., illus.*; **11**:222 *illus.*
Albers, Josef **1**:253
American art and architecture **1**:330
Breuer, Marcel **3**:475
Doesburg, Theo van **6**:213
Eiermann, Egon **7**:91
faculty (Dessau, 1926) **3**:129 *illus.*
furniture **8**:379–380
German art and architecture **9**:128
Gropius, Walter **9**:369
house (in Western architecture) **10**:270
industrial design **11**:155
interior design **11**:214
International Style (Bauhaus art) **11**:222–223
Klee, Paul **12**:95
Lissitzky, El **12**:366
Mies van der Rohe, Ludwig **13**:415
modern architecture **13**:490–491
Moholy-Nagy, László **13**:503
Pevsner, Sir Nikolaus **15**:216
Schlemmer, Oskar **17**:125
Seagram Building **1**:329 *illus.*
suprematism **18**:354
BAÚL, MOUNT
map (17° 38′N 100° 19′W) **13**:357
BAUM, L. FRANK **3**:130
Wizard of Oz, The **20**:195
BAUM, WILLIAM W. **3**:130
BAUMANN PEAK
map (6° 52′N 0° 46′E) **19**:222
BAUMEISTER, WILLI **3**:130 *bibliog.*
Black Dragons **9**:129 *illus.*
BAUMFREE, ISABELLA *see* TRUTH, SOJOURNER
BAUMGARTEN, ALEXANDER GOTTLIEB **3**:130 *bibliog.*
BAUR, FERDINAND CHRISTIAN **3**:130 *bibliog.*
BAUR, JOHN I. H.
Luminism **12**:459
BAURES (Bolivia)
map (13° 35′S 63° 35′W) **3**:366
BAURU (Brazil)
map (22° 19′S 49° 4′W) **3**:460
BAUSCH, PINA
modern dance **13**:498
BAUTZEN (Germany, East and West)
map (51° 11′N 14° 26′E) **9**:140
BAUXITE **3**:130–131 *illus.*
aluminum **1**:316–317 *illus.*
deposits **1**:315 *map*; **14**:424–425 *table*
mining **1**:318 *illus.*
refining **1**:318 *illus.*
Suriname **18**:364
weathering **20**:83
BAUYA (Sierra Leone)
map (8° 11′N 12° 34′W) **17**:296
BAVARIA (West Germany) **3**:131 *map*
art and architecture
Louis II's Bavarian palaces **12**:423
Nymphenburg ware **14**:309
cities
Augsburg **2**:319-320
Bayreuth **3**:134
Berchtesgaden **3**:208
Dachau **6**:4
Munich **13**:641 *illus.*
Oberammergau **14**:315
Regensburg **16**:128
Würzburg **20**:297
Franconia **8**:279
German territories *c*.1176 **9**:149 *map*
Germany in 1648 **9**:151 *map*
Germany 1815–1871 **9**:153 *map*
history **3**:131
Eisner, Kurt **7**:97
Henry the Lion, Duke of Saxony and Bavaria **10**:123
Louis I, King **12**:423
Louis II, King **12**:423
Maximilian, Elector and Duke **13**:239–240
Maximilian I, King **13**:240
Montez, Lola **13**:555
Palatinate **15**:30
Strauss, Franz Josef **18**:294
Wittelsbach (family) **20**:193
BAVARIAN SUCCESSION, WAR OF THE **3**:131
BAWKU (Ghana)
map (11° 5′N 0° 14′W) **9**:164
BAX, SIR ARNOLD **3**:131–132 *bibliog.*
BAXLEY (Georgia)
map (31° 47′N 82° 21′W) **9**:114
BAXTER (county in Arkansas)
map (36° 15′N 92° 20′W) **2**:166
BAXTER (Iowa)
map (41° 49′N 93° 9′W) **11**:244
BAXTER (Tennessee)
map (36° 9′N 85° 38′W) **19**:104
BAXTER, RICHARD **3**:132 *bibliog.*
BAXTER SPRINGS (Kansas)
map (37° 2′N 94° 44′W) **12**:18
BAY see GULF AND BAY
BAY (Arkansas)
map (35° 45′N 90° 34′W) **2**:166
BAY (county in Florida)
map (30° 15′N 85° 45′W) **8**:172
BAY (county in Michigan)
map (43° 45′N 84° 0′W) **13**:377
BAY AREA RAPID TRANSIT (BART)
subway **18**:318–319
BAY TO BREAKERS RACE
running and jogging **16**:346
BAY BULLS (Newfoundland)
map (47° 19′N 52° 49′W) **14**:166
BAY CITY (Michigan) **3**:132
map (43° 36′N 83° 53′W) **13**:377
BAY CITY (Texas)
map (28° 59′N 95° 58′W) **19**:129
BAY ISLANDS
map (16° 20′N 86° 30′W) **10**:218
BAY LEAF **3**:132; **12**:237 *illus.*
BAY MINETTE (Alabama)
map (30° 53′N 87° 47′W) **1**:234

BAY OF PIGS (Cuba)
map (22° 7′N 81° 10′W) **5**:377
BAY OF PIGS INVASION 3:132 *bibliog.*
intelligence gathering **11**:205
Kennedy, John F. **12**:43
United States, history of the **19**:458
BAY PORT (Michigan)
map (43° 51′N 83° 23′W) **13**:377
BAY PSALM BOOK 3:132 *bibliog.*
hymn **10**:346–347
BAY ROBERTS (Newfoundland)
map (47° 36′N 53° 16′W) **14**:166
BAY RUM 3:132
BAY SAINT LOUIS (Mississippi)
map (30° 19′N 89° 20′W) **13**:469
BAY SHORE (New York)
map (40° 44′N 73° 15′W) **14**:149
BAY SPRINGS (Mississippi)
map (31° 53′N 89° 17′W) **13**:469
BAYAMO (Cuba)
map (20° 23′N 76° 39′W) **5**:377
BAYAMÓN (Puerto Rico)
map (18° 24′N 66° 9′W) **15**:614
BAYANO RIVER
map (9° 0′N 79° 6′W) **15**:55
BAYARD (family) 3:132 *bibliog.*
BAYARD (Nebraska)
map (41° 45′N 103° 20′W) **14**:70
BAYARD (New Mexico)
map (32° 46′N 108° 8′W) **14**:136
BAYARD (West Virginia)
map (39° 16′N 79° 22′W) **20**:111
BAYARD, HIPPOLYTE 3:132
BAYBARS I, MAMELUKE SULTAN
Krak des Chevaliers **12**:127
BAYBERRY 3:133 *illus.*
myrtle **13**:692
BAYBORO (North Carolina)
map (35° 9′N 76° 46′W) **14**:242
BAYER, HERBERT
Bauhaus 3:129–130 *illus.*
BAYER, KARL JOSEPH
aluminum **1**:317
BAYER PROCESS
aluminum **1**:317
metallurgy **13**:330
BAYERN *see* BAVARIA (West Germany)
BAYES, NORA
music hall, vaudeville, and burlesque **13**:672
BAYEUX TAPESTRY 3:133 *bibliog., illus.*
comet **5**:134 *illus.*
embroidery **7**:152
needlework **14**:76
Norman Conquest **9**:310 *illus.*; **14**:222 *illus.*; **20**:155 *illus.*
BAYEZID I, SULTAN OF THE OTTOMAN EMPIRE 3:133
BAYEZID II, SULTAN OF THE OTTOMAN EMPIRE 3:133
BAYFIELD (Colorado)
map (37° 14′N 107° 36′W) **5**:116
BAYFIELD (Wisconsin)
map (46° 49′N 90° 49′W) **20**:185
BAYFIELD (county in Wisconsin)
map (46° 30′N 91° 15′W) **20**:185
BAYKAL, LAKE *see* BAIKAL, LAKE
BAYLE, PIERRE 3:133 *bibliog.*
BAYLISS, SIR WILLIAM 3:133–134 *bibliog.*; **20**:378 *illus.*
biology 3:270
Starling, Ernest Henry **18**:227
BAYLOR (county in Texas)
map (33° 38′N 99° 15′W) **19**:129
BAYLOR, ELGIN 3:134
BAYLOR UNIVERSITY 3:134
BAYONET 3:134
socket bayonet **18**:399 *illus.*
weapons **20**:75
BAYONNE (France) 3:134
map (43° 29′N 1° 29′W) **8**:260
BAYONNE (New Jersey) 3:134
map (40° 41′N 74° 7′W) **14**:129
BAYOU *see* SWAMP, MARSH, AND BOG
BAYOU BARTHOLOMEW *see* BARTHOLOMEW, BAYOU
BAYOU BODCAU RESERVOIR
map (32° 53′N 93° 29′W) **12**:430
BAYOU DE VIEW *see* DE VIEW, BAYOU
BAYOU LA BATRE (Alabama)
map (30° 24′N 88° 15′W) **1**:234
BAYOVAR (Peru)
map (5° 50′S 81° 3′W) **15**:193
BAYPORT (Minnesota)
map (45° 1′N 92° 47′W) **13**:453
BAYREUTH (West Germany) 3:134
map (49° 57′N 11° 35′E) **9**:140
BAYREUTH WAGNER FESTIVAL 3:134 *bibliog.*
Wagner, Richard **20**:5
BAYSUNGHUR
Persian art and architecture **15**:186
BAYT AL-MUQADDAS *see* JERUSALEM (Israel)
BAYTOWN (Texas)
map (29° 44′N 94° 58′W) **19**:129
BAZELON, DAVID L. 3:134–135
BAZHENOV, VASILI
Russian art and architecture **16**:362
BAZILLE, FRÉDÉRIC 3:135 *bibliog.*
BAZIN, ANDRÉ 3:135
Cahiers du Cinéma **4**:16
film, history of **8**:80
BAZINE (Kansas)
map (38° 27′N 99° 42′W) **12**:18
BAZIOTES, WILLIAM 3:135 *bibliog.*
BAZOOKA 3:135 *illus.*
BAZZI, GIOVANNI ANTONIO *see* SODOMA, IL
BBC *see* BRITISH BROADCASTING CORPORATION
BCG (Bacille Calmette-Guérin)
immunity **11**:59
tuberculosis **19**:327
BCS THEORY
Nobel Prize
Barden, John **18**:350
Cooper, Leon N. **18**:350
Schrieffer, John R. **18**:350
superconductivity **18**:350
BEACH (North Dakota)
map (46° 55′N 103° 52′W) **14**:248
BEACH, AMY MARCY 3:135 *bibliog.*
BEACH BOYS (musical group) 3:137
BEACH AND COAST 3:135–137 *bibliog., illus.*
beach sand 3:136
berm 3:219
breaker 3:468
changes 3:136
coastal protection **5**:81
coral reef **5**:258–260
erosion cycle **7**:232
erosion and sedimentation **7**:233
estuary **7**:248
floods and flood control **8**:166–167
gulf and bay **9**:402–403
hydrography **10**:341
intertidal life **11**:229 *illus.*
lagoon **12**:165–166
landform evolution **12**:183
longshore drift **12**:409
placer deposit **15**:325
red tide, dinoflagellate **6**:179
river delta **16**:232–233
seaweed **17**:177
sediment, marine **17**:183–184
strandline **18**:288
surf **18**:358
swell **18**:388
transgression, marine **19**:271
upwelling, oceanic **19**:473–474
water wave **20**:57–60 *illus.*
waves and currents 3:136
BEACH HAVEN (New Jersey)
map (39° 34′N 74° 14′W) **14**:129
BEACON 3:137
lighthouse **12**:336–337
BEACON (New York)
map (41° 30′N 73° 58′W) **14**:149
BEACONSFIELD, BENJAMIN DISRAELI, 1ST EARL OF *see* DISRAELI, BENJAMIN, 1ST EARL OF BEACONSFIELD
BEADED LIZARD
Gila monster **9**:178
BEADLE (county in South Dakota)
map (44° 22′N 98° 15′W) **18**:103
BEADLE, GEORGE W. 3:137 *bibliog., illus.*
biology 3:271
fungi **8**:367
Lederberg, Joshua **12**:268
Neurospora **14**:107
Tatum, Edward L. **19**:44
BEADS AND BEADWORK 3:137–138 *bibliog., illus.*
Indians of North America, art of the **11**:138–141
needlework **14**:76
tektites **19**:74
BEAGLE 3:138–139 *bibliog., illus.*; **6**:216 *illus.*
BEAGLE, H. M. S.
Darwin, Charles **6**:41
BEAK
bird 3:289 *illus.*
BEAKER CULTURE 3:139 *bibliog.*
Battle-Axe culture 3:126
drinking vessel **7**:303 *illus.*
European prehistory **7**:303
stone alignments **18**:282
Stonehenge **18**:283
Wessex culture **20**:106
BEALE, EDWARD FITZGERALD 3:139 *bibliog.*
BEAM
bridge (engineering) 3:480 *illus.*
BEAMON, BOB 3:139
BEAN 3:139–140 *bibliog., illus.*; **19**:533 *illus.*
chick-pea **4**:344–345
legume **12**:275
lentil **12**:275
lima bean **12**:342–343
seed **17**:187 *illus.*
soybean **18**:114–115 *illus.*
BEAN, ALAN 2:82 *illus.*; 3:140
Apollo program 2:82 *illus.*
BEAN, ROY 3:140 *bibliog.*
BEAR 2:141 *illus.*; 3:140–141 *bibliog., illus.*
black bear 3:141 *illus.*
brown bear 3:141 *illus.*; **19**:332 *illus.*
cave bear, cave dwellers **4**:224
Eskimo **7**:241
grizzly bear 3:141 *illus.*
Kodiak Island (Alaska) **12**:105
panda **15**:58
polar bear 2:141 *illus.*; 3:141 *illus.*; **13**:105 *illus.*
BEAR, THE (book) 3:141
BEAR CREEK
map (34° 46′N 88° 5′W) **1**:234
BEAR FLAG REPUBLIC 3:141 *bibliog.*
flag **8**:135 *illus.*
BEAR GRASS 3:141–142
BEAR LAKE
map (42° 0′N 111° 20′W) **19**:429
BEAR LAKE (British Columbia)
map (56° 11′N 126° 51′W) 3:491
BEAR LAKE (county in Idaho)
map (42° 20′N 111° 20′W) **11**:26
BEAR RIVER
map (41° 30′N 112° 8′W) **19**:429
BEAR RIVER (Nova Scotia)
map (44° 34′N 65° 39′W) **14**:269
BEARBERRY 3:142
BEARD, CHARLES A. 3:142 *bibliog.*
BEARDED COLLIE 3:142 *bibliog., illus.*; **6**:215 *illus.*
BEARDEN (Arkansas)
map (33° 43′N 92° 37′W) 2:166
BEARDFISH 3:142
BEARDSLEY, AUBREY 3:142–143 *bibliog., illus.*
Ali Baba 3:388 *illus.*
Ascension of St. Rose of Lima, The 3:142 *illus.*
BEARDSTOWN (Illinois)
map (40° 1′N 90° 26′W) **11**:42
BEARDTONGUE (botany) 3:143 *illus.*
BEARDWORM 3:143
Pogonophora **15**:379–380
BEARER BONDS 3:376
BEARING 3:143–144 *bibliog., illus.*
machine **13**:21
BÉARN (France) 3:144
BEARTOOTH PASS
map (44° 58′N 109° 28′W) **20**:301
BEARTOWN MOUNTAIN
map (36° 56′N 81° 56′W) **19**:607
BEAST EPIC *see* ALLEGORY; FABLE; *REYNARD THE FOX* (fable)
BEAT GENERATION 3:144 *bibliog.*
Burroughs, William S. 3:580
Corso, Gregory **5**:277
Duncan, Robert **6**:299
Ferlinghetti, Lawrence **8**:54
Ginsberg, Allen **9**:184–185
"Howl" **10**:285
Kerouac, Jack **12**:59
Snyder, Gary **18**:5–6
On the Road **14**:388
BEATIFICATION *see* CANONIZATION
BEATING OF ACHAN, THE
Blake, William 3:325 *illus.*
BEATITUDE 3:144 *bibliog.*
BEATLES, THE (musical group) 3:144–145 *bibliog., illus.*; **16**:58 *illus.*; **18**:336 *illus.*
rock music **16**:248 *illus.*
Zappa, Frank **20**:356
BEATON, SIR CECIL 3:145 *bibliog.*
BEATRICE 3:145 *bibliog.*
BEATRICE (Alabama)
map (31° 38′N 87° 19′W) **1**:234
BEATRICE (Nebraska)
map (40° 16′N 96° 44′W) **14**:70
BEATRICE, QUEEN OF THE NETHERLANDS 3:145
BEATTIE (Kansas)
map (39° 52′N 96° 25′W) **12**:18
BEATTIE, ANN 3:145
BEATTIE, JAMES 3:145
BEATTY (Nevada)
map (36° 54′N 116° 46′W) **14**:111
BEATTY, DAVID
World War I **20**:232; **20**:235
BEATTY, WARREN 3:145
BEATTYVILLE (Kentucky)
map (37° 35′N 83° 42′W) **12**:47
BEATUS OF LIEBANA
Commentary on the Apocalypse **16**:286 *illus.*
BEAU BASSIN (Mauritius)
map (20° 13′S 57° 27′E) **13**:237
BEAUBOURG 3:145 *bibliog., illus.*
postmodern architecture **15**:464
BEAUCHAMP, KATHERINE MANSFIELD *see* MANSFIELD, KATHERINE
BEAUCHAMP, THOMAS DE, EARL OF WARWICK
Richard II, King of England **16**:210
BEAUCHAMPS, CHARLES LOUIS
Académie Royale de Danse **1**:69
BEAUCHAMPS, PIERRE
ballet 3:42
BEAUFORT (family) 3:146 *bibliog.*
BEAUFORT (North Carolina)
map (34° 43′N 76° 40′W) **14**:242
BEAUFORT (county in North Carolina)
map (35° 20′N 76° 50′W) **14**:242
BEAUFORT (South Carolina) 3:145–146
map (32° 26′N 80° 40′W) **18**:98
BEAUFORT (county in South Carolina)
map (32° 20′N 80° 40′W) **18**:98
BEAUFORT SCALE 3:146
BEAUFORT SEA 3:146
map (73° 0′N 140° 0′W) **4**:70
BEAUFORT WEST (South Africa)
map (32° 18′S 22° 36′E) **18**:79
BEAUHARNAIS (family) 3:146
Josephine **11**:452
BEAUHARNOIS (Quebec)
map (45° 19′N 73° 52′W) **16**:18
BEAUJOYEUX, BALTHAZAR DE
ballet 3:42 *illus.*
BEAUMARCHAIS, PIERRE CARON DE 3:146 *bibliog., illus.*
Barber of Seville, The 3:77
comedy **5**:132
Marriage of Figaro, The **13**:166
BEAUMONT (Mississippi)
map (31° 11′N 88° 55′W) **13**:469
BEAUMONT (Texas) 3:146–147
map (30° 5′N 94° 6′W) **19**:129
BEAUMONT, FRANCIS, AND FLETCHER, JOHN 3:147 *bibliog.*
BEAUMONT, FREDERICK
tunnel **19**:339
BEAUMONT, WILLIAM 3:147 *bibliog.*
BEAUNEVEU, ANDRÉ 3:147
BEAUREGARD (county in Louisiana)
map (30° 40′N 93° 18′W) **12**:430
BEAUREGARD, P. G. T. 3:147 *bibliog.*; **5**:20 *illus.*
Bull Run, Battles of 3:558–559
Civil War, U.S. **5**:20 *illus.*; **5**:21; **5**:30
Petersburg campaign **15**:202
BEAUSÉJOUR (Manitoba)
map (50° 4′N 96° 33′W) **13**:119
BEAUTY BUSH 3:147 *illus.*
BEAUTY LEAF 3:148
laurel **12**:237
BEAUTY PATCH
cosmetics **5**:282 *illus.*
BEAUTY AND THE BEAST (book) 3:147
BEAUTY AND THE BEAST (film)
Cocteau, Jean **5**:89
BEAUVAIS (France)
art
Gothic art and architecture **9**:257
tapestry **19**:33
BEAUVOIR, SIMONE DE 3:148 *bibliog., illus.*
existentialism **7**:332
The Second Sex **17**:178
BEAUX, CECILIA 3:148
BEAUX-ARTS STYLE *see* ÉCOLE DES BEAUX-ARTS
BEAVER 3:148–149 *bibliog., illus.*
habitat 3:149 *illus.*
BEAVER (Alaska)
map (66° 22′N 147° 24′W) **1**:242
BEAVER (Oklahoma)
map (36° 49′N 100° 31′W) **14**:368
BEAVER (county in Oklahoma)
map (36° 45′N 100° 25′W) **14**:368
BEAVER (Pennsylvania)
map (40° 42′N 80° 18′W) **15**:147
BEAVER (county in Pennsylvania)
map (40° 40′N 80° 25′W) **15**:147
BEAVER (Utah)
map (38° 17′N 112° 38′W) **19**:429
BEAVER (county in Utah)
map (38° 18′N 113° 5′W) **19**:429
BEAVER CITY (Nebraska)
map (40° 8′N 99° 50′W) **14**:70
BEAVER COLLEGE 3:149

BEAVER CREEK
  map (46° 15′N 100° 29′W) **14**:248
BEAVER CREEK (Nebraska)
  map (40° 4′N 99° 20′W) **14**:70
BEAVER CREEK (Yukon Territory)
  map (62° 22′N 140° 52′W) **20**:345
BEAVER CROSSING (Nebraska)
  map (40° 47′N 97° 17′W) **14**:70
BEAVER DAM (Kentucky)
  map (37° 24′N 86° 52′W) **12**:47
BEAVER DAM (Wisconsin)
  map (43° 28′N 88° 50′W) **20**:185
BEAVER FALLS (Pennsylvania)
  map (40° 46′N 80° 19′W) **15**:147
BEAVER ISLAND
  map (45° 40′N 85° 31′W) **13**:377
BEAVER RIVER (Pennsylvania)
  map (40° 40′N 80° 18′W) **14**:357
BEAVER RIVER (Saskatchewan)
  map (55° 26′N 107° 45′W) **17**:81
BEAVER RIVER (Utah)
  map (39° 10′N 112° 57′W) **19**:429
BEAVERBROOK, MAX AITKEN, 1ST BARON **3**:149 *bibliog.*
BEAVERHEAD (county in Montana)
  map (45° 10′N 112° 50′W) **13**:547
BEAVERHEAD MOUNTAINS
  map (45° 0′N 113° 20′W) **13**:547
BEAVERHEAD RIVER
  map (45° 31′N 112° 21′W) **13**:547
BEAVERTON (Michigan)
  map (43° 53′N 84° 29′W) **13**:377
BEAVERTON (Oregon)
  map (45° 29′N 122° 48′W) **14**:427
BEBEL, AUGUST **3**:149–150 *bibliog.*
  socialism **18**:21
BEBEY, FRANCIS **3**:150
BEBOP **3**:150 *bibliog.*
  Christian, Charlie **4**:411
  Davis, Miles **6**:52
  Gillespie, Dizzy **9**:182
  jazz **11**:389 *illus.*
  Monk, Thelonious **13**:532
  Parker, Charlie **15**:89–90
  Vaughan, Sarah **19**:528
BECARD **3**:150 *illus.*
BECCAFUMI, DOMENICO **3**:150 *bibliog.*
BECCARIA, CESARE BONESANA **3**:150 *bibliog.*
BEČEJ (Yugoslavia)
  map (45° 37′N 20° 3′E) **20**:340
BÉCHAR (Algeria)
  map (31° 37′N 2° 13′W) **1**:287
BECHE, SIR HENRY THOMAS DE LA *see* DE LA BECHE, SIR HENRY THOMAS
BECHER, JOHANNES R. **3**:150
BECHET, SIDNEY **3**:150 *bibliog.*
BECHUANA *see* TSWANA
BECHUANALAND *see* BOTSWANA
BECHUANALAND PROTECTORATE *see* BOTSWANA
BECK, DAVE
  Teamsters, Chauffeurs, Warehousemen, and Helpers of America, International Brotherhood of **19**:58
BECK, JULIAN
  Living Theatre **12**:376
BECKENBAUER, FRANZ **3**:151
BECKER (county in Minnesota)
  map (46° 55′N 95° 42′W) **13**:453
BECKER, CARL **3**:151 *bibliog.*
BECKER, LYDIA
  suffrage, women's **18**:326
BECKER, PAULA MODERSOHN- *see* MODERSOHN-BECKER, PAULA
BECKET, SAINT THOMAS **3**:151 *bibliog., illus.*
  Great Britain, history of **9**:311
  Henry II, King of England **10**:124
BECKETT, SAMUEL **3**:151–152 *bibliog., illus.*; **11**:268 *illus.*
  Endgame **7**:168
  theater of the absurd **19**:154
  Waiting for Godot **20**:7
    comedy **5**:132
BECKFORD, WILLIAM **3**:152 *bibliog.*
BECKHAM (county in Oklahoma)
  map (35° 15′N 99° 40′W) **14**:368
BECKLEY (West Virginia)
  map (37° 46′N 81° 13′W) **20**:111
BECKMANN, MAX **3**:152 *bibliog., illus.*
  The Night **9**:128 *illus.*
  Self-Portrait with Red Scarf **3**:152 *illus.*
BECKNELL, WILLIAM
  New Mexico **14**:139
BECKWOURTH, JAMES P.
  Pueblo (Colorado) **15**:613
BECQUE, HENRY FRANÇOIS **3**:152
BÉCQUER, GUSTAVO ADOLFO **3**:152
BECQUEREL, ANTOINE HENRI **3**:153 *bibliog.*
  radioactivity **10**:61
  radium **16**:68
BÉCU, JEANNE *see* DU BARRY, JEANNE BÉCU, COMTESSE
BED **3**:153 *bibliog.*
BED LOAD **3**:153 *bibliog.*
  river delta **16**:232
BED-WETTING **3**:153 *bibliog.*
BEDBUG **3**:153 *illus.*
BEDCHAMBER CRISIS
  Victoria, Queen of England, Scotland, and Ireland **19**:574
BEDE, SAINT **3**:153 *bibliog.*
  Great Britain, history of **9**:310
BEDEQUE BAY
  map (46° 22′N 63° 53′W) **15**:548
BEDFORD (England) **3**:153
  map (52° 8′N 0° 29′W) **19**:403
BEDFORD (county in England) *see* BEDFORDSHIRE (England)
BEDFORD (Indiana)
  map (38° 52′N 86° 29′W) **11**:111
BEDFORD (Iowa)
  map (40° 40′N 94° 44′W) **11**:244
BEDFORD (Kentucky)
  map (38° 36′N 85° 19′W) **12**:47
BEDFORD (Massachusetts)
  map (42° 29′N 71° 17′W) **13**:206
BEDFORD (Ohio)
  map (41° 23′N 81° 32′W) **14**:357
BEDFORD (Pennsylvania)
  map (40° 1′N 78° 30′W) **15**:147
BEDFORD (county in Pennsylvania)
  map (40° 0′N 78° 28′W) **15**:147
BEDFORD (county in Tennessee)
  map (35° 30′N 86° 20′W) **19**:104
BEDFORD (Virginia)
  map (37° 20′N 79° 31′W) **19**:607
BEDFORD (county in Virginia)
  map (37° 25′N 79° 30′W) **19**:607
BEDFORDSHIRE (England) **3**:153–154
  Bedford **3**:153
BÉDIER, JOSEPH **3**:154
BEDLAM **3**:154; **15**:599 *illus.*
BEDLINGTON (England)
  map (55° 8′N 1° 35′W) **19**:403
BEDLINGTON TERRIER **3**:154 *bibliog., illus.*; **6**:220 *illus.*
BEDNY, DEMIAN **3**:154
BEDOUIN **2**:103 *illus.*; **3**:154 *bibliog.*
  Jordan **11**:448
  Middle East, history of the **13**:402
BEDROCK
  river and stream **16**:230 *illus.*
BEDSORE **3**:154
  nosocomial **14**:266
BEDSTRAW (botany) **3**:154
BEE **3**:154–159 *bibliog., illus.*; **11**:192 *illus.*
  anatomy **3**:155 *illus.*
  beekeeping **3**:161–162 *illus.*
    Middle Ages **1**:191 *illus.*
  drone and worker bees **3**:158
  habitat **3**:156–158 *illus.*
  life cycle **3**:156 *illus.*
  parthenogenesis **15**:100
  pollination **15**:408–409 *illus.*
  types **3**:155–158
    See also BUMBLEBEE; HONEYBEE
    African killer bee **3**:161–162
    leaf-cutter bee **3**:156–157
    mason bee **3**:157
    mining bee **3**:157
  wax **3**:154; **3**:156–157
BEE (county in Texas)
  map (28° 22′N 97° 45′W) **19**:129
BEE, BERNARD E.
  Civil War, U.S. **5**:21
BEE BALM **3**:159
  balm **3**:53
  bergamot **3**:209
BEE EATER **3**:159 *illus.*; **3**:280 *illus.*
  rainbow bee-eater **10**:5 *illus.*
BEE FLY **8**:189 *illus.*
BEE GEES, THE (musical group) **3**:159
BEEBE (Arkansas)
  map (35° 4′N 91° 53′W) **2**:166
BEEBE, CHARLES W. **3**:159
BEECH **3**:159–160 *bibliog., illus.*
  chestnut **4**:337
  creosote **5**:339
  lumber **12**:456 *illus.*
  oak **14**:311
  tanbark oak **19**:21
  wood **20**:205 *illus.*
BEECH FORK RIVER
  map (37° 46′N 85° 41′W) **12**:47
BEECH GROVE (Indiana)
  map (39° 43′N 86° 3′W) **11**:111
BEECHAM, SIR THOMAS **3**:160 *bibliog.*
BEECHER (family) **3**:160–161 *bibliog.*
BEECHER (Illinois)
  map (41° 21′N 87° 38′W) **11**:42
BEECHER, CATHARINE ESTHER **3**:160–161
BEECHER, HENRY WARD **3**:160
  Beecher's Bibles
    Emigrant Aid Company **7**:156
BEECHER, LYMAN **3**:160
BEEF
  meat and meat packing **13**:257 *table*
  veal **19**:529
BEEF JERKY *see* PEMMICAN
BEEFEATERS **3**:161
BEEFWOOD *see* *CASUARINA*
BEEKEEPING **3**:161–162 *bibliog., illus.*
  bee **3**:158
  honey **10**:220
  pollinator industry **3**:161
BEELZEBUB *see* SATAN
BEER **3**:162–163 *bibliog., illus.*
  See also ALE; MEAD (beverage)
  canning **4**:110 *illus.*
  hops **10**:233
  Incan agricultural production **11**:72
  malt **13**:94
BEER, SIR GAVIN DE *see* DE BEER, SIR GAVIN
BEER, JAKOB LIEBMANN *see* MEYERBEER, GIACOMO
BEER-LAMBERT'S LAW
  absorption, light **1**:63
BE'ER SHEVA *see* BEERSHEBA (Israel)
BEERBOHM, SIR MAX **3**:163 *bibliog.*
BEERHALL PUTSCH *see* MUNICH PUTSCH
BEER'S LAW
  absorption, light **1**:63
BEERSHEBA (Israel) **3**:163
  map (31° 14′N 34° 47′E) **11**:302
BEERSHEBA, BATTLE OF *see* GAZA, BATTLES OF
BEERSHEBA SPRINGS (Tennessee)
  map (35° 28′N 85° 39′W) **19**:104
BEERY, WALLACE **3**:163
BEET **3**:163–164 *illus.*; **19**:534 *illus.*
  sugar beet **18**:327–328
BEETHOVEN, LUDWIG VAN **3**:164–165 *bibliog., illus.*; **9**:130 *illus.*; **13**:665 *illus.*; **16**:293 *illus.*
  Albrechtsberger, Johann Georg **1**:261
  classical period in music **5**:42
  concerto **5**:170
  Diabelli, Anton **6**:148
  fugue **8**:355
  Kreutzer, Rodolphe **12**:129
  orchestra and orchestration **14**:418
  overture **14**:470
  scherzo **17**:119
  string quartet **18**:300
  symphony **18**:405
BEETLE **3**:165–167 *bibliog., illus.*; **11**:191 *illus.*; **11**:192 *illus.*
  bark beetle **3**:82
  carpet beetle **4**:165 *illus.*
  cucumber beetle **9**:300 *illus.*
  dung beetle **6**:300
  firefly **8**:106
  glowworm **9**:210
  ground beetle **8**:228 *illus.*
  grub **9**:381–382
  Japanese beetle **11**:379
  June bug **11**:467
  ladybug **12**:162
  symbolism, Egyptian art and architecture **7**:89
  water beetle **20**:48
  weevil **20**:91
BEETS, NICOLAAS **3**:168
BEEVILLE (Texas)
  map (28° 24′N 97° 45′W) **19**:129
BEF *see* BRITISH EXPEDITIONARY FORCE (BEF)
BEGGAR'S OPERA, THE **3**:168 *bibliog.*
  Threepenny Opera, The **19**:182
BEGGS (Oklahoma)
  map (35° 45′N 96° 4′W) **14**:368
BEGIN, MENACHEM **3**:168 *bibliog., illus.*
  Egypt **7**:80
  Israel **11**:306
BÉGON, MICHEL
  begonia **3**:168
BEGONIA **3**:168 *bibliog., illus.*; **10**:275 *illus.*
BEHAM (family) **3**:168–169 *bibliog.*
BEHAN, BRENDAN **3**:169 *bibliog., illus.*
BEHAR *see* BIHAR (India)
BEHAVIOR, ANIMAL *see* ANIMAL BEHAVIOR
BEHAVIOR, HUMAN
  See also SEXUAL BEHAVIOR
  behavioral genetics **3**:169–170
  compulsive behavior **5**:159
  deviance **6**:143
  hyperactive children **10**:347
  Lorenz, Konrad **12**:414
  natural law **14**:48
  psychology **15**:593–595
  sadism **17**:10
  social behavior
    altruism **1**:314
    conflict theory **5**:178–179
    conformity **5**:179
    evolution **7**:324
    game theory **9**:28
    geographical linguistics **9**:100
    infancy **11**:162
    Nisbet, Robert Alexander **14**:201
    norm, social **14**:219
    prejudice **15**:518
    role **16**:271
    social psychology **18**:12–13
    sociobiology **18**:26–27
    sociology **18**:28–30
    transactional analysis **19**:267
BEHAVIOR MODIFICATION **3**:169 *bibliog.*
  attachment (psychology) **2**:313
  autistic children **2**:355
  cognitive dissonance **5**:94
  emotion **7**:157
  est **7**:245
  group therapy **9**:377
  hallucinogens **10**:24
  hyperactive children **10**:347
  learning theory **12**:260–261
  Pavlov, Ivan Petrovich **15**:120
  psychiatry **15**:588
  psychopathology, treatment of **15**:599–601
  psychopathy **15**:601
  psychotherapy **15**:602–603
  psychotropic drugs **15**:603–605
  Rogers, Carl **16**:269
  Skinner, B. F. **17**:343
  Watson, John B. **20**:68
BEHAVIOR THERAPY *see* BEHAVIOR MODIFICATION
BEHAVIORAL GENETICS **3**:169–170 *bibliog.*
  altruism **1**:314
  animal behavior **2**:13–14; **2**:17–18
  Galton, Sir Francis **9**:22–23
  genetics **9**:90
  handedness **10**:35
  sociobiology **18**:26–27
BEHAVIORAL SCIENCES
  animal behavior **2**:17–18
  attitude and attitude change **2**:315
  catastrophe theory **4**:200
  Center for Advanced Study in the Behavioral Sciences **4**:249
  child development **4**:348–350
  child psychiatry **4**:350–351
  communication **5**:142–144
  conflict theory **5**:178–179
  decision theory **6**:73–74
  developmental psychology **6**:142
  educational psychology **7**:66
  ethology **7**:257
  group dynamics **9**:376
  Harlow, Harry F. **10**:50–51
  political science **15**:403–404
  psycholinguistics **15**:591–592
  psychological measurement **15**:592–593
  psychology **15**:593–595
  queuing theory **16**:24–25
  social psychology **18**:12–13
  sociobiology **18**:26–27
  sociolinguistics **18**:27–28
  sociology **18**:28–30
BEHAVIORISM **3**:170 *bibliog.*
  Bekhterev, Vladimir Mikhailovich **3**:173
  cognitive psychology **5**:94
  compulsive behavior **5**:159
  educational psychology **7**:66
  humanistic psychology **10**:299–300
  learning theory **12**:261
  linguistics **12**:356
  methodological behaviorism **3**:170
  moral awareness **13**:573
  Pavlov, Ivan Petrovich **15**:120
  philosophical behaviorism **3**:170
  psycholinguistics **15**:591
  psychology, history of **15**:597
  psychophysics **15**:601–602
  reasoning **16**:105
  Rogers, Carl **16**:268–269
  Skinner, B. F. **17**:343–344
  Thorndike, Edward L. **19**:179
  Watson, John B. **20**:68
BEHBEHAN (Iran)
  map (30° 35′N 50° 14′E) **11**:250
BEHISTUN (Iran) **3**:171 *bibliog.*
  Darius I, King of Persia **6**:38
  inscription **11**:185

BEHISTUN (cont.)
Rawlinson, Sir Henry Creswicke **16**:95
BEHN, APHRA 3:171 *bibliog.*
BEHRENS, PETER 3:171 *bibliog.*
industrial design **11**:155
BEHRING, EMIL ADOLF VON 3:171 *bibliog.*
Ehrlich, Paul (1854–1915) **7**:91
BEHRMAN, S. N. 3:171 *bibliog.*
BEIDA (Libya) 3:171
map (32° 46′N 21° 43′E) **12**:320
BEIDERBECKE, BIX 3:171–172 *bibliog.*
BEIJERINCK, MARTINUS WILLEM 3:172
BEIJING (China) *see* PEKING (Beijing) (China)
BEILBY, WILLIAM
glassware, decorative **9**:203
BEINECKE LIBRARY **12**:317 *illus.*
BEING AND NOTHINGNESS (book) **3**:172 *bibliog.*
Sartre, Jean Paul **17**:79
BEIRA (Mozambique) *see* SOFALA (Mozambique)
BEIRUT (Lebanon) 3:172 *bibliog.*; **12**:265 *illus., table*
American University of Beirut **1**:367
climate **2**:237 *table*
map (33° 53′N 35° 30′E) **12**:265
BEISAN *see* BETH-SHAN (Beth-Shean) (Israel)
BEISSEL, JOHANN CONRAD 3:172 *bibliog.*
Ephrata **7**:217
BEJA 3:172 *bibliog.*
BEJA (Portugal)
map (38° 1′N 7° 52′W) **15**:449
BÉJA (Tunisia)
map (36° 44′N 9° 11′E) **19**:335
BEJAÏA (Algeria)
map (36° 45′N 5° 5′E) **1**:287
BÉJART, MADELEINE 3:172 *bibliog.*
Molière **13**:508–509
BÉJART, MAURICE 3:173 *bibliog.*
BEJUCO (Panama)
map (8° 36′N 79° 53′W) **15**:55
BÉKÉSCSABA (Hungary)
map (46° 41′N 21° 6′E) **10**:307
BEKHTEREV, VLADIMIR MIKHAILOVICH 3:173 *bibliog.*
BEL AIR (Maryland)
map (39° 32′N 76° 21′W) **13**:188
BEL CANTO 3:173 *bibliog.*
Bellini, Vincenzo **3**:189–190
Callas, Maria **4**:41
Norma **14**:219
opera **14**:400
Patti, Adelina **15**:115–116
Sutherland, Joan **18**:373
voice, singing **19**:626
BEL GEDDES, NORMAN 3:173
BEL AND THE DRAGON 3:173
BELA CRKVA (Yugoslavia)
map (44° 54′N 21° 26′E) **20**:340
BELAFONTE, HARRY 3:173 *bibliog.*
BELAIT RIVER
map (4° 35′N 114° 12′E) **3**:524
BÉLANGER, FRANÇOIS JOSEPH 3:173 *bibliog.*
BELASCO, DAVID 3:173–174 *bibliog., illus.*
Madama Butterfly **13**:39
BELAU, REPUBLIC OF
flag **8**:143 *illus.*
map (7° 30′N 134° 30′E) **14**:334
Pacific Islands, Trust Territory of the **15**:5
sculpture **14**:338 *illus.*
BELAÚNDE TERRY, FERNANDO 3:174
Morales Bermúdez, Francisco **13**:573
Peru **15**:195
BELCHER (Louisiana)
map (32° 45′N 93° 50′W) **12**:430
BELCHER ISLANDS
map (56° 20′N 79° 30′W) **16**:18
BELCHERTOWN (Massachusetts)
map (42° 17′N 72° 24′W) **13**:206
BELCOURT (North Dakota)
map (48° 50′N 99° 45′W) **14**:248
BELDING (Michigan)
map (43° 6′N 85° 14′W) **13**:377
BELED WEYNE (Somalia)
map (4° 47′N 45° 12′E) **18**:60
BELÉM (Brazil) 3:174
map (1° 27′S 48° 29′W) **3**:460
BELÉM (Portugal)
Hieronymites monastery **15**:455 *illus.*
BELEMNITE
Jurassic Period **11**:476 *illus.*
BELEN (New Mexico)
map (34° 40′N 106° 46′W) **14**:136
BELÉN (Uruguay)
map (30° 47′S 57° 47′W) **19**:488
BÉLEP ARCHIPELAGO
New Caledonia **14**:119
BELESAR RESERVOIR
map (42° 45′N 7° 40′W) **18**:140
BELFAST (Maine)
map (44° 27′N 69° 1′W) **13**:70
BELFAST (Northern Ireland) 3:174 *bibliog.*; **14**:255 *illus.*
history **3**:174
Protestant-Catholic fighting **11**:265 *illus.*
map (54° 35′N 5° 55′W) **19**:403
BELFIELD (North Dakota)
map (46° 53′N 103° 12′W) **14**:248
BELFORT (France)
map (47° 38′N 6° 52′E) **8**:260
BELFORT GAP (France) 3:174
BELFRY (Montana)
map (45° 9′N 109° 1′W) **13**:547
BELGAUM (India)
map (15° 52′N 74° 30′E) **11**:80
BELGIAN CONGO *see* ZAIRE
BELGIAN ENDIVE *see* CHICORY
BELGIAN HORSE 3:174 *illus.*; **10**:244 *illus.*
BELGIAN LITERATURE 3:175 *bibliog., illus.*
authors
Crommelynck, Fernand **5**:357
Ghelderode, Michel de **9**:166
Maeterlinck, Maurice **13**:45–46
Mallet-Joris, Françoise **13**:92
Simenon, Georges **17**:314
Verhaeren, Émile **19**:551
BELGIAN MALINOIS 3:175 *bibliog., illus.*; **6**:215 *illus.*
BELGIAN REVOLUTION
Battle for Brussels (September 1830) **12**:442 *illus.*
Low Countries, history of the **12**:441
BELGIAN SHEEPDOG 3:176 *bibliog., illus.*; **6**:215 *illus.*
BELGIAN TERVUREN 3:176 *bibliog., illus.*; **6**:215 *illus.*
BELGIUM 3:176–182 *bibliog., illus., map, table*
art **3**:179
See also FLEMISH ART AND ARCHITECTURE
cities
Antwerp **2**:71 *illus.*
Bruges **3**:522–523
Brussels **3**:526–527 *map*
Charleroi **4**:290
Ghent **9**:166
Liège **12**:326
Mons **13**:543
Namur **14**:12
Ostend **14**:457
Tournai **19**:253
Ypres **20**:337
climate **3**:178 *table*
demography **3**:179
economic activity **3**:179–181
education **3**:179
European universities **7**:307 *table*
flag **3**:176 *illus.*
government **3**:180
historians *see* HISTORY—Belgian historians
history **3**:181–182
Albert I, King **1**:254
Baudouin I, King **3**:129
Brabant, Duchy of **3**:435
Leopold I, King **12**:293–294
Leopold II, King **12**:294
Leopold III, King **12**:294
Low Countries, history of the **12**:438–443 *map*
Ruanda-Urundi **16**:332
Spaak, Paul Henri **18**:118
Tindemans, Leo **19**:206
Van Zeeland, Paul **19**:516
William I, King of the Netherlands **20**:158
World War I *see* WORLD WAR I
World War II **20**:252–253 *map*
Zaire **20**:352
land and resources **3**:177–178 *map*
language **3**:179
Germanic languages **9**:135–137 *table*
literature *see* BELGIAN LITERATURE
manufacturing **3**:179–180
map (50° 50′N 4° 0′E) **7**:268
music
Fétis, François Joseph **8**:63
people **3**:178–179
Walloons **20**:16
religion **3**:179
rivers, lakes, and waterways **3**:178 *illus.*
roads and highways **16**:238
trade **3**:181
transportation **3**:181
vegetation and animal life **3**:178
BELGO-LUXEMBOURG ECONOMIC UNION
trade **3**:181
BELGRADE (Minnesota)
map (45° 27′N 95° 0′W) **13**:453
BELGRADE (Montana)
map (45° 47′N 111° 11′W) **13**:547
BELGRADE (Yugoslavia) 3:182 *illus.*; **20**:339 *illus.*; **20**:342 *illus.*
climate **20**:341 *table*
map (44° 50′N 20° 30′E) **20**:340
BELGRANO, MANUEL 3:182 *bibliog.*
BELHAVEN (North Carolina)
map (35° 33′N 76° 37′W) **14**:242
BELINSKY, VISSARION GRIGORIEVICH 3:182–183 *bibliog.*
BELISARIUS 3:183 *bibliog.*
Procopius of Caesarea **15**:561
BELITUNG ISLAND
map (2° 50′S 107° 55′E) **11**:147
BELIVEAU, JEAN 3:183
BELIZE 3:183–184 *bibliog., map*
cities
Belize City **3**:184
Belmopan **3**:192
economy **3**:184
flag **3**:183 *illus.*
history **3**:184
land **3**:183 *map*
map (17° 15′N 88° 45′W) **14**:225
people **3**:184
Carib **4**:147
BELIZE CITY (Belize) 3:184
climate **14**:228 *table*
map (17° 30′N 88° 12′W) **3**:183
BELIZE RIVER
map (17° 32′N 88° 14′W) **3**:183
BELKNAP (county in New Hampshire)
map (43° 30′N 71° 20′W) **14**:123
BELKNAP, WILLIAM WORTH 3:184
BELKOFSKI (Alaska)
map (55° 5′N 162° 2′W) **1**:242
BELL 3:184–185 *bibliog., illus.*
campanile **4**:64–65
glockenspiel **9**:209 *illus.*
percussion instruments **15**:162 *illus.*
BELL (county in Kentucky)
map (36° 45′N 83° 40′W) **12**:47
BELL (county in Texas)
map (31° 0′N 97° 32′W) **19**:129
BELL, ALEXANDER GRAHAM 3:185 *bibliog., illus.*
Brantford **3**:456
deaf, education of the **6**:66
Gray, Elisha **9**:306
hydrofoil **10**:336
telephone **19**:78–80 *illus.*
BELL, ANDREW 3:185 *bibliog.*
BELL, BERT 3:186
BELL, CLIVE 3:186
BELL, DANIEL 3:186
on capitalism **4**:125
BELL, ELLIS (pseudonym) *see* BRONTË, EMILY
BELL, GERTRUDE 3:186 *bibliog.*
BELL, JOHN (English priest)
Peasants' Revolt **15**:129
BELL, JOHN (physicist)
Bell's theorem **3**:192
BELL, JOHN (politician) 3:186 *bibliog.*
votes received in 1860 election **5**:17 *map*
BELL-BURNELL, JOCELYN
Mullard Radio Astronomy Observatory **13**:636
BELL CURVE
normal distributions **14**:219
BELL JAR, THE (book) 3:186
Plath, Sylvia **15**:359
BELL MAGPIE 3:186 *bibliog.*
BELL TELEPHONE COMPANY *see* AMERICAN TELEPHONE AND TELEGRAPH COMPANY
BELL TELEPHONE COMPANY LABORATORIES
computer music **5**:162
information theory **11**:174
radio astronomy **16**:47
solar cell **18**:40
Telstar **19**:91
transistor **19**:271
BELL VILLE (Argentina)
map (32° 37′S 62° 42′W) **2**:149
BELL X-1 AIRCRAFT **2**:374
BELLA, STEFANO DELLA 3:186 *bibliog.*
BELLA COOLA (American Indians) 3:186
Indians of North America, art of the **11**:139
mask **13**:197 *illus.*
BELLA COOLA (British Columbia)
map (52° 22′N 126° 46′W) **3**:491
BELLA FLOR (Bolivia)
map (11° 9′S 67° 49′W) **3**:366
BELLA VISTA (Argentina)
map (28° 30′S 59° 3′W) **2**:149
BELLA VISTA (Paraguay)
map (22° 8′S 56° 31′W) **15**:77
BELLADONNA (botany) 3:187 *illus.*; **15**:384 *illus.*
atropine **2**:313
medicinal plants **13**:266
nightshade **14**:194
BELLAIRE (Kansas)
map (39° 48′N 98° 40′W) **12**:18
BELLAIRE (Michigan)
map (44° 59′N 85° 13′W) **13**:377
BELLAIRE (Ohio)
map (40° 2′N 80° 45′W) **14**:357
BELLAIRE (Texas)
map (29° 43′N 95° 3′W) **19**:129
BELLAMY (Alabama)
map (32° 22′N 88° 8′W) **1**:234
BELLAMY, EDWARD 3:187 *bibliog.*
socialism **18**:23
BELLARMINE, SAINT ROBERT 3:187 *bibliog.*
BELLAY, JOACHIM DU *see* DU BELLAY, JOACHIM
BELLBIRD 3:187
BELLE (Missouri)
map (38° 17′N 91° 43′W) **13**:476
BELLE BAY
map (47° 36′N 55° 18′W) **14**:166
BELLE ET LA BÊTE, LA (film)
Cocteau, Jean **5**:89
BELLE FOURCHE (South Dakota)
map (44° 40′N 103° 51′W) **18**:103
BELLE FOURCHE RESERVOIR
map (44° 44′N 103° 42′W) **18**:103
BELLE FOURCHE RIVER
map (44° 26′N 102° 19′W) **18**:103
BELLE GLADE (Florida)
map (26° 41′N 80° 40′W) **8**:172
BELLE ISLAND
map (47° 20′N 3° 10′W) **8**:260
BELLE ISLE
map (51° 55′N 55° 20′W) **14**:166
BELLE ISLE, STRAIT OF
map (51° 35′N 56° 30′W) **14**:166
BELLE PLAINE (Iowa)
map (41° 54′N 92° 17′W) **11**:244
BELLE PLAINE (Kansas)
map (37° 24′N 97° 17′W) **12**:18
BELLE PLAINE (Minnesota)
map (44° 37′N 93° 46′W) **13**:453
BELLE-PLAINE (Saskatchewan)
map (50° 24′N 105° 9′W) **17**:81
BELLE ROSE (Louisiana)
map (30° 3′N 91° 3′W) **12**:430
BELLEAU WOOD 3:187 *bibliog.*
World War I **20**:225 *map*
BELLEFONTAINE (Ohio)
map (40° 22′N 83° 46′W) **14**:357
BELLEFONTE (Pennsylvania)
map (40° 55′N 77° 46′W) **15**:147
BELLEMAWR (New Jersey)
map (39° 52′N 75° 6′W) **14**:129
BELLEROPHON 3:187
chimera **7**:260 *illus.*
BELLES LETTRES 3:187
BELLEVIEW (Florida)
map (29° 4′N 82° 3′W) **8**:172
BELLEVILLE (Illinois)
map (38° 31′N 90° 0′W) **11**:42
BELLEVILLE (Kansas)
map (39° 49′N 97° 38′W) **12**:18
BELLEVILLE (New Jersey)
map (40° 48′N 74° 9′W) **14**:129
BELLEVILLE (Ontario)
map (44° 10′N 77° 23′W) **14**:393
BELLEVILLE (Pennsylvania)
map (40° 36′N 77° 43′W) **15**:147
BELLEVILLE (Wisconsin)
map (42° 52′N 89° 32′W) **20**:185
BELLEVUE (Idaho)
map (43° 28′N 114° 16′W) **11**:26
BELLEVUE (Iowa)
map (42° 16′N 90° 26′W) **11**:244
BELLEVUE (Michigan)
map (42° 12′N 83° 29′W) **13**:377
BELLEVUE (Nebraska)
map (41° 9′N 95° 54′W) **14**:70
BELLEVUE (Ohio)
map (41° 17′N 82° 50′W) **14**:357
BELLEVUE (Pennsylvania)
map (40° 30′N 80° 3′W) **15**:147
BELLEVUE (Washington)
map (47° 37′N 122° 12′W) **20**:35
BELLFLOWER 3:188 *illus.*
balloonflower **3**:53
lobelia **12**:384
BELLI, G. G. 3:188 *bibliog.*
BELLI, MELVIN 3:188
BELLIN (Quebec)
map (60° 1′N 70° 1′W) **16**:18

BELLINGHAM (Massachusetts)
  map (42° 5′N 71° 28′W) **13**:206
BELLINGHAM (Washington)
  map (48° 49′N 122° 29′W) **20**:35
BELLINGSHAUSEN, FABIAN GOTTLIEB VON **3**:188
  Antarctica **2**:44 *map*
BELLINGSHAUSEN SEA
  map (71° 0′S 85° 0′W) **2**:40
BELLINI (family) **3**:188–189 *bibliog., illus.*
BELLINI, GENTILE
  Bellini (family) **3**:188
  Mehmed II **13**:405 *illus.*
BELLINI, GIOVANNI
  Bellini (family) **3**:188–189
  The Transfiguration **3**:189 *illus.*
BELLINI, JACOPO
  Bellini (family) **3**:188
BELLINI, VINCENZO **3**:189–190 *bibliog.*
  Italian music **11**:319
  Norma **14**:219
BELLINZONA (Switzerland)
  map (46° 11′N 9° 2′E) **18**:394
BELLMAN, CARL MICHAEL **3**:190 *bibliog.*
BELLO (Colombia)
  map (6° 20′N 75° 33′W) **5**:107
BELLO, ANDRÉS **3**:190 *bibliog.*
BELLO, JOAQUIN EDWARDS
  Chile **4**:355
BELLOC, HILAIRE **3**:190 *bibliog.*
BELLOTTO, BERNARDO **3**:190 *bibliog.*
BELLOW, SAUL **3**:190–191 *bibliog., illus.*
  Adventures of Augie March, The **1**:111
BELLOWS **3**:191; **13**:19 *illus.*
  See also BLACKSMITH; FORGE
BELLOWS, GEORGE **3**:191–192 *bibliog., illus.*
  Both Members of This Club **3**:191 *illus.*
BELLOWS FALLS (Vermont)
  map (43° 8′N 72° 27′W) **19**:554
BELLS (Tennessee)
  map location (35° 43′N 89° 5′W) **19**:104
BELL'S CERATOPHRYS **10**:239 *illus.*
BELL'S INEQUALITY (physics)
  Bell's theorem **3**:192
BELLS OF IRELAND (botany) **3**:192
BELL'S PALSY **15**:52
BELL'S THEOREM (physics) **3**:192 *bibliog.*
BELLUSCHI, PIETRO **3**:192 *bibliog.*
BELLVILLE (Ohio)
  map (40° 37′N 82° 31′W) **14**:357
BELLVILLE (Texas)
  map (29° 57′N 96° 16′W) **19**:129
BELLWOOD (Nebraska)
  map (41° 21′N 97° 14′W) **14**:70
BELLWOOD (Pennsylvania)
  map (40° 36′N 78° 20′W) **15**:147
BELLY DANCE **3**:192
BELMOND (Iowa)
  map (42° 51′N 93° 37′W) **11**:244
BELMONDO, JEAN PAUL **3**:192
BELMONT (Massachusetts)
  map (42° 24′N 71° 10′W) **3**:409
BELMONT (Mississippi)
  map (34° 31′N 88° 13′W) **13**:469
BELMONT (New York)
  map (42° 13′N 78° 2′W) **14**:149
BELMONT (county in Ohio)
  map (40° 0′N 81° 0′W) **14**:357
BELMONT STAKES WINNERS **10**:249 *table*
BELMONTE, JUAN **3**:192
BELMOPAN (Belize) **3**:192
  map (17° 15′N 88° 46′W) **3**:183
BELO HORIZONTE (Brazil) **3**:192
  map (19° 55′S 43° 56′W) **3**:460
BELOEIL (Quebec)
  map (45° 34′N 73° 12′W) **16**:18
BELOIT (Kansas)
  map (39° 28′N 98° 6′W) **12**:18
BELOIT (Wisconsin)
  map (42° 31′N 89° 2′W) **20**:185
BELOIT COLLEGE **3**:192–193
BELORUSSIAN LANGUAGE
  Slavic languages **17**:358
BELORUSSIAN SOVIET SOCIALIST REPUBLIC (USSR) **3**:193 *bibliog.*
  cities
    Brest **3**:474
    Minsk **13**:460
BELOYE MORE *see* WHITE SEA
BELSEN (West Germany) **3**:193
BELSHAZZAR **3**:193
BELT (Montana)
  map (47° 23′N 110° 55′W) **13**:547
BELTER, JOHN HENRY **3**:193 *bibliog.*
  bed **8**:378 *illus.*
BELTON (Missouri)
  map (38° 49′N 94° 32′W) **13**:476
BELTON (South Carolina)
  map (34° 31′N 82° 30′W) **18**:98
BELTON (Texas)
  map (31° 4′N 97° 28′W) **19**:129
BELTON LAKE
  map (31° 8′N 97° 23′W) **19**:129
BELTRAMI (county in Minnesota)
  map (47° 55′N 94° 53′W) **13**:453
BELUGA (sturgeon) **18**:309
BELUGA (whale) **3**:193 *bibliog., illus.*; **20**:120 *illus.*
BELUKHA, MOUNT
  map (49° 48′N 86° 40′E) **19**:388
BELVEDERE **3**:193
BELVIDERE (Illinois)
  map (42° 15′N 88° 50′W) **11**:42
BELVIDERE (New Jersey)
  map (40° 49′N 75° 5′W) **14**:129
BELVOA *see* BILBAO (Spain)
BELY, ANDREI **3**:193–194 *bibliog.*
BELYAYEV, PAVEL IVANOVICH **3**:194
BELZONI (Mississippi)
  map (33° 11′N 90° 29′W) **13**:469
BELZONI, GIOVANNI BATTISTA **3**:194 *bibliog.*
  Valley of the Kings **19**:507
BEMARAHA PLATEAU
  map (20° 0′S 45° 15′E) **13**:38
BEMBA **3**:194 *bibliog.*
BEMBO, PIETRO **3**:194
  De Aetna (book) **3**:385 *illus.*
BEMELMANS, LUDWIG **3**:194 *bibliog.*
  Caldecott Medal **4**:25
BEMENT (Illinois)
  map (39° 55′N 88° 34′W) **11**:42
BEMIDJI (Minnesota)
  map (47° 29′N 94° 53′W) **13**:453
BEMIS (Tennessee)
  map (35° 35′N 88° 49′W) **19**:104
BEMIS, SAMUEL FLAGG **3**:194
BEMIS HEIGHTS, BATTLE OF *see* FREEMAN'S FARM, BATTLES OF
BEN *see* the first element of the name for names not listed below
BEN BELLA, AHMED **3**:194 *bibliog.*
BEN-GURION, DAVID **3**:195 *bibliog., illus.*
  Sharett, Moshe **17**:241
BEN HILL (county in Georgia)
  map (31° 45′N 83° 15′W) **9**:114
BEN HUR (book)
  Wallace, Lew **20**:14
BEN MACDHUI MOUNTAIN
  map (57° 4′N 3° 40′W) **19**:403
BEN NEVIS (mountain) **3**:195
  map (56° 48′N 5° 1′W) **19**:403
BEN-YEHUDAH, ELIEZER **3**:195 *bibliog.*
  Hebrew revival **10**:101
BEN-ZVI, ITZHAK **3**:195
BENALCAZAR, SEBASTIÁN DE
  Quito (Ecuador) **16**:28
BENARES (India) *see* VARANASI (India)
BENAVENTE Y MARTÍNEZ, JACINTO **3**:195 *bibliog.*
  Spanish literature **18**:159
BENAVIDES, ALONSO DE
  Spanish missions **18**:160
BENCH, JOHNNY **3**:196 *bibliog.*
BENCH MARK (surveying) **3**:196 *bibliog.*
  surveying **18**:367–369 *illus.*
BENCHLEY, ROBERT **3**:195 *bibliog.*
BENCZUR, GYULA
  Hungary **10**:309
BEND (Oregon)
  map (44° 3′N 121° 19′W) **14**:427
BENDA, JIŘÍ ANTONÍN **3**:196
BENDA, JULIEN **3**:196
BENDIGO (Australia)
  map (36° 46′S 144° 17′E) **2**:328
BENDIX, VINCENT **3**:196
BENDIX, WILLIAM **3**:196
BENDS **3**:196
  diving, deep-sea **6**:204
  embolism **7**:152
BENE ISRAEL **3**:196 *bibliog.*
BENEDEN, EDOUARD VAN
  zoology **20**:377
BENEDETTI, MARIO **3**:196
  Uruguay **19**:489
BENEDETTO DA MAIANO *see* MAIANO (family)
BENEDICT, SAINT **3**:197 *bibliog., illus.*
  Middle Ages **13**:394
  monastic art and architecture **13**:517–518
  monasticism **13**:521
BENEDICT, RUTH **3**:197 *bibliog.*
  culture **5**:385
  Mead, Margaret **13**:251
BENEDICT BISCOP, SAINT **3**:197
BENEDICT THE BLACK, SAINT **3**:197
BENEDICT XIII, ANTIPOPE **3**:197 *bibliog.*
BENEDICT XIV, POPE
  meeting with Charles III **11**:329 *illus.*
BENEDICT XV, POPE **3**:197 *bibliog.*
BENEDICTINES **3**:197–198 *bibliog.*
  Anselm, Saint **2**:35
  Benedict, Saint **3**:197
  Celestine V, Pope **4**:230
  Cluny **5**:71
  Dix, Dom Gregory **6**:206
  monastic art and architecture **13**:517–518; **13**:520
  Mont-Saint-Michel (France) **13**:544
  Monte Cassino **13**:552
BENELUX (trade union)
  Belgium **3**:181
  Low Countries, history of the **12**:443
  Luxembourg **12**:471
  Netherlands **14**:102
  Spaak, Paul Henri **18**:118
BENEŠ, EDUARD **3**:198 *bibliog., illus.*
  Czechoslovakia **5**:416
BENÉT, STEPHEN VINCENT **3**:198 *bibliog.*
BENÉT, WILLIAM ROSE **3**:198
  Wylie, Elinor **20**:299
BENEVOLI, ORAZIO
  mass (musical setting) **13**:201
BENEWAH (county in Idaho)
  map (47° 15′N 116° 40′W) **11**:26
BENGAL (India) **3**:198–199 *bibliog.*
  Bangladesh **3**:63–66
  Darjeeling **6**:38
  India, history of **11**:92
  Indo-Iranian languages **11**:145
  Santal **17**:68–69
BENGAL, BAY OF **3**:199
  map (15° 0′N 90° 0′E) **11**:80
  Nicobar Islands **14**:183
  Palk Strait **15**:47
BENGAL FAN
  Indian Ocean bottom **11**:105 *map*
BENGEL, J. A. **3**:199
BENGHAZI (Libya) **3**:199
  map (32° 7′N 20° 4′E) **12**:320
BENGLADESH *see* BANGLADESH
BENGUELA (Angola) **3**:199
  map (12° 35′S 13° 25′E) **2**:5
BENGUELA CURRENT
  ocean currents and wind systems, worldwide **14**:322–323 *maps*
  plankton **15**:332
BENHAIM, MARTIN
  globe **9**:208
BENI (department in Bolivia)
  map (14° 0′S 65° 30′W) **3**:366
BENI HASAN (Egypt) **3**:199
BENI-MELLAL (Morocco)
  map (32° 22′N 6° 29′W) **13**:585
BENICIA (California)
  map (38° 3′N 122° 9′W) **4**:31
BENIN **3**:199–201 *illus., map, table*
  art
    bronze plaque **1**:162 *illus.*
  cities
    Cotonou **3**:199–201 *illus., table*; **5**:304
    Porto-Novo **15**:445–446
  economic activities **3**:200
  education **3**:200
    African universities **1**:176 *table*
  flag **3**:199 *illus.*
  government **3**:200
  history **3**:200–201
  land and resources **3**:199–201 *map, table*
  map (9° 30′N 2° 15′E) **1**:136
  people **3**:200
    Ewe **7**:325
    Fon **8**:204
    Yoruba **20**:331
BENIN, BIGHT OF
  map (5° 30′N 3° 0′E) **14**:190
BENIN, KINGDOM OF **3**:201 *bibliog., illus.*
  art
    bronze relief **17**:167 *illus.*
    ivory mask **11**:337 *illus.*
  people
    Edo **7**:58–59
    Fon **8**:204
BENIN CITY (Nigeria)
  map (6° 19′N 5° 41′E) **14**:190
BENIOFF ZONE *see* SUBDUCTION ZONE
BENITEZ PÉREZ, MANUEL *see* EL CORDOBÉS
BENITO (Manitoba)
  map (51° 55′N 101° 31′W) **13**:119
BENITO RIVER
  map (1° 35′N 9° 37′E) **7**:226
BENJAMIN **3**:201
BENJAMIN (Texas)
  map (33° 35′N 99° 48′W) **19**:129
BENJAMIN, ASHER **3**:201 *bibliog.*
BENJAMIN, JUDAH P. **3**:201–202 *bibliog.*
  Civil War, U.S. **5**:31
  Confederate States of America **5**:176
BENJAMIN, WALTER **3**:202 *bibliog.*
BENJAMIN OF TUDELA **3**:202
BENKELMAN (Nebraska)
  map (40° 3′N 101° 32′W) **14**:70
BENN, ANTHONY WEDGWOOD **3**:202 *bibliog.*
  Labour party **12**:157
BENN, GOTTFRIED **3**:202 *bibliog.*
BENNET (Nebraska)
  map (40° 41′N 96° 30′W) **14**:70
BENNETT (county in South Dakota)
  map (43° 15′N 101° 40′W) **18**:103
BENNETT, ARNOLD **4**:202 *bibliog., illus.*
  realism (literature) **16**:104
BENNETT, FLOYD **3**:202
BENNETT, JAMES GORDON **3**:202–203 *bibliog., illus.*
BENNETT, JAMES GORDON, JR. **3**:203 *bibliog.*
BENNETT, MICHAEL **3**:203
BENNETT, RICHARD BEDFORD, VISCOUNT BENNETT **3**:203 *bibliog., illus.*
  Canada, history of **4**:86
BENNETT, RICHARD DYER- *see* DYER-BENNETT, RICHARD
BENNETT, RICHARD RODNEY **3**:203–204 *bibliog.*
  English music **7**:204
BENNETT, WILLIAM STERNDALE **3**:204
BENNETTSVILLE (South Carolina)
  map (34° 37′N 79° 41′W) **18**:98
BENNING, FORT (Georgia) *see* FORT BENNING (Georgia)
BENNINGTON (Kansas)
  map (39° 2′N 97° 36′W) **12**:18
BENNINGTON (Vermont) **3**:204
  map (42° 53′N 73° 12′W) **19**:554
BENNINGTON (county in Vermont)
  map (43° 4′N 73° 7′W) **19**:554
BENNINGTON, BATTLE OF
  American Revolution **1**:360
  Bennington **3**:204
  Green Mountain Boys **9**:348
  Stark, John **18**:227
BENNINGTON COLLEGE **3**:204
  American Dance Festival **1**:338
BENNY, JACK **3**:204 *bibliog.*
BENOIS, ALEKSANDR NIKOLAYEVICH **3**:204 *bibliog.*
  Ballets Russes de Serge Diaghilev **3**:48
BENOIT (Mississippi)
  map (33° 39′N 91° 1′W) **13**:469
BENOIT, JOAN **3**:204
BENOÎT DE SAINTE-MORE **3**:204
BENQUE VIEJO (Belize)
  map (17° 5′N 89° 8′W) **3**:183
BENSLEY (Virginia)
  map (37° 26′N 77° 26′W) **19**:607
BENSON (Arizona)
  map (31° 58′N 110° 18′W) **2**:160
BENSON (Minnesota)
  map (45° 19′N 95° 36′W) **13**:453
BENSON (North Carolina)
  map (35° 23′N 78° 33′W) **14**:242
BENSON (county in North Dakota)
  map (48° 0′N 99° 20′W) **14**:248
BENSON, GEORGE
  jazz **11**:389 *illus.*
BENSON, MARY
  basket **11**:140 *illus.*
BENT (county in Colorado)
  map (38° 0′N 103° 0′W) **5**:116
BENT, CHARLES
  Mexican War **13**:354
BENT, THEODORE
  Zimbabwe Ruins **20**:367
BENTEEN, FREDERICK A.
  Little Bighorn, Battle of the **12**:372
BENTHAM, JEREMY **3**:204–205 *bibliog., illus.*
  law **12**:242
  Mill, John Stuart **13**:425
  socialism **18**:20
  state (in political philosophy) **18**:229; **18**:232
  utilitarianism **19**:497
BENTHONIC ZONE **3**:205 *bibliog.*
  abyssal zone **1**:67
  bathyal zone **3**:123

BENTHONIC ZONE (cont.)
deep-sea life **6**:78; **6**:79
foraminifera **8**:219
littoral zone **12**:373
ocean and sea **14**:331
oceanography **14**:345
paleoecology **15**:34
BENTINCK (family) **3**:205 *bibliog.*
BENTINCK, LORD GEORGE
Bentinck (family) **3**:205
BENTINCK, LORD WILLIAM CAVENDISH
Bentinck (family) **3**:205
BENTINCK, WILLIAM, 1st EARL OF PORTLAND
Bentinck (family) **3**:205
BENTINCK, WILLIAM HENRY CAVENDISH, 3rd DUKE OF PORTLAND
Bentinck (family) **3**:205
BENTLEY, ARTHUR
state (in political philosophy) **18**:232–233
BENTLEY, ERIC **3**:205
BENTLEY, RICHARD **3**:205
BENTLEYVILLE (Pennsylvania)
map (40° 7′N 80° 1′W) **15**:147
BENTON (Arkansas)
map (34° 34′N 92° 35′W) **2**:166
BENTON (county in Arkansas)
map (36° 20′N 94° 15′W) **2**:166
BENTON (Illinois)
map (38° 0′N 88° 55′W) **11**:42
BENTON (county in Indiana)
map (40° 37′N 87° 19′W) **11**:111
BENTON (county in Iowa)
map (42° 5′N 92° 5′W) **11**:244
BENTON (Kentucky)
map (36° 52′N 88° 21′W) **12**:47
BENTON (Louisiana)
map (32° 42′N 93° 44′W) **12**:430
BENTON (county in Minnesota)
map (45° 40′N 94° 0′W) **13**:453
BENTON (county in Mississippi)
map (34° 50′N 89° 10′W) **13**:469
BENTON (Missouri)
map (37° 6′N 89° 34′W) **13**:476
BENTON (county in Missouri)
map (38° 20′N 93° 20′W) **13**:476
BENTON (county in Oregon)
map (44° 30′N 123° 25′W) **14**:427
BENTON (Pennsylvania)
map (41° 12′N 76° 23′W) **15**:147
BENTON (Tennessee)
map (35° 10′N 84° 39′W) **19**:104
BENTON (county in Tennessee)
map (36° 5′N 89° 7′W) **19**:104
BENTON (county in Washington)
map (46° 15′N 119° 35′W) **20**:35
BENTON (Wisconsin)
map (42° 34′N 90° 23′W) **20**:185
BENTON, THOMAS HART (painter) **3**:205–206 *bibliog., illus.*
Jefferson City (Missouri) **11**:393
Threshing Wheat **3**:205 *illus.*
BENTON, THOMAS HART (political leader) **3**:206 *bibliog.*
BENTON CITY (Washington)
map (46° 16′N 119° 29′W) **20**:35
BENTON HARBOR (Michigan)
map (42° 6′N 86° 27′W) **13**:377
BENTONIA (Mississippi)
map (32° 38′N 90° 22′W) **13**:469
BENTONITE
clay minerals **5**:46–47
BENTONVILLE (Arkansas)
map (36° 22′N 94° 13′W) **2**:166
BENTWOOD ROCKING CHAIR **8**:379 *illus.*
BENUE RIVER
map (7° 48′N 6° 46′E) **14**:190
Nigeria **14**:189
BENZ (automobile) **2**:365 *illus.*
BENZ, KARL **3**:206 *bibliog.*
BENZALDEHYDE **3**:206
BENZALKONIUM CHLORIDE
antiseptic **2**:68
BENZEDRINE *see* AMPHETAMINE
BENZENE **3**:206 *bibliog., illus.*
aromatic compounds **2**:186
chemical bond **4**:314 *illus.*
derivatives: Baeyer, Adolf von **3**:20–21
Faraday, Michael **8**:21
molecular structure
Kekulé structure, organic chemistry **14**:435 *illus.*
Kekulé von Stradonitz, Friedrich August **12**:37
phase equilibrium **15**:223 *illus.*
phenyl group **15**:226
pollutants, chemical **15**:410
BENZIE (county in Michigan)
map (44° 40′N 86° 0′W) **13**:377
BENZODIAZEPINES
Librium **12**:319
BENZOIC ACID **3**:207
BENZYLPENICILLIN *see* PENICILLIN
BEOGRAD *see* BELGRADE (Yugoslavia)
BEOWAWE (Nevada)
map (40° 35′N 116° 29′W) **14**:111
BEOWULF (epic) **3**:207 *bibliog.*
Scandinavia, history of **17**:108
BEQUEST *see* TRUST; WILL (law)
BÉRAIN, JEAN **3**:207 *bibliog.*
BÉRANGER, PIERRE JEAN DE **3**:207
BERAT (Albania)
map (40° 42′N 19° 57′E) **1**:250
BERBER LANGUAGES
Afroasiatic languages **1**:179–180 *map*
BERBERA (Somalia)
map (10° 25′N 45° 2′E) **18**:60
BERBÉRATI (Central African Republic)
map (4° 16′N 15° 47′E) **4**:251
BERBERS **1**:145 *illus.*; **3**:207–208 *bibliog., illus.*
Abd el-Krim **1**:54
Afroasiatic **1**:180
Almohads **1**:306
Almoravids **1**:307
Kabyle **12**:4
Libya **12**:321
Moorish art and architecture **13**:570
Moroccan history **13**:586
North Africa **14**:224
Tuareg **19**:325–326
BERBICK, TREVOR
Ali, Muhammad **1**:292
BERCEANU, GEORGHE **20**:287 *illus.*
BERCHEM, NICOLAES PIETERSZOON **3**:208 *bibliog.*
BERCHER, JEAN *see* DAUBERVAL, JEAN
BERCHTESGADEN (West Germany) **3**:208
BERCZY, WILLIAM
Canadian art and architecture **4**:89
BERDYAYEV, NIKOLAI **3**:208 *bibliog.*
BEREA (Kentucky)
map (37° 34′N 84° 17′W) **12**:47
BEREA (Ohio)
map (41° 22′N 81° 52′W) **14**:357
BEREA (South Carolina)
map (34° 53′N 82° 28′W) **18**:98
BEREA COLLEGE **3**:208
BEREGOVOI, GEORGY T. **3**:208
BEREKUM (Ghana)
map (7° 27′N 2° 37′W) **9**:164
BERENGAR OF TOURS **3**:208
BERENICE **3**:208
BERENS RIVER (Manitoba)
map (52° 22′N 97° 2′W) **13**:119
BERENSON, BERNARD **3**:208 *bibliog.*
Gardner Museum **9**:45
BERESFORD (South Dakota)
map (43° 5′N 96° 47′W) **18**:103
BERETTYÓ RIVER
map (46° 59′N 21° 7′E) **10**:307
BEREZNIKI (USSR)
map (59° 24′N 56° 46′E) **19**:388
BERG, ALBAN **3**:208–209 *bibliog., illus.*
BERG EN DAL (Suriname)
map (5° 9′N 55° 4′W) **18**:364
BERGAMO (Italy) **3**:209
map (45° 41′N 9° 43′E) **11**:321
BERGAMOT **3**:209
mint **13**:461
BERGANZA, TERESA **3**:209
BERGEN (Belgium) *see* MONS (Belgium)
BERGEN (county in New Jersey)
map (40° 53′N 74° 3′W) **14**:129
BERGEN (New York)
map (43° 5′N 77° 57′W) **14**:149
BERGEN (Norway) **3**:209
map (60° 23′N 5° 20′E) **14**:261
BERGEN, EDGAR, AND McCARTHY, CHARLIE **3**:209 *bibliog.*
BERGEN-BELSEN (West Germany) *see* BELSEN (West Germany)
BERGEN OP ZOOM (Netherlands)
map (51° 30′N 4° 17′E) **14**:99
BERGENFIELD (New Jersey)
map (40° 55′N 74° 0′W) **14**:129
BERGER, MAURICE *see* BÉJART, MAURICE
BERGER, THOMAS **3**:209
BERGER, VICTOR L. **3**:209–210 *bibliog.*
socialism **18**:23
Socialist party **18**:25
BERGERAC, SAVINIEN CYRANO DE *see* CYRANO DE BERGERAC, SAVINIEN
BERGIUS, FRIEDRICH KARL RUDOLF **3**:210
BERGLAND (Michigan)
map (46° 35′N 89° 34′W) **13**:377
BERGMAN, HJALMAR FREDRIK ELGÉRUS **3**:210
BERGMAN, INGMAR **3**:210 *bibliog., illus.*
film, history of **8**:86
Von Sydow, Max **19**:634
BERGMAN, INGRID **3**:210 *bibliog.*; **9**:287 *illus.*
Bogart, Humphrey **3**:359
BERGMAN, SIR TORBERN **3**:210
BERGMANN, GUSTAV **3**:210
BERGONZI, CARLO **3**:210
BERGOO (West Virginia)
map (38° 29′N 80° 18′W) **20**:111
BERGSON, HENRI **3**:211 *bibliog., illus.*
comedy **5**:132
process philosophy **15**:561
BERIA, LAVRENTI PAVLOVICH **3**:211 *bibliog.*
KGB **12**:64
Khrushchev, Nikita Sergeyevich **12**:69
BERIBERI **3**:211 *bibliog.*
Eijkman, Christiaan **7**:92
nutritional-deficiency diseases **14**:307
thiamine deficiency, vitamins and minerals **19**:619
BERING, VITUS JONASSEN **3**:211 *bibliog., illus.*
Arctic **2**:142 *map*
explorations **7**:336–337 *map*
Northeast Passage **14**:253
Saint Elias, Mount **17**:18
BERING ISLAND
Commander Islands (USSR) **5**:137
BERING LAND BRIDGE **3**:212 *bibliog.*
national parks **14**:38–39 *map, table*
prehistoric humans **15**:512
savanna life **17**:99
BERING SEA **3**:212 *bibliog., map*
Bering Strait **3**:212
islands and island groups
Commander Islands (USSR) **5**:137
Pribilof Islands (Alaska) **15**:534
map (60° 0′N 175° 0′W) **19**:388
shellfish **17**:255
BERING SEA CONTROVERSY **3**:212
BERING STRAIT **3**:212
Bering, Vitus Jonassen **3**:211
map (65° 30′N 169° 0′W) **1**:242
Northeast Passage **14**:253
BERINGIA *see* BERING LAND BRIDGE
BERINGOVA
Commander Islands (USSR) **5**:137
BERIO, LUCIANO **3**:212 *bibliog.*
BERKELEY (California) **3**:212
education
California, state universities and colleges of **4**:38 *table*
map (37° 57′N 122° 18′W) **4**:31
middle schools and junior high schools **13**:412
BERKELEY (Missouri)
map (38° 45′N 90° 20′W) **13**:476
BERKELEY (county in South Carolina)
map (33° 15′N 80° 0′W) **18**:98
BERKELEY (county in West Virginia)
map (39° 25′N 78° 0′W) **20**:111
BERKELEY, BUSBY **3**:213 *bibliog., illus.*; **8**:85 *illus.*
BERKELEY, GEORGE **3**:213 *bibliog., illus.*
idealism **11**:30
philosophy **15**:245
Smibert, John **17**:366
BERKELEY, JOHN, LORD
New Jersey **14**:133
BERKELEY, SIR WILLIAM **3**:213 *bibliog.*
United States, history of the **19**:437
BERKELEY HEIGHTS (New Jersey)
map (40° 41′N 74° 27′W) **14**:129
BERKELEY SPRINGS (West Virginia)
map (39° 38′N 78° 14′W) **20**:111
BERKELIUM **3**:213
actinide series **1**:88
element **7**:130 *table*
metal, metallic element **13**:328
Seaborg, Glenn T. **17**:171
transuranium elements **19**:286
BERKMAN, ALEXANDER
Goldman, Emma **9**:235
BERKNER ISLAND
map (79° 30′S 49° 30′W) **2**:40
BERKS (county in Pennsylvania)
map (40° 20′N 75° 50′W) **15**:147
BERKSHIRE (England) **3**:213–214
BERKSHIRE (county in Massachusetts)
map (42° 27′N 73° 15′W) **13**:206
BERKSHIRE HILLS **3**:214; **5**:195 *illus.*; **13**:208 *illus.*
map (42° 20′N 73° 10′W) **13**:206
BERKSHIRE MUSIC FESTIVAL **3**:214 *bibliog.*
Boston Symphony Orchestra **3**:410
BERLAGE, HENDRIK PETRUS **3**:214 *bibliog.*
BERLE, A. A. **3**:214 *bibliog.*
Liberal parties **12**:312
Roosevelt, Franklin Delano **16**:308
BERLE, MILTON **3**:214
radio and television broadcasting **16**:58 *illus.*
BERLIAWSKY, LOUISE *see* NEVELSON, LOUISE
BERLICHINGEN, GÖTZ VON **3**:214
BERLIN (coach)
coach and carriage **5**:73
BERLIN (Germany, East and West) **3**:214–217 *bibliog., illus., map*; **9**:142–143 *illus., table*
architecture
Schinkel, Karl Friedrich **17**:121
Berlin, Free University of **3**:217
Berlin Wall **3**:217
Brandenburg (East Germany) **3**:453
Brandenburg Gate **3**:453
economy **3**:215–216
Germany, East and West **9**:147
map (52° 31′N 13° 24′E) **9**:140
population **3**:214–215
subway **18**:318 *illus., table*
World War II **20**:275
BERLIN (Maryland)
map (38° 20′N 75° 13′W) **13**:188
BERLIN (New Hampshire)
map (44° 29′N 71° 10′W) **14**:123
BERLIN (New Jersey)
map (39° 48′N 74° 57′W) **14**:129
BERLIN (Ontario) *see* KITCHENER (Ontario)
BERLIN (Pennsylvania)
map (39° 55′N 78° 57′W) **15**:147
BERLIN (Wisconsin)
map (43° 58′N 88° 55′W) **20**:185
BERLIN, CONFERENCE OF (1885)
colonialism **5**:112
Zaire **20**:352
BERLIN, CONGRESS OF (1878) **3**:217 *bibliog.*
Russo-Turkish Wars **16**:374
BERLIN, FREE UNIVERSITY OF **3**:217
BERLIN, IRVING **3**:217 *bibliog., illus.*
BERLIN, SIR ISAIAH **3**:217
BERLIN, TREATY OF (1878)
Berlin, Congress of **3**:217
Russo-Turkish Wars **16**:374
BERLIN AIRLIFT **3**:217 *bibliog.*; **5**:98 *illus.*; **19**:456 *illus.*
Clay, Lucius D. **5**:46
BERLIN LAKE
map (41° 0′N 81° 0′W) **14**:357
BERLIN PAINTER
Pallas Athena (amphora) **4**:257 *illus.*
BERLIN PHILHARMONIC ORCHESTRA **3**:217
Nikisch, Arthur **14**:195
BERLIN WALL **3**:216 *map*; **3**:217 *bibliog.*; **5**:99 *illus.*
Kennedy, John F. **12**:43
BERLIN ZOO **3**:217
See also ZOOLOGICAL GARDEN
BERLINER, EMILE **3**:218 *bibliog.*
phonograph **15**:253
BERLINER ENSEMBLE **3**:218 *bibliog., illus.*
Brecht, Bertolt **3**:471
Deutsches Theater **6**:136–137
Weigel, Helene **20**:92
BERLINGER, MILTON *see* BERLE, MILTON
BERLINGUER, ENRICO **3**:218 *bibliog.*
communism **5**:150
BERLIOZ, HECTOR **3**:218–219 *bibliog., illus.*; **8**:320 *illus.*
kettledrum **12**:62
music, history of Western **13**:666
music criticism **13**:670
orchestra and orchestration **14**:418
symphony **18**:405
BERLITZ SCHOOLS OF LANGUAGE **3**:219
BERM **3**:219 *bibliog.*
beach and coast **3**:136
BERMAN, EUGENE **3**:219 *bibliog.*
BERMAN, LAZAR **3**:219
BERMEJO, BARTOLOMÉ
Isabella I, Queen of Castile **11**:285 *illus.*
BERMEJO PASS
map (32° 50′S 70° 5′W) **4**:355
BERMEJO RIVER
map (26° 51′S 58° 23′W) **2**:149
BERMUDA **3**:219 *bibliog., map*
Hamilton **10**:27
map (32° 20′N 64° 45′W) **3**:219
map (32° 20′N 64° 45′W) **14**:225
BERMUDA AGREEMENT
commercial aviation **2**:372
BERMUDA HIGH

cyclone and anticyclone 5:405
Hadley cell 10:8
high-pressure region 10:162
BERMUDA TRIANGLE 3:219 *bibliog.*
BERMÚDEZ, FRANCISCO MORALES *see* MORALES BERMÚDEZ, FRANCISCO
BERN (Switzerland) 3:220
map (46° 57′N 7° 26′E) 18:394
BERNADETTE, SAINT 3:220 *bibliog.*
Lourdes (France) 12:436
BERNADOTTE, COUNT FOLKE 3:220 *bibliog.*
BERNADOTTE, JEAN BAPTISTE JULES *see* CHARLES XIV JOHN, KING OF SWEDEN
BERNALILLO (New Mexico)
map (35° 18′N 106° 33′W) 14:136
BERNALILLO (county in New Mexico)
map (35° 5′N 106° 40′W) 14:136
BERNANOS, GEORGES 3:220 *bibliog.*
Bresson, Robert 3:474
BERNARD, CLAUDE 3:220 *bibliog.*; 3:271 *illus.*
biology 3:270
homeostasis 10:212
BERNARD, JEAN JACQUES 3:220
BERNARD, TRISTAN 3:220
BERNARD OF CLAIRVAUX, SAINT 3:220–221 *bibliog.*
Abelard, Peter 1:55
Crusades 5:368
monastic art and architecture 13:519 *illus.*
Templars 19:93–94
BERNARD M. BARUCH COLLEGE
New York, City University of 14:154
BERNARD OF MENTHON, SAINT
Saint Bernard Pass 17:16
BERNARDES, DIOGO 3:221 *bibliog.*
BERNARDSVILLE (New Jersey)
map (40° 43′N 74° 34′W) 14:129
BERNART DE VENTADORN 3:221
BERNBURG (Germany, East and West)
map (51° 48′N 11° 44′E) 9:140
BERNE (Indiana)
map (40° 39′N 84° 57′W) 11:111
BERNE (Switzerland) *see* BERN (Switzerland)
BERNE, ERIC
transactional analysis 19:267
BERNER ALPS
map (46° 30′N 7° 30′E) 18:394
BERNESE MOUNTAIN DOG 3:221 *bibliog.*, *illus.*; 6:214 *illus.*
BERNEVILLE, GILLEBERT DE
minstrels, minnesingers, and troubadours 13:460
BERNHARD, THOMAS, 3:221
BERNHARD OF LIPPE-BIESTERFELD 3:221
Juliana, Queen of the Netherlands 11:466
BERNHARDT, SARAH 3:221–222 *bibliog.*, *illus.*
Mucha, Alfons 13:630
BERNICE (Louisiana)
map (32° 49′N 92° 39′W) 12:430
BERNICIA 2:3 *map*
BERNIE (Missouri)
map (36° 40′N 89° 58′W) 13:476
BERNINA PEAK
map (46° 21′N 9° 51′E) 18:394
BERNINI, GIOVANNI LORENZO 3:222–223 *bibliog.*, *illus.*
Apollo and Daphne 11:311 *illus.*
architecture 2:135
Baldachino (St. Peter's Basilica) 3:89 *illus.*
bronzes 3:507–508
caricature 4:149
The Ecstasy of St. Teresa 2:198 *illus.*; 3:222 *illus.*; 17:164 *illus.*
Italian art and architecture 11:311
Saint Peter's Basilica 17:25
Self-Portrait 3:222 *illus.*
BERNOULLI, DANIEL 3:223
kinetic theory of matter 12:78
BERNOULLI, JACQUES 3:223
mathematics, history of 13:225
BERNOULLI, JOHANN
ballistics 3:50
mathematics, history of 13:225
BERNOULLI'S LAW 3:223 *illus.*
carburetor 4:141
BERNOULLI'S THEOREM *see* LARGE NUMBERS, LAW OF
BERNSTEIN, CARL, AND WOODWARD, BOB 3:223 *illus.*
All the President's Men 1:298
BERNSTEIN, EDUARD 3:223–224 *bibliog.*; 18:22 *illus.*
BERNSTEIN, LEONARD 3:224 *bibliog.*, *illus.*
Kennedy Center for the Performing Arts 12:44
West Side Story 13:674 *illus.*
BERNSTEIN, MORRIS *see* LOUIS, MORRIS
BEROUNKA RIVER
map (50° 0′N 14° 24′E) 5:413
BERRA, LAWRENCE PETER *see* BERRA, YOGI
BERRA, YOGI 3:224 *bibliog.*
BERRETTINI, PIETRO *see* CORTONA, PIETRO DA
BERRIEN (county in Georgia)
map (31° 15′N 83° 10′W) 9:114
BERRIEN (county in Michigan)
map (41° 59′N 86° 30′W) 13:377
BERRUGUETE, ALONSO 3:224 *bibliog.*
BERRUGUETE, PEDRO 3:224 *bibliog.*
BERRY
blackberry 3:320 *illus.*
BERRY (Alabama)
map (33° 39′N 87° 36′W) 1:234
BERRY (France) 3:225
BERRY (fruit) 3:225; 8:348 *illus.*
blueberry 3:344 *illus.*
cranberry 5:329 *illus.*
currant 5:393 *illus.*
elderberry 7:103
gooseberry 9:247
huckleberry 10:289
juneberry 11:467
mulberry 13:635 *illus.*
raspberry 16:90 *illus.*
serviceberry 17:211
strawberry 18:295–296 *illus.*
BERRY, CHUCK 3:225 *bibliog.*
rock music 16:248 *illus.*
BERRY, MARTHA McCHESNEY 3:225 *bibliog.*
BERRY, RAYMOND 3:225
BERRYESSA, LAKE
map (38° 35′N 122° 14′W) 4:31
BERRYMAN, CLIFFORD
Nazi-Soviet Pact cartoon 20:250 *illus.*
BERRYMAN, JOHN 3:225 *bibliog.*, *illus.*
BERRYVILLE (Arkansas)
map (36° 22′N 93° 34′W) 2:166
BERRYVILLE (Virginia)
map (39° 9′N 77° 59′W) 19:607
BERSON, SOLOMON
Yalow, Rosalyn Sussman 20:315
BERT AND ERNIE *see* MUPPETS
BERTHA (Minnesota)
map (46° 16′N 95° 4′W) 13:453
BERTHELOT, MARCELIN 3:225; 4:327 *illus.*
chemistry, history of 4:327
BERTHIER, LOUIS ALEXANDRE 3:226
BERTHOLD (North Dakota)
map (48° 19′N 101° 44′W) 14:248
BERTHOLLET, CLAUDE LOUIS, COMTE DE 3:226
chemical nomenclature 4:320
BERTHOUD (Colorado)
map (40° 18′N 105° 5′W) 5:116
BERTHOUD PASS
map (39° 45′N 105° 45′W) 5:116
BERTIE (county in North Carolina)
map (36° 5′N 77° 0′W) 14:242
BERTILLON, ALPHONSE
Bertillon system 3:226
BERTILLON SYSTEM 3:226
BERTIN, ROSE
fashion design 8:31 *illus.*
BERTOIA, HARRY 3:226 *bibliog.*
BERTOLUCCI, BERNARDO 3:226 *bibliog.*
film, history of 8:86
BERTRAM POWERBOAT 3:351 *illus.*
BERTRAND (Nebraska)
map (40° 32′N 99° 38′W) 14:70
BERTRAND, MARCEL ALEXANDRE 3:226 *bibliog.*
BERTRAND DE BORN 3:226
BERTRANDVILLE (Louisiana)
map (29° 46′N 90° 1′W) 12:430
BERWALD, FRANZ 3:226 *bibliog.*
BERWICK (Louisiana)
map (29° 42′N 91° 13′W) 12:430
BERWICK (Maine)
map (43° 16′N 70° 51′W) 13:70
BERWICK (Pennsylvania)
map (41° 3′N 76° 15′W) 15:147
BERWICK (Scotland) 3:226–227
BERWICK, JAMES FITZJAMES, DUKE OF 3:227 *bibliog.*
BERWICKSHIRE (Scotland) *see* BERWICK (Scotland)
BERWYN (Illinois)
map (41° 50′N 87° 47′W) 11:42
BERYL 3:227 *illus.*; 9:74 *illus.*
beryllium 3:227
emerald 7:154
gems 9:74–75
silicate minerals 17:305
BERYLLIOSIS
dust, atmospheric 6:308
BERYLLIUM 3:227
abundances of common elements 7:131 *table*
alkaline earth metals 1:295
beryl 3:227
bronze 3:505
discovery 3:227
element 7:130 *table*
Group IIA periodic table 15:167
metal, metallic element 13:328
silicate minerals 17:304–305
uses 3:227
Vauquelin, Louis Nicolas, discoverer 19:529
BERZELIUS, JÖNS JAKOB 3:227
cerium 4:260
chemical symbolism and notation 4:321
chemistry, history of 4:326
element 7:129
organic chemistry 14:434
selenium 17:190
thorium 19:178
BESANÇON (France) 3:227
map (47° 15′N 6° 2′E) 8:260
BESANT, ANNIE 3:228 *bibliog.*
birth control 3:294
theosophy 19:159–160 *illus.*
BESSARABIA 3:228
Moldavia 13:505
Moldavian Soviet Socialist Republic (USSR) 13:505–506
BESSEL, FRIEDRICH 3:228 *bibliog.*
relativity 16:134
BESSEMER (Alabama)
map (33° 25′N 86° 57′W) 1:234
BESSEMER (Michigan)
map (46° 27′N 89° 24′W) 13:377
BESSEMER (Pennsylvania)
map (40° 59′N 80° 30′W) 15:147
BESSEMER, SIR HENRY 3:228 *bibliog.*
See also BESSEMER PROCESS
iron and steel industry 11:274–276
Kelly, William 12:39
Sheffield (England) 17:250
BESSEMER CITY (North Carolina)
map (35° 17′N 81° 17′W) 14:242
BESSEMER PROCESS
iron and steel industry 11:274–276 *illus.*
Thomas, Sidney Gilchrist 19:174
BESSIE, ALVAH
Hollywood Ten, The 10:204
BESSON, JACQUES
lathe 12:215
BEST, CHARLES 3:228 *bibliog.*
Banting, Sir Frederick G. 3:71
insulin 11:198
MacLeod, John James Rickard 13:33
BEST, GEORGE 3:228 *bibliog.*
BEST FRIEND OF CHARLESTON (locomotive) 3:228 *bibliog.*
locomotive 12:389
BEST-SELLER 3:228–229 *bibliog.*
BESTER, ALFRED 3:229
BESTIARY 3:229 *bibliog.*
iconography 11:22
BETA
B (letter) 3:3
BETA-ALUMINA
ceramics applications 4:259
BETA DECAY 3:229 *bibliog.*
electron capture 3:229
emission 3:229
energy 7:172
fission, nuclear 8:129
neutrino 14:108
nonsymmetry, Wu, Chien-shiung 20:295
radioactivity 16:61
BETA GLUCOSIDASE ENZYMES
laetrile 12:163
BETA-THALASSEMIA MAJOR *see* COOLEY'S ANEMIA
BETA WAVE
brain 3:447
BETANCOURT, RÓMULO 3:229
BETANCUR CUARTUS, BELISARIO
Colombia 5:109
BETATRON 3:229
accelerator, particle 1:73
electromagnetic induction 7:115
BETEL 3:230 *illus.*
stimulant 18:271
BETELGEUSE
Canis Major and Canis Minor 4:108
Orion (astronomy) 14:444
spectrum 18:223 *table*
star 18:221; 18:225 *table*
supergiant 18:351
BETH (letter)
B (letter) 3:3
BETH-SHAN (Beth-Shean) (Israel) 3:230 *bibliog.*
map (32° 30′N 35° 31′E) 11:302
BETH SHEMESH (Israel)
map (31° 47′N 34° 59′E) 11:302
BETHALTO (Illinois)
map (38° 55′N 90° 3′W) 11:42
BETHANY 3:230
BETHANY (Illinois)
map (39° 39′N 88° 44′W) 11:42
BETHANY (Missouri)
map (40° 16′N 94° 2′W) 13:476
BETHANY (Oklahoma)
map (35° 31′N 97° 38′W) 14:368
BETHANY COLLEGE
Campbell, Alexander 4:65
BETHE, HANS 3:230 *bibliog.*
BETHEL (Alaska)
map (60° 48′N 161° 46′W) 1:242
BETHEL (Connecticut)
map (41° 22′N 73° 25′W) 5:193
BETHEL (Maine)
map (44° 25′N 70° 48′W) 13:70
BETHEL (North Carolina)
map (35° 48′N 77° 22′W) 14:242
BETHEL (Palestine) 3:230
BETHEL MANOR (Virginia)
map (37° 6′N 76° 25′W) 19:607
BETHEL SPRINGS (Tennessee)
map (35° 14′N 88° 36′W) 19:104
BETHESDA (Maryland) 3:230
map (38° 59′N 77° 6′W) 13:188
BETHLEHEM (Jordan/Israel) 3:230–231 *bibliog.*
BETHLEHEM (Pennsylvania) 3:231
map (40° 37′N 75° 25′W) 15:147
BETHLEHEM ROYAL HOSPITAL, LONDON *see* BEDLAM
BETHLEN, GÁBOR, PRINCE OF TRANSYLVANIA 3:231
Thirty Years' War 19:171 *map*
BETHLEN, ISTVÁN, COUNT 3:231 *bibliog.*
BETHMANN-HOLLWEG, THEOBALD VON 3:231 *bibliog.*
BETHUNE (South Carolina)
map (34° 25′N 80° 21′W) 18:98
BETHUNE, MARY McLEOD 3:231 *bibliog.*, *illus.*
BÉTHUNE, MAXIMILIEN DE, DUC DE SULLY *see* SULLY, MAXIMILIEN DE BÉTHUNE, DUC DE
BETHUNE-COOKMAN COLLEGE
Bethune, Mary McLeod 3:231
BETI, MONGO 3:231
BETJEMAN, SIR JOHN 3:232 *bibliog.*
BETONY 3:232
BETSIBOKA RIVER
map (16° 3′S 46° 36′E) 13:38
BETSILEO (tribe)
Madagascar 13:38
BETSIMISARAKA (tribe)
Madagascar 13:38
BETSY LAYNE (Kentucky)
map (37° 33′N 82° 38′W) 12:47
BETTA 3:232
Siamese fighting fish 17:290–291
BETTE PEAK
map (22° 0′N 19° 12′E) 12:320
BETTELHEIM, BRUNO 3:232
BETTENDORF (Iowa)
map (41° 32′N 90° 30′W) 11:244
BETTER BUSINESS BUREAU 3:232
BETTERTON, THOMAS
theater, history of the 19:147
BETTI, ENRICO 3:232
BETTI, UGO 3:232
BETTING *see* GAMBLING
BEULAH (Colorado)
map (38° 5′N 104° 59′W) 5:116
BEULAH (Michigan)
map (44° 38′N 86° 6′W) 13:377
BEULAH (North Dakota)
map (47° 16′N 101° 47′W) 14:248
BEULAVILLE (North Carolina)
map (34° 55′N 77° 46′W) 14:242
BEUVE, CHARLES AUGUSTIN SAINTE- *see* SAINTE-BEUVE, CHARLES AUGUSTIN
BEVAN, ANEURIN 3:232 *bibliog.*
Labour party 12:157
BEVERAGES, ALCOHOLIC *see* ALCOHOLIC BEVERAGES
BEVERIDGE, WILLIAM HENRY 3:232 *bibliog.*
BEVERLEY (England) 3:233
BEVERLY (Massachusetts)
map (42° 33′N 70° 53′W) 3:409
BEVERLY (New Jersey)
map (40° 4′N 74° 55′W) 14:129

BEVERLY (Ohio)
map (39° 33′N 81° 38′W) **14**:357
BEVERLY HILLS (California)
map (34° 3′N 118° 26′W) **4**:31
BEVERWIJK (Netherlands)
map (52° 28′N 4° 40′E) **14**:99
BEVIN, ERNEST 3:233 *bibliog.*
BEWICK, THOMAS 3:233
woodcuts and wood engravings **20**:211
BEXAR (county in Texas)
map (28° 25′N 98° 30′W) **19**:129
BEXLEY (Ohio)
map (39° 58′N 82° 56′W) **14**:357
map (39° 58′N 82° 56′W) **14**:357
BEYAZID *see* BAYEZID
BEYLE, HENRI MARIE *see* STENDHAL
BEYOND GOOD AND EVIL (book) 3:233
Nietzsche, Friedrich Wilhelm **14**:186
BEYSEHIR, LAKE
map (37° 40′N 31° 30′E) **19**:343
BEZA, THEODORE 3:233
BÉZIERS (France) 3:233
BEZIQUE 3:233 *bibliog.*
pinochle **15**:307
BHABHA, HOMI JEHANGIR 3:233
BHADGAON (Nepal)
map (27° 42′N 85° 27′E) **14**:86
BHAGALPUR (India)
map (25° 15′N 87° 0′E) **11**:80
BHAGAVAD GITA (poem) 3:233 *bibliog.*
bhakti 3:233–234
Hinduism **10**:173
Vedanta **19**:530
yoga **20**:328
BHAKTI 3:233–234
Buddhism 3:540
Hinduism **10**:173
Indian literature **11**:101–102
BHARAT *see* INDIA
BHARATA NATYAM 3:234
dance **6**:26 *illus.*
BHARHUT (India) 3:234
BHARTRIHARI 3:234
BHAUNAGAR (India)
map (21° 46′N 72° 9′E) **11**:80
BHAVABHUTI 3:234
BHAVE, ACHARYA VINOBA 3:234 *bibliog.*
BHIL 3:234 *bibliog.*
BHIR MOUND
Taxila **19**:48
BHOPAL (India) 3:234
map (23° 16′N 77° 24′E) **11**:80
BHUBANESWAR (India) 3:234
map (20° 14′N 85° 50′E) **11**:80
BHUMIBOL ADULYADEJ
Thailand **19**:140
BHUTAN 3:235–236 *bibliog., illus., map*
economic activities 3:236
flag 3:235 *illus.*
government 3:236
history 3:236
Lamaist art and architecture **12**:172–173
map (27° 30′N 90° 30′E) 2:232
people 3:235–236 *illus.*
Thimbu **19**:169
BHUTTO, BENAZIR
Pakistan **15**:29
BHUTTO, ZULFIKAR ALI 3:236 *bibliog.*
Pakistan **15**:29
BIA *see* INDIAN AFFAIRS, BUREAU OF
BIA, MOUNT
map (18° 59′N 103° 9′E) **12**:203
BIAFRA 3:236 *bibliog.*
Gowon, Yakubu **9**:273
Ibo **11**:6
Ojukwu, Chukemeka Odumegwu **14**:364–365
BIAFRA, BIGHT OF
map (4° 0′N 8° 0′E) **14**:190
BIALIK, HAYYIM NAHMAN 3:236 *bibliog.*; **10**:102 *illus.*
BIAŁYSTOK (Poland)
map (53° 9′N 23° 9′E) **15**:388
BIARRITZ (France) 3:237
map (43° 29′N 1° 34′W) **8**:260
BIATHLON 3:237
skiing **17**:339
BIBB (county in Alabama)
map (33° 0′N 87° 10′W) **1**:234
BIBB (county in Georgia)
map (32° 50′N 83° 40′W) **9**:114
BIBB CITY (Georgia)
map (32° 30′N 84° 59′W) **9**:114
BIBBY, GEOFFREY
Dilmun **6**:176
BIBER, HEINRICH IGNAZ FRANZ VON 3:237
BIBERMAN, HERBERT
Hollywood Ten, The **10**:204
BIBIANI (Ghana)
map (6° 28′N 2° 20′W) **9**:164
BIBIENA (family) *see* GALLI DA BIBIENA (family)
BIBLE 3:237–241 *bibliog., illus., maps, table*
See also names of specific books of the Bible, e.g., ACTS OF THE APOSTLES; DEUTERONOMY, BOOK OF; GENESIS, BOOK OF; etc.
Amorites **1**:376
angel **1**:411–412
apocalyptic literature 2:78–79
Apocrypha 2:79
Apocryphal New Testament 2:79
biblical archaeology 3:241–242
books of the Bible 3:240 *table*
canticle **4**:117
chronology **4**:419
cities *see* PALESTINE
covenant **5**:319
Coverdale, Miles **5**:319–320
fundamentalism **8**:363
God **9**:218
Gutenberg Bible **9**:409
Hebrew Bible *see* BIBLE—Old Testament
Hebrew and Yiddish literature **10**:102
Herod (dynasty) **10**:144
history **10**:184
illuminated manuscripts **11**:47–48
interpretation 3:241
Baur, Ferdinand Christian 3:130
Bengel, J. A. 3:199
Bultmann, Rudolf 3:561
Dead Sea Scrolls **6**:65
Dibelius, Martin **6**:155
Dodd, C. H. **6**:211
Eichhorn, Johann Gottfried **7**:91
Genesis, Book of **9**:78
Ibn Ezra, Abraham ben Meir **11**:5
Levi ben Gershon **12**:303
Masorah **13**:199
midrash **13**:414
Origen **14**:443
Philo of Alexandria **15**:239–240
Rashi **16**:90
Reimarus, Hermann Samuel **16**:131
Renan, Ernest **16**:157
scholasticism **17**:132
Jesus Christ **11**:403
Kralice Bible
Czech literature **5**:412
New Testament 3:239–241
apocalyptic literature 2:78–79
books of the Bible 3:240 *table*
canon 3:240
Epistles 3:240–241
Galilee, Sea of **9**:14
God **9**:218
Gospels 3:240
medieval drama **13**:273–274 *illus.*
slavery **17**:353
Old Testament 3:237–239
apocalyptic literature 2:78–79
Apocrypha 2:79
books of the Bible 3:237–239; 3:240 *table*
canon 3:238–239
Ebla **7**:36
Gaza **9**:64
God **9**:217–218
Masorah **13**:199
messiah **13**:324
Moses **13**:599–600
Pentateuch 3:238; 3:239
prophet 3:239; **15**:571–572
Septuagint **17**:206
slavery **17**:352
Torah **19**:238
Protestantism **15**:576–577
pseudepigrapha **15**:587
revelation **16**:184–185
Samaria **17**:45
translations and versions 3:241
Coverdale, Miles **5**:319–320
Douai (France) **6**:245
Gutenberg Bible **9**:409
Jerome, Saint **11**:398
Lefèvre d'Étaples, Jacques **12**:272
Rogers, John **16**:269
Rosenzweig, Franz **16**:316
Septuagint **17**:206
Tyndale, William **19**:362
Vulgate 3:241; **11**:398
Ussher, James **19**:491
BIBLE LEAF *see* COSTMARY
BIBLE MORALISÉE **12**:316 *illus.*
BIBLE SOCIETIES 3:241
BIBLICAL ARCHAEOLOGY 3:241–242 *bibliog., illus.*
Caesarea **4**:15
Calvary **4**:48
Canaan **4**:68
Dead Sea Scrolls **6**:65
Ebla **7**:36
Gezer **9**:163
Hazor **10**:84–85
Jericho **11**:397
Lachish **12**:160
Masada **13**:194
Megiddo **13**:280
Nimrud **14**:199
Nineveh **14**:199–200
Petrie, Sir Flinders **15**:204
Qumran **16**:28
Rawlinson, Sir Henry Creswicke **16**:95–96
Samaria **17**:45
Sheba **17**:247–248
Smith, George **17**:368
Ugarit **19**:374
Ur **19**:474
Urartu **19**:479
Uruk **19**:490
BIBLIOGRAPHY 3:242–243 *bibliog.*
drug, pharmacopoeia **15**:220–221
Gesner, Konrad von **9**:159
BIBLIOTECA AMBROSIANA *see* AMBROSIAN LIBRARY
BIBLIOTHÈQUE NATIONALE 3:243 *bibliog.*
Labrouste, Henri **12**:157
BIBLIOTHÈQUE SAINTE GENEVIÈVE
Labrouste, Henri **12**:157
BICARBONATE OF SODA *see* SODIUM BICARBONATE
BICAZ, LAKE
map (47° 0′N 26° 0′E) **16**:288
BICENTENNIAL, U.S. 3:243 *bibliog.*
BICHAT, MARIE FRANÇOIS
histology **10**:180
medicine **13**:270
BICHIR 3:243 *illus.*
BICHON FRISE 3:244 *bibliog., illus.*; **6**:219 *illus.*
BICKERDYKE, MARY ANN 3:244
BICKERSTAFF, ISAAC (pseudonym) *see* STEELE, SIR RICHARD
BICKNELL (Indiana)
map (38° 47′N 87° 19′W) **11**:111
BICYCLE 3:244–246 *bibliog., illus.*
gearing systems 3:245 *illus.*
moped **13**:572
motorcycle **13**:612–614 *illus.*
racing
cycling **5**:404
Merckx, Eddy **13**:305
Oldfield, Barney **14**:376
BICYCLE, MOTORIZED *see* MOPED
BIDA (Nigeria)
map (9° 5′N 6° 1′E) **14**:190
Nupe **14**:297
BIDAULT, GEORGES 3:246–247
BIDDEFORD (Maine)
map (43° 30′N 70° 26′W) **13**:70
BIDDLE, JOHN 3:247 *bibliog.*
BIDDLE, NICHOLAS 3:247 *bibliog.*
Bank of the United States 3:67
BIDEN, EDMUND P. *see* STURGES, PRESTON
BIDONVILLE *see* SHANTYTOWN
BIDWELL (Ohio)
map (38° 55′N 82° 18′W) **14**:357
BIÉ (Angola)
map (12° 22′S 16° 56′E) 2:5
BIEBER (California)
map (41° 7′N 121° 8′W) **4**:31
BIEBRZA RIVER
map (53° 37′N 22° 56′E) **15**:388
BIEDERMEIER 3:247 *bibliog., illus.*
furniture **8**:377
Waldmüller, Ferdinand Georg **20**:10
BIEDERMEIER, GOTTLIEB "PAPA"
Biedermeier 3:247
BIEL (Switzerland)
map (47° 10′N 7° 12′E) **18**:394
BIELEFELD (Germany, East and West)
map (52° 1′N 8° 31′E) **9**:140
BIELLA (Italy)
140
map (45° 34′N 8° 3′E) **11**:321
BIELSKO-BIAŁŁA (Poland)
map (49° 49′N 19° 2′E) **15**:388
BIEN HOA (Vietnam)
map (10° 57′N 106° 49′E) **19**:580
BIENNIAL (botany)
flower **8**:181
gardening **9**:43
BIENVILLE (Louisiana)
map (32° 21′N 92° 59′W) **12**:430
BIENVILLE (county in Louisiana)
map (32° 17′N 93° 5′W) **12**:430
BIENVILLE, JEAN BAPTISTE LE MOYNE, SIEUR DE 3:247 *bibliog.*
Mobile (Alabama) **13**:487
New Orleans (Louisiana) **14**:141
BIENVILLE, LAKE
map (55° 5′N 72° 40′W) **16**:18
BIERCE, AMBROSE 3:248 *bibliog.*
BIERSTADT, ALBERT 3:248 *bibliog., illus.*
The Rocky Mountains **12**:191 *illus.*
Sunrise, Yosemite Valley 3:248 *illus.*
BIFACE (hand ax)
Paleolithic Period **15**:38–40 *illus.*
BIG APPLE (dance) 3:248
BIG APPLE (New York City) *see* NEW YORK (city)
BIG BALD MOUNTAIN
map (34° 45′N 84° 19′W) **9**:114
map (34° 45′N 84° 19′W) **19**:104
BIG BANG THEORY 3:248 *bibliog.*
astronomy and astrophysics 2:285
background radiation 3:12
cosmogony **5**:284
cosmology (astronomy) **5**:284–285
creation accounts **5**:335
ether (physics) **7**:250
extragalactic systems **7**:343
Gamow, George **9**:34
Hawking, Stephen William **10**:77
Lemaître, Georges Édouard **12**:280
radio astronomy **16**:50
relativity **16**:136
BIG BAY (Michigan)
map (46° 49′N 87° 44′W) **13**:377
BIG BAY DE NOC
map (45° 46′N 86° 43′W) **13**:377
BIG BEAR (Cree Indian)
Poundmaker **15**:476
BIG BELT MOUNTAINS
map (46° 40′N 111° 25′W) **13**:547
BIG BEN *see* WESTMINSTER PALACE
BIG BEND (Swaziland)
map (26° 50′S 31° 57′E) **18**:380
BIG BEND NATIONAL PARK 3:249; **14**:38 *map, table*; **19**:133 *illus.*
BIG BERTHA
artillery 2:224
BIG BIRD *see* MUPPETS
BIG BLACK RIVER
map (32° 0′N 91° 5′W) **13**:469
BIG BLONDE (short story)
Parker, Dorothy **15**:90
BIG BLUE RIVER
map (39° 50′N 96° 40′W) **14**:70
BIG BOY (locomotive)
locomotive **12**:389 *illus.*; **12**:391
BIG BROTHER AND THE HOLDING COMPANY
Joplin, Janis **11**:446
BIG CHINO WASH
map (34° 52′N 112° 28′W) 2:160
BIG COAL RIVER
map (38° 16′N 81° 47′W) **20**:111
BIG CREEK (British Columbia)
map (51° 44′N 123° 3′W) 3:491
BIG CREEK (California)
map (37° 12′N 119° 9′W) **4**:31
BIG CREEK PEAK
map (44° 28′N 113° 32′W) **11**:26
BIG CYPRESS SWAMP
map (26° 10′N 81° 38′W) **8**:172
BIG DARBY CREEK
map (39° 37′N 82° 58′W) **14**:357
BIG DIPPER 3:249
constellation **5**:212
BIG EAU PLEINE RESERVOIR
map (44° 45′N 89° 50′W) **20**:185
BIG FALLS (Minnesota)
map (48° 12′N 93° 48′W) **13**:453
BIG FORK RIVER
map (48° 31′N 93° 43′W) **13**:453
BIG HOLE RIVER
map (45° 34′N 112° 20′W) **13**:547
BIG HORN (county in Montana)
map (45° 25′N 107° 25′W) **13**:547
BIG HORN (county in Wyoming)
map (44° 27′N 108° 0′W) **20**:301
BIG ISLAND *see* HAWAII (island)
BIG LAKE (Minnesota)
map (45° 20′N 93° 45′W) **13**:453
BIG LAKE (Texas)
map (31° 12′N 101° 28′W) **19**:129
BIG LAKE(Maine)
map (45° 10′N 67° 40′W) **13**:70
BIG LOST RIVER
map (43° 50′N 112° 44′W) **11**:26
BIG PINEY RIVER
map (37° 53′N 92° 4′W) **13**:476
BIG QUILL LAKE
map (51° 55′N 104° 22′W) **17**:81
BIG RAPIDS (Michigan)
map (43° 42′N 85° 29′W) **13**:377
BIG RIVER (Missouri)
map (38° 28′N 90° 37′W) **13**:476

BIG RIVER (Saskatchewan)
map (53° 50′N 107° 1′W) **17**:81
BIG SABLE POINT
map (44° 3′N 86° 31′W) **13**:377
BIG SANDY (Montana)
map (48° 11′N 110° 7′W) **13**:547
BIG SANDY (Tennessee)
map (36° 15′N 88° 5′W) **19**:104
BIG SANDY CREEK
map (38° 6′N 102° 29′W) **5**:116
BIG SANDY RESERVOIR
map (42° 16′N 109° 26′W) **20**:301
BIG SANDY RIVER (Arizona)
map (34° 19′N 113° 31′W) **2**:160
BIG SANDY RIVER (West Virginia)
map (38° 25′N 82° 36′W) **20**:111
BIG SIOUX RIVER
map (42° 30′N 96° 25′W) **18**:103
BIG SNOWY MOUNTAINS
map (46° 50′N 109° 30′W) **13**:547
BIG SPRING (Texas)
map (32° 15′N 101° 28′W) **19**:129
BIG SPRINGS (Nebraska)
map (41° 4′N 102° 5′W) **14**:70
BIG SPRUCE KNOB MOUNTAIN
map (38° 16′N 80° 12′W) **20**:111
BIG STONE (county in Minnesota)
map (45° 22′N 96° 22′W) **13**:453
BIG STONE GAP (Virginia)
map (36° 52′N 82° 47′W) **19**:607
BIG STONE LAKE
map (45° 25′N 96° 40′W) **13**:453
BIG TELESCOPE-ALTAZIMUTH *see* BTA (telescope)
BIG THOMPSON RIVER
map (40° 21′N 104° 45′W) **5**:116
BIG TIMBER (Montana)
map (45° 50′N 109° 57′W) **13**:547
BIG TROUT LAKE
map (53° 45′N 90° 0′W) **14**:393
BIG VALLEY (Alberta)
map (52° 2′N 112° 46′W) **1**:256
BIG WALNUT CREEK
map (40° 2′N 82° 54′W) **14**:357
BIG WELLS (Texas)
map (28° 34′N 99° 34′W) **19**:129
BIG WOOD RIVER
map (42° 52′N 114° 54′W) **11**:26
BIGAMY 3:249
BIGELOW, ERASTUS **19**:450 *illus.*
BIGELOW, JOHN 3:249 *bibliog.*
BIGEYE 3:249
BIGFLAT (Arkansas)
map (36° 0′N 92° 24′W) **2**:166
BIGFOOT *see* SASQUATCH
BIGFORK (Minnesota)
map (47° 45′N 93° 39′W) **13**:453
BIGGAR (Saskatchewan)
map (52° 4′N 108° 0′W) **17**:81
BIGGERS (Arkansas)
map (36° 20′N 90° 48′W) **2**:166
BIGGERS, EARL DERR 3:249
BIGGS, E. POWER 3:249
BIGHORN (sheep) 3:249–250 *illus.*
mountain sheep **13**:624
sheep **17**:248
BIGHORN BASIN
map (44° 15′N 108° 10′W) **20**:301
BIGHORN LAKE
map (45° 6′N 108° 8′W) **13**:547
BIGHORN MEDICINE WHEEL, WYOMING **2**:115 *illus.*
BIGHORN MOUNTAINS
map (44° 0′N 107° 30′W) **20**:301
BIGHORN RIVER
map (46° 9′N 107° 28′W) **19**:419
BIGHT *see* GULF AND BAY
BIGHT, THE (Bahama Islands)
map (24° 19′N 75° 24′W) **3**:23
BIGLOW PAPERS, THE (poem)
Lowell, James Russell **11**:444
BIGOTRY *see* PREJUDICE
BIGTOOTH ASPEN **2**:262
BIHAĆ (Yugoslavia)
map (44° 49′N 15° 52′E) **20**:340
BIHAR (India) 3:250
historic sites
Bodh Gaya **3**:356
Pataliputra **15**:109
map (25° 0′N 86° 0′E) **11**:80
people
Ho **10**:190
Mundari **13**:640
Oraon **14**:416
BIHZAD, KAMAL AL-DIN 3:250 *bibliog.*
Persian art and architecture **15**:186
BIIRGI, JOBST
logarithm **12**:394
BIJAGÓS ARCHIPELAGO
map (11° 25′N 16° 20′W) **9**:399
BIJELJINA (Yugoslavia)
map (44° 45′N 19° 13′E) **20**:340
BIKANER (India)
climate **11**:82 *table*
map (28° 1′N 73° 18′E) **11**:80
BIKILA, ABEBE 3:250
BIKINI (Marshall Islands) 3:250
coral reef **5**:258–259
hydrogen bomb **10**:339–340
BIKO, STEPHEN **10**:298 *illus.*
South Africa **18**:83
BILASPUR (India)
map (22° 5′N 82° 9′E) **11**:80
BILATERIA
classification, biological **2**:9 *illus.*
animal **2**:10
BILAUKTAUNG RANGE
map (13° 0′N 99° 0′E) **19**:139
BILBAO (Spain) 3:250
map (43° 15′N 2° 58′W) **18**:140
BILBO, THEODORE GILMORE 3:250–251 *bibliog.*
BILDERDIJK, WILLEM 3:251 *bibliog.*
BILDUNGSROMAN 3:251
Dickens, Charles **6**:156–157
Goethe, Johann Wolfgang von **9**:223–224
Joyce, James **11**:456–457
Mann, Thomas **13**:123–124
Portrait of the Artist as a Young Man, A **15**:446
Wieland, Christoph Martin **20**:145
BILE
acid
carboxylic acid **4**:141
Wieland, Heinrich Otto **20**:146
digestion, human **6**:170–173
digestive system **6**:173
gallbladder **9**:17
liver **12**:374–375
metabolism **13**:325–327
BILHARZIASIS *see* SCHISTOSOMIASIS
BILINGUAL EDUCATION 3:251 *bibliog.*
Canadian education **4**:91
Hispanic Americans **10**:179 *illus.*
BILINGUALISM
geographical linguistics **9**:100
sociolinguistics **18**:27–28
BILIRUBIN
jaundice **11**:385
BILIVERTI
gold and silver work **9**:230
BILL (proposal of law)
legislative process in the U.S. Congress **5**:186–187
BILL (zoology) *see* BEAK
BILL, MAX 3:251 *bibliog.*
BILL OF EXCHANGE 3:251
See also DRAFT (banking)
negotiable instrument **14**:77–78
BILL OF HEALTH 3:251
BILL OF LADING 3:251
BILL OF PORTLAND
map (50° 31′N 2° 27′W) **19**:403
BILL OF RIGHTS 3:251–254 *bibliog., illus.*
Canadian Bill of Rights **3**:254
civil rights **5**:12
democracy **6**:98
English Bill of Rights **3**:253
freedom of religion **8**:297
freedom of speech **8**:298
freedom of the press **8**:296
French Declaration of the Rights of Man **3**:253–254
human rights **10**:298
privacy, invasion of **15**:556
right to bear arms **16**:222
U.S. Bill of Rights **3**:251–253 *illus.*
See also the specific amendments, e.g., 1ST AMENDMENT; 5TH AMENDMENT; etc.
text **5**:220–221
United States, history of the **19**:442
BILL OF SALE 3:254
BILL WILLIAMS MOUNTAIN
map (35° 17′N 112° 12′W) **2**:160
BILL WILLIAMS RIVER
map (34° 17′N 114° 3′W) **2**:160
BILLAUD-VARENNE, JEAN NICOLAS 3:254 *bibliog.*
BILLBUG *see* WEEVIL
BILLERICA (Massachusetts)
map (42° 34′N 71° 16′W) **3**:409
BILLFISH
spearfish **18**:165
BILLIARDS 3:254–255 *bibliog., illus.*
Hoppe, Willie **10**:232
Mosconi, Willie **13**:596
BILLINGS (Montana) 3:255
map (45° 47′N 118° 27′W) **13**:547
BILLINGS (county in North Dakota)
map (47° 0′N 103° 25′W) **14**:248
BILLINGS (Oklahoma)
map (36° 32′N 97° 27′W) **14**:368
BILLINGS, JOSH 3:255 *bibliog.*
BILLINGS, WILLIAM 3:255–256 *bibliog.*
American music **1**:349
anthem **2**:49
hymn **10**:347
BILLINGS HEIGHTS (Montana)
map (45° 50′N 108° 33′W) **13**:547
BILLROTH, THEODOR
surgery **18**:361
BILLY BUDD (book) 3:256
BILLY THE KID 3:256 *bibliog.*
Garrett, Pat **9**:50
outlaws **14**:468–469 *illus.*
BILOXI (Mississippi) 3:256; **13**:470 *illus.*
map (30° 24′N 88° 53′W) **13**:469
BILTMORE FOREST (North Carolina)
map (35° 32′N 82° 32′W) **14**:242
BILWASKARMA (Nicaragua)
map (14° 45′N 83° 53′W) **14**:179
BIMINI ISLANDS
map (25° 44′N 79° 15′W) **3**:23
BIN (musical instrument)
Indian music **11**:102 *illus.*
BINA (Solomon Islands)
map (8° 55′S 160° 46′E) **18**:56
BINAISA, GODFREY L.
Uganda **19**:373
BINAIYA, MOUNT
map (3° 11′S 129° 26′E) **11**:147
BINARY CODE
telegraph **19**:77 *illus.*
BINARY NUMBER 3:256 *bibliog., illus.*
base **3**:102
bit, computer **3**:300
computer **5**:160c–160d; **5**:160h
computer languages **5**:160o
BINARY STARS 3:256–257 *bibliog., illus.*
Aitken, Robert Grant **1**:228
Algol **1**:291
binary systems **3**:256
Delta Libra, Libra **12**:314
eclipse **7**:40
Kepler's laws **12**:58
mass, transference of **3**:257
multiple systems **3**:256
nova **14**:268
Sirius **17**:328
star **18**:224
Struve, Friedrich Georg Wilhelm von **18**:304
variable star **19**:522
W ursae majoris stars **20**:3
Wolf-Rayet stars **20**:197
X-ray astronomy **20**:306–307 *illus.*
BINCHOIS, GILLES 3:257 *bibliog.*; **8**:320 *illus.*
BINDER (paint)
paint **15**:16–17
BINDESBØLL, MICHAEL GOTTLIEB BIRKNER 3:257 *bibliog.*
BINDING ENERGY 3:257–258 *bibliog.*
See also CHEMICAL ENERGY
conversion electron **5**:233
mass defect **13**:203
BINDURA (Zimbabwe)
map (17° 19′S 31° 20′E) **20**:365
BINDWEED 3:258 *illus.*
BINET, ALFRED 3:258 *bibliog., illus.*
child development **4**:349
psychology, history of **15**:597–598 *illus.*
Stanford-Binet test **18**:217
BINFORD (North Dakota)
map (47° 34′N 98° 21′W) **14**:248
BINFORD, LEWIS R. 3:258
BING, SIR RUDOLF 3:258 *bibliog.*
BINGA, MOUNT
map (19° 45′S 33° 4′E) **20**:365
BINGER (Oklahoma)
map (35° 18′N 98° 21′W) **14**:368
BINGHAM (family) 3:259 *bibliog.*
BINGHAM (county in Idaho)
map (43° 15′N 112° 20′W) **11**:26
BINGHAM (Maine)
map (45° 3′N 69° 53′W) **13**:70
BINGHAM, GEORGE CALEB 3:259 *bibliog., illus.*
Daniel Boone Escorting Settlers through the Cumberland Gap **3**:393 *illus.*
Fur Traders Descending the Missouri **3**:259 *illus.*
BINGHAM, HIRAM
Bingham (family) **3**:259
Machu Picchu **13**:26
BINGHAMTON (New York) 3:259
map (42° 8′N 75° 54′W) **14**:149
BINGO 3:259 *bibliog.*
BINI *see* EDO (African people)
BINI, LUCIO
shock therapy
schizophrenia **17**:124
BINOCULARS 3:259–260 *bibliog., illus.*
faint object detection **8**:8
prism **15**:553 *illus.*
BINOMIAL DISTRIBUTION 3:260 *bibliog., illus.*
de Moivre, Abraham **6**:62
statistics, nonparametric **18**:237
BINOMIAL NOMENCLATURE *see* NOMENCLATURE
BINOMIAL THEOREM 3:260 *bibliog., illus.*
algebra **1**:284
factorial **8**:6
permutation and combination **15**:176
BINT JUBAYL (Lebanon)
map (33° 7′N 35° 26′E) **12**:265
BINTURONG
kinkajou **12**:84
BINZERTE *see* BIZERTE (Tunisia)
BÍO-BÍO RIVER
map (36° 49′S 73° 10′W) **4**:355
BIOCHEMISTRY 3:260–262 *bibliog., illus.*
Abel, John J. **1**:55
active transport **1**:89–90
ATP **2**:312
bacteria **3**:18
Baltimore, David **3**:56
bioluminescence **3**:272
biopotential **3**:275–276
biosensor **3**:276
Bloch, Konrad **3**:334
blood tests **3**:339
carbon compounds **4**:135
cell **4**:232
Chain, Ernst Boris **4**:268
child psychiatry **4**:351
cholesterol **4**:403–404
coenzyme **5**:92–93
Cori, Carl Ferdinand and Gerty Teresa **5**:262
cytology **5**:411
energy conversion **13**:483
fermentation **8**:55
genes: Tatum, Edward L. **19**:44
genetic code **9**:79–82 *illus.*
genetic engineering **9**:84–85
Hoppe-Seyler, Felix **10**:232
hormone, animal **10**:234–237
isoelectric point **11**:299
keratin **12**:58
Krebs cycle **12**:128
Liebig, Justus, Baron von **12**:324
lipid **12**:361–362
Lynen, Feodor **12**:477
macromolecule **13**:36–37
metabolism **13**:325–327
mitochondrion **13**:485
Monod, Jacques Lucien **13**:536
muscle contraction **13**:654–656 *illus.*
nucleic acid **14**:288–291
organic chemistry **14**:438
pharmacology **15**:220
photosynthesis **15**:275–277
protein synthesis **15**:574–576
reactions **12**:128
schizophrenia **17**:124
sleep **17**:360
space medicine **18**:133
Stanley, Wendell Meredith **18**:219
stereochemistry **18**:258–259
Szent-Györgyi, Albert von **18**:416
Tiselius, Arne Wilhelm Kaurin **19**:209
transition elements **19**:274
BIODEGRADATION
Pseudomonas **15**:587
BIOELECTRICITY *see* BIOPOTENTIAL
BIOENERGETICS
metabolism **13**:325–326
BIOENGINEERING
rehabilitation medicine **16**:130
BIOFEEDBACK 3:263 *bibliog.*
analgesic **1**:388
headache **10**:86
BIOGEOGRAPHY **9**:103
BIOGRAPHY 3:263–264 *bibliog.*
See also AUTOBIOGRAPHY
Aubrey, John **2**:316
Boccaccio, Giovanni **3**:353–354
Boswell, James **3**:411–412
Life of Samuel Johnson, The **12**:330
Carlyle, Thomas **4**:152–153
Dobson, Austin **6**:209
Erasmus, Desiderius **7**:227
Erikson, Erik **7**:230–231
Freud, Sigmund **8**:329–330
Gaskell, Elizabeth Cleghorn **9**:54–55
Johnson, Samuel **11**:436
Ludwig, Emil **12**:452
Maurois, André **13**:237
More, Saint Thomas **13**:575–576
Plutarch **15**:372

BIOGRAPHY (cont.)
Sackville-West, Victoria **17**:7
Ssu-ma Ch'ien (Sima Qian) **18**:207
Stone, Irving **18**:280–281
Strachey, Lytton **18**:287
Suetonius **18**:323
Vasari, Giorgio **19**:525
Wallace, Irving **20**:14
Walton, Izaak **20**:20
Zweig, Stefan **20**:383
BIOKO (Equatorial Guinea) **3**:264
Equatorial Guinea **7**:225
Malabo **13**:78
map (3° 30′N 8° 40′E) **7**:226
BIOLOGICAL CHEMISTRY *see* BIOCHEMISTRY
BIOLOGICAL CLASSIFICATION *see* CLASSIFICATION, BIOLOGICAL
BIOLOGICAL CLOCK **3**:264–265 *bibliog.*
bee **3**:159
flower **8**:183
molting **13**:513
pineal gland **15**:306
sleep **17**:359–360
BIOLOGICAL EQUILIBRIUM **3**:265 *bibliog.*
Bárány, Robert **3**:75
ear **7**:6–7
homeostasis **10**:212–213
Meniere's disease **13**:297
motion sickness **13**:610
reflex **16**:120
vertigo **19**:563
vestibular system **3**:265
BIOLOGICAL LOCOMOTION **3**:265–268 *bibliog.*, *illus.*
arthropod **3**:266
basic devices **3**:265–267
bipedalism, prehistoric humans **15**:513
cilia **3**:265
flagella **3**:265; **8**:149
flight **3**:267
muscle contraction **3**:265–266; **13**:654–655
pseudopodia **3**:265
bird
diving birds **6**:204
roadrunner **16**:235
blue-green algae **3**:343
chordate **3**:266–267
fish
flying fish **8**:191
gurnard, flying **8**:191; **9**:406–407
remora **16**:146–147
sea robin **17**:170
insect **11**:193
invertebrate **3**:266
octopus **14**:348
snail **17**:375
squid **18**:203
mammal **13**:102 *illus.*
flying squirrel **8**:191
primate **15**:539
Muybridge, Eadweard **13**:687–688
nervous system **3**:267–268
orthopedics **14**:450
snake **17**:381–382 *illus.*
BIOLOGICAL OCEANOGRAPHY
See also MARINE BIOLOGY
oceanography **14**:344–345
BIOLOGICAL SENSOR *see* BIOSENSOR
BIOLOGICAL WARFARE *see* CHEMICAL AND BIOLOGICAL WARFARE
BIOLOGY **3**:268–271 *bibliog.*, *illus.*
Acetabularia **1**:79
animal experimentation **2**:22
bacteria **3**:14–18
bioelectricity **3**:275
bionics **3**:274–275
biopotential **3**:275
biosatellite **3**:276
branches
biochemistry **3**:260–262
biological oceanography **14**:344–345
biomathematics **3**:272
biophysics **3**:275
biotechnology **3**:277
botany **3**:412–414
comparative anatomy **5**:155
cryobiology **5**:370
cytology **5**:411–412
ecology **7**:42–46
embryology **7**:153–154
genetics **9**:85–90
gnotobiotics **9**:214
hydrobiology, limnology **12**:345
marine biology **13**:153
microbiology **13**:384
ornithology **14**:447
paleoecology **15**:34–35
paleontology **15**:42
photobiological process **15**:259
photochemistry **15**:259
physiology **15**:287
population biology **15**:438
sociobiology **18**:26–27
speleology **18**:177
zoology **20**:375–378
catastrophe theory **4**:200
cell **4**:231–236
evolution **7**:318–325
exploration **3**:269
fundamental disciplines **3**:268
growth **9**:378–381
habitat **10**:4–6
kinship versus **12**:85–86
life **12**:326–327
nomenclature **3**:269
Linnaeus, Carolus **12**:359
origin and early development **3**:268
osmosis **14**:455
oxidation and reduction **14**:475–476
oxygen **14**:477–478
photobiological processes **15**:259
photosynthesis **15**:275–277
population dynamics **15**:438–439
professional and educational organizations **3**:268; **17**:145 *table*
American Institute of Biological Sciences **1**:341
research institutions
Salk Institute for Biological Studies **17**:34
veterinary medicine **19**:566–567
BIOLOGY, HISTORY OF
Agassiz, Louis Rodolphe **1**:182
Andrews, Roy Chapman **1**:408
Baer, Karl Ernst von **3**:20
Bartram, John **3**:98
Beijerinck, Martinus Willem **3**:172
Britton, Nathaniel **3**:499
Buffon, Georges, Comte de **3**:547
Burroughs, John **3**:580
Commoner, Barry **5**:141
Cope, Edward **5**:248
Cuvier, Georges, Baron **5**:399
Darwin, Charles **6**:41–42
Darwin, Erasmus **6**:42
Darwin, Sir Francis **6**:42
De Beer, Sir Gavin **6**:58
Dean, Bashford **6**:67
Dobzhansky, Theodosius **6**:209–210
Ehrlich, Paul (1932–) **7**:90–91
Fabre, Jean Henri **8**:5
Frisch, Karl von **8**:334
Gesner, Konrad von **9**:159
Gray, Asa **9**:306
Grew, Nehemiah **9**:360
Haeckel, Ernst Heinrich **10**:9
Hales, Stephen **10**:19
Hooker (family) **10**:227
Huxley, Sir Julian **10**:324–325
Huxley, Thomas Henry **10**:325
Lamarck, Jean Baptiste **12**:173–174
Leeuwenhoek, Antoni van **12**:271–272
Linnaeus, Carolus **12**:359
Lysenko, Trofim Denisovich **12**:480
Mayr, Ernst **13**:249
Mendel, Gregor Johann **13**:294
Mohl, Hugo von **13**:503
Pliny the Elder **15**:368
Ray, John **16**:96
Simpson, George Gaylord **17**:317
Spallanzani, Lazzaro **18**:149
Vries, Hugo De **19**:639
BIOLUMINESCENCE **3**:272 *bibliog.*, *illus.*
biopotential **3**:276
bristlemouth **3**:488
chemical reactions, nature of **3**:272
comb jelly **5**:130
deep-sea life **6**:78
firefly **8**:106
glowworm **9**:210
habitat **10**:4
hatchetfish **10**:68 *illus.*
invertebrate **11**:236
krill **12**:129–130
lantern fish **12**:200
phosphor **15**:256
pinecone fish **15**:307
types **3**:272
BIOMASS
synthetic fuels **18**:409–410
BIOMATHEMATICS **3**:272 *bibliog.*
medical research **3**:272
BIOME **3**:272–274 *bibliog.*, *map*
biosphere **3**:276
chaparral **4**:283–284
climatic differences **3**:274
desert **6**:126–129
desert life **6**:129–131
ecology **7**:42
forest **8**:228–229
grasslands **9**:299–301
habitat **10**:4–6
intertidal life **11**:229–230
jungle and rain forest **11**:468–470
mountain life **13**:622–623
North American lake **12**:168 *illus.*
ocean and sea **14**:331
paleogeography **15**:35
plant distribution **15**:343
polar life **3**:273–274
productivity
plant **15**:341 *illus.*
savanna life **17**:97–99
steppe life **18**:256–257
swamp, marsh, and bog **18**:376–378
taiga **19**:11
tundra **19**:332–333
BIOMEDICAL ENGINEERING **3**:274
artificial limbs **2**:221–222
artificial organs **2**:222
bionics **3**:274–275
biotechnology **3**:277
prosthetics **15**:573
rehabilitation medicine **16**:130
BIONICS **3**:274–275 *bibliog.*, *illus.*
cybernetics **5**:401
BIOPHARMACEUTICALS **3**:275 *biolog.*
interferon **11**:210
pharmacy **15**:221
BIOPHYSICS **3**:275 *bibliog.*
BIOPOTENTIAL **3**:275–276 *bibliog.*, *illus.*
bioelectricity **3**:275–276
galvanic skin response **9**:23
muscle contraction **13**:654–656 *illus.*
nervous system **14**:91–92
neurophysiology **14**:105–106
BIOPSY **3**:276 *bibliog.*
cancer **4**:104
BIORHYTHM *see* BIOLOGICAL CLOCK
BIOSATELLITE **3**:276
BIOSENSOR **3**:276
BIOSPHERE **3**:276–277 *bibliog.*
characteristics **3**:276
climate **5**:58
composition **3**:276–277
energy forms in **3**:277
forest **8**:227–230
population dynamics **15**:438
BIOT, JEAN BAPTISTE **3**:277
mathematics, history of **13**:226
mineral **13**:439
optical activity **14**:408
BIOTA
Sargasso Sea **17**:77
BIOTECHNOLOGY **3**:277 *bibliog.*
BIOTIN
Du Vigneaud, Vincent **6**:287
Lynen, Feodor **12**:477
vitamins and minerals **19**:620
BIOTITE *see* MICA
BIOTOXINS
poisonous plants and animals **15**:385
BIPEDALISM *see* BIOLOGICAL LOCOMOTION
BIPLANE **2**:370–371 *illus.*
Curtiss Jenny **5**:395–396 *illus.*
BIPONTIUM *see* ZWEIBRÜCKEN (West Germany)
BIPOTENTIAL
acetylcholine **1**:80
'BIR ES SABA *see* BEERSHEBA (Israel)
BIRAN, MAINE DE *see* MAINE DE BIRAN
BIRATNAGAR (Nepal)
map (26° 29′N 87° 17′E) **14**:86
BIRCH **3**:278 *illus.*
filbert **8**:78
hop hornbeam **10**:230
hornbeam **10**:238
BIRCH, JOHN
John Birch Society **11**:424
BIRCH BARK CANOE **4**:113 *illus.*
BIRCH ISLAND (British Columbia)
map (51° 36′N 119° 55′W) **3**:491
BIRCH LEAF MINER
sawfly **17**:104
BIRCH MOUNTAINS
map (57° 30′N 112° 30′W) **1**:256
BIRCH RIVER (Alberta)
map (58° 30′N 112° 15′W) **1**:256
BIRCH RIVER (Manitoba)
map (52° 23′N 101° 6′W) **13**:119
BIRCH TREE (Missouri)
map (37° 0′N 91° 30′W) **13**:476
BIRCHWOOD (Wisconsin)
map (45° 40′N 91° 33′W) **20**:185
BIRCHY BAY (Newfoundland)
map (49° 21′N 54° 44′W) **14**:166
BIRD **3**:278–290 *bibliog.*, *illus.*
See also names of specific birds, e.g., BLUE JAY; CUCKOO
aging **1**:186
altricial and precocial birds **3**:287
anatomy and physiology **3**:282–285 *illus.*
beak **3**:289 *illus.*
body temperature **3**:357–358 *table*
brain **3**:443 *illus.*
development **6**:138 *illus.*
digestive system **6**:173 *illus.*
eye **3**:285 *illus.*
feather **8**:39–40
foot **3**:288 *illus.*
molting **13**:513
musculoskeletal system **3**:283
oil gland **3**:284
reproduction **3**:284–287
respiratory system **16**:179 *illus.*; **16**:181
skeletal system **17**:334 *illus.*
skin **17**:340 *illus.*
syrinx, larynx **12**:209
uric acid **19**:486
urine **19**:486
wing **3**:283
becard **3**:150 *illus.*
Beebe, Charles W. **3**:159
behavior **2**:11–18
animal migration **2**:27–28; **3**:288–289 *illus.*
courtship and mating **2**:20–22; **3**:284–287 *illus.*
imprinting **11**:68
territoriality **19**:121–122
biological locomotion **3**:266–267 *illus.*
bird-watching **3**:290
birds of prey **3**:290–291
classification, biological **3**:279–281 *illus.*; **10**:221
coloration, biological **5**:122
communication **2**:19 *illus.*; **3**:19 *illus.*
birdsong **3**:291–292
echolocation **7**:39
sound frequencies produced **18**:73 *table*
vocalizations **3**:289
diseases, animal **6**:190
aspergillosis **2**:262
psittacosis **15**:588
diving birds **6**:204–205
endangered species **3**:279–282; **7**:166; **7**:167 *illus.*
flight **3**:282–283 *illus.*
game birds **9**:27
habitats
Antarctic life **2**:42–43
Arctic life **2**:139–142
chaparral **4**:283–284
desert life **6**:129–131
forest **8**:227–228
jungle and rain forest **11**:469 *illus.*
mountain life **13**:623
savanna life **17**:98
steppe life **18**:257
tundra **19**:332
hibernation **10**:156
importance of **3**:289–290
maximum life span for some **12**:330 *table*
nest **3**:286–287 *illus.*
oil-soaked bird **15**:412 *illus.*
ornithology **14**:447
painting
Audubon, John James **2**:318–319
Graves, Morris **9**:302
perching birds **15**:161–162
photography
Porter, Eliot **15**:444
pollination **15**:408–409 *illus.*
poultry **15**:473–475
prehistoric **3**:278–279
Archaeopteryx **2**:127
Hesperornis **10**:151
Ichthyornis **11**:19
La Brea Tar Pit **12**:144
Tertiary Period **19**:124 *illus.*
songbirds **18**:64–65
waterfowl **20**:63
BIRD, JOHN (instrument maker)
quadrant **16**:5
BIRD, JOHN MALCOLM (geologist)
plate tectonics **15**:357
BIRD, LARRY **3**:290
BIRD, ROBERT MONTGOMERY **3**:290 *bibliog.*
BIRD ISLAND
map (3° 43′S 55° 12′E) **17**:232
BIRD-OF-PARADISE FLOWER **3**:290 *illus.*

BIRD OF PARADISE 3:290 *bibliog., illus.*
BIRD SANCTUARY *see* WILDLIFE REFUGE
BIRD IN SPACE (Brancusi) 2:201 *illus.*
BIRD SPIDER *see* TARANTULA
BIRD-WATCHING 3:290 *bibliog.*
BIRD WOMAN *see* SACAGAWEA
BIRD'S-FOOT TREFOIL (botany) *see* LOTUS
BIRD'S NEST FUNGUS 3:290
BIRDS OF PREY 3:290–291 *bibliog., illus.*
buzzard **3**:601
condor **5**:173
eagle **7**:3–4
falcon **8**:12
hawk **10**:76–77
jaeger **11**:348
kite (bird) **12**:91–92
osprey **14**:456
owl **14**:472–473
secretary bird **17**:181
shrike **17**:287
skua **17**:344
vulture **19**:640
BIRDSBORO (Pennsylvania)
map (40° 16′N 75° 48′W) **15**:147
BIRDSEYE, CLARENCE 3:291 *bibliog.*
BIRDSONG 3:291–292 *bibliog.*
animal behavior **2**:13
animal communication **2**:19 *illus.*
bird **3**:289
songbirds **18**:65
BIRDUM (Australia)
map (15° 39′S 133° 13′E) **2**:328
BIREFRINGENCE
polarized light **15**:394
BIRENDRA, KING
Nepal **14**:88
BIRGANJ (Nepal)
map (27° 0′N 84° 52′E) **14**:86
BIRGITTA OF SWEDEN *see* BRIDGET OF SWEDEN, SAINT
BIRJAND (Iran)
map (32° 53′N 59° 13′E) **11**:250
BIRKEN (British Columbia)
map (50° 29′N 122° 36′W) **3**:491
BIRKENHEAD (England)
map (53° 24′N 3° 2′W) **19**:403
BIRKENHEAD (New Zealand)
map (36° 49′S 174° 44′E) **14**:158
BIRKENHEAD, F. E. SMITH, 1ST EARL OF 3:292 *bibliog.*
BIRKERØD (Denmark)
map (55° 50′N 12° 26′E) **6**:109
BIRKHOFF, GEORGE DAVID 3:292
BÎRLAD (Romania)
map (46° 14′N 27° 40′E) **16**:288
BIRLING 3:292
BIRMAN CAT
longhaired cats **12**:408
BIRMINGHAM (Alabama) **1**:236 *illus.*; 3:292
map (33° 31′N 86° 49′W) **1**:234
Southern Christian Leadership Conference **18**:112
BIRMINGHAM (England) 3:292–293
map (52° 30′N 1° 50′W) **19**:403
BIRMINGHAM (Iowa)
map (40° 53′N 91° 57′W) **11**:244
BIRMINGHAM (Michigan)
map (42° 33′N 83° 15′W) **13**:377
BIRMINGHAM, UNIVERSITY OF (England) 3:293
BIRNAMWOOD (Wisconsin)
map (44° 56′N 89° 13′W) **20**:185
BIRNBAUM, NATHAN *see* BURNS AND ALLEN
BIRNEY, EARLE 3:293
BIRNEY, JAMES GILLESPIE 3:293 *bibliog.*
Liberty party **12**:314
BIRNIN KEBBI (Nigeria)
map (12° 32′N 4° 12′E) **14**:190
BIRO, LAZLO
pen **15**:140
BIROUGOU MOUNTAINS
map (1° 51′S 12° 20′E) **9**:5
BIRTH *see* PREGNANCY AND BIRTH
BIRTH OF A NATION (film) **8**:82 *illus.*
BIRTH CONTROL 3:293–295 *bibliog.*
abortion **1**:60
Asia **2**:244
Besant, Annie **3**:228
cervicitis **4**:261–262
Griswold v. *Connecticut* **9**:368
India **11**:85
Malthus, Thomas Robert **13**:96
Planned Parenthood Federation of America **15**:333
population **15**:434; **15**:437
population dynamics **15**:438
pregnancy and birth **15**:502
Sanger, Margaret **17**:64–65
sex education **17**:225–226
sex hormones **17**:226
social issues **3**:294–295
vasectomy **19**:525
BIRTH CONTROL PILLS *see* ORAL CONTRACEPTIVES
BIRTH DEFECTS 3:295 *bibliog.*
amniocentesis **1**:375
blue baby **3**:342
bone diseases **3**:377
cerebral palsy **4**:259–260
cleft lip and palate **5**:48
Down's syndrome **6**:252
genetic diseases **9**:82–84
German measles **9**:134
heart diseases **10**:95
hemophilia **10**:119–120
herpes **10**:145
infectious diseases **11**:166
kidney disease **12**:71
life span **12**:331
nervous system, diseases of the **14**:95
pollutants, chemical **15**:410
Siamese twins **17**:291
sickle-cell anemia **17**:293
speech **18**:175
Tay-Sachs disease **19**:48
thalidomide **19**:142
thymus **19**:187
tongue-tie **19**:234
toxoplasmosis **19**:256
BIRTH OF TRAGEDY, THE (book) 3:295
BIRTH OF VENUS, THE (Sandro Botticelli) **3**:418 *illus.*
BIRTHMARK 3:296
mole (birthmark) **13**:507
BIRTHRATE
population **15**:433–437
BIRTHSTONES 3:296 *bibliog., illus., table*
amethyst **1**:368
aquamarine, beryl **3**:227
bloodstone **3**:296
diamond **6**:151–152
emerald **7**:154
garnet **9**:49
moonstone **13**:567
onyx **14**:396
opal **14**:397
pearl **3**:296
peridot **15**:166
ruby **16**:337
sapphire **17**:73
topaz **19**:236
tourmaline **19**:253
turquoise **19**:352
zircon **20**:370
BIRTLE (Manitoba)
map (50° 25′N 101° 3′W) **13**:119
BIRTWISTLE, HARRISON 3:296
Davies, Peter Maxwell **6**:50
English music **7**:203
BISAYAN 3:297 *bibliog.*
BISBEE (Arizona)
map (31° 27′N 109° 55′W) **2**:160
BISBEE (North Dakota)
map (48° 37′N 99° 23′W) **14**:248
BISCAY, BAY OF 3:297
map (44° 0′N 4° 0′W) **7**:268
BISCAYNE BAY
map (25° 33′N 80° 15′W) **8**:172
BISCHOF, WERNER
photojournalism **15**:273
BISCOE (Arkansas)
map (34° 49′N 91° 24′W) **2**:166
BISECTOR
triangle (mathematics) **19**:292
BISHOP 3:297
ministry, Christian **13**:450
BISHOP (California)
map (37° 22′N 118° 24′W) **4**:31
BISHOP (Texas)
map (27° 35′N 97° 48′W) **19**:129
BISHOP, BRIDGET
Salem Witch Trials **17**:31
BISHOP, ELIZABETH 3:297 *bibliog.*
BISHOP, SIR HENRY ROWLEY 3:297 *bibliog.*
BISHOP, ISABEL 3:297 *bibliog.*
BISHOP, ISABELLA LUCY 3:297
BISHOP, JIM 3:297
BISHOP, JOHN PEALE 3:297 *bibliog.*
BISHOP, MAURICE
Grenada **9**:358
BISHOP'S-CAP 3:297
BISHOPS' WARS 3:298 *bibliog.*
Covenanters **5**:319
BISHOPVILLE (South Carolina)
map (34° 13′N 80° 20′W) **18**:98
BISITUN *see* BEHISTUN (Iran)
BISKRA (Algeria)
map (34° 51′N 5° 44′E) **1**:287
BISMARCK (Missouri)
map (37° 46′N 90° 38′W) **13**:476
BISMARCK (North Dakota) 3:298; **14**:251 *illus.*
map (46° 48′N 100° 47′W) **14**:248
BISMARCK (ship)
World War II **20**:256
BISMARCK, OTTO VON 3:298–299 *bibliog., illus.*; **7**:293 *illus.*; **9**:154 *illus.*
Franco-Prussian War **8**:278–279
Germany, history of **9**:152–154
Holstein, Friedrich von **10**:208
Kulturkampf **12**:136
Moltke, Helmuth Karl Bernhard, Graf von **13**:514
Prussia **15**:586
social security **18**:14
World War I **20**:219
BISMARCK ARCHIPELAGO 3:299
islands and island groups
Admiralty Islands **1**:105
New Britain **14**:115
New Ireland **14**:127
map (5° 0′S 150° 0′E) **15**:72
BISMARCK SEA
map (4° 0′S 148° 0′E) **15**:72
World War II **20**:267
BISMARK PLATE
plate tectonics **15**:351 *map*
BISMUTH 3:299 *bibliog.*
element **7**:130 *table*
Group VA periodic table **15**:167
metal, metallic element **13**:328
native elements **14**:47
BISON 3:299 *illus.*; **9**:300 *illus.*
buffalo **3**:546
Catlin's *Buffalo Chase* **11**:129 *illus.*
Folsom culture **8**:204
fossil bones **14**:237 *illus.*
Montana **13**:548
ox **14**:473
Pleistocene Epoch **15**:366–367 *illus.*
Poundmaker **15**:476
Wichita Mountains Wildlife Refuge **14**:369 *illus.*
BISON (South Dakota)
map (45° 31′N 102° 28′W) **18**:103
BISSAU (Guinea-Bissau) 3:299
map (11° 51′N 15° 35′W) **9**:399
BISSET, JACQUELINE **19**:316 *illus.*
BISSETT (Manitoba)
map (51° 2′N 95° 40′W) **13**:119
BISSON, LOUIS AND AUGUSTE 3:299–300
BISSOT, FRANÇOIS MARIE, SIEUR DE VINCENNES *see* VINCENNES, FRANÇOIS MARIE BISSOT, SIEUR DE
BISTCHO LAKE
map (59° 40′N 118° 40′W) **1**:256
BISTINEAU, LAKE
map (32° 25′N 93° 22′W) **12**:430
BISTRIȚA (Romania)
map (47° 8′N 24° 30′E) **16**:288
BISTRIȚA RIVER
map (46° 30′N 26° 57′E) **16**:288
BISUTUN *see* BEHISTUN
BIT, COMPUTER 3:300
binary number **3**:256
byte **3**:603
computer **5**:160c–160d; **5**:160h
computer memory **5**:161
BITES AND STINGS 3:300 *bibliog.*
See also POISONOUS PLANTS AND ANIMALS
bites
asp **2**:261
black widow **3**:319
centipede **4**:250
cobra **5**:84
death adder **6**:68
Gila monster **9**:178
louse **12**:436
mosquito **13**:602–603
pit viper **15**:319
rat **16**:91–92
rattlesnake **16**:93–94
tick **19**:191–192
tsetse fly **19**:323
viper **19**:604
water moccasin **20**:49
diseases
Colorado tick fever **5**:121
filariasis **8**:78
infectious diseases **11**:164–168
malaria **13**:80
Q fever **16**:3
rabies **16**:32
relapsing fever **16**:132
river blindness **16**:232
Rocky Mountain spotted fever **16**:261
scarlet fever **17**:115
trench fever **19**:290
trypanosomiasis **19**:322
typhoid fever **19**:366
yellow fever **20**:322
stings
jellyfish **11**:395
Portuguese man-of-war **15**:457
scorpion **17**:148
scorpion fish **17**:148
stingray **18**:272
types **3**:300
BITHYNIA 3:300 *bibliog.*
Nicaea **14**:178
BITOLA (Yugoslavia)
map (41° 1′N 21° 20′E) **20**:340
BITTEL, KURT
Boğazköy **3**:360
BITTER LAKE
map (45° 17′N 97° 19′W) **18**:103
BITTERFELD (Germany, East and West)
map (51° 37′N 12° 20′E) **9**:140
BITTERN 3:300–301 *illus.*
heron **10**:145
BITTERROOT (botany) 3:301
BITTERROOT RANGE **13**:548 *illus.*
map (47° 6′N 115° 10′W) **11**:26
BITTERROOT RIVER
map (46° 52′N 114° 6′W) **13**:547
BITTERS (beverage) 3:301
BITTERSWEET (botany) 3:301 *illus.*
nightshade **14**:194
BITUMINOUS COAL 3:301
coal and coal mining **5**:76
heat content **8**:353 *table*
Illinois **11**:43
Kentucky **12**:48
sedimentary rock **17**:184–186
BITZIUS, ALBERT *see* GOTTHELF, JEREMIAS
BIVALVE 3:301 *bibliog.*; **13**:510 *illus.*
clam **5**:85
cockle **5**:87
mollusk **13**:510–511
Ordovician Period **14**:422 *illus.*
oyster **14**:479
piddock **15**:294
scallop **17**:107
shell **17**:252 *illus.*
shipworm **17**:277
Silurian Period **17**:310 *illus.*
Triassic Period **19**:293 *illus.*
BIWA LAKE
map (35° 15′N 136° 5′E) **11**:361
BIXBY (Oklahoma)
map (35° 57′N 95° 53′W) **14**:368
BIXBYITE
oxide minerals **14**:476
BIYA, PAUL
Cameroon **4**:61
BIYIDI, ALEXANDRE *see* BETI, MONGO
BIYSK (USSR)
map (52° 34′N 85° 15′E) **19**:388
BIZERTE (Tunisia) 3:301
map (37° 17′N 9° 52′E) **19**:335
BIZET, GEORGES 3:301–302 *bibliog., illus.*
Carmen **4**:153
BJERKNES, VILHELM AND JACOB 3:302
BJÖRLING, JUSSI 3:302
BJØRNSON, BJØRNSTJERNE 3:302–303 *bibliog., illus.*; **14**:265 *illus.*
BJØRNVIG, THORKILD 3:303
BL LACERTAE OBJECTS 3:303
radio astronomy **16**:50
radio galaxies **16**:54
BLACK, DAVIDSON 3:303
Peking man **15**:136
BLACK, HAROLD 3:303
BLACK, HUGO L. 3:303 *bibliog.*; **12**:246 *illus.*
Korematsu v. *United States* **12**:122
Supreme Court of the United States **18**:357
Welsh v. *United States* **20**:102
Youngstown Sheet and Tube Company v. *Sawyer* **20**:337
BLACK, JEREMIAH SULLIVAN 3:303 *bibliog.*
BLACK, JOSEPH 3:303 *bibliog.*
chemistry, history of **4**:325
Watt, James **20**:68
BLACK, MAX 3:303
BLACK AMERICAN LITERATURE 3:303–304 *bibliog.*; 3:311–312
authors
Angelou, Maya **1**:414
Baldwin, James **3**:35
Baraka, Imamu Amiri **3**:75
Bontemps, Arna **3**:382
Brooks, Gwendolyn **3**:511
Brown, Claude **3**:513
Brown, Sterling **3**:516
Bullins, Ed **3**:561
Chesnutt, Charles Waddell **4**:334

BLACK AMERICAN LITERATURE (cont.)
Cleaver, Eldridge 5:47–48
Cullen, Countee 5:384
Davis, Frank Marshall 6:51
Dodson, Owen 6:212
Dumas, Henry 6:297
Dunbar, Paul Laurence 6:298
Ellison, Ralph 7:148
Fisher, Rudolph 8:123
Giovanni, Nikki 9:188
Haley, Alex 10:19
Hansberry, Lorraine 10:40
Hughes, Langston 10:293
Johnson, Fenton 11:432
Jordan, June 11:450
Kelley, William Melvin 11:38
Locke, Alain 11:387
McKay, Claude 13:27
Major, Clarence 13:77
Marshall, Paule 13:173
Mayfield, Julian 13:246
Morrison, Toni 13:589
Murray, Pauli 13:650
Sanchez, Sonia 17:58
Tolson, M. B. 19:227
Toomer, Jean 19:236
Walker, Alice 20:12
Walker, Margaret 20:12
Washington, Booker T. 20:39
Wheatley, Phillis 20:126
Williams, John A. 20:159
Wright, Richard 20:290–291
Harlem Renaissance 10:50
BLACK AMERICANS 3:304–313 *bibliog., illus., maps, table*
See also BLACK AMERICAN LITERATURE; CIVIL RIGHTS; INTEGRATION, RACIAL; names of specific people, e.g., KING, MARTIN LUTHER, JR.; JACKSON, JESSE L.; etc.;
American Colonization Society 1:338
Black Muslims 3:317–318
black nationalism 3:318
Black Panther party 3:318
culture today 3:311–313
education 3:312–313
black colleges 3:314
Central High School (Little Rock, Ark.) 3:310 *illus.*
Up from Slavery 19:471
employment and unemployment 7:159–160
family 3:312
feminism 8:49
folk medicine 8:201
Harlem 10:49–50
historians *see* HISTORY—Black American historians
history 3:305–311 *illus., map*
Civil War, U.S. 5:33
Jim Crow laws 11:418
lynching 12:477
race riots 16:35
Reconstruction 16:108–110
United States, history of the 19:452; 19:457; 19:459
hypertension 10:349
military services
54th Massachusetts Colored Regiment 3:307 *illus.*
music 3:311–312
American music 1:351
gospel music 9:253–254
jazz 11:387–390
Motown 13:616
music hall, vaudeville, and burlesque 13:671 *illus.*
rhythm and blues 16:204–205
soul music 18:71
spirituals 18:189
National Association for the Advancement of Colored People 14:29
population 3:304–305 *maps, table*
Creoles 5:338
migrations from the South 3:305 *map*
mulatto 13:635
North America 14:232
press 3:313
Ebony 7:36
Essence 7:244
race 16:34 *illus.*
racism 16:37
religion 3:307; 3:312
"Roots" (television miniseries)
radio and television broadcasting 16:59
sickle-cell anemia 17:293
SNCC 17:384
sociolinguistics 18:27–28
Southern Christian Leadership Conference 18:112
sports 3:313
Urban League, National 19:480
BLACK-AND-TAN COONHOUND 3:319 *illus.*; 6:216 *illus.*
BLACK BART
outlaws 14:468 *illus.*
BLACK BEAUTY (book) 3:313
Sewell, Anna 17:221
BLACK BUTTE
map (44° 54′N 111° 51′W) 13:547
BLACK CODES 3:313–314 *bibliog.*
Freedmen's Bureau 8:295
BLACK COLLEGES 3:314 *bibliog.*
Fisk University 8:129
Hampton University 10:33
Howard University 10:283
land-grant colleges 12:178
Lincoln University 12:350
Morehouse College 13:577
Spelman College 18:177
Talladega College 19:16
Tuskegee Institute 19:355
United Negro College Fund 19:415
United States, education in the 19:434–435
university 19:469
BLACK COMMUNITY DEVELOPMENT AND DEFENSE ORGANIZATION
Baraka, Imamu Amiri 3:75
BLACK CREEK
map (34° 18′N 79° 37′W) 18:98
BLACK CROOK, THE (play)
musical comedy 13:674
BLACK DEATH (epidemic)
bubonic plague 3:532
Death, Dance of 6:68
Europe, history of 7:285
Florence (Italy) 8:168
infectious diseases 11:164
population 15:433
rat 16:91
BLACK DIAMOND (Washington)
map (47° 18′N 122° 0′W) 20:35
BLACK DWARF 3:314
stellar evolution 18:251
BLACK EAGLE (Montana)
map (47° 31′N 111° 17′W) 13:547
BLACK ENGLISH *see* SOCIOLINGUISTICS
BLACK-EYED PEA *see* COWPEA
BLACK-EYED SUSAN (botany) 3:314–315 *illus.*
BLACK-FIGURE VASES 9:338 *illus.*
Greek art 9:339
BLACK FLY
river blindness 16:232
BLACK FOREST (Colorado)
map (38° 52′N 104° 49′W) 5:116
BLACK FOREST (Germany) 3:315; 9:141 *illus.*
BLACK FOREST MOUNTAINS
map (48° 0′N 8° 15′E) 9:140
BLACK FRIDAY 3:315
Fisk, James 8:128
Gould, Jay 9:265
BLACK HAND 3:315 *bibliog.*
BLACK HAWK (Indian chief)
Black Hawk War 3:315
BLACK HAWK (county in Iowa)
map (42° 30′N 92° 18′W) 11:244
BLACK HAWK WAR 3:315 *bibliog.*; 11:109 *map*
Sauk 17:96
Wabansi 20:3
BLACK HILLS 3:315
Little Bighorn, Battle of the 12:372
map (44° 0′N 104° 0′W) 18:103
mountain 13:619
passion play 15:105
Rushmore, Mount 16:348
South Dakota 18:102 *illus.*
BLACK HOLE (astronomy) 3:315–316 *bibliog., illus.*
Chandrasekhar, Subrahmanyan 4:280
Chandrasekhar limit 4:280
concept 3:315
degenerate matter 6:85
gravitational collapse 9:305
gravitational waves 9:306
Hawking, Stephen William 10:77
neutron star 14:109
observable 3:315
relativity 16:136 *illus.*
Schwarzschild, Karl 17:139
Schwarzschild radius 17:139
sizes 3:315–316
stellar evolution 18:251
temperature 3:316
X-ray astronomy 20:306 *illus.*
BLACK HOLE OF CALCUTTA 3:316
BLACK HUMOR 3:316
Donleavy, J. P. 6:238–239
BLACK KETTLE (Indian chief) 3:316–317 *bibliog.*
Custer, George Armstrong 5:397
BLACK LAKE
map (45° 28′N 84° 15′W) 13:377
BLACK LARCH *see* TAMARACK
BLACK LIGHT
ultraviolet light 19:379
BLACK LUNG 3:317 *bibliog.*
coal and coal mining 5:79
dust, atmospheric 6:308
respiratory system disorders 16:181
BLACK MADONNA
Częstochowa 5:416
BLACK MAMBA 13:96 *illus.*
BLACK MARKET 3:317
BLACK MASK (periodical)
pulp magazines 15:620
BLACK MASS 3:317
satanism 17:84
BLACK MESA (Arizona)
map (36° 35′N 110° 20′W) 2:160
BLACK MESA (Oklahoma)
map (36° 57′N 102° 59′W) 14:368
BLACK MINQUA *see* ERIE (American Indians)
BLACK MOUNTAIN (Kentucky)
map (36° 54′N 82° 54′W) 12:47
BLACK MOUNTAIN (North Carolina)
map (35° 37′N 82° 19′W) 14:242
BLACK MOUNTAIN SCHOOL OF POETRY 3:317 *bibliog.*
Creeley, Robert 5:337
Levertov, Denise 12:303
BLACK MOUNTAINS (Arizona)
map (35° 30′N 114° 30′W) 2:160
BLACK MOUNTAINS (North Carolina) 3:317
Mitchell, Mount 13:483
BLACK MUSLIMS 3:317–318 *bibliog., illus.*
Ali, Muhammad 1:292
black nationalism 3:318
Malcolm X 13:86
Muhammad, Elijah 13:633
BLACK NATIONALISM 3:318 *bibliog.*
Baraka, Imamu Amiri 3:75
black American literature 3:304
Congress of Racial Equality 5:184
Delany, Martin R. 6:87
Garvey, Marcus 9:52
Malcolm X 13:86
BLACK PANTHER (zoology)
leopard 12:292
BLACK PANTHER PARTY 3:318 *bibliog.*
BLACK POWDER *see* GUNPOWDER
BLACK PRINCE, THE *see* EDWARD, THE BLACK PRINCE
BLACK RACER *see* RACER (snake)
BLACK RIVER (Arizona)
map (33° 44′N 110° 13′W) 2:160
BLACK RIVER (Arkansas)
map (35° 38′N 91° 19′W) 2:166
BLACK RIVER (Louisiana)
map (31° 16′N 91° 50′W) 12:430
BLACK RIVER (Michigan)
map (43° 0′N 82° 25′W) 13:377
BLACK RIVER (New York)
map (43° 59′N 76° 4′W) 14:149
BLACK RIVER (Wisconsin)
map (43° 57′N 91° 22′W) 20:185
BLACK RIVER FALLS (Wisconsin)
map (44° 23′N 90° 52′W) 20:185
BLACK ROCK (Arkansas)
map (36° 6′N 91° 6′W) 2:166
BLACK ROCK DESERT
map (41° 10′N 119° 0′W) 14:111
BLACK SEA 3:318–319 *bibliog., map*
Crimea (USSR) 5:347–348 *map*
map (43° 0′N 35° 0′E) 19:388
Russo-Turkish Wars 16:374
seas, gulfs, and bays
Azov, Sea of 2:382
Bosporus 3:407 *map*
Dardanelles 6:37 *map*
Marmara, Sea of 13:161
BLACK STONE (Islam)
Mecca (Saudi Arabia) 13:258 *illus.*
BLACK SUGAR *see* LICORICE
BLACK SWALLOWER (fish) 8:121 *illus.*
BLACK AND TANS 3:319
BLACK VOLTA RIVER
map (8° 41′N 1° 33′W) 9:164
BLACK WARRIOR (ship)
Ostend Manifesto 14:457
BLACK WARRIOR RIVER
map (32° 32′N 87° 51′W) 1:234
BLACK WIDOW 3:319 *bibliog., illus.*
BLACKBEARD 3:319 *bibliog.*
piracy 15:313 *illus.*
BLACKBERRY 3:320 *illus.*; 8:348 *illus.*
BLACKBIRD 3:320 *illus.*
bobolink 3:352
cacique 4:8
cowbird 5:320
grackle 9:276
meadowlark 13:252
BLACKBOARD JUNGLE, THE (book)
Hunter, Evan 10:312
BLACKBODY RADIATION 3:320–321 *bibliog., illus.*
astronomy and astrophysics 2:285
candela 4:106
color index 5:114
history 3:320
Jeans, Sir James 11:390
Kirchhoff, Gustav Robert 12:87
light 12:335
Planck, Max 15:326
Planck's constant 15:327
quantum mechanics 16:9
radio astronomy 16:50
Rayleigh, Lord 16:97
Stefan, Josef 18:245
Wien, Wilhelm Jan 20:146
BLACKBURN (England)
map (53° 45′N 2° 29′W) 19:403
BLACKBURN, MOUNT
map (61° 44′N 143° 26′W) 1:242
BLACKDUCK (Minnesota)
map (47° 44′N 94° 33′W) 13:453
BLACKETT, PATRICK MAYNARD STUART, BARON BLACKETT 3:321
BLACKFOOT (American Indians) 3:321 *bibliog.*
Crowfoot 5:363
Gros Ventres 9:370
Indians of North America, art of the 11:141
medicine man 11:123 *illus.*
Sioux 17:326
tepee 19:114
BLACKFOOT (Idaho)
map (43° 11′N 112° 20′W) 11:26
BLACKFOOT (Montana)
map (48° 34′N 112° 52′W) 13:547
BLACKFOOT RESERVOIR
map (42° 55′N 111° 35′W) 11:26
BLACKFOOT RIVER
map (46° 52′N 113° 53′W) 13:547
BLACKFORD (county in Indiana)
map (40° 27′N 85° 22′W) 11:111
BLACKFRIARS
Chamberlain's Men 4:274
BLACKJACK (card game) 3:321
BLACKLIST 3:321 *bibliog.*
boycott 3:433
film industry 8:89
Hollywood Ten, The 10:204
Hutchins, Robert M. 10:322
Losey, Joseph 12:418
Mostel, Zero 13:605
radio and television broadcasting 16:57
BLACKMAIL 3:321
BLACKMAN, VERNON HERBERT
biology 3:270
BLACKMORE, RICHARD DODDRIDGE 3:321
BLACKMUN, HARRY A. 3:322; 18:355 *illus.*
Roe v. *Wade* and *Doe* v. *Bolton* 16:267–268
BLACKOUT, ELECTRICAL 3:322
major occurrences 3:322
BLACKPOOL (England) 3:322
map (53° 50′N 3° 3′W) 19:403
BLACKS FORK RIVER
map (41° 24′N 109° 38′W) 20:301
BLACKS HARBOUR (New Brunswick) 14:117 *illus.*
map (45° 3′N 66° 47′W) 14:117
BLACKSBURG (South Carolina)
map (35° 7′N 81° 31′W) 18:98
BLACKSBURG (Virginia)
map (37° 14′N 80° 25′W) 19:607
BLACKSHEAR (Georgia)
map (31° 18′N 82° 14′W) 9:114
BLACKSHEAR, LAKE
map (31° 56′N 83° 56′W) 9:114
BLACKSHIRTS 3:322
Himmler, Heinrich 10:168
Hitler, Adolf 10:187
BLACKSMITH 3:322 *bibliog.*; 13:330 *illus.*
shop 8:232 *illus.*
BLACKSTONE (Massachusetts)
map (42° 1′N 71° 30′W) 13:206
BLACKSTONE (Virginia)
map (37° 4′N 78° 0′W) 19:607
BLACKSTONE, SIR WILLIAM 3:322 *bibliog.*
common law 5:140
law, history of 12:246 *illus.*
BLACKSTONE RIVER
map (41° 52′N 71° 23′W) 13:206
BLACKVILLE (South Carolina)
map (33° 22′N 81° 16′W) 18:98

BLACKWATER RESERVOIR
map (43° 22′N 71° 45′W) **14**:123
BLACKWATER RIVER
map (51° 51′N 7° 50′W) **11**:258
BLACKWELL (family) **3**:322–323 *bibliog.*
BLACKWELL (Oklahoma)
map (36° 48′N 97° 17′W) **14**:368
BLACKWELL, ALICE STONE
Blackwell (family) **3**:323
BLACKWELL, ANTOINETTE LOUISA BROWN
Blackwell (family) **3**:323
BLACKWELL, ELIZABETH
Blackwell (family) **3**:322–323
BLACKWELL, HENRY BROWN
Blackwell (family) **3**:323
BLACKWOOD, FREDERICK TEMPLE HAMILTON-TEMPLE-, 1ST MARQUESS OF DUFFERIN AND AVA *see* DUFFERIN AND AVA, FREDERICK TEMPLE HAMILTON-TEMPLE-BLACKWOOD, 1ST MARQUESS OF
BLADDER, URINARY **1**:54 *illus.* **3**:323 *bibliog.*; **7**:328 *illus.*; **12**:72 *illus.*; **16**:163 *illus.*
bed-wetting **3**:153
diseases
cystitis **5**:411
kidney disease **12**:72
trichomoniasis **19**:296
examination, medical **7**:326
urethra **19**:486
BLADDERNUT (botany) **3**:323
BLADDERWORT (botany) **3**:323 *illus.*
BLADE TOOLS
Paleolithic Period **15**:40
BLADEN (county in North Carolina)
map (34° 40′N 78° 35′W) **14**:242
BLADENBORO (North Carolina)
map (34° 33′N 78° 48′W) **14**:242
BLAEU, WILLEM
geography **9**:102 *illus.*
BLAGOEVGRAD (Bulgaria)
map (42° 1′N 23° 6′E) **3**:555
BLAGOVESCHENSK (USSR)
map (50° 17′N 127° 32′E) **19**:388
BLAINE (county in Idaho)
map (43° 25′N 113° 55′W) **11**:26
BLAINE (county in Montana)
map (48° 25′N 108° 55′W) **13**:547
BLAINE (county in Nebraska)
map (41° 55′N 100° 0′W) **14**:70
BLAINE (county in Oklahoma)
map (35° 55′N 98° 25′W) **14**:368
BLAINE, JAMES GILLESPIE **3**:323–324 *bibliog., illus.*
Ingersoll, Robert Green **11**:176
mugwumps **13**:632
Republican party **16**:173
BLAIR (family) **3**:324 *bibliog.*
BLAIR (Nebraska)
map (41° 33′N 96° 8′W) **14**:70
BLAIR (county in Pennsylvania)
map (40° 30′N 78° 25′W) **15**:147
BLAIR, ERIC ARTHUR *see* ORWELL, GEORGE
BLAIR, FRANCIS PRESTON
Blair (family) **3**:324
BLAIR, FRANCIS PRESTON, JR.
Blair (family) **3**:324
BLAIR, JAMES **3**:324 *bibliog.*
BLAIR, MONTGOMERY
Blair (family) **3**:324
Postal Union, Universal **15**:461
BLAIRSVILLE (Georgia)
map (34° 53′N 83° 58′W) **9**:114
BLAIRSVILLE (Pennsylvania)
map (40° 26′N 79° 16′W) **15**:147
BLAIS, MARIE CLAIRE **3**:324 *bibliog.*
Canadian literature **4**:93–94 *illus.*
BLAIZE, HERBERT A.
Grenada **9**:358
BLAKE, EDWARD **3**:324
BLAKE, EUBIE **3**:324 *bibliog.*
BLAKE, EUGENE CARSON **3**:324
BLAKE, HECTOR "TOE" *see* BLAKE, TOE
BLAKE, NICHOLAS (pseudonym) *see* LEWIS, C. DAY
BLAKE, PETER (architect) **3**:325
BLAKE, PETER (painter) **3**:325 *bibliog.*
pop art **15**:429
BLAKE, ROBERT **3**:325 *bibliog.*
BLAKE, TOE **3**:325
BLAKE, WILLIAM **3**:325–326 *bibliog., illus.*; **7**:196 *illus.*
Jacob's Ladder **6**:266 *illus.*; **16**:291 *illus.*
Songs of Innocence and of Experience **18**:65
BLAKE ISLAND
map (47° 32′N 122° 30′W) **20**:35
BLAKELOCK, RALPH ALBERT **3**:326 *bibliog., illus.*
Moonlight Sonata **3**:326 *illus.*
BLAKELY (Georgia)
map (31° 23′N 84° 56′W) **9**:114
BLAKESLEE, ALBERT FRANCIS
fungi **8**:366
BLAMAN, ANNA (pseudonym) *see* VRUGHT, JOHANNA PETRONELLA
BLANC, CAPE
map (37° 20′N 9° 50′E) **19**:335
BLANC, LOUIS **3**:326 *bibliog.*
socialism **18**:20
BLANC, MONT **3**:326
map (45° 50′N 6° 52′E) **18**:394
mountain climbing **13**:621 *illus.*
tunnel **19**:337 *table*
BLANC SABLON (Quebec)
map (51° 25′N 57° 7′W) **16**:18
BLANCA (Colorado)
map (37° 27′N 105° 31′W) **5**:116
BLANCA BAY
map (38° 55′S 62° 10′W) **2**:149
BLANCHARD (Oklahoma)
map (35° 8′N 97° 39′W) **14**:368
BLANCHARD, DOC **3**:326–327
BLANCHARD, FELIX "DOC" *see* BLANCHARD, DOC
BLANCHARD, JEAN **3**:327
BLANCHARD, THOMAS **19**:450 *illus.*
BLANCHARD RIVER
map (41° 2′N 84° 18′W) **14**:357
BLANCHE, JACQUES ÉMILE
Paul, Valéry **19**:506 *illus.*
BLANCHE OF CASTILE **3**:327
Louis IX, King of France **12**:424
BLANCHESTER (Ohio)
map (39° 17′N 83° 55′W) **14**:357
BLANCHISSEUSE (Trinidad and Tobago)
map (10° 47′N 61° 18′W) **19**:300
BLANCO (Texas)
map (30° 6′N 98° 25′W) **19**:129
BLANCO (county in Texas)
map (30° 15′N 98° 25′W) **19**:129
BLANCO, ANTONIO GUZMÁN *see* GUZMÁN BLANCO, ANTONIO
BLANCO, CAPE
map (42° 50′N 124° 34′W) **14**:427
BLAND (Virginia)
map (37° 6′N 81° 7′W) **19**:607
BLAND (county in Virginia)
map (37° 40′N 81° 5′W) **19**:607
BLAND, BOBBY
soul music **18**:71
BLAND-ALLISON ACT **3**:327
BLANDA, GEORGE **3**:327
BLANDING (Utah)
map (37° 37′N 109° 29′W) **19**:429
BLANFORD, HENRY FRANCIS
paleogeography **15**:36
BLANK VERSE **3**:327
Browning, Elizabeth Barrett **3**:518
Eliot, T. S. **7**:139–140
Frost, Robert **8**:345–346
Marlowe, Christopher **13**:161
Shakespeare, William **17**:237
Surrey, Henry Howard, Earl of **18**:366
Thomson, James **19**:175
versification **19**:562
BLANKERS-KOEN, FANNY **3**:327
BLANKET FLOWER **3**:327
BLANQUART-EVRARD, LOUIS DÉSIRÉE **3**:327
albumen print **1**:261
BLANQUI, LOUIS AUGUSTE **3**:327 *bibliog.*
socialism **18**:19
syndicalism **18**:407
BLANSHARD, BRAND **3**:327–328
BLANTYRE (Malawi) **3**:328
map (15° 47′S 35° 0′E) **13**:81
BLARNEY STONE **3**:328
BLASCO-IBÁÑEZ, VICENTE **3**:328
BLASHFIELD, EDWIN HOWLAND **3**:328 *bibliog.*
BLASHKI, PHILIP *see* EVERGOOD, PHILIP
BLASKÓ, BÉLA *see* LUGOSI, BELA
BLAST FURNACE **3**:328 *bibliog.*
fuel, coke **5**:96
furnace **8**:372
iron and steel industry **11**:274
technology, history of **19**:65
Wilkinson, John **20**:153
BLASTEMA
regeneration **16**:127
BLASTING *see* DEMOLITION
BLASTOCYST (embryology)
development **6**:140
BLASTOID **3**:328 *bibliog.*
BLASTOMERE (embryology)
development **6**:137–138; **6**:140
BLASTOMYCOSIS
respiratory system disorders **16**:181
BLASTULA (embryology)
development **6**:137; **6**:138 *illus.*; **6**:140
BLATCH, HARRIOT EATON STANTON **3**:328
BLAUE REITER, DER (art group) **3**:328–329 *bibliog., illus.*
Campendonk, Heinrich **4**:66
expressionism (art) **7**:340
Kandinsky, Wassily **12**:13–14
Klee, Paul **12**:95
Kubin, Alfred **12**:134
Macke, August **13**:27
Marc, Franz **13**:145
Munch, Edvard **13**:640
Münter, Gabriele **13**:644
BLAVATSKY, HELENA PETROVNA **3**:329 *bibliog.*
theosophy **19**:159–160
BLAXLAND, GREGORY
Great Dividing Range **9**:319
BLAZING STAR (botany) **3**:329
BLAZON
heraldry **10**:132
BLEACHES AND BRIGHTENERS **3**:329 *bibliog., illus.*
chlorine
Berthollet, Claude Louis, Comte de **3**:226
chlorine compounds **4**:400
manganese **13**:114
modifiers, bromine **3**:502
paper **15**:68
peroxide **15**:177
Weldon, Walter **20**:97
BLEAK HOUSE (book)
Dickens, Charles **6**:157
BLECKLEY (county in Georgia)
map (32° 25′N 83° 20′W) **9**:114
BLED, LAKE **20**:341 *illus.*
BLEDSOE (county in Tennessee)
map (35° 35′N 85° 15′W) **19**:104
BLEDSOE (Texas)
map (33° 38′N 103° 1′W) **19**:129
BLEECK, OLIVER (pseudonym) *see* THOMAS, ROSS
BLEEDING *see* BLOODLETTING; HEMORRHAGE
BLEEDING HEART (botany) **3**:329–330 *illus.*
BLEGEN, CARL W.
Pylos **15**:634
Troy (archaeological site) **19**:312–313
BLENHEIM (New Zealand)
map (41° 31′S 173° 57′E) **14**:158
BLENHEIM, BATTLE OF **3**:330
Spanish Succession, War of the **18**:162 *map*
BLENHEIM PALACE **3**:330 *bibliog.*
landscape architecture **12**:187 *illus.*
Vanbrugh, Sir John **19**:516–517
BLENNERHASSETT, HARMAN **3**:330
BLENNY **3**:330 *bibliog., illus.*
BLEPHARISMA **3**:330
BLEPHARITIS **3**:330
BLEPHAROPLASTY
plastic surgery **15**:347
BLÉRANCOURT, CHÂTEAU DE
Brosse, Salomon de **3**:512
château **4**:302
BLÉRIOT, LOUIS **3**:330–331
BLESBOK **3**:331 *illus.*
BLEULER, EUGEN **3**:331
schizophrenia **17**:124
BLICHER, STEEN STEENSEN **3**:331 *bibliog.*
BLIDA (Algeria)
map (36° 28′N 2° 50′E) **1**:287
BLIGH, WILLIAM **3**:331 *bibliog.*
Bounty (ship) **3**:422
Tahiti (French Polynesia) **19**:10
BLIGHT
diseases, plant **6**:194
BLIMP *see* AIRSHIP
BLIND, EDUCATION OF THE **3**:331–332 *bibliog.*
Braille, Louis **3**:442
braille system **3**:442
guide dog **9**:394
special education **18**:166–167
BLIND ORATOR, THE *see* GORE, THOMAS P.
BLIND RIVER (Ontario)
map (46° 10′N 82° 58′W) **14**:393
BLIND SNAKE **3**:332
BLINDFISH **3**:332
BLINDNESS **3**:332–333 *bibliog., illus.*
echolocation **7**:39
glaucoma **9**:205
Mace **13**:14
night blindness
vitamin A deficiency, vitamins and minerals **19**:619
Wald, George **20**:9
BLINDSPOT
eye **7**:348–349 *illus.*
BLINK MICROSCOPE **3**:333
comparator **5**:155
Kowal, Charles T. **12**:126
BLISH, JAMES **3**:333
BLISS, SIR ARTHUR **3**:333
BLISS, LILLIE P.
Museum of Modern Art **13**:657
BLITAR (Indonesia)
map (8° 6′S 112° 9′E) **11**:147
BLITHE SPIRIT (play)
Coward, Sir Noel **5**:320
radio and television broadcasting **16**:58 *illus.*
BLITZKRIEG **3**:333 *bibliog.*
Britain, Battle of **3**:488–489
Germany, history of **9**:155
Guderian, Heinz **9**:390
Hitler, Adolf **10**:188
strategy and tactics, military **18**:291
World War II **20**:251–252
BLITZSTEIN, MARC **3**:333
BLIXEN, KAREN *see* DINESEN, ISAK
BLIZZARD **3**:333 *bibliog.*
BLOCH, ERNEST (composer) **3**:333 *bibliog.*
BLOCH, ERNST (philosopher) **3**:334
BLOCH, FELIX **3**:334
BLOCH, KONRAD **3**:334
Lynen, Feodor **12**:477
BLOCH, MARC **3**:334
history **10**:185
BLOCK, ADRIAEN **3**:334
Connecticut River **5**:196
Rhode Island **16**:201
BLOCK, HERBERT LAWRENCE *see* HERBLOCK
BLOCK GRANTS *see* REVENUE SHARING
BLOCK ISLAND
map (41° 11′N 71° 35′W) **16**:198
BLOCK ISLAND (Rhode Island)
map (41° 10′N 71° 34′W) **16**:198
BLOCK ISLAND SOUND
map (41° 10′N 71° 45′W) **16**:198
BLOCK PRINTING **3**:334
graphic arts **9**:291–292
BLOCK AND TACKLE *see* PULLEY
BLOCKADE **3**:334
right of search **16**:222
strategy and tactics, military **18**:291
BLOEMFONTEIN (South Africa) **3**:334–335
map (29° 12′S 26° 7′E) **18**:79
BLOIS (France)
map (47° 35′N 1° 20′E) **8**:260
BLOIS, CHÂTEAU DE **3**:335 *bibliog.*
BLOK, ALEKSANDR ALEKSANDROVICH **3**:335 *bibliog.*
BLONDEL, MAURICE **3**:335
BLONDEL, NICOLAS FRANÇOIS
Chalgrin, Jean François Thérèse **4**:271
BLONDEL DE NESLE **3**:335
BLONDIE (comic strip) **5**:135 *illus.*
Young, Chic **20**:333
BLOOD **3**:335–338 *bibliog., illus.*
antibody **2**:59–60
anticoagulant **2**:60
antigen **2**:61
antitoxin **2**:69
artificial organs **2**:222
Basques **3**:116
biological locomotion **3**:265
blood bank **3**:338
blood substitutes **3**:338; **3**:339
blood tests **3**:339
blood transfusion **3**:339
buffer **3**:547
cell **3**:335–336 *illus.*; **4**:235 *illus.*; **9**:89 *illus.*
aging **1**:185
bone **3**:377
development **6**:139
Legionnaires' disease **12**:274
Swammerdam, Jan **18**:376
circulation
artery **2**:213–214
blood pressure **3**:339
circulatory system **4**:438–442 *illus.*
Harvey, William **10**:65
kidneys **12**:73
liver **12**:374–375
lymphatic system **12**:475–476
respiratory system **16**:178–179
vein **19**:536
diseases
agranulocytosis **1**:188
anemia **1**:409–410

BLOOD (cont.)
arteriosclerosis **2**:213
asphyxia **2**:262
atherosclerosis **2**:291–292
Cooley's anemia **5**:240
cyanosis **5**:400
embolism **7**:152
erythema **7**:236
hemophilia **10**:119–120
hemorrhage **10**:120
hypoglycemia **10**:351
immunodeficiency disease **11**:59–60
infarction **11**:164
infectious diseases **11**:165–166
inflammation **11**:169
jaundice **11**:385
leukemia **12**:300–301
leukocytosis **12**:301
leukopenia **12**:301
methemoglobinemia **13**:343
mononucleosis **13**:537
multiple myeloma **13**:638
phlebitis **15**:248
polycythemia **15**:418
puerperal fever **15**:614
purpura **15**:630
septicemia **17**:206
shock, physiologic **17**:278–279
sickle-cell anemia **17**:293
splenomegaly **18**:191
tetany **19**:127
thrombosis **19**:183
uremia **19**:485
electrophoresis **7**:126
hematology **10**:117
hemoglobin **10**:119
heparin **10**:130
Hoppe-Seyler, Felix **10**:232
immunology **11**:60
insulin **11**:197–198
Landsteiner, Karl **12**:193
parathyroid **15**:83
race **16**:35
Rh factor **16**:192
serum **17**:210
albumin **1**:261
genetic engineering **9**:84
globulin **9**:209
Tiselius, Arne Wilhelm Kaurin **19**:209
space medicine **18**:133
tissue, animal **19**:210
type B, world distribution **9**:89 *map*
urea **19**:485
vitamins and minerals **19**:619
BLOOD (American Indians)
Blackfoot **3**:321
BLOOD, SWEAT AND TEARS (rock group)
rock music **16**:248
BLOOD BANK **3**:338 *bibliog.*
blood tests **3**:339
surgery **18**:362
BLOOD-BRAIN BARRIER
meningitis **13**:298
BLOOD CLOTTING
anticoagulant **2**:60
aspirin **2**:263
blood **3**:337
cardiovascular diseases **4**:145
Dam, Carl Henrik **6**:18
embolism **7**:152
pulmonary embolism **15**:619
Vitamin K **19**:619
BLOOD COUNT *see* BLOOD TESTS
BLOOD MOUNTAIN
map (34° 44′N 83° 56′W) **9**:114
BLOOD OF A POET, THE (film) *see* *SANG D'UN POÈTE, LE* (film)
BLOOD PRESSURE **3**:339 *bibliog.*; **10**:349 *table*
aorta **2**:73
cardiovascular diseases **4**:145
hypertension **10**:348–349
pulse (biology) **15**:621
receptors
heart **10**:94
regulation
electrolyte **7**:115
starvation **18**:228
BLOOD TESTS **3**:339 *bibliog.*
AIDS **1**:201
blood transfusion **3**:339
hematology **10**:117
muscular dystrophy **13**:656
pulmonary function test **15**:620
syphilis **18**:410
BLOOD TRANSFUSION **3**:339
AIDS **1**:201
blood bank **3**:338
blood substitutes **3**:338
Cooley's anemia **5**:240
Rh factor **16**:192
serum **17**:210
BLOOD TYPING *see* BLOOD
BLOOD VESSELS *see* ARTERY; CAPILLARY; CARDIOVASCULAR SYSTEM; CIRCULATORY SYSTEM; VASCULAR SYSTEM; VEIN
BLOODFIN **19**:308 *illus.*
BLOODHOUND **3**:339 *bibliog.*, *illus.*; **6**:216 *illus.*
BLOODLETTING
headache **10**:86
BLOODROOT (botany) **3**:340
BLOODSTONE **3**:340
quartz **16**:14
BLOODSWORTH ISLAND
map (38° 10′N 76° 3′W) **13**:188
BLOODY ASSIZES
Jeffreys, George Jeffreys, 1st Baron **11**:394
BLOODY MARY *see* MARY I, QUEEN OF ENGLAND
BLOODY SUNDAY
Russian Revolution of 1905 **16**:370
BLOOM, ALGAL **3**:340
plankton **15**:332
red tide **16**:114–115
BLOOM, HAROLD **3**:340
BLOOMER (Wisconsin)
map (45° 7′N 91° 29′W) **20**:185
BLOOMER, AMELIA JENKS **3**:340
BLOOMERS (clothing)
Bloomer, Amelia Jenks **3**:340
BLOOMFIELD (Connecticut)
map (41° 50′N 72° 44′W) **5**:193
BLOOMFIELD (Indiana)
map (39° 1′N 86° 56′W) **11**:111
BLOOMFIELD (Iowa)
map (40° 45′N 92° 25′W) **11**:244
BLOOMFIELD (Kentucky)
map (37° 55′N 85° 19′W) **12**:47
BLOOMFIELD (Missouri)
map (36° 53′N 89° 56′W) **13**:476
BLOOMFIELD (New Jersey)
map (40° 48′N 74° 12′W) **14**:129
BLOOMFIELD (New Mexico)
map (36° 43′N 107° 59′W) **14**:136
BLOOMFIELD, LEONARD **3**:340 *bibliog.*
linguistics **12**:356
BLOOMING GROVE (Texas)
map (32° 6′N 96° 43′W) **19**:129
BLOOMINGDALE (New Jersey)
map (41° 0′N 74° 20′W) **14**:129
BLOOMINGTON (Illinois) **3**:340
map (40° 29′N 88° 60′W) **11**:42
BLOOMINGTON (Indiana) **3**:340
map (39° 10′N 86° 32′W) **11**:111
BLOOMINGTON (Minnesota)
map (44° 50′N 93° 17′W) **13**:453
BLOOMINGTON (Texas)
map (28° 39′N 96° 54′W) **19**:129
BLOOMINGTON (Wisconsin)
map (42° 53′N 90° 55′W) **20**:185
BLOOMSBURG (Pennsylvania)
map (41° 0′N 76° 27′W) **15**:147
BLOOMSBURY GROUP **3**:340–341 *bibliog.*
Bell, Clive **3**:186
Forster, E. M. **8**:235
Keynes, John Maynard **12**:63–64
Sackville-West, Victoria **17**:7
Strachey, Lytton **18**:287
Woolf, Virginia **20**:215
BLORA (Indonesia)
map (6° 57′S 111° 25′E) **11**:147
BLOSSBURG (Pennsylvania)
map (41° 41′N 77° 4′W) **15**:147
BLOUNT (county in Alabama)
map (34° 0′N 86° 35′W) **1**:234
BLOUNT (county in Tennessee)
map (35° 45′N 83° 55′W) **19**:104
BLOUNT, WILLIAM **3**:341
BLOUNTSTOWN (Florida)
map (30° 27′N 85° 3′W) **8**:172
BLOUNTSVILLE (Alabama)
map (34° 5′N 86° 35′W) **1**:234
BLOUNTVILLE (Tennessee)
map (36° 31′N 82° 18′W) **19**:104
BLOW, JOHN **3**:341 *bibliog.*
BLOWER
pump **15**:622
BLOWFISH *see* PUFFER
BLOWFLY **3**:341 *bibliog.*; **8**:189 *illus.*
BLOWGUN **3**:341
BLOWTORCH **3**:341 *illus.*
See also BRAZING; WELDING AND SOLDERING
BLUBBER (whale fat) *see* WHALING
BLÜCHER, GEBHARD LEBERECHT VON **3**:341–342 *bibliog.*
Waterloo, Battle of **20**:64–65
BLUDENZ (Austria)
map (47° 9′N 9° 49′E) **2**:348
BLUE ACARA *see* CICHLID
BLUE BABY **3**:342 *bibliog.*
heart diseases **10**:95
surgery **18**:362
BLUE BEECH *see* HORNBEAM (botany)
BLUE BOY, THE (painting) **15**:447
Gainsborough, Thomas **9**:9
BLUE CORDILLERA MOUNTAINS
map (9° 0′S 75° 35′W) **15**:193
BLUE CRAB **5**:325 *illus.*
BLUE CROSS **3**:342
BLUE DAWN FLOWER *see* MORNING GLORY
BLUE EARTH (Minnesota)
map (43° 38′N 94° 6′W) **13**:453
BLUE EARTH (county in Minnesota)
map (44° 3′N 94° 3′W) **13**:453
BLUE EARTH RIVER
map (44° 9′N 94° 2′W) **13**:453
BLUE-EYED GRASS **3**:342
BLUE-GREEN ALGAE **3**:342–343 *bibliog.*, *illus.*
algae **1**:281
Anabaena **1**:387
bacteria **3**:342–343
Gloeocapsa **9**:209
lichen **12**:322
nitrogen cycle **14**:203
Nostoc **14**:266
photosynthesis **3**:342–343
poisonous plants and animals **15**:384
BLUE GROTTO (Italy) **3**:343
BLUE HILL (Maine)
map (44° 25′N 68° 36′W) **13**:70
BLUE HILL (Nebraska)
map (40° 20′N 98° 27′W) **14**:70
BLUE ISLAND (Illinois)
map (41° 40′N 87° 41′W) **11**:42
BLUE JAY **3**:280 *illus.*; **3**:343 *illus.*
jay **11**:386
BLUE LAWS **3**:343 *bibliog.*
Sabbath **17**:5
BLUE MESA RESERVOIR
map (38° 27′N 107° 10′W) **5**:116
BLUE MOUND (Illinois)
map (39° 42′N 89° 7′W) **11**:42
BLUE MOUNTAIN (Mississippi)
map (34° 40′N 89° 2′W) **13**:469
BLUE MOUNTAIN LAKE
map (35° 5′N 93° 40′W) **2**:166
BLUE MOUNTAIN PEAK
map (18° 3′N 76° 35′W) **11**:351
BLUE MOUNTAINS (Jamaica)
map (18° 6′N 76° 40′W) **11**:351
BLUE MOUNTAINS (Oregon) **14**:428 *illus.*
map (45° 30′N 118° 15′W) **14**:427
BLUE NILE *see* NILE RIVER
BLUE NILE RIVER
map (15° 38′N 32° 31′E) **14**:196
BLUE RAPIDS (Kansas)
map (39° 41′N 96° 39′W) **12**:18
BLUE RIDGE (Alberta)
map (54° 8′N 115° 22′W) **1**:256
BLUE RIDGE (Georgia)
map (34° 52′N 84° 20′W) **9**:114
BLUE RIDGE MOUNTAINS **3**:343
Black Mountains **3**:317
Georgia **9**:113
map (37° 0′N 82° 0′W) **2**:86
Maryland **13**:187; **13**:189 *illus.*
South Carolina **18**:100 *illus.*
Virginia **19**:608 *illus.*
BLUE RIVER (British Columbia)
map (52° 5′N 119° 17′W) **3**:491
BLUE SHIELD **3**:343
BLUE SHIFT
red shift **16**:114
BLUE SPOTTED SUNFISH *see* SUNFISH
BLUE SPRINGS (Nebraska)
map (40° 9′N 96° 40′W) **14**:70
BLUE STACK MOUNTAINS
map (54° 50′N 8° 0′W) **11**:258
BLUE WHALE *see* WHALE
BLUEBEARD **3**:344
BLUEBELL (botany) **3**:344 *illus.*
squill **18**:204
Virginia cowslip **19**:612
BLUEBERRY **3**:344 *illus.*
huckleberry **10**:289
BLUEBIRD **3**:344–345 *illus.*
BLUEBOTTLE *see* BLOWFLY
BLUEFIELD (Virginia)
map (37° 15′N 81° 17′W) **19**:607
BLUEFIELD (West Virginia)
map (37° 16′N 81° 13′W) **20**:111
BLUEFIELDS (Nicaragua)
map (12° 0′N 83° 45′W) **14**:179
BLUEFIN
tuna **19**:332 *illus.*
BLUEFISH **3**:345 *illus.*
BLUEGRASS **3**:345 *bibliog.*
steppe life **18**:257 *illus.*
BLUEGRASS MUSIC **3**:345 *bibliog.*
See also COUNTRY AND WESTERN MUSIC
Flatt and Scruggs **8**:156
BLUEPRINT **3**:345 *bibliog.*
BLUES (music) **3**:345–346 *bibliog.*
See also COUNTRY AND WESTERN MUSIC
American music **1**:351
Arlen, Harold **2**:170–171
bluegrass music **3**:345
Fleetwood Mac **8**:159
Handy, W. C. **3**:311 *illus.*; **10**:37
Horne, Lena **10**:239
jazz **11**:388 *illus.*
King, B. B. **12**:80
Memphis (Tennessee) **13**:292
Smith, Bessie **17**:367
BLUESTEM (grass) **3**:346
BLUESTONE LAKE RESERVOIR
map (37° 30′N 80° 50′W) **20**:111
BLUESTONE RIVER
map (37° 34′N 80° 59′W) **20**:111
BLUETHROAT **3**:346 *illus.*
BLUEWATER (New Mexico)
map (35° 15′N 107° 59′W) **14**:136
BLUFF (Utah)
map (37° 17′N 109° 33′W) **19**:429
BLUFF CITY (Tennessee)
map (36° 28′N 82° 16′W) **19**:104
BLUFFS (Illinois)
map (39° 45′N 90° 32′W) **11**:42
BLUFFTON (Indiana)
map (40° 44′N 85° 11′W) **11**:111
BLUFFTON (Ohio)
map (40° 54′N 83° 54′W) **14**:357
BLUFORD, GUION S. **3**:346
BLUM, LÉON **3**:346 *bibliog.*, *illus.*
BLUMBERG, BARUCH S. **3**:346
hepatitis **10**:130
BLUME, JUDY **3**:346–347
BLUME, PETER **3**:347 *bibliog.*, *illus.*
Light of the World **3**:347 *illus.*
BLUMENBACH, JOHANN FRIEDRICH **3**:347
race **16**:33
BLUMENHOF (Saskatchewan)
map (50° 1′N 107° 41′W) **17**:81
BLUMER, HERBERT
sociology **18**:30
BLUNDELL, SIR DENIS **3**:347
BLUNDEN, EDMUND CHARLES **3**:347
BLUNT, ANTHONY
intelligence gathering **11**:205
Philby, H. St. John **15**:231
BLUNT, WILFRID SCAWEN **3**:347
BLUNTSCHLI, JOHANN KASPAR **3**:347
state (in political philosophy) **18**:233
BLY (Oregon)
map (42° 24′N 121° 2′W) **14**:427
BLY, NELLIE **3**:347–348 *bibliog.*, *illus.*
BLY, ROBERT **3**:348
BLYTH (England)
map (55° 7′N 1° 30′W) **19**:403
BLYTHE (California)
map (33° 37′N 114° 36′W) **4**:31
BLYTHE, DAVID GILMOUR **3**:348 *bibliog.*
BLYTHEVILLE (Arkansas)
map (35° 56′N 89° 55′W) **2**:166
BMEWS **3**:348
BMW (Bayernische Motoren Werke)
automotive industry **2**:366
B'NAI B'RITH **3**:348
BO (Sierra Leone)
map (7° 56′N 11° 21′W) **17**:296
BO JU'I *see* PO CHÜ-I (Bo Ju'i)
BO TREE **3**:348
BOA **3**:348–349 *illus.*; **17**:377 *illus.*
anaconda **1**:387
BOA VISTA (Brazil)
map (2° 49′N 60° 40′W) **3**:460
BOA VISTA ISLAND
map (16° 5′N 22° 50′W) **4**:122
BOABDIL **3**:349 *bibliog.*
BOACO (department in Nicaragua)
map (12° 30′N 85° 30′W) **14**:179
BOADICEA **3**:349
BOAR
pig **15**:298
BOARD (lumber) *see* LUMBER
BOARD GAMES *see* DICE GAMES; names of specific games, e.g., BACKGAMMON; MONOPOLY (game); etc.
BOARDMAN (Ohio)
map (41° 2′N 80° 40′W) **14**:357
BOARDSAILING *see* WINDSURFING
BOARFISH **3**:349
BOAS, FRANZ **2**:54 *illus.*; **3**:349 *bibliog.*, *illus.*
Kwakiutl **12**:142
Mead, Margaret **13**:251
BOAT AND BOATING **3**:349–352 *bibliog.*, *illus.*

See also NAVAL VESSELS; SHIP
barnacle **3**:85
history **3**:349–350
transportation **19**:278
iceboating **11**:15–16
Ra expeditions **16**:29
rowing **16**:327–328
types **3**:350–351
barge **3**:80–81 *illus.*
canoe **4**:113
coracle **5**:257
dinghy **6**:178
ferry **8**:59–60
gondola **9**:243
houseboat **10**:274
hydrofoil **10**:335–337
motorboat **13**:612
outrigger **14**:469
PT boat **15**:605
sampan **17**:48
shell **16**:328
steamboat **18**:242
tugboat **19**:329
BOAT PEOPLE
See also REFUGEE
immigration **11**:56
BOAT RACING **3**:351–352
America's Cup **1**:368
motorboat **13**:612 *illus.*
Muncey, Bill **13**:639
rowing **16**:327–328 *illus.*
BOATING *see* BOAT AND BOATING
BOAZ (Alabama)
map (34° 12′N 86° 10′W) **1**:234
"BOBBIES" (London police force)
Peel, Sir Robert **15**:132
BOBBIN LACE **12**:158–159 *illus.*
BOBCAT 3:352 *illus.*
BOBO DIOULASSO (Upper Volta)
climate **19**:473 *table*
map (11° 12′N 4° 18′W) **19**:472
BOBOLI GARDENS
Florence (Italy) **8**:168–169 *map*
landscape architecture **12**:185
Pitti Palace **15**:321
BOBOLINK 3:352–353 *illus.*
blackbird **3**:320
ricebird **16**:209
BOBSLEDDING 3:353
BOBWHITE 3:353 *illus.*
quail **16**:6
BOCA RATON (Florida)
map (26° 21′N 80° 5′W) **8**:172
BOCAS DEL TORO (Panama)
map (9° 20′N 82° 15′W) **15**:55
BOCCACCIO, GIOVANNI 3:353–354 *bibliog., illus.*
Decameron **6**:72
BOCCHERINI, LUIGI 3:354 *bibliog.*
BOCCIE 3:354
lawn bowls **12**:248
BOCCIONI, UMBERTO 3:354–355 *bibliog., illus.*
futurism **8**:384
Unique Forms of Continuity in Space **3**:354 *illus.*; **11**:311 *illus.*
BOCELLI, G.A.
zoology **20**:377
BOCHER, MAIN ROUSSEAU *see* MAINBOCHER
BOCHOLT (Germany, East and West)
map (51° 50′N 6° 36′E) **9**:140
BOCHUM (West Germany) 3:355
BOCK (beer) **3**:163
BOCK, JERRY, AND HARNICK, SHELDON 3:355
BÖCKLIN, ARNOLD 3:355 *bibliog., illus.*
Self-Portrait with Death Playing a Violin **3**:355 *illus.*
BOCSKAY, ISTVÁN, PRINCE OF TRANSYLVANIA 3:355
BODE, JOHANN ELERT 3:355
Astronomisches Jahrbuch **3**:355
BODEGA Y QUADRA, JUAN FRANCISCO DE LA
Washington **20**:38
BODELE (region in Chad)
map (16° 30′N 16° 30′E) **4**:266
BODEN (Sweden)
map (65° 50′N 21° 42′E) **18**:382
BODENHEIM, MAXWELL 3:356
BODENSEE *see* CONSTANCE, LAKE
BODE'S LAW *see* TITIUS-BODE LAW
BODH GAYA (India) 3:356
Anuradhapura **1**:72
Sarnath **17**:78
BODHIDHARMA 3:356
BODHISATTVA 3:356
BODIN, JEAN 3:356 *bibliog.*
law **12**:242
state (in political philosophy) **18**:231–232
BODLEIAN LIBRARY 3:356 *bibliog.*
Duke Humphrey's Library **12**:316 *illus.*
BODMER, KARL 3:356 *bibliog.*
Mandan earth lodge **11**:120 *illus.*
BODØ (Norway)
map (67° 17′N 14° 23′E) **14**:261
BODO LANGUAGE
Sino-Tibetan languages **17**:324
BODONI, GIAMBATTISTA 3:356 *bibliog.*
typeface **19**:364
BODROG RIVER
map (48° 7′N 21° 25′E) **5**:413
BODY CELL *see* SOMATIC CELL
BODY FLUIDS
bile, liver **12**:374–375
blood **3**:335–338
cerebrospinal fluid **18**:184
diagnostic tests **6**:149–150
edema **7**:55
fish **8**:115 *illus.*
hallucinogens **10**:24
hunger and thirst **10**:311
hydrocephaly **10**:331
immunodeficiency disease **11**:59
inflammation **11**:169
kidneys **12**:72–74
lymphatic system **12**:475–476 *illus.*
semen **17**:195
seminal fluids
reproductive system, human **16**:164
serum **17**:210
space medicine **18**:133
spinal cord **18**:184 *illus.*
water **20**:47
BODY LANGUAGE *see* NONVERBAL COMMUNICATION
BODY MARKING 3:356–357 *bibliog., illus.*
Colorado (American Indians) **5**:120
BODY PAINTING *see* BODY MARKING; COSMETICS
BODY SNATCHING 3:357
BODY TEMPERATURE 3:357–358 *bibliog., table*
climate **5**:58
exercise **7**:329
fever **8**:66
fish **8**:114–115
heatstroke **10**:100
hibernation **10**:156
homeotherms **3**:357
hyperthermia **3**:357–358
hypothermia **3**:357; **10**:351
icefish **11**:16
inflammation **11**:169
lizard **12**:380
measure, thermometer **19**:166
metabolism **13**:325
poikilotherms **3**:357
reptile **16**:166
sleep **17**:360
snake **17**:376
of some birds and mammals **3**:357 *table*
tuna **19**:332
BOEHLER, PETER 3:358 *bibliog.*
BOEHM, MARTIN 3:358
Evangelical United Brethren Church **7**:312
BOEHME, JAKOB *see* BÖHME, JAKOB
BOEHMITE
bauxite **3**:131
BOEING, WILLIAM EDWARD 3:358
BOEING COMPANY **1**:128 *table*
aircraft
aviation **2**:372
B-17 Flying Fortress **1**:206–207 *illus.*; **1**:216 *illus.*; **3**:4
B-29 Superfortress **1**:216 *illus.*; **3**:4
B-52 Stratofortress **1**:216 *illus.*; **3**:4
Boeing 707 **1**:210; **2**:372–373 *illus.*
Boeing 747 **1**:128 *illus.*; **2**:372; **2**:374–375 *illus.*
Boeing, William Edward **3**:358
Lunar Rover **12**:461–462 *illus.*
Washington **20**:38
BOEOTIA 3:358
Chaeronea **4**:267
Gla **9**:192
Orchomenos **14**:420
Plataea **15**:351
Thebes (Greece) **19**:155
BOEOTIAN LEAGUE
Boeotia **3**:358
BOER WAR *see* SOUTH AFRICAN WAR
BOERHAAVE, HERMANN 3:358 *bibliog.*
medicine **13**:270
physics, history of **15**:285
BOERNE (Texas)
map (29° 47′N 98° 44′W) **19**:129
BOERS *see* AFRIKANERS
BOETHIUS, ANICIUS MANLIUS SEVERINUS 3:358 *bibliog.*
mathematics, history of **13**:224 *illus.*
scholasticism **17**:132
BOEUF RIVER
map (31° 52′N 91° 47′W) **12**:430
BOFFRAND, GERMAIN 3:358–359 *bibliog.*
Oval Salon, Palais Soubise (Paris) **11**:212 *illus.*
BOG *see* SWAMP, MARSH, AND BOG
BOG COTTON **17**:183 *illus.*
BOG IRON ORE *see* LIMONITE
BOG MOSS *see* PEAT MOSS
BOG ROSEMARY 3:359
BOG TURTLE 3:359
BOGALE (Burma)
map (16° 17′N 95° 24′E) **3**:573
BOGALUSA (Louisiana) 3:359
map (30° 47′N 89° 52′W) **12**:430
BOGAN, LOUISE 3:359
BOGARDE, DIRK 3:359; **12**:418 *illus.*
BOGARDUS, JAMES 3:359 *bibliog.*; **19**:450 *illus.*
American art and architecture **1**:328–329
cast-iron architecture **4**:186
BOGART, HUMPHREY 3:359 *bibliog., illus.*
Bacall, Lauren **3**:9
BOGATA (Texas)
map (33° 28′N 95° 13′W) **19**:129
BOĞAZKÖY (Turkey) 3:359–360 *bibliog.*
Hittite art and architecture **10**:188
Winckler, Hugo **20**:168
BOGOMILS 3:360
Turks **19**:348
BOGOR (Indonesia)
map (6° 35′S 106° 47′E) **11**:147
BOGOTÁ (Colombia) 3:360 *illus.*; **5**:108 *illus.*
Chibcha **4**:340
climate **5**:107 *table*
Jiménez de Quesada, Gonzalo **11**:419
Latin American art and architecture **12**:223
map (4° 36′N 74° 5′W) **5**:107
BOGOTA (New Jersey)
map (40° 53′N 74° 2′W) **14**:129
BOGRA (Bangladesh)
map (24° 51′N 89° 22′E) **3**:64
BOGUE CHITTO (Mississippi)
map (31° 28′N 90° 26′W) **13**:469
BOHÈME, LA (opera) 3:360 *bibliog.*
BOHEMIA (Czechoslovakia) 3:360–361 *map*
boundaries *c.*1360 **7**:285 *map*
cities
Lidice **12**:323
Plzeň **15**:375
Prague **15**:488 *illus.*
Czechoslovakia **5**:416
garnet **9**:49
Germany in 1648 **9**:151 *map*
glassware, decorative **9**:203
history
coin **14**:296 *illus.*
Ferdinand II, Holy Roman Emperor **8**:53
Frederick V, Elector Palatine (the Winter King) **8**:292
George of Poděbrady, King **9**:110
Huss, John **10**:320
Hussites **10**:321
Jagello (dynasty) **11**:348
Maria Theresa, Austrian Archduchess, Queen of Hungary and Bohemia **13**:150
Matthias, Holy Roman Emperor **13**:231–232
Ottokar II, King of Bohemia (Přemysl Ottokar) **14**:464
Palacký, František **15**:29
Přemysl (dynasty) **15**:518
Sigismund, King of Germany and Holy Roman Emperor **17**:299
Slavs **17**:359
Thirty Years' War **19**:170–172
Wenceslas I, King **20**:103
Wenceslas II, King **20**:103
music
Biber, Heinrich Ignaz Franz von **3**:237
Czech music **5**:413
Dvořák, Antonín **6**:317
Smetana, Bedřich **17**:366
BOHEMIAN BRETHREN *see* MORAVIAN CHURCH
BOHEMIAN FOREST MOUNTAINS
map (49° 15′N 12° 45′E) **9**:140
BOHEMIAN UNITY OF BRETHREN *see* MORAVIAN CHURCH
BOHEMOND I, PRINCE OF ANTIOCH 3:361
BOHIER, THOMAS
Chenonceaux, Château de **4**:330
BOHLEN, CHARLES EUSTIS 3:361 *bibliog.*
BÖHLER, OTTO
Richard Wagner **9**:131 *illus.*
BÖHM, GEORG
German and Austrian music **9**:130
BÖHM, GOTTFRIED 3:361
BÖHM, KARL 3:361
BÖHM, THEOBALD
flute **8**:189
BOHMAN, GÖSTA
Sweden **18**:385
BÖHME, JAKOB 3:361 *bibliog.*
BOHOL ISLAND
map (9° 50′N 124° 10′E) **15**:237
BOHR, AAGE NIELS 3:361
BOHR, NIELS 3:361–362 *bibliog., illus.*; **15**:286 *illus.*
atom **2**:305 *illus.*
Bohr's atom **2**:305–306
atomic theory **3**:361–362
chemistry, history of **4**:327–328
physics **15**:281
chemistry, history of **4**:327
element 105 **7**:132
hydrogen spectrum **10**:340–341
quantum mechanics **16**:10
BOHR MAGNETON 3:362
atomic constants **2**:309
BOIARDO, MATTEO MARIA 3:362
BOIELDIEU, FRANÇOIS ADRIEN 3:362 *bibliog.*
BOIESTOWN (New Brunswick)
map (46° 27′N 66° 25′W) **14**:117
BOIGNY, FÉLIX HOUPHOUËT- *see* HOUPHOUËT-BOIGNY, FÉLIX
BOIL (skin infection) 3:362
carbuncle **4**:141
ear disease **7**:7–8
skin diseases **17**:342
BOILEAU-DESPRÉAUX, NICOLAS 3:362 *bibliog.*
BOILER 3:362–363 *illus.*
heat exchanger **10**:98
ship **17**:273–274
steam engine **18**:240–241
valve **19**:509 *illus.*
BOILING POINT 3:363
of solvents **18**:59 *illus.*
water **20**:48
BOILLY, LOUIS LÉOPOLD 3:363
Houdon in his Studio, Working on the Portrait Bust of Laplace, Watched by his Wife and Daughters **10**:263 *illus.*
BOIS, GUY PÈNE DU *see* DU BOIS, GUY PÈNE
BOIS, W. E. B. DU *see* DU BOIS, W. E. B.
BOIS BLANC ISLAND
Mackinac, Straits of **13**:29
map (45° 45′N 84° 28′W) **13**:377
BOIS DE BELLEAU *see* BELLEAU WOOD
BOIS DE BOULOGNE
Haussmann, Georges Eugène, Baron **10**:69
BOIS DE SIOUX RIVER
map (46° 16′N 96° 36′W) **13**:453
BOIS-REYMOND, EMIL DU
zoology **20**:377
BOISE (Idaho) 3:363; **11**:25 *illus.*
map (43° 37′N 116° 13′W) **11**:26
BOISE (county in Idaho)
map (44° 0′N 115° 45′W) **11**:26
BOISE CITY (Oklahoma)
map (36° 44′N 102° 31′W) **14**:368
BOISE RIVER
map (43° 49′N 117° 1′W) **11**:26
BOITO, ARRIGO 3:363
BOJADOR, CAPE
map (26° 8′N 14° 30′W) **13**:585
BOJEADOR, CAPE OF
map (18° 30′N 120° 34′E) **15**:237
BOJER, JOHAN 3:363 *bibliog.*
BOJI PLAIN
map (1° 30′N 39° 45′E) **12**:53
BOJNURD (Iran)
map (37° 28′N 57° 19′E) **11**:250
BOJONEGORO (Indonesia)
map (7° 9′S 111° 52′E) **11**:147
BOK, BART JAN 3:363
BOK, EDWARD WILLIAM 3:363–364 *bibliog.*
BOK-CHOI
Chinese cabbage **4**:388
BOKASSA, JEAN BEDEL 3:364

BOKASSA, JEAN BEDEL (cont.)
Central African Republic **4**:252
Giscard d'Estaing, Valéry **9**:190
BOKCHITO (Oklahoma)
map (34° 1′N 96° 9′W) **14**:368
BOKER, GEORGE HENRY **3**:364
BOKMÅL (language)
Norway **14**:262
BOLAMA (Guinea-Bissau)
climate **9**:399 *table*
map (11° 35′N 15° 28′W) **9**:399
BOLDAVIN (Turkey)
map location (38° 42′N 31° 4′E) **19**:343
BOLDINI, GIOVANNI **3**:364 *bibliog.*
BOLDREWOOD, ROLF *see* BROWNE, THOMAS ALEXANDER
BOLENDER, TODD **3**:364
BOLERO **3**:364
BOLES (Arkansas)
map (34° 47′N 94° 3′W) **2**:166
BOLES, CHARLES E. *see* BLACK BART
BOLESLAV I (Duke of Bohemia)
Přemysl (dynasty) **15**:518
BOLESŁAW I, KING OF POLAND (Bolesław the Brave) **3**:364
Piast (dynasty) **15**:289
BOLESŁAWIEC (Poland)
map (51° 16′N 15° 34′E) **15**:388
BOLETUS **3**:364
BOLEY (Oklahoma)
map (35° 29′N 96° 29′W) **14**:368
BOLEYN, ANNE **3**:364 *bibliog.*
Elizabeth I, Queen of England **7**:141
Henry VIII, King of England **10**:126
BOLGATANGA (Ghana)
map (10° 46′N 0° 52′W) **9**:164
BOLIDE *see* METEOR AND METEORITE
BOLIGEE (Alabama)
map (32° 45′N 88° 2′W) **1**:234
BOLIMOV, BATTLE OF
World War I **20**:227 *map*; **20**:230
BOLING (Texas)
map (29° 16′N 95° 57′W) **19**:129
BOLINGBROKE, HENRY *see* HENRY IV, KING OF ENGLAND
BOLINGBROKE, HENRY ST. JOHN, 1ST VISCOUNT **3**:364 *bibliog.*
BOLINGBROOK (Illinois)
map (41° 42′N 88° 3′W) **11**:42
BOLÍVAR (Argentina)
map (36° 15′S 61° 6′W) **2**:149
BOLÍVAR (Colombia)
map (1° 50′N 76° 58′W) **5**:107
BOLIVAR (county in Mississippi)
map (33° 50′N 90° 50′W) **13**:469
BOLIVAR (Missouri)
map (37° 37′N 93° 25′W) **13**:476
BOLIVAR (New York)
map (42° 4′N 78° 14′W) **14**:149
BOLIVAR (Tennessee)
map (35° 16′N 88° 59′W) **19**:104
BOLÍVAR, SIMÓN **3**:365 *bibliog., illus.*
Ciudad Bolívar (Venezuela) **5**:9
Colombia **5**:109
Latin America, history of **12**:220 *illus.*
Miranda, Francisco de **13**:463
Páez, José Antonio **15**:13
San Martín, José de **17**:57
Santa Marta (Colombia) **17**:68
Santander, Francisco de Paula **17**:69
Sucre, Antonio José de **18**:319
BOLÍVAR PEAK
map (8° 30′N 71° 2′W) **19**:542
BOLIVIA **3**:365–369 *bibliog., illus., map, table*
agriculture **3**:368–369 *illus.*
archaeology
Tiahuanaco **19**:188–189
art
pre-Columbian art and architecture **15**:500
cities
Cochabamba **5**:85
La Paz **12**:147–148 *illus.*
Potosí **15**:467
Santa Cruz **17**:67
Sucre **18**:319
climate **3**:367 *table*
economic activities **3**:368–369 *illus.*
education **3**:367
Latin American universities **12**:233
flag **3**:365 *illus.*
government **3**:368
history **3**:368
Banzer Suárez, Hugo **3**:72
Chaco War **4**:265
Pacific, War of the **15**:5
Santa Cruz, Andrés **17**:67–68
Sucre, Antonio José de **18**:319
land and resources **3**:366–368 *illus., map, table*
literature
Arguedas, Alcides **2**:153
map (17° 0′S 65° 0′W) **18**:85
mining **3**:368 *illus.*
people **3**:367–368 *illus.*
Aymara **2**:379
Bororo **3**:403–404
Quechua **16**:21
tin **19**:205
vegetation and animal life **3**:367
BÖLL, HEINRICH **3**:369–370 *bibliog., illus.*
BOLL WEEVIL **5**:305 *illus.*; **20**:91 *illus.*
BOLLANDISTS **3**:370
hagiography **10**:10
saint **17**:15
BOLLINGEN PRIZE IN POETRY **3**:370
Auden, W. H. **2**:318
Bogan, Louise **3**:359
Cantos, The **4**:118
Fitzgerald, Robert **8**:131
Gregory, Horace **9**:355
Moore, Marianne **13**:569
Roethke, Theodore **16**:268
Schwartz, Delmore **17**:139
Tate, Allen **19**:44
Winters, Yvor **20**:181
BOLLINGER (county in Missouri)
map (37° 20′N 90° 0′W) **13**:476
BOLLNÄS (Sweden)
map (61° 21′N 16° 25′E) **18**:382
BOLMEN LAKE
map (56° 55′N 13° 40′E) **18**:382
BOLOGNA (Italy) **3**:370
cathedral
Quercia, Jacopo della **16**:23
map (44° 29′N 11° 20′E) **11**:321
BOLOGNA, GIOVANNI DA **3**:370–371 *bibliog., illus.*
Mercury **3**:370 *illus.*; **16**:153 *illus.*
BOLOGNA, JACOPO DA
madrigal **13**:45
BOLOGNA, UNIVERSITY OF **3**:371
BOLOGNESI (Peru)
map (6° 35′S 73° 10′W) **15**:193
BOLOMETER **3**:371
Langley, Samuel Pierpont **12**:196
BOLOVEN PLATEAU
map (15° 20′N 106° 20′E) **12**:203
BOLSHEVIK REVOLUTION
Russian Revolutions of 1917 **16**:370–373
BOLSHEVIKS AND MENSHEVIKS **3**:371 *bibliog.*
communism **5**:146–147
Europe, history of **7**:295
Hitler, Adolf **10**:188
Kollantai, Aleksandra **12**:107
Lenin, Vladimir Ilich **12**:282–283
Molotov, Vyacheslav Mikhailovich **13**:513
Pravda **15**:290
Russian Revolutions of 1917 **16**:370–373 *illus.*
Russia/Union of Soviet Socialist Republics, history of **16**:359 *illus.*
socialism **18**:21
Stalin, Joseph **18**:214
Trotsky, Leon **19**:310–311
BOLSHOI BALLET **3**:371–372 *bibliog., illus.*
Godunov, Aleksandr **9**:221
Grigorovich, Yury Nikolayevich **9**:364
Plisetskaya, Maya Mikhailovna **15**:368
Stone Flower **19**:395 *illus.*
BOLT *see* NUTS AND BOLTS
BOLT, ROBERT **3**:372
BOLTON (England) **3**:372
map (53° 35′N 2° 26′W) **19**:403
BOLTON (North Carolina)
map (34° 20′N 78° 25′W) **14**:242
BOLTON, HERBERT EUGENE **3**:372 *bibliog.*
BOLTON-LE-MOORS (England) *see* BOLTON (England)
BOLTWOOD, BERTRAM BORDEN **3**:372
BOLTZMANN, LUDWIG **3**:372
blackbody radiation **3**:320–321
BOLTZMANN CONSTANT **3**:372
atomic constants **2**:309
BOLU (Turkey)
map (40° 44′N 31° 37′E) **19**:343
BOLYAI, JÁNOS **3**:372
hyperbolic geometry
non-Euclidean geometry **14**:216
mathematics, history of **13**:226
BOLZANO (Italy) **3**:373
map (46° 31′N 11° 22′E) **11**:321
BOLZANO, BERNHARD **3**:373
BOM JESUS DA LAPA (Brazil)
map (13° 15′S 43° 25′W) **3**:460
BOMA (Zaire)
map (5° 51′S 13° 3′E) **20**:350
BOMARZO
landscape architecture **12**:185
BOMB **3**:373–374 *bibliog., illus.*
See also WORLD WAR II
atomic bomb **2**:307–308
ballistics **3**:49–51
buzz bomb, V-1 **19**:500
development **3**:373
grenade **9**:358
hydrogen bomb **10**:339–340
impact studies, ballistics **3**:51
neutron bomb **14**:109
stability, ballistics **3**:51
terrorist bombs **3**:374
20th century military use **3**:373–374
weapons **20**:75
BOMBA, KING *see* FERDINAND II, KING OF THE TWO SICILIES
BOMBARD (musical instrument) *see* SHAWM
BOMBAY (India) **3**:374–375 *bibliog., map*; **11**:85 *illus.*
map (18° 58′N 72° 50′E) **11**:80
BOMBAY HOOK ISLAND
map (39° 18′N 75° 27′W) **6**:88
BOMBELLI, RAFAEL
complex number **5**:157
mathematics, history of **13**:224
BOMBER
aircraft **1**:214–216 *illus.*
aviation **2**:370–372
defense, national **6**:82 *table*
Gotha (aircraft) **9**:254
Grumman TBF-1 Avenger **9**:382
nuclear strategy **14**:288
BOMBOIS, CAMILLE **3**:375 *bibliog.*
BON, CAPE
map (37° 5′N 11° 3′E) **19**:335
BON AIR (Virginia)
map (37° 32′N 77° 34′W) **19**:607
BON HOMME (county in South Dakota)
map (43° 0′N 97° 52′W) **18**:103
BON PAYS
Luxembourg (country) **12**:471
BON SECOUR (Alabama)
map (30° 19′N 87° 44′W) **1**:234
BON WIER (Texas)
map (30° 44′N 93° 39′W) **19**:129
BONA DEA **3**:375
BONA FIDE **3**:375
BONAIRE
Netherlands Antilles **14**:103
BONAMPAK (Mexico) **3**:375
murals **13**:244 *illus.*; **15**:497 *illus.*
pre-Columbian art and architecture **15**:497
BONANZA (Nicaragua)
map (14° 1′N 84° 35′W) **14**:179
BONANZA (Oregon)
map (42° 12′N 121° 24′W) **14**:427
BONANZA (Utah)
map (40° 1′N 109° 11′W) **19**:429
BONAO (Dominican Republic)
map (18° 56′N 70° 25′W) **6**:233
BONAPARTE (family) **3**:375–376 *bibliog.*
BONAPARTE, CAROLINE
Bonaparte (family) **3**:375
BONAPARTE, CHARLES LOUIS NAPOLÉON *see* NAPOLEON III, EMPEROR OF THE FRENCH (Louis Napoléon Bonaparte)
BONAPARTE, ÉLISA
Bonaparte (family) **3**:375
BONAPARTE, FRANÇOIS CHARLES JOSEPH (Napoléon II)
Bonaparte (family) **3**:375
BONAPARTE, JÉRÔME (1784–1860)
Bonaparte (family) **3**:375
BONAPARTE, JÉRÔME NAPOLEON
Bonaparte (family) **3**:376
BONAPARTE, JOSEPH
Bonaparte (family) **3**:375
BONAPARTE, LETIZIA RAMOLINO
Bonaparte (family) **3**:375
BONAPARTE, LOUIS
Beauharnais (family) **3**:146
Bonaparte (family) **3**:375
BONAPARTE, LOUIS NAPOLÉON *see* NAPOLEON III, EMPEROR OF THE FRENCH (Louis Napoléon Bonaparte)
BONAPARTE, LUCIEN
Bonaparte (family) **3**:375
BONAPARTE, NAPOLEON *see* NAPOLEON I, EMPEROR OF THE FRENCH (Napoléon Bonaparte)
BONAPARTE, NAPOLÉON JOSEPH CHARLES PAUL
Bonaparte (family) **3**:375–376
BONAPARTE, PAULINE
Bonaparte (family) **3**:375
BONASSE (Trinidad and Tobago)
map (10° 5′N 61° 52′W) **19**:300
BONAVENTURE, SAINT **3**:376 *bibliog.*
innate ideas **11**:179
BONAVENTURE HOTEL (Los Angeles) **10**:261 *illus.*
BONAVISTA (Newfoundland)
map (48° 39′N 53° 7′W) **14**:166
BONAVISTA, CAPE
map (48° 42′N 53° 5′W) **14**:166
BONAVISTA BAY
map (48° 45′N 53° 20′W) **14**:166
BOND (finance) **3**:376 *bibliog.*
Federal Reserve System **8**:42
finance, state and local **8**:92
investment banking **11**:238
mutual fund **13**:687
negotiable instrument **14**:77
savings bond **17**:100–101
Securities and Exchange Commission **17**:181
stock (finance) **18**:273
stock market **18**:274
BOND (county in Illinois)
map (38° 53′N 89° 25′W) **11**:42
BOND, CHEMICAL *see* CHEMICAL BOND
BOND, EDWARD **3**:376 *bibliog.*
BOND, JAMES (fictional character)
Fleming, Ian **8**:159
BOND, JULIAN **3**:376 *bibliog.*
BOND, WARD
Ford, John (film director) **8**:223
BOND, WILLIAM CRANCH **3**:376
BONDERIZING **3**:376
BONDI, HERMANN **3**:376
BONDING, CHEMICAL *see* CHEMISTRY
BONDONE, GIOTTO DI *see* GIOTTO DI BONDONE
BONDOUKOU (Ivory Coast)
map (8° 2′N 2° 48′W) **11**:335
BONDOWOSO (Indonesia)
map (7° 55′S 113° 49′E) **11**:147
BONDSVILLE (Massachusetts)
map (42° 13′N 72° 21′W) **13**:206
BONDUEL (Wisconsin)
map (44° 44′N 88° 27′W) **20**:185
BONE **3**:377 *bibliog., illus.*
See also BONE TOOLS
blood **3**:335; **3**:338
calcium phosphate: Scheele, Carl Wilhelm **17**:115
cartilage **4**:175
collagen **5**:102
connective tissue **5**:196
diseases *see* BONE DISEASES
ear **7**:6 *illus.*
fossil record **8**:243–248
fracture **8**:258–259
horn (biology) **10**:238
joint (in anatomy) **11**:438–440
ligament **12**:333
limb **7**:323 *illus.*
lymphatic system **12**:475
marrow **3**:377
marrow, hemoglobin **10**:119
myositis **13**:691
ossification, growth **9**:379
pelvis **15**:140
phosphorus **15**:256
protein, multiple myeloma **13**:637
radiation injury **16**:42–43
sinusitis **17**:326
skeletal system **17**:334
skeleton, human **17**:334
skull **17**:344–346
BONE BAY
map (4° 0′S 120° 40′E) **11**:147
BONE DISEASES **3**:377–378 *bibliog.*
clubfoot **5**:71
dysplasia **6**:320
geriatrics **9**:122
infectious bone disease
immunodeficiency disease **11**:59
leukemia **12**:301
leukocytosis **12**:301
leukopenia **12**:301
multiple myeloma **13**:638
osteomyelitis **14**:457
injury
dislocation **6**:196
fracture **8**:258–259
metabolic bone diseases
osteoporosis **14**:457–458
Paget's disease **15**:14
rickets **16**:215
myositis **13**:691
orthopedics **14**:450
osteoarthritis **14**:457
treatment **3**:378
vitamins and minerals **19**:619–621
BONE MARROW *see* BONE

BONE TOOLS (prehistoric)
Mesolithic Period **13**:314
Paleolithic Period **15**:38
BONEFISH 3:378
BONESTEEL (South Dakota)
map (43° 4′N 98° 57′W) **18**:103
BONFILS, FREDERICK G. 3:378 *bibliog.*
BONGO (zoology) 3:378 *bibliog., illus.*
BONGO, OMAR
Gabon **9**:5
BONGO DRUM **13**:675 *illus.*; **15**:162 *illus.*
drum (musical instrument) **6**:282
BONHAM (Texas)
map (33° 35′N 96° 11′W) **19**:129
BONHAM, JOHN **16**:249 *illus.*
BONHEUR, ROSA 3:378–379 *bibliog., illus.*
The Horse Fair 3:379 *illus.*
BONHOEFFER, DIETRICH 3:379 *bibliog.*
BONHOMME, MOUNT
map (19° 5′N 72° 18′W) **10**:15
BONHOMME RICHARD (ship) **1**:357 *illus.*; **14**:62 *illus.*
Franklin, Benjamin **8**:284
Jones, John Paul **11**:443
BONIFACE, SAINT 3:379
BONIFACE VIII, POPE 3:379 *bibliog.*
Middle Ages **13**:393
Philip IV, King of France (Philip the Fair) **15**:233
BONIFÁCIO, JOSÉ *see* ANDRADA E SILVA, JOSÉ BONIFÁCIO DE
BONIFACIO, STRAIT OF
map (41° 1′N 14° 0′E) **11**:321
BONIFAY (Florida)
map (30° 48′N 85° 41′W) **8**:172
BONIN ISLANDS 3:379–380
Ring of Fire **16**:225
BONINGTON, RICHARD PARKES 3:380 *bibliog.*
BONITA (Louisiana)
map (32° 55′N 91° 40′W) **12**:430
BONITA SPRINGS (Florida)
map (26° 21′N 81° 47′W) **8**:172
BONITO 3:380 *bibliog., illus.*
BONITO PEAK
map (15° 38′N 86° 55′W) **10**:218
BONN (West Germany) 3:380–381 *bibliog., illus.*
map (50° 44′N 7° 5′E) **9**:140
BONNARD, PIERRE 3:381 *bibliog., illus.*
Nabis **14**:3
Nu dans le bain 3:381 *illus.*
Vuillard, Édouard **19**:640
BONNE TERRE (Missouri)
map (37° 55′N 90° 33′W) **13**:476
BONNEFOUS, JEAN PIERRE 3:381
BONNEFOY, YVES 3:381
BONNER (county in Idaho)
map (48° 20′N 116° 35′W) **11**:26
BONNER DURCHMUSTERUNG 3:381
Argelander, Friedrich Wilhelm August **2**:146
astronomical catalogs and atlases **2**:276
BONNER SPRINGS (Kansas)
map (39° 4′N 94° 53′W) **12**:18
BONNERS FERRY (Idaho)
map (48° 41′N 116° 18′W) **11**:26
BONNEVILLE (county in Idaho)
map (43° 25′N 111° 35′W) **11**:26
BONNEVILLE SALT FLATS 3:381; **19**:495 *illus.*
BONNEY, WILLIAM H. *see* BILLY THE KID
BONNIE AND CLYDE (film) *see* BARROW, CLYDE
BONNIE DOONE (North Carolina)
map (35° 5′N 78° 58′W) **14**:242
"BONNIE DUNDEE" *see* DUNDEE, JOHN GRAHAM OF CLAVERHOUSE, 1st VISCOUNT
BONNIE PRINCE CHARLIE *see* STUART, CHARLES EDWARD (Bonnie Prince Charlie)
BONNY, ANNE
piracy **15**:313 *illus.*
BONONCINI (family) 3:381–382 *bibliog.*
BONOUA (Ivory Coast)
map (5° 16′N 3° 36′W) **11**:335
BONPLAND, AIMÉ
Humboldt, Alexander von **10**:301
BONSAI 3:382 *bibliog., illus.*
BONSHAW (Prince Edward Island)
map (46° 12′N 63° 21′W) **15**:548
BONTECOU, LEE 3:382
BONTEMPELLI, MASSIMO 3:382
BONTEMPS, ARNA 3:382
BONTOK
Igorot **11**:38
BONUS ARMY 3:382
BOOBY 3:382–383 *bibliog.*
Peru **15**:194 *illus.*
BOOGIE-WOOGIE 3:383 *bibliog.*
blues 3:346
BOOJUM TREE 3:383 *bibliog.*
BOOK 3:383–386 *bibliog., illus.*
See also BOOK ILLUSTRATION; FICTION
atlas (book of maps) **2**:297
best-seller 3:228–229
bibliography 3:242–243
book club 3:386
bookbinding 3:389–390
censorship *see* CENSORSHIP
dictionary **6**:159–160
encyclopedia **7**:163–165
Grolier, Jean **9**:368
history
Bay Psalm Book 3:132
block printing 3:334
Book of Hours 3:386
Book of Kells 3:388
Caxton, William **4**:227
Codex Zodche-Nuttall **15**:498 *illus.*
Fust, Johann **8**:383
Gutenberg, Johann **9**:408–409
Gutenberg Bible **9**:409
illuminated manuscripts **11**:46–48
incunabula **11**:77–78
Kelmscott Press **12**:39–40
Manutius, Aldus **13**:134
papyrus **15**:73
pre-Columbian art and architecture **15**:498–499
library **12**:315–318
mass communication **13**:202
paper **15**:68–70
parchment **15**:83
printing **15**:550–553
publishing **15**:611–612
typeface **19**:363–365
BOOK, PAPERBACK *see* PAPERBACK BOOK
BOOK BURNING **4**:246 *illus.*
BOOK OF CHANGES see I CHING (Yijing)
BOOK CLIFFS
map (39° 20′N 109° 0′W) **19**:429
BOOK CLUB 3:386
book-of-the-month club
Canby, Henry Seidel **4**:100
BOOK OF COMMON PRAYER 3:386 *bibliog.*
Cranmer, Thomas **5**:332
Elizabeth I, Queen of England **7**:141
England, Church of **7**:181
Vermigli, Pietro Martire **19**:553
BOOK OF CONCORD 3:386 *bibliog.*
BOOK OF DANIEL, THE
Doctorow, E. L. **6**:210
BOOK OF DURROW **11**:46 *illus.*; **11**:47
BOOK OF HOURS 3:384 *illus.*; 3:386 *bibliog.*
Hesdin, Jacquemart de **10**:151
illuminated manuscripts **11**:48
Limbourg brothers **12**:343
Très Riches Heures du Duc de Berry, Les **7**:284 *illus.*
BOOK ILLUSTRATION 3:386–388 *bibliog., illus.*
Beardsley, Aubrey 3:142–143
Bewick, Thomas 3:233
Blake, William 3:325–326
Blanquart-Evrard, Louis Désirée 3:327
Book of Hours 3:386
Book of Kells 3:388
Bry, Théodore de 3:528
Burne-Jones, Sir Edward 3:576–577
Caldecott Medal **4**:25
calligraphy **4**:41–46
Catherwood, Frederick **4**:210
Celtic art **4**:240 *illus.*
Chagall, Marc **4**:267–268
children's literature **4**:351–354
Cochin (family) **5**:85
Crane, Walter **5**:331
Cruikshank, George **5**:365
Doré, Gustave **6**:241–242
Egyptian art and architecture **7**:89
Furniss, Harry **8**:373
Gorey, Edward **9**:250
Gothic art and architecture **9**:260
Grandville **9**:286
graphic arts **9**:291
Gravelot, Hubert François **9**:302
Greenaway, Kate **9**:349
illuminated manuscripts **11**:46–48
Islamic art and architecture **11**:293
Kent, Rockwell **12**:45
Kupka, František **12**:138
Limbourg brothers **12**:343
Menzel, Adolf von **13**:302
Moreau (family) **13**:576
Moronobu **13**:587
Morris, William **13**:589 *illus.*
Parrish, Maxfield **15**:97
Pennell, Joseph **15**:145
Posada, José Guadalupe **15**:457–458
pre-Columbian art and architecture **15**:498–499
printing **15**:551
Pyle, Howard **15**:633–634
Rackham, Arthur **16**:38
Richter, Adrian Ludwig **16**:214
Rockwell, Norman **16**:261
Rowlandson, Thomas **16**:328
Shepard, Ernest Howard **17**:256
Slevogt, Max **17**:361
Sultan Muhammad **18**:338
Tenniel, Sir John **19**:108
Theophanes the Greek **19**:158
Vedder, Elihu **19**:531
Wolgemut, Michael **20**:199
woodcuts and wood engravings **20**:211
Wyeth, N. C. **20**:299
BOOK OF KELLS 3:384 *illus.*; 3:388 *bibliog.*; **4**:42 *illus.*; **11**:47
BOOK LOUSE 3:389
BOOK OF MORMON *see* MORMONISM
BOOK-OF-THE-MONTH CLUB
book club 3:386
Canby, Henry Seidel **4**:100
BOOK OF THE COURTIER, THE
Castiglione, Baldassare, Conte **4**:188
BOOK OF THE DEAD 3:383 *illus.*; 3:386 *bibliog.*; **4**:41 *illus.*; **10**:159 *illus.*; **20**:292 *illus.*
Egyptian art and architecture **7**:89
embalming **7**:151
BOOKBINDING 3:389–390 *bibliog., illus.*
history, book 3:383
BOOKER (Texas)
map (36° 27′N 100° 32′W) **19**:129
BOOKKEEPING 3:390–392 *bibliog., illus.*
accounting **1**:77–78
assets 3:390
double entry system 3:390
equity 3:390–392
journals 3:391
ledgers 3:391
liabilities 3:390
trial balance 3:391
BOOKMAKING
horse racing **10**:248
BOOLE, GEORGE 3:392–393 *bibliog.*
Boolean algebra 3:393
mathematics, history of **13**:226
BOOLEAN ALGEBRA 3:393 *bibliog., illus.*
Boole, George 3:392–393
mathematics, history of **13**:226
BOOMERANG 3:393 *bibliog.*
BOOMSLANG 3:393 *illus.*; **17**:380 *illus.*
colubrid **5**:124
fang **17**:377 *illus.*
BOONE (county in Arkansas)
map (36° 20′N 93° 5′W) **2**:166
BOONE (county in Illinois)
map (42° 15′N 88° 50′W) **11**:42
BOONE (county in Indiana)
map (40° 3′N 86° 30′W) **11**:111
BOONE (Iowa)
map (42° 4′N 93° 53′W) **11**:244
BOONE (county in Iowa)
map (42° 2′N 93° 55′W) **11**:244
BOONE (county in Kentucky)
map (38° 57′N 84° 45′W) **12**:47
BOONE (county in Missouri)
map (38° 55′N 92° 20′W) **13**:476
BOONE (county in Nebraska)
map (41° 40′N 98° 0′W) **14**:70
BOONE (North Carolina)
map (36° 13′N 81° 41′W) **14**:242
BOONE (county in West Virginia)
map (38° 0′N 81° 45′W) **20**:111
BOONE, DANIEL 3:393–394 *bibliog., illus.*
Henderson, Richard **10**:121
Kentucky **12**:50
Transylvania Company **19**:283
Wilderness Road **20**:150
BOONEVILLE (Arkansas)
map (35° 8′N 93° 55′W) **2**:166
BOONEVILLE (Kentucky)
map (37° 29′N 83° 40′W) **12**:47
BOONEVILLE (Mississippi)
map (34° 39′N 88° 34′W) **13**:469
BOONSBORO (Maryland)
map (39° 30′N 77° 39′W) **13**:188
BOONVILLE (Indiana)
map (38° 3′N 87° 16′W) **11**:111
BOONVILLE (Missouri)
map (38° 58′N 92° 44′W) **13**:476
BOONVILLE (New York)
map (43° 29′N 75° 20′W) **14**:149
BOORSTIN, DANIEL
Library of Congress **12**:319
BOOT **17**:280 *illus.*
BOOT, HENRY A.
radar **16**:39
BOÖTES 3:394
BOOTH (Alabama)
map (32° 30′N 86° 41′W) **1**:234
BOOTH (family) 3:394 *bibliog., illus.*
BOOTH, BALLINGTON
Volunteers of America **19**:632
BOOTH, CHARLES 3:394 *bibliog.*
BOOTH, EDWIN THOMAS
Booth (family) 3:394
BOOTH, SIR FELIX
Boothia Peninsula 3:395
BOOTH, GEORGE AND ELLEN SCRIPPS
Cranbrook Foundation **5**:329
BOOTH, JOHN WILKES
Booth (family) 3:394 *illus.*
Lincoln, Abraham **12**:349
Seward, William H. **17**:228
BOOTH, JUNIUS BRUTUS
Booth (family) 3:394
BOOTH, JUNIUS BRUTUS, JR.
Booth (family) 3:394
BOOTH, WILLIAM 3:394–395 *bibliog., illus.*
Salvation Army **17**:40
BOOTHBAY HARBOR (Maine) **13**:73 *illus.*
map (43° 51′N 69° 38′W) **13**:70
BOOTHIA, GULF OF
map (71° 0′N 91° 0′W) **14**:258
BOOTHIA PENINSULA 3:395
map (70° 30′N 95° 0′W) **14**:258
BOOTH'S THEATER (New York City) 3:394
BOOTHVILLE (Louisiana)
map (29° 19′N 89° 24′W) **12**:430
BOOTLEGGING 3:395 *bibliog.*
prohibition **15**:565
United States, History of the **19**:454 *illus.*
BOP *see* BEBOP
BOPHUTHATSWANA 3:395
flag **8**:136 *illus.*
map (26° 30′S 25° 30′E) **18**:79
BOPP, FRANZ 3:395 *bibliog.*
BOR (Yugoslavia)
map (44° 5′N 22° 7′E) **20**:340
BORA-BORA 3:395; **14**:333 *illus.*
BORAGE 3:395
BORAH, WILLIAM EDGAR 3:395–396 *bibliog.*
BORAH PEAK
map (44° 8′N 113° 48′W) **11**:26
BORANE 3:396
BORÅS (Sweden)
map (57° 43′N 12° 55′E) **18**:382
BORATE MINERALS 3:396 *bibliog.*
BORAX
borate minerals 3:396
Death Valley **6**:70 *illus.*
Payen, Anselme **15**:121
BORAY
boron 3:403
BORBA (Brazil)
map (4° 24′S 59° 35′W) 3:460
BORCH, GERARD TER
Signing of the Peace of Westphalia **19**:171 *illus.*
BORCHARDT, HUGO
pistol **15**:318 *illus.*
BORCHERT, WOLFGANG 3:396
BORCHGREVINK, CARSTEN EGEBERG 3:396
BORDEAUX (France) 3:396
map (44° 50′N 0° 34′W) **8**:260
wine **20**:175
BORDELLO
prostitution **15**:573
BORDEN (Saskatchewan)
map (52° 25′N 107° 13′W) **17**:81
BORDEN (county in Texas)
map (32° 45′N 101° 25′W) **19**:129
BORDEN, GAIL 3:396
BORDEN, LIZZIE 3:396 *bibliog.*
Fall River (Massachusetts) **8**:13
BORDEN, SIR ROBERT L. 3:397 *bibliog., illus.*
Canada, history of **4**:85; **4**:86
BORDENTOWN (New Jersey)
map (40° 9′N 74° 42′W) **14**:129
BORDER COLLIE 3:397 *bibliog., illus.*

BORDER TERRIER 3:397 *bibliog., illus.*; 6:220 *illus.*
BORDERS (Scotland) 3:397 *bibliog.*
Berwick 3:226–227
BORDES, FRANÇOIS 3:398
Combe Grenal 5:130
BORDET, JULES 3:398 *bibliog.*
BORDEWIJK, FERDINAND 3:398
BORDONE, PARIS 3:398
BORDONI, FAUSTINA
Hasse, Johann Adolph 10:67
BORDUAS, PAUL-ÉMILE
Canadian art and architecture 4:90
BORE *see* TIDAL BORE
BOREAL CLIMATE *see* TAIGA CLIMATE
BOREAS 3:398
BOREL, ÉMILE 3:398
mathematics, history of 13:226
BORELLI, GIOVANNI ALFONSO 3:398 *bibliog.*
flight, human-powered 8:164
BORG, BJÖRN 3:398 *illus.*
BORGÅ (Finland) *see* PORVOO (Finland)
BORGER (Texas)
map (35° 39′N 101° 24′W) 19:129
BORGERHOUT (Belgium)
map (51° 13′N 4° 26′E) 3:177
BORGES, JORGE LUIS 3:398–399 *bibliog., illus.*
Ficciones 8:69
BORGESE, GIUSEPPE ANTONIO 3:399
BORGHESE, PAULINE
as *Venus Victrix* 4:115 *illus.*
BORGIA (family) 3:399–400 *bibliog.*
Alexander VI, Pope 1:277
Callistus III, Pope 4:47
Cesare Borgia 3:399 *illus.*
Vatican museums and galleries 19:527–528
BORGIA, SAINT FRANCIS 3:400 *bibliog.*
BORGLUM, GUTZON 3:400 *bibliog., illus.*
Mount Rushmore National Memorial 3:400 *illus.*
Stone Mountain 18:282
BORGNE, LAKE
map (30° 5′N 89° 40′W) 12:430
BORGO MAGGIORE (San Marino)
map (43° 56′N 12° 27′E) 17:56
BORI, LUCREZIA 3:400
BORIC ACID
boron 3:403
BORING (drilling)
machine tools 13:25
BORING, E. G. 3:400
BORINQUÉN *see* PUERTO RICO
BORIS GODUNOV (opera) 3:400–401
Mussorgsky, Modest 1[illegible]:685
BORIS GODUNOV (play) 3:401 *bibliog.*
Pushkin, Aleksandr 15:631–632
BORIS GODUNOV, TSAR OF RUSSIA 3:401 *bibliog.*
Russia/Union of Soviet Socialist Republics, history of 16:353
Time of Troubles 19:202
BORIS I, TSAR OF BULGARIA 3:401 *bibliog.*
BORIS III, TSAR OF BULGARIA 3:401
BORJA (family) *see* BORGIA (family)
BORJA (Peru)
map (4° 26′S 77° 33′W) 15:193
BORK, ROBERT M.
Cox, Archibald 5:322
BORLÄNGE (Sweden)
map (60° 29′N 15° 25′E) 18:382
BORLAUG, NORMAN E.
plant breeding 15:343
BORLAUG, NORMAN ERNEST 1:197 *illus.*; 3:401
green revolution 9:348
BORMAN, FRANK 3:401
Apollo program 2:81
Gemini program 9:72
BORMANN, MARTIN 3:401
Nuremberg Trials 14:297
BORN, MAX 3:401–402 *bibliog.*; 15:286 *illus.*
BÖRNE, LUDWIG 3:402
BORNEAN LIZARD *see* EARLESS MONITOR
BORNEO (Indonesia) 3:402 *bibliog.*; 11:150 *illus.*
cities
Banjarmasin 3:67
history
Brooke, Sir James 3:509
Malayo-Polynesian languages 13:82–83
mask 13:197 *illus.*
money 13:525 *illus.*
people
Dayak 6:56
Sabah (Malaysia) 17:4
Sarawak 17:75
BORNEO (island)
map (0° 30′N 114° 0′E) 11:147
BORNHOLM (Denmark) 3:402
map (55° 10′N 15° 0′E) 6:109
BORNITE 3:402
BORNU *see* KANEM-BORNU
BOROBUDUR (Indonesia) 3:402–403 *bibliog., illus.*
mandala 13:110
Prambanan 15:489
Southeast Asian art and architecture 18:110 *illus.*
temple 19:97–98 *illus.*
BORODIN, ALEKSANDR 3:403 *bibliog.*
Five, The 8:132
Russian music 16:367–368 *illus.*
BORODINO, BATTLE OF
Kutuzov, Mikhail Illarionovich 12:140
Napoleonic Wars 14:19
BORON 3:403 *bibliog., illus.*
abundances of common elements 7:131 *table*
borate minerals 3:396
borax 3:403
element 7:130 *table*
Gay-Lussac, Joseph Louis 9:64
Group IIIA periodic table 15:167
hydrides
chemical nomenclature 4:320
BORON (California)
map (34° 60′N 117° 39′W) 4:31
BORORO (American Indians) 3:403–404 *bibliog.*
BOROSILICATE GLASS
boron 3:403
BOROUGH 3:404
BOROUGH, STEPHEN 3:404
Arctic 2:142 *map*
BOROVIKOVSKY, VLADIMIR
Russian art and architecture 16:362 *illus.*
BOROVSKÝ, KAREL HAVLÍCĚK
Czech literature 5:412
BOROWSKI, TADEUSZ 3:404
BORRELIA
relapsing fever 16:132
BORROMEO, SAINT CHARLES 3:404 *bibliog.*
BORROMINI, FRANCESCO 3:404–405 *bibliog., illus.*
architecture 2:135
Italian art and architecture 11:310
San Carlo alle Quattro Fontane 3:90 *illus.*; 3:404 *illus.*; 17:51
BORROW, GEORGE HENRY 3:405 *bibliog.*
BORU, BRIAN *see* BRIAN BORU
BORZOI 3:405 *bibliog., illus.*; 6:216 *illus.*
BOSANQUET, BERNARD 3:405
BOSASO (Somalia)
map (11° 13′N 49° 8′E) 18:60
BOSBOOM-TOUSSAINT, ANNA LOUISA GEERTRUIDE 3:405
BOSCAWEN, EDWARD
French and Indian Wars 8:313 *map*
BOSCH, CARL 3:405
BOSCH, HIERONYMUS 3:405–406 *bibliog., illus.*
Garden of Earthly Delights, The 3:405–406 *illus.*
Massys, Quentin 13:214
's Hertogenbosch (Netherlands) 17:259
BOSCH, JUAN 3:406
Dominican Republic 6:234
BOSCH, ROBERT 3:406–407
BOSCO, SAINT JOHN 3:407
BOSCOBEL (Wisconsin)
map (43° 8′N 90° 42′W) 20:185
BOSE, SUBHAS CHANDRA 3:407
BOSIO, FRANÇOIS JOSEPH, BARON 3:407
BOSNIA AND HERCEGOVINA (Yugoslavia) 3:407 *map*
map (44° 15′N 17° 30′E) 20:340
Sarajevo 17:74
BOSON 3:407
electroweak theory 7:128
fundamental particles 8:362 *table*
grand unification theories 9:286
unified field theory 19:386
BOSPORUS 3:407 *map*
bridge (engineering) 3:484
BOSPORUS, STRAIT OF
map (41° 6′N 29° 4′E) 19:343
BOSQUE (county in Texas)
map (31° 57′N 97° 35′W) 19:129
BOSS, POLITICAL 3:407–408 *bibliog.*
Cameron, Simon 4:60
Croker, Richard 5:357
Curley, James M. 5:392
Daley, Richard J. 6:11–12
Hague, Frank 10:11
Long (family) 12:405–406
Pendergast, Thomas Joseph 15:142
Platt, Thomas Collier 15:361–362
Tammany Hall 19:20
Tweed, William M. 19:358
Wood, Fernando 20:206
BOSSANGOA (Central African Republic)
map (6° 29′N 17° 27′E) 4:251
BOSSE, ABRAHAM 3:408
BOSSIER (county in Louisiana)
map (32° 37′N 93° 35′W) 12:430
BOSSIER CITY (Louisiana)
map (32° 31′N 93° 43′W) 12:430
BOSSUET, JACQUES BÉNIGNE 3:408 *bibliog.*
BOSSY, MIKE 3:408
BOSTON (Georgia)
map (30° 47′N 83° 47′W) 9:114
BOSTON (Massachusetts) 3:408–410 *bibliog., illus., map*; 13:207 *illus.*
art
Museum of Fine Arts, Boston 13:656
Sargent, John Singer 17:77
clothing industry 5:65
education
Boston College 3:410
Boston Latin School 3:410
Boston University 3:411
Northeastern University 14:254
secondary education 17:179–180
Simmons College 17:314
Wheelock College 20:129
Faneuil Hall 8:20
history
American Revolution 1:354–355 *illus.*
Boston Massacre 3:410
Boston Tea Party 3:410–411 *illus.*
Curley, James M. 5:392
Quincy, Josiah 16:27
map (42° 21′N 71° 4′W) 13:206
music
Boston Pops Orchestra 3:410
Boston Symphony Orchestra 3:410
Caldwell, Sarah 4:27
Mason, Lowell 13:198
subway 18:318 *table*
BOSTON (Texas)
map (33° 26′N 94° 25′W) 19:129
BOSTON BAR (British Columbia)
map (49° 52′N 121° 26′W) 3:491
BOSTON BAY
map (42° 22′N 70° 54′W) 3:409
BOSTON BULLDOG *see* BOSTON TERRIER
BOSTON COLLEGE 3:410
BOSTON COOKING SCHOOL COOKBOOK, THE
Farmer, Fannie 8:24
BOSTON EVENING-POST
Fleet, Thomas 8:159
BOSTON EXCHANGE COFFEE HOUSE
hotel 10:260
BOSTON GLOBE 3:410
BOSTON GROUP
American music 1:350–351
BOSTON LATIN SCHOOL 3:410
BOSTON MARATHON
Rodgers, Bill 16:267
running and jogging 16:346
Switzer, Kathy 18:393
BOSTON MASSACRE 3:410 *bibliog.*
American Revolution 1:354 *illus.*
Attucks, Crispus 2:316
United States, history of the 19:440 *illus.*
BOSTON MOUNTAINS
map (35° 50′N 93° 20′W) 2:166
BOSTON POLICE STRIKE OF 1919
Coolidge, Calvin 5:241
BOSTON POPS ORCHESTRA 3:410
Fiedler, Arthur 8:70
BOSTON PORT ACT *see* INTOLERABLE ACTS
BOSTON POST ROAD 3:410 *bibli g.*
BOSTON SYMPHONY ORCHESTRA 3:410 *bibliog.*
American music 1:350
Berkshire Music Festival 3:214
Boston Pops Orchestra 3:410
Koussevitzky, Serge 12:125–126
Munch, Charles 13:639–640
New England Conservatory of Music 14:121
Ozawa, Seiji 14:480
BOSTON TEA PARTY 3:410–411 *bibliog., illus.*
Adams, Samuel 1:97–98
American Revolution 1:355
United States, history of the 19:440
BOSTON TERRIER 3:411 *bibliog., illus.*; 6:219 *illus.*
BOSTON UNIVERSITY 3:411
Silber, John 17:303
BOSTONIANS, THE (book) 3:411
James, Henry 11:353–354
BOSWELL (Indiana)
map (40° 31′N 87° 23′W) 11:111
BOSWELL (Oklahoma)
map (34° 2′N 95° 52′W) 14:368
BOSWELL (Pennsylvania)
map (40° 10′N 79° 2′W) 15:147
BOSWELL, JAMES 3:411–412 *bibliog., illus.*
Life of Samuel Johnson, The 12:330
biography 3:263
Johnson, Samuel 11:436
BOSWORTH (Missouri)
map (39° 28′N 93° 20′W) 13:476
BOTANICAL GARDEN 3:412 *bibliog., illus.*
aquarium 2:93
Bartram, John 3:98
Brooklyn Botanic Garden and Arboretum 3:510
Dominion Arboretum and Botanic Garden 6:234–235
Kew Gardens 12:62
Padua, University of 15:13
BOTANY 3:412–414 *bibliog., illus.*
diseases, plant 6:194–196
forestry 8:230–232
history 3:413–414
Bailey, Liberty Hyde 3:26
Bartram, John 3:98
Britton, Nathaniel 3:499
Brown, Robert 3:516
Darwin, Charles 6:41–42
Darwin, Sir Francis 6:42
Dioscorides, Pedanius 6:185
Gray, Asa 9:306
Grew, Nehemiah 9:360
Hales, Stephen 10:19
Helmont, Johannes Baptista van 10:116
Hooker (family) 10:227
Humboldt, Alexander von 10:301
Lamarck, Jean Baptiste 12:173
Linnaeus, Carolus 12:359
Mendel, Gregor Johann 13:85
Mohl, Hugo von 13:503
Priestley, Joseph 15:536–537
Schwann, Theodor, and Schleiden, Matthias Jakob 17:138
Theophrastus 19:158
Vries, Hugo De 19:639
horticulture 10:254–255
paleobotany 15:30–32
plant (botany) 15:333–342
research institutions
botanical garden 3:412
Brooklyn Botanic Garden and Arboretum 3:510
Dominion Arboretum and Botanic Garden 6:234–235
United States National Arboretum 19:463
BOTANY BAY 3:414
BOTERO, FERNANDO 3:414
BOTETOURT (county in Virginia)
map (37° 35′N 79° 50′W) 19:607
BOTEV, KHRISTO 3:415
Bulgaria 3:556
Bulgarian literature 3:557
BOTEV MOUNTAIN
map (42° 43′N 24° 55′E) 3:555
BOTFLY 3:415
BOTH YOUR HOUSES (play)
Anderson, Maxwell 1:402
BOTHA, LOUIS 3:415 *bibliog.*
BOTHA, P. W. 3:415
South Africa 18:83
BOTHE, WALTHER WILHELM 3:415
BOTHNIA, GULF OF 3:415
map (63° 0′N 20° 0′E) 18:382
BOTHWELL, JAMES HEPBURN, 4TH EARL OF 3:415
Mary, Queen of Scots 13:186
BOTKINS (Ohio)
map (40° 28′N 84° 11′W) 14:357
BOTO, EZA *see* BETI, MONGO
BOTOŞANI (Romania)
map (47° 45′N 26° 40′E) 16:288
BOTRANGE MOUNTAIN
map (50° 30′N 6° 8′E) 3:177
BOTSWANA 3:415–417 *bibliog., illus., map, table*
cities
Gaborone 3:416 *illus.*; 9:6
economy 3:417
flag 3:415 *illus.*
government 3:417

history **3**:417
land and resources **3**:416–417 *map, table*
map (22° 0′S 24° 0′E) **1**:136
Palace of the National Assembly **3**:416 *illus.*
people **3**:416–417
San **17**:49–50
Tswana **19**:325
physical features
Kalahari Desert **3**:416–417 *table*; **12**:7
Okavango Swamp **14**:365
rivers, lakes, and waterways
Okavango River **3**:416
BOTSWANA (people) *see* TSWANA
BOTTA, PAUL ÉMILE **3**:417
Khorsabad **12**:68
BÖTTGER, JOHANN FRIEDRICH
Meissen ware **13**:283
pottery and porcelain **15**:471
BOTTICELLI, SANDRO **3**:417–418 *bibliog., illus.*
Apelles **2**:76
The Birth of Venus **3**:418 *illus.*
Portrait of St. Augustine **2**:320 *illus.*
Sistine Chapel **17**:329
Venus and Mars **11**:22 *illus.*; **16**:151 *illus.*
BOTTINEAU (North Dakota)
map (48° 50′N 100° 27′W) **14**:248
BOTTINEAU (county in North Dakota)
map (48° 45′N 100° 55′W) **14**:248
BOTTLE **3**:418–419 *bibliog., illus.*; **9**:202 *illus.*
glass **9**:199
BOTTLE TREE **3**:419
BOTTLEBRUSH **3**:419
See also PAPERBARK
BOTULISM **3**:419 *bibliog.*
bacteria **3**:16
canning **4**:111
chemical and biological warfare **4**:312
Clostridium **5**:65
food poisoning and infection **8**:211
spore **18**:195
BOTWOOD (Newfoundland)
map (49° 9′N 55° 21′W) **14**:166
BOUABID, MAATI
Morocco **13**:586
BOUAKÉ (Ivory Coast)
map (7° 41′N 5° 2′W) **11**:335
BOUAR (Central African Republic)
map (5° 57′N 15° 36′E) **4**:251
BOUCHARDON, EDMÉ **3**:419 *bibliog.*
BOUCHER, FRANÇOIS **3**:419–420 *bibliog., illus.*
Nude Lying on a Sofa (Mademoiselle O'Murphy) **3**:419–420 *illus.*
Sèvres ware **17**:221
tapestry **19**:33
BOUCHER DE PERTHES, JACQUES **3**:420
prehistory **15**:517
BOUCICAULT, DION **3**:420 *bibliog.*
Jefferson, Joseph **11**:391
BOUDICCA *see* BOADICEA
BOUDIN, EUGÈNE LOUIS **3**:420 *bibliog.*
Woman in White on the Beach at Trouville **11**:63 *illus.*
BOUDINOT, ELIAS **3**:420 *bibliog.*
BOUGAINVILLE (Solomon Islands) **3**:420
map (6° 0′S 155° 0′E) **15**:72
World War II **20**:267 *illus.*
BOUGAINVILLE, LOUIS ANTOINE DE **3**:420
Bougainville **3**:402
exploration **8**:335
BOUGAINVILLEA (botany) **3**:421 *illus.*
BOUGUEREAU, ADOLPH WILLIAM **3**:421 *bibliog.*
BOUKHAROUBA, MUHAMMAD *see* BOUMEDIENNE, HOUARI
BOULANGER, GEORGES **3**:421 *bibliog.*
BOULANGER, LILI **3**:421 *bibliog.*
BOULANGER, NADIA **3**:421 *bibliog.*
BOULDER (Australia) *see* KALGOORLIE (Australia)
BOULDER (Colorado) **3**:421
map (40° 1′N 105° 17′W) **5**:116
BOULDER (county in Colorado)
map (40° 10′N 105° 20′W) **5**:116
BOULDER (Montana)
map (46° 14′N 112° 7′W) **13**:547
BOULDER CITY (Nevada)
map (35° 59′N 114° 50′W) **14**:111
BOULDER DAM *see* HOOVER DAM
BOULE, MARCELLIN
Neanderthalers **14**:69
BOULÉE, ÉTIENNE LOUIS
pyramids **15**:635
BOULEVARD THEATER **3**:421
BOULEZ, PIERRE **3**:421–422 *bibliog.*; **8**:321 *illus.*
BOULLE, ANDRÉ CHARLES **3**:422 *bibliog.*
furniture **8**:376
BOULLÉE, ÉTIENNE LOUIS **3**:422 *bibliog.*
design for a monument to Sir Isaac Newton **19**:617 *illus.*
visionary architecture **19**:617
BOULOGNE (France) *see* BOULOGNE-SUR-MER (France)
BOULOGNE, JEAN *see* BOLOGNA, GIOVANNI DA
BOULOGNE-SUR-MER (France) **3**:422
map (50° 43′N 1° 37′E) **8**:260
BOULSOVER, THOMAS
Sheffield (England) **17**:250
BOULT, SIR ADRIAN CEDRIC **3**:422 *bibliog.*
BOULTON, MATTHEW **3**:422
Watt, James **20**:68
BOUMEDIENNE, HOUARI **3**:422 *bibliog.*
BOUNDARY (Alaska)
map (64° 4′N 141° 6′W) **1**:242
BOUNDARY (county in Idaho)
map (48° 45′N 116° 30′W) **11**:26
BOUNDARY BAY
map (49° 0′N 122° 58′W) **20**:35
BOUNDARY PEAK
map (37° 51′N 118° 21′W) **14**:111
BOUNTIFUL (Utah)
map (40° 53′N 111° 53′W) **19**:492
BOUNTY (ship) **3**:422 *bibliog.*
Bligh, William **3**:331
mutiny **13**:687
Norfolk Island (Australia) **14**:218
Pitcairn Island **15**:319–320
BOUNTY ISLANDS
map (48° 0′S 179° 30′E) **14**:334
BOURASSA, HENRI **3**:422 *bibliog.*
BOURBAKI, NICOLAS **3**:422–423
BOURBON (dynasty) **3**:423 *bibliog.*; **8**:270 *table*
Bourbon, Charles de Bourbon, Duc De **3**:423
Bourbon, Louis Henri de Bourbon-Condé, Duc de **3**:423
Charles III, King of Spain **4**:296–297
Choiseul, Étienne François, Duc de **4**:403
Condé (family) **5**:172
France, history of **8**:268–269; **8**:271
Henry IV, King of France **10**:128
Latin America, history of **12**:219
Mexico, history of **13**:363
Naples, Kingdom of **14**:15
Orléans (family) **14**:446
Philip V, King of Spain **15**:235
Spain, history of **18**:147
BOURBON (Indiana)
map (41° 18′N 86° 7′W) **11**:111
BOURBON (county in Kansas)
map (37° 50′N 94° 50′W) **12**:18
BOURBON (county in Kentucky)
map (38° 13′N 84° 13′W) **12**:47
BOURBON (Missouri)
map (38° 9′N 91° 15′W) **13**:476
BOURBON, CHARLES DE BOURBON, DUC DE **3**:423
BOURBON, LOUIS HENRI DE BOURBON-CONDÉ, DUC DE **3**:423
BOURBON WHISKEY *see* WHISKEY
BOURBONNAIS (France) **3**:423
BOURDELLE, ÉMILE ANTOINE **3**:423 *bibliog.*
BOURDON, SÉBASTIEN **3**:423–424 *bibliog.*
BOURG (Louisiana)
map (29° 34′N 90° 36′W) **12**:430
BOURG-EN-BRESSE (France)
map (46° 12′N 5° 13′E) **8**:260
BOURGEOIS, LOUIS
Renaissance music **16**:156
BOURGEOIS, LOUISE **3**:424 *bibliog.*
BOURGEOIS GENTLEMAN, THE (play) **3**:424
Molière **13**:509
BOURGEOISIE **3**:424
economics **7**:48–49
France, history of **8**:269
French Revolution **8**:324
BOURGES (France)
cathedral
Gothic art and architecture **9**:257–258
map (47° 5′N 2° 24′E) **8**:260
BOURGET, PAUL **3**:424 *bibliog.*
BOURGOGNE *see* BURGUNDY (France)
BOURGUIBA, HABIB **3**:424
BOURIGNON, ANTOINETTE **3**:424
BOURJAILY, VANCE **3**:424
BOURKE (Australia)
map (30° 5′S 145° 56′E) **2**:328
BOURKE-WHITE, MARGARET **3**:424 *bibliog., illus.*
breadline of the 1930s **19**:454 *illus.*
The Spinner (Mahatma Gandhi) **15**:10 *illus.*
BOURKINA FASSO *see* UPPER VOLTA
BOURNEMOUTH (England) **3**:424
map (50° 43′N 1° 54′W) **19**:403
BOURNONVILLE, AUGUST **3**:425 *bibliog.*
ballet **3**:43
Royal Danish Ballet **16**:330
Royal Swedish Ballet **16**:331
BOUSE (Arizona)
map (33° 56′N 114° 0′W) **2**:160
BOUSSINGAULT, JEAN BAPTISTE **3**:425
BOUTEILLE DE VIEUX MARC (Pablo Picasso) **5**:102 *illus.*
BOUTENS, PIETER CORNELIUS **3**:425
BOUTERWEK, FRIEDRICH **3**:425
BOUTO
dolphin **6**:227 *illus.*; **6**:228
BOUTS, DIRK **3**:425 *bibliog., illus.*
Ecce Homo **11**:405 *illus.*
BOUVIER DES FLANDRES **3**:425–426 *bibliog., illus.*; **6**:215 *illus.*
BOUVINES, BATTLE OF **3**:426
BOUZOUKIA **9**:345 *illus.*
BOVET, DANIELE **3**:426
BOVID **3**:426
See also CATTLE AND CATTLE RAISING; names of specific bovids, e.g., ANTELOPE; OX; etc.
horn (biology) **10**:238
BOVILL (Idaho)
map (46° 51′N 116° 24′W) **11**:26
BOW (music) **3**:426
BOW, CLARA **3**:426
BOW, MUSICAL *see* MUSICAL BOW
BOW AND ARROW **3**:426–427 *bibliog., illus.*
archery **2**:127–128 *illus.*
arrow and arrow releases **3**:426
arrowhead (artifact) **2**:188
bow types **3**:426
Indians, American **11**:119–120
weapons **20**:74
BOW ISLAND (Alberta)
map (49° 52′N 111° 22′W) **1**:256
BOW RIVER
map (49° 56′N 111° 42′W) **1**:256
BOWBELLS (North Dakota)
map (48° 48′N 102° 15′W) **14**:248
BOWDITCH, NATHANIEL **3**:426–427 *bibliog.*
BOWDLE (South Dakota)
map (45° 27′N 99° 39′W) **18**:103
BOWDLER, THOMAS **3**:427 *bibliog.*
BOWDOIN, JAMES **3**:427
BOWDOIN COLLEGE **3**:427
BOWDON (Georgia)
map (33° 32′N 85° 15′W) **9**:114
BOWDON (North Dakota)
map (47° 28′N 99° 43′W) **14**:248
BOWEL *see* INTESTINE
BOWEL MOVEMENT *see* FECES
BOWELL, SIR MACKENZIE **3**:427
BOWEN, ELIZABETH **3**:427 *bibliog.*
BOWEN, IRA SPRAGUE **3**:428
BOWEN, NORMAN LEVI **3**:428
BOWEN-JUDD, SARA *see* WOODS, SARA
BOWEN REACTION SERIES **11**:35 *illus.*
BOWERBIRD **3**:428 *bibliog., illus.*
BOWERY, THE **3**:428
BOWFIN **3**:428
BOWIE (Arizona)
map (32° 19′N 109° 29′W) **2**:160
BOWIE (Maryland)
map (39° 0′N 76° 47′W) **13**:188
BOWIE (Texas)
map (33° 34′N 97° 51′W) **19**:129
BOWIE (county in Texas)
map (33° 25′N 94° 30′W) **19**:129
BOWIE, DAVID **3**:428
BOWIE, JAMES **3**:428 *bibliog.*
Bowie knife **18**:398–399
BOWLER (hat) **7**:275 *illus.*
BOWLES, CHESTER **3**:428
BOWLES, JANE AUER **3**:428
BOWLES, PAUL **3**:428
BOWLES, SAMUEL, III **3**:429 *bibliog.*
BOWLING **3**:429–430 *bibliog., illus., table*
See also LAWN BOWLS (sport)
Anthony, Earl **2**:49
Carter, Don **4**:171
Ladewig, Marion **12**:162
skittles **17**:344
Weber, Dick **20**:87
BOWLING GREEN (Florida)
map (27° 38′N 81° 50′W) **8**:172
BOWLING GREEN (Kentucky)
map (37° 0′N 86° 27′W) **12**:47
BOWLING GREEN (Missouri)
map (39° 20′N 91° 12′W) **13**:476
BOWLING GREEN (Ohio)
map (41° 22′N 83° 39′W) **14**:357
BOWLING GREEN (Virginia)
map (38° 3′N 77° 21′W) **19**:607
BOWLS (game) *see* LAWN BOWLS (sport)
BOWMAN (Georgia)
map (34° 12′N 83° 2′W) **9**:114
BOWMAN (North Dakota)
map (46° 11′N 103° 24′W) **14**:248
BOWMAN (county in North Dakota)
map (46° 10′N 103° 30′W) **14**:248
BOWMAN, ISAIAH **3**:430
BOWMAN, SIR WILLIAM **3**:430
BOWMAN-HALEY LAKE
map (46° 0′N 103° 20′W) **14**:248
BOWNE, BORDEN PARKER **3**:430
BOX BUTTE (county in Nebraska)
map (42° 15′N 103° 10′W) **14**:70
BOX CAMERA **4**:57
BOX ELDER (botany) **3**:430 *illus.*
maple **13**:137
BOX ELDER (Montana)
map (48° 19′N 110° 1′W) **13**:547
BOX ELDER (county in Utah)
map (41° 30′N 113° 0′W) **19**:492
BOX TURTLE **3**:430 *bibliog.*
shell **19**:353 *illus.*
BOXER (dog) **3**:430–431 *bibliog., illus.*; **6**:214 *illus.*
BOXER UPRISING **3**:431 *bibliog.*; **4**:374 *illus.*
Asia, history of **2**:258
McKinley, William **13**:31
Tz'u-hsi, Dowager Empress of China (Cixi) **19**:368
BOXEY (Newfoundland)
map (47° 25′N 55° 34′W) **14**:166
BOXFISH **3**:431
BOXING **3**:431–432 *bibliog., illus.*
Ali, Muhammad **1**:292
Armstrong, Henry **2**:179
Corbett, James J. **5**:261
Dempsey, Jack **6**:105
Durán, Roberto **6**:302
Foreman, George **8**:227
Frazier, Joe **8**:289
heavyweight boxing champions **3**:432 *table*
history **3**:431–432; **18**:197
Holmes, Larry **10**:205
Jeffries, James J. **11**:394
Johnson, Jack **11**:432
Louis, Joe **12**:422
Marciano, Rocky **13**:146
Patterson, Floyd **15**:115
Robinson, Sugar Ray **16**:245–246
rules **3**:431
Sullivan, John L. **18**:337
Tunney, Gene **19**:339
Walker, Mickey **20**:12
weight classes **3**:432
BOXING DAY **3**:433
BOXWOOD (botany) **3**:433 *illus.*
BOY SCOUTS OF AMERICA *see* SCOUTING
BOYARS **3**:433
Ivan IV, Grand Duke of Moscow and Tsar of Russia (Ivan the Terrible) **11**:332–333
BOYCE (Louisiana)
map (31° 23′N 92° 40′W) **12**:430
BOYCE, WILLIAM **3**:433
BOYCEVILLE (Wisconsin)
map (45° 3′N 92° 2′W) **20**:185
BOYCOTT **3**:433 *bibliog.*
blacklist **3**:321
Olympic Games **14**:383–384
syndicalism **18**:407
BOYD (county in Kentucky)
map (38° 25′N 82° 40′W) **12**:47
BOYD (county in Nebraska)
map (42° 55′N 98° 50′W) **14**:70
BOYD (Texas)
map (33° 5′N 97° 34′W) **19**:129
BOYD, BELLE **3**:433
BOYD-ORR, JOHN, 1ST BARON BOYD-ORR OF BRECHIN MEARN **3**:433
BOYDEN, SETH **3**:433–434
BOYDTON (Virginia)
map (36° 40′N 78° 24′W) **19**:607
BOYE, KARIN **3**:434
BOYER, CHARLES **3**:434
BOYER, JEAN PIERRE **3**:434
BOYER RIVER
map (41° 28′N 95° 55′W) **11**:244

BOYERTOWN (Pennsylvania)
  map (40° 20′N 75° 38′W) **15**:147
BOYKINS (Virginia)
  map (36° 35′N 77° 12′W) **19**:607
BOYLE (county in Kentucky)
  map (37° 35′N 84° 50′W) **12**:47
BOYLE, KAY 3:434
BOYLE, RICHARD, 3D EARL OF BURLINGTON *see* BURLINGTON, RICHARD BOYLE, 3D EARL OF
BOYLE, ROBERT 3:434 *bibliog., illus.*
  element **7**:129
  gas laws **9**:53
  physics, history of **15**:282
  qualitative chemical analysis **16**:6
BOYLE, W. A. "Tony"
  United Mine Workers **19**:412
BOYNE, BATTLE OF THE 3:434; **11**:263 *illus.*
  Orangemen **14**:415
BOYNE CITY (Michigan)
  map (45° 13′N 85° 1′W) **13**:377
BOYNE RIVER
  map (53° 43′N 6° 15′W) **11**:258
BOYNTON (Oklahoma)
  map (35° 39′N 95° 39′W) **14**:368
BOYNTON BEACH (Florida)
  map (26° 32′N 80° 3′W) **8**:172
BOYS' CLUBS OF AMERICA 3:434
BOYS TOWN 3:434
  Flanagan, Edward J. **8**:152
BOYSEN-JENSEN, P.
  tropism **19**:309
BOYSEN RESERVOIR
  map (43° 19′N 108° 11′W) **20**:301
BOYUIBE (Bolivia)
  map (20° 25′S 63° 17′W) **3**:366
BOZEMAN (Montana)
  map (45° 41′N 111° 2′W) **13**:547
BOZEMAN TRAIL 3:434 *bibliog.*; **8**:341 *map*; **14**:431 *map*
BOZOUM (Central African Republic)
  map (6° 19′N 16° 23′E) **4**:251
BRABANT, DUCHY OF 3:435
  art
    Floris (family) **8**:176–177
  Low Countries, history of the **12**:440 *map*
BRAČ ISLAND
  map (43° 20′N 16° 40′E) **20**:340
BRACCIOLINI, POGGIO
  Renaissance **16**:149
BRACEGIRDLE, ANNE
  theater, history of the **19**:147
BRACHIOPOD 3:435 *bibliog., illus.*; **15**:35 *illus.*
  Cambrian Period **4**:51–52
  lophophorate **12**:413
  Ordovician Period **14**:422 *illus.*
  Paleozoic Era **15**:43
  shell **17**:250
  Silurian Period **17**:310 *illus.*
  Triassic Period **19**:293 *illus.*
BRACHIOSAURUS 3:435 *bibliog., illus.*
  dinosaur **6**:179–182
BRACKEN (county in Kentucky)
  map (38° 40′N 84° 6′W) **12**:47
BRACKEN, JOHN 3:436
BRACKET FUNGUS 3:436
BRACKETTVILLE (Texas)
  map (29° 19′N 100° 24′W) **19**:129
BRACQUEMOND, FÉLIX 3:436 *bibliog.*
BRACTON, HENRY DE
  common law treatises **5**:140
BRADBURY, RAY 3:436 *illus.*
  Martian Chronicles, The **13**:178
BRADDOCK, EDWARD 3:436 *bibliog.*
  French and Indian Wars **8**:313–314 *map*
  Gage, Thomas **9**:8
  Gist, Christopher **9**:191
BRADENTON (Florida)
  map (27° 29′N 82° 34′W) **8**:172
BRADFORD (Arkansas)
  map (35° 25′N 91° 27′W) **2**:166
BRADFORD (city in England) 3:436
  map (53° 48′N 1° 45′W) **19**:403
BRADFORD (family) 3:436–437 *bibliog.*
BRADFORD (county in Florida)
  map (30° 0′N 82° 10′W) **8**:172
BRADFORD (Illinois)
  map (41° 11′N 89° 39′W) **11**:42
BRADFORD (Ohio)
  map (40° 8′N 84° 26′W) **14**:357
BRADFORD (Pennsylvania)
  map (41° 58′N 78° 39′W) **15**:147
BRADFORD (county in Pennsylvania)
  map (41° 56′N 78° 40′W) **15**:147
BRADFORD (Tennessee)
  map (36° 5′N 88° 51′W) **19**:104
BRADFORD (Vermont)
  map (43° 59′N 72° 9′W) **19**:554
BRADFORD, ANDREW
  Bradford (family) **3**:436
BRADFORD, GAMALIEL 3:437
BRADFORD, THOMAS
  Bradford (family) 3:436–437
BRADFORD, WILLIAM
  Pilgrims **15**:302
  Squanto **18**:202
BRADFORD, WILLIAM (Pilgrim leader) 3:437 *bibliog.*
BRADFORD, WILLIAM (printer, 1663–1752)
  Bradford (family) 3:436
BRADFORD MOUNTAIN
  map (41° 59′N 73° 17′W) **5**:193
BRADLAUGH, CHARLES
  atheism **2**:289
  birth control **3**:294
BRADLEE, BENJAMIN C. 3:437
BRADLEY (Arkansas)
  map (33° 6′N 93° 39′W) **2**:166
BRADLEY (county in Arkansas)
  map (33° 25′N 92° 12′W) **2**:166
BRADLEY (Florida)
  map (27° 48′N 81° 59′W) **8**:172
BRADLEY (Illinois)
  map (41° 9′N 87° 52′W) **11**:42
BRADLEY (South Dakota)
  map (45° 5′N 97° 39′W) **18**:103
BRADLEY (county in Tennessee)
  map (35° 8′N 84° 53′W) **19**:104
BRADLEY, A. C. 3:437 *bibliog.*
BRADLEY, BILL 3:437 *bibliog.*
BRADLEY, FRANCIS HERBERT 3:437 *bibliog.*
  idealism **11**:30
BRADLEY, JAMES 3:437–438
  aberration, stellar **1**:57
  astronomy, history of **2**:280
  light **12**:336
BRADLEY, OMAR N. 3:438 *bibliog., illus.*; **20**:273 *illus.*
BRADLEY, PAT 3:438
BRADLEY, TOM 3:438
BRADLEY v. *SCHOOL BOARD OF THE CITY OF RICHMOND*
  busing, school **3**:590
BRADSHAW (West Virginia)
  map (37° 21′N 81° 49′W) **20**:111
BRADSTREET, ANNE 3:438 *bibliog.*
BRADSTREET, JOHN
  French and Indian Wars **8**:313 *map*
BRADY (Montana)
  map (48° 2′N 111° 51′W) **13**:547
BRADY (Texas)
  map (31° 8′N 99° 20′W) **19**:129
BRADY, DIAMOND JIM 3:438 *bibliog.*
BRADY, MATHEW B. 3:438–439 *bibliog., illus.*
  Cyrus W. Field **8**:71 *illus.*
  Gardner, Alexander **9**:44
  George Armstrong Custer **5**:398 *illus.*
  Kit Carson **4**:170 *illus.*
  Mary Todd Lincoln **12**:350 *illus.*
  Philip H. Sheridan **17**:257 *illus.*
  Ulysses S. Grant **15**:269 *illus.*
BRADYCARDIA *see* HEARTBEAT
BRAEKELEER, HENRI DE
  Inauguration of Leopold I, King of the Belgians **12**:442 *illus.*
BRAGA (Portugal) 3:439
  map (41° 33′N 8° 26′W) **15**:449
BRAGADO (Argentina)
  map (35° 8′S 60° 30′W) **2**:149
BRAGANÇA (dynasty) 3:439 *bibliog.*
  Pereira, Nuno Álvares **15**:163
BRAGANÇA (Portugal)
  map (41° 49′N 6° 45′W) **15**:449
BRAGG, BRAXTON 3:439 *bibliog.*
  Chattanooga, Battles of **4**:303
  Civil War, U.S. **5**:23–25 *map*; **5**:28
  Hill, D. H. **10**:164
BRAGG, FORT (North Carolina) *see* FORT BRAGG (North Carolina)
BRAGG, SIR WILLIAM H. (1862-194[illegible]) 3:439 *bibliog.*; **4**:329 *illus.*
BRAGG, SIR WILLIAM L. (1890-1971) 3:439
  chemistry, history of **4**:329
  X-ray diffraction **20**:308
BRAGG'S LAW
  Bragg, Sir William H. **3**:439
  X-ray diffraction **20**:308
  X rays **20**:310
BRAGI 3:439
BRAGINSKY, VLADIMIR
  gravitational waves **9**:306
BRAHAM (Minnesota)
  map (45° 41′N 93° 28′W) **13**:453
BRAHE, TYCHO 2:278–279 *illus.*; 3:439–440 *bibliog., illus.*
  armillary sphere **2**:173
  astronomy, history of **2**:278
  observatory, astronomical **14**:317
  Uraniborg Observatory **19**:471
BRAHM, OTTO 3:440 *bibliog.*
  Deutsches Theater **6**:136–137
BRAHMA AND BRAHMAN (Hinduism) 3:440
  Hinduism **10**:170
  marriage **13**:165
  philosophy **15**:246
  Vedanta **19**:530
BRAHMAN CATTLE 3:440 *bibliog., illus.*; **4**:216 *illus.*
  zebu cattle **20**:357
BRAHMANBARIA (Bangladesh)
  map (23° 59′N 91° 7′E) **3**:64
BRAHMAPUTRA RIVER 3:440
  map (24° 2′N 90° 59′E) **11**:80
BRAHMIN (caste) 3:440; **10**:170 *illus.*
  caste **4**:186; **4**:187 *illus.*
BRAHMO SAMAJ 3:440 *bibliog.*
  Roy, Rammohun **16**:329
BRAHMS, JOHANNES 3:441 *bibliog., illus.*
  capriccio **4**:128
  Joachim, Joseph **11**:419–420
BRAHUI
  Dravidian languages **6**:263
BRAIDED RUGS
  rugs and carpets **16**:341
BRAIDED STREAM 3:441 *bibliog.*
  floodplain **8**:165–166
  river and stream **16**:231–232
BRAIDWOOD, ROBERT 3:442
  Jarmo **11**:383
BRĂILA (Romania) 3:442
  map (45° 16′N 27° 58′E) **16**:288
BRAILLE, LOUIS 3:442 *bibliog.*
  braille system **3**:442
BRAILLE SYSTEM 3:442 *bibliog., illus.*
  Braille, Louis **3**:442
BRAIN 3:442–448 *bibliog., illus.*
  anatomy **3**:444–447 *illus.*
    circulatory system **4**:440 *illus.*
    Erasistratus **7**:227
    Purkinje, Jan Evangelista **15**:630
  animal behavior **2**:15
  attention **2**:314
  brain bilateralism **3**:448
  Broca, Paul **3**:500
  computer modeling **5**:162 *illus.*
  death and dying **6**:68–69
  disorders
    Alzheimer's disease **1**:320
    aphasia **2**:76–77
    apraxia **2**:91–92
    cerebral palsy **4**:259–260
    coma (unconscious state) **5**:129
    concussion **5**:171
    encephalitis **7**:162
    epilepsy **7**:219 *illus.*
    headache **10**:85
    Huntington's chorea **10**:315
    hydrocephaly **10**:331
    hyperactive children **10**:347
    hypertension **10**:349
    infectious diseases **11**:167
    mastoiditis **13**:217
    meningitis **13**:298
    microcephaly **13**:384
    nervous system, diseases of the **14**:95
    Parkinson's disease **15**:91
    psychosis **15**:602
    schizophrenia **17**:124
    stroke **18**:301–302
    Tay-Sachs disease **19**:48
  dreams and dreaming **6**:266–268
  drug effects **6**:276 *illus.*
  electroencephalograph **7**:113–114
  emotion **7**:157
  eye **7**:350
  Gall, Franz Joseph **9**:16
  hallucinogens **10**:24
  hypnosis **10**:350
  Lashley, Karl S. **12**:213
  memory **13**:290–292
  nervous system **14**:94–95 *illus.*
  neuropharmacology **14**:105
  neurophysiology **14**:105–106
  Olds, James **14**:376
  pattern recognition **15**:114
  PETT **15**:215–216
  phonetics **15**:251
  phrenology **15**:278
  prehistoric humans **15**:513; **15**:515
  psychotropic drugs **15**:604
  Ramón y Cajal, Santiago **16**:81
  sensation **17**:204
  senses **17**:204
  size and weight **3**:442–443
  sleep **17**:360
  speech **18**:173; **18**:175
  sugar **18**:327
  surgery **3**:448; **18**:361
    Cushing, Harvey W. **5**:397
BRAIN, DENNIS 3:448
BRAIN BILATERALISM 3:448 *bibliog., illus.*; **14**:94 *illus.*
  consciousness, separate, theory **3**:448
  evidence **3**:448
  handedness **10**:35
  hemisphere specialization **3**:448
BRAIN DRAIN
  immigration **11**:54
BRAIN DYSFUNCTION, MINIMAL (MBD) *see* HYPERACTIVE CHILDREN
BRAIN TRUST (American history) 3:448–449 *bibliog.*
  Berle, A. A. **3**:214
  cabinet **4**:5
  Roosevelt, Franklin Delano **16**:308
  Tugwell, Rexford G. **19**:329
BRAIN WAVES *see* BRAIN
BRAINARD (Nebraska)
  map (41° 11′N 97° 0′W) **14**:70
BRAINERD (Minnesota)
  map (46° 21′N 94° 12′W) **13**:453
BRAINERD, DAVID 3:449 *bibliog.*
BRAINTREE (Massachusetts)
  map (42° 13′N 71° 0′W) **13**:206
BRAINWASHING 3:449 *bibliog.*
  propaganda **15**:568
  sensory deprivation **17**:205
  techniques **3**:449
BRAKE (device) 3:449–451 *bibliog., illus.*
  automobile **2**:359 *illus.*
  coach and carriage **5**:73
  electromagnet **7**:115
  hydraulic disc brakes **13**:21 *illus.*
  machine **13**:20–21
  motorcycle **13**:614
  trucking industry **19**:315
BRAKHAGE, STAN 3:451
BRALORNE (British Columbia)
  map (50° 47′N 122° 49′W) **3**:491
BRAMAH, JOSEPH 3:451
  lock and key **12**:387
  toilet **19**:222
BRAMANTE, DONATO 3:451–452 *bibliog., illus.*
  cathedrals and churches **4**:207
  Italian art and architecture **11**:309
  Saint Peter's Basilica **17**:25
  Tempietto **16**:152 *illus.*; **19**:93
BRAMBLE 3:452
  blackberry **3**:320
  brier **3**:485
  pollination **15**:408 *illus.*
  raspberry **16**:90
BRAN 3:452
  flour **8**:178
  rice **16**:207–208
  wheat **20**:124
BRANCATI, VITALIANO 3:452
BRANCH (botany) *see* PLANT (botany); SHOOT (botany)
BRANCH (county in Michigan)
  map (41° 55′N 85° 3′W) **13**:377
BRANCH (Newfoundland)
  map (46° 53′N 53° 57′W) **14**:166
BRANCHVILLE (South Carolina)
  map (33° 15′N 80° 49′W) **18**:98
BRANCO RIVER
  map (1° 24′S 61° 51′W) **3**:460
BRANCUSI, CONSTANTIN 3:452–453 *bibliog., illus.*
  Bird in Space **2**:201 *illus.*
  Madmoiselle Pogany **3**:452 *illus.*
  Sleeping Muse **17**:165 *illus.*
BRAND, MAX 3:453
  pulp magazines **15**:620
BRAND, VANCE 3:453
  Apollo-Soyuz Test Project **2**:84
BRAND NAME *see* TRADEMARK
BRANDBERG MOUNTAIN
  map (21° 10′S 14° 33′E) **14**:11
BRANDEIS, LOUIS D. 3:453 *bibliog., illus.*
BRANDEIS UNIVERSITY 3:453
BRANDENBURG (East Germany) 3:453
  See also PRUSSIA
  boundaries *c.*1648 **7**:289 *map*
  expansion of Brandenburg-Prussia, 1415–1815 **15**:585 *map*
  Frederick I, Elector **8**:289
  Frederick I, King of Prussia **8**:291
  Frederick William, Elector of Brandenburg (the Great Elector) **8**:292–293
  German territories *c.*1176 **9**:149 *map*
  Germany, history of **9**:151–152
  Germany in 1648 **9**:151 *map*
  Germany 1815–1871 **9**:153 *map*
  history
    Hohenzollern (dynasty) **10**:199
  map (52° 24′N 12° 32′E) **9**:140

BRANDENBURG (Kentucky)
map (38° 0′N 86° 10′W) **12**:47
BRANDENBURG GATE (East Berlin) **3**:453
Langhans, Carl Gotthard **12**:195
BRANDES, GEORG MORRIS COHEN **3**:454 *bibliog.*
BRANDO, MARLON **3**:454 *bibliog., illus.*
Streetcar Named Desire, A **18**:297
BRANDON (Florida)
map (27° 56′N 82° 17′W) **8**:172
BRANDON (Manitoba) **3**:454
map (49° 50′N 99° 57′W) **13**:119
BRANDON (Mississippi)
map (32° 16′N 89° 59′W) **13**:469
BRANDON (South Dakota)
map (43° 36′N 96° 37′W) **18**:103
BRANDON (Vermont)
map (43° 48′N 73° 5′W) **19**:554
BRANDON (Wisconsin)
map (43° 44′N 88° 47′W) **20**:185
BRANDT, BILL **3**:454
BRANDT, EDGAR
Art Deco **2**:207
BRANDT, GEORG
cobalt **5**:82 *illus.*
BRANDT, WILLY **3**:454–455 *bibliog., illus.*
Germany, East and West **9**:147
BRANDY **3**:455 *bibliog.*
BRANDY STATION, BATTLE OF **3**:455
BRANDYWINE, BATTLE OF THE **3**:455 *bibliog.*
BRANNER, HANS CHRISTIAN **3**:455 *bibliog.*
BRANS, CARL H.
Dicke, Robert **6**:156
BRANS-DICKE THEORY OF GRAVITATION
Dicke, Robert **6**:156
gravitation **9**:305
relativity **16**:135
BRANSFIELD, EDWARD **3**:455
BRANSON (Missouri)
map (36° 39′N 93° 13′W) **13**:476
BRANT *see* GOOSE
BRANT, JOSEPH **3**:455 *bibliog.*
Brantford **3**:456
Mohawk **13**:502
BRANT, SEBASTIAN **3**:456 *bibliog.*
fool **8**:213
BRANT LAKE (New York)
map (43° 41′N 73° 45′W) **14**:149
BRANTFORD (Ontario) **3**:456
map (43° 8′N 80° 16′W) **14**:393
BRANTING, HJALMAR **3**:456
BRANTLEY (Alabama)
map (31° 35′N 86° 22′W) **1**:234
BRANTLEY (county in Georgia)
map (31° 10′N 82° 0′W) **9**:114
BRANTVILLE (New Brunswick)
map (47° 22′N 64° 58′W) **14**:117
BRAQUE, GEORGES **3**:456 *bibliog., illus.*
collage **5**:102
cubism **5**:380
Gris, Juan **9**:366
Picasso, Pablo **15**:291
Still Life with Erik Satie Score **5**:381 *illus.*
Still Life with Playing Cards **8**:308 *illus.*
Violin and Pitcher **3**:456 *illus.*
BRAS D'OR LAKE **3**:456
map (45° 52′N 60° 50′W) **14**:269
BRASENOSE COLLEGE (Oxford University) **14**:474
BRASÍLIA (Brazil) **3**:457 *bibliog., illus.*; **3**:464 *illus.*
architecture
Alvorada Palace **12**:228 *illus.*
Niemeyer, Oscar **14**:185
climate **3**:461 *table*
Costa, Lúcio **5**:290
Kubitschek, Juscelino **12**:134
Latin American art and architecture **12**:228
map (15° 47′S 47° 55′W) **3**:460
BRAŞOV (Romania) **3**:457
map (45° 39′N 25° 37′E) **16**:288
BRASS **3**:457
copper **5**:252
BRASSAÏ **3**:457 *bibliog.*
photography, history and art of **15**:271
BRASSEY MOUNTAINS
map (4° 54′N 117° 30′E) **13**:84
BRASSTOWN BALD MOUNTAIN
map (34° 52′N 83° 48′W) **9**:114
BRATIANU (family) **3**:458
BRATISLAVA (Czechoslovakia) **3**:458
map (48° 9′N 17° 7′E) **5**:413
BRATSK (USSR)
map (56° 5′N 101° 48′E) **19**:388
BRATSK RESERVOIR
map (56° 10′N 102° 10′E) **19**:388
BRATTAIN, WALTER **3**:458
Shockley, William Bradford **17**:279
transistor, inventor **19**:271
BRATTLEBORO (Vermont)
map (42° 51′N 72° 34′W) **19**:554
BRAUDEL, FERNAND **3**:458
history **10**:185
BRAUN, EVA **3**:458
BRAUN, KARL FERDINAND **3**:458
BRAUN, WERNHER VON *see* VON BRAUN, WERNHER
BRAUNSCHWEIG (city in West Germany) **3**:458
map (52° 16′N 10° 31′E) **9**:140
BRAUNSCHWEIG (region in West Germany) *see* BRUNSWICK (region in West Germany)
BRAUTIGAN, RICHARD **3**:458
BRAVA ISLAND
map (14° 52′N 24° 43′W) **4**:122
BRAVAIS, AUGUSTE
crystal **5**:376
mineral **13**:439
BRAVE NEW WORLD (book) **3**:458 *bibliog.*
Huxley, Aldous **10**:324
BRAVO DEL NORTE RIVER
map (25° 55′N 97° 9′W) **13**:357
BRAWLEY (California)
map (32° 59′N 115° 31′W) **4**:31
BRAXTON (county in West Virginia)
map (38° 40′N 80° 45′W) **20**:111
BRAY, THOMAS **3**:458–459 *bibliog.*
BRAYMER (Missouri)
map (39° 35′N 93° 48′W) **13**:476
BRAZEAU, MOUNT
map (52° 33′N 117° 21′W) **1**:256
BRAZIL **3**:459–464 *bibliog., illus., map, table*
art **3**:462
See also the subheading Brazil under specific art forms, e.g., ARCHITECTURE; PAINTING; SCULPTURE; etc.; the subheading Brazil under PRE-COLUMBIAN ART AND ARCHITECTURE
Latin American art and architecture **12**:223–228
cities
Belém **3**:174
Belo Horizonte **3**:192
Brasília **3**:457 *illus.*; **3**:464 *illus.*
Curitiba **5**:392
Fortaleza **8**:238
Manaus **13**:108
Natal **14**:26
Pôrto Alegre **15**:445
Recife **16**:107
Rio de Janeiro **16**:226–227 *map*
Salvador **17**:39
Santos **17**:70
São Paulo **17**:71 *illus.*
climate **3**:459; **3**:461 *table*
culture
Freyre, Gilberto **8**:330
economic activities **3**:462–463 *illus.*
education **3**:461–462
Latin American universities **12**:233 *table*
family **8**:16 *illus.*
flag **3**:459 *illus.*
government **3**:463
history **3**:463–464
Andrada e Silva, José Bonifácio de **1**:406
Bragança (dynasty) **3**:439
Cabral, Pedro Álvarez **4**:7
Figueiredo, João Batista de Oliveira **8**:75
Fonseca, Manuel Deodoro da **8**:205
Geisel, Ernesto **9**:68
Goulart, João **9**:265
John Maurice of Nassau **11**:425
Kubitschek, Juscelino **12**:134
Latin America, history of **12**:217–222
Nabuco, Joaquim **14**:4
Pedro I, Emperor **15**:131
Pedro II, Emperor **15**:131–132
Peixoto, Floriano **15**:134
Portugal, history of **15**:454
Thirty Years' War **19**:171
Tiradentes **19**:207
Tordesillas, Treaty of **19**:239
Triple Alliance, War of the **19**:302
Vargas, Getúlio Dornelles **19**:522
Indians **8**:16 *illus.*
land and resources **3**:459–460 *map*
mica **13**:371
tin **19**:205
language **3**:461
literature *see* BRAZILIAN LITERATURE
map (10° 0′S 55° 0′W) **18**:85
music
Villa-Lobos, Heitor **19**:596–597
people **3**:460–462
Bororo **3**:403–404
Guaraní **9**:386
Indians **11**:132 *map*
Mundurucú **13**:640–641
women in society **20**:204 *table*
Yanomamo **20**:318
philately **15**:230 *illus.*
physical features
Marajó **13**:143
religion **3**:461
Afro-American cults **1**:178
rivers, lakes, and waterways **3**:459–460
Amazon River **1**:323–324 *illus., map*
Araguaia River **2**:108
Iguaçu Falls **11**:38
Madeira River **13**:40
Negro, Rio **14**:78
Parnaíba River **15**:96
Purus River **15**:631
São Francisco River **17**:71
Tocantins River **19**:220
silk **17**:308
sports
Pelé **15**:137
states
Acre **1**:84
Mato Grosso **13**:229
transportation
railroad **16**:73
Trans-Amazonian Highway **19**:267
vegetation and animal life **3**:459
BRAZIL (Indiana)
map (39° 32′N 87° 8′W) **11**:111
BRAZIL BASIN
Atlantic Ocean bottom **2**:295 *map*
BRAZIL CURRENT **3**:464
ocean currents and wind systems, worldwide **14**:322–323 *maps*
BRAZIL NUT **3**:464 *illus.*; **14**:300–301 *illus.*
BRAZILIAN LITERATURE **3**:464 *bibliog.*
authors
Amado, Jorge **1**:320
Anchieta, José de **1**:399
Andrade, Mário de **1**:406
Gonçalves, Dias, Antônio **9**:242
Machado de Assis, Joaquim Maria **13**:17
Matos Guerra, Gregório de **13**:229
Rosa, João Guimarães **16**:312
Veríssimo, Érico **19**:551
Latin American literature **12**:230
BRAZILIAN SHIELD
South America **18**:86–87
BRAZILWOOD **3**:464–465
BRAZING **3**:465
flux, boron **3**:403
BRAZORIA (Texas)
map (29° 3′N 95° 34′W) **19**:129
BRAZORIA (county in Texas)
map (29° 12′N 95° 25′W) **19**:129
BRAZOS (county in Texas)
map (30° 40′N 96° 18′W) **19**:129
BRAZOS RIVER **3**:465
map (28° 53′N 95° 23′W) **19**:129
BRAZZA, PIERRE PAUL FRANÇOIS CAMILLE SAVORGNAN DE **3**:465 *bibliog.*
BRAZZAVILLE (Congo) **3**:465; **5**:182 *illus., table*
Brazza, Pierre Paul François Camille Savorgnan de **3**:465
map (4° 16′S 15° 17′E) **5**:182
BRČKO (Yugoslavia)
map (44° 53′N 18° 48′E) **20**:340
BREA (California)
map (33° 55′N 117° 54′W) **4**:31
BREACH OF CONTRACT
contract (law) **5**:231–232
BREACH OF THE PEACE **3**:465
riot **16**:228
BREAD **3**:465–467 *bibliog., illus.*
baking industry **3**:29
cooking **5**:237–238
flour **8**:178
ingredients **3**:465–466
molds **13**:506
nutrition, human **14**:305–306
production methods **3**:466–467 *illus.*
rye **16**:379–380
wheat **20**:124–126 *illus.*
World War I poster **20**:240 *illus.*
BREADFRUIT **3**:467–468 *bibliog., illus.*
BREADNUT *see* NUT
BREAK DANCING **6**:24 *illus.*
BREAKENRIDGE, MOUNT
map (49° 43′N 121° 56′W) **3**:491
BREAKER **3**:468 *bibliog.*
surf **18**:358
water wave **20**:58 *illus.*
BREAKFAST CEREAL **3**:468 *bibliog.*
Kellogg, W. K. **12**:38
BREAKWATER
coastal protection **5**:81
harbor and port **10**:42; **10**:43 *illus.*
BREAM *see* MINNOW; SUNFISH
BREAM, JULIAN **3**:468
BREAST **3**:468–469 *bibliog., illus.*
breast-feeding **3**:469
cancer **4**:104–106 *illus.*
mammal **13**:97
mastectomy **13**:215
mastitis **13**:217
plastic surgery **15**:347
pregnancy and birth **15**:503
sex change **17**:225
BREAST-FEEDING **3**:469 *bibliog.*
antibody **2**:59–60
mastitis **13**:217
prolactin **15**:567
BREASTED, JAMES HENRY **3**:469–470 *bibliog.*
Fertile Crescent **8**:60
BREASTSTROKE
swimming **18**:390–392 *illus.*
BREATH ANALYZER **3**:470 *bibliog.*
BREATHING
asthma **2**:268
emphysema **7**:158
hyperventilation **10**:349
lungs **12**:464
respiratory system **16**:178–181
speech **18**:173
suffocation **18**:325
BREATHITT (county in Kentucky)
map (37° 35′N 83° 20′W) **12**:47
BREAUX BRIDGE (Louisiana)
map (30° 16′N 91° 54′W) **12**:430
BREBES (Indonesia)
map (6° 53′S 109° 3′E) **11**:147
BRÉBEUF, SAINT JEAN DE **3**:470 *bibliog.*
Jesuit Martyrs of North America **11**:402
BRECCIA **3**:470
fault **8**:38
meteorite craters **13**:338
sedimentary rock **17**:185
BRECHT, BERTOLT **3**:470–471 *bibliog., illus.*; **9**:134 *illus.*
Bentley, Eric **3**:205
Berliner Ensemble **3**:218
Caucasian Chalk Circle, The **4**:217–218
Deutsches Theater **6**:136–137
epic theater **7**:217–218
Fassbinder, Rainer Werner **8**:33
Mother Courage **13**:606
theater, history of the **19**:150–151 *illus.*
theory of acting **1**:86
Threepenny Opera, The **19**:182
Weigel, Helene **20**:92
Weill, Kurt **20**:94
BRECKENRIDGE (Colorado)
map (39° 29′N 106° 3′W) **5**:116
BRECKENRIDGE (county in Kentucky)
map (37° 45′N 86° 25′W) **12**:47
BRECKENRIDGE (Minnesota)
map (46° 16′N 96° 35′W) **13**:453
BRECKENRIDGE (Missouri)
map (39° 44′N 93° 49′W) **13**:476
BRECKENRIDGE (Texas)
map (32° 45′N 98° 54′W) **19**:129
BRECKINRIDGE, JOHN CABELL **3**:471 *bibliog.*
votes in 1860 election **5**:17 *map*
BRECKNOCK *see* POWYS (Wales)
BRECONSHIRE *see* POWYS (Wales)
BREDA (Netherlands) **3**:471
map (51° 35′N 4° 46′E) **14**:99
BREDA, CHARLES VON
James Watt **20**:68 *illus.*
BREDA, PEACE OF (1667)
Anglo-Dutch Wars **2**:3
Suriname **18**:364
BREDENBURY (Saskatchewan)
map (50° 57′N 102° 3′W) **17**:81
BREDERO, GERBRAND ADRIAENSZOON **3**:471
BREEDER REACTOR **3**:471–472 *bibliog., illus.*
construction **3**:471
energy sources **7**:175
nuclear energy **14**:283
plutonium **15**:373
power, generation and transmission of **15**:484

BREEDER REACTOR (cont.)
theory **3**:471
thorium **19**:178
BREEDING *see* ANIMAL COURTSHIP AND MATING; ANIMAL HUSBANDRY; GENETICS; PLANT BREEDING; REPRODUCTION (biology); etc.
BREEDLOVE, CRAIG 3:472
BREEN, JOSEPH J.
film, history of **8**:84
BREER, ROBERT
film, history of **8**:87
BREESE (Illinois)
map (38° 36′N 89° 32′W) **11**:42
BREEZE
mountain and valley winds **13**:624
BREGENZ (Austria) 3:472
map (47° 30′N 9° 46′E) **2**:348
BREIDA FJORD
map (65° 15′N 23° 15′W) **11**:17
BREIZ *see* BRITTANY (France)
BRELAN
poker **15**:386
BREM RIVER (British Columbia)
map (50° 26′N 124° 39′W) **3**:491
BREMEN (Georgia)
map (33° 43′N 85° 9′W) **9**:114
BREMEN (Indiana)
map (41° 27′N 86° 9′W) **11**:111
BREMEN (Ohio)
map (39° 42′N 82° 26′W) **14**:357
BREMEN (West Germany) 3:472
map (53° 4′N 8° 49′E) **9**:140
Town Hall **9**:125 *illus.*
BREMER (county in Iowa)
map (42° 45′N 92° 18′W) **11**:244
BREMER, FREDRIKA 3:472
BREMERHAVEN (West Germany) 3:473
Bremen (West Germany) **3**:472
map (53° 33′N 8° 34′E) **9**:140
BREMERTON (Washington)
map (47° 34′N 122° 38′W) **20**:35
BRENDAN, SAINT 3:473 *bibliog.*
canoe **4**:113
BRENDEL, ALFRED 3:473
BRENHAM (Texas)
map (30° 10′N 96° 24′W) **19**:129
BRENNAN, CHRISTOPHER
Australian literature **2**:343 *illus.*
BRENNAN, WILLIAM JOSEPH, JR. 3:473; **12**:246 *illus.*; **18**:355 *illus.*
Roth v. *United States* **16**:322
Supreme Court of the United States **18**:357
United Steelworkers of America v. *Weber* **19**:465
BRENNER PASS 3:473
map (47° 0′N 11° 30′E) **2**:348
BRENNUS 3:473
BRENT (Alabama)
map (32° 56′N 87° 10′W) **1**:234
BRENT, MARGARET 3:473
BRENTANO, CLEMENS 3:473 *bibliog.*
BRENTANO, FRANZ 3:473 *bibliog.*
BRENTWOOD (New York)
map (40° 47′N 73° 14′W) **14**:149
BRENTWOOD (Tennessee)
map (36° 1′N 86° 47′W) **19**:104
BRESCIA (Italy) 3:473
map (45° 33′N 13° 15′E) **11**:321
BRESLAU WROCLØAW (Poland)
map (51° 6′N 17° 0′E) **15**:388
BRESLIN, JIMMY 3:474
BRESSON, HENRI CARTIER- *see* CARTIER-BRESSON, HENRI
BRESSON, ROBERT 3:474 *bibliog.*
BREST (France) 3:474
map (48° 24′N 4° 29′W) **8**:260
BREST (USSR) 3:474
BREST-LITOVSK, TREATY OF 3:474 *bibliog.*
World War I **20**:238
BRETAGNE *see* BRITTANY (France)
BRETEL, JEHAN
minstrels, minnesingers, and troubadours **13**:460
BRETHREN 3:474 *bibliog.*
Beissel, Johann Conrad **3**:172
Lancaster (Pennsylvania) **12**:177
BRETHREN OF THE COMMON LIFE 3:474
BRÉTIGNY, TREATY OF 3:474
Hundred Years' War **10**:305
John II, King of France (John the Good) **11**:427
BRETON *see* BRITTANY (France); CELTIC LANGUAGES
BRETON (Alberta)
map (53° 7′N 114° 28′W) **1**:256
BRETON, ANDRÉ 3:474 *bibliog.*
surrealism (art) **18**:364
surrealism (film, literature, theater) **18**:366
BRETON, JULES ADOLPHE AIMÉ LOUIS 3:474
BRETÓN, TOMÁS
zarzuela **20**:356
BRETON ISLANDS
map (29° 28′N 89° 11′W) **12**:430
BRETON LITERATURE 3:475
BRETON SOUND
map (29° 30′N 89° 30′W) **12**:430
BRETTON WOODS CONFERENCE 3:475
inflation **11**:170–171
International Monetary Fund **11**:222
World Bank **20**:218
BREU, JORG
Danube school **6**:36
BREUER, MARCEL 3:475 *bibliog., illus.*
Bauhaus **3**:129–130 *illus.*
Whitney Museum of American Art **3**:475 *illus.*; **20**:142
BREUGHEL *see* BRUEGEL (family)
BREUIL, HENRI 3:475 *bibliog.*
BREVARD (county in Florida)
map (28° 18′N 80° 42′W) **8**:172
BREVARD (North Carolina)
map (35° 9′N 82° 44′W) **14**:242
BREVIARY 3:475
Book of Hours **3**:386
BREWER (Maine)
map (44° 48′N 68° 46′W) **13**:70
BREWER, DAVID J. 3:475
BREWING
ale **1**:270
beer **3**:162–163 *illus.*
BREWSTER (Kansas)
map (39° 22′N 101° 23′W) **12**:18
BREWSTER (Nebraska)
map (41° 56′N 99° 52′W) **14**:70
BREWSTER (Ohio)
map (40° 43′N 81° 36′W) **14**:357
BREWSTER (county in Texas)
map (30° 0′N 102° 22′W) **19**:129
BREWSTER (Washington)
map (48° 6′N 119° 47′W) **20**:35
BREWSTER, SIR DAVID 3:475–476
mineral **13**:439
polarized light **15**:394
stereoscope **18**:260
BREWSTER, WILLIAM 3:476 *bibliog.*
Pilgrims **15**:302
BREWTON (Alabama)
map (31° 7′N 87° 4′W) **1**:234
BREYTENBACH, BREYTEN 3:476
BREZHNEV, LEONID ILICH 3:476 *bibliog., illus.*
communism **5**:148
Russia/Union of Soviet Socialist Republics, history of **16**:360
BŘEZINA, OTOKAR
Czech literature **5**:412
BRIA (Central African Republic)
map (6° 32′N 21° 59′E) **4**:251
BRIAN BORU 3:476
Ireland, history of **11**:262
BRIAN HEAD MOUNTAIN
map (37° 41′N 112° 50′W) **19**:492
BRIAND, ARISTIDE 3:476 *bibliog.*; **17**:36 *illus.*
Kellogg-Briand Pact **12**:38
BRIANZA, CARLOTTA
Kirov Ballet **12**:90
BRIAR *see* BRIER
BRIARD 3:476–477 *bibliog., illus.*; **6**:215 *illus.*
BRIBERY 3:477
ABSCAM **1**:62
corporation **5**:275
BRICE, FANNY 3:477 *bibliog.*
BRICELYN (Minnesota)
map (43° 34′N 93° 49′W) **13**:453
BRICK AND BRICKLAYING 3:477–478 *bibliog., illus.*
adobe **1**:105–106
Indus civilization **11**:153
kiln **12**:77
laterite **12**:215
magnesite **13**:53
manufacture **3**:478
patterns **3**:477 *illus.*
refractory brick
firebrick **8**:106
olivine **14**:379
Roman art and architecture **16**:273
BRIDAL WREATH (botany) *see* SPIREA
BRIDALVEIL FALL 3:479
BRIDE *see* MARRIAGE
BRIDE-PRICE 3:479 *bibliog.*
dowry **6**:252
marriage **13**:164
Nguni **14**:176
Southeast Asian art and architecture **18**:108
BRIDGE (card game) 3:479 *bibliog., illus., table*
Culbertson, Ely **5**:383
Goren, Charles H. **9**:251
BRIDGE (dentistry)
dentures **6**:117
BRIDGE (engineering) 3:479–484 *bibliog., illus., table*
Bailey bridge **3**:26
city **5**:4
disasters **3**:482; **3**:484
engineering **7**:178
Ammann, Othmar Hermann **1**:372
Brunel (family) **3**:524
cable **4**:5 *illus.*
caisson **4**:19
Eads, James Buchanan **7**:3
foundation, building **3**:481–482; **8**:249–250
Roebling, John A. and Washington Augustus **16**:268
technology, history of **19**:66 *illus.*
Telford, Thomas **19**:90
Town, Ithiel **19**:255
truss **19**:320
Königsberg bridge problem **12**:108
Maillart, Robert **13**:67
notable bridges **3**:483 *table*
Brooklyn Bridge **3**:510
Clifton Suspension Bridge (England) **19**:66 *illus.*
Delaware Memorial Bridge **6**:89 *illus.*
George Washington Bridge **9**:110
Golden Gate Bridge **4**:32 *illus.*; **9**:232
London Bridge **12**:404–405 *illus.*
Mackinac Bridge **13**:379 *illus.*
Royal Gorge Suspension Bridge **5**:119 *illus.*
Vecchio, Ponte **8**:168–169 *illus., map*
Verrazano-Narrows Bridge **19**:560
Yangtze River Bridge **4**:365 *illus.*
pontoons and pontoon bridges **15**:427
viaduct **19**:567
BRIDGE, DONALD COLEMAN
Bailey bridge **3**:26
BRIDGE, FRANK 3:484
BRIDGE CIRCUIT 3:484 *bibliog.*
BRIDGE OF SAN LUIS REY, THE (book) 3:484
Wilder, Thornton **20**:149–150
BRIDGE OF SIGHS
Doge's Palace **6**:222
BRIDGEPORT (Alabama)
map (34° 57′N 85° 43′W) **1**:234
BRIDGEPORT (California)
map (38° 10′N 119° 13′W) **4**:31
BRIDGEPORT (Connecticut) 3:484
map (41° 11′N 73° 11′W) **5**:193
BRIDGEPORT (Illinois)
map (38° 43′N 87° 46′W) **11**:42
BRIDGEPORT (Nebraska)
map (41° 40′N 103° 6′W) **14**:70
BRIDGEPORT (Texas)
map (33° 13′N 97° 45′W) **19**:129
BRIDGEPORT (Washington)
map (48° 0′N 119° 40′W) **20**:35
BRIDGEPORT (West Virginia)
map (39° 17′N 80° 15′W) **20**:111
BRIDGER, JAMES 3:484 *bibliog.*
frontier **8**:342
Great Salt Lake **9**:322
BRIDGES, CALVIN BLACKMAN
Morgan, Thomas Hunt **13**:579
BRIDGES, HARRY 3:484–485
Bridges v. *California* **3**:485
international longshoremen's unions **11**:222
BRIDGES, ROBERT 3:485 *bibliog.*
BRIDGES* v. *CALIFORNIA 3:485
BRIDGET OF SWEDEN, SAINT 3:485
BRIDGETON (Missouri)
map (38° 47′N 90° 28′W) **13**:476
BRIDGETON (New Jersey)
map (39° 26′N 75° 14′W) **14**:129
BRIDGETOWN (Barbados) 3:485
map (13° 6′N 59° 37′W) **3**:75
BRIDGEVILLE (Delaware)
map (38° 45′N 75° 36′W) **6**:88
BRIDGEWATER (Massachusetts)
map (41° 59′N 70° 58′W) **13**:206
BRIDGEWATER (Nova Scotia)
map (44° 23′N 64° 31′W) **14**:269
BRIDGEWATER (South Dakota)
map (43° 33′N 97° 30′W) **18**:103
BRIDGEWATER (Virginia)
map (38° 18′N 78° 59′W) **19**:607
BRIDGEWATER CANAL 3:485; **19**:407 *illus.*
BRIDGMAN, PERCY WILLIAMS 3:485
BRIDGTON (Maine)
map (44° 3′N 70° 42′W) **13**:70
BRIDIE, JAMES 3:485
BRIDLE *see* RIDING
BRIEF (law) 3:485
amicus curiae **1**:369
BRIENNE, ÉTIENNE CHARLES DE LOMÉNIE DE *see* LOMÉNIE DE BRIENNE, ÉTIENNE CHARLES DE
BRIER 3:485
BRIEUX, EUGÈNE 3:485
BRIG AND BRIGANTINE
See also SAILING SHIPS
ship **17**:268 *illus.*
BRIGADE 3:486
BRIGANTINE (New Jersey)
map (39° 24′N 74° 22′W) **14**:129
BRIGGS (Texas)
map (30° 53′N 97° 56′W) **19**:129
BRIGGS, HENRY 3:486
BRIGGS, W. R.
tropism **19**:310
BRIGHAM CITY (Utah) 3:486
map (41° 31′N 112° 1′W) **19**:492
BRIGHAM YOUNG UNIVERSITY 3:486
BRIGHT, JOHN 3:486 *bibliog.*
BRIGHT, RICHARD 3:486 *bibliog.*
BRIGHTENERS *see* BLEACHES AND BRIGHTENERS
BRIGHTON (Alabama)
map (33° 24′N 86° 57′W) **1**:234
BRIGHTON (Colorado)
map (39° 59′N 104° 49′W) **5**:116
BRIGHTON (England) 3:486
map (50° 50′N 0° 8′W) **19**:403
Royal Pavilion at Brighton **16**:126 *illus.*; **16**:330–331 *illus.*
BRIGHTON (Illinois)
map (39° 2′N 90° 8′W) **11**:42
BRIGHTON (Iowa)
map (41° 10′N 91° 49′W) **11**:244
BRIGHTON (Michigan)
map (42° 32′N 83° 47′W) **13**:377
BRIGHTON (New York)
map (43° 8′N 77° 34′W) **14**:149
BRIGHT'S DISEASE 3:486 *bibliog.*
BRIGUS (Newfoundland)
map (47° 32′N 53° 13′W) **14**:166
BRIKAMA (Gambia)
map (13° 15′N 16° 39′W) **9**:25
BRILL (flounder) **8**:117 *illus.*
BRILL, ABRAHAM ARDEN **15**:598 *illus.*
BRILLAT-SAVARIN, ANTHELME 3:486
BRILLIANT (Alabama)
map (34° 1′N 87° 46′W) **1**:234
BRILLION (Wisconsin)
map (44° 11′N 88° 4′W) **20**:185
BRIMSTONE *see* SULFUR
BRINDISI (Italy)
map (40° 38′N 17° 56′E) **11**:321
BRINDLEY, JAMES
Bridgewater Canal **3**:485
BRINE
pickling **15**:293–294
salt-ice-brine system **15**:224 *illus.*
BRINE SHRIMP 3:486
BRINK, ANDRÉ
South Africa **18**:81
BRINKLEY (Arkansas)
map (34° 53′N 91° 12′W) **2**:166
BRINKLEY, DAVID 3:486–487
BRIOSCO, ANDREA 3:487 *bibliog.*
BRIOT, FRANÇOIS
pewter **15**:217
BRISBANE (Australia) 3:487 *illus.*
climate **2**:332 *table*
education
Griffith University **2**:345 *table*
Queensland University **2**:345 *table*
map (27° 28′S 153° 2′E) **2**:328
BRISBANE, ARTHUR 3:487 *bibliog.*
BRISBANE, SIR THOMAS
Brisbane **3**:487
BRISCOE (county in Texas)
map (34° 30′N 101° 15′W) **19**:129
BRISLING *see* HERRING; SARDINE
BRISSOT DE WARVILLE, JACQUES PIERRE 3:487
BRISTLECONE PINE 3:487–488 *bibliog., illus.*
dendrochronology **6**:106–107
BRISTLEMOUTH 3:488
BRISTLETAIL 3:488
BRISTOL (Connecticut)
map (41° 41′N 72° 57′W) **5**:193
BRISTOL (England) 3:488
Clifton suspension bridge **19**:66 *illus.*
map (51° 27′N 2° 35′W) **19**:403
BRISTOL (Florida)
map (30° 26′N 84° 58′W) **8**:172

BRISTOL (county in Massachusetts)
map (41° 54′N 71° 6′W) **13**:206
BRISTOL (New Hampshire)
map (43° 36′N 71° 45′W) **14**:123
BRISTOL (Pennsylvania)
map (40° 6′N 74° 52′W) **15**:147
BRISTOL (Rhode Island)
map (40° 6′N 74° 52′W) **16**:198
BRISTOL (county in Rhode Island)
map (41° 42′N 71° 18′W) **16**:198
BRISTOL (South Dakota)
map (45° 21′N 97° 45′W) **18**:103
BRISTOL (Tennessee)
map (36° 36′N 82° 11′W) **19**:104
BRISTOL (Vermont)
map (44° 8′N 73° 5′W) **19**:554
BRISTOL (Virginia)
map (36° 36′N 82° 11′W) **19**:607
BRISTOL, UNIVERSITY OF 3:488
BRISTOL BAY
map (58° 0′N 159° 0′W) **1**:242
BRISTOL CHANNEL 3:488
map (51° 20′N 4° 0′W) **19**:403
BRISTOW (Oklahoma)
map (35° 50′N 96° 23′W) **14**:368
BRISTOW, BENJAMIN HELM 3:488
BRITAIN *see* ENGLAND; GREAT BRITAIN; GREAT BRITAIN, HISTORY OF; NORTHERN IRELAND; SCOTLAND; WALES
BRITAIN, BATTLE OF 3:488–489 *bibliog.*
Hitler, Adolf **10**:188
World War II **20**:253–255 *illus., map*
BRITANNIA RAILWAY BRIDGE (Wales) 3:481 *illus.*
BRITANNIA ROYAL NAVAL COLLEGE 3:489
military academies **13**:420
BRITANNICUS
Claudius I, Roman Emperor **5**:44
Rome, ancient **16**:302
BRITISH ANTARCTIC TERRITORY 3:489
BRITISH ANTI-LEWISITE
arsenic **2**:189
BRITISH ASSOCIATION FOR THE ADVANCEMENT OF SCIENCE
Harcourt, William **10**:44
BRITISH BROADCASTING CORPORATION
Bliss, Sir Arthur **3**:333
radio and television broadcasting **16**:60
television, noncommercial **19**:90
BRITISH CAMEROONS **4**:62
BRITISH COLUMBIA (Canada) 3:489–492 *bibliog., illus., map*
cities
Kamloops **12**:10
Prince George **15**:549
Vancouver **19**:517–518 *illus.*
Victoria **19**:573
climate **3**:490
economic activities **3**:490
education
British Columbia, University of **3**:492–493
Simon Fraser University **4**:92 *table*; **17**:315
Vancouver, University of British Columbia at **4**:92 *table*
Victoria, University of **4**:92 *table*; **19**:575
flag **3**:489 *illus.*
fossils **4**:50 *illus.*
Fraser River **3**:489–490; **8**:287
government **3**:492
history **3**:492
Douglas, Sir James **6**:247
land and resources **3**:489–491 *map*
fjord **8**:133
map (54° 0′N 125° 0′W) **4**:70
people **3**:490–492
Bella Coola **3**:186
Carrier Indians **4**:168
Haida **10**:12
Indians, American **11**:124 *map*; **11**:126–127 *illus.*
Kutenai **12**:139–140
Kwakiutl **12**:142
Nootka **14**:217–218
Okanogan **14**:365
Salish **17**:34
Shuswap **17**:289–290
Tlingit **19**:216
Tsimshian **19**:323–324
Queen Charlotte Islands **16**:21–22
Vancouver Island **19**:518
vegetation and animal life **3**:490
BRITISH COLUMBIA, UNIVERSITY OF 3:492–493
BRITISH EAST AFRICA COMPANY *see* EAST AFRICA COMPANY, BRITISH
BRITISH EAST INDIA COMPANY *see* EAST INDIA COMPANY, BRITISH
BRITISH EDUCATION 3:493–495 *bibliog., illus., table*
See also ENGLAND—education
BRITISH EMPIRE 3:495–496 *bibliog., illus., map*
Africa, history of **1**:156–160
Asia, history of **2**:256–259
Australia, history of **2**:339–341
Canada, history of **4**:81–83
colonialism **5**:111–112
Commonwealth of Nations **5**:141
Cromwell, Oliver **5**:358
dominion **6**:234
East India Company, British **7**:31
Europe, history of **7**:292; **7**:293; **7**:298
Fashoda Incident **8**:33
Great Britain, history of **9**:315–317
imperialism **11**:61–62
India, history of **11**:91 *illus., map*; **11**:92–93
Indian Mutiny **11**:103–104
Navigation Acts **14**:61–62
New Zealand, history of **14**:161–162
BRITISH EMPIRE GAMES *see* COMMONWEALTH GAMES
BRITISH ENGLISH *see* ENGLISH LANGUAGE
BRITISH EXPEDITIONARY FORCE (BEF)
French, John, 1st Earl of Ypres **8**:302
World War I **20**:222–224; **20**:231 *illus.*; **20**:236
World War II **20**:254
Ypres, Battles of **20**:337
BRITISH FILM INSTITUTE 3:496
BRITISH GUIANA *see* GUYANA
BRITISH HONDURAS *see* BELIZE
BRITISH INDIAN OCEAN TERRITORY 3:496–497
BRITISH INSTITUTE OF ARCHAEOLOGY, ANKARA
Garstang, John **9**:52
BRITISH INSTITUTE OF MECHANICAL ENGINEERS
mechanical engineering **13**:260
BRITISH INTERPLANETARY SOCIETY 3:497
BRITISH ISLES 3:497
BRITISH KENNEL CLUB
dog **6**:213
BRITISH LANGUAGE *see* CELTIC LANGUAGES
BRITISH LEGION
Veterans' Organizations **19**:566
BRITISH LEYLAND MOTORS CORPORATION
automotive industry **2**:366; **2**:368
BRITISH LIBRARY 3:497
British Museum **3**:497
BRITISH MOTOR CORPORATION
automotive industry **2**:366
BRITISH MUSEUM 3:497 *bibliog., illus.*; **12**:401 *map*
British Library **3**:497
Egyptology **7**:90
Elgin, Thomas Bruce, 7th Earl of **7**:137
Rosetta Stone **16**:317
Smirke, Sir Robert **17**:366
Xanthus **20**:311
BRITISH NATIONAL TRUST OF HISTORIC PLACES
historic preservation **10**:182
BRITISH NORTH AMERICA ACT 3:497 *bibliog.*
See also CONSTITUTION ACT
Canada, history of **4**:83
BRITISH NORTH BORNEO *see* SABAH (Malaysia)
BRITISH OPEN (golf) CHAMPIONS **9**:238 *table*
BRITISH OPEN (WIMBLEDON) CHAMPIONS **19**:110 *table*
BRITISH ORDER OF MERIT
Nightingale, Florence **14**:193 *illus.*; **14**:194
BRITISH SOMALILAND *see* SOMALIA
BRITISH SOUTH AFRICA COMPANY
Lobengula, King of the Ndebele **12**:385
Rhodes, Cecil John **16**:202
Zambia **20**:353
Zimbabwe **20**:365
BRITISH THERMAL UNIT 3:497
BRITISH VIRGIN ISLANDS *see* VIRGIN ISLANDS
BRITSKA
coach and carriage **5**:73
BRITT (Iowa)
map (43° 6′N 93° 48′W) **11**:244
BRITTANY (France) 3:498 *map*
Anne of Brittany **2**:32
bagpipe **3**:22–23
Brest **3**:474
Carnac **4**:154
Celtic languages **4**:241
megalith **13**:278–279
menhir **13**:297
Rennes **16**:157
stone alignments **18**:281–282 *illus.*
BRITTANY SPANIEL 3:498 *bibliog., illus.*; **6**:218 *illus.*
BRITTEN, BENJAMIN 3:498–499 *bibliog., illus.*; **7**:204 *illus.*
Brain, Dennis **3**:448
Bridge, Frank **3**:484
BRITTLE STAR 3:499; **7**:38 *illus.*
BRITTON (South Dakota)
map (45° 48′N 97° 45′W) **18**:103
BRITTON, NATHANIEL 3:499
BRIULLOV, KARL
Russian art and architecture **16**:362
BRNO (Czechoslovakia) 3:499
map (49° 12′N 16° 37′E) **5**:413
BROAD JUMP *see* TRACK AND FIELD
BROAD RIVER
map (34° 0′N 81° 4′W) **18**:98
BROADBENT, DONALD ERIC 3:499
attention **2**:314
cognitive psychology **5**:95
BROADBENT, JOHN EDWARD
Canada **4**:79
BROADBILL 3:499
BROADCASTING *see* RADIO BROADCASTING; TELEVISION BROADCASTING
BROADCLOTH 3:499
BROADMOOR (Colorado)
map (38° 48′N 104° 50′W) **5**:116
BROADUS (Montana)
map (45° 27′N 105° 25′W) **13**:547
BROADWATER (county in Montana)
map (46° 20′N 111° 20′W) **13**:547
BROADWAY 3:499–500 *bibliog.*
Lindsay, Howard, and Crouse, Russel **12**:352
repertory theater **16**:160
BROADWAY (Virginia)
map (38° 38′N 78° 46′W) **19**:607
BROCA, PAUL 3:500
Broca's area **3**:446 *illus.*
BROCADE 3:500
BROCCOLI 3:500 *illus.*; **19**:532 *illus.*
BROCH 3:500
BROCH, HERMANN 3:500 *bibliog.*
BROCHET (Manitoba)
map (57° 53′N 101° 40′W) **13**:119
BROCK, SIR ISAAC 3:500 *bibliog.*
BROCK, LOU 3:501
BROCKDORFF-RANTZAU, ULRICH, GRAF VON
World War I **20**:245–246
BROCKPORT (New York)
map (43° 13′N 77° 56′W) **14**:149
BROCKTON (Massachusetts) 3:501
map (42° 5′N 71° 1′W) **13**:206
BROCKVILLE (Ontario)
map (44° 35′N 75° 41′W) **14**:393
BROCKWAY (Pennsylvania)
map (41° 15′N 78° 47′W) **15**:147
BROCTON (New York)
map (42° 23′N 79° 27′W) **14**:149
BROD, MAX 3:501 *bibliog.*
BRODHEAD (Wisconsin)
map (42° 37′N 89° 22′W) **20**:185
BRODRIBB, JOHN HENRY *see* IRVING, SIR HENRY
BRODSKY, JOSEPH 3:501
BRODZINSKI, KAZIMIERZ
Polish literature **15**:398
BROEDERLAM, MELCHIOR 3:501 *bibliog.*
BROGAN (Oregon)
map (44° 15′N 117° 31′W) **14**:427
BROGLIE, LOUIS DE *see* DE BROGLIE, LOUIS
BROILER (chicken)
poultry **15**:473–475
BROKEN ARROW (Oklahoma)
map (36° 3′N 95° 48′W) **14**:368
BROKEN BOW (Nebraska)
map (41° 24′N 99° 38′W) **14**:70
BROKEN BOW (Oklahoma)
map (34° 2′N 94° 44′W) **14**:368
BROKEN BOW LAKE
map (34° 10′N 94° 40′W) **14**:368
BROKEN HILL (Australia) 3:501
map (31° 57′S 141° 27′E) **2**:328
BROKEN HILL MAN 3:501 *bibliog.*
BROKER, MARRIAGE *see* MARRIAGE
BROKOPONDO (Suriname)
map (5° 4′N 54° 58′W) **18**:364
BROME, RICHARD 3:501
BROMELIAD 3:501–502 *bibliog.*; **11**:469 *illus.*
BROMFIELD, LOUIS 3:502
BROMIDE
halogens **10**:25
sedative **17**:182
BROMINE 3:502 *bibliog., illus.*
abundances of common elements **7**:131 *table*
Balard, Antoine Jérôme **3**:33
chemical properties **3**:502
discovery **3**:502
Dow, Herbert Henry **6**:251
element **7**:130 *table*
Group VIIA periodic table **15**:167
halogens **10**:25
hazards **3**:502
occurrence **3**:502
preparation **3**:502
transition elements **19**:273 *table*
uses **3**:502
BRONC-RIDING
rodeo **16**:266–267
BRONCHIAL TUBE 3:502–503 *bibliog.*; **12**:463 *illus.*
respiratory system **16**:180 *illus.*
respiratory system disorders **16**:181–182
BRONCHIECTASIS
respiratory system disorders **16**:182
BRONCHITIS 3:503 *bibliog.*
emphysema **7**:158
ipecac **11**:248
types **3**:503
BRONCHODILATORS 3:503
BRONCHOSCOPE 3:503 *bibliog.*
photography **15**:266
BRONCK, JONAS
Bronx, the **3**:505
BRONCO *see* MUSTANG (horse); RODEO (contest)
BRØNDERSLEV (Denmark)
map (57° 16′N 9° 58′E) **6**:109
BRONFENBRENNER, URIE 3:503 *bibliog.*
BRONGNIART, ADOLPHE
paleobotany **15**:31
BRONGNIART, ALEXANDRE 3:503
BRONSON (Florida)
map (29° 27′N 82° 38′W) **8**:172
BRONSON (Michigan)
map (41° 52′N 85° 12′W) **13**:377
BRONSON, CHARLES 3:503
BRØNSTED, JOHANNES NICOLAUS 3:503 *bibliog.*
BRØNSTED-LOWRY THEORY
acids and bases **1**:83
BRONSTEIN, LEV DAVIDOVICH *see* TROTSKY, LEON
BRONTË (family) 3:504 *bibliog., illus.*
BRONTË, ANNE **3**:504 *illus.*
BRONTË, CHARLOTTE **3**:504 *illus.*; **7**:200 *illus.*
Gaskell, Elizabeth Cleghorn **9**:54–55
Jane Eyre **11**:358
BRONTË, EMILY **3**:504 *illus.*
Wuthering Heights **20**:297
BRONTOSAURUS 3:504–505 *bibliog., illus.*; **11**:475 *illus.*; **16**:170 *illus., illus.*
dinosaur **6**:179–181
titanothere **19**:211
BRONTOTHERIUM **13**:102 *illus.*
BRONX, THE (New York City) 3:505
housing **10**:278 *illus.*
map (40° 49′N 73° 56′W) **14**:149
BRONX BOTANICAL GARDEN *see* NEW YORK BOTANICAL GARDEN
BRONX RIVER
roads and highways **16**:238
BRONX ZOO 3:505; **20**:375 *illus.*
BRONZE 3:505
Bronze Age **3**:505–506
copper **5**:252–253
tin **19**:204–205
BRONZE AGE 3:505–506 *bibliog., illus.*
Aegean civilization **1**:114–118
African prehistory **1**:174–175
art
Cycladic art **5**:402–403
Minoan art **13**:458–459
prehistoric art **15**:509–510
Spanish art and architecture **18**:151
Asia, history of **2**:249
barrow **3**:95
Chalcolithic Period **4**:270
Chinese archaeology **4**:378
European prehistory **7**:301–305 *illus., map*
house (in Western architecture) **10**:266
Italy, history of **11**:326–327
lake dwelling **12**:171
megalith **13**:279
Scandinavia, history of **17**:108
stone alignments **18**:281

BRONZE AGE (cont.)
sword **18**:398 *illus.*
technology, history of **19**:62
Urnfield culture **19**:487
Wessex culture **20**:106
BRONZE FROG *see* GREEN FROG
BRONZES 3:506–508 *bibliog., illus.*
African art **1**:160–164
Barye, Antoine Louis **3**:99
Benin, Kingdom of **3**:201 *illus.*
Boccioni, Umberto **3**:354–355
Bologna, Giovanni da **3**:370–371
Brancusi, Constantin **3**:452–453
Cellini, Benvenuto **4**:237
Celtic art **4**:239 *illus.*
Chinese art and architecture **4**:383 *illus.*
Donatello **6**:236–237
Etruscans **7**:260 *illus.*
Filarete, Antonio Averlino **8**:78
German art and architecture **9**:126–127
Ghiberti, Lorenzo **9**:168
Gouthière, Pierre Joseph Désiré **9**:267
Greek art **9**:341
Indian art and architecture **11**:97
Leoni (family) **12**:292
Lipchitz, Jacques **12**:360–361
lost-wax process **12**:418–419
Luristan **12**:467
Lysippus **12**:480
Marini, Marino **13**:156
Myron **13**:691
Nadelman, Elie **14**:4
Nakian, Reuben **14**:9
Ottonian art and architecture **14**:467
Pantheon (Rome) **15**:62
Persian art and architecture **15**:183
Pisano, Andrea **15**:316
Remington, Frederic **16**:146
Rodin, Auguste **16**:267
Rogers, Randolph **16**:269
Roman art and architecture **16**:275
Sansovino, Jacopo **17**:66
sculpture **17**:159–165
sculpture techniques **17**:167
steppe art **18**:256 *illus.*
Verrocchio, Andrea del **19**:560–561
Vischer (family) **19**:616
Vries, Adriaen de **19**:639
BRONZINO 3:508–509 *bibliog., illus.*
Allegory (Venus, Cupid, Folly, and Time) **13**:125 *illus.*
Eleonora da Toledo with Her Son **3**:509 *illus.*
BRONZITE *see* PYROXENE
BROOK (Indiana)
map (40° 52′N 87° 22′W) **11**:111
BROOK, ALEXANDER 3:509 *bibliog.*
BROOK, PETER 3:509 *bibliog.*
A Midsummer Night's Dream **19**:151 *illus.*
BROOK FARM 3:509 *bibliog.*
Dana, Charles Anderson **6**:20
Fourier, Charles **8**:253
Hawthorne, Nathaniel **10**:79
Ripley, George **16**:228
BROOK TROUT *see* CHAR
BROOKE (county in West Virginia)
map (40° 18′N 80° 33′W) **20**:111
BROOKE, ALAN FRANCIS, 1ST VISCOUNT ALANBROOKE *see* ALANBROOKE, ALAN FRANCIS BROOKE, 1ST VISCOUNT
BROOKE, EDWARD W. 3:509 *bibliog.*
BROOKE, FRANCES
Canadian literature **4**:93
BROOKE, FULKE GREVILLE, 1ST BARON *see* GREVILLE, FULKE, 1ST BARON BROOKE
BROOKE, SIR JAMES 3:509 *bibliog.*
Sarawak (Malaysia) **17**:75
BROOKE, RUPERT 3:509–510 *bibliog.*
BROOKER, BERTRAM
Canadian art and architecture **4**:90
BROOKFIELD (Illinois)
map (41° 49′N 87° 51′W) **11**:42
BROOKFIELD (Massachusetts)
map (42° 13′N 72° 6′W) **13**:206
BROOKFIELD (Missouri)
map (39° 47′N 93° 4′W) **13**:476
BROOKFIELD (Wisconsin)
map (43° 4′N 88° 9′W) **20**:185
BROOKFIELD ZOO 3:510
BROOKHAVEN (Mississippi)
map (31° 35′N 90° 26′W) **13**:469
BROOKHAVEN NATIONAL LABORATORY 3:510
accelerator, particle **1**:74 *illus.*
BROOKINGS (Oregon)
map (42° 3′N 124° 17′W) **14**:427
BROOKINGS (South Dakota)
map (44° 19′N 96° 48′W) **18**:103
BROOKINGS (county in South Dakota)
map (44° 20′N 96° 50′W) **18**:103
BROOKINGS INSTITUTION 3:510 *bibliog.*
think tanks **19**:169 *table*
Washington, D.C. **20**:41 *map*
BROOKITE
oxide minerals **14**:476
BROOKLAND (Arkansas)
map (35° 55′N 90° 34′W) **2**:166
BROOKLET (Georgia)
map (32° 23′N 81° 40′W) **9**:114
BROOKLINE (Massachusetts) 3:510
map (42° 21′N 71° 7′W) **13**:206
BROOKLYN (Michigan)
map (42° 6′N 84° 15′W) **13**:377
BROOKLYN (Mississippi)
map (31° 3′N 89° 11′W) **13**:469
BROOKLYN (New York city) 3:510
Coney Island **5**:176
BROOKLYN (Nova Scotia)
map (44° 3′N 64° 42′W) **14**:269
BROOKLYN (Ohio)
map (41° 25′N 81° 49′W) **14**:357
BROOKLYN (South Carolina)
map (34° 42′N 80° 47′W) **18**:98
BROOKLYN ACADEMY OF MUSIC
music and concert halls **13**:670
BROOKLYN BOTANIC GARDEN AND ARBORETUM 3:510 *bibliog.*
BROOKLYN BRIDGE 3:481 *illus.*; 3:510 *bibliog.*
New York (city) **14**:145 *map*
Roebling, John A. and Washington Augustus **16**:268
BROOKLYN CENTER (Minnesota)
map (45° 5′N 93° 20′W) **13**:453
BROOKLYN COLLEGE *see* NEW YORK, CITY UNIVERSITY OF
BROOKLYN HANDICAP (horse race) **10**:248 *illus.*
BROOKLYN MUSEUM, THE 3:510 *bibliog.*
BROOKMERE (British Columbia)
map (49° 49′N 120° 53′W) **3**:491
BROOKNEAL (Virginia)
map (37° 3′N 78° 57′W) **19**:607
BROOKS (Alberta)
map (50° 35′N 111° 53′W) **1**:256
BROOKS (county in Georgia)
map (30° 50′N 83° 35′W) **9**:114
BROOKS (Maine)
map (44° 33′N 69° 7′W) **13**:70
BROOKS (county in Texas)
map (27° 0′N 98° 15′W) **19**:129
BROOKS, CLEANTH 3:511
BROOKS, GWENDOLYN 3:511 *bibliog.*
BROOKS, MEL 3:511 *illus.*
BROOKS, MOUNT **14**:226 *illus.*
BROOKS, PHILLIPS 3:511 *bibliog.*
BROOKS, VAN WYCK 3:511 *bibliog.*
BROOKS RANGE 3:511
map (68° 0′N 154° 0′W) **1**:242
BROOKSHIRE (Texas)
map (29° 47′N 95° 57′W) **19**:129
BROOKSIDE (Delaware)
map (39° 40′N 75° 44′W) **6**:88
BROOKSVILLE (Florida)
map (28° 33′N 82° 23′W) **8**:172
BROOKSVILLE (Kentucky)
map (38° 41′N 84° 4′W) **12**:47
BROOKSVILLE (Mississippi)
map (33° 14′N 88° 35′W) **13**:469
BROOKVILLE (Indiana)
map (39° 25′N 85° 1′W) **11**:111
BROOKVILLE (Pennsylvania)
map (41° 9′N 79° 5′W) **15**:147
BROOKVILLE LAKE
map (39° 30′N 85° 0′W) **11**:111
BROOM (botany) 3:511
BROOM, JACOB 3:511–512
BROOM, ROBERT
Australopithecus **2**:345–346
Sterkfontein **18**:260
BROOMCORN *see* SORGHUM
BROOME (Australia)
map (17° 58′S 122° 14′E) **2**:328
BROOME (county in New York)
map (40° 42′N 74° 0′W) **14**:149
BROOMFIELD (Colorado)
map (39° 56′N 105° 4′W) **5**:116
BROOMRAPE (botany) 3:512
BROOTEN (Minnesota)
map (45° 30′N 95° 7′W) **13**:453
BROPHY, BRIGID 3:512
BROPHY, JERE
educational psychology **7**:66
BROSCHI, CARLO *see* FARINELLI
BROSSE, SALOMON DE 3:512 *bibliog.*
château **4**:302
Luxembourg Palace **12**:472
BROTHEL
prostitution **15**:573
BROTHERHOOD OF (labor union) *see* specific union name, e.g., TEAMSTERS, CHAUFFEURS, WAREHOUSEMEN, AND HELPERS OF AMERICA, INTERNATIONAL BROTHERHOOD OF; ELECTRICAL WORKERS, INTERNATIONAL BROTHERHOOD OF; etc.
BROTHERHOOD OF THE NEW LIFE
Harris, Thomas Lake **10**:58
BROTHERS KARAMAZOV, THE (book) 3:512 *bibliog.*
Dostoyevsky, Fyodor Mikhailovich **6**:244–245
BROUGHAM
coach and carriage **5**:73
BROUGHTON, JACK
boxing **3**:432
BROUN, HEYWOOD 3:512 *bibliog.*
BROUNCKER, WILLIAM 3:512
BROUWER, ADRIAEN 3:512–513 *bibliog., illus.*
Pain 3:512 *illus.*
BROUWER, DIRK 3:513
BROUWER, L. E. J. 3:513
mathematics, history of **13**:226
BROWARD (county in Florida)
map (26° 9′N 80° 29′W) **8**:172
BROWDER, EARL 3:513 *bibliog.*
Communist party, U.S.A. **5**:151
BROWN (county in Illinois)
map (39° 59′N 90° 45′W) **11**:42
BROWN (county in Kansas)
map (39° 50′N 95° 30′W) **12**:18
BROWN (county in Minnesota)
map (44° 15′N 94° 40′W) **13**:453
BROWN (county in Nebraska)
map (42° 30′N 99° 55′W) **14**:70
BROWN (county in Ohio)
map (38° 52′N 83° 54′W) **14**:357
BROWN (county in South Dakota)
map (45° 30′N 98° 20′W) **18**:103
BROWN (county in Texas)
map (31° 43′N 99° 0′W) **19**:129
BROWN (county in Wisconsin)
map (44° 27′N 88° 0′W) **20**:185
BROWN, SIR ALFRED R. RADCLIFFE- *see* RADCLIFFE-BROWN, SIR ALFRED R.
BROWN, ARTHUR WHIDDEN
Alcock, Sir John William **1**:264
BROWN, CAPABILITY 3:513 *bibliog.*
Blenheim Palace **3**:330; **12**:187 *illus.*
landscape architecture **12**:187
BROWN, CHARLES BROCKDEN 3:513 *bibliog.*
BROWN, CLAUDE 3:513
BROWN, DEE 3:513
BROWN, EDMUND G. "PAT" 3:514 *illus.*
BROWN, FORD MADOX 3:513–514 *bibliog., illus.*
The Last of England 3:514 *illus.*
Pre-Raphaelites **15**:519
BROWN, GEORGE 3:514 *bibliog.*
BROWN, H. RAP
SNCC **17**:384
BROWN, HABLOT K.
Dickens, Charles **6**:156
BROWN, HELEN GURLEY 3:514
BROWN, HENRY
Plessy v. *Ferguson* **15**:368
BROWN, JACOB JENNINGS 3:514
BROWN, JAMES 3:514
soul music **18**:71
BROWN, JAMES COOKE
languages, artificial **12**:197
BROWN, JERRY 3:514 *bibliog., illus.*
BROWN, JIM 3:514–515 *bibliog., illus.*
BROWN, JOHN 3:515 *bibliog., illus.*; **5**:16 *illus.*
abolitionists **1**:58
Harpers Ferry (West Virginia) **10**:55
Iowa **11**:247
Placid, Lake **15**:325
Springfield (Massachusetts) **18**:200
treason **19**:285
Tubman, Harriet **19**:328
United States, history of the **19**:448
BROWN, JOSEPH ROGERS 3:515
BROWN, KENNETH
Living Theatre **12**:376–377
BROWN, LANCELOT *see* BROWN, CAPABILITY
BROWN, NICHOLAS 3:515
BROWN, NORMAN O. 3:515–516
BROWN, OLYMPIA 3:516
BROWN, PAT *see* BROWN, EDMUND G. "PAT"
BROWN, PAUL EUGENE 3:516 *bibliog.*
BROWN, ROBERT (botanist) 3:516
biology **3**:269
Brownian motion **3**:517–518
zoology **20**:377
BROWN, ROBERT McAFEE (theologian) 3:516
BROWN, ROGER 3:516
BROWN, STERLING 3:516
BROWN, TRISHA
modern dance **13**:498
BROWN, WILLIAM ADAMS 3:516
BROWN ALGAE *see* ALGAE—brown algae
BROWN CITY (Michigan)
map (43° 13′N 82° 59′W) **13**:377
BROWN COAL *see* LIGNITE
BROWN DEER (Wisconsin)
map (43° 10′N 87° 59′W) **20**:185
BROWN DWARF 3:516
BROWN LUNG 3:516–517
dust, atmospheric **6**:308
BROWN-SÉQUARD, CHARLES 3:516 *bibliog.*
BROWN SNAKE *see* EARTH SNAKE
BROWN UNIVERSITY 3:517
Brown, Nicholas **3**:515
Rhode Island School of Design **16**:201
Wayland, Francis **20**:73
BROWN* v. *BOARD OF EDUCATION OF TOPEKA, KANSAS 3:517 *bibliog.*
Davis, John W. **6**:52
National Association for the Advancement of Colored People **14**:29
United States, education in the **19**:435
United States, history of the **19**:457
BROWN* v. *MARYLAND 3:517
Leisy v. *Hardin* **12**:279
BROWNE, CHARLES FARRAR *see* WARD, ARTEMUS
BROWNE, JOHN
English music **7**:202
BROWNE, ROBERT 3:517
BROWNE, SIR THOMAS 3:517 *bibliog.*
BROWNE, THOMAS ALEXANDER 3:517
BROWNE, WILLIAM 3:517
BROWNFIELD (Texas)
map (33° 11′N 102° 16′W) **19**:129
BROWNIAN MOTION 3:517–518
Einstein, Albert **7**:93
kinetic theory of matter **12**:79
noise **14**:213
random walk **16**:83
stochastic process **18**:273
Wiener, Norbert **20**:146
BROWNIE (folklore) 3:518
BROWNING, ELIZABETH BARRETT 3:518 *bibliog., illus.*
Sonnets from the Portuguese **18**:65
BROWNING, JOHN MOSES 3:518
machine gun **13**:23
pistol **15**:318
BROWNING, ROBERT 3:518–519 *bibliog., illus.*; 7:201 *illus.*
Venice (Italy) **19**:544
BROWNING, TOD 3:519
BROWNING AUTOMATIC RIFLE
Browning, John Moses **3**:518
BROWNING SEMIAUTOMATIC PISTOL **15**:318 *illus.*
BROWNLEE RESERVOIR
map (44° 40′N 117° 5′W) **14**:427
BROWNMILLER, SUSAN 3:519
BROWNS MILLS (New Jersey)
map (39° 58′N 74° 34′W) **14**:129
BROWNS VALLEY (Minnesota)
map (45° 36′N 96° 50′W) **13**:453
BROWNSBURG (Indiana)
map (39° 51′N 86° 24′W) **11**:111
BROWNSDALE (Minnesota)
map (43° 44′N 92° 52′W) **13**:453
BROWNSHIRTS *see* SA (*Sturmabteilung*)
BROWNSON, ORESTES 3:519 *bibliog.*
BROWNSTONE 3:519 *bibliog.*
BROWNSTOWN (Illinois)
map (39° 0′N 88° 57′W) **11**:42
BROWNSTOWN (Indiana)
map (38° 53′N 86° 3′W) **11**:111
BROWNSVILLE (Kentucky)
map (37° 12′N 86° 16′W) **12**:47
BROWNSVILLE (Oregon)
map (44° 24′N 122° 59′W) **14**:427
BROWNSVILLE (Pennsylvania)
map (40° 1′N 79° 53′W) **15**:147
BROWNSVILLE (Tennessee)
map (35° 36′N 89° 15′W) **19**:104
BROWNSVILLE (Texas) 3:519
map (25° 54′N 97° 30′W) **19**:129
BROWNSVILLE RAID 3:519 *bibliog.*
BROWNTON (Minnesota)
map (44° 44′N 94° 21′W) **13**:453

BROWNVILLE (Alabama)
map (33° 24′N 87° 52′W) **1**:234
BROWNVILLE (Maine)
map (45° 18′N 69° 2′W) **13**:70
BROWNWOOD (Texas)
map (31° 43′N 98° 59′W) **19**:129
BROXTON (Georgia)
map (31° 38′N 82° 53′W) **9**:114
BROYLE, CAPE (Newfoundland)
map (47° 6′N 52° 57′W) **14**:166
BRUBECK (family) **3**:519 *bibliog.*
BRUBECK, DAVID
Brubeck (family) **3**:519
BRUCE (Mississippi)
map (33° 59′N 89° 21′W) **13**:469
BRUCE (South Dakota)
map (44° 26′N 96° 54′W) **18**:103
BRUCE, SIR DAVID **3**:519 *bibliog.*
BRUCE, JAMES **3**:519–520 *bibliog.*
Africa **1**:157 *map*
BRUCE, JAMES, 8TH EARL OF ELGIN *see* ELGIN, JAMES BRUCE, 8TH EARL OF
BRUCE, LENNY **3**:520 *bibliog., illus.*
BRUCE, MOUNT
map (22° 36′S 118° 8′E) **2**:328
BRUCE, ROBERT *see* ROBERT I, KING OF SCOTLAND (Robert the Bruce)
BRUCE, STANLEY MELBOURNE, 1ST VISCOUNT OF MELBOURNE **3**:520 *bibliog.*
BRUCE, THOMAS, 7TH EARL OF ELGIN *see* ELGIN, THOMAS BRUCE, 7TH EARL OF
BRUCE, WILLIAM SPEIRS **3**:520
BRUCE BAY (New Zealand)
map (43° 35′S 169° 41′E) **14**:158
BRUCE PENINSULA
map (44° 50′N 81° 20′W) **14**:393; **19**:241
BRUCELLOSIS **3**:520
diseases, animal **6**:192
BRUCH, MAX **3**:520
BRÜCKE, DIE (art group) **3**:520–521 *bibliog., illus.*
expressionism (art) **7**:340
German art and architecture **9**:128
graphic arts **9**:294
Heckel, Erich **10**:103
Kirchner, Ernst Ludwig **12**:87
Munch, Edvard **13**:640
Nolde, Emil **14**:214
Pechstein, Max **15**:130
Schmidt-Rottluff, Karl **17**:128
BRUCKNER, ANTON **3**:521 *bibliog., illus.*
Linz (Austria) **12**:360
BRUEGEL (family) **3**:521–522 *bibliog., illus.*
BRUEGEL, PIETER
Bruegel (family) **3**:521–522
Children's Games **19**:256 *illus.*
Hunters in the Snow **12**:190 *illus.*
The Peasant Wedding **8**:161 *illus.*
The Wedding Dance **6**:23 *illus.*
BRUGES (Belgium) **3**:522–523
map (51° 13′N 3° 14′E) **3**:177
Middle Ages **13**:395 *map*
BRUGGE (Belgium) *see* BRUGES (Belgium)
BRUGMANN, KARL **3**:523
BRUHN, ERIK **3**:523 *bibliog.*
BRULE (American Indians) *see* SIOUX (American Indians)
BRULE (county in South Dakota)
map (43° 45′N 99° 7′W) **18**:103
BRÛLÉ, ÉTIENNE **3**:523
Michigan **13**:381
Superior, Lake **18**:352
Toronto (Ontario) **19**:242
BRULE RIVER
map (45° 57′N 88° 12′W) **13**:377
BRUMMELL, BEAU **3**:523
BRUN, CHARLES LE *see* LE BRUN, CHARLES
BRUNDAGE, AVERY **3**:523
San Francisco art museums **17**:54
BRUNDIDGE (Alabama)
map (31° 43′N 85° 49′W) **1**:234
BRUNDTLAND, GRO HARLEM **3**:523
BRUNEAU (Idaho)
map (42° 53′N 115° 48′W) **11**:26
BRUNEAU RIVER
map (42° 57′N 115° 58′W) **11**:26
BRUNEI **3**:523–524 *illus., map*
flag **3**:523 *illus.*
map (4° 30′N 114° 40′E) **2**:232
BRUNEI BAY
map (5° 5′N 115° 18′E) **3**:524
BRUNEL (family) **3**:524 *bibliog., illus.*
ship **17**:273
tunnel **19**:338
viaduct **19**:567
BRUNEL, ISAMBARD KINGDOM
bridge (engineering) **3**:481
Brunel (family) **3**:524
Great Eastern **9**:319
BRUNEL, MARC ISAMBARD
Brunel (family) **3**:524
BRUNELLESCHI, FILIPPO **3**:524–525 *bibliog., illus.*
architecture **2**:134
cathedrals and churches **4**:206
della Robbia (family) **6**:94
dome **6**:230 *illus.*
Florence (Italy) **8**:168
Italian art and architecture **11**:309
Pazzi Chapel (Florence) **2**:195 *illus.*; **3**:524 *illus.*
BRUNER, JEROME SEYMOUR **3**:525 *bibliog.*
concept formation and attainment **5**:169
reasoning **16**:105
BRUNETIÈRE, FERDINAND **3**:525
BRUNHILD **3**:525
BRÜNING, HEINRICH **3**:525
BRÜNNEHILDE *see* BRUNHILD
BRUNNER, EMIL **3**:525 *bibliog.*
BRUNNER, KARL
monetary theory **13**:525
BRUNO, SAINT
Carthusians **4**:174
statue **15**:456 *illus.*
BRUNO, GIORDANO **3**:525 *bibliog.*
astronomy, history of **2**:280
BRUNSWICK (city in West Germany) *see* BRAUNSCHWEIG (city in West Germany)
BRUNSWICK (Georgia)
map (31° 10′N 81° 29′W) **9**:114
BRUNSWICK (Maine)
map (43° 55′N 69° 58′W) **13**:70
BRUNSWICK (Maryland)
map (39° 19′N 77° 37′W) **13**:188
BRUNSWICK (Missouri)
map (39° 26′N 93° 8′W) **13**:476
BRUNSWICK (county in North Carolina)
map (34° 5′N 78° 15′W) **14**:242
BRUNSWICK (Ohio)
map (41° 14′N 81° 50′W) **14**:357
BRUNSWICK (region in West Germany) **3**:525–526
BRUNSWICK (county in Virginia)
map (36° 50′N 77° 50′W) **19**:607
BRUNSWIK, EGON **3**:526
perception **15**:159
BRUS LAGOON
map (15° 50′N 84° 35′W) **10**:218
BRUS LAGUNA (Honduras)
map (15° 47′N 84° 35′W) **10**:218
BRUSH (Colorado)
map (40° 15′N 103° 37′W) **5**:116
BRUSH-TAILED ROCK WALLABY **13**:175 *illus.*
BRUSH TURKEY *see* MEGAPODE
BRUSILOV, ALEKSEI ALEKSEYEVICH **3**:526
World War I **20**:233–234 *illus.*; **20**:238
BRUSSELS (Belgium) **3**:526–527 *map*
climate **3**:178 *table*
government **3**:181
language **3**:179
map (50° 50′N 4° 20′E) **3**:177
subway **18**:318 *table*
BRUSSELS COMPETITION
Berman, Lazar **3**:219
BRUSSELS GRIFFON **3**:527 *illus.*; **6**:217 *illus.*
BRUSSELS SPROUTS **3**:527 *illus.*; **19**:532 *illus.*
BRUSTEIN, ROBERT **3**:527
BRUSTOLON, ANDREA **3**:528 *bibliog.*
BRUT **3**:528
BRUTALISM **3**:528 *bibliog.*
Breuer, Marcel **3**:475 *illus.*
Stirling, James Frazer **18**:272
BRUTUS, DENNIS
South Africa **18**:81
BRUTUS, MARCUS JUNIUS **3**:528 *bibliog.*
Caesar, Gaius Julius **4**:15
Roman coin **16**:301 *illus.*
BRUXELLES *see* BRUSSELS (Belgium)
BRUYÈRE, JEAN DE LA *see* LA BRUYÈRE, JEAN DE
BRY, THÉODORE DE **3**:528
BRYAN (county in Georgia)
map (32° 5′N 81° 30′W) **9**:114
BRYAN (Ohio)
map (41° 28′N 84° 33′W) **14**:357
BRYAN (county in Oklahoma)
map (33° 55′N 96° 15′W) **14**:368
BRYAN (Texas)
map (30° 40′N 96° 22′W) **19**:129
BRYAN, KIRK **3**:528 *bibliog.*
BRYAN, WILLIAM JENNINGS **3**:528–529 *bibliog., illus.*
Democratic party **6**:100–101
free silver **8**:295
Lincoln (Nebraska) **12**:347
Populist party **15**:440
presidential elections **15**:530
Scopes Trial **17**:148
Spanish-American War **18**:150
Wilson, Woodrow **20**:167
BRYAN-CHAMORRO TREATY
Nicaragua Canal **14**:180
BRYANSK (USSR)
map (53° 15′N 34° 22′E) **19**:388
BRYANT (Arkansas)
map (34° 36′N 92° 30′W) **2**:166
BRYANT (South Dakota)
map (44° 35′N 97° 28′W) **18**:103
BRYANT, BEAR **3**:529 *bibliog.*
BRYANT, PAUL W. "BEAR" *see* BRYANT, BEAR
BRYANT, WILLIAM CULLEN **3**:529 *bibliog., illus.*; **6**:303 *illus.*
BRYANT COLLEGE **3**:529
BRYANTVILLE (Massachusetts)
map (42° 3′N 70° 51′W) **13**:206
BRYCE, JAMES BRYCE, 1ST VISCOUNT **3**:529 *bibliog.*
BRYCE CANYON NATIONAL PARK **3**:529; **14**:38 *map, table*; **19**:424 *illus.*; **19**:493 *illus.*
BRYMNER, WILLIAM
Canadian art and architecture **4**:89
BRYN MAWR COLLEGE **3**:529
Seven Sisters Colleges **17**:216
BRYNNER, YUL **3**:529–530
BRYOPHYTE **3**:530 *bibliog.*
hornwort **10**:240
liverwort **12**:376
moss **13**:603–605
plant **15**:333
BRYOZOAN **3**:530 *bibliog.*
invertebrate **11**:235
lophophorate **12**:413
Ordovician Period **14**:421
Paleozoic Era **15**:43
BRYSON (Texas)
map (33° 10′N 98° 23′W) **19**:129
BRYSON CITY (North Carolina)
map (35° 26′N 83° 27′W) **14**:242
BRYTHONIC LANGUAGES
Celtic languages **4**:241
BRYUSOV, VALERY YAKOVLEVICH **3**:530 *bibliog.*
BRZEG (Poland)
map (50° 52′N 17° 27′E) **15**:388
BRZESKA, HENRI GAUDIER- *see* GAUDIER-BRZESKA, HENRI
BRZEZINSKI, ZBIGNIEW **3**:530
BSHARRI (Lebanon)
map (34° 15′N 36° 1′E) **12**:265
BTA (telescope)
Special Astrophysical Observatory **18**:166
BTU *see* BRITISH THERMAL UNIT
BUADA LAGOON
map (0° 31′S 166° 55′E) **14**:51
BUADE, LOUIS DE, COMTE DE FRONTENAC *see* FRONTENAC, LOUIS DE BUADE, COMTE DE
BUBANZA (Burundi)
map (3° 6′S 29° 23′E) **3**:582
BUBASTIS (Egypt) **3**:530–531 *illus.*
BUBBLE CHAMBER **3**:531 *bibliog., illus.*; **14**:286 *illus.*
Alvarez, Luis Walter **1**:319
Glaser, Donald **9**:197
photography **15**:265
BUBER, MARTIN **3**:531–532 *bibliog., illus.*
existentialism **7**:332
BUBIYAN ISLAND
map (29° 47′N 48° 10′E) **12**:141
BUBONIC PLAGUE **3**:532 *bibliog.*
Death, Dance of **6**:68
epidemics **3**:532
Europe, history of **7**:285
flea **8**:158
Florence (Italy) **8**:168
infectious diseases **11**:164
plague pneumonia **3**:532
population **15**:433
rat **16**:91
BUCARAMANGA (Colombia)
map (7° 8′N 73° 9′W) **5**:107
BUCCANEER *see* PIRACY
BUCCHERO
Etruscans **7**:260
BUCEPHALUS **3**:532
BUCER, MARTIN **3**:532 *bibliog.*
BUCHALTER, LOUIS (Lepke) *see* MURDER, INC.
BUCHAN, ALEXANDER
Yamana woman **11**:116 *illus.*
BUCHAN, JOHN, 1ST BARON TWEEDSMUIR **3**:532
BUCHANAN (Georgia)
map (33° 48′N 85° 11′W) **9**:114
BUCHANAN (county in Iowa)
map (42° 30′N 91° 48′W) **11**:244
BUCHANAN (Liberia)
map (5° 57′N 10° 2′W) **12**:313
BUCHANAN (Michigan)
map (41° 50′N 86° 22′W) **13**:377
BUCHANAN (county in Missouri)
map (39° 40′N 94° 45′W) **13**:476
BUCHANAN (Virginia)
map (37° 32′N 79° 41′W) **19**:607
BUCHANAN (county in Virginia)
map (37° 15′N 82° 0′W) **19**:607
BUCHANAN, GEORGE **3**:532 *bibliog.*
BUCHANAN, JAMES **3**:532–534 *bibliog., illus.*
Civil War, U.S. **5**:19
Lancaster (Pennsylvania) **12**:177
Ostend Manifesto **14**:457
Utah War **19**:496
BUCHANS (Newfoundland)
map (48° 49′N 56° 52′W) **14**:166
BUCHAREST (Romania) **3**:534 *illus.*; **16**:287 *illus.*
climate **16**:287 *table*
map (44° 26′N 26° 6′E) **16**:288
BUCHAREST, TREATY OF (1812)
Russo-Turkish Wars **16**:374
BUCHAREST, TREATY OF (1913)
Balkan Wars **3**:38
World War I **20**:222
BUCHENWALD **3**:534
survivors **20**:276 *illus.*
BUCHER, LLOYD M.
Pueblo Incident **15**:614
BUCHINSKY, CHARLES *see* BRONSON, CHARLES
BUCHMAN, FRANK **3**:534
Moral Re-Armament **13**:573
BUCHNER, EDUARD **3**:534
enzyme **7**:213
BÜCHNER, GEORG **3**:534–535 *bibliog.*
BUCHWALD, ART **3**:535
BUCK, PEARL S. **3**:535 *bibliog., illus.*
BUCK MOUNTAIN
map (36° 40′N 81° 15′W) **19**:607
BUCKATUNNA (Mississippi)
map (31° 27′N 88° 32′W) **13**:469
BUCKBOARD
coach and carriage **5**:73
BUCKDANCER'S CHOICE (book)
Dickey, James **6**:157
BUCKEYE (Arizona)
map (33° 22′N 112° 35′W) **2**:160
BUCKEYE (botany) **3**:535 *illus.*
horse chestnut **10**:246
BUCKHANNON (West Virginia)
map (38° 59′N 80° 14′W) **20**:111
BUCKHORN (Arizona)
map (33° 25′N 111° 42′W) **2**:160
BUCKINGHAM (England) *see* BUCKINGHAMSHIRE (England)
BUCKINGHAM (Virginia)
map (37° 32′N 78° 37′W) **19**:607
BUCKINGHAM (county in Virginia)
map (37° 35′N 78° 30′W) **19**:607
BUCKINGHAM, GEORGE VILLIERS, 1ST DUKE OF **3**:535–536 *bibliog.*
Charles I, King of England, Scotland, and Ireland **4**:291
James I, King of England **11**:356
BUCKINGHAM PALACE **3**:536 *illus.*; **12**:401 *map*
Trooping of the Colour **19**:410 *illus.*
BUCKINGHAMSHIRE (England) **3**:536
BUCKLAND (Alaska)
map (66° 16′N 161° 20′W) **1**:242
BUCKLAND, WILLIAM **3**:536
BUCKLE, HENRY THOMAS **3**:536 *bibliog.*
BUCKLEY (Illinois)
map (40° 36′N 88° 2′W) **11**:42
BUCKLEY (Washington)
map (47° 10′N 122° 2′W) **20**:35
BUCKLEY, WILLIAM F., JR. **3**:536–537 *illus.*
BUCKLIN (Kansas)
map (37° 33′N 99° 38′W) **12**:18
BUCKLIN (Missouri)
map (39° 47′N 92° 53′W) **13**:476
BUCKNELL UNIVERSITY **3**:537
BUCKNER, SIMON BOLIVAR, JR. **3**:537 *bibliog.*
BUCKS (county in Pennsylvania)
map (40° 19′N 75° 8′W) **15**:147
BUCKSPORT (Maine)
map (44° 34′N 68° 48′W) **13**:70
BUCKTHORN **3**:537 *illus.*
cascara sagrada **4**:180
coyotillo **5**:323
BUCKWHEAT **3**:537 *illus.*
dock **6**:210

BUCKWHEAT (cont.)
rhubarb **16**:203
smartweed **17**:365
sorrel **18**:69
BUCOVINA **3**:537
BUCTOUCHE (New Brunswick)
map (46° 28′N 64° 43′W) **14**:117
BUCUREȘTI *see* BUCHAREST (Romania)
BUCYRUS (Ohio)
map (40° 48′N 82° 58′W) **14**:357
BUDA *see* BUDAPEST (Hungary)
BUDA (Illinois)
map (41° 20′N 89° 41′W) **11**:42
BUDAPEST (Hungary) **3**:538 *map*; **10**:309 *illus.*
climate **10**:307 *table*
map (47° 30′N 19° 5′E) **10**:307
BUDDH GAYA (India) *see* BODH GAYA (India)
BUDDHA **2**:252 *illus.*; **3**:538–539 *bibliog., illus.*; **3**:541 *illus.*; **11**:95 *illus.*; **11**:375 *illus.*
See also BUDDHISM
Asia, history of **2**:250
bo tree **3**:348
14th century bronze (Thailand) **18**:109 *illus.*
BUDDHISM **3**:63 *illus.*; **3**:539–543 *bibliog., illus., map*; **16**:140 *map*
art and architecture
Ajanta **1**:229
Amitabha Buddha **3**:539 *illus.*
Anuradhapura **1**:72
Ayuthia **2**:379–380
Bamian **3**:59
Bharhut **3**:234
Borobudur **3**:402 *illus.*
Chinese art and architecture **4**:386 *illus.*
Daibutsu (Great Buddha) of Kamakura (Japan) **2**:241 *illus.*
Ellora **7**:148
ema **8**:198 *illus.*
Indian art and architecture **11**:94–95 *illus.*
Japanese art and architecture **11**:373–375
Jocho **11**:421
Lamaist art and architecture **12**:172–173 *illus.*
Liang K'ai (Liang Kai) **12**:311
Lung-men (Longmen) **12**:462
mandala **13**:110
Nara (Japan) **14**:20
pagoda **15**:14
Pegu (Burma) **15**:133
Southeast Asian art and architecture **18**:107–110 *illus.*
stupa **18**:308
temple **19**:97–99 *illus.*
terra-cotta bodhisattva **19**:120 *illus.*
Unkei **19**:470
Asia, history of **2**:250–251
bhakti **3**:540
bodhisattva **3**:356
Buddha **3**:538–539
Buddhist sacred literature **3**:543
Burma **3**:574 *illus.*
China **3**:540–542
Fa-hsien (Faxian) **8**:4
Hsüan-Tsang (Xuanzang) **10**:286–287
dharma **6**:148
dietary laws **6**:165
drama
gigaku **9**:178
God **9**:218
historic sites **3**:542 *map*
Amaravati **1**:321
Bodh Gaya **3**:356
Borobudur **3**:402–403 *illus.*
Lung-men (Longmen) **12**:462
Mandalay **13**:110
Pagan **15**:13
Sanchi **17**:58
Sarnath **17**:78
Tun-huang (Dunhuang) **19**:331
Yün-kang (Yungang) **20**:346
India, history of **11**:89
Japan **3**:541–542; **11**:364 *illus.*
Japan, history of **11**:367; **11**:368
Nichiren **14**:180
Shotoku Taishi **17**:286
Soka-gakkai **18**:39
Kampuchea (Cambodia) **12**:12 *illus.*
karma **3**:539; **12**:28
Kashmir **12**:30
koan **12**:104
Korea, history of **12**:116
Kublai Khan, Mongol Emperor **12**:134
mantra **13**:131
Mon **13**:515
monks **2**:257 *illus.*; **3**:541 *illus.*; **13**:276 *illus.*; **13**:521 *illus.*; **16**:138 *illus.*
Naga (mythological character) **14**:6
nirvana **14**:201
philosophy **3**:539–540; **15**:246–247
Pure Land Buddhism **15**:629
Rangoon (Burma) **16**:85 *illus.*
soul **18**:70
Tantra **19**:25
Tibet
Dalai Lama **6**:11
Tibetan Book of the Dead, The **19**:190
Tibetan Buddhism **19**:190–191
Vietnam War **19**:586 *illus.*
yoga **20**:328–329
Zen Buddhism **20**:358–359
BUDDHIST SACRED LITERATURE **3**:543 *bibliog.*
BUDDING (botany)
grafting **9**:279
BUDDINGTON, ARTHUR FRANCIS **3**:543
BUDE (Mississippi)
map (31° 28′N 90° 51′W) **13**:469
BUDENNY, SEMYON MIKHAILOVICH **3**:543
BUDGE, DON **3**:543
BUDGERIGAR *see* PARAKEET
BUDGET **3**:543–544 *bibliog.*
Management and Budget, U.S. office of **13**:107
zero-based budgeting **20**:361
BUECHEL (Kentucky)
map (38° 12′N 85° 39′W) **12**:47
BUELL, DON CARLOS **3**:544 *bibliog.*
Civil War, U.S. **5**:23 *map*
BUELL, JOHN **3**:544
BUEN RETIRO PALACE **3**:544 *bibliog.*
BUENA (New Jersey)
map (39° 31′N 74° 56′W) **14**:129
BUENA VISTA (Belize)
map (18° 14′N 88° 33′W) **3**:183
BUENA VISTA (Colorado)
map (38° 50′N 106° 8′W) **5**:116
BUENA VISTA (Florida)
map (28° 12′N 82° 45′W) **8**:172
BUENA VISTA (Georgia)
map (32° 19′N 84° 31′W) **9**:114
BUENA VISTA (county in Iowa)
map (42° 43′N 95° 5′W) **11**:244
BUENA VISTA (Virginia)
map (37° 44′N 79° 21′W) **19**:607
BUENA VISTA, BATTLE OF **13**:352–353 *map*
BUENAVENTURA (Colombia) **3**:544
map (3° 53′N 77° 4′W) **5**:107
BUENAVENTURA (Mexico)
map (29° 51′N 107° 29′W) **13**:357
BUENAVISTA, MOUNT
map (9° 33′N 83° 45′W) **5**:291
BUENOS AIRES (Argentina) **2**:150–151 *illus.*; **3**:544–546 *bibliog., map*
climate **2**:148 *table*; **18**:86 *table*
history
Latin America, history of **12**:220
Mendoza, Pedro de **13**:296
Urquiza, Justo José de **19**:487
La Boca **18**:93 *illus.*
map (34° 36′S 58° 27′W) **2**:149
subway **18**:318 *table*
Teatro Colón **18**:92 *illus.*
BUENOS AIRES (province in Argentina)
map (38° 45′N 61° 45′W) **2**:149
BUENOS AIRES (Costa Rica)
map (9° 10′N 83° 20′W) **5**:291
BUENOS AIRES, LAKE
map (46° 35′S 72° 0′W) **2**:149
BUFFALO (Iowa)
map (41° 27′N 90° 43′W) **11**:244
BUFFALO (Kansas)
map (37° 42′N 95° 42′W) **12**:18
BUFFALO (Minnesota)
map (45° 10′N 93° 53′W) **13**:453
BUFFALO (Missouri)
map (37° 39′N 93° 6′W) **13**:476
BUFFALO (county in Nebraska)
map (40° 50′N 99° 5′W) **14**:70
BUFFALO (New York state) **3**:546
map (42° 54′N 78° 53′W) **14**:149
BUFFALO (Oklahoma)
map (36° 50′N 99° 38′W) **14**:368
BUFFALO (South Carolina)
map (34° 43′N 81° 41′W) **18**:98
BUFFALO (South Dakota)
map (45° 35′N 103° 33′W) **18**:103
BUFFALO (county in South Dakota)
map (44° 3′N 99° 10′W) **18**:103
BUFFALO (county in Wisconsin)
map (44° 22′N 91° 45′W) **20**:185
BUFFALO (Wyoming)
map (44° 21′N 106° 42′W) **20**:301
BUFFALO (zoology) **3**:546 *bibliog., illus.*
American buffalo *see* BISON
animal husbandry **2**:23–24 *illus.*
Cape buffalo **17**:98 *illus.*
ox **14**:473
BUFFALO BERRY **3**:546
BUFFALO BILL **3**:546–547 *bibliog., illus.*
Buntline, Ned **3**:565
Sitting Bull **17**:330
BUFFALO BILL RESERVOIR
map (44° 29′N 109° 13′W) **20**:301
BUFFALO BOB
radio and television broadcasting **16**:58 *illus.*
BUFFALO CENTER (Iowa)
map (43° 23′N 93° 57′W) **11**:244
BUFFALO FISH **3**:547
BUFFALO GROVE (Illinois)
map (42° 9′N 87° 58′W) **11**:42
BUFFALO NARROWS (Saskatchewan)
map (55° 51′N 108° 30′W) **17**:81
BUFFALO RIVER (Arkansas) **2**:167 *illus.*
map (36° 10′N 92° 26′W) **2**:166
BUFFALO RIVER (Minnesota)
map (47° 6′N 96° 49′W) **13**:453
BUFFEO
dolphin **6**:228
BUFFER **3**:547 *bibliog.*
pH **15**:218
BUFFER MEMORY (computer term) **5**:161
BUFFET, BERNARD **3**:547 *bibliog.*
BUFFON, GEORGES, COMTE DE **3**:547 *bibliog.*
anatomy **1**:397
BUFORD (Georgia)
map (34° 7′N 84° 0′W) **9**:114
BUG *see* HEMIPTERA
BUG RIVER
map (52° 31′N 21° 5′E) **7**:268
BUGA (Colombia)
map (3° 54′N 76° 17′W) **5**:107
BUGAKU **3**:547; **6**:27 *illus.*
Japanese music **11**:381 *illus.*
BUGANDA
Ganda **9**:34–35
Obote, Milton **14**:316
Uganda **19**:373
BUGATTI, CARLO **3**:547
BUGAYEV, BORIS NIKOLAYEVICH *see* BELY, ANDREI
BUGBANE **3**:547
BUGGY **5**:74 *illus.*
BUGIS **3**:548 *bibliog.*
BUGLE **3**:548
flügelhorn **8**:184
ophicleide **14**:404
BUGLEWEED **3**:548
BUHARI, MOHAMMED **3**:548
BUHL *see* BOULLE, ANDRÉ CHARLES
BUHL (Idaho)
map (42° 36′N 114° 46′W) **11**:26
BUHLER (Kansas)
map (38° 8′N 97° 46′W) **12**:18
BÜHLER, KARL **3**:548
BUIES CREEK (North Carolina)
map (35° 24′N 78° 45′W) **14**:242
BUILDING CONSTRUCTION **3**:548–552 *bibliog., illus.*
caisson **4**:19
carpentry **4**:164
chimney **4**:358
civil engineering **5**:10
cofferdam **5**:94
column-and-beam construction **3**:550 *illus.*
demolition **6**:104
derrick and crane **6**:122
helicopter **10**:112
earth-moving machinery **7**:23–24
electrical wiring **7**:106–107
environmental impact statement **7**:212
fire prevention and control **8**:104
fireplace **8**:106
foundation, building **8**:249–250
house (in Western architecture) **10**:271–272 *illus.*
housing **10**:276–280
industrial archaeology **11**:154
iron and steel industry **11**:272–278
lift-slab construction **3**:551 *illus.*
materials
adobe **1**:105–106
brick and bricklaying **3**:477–478
caulking **4**:219
cement and concrete **4**:243–244
dolomite **6**:226
glass **9**:197–201
granite **9**:287
insulating materials **11**:197
lime (chemical compound) **12**:343
lumber **12**:455 *illus.*
marble **13**:144
mica **13**:371
petrochemicals **15**:205
plywood **15**:374–375
red lauan **16**:112
redwood **16**:117
silicate minerals **17**:304
silicon **17**:305
sinter **17**:325
slate **17**:351
soil **18**:38
soil mechanics **18**:38
spruce **18**:201
tar, pitch, and asphalt **19**:34
wrought iron **20**:295
modular construction **3**:552 *illus.*
pipe and pipeline **15**:310–311
plumbing **15**:371–372
prefabrication **15**:502
roof and roofing **16**:306
skyscraper **17**:348–350
stonemasonry **18**:283
surveying **18**:367–369
technology, history of **19**:62–64 *illus.*; **19**:66
truss **19**:320
window **20**:173
zoning **20**:373–374
BUISSON, FERDINAND ÉDOUARD **3**:552–553
BUJONES, FERNANDO **3**:553
BUJUMBURA (Burundi) **3**:553
map (3° 23′S 29° 22′E) **3**:582
BUKAVU (Zaire)
map (2° 30′S 28° 52′E) **20**:350
BUKHARA (USSR)
map (39° 48′N 64° 25′E) **19**:388
Uzbek Soviet Socialist Republic **19**:499
BUKHARI, AL- **3**:553
BUKHARIN, NIKOLAI IVANOVICH **3**:553 *bibliog.*
Stalin, Joseph **18**:214
BÜKK MOUNTAINS
map (48° 5′N 20° 30′E) **10**:307
BUKOVINA *see* BUCOVINA
BUKOWSKI, CHARLES **3**:553
BULAN (Kentucky)
map (37° 18′N 83° 10′W) **12**:47
BULAWAYO (Zimbabwe) **3**:553
BULB (botany)
See also the names of specific flower bulb plants, e.g., CROCUS; TULIP; etc.
floriculture **8**:170 *illus.*
BULBUL **3**:553
BULERA, LAKE **16**:378 *illus.*
BULFINCH, CHARLES **3**:553 *bibliog.*
Capitol of the United States **4**:126
Faneuil Hall **8**:20
federal style **8**:42
BULFINCH, THOMAS **3**:553
BULGAKOV, MIKHAIL AFANASIEVICH **3**:553–554 *bibliog.*
Moscow Art Theater **13**:599
BULGAKOV, SERGEI NIKOLAYEVICH **3**:554
BULGANIN, NIKOLAI ALEKSANDROVICH **3**:554; **5**:98 *illus.*
Khrushchev, Nikita Sergeyevich **12**:69
BULGARIA **3**:554–557 *bibliog., illus., map, table*
astronaut
Ivanov, Georgy **11**:333
cities
Burgas **3**:568
Plovdiv **15**:369
Ruse **16**:347
Sofia **18**:34–35
Varna **19**:523–524
economy **3**:556
education **3**:556
European universities **7**:307 *table*
flag **3**:554 *illus.*
government **3**:556
history **3**:556–557
Balkan Wars **3**:38
Boris I, Tsar **3**:401
Boris III, Tsar **3**:401
Dimitrov, Georgi Mikhailov **6**:177
Dobruja **6**:209
Ferdinand I, Tsar of Bulgaria **8**:52
Simeon I, Tsar **17**:314
Slavs **17**:359
Stamboliski, Aleksandr **18**:215
Stambolov, Stefan **18**:215
Warsaw Treaty Organization **20**:32
Zhivkov, Todor **20**:362
land and resources **3**:555 *map*

language
Slavic languages **17**:358
map (43° 0′N 25° 0′E) **7**:268
people **3**:555–556
BULGARIAN LITERATURE 3:556; 3:557 *bibliog.*
Botev, Khristo **3**:415
Dimov, Dimitur **6**:177
Vazov, Ivan **19**:529
BULGARS
Bulgaria **3**:555–556
Tatar **19**:43–44
BULGE, BATTLE OF THE 3:557 *bibliog.*
World War II **20**:273–274 *map*
BULGUR *see* WHEAT
BULIMIA 3:557 *bibliog.*
anorexia nervosa **2**:34
BULL, JOHN (composer) 3:557 *bibliog.*
BULL, JOHN (personification) 3:557 *illus.*
BULL, OLAF JACOB MARTIN LUTHER 3:557–558
BULL, OLE 3:558 *bibliog.*
BULL, PAPAL 3:558
BULL, PETER **19**:154 *illus.*
BULL BAY *see* MAGNOLIA
BULL-DOGGING
rodeo **16**:266–267
BULL ISLAND
map (32° 55′N 79° 35′W) **18**:98
BULL MASTIFF 3:558 *bibliog., illus.*
BULL MOOSE PARTY 3:558 *bibliog.*
Johnson, Hiram Warren **11**:432
Progressive party **15**:564
Roosevelt, Theodore **16**:311
BULL-RIDING
rodeo **16**:266–267
BULL-ROARER
musical instruments **13**:677
BULL RUN, BATTLES OF 3:558–559 *bibliog., map*; **5**:21 *illus.*; **5**:24–25 *illus.*; **19**:448 *illus.*
Jackson, Stonewall **11**:344
McDowell, Irvin **13**:14
BULL SHOALS (Arkansas)
map (36° 22′N 92° 37′W) **2**:166
BULL SHOALS LAKE
map (36° 30′N 92° 50′W) **2**:166
BULL SNAKE **5**:124 *illus.*
BULL TERRIER 3:559 *bibliog., illus.*; **6**:220 *illus.*
BULLARD, SIR EDWARD 3:559 *bibliog.*
continental fit **15**:353 *map*
BULLARD, H. G.
radio and television broadcasting **16**:55
BULLDOG 3:559 *bibliog., illus.*; **6**:219 *illus.*
French bulldog **8**:308–309
Staffordshire bull terrier **18**:210
BULLDOZER
earth-moving machinery **7**:23–24 *illus.*
BULLETS **1**:374 *illus.*
dumdum bullet **6**:298
BULLFIGHTING 3:559–560 *bibliog., illus.*
Belmonte, Juan **3**:192
El Cordobés **7**:98
Manolete **13**:126
Pamplona (Spain) **15**:53
Seville (Spain) **17**:220
BULLFROG 3:560 *bibliog., illus.*; **12**:168 *illus.*
BULLHEAD 3:560–561 *bibliog., illus.*; **12**:168 *illus.*
sculpin **17**:159
BULLHEAD (South Dakota)
map (45° 46′N 101° 5′W) **18**:103
BULLHEAD CITY (Arizona)
map (35° 9′N 114° 34′W) **2**:160
BULLINGER, HEINRICH 3:561 *bibliog.*
BULLINS, ED 3:561
BULLITT (county in Kentucky)
map (37° 55′N 85° 40′W) **12**:47
BULLMASTIFF **6**:214 *illus.*
BULLOCH (county in Georgia)
map (32° 25′N 81° 45′W) **9**:114
BULLOCK (county in Alabama)
map (32° 5′N 85° 40′W) **1**:234
BULLOCK, WYNN 3:561 *bibliog.*
BULLOCK'S-HEART *see* CUSTARD APPLE
BULLRUN ROCK
map (44° 21′N 118° 17′W) **14**:427
BULLS BAY
map (32° 59′N 79° 33′W) **18**:98
BULLSHEAD BUTTE
map (49° 55′N 110° 45′W) **1**:256
BULOFF, JOSEPH
musical comedy **13**:674 *illus.*
BÜLOW, BERNHARD HEINRICH MARTIN, FÜRST VON 3:561
BÜLOW, HANS VON 3:561 *bibliog.*
Berlin Philharmonic Orchestra **3**:217
Liszt, Franz **12**:367
BÜLOW, KARL VON
Marne, Battles of the **13**:162
World War I **20**:223
BULRUSH 3:561; **17**:183 *illus.*
BULTMANN, RUDOLF 3:561 *bibliog.*
BULWER, SIR HENRY LYTTON
Clayton-Bulwer Treaty **5**:47
BULWER-LYTTON, EDWARD, 1ST BARON LYTTON 3:562 *bibliog.*
BULWER-LYTTON, EDWARD ROBERT, 1ST EARL OF LYTTON 3:562
BUMBLEBEE **3**:156–157 *illus.*
mimicry **13**:435 *illus.*
BUMBRY, GRACE 3:562
BUMELIA 3:562
BUMPPO, NATTY (fictional character) 3:562
Deerslayer, The **6**:81
BUNAU-VARILLA, PHILIPPE JEAN 3:562 *bibliog.*
BUNBURY (Australia)
map (33° 19′S 115° 38′E) **2**:328
BUNCHBERRY *see* DOGWOOD
BUNCHE, RALPH 3:562 *bibliog., illus.*
BUNCHO 3:562 *bibliog.*
BUNCOMBE (county in North Carolina)
map (35° 35′N 82° 35′W) **14**:242
BUNDABERG (Australia)
map (24° 52′S 152° 21′E) **2**:328
BUNDES BRUDER
B'nai B'rith **3**:348
BUNDESRAT
Germany, East and West **9**:146
BUNDESTAG
Germany, East and West **9**:146
BUNDY, McGEORGE 3:562–563 *illus.*
BUNGO CHANNEL
map (33° 0′N 132° 13′E) **11**:361
BUNIA (Zaire)
map (1° 34′N 30° 15′E) **20**:350
BUNIN, IVAN ALEKSEYEVICH 3:563 *bibliog.*
BUNIONS, CORNS, AND CALLUSES 3:563 *bibliog.*
skin diseases **17**:341
BUNKER *see* FORTIFICATION
BUNKER (Missouri)
map (37° 27′N 91° 13′W) **13**:476
BUNKER, ARCHIE
radio and television broadcasting **16**:59
BUNKER, ELLSWORTH 3:563
BUNKER HILL (Illinois)
map (39° 3′N 89° 57′W) **11**:42
BUNKER HILL (Indiana)
map (40° 40′N 86° 6′W) **11**:111
BUNKER HILL (Nevada)
map (39° 15′N 117° 8′W) **14**:111
BUNKER HILL, BATTLE OF 3:563 *bibliog.*; **19**:319 *illus.*
American Revolution **1**:355–356 *illus.*
Putnam, Israel **15**:632
BUNKIE (Louisiana)
map (30° 57′N 92° 11′W) **12**:430
BUNNELL (Florida)
map (29° 28′N 81° 15′W) **8**:172
BUNNER, H. C. 3:563
BUNNY, JOHN
film, history of **8**:82
BUNRAKU 3:563–564 *bibliog.*
Japanese literature **11**:380
Kabuki **12**:4
BUNSEN, ROBERT WILHELM 3:564 *bibliog.*
bunsen burner **3**:564
cesium **4**:262
BUNSEN BURNER 3:564
Bunsen, Robert Wilhelm **3**:564
BUNSHAFT, GORDON 3:564 *bibliog.*
Beinecke Library **12**:317 *illus.*
Hirshhorn Museum and Sculpture Garden **10**:176
Lever House **2**:137 *illus.*
Skidmore, Owings, and Merrill **17**:337
BUNTING (zoology) 3:564 *illus.*
BUNTLINE, NED 3:565 *bibliog.*
Astor Place Riot **2**:269
BUÑUEL, LUIS 3:565 *bibliog.*
Dalí, Salvador **6**:13
documentary **6**:211
film, history of **8**:86
surrealism (film, literature, theater) **18**:366
Viridiana **3**:565 *illus.*
BUNYA (Swaziland)
map (26° 32′S 31° 1′E) **18**:380
BUNYAN, JOHN 1:299 *illus.*; **3**:565 *bibliog., illus.*; **7**:195 *illus.*
Pilgrim's Progress **15**:302
BUNYAN, PAUL 3:565 *bibliog.*
BUONAROTTI, MICHELANGELO *see* MICHELANGELO
BUONOPARTE, CARLO MARIE
Bonaparte (family) **3**:375
BUOY 3:565–566
BUOYANCY *see* ARCHIMEDES' PRINCIPLE
BUOYANCY, BIOLOGICAL
fish
swim bladder **18**:390
BUR (botany) *see* SANDBUR
BUR REED 3:566
BURAMKUMIN (caste)
Japan **11**:363
BURAO (Somalia)
map (9° 30′N 45° 30′E) **18**:60
BURAS (Louisiana)
map (29° 21′N 89° 32′W) **12**:430
BURAYDA (Saudi Arabia)
map (26° 20′N 43° 59′E) **17**:94
BURBAGE, RICHARD 3:566
acting **1**:87
Chamberlain's Men **4**:274
BURBANK (California)
map (34° 12′N 118° 18′W) **4**:31
BURBANK (Illinois)
map (41° 44′N 87° 45′W) **11**:42
BURBANK, LUTHER 3:566 *bibliog., illus.*
BURBOT 3:566 *illus.*
BURCHFIELD, CHARLES 3:566–567 *bibliog., illus.*
Ice Glare **3**:567 *illus.*
BURCKHARDT, JAKOB 3:567 *bibliog.*
Renaissance **16**:148
BURDEN (Kansas)
map (37° 19′N 96° 45′W) **12**:18
BURDEN, HENRY **19**:450 *illus.*
BURDETT (Kansas)
map (38° 12′N 99° 32′W) **12**:18
BURDIGALA *see* BORDEAUX (France)
BURDOCK 3:567
BUREAU (county in Illinois)
map (41° 22′N 89° 30′W) **11**:42
BUREAU OF INFORMATION OF THE COMMUNIST AND WORKERS PARTIES *see* COMINFORM
BUREAU OF *see under the latter part of the name, e.g.,* CENSUS, U.S. BUREAU OF THE; INDIAN AFFAIRS, BUREAU OF; *etc.*
BUREAUCRACY 3:567–568 *bibliog.*
administrative law **1**:104–105
civil service **5**:14
government **9**:269
Inca **11**:71–72 *illus.*
Parkinson's law **15**:91
Weber, Max (sociologist) **20**:87
BURGAS (Bulgaria) 3:568
map (42° 30′N 27° 28′E) **3**:555
BURGAS BAY
map (42° 30′N 27° 33′E) **3**:555
BURGAW (North Carolina)
map (34° 33′N 77° 56′W) **14**:242
BURGDORF (Switzerland)
map (47° 4′N 7° 37′E) **18**:394
BURGEO (Newfoundland)
map (47° 37′N 57° 37′W) **14**:166
BÜRGER, GOTTFRIED AUGUST 3:568
BURGER, WARREN EARL 3:568–569; **18**:355 *illus.*
Miller v. *California* **13**:428–429
United States v. *Richard M. Nixon* **19**:465
BÜRGERLICHES GESETZBUCH
civil law **5**:12
BURGESS, ANTHONY 3:569 *bibliog., illus.*
BURGESS, GUY
intelligence gathering **11**:205
Philby, H. St. John **15**:231
BURGESSES, HOUSE OF
indentured service **11**:78
Virginia **19**:611
Yeardley, Sir George **20**:320
BURGETTSTOWN (Pennsylvania)
map (40° 23′N 80° 23′W) **15**:147
BURGH, HUBERT DE 3:569
Henry III, King of England **10**:125
BURGHLEY, WILLIAM CECIL, 1ST BARON 3:569 *bibliog.*
BURGIN (Kentucky)
map (37° 45′N 84° 46′W) **12**:47
BURGKMAIR, HANS, THE ELDER 3:569 *bibliog.*
BURGLARY 3:569–570
alarm systems **1**:240
crime **5**:346
BURGOS (Spain) 3:570
map (42° 21′N 3° 42′W) **18**:140
BURGOYNE, JOHN 3:570 *bibliog.*
American Revolution **1**:359–360 *map*
Saratoga, Battles of **17**:75
surrender at Saratoga **1**:361 *illus.*
Ticonderoga **19**:192
BURGUNDIANS *see* ARMAGNACS AND BURGUNDIANS
BURGUNDY (France) 3:570–571 *bibliog., map*
art
Romanesque art and architecture **16**:283 *illus.*
Franche-Comté **8**:273
history
Armagnacs and Burgundians **2**:171
Brabant, Duchy of **3**:435
John the Fearless, Duke **11**:425
Low Countries, history of the **12**:439
Mary of Burgundy **13**:185
Philip the Bold, Duke of Burgundy **15**:231
Philip the Good, Duke of Burgundy **15**:231
wine **20**:175
BURGUNDY GATE (France) *see* BELFORT GAP (France)
BURIAL 3:571 *bibliog.*
See also PASSAGE RITES
art
Chinese art and architecture **4**:384–385; **4**:386
Egyptian art and architecture **7**:85–90
Greek art **9**:338; **9**:342
terra-cotta **19**:119–120
barrow **3**:95
cairn **4**:17
catacombs **4**:197
cemetery **4**:244–245
Cro-Magnon man **5**:353–354
funeral customs **8**:364
mastaba **13**:214
prehistoric and ancient
African prehistory **1**:175 *illus.*
Battle-Axe culture **3**:126
Dowth (Ireland) **6**:252
European prehistory **7**:302–304
Gokstad ship burial **9**:226
Grimaldi man **9**:364
Hallstatt **7**:304 *illus.*; **10**:23
Homo erectus **10**:216
Ipiutak (Alaska) **11**:248
Jericho (Jordan) **11**:397
Mapungubwe (South Africa) **13**:142
Mound Builders **13**:617
Newgrange (Ireland) **14**:168
North American archaeology **14**:238–239 *illus.*
Oseberg ship burial **14**:453
Pazyryk (Siberia) **15**:122
San Agustín (Colombia) **17**:50
Scythians **17**:167
Sutton Hoo ship burial **18**:373–374
Tara (Ireland) **19**:35
Tollund man **19**:227
Urnfield culture **19**:487
Villanovans **19**:597
Vix (France) **19**:623
Wessex culture **20**:106
pyramids **15**:634–636
sarcophagus **17**:75–76
ship burial
Gokstad ship burial **9**:225–226
Oseberg ship burial **14**:453
Sutton Hoo ship burial **18**:373–374
stupa **18**:308
tomb **19**:230–231
tombstone **19**:232
wagon burial
Hallstatt **7**:304 *illus.*; **10**:23
Vix **19**:623
BURIAN, EMIL F.
stage lighting **18**:210
BURIAT LANGUAGE
Altaic languages **19**:476
BURIDAN, JEAN 3:571
BURIN (Newfoundland)
map (47° 2′N 55° 10′W) **14**:166
BURIN (tool)
Paleolithic Period **15**:40
BURIN PENINSULA
map (47° 0′N 55° 40′W) **14**:166
BURJ HAMMUD (Lebanon)
map (33° 53′N 35° 32′E) **12**:265
BURKBURNETT (Texas)
map (34° 6′N 98° 34′W) **19**:129
BURKE (county in Georgia)
map (33° 5′N 82° 0′W) **9**:114

BURKE (county in North Carolina)
  map (35° 50′N 81° 45′W) **14**:242
BURKE (county in North Dakota)
  map (48° 50′N 102° 30′W) **14**:248
BURKE (South Dakota)
  map (43° 11′N 99° 18′W) **18**:103
BURKE, EDMUND 3:571 *bibliog.*
  conservatism **5**:205
  Fourth Estate **8**:255
  Reflections on the Revolution in France **16**:119
  representation **16**:161
  state (in political philosophy) **18**:229
BURKE, KENNETH 3:571 *bibliog.*
BURKE, MARTHA JANE *see* CALAMITY JANE
BURKE, ROBERT O'HARA 3:571–572 *bibliog.*
  Australia, history of **2**:340 *map*
BURKESVILLE (Kentucky)
  map (36° 48′N 85° 22′W) **12**:47
BURKINA FASO *see* UPPER VOLTA
BURKITT, MILES
  Neolithic Period **14**:84
BURL *see* WOOD (botany)
BURLAP *see* JUTE
BURLEIGH (county in North Dakota)
  map (47° 0′N 100° 30′W) **14**:248
BURLESON (Texas)
  map (32° 33′N 97° 19′W) **19**:129
BURLESON (county in Texas)
  map (30° 30′N 96° 43′W) **19**:129
BURLESQUE SHOWS *see* MUSIC HALL, VAUDEVILLE, AND BURLESQUE
BURLESQUE AND TRAVESTY 3:572 *bibliog.*
  See also SATIRE
  mock epic **13**:489
  satyr play **17**:92
BURLETTA 3:572
BURLEY (Idaho)
  map (42° 32′N 113° 48′W) **11**:26
BURLINGAME (California)
  map (37° 35′N 122° 22′W) **4**:31
BURLINGAME (Kansas)
  map (38° 45′N 95° 50′W) **12**:18
BURLINGAME TREATY
  Chinese Exclusion Acts **4**:388
BURLINGTON (Colorado)
  map (39° 18′N 102° 16′W) **5**:116
BURLINGTON (Iowa)
  map (40° 49′N 91° 14′W) **11**:244
BURLINGTON (Kansas)
  map (38° 12′N 95° 45′W) **12**:18
BURLINGTON (Kentucky)
  map (39° 2′N 84° 43′W) **12**:47
BURLINGTON (Maine)
  map (45° 12′N 68° 26′W) **13**:70
BURLINGTON (Massachusetts)
  map (42° 30′N 71° 12′W) **3**:409
BURLINGTON (New Jersey)
  map (40° 4′N 74° 49′W) **14**:129
BURLINGTON (county in New Jersey)
  map (39° 50′N 74° 47′W) **14**:129
BURLINGTON (North Carolina)
  map (36° 4′N 79° 26′W) **14**:242
BURLINGTON (Ontario)
  map (43° 19′N 79° 47′W) **14**:393
BURLINGTON (Vermont) 3:572
  map (44° 29′N 73° 13′W) **19**:554
BURLINGTON (Washington)
  map (48° 28′N 122° 20′W) **20**:35
BURLINGTON (Wisconsin)
  map (42° 41′N 88° 17′W) **20**:185
BURLINGTON (Wyoming)
  map (44° 27′N 108° 26′W) **20**:301
BURLINGTON, RICHARD BOYLE, 3d EARL OF 3:572 *bibliog.*
  Kent, William **12**:45
BURLINGTON JUNCTION (Missouri)
  map (40° 27′N 95° 4′W) **13**:476
BURMA 3:572–575 *bibliog., illus., map, table*
  art
    Shwesandaw cetiya **18**:110 *illus.*
    Southeast Asian art and architecture **18**:109–110 *illus.*
  cities
    Mandalay **13**:110
    Moulmein **13**:616
    Pegu **15**:133
    Rangoon **16**:85 *illus.*
  climate 3:573 *table*
  economic activity 3:574–575
  education 3:574
    Southeast Asian universities **18**:111 *table*
  flag 3:573 *illus.*
  government 3:575
  history 3:575
    Anawratha **1**:398
    Asia, history of **2**:253–254
    Aung San **2**:323
    Ne Win, U **14**:68
    Nu, U **14**:277
    Pagan **15**:13
    Thant, U **19**:142–143
    World War II **20**:260–261 *map*; **20**:266–267; **20**:276–277 *illus., map*
    World WarII **20**:278
  land and resources 3:572–573 *illus., map*
  language
    Sino-Tibetan languages **17**:324–325
    Southeast Asian languages **18**:110–111
  map (22° 0′N 98° 0′E) **2**:232
  missions, Christian
    Judson, Adoniram **11**:464–465
  people 3:574 *illus.*
    Burmese 3:575–576
    Lushai **12**:467
    Mon **13**:515
    Naga (people) **14**:6
  religion 3:574 *illus.*
  rivers, lakes, and waterways
    Irrawaddy River **11**:280
    Salween River **17**:41
BURMA ROAD 3:575
  World War II **20**:260–261 *map*; **20**:266–267; **20**:276–277 *illus., map*; **20**:278
BURMESE (people) 3:575–576 *bibliog.*
  Asia, history of **2**:253
BURMESE CAT 3:576 *illus.*; **4**:195 *illus.*; **17**:284 *illus.*
  longhaired cats **12**:408
BURN 3:576 *bibliog.*
  artificial organs **2**:222
  first aid **8**:109 *illus.*
  plasma transfusion
    serum **17**:210
BURNABY (British Columbia)
  map (49° 15′N 122° 57′W) **3**:491
BURNE-JONES, SIR EDWARD 3:576–577 *bibliog., illus.*
  The Baleful Head 3:576 *illus.*
  Kelmscott Press **12**:39–40
  Morris, William **13**:589
  Pre-Raphaelites **15**:519
  stained glass **18**:212
BURNE-JONES, SIR PHILIP
  Rudyard Kipling **12**:86 *illus.*
BURNELL, JOCELYN BELL
  pulsar **15**:620
BURNET (Texas)
  map (30° 46′N 98° 14′W) **19**:129
BURNET (county in Texas)
  map (30° 45′N 98° 10′W) **19**:129
BURNET, SIR MACFARLANE 3:577 *bibliog.*
  Medawar, Peter Brian **13**:263
BURNET, GILBERT 3:577
BURNETT (county in Wisconsin)
  map (45° 52′N 92° 15′W) **20**:185
BURNETT, CAROL 3:577
BURNETT, FRANCES HODGSON 3:577 *bibliog.*
BURNETT, IVY COMPTON *see* COMPTON-BURNETT, IVY
BURNEY (California)
  map (40° 53′N 121° 40′W) **4**:31
BURNEY, CHARLES 3:577 *bibliog.*
BURNEY, FANNY 3:577 *bibliog.*
BURNHAM (Pennsylvania)
  map (40° 38′N 77° 34′W) **15**:147
BURNHAM, DANIEL HUDSON 3:577 *bibliog.*
  Flatiron Building **8**:156
  Root, John Wellborn **16**:311
  skyscraper **17**:348–350
BURNHAM, FORBES 3:578
  Guyana **9**:411
BURNING BUSH (botany) 3:577–578 *illus.*
  spindle tree **18**:184
BURNS (Oregon)
  map (43° 35′N 119° 3′W) **14**:427
BURNS, ARTHUR F. 3:578 *bibliog.*
BURNS, GEORGE *see* BURNS AND ALLEN
BURNS, ROBERT 3:578–579 *bibliog., illus.*
BURNS AND ALLEN 3:579
BURNS FLAT (Oklahoma)
  map (35° 21′N 99° 10′W) **14**:368
BURNS LAKE (British Columbia)
  map (54° 14′N 125° 46′W) **3**:491
BURNSIDE (Kentucky)
  map (36° 59′N 84° 36′W) **12**:47
BURNSIDE, AMBROSE E. 3:579 *illus.*; **5**:26 *illus.*
BURNSVILLE (Alabama)
  map (32° 28′N 86° 53′W) **1**:234
BURNSVILLE (North Carolina)
  map (35° 55′N 82° 18′W) **14**:242
BURNT GROUND (Bahama Islands)
  map (23° 9′N 75° 17′W) **3**:23
BURR, AARON 3:579–580 *bibliog., illus.*; **6**:293 *illus.*
  Hamilton, Alexander **10**:28
  Jefferson, Thomas **11**:393
  Martin, Luther **13**:179
  treason **19**:285
  Vanderlyn, John **19**:519
  Wilkinson, James **20**:153
BURRO *see* ASS; DONKEY
BURROUGHS, EDGAR RICE 3:580 *bibliog.*
  Tarzan of the Apes **19**:41
BURROUGHS, JOHN 3:580 *bibliog.*; **19**:453 *illus.*
BURROUGHS, WILLIAM S. 3:580 *bibliog., illus.*
BURROW
  mole **13**:507 *illus.*
  prairie dog **15**:489 *illus.*
  rabbit **16**:31 *illus.*
  Tertiary Period **19**:125 *illus.*
BURROWS, LARRY 3:580–581
BURROW'S REPORTS
  common law reports **5**:139
BURRTON (Kansas)
  map (38° 2′N 97° 41′W) **12**:18
BURRUS, SEXTUS AFRANIUS
  Rome, ancient **16**:302
BURRWOOD (Louisiana)
  map (28° 58′N 89° 22′W) **12**:430
BURSA (anatomy)
  muscle **13**:653
BURSA (Turkey) 3:581
  map (40° 11′N 29° 4′E) **19**:343
BURSITIS 3:581
  tendonitis **19**:101
BURSTER
  X-ray astronomy **20**:307
BURT (Iowa)
  map (43° 12′N 94° 13′W) **11**:244
BURT (county in Nebraska)
  map (41° 30′N 96° 20′W) **14**:70
BURT, SIR CYRIL 3:581 *bibliog.*
  behavioral genetics 3:170
BURT LAKE
  map (45° 27′N 84° 40′W) **13**:377
BURTON (Michigan)
  map (43° 2′N 83° 36′W) **13**:377
BURTON, HAROLD
  Morgan v. *Virginia* **13**:579
BURTON, RICHARD (actor) 3:581 *bibliog.*
  Taylor, Elizabeth (actress) **19**:49 *illus.*
BURTON, SIR RICHARD (explorer) 3:581 *bibliog.*
  Africa **1**:157 *map*
  Arabian Nights **2**:100
  exploration **7**:338
  Ruanda-Urundi **16**:332
  Tanganyika, Lake **19**:22
BURTON, ROBERT 3:581 *bibliog.*
  Anatomy of Melancholy, The **1**:398
BURUNDI 3:581–583 *bibliog., map*
  See also RUANDA-URUNDI
  Bujumbura 3:553
  economic activities 3:582–583
  flag 3:582 *illus.*
  government 3:583
  history 3:583
  land 3:582 *map*
  map (3° 15′S 30° 0′E) **1**:136
  people 3:582
    Tutsi **19**:355–356
BURURI (Burundi)
  map (3° 57′S 29° 37′E) 3:582
BURWASH LANDING (Yukon Territory)
  map (61° 21′N 139° 0′W) **20**:345
BURWELL (Nebraska)
  map (41° 47′N 99° 8′W) **14**:70
BURY ST. EDMUNDS (England) 3:583
  Edmund, Saint **7**:58
BURYAT 3:583 *bibliog.*
BUS 3:583–585 *bibliog., illus.*
  coach and carriage **5**:75
  history 3:583–584 *illus.*
  industry 3:584–585
BUSBY (Montana)
  map (45° 32′N 106° 58′W) **13**:547
BUSCH, ADOLF 3:585
BUSCH, WILHELM 3:585
BUSCH STRING QUARTET
  Busch, Adolf 3:585
BUSH, GEORGE 3:585
  president of the United States **15**:525
BUSH, JACK
  Canadian art and architecture **4**:90
BUSH, VANNEVAR 3:585 *bibliog.*
  Manhattan Project **13**:116
BUSH BABY *see* GALAGO
BUSH LOT (Guyana)
  map (6° 12′N 57° 16′W) **9**:410
BUSHEHR (Iran)
  map (28° 59′N 50° 50′E) **11**:250
BUSHIMAIE RIVER
  map (6° 2′S 23° 45′E) **20**:350
BUSHLAND (Texas)
  map (35° 11′N 102° 4′W) **19**:129
BUSHMAN'S CLOCK *see* KOOKABURRA
BUSHMASTER 3:585 *illus.*
BUSHMEN *see* SAN (ethnic group)
BUSHNELL (Florida)
  map (28° 40′N 82° 7′W) **8**:172
BUSHNELL (Illinois)
  map (40° 33′N 90° 30′W) **11**:42
BUSHNELL, DAVID 3:585 *bibliog.*
  submarine **18**:315
  Turtle (submarine) **19**:352
BUSHNELL, HORACE 3:586 *bibliog.*
BUSHRANGERS 3:586 *bibliog.*
  Kelly, Ned **12**:39
BUSHTIT 3:586 *illus.*
BUSINESS ADMINISTRATION 3:586–587 *bibliog.*
  accounting **1**:77–78
  computer crime **5**:160L
  corporation 3:586
  finance 3:587
  government regulation, scope of 3:586–587
  management science **13**:107
  marketing **13**:159
  Minority Business Development Agency **13**:459
  partnership 3:586
    business law 3:589
    joint-stock company **11**:440
  proprietorship 3:586
BUSINESS CYCLE 3:588 *bibliog.*
  Mitchell, Wesley Clair **13**:483–484
  panic, financial **15**:59
  recession **16**:107
  Schumpeter, Joseph A. **17**:137
BUSINESS EDUCATION 3:588 *bibliog.*
BUSINESS LAW 3:588–589 *bibliog.*
  agent **1**:183–184
  arbitration (labor-management and commercial) **2**:110
  bankruptcy 3:70
  contract **5**:231–232
  corporation **5**:272
  Federal Trade Commission **8**:42
  guaranty **9**:386
  law, history of **12**:247
BUSINESS MACHINES 3:589 *bibliog.*
  calculator, electronic **4**:23–24
  cash register
    Kettering, Charles Franklin **12**:61
  computer **5**:160b; **5**:160f
  computer crime **5**:160L
  copying machine **5**:255–256
  microfilm **13**:385
  stock ticker
    Edison, Thomas Alva **7**:58
  typewriter **19**:366
  Watson (family) **20**:67
  xerox machines
    Carlson, Chester Floyd **4**:152
BUSINESS WEEK (periodical) 3:589
BUSING, SCHOOL 3:589–590 *bibliog.*
  Coleman Report **5**:100
BUSNOIS, ANTOINE
  Renaissance music **16**:156
BUSON 3:590 *bibliog.*
BUSONI, FERRUCCIO 3:590 *bibliog.*
BUSRA *see* BASRA (Iraq)
BUSSELTON (Australia)
  map (33° 39′S 115° 20′E) **2**:328
BUSSEY (Iowa)
  map (41° 12′N 92° 53′W) **11**:244
BUSSORA *see* BASRA (Iraq)
BUSSOTTI, SYLVANO
  aleatory music **1**:270
  Italian music **11**:319
BUSSUM (Netherlands)
  map (52° 16′N 5° 10′E) **14**:99
BUSTAMANTE, SIR ALEXANDER 3:590
BUSTAMANTE Y RIVERO, JOSÉ LUÍS
  Peru **15**:195
BUSTARD 3:590–591 *illus.*
BUSTELLI, FRANZ ANTON
  Nymphenburg ware **14**:309
  pottery and porcelain **15**:471
"BUSTER BROWN" (comic strip)
  Outcault, Richard Felton **14**:468
BUTA (Zaire)
  map (2° 48′N 24° 44′E) **20**:350
BUTA RANQUIL (Argentina)
  map (37° 3′S 69° 50′W) **2**:149
BUTADIENE
  rubber **16**:334
BUTANE 3:591
  graphic formula **14**:436 *illus.*
  heat content **8**:353 *table*

hydrocarbon **10**:331 *illus.*
natural gas **14**:47
BUTARE (Rwanda)
map (2° 36′S 29° 44′E) **16**:378
BUTCHER BIRD *see* BELL MAGPIE
BUTCHERS' BENEVOLENT ASSOCIATION v. *CRESCENT CITY LIVESTOCK LANDING AND SLAUGHTERHOUSE CO.* *see* SLAUGHTERHOUSE CASES
BUTE (Scotland) **3**:591
BUTENANDT, ADOLF **3**:591
BUTENE
alkene **1**:297
molecular formula **1**:297 *illus.*
photoisomerization **15**:258
ultraviolet spectrum **18**:172 *illus.*
BUTKUS, DICK **3**:591
BUTLER (Alabama)
map (32° 5′N 88° 13′W) **1**:234
BUTLER (county in Alabama)
map (31° 48′N 86° 40′W) **1**:234
BUTLER (Georgia)
map (32° 34′N 84° 14′W) **9**:114
BUTLER (county in Iowa)
map (42° 43′N 92° 45′W) **11**:244
BUTLER (county in Kansas)
map (37° 45′N 96° 50′W) **12**:18
BUTLER (county in Kentucky)
map (37° 15′N 86° 45′W) **12**:47
BUTLER (Missouri)
map (38° 16′N 94° 20′W) **13**:476
BUTLER (county in Missouri)
map (36° 45′N 90° 25′W) **13**:476
BUTLER (county in Nebraska)
map (41° 15′N 97° 10′W) **14**:70
BUTLER (New Jersey)
map (41° 0′N 74° 21′W) **14**:129
BUTLER (Ohio)
map (40° 35′N 82° 26′W) **14**:357
BUTLER (county in Ohio)
map (39° 26′N 84° 30′W) **14**:357
BUTLER (Oklahoma)
map (35° 38′N 99° 11′W) **14**:368
BUTLER (Pennsylvania)
map (40° 52′N 79° 54′W) **15**:147
BUTLER (county in Pennsylvania)
map (40° 52′N 79° 54′W) **15**:147
BUTLER, ALBAN **3**:591
BUTLER, BENJAMIN FRANKLIN **3**:591 *bibliog.*
BUTLER, JOHN **3**:591
BUTLER, JOSEPH **3**:591
BUTLER, NICHOLAS MURRAY **3**:591–592 *bibliog.*
BUTLER, REG **3**:592 *bibliog.*
BUTLER, SAMUEL (1612–1680) **3**:592 *bibliog.*
BUTLER, SAMUEL (1835–1902) **3**:592 *bibliog.*
Erewhon **7**:228
Way of All Flesh, The **20**:73
BUTLER UNIVERSITY **3**:592
BUTLEROV, ALEKSANDR **3**:592
chemistry, history of **4**:327
BUTNER (North Carolina)
map (36° 8′N 78° 49′W) **14**:242
BUTOR, MICHEL **3**:592 *bibliog.*
BUTTE (county in California)
map (39° 40′N 121° 35′W) **4**:31
BUTTE (county in Idaho)
map (43° 45′N 113° 10′W) **11**:26
BUTTE (land formation) **3**:592
plateau **15**:358
BUTTE (Montana) **3**:592; **13**:550 *illus.*
map (46° 0′N 112° 32′W) **13**:547
BUTTE (Nebraska)
map (42° 58′N 98° 51′W) **14**:70
BUTTE (county in South Dakota)
map (44° 55′N 103° 30′W) **18**:103
BUTTER **3**:592–593 *bibliog., illus.*
churn **4**:427
margarine **13**:149
milk **13**:423
Wisconsin **20**:187 *illus.*
BUTTER-AND-EGGS (botany) *see* TOADFLAX
BUTTER TREE *see* TALLOW TREE
BUTTERCUP (botany) **3**:593 *illus.*; **8**:179 *illus.*; **15**:384 *illus.*
anemone **1**:410
baneberry **3**:62
bugbane **3**:547
clematis **5**:48
columbine **5**:126
larkspur **12**:208
meadow rue **13**:252
BUTTERFIELD (Minnesota)
map (43° 58′N 94° 48′W) **13**:453
BUTTERFIELD, JOHN **3**:593
BUTTERFIELD, WILLIAM **3**:593 *bibliog.*
BUTTERFISH **3**:593
BUTTERFLIES AND MOTHS **3**:594–599 *bibliog., illus.*; **11**:192 *illus.*; **13**:434–436 *illus.*
anatomy **3**:594 *illus.*
animal communication **2**:19 *illus.*
animal courtship and mating **2**:21 *illus.*
antenna **2**:47 *illus.*
classification, biological **3**:594–595
cocoon **3**:595
coloration, biological **5**:122
cutworm **5**:398
distinguishing features **3**:594
emperor moth **15**:226 *illus.*
forest **8**:227–228
gypsy moth **9**:416
importance **3**:595; **3**:599
jungle and rain forest **11**:469 *illus.*
larva **3**:595
caterpillar **4**:202–203
inchworm **11**:74
Mexican jumping bean **13**:351
metamorphosis **3**:595; **11**:190 *illus.*; **13**:333–334 *illus.*
mimicry **13**:434–435 *illus.*
mouth **11**:188 *illus.*
natural selection **14**:49 *illus.*
nun moth **8**:229 *illus.*
peppered moth **14**:49 *map*
pupa **3**:595
silkworm **17**:308
tent caterpillar **19**:113
BUTTERFLY (swimming)
swimming **18**:390 *illus.*; **18**:392
BUTTERFLY BUSH **3**:599
BUTTERFLY FISH **3**:599–600 *illus.*; **8**:116 *illus.*
saddleback butterfly fish **19**:308 *illus.*
BUTTERFLY LILY *see* GINGER LILY
BUTTERFLY WEED **3**:600
milkweed **13**:424
BUTTERNUT (tree) **3**:600 *illus.*
walnut **20**:17
BUTTERNUT (Wisconsin)
map (46° 1′N 90° 30′W) **20**:185
BUTTERWORTH, GEORGE **3**:600 *bibliog.*
BUTTERWORTS
carnivorous plants **4**:157
BUTTON, DICK **3**:600
BUTTON, SIR THOMAS
Manitoba **13**:122
Nelson River **14**:80
Northwest Passage **14**:256
Southampton Island (Northwest Territories) **18**:107
BUTTONBUSH **3**:600
BUTTONWILLOW (California)
map (35° 24′N 119° 28′W) **4**:31
BUTTONWOOD *see* PLANE TREE
BUTTRESS **3**:600–601 *illus.*
cathedrals and churches **4**:206 *illus.*
flying buttress **19**:64–65 *illus.*
BUTTS (county in Georgia)
map (33° 18′N 83° 55′W) **9**:114
BUTZER, MARTIN *see* BUCER, MARTIN
BUXTEHUDE, DIETRICH **3**:601 *bibliog.*
BUXTON (North Carolina)
map (35° 16′N 75° 32′W) **14**:242
BUXTON (North Dakota)
map (47° 36′N 97° 6′W) **14**:248
BUYS BALLOT, CHRISTOPH HENDRIK DIEDERIK **3**:601
BUZĂU (Romania)
map (45° 9′N 26° 49′E) **16**:288
BUZZ BOMB *see* V-1
BUZZARD **3**:601 *illus.*
hawk **10**:76
BUZZARDS BAY **3**:601
map (41° 33′N 70° 47′W) **13**:206
BUZZATI, DINO **3**:601
BWE LANGUAGE
Sino-Tibetan languages **17**:324
BY, JOHN
Ottawa (Ontario) **14**:461
BYBLOS **3**:601–602 *bibliog.*
masks **15**:250 *illus.*
Phoenician art **15**:250
BYDGOSZCZ (Poland) **3**:602
map (53° 8′N 18° 0′E) **15**:388
BYELORUSSIAN SOVIET SOCIALIST REPUBLIC (USSR) *see* BELORUSSIAN SOVIET SOCIALIST REPUBLIC (USSR)
BYKOVSKY, VALERY **3**:602
BYLANY (Czechoslovakia)
Danubian culture **6**:36
BYLAS (Arizona)
map (33° 8′N 110° 7′W) **2**:160
BYLOT, ROBERT
Northwest Passage **14**:256
BYNG, JULIAN HEDWORTH GEORGE, 1ST VISCOUNT BYNG OF VIMY **3**:602
BYNKERSHOEK, CORNELIS VAN
international law **11**:221
BYNUM (Montana)
map (47° 59′N 112° 19′W) **13**:547
BYNUM (North Carolina)
map (35° 47′N 79° 8′W) **14**:242
BYRD, HARRY F. **3**:602
BYRD, RICHARD E. **2**:44 *illus., map*; **3**:602
Ford Tri-motor **8**:223 *illus.*
Ross Ice Shelf (Antarctica) **16**:318
BYRD, ROBERT C. **3**:602 *bibliog.*
BYRD, WILLIAM (composer) **3**:602 *bibliog.*
anthem **2**:49
Tallis, Thomas **19**:17
BYRD, WILLIAM (planter) **3**:602
BYRD, WILLIAM (writer) **3**:602
BYRDSTOWN (Tennessee)
map (36° 34′N 85° 8′W) **19**:104
BYRNES, JAMES FRANCIS **3**:602-603 *bibliog.*
BYRON (Illinois)
map (42° 8′N 89° 15′W) **11**:42
BYRON (Wyoming)
map (44° 48′N 108° 30′W) **20**:301
BYRON, GEORGE GORDON, LORD **3**:603 *bibliog., illus.*; **7**:198 *illus.*; **16**:293 *illus.*
Byronic hero **3**:603
BYRONIC HERO **3**:603 *bibliog.*
BYSSINOSIS *see* BROWN LUNG
BYTE **3**:603
computer **5**:160h
BYTOM (Poland) **3**:603–604
BYUMBA (Rwanda)
map (1° 35′S 30° 4′E) **16**:378
BYURAKAN ASTROPHYSICAL OBSERVATORY **3**:604
BYZANTINE ART AND ARCHITECTURE **3**:604–606 *bibliog., illus.*
Anthemius of Tralles **2**:49
architecture **2**:133 *illus.*
bas-relief **3**:100
cathedrals and churches **4**:204 *illus.*
Coptic art and architecture **5**:255
costume **5**:293–294 *illus.*
dome **6**:229 *illus.*
Early Christian art and architecture **7**:9–11
enamel **7**:162
furniture **8**:374–375
gold and silver work **9**:229
Hagia Sophia **3**:605 *illus.*; **10**:10 *illus.*
icon **11**:20
iconography **11**:21–24
iconostasis **11**:24
illuminated manuscripts **11**:46–47
Isidorus of Miletus **11**:288
ivory and ivory carving **11**:336–337 *illus.*
Mistra **13**:482
mosaic **13**:594–595 *illus.*
mural painting **13**:646
painting **15**:19
Russian art and architecture **16**:361–362
Saint Mark's Basilica **17**:23–24
Saint Savior in the Chora **17**:26
San Vitale **17**:58
sculpture **17**:161–162 *illus.*
BYZANTINE EMPIRE **3**:607–608 *bibliog., illus., map*
See also BYZANTINE ART AND ARCHITECTURE; BYZANTINE MUSIC
Byzantium **3**:608
cathedrals and churches **4**:205
costume **5**:293–294 *illus.*
Decline and Fall of the Roman Empire, The History of the **6**:76
Greece **9**:328
historians *see* HISTORY—Byzantine historians
iconoclasm **11**:20–21
Istanbul (Turkey) **11**:307
Italy, history of **11**:328
Middle Ages **13**:392 *map*
Middle East, history of the **13**:401–402
Ravenna (Italy) **16**:95
Rome, ancient **16**:304
slavery **17**:353
324–610 Early period **3**:607
Arcadius, Roman Emperor in the East **2**:112
Belisarius **3**:183
Constantine I, Roman Emperor **5**:208–209
early period **3**:607
Julian the Apostate, Roman Emperor **11**:466
Justinian I, Emperor (Justinian the Great) **11**:479
Theodora, Byzantine Empress **19**:156
Zeno, Byzantine Emperor **20**:359
610–1081 Middle period **3**:607–608
Basil I, emperor **3**:109
Basil II, emperor **3**:109
Constans II, Emperor **5**:207
Heraclius, Emperor **10**:132
Irene, Empress **11**:265–266
Isaac I Comnenus, Emperor **11**:285
Leo III, Emperor (Leo the Isaurian) **12**:287–288
Leo VI, Emperor (Leo the Wise) **12**:288
middle period **3**:607–608
Zoë, Byzantine Empress **20**:371
1081–1453 Late period **3**:608
Alexius I Comnenus, Emperor **1**:278
Anna Comnena **2**:31
Constantinople, Latin Empire of **5**:209–210 *map*
Crusades **5**:368
Europe, history of **7**:284–285 *map*
Isaac II Angelus, Emperor **11**:285
John II Comnenus, Emperor **11**:426
John V Palaeologus, Emperor **11**:426
John VI Cantacuzenus, Emperor **11**:426
Manuel I Comnenus, Emperor **13**:131
Manuel II Palaeologus, Emperor **13**:131
Michael VIII, Palaeologus, Emperor **13**:371–372
BYZANTINE MUSIC **3**:608 *bibliog.*
hymn **10**:346
BYZANTINE RITE *see* EASTERN RITE CHURCHES; ORTHODOX CHURCH
BYZANTIUM **3**:608 *bibliog.*
B_{17} (vitamin) *see* LAETRILE

C

C (letter) **4**:3 *illus., illus.*
G (letter) **9**:3
C (computer language) **4**:3
computer languages **5**:160p
C-47 SKYTRAIN
DC-3 **6**:57
CA RIVER
map (18° 46′N 105° 47′E) **19**:580
CAABA *see* KAABA
CAB *see* CABRIOLET; HACKNEY CARRIAGE; HANSOM CAB; TAXICAB
CAB *see* CIVIL AERONAUTICS BOARD
CABAIGUAN (Cuba)
map (22° 5′N 79° 30′W) **5**:377
CABALA *see* KABBALAH
CABALLÉ, MONTSERRAT **4**:3
CABALLERO, FERNÁN **4**:3 *bibliog.*
CABALLERO, FERNÁNDEZ
zarzuela **20**:356
CABALLO RESERVOIR
map (32° 58′N 107° 18′W) **14**:136
CABALLOCOHA (Peru)
map (3° 54′S 70° 32′W) **15**:193
CABANATUAN (Philippines)
map (15° 29′N 120° 58′E) **15**:237
CABANO (Quebec)
map (47° 41′N 68° 53′W) **16**:18
CABARET **4**:3–4 *bibliog., illus.*
CABARRUS (county in North Carolina)
map (35° 20′N 80° 35′W) **14**:242
CABBAGE **4**:4 *bibliog., illus.*; **19**:532 *illus.*
broccoli **3**:500
brussels sprouts **3**:527
cauliflower **4**:219
Chinese cabbage **4**:388
collard **5**:103
kale **12**:7
Kerguelen cabbage **12**:59
CABBAGE BUTTERFLY **3**:595–596 *illus.*
CABBAGE PALMETTO **4**:4
CABELL (county in West Virginia)
map (38° 25′N 82° 15′W) **20**:111
CABELL, JAMES B. **4**:4 *bibliog.*
CABET, ÉTIENNE **4**:4 *bibliog.*
socialism **18**:19
CABEZA DE VACA, ÁLVAR NÚÑEZ **4**:5 *bibliog.*
exploration of colonial America **19**:437 *map*
CABEZAS (Bolivia)
map (18° 46′S 63° 24′W) **3**:366

CABEZON (fish)
sculpin 17:159
CABEZÓN, ANTONIO DE
Renaissance music 16:156
CABILDO (Argentina)
map (38° 29′S 61° 54′W) 2:149
CABIMAS (Venezuela)
map (10° 23′N 71° 28′W) 19:542
CABIN CRUISER (boat) 3:351 *illus.*
CABINDA (Angola) 4:5
CABINET (government) 4:5 *bibliog.*
prime minister 15:542
CABINET (United States)
See also articles of specific presidents, e.g., CARTER, JIMMY; WASHINGTON, GEORGE; etc.; names of specific departments, e.g., COMMERCE, U.S. DEPARTMENT OF; TREASURY, U.S. DEPARTMENT OF THE; etc.; names of specific cabinet members, e.g., HARRIS, PATRICIA ROBERTS; WALLACE, HENRY A.; etc.
cabinet (government) 4:5
Kitchen Cabinet 12:91
president of the United States 15:525
CABINET MOUNTAINS
map (48° 8′N 115° 46′W) 13:547
CABLE (communications) 4:5–6 *bibliog., illus.*
Atlantic cable 2:294
Colt, Samuel 5:123–124
Field, Cyrus W. 8:71
MacKay (family) 13:27
power, generation and transmission of 15:484–486
Siemens (family) 17:296
CABLE (Wisconsin)
map (46° 13′N 91° 17′W) 20:185
CABLE, GEORGE WASHINGTON 4:6 *bibliog.*
CABLE CAR 4:6
land reclamation 12:179 *illus.*
San Francisco 17:53 *illus.*
streetcar 18:296 *illus.*
CABLE TV 4:6–7 *bibliog.*
newspaper 14:172
telecommunications 19:76
CABO CAMARÓN, CAPE OF
map (16° 0′N 85° 5′W) 10:218
CABO GRACIAS A DIOS (Nicaragua)
map (14° 59′N 83° 10′W) 14:179
CABO RASO (Argentina)
map (44° 21′S 65° 14′W) 2:149
CABO ROJO (Puerto Rico)
map (18° 5′N 67° 9′W) 15:614
CABOCLO *see* MESTIZO
CABONGA RESERVOIR
map (47° 20′N 76° 35′W) 16:18
CABOOL (Missouri)
map (37° 7′N 92° 6′W) 13:476
CABORA BASSA RESERVOIR
map (15° 40′S 31° 30′E) 13:627
CABOT (Arkansas)
map (34° 58′N 92° 1′W) 2:166
CABOT, JOHN 4:7 *bibliog., illus.*
Canada, history of 4:80–81 *map*
explorations 7:337 *map*
Grand Banks 9:284 *map*
Newfoundland (Canada) 14:168
St. John's (Newfoundland) 17:19
CABOT, SEBASTIAN 4:7 *bibliog.*
Paraná River 15:80
CABRAL, AMILCAR
Guinea-Bissau 9:399
CABRAL, LUIS DE ALMEIDA
Guinea-Bissau 9:399
CABRAL, PEDRO ÁLVAREZ 4:7 *bibliog.*
CABRERA, MANUEL ESTRADA *see* ESTRADA CABRERA, MANUEL
CABRIEL RIVER
map (39° 14′N 1° 3′W) 18:140
CABRILLO, JUAN RODRÍGUEZ 4:7 *bibliog.*
California 4:36
exploration of colonial America 19:437 *map*
San Diego (California) 17:51
Santa Catalina Island 17:67
CABRINI, SAINT FRANCES XAVIER 4:8 *bibliog., illus.*
CABRINI, MOTHER *see* CABRINI, SAINT FRANCES XAVIER
CABRIOLET
coach and carriage 5:73
CABUYA (Costa Rica)
map (9° 36′N 85° 6′W) 5:291
ČAČAK (Yugoslavia)
map (43° 53′N 20° 21′E) 20:340
CACAO (botany) 4:8 *illus.*
chocolate 4:402
cocoa 5:88
CACCIA
music, history of Western 13:665
CACCINI, GIULIO 4:8 *bibliog.*
Italian music 11:318
music, history of Western 13:666
CÁCERES (Brazil)
map (16° 4′S 57° 41′W) 3:460
CÁCERES (Spain)
map (39° 29′N 6° 22′W) 18:140
CACHE (Oklahoma)
map (34° 38′N 98° 38′W) 14:368
CACHE (county in Utah)
map (41° 40′N 111° 45′W) 19:492
CACHE CREEK (British Columbia)
map (50° 48′N 121° 19′W) 3:491
CACHE MEMORY *see* BUFFER MEMORY
CACHE RIVER
map (34° 42′N 91° 20′W) 2:166
CACHEU
map (12° 10′N 16° 21′W) 9:399
CACHUELA ESPERANZA (Bolivia)
map (10° 32′S 65° 38′W) 3:366
CACIQUE 4:8
CACOMISTLE 4:8 *illus.*
CACTI AND OTHER SUCCULENTS 4:9–11 *bibliog., illus.*; 10:275 *illus.*; 15:336 *illus.*
chaparral 4:283–284
characteristics 4:9–10
classification, biological 4:9
desert life 6:129–131
photosynthesis 15:277
varieties 4:10–11
agave 1:183
aloe 1:307
ice plant 11:13
kalanchoe 12:7
peyote 15:217
prickly pear 15:536
stonecrop 18:282–283
yucca 20:338–339
"CACTUS JACK" GARNER *see* GARNER, JOHN NANCE
CACTUS WREN
nest 3:287 *illus.*
CADASTRAL MAP 13:141
CAD/CAM *see* COMPUTER-AIDED DESIGN AND COMPUTER-AIDED MANUFACTURING
CADDIS FLY 4:11 *illus.*; 12:168 *illus.*
CADDO (American Indians) 4:11 *bibliog.*
Indians of North America, music and dance of the 11:143
CADDO (county in Louisiana)
map (32° 32′N 93° 52′W) 12:430
CADDO (Oklahoma)
map (34° 7′N 96° 16′W) 14:368
CADDO (county in Oklahoma)
map (35° 15′N 98° 20′W) 14:368
CADENCE
cadenza 4:11
CADENZA 4:11
CADET 4:11
CADILLAC (automobile) 2:365 *illus.*
CADILLAC (Michigan)
map (44° 15′N 85° 24′W) 13:377
CADILLAC, ANTOINE LAUMET DE LA MOTHE, SIEUR DE 4:11 *bibliog.*
Huron 10:316
CADIZ (Kentucky)
map (36° 52′N 87° 50′W) 12:47
CADIZ (Ohio)
map (40° 16′N 81° 0′W) 14:357
CÁDIZ (Spain) 4:12
map (36° 32′N 6° 18′W) 18:140
CÁDIZ ,GULF OF
map (36° 50′N 7° 10′W) 15:449
CADMAN, CHARLES WAKEFIELD 4:12 *bibliog.*
CADMIUM 4:12 *bibliog.*
abundances of common elements 7:131 *table*
compound
photoelectric cell 15:259
element 7:130 *table*
Group IIB periodic table 15:167
metal, metallic element 13:328
pollutants, chemical 15:410
superconductivity 18:350 *table*
transition elements 19:273
CADMUS 4:12
CADOMIN (Alberta)
map (53° 2′N 117° 20′W) 1:256
CADORNA, LUIGI
Caporetto, Battle of 4:127
World War I 20:229–230; 20:237–238
CADOTT (Wisconsin)
map (44° 57′N 91° 9′W) 20:185
CADUCEUS (computer system)
automata, theory of 2:357
CADUCEUS (mythology) 4:12
CADWELL (Georgia)
map (32° 20′N 83° 3′W) 9:114
CADY, JOSIAH CLEVELAND
Metropolitan Opera 13:348
CAECILIAN 1:377–378 *illus.*
CÆDMON 4:12 *bibliog.*
CAEN (France) 4:12–13
map (49° 11′N 0° 21′W) 8:260
Norman architecture 14:220
Saint-Étienne, Abbey Church of 14:220 *illus.*
CAERE (Etruria) 4:13
Etruscans 7:258–261
sarcophagus from 7:260 *illus.*
Tomb of the Reliefs 19:230 *illus.*
CAERFYRDDIN *see* CARMARTHEN (Wales)
CAERLEON *see* CAMELOT
CAERNARVON (Wales) 4:13
map (53° 8′N 4° 16′W) 19:403
CAERNARVONSHIRE *see* GWYNEDD (Wales)
CAESAR 4:13
CAESAR, GAIUS JULIUS 4:13–15 *bibliog., illus., map*
Brutus, Marcus Junius 3:528
caesar 4:13
calendar 4:28
Cassius Longinus, Gaius 4:185
Cicero, Marcus Tullius 4:428–429
Cleopatra, Queen of Egypt 5:50
cryptology 5:371
Europe, history of 7:281
France, history of 8:265–266
Gallic wars 9:19
La Tène 12:150
military conquests 4:14 *map*
Pompey the Great 15:424–425
Ptolemy XIII, King of Egypt 15:608
Roman expansion under 16:299 *map*
Rome, ancient 16:301 *illus.*
Rubicon River 16:336
CAESAR, GERMANICUS *see* GERMANICUS CAESAR
CAESAR, SID 4:15
CAESAR CREEK LAKE
map (39° 30′N 84° 0′W) 14:357
CAESAREA (Algeria) *see* IOL (Algeria)
CAESAREA (Israel) 4:15 *bibliog.*
CAESURA 4:15
CAETANO, MARCELLO
Portugal 15:452
Portugal, history of 15:455
CAFFEINE 4:15 *bibliog.*
kola nut 12:107
stimulant 18:271
CAGAYAN DE ORO (Philippines)
map (8° 29′N 124° 39′E) 15:237
CAGAYAN RIVER
map (18° 22′N 121° 37′E) 15:237
CAGE, JOHN 4:15–16 *bibliog., illus.*
aleatory music 1:270
happenings 10:41
CAGLIARI (Italy) 4:16
map (39° 20′N 9° 0′E) 11:321
CAGNEY, JAMES 4:16 *bibliog., illus.*; 8:84 *illus.*
CAGUAS (Puerto Rico)
map (18° 14′N 66° 2′W) 15:614
CAHABA RIVER
map (32° 20′N 87° 5′W) 1:234
CAHAN, ABRAHAM 4:16 *bibliog.*
CAHIERS DU CINÉMA (periodical) 4:16
Rohmer, Eric 16:270
CAHOKIA (Illinois)
map (38° 33′N 90° 10′W) 11:42
CAHOKIA MOUNDS 4:16 *bibliog.*; 14:237 *map*
Illinois (American Indians) 11:45
CAI (COMPUTER-ASSISTED INSTRUCTION)
computers in education 5:165–166
teaching machines 19:57
CAIBARIÉN (Cuba)
map (22° 31′N 79° 28′W) 5:377
CAICARA (Venezuela)
map (7° 37′N 66° 10′W) 19:542
CAICOS ISLANDS *see* TURKS AND CAICOS ISLANDS
CAILLAUX, JOSEPH MARIE AUGUSTE 4:16 *bibliog.*
CAILLE, RENÉ
exploration 7:337 *map*
CAILLEBOTTE, GUSTAVE 4:16–17 *bibliog.*
CAILLETET, LOUIS P.
cryogenics 5:370
CAILLOMA (Peru)
map (15° 12′S 71° 46′W) 15:193
CAIMAN 4:17 *bibliog., illus.*; 5:356 *illus.*
CAIN 4:17
CAIN, JAMES M. 4:17 *bibliog.*
CAINE, SIR HALL 4:17 *bibliog.*
CAINE MUTINY, THE (book) 4:17
Wouk, Herman 20:284
CAIRN 4:17
megalith 13:279
stone alignments 18:281
CAIRN TERRIER 4:17 *bibliog., illus.*; 6:220 *illus.*
CAIRNS (Australia)
map (16° 55′S 145° 46′E) 2:328
CAIRO (Egypt) 4:17–19 *bibliog., illus., map*; 7:78 *illus.*
Islamic art and architecture 11:297
map (30° 3′N 31° 15′E) 7:76
CAIRO (Georgia)
map (30° 53′N 84° 12′W) 9:114
CAIRO (Illinois) 4:19
map (37° 0′N 89° 11′W) 11:42
CAIRO (Nebraska)
map (41° 0′N 98° 36′W) 14:70
CAIRO (West Virginia)
map (39° 13′N 81° 9′W) 20:111
CAIRO CONFERENCE 4:19
CAISSON 4:19 *bibliog., illus.*
bridge (engineering) 3:481–482
dike (engineering) 6:175–176
foundation, building 8:249–250
lighthouse 12:337
CAISSON DISEASE *see* BENDS
CAITHNESS (Scotland) 4:19
CAJAL, SANTIAGO RAMÓN Y *see* RAMÓN Y CAJAL, SANTIAGO
CAJAMARCA (Peru)
Inca 11:71
map (7° 10′S 78° 31′W) 15:193
CAJEPUT OIL
paperbark 15:71
CAJEPUT TREE *see* PAPERBARK
CAJETAN 4:19
CAJONES CAYS
map (16° 5′N 83° 12′W) 10:218
CAJUNS 4:19–20 *bibliog.*
Acadia 1:71
Lafayette (Louisiana) 12:163
Louisiana 12:434
CAKE AND PASTRY 4:20–21 *bibliog., illus.*
baking industry 3:29
CAKEWALK (dance) 4:21
CAKOBAO, GEORGE, RATU SIR
Fiji 8:78
ČAKOVEC (Yugoslavia)
map (46° 23′N 16° 26′E) 20:340
CALABAR (Nigeria)
map (4° 57′N 8° 19′E) 14:190
CALABASH 4:21
CALABOZO (Venezuela)
map (8° 56′N 67° 26′W) 19:542
CALABRIA (Italy) 4:21; 7:270 *illus.*; 11:323 *illus.*
Reggio di Calabria 16:128
CALAFATE (Argentina)
map (50° 20′S 72° 18′W) 2:149
CALAH *see* NIMRUD
CALAIS (France) 4:21
Pale 15:30
CALAIS (Maine)
map (45° 11′N 67° 17′W) 13:70
CALAMA (Chile)
map (22° 28′S 68° 56′W) 4:355
CALAMARCA (Bolivia)
map (16° 55′S 68° 9′W) 3:366
CALAMIAN GROUP (ISLANDS)
map (12° 0′N 120° 0′E) 15:237
CALAMITY JANE 4:21 *bibliog.*
Deadwood (South Dakota) 6:65
CĂLĂRAŞI (Romania)
map (44° 11′N 27° 20′E) 16:288
CALAVERAS (county in California)
map (38° 12′N 120° 41′W) 4:31
CALAVERITE 4:21
telluride minerals 19:91
CALCAR, JAN STEPHAN VON
book illustration 3:269 *illus.*
CALCAREOUS ROCK *see* LIMESTONE
CALCASIEU (county in Louisiana)
map (30° 13′N 93° 18′W) 12:430
CALCASIEU LAKE
map (29° 50′N 93° 17′W) 12:430
CALCASIEU RIVER
map (30° 5′N 93° 20′W) 12:430
CALCETA (Ecuador)
map (0° 51′S 80° 10′W) 7:52
CALCHA (Bolivia)
map (21° 6′S 67° 31′W) 3:366
CALCIFICATION
bone, fracture 8:258
CALCINATION 4:21
CALCITE 4:21–22 *bibliog., illus.*; 5:374 *illus.*; 13:440 *illus.*
calcium 4:22
calcium carbonate 4:22–23
carbonate minerals 4:137
cave 4:222

chalk **4**:271
limestone **12**:344–345
polarized light **15**:394 *illus.*
polymorph **15**:421
travertine **19**:284
CALCITONIN *see* THYROCALCITONIN
CALCIUM **4**:22 *bibliog., illus.*
absorption
digestion, human **6**:172
abundances of common elements **7**:131 *table*
alkaline earth metals **1**:295
blood
parathyroid **15**:83
tetany **19**:127
bone **3**:377
carbonate minerals **4**:137
diseases and disorders
arteriosclerosis **2**:213
bursitis **3**:581
endocrine system, diseases of **7**:169
tendonitis **19**:101
element **7**:130 *table*
Group IIA periodic table **15**:167
ion
active transport **1**:89–90
muscle contraction **13**:655
neurophysiology **14**:106
metal, metallic element **13**:328
nutrient cycles **14**:303 *illus.*
reaction, chemical **16**:99–100
transition elements **19**:273 *table*
uranium minerals **19**:478
vitamins and minerals **19**:620
Recommended Daily Allowances **19**:619 *table*
CALCIUM CARBIDE **4**:22
CALCIUM CARBONATE **4**:22–23
antacid **2**:38
calcite **4**:21
coral reef **5**:258
oolite **14**:396
ooze, deep-sea **14**:397
pedocal **15**:131
stonewort **18**:284
CALCIUM CHLORIDE
reduction **4**:22
CALCIUM FLUORIDE **4**:22
CALCIUM MINERALS
perovskite **15**:177
CALCIUM NITRIDE **4**:22
CALCULATOR, ELECTRONIC **4**:23–24 *bibliog., illus.*
adding machine **1**:100
ENIAC: Eckert, John Presper **7**:39
integrated circuit **11**:201–202
liquid crystal **12**:365
microprocessor **13**:387
CALCULUS **4**:24 *bibliog.*
analog computer **1**:389
calculus of variations **4**:24
differential calculus **6**:167–168
differential equations **6**:168
history
Alembert, Jean Le Rond d' **1**:271
Gregory, James **9**:356
Leibniz, Gottfried Wilhelm von **12**:276–277
Maclaurin, Colin **13**:32
mathematics, history of **13**:225–226
Newton, Sir Isaac **14**:173
Taylor, Brook **19**:48
hyperbola **10**:347–348
infinitesimal (mathematics) **11**:168
integral calculus **11**:200–201
limit **12**:345
mathematics **13**:222
maxima and minima **13**:239
Maxwell's equations **13**:241–242
motion, planar **13**:609–610
natural logarithms, e **7**:3
propositional calculus
syllogism **18**:402
series **17**:209
Taylor series **19**:51
tensor
Christoffel, Elwin Bruno **4**:416
Einstein, Albert **7**:93
mathematics, history of **13**:226
CALCULUS OF VARIATIONS **4**:24 *bibliog.*
Bernoulli, Jacques **3**:223
Carathéodory, Constantin **4**:131
Euler, Leonhard **7**:264–265
Lagrange, Joseph Louis de **12**:166
CALCUTTA (India) **4**:24–25 *bibliog., illus.*; **11**:84 *illus.*
climate **11**:82 *table*
map (22° 32′N 88° 22′E) **11**:80
CALDARA, ANTONIO **4**:25 *bibliog.*
CALDAS DA RAINHA (Portugal)
map (39° 24′N 9° 8′W) **15**:449
CALDECOTT MEDAL **4**:25 *bibliog.*
Bemelmans, Ludwig **3**:194
Sendak, Maurice **17**:200
CALDER, ALEXANDER **4**:25 *bibliog., illus.*
fountains **8**:252
kinetic art **12**:78
mobile **13**:487; **14**:33 *illus.*
Red Petals **1**:331 *illus.*; **4**:25 *illus.*
stabile **18**:207
CALDER* v. *BULL **4**:26
CALDERA
volcano **19**:626 *illus.*
CALDERA, RAFAEL
Venezuela **19**:544
CALDERÓN DE LA BARCA, PEDRO **4**:26 *bibliog., illus.*
Spanish literature **18**:158 *illus.*
CALDWELL (Idaho)
map (43° 40′N 116° 41′W) **11**:26
CALDWELL (Kansas)
map (37° 2′N 97° 37′W) **12**:18
CALDWELL (county in Kentucky)
map (37° 10′N 87° 50′W) **12**:47
CALDWELL (county in Louisiana)
map (32° 7′N 92° 8′W) **12**:430
CALDWELL (county in Missouri)
map (39° 40′N 94° 0′W) **13**:476
CALDWELL (county in North Carolina)
map (35° 55′N 81° 35′W) **14**:242
CALDWELL (Ohio)
map (39° 45′N 81° 31′W) **14**:357
CALDWELL (Texas)
map (30° 32′N 96° 42′W) **19**:129
CALDWELL (county in Texas)
map (29° 47′N 97° 40′W) **19**:129
CALDWELL, BILLY **4**:26
CALDWELL, ERSKINE **4**:26 *bibliog., illus.*
Tobacco Road **19**:219
CALDWELL, ROBERT
Dravidian languages **6**:263
CALDWELL, SARAH **4**:27
CALDWELL, TAYLOR **4**:27 *bibliog.*
CALDWELL, ZOE **4**:27
CALE, GUILLAUME
Jacquerie **11**:347
CALEDON RIVER
map (29° 45′S 27° 0′E) **12**:297
CALEDONIA (Minnesota)
map (43° 38′N 91° 29′W) **13**:453
CALEDONIA (New York)
map (42° 58′N 77° 51′W) **14**:149
CALEDONIA (Nova Scotia)
map (44° 22′N 65° 2′W) **14**:269
CALEDONIA (Ohio)
map (40° 38′N 82° 58′W) **14**:357
CALEDONIA (Roman Empire) **4**:27
tartan **19**:40 *illus.*
CALEDONIA (county in Vermont)
map (44° 33′N 72° 5′W) **19**:554
CALEDONIAN GAMES
Highland Games **10**:162
CALENDAR **4**:27–28 *bibliog., illus.*
ancient calendars **4**:27–28
archaeoastronomy **2**:114
astronomy, history of **2**:277
Chinese calendar **4**:388
day **6**:54
Gregorian calendar **4**:28
Gregory XIII, Pope **9**:357
Julian day **11**:466
Maya **13**:245
Meton **13**:345
names of the months **4**:28 *table*
pre-Columbian art and architecture **15**:500
reform **4**:28
sidereal time **17**:294
week **4**:28
year **4**:28; **20**:320
tropical year **19**:309
CALENDULA **4**:28
CALERA (Alabama)
map (33° 6′N 86° 45′W) **1**:234
CALERA (Oklahoma)
map (33° 55′N 96° 26′W) **14**:368
CALEXICO (California)
map (32° 40′N 115° 30′W) **4**:31
CALF-ROPING
rodeo **16**:266–267
CALGARY (Alberta) **4**:28; **4**:76 *illus.*
climate **4**:74 *table*
map (51° 3′N 114° 5′W) **1**:256
rodeo **1**:258 *illus.*; **16**:266
CALGARY, UNIVERSITY OF **4**:28–29
CALHAN (Colorado)
map (39° 2′N 104° 18′W) **5**:116
CALHOUN (county in Alabama)
map (33° 15′N 85° 50′W) **1**:234
CALHOUN (county in Arkansas)
map (33° 35′N 92° 25′W) **2**:166
CALHOUN (county in Florida)
map (30° 25′N 85° 10′W) **8**:172
CALHOUN (Georgia)
map (34° 30′N 84° 57′W) **9**:114
CALHOUN (county in Georgia)
map (31° 32′N 84° 35′W) **9**:114
CALHOUN (county in Illinois)
map (39° 9′N 90° 37′W) **11**:42
CALHOUN (county in Iowa)
map (42° 23′N 94° 37′W) **11**:244
CALHOUN (Kentucky)
map (37° 32′N 87° 16′W) **12**:47
CALHOUN (county in Michigan)
map (42° 14′N 85° 0′W) **13**:377
CALHOUN (county in Mississippi)
map (33° 55′N 89° 20′W) **13**:469
CALHOUN (county in South Carolina)
map (33° 40′N 80° 45′W) **18**:98
CALHOUN (county in Texas)
map (28° 30′N 96° 35′W) **19**:129
CALHOUN (county in West Virginia)
map (38° 50′N 81° 8′W) **20**:111
CALHOUN, JOHN C. **4**:29 *bibliog., illus.*
Civil War, U.S. **5**:15 *illus.*
Jackson, Andrew **11**:341
nullification **14**:292
South Carolina **18**:101
Van Buren, Martin **19**:511
vice-president of the United States **19**:570
Webster, Daniel **20**:88
CALHOUN CITY (Mississippi)
map (33° 51′N 89° 19′W) **13**:469
CALHOUN FALLS (South Carolina)
map (34° 6′N 82° 36′W) **18**:98
CALI (Colombia) **4**:29
map (3° 27′N 76° 31′W) **5**:107
CALIARI, PAOLO *see* VERONESE, PAOLO
CALICHE *see* SOIL
CALICO **4**:29
CALICO (Arkansas)
map (36° 7′N 92° 9′W) **2**:166
CALICO BASS *see* CRAPPIE
CALICUT (India)
map (11° 15′N 75° 46′E) **11**:80
CALIENTE (Nevada)
map (37° 37′N 114° 31′W) **14**:111
CALIFANO, JOSEPH
Health and Human Services, U.S. Department of **10**:86
CALIFORNIA **4**:29–37 *bibliog., illus., map*
agriculture **4**:35
fruit fly **8**:347
Imperial Valley **11**:61
Napa Valley **20**:176 *illus.*
Salinas Valley **19**:531
San Joaquin Valley **12**:185 *illus.*
architecture
Greene and Greene **9**:351
Neutra, Richard **14**:107–108
Schindler, Rudolf M. **17**:121
cities
Alameda **1**:239
Anaheim **1**:388
Bakersfield **3**:28
Berkeley **3**:212
Carmel **4**:153
Eureka **7**:265
Fresno **8**:328
Glendale **9**:207
Huntington Beach **10**:314
Long Beach **12**:406
Los Angeles **4**:32 *illus.*; **12**:416–418 *illus., map*
Monterey **13**:553
Oakland **14**:312
Palm Springs **15**:49
Palo Alto **15**:52
Pasadena **15**:101
Riverside **16**:234
Sacramento **17**:7
San Bernardino **17**:51
San Diego **17**:51–52 *illus.*
San Francisco **17**:52–53 *illus.*
San Jose **17**:54
Santa Ana **17**:66
Santa Barbara **17**:66–67
Santa Clara **17**:67
Santa Cruz **17**:67
Santa Monica **17**:68
Stockton **18**:276
Vallejo **19**:507
climate **4**:32
cultural institutions **4**:34
Death Valley **6**:70 *illus.*
economy **4**:35–36
education **4**:34
California Institute of Technology **4**:38
Claremont Colleges **5**:36
community and junior colleges **5**:151–152
Kerr, Clark **12**:59–60
Mills College **13**:431
open admission **14**:398
Redlands, University of **16**:115
San Francisco, University of **17**:54
Stanford University **18**:218
state universities and colleges of **4**:38 *table*
flag **4**:30 *illus.*
government and politics **4**:34–35
referendum and initiative **16**:119
historic sites **4**:34
history **4**:36–37
Alvarado, Juan Bautista **1**:319
Anza, Juan Bautista de **2**:72–73
Bear Flag Republic **3**:141
Brown, Jerry **3**:514
Cabrillo, Juan Rodríguez **4**:7
Frémont, John C. **8**:302
frontier **8**:342–344
gold rush **9**:228
Indians, American **11**:128–129 *illus.*
Larkin, Thomas Oliver **12**:208
Mexican War **13**:352 *map*; **13**:354–355
Muir, John **13**:635
Nisei **14**:201
Polk, James K. **15**:405
Portoló, Gaspar de **15**:446
Reagan, Ronald **16**:101
Serra, Junípero **17**:210
Spanish missions **18**:160–161
Stanford, Leland **18**:217
Vizcaíno, Sebastián **19**:623
Warren, Earl **20**:31
Yana **20**:317
land and resources **4**:30–33 *map*
Landsat false-color composite photograph **17**:87 *illus.*
landslide and avalanche **12**:193
landscape architecture **12**:188
manufacturing **4**:36
map (37° 30′N 119° 30′W) **19**:419
parks and reserves **4**:35 *illus.*
Death Valley **6**:70
Redwood National Park **16**:117
Sequoia National Park **17**:207
Yosemite National Park **20**:332
people **4**:33
Hupa **10**:315
Indians, American **11**:124 *map*
Indians of North America, art of the **11**:139–140
Mexican-Americans **10**:178
Modoc **13**:499
Mojave **13**:504–505
Paiute **15**:25
Pomo **15**:423
Yuma (Indian tribe) **20**:346
physical features
Colorado Desert **5**:120
Death Valley **6**:70 *illus.*
Donner Pass **6**:240
Imperial Valley **11**:61
La Brea Tar Pit **12**:144–145
Lassen Peak **12**:214
Mojave Desert **13**:505
Monterey submarine canyon **18**:316 *illus.*
San Andreas Fault **17**:50 *illus.*
Shasta, Mount **17**:244
Sierra Nevada **17**:298
Whitney, Mount **20**:142
rivers, lakes, and waterways **4**:30–32
Bridalveil Fall **3**:479
Sacramento River **17**:8
Salton Sea **17**:39
San Francisco Bay **17**:54
San Joaquin River **17**:54
Yosemite Falls **20**:332
Scripps Institution of Oceanography **17**:158
seal, state **4**:30 *illus.*
tax, property **15**:571
tularemia **19**:330
Vandenberg Air Force Base **19**:518
vegetation and animal life **4**:32–33
chaparral **4**:283–284
redwood **16**:117
wine **20**:175
CALIFORNIA (Missouri)
map (38° 38′N 92° 34′W) **13**:476
CALIFORNIA, GULF OF **4**:38
map (28° 0′N 112° 0′W) **13**:357
CALIFORNIA, LOWER *see* BAJA CALIFORNIA (Mexico)
CALIFORNIA, STATE UNIVERSITIES AND COLLEGES OF **4**:38 *bibliog., table*
Kerr, Clark **12**:59–60
Lawrence Berkeley and Lawrence Livermore laboratories **12**:251
Los Alamos National Scientific Laboratory **12**:416
CALIFORNIA BLUEBELL **4**:38
CALIFORNIA CURRENT

CALIFORNIA CURRENT (cont.)
ocean currents and wind systems, worldwide 14:322–323 *maps*
CALIFORNIA INSTITUTE OF TECHNOLOGY 4:38
Jet Propulsion Laboratory 11:407
Palomar Observatory 15:52
CALIFORNIA LAUREL 4:38
CALIFORNIA MOUSE *see* DEER MOUSE
CALIFORNIA PALACE OF THE LEGION OF HONOR
San Francisco art museums 17:54
CALIFORNIA POMPANO *see* BUTTERFISH
CALIFORNIA RAPE *see* CHARLOCK
'CALIFORNIA SOUND'
rock music 16:249
CALIFORNIA TRAIL 14:431 *map*; 19:445 *map*
CALIFORNIAN (ship)
Titanic 19:211
CALIFORNITE *see* IDOCRASE
CALIFORNIUM 4:38–39
actinide series 1:88
element 7:130 *table*
metal, metallic element 13:328
Seaborg, Glenn T. 17:171
transuranium elements 19:286
CALIGULA, ROMAN EMPEROR 4:39 *bibliog.*
Nemi, Lake 14:81
Rome, ancient 16:302
CALIMA
gold pectoral 15:499 *illus.*
CALION ROCK (Arkansas)
map (33° 20′N 92° 32′W) 2:166
CALIPER 4:39 *illus.*
measurement 13:254 *illus.*
CALIPHATE 2:102 *map*; 4:39 *bibliog.*
Abbasids 1:52
Ali 1:292
Almohads 1:306
Almoravids 1:307
Fatimids 8:34
Harun al-Rashid 10:64
imam 11:53–54
Islam 11:289–290
Mamelukes 13:96–97
Middle East, history of the 13:402–404 *map*
Ottoman Empire 14:464
Palestine 15:44
Umayyads 19:380
CALISHER, HORTENSE 3:39
CALISTOGA (California)
map (38° 35′N 122° 35′W) 4:31
CALIXTUS *see* CALLISTUS for Popes of this name
CALL GIRLS *see* PROSTITUTION
CALL OF THE WILD, THE (book) 4:39 *bibliog.*
London, Jack 12:402–403
CALLA 4:40
CALLA LILY 2:226 *illus.*
CALLAGHAN, JAMES 4:40 *bibliog.*, *illus.*
Labour party 12:157
Wilson, Sir Harold 20:164
CALLAGHAN, MORLEY 4:40 *bibliog.*
CALLAHAN (Florida)
map (30° 34′N 81° 49′W) 8:172
CALLAHAN (county in Texas)
map (32° 22′N 99° 22′W) 19:129
CALLAHAN, HARRY M. 4:40 *bibliog.*
CALLANISH (Scotland)
stone alignments 18:281 *illus.*
CALLAO (Peru) 4:40
map (12° 4′S 77° 9′W) 15:193
CALLAS, MARIA 4:40–41 *bibliog.*, *illus.*
CALLAWAY (county in Missouri)
map (38° 50′N 91° 55′W) 13:476
CALLAWAY (Nebraska)
map (41° 17′N 99° 56′W) 14:70
CALLES, PLUTARCO ELÍAS 4:41 *bibliog.*
Mexico, history of 13:365–366
CALLEY, WILLIAM L.
My Lai incident 13:689
CALLIAS 4:41
CALLICRATES 4:41 *bibliog.*
CALLIGRAPHY 4:41–46 *bibliog.*, *illus.*
Carolingian art and architecture 4:161
Chao Meng-fu (Zhao Mengfu) 4:282
Chinese art and architecture 4:379–383; 4:380 *illus.*
Graves, Morris 9:302
illuminated manuscripts 11:46–48
Inca 11:71 *illus.*
Islamic art and architecture 11:294
Japanese art and architecture 11:374
Koetsu 12:105
origin of typeface 19:364
Persian art and architecture 15:186
Sung Hui-tsung (Song Huizong) 18:348
Wang Hsi-chih (Wang Xizhi) 20:22
CALLIMACHUS (poet) 4:46 *bibliog.*
CALLIMACHUS (sculptor) 4:46 *bibliog.*
CALLING LAKE (Alberta)
map (55° 15′N 113° 12′W) 1:256
CALLIOPE 4:46 *bibliog.*
muses 13:656
CALLISTO 4:46 *illus.*; 18:50 *illus.*, *illus.*
Jupiter (planet) 11:472–474 *illus.*, *table*
Voyager 19:638
CALLISTRATUS 4:46
CALLISTUS, SAINT *see* CALLISTUS I, POPE
CALLISTUS I, POPE 4:46
CALLISTUS II, POPE 4:46 *bibliog.*
CALLISTUS III, POPE 4:47 *bibliog.*
CALLOT, JACQUES 4:47 *bibliog.*
graphic arts 9:292
CALLOWAY (county in Kentucky)
map (36° 40′N 88° 15′W) 12:47
CALLOWAY, CAB 4:47 *bibliog.*
CALLUSES *see* BUNIONS, CORNS, AND CALLUSES
CALMAR (Alberta)
map (53° 16′N 113° 49′W) 1:256
CALMAR (Iowa)
map (43° 11′N 91° 52′W) 11:244
CALOMEL
mercury 13:306
CALONNE, CHARLES ALEXANDRE DE 4:47 *bibliog.*
Loménie de Brienne, Étienne Charles de 12:399
CALORIE 4:47
caloric theory
physics, history of 15:285
calorimeter 4:47
dieting 6:165
nutrition, human 14:304–305
CALORIMETER 4:47
Berthelot, Marcelin 3:225
chemical energy 4:315
Joly, John 11:441
CALORIMETRY
calorimeter 4:47
measurement 13:255
CALOTYPE 4:47
Blanquart-Evrard, Louis Désirée 3:327
Hill, D. O., and Adamson, Robert 10:164
photography, history and art of 15:267 *illus.*
Talbot, William Henry, inventor 19:15
CALTANISSETTA (Italy)
map (37° 29′N 14° 4′E) 11:321
CALTECH *see* CALIFORNIA INSTITUTE OF TECHNOLOGY
CALUMET (ceremonial pipe)
See also PEACE PIPE
CALUMET (Michigan)
map (47° 14′N 88° 27′W) 13:377
CALUMET (county in Wisconsin)
map (44° 3′N 88° 15′W) 20:185
CALUMET CITY (Illinois)
map (41° 37′N 87° 31′W) 11:42
CALVARY 4:48
CALVÉ, EMMA 4:48 *bibliog.*
CALVERT (family) 4:48 *bibliog.*
Maryland 13:191–192
CALVERT (county in Maryland)
map (38° 33′N 76° 35′W) 13:188
CALVIN (Oklahoma)
map (34° 58′N 96° 15′W) 14:368
CALVIN, JOHN 4:48–49 *bibliog.*, *illus.*
Calvinism 4:49
Europe, history of 7:287
French literature 8:315
Geneva (Switzerland) 9:91
Geneva, University of 9:91
predestination 15:501–502
Presbyterianism 15:519–520
Reformation 16:122
CALVIN, MELVIN 4:49
biology 3:270
photosynthesis 15:277
CALVINISM 4:49 *bibliog.*
Arminianism 2:173
Beza, Theodore 3:233
Calvin, John 4:48–49
Europe, history of 7:287
Germany, history of 9:151
Huguenots 10:294
hymn 10:346
Knox, John 12:102–103
Nantes, Edict of 14:13
Presbyterianism 15:519–520
Protestant ethic 15:576
Puritanism 15:630
Reformation 16:121–122 *illus.*, *map*
Reformed Church in America 16:123
Reformed churches 16:123
Religion, Wars of 16:141
Remonstrants 16:146
Scotland, Church of 17:152–153
Thirty Years' War 19:171 *map*
CALVINO, ITALO 4:49
CALVO, CARLOS 4:49
CALVO DOCTRINE
Calvo, Carlos 4:49
CALVO SOTELO, JOSÉ
Calvo Sotelo, Leopoldo 4:49
CALVO SOTELO, LEOPOLDO 4:49
CALYPSO (music) 4:49
Belafonte, Harry 3:173
CALYPSO (mythology) 4:49
CALYPSO (North Carolina)
map (35° 9′N 78° 6′W) 14:242
CALZABIGI, RANIERO DE
opera 14:400
CAM *see* COMPUTER-AIDED DESIGN AND COMPUTER-AIDED MANUFACTURING
CAM (CONTENT-ADDRESSABLE MEMORY) (computer term) 5:160g
CAM (machinery) 13:19 *illus.*; 13:20 *illus.*
CAM, DIOGO 4:49
CAM PHA (Vietnam)
map (21° 1′N 107° 19′E) 19:580
CAM RANH (Vietnam)
map (11° 54′N 109° 9′E) 19:580
CAMACHO, MANUEL ÁVILA *see* ÁVILA CAMACHO, MANUEL
CAMAGÜEY (Cuba) 4:49
map (21° 23′N 77° 55′W) 5:377
CAMANÁ (Peru)
map (16° 37′S 72° 42′W) 15:193
CAMARASAURUS 11:475 *illus.*
CAMARGO, MARIE 3:43 *illus.*; 4:50 *bibliog.*
CAMARONES (Argentina)
map (44° 48′S 65° 42′W) 2:149
CAMAS (county in Idaho)
map (43° 30′N 114° 50′W) 11:26
CAMAS (Washington)
map (45° 35′N 122° 24′W) 20:35
CAMBACÉRÈS, JEAN JACQUES RÉGIS DE 4:50; 8:324 *illus.*
Napoleonic Code 14:19
CAMBIO, ARNOLFO DI
Peter, Saint 15:63 *illus.*
CAMBIUM
tree 19:286–287 *illus.*
CAMBODIA *see* KAMPUCHEA
CAMBODIAN COMMUNIST ARMY *see* KHMER ROUGE
CAMBRAI (France) 4:50
Dufay, Guillaume 6:293
CAMBRAI, LEAGUE OF
Italian Wars 11:320
CAMBRAI, TREATY OF
Margaret of Austria 13:149
CAMBRIA (county in Pennsylvania)
map (40° 29′N 79° 16′W) 15:147
CAMBRIAN MOUNTAINS
map (52° 35′N 3° 35′W) 19:403
CAMBRIAN PERIOD 4:50–52 *bibliog.*, *illus.*, *map*
archaeocyathid 2:115
Cambrian rock formations 4:51 *map*
chiton 4:399
continents, estimated positions 15:354 *map*
fossil record 8:245–248
geography 4:50
geologic time 9:103–105
life 4:51–52
Murchison, Roderick Impey 13:647
Nautiloid 14:52
ostracoderm 14:458
Paelozoic Era 15:43
paleotectonics 4:50
polar wandering 15:393 *map*
Precambrian time 15:491–493
Sedgwick, Adam 17:183
CAMBRIDGE (England) 4:52
map (52° 13′N 0° 8′E) 19:403
CAMBRIDGE (Idaho)
map (44° 34′N 116° 41′W) 11:26
CAMBRIDGE (Illinois)
map (41° 18′N 90° 12′W) 11:42
CAMBRIDGE (Maryland)
map (38° 34′N 76° 4′W) 13:188
CAMBRIDGE (Massachusetts) 4:52
education
Harvard University 10:64
Massachusetts Institute of Technology 13:212
map (42° 22′N 71° 6′W) 13:206
CAMBRIDGE (Minnesota)
map (45° 31′N 93° 14′W) 13:453
CAMBRIDGE (Nebraska)
map (40° 17′N 100° 10′W) 14:70
CAMBRIDGE (New York)
map (43° 2′N 73° 23′W) 14:149
CAMBRIDGE (Ohio)
map (40° 2′N 81° 35′W) 14:357
CAMBRIDGE, RICHARD, EARL OF
York (dynasty) 20:330
CAMBRIDGE BAY (Northwest Territories)
map (69° 3′N 105° 5′W) 14:258
CAMBRIDGE CITY (Indiana)
map (39° 49′N 85° 10′W) 11:111
CAMBRIDGE PLATONISTS 4:52 *bibliog.*
Cudworth, Ralph 5:382
More, Henry 13:575
CAMBRIDGE SPRINGS (Pennsylvania)
map (41° 48′N 80° 4′W) 15:147
CAMBRIDGE UNIVERSITY 3:494 *illus.*; 4:52–53 *bibliog.*, *table*
British education 3:495
Cambridge (England) 4:52
Cavendish Laboratory 4:226
Fitzwilliam Museum 8:132
Mullard Radio Astronomy Observatory 13:636
CAMBRIDGESHIRE (England) 4:53
Cambridge 4:52
CAMBYSES I, KING OF PERSIA
Cyrus the Great, King of Persia 5:410
CAMBYSES II, KING OF PERSIA 4:53
CAMDEN (Alabama)
map (31° 59′N 87° 17′W) 1:234
CAMDEN (Arkansas)
map (33° 35′N 92° 50′W) 2:166
CAMDEN (Delaware)
map (39° 7′N 75° 33′W) 6:88
CAMDEN (county in Georgia)
map (31° 0′N 81° 40′W) 9:114
CAMDEN (Maine)
map (44° 12′N 69° 4′W) 13:70
CAMDEN (Mississippi)
map (32° 42′N 89° 50′W) 13:469
CAMDEN (county in Missouri)
map (38° 0′N 92° 45′W) 13:476
CAMDEN (New Jersey) 4:53
map (39° 57′N 75° 7′W) 14:129
CAMDEN (county in New Jersey)
map (39° 57′N 75° 7′W) 14:129
CAMDEN (New York)
map (43° 2′N 75° 45′W) 14:149
CAMDEN (North Carolina)
map (36° 20′N 76° 10′W) 14:242
CAMDEN (county in North Carolina)
map (36° 20′N 76° 11′W) 14:242
CAMDEN (South Carolina)
map (34° 16′N 80° 36′W) 18:98
CAMDEN (Tennessee)
map (36° 4′N 88° 6′W) 19:104
CAMDEN AND AMBOY RAILROAD
John Bull 11:424
CAMDENTON (Missouri)
map (38° 0′N 92° 45′W) 13:476
CAMEL 3:207 *illus.*; 4:53–54 *illus.*; 10:5 *illus.*; 13:105 *illus.*
animal husbandry 2:23; 2:24 *illus.*
Bactrian camel 2:235 *illus.*
caravan 2:241 *illus.*
desert life 6:131
ecological adaptation 13:100 *illus.*
feet 13:102 *illus.*
guanaco 9:385
llama 12:382
Middle East 13:396 *illus.*
Pleistocene Epoch 15:366–367 *illus.*
ruminant 16:345
steppe life 18:257 *illus.*
Tertiary Period 19:125 *illus.*
vicuña 19:576
CAMELOT 4:54
CAMEL'S HAIR 8:67 *illus.*
CAMELS HUMP MOUNTAIN
map (44° 19′N 72° 53′W) 19:554
CAMEO 4:54 *bibliog.*, *illus.*
bas-relief 3:101
enamel 7:162
gem cutting 9:70 *illus.*
jewelry 11:409–411
onyx 14:396
4th-century sardonyx cameo 13:401 *illus.*
CAMERA 4:54–59 *bibliog.*, *illus.*
aerial photography 1:119
astrophotography 2:285
camera lucida
Wollaston, William Hyde 20:199
cinematography 4:432–434
depth of field 6:120
Eastman, George 7:34
exposure meter 15:263
eye 7:349

film, photographic
photography **15**:261–262; **15**:264–265 *illus.*
flash photography **8**:153
lens **12**:286
aperture **2**:76 *illus.*
f-stops **15**:263 *illus.*
photoelectric cell **15**:259
photography **15**:261 *illus.*
photography, history and art of **15**:270–271 *illus.*
polarized light **15**:395
remote sensing **16**:147
stereoscope **18**:260
types **4**:57–59
automated rostrum camera **2**:28–29
Instamatic camera **4**:56 *illus.*
movie camera **4**:58 *illus.*
Polaroid Spectra **4**:58 *illus.*
single-lens reflex camera **4**:54 *illus.*; **15**:261 *illus.*
twin-lens reflex camera **4**:55 *illus.*
view camera **4**:57 *illus.*
video camera **19**:576h–576i *illus.*
video technology **19**:576l–576m *illus.*
CAMERA OBSCURA **4**:59 *bibliog.*; **15**:267 *illus.*
camera **4**:55
Daguerre, Louis J. M. **6**:6
CAMERA WORK (periodical)
Photo-Secession **15**:257
CAMERATA (humanist group)
Italian music **11**:318
CAMERON (Louisiana)
map (29° 48′N 93° 19′W) **12**:430
CAMERON (county in Louisiana)
map (29° 55′N 93° 10′W) **12**:430
CAMERON (Missouri)
map (39° 44′N 94° 14′W) **13**:476
CAMERON (county in Pennsylvania)
map (41° 31′N 78° 14′W) **15**:147
CAMERON (Texas)
map (30° 51′N 96° 59′W) **19**:129
CAMERON (county in Texas)
map (26° 7′N 97° 30′W) **19**:129
CAMERON (West Virginia)
map (39° 50′N 80° 34′W) **20**:111
CAMERON (Wisconsin)
map (45° 25′N 91° 44′W) **20**:185
CAMERON, CHARLES **4**:59 *bibliog.*
Russian art and architecture **16**:362
CAMERON, JULIA MARGARET **4**:59–60 *bibliog.*, *illus.*
photography, history and art of **15**:268 *illus.*
CAMERON, SIMON **4**:60 *bibliog.*
CAMERON, VERNEY LOVETT **4**:60
CAMERON HILLS
map (59° 48′N 118° 0′W) **1**:256
CAMERON MOUNTAINS
map (46° 0′S 167° 0′E) **14**:158
CAMEROON **4**:60–61 *bibliog.*, *illus.*, *map*, *table*
African music **1**:168–171
art
African art **1**:162
cities
Douala **6**:245
Yaoundé **20**:319
climate **4**:60 *table*
economy **4**:61
education
African universities **1**:176 *table*
flag **4**:60 *illus.*
history **4**:61
land **4**:60–61
literature
Bebey, Francis **3**:150
Beti, Mongo **3**:231
map (6° 0′N 12° 0′E) **1**:136
people **4**:61
Bamileke **3**:59
Fang **8**:20
CAMEROONS (West Africa) **4**:62
CAMEROUN, MOUNT
map (4° 12′N 9° 11′E) **4**:61
CAMETÁ (Brazil)
map (2° 15′S 49° 30′W) **3**:460
CAMILLA (Georgia)
map (31° 14′N 84° 12′W) **9**:114
CAMILLE (play) **4**:62 *bibliog.*
Dumas, Alexandre (1824–95) **6**:297
CAMILLUS, MARCUS FURIUS **4**:62
Veii **19**:535
CAMINO (California)
map (38° 44′N 120° 41′W) **4**:31
CAMINO REAL **4**:62 *bibliog.*; **8**:341 *map*
CAMINO Y GALICIA, LEÓN FELIPE
Spanish literature **18**:159
CAMIRI (Bolivia)
map (20° 3′S 63° 31′W) **3**:366
CAMISARDS **4**:62 *bibliog.*
Huguenots **10**:294–295
CAMMANN, GEORGE P.
stethoscope **18**:262
CAMMARANO, SALVATORE
Lucia di Lammermoor **12**:450
Trovatore, Il **19**:312
CAMÕES, LUÍS VAZ DE **4**:62 *bibliog.*
CAMOMILE *see* CHAMOMILE
CAMORRA **4**:62
CAMOUFLAGE **4**:62–63 *bibliog.*
See also COLORATION, BIOLOGICAL; MIMICRY
Thayer, Abbott **19**:143
CAMP (county in Texas)
map (33° 0′N 94° 58′W) **19**:129
CAMP, L. SPRAGUE DE *see* DE CAMP, L. SPRAGUE
CAMP, MAXIME DU *see* DU CAMP, MAXIME
CAMP, WALTER **4**:63 *bibliog.*
football **8**:216
CAMP DAVID **4**:63
CAMP DAVID ACCORDS (1978)
Camp David **4**:63
Egypt **7**:80
West Bank **20**:108
CAMP FIRE GIRLS **4**:63
Gulick, Luther Halsey **9**:404
CAMP HILL (Alabama)
map (32° 43′N 85° 39′W) **1**:234
CAMP HILL (Pennsylvania)
map (40° 14′N 76° 55′W) **15**:147
CAMP MEETINGS **4**:63 *bibliog.*
CAMPAGNOLA, DOMENICO **4**:63 *bibliog.*
CAMPAIGN (Tennessee)
map (35° 46′N 85° 38′W) **19**:104
CAMPAIGN, POLITICAL **4**:63–64 *bibliog.*
advertising **1**:114
campaign issues
presidential elections **15**:531
debate
presidential elections **15**:531
financing
National Conservative Political Action Committee **14**:31
presidential elections **15**:531–532
National Committee for an Effective Congress **14**:30
opinion polls **14**:405–406
political convention **15**:399–400
presidential elections **15**:529–532
primary election **15**:538–539
public opinion **15**:609
special-interest groups **18**:168
CAMPAIGN FOR NUCLEAR DISARMAMENT
pacifism and nonviolent movements **15**:9
CAMPAMENTO (Honduras)
map (14° 33′N 86° 42′W) **10**:218
CAMPANA (Argentina)
map (34° 10′S 58° 57′W) **2**:149
CAMPANA, DINO **4**:64
CAMPANELLA, ROY **4**:64 *bibliog.*
CAMPANELLA, TOMMASO **4**:64 *bibliog.*
CAMPANIA (Italy) **4**:64
Italy, history of **11**:327
Naples **14**:14–15 *illus.*
Salerno **17**:31
CAMPANILE **4**:64–65
Romanesque art and architecture **16**:282
CAMPBELL (clan)
Glencoe, Massacre of **9**:207
CAMPBELL (county in Kentucky)
map (38° 55′N 84° 20′W) **12**:47
CAMPBELL (Missouri)
map (36° 30′N 90° 4′W) **13**:476
CAMPBELL (Nebraska)
map (40° 18′N 98° 44′W) **14**:70
CAMPBELL (Ohio)
map (41° 5′N 80° 36′W) **14**:357
CAMPBELL (county in South Dakota)
map (45° 45′N 100° 0′W) **18**:103
CAMPBELL (county in Tennessee)
map (36° 23′N 84° 7′W) **19**:104
CAMPBELL (county in Virginia)
map (37° 15′N 79° 10′W) **19**:607
CAMPBELL (county in Wyoming)
map (44° 7′N 105° 30′W) **20**:301
CAMPBELL, ALEXANDER **4**:65 *bibliog.*, *illus.*
CAMPBELL, ARCHIBALD
American Revolution **1**:359 *map*
CAMPBELL, CLARENCE **4**:65
CAMPBELL, COLEN **4**:65 *bibliog.*
CAMPBELL, GLEN **4**:65
CAMPBELL, IGNATIUS ROY DUNNACHIE *see* CAMPBELL, ROY
CAMPBELL, J. F.
meteorological instrumentation **13**:340
CAMPBELL, JOHN (journalist) **4**:65
CAMPBELL, JOHN (naval officer)
navigation **14**:60
CAMPBELL, JOHN, 1ST BARON CAMPBELL (jurist) **4**:65
CAMPBELL, MILT
decathlon **6**:72
CAMPBELL, MRS. PATRICK **4**:65 *bibliog.*
Pinero, Sir Arthur Wing **15**:307
CAMPBELL, ROBERT **4**:65–66
Yukon Territory (Canada) **20**:346
CAMPBELL, ROY **4**:66 *bibliog.*
CAMPBELL, THOMAS **4**:66
CAMPBELL, WILFRED **4**:66
CAMPBELL, WILLIAM WALLACE **4**:66
CAMPBELL-BANNERMAN, SIR HENRY **4**:66 *bibliog.*
Liberal parties **12**:311
CAMPBELL HILL
map (40° 22′N 83° 43′W) **14**:357
CAMPBELL ISLAND
map (52° 30′S 169° 5′E) **14**:334
New Zealand **14**:159
CAMPBELL RIVER (British Columbia)
map (50° 1′N 125° 15′W) **3**:491
CAMPBELL-STOKES SUNSHINE RECORDER **13**:340 *illus.*
CAMPBELLITES *see* DISCIPLES OF CHRIST
CAMPBELLSPORT (Wisconsin)
map (43° 36′N 88° 17′W) **20**:185
CAMPBELLSVILLE (Kentucky)
map (37° 21′N 85° 20′W) **12**:47
CAMPBELLTON (Florida)
map (30° 57′N 85° 24′W) **8**:172
CAMPBELLTON (New Brunswick)
map (48° 0′N 66° 40′W) **14**:117
CAMPBELLTON (Prince Edward Island)
map (46° 47′N 64° 18′W) **15**:548
CAMPECHE (city in Mexico) **4**:66
map (19° 51′N 90° 32′W) **13**:357
CAMPECHE (state in Mexico) **4**:66
cities
Campeche (city) **4**:66
CAMPECHE, BAY OF
map (20° 0′N 94° 0′W) **13**:357
CAMPEN, JACOB VAN **4**:66 *bibliog.*
CAMPENDONK, HEINRICH **4**:66 *bibliog.*
Blaue Reiter, Der **3**:328
CAMPHOR **4**:66
CAMPIN, ROBERT **4**:66–67 *bibliog.*
Renaissance art and architecture **16**:153
CAMPINA GRANDE (Brazil)
map (7° 13′S 35° 53′W) **3**:460
CAMPINAS (Brazil)
map (22° 54′S 47° 5′W) **3**:460
CAMPING **4**:67 *bibliog.*
CAMPINI, SECONDO
jet propulsion **11**:407
CAMPINS, LUIS HERRERA *see* HERRERA CAMPINS, LUIS
CAMPION (botany) **4**:67
CAMPION, SAINT EDMUND **4**:67
CAMPION, THOMAS **4**:67 *bibliog.*
CAMPION HALL (Oxford University) **14**:474
CAMPO (Colorado)
map (37° 6′N 102° 35′W) **5**:116
CAMPO FORMIO, TREATY OF **4**:67 *bibliog.*
CAMPO GALLO (Argentina)
map (26° 35′S 62° 51′W) **2**:149
CAMPO GRANDE (Brazil)
map (20° 27′S 54° 37′W) **3**:460
CAMPOAMOR Y CAMPOOSORIO, RAMÓN DE **4**:67 *bibliog.*
CAMPOBASSO (Italy)
map (41° 34′N 14° 39′E) **11**:321
CAMPOBELLO ISLAND (New Brunswick) **4**:67
CAMPOS (Brazil)
map (21° 45′S 41° 18′W) **3**:460
CAMPOS, PEDRO ALBIZU *see* ALBIZU CAMPOS, PEDRO
CAMPTI (Louisiana)
map (31° 54′N 93° 7′W) **12**:430
CAMPTON (Kentucky)
map (37° 44′N 83° 33′W) **12**:47
CAMPTOSAURUS **4**:67–68; **11**:475 *illus.*
CAMROSE (Alberta)
map (53° 1′N 112° 50′W) **1**:256
CAMUS, ALBERT **4**:68 *bibliog.*, *illus.*; **8**:319 *illus.*
alienation **1**:294
existentialism **7**:332
Myth of Sisyphus, The **13**:693
Plague, The **15**:325
Stranger, The **18**:288
theater of the absurd **19**:154
CAN THO (Vietnam)
map (10° 2′N 105° 47′E) **19**:580
CANAAN **4**:68
See also PALESTINE
cities and sites
Beth-shan **3**:230
Gezer **9**:163
Hazor **10**:84–85
Megiddo **13**:280
Shechem **17**:248
Ugarit **19**:374
mythology **13**:698–699
See also NEAR EASTERN MYTHOLOGY
Philistines **15**:239
Phoenician art **15**:250–251
religion
Baal **3**:5
CANAAN (Connecticut)
map (42° 2′N 73° 20′W) **5**:193
CANAAN (Vermont)
map (45° 0′N 71° 32′W) **19**:554
CANAANITE LANGUAGES
Afroasiatic languages **1**:179
Ebla **7**:36
Hebrew language **10**:101
CANADA **4**:68–79 *bibliog.*, *illus.*, *map*, *table*
agriculture **4**:77–78 *illus.*
animal life **4**:74
art *see* CANADIAN ART AND ARCHITECTURE
climate **4**:73–74 *table*
economic activity **4**:77–79 *illus.*
Bank of Canada **3**:67
banking systems **3**:69
North America **14**:234–236 *illus.*
unemployment rate **7**:160
education *see* CANADIAN EDUCATION
fishing **4**:78 *illus.*
flag **4**:69 *illus.*
forestry **4**:78–79 *illus.*
government **4**:76 *illus.*; **4**:79
Bill of Rights **3**:254
British North America Act **3**:497
civil service **5**:14
Constitution Act **5**:212
defense, national **6**:82 *table*
medals and decorations **13**:262 *illus.*
municipal government **13**:642
welfare spending **20**:98 *table*
health **4**:76
history *see* CANADA, HISTORY OF
labor union **12**:153
land **4**:69–72
Canadian Shield **4**:94
meteorite craters **13**:339
language **4**:75
libraries
Canadian Library Association **4**:92–93
manufacturing **4**:77
chemical industry **4**:318
maple syrup and sugar **13**:138
map (60° 0′N 95° 0′W) **14**:225
migration to the United States **11**:55 *map*
mining **4**:77
pipe and pipeline **15**:311
silver **17**:312
Sudbury **18**:322
parks and reserves
Banff National Park **4**:72 *illus.*
Gros Morne National Park (Newfoundland) **14**:167 *illus.*
national parks **14**:36; **14**:38–40 *map*, *table*
people **4**:74–75
Algonquin **1**:291
Bella Coola **3**:186
Blackfoot **3**:321
Carrier Indians **4**:168
Cree **5**:336–337
Crowfoot **5**:363
Eskimo **7**:238–242
Haida **10**:12
Indians, American **11**:124 *map*; **11**:138
Kwakiutl **12**:142
Micmac **13**:384
Nootka **14**:217–218
North America **14**:232
Ojibwa **14**:364
Ottawa **14**:460
Salish **17**:34
Tlingit **19**:216
Tsimshian **19**:323–324
women in society **20**:204 *table*
physical features
Columbia Icefield **5**:125–126
Rocky Mountains **16**:71 *illus.*
police

CANADA (cont.)
Royal Canadian Mounted Police **15**:396; **16**:329–330
political parties **4**:79
Conservative parties **5**:205–206
Liberal parties **12**:311
New Democratic Party **14**:120
Social Credit party **18**:11
provinces and territories
Alberta **1**:254–258 *illus., map*
British Columbia **3**:489–492 *illus., map*
Manitoba **13**:118–122 *illus., map*
New Brunswick **14**:115–118
Newfoundland **14**:165–168 *illus., map*
Northwest Territories **14**:257–259 *illus., map*
Nova Scotia **14**:269–271 *illus., map*
Ontario **14**:391–395 *illus., map*
Prince Edward Island **15**:547–549 *illus., map*
Quebec (province) **16**:16–21 *illus., map*
Saskatchewan **17**:80–83 *illus., map*
Yukon Territory **20**:344–346 *illus., map*
radio and television broadcasting **16**:60
regions
Labrador **12**:157
Maritime Provinces **13**:158
religion **4**:75
Canada, Anglican Church of **4**:87
Canada, United Church of **4**:87
Doukhobors **6**:249
resources **4**:79
Alberta **1**:258
energy and power generation **4**:78
lumber **12**:455
natural resources **4**:74
oil-drilling rights **15**:215
rivers, lakes, and waterways **4**:73–74
Assiniboine River **2**:265
Athabasca, Lake **2**:288
Athabasca River **2**:288
Champlain, Lake **4**:277
Churchill River (Saskatchewan-Manitoba) **4**:427
Hudson Bay **10**:289
James Bay **11**:355
Lake of the Woods **12**:171
Mackenzie River **13**:28–29 *map*
Ottawa River **14**:461
Slave River **17**:351
satellite, artificial
Alouette **1**:308; **11**:242
communications satellite **5**:145
social security **18**:14
soils **4**:72–73
sports
football **8**:218
ice hockey **11**:11
trade **4**:79
North America **14**:235
transportation
Canadian National Railways **4**:94
Canadian Pacific Railway **4**:94
icebreaker **11**:16
railroad **16**:73 *illus.*
roads and highways **16**:238
Trans-Canada Highway **19**:267
urban planning *see* URBAN PLANNING—CANADA
vegetation **4**:74
Dominion Arboretum and Botanic Garden **6**:234–235
maple (tree) **13**:137
CANADA, ANGLICAN CHURCH OF **4**:87
CANADA, HISTORY OF **4**:79–87 *bibliog., illus., maps, tables*
Acadia **1**:71
Canadian art and architecture **4**:88–91
Conservative parties **5**:205–206
ethnic minorities **7**:255–256
governors **4**:85 *table*
Hudson's Bay Company **10**:290–291
political parties **15**:401–402
prime minister **4**:86 *table*
Royal Canadian Mounted Police **16**:329–330
Supreme Court
Davies, Sir Louis Henry **6**:49–50
Duff, Sir Lyman Poore **6**:293
Kerwin, Patrick **12**:60–61
Richards, Sir William Buell **16**:211
Rinfret, Thibaudeau **16**:225
Ritchie, Sir William Johnstone **16**:229
Strong, Sir Samuel Henry **18**:303
Taschereau, Sir Henri **19**:42
c.1000–1763 European Exploration and Colonization **4**:80–81 *map*
Albanel, Charles **1**:248
Cabot, John **4**:7
Cartier, Jacques **4**:174–175
Champlain, Samuel de **4**:277–278
French and Indian Wars **4**:81; **8**:312–314
Frontenac, Louis de Buade, Comte de **8**:340
fur trade **8**:371
Jesuit Martyrs of North America **11**:402
Jogues, Saint Isaac **11**:422
Kelsey, Henry **12**:40
Kirke, Sir David **12**:89
La Vérendrye, Pierre Gaultier de Varennes, Sieur de **12**:151
L'Anse aux Meadows **12**:144
Laval, François de **12**:240
Leif Eriksson **12**:277–278
Louisbourg (Nova Scotia) **12**:429
Montcalm, Louis Joseph, Marquis de **13**:551–552
Monts, Pierre du Gua, Sieur de **13**:560
New France **4**:81; **14**:121
Radisson, Pierre Esprit **16**:67–68
Rupert's Land **16**:347
Talon, Jean **19**:18
Thorfinn Karlsefni **19**:178
Vikings **19**:594–596
Vinland **19**:601
Wolfe, James **20**:197
1763–1867 British rule
American Revolution **1**:358
Baldwin, Robert **3**:35
British Empire **3**:496
British reorganization **7**:81–83 *map*
Brown, George **3**:514
Canada Company **4**:87
Carleton, Guy **4**:151
Caroline affair **4**:160
Douglas, Sir James **6**:247
Durham, John George Lambton, 1st Earl of **6**:306
Elgin, James Bruce, 8th Earl of **7**:137
Family Compact **8**:18
Gosford, Archibald Acheson, 2d Earl of **9**:253
governors **4**:85 *table*
Haldimand, Sir Frederick **10**:18
Hearne, Samuel **10**:90
Henry, Alexander **10**:122
Hincks, Sir Francis **10**:168
Lafontaine, Sir Louis Hippolyte **12**:164
Lansdowne, Henry Charles Keith Petty-Fitzmaurice, 5th Marquess of **12**:199–200
Loyalists **12**:445
Macdonald, John Sandfield **13**:12
Mackenzie, Sir Alexander **13**:27
Mackenzie, William Lyon **13**:28
Murray, James **13**:650
Nelson, Robert **14**:80
North West Company **14**:252–253
Northwest exploration **4**:82
Papineau, Louis Joseph **15**:72
Quebec Act **16**:21
railroads **4**:83
Rebellions of 1837 **16**:105
Red River Settlement **16**:113
Selkirk, Thomas Douglas, 5th Earl of **17**:192
Simpson, Sir George **17**:317
Sydenham, Charles Edward Poulett Thomson, Baron **18**:400
Taché, Sir Étienne Paschal **19**:6
War of 1812 *see* WAR OF 1812
Webster-Ashburton Treaty **20**:89
western fur trade (1821–1870) **10**:291 *map*
1867–1931 Confederation **4**:84–86 *map*
Abbott, Sir John Joseph Caldwell **1**:53
Bering Sea controversy **3**:212
Blake, Edward **3**:324
Borden, Sir Robert L. **3**:397
Bourassa, Henri **3**:422
Bowell, Sir Mackenzie **3**:427
British North America Act **3**:497
Cartier, Sir George Etienne **4**:174
Cartwright, Sir Richard John **4**:178
Crerar, Thomas Alexander **5**:339
Dufferin and Ava, Frederick Temple Hamilton-Temple-Blackwood, 1st Marquess of **6**:293–294
Galt, Sir Alexander Tilloch **9**:22
Grey, Albert, 4th Earl **9**:360
Jesuit Estates Act **11**:402
Laurier, Sir Wilfrid **12**:239
McClung, Nellie **13**:9
Macdonald, Sir John A. **13**:12
Mackenzie, Alexander (1822–92) **13**:28
Meighen, Arthur **13**:281
Monck, Charles Stanley Monck, 4th Viscount **13**:522
Mowat, Sir Oliver **13**:626
Pacific Scandal **15**:8
Red River Rebellion **16**:113
Riel, Louis **16**:218
Strathcona and Mount Royal, Donald Alexander Smith, 1st Baron **18**:291
suffrage, women's **18**:326
Tilly, Sir Samuel Leonard **19**:199
Tupper, Sir Charles **19**:339
World War I **4**:86
1931-present
Aberhart, William **1**:56
Bennett, Richard Bedford, Viscount Bennett **3**:203
Bracken, John **3**:436
Clark, Joseph **5**:38–39
Constitution Act **5**:212
Diefenbaker, John G. **6**:161
Kerwin, Patrick **12**:60–61
King, W. L. Mackenzie **12**:81–82
Léger, Jules **12**:274
Lévesque, René **12**:303
MacEachen, Allan J. **13**:15
Mulroney, Brian **13**:637
Pearson, Lester B. **15**:128
postwar years **4**:86–87
St. Laurent, Louis Stephen **17**:20
Schreyer, Edward Richard **17**:135
Stanfield, Robert Lorne **18**:217
Trudeau, Pierre Elliott **19**:316
World War II **4**:86
CANADA, UNITED CHURCH OF **4**:87
CANADA ACT
Constitution Act **5**:212
CANADA BALSAM
balsam fir **3**:54
CANADA BASIN
map (79° 0'N 145° 0'W) **2**:139
CANADA COMPANY **4**:87
CANADA DE GOMEZ (Argentina)
map (32° 49'S 61° 24'W) **2**:149
CANADA GOOSE
tundra **19**:332 *illus.*
CANADIAN (county in Oklahoma)
map (35° 30'N 98° 0'W) **14**:368
CANADIAN (Texas)
map (35° 55'N 100° 23'W) **19**:129
CANADIAN-AMERICAN CHALLENGE CUP
automobile racing **2**:362
CANADIAN ART AND ARCHITECTURE **4**:76–77; **4**:88–91 *bibliog., illus.*
See also the subheading CANADA under specific art forms, e.g., ARCHITECTURE; PAINTING; SCULPTURE; etc.; names of specific artists, e.g., HÉBERT, LOUIS PHILIPPE; VARLEY, FREDERICK; etc.
colonial styles in North America **5**:111
Group of Seven **9**:376
Indians of North America, art of the **11**:138–139
museums, art **13**:658
CANADIAN BROADCASTING CORPORATION
radio and television broadcasting **16**:60
CANADIAN CID *see* IBERVILLE, PIERRE LE MOYNE, SIEUR D'
CANADIAN EDUCATION **4**:75–76; **4**:91–92 *bibliog., table*
Alberta, University of **1**:259
Canadian Education Association **4**:92
Dalhousie University **6**:12
Laval University **12**:241
McGill University **13**:16
McMaster University **13**:33
Manitoba, University of **13**:122
Manitoba Schools Question **13**:122
Montreal, University of **13**:558–560
Mount Allison University **13**:618
New Brunswick, University of **14**:118
Newfoundland, Memorial University of **14**:168
Ottawa, University of **14**:461
Prince Edward Island, University of **15**:549
Quebec, University of **16**:21
Queen's University at Kingston **16**:22
Saskatchewan, University of **17**:83
Simon Fraser University **17**:315
Toronto, University of **19**:242
Victoria, University of **19**:575
Western Ontario, University of **20**:116
Windsor, University of **20**:174
Winnipeg, University of **20**:180
York University **20**:331
CANADIAN EDUCATION ASSOCIATION **4**:92
CANADIAN ENGLISH *see* ENGLISH LANGUAGE
CANADIAN GROUP OF PAINTERS, THE
Canadian art and architecture **4**:90
CANADIAN LIBRARY ASSOCIATION **4**:92–93
CANADIAN LITERATURE **4**:93–94 *bibliog., illus.*
authors
Atwood, Margaret **2**:316
Avison, Margaret **2**:376
Birney, Earle **3**:293
Blais, Marie Claire **3**:324
Buell, John **3**:544
Callaghan, Morley **4**:40
Campbell, Wilfred **4**:66
Carman, Bliss **4**:153
Charbonneau, Robert **4**:286
Costain, Thomas B. **5**:292
Crawford, Isabella Valancy **5**:333
Crémazie, Octave **5**:338
Davies, Robertson **6**:50
de la Roche, Mazo **6**:61
Drummond, William Henry **6**:283
Engel, Marian **7**:176
Firestone, Shulamith **8**:106
Fréchette, Louis Honoré **8**:289
Gallant, Mavis **9**:16
Garneau, F. X. **9**:48
Garneau, Hector de Saint-Denys **9**:48
Giroux, André **9**:190
Grove, Frederick Philip **9**:378
Haliburton, T. C. **10**:20
Hébert, Anne **10**:101
Hémon, Louis **10**:119
Hood, Hugh John Blagdon **10**:225
Langevin, André **11**:195
Laurence, Margaret **12**:238
Leacock, Stephen **12**:256
MacLennan, Hugh **13**:32
Martin, Claire **13**:179
Millar, Margaret **13**:426
Montgomery, L. M. **13**:556
Morin, Paul **13**:580
Mowat, Farley **13**:626
Nelligan, Émile **14**:79
Parker, Sir Gilbert **15**:90
Pratt, E. J. **15**:490
Raddall, Thomas H. **16**:41–42
Richardson, John **16**:212
Richler, Mordecai **16**:214
Roberts, Sir Charles G. D. **16**:241
Ross, Sinclair **16**:318
Roy,Gabrielle **16**:329
Scott, Duncan Campbell **17**:153
Service, Robert W. **17**:211
Stringer, Arthur **18**:301
Thériault, Yves **19**:160–161
Wilson, Ethel **20**:164
Wiseman, Adele **20**:189
GOVERNOR GENERAL'S AWARD *see* GOVERNOR GENERAL'S AWARD
CANADIAN NATIONAL RAILWAYS **4**:94
turbotrain **16**:75 *illus.*
CANADIAN NORTHERN RAILWAY
Mackenzie, Sir William **13**:28
CANADIAN PACIFIC RAILWAY **3**:490 *illus.*; **4**:94 *bibliog.*; **16**:71 *illus.*
Calgary (Alberta) **4**:28
Canada, history of **4**:84–85
Macdonald, Sir John A. **13**:12
Pacific Scandal **15**:8
Stephen, George **18**:254
CANADIAN RIVER **4**:94
map (35° 27'N 95° 3'W) **14**:368
CANADIAN ROCKIES *see* ROCKY MOUNTAINS

CANADIAN SHIELD **4**:94
Boothia Peninsula **3**:395
Canada **4**:72
Hudson Bay **10**:289
Laurentian Mountains **12**:239
Manitoba **13**:118; **13**:120
North America **14**:226–227
Quebec (province in Canada) **16**:16
CANADICE LAKE
Finger Lakes **8**:93
CANAJOHARIE (New York)
map (42° 54′N 74° 35′W) **14**:149
CANAKKALE, STRAIT OF *see* DARDANELLES
CANAL **4**:94–97 *bibliog., illus.*
drainage systems **6**:255
dredging **6**:268–269
Fulton, Robert **8**:358
harbor and port **10**:42
Leonardo da Vinci **12**:291
lock **4**:95 *illus.*
notable canals
Erie Canal **7**:230 *map*
Grand Canal (China) **9**:284
New York State Barge Canal **14**:156
Nicaragua Canal **14**:179–180
North Sea Canal **14**:252
Panama Canal **15**:56–57 *illus., map*
Sault Sainte Marie Canals **17**:96–97
Suez Canal **18**:323–324 *illus., map*
Welland Ship Canal **20**:99
Thailand **19**:141 *illus.*
transportation **19**:278
United States, 19th century **19**:445 *map*
Venice (Italy) **19**:544
waterway **20**:66
Watson, Elkanah **20**:67
CANAL, GIOVANNI ANTONIO *see* CANALETTO
CANAL POINT (Florida)
map (26° 52′N 80° 38′W) **8**:172
CANAL WINCHESTER (Ohio)
map (39° 51′N 82° 48′W) **14**:357
CANAL ZONE *see* PANAMA CANAL ZONE
CANAL ZONE COLLEGE **4**:97
CANALETTO **4**:98 *bibliog., illus.*
La Salute, Venice **11**:314 *illus.*
CANANDAIGUA (New York)
map (42° 54′N 77° 17′W) **14**:149
CANANDAIGUA LAKE
Finger Lakes **8**:93
map (42° 49′N 77° 16′W) **14**:149
CAÑAR (Ecuador)
map (2° 33′S 78° 56′W) **7**:52
CANARIES BASIN
Atlantic Ocean bottom **2**:295 *map*
CANARIES CURRENT **4**:98
CANARY **4**:99 *bibliog., illus.*
seedeater **17**:187
CANARY ISLANDS **4**:99 *map*
Las Palmas **12**:210
Santa Cruz de Tenerife **17**:68
CANASERAGA (New York)
map (42° 28′N 77° 47′W) **14**:149
CANASTA **4**:99 *bibliog.*
CANASTOTA (New York)
map (43° 10′N 75° 45′W) **14**:149
CANAVERAL, CAPE *see* CAPE CANAVERAL (Florida)
CAÑAZAS (Panama)
map (8° 19′N 81° 13′W) **15**:55
CANBERRA (Australia) **2**:337 *illus.*; **4**:99–100 *map*
architecture
Griffin, Walter Burley **9**:363
education
Australian National University **2**:345 *table*
map (35° 17′S 149° 8′E) **2**:328
CANBY (Minnesota)
map (44° 43′N 96° 16′W) **13**:453
CANBY (Oregon)
map (45° 16′N 122° 42′W) **14**:427
CANBY, EDWARD RICHARD SPRIGG
Kintpuash **12**:86
Mobile (Alabama) **13**:487
CANBY, HENRY SEIDEL **4**:100
CANCAN **4**:100
CANCER (constellation) **4**:100
CANCER (disease) **4**:101–106 *bibliog., illus.*
American Cancer Society **1**:337
bone diseases **3**:378
causes **4**:102–103
acrylonitrile **1**:86
asbestos **2**:227
benzene **3**:206
diseases, occupational **6**:193–194
environmental health **7**:211–212
groundsel **9**:374
herbicide **10**:136
nitrite **14**:202
organic chemistry **14**:438
pollutants, chemical **15**:410–411
radiation injury **16**:42–43
saccharin **17**:6
smoking **17**:373–374
cell **4**:236
diagnosis **4**:104 *illus.*
biopsy **3**:276
mammography **13**:106
Pap test **15**:62
growth **9**:379
Hodgkin's disease **10**:194
immunity **11**:59
kidney disease **12**:71
leukemia **12**:300–301
liver **12**:374
metastasis **13**:335
mole (birthmark) **13**:507
multiple myeloma **13**:638
nervous system, diseases of the **14**:96
pancreas **15**:58
patient psychology and rehabilitation **4**:106
prevention **4**:104
prostate gland **15**:573
remission **4**:106
research **4**:106
embryology **7**:154
Fibiger, Johannes **8**:69
medicine **13**:271
Nathans, Daniel **14**:27
Sloan-Kettering Institute for Cancer Research **17**:363
respiratory system disorders **16**:181–182
sarcoma **17**:75
seven warning signals **4**:103–104 *illus.*
splenomegaly **18**:191
stages **4**:102–104 *illus.*
treatment **4**:104–106 *illus.*
alkaloid **1**:296
biopharmaceuticals **3**:275
chemotherapy **4**:105–106 *illus.*
colchicine **5**:97
genetic engineering **9**:84
hallucinogens **10**:24
hysterectomy **10**:352
interferon **11**:210
laetrile **12**:163
mastectomy **13**:215
megavitamin therapy **13**:280
methadone **13**:343
periwinkle (botany) **15**:172
radiation therapy **4**:105 *illus.*; **16**:43
radon **16**:69
surgery **4**:105 *illus.*
tumor **19**:331
virus **19**:615
herpes **10**:145
retrovirus **16**:184
Rous, Francis Peyton **16**:325
Wistar Institute **20**:190
CANCÚN (Mexico)
map (21° 5′N 86° 46′W) **13**:357
Quintana Roo **16**:27
CANDELA **4**:106
candlepower **4**:107
lumen **12**:458
units, physical **19**:466–467 *table*
CANDELA, FÉLIX **4**:106 *bibliog.*
Latin American art and architecture **12**:228
CANDELABRUM **4**:106
Chanukah **4**:282
CANDELABRUM CACTUS *see* CANDELABRUM TREE
CANDELABRUM TREE **4**:106–107; **17**:98 *illus.*
CANDIA (Crete) *see* IRÁKLION (Greece)
CANDIA, OVANDO
Bolivia **3**:369
CANDIDA (play) **4**:107
Shaw, George Bernard **17**:245
CANDIDAS **4**:107
CANDIDE (book) **4**:107 *bibliog.*
Voltaire **19**:632
CANDIDIASIS **4**:107
diseases, animal **6**:192
fungus diseases **8**:369
leukorrhea **12**:301
CANDLE **4**:107 *bibliog., illus.*
lamp **12**:175–176 *illus.*
tallow tree **19**:17
CANDLEBERRY *see* BAYBERRY
CANDLEFISH **4**:107
smelt **17**:366
CANDLEMAS DAY
Groundhog Day **9**:374
CANDLENUT (botany) **4**:107
CANDLEPOWER **4**:107
candela **4**:106
CANDLER (county in Georgia)
map (32° 25′N 82° 5′W) **9**:114
CANDLEWOOD LAKE
map (41° 32′N 73° 27′W) **5**:193
CANDO (North Dakota)
map (48° 32′N 99° 12′W) **14**:248
CANDOR (New York)
map (42° 14′N 76° 21′W) **14**:149
CANDOR (North Carolina)
map (35° 18′N 79° 45′W) **14**:242
CANDY **4**:108 *bibliog.*
Hershey, Milton Snaveley **10**:148
CANDYTUFT (botany) **4**:108 *illus.*
CANE (botany) *see* SORGHUM
CAÑETE (Peru)
map (13° 5′S 76° 24′W) **15**:193
CANETTI, ELIAS **4**:108
CANEY (Kansas)
map (37° 1′N 95° 56′W) **12**:18
CANEY RIVER
map (36° 20′N 95° 42′W) **14**:368
CANFIELD, DOROTHY *see* FISHER, DOROTHY CANFIELD
CANID *see* DOG FAMILY
CANILLO (Andorra)
map (42° 33′N 1° 36′E) **1**:405
CANINE PARVOVIRAL ENTERITIS *see* PARVOVIRUS
CANINE TEETH **19**:70–72 *illus.*
CANIS MAJOR AND CANIS MINOR **4**:108
Sirius **17**:328
CANISIUS, SAINT PETER **4**:108 *bibliog.*
CANISTEO (New York)
map (42° 16′N 77° 36′W) **14**:149
CANISTOTA (South Dakota)
map (43° 36′N 97° 18′W) **18**:103
CANKAR, IVAN **4**:108
CANKER (animal) **4**:108
herpes **10**:145
CANKER (plant) **4**:108–109
diseases, plant **6**:195
CANMORE (Alberta)
map (51° 5′N 115° 21′W) **1**:256
CANMORE, HOUSE OF
Malcolm III, King of Scotland (Malcolm Canmore) **13**:86
CANNA **4**:109
CANNABICH, JOHANN CHRISTIAN
Mannheim school **13**:125
CANNABIS *see* MARIJUANA
CANNAE, BATTLE OF **4**:109
CANNEL COAL
coal and coal mining **5**:76
CANNES (France) **4**:109
map (43° 33′N 7° 1′E) **8**:260
CANNES FILM FESTIVAL **4**:109
CANNIBALISM **4**:109–110 *bibliog., illus.*
Carib **4**:147
head-hunting **10**:85
Homo erectus **10**:216
CANNING **4**:110–111 *bibliog., illus.*
aluminum **1**:319
Appert, Nicolas **2**:88
food preservation **8**:211–212
packaging **15**:11
pickling **15**:293
CANNING (Nova Scotia)
map (45° 9′N 64° 25′W) **14**:269
CANNING, GEORGE **4**:111 *bibliog., illus.*
Monroe Doctrine **13**:543
Wellington, Arthur Wellesley, 1st Duke of **20**:100
CANNIZZARO, STANISLAO **4**:111
chemistry, history of **4**:326
organic chemistry **14**:435
CANNIZZARRO, STANISLAO
water **20**:48
CANNON **2**:223–224 *illus.*; **4**:111–112 *bibliog., illus.*
Armstrong, William George, Baron Armstrong of Craigside **2**:180
artillery **2**:223–224
development **4**:111–112
firearms **8**:106
howitzer **10**:285
naval vessels **14**:55
weapons **20**:74
Wilkinson, John **20**:153
CANNON (county in Tennessee)
map (35° 48′N 86° 3′W) **19**:104
CANNON, ANNIE JUMP **4**:112
star **18**:222
CANNON, JOSEPH GURNEY **4**:112 *bibliog.*
Norris, George W. **14**:223
CANNON, WALTER B.
homeostasis **10**:212
CANNON BEACH (Oregon)
map (45° 55′N 123° 57′W) **14**:427
CANNON FALLS (Minnesota)
map (44° 31′N 92° 54′W) **13**:453
CANNON RIVER
map (44° 35′N 92° 33′W) **13**:453
CANNONBALL (North Dakota)
map (46° 24′N 100° 38′W) **14**:248
CANNONBALL RIVER
map (46° 26′N 100° 38′W) **14**:248
CANNONBALL TREE **4**:112
CANNONSVILLE RESERVOIR
map (42° 8′N 75° 19′W) **14**:149
CANO, ALONSO **4**:112–113 *bibliog.*
CANO, JUAN SEBASTIÁN DEL **4**:113
exploration **7**:336–337 *map*
Magellan, Ferdinand **13**:47–48 *map*
CANOE **4**:113 *bibliog., illus.*
Canada, history of **4**:82 *illus.*
Carib **4**:147
Kwakiutl **11**:127 *illus.*
outrigger **14**:469; **17**:263 *illus.*
CANOEING AND KAYAKING **4**:113–114 *bibliog., illus.*
CANON (Georgia)
map (34° 21′N 83° 7′W) **9**:114
CANON (music) **4**:114 *bibliog.*
CANON CAMERA **4**:59
CANON CITY (Colorado)
map (38° 27′N 105° 14′W) **5**:116
CANON LAW **4**:114–115 *bibliog.*
Clement V, Pope **5**:49
decretals **6**:76
divorce **6**:205
Gratian **9**:301
Honorius III, Pope **10**:224
law, history of **12**:244
Middle Ages **13**:393
CANONIZATION **4**:115 *bibliog.*
saint **17**:15
CANONSBURG (Pennsylvania)
map (40° 16′N 80° 11′W) **15**:147
CANOOCHEE RIVER
map (31° 59′N 81° 18′W) **9**:114
CANOPIC JARS
mummy **13**:639
CANOPUS, DECREE OF *see* DECREE OF CANOPUS
CANORA (Saskatchewan)
map (51° 37′N 102° 26′W) **17**:81
CANOVA (South Dakota)
map (43° 53′N 97° 30′W) **18**:103
CANOVA, ANTONIO **4**:115 *bibliog., illus.*
Italian art and architecture **11**:311
Pauline Borghese as Venus Victrix **2**:199 *illus.*; **4**:115 *illus.*
pyramids **15**:635
tomb of Vittorio Alfieri **19**:231 *illus.*
CÁNOVAS DEL CASTILLO, ANTONIO
Spain, history of **18**:148
CANSO (Nova Scotia)
map (45° 20′N 61° 0′W) **14**:269
CANSO, STRAIT OF
Cape Breton Island **4**:120
CANTABRIAN MOUNTAINS
map (43° 0′N 5° 0′W) **18**:140
CANTACUZENUS *see* JOHN VI CANTACUZENUS, BYZANTINE EMPEROR
CANTALOUPE **13**:288 *illus.*
CANTATA **4**:115–116 *bibliog.*
aria **2**:153
baroque music **3**:91–92
cantus firmus **4**:118
composers
Bach, Johann Sebastian **3**:11
Carissimi, Giacomo **4**:150
Orff, Carl **14**:432
Telemann, Georg Philipp **19**:78
CANTAURA (Venezuela)
map (9° 19′N 64° 21′W) **19**:542
CANTER (horse)
riding **16**:217 *illus.*
CANTERBURY (England) **4**:116
CANTERBURY (New Brunswick)
map (45° 53′N 67° 29′W) **14**:117
CANTERBURY, ARCHBISHOP OF **4**:116 *bibliog.*
Anselm, Saint **2**:35
Augustine of Canterbury, Saint **2**:321
Becket, Saint Thomas **3**:151
Coggan, Donald **5**:94
Cranmer, Thomas **5**:332
Fisher, Geoffrey Francis **8**:122
Lanfranc **12**:194
Langton, Stephen **12**:196
Laud, William **12**:236
Parker, Matthew **15**:90
Ramsey, Michael **16**:82
Runcie, Robert Alexander Kennedy **16**:345
Temple, William **19**:100
Whitgift, John **20**:139
William I, King of England (William the Conqueror) **20**:155

CANTERBURY CATHEDRAL 4:116 *bibliog.*
William of Sens 20:155
CANTERBURY PLAINS
map (44° 0′S 171° 45′E) 14:158
CANTERBURY TALES, THE (book) 3:385 *illus.*; 4:116–117 *bibliog.*, *illus.*
Chaucer, Geoffrey 4:304
CANTH, MINNA 4:117
CANTHARIDES *see* SPANISH FLY
CANTICLE 4:117
Magnificat 13:60
Song of Solomon 18:64
CÁNTIGAS DE SANTA MARÍA
miniature from 18:144 *illus.*
CANTILEVER 4:117
bridge (engineering) 3:481 *illus.*; 3:483 *table*
CANTINFLAS 4:117
CANTON (Guangzhou) (China) 4:117–118 *illus.*; 4:364 *table*
map (23° 6′N 113° 16′E) 4:362
Zu Shi Miao temple 19:99 *illus.*
CANTON (Georgia)
map (34° 14′N 84° 29′W) 9:114
CANTON (Illinois)
map (40° 33′N 90° 2′W) 11:42
CANTON (Kansas)
map (38° 23′N 97° 26′W) 12:18
CANTON (Massachusetts)
map (42° 9′N 71° 9′W) 13:206
CANTON (Minnesota)
map (43° 32′N 91° 56′W) 13:453
CANTON (Mississippi)
map (32° 37′N 90° 2′W) 13:469
CANTON (New York)
map (44° 36′N 75° 10′W) 14:149
CANTON (North Carolina)
map (35° 32′N 82° 50′W) 14:242
CANTON (Ohio) 4:118
map (40° 48′N 81° 22′W) 14:357
CANTON (Oklahoma)
map (36° 3′N 98° 35′W) 14:368
CANTON (Pennsylvania)
map (41° 39′N 76° 51′W) 15:147
CANTON (South Dakota)
map (43° 18′N 96° 35′W) 18:103
CANTON (Switzerland) 4:118
CANTON (Texas)
map (32° 33′N 95° 52′W) 19:129
CANTON ISLAND
Phoenix Islands 15:251
CANTONESE LANGUAGE *see* YUE LANGUAGE
CANTONMENT (Florida)
map (30° 38′N 87° 19′W) 8:172
CANTOR 4:118
CANTOR, EDDIE 4:118 *bibliog.*
CANTOR, GEORG 4:118 *bibliog.*
mathematics, history of 13:226
CANTOS, THE (poem) 4:118 *bibliog.*
Pound, Ezra 15:476
CANTUS FIRMUS 4:118 *bibliog.*
CANUTE, KING OF ENGLAND, DENMARK, AND NORWAY 4:118 *bibliog.*
Denmark 6:112
CANVAS 4:118
CANYON
landform evolution 12:182 *illus.*
CANYON (county in Idaho)
map (43° 40′N 116° 45′W) 11:26
CANYON (Texas)
map (34° 59′N 101° 55′W) 19:129
CANYON (Yukon Territory)
map (60° 52′N 137° 2′W) 20:345
CANYON CITY (Oregon)
map (44° 23′N 118° 57′W) 14:427
CANYON DE CHELLY NATIONAL MONUMENT 4:119 *bibliog.*; 14:38–39 *map*, *table*
CANYON FERRY LAKE
map (46° 33′N 111° 37′W) 13:547
CANYONVILLE (Oregon)
map (42° 56′N 123° 17′W) 14:427
CANZONE 4:119
CÃO, DIOGO
Zaire 20:351
CAO XUEQIN *see* TS'AO HSÜEH-CH'IN (Cao Xueqin)
CAO YU *see* TS'AO YÜ (Cao Yu)
CAO ZHI *see* TS'AO CHIH (Cao Zhi)
CAP-HAÏTIEN (Haiti) 4:119; 10:16 *illus.*
map (19° 45′N 72° 12′W) 10:15
CAP-PELÉ (New Brunswick)
map (46° 13′N 64° 18′W) 14:117
CAP ROCK *see* SALT DOME
CAPA, ROBERT 4:119 *bibliog.*
photojournalism 15:273 *illus.*
CAPABLANCA, JOSÉ RAÚL 4:119 *bibliog.*
CAPAC, HUAYNA *see* HUAYNA CAPAC
CAPAC NAN see INCA (American Indians)
CAPACITANCE 4:119
capacitor 4:119–120
electromagnetic units 7:118
farad 8:21
materials technology 13:220
measurement
bridge circuit 3:484
CAPACITOR 4:119–120 *bibliog.*
capictance 4:119
circuit, electric 4:437
dielectric 6:161
electricity 7:109
electrolytic
tantalum 19:25
farad 8:21
Leyden jar 4:119
microphone 13:386
types 4:119–120
CAPATÀRIDA (Venezuela)
map (11° 11′N 70° 37′W) 19:542
CAPD *see* CONTINUOUS AMBULATORY PERITONEAL DIALYSIS
CAPE ANN (peninsula)
map (42° 39′N 70° 38′W) 13:206
CAPE BASIN
Atlantic Ocean bottom 2:295 *map*
CAPE BAULD
map (51° 38′N 55° 25′W) 14:166
CAPE BEIRUT
map (33° 54′N 35° 28′E) 12:265
CAPE BRETON ISLAND 4:120; 14:270 *illus.*
Bras d'Or Lake 3:456
Louisbourg (Nova Scotia) 12:429
map (46° 0′N 60° 30′W) 14:269
Sydney (Nova Scotia) 18:401
CAPE CANAVERAL (Florida) 4:120; 8:176 *illus.*
Kennedy Space Center 12:44
map (28° 24′N 80° 37′W) 8:172
map (28° 27′N 80° 32′W) 8:172
CAPE CHARLES (Virginia)
map (37° 16′N 76° 1′W) 19:607
CAPE COAST (Ghana)
map (5° 5′N 1° 15′W) 9:164
CAPE COD (Massachusetts) 4:120 *bibliog.*; 13:208–209 *illus.*
cities
Hyannis 10:327
Provincetown 15:584
Gosnold, Bartholomew 9:253
map (41° 42′N 70° 15′W) 13:206
CAPE COD BAY
map (41° 52′N 70° 22′W) 13:206
CAPE COD CANAL
map (41° 47′N 70° 30′W) 13:206
CAPE COLOUREDS *see* COLOUREDS (South Africa)
CAPE CORAL (Florida)
map (26° 33′N 81° 57′W) 8:172
CAPE DENBIGH (Alaska) 4:120 *bibliog.*; 7:239 *bibliog.*; 14:237 *map*
Eskimo 7:241
Giddings, J. Louis 9:176
CAPE DORSET (Northwest Territories)
map (64° 14′N 76° 32′W) 14:258
CAPE ELIZABETH (Maine)
map (43° 34′N 70° 12′W) 13:70
CAPE FEAR RIVER
map (33° 53′N 78° 0′W) 14:242
CAPE GIRARDEAU (Missouri) 4:120
map (37° 19′N 89° 32′W) 13:476
CAPE GIRARDEAU (county in Missouri)
map (37° 25′N 89° 40′W) 13:476
CAPE OF GOOD HOPE *see* GOOD HOPE, CAPE OF
CAPE OF GOOD HOPE PROVINCE (South Africa) *see* CAPE PROVINCE (South Africa)
CAPE HATTERAS (North Carolina) *see* HATTERAS, CAPE
CAPE HENLOPEN STATE PARK (Delaware) 6:89 *illus.*
CAPE JASMINE 4:120
gardenia 9:42
CAPE JUMPING HARE *see* SPRINGHARE
CAPE KENNEDY (Florida) *see* CAPE CANAVERAL (Florida)
CAPE KRUSENSTERN (Alaska) 4:120 *bibliog.*; 14:237 *map*
Ipiutak 11:248
CAPE MAY (New Jersey) 4:120–121
map (38° 56′N 74° 55′W) 14:129
CAPE MAY (county in New Jersey)
map (38° 56′N 74° 55′W) 14:129
CAPE MAY COURT HOUSE (New Jersey)
map (39° 5′N 74° 50′W) 14:129
CAPE PLATEAU
map (28° 20′S 23° 57′E) 18:79
CAPE PROVINCE (South Africa) 4:121
cities
East London 7:32
Kimberley 12:77
Mafeking 13:46
Port Elizabeth 15:443
map (31° 0′S 23° 0′E) 18:79
CAPE ROJO
map (17° 56′N 67° 11′W) 15:614
CAPE TORMENTINE (New Brunswick)
map (46° 8′N 63° 47′W) 14:117
CAPE TOWN (South Africa) 4:121 *illus.*; 18:79–80 *illus.*, *table*
map (33° 55′S 18° 22′E) 18:79
CAPE VERDE 4:121–122 *bibliog.*, *map*
flag 4:121–122 *illus.*
Guinea-Bissau 9:398–399
map (16° 0′N 24° 0′W) 1:136
CAPE VINCENT (New York)
map (44° 8′N 76° 20′W) 14:149
CAPE YORK PENINSULA (Australia) 4:122
map (14° 0′S 142° 30′E) 2:328
ČAPEK, JOSEF
Čapek, Karel 4:122
ČAPEK, KAREL 4:122 *bibliog.*
CAPELIN
smelt 17:366
CAPER (botany) 4:122 *illus.*
clammyweed 5:36
spiderflower 18:183
CAPERNAUM 4:122
CAPET, HUGH *see* HUGH CAPET, KING OF FRANCE
CAPETIANS *(dynasty)* 4:122–123 *bibliog.*; 8:270 *table*
France, history of 8:267–268
Hugh Capet, King of France 10:292
CAPHARNAUM *see* CAPERNAUM
CAPILLARITY 4:123 *illus.*
CAPILLARY 4:123 *illus.*
circulatory system 4:440 *illus.*; 4:442 *illus.*
dilation
erythema 7:236
lungs 12:463–464 *illus.*
CAPITAL (architecture) 2:131 *illus.*; 4:123 *illus.*
corinthian order
Callimachus (sculptor) 4:46
Doric order 2:131 *illus.*
Greek orders 9:335 *illus.*
Ionic order 4:123 *illus.*
CAPITAL (economics) 4:123 *bibliog.*
balance of payments 3:31–32
equity (finance) 7:226
saving and investment 17:100
CAPITAL, DAS (book) *see KAPITAL, DAS* (book)
CAPITAL PUNISHMENT 4:123–124 *bibliog.*
crime 5:347
Darrow, Clarence S. 6:39
8th Amendment 7:92
electrocution 7:113
Furman v. *Georgia* 8:371–372
garrote 9:51
gas chamber 9:53
guillotine 9:396
hanging 10:38
lethal injection 12:299
murder 13:648
CAPITAL SHIP 14:57 *illus.*
naval vessels 14:56
CAPITALISM 4:124–126 *bibliog.*
corporation 4:125
current problems 4:125
economic planning 7:47
economics 7:48–49
factory system 8:7
government regulation, scope of 4:125
historians
Galbraith, John Kenneth 9:13
Hobson, John A. 10:193
Schumpeter, Joseph A. 17:137
Tawney, Richard Henry 19:45
Weber, Max (sociologist) 20:87
historical development 4:124–125
laissez-faire 12:167
Marxism 13:183–184
modern conceptions 4:125
price system 15:535
profit 15:561–562
Protestant ethic 15:576
socialism 18:20
Wall Street 20:12–13
women in society 20:202
CAPITAN (New Mexico)
map (33° 35′N 105° 35′W) 14:136
CAPITÁN BADO (Paraguay)
map (23° 16′S 55° 32′W) 15:77
CAPITAN BERMÚDEZ (Argentina)
map (32° 49′S 60° 43′W) 2:149
CAPITAN PEAK
map (33° 36′N 105° 16′W) 14:136
CAPITOL OF THE UNITED STATES 4:126 *bibliog.*, *illus.*
art
Crawford, Thomas 5:333
Leutze, Emanuel 12:301
Rogers, Randolph 16:269
Trumbull, John 19:319
Vanderlyn, John 19:519
Bulfinch, Charles 3:553
floor plan 4:126 *illus.*
House Chamber 10:273 *illus.*
Latrobe, Benjamin Henry 12:235
Walter, Thomas U. 20:19
Washington, D.C. 20:41 *map*
CAPITOLINE BRUTUS 17:161 *illus.*
CAPITOLINE HILL 4:126 *bibliog.*
CAPITOLINE TEMPLE
Capitoline Hill 4:126
CAPO D'ISTRIA, GIOVANNI ANTONIO, COUNT 4:126–127
CAPONE, AL 4:127 *bibliog.*
CAPORETTO, BATTLE OF 4:127
World War I 20:238 *map*
CAPOTE, TRUMAN 4:127 *bibliog.*, *illus.*
CAPP, AL 4:127 *illus.*
CAPPADOCIA 4:127–128 *bibliog.*
monasticism 13:521 *illus.*
CAPPADOCIAN FATHERS
Basil the Great, Saint 3:109
Gregory of Nazianzus, Saint 9:356
Gregory of Nyssa, Saint 9:356
CAPPUCCINO, IL *see* STROZZI, BERNARDO
CAPRA, FRANK 4:128 *bibliog.*, *illus.*
documentary 6:211
CAPREOL (Ontario)
map (46° 43′N 80° 56′W) 14:393
CAPRI (Italy) 4:128
Blue Grotto 3:343
map (40° 33′N 14° 13′E) 11:321
CAPRICCIO 4:128
CAPRICORNUS 4:128
CAPRIVI, GEORG LEO, GRAF VON 4:128 *bibliog.*
CAPRIVI STRIP (Namibia) 4:128
CAPSIAN 4:128–129 *bibliog.*
CAPTAIN COOK (Hawaii)
map (19° 30′N 155° 55′W) 10:72
CAPTAIN JACK *see* KINTPUASH
CAPTAIN KIDD *see* KIDD, CAPTAIN
CAPTAINS COURAGEOUS (book) 4:129
Gloucester (Massachusetts) 9:209
Kipling, Rudyard 12:86–87
CAPUCHIN (monkey) 4:129 *illus.*
CAPUCHINS *see* FRANCISCANS
CAPYBARA 4:129 *illus.*; 13:105 *illus.*
CAQUETÁ RIVER
map (1° 35′S 69° 25′W) 5:107
CARA, MARCHETTO
Renaissance music 16:156
CARACAL 4:129 *illus.*
CARACALLA, BATHS OF 4:129–130 *bibliog.*
bath 3:122
CARACALLA, EDICT OF
Italy, history of 11:327
CARACALLA, ROMAN EMPEROR 4:130 *bibliog.*
CARACARA 4:130 *illus.*
CARACAS (Venezuela) 4:130–131 *illus.*; 19:542–543 *illus.*, *table*
Latin America, history of 12:220
map (10° 30′N 66° 56′W) 19:542
Simon Bolivar Center 18:93 *illus.*
CARACTACUS
Cymbeline 5:406
CARAGIALE, ION LUCA 4:131 *bibliog.*
CARAGLIO, GIOVANNI JACOPO 4:131 *bibliog.*
CARANDAITI (Bolivia)
map (20° 45′S 63° 4′W) 3:366
CARANGEOT, ARNOULD
mineral 13:439
CARAQUET (New Brunswick)
map (47° 48′N 64° 57′W) 14:117
CARAT 4:131
diamond 6:151–152
CARATASCA LAGOON
map (15° 23′N 83° 55′W) 10:218
CARATHÉODORY, CONSTANTIN 4:131
CARAUARI (Brazil)
map (4° 52′S 66° 54′W) 3:460
CARAVAGGIO, MICHELANGELO MERISI DA 4:131–132 *bibliog.*, *illus.*
Basket of Fruit 18:269 *illus.*
The Calling of Saint Matthew 11:313 *illus.*
Conversion of Saint Paul 15:21 *illus.*

Gentileschi (family) **9**:95
Honthorst, Gerrit van **10**:224
Italian art and architecture **11**:313
CARAVEL 4:132 *illus.*; **19**:278 *illus.*
ship **17**:266–269 *illus.*
CARAVELA ISLAND
map (11° 30′N 16° 20′W) **9**:399
CARAVELAS (Brazil)
map (17° 45′S 39° 15′W) **3**:460
CARAWAY (Arkansas)
map (35° 46′N 90° 19′W) **2**:166
CARAWAY (spice) **4**:132
CARAWAY, HATTIE WYATT 4:132
CARAYBAMBA (Peru)
map (14° 24′S 73° 9′W) **15**:193
CARBANION 4:132
CARBENICILLIN
antibiotics **2**:59
CARBERRY (Manitoba)
map (49° 52′N 99° 20′W) **13**:119
CARBOHYDRATE 4:132–133 *bibliog.*
Bergius, Friedrich Karl Rudolf **3**:210
carbohydrate chemistry **4**:133
cellulose **4**:238
digestive system **6**:173
diet, human **6**:164
dieting **6**:165
digestion, human **6**:172
digestive system **6**:173–174
function **4**:132
Haworth, Sir Walter Norman **10**:78
lactose **12**:162
liver **12**:374
metabolism **4**:133; **13**:325
diabetes **6**:148–149
hypoglycemia **10**:351
monosaccharide **13**:540
nutrition, human **14**:305
Payen, Anselme **15**:121
polysaccharide **15**:421–422
starch **18**:226
sugar **18**:327
CARBOLIC ACID
Lister, Joseph **12**:366
phenol **15**:225
CARBON 4:133 *bibliog., illus.*
abundances of common elements **7**:131 *table*
alloy
iron **11**:271
atom **5**:306 *illus.*
carbanion **4**:132
carbonium ion **4**:139
characteristics **4**:133–134 *illus.*
stereochemistry **18**:258 *illus.*
biosphere **3**:277
carbon-14
radiochemistry **16**:63
radiometric age-dating **16**:67
compounds **4**:134–135
acetyl group **1**:80
aldehyde **1**:267–268
alicyclic compounds **1**:293
aliphatic compounds **1**:295
alkane **1**:296
alkene **1**:296–297
alkyl group **1**:297
alkyne **1**:297
aromatic compounds **2**:186
aryl group **2**:226
carbonate minerals **4**:137
carbonyl group **4**:139
carboxylic acid **4**:139–140 *table*
cyclic compounds **5**:403–404
ethyl group **7**:257
fluorocarbon **8**:188
heterocyclic compound **10**:153
hydrocarbon **10**:331
ketone **12**:61
methyl group **13**:344–345
nitrile **14**:202
phenyl group **15**:226
diamond **6**:151
element **7**:130 *table*
fixation
photosynthesis **15**:275; **15**:277
forms **4**:134
Group IVA periodic table **15**:167
native elements **14**:47
organic chemistry **14**:434–438
plastics **15**:348–350
polycarbonate, molecular structure **15**:350 *illus.*
socioeconomic role **4**:135
CARBON (county in Montana)
map (45° 15′N 109° 5′W) **13**:547
CARBON (county in Pennsylvania)
map (40° 52′N 75° 45′W) **15**:147
CARBON (county in Utah)
map (38° 38′N 110° 32′W) **19**:492
CARBON (county in Wyoming)
map (41° 45′N 107° 0′W) **20**:301
CARBON BLACK
carbon **4**:134
lampblack **12**:176
CARBON CATION *see* CARBONIUM ION
CARBON CYCLE (astronomy) **4**:135–136 *bibliog., illus.*
CARBON CYCLE (atmosphere) **4**:136 *bibliog., illus.*
biosphere **3**:277
blue-green algae **3**:343
nutrient cycles **14**:303
oxygen **14**:478
soil organisms **18**:39
CARBON DIOXIDE
carbon **4**:135
carbon cycle (atmosphere) **4**:136
carbon-14 age-dating
half-life **10**:20
Libby, Willard Frank **12**:311
radiochemistry **16**:63
radiometric age-dating **16**:67
hemoglobin **10**:119
hyperventilation **10**:349
laser **12**:213 *table*
life-support systems **12**:332
metabolism **13**:325–326
photosynthesis **15**:275–277
receptors, heart **10**:94
septic tank **17**:206
CARBON MONOXIDE
carbon **4**:135
hemoglobin **10**:119
CARBON-NITROGEN-OXYGEN CYCLE *see* CARBON CYCLE (astronomy)
CARBON STAR 4:136–137
CARBON TETRACHLORIDE 4:137
hepatitis **10**:130
Regnault, Henri Victor **16**:129
CARBON-14 DATING *see* CARBON; CARBON DIOXIDE; RADIOMETRIC AGE-DATING
CARBONADO *see* DIAMOND
CARBONARI 4:137
Italy, history of **11**:329
Risorgimento **16**:228 *illus.*
secret societies **17**:181
CARBONATE MINERALS 4:137 *bibliog.*
aragonite **2**:107–108; **4**:137
azurite **2**:384
calcite **4**:21–22; **4**:137
cerussite **4**:261
classes **4**:137–
diamond **6**:151–152
dolomite **6**:226
evaporite **7**:314
geode **9**:97
isomorph **11**:300
limestone **12**:345
magnesite **4**:137; **13**:53
malachite **13**:78–79
Mesozoic Era **13**:322
mineral **13**:443 *table*
rhodochrosite **16**:203
sedimentary rock **17**:184
shale, oil **17**:238
siderite **17**:294
smithsonite **17**:372
talc **19**:15
travertine **19**:284
CARBONATITE
kimberlite **12**:77
ore deposits
major ore deposits **14**:424–425 *table*
CARBONDALE (Colorado)
map (39° 24′N 107° 13′W) **5**:116
CARBONDALE (Illinois)
map (37° 44′N 89° 13′W) **11**:42
CARBONDALE (Kansas)
map (38° 49′N 95° 41′W) **12**:18
CARBONDALE (Pennsylvania)
map (41° 35′N 75° 30′W) **15**:147
CARBONEAR (Newfoundland)
map (47° 45′N 53° 13′W) **14**:166
CARBONELL, ALONSO
Buen Retiro Palace **3**:544
CARBONIA (Italy)
map (39° 11′N 8° 32′E) **11**:321
CARBONIFEROUS PERIOD 4:137–139 *bibliog., illus., map*
coal and coal mining **5**:76
Earth, geological history of **7**:11–15
Edaphosaurus **7**:54
fern **8**:57–58
fossil record **8**:245–246
geologic time **9**:103–105
ice ages **11**:7–11
living organisms **4**:138
Mississippian System **4**:137
paleobotany **15**:30–31 *illus.*
paleoclimatology **15**:32
paleogeography **4**:138
Paleozoic Era **15**:43
Pennsylvania System **4**:137
polar wandering **15**:393 *map, map*
stratigraphy **4**:137
swamp forest **4**:139 *illus.*; **15**:31 *illus.*
tectonics **4**:138
CARBONIUM ION 4:139
CARBONYL GROUP 4:139
aldehyde **1**:267–268
compounds, Grignard reagents **9**:363–364
ketone **12**:61
organic chemistry **14**:437
spectroscopy **18**:170
CARBORUNDUM 4:139
silicon **17**:305
CARBOXYLIC ACID 4:139–141 *bibliog., table*
acetic acid **1**:80
amide **1**:369
amino acid **1**:370
benzoic acid **3**:207
fatty acid **8**:35
formic acid **8**:234
lactic acid **12**:161
maleic acid **13**:87
organic chemistry **14**:437
palmitic acid **15**:51
pyruvic acid **15**:639
CARBUNCLE 4:141
skin diseases **17**:342
CARBURETOR 4:140–141 *bibliog., illus.*
Daimler, Gottlieb **6**:7
internal-combustion engine **11**:215
CARCASSONNE (France) **4**:141
map (43° 13′N 2° 21′E) **8**:260
CARCHEMISH (Turkey) **4**:141 *bibliog.*
Woolley, Sir Leonard **20**:215
CARCINOGEN
cancer **4**:101–103
cyclamates **5**:403
diseases, occupational **6**:193–194
environmental health **7**:211–212
CARCINOMA
cancer **4**:101
tumor **19**:331
CARD DOMINOES
fan-tan (game) **8**:20
CARD GAMES 4:141–143 *bibliog., illus.*
See also names of specific card games, e.g., RUMMY; TAROT; etc.
baccarat **3**:9
bezique **3**:233
blackjack **3**:321
bridge **3**:479
canasta **4**:99
casino **4**:181–182
chemin de fer **4**:323
cribbage **5**:342
euchre **7**:262
fan-tan **8**:20
faro **8**:28
Hoyle, Edmond **10**:286
pinochle **15**:307
playing cards **4**:141–142 *illus.*
poker **15**:386
rummy **16**:345
solitaire **18**:56
tarot **19**:38
types of games **4**:142
whist **20**:133
CARDAMOM 4:143
CARDAMOMES MOUNTAINS
map (12° 0′N 103° 15′E) **12**:11
CARDANO, GEROLAMO 4:143 *bibliog.*
mathematics, history of **13**:224
CARDBOARD *see* PAPER
CARDENAL, ERNESTO
Latin American literature **12**:230
CARDENAL, PEIRE
Provençal literature **15**:583
CÁRDENAS (Cuba)
map (23° 2′N 81° 12′W) **5**:377
CÁRDENAS (Nicaragua)
map (11° 12′N 85° 31′W) **14**:179
CÁRDENAS, GARCIA LÓPEZ DE *see* LÓPEZ DE CÁRDENAS, GARCÍA
CÁRDENAS, LÁZARO 4:143 *bibliog.*
Mexico, history of **13**:366
CARDIAC CATHETERIZATION
Cournand, André **5**:314
heart diseases **10**:96
Richards, Dickinson Woodruff **16**:211
CARDIAC MASSAGE *see* CARDIOPULMONARY RESUSCITATION
CARDIAC MUSCLE *see* MYOCARDIUM
CARDIFF (Wales) **4**:143
map (51° 29′N 3° 13′W) **19**:403
CARDIGAN (Prince Edward Island)
map (46° 14′N 62° 37′W) **15**:548
CARDIGAN BAY (Prince Edward Island)
map (46° 10′N 62° 30′W) **15**:548
CARDIGAN BAY (United Kingdom)
map (52° 30′N 4° 20′W) **19**:403
CARDIGAN WELSH CORGI 4:143 *bibliog., illus.*; **6**:214 *illus.*
CARDIGANSHIRE *see* DYFED (Wales)
CARDIN, PIERRE
fashion design **8**:32
CARDINAL 4:143–144 *illus.*
CARDINAL FISH 4:144
CARDINAL FLOWER *see* LOBELIA
CARDINAL NUMBER *see* NUMBER
CARDINALS, COLLEGE OF 4:144
papacy **15**:63
CARDIOLOGY *see* HEART DISEASES
CARDIOMYOPATHY (heart disease) **10**:95
CARDIOPULMONARY RESUSCITATION 4:144 *bibliog.*; **8**:108 *illus.*
first aid **8**:108–109
heart diseases **10**:96
shock, physiologic **17**:279
CARDIOVASCULAR DISEASES 4:144–145 *bibliog.*
See also CIRCULATORY SYSTEM—diseases and disorders; HEART DISEASES
shock, physiologic **17**:278–279
CARDIOVASCULAR SYSTEM
See also CIRCULATORY SYSTEM; HEART
exercise **7**:330 *table*
reflex **16**:120
space medicine **18**:133
CARDOZO (Uruguay)
map (32° 38′S 56° 21′W) **19**:488
CARDOZO, BENJAMIN N. 4:145 *bibliog.*
CARDS, PLAYING *see* CARD GAMES
CARDSTON (Alberta)
map (49° 12′N 113° 18′W) **1**:256
CARDUCCI, GIOSUÈ 4:145 *bibliog.*
CARDWELL (Missouri)
map (36° 3′N 90° 17′W) **13**:476
CARE (Cooperative for American Relief Everywhere) **4**:145
CAREER EDUCATION 4:146 *bibliog.*
See also VOCATIONAL EDUCATION
Marine Corps, U.S. **13**:155
navy **14**:68
psychological measurement **15**:593
sales **17**:32
service industries **17**:211
technical education **19**:59
CAREER GUIDANCE *see* CAREER EDUCATION
CARÊME, MARIE ANTONIN 4:146
French cooking **5**:239
CAREN, REGINALD *see* HARRISON, REX
CARENCRO (Louisiana)
map (30° 19′N 92° 3′W) **12**:430
CARETAKER, THE (play) **4**:146
Pinter, Harold **15**:308
CAREW, ROD 4:146 *bibliog.*
CAREW, THOMAS 4:146 *bibliog.*
CAREY (Ohio)
map (40° 57′N 83° 23′W) **14**:357
CAREY, HENRY 4:146
CAREY, HUGH 4:146–147
CAREY, S. WARREN
paleogeography **15**:37
CAREY, WILLIAM 4:147 *bibliog.*
CARGO CULTS 4:147 *bibliog., illus.*
CARGO TRANSPORTATION
freighter **8**:301
harbor and port **10**:43–44 *illus.*
railroad **16**:74
ship **17**:274–275 *illus.*
CARIB (American Indians) **4**:147 *bibliog.*
Arawak **2**:110
cannibalism **4**:109
Caribbean Sea **4**:148
passage rites **15**:103
CARIBBEAN CURRENT 4:147
CARIBBEAN INDIANS *see* INDIANS, AMERICAN, CULTURE AREAS
CARIBBEAN SEA 4:147–149 *bibliog., map*
Caribbean plate **15**:351 *map*
climate **4**:148
history **4**:148–149
islands and island groups
Anguilla **2**:7
Antigua and Barbuda **2**:62
Antilles, Greater and Lesser **2**:63
Aruba **2**:225–226
Barbados **3**:75–76 *map*
Cayman Islands **4**:227
Cuba **5**:377–380 *illus., map, table*
Curaçao (Netherlands) **5**:390

CARIBBEAN SEA (cont.)
Dominica **6**:232–233 *illus.*
French West Indies **8**:326
Grenada **9**:357–358 *illus., map*
Grenadine Islands **9**:359
Guadeloupe **9**:385
Hispaniola **10**:180
Isle of Pines **11**:298
Jamaica **11**:351–352 *illus., map, table*
Leeward Islands **12**:272
Martinique **13**:181
Montserrat (island) **13**:560
Netherlands Antilles **14**:103
Puerto Rico **15**:614–616 *illus., map, table*
Saint Kitts-Nevis **17**:20
Saint Lucia **17**:23
Saint Martin (France) **17**:24
Saint Vincent and the Grenadines **17**:27
Trinidad and Tobago **19**:300 *illus., map, table*
Virgin Islands **19**:605–606
West Indies **20**:108–109 *map*
map (15° 0′N 73° 0′W) **4**:148
North America **14**:227
ocean bottom **4**:148
water characteristics **4**:148–149
CARIBOU **2**:140–141 *illus.*; **4**:149 *bibliog., illus.*
animal migration **2**:27
deer **6**:79–81 *illus.*
fossil shinbone **14**:238 *illus.*
reindeer **16**:131
CARIBOU (county in Idaho)
map (42° 45′N 111° 35′W) **11**:26
CARIBOU (Maine)
map (46° 52′N 68° 1′W) **13**:70
CARIBOU MOUNTAIN (Maine)
map (45° 26′N 70° 38′W) **13**:70
CARIBOU MOUNTAINS (Alberta)
map (59° 12′N 115° 40′W) **1**:256
CARIBOU RANGE (Mountain Range)
map (43° 5′N 111° 15′W) **11**:26
CARICATURE **4**:149–150 *bibliog., illus.*
See also SATIRE
art
Beerbohm, Sir Max **3**:163
Bull, John (personification) **3**:557
burlesque and travesty **3**:572
Covarrubias, Miguel **5**:318
Cruikshank, George **5**:365
Daumier, Honoré **6**:45–46
Forain, Jean Louis **8**:219
Furniss, Harry **8**:373
Gillray, James **9**:182
Grandville **9**:286
Grosz, George **9**:371
Posada, José Guadalupe **15**:457–458
Rowlandson, Thomas **16**:328
Tissot, James **19**:209
cartoon (editorial and political) **4**:176–178
drama
Foote, Samuel **8**:219
photography
Carjat, Étienne **4**:151
Nadar **14**:4
CARICATURE (periodical)
Gavarni, Paul **9**:62
CARIES, DENTAL
teeth **19**:71–72 *illus.*
CARILLON **3**:184–185 *illus.*
CARIOCA *see* MESTIZO
CARIPITO (Venezuela)
map (10° 8′N 63° 6′W) **19**:542
CARISSIMI, GIACOMO **4**:150 *bibliog.*
music, history of Western **13**:666
CARJAT, ÉTIENNE **4**:151
CARL JUNCTION (Missouri)
map (37° 11′N 94° 34′W) **13**:476
CARL XVI GUSTAF *see* CHARLES XVI GUSTAV, KING OF SWEDEN
CARLAMANGA
map (4° 20′S 79° 35′W) **7**:52
CARLE, GUILLAUME *see* CALE, GUILLAUME
CARLETON, GUY, 1ST BARON DORCHESTER **4**:151 *bibliog.*
American Revolution **1**:358–359 *map*
Quebec Act **16**:21
CARLETON COLLEGE **4**:151
CARLETON PLACE (Ontario)
map (45° 8′N 76° 9′W) **14**:393
CARLETON UNIVERSITY **4**:151
CARLIN (Nevada)
map (40° 43′N 116° 7′W) **14**:111
CARLINVILLE (Illinois)
map (39° 17′N 89° 53′W) **11**:42
CARLISLE (Arkansas)
map (34° 47′N 91° 45′W) **2**:166
CARLISLE (England) **4**:151
map (54° 54′N 2° 55′W) **19**:403
CARLISLE (Indiana)
map (38° 58′N 87° 25′W) **11**:111
CARLISLE (Iowa)
map (41° 30′N 93° 29′W) **11**:244
CARLISLE (Kentucky)
map (38° 19′N 84° 2′W) **12**:47
CARLISLE (county in Kentucky)
map (36° 50′N 88° 55′W) **12**:47
CARLISLE (Pennsylvania) **4**:151
map (40° 12′N 77° 12′W) **15**:147
CARLISLE BARRACKS
Carlisle (Pennsylvania) **4**:151
CARLISLE BAY
map (13° 5′N 59° 37′W) **3**:75
CARLISLE INDIAN SCHOOL
Carlisle (Pennsylvania) **4**:151
CARLISTS **4**:151 *bibliog.*
Salic law **17**:32
Spain, history of **18**:148
CARLOMAN, KING OF THE FRANKS
Pepin the Short **15**:156
CARLOS, DON **4**:151
Philip II, King of Spain **15**:234
CARLOS, JOHN **14**:383 *illus.*
CARLOS REYLES (Uruguay)
map (33° 3′S 56° 29′W) **19**:488
CARLOTA **4**:151 *bibliog.*
CARLOW (Ireland) **4**:151
CARLSBAD (California)
map (33° 10′N 117° 21′W) **4**:31
CARLSBAD (Czechoslovakia) *see* KARLOVY VARY (Czechoslovakia)
CARLSBAD (New Mexico)
map (32° 25′N 104° 14′W) **14**:136
CARLSBAD (Texas)
map (31° 36′N 100° 38′W) **19**:129
CARLSBAD CAVERNS (New Mexico) **4**:151–152 *bibliog.*
cave **4**:222
national parks **14**:38 *map, table*
CARLSBAD DECREES **4**:152
Karlovy Vary (Czechoslovakia) **12**:28
CARLSBERG RIDGE
plate tectonics **15**:351 *map*
CARLSON, CHESTER FLOYD **4**:152 *bibliog.*
electrostatic printing **7**:127–128
CARLSSON, INGVAR **4**:152
CARLTON (Minnesota)
map (46° 40′N 92° 25′W) **13**:453
CARLTON (county in Minnesota)
map (46° 35′N 92° 40′W) **13**:453
CARLTON (Texas)
map (31° 55′N 98° 10′W) **19**:129
CARLTON, STEVE **4**:152
CARLYLE (Illinois)
map (38° 37′N 89° 22′W) **11**:42
CARLYLE, THOMAS **4**:152–153 *bibliog., illus.*
CARLYLE LAKE
map (38° 40′N 89° 18′W) **11**:42
CARMACKS (Yukon Territory)
map (62° 5′N 136° 18′W) **20**:345
CARMAN, BLISS **4**:153
Fredericton (New Brunswick) **8**:294
CARMANIA
Persia, ancient **15**:182 *map*
CARMANVILLE (Newfoundland)
map (49° 24′N 54° 17′W) **14**:166
CARMARTHEN (Wales) **4**:153
CARMARTHENSHIRE *see* DYFED (wales)
CARMEL (California) **4**:153
map (36° 33′N 121° 55′W) **4**:31
CARMEL (Indiana)
map (39° 59′N 86° 8′W) **11**:111
CARMEL (New York)
map (41° 26′N 73° 41′W) **14**:149
CARMEL, MOUNT **4**:153
CARMEL-BY-THE-SEA (California) *see* CARMEL (California)
CARMELITES **4**:153 *bibliog.*; **13**:396 *illus.*
Honorius III, Pope **10**:224
John of the Cross, Saint **11**:424
Teresa of Ávila, Saint **19**:115–116
CARMELO (Uruguay)
map (34° 0′S 58° 17′W) **19**:488
CARMEN (Oklahoma)
map (36° 35′N 98° 28′W) **14**:368
CARMEN (opera) **4**:153 *bibliog.*
Bizet, Georges **3**:301–302
Calvé, Emma **4**:48
CARMEN DE PATAGONES (Argentina)
map (40° 48′S 62° 59′W) **2**:149
CARMI (Illinois)
map (38° 5′N 88° 10′W) **11**:42
CARMICHAEL, FRANK **4**:153 *bibliog.*
CARMICHAEL, HOAGY **4**:153
CARMICHAEL, STOKELY
SNCC **17**:384
CARMINES, AL
Off-Off Broadway theater **14**:353
CARMONA, ANTÓNIO OSCAR DE FRAGOSO **4**:154
Portugal, history of **15**:455
CARNAC (France) **2**:115 *illus.*; **4**:154 *bibliog.*
megalith **13**:279 *illus.*
stone alignments **18**:281–282 *illus.*
CARNAP, RUDOLF **4**:154 *bibliog.*
ethics **7**:250–251
logical positivism **12**:397
CARNARVON (Australia)
map (24° 53′S 113° 40′E) **2**:328
CARNARVON, GEORGE EDWARD, 5TH EARL OF **4**:154 *bibliog.*
CARNATIC MUSIC
Indian music **11**:103
CARNATION **4**:154 *illus.*; **8**:170 *illus.*
CARNAUBA WAX **4**:154
CARNÉ, MARCEL **4**:155
CARNEADES **4**:155
CARNEGIE (Oklahoma)
map (35° 6′N 98° 36′W) **14**:368
CARNEGIE (Pennsylvania)
map (40° 24′N 80° 6′W) **15**:147
CARNEGIE, ANDREW **4**:155 *bibliog., illus.*
Carnegie Foundations **4**:155
Carnegie Hall **4**:155
Carnegie Institution of Washington **4**:155
Dunfermline (Scotland) **6**:299–300
Pennsylvania **15**:151
CARNEGIE, LAKE
map (26° 10′S 122° 30′E) **2**:328
CARNEGIE CORPORATION OF NEW YORK
Carnegie Foundations **4**:155
CARNEGIE FOUNDATIONS **4**:155
Educational Testing Service **7**:66
Kerr, Clark **12**:59–60
secondary education **17**:179
CARNEGIE HALL **4**:155 *bibliog.*
New York (city) **14**:145 *map*
CARNEGIE INSTITUTION OF WASHINGTON **4**:155
geochemistry **9**:95
Gilman, Daniel Coit **9**:182
Mount Wilson Observatory **13**:618
Palomar Observatory **15**:52
CARNEGIE-MELLON UNIVERSITY **4**:155
CARNEIRO, FRANCISCO SÁ
Portugal **15**:452
CARNELIAN **9**:74 *illus.*
CARNER, JOANNE **4**:155
CARNESVILLE (Georgia)
map (34° 22′N 83° 14′W) **9**:114
CARNEYS POINT (New Jersey)
map (39° 43′N 75° 28′W) **14**:129
CARNIVALS AND FAIRS **4**:156 *bibliog., illus.*
amusement park **1**:386
calliope **4**:46
Ferris wheel **8**:59
Mardi Gras **13**:148
CARNIVORE **4**:156–157 *bibliog., illus., table*
dinosaur **6**:179–180 *table*
mammal **13**:103; **13**:105 *illus.*
CARNIVOROUS PLANTS **4**:157–158 *bibliog., illus.*
CARNOT (family) **4**:158–159 *bibliog.*
Carnot, Hippolite **4**:158
Carnot, Lazare Nicolas Marguerite **4**:158
Carnot, Nicolas Léonard Sadi **4**:158
Carnot, Sadi **4**:158–159
physics, history of **15**:285
CARNOT CYCLE **4**:159 *bibliog.*
Carnot, Sadi **4**:159
heat engine **4**:159
thermodynamics **4**:159
CARNOTITE *see* URANIUM MINERALS
CARNOVSKY, MORRIS **4**:159
CARNSORE POINT
map (52° 10′N 6° 22′W) **11**:258
CARO (Michigan)
map (43° 29′N 83° 24′W) **13**:377
CARO, ANTHONY **4**:159 *bibliog., illus.*
CARO, JOSEPH BEN EPHRAIM **4**:159 *bibliog.*
CAROB **4**:159–160
CAROL (music) **4**:160 *bibliog.*
English music **7**:203
CAROL CITY (Florida)
map (25° 56′N 80° 16′W) **8**:172
CAROL I, KING OF ROMANIA **4**:160
CAROL II, KING OF ROMANIA **4**:160 *illus.*
CAROLINA (Brazil)
map (7° 20′S 47° 28′W) **3**:460
CAROLINA (El Salvador)
map (13° 51′N 88° 19′W) **7**:100
CAROLINA ALLSPICE *see* SWEETSHRUB
CAROLINA BEACH (North Carolina)
map (34° 2′N 77° 54′W) **14**:242
CAROLINE (county in Maryland)
map (38° 53′N 75° 50′W) **13**:188
CAROLINE (county in Virginia)
map (38° 0′N 77° 20′W) **19**:607
CAROLINE AFFAIR **4**:160 *bibliog.*
Van Buren, Martin **19**:511
CAROLINE OF BRUNSWICK
George IV, King of England, Scotland, and Ireland **9**:111
CAROLINE INSTITUTE
Nobel Prize **14**:208
CAROLINE ISLANDS **4**:160
map (8° 0′N 147° 0′E) **14**:334
Pacific Islands, Trust Territory of the **15**:5
World War II **20**:276–277 *map*
Yap **20**:319
CAROLINE LITERATURE
See also CAVALIER POETS
Cowley, Abraham **5**:321
Denham, Sir John **6**:108
CAROLINGIAN ART AND ARCHITECTURE **4**:160–161 *bibliog., illus.*
Alcuin **1**:267
bronzes **3**:507
calligraphy **4**:42 *illus.*
cathedrals and churches **4**:205
Flemish art and architecture **8**:161
French art and architecture **8**:303
German art and architecture **9**:123
Germany, history of **9**:148
illuminated manuscripts **11**:47
mosaic **13**:595
sculpture **17**:162
The Throne of Dagobert **8**:375 *illus.*
CAROLINGIANS (dynasty) **4**:162 *bibliog., illus.*; **8**:270 *table*
Arnulf, Frankish Emperor **2**:186
Charlemagne **4**:289–290
Charles Martel **4**:291
France, history of **8**:266–267
Franks **8**:286
Germany, history of **9**:148
Louis the German, East Frankish King **12**:422
Louis I, Frankish Emperor (Louis the Pious) **12**:429
Pepin the Short, King of the Franks **15**:156
CAROLSFELD, LUDWIG SCHNORR VON
Tristan and Isolde (opera) **19**:303
CAROM BILLIARDS
billiards **3**:254–255 *illus.*
CARONDELET, HÉCTOR, BARON DE **4**:162 *bibliog.*
CARONÍ RIVER
map (8° 21′N 62° 43′W) **19**:542
CAROTENE
algae **1**:281
pigment, skin **15**:300
CAROTENOID **4**:162 *illus.*
blue-green algae **3**:343
chlorophyll **4**:402
Karrer, Paul **12**:29
Kuhn, Richard **12**:135
photosynthesis **15**:276
structure: Heilbron, Sir Ian Morris **10**:108
terpene **19**:118
CAROTHERS, W. H. **4**:162 *bibliog.*
fiber, textile **8**:67
nylon **14**:308–309
CAROTID ARTERY
circulatory system **4**:440 *illus.*
stroke **18**:302
CARP **4**:162–163 *bibliog., illus.*
barbel **3**:77
chub **4**:422
minnow **13**:458
CARPACCIO, VITTORE **4**:163 *bibliog.*
CARPATHIAN MOUNTAINS **4**:163 *map*
map (48° 0′N 24° 0′E) **7**:268
Romania **16**:286
CARPATHO-UKRAINE *see* RUTHENIA (USSR)
CARPE DIEM **4**:163
CARPEAUX, JEAN BAPTISTE **4**:163–164 *bibliog.*
CARPENTARIA, GULF OF **4**:164
map (14° 0′S 139° 0′E) **2**:328
CARPENTER (Wyoming)
map (41° 3′N 104° 22′W) **20**:301
CARPENTER, HARLEAN *see* HARLOW, JEAN
CARPENTER, SCOTT **4**:164 *bibliog.*
Mercury program **13**:308
CARPENTERS AND JOINERS OF AMERICA, UNITED BROTHERHOOD OF **4**:164

CARPENTERSVILLE (Illinois)
map (42° 7′N 88° 17′W) **11**:42
CARPENTIER, ALEJO **4**:164 *bibliog.*
CARPENTIER, HORACE
Oakland (California) **14**:312
CARPENTIER, PIETER
Carpentaria, Gulf of **4**:164
CARPENTRY **4**:164 *bibliog.*
adz **1**:114
nail **14**:7–8
roof and roofing **16**:306
saw **17**:102–103
CARPET BEETLE **4**:165 *illus.*
CARPET INDUSTRY **4**:165 *bibliog., illus.*
Axminster weave **4**:165 *illus.*
Brussels weave **4**:165 *illus.*
carpet inspection **4**:165 *illus.*
nylon **14**:309
rugs and carpets **16**:340–343
Wilton weave **4**:165 *illus.*
CARPETBAGGERS **4**:164–165 *bibliog., illus.*
cartoon depicting **16**:110 *illus.*
Reconstruction **16**:109
CARPETS *see* RUGS AND CARPETS
CARPINCHO *see* CAPYBARA
CARPINI, GIOVANNI DA PIAN DEL **4**:166
exploration **7**:336–337 *map*
CARPINTERIA (California)
map (34° 24′N 119° 31′W) **4**:31
CARPIO (North Dakota)
map (48° 27′N 101° 43′W) **14**:248
CARR, EMILY **4**:166 *bibliog.*
CARR, GERALD **4**:166
Skylab **17**:348
CARR, JOHN DICKSON **4**:166
CARRÀ, CARLO **4**:166 *bibliog., illus.*
Metaphysical Muse, The **4**:166 *illus.*
CARRABELLE (Florida)
map (29° 51′N 84° 40′W) **8**:172
CARRACCI (family) **4**:166–167 *bibliog., illus.*
Italian art and architecture **11**:313
CARRACCI, AGOSTINO
caricature **4**:149–150
Carracci (family) **4**:166–167
CARRACCI, ANNIBALE
Carracci (family) **4**:167
CARRACCI, LUDOVICO
Carracci (family) **4**:166
CARRACK **19**:64 *illus.*
CARRANZA, VENUSTIANO **4**:167 *bibliog.*
Mexico, history of **13**:365
Obregón, Álvaro **14**:317
Villa, Pancho **19**:596
Wilson, Woodrow **20**:167
Zapata, Emiliano **20**:356
CARRARA (Italy)
map (44° 5′N 10° 6′E) **11**:321
CARRAUNTOOHILL MOUNTAIN
map (52° 0′N 9° 45′W) **11**:258
CARRBORO (North Carolina)
map (35° 54′N 79° 4′W) **14**:242
CARRÉ, FERDINAND
refrigeration **16**:124
CARRÉ, JOHN LE *see* LE CARRÉ, JOHN
CARREL, ALEXIS **4**:167 *bibliog.*
surgery **18**:362
CARRERA, JOSÉ RAFAEL **4**:167 *bibliog.*
CARRERA ANDRADE, JORGE **4**:167
CARRERAS, JOSÉ **4**:167–168
CARRÈRE, JOHN MERVEN *see* CARRÈRE AND HASTINGS
CARRÈRE AND HASTINGS **4**:168 *bibliog.*
CARRERIA (Paraguay)
map (21° 59′S 58° 35′W) **15**:77
CARRÉ'S DISEASE *see* DISTEMPER
CARRIACOU ISLAND
Grenadine Islands **9**:359
map (12° 30′N 61° 27′W) **9**:358
CARRIAGE
coach and carriage **5**:73–75 *illus.*
CARRICK-ON-SHANNON (Ireland)
map (53° 57′N 8° 5′W) **11**:258
CARRIE, MOUNT
map (47° 53′N 123° 39′W) **20**:35
CARRIER INDIANS **4**:168 *bibliog.*
CARRIERA, ROSALBA **4**:168 *bibliog., illus.*
pastel **15**:106
Young Girl with Monkey **4**:168 *illus.*
CARRIERE (Mississippi)
map (30° 32′N 89° 39′W) **13**:469
CARRIERS MILLS (Illinois)
map (37° 41′N 88° 38′W) **11**:42
CARRILLO, JULIÁN
Latin American music and dance **12**:232
CARRINGTON (North Dakota)
map (47° 27′N 99° 8′W) **14**:248
CARRINGTON, PETER ALEXANDER RUPERT CARRINGTON, LORD
Thatcher, Margaret **19**:143
CARRION BEETLE **3**:167 *illus.*
CARRION FLOWER **4**:168
CARRIZO MOUNTAINS
map (36° 45′N 109° 10′W) **2**:160
CARRIZO SPRINGS (Texas)
map (28° 31′N 99° 52′W) **19**:129
CARRIZOZO (New Mexico)
map (33° 38′N 105° 53′W) **14**:136
CARROLL (county in Arkansas)
map (36° 22′N 93° 30′W) **2**:166
CARROLL (county in Georgia)
map (33° 35′N 85° 5′W) **9**:114
CARROLL (county in Illinois)
map (42° 5′N 89° 55′W) **11**:42
CARROLL (county in Indiana)
map (40° 36′N 86° 41′W) **11**:111
CARROLL (Iowa)
map (42° 4′N 94° 52′W) **11**:244
CARROLL (county in Iowa)
map (42° 2′N 94° 50′W) **11**:244
CARROLL (county in Kentucky)
map (38° 39′N 85° 6′W) **12**:47
CARROLL (county in Maryland)
map (39° 25′N 77° 0′W) **13**:188
CARROLL (county in Mississippi)
map (33° 30′N 89° 55′W) **13**:469
CARROLL (county in Missouri)
map (39° 25′N 93° 30′W) **13**:476
CARROLL (Nebraska)
map (42° 17′N 97° 17′W) **14**:70
CARROLL (county in New Hampshire)
map (43° 50′N 71° 15′W) **14**:123
CARROLL (county in Ohio)
map (40° 34′N 81° 5′W) **14**:357
CARROLL (county in Tennessee)
map (36° 0′N 88° 25′W) **19**:104
CARROLL (county in Virginia)
map (36° 45′N 80° 45′W) **19**:607
CARROLL, CHARLES **4**:168
CARROLL, JAMES **4**:168
CARROLL, JOHN **4**:168–169 *bibliog.*
CARROLL, LEWIS **4**:169 *bibliog., illus.*
Alice's Adventures in Wonderland **1**:293; **4**:352 *illus.*
Through the Looking-Glass **19**:183
CARROLLTON (Alabama)
map (33° 16′N 88° 5′W) **1**:234
CARROLLTON (Georgia)
map (33° 35′N 85° 5′W) **9**:114
CARROLLTON (Illinois)
map (39° 18′N 90° 24′W) **11**:42
CARROLLTON (Kentucky)
map (38° 41′N 85° 11′W) **12**:47
CARROLLTON (Michigan)
map (43° 27′N 83° 54′W) **13**:377
CARROLLTON (Mississippi)
map (33° 30′N 89° 55′W) **13**:469
CARROLLTON (Missouri)
map (39° 22′N 93° 30′W) **13**:476
CARROLLTON (Ohio)
map (40° 34′N 81° 5′W) **14**:357
CARROLLTOWN (Pennsylvania)
map (40° 36′N 78° 43′W) **15**:147
CARROT **4**:169 *illus.*; **19**:534 *illus.*
caraway **4**:132
chervil **4**:333
cicely **4**:428
coriander **5**:262
dill **6**:176
parsley **15**:99
poison hemlock **15**:382
Queen Anne's lace **16**:21
CARROT RIVER (Saskatchewan)
map (53° 17′N 103° 35′W) **17**:81
CARRY FALLS RESERVOIR
map (44° 25′N 74° 45′W) **14**:149
CARSAMBA (Turkey)
map (41° 12′N 36° 44′E) **19**:343
CARSELAND (Alberta)
map (50° 51′N 113° 28′W) **1**:256
CARSON (North Dakota)
map (46° 25′N 101° 34′W) **14**:248
CARSON (county in Texas)
map (35° 23′N 101° 20′W) **19**:129
CARSON (Washington)
map (45° 44′N 121° 49′W) **20**:35
CARSON, CHRISTOPHER *see* CARSON, KIT
CARSON, SIR EDWARD **4**:169–170
CARSON, JOHNNY **4**:170 *bibliog.*
radio and television broadcasting **16**:59 *illus.*
CARSON, KIT **4**:170 *bibliog., illus.*
Carson City **4**:170
Navajo **14**:53
CARSON, PIRIE, SCOTT STORE **2**:136 *illus.*
CARSON, RACHEL **4**:170 *bibliog.*
DDT **6**:58
Silent Spring **17**:303–304
CARSON CITY (Michigan)
map (43° 11′N 84° 51′W) **13**:377
CARSON CITY (Nevada) **4**:170
map (39° 10′N 119° 46′W) **14**:111
CARSON LAKE
map (39° 19′N 118° 43′W) **14**:111
CARSON RIVER
map (39° 45′N 118° 40′W) **14**:111
CART
coach and carriage **5**:73–74 *illus.*
Sicilian donkey cart **8**:196 *illus.*
CARTAGENA (Colombia) **4**:170; **5**:108 *illus.*; **18**:92 *illus.*
map (10° 25′N 75° 32′W) **5**:107
CARTAGENA (Spain) **4**:170
map (37° 36′N 0° 59′W) **18**:140
CARTE, RICHARD D'OYLY *see* D'OYLY CARTE, RICHARD
CARTE DE VISITE **4**:171
Disdéri, André Adolphe Eugène **6**:190
CARTE DU CIEL
astronomical catalogs and atlases **2**:276
Paris Observatory **15**:88
CARTEL **4**:171
monopoly and competition **13**:540
zaibatsu **20**:348
CARTER (county in Kentucky)
map (38° 20′N 83° 3′W) **12**:47
CARTER (county in Missouri)
map (36° 55′N 91° 0′W) **13**:476
CARTER (county in Montana)
map (45° 25′N 104° 30′W) **13**:547
CARTER (Oklahoma)
map (35° 13′N 99° 30′W) **14**:368
CARTER (county in Oklahoma)
map (34° 15′N 97° 15′W) **14**:368
CARTER (county in Tennessee)
map (36° 17′N 82° 10′W) **19**:104
CARTER, ANGELA **4**:171
CARTER, DON **4**:171
CARTER, ELLIOTT **4**:171 *bibliog.*
CARTER, HOWARD **2**:123 *illus.*; **4**:171 *bibliog.*
Tutankhamen, King of Egypt **19**:355
CARTER, JAMES G.
secondary education **17**:179
CARTER, JIMMY **4**:171–172 *bibliog., illus.*
breeder reactor **3**:472
Egypt **7**:80
human rights **10**:298
Iranian hostage crisis **11**:253–254
Mondale, Walter F. **13**:522
Panama Canal Zone **15**:57
Reagan, Ronald **16**:101
United States, history of the **19**:461
CARTER, LIN **4**:173
CARTER, NICK **4**:173
CARTER DOME MOUNTAIN
map (44° 16′N 71° 12′W) **14**:123
CARTER v. CARTER COAL COMPANY **4**:173
CARTERET (county in North Carolina)
map (35° 0′N 76° 25′W) **14**:242
CARTERET, SIR GEORGE
New Jersey **14**:133
CARTERET, JOHN, 1ST EARL OF GRANVILLE **4**:173 *bibliog.*
CARTERET, PHILIP (colonial governor) **4**:173
New Ireland **14**:127
CARTERS LAKE
map (34° 35′N 84° 35′W) **9**:114
CARTERSVILLE (Georgia)
map (34° 10′N 84° 48′W) **9**:114
CARTERVILLE (Illinois)
map (37° 46′N 89° 5′W) **11**:42
CARTESIAN COORDINATES
coordinate systems (mathematics) **5**:246–247
tangent **19**:22
CARTESIANISM *see* DESCARTES, RENÉ
CARTHAGE (ancient city-state) **4**:173–174 *bibliog., illus., map*
Hamilcar Barca **10**:27
Hannibal **10**:38
Hasdrubal **10**:66
Iol **11**:239
Punic Wars **15**:624–625
Rome, ancient **16**:298
Sicily (Italy) **17**:293
Spain, history of **18**:144
Syracuse (Sicily) **18**:410–411
CARTHAGE (Arkansas)
map (34° 4′N 92° 33′W) **2**:166
CARTHAGE (Illinois)
map (40° 25′N 91° 8′W) **11**:42
CARTHAGE (Indiana)
map (39° 44′N 85° 34′W) **11**:111
CARTHAGE (Mississippi)
map (32° 46′N 89° 32′W) **13**:469
CARTHAGE (Missouri)
map (37° 11′N 94° 19′W) **13**:476
CARTHAGE (New York)
map (43° 59′N 75° 37′W) **14**:149
CARTHAGE (North Carolina)
map (35° 21′N 79° 25′W) **14**:242
CARTHAGE (South Dakota)
map (44° 10′N 97° 43′W) **18**:103
CARTHAGE (Tennessee)
map (36° 15′N 85° 57′W) **19**:104
CARTHAGE (Texas)
map (32° 9′N 94° 20′W) **19**:129
CARTHUSIANS **4**:174
hermit **10**:143
monastic art and architecture **13**:519–520
CARTIER, SIR GEORGE ETIENNE **4**:174 *bibliog.*
CARTIER, JACQUES **4**:174–175 *bibliog., illus.*
Canada, history of **4**:80–81 *map*
exploration **7**:335
landing at Quebec (1542) **4**:80 *map*
Magdalen Islands **13**:46
Prince Edward Island (Canada) **15**:549
Quebec (province in Canada) **16**:20
Saguenay River **17**:12
St. Lawrence, Gulf of **17**:21
St. Lawrence River **17**:21
Saint Pierre and Miquelon (France) **17**:26
scalping **17**:107
CARTIER-BRESSON, HENRI **4**:175 *bibliog., illus.*
photography, history and art of **15**:271 *illus.*
photojournalism **15**:273
CARTILAGE **4**:175
bone **3**:377
collagen **5**:102
connective tissue **5**:196
joint (anatomy) **11**:438; **11**:439
larynx **12**:209
ligament **12**:333
lungs **12**:464
skeletal system **17**:333–334
tissue, animal **19**:210
CARTLAND, BARBARA **4**:175
CARTOGRAPHY *see* MAPS AND MAPMAKING
CARTOON (art) **4**:175–176
animation **2**:28–29
fresco painting **8**:327
Raphael **16**:89
wig **20**:146 *illus.*
CARTOON (comics) *see* COMIC STRIP
CARTOON (editorial and political) **4**:176–178 *bibliog., illus.*
See also COMIC STRIP
Addams, Charles **1**:98
Bull, John (personification) **3**:557
captions **4**:178
caricature **4**:149–150
Democratic party **6**:99 *illus.*; **6**:101 *illus.*
Eastern Question **7**:33 *illus.*
Feiffer, Jules **8**:45
Gillray, James **9**:182
Grandville **9**:286
graphic arts **9**:293
Gropper, William **9**:369
Grosz, George **9**:371
imperialism **11**:62 *illus.*
Nast, Thomas **14**:25–26
New Yorker, The **14**:156
Philipon, Charles **15**:235
Posada, José Guadalupe **15**:457–458
presidential elections **15**:530 *illus.*
Pulitzer Prize **15**:619
Goldberg, Rube **9**:231
Herblock **10**:136
McCutcheon, John T. **13**:11
Mauldin, Bill **13**:233
Oliphant, Patrick **14**:378
Trudeau, Garry **19**:316
Republican party **16**:173 *illus.*
Searle, Ronald **17**:175
Steinberg, Saul **18**:248
style of drawings **4**:177–178
subject content **4**:176–177
Tenniel, Sir John **19**:108
Thurber, James **19**:186
Uncle Sam **19**:381–382 *illus.*
vice-president of the United States **19**:569–570 *illus.*
Villon, Jacques **19**:599
CARTOON, ANIMATED *see* ANIMATION
CARTOONISTS *see* CARTOON; names of specific cartoonists, e.g., MAULDIN, BILL; OLIPHANT, PATRICK; etc.
CARTRIDGE (explosive device)
ammunition **1**:373–375 *illus.*
CARTWRIGHT (Newfoundland)
map (53° 42′N 57° 1′W) **14**:166
CARTWRIGHT, EDMUND **4**:178 *bibliog.*

CARTWRIGHT, PETER 4:178
CARTWRIGHT, SIR RICHARD JOHN 4:178
CARUARU (Brazil)
  map (8° 17′S 35° 58′W) 3:460
CARUCCI DA PONTORMO, JACOPO *see* PONTORMO, JACOPO CARUCCI DA
CARÚPANO (Venezuela)
  map (10° 40′N 63° 14′W) 19:542
CARUSO, ENRICO 4:178 *bibliog.*
CARUTHERSVILLE (Missouri)
  map (36° 11′N 89° 39′W) 13:476
CARVALHO, PEDRO ALEXANDRINO DE
  Portuguese art and architecture 15:456
CARVALHO E MELO, SEBASTIÃO JOSÉ DE, MARQUÊS DE POMBAL *see* POMBAL, SEBASTIÃO JOSÉ DE CARVALHO E MELO, MARQUÊS DE
CARVER (county in Minnesota)
  map (44° 47′N 93° 50′W) 13:453
CARVER, GEORGE WASHINGTON 3:308 *illus.*; 4:178–179 *bibliog., illus.*
  agriculture, history of 1:192
  peanut 15:125
CARVER, JOHN 4:179
  Mayflower (ship) 13:247
CARVER, JONATHAN 4:179
CARVOEIRA, CAPE OF
  map (39° 21′N 9° 24′W) 15:449
CARY (Illinois)
  map (42° 13′N 88° 15′W) 11:42
CARY (North Carolina)
  map (35° 47′N 78° 46′W) 14:242
CARY, ALICE AND PHOEBE 4:179
CARY, JOYCE 4:179 *bibliog.*
CARYATID 4:179
CARYVILLE (Florida)
  map (30° 46′N 85° 49′W) 8:172
CASA GRANDE (Arizona)
  map (32° 53′N 111° 45′W) 2:160
CASA GRANDE NATIONAL MONUMENT
  Hohokam culture 10:199
CASA MILÁ 9:59 *illus.*; 18:155 *illus.*
CASABA *see* MELON
CASABLANCA (Morocco) 4:179–180 *illus.*; 13:586 *illus.*
  climate 13:584 *table*
  map (33° 39′N 7° 35′W) 13:585
CASABLANCA CONFERENCE 4:180
  World War II 20:262–263
CASADESUS, ROBERT 4:180
CASALS, PABLO 4:180 *bibliog.*
  folk dance 8:199
  Puerto Rico 15:615
CASAMANCE RIVER
  map (12° 33′N 16° 46′W) 17:202
CASANOVA DE SEINGALT, GIOVANNI GIACOMO 4:180 *bibliog.*
CASAS, BARTOLOMÉ DE LAS *see* LAS CASAS, BARTOLOMÉ DE
CASAS ADOBES (Arizona)
  map (32° 19′N 110° 59′W) 2:160
CASAZZA, GIULIO GATTI- *see* GATTI-CASAZZA, GIULIO
CASBAH 4:180
CASCABEL 17:377 *illus.*
CASCADE (Idaho)
  map (44° 31′N 116° 2′W) 11:26
CASCADE (Iowa)
  map (42° 18′N 91° 1′W) 11:244
CASCADE (Montana)
  map (47° 16′N 111° 42′W) 13:547
CASCADE (county in Montana)
  map (47° 15′N 111° 15′W) 13:547
CASCADE RANGE 4:180 *bibliog.*
  California 4:30
  Hood, Mount 10:225
  Lassen Peak 12:214
  map (45° 0′N 121° 30′W) 19:419
  national parks 14:38–39 *map, table*
  Oregon 14:428–429 *illus.*
  Rainier, Mount 16:78
  Ring of Fire 16:225
  Shasta, Mount 17:244
CASCADE RESERVOIR
  map (44° 35′N 116° 6′W) 11:26
CASCARA SAGRADA 4:180
CASCARILLA BARK
  croton 5:363
CASCIA, GIOVANNI DA
  madrigal 13:45
CASCO BAY
  map (43° 40′N 70° 0′W) 13:70
CASCUMPEC BAY
  map (46° 45′N 64° 3′W) 15:548
CASE (COMPUTER-AIDED SOFTWARE ENGINEERING)
  computer programming 5:164
A CASE OF NEED (book)
  Crichton, Michael 5:343
CASE WESTERN RESERVE UNIVERSITY 4:180
CASEIN 4:181
  painting techniques 15:24
CASELLA, ALFREDO
  Italian music 11:319
CASEMENT, SIR ROGER 4:181 *bibliog.*
CASERTA (Italy)
  map (41° 4′N 14° 20′E) 11:321
CASERTA PALACE
  Vanvitelli, Luigi 19:521
CASEVILLE (Michigan)
  map (43° 56′N 83° 16′W) 13:377
CASEWORK
  social work 18:18–19
CASEY (Illinois)
  map (39° 18′N 87° 59′W) 11:42
CASEY (Iowa)
  map (41° 31′N 94° 32′W) 11:244
CASEY (county in Kentucky)
  map (37° 20′N 84° 55′W) 12:47
CASEY, WILLIAM J.
  Central Intelligence Agency 3:254
CASH, JOHNNY 4:181 *bibliog.*; 5:313 *illus.*
CASH REGISTER
  adding machine 1:99–100
  Kettering, Charles Franklin 12:61
CASHEW 4:181 *illus.*
  mango 13:115
  smoketree 17:373
CASHIERS (North Carolina)
  map (35° 6′N 83° 6′W) 14:242
CASHMERE 4:181
  fiber, textile 8:67 *illus.*
CASHMERE (Washington)
  map (47° 31′N 120° 28′W) 20:35
CASHTON (Wisconsin)
  map (43° 43′N 90° 47′W) 20:185
CASILDA (Argentina)
  map (33° 3′S 61° 10′W) 2:149
CASIMIR, H. B. G.
  two-fluid model
    superconductivity 18:350
CASIMIR, JOHN *see* JOHN II, KING OF POLAND (John Casimir)
CASIMIR III, KING OF POLAND (Casimir the Great) 4:181
  Piast (dynasty) 15:289
CASIMIR IV, KING OF POLAND 4:181
CASINO (card game) 4:181–182
CASINO (gambling house)
  dice games 6:155
  Las Vegas (Nevada) 12:210
  Monte Carlo (Monaco) 13:552
  roulette 16:324
  solitaire (card game) 18:56
CASIQUIARE RIVER
  map (2° 1′N 67° 7′W) 19:542
CASLON, WILLIAM 4:182 *bibliog.*
  typeface 19:364
CASMA (Peru)
  map (9° 28′S 78° 19′W) 15:193
CASO, ALFONSO 4:182
  Mixtec 13:486
CASONA, ALEJANDRO
  Spanish literature 18:160
CASPER (Wyoming) 4:182
  map (42° 51′N 106° 19′W) 20:301
CASPER, BILLY 4:182 *bibliog.*
CASPIAN DEPRESSION
  map (48° 0′N 52° 0′E) 19:388
CASPIAN SEA 4:182 *map*
  map (42° 0′N 50° 30′E) 19:388
CASS (county in Illinois)
  map (39° 57′N 90° 13′W) 11:42
CASS (county in Indiana)
  map (40° 45′N 86° 21′W) 11:111
CASS (county in Iowa)
  map (41° 17′N 94° 53′W) 11:244
CASS (county in Michigan)
  map (41° 55′N 86° 1′W) 13:377
CASS (county in Minnesota)
  map (47° 0′N 94° 15′W) 13:453
CASS (county in Missouri)
  map (38° 40′N 94° 20′W) 13:476
CASS (county in Nebraska)
  map (40° 55′N 96° 10′W) 14:70
CASS (county in North Dakota)
  map (46° 55′N 97° 15′W) 14:248
CASS (county in Texas)
  map (33° 5′N 94° 20′W) 19:129
CASS, LEWIS 4:182 *bibliog.*
  popular sovereignty 15:433
CASS CITY (Michigan)
  map (43° 36′N 83° 10′W) 13:377
CASS LAKE (Minnesota)
  map (47° 23′N 94° 36′W) 13:453
CASS RIVER
  map (43° 23′N 83° 59′W) 13:377
CASSABANANA 4:183
CASSAI RIVER
  map (3° 2′S 16° 57′E) 2:5
CASSANDER, KING OF MACEDONIA 4:183
CASSANDRA 4:183
CASSATT, MARY 4:183 *bibliog., illus.*
  The Box at the Opera 11:66 *illus.*
  impressionism (art) 11:68
  Young Woman Sewing in the Garden 1:335 *illus.*; 4:183 *illus.*
CASSAVA *see* MANIOC
CASSEGRAINIAN TELESCOPE 4:183–184 *illus.*
CASSELBERRY (Florida)
  map (28° 41′N 81° 20′W) 8:172
CASSELMAN (Ontario)
  map (45° 19′N 75° 5′W) 14:393; 14:461
CASSELTON (North Dakota)
  map (46° 54′N 97° 13′W) 14:248
CASSETTE RECORDER
  tape recorder 19:30
CASSIA *see* CINNAMON
CASSIA (county in Idaho)
  map (42° 20′N 113° 40′W) 11:26
CASSIAN, SAINT JOHN 4:184 *bibliog.*
CASSIAR (British Columbia)
  map (59° 16′N 129° 40′W) 3:491
CASSIAR MOUNTAINS
  map (59° 0′N 129° 0′W) 3:491
CASSIDY, BUTCH
  outlaws 14:468–469 *illus.*
CASSILL, R. V. 4:184
CASSINI (family) 4:184
  maps and mapmaking 13:139
  Rømer, Ole 16:305
CASSINI, GIOVANNI DOMENICO
  ballistics 3:49
  Cassini (family) 4:184
CASSINI, JACQUES
  Cassini (family) 4:184
CASSINI DE THURY, CÉSAR FRANÇOIS
  Cassini (family) 4:184
CASSINO (Italy) 4:184
CASSIODORUS 4:184
CASSIOPEIA (astronomy) 4:184
CASSIOPEIA (mythology)
  Andromeda (mythology) 1:409
CASSIRER, ERNST 4:184–185 *bibliog.*
  state (in political philosophy) 18:232
CASSITERITE *see* OXIDE MINERALS
CASSITES *see* KASSITES
CASSIUS LONGINUS, GAIUS 4:185 *bibliog.*
CASSOPOLIS (Michigan)
  map (41° 55′N 86° 1′W) 13:377
CASSOWARY 3:280 *illus.*; 4:185 *illus.*
CASSVILLE (Missouri)
  map (36° 41′N 93° 52′W) 13:476
CASSVILLE (Wisconsin)
  map (42° 43′N 90° 59′W) 20:185
CAST, FOSSIL *see* FOSSIL RECORD
CAST-IRON ARCHITECTURE 4:185–186 *bibliog., illus.*
  American art and architecture 1:328–329
  architecture 2:136
  Bogardus, James 3:359
  Crystal Palace 5:376
  Guimard, Hector 9:396
  Horta, Victor 10:254
  Labrouste, Henri 12:157
  Paxton, Sir Joseph 15:121
CAST-IRON PLANT *see* ASPIDISTRA
CASTAING, R.
  mineral 13:439
CASTAÑEDA, ALONSO PÉREZ DE
  Cathedral (Mexico City) 12:224 *illus.*
CASTANEDA, CARLOS 4:186 *bibliog.*
CASTANETS 4:186
CASTE 4:186–187 *bibliog., illus.*
  India 4:186–187 *illus.*; 11:84
    Badaga 3:18
    Brahmin 3:440
    cosmetics 5:281
    Hinduism 10:169
    India, history of 11:89
    Maratha 13:143
    Rajput 16:78
    Tamil 19:19
    Untouchables 19:470–471
    women in society 20:203
  Indonesia
    Balinese 3:37
  scheduled castes *see* UNTOUCHABLES
  social structure and organization 18:16
  Sri Lanka 18:205
    Sinhalese 17:323
CASTEL, CHARLES IRÉNÉE, ABBÉ DE SAINT-PIERRE *see* SAINT-PIERRE, CHARLES IRÉNÉE CASTEL, ABBÉ DE
CASTEL SANT'ANGELO 4:187 *bibliog.*
CASTELLACCIO MOUNTAIN
  map (43° 54′N 12° 27′E) 17:56
CASTELLO-BRANCO, CAMILLO 4:187
CASTELLON (Spain) CAVE PAINTING 15:509 *illus.*
CASTELLÓN DE LA PLANA (Spain)
  map (39° 59′N 0° 2′W) 18:140
CASTELNUOVO-TEDESCO, MARIO 4:187 *bibliog.*
CASTELO BRANCO (Portugal)
  map (39° 49′N 7° 30′W) 15:449
CASTELVETRO, LODOVICO 4:187–188
CASTIGLIONE, BALDASSARE, CONTE 4:188 *bibliog.*; 16:89 *illus.*
  portrait (Raphael) 15:447
CASTILE (Spain) 4:188
  cities
    Burgos 3:570
    Cuenca 5:382
    Madrid 13:43–45; 13:44
    Toledo 19:226
  history
    Alfonso VI, King 1:279
    Alfonso X, King 1:279
    Charles V, Holy Roman Emperor 4:294–295
    Ferdinand I, King of Portugal 8:53
    Ferdinand II, King of Aragon 8:52
    Ferdinand III, Spanish King of Castile 8:53
    Isabella I, Queen (Isabella the Catholic) 11:285–286
    Joan the Mad, Queen of Castile 11:420
    Peter I, King (Peter the Cruel) 15:200
    Philip I, King (Philip the Handsome) 15:234
    Portugal, history of 15:453
    Sancho III, King of Navarre (Sancho the Great) 17:58
    Spain, history of 18:145–146 *maps*
CASTILIAN SPANISH
  Romance languages 16:281
CASTILLA (Peru)
  map (5° 12′S 80° 38′W) 15:193
CASTILLA, RAMÓN 4:188 *bibliog.*
  Peru 15:194
CASTILLO, MOUNT
  map (43° 3′S 71° 57′W) 2:149
CASTILLO DE SANTA BARBARA (Spain) 18:139 *illus.*
CASTINE (Maine)
  map (44° 23′N 68° 48′W) 13:70
CASTING 4:188–189 *bibliog., illus.*
  alloy, lost-wax process 12:418–419 *illus.*
  ceramics 4:257
  continuous casting 4:189 *illus.*; 11:277 *illus.*
  foundry 8:251
  metallurgy 13:330
  sand casting 4:188 *illus.*
CASTLE 4:189–191 *bibliog., illus.*
  See also names of specific castles, e.g., LOUIS II'S BAVARIAN PALACES; WINDSOR CASTLE; etc.
  château 4:302
  Edinburgh (Scotland) 7:57 *illus.*
  English art and architecture 7:182–183
  fortification 8:239–240 *illus.*
  interior design 11:211–212
CASTLE, THE (book) 4:191 *bibliog.*
  Kafka, Franz 12:5–6
CASTLE, VERNON AND IRENE 4:191
CASTLE, WILLIAM E.
  population genetics 15:439
CASTLE DALE (Utah)
  map (39° 13′N 111° 1′W) 19:492
CASTLE HARBOR
  map (32° 21′N 64° 40′W) 3:219
CASTLE HOWARD
  Vanbrugh, Sir John 19:516–517
CASTLE MOUNTAIN
  map (64° 32′N 135° 25′W) 20:345
CASTLE OF OTRANTO, THE (book) 4:191 *bibliog.*
  Walpole, Horace, 4th Earl of Orford 20:18
CASTLE PEAK
  map (39° 0′N 106° 55′W) 5:116
CASTLE ROCK (Colorado)
  map (39° 22′N 104° 51′W) 5:116
CASTLE ROCK BUTTE
  map (45° 0′N 103° 27′W) 18:103

CASTLE OF THE NYMPHS *see* NYMPHENBURG PALACE
CASTLEBAR (Ireland)
map (53° 52′N 9° 17′W) **11**:258
CASTLEBERRY (Alabama)
map (31° 17′N 87° 2′W) **1**:234
CASTLEGAR (British Columbia)
map (49° 19′N 117° 40′W) 3:491
CASTLEREAGH, ROBERT STEWART, VISCOUNT **4**:191 *bibliog., illus.*
Canning, George **4**:111
Vienna, Congress of **19**:579
CASTLETON (Vermont)
map (43° 37′N 73° 11′W) **19**:554
CASTNER-KELLNER PROCESS **4**:191
CASTOR (Alberta)
map (52° 13′N 111° 53′W) **1**:256
CASTOR (astronomy) *see* STAR
CASTOR OIL **4**:191
CASTOR AND POLLUX **4**:191
CASTRATION **4**:192
castration complex (psychology) **5**:157
castrato **4**:192
sex change **17**:225
sex hormones **17**:226
CASTRATO **4**:192 *bibliog.*
bel canto **3**:173
CASTRO (Chile)
map (42° 29′S 73° 46′W) **4**:355
CASTRO (county in Texas)
map (34° 30′N 102° 15′W) **19**:129
CASTRO, CIPRIANO **4**:192 *bibliog.*
Gómez, Juan Vicente **9**:241
CASTRO, FIDEL **4**:192–193 *bibliog., illus.*; **9**:392 *illus.*; **16**:188 *illus.*
Central Intelligence Agency **4**:254
communism **5**:150
Cuba **5**:380
Guevara, Che **9**:392
Santiago de Cuba (Cuba) **17**:70
CASTRO, JOSÉ
Mexican War **13**:355
CASTRO VALLEY (California)
map (37° 42′N 122° 4′W) **4**:31
CASTRO Y BELLVÍS, GUILLÉN DE **4**:193 *bibliog.*
CASTROVILLE (California)
map (36° 46′N 121° 45′W) **4**:31
CASUALTY INSURANCE *see* LIABILITY INSURANCE
CASUARINA **4**:193 *illus.*
CASUISTRY **4**:193
CASWELL (county in North Carolina)
map (36° 25′N 79° 20′W) **14**:242
CASWELL, RICHARD
North Carolina **14**:246
CAT **4**:193–196 *bibliog., illus.*
anatomy and physiology **4**:194 *illus.*
brain **3**:443 *illus.*
claws **4**:194 *illus.*
genetics **4**:196
senses **4**:194; **4**:196
sex chromosomes **9**:88 *illus.*
breeding habits **4**:194
breeds **4**:196
Abyssinian **1**:67
American shorthair **1**:366–367
Angora **2**:6
Balinese **3**:37–38 *illus.*
Burmese **3**:576
colorpoint shorthair **5**:122
exotic shorthair **7**:333
Havana brown **10**:71
Himalayan **10**:165–166
Japanese bobtail **11**:379
korat **12**:110–111
longhaired cats **12**:407–408
Maine coon **13**:75 *illus.*
Maltese **4**:195 *illus.*
Manx **13**:134
Russian Blue **16**:364
shorthaired cats **17**:284
Siamese **17**:290
diseases
distemper **6**:200
leukemia **12**:301
parasitic **15**:82
toxoplasmosis **19**:256
distribution **4**:193–194
Egypt, ancient
Bubastis **3**:530–531
health **4**:194
history **4**:193
intelligence **4**:196
phobia **15**:248
scavenger function **4**:194
CAT (COMPUTERIZED AXIAL TOMOGRAPHY) SCANNING
brain **3**:448
examination, medical **7**:326
radiology **16**:64–65 *illus.*
CAT ON A HOT TIN ROOF (play) **4**:197 *bibliog.*
Williams, Tennessee **20**:160–161
CAT FAMILY **4**:196 *bibliog., illus.*
bobcat **3**:352
caracal **4**:129
cat **4**:193
cheetah **4**:309
jaguar **11**:348
jaguarundi **11**:349
Kaffir cat **12**:5
leopard **12**:292–293
lion **12**:360
lynx **12**:477
nomenclature
Linnaeus, Carolus **12**:359
ocelot **14**:346
Pallas's cat **15**:48
puma **15**:621–622
saber-toothed cats **17**:5
serval **17**:210–211
tiger **19**:197
wildcat **20**:148
CAT FEVER *see* DISTEMPER
CAT ISLAND (Bahamas)
map (24° 27′N 75° 30′W) **3**:23
CAT ISLAND (Mississippi)
map (30° 13′N 89° 6′W) **13**:469
CAT WHO WENT TO HEAVEN, THE (book)
Coatsworth, Elizabeth **5**:82
CATABOLISM *see* METABOLISM
CATACOCHA (Ecuador)
map (4° 4′S 79° 38′W) **7**:52
CATACOMB OF PRISCILLA (Rome) **7**:9 *illus.*
CATACOMBS **4**:197 *bibliog., illus.*
CATADIOPTRIC TELESCOPE
Schmidt telescope **17**:128
telescope **19**:80
CATAHOULA (county in Louisiana)
map (31° 47′N 91° 47′W) **12**:430
CATAHOULA LAKE
map (31° 30′N 92° 6′W) **12**:430
ÇATAL HÜYÜK (Turkey) **4**:197–198 *bibliog.*
mother goddess **13**:607
temple **19**:94
CATALAN ART *see* SPANISH ART AND ARCHITECTURE
CATALAN LANGUAGE
Romance languages **16**:280
CATALAN LITERATURE **4**:198 *bibliog.*
Lull, Raymond **12**:454
CATALANS
Spain **18**:142
CATALEPSY
catatonia **4**:201
CATALOG (library)
library **12**:315 *illus.*
CATALOG (retailing) *see* MAIL-ORDER BUSINESS
CATALONIA (Spain) **4**:198 *bibliog.*; **15**:637 *illus.*
cities
Barcelona **3**:79–80 *illus.*
Tarragona **19**:39
CATALPA **4**:198 *illus.*
CATALUFA *see* BIGEYE
CATALUÑA *see* CATALONIA (Spain)
CATALYST **4**:198–199 *bibliog.*
chemical equilibrium and kinetics **4**:316
enzyme **7**:213
inhibitor **11**:178
nickel **14**:183
Ostwald, Wilhelm **14**:459
platinum **15**:360
potassium **15**:465
reaction, chemical **16**:99
Sabatier, Paul **17**:4
synergism **18**:407
CATALYTIC CONVERTER **4**:199 *bibliog., illus.*
exhaust system **7**:331–332
gasoline **9**:55
platinum **15**:360
pollution control **15**:416
CATALYTIC CRACKING
gasoline **9**:55
petroleum **15**:207–209
CATAMARAN **4**:199–200 *illus.*
CATAMARCA (Argentina)
map (28° 28′S 65° 47′W) **2**:149
CATAMARCA (province in Argentina)
map (27° 0′S 67° 0′W) **2**:149
CATAMAYO (Ecuador)
map (3° 59′S 79° 21′W) **7**:52
CATANDUANES ISLAND
map (13° 45′N 124° 15′E) **15**:237
CATANIA (Italy) **4**:200
map (37° 30′N 15° 6′E) **11**:321
CATANZARO (Italy)
map (38° 54′N 16° 36′E) **11**:321
CATAPULT **4**:200 *illus.*
Archimedes **2**:128
fortification **8**:238; **8**:239 *illus.*
CATARACT **4**:200 *bibliog.*
blindness **3**:332–333
radiation injury **16**:42
surgery (16th century) **18**:360 *illus.*
CATARAMA (Ecuador)
map (1° 35′S 79° 28′W) **7**:52
CATASTROPHE (literature)
narrative and dramatic devices **14**:22
CATASTROPHE THEORY **4**:200 *bibliog., illus.*
Thom, René **19**:172
CATASTROPHISM (anatomy)
Cuvier, Georges, Baron **5**:399
CATASTROPHISM (geology) **4**:201 *bibliog., illus.*
Conybeare, W. D. **5**:234
Hutton, James **10**:323–324
Lyell, Sir Charles **12**:474
uniformitarianism **19**:386
CATATONIA **4**:201 *bibliog.*
CATAWBA (American Indians) **4**:201 *bibliog.*
CATAWBA (county in North Carolina)
map (35° 40′N 81° 15′W) **14**:242
CATBIRD **4**:201–202 *illus.*
CATCH-ME-WHO-CAN (locomotive) **19**:279 *illus.*
CATCH-22 (book) **4**:202 *bibliog.*
Heller, Joseph **10**:114–115
CATCHER IN THE RYE, THE (book) **4**:202 *bibliog.*
Salinger, J. D. **17**:32
CATEAU, LE (France)
World War I **20**:223
CATEAU-CAMBRÉSIS, TREATY OF **4**:202
Italian Wars **11**:320
Savoy (dynasty) **17**:102
CATECHISM **4**:202
CATECHU **4**:202
CATEGORICAL GRANTS
finance, state and local **8**:92
CATEGORICAL IMPERATIVE **4**:202
ethics **7**:251
Kant, Immanuel **12**:24
CATEGORY (mathematics) **4**:202 *bibliog.*
CATENARY **4**:202
hyperbolic functions **10**:348
CATERPILLAR **4**:202–203 *illus.*
anatomy **3**:594–595 *illus.*
animal communication **2**:19 *illus.*
butterflies and moths **3**:594–595
cutworm **5**:398
gypsy moth **9**:416 *illus.*
inchworm **11**:74
Lepidoptera **12**:295
metamorphosis **13**:333
Mexican jumping bean **13**:351
silkworm **17**:308
tent caterpillar **19**:113
CATFISH **4**:203 *bibliog., illus.*; **8**:117 *illus.*
bullhead **3**:560–561; **12**:168 *illus.*
coloration, biological **5**:122
fish farming **8**:121
upside-down catfish **4**:203
CATGUT **4**:203
CATHARI *see* ALBIGENSES (Cathari)
CATHARSIS (literature)
narrative and dramatic devices **14**:22
CATHARTIC **4**:204
cascara sagrada **4**:180
castor oil **4**:191
gamboge **9**:26–27
headache **10**:86
senna **17**:203
CATHAY **4**:204
CATHEDRAL OF NOTRE DAME (Paris) *see* NOTRE DAME DE PARIS (cathedral)
CATHEDRALS AND CHURCHES **4**:204–208 *bibliog., illus.*
See also names of specific cathedrals and churches, e.g., AMIENS CATHEDRAL; CHARTRES CATHEDRAL; etc.
abbey **1**:52
altar **1**:311
apse **2**:92
architecture **2**:133–135 *illus.*
baptistery **3**:73 *map*
baroque art and architecture **3**:88–91 *illus.*; **4**:207–208
basilica **3**:109–110
buttress **3**:600–601
Byzantine art and architecture **3**:604; **4**:205
Carolingian art and architecture **4**:160–161
chapel **4**:284
choir stall **8**:375 *illus.*
clerestory **5**:51
cloister **5**:64
Coptic art and architecture **5**:255
crypt **5**:371
dome **6**:229–230
Early Christian art and architecture **4**:204–205; **7**:9–11
early medieval **4**:205
English art and architecture **7**:181–185
Flamboyant Gothic style **8**:150
Flemish art and architecture **8**:162
Florence (Italy) **8**:168 *illus.*
font **8**:205
French art and architecture **8**:303–306
furniture **8**:375
Goodhue, Bertram Grosvenor **9**:246
Gothic art and architecture **4**:205–206; **9**:255–262
Gothic Revival **9**:262–263
ironwork, ornamental **11**:279
Italian art and architecture **11**:308–310
Latin American art and architecture **12**:223–226
in medieval cities **5**:3
Merovingian art and architecture **13**:311
misericord **13**:466
modern (19th and 20th centuries) **4**:208
monastic art and architecture **13**:517–521
Moorish art and architecture **13**:571
nave **14**:58
neoclassical **4**:208
Norman architecture **14**:219–220
Ottonian art and architecture **14**:466–467
Portuguese art and architecture **15**:455–456
Renaissance **4**:206–207
rococo style **4**:207–208; **16**:264 *illus.*
Romanesque art and architecture **4**:205; **16**:282–286 *illus.*
rose window **16**:314
Russian art and architecture **16**:361–362
Scandinavian art and architecture **17**:111–112
Spanish art and architecture **18**:152
stained glass **18**:211–213
technology, history of **19**:64–65 *illus.*
tomb **19**:231
transept **19**:269
triforium **19**:297
CATHER, WILLA **4**:208–209 *bibliog., illus.*
My Ántonia **13**:688–689
CATHERINE, LAKE
map (34° 30′N 93° 0′W) **2**:166
CATHERINE OF ALEXANDRIA, SAINT **4**:209
CATHERINE OF ARAGON **4**:209 *bibliog.*
Cromwell, Thomas, 1st Earl of Essex **5**:358
Henry VIII, King of England **10**:126
Peterborough (England) **15**:202
CATHERINE DE MÉDICIS **4**:209 *bibliog., illus.*
ballet **3**:42 *illus.*
Francis II, King of France **8**:276
French cooking **5**:239
Henry II, King of France **10**:127
Henry III, King of France **10**:127
Saint Bartholomew's Day Massacre **17**:16
tomb **19**:231
CATHERINE THE GREAT *see* CATHERINE II, EMPRESS OF RUSSIA (Catherine the Great)
CATHERINE I, EMPRESS OF RUSSIA **4**:209
Menshikov, Aleksandr Danilovich, Prince **13**:300
Peter I, Emperor of Russia **15**:200–201
CATHERINE II, EMPRESS OF RUSSIA (Catherine the Great) **4**:209–210 *bibliog., illus.*
art
Hermitage Museum **10**:143
National Gallery of Art **14**:33
Cameron Charles **4**:59
meeting with Joseph II of Austria **16**:355 *illus.*
Orlov (family) **14**:446–447
Panin, Nikita Ivanovich, Count **15**:59
Paul I, Emperor of Russia **15**:118

CATHERINE II, EMPRESS OF RUSSIA (cont.)
Potemkin, Grigory Aleksandrovich **15**:466
Pugachev, Yemelian Ivanovich **15**:617
Romanov (dynasty) **16**:290
Russo-Turkish Wars **16**:374
Stanisław II, King of Poland **18**:219
CATHERINE OF SIENA, SAINT **4**:209 *bibliog.*
CATHERINE OF VALOIS
Henry V, King of England **10**:125–126
Tudor (dynasty) **19**:328
CATHERWOOD, FREDERICK **4**:210 *bibliog.*
Stephens, John Lloyd **18**:255
CATHLAMET (Washington)
map (46° 12′N 122° 23′W) **20**:35
CATHODE **4**:210–211
battery **3**:125–126 *illus.*
electrode **7**:113
electrolysis **7**:114–115
electron tube **7**:122
electroplating **7**:126–127 *illus.*
thermionic emission **19**:161
CATHODE RAY **4**:211
chemistry, history of **4**:327
electron **7**:119–120
Perrin, Jean Baptiste **15**:178
Plücker, Julius **15**:370
Thomson, Sir Joseph John **19**:176
CATHODE-RAY TUBE **4**:211 *illus.*
computer, personal **5**:160i
computer graphics **5**:160m–160n
electron optics **7**:122
electron tube **7**:124
electrostatics **7**:128
europium **7**:309
image processing **11**:51
input-output devices **11**:182
oscilloscope **14**:453
phosphorescence **15**:256
radar **16**:38–39 *illus.*
scanning **17**:114
television **19**:85–87
CATHOLIC **4**:211
CATHOLIC APOSTOLIC CHURCH
Irving, Edward **11**:283
CATHOLIC CHURCH *see* ROMAN CATHOLIC CHURCH
CATHOLIC EMANCIPATION **4**:211 *bibliog.*
George III, King of England, Scotland, and Ireland **9**:111
Gordon Riots **9**:249–250
O'Connell, Daniel **14**:346
Wellington, Arthur Wellesley, 1st Duke of **20**:100
CATHOLIC FOREIGN MISSION SOCIETY OF AMERICA *see* MARYKNOLL MISSIONERS
CATHOLIC LEAGUE OF GERMAN PRINCES
Maximilian, Elector and Duke of Bavaria **13**:239
CATHOLIC LEGION OF DECENCY *see* NATIONAL CATHOLIC OFFICE FOR MOTION PICTURES
CATHOLIC UNIVERSITY OF AMERICA **4**:212
Gibbons, James **9**:173
CATHOLIC UNIVERSITY OF PUERTO RICO **4**:212
Illich, Ivan **11**:40
CATHOLIC WORKER MOVEMENT
Day, Dorothy **6**:55
CATHOLIC YOUTH ORGANIZATION, NATIONAL **4**:212
CATILINE **4**:212 *bibliog.*
Caesar, Gaius Julius **4**:14
Cicero, Marcus Tullius **4**:429
CATION **4**:212
carbonium ion **4**:139
chemical nomenclature **4**:320
qualitative chemical analysis **16**:6–7
salt (chemistry) **17**:37
CATKIN (botany) **4**:212; **15**:408 *illus.*
CATLETTSBURG (Kentucky)
map (38° 25′N 82° 36′W) **12**:47
CATLIN (Illinois)
map (40° 4′N 87° 42′W) **11**:42
CATLIN, GEORGE **4**:212 *bibliog., illus.*
Buffalo Chase **11**:129 *illus.*
buffalo hunting **11**:119 *illus.*
Chief Keokuk **11**:121 *illus.*
Comanche village **11**:128 *illus.*
Little Spaniard **5**:130 *illus.*
Mah-to-toh-pa (Four Bears) **13**:111 *illus.*
Mandan scalping his enemy **11**:129 *illus.*
Medicine Man **11**:123 *illus.*
Ojibwa snowshoe dance **11**:142 *illus.*
Old Bear, Mandan shaman **17**:238 *illus.*
Scalp Dance **11**:123 *illus.*
Shawnee Prophet **17**:247
Sioux Bear Dance **6**:21 *illus.*
Strong Wind (Ojibwa chief) **14**:364 *illus.*
The Surrounder, Chief **4**:212 *illus.*
CATNIP (botany) **4**:212
CATO, MARCUS PORCIUS (Cato the Elder) **4**:212–213 *bibliog.*
CATO, MARCUS PORCIUS (Cato the Younger) **4**:213 *bibliog.*
CATO, R. MILTON
Saint Vincent and the Grenadines **17**:27
CATO THE CENSOR *see* CATO, MARCUS PORCIUS (Cato the Elder)
CATO OF UTICA *see* CATO, MARCUS PORCIUS (Cato the Younger)
CATON-THOMPSON, GERTRUDE **4**:213
Nalatale **14**:9
Zimbabwe Ruins **20**:367
CATONSVILLE (Maryland)
map (39° 16′N 76° 44′W) **13**:188
CATOOSA (county in Georgia)
map (34° 55′N 85° 10′W) **9**:114
CATOOSA (Oklahoma)
map (36° 11′N 95° 45′W) **14**:368
CATRIMANI (Brazil)
map (0° 27′N 61° 41′W) **3**:460
CATRON (county in New Mexico)
map (33° 55′N 108° 20′W) **14**:136
CATS, JACOB **4**:213
CAT'S-EYE **4**:213 *illus.*
chrysoberyl **4**:420–421
gems **9**:73–74 *illus.*
quartz **16**:13
CATSKILL (New York)
map (42° 13′N 73° 52′W) **14**:149
CATSKILL MOUNTAINS **4**:213 *bibliog.*
algae **1**:281 *illus.*
map (42° 10′N 74° 30′W) **14**:149
New York (state) **14**:148; **14**:151
CATT, CARRIE CHAPMAN **4**:213 *bibliog.*
suffrage, women's **18**:326
CATTAIL (botany) **4**:214 *illus.*
CATTARAUGUS (New York)
map (42° 20′N 78° 52′W) **14**:149
CATTARAUGUS (county in New York)
map (42° 15′N 78° 40′W) **14**:149
CATTELL, JAMES McKEEN **4**:214 *bibliog.*
psychology, history of **15**:596
CATTERMOLE, GEORGE
The Old Curiosity Shop **14**:274 *illus.*
CATTLE AND CATTLE RAISING **4**:214–217 *bibliog., illus., tables*
anatomy
digestive system **6**:173 *illus.*
embryo **7**:324 *illus.*
teeth **19**:72 *illus.*
animal husbandry **2**:24; **2**:25 *illus.*
artificial insemination **2**:220
breeds **4**:216 *illus.*
beef cattle **4**:215–217 *illus.*
Brahman cattle **3**:440 *illus.*
Brangus cattle **10**:328
buffalo **3**:546 *illus.*
Charolais cattle **4**:299 *illus.*
dairy cattle **4**:215–216 *illus.*
Hereford cattle **12**:20 *illus.*
Holstein-Friesian cattle **4**:216 *illus.*; **6**:7–9 *illus.*; **13**:380 *illus.*
Jersey cattle **4**:216 *illus.*; **6**:7
ox **14**:473 *illus.*
yak **20**:314 *illus.*
zebu cattle **20**:357
dairying **6**:7–10
diseases
cowpox **5**:322
diseases, animal **6**:190
goosefoot **9**:248
mastitis **13**:217
Mycoplasma **13**:690
sneezeweed **18**:3
Dominican Republic **6**:234 *illus.*
factory farming **8**:6
farms and farming **8**:25–27
feedlot **8**:44–45
hybrid **10**:328
manure
dung beetle **6**:300
Masai **13**:194–195
pollutants, chemical **15**:410
products
leather and hides **12**:262–263
meat and meat packing **13**:257–258
milk **13**:423
veal **19**:529
rodeo **16**:266
ruminant **16**:345
savanna life **17**:99
South America **18**:94
Uruguay **19**:489 *illus.*
United States
Chisholm Trail **4**:398
cowboy **5**:321
frontier, U.S. **8**:340–345
Goodnight, Charles **9**:246
Iowa **11**:246 *illus.*
Kansas **12**:20–21 *illus.*
McCoy, Joseph **13**:10
Montana **13**:550 *illus.*
Nebraska **14**:71 *illus.*; **14**:73
Oregon **14**:428 *illus.*
South Dakota **18**:105 *illus.*
Texas **19**:132 *illus.*
Wyoming range wars **20**:304
CATTLE GRUB
botfly **3**:415
CATTLE PLAGUE *see* RINDERPEST
CATTLE RAID OF COOLEY (epic)
Cuchulain **5**:381
CATTON, BRUCE **4**:217 *bibliog.*
CATULLUS **4**:217 *bibliog.*
CATULUS, QUINTUS LUTATIUS **4**:217
CAUCA RIVER
map (8° 54′N 74° 28′W) **5**:107
CAUCASIA **4**:217
Caucasus Mountains **4**:218 *map*
Daghestan **6**:6
rugs and carpets **16**:341–342 *illus.*
folk art **8**:198–199
CAUCASIAN *see* RACE
CAUCASIAN CHALK CIRCLE, THE (play) **4**:217–218 *bibliog.*
Brecht, Bertolt **3**:470
CAUCASIAN LANGUAGES AND LITERATURE **4**:218 *bibliog.*; **12**:355 *map*
Asia **2**:244 *map*
Europe **7**:274 *map*
CAUCASUS MOUNTAINS **4**:218 *illus., map*; **19**:392 *illus., illus.*
Circassians **4**:435
Elbrus, Mount **7**:102
map (43° 30′N 45° 0′E) **4**:218
World War I **20**:231; **20**:234
CAUCHY, AUGUSTIN LOUIS **4**:219 *bibliog.*
mathematics, history of **13**:226
CAUCUS **4**:219
Democratic party **6**:99
CAUDATA (Urodela)
amphibians **1**:378–379 *illus.*
CAUDILLO **4**:219
CAULIFLOWER **4**:219 *illus.*; **19**:532 *illus.*
CAULKING **4**:219
tar, pitch, and asphalt **19**:34
CAUQUENES (Chile)
map (35° 58′S 72° 21′W) **4**:355
CAUSALITY **4**:219 *bibliog.*
Hume, David **10**:301–302
CAUSAPSCAT (Quebec)
map (48° 22′N 67° 14′W) **16**:18
CAUSTIC CHEMICALS **4**:219–220 *bibliog.*
CAUTHEN, STEVE **4**:220 *bibliog., illus.*
CAVAFY, C. P. **4**:220 *bibliog.*
CAVALCANTI, GUIDO **4**:220 *bibliog.*
CAVALEER, CHARLES
North Dakota **14**:251
CAVALIER (North Dakota)
map (48° 48′N 97° 37′W) **14**:248
CAVALIER (county in North Dakota)
map (48° 45′N 98° 30′W) **14**:248
CAVALIER POETS **4**:220 *bibliog.*
Carew, Thomas **4**:146
Herrick, Robert **10**:146
Lovelace, Richard **11**:438
Suckling, Sir John **18**:319
Waller, Edmund **20**:15–16
CAVALIERI, BONAVENTURA **4**:220
mathematics, history of **13**:225
CAVALIERI, EMILIO DE
Italian music **11**:318
CAVALIERS **4**:220
costume **5**:299 *illus.*
shoes **17**:280 *illus.*
English Civil War **7**:189
CAVALLI, PIER FRANCESCO **4**:220 *bibliog.*
CAVALLINI, PIETRO **4**:220–221 *bibliog.*
CAVALLY RIVER
map (4° 22′N 7° 32′W) **12**:313
CAVALRY **4**:221–222 *bibliog., illus.*
battalion **3**:124
Chinese army **4**:371 *illus.*
Cossacks **5**:290
English Civil War **7**:190 *illus.*
hussar **10**:320
Rough riders **16**:324
strategy and tactics, military **18**:290
weapons **20**:74
CAVAN (Ireland) **4**:222
map (54° 0′N 7° 21′W) **11**:258
CAVATELLE **15**:106 *illus.*
CAVAZZONI, MARCO ANTONIO
Renaissance music **16**:156
CAVE **4**:222–224 *bibliog., illus.*; **12**:182 *illus.*
art **4**:222
prehistoric art **15**:507–508 *illus.*
bat **3**:119
Blue Grotto **3**:343
Carlsbad Caverns **4**:151–152
glaciers and glaciation **9**:193 *illus.*
gypsum **9**:415–416
interiors **4**:222
limestone cave **4**:223 *illus.*
Luray Caverns **12**:466
Mammoth Cave **13**:107
niter **14**:201
speleology **18**:177
spelunking **18**:177
stalactite and stalagmite **18**:213
temples
Ajanta **1**:229
Elephanta **7**:134
Ellora **7**:148
Lung-men (Longmen) **12**:462
Tun-huang (Dunhuang) **19**:331
Yün-kang (Yungang) **20**:346
travertine **19**:284
CAVE BEAR *see* BEAR
CAVE BEAR AGE *see* MOUSTERIAN
CAVE CITY (Arkansas)
map (35° 57′N 91° 33′W) **2**:166
CAVE-CREEK (Arizona)
map (33° 50′N 111° 57′W) **2**:160
CAVE DWELLERS **4**:224–225 *bibliog., illus.*
Australopithecus **2**:345–346; **15**:512–513
Basket Makers **1**:393
cave **4**:222
Chou-K'ou-tien (Zhoukoudian) (China) **4**:409–410
cliff dwellers **5**:54–55
Combe Grenal (France) **5**:130
Cro-Magnon man **4**:225; **5**:353–354
Danger Cave (Utah) **6**:31
Meadowcroft Rockshelter (Pennsylvania) **13**:252
Neanderthal caves **4**:224–225
Peking man **15**:136
prehistoric art **15**:506–511
Sandia Cave (New Mexico) **17**:62
Shanidar (Iraq) **17**:240
Tasaday **19**:41
Vallonet Cave (France) **19**:508
CAVE FISH **4**:225; **8**:117 *illus.*
blindfish **3**:332
CAVE IN ROCK (Illinois)
map (37° 29′N 88° 10′W) **11**:42
CAVE RUN LAKE
map (38° 5′N 83° 30′W) **12**:47
CAVE SPRING (Georgia)
map (34° 7′N 85° 20′W) **9**:114
CAVE SPRING (Virginia)
map (37° 14′N 80° 0′W) **19**:607
CAVELIER, ROBERT, SIEUR DE LA SALLE *see* LA SALLE, ROBERT CAVELIER, SIEUR DE
CAVELL, EDITH **4**:225 *bibliog.*
CAVENDISH, HENRY **4**:225–226 *bibliog., illus.*
hydrogen gas **4**:225
water, composition **4**:226
CAVENDISH, THOMAS **4**:226
CAVENDISH LABORATORY **4**:226
CAVERN *see* CAVE
CAVES OF THE THOUSAND BUDDHAS
Tun-huang (Dunhuang) **19**:331
CAVIAR **4**:226
sturgeon **18**:309
CAVITE (Philippines)
map (14° 29′N 120° 55′E) **15**:237
CAVOUR, CAMILLO BENSO, CONTE DI **4**:226 *bibliog., illus.*
Risorgimento **16**:228
Victor Emmanuel II, King of Italy **19**:573
CAVY **4**:226–227 *illus.*
CAWKER CITY (Kansas)
map (39° 30′N 98° 26′W) **12**:18
CAWLEY, EVONNE GOOLAGONG *see* GOOLAGONG, EVONNE
CAXIAS (Brazil)
map (4° 50′S 43° 21′W) **3**:460
CAXIAS DO SUL (Brazil)
map (29° 10′S 51° 11′W) **3**:460
CAXTON, WILLIAM **4**:227 *bibliog.*

book 3:384
effect of printing on English language 7:192
Myrour of the Worlde 12:317 *illus.*
CAYAMBE (Ecuador)
map (0° 3′N 78° 8′W) 7:52
CAYAMBE (volcano)
map (0° 2′N 77° 59′W) 7:52
CAYCE (South Carolina)
map (33° 59′N 81° 4′W) 18:98
CAYENNE (French Guiana) 4:227
climate 8:311 *table*
map (4° 56′N 52° 20′W) 8:311
CAYENNE PEPPER *see* PEPPER (vegetable)
CAYEY (Puerto Rico)
map (18° 7′N 66° 10′W) 15:614
CAYLEY, ARTHUR 4:227 *bibliog.*
mathematics, history of 13:226
non-Euclidean geometry 14:216
CAYMAN ISLANDS 4:227
banking systems 3:69
Georgetown 9:112
map (19° 30′N 80° 40′W) 20:109
CAYO (Belize)
map (17° 10′N 89° 4′W) 3:183
CAYROL, JEAN
Resnais, Alain 16:177
CAYUGA (American Indians) 4:227 *bibliog.*
Iroquois League 11:279–280
Logan, John 12:393
CAYUGA (Indiana)
map (39° 57′N 87° 28′W) 11:111
CAYUGA (county in New York)
map (42° 56′N 76° 34′W) 14:149
CAYUGA HEIGHTS (New York)
map (42° 28′N 76° 30′W) 14:149
CAYUGA LAKE
Finger Lakes 8:93
map (42° 45′N 76° 45′W) 14:149
CAYUSE (American Indians) 4:227 *bibliog.*
Whitman, Marcus 20:140
CAZENOVIA (New York)
map (42° 56′N 75° 51′W) 14:149
CB RADIO *see* CITIZENS BAND RADIO
CBS *see* COLUMBIA BROADCASTING SYSTEM
CCC *see* CIVILIAN CONSERVATION CORPS
CCD *see* CHARGE-COUPLED DEVICE
CCF *see* COOPERATIVE COMMONWEALTH FEDERATION
CD *see* COMPACT DISC
CD-ROM (COMPACT DISC READY-ONLY MEMORY)
compact disc 5:155
computer 5:160h
CEARÁ (Brazil)
map (5° 0′S 40° 0′W) 3:460
CEATHARLACH *see* CARLOW (Ireland)
CEAUSESCU, NICOLAE 4:228
Romania 16:290
CEBALLOS (Mexico)
map (26° 32′N 104° 9′W) 13:357
CEBOLLATI (Uruguay)
map (33° 16′S 53° 47′W) 19:488
CEBU (Philippines) 4:228
map (10° 18′N 123° 54′E) 15:237
CEBU ISLAND 4:228
map (10° 20′N 123° 40′E) 15:237
CECCHETTI, ENRICO
Kirov Ballet 12:90
ČECH, SVATOPLUK 4:228 *bibliog.*
CECIL (county in Maryland)
map (39° 36′N 75° 50′W) 13:188
CECIL, LORD DAVID 4:228 *bibliog.*
CECIL, ROBERT (1563–1612) *see* SALISBURY, ROBERT CECIL, 1ST EARL OF
CECIL, ROBERT (1830–1903) *see* SALISBURY, ROBERT CECIL, 3D MARQUESS OF
CECIL, WILLIAM, 1ST BARON BURGHLEY *see* BURGHLEY, WILLIAM CECIL, 1ST BARON
CECILIA, SAINT 4:228
CECILIA (Kentucky)
map (37° 40′N 85° 57′W) 12:47
CECROPIA MOTH 3:594 *illus.*
CECROPS 4:228
CECUM
intestine 11:230
CEDAR 4:228 *illus.*
arborvitae 2:111
Lebanon 12:266 *illus.*
lumber 12:457 *illus.*
southern white cedar 18:112
wood 20:205 *illus.*
CEDAR (county in Iowa)
map (41° 45′N 91° 8′W) 11:244
CEDAR (county in Missouri)
map (37° 45′N 93° 50′W) 13:476
CEDAR (county in Nebraska)
map (42° 35′N 97° 15′W) 14:70
CEDAR BLUFF RESERVOIR
map (38° 47′N 99° 47′W) 12:18
CEDAR BLUFFS (Nebraska)
map (41° 24′N 96° 37′W) 14:70
CEDAR CITY (Missouri)
map (38° 36′N 92° 11′W) 13:476
CEDAR CITY (Utah)
map (37° 41′N 113° 4′W) 19:492
CEDAR CREEK
map (46° 7′N 101° 18′W) 14:248
CEDAR FALLS (Iowa)
map (42° 32′N 92° 27′W) 11:244
CEDAR GROVE (West Virginia)
map (38° 13′N 81° 26′W) 20:111
CEDAR HARBOR (Bahama Islands)
map (26° 52′N 77° 38′W) 3:23
CEDAR ISLAND
map (37° 39′N 75° 36′W) 19:607
CEDAR LAKE (Indiana)
map (41° 22′N 87° 26′W) 11:111
CEDAR LAKE (Manitoba)
map (53° 15′N 100° 10′W) 13:119
CEDAR RAPIDS (Iowa) 4:229
map (41° 59′N 91° 40′W) 11:244
CEDAR RAPIDS (Nebraska)
map (41° 34′N 98° 9′W) 14:70
CEDAR RIVER
map (41° 17′N 91° 21′W) 11:244
CEDAR SPRINGS (Michigan)
map (43° 13′N 85° 33′W) 13:377
CEDAR VALE (Kansas)
map (37° 6′N 96° 30′W) 12:18
CEDARBURG (Wisconsin)
map (43° 17′N 87° 59′W) 20:185
CEDAREDGE (Colorado)
map (38° 54′N 107° 56′W) 5:116
CEDARTOWN (Georgia)
map (34° 1′N 85° 15′W) 9:114
CEDARVILLE (California)
map (41° 32′N 120° 10′W) 4:31
CEDARVILLE (Michigan)
map (46° 0′N 84° 22′W) 13:377
CEDARVILLE (New Jersey)
map (39° 20′N 75° 12′W) 14:129
CEDILLA
C (letter) 4:3
CEGLÉD (Hungary)
map (47° 10′N 19° 48′E) 10:307
CELA, CAMILO JOSÉ 4:229 *bibliog.*
CELADON 4:229 *bibliog.*
Korean art 12:117
pottery and porcelain 15:469
ČELAKOVSKÝ, F. L.
Czech literature 5:412
CELAN, PAUL 4:229
CELAYA (Mexico)
map (20° 31′N 100° 49′W) 13:357
CELEBES *see* SULAWESI (Indonesia)
CELEBES SEA 4:229
map (3° 0′N 122° 0′E) 11:147
CELEBRATED JUMPING FROG OF CALAVERAS COUNTY, THE (story) 4:229
CELERY 4:229 *illus.*; 19:533 *illus.*
water celery 12:168 *illus.*
CELERY CABBAGE *see* CHINESE CABBAGE
CELESTA 4:229–230 *illus.*
CELESTIAL GOLDFISH 9:234 *illus.*
CELESTIAL MECHANICS 4:230 *bibliog.*
astrolabe 2:270–271
astrometry 2:273
astronautics 2:274–276
astronomy, history of 2:276–277
astronomy and astrophysics 2:281–285
Bessel, Friedrich 3:228
binary stars 3:256–257
Borelli, Giovanni Alfonso 3:398
Brouwer, Dirk 3:513
Campbell, William Wallace 4:66
celestial sphere 4:230
Clairaut, Alexis Claude 5:35
coordinate systems (astronomy) 5:245–246
Copernicus, Nicolaus 5:250
Danjon, André Louis 6:33
development
astronomy, history of 2:278
distance, astronomical 6:198–200
Earth, motions of 7:18–19
Earth, size and shape of 7:19
eclipse 7:41
Eratosthenes of Cyrene 7:227–228
Galaxy, The 9:10
great circle 9:318
Greenwich mean time 9:354
hour angle 10:264
interstellar matter 11:228
Kepler, Johannes 12:57–58
Kepler's laws 12:58
Lagrange, Joseph Louis de 12:166
Laplace, Pierre Simon de 12:205
librations 12:319
motion, circular 13:608
NAVSTAR 14:62
Newcomb, Simon 14:165
Newton, Sir Isaac 14:174
nutation 14:301
occultation 14:320
Oort, Jan Hendrik 14:396
orbital elements 14:417
perturbation 15:191
physics, history of 15:283; 15:285
Poincaré, Henri 15:380
precession of the equinoxes 15:493
Ptolemy 15:606–607
Sacrobosco, Johannes 17:8
Schwarzschild, Karl 17:139
sidereal time 17:294
Slipher, Vesto Melvin 17:362
three-body problem 19:181
CELESTIAL SPHERE 4:230 *illus.*
coordinate systems (astronomy) 5:245 *illus.*
equinox 7:226
precession of the equinoxes 15:493
Pythagoras of Samos 15:639–640
zodiac 20:371
CELESTINA (book) 4:230
CELESTINE V, POPE 4:230
CELESTITE 4:231
CELIAC DISEASE 4:231
sprue 18:201
CELIBACY 4:231 *bibliog.*
CELICA (Ecuador)
map (4° 7′S 79° 59′W) 7:52
CELINA (Ohio)
map (40° 33′N 84° 34′W) 14:357
CELINA (Tennessee)
map (36° 33′N 85° 30′W) 19:104
CELINA (Texas)
map (33° 19′N 96° 47′W) 19:129
CÉLINE, LOUIS FERDINAND 4:231 *bibliog.*
CELJE (Yugoslavia)
map (46° 14′N 15° 16′E) 20:340
CELL 4:231–236 *bibliog., illus.*
aging 1:185–186
atrophy 2:313
biochemistry 3:260–262
biology 3:270 *illus.*
blood 3:335–336 *illus.*
cancer 4:101–103 *illus.*
cell physiology 4:236
cholesterol 4:403
classes 4:231–232
eucaryote 7:262
procaryote 15:560
components 4:233
chloroplast 3:402
cytoplasm 5:412
endoplasmic reticulum 7:171
flagella 8:149
Golgi apparatus 9:240
lysosome 12:480
mitochondrion 13:485
nucleus 14:291
ribosome 16:206
contact inhibition
homeostasis 10:212
cytology 5:411
differentiation
development 6:138–139 *illus.*; 6:141
tissue, animal 19:210
diffusion 6:170
division 4:233–235 *illus.*
meiosis 13:282
mitosis 13:485
growth 9:378–379
histology 10:180
history 4:231
Claude, Albert 5:44
Mohl, Hugo von 13:503
Palade, George Emil 15:29
Swammerdam, Jan 18:376
Wilson, Edmund B. 20:164
immunity 11:57–58
leaf 15:276 *illus.*
life 12:326
membrane
lipid 12:361–362
osmosis 14:455
morphogenesis 4:233
phagocytic cells
infectious diseases 11:165–166
protoplasm 15:579
radiation injury 16:42
reaction, chemical
enzyme 7:212–215
replication
genetic code 9:79–81 *illus.*
nucleic acid 14:288–291
virus 19:614–616 *illus.*
reproduction
cloning 5:64–65
conjugation (biology) 5:191
sex 17:224
theory
Hooke, Robert 10:226; 20:376 *illus.*
Schultze, Max 17:289
Schwann, Theodor, and Schleiden, Matthias Jakob 17:138
Virchow, Rudolf 19:604
tissue culture 4:236; 19:210
Wistar Institute 20:190
CELL, ELECTRIC *see* BATTERY; ELECTROCHEMISTRY
CELL PHYSIOLOGY 4:236 *bibliog.*
active transport 1:89–90
cell 4:232
Claude, Albert 5:44
Commoner, Barry 5:141
cyclic AMP 5:403
cytology 5:411
interferon 11:210
radiation injury 16:42
Schwann, Theodor, and Schleiden, Matthias Jakob 17:138
Warburg, Otto 20:28
CELLA 4:236
Greek architecture 9:334
Mesopotamian art and architecture 13:318–320
CELLE (Germany, East and West)
map (52° 37′N 10° 5′E) 9:140
CELLINI, BENVENUTO 4:236–237 *bibliog., illus.*
gold and silver work 9:230
jewelry 11:410
Perseus with the Head of Medusa 4:237 *illus.*
CELLO 4:237–238 *bibliog., illus.*; 13:677 *illus.*; 18:300–301 *illus.*
performers
Boccherini, Luigi 3:354
Caldara, Antonio 4:25
Casals, Pablo 4:180
Piatigorsky, Gregor 15:289
Rostropovich, Mstislav 16:321
CELLOPHANE 4:238
cellulose 4:238
CELLULAR RADIO 4:238
CELLULAR RESPIRATION *see* METABOLISM
CELLULOID 4:238
Hyatt, John Wesley 10:327–328
plastics 15:347
CELLULOSE 4:238
carbohydrate 4:132
digestive system 6:174
intestine 11:230
monosaccharide 13:540
Payen, Anselme 15:121
polysaccharide 15:421–422
products
guncotton 9:405
lacquer 12:161
paper 15:68–70
plastics 15:347–349
rayon 16:97–98
resin 16:177
wood 20:205
CELLULOSE ACETATE
acetate 1:80
CELSIUS, ANDERS 4:238
Celsius scale 4:238
CELSIUS SCALE 4:238 *bibliog.*
Celsius, Anders 4:238
temperature 19:93
CELSUS 4:238
CELSUS, AULUS CORNELIUS 4:238 *bibliog.*
medicine 13:268
CELTIC ART 4:238–241 *bibliog., illus.*
Book of Kells 3:388
calligraphy 4:42 *illus.*
Celts 4:241–243
European prehistory 7:305
gold and silver work 9:228–229
illuminated manuscripts 11:47
Ireland, history of 11:261
jewelry 11:409
La Tène 12:150
CELTIC CROSS 5:360; 5:361 *illus.*
CELTIC LANGUAGES 4:241
Breton 4:241
Cornish 4:241
languages, extinct 12:198
Gaels 9:7
inscription 11:186
Irish 4:241
Irish literature 11:267–268
Manx 4:241
Scottish Gaelic 4:241
Welsh 4:241
Eisteddfod (literary festival) 7:97
CELTIC LITERATURE

CELTIC LITERATURE (cont.)
Breton literature **3**:475
Cornish literature **5**:269
Irish literature **11**:268
Scottish literature **17**:155
Welsh literature **20**:101–102
CELTIC MYTHOLOGY
Cuchulain **5**:381
Fenian cycle **8**:50
Finn mac Cumhail **8**:98–99
Lug **12**:452
mythology **13**:702–704 *illus.*
CELTIC RENAISSANCE *see* IRISH LITERARY RENAISSANCE
CELTS **4**:241–243 *bibliog., illus., map*
See also CELTIC ART; CELTIC LANGUAGES; CELTIC LITERATURE; CELTIC MYTHOLOGY
Brittany **3**:498
coinage **7**:305 *illus.*
druids **6**:281–282
expansion in Europe **4**:242 *map*
France, history of **8**:266
Gaels **9**:7
Galatia **9**:10
Gaul **9**:60–61
Great Britain, history of **9**:309
Halloween **10**:23
Hallstatt **10**:23
Ireland, history of **11**:261
Iron Age house **10**:265 *illus.*
La Tène **12**:150
lake dwelling **12**:171
Portugal, history of **15**:452
Scotland **17**:151
sword **18**:398 *illus.*
Tara (Ireland) **19**:34–35
United Kingdom **19**:407
Urnfield culture **19**:487
Vix (France) **19**:623
CEMENT (Oklahoma)
map (34° 57′N 98° 9′W) **14**:368
CEMENT AND CONCRETE **4**:243–244 *bibliog., illus.*
bridge (engineering) **3**:482–483 *table*
building construction **3**:550–552
calcination **4**:21
clay minerals **5**:46
gravel **9**:302
marl **13**:160
Morgan, Julia **13**:578
Nervi, Pier Luigi **14**:91
refractory materials **16**:124
reinforced and prestressed concrete **4**:243–244
roads and highways **16**:236 *illus.*; **16**:238–239 *illus.*
Roman art and architecture **16**:273
silica minerals **17**:304
silicon **17**:305
CEMETERY **4**:244–245 *bibliog., illus.*
See also BURIAL; TOMB
barrow **3**:95
catacombs **4**:197
tombstone **19**:232
CÉNACLE **4**:245
CENCI, BEATRICE **4**:245 *bibliog.*
CENDRARS, BLAISE **4**:245 *bibliog.*
CENNI DI PEPI *see* CIMABUE
CENNINI, CENNINO **4**:245 *bibliog.*
CENOZOIC ERA **4**:245–246 *bibliog., table*
Africa **1**:140 *map*
Asia **2**:236 *map*
Australia **2**:331 *map*
continental drift **5**:229
Earth, geological history of **7**:11–15 *illus., map*
Europe **7**:270 *map*
fossil record **8**:245–247
geologic time **9**:104–105 *table*
North America **14**:227 *map*
paleoclimatology **15**:32
paleogeography **4**:245
Pleistocene Epoch **15**:366
Quaternary Period **16**:15
Recent Epoch **16**:106–107
rocks **4**:245
South America **18**:87 *map*
subdivisions of the Cenozoic era **4**:245 *table*
Tertiary Period **19**:122–123
United States **19**:422 *map*
CENSORSHIP **4**:246–248 *bibliog., illus.*
art
Grosz, George **9**:371
MacMonnies, Frederick William **13**:34
Volterra, Daniele da **19**:632
Cato, Marcus Porcius (Cato the Elder) **4**:212–213
film
film, history of **8**:82; **8**:84; **8**:85
Hays, Will **10**:84
1st Amendment **8**:109
Freedom of Information Act **8**:296
freedom of speech **8**:298
freedom of the press **8**:296–297
Index (Roman Catholic) **11**:78
literature
African literature **1**:168
Bowdler, Thomas **3**:427
erotic and pornographic literature **7**:234
Fadeyev, Aleksandr Aleksandrovich **8**:7
Fedin, Konstantin Aleksandrovich **8**:44
Goldfaden, Abraham **9**:233
Gombrowicz, Witold **9**:241
Gorky, Maksim **9**:252–253
Harris, Frank **10**:57
Italian literature **11**:317
Joyce, James **11**:456–457
Lady Chatterley's Lover **12**:162
Lawrence, D. H. **11**:249–250
Matos Guerra, Gregório de **13**:229
Miller, Henry **13**:427
Pasternak, Boris **15**:107
Pilnyak, Boris **15**:303
Radishchev, Aleksandr Nikolayevich **16**:67
Rainbow, The **16**:77–78
samizdat **17**:46
Shvarts, Yevgeny **17**:290
Sinyavsky, Andrei **17**:326
Solzhenitsyn, Aleksandr **18**:59
Tropic of Cancer (book) **19**:307
Ulysses **19**:379
New York Times Company v. *United States* **14**:156
newspaper **14**:172
Pentagon Papers **15**:154
pornography **15**:441–442
CENSUS **4**:248–249 *bibliog.*
Domesday Book **6**:231
CENSUS, U.S. BUREAU OF THE Commerce, U.S. Department of **5**:138
UNIVAC **19**:467
CENTAUR (mythology) **4**:249
Chiron **4**:397
CENTAUR (rocket) **4**:249
CENTAURUS **4**:249
Proxima Centauri **15**:584
CENTENNIAL EXPOSITION **4**:249 *bibliog., illus.*
vocational education **19**:624
CENTER (Colorado)
map (37° 45′N 106° 6′W) **5**:116
CENTER (Nebraska)
map (42° 37′N 97° 53′W) **14**:70
CENTER (North Dakota)
map (47° 7′N 101° 18′W) **14**:248
CENTER (Texas)
map (31° 48′N 94° 11′W) **19**:129
CENTER FOR ADVANCED STUDY IN THE BEHAVIORAL SCIENCES **4**:249
Tyler, Ralph Winfred **19**:362
CENTER CITY (Minnesota)
map (45° 24′N 92° 49′W) **13**:453
CENTER OF GRAVITY **4**:249–250 *bibliog.*
Archimedes **2**:128
centroid **4**:256
CENTER HILL (Florida)
map (28° 38′N 82° 3′W) **8**:172
CENTER HILL LAKE
map (36° 0′N 85° 45′W) **19**:104
CENTER POINT (Alabama)
map (33° 38′N 86° 41′W) **1**:234
CENTER POINT (Iowa)
map (42° 11′N 91° 46′W) **11**:244
CENTER FOR THE STUDY OF DEMOCRATIC INSTITUTIONS **4**:250
Hutchins, Robert M. **10**:322
CENTEREACH (New York)
map (40° 51′N 73° 6′W) **14**:149
CENTERS FOR DISEASE CONTROL **4**:250
epidemiology **7**:219
CENTERVILLE (Iowa)
map (40° 43′N 92° 52′W) **11**:244
CENTERVILLE (Massachusetts)
map (41° 39′N 70° 21′W) **13**:206
CENTERVILLE (Missouri)
map (37° 26′N 90° 58′W) **13**:476
CENTERVILLE (Pennsylvania)
map (41° 44′N 79° 46′W) **15**:147
CENTERVILLE (South Dakota)
map (43° 7′N 96° 58′W) **18**:103
CENTERVILLE (Tennessee)
map (35° 47′N 87° 28′W) **19**:104
CENTERVILLE (Texas)
map (31° 16′N 95° 59′W) **19**:129
CENTERVILLE (Utah)
map (40° 55′N 111° 52′W) **19**:492
CENTIGRADE SCALE *see* CELSIUS SCALE
CENTIMETER
units, physical **19**:466
CENTIMETER-GRAM-SECOND (CGS) UNITS
units, physical **19**:466
CENTIPEDE **2**:217 *illus.*; **4**:250 *illus.*
myriapod **13**:691
soil organisms **18**:39 *illus.*
CENTO *see* CENTRAL TREATY ORGANIZATION
CENTRAL (New Mexico)
map (32° 46′N 108° 9′W) **14**:136
CENTRAL (Scotland) **4**:250
CENTRAL AFRICAN REPUBLIC **4**:250–252 *bibliog., illus., map, table*
cities
Bangui **3**:66
climate **4**:251–252 *table*
economic activities **4**:251
flag **4**:250 *illus.*
government **4**:251–252
history **4**:251–252
Bokassa, Jean Bedel **3**:364
land **4**:251 *map*
map (7° 0′N 21° 0′E) **1**:136
people **4**:251
Azande **2**:380
Pygmy **15**:633 *illus.*
CENTRAL AMERICA **4**:252–253 *bibliog., map*
See also names of specific countries, e.g., COSTA RICA; EL SALVADOR; etc.
economy **4**:253
Keith, Minor Cooper **12**:37
energy consumption and production **7**:174 *table*
exploration *see* EXPLORATION—Central America
history **4**:253
Alvarado, Pedro de **1**:319
Central American Federation **4**:253
Clayton-Bulwer Treaty **5**:47
El Salvador **7**:100–101
Indian languages, American **11**:98–101 *table*
Latin American art and architecture **12**:222–228
North America **14**:224–236 *map*
people **16**:34 *illus.*
See also names of specific Indian tribes, e.g., MAYA; TARASCAN (American Indians); etc.
Indians, American **11**:138
mestizo **13**:324
physical features **4**:252–253
Yucatán Peninsula **20**:338 *map*
rivers, lakes, and waterways
Nicaragua Canal **14**:179–180
truck and bus registration **19**:315 *table*
UNITED PROVINCES OF *see* CENTRAL AMERICAN FEDERATION
CENTRAL AMERICAN COMMON MARKET
Central America **4**:253
El Salvador **7**:100
CENTRAL AMERICAN FEDERATION **4**:253
El Salvador **7**:100
Latin America, history of **12**:220
Morazán, Francisco **13**:575
CENTRAL ARIZONA PROJECT
Colorado River (Colorado) **5**:121
CENTRAL ASIA **4**:253
Islamic art and architecture **11**:293–297
wagon **20**:6
CENTRAL BANK **4**:253–254 *bibliog.*
See also NATIONAL BANK
Bank of Canada **3**:67
Bank of England **3**:67
Bank for International Settlements **3**:67
Federal Reserve System **8**:41–42
inflation **11**:171
CENTRAL BANK OF SWEDEN
Nobel Prize **14**:208
CENTRAL BRAHUI RANGE (Mountain Range)
map (29° 20′N 66° 55′E) **15**:27
CENTRAL CITY (Illinois)
map (41° 14′N 88° 16′W) **11**:42
CENTRAL CITY (Iowa)
map (42° 12′N 91° 31′W) **11**:244
CENTRAL CITY (Kentucky)
map (37° 18′N 87° 7′W) **12**:47
CENTRAL CITY (Nebraska)
map (41° 7′N 98° 0′W) **14**:70
CENTRAL CITY (Pennsylvania)
map (40° 6′N 78° 48′W) **15**:147
CENTRAL CORDILLERA MOUNTAINS (Dominican Republic)
map (18° 45′N 70° 30′W) **6**:233
CENTRAL CORDILLERA MOUNTAINS (Peru)
map (9° 0′S 77° 0′W) **15**:193
CENTRAL CORDILLERA MOUNTAINS (Puerto Rico)
map (18° 10′N 66° 35′W) **15**:614
CENTRAL EUROPE **4**:254
European prehistory **7**:301–302
migration to the United States **11**:55 *map*
CENTRAL FALLS (Rhode Island)
map (41° 54′N 71° 23′W) **16**:198
CENTRAL HIGH SCHOOL (Little Rock, Arkansas) **3**:310 *illus.*
CENTRAL INTELLIGENCE AGENCY **4**:254 *bibliog.*
balloon **3**:52
Dulles, Allen Welsh **6**:295
Eisenhower, Dwight D. **7**:96
Encounter (periodical)
Spender, Stephen **18**:178
intelligence gathering **11**:204–205
National Security Council **14**:46
Radio Free Europe and Radio Liberty **16**:53
CENTRAL ISLIP (New York)
map (40° 47′N 73° 12′W) **14**:149
CENTRAL LAKE (Michigan)
map (45° 4′N 85° 16′W) **13**:377
CENTRAL LIMIT THEOREM **4**:254 *bibliog.*
normal distribution **14**:219
probability **15**:558
CENTRAL MAKRAN RANGE (Mountain Range)
map (26° 40′N 64° 30′E) **15**:27
CENTRAL NERVOUS SYSTEM *see* NERVOUS SYSTEM
CENTRAL PACIFIC RAILROAD
transcontinental railroad **19**:268–269 *map*
CENTRAL PARK (New York City) **4**:254; **14**:145 *map*; **14**:147 *illus.*
Cleopatra's Needles **5**:51
landscape architecture **12**:188
Olmstead, Frederick Law **14**:380
Vaux, Calvert **19**:529
CENTRAL PLACE THEORY **4**:254–255 *bibliog.*
Christaller, Walter **4**:411
Thünen, Johann Heinrich von **19**:185
CENTRAL POINT (Oregon)
map (42° 23′N 122° 57′W) **14**:427
CENTRAL POWERS **4**:255; **7**:294 *map*; **20**:221 *map*
See also WORLD WAR I
CENTRAL PROCESSING UNIT **4**:255 *bibliog.*
computer **5**:160a; **5**:160e; **5**:160h
computer, personal **5**:160i
computer languages **5**:160o–160p
computer memory **5**:161
computer register **5**:164
input-output devices **11**:182–183
microprocessor **13**:387
minicomputer **13**:446
on-line computer **14**:388
CENTRAL RANGE
map (29° 35′S 28° 35′E) **12**:297
CENTRAL SIBERIAN UPLANDS
map (65° 0′N 105° 0′E) **19**:388
CENTRAL TREATY ORGANIZATION **4**:255
CENTRALIA (Illinois)
map (38° 31′N 89° 8′W) **11**:42
CENTRALIA (Kansas)
map (39° 44′N 96° 8′W) **12**:18
CENTRALIA (Missouri)
map (39° 13′N 92° 8′W) **13**:476
CENTRALIA (Washington)
map (46° 43′N 122° 58′W) **20**:35
CENTRE (Alabama)
map (34° 9′N 85° 40′W) **1**:234
CENTRE (county in Pennsylvania)
map (40° 55′N 77° 47′W) **15**:147
CENTRE GEORGES POMPIDOU *see* BEAUBOURG
CENTRE NATIONAL D'ART ET DE CULTURE GEORGES POMPIDOU *see* BEAUBOURG
CENTRE NATIONAL D'ÉTUDES SPATIALES **4**:255
CENTREVILLE (Alabama)
map (32° 56′N 87° 8′W) **1**:234
CENTREVILLE (Maryland)
map (39° 3′N 76° 4′W) **13**:188

CENTREVILLE (Michigan)
map (41° 55′N 85° 32′W) **13**:377
CENTREVILLE (Mississippi)
map (31° 5′N 91° 4′W) **13**:469
CENTRIFUGAL AND CENTRIPETAL FORCES **4**:255 *bibliog.*
centrifuge **4**:255–256
magnitudes **4**:225
Newton, Sir Isaac **14**:174
CENTRIFUGE **4**:255–256 *bibliog., illus.*
casting **4**:189
ultracentrifuge
Svedberg, Theodor **18**:374
CENTRIOLE
cell **4**:232 *illus.*; **4**:233
CENTRIPETAL FORCE *see* CENTRIFUGAL AND CENTRIPETAL FORCES
CENTROID **4**:256
center of gravity **4**:250
triangle (mathematics) **19**:292
CENTURY (Florida)
map (30° 58′N 87° 16′W) **8**:172
CENTURY (West Virginia)
map (39° 6′N 80° 11′W) **20**:111
CENTURY PLANT *see* AGAVE
CEPE *see* BOLETUS
CEPHALIC INDEX **4**:256 *bibliog.*
CEPHALOCHORDATA **4**:256
CEPHALOPOD **4**:256
ammonite **1**:372
cuttlefish **5**:398
mollusk **13**:511–512 *illus.*
nautilus **14**:52–53
octopus **14**:348
CEPHALUS **4**:257
CEPHEIDS **4**:257 *bibliog.*
cosmology (astronomy) **5**:284
extragalactic systems **7**:343
Leavitt, Henrietta Swan **12**:263–264
period-luminosity relation **15**:166
pulsating stars **15**:621
variable star **19**:522–523
W Virginis stars **20**:3
CEPU (Indonesia)
map (7° 9′S 111° 35′E) **11**:147
CERAMICS **4**:257–259 *bibliog., illus.*
See also POTTERY AND PORCELAIN
antique collecting **2**:66
Art Nouveau **2**:211 *illus.*
categories **4**:258–259
cermet **4**:260
chinaware *see* POTTERY AND PORCELAIN
Chinese art and architecture **4**:379–388
clay minerals **5**:47
delftware **6**:92
earthenware *see* POTTERY AND PORCELAIN
feldspar **8**:47
feldspathoid **8**:47
fluorite **8**:188
glass ceramics **9**:201
glaze **9**:206
Japanese art and architecture **11**:372–379
kiln **12**:77
manufacture **4**:257–258 *illus.*
materials **4**:257–258 *illus.*
materials technology **13**:219–221
new applications **4**:259
Persian art and architecture **15**:186
pre-Columbian art and architecture
Chancay **4**:278
Nazca **14**:67
Paracas **15**:74
Vicús **19**:576
refractory materials **16**:124
sintering **17**:325
stoneware **4**:258–259 *illus.*
Victoria and Albert Museum **19**:575
Wedgwood, Josiah **20**:89–90
CERBERUS **4**:259
CERCARIA
schistosomiasis **17**:123
CEREA FLEXIBILITAS *see* CATALEPSY
CEREAL
See also BREAKFAST CEREAL; GRAIN
nutrition, human **14**:305–306
CEREBELLUM
brain **3**:443–446 *illus.*
CEREBRAL CORTEX
brain **3**:446–447 *illus.*
nervous system **14**:94–95 *illus.*
CEREBRAL PALSY **4**:259–260 *bibliog.*
nervous system, diseases of the **14**:95
speech **18**:175
CEREBROSIDE GLYCOLIPID **12**:361 *illus.*
CEREBROSPINAL FLUID
spinal cord **18**:184
CEREBROSPINAL MENINGITIS *see* MENINGITIS
CEREBRUM
brain **3**:443–444 *illus.*
nervous system **14**:95
CERES (astronomy) **4**:260
Gauss, Carl Friedrich **9**:61–62
CERES (mythology) **4**:260
Demeter **6**:96
CERESCO (Nebraska)
map (41° 3′N 96° 39′W) **14**:70
CEREUS *see* CACTI AND OTHER SUCCULENTS
CEREZO, SEBASTIAN
bolero **3**:364
CEREZO ARÉVALO, MARCO VINICIO
Guatemala **9**:389
CERF, BENNETT **4**:260 *bibliog.*
CERIGNOLA (Italy)
map (41° 16′N 15° 54′E) **11**:321
CERINTHUS **4**:260
CERIUM **4**:260
element **7**:130 *table*
Klaproth, Martin Heinrich **12**:95
lanthanide series **12**:200–201
metallic element **13**:328
phosphate minerals **15**:255–256
CERMET **4**:260
CERN *see* EUROPEAN ORGANIZATION FOR NUCLEAR RESEARCH
CERNA MOUNTAIN
map (48° 58′N 13° 48′E) **5**:413
CERNAN, EUGENE **4**:260
Apollo program **2**:81–84
Gemini program **9**:73
CERNUDA, LUIS **4**:260 *bibliog.*
CERRITO, FANNY **4**:260 *bibliog.*
CERRITOS (Mexico)
map (22° 26′N 100° 17′W) **13**:357
CERRO CHATO (Uruguay)
map (33° 6′S 55° 8′W) **19**:488
CERRO COLORADO (Uruguay)
map (33° 52′S 55° 33′W) **19**:488
CERRO DE PASCO (Peru)
map (10° 41′S 76° 16′W) **15**:193
CERRO GORDO (Illinois)
map (39° 53′N 88° 44′W) **11**:42
CERRO GORDO (county in Iowa)
map (43° 7′N 93° 15′W) **11**:244
CERRO GORDO, BATTLE OF
Mexican War **13**:352–354 *map*
CERRO SECHIN (Peru)
pre-Columbian art and architecture **15**:499 *illus.*
CERRO TOLOLO INTER-AMERICAN OBSERVATORY **4**:260–261
CERTIFIED PUBLIC ACCOUNTANT
audit **2**:318
public accounting **1**:78
CERTIORARI
Supreme Court of the United States **18**:355–356
CERTOSA DI PAVIA **4**:261 *bibliog.*
CERULARIUS, MICHAEL *see* MICHAEL CERULARIUS
CERUMEN *see* EARWAX
CERUSSITE **4**:261
CERVANTES SAAVEDRA, MIGUEL DE **4**:261 *bibliog., illus.*; **18**:158 *illus.*
Don Quixote **6**:236
CERVERA, PASQUAL
Spanish-American War **18**:150
CERVETERI *see* CAERE (Etruria)
CERVICITIS **4**:261–262
CERVIN, MONT *see* MATTERHORN
CERVIX (uterus) **16**:163 *illus.*
cervicitis **4**:261–262
Pap test **15**:62
CÉSAIRE, AIMÉ **4**:262 *bibliog.*
CÉSAR **4**:262 *bibliog.*
CESAREAN SECTION **4**:262 *bibliog.*; **15**:505 *illus.*
obstetrics **14**:319
CESENA (Italy)
map (44° 8′N 12° 15′E) **11**:321
CESIUM **4**:262
alkali metals **1**:295
atomic clock **2**:308
element **7**:130 *table*
fallout **8**:14
Group IA periodic table **15**:167
metal **13**:328
ČESKÉ BUDĚJOVICE (Czechoslovakia)
map (48° 59′N 14° 28′E) **5**:413
CESNOLA, LUIGI PALMA DI
Metropolitan Museum of Art, The **13**:348
CÉSPEDES, CARLOS MANUEL DE **4**:262 *bibliog.*
CÉSPEDES, PABLO DE **4**:262
CESTI, MARC ANTONIO **4**:262 *bibliog.*
CESTOS RIVER
map (5° 40′N 9° 10′W) **12**:313
CETA *see* COMPREHENSIVE EMPLOYMENT AND TRAINING ACT
CETACEAN **4**:262 *bibliog.*
CETEWAYO, KING OF THE ZULUS **4**:263 *bibliog.*
CETINJE (Yugoslavia)
map (42° 23′N 18° 55′E) **20**:340
CETONID BEETLE **3**:167 *illus.*
CEUTA (Spanish Possessions in North Africa) **4**:263
map (35° 53′N 5° 19′W) **13**:585
CEYHAN (Turkey)
map (37° 4′N 35° 47′E) **19**:343
CEYLON *see* SRI LANKA
CEYLON (Minnesota)
map (43° 32′N 94° 38′W) **13**:453
CEYLON GRACKLE *see* STARLING
CEYLON ISLAND
map (7° 0′N 81° 0′E) **18**:206
CÉZANNE, PAUL **4**:263–264 *bibliog., illus.*
The Card Players **4**:263 *illus.*; **8**:308 *illus.*
cubism **5**:380–381
The Lake of Annecy **15**:462 *illus.*
Landscape with a Viaduct **11**:65 *illus.*; **12**:192 *illus.*
Mont Sainte-Victoire **4**:263 *illus.*
postimpressionism **15**:462–463
Still Life with a Curtain **11**:65 *illus.*
Still Life with Apples and Oranges **18**:269 *illus.*
Vollard, Ambroise **19**:630
CGS (centimeter-gram-second) UNITS
units, physical **19**:466
CHA CHA (dance) **4**:264
CHABANEL, NOËL
Jesuit Martyrs of North America **11**:402
CHABAZITE *see* ZEOLITE
CHABRIER, EMMANUEL **4**:264 *bibliog.*
CHABROL, CLAUDE **4**:264 *bibliog.*
CHACABUCO (Argentina)
map (34° 38′S 60° 29′W) **2**:149
CHACHALACA **4**:264 *illus.*
CHACHAPOYAS (Peru)
map (6° 13′S 77° 51′W) **15**:193
CHACMOOLS
Tula **19**:330
CHACO (province in Argentina)
map (26° 25′S 60° 30′W) **2**:149
CHACO (South America) **4**:264
Indians, American **11**:132–133 *maps*; **11**:135–136
Paraguay **15**:76; **15**:77
CHACO BOREAL (region in Paraguay)
map (20° 30′S 60° 30′W) **15**:77
CHACO CANYON (New Mexico) **4**:264–265 *bibliog.*; **14**:38–39 *map, table*
CHACO RIVER
map (36° 46′N 108° 39′W) **14**:136
CHACO WAR **4**:265 *bibliog.*
CHACONNE
passacaglia and chaconne **15**:103
CHAD **4**:265–266 *bibliog., illus., map, table*
cities
N'djamena **14**:68
climate **4**:265–266 *table*
economy **4**:265–266
flag **4**:265 *illus.*
history **4**:266
Libya **12**:321
Qaddafi, Muammar al- **16**:3
Tombalbaye, N'Garta **19**:231
land **4**:265–266 *map*
map (15° 0′N 19° 0′E) **1**:136
people **4**:265
Baggara **3**:21
Tibesti Massif **19**:189
CHAD, LAKE **4**:266
map (13° 20′N 14° 0′E) **14**:187
CHADBOURN (North Carolina)
map (34° 19′N 78° 50′W) **14**:242
CHADERA (Israel)
map (32° 26′N 34° 55′E) **11**:302
CHADIC LANGUAGES
Afroasiatic languages **1**:179–180 *map*
CHADLI BENJEDID **4**:266–267
CHADRON (Nebraska)
map (42° 50′N 103° 2′W) **14**:70
CHADWICK, FLORENCE **4**:267
CHADWICK, GEORGE WHITEFIELD **4**:267 *bibliog.*
CHADWICK, SIR JAMES **4**:267
chemistry, history of **4**:328
CHADWICK, JOHN
Ventris, Michael **19**:546
CHADWICK, LYNN **4**:267 *bibliog.*
CHAERONEA **4**:267
CHAETOGNATHA *see* ARROWWORM
CHAFEE, ZECHARIAH **4**:267
CHAFFEE (county in Colorado)
map (38° 45′N 106° 10′W) **5**:116
CHAFFEE (Missouri)
map (37° 11′N 89° 40′W) **13**:476
CHAFFEE, ROGER **4**:267
Apollo program **2**:80
CHAFFINCH
animal communication **2**:19 *illus.*
CHAGALL, MARC **4**:267–268 *bibliog., illus.*
I and the Village **4**:268 *illus.*
Malevich, Kasimir **13**:88
CHAGAS' DISEASE *see* TRYPANOSOMIASIS
CHAGHCHARAN (Afghanistan)
map (34° 32′N 65° 15′E) **1**:133
CHAGOS ARCHIPELAGO
British Indian Ocean Territory **3**:496–497
CHAGUANAS (Trinidad and Tobago)
map (10° 31′N 61° 25′W) **19**:300
CHAIKIN, JOSEPH **4**:268
acting **1**:88
CHAILLU, PAUL BELLONI DU *see* DU CHAILLU, PAUL BELLONI
CHAIN (mathematics) **4**:268
CHAIN (technology) **4**:268
machine **13**:21
CHAIN, ERNST BORIS **4**:268
antibiotics **2**:57
Fleming, Sir Alexander **8**:159
Florey, Sir Howard Walter **8**:169
CHAIN OF BEING **4**:268–269 *bibliog.*
CHAIN REACTION, CHEMICAL **4**:269 *bibliog.*
combustion **5**:131
fire **8**:100–101
free radical **8**:294
inhibitor **11**:178
polymerization **15**:420
CHAIN REACTION, NUCLEAR **4**:269
breeder reactor **3**:471
fission, nuclear **8**:129
fusion, nuclear **8**:381
nuclear energy **14**:278–279
uranium **19**:477
CHAIN SAW **12**:395 *illus.*
CHAIN SNAKE *see* KING SNAKE
CHAIN STORES
retailing **16**:183
CHAIR **4**:269 *bibliog., illus.*
See also FURNITURE
Eames, Charles **7**:5
Hitchcock, Lambert **10**:186–187
Mies van der Rohe, Ludwig **13**:415
misericord **13**:466
Morris, William **13**:589
CHAIRS, THE (play)
Ionesco, Eugène **11**:240–241
CHAISE
coach and carriage **5**:73
CHAITYA *see* TEMPLE
CHAJUL (Guatemala)
map (15° 30′N 91° 2′W) **9**:389
CHAKA *see* SHAKA, KING OF THE ZULUS
CHAKRABARTY, A. M.
genetic engineering **9**:85
CHALATENANGO (El Salvador)
map (14° 3′N 88° 56′W) **7**:100
CHALAZA
egg **7**:72
CHALBAUD, ROMÁN
Venezuela **19**:543
CHALBI DESERT
map (3° 0′N 37° 20′E) **12**:53
CHALCEDON, COUNCIL OF **4**:270
council, ecumenical **5**:310
Eutyches **7**:311
Jacobite church **11**:346
Leo I, Pope **12**:288
Monophysitism **13**:537
CHALCEDONY **4**:270
agate **1**:182–183
bloodstone **3**:340
onyx **14**:396
CHALCHUAPA (El Salvador)
map (13° 59′N 89° 41′W) **7**:100
CHALCIDIAN LEAGUE
Olynthus **14**:385
CHALCIS
Cumae **5**:386
CHALCO, LAKE **2**:382 *map*
CHALCOGENS **4**:270 *bibliog.*
oxygen **14**:476–478
polonium **15**:417
selenium **17**:190
sulfur **18**:334–336
tellurium **19**:91
CHALCOLITHIC PERIOD **4**:270
Battle-Axe culture **3**:126
Bronze Age **3**:506
European prehistory **7**:303
Hacilar **10**:7
temple **19**:94 *illus.*

CHALCOPYRITE **4**:270 *illus.*
tetragonal system **19**:127
CHALDEA **3**:8 *map*; **4**:270–271
Babylonia **3**:8–9
Belshazzar **3**:193
Nebuchadnezzar II, King of Babylonia **14**:74
CHALDEAN LANGUAGE *see* URARTIAN LANGUAGE
CHALDEAN RITE *see* NESTORIAN CHURCH
CHALET **4**:271 *illus.*; **10**:268 *illus.*
CHALEUR BAY
map (48° 0′N 65° 45′W) **14**:117
CHALGRIN, JEAN FRANÇOIS THÉRÈSE **4**:271 *bibliog.*
Arc de Triomphe de l'Étoile **2**:112
CHALIAPIN, FYODOR IVANOVICH **4**:271 *bibliog.*
CHALICE **4**:271
gold and silver work **9**:229 *illus.*
CHALK **4**:271
calcium carbonate **4**:23
drawing **6**:263
foraminifera **8**:219–220
limestone **12**:345
Mesozoic Era **13**:322
CHALLENGER (space shuttle)
Jarvis, Gregory **11**:383
McAuliffe, Christa **13**:6
McNair, Ronald E. **13**:35
Onizuka, Ellison **14**:391
Resnik, Judith A. **16**:177
Scobee, Francis R. **17**:147
Smith, Michael **17**:370
space exploration **18**:130–131 *illus.*
space shuttle **18**:136
CHALLENGER DEEP
Marianas Trench **13**:151
***CHALLENGER* EXPEDITION** **4**:271–272
H.M.S. *Challenger* **14**:345 *illus.*
manganese nodule **13**:114
Murray, Sir John **13**:650
ocean and sea **14**:332
oceanographic instrumentation **14**:342–343 *illus.*
Thomson, Sir Charles Wyville **19**:175
CHALLIS (Idaho)
map (44° 30′N 114° 14′W) **11**:26
CHALLONER, RICHARD **4**:272 *bibliog.*
CHALMERS, THOMAS **4**:272 *bibliog.*
Scotland, Free Church of **17**:153
CHALMETTE (Louisiana)
map (29° 56′N 89° 58′W) **12**:430
CHÂLONS-SUR-MARNE (France)
map (48° 57′N 4° 22′E) **8**:260
CHAM
Champa **4**:276
CHAMA (New Mexico)
map (36° 54′N 106° 35′W) **14**:136
CHAMBAL RIVER
map (26° 29′N 79° 15′E) **9**:37
CHAMBER OF COMMERCE **4**:272
CHAMBER MUSIC **4**:272–273 *bibliog., illus.*
absolute music **1**:62
composers
Bach, Carl Philipp Emanuel **3**:10
Bach, Johann Sebastian **3**:10–11
Beethoven, Ludwig van **3**:164–165
Boccherini, Luigi **3**:354
Brahms, Johannes **3**:441
Caldara, Antonio **4**:25
Carter, Elliott **4**:171
Copland, Aaron **5**:250–251
Couperin (family) **5**:313–314
Davies, Peter Maxwell **6**:50
Dvořák, Antonín **6**:317
Fauré, Gabriel Urbain **8**:38
Haydn, Franz Josef **10**:81
Hindemith, Paul **10**:168
Langgaard, Rued **12**:195
Liszt, Franz **12**:367
Martinů, Bohuslav **13**:181
Nielsen, Carl August **14**:184–185
Purcell, Henry **15**:628
Ravel, Maurice **16**:94
Sammartini, Giovanni Battista **17**:46
Schubert, Franz **17**:135
Telemann, Georg Philipp **19**:78
consort music **5**:206
divertimento **6**:202
Japanese music **11**:380–382 *illus.*
music, history of Western **13**:666
CHAMBER TOMB *see* TOMB
CHAMBERLAIN (South Dakota)
map (43° 49′N 99° 20′W) **18**:103
CHAMBERLAIN, SIR AUSTEN **4**:273 *bibliog.*
CHAMBERLAIN, HOUSTON STEWART **4**:273 *bibliog.*
racism **16**:37
CHAMBERLAIN, JOHN **4**:273 *bibliog.*
CHAMBERLAIN, JOSEPH **4**:273–274 *bibliog., illus.*
Jameson, Sir Leander Starr **11**:357
CHAMBERLAIN, NEVILLE **4**:274 *bibliog., illus.*
Europe, history of **7**:297
Munich Conference **13**:641; **20**:250 *illus.*
CHAMBERLAIN, OWEN **4**:274
CHAMBERLAIN, WILT **3**:113 *illus.*; **3**:311 *illus.*; **4**:274 *bibliog.*
CHAMBERLAIN LAKE
map (46° 17′N 69° 20′W) **13**:70
CHAMBERLAIN'S MEN **4**:274 *bibliog.*
Burbage, Richard **3**:566
Globe Theatre **9**:208–209
Shakespeare, William **17**:236–237
CHAMBERLIN, THOMAS CHROWDER **4**:274 *bibliog.*
CHAMBERS (county in Alabama)
map (32° 55′N 85° 30′W) **1**:234
CHAMBERS (Arizona)
map (35° 11′N 109° 26′W) **2**:160
CHAMBERS (Nebraska)
map (42° 12′N 98° 45′W) **14**:70
CHAMBERS (county in Texas)
map (29° 40′N 94° 43′W) **19**:129
CHAMBERS, EPHRAIM
encyclopedia **7**:164
CHAMBERS, WHITTAKER
Hiss, Alger **10**:180
CHAMBERS, SIR WILLIAM **4**:274–275 *bibliog.*
CHAMBERSBURG (Pennsylvania)
map (39° 56′N 77° 39′W) **15**:147
CHAMBERY (France)
map (45° 34′N 5° 56′E) **8**:260
CHAMBI, MOUNT
map (35° 11′N 8° 42′E) **19**:335
CHAMBLEE (Georgia)
map (33° 54′N 84° 18′W) **2**:292
CHAMBONNIÈRES, JACQUES CHAMPION DE **4**:275 *bibliog.*
CHAMBORD, CHÂTEAU DE **4**:275 *bibliog.*
château **4**:302 *illus.*
CHAMELEON **4**:275 *bibliog., illus.*; **12**:379 *illus.*
coloration, biological **5**:122
CHAMINADE, CÉCILE **4**:275
CHAMISSO, ADELBERT VON **4**:275 *bibliog.*
CHAMOIS (leather) *see* LEATHER AND HIDES
CHAMOIS (Missouri)
map (38° 41′N 91° 46′W) **13**:476
CHAMOIS (zoology) **4**:275–276 *illus.*
CHAMOMILE **4**:276
CHAMORRO **4**:276 *bibliog.*
CHAMPA **4**:276 *bibliog.*
Southeast Asian art and architecture **18**:109 *illus.*
CHAMPAC **4**:276
CHAMPAGNE (France) **4**:276 *map*
wine **20**:175
World War I **20**:229
CHAMPAGNE (wine) **4**:276 *bibliog.*
See also WINE-PRODUCING AREAS
CHAMPAGNE (Yukon Territory)
map (60° 47′N 136° 29′W) **20**:345
CHAMPAIGN (county in Illinois)
map (40° 5′N 88° 12′W) **11**:42
CHAMPAIGN (county in Ohio)
map (40° 8′N 83° 45′W) **14**:357
CHAMPAIGN-URBANA (Illinois) **4**:276–277
map (40° 7′N 88° 12′W) (Urbana) **11**:42
map (40° 7′N 88° 14′W) (Champaign) **11**:42
CHAMPAIGNE, PHILIPPE DE **4**:277 *bibliog.*
CHAMPASAK (Laos)
map (14° 53′N 105° 52′E) **12**:203
CHAMPEAUX, WILLIAM OF *see* WILLIAM OF CHAMPEAUX
CHAMPERTY
barratry **3**:93
CHAMPION (Alberta)
map (50° 14′N 113° 9′W) **1**:256
CHAMPION (Michigan)
map (46° 31′N 87° 58′W) **13**:377
CHAMPLAIN, LAKE **4**:277
map (44° 45′N 73° 15′W) **19**:554
CHAMPLAIN, SAMUEL DE **4**:277–278 *bibliog., illus., map*
Canada, history of **4**:80–81 *map*
exploration **4**:277 *map*; **7**:335–337 *map*
Georgian Bay **9**:118
Great Lakes **9**:319–320 *map*
Quebec (city in Quebec) **16**:16
Saguenay River **17**:12
Saint John (New Brunswick) **17**:19
Trois-Rivières (Quebec) **19**:305
CHAMPLEVÉ
enamel **7**:161–162
CHAMPMESLÉ, LA
theater, history of the **19**:147
CHAMPOLLION, JEAN FRANÇOIS **4**:278 *bibliog.*
hieroglyphics **10**:159–161
Rosetta Stone **16**:317
CHAMPOLLION-FIGEAC, JEAN JACQUES **4**:278
CHAMPOTÓN (Mexico)
map (19° 21′N 90° 43′W) **13**:357
CHAMPS-ÉLYSÉES (Paris) **15**:87 *map*
CHAN, CHARLIE
Biggers, Earl Derr **3**:249
CH'AN BUDDHISM *see* ZEN BUDDHISM
CHAN CHAN (Peru) **4**:278 *bibliog.*
Chimu **4**:359
pre-Columbian art and architecture **15**:501
CHAN-CHIANG (China)
map (21° 16′N 110° 28′E) **4**:362
CH'AN SCHOOL
Mu-ch'i (Muqi) **13**:630
CHANAK CRISIS **4**:278
CHANCAY (Peru) **4**:278
pre-Columbian art and architecture **15**:499
CHANCE *see* PROBABILITY (mathematics)
CHANCE-VOUGHT F4U-1D CORSAIR **5**:277 *illus.*
CHANCELLOR **4**:278
common law and equity **5**:139
CHANCELLOR, JOHN **4**:278
CHANCELLOR, RICHARD **4**:278–279 *bibliog.*
Arctic **2**:142 *map*
CHANCELLORSVILLE, BATTLE OF **4**:279 *bibliog.*
Civil War, U.S. **5**:27–28
Jackson, Stonewall **11**:344
Lee, Robert E. **12**:270
CHANCERY **4**:279
common law **5**:139–140
equity **7**:226
CHANCROID **4**:279
CHANDALAR RIVER
map (66° 36′N 145° 48′W) **1**:242
CHANDELEUR ISLANDS
map (29° 48′N 88° 51′W) **12**:430
CHANDELEUR SOUND
map (29° 55′N 89° 10′W) **12**:430
CHANDELIER **4**:279 *bibliog.*
CHANDELLA RAJPUT
temple
Khajuraho **12**:65
CHANDI LARA JONGGRANG
Prambanan **15**:489
CHANDIGARH (India) **4**:279
Le Corbusier **12**:254
map (30° 44′N 76° 55′E) **11**:80
CHANDLER (Arizona)
map (33° 18′N 111° 50′W) **2**:160
CHANDLER (Indiana)
map (38° 3′N 87° 22′W) **11**:111
CHANDLER (Oklahoma)
map (35° 42′N 96° 53′W) **14**:368
CHANDLER (Quebec)
map (48° 21′N 64° 41′W) **16**:18
CHANDLER, ALBERT BENJAMIN "HAPPY" *see* CHANDLER, HAPPY
CHANDLER, HAPPY **4**:279
CHANDLER, OTIS **4**:279
CHANDLER, RAYMOND T. **4**:279 *bibliog.*
Farewell, My Lovely **8**:23
CHANDLER, ZACHARIAH **4**:279 *bibliog.*
CHANDLERVILLE (Illinois)
map (40° 3′N 90° 9′W) **11**:42
CHANDPUR (Bangladesh)
map (23° 13′N 90° 39′E) **3**:64
CHANDRAGUPTA I, GUPTA KING OF INDIA
Gupta (dynasty) **9**:406
Pataliputra **15**:109
CHANDRAGUPTA II, GUPTA KING OF INDIA
Gupta (dynasty) **9**:406
India, history of **11**:89 *map*
CHANDRAGUPTA MAURYA, EMPEROR OF INDIA **4**:279–280 *bibliog.*
India, history of **11**:89
Maurya (dynasty) **13**:238
CHANDRASEKHAR, SUBRAHMANYAN **4**:280 *bibliog.*
Chandrasekhar limit **4**:280
CHANDRASEKHAR LIMIT **4**:280
degenerate matter **6**:85
stellar evolution **18**:251
CHANEL, COCO **4**:280 *bibliog.*
Art Deco **2**:208
fashion design **8**:31–32 *illus.*
CHANEY, LON **4**:280 *bibliog., illus.*
CHANG, JOHN M. (Chang Myun)
Korea **12**:116
CH'ANG CHIANG *see* YANGTZE RIVER
CH'ANG-CHIH (China)
map (36° 11′N 113° 8′E) **4**:362
CHANG CHIH-TUNG (Zhang Zhidong) **4**:280 *bibliog.*
CH'ANG-CH'UN (Changchun) (China) **4**:280
map (43° 53′N 125° 19′E) **4**:362
CHANG CH'UN-CH'IAO
Gang of Four **9**:36
CHANG E *see* CH'ANG-O (Chang E)
CHANG AND ENG *see* SIAMESE TWINS
CHANG HSUEH-LIANG (Zhang Xueliang) **4**:280–281
CH'ANG-O (Chang E) **4**:281
CH'ANG-SHA (China)
map (28° 11′N 113° 1′E) **4**:362
CHANG TAO-LING (Zhang Daoling) **4**:281
CHANG T'IEN-I (Zhang Tianyi) **4**:281
CHANG TSO-LIN (Zhang Zuolin) **4**:281
CH'ANG-TU (China)
map (31° 11′N 97° 15′E) **19**:190
CHANGCHUN (China) *see* CH'ANG-CH'UN (Changchun) (China)
CHANGE, SOCIAL *see* SOCIAL CHANGE
CHANGE RINGING (bells) **3**:184 *illus.*
CHANNEL ISLANDS (California) *see* SANTA BARBARA ISLANDS
CHANNEL ISLANDS (United Kingdom) **4**:281 *bibliog., illus., map*
Guernsey **9**:391
Jersey **11**:398
map (49° 20′N 2° 20′W) **19**:403
CHANNEL ISLANDS NATIONAL MONUMENT
Santa Barbara Islands **17**:67
CHANNEL-PORT-AUX-BASQUES (Newfoundland)
map (47° 34′N 59° 9′W) **14**:166
CHANNELVIEW (Texas)
map (29° 46′N 95° 7′W) **19**:129
CHANNING (Michigan)
map (46° 9′N 88° 5′W) **13**:377
CHANNING (Texas)
map (35° 41′N 102° 20′W) **19**:129
CHANNING, EDWARD **4**:281
CHANNING, WILLIAM ELLERY **4**:281–282 *bibliog.*
CHANSON **4**:282 *bibliog.*
cabaret **4**:3
chamber music **4**:272
composers
Binchois, Gilles **3**:257
Janequin, Clément **11**:358
CHANSON DE ROLAND (epic) **4**:282 *bibliog.*
Charlemagne cycle **4**:290
French literature **8**:315
Roland **16**:271
CHANSONS DE GESTE **4**:282 *bibliog.*
Chanson de Roland **4**:282
CHANSONS INNOCENTES (poem)
cummings, e. e. **5**:387
CHANT
See also PLAINSONG
Gregory I, Pope **9**:356
Indians of North America, music and dance of the **11**:142
mass (musical setting) **13**:201
CHANTERENE, NICOLAS
Portuguese art and architecture **15**:456
CHANTILLY LACE **12**:159 *illus.*
CHANTY *see* SHANTY (work song)
CHANUKAH **4**:282 *bibliog.*
Maccabees **13**:7
CHANUTE (Kansas)
map (37° 41′N 95° 27′W) **12**:18
CHANUTE, OCTAVE **4**:282
glider **9**:208
CH'AO-AN (China)
map (23° 41′N 116° 38′E) **4**:362
CHAO K'UANG-YIN
Sung (Song) (dynasty) **18**:348
CHAO MENG-FU (Zhao Mengfu) **4**:282 *bibliog.*
CHAO PHRAYA RIVER **3**:63 *illus.*
map (13° 32′N 100° 36′E) **19**:139
CHAO TSU-YANG
China **4**:369
CHAO TZU-YANG (Zhao Ziyang) **4**:282
CHAO WU-CHI *see* ZAO WOU-KI (Chao Wu-Chi)
CHAOS **4**:283
CHAOS THEORY **4**:283

CHAPALA, LAKE
  map (20° 15′N 103° 0′W) **13**:357
CHAPARRAL **4**:283–284 *bibliog., illus.*
  ecology **7**:42
  fire susceptibility **4**:284
  life **4**:283–284
  occurrence **4**:283–284
  savanna life **17**:97–99
  world distribution **3**:273 *map*; **15**:344 *map*
CHAPARRAL COCK *see* ROADRUNNER
CHAPBOOK **4**:284 *bibliog.*
  Eulenspiegel, Till **7**:264
CHAPEL **4**:284 *bibliog.*
  Gothic art and architecture **9**:255–262
  Medici Chapel **13**:265–266
CHAPEL HILL (North Carolina) **4**:284
  map (35° 55′N 79° 4′W) **14**:242
CHAPEL HILL (Tennessee)
  map (35° 38′N 86° 41′W) **19**:104
CHAPELAIN, JEAN **4**:284
CHAPICUY (Uruguay)
  map (31° 39′S 57° 54′W) **19**:488
CHAPIN (Illinois)
  map (39° 46′N 90° 24′W) **11**:42
CHAPLEAU (Ontario)
  map (47° 50′N 83° 24′W) **14**:393
CHAPLIN, CHARLIE **4**:284–285 *bibliog., illus.*
  Cantinflas **4**:117
  film, history of **8**:82–83 *illus.*
CHAPMAN (Barbados)
  map (13° 12′N 59° 33′W) **3**:75
CHAPMAN (Kansas)
  map (38° 58′N 97° 1′W) **12**:18
CHAPMAN (Nebraska)
  map (41° 2′N 98° 9′W) **14**:70
CHAPMAN, GEORGE **4**:285 *bibliog.*
CHAPMAN, GRAHAM
  "Monty Python's Flying Circus" (television series) **13**:560
CHAPMAN, JOHN (artist)
  Davy Crockett **5**:355 *illus.*
CHAPMAN, JOHN (Johnny Appleseed) **4**:285 *bibliog.*
  Fort Wayne (Indiana) **8**:238
CHAPMAN, MARK
  Beatles, The **3**:145
CHAPMAN, SYDNEY
  magnetosphere **13**:60
CHAPMANVILLE (West Virginia)
  map (37° 58′N 82° 1′W) **20**:111
CHAPPAQUIDDICK ISLAND
  map (41° 22′N 70° 29′W) **13**:206
CHAPPE, CLAUDE
  semaphore **17**:194
CHAPPEL, ALONZO
  Stephen Decatur **6**:73 *illus.*
CHAPPELL (Nebraska)
  map (41° 6′N 102° 28′W) **14**:70
CHAPTAL, JEAN ANTOINE **4**:285
CHAPTER HOUSE **4**:285
CHAPULTEPEC **2**:382 *map*; **4**:285
  Mexico City **13**:367 *map*
CHAPULTEPEC, BATTLE OF
  Mexican War **13**:352 *map*; **13**:354
CHAPULTEPEC MOUNTAIN
  map (23° 27′N 103° 4′W) **13**:357
CHAR **4**:285–286 *bibliog., illus.*
CHAR, RENÉ **4**:286 *bibliog.*
CHARACIN **4**:286 *illus.*
  tetra **19**:127
  tropical fish **19**:308
CHARACTER (literature)
  narrative and dramatic devices **14**:22
CHARADES **4**:286 *bibliog.*
CHARAGUA (Bolivia)
  map (19° 48′S 63° 13′W) **3**:366
CHARBONNEAU, ROBERT **4**:286
CHARCOAL **4**:286–287 *illus.*
  carbon **4**:134
  heat content **8**:353 *table*
CHARCOT, JEAN BAPTISTE **4**:287
CHARCOT, JEAN MARTIN **4**:287 *bibliog., illus.*
  Freud, Sigmund **8**:329
  Janet, Pierre **11**:358
  psychopathology, treatment of **15**:599
CHARDIN, JEAN BAPTISTE **4**:287–288 *bibliog., illus.*
  Girl with a Racket and Shuttlecock **4**:287 *illus.*
CHARDIN, PIERRE TEILHARD DE *see* TEILHARD DE CHARDIN, PIERRE
CHARDON (Ohio)
  map (41° 35′N 81° 12′W) **14**:357
CHARDONNET, HILAIRE BERNIGAUD, COMTE DE **4**:288
  fiber, textile **8**:67
  rayon **16**:97
CHARES OF LINDOS
  Colossus of Rhodes **17**:216–218
CHARGAFF, E.
  zoology **20**:378
CHARGE, ELECTRIC **4**:288
  conduction, electric **5**:174
  conservation, laws of **5**:204
  coulomb **5**:308
  Coulomb, Charles Augustin de **5**:308
  Coulomb's law **5**:309
  dipole **6**:186
  direct current **6**:187
  electricity **7**:107–109
  electrochemical equivalent **7**:112
  electromagnetic units **7**:118
  electron **7**:119–120
  electronics **7**:126
  electrostatics **7**:128
  elementary unit, atomic constants **2**:308
  fundamental particles **8**:361; **8**:362 *table*
  ion and ionization **11**:239–240
  isoelectric point **11**:299
  Leyden jar **12**:309
  lightning **12**:339–340
  nuclear physics **14**:285
  static electricity **18**:234
  storage
    capacitance **4**:119
    capacitor **4**:119–120
  Van de Graaff generator **19**:512
CHARGE ACCOUNT *see* CREDIT CARD
CHARGE-COUPLED DEVICE (electronics) **4**:288
  camera **4**:57; **4**:59
  information storage and retrieval **11**:173
CHARGE OF THE LIGHT BRIGADE, THE (poem) **4**:288
  Tennyson, Alfred, Lord **19**:112
CHARI RIVER
  map (12° 58′N 14° 31′E) **4**:266
CHARIOT **4**:288 *bibliog.*
  depicted on a coin **18**:410 *illus.*
  technology, history of **19**:62 *illus.*
  wheel **20**:128
CHARIOT RACING **18**:196 *illus.*
  Pythian Games **15**:640
  stadium **18**:208
CHARISMA **4**:288
CHARISMATIC MOVEMENT **4**:288–289 *bibliog.*
CHARITABLE TRUSTS *see* FOUNDATIONS AND ENDOWMENTS
CHARITON (Iowa)
  map (41° 1′N 93° 19′W) **11**:244
CHARITON (county in Missouri)
  map (39° 30′N 93° 0′W) **13**:476
CHARITON RIVER
  map (39° 19′N 92° 57′W) **13**:476
CHARITY (altruism)
  fund raising **8**:360
  social work **18**:19
CHARITY (Guyana)
  map (7° 24′N 58° 36′W) **9**:410
CHARKA
  cotton gin **5**:307
CHARLEMAGNE, FRANKISH EMPEROR (Charles the Great) **4**:289–290 *bibliog., illus., map*
  bronze equestrian statue of **9**:148 *illus.*
  Carolingian art and architecture **4**:160–161
  Carolingians (dynasty) **4**:162
  cathedrals and churches **4**:205
  coin **8**:266 *illus.*
  conquests 768–814 **8**:285 *map*
  coronation **11**:328 *illus.*; **15**:63 *illus.*
  empire of **4**:289 *map*
  Europe, history of **7**:284
  flag **8**:135 *illus.*
  France, history of **8**:266–267
  Franks **8**:285–286
  Germany, history of **9**:148
  imperialism **11**:61–62
  Italy, history of **11**:327
  Leo III, Pope **12**:288
  plainsong **15**:325–326
  Saxons **17**:104–105
CHARLEMAGNE CYCLE **4**:290 *bibliog.*
CHARLEROI (Belgium) **4**:290
  map (50° 25′N 4° 26′E) **3**:177
CHARLEROI (Pennsylvania)
  map (40° 9′N 79° 57′W) **15**:147
CHARLEROI TO BRUSSELS CANAL
  map (50° 51′N 4° 19′E) **3**:177
CHARLES (county in Maryland)
  map (38° 32′N 76° 59′W) **13**:188
CHARLES, DUKE OF LOWER LORRAINE
  Hugh Capet, King of France **10**:292
CHARLES, EZZARD
  Louis, Joe **12**:422
CHARLES, JACQUES **4**:290
  balloon **3**:51
  gas laws **9**:53
CHARLES, KING OF ROMANIA *see* CAROL I, KING OF ROMANIA
CHARLES, PRINCE OF WALES **4**:290 *bibliog., illus.*
CHARLES, RAY **4**:290
  soul music **18**:71
CHARLES I, EMPEROR OF AUSTRIA-HUNGARY **4**:291
CHARLES I, KING OF ENGLAND, SCOTLAND, AND IRELAND **4**:291 *bibliog., illus.*
  Bishops' Wars **3**:298
  Covenanters **5**:319
  Cromwell, Oliver **5**:357–358
  Eliot, Sir John **7**:139
  English Civil War **7**:189–190
  execution of **9**:314 *illus.*
  Great Britain, history of **9**:314
  Hampden, John **10**:32
  Henrietta Maria **10**:122
  Long Parliament **12**:407
  Milton, John **13**:433
  Northamptonshire (England) **14**:253
  Oxford (England) **14**:474
  portrait
    van Dyck, Sir Anthony **19**:513–514 *illus.*
  Pym, John **15**:634
  Rupert, Prince **16**:346–347
  Strafford, Thomas Wentworth, 1st Earl of **18**:287–288
CHARLES I, KING OF FRANCE AND FRANKISH EMPEROR *see* CHARLEMAGNE, FRANKISH EMPEROR (Charles the Great)
CHARLES I, KING OF HUNGARY (Charles Robert) **4**:296
CHARLES I, KING OF NAPLES (Charles of Anjou) **4**:296
  Italy, history of **11**:329
  Michael VIII Palaeologus, Byzantine Emperor **13**:371
  Naples, Kingdom of **14**:15
  Philip III, King of France (Philip the Bold) **15**:232
  Sicilian Vespers **17**:292
CHARLES I, KING OF PORTUGAL **4**:296 *bibliog.*
CHARLES I, KING OF SPAIN *see* CHARLES V, HOLY ROMAN EMPEROR
CHARLES II, FRANKISH EMPEROR (Charles the Bald) **4**:292
  coronation of **4**:162 *illus.*
  duel **6**:293
  holdings **4**:289 *map*
  Verdun, Treaty of **19**:550
CHARLES II, KING OF ENGLAND, SCOTLAND, AND IRELAND **4**:291–292 *bibliog., illus.*
  Anglo-Dutch Wars **2**:3
  English Civil War **7**:189–190
  Gwynne, Nell **9**:412
  Monmouth, James Scott, Duke of **13**:536
  Oates, Titus **14**:313
  Restoration **16**:182
  Shaftesbury, Anthony Ashley Cooper, 1st Earl of **17**:234
  Test Acts **19**:126
  Whig party (England) **20**:130
  Worcester (city in England) **20**:216
CHARLES II, KING OF NAPLES (Charles the Lame) **4**:296
  Celestine V, Pope **4**:230
CHARLES II, KING OF SPAIN **4**:296 *bibliog.*
  Spain, history of **18**:147
  Spanish Succession, War of the **18**:162
CHARLES III, FRANKISH EMPEROR (Charles the Fat) **4**:292
CHARLES III, KING OF FRANCE (Charles the Simple) **4**:292
CHARLES III, KING OF NAPLES (Charles of Durazzo) **4**:296
CHARLES III, KING OF SPAIN **4**:296–297 *bibliog., illus.*
  meeting with Pope Benedict XIV **11**:329 *illus.*
  Spain, history of **18**:147
CHARLES IV, KING OF FRANCE (Charles the Fair) **4**:292
CHARLES IV, KING OF GERMANY AND HOLY ROMAN EMPEROR **4**:293 *bibliog.*
  Golden Bull **9**:231
  Karlovy Vary (Czechoslovakia) **12**:28
CHARLES IV, KING OF SPAIN **4**:297 *bibliog.*
  Ferdinand VII, King of Spain **8**:54
  Godoy, Manuel de **9**:221
  Spain, history of **18**:147
CHARLES V, HOLY ROMAN EMPEROR **4**:294–295 *bibliog., illus., map*; **9**:150 *illus.*; **10**:210 *illus.*
  empire of **4**:294 *map*
  Ferdinand I, Holy Roman Emperor **8**:52–53
  Francis I, King of France **8**:275
  Habsburg (dynasty) **10**:6 *illus.*
  Italy, history of **11**:329
  Low Countries, history of the **12**:439
  Philip of Hesse **15**:232
  portrait
    Titian **19**:212
  Spain, history of **18**:145–146
  Vesalius, Andreas **19**:564
  Worms (West Germany) **20**:284
CHARLES V, KING OF FRANCE (Charles the Wise) **4**:292–293
CHARLES VI, HOLY ROMAN EMPEROR **4**:295
  Joseph I, Holy Roman Emperor **11**:451
  Maria Theresa, Austrian Archduchess, Queen of Hungary and Bohemia **13**:150
  Polish Succession, War of the **15**:398
  Pragmatic Sanction **15**:487
CHARLES VI, KING OF FRANCE (Charles the Mad or Well-Beloved) **4**:293
  Philip the Bold, Duke of Burgundy **15**:231
CHARLES VII, HOLY ROMAN EMPEROR **4**:295–296
  Wittelsbach (family) **20**:193
CHARLES VII, KING OF FRANCE (Charles the Well-Served) **4**:293 *bibliog., illus.*; **13**:393 *illus.*
  Louis XI, King of France **12**:425
  Pragmatic Sanction **15**:487
CHARLES VIII, KING OF FRANCE **4**:293
  Italian Wars **11**:319
CHARLES IX, KING OF SWEDEN **4**:297 *bibliog.*
  Vaasa (Finland) **19**:501
CHARLES X, KING OF FRANCE **4**:293 *bibliog.*
  July Revolution **11**:466
CHARLES X, KING OF SWEDEN **4**:297 *bibliog.*
  acquisitions 1654–1660 **17**:109 *map*
CHARLES XI, KING OF SWEDEN **4**:297
CHARLES XII, KING OF SWEDEN **4**:297 *bibliog., illus.*
  Mazepa, Ivan Stepanovich **13**:250
  Northern War, Great **14**:256
  Peter I, Emperor of Russia (Peter the Great) **15**:200
  Poltava (USSR) **15**:418
  Stanisław I, King of Poland **18**:218
CHARLES XIII, KING OF SWEDEN
  Scandinavia, history of **17**:110
CHARLES XIV JOHN, KING OF SWEDEN **4**:298 *bibliog.*
  Pau (France) **15**:116
  Scandinavia, history of **17**:110
CHARLES XVI GUSTAV, KING OF SWEDEN **4**:298
CHARLES ALBERT, ELECTOR OF BAVARIA *see* CHARLES VII, HOLY ROMAN EMPEROR
CHARLES ALBERT, KING OF SARDINIA
  Italy, history of **11**:329
  Sardinia, Kingdom of **17**:77
  Savoy (dynasty) **17**:102
CHARLES OF ANJOU *see* CHARLES I, KING OF NAPLES (Charles of Anjou)
CHARLES THE BALD *see* CHARLES II, FRANKISH EMPEROR (Charles the Bald)
CHARLES THE BEWITCHED *see* CHARLES II, KING OF SPAIN
CHARLES THE BOLD, DUKE OF BURGUNDY **4**:290–291 *bibliog.*
CHARLES CITY (Iowa)
  map (43° 4′N 92° 40′W) **11**:244
CHARLES CITY (Virginia)
  map (37° 20′N 77° 4′W) **19**:607
CHARLES CITY (county in Virginia)
  map (37° 20′N 77° 2′W) **19**:607
CHARLES DARWIN FOUNDATION

CHARLES DARWIN FOUNDATION (cont.) FOR THE GALÁPAGOS ISLANDS
wildlife refuge **20**:151
CHARLES THE FAIR *see* CHARLES IV, KING OF FRANCE (Charles the Fair)
CHARLES THE FAT *see* CHARLES III, FRANKISH EMPEROR (Charles the Fat)
CHARLES THE GREAT *see* CHARLEMAGNE, FRANKISH EMPEROR (Charles the Great)
CHARLES ISLAND
map (62° 40′N 74° 15′W) **16**:18
CHARLES THE MAD *see* CHARLES VI, KING OF FRANCE (Charles the Mad or Well-Beloved)
CHARLES MARTEL **4**:291 *bibliog.*
Carolingians (dynasty) **4**:162
France, history of **8**:267
CHARLES MIX (county in South Dakota)
map (43° 10′N 98° 35′W) **18**:103
CHARLES MOUND
map (42° 30′N 90° 14′W) **11**:42
CHARLES RIVER
map (42° 22′N 71° 3′W) **3**:409
CHARLES THE SIMPLE *see* CHARLES III, KING OF FRANCE (Charles the Simple)
CHARLES TOWN (West Virginia)
map (39° 17′N 77° 52′W) **20**:111
CHARLES THE WELL-BELOVED *see* CHARLES VI, KING OF FRANCE (Charles the Mad or Well-Beloved)
CHARLES THE WELL-SERVED *see* CHARLES VII, KING OF FRANCE (Charles the Well-Served)
CHARLES THE WISE *see* CHARLES V, KING OF FRANCE (Charles the Wise)
CHARLESFORT
Ribaut, Jean **16**:205
CHARLES'S LAW
gas laws **9**:53
CHARLESTON (Arkansas)
map (35° 18′N 94° 2′W) **2**:166
CHARLESTON (dance) **4**:298; **6**:30 *illus.*
big apple **3**:248
CHARLESTON (Illinois)
map (39° 30′N 88° 10′W) **11**:42
CHARLESTON (Mississippi)
map (34° 0′N 90° 4′W) **13**:469
CHARLESTON (Missouri)
map (36° 55′N 89° 21′W) **13**:476
CHARLESTON (South Carolina) **4**:298 *illus.*; **18**:99 *illus.*; **19**:417 *illus.*
map (32° 48′N 79° 57′W) **18**:98
Spoleto Festival **18**:192
CHARLESTON (county in South Carolina)
map (32° 45′N 80° 0′W) **18**:98
CHARLESTON (West Virginia) **4**:298; **20**:112 *illus.*
map (38° 21′N 81° 38′W) **20**:111
CHARLESTOWN (Indiana)
map (38° 27′N 85° 40′W) **11**:111
CHARLESTOWN (New Hampshire)
map (43° 14′N 72° 26′W) **14**:123
CHARLESTOWN (Rhode Island)
map (41° 23′N 71° 45′W) **16**:198
CHARLEVILLE-MÉZIÈRES (France)
map (49° 46′N 4° 43′E) **8**:260
CHARLEVOIX (Michigan)
map (45° 19′N 85° 16′W) **13**:377
CHARLEVOIX (county in Michigan)
map (45° 10′N 85° 5′W) **13**:377
CHARLEVOIX, LAKE
map (45° 15′N 85° 8′W) **13**:377
CHARLEVOIX, PIERRE FRANÇOIS XAVIER DE **4**:298
CHARLOCK **4**:298
CHARLOT *see* CHAPLIN, CHARLIE
CHARLOTTE (county in Florida)
map (26° 54′N 81° 58′W) **8**:172
CHARLOTTE (Michigan)
map (42° 36′N 84° 50′W) **13**:377
CHARLOTTE (North Carolina) **4**:299
map (35° 14′N 80° 50′W) **14**:242
CHARLOTTE (Tennessee)
map (36° 11′N 87° 24′W) **19**:104
CHARLOTTE (county in Virginia)
map (37° 0′N 78° 40′W) **19**:607
CHARLOTTE AMALIE (Virgin Islands) **4**:299; **19**:605–606 *illus.*
map (18° 21′N 64° 56′W) **19**:605
CHARLOTTE COURTHOUSE (Virginia)
map (37° 3′N 78° 39′W) **19**:607
CHARLOTTE HARBOR
map (26° 45′N 82° 12′W) **8**:172
CHARLOTTENBURG (Suriname)
map (5° 51′N 54° 46′W) **18**:364
CHARLOTTE'S WEB (book) **4**:299
White, E. B. **20**:134–135
CHARLOTTESVILLE (Virginia) **4**:299
map (38° 2′N 78° 29′W) **19**:607
CHARLOTTETOWN (Prince Edward Island) **4**:299; **15**:549 *illus.*
map (46° 14′N 63° 8′W) **15**:548
CHARLTON (county in Georgia)
map (30° 55′N 82° 10′W) **9**:114
CHARLTON ISLAND
map (52° 0′N 79° 30′W) **14**:393
CHARM (amulet) *see* AMULET
CHARM (quantum mechanics)
quark **16**:12
CHARNOY *see* CHARLEROI (Belgium)
CHAROLAIS CATTLE **4**:216 *illus.*; **4**:299 *bibliog.*, *illus.*
CHARON (astronomy)
Pluto (planet) **15**:373
CHARON (mythology) **4**:299
CHARPENTIER, GUSTAVE **4**:299 *bibliog.*
CHARPENTIER, MARC ANTOINE **4**:299
music, history of Western **13**:666
CHARQUI *see* PEMMICAN
CHART **4**:300
elevation **7**:136
hydrography **10**:341
maps and mapmaking **13**:140
nomogram **14**:215
CHARTER **4**:300
Dartmouth College v. *Woodward* **6**:40
joint-stock company **11**:440
CHARTER OAK **4**:300
CHARTERHOUSE (English school) **4**:300 *bibliog.*
CHARTERHOUSE (monastery)
monastic art and architecture **13**:519
CHARTERHOUSE OF PARMA, THE (book)
Stendhal **18**:253
CHARTERHOUSE OF PAVIA *see* CERTOSA DI PAVIA
CHARTERIS, LESLIE **4**:300
CHARTIER, ALAIN **4**:300
CHARTISM **4**:300 *bibliog.*
radicalism **16**:44
CHARTRES (France) **4**:300
map (48° 27′N 1° 30′E) **8**:260
CHARTRES CATHEDRAL **2**:134 *illus.*; **2**:194 *illus.*; **4**:300–301 *bibliog.*, *illus.*
floorplan **4**:206 *illus.*
Gothic Art and Architecture **9**:256 *illus.*; **9**:258–259 *illus.*
photography
Nègre, Charles **14**:78
sculpture **17**:162 *illus.*
stained glass **18**:211–212 *illus.*
Villard de Honnecourt **19**:598
CHARTREUSE (liqueur)
Carthusians **4**:174
CHARVAKA
philosophy **15**:246
CHARYBDIS *see* SCYLLA AND CHARYBDIS
CHASE (British Columbia)
map (50° 49′N 119° 41′W) **3**:491
CHASE (Kansas)
map (38° 21′N 98° 21′W) **12**:18
CHASE (county in Kansas)
map (38° 20′N 96° 35′W) **12**:18
CHASE (county in Nebraska)
map (40° 30′N 101° 40′W) **14**:70
CHASE, LUCIA **4**:301 *bibliog.*
American Ballet Theatre **1**:337
CHASE, MARTHA
virus **19**:614
CHASE, MARY ELLEN **4**:301
CHASE, MOUNT
map (46° 7′N 68° 29′W) **13**:70
CHASE, SALMON P. **4**:301 *bibliog.*
CHASE, SAMUEL **4**:301
impeachment **11**:61
CHASE, WILLIAM MERRITT **4**:301 *bibliog.*, *illus.*
A Friendly Call **4**:301 *illus.*
CHASE CITY (Virginia)
map (36° 48′N 78° 28′W) **19**:607
CHASIDISM *see* HASIDISM
CHASKA (Minnesota)
map (44° 47′N 93° 35′W) **13**:453
CHASLES, MICHEL
mathematics, history of **13**:226
CHASM **12**:182 *illus.*
CHASSEY CULTURE
European prehistory **7**:302
lake dwelling **12**:171
CHASTITY BELT **4**:301–302
CHAT (bird) **4**:302 *bibliog.*, *illus.*
CHÂTEAU **4**:302 *bibliog.*, *illus.*
See also names of specific chateaux, e.g., BLOIS, CHÂTEAU DE; CHAMBORD, CHÂTEAU DE; etc.
Loire River **12**:398
Luxembourg Palace **12**:472
Touraine **19**:251
CHÂTEAU FRONTENAC (Canada) **4**:88 *illus.*
CHATEAUBRIAND, FRANÇOIS RENÉ, VICOMTE DE **4**:303 *bibliog.*, *illus.*
CHATEAUGAY (New York)
map (44° 56′N 74° 5′W) **14**:149
CHÂTEAUROUX (France)
map (46° 49′N 1° 42′E) **8**:260
CHÂTEAUX
interior design **11**:212
CHÂTELET (Belgium)
map (50° 24′N 4° 31′E) **3**:177
CHÂTELIER, HENRI LOUIS LE *see* LE CHÂTELIER, HENRI LOUIS
CHÂTELLERAULT (France)
map (46° 49′N 0° 33′E) **8**:260
CHÂTELPERRONIAN **4**:303 *bibliog.*
Perigordian **15**:166
CHATHAM (England)
map (51° 23′N 0° 32′E) **19**:403
CHATHAM (county in Georgia)
map (32° 5′N 81° 10′W) **9**:114
CHATHAM (Illinois)
map (39° 40′N 89° 42′W) **11**:42
CHATHAM (Louisiana)
map (32° 19′N 92° 27′W) **12**:430
CHATHAM (Massachusetts)
map (41° 41′N 69° 58′W) **13**:206
CHATHAM (New Brunswick)
map (47° 2′N 65° 28′W) **14**:117
CHATHAM (New Jersey)
map (40° 44′N 74° 23′W) **14**:129
CHATHAM (New York)
map (42° 22′N 73° 36′W) **14**:149
CHATHAM (county in North Carolina)
map (35° 40′N 79° 15′W) **14**:242
CHATHAM (Ontario)
map (42° 24′N 82° 11′W) **14**:393
CHATHAM (Virginia)
map (36° 50′N 79° 24′W) **19**:607
CHATHAM, WILLIAM PITT, 1st EARL OF *see* PITT, WILLIAM (the Elder)
CHATHAM ISLANDS
map (43° 55′S 176° 30′W) **14**:334
New Zealand **14**:159
CHATHAM STRAIT
map (57° 30′N 134° 45′W) **1**:242
CHATOM (Alabama)
map (31° 28′N 88° 16′W) **1**:234
CHATSWORTH (Georgia)
map (34° 46′N 84° 46′W) **9**:114
CHATSWORTH (Illinois)
map (40° 45′N 88° 18′W) **11**:42
CHATTAHOOCHEE (Florida)
map (30° 42′N 84° 51′W) **8**:172
CHATTAHOOCHEE (county in Georgia)
map (32° 20′N 84° 48′W) **9**:114
CHATTAHOOCHEE RIVER **4**:303
map (30° 52′N 84° 57′W) **9**:114
CHATTANOOGA (Tennessee) **4**:303; **19**:105 *map*
map (35° 3′N 85° 19′W) **19**:104
CHATTANOOGA, BATTLES OF **4**:303 *bibliog.*; **5**:28–29 *illus.*
Civil War, U.S. **5**:28
Grant, Ulysses S. **9**:288
CHATTEL
negotiable instrument **14**:77
CHATTERJEE, BANKIM CHANDRA **4**:303–304
CHATTERTON, THOMAS **4**:304 *bibliog.*
literary fraud **12**:370
CHATTI
Franks **8**:285–286
CHATTOOGA (county in Georgia)
map (34° 30′N 85° 20′W) **9**:114
CHATTOOGA RIVER
map (34° 46′N 83° 19′W) **18**:98
CHATZOR HA-GELILITH (Israel)
map (32° 59′N 35° 34′E) **11**:302
CHAU PHU (Vietnam)
map (10° 42′N 105° 7′E) **19**:580
CHAUCER, GEOFFREY **4**:304–305 *bibliog.*, *illus.*; **7**:194 *illus.*
ballade **3**:41
Canterbury Tales, The (book) **3**:385 *illus.*; **4**:116–117
Equatorie of the Planetris, The
cryptology **5**:371
Hoccleve, Thomas **10**:193
CHAUCHOIN, CLAUDETTE *see* COLBERT, CLAUDETTE
CHAUDIÈRE RIVER
map (46° 45′N 71° 17′W) **16**:18
CHAUMONT (France)
map (48° 7′N 5° 8′E) **8**:260
CHAUNCEY (Ohio)
map (39° 24′N 82° 8′W) **14**:357
CHAUNCY, CHARLES **4**:305
CHAUSSON, ERNEST **4**:305
CHAUTAUQUA (adult education programs) **4**:305 *bibliog.*
Vincent, John Heyl **19**:599
CHAUTAUQUA (county in Kansas)
map (37° 10′N 96° 15′W) **12**:18
CHAUTAUQUA (county in New York)
map (42° 15′N 79° 30′W) **14**:149
CHAUTAUQUA LAKE
map (42° 12′N 79° 27′W) **14**:149
CHAUVIN (Alberta)
map (52° 42′N 110° 7′W) **1**:256
CHAVES (county in New Mexico)
map (33° 30′N 104° 30′W) **14**:136
CHAVES (Portugal)
map (41° 44′N 7° 28′W) **15**:449
CHÁVEZ, CARLOS **4**:305 *bibliog.*
CHAVEZ, CESAR **4**:305 *bibliog.*, *illus.*; **10**:178 *illus.*
Chicano **4**:343
migrant labor **13**:417
CHAVIN CULTURE
pre-Columbian art and architecture **15**:499–500 *illus.*
CHAVÍN DE HUÁNTAR (Peru) **4**:306 *bibliog.*
Paracas **15**:74
CHAWK (Burma)
map (20° 54′N 94° 50′E) **3**:573
CHAYEFSKY, PADDY **4**:306 *bibliog.*
Monroe, Marilyn **13**:543
CHAYOTE **4**:306
CHAZY (New York)
map (44° 53′N 73° 26′W) **14**:149
CHEAHA MOUNTAIN
map (33° 30′N 85° 47′W) **1**:234
CHEAT MOUNTAIN
map (38° 40′N 79° 55′W) **20**:111
CHEATHAM (county in Tennessee)
map (36° 15′N 87° 3′W) **19**:104
CHEB (Czechoslovakia)
map (50° 1′N 12° 25′E) **5**:413
CHEBANSE (Illinois)
map (41° 0′N 87° 54′W) **11**:42
CHEBOYGAN (Michigan)
map (45° 39′N 84° 29′W) **13**:377
CHEBOYGAN (county in Michigan)
map (45° 25′N 84° 30′W) **13**:377
CHEBYSHEV, PAFNUTY LVOVICH **4**:306
CHEBYSHEV'S THEOREM *see* LARGE NUMBERS, LAW OF
CHECH ERG DESERT
map (25° 0′N 2° 15′W) **1**:287
CHECHON (Korea)
map (37° 8′N 128° 12′E) **12**:113
CHECK (finance) **4**:306
banking systems **3**:68–69
clearinghouse **5**:47
money **13**:527
negotiable instrument **14**:77
traveler's check **19**:284
CHECKERS (game) **4**:306–307 *bibliog.*, *illus.*, *tables*
champions **4**:306–307 *tables*
Chinese checkers **4**:388
CHECKERSPOTS FRITILLARY BUTTERFLY **3**:595–596 *illus.*
CHECOTAH (Oklahoma)
map (35° 28′N 95° 31′W) **14**:368
CHEDABUCTO BAY
map (45° 23′N 61° 10′W) **14**:269
CHEDDAR MAN **4**:307 *bibliog.*
CHEEKTOWAGA (New York)
map (42° 55′N 78° 46′W) **14**:149
CHEESE **4**:307–309 *bibliog.*, *illus.*, *table*
Edam (Netherlands) **7**:54
milk **13**:423
modern cheesemaking **4**:308–309
molds **13**:506
Netherlands **14**:101 *illus.*
nutritional value **4**:309
processed cheese and cheese spreads **4**:309
varieties of cheese **4**:307–308 *illus.*, *table*
Wisconsin **20**:187 *illus.*
world production **4**:309
CHEETAH **4**:309 *bibliog.*, *illus.*
forelimb **5**:155 *illus.*
feet **13**:102 *illus.*
CHEEVER, JOHN **4**:309–310 *bibliog.*, *illus.*
Cowley, Malcolm **5**:321
CHEFOO (China)
map (37° 33′N 121° 20′E) **4**:362
CHEFOO CONVENTION
Li-Hung-Chang (Li Hongzhang) **12**:310

CHEGUTU (Zimbabwe)
map (18° 10′S 30° 14′E) **20**:365
CHEHALIS (Washington)
map (46° 40′N 122° 58′W) **20**:35
CHEJU ISLAND
map (33° 20′N 126° 30′E) **12**:113
CHEKA (secret police)
Dzerzhinsky, Feliks Edmundovich **6**:320
CHEKHOV, ANTON 4:310 *bibliog., illus.*
Cherry Orchard, The **4**:332
drama **6**:261
Moscow Art Theater **13**:599
Russian literature **16**:366 *illus.*
Stanislavsky, Konstantin **18**:218
Taganrog (USSR) **19**:9
Three Sisters, The **19**:182
Uncle Vanya **19**:382
Yalta (USSR) **20**:315
CHEKIANG (Zhejiang) (China) 4:310–311
Hangchow (Hangzhou) **10**:38
Ning-po (Ningpo) **14**:200
Wen-chow (Wenzhou) **20**:103
CHELAN (Washington)
map (47° 51′N 120° 1′W) **20**:35
CHELAN (county in Washington)
map (47° 56′N 120° 52′W) **20**:35
CHELAN, LAKE
map (48° 5′N 120° 30′W) **20**:35
CHELAN MOUNTAINS
map (47° 55′N 120° 25′W) **20**:35
CHELATION 4:311
food poisoning and infection **8**:211
CHELCICKY, PETER 4:311
CHELEBI, ABDÜLCELIL OF EDIRNE *see* LEVNÎ, RESSAM
CHELLEAN 4:311 *bibliog.*
CHEŁM (Poland)
map (51° 10′N 23° 28′E) **15**:388
CHELMSFORD (England)
map (51° 44′N 0° 28′E) **19**:403
CHELMSFORD (Massachusetts)
map (42° 36′N 71° 21′W) **13**:206
CHELMSFORD, FREDERIC JOHN NAPIER THESIGER, 1ST VISCOUNT 4:311
CHELONIA
turtle **19**:352–354 *illus.*
CHELPIN, HANS VON EULER- *see* EULER-CHELPIN, HANS VON
CHELSEA (Massachusetts)
map (42° 24′N 71° 2′W) **3**:409
CHELSEA (Michigan)
map (42° 19′N 84° 1′W) **13**:377
CHELSEA (Oklahoma)
map (36° 32′N 95° 26′W) **14**:368
CHELSEA (Vermont)
map (43° 59′N 72° 27′W) **19**:554
CHELSEA WARE 4:311 *bibliog.*
pottery and porcelain **15**:471
CHELTENHAM (England)
map (51° 54′N 2° 4′W) **19**:403
CHELYABINSK (USSR) 4:311
map (55° 10′N 61° 24′E) **19**:388
CHEMAKUM (American Indians)
Quileute-Hoh and Chemakum **16**:26
CHEMFET (biosensor) **3**:276
CHEMICAL ANALYSIS
Heyrovský, Jaroslav **10**:155
mass spectrometry **13**:204
mineral **13**:440–441
pH **15**:217–218
qualitative chemical analysis **16**:6–7
quantitative chemical analysis **16**:8–9
titration **19**:215
CHEMICAL AND BIOLOGICAL WARFARE 4:311–313 *bibliog., illus.*
environmental health **7**:210–212
gas mask **9**:53
Haber, Fritz **10**:4
napalm **14**:14
poison gas **15**:382
tear gas **19**:58
Vietnam War **19**:587
weapons **20**:75
World War I **20**:247
CHEMICAL BOND 4:313–315 *bibliog., illus.*
See also REACTION, CHEMICAL
atomic bonds
silicate minerals **17**:305
carbon **4**:133–134
chelation **4**:311
chemical energy **4**:315
chemical symbolism and notation **4**:322
conjugation **5**:191
coordination compounds **5**:247
double
cis-trans isomerism **4**:445
diene **6**:162
electron **7**:120
electron configuration **8**:120
electronegativity **7**:124
energy level **7**:173
hydrogen bond **10**:340
inorganic chemistry **11**:181–182
intermolecular forces **11**:215
ion and ionization **11**:240
Lewis, Gilbert Newton **12**:306
ligand **12**:333–334 *table*
metal **13**:328–329
molecule **13**:507–508
monomer **13**:537
organic chemistry **14**:435–436
resonance (chemistry) **16**:177–178
salt (chemistry) **17**:37
sulfide minerals **18**:333–334
theory
chemistry, history of **4**:326–327
Langmuir, Irving **12**:196
Mulliken, Robert Sanderson **13**:637
Pauling, Linus Carl **15**:119
valence **19**:503
Werner, Alfred **20**:104
CHEMICAL COMBINATION, LAWS OF 4:315 *bibliog.*
atomic weight **2**:311
reaction, chemical **16**:98–100
stoichiometry **18**:276–277
CHEMICAL COMPOUND *see* COMPOUND, CHEMICAL
CHEMICAL ENERGY 4:315 *bibliog.*
combustion **5**:131
electromotive force **7**:119
measurement **4**:315
phosphorus **15**:257
reaction, chemical **16**:99
uses **4**:315
CHEMICAL FIELD EFFECT TRANSISTOR *see* CHEMFET
CHEMICAL HAZARDS *see* DISEASES, OCCUPATIONAL; POLLUTANTS, CHEMICAL
CHEMICAL INDUSTRY 4:315–318 *bibliog., illus., table*
aluminum **1**:316–319
Bhopal (India) **3**:234
calcite **4**:21–22
Castner-Kellner process **4**:191
Chaptal, Jean Antoine **4**:285
cyanide process **5**:400
Dow, Herbert Henry **6**:251
dye **6**:317–318
elastomer **7**:102
electroplating **7**:126–127
epoxy resins **7**:222
ethylene **7**:258
flame retardants **8**:150–151
fluorine industry **8**:187
Freon **8**:326
genetic engineering **9**:85
hydrazine **10**:331
impact on society **4**:324
Keir, James **12**:37
lime (chemical compound) **12**:343
manufacturing **13**:133
materials technology **13**:219–221
Mond (family) **13**:522
organic chemistry **14**:439–440
pesticides **15**:196–199
petrochemicals **15**:205–206
petroleum industry **15**:209–215
pigment **15**:300
plastics **15**:347–351
pollutants, chemical **15**:410–411
process control **15**:560 *illus.*
rayon **16**:97–98
refrigeration **16**:125
resin **16**:177
rubber **16**:332–335
silicones **17**:306
soap and detergent **18**:6–8
soda **18**:31
sodium **18**:33
Solvay, Ernest **18**:58
Solvay process **18**:58
sulfur **18**:335–336
sulfuric acid **18**:336
superphosphate **18**:352–353
synthetic fibers **18**:409
tanker **19**:23–24
technology, history of **19**:68
Teflon **19**:72
toxicology **19**:256
vinyl **19**:601
CHEMICAL INSTRUMENTATION **4**:323–324
bunsen burner **3**:564
calorimeter **4**:47
centrifuge **4**:255–256
chromatography **4**:417–419
colorimeter **5**:122
coulombmeter **5**:308
densitometer **6**:113
electrode **7**:113
electron microscope **7**:120–122
electrophoresis **7**:126
fluorometer **8**:188
fluoroscope **8**:188
indicator **11**:144
ion exchange **11**:240
mass spectrometry **13**:204
molecule **13**:508
pH meter **15**:218
polarimeter **15**:393
polarographic analyzer **15**:395
qualitative chemical analysis **16**:7
quantitative chemical analysis **16**:7–9
spectrophotometer **18**:168–169
spectroscope **18**:169
spectroscopy **18**:170–172
stereoscope **18**:259–260
turbidimeter **19**:339
CHEMICAL KINETICS AND EQUILIBRIUM 4:318–319 *bibliog.*
activity **1**:90
chemical symbolism and notation **4**:322
dissociation **6**:198
Hinshelwood, Sir Cyril Norman **10**:173
physical chemistry **15**:279
thermodynamics **19**:163–164
van't Hoff, Jacobus Henricus **19**:520
CHEMICAL MEDIATOR
inflammation **11**:169
CHEMICAL MINEROLOGY
mineral **13**:440–441
CHEMICAL NOMENCLATURE 4:319–321 *bibliog., illus.*
Berthollet, Claude Louis, Comte de **4**:320
Fourcroy, Antoine François, Comte de **8**:253
International Union of Pure and Applied Chemistry **4**:320
Lavoisier, Antoine Laurent **12**:241–242
lipid **12**:361 *illus.*
polymer **4**:321
CHEMICAL OCEANOGRAPHY
oceanography **14**:344–345
CHEMICAL POLLUTANTS *see* POLLUTANTS, CHEMICAL
CHEMICAL REACTION *see* REACTION, CHEMICAL
CHEMICAL REMANENT MAGNETISM (CRM)
paleomagnetism **15**:42
CHEMICAL SYMBOLISM AND NOTATION 4:321–323 *bibliog., illus.*
CHEMIN DE FER 4:323 *bibliog.*
CHEMIN GRENIER (Mauritius)
map (20° 29′S 57° 27′E) **13**:237
CHEMISORPTION
adsorption **1**:110
CHEMISTRY 4:323–324 *bibliog., illus.*
Annals of Chemistry
Liebig, Justus, Baron von **12**:324
blood
uremia **19**:485–486
branches **4**:323
analytical chemistry **1**:391
astrochemistry **2**:270
biochemistry **3**:260–262
crystal chemistry, mineral **13**:439
electrochemistry **7**:112–113
fossil chemistry, fossil record **8**:247–248
geochemistry **9**:96–97
histochemistry, histology **10**:180
hydrochemistry, limnology **12**:145
inorganic chemistry **11**:181–182
organic chemistry **14**:434–440
photochemistry **15**:257–259
physical chemistry **15**:279
radiochemistry **16**:63
stereochemistry **18**:258–259
thermochemistry **19**:161–162
carbohydrate **4**:132–133
chemical and biological warfare **4**:311–313
chemical bond **4**:313–315
chemical combination, laws of **4**:315
chemical energy **4**:315
chemical equilibrium and kinetics **4**:315–317
chemical industry **4**:317–319
chemical nomenclature **4**:319–321
chemical symbolism and notation **4**:321–323
colloidal state **5**:104–105
compound, chemical **5**:158
crystal **5**:373–374
diagnostic tests **6**:149–150
Earth sciences **7**:24
electrolysis **7**:114–115
electron volt **7**:124
electronegativity **7**:124
element **7**:129–132
emulsion **7**:161
entropy **7**:209
eutectic point **7**:310
evaporation **7**:313–314
examination, medical **7**:326
extraction **7**:341
fractionation **8**:258
free radical **8**:294
gas laws **9**:53
gaseous state **9**:54
glassy state **9**:205
history **4**:324–330
homologous series **10**:216
hydrolysis **10**:342–343
hydrophilic and hydrophobic substances **10**:343
impact on society **4**:324
ion and ionization **11**:239–240
isomer **11**:299
isotope **11**:301
lanthanide series **12**:200–201
liquid **12**:364–365
mole (unit of substance) **13**:507
molecular weight **13**:507
molecule **13**:507–508
monomer **13**:537
neutralization **14**:108
Nobel Prize **14**:208–211 *table*
Alder, Kurt **1**:268
Anfinsen, Christian Boehmer **1**:411
Arrhenius, Svante August **2**:188
Aston, Francis William **2**:268
Baeyer, Adolf von **3**:20–21
Barton, Derek **3**:98
Bergius, Friedrich Karl Rudolf **3**:210
Bosch, Carl **3**:405
Buchner, Eduard **3**:534
Butenandt, Adolf **3**:591
Calvin, Melvin **4**:49
Cornforth, John W. **5**:269
Curie, Marie and Pierre **5**:391–392
Debye, Peter **6**:72
Diels, Otto Paul Hermann **6**:161–162
Du Vigneaud, Vincent **6**:287
Eigen, Manfred **7**:91
Euler-Chelpin, Hans von **7**:265
Fischer, Emil Hermann **8**:110
Fischer, Ernst Otto **8**:110
Fischer, Hans **8**:110
Flory, Paul **8**:177
Giauque, William Francis **9**:172
Grignard, Victor **9**:363
Haber, Fritz **10**:4
Hahn, Otto **10**:11
Harden, Sir Arthur **10**:45
Hassel, Odd **10**:67
Haworth, Sir Walter Norman **10**:78
Herzberg, Gerhard **10**:150
Hevesy, Georg von **10**:154
Hinshelwood, Sir Cyril Norman **10**:173
Hodgkin, Dorothy Crowfoot **10**:194
Joliot-Curie, Frédéric and Irène **11**:441
Karrer, Paul **12**:29
Kendrew, John Cowdery **12**:41
Kuhn, Richard **12**:135
Langmuir, Irving **12**:196
Leloir, Luis Frederico **12**:279
Libby, Willard Frank **12**:311
Lipscomb, William Nunn, Jr. **12**:364
Martin, Archer **13**:179
Merrifield, R. Bruce **13**:312
Mitchell, Peter **13**:483
Moissan, Henri **13**:504
Moore, Stanford **13**:570
Mulliken, Robert Sanderson **13**:637
Natta, Giulio **14**:47
Nernst, Walther **14**:89
Norrish, Ronald George Wreyford **14**:223
Northrop, John Howard **14**:256
Onsager, Lars **14**:391
Ostwald, Wilhelm **14**:459
Pauling, Linus Carl **15**:119
Perutz, Max Ferdinand **15**:196
Porter, George **15**:444
Pregl, Fritz **15**:502
Prelog, Vladimir **15**:518
Prigogine, Ilya **15**:537

CHEMISTRY (cont.)
Ramsay, Sir William **16**:81
Richards, Theodore William **16**:211
Robinson, Sir Robert **16**:245
Rutherford, Sir Ernest **16**:375–376
Ružička, Leopold **16**:377
Sabatier, Paul **17**:4
Sanger, Frederick **17**:64
Seaborg, Glenn T. **17**:171–172
Semenov, Nikolai Nikolayevich **17**:195
Soddy, Frederick **18**:32
Stanley, Wendell Meredith **18**:219
Staudinger, Hermann **18**:239
Stein, William Howard **18**:247
Sumner, James B. **18**:340
Svedberg, Theodor **18**:374
Synge, Richard Laurence Millington **18**:407
Tiselius, Arne Wilhelm Kaurin **19**:209
Todd, Lord Alexander **19**:220
Urey, Harold Clayton **19**:486
van't Hoff, Jacobus Henricus **19**:520
Wallach, Otto **20**:15
Werner, Alfred **20**:104
Wieland, Heinrich Otto **20**:146
Wilkinson, Geoffrey **20**:153
Willstätter, Richard **20**:163
Windaus, Adolf **20**:172
Woodward, Robert B. **15**:639
Woodward, Robert Burns **20**:213
Ziegler, Karl **20**:363
Zsigmondy, Richard Adolf **20**:380
nonmetallic chemistry, inorganic chemistry **11**:182
oceanography **14**:345
osmosis **14**:455
oxidation and reduction **14**:475–476
ozone layer **14**:480
periodic table **15**:166–169 *illus.*
pH **15**:217–218
phase equilibrium **15**:222–224
phlogiston theory **15**:248
phosphor **15**:256
physiological chemistry *see* BIOCHEMISTRY
polymerization **15**:420
precipitation **15**:493
professional and educational organizations
American Chemical Society **1**:337
American Institute of Chemists **1**:341
pyrolysis **15**:637
pyroxene **15**:638
quantitative chemical analysis **16**:7
radical **16**:43
reaction, chemical **16**:98–100
resonance (chemistry) **16**:177–178
saponification **17**:73
saturation **17**:88
solid solution **18**:54
solid state, inorganic chemistry **11**:182
solubility **18**:58
solution **18**:58
solvent **18**:58–59
spectroscopy **18**:170–172
stoichiometry **18**:276–277
sublimation (chemistry) **18**:313
sugar **18**:327
superheavy elements **18**:351
suspension **18**:371
synergism **18**:407
terpene **19**:118
tools **4**:323–324
See also CHEMICAL INSTRUMENTATION
transmutation of elements **19**:276–277
transuranium elements **19**:282
triple point **19**:302
valence **19**:503
vapor pressure **19**:521
CHEMISTRY, HISTORY OF **4**:324–330 *bibliog., illus.*
See also CHEMISTRY
alchemy **1**:263
Andrews, Thomas **1**:405
Avogadro, Amedeo **2**:377
Balard, Antoine Jérôme **3**:33
Bergman, Sir Torbern **3**:210
Berthelot, Marcelin **3**:225
Berzelius, Jöns Jakob **3**:227
Black, Joseph **3**:303
Boyle, Robert **3**:434
Brønsted, Johannes Nicolaus **3**:503
Bunsen, Robert Wilhelm **3**:564
Butlerov, Aleksandr **3**:592
Cannizzaro, Stanislao **4**:111
Cavendish, Henry **4**:225–226
Claisen, Ludwig **5**:35
Crafts, James Mason **5**:328
Cronstedt, Axel Fredrick, Baron **5**:359
Dalton, John **6**:14–15
Davy, Sir Humphry **6**:53–54
Döbereiner, Johann Wolfgang **6**:209
Domagk, Gerhard **6**:229
Draper, John William **6**:263
Dulong, Pierre Louis **6**:296
Dumas, Jean Baptiste André **6**:297
early civilization **4**:324
Erlenmeyer, Richard **7**:231
Faraday, Michael **8**:21–22
First International Chemical Congress (1860)
organic chemistry **14**:435
Fourcroy, Antoine François, Comte de **8**:253
Gadolin, Johan **9**:7
Gay-Lussac, Joseph Louis **9**:64
Gerhardt, Charles Frédéric **9**:122
Gibbs, Josiah Willard **9**:174
Glauber, Johann Rudolf **9**:205
Gmelin, Leopold **9**:213
Graham, Thomas **9**:280–281
Greek philosophers **4**:324
Guldberg, Cato Maximilian **9**:402
Harcourt, William **10**:44
Heilbron, Sir Ian Morris **10**:108
Helmont, Johannes Baptista van **10**:116
Henry, William **10**:123
Heyrovský, Jaroslav **10**:155
Higgins, William **10**:161
Hoffmann, Friedrich **10**:195
Hofmann, August Wilhelm von **10**:196
Kekulé von Stradonitz, Friedrich August **12**:37
Klaproth, Martin Heinrich **12**:95
Laurent, Auguste **12**:238–239
Lavoisier, Antoine Laurent **12**:241–242
Le Châtelier, Henri Louis **12**:253
Lehmann, Johann Gottlob **12**:276
Lewis, Gilbert Newton **12**:306; **19**:503
Liebig, Justus, Baron von **12**:324
Lomonosov, Mikhail Vasilevich **12**:400
Marignac, Jean Charles Galissard de **13**:152
Mendeleev, Dmitry Ivanovich **13**:294–295
Meyer, Lothar **13**:368
Miller, Stanley Lloyd **13**:428
Mitscherlich, Eilhard **13**:485
Moissan, Henri **13**:504
Newlands, John Alexader Reina **14**:169
Nieuwland, Julius Arthur **14**:186
Paracelsus **15**:74
Pelletier, Pierre Joseph **15**:138
Priestley, Joseph **15**:536–537
Proust, Joseph Louis **15**:582
Prout, William **15**:583
Regnault, Henri Victor **16**:129
Scheele, Carl Wilhelm **17**:115
Sidgwick, Nevil Vincent **17**:294–295
Silliman, Benjamin **17**:309
Smithson, James **17**:372
Sørensen, Søren Peter Lauritz **18**:68–69
Stahl, Georg Ernst **18**:211
Stas, Jean Servais **18**:228
Tennant, Smithson **19**:102
Topchiyev, Aleksandr Vasilievich **19**:237
Travers, Morris William **19**:284
van't Hoff, Jacobus Henricus **19**:520
Vauquelin, Louis Nicolas **19**:529
Waage, Peter **20**:3
Walden, Paul **20**:9
Wenzel, Carl Friedrich **20**:104
Wöhler, Friedrich **20**:195
Wollaston, William Hyde **20**:199
Woodward, Robert Burns **20**:213
Wurtz, Charles Adolphe **20**:297
CHEMISTRY, INDUSTRIAL *see* CHEMICAL INDUSTRY
CHEMNITZ (East Germany) *see* KARL-MARX-STADT (East Germany)
CHEMNITZ, MARTIN **4**:329
CHEMOSPHERE **4**:329
CHEMOTAXIS
taxis **19**:48
CHEMOTHERAPY
cancer **4**:105–106 *illus.*
Ehrlich, Paul (1854–1915) **7**:90
leukemia **12**:301
mastectomy **13**:215
psychopathology, treatment of **15**:600–601
stroke **18**:302
CHEMOTROPISM
tropism **19**:310
CHEMULPO (Korea) *see* INCHON (South Korea)
CHEMULT (Oregon)
map (43° 13′N 121° 47′W) **14**:427
CHEMUNG (county in New York)
map (42° 6′N 76° 49′W) **14**:149
CHEN-CHIANG (China)
map (32° 13′N 119° 26′E) **4**:362
CHEN DUXIU *see* CH'EN TU-HSIU (Chen Duxiu)
CH'EN TU-HSIU (Chen Duxiu) **4**:329–330 *bibliog.*
CHENAB RIVER
map (29° 23′N 71° 2′E) **15**:27
CHENANGO (county in New York)
map (42° 32′N 75° 31′W) **14**:149
CHENANGO BRIDGE (New York)
map (42° 10′N 75° 52′W) **14**:149
CHENANGO RIVER
map (42° 5′N 75° 55′W) **14**:149
CHENEY (Kansas)
map (37° 38′N 97° 47′W) **12**:18
CHENEY (Washington)
map (47° 29′N 117° 34′W) **20**:35
CHENEY RESERVOIR
map (37° 45′N 97° 50′W) **12**:18
CHENEYVILLE (Louisiana)
map (31° 1′N 92° 17′W) **12**:430
CHENG-CHOU (Zhengzhou) (China) **4**:330
map (34° 48′N 113° 39′E) **4**:362
CHENG HO (Zheng He) **4**:330
CH'ENG-TE (China)
map (40° 58′N 117° 53′E) **4**:362
CH'ENG TSU *see* YUNG-LO, EMPEROR OF CHINA (Yongle)
CH'ENG-TU (Chengdu) (China) **4**:330
map (30° 39′N 104° 4′E) **4**:362
CHENGDU (China) *see* CH'ENG-TU (Chengdu) (China)
CHÉNIER, ANDRÉ **4**:330 *bibliog.*
CHENILLE PLANT **4**:330 *illus.*
CHENNAULT, CLAIRE L. **4**:330 *bibliog., illus.*
P-40 **15**:3
World War II **20**:260 *illus.*
CHENOA (Illinois)
map (40° 45′N 88° 43′W) **11**:42
CHENONCEAUX, CHÂTEAU DE **4**:330–331
CHEOPS *see* KHUFU, KING OF EGYPT
CHEPÉN (Peru)
map (7° 13′S 79° 27′W) **15**:193
CHEPHREN *see* KHAFRE, KING OF EGYPT
CHEPO (Panama)
map (9° 10′N 79° 6′W) **15**:55
CHEQUAMEGON BAY
map (46° 40′N 90° 50′W) **20**:185
CHERAW (South Carolina)
map (34° 42′N 79° 53′W) **18**:98
CHERBOURG (France) **4**:331
CHERCEL *see* IOL (Algeria)
CHEREMIS LANGUAGE
Uralic languages **19**:475
CHERENKOV, PAVEL ALEKSEYEVICH **4**:331
Cherenkov radiation **4**:331
CHERENKOV RADIATION **4**:331 *bibliog.*
Cherenkov, Pavel Alekseyevich **4**:331
Frank, Ilya Mikhailovich **8**:279
gamma-ray astronomy **9**:34
tachyon **19**:6
CHÉRET, JULES
carnival poster **15**:461 *illus.*
CHERGUI SHATT
map (34° 21′N 0° 30′E) **1**:287
CHERIMOYA *see* CUSTARD APPLE
CHERKESS *see* CIRCASSIANS
CHERLEN RIVER
map (48° 48′N 117° 0′E) **13**:529
CHERNENKO, KONSTANTIN **4**:331 *illus.*
CHERNOBYL (USSR) **4**:331 *bibliog.*
nuclear energy **14**:283
CHERNOZEM **4**:331
distribution, worldwide **18**:37 *map*
CHERNYSHEVSKY, NIKOLAI GAVRILOVICH **4**:331–332 *bibliog.*
CHEROKEE (Alabama)
map (34° 46′N 87° 58′W) **1**:234
CHEROKEE (county in Alabama)
map (34° 10′N 85° 40′W) **1**:234
CHEROKEE (American Indians) **4**:332 *bibliog., illus.*
Chattanooga (Tennessee) **4**:303
Five Civilized Tribes **8**:132
Georgia **9**:117
Houston, Sam **10**:282
Indian treaties **11**:106
Jackson, Andrew **11**:342
Oklahoma **14**:371
removal to Indian Territory **11**:109 *map*
Ross, John **16**:318
Sequoya **17**:207
Shawnee (American Indians) **17**:246
Transylvania Company **19**:283
Watie, Stand **20**:67
writing systems, evolution of **20**:293 *illus.*
CHEROKEE (county in Georgia)
map (34° 15′N 84° 30′W) **9**:114
CHEROKEE (Iowa)
map (42° 45′N 95° 33′W) **11**:244
CHEROKEE (county in Iowa)
map (42° 43′N 95° 35′W) **11**:244
CHEROKEE (Kansas)
map (37° 21′N 94° 49′W) **12**:18
CHEROKEE (county in Kansas)
map (37° 10′N 94° 50′W) **12**:18
CHEROKEE (county in North Carolina)
map (35° 10′N 84° 5′W) **14**:242
CHEROKEE (Oklahoma)
map (36° 45′N 98° 21′W) **14**:368
CHEROKEE (county in Oklahoma)
map (35° 55′N 95° 0′W) **14**:368
CHEROKEE (county in South Carolina)
map (35° 0′N 81° 40′W) **18**:98
CHEROKEE (county in Texas)
map (31° 48′N 95° 10′W) **19**:129
CHEROKEE LAKE
map (36° 16′N 83° 20′W) **19**:104
CHEROKEE NATION v. THE STATE OF GEORGIA
Indian treaties **11**:106
CHEROKEES, LAKE O' THE
map (36° 39′N 94° 49′W) **14**:368
CHERRY (botany) **4**:332 *illus.*; **8**:348 *illus.*; **15**:337 *illus.*
CHERRY (county in Nebraska)
map (42° 30′N 101° 0′W) **14**:70
CHERRY BIRCH *see* MAHOGANY
CHERRY CREEK (Colorado)
map (39° 45′N 105° 1′W) **5**:116
CHERRY CREEK (South Dakota)
map (44° 36′N 101° 30′W) **18**:103
CHERRY HILL (New Jersey)
map (39° 55′N 75° 1′W) **14**:129
CHERRY ORCHARD, THE (play) **4**:332
Chekhov, Anton **4**:310
CHERRY VALLEY (Arkansas)
map (35° 24′N 90° 45′W) **2**:166
CHERRYVALE (Kansas)
map (37° 16′N 95° 33′W) **12**:18
CHERRYVILLE (North Carolina)
map (35° 23′N 81° 23′W) **14**:242
CHERSKIY RANGE (Mountain Range)
map (65° 0′N 145° 0′E) **19**:388
CHERT AND FLINT **4**:332–333 *bibliog., illus.*
chert form **4**:333 *illus.*
flint **4**:332 *illus.*
Folsom culture **14**:237 *illus.*
fossil record **8**:243; **8**:245
Grimes Graves **9**:364–365
Mesolithic Period **13**:314
mining and quarrying **13**:446
mining tools **7**:302 *illus.*
Paleolithic Period **15**:38
prehistoric uses **4**:332
quartz **16**:14
quartzite **16**:14
sedimentary rock **17**:184
CHERUBIM
angel **1**:412
CHERUBINI, LUIGI **4**:333 *bibliog.*
CHERVIL **4**:333
CHESANING (Michigan)
map (43° 11′N 84° 7′W) **13**:377
CHESAPEAKE (ship) **4**:333
CHESAPEAKE (Virginia)
map (36° 43′N 76° 15′W) **19**:607
CHESAPEAKE BAY **4**:333
Bridge-Tunnel **19**:608 *illus.*
fishing industry **13**:189 *illus.*
map (38° 40′N 76° 25′W) **19**:419
CHESAPEAKE BAY RETRIEVER **4**:333–334 *bibliog., illus.*; **6**:219 *illus.*
CHESAPEAKE BEACH (Maryland)
map (38° 41′N 76° 32′W) **13**:188
CHESAPEAKE CITY (Maryland)
map (39° 32′N 75° 49′W) **13**:188
CHESAPEAKE AND DELAWARE CANAL **4**:334
map (39° 34′N 75° 34′W) **6**:88
CHESAPEAKE AND OHIO CANAL **4**:334
CHESHIRE (Connecticut)
map (41° 30′N 72° 54′W) **5**:193
CHESHIRE (England) **4**:334
Chester **4**:336

CHESHIRE (county in New Hampshire)
map (42° 58′N 72° 15′W) **14**:123
CHESLEY (Ontario)
map (44° 17′N 81° 5′W) **14**:393; **14**:461
CHESNEE (South Carolina)
map (35° 9′N 81° 52′W) **18**:98
CHESNUTT, CHARLES WADDELL 4:334 *bibliog.*
black American literature **3**:304
CHESS 4:334–336 *bibliog., illus., tables*
basic layout **4**:335 *illus.*
Capablanca, José Raúl **4**:119
computer chess **4**:336
Fischer, Bobby **8**:110
games **9**:30 *illus.*
games, mathematical **9**:33
history **4**:334–336
Karpov, Anatoly **12**:29
moves of pieces **4**:335 *illus.*
Philidor (family) **15**:231
rules and play **4**:334
Spassky, Boris **18**:165
symbols **4**:335 *illus.*
United States Champions **4**:335 *table*
CHEST 4:336
See also THORAX
breast **3**:468–469
skeleton, human **17**:336
X ray **20**:310 *illus.*
CHEST FISH
ribbonfish **16**:205
CHESTER (California)
map (40° 19′N 121° 14′W) **4**:31
CHESTER (Connecticut)
map (41° 24′N 72° 27′W) **5**:193
CHESTER (England) 4:336
map (53° 12′N 2° 54′W) **19**:403
CHESTER (Illinois)
map (37° 55′N 89° 49′W) **11**:42
CHESTER (Montana)
map (48° 31′N 110° 58′W) **13**:547
CHESTER (Nebraska)
map (40° 1′N 97° 37′W) **14**:70
CHESTER (Oklahoma)
map (36° 13′N 98° 55′W) **14**:368
CHESTER (Pennsylvania) 4:336
map (39° 51′N 75° 21′W) **15**:147
CHESTER (county in Pennsylvania)
map (39° 58′N 75° 36′W) **15**:147
CHESTER (South Carolina)
map (34° 43′N 81° 12′W) **18**:98
CHESTER (county in South Carolina)
map (34° 45′N 81° 10′W) **18**:98
CHESTER (county in Tennessee)
map (35° 27′N 88° 35′W) **19**:104
CHESTER (Vermont)
map (43° 16′N 72° 36′W) **19**:554
CHESTER (Virginia)
map (37° 21′N 77° 27′W) **19**:607
CHESTER BASIN (Nova Scotia)
map (44° 34′N 64° 19′W) **14**:269
CHESTER RIVER
map (38° 58′N 76° 17′W) **13**:188
CHESTERFIELD (England) 4:336
CHESTERFIELD (Indiana)
map (40° 7′N 85° 36′W) **11**:111
CHESTERFIELD (South Carolina)
map (34° 44′N 80° 5′W) **18**:98
CHESTERFIELD (county in South Carolina)
map (34° 40′N 80° 10′W) **18**:98
CHESTERFIELD (Virginia)
map (37° 23′N 77° 31′W) **19**:607
CHESTERFIELD (county in Virginia)
map (37° 20′N 77° 25′W) **19**:607
CHESTERFIELD, PHILIP DORMER STANHOPE, 4TH EARL OF 4:336 *bibliog.*
portrait
Ramsay, Allan **16**:81
CHESTERFIELD INLET (Northwest Territories)
map (63° 21′N 90° 42′W) **14**:258
CHESTERFIELD ISLANDS
New Caledonia **14**:119
CHESTERHILL (Ohio)
map (39° 29′N 81° 52′W) **14**:357
CHESTERTON (Indiana)
map (41° 37′N 87° 4′W) **11**:111
CHESTERTON, G. K. 4:337 *bibliog., illus.*
CHESTERTOWN (Maryland)
map (39° 13′N 76° 4′W) **13**:188
CHESTNUT 4:337 *illus.*; **14**:300 *illus.*
CHESTNUT STREET THEATRE 4:337
CHESUNCOOK LAKE
map (46° 0′N 69° 20′W) **13**:70
CHETEK (Wisconsin)
map (45° 19′N 91° 39′W) **20**:185
CHÉTICAMP (Nova Scotia) **14**:271 *illus.*
map (46° 38′N 61° 1′W) **14**:269
CHETOPA (Kansas)
map (37° 2′N 95° 5′W) **12**:18
CHETUMAL (Mexico) 4:337
CHETWYND (British Columbia)
map (55° 42′N 121° 40′W) **3**:491
CHEVALIER *see* KNIGHT
CHEVALIER, GUILLAUME SULPICE *see* GAVARNI, PAUL
CHEVALIER, MAURICE 4:337 *bibliog.*
Lubitsch, Ernst **12**:447
CHEVERUS, JEAN LOUIS LEFEBVRE DE 4:337–338 *bibliog.*
CHEVES, LANGLON
Bank of the United States **3**:67
CHEVET
Romanesque art and architecture **16**:282 *illus.*
CHEVIOT (Ohio)
map (39° 11′N 84° 35′W) **14**:357
CHEVIOT (zoology) **17**:249 *illus.*
CHEVREUL, MICHEL EUGÈNE
soap and detergent **18**:7
CHEVROTAIN 4:338 *illus.*
ruminant **16**:345
CHEVY CHASE (Maryland)
map (38° 58′N 77° 5′W) **13**:188
CHEWELAH (Washington)
map (48° 17′N 117° 43′W) **20**:35
CHEWING GUM 4:338
chicle **4**:346
sapodilla **17**:73
CHEYENNE (American Indians) 4:338 *bibliog., illus.*
art **11**:141 *illus.*
ghost dance **9**:169
Indian Wars **11**:108–110
Little Bighorn, Battle of the **12**:372
Sand Creek Massacre **17**:59–60
Sun dance **18**:346
tepee **19**:114
CHEYENNE (county in Colorado)
map (38° 45′N 102° 40′W) **5**:116
CHEYENNE (county in Kansas)
map (39° 50′N 101° 45′W) **12**:18
CHEYENNE (county in Nebraska)
map (41° 15′N 103° 0′W) **14**:70
CHEYENNE (Oklahoma)
map (35° 37′N 99° 40′W) **14**:368
CHEYENNE (Wyoming) 4:338–339; **20**:304 *illus.*
map (41° 8′N 104° 49′W) **20**:301
rodeo **16**:266
CHEYENNE RIVER
map (44° 40′N 101° 15′W) **18**:103
CHEYENNE WELLS (Colorado)
map (38° 51′N 102° 11′W) **5**:116
CHEYNE-STOKES RESPIRATION *see* RESPIRATORY SYSTEM DISORDERS
CHI (letter)
X (letter) **20**:305
CH'I-CH'I-HA-ERH (China)
map (47° 19′N 123° 55′E) **4**:362
CHI-HSI (China)
map (45° 17′N 130° 59′E) **4**:362
CHI K'ANG (Ji Kang) 4:339 *bibliog.*
CH'I-LIN LAKE
map (31° 50′N 89° 0′E) **19**:190
CHI-LUNG (Taiwan)
map (25° 8′N 121° 44′E) **19**:13
CH'I PAI-SHIH (Qi Baishi) 4:339 *bibliog.*
CHI RHO CROSS **5**:360; **5**:361 *illus.*
CHI RIVER
map (15° 11′N 104° 43′E) **19**:139
CHI-SQUARE DISTRIBUTION 4:339 *bibliog.*
statistics, nonparametric **18**:238
CHIA-I (Taiwan)
map (23° 29′N 120° 27′E) **19**:13
CHIANG CH'ING (Jiang Qing) 4:339 *bibliog.*
Gang of Four **9**:36
Mao Tse-tung (Mao Zedong) **13**:135
CHIANG CHING-KUO (Jiang Jingguo) 4:339
CHIANG KAI-SHEK 4:339 *bibliog., illus.*
Chang Hsueh-liang (Zhang Xueliang) **4**:280–281
Chiang Ching-kuo (Jiang Jingguo) **4**:339
China, history of **4**:375
Kuomintang (Guomindang) **12**:138
Mao Tse-tung (Mao Zedong) **13**:135
Northern Expedition **14**:254
Soong (family) **18**:66
Stilwell, Joseph W. **18**:270
CHIANG KAI-SHEK, MADAME
Soong (family) **18**:66
CHIANG MAI (city in Thailand) 4:339–340
map (18° 47′N 98° 59′E) **19**:139
CHIANG MAI (kingdom)
Thailand **19**:141
CH'IANG T'ANG
map (34° 0′N 90° 0′E) **19**:190
CHIAPAS (Mexico) 4:340
archaeology
Izapa **11**:338
Palenque **15**:30
art
pre-Columbian art and architecture **15**:496
cities
Tuxtla Gutiérrez **19**:356–357
Indians, American
Lacandón **12**:158
CHIARELLI, LUIGI 4:340
CHIAROSCURO 4:340
Bassano (family) **3**:117–118
drawing **6**:264
graphic arts **9**:291–292
Leonardo da Vinci **12**:290
Rembrandt **16**:145
White, Clarence H. **20**:134
Woman Bathing in a Stream (Rembrandt) **2**:197 *illus.*
CHIBA (Japan)
map (35° 36′N 140° 7′E) **11**:361
CHIBCHA (American Indians) 4:340 *bibliog.*
El Dorado **7**:98
CHIBOUGAMAU (Quebec)
map (49° 55′N 74° 22′W) **16**:18
CHICAGO (Illinois) 4:340–342 *bibliog., illus., map*; **11**:43 *illus.*; **19**:428 *illus.*
architecture
Adler, Dankmar **1**:104
Auditorium Building **2**:318
Burnham, Daniel Hudson **3**:577
Carson, Pirie, Scott Store **2**:136 *illus.*
Chicago School of Architecture **4**:342–343
Goldberg, Bertrand **9**:231
Holabird, William **10**:200
Jenney, William LeBaron **11**:396
John Hancock Center **4**:342 *illus.*; **19**:428 *illus.*
Lake Shore Drive Apartment Towers **13**:415 *illus.*
Robie House **1**:329 *illus.*; **16**:243; **20**:288 *illus.*
Root, John Wellborn **16**:311
Sears Tower **17**:175
skyscraper **17**:348 *illus.*
Sullivan, Louis **18**:337
World's Columbian Exposition of 1893 **20**:281–282
art
Chicago, Art Institute of **4**:342
Brookfield Zoo **3**:510
Chicago, Lyric Opera of **4**:342
Chicago Daily News **4**:342
Chicago Symphony Orchestra **4**:343
Chicago Tribune **4**:343
climate **19**:421 *table*
education
Chicago, University of **4**:342
Northwestern University **14**:260
Parker, Francis Wayland **15**:90
Field Museum of Natural History **8**:72
history
Daley, Richard J. **6**:11–12
Fort Dearborn **8**:236
Haymarket Riot **10**:83
Hull House **10**:296
skyscraper **17**:348–350 *illus.*
Thompson, William Hale **19**:175
housing **10**:276 *illus.*
jazz **11**:388
map (41° 53′N 87° 38′W) **11**:42
subway **18**:318 *table*
CHICAGO, ART INSTITUTE OF 4:342 *bibliog.*
CHICAGO, LYRIC OPERA OF 4:342 *bibliog.*
CHICAGO, UNIVERSITY OF 4:342
Argonne National Laboratory **2**:152
Harper, William Rainey **10**:55
Hutchins, Robert M. **10**:322
Yerkes Observatory **20**:326
CHICAGO BEARS (football team)
Halas, George **10**:17
CHICAGO DAILY NEWS 4:342
Field (family) **8**:71
CHICAGO FIRE (1871)
Chicago **4**:340
CHICAGO HEIGHTS (Illinois)
map (41° 30′N 87° 38′W) **11**:42
CHICAGO NATURAL HISTORY MUSEUM *see* FIELD MUSEUM OF NATURAL HISTORY
CHICAGO OPERA BALLET
Page, Ruth **15**:13
CHICAGO RENAISSANCE
Masters, Edgar Lee **13**:215–216
CHICAGO SCHOOL OF ARCHITECTURE 4:342–343
Adler, Dankmar **1**:104
American art and architecture **1**:329
Auditorium Building **2**:318
Holabird, William **10**:200
Root, John Wellborn **16**:311
skyscraper **17**:348
Sullivan, Louis **18**:337
CHICAGO SEVEN
Kunstler, William **12**:137
CHICAGO SYMPHONY ORCHESTRA 4:343 *bibliog.*
American music **1**:350
Giulini, Carlo Maria **9**:191
Solti, Sir Georg **18**:58
Stock, Frederick **18**:274
CHICAGO TRIBUNE 4:343
McCormick, Robert Rutherford **13**:10
Patterson (family) **15**:115
CHICAGO TRIBUNE-NEW YORK NEWS SYNDICATE
press agencies and syndicates **15**:533
CHICAGO WORLD'S FAIR OF 1893 *see* WORLD'S COLUMBIAN EXPOSITION OF 1893
CHICAGO ZOOLOGICAL PARK *see* BROOKFIELD ZOO
CHICANO 4:343 *bibliog., illus.*
folk medicine **8**:201
Hispanic Americans **10**:177–178 *map*
CHICHAGOF ISLAND
map (57° 30′N 135° 30′W) **1**:242
CHICHÉN ITZÁ 4:343–344 *bibliog., illus.*; **13**:358 *illus.*; **14**:237 *map*
Castillo **15**:498 *illus.*
Maya **13**:243–244
Mayapán **13**:246
pre-Columbian art and architecture **15**:498
Thompson, Edward Herbert **19**:175
Thompson, J. Eric **19**:175
Toltec **19**:229
Tula **19**:329–330
CHICHESTER (England) 4:344
CHICHESTER, SIR FRANCIS 4:344 *bibliog.*
CHICHIMEC
Querétaro (state in Mexico) **16**:23
Tlaxcalan **19**:216
CHICK-PEA 4:344–345 *illus.*
CHICKADEE 4:345 *illus.*
foot **3**:288 *illus.*
CHICKAHOMINY RIVER
map (37° 14′N 76° 53′W) **19**:607
CHICKALOON (Alaska)
map (61° 48′N 148° 28′W) **1**:242
CHICKAMAUGA (Georgia)
map (34° 52′N 85° 18′W) **9**:114
CHICKAMAUGA, BATTLE OF 4:345 *bibliog.*
Civil War, U.S. **5**:28–29
Thomas, George Henry **19**:173
CHICKAMAUGA LAKE
map (35° 22′N 85° 2′W) **19**:104
CHICKASAW (Alabama)
map (30° 46′N 88° 5′W) **1**:234
CHICKASAW (American Indians) 4:345 *bibliog.*
Five Civilized Tribes **8**:132
Mississippian culture **14**:239
Oklahoma **14**:371
removal to Indian Territory **11**:109 *map*
CHICKASAW (county in Iowa)
map (43° 3′N 92° 18′W) **11**:244
CHICKASAW (county in Mississippi)
map (33° 55′N 88° 55′W) **13**:469
CHICKASAWHAY RIVER
map (31° 0′N 88° 45′W) **13**:469
CHICKASHA (Oklahoma)
map (35° 2′N 97° 58′W) **14**:368
CHICKEN 4:345 *bibliog., illus.*
Cornish **4**:345 *illus.*; **15**:474 *illus.*
development **6**:138 *illus.*
diseases
flea **8**:158
leukemia **12**:301
egg **7**:72 *illus.*
embryo **7**:324 *illus.*
imprinting **11**:68
Leghorn **4**:345 *illus.*; **15**:474 *illus.*
parthenogenesis **15**:100
poultry **15**:473–474 *illus.*
Rhode Island Red **15**:474 *illus.*
CHICKEN POX 4:345–346 *bibliog.*
herpes **10**:145
shingles **17**:262
CHICKEN TURTLE 4:346; **14**:167 *illus.*; **16**:167 *illus.*
shell **17**:252 *illus.*

CHICKWEED 4:346
CHICLAYO (Peru)
map (6° 46'S 79° 51'W) **15**:193
CHICLE 4:346
chewing gum **4**:338
sapodilla **17**:73
CHICO (California)
map (39° 44'N 121° 50'W) **4**:31
CHICO RIVER
map (43° 48'S 66° 25'W) **2**:149
CHICOPEE (Georgia)
map (34° 16'N 83° 51'W) **9**:114
CHICOPEE (Massachusetts)
map (42° 10'N 72° 36'W) **13**:206
CHICORY 4:346 *illus.*; **19**:532 *illus.*
CHICOT (county in Arkansas)
map (33° 15'N 91° 17'W) **2**:166
CHICOUTIMI (Quebec) **4**:346
map (48° 26'N 71° 4'W) **16**:18
CHIDLEY, CAPE OF
map (60° 23'N 64° 26'W) **16**:18
CHIEF 4:346 *bibliog.*
CHIEFLAND (Florida)
map (29° 29'N 82° 52'W) **8**:172
CHIEN ANDALOU, UN (film) **18**:366 *illus.*
CHIEN-FO-TUNG *see* CAVES OF THE THOUSAND BUDDHAS
CH'IEN-LUNG (Qianlong) **4**:346–347 *bibliog.*
CHIEN TANG KIANG RIVER
tidal bore **19**:192
CHIETI (Italy)
map (42° 21'N 14° 10'E) **11**:321
CHIFFON 4:347
CHIFLEY, JOSEPH BENEDICT 4:347
Australia, history of **2**:341
CHIGGER 2:106 *illus.*; **4**:347; **13**:484 *illus.*
CHIGI, AGOSTINO
Raphael **16**:89
CHIGNECTO BAY
map (45° 35'N 64° 45'W) **14**:117
CHIGNIK (Alaska)
map (56° 18'N 158° 23'W) **1**:242
CHIHLI, GULF OF
map (38° 30'N 120° 0'E) **4**:362
CHIHUAHUA (dog) **4**:347 *bibliog., illus.*; **6**:217 *illus.*
CHIHUAHUA (Mexico) **4**:347
map (28° 38'N 106° 5'W) **13**:357
CHIHUAHUA (state in Mexico) **4**:347
cities
Chihuahua **4**:347
Ciudad Juárez **5**:9
CHIKAMATSU MONZAEMON 4:347 *bibliog.*
theater, history of the **19**:148
CHILAW (Sri Lanka)
map (7° 34'N 79° 47'E) **18**:206
CHILD, JULIA 4:347
CHILD, LYDIA MARIA 4:348 *bibliog.*
CHILD ABUSE 4:348 *bibliog.*
children's rights **4**:354
CHILD CUSTODY
divorce **6**:206
CHILD DEVELOPMENT 4:348–350 *bibliog., illus.*
adolescence **1**:106–107
anthropometry **2**:55
attachment (psychology) **2**:313
autistic children **2**:355
Bettelheim, Bruno **3**:232
Bruner, Jerome Seymour **3**:525
Bühler, Karl **3**:548
Burt, Sir Cyril **3**:581
child psychiatry **4**:350–351
cognitive psychology **5**:95
complex (psychology) **5**:157
culture **5**:384
Educational Testing Service **7**:66
Erikson, Erik **7**:230
feral children **8**:51
games **9**:31
Gesell, Arnold **9**:159
growth **4**:349 *illus.*
Head Start **10**:85
human body **4**:349 *illus.*
hyperactive children **10**:347
impulses, inner speech **11**:179
infancy **11**:162–163
initiation passage rites **15**:103–104
intelligence **11**:203–204
Luria, Aleksandr Romanovich **12**:466
mental development **4**:348–349
moral awareness **13**:572–573
personality **4**:348–350
Pestalozzi, Johann Heinrich **15**:196
Piaget, Jean **15**:287–288
play **15**:362–363
premature aging **1**:186
preschool education **15**:520–522
primary education **15**:537–538
progressive education **15**:564
psycholinguistics **15**:592
psychological measurement **15**:593
radio and television broadcasting **16**:60
sexual development **17**:229
sexuality: Freud, Sigmund **8**:329
socialization **4**:348; **4**:350
speech development **18**:175
Spock, Benjamin **18**:191–192
tic **19**:191
video game **19**:577
CHILD LABOR 4:350 *bibliog., illus.*; **12**:154 *illus.*
Bailey v. *Drexel Furniture Company* **3**:26
federal child labor act of 1916
Hammer v. *Dagenhart* **10**:30
Kelley, Florence **12**:38
Owen, Robert **14**:471
United States v. *Darby* **19**:465
CHILD PORNOGRAPHY
pornography **15**:441
CHILD PSYCHIATRY 4:350–351 *bibliog.*
child development **4**:348–350
Freud, Anna **8**:328
Freud, Sigmund **8**:329
Klein, Melanie **12**:96
theories **4**:350
types of disturbances **4**:350
CHILD PSYCHOLOGY
child development **4**:348–350
developmental psychology **6**:142–143
juvenile delinquency **11**:480
CHILDBED FEVER *see* PUERPERAL FEVER
CHILDBIRTH *see* PREGNANCY AND BIRTH
CHILDE, V. GORDON 4:351 *bibliog.*
civilization **5**:34
Neolithic Period **14**:84
prehistory **15**:517
Skara Brae **17**:332
CHILDERIC
Franks **8**:286
CHILDERSBURG (Alabama)
map (33° 16'N 86° 21'W) **1**:234
CHILDHOOD DISEASES *see* DISEASES, CHILDHOOD
CHILDREN'S CRUSADE 4:351
CHILDREN'S DISEASES *see* DISEASES, CHILDHOOD
CHILDREN'S HOUR, THE (play)
Hellman, Lillian **10**:115
CHILDREN'S LITERATURE 4:351–354 *bibliog., illus.*
authors
Aiken, Joan **1**:202
Alcott, Louisa May **1**:267
Alexander, Lloyd **1**:273
Alger, Horatio **1**:285–286
Anderson, Hans Christian **1**:401
Armstrong, William **2**:180
Baum, L. Frank **3**:130
Bemelmans, Ludwig **3**:194
Blume, Judy **3**:346–347
Burnett, Frances Hodgson **3**:577
Carroll, Lewis **4**:169
Coatsworth, Elizabeth **5**:82
Collodi, Carlo **5**:104
Crane, Walter **5**:331
Day, Thomas **6**:55
de la Mare, Walter **6**:60
Dodge, Mary Mapes **6**:212
George, Jean Craighead **9**:109
Grahame, Kenneth **9**:281
Greenaway, Kate **9**:349
Grimm, Jacob and Wilhelm **9**:365–366
Hamilton, Virginia **10**:29
Harris, Joel Chandler **10**:57
Hunt, Irene **10**:311
Kipling, Rudyard **11**:86–87
Lagerlöf, Selma **12**:165
Lang, Andrew **12**:194
Le Guin, Ursula **12**:254
Lear, Edward **12**:259
Lewis, C. S. **12**:305
McGinley, Phyllis **13**:16
Milne, A. A. **13**:431
Montgomery, L. M. **13**:556
Nesbit, E. **14**:96
Neville, Emily **14**:115
Potter, Beatrix **15**:467–468
Saint-Exupéry, Antoine de **17**:18
Scarry, Richard **17**:116
Sendak, Maurice **17**:200
Seton, Ernest Thompson **17**:214
Seuss, Dr. **17**:215
Sewell, Anna **17**:221
Speare, Elizabeth **18**:165
Stevenson, Robert Louis **18**:265
Stockton, Frank R. **18**:276
Tolkien, J. R. R. **19**:226–227
White, E. B. **20**:134–135
Whitney, Phyllis **20**:142
Wiggin, Kate Douglas **20**:147
Wilder, Laura Ingalls **20**:149
book illustration **3**:387–388
Caldecott Medal **4**:25
fable **8**:4–5
fairy tale **8**:10–11
fictional characters
Cinderella **4**:432
Drew, Nancy **6**:271
Hardy Boys **10**:48
Tarzan of the Apres **19**:41
Uncle Remus **19**:381
folklore **8**:203
folktale **8**:204
legend **12**:273
literary works
Alice's Adventures in Wonderland **1**:293
Black Beauty **3**:313
Charlotte's Web **4**:299
Peter Pan **15**:200
Grimm's Fairy Tales **9**:366
Heidi **10**:108
Huckleberry Finn **10**:289
Jungle Book, The **11**:468
Mother Goose **13**:607
Pinocchio **15**:307
Robinson Crusoe **16**:246
Swiss Family Robinson, The **18**:393
Tom Sawyer **19**:229
Treasure Island **19**:285
Wind in the Willows, The **20**:172
Wizard of Oz, The **20**:195
Newbery Medal **14**:164
nursery rhymes **14**:298
periodicals
Child, Lydia Maria **4**:348
Dodge, Mary Mapes **6**:212
CHILDREN'S RIGHTS 4:354 *bibliog.*
Hull House **10**:296
minor **13**:459
CHILDRESS (Texas)
map (34° 25'N 100° 13'W) **19**:129
CHILDRESS (county in Texas)
map (34° 30'N 100° 15'W) **19**:129
CHILDS, BARNEY
aleatory music **1**:270
CHILDS, MARQUIS WILLIAM 4:354
"CHILD'S CHRISTMAS IN WALES, A" (poem)
Thomas, Dylan **19**:172
CHILD'S GARDEN OF VERSES, A (book)
Stevenson, Robert Louis **18**:265
CHILE 4:354–357 *bibliog., illus., map, table*
agriculture **4**:356
arts **4**:355–356
Latin American art and architecture **12**:222–228
cities
Antofagasta **2**:69
Arica **2**:154
Concepción **5**:169
Punta Arenas **15**:626
Santiago **17**:69–70 *illus.*
Valparaíso **19**:508
Viña del Mar **19**:599
climate **4**:355; **4**:356 *table*
Easter Island **7**:32–33 *illus., map*
economic activity **4**:356
education **4**:355
Latin American universities **12**:233 *table*
flag **4**:354 *illus.*
government **4**:356–357
history **4**:357
Alessandri, Arturo **1**:272
Allende, Salvador **1**:300–301
Balmaceda, José **3**:53
Frei Montalva, Eduardo **8**:301
Latin America, history of **12**:220–222
Lautaro **12**:240
O'Higgins, Bernardo **14**:356
Pacific, War of the **15**:5
Pinochet Ugarte, Augusto **15**:307
Tacna-Arica Dispute **19**:6
Valdivia, Pedro de **19**:503
land **4**:354–355 *map*
meteorite craters **13**:339
literature
Barrios, Eduardo **3**:95
Donoso, José **6**:240
Huidobro, Vicente **10**:295
Mistral, Gabriela **13**:482
Neruda, Pablo **14**:90
map (30° 0'S 71° 0'W) **18**:85
people **4**:355–356
Araucanians **2**:109–110
physical features
Andes **4**:357 *illus.*
Atacama Desert **2**:286–287
Central Valley **4**:357 *illus.*
Horn, Cape **10**:238
railroad **16**:73
Trans-Andine Railroad **19**:267
resources **4**:355
nitrogen **14**:202
CHILE-PERUVIAN WAR *see* PACIFIC, WAR OF THE
CHILE RISE
plate tectonics **15**:351 *map*
CHILEAN TRENCH
subduction zone **18**:312
CHILECITO (Argentina)
map (29° 10'S 67° 30'W) **2**:149
CHILEMBWE, JOHN 4:357 *bibliog.*
Africa, history of **1**:159
CHILENGUE MOUNTAINS
map (13° 10'S 15° 18'E) **2**:5
CHILETE (Peru)
map (7° 14'S 78° 51'W) **15**:193
CHILI *see* PEPPER (vegetable)
CHILILABOMBWE (Zambia)
map (12° 18'S 27° 43'E) **20**:354
CHILKA LAKE
map (19° 46'N 85° 20'E) **11**:80
CHILLÁN (Chile)
map (36° 36'S 72° 7'W) **4**:355
CHILLICOTHE (Illinois)
map (40° 55'N 89° 29'W) **11**:42
CHILLICOTHE (Missouri)
map (39° 48'N 93° 33'W) **13**:476
CHILLICOTHE (Ohio) **4**:357
map (39° 20'N 82° 59'W) **14**:357
CHILLICOTHE (Texas)
map (34° 10'N 99° 31'W) **19**:129
CHILLIWACK (British Columbia)
map (49° 10'N 121° 57'W) **3**:491
***CHILOMONAS* 4**:357
CHILOPODA *see* CENTIPEDE
CHILOQUIN (Oregon)
map (42° 35'N 121° 52'W) **14**:427
CHILPANCINGO (Mexico) **4**:357–358
map (17° 33'N 99° 30'W) **13**:357
CHILPANCINGO, CONGRESS OF
Morelos y Pavón, José María **13**:577
CHILPANCINGO DE LOS BRAVOS *see* CHILPANCINGO (Mexico)
CHILTON (county in Alabama)
map (32° 55'N 86° 40'W) **1**:234
CHILTON (Wisconsin)
map (44° 2'N 88° 10'W) **20**:185
CHILWA, LAKE
map (15° 12'S 35° 50'E) **13**:81
CHIMAERA (fish) **4**:358 *illus.*
CHIMALTENANGO (Guatemala)
map (14° 40'N 90° 49'W) **9**:389
CHIMAYO (New Mexico)
map (36° 0'N 105° 56'W) **14**:136
CHIMBORAZO (volcano) **4**:358
map (1° 28'S 78° 48'W) **7**:52
CHIMBOTE (Peru)
map (9° 5'S 78° 36'W) **15**:193
CHIMERA (book)
Barth, John **3**:97
CHIMERA (mythology) *see* BELLEROPHON
CHIMES
bell **3**:184
musical instrument **13**:675 *illus.*
percussion instruments **15**:162 *illus.*
CHIMNEY 4:358 *bibliog.*
firebrick **8**:106
CHIMNEY ROCK NATIONAL HISTORIC SITE **14**:72 *illus.*
CHIMOR *see* CHIMU
CHIMPANZEE 2:53 *illus.*; **2**:75 *illus.*; **4**:359 *bibliog., illus.*; **13**:104 *illus.*; **15**:540 *illus.*
animal behavior **2**:17 *illus.*
animal communication **2**:20
ape **2**:74–76
brain **3**:443 *illus.*
Goodall, Jane **9**:245
Ham, space medicine **18**:132 *illus.*
CHIMU 4:359 *bibliog.*
Chan Chan **4**:278
gold funerary mask **15**:501 *illus.*
Inca **11**:70
Latin America, history of **12**:216–217
pre-Columbian art and architecture **15**:500–501
CHIN (Jin) **4**:360 *bibliog.*
CH'IN (Qin) (dynasty) **4**:359 *bibliog.*
Asia, history of **2**:252–253
China, history of **4**:371
Chinese archaeology **4**:379
roads and highways **16**:235
CHIN-CHOU (China)
map (41° 0'N 121° 0'E) **4**:362
CHIN HILLS
map (22° 30'N 93° 30'E) **3**:573
CH'IN-HUANG-TAO (China)
map (39° 56'N 119° 36'E) **4**:362

CHINA 4:360–370 *bibliog., illus., map, table*
See also TAIWAN
agriculture 4:367–368; 4:369 *illus.*
irrigation systems 11:282–283
soybean 18:114–115
tea 19:53–54
alchemy 1:263
animal life 4:365
panda 15:58
archaeology *see* CHINESE ARCHAEOLOGY
art *see* CHINESE ART AND ARCHITECTURE
Burma Road 3:575
Chinese calendar 4:388
cities
Amoy 1:376
An-shan (Anshan) 1:387
Anyang 2:72
Canton (Guangzhou) 4:117–118 *illus.*
Ch'ang-ch'un (Changchun) 4:280
Cheng-chou (Zhengzhou) 4:330
Ch'eng-tu (Chengdu) 4:330
Ching-te-chen (Jingde Zhen) 4:395
Chungking (Chongqing) 4:422–423
Foochow 8:207–208
Fu-shun (Fushun) 8:351
Hangchow (Hangzhou) 10:38
Harbin 10:42
Hofei (Hefei) 10:194
K'ai-feng (Kaifeng) 12:6
Kashgar 4:364 *table*
K'un-ming (Kunming) 12:136
Lan-chou (Lanzhou) 12:177
Lhasa 12:309–310
Lü-shun (Lüshun) 12:446
Lü-ta (Lüda) 12:446
Nanking (Nanjing) 14:12
Ning-po (Ningpo) 14:200
Peking (Beijing) 15:134–136 *illus.*
Shanghai 17:239–240 *illus.*
Shen-yang (Shenyang) 17:255
Sian (Xi'an) 17:291
Soochow (Suzhou) 18:66
Ta-lien (Dalian) 19:3
T'ai-yüan (Taiyuan) 19:11
Tientsin (Tianjin) 19:195
Tsinan (Jinan) 19:324
Tsingtao (Qingdao) 19:324
Wen-chow (Wenzhou) 20:103
Wu-han (Wuhan) 20:296
climate 4:364–365 *table*
communism *see* COMMUNISM
cooking 5:239–240
dance 6:26
Yang-Ko 20:317
demography 4:366 *illus.*
economic activity 4:367–369 *illus.*
Five-Year and Ten-Year Plans 4:367
Kwangtung (Guangdong) 12:142
education 4:366–367 *illus.*; 7:59–62
Chinese universities 4:393–394 *table*
Peking University 15:136
family 8:17
fishing 4:369
flag 4:360 *illus.*; 8:134
foreign occupied areas
Hong Kong 10:221–223 *illus., map, table*
Macao (Portugal) 13:4
forestry 4:368–369
government 4:369
defense, national 6:82 *table*
patriotic rally 2:240 *illus.*
health 4:366–367
acupuncture 1:91
Chinese medicine 4:390–391
history *see* CHINA, HISTORY OF
holidays 4:365 *illus.*
land 4:360–365 *illus., map, table*
continental drifting 15:354 *map*
karst (conical hills) 4:361 *illus.*
North China Plain 4:361 *illus.*
languages 4:365–366
oracle bones 14:413
Sino-Tibetan languages 17:324–325
Southeast Asian languages 18:110–111
syllabaries 20:293
Ural-Altaic languages 19:476
writing systems, evolution of 20:292
literature *see* CHINESE LITERATURE
manufacturing 2:246–247 *illus.*; 4:367
silk 17:307
silk weaving (17th century) 19:136 *illus.*
map (35° 0'N 105° 0'E) 2:232
marriage 13:164
martial arts 13:176–178
money 13:525 *illus.*
newspaper 14:172
People's Daily 15:156
people 4:365–367
Han 10:34
Hui 10:295
Malaysia 13:85; 13:86
Meo 13:303
migration to the United States 11:55 *map*
population 15:434
race 16:34 *illus.*
Tatar 19:43–44
Tungus 19:334
Uzbek 19:499
women in society 20:204 *table*
philosophy *see* CHINA—religion
photography
Thomson, John 19:176
physical features
Hainan 10:14
Kunlun Mountains 12:137
Loess Plateau of China 12:393
Lop Nor 12:412
Ordos Desert 14:420
rift valleys 16:221
Takla Makan Desert 19:15
printing 15:551
prostitution 15:573
provinces and regions 4:360
Anhwei 2:8
Chekiang (Zhejiang) 4:310–311
Fukien (Fujian) 8:356
Honan (Henan) 10:217
Hopei (Hebei) 10:230–231
Hunan 10:304
Hupei (Hubei) 10:315
Inner Mongolia 11:179
Kansu 12:23
Kiangsi (Jiangxi) 12:70
Kiangsu (Jiangsu) 12:70
Kwangsi (Guangxi) 12:142
Kwangtung (Guangdong) 12:142
Kweichow (Guizhou) 2:143
Manchuria 13:109 *map*
Ningsia (Ningxia) 14:200
Shansi (Shanxi) 17:240
Shantung (Shandong) 17:240–241
Shensi (Shenxi) 17:255
Sinkiang (Xinjiang) 17:323
Szechwan (Sichuan) 18:415
Tibet 19:189–190
Tsinghai (Qinghai) 19:324
Yünnan (Yunnan) 20:346–347
religion 4:366
ancestor worship 1:398–399
Buddhism 3:540–541; 3:542 *map*
Confucianism 5:179–180
kitchen gods 12:91
philosophy 15:247
Taoism 19:28–29 *illus.*
Zen Buddhism 20:358–359
resources 4:365
coal and coal mining 5:76–77 *map*
energy and power generation 4:367
jade 11:347
Richtofen, Ferdinand von 16:215
rivers, lakes, and waterways 4:365
Brahmaputra River 3:440
Grand Canal 9:284
Hsi Chiang (Xi Jiang) 10:286
Hwang Ho (Huang He) 10:326–327 *map*
Koko Nor 12:106
Tarim River 19:37
Yangtze River 20:317–318 *map*
rockets and missiles 16:252
Lop Nor (China) 12:412
soils 4:364
theater
Mei Lan-Fang 13:281
Peking Opera 15:136
shadow play 17:234
theater, history of the 19:148
Yüan drama 20:338
trade 4:369
transportation 4:369
Chinese Eastern Railway 4:388
junk 11:470–471
railroad 16:74
sampan 17:48
vegetation 4:365
wagon 20:6
yodel 20:328
CHINA, GREAT WALL OF *see* GREAT WALL OF CHINA
CHINA, HISTORY OF 4:370–377 *bibliog., illus., maps, table*
Bronze Age
Shih-chai-shan (Shizhaishan) 17:261
Cathay 4:204
Chinese archaeology 4:377–379
Chinese historians
Han 10:34
Chinese universities 4:394
communism 5:148–150
Confucianism 5:179–180
dynasties 4:374 *table*
European relations, 1500–1800 2:257–258
foot-binding 8:214
Great Wall of China 9:323
historians *see* HISTORY—Chinese historians
historiography 10:184
Mongolia 13:530
paper 15:68–70
Peking (Beijing) 15:136
socialism 18:22
Sung Hui-tsung (Song Huizong) 18:348
tea 19:53
Vietnam 19:583–584
Vietnam War 19:584
women in society 20:203
zoological gardens 20:374
prior to 221 BC
See also CHINESE ARCHAEOLOGY
Anyang 2:72
Asia, history of 2:251–253; 2:256
Chin (Jin) 4:360
Ch'in (Qin) 4:359; 4:371
Chou (Zhou) (dynasty) 4:409
Chou dynasty and warring states 4:370–371 *map*
Iron Age 11:271
pipe and pipeline 15:310 *illus.*
Shang (dynasty) 4:370; 17:239
Sung (Song) (dynasty) 4:372
221 BC-1279 AD
Han dynasty 4:371 *map*; 10:34
Han Wu Ti 10:34
rockets and missiles 16:251–252 *illus.*
Sui (dynasty) 4:371–372; 18:330
Sung (Song) (dynasty) 18:348
T'ang (Tang) (dynasty) 4:371–372; 19:21–22
T'ang Hsüan-tsung 19:22
Wang Mang, Emperor 20:22
Yellow Emperor 20:322
1279–1644
Korea, history of 12:116–117
Kublai Khan, Mongol Emperor 12:134
Ming (dynasty) 4:372–373; 13:444
money 13:526 *illus.*; 14:296 *illus.*
Mongols 4:372; 13:530 *map*
Nurhachi 14:298
Yüan (Yuan) (dynasty) 20:338
Yung-lo, Emperor (Yongle) 20:346
1644–1912
Boxer Uprising 3:431
Ch'ing (Qing) (dynasty) 4:373–374; 4:395
European expansion in 2:258
K'ang-hsi (Kangxi), Emperor 12:15
K'ang Yu-wei (Kang Youwei) 12:15
Open Door Policy 14:398
opium 14:406
Opium Wars 14:407
Sino-Japanese Wars *see* SINO-JAPANESE WARS
Sun Yat-sen 18:346
Taiping Rebellion *see* TAIPING REBELLION
tea trade 4:373 *illus.*
Tientsin, Treaties of 19:195
Tz'u-hsi, Dowager Empress of China (Cixi) 19:368
White Lotus Rebellion 20:138
1912–present
Chao Tzu-yang (Zhao Ziyang) 4:282–283
Chiang Ch'ing (Jiang Qing) 4:339
Chiang Kai-shek 4:339
Chou En-lai (Zhou Enlai) 4:409
Chu Teh (Zhu De) 4:421
cold war 5:99
communism 5:148–150
Communist Revolution (1934–1949) 4:375–376 *illus., map*
Cultural Revolution 5:384
Feng Yü-hsiang (Feng Yuxiang) 8:50
foreign leased areas 4:375 *map*
Gang of Four 9:36
Great Leap Forward 9:320
Hu Yao-pang (Hu Yaobang) 10:287
Hua Kuo-feng (Hua Guofeng) 10:287
Japan's Twenty-One Demands 11:370
Kashmir 12:30
Korean War *see* KOREAN WAR
Kuomintang (Guomindang) 12:137–138
Lin Piao (Lin Biao) 12:347
Liu Shao-ch'i (Liu Shaoqi) 12:374
Long March 12:406
Manchuria 13:109
Mao Tse-tung (Mao Zedong) 13:134–136
nationalist movement 2:259; 4:374–375
Northern Expedition 14:254
P-40 15:3
People's Republic 4:376–377
refugee 16:125
Sino-Japanese Wars 17:323
Soong (family) 18:66
Taiwan 19:14
Teng Hsiao-p'ing (Deng Xiaoping) 19:101–102
Tibet 19:190
Vietnam 19:583–584 *illus.*
Wang Ching-wei (Wang Jingwei) 20:22
warlords 20:30
Woodcock, Leonard 20:210
World War I *see* WORLD WAR I
World War II *see* WORLD WAR II
Yüan Shih-k'ai (Yuan Shikai) 20:338
CHINA, REPUBLIC OF *see* TAIWAN
CHINA PINK *see* CARNATION
CHINA SEA, EAST 4:377
map (30° 0'N 126° 0'E) 4:362
CHINA SEA, SOUTH 4:377
islands and island groups
Hainan (China) 10:14
map (10° 0'N 113° 0'E) 2:232
seas, gulfs, and bays
Malacca, Strait of 13:78
Manila Bay 13:118
Thailand, Gulf of 19:142
Tonkin, Gulf of 19:234
CHINABERRY 4:377
CHINAGLIA, GIORGIO 4:377
CHINAMECA (El Salvador)
map (13° 30'N 88° 21'W) 7:100
CHINANDEGA (Nicaragua)
map (12° 37'N 87° 9'W) 14:179
CHINATI PEAK
map (29° 57'N 104° 29'W) 19:129
CHINAWARE *see* POTTERY AND PORCELAIN
CHINCH BUG 4:377
CHINCHA ALTA (Peru)
map (13° 27'S 76° 8'W) 15:193
CHINCHILLA 4:377 *illus.*
CHINCOTEAGUE (Virginia)
map (37° 56'N 75° 23'W) 19:607
CHINCOTEAGUE BAY
map (38° 6'N 75° 15'W) 13:188
CHINDE (Mozambique)
map (18° 37'S 36° 24'E) 13:627
CHINDITS
Wingate, Orde 20:179
CHINDWIN RIVER
map (21° 26'N 95° 15'E) 3:573
CHINESE ACADEMY OF SCIENCES 4:377
CHINESE AMERICANS *see* ORIENTAL AMERICANS
CHINESE ARCHAEOLOGY 4:377–379 *bibliog., illus.*
Andersson, Johan Gunnar 1:403
Anyang 2:72
China, history of 4:370
Chou-k'ou-tien (Zhoukoudian) 4:409–410
Lung-men (Longmen) 12:462
Neolithic Period 14:84
oracle bones 14:413
Pan-p'o-ts'un (Banpocun) 15:54
Peking man 15:136
Shih-chai-shan (Shizhaishan) 17:261
Tun-huang (Dunhuang) 19:331
Yün-kang (Yungang) 20:346
CHINESE ART AND ARCHITECTURE 4:370–373 *illus.*; 4:379–388 *bibliog., illus.*
See also the subheading China under specific art forms, e.g., ARCHITECTURE; PAINTING; SCULPTURE; etc.; names of specific artists, e.g., CH'I PAI-SHIH (Qi Baishi); WANG HSI-CHIH (Wang Xizhi); etc.

CHINESE ART AND ARCHITECTURE (cont.)
Asia, history of **2**:251–252 *illus.*
bronze **4**:383 *illus.*
calligraphy **4**:44–45 *illus.*; **4**:379–380
celadon **4**:229
folk art **8**:198
Freer, Charles Lang **8**:300
furniture **8**:374
garden **9**:41 *illus.*
graphic arts **9**:291
Great Wall of China **9**:323
inscription **11**:186
interior design **11**:211
ivory and ivory carving **11**:337
jade **4**:384 *illus.*
Korean art **12**:117–118
lacquer **4**:383–384 *illus.*; **12**:160 *illus.*
Lamaist art and architecture **12**:172–173
landscape painting **12**:188
Lung-men (Longmen) **12**:462
Nanking (Nanjing) (China) **14**:12
Peking (Beijing) **15**:134–136 *illus.*
polychrome ink drawing, dating from early T'ang dynasty **19**:21 *illus.*
pottery and porcelain **4**:384–386 *illus.*; **15**:468–470
Royal Ontario Museum **16**:330
rugs and carpets **16**:342–343 *illus.*
stele **18**:250
Taiwan **19**:13
T'ang (dynasty) **19**:21 *illus.*
temple **19**:98–99 *illus.*
textiles **4**:384 *illus.*
theater **4**:373 *illus.*
tomb **19**:231
Tun-huang (Dunhuang) **19**:331
CHINESE CABBAGE **4**:388 *illus.*
CHINESE CALENDAR **4**:388
CHINESE CHECKERS **4**:388
CHINESE CHIPPENDALE FURNITURE
chinoiserie **4**:395
Chippendale, Thomas **4**:396
CHINESE EASTERN RAILWAY **4**:388 *bibliog.*
CHINESE EXCLUSION ACTS **4**:388–389 *bibliog.*
immigration **11**:56
CHINESE LANGUAGE *see* CHINA—languages
CHINESE LANTERN PLANT **4**:389 *illus.*
CHINESE LITERATURE **4**:389–390 *bibliog.*
authors
Chang T'ien-i (Zhang Tianyi) **4**:281
Chi K'ang (Ji Kang) **4**:339
Ch'ü Yüan (Qu Yuan) **4**:421
Chuang-tzu (Zhuang Zi) **4**:421–422
Juan Chi (Ruan Ji) **11**:457
Kuan Han-ch'ing (Guan Hanqing) **12**:133–134
Kuo Mo-jo (Guo Moruo) **12**:137
Li Po (Li Bo) **12**:310
Li Yü (Li Yu) **12**:310–311
Lu Hsün (Lu Xun) **12**:445–446
Pa Chin (Ba Jin) **15**:3
Po Chü-i (Bo Ju'i) **15**:376
Su Tung-p'o (Su Dongpo) **18**:312
T'ao Yüan-ming (Tao Yuanming) **19**:28
Ts'ao Chih (Cao Zhi) **19**:322
Ts'ao Hsüeh-Ch'in (Cao Xueqin) **19**:322
Ts'ao Yü (Cao Yu) **19**:322
Tu Fu (Du Fu) **19**:325
Wang Wei **20**:22
Wu Ch'eng-en (Wu Chengen) **20**:295–296
Wu Ching-Tzu (Wu Jingzi) **20**:296
biography **3**:263
China, history of **4**:371–372
reformer
Hu Shih (Hu Shi) **10**:287
Sino-Tibetan languages **17**:324
T'ang (Tang) (dynasty) **19**:21
CHINESE LIZARD'S TAIL
lizard's tail **12**:382
CHINESE MEDICINE **4**:390–391 *bibliog.*, *illus.*
acupuncture **1**:91
headache **10**:85
adoption, Western medicine **4**:391
anesthetics **1**:410–411
China **4**:366–367
history **4**:390–391
horn (biology)
saiga **17**:15
immunity (biology) **11**:57
medicine **13**:268
CHINESE MUSIC **4**:391–393 *bibliog.*, *illus.*
instruments **4**:392–393 *illus.*
harmonica **10**:51 *illus.*
sheng **17**:255
Peking Opera **15**:136
theory **4**:391–392
CHINESE MYTHOLOGY
Ch'ang-o (Chang E) **4**:281
door gods **6**:240
Fu-Shou-Lu (Fushoulu) **8**:351
kitchen gods **12**:91
Pa Hsien (Ba Xian) **15**:3
CHINESE PARASOL TREE **4**:393 *illus.*
CHINESE PARSLEY *see* CORIANDER
CHINESE PHILOSOPHY *see* *I CHING* (*Yijing*); PHILOSOPHY; names of specific philosophers, e.g., CONFUCIUS; LAO-TZU (Laozi); etc.
CHINESE SECT OF RIGHT UNITY
Chang Tao-ling (Zhang Daoling) **4**:281
CHINESE UNIVERSITIES **4**:393–394 *bibliog.*, *table*
CHINESE UNIVERSITY OF HONG KONG **4**:394–395
CH'ING (Qing) (dynasty) **4**:395 *bibliog.*, *illus.*
Asia, history of **2**:257
Ch'ien-lung (Qianlong) **4**:346–347
China, history of **4**:373–374
Chinese art and architecture **4**:382–383; **4**:385
Chinese literature **4**:390
flag **8**:135 *illus.*
K'ang-hsi (Kangxi), Emperor of China **12**:15
Korea, history of **12**:116
Manchuria (China) **13**:109
Nurhachi **14**:298
painting
Chu Ta (Zhu Da) **4**:421
Shih-t'ao (Shitao) **17**:261
Shen-yang (Shenyang) (China) **17**:255
shoes **17**:280 *illus.*
silk production **4**:373 *illus.*
Taiping Rebellion **19**:12
temple **19**:98
Tseng Kuo-fan (Zeng Guofan) **19**:322–323
Tso Tsung-t'ang (Zuo Zongtang) **19**:324–325
Tz'u-hsi, Dowager Empress of China (Cixi) **19**:368
Wangs, Four **20**:23
White Lotus Rebellion **20**:138
Yüan Shih-k'ai (Yuan Shikai) **20**:338
CHING HAI *see* KOKO NOR
CHING-TE-CHEN (Jingde Zhen) **4**:395
CHINGOLA (Zambia)
map (12° 32′S 27° 52′E) **20**:354
CHINHOYI (Zimbabwe)
map (17° 22′S 30° 12′E) **20**:365
CHINIT RIVER
map (12° 55′N 105° 35′E) **12**:11
CHINJU (Korea)
map (35° 11′N 128° 5′E) **12**:113
CHINLE (Arizona)
map (36° 9′N 109° 33′W) **2**:160
CHINMEN (Taiwan) *see* QUEMOY (Taiwan)
CHINO (California)
map (34° 1′N 117° 42′W) **4**:31
CHINO VALLEY (Arizona)
map (34° 45′N 112° 27′W) **2**:160
CHINOISERIE **4**:395 *bibliog.*
Regency style **16**:126
Royal Pavilion at Brighton **16**:330–331
CHINOOK (American Indians) **4**:395–396 *bibliog.*
potlatch **15**:467
CHINOOK (fish)
salmon **17**:35
CHINOOK (Montana)
map (48° 35′N 109° 14′W) **13**:547
CHINOOK (wind) **4**:396
mountain climates **13**:621
CHINOOK, LAKE
map (44° 33′N 121° 20′W) **14**:427
CHINQUAPIN (botany) **4**:396 *illus.*
chestnut **4**:337
CHINQUAPIN (North Carolina)
map (34° 50′N 77° 49′W) **14**:242
CHINTZ **4**:396
CHIOGGIA (Italy)
map (45° 13′N 12° 17′E) **11**:321
CHIOS (Greece)
map (38° 22′N 26° 8′E) **9**:325
CHIOS ISLAND
map (38° 22′N 26° 0′E) **9**:325
CHIOU-LUNG (Hong Kong) *see* KOWLOON (Hong Kong)
CHIP (electronics)
biosensor **3**:276
computer **5**:160b *illus.*; **5**:160c; **5**:160d
computer-aided design and computer-aided manufacturing **5**:160L
computer industry **5**:160o
computer memory **5**:161
integrated circuit **11**:201–202 *illus.*
microelectronics **13**:385
microprocessor **13**:387
CHIPATA (Zambia)
map (13° 39′S 32° 40′E) **20**:354
CHIPLEY (Florida)
map (30° 47′N 85° 32′W) **8**:172
CHIPMAN (New Brunswick)
map (46° 11′N 65° 53′W) **14**:117
CHIPMUNK **4**:396 *illus.*; **8**:229 *illus.*
CHIPPENDALE, THOMAS **4**:396 *bibliog.*
furniture **8**:377
CHIPPEWA (American Indians)
Ojibwa **14**:364
Wananikwe **20**:21
CHIPPEWA (county in Michigan)
map (46° 20′N 84° 40′W) **13**:377
CHIPPEWA (county in Minnesota)
map (45° 0′N 95° 32′W) **13**:453
CHIPPEWA (county in Wisconsin)
map (45° 2′N 91° 15′W) **20**:185
CHIPPEWA, LAKE
map (45° 56′N 91° 13′W) **20**:185
CHIPPEWA FALLS (Wisconsin)
map (44° 56′N 91° 24′W) **20**:185
CHIPPEWA RIVER (Minnesota)
map (44° 56′N 95° 44′W) **13**:453
CHIPPEWA RIVER (Wisconsin)
map (44° 25′N 92° 10′W) **20**:185
CHIPUTNETICOOK LAKES
map (45° 40′N 67° 40′W) **13**:70
CHIQUIMULA (Guatemala)
map (14° 48′N 89° 33′W) **9**:389
CHIQUIMULILLA (Guatemala)
map (14° 5′N 90° 23′W) **9**:389
CHIRAC, JACQUES **4**:397
CHIRALIC COMPOUNDS
stereochemistry **18**:258
CHIRAU, JEREMIAH
Zimbabwe (Rhodesia) **20**:365; **20**:366
CHIRICAHUA
Apache **2**:73
CHIRICAHUA PEAK
map (31° 52′N 109° 20′W) **2**:160
CHIRICO, GIORGIO DE **4**:397 *bibliog.*, *illus.*
Böcklin, Arnold **3**:355
Carrà, Carlo **4**:166
Death of a Spirit **18**:365 *illus.*
Hector and Andromeda **4**:397 *illus.*
Piazza d'Italia **11**:314 *illus.*
surrealism (art) **18**:364
CHIRIGUANO
Tupí **19**:339
CHIRIQUÍ GRANDE (Panama)
map (8° 57′N 82° 7′W) **15**:55
CHIRIQUI GULF
map (8° 0′N 82° 20′W) **15**:55
CHIRIQUI LAGOON
map (9° 3′N 82° 0′W) **15**:55
CHIRIQUI VOLCANO
map (8° 48′N 82° 33′W) **15**:55
CHIRON (astronomy) **4**:397
Kowal, Charles T. **12**:126
CHIRON (mythology) **4**:397
CHIROPODY *see* PODIATRY
CHIROPRACTIC **4**:397–398 *bibliog.*
CHIROPTERA
mammal **13**:102; **13**:104 *illus.*
CHIROPTERAN *see* BAT
CHIRPING FROG **4**:398
CHIRRIPÓ MOUNT
map (9° 29′N 83° 30′W) **5**:291
CHIRRIPÓ RIVER
map (10° 41′N 83° 41′W) **5**:291
CHIRU **4**:398
CHISAGO (county in Minnesota)
map (45° 25′N 92° 52′W) **13**:453
CHISAGO CITY (Minnesota)
map (45° 22′N 92° 53′W) **13**:453
CHISANA (Alaska)
map (62° 9′N 142° 10′W) **1**:242
CHISEC (Guatemala)
map (15° 49′N 90° 17′W) **9**:389
CHISHOLM (Maine)
map (44° 29′N 70° 12′W) **13**:70
CHISHOLM (Minnesota)
map (47° 29′N 92° 53′W) **13**:453
CHISHOLM, JESSE
Wichita (Kansas) **20**:144
CHISHOLM, SHIRLEY **3**:312 *illus.*; **4**:398 *illus.*
CHISHOLM MILLS (Alberta)
map (54° 55′N 114° 8′W) **1**:256
CHISHOLM TRAIL **4**:398 *bibliog.*; **8**:341 *map*
CHISHTI, SALIM
Fatehpur Sikri **8**:34
CHÍSINĂU (Romania) *see* KISHINEV (USSR)
CHISTOCHINA (Alaska)
map (62° 34′N 144° 40′W) **1**:242
CHISWICK HOUSE (London)
Burlington, Richard Boyle, 3d Earl of **3**:572
CHITA (USSR)
map (52° 3′N 113° 30′E) **19**:388
CHITARRONE **4**:398
CHITIN **4**:398
CHITINA (Alaska)
map (61° 31′N 144° 27′W) **1**:242
CHITON (mollusk) **4**:398–399 *bibliog.*, *illus.*
mollusk **13**:511 *illus.*
CHITOR (Rajput fortress)
Akbar's seige of **11**:90 *illus.*
CHITRÉ (Panama)
map (7° 58′N 80° 26′W) **15**:55
CHITTAGONG (Bangladesh) **4**:399
climate **3**:65 *table*
map (22° 20′N 91° 50′E) **3**:64
CHITTENDEN (county in Vermont)
map (44° 27′N 73° 3′W) **19**:554
CHITTENDEN, THOMAS **4**:399
CHIUSI (Etruria) **4**:399
Etruscans **7**:258–261
CHIVALRY **4**:399 *bibliog.*
China, history of **4**:370–371
courtly love **5**:317
Don Quixote **6**:236
duel **6**:293
Froissart, Jean **8**:338
knight **12**:99–100
medals and decorations **13**:260–263
Middle Ages **13**:393
CHIVE **4**:399 *illus.*
CHIVILCOY (Argentina)
map (34° 53′S 60° 1′W) **2**:149
CHLÁIR (Ireland) *see* CLARE (Ireland)
CHLAMYDIA **4**:399–400
diseases, animal **6**:192
infectious diseases **11**:164–165
urethritis **11**:167
CHLAMYDOMONAS **4**:400
CHLOR-TRIMETON *see* ANTIHISTAMINE
CHLORAL HYDRATE **4**:400
sedative **17**:182
CHLORAMPHENICOL
antibiotics **2**:57; **2**:58; **2**:59
CHLORDIAZEPOXIDE HYDROCHLORIDE *see* LIBRIUM
CHLORELLA **4**:400 *bibliog.*
algae **1**:283
CHLORFLUOROMETHANES
organic chemistry **14**:439
CHLORIDE **4**:400
ion
neurophysiology **14**:106
Regnault, Henri Victor **16**:129
CHLORINATION
water supply **20**:54
CHLORINE **4**:400–401 *bibliog.*
abundances of common elements **7**:131 *table*
Berthollet, Claude Louis, Comte de **3**:226
chemical industry **4**:318
chemical properties **4**:400
chlorine compounds **4**:400–401
Davy, Sir Humphry **6**:53
element **7**:130 *table*
gas
chemical and biological warfare **4**:311
electrolysis **7**:115
Haber, Fritz **10**:4
poison gas **15**:382
Group VIIA periodic table **12**:167
halite **10**:21
halogens **10**:25
occurrence **4**:400
preparation **4**:400
Scheele, Carl Wilhelm **17**:115
silicate minerals **17**:304–305
toxicity and precautions **4**:400
uses **4**:400
vitamins and minerals **19**:621
CHLORINITY *see* SEAWATER
CHLORITE MINERALS **4**:401 *bibliog.*, *illus.*
clay minerals **5**:46
monoclinic system **13**:536
CHLOROFORM **4**:401
Guthrie, Samuel **9**:409
halide **10**:20

CHLOROGUANIDE
 malaria **13**:80
CHLOROHYDRIN 4:401 *illus.*
CHLOROPHYLL 4:401–402 *bibliog.*
 algae **1**:280–282
 blue-green algae **3**:343
 carotenoid **4**:162
 chloroplast **4**:402
 coloration, biological **5**:122
 Fischer, Hans **8**:110
 heredity **10**:141
 heterocyclic compound **10**:153
 photosynthesis **15**:275–277
 structure: Willstätter, Richard **20**:163
 synthesis: Woodward, Robert Burns **20**:213
CHLOROPHYTA *see* ALGAE, GREEN ALGAE
CHLOROPLAST 4:402
 cell **4**:233
 chlorophyll **4**:401
 cytochrome **5**:411
 genetics **9**:89–90
 photosynthesis **15**:275–277 *illus.*
 Spirogyra **18**:189
CHLOROQUINE
 malaria **13**:80
CHLORPROMAZINE
 psychotropic drugs **15**:604
 tranquilizer **19**:266
CHMIELNICKI, BOHDAN 4:402 *bibliog.*
CHOATE, JOSEPH HODGES 4:402 *bibliog.*
CHOCOLATE 4:402 *bibliog.*
 cocoa **5**:88
 Hershey, Milton Snaveley **10**:148
CHOCOPE (Peru)
 map (7° 47′S 79° 13′W) **15**:193
CHOCRÓN, ISAAC
 Venezuela **19**:543
CHOCTAW (county in Alabama)
 map (32° 0′N 88° 15′W) **1**:234
CHOCTAW (American Indians) 4:402–403 *bibliog.*
 Five Civilized Tribes **8**:132
 Indians of North America, music and dance of the **11**:143
 Oklahoma **14**:371
 removal to Indian Territory **11**:109 *map*
CHOCTAW (county in Mississippi)
 map (33° 20′N 89° 15′W) **13**:469
CHOCTAW (county in Oklahoma)
 map (34° 0′N 95° 35′W) **14**:368
CHOCTAWHATCHEE BAY
 map (30° 25′N 86° 21′W) **8**:172
CHODOWIECKI, DANIEL NIKOLAUS 4:403 *bibliog.*
CH'OE (family)
 Korea, history of **12**:116
CHOELE-CHOEL (Argentina)
 map (39° 16′S 65° 41′W) **2**:149
CHOGA ZANBIL *see* DUR-UNTASH (Iran)
CHOI KYU HAH
 Korea **12**:116
CHOIR
 choral music **4**:405–407
 misericord **13**:466
CHOISEUL, ÉTIENNE FRANÇOIS, DUC DE 4:403 *bibliog.*
CHOISEUL ISLAND
 map (7° 5′S 157° 0′E) **18**:56
CHOIX (Mexico)
 map (26° 43′N 108° 17′W) **13**:357
CHOKE MOUNTAINS
 map (11° 0′N 37° 30′E) **7**:253
CHOKWE 4:403
CHOLECYSTITIS
 gallbladder **9**:17
CHOLECYSTOKININ
 gallbladder **9**:17
 hormone, animal **10**:236 *table*
 intestine **11**:230
CHOLELITHIASIS *see* GALLSTONE
CHOLERA 4:403
 epidemiology **7**:219
 gastrointestinal tract disease **9**:57
 vaccine: Wassermann, August von **20**:46
 Vibrio **19**:567
 water supply **20**:56
CHOLESTEROL 4:403–404 *bibliog., illus.*
 atherosclerosis **2**:291–292
 blood
  fat **8**:33
  heart diseases **10**:96
 gallstone **9**:21
 Goldstein, Joseph L. **9**:236
 hormone, animal **10**:234
 lipid **12**:361–362
 nutrition, human **14**:307
 steroid **18**:261
 sterol **18**:262
 stroke **18**:302
 Windaus, Adolf **20**:172
 Woodward, Robert Burns **20**:213
CHOLIC ACID
 Wieland, Heinrich Otto **20**:146
CHOLINE
 vitamins and minerals **19**:620
CHOLINERGIC
 neostigmine **14**:86
CHOLINESTERASE
 myasthenia gravis **13**:689
CHOLLA CACTUS
 cacti and other succulents **4**:10
CHOLO *see* MESTIZO
CHOLODNY, N.
 tropism **19**:309
CHOLTITZ, DIETRICH VON
 World War II **20**:273
CHOLULA (Mexico) 4:404; **14**:237 *map*
CHOLUTECA (Honduras)
 map (13° 18′N 87° 12′W) **10**:218
CHOMEDEY, PAUL DE, SIEUR DE MAISONNEUVE *see* MAISONNEUVE, PAUL DE CHOMEDEY, SIEUR DE
CHOMETTE, RENÉ *see* CLAIR, RENÉ
CHOMO LHARI MOUNTAIN
 map (27° 50′N 89° 15′E) **3**:235
CHOMSKY, NOAM 4:404 *bibliog.*
 automata, theory of **2**:357
 cognitive psychology **5**:95
 concept formation and attainment **5**:169
 linguistics **12**:357
 psycholinguistics **15**:591–592
 semantics (linguistics) **17**:193
 speech development **18**:176
CHOMUTOV (Czechoslovakia)
 map (50° 28′N 13° 26′E) **5**:413
CHON BURI (Thailand)
 map (13° 22′N 100° 59′E) **19**:139
CHONDRICHTHYES 4:404 *bibliog.*
CHONDRITE 4:404–405
 meteor and meteorite **13**:336–337
 Sorby, Henry Clifton **18**:68
CHONE (Ecuador)
 map (0° 41′S 80° 6′W) **7**:52
CHONG SON 4:405 *bibliog.*
 landscape painting **12**:118 *illus.*
CHONGJIN (Korea)
 map (41° 47′N 129° 50′E) **12**:113
CHONGJU (Korea)
 map (36° 39′N 127° 31′E) **12**:113
CHONGQING (China) *see* CHUNGKING (Chonqing) (China)
CHONJU (Korea)
 map (35° 49′N 127° 8′E) **12**:113
CHOPIN, FRÉDÉRIC 4:405 *bibliog., illus.*; **16**:294 *illus.*
 mazurka **13**:250
 nocturne **14**:212
 polonaise **15**:417
CHOPIN, KATE O'FLAHERTY 4:405
CHOPINE (shoe) **17**:280 *illus.*
CHOPTANK RIVER
 map (38° 38′N 76° 13′W) **13**:188
CHORA MONASTERY (Istanbul) *see* SAINT SAVIOR IN THE CHORA
CHORAL MUSIC 4:405–407 *bibliog., illus.*
 anthem **2**:49
 baton **3**:124
 canon **4**:114
 cantata **4**:115–116
 church music **4**:424
 compilations
  Boyce, William **3**:433
 composers
  Bach, Johann Sebastian **3**:10–11
  Blow, John **3**:341
  Brahms, Johannes **3**:441
  Bruckner, Anton **3**:521
  Davies, Peter Maxwell **6**:50
  Graun, Karl Heinrich **9**:302
  Handel, George Frideric **10**:36
  Mendelssohn, Felix **13**:295–296
  Purcell, Henry **15**:628
  Schütz, Heinrich **17**:138
  Thompson, Randall **19**:175
  Vaughan Williams, Ralph **19**:528–529
  Willaert, Adrian **20**:154
 fuging tune **8**:355
 German and Austrian music **9**:130
 glee **9**:207
 madrigal **13**:45
 medieval music **13**:274–275
 oratorio **14**:416
CHORALE 4:407 *bibliog.*
 composers
  Bach, Johann Sebastian **3**:10–11
  Brahms, Johannes **3**:441
  Pachelbel, Johann **15**:4
 German and Austrian music **9**:129
 hymn **10**:346
CHORD (mathematics)
 sphere **18**:180
CHORD (music) 4:407
 arpeggio **2**:187
 harmony **10**:51–52 *illus.*
CHORDAE TENDINEAE **10**:92 *illus.*
CHORDATE 4:407–408 *bibliog.*
 aging **1**:186
 anatomy
  circulatory system **4**:439–440
  comparative anatomy **5**:155
  endocrine system **7**:168–169
  hoof, nail, and claw **10**:225–226
  hormones **10**:236–237 *table*
  lungs **12**:463–465
  nervous system **14**:92–95
  respiratory system **16**:178–181
  skeletal system **17**:333–334
  spinal cord **18**:184
  teeth **19**:70–71
 biological locomotion **3**:266–267
 characteristics **4**:407
 classification, biological
  amphioxus **1**:381
  animal **2**:10–11
  Cephalochordata **4**:256
  Gnathostomata **9**:213
  Hemichordate **10**:117–118
  invertebrate **11**:235
  vertebrate classes **4**:407
 fossil record **8**:243–248
 nervous system **14**:92
 regeneration **16**:126–127
 tunicate **19**:334
CHORDOPHONES
 musical instruments **13**:677–679 *illus.*
CHOREA 4:408
 Huntington's chorea **10**:315
 rheumatic fever **16**:194
CHOREOGRAPHY 4:408–409 *bibliog., illus.*
 See also BALLET—CHOREOGRAPHERS; MODERN DANCE; MUSICAL COMEDY—choreography
 Ailey, Alvin **1**:202–203
 Berkeley, Busby **3**:213
 Butler, John **3**:591
 Cunningham, Merce **5**:390
 De Mille, Agnes **6**:61
 Dunham, Katherine **6**:300
 Ebreo, Guglielmo **7**:36
 Holm, Hanya **10**:204–205
 Horton, Lester **10**:255
 Humphrey, Doris **10**:303
 Laban, Rudolf von **12**:151
 modern dance **13**:497–498
 Monk, Meredith **13**:532
 Tamiris, Helen **19**:19
 Tharp, Twyla **19**:143
CHORION (embryology)
 development **6**:138 *illus.*; **6**:140 *illus.*
CHOROID
 eye **7**:348–349 *illus.*
CHOROIDITIS
 eye diseases **7**:351
CHORUS (drama) *see* DRAMA
CHORUS (music) *see* CHORAL MUSIC
CHORUS FROG 4:409
CHOSEN *see* KOREA
CHOSEN (Florida)
 map (26° 42′N 80° 41′W) **8**:172
CHOSHUN, MIYAGAWA
 A Beauty **11**:377 *illus.*
CHOSROES *see* KHOSRU I, KING OF PERSIA
CHOTEAU (Montana)
 map (47° 49′N 112° 11′W) **13**:547
CHOTEK, SOPHIE **8**:286 *illus.*
CHOU (Zhou) (dynasty) 4:409 *bibliog.*
 Asia, history of **2**:252
 China, history of **4**:370–371 *map*
 Chinese archaeology **4**:378
 tile from **4**:370 *illus.*
CHOU EN-LAI (Zhou Enlai) 4:409 *bibliog., illus.*; **15**:523 *illus.*
CHOU-K'OU-TIEN (Zhoukoudian) (China) 4:409–410
 Chinese archaeology **4**:378
 Homo erectus **10**:215–216
 Peking man **15**:136
CHOU SHU-JEN (pseudonym) *see* LU HSÜN (Lu Xun)
CHOU TUN-I (Zhou Duni) 4:410 *bibliog.*
CHOUGH 4:410 *illus.*
 Alpine chough **13**:623 *illus.*
CHOUGH, WHITE-WINGED *see* AUSTRALIAN MUDNEST BUILDER
CHOUTEAU (family) 4:410
CHOUTEAU (county in Montana)
 map (47° 55′N 110° 25′W) **13**:547
CHOUTEAU (Oklahoma)
 map (36° 11′N 95° 21′W) **14**:368
CHOUTEAU, AUGUSTE PIERRE
 Chouteau (family) **4**:410
 Oklahoma **14**:370
CHOUTEAU, JEAN PIERRE
 Chouteau (family) **4**:410
CHOUTEAU, RENÉ AUGUSTE
 Chouteau (family) **4**:410
CHOVSGOL, LAKE
 map (51° 0′N 100° 30′E) **13**:529
CHOW CHOW 4:410 *illus.*; **6**:219 *illus.*
CHOWAN (county in North Carolina)
 map (36° 10′N 76° 35′W) **14**:242
CHOWAN RIVER
 map (36° 0′N 76° 40′W) **14**:242
CHOWCHILLA (California)
 map (37° 7′N 120° 16′W) **4**:31
CHRÉTIEN DE TROYES 4:410–411 *bibliog.*
CHRIBI, DRISS
 Morocco **13**:585
CHRISMAN (Illinois)
 map (39° 48′N 87° 41′W) **11**:42
CHRIST (Messiah) 4:411
 See also JESUS CHRIST
CHRIST, JOHANN FRIEDRICH
 iconography **11**:23
CHRIST CHURCH (Oxford University) **14**:474; **19**:408 *illus.*
CHRIST AT EMMAUS (Rembrandt)
 Louvre **12**:437
CHRIST IN MAJESTY (*Godescalc Gospels*) **4**:161 *illus.*
CHRIST THORN *see* CRUCIFIXION THORN
CHRISTADELPHIANS 4:411
CHRISTALLER, WALTER 4:411 *bibliog.*
 central place theory **4**:254–255
CHRISTANSHÅB (Greenland)
 map (68° 50′N 51° 12′W) **9**:353
CHRISTCHURCH (New Zealand) 4:411
 map (43° 32′S 172° 38′E) **14**:158
CHRISTENING *see* BAPTISM
CHRISTENSEN, PARLEY P.
 Farmer-Labor party **8**:24
CHRISTIAN (county in Illinois)
 map (39° 33′N 89° 18′W) **11**:42
CHRISTIAN (county in Kentucky)
 map (36° 55′N 87° 30′W) **12**:47
CHRISTIAN (county in Missouri)
 map (37° 0′N 93° 10′W) **13**:476
CHRISTIAN, CHARLIE 4:411
CHRISTIAN, FLETCHER
 Pitcairn Island **15**:319
CHRISTIAN I, KING OF DENMARK 4:412
 Scandinavia, history of **17**:109
CHRISTIAN II, KING OF DENMARK 4:412
 Scandinavia, history of **17**:109
CHRISTIAN III, KING OF DENMARK 4:412
 Scandinavia, history of **17**:109
CHRISTIAN IV, KING OF DENMARK 4:412 *bibliog.*
 Kristiansand (Norway) **12**:130
 Oslo (Norway) **14**:454
 Thirty Years' War **19**:171 *map*
CHRISTIAN VII, KING OF DENMARK
 Scandinavia, history of **17**:109
CHRISTIAN VIII, KING OF DENMARK
 Scandinavia, history of **17**:110
CHRISTIAN IX, KING OF DENMARK 4:412
CHRISTIAN X, KING OF DENMARK 4:412
CHRISTIAN ART AND ARCHITECTURE, EARLY *see* EARLY CHRISTIAN ART AND ARCHITECTURE
CHRISTIAN BROADCASTING NETWORK
 religious broadcasting **16**:142
CHRISTIAN BROTHERS *see* JOHN BAPTIST DE LA SALLE, SAINT
CHRISTIAN CATHOLIC CHURCH
 Dowie, John Alexander **6**:251
CHRISTIAN CHURCH (Protestant denomination) *see* DISCIPLES OF CHRIST
CHRISTIAN CHURCHES AND CHURCHES OF CHRIST 4:411
CHRISTIAN DEMOCRATIC PARTY (Italy)
 de Gasperi, Alcide **6**:59
 Italy **11**:326
 Italy history of **11**:331

CHRISTIAN DEMOCRATIC UNION (West Germany)
Adenauer, Konrad **1**:102
Germany **9**:146–147
Kohl, Helmut **12**:106
CHRISTIAN ENDEAVOR **4**:411
Clark, Francis Edward **5**:38
CHRISTIAN SCIENCE **4**:411–412 *bibliog.*
church music **4**:424
Eddy, Mary Baker **7**:55
faith healing **8**:11
CHRISTIAN SCIENCE MONITOR, THE **4**:412
CHRISTIAN SOCIALISM **4**:412 *bibliog.*
Maurice, Frederick Denison **13**:234–235
socialism **18**:20
CHRISTIANA (Jamaica)
map (18° 10′N 77° 29′W) **11**:351
CHRISTIANIA (Norway) *see* OSLO (Norway)
CHRISTIANITY **4**:412–414 *bibliog., map*; **16**:140 *map*
See also EARLY CHRISTIAN CHURCH; ORTHODOX CHURCH; PROTESTANTISM; ROMAN CATHOLIC CHURCH; etc.
art and architecture *see* CATHEDRALS AND CHURCHES; EARLY CHRISTIAN ART AND ARCHITECTURE
doctrine and practices
alienation **1**:294
Bible **3**:239–241
catholic **4**:211
cemetery **4**:245
Christmas **4**:415
church **4**:423
creed **5**:337
cross **5**:360–361 *illus.*
dietary laws **6**:165
education **7**:60–62
God **9**:217–219
grace **9**:275
infallibility **11**:161–162
Jesus Christ **11**:403–406
Judgment, Last **11**:464
marriage **13**:166
monasticism **13**:521
National Conference of Christians and Jews **14**:30–31
natural law **14**:48
Neoplatonism **14**:85
original sin **14**:444
passion play **15**:105
patriarch **15**:113
Pentecost **15**:155
philosophy **15**:244
sacrament **17**:7
Second Coming of Christ **17**:178
sin **17**:318
soul **18**:70
Ten Commandments **19**:100
Trinity **19**:300–301
Unitarianism **19**:399–400
usury **19**:491
virgin birth **19**:605
wake **20**:7–8
historiography **10**:184–185
history
Asia, history of **2**:250
cargo cults **4**:147
catacombs **4**:197
charismatic movement **4**:288–289
church and state **4**:424–425
Circassians **4**:435
Constantine I, Roman Emperor **5**:208–209
Crusades **5**:366–369
Decline and Fall of the Roman Empire, The History of the **6**:76
Egypt, ancient **7**:83; **7**:85
Europe, history of **7**:281–283
European expansion **7**:283 *map*
Germany, history of **9**:148
Great Britain, history of **9**:309
heresy **10**:141–142
Ireland, history of **11**:261
Jerusalem (Israel) **11**:399–401 *illus., map*
Julian the Apostate, Roman Emperor **11**:466
Ladislas I, King **12**:162
Latin America, history of **12**:219
law **12**:242
Middle East **13**:398
missions, Christian **13**:467–468
Moriscos **13**:580
Mozarabs **13**:628
Olaf I, King of Norway **14**:372–373
Olaf II, King of Norway (Saint Olaf) **14**:373
pacifism and nonviolent movements **15**:9
Renaissance **16**:149
Russia/Union of Soviet Socialist Republics, history of **16**:351–352
Scandinavia, history of **17**:108
Spain, history of **18**:145–146 *maps*
theater, history of the **19**:145
Turks **19**:347–348
Vladimir I, Grand Duke of Kiev **19**:623
women in society **20**:202
rationalism **16**:93
religion **16**:141
CHRISTIANSBURG (Virginia)
map (37° 8′N 80° 24′W) **19**:607
CHRISTIANSTED (Virgin Islands)
map (17° 45′N 64° 42′W) **19**:605
CHRISTIE, DAME AGATHA **4**:414–415 *bibliog., illus.*
Mallowan, Sir Max **13**:93
CHRISTIE, MANSON & WOODS
auction **2**:317
CHRISTIE, S. H.
Wheatstone bridge **20**:127
CHRISTINA, QUEEN OF SWEDEN **4**:415 *bibliog., illus.*
acquisitions 1632–1654 **17**:109 *map*
Oxenstierna, Axel Count **14**:474
Vasa (dynasty) **19**:525
CHRISTINE DE PISAN
women in society **20**:202
CHRISTMAS **4**:415 *bibliog.*
Christmas tree **11**:73
holly **10**:204
mistletoe **13**:481–482
poinsettia **15**:381
Santa Claus **17**:67
CHRISTMAS CAROL, A (book) **4**:415 *bibliog.*
CHRISTMAS DISEASE
hemophilia **10**:120
CHRISTMAS ISLAND (Indian Ocean) **4**:415
CHRISTMAS ISLAND (Pacific Ocean) **4**:415
CHRISTMAS ROSE *see* HELLEBORE
CHRISTO **4**:415–416 *bibliog., illus.*
Running Fence **4**:416 *illus.*; **13**:496 *illus.*
CHRISTOFF, BORIS **4**:416
CHRISTOFFEL, ELWIN BRUNO **4**:416
CHRISTOPHE, HENRI **4**:416 *illus.*
Cap-Haïtien **4**:119
Pétion, Alexandre Sabès **15**:202
CHRISTOPHER, SAINT **4**:416
CHRISTOPHER (Illinois)
map (37° 58′N 89° 3′W) **11**:42
CHRISTOVAL (Texas)
map (31° 12′N 100° 30′W) **19**:129
CHRIST'S COLLEGE (Cambridge University) **4**:52
CHRISTUS, PETRUS **4**:416 *bibliog.*
CHRISTY, EDWIN P. **4**:416–417 *bibliog.*
American music **1**:349
Foster, Stephen **8**:248
CHRISTY, HENRY
Lartet, Édouard Armand **12**:208
CHRISTY, JAMES W.
Pluto (planet) **15**:373
CHROMATE MINERALS **4**:417 *illus.*
mineral **13**:443 *table*
sulfate minerals **18**:333
sylvite **18**:402
CHROMATIC ABERRATION *see* ABERRATION, CHROMATIC
CHROMATOGRAPHY **4**:417–419 *bibliog., illus.*
adsorption chromatography **4**:417–418
gas chromatography **4**:418–419 *illus.*
Martin, Archer **13**:179
Moore, Stanford **13**:570
qualitative chemical analysis **16**:7
Synge, Richard Laurence **18**:408
thin-layer chromatography **4**:417 *illus.*
Willstätter, Richard **20**:163
CHROMATOPHORE *see* COLORATION, BIOLOGICAL
CHROME
ore, refractory materials **16**:124
CHROMINANCE
television **19**:88
CHROMITE **4**:419
igneous rock **11**:36
major ore deposits **14**:424–425 *table*
oxide minerals **14**:476
CHROMIUM **4**:419 *bibliog.*
abundances of common elements **7**:131 *table*
alloy **4**:419
chromite **4**:419
compounds **4**:419
element **7**:130 *table*
Group VIB periodic table **15**:167
metal, metallic element **13**:328
ore deposits, world distribution **14**:423 *map*
oxide minerals **14**:476
preparation **4**:419
transition elements **4**:419; **19**:273 *table*
uses **4**:419
Vauquelin, Louis Nicolas, discoverer **19**:529
vitamins and minerals **19**:621
CHROMOPHORES
bleaches and brighteners **3**:329
CHROMOSOMAL ABNORMALITIES
birth defects **3**:295
Down's syndrome **6**:252
genetic diseases **9**:82–84
growth **9**:380
hallucinogens **10**:24
Klinefelter's syndrome **12**:98
mutation **13**:686
pregnancy and birth **15**:504
CHROMOSOME
bread wheat development **20**:126 *illus.*
cell **4**:233–235 *illus.*
cytology **5**:412 *illus.*
egg **7**:72
genetic code **9**:80–82 *illus.*
genetics **9**:86–89 *illus.*
heredity **10**:140–141
meiosis **13**:282
mitosis **13**:485
Morgan, Thomas Hunt **13**:579
nucleic acid **14**:289 *illus.*
nucleus **14**:291
parthenogenesis **15**:99–100
radiation injury **16**:42
reproduction **16**:162
Sutton, Walter S. **18**:373
Wilson, Edmund B. **20**:164
zygote **20**:384
CHROMOSPHERE **4**:419; **18**:225 *illus.*
eclipse **7**:41
flash spectrum **8**:154
Lockyer, Sir Joseph Norman **12**:388
plage **15**:325
prominence **15**:567
spicule **18**:181
Sun **18**:342
CHRONIC PAIN *see* PAIN
CHRONICLE PLAY *see* DRAMA; MEDIEVAL DRAMA
CHRONICLES, BOOKS OF **4**:419 *bibliog.*
CHRONOLOGY **4**:419–420 *bibliog.*
Dionysius Exiguus **6**:184
Frere, Sir John **8**:327
prehistory **15**:517
CHRONOMETER **4**:420
Harrison, John **10**:59–60
navigation **14**:60
CHRONOPOTENTIOMETRY
electrochemistry **7**:113
CHROOCOCCUS
blue-green algae **3**:342 *illus.*
CHRYSALIS *see* PUPA
CHRYSANTHEMUM **4**:420 *illus.*
feverfew **8**:66
Shasta daisy **17**:244
CHRYSLER, WALTER PERCY **4**:420 *bibliog.*
CHRYSLER BUILDING (New York City) **4**:420 *bibliog.*; **14**:143 *illus.*
New York (city) **14**:145 *map*
skyscraper **17**:349–350 *illus.*
CHRYSLER CORPORATION
automotive industry **2**:363–368
Chrysler Airflow **2**:365 *illus.*
Iacocca, Lee **11**:3
strike (1937) **12**:155 *illus.*
CHRYSOBERYL **4**:420–421; **9**:74 *illus.*
cat's-eye **4**:213
gems **9**:74–75
CHRYSOCOLLA **4**:421
CHRYSOPHYTA
algae **1**:281–282
diatom **6**:154
CHRYSOPRASE *see* CHALCEDONY
CHRYSOSTOM, SAINT JOHN **4**:421 *bibliog.*
CHRYSOTILE *see* SERPENTINE
CHRYSSA **4**:421 *bibliog.*
CHU CHIANG RIVER
China **4**:365
CHU CHUA (British Columbia)
map (51° 21′N 120° 10′W) **3**:491
CHU HSI (Zhu Xi) **4**:421 *bibliog.*
Confucianism **5**:180
CHU RIVER
map (19° 53′N 105° 45′E) **12**:203
CHU TA (Zhu Da) **4**:421 *bibliog.*
CHU TEH (Zhu De) **4**:421 *bibliog.*
Mao Tse-tung (Mao Zedong) **13**:135
CHU TI *see* YUNG-LO, EMPEROR OF CHINA (Yongle)
CH'Ü YÜAN (Qu Yuan) **4**:421 *bibliog.*
CHU-YÜAN-CHANG *see* HUNG-WU
CHUANG-TZU (Zhuang Zi) **4**:421–422 *bibliog.*
Taoism **19**:29
CHUB **4**:422 *illus.*
CHUBBUCK (Idaho)
map (42° 55′N 112° 28′W) **11**:26
CHUBUT (province in Argentina)
map (44° 0′S 69° 0′W) **2**:149
CHUBUT RIVER
map (43° 20′S 65° 3′W) **2**:149
Patagonia **15**:109
CHUCK-A-LUCK (game)
dice games **6**:155
CHUCK-WILL'S-WIDOW *see* GOATSUCKER (bird)
CHUCUNAQUE RIVER
map (8° 9′N 77° 44′W) **15**:55
CHUECA, FEDERICO
zarzuela **20**:356
CHUFA **4**:422
CHUGACH MOUNTAINS
map (61° 0′N 145° 0′W) **1**:242
CHUGOKU MOUNTAINS
map (34° 58′N 132° 57′E) **11**:361
CHUGWATER (Wyoming)
map (41° 46′N 104° 49′W) **20**:301
CHUKCHI **4**:422 *bibliog.*
CHUKCHI SEA **4**:422
Bering Strait **3**:212
map (69° 0′N 171° 0′W) **1**:242
map (69° 0′N 171° 0′W) **14**:225
CHULA VISTA (California)
map (32° 39′N 117° 5′W) **4**:31
CHULALONGKORN, KING OF SIAM **4**:422 *bibliog.*
Thailand **19**:141
CHULUCANAS (Peru)
map (5° 6′S 80° 10′W) **15**:193
CHUN DOO HWAN **4**:422
Korea **12**:116
CHUNCHI (Ecuador)
map (2° 17′S 78° 55′W) **7**:52
CHUNCHON (Korea)
map (37° 52′N 127° 43′E) **12**:113
CHUNCHULA (Alabama)
map (30° 55′N 88° 12′W) **1**:234
CHUNG-HUA (Taiwan)
map (24° 3′N 120° 33′E) **19**:13
CHUNGJU (Korea)
map (36° 58′N 127° 58′E) **12**:113
CHUNGKING (Chongqing) (China) **4**:422–423
map (29° 39′N 106° 34′E) **4**:362
CHUNGYANG RANGE
map (23° 30′N 121° 0′E) **19**:13
CHUQUICAMATA (Chile)
map (22° 19′S 68° 56′W) **4**:355
CHUR (Switzerland)
map (46° 51′N 9° 32′E) **18**:394
CHURCH **4**:423 *bibliog.*
cathedrals and churches **4**:204–208
tithe **19**:212
CHURCH (Barbados)
map (13° 8′N 59° 29′W) **3**:75
CHURCH, FRANK **4**:423
CHURCH, FREDERICK EDWIN **4**:423 *bibliog., illus.*
Niagara Falls **2**:200 *illus.*
Twilight in the Wilderness **4**:423 *illus.*
CHURCH, SIR RICHARD **4**:423
CHURCH OF CHRIST, SCIENTIST *see* CHRISTIAN SCIENCE
CHURCH OF ENGLAND *see* ENGLAND, CHURCH OF; AUSTRALIA, CHURCH OF ENGLAND IN; etc.
CHURCH HILL (Tennessee)
map (36° 31′N 82° 47′W) **19**:104
CHURCH OF JESUS CHRIST OF THE LATTER-DAY SAINTS *see* MORMONISM
CHURCH MUSIC **4**:424 *bibliog., illus.*
anthem **2**:49
antiphon **2**:65
barrel organ **3**:94
Byzantine music **3**:608
cantata **4**:116
cantus firmus **4**:118
choral music **4**:405–407
chorale **4**:407
composers
Bach, Carl Philipp Emanuel **3**:10
Bach, Johann Christian **3**:10

Bach, Johann Sebastian 3:10–11
Berlioz, Hector 3:218–219
Bruckner, Anton 3:521
Byrd, William 3:602
Caldara, Antonio 4:25
Couperin (family) 5:313–314
Dunstable, John 6:301
Fux, Johann Joseph 8:384
Gibbons, Orlando 9:173
Handel, George Frideric 10:36
Haydn, Michael 10:81–82
Isaac, Heinrich 11:285
Langgaard, Rued 12:195
Liszt, Franz 12:367
Monteverdi, Claudio 13:554
Morley, Thomas 13:581
Mozart, Wolfgang Amadeus 13:628–629
Palestrina, Giovanni Pierluigi da 15:46–47
Praetorius, Michael 15:487
Purcell, Henry 15:628
Scarlatti (family) 17:115
Schütz, Heinrich 17:138
Stravinsky, Igor 18:295
Tallis, Thomas 19:17
Taverner, John 19:45
Tomkins, Thomas 19:232
Victoria, Tomás Luis de 19:574–575
English music 7:202–203
French music 8:320
fuging tune 8:355
gospel music 9:253–254
hymn 10:346–347
Magnificat 13:60
mass (musical setting) 13:201
medieval music 13:274–275 *illus.*
motet 13:606
music, history of Western 13:662–666 *illus.*
oratorio 14:416
plainsong 15:325–326
recitative 16:107–108
Renaissance music 16:156
Spanish music 18:161–162
spirituals 18:189
Te Deum laudamus 19:53
Westminster Choir College 20:118
CHURCH POINT (Louisiana)
map (30° 24′N 92° 13′W) 12:430
CHURCH AND STATE 4:424–425 *bibliog.*
Anselm, Saint 2:35
anti-Semitism 2:68
Becket, Saint Thomas 3:151
blue laws 3:343
Boniface VIII, Pope 3:379
concordat 5:170
Erastianism 7:227
Europe, history of 7:283
flag 8:149
freedom of religion 8:297–298
Holy Roman Empire 10:209–210
Lutheranism 12:469
Marsilius of Padua 13:173
papacy 15:63
Protestantism 15:576–577
Shinto 17:262–263
state (in political philosophy) 18:229–231
CHURCH OF THE BRETHREN *see* BRETHREN
CHURCH OF THE NAZARENE 4:424 *bibliog.*
CHURCH OF THE UNITED BRETHREN IN CHRIST
Boehm, Martin 3:358
CHURCHES OF CHRIST 4:425
Disciples of Christ 6:188
CHURCHILL (Manitoba) 4:425; 13:121 *illus.*
map (58° 46′N 94° 10′W) 13:119
CHURCHILL (county in Nevada)
map (39° 45′N 118° 20′W) 14:111
CHURCHILL, CAPE
map (58° 46′N 93° 12′W) 13:119
CHURCHILL, CHARLES 4:425 *bibliog.*
CHURCHILL, JOHN, 1ST DUKE OF MARLBOROUGH *see* MARLBOROUGH, JOHN CHURCHILL, 1ST DUKE OF
CHURCHILL, LORD RANDOLPH 4:425 *bibliog.*
CHURCHILL, SARAH, DUCHESS OF MARLBOROUGH *see* MARLBOROUGH, SARAH CHURCHILL, DUCHESS OF
CHURCHILL, WINSTON (novelist) 4:425
CHURCHILL, SIR WINSTON (Statesman) 4:425–427 *bibliog., illus.*
Canada, history of 4:87 *illus.*
Churchill River (Newfoundland) 4:427
Fulton (Missouri) 8:358
Iron Curtain 11:272
Westminster College 20:118
Lindemann, Frederick Alexander 12:351
Munich Conference 13:641
Roosevelt, Franklin Delano 16:309
'V for victory' sign 9:318 *illus.*
visit to Jerusalem in 1921 15:45 *illus.*
World War I 20:228
World War II 20:252–275 *illus.*
Yalta Conference 19:455 *illus.*; 20:315 *illus.*
CHURCHILL COLLEGE (Cambridge University) 4:52
CHURCHILL FALLS (Newfoundland) 4:427
map (53° 35′N 64° 27′W) 14:166
CHURCHILL LAKE
map (55° 55′N 108° 20′W) 17:81
CHURCHILL RIVER (Manitoba) 4:427
map (58° 47′N 94° 12′W) 4:70
CHURCHILL RIVER (Newfoundland) 4:427
map (53° 30′N 60° 10′W) 14:166
CHURCHYARD, THOMAS 4:427
CHURN 3:592 *illus.*; 4:427
CHURRIGUERA (family) 4:427 *bibliog.*
retablo, Church of San Esteban 18:154 *illus.*
San Cayetano (Guanajuato, Mexico) 12:225 *illus.*
Spanish art and architecture 18:154
CHURRIGUERESQUE STYLE *see* CHURRIGUERA (family)
CHURUBUSCO (Indiana)
map (41° 14′N 85° 19′W) 11:111
CHURUBUSCO, BATTLE OF
Mexican War 13:354
CHUVASH LANGUAGE
Altaic languages 19:476
CHUY (Uruguay)
map (33° 41′S 53° 27′W) 19:488
CHYLOMICRON *see* LIPOPROTEIN
CHYORNY PEREDEL *see* NARODNIKI
CIA see CENTRAL INTELLIGENCE AGENCY
CIAM *see* CONGRÈS INTERNATIONAL DE L'ARCHITECTURE MODERNE (CIAM)
CIAMIS (Indonesia)
map (7° 20′S 108° 21′E) 11:147
CIANJUR (Indonesia)
map (6° 49′S 107° 8′E) 11:147
CIANO, GALEAZZO, CONTE DI CORTELLAZZO 4:428 *bibliog.*
CIARDI, JOHN 4:428 *bibliog.*
CIBBER, COLLEY 4:428 *bibliog.*
CIBECUE (Arizona)
map (34° 3′N 110° 29′W) 2:160
CIBOLA, SEVEN GOLDEN CITIES OF 4:428 *bibliog.*
Arizona 2:163
Zuñi 20:382
CICADA 4:428 *bibliog., illus.*; 11:192 *illus.*
life cycle 11:190 *illus.*
locust 12:392
mouth 11:188 *illus.*
CICATRIZATION
body marking 3:356–357
CICELY 4:428
CICERO (Illinois)
map (41° 51′N 87° 45′W) 11:42
CICERO, MARCUS TULLIUS 4:428–429 *bibliog., illus.*
Clodius, Publius 5:63–64
Europe, history of 7:281
law 12:242
natural law 14:48
CICHLID 4:429 *illus.*; 8:120 *illus.*
animal communication 2:19 *illus.*
instinct 11:195 *illus.*
CID, EL *see* EL CID
CID, THE (play) 4:429 *bibliog.*
Corneille, Pierre 5:267
CIDER 4:429
CIEGO DE AVILA (Cuba)
map (21° 51′N 78° 46′W) 5:377
CIÉNAGA (Colombia)
map (11° 1′N 74° 15′W) 5:107
CIENFUEGOS (Cuba) 4:429
map (22° 9′N 80° 27′W) 5:377
CIERVA, JUAN DE LA 4:429
autogiro 2:356
C.I.F. 4:430
CIGAR AND CIGARETTE *see* TOBACCO
CIGAR FLOWER 4:430
CILACAP (Indonesia)
map (7° 44′S 109° 0′E) 11:147
CILANTRO *see* CORIANDER
CILÈA, FRANCESCO 4:430
CILIA *see* FLAGELLA
CILIARY BODY
eye 7:348–349 *illus.*
CILIATA 4:430 *bibliog., illus.*
Paramecium 15:79–80 *illus.*
Protozoa 15:579–581 *illus.*
CILICIA 4:430 *bibliog.*
CILIOPHORA *see* CILIATA
CILL CHOINNIGH (Ireland) *see* KILKENNY (city in Ireland)
CIM *see* COMPUTER-AIDED DESIGN AND COMPUTER-AIDED MANUFACTURING
CIMA DA CONEGLIANO 4:430 *bibliog.*
CIMABUE 4:430–431 *bibliog., illus.*
Florence (Italy) 8:168
Madonna with Angels 4:431 *illus.*; 13:185 *illus.*
CIMAROSA, DOMENICO 4:431 *bibliog.*
CIMARRON (Kansas)
map (37° 48′N 100° 21′W) 12:18
CIMARRON (New Mexico)
map (36° 31′N 104° 55′W) 14:136
CIMARRON (county in Oklahoma)
map (36° 45′N 102° 30′W) 14:368
CIMARRON RIVER
map (36° 10′N 96° 17′W) 14:368
CIMBALOM *see* DULCIMER
CIMBRI *see* GERMANIC PEOPLES
CIMETIDINE 4:431
antacid 2:38
antihistamine 2:63
CIMMERIANS 4:431
CIMON 4:431
CINCHONA 4:431 *bibliog.*
quinidine 16:27
quinine 16:27
CINCINNATI (Ohio) 4:431–432 *illus.*; 14:359 *illus.*
map (39° 6′N 84° 31′W) 14:357
CINCINNATI, SOCIETY OF THE 4:432
Knox, Henry 12:102
medals and decorations 13:260
CINCINNATUS, LUCIUS QUINCTIUS 4:432
CINCO PINOS (Nicaragua)
map (13° 14′N 86° 52′W) 14:179
CINDERELLA 4:432
CINEMA *see* FILM, HISTORY OF
CINEMA (British Columbia)
map (53° 11′N 122° 30′W) 3:491
CINÉMA-VÉRITÉ
documentary 6:211
CINEMASCOPE (film technology) 4:433
CINEMATOGRAPHY 4:432–434 *bibliog., illus.*
animation 2:28–29
Friese-Greene, William 8:333
Howe, James Wong 10:284
Jenkins, Charles Francis 11:395
lens 12:286
Marey, Étienne Jules 13:148
Muybridge, Eadweard 13:687
photography 15:265
sound recording and reproduction 18:75 *illus.*
stroboscope 18:301
CINERAMA (film technology) 4:433
CINERARIA 4:434 *illus.*
CINNA, LUCIUS CORNELIUS 4:434 *bibliog.*
CINNABAR 4:434
mercury 13:306
CINNAMON 4:435
CINQ-MARS, MARQUIS DE
Louis XIII, King of France 12:426
CINQUE PORTS 4:435
CINQUEFOIL 4:435 *illus.*
CINTRA (Portugal) *see* SINTRA (Portugal)
CINTRA, PEDRO DE
Sierra Leone 17:296
CIO *see* AMERICAN FEDERATION OF LABOR AND CONGRESS OF INDUSTRIAL ORGANIZATIONS
CIPHER *see* CRYPTOLOGY
CIPHER DISK 5:372 *illus.*
CIPOLLETTI (Argentina)
map (38° 56′S 67° 59′W) 2:149
CIRCADIAN RHYTHM
biological clock 3:264–265
CIRCANNUAL RHYTHM
biological clock 3:264
CIRCASSIANS 4:435
CIRCE 4:435
CIRCLE (Alaska)
map (65° 50′N 144° 4′W) 1:242
CIRCLE (mathematics) 4:435–436 *bibliog., illus.*
arc 2:112
centroid 4:256
conic section 5:188 *illus.*
curvature 5:396
cycloid 5:404–405
eccentricity 7:37
patterned ground 15:115
radian 16:42
secant 17:178
sine 17:319
tangent 19:22
CIRCLE (Montana)
map (47° 25′N 105° 35′W) 13:547
CIRCLE DANCE
folk dance 8:199
CIRCLE IN THE SQUARE 4:436 *bibliog.*
CIRCLEVILLE (Ohio)
map (39° 36′N 82° 57′W) 14:357
CIRCUIT, ELECTRIC 4:436–438 *bibliog., illus.*
See also ELECTRICITY
alarm systems 1:240
alternating current 1:312–313; 4:437–438 *illus.*
ampere 1:377
Ampère, André Marie 1:377
bridge circuit 3:484
circuit breaker 4:438
complex circuits 4:437
coulombmeter 5:308
current, electric
circuit 4:436–438 *illus.*
diode 6:183 *illus.*
electrochemistry 7:112–113
electromagnetic units 7:118
dielectric 6:161
dipole moment, magnetic moment 13:55
direct current 4:436–437 *illus.*; 6:187
electrical values, Kirchhoff's laws 12:87
electrical wiring 7:106–107
electricity 7:109–110 *illus.*
electromagnet 7:115
electron 7:119–120
flow direction, Lenz's law 12:287
fuse 8:381
ground, electrical 9:373
impedance 11:61
inductance 11:151
inductor 11:151–152
measurement, ammeter 1:372
motion, harmonic 13:608
Ohm, Georg Simon 14:363
Ohm's law 14:363
oscillator 14:453
parallel circuit 4:437 *illus.*
printed circuit 15:550
pulse (electronics) 15:621
reactance 16:98
relay 16:137
resistance, electrical 16:177
resistor 16:177
RIC circuit 4:437–438 *illus.*
series circuit 4:436–437 *illus.*
switch, electric 18:393
telephone 19:79
transformer 19:270–271
transistor 19:271–272
Wheatstone bridge 20:127
Zener diode 20:359
CIRCUIT, ELECTRONIC
multivibrator 13:638
oscilloscope 14:453
printed circuit 15:550
thin-film circuits 19:169
voltage regulator 19:631
CIRCUIT BREAKER 4:438 *bibliog.*
electrical wiring 7:107
fuse 8:381
relay 16:137
switch, electric 18:393
CIRCUIT RIDER 4:438 *bibliog.*
Asbury, Francis 2:227
Cartwright, Peter 4:178
CIRCULAR MOTION *see* MOTION, CIRCULAR
CIRCULATORY SHOCK *see* SHOCK, PHYSIOLOGIC
CIRCULATORY SYSTEM 4:438–442 *bibliog., illus.*
American Heart Association 1:340
animal 4:439 *illus.*
aorta 2:73
artery 2:213–214
blood 3:335
blood pressure 3:339
blood vessels 4:442
angiogenin 1:414
capillary 4:123
Chinese medicine 4:390
chordate 4:439–440
coronary artery 5:271
diseases and disorders

CIRCULATORY SYSTEM (cont.)
See also BLOOD DISEASES; HEART DISEASES
aneurysm **1**:411
arteriosclerosis **2**:213
atherosclerosis **2**:291–292
cardiovascular diseases **4**:144–145
embolism **7**:152
gastrointestinal tract disease **9**:57
hemorrhage **10**:120
hypertension **10**:349
inflammation **11**:169
kidney disease **12**:71
nervous system, diseases of the **14**:96
phlebitis **15**:248
Raynaud's disease **16**:97
shock, physiologic **17**:278–279
stroke **18**:301–302
thrombosis **19**:183
varicose vein **19**:523
drug **6**:275–276
earthworm **7**:29
examination, medical **7**:326
exercise **7**:329–330; **7**:330 *table*
fish **8**:114
Harvey, William **10**:65
heart **10**:91–94
heart, artificial **10**:94–95
heart-lung machine **10**:97
hormone, animal **10**:234–235
human body **4**:440–442
insect **11**:187–188 *illus.*
invertebrate **11**:236
kidneys **12**:73
lizard **12**:380
lymphatic system **12**:475–476
pulse (biology) **15**:621
spleen **18**:191
vein **19**:536
CIRCUMCISION **4**:442–443 *bibliog.*
CIRCUMNAVIGATION, WORLD *see* EXPLORATION—world circumnavigation
CIRCUS **4**:443–444 *bibliog., illus.*
See also STADIUM
Astley, Philip **2**:268
Barnum, P. T. **3**:86
calliope **4**:46
clown **5**:70
Franconi (family) **8**:279
Kelly, Emmett **12**:39
Ringling (family) **16**:225–226
showboats **17**:286
Wallenda (family) **20**:15
CIRCUS MAXIMUS
Rome, ancient **16**:300 *map*
stadium **18**:208
CIRE PERDUE *see* LOST-WAX PROCESS
CIREBON (Indonesia)
map (6° 44'S 108° 34'E) **11**:147
CIRQUE **4**:444–445; **12**:182 *illus.*
glaciers and glaciation **9**:193 *illus.*
lake, glacial **12**:169
CIRQUE MOUNTAIN
map (58° 56'N 63° 33'W) **16**:18
CIRRHOSIS **4**:445 *bibliog.*
jaundice **11**:385
liver **12**:374
splenomegaly **18**:191
CIRRUS CLOUDS **4**:445 *bibliog., illus.*; **5**:67–68 *illus.*
mare's tail (cloud) **13**:148
CIS-TRANS ISOMERISM **4**:445 *illus.*
stereochemistry **18**:258 *illus.*
CISCO *see* WHITEFISH
CISCO (Texas)
map (32° 23'N 98° 59'W) **19**:129
CISKEI (tribal homeland)
South Africa **18**:83
CISNE (Illinois)
map (38° 31'N 88° 26'W) **11**:42
CISNEROS, FRANCISCO JIMÉNEZ DE *see* JIMÉNEZ DE CISNEROS, FRANCISCO
CISSNA PARK (Illinois)
map (40° 34'N 87° 54'W) **11**:42
CISSUS **4**:445
CISTERCIANS **4**:445–446 *bibliog.*
Great Britain, history of **9**:310
Harding, Saint Stephen **10**:46
monastic art and architecture **13**:518–520 *illus.*
Trappists **19**:284
CISTICOLA **4**:446
CITHARA *see* KITHARA
CITIZEN KANE (film) **8**:85 *illus.*; **20**:99 *illus.*
cinematography **4**:434
CITIZEN KING, THE *see* LOUIS PHILIPPE, KING OF FRANCE
CITIZENS BAND RADIO **4**:446 *bibliog.*
frequency allocation **8**:326
CITIZENSHIP **4**:446–447 *bibliog., table*
alien **1**:293
allegiance **1**:298
Dred Scott v. *Sandford* **6**:268
expatriation **7**:333
14th Amendment **8**:254
Hull House **10**:296
naturalization **14**:50–51
Plato's *Crito* **5**:352
suffrage **18**:325–326
CITRIC ACID **4**:447
CITRIC ACID CYCLE *see* KREBS CYCLE
CITRINE
amethyst **1**:368
CITROËN (automobile) **2**:365 *illus.*
automotive industry **2**:366–367
CITRON **4**:447
citrus fruits **4**:448
CITRONELLA **4**:447
CITRONELLE (Alabama)
map (31° 6'N 88° 14'W) **1**:234
CITRUS (county in Florida)
map (28° 50'N 82° 30'W) **8**:172
CITRUS FRUITS **4**:447–448 *bibliog., illus., table*
bergamot **3**:209
citron **4**:447
Florida **8**:175 *illus.*
grapefruit **9**:290
kumquat **12**:136
lemon **12**:280
lime **12**:343–344
orange **14**:414–415
production **4**:448 *table*
rue **16**:339
tangerine **19**:22
CITTERN **4**:448 *bibliog.*
CITY **5**:3–8 *bibliog., illus., maps*
contemporary city **5**:4–6
ghetto **9**:167
historic preservation **10**:182
history and development **5**:3–4
hotel **10**:259–260
housing **10**:276–280
human ecology **10**:297
Industrial Revolution **11**:160
inner city **11**:179
Latin America, history of **12**:218
manorialism **13**:127
megalopolis **13**:280
Middle Ages **13**:393
municipal government **13**:642–643
new towns **5**:7; **14**:143
population **15**:434
rise of the megalopolis **5**:6
Rockefeller Center **16**:250–251
suburbs **18**:317
transportation **19**:281
United States, history of the **19**:451
urban anthropology **19**:480
urban climate (meteorology) **19**:480
urban planning **19**:481–485
urban renewal in the U.S. **5**:6–7
CITY OF GOD, THE (book) **5**:8 *bibliog.*
history **10**:184
state (in political philosophy) **18**:230
CITY GOVERNMENT *see* MUNICIPAL GOVERNMENT (local government)
CITY MANAGER **5**:8 *bibliog.*
municipal government **13**:642
CITY OF PARIS (ship) **14**:325 *illus.*
CITY-STATE **5**:9 *bibliog.*
city **5**:3
democracy **6**:98
Europe, history of **7**:280
Greece, ancient **9**:330
Italy, history of **11**:328 *map*
Phoenicia **15**:250
Sparta (Greece) **18**:164–165
state (in political philosophy) **18**:229
CIUDAD ACUÑA (Mexico)
map (29° 18'N 100° 55'W) **13**:357
CIUDAD ALLENDE (Mexico)
map (28° 20'N 100° 51'W) **13**:357
CIUDAD BARRIOS (El Salvador)
map (13° 46'N 88° 16'W) **7**:100
CIUDAD BOLÍVAR (Venezuela) **5**:9
map (8° 8'N 63° 33'W) **19**:542
CIUDAD CAMARGO (Mexico)
map (26° 19'N 98° 50'W) **13**:357
map (27° 40'N 105° 10'W) **13**:357
CIUDAD DE VALLES (Mexico)
map (21° 59'N 99° 1'W) **13**:357
CIUDAD DEL CARMEN (Mexico)
map (18° 38'N 91° 50'W) **13**:357
CIUDAD GUAYANA (Venezuela)
map (8° 22'N 62° 40'W) **19**:542
CIUDAD GUERRERO (Mexico)
map (28° 33'N 107° 30'W) **13**:357
CIUDAD GUZMÁN (Mexico)
map (19° 41'N 103° 29'W) **13**:357
CIUDAD JIMÉNEZ (Mexico)
map (27° 8'N 104° 55'W) **13**:357
CIUDAD JUÁREZ (Mexico) **5**:9
map (31° 44'N 106° 29'W) **13**:357
CIUDAD MANTE (Mexico)
map (22° 44'N 98° 57'W) **13**:357
CIUDAD OBREGÓN (Mexico)
map (27° 29'N 109° 56'W) **13**:357
CIUDAD OJEDA (Venezuela)
map (10° 12'N 71° 19'E) **19**:542
CIUDAD REAL (Spain)
map (38° 59'N 3° 56'W) **18**:140
CIUDAD TRUJILLO (Dominican Republic) *see* SANTO DOMINGO (Dominican Republic)
CIUDAD VICTORIA (Mexico) **5**:9
map (23° 44'N 99° 8'W) **13**:357
CIVET **5**:9 *illus.*
fossa **8**:243
mongoose **13**:531
suricate **18**:363
CIVIL AERONAUTICS *see* AVIATION—general aviation
CIVIL AERONAUTICS BOARD **5**:9
aviation **2**:374
common carrier **5**:138
government regulation **9**:271
CIVIL DEFENSE **5**:9–10 *bibliog.*
fallout shelter **8**:14–15
CIVIL DISOBEDIENCE **5**:10 *bibliog.*
Gandhi, Mahatma **9**:36
King, Martin Luther, Jr. **12**:80
law **12**:242
pacifism and nonviolent movements **15**:9
Russell, Bertrand **16**:349
Thoreau, Henry David **19**:178
CIVIL DISOBEDIENCE (essay)
Thoreau, Henry David **19**:178
CIVIL ENGINEERING **5**:10–11 *bibliog.*
Chanute, Octave **4**:282
engineering **7**:178
soil mechanics **18**:38
technology, history of **19**:66
CIVIL LAW (code law) **5**:11–12 *bibliog.*
See also COMMON LAW
criminal justice **5**:350
Germanic law **9**:137–138
intervention **11**:230
jury **11**:478
Justinian Code **11**:478
law **12**:243
law, history of **12**:244–245 *illus.*
Napoleonic Code **14**:19
parlement **15**:92
Roman law **16**:278–279
women in society **20**:204
CIVIL LAW (noncriminal law)
contract **5**:231–232
desertion **6**:131
equity **7**:226
fraud **8**:288
hypothecation **10**:351
immunity **11**:59
legal aid **12**:272
7th Amendment **17**:219
statute of limitations **18**:239
tort **19**:245–246
trial **19**:292
trover **19**:312
CIVIL LIBERTIES *see* CIVIL RIGHTS
CIVIL RIGHTS **5**:12–13 *bibliog., illus.*
affirmative action **1**:132
Alabama **1**:238
American Civil Liberties Union **1**:337–338
American Indian Movement **1**:340–341
Arkansas **2**:170
black Americans **3**:308–311
Chicano **4**:343
children's rights **4**:354
civil disobedience **5**:10
Civil Rights Acts **5**:13
Civil Rights Cases **5**:13
computers and privacy **5**:166–167
Delaware **6**:91
discrimination **6**:189–190
Dixiecrats **6**:207
Educational Testing Service **7**:66–67
equal opportunity **7**:223
feminism **8**:48–49
15th Amendment **8**:74
14th Amendment **8**:254
freedom of speech **8**:298–299
gay activism **9**:63
Georgia **9**:118
human rights **10**:297–299
integration, racial **11**:202–203
law, history of **12**:246–247
leaders
Abernathy, Ralph David **1**:56–57
Bond, Julian **3**:376
Chafee, Zechariah **4**:267
Chisholm, Shirley **4**:398
Coffin, William Sloane, Jr. **5**:94
Du Bois, W. E. B. **6**:285–286
Evers (family) **7**:316
Gregory, Dick **9**:355
Jackson, Jesse L. **11**:343
Jordan, Barbara **11**:450
Jordan, Vernon **11**:450
King, Martin Luther, Jr. **12**:80–81
Luthuli, Albert John **12**:470
Powell, Adam Clayton, Jr. **15**:480
Randolph, A. Philip **16**:83
White, Walter **20**:136
Wilkins, Roy **20**:152
Young, Andrew **20**:332
lie detector use **12**:324
Mississippi **13**:473
Morgan v. *Virginia* **13**:579
pacifism and nonviolent movements **15**:9–10
patients, mentally ill
Szasz, Thomas **18**:415
prisoners **15**:555
Reconstruction Amendments **5**:220–222
Shelley v. *Kraemer* **17**:253–254
SNCC **17**:384
Southern Christian Leadership Conference **18**:112
Supreme Court of the United States **18**:358
13th Amendment **19**:170
Urban League, National **19**:480
voter registration
Selma (Alabama) **17**:192
Warren, Earl **20**:31
women in society **20**:202; **20**:203–204
CIVIL RIGHTS ACTS **5**:13 *bibliog.*
civil rights **5**:13
Civil Rights Cases **5**:13–14
government regulation **9**:271
Johnson, Lyndon B. **11**:434
signing (1964) **15**:524 *illus.*
United States, history of the **19**:459
CIVIL RIGHTS CASES **5**:13–14 *bibliog.*
Alexander v. *Holmes County (Miss.) Board of Education* **1**:275
Brown v. *Board of Education of Topeka, Kansas* **3**:517
Heart of Atlanta Motel, Inc. v. *United States* **10**:95
Plessy v. *Ferguson* **15**:368
Shelley v. *Kraemer* **17**:253–254
CIVIL RIGHTS COMMISSION
Hesburgh, Theodore M. **10**:150–151
CIVIL RIGHTS ORGANIZATIONS *see* HUMAN RIGHTS ORGANIZATIONS
CIVIL SERVICE **5**:14 *bibliog.*
administrative law **1**:104–105
American Federation of State, County, and Municipal Employees **1**:339
bureaucracy **3**:568
Civil Service Commission **5**:14
Eaton, Dorman Bridgman **7**:34–35
Hatch Acts **10**:68
patronage **15**:114
Pendleton, George Hunt **15**:142
pension **15**:153–154
Roosevelt, Theodore **16**:310
CIVIL SERVICE COMMISSION **5**:14
civil service **5**:14
Eaton, Dorman Bridgman **7**:34–35
CIVIL WAR
foreign policy **8**:226
CIVIL WAR, ENGLISH *see* ENGLISH CIVIL WAR
CIVIL WAR, SPANISH *see* SPANISH CIVIL WAR
CIVIL WAR, U.S. **5**:15–34 *bibliog., illus., maps*
Alabama **1**:237
Andersonville Prison **1**:403
Arkansas **2**:169
background
abolitionists **1**:58
Bleeding Kansas **12**:21
Buchanan, James **3**:532–534
Calhoun, John C. **5**:15
Clay, Henry **5**:15
Compromise of 1850 **5**:158
Crittenden Compromise **5**:352–353
Dred Scott v. *Sandford* **6**:268
Fugitive Slave Laws **8**:355
Kansas-Nebraska Act **12**:22–23
Missouri Compromise **13**:480–481
nullification **14**:292
origins of **5**:15–18
popular sovereignty **15**:433

slavery 17:351–357
battles and campaigns 5:23 *map*
Antietam, Battle of 2:61; 5:25
Appomattox Court House 2:91
Atlanta campaign 2:293; 5:30
Brandy Station, Battle of 3:455
Bull Run, Battles of 3:558–559 *map*; 5:21 *illus.*; 5:23–25 *illus.*, *map*
Carolina campaigns 5:30–31
Chancellorsville, Battle of 4:279; 5:27–28
Chattanooga, Battles of 4:303; 5:28–29
Chickamauga, Battle of 4:345; 5:28–29
Fort Henry and Fort Donelson 8:236
Fort Sumter 5:19–20; 8:237
Fredericksburg, Battle of 5:26; 8:293–294
Georgia campaigns 5:30–31
Gettysburg, Battle of 5:28; 9:160–161
Mobile (Alabama) 13:487
Mobile Bay 5:22
Murfreesboro 5:26
New Orleans (Louisiana) 14:142
Peninsular campaign 5:22–24; 15:144
Perryville 5:25
Petersburg (Virginia) 15:202
Petersburg campaign 15:202
Savannah (Georgia) 17:99
Selma (Alabama) 17:192
Shiloh 5:22
Shiloh, Battle of 17:261
Springfield (Missouri) 18:200
Vicksburg (Mississippi) 5:27; 19:571
Vicksburg Campaign 19:571–572
Virginia campaigns (1864–65) 5:20–30
Wilderness Campaign 20:150
Bickerdyke, Mary Ann 3:244
black Americans 3:307–308
Boyd, Belle 3:433
Chattanooga (Tennessee) 4:303
Columbus (Georgia) 5:126–127
Confederate States of America 5:176–177
Connecticut 5:196
copperheads 5:254
costs of the war 5:33–34
Cumberland River 5:387
Delaware 6:91
Democratic party 6:100
diplomacy and naval policy 5:31–32
Dixiecrats 6:207
Draft Riots 6:254
economic factors 5:32–33
Elmira (New York State) 7:149
Emancipation Proclamation 7:151
finance
greenback 9:349
national bank 14:30
Florida 8:175–176
generals
Beauregard, P. G. T. 3:147; 5:20
Bragg, Braxton 3:439
Buckner, Simon Bolivar, Jr. 3:537
Buell, Don Carlos 3:544
Burnside, Ambrose E. 3:579; 5:26
Butler, Benjamin Franklin 3:591
Cox, Jacob Dolson 5:322
Early, Jubal A. 7:8
Ewell, Richard S. 7:325
Forrest, Nathan Bedford 8:235
Garfield, James A. 9:46
Grant, Ulysses S. 5:21–30; 5:22; 9:287–289
Halleck, Henry W. 5:25; 10:22
Hampton, Wade (1818–1902) 10:32–33
Hancock, Winfield Scott 10:35
Hardee, William J. 10:45
Hill, A. P. 10:163
Hill, D. H. 10:163–164
Hood, John B. 10:225
Hooker, Joseph 5:29; 10:227
Howard, Oliver O. 10:283
Jackson, Stonewall 5:21–24; 5:27; 11:344
Johnston, Albert Sidney 11:437
Johnston, Joseph E. 11:437–438
Kearny, Philip 12:35
Lee, Robert E. 5:24; 12:269–270
Logan, John Alexander 12:393–394
Longstreet, James 12:409
Lyon, Nathaniel 12:478
McClellan, George B. 5:21–29; 13:9
McClernand, John Alexander 13:9
McDowell, Irvin 5:20; 13:14
Meade, George Gordon 5:28; 13:252
Miles, Nelson A. 13:419
Morgan, John Hunt 13:578
Pickett, George E. 15:293
Polk, Leonidas 15:405
Pope, John 15:430
Price, Sterling 15:535
Rosecrans, William S. 5:26; 16:314
Schofield, John McAllister 17:130
Sheridan, Philip H. 17:256–257
Sherman, William Tecumseh 5:29–30; 17:258
Stuart, J. E. B. 18:306
Thomas, George Henry 19:173
Georgia 9:118
Gettysburg Address 9:161–162
Harpers Ferry (West Virginia) 10:55
historians
Catton, Bruce 4:217
Freeman, Douglas Southall 8:299
Illinois 11:45
Indian Wars 11:108
Indiana 11:115
Indians, American
Watie, Stand 20:67
infantry 11:163
journalism 11:455
Kentucky 12:51
leaders and statesmen
Benjamin, Judah P. 3:201–202
Brown, John 3:515
Davis, Jefferson 6:51–52
Fessenden, William Pitt 8:62–63
Lincoln, Abraham 5:17–30; 12:349
Mosby, John Singleton 13:596
Seward, William H. 17:221
Stanton, Edwin M. 18:220
Stevens, Thaddeus 18:263
Toombs, Robert 19:236
locomotive 12:391
Maryland 13:192
Mason-Dixon line 13:199
Massachusetts 13:211
Memphis (Tennessee) 13:292
Meridian (Mississippi) 13:310
Michigan 13:382
military operations 5:20–31 *map*
Mississippi 13:472
Mississippi River 13:474
Missouri 13:479
Montgomery (Alabama) 13:556
naval operations
Farragut, David Glasgow 8:29
Foote, Andrew Hull 8:218–219
Mallory, Stephen Russell 13:92
Monitor and *Merrimack* 13:531–532
navy 14:63
Porter, David Dixon 15:444
Semmes, Raphael 17:198
Welles, Gideon 20:99
Wilkes, Charles 20:151
Winslow, John Ancrum 20:180
Nevada 14:114
New Mexico 14:139–140
Norfolk (Virginia) 14:218
North Carolina 14:246
Ohio 14:362
Oklahoma 14:371
Pennsylvania 15:151
photography 5:15–33 *illus.*; 15:269 *illus.*
Brady, Mathew B. 3:438–439
Gardner, Alexander 9:44
O'Sullivan, Timothy H. 14:459
Quantrill, William C. 16:9
railroad 16:72
Raleigh (North Carolina) 16:79
refrigeration 16:124
Republican Party 16:172–173
Richmond (Virginia) 16:214
secession 5:18
Shreveport (Louisiana) 17:286
South Carolina 18:101
Starr, Belle 18:228
Stewart, Alexander Turney 18:265
strategy and tactics, military 18:291
submarine 18:315
Tennessee 19:106
Tennessee River 19:107
territories prior to the war 19:447 *map*
Texas 19:134
Trent Affair 5:31; 19:290
Tubman, Harriet 19:327–328
uniform 2:182 *illus.*; 19:448–449 *illus.*
Union Leagues 19:387
United States, history of the 19:447–450 *illus.*
Vallandigham, Clement L. 19:506
Vermont 19:558
Virginia 19:612
war reportage
Reid, Whitelaw 16:131
West Virginia 20:114
Wheeler, Joseph 20:129
Zouaves 5:20 *illus.*
CIVILIAN CONSERVATION CORPS 5:34
Job Corps 11:421
Roosevelt, Franklin Delano 16:309
CIVILIZATION 5:34 *bibliog.*
Aegean civilization 1:114–118
Africa, history of 1:151–153
agriculture, history of 1:189–190
Arab history 2:101–102
Asia, history of 2:249
Aztec 2:382–384
China, history of 4:370
city 5:3
culture 5:384–385
diffusion, cultural 6:170
effects of climate on
Huntington, Ellsworth 10:314
Egypt, ancient 7:81–85
Fertile Crescent 8:60
Greece, ancient 9:329–334
Inca 11:69–73
Indus civilization 11:152–154
Maya 13:243–245
Mesopotamia 13:315–317
Middle East, history of the 13:400–410
prehistoric humans 15:517
primitive societies 15:546
Rome, ancient 16:297–304
women in society 20:201–204
writing systems, evolution of 20:291–295
CIVILIZATION AND ITS DISCONTENTS (book) 5:34
CIVITAVECCHIA (Italy)
map (42° 6′N 11° 48′E) 11:321
CIXI, DOWAGER EMPRESS OF CHINA *see* TZ'U-HSI (Cixi), DOWAGER EMPRESS OF CHINA
C.J. STRIKE RESERVOIR
map (42° 57′N 115° 53′W) 11:26
CLACKAMAS (county in Oregon)
map (45° 10′N 122° 16′W) 14:427
CLACKMANNAN (Scotland) 5:34–35
CLACKMANNANSHIRE (Scotland) *see* CLACKMANNAN (Scotland)
CLACTONIAN 5:35 *bibliog.*
CLAESZ, PIETER 5:35 *bibliog.*
memento mori 11:23 *illus.*
CLAFLIN (Kansas)
map (38° 31′N 98° 32′W) 12:18
CLAIBORNE (Alabama)
map (31° 32′N 87° 31′W) 1:234
CLAIBORNE (county in Louisiana)
map (32° 47′N 93° 0′W) 12:430
CLAIBORNE (county in Mississippi)
map (32° 0′N 90° 50′W) 13:469
CLAIBORNE (county in Tennessee)
map (36° 30′N 83° 40′W) 19:104
CLAIMS, COURT OF *see* COURT OF CLAIMS
CLAIR, ARTHUR ST. *see* ST. CLAIR, ARTHUR
CLAIR, RENÉ 5:35 *bibliog.*
Bresson, Robert 3:474
CLAIRAUT, ALEXIS CLAUDE 5:35
astronomy, history of 2:278
CLAIRBORNE, WILLIAM
Maryland 13:191
CLAIRE LAKE
map (58° 35′N 112° 5′W) 1:256
CLAIRON, HIPPOLYTE
theater, history of the 19:147
CLAIRTON (Pennsylvania)
map (40° 18′N 79° 53′W) 15:147
CLAIRVOYANCE 5:35
extrasensory perception 7:346
CLAISEN, LUDWIG 5:35
CLALLAM (American Indians)
medicine-man mask dance 11:122 *illus.*; 13:50 *illus.*
CLALLAM (county in Washington)
map (48° 10′N 123° 49′W) 20:35
CLAM 5:35–36 *bibliog.*, *illus.*; 15:35 *illus.*
coral reef 5:260
geoduck 9:98
intertidal life 11:230
shellfish 17:254 *illus.*
CLAMBAKE 5:36
CLAMMYWEED 5:36
CLAN 5:36 *bibliog.*
genealogy 9:76
Herero 10:141
Ireland, history of c.1170 11:262 *map*
kinship 12:85
matriarchy 13:229
moiety 13:504
tartan 19:40–41 *illus.*
totem 19:249
CLANTON (Alabama)
map (32° 50′N 86° 38′W) 1:234
CLANTON, BILLY
Earp, Wyatt 7:11
CLAPPERTON, HUGH 5:36
Africa, history of 1:157 *map*
CLARABELL THE CLOWN 16:58 *illus.*
CLARE (Ireland) 5:36; 11:259 *illus.*
CLARE (Michigan)
map (43° 49′N 84° 46′W) 13:377
CLARE (county in Michigan)
map (44° 0′N 84° 50′W) 13:377
CLARE, JOHN 5:36 *bibliog.*
CLARE OF ASSISI, SAINT 5:36
Francis of Assisi, Saint 8:274
CLARE COLLEGE (Cambridge University) 4:52
CLARE HALL (Cambridge University) 4:52
CLAREMONT (New Hampshire)
map (43° 23′N 72° 20′W) 14:123
CLAREMONT COLLEGES 5:36
CLAREMORE (Oklahoma)
map (36° 19′N 95° 36′W) 14:368
CLARENCE (Iowa)
map (41° 53′N 91° 4′W) 11:244
CLARENCE CANNON LAKE
map (39° 30′N 91° 45′W) 13:476
CLARENDON (Arkansas)
map (34° 42′N 91° 18′W) 2:166
CLARENDON (Pennsylvania)
map (41° 47′N 79° 6′W) 15:147
CLARENDON (county in South Carolina)
map (33° 40′N 80° 15′W) 18:98
CLARENDON (Texas)
map (34° 56′N 100° 53′W) 19:129
CLARENDON, EDWARD HYDE, 1ST EARL OF 5:36–37
CLARENDON CODE 5:37
Baxter, Richard 3:132
freedom of religion 8:297
Nonconformists 14:216
CLARENVILLE (Newfoundland)
map (48° 10′N 53° 58′W) 14:166
CLARESHOLM (Alberta)
map (50° 2′N 113° 35′W) 1:256
CLARIN *see* ALAS, LEOPOLDO
CLARINDA (Iowa)
map (40° 44′N 95° 2′W) 11:244
CLARINET 5:37 *bibliog.*, *illus.*; 13:676 *illus.*
bass clarinet
bass (music) 3:117
Bechet, Sidney 3:150
sound waves 18:72 *illus.*
wind instruments 20:171 *illus.*
CLARION (Iowa)
map (42° 44′N 93° 44′W) 11:244
CLARION (Pennsylvania)
map (41° 13′N 79° 24′W) 15:147
CLARION (county in Pennsylvania)
map (41° 13′N 79° 24′W) 15:147
CLARION RIVER
map (41° 7′N 79° 41′W) 15:147
CLARISSA (Minnesota)
map (46° 8′N 94° 57′W) 13:453
CLARISSA HARLOWE (book) 5:37 *bibliog.*
Richardson, Samuel 16:213
CLARK (county in Arizona)
map (34° 5′N 93° 10′W) 2:166
CLARK (county in Idaho)
map (44° 20′N 112° 20′W) 11:26
CLARK (county in Illinois)
map (39° 18′N 87° 47′W) 11:42
CLARK (county in Indiana)
map (38° 17′N 85° 44′W) 11:111
CLARK (county in Kansas)
map (37° 15′N 99° 50′W) 12:18
CLARK (county in Kentucky)
map (38° 0′N 84° 10′W) 12:47
CLARK (county in Missouri)
map (40° 25′N 91° 45′W) 13:476
CLARK (county in Nevada)
map (36° 15′N 115° 0′W) 14:111
CLARK (county in Ohio)
map (39° 56′N 83° 49′W) 14:357
CLARK (South Dakota)
map (44° 53′N 97° 44′W) 18:103
CLARK (county in South Dakota)
map (44° 50′N 97° 45′W) 18:103
CLARK (county in Washington)
map (45° 48′N 122° 31′W) 20:35
CLARK (county in Wisconsin)
map (44° 45′N 90° 38′W) 20:185
CLARK, ALVAN GRAHAM 5:37
Dearborn Observatory 6:68

CLARK, BARNEY
heart, artificial **10**:94–95
CLARK, FRANCIS EDWARD 5:38
CLARK, GEORGE ROGERS 5:38 *bibliog.*, *illus.*
American Revolution **1**:359 *map*; **1**:362
land grant issued to **8**:343 *illus.*
Louisville (Kentucky) **12**:436
Vincennes (Indiana) **19**:599
CLARK, GRAHAME 5:38
Star Carr **18**:226
CLARK, JAMES CHICHESTER
Ireland, history of **11**:265
CLARK, JIM 5:38 *bibliog.*
CLARK, JOHN DESMOND 5:38
CLARK, JOHN PEPPER 5:38 *bibliog.*
CLARK, JOSEPH 5:38–39 *illus.*
Canada, history of **4**:87
CLARK, KENNETH B. 5:39
CLARK, KENNETH M. 5:39 *bibliog.*
CLARK, MAE **4**:16 *illus.*
CLARK, MARK W. 5:39
Korean War **12**:122
CLARK, RAMSEY 5:39
CLARK, ROBERT *see* INDIANA, ROBERT
CLARK, TOM CAMPBELL 5:39; **12**:246 *illus.*
CLARK, SIR W. E. LE GROS 5:39
CLARK, WALTER VAN TILBURG 5:39 *bibliog.*
Ox-Bow Incident, The **14**:473
CLARK, WILLIAM 5:39 *bibliog.*
Lewis and Clark Expedition **12**:307–308 *illus.*
CLARK, WILLIAM ANDREWS 5:39 *bibliog.*
Montana **13**:550
CLARK FORK (Idaho)
map (48° 8′N 116° 11′W) **11**:26
CLARK HILL LAKE
map (33° 50′N 82° 20′W) **9**:114
CLARK UNIVERSITY 5:40
Hall, G. Stanley **10**:21
CLARKDALE (Arizona)
map (34° 46′N 112° 3′W) **2**:160
CLARKE (county in Alabama)
map (31° 40′N 87° 50′W) **1**:234
CLARKE (county in Georgia)
map (33° 55′N 83° 20′W) **9**:114
CLARKE (county in Iowa)
map (41° 0′N 93° 45′W) **11**:244
CLARKE (county in Mississippi)
map (32° 0′N 88° 40′W) **13**:469
CLARKE (county in Virginia)
map (39° 5′N 78° 0′W) **19**:607
CLARKE, ARTHUR C. 5:40
CLARKE, AUSTIN 5:40 *bibliog.*
CLARKE, BOBBY 5:40
CLARKE, C. A.
mimicry **13**:436
CLARKE, JAMES FREEMAN 5:40 *bibliog.*
CLARKE, KENNY
Modern Jazz Quartet **13**:498
CLARKE, MARCUS
Australian literature **2**:343
CLARKE, SAMUEL 5:40
CLARKFIELD (Minnesota)
map (44° 48′N 95° 48′W) **13**:453
CLARKS (Louisiana)
map (32° 2′N 92° 8′W) **12**:430
CLARK'S HARBOUR (Nova Scotia)
map (43° 26′N 65° 38′W) **14**:269
CLARKS HILL (Indiana)
map (40° 15′N 86° 43′W) **11**:111
CLARKS POINT (Alaska)
map (58° 51′N 158° 30′W) **1**:242
CLARKSBURG (West Virginia)
map (39° 17′N 80° 21′W) **20**:111
CLARKSDALE (Mississippi)
map (34° 12′N 90° 34′W) **13**:469
CLARKSON (Kentucky)
map (37° 30′N 86° 13′W) **12**:47
CLARKSON (Nebraska)
map (41° 43′N 97° 13′W) **14**:70
CLARKSON, THOMAS
slavery **17**:355 *illus.*
CLARKSTON (Washington)
map (46° 25′N 117° 2′W) **20**:35
CLARKSVILLE (Arkansas)
map (35° 28′N 93° 28′W) **2**:166
CLARKSVILLE (Indiana)
map (38° 17′N 85° 45′W) **11**:111
CLARKSVILLE (Iowa)
map (42° 47′N 92° 40′W) **11**:244
CLARKSVILLE (Tennessee)
map (36° 32′N 87° 21′W) **19**:104
CLARKSVILLE (Texas)
map (33° 37′N 95° 3′W) **19**:129
CLARKSVILLE (Virginia)
map (36° 37′N 78° 34′W) **19**:607
CLARKTON (Missouri)
map (36° 27′N 89° 58′W) **13**:476
CLARKTON (North Carolina)
map (34° 29′N 78° 39′W) **14**:242
CLARY
Salvia **17**:40
CLASS, SOCIAL 5:40–41 *bibliog.*
Africa
Hausa **10**:69
Tutsi **19**:355–356
aristocracy **2**:155
body marking **3**:356–357
bourgeoisie **3**:424
caste **4**:186–187
chief **4**:346
civilization **5**:34
cosmetics **5**:281–282
costume **5**:292–303
effects of technology **19**:60–61
elites **7**:140
funeral customs **8**:364 *illus.*
marriage **13**:164
Marxism **13**:183–184
proletariat **15**:567
Maya **13**:244–245
mestizo **13**:324
middle schools and junior high schools **13**:412
mulatto **13**:635
newspaper **14**:171–172
Ottoman Empire **14**:464
patricians **15**:113
peasant **15**:128–129
plebeians **15**:364
prostitution **15**:573
racism **16**:37–38
role **16**:271
Rome, ancient **16**:297–298
Russia/Union of Soviet Socialist Republics, history of **16**:354
boyars **3**:433
samurai **17**:49
schizophrenia **17**:123
Social Darwinism **18**:12
social structure and organization **18**:16–17
socialism **18**:20
status **18**:238–239
suburbs **18**:317
sumptuary laws **18**:340
tombstone **19**:232
totalitarianism **19**:248
CLASS ACTION 5:41
CLASSICAL MUSIC, MODERN *see* MODERN CLASSICAL MUSIC
CLASSICAL PERIOD IN MUSIC 5:41–42 *bibliog.*, *illus.*
Beethoven, Ludwig van **3**:164–165
Boccherini, Luigi **3**:354
Clementi, Muzio **5**:50
German and Austrian music **9**:130
Haydn, Franz Josef **10**:81
Liszt, Franz **12**:367
Mannheim school **13**:125
Mozart, Wolfgang Amadeus **13**:628–629
music, history of Western **13**:666
opera **14**:400
orchestra and orchestration **14**:418
rondo **16**:305
Sammartini, Giovanni Battista **17**:46
sonata **18**:63
Stamitz (family) **18**:216
symphony **18**:405
trumpet **19**:320
CLASSICAL PHYSICS *see* PHYSICS
CLASSICISM (literature) 5:42 *bibliog.*
See also NEOCLASSICISM (literature)
Addison, Joseph **1**:100
Aubignac, Abbé d' **2**:316
Boileau-Despréaux, Nicolas **3**:362
Corneille, Pierre **5**:267–268
criticism, literary **5**:351
Dryden, John **6**:284–285
French literature **8**:315–316
German literature **9**:132–133
Gibbon, Edward **9**:172–173
Goethe, Johann Wolfgang von **9**:223–224
Herder, Johann Gottfried von **10**:138
Hölderlin, Friedrich **10**:202
Johnson, Samuel **11**:435–436
La Fontaine, Jean de **12**:146
La Rochefoucauld, François, Duc de **12**:148
Lessing, Gotthold **12**:298–299
Molière **13**:509–510
Pascal, Blaise **15**:102
Racine, Jean **16**:36–37
Schiller, Johann Christoph Friedrich von **17**:120–121
CLASSIFICATION, BIOLOGICAL 5:42–44 *bibliog.*, *table*
amphibians **1**:377–379
animal **2**:9 *illus.*; **2**:10–11
Animalia **5**:43
annelid **2**:33
ant **2**:38
antelope **2**:47
arthropod **2**:216
bacteria **3**:15–16
bee **3**:155–158
Berlin Zoo **3**:217
biology **3**:268; **3**:269
birds of prey **3**:290–291
butterflies and moths **3**:594–595
carnivore **4**:157 *table*
cat family **4**:196
Cephalochordata **4**:256
cetacean **4**:262
chordate **4**:407–408
coelenterate **5**:92
Cohn, Ferdinand J. **5**:96
colubrid **5**:124–125
Cope, Edward **5**:248
dog family **6**:222
duck **6**:290–292
echinoderm **7**:38
Euglena **7**:264
eutherian **7**:311
finch **8**:92
five-kingdom **5**:43
flower **8**:183
frog **8**:336
fungi, mushrooms **13**:660–661
Gnathostomata **9**:213
hemichordate **10**:118
humans, modern **5**:43 *table*
insect, Anoplura **2**:34
invertebrate **11**:234–235
Lamarck, Jean Baptiste **12**:173–174
Linnaean system **5**:42–43
Linnaeus, Carolus **5**:42; **12**:359
Lorenz, Konrad **12**:414
lungfish **12**:462
mammal **13**:101–106 *illus.*
Mastigophora **13**:217
Mayr, Ernst **13**:249
mollusk, chiton **4**:399
Monera **5**:43; **13**:523
monkey **13**:532; **13**:534
moss **13**:603
plant **15**:333–335
Plantae **5**:43
primate **15**:542 *table*
Protista **15**:577–578
race **16**:33–34 *illus.*
Ray, John **16**:96
reptile **16**:171
shrub **17**:288–289
slime mold **17**:362
snake **17**:382
spider **18**:182
zoology **20**:376
CLASSIFICATION SYSTEMS (library)
library **12**:315
CLATHRATE COMPOUNDS 5:44 *bibliog.*
CLATSOP (county in Oregon)
map (46° 1′N 123° 41′W) **14**:427
CLAUDE (Texas)
map (35° 7′N 101° 22′W) **19**:129
CLAUDE, ALBERT 5:44
Palade, George Emil **15**:29
CLAUDE, GEORGES
ocean thermal energy conversion **14**:333
CLAUDE LORRAIN *see* LORRAIN, CLAUDE
CLAUDEL, PAUL 5:44 *bibliog.*
CLAUDIUS AELIANUS *see* AELIAN
CLAUDIUS I, ROMAN EMPEROR 5:44 *bibliog.*
Agrippina II **1**:199
Messalina **13**:322
Ostia **14**:458
Rome, ancient **16**:302
CLAUSEN, A. W. 5:44
CLAUSEWITZ, CARL PHILIPP GOTTFRIED VON 5:44–45 *bibliog.*
war **20**:24
CLAUSIUS, RUDOLF 5:45 *bibliog.*
entropy **7**:209
kinetic theory of matter **12**:79
CLAUSSEN, SOPHUS 5:45
CLAUSTROPHOBIA 5:45
phobia **15**:248–249
CLAVER, SAINT PETER 5:45 *bibliog.*
CLAVERHOUSE, JOHN GRAHAM OF *see* DUNDEE, JOHN GRAHAM OF CLAVERHOUSE, 1ST VISCOUNT
CLAVICHORD 5:45 *bibliog.*, *illus.*; **13**:678 *illus.*
Bach, Carl Philipp Emanuel **3**:10
keyboard instruments **12**:63 *illus.*
CLAW *see* HOOF, NAIL, AND CLAW
CLAXTON (Georgia)
map (32° 10′N 81° 55′W) **9**:114
CLAY
See also CLAY MINERALS
alteration, mineral **1**:312
ceramics **4**:257–259
geochemistry **9**:96
phyllite **15**:278
quick clay **16**:25
CLAY (county in Alabama)
map (33° 15′N 85° 50′W) **1**:234
CLAY (county in Arkansas)
map (36° 22′N 90° 30′W) **2**:166
CLAY (county in Florida)
map (30° 0′N 81° 50′W) **8**:172
CLAY (county in Georgia)
map (31° 35′N 85° 0′W) **9**:114
CLAY (county in Illinois)
map (38° 42′N 88° 30′W) **11**:42
CLAY (county in Indiana)
map (39° 25′N 87° 10′W) **11**:111
CLAY (county in Iowa)
map (43° 7′N 95° 5′W) **11**:244
CLAY (county in Kansas)
map (39° 20′N 97° 10′W) **12**:18
CLAY (Kentucky)
map (37° 29′N 87° 49′W) **12**:47
CLAY (county in Kentucky)
map (37° 10′N 83° 45′W) **12**:47
CLAY (county in Minnesota)
map (46° 52′N 96° 30′W) **13**:453
CLAY (county in Mississippi)
map (33° 40′N 88° 50′W) **13**:469
CLAY (county in Missouri)
map (39° 20′N 94° 25′W) **13**:476
CLAY (county in Nebraska)
map (40° 35′N 98° 0′W) **14**:70
CLAY (county in North Carolina)
map (35° 5′N 83° 45′W) **14**:242
CLAY (county in South Dakota)
map (42° 55′N 96° 55′W) **18**:103
CLAY (county in Tennessee)
map (36° 33′N 85° 35′W) **19**:104
CLAY (county in Texas)
map (33° 40′N 98° 15′W) **19**:129
CLAY (West Virginia)
map (38° 28′N 81° 5′W) **20**:111
CLAY (county in West Virginia)
map (38° 27′N 81° 5′W) **20**:111
CLAY, CASSIUS MARCELLUS 5:45 *bibliog.*
CLAY, CASSIUS MARCELLUS, JR. *see* ALI, MUHAMMAD (boxer)
CLAY, HENRY 5:15 *illus.*; 5:46 *bibliog.*, *illus.*
Compromise of 1850 **5**:158 *illus.*
Jackson, Andrew **11**:341–342
Lexington (Kentucky) **12**:309
Missouri Compromise **13**:480–481
War of 1812 **20**:26
Webster, Daniel **20**:88
Whig party (United States) **20**:130–131
CLAY, LUCIUS D. 5:46
CLAY CENTER (Kansas)
map (39° 23′N 97° 8′W) **12**:18
CLAY CENTER (Nebraska)
map (40° 32′N 98° 3′W) **14**:70
CLAY CITY (Indiana)
map (39° 17′N 87° 7′W) **11**:111
CLAY CITY (Kentucky)
map (37° 52′N 83° 55′W) **12**:47
CLAY MINERALS 5:46–47 *bibliog.*
bentonites **5**:46
Carboniferous Period **4**:137–139
industrial mineral **5**:46
industrial uses **5**:46
kaolin clays **5**:46
meerschaum **13**:278
mud cracks **13**:631
other varieties **5**:47
sediment, marine **17**:184
shale **17**:237–238
silicate minerals **17**:305
sillimanite **17**:309
slate **17**:351
CLAY PIGEONS *see* SHOOTING (sport)
CLAY PLUG
oxbow lake **14**:473
CLAY SPRINGS (Arizona)
map (34° 22′N 110° 18′W) **2**:160
CLAYMONT (Delaware)
map (39° 48′N 75° 28′W) **6**:88
CLAYPOOL (Arizona)
map (33° 25′N 110° 51′W) **2**:160
CLAYTON (Alabama)
map (31° 53′N 85° 27′W) **1**:234
CLAYTON (Delaware)
map (39° 17′N 75° 38′W) **6**:88
CLAYTON (Georgia)
map (34° 53′N 83° 23′W) **9**:114
CLAYTON (county in Georgia)
map (33° 35′N 84° 20′W) **9**:114
CLAYTON (Illinois)
map (40° 2′N 90° 57′W) **11**:42

CLAYTON (county in Iowa)
map (42° 52′N 91° 15′W) **11**:244
CLAYTON (Louisiana)
map (31° 44′N 91° 33′W) **12**:430
CLAYTON (Missouri)
map (38° 39′N 90° 20′W) **13**:476
CLAYTON (New Jersey)
map (39° 39′N 75° 6′W) **14**:129
CLAYTON (New Mexico)
map (36° 27′N 103° 11′W) **14**:136
CLAYTON (North Carolina)
map (35° 39′N 78° 28′W) **14**:242
CLAYTON (Oklahoma)
map (34° 35′N 95° 21′W) **14**:368
CLAYTON, JACK
film, history of **8**:86
CLAYTON, JOHN MIDDLETON
Clayton-Bulwer Treaty **5**:47
CLAYTON ANTI-TRUST ACT **5**:47
Federal Trade Commission **8**:42
Sherman Anti-Trust Act **17**:259
CLAYTON-BULWER TREATY **5**:47 *bibliog.*
Hay-Pauncefote Treaty **10**:80
CLEAN AIR ACT OF 1970
pollution control **15**:415–416
CLEANTHES **5**:47
CLEAR CREEK (county in Colorado)
map (39° 40′N 105° 40′W) **5**:116
CLEAR ISLAND
map (51° 26′N 9° 30′W) **11**:258
CLEAR LAKE
map (39° 2′N 122° 50′W) **4**:31
CLEAR LAKE (Iowa)
map (43° 8′N 93° 23′W) **11**:244
CLEAR LAKE (South Dakota)
map (44° 45′N 96° 41′W) **18**:103
CLEAR LAKE (Wisconsin)
map (45° 15′N 92° 16′W) **20**:185
CLEARCHUS **5**:47
CLEARCUTTING
forestry **8**:231
CLEARFIELD (Iowa)
map (40° 48′N 94° 29′W) **11**:244
CLEARFIELD (Pennsylvania)
map (41° 2′N 78° 27′W) **15**:147
CLEARFIELD (county in Pennsylvania)
map (41° 2′N 78° 27′W) **15**:147
CLEARFIELD (Utah)
map (41° 7′N 112° 1′W) **19**:492
CLEARINGHOUSE **5**:47
central bank **4**:253
CLEARMONT (Wyoming)
map (44° 38′N 106° 23′W) **20**:301
CLEARWATER (British Columbia)
map (51° 38′N 120° 2′W) **3**:491
CLEARWATER (Florida)
map (27° 58′N 82° 48′W) **8**:172
CLEARWATER (county in Idaho)
map (46° 40′N 115° 40′W) **11**:26
CLEARWATER (Kansas)
map (37° 30′N 97° 30′W) **12**:18
CLEARWATER (county in Minnesota)
map (47° 37′N 95° 20′W) **13**:453
CLEARWATER (Nebraska)
map (42° 10′N 98° 11′W) **14**:70
CLEARWATER (South Carolina)
map (33° 28′N 81° 55′W) **18**:98
CLEARWATER MOUNTAINS
map (46° 0′N 115° 30′W) **11**:26
CLEARWATER RIVER
map (46° 25′N 117° 2′W) **11**:26
CLEAVAGE (embryology)
development **6**:137–138 *illus.*; **6**:140
embryo **7**:153
embryology **7**:154
CLEAVAGE (mineralogy) **5**:47
mineral identification **13**:441
CLEAVELAND, MOSES
Cleveland (Ohio) **5**:52
CLEAVER, ELDRIDGE **5**:47–48 *bibliog., illus.*
Black Panther party **3**:318
Soul on Ice **18**:71
CLEBURNE (county in Alabama)
map (33° 40′N 85° 35′W) **1**:234
CLEBURNE (county in Arkansas)
map (35° 35′N 92° 5′W) **2**:166
CLEBURNE (Texas)
map (32° 21′N 97° 23′W) **19**:129
CLEESE, JOHN
"Monty Python's Flying Circus" (television series) **13**:560
CLEF **5**:48 *bibliog., illus.*
bass (music) **3**:117
treble **19**:286
CLEFT LIP AND PALATE **5**:48 *bibliog.*
speech **18**:175
CLEISTHENES **5**:48 *bibliog.*
CLEITIAS **5**:48 *bibliog.*
CLELAND, JOHN **5**:48 *bibliog.*
Fanny Hill, or The Memoirs of a Woman of Pleasure **8**:20
CLEMATIS **5**:48 *illus.*
CLEMENCEAU, GEORGES **5**:48–49 *bibliog., illus.*
liberalism **12**:312
Paris Peace Conference **15**:88; **20**:244 *illus.*
Poincaré, Raymond **15**:380
World War I **20**:242
CLEMENS, SAMUEL LANGHORNE *see* TWAIN, MARK
CLEMENS NON PAPA
Renaissance music **16**:156
CLÉMENT, JACQUES
Henry III, King of France **10**:127
CLEMENT OF ALEXANDRIA, SAINT **5**:49 *bibliog.*
CLEMENT I, SAINT **5**:49
Apostolic Fathers **2**:85
CLEMENT OF ROME *see* CLEMENT I, SAINT
CLEMENT V, POPE **5**:49 *bibliog.*
Philip IV, King of France (Philip the Fair) **15**:232
CLEMENT VI, POPE **5**:49
Medici (family) **13**:265
Rienzo, Cola di **16**:219
CLEMENT VII, POPE **5**:49–50
CLEMENT VIII, POPE **5**:50
CLEMENT XI, POPE **5**:50
CLEMENT XIV, POPE **5**:50
CLEMENTE, ROBERTO **5**:50 *bibliog.*
CLEMENTI, MUZIO **5**:50 *bibliog.*
CLEMENTS, WILLIAM P., JR.
Texas **19**:133
CLEMENTSPORT (Nova Scotia)
map (44° 40′N 65° 37′W) **14**:269
CLEMSON (South Carolina)
map (34° 41′N 82° 50′W) **18**:98
CLENDENIN (West Virginia)
map (38° 29′N 81° 21′W) **20**:111
CLEOME
clammyweed **5**:36
CLEOMENES III, KING OF SPARTA **5**:50 *bibliog.*
CLEON **5**:50 *bibliog.*
CLEOPATRA, QUEEN OF EGYPT **5**:50–51 *bibliog., illus.*
Antony, Mark **2**:70–71
asp **2**:261
Caesar, Gaius Julius **16**:301
Ptolemy XIII, King of Egypt **15**:608
Roman coin **16**:301 *illus.*
Tarsus (Turkey) **19**:39–40
CLEOPATRA'S NEEDLES **5**:51 *bibliog.*
obelisk **14**:314–315
CLEP *see* COLLEGE LEVEL EXAMINATION PROGRAM
CLEPSYDRA **5**:51 *bibliog.*; **5**:62 *illus.*
Ctesibius **5**:376
CLERESTORY **5**:51
Gothic art and architecture **9**:255
Romanesque art and architecture **16**:282
CLERGY *see* MINISTRY, CHRISTIAN
CLÉRISSEAU, CHARLES LOUIS **5**:51 *bibliog.*
CLERKE, CHARLES
exploration **7**:336 *map*
CLERMONT (Florida)
map (28° 33′N 81° 46′W) **8**:172
CLERMONT (county in Ohio)
map (39° 5′N 84° 11′W) **14**:357
CLERMONT (steamboat) **5**:51–52 *illus.*
Fulton, Robert **8**:358
ship **17**:272 *illus.*
CLERMONT, ROBERT OF
Bourbon (dynasty) **3**:423
CLERMONT-FERRAND (France) **5**:52
Auvergne **2**:368
map (45° 47′N 3° 5′E) **8**:260
CLEVE, JOOS VAN *see* JOOS VAN CLEVE
CLEVELAND (Alabama)
map (33° 59′N 86° 35′W) **1**:234
CLEVELAND (county in Arkansas)
map (33° 50′N 92° 15′W) **2**:166
CLEVELAND (county in England) **5**:52
CLEVELAND (Georgia)
map (34° 36′N 83° 46′W) **9**:114
CLEVELAND (Mississippi)
map (33° 45′N 90° 50′W) **13**:469
CLEVELAND (county in North Carolina)
map (35° 20′N 81° 35′W) **14**:242
CLEVELAND (Ohio) **5**:52 *bibliog.*
Cleveland Museum of Art **5**:54
Cleveland Orchestra, The **5**:54
Johnson, Tom Loftin **11**:436
map (41° 30′N 81° 41′W) **14**:357
CLEVELAND (Oklahoma)
map (36° 19′N 96° 28′W) **14**:368
CLEVELAND (county in Oklahoma)
map (35° 10′N 97° 20′W) **14**:368
CLEVELAND (Tennessee)
map (35° 10′N 84° 53′W) **19**:104
CLEVELAND (Texas)
map (30° 21′N 95° 5′W) **19**:129
CLEVELAND, GROVER **5**:52–54 *bibliog., illus.*; **6**:100 *illus.*
Democratic party **6**:100
mugwumps **13**:632
Republican party **16**:173–174
United States, history of the **19**:451
CLEVELAND, MOUNT
map (48° 56′N 113° 51′W) **13**:547
CLEVELAND HEIGHTS (Ohio)
map (41° 30′N 81° 34′W) **14**:357
CLEVELAND MUSEUM OF ART **5**:54 *bibliog.*
CLEVELAND ORCHESTRA, THE **5**:54 *bibliog.*
Dohnányi, Christoph von **6**:224
Maazel, Lorin **13**:5
Szell, Georg **18**:416
CLEW BAY
map (53° 50′N 9° 50′W) **11**:258
CLEWISTON (Florida)
map (26° 45′N 80° 56′W) **8**:172
CLIBURN, VAN **5**:54 *bibliog.*
music competitions **13**:669
CLICHY (France) **5**:54
CLICK BEETLE **3**:167 *illus.*
CLIENT-CENTERED THERAPY **5**:54 *bibliog.*
psychotherapy **15**:603
Rogers, Carl **16**:268–269
CLIFF **12**:182 *illus.*
CLIFF DWELLERS **5**:54–55 *bibliog., illus.*
Anasazi **1**:392–394 *illus., illus.*
cave dwellers **4**:225
Mesa Verde National Park (Colorado) **13**:313–314 *illus.*; **14**:239 *illus.*
Montezuma Castle National Monument **13**:555
CLIFF FROG *see* CHIRPING FROG
CLIFFHANGER
film serials **8**:91
CLIFFORD, CLARK **5**:55
Vietnam War **19**:587
CLIFFSIDE PARK (New Jersey)
map (40° 49′N 73° 59′W) **14**:129
CLIFTON (Arizona)
map (33° 3′N 109° 18′W) **2**:160
CLIFTON (Illinois)
map (40° 56′N 87° 56′W) **11**:42
CLIFTON (Kansas)
map (39° 34′N 97° 17′W) **12**:18
CLIFTON (New Jersey)
map (40° 53′N 74° 8′W) **14**:129
CLIFTON (Tennessee)
map (35° 23′N 88° 1′W) **19**:104
CLIFTON FORGE (Virginia)
map (37° 49′N 79° 49′W) **19**:607
CLIMACTERIC *see* MENOPAUSE
CLIMATE **5**:55–58 *bibliog., illus., map*
See also ATMOSPHERIC SCIENCES; METEOROLOGY
Africa **1**:140–141 *map*
agriculture and the food supply **1**:196
arid climate **2**:154
desert **6**:126–129
dust devil **6**:308–309
Asia **2**:236 *map*
Australia **2**:332 *map*
biome **3**:273–274 *map*
blizzard **3**:333
civilization, effects on **5**:58
Huntington, Ellsworth **10**:314
classification **5**:55–57
Köppen, Wladimir Peter **12**:110
Thornthwaite climatic classification **19**:179
climatic change **5**:58
Bryan, Kirk **3**:528
Cenozoic Era **4**:246
Cretaceous Period **5**:341
dinosaur **6**:182
endangered species **7**:165–168
front **8**:339–340
greenhouse effect **9**:351–352
ice ages **11**:7–11
landform evolution **12**:183
Milankovitch theory **13**:418–419
ocean-atmosphere interaction **14**:321
paleoclimatology **15**:32–34
paleoecology **15**:34–35
paleotemperature **15**:42
Pleistocene Epoch, prehistoric humans **15**:511–512
Recent Epoch **16**:107
Tertiary Period **19**:124
Triassic Period **19**:294
weather variation and extremes **20**:81
climatic zones **5**:56 *map*
continental climate **5**:227–228
dew **6**:146
drought **6**:273–274
Earth sciences **7**:24
El Niño (ocean current) **7**:99
Europe **7**:272–273 *map*
evapotranspiration **7**:314–315
fog **8**:193
forest **8**:227
Gulf Stream **9**:403 *illus.*
history **5**:55
horse latitudes **10**:246
Humboldt, Alexander von **10**:301
humidity **10**:302
hydrologic cycle **10**:341–342
inversion **11**:233–234
isotherm **11**:300–301
jet stream **11**:407–408
jungle and rain forest **11**:468–470
lake, glacial **12**:169–170
Lamont-Doherty Geological Observatory **12**:175
littoral zone **12**:373
maritime climate **13**:157
Mediterranean climate **13**:276
microclimate **13**:384–385
mistral **13**:482
monsoon **13**:543–544
mountain climates **13**:620–621
mountain life **13**:622–623
mountain and valley winds **13**:624
North America **14**:227 *map*
orographic precipitation **14**:447
permafrost **15**:173–174
polar climate **15**:392
precipitation **15**:493–495
savanna life **17**:98
semiarid climate **17**:195–196
soil **18**:37
South America **18**:87 *map*
steppe life **18**:256–257
taiga climate **19**:11
temperate climate **19**:92
tropical climate **19**:307
tundra **19**:332
upwelling, oceanic **19**:473–474
urban climate **19**:480
vegetable **19**:531
westerlies **20**:115
wind rose diagram **20**:171
CLIMAX (Colorado)
map (39° 22′N 106° 11′W) **5**:116
molybdenite **13**:514
CLIMAX (literature)
narrative and dramatic devices **14**:22
CLIMAX COMMUNITY **5**:59 *bibliog.*
ecology **7**:43
forest **8**:227–230
CLINCH (county in Georgia)
map (31° 0′N 82° 45′W) **9**:114
CLINCH MOUNTAIN
map (36° 45′N 83° 0′W) **19**:104
CLINCH RIVER
map (35° 53′N 84° 29′W) **19**:104
CLINDAMYCIN
antibiotics **2**:59
CLINGFISH **5**:59
CLINGMAN, THOMAS L.
Great Smoky Mountains **9**:322
CLINGMANS DOME **19**:104 *illus.*
map (35° 35′N 83° 30′W) **19**:104
CLINICAL PATHOLOGY *see* PATHOLOGY
CLINICAL PSYCHOLOGY **5**:59 *bibliog.*
Adler, Alfred **1**:103
client-centered therapy **5**:54
community mental health **5**:152–153
Freud, Sigmund **8**:329–330
history **5**:59
Jung, Carl **11**:467–468
psychiatry **15**:588
psychological tests **5**:59
psychology **15**:595
psychology, history of **15**:598
psychopathology, treatment of **15**:599–601
psychotherapy **5**:59; **15**:603
reasoning **16**:104–105
Rogers, Carl **16**:268–269
CLINID **5**:59
CLINTON (Alabama)
map (32° 55′N 88° 0′W) **1**:234
CLINTON (Arkansas)
map (35° 36′N 92° 28′W) **2**:166
CLINTON (Connecticut)
map (41° 17′N 72° 32′W) **5**:193
CLINTON (family) **5**:59–60 *bibliog., illus.*
CLINTON (Illinois)
map (40° 9′N 88° 57′W) **11**:42
CLINTON (county in Illinois)
map (38° 37′N 89° 22′W) **11**:42
CLINTON (Indiana)
map (39° 40′N 87° 24′W) **11**:111
CLINTON (county in Indiana)
map (40° 18′N 86° 30′W) **11**:111

CLINTON (Iowa)
map (41° 51′N 90° 12′W) **11**:244
CLINTON (county in Iowa)
map (41° 55′N 90° 30′W) **11**:244
CLINTON (Kentucky)
map (36° 40′N 89° 2′W) **12**:47
CLINTON (county in Kentucky)
map (36° 45′N 85° 10′W) **12**:47
CLINTON (Louisiana)
map (30° 52′N 91° 1′W) **12**:430
CLINTON (Maryland)
map (38° 46′N 76° 54′W) **13**:188
CLINTON (Massachusetts)
map (42° 25′N 71° 41′W) **13**:206
CLINTON (county in Michigan)
map (43° 0′N 84° 35′W) **13**:377
CLINTON (Mississippi)
map (32° 20′N 90° 20′W) **13**:469
CLINTON (Missouri)
map (38° 22′N 93° 46′W) **13**:476
CLINTON (county in Missouri)
map (39° 35′N 94° 25′W) **13**:476
CLINTON (New Jersey)
map (40° 38′N 74° 55′W) **14**:129
CLINTON (county in New York)
map (44° 45′N 73° 40′W) **14**:149
CLINTON (North Carolina)
map (35° 0′N 78° 20′W) **14**:242
CLINTON (county in Ohio)
map (39° 27′N 83° 50′W) **14**:357
CLINTON (Oklahoma)
map (35° 31′N 98° 59′W) **14**:368
CLINTON (Ontario)
map (43° 37′N 81° 32′W) **14**:393; **14**:461
CLINTON (county in Pennsylvania)
map (41° 8′N 71° 26′W) **15**:147
CLINTON (South Carolina)
map (34° 29′N 81° 53′W) **18**:98
CLINTON (Tennessee)
map (36° 6′N 84° 8′W) **19**:104
CLINTON (Wisconsin)
map (42° 34′N 88° 52′W) **20**:185
CLINTON, CHARLES
Clinton (family) **5**:59
CLINTON, DEWITT **5**:59–60 *illus.*
Erie Canal **7**:230
CLINTON, GEORGE
Clinton (family) **5**:59
Vermont **19**:558
CLINTON, SIR HENRY **5**:60 *bibliog.*
American Revolution **1**:358–359 *map*; **1**:361–362
Monmouth, Battle of **13**:535–536
Yorktown Campaign **20**:331
CLINTON, JAMES
Clinton (family) **5**:59
CLINTON LABORATORIES *see* OAK RIDGE NATIONAL LABORATORY
CLINTON LAKE
map (38° 55′N 95° 25′W) **12**:18
CLINTON/MINETTE
major ore deposits **14**:424–425 *table*
CLINTONVILLE (Wisconsin)
map (44° 37′N 88° 46′W) **20**:185
CLINTWOOD (Virginia)
map (37° 9′N 82° 27′W) **19**:607
CLIO
muses **13**:656
CLIO (South Carolina)
map (34° 35′N 79° 33′W) **18**:98
CLIPPER SHIP **5**:60–61 *bibliog., illus.*
McKay, Donald **13**:27
ship **17**:269 *illus.*
CLIPPERTON ISLAND
French Polynesia **8**:321–322
map (10° 17′N 109° 13′W) **14**:334
CLITORIS
reproductive system, human **16**:163; **16**:166 *illus.*
CLIVE, KITTY **5**:61
CLIVE, ROBERT **5**:61 *bibliog.*; **11**:92 *illus.*
India, history of **11**:92
CLO-OOSE (British Columbia)
map (48° 40′N 124° 49′W) **3**:491
CLOCK PARADOX **5**:61 *bibliog.*
relativity **16**:134
special relativity **5**:61
CLOCKS AND WATCHES **5**:61–63 *bibliog., illus.*
antique collecting **2**:66 *illus.*
atomic clock **2**:308
chronometer **4**:420
digital instruments **6**:175
Graham, George **9**:279
liquid crystal **12**:365
pendulum **15**:142
Huygens, Christiaan **10**:325
sundial **18**:347
Thomas, Seth **19**:174
water clocks, clepsydra **5**:51
CLODION **5**:63 *bibliog.*
CLODIUS, PUBLIUS **5**:63–64 *bibliog.*
Cicero, Marcus Tullius **4**:428–429
CLODIUS PULCHER *see* CLODIUS, PUBLIUS
CLOETE, STUART **5**:64
CLOG (shoe) **17**:280 *illus.*
CLOG DANCE
folk dance **8**:200 *illus.*
CLOISONNÉ
enamel **7**:161–162 *illus.*
pre-Columbian art and architecture **15**:499
CLOISTER **5**:64
Cloisters, The (New York City) **5**:64
colonnade **5**:112
monastic art and architecture **13**:517–521
CLOISTER AND THE HEARTH, THE (book)
Reade, Charles **16**:100
CLOISTERS, THE (New York City) **5**:64 *bibliog.*
CLONCURRY (Australia)
climate **2**:332 *table*
CLONING **5**:64–65 *bibliog.*
genetic engineering **9**:84–85
horticulture **10**:255
plant breeding **15**:343
plant propagation **15**:345
Protozoa **15**:581
reproduction **16**:161
CLONMEL (Ireland)
map (52° 21′N 7° 42′W) **11**:258
CLOQUET (Minnesota)
map (46° 43′N 92° 28′W) **13**:453
CLOQUET RIVER
map (46° 52′N 92° 35′W) **13**:453
CLOSE, CHUCK **5**:65 *bibliog.*
Portrait of Richard Serra **15**:274 *illus.*
CLOSED SHOP (labor) **5**:65
Labor-Management Relations Act **12**:152
right-to-work laws **16**:222
union shop **19**:387
CLOSET DRAMA *see* DRAMA
CLOSTER (New Jersey)
map (40° 59′N 73° 58′W) **14**:129
CLOSTRIDIUM **5**:65
botulism **3**:419
food poisoning and infection **8**:211
gangrene **9**:37
spore **18**:195
CLOSURE *see* CLOTURE
CLOT *see* THROMBOSIS
CLOTH OF GOLD, FIELD OF THE
meeting of Henry VIII and Francis I **9**:312 *illus.*
CLOTHING *see* COSTUME
CLOTHING INDUSTRY **5**:65–66 *bibliog.*
See also SPINNING; TEXTILE INDUSTRY; WEAVING
anthropometry **2**:55
fashion design **8**:31–33
labor union **5**:65–66
Amalgamated Clothing and Textile Workers Union **1**:321
International Ladies' Garment Workers' Union **11**:221
sewing machine **17**:223–224
CLOTILDA
Clovis **5**:70
CLOTURE **5**:66
filibuster **8**:79
CLOUD **5**:66–68 *bibliog., illus.*
atmosphere **2**:300
cirrus clouds **4**:445
classification **5**:67–68 *illus.*
cumulonimbus clouds **5**:388
cumulus clouds **5**:388
dissipation, weather modification **20**:80
front **8**:340
low-pressure system **20**:76 *illus.*
meteorology **13**:341
nacreous cloud **14**:4
Nimbus **14**:198
noctilucent cloud **14**:212
photography
Stieglitz, Alfred **18**:267 *illus.*
precipitation **15**:494
radar meteorology **16**:41
rain shadow effect **16**:77
seeding
Schaefer, Vincent Joseph **17**:116
weather modification **20**:79–80
sky **17**:346
stratus clouds **18**:293 *illus.*
Strömgren, Bengt Georg Daniel **18**:302
thunderstorm **19**:185
tornado **19**:239–240
waterspout **20**:66
weather map **20**:77 *illus.*
CLOUD (county in Kansas)
map (39° 30′N 97° 40′W) **12**:18
CLOUD, INTERSTELLAR
gas cloud, prominence **15**:567
globule **9**:209
halo, galactic **10**:25
lightning **12**:339–340
Magellanic Clouds **13**:48–49
mare's tail (cloud) **13**:148
nebula **14**:74–75
nebula, interstellar matter **11**:226 *illus.*
CLOUD CHAMBER **5**:68 *bibliog., illus.*
Blackett, Patrick Maynard Stuart, Baron Blackett **3**:321
nuclear physics **14**:285
photography **15**:265
Wilson, Charles Thomson Rees, inventor **20**:164
CLOUD HILL *see* YÜN-KANG (Yungang) (China)
CLOUD PEAK
map (44° 25′N 107° 10′W) **20**:301
CLOUDCROFT (New Mexico)
map (32° 58′N 105° 45′W) **14**:136
CLOUDS, THE (play) **5**:68 *bibliog.*
CLOUET (family) **5**:68–69 *bibliog., illus.*
Francis I on Horseback **16**:155 *illus.*
Portrait of Francis I **5**:69 *illus.*
CLOUGH, ARTHUR HUGH **5**:69 *bibliog.*
CLOVE **5**:69 *illus.*
Pemba (Tanzania) **15**:140
CLOVER (botany) **5**:69–70 *illus.*; **17**:239 *illus.*
CLOVER (South Carolina)
map (35° 7′N 81° 14′W) **18**:98
CLOVERDALE (Alabama)
map (34° 56′N 87° 46′W) **1**:234
CLOVERDALE (California)
map (38° 48′N 123° 1′W) **4**:31
CLOVERDALE (Indiana)
map (39° 31′N 86° 48′W) **11**:111
CLOVIO, GIULIO **5**:70 *bibliog.*
CLOVIS **5**:70 *bibliog.*; **7**:283 *illus.*
coronation of **8**:286 *illus.*
France, history of **8**:266
Franks **8**:285–286 *map*
Germany, history of **9**:148
Merovingians (dynasty) **13**:312
CLOVIS (California)
map (36° 49′N 119° 42′W) **4**:31
CLOVIS (New Mexico)
map (34° 24′N 103° 12′W) **14**:136
CLOWN **4**:443 *illus.*; **5**:70 *bibliog., illus.*
circus **4**:444
Grimaldi, Joseph **9**:364
Grock **9**:368
Harlem Globetrotters **10**:50
Kelly, Emmett **12**:39
CLOWN ANEMONEFISH **8**:116 *illus.*
CLOWNFISH *see* DAMSELFISH
CLUB MOSS **5**:70–71 *illus.*
fossil record **8**:244 *illus.*
plant **15**:334 *illus.*
pteridophyte **15**:606
Triassic Period **19**:294 *illus.*
CLUBFOOT **5**:71 *bibliog.*
CLUJ (Romania) **5**:71
map (46° 47′N 23° 36′E) **16**:288
CLUMBER SPANIEL **5**:71 *bibliog., illus.*; **6**:218 *illus.*
CLUNIES-ROSS (family)
Cocos Islands **5**:89
CLUNY (France) **5**:71 *bibliog.*
French art and architecture **8**:303
iconography **11**:22
Middle Ages **14**:394–396
Romanesque art and architecture **16**:282–283 *illus.*
CLURMAN, HAROLD **5**:71–72
Group Theatre, The **9**:376–377
CLUSTER, GLOBULAR
distance, astronomical **6**:199–200
Galaxy, The **9**:10–13
halo, galactic **10**:25
Shapley, Harlow **17**:241
subgiant **18**:313
X-ray astronomy **20**:306
CLUSTER, STAR **5**:72
Hyades **10**:327
Pleiades (astronomy) **15**:364
CLUSTERS OF GALAXIES **5**:72
Abell, George O. **1**:56
Coma cluster **5**:129
cosmology (astronomy) **5**:285–287
Dreyer, J. L. E. **6**:271
extragalactic systems **7**:344
Local Group of galaxies **12**:385
quasar **16**:15
Virgo cluster of galaxies **19**:613
X-ray astronomy **20**:307
CLUTCH
machine **13**:20 *illus.*
transmission, automotive **19**:275–276 *illus.*
CLWYD (Wales) **5**:72
Flintshire **8**:165
CLYDE (Kansas)
map (39° 36′N 97° 24′W) **12**:18
CLYDE (Northwest Territories)
map (70° 25′N 68° 30′W) **14**:258
CLYDE (Ohio)
map (41° 18′N 82° 59′W) **14**:357
CLYDE, FIRTH OF
map (55° 42′N 5° 0′W) **19**:403
CLYDE, RIVER (Scotland) **5**:72
CLYDE PARK (Montana)
map (45° 53′N 110° 36′W) **13**:547
CLYDE RIVER (Nova Scotia)
map (43° 35′N 65° 25′W) **14**:269
CLYDESDALE **5**:72–73 *bibliog., illus.*; **10**:244 *illus.*
CLYMER (Pennsylvania)
map (40° 40′N 79° 1′W) **15**:147
CLYTEMNESTRA **5**:73
Electra (play) **7**:105
CNES *see* CENTRE NATIONAL D'ÉTUDES SPATIALES
CNIDARIAN *see* COELENTERATE
CNIDOSPORIDIA **5**:73
CNIDUS **5**:73
CNUT *see* CANUTE, KING OF ENGLAND, DENMARK, AND NORWAY
COACH AND CARRIAGE **5**:73–75 *bibliog., illus.*
chariot **4**:288
coach horse **5**:75
stagecoach **18**:210–211
COACH HORSE **5**:75 *bibliog., illus.*
COAHOMA (county in Mississippi)
map (34° 15′N 90° 35′W) **13**:469
COAHUILA (Mexico) **5**:75
cities
Saltillo **17**:38–39
Torreón **19**:244
COAL (county in Oklahoma)
map (34° 35′N 96° 20′W) **14**:368
COAL AGE *see* CARBONIFEROUS PERIOD
COAL CITY (Illinois)
map (41° 17′N 88° 17′W) **11**:42
COAL AND COAL MINING **5**:75–79 *bibliog., illus., map*
anthracite coal **5**:76–77 *illus., map*
bituminous coal **3**:301
black lung **3**:317
'breaker' boys **12**:154 *illus.*
carbon cycle (atmosphere) **4**:136
carbonaceous rock, sedimentary rock **17**:185
Carboniferous Period **4**:137
coal gasification **5**:79
coal tar **5**:79–80
coke **5**:96
consumption
fuel **8**:353 *table*
principal consuming nations, worldwide **5**:77 *map*
distillation, coal tar **5**:79–80
Earth, geological history of **7**:12
energy sources **7**:175 *table*
North America **14**:228
nuclear energy **14**:283–284
environmental considerations **5**:79
acid rain **1**:82
floodwater removal: Newcomen, Thomas **14**:165
fluidized bed combustion **8**:185
formation of **5**:75–76
grades of coal **5**:75–76
heat content **8**:353 *table*
Indians, American **11**:138
industrial archaeology **11**:154
Industrial Revolution **11**:158 *illus.*
jet **11**:406
labor union
United Mine Workers of America **19**:411–412
lignite **12**:340
liquefaction of coal: Bergius, Friedrich Karl Rudolf **3**:210
machinery **5**:77–78 *illus.*
Max Planck Institute for Coal Research
Ziegler, Karl **20**:363
mining of coal **5**:76–79 *illus.*
molasse **13**:505
Molly Maguires **13**:512
natural gas **14**:48
oceanic mineral resources **14**:340
paleogeography **15**:38
Paleozoic Era **15**:43
peat **15**:129
production and distribution **5**:79
Donets Basin (USSR) **6**:237–238
Europe **7**:274

Kentucky **12**:48–49 *illus.*
Kuznetsk Basin (USSR) **12**:142
major generation stations, U.S. **15**:482 *map*
Ohio **14**:360
Pennsylvania **15**:149
principal producing nations, worldwide **5**:77 *map*
Ruhr Valley (West Germany) **16**:343
Svalbard (Norway) **18**:374
United Kingdom **19**:410
Wales **20**:10 *illus.*
West Virginia **20**:112; **20**:113 *illus.*; **20**:114
safety **5**:79
surface mining **5**:78–79
land reclamation **12**:179–180
synthetic fuels **18**:409
tar, pitch, and asphalt **19**:34
COAL FORK (West Virginia)
map (38° 19′N 81° 32′W) **20**:111
COAL GASIFICATION
coal and coal mining **5**:79
coal gas
heat content **8**:353 *table*
Murdock, William **13**:648
producer gas **15**:561
COAL GROVE (Ohio)
map (38° 30′N 82° 39′W) **14**:357
COAL HILL (Arkansas)
map (35° 26′N 93° 40′W) **2**:166
COAL MINING *see* COAL AND COAL MINING
COAL OIL *see* KEROSENE
COAL RIVER (British Columbia)
map (59° 45′N 126° 55′W) **3**:491
COAL RIVER (West Virginia)
map (38° 22′N 81° 50′W) **20**:111
COAL TAR 5:79–80 *bibliog.*
coal and coal mining **5**:76
coal tar pitch **5**:80
creosote **5**:339
naphtha **14**:14
naphthalene **14**:14
tar, pitch, and asphalt **19**:34
COALDALE (Alberta)
map (49° 43′N 112° 37′W) **1**:256
COALGATE (Oklahoma)
map (34° 32′N 96° 13′W) **14**:368
COALINGA (California)
map (36° 9′N 120° 21′W) **4**:31
COALMONT (British Columbia)
map (49° 31′N 120° 41′W) **3**:491
COALPORT (Pennsylvania)
map (40° 45′N 78° 32′W) **15**:147
COALVILLE (Utah)
map (40° 55′N 111° 24′W) **19**:492
COAMO (Puerto Rico)
map (18° 5′N 66° 22′W) **15**:614
COARI (Brazil)
map (4° 5′S 63° 8′W) **3**:460
COAST *see* BEACH AND COAST
COAST AND GEODETIC SURVEY, U.S. *see* NATIONAL OCEAN SURVEY (U.S.)
COAST GUARD, U.S. 5:80 *bibliog.*, *illus.*
cutter **5**:398
flag **8**:148 *illus.*
International Ice Patrol **11**:220
rank, military **16**:86 *table*
Shore Patrol **17**:283
smuggling **17**:374
United States Coast Guard Academy **19**:462
COAST RANGES 5:80
California **4**:30
map (41° 0′N 123° 30′W) **19**:419
Oregon **14**:428
Saint Elias, Mount **17**:18
COAST SALISH *see* SALISH (American Indians)
COASTAL PLAIN 5:80–81 *bibliog.*
lagoon **12**:165–166
land reclamation **12**:178–181
map (35° 0′N 77° 30′W) **14**:242
COASTAL PROTECTION 5:81 *bibliog.*, *illus.*
harbor and port **10**:42–43 *illus.*
longshore drift **12**:409
COATBRIDGE (Scotland) 5:81
map (55° 52′N 4° 1′W) **19**:403
COATEPEQUE (Guatemala)
map (14° 42′N 91° 52′W) **9**:389
COATES, ALBERT 5:82 *bibliog.*
COATES, JOSEPH GORDON 5:82
COATESVILLE (Pennsylvania)
map (39° 59′N 75° 49′W) **15**:147
COATICOOK (Quebec)
map (45° 8′N 71° 48′W) **16**:18
COATIMUNDI 5:82 *illus.*
COATS, GEORGE
radio and television broadcasting **16**:55
COATS OF ARMS
guilds **9**:395 *illus.*
heraldry **10**:132–134
COATS ISLAND
map (62° 30′N 83° 0′W) **14**:258
COATS LAND (region in Antarctica)
map (77° 0′S 28° 0′W) **2**:40
COATSWORTH, ELIZABETH 5:82
COATZACOALCOS (Mexico)
map (18° 9′N 94° 25′W) **13**:357
COAXIAL CABLE
cable **4**:6 *illus.*
COBALT 5:82–83 *bibliog.*, *illus.*
abundances of common elements **7**:131 *table*
chemical properties **5**:82
cobalt isotopes **5**:82
element **7**:130 *table*
Group VIII periodic table **12**:167
Lehmann, Johann Gottlob **12**:276
metal, metallic element **13**:328
occurrence **5**:82
ore deposits
cobaltite **5**:83
world distribution **14**:423 *map*
sulfide minerals **18**:333
transition elements **5**:82; **19**:273 *table*
uranium minerals **19**:478
uses **5**:82
COBALT (Ontario)
map (47° 24′N 79° 41′W) **14**:393
COBALTITE 5:83
COBB (county in Georgia)
map (33° 55′N 84° 35′W) **9**:114
COBB, IRVIN S. 5:83
COBB, LEE J. 5:83
Death of a Salesman **19**:150 *illus.*
COBB, TY 3:106 *illus.*; 5:83 *bibliog.*, *illus.*
COBBE, A. S.
World War I **20**:244
COBBETT, WILLIAM 5:83–84 *bibliog.*, *illus.*
COBBLE 5:84
COBDEN, RICHARD 5:84
COBEQUID MOUNTAINS
map (45° 30′N 63° 30′W) **14**:269
COBIA 5:84
COBIJA (Bolivia)
map (11° 2′S 68° 44′W) **3**:366
COBLENZ (West Germany) *see* KOBLENZ (West Germany)
COBLESKILL (New York)
map (42° 41′N 74° 29′W) **14**:149
COBOL 5:84
computer languages **5**:160o
COBOURG (Ontario)
map (43° 58′N 78° 10′W) **14**:393; **14**:461
COBRA **15**:384 *illus.*
spitting cobra **16**:167 *illus.*
COBRA (artists' group) 5:84 *bibliog.*
Alechinsky, Pierre **1**:270
Appel, Karel **2**:87
Dutch art and architecture **6**:313
COBRA (snake) 5:84 *bibliog.*, *illus.*; **17**:377 *illus.*
copperhead **5**:254
death adder **6**:68
fang **17**:380 *illus.*
COBURG (Germany, East and West)
map (50° 15′N 10° 58′E) **9**:140
COBURN, ALVIN LANGDON 5:84 *bibliog.*
COBURN MOUNTAIN
map (45° 28′N 70° 6′W) **13**:70
COCA 5:84–85
drug trafficking **6**:281
stimulant **18**:271
COCAINE 5:85 *bibliog.*
anesthetics **1**:410
drug abuse **6**:279; **6**:280
drug trafficking **6**:281
procaine **15**:559
psychotropic drugs **15**:604
stimulant **18**:271
COCAMA
Tupí **19**:339
COCCIDIOIDOMYCOSIS 5:85
respiratory system disorders **16**:181
COCCIDIOSIS 5:85
diseases, animal **6**:192
COCCYX
spine **18**:185 *illus.*
COCHABAMBA (Bolivia) 5:85
map (17° 24′S 66° 9′W) **3**:366
COCHECO RIVER
map (43° 11′N 70° 50′W) **14**:123
COCHIN (family) 5:85 *bibliog.*
COCHIN (India) 5:85
climate **2**:237 *table*; **11**:82 *table*
map (9° 58′N 76° 15′E) **11**:80
COCHIN CHINA 5:85
COCHINEAL 5:85
COCHISE (county in Arizona)
map (31° 50′N 109° 50′W) **2**:160
COCHISE (Indian leader) 5:85–86 *bibliog.*
Mangas Coloradas **13**:115
COCHITUATE (Massachusetts)
map (42° 19′N 71° 22′W) **3**:409
COCHLEA **7**:6–7 *illus.*
ear **7**:6
COCHRAN (Georgia)
map (32° 23′N 83° 21′W) **9**:114
COCHRAN (county in Texas)
map (33° 38′N 102° 48′W) **19**:129
COCHRAN, SIR CHARLES BLAKE 5:86
COCHRAN, JACQUELINE 5:86 *bibliog.*
COCHRANE (Alberta)
map (51° 11′N 114° 28′W) **1**:256
COCHRANE (Ontario)
map (49° 4′N 81° 1′W) **14**:393
COCHRANE RIVER
map (57° 52′N 101° 38′W) **17**:81
COCHRANTON (Pennsylvania)
map (41° 31′N 80° 3′W) **15**:147
COCK-OF-THE-ROCK 5:86
COCKATOO 5:86 *bibliog.*, *illus.*; **15**:97 *illus.*
COCKBURN ISLAND
map (45° 55′N 83° 42′W) **13**:377
COCKCROFT, SIR JOHN DOUGLAS 2:311 *illus.*; 5:86
COCKER SPANIEL 5:86–87 *bibliog.*, *illus.*; **6**:219 *illus.*
English cocker spaniel **7**:190
COCKERELL, CHARLES ROBERT 5:87 *bibliog.*
COCKERELL, SIR CHRISTOPHER
air-cushion vehicle **1**:204
COCKEYSVILLE (Maryland)
map (39° 29′N 76° 39′W) **13**:188
COCKFIGHTING 5:87
COCKLE 5:87; **13**:510 *illus.*
shell **17**:251 *illus.*
COCKLEBUR 5:87
flower **8**:182
COCKNEY 5:87 *bibliog.*
COCKPIT COUNTRY (region in Jamaica)
map (18° 18′N 77° 43′W) **11**:351
COCKROACH 5:87–88 *bibliog.*, *illus.*
biological locomotion **3**:266 *illus.*
digestive system **6**:173 *illus.*
reproductive system **11**:190 *illus.*
roach **16**:234–235
COCKSCOMB (botany) 5:88
COCO RIVER
map (15° 0′N 83° 10′W) **10**:218
COCOA (botany) 5:88 *illus.*
cacao **4**:8
stimulant **18**:271
COCOA (Florida)
map (28° 21′N 80° 44′W) **8**:172
COCOA BEACH (Florida)
map (28° 19′N 80° 36′W) **8**:172
COCONINO (county in Arizona)
map (35° 30′N 111° 55′W) **2**:160
COCONUT 5:88 *bibliog.*, *illus.*
copra **5**:254–255
fats and oils source **8**:35
palm **15**:49
COCOON 5:88
butterflies and moths **3**:595
silk **17**:306–307
COCOS ISLANDS (Australia) 5:89
COCOS PLATE
plate tectonics **15**:351 *map*
COCTEAU, JEAN 5:89 *bibliog.*, *illus.*
COD 5:89–90 *bibliog.*, *illus.*; **8**:124 *illus.*
burbot **3**:566
world fishing grounds **8**:125 *map*
CODAJÁS (Brazil)
map (3° 50′S 62° 5′W) **3**:460
CODDINGTON, WILLIAM 5:90
Rhode Island **16**:201
CODE, SECRET *see* CRYPTOLOGY
CODE CIVIL *see* NAPOLEONIC CODE
CODE OF HANDSOME LAKE *see* *KAIWI:YO:H*
CODE LAW *see* CIVIL LAW (code law)
CODE OF MANU
Hinduism **10**:172–173
manu **13**:131
CODE NAPOLÉON *see* NAPOLEONIC CODE
CODEINE 5:90 *bibliog.*
heroin **10**:145
opium **14**:406
CODES AND CIPHERS *see* CRYPTOLOGY
CODEX, DRESDEN
Maya **13**:244 *illus.*
CODEX BORBONICUS **12**:223 *illus.*
CODEX MENDOZA
Aztec **2**:382
CODEX ZOUCHE-NUTTALL **15**:498 *illus.*
CODINGTON (county in South Dakota)
map (44° 55′N 97° 12′W) **18**:103
CODOMANNUS *see* DARIUS III CODOMANNUS, KING OF PERSIA
CODON
genetic code **9**:79–82 *illus.*
genetics **9**:88–89
protein synthesis **15**:575–576
CODROY (Newfoundland)
map (47° 53′N 59° 24′W) **14**:166
CODROY POND (Newfoundland)
map (48° 4′N 58° 52′W) **14**:166
CODUSSI, MAURO 5:90 *bibliog.*
Venice (Italy) **19**:544
CODY (Wyoming)
map (44° 32′N 109° 3′W) **20**:301
CODY, JOHN PATRICK 5:90
CODY, WILLIAM F. *see* BUFFALO BILL
COE, SEBASTIAN 5:90
COE, TUCKER *see* WESTLAKE, DONALD E.
COEDUCATION 5:90–91 *bibliog.*
Bates College **3**:121
Mulcaster, Richard **13**:635
COEHLO, GONÇALO
Rio de Janeiro (Brazil) **16**:226–227
COELACANTH 5:91 *bibliog.*, *illus.*
COELENTERATE 5:91–92 *bibliog.*, *illus.*
anatomy **5**:91
coral **5**:257–258
Huxley, Thomas Henry **10**:325
hydra **10**:329–330
invertebrate **11**:235
jellyfish **11**:395
reproduction **5**:91–92
sea anemone **17**:168
sea pen **17**:170
COELOM 5:92
circulatory system **4**:438–439
COELOSTAT 5:92 *illus.*
COENZYME 5:92–93 *bibliog.*; **7**:214 *illus.*
enzyme **7**:213; **7**:214 *illus.*
Euler-Chelpin, Hans von **7**:265
Lipmann, Fritz Albert **12**:362
synthesis: Todd, Lord Alexander **19**:220
COERCIVE ACTS *see* INTOLERABLE ACTS
COEROENI RIVER
map (3° 21′N 57° 31′W) **18**:364
COESITE 5:93
meteorite craters **13**:338
silica minerals **17**:304
COETIVY ISLAND
map (7° 8′S 56° 16′E) **17**:232
COETZEE, J. M. 5:93
COEUR D'ALENE (Idaho) **11**:27 *illus.*
map (47° 41′N 116° 46′W) **11**:26
COEUR D'ALENE LAKE
map (47° 32′N 116° 48′W) **11**:26
COEUR D'ALENE MOUNTAINS
map (47° 50′N 116° 5′W) **11**:26
COEUR D'ALENE RIVER
map (47° 28′N 116° 48′W) **11**:26
COFFEE 3:462 *illus.*; 5:93–94 *bibliog.*, *illus.*, *table*
consumption and marketing **5**:94
cultivation **5**:93–94
Kentucky coffee tree **12**:52
Kenya **12**:55
plantation **5**:291 *illus.*
processing **5**:94
production **5**:93 *table*
stimulant **18**:271
COFFEE (county in Alabama)
map (31° 25′N 86° 0′W) **1**:234
COFFEE (county in Georgia)
map (31° 35′N 82° 50′W) **9**:114
COFFEE (county in Tennessee)
map (35° 30′N 86° 5′W) **19**:104
COFFEEN (Illinois)
map (39° 5′N 89° 24′W) **11**:42
COFFEEVILLE (Mississippi)
map (33° 59′N 89° 40′W) **13**:469
COFFERDAM 5:94
bridge (engineering) **3**:480–481
COFFEY (county in Kansas)
map (38° 15′N 95° 45′W) **12**:18
COFFEYVILLE (Kansas)
map (37° 2′N 95° 37′W) **12**:18
COFFIN *see* BURIAL; FUNERAL CUSTOMS; FUNERAL INDUSTRY; etc.
COFFIN, HENRY SLOANE 5:94 *bibliog.*
COFFIN, WILLIAM SLOANE, JR. 5:94
COG (ship) **17**:266 *illus.*
COGENERATION 5:94
COGGAN, DONALD 5:94
COGGON (Iowa)
map (42° 17′N 91° 32′W) **11**:244

COGITO, ERGO SUM
Descartes, René **6**:126
Discourse on Method **6**:189
COGNAC *see* WINE
COGNAC (France)
map (45° 42′N 0° 20′W) **8**:260
COGNAC, LEAGUE OF
Italian Wars **11**:320
COGNITIVE DEVELOPMENT
adolescence **1**:106
Bruner, Jerome Seymour **3**:525
concept formation and attainment **5**:169
hyperactive children **10**:347
infancy **11**:163
Piaget, Jean **15**:287–288
COGNITIVE DISSONANCE 5:94 *bibliog.*
attitude and attitude change **2**:315
motivation **13**:610
COGNITIVE PSYCHOLOGY 5:94–95 *bibliog.*
adolescence **1**:106
artificial intelligence **2**:221
attention **5**:95
cognition, children **5**:95
concept formation and attainment **5**:169
developmental psychology **6**:142
educational psychology **7**:66
ethics **7**:250–251
experimental methods **5**:94
inner speech **11**:179
memory **5**:95
pattern recognition **5**:95
personality **15**:189–190
Piaget, Jean **15**:287–288
problem solving **5**:95; **15**:559
psycholinguistics **5**:95
psychology **15**:594
psychotherapy **15**:603
reasoning **16**:104
Simon, Herbert A. **17**:315
social psychology **18**:13
COGSWELL (North Dakota)
map (46° 7′N 97° 47′W) **14**:248
COHAN, GEORGE M. 5:95 *bibliog.*
musical comedy **13**:674
COHASSET (Massachusetts)
map (42° 14′N 70° 48′W) **13**:206
COHEN, LEONARD
Canadian literature **4**:94
COHEN, MORRIS RAPHAEL 5:95 *bibliog.*
COHENS* v. *VIRGINIA 5:95–96
Marshall, John **13**:172
COHERENT LIGHT 5:96; **12**:334
holography **10**:208
interference **11**:209
laser and maser **12**:210–213
optics **14**:412–413
COHESION 5:96
COHL, ÉMILE
animation **2**:28
COHN, EDWIN
Minot, George **13**:460
COHN, FERDINAND J. 5:96
COHOCTON RIVER
map (42° 9′N 77° 5′W) **14**:149
COHOES (New York)
map (42° 46′N 73° 42′W) **14**:149
COIMBATORE (India)
map (11° 0′N 76° 58′E) **11**:80
COIMBRA (Portugal) 5:96
map (40° 12′N 8° 25′W) **15**:449
Portuguese art and architecture **15**:455–456
COIN AIRCRAFT
aircraft, military **1**:214
COIN COLLECTING *see* NUMISMATICS
COINCIDENCE METHOD
Bothe, Walther Wilhelm **3**:415
COIPASA, LAKE
map (19° 12′S 68° 7′W) **3**:366
COIT, STANTON
Ethical Culture **7**:250
COITUS
fertilization **8**:61
impotence **11**:62
menopause **13**:299–300
polygamy **15**:419
sexual intercourse **17**:230–231
COJBALSAN (Mongolia)
map (48° 34′N 114° 50′E) **13**:529
COKE 5:96
bituminous coal **3**:301
carbon **4**:134
coal and coal mining **5**:76
heat content **8**:353 *table*
producer gas **15**:561
technology, history of **19**:65
COKE (county in Texas)
map (31° 55′N 100° 35′W) **19**:129
COKE, SIR EDWARD 5:96 *bibliog.*
common law **5**:140
COKE, THOMAS 5:96–97 *bibliog.*
common law **5**:138–141
COKER v. *GEORGIA*
capital punishment **4**:124
COLATINA (Brazil)
map (19° 32′S 40° 37′W) **3**:460
COLBATH, JEREMIAH JONES *see* WILSON, HENRY
COLBERT (county in Alabama)
map (34° 40′N 87° 45′W) **1**:234
COLBERT (Oklahoma)
map (33° 51′N 96° 30′W) **14**:368
COLBERT, CLAUDETTE 5:96–97
COLBERT, JEAN BAPTISTE 5:97 *bibliog., illus.*
Louis XIV, King of France **12**:426
mercantilism **13**:303
COLBY (Kansas)
map (39° 24′N 101° 3′W) **12**:18
COLBY (Wisconsin)
map (44° 55′N 90° 19′W) **20**:185
COLCHESTER (Connecticut)
map (41° 34′N 72° 20′W) **5**:193
COLCHESTER (England) 5:97
map (51° 54′N 0° 54′E) **19**:403
COLCHESTER (Illinois)
map (40° 25′N 90° 48′W) **11**:42
COLCHICINE 5:97
gout **9**:267
meadow saffron **13**:252
COLCHIS 5:97
COLD, COMMON 5:97 *bibliog.*
ascorbic acid (Vitamin C)
Pauling, Linus Carl **15**:119
vitamins and minerals **19**:620
respiratory system disorders **16**:181
virus, rhinitis **16**:196
COLD-BLOODED ANIMAL *see* BODY TEMPERATURE
COLD AND COLDNESS *see* CRYOBIOLOGY; CRYOGENICS; HEAT AND HEAT TRANSFER; TEMPERATURE
COLD CREAM
cosmetics **5**:282–283
COLD FRONT
front **8**:339–340 *illus.*
COLD HARBOR, BATTLE OF
Wilderness Campaign **20**:150
COLD SORE *see* CANKER
COLD SPRING (Minnesota)
map (45° 27′N 94° 26′W) **13**:453
COLD SPRING HARBOR
map (40° 53′N 73° 28′W) **5**:193
COLD TYPE *see* TYPESETTING
COLD WAR 5:98–99 *bibliog., illus.*
Acheson, Dean **5**:149
communism **5**:149
defense, national **6**:82
détente **6**:134
Dulles, John Foster **6**:295–296
Eisenhower, Dwight D. **7**:96
foreign policy **8**:226
Germany, history of **9**:156
Hiss, Alger **10**:180
intelligence gathering **11**:204–205
Kennan, George F. **12**:41
Kennedy, John F. **12**:43
Khrushchev, Nikita Sergeyevich **12**:68–69
Korean War **12**:119–122
McCarran Act **13**:7–8
McCarthy, Joseph R. **13**:8
North Atlantic Treaty Organization **14**:240
Potsdam Conference **15**:467
Rosenberg, Julius and Ethel **16**:315
Russia/Union of Soviet Socialist Republics, history of **16**:360
Truman, Harry S. **19**:317–318
United States, history of the **19**:456
Vietnam War **19**:585–586
war **20**:24
COLDSPRING (Texas)
map (30° 36′N 95° 8′W) **19**:129
COLDWATER (Kansas)
map (37° 16′N 99° 19′W) **12**:18
COLDWATER (Michigan)
map (41° 57′N 84° 60′W) **13**:377
COLDWATER (Mississippi)
map (34° 41′N 89° 59′W) **13**:469
COLDWATER (Ohio)
map (40° 29′N 84° 38′W) **14**:357
COLE (county in Missouri)
map (38° 30′N 92° 15′W) **13**:476
COLE, GEORGE DOUGLAS HOWARD
socialism **18**:21
COLE, HENRY
industrial design **11**:155
COLE, JACK
modern dance **13**:498
COLE, LESTER
Hollywood Ten, The **10**:204
COLE, NAT KING 5:99 *bibliog.*
COLE, THOMAS 5:99–100 *bibliog., illus.*; **6**:303 *illus.*
Church, Frederick Edwin **4**:423
Hudson River school **10**:290
Kaaterskill Falls **5**:100 *illus.*
COLE, TIMOTHY 5:100 *bibliog.*
COLE CAMP (Missouri)
map (38° 28′N 93° 12′W) **13**:476
COLEBROOK (New Hampshire)
map (44° 54′N 71° 30′W) **14**:123
COLEMAN (Michigan)
map (43° 46′N 84° 35′W) **13**:377
COLEMAN (Texas)
map (31° 50′N 99° 26′W) **19**:129
COLEMAN (county in Texas)
map (31° 45′N 99° 28′W) **19**:129
COLEMAN, JAMES S.
Coleman Report **5**:100
COLEMAN, ORNETTE
jazz **11**:389
COLEMAN REPORT 5:100 *bibliog.*
COLEMANITE
borate minerals **3**:396
COLEOPTERA *see* BEETLE
COLERAINE (Minnesota)
map (47° 17′N 93° 27′W) **13**:453
COLERIDGE (Nebraska)
map (42° 30′N 97° 13′W) **14**:70
COLERIDGE, SAMUEL TAYLOR 5:100–101 *bibliog., illus.*
conservatism **5**:205
Encyclopaedia Metropolitana **7**:164
Lake District (England) **12**:171
Lyrical Ballads **12**:479
Rime of the Ancient Mariner, The **16**:224
Southey, Robert **18**:112
Wordsworth, William **20**:216–217
COLES (county in Illinois)
map (39° 30′N 88° 15′W) **11**:42
COLET, JOHN
Renaissance **16**:149
COLETTE 5:101 *bibliog., illus.*; **8**:319 *illus.*
COLEUS 5:101
COLFAX (Illinois)
map (40° 34′N 88° 37′W) **11**:42
COLFAX (Indiana)
map (40° 12′N 86° 40′W) **11**:111
COLFAX (Iowa)
map (41° 41′N 93° 14′W) **11**:244
COLFAX (Louisiana)
map (31° 31′N 92° 42′W) **12**:430
COLFAX (county in Nebraska)
map (41° 35′N 97° 5′W) **14**:70
COLFAX (county in New Mexico)
map (36° 40′N 104° 40′W) **14**:136
COLFAX (Washington)
map (46° 53′N 117° 22′W) **20**:35
COLFAX (Wisconsin)
map (45° 0′N 91° 44′W) **20**:185
COLFAX, SCHUYLER 5:101
COLGATE UNIVERSITY 5:101
COLGRASS, MICHAEL 5:101
COLIC 5:101
Hoffman, Friedrich **10**:195
COLIGNY, GASPARD DE, SEIGNEUR DE CHÂTILLON 5:101–102 *bibliog.*
Saint Bartholomew's Day Massacre **17**:16
COLIMA (Mexico) 5:102
map (19° 14′N 103° 43′W) **13**:357
COLIMA (state in Mexico) 5:102
COLINET (Newfoundland)
map (47° 13′N 53° 33′W) **14**:166
COLISTIN
antibiotics **2**:57
COLITIS 5:102
enteritis **7**:208
gastrointestinal tract disease **9**:57
COLLAGE 5:102 *bibliog., illus.*
See also ASSEMBLAGE (art)
Arp, Jean **2**:187
constructivism **5**:224
Cornell, Joseph **5**:268
cubism **5**:381
Dada **6**:4–5
Ernst, Max **7**:231
Hamilton, Richard **10**:29
Marca-Relli, Conrad **13**:145
Motherwell, Robert **13**:607
Picasso, Pablo **15**:291
Rauschenberg, Robert **16**:94
Schwitters, Kurt **17**:141
surrealism (art) **18**:365
COLLAGEN 5:102
bone **3**:377
cartilage **4**:175
connective tissue **5**:196
scar **17**:115
COLLAGEN DISEASE 5:102–103 *bibliog.*
arthritis **5**:102
connective tissue diseases **5**:102–103
lupus erythematosus **12**:466
COLLARD 5:103 *illus.*
COLLBRAN (Colorado)
map (39° 14′N 107° 57′W) **5**:116
COLLECTIVE BARGAINING
arbitration (labor-management and commercial) **2**:110
game theory **9**:27–29
industrial relations **11**:158
labor union **12**:153–154
COLLECTIVE FARM
agriculture and the food supply **1**:195
cooperative **5**:245
Hungary **10**:309
Kibbutz **12**:70
Union of Soviet Socialist Republics **19**:396
COLLECTOR v. *DAY*
income tax **11**:76
COLLECTORS *see* ART COLLECTORS AND PATRONS
COLLEGE *see* UNIVERSITY
COLLEGE (Alaska)
map (64° 51′N 147° 47′W) **1**:242
COLLEGE ENTRANCE EXAMINATION BOARD
Educational Testing Service **7**:66
COLLEGE ENTRANCE EXAMINATIONS *see* EDUCATIONAL MEASUREMENT
COLLEGE LEVEL EXAMINATION PROGRAM 5:103
COLLEGE PARK (Georgia)
map (33° 39′N 84° 27′W) **9**:114
COLLEGE PARK (Maryland)
map (39° 0′N 76° 55′W) **13**:188
COLLEGE PLACE (Washington)
map (46° 3′N 118° 23′W) **20**:35
COLLEGE SCHOLARSHIP SERVICE
scholarships, fellowships, and loans **17**:130
COLLEGE STATION (Texas)
map (30° 37′N 96° 21′W) **19**:129
COLLEGE WORK-STUDY
scholarships, fellowships, and loans **17**:130
COLLEGEDALE (Tennessee)
map (35° 4′N 85° 3′W) **19**:104
COLLEGIA *see* GUILDS
COLLEMBOLA *see* SPRINGTAIL
COLLEONI, BARTOLOMEO **2**:195 *illus.*
COLLEONI MONUMENT
Verrocchio, Andrea del **19**:561
COLLETON (county in South Carolina)
map (32° 50′N 80° 45′W) **18**:98
COLLIE 5:103 *bibliog., illus.*; **6**:215 *illus.*
bearded collie **3**:142
border collie **3**:397
COLLIER (county in Florida)
map (26° 10′N 81° 22′W) **8**:172
COLLIER, JEREMY 5:103
COLLIER, JOHN PAYNE
literary fraud **12**:370
COLLIER'S (periodical)
muckrakers **13**:630–631
periodical **15**:170 *illus.*
COLLIERVILLE (Tennessee)
map (35° 3′N 89° 40′W) **19**:104
COLLIN (county in Texas)
map (33° 10′N 96° 35′W) **19**:129
COLLINGDALE (Pennsylvania)
map (39° 55′N 75° 17′W) **15**:147
COLLINGSWORTH (county in Texas)
map (34° 57′N 100° 15′W) **19**:129
COLLINS (Georgia)
map (32° 11′N 82° 7′W) **9**:114
COLLINS (Mississippi)
map (31° 39′N 89° 33′W) **13**:469
COLLINS, EDDIE 5:104 *bibliog.*
COLLINS, JUDY 5:104
COLLINS, MICHAEL (astronaut) 5:104 *illus.*
COLLINS, MICHAEL (Irish statesman) 5:104 *bibliog.*
COLLINS, WILKIE 5:104 *bibliog.*
COLLINS, WILLIAM 5:104 *bibliog.*
COLLINSVILLE (Alabama)
map (34° 16′N 85° 52′W) **1**:234
COLLINSVILLE (Illinois)
map (38° 41′N 89° 51′W) **11**:42
COLLINSVILLE (Mississippi)
map (32° 30′N 88° 51′W) **13**:469
COLLINSVILLE (Oklahoma)
map (36° 22′N 95° 51′W) **14**:368
COLLINSVILLE (Virginia)
map (36° 43′N 79° 54′W) **19**:607

COLLINWOOD (Tennessee)
map (35° 10′N 87° 44′W) **19**:104
COLLIP, J. B.
MacLeod, John James Rickard **13**:33
COLLISTER (Idaho)
map (43° 38′N 116° 15′W) **11**:26
COLLODI, CARLO 5:104
Pinocchio (fictional character) **15**:307
COLLOIDAL CHEMISTRY
Graham, Thomas **9**:280–281
COLLOIDAL PARTICLE
Perrin, Jean Baptiste **15**:178
COLLOIDAL STATE 5:104–105
emulsion **7**:161
gel **9**:69
phase equilibrium **15**:222 *illus.*
smoke **17**:373
sol **18**:40
Svedberg, Theodor **18**:374
Zsigmondy, Richard Adolf **20**:380
COLLOPHANE
apatite **2**:74
COLLOQUIAL LANGUAGE *see* SLANG; SOCIOLINGUISTICS
COLLOTYPE 5:105
COLLUSION 5:105
conspiracy **5**:206
COLMAN (South Dakota)
map (43° 59′N 96° 49′W) **18**:103
COLMAN, RONALD 5:105 *bibliog.*
COLMAR (France) 5:105
map (48° 5′N 7° 22′E) **8**:260
COLOANE
Macao (Portugal) **13**:4
COLOGNE (West Germany) 5:105 *illus.*
cathedral **2**:191 *illus.*; **5**:105 *illus.*; **9**:124 *illus.*
Danubian culture **6**:36
map (50° 56′N 6° 59′E) **9**:140
World War II **20**:273 *illus.*
COLOMA (Michigan)
map (42° 11′N 86° 19′W) **13**:377
COLOMBE (family) 5:106 *bibliog.*
COLOMBIA 5:106–109 *bibliog., illus., map, table*
art
gold and silver work **9**:229 *illus.*
Latin American art and architecture **12**:222–228
San Agustín **17**:50
cities
Barranquilla **3**:93
Bogotá **3**:360 *illus.*
Buenaventura **3**:544
Cali **4**:29
Cartagena **4**:170
Medellín **13**:263
Santa Marta **17**:68
climate **5**:106–107 *table*
drug trafficking **6**:281
economic activity **5**:107–108 *illus.*
education **5**:107
Latin American universities **12**:233 *table*
flag **5**:106 *illus.*
government **5**:108
history **5**:108–109
Latin America, history of **12**:220
Nariño, Antonio **14**:21
New Granada **14**:121
Panama Canal **15**:56–57
Santander, Francisco de Paula **17**:69
land **5**:106–107 *map*
literature
García Márquez, Gabriel **9**:39
Silva, José Asunción **17**:312
Magdalena River **13**:46
map (4° 0′N 72° 0′W) **18**:85
people **5**:106–107
Chibcha **4**:340
COLOMBO (Sri Lanka) 5:109; **18**:205–206 *illus., table*
map (6° 56′N 79° 51′E) **18**:206
COLOMBO PLAN 5:109
COLOME (South Dakota)
map (43° 15′N 99° 43′W) **18**:103
COLON (biology) *see* INTESTINE
COLÓN (Cuba)
map (22° 43′N 80° 54′W) **5**:377
COLÓN (Panama) 5:109
map (9° 22′N 79° 54′W) **15**:55
COLÓN (Uruguay)
map (33° 53′S 54° 43′W) **19**:488
COLONIA (New Jersey)
map (40° 35′N 74° 18′W) **14**:129
COLONIA DEL SACRAMENTO (Uruguay)
map (34° 28′S 57° 51′W) **19**:488
COLONIA LAS HERAS (Argentina)
map (46° 33′S 68° 57′W) **2**:149
COLONIA LAVALLESA (Uruguay)
map (31° 6′S 57° 1′W) **19**:488
COLONIA PROVIDENCIA (Puerto Rico)
map (17° 59′N 66° 0′W) **15**:614
COLONIAL BEACH (Maryland)
map (38° 15′N 76° 58′W) **13**:188
COLONIAL BEACH (Virginia)
map (38° 15′N 76° 58′W) **19**:607
COLONIAL HEIGHTS (Virginia)
map (37° 15′N 77° 25′W) **19**:607
COLONIAL PERIOD (United States) *see* UNITED STATES, HISTORY OF THE
COLONIAL STYLES IN NORTH AMERICA 5:109–111 *bibliog., illus.*
Benjamin, Asher **3**:201
Canada **5**:111
Copley, John Singleton **5**:251
Feke, Robert **8**:45
Harrison, Peter **10**:60
house (in Western architecture) **10**:270 *illus.*
Independence Hall **11**:78
limners **12**:345
middle colonies **5**:110
Monticello **13**:557
Mount Vernon (Washington's home) **13**:618
needlework **14**:76
New England **5**:110–111
Peale (family) **15**:124
pewter **15**:217 *illus.*
southern colonies **5**:110
COLONIALISM 5:111–112 *bibliog.*
Africa, history of **1**:156–159
Asia, history of **2**:256–259
British Empire **3**:495–496 *map*
Dutch West India Company **6**:315
East India Company, British **7**:31
East India Company, Dutch **7**:31–32
East India Company, French **7**:32
French colonial empire **8**:309–310
governor general **9**:272
Greece, ancient **9**:330 *map*
imperialism **11**:62
mercantilism **13**:303
Nigeria **14**:192
primitive societies **15**:546
slavery **17**:353–355
United Nations **19**:412–413
viceroy **19**:571
Wakefield, Edward Gibbon **20**:8
COLONIZATION *see* EXPLORATION
COLONNADE 5:112
entablature **7**:208
Saint Peter's Basilica **17**:25 *illus.*
COLONY (Kansas)
map (38° 4′N 95° 22′W) **12**:18
COLOPHONY *see* ROSIN
COLOR (optics) 5:112–113 *bibliog., illus., table*
aberration
lens **12**:286 *illus.*
coloration, biological **5**:121–122
dispersion (physics) **6**:197
film, photographic **8**:87–88 *illus.*
film processing **8**:90
index of refraction **11**:79
interference **11**:207–209
measurement
colorimeter **5**:122
paint **15**:16–17
photography **15**:263–265
pigment **15**:300
radio and television broadcasting **16**:59
rainbow **16**:77
spectral colors wavelengths **5**:113 *table*
ultramarine **19**:377
COLOR (quantum chromodynamics)
fundamental particles **8**:361; **8**:363
gluon **9**:212
hadron **10**:9
quantum chromodynamics **16**:9
quark **16**:12
COLOR BLINDNESS 5:113–114 *illus.*
COLOR-FIELD PAINTING 5:114
abstract expressionism **1**:66
Dzubas, Friedel **6**:320
Frankenthaler, Helen **8**:280 *illus.*
Gottlieb, Adolph **9**:264 *illus.*
Hartung, Hans **10**:64
Louis, Morris **12**:422 *illus.*
modern art **13**:494
Newman, Barnett **14**:169 *illus.*
Noland, Kenneth **14**:213–214 *illus.*
painting **15**:23
Rothko, Mark **16**:322 *illus.*
Stamos, Theodoros **18**:216
Still, Clyfford **18**:268 *illus.*
COLOR INDEX 5:114 *bibliog.*
star **18**:221
COLOR PERCEPTION 5:114–115 *bibliog.*; 7:350 *illus.*
See also COLOR
bee **2**:11 *illus.*
color blindness **5**:113–114
eye **7**:348
film, photographic **8**:88
film processing **8**:90
gull **2**:12 *illus.*
Helmholtz, Hermann Ludwig Ferdinand von **10**:115–116
illusions **11**:49
stickleback **2**:12 *illus.*
synesthesia **18**:407
television **19**:87
theories **5**:114
Land, Edwin **12**:178
types **5**:114
COLOR PHOTOGRAPHY *see* PHOTOGRAPHY
COLORADO 5:115–119 *bibliog., illus., map*
cities
Aspen **2**:262
Boulder **3**:421
Colorado Springs **5**:121
Denver **6**:117 *illus.*
Durango **6**:303
Pueblo **15**:613
climate **5**:115
cultural institutions **5**:117
economy **5**:118 *illus.*
education **5**:117
Colorado, state universities and colleges of **5**:120
Denver, University of **6**:117
United States Air Force Academy **19**:462
flag **5**:115 *illus.*
government and politics **5**:118–119
historic sites and recreation **5**:117–118
history **5**:119
Jefferson, Territory of **11**:391
Sand Creek Massacre **17**:59–60
Tabor, Horace W. **19**:5
land **5**:115–117 *map*
map (41° 0′N 107° 0′W) **19**:419
people **5**:117–118
Indians of North America, art of the **11**:140
Ute **19**:496
physical features
Elbert, Mount **7**:102
Grand Canyon **18**:316 *illus.*
Mesa Verde National Park **13**:313–314 *illus.*
Pikes Peak **15**:301
Rocky Mountains **16**:261–263 *illus., map*
Royal Gorge **16**:330
resources **5**:117
sylvanite **18**:402
uranium minerals **19**:478
rivers, lakes, and waterways **5**:115
Colorado River **5**:120–121 *map*
seal, state **5**:115 *illus.*
vegetation and animal life **5**:117
COLORADO (American Indians) 5:120 *bibliog.*
COLORADO (Costa Rica)
map (10° 46′N 83° 35′W) **5**:291
COLORADO (county in Texas)
map (29° 40′N 96° 30′W) **19**:129
COLORADO, STATE UNIVERSITIES AND COLLEGES OF 5:120
COLORADO CITY (Arizona)
map (36° 58′N 112° 58′W) **2**:160
COLORADO CITY (Texas)
map (32° 24′N 100° 52′W) **19**:129
COLORADO DESERT 5:120
Imperial Valley **11**:61
map (33° 10′N 117° 20′W) **4**:31
COLORADO PLATEAU 5:120
cliff dwellers **5**:54
Colorado **5**:115
Painted Desert (Arizona) **15**:17
COLORADO POTATO BEETLE **3**:167 *illus.*
COLORADO RIVER
North America **14**:236
COLORADO RIVER (Argentina)
map (39° 50′S 62° 8′W) **2**:149
COLORADO RIVER (Colorado) 5:120–121 *map*
Arizona **2**:161
map (31° 54′N 114° 57′W) **5**:120
Mead, Lake **13**:251
Powell, John Wesley **15**:481
COLORADO RIVER (Texas) 5:121
map (28° 36′N 95° 58′W) **19**:129
COLORADO RIVER AQUEDUCT
map (33° 50′N 117° 23′W) **4**:31
COLORADO SPRINGS (Colorado) 5:121
map (38° 50′N 104° 49′W) **5**:116
COLORADO TICK FEVER 5:121
COLORATION, BIOLOGICAL 5:121–122 *bibliog., illus.*
animal communication **2**:19 *illus.*; **2**:21 *illus.*
blenny **3**:330
butterflies and moths **3**:594–595 *illus.*
carotenoid **4**:162
chameleon **4**:275 *illus.*
feather **8**:39–40
flounder **8**:178
horse **10**:244
hummingbird **10**:303
lizard **12**:380
mimicry **13**:434–436
stickleback **2**:12 *illus.*
COLORATURA
soprano **18**:68
COLORIMETER 5:122
COLORPOINT SHORTHAIR CAT 4:195 *illus.*; **5**:122 *illus.*
COLOSSEUM 2:132 *illus.*; **5**:122–123 *bibliog., illus.*
Roman art and architecture **16**:273–274 *illus.*
Rome, ancient **16**:300 *map*
stadium **18**:208 *illus.*
COLOSSIANS, EPISTLE TO THE 5:123 *bibliog.*
COLOSSUS OF RHODES
Seven Wonders of the World **17**:217–218 *illus.*
COLOSTRUM
breast-feeding **3**:469
COLOUREDS (South Africa) 5:123 *bibliog.*; **16**:34 *illus.*
apartheid **2**:74
Khoikhoi **12**:67
South Africa **18**:80; **18**:81; **18**:82; **18**:83
COLQUECHACA (Bolivia)
map (18° 40′S 66° 1′W) **3**:366
COLQUITT (Georgia)
map (31° 10′N 84° 44′W) **9**:114
COLQUITT (county in Georgia)
map (31° 10′N 83° 40′W) **9**:114
COLSTRIP (Montana)
map (45° 53′N 106° 38′W) **13**:547
COLT (Arkansas)
map (35° 8′N 90° 49′W) **2**:166
COLT, SAMUEL 5:123–124 *bibliog., illus.*; **19**:450 *illus.*
Paterson (New Jersey) **15**:111
pistol **15**:317–318 *illus.*
revolver **16**:189–190 *illus.*
COLTA (Peru)
map (15° 10′S 73° 18′W) **15**:193
COLTER, JOHN 5:124 *bibliog.*
Teton Range **19**:127
Yellowstone National Park **20**:323
COLTRANE, JOHN 5:124 *bibliog.*
jazz **11**:389 *illus.*
COLUBRID 5:124–125 *bibliog., illus.*; **17**:376–377 *illus.*
COLUGO 5:125 *illus.*; **13**:104 *illus.*
COLUM, PADRAIC 5:125 *bibliog.*
COLUMBA, SAINT 5:125 *bibliog.*
Loch Ness monster **12**:386
COLUMBAN, SAINT 5:125 *bibliog.*
COLUMBIA (county in Arkansas)
map (33° 15′N 93° 18′W) **2**:166
COLUMBIA (county in Florida)
map (30° 15′N 82° 35′W) **8**:172
COLUMBIA (county in Georgia)
map (33° 35′N 82° 15′W) **9**:114
COLUMBIA (Illinois)
map (38° 27′N 90° 12′W) **11**:42
COLUMBIA (Kentucky)
map (37° 6′N 85° 18′W) **12**:47
COLUMBIA (Louisiana)
map (32° 6′N 92° 5′W) **12**:430
COLUMBIA (Maryland)
map (39° 13′N 76° 52′W) **13**:188
COLUMBIA (Mississippi)
map (31° 15′N 89° 56′W) **13**:469
COLUMBIA (Missouri)
map (38° 57′N 92° 20′W) **13**:476
COLUMBIA (county in New York)
map (42° 15′N 73° 47′W) **14**:149
COLUMBIA (North Carolina)
map (35° 55′N 76° 15′W) **14**:242
COLUMBIA (county in Oregon)
map (45° 57′N 123° 3′W) **14**:427
COLUMBIA (Pennsylvania)
map (40° 2′N 76° 30′W) **15**:147
COLUMBIA (county in Pennsylvania)
map (41° 0′N 76° 28′W) **15**:147
COLUMBIA (South Carolina) 5:125
capitol building **18**:97 *illus.*
map (34° 0′N 81° 3′W) **18**:98
COLUMBIA (Space Shuttle)
space exploration **18**:130–131 *illus.*
Space Shuttle **18**:135–136 *illus.*
COLUMBIA (symbol of the United States) **8**:340 *illus.*

COLUMBIA (Tennessee)
map (35° 37′N 87° 2′W) **19**:104
COLUMBIA (county in Washington)
map (46° 18′N 117° 50′W) **20**:35
COLUMBIA (county in Wisconsin)
map (43° 27′N 89° 17′W) **20**:185
COLUMBIA, MOUNT
map (52° 9′N 117° 25′W) **1**:256
COLUMBIA BROADCASTING SYSTEM
radio and television broadcasting **16**:55–59
COLUMBIA BROADCASTING SYSTEM HEADQUARTERS
Saarinen, Eero **17**:4
COLUMBIA CITY (Indiana)
map (41° 10′N 85° 29′W) **11**:111
COLUMBIA FALLS (Maine)
map (44° 39′N 67° 44′W) **13**:70
COLUMBIA FALLS (Montana)
map (48° 23′N 114° 11′W) **13**:547
COLUMBIA ICEFIELD 5:125–126; **14**:226 *illus.*
COLUMBIA MOUNTAINS
map (51° 30′N 118° 30′W) **3**:491
COLUMBIA RIVER 5:126 *bibliog., map*
Gray, Robert **9**:306
Indians of North America, art of the **11**:139
Oregon **14**:428–429 *illus.*
COLUMBIA RIVER PLATEAU
zeolite **20**:360
COLUMBIA UNIVERSITY 5:126 *bibliog.*
architecture
McKim, Mead, and White **13**:29
Barnard, Frederick Augustus Porter **3**:86
Barnard College **3**:86
Butler, Nicholas Murray **3**:592
Dewey, John **6**:146
Johnson, Samuel (philosopher) **11**:435
Low, Seth **12**:438
oral history **14**:414
Pulitzer Prize **15**:618–619
School of Journalism
Pulitzer, Joseph **15**:618
Teachers College *see* TEACHERS COLLEGE, COLUMBIA UNIVERSITY
COLUMBIAN CENTINEL
Russel, Benjamin **16**:348
COLUMBIANA (Alabama)
map (33° 11′N 86° 36′W) **1**:234
COLUMBIANA (Ohio)
map (40° 53′N 80° 42′W) **14**:357
COLUMBIANA (county in Ohio)
map (40° 47′N 80° 46′W) **14**:357
COLUMBINE (botany) 5:126 *illus.*
COLUMBINE (*commedia dell'arte*) **5**:137 *illus.*
COLUMBITE *see* OXIDE MINERALS
COLUMBITE-TANTALITE
tantalum **19**:25
COLUMBUS (Georgia) 5:126–127
map (32° 29′N 84° 59′W) **9**:114
COLUMBUS (county in Georgia)
map (32° 30′N 84° 50′W) **9**:114
COLUMBUS (Indiana)
Indiana **11**:112
map (39° 13′N 85° 55′W) **11**:111
COLUMBUS (Kansas)
map (37° 10′N 94° 50′W) **12**:18
COLUMBUS (Mississippi)
map (33° 30′N 88° 25′W) **13**:469
COLUMBUS (Montana)
map (45° 38′N 109° 15′W) **13**:547
COLUMBUS (Nebraska)
map (41° 25′N 97° 22′W) **14**:70
COLUMBUS (New Mexico)
map (31° 50′N 107° 38′W) **14**:136
COLUMBUS (North Carolina)
map (35° 15′N 82° 12′W) **14**:242
COLUMBUS (county in North Carolina)
map (34° 15′N 78° 40′W) **14**:242
COLUMBUS (Ohio) 5:127
map (39° 57′N 83° 0′W) **14**:357
COLUMBUS (Texas)
map (29° 42′N 96° 33′W) **19**:129
COLUMBUS (Wisconsin)
map (43° 21′N 89° 1′W) **20**:185
COLUMBUS, CHRISTOPHER 5:127–129 *bibliog., illus., map*; **7**:286 *illus.*; **19**:436 *illus.*
caravel **4**:132
Caribbean Sea **4**:148
explorations **7**:334–337 *map*
flag **8**:135 *illus.*
Indians, American **11**:115
Latin America, history of **12**:217; **12**:218
maps and mapmaking **13**:139 *illus.*
Maya **13**:245
Pinzón, Martín Alonso **15**:309
COLUMBUS GROVE (Ohio)
map (40° 55′N 84° 4′W) **14**:357
COLUMBUS JUNCTION (Iowa)
map (41° 17′N 91° 22′W) **11**:244
COLUMN 2:131 *illus.*; **5**:129
architecture **2**:130; **2**:131
capital **4**:123
colonnade **5**:112
Colosseum **5**:123
Column of Trajan **5**:129
entablature **7**:208
Greek architecture **9**:335; **9**:336–337
house (in Western architecture) **10**:264
Rome, ancient **16**:303 *illus.*
COLUMN, TRIUMPHAL *see* TRIUMPHAL COLUMN
COLUMN OF TRAJAN 5:129 *bibliog.*; **16**:303 *illus.*
COLUSA (California)
map (39° 13′N 122° 1′W) **4**:31
COLUSA (county in California)
map (39° 13′N 122° 1′W) **4**:31
COLVILLE (Washington)
map (48° 33′N 117° 54′W) **20**:35
COLVILLE, ALEX
Canadian art and architecture **4**:91
COLVOS PASSAGE
map (47° 27′N 122° 31′W) **20**:35
COLWICH (Kansas)
map (37° 47′N 97° 32′W) **12**:18
COLY 5:129
mousebird **13**:626
COMA (optics) 5:129
COMA (unconscious state) 5:129 *bibliog.*
death and dying **6**:69
diabetes **6**:148
hypoglycemia **10**:351
shock therapy **17**:279
stroke **18**:302
COMA CLUSTER 5:129
clusters of galaxies **5**:72
galaxies **5**:129
COMA PEDROSA PEAK
map (42° 35′N 1° 26′E) **1**:405
COMAL (Indonesia)
map (6° 55′S 109° 31′E) **11**:147
COMAL (county in Texas)
map (29° 47′N 98° 15′W) **19**:129
COMANCHE (American Indians) **5**:129–130 *bibliog., illus.*
Kiowa **12**:86
Parker, Quanah **15**:90–91
Shoshoni **17**:285
village **11**:128 *illus.*
Wichita (American Indians) **20**:144
COMANCHE (county in Kansas)
map (37° 15′N 99° 15′W) **12**:18
COMANCHE (Oklahoma)
map (34° 22′N 97° 58′W) **14**:368
COMANCHE (county in Oklahoma)
map (34° 40′N 98° 25′W) **14**:368
COMANCHE (Texas)
map (31° 54′N 98° 36′W) **19**:129
COMANCHE (county in Texas)
map (31° 57′N 98° 35′W) **19**:129
COMANECI, NADIA 5:130 *bibliog., illus.*; **14**:383 *illus.*
COMAYAGUA (Honduras)
map (14° 25′N 87° 37′W) **10**:218
COMB JELLY 5:130 *illus.*
COMBAHEE RIVER
map (32° 30′N 80° 31′W) **18**:98
COMBAT NEUROSIS
neurosis **14**:107
COMBE GRENAL (France) 5:130 *bibliog.*
Bordes, François **3**:398
COMBINATION (mathematics) *see* PERMUTATION AND COMBINATION
COMBINE (farm machinery) **1**:192 *illus.*; **5**:130–131 *bibliog., illus.*; **20**:125 *illus.*
COMBINE ART *see* ASSEMBLAGE (art)
COMBINING WEIGHT, LAW OF
chemical combination, laws of **4**:315
COMBRETUM *see* MANGROVE
COMBUSTION 5:131
See also FIRE; FLAME
Berthollet, Claude Louis, Comte de **3**:226
chain reaction, chemical **4**:269
fluidized bed combustion **8**:185
furnace **8**:372
Gadolin, Johan **9**:7
heat of, thermochemistry **19**:161 *table*
oxidation and reduction **14**:475–476
oxygen **14**:477
phlogiston theory **15**:248
reaction, chemical **16**:99
smoke **17**:373
spontaneous combustion **18**:194
COMDEN, BETTY, AND GREEN, ADOLPHE 5:131 *bibliog.*
COME LIVE WITH ME AND BE MY LOVE (poem)
Marlowe, Christopher **13**:161
COMECON *see* COUNCIL FOR MUTUAL ECONOMIC ASSISTANCE
COMÉDIE FRANÇAISE, LA 1:86–87 *illus.*; **5**:131 *bibliog.*
Barrault, Jean Louis **3**:93
Bernhardt, Sarah **3**:221–222
Coquelin, Constant **5**:257
COMÉDIE HUMAINE, LA (literary series) 5:131–132 *bibliog.*
Balzac, Honoré de **3**:57–58
COMÉDIE ITALIENNE, LA 5:132
Hôtel de Bourgogne, Théâtre de L' **10**:262
COMEDY 5:132 *bibliog.*
See also specific literary works, e.g., *CELEBRATED JUMPING FROG OF CALAVERAS COUNTY, THE;* GARGANTUA AND PANTAGRUEL; etc.
drama **6**:257–260
forms
black humor **3**:316
farce **8**:22–23
slapstick **17**:350
tragicomedy **19**:265
wit **20**:190–191
literature
Aristophanes **2**:155–156
Congreve, William **5**:188
Coward, Sir Noel **5**:320
Cratinus **5**:333
Dekker, Thomas **6**:86
erotic and pornographic literature **7**:234
Eupolis **7**:265
Farquhar, George **8**:29
Fredro, Alexander, Count **8**:294
Goldoni, Carlo **9**:235
Goldsmith, Oliver **9**:236
Jonson, Ben **11**:445–446
Leacock, Stephen **12**:256
Menander **13**:292–293
Molière **13**:509–510
Nestroy, Johann **14**:97
Philemon **15**:231
Plautus **15**:362
satyr play **17**:92
Shakespeare, William **17**:237
Shaw, George Bernard **17**:245–246
Sheridan, Richard Brinsley **17**:257
Terence **19**:115
Vega, Lope de **19**:531
Wilde, Oscar **20**:148–149
Wycherley, William **20**:298
stage, film, radio, television
See also COMIC OPERA; *COMMEDIA DELL'ARTE;* MUSIC HALL, VAUDEVILLE, AND BURLESQUE; MUSICAL COMEDY
Abbott and Costello **1**:53
Allen, Fred **1**:299
Allen, Woody **1**:300
Amos 'n' Andy **1**:376
Ball, Lucille **3**:40
Benny, Jack **3**:204
Berle, Milton **3**:214
Brice, Fanny **3**:477
Brooks, Mel **3**:511
Bruce, Lenny **3**:520
Burnett, Carol **3**:577
Burns and Allen **3**:579
Caesar, Sid **4**:15
Cantor, Eddie **4**:118
Carson, Johnny **4**:170
Chaplin, Charlie **4**:284–285
Clive, Kitty **5**:61
Cosby, Bill **5**:280
Coward, Sir Noel **5**:320
Fields, W. C. **8**:73–74
film, history of **8**:82–83
Gregory, Dick **9**:355
Gwynne, Nell **9**:412
Hope, Bob **10**:230
Kaye, Danny **12**:33
Keaton, Buster **12**:35
Keystone Kops **12**:64
Kyogen (Japan) **12**:143
Laurel and Hardy **12**:238
Lear, Norman **12**:259
Lloyd, Harold **12**:383
Lunt, Alfred, and Fontanne, Lynn **12**:465
Marx Brothers **13**:182–183
Mathews, Charles and Charles James **13**:228
"Monty Python's Flying Circus" (television series) **13**:560
Moore, Mary Tyler **13**:569
Mostel, Zero **13**:605
Nichols, Mike **14**:182
radio and television broadcasting **16**:56; **16**:59
Rogers, Will **16**:269
Sellers, Peter **17**:192
Sennett, Mack **17**:204
Simon, Neil **17**:315
Tati, Jacques **19**:44
theater, history of the **19**:144
Weber, Joseph, and Fields, Lew **20**:87
Wilder, Billy **20**:149
COMEDY OF ERRORS, THE (play)
Shakespeare, William **17**:237
COMEDY OF MANNERS
comedy **5**:132
COMENIUS, JOHN AMOS 5:132–133 *bibliog.*
Czech literature **5**:412
COMER (Georgia)
map (34° 4′N 83° 8′W) **9**:114
COMERÍO (Puerto Rico)
map (18° 13′N 66° 14′W) **15**:614
COMET 5:133–134 *bibliog., illus.*
Encke, Johann Franz **7**:162
Halley, Edmond **10**:22
Halley's comet **10**:23
Mitchell, Maria **13**:483
Moon **13**:563
Oort, Jan Hendrik **14**:396
solar system **18**:50–51
Tunguska fireball **19**:334
Whipple, Fred Lawrence **20**:131
COMFORT (North Carolina)
map (35° 0′N 77° 30′W) **14**:242
COMFORT (Texas)
map (29° 58′N 98° 49′W) **19**:129
COMFORT, CHARLES
Canadian art and architecture **4**:90
COMFREY 5:135
COMIC OPERA 5:135 *bibliog.*
See also OPERETTA
Barber of Seville, The **3**:77
composers
Auber, Daniel François Esprit **2**:316
Boieldieu, François Adrien **3**:362
Cimarosa, Domenico **4**:431
Donizetti, Gaetano **6**:238
Galuppi, Baldassare **9**:23
Gilbert and Sullivan **9**:179
Grétry, André **9**:359
Mozart, Wolfgang Amadeus **13**:628–629
Nicolai, Otto **14**:183
Paisiello, Giovanni **15**:25
Pergolesi, Giovanni Battista **15**:165
Rossini, Gioacchino **16**:319–320
French music **8**:320–321
libretto
Schikaneder, Emanuel **17**:120
Magic Flute, The **13**:50–51
Marriage of Figaro, The **13**:166
opera **14**:400
Russell, Lillian **16**:351
Zarzuela **20**:356
COMIC RELIEF
narrative and dramatic devices **14**:22
COMIC STRIP 5:135–136 *bibliog., illus.*
Busch, Wilhelm **3**:585
Capp, Al **4**:127
caricature **4**:150
Gould, Chester **9**:265
Lichtenstein, Roy **12**:322
Outcault, Richard Felton **14**:468
Schulz, Charles M. **17**:136
yellow journalism **20**:322
Young, Chic **20**:333
COMILLA (Bangladesh)
map (23° 27′N 91° 12′E) **3**:64
COMINFORM 5:136
communism in Eastern Europe **5**:148
COMINO, CAPE
map (40° 31′N 9° 50′E) **11**:321
COMINO ISLAND
map (36° 0′N 14° 20′E) **13**:94
COMINTERN 5:136
Communist party, U.S.A. **5**:151
International, Socialist **11**:218
Lenin, Vladimir Ilich **12**:282–283
Leninism **5**:146–147
Radek, Karl **16**:142
Zinoviev, Grigory Yevseyevich **20**:369
COMMAGER, HENRY STEELE 5:136–137

COMMAND AND SERVICE MODULE
Apollo program **2**:80–84
COMMANDER ISLANDS (USSR) **5**:137
COMMANDMENTS, TEN *see* TEN COMMANDMENTS
COMMANDO **5**:137
Entebbe **7**:208
knife **18**:399 *illus.*
COMMEDIA DELL'ARTE **5**:137–138 *bibliog., illus.*
acting **1**:87
Comédie Italienne, La **5**:132
comedy **5**:132
drama **6**:258
Fo, Dario **8**:192
Gillot, Claude **9**:182
Goldoni, Carlo **9**:235
Harlequin **10**:50
mime and pantomime **13**:434
Pierrot **15**:297
theater, history of the **19**:147 *illus.*
COMMENSAL ORGANISM
symbiosis **18**:402
COMMERCE *see* FREE TRADE; INTERNATIONAL TRADE
COMMERCE (Georgia)
map (34° 12′N 83° 28′W) **9**:114
COMMERCE (Oklahoma)
map (36° 56′N 94° 53′W) **14**:368
COMMERCE (Texas)
map (33° 15′N 95° 54′W) **19**:129
COMMERCE, U.S. DEPARTMENT OF **5**:138
Minority Business Development Agency **13**:459
National Oceanic and Atmospheric Administration **14**:35
patent **15**:110
secretary of commerce
See also articles of specific presidents, e.g., KENNEDY, JOHN F.; TRUMAN, HARRY S.; etc.; names of specific secretaries of commerce, e.g.,
flag **8**:148 *illus.*
Washington, D.C. **20**:41 *map*
COMMERCIAL ART *see* GRAPHIC ARTS; INDUSTRIAL DESIGN
COMMERCIAL AVIATION *see* AVIATION
COMMERCIAL BANK *see* BANKING SYSTEMS
COMMERCIAL LAW *see* BUSINESS LAW
COMMITTEE FOR ECONOMIC DEVELOPMENT **5**:138
COMMITTEE ON EDUCATIONAL PRACTICES OF THE NATIONAL ASSOCIATION OF INDEPENDENT SCHOOLS
sex education **17**:225
COMMITTEE FOR INDUSTRIAL ORGANIZATION *see* AMERICAN FEDERATION OF LABOR AND CONGRESS OF INDUSTRIAL ORGANIZATIONS
COMMITTEE OF PUBLIC SAFETY
French Revolution **8**:323
COMMODITY MARKET *see* FUTURES
COMMODUS, ROMAN EMPEROR **5**:138
Rome, ancient **16**:303
COMMON BUSINESS ORIENTED LANGUAGE *see* COBOL
COMMON CARRIER **5**:138 *bibliog.*
government regulation **9**:270–271
integration, racial
Morgan v. *Virginia* **13**:579
telegraph **19**:77
telephone **19**:80
television **19**:85
trucking industry **19**:314
COMMON CAUSE **5**:138 *bibliog.*
Gardner, John W. **9**:45
COMMON COLD *see* COLD, COMMON
COMMON DOCTOR *see* AQUINAS, SAINT THOMAS
COMMON LAW **5**:138–141 *bibliog.*
See also CIVIL LAW
actions **5**:139
adversary procedure **1**:111
Blackstone, Sir William **3**:322
Coke, Sir Edward **5**:96
court **5**:315
court of common pleas **5**:316
development **5**:139
equity **5**:139–140; **7**:226
escheat **7**:237
expansion in the United States **5**:140
felony **8**:48
Great Britain, history of **9**:311
Henry II, King of England **10**:124
inheritance **11**:177
jury **5**:139
7th Amendment **17**:219
King's Court **5**:139
law, history of **12**:244–246
legal procedure **12**:272
marriage **13**:165
personal property **15**:188
records of cases **5**:139
sodomy **18**:34
tort **19**:245
treatises **5**:140
trust **19**:321
women in society **20**:204
COMMON MARKET *see* BENELUX (trade union); CENTRAL AMERICAN COMMON MARKET; EUROPEAN ECONOMIC COMMUNITY; EUROPEAN FREE TRADE ASSOCIATION; LATIN AMERICAN FREE TRADE ASSOCIATION
COMMON PLEAS, COURT OF *see* COURT OF COMMON PLEAS
COMMON PRAYER, BOOK OF *see* BOOK OF COMMON PRAYER
COMMON SENSE (book) **5**:141
Paine, Thomas **15**:16
COMMON STOCK *see* STOCK (finance)
COMMON THORN APPLE *see* JIMSONWEED
COMMONER, BARRY **5**:141
COMMONFORT, IGNACIO
Mexico, history of **13**:364
COMMONS, HOUSE OF
Parliament **15**:92–93
COMMONS, JOHN R. **5**:141
COMMONS, THE *see* THIRD ESTATE
COMMONWEAL OF CHRIST *see* COXEY'S ARMY
COMMONWEALTH GAMES **5**:141
COMMONWEALTH OF NATIONS **5**:141 *bibliog., table*
British Empire **3**:496 *map*
dominion **6**:234
governor general **9**:272
COMMUNAL LIVING **5**:141–142 *bibliog.*
Brook Farm **3**:509
China **4**:367–368
Ephrata (Pennsylvania) **7**:217
family **8**:18
Fourier, Charles **8**:253
Indiana **11**:114
Iowa **11**:247–248
Israel **11**:304
Kibbutz **12**:70
Nazarenes (art group) **14**:66
New Harmony (Indiana) **14**:126
Noyes, John Humphrey **14**:277
Oneida Community **14**:389
Owen, Robert **14**:471
Utopia **19**:497
COMMUNE (group living unit) *see* COMMUNAL LIVING
COMMUNE (medieval municipality) **5**:142 *bibliog.*
COMMUNE OF PARIS **5**:142 *bibliog., illus.*
Blanqui, Louis Auguste **3**:327
Clemenceau, Georges **5**:49
French Revolution **8**:323
COMMUNICABLE DISEASE CENTER *see* CENTERS FOR DISEASE CONTROL
COMMUNICABLE DISEASES *see* INFECTIOUS DISEASES
COMMUNICATION **5**:142–144 *bibliog., illus.*
See also ANIMAL COMMUNICATION; MASS COMMUNICATION; TELECOMMUNICATIONS
artificial intelligence **2**:221
cable **4**:6 *illus.*
cryptology **5**:371–373
cybernetics **5**:400–401
De Forest, Lee **6**:58
diffusion, cultural **6**:170
facsimile transmission **8**:5–6
feedback **8**:44
folklore **8**:203
inductor **11**:152
infancy **11**:163
information theory **11**:174–175
inner speech **11**:179
interpersonal **5**:143–144
language and verbal behavior **5**:144
languages, artificial **12**:197–198
lingua franca **12**:354
McLuhan, Marshall **13**:33
mass communication **13**:201–203
models **5**:143 *illus.*
newspaper **14**:171–173
nonverbal communication **14**:217
pigeon **15**:300
radio and television broadcasting **16**:54–60
receiver (communications) **16**:106
rhetoric and oratory **16**:194
Sarnoff, David **17**:78
semaphore **17**:194–195
semiotics **17**:197
Shannon, Claude Elwood **17**:240
sign language **17**:299–300
signaling **17**:300–301
social psychology **18**:12
speech **18**:173–175
technology, history of **19**:68
telecommunications **19**:75–76
telegraph **19**:76–78
telemetry **19**:78
telephone **19**:78–80
transmitter **19**:276
writing systems, evolution of **20**:291–292
COMMUNICATION WORKERS OF AMERICA **5**:142
COMMUNICATIONS SATELLITE **5**:144–145 *bibliog., illus.*
antenna (electronics) **2**:47–48
cable TV **4**:7
European Space Agency **7**:306
mass communication **13**:202–203
satellite, artificial **17**:86
Applications Technology Satellite **2**:89–90
Early Bird **7**:8
Echo **7**:39
Intelsat **11**:205–206
Molniya **13**:512
Relay **16**:137
Syncom **18**:406
Telstar **19**:91
space exploration **18**:123
space law **18**:132
telephone **19**:79–80 *map*
COMMUNICATIONS SATELLITE CORPORATION *see* COMSAT
COMMUNION *see* EUCHARIST; MASS (liturgy)
COMMUNISM **5**:146–150 *bibliog., illus.*
See also COMMUNIST PARTY, SOVIET; COMMUNIST PARTY, U.S.A.
Albania **1**:249; **1**:251
arts **19**:395
Asia, history of **2**:258 *illus.*; **2**:259; **2**:260
Babeuf, François Noël **3**:6
birth control **3**:295
Bolsheviks and Mensheviks **3**:371
Bulgaria **3**:556–557
China **5**:148–149
brainwashing **3**:449
Chao Tzu-yang (Zhao Ziyang) **4**:282–283
China, history of **4**:375–377 *map*
Chou En-lai (Zhou Enlai) **4**:409
Confucianism **5**:180
government of China **4**:369
Hu Yao-pang (Hu Yaobang) **10**:287
Hua Kuo-feng (Hua Guofeng) **10**:287
Lin Piao (Lin Biao) **12**:347
Liu Shao-ch'i (Liu Shaoqi) **12**:374
Long March **12**:406
Mao Tse-tung (Mao Zedong) **13**:134–136
Teng Hsiao-p'ing (Deng Xiaoping) **19**:101–102
universities **4**:394
Yang-Ko **20**:317
Cominform **5**:136
Comintern **5**:136
Communist party worldwide relations **5**:150
criminal justice **5**:350
Cuba **5**:150; **5**:380
Cultural Revolution **5**:384
Czechoslovakia **5**:416
Dubček, Alexander **6**:287
dictatorship of the proletariat **6**:159
disunity **5**:150
EAM-ELAS **7**:5
early forms **5**:146
Eastern Europe **5**:148
economic planning **7**:47
Engels, Friedrich **7**:176–177
Eurocommunism **5**:150
Europe, history of **7**:295; **7**:298
France **5**:150
Duclos, Jacques **6**:292
socialism **18**:23
freedom of the press **8**:297
Friendship of the Nations (poster) **7**:295 *illus.*
Germany
Germany, history of **9**:155
Honecker, Erich **10**:220
Luxemburg, Rosa **12**:473
Ulbricht, Walter **19**:376
Zetkin, Clara **20**:361–362
housing **10**:279
Hungary **5**:148 *illus.*; **10**:309; **10**:310
Hungarian Revolution **10**:306
Kun, Béla **12**:136
Rákosi, Mátyás **16**:79
India
Kerala **12**:58
International, Socialist **11**:218
Italy
Berlinguer, Enrico **3**:218
communism **5**:150
Gramsci, Antonio **9**:283
Nono, Luigi **14**:217
socialism **18**:23
Togliatti, Palmiro **19**:221
Kampuchea (Cambodia) **12**:12–13
Korea
Korea, history of **12**:117
Korea, North **5**:149; **12**:115–116
Laos **12**:204
Leninism **5**:146–147
Malaysia **13**:86
Maoism **5**:148
Marx, Karl **13**:181–182
Marxism **5**:146; **13**:184
Mongolia **13**:529
newspaper **14**:172
Poland **15**:389–391
politburo **15**:398
publications
Communist Manifesto **5**:151
Kapital, Das **12**:25
Romania **16**:289–290
Singapore **17**:322
Sino-Soviet split **5**:149
socialism **18**:20
socialist law **18**:25
Southeast Asia **5**:149–150
Khmer Rouge **12**:67
Stalinism **5**:147–148
Sudan **18**:322
totalitarianism **19**:248
Union of Soviet Socialist Republics **5**:146–148
Khrushchev, Nikita Sergeyevich **12**:68–69
Lenin, Vladimir Ilich **12**:282–283
Pravda **15**:490
Russian Revolutions of 1917 **16**:370–373
Russia/Union of Soviet Socialist Republics, history of **16**:359–360
United Kingdom **19**:411
United States
See also COMMUNIST PARTY, U.S.A.
academic freedom **1**:69
McCarran Act **13**:7–8
McCarthy, Joseph R. **13**:8
Marcantonio, Vito **13**:145
Socialist Workers' party **18**:25–26
Vietnam **19**:583–584
Ho Chi Minh **10**:190
Viet Cong **19**:579
Viet Minh **19**:579
Vietnam War **19**:584–591
Vo Nguyen Giap **19**:624
Western Europe **5**:150
women in society **20**:204
Yugoslavia **5**:148; **20**:343–344
Djilas, Milovan **6**:208
Tito **19**:214–215
COMMUNISM PEAK **5**:150
map (38° 57′N 72° 1′E) **19**:388
COMMUNIST INTERNATIONAL *see* COMINTERN
COMMUNIST LABOR PARTY (U.S.)
Reed, John **16**:118
COMMUNIST MANIFESTO (pamphlet) **5**:151
Engels, Friedrich **7**:176
Europe, history of **7**:293
Marx, Karl **13**:182
rise of Marxism **5**:146
socialism **18**:20
COMMUNIST PARTY (China) *see* COMMUNISM—China
COMMUNIST PARTY (France) *see* COMMUNISM—France
COMMUNIST PARTY (Germany) *see* COMMUNISM—Germany
COMMUNIST PARTY (Italy) *see* COMMUNISM—Italy
COMMUNIST PARTY, SOVIET
politburo **15**:398

COMMUNIST PARTY, SOVIET (cont.)
Union of Soviet Socialist Republics **19**:398
COMMUNIST PARTY, U.S.A. 5:151 *bibliog.*
See also COMMUNISM, UNITED STATES
Browder, Earl **3**:513
Daily Worker **6**:7
Dennis v. *United States* **6**:113
Flynn, Elizabeth Gurley **8**:191
Foster, William Z. **8**:248
Smith Act
sedition **17**:186
COMMUNIST POLITICAL ASSOCIATION
Communist party, U.S.A. **5**:151
COMMUNITY ANTENNA TELEVISION *see* CABLE TV
COMMUNITY CHEST *see* FUND RAISING
COMMUNITY ECOLOGY *see* BIOME
COMMUNITY AND JUNIOR COLLEGES 5:151–152 *bibliog.*
Canadian education **4**:91–92
curriculum **5**:152
enrollment **5**:152
faculty **5**:152
Harper, William Rainey **10**:55
history **5**:151–152
professional and educational organizations
American Association of Community and Junior Colleges **1**:336
university **19**:468–469
COMMUNITY MENTAL HEALTH 5:152–153 *bibliog.*
COMMUNITY ORGANIZATION
social work **18**:18–19
COMMUNITY OF PEACE PEOPLE
Corrigan, Mairead, and Williams, Betty **5**:276
COMMUNITY PROPERTY 5:153
inheritance **11**:177
COMMUTATIVE LAW 5:153
algebra **1**:284–285
arithmetic **2**:158
group theory **9**:377
COMMUTATOR *see* GENERATOR
COMNENUS (dynasty)
Alexius I Comnenus, Byzantine Emperor **1**:278
Anna Comnena **2**:31
Isaac I Comnenus, Byzantine Emperor **11**:285
John II Comnenus, Byzantine Emperor **11**:426
Manuel I Comnenus, Byzantine Emperor **13**:131
COMO (Italy) 5:153
map (45° 47′N 9° 5′E) **11**:321
COMO (Mississippi)
map (34° 31′N 90° 3′W) **13**:469
COMO, LAKE 5:153
map (46° 0′N 9° 20′E) **11**:321
COMODORO RIVADAVIA (Argentina)
map (45° 52′S 67° 30′W) **2**:149
COMONFORT, IGNACIO
Juárez, Benito **11**:458
COMORIN, CAPE OF
map (8° 4′N 77° 34′E) **11**:80
COMOROS 5:153–154 *illus., map*
cities
Moroni **13**:587
flag **5**:153 *illus.*; **8**:136 *illus.*
map (12° 10′S 44° 15′E) **1**:136
Mayotte (France) **13**:248
COMOX (British Columbia)
map (49° 40′N 124° 55′W) **3**:491
COMPACT DISC 5:154–155 *bibliog., illus.*
information storage and retrieval **11**:173
sound recording and reproduction **18**:76–77
COMPADRAZGO
kinship **12**:86
COMPANY TOWN
housing **10**:276
COMPARATIVE ANATOMY 5:155 *bibliog., illus.*
Agassiz, Louis Rodolphe **1**:182
anatomy **1**:396–397
Buffon, Georges, Comte de **3**:547
Cuvier, Georges, Baron **5**:399
echinoderm **7**:37
gastropod **9**:57
gill **9**:180
grasshopper **9**:298
Grew, Nehemiah **9**:360
invertebrate **11**:235–237
nervous system **14**:92
phylogeny **15**:279
rodent **16**:265–266
COMPARATIVE LINGUISTICS *see* HISTORICAL LINGUISTICS
COMPARATIVE PSYCHOLOGY 5:155 *bibliog.*
ethology **7**:257
Morgan, Conway Lloyd **13**:578
psychology **15**:594
Yerkes, Robert Mearns **20**:326
COMPARATOR 5:155
COMPASS, MATHEMATICAL 5:155
COMPASS, NAVIGATIONAL 5:155–156 *bibliog., illus.*
gyroscope **9**:416
liquid compass **14**:58–59 *illus.*
magnetism **13**:56
COMPASS PLANT *see* ROSINWEED
COMPENSATION LAWS *see* UNEMPLOYMENT INSURANCE; WORKERS' COMPENSATION
COMPENSATORY EDUCATION 5:156
Head Start **10**:85
reading education **16**:101
COMPETENCE (law)
contract **5**:231
COMPETENCE (linguistics)
anthropological linguistics **2**:51
ethnography of speaking **18**:28
grammar **9**:282
psycholinguistics **15**:591
COMPETITION (business) *see* MONOPOLY AND COMPETITION (economics)
COMPILER (computer program) 5:156–157 *bibliog.*
computer **5**:160f; **5**:160h
computer languages **5**:160o
computer software **5**:164; **5**:165
interpreter **11**:225
COMPLAINT (law) 5:157
legal procedure **12**:273
COMPLEAT ANGLER, THE (book)
Walton, Izaak **20**:20
COMPLEMENT (blood plasma)
infectious diseases **11**:165
inflammation **11**:169
COMPLEX (chemistry)
coordination compounds **5**:247–248
isomer **11**:299
ligand **12**:333–334
COMPLEX (psychology) 5:157 *bibliog.*
inferiority complex
Adler, Alfred **1**:103
Oedipus complex
Freud, Sigmund **8**:329
psychoanalysis **15**:589
sexual development **17**:230
COMPLEX NUMBER 5:157 *bibliog.*
algebra **1**:284
Bolyai, János **3**:372
mathematics, history of **13**:225
COMPLUTENSIAN POLYGLOT BIBLE
Jiménez de Cisneros, Francisco **11**:419
COMPOSITE FAMILY (botany) *see* DAISY (botany); SUNFLOWER
COMPOSITE FAMILY (social unit) *see* EXTENDED FAMILY
COMPOST 5:157–158
fertilizer **8**:61
manure **13**:134
COMPOUND, CHEMICAL 5:158 *bibliog.*
acids and bases **1**:82–83
anhydride **2**:8
biochemical
amide **1**:369
amine **1**:370
amino acid **1**:370–371
ascorbic acid **2**:228
benzoic acid **3**:207
fats and oils **8**:34
fatty acid **8**:35
formic acid **8**:234
glycerol **9**:212
glycol **9**:212
glycoside **9**:212
hydrophilic and hydrophobic substances **10**:343
lactic acid **12**:161
lactose **12**:162
monosaccharide **13**:540
peptide **15**:157
polysaccharide **15**:421–422
pyruvic acid **15**:639
starch **18**:226
sterol **18**:262
sugar **18**:327
bromine **3**:502
buffer **3**:547
butane **3**:591
carbon **4**:134–135
chelation **4**:311
chemical bond **4**:313–315
chemical combination, laws of **4**:315
chemical nomenclature **4**:319–321
chemical symbolism and notation **4**:321–323
chlorine **4**:400–401
clathrate compounds **5**:44
configuration **5**:178
coordination compounds **5**:247–248
decomposition
Faraday's laws of electrolysis **8**:22
double salt **6**:246
electrolyte **7**:115
element **7**:129
equivalent weight **7**:227
extraction **7**:341
fluorine **8**:187–188
free radical **8**:294
halide **10**:20
heat of formation
thermochemistry **19**:161 *table*
Higgins, William **10**:161
hydrogen **10**:338
identification
mass spectrometry **13**:204
qualitative chemical analysis **16**:6–7
quantitative chemical analysis **16**:7–9
spectroscopy **18**:170–172
industrial
chemical industry **4**:317–319
cyanide process **5**:400
epoxy resins **7**:222
flame retardants **8**:150–151
Freon **8**:326
mineral oil **13**:444
pesticides **15**:196–199
pigment **15**:300
plastics **15**:347–351
rayon **16**:97–98
resin **16**:176–177
rubber **16**:332–335
soap and detergent **18**:6–8
Solvay process **18**:58
superphosphate **18**:352–353
synthetic fibers **18**:409
Teflon **19**:72
inorganic
alum **1**:314–315
amphoteric compounds **1**:382
beryllium **3**:227
boron **3**:403
calcium **4**:22
chalcogens **4**:270
chromium **4**:419
cobalt **5**:83
copper **5**:253–254
gallium **9**:21
germanium **9**:138
hydrate **10**:330
hydrochloric acid **10**:331–332
inorganic chemistry **11**:181–182
iodine **11**:239
lime **12**:343
lithium **12**:370–371
manganese **13**:114
mineral acid **13**:444
nitric acid **14**:202
oxygen **14**:477–478
plutonium **15**:373
radium **16**:68
rubidium **16**:336
salt (chemistry) **17**:37
selenium **17**:190
sodium **18**:32–33
sulfur **18**:335–336
sulfuric acid **18**:336
thallium **19**:142
tin **19**:204–205
titanium **19**:211
tungsten **19**:333–334
uranium **19**:477
zinc **20**:368
ion and ionization **11**:239–240
iron **11**:271
isomer **11**:299
lead **12**:256
ligand **12**:333–334
macromolecule **13**:36–37
magnesium **13**:54
mercury **13**:306
molecular weight **13**:507
molecule **13**:507–508
nitrogen **14**:202–203
optical activity **14**:408
organic
acetaldehyde **1**:79
acetate **1**:80
acetic acid **1**:80
acetone **1**:80
acetyl group **1**:80
acetylene **1**:80
alcohol **1**:264
aldehyde **1**:267–268
alicyclic compounds **1**:293
aliphatic compounds **1**:295
alkane **1**:296
alkene **1**:296–297
alkyl group **1**:297
alkyne **1**:297
aniline **2**:8
aromatic compounds **2**:186
aryl group **2**:226
azo group **2**:381
benzaldehyde **3**:206
benzene **3**:206
carbonyl group **4**:139
carboxylic acid **4**:139–140 *table*
chlorohydrin **4**:401
copolymer **5**:251
cyclic compounds **5**:403–404
diene **6**:162
ester **7**:246
ethane **7**:249
ether (chemistry) **7**:249–250
ethyl alcohol **7**:257
ethyl ether **7**:257
ethyl group **7**:257
ethylene **7**:258
fluorocarbon **8**:188
formaldehyde **8**:234
heterocyclic compound **10**:153
homologous series **10**:216
homopolymer **10**:216
hydrazine **10**:331
hydrocarbon **10**:331
hydroquinone **10**:344
hydroxyl group **10**:344
ketone **12**:61
lactone **12**:161–162
maleic acid **13**:87
methane **13**:343
methyl alcohol **13**:344
methyl group **13**:344–345
methylene **13**:345
monohydric alcohol **13**:536
naphthalene **14**:14
nitrile **14**:202
nitrogen compounds **14**:202
organic chemistry **14**:436–438
palmitic acid **15**:51
pentane **15**:155
phenol **15**:225
phenyl group **15**:226
polyester **15**:418–419
polyhydric alcohol **15**:420
propane **15**:569
pyrrole **15**:639
quinone **16**:27
silicones **17**:306
terpene **19**:118
peroxide **15**:177
phosphorus **15**:256–257
poison **15**:381–382
polymorph **15**:420–421
potassium **15**:465
Proust, Joseph Louis **15**:582
reaction, chemical **16**:98–100
silicon **17**:305
solvent **18**:58–59
stereochemistry **18**:258–259
stoichiometry **18**:276–277
valence **19**:503
water **20**:47–48
Wilkinson, Geoffrey **20**:153
X-ray diffraction **20**:309
zwitterion **20**:384
COMPREHENSION LOSS
stroke **18**:302
COMPREHENSIVE EMPLOYMENT AND TRAINING ACT
career education **4**:146
Job Corps **11**:421
COMPRESSED AIR *see* PNEUMATIC SYSTEMS
COMPRESSOR 5:158
pneumatic systems **15**:375
pump **15**:622–623
refrigeration **16**:124–125
turbine **19**:340
COMPROMISE OF 1850 5:158 *bibliog., illus.*
Civil War, U.S. **5**:15–16
Fillmore, Millard **8**:80
popular sovereignty **15**:433
Webster, Daniel **20**:88
Whig party (United States) **20**:131
COMPROMISE OF 1877
Hayes, Rutherford B. **10**:83
COMPSOGNATHUS 5:158 *bibliog.*; **11**:476 *illus.*
dinosaur **6**:179–182
COMPTON (California)
map (33° 54′N 118° 13′W) **4**:31
COMPTON, ARTHUR HOLLY 5:159 *bibliog.*; **15**:286 *illus.*
Compton effect **5**:159

COMPTON, JOHN
Saint Lucia **17**:23
COMPTON-BURNETT, IVY 5:159 *bibliog.*
COMPTON EFFECT 5:159 *bibliog.*
Compton, Arthur Holly **5**:159
gamma rays **9**:34
COMPTROLLER OF THE CURRENCY, OFFICE OF THE 5:159
Treasury, U.S. Department of the **19**:285
COMPULSIVE BEHAVIOR 5:159
neurosis **14**:107
COMPUTER 5:159–160i *bibliog., illus.*
See also ANALOG DEVICES—computers
analog-to-digital converter **1**:389
applications **5**:160f–160g
applications software **5**:164–165
automotive instrumentation **2**:368
business machines **3**:589
computer-aided design and computer-aided manufacturing **5**:160j–160L
computer chess **4**:336
computer graphics **5**:160L–160n
computer modeling **5**:161–162
computer music **5**:162–163
computers in education **5**:165–166
cryptology **5**:373
digital technology **6**:175
electronic mail **7**:124
food industry **8**:210
games, mathematical **9**:33
image processing **11**:51–53
linguistics **12**:358
newspaper **14**:172
phototypesetting **15**:278
problem solving **15**:559
process control **15**:560
radio astronomy **16**:52
space exploration **18**:122
video game **19**:576i–576j
videotex **19**:576p–577
artificial intelligence **2**:221–222
automata, theory of **2**:356–357
automation **2**:357; **2**:358
binary number **3**:256
bit, computer **3**:300
byte **3**:603
calculator, electronic **4**:23–24
cathode-ray tube **4**:211
central processing unit **4**:255
computer, personal **5**:160i–160
computer crime **5**:160L
computer industry **5**:160n–160o
computer languages **5**:160o–160p
computer memory **5**:160p–161
computer networking **5**:163
computer programming **5**:163
computer register **5**:164
computer software **5**:164–165
computer terminal **5**:165
computers and privacy **5**:166–167
cybernetics **5**:401
database **6**:43–44
digital technology **6**:175
digital-to-analog converter **6**:175
electronics industry **7**:126
glossary **5**:160h–160i
history **5**:160–160c
Aiken, Howard Hathaway **1**:202
Atanasoff, John V. **2**:287
Babbage, Charles **3**:5
Bush, Vannevar **3**:585
computer languages **5**:160o–160p
Eckert, John Presper **7**:39
Forrester, Jay Wright **8**:235
Hollerith, Herman **10**:204
Mauchly, John William **13**:232
Simon, Herbert A. **17**:315
technology, history of **19**:69
UNIVAC **19**:467
Watson (family) **20**:67
hybrid computer **10**:328–329
information science **11**:172
information storage and retrieval **11**:173–174
input-output devices **11**:182–183
paintbox **15**:17
microcomputer **13**:385
microprocessor **13**:387
minicomputer **13**:446
modem **13**:490
multiplexer **13**:638
on-line computer **14**:388
parallel processing **15**:79
pulse (electronics) **15**:621
punched card **15**:623–624
reasoning **16**:105
COMPUTER, PERSONAL 5:160i–160j *bibliog., illus.*
BASIC **3**:108
computer **5**:160c; **5**:160f–160g; **5**:160i
computer crime **5**:160L
computer graphics **5**:160m
computer industry **5**:160o
computers in education **5**:165
microcomputer **13**:385
programming languages **5**:160o
COMPUTER-AIDED DESIGN AND COMPUTER-AIDED MANUFACTURING 5:160j–160L *bibliog., illus.*
computer graphics **5**:160n
computer modeling **5**:162
process control **15**:560–561
COMPUTER ART *see* COMPUTER GRAPHICS
COMPUTER-ASSISTED INSTRUCTION *see* CAI
COMPUTER CRIME 5:160L *bibliog.*
COMPUTER GRAPHICS 5:160L–160n *bibliog., illus.*
animation **2**:29
cinematography **4**:433
computer, personal **5**:160i–160j
computer-aided design and computer-aided manufacturing **5**:160k
computer modeling **5**:162
input-output devices **11**:182
paintbox **15**:17
COMPUTER HARDWARE 5:160h
central processing unit **4**:255
computer memory **5**:160p–161
computer software **5**:164–165
input-output devices **11**:182–183
COMPUTER INDUSTRY 5:160n–160o *bibliog.*
computer, personal **5**:160i
computer software **5**:165
history **5**:160a–160c
COMPUTER LANGUAGES 5:160o–160p *bibliog.*
Ada **1**:91
ALGOL **1**:290–291
BASIC **3**:108
C **4**:3
COBOL **5**:84
compiler **5**:156–157
computer **5**:160b; **5**:160c; **5**:160f; **5**:160h
computer programming **5**:163–164
computer software **5**:164–165
FORTRAN **8**:241
interpreter **11**:225
Pascal **15**:101
PROLOG **15**:567
SNOBOL **18**:3
COMPUTER MEMORY 5:160p–161 *bibliog.*
byte **3**:603
compact disc **5**:155
computer **5**:160a *illus.*; **5**:160b; **5**:160d; **5**:160e–160f; **5**:160g; **5**:160h
computer, personal **5**:160i
computer graphics **5**:160m
computer register **5**:164
computer software **5**:165
Forrester, Jay Wright **8**:235
information storage and retrieval **11**:173
Josephson effect **18**:350
magnetism **13**:58
memory **13**:291
COMPUTER MODELING 5:161–162 *bibliog., illus.*
computer-aided design and computer-aided manufacturing **5**:160j–160L
operations research **14**:403
COMPUTER MUSIC 5:162–163 *bibliog.*
electronic music **7**:125; **7**:126
COMPUTER NETWORKING 5:163
computer **5**:160f; **5**:160h
computer, personal **5**:160j
COMPUTER PROGRAMMING 5:163–164 *bibliog.*
calculator, electronic **4**:23
compiler **5**:156–157
computer **5**:159–160; **5**:160a–160b; **5**:160e–160f; **5**:160i
computer languages **5**:160o–160p
computer modeling **5**:162
computer software **5**:164–165
flowchart **8**:178
interpreter **11**:225
problem solving **15**:563
COMPUTER REGISTER 5:164 *bibliog.*
central processing unit **4**:255
computer **5**:160e
COMPUTER SOFTWARE 5:164–165 *bibliog.*
compiler **5**:156–157
computer **5**:160c; **5**:160f; **5**:160i
computer, personal **5**:160i–160j
computer-aided design and computer-aided manufacturing **5**:160j–160L
computer graphics **5**:160L–160n
computer languages **5**:160o–160p
computer programming **5**:163–164
cybernetics **5**:401
information storage and retrieval **11**:174
COMPUTER TERMINAL 5:165
input-output devices **11**:182
keyboard, computer **12**:62
modem **13**:490
printer, computer **15**:550
COMPUTERIZED AXIAL TOMOGRAPH *see* CAT (COMPUTERIZED AXIAL TOMOGRAPHY) SCANNING
COMPUTERS IN EDUCATION 5:165–166 *bibliog., illus.*
teaching **19**:56–57
teaching machine **19**:57
COMPUTERS AND PRIVACY 5:166–167 *bibliog.*
COMSAT (Communications Satellite Corporation)
communications satellite **5**:144–145
INTELSAT **11**:204
COMSTOCK (Texas)
map (29° 41′N 101° 11′W) **19**:129
COMSTOCK, ANTHONY 5:167
pornography **15**:441
COMSTOCK LODE 5:167 *bibliog.*
Virginia City (Nevada) **14**:112 *illus.*
COMTAT (France) 5:167
COMTAT-VENAISSIN (France) *see* COMTAT (France)
COMTE, AUGUSTE 5:168 *bibliog.*
altruism **1**:314
positivism **15**:458
sociology **18**:28 *illus.*; **18**:30
COMYN, JOHN
Robert I, King of Scotland (Robert the Bruce) **16**:241
COMYN, MICHAEL
Irish literature **11**:268
CON SON ISLAND
map (8° 43′N 106° 36′E) **19**:580
CONABLE, BARBER B. 5:168
CONAKRY (Guinea) 5:168; **9**:398 *illus., table*
map (9° 31′N 13° 43′W) **9**:397
CONANICUT ISLAND (Rhode Island) **16**:199 *illus.*
map (41° 32′N 71° 21′W) **16**:198
CONANT, JAMES BRYANT 5:168 *bibliog.*
secondary education **17**:179
CONCEIT (literature) 5:168 *bibliog.*
Cowley, Abraham **5**:321
Donne, John **6**:239
metaphysical poetry **13**:334
CONCENTRATION (chemistry) 5:168–169 *bibliog.*
active transport **1**:89–90
saturation **17**:88
solution **18**:58
CONCENTRATION (industrial)
monopoly and competition **13**:538–539
CONCENTRATION CAMP 5:169 *bibliog.*
Auschwitz **2**:325
Belsen **3**:193
Buchenwald **3**:534
Dachau **6**:4
gas chamber **9**:53
Gestapo **9**:159
Gulag **9**:402
gypsies **9**:415
Holocaust **10**:206
Lublin (Poland) **12**:447
Treblinka **19**:286
World War II **20**:275
CONCEPCIÓN (Argentina)
map (27° 20′S 65° 35′W) **2**:149
CONCEPCIÓN (Bolivia)
climate **3**:367 *table*
map (16° 15′S 62° 4′W) **3**:366
CONCEPCIÓN (Chile) 5:169
map (36° 50′S 73° 3′W) **4**:355
Valdivia, Pedro de **19**:503
CONCEPCIÓN (Panama)
map (8° 31′N 82° 37′W) **15**:55
CONCEPCIÓN (Paraguay)
map (23° 25′S 57° 17′W) **15**:77
CONCEPCÍON DEL ORO (Mexico)
map (24° 38′N 101° 25′W) **13**:357
CONCEPCIÓN DEL URUGUAY (Argentina)
map (32° 29′S 58° 14′W) **2**:149
CONCEPT FORMATION AND ATTAINMENT 5:169 *bibliog.*
Bruner, Jerome Seymour **3**:525
Hull, Clark **10**:296
learning theory **12**:260–261
Piaget, Jean **15**:287–288
problem solving **15**:559
reasoning **16**:104
Skinner, B. F. **17**:343–344
CONCEPTION *see* FERTILIZATION
CONCEPTION BAY
map (47° 45′N 53° 0′W) **14**:166
CONCEPTUAL ART 5:170 *bibliog.*
Christo **4**:415–416
drawing **6**:265
LeWitt, Sol **12**:308
modern art **13**:495
Morris, Robert (artist) **13**:588
CONCERT OF EUROPE
congress system **5**:188
CONCERTGEBOUW ORCHESTRA 5:170
Haitink, Bernard **10**:16
CONCERTINA 5:170 *illus.*
See also ACCORDION
CONCERTO 5:170 *bibliog.*
absolute music **1**:62
baroque music **3**:91–92
cadenza **4**:11
classical period in music **5**:41
composers
Bach, Johann Christian **3**:10
Bach, Johann Sebastian **3**:11
Barber, Samuel **3**:77
Bartók, Béla **3**:98
Beethoven, Ludwig van **3**:164–165
Brahms, Johannes **3**:441
Corelli, Arcangelo **5**:262
Gabrieli (family) **9**:6
MacDowell, Edward **13**:14
Martinů, Bohuslav **13**:181
Mennin, Peter **13**:298
Rachmaninoff, Sergei **16**:36
Tchaikovsky, Peter Ilich **19**:51–52
Torelli, Giuseppe **19**:239
Vaughan Williams, Ralph **19**:528–529
Viotti, Giovanni Battista **19**:603–604
Vivaldi, Antonio **19**:622
Italian music **11**:318
music, history of Western **13**:666
CONCH 5:170
mollusk **13**:510
shell **17**:250–251 *illus.*
CONCHAS DAM (New Mexico)
map (35° 22′N 104° 11′W) **14**:136
CONCHAS LAKE
map (35° 25′N 104° 14′W) **14**:136
CONCHE (Newfoundland)
map (50° 53′N 55° 54′W) **14**:166
CONCHITI RESERVOIR
map (35° 35′N 106° 20′W) **14**:136
CONCHO (Arizona)
map (34° 28′N 109° 36′W) **2**:160
CONCHO (county in Texas)
map (31° 15′N 99° 50′W) **19**:129
CONCILIARISM 5:170
Basel, Council of **3**:108
Constance, Council of **5**:207
council, ecumenical **5**:309–310
Gallicanism **9**:19
Gerson, Jean le Charlier de **9**:159
Nicholas of Cusa **14**:181
CONCINI, CONCINO *see* ANCRE, CONCINO CONCINI, MARQUIS D′
CONCONULLY (Washington)
map (48° 34′N 119° 45′W) **20**:35
CONCORD (California)
map (37° 59′N 122° 2′W) **4**:31
CONCORD (Massachusetts) 5:171
map (42° 27′N 71° 21′W) **13**:206
CONCORD (Missouri)
map (38° 31′N 90° 23′W) **13**:476
CONCORD (New Hampshire) 5:171
map (43° 12′N 71° 32′W) **14**:123
CONCORD (North Carolina)
map (35° 25′N 80° 35′W) **14**:242
CONCORD, BATTLE OF *see* LEXINGTON AND CONCORD, BATTLE OF
CONCORD RIVER
map (42° 39′N 71° 18′W) **13**:206
CONCORDAT 5:171
CONCORDAT OF 1801 **5**:171
CONCORDAT OF WORMS (1122) **5**:171
Henry V, King of Germany and Holy Roman Emperor **10**:129
CONCORDAT OF 1754
Ferdinand VI, King of Spain **8**:53
CONCORDE 2:372–373 *illus.*; **5**:171 *bibliog.* **19**:281 *illus.*
airport noise **1**:225
supersonic transport **18**:353 *illus.*
CONCORDIA (Argentina)
map (31° 24′S 58° 2′W) **2**:149

CONCORDIA (Kansas)
map (39° 34′N 97° 39′W) **12**:18
CONCORDIA (county in Louisiana)
map (31° 28′N 91° 37′W) **12**:430
CONCORDIA (Missouri)
map (38° 59′N 93° 34′W) **13**:476
CONCORDIA COLLEGES **5**:171
CONCRETE *see* CEMENT AND CONCRETE
CONCRETE COMPUTER MUSIC **5**:163
CONCRETE POETRY **5**:171 *bibliog.*
CONCRETION **5**:171
hematite **10**:117
CONCUBINAGE **5**:172 *bibliog.*
CONCUSSION **5**:172
CONDÉ (family) **5**:172 *bibliog.*
Bourbon, Louis Henri de Bourbon-Condé, Duc de **3**:423
Fronde **8**:339
CONDE (South Dakota)
map (45° 9′N 98° 6′W) **18**:103
CONDÉ, LOUIS II, PRINCE DE
Condé (family) **5**:172
Montpensier, Anne Marie Louise d'Orléans, Duchesse de **13**:558
Turenne, Henri de La Tour d'Auvergne, Vicomte de **19**:341
CONDENSATION
distillation **6**:200
polymerization **15**:420
refrigeration **16**:124–125
CONDENSER (electrical) *see* CAPACITOR
CONDENSER (heat exchanger) **5**:172
cooling tower **5**:242
heat exchanger **10**:97–98
CONDILLAC, ÉTIENNE BONNOT DE **5**:172 *bibliog.*
CONDITIONING (psychology) **5**:172
animal behavior **2**:13
behavior modification **3**:169
learning theory **12**:260–261
Pavlov, Ivan Petrovich **15**:120
psychology, history of **15**:597
reflex **16**:120
Skinner, B. F. **17**:343–344
Skinner box **17**:344
Watson, John B. **20**:68
CONDOM
birth control **3**:293
CONDOMINIUM **5**:172–173 *bibliog.*
housing **10**:278
CONDON (Oregon)
map (45° 14′N 120° 11′W) **14**:427
CONDON, RICHARD **5**:173
CONDOR **5**:173 *bibliog., illus.*
CONDORCET, MARIE JEAN ANTOINE NICOLAS CARITAT, MARQUIS DE **5**:173 *bibliog.*
CONDOTO (Colombia)
map (5° 6′N 76° 37′W) **5**:107
CONDOTTIERI **5**:173 *bibliog.*
Hawkwood, Sir John **10**:78
CONDUCTING (music) **5**:173–174 *bibliog., illus.*
Abbado, Claudio **1**:51–52
Barenboim, Daniel **3**:80
baton **3**:124
Beecham, Sir Thomas **3**:160
Böhm, Karl **3**:361
Boulez, Pierre **3**:421–422
Boult, Sir Adrian Cedric **3**:422
Bülow, Hans von **3**:561
Davis, Colin **6**:50–51
Dohnányi, Christoph von **6**:224
Dorati, Antal **6**:241
Fiedler, Arthur **8**:70
Foss, Lukas **8**:242–243
Furtwängler, Wilhelm **8**:380–381
Giulini, Carlo Maria **9**:191
Goossens, Sir Eugene **9**:247
Haitink, Bernard **10**:16
Hallé, Sir Charles **10**:22
Henschel, Sir George **10**:130
Irving, Robert **11**:284
Jochum, Eugen **11**:421
Karajan, Herbert von **12**:26
Klemperer, Otto **12**:96
Koussevitzky, Serge **12**:125–126
Leinsdorf, Erich **12**:278
Levine, James **12**:304
Maazel, Lorin **13**:5
Maderna, Bruno **13**:40
Mehta, Zubin **13**:281
Mitropoulos, Dimitri **13**:485
Monteux, Pierre **13**:554
Munch, Charles **13**:639–640
Muti, Riccardo **13**:687
Nikisch, Arthur **14**:195
Ormandy, Eugene **14**:447
Ozawa, Seiji **14**:480
Previn, André **15**:534
Rostropovich, Mstislav **16**:321
Sargent, Sir Malcolm **17**:78
Schippers, Thomas **17**:122
Slatkin, Leonard **17**:351
Solti, Sir Georg **18**:57–58
Spohr, Louis **18**:192
Steinberg, William **18**:248
Stock, Frederick **18**:274
Stokowski, Leopold **18**:278
Strauss (family) **18**:293–294
Szell, Georg **18**:416
Thomas, Michael Tilson **19**:173
Toscanini, Arturo **19**:247–248
Walter, Bruno **20**:19
Weingartner, Felix **20**:95
CONDUCTION, ELECTRIC **5**:174 *bibliog.*
aluminum **1**:316
circuit, electric **4**:436–438
contact potential **5**:227
electrostatics **7**:128
glass **9**:201
ground, electrical **9**:373
heat and heat transfer **10**:98
insulator **11**:197
Josephson, Brian David **11**:452
liquid **12**:365
photoelectric cell **15**:259
photoelectric effect **15**:260
physics, history of **15**:283–284
plasma physics **15**:345–346
printed circuit **15**:550
resistivity **16**:177
semiconductor **17**:196–197
solid-state physics **18**:54
superconductivity **18**:350
CONE (botany) *see* POLLEN CONE; SEED CONE
CONE (mathematics) **5**:174–175 *illus.*
conic sections **5**:188–189 *illus.*
volume **19**:632
CONECUH (county in Alabama)
map (31° 30′N 87° 0′W) **1**:234
CONECUH RIVER
map (30° 58′N 87° 14′W) **1**:234
CONEFLOWER **5**:175 *illus.*
CONEJOS (Colorado)
map (37° 5′N 106° 1′W) **5**:116
CONEJOS (county in Colorado)
map (37° 15′N 106° 20′W) **5**:116
CONEJOS RIVER
map (37° 18′N 105° 44′W) **5**:116
CONEMAUGH RIVER
map (40° 28′N 79° 17′W) **15**:147
CONES (eye)
eye **7**:349–350 *illus.*
CONESTOGA (American Indians) *see* SUSQUEHANNA (American Indians)
CONESTOGA (wagon) **5**:175–176 *illus.*; **19**:444 *illus.*
wagon **20**:6
CONESUS LAKE
Finger Lakes **8**:93
CONEY *see* HYRAX
CONEY ISLAND (New York City) **5**:176
CONFEDERATE STATES OF AMERICA **5**:176–177 *bibliog., illus., map*
Benjamin, Judah P. **3**:201–202
Civil War, U.S. **5**:17–19 *map*; **5**:31–32
Civil War, U.S. uniform **19**:448–449 *illus.*
Davis, Jefferson **6**:51–52
flag **8**:135 *illus.*
Gordon, John Brown **9**:249
Mallory, Stephen Russell **13**:92
Mason, James Murray **13**:199
Memminger, Christopher Gustavus **12**:290
Montgomery (Alabama) **13**:556
original cabinet **5**:18 *illus.*
Stephens, Alexander Hamilton **18**:254
Toombs, Robert **19**:236
United States, history of the **19**:448
Yancey, William Lowndes **20**:317
CONFEDERATION
federalism **8**:43
government **9**:268
CONFEDERATION, ARTICLES OF *see* ARTICLES OF CONFEDERATION
CONFEDERATION, CANADIAN *see* CANADA, HISTORY OF
CONFEDERATION OF THE BAR
Poland **15**:391
CONFESSION (law) **5**:177
self-incrimination **17**:191
torture **19**:247
CONFESSION (religion) **5**:177
Columban, Saint **5**:125
CONFESSION, THE (film)
Costa-Gavras, Henri **5**:291
CONFESSIONAL LITERATURE **5**:177 *bibliog.*
autobiography **2**:355
Confessions, Les **5**:177
Confessions of St. Augustine, The **5**:178
Sexton, Anne **17**:228
CONFESSIONS, LES (book) **5**:177
Rousseau, Jean Jacques **16**:325–327
CONFESSIONS OF AN ENGLISH OPIUM EATER (book)
De Quincey, Thomas **6**:62
CONFESSIONS OF FAITH **5**:177
articles of religion **2**:220
Augsburg Confession **2**:320
Heidelberg (West Germany) **10**:107
Luther, Martin **12**:468–469
CONFESSIONS OF ST. AUGUSTINE, THE (books) **5**:178 *bibliog.*
Augustine, Saint **2**:321
CONFESSORS OF THE GLORY OF CHRIST
Schwenkfeld von Ossig, Kaspar **17**:140
CONFIDENCE GAME **5**:178 *bibliog.*
fraud **8**:288
CONFIGURATION (chemistry) **5**:178 *bibliog.*
compounds, chemical **5**:178
isomers **5**:178
optical activity **5**:178
stereochemistry **18**:258
CONFIGURATION, ELECTRONIC *see* ELECTRON CONFIGURATION
CONFINEMENT REARING *see* FACTORY FARMING
CONFIRMATION **5**:178
See also BAR MITZVAH
CONFLICT THEORY **5**:178–179 *bibliog.*
frustration **8**:350
CONFLUENCE (Pennsylvania)
map (39° 49′N 79° 21′W) **15**:147
CONFORMITY **5**:179 *bibliog.*
attitude and attitude change **2**:315
cognitive dissonance **5**:94
deviance **6**:143
group dynamics **9**:376
CONFUCIANISM **5**:179–180 *bibliog., illus.*; **16**:140 *map*
China, history of **4**:371–375
Chinese literature **4**:389
Chou Tun-i (Zhou Duni) **4**:410
Chu Hsi (Zhu Xi) **4**:421
I Ching (Yijing) **11**:3
Korea, history of **12**:116
Mencius **13**:293
philosophy **15**:247
Sung (Song) (dynasty) **18**:348
Wang An-shih (Wang Anshi) **20**:22
Wang Yang-ming **20**:22
women in society **20**:203
CONFUCIUS **2**:252 *illus.*
Asia, history of **2**:252
Confucianism **5**:179–180 *illus.*
philosophy **15**:247
Shantung (Shandong) (China) **17**:241
CONGAREE RIVER
map (33° 45′N 80° 37′W) **18**:98
CONGENITAL DISEASES
diseases, human **6**:193
CONGENITAL MALFORMATIONS *see* BIRTH DEFECTS
CONGER EEL **7**:71 *illus.*
eel **7**:70
CONGLOMERATE (business) **5**:180–181 *bibliog.*
See also MERGER (business)
monopoly and competition **13**:539–540
CONGLOMERATE (geology) **5**:181 *bibliog., illus.*
classifications **5**:181
ice ages **11**:8
sedimentary rock **17**:185
stratigraphy **18**:292 *illus.*
till and tillite **19**:199
CONGO **5**:181–183 *bibliog., illus., map, table*
African art **1**:163
African music **1**:168–171 *illus.*
cities
Brazzaville **3**:465
climate **5**:181–182 *table*
economic activity **5**:182
education **5**:182
African universities **1**:176 *table*
flag **5**:181 *illus.*
government **5**:182–183
history **5**:182–183
United Nations **19**:414
land and resources **5**:181–182 *map*
map (1° 0′S 15° 0′E) **1**:136
people **5**:181–182
Lunda **12**:462
CONGO, REPUBLIC OF THE *see* ZAIRE
CONGO-BRAZZAVILLE *see* CONGO
CONGO CRISIS **5**:183 *bibliog.*
Lumumba, Patrice **12**:459
CONGO FREE STATE *see* ZAIRE
CONGO-KINSHASA *see* ZAIRE
CONGO-LEOPOLDVILLE *see* ZAIRE
CONGO RIVER **5**:183–184 *bibliog., illus., map*; **20**:351 *illus.*
jungle and rain forest **11**:469
map (6° 4′S 12° 24′E) **20**:350
Stanley, Sir Henry Morton **18**:219
CONGREGATION OF THE ORATORY
Neri, Saint Philip **14**:89
CONGREGATIONALISM **5**:184 *bibliog.*
Browne, Robert **3**:517
Cotton, John **5**:307
Mather (family) **13**:227–228
Puritanism **15**:630
United Church of Christ **19**:401
CONGRÈS INTERNATIONAL DE L'ARCHITECTURE MODERNE (CIAM)
modern architecture **13**:491
CONGRESS (Saskatchewan)
map (49° 46′N 106° 0′W) **17**:81
CONGRESS, LIBRARY OF *see* LIBRARY OF CONGRESS
CONGRESS OF INDUSTRIAL ORGANIZATIONS *see* AMERICAN FEDERATION OF LABOR AND CONGRESS OF INDUSTRIAL ORGANIZATIONS
CONGRESS OF RACIAL EQUALITY **5**:184
CONGRESS SYSTEM **5**:187–188 *bibliog.*
balance of power **3**:32
Europe, history of **7**:292
Holy Alliance **10**:209
Metternich, Klemens, Fürst von **13**:349–350
Quadruple Alliance **16**:5
CONGRESS OF THE UNITED STATES **5**:184–187 *bibliog., illus.*
ABSCAM **1**:62
budget **3**:544
committees **5**:187
constitution of the united states **5**:214–220
Bill of Rights **3**:252–253
20th Amendment **5**:222; **19**:359
25th Amendment **19**:359
elections **5**:185
District of Columbia **6**:201
presidential elections **15**:531–532
framework of the Constitution **5**:214
General Accounting Office **9**:77
House of Representatives of the United States **10**:272–274
impeachment **11**:60–61
lame duck **12**:174
legislative process **5**:186–187
legislature **12**:275
Library of Congress **12**:318–319
lobbyist **12**:384
Luther v. *Borden* **12**:469
McCulloch v. *Maryland* **13**:11
Marbury v. *Madison* **13**:144
membership **5**:185
organization **5**:185–186
president of the United States **15**:522; **15**:524; **15**:527–528
presidential elections **15**:529; **15**:531–532
Reconstruction **16**:108–110
Senate of the United States **17**:198–199
special-interest groups **18**:168
United States, history of the **19**:442 *illus.*
veto **19**:567
vice-president of the United States **19**:569
whip **20**:131
CONGRESSIONAL MEDAL OF HONOR
medals and decorations **13**:260–263 *illus.*
CONGRESSIONAL RECORD **5**:188
CONGREVE, SIR WILLIAM (artillerist)
rockets and missiles **16**:252 *illus.*
CONGREVE, WILLIAM (playwright) **5**:188 *bibliog., illus.*
Way of the World, The **20**:73
comedy **5**:132
CONGRUENCE
number theory **14**:294
CONGRUENT FIGURES **5**:188
geometry **9**:107
CONIC SECTIONS **5**:188–189 *bibliog., illus.*
Apollonius of Perga **2**:84
circle **4**:435–436 *illus.*

cone 5:174–175
Desargues, Gérard 6:125
eccentricity 7:37
ellipse 7:147
hyperbola 10:347–348
parabola 15:74
CONIFER 5:189–191 *bibliog., illus.*; 15:335 *illus.*
cedar 4:228
cypress 5:407
deciduous plant 6:73
distribution 5:184–191
Douglas fir 6:248
fir 8:99–100
forest 8:229 *illus.*
gymnosperm 9:414
hemlock 10:119
juniper 11:470
Jurassic Period 11:475 *illus.*
larch 12:206
life span 12:330 *table*
monkey puzzle tree 13:535
Norfolk Island pine 14:219
petrified wood 15:205
pine 15:305
podocarp 15:377
pollen cone 15:407
redwood 16:117
seed cone 17:187
spruce 18:200–201
tamarack 19:18
tree 19:286–287 *illus.*
Triassic Period 19:294 *illus.*
yew 20:327
CONJUGATE ACID
acids and bases 1:83
CONJUGATE BASE
acids and bases 1:83
CONJUGATION (biology) 5:191
Paramecium 15:79
Spirogyra 18:189
CONJUGATION (chemistry) 5:191
diene 6:162
CONJUNCTION
parts of speech 15:101
CONJUNCTION (astronomy) 5:191
CONJUNCTIVA
eye 7:348 *illus.*
CONJUNCTIVITIS 5:191
CONJURING *see* MAGIC ACTS
CONKLIN (Alberta)
map (55° 38′N 111° 5′W) 1:256
CONKLING, ROSCOE 5:191 *bibliog.*
Garfield, James A. 9:46
Hayes, Rutherford B. 10:83
CONN, LAKE
map (54° 4′N 9° 20′W) 11:258
CONNACHT (Ireland) 5:191
CONNALLY, JOHN B. 5:191 *bibliog.*
CONNALLY, TOM 5:191 *bibliog.*
CONNALLY RESOLUTION
Connally, Tom 5:191
CONNAUGHT (Ireland) *see* CONNACHT (Ireland)
CONNEAUT (Ohio)
map (41° 57′N 80° 34′W) 14:357
CONNEAUTVILLE (Pennsylvania)
map (41° 36′N 80° 18′W) 15:147
CONNECTICUT 5:191–196 *bibliog., illus., map*
Berkshire Hills 3:214
cities
Bridgeport 3:484
Danbury 6:21
Greenwich 9:354
Groton 9:372
Hartford 10:62
New Haven 14:126–127
New London 14:134
Norwalk 14:260
Stamford 18:215–216
Waterbury 20:60–61
climate 5:192
cultural institutions 5:194
economy 5:194–195 *illus.*
education 5:194
Barnard, Henry 3:86
Connecticut, state university and colleges of 5:196
Connecticut College 5:196
Trinity College (Hartford, Conn.) 19:301
United States Coast Guard Academy 19:462
Wesleyan University 20:105–106
Yale University 20:315
flag 5:192 *illus.*
government and politics 5:195
historical sites 5:194
history 5:195–196
Charter Oak 4:300
Fundamental Orders 8:361
Ludlow, Roger 12:451–452
United States, history of the 19:436
Winthrop (family) 20:182
Wolcott (family) 20:195
land and resources 5:192–193 *map*
map (41° 45′N 72° 45′W) 19:419
people 5:192; 5:194
Pequot 15:158
rivers, lakes, and waterways 5:192
Housatonic River 10:264
seal, state 5:192 *illus.*
vegetation and animal life 5:192
CONNECTICUT, STATE UNIVERSITY AND COLLEGES OF 5:196
CONNECTICUT COLLEGE 5:196
American Dance Festival 1:338
CONNECTICUT COMPROMISE
Sherman, Roger 17:258
CONNECTICUT RIVER 5:196
map (41° 17′N 72° 21′W) 19:419
CONNECTICUT WITS 5:196 *bibliog.*
Barlow, Joel 3:84–85
Dwight, Timothy 6:317
CONNECTICUT YANKEE IN KING ARTHUR'S COURT (book)
Twain, Mark 19:357
CONNECTIVE TISSUE 5:196 *bibliog.*
cartilage 4:175
collagen 5:102
diseases
arthritis 2:214–216
collagen disease 5:102
gout 9:266–267
lupus erythematosus 12:466
rheumatism 16:194–195
sarcoma 17:75
hair 10:14 *illus.*
ligaments 12:333
tendon 19:101
CONNELL (Washington)
map (46° 40′N 118° 52′W) 20:35
CONNELL, EVAN S., JR. 5:196–197
CONNELLSVILLE (Pennsylvania)
map (40° 1′N 79° 35′W) 15:147
CONNELLY, CORNELIA 5:197 *bibliog.*
CONNELLY, MARC 5:197 *bibliog.*
CONNEMARA (region in Ireland)
map (53° 25′N 9° 45′W) 11:258
CONNEMARA PONY
pony 15:428
CONNERSVILLE (Indiana)
map (39° 39′N 85° 8′W) 11:111
CONNOLLY, CYRIL 5:197
CONNOLLY, MAUREEN 5:197 *bibliog.*
CONNORS, JIMMY 5:197 *bibliog., illus.*
CONN'S SYNDROME
endocrine system, diseases of the 7:170
CONOCOCHEAGUE RIVER
map (39° 37′N 77° 50′W) 13:188
CONODONT 5:197 *bibliog.*
Paleozoic Era 15:43
CONOVER (North Carolina)
map (35° 42′N 81° 12′W) 14:242
CONQUISTADORS 5:197
Almagro, Diego de 1:306
Balboa, Vasco Núñez de 3:33
Cortés, Hernán 5:278
de Soto, Hernando 6:63
historians
Prescott, William H. 15:522
Latin America, history of 12:218–219
Mendoza, Pedro de 13:296
Mexico, history of 13:362
Narváez, Pánfilo de 14:23
Pizarro, Francisco 15:324–325
slavery 17:353
CONRAD (Iowa)
map (42° 14′N 92° 52′W) 11:244
CONRAD (Montana)
map (48° 10′N 111° 57′W) 13:547
CONRAD, CHARLES, JR. *see* CONRAD, PETE
CONRAD, FRANK
radio and television broadcasting 16:54
CONRAD, JOSEPH 5:198 *bibliog., illus.*
Heart of Darkness 10:95
CONRAD, PAUL 5:198
cartoon (editorial and political) 4:177 *illus.*
CONRAD, PETE 5:198–199
Apollo program 2:82
Gemini program 9:72–73
Skylab 17:347–348
space medicine 18:133 *illus.*
CONRAD I, KING OF GERMANY 5:199
CONRAD II, KING OF GERMANY AND HOLY ROMAN EMPEROR 5:199 *bibliog.*
CONRAD III, KING OF GERMANY AND HOLY ROMAN EMPEROR 5:199 *bibliog.*
Welf (family) 20:97
CONRAD IV, KING OF GERMANY 5:199
CONRAIL
railroad 16:73
CONRIED, HEINRICH
Metropolitan Opera 13:348
CONROE (Texas)
map (30° 19′N 95° 27′W) 19:129
CONROY, JACK 5:199 *bibliog.*
CONSANGUINEAL FAMILY *see* EXTENDED FAMILY
CONSCIENCE 5:199 *bibliog.*
moral awareness 13:572–573
CONSCIENCE, HENDRIK 5:199
CONSCIENTIOUS OBJECTOR 5:200 *bibliog.*
American Friends Service Committee 1:340
civil disobedience 5:10
pacifism and nonviolent movements 15:8
Welsh v. *United States* 20:102
CONSCIOUSNESS, STATES OF 5:200 *bibliog.*
altered states 5:200
brain bilateralism 3:448
coma (unconscious state) 5:129
concept 5:200
defense mechanisms 6:83
dreams and dreaming 6:266–268
epilepsy 7:220
Freud, Sigmund 8:329
hallucinogens 10:24
humanistic psychology 10:299
hypnosis 10:350
inner speech 11:179
physiology 5:200
synesthesia 18:407
trance 19:266
unconscious 19:382–383
CONSCIOUSNESS-RAISING GROUPS *see* GROUP THERAPY
CONSCRIPTION 5:201 *bibliog.*
conscientious objector 5:200
defense, national 6:82
feudalism 8:64–65
Scharnhorst, Gerhard Johann David von 17:117
Welsh v. *United States* 20:102
CONSEIL EUROPÉEN POUR LA RECHERCHE NUCLÉAIRE *see* EUROPEAN ORGANIZATION FOR NUCLEAR RESEARCH
CONSERVATION 5:201–204 *bibliog., illus.*
See also POLLUTION, ENVIRONMENTAL
Audubon Society, National 2:319
Civilian Conservation Corps 5:34
conservation movement 5:203–204
endangered species 7:165–168
environmental impact statement 7:212
game laws 9:27
hunting 10:313–314
Interior, United States Department of the 11:210
Leopold, Aldo 12:293
Marsh, George Perkins 13:171
mountain climbing 13:621–622
Muir, John 13:635
national parks 14:44
photography
Porter, Eliot 15:444
Pinchot, Gifford 15:304
recycling of materials 16:111
Roosevelt, Franklin Delano 16:309
Roosevelt, Theodore 16:310
Tennessee Valley Authority 19:107–108
wildlife refuge 20:150–151
CONSERVATION, HISTORIC *see* HISTORIC PRESERVATION
CONSERVATION, LAWS OF 5:204–205 *bibliog., illus.*
See also KIRCHHOFF'S LAWS
angular momentum 2:7
Bothe, Walther Wilhelm 3:415
charge, electric 5:204–205
ecology 7:43
electrostatics 7:128
energy 5:204
energy conversion 7:172
fundamental particles 8:362
Helmholtz, Hermann Ludwig Ferdinand von 10:115–116
neutrino 14:108
symmetry 5:204
symmetry (physics) 18:404
theoretical physics 19:159
thermodynamics 19:163–165
CONSERVATION ARCHAEOLOGY *see* SALVAGE ARCHAEOLOGY
CONSERVATION OF MASS AND ENERGY *see* CONSERVATION, LAWS OF
CONSERVATION AND RESTORATION
pollution, environmental 15:415
CONSERVATISM 5:205 *bibliog.*
Burke, Edmund 3:571
Disraeli, Benjamin, 1st Earl of Beaconsfield 6:197–198
totalitarianism 19:248
United States
evangelicalism 7:312
Moral Majority 13:573
National Conservative Political Action Committee 14:31
CONSERVATIVE PARTIES 5:205–206 *bibliog.*
Canada 5:205–206
Bennett, Richard Bedford, Viscount Bennett 3:203
Borden, Sir Robert 3:397
Bracken, John 3:436
Canada, History of 4:86–87
Clark, Joseph 5:38–39
Diefenbaker, John 6:161
Macdonald, Sir John A. 13:12
Great Britain
Churchill, Sir Winston 4:425–427
Disraeli, Benjamin, 1st Earl of Beaconsfield 6:197–198
Great Britain, history of 9:317–318
Law, Andrew Bonar 12:247
Macmillan, Harold 13:34
Peel, Sir Robert 15:132
Salisbury, Robert Cecil, 3d Marquess of 17:33
Thatcher, Margaret 19:143
Tory party 19:247
United States
Republican party 16:172–176
CONSERVATOR *see* GUARDIAN
CONSIDERANT, VICTOR PROSPER 5:206
CONSIDERATION (law)
contract 5:231
CONSIDINE, BOB 5:206
CONSOLIDATED B-24D LIBERATOR AIRCRAFT *see* B-24 LIBERATOR
CONSOLIDATED RAIL CORPORATION *see* CONRAIL
CONSONANCE (music)
dissonance (music) 6:198
CONSONANTS (phonetics)
positions of mouth and tongue 18:174 *illus.*
CONSORT MUSIC 5:206 *bibliog.*
Byrd, William 3:602
English music 7:203 *illus.*
viol 19:602
CONSPICUOUS CONSUMPTION 5:206
CONSPIRACY 5:206
collusion 5:105
CONSTABLE, HENRY 5:206
CONSTABLE, JOHN 5:206–207 *bibliog., illus.*
Boatbuilding near Flatford Mill 5:207 *illus.*
Stonehenge 15:24 *illus.*; 20:61 *illus.*
View of Salisbury Cathedral 7:187 *illus.*
CONSTANCE, COUNCIL OF 5:207 *bibliog.*
conciliarism 5:170
Gerson, Jean le Charlier de 9:159
Huss, John 10:320
John XXIII, "Antipope" 11:429
Martin V, Pope 13:180
Sigismund, King of Germany and Holy Roman Emperor 17:299
CONSTANCE, LAKE 5:207
map (47° 35′N 9° 25′E) 18:394
CONSTANS II POGONATUS, BYZANTINE EMPEROR 5:207
CONSTANT (mathematics) 5:207
pi 15:287
CONSTANT, BENJAMIN 5:207–208 *bibliog.*
aestheticism 1:130
French literature 8:317
Staël, Madame de 18:209
CONSTANT COMPOSITION, LAW OF
chemical combination, laws of 4:315
CONSTANȚA (Romania) 5:208
map (44° 11′N 28° 39′E) 16:288
CONSTANTINE (Algeria) 5:208
map (36° 22′N 6° 37′E) 1:287
CONSTANTINE, BASILICA OF (Rome) 16:274 *illus.*
CONSTANTINE I, KING OF GREECE 5:208
Venizélos, Eleuthérios 19:546
World War I 20:230; 20:238

CONSTANTINE I, ROMAN EMPEROR (Constantine the Great) **5**:208–209 *bibliog., illus.*
architecture **2**:133
basilica **16**:274 *illus.*
Byzantine Empire **3**:607
cathedrals and churches **4**:204
Constanța (Romania) **5**:208
Constantine (Algeria) **5**:208
Europe, history of **7**:282
Italy, history of **11**:327
Licinius, Roman Emperor **12**:323
Maximian, Roman Emperor **13**:239
Praetorian guard **15**:487
Rome, ancient **16**:304
Senate, Roman **17**:200
CONSTANTINE II, KING OF GREECE **5**:208
Greece **9**:328
CONSTANTINE VI, BYZANTINE EMPEROR
Irene, Empress **11**:265–266
CONSTANTINE VIII, BYZANTINE EMPEROR
Basil II, Byzantine emperor **3**:109
CONSTANTINOPLE (Turkey) *see* ISTANBUL (Turkey)
CONSTANTINOPLE, COUNCILS OF **5**:209
Holy Spirit **10**:211
Theodosius I, Roman Emperor (Theodosius the Great) **19**:156
CONSTANTINOPLE, LATIN EMPIRE OF **5**:209–210 *bibliog., map*
Byzantine Empire **3**:607–608
Crusades **5**:369
Italy, history of **11**:327
Michael VIII, Palaeologus, Byzantine Emperor **13**:371
Middle East, history of the **13**:401–402
CONSTANTINOPLE, TREATY OF
World War I **20**:222
CONSTANTINUS, FLAVIUS VALERIUS *see* CONSTANTINE I, ROMAN EMPEROR (Constantine the Great)
CONSTANTIUS I, ROMAN EMPEROR **5**:210
Constantine I, Roman Emperor **5**:208
CONSTANTIUS II, ROMAN EMPEROR **5**:210
CONSTELLATION (astronomy) **5**:210–212 *bibliog., illus.*
Aquarius **2**:93
Aquila **2**:94
Argo **2**:152
Aries **2**:154
Auriga **2**:324
Big Dipper **3**:249
Boötes **3**:394
Cancer **4**:100
Canis Major and Canis Minor **4**:108
Capricornus **4**:128
Centaurus **4**:249
Crab nebula **5**:325
Crux **5**:370
Cygnus **5**:406
Galaxy, The **9**:11
Gemini **9**:71
Leo **12**:287
Libra **12**:314
Lyra **12**:479
Orion (astronomy) **14**:444
Pisces **15**:317
Pleiades **15**:364
Sagittarius **17**:12
Scorpius **17**:149
star **18**:221
Taurus **19**:45
Ursa Major
Big Dipper **3**:249
Ursa Minor
Little Dipper **12**:372
Virgo **19**:613
zodiac **20**:371
CONSTELLATION (ship) **5**:211
CONSTIPATION **5**:212 *bibliog.*
cascara sagrada **4**:180
cathartic **4**:204
gastrointestinal tract disease **9**:56
hemorrhoids **10**:120
intestine **11**:231
pregnancy and birth **15**:503
CONSTITUTION (body of precedents) **5**:212 *bibliog.*
Bill of Rights **3**:251
first written in Europe
Stanisław II, King of Poland **18**:219
Germany
Frederick William IV, King of Prussia **8**:293
Weimar Republic **20**:94–95
government **9**:267
Great Britain
Great Britain, history of **9**:311
Magna Carta **13**:52–53
judicial review **11**:464
monarchy
king **12**:80
CONSTITUTION (ship) **5**:212 *bibliog.*; **14**:55 *illus.*
Hull, Isaac **10**:296
War of 1812 **20**:26 *illus.*
CONSTITUTION ACT (Canada) **5**:212
CONSTITUTION OF THE UNITED STATES **5**:212–223 *bibliog., illus.*
See also the specific amendments, e.g., 1ST AMENDMENT; 2D AMENDMENT; 20TH AMENDMENT; etc.
American Revolution **1**:365
Anti-Federalists **2**:61
attainder, bill of **2**:313
Bill of Rights **3**:252–253
commerce clause
Brown v. *Maryland* **3**:517
Heart of Atlanta Motel, Inc. v. *United States* **10**:95
Schechter Poultry Corporation v. *United States* **17**:117
Constitutional Convention **5**:223–224
drafting of **1**:365 *illus.*; **5**:212–214
electoral college **7**:104–105
Equal Rights Amendment **7**:224
Federalist, The **8**:43
framework
federalism as a basis **5**:214
governmental power limited and circumscribed **5**:214
popular control but not majority rule **5**:214
three coordinate branches of government **5**:214–215
genesis and ratification **5**:212–214
habeas corpus **10**:3–4
impeachment **11**:60–61
implied power
McCulloch v. *Maryland* **13**:11
Iroquois League **11**:280
judicial review **11**:464
maritime law **13**:158
military justice **13**:421
patent **15**:110
political philosophy of the framers **5**:213
president of the united states **15**:524; **15**:526–527
presidential elections **15**:529
privacy, invasion of **15**:556
proposed amendments **5**:223
Senate of the United States **17**:198
separation of powers **17**:206
signatories **5**:220
Rutledge, John **16**:376–377
state rights **18**:233
supremacy clause **5**:220
Supreme Court of the United States **18**:355
taxation
Pollock v. *Farmers' Loan and Trust Co.* **15**:409–410
text and commentary **5**:215–223
titles of nobility and honor **19**:213
treason **19**:285
trial **19**:292
United States, history of the **19**:442
veto **19**:567
vice-president of the United States **19**:568–570
CONSTITUTIONAL CONVENTION **1**:365 *illus.*; **5**:213 *illus.*; **5**:223–224 *bibliog.*
American Revolution **1**:365
Connecticut **5**:196
Ellsworth, Oliver **7**:149
Fitzsimons, Thomas **8**:132
genesis of the Constitution **5**:213
Hamilton, Alexander **10**:28
Johnson, William Samuel **11**:437
King, Rufus **12**:81
Madison, James **13**:41–42
Mason, George **13**:198–199
Paterson, William **15**:111
Randolph (family) **16**:82–83
Rutledge, John **16**:377
Sherman, Roger **17**:258
United States, history of the **19**:442
Washington, George **20**:43
CONSTITUTIONAL GOVERNMENT AND POLITICS (book)
Friedrich, Carl J. **8**:332
CONSTITUTIONAL UNION PARTY **5**:224
CONSTRICTORS (snake) **17**:377 *illus.*; **17**:379–380 *illus.*
CONSTRUCTION
salvage archaeology **17**:40
underwater construction
cofferdam **5**:94
CONSTRUCTION, BUILDING *see* BUILDING CONSTRUCTION; HOUSE (in Western architecture)
CONSTRUCTIVISM **5**:224–225 *bibliog., illus.*
Albers, Josef **1**:253
Baumeister, Willi **3**:130
Gabo, Naum **9**:3–4
kinetic art **12**:78
Lippold, Richard **12**:363
Lissitzky, El **12**:366
mobile **13**:487
modern architecture **13**:491
Moholy-Nagy, László **13**:503
Pevsner, Antoine **15**:216
Rickey, George W. **16**:216
Rodchenko, Aleksandr Mikhailovich **16**:265
Roszak, Theodore **16**:321
sculpture **17**:165
Stella, Frank **18**:250
Tatlin, Vladimir Yevgrafovich **19**:44
CONSUL (ancient Roman history) **5**:225
CONSUL (modern government official) **5**:225
foreign service **8**:226–227
CONSULATE **5**:225; **8**:324 *illus.*
French Revolution **8**:324
Napoleon I, Emperor of the French (Napoléon Bonaparte) **14**:16–17
CONSUMER
computers and privacy **5**:167
price system **15**:535
retailing **16**:183
supply and demand **18**:353–354
value-added tax **19**:508–509
CONSUMER COOPERATIVE
cooperative **5**:245
CONSUMER CREDIT **5**:225 *bibliog.*
credit agency **5**:336
credit card **5**:336
finance company **8**:92
installment plan **11**:194
interest **11**:207
CONSUMER CREDIT PROTECTION ACT
class action **5**:41
CONSUMER EDUCATION
nutrition, human **14**:307
CONSUMER PRICE INDEX **5**:225
inflation **11**:170–171 *table*
CONSUMER PRODUCT SAFETY COMMISSION **5**:225
CONSUMER PROTECTION **5**:226 *bibliog.*
advertising **1**:113
Better Business Bureau **3**:232
class action **5**:41
Consumer Product Safety Commission **5**:225
government regulation **9**:271–272
Nader, Ralph **14**:5 *illus.*
Underwriters' Laboratories **19**:383
CONSUMERS UNION *see* CONSUMER PROTECTION
CONSUMPTION (disease) *see* TUBERCULOSIS
CONTACT (touch)
thigmotaxis
taxis **19**:48
CONTACT LENS **5**:226–227
CONTACT METAMORPHISM *see* METAMORPHIC ROCK
CONTACT POTENTIAL **5**:227
CONTAGIOUS DISEASES *see* INFECTIOUS DISEASES
CONTAINERIZATION **5**:227 *bibliog., illus.*
harbor and port **10**:43; **10**:44 *illus.*
CONTAINERS *see* PACKAGING
CONTAINMENT *see* COLD WAR
CONTAMANA (Peru)
map (7° 15′S 74° 54′W) **15**:193
CONTAMIN, VICTOR
Halle des Machines **4**:185 *illus.*
CONTEMPLATION *see* MEDITATION
CONTEMPORARY ART SOCIETY
Canadian art and architecture **4**:90
CONTEMPT **5**:227
Bridges v. *California* **3**:485
injunction **11**:178
CONTINENT
continental drift **5**:228–229
continental shelf and slope **5**:230
continental shield **5**:230
Earth, geological history of **7**:11–15
estimated position of continents
Ordovician Period **14**:421 *map*
Permian Period **15**:175 *map*
Tertiary Period **19**:123 *map*
Triassic Period **19**:295 *map*
Gondwanaland **9**:243
isostasy **11**:300
plate tectonics **15**:351–357
continental crust **15**:351 *map*
fit of continents around Mid-Atlantic Ridge **15**:353 *map*
CONTINENTAL CLIMATE **5**:227–228 *bibliog.*
CONTINENTAL CONGRESS **5**:228 *bibliog., illus.*
Declaration of Independence **6**:74
Dickinson, John **6**:158
Galloway, Joseph **9**:21
Hanson, John **10**:41
McKean, Thomas **13**:27
Princeton, New Jersey **14**:130 *illus.*
United States, history of the **19**:440–441 *illus.*
CONTINENTAL DIVIDE **5**:228
Rocky Mountains **16**:262
CONTINENTAL DRIFT (geology) **5**:228–229 *bibliog., illus., map*
See also CONTINENTAL SHIELD
Bullard, Sir Edward **3**:559
Carboniferous Period **4**:138 *map*
convection cell **5**:232
Cretaceous Period **5**:340 *map*
Devonian Period **6**:144 *map*
dinosaur **6**:182
Earth, geological history of **7**:14
Earth, structure and composition of **7**:20; **7**:23
geology **9**:106
geophysics **9**:108
Hess, H. H. **10**:151–152
Holmes, Arthur **10**:205
ice ages **11**:10–11
Jurassic Period **11**:474
mantle **13**:130
Mesozoic Era **13**:322
ocean and sea **14**:327
orogeny **14**:447
paleoclimatology **15**:33
paleogeography **15**:36–38 *map*
plate tectonics **15**:353–354 *map*
polar wandering **15**:393
seafloor spreading **17**:172 *illus.*
theory **5**:228
Vine, F. J. **19**:600
Wegener, Alfred Lothar **20**:91
CONTINENTAL RISE
Atlantic Ocean bottom **2**:295 *map*
Indian Ocean bottom **11**:105 *map*
CONTINENTAL SHELF AND SLOPE **5**:230 *bibliog., illus.*
bathyal zone **3**:123
benthonic zone **3**:205
Canaries Current **4**:98
coastal plain **5**:81
Earth, structure and composition of **7**:21
epipelagic zone **7**:220
fishing industry **8**:124–127
habitat **10**:4
littoral zone **12**:373
Lomonosov Ridge **12**:400
neritic zone **14**:89
ocean and sea **14**:331
oceanic mineral resources **14**:340
Ordovician Period **14**:421
plate tectonics
fit of continents around Mid-Atlantic Ridge **15**:353 *map*
sediment, marine **17**:183 *illus.*
submarine canyon **18**:316
territorial waters **19**:121
Triassic Period **19**:293
CONTINENTAL SHIELD **5**:230
See also CONTINENTAL DRIFT (geology)
basement rock **3**:108
Cambrian Period **4**:51
Canadian Shield **4**:94
Earth, geological history of **7**:14
CONTINENTAL SYSTEM **5**:230 *bibliog.*
Napoleon I, Emperor of the French (Napoléon Bonaparte) **14**:17; **14**:18
CONTINUING EDUCATION *see* ADULT EDUCATION
CONTINUITY **5**:230–231 *bibliog., illus.*
Baire, René **3**:27
Dedekind, Richard **6**:76–77
topology **19**:238
CONTINUOUS AMBULATORY PERITONEAL DIALYSIS
kidney, artificial **12**:71
CONTINUOUS CASTING
iron and steel industry **11**:277 *illus.*

CONTOOCOOK (New Hampshire)
map (43° 13′N 71° 43′W) **14**:123
CONTOOCOOK RIVER
map (43° 27′N 71° 35′W) **14**:123
CONTOUR PLOWING **20**:187 *illus.*
CONTRA COSTA (county in California)
map (37° 55′N 121° 55′W) **4**:31
CONTRA DANCE
folk dance **8**:199
CONTRABAND 5:231
right of search **16**:222
CONTRABASS *see* DOUBLE BASS
CONTRABASSOON 5:231 *bibliog.*
CONTRACEPTION *see* BIRTH CONTROL
CONTRACT (law) 5:231–232 *bibliog.*
age of consent **1**:183
arbitration (labor-management and commercial) **2**:110
assignment **2**:265
bill of lading **3**:251
business law **3**:588
children's rights **4**:354
Constitution of the United States **5**:217
covenant (law) **5**:319
Dartmouth College v. *Woodward* **6**:40
feudalism **8**:64–65
Fletcher v. *Peck* **8**:163
franchise (business) **8**:273
indentured service **11**:78
insurance **11**:199
lease **12**:261
liability **12**:311
Lochner v. *New York* **12**:386
marriage **13**:165–166
misrepresentation **13**:467
remedies for breach of contract **5**:232
requirements of a valid contract **5**:231–232
Roman law **16**:279
socialist law **18**:25
surety **18**:358
yellow-dog contract **20**:322
CONTRACTIONS, PREMATURE (heart)
heart diseases **10**:96
CONTRALTO 5:232
castrato **4**:192
CONTRERAS, BATTLE OF 5:232
Mexican War **13**:354
CONTROL SYSTEMS *see* AUTOMATION; FEEDBACK; PROCESS CONTROL
CONTROL UNIT (computer term) **5**:160d; **5**:160e
CONVECTION 5:232 *bibliog.*
atmosphere **2**:300–302 *illus.*
Earth, heat flow in **7**:17–18
Earth, structure and compostion of **7**:20 *illus.*
ground temperature **9**:373
heat and heat transfer **10**:98
CONVECTION CELL 5:232 *bibliog.*
continental drift **5**:229
Earth, heat flow in **7**:17–18
Ferrel cell **8**:59
flash flood **8**:153
geochemistry **9**:96
Hadley cell **10**:8
hurricane and typhoon **10**:317–319
sandstorm and dust storm **17**:63–64
seafloor spreading **17**:172
solar convection, Sun **18**:341
CONVENT 5:232–233
CONVENT (Louisiana)
map (30° 6′N 90° 50′W) **12**:430
CONVENTICLE ACT OF 1664
Clarendon Code **5**:37
CONVENTION, POLITICAL *see* POLITICAL CONVENTION
CONVERGENCE (mathematics) 5:233 *illus.*
Cauchy, Augustin Louis **4**:219
Dirichlet, Peter Gustav Lejeune **6**:188
function **8**:359
limit **12**:345
Maclaurin, Colin **13**:32
mathematics, history of **13**:225
series **17**:209
CONVERSE (Indiana)
map (40° 35′N 85° 52′W) **11**:111
CONVERSE (county in Wyoming)
map (42° 52′N 105° 30′W) **20**:301
CONVERSE, FREDERICK SHEPHERD 5:233 *bibliog.*
CONVERSION (law) 5:233
personal property
tort **19**:246
trover **19**:312
CONVERSION ELECTRON 5:233
CONVERTIBLE (automobile)
body design **2**:359
CONVEYOR 5:233–234 *bibliog.*
grain elevator **9**:282
mass production **13**:203–204
CONVOLVULUS *see* MORNING GLORY
CONVOY (Ohio)
map (40° 55′N 84° 42′W) **14**:357
CONVULSION 5:234 *bibliog.*
barbiturate **6**:276 *illus.*
eclampsia **7**:39–40
epilepsy **7**:220
shock therapy **17**:279
CONWAY (Arkansas)
map (35° 5′N 92° 26′W) **2**:166
CONWAY (county in Arkansas)
map (35° 15′N 92° 40′W) **2**:166
CONWAY (Missouri)
map (37° 30′N 92° 49′W) **13**:476
CONWAY (New Hampshire)
map (43° 59′N 71° 7′W) **14**:123
CONWAY (Prince Edward Island)
map (46° 40′N 63° 59′W) **15**:548
CONWAY (South Carolina)
map (33° 50′N 79° 3′W) **18**:98
CONWAY, THOMAS
Conway Cabal **5**:234
CONWAY CABAL 5:234
Washington, George **20**:43
CONWAY SPRINGS (Kansas)
map (37° 24′N 97° 39′W) **12**:18
CONY *see* PIKA
CONYBEARE, W. D. 5:234 *bibliog.*
CONYERS (Georgia)
map (33° 40′N 84° 1′W) **9**:114
COOGAN, JACKIE 5:234
COOK (county in Georgia)
map (31° 10′N 83° 25′W) **9**:114
COOK (county in Illinois)
map (41° 53′N 87° 38′W) **11**:42
COOK (Minnesota)
map (47° 51′N 92° 41′W) **13**:453
COOK (county in Minnesota)
map (47° 55′N 90° 25′W) **13**:453
COOK, CAPE
map (50° 8′N 127° 55′W) **3**:491
COOK, EBENEZER 5:234
COOK, FREDERICK A.
Peary, Robert Edwin **15**:128
COOK, GEORGE CRAM 5:234 *bibliog.*
Provincetown Players **15**:584
COOK, JAMES 5:234–237 *bibliog., illus., map*
Antarctica **2**:44 *map*
Australia, history of **2**:340 *map*
Canada, exploration of **4**:80 *map*
Cook Islands **5**:237
explorations **7**:336–337 *map*
Maori **13**:136
Melanesia **13**:284
New Zealand, history of **14**:161
Tasman Sea **19**:42
COOK, MOUNT 5:237
map (43° 36′S 170° 10′E) **14**:158
COOK, PETER
postmodern architecture **15**:464 *illus.*
COOK, THOMAS
tourism **19**:252
COOK, WILLIAM *see* TUDOR, ANTONY
COOK INLET
map (60° 30′N 152° 0′W) **1**:242
tidal energy **19**:193
COOK ISLANDS 5:237
flag **8**:143 *illus.*
map (20° 0′S 158° 0′W) **14**:334
COOK STRAIT 5:237
map (41° 15′S 174° 30′E) **14**:158
COOKE (county in Texas)
map (33° 37′N 97° 12′W) **19**:129
COOKE, ALISTAIR 5:237 *illus.*
COOKE, GEORGE FREDERICK 5:237 *bibliog.*
COOKE, JAY 5:237
COOKE, SAM
soul music **18**:71
COOKE, TERENCE J. 5:237
COOKEVILLE (Tennessee)
map (36° 10′N 85° 31′W) **19**:104
COOKIE
cake and pastry **4**:20–21
COOKIE MONSTER *see* MUPPETS
COOKING 5:237–240 *bibliog., illus.*
Brillat-Savarin, Anthelme **3**:486
Carême, Marie Antonin **4**:146
Child, Julia **4**:347
clambake **5**:36
cordon bleu **5**:261–262
Escoffier, Auguste **7**:237–238
Farmer, Fannie **8**:24
history
earliest types **5**:237–238
Indians, American **11**:120
midden **13**:390
Joy of Cooking **11**:456
modern cuisines **5**:238–240
oriental **5**:239–240
five-spice powder **8**:132
oven **14**:469
stove **18**:286
Teflon **19**:72
COOK'S HARBOUR (Newfoundland)
map (51° 36′N 55° 52′W) **14**:166
COOKTOWN (Australia)
map (15° 28′S 145° 15′E) **2**:328
COOL JAZZ **11**:389 *illus.*
COOLANT
cooling system, engine **5**:241–242
COOLEY, AARON *see* *COOLEY* v. *BOARD OF PORT WARDENS*
COOLEY, CHARLES HORTON 5:240 *bibliog.*
COOLEY, DENTON A. 5:240 *bibliog.*
COOLEY* v. *BOARD OF PORT WARDENS 5:240
Cooley rule **5**:240
Leisy v. *Hardin* **12**:279
COOLEY'S ANEMIA 5:240
malaria **13**:80
COOLIDGE (Arizona)
map (32° 59′N 111° 31′W) **2**:160
COOLIDGE (Georgia)
map (31° 1′N 83° 52′W) **9**:114
COOLIDGE (Texas)
map (31° 45′N 96° 39′W) **19**:129
COOLIDGE, CALVIN 5:240–241 *bibliog., illus.*
as president **5**:241
early career **5**:240–241
Northampton (Massachusetts) **14**:253
Republican party **16**:174–175 *illus.*
COOLING *see* REFRIGERATION
COOLING SYSTEM, ENGINE 5:241–242 *bibliog., illus.*
antifreeze **2**:61
expansion tank **5**:242
internal-combustion engine **11**:216
radiator **5**:242 *illus.*
sealed systems **5**:242
temperature indicators **5**:242
thermostat **5**:241–242 *illus.*; **19**:167
water pump and fan **5**:242 *illus.*
COOLING TOWER 5:242
COOMARASWAMY, ANANDA KENTISH 5:242–243 *bibliog.*
COON, CARLETON 5:243 *bibliog.*
COON RAPIDS (Iowa)
map (41° 52′N 94° 41′W) **11**:244
COON RAPIDS (Minnesota)
map (45° 9′N 93° 18′W) **13**:453
COONHOUND *see* BLACK-AND-TAN COONHOUND
COOPER (county in Missouri)
map (38° 50′N 92° 50′W) **13**:476
COOPER (Texas)
map (33° 23′N 95° 35′W) **19**:129
COOPER, ALICE
rock music **16**:249
COOPER, ANTHONY ASHLEY (1621–1683) *see* SHAFTESBURY, ANTHONY ASHLEY COOPER, 1ST EARL OF
COOPER, ANTHONY ASHLEY (1671–1713) *see* SHAFTESBURY, ANTHONY ASHLEY COOPER, 3D EARL OF
COOPER, ANTHONY ASHLEY (1801–1885) *see* SHAFTESBURY, ANTHONY ASHLEY COOPER, 7TH EARL OF
COOPER, FRANK JAMES *see* COOPER, GARY
COOPER, GARY 5:243 *illus.*
COOPER, JAMES FENIMORE 5:243–244 *bibliog., illus.*
Bumppo, Natty **3**:562
Deerslayer, The **6**:81
Leatherstocking Tales, The **12**:263
Mohegan **13**:503
COOPER, KENNETH H.
exercise **7**:330
COOPER, LEON N. 5:244
superconductivity **18**:350
COOPER, LEROY GORDON, JR. 5:244
Mercury program **13**:308
COOPER, PETER 5:244 *bibliog.*; **19**:450 *illus.*
Cooper Union **5**:244
Tom Thumb (locomotive) **19**:229
COOPER, SAMUEL 5:244 *bibliog.*
COOPER CREEK
map (28° 29′S 137° 46′E) **2**:328
COOPER-HEWITT MUSEUM 5:245
New York (city) **14**:145 *map*
COOPER RIVER
map (32° 46′N 79° 57′W) **18**:98
COOPER UNION 5:244
Cooper, Peter **5**:244
COOPERATIVE (agriculture)
See also COLLECTIVE FARM
Grange, National **9**:286
COOPERATIVE (business organization) 5:244–245 *bibliog.*
credit union **5**:336
retailing **16**:183
Saskatchewan (Canada) **17**:82
COOPERATIVE FOR AMERICAN RELIEF EVERYWHERE *see* CARE (Cooperative for American Relief Everywhere)
COOPERATIVE COMMONWEALTH FEDERATION
Canada, history of **4**:86
COOPERATIVE EDUCATION
Bennington College **3**:204
COOPERATIVE EXTENSION SERVICE, U.S.
agricultural extension service **1**:189
Agriculture, U.S. Department of **1**:194
COOPERATIVE MARKETING ACT
Volstead, Andrew J. **19**:631
COOPERATIVE REPUBLIC OF GUYANA *see* GUYANA
COOPERS (Alabama)
map (32° 46′N 86° 33′W) **1**:234
COOPER'S 12-MINUTE TEST (running) **7**:330 *table*
COOPERSTOWN (New York) 5:245
map (42° 42′N 74° 56′W) **14**:149
COOPERSTOWN (North Dakota)
map (47° 27′N 98° 7′W) **14**:248
COOPERSVILLE (Michigan)
map (40° 31′N 75° 23′W) **13**:377
COORDINATE GEOMETRY *see* ANALYTIC GEOMETRY
COORDINATE PLANE *see* COORDINATE SYSTEMS (mathematics)
COORDINATE SYSTEMS (astronomy) 5:245–246 *bibliog., illus.*
astrometry **2**:273
celestial sphere **4**:230
galactic coordinates **5**:246
COORDINATE SYSTEMS (mathematics) 5:246–247 *bibliog., illus.*
See also ANALYTIC GEOMETRY
axis **2**:378
Descartes, René **6**:126
differential geometry **6**:169
geometry **9**:107
parameter **15**:80
point **15**:381
scalar **17**:106
spherical trigonometry **18**:180
three dimensions **5**:247
translation (mathematics) **19**:274
trigonometry **19**:298
two dimensions **5**:246
COORDINATION COMPOUNDS 5:247–248 *bibliog.*
cadmium **4**:12
chemical nomenclature **4**:320–321
chemistry, history of **4**:328–329
cobalt **5**:83
geometric isomers **5**:247
gold **9**:226
hemoglobin *see* HEMOGLOBIN
isomer *see* ISOMER
ligand **12**:333–334
monofunctional ligands **12**:334 *table*
optical isomers **5**:248
states **5**:247
transition elements **19**:273
inorganic chemistry **11**:182
COOS (county in New Hampshire)
map (44° 45′N 71° 15′W) **14**:123
COOS (county in Oregon)
map (43° 15′N 124° 5′W) **14**:427
COOS BAY (Oregon)
map (43° 22′N 124° 13′W) **14**:427
COOSA (county in Alabama)
map (32° 55′N 86° 10′W) **1**:234
COOSA RIVER
map (32° 30′N 86° 16′W) **1**:234
COOSAWHATCHIE RIVER
map (32° 32′N 80° 52′W) **18**:98
COOT 5:248 *illus.*
See also RAIL (bird)
foot **3**:288 *illus.*
gallinule **9**:19–20
COOVER, ROBERT 5:248
COOWESCOOWE *see* ROSS, JOHN (Cherokee Indian)
COPAL *see* KAURI PINE
COPÁN (Honduras) 5:248 *bibliog.*; **10**:219 *illus.*; **14**:237 *map*
map (14° 50′N 89° 9′W) **10**:218
Quiriguá **16**:27
Stephens, John Lloyd **18**:255
COPAN (Oklahoma)
map (36° 54′N 95° 56′W) **14**:368

COPE (Colorado)
map (39° 40′N 102° 51′W) 5:116
COPE, EDWARD 5:248 *bibliog.*
COPEAU, JACQUES 5:248–249 *bibliog.*
COPELAND (Florida)
map (25° 57′N 81° 22′W) 8:172
COPENHAGEN (Denmark) 5:249–250 *map*; 6:110 *illus., table*
map (55° 40′N 12° 35′E) 6:109
Thorvaldsen, Bertel 19:180
COPENHAGEN, BATTLE OF 17:110 *illus.*
COPENHAGEN, PEACE OF
Thirty Years' War 19:171
COPEPOD 5:250; 15:331 *illus.*
plankton 15:332
COPERNICAN THEORY
astronomy, history of 2:278
Digges, Thomas 6:174
Galileo Galilei 9:15
COPERNICUS (artificial satellite)
OAO 14:313
COPERNICUS, NICOLAUS 5:250 *bibliog., illus.*; 15:283 *illus.*
astronomy, history of 2:278
geocentric world system 9:95
heliocentric theory
Rheticus 16:194
heliocentric world system 10:112
solar system 18:44–45 *illus.*
COPIAH (county in Mississippi)
map (31° 50′N 90° 25′W) 13:469
COPIAPO (Chile)
map (27° 19′S 70° 56′W) 4:355
COPLAND, AARON 1:351 *illus.*; 5:250–251 *bibliog., illus.*
Berkshire Music Festival 3:214
COPLEY, JOHN SINGLETON 5:251 *bibliog., illus.*
colonial styles in North America 5:111
Henry Laurens 12:238 *illus.*
John Hancock 10:34 *illus.*
Paul Revere 1:332 *illus.*; 16:186 *illus.*
Watson and the Shark 5:251 *illus.*
COPOLYMER 5:251
plastics 15:348
COPPENAME RIVER
map (5° 48′N 55° 55′W) 18:364
COPPER 5:251–254 *bibliog., illus., table*
abundances of common elements 7:131 *table*
azurite 2:384
bornite, deposit 3:402
brass 3:457
bronze 3:505
carbonate minerals 4:137
chalcopyrite 4:270
chrysocolla 4:421
cuprite 5:390
Daly, Marcus 6:15
electrolysis 7:114–115
electroplating 7:127 *illus.*
element 7:130 *table*
enargite 7:162
Enkomi, trading post 7:206
extraction: Weldon, Walter 20:97
Group IB periodic table 15:167
malachite 13:78–79
metal, metallic element 13:328
metallurgy 13:329–330
Beaker culture 3:139
native elements 14:47
nervous system, diseases of the 14:96
ore deposits
major ore deposits 14:424–425 *table*
Montana 13:550 *illus.*
world distribution 14:423 *map*
Zambia 20:353–354 *illus.*
oxide minerals 14:476
phytoplankton, plankton 15:332
printed circuit 15:550
pyrite 15:637
qualitative chemical analysis 16:6 *illus.*
refining, silver from 17:312
roof and roofing 16:306
smelting, Chalcolithic Period 4:270
sulfide minerals 18:334
technology, history of 19:62
tetrahedrite 19:127
transition elements 19:273 *table*
uranium minerals 19:478
vitamins and minerals 19:621
COPPER AGE *see* CHALCOLITHIC PERIOD
COPPER BEECH (tree) 3:160
COPPER BUTTE
map (48° 42′N 118° 28′W) 20:35
COPPER CENTER (Alaska)
map (61° 58′N 145° 19′W) 1:242
COPPER HARBOR (Michigan)
map (47° 27′N 87° 53′W) 13:377
COPPER MOUNTAIN (British Columbia)
map (49° 20′N 120° 33′W) 3:491
COPPER RIVER
map (60° 30′N 144° 50′W) 1:242
COPPERAS COVE (Texas)
map (31° 8′N 97° 54′W) 19:129
COPPERHEAD (snake) 5:254 *bibliog., illus.*
COPPERHEADS (U.S. history) 5:254 *bibliog.*
Vallandigham, Clement L. 19:506
COPPERMINE (Northwest Territories)
map (67° 50′N 115° 5′W) 14:258
COPPOLA, FRANCIS FORD 5:254
COPRA 5:254–255; 14:335 *illus.*
Samoans 17:46
COPROLITE 5:255
midden 13:390
sedimentary rock 17:185
COPTIC ART AND ARCHITECTURE 5:255 *bibliog., illus.*
ivory carving 5:255 *illus.*
Lalibela (churches) 12:171
mandorla 13:112
tapestry 19:31 *illus.*
COPTIC CHURCH 5:255 *bibliog.*
circumcision 4:442–443
Ethiopia
Amhara 1:368–369
Monastery of Saint Jeremiah
Saqqara 17:74
Monophysitism 13:537
COPTIC LANGUAGE
Afroasiatic languages 1:179
COPTS
Egyptology 7:90
COPYING MACHINE 5:255–256 *bibliog.*
business machines 3:589
electrostatic printing 7:127–128
mimeograph 13:434
COPYRIGHT 5:256 *bibliog.*
computer software 5:165
Library of Congress 12:318–319
COQUELIN, CONSTANT 5:257
COQUILLE (Oregon)
map (43° 11′N 124° 11′W) 14:427
COQUINA 5:257
limestone 12:345
COR PULMONALE 5:257
cardiovascular diseases 4:145
CORACLE 5:257
CORAL 5:257–258 *bibliog., illus.*
coral reef 5:258–260
fossil record 8:244 *illus.*
oceanic mineral resources 14:340
Paleozoic Era 15:43
Precambrian time 15:491 *illus.*
Silurian Period 17:310 *illus.*
CORAL GABLES (Florida) 5:258
map (25° 45′N 80° 16′W) 8:172
CORAL HARBOUR (Northwest Territories)
map (64° 8′N 83° 10′W) 14:258
CORAL REEF 5:258–260 *bibliog., illus.*; 14:333 *illus.*
atolls 5:258 *illus.*
coral 5:258–260
Crustacea 5:260
echinoderms 5:260
fauna and flora 5:259–260 *illus.*
fish 5:260
formation 5:258
Great Barrier Reef 9:308 *illus.*
lagoon 12:165–166 *illus.*
life 5:259–260
limestone 12:345
Lithothamnion 12:371
location indicating Permian climates 15:33 *map*
oil and gas fields 5:259
paleoclimatology 15:33 *map*
Recent Epoch 16:107
seamount 17:174
weapons testing 5:259
CORAL SEA 5:260
Great Barrier Reef 9:308 *illus.*
map (20° 0′S 158° 0′E) 14:334
Torres Strait 19:244
World War II 20:266
CORAL SNAKE 5:260 *bibliog., illus.*; 17:377 *illus.*
mimicry 13:435 *illus.*
CORAL TREE 5:260
CORALBELLS (botany) 5:260–261
CORALROOT (botany) 5:261
CORALVILLE (Iowa)
map (41° 40′N 91° 35′W) 11:244
CORALVILLE LAKE
map (41° 47′N 91° 48′W) 11:244
CORAM (Montana)
map (48° 36′N 114° 2′W) 13:547
CORANTIJN RIVER
map (5° 55′N 57° 5′W) 18:364
CORBETT, JAMES J. 5:261
CORBIN (Kentucky)
map (36° 57′N 84° 5′W) 12:47
CORBUSIER, LE *see* LE CORBUSIER
CORCAIGH (Ireland) *see* CORK (county in Ireland)
CORCORAN (California)
map (36° 6′N 119° 33′W) 4:31
CORCORAN GALLERY OF ART 5:261
Washington, D.C. 20:41 *map*
CORCOVADO GULF
map (43° 30′S 73° 30′W) 4:355
CORDAY, CHARLOTTE 5:261
CORDED WARE CULTURE
European prehistory 7:302–303
CORDELE (Georgia)
map (31° 58′N 83° 47′W) 9:114
CORDELIERS 5:261
CORDELL (Oklahoma)
map (35° 17′N 98° 59′W) 14:368
CORDELL HULL RESERVOIR
map (36° 25′N 85° 40′W) 19:104
CORDER (Missouri)
map (39° 6′N 93° 38′W) 13:476
CORDERO, ANGEL 5:261
CORDIERITE 5:261
CORDILLERA CENTRAL MOUNTAINS
map (18° 30′S 64° 55′W) 3:366
CORDILLERA DARWIN (Tierra del Fuego) 18:92 *illus.*
CORDILLERA ISABELIA MOUNTAINS
map (13° 45′N 85° 15′W) 14:179
CORDILLERA REAL MOUNTAINS
map (17° 0′S 67° 10′W) 3:366
CORDILLERAN MOUNTAIN BELTS
mountain 13:619
plate tectonics 15:355; 15:356
CORDILLERAN REGION (Canada)
Canada 4:72
CÓRDOBA (Argentina) 5:261
map (31° 24′S 64° 11′W) 2:149
CÓRDOBA (province in Argentina)
map (32° 0′S 64° 0′W) 2:149
CÓRDOBA (Spain) 5:261
Abd al-Rahman I 1:53–54
Great Mosque 13:570 *illus.*; 18:152 *illus.*
map (37° 53′N 4° 46′W) 18:140
Moorish art and architecture 13:570 *illus.*
Spain, history of 18:146 *map*
Spanish art and architecture 18:152
CÓRDOBA, FRANCISCO HERNÁNDEZ DE *see* HERNÁNDEZ DE CÓRDOBA, FRANCISCO
CÓRDOBA, GONZALO FERNÁNDEZ DE *see* FERNÁNDEZ DE CÓRDOBA, GONZALO
CORDOBÉS, EL *see* EL CORDOBÉS
CORDON BLEU (bird) 5:261
CORDON BLEU (cooking) 5:261–262
CORDOVA (Alabama)
map (33° 46′N 87° 11′W) 1:234
CORDOVA (Alaska)
map (60° 33′N 145° 46′W) 1:242
CORDOVA (Illinois)
map (41° 41′N 90° 19′W) 11:42
CORDOVA (Spain) *see* CÓRDOBA (Spain)
CORDOVA, ROBERTO SUAZO *see* SUAZO CORDOVA, ROBERTO
CORDUROY 5:262
CORDUS, VALERIUS
pharmacopoeia 15:220
CORE *see* CONGRESS OF RACIAL EQUALITY
CORE TOOLS
Paleolithic Period 15:38–39
COREA, CHICK
jazz 11:389 *illus.*
CORELLI, ARCANGELO 5:262 *bibliog.*
chamber music 4:272
CORELLI, FRANCO 5:262 *bibliog.*
CORFU (Greece) 5:262
map (39° 40′N 19° 42′E) 9:325
CORGI, CARDIGAN WELSH *see* CARDIGAN WELSH CORGI
CORI, CARL FERDINAND AND GERTY TERESA 5:262
CORIANDER 5:262 *illus.*
CORINNA (Maine)
map (44° 55′N 69° 16′W) 13:70
CORINNA (poetess) 5:262
CORINNE (Utah)
map (41° 35′N 112° 7′W) 19:492
CORINTH (Greece) 5:263
Greek art 9:339
history
Peloponnesian War 15:139
Periander, Tyrant of Corinth 15:165
Isthmian Games 11:308
CORINTH (Mississippi)
map (34° 56′N 88° 31′W) 13:469
CORINTH (New York)
map (43° 15′N 73° 49′W) 14:149
CORINTH, GULF OF
map (38° 19′N 22° 4′E) 9:325
CORINTH, ISTHMUS OF 5:263
map (37° 55′N 23° 0′E) 9:325
CORINTH, LOVIS 5:263 *bibliog.*
CORINTH CANAL 4:97 *illus.*
Corinth, Isthmus of 5:263
CORINTHIAN ORDER 2:131 *illus.*; 9:335 *illus.*
Greek architecture 9:337
Greek art 9:340–342
CORINTHIANS, EPISTLES TO THE 5:263 *bibliog.*
Clement I, Saint 5:49
CORINTO (El Salvador)
map (13° 49′N 87° 58′W) 7:100
CORIOLANUS, GNAEUS MARCIUS 5:263
CORIOLIS, GASPARD GUSTAV DE
mathematics, history of 13:226
CORIOLIS EFFECT 5:263; 14:322 *illus.*
atmosphere 2:301
cyclone and anticyclone 5:405
Ekman, Vagn Walfrid 7:98
jet stream 11:407
meteorology 13:341
monsoon 13:543–544
ocean currents 14:322 *illus.*
polar easterlies 15:393
Rossby waves 16:319
upwelling, oceanic 19:474
water wave 20:59
wind 20:169
CORK (botany) 3:269 *illus.*; 5:264 *illus.*
oak 14:311
CORK (city in Ireland) 5:263–264
map (51° 54′N 8° 28′W) 11:258
CORK (county in Ireland) 5:264
cities
Cork 5:263–264
CORK OAK 5:264 *illus.*
CORK TREE 5:264 *illus.*
CORMORANT 2:42–43 *illus.*; 5:264–265 *illus.*; 6:204 *illus.*
foot 3:288 *illus.*
Galápagos Islands 9:10
CORN (botany) 5:265–267 *bibliog., illus.*; 9:281 *illus.*; 14:235 *illus.*; 19:532 *illus.*
commercial uses 5:267
farms and farming 8:25–27
cultivation 5:265–266
fodder 8:192–193
harvester 10:65
gene bank 9:76
grass 9:295
hybrids 5:266–267
Inca 11:72
Nebraska 14:73 *illus.*
parasite
witchweed 20:192
plant breeding 15:342–343 *illus.*
starch 18:226
whiskey 20:133
CORN DANCE 5:267 *bibliog.*
Creek (American Indians) 5:337
CORN ISLANDS
Nicaragua Canal 14:180
CORN LAWS 5:267 *bibliog.*
Cobden, Richard 5:84
Peel, Sir Robert 15:132
CORN SALAD (botany) 5:267
CORN SNAKE 5:124 *illus.*
CORNEA
eye 7:348–349 *illus.*
eye diseases 7:351
keratography
photography 15:266
CORNEILLE, PIERRE 5:267–268 *bibliog., illus.*; 8:316 *illus.*
Cid, The 4:429
drama 6:259
CORNELIA (Georgia)
map (34° 31′N 83° 32′W) 9:114
CORNELIUS, PETER 5:268
CORNELL (Wisconsin)
map (45° 10′N 91° 9′W) 20:185
CORNELL, EZRA 5:268 *bibliog.*
Cornell University 5:268
CORNELL, JOSEPH 5:268 *bibliog., illus.*
Pipe and Glass Box (Eclipse Series) 5:268 *illus.*
CORNELL, KATHARINE 5:268
CORNELL UNIVERSITY 5:268
Arecibo Observatory 2:145
Cornell, Ezra 5:268
White, Andrew Dickson 20:134

CORNER BROOK (Newfoundland) 5:268; 14:167 *illus.*
map (48° 57′N 57° 57′W) 14:166
CORNET 5:268–269 *bibliog., illus.*
See also TRUMPET
Armstrong, Louis 2:179
Beiderbecke, Bix 3:171–172
CORNETFISH 5:269
CORNETI GAUDI, ANTONIO *see* GAUDÍ, ANTONIO
CORNETT 5:269 *bibliog.*
CORNFLOWER 8:179 *illus.*
See also BACHELOR'S BUTTON
CORNFORTH, JOHN W. 5:269
CORNICE 2:131 *illus.*; 5:269
CORNING (Arkansas)
map (36° 24′N 90° 26′W) 2:166
CORNING (California)
map (39° 56′N 122° 11′W) 4:31
CORNING (Iowa)
map (40° 59′N 94° 44′W) 11:244
CORNING (New York)
map (42° 9′N 77° 4′W) 14:149
CORNING (Ohio)
map (39° 36′N 82° 5′W) 14:357
CORNING, ERASTUS 5:269 *bibliog.*
CORNING GLASS COMPANY
glassware, decorative 9:204
CORNISH (fowl) *see* CHICKEN
CORNISH (Maine)
map (43° 48′N 70° 48′W) 13:70
CORNISH LANGUAGE *see* CELTIC LANGUAGES
CORNISH LITERATURE 5:269 *bibliog.*
CORNPLANTER (Seneca Indian) 5:269 *bibliog.*
scalping 17:107
CORNS *see* BUNIONS, CORNS, AND CALLUSES
CORNSTALK (Shawnee Indian) 5:269 *bibliog.*
CORNUCOPIA 5:269
CORNWALL (England) 5:270; 19:409 *illus.*
cities
Penzance 15:155
Cornish literature 5:269
Land's End 12:184
CORNWALL (Ontario)
map (45° 2′N 74° 44′W) 14:393
CORNWALL, PETER BRUCE
Dilmun 6:176
CORNWALLIS, CHARLES CORNWALLIS, 1ST MARQUESS 5:270 *bibliog., illus.*
American Revolution 1:359 *map*; 1:363
East India Company, British 7:31
India, history of 11:92
surrender at Yorktown 1:363 *illus.*
Yorktown Campaign 20:331
CORNWELL, DAVID *see* LE CARRÉ, JOHN
CORNYSH, WILLIAM
English music 7:203
CORO (Venezuela)
map (11° 25′N 69° 41′W) 19:542
COROCORO (Bolivia)
map (17° 12′S 68° 29′W) 3:366
COROCORO ISLAND
map (8° 30′N 60° 10′W) 9:410
COROICO (Bolivia)
map (16° 10′S 67° 44′W) 3:366
CORONA 5:270 *bibliog.*; 7:40 *illus.*; 18:225 *illus.*
chromosphere 4:419
coronagraph 5:270–271
Lyot, Bernard Ferdinand 12:479
Menzel, Donald Howard 13:303
OSO 14:456
radio astronomy 16:48
solar wind 18:53
spicule 18:181
Sun 18:343–345 *illus.*
CORONA (California)
map (33° 52′N 117° 34′W) 4:31
CORONA (New Mexico)
map (34° 15′N 105° 36′W) 14:136
CORONADO, FRANCISCO VÁZQUEZ DE 5:270 *bibliog.*
Cibola, Seven Golden Cities of 4:428
exploration of colonial America 7:336 *map*; 19:437 *map*
Kansas 12:21
Wichita (American Indians) 20:144
CORONAGRAPH 5:270–271 *bibliog.*
corona 5:270
Lyot, Bernard Ferdinand 12:479
Sun 18:343
CORONARY ARTERY 5:271 *illus.*
heart 10:92
heart diseases 10:96
CORONARY DISEASE *see* HEART DISEASES
CORONATION 5:271
CORONATION (Alberta)
map (52° 5′N 111° 27′W) 1:256
CORONEL (Chile)
map (37° 1′S 73° 8′W) 4:355
CORONEL BRANDSEN (Argentina)
map (35° 10′S 58° 14′W) 2:149
CORONEL DORREGO (Argentina)
map (38° 42′S 61° 17′W) 2:149
CORONEL PRINGLES (Argentina)
map (37° 58′S 61° 22′W) 2:149
CORONEL VIDAL (Argentina)
map (37° 27′S 57° 43′W) 2:149
CORONELES SÁNCHEZ FORTÍN PAREDES (Paraguay)
map (19° 20′S 59° 58′W) 15:77
CORONER 5:271
inquest 11:183
CORONETS *see* CROWNS AND CORONETS
COROPUNA MOUNTAIN
map (15° 31′S 72° 42′W) 15:193
COROT, JEAN BAPTISTE CAMILLE 5:271–272 *bibliog., illus.*
The Bridge at Narni 11:63 *illus.*; 12:192 *illus.*
Chartres Cathedral 5:272 *illus.*
COROZAL (Belize)
map (18° 24′N 88° 24′W) 3:183
CORPORA ALLATA
endocrine system 7:168
CORPORATION 5:272–275 *bibliog., table*
bond 3:376
business administration 3:586
capitalism 4:125
conglomerate (business) 5:180–181
financial statement 3:391–392 *illus.*
Fortune 50 5:273 *table*
Fortune 500 8:242
history 5:272–274
holding company 10:202
income tax 11:76–77
joint-stock company 11:440
merger 13:310
monopoly and competition 13:538–540
mortmain 13:592
multinational corporation 5:274–275
Watson (family) 20:67
ownership
institutional stockholders 5:274
stockholders 5:272–274
petroleum industry 15:214
pharmaceutical industry 15:219–220
public relations 15:610
Rockefeller (family) 16:250
role 16:271
stock (finance) 18:273–274
stock market 18:274–275
trustee 19:322
CORPORATION ACT OF 1661
Clarendon Code 5:37
CORPORATION FOR PUBLIC BROADCASTING
television, noncommercial 19:90
CORPORATIONS, BUREAU OF
Roosevelt, Theodore 16:310
CORPORATISM
representation 16:161
CORPSE
autopsy 2:368
funeral customs 8:363–364
CORPSE PLANT *see* INDIAN PIPE
CORPUS ARISTOTELICUM (treatise)
Aristotle 2:156
CORPUS CARDIACUM HORMONE
hormone, animal 10:237 *table*
CORPUS CHRISTI (Texas) 5:275
map (27° 48′N 97° 24′W) 19:129
CORPUS CHRISTI BAY 19:131 *illus.*
CORPUS CHRISTI COLLEGE (Cambridge University) 4:52
Thomson, Sir George Paget 19:175
CORPUS CHRISTI COLLEGE (Oxford University) 14:474
CORPUS CHRISTI CYCLE *see* MEDIEVAL DRAMA
CORPUS JURIS CIVILIS *see* JUSTINIAN CODE
CORPUS LUTEUM
menstruation 13:301
CORQUE (Bolivia)
map (18° 21′S 67° 42′W) 3:366
CORQUÍN (Honduras)
map (14° 34′N 88° 52′W) 10:218
CORRECTIONVILLE (Iowa)
map (42° 28′N 95° 47′W) 11:244
CORREGGIO 5:275–276 *bibliog., illus.*
ceiling fresco (San Giovanni Evangelista, Parma) 5:275 *illus.*
CORREGIDOR (Philippines) 5:276
CORRELATION AND REGRESSION 5:276 *bibliog.*
statistics 18:237
CORRELL, CHARLES *see* AMOS 'N' ANDY (radio comedy team)
CORRENS, KARL
biology 3:271
heredity 10:141
Mendel, Gregor Johann 13:294
CORRESPONDENCE PRINCIPLE 5:276
CORRESPONDENCE SCHOOL 5:276 *bibliog.*
Chautauqua 4:305
Open University 14:399
CORRIB, LAKE
map (53° 5′N 9° 10′W) 11:258
CORRIENTES (Argentina)
map (27° 28′S 58° 50′W) 2:149
CORRIENTES (province in Argentina)
map (29° 0′S 58° 0′W) 2:149
CORRIENTES, CAPE
map (20° 25′N 105° 42′W) 13:357
CORRIGAN, MAIREAD, AND WILLIAMS, BETTY 5:276 *bibliog.*
CORROSION 5:276–277 *bibliog.*
aluminum 1:316
iron 11:270
lubrication 12:447
magnesium 13:53–54
materials technology 13:220
nickel 14:183
oxidation and reduction 14:475–476
oxygen 14:477
reaction, chemical 16:99
tin 19:205
CORRY (Pennsylvania)
map (41° 56′N 73° 39′W) 15:147
CORSAIR (aircraft) 5:277 *illus.*
CORSAIR (pirate) *see* PIRACY
CORSE, CAPE
map (43° 0′N 9° 25′E) 8:260
CORSI, JACOPO
opera 14:399
CORSICA (France) 5:277 *illus.*
cities
Ajaccio 1:229
history
Bonaparte (family) 3:375–376
Paoli, Pasquale 15:62
map (42° 0′N 9° 0′E) 8:260
CORSICANA (Texas)
map (32° 6′N 96° 28′W) 19:129
CORSICO ISLAND
map (0° 53′N 9° 20′E) 7:226
CORSO, GREGORY 5:277 *bibliog.*
CORSON (county in South Dakota)
map (45° 43′N 101° 5′W) 18:103
CORT, HENRY 5:277–278 *bibliog.*
CORTAILLOD CULTURE
lake dwelling 12:171
CORTÁZAR, JULIO 5:278 *bibliog.*
CORTE REAL, MIGUEL
Rhode Island 16:201
CORTÉS, HERNÁN 5:278 *bibliog., illus.*
Aztec 2:383; 11:134 *illus.*
chocolate 4:402
Cuauhtémoc 5:377
Latin America, history of 12:216
Mexico, history of 13:362–363 *illus.*
Montezuma II 13:555
mustang 13:685–686
routes 5:278 *map*
slavery in the New World 17:353
Tenochtitlán 19:112 *illus.*
Tlaxcala (city in Mexico) 19:216
Tlaxcala (state in Mexico) 19:216
Velázquez de Cuéllar, Diego 19:537
Veracruz (city in Mexico) 19:548–549
CORTEZ (Colorado)
map (37° 21′N 108° 35′W) 5:116
CORTEZ MOUNTAINS
map (40° 20′N 116° 20′W) 14:111
CORTI, ORGAN OF *see* ORGAN OF CORTI
CORTICOID 5:278 *bibliog.*
adrenal gland 1:108
cholesterol 4:404
hormone, animal 10:236 *table*
steroid 18:261
CORTICOSTEROID *see* CORTICOID
CORTISOL *see* GLUCOCORTICOID
CORTISONE
Woodward, Robert Burns 20:213
CORTLAND (New York)
map (42° 36′N 76° 11′W) 14:149
CORTLAND (county in New York)
map (42° 36′N 76° 11′W) 14:149
CORTLAND (Ohio)
map (41° 20′N 80° 44′W) 14:357
CORTONA, DOMENICO DA
Chambord, Château de 4:302 *illus.*
CORTONA, PIETRO DA 5:279 *bibliog.*
Triumph of Divine Providence 3:89 *illus.*
CORTOT, ALFRED 5:279
CORUBAL RIVER
map (11° 57′N 15° 6′W) 9:399
CORUM (Turkey)
map (40° 33′N 34° 58′E) 19:343
CORUMBÁ (Brazil)
map (19° 1′S 57° 39′W) 3:460
CORUNDUM 5:279 *illus.*
birthstones 3:296 *table*
emery 7:155
gems 9:74–75
oxide minerals 14:476
ruby 16:337
sapphire 17:73
CORUNNA (Michigan)
map (42° 59′N 84° 7′W) 13:377
CORVALLIS (Oregon)
map (44° 34′N 123° 16′W) 14:427
CORVINUS, JAKOB (pseudonym) *see* RAABE, WILHELM
CORVINUS, MATTHIAS *see* MATTHIAS CORVINUS, KING OF HUNGARY
CORVISART, J.N.
examination, medical 7:326
CORVO (Portugal)
Azores 2:381–382 *map*
CORWIN, NORMAN
radio and television broadcasting 16:56
CORYDALIS 5:279
CORYDON (Indiana)
map (38° 13′N 86° 7′W) 11:111
CORYDON (Iowa)
map (40° 45′N 93° 19′W) 11:244
CORYDON (Kentucky)
map (37° 44′N 87° 43′W) 12:47
CORYELL (county in Texas)
map (31° 20′N 97° 50′W) 19:129
CORYNEBACTERIUM 5:279
CORYTHOSAURUS 5:279–280 *bibliog., illus.*
COS (Greece)
Dodecanese 6:212
COSA, JUAN DE LA 5:280
COSBY, BILL 5:280
COSECANT
trigonometry 19:298–299
COSELL, HOWARD 5:280 *bibliog.*
COSENZA (Italy) 5:280
map (39° 17′N 16° 15′E) 11:321
COSGRAVE (family) 5:280
Ireland, history of 11:264–265
COSHOCTON (Ohio)
map (40° 16′N 81° 51′W) 14:357
COSHOCTON (county in Ohio)
map (40° 16′N 81° 51′W) 14:357
COSIMO, PIERO DI
Sistine Chapel 17:329
COSINE 5:280 *illus.*
Taylor series 19:51
trigonometry 19:298
COSMAS AND DAMIAN, SAINTS 5:280
COSMATI WORK *see* MOSAIC
COSMETIC SURGERY *see* PLASTIC SURGERY
COSMETICS 5:280–283 *bibliog., illus., table*
costume 5:292–303
costume and makeup, theatrical 5:303
Food and Drug Administration 8:208
henna 10:121–122
hexachlorophene 10:154
history 5:280–282
lanolin 12:199
modern cosmetics 5:282–283
myrrh 13:691
perfume 15:164
peroxide 15:177
pure food and drug laws 15:628–629
retail sales 5:282 *table*
sandalwood 17:61
stibnite, antimony 2:63
talc 19:15
U.S. cosmetics industry 5:283
COSMIC RAYS 5:283–284 *bibliog., illus.*
Anderson, Carl David 1:401
Bothe, Walther Wilhelm 3:415
fallout 8:14
frequency, electromagnetic 7:117 *table*
Hess, Victor 10:152
High Energy Astronomical Observatory 10:161
Landau, Lev 12:181
photography
Blackett, Patrick Maynard Stuart, Baron Blackett 3:321
Van Allen radiation belts 19:510
wavelength, electromagnetic 7:117 *table*

COSMOGONY 5:284
Darwin, Sir George Howard **6**:42
COSMOLEDO GROUP (Islands)
map (9° 43′S 47° 35′E) **17**:232
COSMOLOGICAL DISTANCE *see* DISTANCE, COSMOLOGICAL
COSMOLOGY (astronomy) 5:284–289 *bibliog., illus.*
age of the universe **5**:286–287
Hubble's constant **10**:288
astronomy, history of **2**:280
background radiation **3**:12
Battani, al- **3**:125
big bang theory **3**:248
binary stars **3**:256
BL Lacertae objects **3**:303
black dwarf **3**:314
black hole **3**:315–316
Bondi, Hermann **3**:376
Boötes **3**:394
Bowen, Ira Sprague **3**:428
brown dwarf **3**:516
Chamberlin, Thomas Chrowder **4**:274
constitution of the universe **5**:285–286
Copernicus, Nicolaus **5**:250
corona **5**:270
cosmic rays **5**:283–284
cosmogony **5**:284
Dicke, Robert **6**:156
Earth, geological history of **7**:11
Earth sciences **7**:24
Eddington, Sir Arthur **7**:55
extragalactic systems **7**:345
astronomy and astrophysics **2**:284–285
Friedmann, Aleksandr **8**:332
future of the universe **5**:289
gamma-ray astronomy **9**:33–34
gravitation **9**:305
gravitational collapse **9**:305
Hawking, Stephen William **10**:77
heliocentric world system **10**:112
history of cosmology **5**:284–285
inflationary theory **11**:171
island universe theory
Hubble, Edwin **10**:288
Kepler, Johannes **12**:57–58
Lemaître, Georges Édouard **12**:280
life, extraterrestrial **12**:327–329
Local Group of galaxies **12**:385
Milne, Edward Arthur **13**:431
nebula **14**:74–75
non-Euclidean geometry **14**:216
Olbers's paradox **14**:373
origin of the universe **5**:288–289
Orion nebula **14**:444–445
planets **15**:329–331
quasar **16**:14–15
radio galaxies **16**:53–54
red shift **16**:114
relativity **16**:136–137
Sitter, Willem de **17**:330
solar system **18**:44–53
steady-state theory **18**:240
Gold, Thomas **9**:228
Hoyle, Sir Fred **10**:286
structure of the universe **5**:287
X-ray astronomy **20**:307
COSMOLOGY (philosophy)
See also METAPHYSICS
Confucianism **5**:179 *illus.*
creation accounts **5**:334–335
heaven **10**:100
hell **10**:113
COSMONAUTS, NON-SOVIET
Ivanov, Georgy (Bulgaria) **11**:333
Jähn, Sigmund (East Germany) **11**:349
Remek, Vladimir (Czechoslovakia) **16**:145
COSMONAUTS, SOVIET
Aksenov, Vladimir **1**:232
Belyayev, Pavel Ivanovich **3**:194
Beregovoi, Georgy T. **3**:208
Bykovsky, Valery **3**:602
Demin, Lev Stepanovich **6**:97
Dobrovolsky, Georgy T. **6**:209
Dzhanibekov, Vladimir **6**:320
Feoktistov, Konstantin P. **8**:51
Filipchenko, Anatoly V. **8**:79
Gagarin, Yuri **9**:8
Glazkov, Yury Nikolayevich **9**:206
Grechko, Georgy Mikhailovich **9**:324
Gubarev, Aleksei **9**:390
Ivanchenkov, Aleksandr **11**:333
Khrunov, Yevgeny **12**:68
Klimuk, P. I. **12**:97
Komarov, Vladimir **12**:107
Kovalenok, Vladimir **12**:126
Kubasov, Valery N. **12**:134
Laika (dog) **12**:167
Lazarev, V. G. **12**:252
Lebedev, Valentin **12**:267
Leonov, Aleksei **12**:292
Lyakhov, Vladimir **12**:473
Makarov, Oleg **13**:77
Nikolayev, Andrian **14**:195
Patsayev, Viktor **15**:114
Popovich, Pavel Romanovich **15**:431–432
Romanenko, Yury Viktorovich **16**:281
Rozhdestvensky, Valery **16**:332
Rukavishnikov, Nikolay **16**:344
Ryumin, Valery **16**:380
Sarafanov, Gennady Vasilievich **17**:74
Sevastianov, Vitaly I. **17**:215
Shatalov, Vladimir A. **17**:244–245
Shonin, Georgy Stepanovich **17**:281
Tereshkova, Valentina Vladimirovna Nikolayeva **19**:116
Titov, Gherman S. **19**:215
Volkov, Vladislav Nikolayevich **19**:629
Volynov, Boris Valentinovich **19**:633
Yegorov, Alekesi Stanislavonich **20**:322
Yegorov, Boris B. **20**:322
Yeliseyev, Aleksei Stanislavovich **20**:322
Zholobov, Vitaly **20**:362
Zudov, Vyacheslav Dmitriyevich **20**:381
COSMOPOLITAN WHOOPER *see* WATERFOWL
COSMOS (botany) 5:290 *illus.*
COSMOS (Minnesota)
map (44° 56′N 94° 43′W) **13**:453
COSMOS (satellite programs) 5:289–290
military warning and detection systems **13**:422
Salyut **17**:42 *table*; **17**:43 *table*; **17**:44
Venus probes **19**:539 *table*
COSSACKS 5:290 *bibliog.*
Chmielnicki, Bohdan **4**:402
Don Cossacks **6**:235
Mazepa, Ivan Stepanovich **13**:250
Razin, Stenka **16**:98
Russia/Union of Soviet Socialist Republics, history of **16**:355
Yermak Timofeyevich **20**:327
COST, INSURANCE, AND FREIGHT *see* C.I.F
COST ACCOUNTING *see* ACCOUNTING
COST-BENEFIT ANALYSIS 5:290 *bibliog.*
accounting **1**:78
decision theory **6**:73–74
COST OF LIVING *see* CONSUMER PRICE INDEX
COSTA, LÚCIO 5:290 *bibliog.*
Brasília **3**:457
Latin American art and architecture **12**:228
Neimeyer, Oscar **14**:185
COSTA, MANUEL PINTO DA
São Tomé and Príncipe **17**:72
COSTA BRAVA (Spain) **18**:142 *illus.*
map (41° 45′N 3° 4′E) **18**:140
COSTA DE MOSQUITOS
map (13° 0′N 83° 45′W) **14**:179
COSTA DEL SOL
map (36° 30′N 4° 30′W) **18**:140
COSTA DEL SOL (Spain)
Almería **1**:306
COSTA-GAVRAS, HENRI 5:291
COSTA MESA (California)
map (33° 39′N 117° 55′W) **4**:31
COSTA RICA 5:291–292 *bibliog., illus., map, table*
cities
San José **17**:55
economic activity **5**:291–292 *illus.*
education **5**:291
Latin American universities **12**:233 *table*
flag **5**:291 *illus.*; **8**:134
government **5**:292
history **5**:292
land and climate **5**:291–292 *map, table*
map (10° 0′N 84° 0′W) **14**:225
people **5**:291
pre-Columbian art and architecture **15**:496
COSTAIN, THOMAS B. 5:292
COSTELEY, GUILLAUME
Renaissance music **16**:156
COSTELLO, JOHN A.
Ireland, history of **11**:265
COSTELLO, LOU *see* ABBOTT AND COSTELLO
COSTER, ANNE VALLAYER- *see* VALLAYER-COSTER, ANNE
COSTER, CHARLES DE
Belgian literature **3**:175
COSTER, DIRK
hafnium **10**:9
COSTILLA (county in Colorado)
map (37° 15′N 105° 30′W) **5**:116
COSTILLA (New Mexico)
map (36° 59′N 105° 32′W) **14**:136
COSTILLA, MIGUEL HIDALGO Y *see* HIDALGO Y COSTILLO, MIGUEL
COSTMARY 5:292
COSTUME 5:292–303 *bibliog., illus.*
See also UNIFORM
Aegean civilization **1**:115 *illus.*
ancient times **5**:292–294 *illus.*
Arabs **2**:103–105 *illus.*; **2**:106
Balenciaga, Cristóbal **3**:36
Baroque Era **5**:297–298 *illus.*
bloomers
Bloomer, Amelia Jenks **3**:340
Chanel, Coco **4**:280
cowboy **5**:320 *illus.*
18th century **5**:298–301 *illus.*
Eskimo **7**:240
fashion design **8**:31–33
feather
hummingbird **10**:303
folk art **8**:196–198 *illus.*
folk dance **8**:200
gloves **9**:210
Indians, American **11**:121 *illus.*
Indians of North America, music and dance of the **11**:142–144 *illus.*
jewelry **11**:408–411 *illus.*
Middle Ages **5**:294–297 *illus.*
moccasin **13**:488
netsuke **14**:104
19th century **5**:299–303 *illus.*
Oceanic art **14**:337–338
ready-to-wear clothing
clothing industry **5**:65
Renaissance Era **5**:295–297 *illus.*
shoes **17**:279–280 *illus.*
tartan **19**:40–41
20th century **5**:302–303 *illus.*
umbrella **19**:380
wig **20**:146–147
zipper **20**:370
COSTUME AND MAKEUP, THEATRICAL 5:303 *bibliog.*
See also BALLET
design
Aronson, Boris **2**:186–187
Beaton, Sir Cecil **3**:145
Gris, Juan **9**:366
Kabuki **12**:4 *illus.*
Talma, François Joseph **19**:17
theater, history of the **19**:144; **19**:147
COSWAY, RICHARD 5:303–304 *bibliog.*
COTABAMBAS (Peru)
map (13° 45′S 72° 21′W) **15**:193
COTANGENT
trigonometry **19**:298–299
CÔTE, M. A. DE FOY SUZOR- *see* SUZOR-CÔTE, M. A. DE FOY
CÔTE D'AZUR (France) 5:304
cities
Nice **14**:180 *illus.*
CÔTE D'OR (France)
Burgundy **3**:570
COTEAU DES PRAIRIES
map (44° 30′N 96° 45′W) **18**:103
COTEAUX (Haiti)
map (18° 12′N 74° 2′W) **10**:15
COTINGAS 5:304
bellbird **3**:187
COTMAN, JOHN SELL 5:304 *bibliog.*
COTOCA (Bolivia)
map (17° 49′S 63° 3′W) **3**:366
COTONEASTER 5:304; **17**:288 *illus.*
COTONOU (Benin) **3**:199–201 *illus., table*; **5**:304
climate **3**:201 *table*
map (6° 21′N 2° 26′E) **3**:200
COTOPAXI 5:304; **18**:86 *illus.*
map (0° 40′S 78° 26′W) **7**:52
COTSWOLD HILLS
map (51° 45′N 2° 10′W) **19**:403
COTSWOLD-SEVERN 5:304 *bibliog.*
COTTAGE GROVE (Oregon)
map (43° 48′N 123° 3′W) **14**:427
COTTBUS (Germany, East and West)
map (51° 45′N 14° 19′E) **9**:140
COTTE, ROBERT DE 5:304 *bibliog.*
COTTER (Arkansas)
map (36° 16′N 92° 32′W) **2**:166
COTTLE (county in Texas)
map (34° 2′N 100° 15′W) **19**:129
COTTON 5:305–307 *bibliog., illus.*
Alabama **1**:237 *illus.*
cellulose **4**:238
cotton gin **5**:307
Whitney, Eli **20**:141
cotton market **5**:306
Memphis (Tennessee) **13**:292
cultivation **5**:305–306
Egypt **7**:78 *illus.*
farms and farming
harvester **10**:65
Mississippi **13**:472 *illus.*
slavery **17**:355 *illus.*
South Carolina **18**:101
Sudan **18**:322 *illus.*
Syria **18**:413 *illus.*
Texas **19**:132 *illus.*
textile industry **19**:136
calico **4**:29
Fall River (Massachusetts) **8**:13
fiber, textile **8**:67–68 *illus., map*
Gregg, William **9**:355
indigo **11**:144
Lowell, Francis Cabot **12**:444
madras **13**:43
Mercer, John **13**:304
muslin **13**:683
weevil **20**:91
COTTON (county in Oklahoma)
map (34° 20′N 98° 20′W) **14**:368
COTTON, JOHN 5:307 *bibliog.*
COTTON GIN 5:306 *illus.*; **5**:307 *bibliog., illus.*
slavery **17**:352
Whitney, Eli **20**:141
COTTON PLANT (Arkansas)
map (35° 0′N 91° 15′W) **2**:166
COTTON VALLEY (Louisiana)
map (32° 49′N 93° 25′W) **12**:430
COTTONDALE (Alabama)
map (33° 11′N 87° 27′W) **1**:234
COTTONDALE (Florida)
map (30° 48′N 85° 23′W) **8**:172
COTTONMOUTH *see* WATER MOCCASIN
COTTONPORT (Louisiana)
map (30° 59′N 92° 3′W) **12**:430
COTTONWOOD (Arizona)
map (34° 45′N 112° 1′W) **2**:160
COTTONWOOD (botany) 5:307 *illus.*
poplar **15**:431
COTTONWOOD (Idaho)
map (46° 3′N 116° 21′W) **11**:26
COTTONWOOD (county in Minnesota)
map (44° 0′N 95° 10′W) **13**:453
COTTONWOOD FALLS (Kansas)
map (38° 22′N 96° 32′W) **12**:18
COTTONWOOD RIVER
map (38° 23′N 96° 3′W) **12**:18
COTUÍ (Dominican Republic)
map (19° 3′N 70° 9′W) **6**:233
COTULLA (Texas)
map (28° 26′N 99° 14′W) **19**:129
COTYLEDON 5:307–308
flower **8**:183
seed **17**:187 *illus.*
COUBERTIN, PIERRE DE *see* DE COUBERTIN, PIERRE
COUDÉ TELESCOPE 5:308 *illus.*
COUDERSPORT (Pennsylvania)
map (41° 46′N 78° 1′W) **15**:147
COUGAR *see* PUMA
COUGHLIN, CHARLES E. 5:308 *bibliog.*
Union party **19**:387
COULEE CITY (Washington)
map (47° 37′N 119° 17′W) **20**:35
COULEE DAM (Washington)
map (47° 58′N 118° 59′W) **20**:35
COULOMB 5:308
charge, electrical **4**:288
coulombmeter **5**:308
electrochemistry **7**:113
units, physical **19**:466–467 *tables*
COULOMB, CHARLES AUGUSTIN DE 5:308 *bibliog., illus.*; **7**:107 *illus.*
Coulomb's law **5**:309
physics, history of **15**:283–284
COULOMBMETER 5:308
COULOMB'S LAW 5:309; **7**:108
charge, electrical **4**:288
electromagnetic units **7**:118–119
electrostatics **7**:128
Maxwell's equations **13**:242
potential, electric **15**:466
COULOMETRY
electrochemistry **7**:113
COULTERVILLE (California)
map (37° 43′N 120° 12′W) **4**:31
COULTERVILLE (Illinois)
map (38° 11′N 89° 36′W) **11**:42
COUNCE (Tennessee)
map (35° 3′N 88° 16′W) **19**:104

COUNCIL (Idaho)
map (44° 44′N 116° 26′W) **11**:26
COUNCIL, ECUMENICAL 5:309–310 *bibliog., illus., table*
Basel, Council of **3**:108
Chalcedon, Council of **4**:270
conciliarism **5**:170
Constance, Council of **5**:207
Constantinople, councils of **5**:209
Ephesus, Council of **7**:216
Ferrara-Florence, Council of **8**:58
heresy **10**:141
Lateran councils **12**:215
Lyon, councils of **12**:478
Nicaea, councils of **14**:178
Trent, Council of **19**:290
Vatican Council, First **19**:527
Vatican Council, Second **19**:527
COUNCIL BLUFFS (Iowa) 5:310
map (41° 16′N 95° 52′W) **11**:244
COUNCIL OF ECONOMIC ADVISERS 5:310
Heller, Walter **10**:115
president of the United States **15**:525
COUNCIL OF EUROPE 5:310
COUNCIL GROVE (Kansas)
map (38° 40′N 96° 29′W) **12**:18
COUNCIL MANAGER *see* CITY MANAGER
COUNCIL FOR MUTUAL ECONOMIC ASSISTANCE 5:310
COUNCIL OF NEW ENGLAND *see* NEW ENGLAND, COUNCIL OF
COUNCIL OF TRENT *see* TRENT, COUNCIL OF
COUNT (title) *see* TITLES OF NOBILITY AND HONOR
COUNT OF MONTE CRISTO, THE (book) 5:310
COUNTER-REFORMATION 5:310–311 *bibliog., illus.*
Bellarmine, Saint Robert **3**:187
Borromeo, Saint Charles **3**:404
Cajetan **4**:19
Canisius, Saint Peter **4**:108
education **7**:61
Europe, history of **7**:287
Francis de Sales, Saint **8**:274
Holy Roman Empire **10**:211
Ignatius Loyola, Saint **11**:32–33
Jesuits **11**:402
Neri, Saint Philip **14**:89
papacy **15**:65
Paul III, Pope **15**:118
Pole, Reginald **15**:395
Sixtus V, Pope **17**:331
Trent, Council of **19**:290
COUNTERCULTURE 5:311–312 *bibliog.*
communal living **5**:142
rock music **16**:249
On the Road **14**:388
Woodstock Festival **20**:213
young people **20**:335
COUNTERFEITING 5:312 *bibliog.*
forgery **8**:233
gems **9**:75
COUNTERFORCE STRATEGY *see* NUCLEAR STRATEGY
COUNTERINSURGENCY AIRCRAFT *see* COIN AIRCRAFT
COUNTERPOINT 5:312 *bibliog.*
See also ORGANUM
Albrechtsberger, Johann Georg **1**:261
Bach, Johann Sebastian **3**:11
Brahms, Johannes **3**:441
canon **4**:114
fugue **8**:355
Fux, Johann Joseph **8**:384
polyphony **15**:421
COUNTERTENOR 5:312
Deller, Alfred **6**:94
COUNTRY BUILDER'S ASSISTANT, THE (book)
Benjamin, Asher **3**:201
COUNTRY GENTLEMEN (periodical)
Curtis, Cyrus H. K. **5**:395
COUNTRY HOMES (Washington)
map (47° 45′N 117° 24′W) **20**:35
COUNTRY JOE AND THE FISH
rock music **16**:249
COUNTRY AND WESTERN MUSIC 5:312–313 *bibliog., illus.*
See also BLUEGRASS MUSIC
Campbell, Glen **4**:65
Cash, Johnny **4**:181
Denver, John **6**:117
Grand Ole Opry **9**:285
Nashville (Tennessee) **14**:24
Presley, Elvis **15**:532
Williams, Hank **20**:159
COUNTY 5:313 *bibliog.*
sheriff **17**:257
COUNTY FAIR *see* CARNIVALS AND FAIRS
COUNTY OF WASHINGTON v. GUNTHER
equal opportunity **7**:223
COUP D'ÉTAT
junta **11**:471
COUPER, ARCHIBALD SCOTT
chemistry, history of **4**:327
organic chemistry **14**:435
COUPERIN (family) 5:313–314 *bibliog.*
Chambonnières, Jacques Champion de **4**:275
COUPERUS, LOUIS
Dutch and Flemish literature **6**:314
COUPEVILLE (Washington)
map (48° 13′N 122° 41′W) **20**:35
COUPLET
versification **19**:562
COUPLING, HYDRAULIC
hydraulic systems **10**:331
COUPON BONDS *see* BEARER BONDS
COURAGEOUS, THE (yacht) **3**:352 *illus.*
COURANTYNE RIVER
map (5° 55′N 57° 5′W) **9**:410
COURBET, GUSTAVE 5:314 *bibliog., illus.*
The Artist's Studio **16**:103 *illus.*
Bonjour, Monsieur Courbet! (The Meeting) **5**:314 *illus.*
French art and architecture **8**:306
Proudhon and his Children **18**:21 *illus.*
social realism **18**:13
COURCELLES (Belgium)
map (50° 28′N 4° 22′E) **3**:177
COUREUR DE BOIS **7**:81 *illus.*
fur trade **8**:371
COURLAN *see* LIMPKIN
COURNAND, ANDRÉ 5:314
Richards, Dickinson Woodruff **16**:211
COURRÈGES, ANDRÉ
fashion design **8**:32
COURSER (bird)
shorebirds **17**:283
COURSING
dog racing **6**:222
COURT 5:314–316
advocate **1**:114
chancery **4**:279
equity **7**:226
common-law courts **5**:315
contempt **5**:227
court of appeals **5**:316
court of claims **5**:316
court of common pleas **5**:316
court-martial **5**:316
courts in civil-law countries **5**:316
criminal justice **5**:349–350
district court **6**:201
habeas corpus **10**:3–4
impeachment **11**:61
International Court of Justice **11**:219
judgment **11**:464
judicial review **11**:464
jurisdiction
Constitution of the United States **5**:219
jury **11**:477–478
justice of the peace **11**:478
King's Bench (15th century) **12**:245 *illus.*
King's Court **5**:139
legal procedure **12**:273
military justice **13**:421
parlement **15**:92
self-incrimination **17**:191
Supreme Court (U.S.) *see* SUPREME COURT OF THE UNITED STATES
Tax Court, U.S. **19**:45
trial **19**:291–292
will (law) **20**:153
witness **20**:192–193
work of the courts **5**:314–315
COURT, MARGARET SMITH 5:316
COURT OF APPEALS 5:316
appeal **2**:87
Hand, Learned **10**:35
legal procedure **12**:273
Supreme Court of the United States **18**:355
COURT OF CLAIMS 5:316
COURT OF COMMON PLEAS 5:316
development of common law **5**:139
COURT-MARTIAL 5:316 *bibliog.*
military justice **13**:421
COURT OF MILITARY APPEALS *see* MILITARY JUSTICE
COURT TENNIS *see* TENNIS
COURTAULD INSTITUTE OF ART 5:316 *bibliog.*
COURTELINE, GEORGES 5:316–317
COURTENAY (British Columbia)
map (49° 41′N 125° 0′W) **3**:491
COURTLAND (Alabama)
map (34° 40′N 87° 18′W) **1**:234
COURTLAND (Virginia)
map (36° 43′N 77° 4′W) **19**:607
COURTLY LOVE 5:317 *bibliog.*
Chrétien de Troyes **4**:410
French literature **8**:315
Guillaume de Lorris **9**:395
Marie de France **13**:151
minstrels, minnesingers, and troubadours **13**:460
Provençal literature **15**:583
Roman de la Rose, Le **16**:278
women in society **20**:202
COURTOIS, BERNARD
iodine **11**:238
COURTSHIP
animal courtship and mating **2**:20–22
marriage **13**:164
COUSHATTA (Louisiana)
map (32° 0′N 93° 21′W) **12**:430
COUSIN, JEAN 5:317 *bibliog.*
COUSIN, VICTOR 5:317 *bibliog.*
COUSINS, NORMAN 5:317
COUSTEAU, JACQUES-YVES 5:317–318 *bibliog., illus.*
skin diving **17**:342
COUSTOU (family) 5:318 *bibliog.*
Coysevox, Antoine **5**:323
COUSY, BOB 3:113 *illus.*; 5:318 *bibliog.*
COUTURE, THOMAS 5:318 *bibliog.*
COUVADE 5:318 *bibliog.*
passage rites **15**:103
COUZENS, JAMES 5:318 *bibliog.*
COVALENT BOND *see* CHEMICAL BOND
COVARIANCE *see* VARIANCE AND COVARIANCE
COVARRUBIAS, MIGUEL 5:318 *bibliog.*
COVE (Oregon)
map (45° 18′N 117° 49′W) **14**:427
COVELO (California)
map (39° 48′N 123° 15′W) **4**:31
COVENANT (law) 5:319
encumbrance **7**:163
COVENANT (religion) 5:319 *bibliog.*
Genesis, Book of **9**:78
Last Supper **12**:214
Moses **13**:600
Noah **14**:207
COVENANTERS 5:319 *bibliog.*
Charles II, King of England, Scotland, and Ireland **4**:291–292
Henderson, Alexander **10**:121
Montrose, James Graham, 1st Marquess of **13**:560
COVENT GARDEN 5:319 *bibliog.*; 12:401 *map*
Cooke, George Frederick **5**:237
Kemble (family) **12**:41
Royal Ballet, The **16**:329
COVENTRY (England) 5:319
map (52° 25′N 1° 30′W) **19**:403
COVENTRY (Rhode Island)
map (41° 41′N 71° 34′W) **16**:198
COVENTRY CATHEDRAL 5:319 *bibliog.*
Spence, Sir Basil **18**:177
COVERDALE, MILES 5:319–320 *bibliog.*
COVERED WAGON *see* CONESTOGA (wagon); WAGON
COVERED WELLS (Arizona)
map (32° 10′N 112° 8′W) **2**:160
COVILHA (Portugal)
map (40° 17′N 7° 30′W) **15**:449
COVINGTON (county in Alabama)
map (31° 20′N 86° 30′W) **1**:234
COVINGTON (Georgia)
map (33° 35′N 83° 53′W) **9**:114
COVINGTON (Indiana)
map (40° 9′N 87° 24′W) **11**:111
COVINGTON (Kentucky)
map (39° 5′N 84° 30′W) **12**:47
COVINGTON (Louisiana)
map (30° 29′N 90° 6′W) **12**:430
COVINGTON (county in Mississippi)
map (31° 40′N 89° 35′W) **13**:469
COVINGTON (Ohio)
map (40° 7′N 84° 21′W) **14**:357
COVINGTON (Oklahoma)
map (36° 18′N 97° 35′W) **14**:368
COVINGTON (Tennessee)
map (35° 34′N 89° 38′W) **19**:104
COVINGTON (Virginia)
map (37° 47′N 79° 59′W) **19**:607
COW *see* CATTLE AND CATTLE RAISING; DAIRYING
COW HEAD (Newfoundland)
map (49° 55′N 57° 48′W) **14**:166
COWAN, CLYDE L.
neutrino **14**:108
COWAN, LOUIS G.
radio and television broadcasting **16**:58
COWANSVILLE (Quebec)
map (45° 12′N 72° 45′W) **16**:18
COWARD, SIR NOEL 5:320 *bibliog., illus.*
Lean, David **12**:259
COWBIRD 5:320 *illus.*
COWBOY 5:320–321 *bibliog., illus.*; 8:342 *illus.*
Argentina **2**:150 *illus.*
frontier **8**:342
Hickok, Wild Bill **10**:157
rodeo **16**:266
Rogers, Will **16**:269
COWCATCHER
locomotive **12**:389
COWDEN (Illinois)
map (39° 15′N 88° 52′W) **11**:42
COWELL, HENRY 5:321 *bibliog.*
COWEN (West Virginia)
map (38° 25′N 80° 34′W) **20**:111
COWEN, SIR ZELMAN 5:321
COWETA (county in Georgia)
map (33° 25′N 84° 45′W) **9**:114
COWFISH *see* BOXFISH
COWLES, GARDNER 5:321
COWLEY (county in Kansas)
map (37° 15′N 96° 50′W) **12**:18
COWLEY, ABRAHAM 5:321 *bibliog.*
COWLEY, MALCOLM 5:321
COWLITZ (county in Washington)
map (46° 7′N 122° 43′W) **20**:35
COWLITZ RIVER
map (46° 5′N 122° 53′W) **20**:35
COWPEA 5:321 *illus.*
COWPEN MOUNTAIN
map (34° 54′N 84° 33′W) **9**:114
COWPENS (South Carolina)
map (35° 1′N 81° 48′W) **18**:98
COWPENS, BATTLE OF 5:322
Greene, Nathanael **9**:350–351
COWPER, WILLIAM 5:322 *bibliog., illus.*
COWPER'S GLAND **16**:163 *illus.*
COWPOX 5:322 *bibliog.*
diseases, animal **6**:190–191
smallpox **17**:365
Jenner, Edward **11**:396
vaccinia **19**:502
COWRIE 5:322
shell **17**:251 *illus.*
COWSLIP (botany) 5:322
Virginia cowslip (botany) **19**:612
COX, ARCHIBALD 5:322
Common Cause **5**:138
Nixon, Richard M. **14**:206
Watergate **20**:64
COX, HARVEY 5:322
COX, JACOB DOLSON 5:322
COX, JAMES M. 5:322–323 *bibliog.*
COXCATLÁN
Tehuacán Valley **19**:73
COXE, TENCH 5:323 *bibliog.*
COXEY, JACOB S.
Coxey's Army **5**:323
COXEY'S ARMY 5:323 *bibliog.*
COXIM (Brazil)
map (18° 30′S 54° 45′W) **3**:460
COX'S COVE (Newfoundland)
map (49° 7′N 58° 5′W) **14**:166
COXSACKIE (New York)
map (42° 21′N 73° 48′W) **14**:149
COYOTE 5:323 *bibliog., illus.*; 9:300 *illus.*
COYOTE (mythological character)
folklore **8**:203
COYOTILLO 5:323
COYPEL (family) 5:323 *bibliog.*
COYPU *see* NUTRIA
COYSEVOX, ANTOINE 5:323 *bibliog.*
Coustou (family) **5**:318
COYUCA DE CATALÁN (Mexico)
map (18° 20′N 100° 39′W) **13**:357
COZAD (Nebraska)
map (40° 52′N 99° 59′W) **14**:70
COZENS (family) 5:323–324 *bibliog.*
COZUMEL (Mexico)
map (20° 31′N 86° 55′W) **13**:357
Quintana Roo **16**:27
COZYMASE
Euler-Chelpin, Hans von **7**:265
COZZENS, JAMES GOULD 5:324
CPA *see* CERTIFIED PUBLIC ACCOUNTANT
CPB *see* CORPORATION FOR PUBLIC BROADCASTING
CPR *see* CARDIOPULMONARY RESUSCITATION
CPU *see* CENTRAL PROCESSING UNIT

CPUSA *see* COMMUNIST PARTY, U.S.A.
CRAB 5:324–325 *bibliog., illus.*
arthropod 2:217–218 *illus.*
crustacean 5:369–370
fiddler crab 8:70; 11:229 *illus.*
hermit crab 10:143; 11:229 *illus.*
horseshoe crab 10:252
intertidal life 11:230
Maryland 13:191
plankton 15:332
rock crab 11:229 *illus.*
shellfish 17:254–255 *illus.*
CRAB APPLE 5:325
CRAB HILL (Barbados)
map (13° 19′N 59° 38′W) 3:75
CRAB LOUSE
skin diseases 17:342
CRAB NEBULA 5:325–326 *bibliog., illus.*
Friedman, Herbert 8:331
pulsar 15:621 *illus.*
radio astronomy 16:49
supernova 18:352
Taurus 19:45
x-ray astronomy 20:307 *illus.*
CRAB ORCHARD (Kentucky)
map (37° 28′N 84° 30′W) 12:47
CRAB ORCHARD (Tennessee)
map (35° 55′N 84° 53′W) 19:104
CRAB ORCHARD LAKE
map (37° 43′N 89° 5′W) 11:42
CRABBE, GEORGE 5:326 *bibliog.*
CRABEATER SEAL
Antarctica 2:43
CRABPLOVER
shorebirds 17:283
CRACKING PROCESS (chemistry)
petroleum industry 15:205 *illus.*; 15:206 *illus.*; 15:214 *illus.*
pyrolysis 15:637
CRACOW (Poland) *see* KRAKÓW (Poland)
CRADLE OF LIBERTY *see* FANEUIL HALL
CRADOCK, SIR CHRISTOPHER
World War I 20:228
CRAFT 5:326–328 *bibliog., illus.*
See also DECORATIVE ARTS
CRAFT UNION
labor union 12:155
CRAFTS, JAMES MASON 5:328
CRAGUN, RICHARD ALLAN 5:328
CRAIG (Colorado)
map (40° 31′N 107°33′W) 5:116
CRAIG (county in Oklahoma)
map (36° 45′N 95° 15′W) 14:368
CRAIG (county in Virginia)
map (37° 30′N 80° 10′W) 19:607
CRAIG, GORDON 5:328 *bibliog.*
Duncan, Isadora 6:299
puppet 15:627
Terry, Dame Ellen Alice 19:122
The Vikings at Helgeland set 19:151 *illus.*
CRAIG, SIR JAMES 5:328
CRAIGHEAD (county in Arkansas)
map (35° 50′N 90° 40′W) 2:166
CRAIGMYLE (Alberta)
map (51° 40′N 112° 15′W) 1:256
CRAIOVA (Romania) 5:328
map (44° 19′N 23° 48′E) 16:288
CRAKOW (shoe) 17:280 *illus.*
CRAM, RALPH ADAMS 5:328 *bibliog.*
Saint John the Divine, Cathedral of 17:19
CRAMER, JOHANN BAPTIST 5:328 *bibliog.*
CRAMER'S RULE 5:328 *illus.*
CRANACH, LUCAS, THE ELDER 5:329 *bibliog., illus.*
Caritas 5:329 *illus.*
Freiburg im Breisgau (West Germany) 8:301
Venus and Cupid 9:126 *illus.*
Wittenberg (East Germany) 20:193
CRANACH, LUCAS, THE YOUNGER
Crucifixion 7:287 *illus.*
CRANBERRY 5:329
harvest 13:210 *illus.*
CRANBERRY PORTAGE (Manitoba)
map (54° 35′N 101° 23′W) 13:119
CRANBROOK (British Columbia)
map (49° 31′N 115° 46′W) 3:491
CRANBROOK FOUNDATION 5:329
CRANDON (Wisconsin)
map (45° 34′N 88° 54′W) 20:185
CRANE (bird) 3:280 *illus.*; 5:330 *bibliog., illus.*
crowned crane 5:330 *illus.*
demoiselle 18:257 *illus.*
limpkin 12:347
sandhill crane 5:330 *illus.*
whooping crane 20:143–144
CRANE (machine) *see* DERRICK AND CRANE
CRANE (Missouri)
map (36° 54′N 93° 34′W) 13:476
CRANE (Texas)
map (31° 24′N 102° 21′W) 19:129
CRANE (county in Texas)
map (31° 23′N 102° 30′W) 19:129
CRANE, HART 5:330 *bibliog.*
CRANE, STEPHEN 1:346 *illus.*; 5:330–331 *bibliog., illus.*
Red Badge of Courage, The 16:112
CRANE, WALTER 5:331 *bibliog.*
CRANE FLY 5:331 *illus.*
CRANESBILL (botany) *see* GERANIUM
CRANFORD (New Jersey)
map (40° 39′N 74° 19′W) 14:129
CRANIAL CAPACITY
Homo sapiens 10:215 *illus.*
Peking man 10:215 *illus.*
CRANIAL NERVE
brain 3:445
nervous system 14:93 *illus.*
peripheral nervous system 15:171
CRANK
machine 13:19–20 *illus.*
CRANKO, JOHN 5:331 *bibliog.*
Haydée, Marcia 10:80
Stuttgart Ballet 18:310
CRANMER, THOMAS 5:331–332 *bibliog., illus.*
Oxford (England) 14:474
CRANNOG
lake dwelling 12:171
CRANSTON (Rhode Island) 5:332
map (41° 47′N 71° 26′W) 16:198
CRAPE MYRTLE 5:332 *illus.*
CRAPPIE 5:332 *illus.*
CRAPS (game) 14:132 *illus.*
dice games 6:155 *illus.*
CRASHAW, RICHARD 5:332 *bibliog.*
CRASKE, LEONARD
Gloucester (Massachusetts) 9:209
CRASSUS, MARCUS LICINIUS 5:332–333 *bibliog.*
Caesar, Gaius Julius 4:14
Pompey the Great 15:425
Spartacus 18:165
CRATER
See also METEOR CRATERS; METEOR AND METEORITE; VOLCANO
Moon, far side 13:565 *map*
CRATER LAKE 5:333
map (42° 56′N 122° 6′W) 14:427
national parks 14:38 *map, table*
CRATERS OF THE MOON NATIONAL MONUMENT 5:333; 11:29 *illus.*; 14:38–39 *map, table*
CRATES OF MALLUS
globe 9:208
CRATÉUS (Brazil)
map (5° 10′S 40° 40′W) 3:460
CRATINUS 5:333
CRATO (Brazil)
map (7° 14′S 39° 23′W) 3:460
CRAVEN (county in North Carolina)
map (35° 15′N 77° 10′W) 14:242
CRAWFISH *see* CRAYFISH
CRAWFORD (county in Arkansas)
map (35° 35′N 94° 15′W) 2:166
CRAWFORD (Colorado)
map (38° 42′N 107° 37′W) 5:116
CRAWFORD (county in Georgia)
map (32° 40′N 84° 0′W) 9:114
CRAWFORD (county in Illinois)
map (39° 0′N 87° 45′W) 11:42
CRAWFORD (county in Indiana)
map (38° 20′N 86° 25′W) 11:111
CRAWFORD (county in Iowa)
map (42° 2′N 94° 22′W) 11:244
CRAWFORD (county in Kansas)
map (37° 30′N 94° 50′W) 12:18
CRAWFORD (county in Michigan)
map (44° 40′N 84° 35′W) 13:377
CRAWFORD (Mississippi)
map (33° 18′N 88° 37′W) 13:469
CRAWFORD (county in Missouri)
map (38° 0′N 91° 20′W) 13:476
CRAWFORD (Nebraska)
map (42° 41′N 103° 25′W) 14:70
CRAWFORD (county in Ohio)
map (40° 48′N 82° 58′W) 14:357
CRAWFORD (county in Pennsylvania)
map (41° 39′N 80° 10′W) 15:147
CRAWFORD (county in Wisconsin)
map (43° 15′N 90° 58′W) 20:185
CRAWFORD, CHERYL 5:333
Actors Studio 1:90
Group Theatre, The 9:376–377
CRAWFORD, FRANCIS MARION 5:333
CRAWFORD, ISABELLA VALANCY 5:333
CRAWFORD, JOAN 5:333 *bibliog.*
CRAWFORD, THOMAS 5:333 *bibliog.*
CRAWFORD, WILLIAM H. 5:333 *bibliog.*
CRAWFORD NOTCH
map (43° 11′N 71° 24′W) 14:123
CRAWFORDSVILLE (Indiana)
map (40° 2′N 86° 54′W) 11:111
CRAWFORDVILLE (Florida)
map (30° 11′N 84° 23′W) 8:172
CRAWFORDVILLE (Georgia)
map (33° 33′N 82° 54′W) 9:114
CRAWL (swimming)
swimming and diving 18:390–391 *illus.*
CRAXI, BETTINO 5:333
Italy, history of 11:331
CRAYENCOUR, MARGUERITE DE *see* YOURCENAR, MARGUERITE
CRAYFISH 5:333–334 *bibliog.*, 12:168 *illus.*
anatomy 5:370 *illus.*
arthropod 2:216–218
circulatory system 4:439 *illus.*
crustacean 5:369–370 *illus.*
CRAYON
drawing 6:263
CRAZY HORSE (Sioux Indian) 5:334 *bibliog.*
Gall 9:16
Sitting Bull 17:330
CRAZY MOUNTAINS
map (46° 8′N 110° 20′W) 13:547
CRAZY WIDOW *see* LIMPKIN
CREAM *see* ICE CREAM; MILK
CREAM, THE 5:334
CREAMCUPS (botany) 5:334
CREASEY, JOHN 5:334
CREATINE KINASE
muscular dystrophy 13:656
CREATION ACCOUNTS 5:334–335 *bibliog.*
Enuma Elish 7:209
Genesis, Book of 9:78
Kabbalah 12:3
mythology 5:334–335; 13:695
origin of life 12:327
scientific 5:335
women in society 20:201
CREATION OF ADAM (Michelangelo) 2:190 *illus.*
CREATION SOCIETY (literary group)
Kuo Mo-jo (Guo Moruo) 12:137
CREATIONISM 5:335–336
censorship 4:248
CREATIVITY
aesthetics 1:130–131
humanistic psychology 10:299
CRÉBILLON 5:336
CRÈCHE
doll 6:224–225
CRÉCY, BATTLE OF 5:336 *bibliog.*; 7:285 *illus.*; 9:312 *illus.*
Hundred Years' War 10:304–305
CREDI, LORENZO DI *see* LORENZO DI CREDI
CREDIT, LETTER OF *see* LETTER OF CREDIT
CREDIT AGENCY 5:336
See also CONSUMER CREDIT
Tappan brothers 19:34
CREDIT CARD 5:336 *bibliog.*
consumer credit 5:225
installment plan 11:194
CRÉDIT MOBILIER OF AMERICA 5:336
Colfax, Schuyler 5:101
Durant, Thomas Clark 6:303
transcontinental railroad 19:269
CREDIT UNION 5:336 *bibliog.*
banking systems 3:68
cooperative 5:244
finance company 8:92
money 13:527
CREE (American Indians) 5:336–337 *bibliog.*
Indians of North America, art of the 11:141
Man Who Gives the War Whoop 11:126 *illus.*
Poundmaker 15:476
CREE LAKE
map (57° 30′N 106° 30′W) 17:81
CREED 5:337 *bibliog.*
Nicene Creed
Jesus Christ 11:403; 11:406
Nicaea, Councils of 14:178
Trinity 19:300–301
CREEDE (Colorado)
map (37° 51′N 106° 56′W) 5:116
CREEK (American Indians) 5:337 *bibliog.*
Apalachee 2:74
Five Civilized Tribes 8:132
Georgia 9:117
Jackson, Andrew 11:341
McGillivray, Alexander 13:16
Mississippian culture 14:239
Oklahoma 14:371
removal to Indian Territory 11:109 *map*
Seminole 17:197
Shawnee (American Indians) 17:246
Tuscaloosa (Alabama) 19:354
Weatherford, William 20:82
CREEK (county in Oklahoma)
map (35° 55′N 96° 20′W) 14:368
CREEL (Mexico)
map (27° 45′N 107° 38′W) 13:357
CREELEY, ROBERT 5:337 *bibliog.*
CREEPER (bird) 5:337 *illus.*
See also PHILIPPINE CREEPER (bird)
CREEPING CHARLIE *see* MONEYWORT
CREEPING JENNY *see* MONEYWORT
CREIGHTON (Nebraska)
map (42° 28′N 97° 54′W) 14:70
CREIGHTON, JAMES EDWIN 5:337–338
CREMATION 5:338 *bibliog.*
Bali 8:364 *illus.*
burial 3:571
cemetery 4:245
Chiusi 4:399
European prehistory 7:304 *illus.*
funeral customs 8:364
funeral industry 8:365
CRÉMAZIE, OCTAVE 5:338
Canadian literature 4:93
CREMIN, LAWRENCE ARTHUR 5:338
CREMONA (Alberta)
map (51° 33′N 114° 29′W) 1:256
CREMONA (Italy) 5:338
map (45° 7′N 10° 2′E) 11:321
CRENSHAW (county in Alabama)
map (31° 45′N 86° 20′W) 1:234
CRENSHAW (Mississippi)
map (34° 30′N 90° 12′W) 13:469
CREOLE (linguistics) 5:338 *bibliog.*
See also LINGUA FRANCA; PIDGIN
Romance languages 16:280
sociolinguistics 18:27
CREOLES (people) 5:338–339 *bibliog.*
Latin America, history of 12:219
Mexico, history of 13:363
Sierra Leone 17:297; 17:298
CREOSOTE 5:339
CREOSOTE BUSH 5:339
CRERAR, HENRY 5:339
CRERAR, THOMAS ALEXANDER 5:339
CRES ISLAND
map (44° 50′N 14° 25′E) 20:340
CRESAPTOWN (Maryland)
map (39° 36′N 78° 50′W) 13:188
CRESCENT (Oklahoma)
map (35° 57′N 97° 36′W) 14:368
CRESCENT CITY (California)
map (41° 45′N 124° 12′W) 4:31
CRESCENT CITY (Florida)
map (29° 26′N 81° 30′W) 8:172
CRESCENT LAKE (Oregon)
map (43° 29′N 121° 59′W) 14:427
CRESCO (Iowa)
map (43° 22′N 92° 7′W) 11:244
CRESS 5:339
peppergrass 15:157
CRESSKILL (New Jersey)
map (40° 57′N 73° 57′W) 14:129
CRESSON (Pennsylvania)
map (40° 28′N 78° 35′W) 15:147
CRESSON (Texas)
map (32° 32′N 97° 37′W) 19:129
CRESTA RACING *see* TOBOGGANING
CRESTED BUTTE (Colorado)
map (38° 52′N 106° 59′W) 5:116
CRESTFISH 5:339
CRESTON (British Columbia)
map (49° 6′N 116° 31′W) 3:491
CRESTON (Iowa)
map (41° 4′N 94° 22′W) 11:244
CRESTONE PEAK
map (37° 58′N 105° 36′W) 5:116
CRESTVIEW (Florida)
map (30° 46′N 86° 34′W) 8:172
CRESTWOOD (Kentucky)
map (38° 19′N 85° 28′W) 12:47
CRESWELL (Oregon)
map (43° 55′N 123° 1′W) 14:427
CRESWELLIAN 5:339 *bibliog.*
CRETACEOUS PERIOD 5:339–341 *bibliog., illus., map*
chalk 4:271
climate 5:341
coal and coal mining 5:76
continental drift 5:228
dinosaurs 5:341 *illus.*
Allosaurus 1:303
Corythosaurus 5:279–280
Gorgosaurus 9:251
hadrosaurs 5:341
hesperornis 10:151
Iguanadon 11:39
mosasaur 13:596
Pachycephalosaurus 15:5

Palaeoscincus 15:29
Protoceratops 15:578
Struthiomimus 18:303–304
Styracosaurus 18:311
Trachodon 19:258
Triceratops 19:296
Tyrannosaurus 19:367
fern 8:58
fossil record 5:341; 8:245–247
kimberlite 12:77
Mesozoic Era 5:339; 13:322
mineral formations 5:339
paleogeography 5:339
plate tectonics 15:354 *map*
polar wandering 15:393 *map*
rock formations 5:340 *map*
CRETE (Greece) 5:342 *bibliog., illus.*; 9:326 *illus.*
archaeology
Evans, Sir Arthur 7:312
Knossos 12:101–102
Minoan art 13:458–459 *illus.*
Phaistos 15:218
history
Aegean civilization 1:114–118
costume 5:293 *illus.*
women in society 20:201
World War II 20:256
Iráklion 11:249
map (35° 29′N 24° 42′E) 9:325
writing systems, evolution of 20:292
syllabaries 20:293
CRETE (Nebraska)
map (40° 38′N 96° 58′W) 14:70
CRETE, SEA OF
map (35° 46′N 23° 54′E) 9:325
CRETINISM
endocrine system, diseases of the 7:170
CREUS, CAPE OF
map (42° 19′N 3° 19′E) 18:140
CREUTZFELDT-JAKOB DISEASE
hormone, animal 10:237
nervous system, diseases of the 14:96
CREVASSE
cirque 4:444–445
glaciers and glaciation 9:193 *illus.*
CREVE COEUR (Illinois)
map (40° 39′N 89° 35′W) 11:42
CRÈVECOEUR, MICHEL GUILLAUME JEAN DE 5:342 *bibliog.*
CREWE (England)
map (53° 5′N 2° 27′W) 19:403
CREWEL WORK *see* EMBROIDERY
CRIB DEATH 5:342 *bibliog.*
CRIBBAGE 5:342 *bibliog.*
CRICHTON, MICHAEL 5:343
CRICK, FRANCIS 5:343 *bibliog.*; 20:378 *illus.*
biology 3:271 *illus.*
genetics 9:88
nucleic acid 14:289
Watson, James D. 20:67
Wilkins, Maurice 20:152
CRICKET (game) 5:343–344 *bibliog., illus.*
CRICKET (insect) 5:344 *bibliog., illus.*
soil organisms 18:39 *illus.*
CRICKET FROG 5:344
CRIME 5:344–347 *bibliog., table*
See also CRIMINAL JUSTICE
airplane hijacking 1:222
arson 2:190
assault and battery 2:264
barratry 3:93
Bertillon system 3:226
Black Hand 3:315
causes of crime 5:346–347
classification of crime 5:345–346
computer crime 5:160L
control of crime 5:347
crimes against the person 5:345
crimes against property 5:345
criminal justice 5:349–350
deportation 6:118
deviance 6:143
drug trafficking 6:281
euthanasia 7:311
felony 8:48
fingerprinting 8:93
forensic science 8:227
forgery 8:233
fraud 8:288
gambling 9:26
genocide 9:93
gun control 9:405
homicide 10:214–215
homosexuality 10:217
juvenile delinquency 11:480
kidnapping 12:71
larceny 12:206
Lombroso, Cesare 12:399
lynching 12:476–477
Mafia 13:46
manslaughter 13:128
marijuana 13:153
mayhem 13:248
measurement of crime 5:346
misdemeanor 13:466
murder 13:647–648
Murder, Inc. 13:648
organized crime 14:441
outlaws (U.S. history) 14:468–469
police 15:396
prevention, surveillance systems 18:366
psychopathy 15:601
radio and television broadcasting 16:60
rape 16:88
robbery 16:240
sociology 18:29
solicitation 18:54
statistics 5:346 *table*
syndicate 18:407
Union of Soviet Socialist Republics 15:554–555
white-collar crime 20:136–137
CRIME LABORATORY
chemistry 4:324
forensic science 8:227
CRIME AND PUNISHMENT (book) 5:347 *bibliog.*; 14:274 *illus.*
Dostoyevsky, Fyodor Mikhailovich 6:245
CRIME SHOWS *see* MYSTERY, SUSPENSE, AND DETECTIVE SHOWS
CRIMEA (USSR) 5:347–348 *map*
history
Cimmerians 4:431
Crimean War 5:348–349
map (45° 0′N 34° 0′E) 19:388
CRIMEAN ASTROPHYSICAL OBSERVATORY 5:348
CRIMEAN WAR 5:348–349 *bibliog., illus., map*
Balaklava, Battle of 3:30
Charge of the Light Brigade, The 4:288
causes
Nesselrode, Karl Robert, Count 14:97
nursing
Nightingale, Florence 14:193
Paris, treaties of 15:87
photography
Fenton, Roger 8:51
Russia/Union of Soviet Socialist Republics, history of 16:357
Russo-Turkish Wars 16:374
Sevastopol (USSR) 17:215
war reportage
Russell, Sir William Howard 16:351
CRIMINAL JUSTICE 5:349–350 *bibliog.*
accessory 1:76
accomplice 1:76
amnesty 1:375
arraignment 2:188
bail 3:26
Beccaria, Cesare Bonesana 3:150
capital punishment 4:123–124
Furman v. *Georgia* 8:371–372
complaint 5:157
confession (law) 5:177
contempt 5:227
counterfeiting 5:312
crime 5:344–347
defense counsel 6:83
embezzlement 7:151
entrapment 7:208–209
ex post facto law 7:326
extradition 7:341
felony 8:48
forfeiture 8:232
Hammurabi, Code of 10:31
immunity 11:59
indictment 11:144
insanity, legal 11:185
Bazelon, David L. 3:134
institutionalization 11:196; 11:197
jury 11:478
juvenile delinquency 11:480
law 12:243
legal aid 12:272
lie detector 12:324
lynching 12:477
manslaughter 13:128
mayhem 13:248
mens rea 13:300
military justice 13:421
misdemeanor 13:466
misprision 13:467
murder 13:647–648
nolo contendere 14:214
parlement 15:92
parole 15:97
plea bargaining 15:363–364
prison 15:554–555
prisoners' rights 15:555
prosecuting attorney 15:572
punishment 15:625–626
robbery 16:240
sentence 17:205
6th Amendment 17:331
socialist law 18:25
statute of limitations 18:239
tort 19:245
trial 19:292
CRIMINAL LAW *see* CRIMINAL JUSTICE
CRIMINALISTICS
forensic science 8:227
CRIMINALS *see* CRIME
CRIMINOLOGY *see* CRIME
CRINOID 2:350; 7:38 *illus.*; 15:34 *illus.*
cystoid 5:411
Ordovician Period 14:422 *illus.*
Triassic Period 19:293 *illus.*
CRIOLLE *see* MESTIZO
CRIPPEN, ROBERT 5:350
Space Shuttle 18:135–136 *illus.*
CRIPPLE CREEK (Colorado)
map (38° 45′N 105° 11′W) 5:116
CRIPPS, SIR STAFFORD 5:350–351 *bibliog., illus.*
CRISFIELD (Maryland)
map (37° 59′N 75° 51′W) 13:188
CRISIS, THE (periodical)
Du Bois, W. E. B. 6:285
CRISP (county in Georgia)
map (31° 55′N 83° 45′W) 9:114
CRISPI, FRANCESCO 5:351 *bibliog.*
CRISTAL MOUNTAINS
map (0° 30′N 10° 30′E) 9:5
CRISTILLO, LOUIS F. *see* ABBOTT AND COSTELLO
CRISTÓBAL COLÓN PEAK
map (10° 50′N 73° 41′W) 5:107
CRISTOBALITE 5:351
silica minerals 17:304
CRISTOFORI, BARTOLOMMEO
piano 15:288–289 *illus.*
CRITICAL ANGLE
refraction 16:124
CRITICAL CONSTANTS 5:351 *bibliog.*
van der Waals equation 19:513
CRITICAL MASS *see* CHAIN REACTION, NUCLEAR
CRITICISM, ART *see* ART CRITICISM
CRITICISM, DRAMA *see* DRAMA—criticism
CRITICISM, FILM *see* FILM, HISTORY OF—criticism, film
CRITICISM, LITERARY 5:351–352 *bibliog.*
American literature 1:345–347
Aiken, Conrad 1:202
Allen, Hervey 1:299
Anderson, Sherwood 1:402
Babbitt, Irving 3:5
Berryman, John 3:225
Blish, James 3:333
Bloom, Harold 3:340
Bogan, Louise 3:359
Brooks, Cleanth 3:511
Brooks, Van Wyck 3:511
Broun, Heywood 3:512
Brown, Charles Brockden 3:513
Brown, Sterling 3:516
Bryant, William Cullen 3:529
Burke, Kenneth 3:571
Calisher, Hortense 4:39
Canby, Henry Seidel 4:100
Chase, Mary Ellen 4:301
Cowley, Malcolm 5:321
Deutsch, Babette 6:136
Erskine, John 7:235
Fiedler, Leslie A. 8:70–71
Fuller, Margaret 8:357
Gass, William H. 9:56
Hardwick, Elizabeth 10:47
Howe, Irving 10:284
Kazin, Alfred 11:34
Matthiessen, F. O. 13:232
Mencken, H. L. 13:293
Olson, Charles 14:381
Parrington, Vernon L. 15:97
Poe, Edgar Allan 15:377–378
Ransom, John Crowe 16:88
Stedman, Edmund Clarence 18:243
Tate, Allen 19:44
Trilling, Lionel 19:299
Van Doren, Carl 19:513
Warren, Robert Penn 20:31
Wilson, Edmund 20:164
Winters, Yvor 20:181
Woollcott, Alexander 20:215
Danish literature
Brandes, Georg Morris Cohen 3:454
Dutch and Flemish literature 6:314
English literature
Abercrombie, Lascelles 1:56
Aldington, Richard 1:269
Alvarez, A. 1:319
Amis, Kingsley 1:372
Arnold, Matthew 2:185
Beerbohm, Sir Max 3:163
Bentley, Richard 3:205
Bradley, A. C. 3:437
Brooke, Rupert 3:509–510
Burgess, Anthony 3:569
Cecil, Lord David 4:228
Chesterton, G. K. 4:337
Coleridge, Samuel Taylor 5:100–101
Collier, Jeremy 5:103
Connolly, Cyril 5:197
Croker, John Wilson 5:357
Daiches, David 6:7
Dryden, John 6:284–285
Eliot, T. S. 7:139–140
Frye, Northrop 8:351
Gifford, William 9:177
Graves, Robert 9:302–303
Jeffrey, Francis 11:394
Johnson, Samuel 11:435–436
Lamb, Charles 11:174
Leavis, F. R. 12:263
Lewis, C. S. 12:305
Muir, Edwin 13:634
Pound, Ezra 15:475–476
Richards, I. A. 16:211
Rymer, Thomas 16:380
Shakespeare, William 17:237
Sidney, Sir Philip 17:295
Swinburne, Algernon Charles 18:392
Woolf, Virginia 20:214–215
French literature
Aubignac, Abbé d' 2:316
Banville, Théodore de 3:71
Barbey d'Aurevilly, Jules Amédée 3:78
Barthes, Roland 3:97
Becque, Henry François 3:152
Bonnefoy, Yves 3:381
Breton, André 3:474
Bruntière, Ferdinand 3:525
Chapelain, Jean 4:282
Cocteau, Jean 5:89
Gourmont, Remy de 9:266
Proust, Marcel 15:582–583
Sainte-Beuve, Charles Augustin 17:27
Staël, Madame de 18:209
German literature
Auerbach, Erich 2:319
Benjamin, Walter 3:202
Bouterwek, Friedrich 3:425
Herder, Johann Gottfried 10:138
Kraus, Karl 12:127
Lessing, Gotthold 12:298–299
Schlegel, Friedrich von 17:124
history of 5:351–352
Italian literature
Carducci, Giosuè 4:144
Castelvetro, Lodovico 4:187–188
De Sanctis, Francesco 6:62–63
Japanese literature
Tsubouchi Shoyo 19:325
narrative and dramatic devices 14:22–23
New Criticism 14:119
Russian literature
Aksakov, Konstantin Sergeyevich 1:232
Belinsky, Vissarion Grigorievich 3:182–183
Bely, Andrei 3:193–194
Brodsky, Joseph 3:501
Merezhkovsky, Dmitry Sergeyevich 13:309
Spanish literature
Alas, Leopoldo 1:240
CRITICISM, MUSIC *see* MUSIC CRITICISM
CRITIQUE OF PURE REASON (book) 5:352 *bibliog.*
Kant, Immanuel 12:23–24
CRITO (book) 5:352 *bibliog.*
CRITTENDEN (county in Arkansas)
map (35° 10′N 90° 20′W) 2:166
CRITTENDEN (county in Kentucky)
map (37° 20′N 88° 5′W) 12:47
CRITTENDEN COMPROMISE 5:352–353 *bibliog.*
Civil War, U.S. 5:19
CRIVELLI, CARLO 5:353 *bibliog.*
CRIVITZ (Wisconsin)
map (45° 14′N 88° 1′W) 20:185
CRO-MAGNON MAN 2:53 *illus.*; 5:353–354 *bibliog., illus.*

CRO-MAGNON MAN (cont.)
Altamira **1**:311
archaeology **2**:125
cave dwellers **4**:225
Lascaux **12**:210
Neanderthalers **14**:69
prehistoric art **15**:507–508
CROAKER *see* DRUM (fish)
CROATIA (Yugoslavia) 5:354–355 *map*
cities
Dubrovnik **6**:289
Pula **15**:618
Rijeka **16**:223
Šibenik **17**:291
Split **18**:191
Zadar **20**:348
Zagreb **20**:348
Dalmatia **6**:14
history
Yugoslavia **20**:343–344
Istria **11**:308
map (45° 10′N 15° 30′E) **20**:340
Plitvice Lakes **20**:341 *illus.*
CROATS
Croatia (Yugoslavia) **5**:354–355
literature
Yugoslavia **20**:342
CROCE, ARLENE 5:355 *bibliog.*
CROCE, BENEDETTO 5:355 *bibliog.*
CROCHET 5:355 *bibliog., illus.*
CROCKER (Missouri)
map (37° 57′N 92° 16′W) **13**:476
CROCKER, CHARLES
California **4**:37
CROCKER MOUNTAINS
map (5° 40′N 116° 14′E) **13**:84
CROCKETT (county in Tennessee)
map (35° 50′N 89° 10′W) **19**:104
CROCKETT (Texas)
map (31° 19′N 95° 28′W) **19**:129
CROCKETT (county in Texas)
map (30° 40′N 101° 20′W) **19**:129
CROCKETT, DAVY 5:355–356 *bibliog., illus.*
CROCODILE 5:356 *bibliog., illus.*; **11**:475 *illus.*; **16**:167 *illus.*
caiman **4**:17
Egypt, ancient
Ombos **14**:387
gavial **9**:62–63
Jurassic Period **11**:476 *illus.*
Tertiary Period **19**:124 *illus.*
CROCODILE RIVER *see* LIMPOPO RIVER
CROCODYLIA
crocodile **5**:356 *illus.*
CROCOITE **4**:417 *illus.*
CROCUS 5:356–357 *illus.*; **8**:170 *illus.*
meadow saffron **13**:252
saffron **17**:11
CROESUS, KING OF LYDIA 5:357
Herodotus **10**:144
Sardis **17**:77
Temple of Artemis at Ephesus **17**:217
CROFT, WILLIAM
English music **7**:203
CROFTON (Kentucky)
map (37° 3′N 87° 29′W) **12**:47
CROFTON (Maryland)
map (39° 1′N 76° 42′W) **13**:188
CROFTON (Nebraska)
map (42° 44′N 97° 30′W) **14**:70
CROGHAN (New York)
map (43° 54′N 75° 24′W) **14**:149
CROHN'S DISEASE *see* COLITIS
CROIX DE GUERRE (France)
medals and decorations **13**:262–263 *illus.*
CROKER, CAPE
map (44° 58′N 80° 59′W) **14**:393; **19**:241
CROKER, JOHN WILSON 5:357
CROKER, RICHARD 5:357
Tammany Hall **19**:20
CROKER, THOMAS CROFTON 5:357
CROMARTY (Scotland) *see* ROSS AND CROMARTY (Scotland)
CROME, JOHN 5:357 *bibliog.*
CROMER, EVELYN BARING, 1st EARL OF 5:357 *bibliog.*
CROMLECH *see* MEGALITH
CROMMELYNCK, FERNAND 5:357
CROMPTON, SAMUEL 5:357
Bolton **3**:372
spinning **18**:186
CROMWELL (Alabama)
map (32° 14′N 88° 17′W) **1**:234
CROMWELL (Connecticut)
map (41° 36′N 72° 39′W) **5**:193
CROMWELL, OLIVER 5:357–358 *bibliog., illus.*
English Civil War **7**:189
Great Britain, history of **9**:314
Ireland, history of **11**:263
Long Parliament **12**:407
Waterford (city in Ireland) **20**:63
Wexford (Ireland) **20**:119
Worcester (city in England) **20**:216
CROMWELL, RICHARD 5:358
CROMWELL, THOMAS, 1st EARL OF ESSEX 5:358 *bibliog., illus.*
Henry VIII, King of England **10**:126
CRONIN, A. J. 5:359
CRONKITE, WALTER 5:359 *bibliog.*
radio and television broadcasting **16**:57 *illus.*
CRONSTEDT, AXEL FREDRIK, BARON 5:359
CRONUS 5:359
mythology **13**:700
CRONYN, HUME 5:359
CROOK (Colorado)
map (40° 51′N 102° 48′W) **5**:116
CROOK (county in Oregon)
map (44° 5′N 120° 20′W) **14**:427
CROOK (county in Wyoming)
map (44° 30′N 104° 35′W) **20**:301
CROOK, GEORGE 5:359 *bibliog.*; **19**:451 *illus.*
Crazy Horse **5**:334
Geronimo **9**:158
CROOKED ISLAND
map (22° 45′N 74° 13′W) **3**:23
CROOKED LAKE
map (48° 13′N 91° 50′W) **13**:453
CROOKED RIVER (Saskatchewan)
map (52° 51′N 103° 44′W) **17**:81
CROOKES, SIR WILLIAM 5:359 *bibliog.*
CROOKSTON (Minnesota)
map (47° 47′N 96° 37′W) **13**:453
CROOKSVILLE (Ohio)
map (39° 46′N 82° 6′W) **14**:357
CROP DUSTING **1**:197 *illus.*
helicopter **10**:112
CROPSEY, JASPAR 5:359 *bibliog.*
CROQUET 5:359–360 *bibliog., illus.*
CROSBY (Minnesota)
map (46° 28′N 93° 57′W) **13**:453
CROSBY (Mississippi)
map (31° 17′N 91° 4′W) **13**:469
CROSBY (North Dakota)
map (48° 55′N 103° 18′W) **14**:248
CROSBY (county in Texas)
map (33° 38′N 101° 15′W) **19**:129
CROSBY, BING 5:360 *bibliog.*
Hope, Bob **10**:230
CROSBY, STILLS, AND NASH (musical group) **1**:352 *illus.*
CROSBYTON (Texas)
map (33° 40′N 101° 14′W) **19**:129
CROSS 5:360–361 *bibliog., illus.*
Early Christian art and architecture **7**:9–10
English art and architecture **7**:182
Gothic art and architecture **9**:260
inscription **11**:185
medals and decorations **13**:260–263 *illus.*
CROSS (county in Arkansas)
map (35° 20′N 90° 18′W) **2**:166
CROSS, WILBUR L.
Connecticut **5**:196
CROSS CITY (Florida)
map (29° 39′N 83° 7′W) **8**:172
CROSS-COUNTRY RUNNING *see* ORIENTEERING; RUNNING AND JOGGING; TRACK AND FIELD
CROSS-COUNTRY SKIING *see* SKIING
CROSS-DATING
prehistory **15**:517
CROSS-EYE *see* STRABISMUS
CROSS LAKE (Manitoba)
map (54° 37′N 97° 47′W) **13**:119
CROSS-POLLINATION *see* PLANT BREEDING; POLLINATION, SELF-POLLINATION
CROSS RIVER
map (4° 42′N 8° 21′E) **14**:190
CROSS-SECTION 5:361
gadolinium **9**:7
CROSS STAFF *see* JACOB'S STAFF
CROSSBILL 5:361–362 *illus.*; **8**:229 *illus.*
beak **3**:289 *illus.*
CROSSBOW
bow and arrow **3**:426–427 *illus.*
CROSSBREEDING *see* HYBRID
CROSSETT (Arkansas)
map (33° 8′N 91° 58′W) **2**:166
CROSSFIELD (Alberta)
map (51° 26′N 114° 2′W) **1**:256
CROSSFIELD, A. SCOTT
X-15 **20**:311
CROSSMAN, RICHARD 5:362
CROSSVILLE (Illinois)
map (38° 10′N 88° 4′W) **11**:42
CROSSVILLE (Tennessee)
map (35° 58′N 85° 2′W) **19**:104
CROSSWORD PUZZLE 5:362 *bibliog., illus.*
CROSWELL (Michigan)
map (43° 16′N 82° 37′W) **13**:377
CROTALARIA 5:362 *illus.*
CROTCH, WILLIAM
English music **7**:203
CROTHERS, RACHEL 5:363
CROTHERSVILLE (Indiana)
map (38° 48′N 85° 50′W) **11**:111
CROTON (botany) 5:363 *illus.*
CROTON BUG *see* COCKROACH
CROTON FALLS RESERVOIR
map (41° 21′N 73° 41′W) **5**:193
CROTONE (Italy)
map (39° 5′N 17° 7′E) **11**:321
CROUCHBACK, EDMUND
Lancaster (dynasty) **12**:177
CROUP 5:363
CROUSE, RUSSEL
Lindsay, Howard, and Crouse, Russel **12**:352
CROW (American Indians) 5:363 *bibliog.*
Hidatsa **10**:158
Indians of North America, art of the **11**:141
Montana **13**:548
tepee **19**:114
CROW (bird) 5:363 *illus.*
blue jay **3**:343
instinct **11**:195 *illus.*
nutcracker **14**:302
raven **16**:95
CROW, JIM *see* JIM CROW
CROW AGENCY (Montana)
map (45° 36′N 107° 27′W) **13**:547
CROW RIVER
map (45° 15′N 93° 31′W) **13**:453
CROW WING (county in Minnesota)
map (46° 25′N 94° 3′W) **13**:453
CROW WING RIVER
map (46° 19′N 94° 20′W) **13**:453
CROWBERRY 5:363
rosemary **16**:314
CROWDER (Mississippi)
map (34° 10′N 90° 6′W) **13**:469
CROWDER (Oklahoma)
map (35° 7′N 95° 40′W) **14**:368
CROWELL (Texas)
map (33° 59′N 99° 43′W) **19**:129
CROWFOOT (Blackfoot Indian) 5:363 *bibliog.*
CROWLEY (county in Colorado)
map (38° 20′N 103° 45′W) **5**:116
CROWLEY (Louisiana)
map (30° 13′N 92° 22′W) **12**:430
CROWLEY RIDGE
map (35° 45′N 90° 45′W) **2**:166
CROWN GALL
diseases, plant **6**:195
CROWN MOUNTAIN (Virgin Islands)
map (18° 21′N 64° 58′W) **19**:605
CROWN POINT (Indiana)
map (41° 25′N 87° 22′W) **11**:111
CROWN POINT (New York) 5:364
French and Indian Wars **8**:313
map (43° 57′N 73° 25′W) **14**:149
CROWN OF THORNS (botany) 5:364 *illus.*
CROWN OF THORNS (religion)
sainte-chapelle **17**:28
Gothic art and architecture **9**:257
CROWNPOINT (New Mexico)
map (35° 40′N 108° 10′W) **14**:136
CROWNS AND CORONETS 5:364 *bibliog., illus.*
Monza (Italy) **13**:560
CROWS NEST PEAK
map (44° 3′N 103° 58′W) **18**:103
CROWTHER, GEOFFREY
Economist, The **7**:49
CROZET (Virginia)
map (38° 4′N 78° 42′W) **19**:607
CROZET ISLANDS
French Southern and Antarctic Territories **8**:326
CRT *see* CATHODE-RAY TUBE
CRUCES (Cuba)
map (22° 21′N 80° 16′W) **5**:377
CRUCIBLE, THE (play)
Miller, Arthur **13**:427
CRUCIFIX
cross **5**:361
CRUCIFIXION 5:364; **7**:287 *illus.*
Passion cycle **15**:105
reliquary **16**:144
stations of the cross **18**:235
stigmata **18**:268
CRUCIFIXION THORN (botany) 5:364–365
CRUDE OIL *see* PETROLEUM
CRUEL AND UNUSUAL PUNISHMENT (U.S. Constitution) *see* 8TH AMENDMENT
CRUELTY TO ANIMALS ACT (Great Britain)
vivisection **19**:622–623
CRUGER (Mississippi)
map (33° 14′N 90° 14′W) **13**:469
CRUIKSHANK, GEORGE 5:365 *bibliog.*
The Battle Royal in the Churchyard **14**:273 *illus.*
CRUISE MISSILE 5:365–366 *bibliog., illus.*
rockets and missiles **16**:256
CRUISER (ship) 5:366 *bibliog., illus.*
naval vessels **14**:56–57 *illus.*
nuclear-power guided-missile **14**:57 *illus.*
CRUMB, GEORGE 5:366 *bibliog.*
CRUMB, ROBERT
comic strip **5**:136
CRUMHORN *see* KRUMMHORN
CRUMP, EDWARD H. "BOSS"
Memphis (Tennessee) **13**:292
CRUSADES 5:366–369 *bibliog., illus., map*; **7**:284 *illus.*
Asia, history of **2**:255
Bernard of Clairvaux, Saint **3**:220–221
Bohemond I, Prince of Antioch **3**:361
campaigns **5**:368–369
causes **5**:366–368
Children's Crusade **4**:351; **5**:369
Constantinople, Latin Empire of **5**:209–210
Europe, history of **7**:284–285
exploration **7**:334
fortresses **5**:368 *illus.*
Krak des Chevaliers **12**:126–127
France, history of **8**:268
Godfrey of Bouillon **9**:220–221
Hospitalers **10**:258–259
Jerusalem, Latin Kingdom of **11**:401–402
Joinville, Jean, Sire de **11**:440
knight **12**:100
Louis IX, King of France **12**:424–425
Middle Ages **13**:391
Middle East, history of the **13**:404 *illus.*
Nur al-Din **14**:297
papacy **15**:63–65
Peter the Hermit **15**:200
Philip II, King of France (Philip Augustus) **15**:232
principal routes **5**:367 *map*
reliquary **16**:144
results **5**:369
Richard I, King of England **16**:209–210
Saladin **17**:29
Sigismund, King of Germany and Holy Roman Emperor **17**:299
slavery **17**:353
Templars **19**:93–94
Teutonic Knights **19**:127–128
Turks **19**:348
Villehardouin, Geoffroi de **19**:598
CRUST (biology)
skin diseases **17**:341–342
CRUST (geology) *see* EARTH, STRUCTURE AND COMPOSITION OF
CRUSTACEAN 5:369–370 *bibliog., illus.*
abdomen **1**:54
amphipod **1**:382
anatomy **5**:369–370
barnacle **3**:85
brine shrimp **3**:486
copepod **5**:250
coral reef **5**:260
crab **5**:324–325
crayfish **5**:333–334
deep-sea life **6**:78
fiddler crab **8**:70
gribble **9**:361
hermit crab **10**:143
hormone, animal **10**:237 *table*
horseshoe crab **10**:252
isopod **11**:300
krill **12**:129–130
lobster **12**:385
louse **12**:436
metamorphosis **13**:334
ostracod **14**:458
pill bug **15**:303
plankton **15**:331
shell **17**:250
shellfish **17**:254–255 *illus.*
shrimp **17**:287
skeletal system **17**:333
water flea **20**:48
zooplankton **20**:378
CRUX (constellation) 5:370
CRUX ANSATA (cross) **5**:360; **5**:361 *illus.*
CRUYFF, JOHAN 5:370 *bibliog.*

CRUZ, CAPE OF
map (19° 51′N 77° 44′W) **5**:377
CRUZ, RAMÓN DE LA
Spanish literature **18**:159
CRUZ, SOR JUANA INÉS DE LA *see* JUANA INÉS DE LA CRUZ, SOR
CRUZ ALTA (Argentina)
map (33° 1′S 61° 49′W) **2**:149
CRUZ BAY (Virgin Islands)
map (18° 20′N 64° 48′W) **19**:605
CRUZ DEL EJE (Argentina)
map (30° 44′S 64° 48′W) **2**:149
CRUZ-DIEZ, CARLOS
Venezuela **19**:543
CRUZADO *see* MESTIZO
CRUZEIRO DO SUL (Brazil)
map (7° 38′S 72° 36′W) **3**:460
CRY, THE BELOVED COUNTRY (book) **5**:370
Paton, Alan **15**:112
CRYING BIRD *see* LIMPKIN
CRYOBIOLOGY **5**:370 *bibliog.*
cryogenics **5**:370–371
CRYOGENICS **5**:370–371 *bibliog.*
absolute zero **1**:63
applications **5**:371
frozen storage, tissues and organs **5**:370
cryobiology **5**:370
cryopumping **5**:371
dysprosium **6**:320
Giauque, William Francis **9**:172
helium **10**:113
inert gases **11**:161
Kamerlingh Onnes, Heike **12**:10
Kapitza, Peter **12**:25
neon **14**:85
nitrogen **14**:202
superconductivity **18**:350
superfluidity **18**:351
vacuum **19**:502
CRYOLITE **5**:371
halide minerals **10**:21
CRYONICS
cryobiology **5**:370
CRYPT **5**:371
See also TOMB
CRYPTOCOCCOSIS
fungus diseases **8**:369
CRYPTOLOGY **5**:371–373 *bibliog., illus.*
ciphers **5**:372
codes **5**:372
early history **5**:371–372
technical aspects
cryptanalysis **5**:372–373
cryptography **5**:372
Ventris, Michael **19**:546
World War II **20**:266; **20**:272
CRYPTOLOGY (geology)
geode **9**:97
CRYPTOMONAD **5**:373
CRYSTAL **5**:373–376 *bibliog., illus.*
Bragg, Sir William H. **3**:439
Bragg, Sir William L. **3**:439
cleavage **5**:47
diamond **6**:151 *illus.*
dichroism **6**:156
Friedel, Georges **8**:331
geode **9**:97
hardness, mineral **10**:47
Haüy, René-Just **10**:69–70
ice, river and lake **11**:7
ion and ionization **11**:240
isomorph **11**:300
laser and maser **12**:213 *table*
liquid crystal **12**:365
metal **13**:329
mineral **13**:439–440 *illus.*
optical activity **14**:408
optical mineralogy **14**:408–409
phenocryst **15**:225
piezoelectricity **15**:298
pitchstone **15**:320
polarized light **15**:394
polymorph **15**:420–421
porphyry **15**:442
quartz **16**:13
rock **16**:247
metamorphic rock **13**:331–333
petrology **15**:215
silicate minerals **17**:304–305
snow and snowflake **18**:4 *illus., table*
solid solution **18**:54
stalactite and stalagmite **18**:213
systems **5**:375 *illus.*
cubic system **5**:374 *illus.*
hexagonal system **10**:154–155
isometric system **11**:299
monoclinic system **13**:536
orthorhombic system **14**:451
rhombic system **5**:375 *illus.*
rhombohedral system **5**:375 *illus.*
tetragonal system **19**:127
triclinic system **19**:296
trigonal system **5**:375 *illus.*
Wollaston, William Hyde **20**:199
X-ray diffraction **20**:308–309
X rays **20**:310
CRYSTAL (North Dakota)
map (48° 36′N 97° 40′W) **14**:248
CRYSTAL CITY (Manitoba)
map (49° 9′N 98° 56′W) **13**:119
CRYSTAL CITY (Missouri)
map (38° 13′N 90° 23′W) **13**:476
CRYSTAL CITY (Texas)
map (28° 41′N 99° 50′W) **19**:129
CRYSTAL FALLS (Michigan)
map (46° 5′N 88° 20′W) **13**:377
CRYSTAL LAKE (Illinois)
map (42° 14′N 88° 19′W) **11**:42
CRYSTAL PALACE **2**:200 *illus.*; **5**:376 *bibliog., illus.*
Arts and Crafts movement **2**:225
Grove, Sir George **9**:378
industrial design **11**:155
Paxton, Sir Joseph **15**:121
CRYSTAL RIVER (Florida)
map (28° 54′N 82° 36′W) **8**:172
CRYSTAL SPRINGS (Mississippi)
map (31° 59′N 90° 21′W) **13**:469
CRYSTAL VIOLET *see* GENTIAN VIOLET
CT SCANNING *see* CAT (COMPUTERIZED AXIAL TOMOGRAPHY) SCANNING
CTENOPHORA *see* COMB JELLY
CTESIBIUS **5**:376
clepsydra **5**:51
CTESIPHON (Iraq) **5**:377 *bibliog.*
CUANDO RIVER
map (18° 27′S 23° 32′E) **2**:5
CUANGO RIVER
map (18° 50′S 22° 25′E) **2**:5
CUANZA RIVER
map (9° 19′S 13° 8′E) **2**:5
CUAUHTÉMOC **5**:377 *bibliog.*
CUBA **5**:377–380 *bibliog., illus., map, table*
arts **5**:378
ballistic missile installations **5**:380 *illus.*
cities
Camagüey **4**:49
Cienfuegos **4**:429
Guantánamo **9**:386
Havana **10**:70 *map*
Santiago de Cuba **17**:70
climate **5**:378 *table*
communications satellite
Molniya **5**:145
dance
Alonso, Alicia **1**:307
cha cha **4**:264
tango **19**:23
economic activity **5**:378–380 *illus.*
education **5**:378
Latin American universities **12**:233 *table*
flag **5**:377 *illus.*
government **5**:379
Guantánamo Bay **9**:386
history **5**:379–380
Batista, Fulgencio **3**:124
Bay of Pigs invasion **3**:132
Castro, Fidel **4**:192–193
Céspedes, Carlos Manuel de **4**:262
communism **5**:150
concentration camp **5**:169
Estrada Palma, Tomás **7**:247–248
Grau San Martín, Ramón **9**:301–302
Guevara, Che **9**:392
Havana street scene (c.1515) **12**:218 *illus.*
Khrushchev, Nikita Sergeyevich **12**:68–69
Latin America, history of **12**:218 *illus.*
Machado y Morales, Gerardo **13**:18
McKinley, William **13**:31
Martí, José **13**:176
Ostend Manifesto **14**:457
Platt Amendment **15**:362
refugee **16**:125
Spanish-American War **18**:149–150
Ten Years' War **19**:101
Velázquez de Cuéllar, Diego **19**:537
integration, racial **11**:203
Isle of Pines **11**:298
land and resources **5**:377–378 *map, table*
literature
Carpentier, Alejo **4**:164
Gillén, Nicolás **9**:396
Martí, José **13**:176
map (21° 30′N 80° 0′W) **20**:109
migration to the United States **11**:55 *map*
people **5**:378
refugees in Florida **8**:176
settlement in the United States **10**:177 *map*; **10**:179
trade **5**:379
CUBA (Alabama)
map (32° 26′N 88° 23′W) **1**:234
CUBA (Illinois)
map (40° 30′N 90° 12′W) **11**:42
CUBA (Kansas)
map (39° 48′N 97° 27′W) **12**:18
CUBA (Missouri)
map (38° 4′N 91° 24′W) **13**:476
CUBA (New Mexico)
map (36° 1′N 107° 4′W) **14**:136
CUBA (New York)
map (42° 13′N 78° 17′W) **14**:149
CUBAN MISSILE CRISIS **5**:99 *illus.*; **5**:380 *bibliog., illus.*; **15**:525 *illus., illus.*
intelligence gathering **11**:205
Kennedy, John F. **12**:43
navy **14**:65
U-2 **19**:369
CUBAN TREE FROG **5**:380
CUBANGO RIVER
map (18° 50′S 22° 25′E) **2**:5
CUBE **5**:380
polyhedron **15**:419–420 *illus.*
CUBIC SYSTEM
crystal **5**:375 *illus.*
isometric system **11**:299
CUBILLAS, TEOFILO
soccer **18**:11
CUBISM **5**:380–381 *bibliog., illus.*
See also ORPHISM
Apollinaire, Guillaume **2**:79
Archipenko, Aleksandr **2**:129
Art Deco **2**:207–208
Balla, Giacomo **3**:40
Boccioni, Umberto **3**:354–355
Braque, Georges **3**:456
Davis, Stuart **6**:52–53
Delaunay, Robert **6**:87
Demuth, Charles **6**:105
Duchamp-Villon, Raymond **6**:290
expressionism (art) **7**:340
Feininger, Lyonel **8**:45
Giacometti, Alberto **9**:171
Gleizes, Albert **9**:207
Gris, Juan **9**:366–367
La Fresnaye, Roger de **12**:146
landscape painting **12**:192
Laurens, Henri **12**:238
Léger, Fernand **12**:274
Lipchitz, Jacques **12**:360–361
Malevich, Kasimir **13**:88
modern art **13**:493–494
Mondrian, Piet **13**:523
painting **15**:22
photography
Jacobi, Lotte **11**:345
Picasso, Pablo **15**:291
sculpture **17**:165
Sheeler, Charles **17**:248
Storrs, John Bradley **18**:285
Three Dancers (Picasso) **2**:202 *illus.*
Villon, Jacques **19**:599
Weber, Max (painter) **20**:87
CUBIT
weights and measures **20**:93
CUCHULAIN **5**:381
mythology **13**:703–704
CUCHUMATANES MOUNTAINS
map (15° 35′N 91° 25′W) **9**:389
CUCKOO **5**:381–382 *illus.*
ani **2**:8
hoatzin **10**:191
CUCKOO SHRIKE **5**:382
minivet **13**:451
CUCUÍ (Brazil)
map (1° 12′N 66° 50′W) **3**:460
CUCUMBER **5**:382 *illus.*; **8**:348 *illus.*; **19**:532 *illus.*
watermelon **20**:65
CUCUMBER TREE *see* MAGNOLIA
CÚCUTA (Colombia)
map (7° 54′N 72° 31′W) **5**:107
CUCUTENI-TRIPOLYE CULTURE **14**:83 *illus.*
painted vase **14**:84 *illus.*
CUD
ruminant **16**:345
CUDAHY (Wisconsin)
map (42° 57′N 87° 52′W) **20**:185
CUDWORTH, RALPH **5**:382
CUELLO (Belize)
Maya **13**:243
CUENCA (Ecuador) **5**:382
map (2° 53′S 78° 59′W) **7**:52
open-air market **18**:95 *illus.*
CUENCA (Spain)
map (40° 4′N 2° 8′W) **18**:140
CUENCAMÉ (Mexico)
map (24° 53′N 103° 42′W) **13**:357
CUERNAVACA (Mexico) **5**:382–383
map (18° 55′N 99° 15′W) **13**:357
CUERO (Texas)
map (29° 6′N 97° 18′W) **19**:129
CUEVA, JUAN DE LA **5**:383 *bibliog.*
CUEVAS, JOSÉ LUIS **5**:383 *bibliog.*
CUEVAS, MARQUIS GEORGE DE *see* DE CUEVAS, MARQUIS GEORGE
CUFFE, PAUL
black nationalism **3**:318
CUI, CÉSAR **5**:383 *bibliog.*
Five, The **8**:132
CUIABÁ (Brazil)
map (15° 35′S 56° 5′W) **3**:460
CUILO RIVER
map (3° 22′S 17° 22′E) **2**:5
CUIRASSIER **7**:190 *illus.*
CUISENAIRE METHOD **5**:383
CUISINE *see* COOKING
CUITO RIVER
map (18° 1′S 20° 48′E) **2**:5
CUITZEO, LAKE
map (19° 55′N 101° 5′W) **13**:357
CUKOR, GEORGE **5**:383 *bibliog., illus.*
CULBERSON (county in Texas)
map (30° 25′N 104° 30′W) **19**:129
CULBERTSON (Montana)
map (48° 9′N 104° 31′W) **13**:547
CULBERTSON (Nebraska)
map (40° 14′N 100° 50′W) **14**:70
CULBERTSON, ELY **5**:383 *bibliog.*
CULEBRA ISLAND
map (18° 19′N 65° 17′W) **15**:614
CULEBRA PEAK
map (37° 7′N 105° 11′W) **5**:116
CULIACÁN (Mexico) **5**:383
map (24° 48′N 107° 24′W) **13**:357
CULINARY TECHNIQUES *see* COOKING
CULLEN, COUNTEE **5**:384 *bibliog.*
CULLEN, MAURICE
Canadian art and architecture **4**:89
CULLEN, WILLIAM
refrigeration **16**:124
CULLEOKA (Tennessee)
map (35° 29′N 86° 59′W) **19**:104
CULLMAN (Alabama)
map (34° 11′N 86° 51′W) **1**:234
CULLMAN (county in Alabama)
map (34° 5′N 86° 50′W) **1**:234
CULLMANN, OSCAR **5**:384
CULLODEN MOOR, BATTLE OF **17**:152 *illus.*
Stuart, Charles Edward (Bonnie Prince Charlie) **18**:305 *illus.*
CULLOM (Illinois)
map (40° 53′N 88° 16′W) **11**:42
CULLOWHEE (North Carolina)
map (35° 19′N 83° 11′W) **14**:242
CULPEPER (Virginia)
map (38° 28′N 77° 53′W) **19**:607
CULPEPER (county in Virginia)
map (38° 30′N 78° 0′W) **19**:607
CULTS *see* RELIGIOUS CULTS
CULTURAL ANTHROPOLOGY *see* ANTHROPOLOGY
CULTURAL BIAS *see* ETHNOCENTRISM
CULTURAL DIFFERENCES
illusions **11**:49
CULTURAL GEOGRAPHY **9**:103
CULTURAL REVOLUTION **5**:384 *bibliog.*
Chao Tzu-yang (Zhao Ziyang) **4**:283
Chiang Ch'ing (Jiang Qing) **4**:339
China **4**:366
China, history of **4**:377
Chinese Academy of Sciences **4**:377
Chinese literature **4**:390
Chinese universities **4**:394
communism **5**:149
Confucianism **5**:180
Gang of Four **9**:36
Hu Yao-pang (Hu Yaobang) **10**:287
Lin Piao (Lin Biao) **12**:347
Liu Shao-ch'i (Liu Shaoqi) **12**:374
Mao Tse-tung (Mao Zedong) **13**:135–136
Teng Hsiao-p'ing (Deng Xiaoping) **19**:102
CULTURE **5**:384–385 *bibliog.*
anthropological linguistics **2**:50–51
anthropology **2**:52
Benedict, Ruth **3**:197
Burckhardt, Jakob **3**:567
civilization **5**:34
Civilization and Its Discontents **5**:34
communication **5**:144

CULTURE (cont.)
Cro-Magnon man 5:353–354 *illus.*
definition 18:28
diffusion, cultural 6:170
ethics 7:251
ethnocentrism 7:256
ethnohistory 7:257
folklore 8:203
Fromm, Erich 8:339
handedness 10:35
Kluckhohn, Clyde 12:98
Kroeber, Alfred L. 12:130
language and literature 12:196–197
Leach, Sir Edmund 12:256
Mead, Margaret 13:251–252
Montagu, Ashley 13:544
norm, social 14:219
primitive art 15:543
racism 16:37–38
speech patterns 9:98–100
Tylor, Sir Edward B. 19:362
CULTURE AND ANARCHY (book) 5:385
Arnold, Matthew 2:185
CULTURE AREA 5:385–386 *bibliog.*
archaeology 2:116–126
CULTURE LAG 5:386 *bibliog.*
CULTURE SHOCK 5:386
feral children 8:51
CULVER (Indiana)
map (41° 13′N 86° 25′W) 11:111
CULVER (Oregon)
map (44° 32′N 121° 13′W) 14:427
CULVER'S ROOT *see* FIGWORT
CUMAE 5:386
sibyl 17:292
CUMANÁ (Venezuela)
map (10° 28′N 64° 10′W) 19:542
CUMANS 5:386
CUMBAL VOLCANO
map (0° 57′N 77° 52′W) 5:107
CUMBERLAND (county in Illinois)
map (39° 17′N 88° 15′W) 11:42
CUMBERLAND (Iowa)
map (41° 16′N 94° 52′W) 11:244
CUMBERLAND (Kentucky)
map (36° 59′N 82° 59′W) 12:47
CUMBERLAND (county in Kentucky)
map (36° 45′N 85° 25′W) 12:47
CUMBERLAND (county in Maine)
map (43° 52′N 70° 25′W) 13:70
CUMBERLAND (Maryland)
map (39° 39′N 78° 46′W) 13:188
CUMBERLAND (county in New Jersey)
map (39° 26′N 75° 14′W) 14:129
CUMBERLAND (county in North Carolina)
map (35° 0′N 78° 55′W) 14:242
CUMBERLAND (county in Pennsylvania)
map (40° 12′N 77° 12′W) 15:147
CUMBERLAND (county in Tennessee)
map (35° 55′N 85° 0′W) 19:104
CUMBERLAND (Virginia)
map (37° 30′N 78° 15′W) 19:607
CUMBERLAND (county in Virginia)
map (37° 30′N 78° 15′W) 19:607
CUMBERLAND (Wisconsin)
map (45° 32′N 92° 1′W) 20:185
CUMBERLAND, LAKE
map (36° 57′N 84° 55′W) 12:47
CUMBERLAND, RICHARD 5:387 *bibliog.*
CUMBERLAND CITY (Tennessee)
map (36° 23′N 87° 38′W) 19:104
CUMBERLAND GAP 5:387; 12:49 *illus.*
CUMBERLAND HILL (Rhode Island)
map (41° 59′N 71° 28′W) 16:198
CUMBERLAND HOUSE (Saskatchewan)
Hearne, Samuel 10:90
map (53° 58′N 102° 16′W) 17:81
CUMBERLAND MOUNTAINS
Cumberland Plateau 5:387
CUMBERLAND PLATEAU 5:387
Cumberland Gap 5:387
Georgia 9:113
Tennessee 19:102
CUMBERLAND RIVER 5:387
map (37° 9′N 88° 25′W) 19:419
CUMBERLAND ROAD
National Road 14:45
roads and highways 16:237
CUMBRIA (England) 5:387
cities
Carlisle 4:151
Lake District 12:170
CUMIN 5:387
CUMING (county in Nebraska)
map (41° 55′N 96° 45′W) 14:70
CUMMING (Georgia)
map (34° 13′N 84° 8′W) 9:114
CUMMING, ALEXANDER
toilet 19:222
CUMMINGS, E. E. 5:387–388 *bibliog., illus.*
CUMULONIMBUS CLOUDS 5:67–68 *illus.*; 5:388 *bibliog., illus.*
hail and hailstones 10:12–13 *illus.*
lightning 12:339
thunderstorm 19:185
waterspout 20:66
CUMULUS CLOUDS 5:67–68 *illus.*; 5:388 *bibliog., illus.*
CUNA (American Indians) 5:388 *bibliog.*
CUNARD, SIR SAMUEL 5:389 *bibliog.*
ship 17:274
CUNAXA, BATTLE OF
Cyrus the Younger 5:410
CUNCO (Chile)
map (38° 55′S 72° 2′W) 4:355
CUNDINAMARCA
Nariño, Antonio 14:21
CUNEIFORM 5:389 *bibliog., illus.*; 19:62 *illus.*
archives 12:316 *illus.*
Boğazköy 3:360
Ebla 7:36
Mari 13:149–150
Nineveh 14:200
Nippur 14:201
Sippar 17:327
Ugarit 19:374
Grotefend, Georg Friedrich 9:372
inscription 11:185
Behistun 3:171
languages, extinct 12:198
Rawlinson, Sir Henry Creswicke 16:95
Smith, George 17:368
Sumerian 20:292 *illus.*
syllabaries 20:293
writing systems, evolution of 20:292 *illus.*
CUNENE RIVER
map (17° 20′S 11° 50′E) 2:5
CUNEO (Italy)
map (44° 23′N 7° 32′E) 11:321
CUNHA, TRISTAO DA 5:389
CUNHAL, ALVARO
Portugal 15:452
CUNNINGHAM (Kansas)
map (37° 39′N 98° 26′W) 12:18
CUNNINGHAM, SIR ALEXANDER 5:389
Taxila 19:48
CUNNINGHAM, GLENN 5:390 *bibliog.*
CUNNINGHAM, IMOGEN 5:390 *bibliog.*
Weston, Edward 20:118
CUNNINGHAM, MERCE 5:390 *bibliog.*
ballet company 3:44 *illus.*
happenings 10:41
modern dance 13:497–498 *illus.*
CUNNINGHAM, R. WALTER 5:390
Apollo program 2:81
CUNNINGHAM LAKE
map (25° 4′N 77° 26′W) 3:23
CUNOBELINUS *see* CYMBELINE
CUNY *see* NEW YORK, CITY UNIVERSITY OF
CUOMO, MARIO 5:390
CUP FUNGUS 5:390 *bibliog.*
fungi 8:368
CUPAR (Saskatchewan)
map (50° 57′N 104° 12′W) 17:81
CUPBOARD 8:195 *illus.*
CUPID *see* EROS (mythology)
CUPOLA *see* DOME (architecture)
CUPRITE 5:390
CUQUENÁN FALLS *see* KUKENAAM FALLS
CURAÇAO (Netherlands Antilles) 5:390
cities
Willemstad 20:154
CURARE 5:390–391
CURASSOW 5:391 *bibliog., illus.*
CURCI, AMELITA GALLI- *see* GALLI-CURCI, AMELITA
CUREPIPE (Mauritius)
map (20° 19′S 57° 31′E) 13:237
CURIA, ROMAN 5:391
CURIA REGIS *see* KING'S COURT
CURIAPO (Venezuela)
map (8° 33′N 61° 0′W) 19:542
CURICÓ (Chile)
map (34° 59′S 71° 14′W) 4:355
CURIE (unit of measure)
radioactivity 16:62
CURIE, FRÉDÉRIC AND IRÈNE JOLIOT- *see* JOLIOT-CURIE, FRÉDÉRIC AND IRÈNE
CURIE, MARIE AND PIERRE 4:328 *illus.*; 5:391–392 *bibliog., illus.*; 15:286 *illus.*
polonium 15:417
radioactivity 16:60–61 *illus.*
radium 16:68
CURIE TEMPERATURE 5:392
Curie, Marie and Pierre 5:391
magnetism 13:56
CURITIBA (Brazil) 5:392
map (25° 25′S 49° 15′W) 3:460
CURIUM 5:392
actinide series 1:88
element 7:130 *table*
metal, metallic element 13:328
Seaborg, Glenn T. 17:171–172
transuranium elements 19:286
CURLEW 5:392 *illus.*
Hudsonian curlew 19:332 *illus.*
CURLEW (Washington)
map (48° 53′N 118° 36′W) 20:35
CURLEY, JAMES M. 5:392 *bibliog.*
CURLING (sport) 5:392 *bibliog.*
CURLING'S ULCER *see* ULCER, stress ulcer
CURLY-COATED RETRIEVER 5:392–393 *bibliog., illus.*; 6:218 *illus.*
CURONIAN LANGUAGE
Baltic languages 3:54–55
CURRAGH (boat)
canoe 4:113
CURRANT 5:393 *illus.*
CURRENCY
See also MONEY; NUMISMATICS
parity (economics) 15:88
CURRENT (water)
ocean currents 14:322–323
water mass 20:49
CURRENT, ELECTRIC
See also CIRCUIT, ELECTRIC; ELECTRICITY
alternating current 1:312–313
direct current 6:187
disturbances, magnetic storms 13:55
electromagnet 7:115
measurement 13:255–256
units, physical 19:466
silicon-controlled rectifier 17:305
thyratron 19:187
CURRICLE
coach and carriage 5:73
CURRICULUM 5:393–394 *bibliog.*
censorship 4:248
community and junior colleges 5:152
creationism 5:335–336
educational psychology 7:66
Eliot, Charles William 7:138
Great Books Program 9:309
humanities, education in the 10:300
law
Hutchins, Robert M. 10:322
mathematics, education in 13:222–223
mathematics, new 13:227
middle schools and junior high schools 13:412–413
military academies 13:420–421
Mulcaster, Richard 13:635
Parker, Francis Wayland 15:90
physical education, teaching of 15:279–280
physics, history of 15:282
preschool education 15:521
secondary education 17:179–180
Soviet education 18:113–114
teacher education 19:54
Tyler, Ralph Winfred 19:362
United States Military Academy 19:463
university 19:468–469
Wayland, Francis 20:73
White, Andrew Dickson 20:134
Yale Report of 1828 20:315
CURRIE (Minnesota)
map (43° 59′N 95° 40′W) 13:453
CURRIE, SIR ARTHUR W. 5:394
CURRIER, NATHANIEL *see* CURRIER AND IVES
CURRIER AND IVES 5:394 *bibliog., illus.*
Full Cry 10:313 *illus.*
Kearsarge 5:32 *illus.*
Rocky Mountains 5:394 *illus.*
CURRITUCK (North Carolina)
map (36° 27′N 76° 1′W) 14:242
CURRITUCK (county in North Carolina)
map (36° 20′N 76° 0′W) 14:242
CURRY (Alaska)
map (62° 37′N 150° 1′W) 1:242
CURRY (condiment) 5:394
fenugreek 8:51
turmeric 19:349
CURRY (county in New Mexico)
map (34° 30′N 103° 20′W) 14:136
CURRY (county in Oregon)
map (42° 30′N 124° 10′W) 14:427
CURRY, JOHN STEUART 5:394 *bibliog., illus.*
The Flying Codonas 5:394 *illus.*
CURSOR (computer term) 5:160h
CURTIN, JOHN 5:394
Australia, history of 2:341
CURTINA (Uruguay)
map (32° 9′S 56° 7′W) 19:488
CURTIS (Arkansas)
map (34° 0′N 93° 6′W) 2:166
CURTIS (Nebraska)
map (40° 38′N 100° 31′W) 14:70
CURTIS, BENJAMIN ROBBINS 5:395 *bibliog.*
Cooley v. *Board of Port Wardens* 5:240
CURTIS, CHARLES (political figure) 5:395 *bibliog.*
CURTIS, CHARLES G. (inventor)
turbine 19:340
CURTIS, CYRUS H. K. 5:395 *bibliog.*
periodical 15:169
CURTIS, GEORGE WILLIAM 5:395 *bibliog.*
CURTIS, HEBER DOUST 5:395
astronomy, history of 2:281
CURTIS CUP
golf 9:239–240
CURTIS INSTITUTE OF MUSIC, THE 5:395
Hofmann, Josef Casimir 10:196
Serkin, Rudolf 17:209
CURTIS ISLAND
map (23° 38′S 151° 9′E) 2:328
CURTIS PUBLISHING COMPANY
Curtis, Cyrus H. K. 5:395
CURTISS, GLENN HAMMOND 5:395 *bibliog.*
CURTISS JENNY 5:395–396 *illus.*
CURTIUS, ERNST ROBERT 5:396 *bibliog.*
CURUZÚ-CUATIÁ (Argentina)
map (29° 47′S 58° 3′W) 2:149
CURVATURE (mathematics) 5:396
differential geometry 6:169
CURVATURE (space)
cosmology (astronomy) 5:287–288 *illus.*
relativity 16:134
CURVE (mathematics) 5:396 *bibliog.*
asymptote 2:286
catenary 4:202
circle 4:435–436 *illus.*
curvature 5:396
cycloid 5:404–405
eccentricity 7:37
hyperbola 10:347–348
Jordan, Camille 11:450
least-squares method 12:262
normal distribution 14:219
parabola 15:74
plane
line 12:352–353
secant 17:178
spiral 18:188
tangent 19:22
CURWENSVILLE (Pennsylvania)
map (40° 58′N 78° 32′W) 15:147
CURWOOD, MOUNT
map (46° 42′N 88° 14′W) 13:377
CURZON, GEORGE NATHANIEL CURZON, 1ST MARQUESS 5:396 *bibliog., illus.*
CUSCO *see* CUZCO (Peru)
CUSCUS 5:396–397 *illus.*
phalanger 15:218
CUSH 5:397
Egypt, ancient 7:83
Meroë 13:311
Nubia 14:277
CUSHING (Oklahoma)
map (35° 59′N 96° 46′W) 14:368
CUSHING, CALEB 5:397 *bibliog.*
CUSHING, HARVEY W. 5:397
surgery 18:362
CUSHING, RICHARD JAMES 5:397 *bibliog.*
CUSHING'S DISEASE
endocrine system, diseases of the 7:170
CUSHING'S SYNDROME
endocrine system, diseases of the 7:170
osteoporosis 14:458
CUSHING'S ULCER *see* NERVOUS SYSTEM, DISEASES OF THE; ULCER
CUSHITES
Engaruka 7:176
CUSHITIC LANGUAGES
Afroasiatic languages 1:179–180 *map*
CUSHMAN, CHARLOTTE SAUNDERS 5:397 *bibliog.*
Walnut Street Theatre 20:18

CUSICK (Washington)
map (48° 20′N 117° 18′W) **20**:35
CUSK EEL 5:397
CUSSETA (Georgia)
map (32° 18′N 84° 47′W) **9**:114
CUSTARD APPLE 5:397 *illus.*
CUSTER (county in Colorado)
map (38° 5′N 105° 25′W) **5**:116
CUSTER (county in Idaho)
map (44° 15′N 114° 15′W) **11**:26
CUSTER (Michigan)
map (43° 58′N 86° 14′W) **13**:377
CUSTER (county in Montana)
map (46° 10′N 105° 35′W) **13**:547
CUSTER (county in Nebraska)
map (41° 20′N 99° 50′W) **14**:70
CUSTER (county in Oklahoma)
map (35° 40′N 99° 0′W) **14**:368
CUSTER (South Dakota)
map (43° 46′N 103° 36′W) **18**:103
CUSTER (county in South Dakota)
map (43° 40′N 103° 30′W) **18**:103
CUSTER, GEORGE ARMSTRONG 5:397–398 *bibliog., illus.*
Cheyenne (American Indians) **4**:338
Crazy Horse **5**:334
Gall **9**:16
Indian Wars **11**:110
Little Bighorn, Battle of the **11**:108 *illus.*; **12**:372
CUSTER'S LAST STAND *see* LITTLE BIGHORN, BATTLE OF THE
CUSTIS, DANIEL PARKE
Washington, Martha **20**:44
CUSTODY
divorce **6**:206
CUSTOMS (duty)
police **15**:396
port of entry **15**:443
smuggling **17**:374
CUSTOMS, BUREAU OF
Treasury, U.S. Department of the **19**:285
CUSTOMS UNION 5:398
See also FREE TRADE
CUT BANK (Montana)
map (48° 38′N 112° 20′W) **13**:547
CUTCH *see* CATECHU
CUTHBERT, SAINT 5:398
CUTHBERT (Georgia)
map (31° 46′N 84° 48′W) **9**:114
CUTLASS FISH 5:398
CUTLER (Maine)
map (44° 40′N 67° 12′W) **13**:70
CUTLER, MANASSEH 5:398
Ohio Company of Associates **14**:362
CUTLERY
sword and knife **18**:398
CUTS-SAH-NEM *see* YAKIMA (American Indians)
CUTTACK (India)
map (20° 30′N 85° 50′E) **11**:80
CUTTER (sailing ship) 5:398
CUTTING, FRANCIS
English music **7**:203
CUTTLEFISH 5:398 *illus.*
mollusk **13**:511–512 *illus.*
CUTTY SARK (ship)
clipper ship **5**:61
CUTWORM 5:398
CUVIER, GEORGES, BARON 4:201 *illus.*; **5**:399 *bibliog.*; **20**:376 *illus.*
anatomy **1**:397
baron **3**:269
comparative anatomy **5**:155
CUVILLIÉS, FRANÇOIS 5:399 *bibliog.*
Amalienburg Pavilion **1**:321; **16**:264 *illus.*
CUVO RIVER
map (10° 50′S 13° 47′E) **2**:5
CUXHAVEN (West Germany)
map (53° 52′N 8° 42′E) **9**:140
CUYAHOGA (county in Ohio)
map (41° 30′N 81° 41′W) **14**:357
CUYAHOGA FALLS (Ohio)
map (41° 8′N 81° 29′W) **14**:357
CUYAHOGA RIVER
map (41° 30′N 81° 42′W) **14**:357
CUYP, AELBERT 5:399 *bibliog., illus.*
River Landscape **5**:399 *illus.*
The River Maas Near Dordrecht **6**:310 *illus.*
CUYPERS, PETRUS 5:399 *bibliog.*
CUYUNI RIVER
map (6° 23′N 58° 41′W) **9**:410
CUZA, ALEXANDRU ION 5:399
CUZCO (Peru) 5:399–400 *bibliog.*
art and architecture
Compañia de Jesús (1651–68) **12**:225 *illus.*
Latin American art and architecture **12**:223
pre-Columbian art and architecture **15**:501
Sacsahuaman **17**:8
history **11**:117 *illus.*
Latin America, history of **12**:217
Pizarro, Francisco **15**:324
Inca **11**:69–73
map (13° 31′S 71° 59′W) **15**:193
CY YOUNG AWARD **3**:105 *table*
Young, Cy **20**:333
CYANATE SALTS
Wöhler, Friedrich, discoverer **20**:195
CYANGUGU (Rwanda)
map (2° 29′S 28° 54′E) **16**:378
CYANIDE 5:400 *bibliog.*
compounds, chemical **5**:400
laetrile **12**:163
poison **5**:400
poison gas **15**:382
CYANIDE PROCESS 5:400
CYANIDING
hardening **10**:45
CYANOCOBALAMIN (Vitamin B_{12})
blood **3**:338
digestion, human **6**:171
hemoglobin **10**:119
Hodgkin, Dorothy Crawfoot **10**:194
Minot, George **13**:460
vitamins and minerals **19**:620
Recommended Daily Allowances **19**:618 *table*
CYANOPHYTA *see* BLUE-GREEN ALGAE
CYANOSIS 5:400
blue baby **3**:342
heart diseases, congenital **10**:95
CYAXARES, KING OF MEDIA 5:400
CYBELE 5:400
mother goddess **13**:607
CYBERNETICS 5:400–401 *bibliog.*
artificial intelligence **2**:221; **5**:401
automata theory **5**:401
bionics **3**:274–275
communication and control **5**:400–401
computers, use **5**:401
heuristics **5**:401
history **5**:401
homeostasis **10**:212
information theory **11**:174
McLuhan, Marshall **13**:33
negative feedback **5**:401
pattern recognition **5**:401
systems **5**:401
Wiener, Norbert, founder **20**:146
CYCAD 5:402 *bibliog., illus.*
fern **8**:58
gymnosperm **9**:414
Jurassic Period **11**:474 *illus.*; **11**:477
petrified wood **15**:205
plant **15**:334–335 *illus.*
sago **17**:12
Triassic Period **19**:294 *illus.*
CYCLADES (Greece) 5:402; **7**:271 *illus.*
Aegean civilization **1**:114–118
Cycladic art **5**:402–403
Delos **6**:94–95
map (37° 30′N 25° 0′E) **9**:325
Melos **13**:288
Naxos **14**:66
Thera **19**:160
CYCLADIC ART 5:402–403 *bibliog., illus.*
sculpture **17**:160
CYCLAMATES 5:403
sugar **18**:327
CYCLAMEN 5:403 *illus.*; **8**:170 *illus.*
CYCLIC AMP 5:403 *bibliog.*
hormone, animal **10**:235
slime mold **17**:362
Sutherland, Earl W., Jr. **18**:372
CYCLIC COMPOUNDS 5:403–404 *bibliog., illus.*
See also COMPOUND, CHEMICAL
alicyclic compounds **1**:293
aromatic compounds **2**:186
heterocyclic compound **10**:153
photocycloaddition
photochemistry **15**:258–259
synthesis
Ružička, Leopold **16**:377
CYCLIC PHOSPHORYLATION *see* PHOSPHORYLATION
CYCLING 5:404 *bibliog., illus.*
Merckx, Eddy **13**:305
youth hostel **20**:337
CYCLITIS
eye diseases **7**:351
CYCLOHEXANE 5:404
CYCLOID 5:404–405 *illus.*
calculus of variations **4**:24
CYCLONE AND ANTICYCLONE 2:298 *illus.*; **5**:405–406 *bibliog., illus.*
atmosphere **2**:303
blizzard **3**:333
climate **5**:57
cloud **5**:68
front **8**:340
high-pressure region **10**:162
hurricane and typhoon **10**:317–319
low-pressure region **12**:443
Mediterranean climate **13**:276
meteorology **13**:342
ocean currents **14**:322–324
polar climate **15**:392
precipitation **15**:495
radar meteorology **16**:41
thunderstorm **19**:185
tornado **19**:239–240
weather forecasting **20**:76–78
wind
seasonal variation, worldwide **20**:169 *map*
CYCLOPROPANE
cyclic compounds **5**:403
CYCLOPS 5:406
Polyphemus **15**:421
Tiryns **19**:209
CYCLOSPORINE 5:406
CYCLOTRON
accelerator, particle **1**:74–75
fusion energy **8**:382
Lawrence, Ernest Orlando **12**:250
nuclear physics **14**:285
plasma physics **15**:346
CYGNUS 5:406
CYGNUS A 5:406 *bibliog.*
CYLINDER 5:406 *illus.*
hydraulic systems **10**:330–331
volume **19**:632
CYLINDER PRESS *see* FLATBED CYLINDER PRESS
CYLINDER SEAL
Mesopotamian art and architecture **13**:317–319 *illus.*
CYMBALS 5:406 *bibliog.*; **6**:282 *illus.*; **13**:675 *illus.*
percussion instruments **15**:162 *illus.*
CYMBELINE 5:406
CYMRU *see* WALES
CYNEWULF 5:406 *bibliog.*
CYNGHANEDD (rhyme)
Dafydd ap Gwilym **6**:6
CYNICS 5:406–407 *bibliog.*
Antisthenes **2**:68–69
Diogenes of Sinope **6**:184
CYNTHIA (Greek goddess) *see* ARTEMIS
CYNTHIANA (Kentucky)
map (38° 23′N 84° 18′W) **12**:47
CYO *see* CATHOLIC YOUTH ORGANIZATION, NATIONAL
CYPRESS 5:407 *bibliog., illus.*; **8**:173 *illus.*
See also REDWOOD
bald cypress **3**:33
incense cedar **11**:73
juniper **11**:470
southern white cedar **18**:112
CYPRESS HILLS
map (49° 40′N 109° 30′W) **17**:81
CYPRIAN, SAINT 5:407 *bibliog.*
CYPRUS 5:407–409 *bibliog., illus., map, table*
archaeology
Enkomi **7**:206
cities
Nicosia **14**:184
climate **5**:407–408 *table*
economy **5**:408 *illus.*
flag **5**:408 *illus.*
history and government **5**:409
EOKA **7**:215
Makarios III **13**:77
Salamis (city) **17**:30
Turkey **19**:346
United Nations **19**:414
land **5**:407
language
ancient syllabary **20**:293
Greek language **9**:342
map (35° 0′N 33° 0′E) **2**:232
people **5**:407
CYPRUS FEVER *see* BRUCELLOSIS
CYRAN, ABBÉ DE SAINT- *see* SAINT-CYRAN, ABBÉ DE
CYRANKIEWICZ, JÓZEF
Poland **15**:390
CYRANO DE BERGERAC (play) 5:409
Rostand, Edmond **16**:320
CYRANO DE BERGERAC, SAVINIEN 5:409 *bibliog.*
Cyrano de Bergerac (play) **5**:409
CYRENAICA 5:409
flag **8**:134
map (31° 0′N 22° 30′E) **12**:320
modern history
Idris, King of Libya **11**:32
CYRENAICS 5:409 *bibliog.*
Aristippus **2**:155
CYRENE (Libya) 5:409–410 *bibliog.*
CYRIL (Oklahoma)
map (34° 54′N 98° 12′W) **14**:368
CYRIL OF ALEXANDRIA, SAINT 5:410 *bibliog.*
CYRIL OF JERUSALEM, SAINT 5:410
CYRIL AND METHODIUS, SAINTS 5:410 *bibliog.*
Bulgaria **3**:556
Old Church Slavonic **17**:358
CYRILLIC ALPHABET 5:410; **20**:294 *table*
CYRÖN RIVER
map (63° 14′N 21° 45′E) **8**:95
CYRUS THE GREAT, KING OF PERSIA 5:410 *bibliog.*
Pasargadae **15**:101
Persia, Ancient **15**:181
Persian Wars **15**:187
CYRUS THE YOUNGER 5:410–411 *bibliog.*
Tissaphernes, Persian Satrap **19**:209
CYST 5:411
kidney disease **12**:71
CYSTIC FIBROSIS 5:411 *bibliog.*
respiratory system disorders **16**:182
CYSTINURIA 5:411
CYSTITIS 5:411 *bibliog.*
urogenital diseases **19**:487
CYSTOID 5:411 *bibliog.*
CYTOCHROME 5:411
effect of cyanide **5**:400
photosynthesis **15**:277
CYTOKINESIS *see* MITOSIS
CYTOKININ 5:411
CYTOLOGY 5:411–412 *bibliog., illus.*
cell **4**:232 *illus.*; **4**:233
cell physiology **4**:236
history **5**:411–412
biology **3**:269–270
Claude, Albert **5**:44
Hooke, Robert **10**:226–227
Mohl, Hugo von **13**:503
Palade, George Emil **15**:29
Schultze, Max **17**:289
Schwann, Theodor, and Schleiden, Matthias Jakob **17**:138
Virchow, Rudolf **19**:604
Wilson, Edmund B. **20**:164
zoology **20**:376–377
CYTOMEGALOVIRUS
herpes **10**:145
CYTOPLASM 5:412 *bibliog.*
See also PROTOPLASM
aging **1**:185
cell **4**:232 *illus.*; **4**:233
cytoplasmic chromosome, heredity **10**:141
Golgi apparatus **9**:240
plant, chloroplast **4**:402
Sonneborn, Tracy Morton **18**:65
CYTOSINE
genetic code **9**:79–81 *illus.*
mutation **13**:686
nucleic acid **14**:289 *illus.*
protein synthesis **15**:575
pyrimidine **15**:637
CZARTORYSKI, ADAM JERZY 5:412 *bibliog.*
CZECH LITERATURE 5:412–413 *bibliog.*
Čapek, Karel **4**:122
Čech, Svatopluk **4**:228
Hašek, Jaroslav **10**:66
Havel, Václav **10**:71
Kafka, Franz **12**:5–6
Mácha, Karel Hynek **13**:17
CZECH MUSIC 5:413 *bibliog.*
Biber, Heinrich Ignaz Franz von **3**:237
Dvořák, Antonín **6**:317
Janáček, Leoš **11**:358
Martinů, Bohuslav **13**:181
Smetana, Bedřich **17**:366
Weinberger, Jaromír **20**:95
CZECH SOCIALIST REPUBLIC *see* CZECHOSLOVAKIA
CZECHOSLOVAKIA 5:413–416 *bibliog., illus., map, table*
archaeology
Dolní Věstonice **6**:226
arts **5**:415
See also the subheading Czechoslovakia under ARCHITECTURE; GRAPHIC ARTS; PAINTING; PREHISTORIC ART
cities
Bratislava **3**:458
Brno **3**:499
Karlovy Vary **12**:28
Košice **12**:124
Lidice **12**:323

CZECHOSLOVAKIA (cont.)
Ostrava **14**:458
Plzeň **15**:375
Prague **15**:488 *illus.*
climate **5**:414 *table*
communism *see* COMMUNISM
economic activity **5**:415–416 *illus.*
education **5**:415
European universities **7**:307 *table*
farmhouse **10**:269 *illus.*
flag **5**:413 *illus.*
government **5**:416
history **5**:416
annexed by Germany 1938–1939 **9**:156 *map*
Beneš, Eduard **3**:198
communism **5**:148
Dubček, Alexander **6**:287
Gottwald, Klement **9**:264
Hitler, Adolf **10**:188
Husák, Gustav **10**:319
Huss, John **10**:320
Hussites **10**:321
Little Entente **12**:372–373
Masaryk, Jan **13**:195
Masaryk, Tomáš **13**:195
Přemysl (dynasty) **15**:518
Teschen **19**:126
Warsaw Treaty Organization **20**:32
World War II **20**:250 *illus.*
land and resources **5**:414 *map, table*
uranium minerals **19**:478
language
Slavic languages **17**:358
literature *see* CZECH LITERATURE
map (49° 30′N 17° 0′E) **7**:268
music *see* CZECH MUSIC
people **5**:414–415
regions
Bohemia **3**:360–361 *map*
Moravia **13**:574 *map*
Silesia **17**:304
Slovakia **17**:363–364 *map*
Sudetenland **18**:323 *map*
religion **5**:415
John Nepomucene, Saint **11**:425
rivers, lakes, and waterways **5**:414
vegetation and animal life **5**:414
CZERNY, CARL **5**:416 *bibliog.*
CZĘSTOCHOWA (Poland) **5**:416
map (50° 49′N 19° 6′E) **15**:388
CZOLGOSZ, LEON
McKinley, William **13**:31

D

D (letter) **6**:3 *illus.*
D LAYER *see* IONOSPHERE
DA *see* the last element of the name for names not listed below or for those names that are treated as one word
DA LAT (Vietnam)
map (11° 56′N 108° 25′E) **19**:580
DA NANG (Vietnam) **6**:3
map (16° 4′N 108° 13′E) **19**:580
DA PONTE, FRANCESCO, THE ELDER
Bassano (family) **3**:117–118
DA PONTE, LORENZO **6**:3 *bibliog.*
Marriage of Figaro, The **13**:166
DA RIVER
map (21° 15′N 105° 20′E) **19**:580
DA VINCI, LEONARDO *see* LEONARDO DA VINCI
DAB **8**:155 *illus.*
DABCHICK *see* GREBE
DABOLA (Guinea)
map (10° 45′N 11° 7′W) **9**:397
DAC LAC PLATEAU
map (12° 50′N 108° 5′E) **19**:580
DACCA (Bangladesh) **3**:65 *illus.*; **6**:3–4 *illus.*
map (23° 43′N 90° 25′E) **3**:64
DACE **6**:4 *illus.*
DACHAU (West Germany) **6**:4 *bibliog.*
concentration camp **5**:169
map (48° 15′N 11° 27′E) **9**:140
DACHSBRACKE
drever **6**:271
DACHSHUND **6**:4 *bibliog., illus.*; **6**:216 *illus.*
DACIAN LANGUAGE
languages, extinct **12**:198
DACITE **6**:4
DACKO, DAVID
Central African Republic **4**:251–252
DACRON *see* SYNTHETIC FIBERS
DACTYL
versification **19**:562
DADA **6**:4–5 *bibliog., illus.*
Arp, Jean **2**:187
collage **5**:102
Dix, Otto **6**:206–207
Duchamp, Marcel **6**:290
Ernst, Max **7**:231–232
Lissitzky, El **12**:366
modern art **13**:493–494
Picabia, Francis **15**:290
Ray, Man **16**:96
Schwitters, Kurt **17**:141
surrealism (art) **18**:365
Tzara, Tristan **19**:368
DADANAWA (Guyana)
map (2° 50′N 59° 30′W) **9**:410
DADD, RICHARD **6**:5 *bibliog.*
DADDAH, MOKTAR OULD **6**:5
Mauritania **13**:237
DADDI, BERNARDO **6**:5 *bibliog.*
DADDY LONGLEGS **2**:106 *illus.*; **6**:5 *bibliog., illus.*
arachnid **2**:106–107
DADE (county in Florida)
map (25° 33′N 80° 32′W) **8**:172
DADE (county in Georgia)
map (34° 55′N 85° 30′W) **9**:114
DADE (county in Missouri)
map (37° 25′N 93° 50′W) **13**:476
DADE CITY (Florida)
map (28° 22′N 82° 12′W) **8**:172
DADEVILLE (Alabama)
map (32° 50′N 85° 46′W) **1**:234
DADRA AND NAGAR HAVELI TERRITORY
map (20° 5′N 73° 0′E) **11**:80
DAEDALUS (journal) **6**:5
DAEDALUS (mythology) **6**:5–6
Knossos **12**:102
DAFFODIL **6**:6 *illus.*; **8**:170 *illus.*
narcissus **14**:21
Sternbergia **18**:261 *illus.*
DAFYDD AP GWILYM **6**:6 *bibliog.*
DAGESTAN (USSR) *see* DAGHESTAN (USSR)
DAGGER **18**:399 *illus.*
DAGGETT (county in Utah)
map (40° 55′N 109° 30′W) **19**:492
DAGHESTAN (USSR) **6**:6
DAGOBERT I, FRANKISH KING
Merovingians (dynasty) **13**:312
DAGON **6**:6
D'AGOULT, MARIE **16**:293 *illus.*
DAGUERRE, LOUIS J. M. **6**:6 *bibliog., illus.*; **15**:267 *illus.*
book **3**:385
daguerreotype **6**:6–7
Niepce, Joseph Nicéphore **14**:185
DAGUERREOTYPE **6**:6–7 *bibliog.*
camera **4**:55
Daguerre, Louis J. M. **6**:6
Fizeau, Armand Hippolyte Louis **8**:133
Southworth, Albert Sands, and Hawes, Josiah Johnson **18**:112–113
DAGUR LANGUAGE
Ural-Altaic languages **19**:476
DAGWOOD BUMSTEAD (fictional character)
Young, Chic **20**:333
DAHL, JOHANN CHRISTIAN
Scandinavian art and architecture **17**:113
DAHL, ROBERT
elites **7**:140
DAHLAK ARCHIPELAGO
map (15° 45′N 40° 30′E) **7**:253
DAHLBERG, EDWARD **6**:7 *bibliog.*
DAHLGREN (Illinois)
map (38° 12′N 88° 41′W) **11**:42
DAHLIA **6**:7 *illus.*; **8**:170 *illus.*
DAHLONEGA (Georgia)
map (34° 32′N 89° 59′W) **9**:114
DAHOMEY *see* BENIN
DAHOMEY (people) *see* FON
DAHOMEY, KINGDOM OF **3**:200
DAHUNI (Papua New Guinea)
map (10° 31′S 149° 55′E) **15**:72
DAI JIN *see* TAI CHIN (Dai Jin)
DAICHES, DAVID **6**:7 *bibliog.*
DAIKON *see* RADISH
DÁIL ÉIREANN
Ireland **11**:261
Ireland, history of **11**:264
Sinn Fein **17**:323
D'AILLY, PIERRE *see* AILLY, PIERRE D'
DAILY WORKER **6**:7
DAIMLER, GOTTLIEB **6**:7 *bibliog.*
bicycle **3**:246
Maybach, Wilhelm **13**:246
motorcycle **13**:614
DAIMYO
Japan, history of **11**:368
DAINGERFIELD (Texas)
map (33° 2′N 94° 44′W) **19**:129
DAIREAUX (Argentina)
map (36° 36′S 61° 45′W) **2**:149
DAIREN (China) *see* LÜ-TA (Lüda) (China); TA-LIEN (Dalian) (China)
DAIRYING **6**:7–10 *bibliog., illus.*; **13**:380 *illus.*
Babcock, Stephen Moulton **3**:6
breeding **6**:9
buttermilk
Lactobacillus **12**:161
cattle and cattle raising **4**:216
artificial insemination **2**:220
diseases, animal **6**:190
feed **6**:8–9
goat **9**:215
lactation **6**:7
milk **13**:423
marketing **6**:9–10
pricing **6**:10
milking **6**:7–8
record keeping **6**:8
veal **19**:529
Wisconsin **20**:187 *illus.*
DAISY (botany) **6**:10 *illus.*
black-eyed Susan **3**:314
calendula **4**:28
chamomile **4**:276
chrysanthemum **4**:420
cosmos **5**:290
feverfew **8**:66
fleabane **8**:158
flower **8**:181
paper daisy **10**:5 *illus.*
ragweed **16**:70
safflower **17**:11
Shasta daisy **17**:244
strawflower **18**:296
sunflower **18**:348
yarrow **20**:319
zinnia **20**:369
DAISY MILLER (book) **6**:10 *bibliog.*
James, Henry **11**:354
DAJABÓN (Dominican Republic)
map (19° 33′N 71° 42′W) **6**:233
DAJAK *see* DAYAK
DAJARRA (Australia)
map (21° 41′S 139° 31′E) **2**:328
DAKAR (Senegal) **6**:10–11 *illus.*; **17**:202 *illus.*
climate **17**:202 *table*
Faidherbe, Louis Léon César **8**:8
map (14° 40′N 17° 26′W) **17**:202
DAKHIN SHAHBAZPUR ISLAND
map (22° 30′N 90° 45′E) **3**:64
DAKHLA (Mauritania)
map (23° 43′N 15° 57′W) **13**:236
DAKOTA (American Indians) *see* SIOUX (American Indians)
DAKOTA (county in Minnesota)
map (44° 40′N 93° 5′W) **13**:453
DAKOTA (county in Nebraska)
map (42° 25′N 96° 35′W) **14**:70
DAKOTA CITY (Iowa)
map (42° 43′N 94° 12′W) **11**:244
DAKOTA CITY (Nebraska)
map (42° 25′N 96° 25′W) **14**:70
DAKOVO (Yugoslavia)
map (45° 19′N 18° 25′E) **20**:340
DALADIER, ÉDOUARD **6**:11 *bibliog.*
DALAI LAMA **6**:11 *bibliog., illus.*
Lhasa (Tibet) **12**:309–310
Lhasa apso **12**:310
Potala palace **19**:190 *illus.*
Tibetan Buddhism **19**:190–191
DALATANDO (Angola)
map (9° 18′S 14° 54′E) **2**:5
D'ALBERT, EUGEN *see* ALBERT, EUGEN D'
DALCROZE, ÉMILE JAQUES **6**:11 *bibliog.*
eurhythmics **7**:265–266
DALE (county in Alabama)
map (31° 27′N 85° 37′W) **1**:234
DALE (Indiana)
map (38° 10′N 86° 59′W) **11**:111
DALE, CHESTER
National Gallery of Art **14**:33
DALE, SIR HENRY HALLETT **6**:11 *bibliog.*
DALE, SIR THOMAS
Virginia **19**:611
DALE CITY (Virginia)
map (38° 38′N 77° 18′W) **19**:607
DALE HOLLOW LAKE
map (36° 36′N 85° 19′W) **19**:104
D'ALEMBERT, JEAN LE ROND *see* ALEMBERT, JEAN LE ROND D'
DALETH (letter)
D (letter) **6**:3
DALEVILLE (Alabama)
map (31° 17′N 85° 44′W) **1**:234
DALEVILLE (Indiana)
map (40° 7′N 85° 33′W) **11**:111
DALEY, ARTHUR **6**:11
DALEY, RICHARD J. **6**:11–12 *bibliog., illus.*
DALHART (Texas)
map (36° 4′N 102° 31′W) **19**:129
DALHOUSIE (New Brunswick)
map (48° 4′N 66° 23′W) **14**:117
DALHOUSIE, JAMES ANDREW BROUN RAMSAY, 1ST MARQUESS OF **6**:12 *bibliog.*
DALHOUSIE UNIVERSITY **6**:12
DALÍ, SALVADOR **6**:12–13 *bibliog., illus.*
Buñuel, Luis **3**:565
Chromosome of a Highly Colored Fish's Eye Starting the Harmonious Disintegration of the Persistence of Memory **6**:12 *illus.*
Discovery of America by Christopher Columbus **18**:155 *illus.*
film, history of **8**:84
Soft Construction with Boiled Beans: Premonition of Civil War **15**:23 *illus.*
Spanish art and architecture **18**:156
surrealism (art) **18**:364
Temptation of Saint Anthony **18**:365 *illus.*
DALIAN (China) *see* TA-LIEN (Dalian) (China)
DALIN, OLOF VON **6**:13
DALLAM (county in Texas)
map (36° 15′N 102° 38′W) **19**:129
DALLAPICCOLA, LUIGI **6**:13 *bibliog.*
Italian music **11**:319
DALLAS (county in Alabama)
map (32° 20′N 87° 10′W) **1**:234
DALLAS (county in Arkansas)
map (34° 0′N 92° 45′W) **2**:166
DALLAS (Georgia)
map (33° 55′N 84° 51′W) **9**:114
DALLAS (county in Iowa)
map (41° 38′N 94° 0′W) **11**:244
DALLAS (county in Missouri)
map (37° 40′N 93° 0′W) **13**:476
DALLAS (Oregon)
map (44° 55′N 123° 19′W) **14**:427
DALLAS (Texas) **6**:13–14 *illus.*
map (32° 47′N 96° 48′W) **19**:129
DALLAS (county in Texas)
map (32° 17′N 96° 47′W) **19**:129
DALLAS, GEORGE MIFFLIN **6**:14 *bibliog.*
DALLAS CENTER (Iowa)
map (41° 41′N 93° 58′W) **11**:244
DALLES DAM **6**:17 *illus.*
DALMANE
sedative **17**:182
DALMATIA (Yugoslavia) **6**:14
archaeology
Evans, Sir Arthur **7**:312
cities
Split **18**:191
DALMATIAN (dog) **6**:14 *bibliog., illus.*; **6**:219 *illus.*
DALMATIAN LANGUAGE
languages, extinct **12**:198
Romance languages **16**:280
DALOA (Ivory Coast)
map (6° 53′N 6° 27′W) **11**:335
DALOU, AIMÉ JULES **6**:14 *bibliog.*
DALRIADA (kingdom)
Scotland **17**:151
DALRYMPLE, JOHN
Glencoe, Massacre of **9**:207
DALTON (Georgia)
carpet industry **4**:165
map (34° 47′N 84° 58′W) **9**:114
DALTON (Massachusetts)
map (42° 29′N 73° 9′W) **13**:206
DALTON (Nebraska)
map (41° 25′N 102° 58′W) **14**:70
DALTON, JOHN **4**:326 *illus.*; **6**:14–15 *bibliog., illus.*
atomic theory **2**:304–305 *illus.*
chemistry, history of **4**:325
element **7**:129
chemical combination, laws of **4**:315
Dalton's law **6**:15
DALTON GARDENS (Idaho)
map (47° 44′N 116° 46′W) **11**:26
DALTON PLAN **6**:15
DALTON'S LAW **6**:15
DALTREY, ROGER
Who, The **20**:143
DALY, AUGUSTIN **6**:15 *bibliog.*
Elliott, Maxine **7**:147
DALY, MARCUS **6**:15
Montana **13**:550
DALY, REGINALD
coral reef **5**:258
DALY CITY (California) **10**:278 *illus.*
map (37° 42′N 122° 29′W) **4**:31

DALY RIVER
map (13° 20′S 130° 19′E) **2**:328
DAM **6**:15–18 *bibliog., illus.*
Aswan High Dam **2**:286
beaver dam **3**:148–149 *illus.*
concrete dam **6**:17
Delta Plan **6**:95–96
design and structure **6**:16–17 *illus.*
dike (engineering) **6**:175
disasters
Fréjus **8**:301
Vaiont Dam **19**:503
earth-filled dam **6**:16 *illus.*
fish ladder **6**:17
floods and flood control **8**:167
foundation, building **8**:250
gates **6**:17
Glen Canyon Dam **2**:163 *illus.*; **6**:17 *illus.*
Grand Coulee Dam **9**:285
Hoover Dam **10**:230
hydroelectric power **10**:332–335
irrigation **11**:281
Kaiser, Henry John **12**:7
Nile River **14**:197
overflow and nonoverflow dams **6**:15
reservoir **6**:17
rock-filled dam **6**:16–17 *illus.*
soil mechanics **18**:38
Teton Dam **19**:127
types **6**:16–17 *illus.*
DAM, CARL HENRIK **6**:18 *bibliog.*
Doisy, Edward **6**:224
DAMAGES (law) **6**:18
contract **5**:232
trover **19**:312
DAMAN *see* GOA, DAMAN, AND DIU
DAMANHUR (Egypt)
map (31° 2′N 30° 28′E) **7**:76
DAMAS, LÉON GONTRAN **6**:18 *bibliog.*
DAMASCUS (Arkansas)
map (35° 22′N 92° 25′W) **2**:166
DAMASCUS (Georgia)
map (31° 18′N 84° 43′W) **9**:114
DAMASCUS (Maryland)
map (39° 17′N 77° 12′W) **13**:188
DAMASCUS (Syria) **6**:18–19 *bibliog., illus.*; **18**:412 *illus., table*
history **6**:18–19
map (33° 30′N 36° 18′E) **18**:412
mosaic **13**:596
DAMASK **6**:19
DAMASKINÓS **6**:19
DAMASUS I, POPE **6**:19
DAMAVAND, MOUNT *see* DEMAVEND, MOUNT
D'AMBOISE, JACQUES **6**:19
DAME AUX CAMÉLIAS, LA (play) *see* *CAMILLE* (play)
DAMIAN, SAINT *see* COSMAS AND DAMIAN, SAINTS
DAMIEN, FATHER **6**:19 *bibliog.*
DAMMARTIN, GUY DE
Flamboyant Gothic style **8**:150
DAMOCLES **6**:19
DAMON, WILLIAM
moral awareness **13**:573
DAMON AND PYTHIAS **6**:19
DAMPIER (Australia)
map (20° 39′S 116° 45′E) **2**:328
DAMPIER, WILLIAM **6**:19 *bibliog.*
Australia, history of **2**:340 *map*
DAMPING **6**:19
DAMPING OFF (botany)
diseases, plant **6**:195
DAMROSCH (family) **6**:20 *bibliog.*
DAMROSCH, FRANK HEINO
Damrosch (family) **6**:20
Juilliard School, The **11**:465
DAMROSCH, WALTER
Damrosch (family) **6**:20
DAMSELFISH **6**:20 *illus.*
DAMSELFLY **6**:20 *bibliog.*
Odonata **14**:350
DAN (biblical character) **6**:20
DAN RIVER
map (36° 42′N 78° 45′W) **19**:607
DANA (Indiana)
map (39° 48′N 87° 30′W) **11**:111
DANA, CHARLES ANDERSON **6**:20 *bibliog.*
DANA, JAMES DWIGHT **6**:20 *bibliog.*
geosyncline **9**:119
mineral **13**:439
paleogeography **15**:35–36
DANA, RICHARD HENRY **6**:21 *bibliog.*
DANA, WILLIAM
X-15 **20**:311
DANAË **6**:21
DANAKIL DEPRESSION (Ethiopia) **7**:254 *illus.*
DANAKIL PLAIN
map (12° 25′N 40° 30′E) **7**:253
DANANÉ (Ivory Coast)
map (7° 16′N 8° 9′W) **11**:335
DANAUS **6**:21
DANBURY (Connecticut) **6**:21
map (41° 23′N 73° 27′W) **5**:193
DANBURY (Iowa)
map (42° 14′N 95° 43′W) **11**:244
DANBURY (Nebraska)
map (40° 3′N 100° 24′W) **14**:70
DANBURY (North Carolina)
map (36° 24′N 80° 12′W) **14**:242
DANBURY (Texas)
map (29° 14′N 95° 21′W) **19**:129
DANBY, THOMAS OSBORNE, 1st EARL OF **6**:21 *bibliog.*
DANCE **6**:21–28 *bibliog., illus.*
See also the subheading dance under names of specific countries, e.g., ITALY; SPAIN; etc.; names of specific choreographers and dancers, e.g., NIJINSKY, VASLAV; THARP, TWYLA; etc.
ballade **3**:40–41
ballet **3**:41–47
big apple **3**:248
bolero **3**:364
cakewalk **4**:21
calypso **4**:49
cancan **4**:100
cha cha **4**:264
Charleston (dance) **4**:298
choreography **4**:408–409 *illus.*
criticism
Barnes, Clive **3**:86
Croce, Arlene **5**:355
Terry, Walter **19**:122
dance, social **6**:29–30
Death, Dance of **6**:68
disco music **6**:189
education
arts, education in the **2**:224–225
Denishawn **6**:108
eurhythmics **7**:265–266
Juilliard School, The **11**:465
Laban, Rudolf von **12**:151
Volkova, Vera **19**:629–630
fado **8**:7
fandango **8**:20
fertility rites **8**:60
flamenco **8**:151
folk dance **8**:199–201
fox-trot **8**:257
gavotte **9**:63
historians and scholars
Kirstein, Lincoln **12**:90
hula **10**:295
Indians, American
ghost dance **9**:169
Indians of North America, music and dance of the **11**:142–144 *illus.*
jitterbug **11**:419
Latin American music and dance **12**:231
masque **13**:200
Maypole dance **13**:248–249
minuet **13**:461
modern dance **13**:496–498
morris dance **13**:589
music hall, vaudeville, and burlesque **13**:671–673 *illus.*
musical comedy **13**:673–675
passacaglia and chaconne **15**:103
saraband **17**:74
square dance **18**:202
swing **18**:392–393
sword dance **18**:399
tango **19**:23
tap dancing **19**:29
tarantella **19**:35
theatricalism
Fuller, Loie **8**:357
waltz **20**:21
DANCE, GEORGE **6**:28 *bibliog.*
DANCE, SOCIAL **6**:29–30 *bibliog., illus.*
big apple **3**:248
cakewalk **4**:21
Castle, Vernon and Irene **4**:191
cha cha **4**:264
Charleston **4**:298
dance **6**:23–24 *illus.*
fox-trot **8**:257
Indians of North America, music and dance of the **11**:143
minuet **13**:461
tango **19**:23
waltz **20**:21
DANCE OF DEATH *see* DEATH, DANCE OF
DANCE INDEX (periodical)
Kirstein, Lincoln **12**:90
DANCE MARATHON **6**:30 *bibliog., illus.*
DANCE OF THE SEVEN DEADLY SINS, THE (poem)
Dunbar, William **6**:298
DANCE THEATRE OF HARLEM **6**:30
Mitchell, Arthur **13**:482
DANCEMAGAZINE **6**:30
DANCHENKO, VLADIMIR IVANOVICH NEMIROVICH *see* NEMIROVICH-DANCHENKO, VLADIMIR IVANOVICH
DANCING RABBIT CREEK, TREATY OF
Choctaw **4**:403
DANDARAH *see* DENDERA (Egypt)
DANDELION **6**:30–31 *illus.*
DANDIE DINMONT TERRIER **6**:31 *illus.*; **6**:220 *illus.*
DANDOLO, ENRICO
doge **6**:222
D'ANDRADE, FRANCISCO **14**:400 *illus.*
DANDRIDGE (Tennessee)
map (36° 1′N 83° 25′W) **19**:104
DANDRUFF **6**:31
DANE (county in Wisconsin)
map (43° 7′N 89° 28′W) **20**:185
DANELAW **6**:31
East Anglia **7**:31
DANEMAN, PAUL **19**:154 *illus.*
DANFORTH (Maine)
map (45° 40′N 67° 52′W) **13**:70
DANFORTH, THOMAS **6**:31 *bibliog.*
DANFORTH FOUNDATION **6**:31
DANFORTH HILLS
map (40° 15′N 108° 0′W) **5**:116
DANGER CAVE (Utah) **6**:31 *bibiliog.*; **14**:237 *map*
DANGRAEK MOUNTAINS
map location map (14° 25′N 103° 30′E) **19**:139
DANHAUSER, JOSEF
leading figures of the Romantic movement **16**:293 *illus.*
DANIEL (prophet) **12**:226 *illus.*
DANIEL (Wyoming)
map (42° 52′N 110° 4′W) **20**:301
DANIEL, ANTOINE
Jesuit Martyrs of North America **11**:402
DANIEL, ARNAUT **6**:31
DANIEL, BOOK OF **6**:31–32
DANIEL, SAMUEL **6**:32 *bibliog.*
masque **13**:200
DANIEL, YULI **6**:32 *bibliog.*
DANIELL, JOHN FREDERIC **6**:32
DANIELL CELL
battery **3**:125
DANIELS (county in Montana)
map (48° 50′N 105° 28′W) **13**:547
DANIELS, CONRAD
darts **6**:40
DANIELS, JONATHAN WORTH **6**:32 *bibliog.*
DANIELS, JOSEPHUS **6**:32 *bibliog.*
DANIEL'S HARBOUR (Newfoundland)
map (50° 14′N 57° 35′W) **14**:166
DANIELSON (Connecticut)
map (41° 48′N 71° 53′W) **5**:193
DANIELSVILLE (Georgia)
map (34° 7′N 83° 13′W) **9**:114
DÄNIKEN, ERICH VON *see* VON DÄNIKEN, ERICH
DANILOVA, ALEXANDRA **6**:32 *bibliog.*
Ballets Russes de Monte Carlo **3**:48
DANISH ART AND ARCHITECTURE *see* SCANDINAVIAN ART AND ARCHITECTURE
DANISH LANGUAGE
Germanic languages **9**:135–137 *tables*
DANISH LITERATURE **6**:32–33 *bibliog.*
Aakjaer, Jeppe **1**:49
Abell, Kjeld **1**:56
Andersen, Hans Christian **1**:401
Bang, Herman **3**:62–63
Bjørnvig, Thorkild **3**:303
Blicher, Steen Steensen **3**:331
Brandes, George Morris Cohen **3**:454
Branner, Hans Christian **3**:455
Claussen, Sophus **5**:45
Dinesen, Isak **6**:178
Drachmann, Holger Henrik Herholdt **6**:253–254
Ewald, Johannes **7**:325
Gjellerup, Karl Adolph **9**:192
Goldschmidt, Meyer Aron **9**:236
Grundtvig, Nicolai Frederik Severin **9**:382
Hauch, Johannes Carsten **10**:68
Heidberg, Johan Ludvig **10**:106
Holberg, Ludvig, Baron **10**:202
Jacobsen, Jens Peter **11**:346–347
Jensen, Johannes Vilhelm **11**:396
Kierkegaard, Søren **12**:75
Munk, Kaj **13**:643
Nexø, Martin Andersen- **14**:175
Oehlenschläger, Adam Gottlob **14**:352
Paludin-Müller, Frederik **15**:52–53
Pontoppidan, Henrik **15**:427
Saxo Grammaticus **17**:104
Soya, Carl Erik Martin **18**:114
Wied, Gustav **20**:145
Winther, Christian **20**:181
DANJON, ANDRÉ LOUIS **6**:33
DANJURO, ICHIKAWA
Ichikawa (family) **11**:19
DANLI (Honduras)
map (14° 0′N 86° 35′W) **10**:218
DANNAY, FREDERIC *see* QUEEN, ELLERY
DANNEBROG (Nebraska)
map (41° 7′N 98° 33′W) **14**:70
DANNECKER, JOHANN HEINRICH VON **6**:33
DANNEMORA (New York)
map (44° 43′N 73° 43′W) **14**:149
D'ANNUNZIO, GABRIELE **6**:33–34 *bibliog., illus.*; **11**:316 *illus.*
Duse, Eleonora **6**:307
Pizzetti, Ildebrando **15**:325
Rijeka (Yugoslavia) **16**:223
DANSE DES MORTS *see* DEATH, DANCE OF
DANSE MACABRE *see* DEATH, DANCE OF
DANSVILLE (New York)
map (42° 34′N 77° 42′W) **14**:149
DANTE ALIGHIERI **6**:34 *bibliog., illus.*; **11**:315 *illus.*
Beatrice **3**:145
Divine Comedy, The **6**:203
state (in political philosophy) **18**:230
DANTON, GEORGES JACQUES **6**:34–35 *bibliog., illus.*
French Revolution **8**:323 *illus.*
D'ANTONGUOLLA, RODOLFO *see* VALENTINO, RUDOLPH
DANTZIG, RUDI VAN **6**:35
Dutch National Ballet **6**:314
DANUBE RIVER **6**:35–36 *bibliog., map*
dam **16**:289 *illus.*
economic development **6**:36
Inn River **11**:179
Iron Gate **11**:272
map (45° 20′N 29° 40′E) **6**:35
DANUBE SCHOOL (art group) **6**:36 *bibliog.*
Altdorfer, Albrecht **1**:311–312
Cranach, Lucas, the Elder **5**:329
Huber, Wolf **10**:288
Renaissance art and architecture **16**:154
DANUBIAN CULTURE **6**:36 *bibliog.*
European prehistory **7**:302
DANVERS (Massachusetts)
map (42° 34′N 70° 56′W) **13**:206
DANVILLE (Arkansas)
map (35° 3′N 93° 24′W) **2**:166
DANVILLE (Georgia)
map (32° 37′N 83° 15′W) **9**:114
DANVILLE (Illinois)
map (40° 8′N 87° 37′W) **11**:42
DANVILLE (Indiana)
map (39° 46′N 86° 32′W) **11**:111
DANVILLE (Kentucky)
map (37° 39′N 84° 46′W) **12**:47
DANVILLE (Pennsylvania)
map (40° 57′N 76° 37′W) **15**:147
DANVILLE (Vermont)
map (44° 25′N 66° 9′W) **19**:554
DANVILLE (Virginia)
map (36° 35′N 79° 24′W) **19**:607
DANVILLE (Washington)
map (48° 59′N 118° 30′W) **20**:35
DANZIG *see* GDAŃSK (Poland)
DAODE JING *see* *TAO TE CHING* (Daode Jing)
DAPHNE (Alabama)
map (30° 36′N 87° 54′W) **1**:234
DAPHNE (botany) **6**:36
DAPHNE (mythology) **6**:36
DAPHNIA *see* WATER FLEA
DAPHNIS (mythology) **6**:36
DAPSONE
leprosy **12**:295
DAQIQI
Persian literature **15**:187
DAR *see* DAUGHTERS OF THE AMERICAN REVOLUTION, NATIONAL SOCIETY OF THE
DAR ES SALAAM (Tanzania) **1**:147 *illus.*; **6**:37; **19**:27 *illus.*
climate **19**:27 *table*
map (6° 48′S 39° 17′E) **19**:27
DARA (Syria)
map (32° 37′N 36° 6′E) **18**:412
DARAVICA MOUNTAIN
map (42° 32′N 20° 8′E) **20**:340

D'ARBONNE, LAKE
 map (32° 45′N 92° 25′W) **12**:430
DARBY (family) **6**:37
 Coalbrookdale ironworks **19**:66 *illus.*
D'ARCY (British Columbia)
 map (50° 33′N 122° 29′W) **3**:491
DARCY, HENRY PHILIBERT GASPARD **6**:37
 permeability, rock **15**:174
DARDANELLE (Arkansas)
 map (35° 13′N 93° 9′W) **2**:166
DARDANELLE (California)
 map (38° 20′N 119° 50′W) **4**:31
DARDANELLE LAKE
 map (35° 25′N 93° 20′W) **2**:166
DARDANELLES **6**:37 *map*
 map (40° 15′N 26° 25′E) **19**:343
 World War I **20**:228; **20**:231
DARDANUS **6**:37
DARE (county in North Carolina)
 map (35° 50′N 75° 50′W) **14**:242
DARE, VIRGINIA **6**:37
D'AREZZO, GUIDO
 staff (music) **18**:209
DARFUR **6**:37 *bibliog.*
 Fur **8**:369
DARGOMYZHSKY, ALEKSANDR SERGEYEVICH **6**:37 *bibliog.*
 Russian music **16**:367
DARHAN (Mongolia)
 map (49° 28′N 105° 56′E) **13**:529
DARIE HILLS
 map (8° 15′N 47° 25′E) **18**:60
DARIEN (Connecticut)
 map (41° 5′N 73° 28′W) **5**:193
DARIEN (Georgia)
 map (31° 22′N 81° 26′W) **9**:114
DARIEN CORDILLERA MOUNTAINS
 map (12° 55′N 85° 30′W) **14**:179
DARIEN MOUNTAINS
 map (8° 20′N 77° 22′W) **15**:55
DARIEN SCHEME
 Panama **15**:56
DARÍO, RUBÉN **6**:37–38 *bibliog.*
 Latin American literature **12**:229
 León (Nicaragua) **12**:289
DARIUS I, KING OF PERSIA
 palace relief **15**:184 *illus.*
DARIUS I, KING OF PERSIA (Darius the Great) **6**:38 *bibliog., illus.*
 archers from army of **2**:249 *illus.*
 Behistun **3**:171
 Greece, ancient **9**:331
 Persepolis **15**:180
 Persia, ancient **15**:181–182 *map*
 Persian Wars **15**:187–188
 Susa **18**:370
 Xerxes I, King of Persia **20**:312
DARIUS III CODOMANNUS, KING OF PERSIA **6**:38
DARJEELING (India) **6**:38; **11**:81–82 *illus., table*
 Sherpa **17**:259
 tea **19**:53 *illus.*
DARK AGES **6**:38
DARK CRIMSON UNDERWING MOTH **3**:598–599 *illus.*
DARK HORSE **6**:38
 political convention **15**:399
DARKE (county in Ohio)
 map (40° 8′N 84° 38′W) **14**:357
DARKNESS AT NOON (book) **6**:38–39
 Koestler, Arthur **11**:105
DARLAN, JEAN FRANÇOIS **6**:39
DARLING (Mississippi)
 map (34° 22′N 90° 23′W) **13**:469
DARLING, JAY NORWOOD **6**:39 *bibliog.*
DARLING RANGE
 map (32° 0′S 116° 30′E) **2**:328
DARLING RIVER **6**:39
 map (34° 7′S 141° 55′E) **2**:328
DARLINGTON (England) **6**:39
 map (54° 31′N 1° 34′W) **19**:403
DARLINGTON (South Carolina)
 map (34° 18′N 79° 52′W) **18**:98
DARLINGTON (county in South Carolina)
 map (34° 20′N 79° 55′W) **18**:98
DARLINGTON (Wisconsin)
 map (42° 41′N 90° 7′W) **20**:185
DARMSTADT (West Germany) **6**:39
 haggadah **11**:461 *illus.*
 map (49° 53′N 8° 40′E) **9**:140
DARNA (Libya)
 map (32° 46′N 22° 39′E) **12**:320
DARNLEY, HENRY STEWART, LORD **6**:39
 Mary, Queen of Scots **13**:186
 Stuart (family) **18**:304
DARRIEUS ROTOR
 windmills and wind power **20**:172–173 *illus.*
DARROW, CLARENCE S. **6**:39 *bibliog., illus.*
 Scopes Trial **17**:148
DART, RAYMOND **6**:39 *bibliog.*
 Australopithecus **2**:345–346
 Makapansgat **13**:77
 Taung skull **19**:45
DART, RICHARD POUSETTE- *see* POUSETTE-DART, RICHARD
DARTER (bird) *see* ANHINGA
DARTER (fish) **6**:40
DARTMOOR (England) **6**:40
DARTMOUTH (Nova Scotia) **6**:40
 map (44° 40′N 63° 34′A) **14**:269
DARTMOUTH COLLEGE **6**:40
 Wheelock, Eleazar **20**:129
DARTMOUTH COLLEGE* v. *WOODWARD **6**:40
 Marshall, John **13**:172
DARTS (game) **6**:40 *illus.*
DARVON **6**:40
 analgesic **1**:388
 respiratory system disorders **16**:182
DARWIN (Australia) **6**:40–41
 climate **2**:332 *table*
 map (12° 28′S 130° 50′E) **2**:328
DARWIN, CHARLES **3**:270 *illus.*; **6**:41–42 *bibliog., illus.*; **7**:319 *illus.*
 animal behavior **2**:11
 biology **3**:269
 classification, biological **5**:42
 coral reef **5**:258
 Darwin's finches **6**:42–43
 De Beer, Sir Gavin **6**:58
 emotion **7**:157
 eugenics **7**:263
 evolution **7**:318–319; **7**:324
 exploration **8**:335
 fossil record **8**:247
 Galápagos Islands **9**:10
 Galton, Sir Francis **9**:22–23
 geologic time **9**:103
 Haeckel, Ernst Heinrich **10**:9
 heredity **10**:140
 Hooker (family) **10**:227
 Huxley, Thomas Henry **10**:325
 Lamarck, Jean Baptiste **12**:173
 Lyell, Sir Charles **12**:475
 natural selection **14**:49
 Neanderthalers **14**:69
 Origin of Species, On the **14**:443–444
 population dynamics **15**:438
 Scopes Trial **17**:148
 sexual selection **17**:231
 Social Darwinism **18**:11
 tropism **19**:309
 unconformity **19**:382
 Wallace, Alfred Russel **20**:13
DARWIN, ERASMUS **6**:42 *bibliog.*
 Darwin, Charles **6**:41
DARWIN, SIR FRANCIS **6**:42
 tropism **19**:309
DARWIN, SIR GEORGE HOWARD **6**:42
DARWIN COLLEGE (Cambridge University) **4**:52
DARWINISM
 Darwin, Charles **6**:41
 Social Darwinism **18**:11–12
DARWIN'S FINCHES **6**:42–43 *bibliog.*; **7**:320 *illus.*
 adaptive radiation **1**:98
 Darwin, Charles **6**:41
 evolution **7**:320
DAS ISLAND
 map (25° 9′N 52° 53′E) **19**:401
DAS KAPITAL see KAPITAL, DAS (book)
DASHEEN *see* TARO
DASHEN, MOUNT
 map (13° 10′N 38° 26′E) **7**:253
DASHT RIVER
 map (25° 10′N 61° 40′E) **15**:27
DASS, PETTER **6**:43
 Norwegian literature **14**:265
DASSAULT MIRAGE III-C AIRCRAFT *see* MIRAGE (aircraft)
DASSEL (Minnesota)
 map (45° 5′N 94° 19′W) **13**:453
DASSIE *see* HYRAX
DASYURE *see* HYRAX
DATA PROCESSING
 automata, theory of **2**:356–357
 information science **11**:172
 information storage and retrieval **11**:173–174
 input-output devices **11**:182–183
DATA TERMINAL *see* COMPUTER TERMINAL
DATABASE **6**:43–44 *bibliog.*
 computer networking **5**:163
 computers and privacy **5**:166–167
 expert system **7**:334
 information science **11**:172–173
 information storage and retrieval **11**:173–174
DATE AND DATE PALM **6**:44–45 *bibliog., illus.*
DATING SYSTEMS *see* CHRONOLOGY
DATOLITE *see* ZEOLITE
DATU, CAPE
 map (2° 6′N 109° 39′E) **13**:84
DATU PIANG (Philippines)
 map (7° 1′N 124° 30′E) **15**:237
DATURA **6**:45
 medicinal plants **13**:266
DAUBERVAL, JEAN **6**:45
D'AUBIGNAC, ABBÉ *see* AUBIGNAC, ABBÉ D'
D'AUBIGNÉ, AGRIPPA *see* AUBIGNÉ, AGRIPPA D'
DAUBIGNY, CHARLES FRANÇOIS **6**:45 *bibliog.*
DAUD, MUHAMMAD
 Afghanistan **1**:135
DAUDET, ALPHONSE **6**:45 *bibliog.*
DAUDET, LÉON **6**:45
DAUGHERTY, HARRY M. **6**:45 *bibliog.*
DAUGHTERS OF THE AMERICAN REVOLUTION, NATIONAL SOCIETY OF THE **6**:45
DAULATABAD (Afghanistan)
 map (36° 26′N 64° 55′E) **1**:133
DAULE (Ecuador)
 map (1° 50′S 79° 56′W) **7**:52
DAULE (towns in Ecuador)
 map (0° 24′N 80° 0′W) **7**:52
DAULE RIVER
 map (2° 10′S 79° 52′W) **7**:52
DAUM, AUGUSTE AND ANTONIN *see* DAUM FRÈRES
DAUM FRÈRES
 Art Deco **2**:207
DAUMIER, HONORÉ **6**:45–46 *bibliog., illus.*
 caricature **4**:150
 Carjat, Étienne **4**:151
 Crispino and Scapino **6**:46 *illus.*
 Don Quixote and Sancho Panza **14**:273 *illus.*
 graphic arts **9**:293
DAUPHIN **6**:46
DAUPHIN (Manitoba)
 map (51° 9′N 100° 3′W) **13**:119
DAUPHIN (county in Pennsylvania)
 map (40° 15′N 76° 52′W) **15**:147
DAUPHIN ISLAND (Alabama)
 map (30° 15′N 88° 7′W) **1**:234
DAUPHIN LAKE
 map (51° 17′N 99° 48′W) **13**:119
DAUPHINÉ (France) **6**:46
D'AUREVILLY, JULES AMÉDÉE BARBEY *see* BARBEY D'AUREVILLY, JULES AMÉDÉE
DAUSSET, JEAN **6**:46
DAVANT (Louisiana)
 map (29° 37′N 89° 51′W) **12**:430
DAVAO (Philippines) **6**:46
 map (7° 4′N 125° 36′E) **15**:237
DAVENANT, SIR WILLIAM **6**:46 *bibliog.*
 masque **13**:200
DAVENPORT (Iowa) **6**:46; **11**:245 *illus.*
 map (41° 32′N 90° 41′W) **11**:244
DAVENPORT (Nebraska)
 map (40° 19′N 97° 49′W) **14**:70
DAVENPORT (Oklahoma)
 map (35° 42′N 96° 46′W) **14**:368
DAVENPORT (Washington)
 map (47° 39′N 118° 9′W) **20**:35
DAVENPORT, CHARLES **6**:46
DAVENPORT, FANNY **6**:46
DAVENPORT, HOMER (cartoonist)
 Mark Hanna cartoon **4**:176 *illus.*
DAVENPORT, JOHN **6**:47
DAVENPORT, WILLIE (athlete) **14**:384 *illus.*
DAVEY, MARIE AUGUSTA *see* FISKE, MINNIE MADDERN
DAVID (Panama)
 map (8° 26′N 82° 26′W) **15**:55
DAVID (sculpture) **6**:47 *bibliog.*
 Donatello **3**:508 *illus.*; **6**:237 *illus.*; **16**:150 *illus.*
 Michelangelo **11**:311 *illus.*; **13**:373; **17**:163 *illus.*
DAVID, FÉLICIEN CÉSAR **6**:47
DAVID, GERARD **6**:47 *bibliog., illus.*
 Virgin and Child **6**:47 *illus.*
DAVID, HENRY WINTER
 Wade, Benjamin Franklin **20**:4
DAVID, JACQUES LOUIS **6**:47–48 *bibliog., illus.*
 Antoine Laurent Lavoisier **12**:241 *illus.*
 The Battle of the Romans and the Sabines **11**:23 *illus.*
 Death of Marat **13**:143 *illus.*
 French art and architecture **8**:306
 Leonidas at Thermopylae **14**:81 *illus.*
 Madame Récamier **7**:159 *illus.*; **8**:306 *illus.*
 Napoléon Bonaparte **8**:271 *illus.*
 Oath of the Horatii **6**:48 *illus.*
DAVID, KING OF ISRAEL **6**:48 *bibliog.*
DAVID, SAINT **6**:48
DAVID I, KING OF SCOTLAND **6**:49 *bibliog.*
DAVID II, KING OF SCOTLAND **6**:49 *bibliog.*
DAVID CITY (Nebraska)
 map (41° 15′N 97° 8′W) **14**:70
DAVID COPPERFIELD (book) **6**:48–49 *bibliog.*
 Dickens, Charles **6**:156
DAVIDOVSKY, MARIO **6**:49 *bibliog.*
DAVIDSON (North Carolina)
 map (35° 30′N 80° 51′W) **14**:242
DAVIDSON (county in North Carolina)
 map (35° 50′N 80° 15′W) **14**:242
DAVIDSON (Saskatchewan)
 map (51° 18′N 106° 59′W) **17**:81
DAVIDSON (county in Tennessee)
 map (36° 10′N 86° 45′W) **19**:104
DAVIDSON, BRUCE **6**:49
DAVIDSON, JO **6**:49
DAVIDSON, JOHN **6**:49 *bibliog.*
DAVIDSON, N. R.
 theater of fact **19**:153
DAVIDSON COLLEGE **6**:49
DAVIE (county in North Carolina)
 map (35° 55′N 80° 35′W) **14**:242
DAVIES, ARTHUR B. **6**:49 *bibliog.*
DAVIES, SIR JOHN **6**:49
DAVIES, SIR LOUIS HENRY **6**:49–50
DAVIES, PETER MAXWELL **6**:50
 English music **7**:204
DAVIES, ROBERTSON **6**:50 *bibliog.*
 Canadian literature **4**:93–94 *illus.*
DAVIES, SAMUEL **6**:50 *bibliog.*
DAVIES, THOMAS
 View of the Bridge on the River La Puce **4**:88 *illus.*
DAVIES, WILLIAM HENRY **6**:50
DAVIESS (county in Indiana)
 map (38° 45′N 87° 5′W) **11**:111
DAVIESS (county in Kentucky)
 map (37° 40′N 87° 5′W) **12**:47
DAVIESS (county in Missouri)
 map (39° 55′N 94° 0′W) **13**:476
DAVIS (California)
 map (38° 33′N 121° 44′W) **4**:31
DAVIS (county in Iowa)
 map (40° 45′N 92° 22′W) **11**:244
DAVIS (North Carolina)
 map (34° 48′N 76° 28′W) **14**:242
DAVIS (Oklahoma)
 map (34° 30′N 97° 3′W) **14**:368
DAVIS (county in Utah)
 map (41° 0′N 112° 5′W) **19**:492
DAVIS, ALEXANDER JACKSON **6**:50 *bibliog.*
DAVIS, BENJAMIN O. **6**:50 *bibliog.*
DAVIS, BETTE **6**:50 *bibliog., illus.*
DAVIS, COLIN **6**:50–51
DAVIS, DAVID **6**:51 *bibliog.*
DAVIS, ELMER **6**:51 *bibliog.*
DAVIS, FRANK MARSHALL **6**:51
DAVIS, GLENN **6**:51
DAVIS, HENRY WINTER **6**:51 *bibliog.*
DAVIS, JEFFERSON **5**:176 *illus.*; **6**:51–52 *bibliog., illus.*
 Civil War, U.S. **5**:18–30 *illus.*
 Confederate States of America **5**:177
 Fort Sumter **8**:237
 Montgomery (Alabama) **13**:556
 Richmond (Virginia) **16**:214
 Stone Mountain **18**:282
 Virginia **19**:609
DAVIS, JOHN **6**:52
DAVIS, JOHN W. **6**:52 *bibliog.*
 political convention **15**:399
DAVIS, MILES **6**:52 *bibliog.*
 jazz **11**:389 *illus.*
DAVIS, MOUNT
 map (39° 47′N 79° 10′W) **15**:147
DAVIS, OSSIE **6**:52 *bibliog.*
DAVIS, PAULINA WRIGHT **6**:52
DAVIS, RENNIE
 counterculture **5**:311
DAVIS, RICHARD HARDING **6**:52 *bibliog.*
DAVIS, STUART **6**:52–53 *bibliog., illus.*
 Place Pasdeloupe **6**:53 *illus.*
DAVIS, WILLIAM MORRIS **6**:53
DAVIS COVE (Newfoundland)
 map (47° 40′N 54° 18′W) **14**:166
DAVIS CUP
 tennis **19**:109
DAVIS MOUNTAINS
 map (30° 35′N 104° 0′W) **19**:129

DAVIS SEA
  map (66° 0′S 92° 0′E) **2**:40
DAVIS STRAIT **6**:53
  map (67° 0′N 57° 0′W) **4**:70
DAVISBORO (Georgia)
  map (32° 59′N 82° 36′W) **9**:114
DAVISON (county in South Dakota)
  map (43° 40′N 98° 10′W) **18**:103
DAVISON, GEORGE
  Linked Ring Brotherhood **12**:358
DAVISSON, CLINTON **6**:53
  chemistry, history of **4**:328
  quantum mechanics **16**:10
DAVITT, MICHAEL **6**:53 *bibliog.*
DAVOS (Switzerland) **6**:53
  map (46° 48′N 9° 50′E) **18**:394
DAVOUT, LOUIS NICOLAS **6**:53
DAVY, SIR HUMPHRY **6**:53–54 *bibliog., illus.*
  anesthetics **1**:410
  calcium **4**:22
  discharge, electrical **6**:188
  electrochemistry **7**:112
  fuel cell **8**:354
DAVYS, JOHN *see* DAVIS, JOHN
DAWA RIVER
  map (4° 11′N 42° 6′E) **7**:253
DAWES (county in Nebraska)
  map (42° 45′N 103° 10′W) **14**:70
DAWES, CHARLES G. **6**:54 *bibliog.*
DAWES, HENRY LAURENS
  Dawes Act (1887) **6**:54
  Oklahoma **14**:370
DAWES, WILLIAM **6**:54
DAWES ACT (1887) **6**:54
  Fletcher, Alice **8**:163
  Indians, American **11**:137
  United States, history of the **19**:450
  Washo **20**:45
DAWES PLAN
  reparations **16**:160
  Young, Owen D. **20**:334
DAWN HORSE *see* EOHIPPUS
DAWN REDWOOD **6**:54
DAWSON (Georgia)
  map (31° 47′N 84° 26′W) **9**:114
DAWSON (county in Georgia)
  map (34° 25′N 84° 10′W) **9**:114
DAWSON (Minnesota)
  map (44° 56′N 96° 3′W) **13**:453
DAWSON (county in Montana)
  map (47° 15′N 104° 50′W) **13**:547
DAWSON (Nebraska)
  map (40° 8′N 95° 50′W) **14**:70
DAWSON (county in Nebraska)
  map (40° 50′N 99° 50′W) **14**:70
DAWSON (Texas)
  map (31° 54′N 96° 43′W) **19**:129
DAWSON (county in Texas)
  map (32° 45′N 101° 58′W) **19**:129
DAWSON (Yukon Territory)
  map (64° 4′N 139° 25′W) **20**:345
DAWSON, CHARLES
  Piltdown man **15**:303
DAWSON CREEK (British Columbia)
  map (55° 46′N 120° 14′W) **3**:491
DAWSON RANGE (Mountain Range)
  map (62° 40′N 139° 0′W) **20**:345
DAWSON SPRINGS (Kentucky)
  map (37° 10′N 87° 41′W) **12**:47
DAWSONVILLE (Georgia)
  map (34° 25′N 84° 7′W) **9**:114
DAY **6**:54 *bibliog.*
  calendar **4**:28
  dog days **6**:221
  Julian day **11**:466
  sidereal time **17**:294
  time **19**:201–202
  variations in length **6**:54
DAY (county in South Dakota)
  map (45° 20′N 97° 38′W) **18**:103
DAY, BENJAMIN HENRY **6**:55 *bibliog.*
  journalism **11**:455
DAY, CLARENCE **6**:55 *bibliog.*
DAY, DOROTHY **6**:55 *bibliog.*
DAY, J. EDWARD **15**:526 *illus.*
DAY, STEPHEN **6**:55
DAY, THOMAS **6**:55 *bibliog.*
DAY OF ATONEMENT (Judaism) *see* YOM KIPPUR
DAY-CARE CENTER **6**:55 *bibliog.*
  Head Start **10**:85
  preschool education **15**:520–522
DAY-LEWIS, C. **6**:55 *bibliog.*
  Spender, Stephen **18**:177–178
DAY LILY **6**:55–56 *illus.*
DAY OF THE LOCUST, THE (book) **6**:56 *bibliog.*
DAYAK **6**:56 *bibliog.*
  head-hunting **10**:85
DAYALA, JOSEFA
  Portuguese art and architecture **15**:456
DAYAN, MOSHE **6**:56 *bibliog., illus.*
DAYANANDA SARASVATI **6**:56 *bibliog.*
DAYFLOWER **6**:56
DAYGLOW *see* AIRGLOW
DAYLIGHT SAVING TIME **6**:56–57 *bibliog.*
DAYR AL-BAHRI *see* DEIR EL-BAHRI (Egypt)
DAYR AL-ZAWR (Syria)
  map (35° 20′N 40° 9′E) **18**:412
DAYTON (Ohio) **6**:57
  map (39° 45′N 84° 15′W) **14**:357
DAYTON (Tennessee)
  map (35° 30′N 85° 0′W) **19**:104
DAYTON (Texas)
  map (30° 3′N 94° 54′W) **19**:129
DAYTON (Washington)
  map (46° 19′N 117° 59′W) **20**:35
DAYTON (Wyoming)
  map (44° 53′N 107° 16′W) **20**:301
DAYTON, WILLIAM **16**:172 *illus.*
DAYTONA BEACH (Florida) **6**:57
  map (29° 12′N 81° 0′W) **8**:172
DAYVILLE (Oregon)
  map (44° 28′N 119° 32′W) **14**:427
DAZAI OSAMU **6**:57
DC *see* DIRECT CURRENT
DC-3 **2**:370–372 *illus.*; **6**:57 *illus.*
  Douglas, Donald Wills **6**:247
DC-10
  Douglas, Donald Wills **6**:247
DDT **6**:57–58 *bibliog., illus.*
  conservation **5**:202
  environmental health **7**:211
  fly **8**:190
  louse **12**:436
  malaria **13**:80
    medicine **13**:271
  Müller, Paul **13**:637
  nutrient cycles **14**:304
  organic chemistry **14**:438–439
  pesticides **15**:197
  pollution, environmental **15**:413 *illus.*
DE *see* the last element of the name for names not listed below
DE AAR (South Africa)
  map (30° 39′S 24° 0′E) **18**:79
DE ARCHITECTURA (book)
  Vitruvius **19**:621
DE BACA (county in New Mexico)
  map (34° 20′N 104° 30′W) **14**:136
DE BARY (Florida)
  map (28° 52′N 81° 15′W) **8**:172
DE BEER, SIR GAVIN **6**:58
  Huxley, Sir Julian **10**:324
DE BEQUE (Colorado)
  map (39° 20′N 108° 13′W) **5**:116
DE BROGLIE, LOUIS **6**:58 *bibliog.*; **15**:286 *illus.*
  chemistry, history of **4**:328
  de Broglie wavelength **6**:58
DE BROGLIE WAVELENGTH **6**:58 *bibliog., illus.*
  quantum mechanics **16**:10
  Thomson, Sir George Paget **19**:175
DE BRUGES, HENNEQUIN
  tapestry **19**:33
DE CAMP, L. SPRAGUE **6**:58
DE COUBERTIN, PIERRE
  Olympic Games **14**:382 *illus.*
DE CUEVAS, MARQUIS GEORGE **6**:58
DE DUVE, CHRISTIAN
  Palade, George Emil **15**:29
DE FILIPPO, EDUARDO **6**:58 *bibliog.*
DE FLANDES, JUAN
  Annunciation, The **2**:206 *illus.*
DE FOREST (Wisconsin)
  map (43° 15′N 89° 20′W) **20**:185
DE FOREST, JOHN WILLIAM **6**:58 *bibliog.*
DE FOREST, LEE **6**:58 *bibliog.*; **16**:44 *illus.*
  electron tube, inventor **7**:122
  triode, inventor **19**:301
DE FUNIAK SPRINGS (Florida)
  map (30° 43′N 86° 7′W) **8**:172
DE GASPERI, ALCIDE **6**:59 *bibliog.*
  Italy, history of **11**:331
DE GAULLE, CHARLES **6**:59 *bibliog., illus.*
  Algerian War **1**:290
  Europe, history of **7**:298
  France, history of **8**:272
  Pompidou, Georges **15**:425
DE GIOVANNI, STEFANO *see* SASSETTA
DE GRAY LAKE
  map (34° 15′N 93° 15′W) **2**:166
DE GREY RIVER
  map (20° 12′S 119° 11′E) **2**:328
DE GUICHE, DOROTHY AND LILLIAN *see* GISH, DOROTHY AND LILLIAN
DE HAVILLAND, OLIVIA **6**:60
DE HAVILLAND D.H.98 MOSQUITO B.M.K.IV AIRCRAFT *see* MOSQUITO (aircraft)
DE KALB (county in Alabama)
  map (34° 30′N 85° 50′W) **1**:234
DE KALB (county in Georgia)
  map (33° 45′N 84° 10′W) **9**:114
DE KALB (Illinois)
  map (41° 59′N 88° 41′W) **11**:42
DE KALB (county in Illinois)
  map (41° 59′N 88° 41′W) **11**:42
DE KALB (county in Indiana)
  map (41° 22′N 85° 4′W) **11**:111
DE KALB (Mississippi)
  map (32° 46′N 88° 39′W) **13**:469
DE KALB (county in Missouri)
  map (39° 55′N 94° 25′W) **13**:476
DE KALB (county in Tennessee)
  map (36° 0′N 85° 50′W) **19**:104
DE KEYSER, HENDRICK
  Westerkerk, The **6**:312 *illus.*
DE KOONING, WILLEM **6**:60 *bibliog., illus.*
  Untitled V **6**:60 *illus.*
  Woman, Sag Harbor **1**:65 *illus.*
  Woman I **13**:495 *illus.*
DE KRUIF, PAUL **6**:60
DE LA BECHE, SIR HENRY THOMAS **6**:60
  Sedgwick, Adam **17**:183
DE LA ESPRIELLA, RICARDO
  Panama **15**:56
DE LA MADRID HURTADO, MIGUEL **6**:60
  Mexico, history of **13**:361; **13**:366
DE LA MARE, WALTER **6**:60 *bibliog.*
DE LA RAMÉE, LOUISE *see* OUIDA
DE LA ROCHE, MAZO **6**:61 *bibliog.*
DE LA TORRE, VICTOR RAÚL HAYA
  Peru **15**:195
DE LA WARR, THOMAS WEST, 12th BARON **6**:61
  Virginia **19**:611
DE LAMERIE, PAUL
  gold and silver work **9**:230
DE LANCEY (family) **6**:61
DE LANCEY, JAMES (1703–60)
  De Lancey (family) **6**:61
DE LANCEY, JAMES (1732–1800)
  De Lancey (family) **6**:61
DE LANCEY, OLIVER
  De Lancey (family) **6**:61
DE LAND (Florida)
  map (29° 2′N 81° 18′W) **8**:172
DE LARGE, ROBERT C. **16**:185 *illus.*
DE LAVAL, CARL GUSTAF
  turbine **19**:340
DE LEON, DANIEL **6**:61 *bibliog.*
  Industrial Workers of the World **11**:160
  socialism **18**:23
  Socialist Labor party **18**:24–25
DE LEON SPRINGS (Florida)
  map (29° 7′N 81° 21′W) **8**:172
DE LONG, GEORGE WASHINGTON **6**:61 *bibliog.*
  Arctic **2**:142 *map*
DE LOS ANGELES, VICTORIA **6**:61
DE MILLE, AGNES **6**:61
DE MILLE, CECIL B. **6**:61–62 *bibliog., illus.*
  film, history of **8**:83 *illus.*
DE MOIVRE, ABRAHAM **6**:62 *bibliog.*
DE MOIVRE'S THEOREM
  de Moivre, Abraham **6**:62
DE NIRO, ROBERT **6**:62
DE NOBILI, ROBERTO **6**:62
DE PAUW UNIVERSITY **6**:62
DE PERE (Wisconsin)
  map (44° 27′N 88° 4′W) **20**:185
DE QUEEN (Arkansas)
  map (34° 2′N 94° 21′W) **2**:166
DE QUINCEY, THOMAS **6**:62 *bibliog., illus.*
DE QUINCY (Louisiana)
  map (30° 27′N 93° 26′W) **12**:430
DE RE AEDIFICATORIA (book)
  Alberti, Leon Battista **1**:259
DE RE METALLICA (book) **6**:62
DE RERUM NATURA (poem) **6**:62
  Lucretius **12**:451
DE RIDDER (Louisiana)
  map (30° 51′N 93° 17′W) **12**:430
DE ROBECK, JOHN
  World War I **20**:231
DE SANCTIS, FRANCESCO **6**:62–63 *bibliog.*
DE SICA, VITTORIO **6**:63; **8**:86 *illus.*
DE SMET (South Dakota)
  map (44° 23′N 97° 33′W) **18**:103
DE SMET, PIERRE JEAN **6**:63 *bibliog.*
  Montana **13**:550
DE SOTO (county in Florida)
  map (27° 11′N 81° 48′W) **8**:172
DE SOTO (Kansas)
  map (38° 59′N 94° 58′W) **12**:18
DE SOTO (county in Louisiana)
  map (32° 5′N 93° 42′W) **12**:430
DE SOTO (county in Mississippi)
  map (34° 55′N 90° 0′W) **13**:469
DE SOTO (Missouri)
  map (38° 8′N 90° 33′W) **13**:476
DE SOTO, HERNANDO **6**:63 *bibliog., illus.*
  exploration **7**:336 *map*
  exploration of colonial America **19**:437 *map*
  Georgia **9**:117
  Hakluyt, Richard **10**:17
  Mississippi River **13**:473
  Quapaw **16**:12
  Tallahassee (Florida) **19**:16
  Tennessee **19**:106
DE STIJL (art group)
  Agam, Yaacov **1**:181
  Dutch art and architecture **6**:313
  modern architecture **13**:491
  Mondrian, Piet **13**:523
DE STIJL (periodical) **6**:63–64 *bibliog.*
  Oud, Jacobus Johannes Pieter **14**:467
  Rietveld, Gerrit Thomas **16**:219
DE TOUR VILLAGE (Michigan)
  map (46° 0′N 83° 53′W) **13**:377
DE VALERA, EAMON **6**:64 *bibliog., illus.*
  Fianna Fáil (political party) **8**:67
  Ireland, history of **11**:264–265 *illus.*
DE VALLS BLUFF (Arkansas)
  map (34° 47′N 91° 28′W) **2**:166
DE VIEW, BAYOU
  map (34° 48′N 91° 18′W) **2**:166
DE VOTO, BERNARD **6**:64 *bibliog.*
DE VRIES, PETER **6**:64 *bibliog.*
DE WITT (Arkansas)
  map (34° 18′N 91° 20′W) **2**:166
DE WITT (county in Illinois)
  map (40° 10′N 89° 0′W) **11**:42
DE WITT (Iowa)
  map (41° 49′N 90° 33′W) **11**:244
DE WITT (Michigan)
  map (42° 51′N 84° 34′W) **13**:377
DE WITT (Nebraska)
  map (40° 24′N 96° 55′W) **14**:70
DE WITT (county in Texas)
  map (29° 7′N 97° 20′W) **19**:129
DE YOUNG (M.H.) MEMORIAL MUSEUM
  San Francisco art museums **17**:54
DEACON
  ministry, Christian **13**:450
DEAD, BURIAL OF *see* BURIAL
DEAD-LEAF BUTTERFLY **3**:595–596 *illus.*
DEAD RECKONING **14**:61 *illus.*
DEAD SEA **6**:64–65; **11**:303 *illus.*; **13**:397 *illus.*
  map (31° 30′N 35° 30′E) **11**:302
  rift valleys **16**:221
DEAD SEA SCROLLS **3**:242 *illus.*; **6**:65 *bibliog., illus.*
  Essenes **7**:244
  Habakkuk, Book of **10**:3
  Qumran **16**:28
DEAD SOULS (book) **6**:65 *bibliog.*
  Gogol, Nikolai **9**:225
DEADLY NIGHTSHADE *see* BELLADONNA
DEADMANS CAY (Bahama Islands)
  map (23° 14′N 75° 14′W) **3**:23
DEADWOOD (South Dakota) **6**:65
  map (44° 23′N 103° 44′W) **18**:103
DEAF, EDUCATION OF THE **6**:65–66 *bibliog., illus.*
  Gallaudet (family) **9**:17
  Gallaudet College **9**:17
  history **6**:64
  special education **18**:166–167
DEAF SMITH (county in Texas)
  map (34° 57′N 102° 38′W) **19**:129
DEAFNESS **6**:66–67 *bibliog., illus.*
  ear disease **7**:7
  environmental health **7**:212
  hearing aid **10**:89
  sign language **17**:300
  speech **18**:175
DEÁK, FERENC **6**:67
DEAKIN, ALFRED **6**:67 *bibliog.*
DEAL ISLAND (Maryland)
  map (38° 9′N 75° 56′W) **13**:188
DEALE (Maryland)
  map (38° 47′N 76° 33′W) **13**:188
DEALFISH
  ribbonfish **16**:205
DEAN, BASHFORD **6**:67 *bibliog.*
DEAN, DIZZY **6**:67 *bibliog.*
DEAN, JAMES **6**:67 *bibliog., illus.*
DEAN, JAY HANNA *see* DEAN, DIZZY

DEAN, JOHN W. III 6:67 *bibliog.*
Watergate 20:64 *illus.*
DEÁN FUNES (Argentina)
map (30° 26′S 64° 21′W) 2:149
DEANE, SILAS 6:68 *bibliog.*
Franklin, Benjamin 8:284
DEARBORN (county in Indiana)
map (39° 6′N 84° 51′W) 11:111
DEARBORN (Michigan) 6:68
map (42° 18′N 83° 10′W) 13:377
DEARBORN, FORT *see* FORT DEARBORN (Illinois)
DEARBORN, HENRY 6:68
Fort Dearborn 8:236
DEARBORN OBSERVATORY 6:68
DEASE, PETER WARREN 6:68
DEATH, DANCE OF 6:68 *bibliog.*
Holbein, Hans, the Younger 10:201
DEATH OF A SALESMAN (play) 6:69–70 *bibliog.*; 19:150 *illus.*
Miller, Arthur 13:427
DEATH ADDER 6:68
DEATH CAMP *see* CONCENTRATION CAMP
DEATH DUTY *see* INHERITANCE TAX
DEATH AND DYING 6:68–69 *bibliog.*
See also TOMB
autopsy 2:368
coroner 5:271
Death, Dance of 6:68
euthanasia 7:310–311
fertility rites 8:60
forensic science 8:227
funeral customs 8:363–365
homicide 10:214–215
hospice 10:256
immortality 11:56
infancy
hyaline membrane disease 10:327
whooping cough 20:143
leukemia 12:300–301
life span 12:330–331
mistaken death, hypothermia 10:351
music
Dies irae 6:163
necrosis 14:75
passage rites 15:104
pathology 15:112
phobia 15:248
poison 15:381–382
poisonous plants and animals 15:385
shock, physiologic 17:279
suicide 18:330–331
suttee 18:373
tombstone 19:232
typhus 19:366–367
unnatural causes, inquest 11:183
venom 19:546
water mold 20:49
yellow fever 20:322
DEATH PENALTY *see* CAPITAL PUNISHMENT
DEATH RATE
population 15:433–434
DEATH IN THE FAMILY, A (book)
Agee, James 1:183
DEATH VALLEY (California) 4:33 *illus.*; 6:70 *bibliog.*, *illus.*; 14:229 *illus.*; 19:420 *illus.*
map (36° 30′N 117° 0′W) 4:31
national parks 14:38–39 *map*, *table*
DEATH IN VENICE (book) 6:70
Mann, Thomas 13:123–124
DEATH'S-HEAD MOTH 3:598–599 *illus.*
DeBAKEY, MICHAEL 6:70
heart, artificial 10:95
DEBATE
presidential elections 15:531 *illus.*
DEBAYLE, ANASTASIO SOMOZA
Somoza (family) 18:62
DÉBÉ (Trinidad and Tobago)
map (10° 12′N 61° 27′W) 19:300
DEBENTURE
bond 3:376
DEBORAH 6:70
DEBRÉ, MICHEL 6:70
DEBRE MARKOS (Ethiopia)
map (10° 20′N 37° 45′E) 7:253
DEBRECEN (Hungary) 6:70
map (47° 32′N 21° 38′E) 10:307
DEBS, EUGENE V. 6:70–71 *bibliog.*, *illus.*
campaign poster (1904) 18:23 *illus.*
Industrial Workers of the World 11:160
Pullman Strike 15:619
Socialist party 18:25
Terre Haute (Indiana) 19:121
DEBT 6:71
amortization 1:376
bankruptcy 3:70
hypothecation 10:351
lien 12:326
moratorium 13:574
mortgage 13:591–592
DEBT, NATIONAL *see* NATIONAL DEBT
DEBT, PUBLIC *see* NATIONAL DEBT
DEBT PEONAGE *see* SLAVERY
DEBUGGING (computer term) 5:160f; 5:160h
DEBURAU, JEAN GASPARD 6:71
DEBUSSY, CLAUDE 6:71–72 *bibliog.*, *illus.*; 8:321 *illus.*
Afternoon of a Faun, The 1:181
impressionism (music) 11:68
Satie, Erik 17:87
DEBYE, PETER 6:72
ion and ionization 11:240
DEBYE LENGTH
plasma physics 15:346
DECADENCE 6:72 *bibliog.*
Balmont, Konstantin Dmitriyevich 3:54
Beardsley, Aubrey 3:142–143
Dowson, Ernest 6:252–253
Verlaine, Paul 19:551–552
DECAGON 15:419 *illus.*
polygon 15:419 *illus.*
DECAMERON (book) 6:72 *bibliog.*
Boccaccio, Giovanni 3:353–354
book illustration
Gravelot, Hubert François 9:302
DECATHLON 6:72 *bibliog.*
Jenner, Bruce 11:396
Johnson, Rafer 11:435
Mathias, Bob 18:228
Thorpe, Jim 19:180
DECATUR (Alabama)
map (34° 36′N 86° 59′W) 1:234
DECATUR (Georgia)
map (33° 46′N 84° 18′W) 9:114
DECATUR (county in Georgia)
map (30° 55′N 84° 35′W) 9:114
DECATUR (Illinois) 6:72
map (39° 51′N 89° 32′W) 11:42
DECATUR (Indiana)
map (40° 50′N 84° 56′W) 11:111
DECATUR (county in Indiana)
map (39° 20′N 85° 29′W) 11:111
DECATUR (county in Iowa)
map (40° 45′N 93° 45′W) 11:244
DECATUR (county in Kansas)
map (39° 45′N 100° 30′W) 12:18
DECATUR (Michigan)
map (42° 17′N 85° 58′W) 13:377
DECATUR (Mississippi)
map (32° 26′N 89° 7′W) 13:469
DECATUR (Nebraska)
map (42° 0′N 96° 15′W) 14:70
DECATUR (Tennessee)
map (35° 31′N 84° 47′W) 19:104
DECATUR (county in Tennessee)
map (35° 35′N 88° 10′W) 19:104
DECATUR (Texas)
map (33° 14′N 97° 35′W) 19:129
DECATUR, STEPHEN 6:72–73 *bibliog.*, *illus.*
Tripolitan War 19:303
DECATURVILLE (Tennessee)
map (35° 35′N 88° 7′W) 19:104
DECCA NAVIGATION SYSTEM 14:61 *illus.*
DECCAN PLATEAU 6:73
map (14° 0′N 77° 0′E) 11:80
DECEMBER
birthstones 3:296 *illus.*, *table*
calendar 4:28
DECEMBRISTS 6:73 *bibliog.*
Nicholas I, Emperor of Russia 14:181
DECEPTION, MOUNT
map (47° 49′N 123° 14′W) 20:35
DECHERD (Tennessee)
map (35° 13′N 86° 5′W) 19:104
DECIBEL *see* SOUND AND ACOUSTICS
DECIDUOUS PLANT 6:73
annual growth cycle 19:287 *illus.*
DECIMAL 6:73
duodecimal system 6:301–302
scientific notation 17:145
DĚČIN (Czechoslovakia)
map (50° 48′N 14° 13′E) 5:413
DECISION MAKING
cognitive dissonance 5:94
DECISION THEORY 6:73–74 *bibliog.*, *illus.*
See also GAME THEORY; PROBABILITY (mathematics)
management science 13:107
Neyman, Jerzy 14:175
DECKER, MARY 6:74
DECKERVILLE (Michigan)
map (43° 32′N 82° 44′W) 13:377
DECLARATION (law) *see* COMPLAINT (law)
DECLARATION OF HUMAN RIGHTS (1945)
slavery 17:357
DECLARATION OF INDEPENDENCE 6:74–76 *bibliog.*
presentation to Continental Congress 1:357 *illus.*; 19:440 *illus.*
signers
Adams, John 1:94–95
Adams, Samuel 1:97–98
Chase, Samuel 4:301
Franklin, Benjamin 8:282–284
Gerry, Elbridge 9:158
Hancock, John 10:34
Hopkins, Stephen 10:232
Jefferson, Thomas 11:391
Lee (family) 12:269
Livingston (family) 12:377
McKean, Thomas 13:27
Morris (family) 13:588
Morris, Robert (merchant) 13:588
Rush, Benjamin 16:347
Sherman, Roger 17:258
Wilson, James 20:165
Witherspoon, John 20:192
Wolcott (family) 20:195
Wythe, George 20:305
text and signatories 6:75
typeface 19:364
DECLARATION OF SENTIMENTS
Seneca Falls Convention 17:200
DECLARATION OF THE RIGHTS OF MAN AND OF THE CITIZEN (1789)
Bill of Rights 3:253–254
civil rights 5:12
Europe, history of 7:291
DECLARATORY ACT
Rockingham, Charles Watson-Wentworth, 2d Marquess of 16:260
Stamp Act 18:216
United States, history of the 19:439
DECLINATION (astronomy) 6:76
astrometry 2:273
DECLINE AND FALL OF THE ROMAN EMPIRE, THE HISTORY OF THE (book) 6:76 *bibliog.*
Gibbon, Edward 9:172–173
DECLINE OF THE WEST, THE (book) 6:76 *bibliog.*
DECOMPOSITION (chemistry) 6:76 *illus.*
electrolysis 7:114–115
hydrolysis 10:342–343
oxygen 14:477
pyrolysis 15:637
DECOMPRESSION SICKNESS *see* BENDS
DECONGESTANT DRUGS 6:76
DECORAH (Iowa)
map (43° 18′N 91° 48′W) 11:244
DECORATION DAY *see* MEMORIAL DAY
DECORATIONS *see* MEDALS AND DECORATIONS
DECORATIVE ARTS 6:76 *bibliog.*
antique collecting 2:65–68 *illus.*
appliqué 2:91
armor 2:174–175
Art Deco 2:207–208
Art Nouveau 2:209–212 *illus.*
Arts and Crafts movement 2:225
Austria
Wiener Werkstätte 20:146
bark cloth 3:82–83 *illus.*
basketry 3:115–116
batik 3:123–124
Bauhaus 3:129–130
beads and beadwork 3:137–138
Belgium
Van de Velde, Henry 19:512
block printing 3:334
bookbinding 3:389–390
candelabrum 4:106
celadon 4:229
Celtic art 4:238–241
chandelier 4:279
Chinese art and architecture 4:379–386
chinoiserie 4:395
costume 5:292–303 *illus.*
craft 5:26–28
crochet 5:355
delftware 6:92
Egyptian art and architecture 7:89–90
embroidery 7:152
enamel 7:161–162
faïence 8:8
France
Directoire style 6:187
Empire Style 7:158–159
Gobelins 9:216
Guimard, Hector 9:396–397
Limoges ware 12:346
Lurçat, Jean 12:466
Meissonier, Juste Aurèle 13:283
Merovingian art and architecture 13:311
Palissy, Bernard 15:47
furniture 8:373
Gallé, Émile 9:17
Germany
Meissen ware 13:283
Nymphenburg ware 14:309
gilding 9:180
glassblowing 9:202
glassware, decorative 9:202–204
gold and silver work 9:230
Gothic art and architecture 9:260
graphic arts 9:291–294
Great Britain
Burne-Jones, Sir Edward 3:576–577
Chippendale, Thomas 4:396
Georgian style 9:119
Minton ware 13:461
Morris, William 13:589
Queen Anne style 16:21
Regency Style 16:126
Staffordshire ware 18:210
Victorian style 19:575–576
Worcester ware 20:216
Greece
Greek art 9:337–342
Minoan Art 13:458
guilds 9:395
illuminated manuscripts 11:46–48
Indian art and architecture 11:94–98
Indians of North America, art of the 11:139
intaglio (art) 11:199
interior design 11:210–214
ironwork, ornamental 11:279
Islamic art and architecture 11:293–297
Japan
Koetsu 12:105
Korin 12:122–123
Masanobu (1434–1530) 13:195
netsuke 14:104
jewelry 11:408–411
Korean art 12:117–118 *illus.*
lost-wax process 12:418–419
macrame 13:36
marquetry 13:163
Merovingian art and architecture 13:311
mosaic 13:593–595
needlework 14:76
embroidery 7:152
lace 12:158–160
quilting 14:26
neoclassicism (art) 14:82
paper folding 15:70–71
papier-mâché 15:71
Persian art and architecture 15:183–187
pewter 15:217
Phoenician art 15:250–251
pottery and porcelain 15:468–472
pre-Columbian art and architecture 15:495–501
rococo style 16:263–265
Roman art and architecture 16:277
Royal Copenhagen ware 16:330
rugs and carpets 16:340
Russia
Fabergé, Peter Carl 8:4
steppe art 18:255–256
Scandinavian art and architecture 17:114
scrimshaw 17:158
Southeast Asian art and architecture 18:108
spinning 18:186
stained glass 18:211–213
tapestry 19:33
terra-cotta 19:119–120
United States
colonial styles in North America 5:109–111
National Collection of Fine Arts 14:30
Philadelphia Museum of Art 15:229
Tiffany, Louis Comfort 19:196
Winterthur Museum 20:181
wallpaper 20:16–17
weaving 20:83–85
DECORUM (literature)
narrative and dramatic devices 14:22
DECOUPAGE
collage 5:102

DECREE OF CANOPUS
  Tanis **19**:23
DECRETALS **6**:76 *bibliog.*
  canon law **4**:114
DECROUX, ÉTIENNE
  mime and pantomime **13**:434 *illus.*
DEDEKIND, RICHARD **6**:76–77
  mathematics, history of **13**:226
DEDHAM (Massachusetts)
  map (42° 15′N 71° 10′W) **13**:206
DEDUCTION **6**:77 *bibliog.*
  See also INDUCTION (reasoning process)
  educational psychology **7**:66
  logic **12**:396
  proof, mathematical **15**:568
  reasoning **16**:104
  theoretical physics **19**:159
DEDUCTIVE METHOD *see* DEDUCTION
DEE, JOHN **6**:77
DEE, RUBY **6**:77
DEED (real estate) **6**:77 *bibliog.*
  property **15**:571
  title **19**:213
DEEP CREEK LAKE
  map (39° 30′N 79° 19′W) **13**:188
DEEP GAP (pass)
  map (36° 14′N 81° 30′W) **14**:242
DEEP RIVER (Connecticut)
  map (41° 23′N 72° 26′W) **5**:193
DEEP RIVER (Iowa)
  map (41° 35′N 92° 22′W) **11**:244
DEEP-SEA DRILLING PROJECT **6**:77 *bibliog.*
  Glomar Challenger **14**:345 *illus.*
  JOIDES **11**:438
  Mohole Project **13**:503
  ocean and sea **14**:332
DEEP-SEA LIFE **6**:77–79 *bibliog., illus.*
  ocean and sea **14**:330 *illus.*
  oceanography **14**:345
DEEPWATER (Missouri)
  map (38° 16′N 93° 47′W) **13**:476
DEER **6**:79–81 *bibliog., illus.*; **8**:228 *illus.*; **11**:469 *illus.*
  caribou **4**:149
  elk **7**:146
  horn (biology) **10**:238
  Irish elk **11**:266
  key deer **6**:79
  moose **13**:571–572
  mule deer **6**:80 *illus.*
  muntjac **13**:644
  musk deer **13**:681
  pronghorn **15**:567–568 *illus.*
  pudu **6**:79–80 *illus.*
  red deer **6**:80 *illus.*
  reindeer **16**:131
  ruminant **16**:345
  venison **19**:546
  wapiti **20**:24
  white-tailed deer **6**:79–80 *illus.*
    early years mortality **12**:331 *table*
DEER CREEK
  map (39° 27′N 83° 0′W) **14**:357
DEER ISLAND (Massachusetts)
  map (42° 21′N 70° 58′W) **3**:409
DEER ISLAND (Mississippi)
  map location (30° 25′N 88° 55′W) **13**:469
DEER LAKE (Newfoundland)
  map (49° 10′N 57° 26′W) **14**:166
DEER LODGE (Montana)
  map (46° 24′N 112° 44′W) **13**:547
DEER LODGE (county in Montana)
  map (46° 5′N 113° 5′W) **13**:547
DEER MOUSE **4**:283 *illus.*; **6**:81 *illus.*; **9**:300 *illus.*
DEER PARK (Alabama)
  map (31° 13′N 88° 19′W) **1**:234
DEER PARK (Washington)
  map (47° 57′N 117° 28′W) **20**:35
DEER RIVER (Minnesota)
  map (47° 20′N 93° 48′W) **13**:453
DEER TRAIL (Colorado)
  map (39° 37′N 104° 2′W) **5**:116
DEERE, JOHN **6**:81
  plow **1**:192 *illus.*; **15**:370
DEERFIELD (Illinois)
  map (42° 10′N 87° 51′W) **11**:42
DEERFIELD (Kansas)
  map (37° 59′N 101° 8′W) **12**:18
DEERFIELD BEACH (Florida)
  map (26° 19′N 80° 6′W) **8**:172
DEERFIELD RIVER
  map (42° 35′N 72° 35′W) **13**:206
DEERFLY **6**:81 *illus.*
DEERHOUND
  Scottish deerhound **17**:155
DEERING (Alaska)
  map (66° 5′N 162° 43′W) **1**:242
DEERSLAYER, THE (book) **6**:81
DEERWOOD (Minnesota)
  map (46° 28′N 93° 54′W) **13**:453
DEFAMATION **6**:81
  freedom of the press **8**:296
  New York Times Company v. *Sullivan* **14**:156
  tort **19**:246
  Zenger, John Peter **20**:359
DEFAULT, JUDGEMENT BY
  judgement **11**:464
  legal procedure **12**:273
DEFECATION *see* EXCRETORY SYSTEM; FECES
DEFENDANT (law)
  attachment **2**:313
  defense counsel **6**:83
  legal procedure **12**:273
  prosecuting attorney **15**:572
  trial **19**:291–292
DEFENESTRATION OF PRAGUE
  Thirty Years' War **19**:170
DEFENSE, NATIONAL **6**:81–82 *bibliog., table*
  air force **1**:206–209
  aircraft, military **1**:214–220
  arms control **2**:178
  army **2**:180–183
  civil defense **5**:9–10
  cold war **5**:98–99
  conscription **5**:201
  intelligence gathering **11**:204–205
  military-industrial complex **13**:422
  military warning and detection systems **13**:421–422
  navy **14**:62–66
  nuclear strategy **14**:288
  strategy and tactics, military **18**:289–291
DEFENSE, U.S. DEPARTMENT OF **6**:82–83 *bibliog.*
  See also AIR FORCE; ARMY; MARINE CORPS, U.S.; NAVY
  Ada (computer language) **1**:91
  military-industrial complex **13**:422
  National Security Agency **14**:45–46
  Pentagon, The **15**:154
  secretary of defense
    See also articles of specific presidents, e.g., NIXON, RICHARD M.; TRUMAN, HARRY S.; etc.; names of specific secretaries of defense, e.g., McNAMARA, ROBERT S.; ROOT, ELIHU; etc.
  flag **8**:148 *illus.*
DEFENSE ADVANCED PROJECTS AGENCY (U.S.)
  Vela (artificial satellite) **19**:536
DEFENSE BOND *see* SAVINGS BOND
DEFENSE COUNSEL **6**:83
  legal aid **12**:272
DEFENSE INTELLIGENCE AGENCY
  intelligence gathering **11**:205
DEFENSE MECHANISMS (psychology) **6**:83 *bibliog.*
  ego **7**:73–74
  emotion **7**:157
  frustration **8**:350
  psychoanalysis **15**:589
DEFIANCE (Iowa)
  map (41° 49′N 95° 20′W) **11**:244
DEFIANCE (Ohio)
  map (41° 17′N 84° 22′W) **14**:357
DEFIANCE (county in Ohio)
  map (41° 19′N 84° 30′W) **14**:357
DEFINITE PROPORTIONS, LAW OF
  chemical combination, laws of **4**:315
DEFOE, DANIEL **6**:83–84 *bibliog., illus.*
  Moll Flanders **13**:509–510
  Robinson Crusoe **16**:246
DEFOLIANT
  chemical and biological warfare **4**:312
  herbicide **10**:135–136 *illus.*
  pollutants, chemical **15**:410
  Vietnam War **19**:591
DEFORESTATION
  conservation **5**:203
DEGANAWIDAH
  Iroquois League **11**:280
  Mohawk **13**:502
DEGAS, EDGAR **6**:84 *bibliog., illus.*
  Absinthe **6**:84 *illus.*
  Ballerina Posing for a Photograph **11**:65 *illus.*
  Blue Dancers **8**:307 *illus.*
  Cassatt, Mary **4**:183
  Dancer with a Fan **6**:84 *illus.*
  Rehearsal on the Stage **6**:24 *illus.*
  The Star Bowing **15**:107 *illus.*
DEGÉE, OLIVER *see* TOUSSEUL, JEAN (pseudonym)
DEGEMA (Nigeria) **14**:190 *illus.*
DEGENERATE MATTER **6**:85
  neutron star **14**:109
DEGENERATIVE DISEASES
  amyotrophic lateral sclerosis **1**:386–387
  nervous system, diseases of the **14**:95
  osteoarthritis **14**:457
DEGREE, ACADEMIC **6**:85 *bibliog.*
  graduate education **9**:276–277
  open admission **14**:398
DEHIWALA-MOUNT LAVINIA (Sri Lanka)
  map (6° 51′N 79° 52′E) **18**:206
DEHRA DUN (India)
  map (30° 19′N 78° 2′E) **11**:80
DEHYDRATION **6**:85
DEHYDRATION OF FOOD **6**:85 *bibliog.*
  food preservation **8**:212
  freeze-drying **6**:85
DEIMOS (astronomy) **6**:85
DEINEKA, ALEKSANDR
  Russian art and architecture **16**:364
DEINSTITUTIONALIZATION *see* INSTITUTIONALIZATION
DEIR EL-BAHRI (Egypt) **6**:85–86
  Maspero, Sir Gaston **13**:199
  Senmut **17**:203
  temple **19**:94
DEIRA **2**:3 *map*
  Northumbria **14**:256
DEISM **6**:86 *bibliog.*
DEJ (Romania)
  map (47° 9′N 23° 52′E) **16**:288
DEJ, GHEORGHE GHEORGHIU- *see* GHEORGHIU-DEJ, GHEORGHE
DÉJA VU (musical composition)
  Colgrass, Michael **5**:101
DÉJÀ VU PHENOMENON
  consciousness, states of **5**:200
DÉJEUNER SUR L'HERBE
  Manet, Édouard **13**:112
DEKEN, AGATHA
  Wolff, Elizabeth **20**:198
DEKKER, EDUARD DOUWES *see* MULTATULI (pseudonym)
DEKKER, THOMAS **6**:86 *bibliog.*
  Webster, John **20**:89
DEL *see* the element of the name following DEL, except for names listed below
DEL CITY (Oklahoma)
  map (35° 27′N 97° 27′W) **14**:368
DEL MURRONE, PIETRO *see* CELESTINE V, POPE
DEL NORTE (county in California)
  map (41° 45′N 123° 55′W) **4**:31
DEL NORTE (Colorado)
  map (37° 41′N 106° 21′W) **5**:116
DEL RAY ISLAND
  map (8° 22′N 78° 55′W) **15**:55
DEL RIO (Texas)
  map (29° 22′N 100° 54′W) **19**:129
DELACROIX, EUGÈNE **6**:86–87 *bibliog., illus.*
  Bonington, Richard Parkes **3**:380
  The Death of Sardanapalus **16**:292 *illus.*
  Liberty Leading the People **6**:86 *illus.*
DELANCO (New Jersey)
  map (40° 3′N 74° 57′W) **14**:129
DELANEY AMENDMENT *see* PURE FOOD AND DRUG LAWS
DELANO (California)
  map (35° 41′N 119° 15′W) **4**:31
DELANO PEAK
  map (38° 22′N 112° 23′W) **19**:492
DELANY, MARTIN R. **6**:87 *bibliog.*
DELAUNAY, ROBERT **6**:87 *bibliog., illus.*
  orphism **14**:448
  Simultaneous Windows **6**:87 *illus.*
DELAVAN (Illinois)
  map (40° 22′N 89° 33′W) **11**:42
DELAVAN (Wisconsin)
  map (42° 38′N 88° 39′W) **20**:185
DELAWARE **6**:87–91 *bibliog., illus., map*
  cities
    Dover **6**:250
    Newark **14**:164
    Wilmington **20**:163
  climate **6**:89
  cultural institutions **6**:90
  economic activity **6**:90
  education **6**:90
    Delaware, state university and college **6**:91
  flag **6**:87 *illus.*
  geographical linguistics **9**:99 *map*
  government **6**:90
  historical sites and recreation **6**:90
  history **6**:90–91
    New Sweden **14**:142
  land and resources **6**:89
  map (39° 10′N 75° 30′W) **19**:419
  people **6**:89–90
  rivers, lakes, and waterways **6**:89
  seal, state **6**:87 *illus.*
  vegetation and animal life **6**:89
DELAWARE (American Indians) **6**:91 *bibliog.*
  Chief Tishcohan **11**:119 *illus.*
  Delaware Prophet **6**:91
  Mahican **13**:65
  Susquehanna (American Indians) **18**:372
  treaty with William Penn **19**:437 *illus.*
DELAWARE (county in Indiana)
  map (40° 13′N 85° 25′W) **11**:111
DELAWARE (county in Iowa)
  map (42° 30′N 91° 20′W) **11**:244
DELAWARE (county in New York)
  map (42° 17′N 74° 55′W) **14**:149
DELAWARE (Ohio)
  map (40° 18′N 83° 4′W) **14**:357
DELAWARE (county in Ohio)
  map (40° 18′N 83° 4′W) **14**:357
DELAWARE (Oklahoma)
  map (36° 47′N 95° 38′W) **14**:368
DELAWARE (county in Oklahoma)
  map (36° 25′N 94° 50′W) **14**:368
DELAWARE (county in Pennsylvania)
  map (39° 55′N 75° 23′W) **15**:147
DELAWARE, STATE UNIVERSITY AND COLLEGE **6**:91
  Winterthur Museum **20**:181
DELAWARE BAY **6**:91
  map (39° 5′N 75° 15′W) **6**:88
DELAWARE CITY (Delaware)
  map (39° 34′N 75° 36′W) **6**:88
DELAWARE MEMORIAL BRIDGE **6**:89 *illus.*
DELAWARE PROPHET **6**:91 *bibliog.*
DELAWARE RIVER **6**:91
  Delaware Water Gap **6**:91
  Fitch, John **8**:129
  map (39° 20′N 75° 25′W) **15**:147
DELAWARE RIVER (Kansas)
  map (39° 3′N 95° 24′W) **12**:18
DELAWARE WATER GAP **6**:91
DELBRÜCK, MAX **6**:91–92
  Hershey, Alfred Day **10**:148
  Luria, Salvador **12**:467
DELCASSÉ, THÉOPHILE **6**:92 *bibliog.*
DELDERFIELD, R. F. **6**:92
DELEDDA, GRAZIA **6**:92
DELÉMONT (Switzerland)
  map (47° 22′N 7° 21′E) **18**:394
DELFE, JOCOPO *see* BILIVERTI
DELFT (Netherlands) **6**:92; **14**:101 *illus.*
  Hooch, Pieter de **10**:224–225
  map (52° 0′N 4° 21′E) **14**:99
DELFT, TREATY OF
  Jacqueline of Hainaut **11**:347
DELFTWARE **6**:92 *bibliog., illus.*
  Delft (Netherlands) **6**:92
  faïence **8**:8
  pottery and porcelain **15**:471
DELFZIJL (Netherlands)
  map (53° 19′N 6° 46′E) **14**:99
DELGADO, CAPE
  map (10° 40′S 40° 35′E) **13**:627
DELHI (India) *see* NEW DELHI (India
DELHI (Iowa)
  map (42° 26′N 91° 20′W) **11**:244
DELHI (Louisiana)
  map (32° 27′N 91° 30′W) **12**:430
DELHI (New York)
  map (42° 17′N 74° 55′W) **14**:149
DELHI SULTANATE **6**:92
  art
    Qutb Minar **16**:28
  India, history of **11**:91
DELHI TERRITORY
  map (28° 37′N 77° 10′E) **11**:80
DELIAN LEAGUE **6**:92–93 *bibliog.*
  Aristides **2**:155
  Cimon **4**:431
  Ionia **11**:241
DELIBES, LÉO **6**:93 *bibliog.*
DELICATE BALANCE, A (play)
  Albee, Edward **1**:253
DELICIAS (Mexico)
  map (28° 13′N 105° 28′W) **13**:357
DELIGHT (Arkansas)
  map (34° 2′N 93° 30′W) **2**:166
DELILAH (biblical character) **6**:93
DELIMARA POINT
  map (35° 49′N 14° 33′E) **13**:94
DELINQUENCY *see* CRIME
DELIQUESCENCE
  hygroscopicity **10**:345
DELIRIUM **6**:93
DELIRIUM TREMENS
  alcohol consumption **1**:265
DELIUS, FREDERICK **6**:93 *bibliog., illus.*
  symphonic poem **18**:405

DELIVERANCE (book)
Dickey, James **6**:157
DELL RAPIDS (South Dakota)
map (43° 50′N 96° 43′W) **18**:103
DELLA BELLA, STEFANO *see* BELLA, STEFANO DELLA
DELLA-CRUSCANS 6:93 *bibliog.*
DELLA FRANCESCA, PIERO *see* PIERO DELLA FRANCESCA
DELLA GATTA, BARTOLOMMEO
Sistine Chapel **17**:329
DELLA NOTTE, GERARDO *see* HONTHORST, GERRIT VAN
DELLA PORTA, GIACOMO
Il Gesù, Church of **4**:207 *illus.*
DELLA ROBBIA (family) **6**:94 *bibliog., illus.*
della Robbia, Luca
Florence (Italy) **8**:168
Madonna in the Rose Garden **19**:120 *illus.*
Italian art and architecture **11**:311
pottery and porcelain **15**:470–471
Singing Angels **6**:94 *illus.*
DELLENBAUGH, MOUNT
map (36° 7′N 113° 32′W) **2**:160
DELLER, ALFRED 6:94 *bibliog.*
DELLO JOIO, NORMAN 6:94 *bibliog.*
DELMAR (Delaware)
map (38° 27′N 75° 34′W) **6**:88
DELMAR (Iowa)
map (42° 0′N 90° 37′W) **11**:244
DELMARVA PENINSULA 6:94
DELMENHORST (Germany, East and West)
map (53° 3′N 8° 38′E) **9**:140
DELMONT (South Dakota)
map (43° 16′N 98° 10′W) **18**:103
DELORAINE (Manitoba)
map (49° 12′N 100° 29′W) **13**:119
DELORME, PHILIBERT 6:94 *bibliog.*
Tuileries **19**:329
DELOS (Greece) **6**:94–95
DELPHI 6:95 *bibliog.*
Greece, ancient **9**:330
Pythian Games **15**:640
sanctuary of Athena Pronaia **19**:96 *illus.*
DELPHI (Indiana)
map (40° 36′N 86° 41′W) **11**:111
DELPHIC ORACLE
Apollo **2**:80
Delphi **6**:95
DELPHINIUM 6:95 *illus.*
larkspur **12**:208
DELPHOS (Kansas)
map (39° 16′N 97° 46′W) **12**:18
DELPHOS (Ohio)
map (40° 50′N 84° 20′W) **14**:357
DELSARTE, FRANÇOIS 6:95 *bibliog.*
DELTA (Colorado)
map (38° 44′N 108° 4′W) **5**:116
DELTA (county in Colorado)
map (38° 50′N 107° 50′W) **5**:116
DELTA (letter)
D (letter) **6**:3
DELTA (Michigan)
map (46° 0′N 86° 50′W) **13**:377
DELTA (river) *see* RIVER DELTA
DELTA (rocket) **6**:95
GEOS (artificial satellite) **9**:119
GOES (artificial satellite) **9**:222
rockets and missiles **16**:256–257 *illus.*
Thor (rocket) **19**:177 *illus.*
DELTA (county in Texas)
map (33° 20′N 95° 43′W) **19**:129
DELTA (Utah)
map (39° 21′N 112° 35′W) **19**:492
DELTA BEACH (Manitoba)
map (50° 11′N 98° 19′W) **13**:119
DELTA PLAN 6:95–96
floods and flood control **8**:167
land reclamation **12**:179 *illus.*
DELTA WAVE
brain **3**:447
DELTONA (Florida)
map (28° 54′N 81° 16′W) **8**:172
DELUGE 6:96 *bibliog.*
ark **2**:164
Gilgamesh, Epic of **9**:180
Noah **14**:207
DELUSION *see* PARANOIA; SCHIZOPHRENIA
DELVAUX, PAUL 6:96 *bibliog., illus.*
Hands **6**:96 *illus.*
DELVINE (Albania)
map (39° 57′N 20° 6′E) **1**:250
DEMAND (economics) *see* SUPPLY AND DEMAND
DEMAND DEPOSIT 6:96
DEMAREST (New Jersey)
map (40° 57′N 73° 58′W) **14**:129
DEMAVEND, MOUNT 6:96
map (35° 56′N 52° 8′E) **11**:250
DEMENTIA 6:96
nervous system, diseases of the **14**:95
DEMENTIA PRAECOX *see* SCHIZOPHRENIA
DEMERARA RIVER
map (6° 48′N 58° 10′W) **9**:410
DEMEROL 6:96
heroin **10**:145
morphine **13**:587
opium **14**:406
DEMETER 6:96
Eleusis **7**:135
fertility rites **8**:60
DEMETRIUS (Russian ruler) *see* DMITRY
DEMETRIUS I POLIORCETES, KING OF MACEDONIA 6:96–97
DEMETRIUS I SOTER, SELEUCID KING 6:97
DEMIN, LEV STEPANOVICH 6:97
DEMING (New Mexico)
map (32° 16′N 107° 45′W) **14**:136
DEMIREL, SÜLEYMAN 6:97
DEMIURGE 6:97
DEMMITT (Alberta)
map (55° 26′N 119° 54′W) **1**:256
DEMOCRACY 6:97–99 *bibliog.*
Europe, history of **7**:280; **7**:292
government **9**:267
pluralism **15**:372
political parties **15**:400–403
representation **16**:161
socialism **18**:20
subversion **18**:317
town meeting **19**:255
DEMOCRACY IN AMERICA (book)
Tocqueville, Alexis de **19**:220
DEMOCRATIC-FARMER LABOR PARTY *see* FARMER-LABOR PARTY
DEMOCRATIC KAMPUCHEA *see* KAMPUCHEA
DEMOCRATIC PARTY 6:99–103 *bibliog., illus.*
Bryan, William Jennings **3**:528–529
Civil War, U.S. **5**:18
congressional membership and organization **5**:185–186
copperheads **5**:254
Davis, John W. **6**:52
Democratic Republicans **6**:99
Dixiecrats **6**:207
Federalist party **8**:43–44
Hunkers and Barnburners **10**:311
Jackson, Andrew **11**:341–342
Lincoln, Abraham **12**:349
Madison, James **13**:42
National Convention (1976) **7**:104 *illus.*
political parties **15**:400
Reconstruction **16**:108–110
Roosevelt, Franklin Delano **16**:307–309
symbol
Nast, Thomas **14**:25–26
Tammany Hall **19**:19–20
Tweed, William M. **19**:358
United States, history of the **19**:443–444; **19**:446
DEMOCRATIC PEOPLE'S REPUBLIC OF KOREA *see* KOREA
DEMOCRATIC AND POPULAR REPUBLIC OF ALGERIA *see* ALGERIA
DEMOCRATIC REPUBLIC OF AFGHANISTAN *see* AFGHANISTAN
DEMOCRATIC REPUBLIC OF MADAGASCAR *see* MADAGASCAR
DEMOCRATIC REPUBLIC OF SÃO TOMÉ AND PRINCIPE *see* SÃO TOMÉ AND PRINCIPE
DEMOCRATIC REPUBLIC OF THE CONGO *see* ZAIRE
DEMOCRATIC REPUBLIC OF THE SUDAN *see* SUDAN
DEMOCRATIC REPUBLICAN PARTY *see* DEMOCRATIC PARTY
DEMOCRATIC SOCIALIST REPUBLIC OF SRI LANKA *see* SRI LANKA
DEMOCRITUS 6:103 *bibliog.*
atom **2**:304
atomism **2**:312
materialism **13**:219
pre-Socratic philosophy **15**:533
skepticism **17**:337
theory **2**:304
DEMOCRITUS JUNIOR *see* BURTON, ROBERT
DEMOGRAPHY 6:103–104 *bibliog.*
census **4**:248–249
de Moivre, Abraham **6**:62
fertility, human **8**:60
human ecology **10**:297
North America **14**:232–233 *map*
old age **14**:373–374
population **15**:433–436 *maps*
population dynamics **15**:438
sociology **18**:29
DEMOISELLEFISH *see* DAMSELFISH
DEMOLITION 6:104 *bibliog.*
dynamite **6**:319
salvage archaeology **17**:40
DEMOLITION DERBY 6:104
DEMON 6:104 *bibliog.*
exorcism **7**:333
DEMOPOLIS (Alabama)
map (32° 31′N 87° 50′W) **1**:234
DEMOREST (Georgia)
map (34° 31′N 83° 32′W) **9**:114
DEMOSTHENES 6:104–105 *bibliog., illus.*
Aeschines **1**:128
Callistratus **4**:46
DEMOTIC EGYPTIAN LANGUAGE
Afroasiatic languages **1**:179
DEMOTTE (Indiana)
map (41° 12′N 87° 12′W) **11**:111
DEMPSEY, JACK 3:432 *illus.*; **6**:105 *bibliog., illus.*
Tunney, Gene **19**:339
DEMPSTER, ARTHUR JEFFREY 6:105
DEMURRER 6:105
DEMUTH, CHARLES 6:105–106 *bibliog., illus.*
At a House in Harley Street **14**:275 *illus.*
My Egypt **6**:106 *illus.*
DEMYTHOLOGIZATION *see* BULTMANN, RUDOLF
DEN BOSCH (Netherlands) *see* 'S HERTOGENBOSCH (Netherlands)
DEN HELDER (Netherlands)
map (52° 54′N 4° 45′E) **14**:99
DENALI NATIONAL PARK (Alaska) **14**:226 *illus.*
map (63° 44′N 148° 54′W) **1**:242
DENARIUS 6:106
DENATURED ALCOHOL 6:106 *bibliog.*
ethyl alcohol **7**:257
DENBIGH FLINT COMPLEX
Cape Denbigh **4**:120
Cape Krusenstern **4**:120
DENBIGHSHIRE *see* CLWYD (Wales)
DENBY, EDWIN
modern dance **13**:497
DENDERA (Egypt) **6**:106
DENDRITE *see* NERVE CELL
DENDROCHRONOLOGY 2:120 *illus.*; **6**:106–107 *bibliog., illus.*
archaeology **2**:121
bark **3**:82
bristlecone pine **3**:488
Douglass, Andrew Ellicott **6**:106; **6**:248
geologic time **9**:103–105
growth **9**:381
paleoclimatology **15**:33
tree-ring age dating **6**:106–107
DENDROGRAM *see* TREE DIAGRAM
DENG XIAOPING *see* TENG HSIAO-P'ING (Deng Xiaoping)
DENGAKU 6:107
DENGUE FEVER 6:108
DENHAM, SIR JOHN 6:108
DENHAM, MOUNT
map (18° 13′N 77° 32′W) **11**:351
DENHAM SPRINGS (Louisiana)
map (30° 29′N 90° 57′W) **12**:430
DENIAL (psychology)
defense mechanisms **6**:83
DENIKIN, ANTON
Russian Revolutions of 1917 **16**:372
DENIM 6:108
DENIS *see* DINIS, KING OF PORTUGAL
DENIS, SAINT 6:108
DENIS, MAURICE 6:108 *bibliog.*
Nabis **14**:3
DENIS, RUTH ST. *see* ST. DENIS, RUTH
DENISHAWN 6:108 *bibliog.*
dance **6**:28
Graham, Martha **9**:280
Humphrey, Doris **10**:303
modern dance **13**:497
St. Denis, Ruth **17**:17–18
DENISON (Iowa)
map (42° 1′N 95° 21′W) **11**:244
DENISON (Texas)
map (33° 45′N 96° 33′W) **19**:129
DENISON UNIVERSITY 6:108
DENISOV, EDISON
Russian music **16**:369
DENIZLI (Turkey)
map (37° 46′N 29° 6′E) **19**:343
DENMARK 6:108–113 *bibliog., illus., map, table*
agriculture **6**:111
archaeology
Ertebølle culture **7**:235
human remains **18**:378
Tollund man **19**:227
Trelleborg **19**:290
art **6**:111
See also the subheading Denmark under specific art forms, e.g., ARCHITECTURE; PAINTING; POTTERY AND PORCELAIN; SCULPTURE; etc.; the subheading Denmark under NEOCLASSICISM (art)
Scandinavian art and architecture **17**:112–114 *illus.*
ballet **3**:42–43
Bournonville, August **3**:425
cities
Ålborg **1**:261
Århus **2**:153
Copenhagen **5**:249–250 *map*
Odense **14**:348–349
Roskilde **16**:317–318
climate **6**:110 *table*
economy **6**:110–112 *illus.*
Copenhagen **5**:249–250
education **6**:111
European universities **7**:307 *table*
fishing **6**:110–112 *illus.*
flag **6**:108 *illus.*
Scandinavia, history of **17**:108
government **6**:112
health **6**:111
historians *see* HISTORY—Danish historians
history **6**:112–113
Christian I, King **4**:412
Christian II, King **4**:412
Christian III, King **4**:412
Christian IV, King **4**:412
Christian IX, King **4**:412
Christian X, King **4**:412
Copenhagen **5**:250
Copenhagen, Battle of **17**:110 *illus.*
Frederick III, King **8**:289
Frederick IV, King **8**:289–290
Frederick VI, King **8**:290
Frederick VII, King **8**:290
German possessions in 1648 **9**:151 *map*
Margaret I, Queen of Denmark, Norway, and Sweden **13**:149
Margaret II, Queen of Denmark **13**:149
Scandinavia, history of **17**:107–111 *maps*
Schleswig-Holstein **17**:126 *map*
Sweyn, King **18**:388
Thirty Years' War *see* THIRTY YEARS' WAR
Virgin Islands **19**:605–606
World War II **20**:252–253 *map*
house (in Western architecture) **10**:268 *illus.*
land and resources **6**:109–110
language
Germanic languages **9**:135–137 *tables*
literature *see* DANISH LITERATURE
map (56° 0′N 10° 0′E) **7**:268
music
Gade, Niels **9**:7
Grundtvig, Nicolai Frederik Severin **9**:382
Langgaard, Rued **12**:195
Nielsen, Carl August **14**:184–185
people **6**:110–111
Eskimo **7**:242
physical features
Faeroe Islands **8**:7
Frisian Islands **8**:334
Jutland **11**:479
Zealand **20**:357
pornography **15**:441
prostitution **15**:573
regions
Bornholm **3**:402
Fyn **6**:112 *illus.*
Greenland **9**:352–353 *illus., map*
rivers, lakes, and waterways **6**:110
trade **6**:112
transportation **6**:111–112
vegetation and animal life **6**:110
DENMARK (Australia)
map (34° 57′S 117° 21′E) **2**:328
DENMARK (South Carolina)
map (33° 19′N 81° 9′W) **18**:98
DENMARK (Wisconsin)
map (44° 21′N 87° 50′W) **20**:185
DENMARK STRAIT
map (67° 0′N 25° 0′W) **14**:225
DENNIE, JOSEPH 6:113 *bibliog.*
DENNIS, RUTH *see* ST. DENIS, RUTH

DENNIS PORT (Massachusetts)
map (41° 39′N 70° 8′W) **13**:206
DENNIS v. UNITED STATES **6**:113
freedom of speech **8**:298
Smith Act **17**:371
DENNISON (Ohio)
map (40° 24′N 81° 19′W) **14**:357
DENOMINATOR *see* FRACTION
DENOUEMENT (literature)
narrative and dramatic devices **14**:22
DENPASAR (Indonesia)
map (8° 39′S 115° 13′E) **11**:147
DENSITOMETER **6**:113
DENSITY **6**:113–114 *tables*
Cavendish, Henry **4**:225
measurement **13**:255
phase equilibrium **15**:222–224 *illus.*
specific gravity **18**:168
DENSITY (biology)
population dynamics **15**:438
DENSITY CURRENT **6**:114 *bibliog.*
earthquake generations **6**:114
erosion and sedimentation **7**:233
graywacke **9**:307
lake (body of water) **12**:168
ocean and sea **6**:114
turbidity currents **6**:114
volcanic eruptions **6**:114
DENT (county in Missouri)
map (37° 35′N 91° 35′W) **13**:476
DENT, EDWARD JOSEPH **6**:114
DENTIN
teeth **19**:70 *illus.*
DENTISTRY **6**:114–116 *bibliog., illus.*
anesthetics **6**:116
nitrous oxide, nitrogen **14**:202
Procaine **15**:559
sodium pentothal **18**:33
antibiotics **6**:116
dentures **6**:117
education **6**:116
forensic science **8**:227
history **6**:115–116 *illus.*
hypnosis **10**:350
laser and maser **12**:212 *illus.*
modern dental practice **6**:116
orthodontics **14**:449
periodontics **15**:170
ginginitis **9**:184
pyorrhea **15**:634
professional and educational organizations
American Dental Association **1**:338
specialized fields **6**:116
teeth **19**:71–72
bacteria **6**:116
fillings **6**:115–116
DENTON (Maryland)
map (38° 53′N 75° 50′W) **13**:188
DENTON (Montana)
map (47° 19′N 109° 57′W) **13**:547
DENTON (North Carolina)
map (35° 38′N 80° 6′W) **14**:242
DENTON (Texas)
map (33° 13′N 97° 8′W) **19**:129
DENTON (county in Texas)
map (33° 10′N 97° 10′W) **19**:129
D'ENTRECASTEAUX ISLANDS
Kula Ring **12**:135
DENTSVILLE (South Carolina)
map (34° 4′N 80° 57′W) **18**:98
DENTURES **6**:117 *bibliog.*
DENVER (Colorado) **5**:118 *illus.*; **6**:117 *bibliog., illus.*; **19**:417 *illus.*
map (39° 43′N 105° 1′W) **5**:116
DENVER (Iowa)
map (42° 40′N 92° 20′W) **11**:244
DENVER, JOHN **6**:117
DENVER, UNIVERSITY OF **6**:117
DENVER CITY (Texas)
map (32° 58′N 102° 50′W) **19**:129
DENVER POST
Bonfils, Frederick G. **3**:378
DENVILLE (New Jersey)
map (40° 53′N 74° 29′W) **14**:129
DEODAR *see* CEDAR
DEODORIZER **6**:117–118
DEONTOLOGY
ethics **7**:251
DEOXYRIBONUCLEIC ACID *see* DNA
DEOXYRIBOSE
sugar **18**:327
DEPARTMENT OF *see under the latter part of the name, e.g.,* AGRICULTURE, U.S. DEPARTMENT OF; COMMERCE, U.S. DEPARTMENT OF; *etc.*
DEPARTMENT STORE **6**:118 *bibliog.*
discount house **6**:189
Field (family) **8**:71
Filene, Edward Albert **8**:78–79
Penney, J. C. **15**:145
retailing **16**:183
Ward, Montgomery **20**:29
Wood, Robert E. **20**:207
DEPEW (New York)
map (42° 54′N 78° 42′W) **14**:149
DEPEW (Oklahoma)
map (35° 48′N 96° 31′W) **14**:368
DEPILATORY **6**:118
D'ÉPINAY, LOUISE FLORENCE PÉTRONILLE DE LA LIVE *see* ÉPINAY, LOUISE FLORENCE PÉTRONILLE DE LA LIVE D'
DEPORTATION **6**:118
Alien and Sedition Acts **1**:293–294
DEPOSIT (finance)
banking systems **3**:68–69
credit union **5**:336
demand deposit **6**:96
savings bank **17**:100
savings and loan association **17**:100
DEPOSIT (New York)
map (42° 4′N 75° 25′W) **14**:149
DEPOSITION **6**:118
DEPOSITION OF CHRIST (Caravaggio) **4**:131 *illus.*
DEPRECIATION
amortization **1**:376
DEPRESSANT *see* SEDATIVE
DEPRESSION (economics)
See also DEPRESSION OF THE 1930S
Say, Jean Baptiste **17**:106
DEPRESSION (psychology) **6**:118–119 *bibliog.*
antidepressants **2**:60; **6**:276 *illus.*
barbiturate **3**:78
culture shock **5**:386
emotional expressions **7**:157
geriatrics **9**:122
headache **10**:85
Huntington's chorea **10**:315
manic-depressive psychosis **13**:116
psychotropic drugs **15**:604
sedative **17**:182
shock therapy **17**:279
suicide **18**:331
DEPRESSION OF THE 1930S **6**:119–120 *bibliog., illus.*
American literature **1**:346–347
Australia, history of **2**:341
automotive industry **2**:364
dance marathon **6**:30
Europe, history of **7**:296
Federal Theatre Project **8**:42
Federal Writers' Project **8**:42–43
Hitler, Adolf **10**:187
Hoover, Herbert **10**:228–229
housing **10**:277
Keynes, John Maynard **12**:64
middle schools and junior high schools **13**:412
National Recovery Administration **14**:45
New Deal **14**:119–120
panic, financial **15**:59
photography
Lange, Dorothea **12**:195 *illus.*
photography, history and art of **15**:271–272 *illus.*
photojournalism **15**:273
Stryker, Roy **18**:304
radio and television broadcasting **16**:56
Roosevelt, Franklin Delano **16**:308
United States, history of the **19**:454–455 *illus.*
World War II **20**:249
DEPTH CHARGE **6**:120
submarine **18**:315
DEPTH OF FIELD **6**:120 *bibliog.*
cinematography **4**:434
DEPTH PERCEPTION *see* PERCEPTION
DEPUE (Illinois)
map (41° 19′N 89° 19′W) **11**:42
DER STERN see STERN, DER (periodical)
DERA GHAZI KHAN
map (30° 3′N 70° 38′E) **15**:27
DERA ISMAIL KHAN
map (31° 50′N 70° 54′E) **15**:27
DERAIN, ANDRÉ **6**:121 *bibliog., illus.*
Westminster Bridge **6**:121 *illus.*
DERBY (Connecticut)
map (41° 19′N 73° 5′W) **5**:193
DERBY (England) **6**:121
map (52° 55′N 1° 29′W) **19**:403
DERBY (Kansas)
map (37° 33′N 97° 16′W) **12**:18
DERBY, ABRAHAM
Salop (England) **17**:36
DERBY, EDWARD STANLEY, 14th EARL OF **6**:121 *bibliog.*
DERBY, THE **6**:121
DERBY LINE (Vermont)
map (45° 0′N 72° 6′W) **19**:554
DERBYSHIRE (England) **6**:121
cities
Chesterfield **4**:336
Derby **6**:121
DEREGULATION
airline deregulation **1**:225
consumer protection **5**:226
government regulation **9**:271–272
railroad **16**:73
trucking industry **19**:314–315
DERG, LAKE
map (53° 0′N 8° 20′W) **11**:258
DERIVATIVE (mathematics) *see* CALCULUS; DIFFERENTIAL CALCULUS; INTEGRAL CALCULUS
DERLETH, AUGUST **6**:121
DERMAPTERA *see* EARWIG
DERMATITIS **6**:121–122 *bibliog.*
eczema **7**:54
immunity **11**:58
incense cedar **11**:73
poison ivy **15**:383
skin diseases **17**:341–342
vitamins and minerals **19**:619–620
DERMATITIS, SEBHORRHEIC *see* DANDRUFF
DERMATOLOGY **6**:122 *bibliog.*
DERMATOMYOSITIS
collagen disease **5**:102–103
DERMATOPHYTE *see* FUNGUS DISEASES
DERMIS
epidermis **7**:219
hair **10**:14 *illus.*
skin **17**:340–341 *illus.*
DERMOCARPA
blue-green algae **3**:342 *illus.*
DERMOPTERA
mammal **13**:102; **13**:104 *illus.*
DERMOT, JESSICA *see* ELLIOTT, MAXINE
DERMOTT (Arkansas)
map (33° 32′N 91° 26′W) **2**:166
DE'ROBERTI, ERCOLE
Renaissance music **16**:156 *illus.*
DEROBURT, HAMMER
Nauru **14**:51
DERRICK AND CRANE **6**:122 *bibliog., illus.*
containerization **5**:227 *illus.*
harbor and port **10**:44 *illus.*
DERRIDA, JACQUES **6**:122
DERRINGER (pistol) **6**:123 *bibliog., illus.*
DERRIS **6**:123
DERRY (New Hampshire)
map (42° 53′N 71° 19′W) **14**:123
DERRY (Pennsylvania)
map (40° 20′N 79° 18′W) **15**:147
DERUTA (Italy)
majolica **13**:76
DERVENTA (Yugoslavia)
map (44° 58′N 17° 55′E) **20**:340
DERVISH **6**:123 *bibliog., illus.*
fakir **8**:11
Konya (Turkey) **12**:109
Uighur **19**:374
DÉRY, TIBOR **6**:123 *bibliog.*
DERZHAVIN, GAVRILA ROMANOVICH **6**:123 *bibliog.*
DES *see under the element of the name following* DES, *except for names listed below*
DES (data encryptian standard)
cryptology **5**:373
DES (pharmaceutical) **6**:123 *bibliog., illus.*
cattle and cattle raising **4**:217
gynecological disorders, hormone **6**:123
organic chemistry **14**:438
DES ALLEMANDS (Louisiana)
map (29° 50′N 90° 28′W) **12**:430
DES ALLEMANDS, BAYOU
map (29° 42′N 90° 21′W) **12**:430
DES ARC (Arkansas)
map (34° 58′N 91° 30′W) **2**:166
DES MOINES (Iowa) **6**:123–124; **11**:245 *illus.*
map (41° 35′N 93° 37′W) **11**:244
DES MOINES (county in Iowa)
map (40° 55′N 91° 8′W) **11**:244
DES MOINES (Washington)
map (47° 24′N 122° 19′W) **20**:35
DES MOINES RIVER
map (40° 22′N 91° 26′W) **19**:419
DES PLAINES (Illinois)
map (42° 2′N 87° 54′W) **11**:42
DES PLAINES RIVER
map (41° 24′N 88° 16′W) **11**:42
DESAI, MORARJI RANDCHHADJI **6**:124
India **11**:88
DESALINATION **6**:124–125 *bibliog., illus.*
water supply **20**:54
DESARGUES, GÉRARD **6**:125
descriptive geometry **6**:126
DESCARTES, RENÉ **6**:125–126 *bibliog., illus.*
causality **4**:219
coordinate systems (mathematics) **5**:246–247
Discourse on Method **6**:189
dualism **6**:287
epistemology **7**:221–222
innate ideas **11**:179
light **12**:335
mathematics, history of **13**:225
philosophy **15**:242 *illus.*; **15**:244–245
physics, history of **15**:282–284 *illus.*
psychology, history of **15**:596 *illus.*
rationalism **16**:92; **16**:93
science, philosophy of **17**:141
skepticism **17**:337
Snell, Willebrord van Roijen **18**:3
Spinoza, Baruch **18**:187
Vico, Giambattista **19**:572
woodcut diagram, sensory impression **15**:596 *illus.*
DESCENT GROUP *see* KINSHIP
DESCHAMBAULT LAKE (Saskatchewan)
map (54° 55′N 103° 22′W) **17**:81
DESCHAMPS, EUSTACHE **6**:126
DESCHUTES (county in Oregon)
map (43° 50′N 121° 20′W) **14**:427
DESCHUTES RIVER
map (45° 38′N 120° 54′W) **14**:427
DESCHUTES-UMATILLA PLATEAU
Oregon **14**:428
DESCRIPTIVE GEOMETRY **6**:126
geometry **9**:107
Monge, Gaspard, founder **13**:527–528
projective geometry **15**:565
DESE (Ethiopia)
map (11° 5′N 39° 41′E) **7**:253
DESEGREGATION *see* INTEGRATION, RACIAL
DESENSITIZATION
allergy **1**:302
DESERET *see* UTAH
DESERET PEAK
map (40° 28′N 112° 38′W) **19**:492
DESERT **6**:126–129 *bibliog., illus., map*
Arabian Desert **2**:98–99
Atacama Desert **2**:286–287
Bonneville Salt Flats **3**:381
climate
arid climate **2**:154
dust devil **6**:308–309
horse latitudes, tropical climate **10**:246
semiarid climate **17**:196
Death Valley **4**:33 *illus.*
desert life **6**:129–131
erosion and sedimentation **7**:232–234
flash flood **8**:153
Gobi Desert **2**:235 *illus.*; **9**:216–217 *illus., map*
Great Victoria Desert **9**:323
Kalahari Desert **12**:7
Kara Kum (USSR) **12**:26
Kyzyl Kum Desert **12**:143
land reclamation **12**:178–181
landforms **6**:128–129
landform evolution **12**:183
Mojave Desert **13**:505
mudflow **13**:631
Namib Desert **14**:10
Negev Desert **14**:77
Nubian Desert **14**:278
Ordos Desert **14**:420
Painted Desert (Arizona) **15**:17
paleoclimatology **15**:33
pavement **12**:182 *illus.*
permanence of deserts **6**:129
playa **15**:363
Sahara Desert (Africa) **17**:13–14 *illus., map*
sand dune **17**:60
sandstone deposits, location indicating Permian climates **15**:33 *map*
sandstorm and dust storm **17**:63–64
Saudi Arabia **17**:93–94
Simpson Desert **17**:317
Sinai Desert **17**:318 *illus.*
Takla Makan Desert **19**:15
types **6**:126
water sources **6**:127–128
world distribution **3**:273 *map*; **6**:126–128 *map*; **15**:344 *map*
DESERT FOX, THE *see* ROMMEL, ERWIN
DESERT LIFE **6**:129–131 *bibliog., illus.*

DESERT LIFE (cont.)
See also NOMAD; names of specific plants and animals, e.g., PRICKLY PEAR; GECKO; etc.
Bedouin **3**:154
Beja **3**:172
Berbers **3**:207–208
habitat **10**:5 *illus.*
Namib Desert **14**:11 *illus.*
Triassic Period **19**:294 *illus.*
DESERT LILY 6:131
DESERT LYNX *see* CARACAL
DESERTION 6:131 *bibliog.*
DESEXUALIZATION *see* SUBLIMATION (psychology)
DESHA (county in Arkansas)
map (33° 45′N 91° 17′W) **2**:166
DESHAYES, GERARD PAUL 6:131
DESHLER (Nebraska)
map (40° 8′N 97° 44′W) **14**:70
DESHLER (Ohio)
map (41° 12′N 83° 54′W) **14**:357
DESIDERIO DA SETTIGNANO 6:131 *bibliog., illus.*
Laughing Child **6**:131 *illus.*
DESIGN, COMPUTER-AIDED *see* COMPUTER-AIDED DESIGN AND COMPUTER-AIDED MANUFACTURING
DESIGN, INDUSTRIAL *see* INDUSTRIAL DESIGN
DESIO, ARDITO
Godwin Austen **9**:221
DESIRE UNDER THE ELMS (play)
O'Neill, Eugene **14**:389–390
DESKEY, DONALD
Radio City Music Hall **16**:53
DESKTOP PUBLISHING
computer **5**:160g
computer, personal **5**:160i–160j
DESLOGE (Missouri)
map (37° 53′N 90° 33′W) **13**:476
DESMAN 6:132 *illus.*
DESMAREST, NICOLAS 6:132 *bibliog.*
DESMID 6:132
DESNOS, ROBERT 6:132
DESOXYN *see* AMPHETAMINE
DESPEÑAPERROS PASS
map (38° 24′N 3° 30′W) **18**:140
DESPENSER, HUGH
Edward II, King of England **7**:68
DESPOTISM 6:132 *bibliog.*
DESPRÉAUX, NICOLAS BOILEAU- *see* BOILEAU-DESPRÉAUX, NICOLAS
DESSALINES, JEAN JACQUES 6:132
Pétion, Alexandre Sabès **15**:202
DESSAU (East Germany) **6**:132
Bauhaus **3**:130; **11**:222 *illus.*
map (51° 50′N 12° 14′E) **9**:140
DESSOSIERS, C.
Art Nouveau brooch **2**:210 *illus.*
D'ESTAING, VALÉRY GISCARD *see* GISCARD D'ESTAING, VALÉRY
DESTROYER (warship) **6**:132–133 *bibliog., illus.*
naval vessels **14**:55–57 *illus.*
DESTRUCTIVE DISTILLATION *see* PYROLYSIS
DESTUTT DE TRACY, ANTOINE LOUIS CLAUDE, COMTE 6:133
DESY LABORATORY 6:133
D'ÉTAPLES, JACQUES LEFÈVRE *see* LEFÈVRE D'ÉTAPLES, JACQUES
DETECTIVE FICTION *see* MYSTERY, SUSPENSE, AND DETECTIVE FICTION
DETECTIVE STORY (periodical)
pulp magazines **15**:620
DETECTOR
alarm systems **1**:240
gravitational waves **9**:306
metal detector **13**:329
smoke detector **17**:373
DETECTOR, PARTICLE 6:133–134 *illus.*
Cherenkov radiation **4**:331
nuclear physics **14**:285
types **6**:133–134
bubble chamber **3**:531
cloud chamber **5**:68
Geiger counter **9**:68
scintillation counter **17**:146–147
spark chamber **18**:163
DÉTENTE 6:134
arms control **2**:178
balance of power **3**:32
cold war **5**:99
Nixon, Richard M. **14**:205
United States, history of the **19**:458
DETERGENT *see* SOAP AND DETERGENT
DETERMINANT (mathematics) **6**:134
Cramer's rule **5**:328
matrix **13**:230
DETERMINISM (geography) **9**:102
DETERMINISM (philosophy) **6**:134 *bibliog.*
Hobbes, Thomas **10**:192
will (philosophy) **20**:153–154
DETERRENCE (political science)
nuclear strategy **14**:288
DETRITAL REMANENT MAGNETISM (DRM)
paleomagnetism **15**:41
DETROIT (Michigan) **6**:134–136 *bibliog., map*; **13**:381 *illus.*
automotive industry **2**:363
Cadillac, Antoine Laumet de La Mothe, Sieur de **4**:11
map (42° 20′N 83° 3′W) **13**:377
DETROIT (Texas)
map (33° 40′N 95° 16′W) **19**:129
DETROIT, UNIVERSITY OF 6:136
***DETROIT FREE PRESS* 6**:136
DETROIT INSTITUTE OF ARTS, THE 6:136 *bibliog.*
mural (Diego Rivera) **13**:646 *illus.*
DETROIT LAKES (Minnesota)
map (46° 49′N 95° 51′W) **13**:453
DETROIT RESERVOIR
map (44° 42′N 122° 10′W) **14**:427
DETROIT RIVER
map (42° 6′N 83° 8′W) **13**:377
DETSKOYE SELO (USSR) *see* PUSHKIN (USSR)
DEUCALION 6:136
DEUEL (county in Nebraska)
map (41° 5′N 102° 20′W) **14**:70
DEUEL (county in South Dakota)
map (44° 45′N 97° 40′W) **18**:103
DEURNE (Belgium)
map (51° 13′N 4° 28′E) **3**:177
DEUS EX MACHINA
narrative and dramatic devices **14**:22
DEUTERIUM 6:136
deuteron **6**:136
fusion, nucler **8**:381–382 *illus.*
heavy water **10**:100
hydrogen **10**:337
hydrogen bomb **10**:339
hydrogen isotope **6**:136
proton-proton reaction **15**:578–579
Urey, Harold Clayton **19**:486
DEUTEROCANONICAL BOOKS *see* APOCRYPHA
DEUTERON 6:136
binding energy **3**:258
fusion, nuclear **8**:381–382
DEUTERONOMY, BOOK OF 6:136 *bibliog.*
DEUTSCH, BABETTE 6:136
DEUTSCHE BAY
map (54° 30′N 7° 30′E) **9**:140
DEUTSCHE BUCHGEMEINSCHAFT
book club **3**:386
DEUTSCHES ELEKTRONEN SYNCHROTRON LABORATORY *see* DESY LABORATORY
DEUTSCHES MUSEUM (Munich) **13**:659
DEUTSCHES THEATER 6:136–137 *bibliog.*
Brahm, Otto **3**:440
DEUTSCHES WERKBUND
Secession movement **17**:178
DEUTZIA 6:137 *illus.*
DEUXPONTS *see* ZWEIBRÜCKEN (West Germany)
DEVA (Romania)
map (45° 53′N 22° 55′E) **16**:288
DEVALUATION 6:137
DEVANAGARI SCRIPT
Indo-Iranian languages **11**:145
Sino-Tibetan writing systems **17**:325
DEVANTER, WILLIS VAN *see* VAN DEVANTER, WILLIS
DEVELOPING COUNTRIES *see* THIRD WORLD
DEVELOPMENT 6:137–142 *bibliog., illus.*
egg **7**:72
parthenogenesis **15**:99–100
embryo **7**:152–153
Spemann, Hans **18**:177
embryology **7**:153–154
evolution **7**:318–325
fertilization **8**:60–61
genetics **9**:89
gestation **9**:160
gonadotropin **9**:242
growth **9**:378–381
growth hormone **9**:381
heredity **10**:139
hormone, animal **10**:234
kidney **12**:74
larva **12**:208
meiosis **13**:282
mitosis **13**:485
molting **13**:513
neoteny **14**:86
nervous system, diseases of the **14**:95
ontogeny **14**:396
phylogeny **15**:279
precocial animal **15**:495
pregnancy and birth **15**:502–506
sex hormones **17**:226
sexual development **17**:228–230
DEVELOPMENT (economics) *see* ECONOMIC PLANNING
DEVELOPMENTAL PSYCHOLOGY 6:142–143 *bibliog.*
child development **4**:348–350
cognitive psychology **5**:94–95
educational psychology **7**:66
Erikson, Erik **7**:230
fixation **8**:132
Gesell, Arnold **9**:159
Hall, G. Stanley **10**:21
humanistic psychology **10**:299
infancy **11**:162–163
Koffka, Kurt **12**:106
moral awareness **13**:572
personality **15**:189
Piaget, Jean **15**:287–288
primary education **15**:538
psychology **15**:595
reasoning **16**:104–105
speech development **18**:176
DEVENTER (Netherlands)
map (52° 15′N 6° 10′E) **14**:99
DEVEREUX, ROBERT, 2D EARL OF ESSEX *see* ESSEX, ROBERT DEVEREUX, 2D EARL OF
DEVI
Durga **6**:305
DEVIANCE 6:143 *bibliog.*
conformity **5**:179
group dynamics **9**:376
DEVIL *see* DEMON; SATAN
DEVIL DOGS *see* MARINE CORPS, U.S.
DEVIL FISH *see* STINGRAY
DEVILLE, HENRI SAINT-CLAIRE
extraction of aluminum **1**:317
DEVIL'S ADVOCATE *see* CANONIZATION
DEVIL'S ISLAND (French Guiana) **6**:143
French Guiana **8**:310–311
map (5° 17′N 52° 35′W) **8**:311
DEVILS LAKE (North Dakota)
map (48° 7′N 98° 59′W) **14**:248
DEVIL'S TOWER
Wyoming **20**:303 *illus.*
DEVIL'S TRIANGLE *see* BERMUDA TRIANGLE
DEVIL'S-WALKING-STICK *see* ANGELICA TREE; HERCULES' CLUB (botany)
DEVILWOOD 6:143
DEVINE (British Columbia)
map (50° 32′N 122° 30′W) **3**:491
DEVINE (Texas)
map (29° 8′N 98° 54′W) **19**:129
DEVINE, GEORGE 6:143
DEVOLUTION, WAR OF 6:143
Aix-la-Chapelle, Treaties of **1**:229
Louis XIV, King of France **12**:426
DEVON (England) **6**:143–144 *bibliog.*
cities
Exeter **7**:331
Plymouth **15**:373–374
Dartmoor **6**:40
DEVON ISLAND
map (75° 0′N 87° 0′W) **14**:258
DEVONIAN PERIOD 6:144–146 *bibliog., illus., map*
coelacanth **5**:91
continents, estimated positions **15**:354 *map*
fern **8**:57
fossil record **8**:245–246
geologic time **9**:103–105
life **6**:145–146
lungfish **12**:463
Murchison, Roderick Impey **13**:647
paleoclimatology **15**:32
paleotectonics and geography **6**:144–145
Paleozoic Era **15**:43
polar wandering **15**:393 *map*
rock formations **6**:144 *map*
Sedgwick, Adam **17**:183
DEVONPORT (New Zealand)
map (36° 49′S 174° 48′E) **14**:158
DEVONSHIRE (England) *see* DEVON (England)
DEVRIES, WILLIAM C.
heart, artificial **10**:94; **10**:95
DEVSHIRME SYSTEM
Ottoman Empire **14**:464
DEVSNER, ANTOINE
Oval Fresco **5**:224 *illus.*
DEW (geology) **6**:146
fog **8**:193
hoarfrost **10**:191
DEW LINE *see* BMEWS
DEWAR, SIR JAMES 6:146
cryogenics **5**:370–371
vacuum bottle
vacuum **19**:502
DEWEY (Oklahoma)
map (36° 48′N 95° 56′W) **14**:368
DEWEY (county in Oklahoma)
map (36° 0′N 99° 0′W) **14**:368
DEWEY (Puerto Rico)
map (18° 18′N 65° 18′W) **15**:614
DEWEY (county in South Dakota)
map (45° 8′N 100° 47′W) **18**:103
DEWEY, GEORGE 6:146 *bibliog.*
Spanish-American War **18**:149–150
DEWEY, JOHN 6:146–147 *bibliog., illus.*
aesthetics **1**:131
ethics **7**:251
pragmatism **15**:487
primary education **15**:538
progressive education **15**:564
psychology, history of **15**:596
DEWEY, JOHN FREDERICK
plate tectonics **15**:357
DEWEY, MELVIL 6:147 *bibliog., table*
DEWEY, THOMAS E. 6:147 *bibliog.*
Truman, Harry S. **19**:318
DEWEY BEACH (Delaware)
map (38° 42′N 75° 5′W) **6**:88
DEWEY DECIMAL SYSTEM OF CLASSIFICATION **6**:147 *table*
DEWHURST, COLLEEN 6:147
DEWING, THOMAS WILMER 6:147
DEXEDRINE *see* AMPHETAMINE
DEXTER (Maine)
map (45° 1′N 69° 18′W) **13**:70
DEXTER (Missouri)
map (36° 48′N 89° 57′W) **13**:476
DEXTER (New Mexico)
map (33° 12′N 104° 22′W) **14**:136
DEXTER (New York)
map (44° 1′N 76° 3′W) **14**:149
DEXTROSE
animal metabolism **13**:327
carbohydrate **4**:133
Cori, Carl Ferdinand and Gerty Teresa **5**:262
fermentation **8**:55
glycoside **9**:212
starch **18**:226
sugar **18**:327
DEZFUL (Iran)
map (32° 23′N 48° 24′E) **11**:250
DEZHNEV, SEMYON
Arctic **2**:142 *map*
Bering, Vitus Jonassen **3**:211
Bering Sea **3**:212
Bering Strait **3**:212
DHAHRAN (Saudi Arabia) **6**:148
DHAKA (Bangladesh) *see* DACCA (Bangladesh)
DHAMAR (Yemen) (Sana)
map (14° 46′N 44° 23′E) **20**:325
DHARMA 6:148
Buddhism **3**:540
Hinduism **10**:170
DHAULAGIRI MOUNTAIN
map (28° 42′N 83° 30′E) **14**:86
D'HOLBACH, PAUL HENRI DIETRICH, BARON *see* HOLBACH, PAUL HENRI DIETRICH, BARON D'
DHOLE 6:148 *illus.*
D'HONDECOETER, MELCHIOR *see* HONDECOETER, MELCHIOR D'
DI *see* the element of the name following DI, except for names listed below
DI BORGOGNE, GUIDO *see* CALLISTUS II, POPE
DI PACE, DOMENICO *see* BECCAFUMI, DOMENICO
DI SUVERO, MARK 6:148
DIABASE 6:148
dikes **6**:148
DIABELLI, ANTON 6:148
DIABETES 6:148–149 *bibliog.*
acetone breath **1**:80
Banting, Sir Frederick G. **3**:71
Best, Charles **3**:228
diabetes insipidus **6**:148
antidiuretic hormone **2**:61
endocrine system, diseases of the **7**:170
pituitary gland **15**:322
diabetes mellitus **6**:148–149
autoimmune diseases **2**:356
endocrine system, diseases of the **7**:171

eye diseases **7**:350
fungus diseases **8**:369
gangrene **9**:37
gingivitis **9**:184
glucose tolerance test **9**:211
heart diseases **10**:96
infectious diseases **11**:164
insulin **11**:198
kidney disease **12**:71–72
MacLeod, John James Rickard **13**:33
metabolism **13**:327
obesity **14**:315–316
pancreas **15**:58
pregnancy and birth **15**:504
saccharin **17**:6
treatment **6**:148–149
ulcer **19**:376
DIABLE, ÎLE DU *see* DEVIL'S ISLAND (French Guiana)
DIABLO, MOUNT
map (37° 53′N 121° 55′W) **4**:31
DIABLO LAKE
map (48° 43′N 121° 8′W) **20**:35
DIABLO RANGE
map (37° 0′N 121° 20′W) **4**:31
DIACHRONIC LINGUISTICS *see* HISTORICAL LINGUISTICS; SYNCHRONIC LINGUISTICS
DIADEM
crowns and coronets **5**:364
DIADOCHI **6**:149
DIADOCHY *see* SOLID SOLUTION
DIAGHILEV, SERGE PAVLOVICH **6**:149 *bibliog., illus.*
ballet **3**:43
Ballets Russes de Serge Diaghilev **3**:48–49
Gris, Juan **9**:366
Larionov, Mikhail Fyodorovich **12**:207
Russian art and architecture **16**:363
Russian music **16**:368–369 *illus.*
DIAGNOSTIC TESTS **6**:149–150 *bibliog.*
allergy **1**:301
autopsy **2**:368
biopsy **3**:276
blood tests **3**:339
bronchoscope **3**:503
drug **6**:274–279
electrocardiograph **7**:111–112
electroencephalograph **7**:113–114
endoscope **7**:171
examination, medical **7**:326
expert system **7**:334
fetus
amniocentesis **1**:375
pregnancy and birth **15**:505
fluoroscope **8**:188
gastroscope **9**:58
genetic diseases **9**:84
glucose tolerance test **9**:211
gynecology **9**:414
heart diseases **10**:95; **10**:96
hematology **10**:117
leukemia **12**:301
mammography **13**:106
meningitis **13**:298
microbiology **13**:384
mycology **13**:690
nervous system, diseases of the **14**:96
nuclear magnetic resonance imaging **14**:284
nystagmus **14**:310
ophthalmoscope **14**:404–405
Pap test **15**:62
PETT **15**:215–216
projective tests **15**:566
pulmonary function test **15**:620
radiography **16**:63
radioimmunoassay **16**:63
radiology **16**:64–65
Schick test **17**:120
scintillation counter **17**:146–147
stethoscope **18**:262
syphilis **18**:410
technetium **19**:59
thyroid function test **19**:187–188
tuberculin test **19**:326–327
ultrasonics **19**:378
urinalysis
urine **19**:487
venereal disease **19**:541
Wassermann, August von **20**:46
X rays **20**:310 *illus.*
surgery **18**:361
DIAGONAL (Iowa)
map (40° 48′N 94° 20′W) **11**:244
DIAKA
map (15° 13′N 4° 14′W) **13**:89
DIAL, THE (periodical) **6**:150
Ripley, George **16**:228
DIALECT *see* GEOGRAPHICAL LINGUISTICS
DIALECTIC **6**:150
dialectical materialism **6**:150
Hegel, Georg Wilhelm Friedrich **10**:105
Hugh of Saint Victor **10**:292
Plato **15**:361
Zeno of Elea **20**:359
DIALECTIC OF SEX (book) **6**:150
DIALECTICAL MATERIALISM **6**:150 *bibliog.*
dialectic **6**:150
Marx, Karl **13**:182
Marxism **13**:183
materialism **13**:218–219
DIALECTICAL PSYCHOLOGY *see* DEVELOPMENTAL PSYCHOLOGY
DIALECTICAL THEATER *see* EPIC THEATER
DIALECTOLOGY *see* GEOGRAPHICAL LINGUISTICS
DIALOGUE (literature)
narrative and dramatic devices **14**:22
***DIALOGUES* OF PLATO** **6**:150 *bibliog.*
Plato **15**:360–361
DIALYSIS **6**:150–151 *bibliog.*
desalination **6**:125
hemodialysis
kidney, artificial **12**:71
uremia **19**:485
macromolecule **13**:37
DIAMAGNETISM
Oersted, Hans Christian **14**:352
DIAMANT (rocket) **6**:151
DIAMANTE (Argentina)
map (32° 4′S 60° 39′W) **2**:149
DIAMANTINA RIVER
map (26° 45′S 139° 10′E) **2**:328
DIAMANTINO (Brazil)
map (14° 25′S 56° 27′W) **3**:460
DIAMETER
sphere **18**:180
DIAMOND **6**:151–152 *bibliog., illus.*
birthstones **3**:296 *illus., table*
Brady, Diamond Jim **3**:438
carat **4**:131
carbon **4**:134 *illus.*
cyclic compounds **5**:403
gems **9**:73–75 *illus.*
gemstones **6**:151–152 *illus.*
index of refraction **11**:79
industrial uses **6**:152
jewelry **11**:408–411
mining and production **6**:152; **13**:449 *illus.*
Africa **1**:149 *map*
Kimberley (South Africa) **12**:77
Namibia **14**:12 *illus.*
Rhodes, Cecil John **16**:202
Tennant, Smithson **19**:102
DIAMOND CORNER (Barbados)
map (13° 17′N 59° 35′W) **3**:75
DIAMOND HEAD CRATER
map (21° 16′N 157° 49′W) **10**:72
DIAMOND HILL (Rhode Island)
map (41° 59′N 71° 25′W) **16**:198
DIAMOND LAKE
map (43° 10′N 122° 9′W) **14**:427
DIAMOND NECKLACE, AFFAIR OF THE **6**:152 *bibliog.*
DIAMOND PEAK (Idaho)
map (44° 9′N 113° 5′W) **11**:26
DIAMOND PEAK (Oregon)
map (43° 33′N 122° 9′W) **14**:427
DIAMONDVILLE (Wyoming)
map (41° 47′N 110° 32′W) **20**:301
DIANA **6**:153
Nemi, Lake **14**:81
DIANE DE POITIERS **6**:153
Chenonceaux, Château de **4**:330
DIAPHRAGM (anatomy) **1**:54 *illus.*; **6**:153 *illus.*
DIAPHRAGM (camera) **4**:56
DIAPHRAGM (contraceptive device)
birth control **3**:293
DIAPIR
salt dome **17**:37
DIARRHEA **6**:153
diseases, childhood **6**:193
dysentery **6**:320
gastrointestinal tract disease **9**:57
intestine **11**:231
paregoric **15**:84
starvation **18**:228
DIARY **6**:153 *bibliog.*
Evelyn, John **7**:315
Gadda, Carlo Emilio **9**:6
Gide, André **9**:176
Nin, Anaïs **14**:199
Pepys, Samuel **15**:157–158
Sei Shonagon **17**:189
DIARY OF ANNE FRANK, THE see FRANK, ANNE
DIAS, ANTÔNIO GONÇALVES *see* GONÇALVES DIAS, ANTÔNIO
DIAS, BARTOLOMEU **6**:153
Africa **1**:157 *map*
exploration **7**:337 *map*
Good Hope, Cape of **9**:245
DIAS, DIOGO
Madagascar **13**:39
DIASPORA **6**:153
ghetto **9**:167
Jews **11**:414; **11**:417
DIASPORE
bauxite **3**:131
DIASTASE **6**:153
Payen, Anselme **15**:121
DIASTOLE
blood pressure **3**:339
heart **10**:93 *illus.*
DIASTROPHISM **6**:153
erosion and sedimentation **7**:232
landform evolution **12**:183
Lugeon, Maurice **12**:452–453
Mesozoic Era **13**:322
orogeny **14**:447
Recent Epoch **16**:106–107
DIATHERMY **6**:153–154 *bibliog.*
DIATOM **1**:282 *illus.*; **6**:154 *bibliog., illus.*
algae **1**:281
micropaleontology **13**:386
sediment, marine **17**:184
DIATONIC SCALE
scale (music) **17**:106–107
DIATRYMA (bird) **3**:279 *illus.*
DIAZ (Arkansas)
map (35° 40′N 91° 18′W) **2**:166
DIAZ, BARTHOLOMEU *see* DIAS, BARTOLOMEU
DÍAZ, PORFIRIO **6**:154 *bibliog., illus.*
Madero, Francisco I. **13**:41
Mexico, history of **13**:364–365 *illus.*
DIAZ DE LA PEÑA, NARCISSE VIRGILE **6**:155 *bibliog.*
DÍAZ DE SOLÍS, JUAN *see* SOLÍS, JUAN DÍAZ DE
DIAZ DE VIVAR, RODRIGO *see* EL CID
DÍAZ DEL CASTILLO, BERNAL
Latin American literature **12**:229
DÍAZ MIRÓN, SALVADOR **6**:155
DIAZ ORDAZ, GUSTAVO **6**:155
Mexico, history of **13**:366
DÍAZ SÁNCHEZ, RAMÓN
Venezuela **19**:543
DIAZEPAM *see* VALIUM
DIAZO PROCESS
blueprint **3**:345
DIBELIUS, MARTIN **6**:155
D'IBERVILLE (Mississippi)
map (30° 26′N 88° 54′W) **13**:469
DIBOLL (Texas)
map (31° 11′N 94° 47′W) **19**:129
DIBRE (Albania)
map (41° 41′N 20° 26′E) **1**:250
DICE GAMES **6**:155 *bibliog., illus.*; **9**:29 *illus.*; **9**:30
gambling **9**:26
DICED SNAKE **17**:381 *illus.*
DICHROISM **6**:155
optical mineralogy **14**:408
polarized light **15**:394–395
DICK, PHILIP K. **6**:156 *bibliog.*
DICK ACT (1903)
National Guard **14**:34
"DICK TRACY" **5**:135 *illus.*
Gould, Chester **9**:265
DICKCISSEL **6**:156 *illus.*
DICKE, ROBERT **6**:156
radiometer **16**:65
relativity **16**:135
DICKENS (Texas)
map (33° 37′N 100° 50′W) **19**:129
DICKENS (county in Texas)
map (33° 38′N 100° 47′W) **19**:129
DICKENS, CHARLES **6**:156–157 *bibliog., illus.*; **7**:199 *illus.*
Christmas Carol, A **4**:415
Scrooge **17**:158
David Copperfield **6**:48–49
film adaptations
Lean, David **12**:259
Great Expectations **9**:319
Hard Times **10**:45
The Old Curiosity Shop **14**:274 *illus.*
Oliver Twist **14**:379
Pickwick Papers, The **15**:294
Portsmouth (England) **15**:448
Tale of Two Cities, A **19**:16
DICKENSON (county in Virginia)
map (37° 5′N 82° 20′W) **19**:607
DICKEY (county in North Dakota)
map (46° 5′N 98° 30′W) **14**:248
DICKEY, BILL **6**:157
DICKEY, JAMES **6**:157 *bibliog.*
DICKINSON (county in Iowa)
map (43° 23′N 95° 5′W) **11**:244
DICKINSON (county in Kansas)
map (38° 55′N 97° 10′W) **12**:18
DICKINSON (county in Michigan)
map (46° 0′N 87° 50′W) **13**:377
DICKINSON (North Dakota)
map (46° 53′N 102° 47′W) **14**:248
DICKINSON, EDWIN **6**:157 *bibliog.*
DICKINSON, EMILY **6**:157–158 *bibliog., illus.*
Higginson, Thomas Wentworth **10**:161
DICKINSON, JOHN **6**:158 *bibliog.*
DICKINSON, JONATHAN **6**:158
DICKINSON COLLEGE **6**:158
Dickinson, John **6**:158
DICKSON (Tennessee)
map (36° 5′N 87° 23′W) **19**:104
DICKSON (county in Tennessee)
map (36° 10′N 87° 20′W) **19**:104
DICKSON, BRIAN **6**:158
DICKSON, CARTER (pseudonym) *see* CARR, JOHN DICKSON
DICKSON, GORDON R. **6**:158–159
DICKSON, LEONARD **6**:159
DICKSON, WILLIAM KENNEDY LAURIE
film, history of **8**:81 *illus.*; **8**:84
DICKSON CITY (Pennsylvania)
map (41° 27′N 75° 37′W) **15**:147
DICOT
flower **8**:183
plant **15**:335 *illus.*
DICOTYLEDON *see* DICOT
DICTATING MACHINES **3**:589
DICTATORSHIP **6**:159 *bibliog.*
caudillo **4**:219
government **9**:267–268
totalitarianism **19**:248
DICTATORSHIP OF THE PROLETARIAT **6**:159
DICTION (literature)
narrative and dramatic devices **14**:22
DICTIONARY **6**:159–160 *bibliog.*
applied linguistics **2**:90
English language
Fowler, H. W. **8**:255
Harris, William Torrey **10**:58
Johnson, Samuel (writer) **11**:435–436
Murray, Sir James **13**:650
Oxford English Dictionary, The **14**:474–475
Porter, Noah **15**:445
Webster, Noah **20**:89
French language
Larousse, Pierre **12**:208
German language
Grimm, Jacob and Wilhelm **9**:365–366
lexicology and lexicography **12**:308–309
DICTIONARY OF NATIONAL BIOGRAPHY
Stephen, Sir Leslie **18**:254
DICUMAROL
anticoagulant **2**:60
DIDACHE **6**:160
Apostolic Fathers **2**:85
DIDELOT, CHARLES LOUIS
Kirov Ballet **12**:89
DIDEROT, DENIS **6**:160 *bibliog., illus.*; **7**:164 *illus.*; **8**:317 *illus.*
drame bourgeois **6**:262
encyclopedia **7**:164
Enlightenment **7**:207
DIDINIUM **6**:160
DIDION, JOAN **6**:160–161 *illus.*
DIDO **6**:161
DIDRIKSON, BABE *see* ZAHARIAS, BABE DIDRIKSON
DIDSBURY (Alberta)
map (51° 40′N 114° 8′W) **1**:256
DIE ZEIT see ZEIT, DIE
DIEBENKORN, RICHARD **6**:161
DIEFENBAKER, JOHN G. **6**:161 *bibliog., illus.*
Canada, history of **4**:87
DIEFENBAKER, LAKE
map (51° 0′N 106° 55′W) **17**:81
DIEFFENBACHIA **6**:161 *illus.*
DIEGO GARCIA
British Indian Ocean Territory **3**:496–497
DIEGO-SUAREZ (Madagascar)
map (12° 16′S 49° 17′E) **13**:38
DIELECTRIC **6**:161
capacitance **4**:119
capacitor **4**:119
constant, atomic constants **2**:308
DIELS, OTTO PAUL HERMANN **6**:161–162 *bibliog.*
DIEM, NGO DINH *see* NGO DINH DIEM

DIEN BIEN PHU, BATTLE OF **6**:162 *bibliog.*
Vietnam War **19**:585 *map*
DIENE (chemistry) **6**:162 *bibliog., illus.*
Alder, Kurt **1**:268
isoprene **11**:300
synthesis reaction
Diels, Otto Paul Hermann **6**:161–162
DIENTZENHOFER (family) **6**:162 *bibliog.*
DIEPPE (France) **6**:162
map (49° 56′N 1° 5′E) **8**:260
DIEPPE (New Brunswick)
map (46° 6′N 64° 45′W) **14**:117
DIERKS (Arkansas)
map (34° 7′N 94° 1′W) **2**:166
DIES, MARTIN **6**:162–163 *bibliog.*
Un-American Activities, House Committee on **19**:380
DIES AND DIEMAKING *see* TOOL AND DIEMAKING
DIES IRAE **6**:163
DIESEL, RUDOLF **6**:163 *bibliog.*
diesel engine **6**:163 *illus.*
DIESEL-ELECTRIC LOCOMOTIVE **16**:75 *illus.*
DIESEL ENGINE **6**:163 *bibliog., illus.*
automotive industry **2**:367
Diesel, Rudolf, inventor **6**:163
engine **7**:177
ignition system **11**:36
internal-combustion engine **11**:217 *illus.*
Kettering, Charles Franklin **12**:61
locomotive **12**:390–391 *illus.*
motorboat **13**:612
railroad **16**:73
ship **17**:273–274 *illus.*
trucking industry **19**:314
DIESKAU, DIETRICH FISCHER- *see* FISCHER-DIESKAU, DIETRICH
DIESKAU, LUDWIG AUGUST
French and Indian Wars **8**:313 *map*
DIET (council)
Worms (West Germany) **20**:284
DIET (legislative body)
Japan **11**:366
DIET, ANIMAL
grass **9**:295
kudzu **12**:135
sorghum **18**:69
soybean **18**:115
DIET, HUMAN **6**:163–164 *bibliog.*
cheese **4**:309
cholesterol controversy **14**:307
consumer education **14**:307
cooking **5**:237–240
dietary laws **6**:164–165
dieting **6**:165–166
federal guidelines **14**:306–307
fruits and fruit cultivation **8**:347–349
grass **9**:295
health foods **10**:89
iguana **11**:38
lipid **12**:362
nutrition, human **14**:304–307
nutritional-deficiency diseases **14**:308
megavitamin therapy **13**:280
obesity **14**:316
orthomolecular medicine **14**:450
protein **15**:574
Recommended Dietary Allowances **14**:306
rice **16**:208
salt (sodium chloride) **17**:37
sorghum **18**:69
soybean **18**:115
starch **18**:226
starvation **18**:228
vegetable **19**:531
vegetarianism **19**:535
wheat **20**:125
DIETARY LAWS **6**:164–165
DIETETICS
nutrition, human **14**:304
DIETHYL ETHER *see* ETHYL ETHER
DIETHYLSTILBESTROL *see* DES (pharmaceutical)
DIETING **6**:165–166 *bibliog.*
obesity **14**:315–316
DIETRICH (Idaho)
map (42° 55′N 114° 16′W) **11**:26
DIETRICH, MARLENE **6**:166 *bibliog., illus.*; **8**:84 *illus.*
Sternberg, Josef von **18**:260
DIFFERDANGE (Luxembourg)
map (49° 32′N 5° 52′E) **12**:472
DIFFERENTIAL (device) **6**:166 *bibliog., illus.*
automobile **2**:359 *illus.*
DIFFERENTIAL AMPLIFIER
amplifier **1**:383
DIFFERENTIAL ANALYZER **6**:166
Bush, Vannevar **3**:585
hybrid computer **10**:328–329
DIFFERENTIAL CALCULUS **6**:167–168 *bibliog., illus., table*
calculus **4**:24
computer **5**:160
differential equations **6**:168; **7**:224–225
differential geometry **6**:169
Euler, Leonhard **7**:264–265
infinitesimal (mathematics) **11**:168
mathematics, history of **13**:225
maxima and minima **13**:239
Newton, Sir Isaac **14**:173
DIFFERENTIAL EQUATIONS **6**:168 *bibliog.*
Alembert, Jean Le Rond d′ **1**:271
Birkhoff, George David **3**:292
Boole, George **3**:392–393
Cauchy, Augustin Louis **4**:219
complex number **5**:157
differential analyzer **6**:166
Duhamel, Jean **6**:294
equation **7**:224–225
Fredholm, Erik Ivar **8**:294
Hermite, Charles **10**:143
Lagrange, Joseph Louis de **12**:166
mathematics, history of **13**:225
Maxwell′s equations **13**:241–242
numerical analysis **14**:295
DIFFERENTIAL GEOMETRY **6**:169 *bibliog.*
geometry **9**:107
mathematics, history of **13**:226
Veblen, Oswald **19**:529
DIFFERENTIATION (embryology)
development **6**:138–139; **6**:141
embryology **7**:154
growth **9**:379
DIFFLUGIA **6**:169
DIFFRACTION (physics) **6**:169 *bibliog., illus.*
Airy disk **1**:228
electron optics **7**:122
gems **9**:73
Grimaldi, Francesco Maria **9**:364
light **12**:335–336
optics **14**:412
sound and acoustics **18**:73
types **6**:169
X-ray diffraction **20**:308–309
DIFFRACTION GRATING **6**:169–170 *illus.*
Michelson, Albert Abraham **13**:375–376
optics **14**:411–412 *illus.*
Rowland, Henry Augustus, inventor **16**:328
Siegbahn, Manne **17**:295
spectrum **18**:172–173
star **18**:222
stellar spectrum **18**:252
DIFFUSION **6**:170 *bibliog.*
osmosis **14**:455
DIFFUSION, CULTURAL **6**:170 *bibliog.*
culture **5**:385
culture area **5**:386
Graebner, Fritz **9**:278
Heine-Geldern, Robert **10**:109
Heyerdahl, Thor **10**:155
Perry, W. J. **15**:179
prehistory **15**:517
Ra expeditions **16**:29
Smith, Sir Elliot **17**:368
DIGAMMA (letter)
V (letter) **19**:500
DIGBY (Nova Scotia)
map (44° 37′N 65° 46′W) **14**:269
DiGEORGE′S SYNDROME
immunodeficiency disease **11**:60
DIGESTION, HUMAN **6**:170–173 *bibliog., illus.*
amino acid **1**:370–371
Beaumont, William **3**:147
gallbladder **9**:17
intestine **11**:230–231
pancreas **15**:57–59
salivary glands **17**:34
tongue **19**:234
DIGESTIVE SYSTEM **6**:173–174 *bibliog., illus.*
colic **5**:101
digestion, human **6**:170–173
duodenum **6**:302
esophagus **7**:242
excretory system **7**:327
gallbladder **9**:17
gastrointestinal tract disease **9**:56–57
horse **10**:241
insect **11**:187–188 *illus.*
intestine **11**:230–231
physiology
Bayliss, Sir William **3**:133–134
liver **12**:374
pancreas **15**:57
Pavlov, Ivan Petrovich **15**:120
peristalsis **15**:171–172
ruminant **16**:345
salivary glands **17**:34
snake **17**:379–381
sterol **18**:262
stomach **18**:279–280 *illus.*
tissue, animal **19**:210
Trichomonas **19**:296
DIGGER INDIANS *see* PAIUTE (American Indians); SHOSHONI (American Indians)
DIGGER WASP **6**:174 *bibliog., illus.*
animal behavior **2**:13 *illus.*
DIGGERS(political movement)
Levelers **12**:302
DIGGES, THOMAS **6**:174
astronomy, history of **2**:280
DIGHTON (Kansas)
map (38° 29′N 100° 28′W) **12**:18
DIGITAL TECHNOLOGY **6**:175 *bibliog.*
analog devices **1**:389
analog-to-digital converter **1**:389
compact disc **5**:154–155
computer *see* COMPUTER
digital-to-analog converter **6**:175
liquid crystal **12**:365
sound recording and reproduction **18**:76
tape recorder **19**:30
DIGITAL-TO-ANALOG CONVERTER **6**:175 *bibliog.*
DIGITALIS **6**:175
drug **6**:275
folk medicine **8**:201
foxglove **8**:257
heart failure **10**:96
medicinal plants **13**:266
shock, physiologic **17**:278
steroid **18**:261
DIGLOSSIA
geographical linguistics **9**:100
DIHANG RIVER
Brahmaputra River **3**:440
DIJON (France) **6**:175
map (47° 19′N 5° 1′E) **8**:260
DIK-DIK *see* ANTELOPE
DIKE (engineering) **6**:175–176
Delta Plan **6**:95
floods and flood control **8**:167
polder **15**:395
DIKE (geology) **6**:176 *bibliog., illus.*
basalt **3**:101
diabase **6**:148
Earth, structure and composition of **7**:22
felsite **8**:48
granite **9**:287
lamprophyre **12**:176
latite **12**:234
mid-oceanic ridge **13**:390
porphyry **15**:442
DILI (Indonesia)
map (8° 33′S 125° 35′E) **11**:147
DILIGENTE (sailing ship)
ship **17**:268 *illus.*
DILKE, SIR CHARLES **6**:176
DILL **6**:176 *illus.*
DILL CITY (Oklahoma)
map (35° 17′N 99° 8′W) **14**:368
DILLARD, ANNIE **6**:176
DILLINGER, JOHN **6**:176 *bibliog.*
DILLINGHAM (Alaska)
map (59° 2′N 158° 29′W) **1**:242
DILLON (Montana)
map (45° 13′N 112° 38′W) **13**:547
DILLON (South Carolina)
map (34° 25′N 79° 22′W) **18**:98
DILLON (county in South Carolina)
map (34° 20′N 79° 25′W) **18**:98
DILLON, C. DOUGLAS **6**:176; **15**:526 *illus.*
DILLON, JOHN (Irish nationalist) **15**:96 *illus.*
DILLON LAKE
map (40° 2′N 82° 10′W) **14**:357
DILLWYN (Virginia)
map (37° 32′N 78° 27′W) **19**:607
DILMUN **6**:176
DILTHEY, WILHELM **6**:176–177 *bibliog.*
DiMAGGIO, JOE **3**:106 *illus.*; **6**:177 *bibliog., illus.*
Monroe, Marilyn **13**:542
DIMAGNETISM *see* MAGNETISM
DIMANTINA FRACTURE ZONE
Indian Ocean bottom **11**:105 *map*
DIMASHQ (Syria) *see* DAMASCUS (Syria)
DIMBOKRO (Ivory Coast)
map (6° 39′N 4° 42′W) **11**:335
DÎMBOVIȚA RIVER
map (44° 14′N 26° 27′E) **16**:288
DIMENSION THEORY
Cantor, Georg **4**:118
DIMETHYLKETONE *see* ACETONE
DIMETRODON **6**:177 *bibliog.*
DIMITROV, GEORGI MIKHAILOV **6**:177
Bulgaria **3**:557
Sofia (Bulgaria) **18**:34
DIMITROVA, BLAGA
Bulgarian literature **3**:557
DIMITROVGRAD (Bulgaria)
map (42° 3′N 25° 36′E) **3**:555
DIMITRY DONSKOI, GRAND DUKE OF MOSCOW **6**:177
DIMLANG MOUNTAIN
map (8° 24′N 11° 47′E) **14**:190
DIMMIT (county in Texas)
map (28° 27′N 99° 45′W) **19**:129
DIMMITT (Texas)
map (34° 33′N 102° 19′W) **19**:129
DIMONA (Israel)
map (31° 4′N 35° 2′E) **11**:302
DIMOV, DIMITUR **6**:177
DINAJPUR (Bangladesh)
map (25° 38′N 88° 38′E) **3**:64
DINARA PLANINA *see* DINARIC ALPS
DINARIC ALPS **6**:178
map (43° 50′N 16° 35′E) **20**:340
Yugoslavia **20**:340
DINCHERLE, ALBERTO *see* MORAVIA, ALBERTO (pseudonym)
DINDSEANCHES
Tara (Ireland) **19**:34
D′INDY, VINCENT *see* INDY, VINCENT D′
DINE, JIM **6**:178 *bibliog., illus.*
happenings **10**:41
Palette of Pleasure **6**:178 *illus.*
DINE, S. S. VAN *see* VAN DINE, S. S.
DINESEN, ISAK **6**:178 *bibliog., illus.*
DING (cartoonist)
Darling, Jay Norwood **6**:39
DINGHY **6**:178
DINGLE BAY
map (52° 5′N 10° 15′W) **11**:258
DINGLE PENINSULA
map (52° 10′N 10° 5′W) **11**:258
DINGLINGER, JOHANN MELCHIOR
gold and silver work **9**:230
DINGO **6**:178–179 *illus.*; **10**:5 *illus.*
DINGWALL (Nova Scotia)
map (46° 54′N 60° 28′W) **14**:269
DINIS, KING OF PORTUGAL **6**:179
Portugal, history of **15**:453
DINIS DA CRUZ E SILVA, ANTÔNIO
Portuguese literature **15**:457
DINKELOO, JOHN *see* ROCHE, KEVIN
DINOFLAGELLATE **6**:179 *bibliog.*; **15**:331 *illus.*
algae **1**:282
bioluminescence **3**:272
poisonous plants and animals **15**:384
red tide **16**:114
DINOHYUS
Miocene Epoch **19**:125 *illus.*
DINOSAUR **6**:179–182 *bibliog., illus.*
Allosaurus **1**:303
Anchisaurus **1**:399
Brachiosaurus **3**:435
Brontosaurus **3**:504–505
Camptosaurus **4**:67–68
Compsognathus **5**:158
Corythosaurus **5**:279–280
Cretaceous Period **5**:341 *illus.*
crocodile **5**:356
Dimetrodon **6**:177
Diplodocus **6**:185–186
Edaphosaurus **7**:54
evolution **7**:318–325; **16**:170 *illus., table*
fossil record **8**:245 *illus.*
Gorgosaurus **9**:251
Hallopus **10**:23
Iguanodon **11**:39
Jurassic Period **11**:475–476 *illus.*
Marsh, Othniel Charles **13**:171
Mesozoic Era **13**:322
Nanosaurus **14**:13
Ornithischia **6**:180–181 *illus.*
Ornitholestes **14**:447
Pachycephalosaurus **15**:5
Palaeoscincus **15**:29
paleoclimatology **15**:33
Plateosaurus **15**:358–359
Plesiosaur **15**:367–368 *illus.*
Podokesaurus **15**:377
Procompsognathus **15**:561
Protoceratops **15**:578
reptile classification **6**:179
Saurischia **6**:179–180 *illus.*
sauropods **6**:180
Stegosaurus **18**:246
Struthiomimus **18**:303
Styracosaurus **18**:311

therapods 6:179–180
Trachodon 19:258
Triassic Period 19:292–295 *illus.*
Triceratops 19:296
Tyrannosaurus 19:367
DINOSAUR (Colorado)
map (40° 15′N 109° 1′W) 5:116
DINOSAUR NATIONAL MONUMENT 6:182; 14:38–39 *map, table*
DINUBA (California)
map (36° 32′N 119° 23′W) 4:31
DINWIDDIE (Virginia)
map (37° 5′N 77° 35′W) 19:607
DINWIDDIE (county in Virginia)
map (37° 10′N 77° 20′W) 19:607
DINWIDDIE, ROBERT 6:182 *bibliog.*
DIOCLETIAN, BATHS OF 6:182 *bibliog.*
DIOCLETIAN, ROMAN EMPEROR 6:182–183 *bibliog., illus.*
Rome, ancient 16:304
Split (Yugoslavia) 18:191
DIOCLETIAN'S PALACE 2:132 *illus.*; 6:183 *bibliog.*; 16:275 *illus.*
DIODE 6:183 *bibliog., illus.*
applications 6:183
bridge circuit 3:484
electroluminescence 7:114
electron tube 7:122
Esaki, Leo 7:236
junction diodes 17:196
laser and maser 12:213 *table*
light-emitting diode 17:197
photoelectric cell 15:259–260
photoelectric effect 15:260
semiconductor 17:196–197
vacuum tube 19:502
Zener diode 17:196–197; 20:359
DIODORUS
Seven Wonders of the World 17:216
DIOGENES OF APOLLONIA 6:183–184
DIOGENES LAËRTIUS 6:184
DIOGENES OF SINOPE 6:184 *bibliog.*
DIOGO CAO *see* CAM, DIOGO
DIOMEDES 6:184
DION OF SYRACUSE 6:184
Dionysius the Younger 6:184
DIONE (astronomy)
Saturn (astronomy) 17:89–91 *illus., table*
DIONYSIUS THE ELDER, TYRANT OF SYRACUSE 6:184
Plato 15:360
Syracuse (Sicily) 18:411
Taormina (Italy) 19:29
DIONYSIUS EXIGUUS 6:184 *bibliog.*
DIONYSIUS THE GREAT 6:184
DIONYSIUS THE PSEUDO-AREOPAGITE 6:184
DIONYSIUS THRAX 6:184 *bibliog.*
linguistics 12:354
DIONYSIUS THE YOUNGER, TYRANT OF SYRACUSE 6:184
Plato 15:360
Syracuse (Sicily) 18:411
Timoleon 19:203
DIONYSUS (Greek god) 6:184–185; 13:593 *illus.*; 13:701 *illus.*
animal procession 20:374 *illus.*
dance 6:23
Delphi 6:95
Greek music 9:345
initiation rites 13:645 *illus.*
mythology 13:700–701 *illus.*
theater, history of the 19:144
DIOP, BIRAGO ISMAEL 6:185 *bibliog.*
DIOP, DAVID 6:185 *bibliog.*
DIOPHANTINE EQUATIONS 6:185 *bibliog.*
Diophantus 6:185
number theory 14:294
Poincaré, Henri 15:380
DIOPHANTUS 6:185
Diophantine equations 6:185
DIOPSIDE
pyroxene 15:638
DIOR, CHRISTIAN 6:185 *bibliog.*
fashion design 8:32
Saint Laurent, Yves 17:20
DIORI, HAMANI
Niger 14:188
DIORITE 6:185 *bibliog.*
igneous rock 6:185
DIOSCORIDES, PEDANIUS 6:185
botany 3:413
medicinal plants 13:266
DIOSCURI (Sons of Zeus) *see* CASTOR AND POLLUX
DIOURBEL (Senegal)
map (14° 40′N 16° 15′W) 17:202
DIOXIN
pollutants, chemical 15:410
DIPHTHERIA 6:185
antitoxin
Ehrlich, Paul (1854–1915) 7:91
Corynebacterium 5:279
Fothergill, John 8:248
poisonous plants and animals 15:383
Roux, Pierre Paul Émile 16:327
Schick test 17:120
vaccination 19:501
Wassermann, August von 20:46
DIPLOCOCCUS 6:185
pneumococcus 15:375
pneumonia 15:376
DIPLODOCUS 6:185–186 *bibliog., illus.*
dinosaur 6:180–181
fossil record 8:245 *illus.*
DIPLOMACY *see* FOREIGN SERVICE
DIPLOMATIC IMMUNITY
immunity (law) 11:59
DIPLOPODA *see* MILLIPEDE
DIPLURA 6:186
DIPOLE 6:186
chemical bonds 4:314
electret 7:105
intermolecular forces 11:215
moment
dielectric 6:161
magnetic moment 13:55
DIPPER (bird) 6:186 *illus.*
DIPTERA *see* FLY
DIPYLON KRATER, THE 9:338 *illus.*
DIRAC, PAUL 6:186–187 *bibliog., illus.*; 15:286 *illus.*
Dirac equation 6:186–187
Schrödinger, Erwin 17:135
DIRE DAWA (Ethiopia)
map (9° 37′N 41° 52′E) 7:253
DIRECT CURRENT 6:187
See also ALTERNATING CURRENT; ELECTRICITY
circuit, electric 4:436–438
diode 6:183
first generator 15:481 *illus.*
Josephson effect
superconductivity 18:350
motor 13:611–612 *illus.*
oscillator 14:453
rectifier 16:110–111
DIRECT MAIL 6:187 *bibliog.*
advertising 1:111; 1:112; 1:113
special-interest groups 18:168
DIRECT MARKETING *see* MAIL-ORDER BUSINESS
DIRECT PRIMARY *see* PRIMARY ELECTION
DIRECT TAXES *see* TAXATION
DIRECTING (film, theater) 6:187 *bibliog.*
See also the subheading theater under specific countries, e.g., FRANCE; UNITED STATES; etc.; names of specific directors, e.g., FELLINI, FEDERICO; FORD, JOHN (film director); etc.
cinematography 4:432; 4:434
film, history of 8:80–89
film production 8:90
theater, history of the 19:147; 19:149
DIRECTION COSINE
analytic geometry 1:391
DIRECTOIRE STYLE 6:187 *bibliog.*
furniture 8:377
Riesener, Jean Henri 16:219
DIRECTORY 6:187–188
Barras, Paul François, Vicomte de 3:93
Directoire style 6:187
French Revolution 8:324
Sieyès, Emmanuel Joseph 17:298
DIRIAMBA (Nicaragua)
map (11° 51′N 86° 14′W) 14:179
DIRICHLET, PETER GUSTAV LEJEUNE 6:188
mathematics, history of 13:226
DIRIGIBLE *see* AIRSHIP
DIRKEN, EVERETT M. 15:524 *illus.*
DIRKS, RUDOLPH 6:188
comic strip 5:135
DIRKSEN, EVERETT M. 6:188 *bibliog.*
DIRT BIKE *see* MOTORCYCLE
DIRTY DEVIL RIVER
map (37° 53′N 110° 24′W) 19:492
DISABILITY INSURANCE
social security 18:15
DISABLED AMERICAN VETERANS (organization) 6:188
DISABLED PERSONS *see* HANDICAPPED PERSONS; REHABILITATION MEDICINE
DISACCHARIDE
carbohydrate 4:133
sugar 18:327
DISAPPOINTMENT, CAPE
map (46° 18′N 124° 3′W) 20:35
DISAPPOINTMENT, LAKE
map (23° 30′S 122° 50′E) 2:328
DISAPPOINTMENT CREEK
map (38° 1′N 108° 51′W) 5:116
DISARMAMENT *see* ARMS CONTROL
DISC CAMERA 4:59
DISCHARGE, ELECTRICAL 6:188 *bibliog.*
X rays 20:310
DISCIPLES OF CHRIST 6:188 *bibliog.*
Campbell, Alexander 4:65
church music 4:424
Stone, Barton Warren 18:280
DISCO MUSIC 6:189
hustle 10:321
DISCOBOLUS
Myron 13:691
DISCOID LUPUS ERYTHEMATOSUS (DLE) *see* LUPUS ERYTHEMATOSUS
DISCONTINUITY (mathematics)
continuity 5:231
DISCOUNT HOUSE 6:189
DISCOUNT RATE 6:189
Federal Reserve System 8:42
DISCOURSE ON METHOD (book) 6:189
DISCOVERER (artificial satellite) 6:189
DISCOVERY (ship)
Cook, James 5:236
Hudson, Henry 10:289
DISCRIMINANT (mathematics) 6:189 *bibliog., illus.*
equation 7:224
quadratic function 16:5
DISCRIMINATION 6:189–190 *bibliog.*
See also RIGHT TO COUNSEL (law)
affirmative action 1:132
anti-Semitism 2:68
apartheid 2:74
black Americans 3:306–309
black codes 3:313–314
blacklist 3:321
civil rights 5:12–13
Civil Rights Cases 5:13–14
Civil War 5:33
equal opportunity 7:223
equal protection of the laws 7:224
ethnic minorities 7:255–256
gay activism 9:63
ghetto 9:167
grandfather clause 9:286
Gray Panthers 9:307
Indians, American 11:137–138
integration, racial 11:202–203
intelligence, tests 11:204
Jensen, Arthur 11:396
National Association for the Advancement of Colored People 14:29
Oriental Americans 14:441–442
pacifism and nonviolent movements 15:10
prejudice 15:518
racism 16:37–38
sexism 17:227
Equal Rights Amendment 7:224
feminism 8:48–49
women in society 20:201–204
13th Amendment 19:170
voter registration 19:637
zoning 20:374
DISCUS THROW
track and field 19:261
DISDÉRI, ANDRÉ ADOLPHE EUGÈNE 6:190
carte de visite 4:171
DISEASES, ANIMAL 6:190–192 *bibliog.*
anthrax 2:50
ape 2:75
aspergillosis 2:262
brucellosis 3:520
cat 4:194
chigger 4:347
coccidiosis 5:85
cowpox 5:322
distemper 6:200
dog 6:221
environmental health 7:212
examination, medical 7:326
foot-and-mouth disease 8:214
fungus diseases 8:369
glanders 9:197
horse 10:241–244
housefly 10:274
infectious diseases 11:164–168
leishmaniasis 12:279
leptospirosis 12:296
parasitic diseases 15:82
psittacosis 15:588
Q fever 16:3
quarantine 16:12
rabies 16:32
red tide 16:114
significance 6:190–191
Streptococcus 18:297
tapeworm 19:33–34 *illus.*
teeth 19:72
tick 19:192
toxoplasmosis 19:256
trichinosis 19:296
trypanosomiasis 19:322
tuberculosis 19:327
veterinary medicine 19:566–567
virus 19:615
DISEASES, CHILDHOOD 6:192-193 *bibliog.*
asthma 2:268
cerebral palsy 4:259–260
chicken pox 4:345–346
child psychiatry 4:350–351
cold, common 5:97
crib death 5:342
croup 5:363
cystic fibrosis 5:411
deafness 6:66
diabetes 6:148–149
Down's syndrome 6:252
fifth disease 8:74
galactosemia 9:9
genetic diseases 9:82–84
heart diseases 10:95
hookworm 10:227
hydrocephaly 10:331
immunodeficiency disease 11:59–60
impetigo 11:62
infectious diseases 11:166
Kawasaki disease 12:32
kwashiorkor 12:142–143
leukemia 12:300
mumps 13:639
muscular dystrophy 13:656
mycoplasmal pneumonia 13:690
orthopedics 14:450
osteomyelitis 14:457
parasitic diseases 15:82
pediatrics 15:131
phenylketonuria 15:226
pinworm 15:308
poison 15:381
respiratory system disorders 16:182
Reye's syndrome 16:190
rheumatic fever 16:194
rickets 16:215
scarlet fever 17:115
scoliosis 17:147
strabismus 18:287
strep throat 18:297
Tay-Sachs disease 19:48
Tourette's syndrome 19:251
whooping cough 20:143
DISEASES, HUMAN
See also DISEASES, CHILDHOOD; DISEASES, OCCUPATIONAL; MEDICINE; names of specific diseases, e.g., DIPHTHERIA; PNEUMONIA; etc.; names of specific disorders, e.g., HYPOTHERMIA; NAUSEA; etc.
allergy 1:301–302
autoimmune diseases 2:356
bites and stings 3:300
blood 3:337–338
bone diseases 3:377–378
bubonic plague 3:532
cause
bacteria 3:16–18
chigger 4:347
diseases, animal 6:190
flea 8:158
fly 8:189–190
housefly 10:274
insect 11:193
louse 12:436
mosquito 13:602
mouse 13:626
rodent 16:265
Siphonaptera 17:326
Staphylococcus 18:220
Streptococcus 18:297
tick 19:191–192
virus 19:615
Centers for Disease Control 4:249–250
collagen disease 5:102–103
diagnostic tests 6:149–150
diseases, occupational 6:193–194
ear disease 7:7–8
endocrine system, diseases of the 7:169–171
environmental health 7:210–212
enzyme 7:214–215
epidemiology 7:219
examination, medical 7:326
exercise 7:330
eye diseases 7:350–351
fever 8:66
food poisoning and infection 8:211

DISEASES, HUMAN (cont.)
fungus diseases 8:369
gastrointestinal tract disease 9:56–57 *illus.*
genetic diseases 9:82–84
geriatrics 9:122
heart diseases 10:95–96
hospital diseases, nosocomial 14:266
hypochondria 10:351
immunity 11:56–59
immunodeficiency disease 11:59–60
infectious diseases 11:164–168
kidney disease 12:71–72
liver 12:374
lymphatic system 12:475–476
motion sickness 13:610
naturopathy 14:51
nervous system, diseases of the 14:95–96
nutritional-deficiency diseases 14:307–308
parasitic diseases 15:82
poisonous plants and animals 15:383–385 *illus.*
primitive societies 15:546
protozoal diseases 15:581
pschyosomatic disorders 15:602
public health 15:608
quarantine 16:12
research institutions
National Institutes of Health 14:34
respiratory system disorders 16:181–182
Rockefeller Foundation 16:251
skin diseases 17:341–342
tapeworm 19:33–34
teeth 19:71–72 *illus.*
toxicology 19:256
urogenital diseases 19:487
venereal disease 19:539–541
DISEASES, OCCUPATIONAL 6:193–194 *bibliog.*
anthrax 2:50
asbestos 2:227
black lung 3:317
brown lung 3:516–517
cancer 4:102
coal and coal mining 5:79
cor pulmonale 5:257
dust, atmospheric 6:308
dust diseases 6:193
environmental health 7:210–212
Hamilton, Alice 10:28–29
hazards 6:193
mining and quarrying 13:448–449
National Institute of Occupational Safety and Health 6:194
necrosis, match manufacture 13:218
Occupational Safety and Health Administration 14:321
pollution, environmental 15:413–415
radiation injury 16:42–43
respiratory system disorders 16:181
silicosis 6:193–194
stress, biological 18:297
synergism 6:193–194; 18:407
U.S. law 6:194
workers' compensation 20:217
zinc overingestion 19:621
DISEASES, PLANT 6:194–196 *bibliog.*
canker (plant) 4:108–109
causes
broomrape 3:512
dodder 6:211–212
midge 13:413
pathogens 6:194–195
witchweed 20:192
control of disease 6:195–196
gardening 9:44
gene bank 9:76
gibberellins 9:172
ergot 7:228
fungi 8:366–368 *illus.*
fungus diseases 8:369
mildew 13:419
parasitic diseases 15:83
symptoms 6:194
tree 19:288
wheat 20:125
wine 20:175
DISINFECTANT *see* ANTISEPTIC
DISK BRAKE
brake 3:449–451
computer-aided design 5:160k *illus.*
DISK DRIVE (computer term) 5:160h
DISK OPERATING SYSTEM *see* DOS
DISKETTE *see* FLOPPY DISK
DISKO BAY
map (69° 15′N 52° 0′W) 9:353
DISKO ISLAND
map (69° 50′N 53° 30′W) 9:353
DISLOCATION (medicine) 6:196
DISMAL PEAK
map (37° 15′N 80° 56′W) 19:607
DISMAL SWAMP 6:196
DISNEY, WALT 6:196–197 *bibliog., illus.*
animation 2:28–29
film, history of 8:84
Mickey Mouse 13:383
DISNEYLAND AND WALT DISNEY WORLD 6:197
DISORDERLY CONDUCT *see* BREACH OF THE PEACE
DISPERSION (physics) 6:197
gems 9:73
intermolecular forces 11:215
rainbow 16:77
DISPLACED PERSON *see* REFUGEE
DISPLACEMENT (psychology)
defense mechanisms 6:83
DISPUR (India)
map (26° 9′N 91° 46′E) 11:80
DISRAELI, BENJAMIN, 1ST EARL OF BEACONSFIELD 6:197–198 *bibliog., illus.*
British Conservative party 5:205
Great Britain, history of 9:318
Victoria, Queen of England, Scotland, and Ireland 19:574
D'ISRAELI, ISAAC 6:198
DISSECTION
Erasistratus 7:227
DISSENT (periodical)
Howe, Irving 10:284
DISSOCIATION
ion and ionization 11:239–240
DISSOCIATION (chemistry) 6:198 *illus.*
acids and bases 1:83
chemical equilibrium and kinetics 4:316
oxygen 14:477
photodissociation
photochemistry 15:258
Theory of Electrolytic Dissociation 6:198
DISSOCIATION (psychology) 6:198
hallucinogens 10:24
DISSONANCE (music) 6:198
jazz 11:390
DISSONANCE (psychology) *see* COGNITIVE DISSONANCE
DISSTON, HAMILTON
Florida 8:176
DISTANCE, ASTRONOMICAL 6:198–200 *bibliog., illus.*
Aristarchus of Samos 2:155
Cassini (family) 4:184
declination 6:76
determining
direct methods 6:199
indirect methods 6:199
Hyades 10:327
Kapteyn, Jacobus Cornelius 12:25–26
light-year 12:336
moon 13:561
parallax 15:78–79
parsec 15:98
period-luminosity relationship
Magellanic Clouds 13:48–49
quasar 16:14–15
radar astronomy 16:40
red shift 16:114
Roche's limit 16:247
RR Lyrae stars 16:332
Schlesinger, Frank 17:125–126
Shapley, Harlow 17:241
star 18:221
Struve, Friedrich Georg Wilhelm von 18:304
Titius-Bode law 19:213 *table*
DISTANT EARLY WARNING LINE *see* BMEWS
DISTELL, MARTHE
cordon bleu (cooking) 5:261
DISTEMPER 6:200
diseases, animal 6:191
DISTILLATION 6:200 *bibliog., illus.*
desalination 6:124 *illus.*
extraction 7:341
fractionation 8:258
DISTILLERY 20:133 *illus.*
DISTILLING *see* WHISKEY
DISTINGUISHED SERVICE CROSS
medals and decorations 13:261–263 *illus.*
DISTRIBUTION (economics) 6:200 *bibliog.*
economics 7:49
marketing 13:159
retailing 16:183–184
wholesaling 20:143
DISTRIBUTION (statistics) 6:200–201 *bibliog.*
binomial distribution 3:260
central limit theorem 4:254
histogram 10:180
inference (mathematics) 11:168
normal distribution 14:219
Poisson distribution 15:385
retailing 16:183
DISTRIBUTION-FREE STATISTICAL METHODS *see* STATISTICS, NONPARAMETRIC
DISTRIBUTIVE LAW 6:201
algebra 1:283
arithmetic 2:158
DISTRIBUTOR (electrical)
ignition system 11:36–38 *illus.*
DISTRICT ATTORNEY *see* PROSECUTING ATTORNEY
DISTRICT OF COLUMBIA 6:201 *bibliog., map*
See also WASHINGTON, D.C.
history
Banneker, Benjamin 3:70
map (38° 54′N 77° 1′W) 13:188
presidential elections
District of Columbia Amendment 5:223
23d Amendment 19:360
DISTRICT OF COLUMBIA, UNIVERSITY OF THE 6:201
DISTRICT COURT 6:201
DISTRITO FEDERAL (district in Brazil)
map (15° 45′S 47° 45′W) 3:460
DISTURBING THE PEACE *see* BREACH OF THE PEACE
DISULFIRAM 6:201–202
DISUQ (Egypt)
map (31° 8′N 30° 39′E) 7:76
DITHYRAMB 6:202
DITTANY 6:202
DITTERSDORF, KARL DITTERS VON 6:202 *bibliog.*
DIU *see* GOA, DAMAN, AND DIU
DIURETIC DRUGS 6:202 *bibliog.*
edema 7:55
gout 9:266–267
DIVER (bird) *see* LOON (bird)
DIVERNON (Illinois)
map (39° 34′N 89° 39′W) 11:42
DIVERTICULOSIS 6:202 *bibliog.*; 9:56 *illus.*
enteritis 7:208
DIVERTIMENTO 6:202
See also SERENADE
DIVIDE (county in North Dakota)
map (48° 50′N 103° 30′W) 14:248
DIVIDEND *see* STOCK (finance)
DIVINATION 6:202–203 *bibliog.*
fortune-telling 8:241
oracle bones 14:413
DIVINE, FATHER 6:202 *bibliog.*
DIVINE COMEDY, THE (epic) 6:203 *bibliog.*
Beatrice 3:145
book illustration
Blake, William 3:326
Dante Alighieri 6:34
Vergil 19:551 *illus.*
DIVINE OFFICE 6:203
Book of Common Prayer 3:386
breviary 3:475
DIVINE RIGHT 6:203 *bibliog.*
king 12:80
monarchy 13:517
social contract 18:11
DIVING 6:203 *bibliog., illus.*
Louganis, Greg 12:421
McCormack, Patricia 13:10
DIVING, DEEP-SEA 6:203–204 *bibliog., illus.*
archaeology 2:119 *illus.*
bathyscaphe 3:123
Beebe, Charles W. 3:159
bends 3:196
Cousteau, Jacques-Yves 5:317–318
helium 10:113
sensory deprivation 17:205
DIVING, SKIN *see* SKIN DIVING
DIVING BEETLE 3:167 *illus.*
DIVING BIRDS 6:204–205 *bibliog., illus.*
DIVINING ROD *see* DOWSING
DIVISION (mathematics)
arithmetic
DIVISION (military) 6:205
DIVISIONISM
neoimpressionism 14:83
DIVO (Ivory Coast)
map (5° 50′N 5° 22′W) 11:335
DIVORCE 6:205–206 *bibliog.*
abandonment 1:51
alimony 1:294
bigamy 3:249
Constitution of the United States 5:219
desertion 6:131
family 8:17–18
marriage 13:165
Milton, John 13:433
Nevada 14:113
D'IVRY, PIERRE CONTANT
ironwork, ornamental 11:279
DIX, DOROTHEA 6:206 *bibliog.*
psychopathology, treatment of 15:599
DIX, DOROTHY 6:206 *bibliog.*
DIX, FORT (New Jersey) *see* FORT DIX (New Jersey)
DIX, DOM GREGORY 6:206
DIX, OTTO 6:206–207 *illus.*
Grosstadt 4:3 *illus.*
Portrait of a Journalist 6:207 *illus.*
DIXFIELD (Maine)
map (44° 32′N 70° 27′W) 13:70
DIXIE (county in Florida)
map (29° 35′N 83° 10′W) 8:172
DIXIECRATS 6:207 *bibliog.*
DIXIELAND
jazz 11:388 *illus.*
DIXON (Illinois)
map (41° 50′N 89° 29′W) 11:42
DIXON (Kentucky)
map (37° 31′N 87° 41′W) 12:47
DIXON (Missouri)
map (37° 60′N 92° 6′W) 13:476
DIXON (county in Nebraska)
map (42° 30′N 96° 50′W) 14:70
DIXON (New Mexico)
map (36° 12′N 105° 53′W) 14:136
DIXON, FRANKLIN W.
Hardy Boys 10:48
DIXON, JEREMIAH
Mason-Dixon line 13:199
DIXON, JOSEPH 6:207
DIXON ENTRANCE, STRAIT OF
map (54° 25′N 132° 30′W) 3:491
DIXON ENTRANCE SOUND
map (54° 25′N 132° 30′W) 1:242
DIXONS MILLS (Alabama)
map (32° 4′N 87° 47′W) 1:234
DIXVILLE NOTCH (pass)
map (44° 51′N 71° 14′W) 14:123
DIYARBAKIR (Turkey)
map (37° 55′N 40° 14′E) 19:343
DIZZINESS *see* VERTIGO (dizziness)
DJAKARTA (Indonesia) *see* JAKARTA (Indonesia)
DJAMBALA (Congo)
map (2° 33′S 14° 45′E) 5:182
DJEBU *see* EDFU (Egypt)
DJEDI WADI
map (34° 28′N 6° 5′E) 1:287
DJEMAL PASHA
World War I 20:232
DJERBA ISLAND
map (33° 48′N 10° 54′E) 19:335
marriage 13:164 *illus.*
DJIBOUTI (city in Djibouti) 6:207
map (11° 36′N 43° 9′E) 6:208
DJIBOUTI (country) 6:207–208 *bibliog., illus., map*
cities
Djibouti 6:207
flag 6:207 *illus.*
government 6:208
history 6:208
land and economy 6:208 *map*
map (11° 30′N 43° 0′E) 1:136
people 6:208
DJILAS, MILOVAN 6:208
DJOUA RIVER
map (1° 13′S 13° 12′E) 9:5
DJUGASHVILI, JOSEPH VISSARIONOVICH *see* STALIN, JOSEPH
DMITRY I, RUSSIAN RULER
Time of Troubles 19:202
DMITRY II, RUSSIAN RULER
Time of Troubles 19:202
DMOWSKI, ROMAN 6:208
DMYTRYK, EDWARD
Hollywood Ten, The 10:204
DNA
See also NUCLEIC ACID
Arber, Werner 2:110
Avery, Oswald T. 2:370
biochemistry 3:261
cancer 4:102
cell 4:233; 4:234; 4:235
cloning 5:64
Crick, Francis 5:343
enzyme 7:212
evolution 7:320
Franklin, Rosalind 8:285
genetic engineering 9:84–85 *illus.*
heredity 10:140
herpes 10:145
Hershey, Alfred Day 10:148
Kornberg, Arthur 12:123
McCarty, Maclyn 13:9
MacLeod, Colin M. 13:32
medicine 13:272

Miescher, Johann **13**:416
Monera **13**:523
mutation **13**:686–687
Nathans, Daniel **14**:27
photosynthesis **15**:276
plasmid **15**:347
protein synthesis **15**:575
retrovirus **16**:183–184
Sanger, Frederick **17**:64
Smith, Hamilton **17**:368
Watson, James D. **20**:67
Wilkins, Maurice **20**:152
DNEPR RIVER **6**:208
map (46° 30′N 32° 18′E) **19**:388
DNEPROPETROVSK (USSR) **6**:208
map (48° 27′N 34° 59′E) **19**:388
DNESTR RIVER **6**:208–209
map (46° 18′N 30° 17′E) **19**:388
DNIEPER RIVER *see* DNEPR RIVER
DNIESTER RIVER *see* DNESTR RIVER
DO-NE-HO-GA-WA *see* PARKER, ELY S.
DOBELL, SIR CHARLES M.
World War I **20**:239
DÖBELN (Germany, East and West)
map (51° 7′N 13° 7′E) **9**:140
DOBERAI PENINSULA
map (1° 30′S 132° 30′E) **11**:147
DÖBEREINER, JOHANN WOLFGANG **6**:209
DOBERMAN PINSCHER **6**:209 *bibliog., illus.*; **6**:215 *illus.*
DÖBLIN, ALFRED **6**:209 *bibliog.*
DOBROGEA *see* DOBRUJA
DOBROVOLSKY, GEORGY T. (cosmonaut) **6**:209
DOBRUDZHANSKO PLATEAU
map (43° 32′N 27° 50′E) **3**:555
DOBRUJA **6**:209
map (43° 50′N 28° 0′E) **3**:555
DOBSON (North Carolina)
map (36° 24′N 80° 43′W) **14**:242
DOBSON, AUSTIN **6**:209
DOBSONFLY **6**:209
DOBZHANSKY, THEODOSIUS **6**:209–210 *bibliog.*
biology **3**:271
DOCETISM **6**:210
Jesus Christ **11**:406
Valentinus **19**:505
DOCK (botany) **6**:210
rhubarb **16**:203–204
DOCK (marine) **17**:276 *illus.*
harbor and port **10**:42–44 *illus.*
DOCK WORKERS' UNIONS *see* INTERNATIONAL LONGSHOREMEN'S UNIONS
DOCTOR *see* MEDICINE
DOCTOR FAUSTUS (play) **6**:210 *bibliog.*; **7**:143 *illus.*
Alleyn, Edward **1**:302
Marlowe, Christopher **13**:161
DR. JEKYLL AND MR. HYDE **(book)** **6**:210 *bibliog.*
Stevenson, Robert Louis **18**:265
DOCTOR-PATIENT PRIVILEGE
evidence **7**:317
DOCTOR ZHIVAGO (book) **6**:210 *bibliog.*
Pasternak, Boris **15**:107
DOCTOROW, E. L. **6**:210 *illus.*
DOCTORS OF THE CHURCH **6**:210
Ambrose, Saint **1**:325
Anselm, Saint **2**:35
Aquinas, Saint Thomas **2**:95
Augustine, Saint **2**:320–321
Basil the Great, Saint **3**:109
Bede, Saint **3**:153
Bellarmine, Saint Robert **3**:187
Bernard of Clairvaux, Saint **3**:220–221
Canisius, Saint Peter **4**:108
Catherine of Siena, Saint **4**:209
Cyril of Alexandria, Saint **5**:410
Cyril of Jerusalem, Saint **5**:410
Ephraem the Syrian, Saint **7**:216–217
Fathers of the Church **8**:34
Francis de Sales, Saint **8**:274
Gregory I, Pope **9**:356
Hilary of Poitiers, Saint **10**:163
Jerome, Saint **11**:398
John of the Cross, Saint **11**:424
Leo I, Pope **12**:288
Peter Chrysologus, Saint **15**:200
Peter Damian, Saint **15**:200
Teresa of Ávila, Saint **19**:115–116
DOCUMENTARY **6**:210–211 *bibliog., illus.*
See also PHOTOJOURNALISM
Dovzhenko, Alexander **6**:251
film, history of **8**:87
Flaherty, Robert Joseph **8**:150
Jutra, Claude **11**:479
National Film Board of Canada **14**:32
Ophuls, Marcel **14**:405
Resnais, Alain **16**:177
Riefenstahl, Leni **16**:218
theater of fact **19**:153
Vertov, Dziga **19**:563
Winogrand, Garry **20**:180
Wiseman, Fred **20**:189
DODD, C. H. **6**:211 *bibliog.*
DODD, THOMAS
Pearson, Drew **15**:128
DODD, WILLIAM EDWARD **6**:211 *bibliog.*
DODDER (botany) **6**:211–212
DODDRIDGE (Arkansas)
map (33° 6′N 93° 54′W) **2**:166
DODDRIDGE (county in West Virginia)
map (39° 15′N 80° 42′W) **20**:111
DODECAHEDRON **15**:419 *illus.*
DODECANESE (Greece) **6**:212
map (36° 30′N 27° 0′E) **9**:325
Rhodes **16**:201–202
DODERER, HEIMITO VON **6**:212
DODGE (county in Georgia)
map (32° 10′N 83° 10′W) **9**:114
DODGE (county in Minnesota)
map (44° 0′N 92° 50′W) **13**:453
DODGE (Nebraska)
map (41° 43′N 96° 52′W) **14**:70
DODGE (county in Nebraska)
map (41° 35′N 96° 40′W) **14**:70
DODGE (county in Wisconsin)
map (43° 22′N 88° 43′W) **20**:185
DODGE, CHARLES
computer music **5**:163
DODGE, HENRY
Wisconsin **20**:188
DODGE, JOHN ADAMS
sewing machine **17**:223
DODGE, MARY MAPES **6**:212
DODGE, NEHEMIAH
Rhode Island **16**:201
DODGE BROTHERS
automotive industry **2**:363
DODGE CENTER (Minnesota)
map (44° 2′N 92° 51′W) **13**:453
DODGE CITY (Kansas) **6**:212
map (37° 45′N 100° 1′W) **12**:18
DODGEVILLE (Wisconsin)
map (42° 58′N 90° 8′W) **20**:185
DODGSON, CHARLES LUTWIDGE *see* CARROLL, LEWIS
DODO BIRD **6**:212 *bibliog., illus.*
solitaire (bird) **18**:55
DODOMA (Tanzania)
map (6° 11′S 35° 45′E) **19**:27
DODONA **6**:212
Epirus **7**:220
DODSON (Louisiana)
map (32° 5′N 92° 39′W) **12**:430
DODSON (Montana)
map (48° 24′N 108° 15′W) **13**:547
DODSON, OWEN **6**:212
DOE, JOHN OR JANE **6**:212
DOE, SAMUEL K. **6**:212
Liberia **12**:313
DOE v. *BOLTON* *see* *ROE* v. *WADE* AND *DOE* v. *BOLTON*
DOENITZ, KARL **6**:212–213
Nuremberg Trials **14**:297
DOERUN (Georgia)
map (31° 19′N 83° 55′W) **9**:114
DOESBURG, THEO VAN **6**:213 *bibliog.*
de Stijl (periodical) **6**:63–64
modern architecture **13**:491
DOETINCHEM (Netherlands)
map (51° 58′N 6° 17′E) **14**:99
DOG **6**:213–221 *bibliog., illus.*
breeds of dog not recognized by the American Kennel Club are listed here. For AKC breeds *see* HOUND; NONSPORTING DOG; SPORTING DOG; TERRIER; TOY DOG; WORKING DOG; names of specific breeds of dogs, e.g., COCKER SPANIEL; POODLE; etc.
African hunting dog **1**:164–165
American Kennel Club **1**:341
anatomy **6**:213 *illus.*
border collie **3**:397
characteristics **6**:221
conditioning
Pavlov, Ivan Petrovich **15**:120
diseases **6**:221
diseases, animal **6**:191; **6**:192
distemper **6**:200
parvovirus **15**:101
dogsled **6**:223
drever **6**:271
Eskimo dog **7**:242
Finnish spitz **8**:99
German longhaired pointer **9**:134
guide dog **9**:394
jaw **13**:99 *illus.*
Mexican hairless dog **13**:350–351
Nova Scotia duck tolling retriever **14**:271
Portuguese water dog **15**:457
pudelpointer **15**:613
reproduction **6**:221
senses **6**:221
sound frequencies produced **18**:73 *table*
spaceflight
Laika **12**:167
space medicine **18**:132
Sputnik **18**:201
Tahltan bear dog **19**:10
teeth **19**:72 *illus.*
usefulness **6**:213–221
DOG CART
coach and carriage **5**:73
DOG DAYS **6**:221
DOG FAMILY **6**:221–222 *bibliog.*
coyote **5**:323
dhole **6**:148
dingo **6**:178–179
fox **8**:255–256
hyena **10**:344
jackal **11**:340
wolf **20**:195–196
DOG FENNEL *see* CHAMOMILE
DOG RACING **6**:222 *bibliog.*
greyhound **9**:361
whippet **20**:131
DOG SHOWS **6**:221
DOG STAR *see* SIRIUS
DOGBANE **6**:222 *illus.*
medicinal plants **13**:266
oleander **13**:377
periwinkle (botany) **15**:172
strophanthus **18**:303
DOGE **6**:222
DOGE'S PALACE **6**:222 *bibliog.*; **19**:545 *illus.*
DOGFACE BUTTERFLY **3**:595–596 *illus.*
DOGFISH **6**:222–223
skeleton **8**:112 *illus.*
swimming motions **8**:115 *illus.*
DOGGER BANK **6**:223
DOGGEREL **6**:223
DOGON **6**:223 *bibliog.*
DOGSLED **6**:223 *bibliog.*
Eskimo **7**:240
snowmobile **18**:5
DOGWOOD **6**:223 *illus.*
DOHA (Qatar) **6**:224; **16**:4 *illus.*
map (25° 17′N 51° 32′E) **16**:4
DOHNÁNYI, CHRISTOPH VON **6**:224
DOHNÁNYI, ERNST VON **6**:224
DOISY, EDWARD **6**:224
D'OKEGHEM, JEAN *see* OKEGHEM, JEAN D'
DOLAN, JOHN (TERRY)
National Conservative Political Action Committee **14**:31
DOLAND (South Dakota)
map (44° 54′N 98° 6′W) **18**:103
DOLBEAU (Quebec)
map (48° 53′N 72° 14′W) **16**:18
DOLBY LABS
cinematography **4**:433
DOLDRUMS (climate) **6**:224
Hadley cell **10**:8
low-pressure region **12**:443
Pacific Ocean **15**:7
DOLE, ROBERT J. **6**:224
DOLE, SANFORD BALLARD **6**:224 *bibliog.*
Hawaii (state) **10**:76
DOLGEVILLE (New York)
map (43° 6′N 74° 46′W) **14**:149
DOLIN, ANTON **6**:224 *bibliog.*
DOLL **6**:224–225 *bibliog., illus.*
See also PUPPET
fashion design **8**:31
kachina **12**:4
Peruvian doll (Hilario Mendivil) **12**:226 *illus.*
DOLL HOUSE **6**:225 *illus.*
DOLLAR **6**:225 *bibliog.*
Jefferson, Thomas **11**:392
DOLLAR AVERAGING **6**:225
"DOLLAR DIPLOMACY"
Knox, Philander Chase **12**:103
United States, history of the **19**:452
DOLLFUSS, ENGELBERT **6**:226 *bibliog.*
Austria **2**:351
DOLLHOUSE
toy **19**:256
DÖLLINGER, IGNAZ VON **6**:226
DOLLOND, JOHN **6**:226
DOLL'S HOUSE, A (play) **6**:226
Ibsen, Henrik **11**:6–7
DOLMEN *see* MEGALITH
DOLNÍ VĚSTONICE **6**:226
Gravettian **9**:303
Venus figurines **15**:40 *illus.*
DOLOMITE (Alabama)
map (33° 28′N 86° 58′W) **1**:234
DOLOMITE (geology) **6**:226 *bibliog.*
calcium **4**:22
carbonate minerals **4**:137
Dolomites (mountain group) **6**:226
evaporite **7**:314
galena **9**:13
magnesium from **13**:53–54 *illus.*
marble **13**:144
refractory materials **16**:124
sedimentary rock **17**:184
DOLOMITES (mountain group) **6**:226; **11**:322 *illus.*
dolomite **6**:226
map (46° 25′N 11° 50′E) **11**:321
DOLORES (Argentina)
map (36° 20′S 57° 40′W) **2**:149
DOLORES (Colorado)
map (37° 28′N 108° 30′W) **5**:116
DOLORES (county in Colorado)
map (37° 45′N 108° 30′W) **5**:116
DOLORES (Guatemala)
map (16° 31′N 89° 25′W) **9**:389
DOLORES (Uruguay)
map (33° 33′S 58° 13′W) **19**:488
DOLORES RIVER
map (38° 49′N 109° 17′W) **5**:116
DOLPHIN **6**:226–229 *bibliog., illus.*; **13**:105 *illus.*
brain **3**:443 *illus.*
cetacean **4**:262
forelimb **5**:155 *illus.*
skin **17**:340 *illus.*
DOLPHIN FISH *see* DORADO
DOLTON (Illinois)
map (41° 39′N 87° 37′W) **11**:42
DOM PÉRIGNON
champagne **4**:276
DOMAGK, GERHARD **6**:229
chemistry, history of **4**:329
20th century medicine **13**:271
DOME (architecture) **6**:229–230 *bibliog., illus.*
Brunelleschi, Filippo **3**:524
cathedrals and churches **4**:205
geodesic **9**:97 *illus.*
Guarini, Guarino **9**:387
Hagia Sophia **10**:10
Isidorus of Miletus **11**:288
Pantheon (Rome) **15**:61–62 *illus.*
Radcliffe Camera (Oxford University) **9**:174 *illus.*
Roman art and architecture **16**:273
Russian art and architecture **16**:361 *illus.*
Sinan **17**:318
stadium **18**:208–209
Villa Rotonda **15**:48 *illus.*
DOMENICHINO **6**:230–231 *bibliog.*
DOMENICO VENEZIANO **6**:231 *bibliog.*
DOMESDAY BOOK **6**:231 *bibliog.*
Great Britain, history of **9**:310
Normans **14**:222
William I, King of England (William the Conqueror) **20**:155
DOMESTIC ARCHITECTURE *see* HOUSE (in Western architecture)
DOMESTIC COUNCIL **6**:231
DOMESTIC SERVICE **6**:231–232 *bibliog., illus., table*
slavery **17**:351–354
DOMESTIC SHORTHAIR CAT *see* AMERICAN SHORTHAIR CAT
DOMESTICATION OF PLANTS AND ANIMALS *see* AGRICULTURE, HISTORY OF; ANIMAL HUSBANDRY; PLANT BREEDING
DOMINGO, PLACIDO **6**:232 *bibliog.*
DOMÍNGUEZ, FRANCISCO ATANASIS
Utah **19**:495
DOMINIC, SAINT **6**:232 *bibliog.*
Dominicans **6**:234
DOMINICA **6**:232–233 *illus.*
flag **6**:232 *illus.*; **8**:142 *illus.*
map (15° 30′N 61° 20′W) **20**:109
DOMINICAL (Costa Rica)
map (9° 13′N 83° 51′W) **5**:291
DOMINICAN REPUBLIC **6**:233–234 *bibliog., illus., map, table*
cities
Santiago de los Caballeros **17**:70
Santo Domingo **17**:70
economy **6**:233–234 *illus.*
education **6**:234
Latin American universities **12**:233 *table*
flag **6**:233 *illus.*
government **6**:234
history **6**:233–234

DOMINICAN REPUBLIC (cont.)
Balaguer, Joaquín 3:30
Bosch, Juan 3:406
civil war (1965) 12:221 *illus.*
Latin America, history of 12:221
Trujillo, Rafael 19:317
land and people 6:233–234 *map, table*
Latin American art and architecture 12:222–228
map (19° 0′N 70° 40′W) 20:109
DOMINICANS (religious order) 6:234 *bibliog.*
Albertus Magnus, Saint 1:259–260
Aquinas, Saint Thomas 2:94–95
Dominic, Saint 6:232
Honorius III, Pope 10:224
Middle Ages 14:394–396 *illus.*
monastic art and architecture 13:518; 13:520
DOMINION 6:234
DOMINION (Nova Scotia)
map (46° 13′N 60° 1′W) 14:269
DOMINION ARBORETUM AND BOTANIC GARDEN 6:234–235
DOMINION EDUCATION ASSOCIATION *see* CANADIAN EDUCATION ASSOCIATION
DOMINOES 6:235 *bibliog., illus.*
DOMITIAN, ROMAN EMPEROR 6:235 *bibliog.*
Juvenal 11:480
Rome, ancient 16:303
DOMS *see* PAHARI
DOMUS (periodical)
Ponti, Gio 15:427
DON BENITO (Spain)
map (38° 57′N 5° 52′W) 18:140
DON COSSACKS 6:235 *bibliog.*
Cossacks 5:290
Pugachev, Yemelian Ivanovich 15:617
Razin, Stenka 16:98
***DON GIOVANNI* (opera)** 6:235 *bibliog.*; 14:400 *illus.*
DON JUAN 6:236 *bibliog.*
Don Giovanni (opera) 6:235
DON QUIXOTE (ballet)
Bolshoi Ballet 3:371–372
DON QUIXOTE (book) 6:236 *bibliog., illus.*; 14:273 *illus.*
Cervantes Saavedra, Miguel de 4:261
Don Quixote (Gustave Doré) 3:387 *illus.*
Jiménez de Quesada, Gonzalo 11:419
Spanish literature 18:158
DON RIVER 6:236
map (47° 4′N 39° 18′E) 19:388
DONA ANA (New Mexico)
map (32° 23′N 106° 49′W) 14:136
DONA ANA (county in New Mexico)
map (32° 20′N 106° 50′W) 14:136
DONALDA (Alberta)
map (52° 35′N 112° 34′W) 1:256
DONALDSON (Arkansas)
map (34° 14′N 92° 55′W) 2:166
DONALDSONVILLE (Louisiana)
map (30° 6′N 90° 59′W) 12:430
DONALSONVILLE (Georgia)
map (31° 3′N 84° 53′W) 9:114
DONATELLO 6:236–237 *bibliog., illus.*
bronzes 3:507
David 3:508 *illus.*; 6:237 *illus.*; 16:150 *illus.*
Florence (Italy) 8:168
Italian art and architecture 11:310–311
Janson, H. W. 11:359
monument to Gattamelata 17:163 *illus.*
Padua (Italy) 15:12
DONATISTS 6:237 *bibliog.*
Timgad 19:203
DONATUS, AELIUS 6:237
DONAU RIVER *see* DANUBE RIVER
DONCASTER (England) 6:237
map (53° 32′N 1° 7′W) 19:403
DONCK, ADRIAEN CORNELISSEN VAN DER
Yonkers (New York) 20:330
DONDRA HEAD
map (5° 55′N 80° 35′E) 18:206
DONEGAL (Ireland) 6:237
map (54° 39′N 8° 7′W) 11:258
DONEGAL BAY
map (54° 30′N 8° 30′W) 11:258
DONELSON, FORT (Kentucky) *see* FORT HENRY AND FORT DONELSON (Kentucky)
DONEN, STANLEY
film, history of 8:85
DONETS BASIN 6:237–238
DONETS RIVER 6:238
DONETSK (USSR) 6:238
map (48° 0′N 37° 48′E) 19:388
DONG, PHAM VAN *see* PHAM VAN DONG
DONG QICHANG *see* TUNG CH'I-CH'ANG (Dong Qichang)
DONG-SON CULTURE
Shih-chai-shan (Shizhaishan) 17:261
Southeast Asian art and architecture 18:108
DONGEN, KEES VAN 6:238 *bibliog.*
DONIPHAN (county in Kansas)
map (39° 50′N 95° 10′W) 12:18
DONIPHAN (Missouri)
map (36° 37′N 90° 50′W) 13:476
DONIPHAN, ALEXANDER WILLIAM
Mexican War 13:352 *map*; 13:354–355
DÖNITZ, KARL *see* DOENITZ, KARL
DONIZETTI, GAETANO 6:238 *bibliog., illus.*
Italian music 11:318–319 *illus.*
La Favorita 14:401 *illus.*
Lucia di Lammermoor 12:450
DONKEY 6:238
ass 2:263
diseases
glanders 9:197
horse 10:245
hybrid 10:328
mule 13:636
DONLEAVY, J. P. 6:238–239 *bibliog., illus.*
DONLEY (county in Texas)
map (34° 57′N 100° 50′W) 19:129
DONNE, JOHN 6:239 *bibliog., illus.*; 7:195 *illus.*
DONNELLY (Alberta)
map (55° 44′N 117° 6′W) 1:256
DONNELLY (Idaho)
map (44° 44′N 116° 5′W) 11:26
DONNER, GEORG RAPHAEL 6:239–240 *bibliog.*
DONNER, JACOB AND GEORGE *see* DONNER PARTY
DONNER PARTY 6:240 *bibliog.*
DONNER PASS 6:240
map (39° 19′N 120° 20′W) 4:31
DONORA (Pennsylvania)
map (40° 11′N 79° 52′W) 15:147
pollution, environmental 15:411
DONOSO, JOSÉ 6:240 *bibliog.*
DONSKOI, DIMITRY *see* DIMITRY DONSKOI, GRAND DUKE OF MOSCOW
DOOLEY, MR.
Dunne, Finley Peter 6:301
DOOLEY, THOMAS 6:240 *bibliog.*
DOOLITTLE, HILDA (H. D.) 6:240 *bibliog.*
DOOLITTLE, JAMES 6:240
World War II 20:264–266 *illus.*
DOOLY (county in Georgia)
map (32° 10′N 83° 50′W) 9:114
DOOMESDAY BOOK *see* DOMESDAY BOOK
DOONERAK, MOUNT
map (67° 56′N 150° 37′W) 1:242
DOONESBURY (cartoon)
Trudeau, Garry 19:316
DOOR (county in Wisconsin)
map (44° 52′N 87° 17′W) 20:185
DOOR GODS 6:240
DOOR PENINSULA
map (44° 55′N 87° 20′W) 20:185
DOORNIK (Belgium) *see* TOURNAI (Belgium)
DOOXO NUGAALEED VALLEY
map (8° 35′N 48° 35′E) 18:60
DOPAMINE
levodopa 12:305
nervous system, diseases of the 14:95
schizophrenia 17:124
sleep 17:360
DOPING (computer term) 5:160h
DOPPELGÄNGER *see* DOUBLE (in literature)
DOPPLER, CHRISTIAN JOHANN 6:240
Doppler effect 6:240–241
DOPPLER EFFECT 6:240–241 *bibliog., illus.*
See also ASTROMETRY; ASTRONOMY, HISTORY OF; CELESTIAL MECHANICS
background radiation 3:12
binary stars 3:257
Doppler, Christian Johann 6:240
practical applications 6:241
pulsating stars 15:621
radar 16:39
radar astronomy 16:40
radar meteorology 16:41
red shift 16:114
DOPPLER SHIFT *see* DOPPLER EFFECT
DOR (Israel)
map (32° 37′N 34° 55′E) 11:302
DORADO 6:241; 8:117 *illus.*
dolphin 6:228
DORAIS, GUS
football 8:216–217
DORATI, ANTAL 6:241
DORAVILLE (Georgia)
map (33° 54′N 84° 17′W) 2:292
DORCHESTER (county in Maryland)
map (38° 34′N 76° 4′W) 13:188
DORCHESTER (New Brunswick)
map (45° 54′N 64° 31′W) 14:117
DORCHESTER (county in South Carolina)
map (33° 0′N 80° 20′W) 18:98
DORCHESTER (Wisconsin)
map (45° 0′N 90° 20′W) 20:185
DORCHESTER, GUY CARLTON, 1ST BARON *see* CARLETON, GUY, 1ST BARON DORCHESTER
DORCHESTER COMPANY
Massachusetts 13:210
DORDOGNE RIVER 7:270 *illus.*
map (45° 2′N 0° 35′W) 8:260
DORDRECHT (Netherlands) 6:241; 14:102 *illus.*
map (51° 49′N 4° 40′E) 14:99
DORDT (Netherlands) *see* DORDRECHT (Netherlands)
DORÉ, GUSTAVE 6:241–242 *bibliog., illus.*
book illustration 3:388
Don Quixote 3:387 *illus.*; 6:236 *illus.*
Gargantua 6:242 *illus.*
Little Red Riding Hood 8:10 *illus.*
Russian gentry wager serfs during a card game (engraving) 16:370 *illus.*
Sleeping Beauty 8:10 *illus.*
DORÉ LAKE
map (54° 46′N 107° 17′W) 17:81
DOREN, CARL VAN *see* VAN DOREN, CARL
DOREN, MARK VAN *see* VAN DOREN, MARK
DORENA (Oregon)
map (43° 47′N 122° 55′W) 14:427
DORIA, ANDREA 6:242
DORIANS 6:242 *bibliog.*
Europe, history of 7:280
Greece, ancient 9:329–330 *map*
DORIC ORDER (architecture) 2:131 *illus.*; 9:335 *illus.*
Greek art 9:337–342
temple 19:95–97
Temple of Hera 9:335 *illus.*
Temple of Poseidon 19:63
DORIDEN
sedative 17:182
DORION, SIR ANTOINE AIMÉ 6:242
DORMANCY (botany) 6:242–243 *bibliog.*
fruits and fruit cultivation 8:349
DORMANCY (zoology)
hibernation 10:156
DORMOUSE 6:243 *illus.*; 13:625 *illus.*
DORNIER, CLAUDE
aviation 2:374
DORNIER DO 17E-1 AIRCRAFT 20:255 *illus.*
DORPAT (USSR) *see* TARTU (USSR)
DÖRPFELD, WILHELM 6:243
Tiryns 19:209
Troy (archaeological site) 19:312–313
DORR, THOMAS WILSON *see* DORR'S REBELLION
DORRANCE (Kansas)
map (38° 51′N 98° 35′W) 12:18
DORR'S REBELLION 6:243 *bibliog.*
Luther v. *Borden* 12:469
treason 19:285
DORSET (Canada)
Indians of North America, art of the 11:139
DORSET (England) 6:243 *bibliog.*
cities
Bournemouth 3:424
Maiden Castle 13:66
DORSET CULTURE 7:239 *map*
Eskimo 7:241
DORSETSHIRE (England) *see* DORSET (England)
DORSEY, JIMMY AND TOMMY 6:243 *bibliog.*
DORT (Netherlands) *see* DORDRECHT (Netherlands)
DORTMUND (West Germany) 6:243
map (51° 31′N 7° 28′E) 9:140
DORYPHORUS
Polyclitus 15:418
DOS (DISK OPERATING SYSTEM) (computer term) 5:160h
DOS BAHÍAS, CAPE
map (44° 55′S 65° 32′W) 2:149
DOS PALOS (California)
map (36° 59′N 120° 37′W) 4:31
DOS PASSOS, JOHN 6:243–244 *bibliog., illus.*
U.S.A. 19:491
DOSIMETER 6:244 *illus.*
DOSSENA, ALCEO
forgery in art 8:233 *illus.*
DOSSI, DOSSO 6:244 *bibliog.*
DOSTOYEVSKY, FYODOR MIKHAILOVICH 6:244–245 *bibliog., illus.*
Brothers Karamazov, The 3:512
Crime and Punishment 5:347
Idiot, The 11:31
Notes from the Underground 14:267
Possessed, The 15:458
Russian literature 16:365–366 *illus.*
DOTHAN (Alabama)
map (31° 13′N 85° 24′W) 1:234
DOTING COVE (Newfoundland)
map (49° 27′N 53° 57′W) 14:166
DOTY, JAMES
Wisconsin 20:188
DOU, GERARD 6:245 *bibliog.*
DOUAI (France) 6:245
DOUALA (Cameroon) 4:60 *table*; 4:61 *illus.*; 6:245
climate 1:142 *table*
map (4° 3′N 9° 42′E) 4:61
DOUBLE (in literature) 6:245–246 *bibliog.*
Dr. Jekyll and Mr. Hyde 6:210
DOUBLE BASS 6:246 *bibliog., illus.*
bass (music) 3:117
Koussevitzky, Serge 12:125
Mingus, Charles 13:444
DOUBLE BASSOON *see* CONTRABASSOON
DOUBLE BOND *see* CHEMICAL BOND
DOUBLE EAGLE II (balloon) 3:51 *illus.*
DOUBLE ENTRY *see* BOOKKEEPING
DOUBLE HELIX *see* NUCLEIC ACID, DNA
DOUBLE HORN
French horn 8:311–312 *illus.*
DOUBLE JEOPARDY 6:246
5th Amendment 8:74
military justice 13:421
DOUBLE SALT (chemistry) 6:246 *bibliog.*
salt (chemistry) 17:37
DOUBLE SPRINGS (Alabama)
map (34° 9′N 87° 24′W) 1:234
DOUBLE STAR *see* BINARY STARS
DOUBLE TAXATION
income tax 11:76–77
DOUBLEDAY, ABNER 6:246 *bibliog.*
baseball 3:102
DOUBLEDAY AND CO., INC.
O. Henry Award 14:311
DOUBLOON 14:296 *illus.*
DOUÉ
map (16° 38′N 15° 2′W) 17:202
DOUGHBOY (World War I) 11:164 *illus.*
DOUGHERTY (county in Georgia)
map (31° 32′N 84° 15′W) 9:114
DOUGHTY, CHARLES MONTAGU 6:246
DOUGHTY, THOMAS 6:246 *bibliog.*
DOUGLAS (Arizona)
map (31° 21′N 109° 33′W) 2:160
DOUGLAS (county in Colorado)
map (39° 20′N 105° 0′W) 5:116
DOUGLAS (family) 6:246–247 *bibliog.*
James V, King of Scotland 11:357
DOUGLAS (Georgia)
map (31° 31′N 82° 51′W) 9:114
DOUGLAS (county in Georgia)
map (33° 45′N 84° 45′W) 9:114
DOUGLAS (county in Illinois)
map (39° 48′N 88° 14′W) 11:42
DOUGLAS (Isle of Man)
map (54° 9′N 4° 28′W) 19:403
DOUGLAS (county in Kansas)
map (38° 55′N 95° 15′W) 12:18
DOUGLAS (county in Minnesota)
map (45° 55′N 95° 30′W) 13:453
DOUGLAS (county in Missouri)
map (36° 55′N 92° 30′W) 13:476
DOUGLAS (county in Nebraska)
map (41° 15′N 96° 10′W) 14:70
DOUGLAS (county in Nevada)
map (38° 55′N 119° 39′W) 14:111
DOUGLAS (North Dakota)
map (47° 51′N 101° 30′W) 14:248

DOUGLAS (county in Oregon)
map (43° 20′N 123° 10′W) **14**:427
DOUGLAS (county in South Dakota)
map (43° 22′N 98° 20′W) **18**:103
DOUGLAS (county in Washington)
map (47° 40′N 119° 40′W) **20**:35
DOUGLAS (county in Wisconsin)
map (46° 22′N 91° 57′W) **20**:185
DOUGLAS (Wyoming)
map (42° 45′N 105° 24′W) **20**:301
DOUGLAS, DONALD WILLS **6**:247
DOUGLAS, GAWIN **6**:247 *bibliog.*
DOUGLAS, SIR JAMES **6**:247 *bibliog.*
Victoria (British Columbia) **19**:573
DOUGLAS, NORMAN **6**:247 *bibliog.*
DOUGLAS, STEPHEN A. **6**:247–248 *bibliog., illus.*
Civil War, U.S. **5**:16–18
election of 1860 **5**:17 *illus., map*
Kansas-Nebraska Act **12**:23
Lincoln, Abraham **12**:348–349
DOUGLAS T. C. **6**:248
DOUGLAS, THOMAS, 5TH EARL OF SELKIRK *see* SELKIRK, THOMAS DOUGLAS, 5TH EARL OF
DOUGLAS, WILLIAM O. **6**:248 *bibliog., illus.*; **12**:246 *illus.*
DOUGLAS FIR **6**:248 *illus.*
wood **20**:205 *illus.*
DOUGLAS-HOME, SIR ALEC **6**:248 *bibliog.*
DOUGLASS (Kansas)
map (37° 31′N 97° 1′W) **12**:18
DOUGLASS, ANDREW ELLICOTT **6**:248
dendrochronology **6**:106–107
DOUGLASS, FREDERICK **3**:307 *illus.*; **6**:248–249 *bibliog., illus.*
Rochester (New York) **16**:247
slavery **17**:357 *illus.*
DOUGLASVILLE (Georgia)
map (33° 45′N 84° 45′W) **9**:114
DOUKHOBORS **6**:249 *bibliog.*
civil disobedience **5**:10
conscientious objector **5**:200
DOUMERGUE, GASTON **6**:249 *bibliog.*
DOURA-EUROPOS (Syria) **6**:249 *bibliog.*
DOURIS **6**:249 *bibliog.*
DOURO RIVER **6**:249–250
map (41° 8′N 8° 40′W) **18**:140
DOUX, JEAN PICART LE
tapestry **19**:33
DOVAY (France) *see* DOUAI (France)
DOVE **6**:250 *illus.*
game birds **9**:27
pigeon **15**:299 *illus.*
DOVE, ARTHUR **6**:250 *bibliog., illus.*
The Moon **6**:250 *illus.*
DOVE CREEK (Colorado)
map (37° 46′N 108° 54′W) **5**:116
DOVEKIE
auk **2**:322–323
DOVER (Arkansas)
map (35° 24′N 93° 7′W) **2**:166
DOVER (Delaware) **6**:250
map (39° 10′N 75° 32′W) **6**:88
DOVER (England) **6**:250; **7**:180 *illus.*
foraminifera **8**:219
DOVER (Massachusetts)
map (42° 15′N 71° 17′W) **3**:409
DOVER (New Hampshire)
map (43° 12′N 70° 56′W) **14**:123
DOVER (New Jersey)
map (40° 53′N 74° 34′W) **14**:129
DOVER (North Carolina)
map (35° 13′N 77° 26′W) **14**:242
DOVER (Ohio)
map (40° 32′N 81° 29′W) **14**:357
DOVER (Tennessee)
map (36° 29′N 87° 50′W) **19**:104
DOVER, STRAIT OF **4**:281 *map*; **6**:250
map (51° 0′N 1° 30′E) **19**:403
DOVER, TREATY OF
Charles II, King of England, Scotland, and Ireland **4**:292
DOVER AIR FORCE BASE
map (39° 8′N 75° 28′W) **6**:88
DOVER BEACH (poem) **6**:250–251
DOVER CASTLE (England) **4**:190 *illus.*
DOVER-FOXCROFT (Maine)
map (45° 11′N 69° 13′W) **13**:70
DOVZHENKO, ALEXANDER **6**:251 *bibliog.*
DOW, ARTHUR
Fenollosa, Ernest Francisco **8**:51
DOW, HERBERT HENRY **6**:251 *bibliog.*
DOW, NEAL
temperance movement **19**:92
DOW-JONES AVERAGE **6**:251 *bibliog.*
DOWAGIAC (Michigan)
map (41° 59′N 86° 6′W) **13**:377
DOWELL, ANTHONY **6**:251 *bibliog.*
DOWER **6**:251
inheritance **11**:177
DOWIE, JOHN ALEXANDER **6**:251
DOWITCHER **6**:251 *illus.*
DOWLAND, JOHN **6**:251–252 *bibliog.*
DOWLAT AL KUWAIT *see* KUWAIT (country)
DOWN (Northern Ireland) **6**:252
DOWN FEATHER
feather **8**:39–40 *illus.*
DOWN SYNDROME *see* DOWN'S SYNDROME
DOWNERS GROVE (Illinois)
map (41° 48′N 88° 1′W) **11**:42
DOWNEY (Idaho)
map (42° 26′N 112° 7′W) **11**:26
DOWNHILL SKIING *see* SKIING
DOWNIEVILLE (California)
map (39° 34′N 120° 50′W) **4**:31
DOWNING (Missouri)
map (40° 29′N 92° 22′W) **13**:476
DOWNING, ANDREW JACKSON **6**:252
American art and architecture **1**:328
house (in Western architecture) **10**:270
landscape architecture **12**:188
DOWNING COLLEGE (Cambridge University) **4**:52
DOWNS (Kansas)
map (39° 30′N 98° 33′W) **12**:18
DOWNS MOUNTAIN
map (43° 18′N 109° 40′W) **20**:301
DOWN'S SYNDROME **6**:252 *bibliog. illus.*
diagnostic tests
amniocentesis **1**:375
genetic diseases **9**:83–84
mental retardation **13**:302
nervous system, diseases of the **14**:95
speech **18**:175
DOWNSVILLE (New York)
map (42° 5′N 75° 0′W) **14**:149
DOWNTOWN ATHLETIC CLUB (New York City)
Heisman Trophy **10**:110
DOWNY MILDEW *see* DISEASES, PLANT
DOWRY **6**:252
DOWS (Iowa)
map (42° 39′N 93° 30′W) **11**:244
DOWSING **6**:252
DOWSON, ERNEST **6**:252–253 *bibliog.*
decadence **6**:72
DOWTH **6**:253 *bibliog.*
DOXOLOGY **6**:253
DOYLE (California)
map (40° 2′N 120° 6′W) **4**:31
DOYLE, SIR ARTHUR CONAN **6**:253 *bibliog., illus.*
Holmes, Sherlock **10**:206
Houdini, Harry **10**:263
Hound of the Baskervilles, The **10**:264
DOYLESTOWN (Pennsylvania)
map (40° 19′N 75° 8′W) **15**:147
D'OYLY CARTE, RICHARD **6**:253 *bibliog.*
D'OYLY CARTE OPERA COMPANY
D'Oyly Carte, Richard **6**:253
Gilbert and Sullivan **9**:179
DPT (vaccine)
diseases, childhood **6**:193
DR. *see* DOCTOR for names beginning with DR.
DRA DESERT
map (29° 0′N 6° 45′W) **1**:287
DRABBLE, MARGARET **6**:253
DRACAENA (botany) **6**:253
DRACHMANN, HOLGER HENRIK HERHOLDT **6**:253–254 *bibliog.*
DRACHTEN (Netherlands)
map (53° 6′N 6° 5′E) **14**:99
DRACO **6**:254
DRACULA (book) **6**:254 *bibliog.*
Stoker, Bram **18**:278
DRACULA (film) **12**:453 *illus.*
film, history of **8**:88
DRACULA (legend)
Vlad the Impaler, Prince of Walachia **19**:623
DRACUT (Massachusetts)
map (42° 40′N 71° 18′W) **13**:206
DRAFT (banking) **6**:254
See also BILL OF EXCHANGE
negotiable instrument **14**:77
DRAFT (military) *see* CONSCRIPTION
DRAFT HORSE **6**:254 *bibliog., illus.*; **10**:244 *illus.*
Belgian horse **3**:174 *illus.*
Clydesdale **5**:72–73
coach horse **5**:75
harness **10**:52–53 *illus.*
horse **10**:244
Percheron **15**:161
Shire **17**:277
Suffolk **18**:325
wagon **20**:6 *illus.*
DRAFT RIOTS **6**:254 *bibliog.*
Greeley, Horace **9**:346
race riots **16**:35
Seymour, Horatio **17**:233
United States, history of the **19**:449
DRAFTING, COMPUTERIZED
computer-aided design and computer-aided manufacturing **5**:160k
computer graphics **5**:160m-160n
DRAG
aerodynamics **1**:123
DRAG (coach)
coach and carriage **5**:73
DRAG RACING **6**:254
automobile racing **2**:362
dragster **2**:362 *illus.*
DRAGO, LUIS MARÍA **6**:254–255
DRAGO DOCTRINE *see* DRAGO, LUIS MARÍA
DRAGON **6**:255
DRAGONET **6**:255
DRAGONFLY **6**:255 *bibliog., illus.*; **11**:192 *illus.*
Odonata **14**:350
DRAGONHEAD (botany) **6**:255
DRAGON'S-MOUTH (botany) **6**:255
DRAGONS MOUTH, STRAIT OF
map (10° 45′N 61° 46′W) **19**:300
DRAGOON (Arizona)
map (32° 2′N 110° 2′W) **2**:160
DRAHTHAAR *see* GERMAN WIREHAIRED POINTER
DRAIN (Oregon)
map (43° 40′N 123° 19′W) **14**:427
DRAINAGE BASIN *see* RIVER AND STREAM
DRAINAGE SYSTEMS **6**:255 *bibliog.*
canal **4**:94–95
oxbow lake **14**:473
plumbing **15**:371 *illus.*
roads and highways **16**:236 *illus.*; **16**:238 *illus.*
DRAIS, KARL VON
bicycle **3**:244
DRAKE (North Dakota)
map (47° 55′N 100° 23′W) **14**:248
DRAKE (zoology) *see* DUCK
DRAKE, EDWIN L. **6**:256 *bibliog.*
oil well **15**:212 *illus.*
DRAKE, SIR FRANCIS **6**:256–257 *bibliog., illus.*
California **4**:36
Drake Passage **6**:257
exploration **7**:336–337 *map*
Golden Hind **17**:267 *illus.*
Horn, Cape **10**:238
naval vessels **14**:55
San Francisco Bay **17**:54
Vigo (Spain) **19**:592
world circumnavigation **6**:256 *map*
DRAKE, JOSEPH RODMAN **6**:257
DRAKE PASSAGE **6**:257
DRAKE PEAK
map (42° 19′N 120° 7′W) **14**:427
DRAKE UNIVERSITY **6**:257
DRAKENSBERG **6**:257
map (27° 0′S 30° 0′E) **18**:79
DRAKESBORO (Kentucky)
map (37° 13′N 87° 3′W) **12**:47
DRAM (DYNAMIC RANDOM ACCESS MEMORY)
computer **5**:160h
computer memory **5**:161
DRAMA **6**:257–262 *bibliog., illus.*
See also RADIO DRAMA; THEATER, HISTORY OF THE
African literature **1**:167–168
See also national subheadings under DRAMA, e.g., DRAMA—Nigerian literature; DRAMA—South African literature; etc.
Césaire, Aimé **4**:262
American literature **1**:346–347
Abbott, George **1**:53
Aiken, Joan **1**:202
Albee, Edward **1**:252
Allen, Woody **1**:300
Anderson, Maxwell **1**:402
Angelou, Maya **1**:414
Ardrey, Robert **2**:144
Ashbery, John **2**:229
Auden, W. H. **2**:317–318
Baldwin, James **3**:35
Baraka, Imamu Amiri **3**:75
Barnes, Djuna **3**:86
Barry, Philip **3**:96
Behrman, S. N. **3**:171
Bellow, Saul **3**:190
Bird, Robert Montgomery **3**:290
black American literature **3**:304
Bodenheim, Maxwell **3**:356
Boucicault, Dion **3**:420
Bunner, H. C. **3**:563
Burrows, Abe **3**:580
Chayefsky, Paddy **4**:306
Cohan, George M. **5**:95
Connelly, Marc **5**:197
Crothers, Rachel **5**:363
Dunlap, William **6**:300–301
Federal Theatre Project **8**:42
Ferber, Edna **8**:52
Fitch, Clyde **8**:129
Gelber, Jack **9**:69
Glaspell, Susan **9**:197
Gordon, Ruth **9**:249
Green, Paul **9**:347
Guare, John **9**:387
Hansberry, Lorraine **10**:40
Hart, Moss **10**:61
Hecht, Ben **10**:103
Hellman, Lillian **10**:115
Horovitz, Israel **10**:241
Howard, Bronson **10**:282
Howard, Sidney Coe **10**:283
Inge, William **11**:176
Kaufman, George S. **12**:31–32
Lindsay, Howard, and Crouse, Russel **12**:352
Loos, Anita **12**:411
MacKaye, Steele **13**:27
Mamet, David **13**:97
Miller, Arthur **13**:427
Moody, William Vaughn **13**:561
Odets, Clifford **14**:350
O'Neill, Eugene **14**:389–390
Payne, John Howard **15**:122
Rabe, David **16**:31
Rice, Elmer **16**:208–209
Saroyan, William **17**:78–79
Sheldon, Edward **17**:250
Shepard, Sam **17**:256
Sherwood, Robert E. **17**:259
Simon, Neil **17**:315
Thomas, Augustus **19**:172
Torrence, Ridgely **19**:243
Tyler, Royall **19**:362
Van Druten, John **19**:513
Van Itallie, Jean Claude **19**:515
Vidal, Gore **19**:576–577
Wilder, Thornton **20**:149–150
Williams, Tennessee **20**:160–161
Woodworth, Samuel **20**:213
Arabic literature
Hakim, Tawfiq al- **10**:17
Australian literature
Bernhard, Thomas **3**:221
Stewart, Douglas Alexander **18**:265
Austrian literature **2**:354
Grillparzer, Franz **9**:364
Handke, Peter **10**:37
Kraus, Karl **12**:127
Nestroy, Johann **14**:97
Schnitzler, Arthur **17**:129
Werfel, Franz **20**:104
Belgian literature
Crommelynck, Fernand **5**:357
Ghelderode, Michel de **9**:166
Maeterlinck, Maurice **13**:45–46
Breton literature **3**:475
Bulgarian literature
Canetti, Elias **4**:108
Vazov, Ivan **19**:529
Canadian literature **4**:93
Chinese literature **4**:390
Kuan Han-ch'ing (Guan Hanqing) **12**:133–134
Ts'ao Yü (Cao Yu) **19**:322
Yüan drama **20**:338
chorus
theater, history of the **19**:144
criticism
Adler, Renata **1**:104
Agee, James **1**:183
Atkinson, Brooks **2**:269
Barnes, Clive **3**:86
Bazin, André **3**:135
Benchley, Robert **3**:196
Bentley, Eric **3**:205
Brown, John Mason **3**:515
Brustein, Robert **3**:527
Clurman, Harold **5**:71–72
Fergusson, Francis **8**:54
Nathan, George Jean **14**:27
Poetics of Aristotle **15**:378
Simon, John **17**:315
Tynan, Kenneth **19**:362
Woollcott, Alexander **20**:215
Czech literature
Čapek, Karel **4**:122
Havel, Václav **10**:71
Danish literature **6**:32–33

DRAMA (cont.)
Abell, Kjeld **1**:56
Branner, Hans Christian **3**:455
Drachmann, Holger Henrik Herholdt **6**:253–254
Ewald, Johannes **7**:325
Gjellerup, Karl Adolph **9**:192
Hauch, Johannes Carsten **10**:68
Heiberg, Johan Ludvig **10**:106
Holberg, Ludvig, Baron **10**:202
Munk, Kaj **13**:643
Soya, Carl Erik Martin **18**:114
Wied, Gustav **20**:145
Dutch and Flemish literature **6**:314
Bredero, Gerbrand Adriaenszoon **3**:471
Heijermans, Herman **10**:108
Rederijkers (literary groups) **16**:115
Vondel, Joost van den **19**:634
education *see* ACTING
English literature **7**:194–198
Bagnold, Enid **3**:22
Bale, John **3**:36
Beaumont, Francis, and Fletcher, John **3**:147
Behn, Aphra **3**:171
Bennett, Arnold **3**:202
Bolt, Robert **3**:372
Bond, Edward **3**:376
Brome, Richard **3**:501
burlesque and travesty **3**:572
Caine, Sir Hall **4**:17
Carey, Henry **4**:146
Chapman, George **4**:285
Christie, Dame Agatha **4**:414–415
Cibber, Colley **4**:428
Coward, Sir Noel **5**:320
Cumberland, Richard **5**:387
Davenant, Sir William **6**:46
Dekker, Thomas **6**:86
Drinkwater, John **6**:273
Dryden, John **6**:284–285
Eliot, T. S. **7**:139–140
Etherege, George **7**:250
Farquhar, George **8**:29
Fielding, Henry **8**:73
Foote, Samuel **8**:219
Ford, John (playwright) **8**:223
Fry, Christopher **8**:350
Galsworthy, John **9**:21–22
Gascoigne, George **9**:53–54
Gay, John **9**:63
Goldsmith, Oliver **9**:236
Gray, Simon **9**:307
Greene, Graham **9**:350
Hartog, Jan de **10**:63
Heywood, John **10**:155–156
Heywood, Thomas **10**:156
Jellicoe, Ann **11**:394–395
Jerrold, Douglas William **11**:398
Jones, Henry Arthur **11**:442
Jonson, Ben **11**:445–446
Kyd, Thomas **12**:143
Lillo, George **12**:341
Lyly, John **12**:475
Marlowe, Christopher **13**:161
Marston, John **13**:174
Massinger, Philip **13**:213–214
Maugham, W. Somerset **13**:233
Medwall, Henry **13**:278
Middleton, Thomas **13**:413
Mortimer, John **13**:592
Orton, Joe **14**:451
Osborne, John **14**:452
Otway, Thomas **14**:467
Pinero, Sir Arthur Wing **15**:307
Pinter, Harold **15**:308
Priestly, J. B. **15**:536
Rattigan, Terence **16**:93
Restoration drama **16**:182
Rowe, Nicholas **16**:327
Shaffer, Peter **17**:234
Shakespeare, William **17**:236–237
Shaw, George Bernard **17**:245–246
Sheridan, Richard Brinsley **17**:257
Shirley, James **17**:277
Stoppard, Tom **18**:284
Tourneur, Cyril **19**:253
Udall, Nicholas **19**:370
University Wits **19**:470
Vanbrugh, Sir John **19**:516–517
Waterhouse, Keith **20**:64
Webster, John **20**:89
Wesker, Arnold **20**:105
Whiting, John **20**:140
Wilde, Oscar **20**:148–149
Wodehouse, Sir P. G. **20**:195
Wycherley, William **20**:298
Finnish literature
Canth, Minna **4**:117
forms
Bunraku **3**:563–564
burlesque and travesty **3**:572
burletta **3**:572
comedy **5**:132
commedia dell'arte **5**:137–138
Dengaku **6**:107
drame bourgeois **6**:262
epic theater **7**:217–218
farce **8**:22–23
happenings **10**:41
Kabuki **12**:4
masque **13**:200
melodrama **13**:287–288
mumming play **13**:638–639
No drama **14**:207
passion play **15**:105
satire **17**:88
satyr play **17**:92
soap opera **18**:8
theater of fact **19**:153
theater of the absurd **19**:154
tragedy **19**:265
tragicomedy **19**:265
ventriloquism **19**:546
well-made play **20**:99
French literature **8**:314–320
Adam de la Halle **1**:93
Adamov, Arthur **1**:93
Anouilh, Jean **2**:34–35
Antoine, André **2**:69
Apollinaire, Guillaume **2**:79
Artaud, Antonin **2**:212
Audiberti, Jacques **2**:318
Augier, Émile **2**:319
Aymé, Marcel **2**:379
Banville, Théodore de **3**:71
Bataille, Henry **3**:121
Beaumarchais, Pierre Caron de **3**:146
Becque, Henry Françoise **3**:152
Bernanos, Georges **3**:220
Bernard, Jean Jacques **3**:220
Bernard, Tristan **3**:220
Brieux, Eugène **3**:485
Camus, Albert **4**:68
Cid, The **4**:429
Claudel, Paul **5**:44
Cocteau, Jean **5**:89
Corneille, Pierre **5**:267–268
Courteline, Georges **5**:316–317
Crébillon **5**:336
Dumas, Alexandre (1824–95) **6**:297
Feydeau, Georges **8**:66
Fort, Paul **8**:236
Garnier, Robert **9**:49
Genet, Jean **9**:79
Giraudoux, Jean **9**:189
Guitry, Sacha **9**:401
Hardy, Alexandre **10**:47
Hugo, Victor **10**:294
Ionesco, Eugène **11**:240–241
Jarry, Alfred **11**:383
Labiche, Eugène Marin **12**:151
Lesage, Alain René **12**:296
Mairet, Jean **13**:76
Margaret of Navarre **13**:149
Marivaux, Pierre Carlet de Chamblain de **13**:158
Molière **13**:508–509
Pagnol, Marcel **15**:14
Racine, Jean **16**:36–37
Romains, Jules **16**:272–273
Rostand, Edmond **16**:320
Salacrou, Armand **17**:29
Sardou, Victorien **17**:77
Scribe, Eugène **17**:158
Tardieu, Jean **19**:35–36
Vauthier, Jean **19**:529
Vildrac, Charles **19**:596
Vitrac, Roger **19**:621
Voltaire **19**:632
well-made play **20**:99
German literature **9**:132–134
Brecht, Bertolt **3**:470–471
Bretano, Clemens **3**:473
Büchner, Georg **3**:534–535
Freytag, Gustav **8**:330
Goethe, Johann Wolfgang von **9**:223–224
Grabbe, Christian Dietrich **9**:275
Grass, Günter **9**:297–298
Hauptmann, Gerhart **10**:69
Hebbel, Christian Friedrich **10**:100
Hochhuth, Roth **10**:193
Hofmannsthal, Hugo von **10**:196–197
Horváth, Ödön von **10**:255
Jahnn, Hans Henny **11**:349
Kaiser, Georg **12**:6–7
Lessing, Gotthold **12**:298–299
Sachs, Hans **17**:7
Schiller, Johann Christoph Friedrich von **17**:120–121
Sternheim, Carl **18**:261
Sudermann, Hermann **18**:322–323
Toller, Ernst **19**:227
Wedekind, Frank **20**:89
Weiss, Peter **20**:95–96
Zuckmayer, Carl **20**:381
Greek literature, ancient **9**:343–344
Aeschylus **1**:128–129
Aristophanes **2**:155–156
Bacchae, The **3**:9
Clouds, The **5**:68
Cratinus **5**:333
dithyramb **6**:202
Electra **7**:105
Eupolis **7**:265
Euripides **7**:266
Lysistrata **12**:480
Medea **13**:263
Menander **13**:292–293
Oedipus Rex **14**:351
Oresteia **14**:432
Philemon **15**:231
satyr play **17**:92
Sophocles **18**:67–68
tragedy **19**:265
Trojan Woman, The **19**:305
Greek literature, modern
Xenopoulos, Gregorios **20**:312
Hebrew and Yiddish literature **10**:102
Ansky, Shloime **2**:35
Asch, Sholem **2**:228
Goldfaden, Abraham **9**:233
Gordin, Jacob **9**:248
Peretz, Y.L. **15**:163
Hungarian literature
Déry, Tibor **6**:123
Molnár, Ferenc **13**:512
Orkeny, Istvan **14**:445
Icelandic literature
Sigurjónsson, Jóhann **17**:302
Thórdarson, Agnar **19**:177–178
Indian literature **11**:101
Bhavabhuti **3**:234
Kalidasa **12**:8
Tagore, Sir Rabindranath **19**:10
Irish literature **11**:268
Abbey Theatre **1**:52–53
Beckett, Samuel **3**:151–152
Behan, Brendan **3**:169
Colum, Padraic **5**:125
Dunsany, Lord **6**:301
Ervine, St. John Greer **7**:235
Fitzmaurice, George **8**:131
Friel, Brian **8**:332
Gregory, Isabella Augusta, Lady **9**:355
Hyde, Douglas **10**:329
Johnston, Denis **11**:437
O'Casey, Sean **14**:319–320
Synge, John Millington **18**:407
Yeats, William Butler **20**:321
Italian literature **11**:315–317
Alamanni, Luigi **1**:239
Alfieri, Vittorio **1**:279
Betti, Ugo **3**:232
Buzzati, Dino **3**:601
Chiarelli, Luigi **4**:340
commedia dell'arte **5**:137–138
D'Annunzio, Gabriele **6**:33
De Filippo, Eduardo **6**:58
Fo, Dario **8**:192
Goldoni, Carlo **9**:235–236
Gozzi, Carlo, Conte **9**:274–275
Marinetti, Filippo Tommaso **13**:156
Pirandello, Luigi **15**:314
Japanese literature **11**:380
Abe Kobo **1**:55
Bunraku **3**:563–564
Chikamatsu Monzaemon **4**:347
Kabuki **12**:4
No drama **14**:207
Zeami Motokiyo **20**:357
Kleist Prize *see* KLEIST PRIZE
Latin literature **12**:234
Livius Andronicus **12**:378
Naevius, Gnaeus **14**:5
Plautus **15**:362
satire **17**:88
Terence **19**:115
medieval
Dengaku **6**:107
Everyman **7**:316
Hroswitha von Gandersheim **10**:286
Mexican literature
Juana Inés de la Cruz, Sor **11**:457–458
Usigli, Rodolfo **19**:490
Villaurrutia, Xavier **19**:598
narrative and dramatic devices **14**:22–23
naturalism **14**:49–50
Nigerian literature
Clark, John Pepper **5**:38
Soyinka, Wole **18**:115
Norwegian literature
Bjørnson, Bjørnstjerne **3**:302–303
Grieg, Nordahl Brun **9**:362
Ibsen, Henrik **11**:6–7
Polish literature
Fredro, Alexander, Count **8**:294
Gombrowicz, Witold **9**:241
Mrożwek, Sławomir **13**:629
Słowacki, Juliusz **17**:364
Witkiewicz, Stanisław Ignacy **20**:192
Wyspiański, Stanisław **20**:305
Portuguese literature
Garrett, João Baptista de Almeida **9**:50
Sá de Miranda, Francisco de **17**:3
Silva, António José da **17**:312
Vicente, Gil **19**:571
professional and educational associations
American Educational Theatre Association **1**:338
American National Theater and Academy **1**:352
Pulitzer Prize *see* LITERATURE—Pulitzer Prize
radio and television broadcasting **16**:58 *illus.*
Romanian literature
Alecsandri, Vasile **1**:270
Caragiale, Ion Luca **4**:131
Russian literature **16**:364–367
Aksakov, Konstantin Sergeyevich **1**:232
Andreyev, Leonid Nikolayevich **1**:408
Artsybashev, Mikhail Petrovich **2**:225
Boris Godunov (play) **3**:401
Bulgakov, Mikhail Afanasievich **3**:553–554
Chekhov, Anton **4**:310
Evreinov, Nikolai Nikolaevich **7**:325
Fonvizin, Denis Ivanovich **8**:207
Griboyedov, Aleksandr Sergeyevich **9**:361
Ostrovsky, Aleksandr Nikolayevich **14**:459
Shvarts, Yevgeny **17**:290
Turgenev, Ivan **19**:341
Scottish literature
Barrie, Sir James **3**:94
Bridie, James **3**:485
Lindsay, Sir David **12**:352
set design *see* THEATER ARCHITECTURE AND STAGING
South African literature
Fugard, Athol **8**:355
Spanish literature **18**:157–160
Álvarez Quintero, Serafín and Joaquín **1**:319–320
Arrabal, Fernando **2**:187
Benavente y Martínez, Jacinto **3**:195
Calderón de la Barca, Pedro **4**:26
Castro y Bellvís, Guillén de **4**:193
Cueva, Juan de la **5**:383
Echegaray y Eizaguirre, José **7**:37
Encina, Juan del **7**:162
García Lorca, Federico **9**:38–39
Martínez Sierra, Gregorio **13**:180
Rojas Zorrilla, Francisco de **16**:270
Rueda, Lope de **16**:339
Ruiz, José Martínez **16**:344
Ruiz de Alarcón y Mendoza, Juan **16**:344
Sastre, Alfonso **17**:84
Tirso de Molina **19**:209
Vallejo, Antonio Buero **19**:507
Vega, Lope de **19**:531
Zorilla y Moral, José **20**:380
Swedish literature **18**:386–387
Bergman, Hjalmar Fredrik Elgérus **3**:210
Strindberg, August **18**:299
Swiss literature
Dürrenmatt, Friedrich **6**:307
Frisch, Max **8**:334
theater festivals **19**:153
theory
Artaud, Antonin **2**:213
Brecht, Bertolt **3**:470–471
Cueva, Juan de la **5**:383
Poetics of Aristotle **15**:378
Welsh literature
Thomas, Dylan **19**:172–173
Yugoslav literature
Cankar, Ivan **4**:108

DRÁMA (Greece)
map (41° 9′N 24° 8′E) **9**:325
DRAMAMINE **6**:262
DRAMATIC IRONY
narrative and dramatic devices **14**:22
DRAMATIC MONOLOGUE
narrative and dramatic devices **14**:22
DRAME BOURGEOIS **6**:262 *bibliog.*
DRAMMEN (Norway)
map (59° 44′N 10° 15′E) **14**:261
DRANE AND ALEXANDER
music hall, vaudeville, and burlesque **13**:672 *illus.*
DRANG NACH OSTEN **6**:262
Albert I, Margrave of Brandenburg **1**:254
DRANGIANA
Persia, ancient **15**:182 *map*
DRAPER, HENRY **6**:262–263
astronomical catalogs and atlases **2**:276
Henry Draper Catalogue **10**:123
DRAPER, JOHN WILLIAM **6**:263 *bibliog.*
photochemistry **15**:257
DRAPER, RUTH **6**:263
DRAU (DRAVA) RIVER
map (45° 33′N 18° 55′E) **6**:35
DRAUGHTS (game) *see* CHECKERS
DRAVA (DRAU) RIVER
map (45° 33′N 18° 55′E) **6**:35
DRAVIDIAN LANGUAGES **6**:263 *bibliog.*; **12**:355 *map*
Asia **2**:244 *map*
India **11**:84
India, history of **11**:89
Khond **12**:68
Tamil **19**:19
DRAVIDIANS **2**:242 *illus.*; **16**:34 *illus.*
India, history of **11**:89–90
DRAW POKER (card game)
poker **15**:386
DRAWBRIDGE *see* BASCULE BRIDGE; SWINGING DRAWBRIDGE
DRAWING **6**:263–265 *bibliog.*, *illus.*
Bartlett, Jennifer **3**:97
Cozens, Alexander **5**:324
Greek art **9**:338–342
Guys, Constantin **9**:411
Leonardo da Vinci **12**:289–291
Lorraine, Claude **12**:412–416
Moreau (family) **13**:576
Pascin, Jules **15**:102
pastel **15**:106–107
Pisanello, Antonio **15**:316
Rackham, Arthur **16**:38
Rowlandson, Thomas **16**:328
silverpoint **17**:313
Steinberg, Saul **18**:248
DRAWING AND QUARTERING **6**:265
DRAYTON (North Dakota)
map (48° 38′N 97° 11′W) **14**:248
DRAYTON (South Carolina)
map (34° 58′N 81° 54′W) **18**:98
DRAYTON, MICHAEL **6**:265 *bibliog.*
DRAYTON PLAINS (Michigan)
map (42° 41′N 83° 23′W) **13**:377
DRAYTON VALLEY (Alberta)
map (53° 13′N 114° 59′W) **1**:256
DREADNOUGHT (battleship) **6**:266 *bibliog.*, *illus.*
Fisher of Kilverstone, John Arbuthnot Fisher,1st Baron **8**:123
naval vessels **14**:55 *illus.*
DREAM DANCERS
Smohalla **17**:373
Wananikwe **20**:21
DREAM PLAY, A (play) **6**:266 *bibliog.*
DREAM OF THE RED CHAMBER, THE (book) **6**:266 *bibliog.*
Ts'ao Hsüeh-Ch'in (Cao Xueqin) **19**:322
DREAMS AND DREAMING **6**:266–268 *bibliog.*, *illus.*
consciousness, states of **5**:200
Freud, Sigmund **8**:329
Interpretation of Dreams, The **11**:225
Jung, Carl **11**:467
psychoanalysis **15**:590
sleep **17**:360
surrealism (art) **18**:364–365
DREBBEL, CORNELIS **6**:268
submarine **18**:313
DRED SCOTT* v. *SANDFORD **6**:268 *bibliog.*, *illus.*; **13**:477
black Americans **3**:306–307
Civil War, U.S. **5**:16
Curtis, Benjamin Robbins **5**:395
Missouri **13**:479
Taney, Roger B. **19**:21
United States, history of the **19**:447
DREDGING **6**:268–269 *bibliog.*, *illus.*
gold **9**:227
harbor and port **10**:42
oceanographic instrumentation **14**:343 *illus.*
DREIER, KATHERINE
Guggenheim Museum **9**:393
DREISER, THEODORE **6**:269–270 *bibliog.*, *illus.*
American Tragedy, An **1**:367
Sister Carrie **17**:329
DRESDEN (East Germany) **6**:270 *illus.*
map (51° 3′N 13° 44′E) **9**:140
DRESDEN (Ohio)
map (40° 7′N 82° 1′W) **14**:357
DRESDEN (Tennessee)
map (36° 18′N 88° 42′W) **19**:104
DRESDEN CODEX
Maya **13**:244 *illus.*
DRESDEN STATE ART COLLECTIONS **6**:270–271 *bibliog.*
Permoser, Balthasar **15**:176
Pöpplemann, Matthäus Daniel **15**:432
Zwinger, The **9**:126 *illus.*
DRESDEN WARE *see* MEISSEN WARE
DRESS *see* COSTUME; UNIFORM
DRESSAGE
horse show **10**:250
riding **16**:217
DRESSLER, MARIE **6**:271
DRESSMAKING
clothing industry **5**:65
DREVER **6**:271
DREW (county in Arkansas)
map (33° 37′N 91° 45′W) **2**:166
DREW (Mississippi)
map (33° 49′N 90° 32′W) **13**:469
DREW, DANIEL **6**:271 *bibliog.*
Fisk, James **8**:128
Gould, Jay **9**:265
DREW, GEORGIANNA
Barrymore (family) **3**:96
DREW, NANCY (fictional character) **6**:271
DREW UNIVERSITY **6**:271
DREXEL (family) **6**:271 *bibliog.*
DREXEL FURNITURE COMPANY
Bailey v. *Drexel Furniture Company* **3**:26
DREXEL HILL (Pennsylvania)
map (39° 57′N 75° 19′W) **15**:147
DREYER, CARL THEODOR **6**:271 *bibliog.*
DREYER, J. L. E. **6**:271
DREYFUS, ALFRED **6**:272 *illus.*
Devil's Island **6**:143
DREYFUS AFFAIR **6**:271–272 *bibliog.*, *illus.*
Clemenceau, Georges **5**:49
Proust, Marcel **15**:582
Waldeck-Rousseau, René **20**:9
Zola, Émile **20**:372
DREYFUSS, HENRY **6**:272
industrial design **11**:156
DRIESCH, HANS ADOLF EDUARD **6**:272
DRIFFIELD, VERO CHARLES *see* HURTER, FERDINAND, AND DRIFFIELD, VERO C.
DRIFT (genetics)
population genetics **15**:440
DRIFT, GLACIAL **6**:272
erratic, glacial **7**:234–235
esker **7**:238
landform evolution **12**:183
rock material **6**:272
DRIFTLESS AREA **6**:272
DRIGGS (Idaho)
map (43° 44′N 111° 14′W) **11**:26
DRILL (monkey) **6**:272 *illus.*
DRILLING **6**:272–273 *bibliog.*
See also HAND TOOLS; MINING AND QUARRYING; PETROLEUM INDUSTRY
deep-sea drilling project **6**:77
derrick and crane **6**:122
machine tools **13**:24–25 *illus.*
oceanic oil drilling rig **14**:340 *illus.*; **15**:212 *illus.*
petroleum **15**:209
petroleum industry **15**:210
seabed corer **14**:344 *illus.*
tunnel **19**:338–339
water well **20**:60
DRINA RIVER
map (44° 53′N 19° 21′E) **20**:340
World War I **20**:226–227 *map*
DRINIT, BAY OF
map (41° 45′N 19° 28′E) **1**:250
DRINK RIVER
map (41° 45′N 19° 34′E) **1**:250
DRINKING (alcohol) *see* ALCOHOL CONSUMPTION
DRINKING STRAW
vacuum **19**:502
DRINKWATER, JOHN **6**:273
DRIPSTONE *see* STALACTITE AND STALAGMITE
DRISKILL MOUNTAIN
map (32° 25′N 92° 54′W) **12**:430
DRIVE SHAFT **2**:359 *illus.*
DROBETA-TURNU-SEVERIN (Romania)
map (44° 38′N 22° 39′E) **16**:288
DROESHOUT, MARTIN
William Shakespeare **17**:236 *illus.*
DROGHEDA (Ireland)
map (53° 43′N 6° 21′W) **11**:258
DROMEDARY CAMEL
camel **4**:53–54 *illus.*
DRONE (bee) **3**:158–159 *illus.*
DRONGO **6**:273
DROPSY
edema **7**:55
medicinal plants **13**:266
poppy **15**:432
DROSOPHILA
fruit fly **8**:347
DROSTE-HÜLSHOFF, ANNETTE ELISABETH, VON **6**:273 *bibliog.*
DROTTNINGHOLM THEATRE AND MUSEUM **6**:273
DROUGHT **6**:273–274 *bibliog.*
famine **8**:18–19
groundwater **9**:374
hydrologic cycle **10**:341
invisible droughts **6**:274
paleoclimatology **15**:33
Sahel (Africa) **17**:14–15
semiarid climate **17**:196
DROWNING **6**:274 *bibliog.*
lifesaving and water safety **12**:333
DROYSEN, JOHANN GUSTAV **6**:274
Diadochi **6**:149
DRUG **6**:274–279 *bibliog.*, *illus.*
See also names of specific drugs, e.g., ASPIRIN; VALIUM; etc.
administration **6**:275–276
adverse reactions **6**:277
respiratory system disorders **16**:182
analgesic **1**:388
anesthetics **1**:410–411
animal experimentation **2**:22
antacid **2**:38
anthelmintic drugs **2**:49
antibiotics **2**:57–59
anticoagulant **2**:60
antidepressants **2**:60–61
antihistamine **2**:63
antiseptic **2**:68
antitoxin **2**:69
aphrodisiac **2**:78
apothecary **2**:85
astringent **2**:270
barbiturate **3**:78
biopharmaceuticals **3**:275
birth control **3**:294
bronchodilators **3**:503
cancer **4**:105–106
cathartic **4**:204
decongestant drugs **6**:76
detoxification drugs **6**:274–279
dieting **6**:165
diuretic drugs **6**:202
drug **6**:277
emetic **7**:155
environmental health **7**:211
ergot **7**:228
excretion **6**:276
fertility, human **8**:60
gelatin **9**:69
hallucinogens **10**:24
headache **10**:85–86
hexachlorophene **10**:154
history **6**:274–275
Dioscorides, Pedanius **6**:185
Paracelsus **15**:74
hormone, animal **10**:237
hypertension **10**:349
interaction **6**:277
synergism **18**:407
magnesium **13**:54
medicinal plants **13**:266
metabolism **6**:276
opiate receptor **14**:405
patent medicine **15**:110
pharmaceutical industry **15**:219–220
pharmacology **15**:220
neuropharmacology **14**:105
pharmacopoeia **15**:220–221
pharmacy **15**:221–222
placebo **15**:325
protozoal diseases **15**:581
psychotropic drugs **15**:603–605
regulation **6**:278
Food and Drug Administration **8**:208
government regulation **9**:271
pure food and drug laws **15**:628–629
scientific research **6**:278–279
sedative **17**:181–182
shock, physiologic **17**:278–279
smelling salts **17**:365
steroid **18**:261–262
stimulant **18**:271
sulfa drugs **18**:333
toxicology **6**:277–278; **19**:256
tranquilizer **19**:266
tuberculosis **19**:327
withdrawal symptoms **20**:192
DRUG ABUSE **6**:279–281 *bibliog.*
AIDS **1**:201
alcoholism **1**:265–266
amphetamine **1**:377
amyl nitrite **1**:386–387
angel dust **1**:412
barbiturate **3**:78
cocaine **5**:85
codeine **5**:90
counterculture **5**:311
crime **5**:345
Darvon **6**:40
delirium **6**:93
drug trafficking **6**:281
hepatitis **10**:130
heroin **10**:145
LSD **12**:445
methadone **13**:343
morphine **13**:587
nalorphine **14**:9
opium **14**:406
paraldehyde **15**:78
pharmacy **15**:221
psychotropic drugs **15**:604
respiratory system disorders **16**:182
sedative **17**:182
stimulant **18**:271
Valium **19**:506
vertigo **19**:563
withdrawal symptoms **20**:192
young people **20**:336
DRUG TRAFFICKING **6**:281 *bibliog.*
DRUIDS **6**:281–282 *bibliog.*
Celts **4**:241
Stonehenge **18**:283
Stukeley, William **18**:308
DRUM (fish) **6**:282
spot **18**:198
DRUM (musical instrument) **6**:282 *bibliog.*, *illus.*
African music **1**:168–170 *illus.*
Chinese music **4**:392–393 *illus.*
Indian music **11**:102–103 *illus.*
Japanese music **11**:381–382 *illus.*
kettledrum **12**:61–62 *illus.*
Latin American music and dance **12**:231 *illus.*
musical instruments **13**:675–676 *illus.*
percussion instruments **15**:162 *illus.*
snare drum **17**:384
Southeast Asian art and architecture **18**:108
DRUM REBELLION *see* DREAM DANCERS
DRUMEV, VASSIL
Bulgaria **3**:556
DRUMHELLER (Alberta)
map (51° 28′N 112° 42′W) **1**:256
DRUMLIN **6**:282
erosion and sedimentation **7**:232
glaciers and glaciation **9**:192–195
DRUMMOND (Montana)
map (46° 40′N 113° 9′W) **13**:547
DRUMMOND (Wisconsin)
map (46° 20′N 91° 15′W) **20**:185
DRUMMOND, ROSCOE **6**:282
DRUMMOND, THOMAS **6**:282
DRUMMOND, WILLIAM **6**:282
DRUMMOND, WILLIAM HENRY **6**:283
DRUMMOND ISLAND
Manitoulin Islands **13**:122
map (46° 0′N 83° 40′W) **13**:377
DRUMMONDVILLE (Quebec)
map (45° 53′N 72° 29′W) **16**:18
DRUMRIGHT (Oklahoma)
map (35° 59′N 96° 36′W) **14**:368
DRUMS IN THE NIGHT (play)
Brecht, Bertolt **3**:470
DRUPE **17**:251 *illus.*
fruits and fruit cultivation **8**:348–349
DRURY, ALLEN **6**:283
DRURY LANE THEATRE **6**:283
Clive, Kitty **5**:61
Garrick, David **9**:50–51
Loutherbourg, Philippe Jacques de **12**:437
Sheridan, Richard Brinsley **17**:257
DRUSES see DRUZES
DRUSUS (family) **6**:283

DRUTEN, JOHN VAN *see* VAN DRUTEN, JOHN
DRUZES 6:283 *bibliog.*
DRY CELL 3:125–126 *illus.*
DRY CLEANING 6:283–284 *bibliog.*
carbon tetrachloride 4:137
DRY DOCK (shipping) 6:284 *illus.*
DRY PRONG (Louisiana)
map (31° 35′N 92° 32′W) 12:430
DRY RIDGE (Kentucky)
map (38° 41′N 84° 35′W) 12:47
DRY TORTUGAS (Florida) 6:284
DRYADS *see* NYMPHS (mythology)
DRYDEN (Ontario)
map (49° 47′N 92° 50′W) 14:393
DRYDEN, JOHN 6:284–285 *bibliog., illus.*
Alexander's Feast
dithyramb 6:202
Essay on Dramatic Poesy, An
neoclassicism (literature) 14:82
satire 17:88
DRYING OF FOOD *see* DEHYDRATION OF FOOD; FREEZE-DRYING
DRYOPITHECUS 6:285
prehistoric human origins 15:512
Proconsul 15:561
DRYPOINT 6:285 *bibliog.*
engraving 7:205–206
etching 7:248–249
graphic arts 9:291–293
Master of the Housebook 13:215
DU *see* the element of the name following DU, except for names listed below
DU BARRY, JEANNE BÉCU, COMTESSE 6:285 *bibliog.*
DU BELLAY, JOACHIM 6:285 *bibliog.*
DU BOIS (Pennsylvania)
map (41° 7′N 78° 46′W) 15:147
DU BOIS, GUY PÈNE 6:285 *bibliog.*
DU BOIS, W. E. B. 3:308 *illus.*; 6:285–286 *bibliog., illus.*
National Association for the Advancement of Colored People 14:29
United States, history of the 19:452
DU CAMP, MAXIME 6:286
DU CHAILLU, PAUL BELLONI 6:286 *bibliog.*
DU FU *see* TU FU (Du Fu)
DU GARD, ROGER MARTIN *see* MARTIN DU GARD, ROGER
DU GUESCLIN, BERTRAND 6:286
DU LOCLE, CAMILLE
Aïda 1:201
DU MAURIER, DAPHNE 6:286 *bibliog.*
DU MAURIER, GEORGE 6:286 *bibliog.*
DU PAGE (county in Illinois)
map (41° 52′N 88° 6′W) 11:42
DU PARC, THÉRÈSE
theater, history of the 19:147
DU PONT (family) 6:286–287 *bibliog., illus.*
nylon 14:308
Winterthur Museum 20:181
DU PONT COMPANY
mills (c.1880) 19:450 *illus.*
Wilmington (Delaware) 20:163
DU PONT DE NEMOURS, ÉLEUTHÈRE IRÉNÉE 6:286 *illus.*
Delaware 6:90–91
DU TOIT, ALEXANDER L.
plate tectonics 15:357
DU VIGNEAUD, VINCENT 6:287
DUAL MONARCHY *see* AUSTRIA-HUNGARY
DUAL ORGANIZATION *see* MOIETY
DUALISM 6:287 *bibliog.*
Albigenses 1:260
Avicenna 2:376
Bogomils 3:360
Descartes, René 6:126
Docetism 6:210
gnosticism 9:213–214
Manichaeism 13:116–117
metaphysics 13:334
Satan 17:84
Zorastrianism 20:379–380
DUARTE, EVA *see* PERÓN, EVA
DUARTE, JOSÉ NAPOLEÓN 6:287
El Salvador 7:101
DUARTE PEAK
map (19° 2′N 70° 59′W) 6:233
DUBACH (Louisiana)
map (32° 42′N 92° 39′W) 12:430
DUBAI (United Arab Emirates) 6:287
harbor and port 10:42
map (25° 18′N 55° 18′E) 19:401
United Arab Emirates 19:400
DUBBO (Australia)
map (32° 15′S 148° 36′E) 2:328
DUBČEK, ALEXANDER 6:287 *bibliog.*
Czechoslovakia 5:416
DUBINSKY, DAVID 6:287 *bibliog.*
International Ladies' Garment Workers' Union 11:221
Liberal parties 12:312
DUBLIN (city in Ireland) 6:287–288 *bibliog., illus.*; 11:257 *illus., table*
history
Easter Rising 7:33 *illus.*
Vikings 19:595
map (53° 20′N 6° 15′W) 11:258
DUBLIN (county in Ireland) 6:288
cities
Dublin 6:287–288 *illus.*
Dún Laoghaire 6:298
DUBLIN (Georgia)
map (32° 32′N 82° 54′W) 9:114
DUBLIN (Texas)
map (32° 5′N 98° 21′W) 19:129
DUBLINERS (book) 6:288 *bibliog.*
Joyce, James 11:456–457
DUBNOW, SIMON 6:288–289 *bibliog.*
DUBOIS (Idaho)
map (44° 10′N 112° 14′W) 11:26
DUBOIS (Indiana)
map (38° 27′N 86° 48′W) 11:111
DUBOIS (county in Indiana)
map (38° 20′N 87° 5′W) 11:111
DUBOIS, EUGÈNE 6:289
Homo erectus 10:215
Java man 11:385
DUBOS, RENE 6:289 *bibliog.*
antibiotics 2:57
DUBREKA (Guinea)
map (9° 48′N 13° 31′W) 9:397
DUBROVNIK (Yugoslavia) 6:289
map (42° 38′N 18° 7′E) 20:340
DUBUFFET, JEAN 6:289 *bibliog., illus.*
art brut 2:203
The Hare Path 6:289 *illus.*
DUBUQUE (Iowa) 6:289
map (42° 30′N 90° 41′W) 11:244
DUBUQUE (county in Iowa)
map (42° 30′N 90° 50′W) 11:244
DUBUQUE, JULIEN 6:289
DUCCIO DI BUONINSEGNA 6:289–290 *bibliog.*
Italian art and architecture 11:312
Maestà altarpiece 2:194 *illus.*
DUCE, IL *see* MUSSOLINI, BENITO
DUCHAMP, MARCEL 6:290 *bibliog., illus.*
Bicycle Wheel 6:290 *illus.*; 17:165 *illus.*
film, history of 8:84
Guggenheim, Peggy 9:392
kinetic art 12:78
L.H.O.O.Q. 6:5 *illus.*
Marey, Étienne Jules 13:148
Nude Descending a Staircase
Armory Show 2:177
futurism 8:384
Philadelphia Museum of Art 15:229
Villon, Jacques 19:599
DUCHAMP-VILLON, RAYMOND 6:290 *bibliog.*
DUCHENNE, GUILLAUME B. A.
muscular dystrophy 13:656
DUCHESNE (Utah)
map (40° 10′N 110° 24′W) 19:492
DUCHESNE (county in Utah)
map (40° 20′N 110° 22′W) 19:492
DUCHESNE, ANDRÉ 6:290
DUCHESNE RIVER
map (40° 5′N 109° 41′W) 19:492
DUCIE ISLAND
Pitcairn Island 15:319
DUCK (zoology) 3:280 *illus.*; 6:290–292 *bibliog., illus.*
American ruddy duck 6:291–292 *illus.*
Australian freckled duck 6:291
canvasback 6:292
dabbling duck 6:291
diving duck 6:292
duck hunting 10:314 *illus.*
egg 7:72
eider duck 6:291–292 *illus.*; 19:332 *illus.*
hybrid 10:328
imprinting 11:68
mallard 13:91 *illus.*
merganser 13:309–310
muscovy duck 6:292; 15:474 *illus.*
perching duck 6:291
pintail duck 19:332 *illus.*
pochard 6:292
poultry 15:474–475 *illus., illus.*
respiratory system 16:179 *illus.*
ruddy duck 6:291–292 *illus.*
shelduck 17:250
steamer duck 6:291
whistling duck 6:291
White Pekin duck 15:474–475 *illus.*
widgeon 20:145
wood duck 6:291 *illus.*
DUCK BAY (Manitoba)
map (52° 10′N 100° 9′W) 13:119
DUCK-BILLED PLATYPUS 6:292 *illus.*; 13:104 *illus.*; 13:541 *illus.*
DUCK HAWK *see* FALCON
DUCK HILL (Mississippi)
map (33° 38′N 89° 43′W) 13:469
DUCK LAKE (Saskatchewan)
map (52° 47′N 106° 13′W) 17:81
DUCK RIVER
map (36° 2′N 87° 52′W) 19:104
DUCKTOWN (Tennessee)
map (35° 3′N 84° 23′W) 19:104
DUCKWEED 6:292
Arales 2:108
DUCLOS, JACQUES 6:292
DUCOS, PIERRE ROGER
Sieyès, Emmanuel Joseph 17:298
DUCTILITY
materials technology 13:220 *table*
DUCTLESS GLANDS *see* ENDOCRINE SYSTEM; HORMONE, ANIMAL
DUDELANGE (Luxembourg)
map (49° 28′N 6° 5′E) 12:472
DUDEVANT, AURORE *see* SAND, GEORGE
DUDLEY (England)
map (52° 30′N 2° 5′W) 19:403
DUDLEY (Massachusetts)
map (42° 3′N 71° 56′W) 13:206
DUDLEY, LORD GUILDFORD
Grey, Lady Jane 9:360
DUDLEY, JOHN, DUKE OF NORTHUMBERLAND *see* NORTHUMBERLAND, JOHN DUDLEY, DUKE OF
DUDLEY, ROBERT, EARL OF LEICESTER *see* LEICESTER, ROBERT DUDLEY, EARL OF
DUDRICK, STANLEY
gastrointestinal tract disease 9:57
DUE PROCESS 6:292–293
See also 14TH AMENDMENT; 6TH AMENDMENT
administrative law 1:105
Argersinger v. *Hamlin* 2:152
arrest 2:188
attainder, bill of 2:313
Bill of Rights 3:253
defense counsel 6:83
Escobedo v. *Illinois* 7:237
5th Amendment 8:74
Fortas, Abe 8:238
Gideon v. *Wainwright* 9:177
Griswold v. *Connecticut* 9:367–368
habeas corpus 10:3–4
human rights 10:298
juvenile delinquency 11:480
law, history of 12:246–247
Magna Carta 13:53
Mapp v. *Ohio* 13:138
Miranda v. *Arizona* 13:463
Munn v. *Illinois* 13:643
Powell v. *Alabama* 15:481
Reconstruction Amendments 5:221–222
Slaughterhouse Cases 17:351
Twining v. *New Jersey* 19:360
Watkins v. *United States* 20:67
witness 20:192–193
DUÉKOUÉ (Ivory Coast)
map (6° 45′N 7° 21′W) 11:335
DUEL 6:293 *bibliog.*
fencing 8:49
trial by combat 19:292
DUER, WILLIAM 6:293
DUFAY, C. F.
physics, history of 15:283
DUFAY, GUILLAUME 6:293 *bibliog.*; 8:320 *illus.*
music, history of Western 13:665
DUFF, ALEXANDER 6:293
DUFF, SIR LYMAN POORE 6:293
DUFFERIN AND AVA, FREDERICK TEMPLE HAMILTON-TEMPLE-BLACKWOOD, 1ST MARQUESS OF 6:293–294 *bibliog.*
DUFUR (Oregon)
map (45° 27′N 121° 8′W) 14:427
DUFY, RAOUL 6:294 *bibliog., illus.*
Le Café à l'Estaque 6:294 *illus.*
DUGGER (Indiana)
map (39° 4′N 87° 16′W) 11:111
DUGONG
sirenia 17:327–328
DUGOUT (boat) 4:113 *illus.*
DUHAMEL, GEORGES 6:294 *bibliog.*
DUHAMEL, JEAN 6:294
DÜHRING, KARL EUGEN 6:294
DUIKER 6:294 *illus.*
DUISBURG (West Germany) 6:294–295
map (51° 25′N 6° 46′E) 9:140
DUITAMA (Colombia)
map (5° 50′N 73° 2′W) 5:107
DUKAS, PAUL 6:295 *bibliog.*
DUKE (title)
titles of nobility and honor 19:213
DUKE, CHARLES, JR. 6:295
Apollo program 2:84
DUKE, JAMES BUCHANAN 6:295 *bibliog.*
DUKE ENDOWMENT 6:295
DUKE UNIVERSITY 6:295
American Dance Festival 1:338
Duke, James Buchanan 6:295
Rhine, J. B. 16:195
DUKENFIELD, WILLIAM CLAUDE *see* FIELDS, W.C.
DUKES (county in Massachusetts)
map (41° 23′N 70° 31′W) 13:206
DUKHAN (Qatar)
map (25° 25′N 50° 48′E) 16:4
DUKHOBORS *see* DOUKHOBORS
DULBECCO, RENATO 6:295
Baltimore, David 3:56
DULCE (New Mexico)
map (36° 56′N 107° 0′W) 14:136
DULCE GULF
map (8° 32′N 83° 14′W) 5:291
DULCIMER 6:295 *bibliog.*
DULLES, ALLEN WELSH 6:295 *bibliog.*
DULLES, JOHN FOSTER 5:98 *illus.*; 6:295–296 *bibliog., illus.*
Eisenhower, Dwight D. 7:96
Southeast Asia Treaty Organization 18:107
United States, history of the 19:458
DULLIN, CHARLES 6:296
DULONG, PIERRE LOUIS 6:296
chemistry, history of 4:326
DULSE 6:296
seaweed 17:177
DULUTH (Georgia)
map (34° 0′N 84° 9′W) 9:114
DULUTH (Minnesota) 6:296; 13:456 *illus.*
map (46° 47′N 92° 6′W) 13:453
DULUTH, DANIEL GREYSOLON, SIEUR 6:296
DULWICH ART GALLERY
Soane, Sir John 18:6
DUMA 6:296 *bibliog.*
Nicholas II, Emperor of Russia 14:182
Russia/Union of Soviet Socialist Republics, history of 16:358
DUMA (Syria)
map (33° 35′N 36° 24′E) 18:412
DUMAGUETE (Philippines)
map (9° 18′N 123° 18′E) 15:237
DUMAS (Arkansas)
map (33° 53′N 91° 29′W) 2:166
DUMAS (Texas)
map (35° 52′N 101° 58′W) 19:129
DUMAS, ALEXANDRE (1802–70) 6:296–297 *bibliog., illus.*; 16:293 *illus.*
Count of Monte Cristo, The 5:310
Montez, Lola 13:555
Three Musketeers, The 19:182
DUMAS, ALEXANDRE (1824–95) 6:297 *bibliog.*
Camille (play) 4:62
Traviata, La (opera) 19:284
DUMAS, HENRY 6:297
DUMAS, JEAN BAPTISTE ANDRÉ 6:297 *bibliog.*
organic chemistry 14:434
DUMAS FILS *see* DUMAS, ALEXANDRE (1824–95)
DUMAS PÈRE *see* DUMAS, ALEXANDRE (1802–70)
DUMB SHOW 6:297
DUMBARTON (Scotland) *see* DUNBARTON (Scotland)
DUMBARTON OAKS 6:297–298
DUMBELL (weight lifting) *see* WEIGHT LIFTING (sport)
DUMDUM BULLET 6:298
DUMÉZIL, GEORGES
mythology 13:694; 13:701
DUMFRIES AND GALLOWAY (Scotland) 6:298
map (55° 4′N 3° 37′W) 19:403
DUMMER'S WAR
French and Indian Wars 8:313
DUMONT (Iowa)
map (42° 45′N 92° 58′W) 11:244
DUMONT (New Jersey)
map (40° 56′N 74° 0′W) 14:129
DUMONT, ALBERTO SANTOS- *see* SANTOS-DUMONT, ALBERTO
DUMONT D'URVILLE, JULES SÉBASTIAN CÉSAR 6:298
Oceania 14:333

DUMOURIEZ, CHARLES FRANÇOIS DU PERIER 6:298
DUMPING *see* INTERNATIONAL TRADE
DUMPS, CHEMICAL **15**:410; **15**:411
DUMUZI
mythology **13**:696
DUMYAT (Egypt)
map (31° 25′N 31° 48′E) **7**:76
DUN AND BRADSTREET
credit agency **5**:336
Tappan brothers **19**:34
DÚN LAOGHAIRE (Ireland) **6**:298
map (53° 17′N 6° 8′W) **11**:258
DUNANT, JEAN HENRI **6**:298 *bibliog.*
Red Cross **16**:112
DUNAÚJVÁROS (Hungary)
map (46° 58′N 18° 57′E) **10**:307
DUNAWAY, FAYE **6**:298
DUNBAR (West Virginia)
map (38° 22′N 81° 45′W) **20**:111
DUNBAR, PAUL LAURENCE **6**:298
DUNBAR, WILLIAM **6**:298–299 *bibliog.*
DUNBARTON (Scotland) **6**:299
DUNCAN (British Columbia)
map (48° 47′N 123° 42′W) **3**:491
DUNCAN (Mississippi)
map (34° 3′N 90° 45′W) **13**:469
DUNCAN (Oklahoma)
map (34° 30′N 97° 57′W) **14**:368
DUNCAN, DAVID DOUGLAS
photojournalism **15**:273
DUNCAN, ISADORA **6**:299 *bibliog., illus.*
ballet **3**:43 *illus.*
choreography **4**:408–409
dance **6**:28 *illus.*
Yesenin, Sergei Aleksandrovich **20**:327
DUNCAN, JOHN
sewing machine **17**:223
DUNCAN, ROBERT **6**:299
DUNCAN, WILLIAM
Tsimshian **19**:324
DUNCANNON (Pennsylvania)
map (40° 23′N 77° 2′W) **15**:147
DUNCANSBY HEAD
map (58° 39′N 3° 1′W) **19**:403
DUNCANVILLE (Texas)
map (32° 39′N 96° 55′W) **19**:129
DUNCKER, KARL
problem solving **15**:559
DUNDALK (Ireland)
map (54° 1′N 6° 25′W) **11**:258
DUNDALK (Maryland)
map (39° 15′N 76° 31′W) **13**:188
DUNDEE (Michigan)
map (41° 57′N 83° 40′W) **13**:377
DUNDEE (New York)
map (42° 31′N 76° 59′W) **14**:149
DUNDEE (Scotland) **6**:299
map (56° 28′N 3° 0′W) **19**:403
DUNDEE, JOHN GRAHAM OF CLAVERHOUSE, 1ST VISCOUNT **6**:299
DUNDY (county in Nebraska)
map (40° 10′N 101° 40′W) **14**:70
DUNE *see* SAND DUNE
DUNEDIN (Florida)
map (28° 0′N 82° 47′W) **8**:172
DUNEDIN (New Zealand) **6**:299
map (45° 52′S 170° 30′E) **14**:158
DUNFERMLINE (Scotland) **6**:299–300
map (56° 4′N 3° 29′W) **19**:403
DUNG BEETLE **6**:300 *illus.*
DUNGARVAN (Ireland)
map (52° 5′N 7° 37′W) **11**:258
DUNGEONS AND DRAGONS (game) **9**:31
DUNHAM, KATHERINE **6**:300 *bibliog.*
DUNITE **6**:300 *bibliog.*
olivine **14**:380
DUNIWAY, ABIGAIL SCOTT **6**:300
DUNKERQUE (France) **6**:300
map (51° 3′N 2° 22′E) **8**:260
World War II **20**:253–254 *illus., map*
DUNKERS *see* BRETHREN
DUNKIRK (France) *see* DUNKERQUE (France)
DUNKIRK (Indiana)
map (40° 23′N 85° 13′W) **11**:111
DUNKIRK (New York)
map (42° 29′N 79° 20′W) **14**:149
DUNKIRK (Ohio)
map (40° 48′N 83° 39′W) **14**:357
DUNKLIN (county in Missouri)
map (36° 20′N 90° 0′W) **13**:476
DUNLAP (Iowa)
map (41° 51′N 95° 36′W) **11**:244
DUNLAP (Tennessee)
map (35° 23′N 85° 23′W) **19**:104
DUNLAP, WILLIAM **6**:300–301 *bibliog.*
American art and architecture **1**:332
DUNLEARY (Ireland) *see* DÚN LAOGHAIRE (Ireland)
DUNLOP, JOHN **6**:301
DUNMORE (Pennsylvania)
map (41° 25′N 75° 38′W) **15**:147
DUNMORE, JOHN MURRAY, 4th EARL OF **6**:301
DUNMORE'S WAR, LORD *see* DUNMORE, JOHN MURRAY, 4TH EARL OF
DUNN (North Carolina)
map (35° 19′N 78° 37′W) **14**:242
DUNN (county in North Dakota)
map (47° 30′N 102° 30′W) **14**:248
DUNN (county in Wisconsin)
map (44° 57′N 91° 57′W) **20**:185
DUNNE, FINLEY PETER **6**:301 *bibliog.*
DUNNELLON (Florida)
map (29° 3′N 82° 28′W) **8**:172
DUNNING (Nebraska)
map (41° 50′N 100° 6′W) **14**:70
DUNNING, WILLIAM ARCHIBALD **6**:301 *bibliog.*
DUNNOCK *see* HEDGE SPARROW
DUNNOCK, MILDRED
Death of a Salesman **19**:150 *illus.*
DUNOIS, JEAN, COMTE DE (the Bastard of Orléans) **6**:301
DUNS SCOTUS, JOHN **6**:301 *bibliog.*
scholasticism **17**:131–132 *illus.*
DUNSANY, LORD **6**:301
DUNSEITH (North Dakota)
map (48° 50′N 100° 2′W) **14**:248
DUNSMUIR (California)
map (41° 13′N 122° 16′W) **4**:31
DUNSTABLE, JOHN **6**:301 *bibliog.*
music, history of Western **13**:665
DUNSTAN, SAINT **6**:301
Edgar, King of England **7**:56
DUNVILLE (Newfoundland)
map (47° 16′N 53° 54′W) **14**:166
DUODECIMAL SYSTEM **6**:301–302 *bibliog.*
base **2**:102
DUODENUM **6**:302
digestion, human **6**:171
gallbladder **9**:17
intestine **11**:230
ulcer **9**:56 *illus.*; **19**:376
DUOMO OF FLORENCE *see* SANTA MARIA DEL FIORE (Florence)
DUPARC, HENRI **6**:302 *bibliog.*
DUPIN, C.
mathematics, history of **13**:226
DUPLEIX, JOSEPH FRANÇOIS **6**:302 *bibliog.*
East India Company, French **7**:32
DUPLESSIS, J. S.
Louis XVI, King of France **12**:427 *illus.*
DUPLESSIS, MAURICE LE NOBLET **6**:302
Canada, history of **4**:86
DUPLESSIS-MORNAY, PHILIPPE *see* MORNAY, PHILIPPE DE
DUPLICATING MACHINE *see* ELECTROSTATIC PRINTING
DUPLIN (county in North Carolina)
map (34° 55′N 77° 55′W) **14**:242
DUPONT MANOR (Delaware)
map (39° 12′N 75° 34′W) **6**:88
DUPREE (South Dakota)
map (45° 3′N 101° 36′W) **18**:103
DUPREZ, GILBERT-LOUIS
Lucia di Lammermoor **12**:450
DUQUESNE, FORT *see* FORT DUQUESNE (Pennsylvania)
DUQUESNOY, FRANÇOIS **6**:302 *bibliog.*
DUQUOIN (Illinois)
map (38° 1′N 89° 14′W) **11**:42
DUR SHARRUKIN (Iraq)
Khorsabad **12**:68
Mesopotamian art and architecture **13**:320–321 *illus.*
DUR-UNTASH (Iran) **6**:302; **15**:183 *illus.*
Elam **7**:101
DURA-EUROPUS *see* DOURA-EUROPOS (Syria)
DURÁN, ROBERTO **6**:302
DURAND (Illinois)
map (42° 26′N 89° 20′W) **11**:42
DURAND (Michigan)
map (42° 55′N 83° 59′W) **13**:377
DURAND (Wisconsin)
map (44° 38′N 91° 58′W) **20**:185
DURAND, ASHER BROWN **6**:302–303 *bibliog., illus.*
Hudson River school **10**:290
Kindred Spirits **1**:333 *illus.*; **6**:303 *illus.*
DURAND, CAPTAIN
Dilmun **6**:176
DURAND-RUEL, PAUL
Walters Art Gallery **20**:20
DURANGO (Colorado) **6**:303
map (37° 16′N 107° 53′W) **5**:116
DURANGO (Mexico) **6**:303
map (24° 2′N 104° 40′W) **13**:357
DURANGO (state in Mexico) **6**:303
DURANT (Mississippi)
map (33° 4′N 89° 51′W) **13**:469
DURANT (Oklahoma)
map (34° 0′N 96° 23′W) **14**:368
DURANT, THOMAS CLARK **6**:303 *bibliog.*
railroad **16**:72
DURANT, WILL AND ARIEL **6**:303 *bibliog.*
DURANT, WILLIAM CRAPO **6**:303 *bibliog.*
automotive industry **2**:363
DURANTE, JIMMY **6**:303 *bibliog.*
DURAS, MARGUERITE **6**:304 *bibliog.*
Resnais, Alain **16**:177
DURAZNO (Uruguay)
map (33° 22′S 56° 31′W) **19**:488
DURAZZO (Albania) *see* DURRËS (Albania)
DURBAN (South Africa) **6**:304
climate **1**:142 *table*; **18**:80 *table*
map (29° 55′S 30° 56′E) **18**:79
DURBIN (West Virginia)
map (38° 33′N 79° 50′W) **20**:111
DÜREN (Germany, East and West)
map (50° 48′N 6° 28′E) **9**:140
DÜRER, ALBRECHT **6**:304–305 *bibliog., illus.*
book illustration **3**:387
The Four Horsemen of the Apocalypse **3**:387 *illus.*; **16**:155 *illus.*; **20**:211 *illus.*
German art and architecture **9**:125–126
The Great Piece of Turf **20**:61 *illus.*
Grünewald, Matthias **9**:382–383
Knight, Death and the Devil **2**:197 *illus.*; **7**:205 *illus.*
Kulmbach, Hans von **12**:136
Lucas van Leyden **12**:448–449
Nuremberg (West Germany) **14**:297
Passion cycle **15**:105
Paumgärtner Altarpiece **6**:305 *illus.*
Renaissance art and architecture **16**:154
rhinoceros **9**:291 *illus.*
Self-Portrait with Wig **6**:304 *illus.*
watercolor **20**:61
Wolgemut, Michael **20**:199
DURGA **6**:305
DURHAM (California)
map (39° 44′N 121° 48′W) **4**:31
DURHAM (England) **6**:305
DURHAM (county in England) **6**:305–306 *bibliog.*
cities
Darlington **6**:39
Durham **6**:305
DURHAM (New Hampshire)
map (43° 8′N 70° 56′W) **14**:123
DURHAM (North Carolina) **6**:305
map (35° 59′N 78° 54′W) **14**:242
DURHAM (county in North Carolina)
map (36° 5′N 78° 50′W) **14**:242
DURHAM, JOHN GEORGE LAMBTON, 1ST EARL OF **6**:306 *bibliog., illus.*
Canada, history of **4**:83
Rebellions of 1837 **16**:105
DURHAM CATHEDRAL **2**:133 *illus.*; **6**:306 *bibliog.*
architecture **2**:133
cathedrals and churches **4**:205
English art and architecture **7**:182
Norman architecture **14**:220 *illus.*
Romanesque art and architecture **16**:282
DURHAM RULE
Bazelon, David L. **3**:134–135
DURIAN **6**:306
DURKHEIM, ÉMILE **6**:306 *bibliog.*
alienation **1**:294
bureaucracy **3**:567
crime **5**:345
magic **13**:50
Mauss, Marcel **13**:238
primitive religion **15**:543
Radcliffe-Brown, Sir Alfred R. **16**:41
sociology **18**:29 *illus.*
suicide **18**:331
totem **19**:249
DUROCHER, LEO **6**:306–307 *bibliog.*
DURRELL, LAWRENCE **6**:307 *bibliog., illus.*
DÜRRENMATT, FRIEDRICH **6**:307 *bibliog., illus.*
DURRËS (Albania) **6**:307
map (41° 19′N 19° 26′E) **1**:250
D'URVILLE, JULES SÉBASTIAN CÉSAR DUMONT *see* DUMONT D'URVILLE, JULES SÉBASTIAN CÉSAR
DURYEA, CHARLES E. AND J. FRANK **6**:307 *bibliog.*
automobile racing **2**:362
Springfield (Massachusetts) **18**:200
DUSAN, STEPHEN *see* STEPHEN DUŠAN, KING OF SERBIA
DUSE, ELEONORA **6**:307 *bibliog.*
D'Annunzio, Gabriele **6**:33
DUSHANBE (USSR) **6**:308
map (38° 35′N 68° 48′E) **19**:388
DUSHORE (Pennsylvania)
map (41° 31′N 76° 24′W) **15**:147
DUSON (Louisiana)
map (30° 12′N 92° 11′W) **12**:430
DÜSSELDORF (West Germany) **6**:308
map (51° 12′N 6° 47′E) **9**:140
DÜSSELDORF AKADEMIE **6**:308 *bibliog.*
DUST, ATMOSPHERIC **6**:308
gas mask **9**:53
respiratory system disorders **16**:181
sources, artificial and natural **6**:308
DUST, INTERSTELLAR
Galaxy, The **9**:10; **9**:13
interstellar matter **11**:225–228
DUST, STELLAR
origin of life **12**:327
DUST BOWL **5**:202 *illus.*; **6**:308 *bibliog., illus.*
conservation **5**:202
Nebraska **14**:74
DUST DEVIL **6**:308–309
DUST STORM *see* SANDSTORM AND DUST STORM
DUST WHICH IS GOD, THE (poem)
Benét, William Rose **3**:198
DUSTY MILLER (botany) **6**:309
DUTCH, THE *see* NETHERLANDS
DUTCH ART AND ARCHITECTURE **6**:309–313 *bibliog., illus.*
See also the subheading Netherlands under specific art forms, e.g., ARCHITECTURE; SCULPTURE; etc.; the subheading Netherlands under specific historic periods, e.g., BAROQUE ART AND ARCHITECTURE; RENAISSANCE ART AND ARCHITECTURE; etc.; names of specific artists, e.g., ESCHER, MAURITS CORNEILLE; VERMEER, JAN; etc.
Campen, Jacob van **4**:66
cathedrals and churches **4**:207–208
Flemish art and architecture **8**:161
history
Mander, Carel van **13**:111
landscape painting **12**:189–190
modern architecture **13**:491
museums, art **13**:658
Netherlands **14**:100
Renaissance **16**:153–154
Rijksmuseum **16**:223
still-life painting **18**:269 *illus.*
DUTCH BARGE DOG *see* KEESHOND
DUTCH EAST INDIA COMPANY *see* EAST INDIA COMPANY, DUTCH
DUTCH EAST INDIES *see* INDONESIA
DUTCH ELM DISEASE
bark beetle **3**:82
disease, plant **6**:195
elm **7**:149
fungi **8**:367
DUTCH AND FLEMISH LITERATURE **6**:313–314 *bibliog.*
authors
Beets, Nicolaas **3**:168
Bilderdijk, Willem **3**:251
Bordewijk, Ferdinand **3**:398
Bosboom-Toussaint, Anna Louisa Geertruide **3**:405
Boutens, Pieter Cornelius **3**:425
Bredero, Gerbrand Adriaenszoon **3**:471
Cats, Jacob **4**:213
Conscience, Hendrik **5**:199
Erasmus, Desiderius **7**:227
Gezelle, Guido **9**:163
Gijsen, Marnix **9**:178
Heijermans, Herman **10**:108
Hooft, Pieter Corneliszoon **10**:226
Huygens, Constantijn **10**:325
Nijhoff, Martinus **14**:194
Ruysbroeck, John **16**:377
Streuvels, Stijn **18**:298
Teirlinck, Herman **19**:74
Timmermans, Felix **19**:203

DUTCH AND FLEMISH LITERATURE (cont.)
Vermeylen, August **19**:553
Verwey, Albert **19**:563
Vestdijk, Simon **19**:565
Vondel, Joost van den **19**:634
Vrught, Johanna Petronella **19**:639
Woestijne, Karel van de **20**:195
Wolff, Elizabeth **20**:198
Wolkers, Jan **20**:199
Everyman **7**:316
Rederijkers (literary groups) **16**:115
DUTCH GUIANA *see* SURINAME
DUTCH LANGUAGE
Germanic languages **9**:135–137 *table*
DUTCH NATIONAL BALLET **6**:314
Dantzig, Rudi Van **6**:35
DUTCH REFORMED CHURCH
South Africa **18**:80
DUTCH REVOLT **6**:314–315 *bibliog., illus.*; **12**:439–440 *illus.*
Brabant, Duchy of **3**:435
Council of Troubles **12**:439 *illus.*
Europe, history of **7**:287
historians
Motley, John Lothrop **13**:611
Low Countries, history of the **12**:439–440
Maastricht (Netherlands) **13**:3
Oldenbarnevelt, Johan van **14**:375
Philip II, King of Spain **15**:234
's Hertogenbosch (Netherlands) **17**:259
William I, Prince of Orange (William the Silent) **20**:158
DUTCH RUSH *see* HORSETAIL (botany)
DUTCH WARS *see* ANGLO-DUTCH WARS
DUTCH WEST INDIA COMPANY **6**:315 *bibliog.*
Delaware **6**:90
Hudson River **10**:290
Netherlands **14**:102
New Netherland **14**:140
New York (state) **14**:153
patroons **15**:114
Yonkers (New York) **20**:330
DUTCH WEST INDIES *see* NETHERLANDS ANTILLES
DUTCHESS (county in New York)
map (41° 42'N 73° 56'W) **14**:149
DUTCHMAN (play)
Baraka, Imamu Amiri **3**:75
DUTCHMAN'S-BREECHES (botany) **6**:315
DUTCHMAN'S-PIPE (botany) **6**:315 *illus.*
DUTERT, C. L. F.
Halle des Machines **4**:185 *illus.*
DUTTON (Montana)
map (47° 51'N 111° 43'W) **13**:547
DUTTON, CLARENCE EDWARD **6**:315–316 *bibliog., illus.*
DUTTON, MOUNT (Utah)
map (38° 1'N 112° 13'W) **19**:492
DUTY (tax) *see* TARIFF
DUUN, OLAV **6**:316 *bibliog.*
DUVAL (county in Florida)
map (30° 20'N 81° 40'W) **8**:172
DUVAL (county in Texas)
map (27° 42'N 98° 32'W) **19**:129
DUVALIER, FRANÇOIS **6**:316 *bibliog., illus.*
DUVALIER, JEAN CLAUDE **6**:316
DUVE, CHRISTIAN DE *see* DE DUVE, CHRISTIAN
DUVEEN, JOSEPH, BARON DUVEEN OF MILLBANK **6**:316 *bibliog.*
DUVENECK, FRANK **6**:316 *bibliog.*
DUVERGIER DE HAURANNE, JEAN *see* SAINT-CYRAN, ABBÉ DE
DUWEIR, TELL EL- *see* LACHISH (Israel)
DUXBURY (Massachusetts)
map (42° 2'N 70° 40'W) **13**:206
DVARAVATI (kingdom)
Southeast Asian art and architecture **18**:109
Thailand **19**:141
DVINA RIVER, NORTHERN **6**:317
DVINA RIVER, WESTERN **6**:317
DVOŘÁK, ANTONÍN **6**:317 *bibliog., illus.*
Czech music **5**:413
DWARF GECKO **6**:317
DWARF GOURAMI **19**:308 *illus.*
DWARF SPANIEL *see* PAPILLON (dog)
DWARF STAR
black dwarf **3**:314
flare star **8**:153
Proxima Centauri **15**:584
white dwarf **20**:137
DWARFISM
endocrine system, diseases of the **7**:170; **7**:171
growth hormone **9**:381
DWIGHT (Illinois)
map (41° 5'N 88° 26'W) **11**:42
DWIGHT, REGINALD KENNETH *see* JOHN, ELTON
DWIGHT, TIMOTHY **6**:317 *bibliog.*
DWINGELOO RADIO OBSERVATORY
Westerbork Observatory **20**:115
DWORKIN, RONALD
legal realism **12**:243
DWORSHAK RESERVOIR
map (46° 45'N 116° 0'W) **11**:26
DYAK *see* DAYAK
DYCK, SIR ANTHONY VAN *see* VAN DYCK, SIR ANTHONY
DYE **6**:317–318 *bibliog., illus.*
alizarin **1**:295
annatto tree **2**:32
arbutus **2**:111–112
azo group **2**:381
azobenzene **2**:381
Baeyer, Adolf von **3**:20–21
batik **3**:123–124
benzene **3**:206
bromine **3**:502
catechu **4**:202
chemical industry **4**:318
cobalt **5**:83
cochineal **5**:85
color **5**:113
colorimeter **5**:122
cosmetics **5**:281–283
gentian violet **9**:94
goldenrod **9**:233
heath **10**:99
heather **10**:99
henna **10**:121–122
Hofmann, August Wilhelm von **10**:196
indigo **11**:144
lake (dye) **12**:169
laser and maser **12**:213 *table*
logwood **12**:397–398
oak **14**:311
organic chemistry **14**:438–439
Perkin, Sir William Henry **15**:172
pokeweed **15**:387
safflower **17**:11
saffron **17**:11
tamarind **19**:18
textile industry **19**:137
turmeric **19**:349
Tyrian purple **19**:367
woad **20**:195
yellowwood **20**:323
DYER (Tennessee)
map (36° 4'N 88° 59'W) **19**:104
DYER (county in Tennessee)
map (36° 5'N 89° 25'W) **19**:104
DYER, MARY **6**:318–319 *bibliog.*
DYER-BENNETT, RICHARD **6**:319 *bibliog.*
DYERSBURG (Tennessee)
map (36° 3'N 89° 23'W) **19**:104
DYERSVILLE (Iowa)
map (42° 29'N 91° 8'W) **11**:244
DYFED (Wales) **6**:319
Carmarthen **4**:153
DYING *see* DEATH AND DYING
DYING GAUL **6**:319
DYJE RIVER
map (48° 37'N 16° 56'E) **5**:413
DYLAN, BOB **6**:319 *bibliog.*
rock music **16**:248
"DYMAXION" PRINCIPLES
Fuller, R. Buckminster **8**:357–358
DYNAMIC RANDOM ACCESS MEMORY *see* DRAM
DYNAMICS (geology)
Earth, heat flow in **7**:17–18
earthquakes **7**:25–27
force **8**:220
plate tectonics **15**:351–357
volcano **19**:626–628
water wave **20**:57–60
waves and wave motion **20**:71–72
DYNAMICS (mechanical) **6**:319 *bibliog.*
See also MECHANICAL ENGINEERING
DYNAMITE **6**:319
explosives **7**:339
nitroglycerin **14**:203
Nobel, Alfred **14**:208
DYNAMO *see* GENERATOR
DYNAMO THEORY **6**:319
Earth, geomagnetic field of **7**:15–16
DYNAMOMETER **6**:319–320
Froude, William **8**:346
DYNE **6**:320
erg **7**:228
DYNEIN
biological locomotion **3**:265
DYSENTERY **6**:320
amebiasis **1**:326
amoeba **1**:376
colitis **5**:102
Entamoeba **7**:208
food poisoning and infection **8**:211
gastrointestinal tract disease **9**:57
parasitic cycle **15**:83 *illus.*
protozoal diseases **15**:581
Shigella **17**:260
DYSLEXIA **6**:320 *bibliog.*
DYSMENORRHEA **6**:320
DYSPAREUNIA
menopause **13**:299
DYSPEPSIA *see* INDIGESTION
DYSPLASIA **6**:320
bone diseases **3**:377
DYSPROSIUM **6**:320
element **7**:130 *table*
lanthanide series **6**:320; **12**:200–201
metal, metallic element **13**:328
metallic element **6**:320
DYSTHEMIA *see* DEPRESSION (psychology)
DYUSHAMBE *see* DUSHANBE (USSR)
DZAOUDZI (Mayotte)
map (12° 47'S 45° 17'E) **5**:153
DZERZHINSKY, FELIKS EDMUNDOVICH **6**:320
KGB **12**:64
DZHANIBEKOV, VLADIMIR (cosmonaut) **6**:320
DZIERŻONIÓW (Poland)
map (50° 44'N 16° 39'E) **15**:388
DZUBAS, FRIEDEL **6**:320
DZUNGARIAN BASIN
map (45° 0'N 88° 0'E) **13**:529

E

E (letter) **7**:3 *illus.*
H (letter) **10**:3
e (mathematics) **7**:3 *illus.*
irrational number **11**:280
logarithm **12**:394
mathematics, history of **13**:226
Millikan's oil-drop experiment **13**:430
E LAYER *see* IONOSPHERE
E PLURIBUS UNUM **7**:3
EA **7**:3
Eridu **7**:229
mythology **13**:696
EADS (Colorado)
map (38° 29'N 102° 47'W) **5**:116
EADS, JAMES BUCHANAN **7**:3
bridge (engineering) **3**:481
EAGAR (Arizona)
map (34° 6'N 109° 11'W) **2**:160
EAGELS, JEANNE **7**:3 *bibliog.*
EAGLE **7**:3–4 *bibliog., illus.*
bald eagle **3**:280 *illus.*
beak **3**:289 *illus.*
golden eagle **3**:291 *illus.*; **13**:623 *illus.*
foot **3**:288 *illus.*
tawny eagle **17**:98 *illus.*
EAGLE (Alaska)
map (64° 46'N 141° 16'W) **1**:242
EAGLE (Colorado)
map (39° 39'N 106° 50'W) **5**:116
EAGLE (county in Colorado)
map (39° 40'N 106° 40'W) **5**:116
EAGLE BAY (British Columbia)
map (50° 56'N 119° 12'W) **3**:491
EAGLE BUTTE (South Dakota)
map (45° 0'N 101° 14'W) **18**:103
EAGLE CREEK (Indiana)
map (39° 50'N 86° 18'W) **11**:111
EAGLE CREEK (Kentucky)
map (38° 36'N 85° 4'W) **12**:47
EAGLE GROVE (Iowa)
map (42° 40'N 93° 54'W) **11**:244
EAGLE LAKE (Maine)
map (47° 2'N 68° 36'W) **13**:70
EAGLE LAKE (Texas)
map (29° 35'N 96° 20'W) **19**:129
EAGLE MOUNTAIN (Minnesota)
map (47° 54'N 90° 33'W) **13**:453
EAGLE MOUNTAIN (Texas)
map (30° 55'N 105° 5'W) **19**:129
EAGLE NEST BUTTE (South Dakota)
map (43° 27'N 101° 39'W) **18**:103
EAGLE PASS (Texas)
map (28° 43'N 100° 30'W) **19**:129
EAGLE PEAK (California)
map (41° 17'N 120° 12'W) **4**:31
EAGLE RIVER (Michigan)
map (47° 24'N 88° 18'W) **13**:377
EAGLE RIVER (Wisconsin)
map (45° 55'N 89° 15'W) **20**:185
EAGLETON, THOMAS F. **7**:4
EAKINS, THOMAS **7**:4–5 *bibliog., illus.*
American art and architecture **1**:333
Marey, Étienne Jules **13**:148
Max Schmitt in a Single Scull **7**:5 *illus.*
Philadelphia Museum of Art **15**:229
Tanner, Henry **19**:24
EAM-ELAS **7**:5
Greece **9**:328
EAMES, CHARLES **7**:5 *bibliog.*
chair **8**:379 *illus.*
EAMES, EMMA **7**:5–6 *bibliog.*
EANES, ANTÓNIO DOS SANTOS RAMALHO **7**:6
EANNA
Uruk **19**:490
EAR **7**:6–7 *bibliog., illus.*
audio frequency **2**:318; **18**:73 *table*
ear disease **7**:7–8
earwax **7**:30
eustachian tube **7**:310
hearing aid **10**:89
lizard **12**:380
mammal **13**:97
motion sickness **13**:610
owl **14**:473
physiology
Bárány, Robert **3**:75
Helmholtz, Hermann Ludwig Ferdinand von **10**:115–116
reptile **16**:171
senses **17**:204
snake **17**:378
space medicine **18**:133
surgery **18**:362
tinnitus **19**:206
vestibular system **3**:265
vertigo **19**:563
EAR DISEASE **7**:7–8 *bibliog.*
deafness **6**:66–67
environmental health **7**:210–212
mastoiditis **13**:217
Meniere's disease **13**:297
EAR SHELL *see* ABALONE
EARHART, AMELIA **7**:8 *bibliog.*
EARL (title)
titles of nobility and honor **19**:213
EARL, RALPH **7**:8 *bibliog.*
EARLE (Arkansas)
map (35° 16'N 90° 28'W) **2**:166
EARLESS MONITOR **7**:8
EARLIMART (California)
map (35° 53'N 119° 16'W) **4**:31
EARLINGTON (Kentucky)
map (37° 16'N 87° 30'W) **12**:47
EARLVILLE (New York)
map (42° 44'N 75° 33'W) **14**:149
EARLY (county in Georgia)
map (31° 20'N 84° 55'W) **9**:114
EARLY, JUBAL A. **7**:8 *bibliog., illus.*
Civil War, U.S. **5**:30
EARLY AUTUMN (book)
Bromfield, Louis **3**:502
EARLY BIRD (artificial satellite) **7**:8–9; **18**:123 *illus.*
communications satellite **5**:144–145
EARLY CHRISTIAN ART AND ARCHITECTURE **2**:193–194; **7**:9–11 *bibliog., illus.*
altar **1**:311
Anthemius of Tralles **2**:49
apse **2**:92
architecture **2**:133
atrium **2**:313
baptistery **3**:73
basilica **3**:109–110
Byzantine art and architecture **3**:604–606
catacombs **4**:197
cathedrals and churches **4**:204 *illus.*
Celtic art **4**:238–241
chalice **4**:271
cloister **5**:64
Coptic art and architecture **5**:255
cross **5**:360–361
Galla Placidia, Mausoleum of **9**:16
icon **11**:20
iconography **11**:21
illuminated manuscripts **11**:46–47
ivory and ivory carving **11**:337
Merovingian art and architecture **13**:311
monastic art and architecture **13**:517–521
mosaic **13**:594–595
mural painting **13**:646
painting **15**:19
Passion cycle **15**:105
reliquary **16**:143–144
Saint Mark's Basilica **17**:23–24
San Vitale **17**:58
Santa Costanza **17**:67
Sant'Ambrogio **17**:69
sarcophagus **17**:75–76
sculpture **17**:161–162 *illus.*

tomb **19**:231
triumphal arch **19**:304
EARLY CHRISTIAN CHURCH
Acts of the Apostles **1**:90–91
adoptionism **1**:107
Ambrose, Saint **1**:325
Antioch (Turkey) **2**:64
Apocryphal New Testament **2**:79
Apostolic Fathers **2**:85
apostolic succession **2**:85
Athanasius, Saint **2**:288
Augustine, Saint **2**:320–321
cathedrals and churches **4**:204
christological controversy
Apollinarianism **2**:79
Arianism **2**:153–154
Docetism **6**:210
Eutyches **7**:311
Jesus Christ **11**:405–406
Monarchianism **13**:517
Monophysitism **13**:537
Monothelitism **13**:540
Sabellianism **17**:5
Clement of Alexandria, Saint **5**:49
Clement I, Saint **5**:49
council, ecumenical **5**:309–310
Chalcedon, Council of **4**:270
Constantinople, Councils of **5**:209
Ephesus, Council of **7**:216
Cyprian, Saint **5**:407
Cyril of Alexandria, Saint **5**:410
Cyril of Jerusalem, Saint **5**:410
Didache **6**:160
Dionysius the Great **6**:184
Donatists **6**:237
Ebionites **7**:35–36
Eusebius of Caesarea **7**:310
Eusebius of Nicomedia **7**:310
Fathers of the Church **8**:34
Gregory VII, Pope **9**:357
hymn **10**:346
Ignatius of Antioch, Saint **11**:33
Irenaeus, Saint **11**:265
Jerome, Saint **11**:398
Justin Martyr, Saint **11**:478
Lactantius, Lucius Caecilius Firmianus **12**:161
Leo I, Pope **12**:288
Macarius the Egyptian, Saint **13**:5
Marcion **13**:147
Martin of Tours, Saint **13**:179–180
Maximus, Saint **13**:241
Meletius of Antioch, Saint **13**:287
Montanism **13**:551
Nag Hammadi Papyri **14**:5
Neoplatonism **14**:85
Nestorianism **14**:97
Novatian **14**:272
Origen **14**:443
Palladius, Saint **15**:48
Papias of Hierapolis **15**:71
patristic literature **15**:113–114
Paul, Saint **15**:116–117
Paulicians **15**:119
Pelagianism **15**:137
Peter, Saint **15**:199–200
Peter Damian, Saint **15**:200
Polycarp, Saint **15**:418
Priscillian **15**:553
pseudepigrapha **15**:587
Simon Magus **17**:315
Tatian **19**:44
Tertullian **19**:125
Theodore of Mopsuestia **19**:156
Theodoret **19**:156
Valentinus **19**:505
Vincent of Lérins, Saint **19**:600
EARLY MAN *see* PREHISTORIC HUMANS
EARNED INCOME *see* INCOME, PERSONAL; WAGES
EARP, WYATT 7:11 *bibliog.*
EARTH, GEOLOGICAL HISTORY OF 7:11–15 *bibliog., illus., map*
catastrophism **4**:201
continental drift **5**:228–229
Conybeare, W. D. **5**:234
Desmarest, Nicolas **6**:132
Earth, structure and composition of 7:19–23
fossil record **8**:243–248
geochemistry **9**:95–97
geologic time **9**:103–105
geology **9**:105–106
Gondwanaland **9**:243
Holmes, Arthur **10**:205
Hurley, Patrick Mason **10**:316
Hutton, James **10**:323–324
ice ages **11**:7–11
igneous rock **11**:33–36
Joly, John **11**:441
Lehmann, Johann Gottlob **12**:276
Lyell, Sir Charles **12**:474–475
mid-oceanic ridge **13**:389–390
Miller, Stanley Lloyd **13**:428
Oppel, Albert **14**:407
Orbigny, Alcide Dessalines D' **14**:416
paleobotany **15**:30–32
paleoclimatology **15**:32–34
paleoecology **15**:34–35
paleogeography **15**:35–38
paleomagnetism **15**:41–42
paleontology **15**:42
paleotemperature **15**:42
polar wandering **15**:393
radiometric age-dating **16**:65–67
unconformity **19**:382
uniformitarianism **19**:386
valley and ridge province **19**:507–508
EARTH, GEOMAGNETIC FIELD OF 7:15–17 *bibliog., illus., map*
convection cell **5**:232
distribution 7:15
dynamo theory **6**:319
geophysics **9**:108
GEOS (artificial satellite) **9**:119
Lomond, Loch **12**:400
magnetic declination worldwide 7:16 *map*
magnetic poles **16**:318
magnetic poles reversal **15**:42 *table*
magnetic storm **13**:55
magnetism **13**:56
Gilbert, William **9**:179
magnetosphere **13**:59–60 *illus.*
OGO (artificial satellite) **14**:355
paleomagnetism **15**:41–42
plate tectonics **15**:353; **15**:357
polar wandering **15**:393
Ross, Sir James Clark **16**:318
Van Allen radiation belts **19**:510
variation with time 7:16
EARTH, GRAVITATIONAL FIELD OF 7:17 *bibliog., illus.*
density current **6**:114
geoid and gravity anomalies 7:17
geophysics **9**:108
GEOS (artificial satellite) **9**:119
hill regions
three-body problem **19**:182
peturbation **15**:191
tide **19**:193–194 *illus.*
value of gravity 7:17
EARTH, HEAT FLOW IN 7:17–18 *bibliog.*
convection 7:17–18
convection cell **5**:232
Fourier, Joseph **8**:253
geochemistry **9**:96–97
geothermal energy **9**:120–121
ground temperature **9**:373
Hall, Sir James **10**:22
Jeffreys, Sir Harold **11**:394
lithosphere **12**:371
magma **13**:51–52
paleogeography **15**:37
plate tectonics **15**:356–357
EARTH, MOTIONS OF 7:18–19 *bibliog., illus.*
celestial sphere **4**:230
Coriolis effect **5**:263
day **6**:54
earthquakes 7:25–28
geophysics **9**:108
Heracleides Ponticus **10**:131
nutation **14**:301
occultation **14**:320
paleomagnetism **15**:41–42
parallax **15**:78–79
parsec **15**:98
radar astronomy **16**:40
revolution of 7:18 *illus.*
rotation of 7:18 *illus.*
subsidence **18**:316
time (physics) **19**:201
volcano **19**:626–628
Von Arx, William S. **19**:633
year **20**:320
zodiac **20**:371
EARTH, SIZE AND SHAPE OF 7:19 *bibliog., illus.*
Clairaut, Alexis Claude **5**:35
continental drift **5**:228–229
Eratosthenes of Cyrene 7:227–228
geomorphology **9**:107
geophysics **9**:108
GEOS (artificial satellite) **9**:119
geosyncline **9**:119–120
hypsographic curve **10**:351
landform evolution **12**:182–183 *illus.*
latitude **12**:234–235
longitude **12**:409
maps and mapmaking **13**:138–142
North Pole **14**:252
ocean and sea **14**:325–332
oceanic trenches **14**:341–342
paleogeography **15**:35–38
physiography **15**:287
Picard, Jean **15**:290
plateau **15**:358
South Pole **18**:106
submarine canyon **18**:316
Vening Meinesz, Felix **19**:545
EARTH, STRUCTURE AND COMPOSITION OF 7:19–23 *bibliog., illus.*
atmosphere **2**:298–304
atmospheric refraction **2**:304
exosphere 7:333
greenhouse effect **9**:351–352
ionosphere **11**:241–242
basement rock **3**:108
crater impact modification 7:23
crust 7:19–23
chlorine **4**:400
diastrophism **6**:153
fault **8**:36–38
feldspar **8**:46–47
fold **8**:194–195
fossil record **8**:243
horst and graben **10**:253–254
isostasy **11**:300
lithosphere **12**:371
mid-oceanic ridge **13**:390
nickel **14**:183
orogeny **14**:447
plate tectonics **15**:351–357 *map*
Precambrian time **15**:492
silicate minerals **17**:304–305
structural geology **18**:303
subduction zone **18**:312–313
submarine canyon **18**:316
Tertiary Period **19**:122–124
transform fault **19**:269–270
Vening Meinesz, Felix **19**:545
Dalton, John **6**:14–15
Dana, James Dwight **6**:20
Deep-Sea Drilling Project **6**:77
density
Cavendish, Henry **4**:225
Earth, geological history of 7:11–15
Earth, geomagnetic field of 7:16
Earth, heat flow in 7:17–18
earthquakes 7:25–28
erosion cycle 7:232
evaporation 7:313
feldspar **8**:46–47
fossil record **8**:243–248
fumarole **8**:358
geochemistry **9**:95–97
geology, dynamical **9**:105
geophysics **9**:108
granite **9**:287
Gutenberg, Beno **9**:408
Hall, Sir James **10**:22
igneous rock **11**:33–36
island arc **11**:297–298
isostasy **11**:300
Jeffreys, Sir Harold **11**:394
kimberlite **12**:77
landform evolution **12**:181–183
lithosphere **12**:371
magma **13**:51–52
mantle **13**:130 *illus.*
mineral **13**:438–444
Mohorovičić discontinuity **13**:503
native elements **14**:47
natural gas **14**:47–48
olivine **14**:379
orogeny **14**:447
periodic table **15**:166–169
petrology **15**:215
plate tectonics 7:21–22; **15**:351–357
rock **16**:247
sand dune **17**:60
sedimentary rock **17**:184–186
seismometer **17**:189–190 *illus.*
silicate minerals **17**:305
soil **18**:36–38
soil mechanics **18**:38
stage **18**:210
stishovite **18**:273
Strachey, John **18**:287
stromatolite **18**:302
structural geology **18**:303
subduction zone **18**:312–313
syncline and anticline **18**:406
theory of origin 7:20
unconformity **19**:382
geology **9**:105 *illus.*
uniformitarianism **19**:386
volcano **19**:626–628
water **20**:47
hydrologic cycle **10**:341–342
hydrologic sciences **10**:342
hydrosphere **10**:344
water resources **20**:51–52
EARTH-MOVING MACHINERY 7:23–24 *illus.*
dredging **6**:268–269
roads and highways **16**:239 *illus.*
EARTH PIG *see* AARDVARK
EARTH RESOURCES TECHNOLOGY SATELLITE *see* LANDSAT (artificial satellite)
EARTH SCIENCES 7:24 *bibliog.*
astronomy and astrophysics 7:24
chemistry 7:24
convection cell **5**:232
cosmology 7:24
Earth, geomagnetic field of 7:15–17
Earth, structure and composition of 7:21
ecology 7:24
erosion and sedimentation 7:232–234
Ewing, Maurice 7:325
geochemistry **9**:95–97
geologic time **9**:103–105
geology 7:24; **9**:105–106
geophysics **9**:107–108
glaciers and glaciation **9**:192–195
hydrologic cycle **10**:341–342
hydrologic sciences 7:24
laccolith **12**:158
Landsat **12**:184–185
landslide and avalanche **12**:192
Meteor Crater **13**:337
meteorology 7:24
oceanography 7:24
pack ice **15**:10–11
paleogeography **15**:35–38
physics 7:24
plate tectonics **15**:351–357
pollution, environmental **15**:411–415
professional and educational organizations **17**:145 *table*
Sorby, Henry Clifton **18**:68
United States Geological Survey **19**:462
volcano **19**:626–628
weathering **20**:82–83
EARTH SNAKE 7:24
EARTH TIDE (geology) 7:25 *bibliog.*
EARTH WOLF *see* AARDWOLF
EARTH-WORSHIP
Dogon **6**:223
EARTHENWARE *see* DELFTWARE; FAÏENCE; POTTERY AND PORCELAIN
EARTHQUAKES 7:25–28 *bibliog., illus., map, tables*
Concepción (Chile) **5**:169
density current **6**:114
Dutton, Clarence Edward **6**:315–316
Ewing, Maurice 7:325
fault **8**:36–38
fold **8**:194–195
geology **9**:106
geophysics **9**:108
great earthquakes 7:28 *table*
hazard reduction 7:27
Huascarán **10**:287
Jeffreys, Sir Harold **11**:394
landslide and avalanche **12**:193
Managua (Nicaragua) **13**:108
measurement 7:25–27
Gutenberg, Beno **9**:408
Lamont-Doherty Geologic Observatory **12**:175
Richter scale **16**:215
seismogram **17**:189
seismometer **17**:189–190 *illus.*
microseism **13**:388
Mohorovičic discontinuity **13**:503
oceanic fracture zones **14**:339
orogeny **14**:447
plate tectonics **15**:352; **15**:357
prediction 7:27–28
inert gases **11**:161
rift valleys **16**:221
San Andreas Fault **17**:50
size 7:25–27
subduction zone **18**:312–313
transform fault **19**:269
tsunami **19**:325
Valparaíso (Chile) **19**:508
world distribution 7:26 *map*
EARTHSHINE 7:28
EARTHSTAR 7:28; **8**:368 *illus.*
EARTHWORKS 7:28 *bibliog., illus.*
Avebury **2**:369
environmental art 7:209–210
modern art **13**:495
Mound Builders **13**:617 *illus.*
North American archaeology **14**:239
Offa's Dyke **14**:353
Smithson, Robert **17**:372
Spiral Jetty (Robert Smithson) **2**:202 *illus.*
Stonehenge **18**:283
Tara **19**:34–35
EARTHWORM 7:29–30 *bibliog., illus.*
anatomy 7:29 *illus.*
annelid **2**:33

EARTHWORM (cont.)
biological locomotion **3**:266
skeletal system **17**:333
soil organisms **18**:39 *illus.*
worm **20**:283 *illus.*
EARWAX 7:30
EARWIG 7:30 *illus.*; **11**:192 *illus.*
soil organisms **18**:39 *illus.*
EASEMENT (law) 7:30
encumbrance 7:163
title **19**:213
EASLEY (South Carolina)
map (34° 50′N 82° 36′W) **18**:98
EAST AFRICA 7:30
See also BURUNDI; KENYA; RWANDA; SOMALIA; TANZANIA; UGANDA
EAST AFRICA COMPANY, BRITISH
Kampala (Uganda) **12**:10
Kenya **12**:56
EAST AFRICA COMPANY, GERMAN
Kenya **12**:56
EAST AFRICAN RIFT SYSTEM 7:30–31 *bibliog.*
Edward, Lake 7:67
Ethiopia 7:252
Great Rift Valley **9**:321–322 *illus.*
horst and graben **10**:254
igneous rock **11**:34
Malawi **13**:81
Nyasa, Lake **14**:308
plate tectonics **15**:351 *map*; **15**:353
rift valleys **16**:221
Rwanda **16**:378 *illus.*
EAST ANGLIA (England) **2**:3 *map*; 7:31 *bibliog.*
See also NORFOLK (England); SUFFOLK (county in England)
Danelaw **6**:31
EAST ASIA *see* ASIA; SOUTHEAST ASIA
EAST BATON ROUGE (county in Louisiana)
map (30° 30′N 91° 5′W) **12**:430
EAST BENGAL *see* BANGLADESH
EAST BERLIN *see* BERLIN (Germany, East and West)
EAST BERLIN (Pennsylvania)
map (39° 56′N 76° 59′W) **15**:147
EAST BREWTON (Alabama)
map (31° 5′N 87° 4′W) **1**:234
EAST BRIMFIELD LAKE
map (42° 6′N 72° 10′W) **13**:206
EAST BROOKLYN (Connecticut)
map (41° 48′N 71° 54′W) **5**:193
EAST BRUNSWICK (New Jersey)
map (40° 25′N 74° 23′W) **14**:129
EAST CAPE
map (37° 41′S 178° 33′E) **14**:158
EAST CARROLL (county in Louisiana)
map (32° 40′N 91° 15′W) **12**:430
EAST CHICAGO (Indiana)
map (41° 38′N 87° 27′W) **11**:111
EAST CHINA SEA *see* CHINA SEA, EAST
EAST CLEVELAND (Ohio)
map (41° 32′N 81° 35′W) **14**:357
EAST DISMAL SWAMP
map (35° 45′N 76° 35′W) **14**:242
EAST DOUGLAS (Massachusetts)
map (42° 4′N 71° 43′W) **13**:206
EAST ELY (Nevada)
map (39° 15′N 114° 53′W) **14**:111
EAST END (Virgin Islands)
map (18° 21′N 64° 40′W) **19**:605
EAST FALKLAND ISLAND
map (51° 55′S 59° 0′W) **2**:149
EAST FALMOUTH (Massachusetts)
map (41° 35′N 70° 34′W) **13**:206
EAST FELICIANA (county in Louisiana)
map (30° 52′N 91° 2′W) **12**:430
EAST FLEVOLAND (region in Netherlands)
map (52° 30′N 5° 45′E) **14**:99
EAST FRISIAN ISLANDS
map (53° 44′N 7° 25′E) **9**:140
EAST GERMANY *see* GERMANY, EAST AND WEST
EAST GLACIER PARK (Montana)
map (48° 27′N 113° 13′W) **13**:547
EAST GRAND FORKS (Minnesota)
map (47° 56′N 97° 1′W) **13**:453
EAST GREENWICH (Rhode Island)
map (41° 40′N 71° 27′W) **16**:198
EAST HARTFORD (Connecticut)
map (41° 46′N 72° 39′W) **5**:193
EAST HAVEN (Connecticut)
map (41° 17′N 72° 52′W) **5**:193
EAST HELENA (Montana)
map (46° 35′N 111° 56′W) **13**:547
EAST INDIA COMPANY, BRITISH **2**:256 *illus.*; 7:31 *bibliog.*, *illus.*
Asia, history of **2**:257
British Empire **3**:495–496 *illus.*
Calcutta (India) **4**:25
Clive, Robert **5**:61
Great Britain, history of **9**:313
India, history of **11**:92
joint-stock company **11**:440
tea **19**:53
EAST INDIA COMPANY, DUTCH 7:31–32 *bibliog.*
Asia, history of **2**:257
Netherlands **14**:102
spice trade **18**:181
EAST INDIA COMPANY, FRENCH 7:32 *bibliog.*
Asia, history of **2**:257
India, history of **11**:92
EAST INDIAMAN (merchant vessel) 7:31 *illus.*
ship **17**:268–269 *illus.*
EAST INDIES 7:32
spice trade **18**:180–181
EAST LANSING (Michigan)
map (42° 44′N 84° 29′W) **13**:377
EAST LAS VEGAS (Nevada)
map (36° 6′N 115° 3′W) **14**:111
EAST LAURINBURG (North Carolina)
map (34° 46′N 79° 27′W) **14**:242
EAST LIVERPOOL (Ohio)
map (40° 38′N 80° 35′W) **14**:357
EAST LONDON (South Africa) 7:32
map (33° 0′S 27° 55′E) **18**:79
EAST LONGMEADOW (Massachusetts)
map (42° 4′N 72° 31′W) **13**:206
EAST LOS ANGELES (California)
map (34° 1′N 118° 9′W) **4**:31
EAST LYNN LAKE
map (38° 5′N 82° 20′W) **20**:111
EAST MILLINOCKET (Maine)
map (45° 37′N 68° 35′W) **13**:70
EAST MOLINE (Illinois)
map (41° 31′N 90° 25′W) **11**:42
EAST NAPLES (Florida)
map (26° 8′N 81° 46′W) **8**:172
EAST NISHNABOTNA RIVER
map (40° 39′N 95° 37′W) **11**:244
EAST ORANGE (New Jersey)
map (40° 46′N 74° 13′W) **14**:129
EAST PAKISTAN *see* BANGLADESH
EAST PALATKA (Florida)
map (29° 40′N 81° 35′W) **8**:172
EAST PALESTINE (Ohio)
map (40° 50′N 80° 33′W) **14**:357
EAST PEPPERELL (Massachusetts)
map (42° 40′N 71° 34′W) **13**:206
EAST PINE (British Columbia)
map (55° 43′N 121° 13′W) **3**:491
EAST POINT (Georgia)
map (33° 40′N 84° 27′W) **9**:114
EAST POINT (Massachusetts)
map (42° 25′N 70° 54′W) **3**:409
EAST POINT (Prince Edward Island)
map (46° 27′N 61° 58′W) **15**:548
EAST PRAIRIE (Missouri)
map (36° 47′N 89° 23′W) **13**:476
EAST PROVIDENCE (Rhode Island)
map (41° 49′N 71° 23′W) **16**:198
EAST RIDGE (Tennessee)
map (35° 0′N 85° 15′W) **19**:104
EAST RIVER
map (40° 48′N 73° 48′W) **14**:129
EAST RUTHERFORD (New Jersey)
map (40° 51′N 74° 6′W) **14**:129
EAST SAINT LOUIS (Illinois)
map (38° 38′N 90° 9′W) **11**:42
EAST SIBERIAN SEA
map (74° 0′N 166° 0′E) **19**:388
EAST SPENCER (North Carolina)
map (35° 41′N 80° 26′W) **14**:242
EAST SUDBURY (Massachusetts)
map (42° 24′N 71° 24′W) **3**:409
EAST SULLIVAN (Maine)
map (44° 30′N 68° 9′W) **13**:70
EAST SUSSEX (England) *see* SUSSEX (England)
EAST TAWAS (Michigan)
map (44° 17′N 83° 29′W) **13**:377
EAST WALKER RIVER
map (38° 53′N 119° 10′W) **14**:111
EAST WALPOLE (Massachusetts)
map (42° 10′N 71° 13′W) **3**:409
EASTBOROUGH (Kansas)
map (37° 41′N 97° 16′W) **12**:18
EASTBOURNE (England)
map (50° 46′N 0° 17′E) **19**:403
EASTBOURNE (New Zealand)
map (41° 18′S 174° 54′E) **14**:158
EASTER 7:32 *bibliog.*
Egg (Fabergé) **16**:363 *illus.*
Good Friday **9**:245
Jesus Christ **11**:403–405
resurrection **16**:183
EASTER ISLAND 7:32–33 *bibliog.*, *illus.*, *map*
Heyerdahl, Thor **10**:155
hieroglyphics
Malayo-Polynesian languages **13**:83
history 7:33
map (27° 7′S 109° 22′W) **14**:334
Oceanic art **14**:338 *illus.*
EASTER RISING 7:33 *bibliog.*, *illus.*
Ireland, history of **11**:264 *illus.*
Irish Republican Army **11**:269
EASTERN AUSTALIAN NATIVE CAT **13**:175 *illus.*
EASTERN BAY (Chesapeake Bay)
map (38° 51′N 76° 19′W) **13**:188
EASTERN CHURCH *see* ORTHODOX CHURCH
EASTERN CORDILLERA MOUNTAINS (Bolivia)
map (17° 30′S 64° 30′W) **3**:366
EASTERN CORDILLERA MOUNTAINS (Colombia)
map (6° 0′N 73° 0′W) **5**:107
EASTERN CORDILLERA MOUNTAINS (Peru)
map (11° 0′S 74° 0′W) **15**:193
EASTERN DESERT *see* ARABIAN DESERT
EASTERN EUROPE 7:33
See also BULGARIA; CZECHOSLOVAKIA; ESTONIAN SOVIET SOCIALIST REPUBLIC (USSR); HUNGARY; LATVIAN SOVIET SOCIALIST REPUBLIC (USSR); LITHUANIAN SOVIET SOCIALIST REPUBLIC (USSR); POLAND; ROMANIA; YUGOSLAVIA
art
folk art **8**:196 *illus.*
chemical industry **4**:319
Council for Mutual Economic Assistance **5**:310
history
cold war **5**:98–99
communism **5**:148
Europe, history of 7:289–290
migration to the United States **11**:55 *map*
neolithic period
European prehistory 7:301–302
physical features
Carpathian Mountains **4**:163 *map*
regions
Balkans **3**:38–40 *map*
Baltic States **3**:55 *map*
Bessarabia **3**:228
Bucovina **3**:537
Macedonia **13**:15 *map*
Moldavia **13**:505
Ruthenia **16**:375
Silesia **17**:304
Walachia **20**:8–9
Slavs **17**:359
theater
puppet **15**:627
Warsaw Treaty Organization **20**:32
EASTERN GHATS (mountains)
map (14° 0′N 78° 50′E) **11**:80
EASTERN ORTHODOX CHURCH *see* ORTHODOX CHURCH
EASTERN QUESTION 7:33–34 *bibliog.*, *illus.*
Crimean War **5**:348
Ottoman Empire **14**:466
EASTERN RITE CHURCHES 7:34 *bibliog.*, *table*
canon law **4**:114; **4**:115
icon **11**:20
iconography **11**:21–22
iconostasis **11**:24
Maronites **13**:162
monks **16**:138 *illus.*
Sigismund III, King of Poland **17**:299
EASTERN ROMAN EMPIRE *see* BYZANTINE EMPIRE
EASTHAM (Massachusetts)
map (41° 50′N 69° 58′W) **13**:206
EASTHAMPTON (Massachusetts)
map (42° 16′N 72° 40′W) **13**:206
EASTLAKE (Michigan)
map (44° 15′N 86° 18′W) **13**:377
EASTLAND (Texas)
map (32° 24′N 98° 49′W) **19**:129
EASTLAND (county in Texas)
map (32° 18′N 98° 52′W) **19**:129
EASTLAND, JAMES O. 7:34
EASTMAIN (Quebec)
map (52° 15′N 78° 30′W) **16**:18
EASTMAIN RIVER
map (52° 15′N 78° 35′W) **16**:18
EASTMAN (Georgia)
map (32° 12′N 83° 11′W) **9**:114
EASTMAN, GEORGE 7:34 *bibliog.*; **15**:270 *illus.*
Eastman School of Music 7:34
George Eastman House **9**:109–110
Rochester (New York) **16**:247
EASTMAN, MAX 7:34 *bibliog.*
EASTMAN, SETH
pioneers atttacked by Comanche Indians **8**:344 *illus.*
tribal council **11**:117 *illus.*
EASTMAN KODAK COMPANY
camera **4**:55
Eastman, George 7:34
EASTMAN SCHOOL OF MUSIC 7:34
EASTON (Maryland)
map (38° 46′N 76° 4′W) **13**:188
EASTON (Pennsylvania)
map (40° 42′N 75° 12′W) **15**:147
EASTON, DAVID 7:34
EASTPORT (Idaho)
map (48° 59′N 116° 11′W) **11**:26
EASTPORT (Maine)
map (44° 54′N 67° 0′W) **13**:70
EASTVILLE (Virginia)
map (37° 21′N 75° 57′W) **19**:607
EASTWOOD, CLINT 7:34 *bibliog.*
EATING DISORDERS
anorexia nervosa **2**:34
bulimia **3**:557
EATON (Colorado)
map (40° 32′N 104° 42′W) **5**:116
EATON (county in Michigan)
map (42° 35′N 84° 50′W) **13**:377
EATON (Ohio)
map (39° 45′N 84° 38′W) **14**:357
EATON, DORMAN BRIDGMAN 7:34–35
EATON, JOHN HENRY 7:35
EATON, MARGARET (Peggy) O'NEALE
Calhoun, John C. **4**:29
Eaton, John Henry 7:35
EATON, THEOPHILUS 7:35
EATON, WILLIAM
Tripolitan War **19**:303
EATON RAPIDS (Michigan)
map (42° 36′N 84° 39′W) **13**:377
EATONTON (Georgia)
map (33° 20′N 83° 23′W) **9**:114
EATONTOWN (New Jersey)
map (40° 18′N 74° 7′W) **14**:129
EAU CLAIRE (Wisconsin)
map (44° 49′N 91° 31′W) **20**:185
EAU CLAIRE (county in Wisconsin)
map (44° 45′N 91° 15′W) **20**:185
EAU CLAIRE RIVER
map (44° 55′N 89° 37′W) **20**:185
EBAN, ABBA 7:35
EBBINGHAUS, HERMANN 7:35 *bibliog.*, *illus.*
memory **13**:291
psychology, history of **15**:596
EBBITT HOUSE (District of Columbia) **10**:260 *illus.*
EBBO GOSPELS **12**:316 *illus.*
EBELING, GERHARD 7:35
EBENSBURG (Pennsylvania)
map (40° 29′N 78° 44′W) **15**:147
EBER
Ebla 7:36
EBERHART, RICHARD 7:35 *bibliog.*
EBERSWALDE (Germany, East and West)
map (52° 50′N 13° 49′E) **9**:140
EBERT, FRIEDRICH 7:35 *bibliog.*
EBIONITES 7:35–36
EBLA (Syria) 7:36 *bibliog.*
EBOLA RIVER
map (3° 20′N 20° 57′E) **20**:350
EBONY (botany) 7:36
EBONY (periodical) 7:36
Johnson, John Harold **11**:432–433
EBREO, GUGLIELMO 7:36 *bibliog.*
EBRIUM
Ebla 7:36
EBRO DELTA
map (40° 43′N 0° 54′E) **18**:140
EBRO RESERVOIR
map (43° 0′N 3° 58′W) **18**:140
EBRO RIVER 7:36
map (42° 15′N 1° 57′W) **18**:140
EÇA DE QUEIROZ, JOSÉ MARIA 7:36
Portuguese literature **15**:457
ECBATANA 7:37
See also HAMADAN
ECCE HOMO (Dirk Bouts) **3**:425 *illus.*
ECCENTRICITY (mathematics) 7:37
conic sections **5**:188
ellipse 7:147
hyperbola **10**:348
parabola **15**:74
ECCLES, SIR JOHN 7:37
ECCLESIASTES, BOOK OF 7:37
ECCLESIASTICAL ARCHITECTURE *see* CATHEDRALS AND CHURCHES
ECCLESIASTICAL COSTUME *see* VESTMENTS

ECCLESIASTICUS *see* SIRACH, BOOK OF
ECDYSONE
hormone, animal **10**:237 *table*
molting **13**:513
ECHAURREN, ROBERTO SEBASTIÁN MATTA *see* MATTA ECHAURREN, ROBERTO SEBASTIÁN
ECHEGARAY Y EIZAGUIRRE, JOSÉ 7:37
ECHEVE IBIA, BALTASAR DE
Latin American art and architecture **12**:226
ECHEVERRÍA, ESTEBAN 7:37
ECHEVERRÍA ÁLVAREZ, LUIS 7:37 *bibliog.*
Mexico, history of **13**:366
ECHIDNA *see* SPINY ANTEATER
ECHINODERM 7:37–39 *bibliog., illus.*; **15**:35 *illus.*
anatomy 7:37–38 *illus.*
blastoid **3**:328
brittle star **3**:499
coral reef **5**:260
crinoid **2**:350
Devonian Period **6**:146
invertebrate **11**:235
Ordovician Period **14**:421
Paleozoic Era **15**:43
sea cucumber **17**:168
shell **17**:250
Silurian Period **17**:310 *illus.*
skeletal system **17**:333
starfish **18**:226–227
ECHINUS **2**:131 *illus.*
ECHO (Minnesota)
map (44° 37′N 95° 25′W) **13**:453
ECHO (mythology) 7:39
ECHO (satellite) 7:39
ECHOLALIA *see* CATATONIA
ECHOLOCATION 7:39 *bibliog.*
bat **3**:119; **3**:120 *illus.*; **3**:121
ear 7:6
seal **17**:174
ECHOLS (county in Georgia)
map (30° 45′N 82° 55′W) **9**:114
ECHOPRAXIA *see* CATATONIA
ECHYNODERM
cystoid **5**:411
ÉCIJA (Spain)
map (37° 32′N 5° 5′W) **18**:140
ECK, JOHANN 7:39
Leipzig (East Germany) **12**:278
ECKERMANN, JOHANN PETER 7:39
ECKERSBERG, C.W.
Scandinavian art and architecture **17**:113
ECKERT, JOHN PRESPER 7:39
computer **5**:160a *illus.*
computer industry **5**:160n
Mauchly, John William **13**:232
UNIVAC **19**:467
ECKHART, MEISTER 7:39 *bibliog.*
ECLAMPSIA 7:39–40
ECLECTIC (Alabama)
map (32° 37′N 86° 2′W) **1**:234
ECLECTICISM (art) 7:40
house (in Western architecture) **10**:270
Pope, John Russell **15**:430–431
Post, George Browne **15**:458–459
Saint Joseph's Fountain **15**:464 *illus.*
ECLECTICISM (philosophy) 7:40
ECLIPSE 7:40–41 *bibliog., illus., table*
dates of occurrence 1980–89 7:41 *table*
flash spectrum **8**:154
lunar eclipse 7:40–41 *illus., table*
pulsar **15**:621
saros **17**:78
solar eclipse 7:40–41 *illus.*; **18**:344 *illus.*
ECLIPSING BINARY STAR *see* BINARY STARS
ECLIPTIC 7:41
celestial sphere **4**:230
coordinate systems (astronomy) **5**:246
equinox 7:226
zodiac **20**:371
zodiacal light **20**:371
ECLOGITE 7:41–42 *bibliog.*
facies, metamorphic rock **13**:332 *table*
ECLOGUE 7:42
Barclay, Alexander **3**:80
Encina, Juan del 7:162
Vergil **19**:551
ECOGEOGRAPHY **9**:103
ÉCOLE DES ARTS ET MÉTIERS
Canadian art and architecture **4**:88
ÉCOLE DES BEAUX-ARTS 7:42 *bibliog.*
academies of art **1**:69–70
Bouguereau, Adolph William **3**:421
Carrère and Hastings **4**:168
Grand Central Terminal **9**:285
Hunt, Richard Morris **10**:312
Institut de France **11**:195
World's Columbian Exposition of 1893 **20**:282
ECOLOGY 7:42–46 *bibliog., illus.*
See also ENVIRONMENT; HUMAN ECOLOGY
archaeology **2**:120
biology **3**:268
biome **3**:272–274
biosphere **3**:276–277
carbon cycle (atmosphere) **4**:136
Carson, Rachel **4**:170
chaparral **4**:283–284
climate **5**:55–58
communities 7:42–43
climax community **5**:59
conservation **5**:201–204
coral reef **5**:258–260
desert life **6**:129–131
diseases, animal **6**:190
drought **6**:273–274
Earth sciences 7:24
ecological niches
grass **9**:297
Hutchinson, George Evelyn **10**:322–323
ecosystems 7:43–45 *illus.*
Elton, Charles 7:150
Odum, Eugene P. **14**:350
endangered species 7:165–168
eutrophication 7:311
evolution and adaptation 7:46
food chain 7:44–45 *illus.*
aquatic 7:43 *illus.*
marine food chain **14**:330 *illus.*
pesticides **15**:198 *illus.*
plankton **15**:332–333
forest **8**:227–230
grasslands **9**:299–301
habitat **10**:4–6
hydrologic cycle **10**:342
infectious diseases **11**:166
intertidal life **11**:229–230
jungle and rain forest **11**:468–470
lake (body of water) **12**:167–169
landfill **12**:181
mathematical models 7:46
mountain life **13**:622–623
national parks **14**:44
nutrient cycles **14**:302–304
oceanic nutrients **14**:341
oil spills **14**:363–364
organisms, ecological classification of organisms 7:42
paleoecology **15**:34–35
poisonous plants and animals **15**:385
polar life 7:43–46
population dynamics **15**:438–439
remote sensing **16**:147
savanna life **17**:97–99
steppe life **18**:257
swamp, marsh, and bog **18**:376–378
tundra **19**:332–333
water quality **20**:50–51
ECONOMETRICS 7:46–47 *bibliog.*
Frisch, Ragnar **8**:334
Kantorovich, Leonid V. **12**:24
Koopmans, Tjalling C. **12**:110
Tinbergen, Jan **19**:206
ECONOMIC ADVISERS, COUNCIL OF *see* COUNCIL OF ECONOMIC ADVISERS
ECONOMIC ANALYSIS, BUREAU OF
Commerce, U.S. Department of **5**:138
ECONOMIC COOPERATION ADMINISTRATION
Marshall Plan **13**:173
ECONOMIC DEVELOPMENT
Agency for International Development **1**:183
foreign aid **8**:224–225
International Development Association **11**:220
International Finance Corporation **11**:220
Third World **19**:170
United Nations **19**:412–413
World Bank **20**:218
ECONOMIC GEOGRAPHY **9**:103
Thünen, Johann Heinrich von **19**:185
ECONOMIC GEOLOGY **9**:105
geochemistry **9**:95
ECONOMIC OPPORTUNITY ACT
War on Poverty **20**:28
ECONOMIC PLANNING 7:47 *bibliog.*
Colombo Plan **5**:109
Council of Economic Advisers **5**:310
Council for Mutual Economic Assistance (USSR) **5**:310
economy, national 7:49–51
fiscal policy **8**:109–110
mixed economy **13**:486
monetary policy **13**:524
Organization for Economic Cooperation and Development **14**:440
ECONOMIC AND SOCIAL COUNCIL (UN)
United Nations **19**:413
ECONOMICS 7:47–49 *bibliog.*
banking systems **2**:68–69
basic concepts 7:47–48
capital **4**:123
capitalism **4**:124–126
class, social **5**:40–41
computer modeling **5**:162
conservation **5**:203–204
distribution (economics) **6**:200
econometrics 7:46–47
economic planning 7:47
economists
Bagehot, Walter **3**:21
Baruch, Bernard M. **3**:99
Burns, Arthur F. **3**:578
Commons, John R. **5**:141
Fisher, Irving **8**:122
Friedman, Milton **8**:331–332
Galbraith, John Kenneth **9**:13
Heller, Walter **10**:115
Hobson, John A. **10**:193
Kantorovich, Leonid V. **12**:24
Keynes, John Maynard **12**:63–64
Lewis, Sir Arthur **12**:305
Malthus, Thomas Robert **13**:96
Marshall, Alfred **13**:171
Mitchell, Wesley Clair **13**:483–484
Ricardo, David **16**:206
Say, Jean Baptiste **17**:106
Schumpeter, Joseph A. **17**:137
Smith, Adam **17**:366–367
Turgot, Anne Robert Jacques **19**:341–342
Veblen, Thorstein B. **19**:529
Volcker, Paul **19**:628
foreign policy **8**:225–226
game theory **9**:27–29
gross national product **9**:371
history 7:48–49
laissez-faire **12**:167
manorialism **13**:126–127
mercantilism **13**:303
physiocrats **15**:286–287
inflation **11**:169–171
input-output analysis **11**:182
interest **11**:207
international organizations
Bank for International Settlements **3**:67
Council for Mutual Economic Assistance **5**:310
European Economic Community 7:299–300
European Free Trade Association 7:300–301
International Monetary Fund **11**:222
Latin American Integration Association **12**:228
Organization for Economic Cooperation and Development **14**:440
Organization of Petroleum Exporting Countries **14**:440
World Bank **20**:218
international trade **11**:223–224
macroeconomics 7:47–49
Marxism **13**:183–184
microeconomics 7:47–49
mixed economy **13**:486
monetary theory **13**:524–525
money **13**:525–527
monopoly and competition (economics) **13**:537–540
neoclassical tradition 7:49
Nobel Prize **14**:208 *table*
Arrow, Kenneth Joseph **2**:188
Frisch, Ragnar **8**:334
Hayek, Friedrich August von **10**:82
Hicks, Sir John Richard **10**:158
Koopmans, Tjalling C. **12**:110
Kuznets, Simon S. **12**:142
Leontief, Wassily **12**:292
Lewis, Sir Arthur **12**:305
Myrdal, Gunnar **13**:691
Ohlin, Bertil **14**:363
Samuelson, Paul A. **17**:49
Simon, Herbert A. **17**:315
Tinbergen, Jan **19**:206
price system **15**:535
professional and research organizations
Brookings Institution **3**:510
Committee for Economic Development **5**:138
profit **15**:561–562
recession **16**:107
saving and investment **17**:100
stagflation **18**:211
supply and demand **18**:353–354
supply-side economics 7:49
zaibatsu **20**:348
ECONOMIST, THE (periodical) 7:49
Bagehot, Walter **3**:21
ECONOMY, NATIONAL 7:49–51 *bibliog., illus.*
econometrics 7:46–47
economic planning 7:47
economics 7:48–49
Egypt, ancient 7:84
finance, state and local **8**:92
fiscal policy **8**:109–110
income, national **11**:74–75
inflation **11**:169–171
laissez-faire **12**:167
mixed economy **13**:486
monetary policy **13**:524
monetary theory **13**:524–525
money **13**:526–527
multiplier effect **13**:638
national debt **14**:31–32
price system **15**:535
recession **16**:107
saving and investment **17**:100
service industries **17**:211
stagflation **18**:211
supply and demand **18**:353–354
Tinbergen, Jan **19**:206
ECOSPHERE
biome **3**:272–274
biosphere **3**:276–277
life, extraterrestrial **12**:327–328
ECOSYSTEM *see* ECOLOGY
ECT (electroconvulsive therapy) *see* SHOCK THERAPY
ECTHYMA *see* IMPETIGO
ECTOCARPUS 7:51
ECTODERM
development **6**:138; **6**:141 *illus.*
growth **9**:379
ECTOPIC PREGNANCY
pregnancy and birth **15**:504
ECTOR (county in Texas)
map (31° 48′N 102° 33′W) **19**:129
ECTOTHERM
body temperature **3**:357
ECUADOR 7:51–54 *bibliog., illus., map, table*
art
See also the subheading Ecuador under ARCHITECTURE
Latin American art and architecture **12**:222–228
pre-Columbian art and architecture **15**:495–501
cities
Cuenca **5**:382
Guayaquil **9**:390
Quito **16**:28
climate 7:51–52 *table*
economic activity 7:53
education 7:52–53
Latin American universities **12**:233
flag 7:51 *illus.*
Galápagos Islands **9**:10 *map*
government 7:53
history 7:53
Flores, Juan José **8**:169
García Moreno, Gabriel **9**:39
Latin America, history of **12**:220–221
New Granada **14**:121
Rocafuerte, Vicente **16**:246
Sucre, Antonio José de **18**:319–320
Velasco Ibarra, José María **19**:536
land 7:51–52 *map, table*
literature
Carrera Andrade, Jorge **4**:167
Icaza, Jorge **11**:7
Montalvo, Juan **13**:545–546
map (2° 0′S 77° 30′W) **18**:85
people 7:52–53 *illus.*; **18**:95 *illus.*
Colorado (American Indians) **5**:120
Jívaro **11**:419
physical features
Chimborazo **4**:358
Cotopaxi **5**:304
ECUM SECUM (Nova Scotia)
map (44° 58′N 62° 8′W) **14**:269
ECUMENICAL COUNCIL *see* COUNCIL, ECUMENICAL
ECUMENICAL MOVEMENT 7:54 *bibliog.*
Athenagoras **2**:289
Blake, Eugene Carson **3**:324

ECUMENICAL MOVEMENT (cont.)
Brown, Robert McAfee **3**:516
Brown, William Adams **3**:516
council, ecumenical **5**:309–310
Mott, John R. **13**:616
National Conference of Christians and Jews **14**:30–31
National Council of Churches **14**:31
Söderblom, Nathan **18**:32
South India, Church of **18**:106
Visser 'T Hooft, Willem Adolf **19**:617
World Council of Churches **20**:218
ECZEMA 7:54 *bibliog.*
dermatitis **6**:122
EDAM (Netherlands) 7:54
EDAPHIC CLIMAX *see* CLIMAX COMMUNITY
EDAPHOSAURUS 7:54 *bibliog., illus.*
EDB (chemical) 7:54–55 *bibliog.*
EDDA (book) 7:55 *bibliog.*
Snorri Sturluson **18**:3
EDDINGTON, SIR ARTHUR 7:55 *bibliog.*
astronomy, history of **2**:279
relativity **16**:133
EDDY (county in New Mexico)
map (32° 30′N 104° 15′W) **14**:136
EDDY (county in North Dakota)
map (47° 45′N 98° 50′W) **14**:248
EDDY, MARY BAKER 7:55 *bibliog., illus.*
Christian Science **4**:411–412
Lynn (Massachusetts) **12**:477
EDDY, NELSON, AND MacDONALD, JEANETTE 7:55 *bibliog.*
EDDYSTONE LIGHTHOUSE **12**:336–337 *illus.*
EDDYVILLE (Iowa)
map (41° 9′N 92° 38′W) **11**:244
EDDYVILLE (Kentucky)
map (37° 3′N 88° 4′W) **12**:47
EDE (Netherlands)
map (52° 3′N 5° 40′E) **14**:99
EDELFELT, ALBERT
Finland **8**:97
EDELWEISS 7:56
EDEMA 7:56
cardiovascular diseases **4**:145
diuretic drugs **6**:202
frostbite **8**:346
heart failure **10**:96
inflammation **11**:169
respiratory system disorders **16**:182
uremia **19**:485
EDEN (Mississippi)
map (32° 59′N 90° 20′W) **13**:469
EDEN (North Carolina)
map (36° 29′N 79° 46′W) **14**:242
EDEN (Texas)
map (31° 13′N 99° 51′W) **19**:129
EDEN (Wyoming)
map (42° 3′N 109° 26′W) **20**:301
EDEN, SIR ANTHONY 7:56 *bibliog., illus.*
EDEN, GARDEN OF 7:56
EDEN VALLEY (Minnesota)
map (45° 19′N 94° 33′W) **13**:453
EDENTATES 7:56 *bibliog.*
mammal **13**:103–104 *illus.*
EDENTON (North Carolina)
map (36° 4′N 76° 39′W) **14**:242
EDERLE, GERTRUDE 7:56 *bibliog.*
English Channel 7:189
EDFU (Egypt) 7:56
map (24° 58′N 32° 52′E) 7:76
EDGAR (county in Illinois)
map (39° 40′N 87° 45′W) **11**:42
EDGAR (Nebraska)
map (40° 22′N 97° 58′W) **14**:70
EDGAR, KING OF ENGLAND 7:57
Wessex **20**:106
EDGAR ALLAN POE AWARD
Ambler, Eric **1**:325
Chandler, Raymond T. **4**:279
Creasey, John **5**:334
Crichton, Michael **5**:343
Millar, Margaret **13**:426
Symons, Julian **18**:404
Thomas, Ross **19**:174
Whitney, Phyllis **20**:142
EDGAR ATHELING
Margaret of Scotland, Saint **13**:149
EDGARD (Louisiana)
map (30° 3′N 90° 34′W) **12**:430
EDGARTOWN (Massachusetts)
map (41° 23′N 70° 31′W) **13**:206
EDGE, C. N.
wildlife refuge **20**:151
EDGE ISLAND
map (76° 35′N 25° 10′E) **14**:261
EDGECOMBE (county in North Carolina)
map (35° 55′N 77° 35′W) **14**:242
EDGEFIELD (South Carolina)
map (33° 47′N 81° 56′W) **18**:98
EDGEFIELD (county in South Carolina)
map (33° 45′N 82° 0′W) **18**:98
EDGELEY (North Dakota)
map (46° 22′N 98° 43′W) **14**:248
EDGEMERE (Maryland)
map (39° 14′N 76° 27′W) **13**:188
EDGEMONT (South Dakota)
map (43° 18′N 103° 50′W) **18**:103
EDGERTON (Minnesota)
map (43° 53′N 96° 8′W) **13**:453
EDGERTON (Ohio)
map (41° 27′N 84° 45′W) **14**:357
EDGERTON (Wisconsin)
map (42° 50′N 89° 4′W) **20**:185
EDGERTON (Wyoming)
map (43° 25′N 106° 15′W) **20**:301
EDGERTON, HAROLD EUGENE 7:57 *bibliog.*
EDGEWATER (Alabama)
map (33° 32′N 86° 57′W) **1**:234
EDGEWATER (Florida)
map (29° 0′N 80° 54′W) **8**:172
EDGEWOOD (British Columbia)
map (49° 47′N 118° 8′W) **3**:491
EDGEWOOD (Illinois)
map (38° 55′N 88° 40′W) **11**:42
EDGEWOOD (Maryland)
map (39° 25′N 76° 18′W) **13**:188
EDGEWORTH, MARIA 7:57
EDIACARAN FAUNA 7:57
EDICT OF *see under the latter part of the name, e.g.,* NANTES, EDICT OF; RESTITUTION, EDICT OF (1629); *etc.*
EDINA (Missouri)
map (40° 10′N 92° 11′W) **13**:476
EDINBORO (Pennsylvania)
map (41° 52′N 80° 8′W) **15**:147
EDINBURG (Illinois)
map (39° 39′N 89° 23′W) **11**:42
EDINBURG (Indiana)
map (39° 21′N 85° 58′W) **11**:111
EDINBURG (Mississippi)
map (32° 48′N 89° 20′W) **13**:469
EDINBURG (North Dakota)
map (48° 30′N 97° 52′W) **14**:248
EDINBURG (Texas)
map (26° 18′N 98° 10′W) **19**:129
EDINBURGH (Scotland) 7:57 *bibliog., illus.*; **19**:406 *illus.*
castle **17**:149 *illus.*
map (55° 57′N 3° 13′W) **19**:403
EDINBURGH, PHILIP MOUNTBATTEN, DUKE OF 7:57 *bibliog.*
EDINBURGH, UNIVERSITY OF 7:57–58
EDINBURGH REVIEW (periodical)
Jeffrey, Francis **11**:394
Smith, Sydney **17**:370
EDIRNE (Turkey) 7:58
map (41° 40′N 26° 34′E) **19**:343
EDISON (New Jersey)
map (40° 31′N 74° 24′W) **14**:129
EDISON, THOMAS ALVA 7:58 *bibliog., illus.*; **19**:453 *illus.*
Farmer, Moses **8**:24
film, history of **8**:80–82 *illus.*
first direct-current generator **15**:481 *illus.*
Insull, Samuel **11**:198
lighting devices **12**:338
incandescent lamp **11**:73
New York City electric power station **19**:67 *illus.*
phonograph **15**:253 *illus.*
Schenectady (New York) **17**:119
telephone **19**:80
thermionic emission, Edison effect **19**:161
EDISTO ISLAND (South Carolina)
map (32° 34′N 80° 17′W) **18**:98
EDISTO RIVER
map (32° 39′N 80° 24′W) **18**:98
EDMOND (Oklahoma)
map (35° 39′N 97° 29′W) **14**:368
EDMONDS (Washington)
map (47° 48′N 122° 22′W) **20**:35
EDMONSON (county in Kentucky)
map (37° 10′N 86° 15′W) **12**:47
EDMONT, EDMOND
linguistic atlases **9**:98
EDMONTON (Alberta) **1**:258 *illus.*; 7:58
map (53° 33′N 113° 28′W) **1**:256
EDMONTON (Kentucky)
map (36° 59′N 85° 37′W) **12**:47
EDMORE (Michigan)
map (43° 25′N 85° 3′W) **13**:377
EDMORE (North Dakota)
map (48° 25′N 98° 27′W) **14**:248
EDMUND, SAINT 7:58
EDMUND IRONSIDE, KING OF ENGLAND
Canute, King **4**:118
EDMUNDS (county in South Dakota)
map (45° 25′N 99° 15′W) **18**:103
EDMUNDS, GEORGE FRANKLIN 7:59
EDMUNDS ACT (1882)
Edmunds, George Franklin 7:58
EDMUNDSTON (New Brunswick)
map (47° 22′N 68° 20′W) **14**:117
EDNA (Kansas)
map (37° 4′N 95° 22′W) **12**:18
EDNA (Texas)
map (28° 59′N 96° 39′W) **19**:129
EDO (African people) 7:59 *bibliog.*
Benin, Kingdom of **3**:201
EDO (Japan)
Japan, history of **11**:369
Japanese art and architecture **11**:376–377
Tokyo (Japan) **19**:223–225
Ukiyo-e **19**:375
EDOM 7:59
EDSON (Alberta)
map (53° 35′N 116° 26′W) **1**:256
EDSON, LEWIS
fuging tune **8**:355
EDUARDO CASTEX (Argentina)
map (35° 54′S 64° 18′W) **2**:149
EDUCATION 7:59–64 *bibliog.*
See also UNITED STATES, EDUCATION IN THE; *names of specific types of education, e.g.,* ART EDUCATION; WORK STUDY EDUCATIONAL PROGRAMS; *etc.; names of specific instructional program levels, e.g.,* COMMUNITY AND JUNIOR COLLEGES; PRESCHOOL EDUCATION; *etc.; the subheading* education *under the names of specific countries and states, e.g.,* FRANCE; MISSISSIPPI; *etc.; names of specific schools,*
academic freedom **1**:68–69
academy **1**:70–71
accreditation of schools and colleges **1**:79
black Americans **3**:312–313
blind, education of the **3**:331–332
career education **4**:144–146
censorship **4**:248
child development **4**:348–350
church-related school systems *see names of specific religious sects, e.g.,* JUDAISM; ROMAN CATHOLIC CHURCH; *etc.*
coeducation **5**:90–91
compensatory education **5**:156
computers in education **5**:165–166
correspondence school **5**:276
curriculum **5**:393–394
secondary education **17**:179–180
educational measurement 7:64–66
educational philosophy 7:62–64
educational psychology 7:66
Educational Testing Service 7:66–67
equal opportunity 7:223
exchange programs
Fulbright Exchange Program **8**:357
financial aid
Educational Testing Service 7:66–67
Elementary and Secondary Education Act of 1965 7:133
scholarships, fellowships, and loans **17**:130–131
foundations and endowments
Danforth Foundation **6**:31
Duke Endowment **6**:295
Ford Foundation **8**:223
Kresge Foundation **12**:129
Mellon Foundation **13**:287
Nuffield Foundation **14**:291
Rosenwald, Julius **16**:316
Sloan Foundation **17**:363
free schools **8**:294–295
freedom of religion **8**:298
fund raising **8**:360
United Negro College Fund **19**:415
graduate education **9**:276–277
Great Books Program **9**:309
history 7:59–62
ancient education 7:59–60
early modern period (1400 to 1800) 7:60–61
Erasmus, Desiderius 7:227
medieval education (600 to 1400) 7:60
Middle Ages **13**:394–396
19th century 7:61–62
20th century 7:62
honor system **10**:223–224
humanism **10**:299
humanities, education in the **10**:300
Indian schools, American **11**:106
industrial arts programs **11**:154–155
leaders
Adams, Herbert Baxter **1**:94
Allen, James Edward, Jr. **1**:299
Arnold, Thomas **2**:185
Barnard, Henry **3**:86
Barzun, Jacques **3**:99–100
Beecher, Catharine Esther **3**:160–161
Bell, Andrew **3**:185
Butler, Nicholas Murray **3**:591–592
Comenius, John Amos **5**:132–133
Conant, James Bryant **5**:168
Cremin, Lawrence Arthur **5**:338
Dewey, John **6**:146–147
Eliot, Charles William 7:138
Flexner, Abraham **8**:163–164
Froebel, Friedrich Wilhelm August **8**:335–336
Gilman, Daniel Coit **9**:182
Hale, Sarah Josepha **10**:19
Harper, William Rainey **10**:55
Harris, William Torrey **10**:58
Herbart, Johann Friedrich **10**:134–135
Jencks, Christopher **11**:395
John Baptist de la Salle, Saint **11**:424
Keppel, Francis **12**:58
Kerr, Clark **12**:59–60
Kilpatrick, William Heard **12**:77
Lancaster, Joseph **12**:177
Langdell, Christopher Columbus **12**:195
McCosh, James **13**:10
McGuffey, William Holmes **13**:17
Mann, Horace **13**:122–123 *bibliog.*
Montessori, Maria **13**:553
Moton, Robert Russa **13**:611
Mulcaster, Richard **13**:635
Nott, Eliphalet **14**:268
Palmer, Alice Freeman **15**:50
Parker, Francis Wayland **15**:90
Peabody, Elizabeth **15**:122–123
Pestalozzi, Johann Heinrich **15**:196
Porter, Noah **15**:445
Seton, Saint Elizabeth Ann Bayley **17**:214
Silberman, Charles **17**:303
Tyler, Ralph Winfred **19**:362
Washington, Booker T. **20**:39
Wayland, Francis **20**:73
Willard, Emma Hart **20**:154
learning disabilities **12**:259–260
legislation
blind, education of the **3**:332
career education **4**:146
Elementary and Secondary Education Act of 1965 7:133
G.I. Bill of Rights **9**:170
land-grant colleges **12**:178
learning disabilities **12**:259–260
Mann, Horace **13**:122–123
Morrill Acts **13**:588
National Defense Education Act **14**:32
Right-to-Read Program **16**:222
Scopes Trial **17**:148
Smith-Hughes Act **17**:372
Smith-Lever Act of 1914 **17**:372
literacy and illiteracy **12**:368–370
lycée **12**:474
Montessori method **13**:554
nutrition, human **14**:307
open classroom **14**:398
philosophy
behaviorism 7:63
existentialist humanism 7:63
Marxism 7:63
nature of knowledge 7:63
nature of society 7:63–64
Platonic idealism 7:63
photography, Parsons School of Design **15**:99
physical education, teaching of **15**:279–280
professional and educational organizations
American Association of Community and Junior Colleges **1**:336
American Association for Higher Education **1**:336
American Council on Education **1**:338
Canadian Education Association **4**:92
Education Commission of the States 7:64
ERIC Clearinghouses 7:228–229

National Education Association 14:32
National Honor Society 14:34
National Institute of Education 14:34
Parents and Teachers, National Congress of 15:84
Phi Beta Kappa 15:226
special-interest groups 18:167–168
United States Student Association 19:464
progressive education 15:564
religion
catechism 4:202
Illich, Ivan 11:40
scholasticism 17:131–132
sex education 17:225–226
socialization 18:26
special education 18:166–167
deaf, education of the 6:65–66
student movements 18:307–308
surveying 18:369
teacher education 19:54
teaching machines 19:55–56
teaching methods 19:56–57
technology transfer 19:60
university 19:467–469
vocational education 19:624–625
Winnetka Plan 20:180
women in society 20:204 *table*
work study programs *see* WORK STUDY EDUCATIONAL PROGRAMS
Yale Report of 1828 20:315
young people 20:335
EDUCATION, ELEMENTARY *see* PRIMARY EDUCATION
EDUCATION, PRIMARY *see* PRIMARY EDUCATION
EDUCATION, SECONDARY *see* SECONDARY EDUCATION
EDUCATION, U.S. BUREAU OF *see* EDUCATION, U.S. DEPARTMENT OF
EDUCATION, U.S. DEPARTMENT OF 7:64
Barnard, Henry 3:86
Coleman Report 5:100
Health and Human Services, U.S. Department of 10:86–87
National Education Association 14:32
EDUCATION, U.S. OFFICE OF *see* EDUCATION, U.S. DEPARTMENT OF
EDUCATION, VOCATIONAL *see* VOCATIONAL EDUCATION
EDUCATION COMMISSION OF THE STATES 7:64
National Assessment of Educational Progress 14:29
EDUCATION OF HENRY ADAMS, THE (book) 7:64 *bibliog.*
Adams, Henry 1:94
EDUCATION OF THE EXCEPTIONAL *see* SPECIAL EDUCATION
EDUCATION OF THE HANDICAPPED *see* SPECIAL EDUCATION
EDUCATIONAL MEASUREMENT 7:64–66 *bibliog.*
admissions tests 7:64–65
Advanced Placement Program 1:110
Cattell, James McKeen 4:214
college entrance examinations 7:65
racism 16:37
secondary education 17:179
College Level Examination Program 5:103
computers in education 5:166
Educational Testing Service 7:66–67
ethnic minorities 7:64–66
Graduate Record Examination 9:277
Hutchins, Robert M. 10:322
intelligence 11:203–204
literacy and illiteracy 12:368–370
National Assessment of Educational Progress 14:29
normal distribution 14:219
psychological measurement 15:593
standardized tests 7:65
Stanford-Binet test 18:217–218
Tyler, Ralph Winfred 19:362
EDUCATIONAL PSYCHOLOGY 7:66 *bibliog.*
brainwashing 3:449
Bronfenbrenner, Urie 3:503
Burt, Sir Cyril 3:581
Hall, G. Stanley 10:21
Herbart, Johann Friedrich 10:134–135
Jensen, Arthur 11:396
origins 7:66
primary education 15:538
psychology 15:595
theory and practice 7:66
Thorndike, Edward L. 19:179
EDUCATIONAL RESOURCES INFORMATION CENTER *see* ERIC CLEARINGHOUSES
EDUCATIONAL TELEVISION *see* TELEVISION, NONCOMMERCIAL
EDUCATIONAL TESTING SERVICE 7:66–67
Graduate Record Examination 9:277
EDVAC (computer) 5:160b
Mauchly, John William 13:232
EDWARD, THE BLACK PRINCE 7:67 *bibliog., illus.*
Edward III, King of England 7:68
map (0° 25′S 29° 30′E) 19:372
EDWARD, LAKE 7:67
EDWARD I, KING OF ENGLAND 7:67–68 *bibliog., illus.*; 9:311 *illus.*
actions in common law 5:139
Great Britain, history of 9:312
Harlech Castle (Wales) 20:11 *illus.*
Kincardine (Scotland) 12:78
Parliament 15:92 *illus.*
Robert I, King of Scotland (Robert the Bruce) 16:241
Wallace, Sir William 20:14–15
EDWARD II, KING OF ENGLAND 7:68 *bibliog.*
Gloucester (England) 9:209
Mortimer (family) 13:592
EDWARD III, KING OF ENGLAND 7:68 *bibliog., illus.*
dominions c.1360 7:285 *map*
Hundred Years' War 10:304
Mortimer (family) 13:592
Philip VI, King of France 15:233
EDWARD IV, KING OF ENGLAND 7:68 *bibliog.*
Richard III (play) 16:209
Roses, Wars of the 16:316
Warwick, Richard Neville, Earl of 20:33
Woodville, Elizabeth 20:213
York (dynasty) 20:330
EDWARD V, KING OF ENGLAND 7:68
Richard III, King of England 16:210
Roses, Wars of the 16:316
York (dynasty) 20:330
EDWARD VI, KING OF ENGLAND 7:68 *bibliog.*
Northumberland, John Dudley, Duke of 14:256
Somerset, Edward Seymour, 1st Duke of 18:61
EDWARD VII, KING OF ENGLAND, SCOTLAND, AND IRELAND 7:69 *bibliog., illus.*
Langtry, Lillie 12:196
EDWARD VIII, KING OF ENGLAND, SCOTLAND, AND IRELAND 7:69 *bibliog.*
EDWARD THE CONFESSOR, KING OF ENGLAND 7:67 *bibliog.*
EDWARD THE ELDER, KING OF WESSEX 7:67 *bibliog.*
ÆthelflÆd 1:131
Danelaw 6:31
EDWARD THE MARTYR, KING OF ENGLAND
Æthelred II, King of England 1:131
EDWARDES, GEORGE
musical comedy 13:674
EDWARDES, JOHN
Sealyham terrier 17:174
EDWARDIAN LITERATURE 7:69 *bibliog.*
Austin, Alfred 2:327
Barrie, James 3:94–95
Beerbohm, Sir Max 3:163
Bennett, Arnold 4:202
Butler, Samuel 3:592
Conrad, Joseph 5:198
Eliot, T. S. 7:139–140
Forster, E. M. 8:235
Galsworthy, John 9:21–22
Hardy, Thomas 10:47–48
Irish Literary Renaissance 11:267
Joyce, James 11:456–457
Kipling, Rudyard 12:86–87
Lawrence, D. H. 11:249–250
Shaw, George Bernard 17:245–246
Wells, H. G. 20:101
Yeats, William Butler 20:321
EDWARDS (county in Illinois)
map (38° 25′N 88° 5′W) 11:42
EDWARDS (county in Kansas)
map (37° 50′N 99° 15′W) 12:18
EDWARDS (New York)
map (44° 20′N 75° 15′W) 14:149
EDWARDS (county in Texas)
map (30° 0′N 100° 15′W) 19:129
EDWARDS, JAMES B.
South Carolina 18:100
EDWARDS, JOHN PAUL
Weston, Edward 20:118
EDWARDS, JONATHAN 7:69–70 *bibliog., illus.*
Great Awakening 9:308
EDWARDS, ROBERT G.
artificial insemination 2:221
EDWARDS AIR FORCE BASE
Space Shuttle 18:135–136 *illus.*
EDWARDS BELLO, JOAQUIN *see* BELLO, JOAQUIN EDWARDS
EDWARDS PLATEAU
map (31° 20′N 101° 0′W) 19:129
EDWARD'S SYNDROME
genetic diseases 9:83
EDWARDSVILLE (Illinois)
map (38° 49′N 89° 58′W) 11:42
EEC *see* EUROPEAN ECONOMIC COMMUNITY
EEG *see* ELECTROENCEPHALOGRAPH
EEK (Alaska)
map (60° 12′N 162° 15′W) 1:242
EEKLO (Belgium)
map (51° 11′N 3° 34′E) 3:177
EEL 7:70–71 *bibliog., illus.*; 8:115–117 *illus.*
animal migration 2:27
electric eel 7:105–106
freshwater eel 12:168 *illus.*
life history 7:70 *illus.*
moray eel 13:575
EEL RIVER (California)
map (40° 40′N 124° 20′W) 4:31
EEL RIVER (Indiana)
map (39° 7′N 86° 57′W) 11:111
EELGRASS 7:71
EELPOUT 7:71
EELWORM 18:39 *illus.*
EFATE
Vanuatu 19:520
EFFINGHAM (county in Georgia)
map (32° 20′N 81° 20′W) 9:114
EFFINGHAM (Illinois)
map (39° 7′N 88° 33′W) 11:42
EFFINGHAM (county in Illinois)
map (39° 3′N 88° 40′W) 11:42
EFFINGHAM (Kansas)
map (39° 31′N 95° 24′W) 12:18
EFFNER, JOSEF
Nymphenburg Palace 14:309
EFREMOV, OLEG
Moscow Art Theater 13:599
EFTA *see* EUROPEAN FREE TRADE ASSOCIATION
EGADI ISLANDS
map (37° 56′N 12° 16′E) 11:321
EGAN RANGE
map (39° 0′N 115° 0′W) 14:111
EGANVILLE (Ontario)
map (45° 32′N 77° 6′W) 14:393; 14:461
EGAS, ENRIQUE 7:71 *bibliog.*
EGAS MONIZ, ANTÓNIO
brain 3:448
schizophrenia 17:124
EGBERT, KING OF WESSEX 7:71–72
EGEDE, HANS
Godthåb (Greenland) 9:221
EGEGIK (Alaska)
map (58° 13′N 157° 22′W) 1:242
EGER (Hungary)
map (47° 54′N 20° 23′E) 10:307
EGERIA 7:72
EGG 7:72 *bibliog., illus.*
bird 3:286–287
butterflies and moths 3:595
chicken 4:345
development 6:137–141 *illus.*
embryo 7:153
fish 8:119–120
frog 8:337 *illus.*
Hertwig, Oscar 10:148
oviparity 14:471
parthenogenesis 15:99–100
plover 5:121 *illus.*
pregnancy and birth 15:502
reproduction 16:161
reproductive system, human 16:163–166 *illus.*
reptile 16:168–169 *illus.*
snake 17:381–381 *illus.*
viviparity 19:622
EGG PRODUCTION 7:72 *bibliog.*
chicken 4:345
poultry 15:473–475
EGGAN, FRED
social anthropology 18:11
EGGLESTON, EDWARD 7:73 *bibliog.*
EGGLESTON, WILLIAM
photography, history and art of 15:272
EGGPLANT 7:73 *illus.*; 19:533 *illus.*
EGK, WERNER 7:73 *bibliog.*
EGLANTINE 7:73
EGLEVSKY, ANDRÉ 7:73 *bibliog.*
Ballets Russes de Monte Carlo 3:48
EGMONT, CAPE OF
map (46° 24′N 64° 8′W) 15:548
EGMONT, LAMORAAL, GRAAF VAN 7:73
EGMONT, MOUNT
map (39° 18′S 174° 4′E) 14:158
EGMONT BAY
map (46° 35′N 64° 12′W) 15:548
EGO 7:73–74 *bibliog.*
anxiety 2:72
Erikson, Erik 7:230–231
Fichte, Johann Gottlieb 8:70
Freud, Anna 8:328
Freud, Sigmund 8:329–330
personality 15:189–190
psychoanalysis 15:589–590
superego 18:351
EGOCENTRISM *see* SPATIAL RELATIONSHIP
EGOISM 7:74 *bibliog.*
ethics 7:251
Narcissus (mythology) 14:21
EGRET 7:74 *illus.*; 14:37 *illus.*
heron 10:145
EGRIDIR, LAKE
map (38° 2′N 30° 53′E) 19:343
EGYPT 7:74–81 *bibliog., illus., map, tables*
agriculture 7:78–79 *illus.*; 13:398 *illus.*
fellahin 8:47
irrigation 11:283
arts 7:77
See also EGYPTIAN ART AND ARCHITECTURE
Aswan High Dam 2:286
cities
al-Faiyum 1:232
al-Minya 1:232
Alexandria 1:277
Aswan 2:286
Asyut 2:286
Cairo 4:17–19 *illus., map*
Giza 9:192
Port Said 15:443
Suez 18:323
climate 7:75; 7:77 *table*
economic activity 7:77–79 *illus.*
education 7:77–78 *illus.*
Middle Eastern universities 13:410–412 *table*
flag 7:75 *illus.*
government 7:79
defense, national 6:82 *table*
health 7:77
history before 600 AD *see* EGYPT, ANCIENT
history 600 AD-present 7:79–81 *illus.*
Arab-Israeli Wars 2:96–98 *map*
Cromer, Evelyn Baring, 1st Earl of 5:357
Farouk, King 8:28–29
Fatimids 8:34
Fuad I, King 8:351
Gaza Strip 9:64
Ismail Pasha 11:298
Mamelukes 13:97
Middle East, history of the 13:404–410
Muhammad Ali Pasha 13:633
Napoleon I, Emperor of the French (Napoléon Bonaparte) 14:16
Nasser, Gamal Abdel 14:25
Sadat, Anwar al- 17:8
Saladin 17:29
Suez Crisis 18:325
Tawfiq Pasha 19:45
United Arab Republic 19:401
Wafd 20:4
World War I 20:232; 20:234
World War II 20:258; 20:263 *map*
land and resources 7:74–77 *illus., map, table*
language 7:76
Afroasiatic languages 1:178–179 *map*
literature
biography 3:263
Hakim, Tawfiq al- 10:17
Mahfuz, Najib 13:64
Taha Husayn 19:10
map (27° 0′N 30° 0′E) 1:136
numeral 14:294
people 7:76–77 *illus.*
fellahin 8:47
women in society 20:204 *table*
physical features
Arabian Desert 2:98–99
Qattara Depression 16:4
Sinai 17:318
political parties 7:79

EGYPT (cont.)
Wafd **20**:4
religion 7:76
Coptic church **5**:255
rivers, lakes, and waterways **7**:75
Nasser, Lake **14**:25
Suez Canal **18**:323–324 *illus., map*
vegetation and animal life 7:75–76
EGYPT (Massachusetts)
map (42° 13′N 70° 46′W) **3**:409
EGYPT, ANCIENT 7:81–85 *bibliog., illus., map, table*
See also EGYPTIAN ART AND ARCHITECTURE; EGYPTOLOGY
Abyssinian cat **1**:67
agriculture, history of **1**:189–190 *illus.*
plow **15**:370 *illus.*
wine **20**:174 *illus.*
alchemy **1**:263
animal worship
asp **2**:261
baboon **3**:7 *illus.*
Bubastis **3**:530–531
cat **4**:193
dung beetle **6**:300
ibis **11**:4
astronomy, history of **2**:277 *illus.*
circumcision **4**:442–443
cities 7:81 *map*
Abydos **1**:67
Amarna, Tell el- **1**:321–322
Bubastis **3**:530–531
Dendera **6**:106
Edfu 7:56
Heliopolis **10**:112–113
Hierakonpolis **10**:159
Luxor **12**:473
Memphis **13**:292
Ombos **14**:387
Oxyrhynchus **14**:478–479
Tanis **19**:23
Thebes (Egypt) **19**:154–155
Ugarit **19**:374
costume **5**:292 *illus.*
cosmetics **5**:281 *illus.*
jewelry **11**:408 *illus.*
shoes **17**:280 *illus.*
cultural diffusion
Perry, W. J. **15**:179
Ra expeditions **16**:29
dance **6**:22–23 *illus.*
dynasties 7:82 *table*
engineering 7:177
roads and highways **16**:235
surveying **18**:367 *illus.*
funeral customs
embalming 7:151
mummy **13**:639
myrrh **13**:691
greyhound **9**:361
language
Afroasiatic languages **1**:178 *map*
hieroglyphics **10**:159–161
Rosetta Stone **16**:317 *illus.*
writing systems, evolution of **20**:292–293 *illus.*
law, history of **12**:244
literature
book **3**:383
lotus **12**:420–421
maps and mapmaking **13**:139
mathematics, history of **13**:223
medicine **13**:267
biology **3**:268
metallurgy **13**:329
Middle East, history of the **13**:400–401; **13**:404
mythology *see* EGYPTIAN MYTHOLOGY
Nubia **14**:277–278
Palermo Stone **15**:43
pharaoh **15**:219
incest **11**:74
printing **15**:551
religion
See also EGYPT, ANCIENT, ANIMAL-WORSHIP; EGYPTIAN MYTHOLOGY
Book of the Dead **3**:386
ship **17**:263 *illus.*
slavery **17**:352 *illus.*
textile industry
loom **12**:410
weights and measures **20**:93
wrestling **20**:287
3200–2000 BC Old Kingdom
dynasties 7:81–82 *table*
Menes, King **13**:297
Snefru, King **18**:3
2000–1800 BC Middle Kingdom
Amenemhet I, King **1**:326
dynasties 7:82 *table*
Sesostris I, King **17**:212
Sesostris III, King **17**:212
1800-1570 BC Hyksos domination
dynasties 7:82 *table*
Hyksos **10**:345
1570–1090 BC New Kingdom
Ahmose I, King **1**:201
Akhenaten **1**:230
Amarna, Tell el- **1**:322
Amenhotep I, King **1**:326
Amenhotep II, King **1**:326
Amenhotep III, King **1**:326
dynasties 7:82–83 *table*
Hatshepsut, Queen of Egypt **10**:68
Nefertiti **14**:77
Ramses I, King of Egypt **16**:81
Ramses II, King of Egypt **16**:81–82
Ramses III, King of Egypt **16**:82
Seti I, King **17**:214
Thutmose I, King **19**:186
Thutmose II, King **19**:186
Thutmose III, King **19**:186
Tutankhamen, King **19**:355
1090–333 BC decline
Ahmose II, King **1**:201
dynasties 7:82 *table*
Necho II, King of Egypt **14**:75
Psamtik I, King **15**:587
Sheshonk I, King **17**:259
333–323 BC Alexander the Great foreign domination 7:83
323–30 BC Ptolemaic kings
Cleopatra, Queen **5**:50–51
Ptolemy I, King (Ptolemy Soter) **15**:607
Ptolemy II, King (Ptolemy Philadelphus) **15**:607
Ptolemy III, King (Ptolemy Eueregetes) **15**:607
Ptolemy IV, King (Ptolemy Philopater) **15**:607
Ptolemy V, King (Ptolemy Epiphanes) **15**:607
Ptolemy VI, King (Ptolemy Philometor) **15**:607
Ptolemy VIII, King (Ptolemy Euergetes) **15**:607
Ptolemy XII, King (Ptolemy Auletes) **15**:607
Ptolemy XIII, King **15**:608
EGYPT, LAKE OF
map (37° 35′N 88° 55′W) **11**:42
EGYPTIAN, THE (book)
Waltari, Mika **20**:19
EGYPTIAN APE *see* *AEGYPTOPITHECUS*
EGYPTIAN ARCHAEOLOGY *see* EGYPTOLOGY
EGYPTIAN ART AND ARCHITECTURE **2**:192 *illus.*; 7:82–84 *illus.*; 7:85–90 *bibliog., illus.*
architecture **2**:130–131
bas-relief **3**:100; **5**:51 *illus.*
Cleopatra's Needles **5**:51
Coptic art and architecture **5**:255
costume **5**:292–293 *illus.*
Egyptology 7:90
furniture **8**:373–374
glassware, decorative **9**:203 *illus.*
gold and silver work **9**:228
illuminated manuscripts **11**:46
Imhotep **11**:54
interior design **11**:211
ivory and ivory carving **11**:336
jewelry **11**:408 *illus.*
Khafre, King of Egypt **12**:64
Khufu, King of Egypt **12**:69
landscape architecture **12**:186 *illus.*
Louvre **12**:437
mastaba **13**:214
Memphis (Egypt) **13**:292
Metropolitan Museum of Art, The **13**:348
mummy **13**:639 *illus.*
mural painting **13**:646
museums, art **13**:658
Nefertiti **14**:77 *illus.*
obelisk **14**:314–315
painting **15**:18 *illus.*
technology, history of **19**:61 *illus.*
post and lintel **15**:459
sarcophagus **17**:76
sculpture **17**:159 *illus.*
Senmut **17**:203
Seven Wonders of the World **17**:216–218
sphinx **18**:180
stele **18**:250
temples 7:85–86 *illus.*; **19**:94–95 *illus.*
Abu Simbel **1**:66–67
Beth-shan **3**:230
Deir el-Bahri **6**:85–86
Dendera **6**:106
Edfu 7:56
Karnak **12**:28
Luxor **12**:473
Ombos **14**:387
Philae **15**:229
Temple of Amon-re at Thebes **19**:155 *illus.*
tombs **19**:230
Beni Hasan **3**:199
pyramids **15**:634–636
Saqqara **17**:74
Tutankhamen's gold funerary mask **19**:355 *illus.*
Valley of the Kings **19**:507
EGYPTIAN BOOK OF THE DEAD **4**:41 *illus.*; **20**:292 *illus.*
EGYPTIAN MYTHOLOGY 7:84 *illus.*; **13**:695 *illus.*
Amon-Re **1**:376
Anubis **2**:72
Apis **2**:78
Book of the Dead **3**:386
Hathor **10**:68
Heliopolis **10**:112–113
Horus **10**:255
Isis **11**:288
Maat **12**:244 *illus.*
mythology **13**:697–698
Osiris **14**:454
Oxyrhynchus **14**:478
Ptah **15**:605
Serapis **17**:207
Set **17**:213
Thoth **19**:180
EGYPTIAN PEA *see* CHICK-PEA
EGYPTOLOGY 7:90 *bibliog.*
See also EGYPT, ANCIENT; EGYPTIAN ART AND ARCHITECTURE
archaeology **2**:122
Belzóni, Giovanni Battista **3**:194
Breasted, James Henry **3**:469–470
Carnarvon, George Edward, 5th Earl of **4**:154
Carter, Howard **4**:171
Champollion, Jean François **4**:278
Champollion-Figeac, Jean Jacques **4**:278
Mariette, Auguste **13**:152
Maspero, Sir Gaston **13**:199
Petrie, Sir Flinders **15**:204
EHA-AMUFU (Nigeria)
map (6° 40′N 7° 46′E) **14**:190
EHRENBERG (Arizona)
map (33° 36′N 114° 31′W) **2**:160
EHRENBERG, ILYA GRIGORIEVICH 7:90
EHRENFEST, PAUL 7:90 *bibliog.*
EHRENSTRAHL, DAVID KLÖCKER
Scandinavian art and architecture **17**:112
EHRHARDT (South Carolina)
map (33° 6′N 81° 1′W) **18**:98
EHRICKE, KRAFFT A.
space station **18**:136
EHRLICH, PAUL (1854–1915) 7:90 *bibliog.*
biology **3**:269
chemistry, history of **4**:329
immunity **11**:57
magic bullets 7:90
medicine **13**:271
Metchnikoff, Elie **13**:335
Nobel Prize 7:90
EHRLICH, PAUL (1932–) 7:90–91
environmental movement 7:90–91
natural resources, nonrenewable 7:90–91
overpopulation 7:90–91
EHRLICHMAN, JOHN 7:91
Watergate **20**:64
EHURSAG *see* UR (Iraq)
ÉIBAR (Spain)
map (43° 11′N 2° 28′W) **18**:140
EICHENBERG, FRITZ
Before the Murder **14**:274 *illus.*
EICHENDORFF, JOSEPH, FREIHERR VON 7:91 *bibliog.*
EICHHORN, JOHANN GOTTFRIED 7:91
EICHMANN, ADOLF 7:91 *bibliog.*
EICHRODT, LUDWIG
Biedermeier **3**:247
EIDER DUCK **6**:291–292 *illus.*; **19**:332 *illus.*
tundra **19**:332 *illus.*
EIDSVOLL CONSTITUTION
Scandinavia, history of **17**:110
EIERMANN, EGON 7:91 *bibliog.*
EIFFEL, ALEXANDRE GUSTAVE 7:91 *bibliog.*
Eiffel Tower 7:91
Statue of Liberty **18**:238
EIFFEL TOWER 7:91 *bibliog.*; 7:276 *illus.*; **15**:85–86 *illus., map*
Eiffel, Alexandre Gustave 7:91
EIGEN, MANFRED 7:91
EIGHT, THE (art group) *see* ASHCAN SCHOOL (art group)
EIGHT DEGREE CHANNEL
map (8° 0′N 73° 0′E) **11**:80
18TH AMENDMENT 7:91
prohibition **15**:565
temperance movement **19**:92
text **5**:222
21st Amendment **19**:359
Volstead, Andrew J. **19**:631
8TH AMENDMENT 7:92
Furman v. *Georgia* **8**:371–372
text **5**:221
EIJKMAN, CHRISTIAAN 7:92
EILAT *see* ELAT (Israel)
EILSHEMIUS, LOUIS MICHEL 7:92
EINAUDI, LUIGI 7:92 *bibliog.*
EINDHOVEN (Netherlands) 7:92
map (51° 26′N 5° 28′E) **14**:99
EINEM, GOTTFRIED VON 7:92
EINHARD
Germany, history of **9**:148
EINHORN, DAVID 7:92
EINKORN **20**:126 *illus.*
EINSIEDELN (Switzerland)
map (47° 8′N 8° 45′E) **18**:394
Moosbrugger, Caspar **13**:571
EINSTEIN, ALBERT 7:92–94 *bibliog., illus.*; **15**:286 *illus.*
atomic bomb **2**:307
Bell's theorem **3**:192
Brownian motion **3**:518
clock paradox **5**:61
cosmology (astronomy) **5**:284; **5**:287–289
gravitation **9**:304–305
photochemistry **15**:257
photoelectric effect **15**:260
quantum mechanics **16**:9–10
relativity **16**:132–135 *illus.*
unified field theory **19**:385–386
EINSTEIN EQUIVALENCE PRINCIPLE (EEP)
relativity **16**:134–136
EINSTEIN OBSERVATORY
High Energy Astronomical Observatory (artificial satellite) **10**:161
EINSTEIN TOWER **13**:295 *illus.*
EINSTEINIUM (element) 7:94
actinide series **1**:88
element 7:130 *table*
metal, metallic element **13**:328
Seaborg, Glenn T. **17**:171–172
transuranium elements **19**:286
EINTHOVEN, WILLEM 7:94
electrocardiograph 7:111–112
EIRE *see* IRELAND
EIRUNEPÉ (Brazil)
map (6° 40′S 69° 52′W) **3**:460
EISAKU, SATO *see* SATO EISAKU
EISELE, DONN F. 7:94
Apollo program **2**:81
EISELEY, LOREN 7:94
EISENACH (Germany, East and West)
map (50° 59′N 10° 19′E) **9**:140
EISENBERG-BERG, NANCY
moral awareness **13**:573
EISENERZER ALPS (Mountains)
map (47° 28′N 14° 45′E) **2**:348
EISENHOWER, DWIGHT D. 7:94–96 *bibliog., illus.*
as president 7:95–96
Dulles, John Foster **6**:295–296
early life and career 7:94
Gettysburg (Pennsylvania) **9**:160
military-industrial complex **13**:422
Nixon, Richard M. **14**:204–205
Normandy Invasion **14**:221
presidential elections **15**:529–530
Republican party **16**:175 *illus.*
State of the Union address (1957) **15**:523 *illus.*
United States, history of the **19**:457–458 *illus.*
Vietnam War **19**:585
World War II 7:94–95; **20**:262–263; **20**:272–273 *illus.*; **20**:275
EISENHÜTTENSTADT (Germany, East and West)
map (52° 10′N 14° 39′E) **9**:140
EISENMAN, PETER 7:96 *bibliog.*
EISENSTADT (Austria)
map (47° 51′N 16° 32′E) **2**:348
EISENSTAEDT, ALFRED 7:96 *illus.*
V-J Day 7:96 *illus.*
EISENSTEIN, SERGEI MIKHAILOVICH 7:97 *bibliog., illus.*

constructivist theater **5**:224–225
film, history of **8**:80
EISLEBEN (Germany, East and West)
map (51° 31′N 11° 32′E) **9**:140
EISNER, KURT 7:97 *bibliog.*
EISTEDDFOD (Welsh festival) 7:97
EITOKU 7:97 *bibliog.*
Japanese art and architecture **11**:376
Pine Trees and Eagle **11**:376 *illus.*
EJACULATION
semen **17**:195
sexual intercourse **17**:230–231
EJECTION SEAT (aircraft)
parachute **15**:75
EJURA (Ghana)
map (7° 23′N 1° 22′W) **9**:164
EKALAKA (Montana)
map (45° 53′N 104° 33′W) **13**:547
EKELÖF, GUNNAR 7:97 *bibliog.*
EKHOF, KONRAD
theater, history of the **19**:147–148
EKMAN, VAGN WALFRID 7:98
ocean currents **14**:322–324
EKWENSI, CYPRIAN 7:98 *bibliog.*
EKWOK (Alaska)
map (59° 22′N 157° 30′W) **1**:242
EL *see* under the second element of the name except for names listed below
EL (Semite deity)
mythology **13**:698
EL AAIÚN (Morocco)
map (27° 9′N 13° 12′W) **13**:585
EL ASNAM (Algeria)
map (36° 10′N 1° 20′E) **1**:287
EL BANCO (Colombia)
map (9° 0′N 73° 58′W) **5**:107
EL BAÚL (Venezuela)
map (8° 57′N 68° 17′W) **19**:542
EL CAJON (California)
map (32° 48′N 116° 58′W) **4**:31
EL CAMPO (Texas)
map (29° 12′N 96° 16′W) **19**:129
EL CAPITAN MOUNTAIN
map (46° 1′N 114° 23′W) **13**:547
EL CARRICITO (Mexico)
map (28° 24′N 103° 23′W) **13**:357
EL CEDRAL (Guatemala)
map (16° 26′N 90° 3′W) **9**:389
EL CENTRO (California)
map (32° 48′N 115° 34′W) **4**:31
EL CERRITO (California)
map (37° 55′N 122° 18′W) **4**:31
EL CERRO (Bolivia)
map (17° 31′S 61° 34′W) **3**:366
EL CERRO DEL ARIPO MOUNTAIN
map (10° 43′N 61° 15′W) **19**:300
EL CHARCO LARGO (Mexico)
map (24° 10′N 97° 58′W) **13**:357
EL CHICHÓN 7:98
EL CID 7:98; **18**:145 *illus.*
Cid, The (play) **4**:429
Corneille, Pierre **5**:267
Poem of the Cid, The
Spanish literature **18**:157
EL COLORADO (Argentina)
map (26° 18′S 59° 22′W) **2**:149
EL CORÁZÓN (Ecuador)
map (1° 12′S 79° 6′W) **7**:52
EL CORDOBÉS 3:559 *illus.*; 7:98 *bibliog.*
EL CUCO (El Salvador)
map (13° 10′N 88° 7′W) **7**:100
EL CUY (Argentina)
map (39° 56′S 68° 20′W) **2**:149
EL DESEMBOQUE (Mexico)
map (30° 30′N 112° 59′W) **13**:357
EL DJOUF DESERT
map (21° 25′N 6° 40′W) **13**:236
EL DORADO 7:98 *bibliog.*
Jiménez de Quesada, Gonzalo **11**:419
EL DORADO (Arkansas)
map (33° 13′N 92° 40′W) **2**:166
EL DORADO (county in California)
map (38° 43′N 120° 48′W) **4**:31
EL DORADO (Kansas)
map (37° 49′N 96° 52′W) **12**:18
EL DORADO (Venezuela)
map (6° 44′N 61° 38′W) **19**:542
EL DORADO SPRINGS (Missouri)
map (37° 52′N 94° 1′W) **13**:476
EL ENCANTO (Colombia)
map (1° 37′S 73° 14′W) **5**:107
EL ENCANTO (Guatemala)
map (17° 17′N 89° 34′W) **9**:389
EL ESTOR (Guatemala)
map (15° 32′N 89° 21′W) **9**:389
EL FERROL DEL CAUDILLO (Spain)
map (43° 29′N 8° 14′W) **18**:140
EL GOLÉA (Algeria)
map (30° 30′N 2° 50′E) **1**:287
EL GRAN CAPITÁN *see* FERNÁNDEZ DE CÓRDOBA, GONZALO
EL GRECO 7:98–99 *bibliog., illus.*
Christ Carrying the Cross **18**:154 *illus.*
Laocoon **15**:20 *illus.*
The Purification of the Temple **7**:99 *illus.*
Spanish art and architecture **18**:153
EL HANK (cliff)
map (24° 30′N 7° 0′W) **13**:89
EL-KEDAH, TELL *see* HAZOR (Israel)
EL MAYOCO (Argentina)
map (42° 39′S 70° 59′W) **2**:149
EL MÉDANO (Mexico)
map (24° 25′N 111° 30′W) **13**:357
EL MIRAGE (Arizona)
map (33° 36′N 112° 19′W) **2**:160
EL NEVADO, MOUNT
map (3° 59′N 74° 4′W) **5**:107
EL NIÑO (hydrology) 7:99 *bibliog.*
ocean-atmosphere interaction **14**:321
EL OSO (Venezuela)
map (4° 59′N 65° 25′W) **19**:542
EL PASO (county in Colorado)
map (39° 50′N 104° 30′W) **5**:116
EL PASO (Illinois)
map (40° 44′N 89° 1′W) **11**:42
EL PASO (Texas) 7:99–100
climate **14**:228 *table*; **19**:421 *table*
map (31° 45′N 106° 29′W) **19**:129
EL PASO (county in Texas)
map (31° 45′N 106° 15′W) **19**:129
EL PASO DEL NORTE (Mexico) *see* CIUDAD JUÁREZ (Mexico)
EL PORVENIR (Mexico)
map (31° 15′N 105° 51′W) **13**:357
EL PROGRESO (Ecuador)
map (0° 54′S 89° 33′W) **7**:52
EL PROGRESO (Honduras)
map (15° 21′N 87° 49′W) **10**:218
EL REAL (Panama)
map (8° 8′N 77° 43′W) **15**:55
EL RENO (Oklahoma)
map (35° 32′N 97° 57′W) **14**:368
EL SALTO (Mexico)
map (23° 47′N 105° 22′W) **13**:357
EL SALVADOR 7:100–101 *bibliog., illus., map, table*
cities
San Salvador **17**:57
Santa Ana **17**:66
climate **7**:100–101 *table*
economic activity **7**:100
education
Latin American universities **12**:233 *table*
flag **7**:100 *illus.*
government **7**:100–101
history **7**:100–101
Duarte, José Napoleón **6**:287
land and resources **7**:100–101 *map, table*
map (13° 50′N 88° 55′W) **14**:225
people **7**:100
pre-Columbian art and architecture **15**:496
refugee **16**:125
EL SAMÁN DE APURE (Venezuela)
map (7° 55′N 68° 44′W) **19**:542
EL SAUZ (Mexico)
map (29° 2′N 106° 16′W) **13**:357
EL SEIBO (Dominican Republic)
map (18° 46′N 69° 2′W) **6**:233
EL TAJÍN (Mexico) 7:101 *bibliog.*; **14**:237 *map*
Remojadas **16**:146
Teotihuacán **19**:113
EL TIGRE (Venezuela)
map (8° 55′N 64° 15′W) **19**:542
EL TURBIO (Argentina)
map (51° 41′S 72° 5′W) **2**:149
EL VIEJO (Nicaragua)
map (12° 40′N 87° 10′W) **14**:179
EL ZANJÓN, PACT OF
Ten Years' War **19**:101
ELAGABALUS *see* HELIOGABALUS, ROMAN EMPEROR
ELAINE (Arkansas)
map (34° 18′N 90° 51′W) **2**:166
ELAM 7:101–102 *bibliog.*
Dur-Untash **6**:302
Fertile Crescent **8**:60
Mesopotamia **13**:316 *map*
Persia, ancient **15**:181
Susa **18**:370
Ur **19**:474
ELAMITE LANGUAGE
languages, extinct **12**:198
writing systems, evolution of **20**:292
ELAND 7:102 *illus.*
bongo **3**:378
ELAS *see* EAM-ELAS
ELASTICITY
Euler, Leonhard **7**:264–265
materials technology **13**:220
mathematical theory
Cauchy, Augustin Louis **4**:219
ELASTOMER 7:102 *bibliog.*
rubber **16**:332–335
synthetic fibers **18**:409
ELAT (Israel) 7:102
Ezion-geber **7**:352
map (29° 33′N 34° 57′E) **11**:302
ELATH *see* ELAT (Israel)
ELAVIL *see* TRICYCLICS
ELAZIG (Turkey)
map (38° 41′N 39° 14′E) **19**:343
ELBA (Alabama)
map (31° 25′N 86° 4′W) **1**:234
ELBA (Italy) 7:102
map (42° 46′N 10° 17′E) **11**:321
ELBASAN (Albania)
map (41° 6′N 20° 5′E) **1**:250
ELBE RIVER 7:102
map (53° 50′N 9° 0′E) **7**:268
ELBERFELD (West Germany) *see* WUPPERTAL (West Germany)
ELBERT (Colorado)
map (39° 13′N 104° 32′W) **5**:116
ELBERT (county in Colorado)
map (39° 20′N 104° 10′W) **5**:116
ELBERT (county in Georgia)
map (34° 10′N 82° 50′W) **9**:114
ELBERT, MOUNT 7:102
map (39° 7′N 106° 27′W) **5**:116
ELBERTA (Michigan)
map (44° 37′N 86° 14′W) **13**:377
ELBERTON (Georgia)
map (34° 7′N 82° 52′W) **9**:114
ELBLĄG (Poland)
map (54° 10′N 19° 25′E) **15**:388
ELBOW **11**:439 *illus.*
ELBOW (Saskatchewan)
map (51° 7′N 106° 35′W) **17**:81
ELBOW LAKE (Minnesota)
map (45° 59′N 95° 58′W) **13**:453
ELBRUS, MOUNT 7:102; **19**:392 *illus.*
map (43° 21′N 42° 26′E) **4**:218
ELBURZ MOUNTAINS 7:102–103
Demavend, Mount **6**:96
map (36° 0′N 53° 0′E) **11**:250
ELCHE (Spain) 7:103
map (38° 15′N 0° 42′W) **18**:140
ELCHO (Wisconsin)
map (45° 26′N 89° 11′W) **20**:185
ELDA (Spain)
map (38° 29′N 0° 47′W) **18**:140
ELDER (church officer) *see* MINISTRY, CHRISTIAN
ELDERBERRY 7:103
ELDERLY *see* OLD AGE
ELDON (Iowa)
map (40° 55′N 92° 13′W) **11**:244
ELDON (Missouri)
map (38° 21′N 92° 35′W) **13**:476
ELDORA (Iowa)
map (42° 19′N 93° 26′W) **11**:244
ELDORADO (Illinois)
map (37° 49′N 88° 26′W) **11**:42
ELDORADO (Oklahoma)
map (34° 28′N 99° 39′W) **14**:368
ELDORADO (Texas)
map (30° 52′N 100° 36′W) **19**:129
ELDORET (Kenya)
map (0° 31′N 35° 17′E) **12**:53
ELDRED (Pennsylvania)
map (41° 57′N 78° 23′W) **15**:147
ELDREDGE, NILES
evolution **7**:324
ELDRIDGE (Iowa)
map (41° 39′N 90° 35′W) **11**:244
ELDRIDGE, FLORENCE 7:103
ELEANOR OF AQUITAINE 7:103 *bibliog.*
Aquitaine **2**:95–96
Henry II, King of England **10**:124–125
Louis VII, King of France (Louis the Young) **12**:424
ELEATIC SCHOOL 7:103 *bibliog.*
Parmenides **15**:95
pre-Socratic philosophy **15**:532–533
Zeno of Elea **20**:359
ELECTION 7:103–104 *bibliog., illus.*
absentee voting **1**:62
ballot **3**:53
campaign, political **4**:63–64
caucus **4**:219
Congress of the United States **5**:185
electoral college **7**:104–105
favorite son **8**:39
framework of the Constitution **5**:214
lame duck **12**:174
National Conservative Political Action Committee **14**:31
plebiscite **15**:364
political convention **15**:399–400
political parties **15**:400–403
poll tax **15**:405
presidential elections **15**:529–532
primary election **15**:538–539
public opinion **15**:609
recall **16**:106
referendum and initiative **16**:118–119
representation **16**:160–161
Baker v. *Carr* **3**:28
gerrymander **9**:158
proportional representation **15**:572
suffrage
15th Amendment **8**:325–326
19th Amendment **14**:199
26th Amendment **19**:359–360
voter registration **19**:637
voting machine **19**:637
write-in candidate **20**:291
ELECTION, PRIMARY *see* PRIMARY ELECTION
ELECTORAL COLLEGE 7:104–105 *bibliog.*
Constitution of the United States **5**:217–218
framework of the Constitution **5**:214
presidential elections **15**:531
12th Amendment **5**:221; **19**:358
Wilson, James **20**:165
ELECTRA (mythology) 7:105
ELECTRA (play) 7:105 *bibliog.*
Sophocles **18**:67
ELECTRA COMPLEX (psychology) **5**:157
ELECTRET (physics) 7:105
ELECTRIC ARC *see* ARC, ELECTRIC
ELECTRIC CAR 7:105 *bibliog.*
automotive industry **2**:363
history **7**:105
hybrid electric car **7**:105
technology **7**:105
ELECTRIC CHARGE *see* CHARGE, ELECTRIC
ELECTRIC CIRCUIT *see* CIRCUIT, ELECTRIC
ELECTRIC CURRENT *see* CIRCUIT, ELECTRIC
ELECTRIC EEL 7:105–106 *bibliog.*
gymnotid **9**:414
ELECTRIC EYE *see* PHOTOELECTRIC CELL
ELECTRIC FIELD
dielectric **6**:161
Maxwell's equations **13**:241–242
physics, history of **15**:283–284
ELECTRIC FISH
biopotential **3**:276
catfish **4**:203
ELECTRIC FURNACE 7:106 *bibliog.*
furnace **8**:372
iron and steel industry **11**:276–277
ELECTRIC GUITAR *see* GUITAR
ELECTRIC LIGHT BUG *see* WATER BUG
ELECTRIC LIGHTING
lamp **12**:175 *illus.*
lighting devices **12**:338–339
Swan, Sir Joseph Wilson **18**:379
ELECTRIC ORGAN
electronic music **7**:125 *illus.*
ELECTRIC POWER, GENERATION AND TRANSMISSION *see* POWER, GENERATION AND TRANSMISSION OF
ELECTRICAL, RADIO AND MACHINE WORKERS, INTERNATIONAL UNION OF 7:106
ELECTRICAL AND ELECTRONIC ENGINEERING 7:106 *bibliog.*
See also ELECTRONICS
Black, Harold **3**:303
contact potential **5**:227
education and training **7**:106
Fleming, Sir Ambrose **8**:159
Hammond, John Hays, Jr. **10**:31
image processing **11**:51–53 *illus.*
laser and maser **12**:210–213
modulation **13**:499–500
oscilloscope **14**:453
pattern recognition **15**:114–115
phonograph **15**:253–254
photography **15**:261–266
professional and educational organizations
Institute of Electrical and Electronic Engineers **7**:106
Pupin, Michael Idvorsky **15**:626
reactance **16**:98
rectifier **16**:110
resistance, electrical **16**:177
resistivity **16**:177
semiconductor **17**:196–197
signal generator **17**:300
silver **17**:313

ELECTRICAL AND ELECTRONIC ENGINEERING (cont.)
solid-state physics **18**:54–55
sound recording and reproduction **18**:74–77
Sprague, Frank Julian **18**:198
static **18**:234
Steinmetz, Charles Proteus **18**:249
stroboscope **18**:301
superconductivity **18**:350
switch, electric **18**:393
technology, history of **19**:69
telecommunications **19**:75–76
thermionic emission **19**:161
transformer **19**:270–271
tuner **19**:333
tungsten **19**:334
vacuum **19**:502
video recording **19**:577
videodisk **19**:577
volt **19**:631
X-ray tube **20**:309
ELECTRICAL AND ELECTRONIC TECHNOLOGY
actinometer **1**:88–89
ammeter **1**:372
amplifier **1**:382–383
analog-to-digital computer **1**:389
aperture **2**:76
biosensor **3**:276
calculator, electronic **4**:23–24
camera **4**:54–59
capacitor **4**:119–120
cathode-ray tube **4**:211
charge-coupled device **4**:288
circuit breaker **4**:438
compact disc **5**:154–155
computer **5**:159–160i
computer-aided design and computer-aided manufacturing **5**:160j–160L
copy machine **5**:255–256
densitometer **6**:113
digital technology **6**:175
diode **6**:183
electrode **7**:113
electromagnetic pulse **7**:116
electron tube **7**:122–124
electrotype **7**:128
enlarger **7**:206
filter, electronic **8**:91
flatbed cylinder press **8**:154
galvanometer **9**:23
grid **9**:361
hybrid computer **10**:328–329
incandescent lamp **11**:73
inductor **11**:151–152
input-output devices **11**:182–183
klystron **12**:98–99
laser and maser **12**:210–213
Leyden jar **12**:309
Linotype **12**:359
loudspeaker **12**:421
magnetron **13**:60
metal detector **13**:329
microphone **13**:386–387
microprocessor **13**:387
mimeograph **13**:434
mimicomputer **13**:446
Monotype **13**:541
multiplexer **13**:638
multivibrator **13**:638
on-line computer **14**:388
oscillator **14**:453
photoelectric cell **15**:259–260
polarographic analyzer **15**:395
radar **16**:38–40
radio **16**:44–47
receiver (communications) **16**:106
rectifier **16**:110–111
relay (control device) **16**:137
resistor **16**:177
rheostat **16**:193
rotary press **16**:321
sensitometer **17**:205
sheet-fed press **17**:249–250
signal generator **17**:300
silicon-controlled rectifier **17**:305
solenoid **18**:53
sonar **18**:62
stroboscope **18**:301
switch, electric **18**:393
tape recorder **19**:30–31
telegraph **19**:76–78
telephone **19**:78–80
television **19**:83–89
thermistor **19**:161
thyratron **19**:187
transducer **19**:269
transistor **19**:271–272
transmitter **19**:276
traveling-wave tube **19**:284
triode **19**:301
tuner **19**:333
typesetting **19**:365
typewriter **19**:365–366
UNIVAC **19**:467
vacuum tube **19**:502
vocoder **19**:625
voltage regulator **19**:631
voltmeter **19**:632
waveguide **20**:70
web-fed press **20**:85–86
Wheatstone bridge **20**:127
X-ray tube **20**:309
Zener diode **20**:359
ELECTRICAL NUMERICAL INTEGRATOR AND CALCULATOR *see* ENIAC
ELECTRICAL SYSTEM, AUTOMOTIVE *see* IGNITION SYSTEM
ELECTRICAL WIRING 7:106–107 *bibliog.*
circuit breaker **4**:438
ELECTRICAL WORKERS, INTERNATIONAL BROTHERHOOD OF 7:107
ELECTRICITY 7:107–111 *bibliog., illus.* *See also* ELECTRICAL AND ELECTRONIC TECHNOLOGY
alternating current **1**:312–313
armature **2**:171
biopotential **3**:275
blackout, electrical **3**:322
charge, electric **4**:288
circuit **4**:436–438 *illus.*
conduction, electric **5**:174
Coulomb, Charles Augustin de **5**:308
current, electric **7**:109–110
direct current **6**:187
discharge, electrical **6**:188
electromotive force **7**:119
electron **7**:120
electrostatics **7**:128
Faraday, Michael **8**:21–22
Franklin, Benjamin **8**:283
fuel cell **8**:354
Galvani, Luigi **9**:23
generation **15**:481–485 *illus., map, table*
hydroelectric power **10**:332–335
incinerator **11**:74
magnetohydrodynamics **13**:59 *illus.*
nuclear energy **14**:278–284
thermoelectricity **19**:165
tidal energy **19**:192–193
Gilbert, William **9**:179
insulator **11**:197
Kirchhoff's laws **12**:87
Laplace, Pierre Simon de **12**:205
Lenz's law **12**:287
Leyden jar **12**:309
lighting devices **12**:338 *illus.*
locomotive **12**:390–391 *illus.*
magnetism **13**:55–58
Maxwell, James Clerk **13**:241
Maxwell's equations **13**:242
measurement **13**:255–256
coulombmeter **5**:308
galvanometer **9**:23
potentiometer **15**:467
units, physical **19**:467
volt **19**:631
voltmeter **19**:632
watt **20**:68
new ceramics applications **4**:259
noise **14**:213
Ohm's law **14**:363
parity (physics) **15**:89
photoelectric effect **15**:260
physics **15**:281
physics, history of **15**:283–284
piezoelectricity **15**:298
potential, electric **15**:466
Priestley, Joseph **15**:536
production, countries worldwide **15**:485 *table*
production and transmission of, United States **15**:482 *map, table*
pulse (electronics) **15**:621
rheostat **16**:193
rockets and missiles **16**:260
Siemens (family) **17**:295–296
solar cell **18**:40
speed of **7**:110
static electricity **18**:234
Steinmetz, Charles Proteus **18**:249
storm static **18**:234
theory of matter **7**:110
transmission **15**:484–486 *illus.*
unanswered problems **7**:110–111
Weber, Wilhelm Eduard **20**:88
Wollaston, William Hyde **20**:199
ELECTROCARDIOGRAPH 7:111–112 *bibliog., illus.*
Einthoven, Willem **7**:94
examination, medical **7**:326
heart **10**:94
heart diseases **10**:96
oscilloscope **14**:453
ELECTROCHEMICAL EQUIVALENT 7:112
ELECTROCHEMICAL SERIES *see* ELECTROMOTIVE SERIES
ELECTROCHEMISTRY 7:112–113 *bibliog., illus.*
Debye, Peter **6**:72
electrolysis **7**:114–115
electromagnetic units **7**:118–119
electromotive force **7**:119
Faraday's laws of electrolysis **8**:22
fuel cell **8**:354
ion and ionization **11**:239–240
physical chemistry **15**:279
physics, history of **15**:283–284
ELECTROCONVULSIVE THERAPY *see* SHOCK THERAPY
ELECTROCUTION 7:113
ELECTRODE 7:113
cathode **4**:210–211
cathode ray **4**:211
electrochemistry **7**:112–113
electron tube **7**:122–124
grid **9**:361
pH meter **15**:217–218
ELECTRODIALYSIS
dialysis **6**:150–151
ELECTRODYNAMICS
Dirac, Paul **6**:186–187
Hertz, Heinrich Rudolph **10**:149
relativity **16**:134
ELECTRODYNAMOMETER
ammeter **1**:372
galvanometer **9**:23
measurement **13**:255–256
voltmeter **19**:632
ELECTROENCEPHALOGRAPH 6:267 *illus.*; 7:113–114 *bibliog., illus.*; 7:219 *illus.*
brain **3**:447
death and dying **6**:69
dreams and dreaming **6**:266–267
electrode **7**:113
oscilloscope **14**:453
psychopathy **15**:601
sleep **17**:360
ELECTROFAX PROCESS
electrostatic printing **7**:128
ELECTROGASDYNAMICS
power, generation and transmission of **15**:483
ELECTROLUMINESCENCE (physics) 7:114 *bibliog.*
ELECTROLYSIS 7:114–115 *bibliog.*
anion **2**:29
Arrhenius, Svante August **2**:188
cathode **4**:210–211
cation **4**:212
chemical industry **4**:318
chemistry, history of **4**:325–326
chlorine preparation **4**:400
depilatory **6**:118
dissociation (chemistry) **6**:198
electrochemical equivalent **7**:112
electrochemistry **7**:112–113
electrode **7**:113
electrolyte **7**:115
electroplating **7**:126–127 *illus.*
Faraday, Michael **8**:21–22
Faraday's laws of electrolysis **8**:22
potassium production **15**:465
reaction, chemical **16**:99
ELECTROLYTE 7:115
Debye, Peter **6**:72
digestion, human **6**:172
diuretic drugs **6**:202
electrochemistry **7**:112–113
electroplating **7**:126–127
space medicine **18**:133
sulfuric acid **18**:336
ELECTROMAGNET 7:115 *illus.*
circuit breaker **4**:438
electromagnetic induction **7**:115–116
magnet **13**:54
Morse, Samuel F. B. **13**:590
motor **13**:611–612
ELECTROMAGNETIC INDUCTION 7:115–116 *bibliog.*
electromagnetic units **7**:118
Faraday, Michael **8**:21–22
generator **9**:78
Henry, Joseph **10**:122
inductor **11**:151–152
Lenz's law **12**:287
Maxwell's equations **13**:242
microphone **13**:386
Oersted, Hans Christian, discoverer **14**:352
physics, history of **15**:284
transformer **19**:270
ELECTROMAGNETIC PULSE 7:116 *bibliog.*
nuclear strategy **14**:288
ELECTROMAGNETIC RADIATION 7:116–118 *bibliog., illus., table*
antenna (electronics) **2**:47–48
background radiation **3**:12
color **5**:112–113
Compton effect **5**:159
Einstein, Albert **7**:92–94
electromagnetic field **7**:116–117
electromagnetic induction **7**:115–116
electromagnetic pulse **7**:116
electromagnetic spectrum **7**:117 *table*
energy transport **7**:172–173
ether (physics) **7**:250
frequency allocation **8**:326–327
frequency radiation **7**:116–118
gamma-ray astronomy **9**:33–34
gamma rays **9**:34
infrared radiation **11**:175
interaction with matter **7**:117–118
Kirchhoff, Gustav Robert **12**:87
laser and maser **12**:210–213
light **12**:334–336
Lorentz, Hendrik Antoon **12**:413–414
Maxwell, James Clerk **13**:241
Maxwell's equations **13**:242
microwaves **13**:389
modulation **13**:499–500
noise **14**:213
photoelectric effect **15**:260
photomultiplier **15**:274
quantum electrodynamics **7**:118
radar **16**:38–40
radiation **16**:42
radio **16**:44–47
radio astronomy **16**:47–53
spectrum **18**:172–173
synchrotron radiation **18**:406
telecommunications **19**:75–76
television transmission **19**:85
ultraviolet light **19**:379
waves and wave motion **20**:71–72
whistler **20**:134
X-ray tube **20**:309
X rays **20**:309–311
ELECTROMAGNETIC SPECTRUM 7:117 *table*
infrared radiation **11**:175
spectrum **18**:172–173
X-ray astronomy **20**:305
ELECTROMAGNETIC UNITS 7:118–119 *table*
ampere **1**:377
coulomb **5**:308
farad **8**:21
Gaussian units **7**:118
henry **10**:122
metric system **13**:345–347
MKSA units **7**:118
ohm **14**:363
units, physical **19**:465–467
volt **19**:631
ELECTROMAGNETISM *see* MAGNETISM—electromagnetism
ELECTROMECHANICAL DEVICE
solenoid **18**:53
ELECTROMETER 7:119
ELECTROMOTIVE FORCE (emf) (physics) 7:119
circuit, electric **4**:436–438
ELECTROMOTIVE SERIES 7:119 *bibliog., table*
ELECTROMYOGRAPHY
phonetics **15**:252
ELECTRON 7:119–120 *bibliog.*
annihilation **2**:33
atom, relation to **7**:120
atom **2**:305–06
conversion electron **5**:233
electron configuration **7**:120
transition elements **19**:273 *table*
charge-to-mass ratio
atomic constants **2**:309
Zeeman, Pieter **20**:358
chemical bonding **7**:120
aromatic compounds **2**:186
chemical bond **4**:313–315
discovery **7**:119
electricity **7**:110; **7**:120
charge, electric **4**:288
circuit, electric **4**:436–438
discharge, electrical **6**:188
electrochemistry **7**:112
electronics **7**:126
Millikan, Robert **13**:430

Millikan's oil-drop experiment **13**:430
electromagnetic radiation 7:116–118
whistler **20**:134
electron emission
beta decay **3**:229
laser and maser **12**:211 *illus.*
photoelectric cell **15**:259
photoelectric effect **15**:260
thermionic emission **19**:161
energy level 7:173
exclusion principle 7:250
exoelectron 7:333
free radical **8**:294
fundamental particles **8**:361
gamma rays **9**:34
ion and ionization **11**:239–240
Lenard, Philipp Eduard Anton **12**:281
neutrino **14**:108
orbital **14**:416–417
oxidation and reduction **14**:475
oxidation and reduction reactions
electromotive series 7:119
plasma physics **15**:345–346
positron **15**:458
Tamm, Igor Yevgenievich **19**:19
theory
Einstein, Albert 7:93
Lorentz, Hendrik Antoon **12**:413–414
Thomson, Sir Joseph John, discoverer **19**:176
valence **19**:503
wave mechanics 7:120
Davisson, Clinton **6**:53
de Broglie, Louis **6**:58
de Broglie wavelength **6**:58
Thomson, Sir George Paget **19**:175
Wu, Chien-shiung **20**:295
ELECTRON BEAM
cathode-ray tube **4**:211
electron microscope 7:120–122
electron optics 7:122
interference **11**:207–209
ELECTRON CONFIGURATION 7:120
aromatic compounds **2**:186
atom **2**:305–306
ELECTRON MICROPROBE
mineral **13**:440
ELECTRON MICROSCOPE 7:120–122 *bibliog., illus.*
crystal **5**:376
electron optics 7:122
metallurgy **13**:331
microbiology **13**:384
micropaleontology **13**:386
photomicrograph 7:121 *illus.*
Ruska, Ernst August Friedrich **16**:348
Scanning electron microscope 7:120–122
transmission electron microscope 7:120–122
Zworykin, Vladimir Kosma **20**:372
ELECTRON OPTICS 7:122 *bibliog.*
See also LIGHT
ELECTRON TRANSPORT
metabolism **13**:326
ELECTRON TUBE 7:122–124 *bibliog., illus.*
See also TRANSISTOR
cathode **4**:210–211
thermionic emission **19**:161
cathode-ray tube **4**:211
classification 7:123 *illus.*
development 7:122–123
diode **6**:183
electrode 7:113
Fleming, Sir Ambrose **8**:159
grid **9**:361
klystron **12**:99–98
microwaves **13**:389
nickel **14**:183
radio **16**:45
thyratron **19**:187
transistor replacing
remaining tube uses 7:123–124
traveling-wave tube **19**:284
triode **19**:301
types of tubes 7:122–124
vacuum **19**:502
vacuum tube **19**:502
ELECTRON VOLT (physics) 7:124
ELECTRONEGATIVITY 7:124
chemical bonds **4**:314
element 7:132
oxidation and reduction **14**:475
ELECTRONIC BANKING *see* ELECTRONIC FUNDS TRANSFER SYSTEMS
ELECTRONIC CHURCH *see* RELIGIOUS BROADCASTING
ELECTRONIC COMMUNICATION *see* TELECOMMUNICATIONS
ELECTRONIC FLASH
flash photography **8**:153
ELECTRONIC FUNDS TRANSFER SYSTEMS
banking systems **3**:69
ELECTRONIC IGNITION SYSTEM
ignition system **11**:38
ELECTRONIC INFORMATION SERVICES
cable TV **4**:7
computer networking **5**:163
computers and privacy **5**:166–167
newspaper **14**:172
press agencies and syndicates **15**:533
telecommunications **19**:76
videotext **19**:577
ELECTRONIC JOURNALISM *see* RADIO BROADCASTING; TELEVISION BROADCASTING
ELECTRONIC MAIL 7:124
ELECTRONIC MUSIC 7:124–126 *bibliog., illus.*
composers
Babbitt, Milton **3**:5–6
Berio, Luciano **3**:212
Davidovsky, Mario **6**:49
Maderna, Bruno **13**:40
Nono, Luigi **14**:216–217
Stockhausen, Karlheinz **18**:275
Wuorinen, Charles **20**:296–297
Xenakis, Yannis **20**:311
computer music **5**:162–163
instruments 7:124–126
theremin **19**:160
rock music **16**:249
ELECTRONIC PUBLISHING
computer **5**:160g
computer, personal **5**:160i–160j
ELECTRONIC SURVEILLANCE *see* SURVEILLANCE SYSTEMS; WIRETAPPING
ELECTRONICS 7:126 *bibliog.*
See also ELECTRICAL AND ELECTRONIC TECHNOLOGY; MICROELECTRONICS
conduction, electric **5**:174
cryogenics **5**:371
electromagnetic pulse 7:116
electron tube 7:122–124
ferrite **8**:59
filter, electronic **8**:91
gating circuit **9**:58
guidance and control systems **9**:393–394
high fidelity **10**:161
impedance **11**:61
integrated circuit **11**:201–202
klystron **12**:98–99
magnetron **13**:60
microelectronics **13**:385
microwaves **13**:389
naval vessels **14**:56
noise **14**:213
piezoelectricity **15**:298
printed circuit **15**:550
pulse (electronics) **15**:621
radar **16**:38–40
relay (control device) **16**:137
research institutions
Lincoln Laboratory **12**:350
rhenium **16**:193
semiconductor **17**:196–197
solid-state physics **18**:54–55
indium **11**:144
telecommunications **19**:75–76
thermistor **19**:161
thin-film circuits **19**:169
Townes, Charles Hard **19**:255
transistor **19**:271–272
tubes, molybdenum **13**:514
vocoder **19**:625
Zener diode **20**:359
ELECTRONICS INDUSTRY 7:126
computer industry **5**:160n–160o
ELECTROPHORESIS 7:126 *bibliog.*
densitometer **6**:113
globulin **9**:209
isoelectric point **11**:299
Tiselius, Arne Wilhelm Kaurin **19**:209
ELECTROPHYSIOLOGY
neurophysiology **14**:105–106
sensation **17**:204
ELECTROPLATING 7:126–127 *bibliog., illus.*
anodizing **2**:34
cadmium **4**:12
chromium **4**:419
electrode 7:113
electrolysis 7:115
Farmer, Moses **8**:24
galvanizing, zinc **20**:367
gilding **9**:180
machine 7:127 *illus.*
nickel **14**:183
Siemens (family) **17**:296
tin **19**:205
ELECTROSHOCK TREATMENT *see* SHOCK THERAPY
ELECTROSTATIC PRINTING 7:127–128 *bibliog., illus.*
business machines **3**:589
Carlson, Chester Floyd **4**:152
copying machine **5**:255–256
photocopy process 7:127–128
ELECTROSTATICS 7:128 *bibliog.*
charge, electrical **4**:288
dielectric constant
atomic constants **2**:308
discharge, electrical **6**:188
electrostatic printing 7:127–128
force law *see* COULOMB'S LAW
generator
Van de Graaff, Robert Jemison **19**:512
physics, history of **15**:283–284
plasma physics **15**:346
potential, electric **15**:466
static electricity **18**:234
ELECTROTYPE 7:128 *bibliog.*
ELECTROWEAK THEORY 7:128
Glashow, Sheldon **9**:197
ELECTRUM *see* AMBER
ELEGY 7:129 *bibliog.*
Adonais **1**:107
Donne, John **6**:239
"Elegy Written in a Country Churchyard" 7:129
Gray, Thomas **9**:307
Propertius, Sextus **15**:570
Shelley, Percy Bysshe **17**:253
Tennyson, Alfred Lord **19**:111–112
Tibullus **19**:191
Whitman, Walt **20**:140–141
"ELEGY WRITTEN IN A COUNTRY CHURCHYARD" (poem) 7:129 *bibliog.*
Gray, Thomas **9**:307
ELEMENT 7:129–132 *bibliog., illus., tables*
See also names of specific elements, e.g., EINSTEINIUM; HYDROGEN; etc.
abundances of common elements 7:131 *table*
actinide series **1**:88
atom **2**:304–306
atomic number **2**:311
atomic weight **2**:311–312
Marignac, Jean Charles Galissard de **13**:152
chemical properties 7:131–132
classification 7:129–131
Döbereiner, Johann Wolfgang **6**:209
compound, chemical **5**:158
defined
chemistry, history of **4**:325
discovery 7:129–131
distribution and migration of
geochemistry **9**:95
electromotive series 7:119
gaseous elements
inert gases **11**:161
identification and quantity
radiochemistry **16**:63
ion substitution
solid solution **18**:54
lanthanide series **12**:200–201
mass number **13**:203
mineral **13**:438–444
native elements **14**:47
nuclear charge **13**:599
nutrient cycles **14**:302–304
origin 7:132
periodic table **15**:166–169
physical properties 7:131
radiometric age-dating **16**:65
spectral lines
Zeeman, Pieter **20**:357–358
stoichiometry **18**:276–278
superconductivity **18**:350 *table*
superheavy elements **18**:351
systematization
chemistry, history of **4**:325–326
transition elements **19**:273–274
transmutation of elements **19**:276–277
transuranium elements **19**:282
ELEMENT 104 7:132
superheavy elements **18**:351
ELEMENT 105 7:132
superheavy elements **18**:351
ELEMENT 106 7:132
superheavy elements **18**:351
ELEMENT 107 7:132–133
ELEMENT 108 7:133
ELEMENT 109 7:133
ELEMENT 112
superheavy elements **18**:351
ELEMENT 114
superheavy elements **18**:351
ELEMENT 126
superheavy elements **18**:351
ELEMENTARY EDUCATION *see* PRIMARY EDUCATION
ELEMENTARY PARTICLES *see* FUNDAMENTAL PARTICLES
ELEMENTARY AND SECONDARY EDUCATION ACT OF 1965 7:133
United States, education in the **19**:435
ELEMENTS, TRANSMUTATION OF *see* TRANSMUTATION OF ELEMENTS
ELEPHANT 7:133–134 *bibliog., illus.*; **13**:105 *illus.*
circus **4**:443–444 *illus.*
Indian elephant **2**:246 *illus.*
ivory and ivory carving **11**:336
Jumbo **11**:466
mammoth (animal) **13**:106–107
mastodon **13**:217
proboscidean **15**:559
skull 7:133–134 *illus.*
ELEPHANT BEETLE *see* WEEVIL
ELEPHANT BUTTE RESERVOIR
map (33° 19′N 107° 10′W) **14**:136
ELEPHANT MOUNTAIN (Maine)
map (44° 46′N 70° 46′W) **13**:70
ELEPHANT RANGE (Kampuchea)
map (11° 0′N 104° 5′E) **12**:11
ELEPHANT SEAL *see* SEAL (zoology)
ELEPHANTA (India) 7:134
ELEPHANTFISH 7:134
ELEPHANTIASIS
filariasis **8**:78
ELEPHANT'S-EAR (botany) 7:134
taro **19**:38
ELEUSINIAN MYSTERIES 7:134–135 *bibliog.*
Demeter **6**:96
mother goddess **13**:607
mystery cults **13**:693
Persephone **15**:180
ELEUSIS (Greece) 7:135
ELEUTHERA ISLAND
Bahama Islands **3**:23
map (25° 10′N 76° 14′W) **3**:23
ELEVATED RAILROAD 7:135–136 *bibliog.*
history 7:135
ELEVATION (geography and astronomy) 7:136
ELEVATOR 7:136–137 *bibliog., illus.*
Chicago school of architecture **4**:342
grain elevator **9**:282
Post, George Browne **15**:458–459
Sprague, Frank Julian **18**:198
ELEVEN EXECUTIONERS **4**:4 *illus.*
11TH AMENDMENT 7:137
text **5**:221
ELF *see* FAIRY
ELFIN COVE (Alaska)
map (58° 12′N 136° 20′W) **1**:242
ELGAR, SIR EDWARD 7:137 *bibliog., illus.*
ELGIN (Illinois)
map (42° 2′N 88° 17′W) **11**:42
ELGIN (Minnesota)
map (44° 8′N 92° 15′W) **13**:453
ELGIN (Nebraska)
map (41° 59′N 98° 5′W) **14**:70
ELGIN (North Dakota)
map (46° 24′N 101° 51′W) **14**:248
ELGIN (Oklahoma)
map (34° 48′N 98° 18′W) **14**:368
ELGIN (Oregon)
map (45° 34′N 117° 55′W) **14**:427
ELGIN (Texas)
map (30° 21′N 97° 22′W) **19**:129
ELGIN, JAMES BRUCE, 8TH EARL OF 7:137 *bibliog.*
ELGIN, THOMAS BRUCE, 7TH EARL OF 7:137
Elgin Marbles 7:137
ELGIN MARBLES 7:137
Canova, Antonio **4**:115
Elgin, Thomas Bruce, 7th Earl of 7:137
neoclassicism (art) **14**:81
ELGINSHIRE (Scotland) *see* MORAY (Scotland)
ELGON, MOUNT 7:137
map (1° 8′N 34° 33′E) **19**:372
ELIA (Cuba)
map (20° 59′N 77° 26′W) **5**:377
ELIADE, MIRCEA 7:138 *bibliog.*
ELÍAS PIÑA (Dominican Republic)
map (18° 53′N 71° 42′W) **6**:233

ELIDA (New Mexico)
map (33° 57′N 103° 39′W) **14**:136
ELIJAH 7:138 *bibliog.*
ELIJAH BEN SOLOMON 7:138
ELIJAH MUHAMMAD *see* MUHAMMAD, ELIJAH
ELIOT, CHARLES WILLIAM 7:138 *bibliog.*
secondary education **17**:179
ELIOT, GEORGE 7:138–139 *bibliog., illus.*; 7:200 *illus.*
Adam Bede **1**:92
Middlemarch **13**:413
Mill on the Floss, The **13**:426
realism (literature) **16**:104
Silas Marner **17**:303
ELIOT, SIR JOHN (English parliamentarian) 7:139
ELIOT, JOHN (missionary) 7:139 *bibliog.*
ELIOT, T. S. **1**:346 *illus.*; 7:139–140 *bibliog., illus.*
Four Quartets **8**:253
Love Song of J. Alfred Prufrock, The **7**:139
Murder in the Cathedral 7:140
Pizzetti, Ildebrando **15**:325
Pound, Ezra **15**:475–476
Waste Land, The **20**:47
ELISABETHVILLE (Belgian Congo) *see* LUBUMBASHI (Zaire)
ELISHA 7:140
ELITES 7:140–141 *bibliog.*
Mosca, Gaetano **13**:596
Pareto, Vilfredo **15**:84
ELIZABETH, SAINT 7:141
ELIZABETH (Australia)
map (34° 43′S 138° 40′E) **2**:328
ELIZABETH (Colorado)
map (39° 22′N 104° 36′W) **5**:116
ELIZABETH (Louisiana)
map (30° 52′N 92° 48′W) **12**:430
ELIZABETH (New Jersey) 7:141
harbor and port **10**:43
map (40° 40′N 74° 11′W) **14**:129
ELIZABETH (West Virginia)
map (39° 4′N 81° 24′W) **20**:111
ELIZABETH, EMPRESS OF AUSTRIA 7:141
ELIZABETH, EMPRESS OF RUSSIA 7:142–143 *bibliog.*
ELIZABETH CITY (North Carolina)
map (36° 18′N 76° 14′W) **14**:242
ELIZABETH OF HUNGARY, SAINT 7:142
ELIZABETH I, QUEEN OF ENGLAND 7:141–142 *bibliog., illus.*; 7:144 *illus.*; **9**:312 *illus.*
Burghley, William Cecil, 1st Baron **3**:569
Elizabethan Age 7:143
Elizabethan style 7:146
Eric XIV, King of Sweden 7:229
Essex, Robert Devereux, 2d Earl of 7:245
Irish settlements **11**:262 *map*
Leicester, Robert Dudley, Earl of **12**:277
Mary, Queen of Scots **13**:186–187
Raleigh, Sir Walter **16**:79
Salisbury, Robert Cecil, 1st Earl of **17**:33
Walsingham, Sir Francis **20**:19
ELIZABETH II, QUEEN OF ENGLAND, SCOTLAND, AND NORTHERN IRELAND 7:142 *bibliog., illus.*; 7:180 *illus.*; **19**:410 *illus.*
Edinburgh, Philip Mountbatten, Duke of 7:57
Windsor (dynasty) **20**:174
ELIZABETH ISLANDS
map (41° 27′N 70° 47′W) **13**:206
ELIZABETHAN AGE 7:143–144 *bibliog., illus.*
See also ELIZABETH I, QUEEN OF ENGLAND; ELIZABETHAN LITERATURE; ELIZABETHAN PLAYHOUSE; ELIZABETHAN STYLE (architecture)
cosmetics **5**:282 *illus.*
English music 7:203 *illus.*
Great Britain, history of **9**:313
madrigal **13**:45
shoes **17**:280 *illus.*
Sidney, Sir Philip **17**:295
ELIZABETHAN LITERATURE
comedy **5**:132
Dekker, Thomas **6**:86
drama **6**:258–259
English literature 7:195
Heywood, John **10**:155–156
Jonson, Ben **11**:445–446
Kyd, Thomas **12**:143
Lodge, Thomas **12**:392–393
Lyly, John **12**:475
Marlowe, Christopher **13**:161
Shakespeare, William **17**:236–237
Sidney, Sir Philip **17**:295
Spenser, Edmund **18**:178–179
supernatural literature **18**:352
Tourneur, Cyril **19**:253
University Wits **19**:470
ELIZABETHAN PLAYHOUSE 7:145–146 *bibliog., illus.*
acting **1**:87
Admiral's Men **1**:105
Alleyn, Edward **1**:302
Chamberlain's Men **4**:274
Fortune Theatre **8**:241–242
Globe Theatre **9**:208–209
Swan Theatre **18**:379
Tarlton, Richard **19**:37
theater, history of the **19**:145–146 *illus.*
theater architecture and staging **19**:152
ELIZABETHAN POOR LAW ACT
poor laws **15**:429
ELIZABETHAN SETTLEMENT (Church of England)
Elizabeth I, Queen of England 7:142
Elizabethan Age 7:143
ELIZABETHAN STYLE (architecture) 7:146 *bibliog., illus.*
house (in Western architecture) **10**:266
ELIZABETHTON (Tennessee)
map (36° 21′N 82° 13′W) **19**:104
ELIZABETHTOWN (Illinois)
map (37° 27′N 88° 18′W) **11**:42
ELIZABETHTOWN (Kentucky)
map (37° 42′N 85° 52′W) **12**:47
ELIZABETHTOWN (New York)
map (44° 13′N 73° 36′W) **14**:149
ELIZABETHTOWN (North Carolina)
map (34° 38′N 78° 37′W) **14**:242
ELIZABETHTOWN (Pennsylvania)
map (40° 9′N 76° 36′W) **15**:147
ELK **6**:80 *illus.*; 7:146 *illus.*
deer **6**:79
Irish elk **11**:266
Jackson Hole (Wyoming) **11**:344
moose **13**:571–572
mountain life **13**:623
wapiti **20**:24
ELK (county in Kansas)
map (37° 25′N 96° 15′W) **12**:18
ELK (county in Pennsylvania)
map (41° 26′N 78° 43′W) **15**:147
ELK (Poland)
map (53° 50′N 22° 22′E) **15**:388
ELK CITY (Oklahoma)
map (35° 25′N 99° 25′W) **14**:368
ELK CITY LAKE
map (37° 25′N 95° 55′W) **12**:18
ELK GROVE VILLAGE (Illinois)
map (42° 1′N 87° 59′W) **11**:42
ELK HORN (Iowa)
map (41° 36′N 95° 3′W) **11**:244
ELK MOUNTAIN (Wyoming)
map (41° 41′N 106° 25′W) **20**:301
ELK MOUNTAINS (Colorado)
map (39° 5′N 107° 5′W) **5**:116
ELK POINT (Alberta)
map (53° 34′N 110° 54′W) **1**:256
ELK POINT (South Dakota)
map (42° 41′N 96° 41′W) **18**:103
ELK RAPIDS (Michigan)
map (44° 54′N 85° 25′W) **13**:377
ELK RIVER (Idaho)
map (46° 47′N 116° 11′W) **11**:26
ELK RIVER (Maryland)
map (39° 24′N 76° 5′W) **13**:188
ELK RIVER (Minnesota)
map (45° 18′N 93° 35′W) **13**:453
ELK RIVER (West Virginia)
map (38° 21′N 81° 38′W) **20**:111
ELKADER (Iowa)
map (42° 51′N 91° 24′W) **11**:244
ELKHART (Indiana)
map (41° 41′N 85° 58′W) **11**:111
ELKHART (county in Indiana)
map (41° 35′N 85° 50′W) **11**:111
ELKHART (Kansas)
map (37° 0′N 101° 54′W) **12**:18
ELKHART LAKE (Wisconsin)
map (43° 50′N 88° 1′W) **20**:185
ELKHEAD MOUNTAINS (Colorado)
map (40° 50′N 107° 5′W) **5**:116
ELKHORN (Manitoba)
map (49° 58′N 101° 14′W) **13**:119
ELKHORN (Nebraska)
map (41° 17′N 96° 14′W) **14**:70
ELKHORN (Wisconsin)
map (42° 40′N 88° 33′W) **20**:185
ELKHORN CITY (Kentucky)
map (37° 18′N 82° 21′W) **12**:47
ELKHORN RIVER (Nebraska)
map (41° 7′N 96° 19′W) **14**:70
ELKIN (North Carolina)
map (36° 16′N 80° 51′W) **14**:242
ELKINS BILL
Roosevelt, Theodore **16**:310
ELKINS PARK (Pennsylvania)
map (40° 5′N 75° 8′W) **15**:147
ELKLAND (Pennsylvania)
map (41° 59′N 77° 21′W) **15**:147
ELKO (British Columbia)
map (49° 18′N 115° 7′W) **3**:491
ELKO (Nevada) 7:146
map (40° 50′N 115° 46′W) **14**:111
ELKO (county in Nevada)
map (41° 0′N 115° 30′W) **14**:111
ELKTON (Kentucky)
map (36° 49′N 87° 9′W) **12**:47
ELKTON (Maryland)
map (39° 36′N 75° 50′W) **13**:188
ELKTON (South Dakota)
map (44° 14′N 96° 29′W) **18**:103
ELKTON (Virginia)
map (38° 25′N 78° 38′W) **19**:607
ELKVILLE (Illinois)
map (37° 55′N 89° 14′W) **11**:42
ELLÁS *see* GREECE
ELLAVILLE (Georgia)
map (32° 15′N 84° 18′W) **9**:114
ELLEN, MOUNT (Utah)
map (38° 7′N 110° 49′W) **19**:492
ELLENDALE (Louisiana)
map (29° 38′N 90° 49′W) **12**:430
ELLENDALE (Minnesota)
map (43° 52′N 93° 18′W) **13**:453
ELLENDALE (North Dakota)
map (46° 6′N 98° 32′W) **14**:248
ELLENSBURG (Washington)
map (47° 0′N 120° 32′W) **20**:35
ELLENVILLE (New York)
map (41° 43′N 74° 28′W) **14**:149
ELLERBEE (North Carolina)
map (35° 4′N 79° 46′W) **14**:242
ELLESMERE ISLAND (Northwest Territories) **4**:69 *illus.*; 7:146–147
map (81° 0′N 80° 0′W) **14**:258
ELLETTSVILLE (Indiana)
map (39° 14′N 86° 37′W) **11**:111
ELLICE ISLANDS *see* TUVALU
ELLICOTT, ANDREW
Banneker, Benjamin **3**:70
ELLICOTT, JOSEPH
Buffalo (New York) **3**:546
ELLICOTT CITY (Maryland)
map (39° 16′N 76° 48′W) **13**:188
ELLICOTTVILLE (New York)
map (42° 17′N 78° 40′W) **14**:149
ELLIJAY (Georgia)
map (34° 42′N 84° 28′W) **9**:114
ELLINGTON (Missouri)
map (37° 14′N 90° 58′W) **13**:476
ELLINGTON, DUKE 7:147 *bibliog., illus.*
jazz **11**:388 *illus.*
ELLINWOOD (Kansas)
map (38° 21′N 98° 35′W) **12**:18
ELLIOT, GILBERT, 4TH EARL OF MINTO *see* MINTO, GILBERT ELLIOT, 4TH EARL OF
ELLIOT LAKE (Ontario)
map (46° 23′N 82° 39′W) **14**:393
ELLIOTT (county in Kentucky)
map (38° 5′N 83° 5′W) **12**:47
ELLIOTT (Mississippi)
map (33° 40′N 89° 44′W) **13**:469
ELLIOTT, HERB 7:147 *bibliog.*
ELLIOTT, MAXINE 7:147 *bibliog.*
ELLIOTT, ROBERT B. **16**:185 *illus.*
ELLIPSE (mathematics) 7:147 *illus.*
conic section **5**:188 *illus.*
eccentricity 7:37
focal property 7:147
ELLIPSOID (mathematics) 7:148
plane section 7:148
ELLIPTIC GEOMETRY
geometry **9**:107
non-Euclidean geometry **14**:215–216
ELLIPTICAL MOTION
motion, harmonic **13**:609
ELLIS (Kansas)
map (38° 56′N 99° 34′W) **12**:18
ELLIS (county in Kansas)
map (38° 55′N 99° 15′W) **12**:18
ELLIS (county in Oklahoma)
map (36° 15′N 99° 45′W) **14**:368
ELLIS (county in Texas)
map (32° 20′N 96° 48′W) **19**:129
ELLIS, HAVELOCK 7:148 *bibliog.*
ELLIS, PERRY
fashion design **8**:32
ELLIS ISLAND (New York City) 7:148; **11**:54 *illus.*
ELLISON, RALPH 7:148 *bibliog., illus.*
Invisible Man **11**:238
ELLISVILLE (Mississippi)
map (31° 36′N 89° 12′W) **13**:469
ELLORA (India) 7:148–149
Indian art and architecture **11**:96 *illus.*
ELLOREE (South Carolina)
map (33° 32′N 80° 34′W) **18**:98
ELLSBERG, DANIEL **4**:248 *illus.*
Pentagon Papers **15**:154
ELLSWORTH (Kansas)
map (38° 44′N 98° 14′W) **12**:18
ELLSWORTH (county in Kansas)
map (38° 40′N 98° 15′W) **12**:18
ELLSWORTH (Maine)
map (44° 33′N 68° 26′W) **13**:70
ELLSWORTH (Wisconsin)
map (44° 44′N 92° 29′W) **20**:185
ELLSWORTH, LINCOLN 7:149
Vinson Massif **19**:601
ELLSWORTH, OLIVER 7:149
ELLSWORTH LAND (region in Antarctica)
map (75° 30′S 80° 0′W) **2**:40
ELLSWORTH MOUNTAINS
map (79° 0′S 85° 0′W) **2**:40
ELLUL, JACQUES
technology **19**:59–60
ELLWOOD, CRAIG 7:149 *bibliog.*
ELLWOOD CITY (Pennsylvania)
map (40° 50′N 80° 17′W) **15**:147
ELM 7:149 *illus.*
biological classification plant **15**:333
hackberry **10**:7
nettle **14**:104
ELM CITY (North Carolina)
map (35° 48′N 77° 52′W) **14**:242
ELM CREEK (Manitoba)
map (49° 41′N 98° 0′W) **13**:119
ELM CREEK (Nebraska)
map (40° 43′N 99° 22′W) **14**:70
ELM GROVE (Wisconsin)
map (43° 3′N 88° 4′W) **20**:185
ELMA (Washington)
map (47° 0′N 123° 25′W) **20**:35
ELMAN, MISCHA 7:149 *bibliog.*
ELMER (New Jersey)
map (39° 36′N 75° 10′W) **14**:129
ELMER GANTRY (book) 7:149 *bibliog.*
Lewis, Sinclair **11**:306–307
ELMHURST (Illinois)
map (41° 53′N 87° 56′W) **11**:42
ELMIRA (New York) 7:149
map (42° 6′N 76° 49′W) **14**:149
ELMIRA (Prince Edward Island)
map (46° 27′N 62° 4′W) **15**:548
ELMIRA COLLEGE 7:150
ELMORE (county in Alabama)
map (32° 35′N 86° 10′W) **1**:234
ELMORE (county in Idaho)
map (43° 25′N 115° 30′W) **11**:26
ELMORE (Minnesota)
map (43° 30′N 94° 5′W) **13**:453
ELMORE CITY (Oklahoma)
map (34° 37′N 97° 24′W) **14**:368
ELMSHORN (Germany, East and West)
map (53° 45′N 9° 39′E) **9**:140
ELMWOOD (Nebraska)
map (40° 50′N 96° 18′W) **14**:70
ELMWOOD (Wisconsin)
map (44° 47′N 92° 9′W) **20**:185
ELMWOOD PARK (Illinois)
map (41° 55′N 87° 49′W) **11**:42
ELMWOOD PARK (New Jersey)
map (40° 54′N 74° 7′W) **14**:129
ELNORA (Indiana)
map (38° 53′N 87° 5′W) **11**:111
ELODEA 7:150
ELOISE (Florida)
map (28° 0′N 81° 44′W) **8**:172
ELORTONDO (Argentina)
map (33° 42′S 61° 37′W) **2**:149
ELORZA (Venezuela)
map (7° 3′N 69° 31′W) **19**:542
ELOY (Arizona)
map (32° 45′N 111° 33′W) **2**:160
ELOY BLANCO, ANDRES
Venezuela **19**:543
ELROY (Wisconsin)
map (43° 45′N 90° 16′W) **20**:185
ELSASSER, WALTER MAURICE 7:150
ELSEVIER, LOUIS *see* ELZEVIR, LOUIS
ELSHEIMER, ADAM 7:150 *bibliog.*
ELSIE (Michigan)
map (43° 5′N 84° 23′W) **13**:377
ELSKAMP, MAX
Belgian literature **3**:175
ELSMERE (Delaware)
map (39° 44′N 75° 36′W) **6**:88
ESSLER, FANNY 7:150 *bibliog.*
ELTON (Louisiana)
map (30° 29′N 92° 42′W) **12**:430
ELTON, CHARLES 7:150
ÉLUARD, PAUL 7:150
ELVAS (Portugal)
map (38° 53′N 7° 10′W) **15**:449

ELVIRA (Argentina)
map (35° 14′S 59° 29′W) 2:149
ELWOOD (Indiana)
map (40° 17′N 85° 50′W) 11:111
ELWOOD PARK (Florida)
map (27° 28′N 82° 29′W) 8:172
ELY (Minnesota)
map (47° 54′N 91° 51′W) 13:453
ELY (Nevada)
map (39° 15′N 114° 53′W) 14:111
ELY, EUGENE
aircraft carrier 1:220
ELY CATHEDRAL 16:283 *illus.*
ELYRIA (Ohio)
map (41° 22′N 82° 6′W) 14:357
ELYSIAN FIELDS 7:150
ELYTIS, ODYSSEUS 7:150
ELZEVIR, LOUIS 7:150 *bibliog.*
EMA (folk art) 8:198 *illus.*
EMANATIONISM 7:150–151
Iamblichus 11:3
EMANCIPATION PROCLAMATION (Russian history)
Alexander II, Emperor of Russia 1:276
Russia/Union of Soviet Socialist Republics, history of 16:357
EMANCIPATION PROCLAMATION (U.S. history) 5:29 *illus.*; 7:151 *bibliog., illus.*
black Americans 3:307
Civil War, U.S. 5:31
Lincoln, Abraham 12:349
13th Amendment 19:170
EMANUEL (county in Georgia)
map (32° 35′N 82° 20′W) 9:114
EMBALMING 7:151 *bibliog.*
funeral customs 8:363
mummy 13:639
EMBARGO 7:151
United States v. *Curtiss-Wright Export Corporation* 19:464
EMBARGO ACT 7:151 *bibliog.*
Jefferson, Thomas 11:393
Madison, James 13:42
War of 1812 20:26
EMBARRAS RIVER
map (38° 39′N 87° 37′W) 11:42
EMBARRASS (Wisconsin)
map (44° 40′N 88° 42′W) 20:185
EMBASSY
ambassador 1:324
foreign service 8:226–227
EMBEZZLEMENT 7:151
fraud 8:288
EMBIOPTERA 7:151–152
web spinner 20:86 *illus.*
EMBLEM BOOK 7:152
EMBOLISM 7:152 *bibliog.*
blood 3:338
nervous system, diseases of the 14:96
pulmonary embolism 15:619
shock, physiologic 17:279
stroke 18:302
thrombosis 19:183
EMBROIDERY 7:152 *bibliog., illus.*
needlework 14:76
Paracas 15:74
stitches 7:152 *illus.*
Transylvanian sheepskin vest 8:196 *illus.*
EMBRYO 7:152–153 *bibliog., illus.*
See also SEED
anthropometry 2:55
cloning 5:64
development 6:137–141 *illus.*
Spemann, Hans 18:177
thalidomide 19:142
egg 7:72
evolution 7:324 *illus.*
frog 8:337 *illus.*
gestation 9:160
growth 9:378–381
heart 10:92
His (family) 10:177
homonculus 10:139 *illus.*
phylogeny 15:279
pregnancy and birth 15:502
pregnancy test 15:506
reproduction 16:163
suffocation 18:325
umbilical cord 19:380
EMBRYOLOGY 7:153–154 *bibliog.*
comparative anatomy 5:155
development 6:137–142 *illus.*
developmental anatomy 1:397–398
gestation 9:160
history
anatomy 1:397–398
Baer, Karl Ernst von 3:20
biology 3:270–271
De Beer, Sir Gavin 6:58
Driesch, Hans Adolf Eduard 6:272
Fabricius ab Aquapendente, Hieronymus 8:5
Hertwig, Oscar 10:148
Pander, Christian Heinrich 15:58
Wilson, Edmund B. 20:164
Wolff, Caspar Friedrich 20:198
zoology 20:377
EMBRYOPHYTE
plant 15:333–334
EMBURY, PHILIP 7:154
EMDEN (Germany, East and West)
map (53° 22′N 7° 12′E) 9:140
EMDEN (ship)
World War I 20:228
EMELLE (Alabama)
map (32° 44′N 88° 19′W) 1:234
EMERADO (North Dakota)
map (47° 55′N 97° 22′W) 14:248
EMERALD 3:296 *illus., table*; 7:154 *bibliog., illus.*; 9:74 *illus.*
gems 9:74–75
prehnite 15:518
EMERGENCY MEDICINE
hospital 10:258
technicians
ambulance 1:326
paramedic 15:80
EMERSON (Arkansas)
map (33° 6′N 93° 11′W) 2:166
EMERSON (Nebraska)
map (42° 17′N 96° 44′W) 14:70
EMERSON (New Jersey)
map (40° 58′N 74° 2′W) 14:129
EMERSON, PETER HENRY 7:154 *bibliog.*
photography, history and art of 15:270
EMERSON, RALPH WALDO 7:154–155 *bibliog., illus.*
American Scholar, The (speech) 1:366
Thoreau, Henry David 19:178
transcendentalism 19:268
EMERSON, ROY
Borg, Björn 3:398
EMERY (geology) 7:155
corundum 5:279
EMERY (Utah)
map (38° 55′N 111° 15′W) 19:492
EMERY (county in Utah)
map (38° 55′N 110° 42′W) 19:492
EMESA *see* HOMS (Syria)
EMETIC 7:155
ipecac 11:248
EMF *see* ELECTROMOTIVE FORCE (emf) (physics)
EMI KOUSSI PEAK
map (19° 50′N 18° 30′E) 4:266
EMIGRANT AID COMPANY 7:156 *bibliog.*
EMIGRATION, ANIMAL *see* ANIMAL MIGRATION
ÉMIGRÉS 7:156
refugee 16:125
ÉMILE (book)
Rousseau, Jean Jacques 16:326
EMILIA-ROMAGNA (Italy) 7:156
cities
Bologna 3:370
Ferrara 8:58
Modena 13:490
Parma 15:95
Piacenza 15:287
Ravenna 16:95
Reggio nell'Emilia 16:128
Rimini 16:224
Italian unification 11:330 *map*
EMILIO SOJO, VICENTE
Venezuela 19:543
EMIN PASHA 7:156 *bibliog.*
EMINENCE (Kentucky)
map (38° 22′N 85° 11′W) 12:47
EMINENCE (Missouri)
map (37° 9′N 91° 22′W) 13:476
EMINENT DOMAIN 7:156 *bibliog.*
5th Amendment 8:74
property 15:571
EMINESCU, MIHAIL 7:156 *bibliog.*
EMIR 7:156
EMISSION
spectrum 18:172 *illus.*
EMLEMBE
map (25° 57′S 31° 11′E) 18:380
EMLENTON (Pennsylvania)
map (41° 11′N 79° 43′W) 15:147
EMMA (book) 7:156 *bibliog.*
Austen, Jane 2:326
EMMANUEL COLLEGE (Cambridge University) 4:52
EMMANUEL PHILIBERT, DUKE OF SAVOY
Savoy (dynasty) 17:102
EMMAUS (Pennsylvania)
map (40° 32′N 75° 30′W) 15:147
EMMEN (Netherlands)
map (52° 47′N 7° 0′E) 14:99
EMMER 20:126 *illus.*
EMMET (Arkansas)
map (33° 44′N 93° 28′W) 2:166
EMMET (county in Iowa)
map (43° 23′N 94° 38′W) 11:244
EMMET (county in Michigan)
map (45° 35′N 84° 55′W) 13:377
EMMET, ROBERT 7:156 *bibliog.*
EMMETSBURG (Iowa)
map (43° 7′N 94° 41′W) 11:244
EMMETT (Idaho)
map (43° 52′N 116° 30′W) 11:26
EMMETT, DANIEL DECATUR
American music 1:349
EMMITSBURG (Maryland)
map (39° 42′N 77° 20′W) 13:188
EMMONS (county in North Dakota)
map (46° 20′N 100° 15′W) 14:248
EMMY AWARDS 7:156–157
Cosby, Bill 5:280
Davis, Ossie 6:52
Harris, Julie 10:57
Houseman, John 10:274
Muppets 13:644
Newman, Edwin 14:169
Stanwyck, Barbara 18:220
Streep, Meryl 18:296
Ustinov, Peter 19:491
Villella, Edward 19:598
EMORY (Texas)
map (32° 52′N 95° 46′W) 19:129
EMORY PEAK
map (29° 13′N 103° 17′W) 19:129
EMORY UNIVERSITY 7:157
EMOTION 7:157 *bibliog.*
anxiety 2:72
biopsychological reactions 7:157
depression 6:118–119
drug 6:276 *illus.*
eczema 7:54
Erikson, Erik 7:230
ethics 7:250–251
expressions 7:157
fear 8:39
Freud, Sigmund 8:329–330
frustration 8:350
grief, funeral customs 8:364
hallucinogens 10:24
headache 10:85
humanistic psychology 10:300
hypertension 10:349
hysteria 10:352
learning theory 12:261
menopause 13:299
moral awareness 13:573
pain 15:15
palpitation 15:52
psychology 15:594
psychopathy 15:601
psychosomatic disorders 15:602
psychotherapy 15:603
schizophrenia 17:123
senility 17:203
sensory deprivation 17:205
speech 18:175
stress, biological 18:297
theories 7:157
ulcer 19:376
EMPAQUETAGE
Christo 4:416
EMPATHY
humanistic psychology 10:299–300
EMPEDOCLES 7:157–158 *bibliog.*
pre-Socratic philosophy 15:533
EMPEROR
caesar 4:13
titles of nobility and honor 19:213
EMPEROR JONES, THE (play) 7:158 *bibliog.*
EMPEROR MOTH
antenna 2:47 *illus.*
EMPEROR PENGUIN
Antarctica 2:43
EMPHYSEMA 7:158 *bibliog.*
bronchitis 3:503
EMPIRE 7:158
See also COLONIALISM
Aztec 2:382–383
Byzantine Empire 3:607–608
Holy Roman Empire 10:209–211
imperialism 11:61–62
Inca 11:69–73
Rome, ancient 16:297–304
EMPIRE (Nevada)
map (40° 37′N 119° 21′W) 14:111
EMPIRE (Oregon)
map (43° 23′N 124° 17′W) 14:427
EMPIRE STATE BUILDING 7:158 *bibliog.*; 14:143 *illus.*
skyscraper 17:349–350 *illus.*
EMPIRE STATE MALL (Albany)
architecture
Harrison, Wallace K. 10:60
EMPIRE STYLE 7:158–159 *illus.*
furniture 8:377
jewelry 11:411
Malmaison 13:93
Percier, Charles 15:162
EMPIRICISM 7:159 *bibliog.*
associationism 2:265
Berkeley, George 3:213
Condillac, Étienne Bonnot de 5:172
Enlightenment 7:206
epistemology 7:222
Hume, David 10:301–302
Kant, Immanuel 12:23–24
Locke, John 12:387–388
logical positivism 12:397
Maine de Biran 13:75
metaphysics 13:335
Mill, John Stuart 13:425
philosophy 15:245
positivism 15:458
pragmatism 15:487
rationalism 16:93
science, philosophy of 17:142
sensationalism 17:204
utilitarianism 19:497
Vives, Juan Luis 19:622
EMPLOYEE RETIREMENT INCOME SECURITY ACT
pension 15:154
EMPLOYMENT AND UNEMPLOYMENT 7:159–160 *bibliog.*
career education 4:146
Coxey's Army 5:323
domestic service 6:231–232
economics 7:48–49
economy, national 7:49–51
equal opportunity 7:223
affirmative action 1:132
discrimination 6:189–190
integration, racial 11:202–203
race riots 16:35
Randolph, A. Philip 16:83
sexism 17:227
United Steelworkers of America v. *Weber* 19:465
fiscal policy 8:109–110
industrial engineering 11:156
industrial psychology 11:157
industrial relations 11:157
inflation 11:170–171
Job Corps 11:421
Keynes, John Maynard 12:63–64
Labor, U.S. Department of 12:151–152
labor force 12:152
labor union 12:152–156
Lochner v. *New York* 12:386
migrant labor 13:417
minimum wage 13:446
open shop 14:398
pension 15:153–154
poverty 15:478–479
prison work programs 15:554
right-to-work laws 16:222
secondary education 17:180
service industries 17:211
social security 18:14–16
suburbs 18:317
suicide 18:331
trucking industry 19:316
underemployment 19:383
unemployment insurance 19:383–384
union shop 19:387
university 19:468 *bibliog.*
welfare state 20:97–98
women in society 20:203–204 *table*
workers' compensation 20:217
Works Progress Administration 20:217–218
yellow-dog contract 20:322
young people 20:335–336
EMPOLI (Italy)
map (43° 43′N 10° 57′E) 11:321
EMPOLI, JACOPO DA
Catherine de Médicis 4:209 *illus.*
EMPORIA (Kansas)
map (38° 24′N 96° 11′W) 12:18
EMPORIA (Virginia)
map (36° 41′N 77° 32′W) 19:607
EMPORIA GAZETTE
White, William Allen 20:136
EMPORIUM (Pennsylvania)
map (41° 31′N 78° 14′W) 15:147
EMPRESS (Alberta)
map (50° 57′N 110° 0′W) 1:256
EMPSON, WILLIAM
pastoral literature 15:109
EMPTY QUARTER RUB AL-KHALI DESERT
map (20° 0′N 51° 0′E) 17:94
EMRE, YUNUS *see* YUNUS EMRE
EMS RIVER
map (53° 30′N 7° 0′E) 9:140

EMSHWILLER, ED
Galaxy magazine cover 17:144 *illus.*
EMU 7:160 *illus.*
EMU WREN 7:160–161
EMULSION (chemistry) 7:161
cosmetics 5:282–283
ENAMEL (anatomy)
teeth 19:70 *illus.*
ENAMEL (art) 7:161–162 *bibliog., illus.*
Bartlett, Jennifer 3:97
Byzantine art and architecture 3:606
jewelry 11:410–411
Limosin, Léonard 12:346
ENANTIOMER
stereochemistry 18:258 *illus.*
ENARGITE (geology) 7:162
sulfosalts 18:334
ENCAMP (Andorra)
map (42° 32′N 1° 35′E) 1:405
ENCAMPMENT (Wyoming)
map (41° 12′N 106° 47′W) 20:301
ENCARNACIÓN (Paraguay)
map (27° 20′S 55° 54′W) 15:77
ENCAUSTIC PAINTING 7:162 *bibliog.*
ENCELADUS (astronomy)
Saturn (astronomy) 17:90–91 *illus., table*
ENCEPHALITIS 7:162 *bibliog.*
herpes 10:146
nervous system, diseases of the 14:96
ENCHANTER'S NIGHTSHADE (botany) 7:162
ENCHI FUMIKO 7:162
ENCICLOPEDIA ITALIANA DI SCIENZE, LETTERE ED ARTI
encyclopedia 7:165
ENCICLOPEDIA UNIVERSAL ILUSTRADA EUROPEO-AMERICANA
encyclopedia 7:165
ENCINA, JUAN DEL 7:162 *bibliog.*
ENCINITAS (California)
map (33° 3′N 117° 17′W) 4:31
ENCINO (Texas)
map (26° 57′N 98° 8′W) 19:129
ENCKE, JOHANN FRANZ 7:162
comet 5:133–134
ENCLOSURE 7:163 *bibliog.*
agriculture, history of 1:190–191
Industrial Revolution 11:158
manorialism 13:127
ENCOMIENDA 7:163 *bibliog.*
Latin America, history of 12:218
Mexico, history of 13:363
slavery 17:353
ENCOUNTER (periodical)
Spender, Stephen 18:178
ENCOUNTER GROUPS *see* GROUP THERAPY
ENCULTURATION *see* SOCIALIZATION
ENCUMBRANCE (law) 7:163
ENCYCLICAL 7:163
ENCYCLOPAEDIA BRITANNICA
Adler, Mortimer J. 1:104
encyclopedia 7:164
ENCYCLOPEDIA 7:163–165 *bibliog., illus.*
Alembert, Jean Le Rond d' 7:164
Diderot, Denis 6:160
Larousse, Pierre 12:208
Pliny the Elder 15:368
Vincent of Beauvais 19:600
ENCYCLOPEDIA AMERICANA
encyclopedia 7:165
ENCYCLOPEDIA UNIVERSALIS
encyclopedia 7:165
ENCYCLOPÉDIE
Alembert, Jean Le Rond d' 1:271
Diderot, Denis 6:160
encyclopedia 7:164
Helvétius, Claude Adrien 10:117
Holbach, Paul Henri Dietrich, Baron d' 10:200
END OF THE TRAIL, THE
Fraser, James Earle 8:287
ENDAMOEBA *see* ENTAMOEBA
ENDANGERED SPECIES 7:165–168 *bibliog., illus.*
bird 3:279–282
condor 5:173
cormorant 5:264–265
crane (bird) 5:330
eagle 7:3
egret 7:74
emu 7:160
falcon 8:12
game birds 9:27
lyrebird 12:479
pheasant 15:225
puffin 15:616 *illus.*
rockfowl 16:260
scrubbird 17:158
solitaire 18:55
spoonbill 18:194
vulture 19:640
whooping crane 20:143–144
woodpecker 20:212
conservation 5:203
DDT 6:57–58
ecology 7:42–46
fish 8:128
darter 6:40
fur-bearing animals 8:370
game laws 9:27
horn (biology) 10:238
Kenya 12:54
mammal
desman 6:132
false paca 8:15
ferret 8:59
gorilla 9:251
ibex 11:4
indri 11:150
koala 12:103–104
kouprey 14:473 *illus.*
leopard 12:292–293
numbat 14:292
orangutan 14:416
oryx 14:451
puma 15:622
rhinoceros 16:196
sea otter 17:169
seal 17:173 *illus.*
sirenia 17:328
solenodon 18:53
Tahltan bear dog 19:10
Tasmanian wolf 19:42–43
tiger 19:197
vicuña 19:576
wapiti 20:24
whale 20:122
whaling 20:123
wildebeest 20:149
pesticides 15:196–199
Red Data Book 16:112
reptile
bog turtle 3:359
earless monitor 7:8
gavial 9:63
Indo-Pacific ridley 16:218 *illus.*
Komodo dragon 12:108
leatherback turtle 12:263
tuatara 19:326
turtle 19:354
wildlife refuge 20:150–151
ENDANGERED SPECIES PRESERVATION ACT (United States)
wildlife refuge 20:150
ENDEAVOUR (ship) 5:235 *illus.*
Cook, James 5:236
ENDECOTT, JOHN 7:168 *bibliog.*
Pequot War 15:158
ENDER, KORNELIA 14:384 *illus.*
ENDERBURY ISLAND
Phoenix Islands 15:251
ENDERBY LAND (region in Antarctica)
map (67° 30′S 53° 0′E) 2:40
ENDERLIN (North Dakota)
map (46° 37′N 97° 36′W) 14:248
ENDERS, JOHN F. 7:168
ENDERS RESERVOIR
map (40° 25′N 101° 31′W) 14:70
ENDGAME (play) 7:168
ENDICOTT (New York)
map (42° 6′N 76° 3′W) 14:149
ENDICOTT (Washington)
map (46° 56′N 117° 41′W) 20:35
ENDIVE 7:168 *illus.*; 19:532 *illus.*
ENDIVE, BELGIAN OR FRENCH *see* CHICORY
ENDLESS HOUSE
Kiesler, Frederick John 12:75
ENDO, MITSUYE
Nisei 14:201
ENDO SHUSAKU 7:168
ENDOCARDITIS 7:168
causes, dentistry 6:114
heart diseases 10:96
ENDOCRINE SYSTEM 7:168–169 *bibliog., illus.*
adrenal gland 1:108
Brown-Séquard, Charles 3:516
duodenum, intestine 11:230
gland 9:196–197
homeostasis 10:212
hormone, animal 10:234–237
insect, juvenile hormone 11:480
insulin 11:197–198
liver 12:374
metabolism 13:327
pancreas 15:57–58
parathyroid 15:83
pineal gland 15:306
pituitary gland 15:322
prostaglandins 15:572–573
sex hormones 17:226–227
thyroid gland 19:188
ENDOCRINE SYSTEM, DISEASES OF THE 7:169–171 *bibliog.*
Addison's disease 1:101
amenorrhea 1:326
diabetes 6:148–149
diabetes insipidus 6:148
goiter 9:225
growth hormone 9:381
hypoglycemia 10:351
myasthenia gravis 13:689
nutritional-deficiency diseases 14:307
obesity 14:315
osteoporosis 14:458
parathyroid 15:83
pituitary gland 15:322
sex change 17:225
sex hormones 17:226
ENDODERM
development 6:138; 6:141 *illus.*
ENDOGAMY 7:171
exogamy 7:333
incest 11:74
women in society 20:203
ENDOMETRIUM
uterus 19:497
ENDOPLASMIC RETICULUM 7:171
cell 4:232 *illus.*; 4:233
cytochrome 5:411
Golgi apparatus 9:240
ENDORPHIN
opiate receptor 14:405
ENDOSCOPE 7:171
bronchoscope 3:503
endoscopic photography 15:266
examination, medical 7:326
gastroscope 9:58
ENDOSPERM
seed 17:186
ENDOTHERM
body temperature 3:357
ENDOTHERMIC AND EXOTHERMIC REACTIONS (chemistry) 7:171 *bibliog.*
Hess's law 10:151
hydrogenation 10:341
ENDOWMENT *see* FOUNDATIONS AND ENDOWMENTS
ENDOWMENT INSURANCE
life insurance 12:329
ENDURO *see* MOTORCYCLING
ENDYMION (mythology) 7:171
ENDYMION (poem) 7:171
Keats, John 12:36
ENEMA
cathartic 4:204
ENEMY OF THE PEOPLE, AN (play) 7:171–172
ENERGY 7:172–173 *bibliog.*
binding energy 3:257–258
biologic
metabolism 13:325–327
Mitchell, Peter 13:483
nutrition, human 14:304–306 *illus.*
biosphere 3:277
chemical equilibrium and kinetics 4:316–317
conservation, laws of 5:204–205 *illus.*
conversion 7:172
chemical energy 4:315
engine 7:177
mechanical engineering 13:259–260
plasma physics 15:346
turbine 19:340
cosmic rays 5:283
electricity 7:107–111
electron volt 7:124
enthalpy 7:208
entropy 7:173; 7:209
exchange
Boltzmann, Ludwig 3:372
forms of 7:172
free energy
chemical equilibrium and kinetics 4:316
fusion, nuclear 8:381
fusion energy 8:382–383
ground temperature 9:373
ion and ionization 11:240 *illus.*
kinetic energy 12:78
light energy
light 12:334
photochemistry 15:257–259
machine 13:19–21
mass relationship
Einstein, Albert 7:93
phosphorescence 15:256
photoelectric effect 15:260
photon energy
photoelectric cell 15:259–260
photon 15:274
potential, electric 15:466
potential energy 15:466
quantum mechanics 16:9–11
radiation 16:42
electromagnetic radiation 7:116–118
research institutions
Lawrence Berkeley and Lawrence Livermore laboratories 12:251
Oak Ridge National Laboratory 14:312
resonance (physics) 16:178
solar energy 18:41–44
spectral distribution, blackbody radiation 3:320 *illus.*
spectrum 18:173
storage, flywheel 8:191–192
thermal
heat and heat transfer 10:98
ocean thermal energy conversion 14:333
thermodynamics 19:162–165
tidal energy 19:192–193
transducer 19:269
transfer
isothermal process 11:301
transformer 19:270–271
transport 7:172–173
kinetic theory of matter 12:79
pipe and pipeline 15:310–311
unit of measurement
British thermal unit 3:497
calorie 4:47
erg 7:228
joule 11:453
units, physical 19:467
work (physics) 20:217
ENERGY (psychic)
libido 12:314
ENERGY, U.S. DEPARTMENT OF 7:173
Atomic Energy Commission
Libby, Willard Frank 12:311
Rickover, Hyman 16:216
Seaborg, Glenn T. 17:171–172
Fermi Award
Teller, Edward 19:90
von Neumann, John 19:634
hydrogen bomb 10:339
Lilienthal, David 12:340
radioactive waste disposal 14:282
research institutions
Argonne National Laboratory 2:152
Brookhaven National Laboratory 3:510
Fermi National Accelerator Laboratory 8:56
Lawrence Berkeley and Lawrence Livermore laboratories 12:251
Los Alamos National Scientific Laboratory 12:416
Oak Ridge National Laboratory 14:312
Stanford Linear Accelerator Center 18:218
secretary of energy
flag 8:148 *illus.*
ENERGY CONSERVATION
aluminum 1:319
conservation, laws of 5:204–205
Daylight Saving Time 6:56–57
flywheel 8:192
recycling of materials 16:111
symmetry (physics) 18:404
thermodynamics 19:162; 19:164
ENERGY LEVEL (physics) 7:173
electron configuration 7:120
laser and maser 12:210–211
metal 13:329
semiconductor 17:196
ENERGY RESEARCH AND DEVELOPMENT ADMINISTRATION
Energy, U.S. Department of 7:173
ENERGY SOURCES 7:173–175 *bibliog., tables*
See also ENERGY TECHNOLOGY
Africa 1:149 *map*
agriculture and the food supply 1:196–197
ATP 2:312
bituminous coal 3:301
breeder reactor 3:471–472; 7:175
coal and coal mining 5:75–79; 7:175
coal gasification 5:79
consumption, worldwide 7:174–175 *tables*
conversion to new sources 7:175
ecology 7:42–46
energy recovery
waste disposal systems 20:47
fuel 8:352–354
synthetic fuels 18:409–410
fuel cell 8:354
fusion energy 7:175; 8:382–383

gasohol **9**:55
gasoline **9**:55
geothermal energy 7:174–175; **9**:120–121
hot springs **10**:259
hydroelectric power **10**:335
impact of chemistry **4**:324
kerosene **12**:59
natural gas 7:174–175; **14**:48
nonrenewable resources 7:174–175
North America **14**:228–230
nuclear energy 7:175; **14**:278–284
ocean-atmosphere interaction **14**:321
ocean and sea **14**:331–332
ocean thermal energy conversion **14**:333
peat 7:174–175; **15**:129
petroleum 7:173–175
petroleum industry **15**:209–215
power, generation and transmission of **15**:481–486
problems 7:173
producer gas **15**:561
production, worldwide 7:174 *tables*
propane **15**:569
renewable resources 7:173–175
shale, oil **17**:238
solar energy 7:175; **18**:41–44
tar sands **19**:34
thermodynamics **19**:164–165
Trans-Alaska Pipeline **19**:266–267
United States, manufacturing **13**:132–133
windmills and wind power **20**:172–173
ENERGY TECHNOLOGY
See also NUCLEAR REACTOR; POWER, GENERATION AND TRANSMISSION OF
armature **2**:171
battery **3**:125–126
bellows **3**:191
boiler **3**:362–363
breeder reactor **3**:471–472
catalytic converter **4**:199
compressor **5**:158
condenser **5**:172
electromagnet 7:115
engine 7:177
flywheel **8**:191–192
fuel cell **8**:354
fuse **8**:381
gear **9**:65–66
generator **9**:78
heat engine **10**:97
heat exchanger **10**:97–98
heat pump **10**:98–99
heating systems **10**:99–100
internal-combustion engine **11**:215–218
lever **12**:302
machine **13**:19–21
magnet **13**:54–55
mill **13**:424–425
motor **13**:611–612
nuclear energy **14**:278–284
perpetual motion machine **15**:178
pulley **15**:619
pump **15**:622–623
solar cell **18**:40
solar collectors **18**:40–41
stator **18**:238
steam engine **18**:240–241
Stirling engine **18**:272–273
tokamak **19**:223
transformer **19**:270–271
treadmill **19**:285
turbine **19**:340
Wankel engine **20**:23–24
waterwheel **20**:66–67
windmills and wind power **20**:172–172
ENESCO, GEORGES 7:176
ENFANTIN, BARTHÉLÉMY PROSPER 7:176
ENFIELD (Connecticut)
map (41° 58′N 72° 36′W) **5**:193
ENFIELD (New Hampshire)
map (43° 34′N 71° 57′W) **14**:123
ENFIELD (North Carolina)
map (36° 11′N 77° 47′W) **14**:242
ENFLURANE
anesthetics **1**:410
ENG AND CHANG *see* SIAMESE TWINS
ENGARUKA (Tanzania) 7:176
ENGEL, MARIAN 7:176
ENGEL* v. *VITALE 7:176 *bibliog.*
classroom prayer 7:176
ENGELHARD (North Carolina)
map (35° 31′N 76° 2′W) **14**:242
ENGELS, FRIEDRICH 7:176–177 *bibliog., illus.*
communism **5**:146
Communist Manifesto **5**:151
dialectical materialism **6**:150
law **12**:242–243
Marx, Karl **13**:181–182
membership card for International Workingmen's Association **18**:21 *illus.*
socialism **18**:19–20
ENGINE 7:177
automobile **2**:358
cooling system, engine **5**:241–242 *illus.*
Carnot engine
Carnot, Nicolas Léonard Sadi **4**:158
diesel engine **6**:163 *illus.*
energy conversion, other forms 7:177
external-combustion engine
Stirling engine **18**:272–273
flywheel **8**:192
heat engine **10**:97
heat exchanger **10**:98
internal-combustion engine **11**:215–218
jet
compressor **5**:158
jet propulsion **11**:406–407
ramjet **16**:80–81
turbojet **11**:406 *illus.*
Zwicky, Fritz **20**:384
knock, gasoline **9**:55
locomotive **12**:388–392
mechanical engineering **13**:259–260
motor **13**:611–612
motorboat **13**:612 *illus.*
Rolls-Royce **16**:272
steam engine **18**:240–241
turbine **19**:340
turbofan **11**:406 *illus.*
Wankel engine 7:177; **20**:23–24
ENGINEERING 7:177–178 *bibliog.*
branches 7:178
astronautics **2**:274–276
bioengineering **16**:130
biomedical engineering **3**:274
biotechnology **3**:277
civil engineering **5**:10–11
electrical and electronic engineering 7:106
fire protection **8**:104
genetic engineering **9**:84–85
human factors engineering **10**:297
industrial engineering **11**:156
materials technology **13**:219–221
mechanical engineering **13**:259–260
process control **15**:560–561
systems engineering **18**:414–415
computer-aided design and computer-aided manufacturing **5**:160j–160L
computer modeling **5**:162
draftsman **13**:259 *illus.*
flume studies **8**:186
geology **9**:105
history 7:177–178
Baker, Sir Benjamin **3**:27
Eupalinus 7:265
Frontinus, Sextus Julius **8**:345
Gilbreth, Frank and Lillian **9**:180
Hero of Alexandria **10**:144
Rankine, William John Macquorn **16**:88
technology, history of **19**:61–69 *illus.*
Telford, Thomas **19**:90
Terzaghi, Karl **19**:125
Vitruvius **19**:621
irrigation **11**:280–283
labor union
United Auto Workers **19**:401
machine **13**:19–21
modern era 7:178
pipe and pipeline **15**:310–311
professional and educational organizations **17**:145 *table*
American Chemical Society **1**:337
American Institute of Aeronautics and Astronautics **1**:341
American Institute of Chemists **1**:341
National Academy of Sciences **14**:27
roads and highways **16**:235–239 *illus.*
soil **18**:38
truss **19**:320
vector analysis **19**:530
waste disposal systems **20**:46
ENGINEERING TECHNOLOGY
alarm systems **1**:240
automation **2**:357–358
blueprint **3**:345
breath analyzer **3**:470
dynamometer **6**:319–320
fire extinguisher **8**:102
fire prevention and control **8**:103–105
incinerator **11**:74
instrumentation **11**:196–197
invention **11**:232–233
lie detector **12**:323–324
pantograph **15**:62
rangefinder **16**:84
robot **16**:246
smoke detector **17**:373
ENGINEERS, CORPS OF 7:178
ENGLAND 7:178–181 *bibliog., illus., map*
See also GREAT BRITAIN, HISTORY OF; UNITED KINGDOM
aircraft, military *see* AIRCRAFT, MILITARY—Great Britain
archaeology
Avebury **2**:369
Celts **4**:241–242
Clark, Grahame **5**:38
Cotswold-Severn **5**:304
Creswellian **5**:339
European prehistory 7:301 *map*
Grimes Graves **9**:364–365
Hadrian's Wall **10**:8
lake dwelling **12**:171
Maiden Castle **13**:66
megalith **13**:278–279
Star Carr **18**:226
stone alignments **18**:281
Stonehenge **18**:283 *illus.*
Sutton Hoo ship burial **18**:373–374
Wessex culture **20**:106
Woodhenge **20**:211
art *see* ENGLISH ART AND ARCHITECTURE
censorship **4**:247
cities
Bath **3**:121–122
Bedford **3**:153
Beverley **3**:233
Birmingham **3**:292–293
Blackpool **3**:322
Bolton **3**:372
Bournemouth **3**:424
Bradford **3**:436
Brighton **3**:486
Bristol **3**:488
Bury St. Edmunds **3**:583
Cambridge **4**:52
Canterbury **4**:116
Carlisle **4**:151
Chester **4**:336
Chesterfield **4**:336
Chichester **4**:344
Colchester **5**:97
Coventry **5**:319
Darlington **6**:39
Derby **6**:121
Doncaster **6**:237
Dover **6**:250
Durham **6**:305
Exeter 7:331
Gateshead **9**:58
Gloucester **9**:209
Grimsby **9**:366
Harrogate **10**:61
Hartlepool **10**:62
Harwich **10**:65
Hastings **10**:67
Hull **10**:295
Leeds **12**:271
Leicester **12**:277
Lincoln **12**:347
Liverpool **12**:375–376
London **12**:400–402 *illus., map*
Maidstone **13**:66–67
Manchester **13**:108
Newcastle upon Tyne **14**:164–165
Northampton **14**:253
Norwich **14**:266
Nottingham **14**:268
Oxford **14**:474
Penzance **15**:155
Peterborough **15**:202
Plymouth **15**:373–374
Portsmouth **15**:448
Reading **16**:100
Saint Albans **17**:15–16
Salisbury **17**:33
Scarborough **17**:115
Sheffield **17**:250
Southampton **18**:107
Stoke-on-Trent **18**:278
Stratford-on-Avon **18**:291
Wakefield **20**:8
Winchester **20**:168
Worcester **20**:216
Worsley **19**:407 *illus.*
York **20**:330
climate 7:178; 7:180
cosmetics **5**:282
counties
Avon **2**:377
Bedfordshire **3**:153–154
Berkshire **3**:213–214
Buckinghamshire **3**:536
Cambridgeshire **4**:53
Cheshire **4**:334
Cleveland **5**:52
Cornwall **5**:270
Cumbria **5**:387
Derbyshire **6**:121
Devon **6**:143–144
Dorset **6**:243
Durham **6**:305–306
Essex 7:245
Gloucestershire **9**:210
Hampshire **10**:32
Hereford and Worcester **10**:141
Hertfordshire **10**:148
Humberside **10**:300
Isle of Wight **11**:298
Kent **12**:45
Lancashire **12**:177
Leicestershire **12**:277
Lincolnshire **12**:350
Norfolk **14**:218
Northamptonshire **14**:253
Nottinghamshire **14**:268
Oxfordshire **14**:475
Salop **17**:36
Somerset **18**:61
Staffordshire **18**:209–210
Suffolk **18**:325
Surrey **18**:366
Sussex **18**:372
Warwickshire **20**:33
Wiltshire **20**:167
Yorkshire **20**:331
crime **5**:346 *table*
crown **5**:364 *illus.*
dance
minuet **13**:461
morris dance **13**:589
domestic service **6**:232 *table*
economic activities 7:180
automotive industry **2**:366 *table*
Bank of England **3**:67
banking systems **3**:68–69
Great Britain, history of **9**:318
London **12**:400
Ricardo, David **16**:206
unemployment rate 7:160
education 7:61
academy **1**:71
Arnold, Matthew **2**:185
Ascham, Roger **2**:228
Bell, Andrew **3**:185
Birmingham, University of **3**:293
Bristol, University of **3**:488
Britannia Royal Naval College **3**:489
British education **3**:493–495
Cambridge University **4**:52–53
Charterhouse **4**:300
Eton College 7:258
Harrow School **10**:61
Lancaster, Joseph **12**:177
London, University of **12**:403–404
Manchester, Victoria University of **13**:108–109
Mulcaster, Richard **13**:635
open classroom **14**:398
Open University **14**:399
Oxford, University of **14**:474
Rugby School **16**:340
Sandhurst, Royal Military Academy at **17**:62
Summerhill **18**:339
Sunday school **18**:347
universities **3**:493 *table*
Winchester College **20**:168
forest **8**:228 *illus.*
gardens
Hooker (family) **10**:227
government and politics **19**:411
Conservative parties **5**:205–206
Great Britain, history of **9**:317
intelligence gathering **11**:204–205
Labour party **12**:156–157
Liberal parties **12**:311
Parliament **15**:92
Tory party **19**:247
Whig party **20**:130
health-care systems **10**:88
history 7:180–181
See also GREAT BRITAIN, HISTORY OF
Industrial Revolution **11**:158–159
political parties **15**:400
state (in political philosophy) **18**:232
labor union

ENGLAND (cont.)
Trades Union Congress **19**:264
Transport and General Workers' Union **19**:277
land 7:178–180 *map*; **19**:404–405 *illus.*
language
See also ENGLISH LANGUAGE
Celtic languages **4**:241
law
See also COMMON LAW; UNITED KINGDOM—legal system
adoption **1**:107
capital punishment **4**:123–124
inheritance **11**:177
law, history of **12**:245–246
libraries
Bodleian Library **3**:356
British Library **3**:497
literature *see* ENGLISH LITERATURE
map (52° 30′N 1° 30′W) **19**:403
mining and quarrying **13**:446
money
Offa, King of Mercia **14**:353
pound sterling **15**:476
patron saint
George, Saint **9**:109
people 7:180; 7:275 *illus.*
Anglo-Saxons **2**:3 *map*
class, social **5**:40
migration to the United States **11**:55 *map*
physical features
Land's End **12**:184
Pennines **15**:145
Scilly Islands **17**:146
pistol **15**:318 *illus.*
radio and television broadcasting **16**:60
regions
Dartmoor **6**:40
East Anglia 7:31
Fens, The **8**:51
Lake District **12**:170
Middlesex **13**:413
Midlands **13**:414
rivers, lakes, and waterways
Avon, River **2**:377
Bridgewater Canal **3**:485
Humber, River **10**:300
Mersey, River **13**:312
Severn, River **17**:220
Thames, River **19**:142
Trent, River **19**:290
social security **18**:14
socialism *see* SOCIALISM
sports
soccer **18**:9–10 *illus.*
tennis **19**:108–109
theater
See also ELIZABETHAN AGE; JACOBEAN THEATER; MEDIEVAL DRAMA
Bancroft, Sir Squire **3**:61
burletta **3**:572
Clive, Kitty **5**:61
Cochran, Sir Charles Blake **5**:86
Devine, George **6**:143
D'Oyly Carte, Richard **6**:253
Drury Lane Theatre **6**:283
Foote, Samuel **8**:219
Garrick, David **9**:50–51
Gielgud, Sir John **9**:177
Granville-Barker, Harley **9**:289
Grein, J. T. **9**:357
Gwynne, Nell **9**:412
Hall, Peter **10**:22
Haymarket Theatre **10**:83
interlude **11**:214
Irving, Sir Henry **11**:284
Kean (family) **12**:34–35
Macready, William Charles **13**:36
masque **13**:200
Mathews, Charles James (1803–1878) **13**:228
mumming play **13**:638–639
music hall, vaudeville, and burlesque **13**:671–673
musical comedy **13**:673–675
National Theatre **14**:46
Old Vic Theatre **14**:375
Olivier, Laurence Kerr, Baron Olivier of Brighton **14**:379
Redgrave (family) **16**:115
Royal Shakespeare Company **16**:331
Siddons, Sarah **17**:294
theater, history of the **19**:145–146; **19**:149; **19**:150
theater architecture and staging **19**:152
Vestris, Madame **19**:565
titles of nobility **19**:214 *table*
transportation
locomotive **12**:388–390 *illus.*
railroad **16**:73; **16**:75 *illus.*
roads and highways **16**:235–238
turnpike **19**:351
Yorkshire wagon **20**:6 *illus.*
urban planning *see* URBAN PLANNING
water supply **20**:56–57
ENGLAND (Arkansas)
map (34° 33′N 91° 58′W) **2**:166
ENGLAND, CHURCH OF 7:181 *bibliog.*
Andrewes, Lancelot **1**:407–408
Anglican Communion **1**:416
anthem **2**:49
Book of Common Prayer **3**:386
Canterbury **4**:116
Canterbury, archbishop of **4**:116
Clarendon Code **5**:37
Cranmer, Thomas **5**:331–332
Cromwell, Thomas, 1st Earl of Essex **5**:358
Elizabeth I, Queen of England 7:141
Elizabethan Age 7:143
Europe, history of 7:287
Great Britain, history of **9**:313; **9**:317
Henry VIII, King of England **10**:126
Hooker, Richard **10**:227
hymn **10**:346
James II, King of England, Scotland, and Ireland **11**:356
Laud, William **12**:236
Oxford movement **14**:475
Puritanism **15**:630
Reformation **16**:121 *map*
Test Acts **19**:126
Thirty-nine Articles **19**:170
United States, history of the **19**:439
ENGLAND, JOHN 7:181 *bibliog.*
ENGLE, JOE H.
Space Shuttle **18**:136
ENGLEE (Newfoundland)
map (50° 44′N 56° 6′W) **14**:166
ENGLEWOOD (Colorado)
map (39° 39′N 104° 59′W) **5**:116
ENGLEWOOD (Florida)
map (26° 58′N 82° 21′W) **8**:172
ENGLEWOOD (Kansas)
map (37° 2′N 100° 1′W) **12**:18
ENGLEWOOD (New Jersey)
map (40° 54′N 73° 59′W) **14**:129
ENGLEWOOD CLIFFS (New Jersey)
map (40° 53′N 73° 57′W) **14**:129
ENGLISH (Indiana)
map (38° 20′N 86° 28′W) **11**:111
ENGLISH ART AND ARCHITECTURE 7:181–188 *bibliog., illus.*
See also the subheading Great Britain under names of specific art forms, movements, and historic periods, e.g., ARCHITECTURE; DECORATIVE ARTS; NEOCLASSICISM (art); BAROQUE ART AND ARCHITECTURE; etc.; names of specific artists, e.g., BACON, FRANCIS; HOGARTH, WILLIAM; etc.
Anglo-Saxon 7:181–182
Art Nouveau **2**:209–210
calligraphy **4**:43
cathedrals and churches **4**:207 *illus.*; **4**:208
Celtic art **4**:238–241
costume **5**:299–303 *illus.*
Elizabethan style 7:146
folk art **8**:196
Georgian style **9**:119
glassware, decorative **9**:203 *illus.*
Gothic art and architecture **9**:258; **9**:261–262
Gothic Revival **9**:262–263
Greek Revival **9**:345–346
history
Pevsner, Sir Nikolaus **15**:216
house (in Western architecture) **10**:266–267 *illus.*
illuminated manuscripts **11**:47–48
interior design **11**:212–214 *illus.*
Jacobean style **11**:345
jewelry **11**:410 *illus.*
landscape architecture **12**:186–187; **12**:187 *illus.*
garden **9**:40–41 *illus.*
landscape painting **12**:190
museums, art **13**:658
Norman architecture **14**:220
painting **15**:21–22
Perpendicular Gothic style **15**:177
pottery and porcelain **15**:471–472
Pre-Raphaelites **15**:519
Queen Anne Style **16**:21
Regency style **16**:126
Romanesque art and architecture **16**:282–283 *illus.*
rugs and carpets **16**:343
social realism **18**:13
stained glass **18**:212
Tate Gallery, The **19**:44
Tudor style **19**:329
Victorian style **19**:575–576 *illus.*
ENGLISH BILLIARDS **3**:255 *illus.*
ENGLISH CHANNEL 7:188–189 *bibliog.*
Channel Islands **4**:281 *map*
Dover, Strait of **6**:250
Eddystone Lighthouse **12**:337 *illus.*
flight, human-powered **8**:165 *illus.*
map (50° 20′N 1° 0° W) **19**:403
swimmers
Chadwick, Florence **4**:267
Ederle, Gertrude 7:56
tunnel **19**:339
ENGLISH CIVIL WAR 7:189–190 *bibliog., illus., map*
Cavaliers **4**:220
Charles I, King of England, Scotland, and Ireland **4**:291
Covenanters **5**:319
Cromwell, Oliver **5**:357–358
Europe, history of 7:288
Great Britain, history of **9**:313–314
Henderson, Alexander **10**:121
historians
Gardiner, Samuel Rawson **9**:44
Ireland, history of **11**:263
Levelers **12**:302
Long Parliament **12**:407
major battles **9**:314 *map*
Montrose, James Graham, 1st Marquess of **13**:560
Nottinghamshire (England) **14**:268
political sympathies 7:189 *map*
Puritanism **15**:630
Roundheads **16**:325
Saint Albans **17**:16
Somerset (England) **18**:61
uniform **4**:221 *illus.*; 7:190 *illus.*
women in society **20**:202
Worcester (city in England) **20**:216
ENGLISH COCKER SPANIEL **6**:219 *illus.*; 7:190 *bibliog., illus.*
cocker spaniel **5**:87
ENGLISH DERBY *see* DERBY, THE
ENGLISH FOXHOUND **6**:216 *illus.*; 7:190 *bibliog., illus.*
harrier (dog) **10**:56
ENGLISH HORN 7:190–191 *bibliog.*
oboe **14**:316 *illus.*
ENGLISH LANGUAGE 7:191–193 *bibliog.*
See also BASIC ENGLISH
American language 7:193
as a second language 7:192
cockney **5**:87
correct usage
Newman, Edwin **14**:169
dictionaries **6**:159–160
Fowler, H.W. **8**:255
effect of printing on 7:192
English-based creoles **5**:338
lingua franca **12**:354
Middle English 7:191–192; **13**:412
Modern English 7:192–193
Old English 7:191; **14**:374–375
origins 7:191
parts of speech **15**:100–101
reading education
Initial Teaching Alphabet **11**:178
sign language **17**:300
slang **17**:350
writing systems, evolution of **20**:294
ENGLISH LITERATURE 7:193–202 *bibliog., illus.*
See also AUSTRALIAN LITERATURE; CANADIAN LITERATURE; IRISH LITERATURE; SCOTTISH LITERATURE; WELSH LITERATURE; the subheading English literature under CRITICISM, LITERARY; DRAMA; NOVEL; POETRY; etc.; names of specific authors, e.g., CHAUCER, GEOFFREY; WOOLF, VIRGINIA; etc.; titles of specific literary works, e.g., *PARADISE LOST* (poem); *TO THE LIGHTHOUSE* (book); etc.
aestheticism **1**:130
Anglo-Norman period 7:194–195
Anglo-Saxon period 7:193–194
Anglo-Saxon Chronicle, The **2**:3
Angry Young Men **2**:7
Arthur and Arthurian legend **2**:219
biography **3**:263–264
Bloomsbury group **3**:340–341
Cavalier poets **4**:220
chapbook **4**:284
decadence **6**:72
Edwardian literature 7:69
Elizabethan Age 7:143–144; 7:195
Georgian poetry **9**:118
Jacobean literature **11**:345
Middle English 7:191–192
Chaucer, Geoffrey **4**:304
Langland, William **12**:196
Lydgate, John **12**:474
Sir Gawain and the Green Knight **17**:327
Old English 7:193
Ælfric **1**:118
English language 7:191
Exeter Book 7:331
Tolkien, J. R. R. **19**:266–267
poet laureate **15**:378
realism (literature) **16**:104
romanticism (literature) **16**:292
Victorian literature **19**:575
17th century 7:195–196
18th century 7:196–198
19th century 7:198–201
20th century 7:201–202
ENGLISH MUSCOVY COMPANY *see* MUSCOVY COMPANY
ENGLISH MUSIC 7:202–204 *bibliog., illus.*
See also names of specific composers, e.g., BRITTEN, BENJAMIN; PURCELL, HENRY; etc.
consort music **5**:206
Deller, Alfred **6**:94
French influence 7:202–203
fuging tune **8**:355
glee **9**:207
hymn **10**:346
madrigal **13**:45
medieval music **13**:275
music, history of Western **13**:665–667
music festivals **13**:670
opera **14**:401
rock music **16**:248
song **18**:64
viol **19**:602
virginal **19**:606
ENGLISH SETTER **6**:218 *illus.*; 7:204 *bibliog., illus.*
ENGLISH SPARROW *see* SPARROW
ENGLISH SPRINGER SPANIEL **6**:218 *illus.*; 7:204 *bibliog., illus.*
ENGLISH TOY SPANIEL **6**:217 *illus.*; 7:204–205 *bibliog., illus.*
ENGLISH WARS *see* ANGLO-DUTCH WARS
ENGRAVING 7:205–206 *bibliog., illus.*
Barbari, Jacopo de' **3**:76
Bartolozzi, Francesco **3**:98
Bartsch, Adam von **3**:98–99
Bella, Stefano della **3**:186
Blake, William **3**:325
book illustration **3**:387
Bosse, Abraham **3**:408
Bry, Théodore de **3**:528
Caraglio, Giovanni Jacopo **4**:131
Cochin (family) **5**:85
drypoint **6**:285
etching 7:248–249
Gillray, James **9**:182
Goltzius, Hendrik **9**:241
graphic arts **9**:292
Hogarth, William **10**:198
Indians of North America, art of the **11**:139
intaglio (art) **11**:199
intaglio (printing) **11**:199
Lucas van Leyden **12**:448–449
Master E. S. **13**:215
Master of the Housebook **13**:215
Master of the Playing Cards **13**:215
Merian (family) **13**:310
Nanteuil, Robert **14**:13
Saint-Aubin (family) **17**:16
Schongauer, Martin **17**:133
scrimshaw **17**:158
tools 7:205 *illus.*
woodcuts and wood engravings **20**:210–211
ENIAC (computer) **5**:160a
Atanasoff, John V. **2**:287
computer industry **5**:160n
Eckert, John Presper, designer 7:39
Mauchly, John William **13**:232
ENID (Oklahoma) 7:206
map (36° 19′N 97° 48′W) **14**:368
ENID LAKE
map (34° 10′N 89° 50′W) **13**:469
ENIGMA (cryptograph machine)
cryptology **5**:373 *illus.*
ENIWETOK (Marshall Islands) 7:206

coral reef **5**:258–259
hydrogen bomb **10**:339 *illus.*
ENJAMBMENT
versification **19**:562
ENKHUIZEN (Netherlands)
map (52° 42′N 5° 17′E) **14**:99
ENKI *see* EA
ENKIDU
mythology **13**:697
ENKOMI (Cyprus) 7:206 *bibliog.*
ENLARGER (photography) 7:206 *bibliog.*
lens **12**:286
ENLIGHTENMENT 7:206–207 *bibliog.*
Alembert, Jean Le Rond d' **1**:271
Baumgarten, Alexander Gottlieb **3**:130
Bayle, Pierre **3**:133
Catherine II, Empress (Catherine the Great) **4**:209–210
Condillac, Étienne Bonnot de **5**:273
Condorcet, Marie Jean Antoine Nicolas Caritat, Marquis de **5**:173
Dalin, Olof von **6**:13
deism **6**:86
Diderot, Denis **6**:160
Épinay, Louise Florence Pétronille de la Live d' 7:220
Europe, history of 7:290
family **8**:17
Fénelon, François de Salignac de la Mothe **8**:50
Fontenelle, Bernard le Bovier de **8**:207
France, history of **8**:269
French literature **8**:316–317
history **10**:185
Holbach, Paul Henri Dietrich, Baron d' **10**:200
Holberg, Ludvig, Baron **10**:202
humanism **10**:299
Leibniz, Gottfried Wilhelm von **12**:276–277
Lessing, Gotthold **12**:299
Montesquieu, Charles Louis de Secondat, Baron de la Brède et de **13**:553
philosophes (intellectual group) **15**:240
Reimarus, Hermann Samuel **16**:131
Rousseau, Jean Jacques **16**:326–327
Spain, history of **18**:147
Voltaire **19**:631–632
Wieland, Christoph Martin **20**:145
Wolff, Christian **20**:198
women in society **20**:202
ENLIL *see* MARDUK (Mesopotamian deity)
ENMEBARAGESI, KING OF KISH
Kish **12**:90
ENMORE (Guyana)
map (6° 46′N 57° 59′W) **9**:410
ENNA (Italy)
map (37° 34′N 14° 17′E) **11**:321
ENNEDI MOUNTAINS (plateau)
map (17° 15′N 22° 0′E) **4**:266
ENNIS (Montana)
map (45° 21′N 111° 44′W) **13**:547
ENNIS (Texas)
map (32° 20′N 96° 38′W) **19**:129
ENNIUS, QUINTUS 7:207 *bibliog.*
ENNS RIVER
map (48° 14′N 14° 32′E) **2**:348
ENO, BRIAN
rock music **16**:249 *illus.*
ENOCH 7:207
ENOCH, BOOKS OF *see* PSEUDEPIGRAPHA
ENOREE RIVER
map (34° 26′N 81° 25′W) **18**:98
ENOS, WILLIAM BERKELEY *see* BERKELEY, BUSBY
ENOSBURG FALLS (Vermont)
map (44° 55′N 72° 48′W) **19**:554
ENRIQUILLO (Dominican Republic)
map (17° 54′N 71° 14′W) **6**:233
ENRIQUILLO, LAKE
map (18° 27′N 71° 39′W) **6**:233
ENSCHEDE (Netherlands)
map (52° 12′N 6° 53′E) **14**:99
ENSENADA (Argentina)
map (34° 51′S 57° 55′W) **2**:149
ENSENADA (Mexico)
map (31° 52′N 116° 37′W) **13**:357
ENSENADA, ZENÓN DE SOMODEVILLA, MARQUÉS DE LA 7:207
ENSOR, JAMES
Les Masques singuliers 7:207 *illus.*
ENSTATITE *see* PYROXENE
ENTABLATURE **2**:131 *illus.*; 7:208
architrave **2**:137
cornice **5**:269
frieze **8**:333
Greek architecture **9**:335 *illus.*
Temple of Zeus **17**:160 *illus.*
ENTAIL 7:208
inheritance **11**:177
ENTAMOEBA 7:208
amebiasis **1**:326
amoeba **1**:376
colitis **5**:102
dysentery
parasitic cycle **15**:83 *illus.*
food poisoning and infection **8**:211
ENTASIS **2**:131 *illus.*
ENTEBBE (Uganda) 7:208; **19**:373 *illus.*
map (0° 4′N 32° 28′E) **19**:372
ENTENTE CORDIALE *see* TRIPLE ENTENTE
ENTERITIS 7:208; **9**:56 *illus.*
clinical forms 7:208
ENTEROBACTER 7:208
ENTEROGASTRONE
intestine **11**:230
ENTERPRISE (aircraft carrier) **1**:221 *illus.*; **20**:266 *illus.*
ENTERPRISE (Alabama)
map (31° 19′N 85° 51′W) **1**:234
ENTERPRISE (Guyana)
map (6° 56′N 58° 24′W) **9**:410
ENTERPRISE (Kansas)
map (38° 54′N 97° 7′W) **12**:18
ENTERPRISE (Oregon)
map (45° 25′N 117° 17′W) **14**:427
ENTERPRISE, THE (yacht) **3**:352 *illus.*
ENTHALPY 7:208 *illus.*
measurement 7:208
thermodynamics **19**:163
ENTOMOLOGY *see* INSECT
ENTOPROCT 7:208
worm **20**:283
ENTRAPMENT 7:208
ABSCAM **1**:62
ENTRE RÍOS (province in Argentina)
map (32° 0′S 59° 0′W) **2**:149
ENTRE RÍOS CORDILLERA
map (14° 19′N 85° 26′W) **10**:218
ENTROPY (information)
communication **5**:142–144
information theory **11**:174
Shannon, Claude Elwood **17**:240
ENTROPY (physics) 7:209 *bibliog.*
Clausius, Rudolf **5**:45
disorder in systems 7:209
energy 7:173
physics, history of **15**:285–286
reversible and irreversible processes **16**:186
thermochemistry **19**:162
thermodynamics **19**:163
ENTSY *see* SAMOYED (people)
ENTWISTLE, JOHN
Who, The **20**:143
ENUGU (Nigeria)
map (6° 27′N 7° 27′E) **14**:190
ENUMA ELISH 7:209 *bibliog.*
creation accounts **5**:335
Marduk **13**:148
mythology **13**:696 *illus.*
ENUMCLAW (Washington)
map (47° 12′N 121° 59′W) **20**:35
ENURESIS *see* BED-WETTING
ENVALIRA PASS
map (42° 32′N 1° 42′E) **1**:405
ENVER PASHA
Ottoman Empire **14**:466
Young Turks **20**:336
ENVIRONMENT
computer modeling **5**:162
conservation **5**:201–204
dendrochronology **6**:107
desert **6**:128–129
environmental toxicology **19**:256
human environment
behavioral genetics **3**:169–170
child development **4**:348
child psychiatry **4**:350–351
infancy **11**:162–163
Köppen, Wladimir Peter **12**:110
microclimate **13**:384–385
mountain climates **13**:620–621
nutrient cycles **14**:302–304
paleoclimatology **15**:32–34
urban climate **19**:480
ENVIRONMENTAL ART 7:209 *bibliog.*
Christo **4**:415–416
earthworks 7:28
Ferber, Herbert **8**:52
Kaprow, Allan **12**:25
Kienholz, Edward **12**:74–75
Klein, Yves **12**:96
modern art **13**:495
Morris, Robert (artist) **13**:588
Oldenburg, Claes **14**:376
Segal, George **17**:187–188
Smithson, Robert **17**:372
ENVIRONMENTAL BIOLOGY *see* ECOLOGY
ENVIRONMENTAL CHEMISTRY
chemistry **4**:323
ENVIRONMENTAL GEOLOGY **9**:105
ENVIRONMENTAL HEALTH 7:210–212 *bibliog.*
chemical and biological warfare **4**:312–313
diseases 7:210–212
cancer **4**:104
infectious 7:210
occupational **6**:193–194; 7:212
food and drug contamination 7:211–212
geochemistry **9**:97
pesticides **15**:198
pollutants, chemical **15**:410–411
pollution, effects of 7:211
pollution, environmental **15**:411–415
race **16**:35
toxicology **19**:256
transportation **19**:281–282
weather modification **20**:79
ENVIRONMENTAL IMPACT STATEMENT 7:212
ENVIRONMENTAL MOVEMENT
Arctic **2**:144
Audubon Society, National **2**:319
Carson, Rachel **4**:170
conservation **5**:202–203
Ehrlich, Paul (1932–) 7:90–91
environmental impact statement 7:212
Greenpeace **9**:354
national parks **14**:44
nuclear energy **14**:283 *illus.*
packaging **15**:12
pesticides **15**:198
petroleum industry **15**:215
pollution, environmental **15**:411
roads and highways **16**:238
Sierra Club **17**:296
state programs
Colorado **5**:119
Massachusetts **13**:207
New York (state) **14**:153
Pennsylvania **15**:148
Vermont **19**:556
surveillance systems **18**:366
United Nations **19**:415
ENVIRONMENTAL PROTECTION AGENCY 7:212
acid rain **1**:82
conservation **5**:202–203
environmental health 7:210
pollutants, chemical **15**:410–411
pollution control **15**:416
public health **15**:608
ENVIRONMENTAL THEATER
Schechner, Richard **17**:117
ENZYME 7:212–215 *bibliog., illus.*
Anfinsen, Christian Boehmer **1**:411
Arber, Werner **2**:110
ascorbic acid
scurvy **17**:167
Baltimore, David **3**:56
catalyst **4**:199; 7:213
coenzyme **5**:92–93
crystallization
Sumner, James B. **18**:340
deficiency
diseases 7:214–215
diastase **6**:153
digestive system **6**:174
pancreatitis **15**:58
feedback inhibition
homeostasis **10**:212
functioning 7:213–214
genetic code **9**:79–82
genetic engineering **9**:84–85 *illus.*
hormone, animal **10**:235
inflammation **11**:169
lysosome **12**:480
lysozyme
Fleming, Sir Alexander **8**:159
metabolism 7:214
drug **6**:276
mitochondrion **13**:485
molting **13**:513
mutation **13**:687
Neurospora **14**:107
operon **14**:403–404
pancreas **15**:57–58
pepsin
Northrop, John Howard **14**:256
protein **15**:574
protein synthesis **15**:575
reverse transcriptase
Temin, Howard Martin **19**:91
Smith, Hamilton **17**:368
Warburg, Otto **20**:28
EOCENE EPOCH
Eohippus **10**:245 *illus.*
extinct mammals **13**:102–103 *illus.*
geologic time **9**:104 *table*
paleomagnetism **15**:41 *map*
polar wandering **15**:393 *map*
Tertiary Period **19**:122–124 *illus.*, *table*
EOHIPPUS 7:215 *bibliog., illus.*; **10**:245 *illus.*; **13**:102 *illus.*
Tertiary Period **19**:124 *illus.*
EOKA 7:215
EOLIE ISLANDS
map (38° 30′N 15° 0′E) **11**:321
EOS 7:215
EÖTVÖS, JOZSEF, BARON VON VÁSÁROSNEMÉNY 7:215
EÖTVÖS, LÓRÁNT, BARON VON VÁSÁROSNEMÉNY 7:215
relativity **16**:134
EPAMINONDAS 7:215 *bibliog.*
Messene **13**:322
Pelopidas **15**:138–139
Thebes (Greece) **19**:155
EPANO ENGLIANOS *see* PYLOS (Greece)
EPAZOTE, MOUNT
map (24° 35′N 105° 7′W) **13**:357
EPCOT CENTER
cinematography **4**:434
Walt Disney World **6**:197
EPE (Nigeria)
map (6° 37′N 3° 59′E) **14**:190
EPHEDRA 7:215–216
EPHEDRINE 7:216 *illus.*
Chinese medicine **4**:391
EPHEMERIS 7:216
celestial mechanics **4**:230
EPHEMERIS TIME 7:216
time (physics) **19**:201
United States Naval Observatory **19**:464
EPHESIANS, EPISTLE TO THE 7:216 *bibliog.*
EPHESUS 7:216 *bibliog.*
temple of Artemis **17**:217 *illus.*
EPHESUS, COUNCIL OF 7:216
Immaculate Conception **11**:54
EPHORS 7:216
EPHRAEM THE SYRIAN, SAINT 7:216–217
EPHRAIM 7:217
EPHRAIM (Utah)
map (39° 22′N 111° 35′W) **19**:492
EPHRATA (Pennsylvania) 7:217; **15**:151 *illus.*
Beissel, Johann Conrad **3**:172
map (40° 11′N 76° 10′W) **15**:147
EPHRATA (Washington)
map (47° 19′N 119° 33′W) **20**:35
EPIC 7:217 *bibliog., illus.*
American literature
Cantos, The **4**:118
Crane, Hart **5**:330
Dos Passos, John **6**:243
Melville, Herman **13**:289–290
Pound, Ezra **15**:475–476
Song of Hiawatha, The **18**:64
Williams, William Carlos **20**:161
Austrian literature **2**:354
Czech literature
Mácha, Karel Hynek **13**:17
Danish literature
Oehlenschläger, Adam Gottlob **14**:352
Dutch and Flemish literature **6**:314
English literature
Beowulf **3**:207
Browning, Robert **3**:518–519
Byron, George Gordon, Lord **3**:603
Daniel, Samuel **6**:32
Eliot, T. S. 7:139–140
Faerie Queene, The **8**:7 *bibliog.*
Milton, John **13**:432–433
Tennyson, Alfred, Lord **19**:111–112
Wordsworth, William **20**:216–217
Finnish literature
Kalevala **12**:7–8
French literature
Chanson de Roland **4**:282
chansons de geste **4**:282
German literature
Brecht, Bertolt **3**:470–471
Goethe, Johann Wolfgang von **9**:223–224
Klopstock, Friedrich Gottlieb **12**:98
Nibelungenlied **14**:177–178
Gilgamesh **9**:180
Greek literature, ancient
Homer **10**:213
Iliad **11**:40
Odyssey **14**:351
Hungarian literature
Arany, János **2**:109
Indian literature
Mahabarata, The **13**:64

EPIC (cont.)
Ramayana **16**:80
Irish literature
Cuchulain **5**:381
Joyce, James **11**:456–457
Italian literature
Ariosto, Ludovico **2**:154
Boccaccio, Giovanni **3**:353
Dante Alighieri **6**:34
Divine Comedy, The **6**:203
Tasso, Torquato **19**:43
Latin literature
Aeneid **1**:119
Ennius, Quintus 7:207
Lucan **12**:448
Ovid **14**:470–471
Statius **18**:238
Vergil **19**:551
mock epic **13**:489
oral literature **14**:414
Persian literature **15**:187
Attar, Farid al-Din Abu Hamid **2**:314
Firdawsi **8**:100
Shah Namah (poem) **17**:235
Portuguese literature
Camões, Luís Vaz de **4**:62
Russian literature
Dostoyevsky, Fyodor Mikhailovich **6**:244–245
Pasternak, Boris **15**:107
Solzhenitsyn, Aleksandr **18**:59
Tolstoi, Count Leo **19**:228
Spanish literature
Cervantes Saavedra, Miguel de **4**:261
Swedish literature
Tegnér, Esaias **19**:72
EPIC THEATER 7:217–218 *bibliog.*
acting **1**:86
English literature
Shaw, George Bernard **17**:245
German literature
Brecht, Bertolt **3**:470–471
Piscator, Erwin **15**:316
Wedekind, Frank **20**:89
EPICHARMUS
theater, history of the **19**:144
EPICTETUS (painter) 7:218 *bibliog.*
EPICTETUS (philosopher) 7:218 *bibliog.*
EPICUREANISM 7:218 *bibliog.*
De re natura **6**:62
Epicurus 7:218
Gassendi, Pierre **9**:56
Lucretius **12**:451
EPICURUS 7:218 *bibliog.*
Lucretius **12**:451
materialism **13**:219
EPIDAURUS (Greece) 7:218–219 *bibliog., illus.*
theater 7:218 *illus.*
EPIDEMIC
AIDS **1**:201
bubonic plague **3**:532
epidemiology 7:219
infectious diseases **11**:166
influenza **11**:171–172
measles **13**:253
meningitis **13**:298
meningococcus **13**:298
mycoplasmal pneumonia **13**:690
swine flu **18**:392
typhus **19**:366
EPIDEMIOLOGY 7:219 *bibliog.*
influenza **11**:171
Sydenham, Thomas **18**:400
EPIDERMIS 7:219 *bibliog.*
feather **8**:39–40
hair **10**:14 *illus.*
hoof, nail, and claw **10**:225–226
horn (biology) **10**:238
molting **13**:513
regeneration **16**:127
skin **17**:340–341 *illus.*
EPIDOTE (geology) 7:219
facies, metamorphic rock **13**:332 *table*
monoclinic system **13**:536
EPIGENESIS
heredity **10**:139
EPIGLOTTIS **12**:209; **18**:174 *illus.*
EPIGRAM 7:219
Martial **13**:176
EPIGRAPHY *see* INSCRIPTION
EPILEPSY 7:219–220 *bibliog., illus.*
brain bilateralism **3**:448
nervous system diseases of the **14**:96
sedative **17**:182
EPILIMNION *see* LAKE (body of water)
ÉPINAY, LOUISE FLORENCE PÉTRONILLE DE LA LIVE D' 7:220
EPINEPHRINE *see* ADRENALINE
EPIPELAGIC ZONE 7:220
ocean and sea **14**:331
pelagic zone **15**:137
EPIPHANY (literature) 7:220 *bibliog.*
Joyce, James **11**:456–457
EPIPHANY (theology) 7:220 *bibliog.*
magi **13**:49
EPIPHYTE 7:220 *bibliog.*
fern **8**:56
hornwort **10**:240
jungle and rain forest **11**:469 *illus.*
vanilla **19**:519–520
EPIRUS 7:220–221 *bibliog.*
Pyrrhus, King **15**:639
EPISCOPAL CHURCH 7:221 *bibliog.*
General Theological Seminary **9**:78
Scotland **17**:151
Seabury, Samuel **17**:172
South, University of the **18**:78
White, William **20**:136
EPISTEMOLOGY 7:221–222 *bibliog.*
agnosticism **1**:187
analytic and linguistic philosophy **1**:389
Aristotle 7:221–222
Ayer, Sir Alfred Jules **2**:378
Bolzano, Bernhard **3**:373
Cassirer, Ernst **4**:184
causality **4**:219
Descartes, René **6**:126
dualism **6**:287
empiricism 7:159
Hume, David **10**:301–302
idealism **11**:30
Kant, Immanuel **12**:23–24
Locke, John **12**:387–388
metaphysics **13**:335
Mill, John Stuart **13**:425
monism **13**:531
Moore, G. E. **13**:567–568
phenomenology **15**:225
philosophy **15**:243
Plato 7:221
pragmatism **15**:487
Protagoras 7:221
rationalism **16**:92–93
realism (philosophy) **16**:104
Russell, Bertrand **16**:349
sensationalism **17**:204
skepticism **17**:337
Socrates 7:221
Sophists 7:221
Wittgenstein, Ludwig **20**:193–194
EPISTLE (literature) 7:222
See also COLOSSIANS, EPISTLE TO THE; under the latter element of the name for other epistles of the New Testament
Horace **10**:233–234
Pliny the Younger **15**:368
Pope, Alexander **15**:430
EPITAPH 7:222
EPITAXY 7:222
computer **5**:160h
EPITHELIAL CELL **4**:235 *illus.*
aging **1**:185–186
Henle, Friedrich **10**:121
EPITHELIAL TISSUE
tissue, animal **19**:210
EPITHERMAL DEPOSIT *see* ORE DEPOSITS
EPOXY RESINS 7:222
adhesive **1**:102
EPPING (New Hampshire)
map (43° 2′N 71° 4′W) **14**:123
EPROM (ERASABLE PROGRAMMED READ-ONLY MEMORY)
computer **5**:160h
computer memory **5**:161
EPSILON (letter)
E (letter) 7:3
H (letter) **10**:3
EPSILON LYRAE *see* LYRA
EPSOM DOWNS (England)
Derby, The **6**:121
EPSOM SALTS 7:222
magnesium **13**:54
EPSTEIN, ARNOLD LEONARD 7:223
EPSTEIN, JACOB 7:223 *bibliog.*
EPSTEIN-BARR VIRUS
cancer **4**:102
herpes **10**:145
EQUAL EMPLOYMENT OPPORTUNITY COMMISSION
Civil Rights Acts **5**:13
equal opportunity 7:223
EQUAL OPPORTUNITY 7:223–224 *bibliog.*
See also AFFIRMATIVE ACTION
Brown v. *Board of Education of Topeka, Kansas* **3**:517
Civil Rights Acts **5**:13
feminism **8**:48–49
integration, racial **11**:203
Randolph, A. Philip **16**:83
United States, education in the **19**:434–435
United Steelworkers of America v. *Weber* **19**:465
University of California v. *Bakke* **19**:470
Urban League, National **19**:480
women in society **20**:204
EQUAL PROTECTION OF THE LAWS 7:224 *bibliog.*
Brown v. *Board of Education of Topeka, Kansas* **3**:517
feminism **8**:48–49
14th Amendment **8**:254
Powell v. *Alabama* **15**:481
Reconstruction Amendments **5**:221–222
Shelley v. *Kraemer* **17**:253–254
Slaughterhouse Cases **17**:351
U.S. Bill of Rights **3**:253
EQUAL RIGHTS AMENDMENT 7:224 *bibliog.*
Constitution of the United States **5**:220
demonstration **20**:203 *illus.*
National Organization for Women **14**:36
text **5**:223
women in society **20**:204
EQUALITY (Illinois)
map (37° 44′N 88° 20′W) **11**:42
EQUALITY OF EDUCATIONAL OPPORTUNITY
Coleman Report **5**:100
EQUANIL
tranquilizer **19**:266
EQUATION 7:224–225 *bibliog., illus.*
algebra **1**:284
algebraic geometry **1**:285
of circle, analytic geometry **1**:390
complex number **5**:157
of curve, analytic geometry **1**:390
differential equations **6**:168
Diophantine equations **6**:185
Dirac equation **6**:186–187
discriminant **6**:189
Fibonacci sequence **8**:69
function **8**:359
graph **9**:290
inequality **11**:161
of line, analytic geometry **1**:391
linear equation **12**:354
parameter **15**:80
of plane, analytic geometry **1**:390
of plane curve, analytic geometry **1**:390
polynomial equation **15**:421
quadratic equation
quadratic function **16**:5
quartic equation
Ferrari, Lodovico **8**:59
quintic equation
Galois, Evariste **9**:21
root (mathematics) **16**:311
systems of equations 7:224
van der Walls equation **19**:512–513
EQUATION OF TIME 7:225
day **6**:54
EQUATOR 7:225
coordinate systems (astronomy) **5**:245
doldrums **6**:224
Earth, motions of 7:18
great circle **9**:318
Greenwich mean time **9**:354
Hadley cell **10**:8
jungle and rain forest **11**:468 *map*
latitude **12**:234–235
precession of the equinoxes **15**:493
tropical climate **19**:307
EQUATORIAL CHANNEL
map (0° 0′ 73° 10′E) **13**:87
EQUATORIAL CURRENTS
Gulf Stream **9**:403
ocean currents and wind systems, worldwide **14**:322–323 *maps*
EQUATORIAL GUINEA 7:225–226 *bibliog., map*
cities
Malabo **13**:78
flag 7:225 *illus.*; **8**:136 *illus.*
history 7:225–226
land and people 7:225–226 *map*
map (2° 0′N 9° 0′E) **1**:136
provinces
Bioko **3**:264
Mbini **13**:251
EQUATORIUM 7:226
EQUESTRIAN ARTS *see* RIDING
EQUILIBRIUM *see* BIOLOGICAL EQUILIBRIUM; CHEMICAL KINETICS AND EQUILIBRIUM; PHASE EQUILIBRIUM; STATICS
EQUINE EQUIPMENT *see* RIDING
EQUINOX 7:226
celestial sphere **4**:230
Earth, motions of 7:18
Greenwich mean time **9**:354
tropical year **19**:309
EQUITATION
horse show **10**:250
riding **16**:217
EQUITY (finance) 7:226
stock (finance) **18**:273–274
EQUITY (law) 7:226–227 *bibliog.*
chancery **4**:279
common law **5**:139–140
injunction **11**:178
law, history of **12**:245
legal procedure **12**:272–273
remedies 7:226
writ of assistance **20**:291
EQUIVALENT WEIGHT (chemistry) 7:227
concentration **5**:168–169
neutralization product **14**:108
ER *see* ENDOPLASMIC RETICULUM
ER RIF *see* RIF
ERA (Equal Rights Amendment) *see* EQUAL RIGHTS AMENDMENT
ERA (geology) *see* GEOLOGIC TIME
ERA OF GOOD FEELINGS *see* MONROE, JAMES
ERASABLE PROGRAMMED READ-ONLY MEMORY *see* EPROM
ERASISTRATUS 7:227 *bibliog.*
anatomy **1**:395
ERASMUS, DESIDERIUS 7:227 *bibliog., illus.*; **16**:149 *illus.*
educational psychology 7:66
fool **8**:313
Holbein, Hans, the Younger **10**:200
humanism **10**:299
humanities, education in the **10**:300
Praise of Folly, The **15**:489
Renaissance **16**:149
ERASTIANISM 7:227
ERATH (Louisiana)
map (29° 58′N 92° 2′W) **12**:430
ERATH (county in Texas)
map (32° 17′N 98° 15′W) **19**:129
ERATO
muses **13**:656
ERATOSTHENES OF CYRENE 7:227–228
Earth, size and shape of 7:19
geography **9**:101
prime number **15**:542
ERBEN, KAREL JAROMIR
Czech literature **5**:412
ERBIUM 7:228
element 7:130 *table*
lanthanide series **12**:200–201
metallic element **13**:328
ERCILLA Y ZÚÑIGA, ALONSO DE
Lautaro **12**:240
ERCOLE I
Este (family) 7:246
EREBUS 7:228
EREBUS, MOUNT **2**:41 *illus.*; 7:228
map (77° 32′S 167° 9′E) **2**:40
Mawson, Sir Douglas **13**:238
ERECH *see* URUK (Iraq)
ERECHTHEUM
acropolis **1**:84–85
caryatid **4**:179
Elgin, Thomas Bruce, 7th Earl of 7:137
ERECHTHEUS 7:228
ERECTION (penis)
abnormalities
priapism **15**:534
EREGLI (Turkey)
map (37° 31′N 34° 4′E) **19**:343
EREWHON (book) 7:228 *bibliog.*
ERFURT (East Germany) 7:228
map (50° 58′N 11° 1′E) **9**:140
ERG (physics) 7:228
ERGONOMICS *see* HUMAN FACTORS ENGINEERING
ERGOSTEROL
sterol **18**:262 *illus.*
ERGOT 7:228
fungus diseases **8**:369
rye **16**:380
fungi **8**:367
ERGOTAMINE TARTRATE
headache **10**:86
ERHARD, LUDWIG 7:228 *bibliog.*
ERHARD, WERNER
est 7:245
ERHARD SEMINARS TRAINING *see* EST (psychology)
ERIC CLEARINGHOUSES 7:228–229
ERIC THE RED 7:229 *bibliog.*
Canada, history of **4**:80
ERIC XIV, KING OF SWEDEN 7:229 *bibliog.*
ERICHSEN, VIRGILIUS

Catherine II, Empress of Russia **4**:210 *illus.*
ERICKSON, ARTHUR
Canadian art and architecture **4**:91
ERICSSON, JOHN 7:229 *bibliog.*; **19**:450 *illus.*
Monitor and *Merrimack* **13**:532
propeller **15**:570
ship **17**:273
ERICSSON, LEIF *see* LEIF ERIKSSON
ERIDU (Iraq) 7:229
Mesopotamian art and architecture **13**:318
ziggurat **20**:363
ERIE (American Indians) 7:229
ERIE (Colorado)
map (40° 3′N 105° 3′W) **5**:116
ERIE (Illinois)
map (41° 39′N 90° 5′W) **11**:42
ERIE (Kansas)
map (37° 34′N 95° 15′W) **12**:18
ERIE (county in New York)
map (42° 50′N 78° 45′W) **14**:149
ERIE (county in Ohio)
map (41° 27′N 82° 42′W) **14**:357
ERIE (Pennsylvania) 7:229
map (42° 8′N 80° 4′W) **15**:147
ERIE (county in Pennsylvania)
map (42° 8′N 80° 4′W) **15**:147
ERIE, LAKE 7:229–230 *map*
map (42° 15′N 81° 0′W) **9**:320
pollution, environmental **5**:201 *illus.*
ERIE CANAL 4:96; 7:230 *bibliog.*, *map*
ERIGENA, JOHN SCOTUS 7:230 *bibliog.*
ERIKSON, ERIK 7:230–231 *bibliog.*
developmental psychology **6**:142
ego **7**:73
history **10**:185
middle age **13**:391
psychoanalysis, personality **15**:189
psychohistory **15**:591
ERIKSSON, LEIF *see* LEIF ERIKSSON
ERIN (Tennessee)
map (36° 19′N 87° 46′W) **19**:104
ERIS 7:231
ERITREA (Ethiopia) 7:231 *bibliog.*
art
Lalibela **12**:171
cities
Asmara **2**:261
ERKEL, FERENC
Hungarian music **10**:306
ERLACH, JOHANN BERNARD FISCHER VON *see* FISCHER VON ERLACH, JOHANN BERNHARD
ERLANDER, TAGE 7:231
ERLANGEN (Germany, East and West)
map (49° 36′N 11° 1′E) **9**:140
ERLENMEYER, RICHARD 7:231
ERLING, LAKE
map (33° 5′N 93° 35′W) **2**:166
ERMAK
icebreaker **11**:16
ERMINE 7:231 *illus.*
ERNIE AND BERT *see* MUPPETS
ERNST, MAX 7:231–232 *bibliog.*, *illus.*
Elephant of the Celebes 7:231 *illus.*
Guggenheim, Peggy **9**:392
Rendez-vous of the Friends **18**:365 *illus.*
surrealism (art) **18**:364–365
EROS (astronomy) 7:232
EROS (mythology) 7:232
Cupid **9**:192 *illus.*
EROSION (biology)
skin diseases **17**:341
EROSION CYCLE 7:232 *bibliog.*
butte **3**:592
erosion and sedimentation 7:232–234
igneous rock **11**:34
landform evolution **12**:183
paleoclimatology **15**:32
EROSION AND SEDIMENTATION 7:232–234 *bibliog.*, *illus.*
alluvial fans **1**:305
Asia, history of **2**:249
baselevel **3**:108
basin and range province **3**:110
beach and coast **3**:135–136
bed load **3**:153
braided stream **3**:441
coastal protection **5**:81
conservation **5**:203 *illus.*
contour plowing **13**:479 *illus.*
desert **6**:128
Earth sciences 7:24
erosion cycle 7:232
erratic, glacial 7:234–235
escarpment 7:237
evaporite 7:314
flash flood **8**:153
floodplain **8**:165–166
flume studies **8**:186
geochemistry **9**:96–97
geology **9**:106
glaciers and glaciation **9**:194
horst and graben **10**:253–254
Jurassic Period **11**:475–477
kudzu **12**:135
lake (body of water) **12**:168–169
lake, glacial **12**:169–170
landform evolution **12**:182–183 *illus.*
landslide and avalanche **12**:192–193
laterite **12**:215
loess **12**:393
mangrove **13**:116
meander, river **13**:253
modes of 7:232–233
monadnock **13**:517
mountain **13**:619–620
mud cracks **13**:631
Ninetyeast Ridge **14**:199
oceanic mineral resources **14**:340–342
Ordovician Period **14**:421
oxbow lake **14**:473
paleoecology **15**:34
peneplain **15**:143
plate tectonics **15**:351–357
plateau **15**:358
processes 7:233–234
Recent Epoch **16**:106–107
red beds **16**:112
regolith **16**:129
regression, marine **16**:129
river delta **16**:232–233
river and stream **16**:230–232 *illus.*
sandstone **17**:63
sea level **17**:169
seawater **17**:177
sedge **17**:183
sediment, marine **17**:183–184
shale **17**:237–238
stage **18**:210
strandline **18**:288
stromatolite **18**:302
subsidence **18**:316–317
syncline and anticline **18**:406
talus **19**:18
Tertiary Period **19**:122–125
till and tillite **19**:199
unconformity **19**:382
valley and ridge province **19**:507–508
varved deposit **19**:524
water supply **20**:53
water wave **20**:60
waterfall **20**:63
weathering **20**:82–83
wind action **20**:170
EROTIC AND PORNOGRAPHIC LITERATURE 7:234 *bibliog.*
See also CENSORSHIP; LITERATURE
Aretino, Pietro **2**:146
Aristophanes **2**:155–156
Beardsley, Aubrey **3**:142–143
Boccaccio, Giovanni **3**:353–354
Casanova de Seingalt, Giovanni Giacomo **4**:180
Chaucer, Geoffrey **4**:304–305
Cleland, John **5**:48
Fanny Hill, or The Memoirs of a Woman of Pleasure **8**:20
Harris, Frank **10**:57
Lawrence, D. H. **12**:249–250
Miller, Henry **13**:427–428
Miller v. *California* **13**:428–429
Ovid **14**:470–471
Petronius Arbiter **15**:215
Rabelais, François **16**:31–32
Sade, Marquis de **17**:9
ERRATIC, GLACIAL 7:234–235
ice ages **11**:8
paleoclimatology **15**:32
ERROR (mathematics) 7:235
measurement **13**:256–257
numerical analysis **14**:294–295
ERSHAD, HUSSAIN MUHAMMAD 7:235
Bangladesh **3**:66
ERSKINE (Minnesota)
map (47° 40′N 96° 0′W) **13**:453
ERSKINE, JOHN 7:235
ERSKINE, RALPH 7:235
ERSKINE, THOMAS, 1st BARON ERSKINE 7:235 *bibliog.*
ERTEBØLLE CULTURE 7:235 *bibliog.*
European prehistory 7:302
midden **13**:390
ERTS *see* LANDSAT (artificial satellite)
ERVIN, SAM, JR. 7:235
Watergate **20**:64
ERVINE, ST. JOHN GREER 7:235
ERVING, JULIUS 3:113 *illus.*; 7:235
ERWIN (North Carolina)
map (35° 20′N 78° 41′W) **14**:242
ERWIN (Tennessee)
map (36° 9′N 82° 25′W) **19**:104
ERYSIPELAS
skin diseases **17**:342
ERYTHEMA 7:236
inflammation **11**:169
skin redness 7:236
ERYTHROBLASTOSIS FETALIS
jaundice **11**:385
Rh factor **16**:192
ERYTHROCYTE (red blood cell)
blood **3**:335–336
ERYTHROMYCIN
antibiotics **2**:59
ERYTHROPOIETIN
hormone, animal **10**:236 *table*
ERZICAN (Turkey)
map (39° 44′N 39° 29′E) **19**:343
ERZURUM (Turkey)
map (39° 55′N 41° 17′E) **19**:343
ESAKI, LEO 7:236
ESALEN INSTITUTE 7:236
ESARHADDON, KING OF ASSYRIA 7:236
Nineveh **14**:200
ESAU 7:236
ESBJERG (Denmark)
map (55° 28′N 8° 27′E) **6**:109
ESCALANTE (Utah)
map (37° 47′N 111° 36′W) **19**:492
ESCALANTE, SILVESTRE VÉLEZ DE 7:236 *bibliog.*
exploration of colonial America **19**:437 *map*
ESCALANTE DESERT
map (37° 50′N 113° 30′W) **19**:492
ESCALANTE RIVER
map (37° 17′N 110° 53′W) **19**:492
ESCALATOR 7:236 *bibliog.*
ESCALLONIA 7:236 *illus.*
ESCAMBIA (county in Alabama)
map (31° 10′N 87° 10′W) **1**:234
ESCAMBIA (county in Florida)
map (30° 40′N 87° 20′W) **8**:172
ESCANABA (Michigan)
map (45° 45′N 87° 4′W) **13**:377
ESCAPE ARTIST *see* MAGIC ACTS
ESCAPE VELOCITY 7:236–237 *table*
ESCAROLE *see* ENDIVE
ESCARPADA POINT
map (18° 31′N 122° 13′E) **15**:237
ESCARPMENT (geology) 7:237
fault **8**:37
Moon, far side **13**:565 *map*
river and stream **16**:230–231 *illus.*
ESCH (Luxembourg)
map (49° 30′N 5° 59′E) **12**:472
ESCHATOLOGY 7:237 *bibliog.*
Antichrist **2**:60
Bosch, Hieronymus **3**:405–406
Dodd, C. H. **6**:211
Judgment, Last **11**:464
ESCHEAT 7:237
will (law) **20**:153
ESCHEN (Liechtenstein)
map (47° 13′N 9° 31′E) **12**:325
ESCHENBACH, WOLFRAM VON *see* WOLFRAM VON ESCHENBACH
ESCHER, MAURITS CORNEILLE 7:237 *bibliog.*
graphic arts **9**:293
ESCHERICHIA 7:237
genetic engineering **9**:85 *illus.*
induction, enzyme 7:214
operon **14**:404
reproduction **16**:162
Tatum, Edward L. **19**:44
ESCHWEILER (Germany, East and West)
map (50° 49′N 6° 16′E) **9**:140
ESCOBEDO* v. *ILLINOIS 7:237
right to counsel 7:237
ESCOFFIER, AUGUSTE 7:237–238 *bibliog.*
ESCOLAR *see* SNAKE MACKEREL
ESCONDIDO (California)
map (33° 7′N 117° 5′W) **4**:31
ESCONDIDO RIVER
map (12° 4′N 83° 45′W) **14**:179
ESCORIAL 7:238 *bibliog.*
Giordano, Luca **9**:186
Spanish art and architecture **18**:152–153 *illus.*
ESCROW 7:238
ESCUINAPA DE HIDALGO (Mexico)
map (22° 51′N 105° 48′W) **13**:357
ESCUINTLA (Guatemala)
map (14° 18′N 90° 47′W) **9**:389
ESDRAELON, PLAIN OF 7:238
ESDRAS *see* PSEUDEPIGRAPHA
ESEA *see* ELEMENTARY AND SECONDARY EDUCATION ACT OF 1965
ESENIN, SERGEI ALEKSANDROVICH *see* YESENIN, SERGEI ALEKSANDROVICH
ESFAHAN (Iran) *see* ISFAHAN (Iran)
ESHERICK, JOSEPH 7:238 *bibliog.*
ESHKOL, LEVI 7:238 *bibliog.*
ESKDALE (West Virginia)
map (38° 5′N 81° 27′W) **20**:111
ESKER 7:238
glaciers and glaciation **9**:192–195
ESKILSTUNA (Sweden)
map (59° 22′N 16° 30′E) **18**:382
ESKIMO 7:238–242 *bibliog.*, *illus.*, *map*; **11**:116 *illus.*; **14**:232 *illus.*
Aleut **1**:272
archaeology
Cape Denbigh **4**:120
Cape Krusenstern **4**:120
cultures 7:239 *map*
Ipiutak **11**:248
Okvik **14**:372
Arctic **2**:143
art 7:241
Indians of North America, art of the **11**:138–139
Indians of North America, music and dance of the **11**:143–144
ivory and ivory carving **11**:337
scrimshaw **17**:158
soapstone carving 7:241 *illus.*; **11**:139 *illus.*
clothing 7:240
documentary **6**:211
education
Indian schools, American **11**:106
ethnology
Rasmussen, Knud **16**:90
Stefansson, Vilhjalmur **18**:245
history 7:241–242
hunter-gatherers **2**:138 *illus.*; 7:239–241 *illus.*; **10**:313
infanticide **11**:163
Ingalik, relations with **11**:175–176
life today 7:242
present habitats 7:239 *map*
marriage **13**:164
race **16**:34 *illus.*
religion 7:241
shaman **17**:239
settlement 7:239–240 *illus.*
igloo **11**:126 *illus.*
Northwest Territories **14**:259 *illus.*
social organization 7:240–241
primitive societies **15**:546
subsistence 7:239–240
walrus **20**:18
transportation 7:240
ESKIMO-ALEUT LANGUAGES **12**:355 *map*
Asia **2**:244 *map*
Indian languages, American **11**:98–101 *table*
North America **14**:234 *map*
Ural-Altaic languages **19**:476
ESKIMO DOG 7:240; 7:242
ESKIMO PEOPLE'S CIRCUMPOLAR CONFERENCE *see* INUIT CIRCUMPOLAR CONFERENCE
ESKIMO POINT (Northwest Territories)
map (61° 7′N 94° 3′W) **14**:258
ESKISEHIR (Turkey)
map (39° 46′N 30° 32′E) **19**:343
ESKRIDGE (Kansas)
map (38° 52′N 96° 6′W) **12**:18
ESLA RIVER
map (41° 29′N 6° 3′W) **18**:140
ESMERALDA (Cuba)
map (21° 51′N 78° 7′W) **5**:377
ESMERALDA (county in Nevada)
map (37° 45′N 117° 45′W) **14**:111
ESMERALDA (Venezuela)
map (3° 10′N 65° 33′W) **19**:542
ESMERALDAS (Ecuador)
map (0° 59′N 79° 42′W) 7:52
ESMERALDAS RIVER
map (0° 58′N 79° 38′W) 7:52
ESMOND (North Dakota)
map (48° 2′N 99° 46′W) **14**:248
ESOBAR, MARISOL *see* MARISOL
ESOPHAGUS 7:242
heartburn **10**:97
ESP *see* EXTRASENSORY PERCEPTION
ESPALIER 7:242–243
ESPANOLA (New Mexico)
map (36° 6′N 106° 2′W) **14**:136
ESPERANÇA (Brazil)
map (4° 24′S 69° 52′W) **3**:460
ESPERANTO 7:243 *bibliog.*
languages, artificial **12**:197
ESPERANZA (Puerto Rico)
map (18° 6′N 65° 28′W) **15**:614
ESPICHEL, CAPE OF
map (38° 25′N 9° 13′W) **15**:449

ESPINEL, VICENTE MARTÍNEZ 7:243 *bibliog.*
ESPIONAGE 7:243–244 *bibliog.*
Central Intelligence Agency **4**:254
famous spies
André, John **1**:407
Hale, Nathan **10**:18
Mata Hari **13**:218
Philby, H. (Kim) **15**:231
Rosenberg, Julius and Ethel **16**:315
intelligence operations **11**:204–205
KGB **12**:64
McCarran Act **13**:7–8
ESPIRITO SANTO (Brazil)
map (19° 30′S 40° 30′W) **3**:460
ESPIRITU
Vanuatu **19**:520–521
ESPOO (Finland)
map (60° 13′N 24° 40′E) **8**:95
ESPOSITO, PHIL 7:244 *bibliog.*
ESPRONCEDA, JOSÉ DE
Spanish literature **18**:159
ESPUNDIA
leishmaniasis **12**:279
ESQUEL (Argentina)
map (42° 54′S 71° 19′W) **2**:149
ESQUIMALT (British Columbia)
map (48° 26′N 123° 24′W) **3**:491
ESQUIRE (magazine) 7:244
ESQUIVEL, ADOLFO PÉREZ *see* PÉREZ ESQUIVEL, ADOLFO
ESSAOUIRA (Morocco)
map (31° 30′N 9° 47′W) **13**:585
ESSAY 7:244 *bibliog.*
American literature **1**:343
Adler, Renata **1**:104
Aiken, Conrad **1**:201
Auden, W. H. **2**:317–318
Austin, Mary Hunter **2**:327
Baker, Ray Stannard **3**:28
Baldwin, James **3**:35
Barth, John **3**:96–97
Bishop, John Peale **3**:297
Brakhage, Stan **3**:451
Brustein, Robert **3**:527
Chesnutt, Charles Waddell **4**:334
Cleaver, Eldridge **5**:47–48
Cousins, Norman **5**:317
Emerson, Ralph Waldo 7:154–155
Fisher, M. F. K. **8**:122
Holmes, Oliver Wendell **10**:205
McCarthy, Mary **13**:8–9
McGinley, Phyllis **13**:16
Mailer, Norman **13**:67
Pound, Ezra **15**:475–476
Sontag, Susan **18**:66
Thoreau, Henry David **19**:178
Thurber, James **19**:186
Twain, Mark **19**:357
White, E. B. **20**:134–135
Argentine literature
Mallea, Eduardo **13**:92
Austrian literature
Kraus, Karl **12**:127
Chinese literature
Chuang-tzu (Zhuang Zi) **4**:421–422
Dutch and Flemish literature
Beets, Nicolaas **3**:168
English literature 7:200
Addison, Joseph **1**:100
Arnold, Matthew **2**:185
Bacon, Francis **3**:13–14
Beerbohm, Sir Max **3**:163
Brophy, Brigid **3**:512
Burgess, Anthony **3**:569
Chesterton, G. K. **4**:337
Cobbett, William **5**:83–84
Coleridge, Samuel Taylor **5**:100–101
Connolly, Cyril **5**:197
Conrad, Joseph **5**:198
Cowley, Abraham **5**:321
De Quincey, Thomas **6**:62
Dryden, John **6**:284–285
Eliot, T. S. 7:139–140
Goldsmith, Oliver **9**:236
Hazlitt, William **10**:84
Huxley, Aldous **10**:324
Johnson, Samuel **11**:435–436
Lamb, Charles **12**:174
Macaulay, Thomas Babington **13**:6
Pope, Alexander **15**:430
Shaw, George Bernard **17**:245–246
Steele, Sir Richard **18**:243
Swift, Jonathan **18**:389
Temple, Sir William (essayist) **19**:100
Wilde, Oscar **20**:148–149
Wilson, Colin **20**:164
French literature
Apollinaire, Guillaume **2**:79
Aymé, Marcel **2**:379
Barrès, Maurice **3**:94
Barthes, Roland **3**:97
Benda, Julien **3**:196
Boileau-Despreaux, Nicolas **3**:362
Bonnefoy, Yves **3**:381
Bourget, Paul **3**:424
Breton, André **3**:474
Butor, Michel **3**:592
Camus, Albert **4**:68
Claudel, Paul **5**:44
Cocteau, Jean **5**:89
Colette **5**:101
Giraudoux, Jean **9**:189
Montaigne, Michel de **13**:545
Sainte-Beuve, Charles Augustin **17**:27
Sartre, Jean-Paul **17**:79–80
Valéry, Paul **19**:505–506
Voltaire **19**:632
German literature
Benn, Gottfried **3**:202
Börne, Ludwig **3**:402
Hungarian literature
Eötvös, Jozsef, Baron von Vásárosnemény 7:215
Italian literature
Borgese, Giuseppe Antonio **3**:399
Latin literature
Cicero, Marcus Tullius **4**:428–429
Seneca, Lucius Annaeus **17**:200
Russian literature
Aldanov, M. A. **1**:267
Scottish literature
Beattie, James **3**:145
Carlyle, Thomas **4**:152–153
Spanish literature
Ortega y Gasset, José **14**:449
Ruiz, José Martínez **16**:344
Unamuno, Miguel de **19**:381
Yugoslav literature
Andríc, Ivo **1**:408
ESSAY ON MAN, AN (poem) 7:244 *bibliog.*
Pope, Alexander **15**:430
ESSAYS OF MONTAIGNE (book) 7:244 *bibliog.*
Montaigne, Michel de **13**:545
ESSEN (West Germany) 7:244
map (51° 28′N 7° 1′E) **9**:140
ESSENCE (magazine) 7:245
ESSENES 7:245 *bibliog.*
Dead Sea Scrolls **6**:65
Qumran **16**:28
ESSENTIAL OILS 7:245
bergamot **3**:209
caraway **4**:132
clove **5**:69
cumin **5**:387
flavors and fragrances **8**:157
herbs and spices **10**:137
jasmine **11**:384
Kerguelen cabbage **12**:59
mint (botany) **13**:461
patchouli **15**:109
peppermint **15**:157
perfume **15**:164
terpene **19**:118
thyme **19**:187
tung oil **19**:333
ESSEQUIBO RIVER
map (6° 59′N 58° 23′W) **9**:410
ESSEX (Connecticut)
map (41° 21′N 72° 24′W) **5**:193
ESSEX (England) **2**:3 *map*; 7:245
cities
Colchester **5**:97
ESSEX (Iowa)
map (40° 50′N 95° 18′W) **11**:244
ESSEX (Maryland)
map (39° 18′N 76° 29′W) **13**:188
ESSEX (Massachusetts)
map (42° 38′N 70° 47′W) **13**:206
ESSEX (county in Massachusetts)
map (42° 40′N 70° 55′W) **13**:206
ESSEX (Missouri)
map (36° 49′N 95° 52′W) **13**:476
ESSEX (county in New Jersey)
map (40° 48′N 74° 12′W) **14**:129
ESSEX (county in New York)
map (44° 5′N 73° 45′W) **14**:149
ESSEX (Ontario)
map (42° 10′N 82° 49′W) **14**:393; **19**:241
ESSEX (county in Vermont)
map (44° 42′N 71° 45′W) **19**:554
ESSEX (county in Virginia)
map (37° 55′N 76° 55′W) **19**:607
ESSEX, ROBERT DEVEREUX, 2D EARL OF 7:245 *bibliog., illus.*
Elizabeth I, Queen of England 7:142
ESSEX, THOMAS CROMWELL, 1ST EARL OF *see* CROMWELL, THOMAS, 1ST EARL OF ESSEX
ESSEX JUNCTION (Vermont)
map (44° 29′N 73° 7′W) **19**:554
ESSEXVILLE (Michigan)
map (43° 37′N 83° 50′W) **13**:377
ESSLINGEN (Germany, East and West)
map (48° 45′N 9° 16′E) **9**:140
est (psychology) 7:245
ESTAING, JEAN BAPTISTE CHARLES HENRI HECTOR, COMTE D′ 7:246 *bibliog.*
American Revolution **1**:359 *map*
ESTAING, VALÉRY GISCARD D′ *see* GISCARD D′ESTAING, VALÉRY
ESTANCIA (New Mexico)
map (34° 45′N 106° 4′W) **14**:136
ESTANYO PEAK
map (42° 37′N 1° 36′E) **1**:405
ESTATE 7:246 *bibliog.*
administrator **1**:105
entail 7:208
escheat 7:237
fee **8**:44
inheritance **11**:177
inheritance tax **11**:177–178
primogeniture **15**:547
trust 7:246
types 7:246
will (law) **20**:153
ESTATES-GENERAL *see* STATES-GENERAL
ESTE (family) 7:246 *bibliog.*
Modena (Italy) **13**:490
Pisanello, Antonio **15**:316
Reggio nell′Emilia (Italy) **16**:128
Tura, Cosimo **19**:339
ESTEBAN (explorer)
New Mexico **14**:139
ESTELÍ (Nicaragua)
map (13° 5′N 86° 23′W) **14**:179
ESTENSSORO, VICTOR PAZ *see* PAZ ESTENSSORO, VICTOR
ESTER 7:246 *bibliog.*
carboxylic acid **4**:140
fats and oils **8**:34–35
lactone **12**:161–162
lipid **12**:362
organic chemistry **14**:437
polyester **15**:418–419
polymerization **15**:420
saponification **17**:73
ESTERHÁZY (family) 7:246
Haydn, Franz Josef **10**:81
ESTERHAZY (Saskatchewan)
map (50° 40′N 102° 8′W) **17**:81
ESTERHAZY, FERDINAND
Dreyfus affair **6**:271–272
ESTES, RICHARD 7:246
ESTES, WILLIAM KAYE 7:246
psychology, history of **15**:597
ESTES PARK (Colorado)
map (40° 23′N 105° 31′W) **5**:116
ESTEVAN (Saskatchewan)
map (49° 7′N 103° 5′W) **17**:81
ESTHER, BOOK OF 7:246–247 *bibliog.*
ESTHERVILLE (Iowa)
map (43° 24′N 94° 50′W) **11**:244
ESTHETICS *see* AESTHETICS
ESTILL (county in Kentucky)
map (37° 40′N 84° 0′W) **12**:47
ESTILL (South Carolina)
map (32° 45′N 81° 14′W) **18**:98
ESTIVATION
hibernation **10**:156
ESTON (Saskatchewan)
map (51° 10′N 108° 46′W) **17**:81
ESTONIAN LANGUAGE
Uralic languages **19**:475
ESTONIAN SOVIET SOCIALIST REPUBLIC (USSR) 7:247 *bibliog., map*
cities
Narva **14**:23
Tallinn **19**:17
Tartu **19**:41
history 7:247
Livonia **12**:378
meteorite craters **13**:339
people 7:247
ESTRADA CABRERA, MANUEL 7:247 *bibliog.*
ESTRADA PALMA, TOMÁS 7:247–248
ESTRELA MOUNTAINS
map (40° 20′N 7° 38′W) **15**:449
ESTREMADURA (Portugal) 7:248
ESTROGEN
DES **6**:123
hormone, animal **10**:236 *table*
menopause **13**:299–300
menstruation **13**:300–301 *illus.*
sex hormones **17**:226
ESTROUS CYCLE 7:248 *bibliog.*
menstruation **13**:300–302
reproduction **16**:163
reproductive system, human **16**:164–166
sex hormones **17**:226
ESTUARY 7:248 *bibliog.*
beach and coast **3**:135
fresh water **8**:328
gulf and bay **9**:402–403
habitat **10**:4
intertidal life **11**:230
lagoon **12**:165–166
ESZTERGOM (Hungary) 7:248
ETA (caste)
Japan **11**:363
ETA (letter)
H (letter) **10**:3
ÉTATS-GENERAUX *see* STATES-GENERAL
ETCHING 7:248–249 *bibliog., illus.*
aquatint **2**:93
drypoint **6**:285
engraving 7:205–206
graphic arts **9**:292
intaglio (printing) **11**:199
photoengraving **15**:260
Picasso, Pablo **15**:290–292
tools 7:249 *illus.*
ETEMENAKI (ziggurat) **19**:95 *illus.*
ETEN (Peru)
map (6° 54′S 79° 52′W) **15**:193
ETHAN FROME (book) 7:249 *bibliog.*
Wharton, Edith **20**:124
ETHANAL
acetaldehyde **1**:79
aldehyde **1**:268
ETHANE (chemistry) 7:249
ethyl group 7:257
graphic formula **14**:435 *illus.*
natural gas **14**:47
ETHANOL *see* ETHYL ALCOHOL
ETHEL (Mississippi)
map (33° 7′N 89° 34′W) **13**:469
ETHELBERT *see* ÆTHELBERT, KING OF KENT
ETHELBERT (Manitoba)
map (51° 31′N 100° 22′W) **13**:119
ETHELRED II *see* ÆTHELRED II, KING OF ENGLAND (Æthelred the Unready)
ETHENE *see* ETHYLENE
ETHER (chemistry) 7:249–250
administration **18**:361 *illus.*
dentistry **6**:116
ethyl ether 7:257
history
Morton, William **13**:593
isomer **11**:299
surgery **18**:361 *illus.*
ETHER (physics) 7:250
Einstein, Albert 7:93
light **12**:335–336
Michelson-Morley experiment **13**:376
physics, history of **15**:284–285
relativity **16**:134
ETHEREGE, SIR GEORGE 7:250 *bibliog.*
ETHICAL CULTURE 7:250
Adler, Felix **1**:104
ETHICAL DRUG
pharmaceutical industry **15**:220
ETHICS 7:250–252 *bibliog.*
Aristotle **2**:157–158
categorical imperative **4**:202
Cicero, Marcus Tullius **4**:429
civil disobedience **5**:10
conscience **5**:199
Dewey, John **6**:146–147
egoism 7:74
folklore **8**:203
hypnosis **10**:350
Kant, Immanuel **12**:24
metaethics 7:250–251
Moore, G. E. **13**:568
moral awareness **13**:572–573
new fields 7:252
normative ethics 7:251
professional ethics 7:251–252
religion **16**:139
religious ethics 7:251
Santayana, George **17**:69
Schopenhauer, Arthur **17**:134
Seneca, Lucius Annaeus **17**:194
situation ethics 7:251
social ethics 7:251
Spinoza, Baruch **18**:187–188
Troeltsch, Ernst **19**:304
will (philosophy) **20**:153–154
ETHICS, BUSINESS
Better Business Bureau **3**:232
ETHICS, MEDICAL *see* MEDICAL ETHICS
ETHIOPIA 7:252–255 *bibliog., illus., map, table*
African music **1**:168–171
archaeology **1**:172 *map*
Omo **14**:387–388

architecture
Lalibela **12**:171
cities
Addis Ababa **1**:100
Aksum **1**:232
Asmara **2**:261
Gonder **9**:243
Harar **10**:42
climate 7:252; 7:254 *table*
economic activity 7:254
education 7:253
African universities **1**:176 *table*
Eritrea 7:231
flag 7:252 *illus.*
government 7:254
history 7:254–255
Haile Selassie, Emperor **10**:13–14
Laval, Pierre **12**:240
League of Nations **12**:258
Menelik II, Emperor **13**:297
Mengistu Haile Mariam **13**:297
Somalia **18**:61
World War II **20**:249
land and resources 7:252–254 *illus., map, table*
plate tectonics **15**:352
languages
Afroasiatic languages **1**:180
Amhara **1**:368
Tigré **19**:197
map (9° 0′N 39° 0′E) **1**:136
people 7:253
Amhara **1**:368–369
Galla **9**:16
Semites **17**:197
Sidamo **17**:294
Tigré **19**:197
religion
Amhara **1**:368–369
Coptic church **5**:255
Falashas **8**:11–12
rivers, lakes, and waterways 7:252; 7:254 *illus.*
Tana, Lake **19**:20
ETHNIC DANCE
See also FOLK DANCE
dance **6**:23; **6**:26–27 *illus.*
Dunham, Katherine **6**:300
La Meri **12**:147
ETHNIC MINORITIES 7:255–256 *bibliog.*
affirmative action **1**:132
Apartheid **2**:74
black Americans **3**:304–313
Chicano **4**:343
class, social **5**:40
discrimination **6**:189–190
educational measurement 7:64–66
equal opportunity 7:223
ethnocentrism 7:255
family **8**:17
folk music **8**:202–203
generations of 7:256
Hispanic Americans **10**:177–180
housing **10**:278; **10**:279
immigration **11**:54–56 *map*
Indians, American **11**:137–138
inner city **11**:179
Minority Business Development Agency **13**:459
newspaper **14**:171
Oriental Americans **14**:441–443
poverty, United States **15**:478
racism **16**:37–38
social structure and organization **18**:16–17
South Africa **18**:80–83
tribe **19**:295
types in North America 7:255–256
types worldwide 7:256
ETHNOASTRONOMY
archaeoastronomy **2**:114
ETHNOCENTRISM 7:256 *bibliog.*
civilization **5**:34
ethnic minorities 7:255
racism **16**:37
ETHNOGRAPHY 7:256–257 *bibliog.*
See also AFRICA—people; ASIA—people; INDIANS, AMERICAN—tribes, Middle and South American; INDIANS, AMERICAN—tribes, North American; RACE; names of specific peoples, e.g., AINU; LAPPS; YORUBA; etc.
anthropological linguistics **2**:50–51
anthropology **2**:52
ethnography of speaking **18**:28
ethnohistory 7:257
Evans-Pritchard, Sir Edward 7:313
Graebner, Fritz **9**:278
Malinowski, Bronislaw **13**:91
ETHNOHISTORY 7:257 *bibliog.*
ETHNOLINGUISTICS *see* ANTHROPOLOGICAL LINGUISTICS
ETHNOLOGY *see* ANTHROPOLOGY
ETHOGRAM
ethology 7:257
ETHOLOGY 7:257 *bibliog.*
animal behavior **2**:11–12
animal communication **2**:18–20
animal courtship and mating **2**:20–22
Frisch, Karl von **8**:334
imprinting **11**:68–69
instinct **11**:194–195
Lorenz, Konrad **12**:414
sociobiology **18**:26–27
territoriality **19**:121–122
Tinbergen, Nikolaas **19**:206
ETHRIDGE (Montana)
map (48° 34′N 112° 7′W) **13**:547
ETHRIDGE (Tennessee)
map (35° 19′N 87° 18′W) **19**:104
ETHROG
citron **4**:447
ETHYL ALCOHOL 7:257 *bibliog.*
acetic acid **1**:80
Acetobacter **1**:80
antifreeze **2**:61
denatured alcohol **6**:106
gasohol **9**:55
genetic engineering **9**:85
heat content **8**:353 *table*
nuclear magnetic resonance spectrum **18**:171 *illus.*
phase equilibrium **15**:223 *illus.*
sedative **17**:182
ETHYL ETHER 7:257
refrigeration **16**:124
ETHYL GROUP 7:257
ethyl alcohol 7:257
ethyl ether 7:257
ETHYLENE 7:258
chlorohydrin **4**:401
ethane 7:249
ethyl alcohol 7:257
graphic formula **14**:437 *illus.*
methylene **13**:345
petrochemicals **15**:205
plastics **15**:349
pyrolysis **15**:637
ETHYLENE DIBROMIDE *see* EDB
ETHYLENE GLYCOL **9**:212
antifreeze **2**:61
polyhydric alcohol **15**:420
synthesis
Wurtz, Charles Adolphe **20**:297
ETHYNE *see* ACETYLENE
ETIOLATION 7:258
ETIQUETTE 7:258 *bibliog.*
flag **8**:134; **8**:149
Post, Emily **15**:458
ETNA (California)
map (41° 27′N 122° 54′W) **4**:31
ETNA (Wyoming)
map (43° 2′N 111° 0′W) **20**:301
ETNA, MOUNT 7:258; **17**:293 *illus.*
map (37° 46′N 15° 0′E) **11**:321
ETOBICOKE (Ontario)
map (43° 39′N 79° 34′W) **19**:241
map (43° 39′N 79° 34′W) **14**:393
ETON COLLEGE 7:258 *bibliog.*; **19**:408 *illus.*
ETOWAH (county in Alabama)
map (34° 5′N 86° 5′W) **1**:234
ETOWAH (Tennessee)
map (35° 20′N 84° 32′W) **19**:104
ETOWAH MOUNDS (Georgia) 7:258 *bibliog.*; **14**:237 *map*
ETRURIA *see* ETRUSCANS
ETRUSCANS 7:258–261 *bibliog., illus., map*
architecture **2**:132
art 7:259–261 *illus.*
clay plaque in Orientalizing phase **11**:327 *illus.*
jewelry **11**:409
Roman art and architecture **16**:273
sarcophagus **17**:76 *illus.*
sculpture **17**:160
cities
Caere **4**:13
Chiusi **4**:399
Spina **18**:183
Tarquinia **19**:39
Veii **19**:535–536
costume **5**:293 *illus.*
dentures **6**:117
history and trade 7:259
Italy, history of **11**:327
language 7:258
languages, extinct **12**:198
writing systems, evolution of **20**:293–294 *illus., table*
Lars Porsena, King of Clusium **12**:208
origin 7:258
Rome, ancient **16**:297
settlement 7:259 *map*
Tomb of the Reliefs **19**:230–231 *illus.*
Villanovans **19**:597
ETTINGER, SOLOMON
Yiddish theater **20**:328
ETTWEIN, JOHN 7:261 *bibliog.*
ETTY, WILLIAM 7:261 *bibliog.*
ÉTUDE 7:261
Chopin, Frédéric **4**:405
ETYMOLOGY
See also HISTORICAL LINGUISTICS
dictionary **6**:159–160
lexicology and lexicography **12**:308–309
EUA ISLAND
map (21° 22′S 174° 56′W) **19**:233
EUBACTERIA
See also BACTERIA
Vibrio **19**:567
EUBOEA (Greece) 7:261
map (38° 34′N 23° 50′E) **9**:325
EUCALYPTUS 7:261–262 *bibliog., illus.*; **10**:5 *illus.*
koala **12**:103–104
mahogany **13**:66
EUCARYOTE 7:262
bacteria **3**:15
cell **4**:231–232 *illus.*; **4**:233–234
cytoplasm **5**:412
endoplasmic reticulum 7:171
genetics **9**:88
Golgi apparatus **9**:240
plant evolution **15**:334–335 *illus.*
Precambrian time **15**:493
ribosome **16**:206
EUCHARIST 7:262 *bibliog.*
chalice **4**:271
Last Supper **12**:214
Lateran councils **12**:215
Mass **13**:200
EUCHRE (card game) 7:262 *bibliog.*
EUCKEN, RUDOLF CHRISTOPH 7:262
EUCLID 7:262–263 *bibliog., illus.*
Dee, John **6**:77
Euclidean geometry 7:263
geometry **9**:106
mathematics, history of **13**:223 *illus.*
EUCLID (Ohio)
map (41° 34′N 81° 32′W) **14**:357
EUCLIDEAN GEOMETRY 7:263 *bibliog.*
See also NON-EUCLIDEAN GEOMETRY
Cayley, Arthur **4**:227
Euclid 7:262–263
geometry **9**:106–107
Hilbert, David **10**:163
logical structure **9**:107
parallel **15**:79
point **15**:381
Pythagoras, theorem of **15**:639
EUDORA (Arkansas)
map (33° 7′N 91° 16′W) **2**:166
EUDORA (Kansas)
map (38° 57′N 95° 6′W) **12**:18
EUDORINA 7:263
EUDOXUS OF CNIDUS 7:263 *bibliog.*
mathematics, history of **13**:223
EUFAULA (Alabama)
map (31° 54′N 85° 9′W) **1**:234
EUFAULA (Oklahoma)
map (35° 17′N 95° 35′W) **14**:368
EUFAULA LAKE
map (35° 17′N 95° 31′W) **14**:368
EUGENE (Oregon) 7:263
map (44° 2′N 123° 5′W) **14**:427
EUGENE, FRANK **15**:257 *illus.*
EUGENE III, POPE 7:263
EUGENE IV, POPE
Basel, Council of **3**:108
EUGENE ONEGIN (book)
Pushkin, Aleksandr **15**:631–632
EUGENE OF SAVOY 7:263 *bibliog.*
Spanish Succession, War of the **18**:162–163
EUGENICS 7:263–264 *bibliog.*
amniocentesis **1**:375
behavioral genetics **3**:169–170
Darwin, Charles **6**:42
Davenport, Charles **6**:46
Galton, Sir Francis **9**:23
genetic diseases **9**:82–84
genetic engineering **9**:84–85
reproductive programs 7:263
selection modification, genetic change 7:263
EUGÉNIE 7:264
EUGEOSYNCLINE
geosyncline **9**:119–120
EUGLENA 7:264; **15**:579 *illus.*
algae **1**:282 *illus.*
biological locomotion **3**:265
eye 7:348
reproduction **15**:581 *illus.*
EUKARYOTIC CELL *see* EUCARYOTE
EUKINETICS
Laban, Rudolf von **12**:151
EULENSPIEGEL, TILL 7:264
EULER, LEONHARD 7:264–265 *bibliog., illus.*
astronomy, history of **2**:278
ballistics **3**:50
Königsberg bridge problem **12**:108–109
magic square **13**:51
three-body problem **19**:181
EULER, ULF SVANTE VON
Katz, Sir Bernard **12**:31
EULER-CHELPIN, HANS VON 7:265
EUMENES 7:265
EUMENES II, KING OF PERGAMUM 7:265
EUMENIDES *see* FURIES
EUNDA
Ovambo **14**:469
EUNICE (Louisiana)
map (30° 30′N 92° 25′W) **12**:430
EUNICE (New Mexico)
map (32° 26′N 103° 9′W) **14**:136
EUNOMIUS 7:265
EUNUCH *see* CASTRATION
EUPALINUS 7:265
EUPHONIUM
tuba **19**:326
EUPHRATES RIVER 7:265
Iraq **11**:254
map (31° 0′N 47° 25′E) **2**:232
EUPHRONIUS 7:265 *bibliog.*
Onesimos **14**:390
pottery **15**:470 *illus.*
EUPOLIS 7:265
EUPORA (Mississippi)
map (33° 32′N 89° 16′W) **13**:469
EURASIA
See also ASIA; EUROPE
Central Asia **4**:253
earthquakes 7:26
plate tectonics
continental drifting **15**:354 *map*
Eurasian plate **15**:351 *map*
savanna life **17**:97–99
steppe life **18**:256–257
EURATOM (European Atomic Energy Community) *see* EUROPEAN ATOMIC ENERGY COMMUNITY
EUREKA (California) 7:265
map (40° 47′N 124° 9′W) **4**:31
EUREKA (Illinois)
map (40° 43′N 89° 16′W) **11**:42
EUREKA (Kansas)
map (37° 49′N 96° 17′W) **12**:18
EUREKA (Montana)
map (48° 53′N 115° 3′W) **13**:547
EUREKA (Nevada)
map (39° 31′N 115° 58′W) **14**:111
EUREKA (county in Nevada)
map (40° 0′N 116° 15′W) **14**:111
EUREKA (South Dakota)
map (45° 46′N 99° 38′W) **18**:103
EUREKA (Utah)
map (39° 57′N 112° 7′W) **19**:492
EUREKA SPRINGS (Arkansas)
map (36° 24′N 93° 44′W) **2**:166
EURHYTHMICS 7:265–266 *bibliog.*
Dalcroze, Émile Jaques **6**:11
Laban, Rudolf von **12**:151
EURIPIDES 7:266 *bibliog., illus.*
Bacchae, The **3**:9
cyclops
satyr play **17**:92
drama **6**:257–258
Medea **13**:263
Trojan Women, The **19**:305
EUROCOMMUNISM
Berlinguer, Enrico **3**:218
communism **5**:150
socialism **18**:23
EURODOLLAR 7:267 *bibliog.*
banking systems **3**:69
EUROPA (astronomy) 7:267
Jupiter (planet) **11**:472–474 *illus., table*
Voyager **19**:638
EUROPA (mythology) 7:267
EUROPA POINT
map (36° 6′N 5° 21′W) **9**:174
EUROPE 7:267–280 *bibliog., illus., maps, table*
agriculture 7:278–279 *illus., map*
arable land 7:274
food production **1**:197 *table*
animal life 7:273–274
archaeology *see* EUROPEAN PREHISTORY

EUROPE (cont.)
climate 7:272–273 *maps, tables*
maritime climate 13:157
weather variation and extremes 20:80–81 *tables*
colonialism 5:111
Council of Europe 5:310
economic development and commerce 7:277–280 *illus., map*
European Community 7:299
European Economic Community 7:299–300
European Free Trade Association 7:300–301
inflation 11:171
Rothschild (family) 16:322
education 7:59–62; 7:276
degree, academic 6:85
European universities 7:306–309
graduate education 9:276–277
Gymnasium 9:412
Herbart, Johann Friedrich 10:134–135
literacy and illiteracy 12:368
student movements 18:307–308
university 19:468–469
exploration *see* EXPLORATION—Europe
fishing 7:279
forests 7:274; 7:279
geologic time
Bordes, François 3:398
Ordovician Period 14:421 *map*
Permian Period 15:174–175 *map*
Precambrian rock formations 15:492 *map*
Silurian Period 17:310–311
Tertiary Period 19:123 *map*
Triassic Period 19:292–293 *illus.*
geology and landforms 7:269–272 *illus., map*
glaciers and glaciation 9:193–194
mountains, highest 13:620 *table*
head-hunting 10:85
health 7:276
health-care systems 10:88
history *see* EUROPE, HISTORY OF; EUROPEAN PREHISTORY; names of specific countries, e.g., FRANCE; SPAIN; etc.
industrial development 7:277–278 *illus.*
automotive industry 2:366 *table*
chemical industry 4:318–319
languages 7:274–276 *map*
Basque language 3:116
Gemanic languages 9:135–137 *table*
geographical linguistics 9:100
Greek language 9:342–343
Indo-European languages 11:145
Latin language 12:233–234
Romance languages 16:280–281
migration to the United States 11:55 *map*
music competitions 13:669
music festivals 13:670–671
national parks 14:41–43 *map, table*
people 7:275–277 *illus., map*
Celts 4:241–243
demography 7:276–277 *illus., map*
Germanic peoples 9:138
race 16:33–35 *illus., map*
Slavs 17:359
Turks 19:348
women in society 20:204 *table*
physical features
Alps 1:309–310 *illus., map*
Carpathian Mountains 4:163 *map*
Elbrus, Mount 7:102
Iberian Peninsula 11:3–4
Iron Gate 11:272
Jura (mountain range) 11:474
Pripet Marshes (USSR) 15:553
Pyrenees 15:636–637 *illus.*
rift valleys 16:221
Sudeten Mountains 18:323
regions
Ardennes 2:144
Balkans 3:38–40 *map*
Baltic States 3:55
Central Europe 4:254
Eastern Europe 7:33
Riviera 16:234
Western Europe 20:116
religions 7:276
resources 7:274–275
electrical production 15:485 *table*
energy consumption and production 7:174 *table*
mineral resources 7:274; 7:278 *map, map*
oil and gas reserves 15:209 *table*
petroleum industry 15:210 *table*
water resources 7:274; 20:51 *table*
rivers, lakes, and waterways 7:273
Black Sea 3:318–319 *map*
canal 4:96–97
Constance, Lake 5:207
Danube River 6:35–36 *map*
Elbe River 7:102
Geneva, Lake 9:91
Inn River 11:179
Meuse River 13:350
Moselle River 13:599
Rhine River 16:195–196
Scheldt River 17:118
sports
soccer 18:10
trade 7:279–280
transportation 7:279
railroad 16:73–74
roads and highways 16:238
truck and bus registration 19:315 *table*
vegetation and soils 7:273 *map*
Western European Union 20:116
EUROPE, HISTORY OF 7:280–299 *bibliog., illus., maps*
See also AEGEAN CIVILIZATION; EUROPEAN PREHISTORY; the subheading history under names of specific countries, e.g., BULGARIA; NORWAY; etc.; names of specific articles for specific countries and areas, e.g., ITALY, HISTORY OF; SCANDINAVIA, HISTORY OF; etc.
balance of power 3:32
colonialism 5:111–112
Holy Roman Empire 10:209–211
Magyars 13:62–63
medicine 13:269–270
papacy 15:62–66
Slavs 17:359
technology, history of 19:63–65
prior to 500 AD
Alexander the Great, King of Macedonia 7:280
Celts 4:241–243
Germanic peoples 9:138
Greece, ancient 7:280
Huns 10:311
Rome, ancient 7:280–281
Slavs 17:359
500–1350 Middle Ages 7:282–286
Angevins (dynasties) 1:414
Avars 2:369
Carolingians (dynasty) 4:162
Charlemagne, Frankish emperor 4:289–290 *map*
Charles Martel 4:291
chivalry 4:399
Christianity 7:281–285 *map*
commerce 13:395 *map*
commune 5:142
Crusades 5:366–369
Dark Ages 6:38
Drang nach Osten 6:262
enclosure 7:163
feudalism 8:64–65
Germanic peoples 9:138
guilds 9:395
heraldry 10:132–134
Khazars 12:66
knight 12:99–100
manorialism 13:126–127
Merovingians (dynasty) 13:312
Middle Ages 13:391–396
Muslim and other invasions 7:283–284
Normans 14:221–222
Saxons 17:104–105
sumptuary laws 18:340
urban planning 19:481
Verdun, Treaty of 19:550
1350–1600
Hundred Years' War 10:304–305
overseas expansion 7:286
piracy 15:312
Pragmatic Sanction 15:487
Reformation 7:287; 16:121–123 *map*
Renaissance 7:286–287; 16:148–149
rise of national monarchies 7:285–286 *map*
1600–1800
absolutism 7:288–289
Aix-la-Chapelle, Treaties of 1:229
Augsburg, League of 2:320
Austrian Succession, War of the 2:354
divine right 6:203
Eastern Europe 7:289–290
Enlightenment 7:290
French Revolution 7:290–291
French Revolutionary Wars 8:325–326
Industrial Revolution 11:158
Northern War, Great 14:256
privateering 15:557–558
Quadruple Alliance 16:5
Spanish Succession, War of the 18:162–163 *map*
Thirty Years' War 19:171 *map*
Triple Alliance 19:301–302
Westphalia, Peace of 20:119
1800–1900
Berlin, Congress of 3:217
congress system 5:187–188
Continental System 5:230
Eastern Question 7:33–34
growth of nationalism 7:291–292 *map*
Holy Alliance 10:209
imperialism 7:293
Industrial Revolution 7:292
Metternich, Klemens, Fürst von 13:349–350
Napoleonic Wars 14:19–20
national unification 7:292
Revolutions of 1848 16:188
socialism 7:293
Triple Alliance 19:301–302
Vienna, Congress of 19:579
1900-present
fascism 7:295–297
Hague conferences 10:11
Marshall Plan 13:173
nazism 14:67–68
Oder-Neisse line 14:349 *map*
Russian Revolutions of 1917 7:295
suffrage, women's 18:326
World War I *see* WORLD WAR I
World War II *see* WORLD WAR II
1914 cartoon 20:220 *illus., illus., map, map*
EUROPEAN ATOMIC ENERGY COMMUNITY
European Community 7:299
EUROPEAN COAL AND STEEL COMMUNITY
European Community 7:299
EUROPEAN COMMISSION
Council of Europe 5:310
EUROPEAN COMMUNITY 7:299 *bibliog.*
Belgium 3:181
central institutions 7:299
European Economic Community 7:299–300
Monnet, Jean 13:536
Thorn, Gaston 19:178
Veil, Simone 19:536
EUROPEAN CONVENTION ON THE SUPPRESSION OF TERRORISM
Council of Europe 5:310
EUROPEAN COUNCIL
European Community 7:299
EUROPEAN COURT OF HUMAN RIGHTS
Council of Europe 5:310
EUROPEAN ECONOMIC COMMUNITY 7:297–298 *illus., map*; 7:299–300 *bibliog.*
Bank for International Settlements 3:67
customs union 5:398
European Community 7:299
European Free Trade Association 7:300–301
headquarters 3:180 *illus.*
international trade 11:224 *table*
Ireland, history of 11:265
Monnet, Jean 13:536
Netherlands 14:102
Schuman, Robert 17:136
Spaak, Paul Henri 18:118
taxation
value-added tax 19:509
Wilson, Sir Harold 20:164
EUROPEAN FENCE LIZARD *see* LACERTID
EUROPEAN FOOTBALLER OF THE YEAR AWARD
Matthews, Sir Stanley 13:231
EUROPEAN FREE TRADE ASSOCIATION 7:300–301 *bibliog.*
customs union 5:398
EUROPEAN ORGANIZATION FOR NUCLEAR RESEARCH 7:301
accelerator, particle 1:74–75 *illus.*
EUROPEAN PARLIAMENT *see* EUROPEAN COMMUNITY; 7:299
EUROPEAN PREHISTORY 7:301–306 *bibliog., illus., map*
archaeology 2:123–124
barrow 3:95
Battle-Axe culture 3:126
Beaker culture 3:139
broch 3:500
Bronze Age 3:506
bronze industries 7:303–304
metallurgy 7:302–303
social developments 7:304–305
Urnfield culture 19:487
Wessex culture 20:106
burial 7:304 *illus.*
Celts 4:241–243
Danubian culture 6:36
house (in Western architecture) 10:264–266 *illus.*
Iron Age 11:271
Hallstatt 10:23
La Tène period 12:150
Tollund man 19:227
Villanovans 19:597
lake dwelling 12:171
megalith 13:278–279
menhir 13:297
Mesolithic Period 13:314
Neanderthalers 14:68–69; 15:515 *illus.*
Neolithic Period 14:83–84
Central Europe 7:301–302
Eastern Europe 7:301–302
megalithic culture 7:302
Western Europe 7:302
Paleolithic Period 15:38–41
Lower Paleolithic camp 15:39 *illus.*
Mousterian 13:626
Perigordian 15:166
prehistoric art 15:506–510
prehistoric humans 15:511–517
prehistory 15:517
stone alignments 18:281–282
tomb 19:230
Venus figurines 15:40 *illus.*
EUROPEAN PRIMROSE *see* COWSLIP (botany)
EUROPEAN RECOVERY PROGRAM *see* MARSHALL PLAN
EUROPEAN SMOOTH SNAKE 17:377 *illus.*; 17:381 *illus.*
EUROPEAN SOUTHERN OBSERVATORY 7:306
EUROPEAN SPACE AGENCY 7:306
Ariane 2:153
GEOS (artificial satellite) 9:119
satellite, artificial 17:85
space exploration 18:121
Space Telescope 18:137
Spacelab 18:138; 19:69 *illus.*
EUROPEAN SPRAT *see* HERRING; SARDINE
EUROPEAN SWALLOWTAIL BUTTERFLY
life cycle 3:595 *illus.*
EUROPEAN UNIVERSITIES 7:306–309 *bibliog., table*
British education 3:493–495
graduate education 9:276–277
history 7:306–309
library 12:315 *illus.*
Union of Soviet Socialist Republics, universities of the 19:398–399
EUROPEAN VIPER
adder 1:99
EUROPIUM 7:309
element 7:130 *table*
lanthanide series 12:200–201
metal, metallic element 13:328
EUROPOS *see* DOURA-EUROPOS (Syria)
EURPHORBIA *see* SPURGE
EURYDICE *see* ORPHEUS
EURYNOME 7:309–310
EURYPTERID 7:310 *bibliog., illus.*
Silurian Period 17:310 *illus.*
EUSEBIUS OF CAESAREA 7:310 *bibliog.*
EUSEBIUS OF NICOMEDIA 7:310
EUSKALDUNAK *see* BASQUES
EUSKARA *see* BASQUE LANGUAGE
EUSTACE, SAINT 7:310
EUSTACHIAN TUBE 7:6 *illus.*; 7:310
ear 7:6
ear disease 7:7
EUSTACHIO, BARTOLOMMEO
dentistry 6:115
EUSTIS (Florida)
map (28° 51′N 81° 41′W) 8:172
EUTAW (Alabama)
map (32° 50′N 87° 53′W) 1:234

EUTECTIC POINT (chemistry) 7:310
phase equilibrium **15**:224
EUTERPE
muses **13**:656
EUTHANASIA 7:310–311 *bibliog.*
death and dying **6**:69
medical ethics **13**:264
EUTHERIAN 7:311
EUTHYMIDES 7:311 *bibliog.*
EUTROPHICATION 7:311 *bibliog.*
fertilizer **8**:62
lake (body of water) **12**:169
pollution, environmental **15**:412
soap and detergent **18**:8
EUTYCHES 7:311
Monophysitism **13**:537
EVA (Alabama)
map (34° 20′N 86° 46′W) **1**:234
EVAGORAS, DESPOT OF CYPRUS 7:311
EVAN-THOMAS, HUGH
World War I **20**:235
EVANGELICAL ALLIANCE *see* NATIONAL COUNCIL OF CHURCHES
EVANGELICAL AND REFORMED CHURCH *see* UNITED CHURCH OF CHRIST
EVANGELICAL UNITED BRETHREN CHURCH 7:312 *bibliog.*
Albright, Jacob **1**:261
Methodism **13**:344
Otterbein, Philip William **14**:462
EVANGELICALISM 7:312 *bibliog.*
Falwell, Jerry **8**:15
fundamentalism **8**:363
Graham, Billy **9**:279
Great Awakening **9**:308
Great Britain, history of **9**:317
Moody, Dwight L. **13**:561
Moral Re-Armament **13**:573
Moravian Church **13**:574–575
Pentecostalism **15**:155
pietism **15**:297–298
religious broadcasting **16**:142
revivalism **16**:186–187
Roberts, Oral **16**:242
Salvation Army **17**:40
Tennant, William **19**:102
Truth, Sojourner **19**:322
Whitefield, George **20**:138
EVANGELINE (county in Louisiana)
map (30° 45′N 92° 22′W) **12**:430
EVANGELINE (poem)
Longfellow, Henry Wadsworth **11**:407
EVANS (Colorado)
map (40° 22′N 104° 40′W) **5**:116
EVANS (county in Georgia)
map (32° 10′N 81° 55′W) **9**:114
EVANS, SIR ARTHUR 2:122 *illus.*; 7:312 *bibliog., illus.*
Aegean civilization **1**:114–115
Knossos **12**:102
EVANS, DAME EDITH 7:312 *bibliog.*
EVANS, FREDERICK HENRY 7:312 *bibliog.*
EVANS, SIR JOHN 7:312–313
EVANS, MARY ANNE *see* ELIOT, GEORGE
EVANS, MAURICE 7:313
EVANS, MORTIMER
Friese-Greene, William **8**:333
EVANS, MOUNT
map (39° 35′N 105° 38′W) **5**:116
EVANS, OLIVER 7:313 *bibliog.*
manufacturing **13**:132
mass production **13**:203–204
EVANS, RICHARD
Henri Christophe **4**:416 *illus.*
EVANS, RONALD 7:313
Apollo program **2**:84
EVANS, ROWLAND, JR., AND NOVAK, ROBERT 7:313
EVANS, WALKER 7:313 *bibliog.*
photography, history and art of **15**:272 *illus.*
EVANS-PRITCHARD, SIR EDWARD 7:313 *bibliog.*
magic **13**:50
EVANSDALE (Iowa)
map (42° 30′N 92° 17′W) **11**:244
EVANSTON (Illinois) 7:313
map (42° 3′N 87° 42′W) **11**:42
EVANSTON (Wyoming)
map (41° 16′N 110° 58′W) **20**:301
EVANSVILLE (Indiana) 7:313
map (37° 58′N 87° 35′W) **11**:111
EVANSVILLE (Minnesota)
map (46° 0′N 95° 40′W) **13**:453
EVANSVILLE (Wisconsin)
map (42° 47′N 89° 18′W) **20**:185
EVANSVILLE (Wyoming)
map (42° 52′N 106° 16′W) **20**:301
EVAPORATION 7:313–314
cooling tower **5**:242
desalination **6**:124 *illus.*
desert **6**:126
evapotranspiration **7**:314–315
in extraction **7**:341
meteorological instrumentation **13**:340
meteorology **13**:342
refrigeration **16**:124
salt (sodium chloride) **17**:37
sedimentary rock **17**:185
EVAPORITE 7:314 *bibliog., illus.*
anhydrite **2**:8
aragonite **2**:107–108
borate minerals **3**:396
desert **6**:128
economic importance **7**:314
glauberite **9**:205
gypsum **9**:415–416
halite **10**:21
limestone **12**:344–345
mining, chloride **4**:400
oceanic mineral resources **14**:340
paleoclimatology **15**:33
paleogeography **15**:38
playa **15**:363
polyhalite **15**:419
saline or alkaline waters **7**:314
sedimentary rock **17**:184–185 *illus.*
sites **7**:314
sulfate minerals **18**:333
sylvite **18**:402
EVAPOTRANSPIRATION 7:314–315 *bibliog.*
hydrologic cycle **10**:341–342
Thornthwaite climate classification **19**:179
water resources **20**:51
EVART (Michigan)
map (43° 54′N 85° 8′W) **13**:377
EVARTS, WILLIAM MAXWELL 7:315 *bibliog.*
EVATT, HERBERT VERE 7:315 *bibliog.*
EVE 7:315
EVELETH (Minnesota)
map (47° 28′N 92° 32′W) **13**:453
EVELYN, JOHN 7:315 *bibliog.*
EVEN (people)
Tungus **19**:334
EVENING PRIMROSE 7:315 *illus.*
mutation **13**:686
EVENING SHADE (Arkansas)
map (36° 4′N 91° 37′W) **2**:166
EVENING STAR
Castor and Pollux **4**:191
EVENK
Tungus **19**:334
EVER-VICTORIOUS ARMY
Gordon, Charles George **9**:249
EVEREST, SIR GEORGE
Everest, Mount **7**:315
EVEREST, MOUNT 7:315 *bibliog.*
Hillary, Sir Edmund **10**:164 *illus.*
map (27° 59′N 86° 56′E) **14**:86
mountain climbing **13**:621–622
mountain life **13**:623
EVERETT (Massachusetts)
map (42° 24′N 71° 3′W) **3**:409
EVERETT (Pennsylvania)
map (40° 1′N 78° 23′W) **15**:147
EVERETT (Washington)
map (47° 59′N 122° 31′W) **20**:35
EVERETT, EDWARD 7:315 *bibliog.*
EVERETT LAKE
map (43° 6′N 71° 40′W) **14**:123
EVERGLADES 7:316 *bibliog., illus.*
flora and fauna
swamp, marsh, and bog **18**:377 *illus.*
map (26° 0′N 80° 40′W) **8**:172
national parks **14**:37–38 *illus., map, table*
EVERGOOD, PHILIP 7:316 *bibliog.*
EVERGREEN (Alabama)
map (31° 26′N 86° 57′W) **1**:234
EVERGREEN (botany) 7:316
See also CONIFER
Gnetum **9**:213
gymnosperm **9**:414
jungle and rain forest **11**:469–470
seed cone **17**:187
EVERLASTING (botany) 7:316
EVERS (family) 7:316 *bibliog.*
EVERT, CHRIS *see* LLOYD, CHRIS EVERT
EVERYMAN (play) 7:316 *bibliog.*
Dutch and Flemish literature **6**:314
Hofmannsthal, Hugo von **10**:196–197
medieval drama **13**:274
Salzburg Festival **17**:45
EVIDENCE 7:316–318 *bibliog.*
admissible
evidence obtained illegally 7:317–318
hearsay **7**:317
incompetence **11**:77
privilege **7**:317
circumstantial **7**:317
constitutional safeguards **7**:317–318
direct **7**:317
fingerprinting **8**:93
forensic science **8**:227
inadmissible **7**:317–318
incompetence **11**:77
inquest **11**:183
legal procedure **12**:273
Mapp v. *Ohio* **13**:138
Miranda v. *Arizona* **13**:463
pathology, forensic **15**:112
search warrant **17**:175
self-incrimination **17**:191
wiretapping **20**:183
witness **20**:192–193
EVIL EYE 7:318 *bibliog.*
EVINAYONG (Equatorial Guinea)
map (1° 27′N 10° 34′E) **7**:226
EVITA *see* PERÓN, EVA
EVOLUTION 7:318–325 *bibliog., illus., tables*
adaptive radiation **1**:98
Agassiz, Louis Rodolphe **1**:182
altruism **1**:314
amphibians **7**:321–323
amphioxus **1**:381
animal **2**:8–11; **2**:9 *illus.*
animal behavior **2**:15–17; **7**:324
ant **2**:38
Archaeopteryx **2**:127
arthropod **2**:216–218
biology **3**:268
bird **3**:278–279
blue-green algae **3**:343
Cambrian Period **4**:50–52
cat family **4**:196
catastrophism **4**:201
chordate **4**:407
classification, biological **5**:42–43
coelacanth **5**:91
comparative anatomy **5**:155
controversy **7**:324
creation accounts **5**:334–335
creationism **5**:335–336
Cuvier, Georges, Baron **5**:399
Darwin, Charles **6**:41–42
Darwin, Erasmus **6**:42
De Beer, Sir Gavin **6**:58
developmental psychology **6**:142
dinosaur **6**:179–182
dog family **6**:222
ear **7**:6
Earth, geological history of **7**:12
ecology **7**:42–46
Eiseley, Loren **7**:94
elephant **7**:133–134
embryo **7**:324 *illus.*
eugenics **7**:263
evidence **7**:320–324
eye **7**:348
fish **7**:321–323; **8**:120–121
flower **8**:183
fossil record **8**:243–248
fungi **8**:365
genetics **7**:318–319
geology **9**:106
Haeckel, Ernst Heinrich **10**:9
Haldane, J. B. S. **10**:17
heart **10**:94
heredity **10**:140
history **7**:318–319
hoof, nail, and claw **10**:225
hormones **10**:236
horse **10**:245 *illus.*
human, prehistoric humans **15**:511–517
Huxley, Sir Julian **10**:325 *illus.*
Huxley, Thomas Henry **10**:325
Hyatt, Alpheus **10**:327
insect **11**:193
Jurassic Period **11**:477
kidneys **12**:74
Lamarck, Jean Baptiste **12**:173
landform evolution **12**:182–183
life span and **12**:331
lizard **12**:382
Lubbock, John, 1st Baron Avebury **12**:446
lungs **12**:464
McCosh, James **13**:10
mammal **7**:323–324; **13**:99–101; **13**:103 *illus.*
marsupial **13**:174
Mayr, Ernst **13**:249
Mendel, Gregor Johann **13**:294
Mesozoic Era **13**:322
Miller, Stanley Lloyd **13**:428
mimicry **13**:435–436
molecular basis **7**:320
monkey **13**:535
mutation **13**:686–687
natural selection **14**:49
new species **7**:320
Oparin, Aleksandr Ivanovich **14**:397
origin of life **12**:327
Origin of Species, On the **14**:443–444
paleoclimatology **15**:33
paleontology **15**:42
Paleozoic Era **15**:42–43
phylogeny **15**:278–279
plankton **15**:331–332
plant **7**:320; **15**:334–335 *illus.*
flower **8**:182 *illus.*
Plesiosaur **15**:367–368
population genetics **15**:439–440
prehistoric humans **2**:53 *illus.*
primate **7**:324; **15**:539–541 *illus.*
primitive societies **15**:546
race **16**:33–35
reproduction **16**:161; **16**:163
reptile **7**:323; **16**:170–171 *table*
rodent **16**:266
savanna life **17**:98–99
Scopes Trial **17**:148
sex **17**:224
sexual selection **17**:231
Simpson, George Gaylord **17**:317
social behavior **7**:324
Social Darwinism **18**:11–12
sociobiology **18**:26–27
sponge **18**:193
structural geology **18**:303
teeth **19**:71
Teilhard de Chardin, Pierre **19**:73–74
Tertiary Period **19**:122–125
uniformitarianism **19**:386
Wallace, Alfred Russel **20**:13
Weismann, August **20**:95
EVOLUTION, HUMAN *see* PREHISTORIC HUMANS
ÉVORA (Portugal) 7:325
map (38° 34′N 7° 54′W) **15**:449
EVRARD, LOUIS DÉSIRÉE BLANQUART- *see* BLANQUART-EVRARD, LOUIS DÉSIRÉE
EVREINOV, NIKOLAI NIKOLAEVICH 7:325
EVREN, KENAN 7:325
EVREUX (France)
map (49° 1′N 1° 9′E) **8**:260
EVROS RIVER
map (40° 52′N 26° 12′E) **9**:325
EVTUSHENKO, YEVGENY ALEKSANDROVICH *see* YEVTUSHENKO, YEVGENY ALEKSANDROVICH
ÉVVOIA *see* EUBOEA (Greece)
EWA (Hawaii)
map (21° 21′N 158° 2′W) **10**:72
EWALD, JOHANNES 7:325 *bibliog.*
EWE (people) 7:325 *bibliog.*
EWELL, LAKE
map (48° 20′N 111° 15′W) **13**:547
EWELL, RICHARD S. 7:325 *bibliog.*
EWEN (Michigan)
map (46° 32′N 89° 17′W) **13**:377
EWING (Nebraska)
map (42° 16′N 98° 21′W) **14**:70
EWING (Virginia)
map (36° 38′N 83° 26′W) **19**:607
EWING, MAURICE 7:325 *bibliog.*
EWING TOWNSHIP (New Jersey)
map (40° 17′N 74° 47′W) **14**:129
EX PARTE GARLAND *see* GARLAND, AUGUSTUS HILL
EX PARTE MERRYMAN
habeas corpus **10**:4
EX PARTE MILLIGAN 7:325
habeas corpus **10**:4
military force against civilians **7**:325–326
military justice **13**:421
president of the United States **15**:527
statute of limitations **18**:239
EX POST FACTO LAW 7:326
Calder v. *Bull* **4**:26
Constitution of the United States **5**:217–219
Garland, Augustus Hill **9**:48
EX-VOTOS
Latin American art and architecture **12**:227
EXALTACIÓN (Bolivia)
map (13° 16′S 65° 15′W) **3**:366
EXAMINATION, EDUCATIONAL *see* EDUCATIONAL MEASUREMENT
EXAMINATION, MEDICAL 7:326 *bibliog.*
autopsy **2**:368
biopsy **3**:276
blood tests **3**:339

EXAMINATION, MEDICAL (cont.)
diagnostic tests 6:149–150
heart 10:94
photography 15:266
endoscopic photography 15:266
eye 15:266
X rays 15:266
EXCAVATING MACHINERY
earth-moving machinery 7:24
EXCELSIOR SPRINGS (Missouri)
map (39° 20′N 94° 13′W) 13:476
EXCESS PROFITS TAX 7:326
EXCHANGE RATE 7:326–327 *bibliog.*
balance of payments 3:32
central bank 4:254
dollar 6:225
International Monetary Fund 11:222
parity (economics) 15:88
traveler's check 19:284
EXCHEQUER (court) *see* KING'S COURT
EXCHEQUER (department) 7:327
EXCISE *see* SALES TAX
EXCLUSION PRINCIPLE (physics) 7:327
fermion 8:56
orbital 14:417
Pauli, Wolfgang 15:118–119
EXCLUSIONARY RULE 7:327
Mapp v. *Ohio* 13:138
EXCOMMUNICATION 7:327
EXCRETORY SYSTEM 7:327–328 *bibliog., illus.*
See also FECES
bladder, urinary 3:323
endocrine system, diseases of the 7:169
intestine 11:231
invertebrate 11:236
kidneys 12:72–74
reptile 16:169
tissue, animal 19:210
urea 19:485
ureter 19:486
urethra 19:486
urinary system 19:486 *illus.*
urogenital diseases 19:487
EXCURSION INLET (Alaska)
map (58° 25′N 135° 27′W) 1:242
EXECUTION *see* CAPITAL PUNISHMENT
EXECUTIVE BRANCH 7:328; 15:525 *table*
cabinet 4:5
Constitution of the United States 5:217–219
executive privilege 7:328–329
president of the United States 15:522–528
vice-president of the United States 19:568–570
EXECUTIVE PRIVILEGE 7:328–329 *bibliog.*
Constitution of the United States 5:219
law, history of 12:247
president of the United States 15:527
United States v. *Richard M. Nixon* 19:465
Watergate 20:64
EXECUTIVES
stress, biological 18:298
EXEKIAS 7:329 *bibliog.*
Attic amphora 9:338–339 *illus.*
EXEMPLUM (literature) 7:329
EXEQUATUR
consul (modern government official) 5:225
EXERCISE 7:329–331 *bibliog., illus., tables*
adaptation and training 7:330
body temperature 7:329
cardiovascular system 7:330 *table*
Chinese medicine 4:391
circulatory system 4:441
diseases 7:330
fat 7:331
gymnasium 9:412
gymnastics 9:412
inactivity versus 7:329–330
isometrics 11:299–300
muscle 7:331
physical benefits 7:329
posture 7:331
programs 7:330–331
relaxation 7:331
running and jogging 16:346
sports medicine 18:197
stress, biological 18:298
weight lifting 20:92
EXETER (California)
map (36° 18′N 119° 9′W) 4:31
EXETER (England) 7:331
map (50° 43′N 3° 31′W) 19:403
EXETER (Nebraska)
map (40° 39′N 97° 27′W) 14:70
EXETER (New Hampshire) 7:331
map (42° 59′N 70° 57′W) 14:123
EXETER (Ontario)
map (43° 21′N 81° 29′W) 14:393; 19:241
EXETER BOOK 7:331 *bibliog.*
EXETER COLLEGE (Oxford University) 14:474
EXETER RIVER
map (43° 2′N 70° 55′W) 14:123
EXFOLIATION 7:331
EXHALATION
respiratory system 16:180 *illus.*
EXHAUST SYSTEM 7:331–332 *illus.*
catalytic converter 4:199
internal-combustion engine 11:216
EXHIBITIONISM (psychology) 7:332 *bibliog.*
EXIMBANK *see* EXPORT-IMPORT BANK
EXISTENTIALISM 7:332 *bibliog.*
absurdism 1:66
alienation 1:294
Beauvoir, Simone de 3:148
Beckett, Samuel 3:152
Endgame 7:168
Berdyayev, Nikolai 3:208
Buber, Martin 3:531–532
Camus, Albert 4:68
Dostoyevsky, Fyodor Mikhailovich 6:244–245
educational philosophy 7:63
French literature 8:319
Heidegger, Martin 10:106–107
Jaspers, Karl 11:384–385
Kierkegaard, Søren 12:75
Marcel, Gabriel 13:145–146
metaphysics 13:335
Nietzsche, Friedrich Wilhelm 14:185–186
personality 15:189
phenomenology 15:255
Sartre, Jean Paul 17:79–80
Being and Nothingness 3:172
Nausea 14:51
No Exit 14:207
Unamuno, Miguel de 19:381
EXISTENTIALISM, NEW *see* NEW EXISTENTIALISM
EXMOOR PONY
pony 15:428
EXOBIOLOGY *see* LIFE, EXTRATERRESTRIAL
EXODUS, BOOK OF 7:332–333 *bibliog.*
Passover 15:105–106
slavery 17:352
Ten Commandments 7:332–333
EXOELECTRON (physics) 7:333
EXOGAMY 7:333
endogamy 7:171
incest 11:74
EXORCISM 7:333 *bibliog.*
demon 6:104
EXOSPHERE 7:333
EXOTHERMIC REACTION *see* ENDOTHERMIC AND EXOTHERMIC REACTIONS (chemistry)
EXOTIC SHORTHAIR CAT 4:195 *illus.*; 7:333 *illus.*
EXPATRIATION 7:333
citizenship 4:447
EXPECTED VALUE (mathematics) 7:333–334
large numbers, law of 12:207
EXPERIMENT (Georgia)
map (33° 16′N 84° 17′W) 9:114
EXPERIMENT (locomotive)
locomotive 12:389
EXPERIMENTAL EDUCATION *see* EDUCATION
EXPERIMENTAL EVOLUTION, STATION FOR *see* CARNEGIE INSTITUTION OF WASHINGTON
EXPERIMENTAL PHYSICS
physics 15:280
physics, history of 15:286
EXPERIMENTAL PSYCHOLOGY 7:334 *bibliog.*
Boring, E. G. 3:400
Cattell, James McKeen 4:214
Ebbinghaus, Hermann 7:35
Hull, Clark 10:296
psychology 15:595
psychophysics 15:601–602
Wundt, Wilhelm, founder 20:296
EXPERIMENTAL THEATER *see* IMPROVISATIONAL AND EXPERIMENTAL THEATER
EXPERIMENTS
animal experimentation 2:22
behavioral genetics 3:170
genetic engineering 9:84–85; 9:85
Hawthorne studies 10:79
EXPERT SYSTEM (computers) 7:334
artificial intelligence 2:221–222
automata, theory of 2:357
computer 5:160g; 5:160h
computer-aided design and computer-aided manufacturing 5:160L
EXPLOITS DAM
map (48° 45′N 56° 30′W) 14:166
EXPLORATION 7:334–338 *bibliog., map*
See also NORTHEAST PASSAGE; NORTHWEST PASSAGE; SPACE EXPLORATION
Africa 1:157 *map*
Abruzzi, Luigi Amedeo, Duca degli 1:62
Baker, Sir Samuel White 3:28
Barth, Heinrich 3:96
Brazza, Pierre Paul François Camille Savorgnan de 3:465
Bruce, James 3:519–520
Burton, Sir Richard 3:581
Cam, Diogo 4:49
Cameron, Verney Lovett 4:60
Clapperton, Hugh 5:36
Dias, Bartolomeu 6:153
Du Chaillu, Paul Belloni 6:286
Emin Pasha 7:156
exploration 7:334; 7:335–338
Gama, Vasco da 9:24
Henry the Navigator 10:123–124
Livingstone, David 12:377–378
Nachtigal, Gustav 14:4
Park, Mungo 15:89
Speke, John Hanning 18:176–177
Stanley, Sir Henry Morton 18:219
Thomson, Joseph 19:176
Age of Discovery 7:334–335
ancient and medieval 7:334
Antarctica 2:43–45 *illus., map*
Amundsen, Roald 1:386
Bellingshausen, Fabian Gottlieb von 3:188
Borchgrevink, Carsten Egeberg 3:396
Bransfield, Edward 3:455
Bruce, William Speirs 3:520
Byrd, Richard E. 2:44; 3:602
Charcot, Jean Baptiste 4:287
Cook, James 5:236
Dumont d'Urville, Jules Sébastian César 6:298
Ellsworth, Lincoln 7:149
exploration 7:338
Fuchs, Sir Vivian 8:351–352
Gerlache de Gomery, Adrien de, Baron 9:123
Hillary, Sir Edmund 10:164
Mawson, Sir Douglas 13:238
Nordenskjöld, Otto 14:218
Palmer, Nathaniel Brown 15:50–51
Ross, Sir James Clark 16:318
Scott, Robert Falcon 2:44; 17:153–154
Shackleton, Sir Ernest Henry 17:233
Wilkes, Charles 20:151
Wilkins, Sir George Hubert 20:152
anthropological
Heyerdahl, Thor 10:155
Kon-Tiki 12:108
Ra expeditions 16:29
Arctic 2:142–144 *illus., map*
Amundsen, Roald 1:386
Baffin, William 3:21
Barents, Willem 3:80
Barrow, Sir John 3:95
Bennett, Floyd 3:202
Davis, John 6:52
De Long, George Washington 6:61
Ellsworth, Lincoln 7:149
exploration 7:338
Greely, Adolphus Washington 9:347
Hall, Charles Francis 10:21
Kotzebue, Otto von 12:125
MacMillan, Donald Baxter 13:33
Nansen, Fridtjof 14:13
Nobile, Umberto 14:211
Parry, Sir William Edward 15:98
Peary, Robert Edwin 15:128
Rasmussen, Knud 16:90
Simpson, Thomas 17:317
Stefansson, Vilhjalmur 18:245
Sverdrup, Otto Neumann 18:375
Sverdrup, Harald Ulrik 18:375
Wilkins, Sir George Hubert 20:152
Asia
Andrews, Roy Chapman 1:408
Benjamin of Tudela 3:202
Chancellor, Richard 4:278–279
Cheng Ho (Zheng He) 4:330
exploration 7:338
Hedin, Sven Anders 10:104
Ibn Battuta 11:5
La Pérouse, Jean François de Galaup, Comte de 12:148
Northeast Passage 14:253
Odoric of Pordenone 14:350
Philby, H. St. John 15:231
Polo, Marco 15:417
Stein, Sir Aurel 18:246
Younghusband, Sir Francis Edward 20:336
Australia
Australia, history of 2:340 *illus., map*
Burke, Robert O'Hara 3:571–572
Cook, James 5:236
Dampier, William 6:19
exploration 7:338
exploration and settlement 2:340 *map*
Eyre, Edward John 7:352
Flinders, Matthew 8:165
Forrest, John, 1st Baron Forrest 8:235
Stuart, John McDouall 18:306
Sturt, Charles 18:309
Tasman, Abel Janszoon 19:42
Central America
Alvarado, Pedro de 1:319
Stephens, John Lloyd 18:255
Europe
exploration 7:334
land exploration 8:335–338
later maritime explorations 7:335
Latin America
Latin America, history of 12:217–219
New Zealand
Cook, James 5:236
New Zealand, history of 14:161
Tasman, Abel Janszoon 14:161 *map*
North America
Abruzzi, Luigi Amedeo, Duca degli 1:62
Albanel, Charles 1:248
Anza, Juan Bautista de 2:72–73
Ayllón, Lucas Vásquez de 2:379
Bering, Vitus Jonassen 3:211
Block, Adriaen 3:334
Brûlé, Étienne 3:523
Cabeza de Vaca, Álvar Núñez 4:5
Cabot, John 4:7
Cabot, Sebastian 4:7
Cabrillo, Juan Rodríguez 4:7
Campbell, Robert 4:65–66
Canada, history of 4:80 *map*
Cartier, Jacques 4:174–175
Carver, Jonathan 4:179
Champlain, Samuel de 4:277–278 *map*
Charlevoix, Pierre François Xavier de 4:298
Clark, William 5:39
Columbus, Christopher 5:127–129
conquistadors 5:197
Cook, James 5:234–237
Coronado, Francisco Vázquez de 5:270
Cortés, Hernán 5:278
de Soto, Hernando 6:63
Dease, Peter Warren 6:68
Duluth, Daniel Greysolon, Sieur 6:296
Eric the Red 7:229
Escalante, Silvestre Vélez de 7:236
exploration 7:335
Franklin, Sir John 8:284–285
Fraser, Simon 8:287
Frémont, John C. 8:302
Frobisher, Sir Martin 8:335
fur trade 8:371
Gilbert, Sir Humphrey 9:179
Gist, Christopher 9:191
Gosnold, Bartholomew 9:253
Great Britain, history of 9:313
Hakluyt, Richard 10:17
Hearne, Samuel 10:90
Hennepin, Louis 10:122
Hudson, Henry 10:289
Iberville, Pierre Le Moyne, Sieur d' 11:4
James, Thomas 11:354
Jolliet, Louis 11:441
Kelsey, Henry 12:40
Kino, Eusebio Francisco 12:84–85

La Salle, Robert Cavelier, Sieur de **12**:149 *map*
La Vérendrye, Pierre Gaultier de Varennes, Sieur de **12**:151
Leif Eriksson **12**:277–278
Lewis, Meriwether **12**:306
Lewis and Clark Expedition **12**:307–308 *map*
Long, Stephen H. **12**:406
Mackenzie, Sir Alexander (1764–1820) **13**:27
Marquette, Jacques **13**:163
Meares, John **13**:253
Menéndez de Avilés, Pedro **13**:297
Monts, Pierre du Gua, Sieur de **13**:560
mountain men **13**:623–624
Nicolet, Jean **14**:184
North West Company **14**:252–253
Northwest Passage **14**:256–257 *map*
Oñate, Juan de **14**:389
Perrot, Nicolas **15**:178–179
Pike, Zebulon Montgomery **15**:301
Pinzón, Martín Alonso **15**:309
Ponce de León, Juan **15**:425–426
Portolá, Gaspar de **15**:446
Radisson, Pierre Esprit **16**:67–68
Ribaut, Jean **16**:205
Smith, Jedediah Strong **17**:369
Thompson, David **19**:174
Thorfinn Karlsefni **19**:178
Tonty, Henri de **19**:235–236
United States, history of the **19**:437 *map*
Vancouver, George **19**:518
Verrazano, Giovanni da **19**:560
Vizcaíno, Sebastián **19**:623
ocean deeps
bathyscaphe **3**:123 *illus.*
Piccard, Auguste **15**:292
Pacific Ocean
Bingham (family) **3**:259
Bougainville, Louis Antoine de **3**:420
Cook, James **5**:234–237
exploration 7:335
petroleum **15**:208
polar expeditions 7:338
professional and educational organizations
National Geographic Society **14**:33
South America
Aguirre, Lope de **1**:200
Almagro, Diego de **1**:306
Balboa, Vasco Núñez de **3**:33
Bingham (family) **3**:259
Cabral, Pedro Álvarez **4**:7
Cavendish, Thomas **4**:226
El Dorado **7**:98
exploration 7:335
Humboldt, Alexander von **10**:301 *illus.*
Jiménez de Quesada, Gonzalo **11**:419
Orellana, Francisco de **14**:432
Pizarro, Francisco **15**:324 *map*
Ursúa, Pedro de **19**:487
Valdivia, Pedro de **19**:503
Vespucci, Amerigo **19**:564
world circumnavigation
Cano, Juan Sebastian del **4**:113
Cavendish, Thomas **4**:226
Cook, James **5**:236
Drake, Sir Francis **6**:256–257
Gray, Robert **9**:306
Krusenstern, Adam Johann **12**:132
Magellan, Ferdinand **13**:47–48 *map*
EXPLORER (artificial satellite) 7:338–339 *bibliog.*; **17**:85 *illus.*
IMP **11**:60
International Geophysical Year **11**:220
Jupiter (rocket) **11**:474
magnetosphere **13**:60
National Aeronautics and Space Administration **14**:28
Redstone **16**:117
space exploration **18**:119–120 *illus.*
Uhuru **19**:374
Van Allen radiation belts **19**:510
Vanguard **19**:519
EXPLOSION
shock wave **17**:279
star **18**:224
supernova **18**:352
EXPLOSIVES 7:339 *bibliog.*
Abel, Sir Frederick Augustus **1**:55
ammunition **1**:373–375 *illus.*
azide **2**:381
ballistics **3**:51
bomb **3**:373–374
chemical industry **4**:318
coal and coal mining **5**:79
demolition **6**:104
depth charge **6**:120
detonator
lead **12**:256
Dewar, Sir James **6**:146
dynamite **6**:319
fireworks **8**:107
flash point **8**:154
grenade **9**:358 *illus.*
guncotton **9**:405
gunpowder **9**:405–406
history and development 7:339
Maxim (family) **13**:239
mine **13**:437–438
nitrogen **14**:203
Nobel, Alfred **14**:208
plutonium **15**:373
RDX **16**:98
shrapnel **17**:286
TNT **19**:216
tunnel **19**:338–339
weapons **20**:75
World War I **20**:247
EXPO '67 (Montreal) **16**:17 *illus.*
EXPONENT 7:339 *bibliog., table*
binomial theorem **3**:260
exponential functions 7:339–340
logarithm **12**:394
mathematical tables **13**:221
EXPONENTIAL FUNCTIONS 7:339–340 *illus.*
e 7:3
exponent 7:339
hyperbolic functions **10**:348
EXPONENTIAL NOTATION
scientific notation **17**:146
EXPORT-IMPORT BANK 7:340
EXPORT AND IMPORT TRADE *see* INTERNATIONAL TRADE
EXPOSITION (fair) *see* WORLD'S FAIRS
EXPOSITION (literature)
narrative and dramatic devices **14**:22
EXPOSITION UNIVERSELLE OF 1889 (Paris)
Halle des Machines **4**:185 *illus.*
EXPOSURE METER *see* ACTINOMETER
EXPRESSIONISM 7:340 *bibliog., illus.*
art
See also ABSTRACT EXPRESSIONISM
Barlach, Ernst **3**:83–84
Beckmann, Max **3**:152
Blaue Reiter, Der **3**:328
Brücke, Die **3**:520–521
Ensor, James 7:207–208
German art and architecture **9**:128
Heckel, Erich **10**:103
Hofmann, Hans **10**:196
Jawlensky, Alexey von **11**:386
Kirchner, Ernst Ludwig **12**:87
Kokoschka, Oskar **12**:106
Macke, August **13**:27
Marc, Franz **13**:144–145
Mendelsohn, Eric **13**:295
Munch, Edvard **13**:640
Münter, Gabriele **13**:644
Nolde, Emil **14**:214
Orozco, José Clemente **14**:448
painting **15**:22
Pechstein, Max **15**:130
Rodin, Auguste **16**:267
Balzac (statue) **2**:200 *illus.*
Scandinavian art and architecture **17**:113–114
Schiele, Egon **17**:120
Schmidt-Rottluff, Karl **17**:128
sculpture **17**:165
Soutine, Chaim **18**:113
film, history of **8**:83
Lang, Fritz **12**:194–195
literature and theater
Becher, Johannes R. **3**:150
Benn, Gottfried **3**:202
Döblin, Alfred **6**:209
drama **6**:261
epic theater 7:217–218
German literature **9**:133–134
Jessner, Leopold **11**:402
Kaiser, Georg **12**:6–7
Toller, Ernst **19**:227
Trakl, Georg **19**:266
EXPRESSWAY *see* ROADS AND HIGHWAYS
EXTENDED FAMILY 7:340
family **8**:16–17 *illus.*
lineage **12**:353
nuclear family **14**:284
EXTERNAL-COMBUSTION ENGINES
Stirling engine **18**:272–273 *illus.*
EXTINCT SPECIES
See also FOSSIL RECORD
bird
Archaeopteryx **2**:127
auk **2**:322
curlew **5**:392
diving birds **6**:204–205
dodo bird **6**:212
falcon **8**:12
flamingo **8**:151
game birds **9**:27
grebe **9**:323
Hawaiian honeycreeper **10**:76
merganser **13**:310
moa **13**:486–487
New Zealand wattlebird **14**:163
New Zealand wren **14**:163–164
owl **14**:472–473
parakeet **15**:78
parrot **15**:98
pigeon **15**:299–300
rail **16**:71
solitaire **18**:55
carnivore **4**:157
evolution 7:320–324
fish **8**:120–121
arthrodire **2**:216
coelacanth **5**:91
lamprey **12**:176
ostracoderm **14**:458
fossil record **8**:243–248
geologic time
Cambrian Period **4**:50–52 *illus.*
Carboniferous Period **4**:138–139 *illus.*
Cretaceous Period **5**:341
Devonian Period **6**:145–146 *illus.*
Jurassic Period **11**:475–477 *illus.*
Ordovician Period **14**:420–422
Permian Period **15**:174 *illus.*
Pleistocene Epoch **15**:366
Silurian Period **17**:310–312 *illus.*
Tertiary Period **19**:124–125 *illus.*
Triassic Period **19**:294 *illus.*
graptolite **9**:294
hunting **10**:313
invertebrate **11**:234
echinoderm 7:37
trilobite **19**:299
mammal **13**:99–103
See also PREHISTORIC HUMANS
ape, Proconsul **15**:561
Baluchitherium **3**:57
Barylambda **3**:99
Brontotherium **13**:102 *illus.*
cat family **4**:196
cave bear **4**:224
edentates 7:56
eohippus 7:215
flat-coated retriever **8**:154
Irish elk **11**:266
mammoth **13**:106–107
mastodon **13**:217 *illus.*
moeritherium 7:134 *illus.*
proboscidean **15**:559
quagga **16**:5
rodent **16**:265–266
saber-toothed cats **17**:5
seal **17**:174
Sirenia **17**:327
sloth **17**:363
tarpan **19**:38
titanothere **19**:211
Triconodon **13**:102 *illus.*
trilophodon 7:134 *illus.*
Tritemnodon **13**:102 *illus.*
whale **20**:119
woolly rhinoceros **13**:102 *illus.*
reptile **16**:166
crocodile **5**:356
dinosaur **6**:179–182
pterodactyl **15**:606
EXTINCTION (astronomy) 7:340
EXTINCTION (geology) 7:340–41 *bibliog.*
See also EXTINCT SPECIES
EXTORTION *see* BLACKMAIL
EXTRACTION 7:341 *bibliog.*
fats and oils **8**:35
gold **9**:227
medium, ethyl ether 7:257
solvent **18**:58–59
EXTRADITION 7:341
international 7:341
interstate 7:341
right of asylum **16**:222
EXTRAGALACTIC ASTRONOMY
Hubble, Edwin **10**:288
Uhuru **19**:374
EXTRAGALACTIC MATTER
period-luminosity relation **15**:166
EXTRAGALACTIC SYSTEMS **5**:286 *illus.*; 7:341–346 *bibliog., illus.*
Baade, Walter **3**:4
characteristics 7:344–345
classification 7:344 *illus.*
comet **5**:133–134
cosmic rays **5**:283–284
cosmology (astronomy) **5**:284–289
Crab nebula **5**:325–326
distance, astronomical **6**:200
distance measurements 7:343–344
evidence 7:341
galaxies
clusters of galaxies **5**:72
Coma cluster **5**:129
mass of galaxies 7:346
normal galaxies 7:345
radio galaxies **16**:53–54
Seyfert galaxies **17**:232–233
Virgo cluster of galaxies **19**:613
X-ray galaxies **20**:309
High Energy Astronomical Observatory (artificial satellite) **10**:161
Hubble, Edwin 7:343–344; **10**:288
Hubble's constant **10**:288
Hubble's law 7:344
Humason, Milton La Salle **10**:300
interstellar matter **11**:225–228
Lundmark, Knut **12**:462
parallax **15**:78–79
planetary nebula **15**:329
population, stellar **15**:437
quasar **16**:14–15
radio astronomy **16**:49–53 *illus.*
red shift **16**:114
role of Cepheids 7:343
Virgo **19**:613
X-ray astronomy **20**:306
EXTRAPOLATION *see* INTERPOLATION
EXTRASENSORY PERCEPTION 7:346 *bibliog.*
clairvoyance **5**:35
parapsychology **15**:81
EXTRATERRESTRIAL LIFE *see* LIFE, EXTRATERRESTRIAL
EXTRATERRESTRIAL SYSTEMS *see* ASTROGEOLOGY; PLANETARY SYSTEMS; SOLAR SYSTEM; etc.
EXTRATERRITORIALITY 7:346
Opium Wars **14**:407
right of asylum **16**:222
EXTRAVERSION-INTROVERSION (psychology) 7:346 *bibliog.*
EXTREME UNCTION *see* ANOINTING OF THE SICK
EXTRUSION 7:346–347 *illus.*
process 7:347 *illus.*
EXTRUSIVE ROCK *see* IGNEOUS ROCK
EXUMA SOUND
map (24° 15′N 76° 0′W) **3**:23
EXUPÉRY, ANTOINE DE SAINT- *see* SAINT-EXUPÉRY, ANTOINE DE
EYADEMA, GNASSINGBE
Togo **19**:222
EYCK, JAN VAN 7:347–348 *bibliog., illus.*
Arnolfini wedding portrait 7:347 *illus.*; **15**:19 *illus.*
Christus, Petrus **4**:416
Ghent Altarpiece **16**:154 *illus.*
Madonna with Chancellor Rolin **8**:160 *illus.*
Renaissance art and architecture **16**:153
EYE 7:348–350 *bibliog., illus.*
afterimages **1**:181
anatomy 7:348–349 *illus.*
bird **3**:285 *illus.*
blindness **3**:332–333
Bowman, Sir William **3**:430
brain, role of 7:350
camera 7:349
color perception **5**:114–115; 7:350 *illus.*
cosmetics **5**:281–283 *table*
diseases *see* EYE DISEASES
examination, medical 7:326
flatfish **8**:154
folklore, evil eye 7:318
four-eyed fish **8**:252–253
insect **11**:188–189 *illus.*
light detection 7:348
lizard **12**:380
ophthalmology **14**:404
owl **14**:473
perception **15**:158–160
photographic study of **15**:266
plastic surgery **15**:347
primate **15**:539
Purkinje, Jan Evangelista **15**:630
rapid eye movement sleep **17**:360
reflex **16**:120

EYE (cont.)
reptile **16**:171
senses **17**:204
sinus **17**:325
snake **17**:378–379 *illus.*
stereoscopy **7**:350 *illus.*
tears **19**:58
visual memory
television **19**:83
Wald, George **20**:9
EYE, ARTIFICIAL **7**:350
EYE DISEASES **7**:350–351 *bibliog.*
blepharitis **3**:330
blindness **3**:332–333
cataract **4**:200
radiation injury **16**:42–43
color blindness **5**:114
conjunctivitis **5**:191
eye worm **7**:351
glaucoma **9**:205
goiter **9**:225
hyperopia **10**:348
hypertension **10**:349
jaundice **11**:385
myopia **13**:691
nystagmus **14**:310
ophthalmoscope **14**:404–405
river blindness **16**:232
strabismus **18**:287
sty **18**:311
trachoma **19**:258
treatment **7**:351
contact lens **5**:226–227
eyeglasses **7**:351–352
laser and maser **12**:213
surgery **18**:362 *illus.*
ultraviolet light, exposure **19**:379
EYE WORM **7**:351
EYEGLASSES **7**:351–352 *bibliog., illus.*
contact lens **5**:226–227
sunglasses
dichroism **6**:156
polarized light **15**:395
EYELASH
sty **18**:311
EYELID
blepharitis **3**:330
eye **7**:349
plastic surgery **15**:347
sty **18**:311
EYLAU, BATTLE OF **16**:356 *illus.*
EYOTA (Minnesota)
map (43° 59′N 92° 14′W) **13**:453
EYRA *see* JAGUARUNDI
EYRE, EDWARD JOHN **7**:352 *bibliog.*
Australia, history of **2**:340 *map*
EYRE, LAKE **7**:352
map (28° 30′S 137° 20′E) **2**:328
EYRE COURT *see* KING'S COURT
EYRING, HENRY
chemistry, history of **4**:328
EYSENCK, H. J. **7**:352 *bibliog.*
EZEKIEL, BOOK OF **7**:352 *bibliog.*
EZION-GEBER (Israel) **7**:352 *bibliog.*
EZRA, ABRAHAM BEN MEIR IBN *see* IBN EZRA, ABRAHAM BEN MEIR
EZRA AND NEHEMIAH, BOOKS OF **7**:352 *bibliog.*

F

F (letter) **8**:3 *illus.*
V (letter) **19**:500
F-NUMBER **15**:263 *illus.*
aperture **2**:76
camera **4**:56
lens **12**:286
F-15 EAGLE (aircraft) **1**:215 *illus.*; **8**:3 *illus.*
F-16 FIGHTING FALCON (aircraft) **8**:3
F-86 SABRE (aircraft) **1**:215 *illus.*; **8**:3
F-100 SUPER SABRE (aircraft)
aviation **2**:374
FA-HSIEN (Faxian) **8**:4 *bibliog.*
FAA *see* FEDERAL AVIATION ADMINISTRATION
FABBRI, DIEGO
Italian literature **11**:317
FABENS (Texas)
map (31° 30′N 106° 10′W) **19**:129
FABER, CECILIA BÖHL DE *see* CABALLERO, FERNÁN
FABERGÉ, PETER CARL **8**:4 *bibliog.*
jewelry **11**:411
Russian art and architecture **16**:362–363 *illus.*
FABI, THE *see* FABIUS (family)
FABIAN SOCIETY **8**:4 *bibliog.*
Labour party **12**:156
Nesbit, E. **14**:96
Shaw, George Bernard **17**:246
socialism **18**:20
Wallas, Graham **20**:15
Webb, Sidney and Beatrice **20**:86
FABIUS (family) **8**:4
Veii **19**:535
FABIUS, LAURENT **8**:4
FABIUS MAXIMUS
Punic Wars **15**:625
FABIUS MAXIMUS AEMILIANUS, QUINTUS
Fabius (family) **8**:4
FABIUS MAXIMUS VERROCUS, QUINTUS
Fabius (family) **8**:4
FABIUS PICTOR, QUINTUS
Fabius (family) **8**:4
FABLE **8**:4–5 *bibliog., illus.*
Aesop **1**:130
African music **1**:170
bestiary **3**:229
Ibn al-Muqaffa **11**:5
Krylov, Ivan Andreyevich **12**:132
La Fontaine, Jean de **12**:146
Orwell, George **14**:451
Animal Farm **2**:22
Reynard the Fox **16**:191
Thurber, James **19**:186
FABLIAU **8**:5 *bibliog.*
Boccaccio, Giovanni **3**:353–354
Decameron **6**:72
Chaucer, Geoffrey **4**:304–305
FABRE, JEAN HENRI **8**:5 *bibliog.*
FABRIANO (Italy)
map (43° 20′N 12° 54′E) **11**:321
FABRIANO, GENTILE DA *see* GENTILE DA FABRIANO
FABRIC *see* FIBER, TEXTILE; TEXTILES; TEXTILE INDUSTRY
FABRICIUS, DAVID **8**:5
FABRICIUS AB AQUAPENDENTE, HIERONYMUS **8**:5
medicine **13**:269
FACADE **8**:5
FACE
cosmetics **5**:280–283
muscle **13**:653
skeleton, human **17**:336
skull **17**:345 *illus.*
FACE-LIFT *see* PLASTIC SURGERY
FACKEL, DIE (periodical)
Kraus, Karl **12**:127
FACSIMILE **8**:5–6 *bibliog., illus.*
telecommunication transmission **8**:5
telephone **19**:80
FACTOR (mathematics) **8**:6
equation **7**:224
exponent **7**:339
laplace coefficients
LaPlace, Pierre Simon de **12**:205
FACTOR ANALYSIS **8**:6 *bibliog.*
Burt, Sir Cyril **3**:581
Eysenck, H. J. **7**:352
psychological measurement **15**:592
FACTORIAL **8**:6
permutation and combination **15**:176
FACTORY FARMING **8**:6 *bibliog.*
cattle and cattle raising **4**:215 *illus.*; **4**:217
dairying **6**:7–9 *illus.*
egg production **7**:72
feedlot **8**:44–45
fish farming **8**:121–122
poultry **15**:473
FACTORY SYSTEM **8**:6–7 *bibliog.*
Europe, history of **7**:292
Industrial Revolution **11**:158–160
labor force, photojournalism **15**:273
manufacturing **13**:132
mass production **13**:203
textile industry **19**:137
FACTORYVILLE (Pennsylvania)
map (41° 34′N 75° 47′W) **15**:147
FACULA **8**:7
FACULAE
solar cycle **18**:41
solar flare **18**:41
FADA NGOURMA
map (12° 4′N 0° 21′E) **19**:472
FADEYEV, ALEKSANDR ALEKSANDROVICH **8**:7 *bibliog.*
FADO **8**:7 *bibliog.*
FAENZA (Italy)
faïence **8**:8
majolica **13**:76
map (44° 17′N 11° 53′E) **11**:321
FAERIE QUEENE, THE (poem) **8**:7 *bibliog.*
Spenser, Edmund **18**:178
FAEROE ISLANDS **8**:7
flag **8**:140 *illus.*
Germanic languages **9**:135–137 *table*
map (62° 0′N 7° 0′W) **7**:268
FAFNIR **8**:7–8
FAGAMALO (Western Samoa)
map (13° 25′S 172° 21′W) **20**:117
FAGAN, ELEANORA *see* HOLIDAY, BILLIE
FAGEOL, FRANK
bus **3**:583
FAGEOL, WILLIAM
bus **3**:583
FAGERSTA (Sweden)
map (60° 0′N 15° 47′E) **18**:382
FAGUIBINE, LAKE
map (16° 45′N 3° 54′W) **13**:89
FAHD, KING OF SAUDI ARABIA **8**:8
FAHRENHEIT, GABRIEL DANIEL **8**:8
FAHRENHEIT SCALE **8**:8 *bibliog.*
Celsius scale and **4**:238
temperature **19**:93
FAIAL (Portugal)
Azores **2**:381–382 *map*
FAIDHERBE, LOUIS LÉON CÉSAR **8**:8
FAÏENCE **8**:8 *bibliog.*
Minoan art **13**:458
FAINT OBJECT DETECTION **8**:8 *bibliog.*
astronomy and astrophysics **2**:281
infrared radiation **11**:175
magnitude **13**:60–61
National Geographic Society–Palomar Observatory Sky Survey **14**:34
FAINTING **8**:8
first aid **8**:108–109 *illus.*
smelling salts **17**:365
FAIR, A. A. (pseudonym) *see* GARDNER, ERLE STANLEY
FAIR BLUFF (North Carolina)
map (34° 19′N 79° 2′W) **14**:242
FAIR DEAL **8**:8–9 *bibliog.*
Truman, Harry S. **19**:317
FAIR EMPLOYMENT PRACTICES *see* EQUAL OPPORTUNITY
FAIR EMPLOYMENT PRACTICES ACT
integration, racial **11**:202
FAIR HAVEN (New Jersey)
map (40° 23′N 74° 3′W) **14**:129
FAIR HAVEN (Vermont)
map (43° 36′N 73° 16′W) **19**:554
FAIR LABOR STANDARDS ACT
United States v. *Darby* **19**:465
FAIR LAWN (New Jersey)
map (40° 56′N 74° 7′W) **14**:129
FAIR OAKS (Georgia)
map (33° 55′N 84° 32′W) **2**:292
FAIRBAIRN, SIR WILLIAM **8**:9
FAIRBANK (Iowa)
map (42° 38′N 92° 3′W) **11**:244
FAIRBANKS (Alaska) **8**:9
map (64° 51′N 147° 43′W) **1**:242
FAIRBANKS, CHARLES WARREN **8**:9
FAIRBANKS, DOUGLAS **8**:9 *bibliog.*
FAIRBANKS, DOUGLAS, JR.
Fairbanks, Douglas **8**:9
FAIRBANKS, THADDEUS **8**:9
FAIRBORN (Ohio)
map (39° 49′N 84° 2′W) **14**:357
FAIRBURN (Georgia)
map (33° 34′N 84° 35′W) **9**:114
FAIRBURY (Illinois)
map (40° 45′N 88° 31′W) **11**:42
FAIRBURY (Nebraska)
map (40° 8′N 97° 11′W) **14**:70
FAIRCHILD, DAVID GRANDISON **8**:9
FAIRCHILD, SHERMAN MILLS **8**:9
FAIRDALE (Kentucky)
map (38° 6′N 85° 46′W) **12**:47
FAIRFAX (Alabama)
map (32° 48′N 85° 11′W) **1**:234
FAIRFAX (Minnesota)
map (44° 32′N 94° 31′W) **13**:453
FAIRFAX (Missouri)
map (40° 22′N 95° 24′W) **13**:476
FAIRFAX (Oklahoma)
map (36° 34′N 96° 42′W) **14**:368
FAIRFAX (South Carolina)
map (33° 1′N 81° 18′W) **18**:98
FAIRFAX (South Dakota)
map (43° 2′N 98° 54′W) **18**:103
FAIRFAX (Vermont)
map (44° 40′N 73° 1′W) **19**:554
FAIRFAX (Virginia)
map (38° 51′N 77° 18′W) **19**:607
FAIRFAX (county in Virginia)
map (38° 45′N 77° 15′W) **19**:607
FAIRFAX, THOMAS, 3d BARON FAIRFAX OF CAMERON
English Civil War **7**:189
FAIRFAX OF CAMERON, THOMAS FAIRFAX, 6th BARON **8**:9 *bibliog.*
FAIRFAX ISLAND (Australia)
Great Barrier Reef **9**:308 *illus.*
FAIRFAX RESOLVES
Mason, George **13**:198
FAIRFIELD (Alabama)
map (33° 29′N 86° 55′W) **1**:234
FAIRFIELD (California)
map (38° 15′N 122° 3′W) **4**:31
FAIRFIELD (Connecticut)
map (41° 9′N 73° 15′W) **5**:193
FAIRFIELD (county in Connecticut)
map (41° 11′N 73° 11′W) **5**:193
FAIRFIELD (Idaho)
map (43° 21′N 114° 48′W) **11**:26
FAIRFIELD (Illinois)
map (38° 23′N 88° 22′W) **11**:42
FAIRFIELD (Iowa)
map (40° 56′N 91° 57′W) **11**:244
FAIRFIELD (Maine)
map (44° 35′N 69° 36′W) **13**:70
FAIRFIELD (Montana)
map (47° 37′N 111° 59′W) **13**:547
FAIRFIELD (Nebraska)
map (40° 26′N 98° 6′W) **14**:70
FAIRFIELD (Ohio)
map (39° 20′N 84° 33′W) **14**:357
FAIRFIELD (county in Ohio)
map (39° 45′N 82° 38′W) **14**:357
FAIRFIELD (county in South Carolina)
map (34° 25′N 81° 5′W) **18**:98
FAIRFIELD (Texas)
map (31° 44′N 96° 10′W) **19**:129
FAIRGOULE, LOUIS *see* ROMAINS, JULES
FAIRGROVE (Michigan)
map (43° 31′N 83° 33′W) **13**:377
FAIRHAVEN (Massachusetts)
map (41° 39′N 70° 54′W) **13**:206
FAIRHOPE (Alabama)
map (30° 31′N 87° 54′W) **1**:234
FAIRLAND (Indiana)
map (39° 35′N 85° 52′W) **11**:111
FAIRLAND (Oklahoma)
map (36° 45′N 94° 51′W) **14**:368
FAIRLAWN (Virginia)
map (37° 8′N 80° 35′W) **19**:607
FAIRLEIGH DICKINSON UNIVERSITY **8**:9
FAIRLESS, BENJAMIN **8**:9
FAIRMONT (Minnesota)
map (43° 39′N 94° 28′W) **13**:453
FAIRMONT (Nebraska)
map (40° 38′N 97° 35′W) **14**:70
FAIRMONT (North Carolina)
map (34° 30′N 79° 7′W) **14**:242
FAIRMONT (West Virginia)
map (39° 29′N 80° 9′W) **20**:111
FAIRMOUNT (Georgia)
map (34° 26′N 84° 42′W) **9**:114
FAIRMOUNT (Illinois)
map (40° 3′N 87° 56′W) **11**:42
FAIRMOUNT (Indiana)
map (40° 25′N 85° 39′W) **11**:111
FAIRMOUNT (North Dakota)
map (46° 3′N 96° 36′W) **14**:248
FAIRPLAY (Colorado)
map (39° 19′N 105° 60′W) **5**:116
FAIRS *see* CARNIVALS AND FAIRS; TRADE FAIRS; WORLD'S FAIRS
FAIRSERVIS, WALTER **8**:9
FAIRVIEW (Alberta)
map (56° 4′N 118° 23′W) **1**:256
FAIRVIEW (Illinois)
map (40° 38′N 90° 10′W) **11**:42
FAIRVIEW (Montana)
map (47° 51′N 104° 3′W) **13**:547
FAIRVIEW (New Jersey)
map (40° 49′N 74° 0′W) **14**:129
FAIRVIEW (Oklahoma)
map (36° 16′N 98° 29′W) **14**:368
FAIRVIEW (Tennessee)
map (35° 59′N 87° 7′W) **19**:104
FAIRVIEW (West Virginia)
map (39° 36′N 80° 15′W) **20**:111
FAIRVIEW HEIGHTS (Illinois)
map (38° 36′N 90° 0′W) **11**:42
FAIRWEATHER, MOUNT
map (58° 54′N 137° 32′W) **1**:242
map (58° 54′N 137° 32′W) **3**:491
FAIRY **8**:9–10 *bibliog., illus.*
brownie **3**:518
FAIRY BLUEBIRD **8**:10
FAIRY RING MUSHROOM **8**:10
mushrooms **13**:660–661
FAIRY SLIPPER (botany) **8**:10
FAIRY TALE **8**:10–11 *bibliog., illus.*
Andersen, Hans Christian **1**:401
Basile, Giovanni Battista **3**:109
Beauty and the Beast (book) **3**:147
Bettelheim, Bruno **3**:232
Bluebeard **3**:344
children's literature **4**:351
Croker, Thomas Crofton **5**:357
folktale **8**:204
Grimm, Jacob and Wilhelm **9**:365–366

Grimm's Fairy Tales **9**:366
Lang, Andrew **12**:194
Mother Goose **13**:607
Pushkin, Aleksandr **15**:631–632
FAISAL, KING OF SAUDI ARABIA **8**:11 *bibliog.*
Khalid, King of Saudi Arabia **12**:65
FAISAL I, KING OF IRAQ **8**:11 *bibliog.*
Lawrence, T. E. **12**:250
Palestine **15**:45
World War I **20**:243
FAITH *see* RELIGION
FAITH (South Dakota)
map (45° 2′N 102° 2′W) **18**:103
FAITH OF CHALCEDON *see* CHALCEDON, COUNCIL OF
FAITH HEALING **8**:11 *bibliog.*
anointing of the sick **2**:34
folk medicine **8**:201
Roberts, Oral **16**:242
FAIYUM *see* AL-FAIYUM (Egypt)
FAJARDO (Puerto Rico)
map (18° 20′N 65° 39′W) **15**:614
FAKAOFO
Tokelau **19**:223
FAKE ART *see* FORGERY IN ART
FAKHR AL-DIN **8**:11 *bibliog.*
FAKIR **8**:11
FAKSE BAY
map (55° 10′N 12° 15′E) **6**:109
FALABELLA
pony **15**:428
FALAISE, TREATY OF
William the Lion, King of Scotland **20**:154
FALAISE DE L'ÎLE-DE-FRANCE
Champagne **4**:276
FALASHAS **8**:11–12 *bibliog.*
FALCO, LOUIS **8**:12
FALCON **2**:140–141 *illus.*; **8**:12 *bibliog.*, *illus.*
caracara **4**:130
falconry **8**:12–13
hawk **10**:76
naukeen kestrel **10**:5 *illus.*
FALCON RESERVOIR
map (26° 37′N 99° 11′W) **19**:129
FALCONET, ÉTIENNE MAURICE **8**:12 *bibliog.*
FALCONRY **8**:12–13 *bibliog.*
eagle **7**:3
hawk **10**:76
FALELIMA (Western Samoa)
map (13° 32′S 172° 41′W) **20**:117
FALÉMÉ RIVER
map (14° 46′N 12° 14′E) **17**:202
FALEVAI (Western Samoa)
map (13° 55′S 171° 59′W) **20**:117
FALFURRIAS (Texas)
map (27° 14′N 98° 9′W) **19**:129
FALIERO, MARINO
doge **6**:222
FALKENHAYN, ERICH VON **8**:13 *bibliog.*
Verdun, Battle of **19**:550
World War I **20**:232–233
FALKENSEE (Germany, East and West)
map (52° 33′N 13° 4′E) **9**:140
FALKIRK (Scotland)
map (56° 0′N 3° 48′W) **19**:403
FALKLAND ISLANDS **8**:13
map (51° 45′S 59° 0′W) **18**:85
World War I **20**:228 *illus.*
FALL, ALBERT B.
Teapot Dome **19**:58
FALL CITY (Washington)
map (47° 34′N 121° 53′W) **20**:35
FALL CREEK
map (39° 47′N 86° 11′W) **11**:111
FALL LINE **8**:13 *map*
Georgia **9**:113
FALL RIVER (Kansas)
map (37° 24′N 95° 40′W) **12**:18
map (37° 36′N 96° 2′W) **12**:18
FALL RIVER (Massachusetts) **8**:13
map (41° 43′N 71° 8′W) **13**:206
FALL RIVER (county in South Dakota)
map (43° 15′N 103° 30′W) **18**:103
FALL RIVER (Wisconsin)
map (43° 23′N 89° 3′W) **20**:185
FALL RIVER LAKE
map (37° 42′N 96° 8′W) **12**:18
"FALL OF THE HOUSE OF USHER, THE" (short story) **8**:13 *bibliog.*
Poe, Edgar Allan **15**:378
FALL ZONE *see* FALL LINE
FALLA, MANUEL DE **8**:13–14 *bibliog.*
Three-Cornered Hat, The **18**:161 *illus.*
FALLACY **8**:14 *bibliog.*
science, philosophy of **17**:142
FALLBROOK (California)
map (33° 23′N 117° 15′W) **4**:31
FÄLLDIN, THORBJÖRN **8**:14 *illus.*
FALLEN TIMBERS, BATTLE OF **8**:14 *bibliog.*
Wayne, Anthony **20**:73
FALLING STAR *see* METEOR AND METEORITE; STAR
FALLINGWATER (house) **2**:137 *illus.*
cantilever **4**:117
FALLODON, 1st VISCOUNT GREY OF *see* GREY, SIR EDWARD
FALLON (Montana)
map (46° 50′N 105° 7′W) **13**:547
FALLON (county in Montana)
map (46° 20′N 104° 20′W) **13**:547
FALLON (Nevada)
map (39° 28′N 118° 47′W) **14**:111
FALLOPIAN TUBES **16**:163 *illus.*
menstruation **13**:301
FALLOPIUS, GABRIEL
medicine **13**:269
FALLOUT **8**:14 *bibliog.*
cesium **4**:262
Chernobyl (USSR) **4**:331
fallout shelter **8**:14–15
hydrogen bomb **10**:339–340
Pauling, Linus Carl **15**:119
strontium **18**:303
FALLOUT SHELTER **8**:14–15 *bibliog.*
civil defense **5**:10
FALLS (county in Texas)
map (31° 17′N 96° 55′W) **19**:129
FALLS CHURCH (Virginia)
map (38° 53′N 77° 11′W) **19**:607
FALLS CITY (Nebraska)
map (40° 3′N 95° 36′W) **14**:70
FALLS OF CLYDE
Clyde, River **5**:72
FALMININUS, TITUS QUINCTIUS
Philip V, King of Macdonia **15**:234
FALMOUTH (Jamaica)
map (18° 30′N 77° 39′W) **11**:351
FALMOUTH (Kentucky)
map (38° 40′N 84° 20′W) **12**:47
FALMOUTH (Maine)
map (43° 39′N 70° 16′W) **13**:70
FALMOUTH (Massachusetts)
map (41° 34′N 70° 38′W) **13**:206
FALMOUTH (Virginia)
map (38° 19′N 77° 28′W) **19**:607
FALSE BAY
map (34° 12′S 18° 40′E) **18**:79
FALSE PACA **8**:15 *illus.*
FALSE SUNBIRD **8**:15
FALSE TEETH *see* DENTURES
FALSE WATER COBRA
colubrid **5**:124
FALSETTO **8**:15
FALSTAFF (fictional character) **8**:15 *bibliog.*
Henry IV (Parts 1 and 2) **10**:124
Merry Wives of Windsor, The **13**:312
FALSTAFF (opera)
Boito, Arrigo **3**:363
Verdi, Giuseppe **19**:549–550
FALSTER ISLAND
map (54° 48′N 11° 58′E) **6**:109
FALUN (Sweden)
map (60° 36′N 15° 38′E) **18**:382
FALWELL, JERRY **8**:15
Moral Majority **13**:573
FAMAGUSTA (Cyprus)
map (35° 7′N 33° 57′E) **5**:409
FAMAGUSTA BAY
map (35° 15′N 34° 10′E) **5**:409
FAMILISTS **8**:15
FAMILY **8**:15–18 *bibliog.*, *illus.*
See also ADOPTION AND FOSTER CARE; MARRIAGE; PARENT; etc.
adolescence **1**:107
adoption and foster care **1**:107
alternatives to family living **8**:18
Arabs **2**:104–105
Basques **3**:116
birth control **3**:293–295
black Americans **3**:312
Cameroon, Bamileke **3**:60
child abuse **4**:348
communal living **5**:141–142
contemporary family life patterns **8**:17–18
culture **5**:385
exogamy **7**:333
extended family **7**:341
family structure **8**:16–17
family support programs **8**:18
functioning **8**:17
genealogy **9**:76
human ecology **10**:297
incest **11**:73–74
kinship **12**:85
matriarchy **13**:229
menopause **13**:299
next of kin **14**:175
nuclear family **14**:284
passage rites of birth **15**:103
Planned Parenthood Federation of America **15**:333
population **15**:437
population genetics **15**:439–440
preschool education **15**:520–522
primary education **15**:537
social structure and organization **18**:16–17
Westermarck, Edward Alexander **20**:115
women in society **20**:201; **20**:202; **20**:203
young people **20**:335–336
FAMILY COMPACT **8**:18
Choiseul, Étienne François, Duc de **4**:403
FAMILY MEDICAL PRACTICE
medicine **13**:272
medicine, education in **13**:273
FAMILY PLANNING *see* BIRTH CONTROL
FAMILY THERAPY
psychotherapy **15**:603
FAMINE **8**:18–19 *bibliog.*, *table*
diseases, plant **6**:194
Ireland, history of **11**:263–264 *illus.*
dulse **6**:296
nutritional-deficiency diseases **14**:308
relief assistance
Agency for International Development **1**:183
starvation **18**:228
FAN **8**:19 *bibliog.*, *illus.*
automotive
cooling system, engine **5**:242
trucking industry **19**:315–316
FAN K'UAN (Fan Kuan) **8**:20
Traveling amid Mountains and Streams **12**:188 *illus.*
FAN SI PAN MOUNTAIN
map (22° 15′N 103° 46′E) **19**:580
FAN-TAN (card game) **8**:20 *bibliog.*
FANAKALO (lingua franca)
South Africa **18**:80
FANALOKA
fossa **8**:243
FANCONI SYNDROME
kidney disease **12**:71
FANDAN *see* FAN-TAN (card game)
FANDANGO **8**:20 *bibliog.*
FANEUIL, PETER *see* FANEUIL HALL
FANEUIL HALL **8**:20 *bibliog.*; **13**:207 *illus.*
FANFANI, AMINTORE **8**:20 *illus.*
FANG (anatomy)
snake **17**:380 *illus.*
FANG (people) **8**:20 *bibliog.*
African music **1**:169
FANGIO, JUAN MANUEL **8**:20 *bibliog.*
FANNIE FARMER COOKBOOK, THE
Farmer, Fannie **8**:24
FANNIE MAE *see* FEDERAL NATIONAL MORTGAGE ASSOCIATION
FANNIN (county in Georgia)
map (34° 56′N 84° 20′W) **9**:114
FANNIN (county in Texas)
map (33° 33′N 96° 10′W) **19**:129
FANNY HILL, OR THE MEMOIRS OF A WOMAN OF PLEASURE (book) **8**:20
FANO (Italy)
map (43° 50′N 13° 1′E) **11**:321
FANON, FRANTZ **8**:20–21 *bibliog.*
FANTASY (literature)
See also SUPERNATURAL LITERATURE
Alexander, Lloyd **1**:273
De Camp, L. Sprague **6**:58
Dunsany, Lord **6**:301
Lewis, C. S. **12**:305
Lovecraft, H. P. **12**:438
Tolkien, J. R. R. **19**:226–227
White, T.H. **20**:136
FANTASY (psychology) **8**:21
games **9**:31
humanistic psychology **10**:300
hypnosis **10**:350
surrealism (art) **18**:364–365
FANTI **8**:21
FANTIN-LATOUR, HENRI **8**:21 *bibliog.*
Verlaine and Rimbaud **19**:552 *illus.*
FAR EAST **8**:21
See also names of specific countries, e.g., CHINA; MONGOLIA; etc.
folk art **8**:198
food production **1**:197 *table*
herbs and spices **10**:137
music, non-Western **13**:667–668
petroleum industry **15**:210 *table*
Polo, Marco **15**:417
sampan **17**:48
spice trade **18**:180–181
FAR FROM THE MADDING CROWD **8**:21 *bibliog.*
FARABI, AL- **8**:21 *bibliog.*
FARAD (physics) **8**:21
units, physical **19**:466–467 *tables*
FARADAY, MICHAEL **4**:326 *illus.*; **8**:21–22 *bibliog.*, *illus.*
chemistry, history of **4**:325
electrochemistry **7**:112 *illus.*
electromagnetic induction **7**:115
farad **8**:21
Faraday's laws of electrolysis **8**:22
generator **9**:78
glass **9**:198
ion and ionization **11**:239
magnetism **13**:56
magnetohydrodynamics **13**:58
Maxwell's equations **13**:241–242
motor **13**:611
physics, history of **15**:284 *illus.*
FARADAY'S LAWS OF ELECTROLYSIS **8**:22 *bibliog.*
coulombmeter **5**:308
electrochemistry **7**:112
FARAFANGANA (Madagascar)
map (22° 49′S 47° 50′E) **13**:38
FARAH (Afghanistan)
map (32° 22′N 62° 7′E) **1**:133
FARBER, MYRON
freedom of the press **8**:297
FARCE **8**:22–23 *bibliog.*
See also SATIRE
Anouilh, Jean **2**:34–35
commedia dell'arte **5**:137–138
Courteline, Georges **5**:316
drama **6**:258
Feydeau, Georges **8**:66
Foote, Samuel **8**:219
Labiche, Eugène Marin **12**:151
Lesage, Alain René **12**:296
Orton, Joe **14**:451
Rueda, Lope de **16**:339
FARCY *see* GLANDERS
FARD, WALLACE D.
Black Muslims **3**:317
FAREL, GUILLAUME **8**:23
FAREWELL, CAPE
map (40° 30′S 172° 41′E) **14**:158
FAREWELL, MY LOVELY (book) **8**:23
FAREWELL TO ARMS, A (book) **8**:23 *bibliog.*
FARGE, JOHN LA *see* LA FARGE, JOHN
FARGE, OLIVER HAZARD PERRY LA *see* LA FARGE, OLIVER HAZARD PERRY
FARGO (North Dakota) **8**:23
map (46° 52′N 96° 48′W) **14**:248
FARGO, WILLIAM GEORGE **8**:23 *bibliog.*
FARGUE, LÉON PAUL **8**:23
FARIAS, VALENTÍN GÓMEZ
Mexican War **13**:353
FARIBAULT (Minnesota)
map (44° 18′N 93° 16′W) **13**:453
FARIBAULT (county in Minnesota)
map (43° 38′N 93° 55′W) **13**:453
FARIDPUR (Bangladesh)
map (23° 36′N 89° 50′E) **3**:64
FARINA (Illinois)
map (38° 50′N 88° 46′W) **11**:42
FARINELLI **8**:23 *bibliog.*
FARLEY, JAMES A. **8**:23
FARM BUREAU *see* AMERICAN FARM BUREAU FEDERATION
FARM CREDIT ADMINISTRATION **8**:23–24 *bibliog.*
Roosevelt, Franklin Delano **16**:309
FARM PRICES
National Farmers Organization **14**:32
National Farmers Union **14**:32
parity (economics) **15**:88
FARM SECURITY ADMINISTRATION
photography, history and art of **15**:271–272
Stryker, Roy **18**:304
FARMER, FANNIE **8**:24 *bibliog.*, *illus.*
FARMER, JAMES
Congress of Racial Equality **5**:184
FARMER, MOSES **8**:24
FARMER CITY (Illinois)
map (40° 15′N 88° 39′W) **11**:42
FARMER-LABOR PARTY **8**:24 *bibliog.*
FARMERSBURG (Indiana)
map (39° 15′N 87° 23′W) **11**:111
FARMERVILLE (Louisiana)
map (32° 47′N 92° 24′W) **12**:430
FARMINGTON (Illinois)
map (40° 42′N 90° 0′W) **11**:42
FARMINGTON (Iowa)
map (40° 38′N 91° 44′W) **11**:244
FARMINGTON (Maine)
map (44° 40′N 70° 9′W) **13**:70
FARMINGTON (Michigan)
map (42° 28′N 83° 22′W) **13**:377

FARMINGTON (Minnesota)
map (44° 38′N 93° 8′W) **13**:453
FARMINGTON (Missouri)
map (37° 47′N 90° 25′W) **13**:476
FARMINGTON (New Hampshire)
map (43° 24′N 71° 4′W) **14**:123
FARMINGTON (New Mexico)
map (36° 44′N 108° 12′W) **14**:136
FARMINGTON (Utah)
map (40° 59′N 111° 53′W) **19**:492
FARMINGTON RIVER
map (41° 51′N 72° 38′W) **5**:193
FARMS AND FARMING **8**:24–28 *bibliog.*, *illus.*
See also AGRIBUSINESS; AGRICULTURE, HISTORY OF; AGRICULTURE AND THE FOOD SUPPLY
agricultural extension service **1**:189
barn **3**:85
Canada **4**:77–78 *illus.*
cattle and cattle raising **4**:214–217
Communist countries
socialist law **18**:25
computer **5**:160f
contour plowing **13**:479 *illus.*
cost-price squeeze **8**:28
drainage systems **6**:255
Europe **7**:279 *illus.*
Danubian culture **6**:36
factory farming **8**:6
family farm **8**:25
farm specialization **8**:25–27
farmhouses **10**:268–269 *illus.*
India **11**:85–86 *illus.*
irrigation **11**:280–283
Landsat (artificial satellite) **12**:185 *illus.*
machines and implements
combine **5**:130–131 *illus.*
Deere, John **6**:81
draft horse **6**:254
harrow **10**:61
harvester **1**:192–193 *illus.*; **10**:65; **13**:457 *illus.*
helicopter, crop dusting **10**:112
plow **15**:369–370 *illus.*
reaper **16**:104 *illus.*
seed drill **19**:330–331 *illus.*
tomato-picking machine **1**:195 *illus.*
tractor **19**:262
tractor (steam) **1**:193 *illus.*
wagon **20**:6 *illus.*
organizations
American Farm Bureau Federation **1**:338
4-H program **8**:253
Future Farmers of America **8**:383
Grange, National **9**:286
National Farmers Organization **14**:32
National Farmers Union **14**:32
special-interest groups **18**:168
peat **15**:129
photography
photography, history and art of **15**:271–272
price stabilization **8**:27–28
rice **16**:207–208 *illus.*
sandstorm and dust storm **17**:64
soil **18**:36–38
tenant farming
slavery **17**:353
terrace farming **1**:194 *illus.*; **4**:369 *illus.*
Igorot **11**:38
Inca **11**:72
United States **8**:24–28
California **4**:35
frontier **8**:343 *illus.*
Iowa **11**:247–248
Kansas **12**:22
Nonpartisan League **14**:217
Texas **19**:131–132
Watson, Elkanah **20**:67
wheat **20**:125 *illus.*
FARMVILLE (North Carolina)
map (35° 36′N 77° 35′W) **14**:242
FARMVILLE (Virginia)
map (37° 18′N 78° 24′W) **19**:607
FARNABY, GILES
English music **7**:203
FARNAM (Nebraska)
map (40° 42′N 100° 13′W) **14**:70
FARNESE, ALESSANDRO **8**:28 *bibliog.*
FARNESE, ELIZABETH **8**:28
FARNESE HERACLES **8**:28 *bibliog.*
FARNESE PALACE (Rome) **4**:167 *illus.*; **8**:28 *bibliog.*
Michelangelo **13**:375
FARNHAMVILLE (Iowa)
map (42° 17′N 94° 24′W) **11**:244
FARNSWORTH, PHILO TAYLOR **8**:28
FARO (card game) **8**:28 *bibliog.*
FAROE ISLANDS *see* FAEROE ISLANDS
FAROUK, KING OF EGYPT **8**:28–29 *bibliog.*
FARQUHAR, GEORGE **8**:29
FARQUHAR GROUP (Islands)
map (10° 10′S 51° 10′E) **17**:232
FARRAGUT (Iowa)
map (40° 43′N 95° 29′W) **11**:244
FARRAGUT, DAVID GLASGOW **8**:29 *bibliog.*, *illus.*
Civil War, U.S. **5**:22–23 *illus.*, *map*
New Orleans (Louisiana) **14**:142
statue **17**:18 *illus.*
FARRAR, GERALDINE **8**:29 *bibliog.*
FARRAR, MARGARET
crossword puzzle **5**:362
FARRELL (Pennsylvania)
map (41° 13′N 80° 30′W) **15**:147
FARRELL, JAMES T. **8**:29 *bibliog.*, *illus.*
FARRELL, SUZANNE **8**:30
Martins, Peter **13**:181
FARSIGHTEDNESS *see* HYPEROPIA
FARVEL, CAPE
map (59° 45′N 44° 0′W) **9**:353
FARWELL (Texas)
map (34° 23′N 103° 2′W) **19**:129
FAS (Morocco) *see* FEZ (Morocco)
FASCES **8**:30
Etruscans **7**:259
Roman **16**:278 *illus.*; **18**:229 *illus.*
FASCI DI COMBATTIMENTO
Mussolini, Benito **13**:684
FASCISM **8**:30 *bibliog.*, *illus.*
Austria **2**:351
authoritarian personality **2**:354
Europe, history of **7**:295–297
fasces **8**:30
Iron Guard **11**:272
Italy
Blackshirts **3**:322
Gentile, Giovanni **9**:94
Italy, history of **11**:330–331
Milan (Italy) **13**:418
Mussolini, Benito **13**:684
Mosley, Sir Oswald **13**:601
radicalism **16**:44
representation **16**:161
Spain
Carlists **4**:151Franco, Francisco **8**:277–278
Primo de Rivera, José Antonio **15**:546
Spanish Civil War **18**:156-157
totalitarianism **19**:248
FASCIST ART **8**:30–31 *bibliog.*
FASHION DESIGN **8**:31–33 *bibliog.*, *illus.*
See also COSTUME
Art Deco **2**:208 *illus.*
Balenciaga, Cristóbal **3**:36
Chanel, Coco **4**:280
clothing industry **5**:66
Dior, Christian **6**:185
education
Parsons School of Design **15**:99
Pratt Institute **15**:490
fan **8**:19
fashion photography **8**:33
Lanvin, Jeanne **12**:201
McCardell, Claire **13**:7
Mainbocher **13**:69
Patou, Jean **15**:112
Poiret, Paul **15**:381
Saint Laurent, Yves **17**:20
Schiaparelli, Elsa **17**:119–120
Worth, Charles Frederick **20**:284
FASHION INSTITUTE OF TECHNOLOGY
New York, State University of **14**:154
FASHION PHOTOGRAPHY **8**:33 *bibliog.*
Avedon, Richard **2**:369
Penn, Irving **15**:144
FASHODA INCIDENT **8**:33
FASSBINDER, RAINER WERNER **8**:33
FAST, HOWARD **8**:33
FAST FOODS *see* FOOD SERVICE SYSTEMS
FAST-PITCH SOFTBALL
softball **18**:35
FASTING **8**:33
FAT **8**:33–34
diet, human **6**:164
dieting **6**:165
digestion, human **6**:172
digestive system **6**:174
exercise **7**:331
fats and oils **8**:34–35; **8**:35
fatty acid **8**:35
gallbladder **9**:17
hibernation **10**:156
hypoglycemia **10**:351
insulin **11**:197
lipid **12**:362
metabolism **13**:325
nutrition, human **14**:305
obesity **14**:315–316
plant (botany) **13**:327
pyruvic acid **15**:639
starvation **18**:228
steatopygia **18**:242–243
tissue, animal **19**:210
FATA MORGANA **8**:34
FATEHPUR SIKRI (India) **8**:34
Indian art and architecture **11**:97
Islamic art and architecture **11**:297
Mogul art and architecture **13**:500–501 *illus.*
FATES **8**:34
FATH, JACQUES
fashion design **8**:32
FATHER DIVINE *see* DIVINE, FATHER
"FATHER OF THE U.S. CAVALRY" *see* KEARNY, STEPHEN WATTS
FATHERS AND SONS (book) **8**:34 *bibliog.*
nihilism **14**:194
Turgenev, Ivan **19**:341
FATHERS OF THE CHURCH **8**:34
Ambrose, Saint **1**:325
Athanasius, Saint **2**:288
Augustine, Saint **2**:320–321
Chrysostom, Saint John **4**:421
Clement of Alexandria, Saint **5**:49
Dionysius the Great **6**:184
Gregory I, Pope **9**:356
Gregory of Nazianzus, Saint **9**:356
Gregory of Nyssa, Saint **9**:356
Gregory Thaumaturgus, Saint **9**:356
Isidore of Seville, Saint **11**:287
Jerome, Saint **11**:398
John Damascene, Saint **11**:424
patristic literature **15**:113–114
FATIGUE (biology)
headache **10**:85
FÁTIMA (city in Portugal) **8**:34
FATIMA (daughter of Muhammad) **8**:34
Ali **1**:292
Fatimids **8**:34
FATIMAH
Qum (Iran) **16**:28
FATIMIDS **8**:34
FATS AND OILS **8**:34–35 *bibliog.*
carboxylic acid **4**:140
chemistry of **8**:34
essential oils **7**:244–245
fat **8**:33
function, physiological **8**:35
glycerol **9**:212
hydrogenation **10**:341
jojoba **11**:440
lighting, lamp **12**:175–176
lipid **12**:361–362
lubrication **12**:447–448
nut **14**:301
perfume **15**:164
plant **15**:341
processing **8**:35
safflower **17**:11
saponification **17**:73
soap and detergent **18**:6
sources **8**:35
whaling **20**:123 *illus.*
sperm oil **18**:179
stearin **18**:242
varnish **19**:524
vegetable oils **19**:534–535
whale **20**:121
FATTY ACID **8**:35 *illus.*, *table*; **12**:361 *illus.*
carboxylic acid **4**:139–141
cholesterol **4**:404
fat **8**:33
fats and oils **8**:34
lipid **12**:361–362
metabolism **13**:327
palmitic acid **15**:51
prostaglandins **15**:572–573
FAUBUS, ORVAL
black Americans **3**:310 *illus.*
FAUCET, WATER **15**:372 *illus.*
valve **19**:509 *illus.*
FAUCHARD, PIERRE
dentistry **6**:115
FAUCHER, CLAIRE *see* MARTIN, CLAIRE
FAULK (county in South Dakota)
map (45° 5′N 99° 8′W) **18**:103
FAULKNER (county in Arkansas)
MAP LOCATION 3510N09212W)map (35° 10′N 92° 12′W) **2**:166
FAULKNER, BRIAN **8**:36
Ireland, history of **11**:265
FAULKNER, WILLIAM **1**:347 *illus.*; **8**:36 *bibliog.*, *illus.*
Absalom, Absalom! **1**:62
As I Lay Dying **2**:226
Bear, The **3**:141
Sound and the Fury, The **18**:74
FAULKTON (South Dakota)
map (45° 2′N 99° 8′W) **18**:103
FAULT (geology) **8**:36–38 *bibliog.*, *illus.*
basin and range province **3**:110
construction along **8**:37–38
diastrophism **6**:153
Earth, geological history of **7**:13
earthquakes **7**:28
East African Rift System **7**:30
escarpment **7**:237
horst and graben **10**:253–254
line
Moon, far side **13**:565 *map*
mountain **13**:619–620 *illus.*
movement, measurement of rate **8**:37
orogeny **14**:447
rift valleys **16**:221
San Andreas Fault **17**:50 *illus.*
structural geology **18**:303
transform fault
Earth, structure and composition of **7**:21
types **8**:37
zones
oceanic fracture zones **14**:339
zones, mylonite **13**:690
FAUN, HOUSE OF THE
The Battle of Issus **16**:277 *illus.*
mosaic **9**:333 *illus.*
Pompeii **15**:424
FAUNA (mythology) *see* BONA DEA
FAUNTROY, WALTER E.
District of Columbia **6**:201
FAUNUS **8**:38
FAUQUIER (county in Virginia)
map (38° 35′N 77° 35′W) **19**:607
FAURÉ, GABRIEL URBAIN **8**:38 *bibliog.*
FAURESMITH CULTURE
prehistoric humans **15**:515
FAUST (opera)
Bolshoi ballet **3**:371 *illus.*
Gounod, Charles **9**:266
FAUST (poem) **8**:38 *bibliog.*
Goethe, Johann Wolfgang von **9**:223–224
FAUST, FREDERICK *see* BRAND, MAX
FAUST, JOHANN **8**:38 *bibliog.*
Doctor Faustus (play) **6**:210
Faust (poem) **8**:38
FAUSTUS *see* *DOCTOR FAUSTUS* (play); *FAUST, JOHANN*
FAUVISM **8**:38–39 *bibliog.*, *illus.*
Braque, Georges **3**:456
Derain, André **6**:121
Dongen, Kees van **6**:238
Dufy, Raoul **6**:294
landscape painting **12**:192
Matisse, Henri **13**:229
painting **15**:22
Rouault, Georges **16**:324
Vlaminck, Maurice de **19**:624
FAVART, CHARLES SIMON
theater, history of the **19**:147
FAVORITA, LA (opera) **14**:401 *illus.*
FAVORITE SON **8**:39
FAVRE, ANTOINE
music box **13**:669
FAVRE, LOUIS
Saint Gotthard Tunnel **17**:19
FAWCETT (Alberta)
map (54° 32′N 114° 5′W) **1**:256
FAWCETT, MILLICENT GARRET
suffrage, women's **18**:326
FAWKES, GUY **8**:39 *bibliog.*
FAXA BAY
map (64° 25′N 23° 0′W) **11**:17
FAXIAN *see* FA-HSIEN (Faxian)
FAYALITE
olivine **14**:380 *table*
FAYE, DOROTHY *see* DUNAWAY, FAYE
FAYETTE (Alabama)
map (33° 42′N 87° 50′W) **1**:234
FAYETTE (county in Alabama)
map (33° 45′N 87° 45′W) **1**:234
FAYETTE (county in Georgia)
map (33° 25′N 84° 30′W) **9**:114
FAYETTE (county in Illinois)
map (38° 58′N 89° 6′W) **11**:42
FAYETTE (county in Indiana)
map (39° 39′N 85° 8′W) **11**:111
FAYETTE (county in Iowa)
map (42° 52′N 91° 48′W) **11**:244
FAYETTE (county in Kentucky)
map (38° 2′N 84° 28′W) **12**:47
FAYETTE (Mississippi)
map (31° 42′N 91° 4′W) **13**:469
FAYETTE (Missouri)
map (39° 9′N 92° 41′W) **13**:476

FAYETTE (Ohio)
map (41° 40′N 84° 20′W) **14**:357
FAYETTE (county in Ohio)
map (39° 32′N 83° 26′W) **14**:357
FAYETTE (county in Pennsylvania)
map (39° 55′N 79° 40′W) **15**:147
FAYETTE (county in Tennessee)
map (35° 15′N 89° 25′W) **19**:104
FAYETTE (county in Texas)
map (29° 50′N 96° 57′W) **19**:129
FAYETTE (county in West Virginia)
map (38° 0′N 81° 5′W) **20**:111
FAYETTEVILLE (Arkansas)
map (36° 4′N 94° 10′W) **2**:166
FAYETTEVILLE (Georgia)
map (33° 27′N 84° 27′W) **9**:114
FAYETTEVILLE (North Carolina) **8**:39
map (35° 3′N 78° 54′W) **14**:242
FAYETTEVILLE (Tennessee)
map (35° 9′N 86° 35′W) **19**:104
FAYETTEVILLE (West Virginia)
map (38° 3′N 81° 6′W) **20**:111
FAYLAKA ISLAND
map (29° 25′N 48° 22′E) **12**:141
FAYRFAX, ROBERT
English music **7**:202–203
FBI *see* FEDERAL BUREAU OF INVESTIGATION
FCC *see* FEDERAL COMMUNICATIONS COMMISSION
FDA *see* FOOD AND DRUG ADMINISTRATION
FDIC *see* FEDERAL DEPOSIT INSURANCE CORPORATION
FEAR **8**:39 *bibliog.*
anxiety **2**:72
phobia **15**:248–249
symptoms **8**:39
vertigo **19**:563
zoophobia **20**:378
FEAR, CAPE
map (33° 50′N 77° 58′W) **14**:242
FEARING, KENNETH **8**:39 *bibliog.*
FEAST OF DEDICATION *see* CHANUKAH
FEAST OF MACCABEES *see* CHANUKAH
FEAST OF WEEKS *see* PENTECOST
FEATHER **3**:283 *illus.*; **8**:39–40 *bibliog., illus.*
bird **3**:282–283
egret **7**:74
goose **9**:247
grouse **9**:378
hummingbird **10**:303
molting **13**:513
ostrich **14**:458
sand grouse **17**:61
FEATHER ART
Oceanic art **14**:338
FEATHER STAR **8**:40
FEATHERBACK (fish) *see* KNIFE FISH
FEATHERBEDDING **8**:40
FEBRUARY
birthstones **3**:296 *illus., table*
calendar **4**:28
FEBVRE, LUCIEN
history **10**:185
FECES
bacterial pollution
Enterobacter **7**:208
constipation **5**:212
diarrhea **6**:153
excretory system **7**:327
hippopotamus **10**:175
toxoplasmosis **19**:256
FECHNER, GUSTAV THEODOR **8**:40
Ebbinghaus, Hermann **7**:35
psychology, history of **15**:596
psychophysics **15**:601–602
FECUNDITY *see* REPRODUCTION
FEDCHENKO, A. P.
Pamirs **15**:53
FEDERAL AVIATION ADMINISTRATION **8**:40
airport **1**:225
aviation **2**:374
FEDERAL BUREAU OF INVESTIGATION **8**:40–41 *bibliog.*
ABSCAM **1**:62
crime statistics **5**:346
fingerprinting **8**:93
Hoover, J. Edgar **10**:229–230
intelligence gathering **11**:205
Washington, D.C. **20**:41 *map*
FEDERAL COMMUNICATIONS COMMISSION **8**:41
cable TV **4**:7
citizens band radio **4**:446
common carrier **5**:138
frequency allocation **8**:326–327
government regulation **9**:271
radio and television broadcasting **16**:56–57
Washington, D.C. **20**:41 *map*
FEDERAL DEPOSIT INSURANCE CORPORATION **8**:41
banking systems **3**:68
Comptroller of the Currency, Office of the **5**:159
Glass, Carter **9**:201
moratorium **13**:574
FEDERAL ENERGY ADMINISTRATION
Energy, U.S. Department of **7**:173
FEDERAL HOME LOAN BANK BOARD **8**:41
mortgage **13**:591–592
FEDERAL HOUSING ADMINISTRATION **8**:41
condominium **5**:173
housing **10**:277
mortgage **13**:592
FEDERAL MEDIATION AND CONCILIATION SERVICE **8**:41
mediation **13**:264
FEDERAL NATIONAL MORTGAGE ASSOCIATION **8**:41
mortgage **13**:592
FEDERAL POWER COMMISSION
Energy, U.S. Department of **7**:173
government regulation **9**:271
FEDERAL REPUBLIC OF GERMANY (West Germany) *see* GERMANY, EAST AND WEST
FEDERAL RESERVE SYSTEM **8**:41–42 *bibliog.*
banking systems **3**:68–69
Burns, Arthur F. **3**:578
central bank **4**:253
check **4**:306
Glass, Carter **9**:201
government regulation **9**:270–271
inflation **11**:171
interest **11**:207
monetary policy **13**:524
money **13**:527
national bank **14**:30
Volcker, Paul **19**:628
Warburg, Paul Moritz **20**:28
FEDERAL SAVINGS AND LOAN INSURANCE CORPORATION *see* FEDERAL HOME LOAN BANK BOARD
FEDERAL SECURITY AGENCY
Health and Human Services, U.S. Department of **10**:86–87
FEDERAL STYLE **8**:42 *bibliog.*
Bulfinch, Charles **3**:553
house (in Western architecture) **10**:270
FEDERAL THEATRE PROJECT **8**:42 *bibliog.*
FEDERAL TRADE COMMISSION **8**:42 *bibliog.*
funeral industry **8**:365
government regulation **9**:270; **9**:272
Sherman Anti-Trust Act **17**:259
Washington, D.C. **20**:41 *map*
FEDERAL WRITERS' PROJECT **8**:42–43 *bibliog.*
FEDERALISM **8**:43 *bibliog.*
Australia, history of **2**:340–341
Federalist party **8**:43–44
framework of the Constitution **5**:214
government **9**:268
Supreme Court of the United States **18**:355
FEDERALIST, THE (essays) **8**:43 *bibliog., illus.*
genesis and framework of the Constitution **5**:213–214
Hamilton, Alexander **10**:28
FEDERALIST PAPERS see FEDERALIST, THE (essays)
FEDERALIST PARTY **8**:43–44 *bibliog.*
Alien and Sedition Acts **1**:293–294
Bill of Rights **3**:252
conservatism **5**:205
Hartford Convention **10**:62
Jefferson, Thomas **11**:393
King, Rufus **12**:81
Madison, James **13**:41–42
Marshall, John **13**:172
political parties **15**:400
Russel, Benjamin **16**:348–349
United States, history of the **19**:443
FEDERALSBURG (Maryland)
map (38° 42′N 75° 47′W) **13**:188
FEDERATED MALAY STATES *see* MALAYSIA
FEDERATED STATES OF MICRONESIA *see* MICRONESIA, FEDERATED STATES OF
FEDERATION *see* FEDERALISM
FÉDÉRATION AÉRONAUTIQUE INTERNATIONALE
aerial sports **1**:121
FEDERATION OF AMERICAN SCIENTISTS **8**:44
FÉDÉRATION INTERNATIONAL DES LUTTES AMATEURS (FILA)
wrestling **20**:287
FÉDÉRATION INTERNATIONALE DE FOOTBALL ASSOCIATIONS (FIFA)
soccer **18**:8; **18**:10
FÉDÉRATION INTERNATIONALE DE L'AUTOMOBILE
automobile racing **2**:360
FÉDÉRATION INTERNATIONALE DE ROLLER-SKATING
roller-skating **16**:272
FÉDÉRATION INTERNATIONALE MOTOCYCLISTE (FIM)
motorcycling **13**:615
FEDERATION OF MALAYSIA *see* MALAYSIA
FEDERATION OF RHODESIA AND NYASALAND
Malawi **13**:82
Zambia **20**:354
Zimbabwe (Rhodesia) **20**:365–366
FEDERATION OF SOUTH ARABIA *see* YEMEN (Aden)
FEDERATIVE REPUBLIC OF BRAZIL *see* BRAZIL
FEDERMANN, NIKOLAUS
Venezuela **19**:544
FEDEROV, EVGRAF STEPANOVICH
crystal **5**:376
FEDIN, KONSTANTIN ALEKSANDROVICH **8**:44 *bibliog.*
FËDOR, TSAR OF RUSSIA *see* FYODOR III, TSAR OF RUSSIA
FEDOROV, EVGRAF STEPANOVICH
crystal **5**:376
mineral **13**:439
FEDOTOV, PAVEL
Russian art and architecture **16**:362
FEE (property law) **8**:44
entail **7**:208
estate **7**:246
FEED, ANIMAL
antibiotics **2**:58
cattle and cattle raising **4**:217
FEEDBACK **8**:44 *bibliog., illus.*
See also BIOFEEDBACK
Armstrong, Edwin **2**:179
automation **2**:357
Black, Harold **3**:303
communication **5**:143
control system
servomechanism **17**:212
cybernetics **5**:400–401
negative feedback **8**:44
Nyquist criterion
Nyquist, Harry **14**:310
oscillator **14**:453
output return for operation **8**:44
process control **15**:560
FEEDBACK INHIBITION
enzyme **7**:214
homeostasis **10**:212
FEEDLOT **4**:215 *illus.*; **8**:44–45
factory farming **8**:6
FEHMARN ISLAND
map (54° 28′N 11° 8′E) **9**:140
FEIFFER, JULES **8**:45
FEIJÓO Y MONTENEGRO, BENITO JERONIMO
Spanish literature **18**:159
FEINBERG, GERALD
tachyon **19**:6
FEINGOLD, BEN F.
hyperactive children **10**:347
FEININGER, LYONEL **8**:45 *bibliog., illus.*
Bauhaus **3**:129–130 *illus.*
comic strip **5**:135
Woman in Mauve **8**:45 *illus.*
FEIRA DE SANTANA (Brazil)
map (12° 15′S 38° 57′W) **3**:460
FEKE, ROBERT **8**:45 *bibliog., illus.*
Isaac Royall and His Family **8**:45 *illus.*
FELD, ELIOT **8**:45–46
FELDBERG MOUNTAIN
map (47° 52′N 7° 59′E) **9**:140
FELDSPAR **8**:46–47 *bibliog., illus.*; **9**:74 *illus.*
alkali feldspar **8**:46–47
alteration, mineral **1**:312
dacite **6**:4
diabase **6**:148
diorite **6**:185
facies, metamorphic rock **13**:332 *table*
felsite **8**:48
gneiss **9**:213
granite **9**:287
granodiorite **9**:287
igneous rock **11**:33–34
latite **12**:234
microcline **8**:46
monzonite **13**:560
moonstone **13**:567
mylonite **13**:690
plagioclase feldspar **8**:46–47 *illus.*
andesite **1**:404
gabbro **9**:3
sandstone **17**:63 *table*
silicate minerals **17**:305
solid solution **18**:54
syenite **18**:401
trachyte **19**:258
triclinic system **19**:296
FELDSPATHOID **8**:47 *bibliog., illus.*
lapis lazuli **12**:205
leucite **8**:47
nepheline **8**:47
scapolite **17**:115
silicate minerals **17**:305
sodalite **18**:32
FELDSTEIN, MARTIN
Council of Economic Advisers **5**:310
FELIDU ATOLL
map (3° 30′N 73° 30′E) **13**:87
FELINE DISTEMPER
distemper **6**:200
FELINE FAMILY *see* CAT; CAT FAMILY
FELINE LEUKEMIA
cat **4**:194
FELINE VIRAL RHINOTRACHEITIS *see* RHINOTRACHEITIS, FELINE VIRAL
FELIX V, POPE
Basel, Council of **3**:108
FELL PONY
pony **15**:428
FELLAHIN **7**:78 *illus.*; **8**:47 *bibliog.*
FELLER, BOB **8**:47–48
FELLIG, ARTHUR *see* WEEGEE
FELLINI, FEDERICO **8**:48 *bibliog., illus.*
film, history of **8**:86
FELLOWS, SIR CHARLES
Xanthus **20**:311
FELLOWSHIPS *see* SCHOLARSHIPS, FELLOWSHIPS, AND LOANS
FELLSMERE (Florida)
map (27° 46′N 80° 36′W) **8**:172
FELONY **8**:48
criminal justice **5**:350
larceny **12**:206
perjury **15**:172
riot **16**:228
robbery **16**:240
sodomy **18**:34
FELS PLANETARIUM
Franklin Institute **8**:285
FELSITE **8**:48
FELT **8**:48
FELTON, REBECCA LATIMER *see* FELTON, WILLIAM HARRELL
FELTON, WILLIAM HARRELL **8**:48
FELUCCA **13**:397 *illus.*
FEMALE *see* WOMEN (biology); WOMEN IN SOCIETY
FEMALE EUNUCH, THE (book)
Greer, Germaine **9**:355
FEMININE MYSTIQUE, THE (book)
Friedan, Betty **8**:331
FEMINISM **8**:48–49 *bibliog.*
See also WOMEN'S RIGHTS MOVEMENTS
women in society **20**:202; **20**:204
FEMORAL ARTERY
circulatory system **4**:440 *illus.*
FEMUNDEN LAKE
map (62° 12′N 11° 52′E) **14**:261
FENCE (barrier)
barbed wire **3**:76–77
FENCING (sport) **8**:49–50 *bibliog., illus.*
pentathlon **15**:155
sword and knife **18**:397–399
target areas **8**:49–50 *illus.*
weapons **8**:49 *illus.*
FÉNELON, FRANÇOIS DE SALIGNAC DE LA MOTHE **8**:50 *bibliog.*
quietism **16**:26
FÉNÉON, FÉLIX
neoimpressionism **14**:83
FENG MENG-LUNG (Feng Menglong)
Chinese literature **4**:390
FENG YÜ-HSIANG (Feng Yuxiang) **8**:50 *bibliog.*
FENG YUXIANG *see* FENG YÜ-HSIANG (Feng Yuxiang)
FENIAN CYCLE (tales) **8**:50
Finn mac Cumhail **8**:98–99
Irish literature **11**:267–268
FENIANS **8**:50 *bibliog.*
Davitt, Michael **6**:53
FENNEL **8**:50

FENNIMORE (Wisconsin)
  map (42° 59′N 90° 39′W) **20**:185
FENNVILLE (Michigan)
  map (42° 36′N 86° 6′W) **13**:377
FENOLLOSA, ERNEST FRANCISCO **8**:50–51 *bibliog.*
FENRIR **8**:51
FENS, THE **8**:51
FENTON (Michigan)
  map (42° 48′N 83° 42′W) **13**:377
FENTON, ROGER **8**:51 *bibliog.*
FENTON v. *REED*
  common law **5**:140
FENTRESS (county in Tennessee)
  map (36° 20′N 84° 55′W) **19**:104
FENUGREEK **8**:51
FEODOR *see* FYODOR
FEOKTISTOV, KONSTANTIN P. **8**:51
FER-DE-LANCE **8**:51 *illus.*
FERAL CHILDREN **8**:51–52 *bibliog.*
FERASSIE, LA *see* LA FERASSIE (France)
FERBER, EDNA **8**:52
FERBER, HERBERT **8**:52 *bibliog.*
FERDINAND (Indiana)
  map (38° 14′N 86° 52′W) **11**:111
FERDINAND, ARCHDUKE OF AUSTRIA *see* FRANZ FERDINAND, AUSTRIAN ARCHDUKE
FERDINAND, KING OF ROMANIA **8**:53
  Marie **13**:151
FERDINAND, SAINT *see* FERDINAND III, SPANISH KING OF CASTILE
FERDINAND I, EMPEROR OF AUSTRIA **8**:52
FERDINAND I, HOLY ROMAN EMPEROR **8**:52–53 *bibliog.*
  Habsburg (dynasty) **10**:6 *illus.*
  John I, King of Hungary (John Zápolya) **11**:427
  Suleiman I, Sultan of the Ottoman Empire (Suleiman the Magnificent) **18**:333
FERDINAND I, KING OF CASTILE
  Coimbra **5**:96
FERDINAND I, KING OF NAPLES **8**:53
FERDINAND I, KING OF PORTUGAL **8**:53
FERDINAND I, KING OF THE TWO SICILIES **8**:54
  Sicily (Italy) **17**:293
FERDINAND I, TSAR OF BULGARIA **8**:52 *bibliog.*
FERDINAND III, SPANISH KING OF CASTILE **8**:53 *bibliog.*
  Maximilian, Elector and Duke of Bavaria **13**:239
  Thirty Years' War **19**:170
  Wallenstein, Albrecht Wenzel von **20**:15
FERDINAND II, KING OF ARAGON (Ferdinand the Catholic) **8**:52 *bibliog., illus.*
  Ferdinand and Isabella **18**:146 *illus.*
  Isabella I, Queen of Castile (Isabella the Catholic) **11**:285–286
  Louis XII, King of France **12**:425
  Philip I, King of Castile (Philip the Handsome) **15**:234
  Spain, history of **18**:145
FERDINAND II, KING OF THE TWO SICILIES **8**:54 *bibliog.*
FERDINAND III, HOLY ROMAN EMPEROR **8**:53 *bibliog.*
FERDINAND III, SPANISH KING OF CASTILE
  Córdoba (Spain) **5**:261
  Seville (Spain) **17**:220–221
FERDINAND V, KING OF CASTILE
  See also FERDINAND II, KING OF ARAGON (Frederick the Catholic)
FERDINAND VI, KING OF SPAIN **8**:53
  Spain, history of **18**:147
FERDINAND VII, KING OF SPAIN **8**:54 *bibliog., illus.*
  Spain, history of **18**:147–148
FERDINAND THE CATHOLIC *see* FERDINAND II, KING OF ARAGON (Ferdinand the Catholic)
FERDOWSI *see* FIRDAWSI
FERENCZI, SANDOR **15**:598 *illus.*
FERGUS (county in Montana)
  map (47° 15′N 109° 15′W) **13**:547
FERGUS FALLS (Minnesota)
  map (46° 17′N 96° 4′W) **13**:453
FERGUSON (Missouri)
  map (38° 46′N 90° 19′W) **13**:476
FERGUSON, JAMES EDWARD **8**:54
FERGUSON, "MA AND PA" *see* FERGUSON, JAMES EDWARD
FERGUSON, MIRIAM A. WALLACE *see* FERGUSON, JAMES EDWARD
FERGUSSON, FRANCIS **8**:54
FERGUSSON, ROBERT **8**:54
FERKÉSSÉDOUGOU (Ivory Coast)
  map (9° 36′N 5° 12′W) **11**:335
FERLINGHETTI, LAWRENCE **8**:54 *bibliog.*
FERMANAGH (Northern Ireland) **8**:55
FERMAT, PIERRE DE **8**:55 *bibliog., illus.*
  light **12**:335
  mathematics, history of **13**:225
FERMAT'S LAST THEOREM
  number theory **14**:294
FERMENTATION **8**:55 *bibliog.*
  anaerobe **1**:387
  beer **3**:162–163
  biochemistry **3**:261
  Buchner, Eduard **3**:534
  fungi **8**:365
  Harden, Sir Arthur **10**:45
  milk
    lactic acid **12**:161
    Lactobacillus **12**:161
  Pasteur, Louis **15**:107
  ruminant **16**:345
  sake **17**:28
  synthetic fuels **18**:410
  vinegar **19**:600
  whiskey **20**:132–133
  wine **20**:177
  yeast **20**:320
FERMI, ENRICO **8**:55–56 *bibliog., illus.*
  atomic bomb **2**:307
  fermium **8**:56
  neutrino **14**:108
  nuclear energy **14**:279
FERMI AWARD
  Oppenheimer, J. Robert **14**:407–408
  Wigner, Eugene Paul **20**:147
FERMI-DIRAC PRINCIPLE
  solid-state physics **18**:55
FERMI NATIONAL ACCELERATOR LABORATORY **8**:56; **14**:286 *illus.*
FERMION **8**:56
  exclusion principle **7**:327
FERMIUM **8**:56
  actinide series **1**:88
  element **6**:130 *table*
  metal, metallic element **13**:328
  Seaborg, Glenn T. **17**:171–172
  transuranium elements **19**:286
FERN **8**:56–58 *bibliog., illus.*
  Carboniferous Period **15**:30 *illus.*
  evolution **8**:57–58
  houseplants **10**:274
  plant **15**:334 *illus.*; **15**:336 *illus.*
  pteridophyte **15**:606
  reproduction **16**:162
    reproductive cycle **8**:56–57
    spore **18**:195
    vegetative reproduction **8**:57
  seed fern **15**:174 *illus.*
  Triassic Period **19**:294 *illus.*
FERN CREEK (Kentucky)
  map (38° 9′N 85° 36′W) **12**:47
FERNÁNDEZ (Argentina)
  map (27° 55′S 63° 54′W) **2**:149
FERNÁNDEZ, GREGORIO **8**:58 *bibliog.*
FERNÁNDEZ DE CÓRDOBA, FRANCISCO
  Granada (city in Nicaragua) **9**:283
FERNÁNDEZ DE CÓRDOBA, GONZALO **8**:58 *bibliog.*
FERNÁNDEZ DE LIZARDI, JOSÉ JOAQUÍN **8**:58
FERNANDEZ DE MORATIN, LEANDRO *see* MORATIN, LEANDRO FERNANDEZ DE
FERNANDINA BEACH (Florida)
  map (30° 40′N 81° 27′W) **8**:172
FERNANDO DE LA MORA (Paraguay)
  map (25° 19′S 57° 36′W) **15**:77
FERNANDO PO *see* BIOKO (Equatorial Guinea)
FERNDALE (Washington)
  map (48° 51′N 122° 36′W) **20**:35
FERNLEY (Nevada)
  map (39° 36′N 119° 15′W) **14**:111
FERNWOOD (Idaho)
  map (47° 7′N 116° 23′W) **11**:26
FERRAR, NICHOLAS **8**:58 *bibliog.*
FERRARA (Italy) **8**:58
  Este (family) **7**:246
  Italian city-state **11**:328 *map*
  map (44° 50′N 11° 35′E) **11**:321
FERRARA-FLORENCE, COUNCIL OF **8**:58 *bibliog.*
FERRARI, BENEDETTO
  opera houses **14**:401
FERRARI, ERMANNO WOLF- *see* WOLF-FERRARI, ERMANNO
FERRARI, GIUSEPPE **8**:58
FERRARI, LODOVICO **8**:58
FERRARIS METERS
  measurement **13**:256
FERRARO, GERALDINE **6**:103 *illus.*; **8**:59
FERRARO, V. C. A.
  magnetosphere **13**:60
FERREL CELL **8**:59
  Hadley cell **10**:8
FERREÑAFE (Peru)
  map (6° 38′S 79° 45′W) **15**:193
FERRER, JOSÉ **8**:59
FERRET **8**:59 *illus.*
FERRIC AMMONIUM SULFATE *see* ALUM
FERRIDAY (Louisiana)
  map (31° 38′N 91° 33′W) **12**:430
FERRIER, KATHLEEN **8**:59 *bibliog.*
FERRIS WHEEL **8**:59
FERRISS, HUGH **8**:59 *bibliog.*
FERRITE **8**:59
  computer memory **5**:161
  magnetism **13**:57
  new ceramics applications **4**:259
  oxygen **14**:478
FERRO, SCIPIONE
  mathematics, history of **13**:224
FERROCENE *see* IRON
FERROMAGNETISM *see* MAGNETISM
FERRON (Utah)
  map (39° 5′N 111° 8′W) **19**:492
FERROTYPE **8**:59
FERRY **8**:59–60
  air-cushion vehicle **1**:204–205
  hydrofoil **10**:337
  Stevens, Robert Livingston **18**:263
FERRY (county in Washington)
  map (48° 20′N 118° 30′W) **20**:35
FERRY, JULES FRANÇOIS CAMILLE **8**:60 *bibliog.*
FERTILE (Minnesota)
  map (47° 32′N 96° 17′W) **13**:453
FERTILE CRESCENT **8**:60 *bibliog.*
  Breasted, James Henry **3**:469–470
  Mesopotamia **13**:315–317 *illus.*
  Neolithic Period **14**:84
FERTILITY, HUMAN **8**:60 *bibliog.*
  artificial insemination **2**:220–221
  birth control **3**:293–295
  genetic engineering **9**:84
  multiple birth **13**:637
  pregnancy and birth **15**:502
  radiation injury **16**:42
  vasectomy **19**:525
FERTILITY RITES **8**:60 *bibliog.*
  head-hunting **10**:85
  Japanese figurine **11**:372 *illus.*
  Lupercalia **12**:465–466
  Maypole dance **13**:248–249
  mumming play **13**:638–639
  prehistoric art **15**:509–510
  snake ceremony, Hopi **11**:131 *illus.*
  Venus of Willendorf **19**:548
FERTILIZATION **8**:60–61 *bibliog., illus.*
  See also REPRODUCTION, PLANT
  artificial insemination **2**:220–221
  basic patterns **8**:60–61
  birth control **3**:293–295
  development **6**:137; **6**:140
  egg **7**:72
  embryo **7**:152–153
  embryology **7**:154
  genetics **9**:86 *illus.*
  heredity **10**:140
  Hertwig, Oscar **10**:148
  hybrid **10**:328 *illus.*
  lysosome **12**:480
  menstruation **13**:301
  pregnancy and birth **15**:502
  reproduction **16**:162–164 *illus.*
  reproductive system, human **16**:164 *illus.*
  reptile **16**:168
  sexual intercourse **17**:230
  zygote **20**:384
FERTILIZER **8**:61–62 *bibliog., table*
  agriculture and the food supply **1**:196
  ammonia **1**:372
  apatite **2**:74
  bacteria **3**:16
  boron **3**:403
  calcium phosphate **4**:22
  Carson, Rachel
    Silent Spring **17**:303–304
  chemical industry **4**:318
  compost **5**:157–158
  consumption **8**:62 *table*
  environmental health **7**:212
  gardening **9**:42–43
  genetic engineering **9**:84
  guano **9**:386
  Lawes, Sir John Bennett **12**:248
  manganese **13**:114
  marl **13**:160
  mining and quarrying **13**:446
  molybdenum **13**:514
  nitrate minerals **14**:201
  nitrogen **14**:202
  nitrogen cycle **14**:203
  petrochemicals **15**:205
  phosphate minerals **15**:256
  phosphorite **15**:256
  phosphorus **15**:256
  production **8**:62 *table*
  saltpeter **17**:39
  seaweed **17**:177
  superphosphate **18**:352–353
FÈS (Morocco) *see* FEZ (Morocco)
FESCUE **8**:62
FESSENDEN (North Dakota)
  map (47° 39′N 99° 38′W) **14**:248
FESSENDEN, REGINALD AUBREY **8**:62 *bibliog.*
FESSENDEN, WILLIAM PITT **8**:62–63 *bibliog.*
FESTA, COSTANZO
  Italian music **11**:317
  madrigal **13**:45
  Renaissance music **16**:156
FESTINGER, LEON
  cognitive dissonance **5**:94
  motivation **13**:610
FESTIVAL OF LIGHTS *see* CHANUKAH
FESTIVAL PLAYS *see* MEDIEVAL DRAMA
FESTIVALS, THEATER *see* THEATER FESTIVALS
FESTSPIELHAUS (Richard Wagner) **13**:666
  opera houses **14**:402
FÉTIS, FRANÇOIS JOSEPH **8**:63
FETISH **8**:63 *bibliog.*
  African art **1**:161–164 *illus.*
  headhunters' skull fetish **13**:49 *illus.*
FETISHISM **8**:63 *bibliog.*
FETTERBUSH **8**:63
FETTERMAN, WILLIAM JUDD
  See also FETTERMAN MASSACRE OF 1866
  Bozeman Trail **3**:434
  Wyoming **20**:304
FETTERMAN MASSACRE OF 1866
  Indian Wars **11**:108–109 *map*
FETTI, DOMENICO
  Claudio Monteverdi **11**:318; **13**:554 *illus.*
FETUS
  abortion **1**:60
  development **6**:141–142 *illus.*
  embryo **7**:152–153 *illus.*
  pregnancy and birth **15**:502–503 *illus.*
FEUCHTMAYER, JOSEPH ANTON **8**:63 *bibliog.*
FEUCHTWANGER, LION **8**:63 *bibliog.*
FEUD **8**:63 *bibliog.*
FEUDALISM **8**:64–65 *bibliog., illus.*
  castle **4**:189–190
  chivalry **4**:399
  common law **5**:139
  decline of **8**:64–65
  Europe, history of **7**:284–286
  France, history of **8**:267
  Great Britain
    Henry I, King of England **10**:124
    Peasants' Revolt **15**:129
    William I, King of England (William the Conqueror) **20**:155
  historical significance **8**:65
  institutions **8**:64
  Ireland, history of **11**:262
  Japan
    Japan, history of **11**:368
    samurai **17**:49
    Shogun **17**:281
    Tokugawa (family) **19**:223
  knight **12**:100
  law, history of **12**:244–246
  manorialism **13**:126–127
  Middle Ages **13**:392
  origins **8**:64
  peasant **15**:129
  Peasants' War **15**:129
  property **15**:570–571
FEUERBACH, ANSELM **8**:65 *bibliog., illus.*
  Iphigenia **8**:65 *illus.*
FEUERBACH, LUDWIG **8**:65–66 *bibliog.*
  alienation **1**:294
  Marx, Karl **13**:182
  socialism **18**:19
FEUILLADE, LOUIS **8**:66
FEUILLANTS **8**:66
FEUILLET, RAOUL AUGER
  Académie Royale de Danse **1**:69
FEURÉ, GEORGES DE
  Art Deco vase **2**:208 *illus.*

FEVER 8:66 *bibliog.*
aspirin 2:262
body temperature 3:358
brucellosis 3:520
Colorado tick fever 5:121
delirium 6:93
dengue fever 6:108
feverfew 8:66
leptospirosis 12:296
parrot fever, psittacosis 15:588
puerperal fever 15:614
Q fever 16:3
rabbit fever, tularemia 19:330
red fever, *Babesia* 3:6
relapsing fever 16:132
rheumatic fever 16:194
Rocky Mountain spotted fever 16:261
scarlet fever 17:115
Streptococcus 18:297
trench fever 19:290
typhoid fever 19:366
yellow fever 16:118; 20:322
FEVERFEW 8:66 *illus.*
FEVERWORT 8:66
FEYDEAU, GEORGES 8:66 *bibliog.*
FEYNMAN, RICHARD PHILLIPS 8:66
Tomonaga, Sin-Itiro 19:232
FEYZABAD (Afghanistan)
map (37° 6′N 70° 34′E) 1:133
FEZ (Morocco) 8:66
map (34° 5′N 4° 57′W) 13:585
Moorish art and architecture 13:571
FEZZAN (region in Libya)
map (26° 0′N 14° 0′E) 12:320
FHA *see* FEDERAL HOUSING ADMINISTRATION; FUTURE HOMEMAKERS OF AMERICA
FIAMBALÁ (Argentina)
map (27° 41′S 67° 38′W) 2:149
FIANARANTSOA (Madagascar)
map (21° 26′S 47° 5′E) 13:38
FIANNA (revolutionary society, l9th century) *see* FENIANS
FIANNA (warrior band, 100–200 AD)
Fenian cycle 8:50
Irish literature 11:268
FIANNA FÁIL (political party) 8:67
de Valera, Eamon 6:64
Ireland 11:261
Ireland, history of 11:265
FIAT (automobile)
automotive industry 2:367
FIBER, TEXTILE 8:67–68 *bibliog., illus., map*
See also TEXTILES
carpet industry 4:165
Chardonnet, Hilaire Bernigaud, Comte de 4:288
fabrics
bark cloth 3:82–83 *illus.*
batik 3:123–124 *illus.*
broadcloth 3:499
brocade 3:500
calico 4:29
canvas 4:118
chiffon 4:347
chintz 4:396
corduroy 5:262
damask 6:19
denim 6:108
flannel 8:153
foulard 8:249
gingham 9:184
jersey 11:398
jute 11:479
khaki 12:65
lace 12:158–160
madras 13:43
muslin 13:683
paisley 15:25
ramie 16:80
satin 17:88
taffeta 19:7
tartan 19:40–41 *illus.*
tweed 19:358
twill 19:360
velvet 19:538
fibers
angora 2:6
cashmere 4:181
cotton 5:305–307
felt 8:48
hemp 10:120
linen 12:354
nylon 14:308–309
ramie 16:80
rayon 16:97–98
silk 17:306–308
synthetic fibers 18:409
wool 20:213–214
folk art 8:198
spinning 18:186
textile industry 19:135–136
thread 19:181
weaving 20:84–85
FIBER OPTICS 8:68–69 *bibliog.*
electromagnetic pulse 7:116
glass 9:201
laser and maser 12:212
multiplexer 13:638
telecommunications 19:76
FIBERGLASS 8:69 *bibliog.*
FIBIGER, JOHANNES 8:69
FIBONACCI, LEONARDO *see* LEONARDO PISANO
FIBONACCI SEQUENCE 8:69 *bibliog.*
golden ratio
golden section 9:233 *illus.*
Leonardo Pisano 12:291
FIBRILLATION
palpitation 15:52
FIBRINOGEN
serum 17:210
FICCIONES (book) 8:69 *bibliog.*
FICHANDLER, ZELDA
repertory theater 16:160
FICHTE, JOHANN GOTTLIEB 8:69–70 *bibliog.*
idealism 11:30
FICHTELBERG MOUNTAIN
map (50° 26′N 12° 57′E) 9:140
FICINO, MARSILIO 8:70 *bibliog.*; 16:148 *illus.*
Renaissance 16:149
FICKE, ARTHUR DAVISON 8:70 *bibliog.*
FICTION
Gothic romance 9:263
mystery, suspense, and detective fiction 13:692–693
narrative and dramatic devices 14:22–23
novel 14:272–276
novella and novelette 14:276
periodical 15:169–170
picaresque novel 15:290
pulp magazines 15:620
romance 16:280
science fiction 17:143–144
short story 17:283–284
supernatural literature 18:352
FIDALGO ISLAND
map (48° 28′N 122° 36′W) 20:35
FIDDLER CRAB 8:70 *bibliog., illus.*
shell 17:252 *illus.*
FIDDLER ON THE ROOF (musical)
score
Bock, Jerry, and Harnick, Sheldon 3:355
FIEDLER, ARTHUR 8:70 *bibliog., illus.*
FIEDLER, LESLIE A. 8:70–71 *bibliog.*
FIEF *see* FEUDALISM
FIELD (family) 8:71 *bibliog.*
Marshall Field Wholesale Store 1:328 *illus.*; 16:212 *illus.*
FIELD (mathematics) 8:71
arithmetic 2:158
FIELD, CYRUS W. 8:71 *bibliog., illus.*
Atlantic cable 2:294
FIELD, DAVID DUDLEY, JR. 8:71 *bibliog.*
legal procedure 12:272
FIELD, EUGENE 8:71 *bibliog.*
FIELD, JOHN 8:72 *bibliog.*
FIELD, MARSHALL *see* FIELD (family)
FIELD, ROBERT
Canadian art and architecture 4:89
FIELD, STEPHEN JOHNSON 8:72 *bibliog.*
Slaughterhouse Cases 17:351
FIELD ARTILLERY *see* ARTILLERY
FIELD EFFECT TRANSISTOR
transistor 19:272 *illus.*
FIELD HOCKEY 8:72 *bibliog., illus.*
FIELD MUSEUM OF NATURAL HISTORY 8:72
Field (family) 8:71
Putnam, Frederic Ward 15:632
FIELD SPANIEL 6:219 *illus.*; 8:72 *bibliog., illus.*
FIELD THEORY (psychology)
Lewin, Kurt 12:305
FIELDING, HENRY 8:73 *bibliog., illus.*
Joseph Andrews 11:451
Pamela 15:53
Tom Jones 19:229
FIELDING, WILLIAM STEVENS 8:73
FIELDS, DOROTHY 8:73
FIELDS, HERBERT
Fields, Dorothy 8:73
FIELDS, LEW
Weber, Joseph, and Fields, Lew 20:87
FIELDS, W. C. 8:73–74 *bibliog., illus.*
FIENNES, WILLIAM, 1ST VISCOUNT SAYE AND SELE *see* SAYE AND SELE, WILLIAM FIENNES, 1ST VISCOUNT
FIER (Albania)
map (40° 43′N 19° 34′E) 1:250
FIERY SEARCHER GROUND BEETLE 3:167 *illus.*
FIESOLE, MINO DA *see* MINO DA FIESOLE
FIFE (musical instrument) 8:74
FIFE (Scotland) 8:74
Saint Andrews 17:16
15TH AMENDMENT 8:74
Reconstruction 16:109
Stewart, William Morris 18:266
suffrage
suffrage, women's 18:326
24th Amendment 19:359
text 5:222
5TH AMENDMENT 8:74 *bibliog.*
double jeopardy 6:246
due process 6:292–293
evidence 7:99
grand jury 9:285
indictment 11:144
jury 11:477
self-incrimination 17:191
evidence 7:317
Griswold v. *Connecticut* 9:368
Twining v. *New Jersey* 19:360
wiretapping 20:183
witness 20:192–193
text 5:221
FIFTH CATARACT
map (18° 23′N 33° 47′E) 18:320
FIFTH DISEASE 8:74 *bibliog.*
FIFTH REPUBLIC *see* FRANCE, HISTORY OF
FIFTY-FOUR FORTY OR FIGHT *see* OREGON QUESTION
54th MASSACHUSETTS COLORED REGIMENT 3:307 *illus.*
Douglass, Frederick 6:249
FIG 8:74–75 *bibliog., illus.*; 8:348 *illus.*
banyan 3:72
bo tree 3:348
caprifig 8:75
fig cultivation 8:75
FIG WASP
fig 8:75
FIGARO, LE (newspaper) 8:75
FIGEAC, JEAN JACQUES CHAMPOLLION- *see* CHAMPOLLION-FIGEAC, JEAN JACQUES
FIGG, JAMES
boxing 3:432
FIGGIS, JOHN N.
state (in political philosophy) 18:232
FIGHTER AIRCRAFT 1:214–217 *illus.*
See also AIRCRAFT, MILITARY; names of specific aircraft types, e.g., MIG; SPITFIRE (aircraft); etc.
aircraft manufacture 2:374
FIGHTIN JOE *see* WHEELER, JOSEPH
FIGHTING *see* FEUD
FIGHTING FISH *see* BETTA
FIGUEIRA DA FOZ (Portugal)
map (40° 9′N 8° 52′W) 15:449
FIGUEIREDO, JOÃO BATISTA DE OLIVEIRA 8:75
FIGUEROA (family) 8:75 *bibliog.*
FIGURE SKATING *see* ICE SKATING; ROLLER SKATING
FIGURED BASS 8:75 *bibliog.*
baroque music 3:91–92
cello 4:237–238
German and Austrian music 9:129
harmony 10:52
FIGUREHEAD 8:75–76 *bibliog.*; 8:197 *illus.*
Rush, William 16:347
Skillin (family) 17:339
FIGURES OF SPEECH 8:76 *bibliog.*
conceit 5:168
metaphor 13:334
simile 17:314
FIGWORT 8:76
FIJI 8:76–78 *bibliog., illus., map*
cities
Suva 18:374
economic activity 8:77
flag 8:77 *illus.*
history 8:77–78
land and people 8:77
map (18° 0′S 175° 0′E) 14:334
money 13:525 *illus.*
FIJI PLATE
plate tectonics 15:351 *map*
FIKRET, TEVFIK *see* TEVFIK FIKRET
FILAMENT (muscle) 13:655 *illus.*
muscle contraction 13:655
FILAMENTOUS GROWTH *see* GROWTH
FILARETE, ANTONIO AVERLINO 8:78 *bibliog.*
FILARIASIS 8:78 *bibliog.*
eye worm 7:351
lymphatic system 12:476
FILBERT 8:78 *illus.*; 8:228 *illus.*; 14:300–301 *illus.*
FILCHNER ICE SHELF
map (79° 0′S 40° 0′W) 2:40
FILE SHELL 17:251 *illus.*
FILEFISH 8:78 *illus.*
FILENE, EDWARD ALBERT 8:78–79
FILER (Idaho)
map (42° 34′N 114° 37′W) 11:26
FILIBUSTER 8:79 *bibliog.*
cloture 5:66
Senate of the United States 17:199
FILIPCHENKO, ANATOLY V. 8:79
FILIPINO AMERICANS *see* ORIENTAL AMERICANS
FILIPPO, EDUARDO DE *see* DE FILIPPO, EDUARDO
FILLINGS (teeth)
dentistry 6:115–116
FILLMORE (California)
map (34° 24′N 118° 55′W) 4:31
FILLMORE (county in Minnesota)
map (43° 38′N 92° 5′W) 13:453
FILLMORE (county in Nebraska)
map (40° 30′N 97° 35′W) 14:70
FILLMORE (Utah)
map (38° 58′N 112° 20′W) 19:492
FILLMORE, MILLARD 8:79–80 *bibliog., illus.*
as vice-president 8:80
early career 8:79–80
FILM, HISTORY OF 8:80–89 *bibliog., illus.*
See also names of specific actors and actresses, e.g., DAVIS, BETTE; HOFFMAN, DUSTIN; etc.
animation 2:28–29
Canada
Jutra, Claude 11:479
McLaren, Norman 13:31–32
National Film Board of Canada 14:32
criticism, film
Gilliatt, Penelope 9:182
Kael, Pauline 12:4–5
Simon, John 17:315
Czechoslovakia
Forman, Milos 8:234
Denmark
Dreyer, Carl Theodor 6:271
documentary 6:210–211
England
Korda, Sir Alexander 12:111
Lean, David 12:259
Losey, Joseph 12:418
Muybridge, Eadweard 13:687–688
Reed, Sir Carol 16:117–118
Richardson, Tony 16:213
Schlesinger, John 17:126
France
Bresson, Robert 3:474
Cahiers du Cinéma (periodical) 4:16
Carné, Marcel 4:155
Chabrol, Claude 4:264
Clair, René 5:35
Cocteau, Jean 5:89
Costa-Gavras, Henri 5:291
Feuillade, Louis 8:66
Gance, Abel 9:34
Godard, Jean Luc 9:219
Lumière, Louis and Auguste 12:458
Malle, Louis 13:91–92
Marey, Étienne Jules 13:148
Méliès, Georges 13:287
Moreau, Jeanne 13:576–577
New Wave, 14:143
Ophuls, Marcel 14:405
Pagnol, Marcel 15:14
Pathé, Charles 15:111
Ray, Man 16:96
Renoir, Jean 16:157–158 *illus.*
Resnais, Alain 16:177
Rohmer, Eric 16:270
Truffaut, François 19:316–317
Vigo, Jean 19:592
Germany
Fassbinder, Rainer Werner 8:33
Fischinger, Oskar 8:111
Herzog, Werner 10:150
Jannings, Emil 11:359
Kracauer, Siegfried 12:126
Lang, Fritz 12:194–195
Murnau, F. W. 13:649
Ophuls, Max 14:405
Pabst, G. W. 15:4
Richter, Hans 16:214

FILM, HISTORY OF (cont.)
Riefenstahl, Leni **16**:218
Straub, Jean Marie **18**:293
Greece
Theodorakis, Mikis **19**:156
iconography **11**:24
India
Ray, Satyajit **16**:96
Italy
Antonioni, Michelangelo **2**:70
Bertolucci, Bernardo **3**:226
De Sica, Vittorio **6**:63
Fellini, Federico **8**:48
neorealism **14**:85–86
Pasolini, Pier Paolo **15**:103
Rossellini, Roberto **16**:319
Visconti, Luchino **19**:616
Wertmuller, Lina **20**:105
Japan
Kurosawa, Akira **12**:139
Mizoguchi, Kenji **13**:486
Ozu, Yasujiro **14**:480
newsreel **14**:173
Poland
Polanski, Roman **15**:392
Wajda, Andrzej **20**:7
professional institutes and awards
Academy Awards **1**:71
American Film Institute **1**:339
British Film Institute **3**:496
Cannes Film Festival **4**:109
Russia
Dovzhenko, Alexander **6**:251
Eisenstein, Sergei Mikhailovich **7**:97
Kozintsev, Grigory **12**:126
Pudovkin, Vsevolod I. **15**:613
Vertov, Dziga **19**:563
Senegal
Sembene, Ousmane **17**:195
Spain
Buñuel, Luis **3**:565
Dalí, Salvador **6**:13
surrealism (film, literature, theater) **18**:366
Sweden
Bergman, Ingmar **3**:210
United States
Aldrich, Robert **1**:269
Allen, Woody **1**:300
Altman, Robert B. **1**:313–314
Berkeley, Busby **3**:213
Brakhage, Stan **3**:451
Brooks, Mel **3**:511
Browning, Tod **3**:519
Capra, Frank **4**:128
censorship **4**:248
Chaplin, Charlie **4**:284–285
Coppola, Francis Ford **5**:254
Cukor, George **5**:383
DeMille, Cecil B. **6**:61–62
Disney, Walt **6**:196–197
Edison, Thomas Alva **7**:58
film noir **8**:90
film serials **8**:91
Flaherty, Robert Joseph **8**:150
Ford, John (film director) **8**:222–223
Frank, Robert **8**:280
Goldwyn, Samuel **9**:237
Griffith, D. W. **9**:363
Hawks, Howard **10**:78
Hays, Will **10**:84
Hecht, Ben **10**:103
Hitchcock, Alfred **10**:186
Hollywood (California) **10**:204
Hollywood Ten, The **10**:204
Hopper, Hedda **10**:233
Hughes, Howard **10**:292
Huston, John **10**:322
Keaton, Buster **12**:35
Kubrick, Stanley **12**:134–135
Lange, Fritz **12**:194–195
Lubitsch, Ernst **12**:447
Lucas, George **12**:448
Lumet, Sidney **12**:458
Mayer, Louis B. **13**:246
music hall, vaudeville, and burlesque **13**:672–673
Nichols, Mike **14**:182
Peckinpah, Sam **15**:130
Penn, Arthur **15**:144
Porter, Edwin S. **15**:444
Preminger, Otto **15**:518
Selznick, David O. **17**:193
Sennett, Mack **17**:204
Speilberg, Stephen **18**:183
Stroheim, Erich von **18**:301
Sturges, Preston **18**:309
Vidor, King **19**:577–578
Walsh, Raoul **20**:19
Warhol, Andy **20**:30
Welles, Orson **20**:99
Wellman, William **20**:100–101
Wilder, Bily **20**:140
Wyler, William **20**:299
Zanuck, Darryl F. **20**:355
Zinnemann, Fred **20**:368–369
Zukor, Adolph **20**:381
FILM, PHOTOGRAPHIC
black-and-white film composition **15**:261 *illus.*
camera **4**:54–55
celluloid **4**:238
cinematography **4**:432
color film composition **15**:265 *illus.*
Eastman, George **7**:34
photography **15**:221–262 *illus.*
silver **17**:312–313
FILM NOIR **8**:89 *bibliog.*
Truffaut, François **19**:316–317
FILM PROCESSING *see* PHOTOGRAPHY—film processing
FILM PRODUCTION **8**:89–91 *bibliog., illus.*
See also CINEMATOGRAPHY
FILM SERIALS **8**:91 *bibliog.*
FILMER, SIR ROBERT
divine right **6**:203
FILMS, SILENT *see* FILM, HISTORY OF
FILOPLUME
feather **8**:39–40 *illus.*
FILTER, ELECTRONIC **8**:91 *bibliog.*
capacitor **4**:120
FILTRATION **8**:91
charcoal **4**:286–287
water supply **20**:53
FIN DE SIÈCLE **8**:91–92 *bibliog.*
FINANCE, BUSINESS
arbitrage **2**:110
bond **3**:376
capital **4**:123
Cooke, Jay **5**:237
credit union **5**:336
Drew, Daniel **6**:271
equity (finance) **7**:226
Fisk, James **8**:128
gold standard **9**:230
Green, Hetty **9**:347
Harriman (family) **10**:56–57
Juilliard, Augustus D. **11**:465
Law, John **12**:247
management science **13**:107
Mellon, Andrew W. **13**:287
Morgan (family) **13**:577
panic, financial **15**:59
Rockefeller(family) **16**:250
Rothschild (family) **16**:322
Sage, Russell **17**:12
stock market **18**:274–275
Wall Street **20**:12–13
FINANCE, GOVERNMENT *see* BUDGET; INCOME, NATIONAL
FINANCE, STATE AND LOCAL **8**:92 *bibliog.*
bond **3**:376
municipal government **13**:642
property tax **15**:571
revenue sharing **16**:185
sales tax **17**:32
FINANCE COMPANY **8**:92
credit union **5**:336
installment plan **11**:194
FINANCIAL AID *see* EDUCATION; LOANS
FINANCIAL STATEMENT
accounting **1**:77–78 *illus.*
audit **2**:318
bookkeeping **3**:391–392 *illus.*
FINBARR, SAINT
Cork (city) **5**:263–264
FINCASTLE (Virginia)
map (37° 30′N 79° 53′W) **19**:607
FINCH **8**:92–93 *bibliog., illus.*
bunting **3**:564
cardinal **4**:143–144
cordon bleu (bird) **5**:261
crossbill **5**:362
Darwin's finches **6**:42–43
dickcissel **6**:156
goldfinch **9**:233–234
grass finch **9**:298
grosbeak **9**:370
Hawaiian honeycreeper **10**:76
junco **11**:467
longspur **12**:409
parrot finch **15**:98
plush-capped tanager **15**:372
seedeater **17**:187
siskin **17**:328
songbirds **18**:64–65
waxbill **20**:72–73
weaver finch **20**:83
FINCK, HEINRICH
German and Austrian music **9**:129
FINDLAY (Illinois)
map (39° 31′N 88° 45′W) **11**:42
FINDLAY (Ohio)
map (41° 2′N 83° 39′W) **14**:357
FINE GAEL (political party) **8**:93
Ireland **11**:261
Ireland, history of **11**:265
FINES HERBES
chervil **4**:333
parsley **15**:99
tarragon **19**:39
FINFOOT **8**:93 *illus.*
FINGAL (North Dakota)
map (46° 46′N 97° 47′W) **14**:248
FINGER
hoof, nail, and claw **10**:225
FINGER LAKES **8**:93; **14**:150 *illus.*
FINGER SPELLING **6**:66 *illus.*
FINGERPRINTING **8**:93 *bibliog., illus.*
photography **15**:266
FINI, LEONOR **8**:94 *bibliog.*
FINIGUERRA, MASO **8**:94 *bibliog.*
FINISTERRE, CAPE **8**:94
map (42° 53′N 9° 16′W) **18**:140
FINK, MIKE **8**:94 *bibliog.*
FINKE RIVER
map (27° 0′S 136° 10′E) **2**:328
FINLAND **8**:94–98 *bibliog., illus., map, table*
art **8**:96–97
See also the subheading Finland under ARCHITECTURE; MODERN ARCHITECTURE
Scandinavian art and architecture **17**:111–114
cities
Helsinki **10**:116–117 *illus.*
Porvoo **15**:457
Tampere **19**:20
Turku **19**:349
Vaasa **19**:501
climate **8**:94; **8**:96 *table*
economic activity **8**:97–98 *illus.*
education **8**:96
European universities **7**:307 *table*
Finnish spitz (dog) **8**:99
flag **8**:94 *illus.*; **8**:140 *illus.*
forestry **8**:97 *illus.*
government **8**:98
health **8**:96
history **8**:98
Karelia (USSR) **12**:27
Kekkonen, Urho K. **12**:37
Mannerheim, Carl Gustaf Emil **13**:124
Russo-Finnish War **16**:373
Scandinavia, history of **17**:107–111 *maps*
World War II **20**:251
land and resources **8**:94–96 *illus., map*
language
Ural-Altaic languages **19**:475
literature *see* FINNISH LITERATURE
map (64° 0′N 26° 0′E) **7**:268
mineral resources **8**:95; **8**:97 *illus.*
music
Sibelius, Jean **17**:291
people **8**:95–98 *illus.*
rivers, lakes, and waterways **8**:94–96 *illus.*
trade **8**:97–98
vegetation and animal life **8**:95
FINLAND, GULF OF **8**:98
map (60° 0′N 27° 0′E) **7**:268
FINLEY (North Dakota)
map (47° 31′N 97° 50′W) **14**:248
FINLEY, ROBERT **8**:98
FINMOORE (British Columbia)
map (53° 59′N 123° 37′W) **3**:491
FINN MAC CUMHAIL **8**:98–99 *bibliog.*
FINN RIVER
map (54° 50′N 7° 29′W) **11**:258
FINNAN HADDIE *see* HADDOCK
FINNBOGADÓTTIR, VIGDÍS
Iceland **11**:18
FINNEGANS WAKE **(book)** **8**:99 *bibliog.*
Joyce, James **11**:456–457
FINNEY (county in Kansas)
map (38° 5′N 100° 45′W) **12**:18
FINNEY, ALBERT **8**:99
FINNEY, CHARLES G. **8**:99 *bibliog.*
Great Awakening **9**:308
FINNIGAN (Alberta)
map (51° 7′N 112° 5′W) **1**:256
FINNISH LITERATURE **8**:99 *bibliog.*
authors
Canth, Minna **4**:117
Haavikko, Paavo **10**:3
Runeberg, Johan Ludvig **16**:345–346
Sillanpää, Frans Eemil **17**:309
Södergran, Edith **18**:32
Waltari, Mika **20**:19
Finland **8**:96
Kalevala **12**:7–8
FINNISH-RUSSIAN WAR *see* RUSSO-FINNISH WAR
FINNISH SPITZ **8**:99
FINSCHHAFEN (Papua New Guinea)
map (6° 35′S 147° 50′E) **15**:72
FIORD *see* FJORD
FIORDLAND NATIONAL PARK (New Zealand) **14**:157 *illus.*
FIORELLI, GIUSEPPE **8**:99
FIORENTINO, ROSSO *see* ROSSO FIORENTINO
FIR **8**:99–100 *illus.*
balsam fir **3**:54
conifer **5**:189–191
lumber **12**:457 *illus.*
FIRBANK, RONALD **8**:100 *bibliog.*
FIRDAWSI **8**:100 *bibliog.*
Shah Namah **17**:235
FIRE **8**:100–101 *illus.*
See also FLAME
cave dwellers **4**:224
chaparral **4**:284
classes of fire **8**:102
fire extinguisher **8**:102
flash point, hazards **8**:154
grain elevator **9**:282
grasslands, environment **9**:299
Greek fire, weapon **9**:342
Homo erectus **10**:216
ignition, woodchips **8**:100 *illus.*
match **13**:218
napalm **14**:14
use, history **8**:100–101
FIRE ALARM *see* ALARM SYSTEMS
FIRE ANT *see* ANT
FIRE-EATERS
Yancey, William Lowndes **20**:317
FIRE ENGINE **8**:101–102 *bibliog., illus.*
fire fighting equipment **8**:101–102
fire prevention and control **8**:101–102; **8**:103
history and development **8**:101–102
FIRE EXTINGUISHER **8**:102 *bibliog.*
bromine **3**:502
carbon tetrachloride **4**:137
extinguishing agents **8**:102
suitability, Class A-D fires **8**:102
FIRE FIGHTING *see* FIRE PREVENTION AND CONTROL
FIRE INSURANCE **8**:102
FIRE ISLAND
map (40° 40′N 73° 11′W) **5**:193
FIRE NEXT TIME, THE **(book)** **8**:103 *bibliog.*
FIRE PREVENTION AND CONTROL **8**:103–105 *bibliog., illus.*
alarm systems **1**:240
building construction **3**:549
chimney **4**:358
fire departments **8**:103
fire engine **8**:101–102
fire extinguisher **8**:102
fire hose
Heyden, Jan van der **10**:155
flame retardants **8**:150–151
forest fires **8**:104
helicopter **10**:112
hotel **10**:262
safety codes and standards **8**:104
smoke detector **17**:373
spontaneous combustion **18**:194
FIRE THORN **8**:105
FIRE TUBE BOILER
boiler **3**:362–363
FIREARMS **8**:105–106 *bibliog., illus.*
ammunition **1**:373–374
automatic weapons **8**:106
ballistics **3**:49–50; **3**:51
Browning, John Moses **3**:518
cannon **4**:111–112 *illus.*
Carl-Gustav M2 **16**:108 *illus.*
Caslon, William **4**:182
Colt, Samuel **5**:123–124
derringer **6**:123 *illus.*
dumdum bullet **6**:298
explosives **7**:339
firing mechanism **8**:105
Garand, John Cantius **9**:38
Gatling, Richard Jordan **9**:58
gun control **9**:405
guncotton **9**:405
gunpowder **9**:405–406
machine gun **13**:21–23
manufacturing **13**:132
mass production **13**:204
Maxim (family) **13**:239
musket **13**:682–683
night sights **14**:193
pistol **15**:317–318
recoilless rifle **16**:108
revolver **16**:189–190
rifle **16**:219–221
rifling **8**:106
right to bear arms **16**:222
shooting **17**:282

shotgun **17**:285–286
strategy and tactics, military **18**:291
technology, history of **19**:65
weapons **20**:75
FIREBALL *see* METEOR AND METEORITE
FIREBRAT *see* BRISTLETAIL
FIREBRICK **8**:106
FIREFLY **3**:167 *illus.*; **8**:106 *illus.*
bioluminescence **3**:272 *illus.*
instinct **11**:195 *illus.*
FIRENZE (Italy) *see* FLORENCE (Italy)
FIREPLACE **8**:106 *bibliog.*
firebrick **8**:106
FIREPROOFING *see* FIRE PREVENTION AND CONTROL; FLAME RETARDANTS
FIRES OF LONDON (instrumental group)
Davies, Peter Maxwell **6**:50
FIRESTONE, HARVEY **19**:453 *illus.*
FIRESTONE, HARVEY S. **8**:106 *bibliog.*
Liberia **12**:314 *illus.*
FIRESTONE, SHULAMITH **8**:106
Dialectic of Sex **6**:150
FIREWEED **8**:107
tundra **19**:332 *illus.*
FIREWORKS **8**:107 *bibliog.*, *illus.*
Independence Day **11**:78
military **8**:107
saltpeter **17**:39
FIRN **8**:108
FIRST AID **8**:108–109 *bibliog.*, *illus.*
bleeding **8**:108 *illus.*
burns **8**:109 *illus.*
cardiopulmonary resuscitation **4**:144; **8**:108
Heimlich maneuver **8**:109 *illus.*
mouth-to-mouth artifical respiration **8**:108 *illus.*
shock, physiologic **17**:279
1ST AMENDMENT **8**:109 *bibliog.*
Bill of Rights **3**:253
censorship **4**:246
Engel v. *Vitale* **7**:176
14th Amendment **8**:254
freedom of religion **8**:297
freedom of speech **8**:298
Gitlow v. *New York* **9**:191
freedom of the press **8**:296
lobbyist **12**:384
Miller v. *California* **13**:428–429
New York Times Company v. *Sullivan* **14**:156
New York Times Company v. *United States* **14**:156
right of association
Griswold v. *Connecticut* **9**:368
Roth v. *United States* **16**:321–322
Schenck v. *United States* **17**:119
sedition **17**:186
text **5**:220
Zenger, John Peter **20**:359
FIRST CATARACT RAPIDS
map (24° 1′N 21° 52′E) **7**:76
FIRST CONNECTICUT LAKE
map (45° 5′N 71° 15′W) **14**:123
FIRST INTERNATIONAL *see* INTERNATIONAL, SOCIALIST
FIRST REPUBLIC *see* FRANCE, HISTORY OF; FRENCH REVOLUTION
FIRTH (Nebraska)
map (40° 33′N 96° 37′W) **14**:70
FIRTH, SIR RAYMOND **8**:109
social anthropology **18**:11
FIRTH OF FORTH
Forth, River **8**:238
map (56° 5′N 2° 55′W) **19**:403
FIRTH OF LORNE
map (56° 20′N 5° 40′W) **19**:403
FISCAL POLICY **8**:110 *bibliog.*
economics **7**:49
economy, national **7**:50
Keynes, John Maynard **12**:63–64
recession **16**:107
stagflation **18**:211
taxation **19**:47
FISCHART, JOHANN BAPTIST **8**:110
FISCHBACHER ALPS (mountains)
map (47° 28′N 15° 30′E) **2**:348
FISCHER, BOBBY **8**:110 *bibliog.*
chess **4**:336 *illus.*
Karpov, Anatoly **12**:29
FISCHER, EMIL HERMANN **8**:110 *bibliog.*, *illus.*
enzyme **7**:213
stereochemistry **18**:258–259
Walden, Paul **20**:9
FISCHER, ERNST
Wilkinson, Geoffrey **20**:153
FISCHER, ERNST OTTO **8**:110
FISCHER, HANS **8**:110
FISCHER, JOHANN MICHAEL **8**:110–111 *bibliog.*
Abbey Church of Ottobeuren **16**:264 *illus.*
FISCHER-DIESKAU, DIETRICH **8**:111 *bibliog.*
FISCHER VON ERLACH, JOHANN BERNHARD **8**:111 *bibliog.*
Austrian art and architecture **2**:352–353
Schönbrunn Palace **17**:133
FISCHINGER, OSKAR **8**:111
animation **2**:29
FISH **8**:111–121 *bibliog.*, *illus.*
See also FISHING INDUSTRY; specific types of fish, e.g., TROPICAL FISH; names of specific fish, e.g., CRAPPIE; ELECTRIC EEL; PERCH; TROUT; etc.; names of specific families of fish, e.g., GAR; STURGEON; etc.
aging **1**:186
anatomy and physiology **8**:112–114 *illus.*
body fluids **8**:115
body temperature **8**:114–115
circulatory system **4**:439 *illus.*
egg **7**:72
embryo **7**:324 *illus.*
eye, flatfish **8**:154
gas bladder **8**:118 *illus.*
gill **9**:180–181
intestine **11**:230
kidneys **12**:74
lateral line system **8**:118–119 *illus.*
lungs **12**:463–465
pigment, skin **15**:301
respiratory system **16**:179
scale **8**:113–114 *illus.*
senses **8**:119 *illus.*
skeletal system **17**:334 *illus.*
skin **17**:340 *illus.*
swim bladder **18**:390
teeth **19**:71
animal migration **2**:27; **2**:28
biological locomotion **3**:266–267 *illus.*
bioluminescence **3**:272
classification, biological **4**:285–286; **8**:121
coloration, biological **3**:330; **5**:122
cooking **5**:238–239
deep-sea life **6**:78 *illus.*; **6**:79 *illus.*
diseases
water mold **20**:49
distribution **8**:112
ecology, aquarium **2**:93
evolution **7**:321–323; **8**:120–121
fish ladders, dam **6**:17
fish meal **8**:122
food, algal mat **1**:283
fossil record
Agassiz, Louis Rodolphe **1**:182
Devonian Period **6**:145–146 *illus.*
fossil **8**:243 *illus.*
Paleozoic Era **15**:43
Triassic Period **19**:293 *illus.*
ichthyology **11**:19
leather and hides **12**:262–263
life cycle **8**:120 *illus.*
flatfish **8**:155
liver oils
vitamin A, vitamins and minerals **19**:619
maximum life span for some **12**:330 *table*
molting **13**:513
Osteichthyes **14**:456–457
parental care **8**:120 *illus.*
pollutants, chemical **15**:410
swimming and diving **8**:115 *illus.*; **8**:118
teleost **19**:78
FISH (family) **8**:111 *bibliog.*
FISH, HAMILTON
Fish (family) **8**:111
FISH, ROBERT L. **8**:121
FISH FARMING **8**:121–122 *bibliog.*, *illus.*
bivalve **3**:301
carp **4**:162–163
fishing industry **8**:127
mullet **13**:637
plankton **15**:332
FISH FLOUR *see* FISH MEAL
FISH HAWK *see* OSPREY
FISH MEAL **8**:122
FISH RIVER
map (28° 7′S 17° 45′E) **14**:11
FISH-SKIN DISEASE
xeroderma **20**:312
FISH AND WILDLIFE ACT (United States)
wildlife refuge **20**:150
FISH AND WILDLIFE SERVICE, U.S.
Interior, United States Department of the **11**:210
wildlife refuge **20**:150
FISHER (animal)
marten **13**:175
FISHER (Arkansas)
map (35° 30′N 90° 58′W) **2**:166
FISHER (Illinois)
map (40° 19′N 88° 21′W) **11**:42
FISHER (Louisiana)
map (31° 30′N 93° 28′W) **12**:430
FISHER (county in Texas)
map (32° 43′N 100° 22′W) **19**:129
FISHER, ANDREW **8**:122
FISHER, DOROTHY CANFIELD **8**:122 *bibliog.*
FISHER, GEOFFREY FRANCIS **8**:122
FISHER, IRVING **8**:122
monetary theory **13**:525
FISHER, SAINT JOHN **8**:122 *bibliog.*
FISHER, M. F. K. **8**:122
FISHER, SIR RONALD AYLMER **8**:122–123 *bibliog.*
mimicry **13**:436
FISHER, RUDOLPH **8**:123 *bibliog.*
FISHER, VARDIS **8**:123 *bibliog.*
FISHER OF KILVERSTONE, JOHN ARBUTHNOT FISHER, 1st BARON **8**:123 *bibliog.*
World War I **20**:220
FISHERIES *see* FISHING INDUSTRY
FISHERS ISLAND
map (41° 16′N 72° 2′W) **14**:149
FISHER'S ISLAND SOUND
map (41° 18′N 72° 0′W) **5**:193
FISHFLY *see* DOBSONFLY
FISHING (sport) **8**:123–124 *bibliog.*, *illus.*
See also FISHING INDUSTRY
Indians, American **11**:118 *illus.*; **11**:119
North America c.1500 **11**:125 *map*
lures **8**:123–124 *illus.*
methods **8**:123–124 *illus.*
perch **15**:161
types of fish **8**:123
FISHING CREEK (Maryland)
map (38° 20′N 76° 14′W) **13**:188
FISHING FROG *see* GOOSEFISH
FISHING INDUSTRY **8**:124–128 *bibliog.*, *illus.*, *map*, *tables*
See also WHALING
Asia
Japan **11**:366 *illus.*
causes of diminishing catches **8**:128
coracle **5**:257
Europe **7**:279
Basques **3**:116
Dogger Bank **6**:223
Portugal **15**:451 *illus.*
fish **8**:111–112
carp **4**:162–163
char **4**:285
eel **7**:71
flounder **8**:178
greenling **9**:353
grouper **9**:377 *illus.*
haddock **10**:7
hake **10**:17
halibut **10**:20
herring **10**:146–147
John Dory (fish) **11**:425
mullet **13**:637
perch **15**:161
plaice **15**:325
porgy **15**:441
salmon **17**:34–35
sandfish **17**:62
sardine **17**:76
saury **17**:97
scorpion fish **17**:148
sea bass **17**:168
sea snake **17**:170
shad **17**:234
shark **17**:244
shellfish **17**:254–255
shrimp **17**:287
smelt **17**:365
snapper **17**:384
sole **18**:53
spadefish **18**:138
sprat **18**:199
squirrelfish **18**:205
trout **19**:311–312
tuna **19**:331–332
turbot **19**:341
weakfish **20**:74
whitefish **20**:138
world catches of fish by species group **8**:125 *map*, *table*
wrasse **20**:285
fish catches of six major fishing countries **8**:125 *table*
fish farming **8**:121–122
fisheries management **8**:127–128
food poisoning and infection **8**:211
future possibilities **8**:128
history **8**:125–126
hunter-gatherers **10**:313
Indians, American **11**:126–127
South America c.1500 **11**:133 *map*
Maryland **13**:191
North America
California **4**:35
Canada **3**:492 *illus.*; **4**:78 *illus.*
Caribbean Sea **4**:149
Grand Banks **9**:284 *map*
Louisiana **12**:431 *illus.*
Maryland **13**:189 *illus.*
Newfoundland (Canada) **14**:167
ocean and sea **14**:331
pollutants, chemical **15**:410
principal fisheries **8**:125–127 *map*
Sea, Law of the **17**:167
snail **17**:375
submarine canyon **18**:316
technologies **8**:127 *illus.*
territorial waters **19**:121
turtle **19**:354
world's largest fishing fleets **8**:125 *table*
FISK, JAMES **8**:128 *bibliog.*, *illus.*
FISK UNIVERSITY **8**:129
Johnson, Charles Spurgeon **11**:431
FISKDALE (Massachusetts)
map (42° 7′N 72° 7′W) **13**:206
FISKE, JOHN **8**:129 *bibliog.*
FISKE, MINNIE MADDERN **8**:129 *bibliog.*
FISSION, NUCLEAR **8**:129 *bibliog.*, *illus.*
atomic bomb **2**:307
binding energy **3**:258
breeder reactor **3**:471–472
californium **4**:39
chain reaction, nuclear **4**:269
Fermi, Enrico **8**:55–56
fuel **8**:352; **14**:278
Hahn, Otto **10**:11
Meitner, Lise **13**:283
modes of fission **8**:129
nuclear energy **14**:278–284 *illus.*
promethium **15**:567
radiometric age-dating **16**:66
transmutation of elements, discovery **19**:276–277
uranium **19**:477
FISSION OF CELLS *see* GROWTH; MEIOSIS; MITOSIS
FISSURE (biology)
skin diseases **17**:341
FITCH *see* POLECAT
FITCH, CLYDE **8**:129
FITCH, JOHN **8**:129 *bibliog.*
steamboat **18**:242; **19**:67 *illus.*
FITCHBURG (Massachusetts)
map (42° 35′N 71° 48′W) **13**:206
FITNESS, PHYSICAL *see* EXERCISE; RUNNING AND JOGGING
FITO, MOUNT
map (13° 55′S 171° 44′W) **20**:117
FITZ, HENRY **8**:130
FITZGERALD (Georgia)
map (31° 43′N 83° 15′W) **9**:114
FITZGERALD, EDWARD **8**:130 *bibliog.*
Rubaiyat of Omar Khayyam **16**:332
FITZGERALD, ELLA **8**:130
FITZGERALD, F. SCOTT **1**:346 *illus.*; **8**:130–131 *bibliog.*, *illus.*
Great Gatsby, The **9**:319
Tender Is the Night **19**:101
FITZGERALD, GARRET **8**:131
Ireland **11**:261
Ireland, history of **11**:265
FITZGERALD, GEORGE FRANCIS **8**:131
relativity **16**:134
FITZGERALD, LIONEL LEMOINE **8**:131 *bibliog.*
FITZGERALD, ROBERT **8**:131
FITZGERALD, ROBERT DAVID **8**:131 *bibliog.*
FITZGERALD, ZELDA SAYRE **8**:131 *bibliog.*
FITZGERALD-LORENTZ CONTRACTION (physics) **8**:131 *bibliog.*
Einstein, Albert **7**:93
Fitzgerald, George Francis **8**:131
Lorentz, Hendrik Antoon **12**:413
relativity **16**:134
FITZMAURICE, GEORGE **8**:131 *bibliog.*
FITZMAURICE, HENRY CHARLES KEITH PETTY-, 5TH MARQUESS OF LANSDOWNE *see* LANSDOWNE, HENRY CHARLES KEITH PETTY-FITZMAURICE, 5TH MARQUESS OF

FITZMAURICE, WILLIAM PETTY, 2D EARL OF SHELBURNE *see* SHELBURNE, WILLIAM PETTY FITZMAURICE, 2D EARL OF
FITZPATRICK, SIR CHARLES **8**:131
FITZPATRICK, DANIEL
- Battle of Stalingrad cartoon **20**:264 *illus.*

FITZPATRICK, THOMAS **8**:131–132 *bibliog.*
FITZROY, MOUNT
- map (49° 17′S 73° 5′W) **2**:149

FITZROY CROSSING (Australia)
- map (18° 11′S 125° 35′E) **2**:328

FITZROY RIVER
- map (17° 31′S 123° 35′E) **2**:328

FITZSIMMONS, FRANK EDWARD **8**:132
- Teamsters, Chauffeurs, Warehousemen, and Helpers of America, International Brotherhood of **19**:58

FITZSIMONS, THOMAS **8**:132
FITZWILLIAM COLLEGE (Cambridge University) **4**:52–53
FITZWILLIAM MUSEUM **8**:132
FIUME (Yugoslavia) *see* RIJEKA (Yugoslavia)
FIVE, THE (musical group) **8**:132 *bibliog.*
- Balakirev, Mily Alekseyevich **3**:30
- Borodin, Aleksandr **3**:403
- Cui, César **5**:383
- Mussorgsky, Modest **13**:685
- Rimsky-Korsakov, Nikolai Andreyevich **16**:224–225
- Russian music **16**:367
- Tchaikovsky, Peter Ilich **19**:52

FIVE CIVILIZED TRIBES **8**:132 *bibliog.*
- Cherokee **4**:332
- Chickasaw **4**:345
- Choctaw **4**:403
- Creek **5**:337
- Indian Territory **11**:106
- Oklahoma **14**:371
- Seminole **17**:197
- Wichita **20**:144

FIVE MILE ACT OF 1665
- Clarendon Code **5**:37

FIVE NATIONS *see* IROQUOIS LEAGUE
FIVE POWER NAVAL ARMAMENTS TREATY (1922)
- Washington Conference **20**:44

FIVE-SPICE POWDER **8**:132
FIVE-YEAR PLANS
- China **4**:367
- economic planning **7**:47

"FIVES" (game)
- handball **10**:35

FIXATION **8**:132 *bibliog.*
FIXER, THE (book)
- Malamud, Bernard **13**:79

FIZEAU, ARMAND HIPPOLYTE LOUIS **8**:133
- speed of light **12**:335 *illus.*

FJORD **8**:133 *bibliog.*; **14**:264 *illus.*
- gulf and bay **9**:403

FLACIUS ILLYRICUS, MATTHIAS **8**:133
FLACK, AUDREY **8**:133 *bibliog.*
FLAG **8**:133–149 *bibliog., illus.*
- *See also* the fact box in each country and state article, e.g., NETHERLANDS; NEW YORK (state); etc.
- International Flag Code **17**:300–301 *illus.*
- Ross, Betsy **16**:318
- semaphore **17**:194–195
- Union Jack **19**:387

FLAG (botany) *see* IRIS (botany)
FLAG OF CONVENIENCE **8**:149
FLAGELLA **8**:149
- bacteria **3**:15 *illus.*
- biological locomotion **3**:265
- cell movement **8**:149
- dinoflagellate **6**:179
- *Euglena* **7**:264
- stentor **18**:253

FLAGELLANTS **8**:149 *bibliog.*
FLAGELLATA
- *See also* MASTIGOPHORA
- Protozoa **15**:579

FLAGEOLET **8**:149
FLAGET, BENEDICT JOSEPH **8**:149 *bibliog.*
FLAGG, ERNEST **8**:149–150
FLAGG, JAMES MONTGOMERY
- *I Want You* (poster) **15**:462 *illus.*
- Uncle Sam **19**:382
- World War I propaganda poster **15**:569 *illus.*

FLAGG, JOSIAH
- American music **1**:350

FLAGLER (Colorado)
- map (39° 18′N 103° 4′W) **5**:116

FLAGLER (county in Florida)
- map (29° 25′N 81° 20′W) **8**:172

FLAGLER, HENRY M.
- Florida **8**:176
- Miami (Florida) **13**:370
- Palm Beach **15**:49

FLAGLER BEACH (Florida)
- map (29° 29′N 81° 7′W) **8**:172

FLAGSTAD, KIRSTEN **8**:150 *bibliog.*
FLAGSTAFF (Arizona) **8**:150
- map (35° 12′N 111° 39′W) **2**:160
- remote sensing **16**:147 *illus., map*

FLAGSTAFF LAKE
- map (45° 10′N 70° 15′W) **13**:70

FLAGSTONE **16**:306 *illus.*
FLAHERTY, ROBERT JOSEPH **8**:150 *bibliog.*
- documentary **6**:211

FLAKE TOOLS
- Paleolithic Period **15**:38–40

FLAMBEAU FLOWAGE RESERVOIR
- map (46° 5′N 90° 11′W) **20**:185

FLAMBOYANT GOTHIC STYLE **8**:150 *bibliog.*
- Gothic art and architecture **9**:261

FLAME **8**:150 *bibliog.*
- *See also* FIRE
- Greek fire **9**:342
- napalm **14**:14
- premixed and diffusive types **8**:150

FLAME RETARDANTS **8**:150–151
- boron **3**:403
- bromine **3**:502
- fire prevention and control **8**:104
- pollutants, chemical **15**:410

FLAME TEST
- qualitative chemical analysis **16**:6 *illus.*

FLAME TREE **8**:151
FLAMENCO **6**:27 *illus.*; **8**:151 *bibliog.*
FLAMING GORGE RESERVOIR
- map (41° 15′N 109° 30′W) **20**:301

FLAMINGO **8**:151 *bibliog., illus.*; **12**:55 *illus.*
- American flamingo **18**:377 *illus.*
- beak **3**:289 *illus.*

FLAMININUS, TITUS QUINCTIUS **8**:151 *bibliog.*
- Rome, ancient **16**:300

FLAMMARION, CAMILLE **8**:151
FLAMSTEED, JOHN **8**:151–152 *bibliog., illus.*
- astronomy, history of **2**:278

FLANAGAN (Illinois)
- map (40° 53′N 88° 52′W) **11**:42

FLANAGAN, EDWARD J. **8**:152 *bibliog.*
- Boys Town **3**:434

FLANAGAN, HALLIE
- Federal Theatre Project **8**:42

FLANDERS (historic region of the Low Countries) **8**:152 *bibliog.*
- boundaries during 1154–1180 **8**:267 *map*
- boundaries under Louis XIV **8**:269 *map*
- Bruges **3**:522–523
- Flemish art and architecture **8**:159–162
- government **3**:181
- history
  - Artevelde (family) **2**:214
  - Dutch Revolt **6**:315
  - Low Countries, history of the **12**:438–443 *map*
  - Philip II, King of France (Philip Augustus) **15**:232
- language **3**:179
- literature *see* DUTCH AND FLEMISH LITERATURE
- music
  - Isaac, Heinrich **11**:285
- people **3**:178–179

FLANDERS (province in France) **8**:152 *map*
FLANDREAU (South Dakota)
- map (44° 3′N 96° 36′W) **18**:103

FLANNAGAN, JOHN B. **8**:152–153 *bibliog.*
FLANNEL **8**:153
FLANNELBUSH **8**:153
FLAP-FOOTED LIZARD **8**:153
FLARE, SOLAR *see* SOLAR FLARE
FLARE STAR **8**:153
- dwarf star **8**:153
- Proxima Centauri **15**:584
- star **18**:224
- variable star **19**:522
- X-ray astronomy **20**:306

FLASH FLOOD **8**:153 *bibliog.*
- desert **6**:127–128; **6**:128 *illus.*
- erosion and sedimentation **7**:232
- semiarid climate **17**:196
- thunderstorm **19**:185

FLASH PHOTOGRAPHY **8**:153 *bibliog., illus.*
- capacitor **4**:120
- Edgerton, Harold Eugene **7**:56–57
- photography **15**:263; **15**:265
- types of flash **8**:153

FLASH POINT **8**:154
- fire **8**:100–101

FLASH SPECTRUM **8**:154
FLASHBULB
- flash photography **8**:153 *illus.*

FLASHER (North Dakota)
- map (46° 27′N 101° 14′W) **14**:248

FLAT (Alaska)
- map (62° 27′N 158° 1′W) **1**:242

FLAT-COATED RETRIEVER **6**:218 *illus.*; **8**:154 *illus.*
FLAT ISLAND
- map (19° 52′S 57° 40′E) **13**:237

FLAT LICK (Kentucky)
- map (36° 50′N 83° 46′W) **12**:47

FLAT RIVER (Missouri)
- map (37° 51′N 90° 31′W) **13**:476

FLAT RIVER RESERVOIR
- map (41° 42′N 71° 37′W) **16**:198

FLAT ROCK (Alabama)
- map (34° 46′N 85° 42′W) **1**:234

FLAT ROCK (Illinois)
- map (38° 54′N 87° 40′W) **11**:42

FLAT TOPS MOUNTAINS
- map (40° 0′N 107° 10′W) **5**:116

FLATBED CYLINDER PRESS **8**:154 *bibliog.*; **15**:550 *illus.*
- letterpress **12**:300–301 *illus.*

FLATFISH **8**:154–155 *bibliog., illus.*
- flounder **8**:177–178
- halibut **10**:20
- plaice **15**:325
- sole **18**:53
- turbot **19**:340–341

FLATHEAD (American Indians) **8**:155 *bibliog.*
- Salish **17**:34
- Spokan **18**:192

FLATHEAD (county in Montana)
- map (48° 15′N 114° 0′W) **13**:547

FLATIRON BUILDING **8**:156 *bibliog.*
- Burnham, Daniel Hudson **3**:577
- skyscraper **17**:348–350
- Steichen, Edward **18**:246 *illus.*

FLATONIA (Texas)
- map (29° 47′N 97° 6′W) **19**:129

FLATT AND SCRUGGS **8**:156 *bibliog.*
- bluegrass music **3**:345

FLATTERY, CAPE **8**:156
- map (48° 23′N 124° 43′W) **20**:35

FLATTS VILLAGE, THE (Bermuda)
- map (32° 19′N 64° 43′W) **3**:219

FLATWARE **8**:156 *bibliog.*
FLATWOODS (Kentucky)
- map (38° 31′N 82° 43′W) **12**:47

FLATWORM **8**:156 *bibliog.*
- diseases, animal **6**:192
- fluke **8**:186
- invertebrate **11**:235
- planaria **15**:326
- schistosomiasis **17**:123
- tapeworm **19**:33–34
- worm **20**:283 *illus., illus.*

FLAUBERT, GUSTAVE **8**:156–157 *bibliog., illus.*
- Du Camp, Maxime **6**:286
- *Madame Bovary* **13**:39
- realism (literature) **16**:104

FLAVIAN AMPHITHEATER *see* COLOSSEUM
FLAVIAN DYNASTY
- Domitian, Roman Emperor **6**:235
- Rome, ancient **16**:303
- Titus, Roman Emperor **19**:215
- Vespasian, Roman Emperor **19**:564

FLAVIN, DAN **8**:157 *bibliog.*
FLAVIO (opera) **14**:399 *illus.*
FLAVORS AND FRAGRANCES **8**:157 *bibliog.*
- ambergris **1**:325
- bay rum **3**:132
- bergamot **3**:209
- champac **4**:276
- citronella **4**:447
- cosmetics **5**:281–282
- essential oils **7**:244–245
- fennel **8**:50
- fenugreek **8**:51
- feverfew **8**:66
- food additives **8**:208
- food technology **8**:213
- frankincense **8**:282
- garlic **9**:48
- ginger **9**:184
- heather **10**:99
- herbs and spices **10**:136–137
- hibiscus **10**:157
- horehound **10**:234
- horseradish **10**:251
- hyacinth **10**:327
- hyssop **10**:352
- jasmine **11**:384
- juniper **11**:470
- kola nut **12**:107
- laurel **12**:237
- licorice **12**:323
- lovage **12**:437
- mace **13**:14–15
- marjoram **13**:158
- mint **13**:460–461
- musk **13**:681
- mustard **13**:686
- myrrh **13**:691
- myrtle **13**:691
- nutmeg **14**:302
- orchid **14**:419–420
- oregano **14**:426
- pepper (vegetable) **15**:156–157
- peppermint **15**:157
- perfume **15**:164
- pomegranate **15**:422
- rose **16**:313
- rosemary **16**:314
- saffron **17**:11
- *Salvia* **17**:40
- sandalwood **17**:61
- sarsaparilla **17**:79
- sassafras **17**:83
- savory **17**:101
- shallot **17**:238
- sorrel **18**:69–70
- spearmint **18**:165–166
- spikenard **18**:183
- sweet gum **18**:387
- tamarind **19**:18
- tansy **19**:25
- tarragon **19**:39
- thyme **19**:187
- tuberose **19**:327
- turmeric **19**:349
- vanilla **19**:519–520
- violet **19**:602
- woodruff **20**:212

FLAX **8**:67–68 *illus., map*; **8**:157–158 *bibliog., illus.*
- cellulose **4**:238
- linen **12**:354
- linseed oil **12**:359

FLAXMAN, JOHN **8**:158 *bibliog.*
FLEA **8**:158 *bibliog., illus.*; **11**:192 *illus.*
- bubonic plague **3**:532
- cat **4**:194
- life cycle **8**:158 *illus.*
- Siphonaptera **17**:326

FLEABANE (botany) **8**:158–159
FLEET, JAMES ALWARD VAN *see* VAN FLEET, JAMES ALWARD
FLEET, THOMAS **8**:159
FLEETWOOD (Pennsylvania)
- map (40° 27′N 75° 49′W) **15**:147

FLEETWOOD HILL, BATTLE OF *see* BRANDY STATION, BATTLE OF
FLEETWOOD MAC **8**:159
FLEMING (Colorado)
- map (40° 41′N 102° 50′W) **5**:116

FLEMING (county in Kentucky)
- map (38° 21′N 83° 42′W) **12**:47

FLEMING, SIR ALEXANDER **8**:159 *bibliog., illus.*
- biology **3**:269
- Chain, Ernst Boris **4**:268
- Florey, Sir Howard Walter **8**:169
- penicillin **15**:143
  - antibiotics **2**:57
  - medicine **13**:271

FLEMING, SIR AMBROSE **8**:159 *bibliog.*
- electron tube, inventor **7**:122

FLEMING, SIR ARTHUR PERCY MORRIS **8**:159
FLEMING, IAN **8**:159 *bibliog.*
FLEMING, PEGGY **8**:159
FLEMINGS
- Belgium **3**:178–179

FLEMINGSBURG (Kentucky)
- map (36° 25′N 83° 44′W) **12**:47

FLEMINGTON (New Jersey)
- map (40° 31′N 74° 52′W) **14**:129

FLEMISH ART AND ARCHITECTURE **8**:159–163 *bibliog., illus.*

See also the subheading Belgium under specific art forms, e.g., PAINTING; SCULPTURE; etc.; the subheading Belgium under BAROQUE ART AND ARCHITECTURE; RENAISSANCE ART AND ARCHITECTURE; names of specific artists, e.g., BOSCH, HIERONYMUS; VAN DE VELDE, HENRY; etc.
art history
Mander, Carel van **13**:111
delftware **6**:92
Dutch art and architecture **6**:309–313
graphic arts **9**:292
lace **12**:159 *illus.*
perspective **15**:190
Rijksmuseum **16**:223
Romanesque art and architecture **16**:284
tapestry **19**:33
FLEMISH LANGUAGE
Germanic languages **9**:135–137 *table*
FLEMISH LITERATURE *see* BELGIAN LITERATURE; DUTCH AND FLEMISH LITERATURE
FLENSBURG (Germany, East and West)
map (54° 47′N 9° 26′E) **9**:140
FLEROV, GEORGY N.
element 104 **7**:132
FLETCHER (North Carolina)
map (35° 26′N 82° 30′W) **14**:242
FLETCHER, ALICE **8**:163 *bibliog.*
FLETCHER, GILES **8**:163
FLETCHER, ISAAC
industrial archaeology **11**:154
FLETCHER, JOHN *see* BEAUMONT, FRANCIS, AND FLETCHER, JOHN
FLETCHER, JOHN GOULD **8**:163
FLETCHER, PHINEAS **8**:163
FLETCHER HENDERSON'S NEW YORK BAND
Armstrong, Louis **2**:179
FLETCHER v. PECK **8**:163
Marshall, John **13**:172
Yazoo Land Fraud **20**:320
FLETCHER'S ICE ISLAND **8**:163 *bibliog.*
iceberg **11**:15
FLETTNER, PETER *see* FLÖTNER, PETER
FLEUR-DE-LIS (botany) **8**:163
See also IRIS (botany)
FLEUR-DE-LYS (Newfoundland)
map (50° 7′N 56° 8′W) **14**:166
FLEURY, ANDRÉ HERCULE DE **8**:163 *bibliog.*
FLEXAGON
paper folding **15**:71
FLEXNER, ABRAHAM **8**:163–164 *bibliog.*
Institute for Advanced Study **11**:195
FLEXOGRAPHY
printing **15**:553
FLICKER **8**:164 *bibliog., illus.*
FLIGHT **8**:164 *bibliog.*
See also AIRCRAFT; AIRSHIP; AVIATION; BALLOON; GLIDER; HELICOPTER; ROCKETS AND MISSILES
biological locomotion **3**:267
bird **3**:278–290
Borelli, Giovanni Alfonso **3**:398
insect **11**:191 *illus.*
Mach number **13**:17
FLIGHT, HUMAN-POWERED **8**:164–165 *bibliog., illus.*
glider **9**:207–208
Leonardo da Vinci **12**:291
FLIGHT SIMULATOR *see* TEACHING MACHINES
FLIN FLON (Manitoba)
map (54° 46′N 101° 53′W) **13**:119
FLINDERS, MATTHEW **8**:165 *bibliog.*
Australia, history of **2**:340 *map*
FLINDERS ISLAND
map (40° 0′S 148° 0′E) **2**:328
FLINDERS RANGE **8**:165
map (31° 0′S 139° 0′E) **2**:328
FLINDERS RIVER
map (17° 36′S 140° 36′E) **2**:328
FLINDT, FLEMMING **8**:165
Royal Danish Ballet **16**:330
FLINT *see* CHERT AND FLINT
FLINT (Michigan) **8**:165
map (43° 1′N 83° 41′W) **13**:377
FLINT, RICHARD FOSTER **8**:165
FLINT AND CHERT *see* CHERT AND FLINT
FLINT COMPLEX, DENBIGH *see* DENBIGH FLINT COMPLEX
FLINT HILLS
map (38° 50′N 100° 0′W) **12**:18
FLINT RIVER (Alabama)
map (34° 30′N 86° 31′W) **1**:234
FLINT RIVER (Georgia)
map (30° 52′N 84° 38′W) **9**:114
FLINTLOCK
English pistol **15**:318 *illus.*
musket **13**:682–683 *illus.*
FLINTSHIRE (Wales) **8**:165
FLINTVILLE (Tennessee)
map (34° 59′N 86° 25′W) **19**:104
FLIVVER *see* MODEL T (automobile)
FLOATATION *see* ARCHIMEDES' PRINCIPLE
FLOCCULATION
water supply **20**:53
FLOODPLAIN **8**:165–166 *bibliog.*
floods and flood control **8**:167–168
meander, river **13**:253
mud cracks **13**:631
oxbow lake **14**:473
FLOODS AND FLOOD CONTROL **8**:166–168 *bibliog., illus., table*
Asia, history of **2**:249
dam **6**:15–18
Delta Plan **6**:95–96
dike (engineering) **6**:175–176
flash flood **8**:153
floodplain **8**:165–166
Florence (Italy) **8**:169
Fréjus **8**:301
irrigation **11**:281
Johnstown (Pennsylvania) **11**:438
levee **12**:302
major floods, 1880–1980 **8**:167 *table*
Mississippi River **13**:473
Netherlands **14**:98–99
Ordovician Period **14**:421
river and stream **16**:230–231 *illus.*
Tennessee Valley Authority **19**:107–108
FLOODWOOD (Minnesota)
map (46° 55′N 92° 56′W) **13**:453
FLOPPY DISK
computer **5**:160h
computer, personal **5**:160i
computer software **5**:165
FLOPS (computer term) **5**:160h
FLORA (Illinois)
map (38° 40′N 88° 29′W) **11**:42
FLORA (Indiana)
map (40° 33′N 86° 31′W) **11**:111
FLORA (mythology) **8**:168
FLORA VISTA (New Mexico)
map (36° 48′N 108° 2′W) **14**:136
FLORADORA SEXTET
tap dancing **19**:29
FLORALA (Alabama)
map (31° 0′N 86° 20′W) **1**:234
FLORENCE (Alabama)
map (34° 49′N 87° 40′W) **1**:234
FLORENCE (Arizona)
map (33° 2′N 111° 23′W) **2**:160
FLORENCE (Colorado)
map (38° 23′N 105° 8′W) **5**:116
FLORENCE (Italy) **8**:168–169 *bibliog., illus., map*
architecture **2**:134
Ammanati, Bartolommeo **1**:372
Baptistery **11**:311 *illus.*
Brunelleschi, Filippo **3**:524–525
cathedral **2**:135 *illus.*; **6**:230 *illus.*; **8**:168 *illus.*; **16**:150 *illus.*
Italian art and architecture **11**:308–314
Michelozzo **13**:375
Sangallo (family) **17**:64
art
Andrea da Firenze **2**:94 *illus.*
artistic heritage **8**:168 *illus.*
Baldovinetti, Alesso **3**:34
Bandinelli, Baccio **3**:62
Bargello (museum) **3**:81
Bartolommeo, Fra **3**:98
Bronzino **3**:508–509
Cimabue **4**:430–431
Gaddi (family) **9**:6–7
Ghiberti, Lorenzo **9**:168
Giotto di Bondone **9**:187
Maiano (family) **13**:66
Masaccio **13**:193–194
Nanni di Banco **14**:12–13
Pisano, Andrea **15**:316
Renaissance art and architecture **16**:151–152
Rossellino (family) **16**:319
Uffizi **19**:371
bridge (engineering) **3**:480
history **8**:168–169
Hawkwood, Sir John **10**:78
Italian city-state **11**:328 *map*
Machiavelli, Niccolò **13**:18
Medici (family) **13**:265
Renaissance **16**:149
Savonarola, Girolamo **17**:101
library
Laurentian Library **12**:239
map (43° 46′N 11° 15′E) **11**:321
Platonic tradition **15**:361
FLORENCE (Kansas)
map (38° 15′N 96° 56′W) **12**:18
FLORENCE (Oregon)
map (43° 58′N 124° 7′W) **14**:427
FLORENCE (South Carolina)
map (34° 12′N 79° 46′W) **18**:98
FLORENCE (county in South Carolina)
map (34° 0′N 79° 40′W) **18**:98
FLORENCE (Texas)
map (30° 51′N 97° 48′W) **19**:129
FLORENCE (Wisconsin)
map (45° 56′N 88° 7′W) **20**:185
FLORENCE (county in Wisconsin)
map (45° 50′N 88° 23′W) **20**:185
FLORENCIA (Colombia)
map (1° 36′N 75° 36′W) **5**:107
FLORENCIO SANCHEZ (Uruguay)
map (33° 53′S 57° 24′W) **19**:488
FLORES (Guatemala)
map (16° 56′N 89° 53′W) **9**:389
FLORES (Portugal)
Azores **2**:381–382 *map*
FLORES, JOSÉ MARIA
Mexican War **13**:355
FLORES, JUAN JOSÉ **8**:169 *bibliog.*
Rocafuerte, Vicente **16**:246
FLORESVILLE (Texas)
map (29° 8′N 98° 10′W) **19**:129
FLOREY, SIR HOWARD WALTER **8**:169 *bibliog.*
antibiotics **2**:57
Chain, Ernst Boris **4**:268
Fleming, Sir Alexander **8**:159
penicillin **15**:143
FLORHAM PARK (New Jersey)
map (40° 47′N 74° 23′W) **14**:129
FLORIANO (Brazil)
map (6° 47′S 43° 1′W) **3**:460
FLORIANÓPOLIS (Brazil)
map (27° 35′S 48° 34′W) **3**:460
FLORICULTURE **8**:169–170 *bibliog., illus.*
commerical bulb growing **8**:170
gardening **9**:42–44
greenhouse floriculture **8**:169–170
transport **8**:170
FLORIDA **8**:171–176 *bibliog., illus., map*
agriculture **8**:174–175 *illus.*
animal life **8**:173
cities
Coral Gables **5**:258
Daytona Beach **6**:57
Fort Lauderdale **8**:237
Hialeah **10**:156
Jacksonville **11**:344
Key West **12**:62
Miami **13**:369–370
Miami Beach **13**:370 *illus.*
Orlando **14**:445
Palm Beach **15**:49
Pensacola **15**:153
Saint Augustine **17**:16
Saint Petersburg **17**:26
Sarasota **17**:75
Tallahassee **19**:16
Tampa **19**:20
West Palm Beach **20**:109
climate **8**:171; **8**:173
cultural institutions **8**:173–174
economic activity **8**:174
education **8**:173
Florida, state universities of **8**:176
flag **8**:171 *illus.*
government and politics **8**:174–175
historical sites **8**:174
history **8**:175–176
de Soto, Hernando **6**:63
French and Indian Wars **8**:312
Jackson, Andrew **11**:341
Laudonnière, René Goulaine de **12**:236
Menéndez de Avilés, Pedro **13**:297
Ponce de León, Juan **15**:425–426
Ribaut, Jean **16**:205
Seminole Wars **17**:197
Spanish missions **18**:160
land and resources **8**:171–173 *illus., map*
map (29° 0′N 82° 0′W) **19**:419
people **8**:173–174
Apalachee **2**:74
Seminole **17**:197
physical features
Cape Canaveral **4**:120
Dry Tortugas **6**:284
Everglades **7**:316 *illus.*; **18**:377 *illus.*
Florida Keys **8**:176
Sable, Cape **17**:6
rivers, lakes, and waterways **8**:171
Okeechobee, Lake **14**:365
Suwannee River **18**:374
seal, state **8**:171 *illus.*
sports and outdoor recreation **8**:174
dog racing **6**:222
tourism **8**:174
vegetation **8**:173
FLORIDA (Cuba)
map (21° 32′N 78° 14′W) **5**:377
FLORIDA (Uruguay)
map (34° 6′S 56° 13′W) **19**:488
FLORIDA, STATE UNIVERSITIES OF **8**:176
FLORIDA, STRAITS OF **8**:176
Gulf Stream **9**:403
FLORIDA BAY
map (25° 0′N 80° 45′W) **8**:172
FLORIDA CITY (Florida)
map (25° 27′N 80° 29′W) **8**:172
FLORIDA CURRENT
Caribbean Current **4**:147
Gulf Stream **9**:403
FLORIDA KEYS (Islands) **8**:176
map (24° 45′N 81° 0′W) **8**:172
FLORIEN (Louisiana)
map (31° 27′N 93° 27′W) **12**:430
FLORIN (coin) **14**:296 *illus.*
FLORIO, JOHN **8**:176
FLORIS (family) **8**:176–177 *bibliog.*
FLORIS, CORNELIS
The Town Hall of Antwerp **8**:162 *illus.*
FLORISSANT (Missouri)
map (38° 48′N 90° 20′W) **13**:476
FLORY, PAUL **8**:177
FLOSSFLOWERS *see* AGERATUM
FLOTATION PROCESS **8**:177
FLÖTNER, PETER **8**:177 *bibliog.*
FLOTOW, FRIEDRICH VON **8**:177
FLOTSAM, JETSAM, AND LAGAN **8**:177
FLOUNDER **8**:155 *illus.*; **8**:177–178 *illus.*
flatfish **8**:154
FLOUR **8**:178 *bibliog.*
grain **9**:281
rice **16**:208
wheat **20**:126
FLOWCHART **8**:178 *bibliog., illus.*
computer **5**:160h
FLOWER **8**:178–184 *bibliog., illus.*
See also names of specific flowers, e.g., COLUMBINE (botany); DAISY (botany); etc.
arrangement on the plant **8**:180–181
biological clock **8**:183
classification, biological **8**:183
coloration, biological **5**:122
floriculture **8**:169–170
flowering time **8**:181
formation **8**:181
gardening **9**:43
importance **8**:183–184
Linnaeus, Carolus **12**:359
perfume **15**:164
photoperiodism **8**:182–183
plant **15**:335–337 *illus.*
pollination **15**:408–409 *illus.*
seed and fruit **8**:181
structure **8**:179 *illus.*
temperature and light **8**:181–182
FLOWER-CHILDREN *see* HAIGHT-ASHBURY (California)
FLOWERING OF NEW ENGLAND, THE (book)
Brooks, Van Wyck **3**:511
FLOWERING RUSH (botany) **8**:184
FLOWERPECKER (bird) **8**:184
FLOWERPOT SNAKE **8**:184
FLOWER'S COVE (Newfoundland)
map (51° 18′N 56° 44′W) **14**:166
FLOWERS OF EVIL, THE (book) **8**:184 *bibliog.*
Baudelaire, Charles **3**:128–129
FLOWERY BRANCH (Georgia)
map (34° 11′N 83° 55′W) **9**:114
FLOWMETER **8**:184
FLOWSTONE *see* TRAVERTINE
FLOYD (county in Georgia)
map (34° 20′N 85° 15′W) **9**:114
FLOYD (county in Indiana)
map (38° 18′N 85° 49′W) **11**:111
FLOYD (county in Iowa)
map (43° 3′N 92° 45′W) **11**:244
FLOYD (county in Kentucky)
map (37° 30′N 82° 45′W) **12**:47
FLOYD (New Mexico)
map (34° 13′N 103° 35′W) **14**:136
FLOYD (county in Texas)
map (34° 2′N 101° 15′W) **19**:129
FLOYD (Virginia)
map (36° 55′N 80° 19′W) **19**:607

FLOYD (county in Virginia)
map (36° 55′N 80° 25′W) **19**:607
FLOYD, CARLISLE 8:184
FLOYD, JOHN BUCHANAN 8:184
FLOYD, PRETTY BOY 8:184 *bibliog.*
FLOYD RIVER
map (42° 29′N 96° 23′W) **11**:244
FLOYDADA (Texas)
map (33° 59′N 101° 20′W) **19**:129
FLU *see* INFLUENZA
FLÜGELHORN 8:184 *illus.*
FLUID *see* BODY FLUIDS; LIQUID
FLUID DYNAMICS *see* FLUID MECHANICS (physics); HYDRODYNAMICS
FLUID FILM BEARING
bearing **3**:144
FLUID MECHANICS (physics) 8:184–185 *bibliog., illus.*
aerodynamics **1**:123–124
Bernoulli, Daniel **3**:223
Bernoulli's law **3**:223
Kármán, Theodore von **12**:28
liquid **12**:364–365
Pascal's law **15**:102
turbine **19**:340
FLUIDIZED BED COMBUSTION 8:185
FLUKE (flatworm) 8:186
diseases, animal **6**:192
FLUME STUDIES 8:186 *bibliog.*
Gilbert, Grove Karl **9**:178–179
FLUORESCENCE (physics) 8:186 *bibliog.*
fluorometer **8**:188
phosphor **15**:256
photochemistry **15**:258
Stokes, Sir George Gabriel **18**:278
FLUORESCENCE, MINERAL 8:186 *illus.*
luminescence, mineral **12**:458
FLUORESCENT LIGHT 8:186–187 *bibliog.*
argon **2**:152
ballast, inductor **11**:151–152
lamp
circuit, electric **4**:437 *illus.*
lanthanum **12**:201
lighting devices **12**:338–339
FLUORIDATION 8:187 *bibliog.*
dentistry **6**:114
FLUORIDE
fluoridation **8**:187
Moissan, Henri **13**:504
FLUORINE 8:187–188 *bibliog.*
abundances of common elements **7**:131 *table*
compounds
calcium **4**:22
fluorocarbon **8**:188
inorganic chemistry **11**:182
element **7**:130 *table*
gas **8**:187–188
geologic time
Oakley, Kenneth **14**:312
Group VIIA periodic table **15**:167
halide minerals **10**:21
halogens **10**:25
industry **8**:187–188
Moissan, Henri, discoverer **13**:504
natural occurrence **8**:187
reducing potential
electromotive series **7**:119
vitamins and minerals **19**:621
FLUORITE 8:188 *illus.*
calcium fluoride **8**:188
fluorine **8**:187
FLUOROCARBON 8:188
aerosol **1**:125
fluorine **8**:187
Freon **8**:326
FLUOROMETER 8:188
FLUOROSCOPE 8:188 *bibliog.*
FLUSHING (Michigan)
map (43° 4′N 83° 51′W) **13**:377
FLUSHING (Ohio)
map (40° 9′N 81° 4′W) **14**:357
FLUTE 8:188–189 *bibliog., illus.*
African **1**:169–170 *illus.*
Chinese music **4**:392
fife **8**:74
flageolet **8**:149
Japanese music **11**:381–382 *illus.*
musical instruments **13**:676–677
nay **2**:100
performers
Galway, James **9**:23–24
Quantz, Johann Joachim **16**:11–12
Rampal, Jean Pierre **16**:81
piccolo **15**:292
recorder **16**:110
sound waves **18**:72 *illus.*
FLUVANNA (county in Virginia)
map (37° 50′N 78° 15′W) **19**:607
FLUX 8:189
Olbers's paradox **14**:373
FLY 8:189–190 *bibliog., illus.*
blowfly **3**:341
botfly **3**:415
crane fly **5**:331
deerfly **6**:81
eye **11**:189 *illus.*
fruit fly **8**:347
horsefly **10**:250–251
housefly **10**:274
larva
myiasis **13**:690
midge **13**:413
mosquito **13**:602–603
salivary glands
chromosome **14**:290 *illus.*
tsetse fly **19**:323
FLY, JAMES L.
radio and television broadcasting **16**:57
FLY AGARIC (mushroom) **15**:384 *illus.*
FLYCATCHER (bird) 8:190–191 *bibliog., illus.*
pewee **15**:217
phoebe **15**:249
robin **16**:243
silky flycatcher **17**:308
FLYCATCHER (botany)
carnivorous plants **4**:157
FLYING *see* AVIATION
FLYING BOAT
airport **1**:223
commercial aviation **2**:372
FLYING BUTTRESS *see* BUTTRESS
FLYING CLOUD (ship)
clipper ship **5**:60
FLYING DRAGON **12**:381 *illus.*
FLYING DUTCHMAN, THE (opera) 8:191
FLYING DUTCHMAN, THE (painting) (Howard Pyle) **3**:388 *illus.*
FLYING FISH 8:116 *illus.*; **8**:191 *illus.*
characin **4**:286
halfbeak **10**:20
hatchetfish **10**:68
FLYING FISH (ship)
clipper ship **5**:60
FLYING FORTRESS *see* B-17 FLYING FORTRESS
FLYING GURNARD 8:191
FLYING LEMUR *see* COLUGO
FLYING SAUCER *see* UNIDENTIFIED FLYING OBJECT
FLYING SHUTTLE
Kay, John **12**:32–33
FLYING SQUIRREL 8:191; **18**:204 *illus.*
FLYING TIGERS
Chennault, Claire L. **4**:330
P-40 **15**:3
World War II **20**:260
FLYNN, ELIZABETH GURLEY 8:191 *bibliog.*
FLYNN, ERROL 8:191 *bibliog.*
FLYNN, LESLIE THOMAS *see* FLYNN, ERROL
FLYWHEEL 8:191–192
FM *see* FREQUENCY MODULATION
FM RADIO 8:192 *bibliog.*
wavelength and frequency, electromagnetic **7**:117 *table*
FO, DARIO 8:192
Italian literature **11**:317
FOARD (county in Texas)
map (34° 0′N 99° 42′W) **19**:129
FOB 8:192
FOCAL LENGTH (photography)
camera **4**:55
lens **12**:285–286
FOCAL POINT (optics) 8:192
camera **4**:54
coma (optics) **5**:129
mirror **13**:464–465 *illus.*
FOCH, FERDINAND 8:192 *bibliog., illus.*
Somme, Battles of the **18**:62
World War I **20**:241–243 *illus.*
FOCILLON, HENRY 8:192 *bibliog.*
FOCŞANI (Romania)
map (45° 41′N 27° 11′E) **16**:288
FOCUS (mathematics)
ellipse **7**:147
FOCUS (photography)
camera **4**:54; **4**:55; **4**:56–57
depth of field **6**:120
FODDER 8:192–193
FOEHN 8:193
mountain climates **13**:621
Rocky Mountains
chinook **4**:396
zonda **20**:373
FOG 8:193 *bibliog.*
cloud **5**:68
London fog
pollution, environmental **15**:414
mist **13**:481
sirocco **17**:328
stratus clouds **18**:293
upwelling, oceanic **19**:473–474
weather modification **20**:80
FOGAZZARO, ANTONIO 8:193 *bibliog.*
FOGGIA (Italy) 8:193
map (41° 27′N 15° 34′E) **11**:321
FOGGY MOUNTAIN BOYS
Flatt and Scruggs **8**:156
FOGO (Newfoundland)
map (49° 43′N 54° 17′W) **14**:166
FOGO ISLAND (Cape Verde Islands)
map (14° 55′N 24° 25′W) **4**:122
FOGO ISLAND (Newfoundland)
map (49° 40′N 54° 13′W) **14**:166
FOHNSDORF (Austria)
map (47° 13′N 14° 41′E) **2**:348
FÖHR ISLAND
map (54° 43′N 8° 30′E) **9**:140
FOIL (aerodynamics)
hydrofoil **10**:335–337 *illus.*
FOIX (France) 8:193
FOKINE, MIKHAIL 8:193 *bibliog.*
ballet **3**:43 *illus.*
Ballets Russes de Serge Diaghilev **3**:48
choreography **4**:408–409 *illus.*
Pavlova, Anna **15**:121
Royal Swedish Ballet **16**:331
FOKKER, ANTHONY HERMANN GERARD 8:193 *bibliog.*
FOKKER D-VII AIRCRAFT 1:215 *illus.*; **8**:194 *illus.*
FOKKER E-III AIRCRAFT **2**:370–371 *illus.*
FOLD (geology) 8:194–195 *bibliog., illus.*
diastrophism **6**:153
Earth, geological history of **7**:13
geosyncline **9**:119–120
mountain **13**:619–620 *illus.*
nappe **14**:20
structural geology **18**:303
syncline and anticline **18**:406
FOLDING-ROLL FILM CAMERA **4**:57
FOLEY (Alabama)
map (30° 25′N 87° 41′W) **1**:234
FOLEY (Minnesota)
map (45° 40′N 93° 55′W) **13**:453
FOLGER SHAKESPEARE LIBRARY 8:195
FOLIATION 8:195 *bibliog.*
FOLIC ACID
coenzyme **5**:92
deficiency
sprue **18**:201
hemoglobin **10**:119
vitamins and minerals **19**:620
Recommended Dietary Allowances **19**:618 *table*
FOLIES-BERGÈRE 8:195
FOLIGNO (Italy)
map (42° 57′N 12° 42′E) **11**:321
FOLIO 8:195
FOLK ART 8:195–199 *bibliog., illus.*
antique collecting **2**:66
bark cloth **3**:82–83 *illus.*
basketry **3**:115–116
beads and beadwork **3**:137–138
craft **5**:326
figurehead **8**:75–76
Korean art **12**:118
Latin American art and architecture **12**:226–227 *illus.*
limners **8**:197–198 *illus.*; **12**:345
Mexico **12**:226–227 *illus.*
needlework **14**:76
Pennsylvania Dutch **15**:152 *illus.*
primitive art **15**:543
scrimshaw **17**:158
tombstone **19**:232 *illus.*
wood carving **20**:207–208 *illus.*
FOLK DANCE 8:199–201 *bibliog., illus.*
costume and accessories **8**:200
dance **6**:23 *illus.*; **6**:27 *illus.*
hasapikos **10**:66
hora **10**:233
jig **11**:417
mazurka **13**:250
Moiseyev, Igor Aleksandrovich **13**:504
steps **8**:199–200 *illus.*
tarantella **19**:35
FOLK HISTORY *see* ETHNOHISTORY
FOLK LITERATURE *see* FOLKLORE
FOLK MEDICINE 8:201 *bibliog.*
American **8**:201
hallucinogens **10**:24
herbs and spices **10**:137
hot-cold theory **8**:201
medicinal plants **13**:266
medicine **13**:267
opium **14**:406
poisonous plants and animals **15**:383
practices today **8**:201
sausage tree **17**:97
snakeroot **17**:383
FOLK MUSIC 8:202–203 *bibliog., illus.*
See also CALYPSO
bagpipe **3**:22–23 *illus.*
dulcimer **6**:295
England
Butterworth, George **3**:600
Grainger, Percy **9**:282
Holst, Gustav **10**:208
Vaughan Williams, Ralph **19**:528–529
Hungary
Bartók, Béla **3**:98
Hungarian music **10**:306
Kodály, Zoltán **12**:105
India
Indian literature **11**:101
Ireland
Stanford, Sir Charles Villiers **18**:217
Japan
Dengaku **6**:107
mandolin **13**:111–112 *illus.*
Norway
Grieg, Edvard **9**:361–362
Poland
Lutosławski, Witold **12**:470
Portugal
fado **8**:7
Russia
Balakirev, Mily Alekseyevich **3**:30
Rimsky-Korsakov, Nikolai Andreyevich **16**:224–225
song **18**:64
United States
Baez, Joan **3**:21
Collins, Judy **5**:104
Denver, John **6**:117
Dyer-Bennett, Richard **6**:319
Dylan, Bob **6**:319
Foster, Stephen **8**:248
Grainger, Percy **9**:282
Guthrie, Woody and Arlo **9**:409
Ives, Burl **11**:333
Leadbelly **12**:256
Lomax (family) **12**:398
Mitchell, Joni **13**:483
Odetta **14**:350
Ritchie (family) **16**:229
Seeger, Pete **17**:187
Simon and Garfunkel **17**:315
yodel **20**:328
zither **20**:370–371
FOLK-ROCK
rock music **16**:248
FOLK SONG *see* FOLK MUSIC
FOLKESTONE (England)
map (51° 5′N 1° 11′E) **19**:403
FOLKLORE 8:203 *bibliog.*
See also FOLK ART; FOLK DANCE; FOLK MEDICINE; FOLK MUSIC; FOLKTALE; FOLKWAYS; LEGEND; MYTHOLOGY
aphorism, maxim, and proverb **2**:77
Arabic literature **2**:101
Ibn al-Muqaffa **11**:5
Jahiz, Abu Uthman Amr al- **11**:349
banshee **3**:71
brownie **3**:518
Bunyan, Paul **3**:565
Chapman, John **4**:285
Crockett, Davy **5**:355–356
fairy **8**:9–10
Fink, Mike **8**:94
frontier **8**:342–344
Geoffrey of Monmouth **9**:98
giants **9**:171
Ginzberg, Louis **9**:185
Groundhog Day **9**:374
Horatii **10**:234
Hurston, Zora Neale **10**:319
incubus **11**:77
Irish literature **11**:268
Fenian cycle **8**:50
Finn mac Cumhail **8**:98–99
jinni **11**:419
John Henry **11**:425
Jones, Casey **11**:442
Lang, Andrew **12**:194
Library of Congress **12**:318
Loch Ness monster **12**:386
mermaid **13**:311
nix **14**:204
omen **14**:387
oni **14**:390
Pecos Bill **15**:130
shamrock **17**:239
supernatural literature **18**:352
tengu **19**:102
vampire **19**:510
werewolf **20**:104

FOLKSTON (Georgia)
map (30° 50′N 82° 1′W) 9:114
FOLKTALE 8:204 *bibliog.*
See also FABLE; FAIRY TALE; LEGEND
Afanasiev, Aleksandr Nikolayevich 1:132
Arnim, Achim and Bettina von 2:184
Asbjørnsen, Peter Christen 2:227
Breton literature 3:475
Cinderella 4:432
Diop, Birago Ismael 6:185
Gregory, Isabella Augusta, Lady 9:355
Moe, Jørgen Engebretsen 13:500
FOLKWAYS 8:204 *bibliog.*
norm, social 14:219
Sumner, William Graham 18:340
FOLLANSBEE (Ohio)
map (40° 20′N 80° 36′W) 14:357
FOLLETTE, ROBERT M. LA *see* LA FOLLETTE, ROBERT M.
FOLLICLE, OVARIAN
menstruation 13:300–301
FOLLICLE-STIMULATING HORMONE (FSH)
endocrine system, diseases of the 7:171
gonadotropin 9:242
hormones 10:236
pituitary gland 15:322
FOLLICULITIS
skin diseases 17:342
FOLLY BEACH (South Carolina)
map (32° 39′N 79° 56′W) 18:98
FOLSOM (California)
map (38° 41′N 121° 15′W) 4:31
FOLSOM CULTURE 8:204
flint spear point 14:237 *illus.*
North American archaeology 14:236–237
Pleistocene Epoch 15:366
Sandia Cave 17:62
FOLSON (New Jersey)
map (39° 38′N 74° 51′W) 14:129
FON 8:204 *bibliog.*
Ewe 8:325
FOND DU LAC (Saskatchewan)
map (59° 19′N 107° 10′W) 17:81
FOND DU LAC (Wisconsin)
map (43° 47′N 88° 27′W) 20:185
FOND DU LAC (county in Wisconsin)
map (43° 45′N 88° 28′W) 20:185
FONDA (family) 8:204–205 *bibliog., illus.*
FONDA (Iowa)
map (42° 35′N 94° 51′W) 11:244
FONDA (New York)
map (42° 57′N 74° 22′W) 14:149
FONDA, HENRY
Fonda (family) 8:204–205 *illus.*
Ford, John (film director) 8:223
FONDA, JANE
Fonda (family) 8:204–205 *illus.*
FONDA, PETER
Fonda (family) 8:204–205 *illus.*
FONSECA, GULF OF
map (13° 10′N 87° 40′W) 10:218
Nicaragua Canal 14:180
FONSECA, MANUEL DEODORO DA 8:205
FONT (baptism) 8:205
Church of Saint Barthélemy (Liège) 16:285 *illus.*
FONT DE GAUME (France) 8:205
FONTAINE, JEAN DE LA *see* LA FONTAINE, JEAN DE
FONTAINE, PIERRE FRANÇOIS LÉONARD 8:205
Malmaison 13:93
Percier, Charles 15:162
FONTAINEBLEAU (France) 8:205
FONTAINEBLEAU, CHÂTEAU DE 8:205; 16:155 *illus.*
FONTAINEBLEAU, SCHOOL OF 8:205–206 *bibliog., illus.*
Cellini, Benvenuto 4:237
French art and architecture 8:305
Primaticcio, Francesco 15:542
Renaissance art and architecture 16:155
Rosso Fiorentino 16:320
FONTANA, CARLO 8:206 *bibliog.*
FONTANA, DOMENICO 8:206 *bibliog.*
FONTANA, FERDINANDO
Puccini, Giacomo 15:612
FONTANA, LAVINIA 8:206 *bibliog.*
FONTANA, LUCIO 8:206 *bibliog.*
FONTANA MAGGIORE
fountains 8:252
FONTANE, THEODOR 8:206–207 *bibliog., illus.*
FONTANELLE (Iowa)
map (41° 17′N 94° 34′W) 11:244
FONTANNE, LYNN
Lunt, Alfred, and Fontanne, Lynn 12:465
FONTE BOA (Brazil)
map (2° 32′S 66° 1′W) 3:460
FONTÉCHEVADE MAN 8:207 *bibliog.*
FONTENELLE, BERNARD LE BOVIER DE 8:207
FONTENELLE RESERVOIR
map (42° 5′N 110° 6′W) 20:301
FONTEYN, DAME MARGOT 8:207 *bibliog., illus.*
Karsavina, Tamara Platonovna 12:29
Nureyev, Rudolf 14:297
FONTUR
map (66° 23′N 14° 30′W) 11:17
FONVIZIN, DENIS IVANOVICH 8:207 *bibliog.*
FONZ, THE *see* WINKLER, HENRY
FOOCHOW (Fuzhou) (China) 8:207–208
map (26° 6′N 119° 17′E) 4:362
FOOD *see* AGRICULTURE AND THE FOOD SUPPLY; COOKING; DIET, HUMAN; FOOD ADDITIVES; FOOD INDUSTRY; FOOD PRESERVATION; FOOD SERVICE SYSTEMS; FOOD TECHNOLOGY; HEALTH FOODS; articles on specific foods, e.g., APPLE; HONEY; etc.
FOOD, DRUG, AND COSMETIC ACT *see* PURE FOOD AND DRUG LAWS
FOOD ADDITIVES 8:208 *bibliog.*
antioxidants 2:64–65
benzoic acid 3:207
cattle and cattle raising 4:217
environmental health 7:211–212
flavors and fragrances 8:157
food preservation 8:212
hyperactive children 10:347
monosodium glutamate 13:540
nitrite 14:202
nutrition, human 14:307
propionates 15:572
saccharin 17:6
sausage 17:97
sulfites 18:334
FOOD ADDITIVES AMENDMENT *see* PURE FOOD AND DRUG LAWS
FOOD AND AGRICULTURE ORGANIZATION 8:208 *bibliog.*
nutritional-deficiency diseases 14:308
FOOD AID CONVENTION
agriculture and the food supply 1:198–199
FOOD CHAIN *see* ECOLOGY
FOOD AND DRUG ADMINISTRATION 8:208 *bibliog.*
cyclamates 5:403
drug 6:278
environmental health 7:210
flavors and fragrances 8:157
food additives 8:208
nitrite 14:202
saccharin 17:6
sulfites 18:334
government regulation 9:271
hexachlorophene 10:154
hyperactive children 10:347
ice cream 11:11
laetrile 12:163
patent medicine 15:110
pharmaceutical industry 15:220
pharmacy 15:221
public health 15:608
pure food and drug laws 15:628–629
sugar 18:327
Washington, D.C. 20:41 *map*
FOOD INDUSTRY 8:208–211 *bibliog., illus., tables*
See also AGRIBUSINESS; AGRICULTURE AND THE FOOD SUPPLY; FARMS AND FARMING; FOOD PRESERVATION; FOOD TECHNOLOGY; names of specific foods, e.g., CORN (botany); POULTRY; etc.
antibiotics 8:212
baking industry 3:29
cattle and cattle raising 4:214–217
energy utilization 8:210–211
fishing industry 8:124–128
flow of goods in food industry 8:209 *illus.*
Food and Drug Administration 8:208
food labeling
nutrition, human 14:307
food processing 8:209–210 *table*
diet, human 6:164
frozen food 8:346–347
Heinz, Henry John 10:109
Lipton, Sir Thomas 12:364
meat and meat packing 13:257–258
packaging 15:11–12
pasteurization 15:108
quality control and testing 8:209–210
refrigeration 16:124–125
sugar production 18:328–330
food retailing 8:210
Hartford, Huntington 10:62
Poland 15:391
price structure 8:210
retail cost factors 8:210 *table*
supermarket 18:352
food service systems 8:212
fruits and fruit cultivation 8:349–350
government regulation 8:211
history 8:208–209
organic chemistry 14:439
petrochemicals 15:205
pure food and drug laws 15:628–629
radiation 8:212
FOOD AND NUTRITION BOARD, U.S.
cholesterol 4:404
cholesterol controversy 14:307
nutritional-deficiency diseases 14:308
Recommended Dietary Allowances 14:306
FOOD AND NUTRITION SERVICE, U.S.
Agriculture, U.S. Department of 1:194
FOOD FOR PEACE
Agency for International Development 1:183
agriculture and the food supply 1:195
foreign aid 8:224
FOOD POISONING AND INFECTION 8:211 *bibliog.*
dinoflagellate 6:179
infectious diseases 11:167
metals 8:211
microorganisms 8:211
natural poisons 8:211
parasitic diseases 15:82
poisonous plants and animals 15:384–385
ptomaine poisoning 15:608
red tide 16:114
Salmonella 17:36
Staphylococcus 18:220
symptoms 8:211
FOOD PRESERVATION 8:211–212 *bibliog.*
aluminum 1:319
canning 4:110–111 *illus.*
cooking 5:237–240
dehydration of food 6:85; 8:212
fishing industry 8:127–128 *illus.*
food additives 8:208; 8:212
food industry 8:208–209
food technology 8:213
freeze-drying 8:300
frozen food 8:346–347
fruits and fruit cultivation 8:350
heat processing 8:211–212
honey 10:220
Inca 11:72
jam and jelly 12:351
milk 13:423
Borden, Gail 3:396
nitrite 14:202
packaging 15:11–12
pickling 15:293
propionates 15:572
pure food and drug laws 15:628–629
refrigeration 8:212; 16:124–125
saltpeter 17:39
sulfites 18:334
FOOD SERVICE SYSTEMS 8:212 *bibliog.*
food industry 8:209
restaurant 16:182
FOOD STAMP PROGRAM 8:212 *bibliog.*
FOOD TECHNOLOGY 8:213 *bibliog.*
algae 1:283
fermentation 8:55
food industry 8:208–211
food preservation 8:213
food service systems 8:212
meat imitations 13:257
new foods 8:213
space-food technology 8:213
FOOD WEB *see* ECOLOGY
FOOL 8:213 *bibliog.*
FOOLS, FEAST OF 8:213
FOOL'S GOLD *see* PYRITE
FOOT (anatomy)
bird 3:288 *illus.*
diving birds 6:204
bunions, corns, and calluses 3:563
cat 4:194 *illus.*
cat family 4:196
clubfoot 5:71
fungus diseases 8:369
human body 10:296e *illus.*
grouse 9:378
mammal 13:102 *illus.*
muscle 13:654
podiatry 15:377
FOOT (measure)
weights and measures 20:93
FOOT (versification) 19:562
FOOT, MICHAEL 8:214
FOOT-AND-MOUTH DISEASE 8:214
diseases, animal 6:190; 6:191
FOOT-BINDING 8:214; 20:202 *illus.*
FOOTBALL 8:214–218 *bibliog., illus., tables*
American Football League 8:217–218 *table*
commissioners
Rozelle, Pete 16:331
equipment 8:215–216 *illus.*
football field 8:215 *illus.*
Heisman Trophy *see* HEISMAN TROPHY
history 8:216–218; 18:196 *illus.*
line of scrimmage 8:217 *illus.*
National Collegiate Athletic Association 14:30
National Football League 8:217–218 *table*
players and coaches
Baugh, Sammy 3:129
Bell, Bert 3:186
Berry, Raymond 3:225
Blanchard, Doc 3:326–327
Blanda, George 3:327
Brown, Jim 3:514–515
Brown, Paul Eugene 3:516
Bryant, Bear 3:529
Butkus, Dick 3:591
Camp, Walter 4:63
Davis, Glenn 6:51
Graham, Otto 9:280
Grange, Red 9:286–287
Griese, Bob 9:362
Groza, Lou 9:381
Halas, George 10:17
Hornung, Paul 10:240
Hutson, Don 10:323
Lombardi, Vince 12:398–399
Nagurski, Bronko 14:6–7
Namath, Joe 14:9
Robinson, Eddie 16:243
Rockne, Knute 16:260
Sayers, Gale 17:106
Simpson, O. J. 17:317
Stabler, Ken 18:207–208
Stagg, Amos Alonzo 18:211
Starr, Bart 18:227–228
Staubach, Roger 18:239
Tarkenton, Fran 19:37
Thorpe, Jim 19:180
Unitas, Johnny 19:400
Warner, Pop 20:30
Wilkinson, Bud 20:152–153
Pop Warner football 15:430
professional football 8:217–218 *tables*
rugby 16:339–340
rules 8:214–217 *illus.*
soccer 18:8
sports medicine 18:198
stadium 18:208–209
Super Bowl 8:218 *table*
FOOTE, ANDREW HULL 8:219
FOOTE, ROBERT BRUCE 8:219
FOOTE, SAMUEL 8:219 *bibliog.*
FOOTHILLS (Alberta)
map (53° 4′N 116° 48′W) 1:256
FOOTRACING *see* TRACK AND FIELD
FOR WHOM THE BELL TOLLS (book) 8:219 *bibliog.*
FORAIN, JEAN LOUIS 8:219
FORAMINIFERA 8:219–220 *bibliog., illus.*
age dating 8:220
chalk 8:219–220
distribution 8:219
fossil record 8:247
ice ages 11:10
marine protozoa 8:219
micropaleontology 13:386
paleoclimatology 15:33
paleotemperature 15:42
Protozoa 15:580

FORAMINIFERA (cont.)
Rhizopoda **16**:197
rock formation components **8**:219–220
sediment, marine **17**:184
FORAMS *see* FORAMINIFERA
FORBES (magazine) **8**:220
FORBES, BERTIE CHARLES
Forbes (magazine) **8**:220
FORBES, JOHN **8**:220 *bibliog.*
French and Indian Wars **8**:313 *map*
FORBES, ROBERT BENNET **8**:220
FORBES-ROBERTSON, SIR JOHNSTON **8**:220 *bibliog.*
FORBIDDEN CITY **4**:387 *illus.*; **8**:220
Lhasa (Tibet/China) **12**:309–310
Peking (Beijing) (China) **15**:135–136 *illus.*
FORCE (physics) **8**:220 *bibliog.*
centrifugal and centripetal forces **4**:255
dyne **6**:320
electric **7**:108
electromotive force **7**:119
friction **8**:330–331
fundamental interactions **8**:360–361
gravitation **9**:304–305
laws of motion **12**:251
measurement **13**:255
units, physical **19**:466 *table*
mechanics **8**:220
motion, harmonic **13**:608–609
nuclear force
nuclear physics **14**:287
pound **15**:475
statics **18**:234–235
FORCE ACT
nullification **14**:292
FORD (family) **8**:220–221 *bibliog.*, *illus.*
FORD (county in Illinois)
map (40° 27′N 88° 6′W) **11**:42
FORD (county in Kansas)
map (37° 40′N 99° 55′W) **12**:18
FORD, EDSEL
Ford (family) **8**:220–221
FORD, EDWARD CHARLES "WHITEY" *see* FORD, WHITEY
FORD, FORD MADOX **8**:221 *bibliog.*
FORD, GERALD R. **8**:221–222 *bibliog.*, *illus.*; **15**:528 *illus.*
Dole, Robert J. **6**:224
Kissinger, Henry A. **12**:90–91
Nixon, Richard M. **14**:206
Republican party **16**:175
swine flu **18**:392
Tokyo Rose **19**:226
FORD, HENRY **19**:453 *illus.*
assembly line **2**:265
automotive industry **2**:363–364
Dearborn (Michigan) **6**:68
Ford (family) **8**:220–221 *illus.*
Industrial Revolution **11**:159
Kahn, Albert **12**:6
manufacturing **13**:133
mass production **13**:204
FORD, HENRY II
Ford (family) **8**:221
FORD, JOHN (film director) **8**:222–223 *bibliog.*, *illus.*
Wayne, John **20**:73–74
FORD, JOHN (playwright) **8**:223 *bibliog.*
FORD, JOHN THOMSON
Ford's Theatre **8**:224
FORD, PAUL LEICESTER **8**:223 *bibliog.*
FORD, WHITEY **8**:223 *bibliog.*
FORD CITY (California)
map (35° 9′N 119° 27′W) **4**:31
FORD CITY (Pennsylvania)
map (40° 46′N 79° 32′W) **15**:147
FORD FOUNDATION **8**:223 *bibliog.*
Bundy, McGeorge **3**:562–563
Center for Advanced Study in the Behavioral Sciences **4**:249
Ford (family) **8**:221
FORD MOTOR COMPANY **2**:363–368 *illus.*
See also FORD, HENRY
assembly line **19**:67 *illus.*; **19**:432 *illus.*
automobile models **2**:365 *illus.*
Couzens, James **5**:318
Dearborn (Michigan) **6**:68
Ford (family) **8**:220–221
Ford Tri-motor **8**:223–224
Iacocca, Lee **11**:3
McNamara, Robert S. **13**:35
Model T **13**:490
FORD RIVER
map (45° 40′N 87° 9′W) **13**:377
FORD TRI-MOTOR **2**:370–372 *illus.*; **8**:223–224 *illus.*
FORDHAM UNIVERSITY **8**:224
FORD'S THEATRE **8**:224
Washington, D.C. **20**:41 *map*
FORDSVILLE (Kentucky)
map (37° 38′N 86° 43′W) **12**:47
FORDVILLE (North Dakota)
map (48° 13′N 97° 47′W) **14**:248
FORDYCE (Arkansas)
map (33° 49′N 92° 25′W) **2**:166
FORE STAFF *see* JACOB'S STAFF
FORECLOSURE *see* MORTGAGE
FOREIGN AFFAIRS (journal) **8**:224
FOREIGN AGRICULTURAL SERVICE, U.S.
Agriculture, U.S. Department of **1**:193–194
FOREIGN AID **8**:224–225 *bibliog.*, *table*
Agency for International Development **1**:183
technology transfer **19**:60
United States
Lend-Lease **12**:281
Marshall Plan **13**:173
Point Four Program **15**:381
FOREIGN EXCHANGE *see* EXCHANGE RATE
FOREIGN-LANGUAGE PRESS IN THE UNITED STATES *see* NEWSPAPER
FOREIGN LANGUAGES, TEACHING OF **8**:225 *bibliog.*
applied linguistics **2**:90–91
Berlitz Schools of Language **3**:219
linguistics **12**:354; **12**:356
FOREIGN LEGION *see* FRENCH FOREIGN LEGION
FOREIGN POLICY **8**:225–226 *bibliog.*
alliance **1**:302
arms control **2**:178
balance of power **3**:32
boycott **3**:433
Clausewitz, Carl Philipp Gottfried von **5**:44–45
cold war **5**:98–99
conflict theory **5**:178–179
Congress of the United States **5**:187
defense, national **6**:81–82
extradition **7**:341
foreign aid **8**:224–225
geopolitics **9**:108–109
intelligence gathering **11**:204
irredentism **11**:280
isolationism **11**:299
mediation **13**:264
political science **15**:403
president of the United States **15**:522–523
treaty **19**:285–286
treaty ratification
Senate of the United States **17**:198–199
war **20**:24–25
FOREIGN SERVICE **8**:226–227 *bibliog.*
ambassador **1**:324
consul (modern government official) **5**:225
extraterritoriality **7**:346
international law **11**:221–222
FOREIGN TRADE *see* INTERNATIONAL TRADE
FOREIGN-TRADE ZONE *see* FREE PORT
FOREL, MOUNT
map (67° 0′N 37° 0′W) **9**:353
FOREMAN, GEORGE **8**:227
FOREMAN, RICHARD **2**:227 *bibliog.*
FOREMOST (Alberta)
map (49° 29′N 111° 25′W) **1**:256
FORENSIC SCIENCE **8**:227 *bibliog.*
autopsy **2**:368
coroner **5**:271
pathology **15**:112
toxicology **19**:256
FOREST **8**:227–230 *bibliog.*, *illus.*
See also FORESTRY; NATIONAL FOREST SYSTEM (U.S.)
conservation **5**:201; **5**:203
ecology
food web **7**:42 *illus.*
economic importance **8**:229–230
England **19**:406
fire prevention and control **8**:104
habitat **10**:5
jungle and rain forest **11**:468–470
Pygmy **15**:633
taiga climate **19**:11
tree **19**:288
world distribution **3**:273 *map*; **15**:344 *map*
FOREST (Mississippi)
map (32° 22′N 89° 28′W) **13**:469
FOREST (Ohio)
map (40° 48′N 83° 31′W) **14**:357
FOREST (county in Pennsylvania)
map (41° 29′N 79° 27′W) **15**:147
FOREST (county in Wisconsin)
map (45° 40′N 88° 47′W) **20**:185
FOREST, JOHN WILLIAM DE *see* DE FOREST, JOHN WILLIAM
FOREST, LEE DE *see* DE FOREST, LEE
FOREST OF ARDENNES *see* ARDENNES
FOREST CITY (Iowa)
map (43° 16′N 93° 39′W) **11**:244
FOREST CITY (North Carolina)
map (35° 20′N 81° 52′W) **14**:242
FOREST CITY (Pennsylvania)
map (41° 39′N 75° 28′W) **15**:147
FOREST GROVE (Oregon)
map (45° 31′N 123° 7′W) **14**:427
FOREST HILLS CHAMPIONS (tennis) **19**:111 *table*
FOREST HOME (Alabama)
map (31° 52′N 86° 50′W) **1**:234
FOREST LAKE (Minnesota)
map (45° 17′N 92° 59′W) **13**:453
FOREST SERVICE, U.S. *see* NATIONAL FOREST SYSTEM (U.S.)
FORESTBURG (Alberta)
map (52° 35′N 112° 4′W) **1**:256
FORESTER, C. S. **8**:230 *bibliog.*
FORESTRY **8**:230–232 *bibliog.*, *illus.*
Canada **4**:78–79 *illus.*
fire
chaparral **4**:284
lightning **12**:340
forest protection **8**:231–232
logging **12**:394
lumber **12**:455–457
Muir, John **13**:635
Pinchot, Gifford **15**:304
remote sensing **16**:147
FORESTVILLE (Quebec)
map (48° 45′N 69° 6′W) **16**:18
FORFARSHIRE (Scotland) *see* ANGUS (Scotland)
FORFEITURE **8**:232
FORGAN (Oklahoma)
map (36° 54′N 100° 32′W) **14**:368
FORGE **8**:232–233 *bibliog.*, *illus.*
annealing **2**:33
extrusion **7**:347
metallurgy **13**:329–330
FORGERY **8**:233
anthropology
Kensington Rune Stone **12**:45
Oakley, Kenneth **14**:312
Piltdown man **15**:303
counterfeiting **5**:312
fraud **8**:288
uttering **8**:233
van Meegeren, Hans **8**:233 *illus.*
FORGERY, LITERARY *see* LITERARY FRAUD
FORGERY IN ART **8**:233–234 *bibliog.*, *illus.*
FORGET-ME-NOT (botany) **8**:234 *illus.*
tundra **19**:332 *illus.*
FORGETTING
memory **13**:291
FORKED RIVER (New Jersey)
map (39° 51′N 74° 12′W) **14**:129
FORLI **8**:234
FORLI, MELOZZO DA *see* MELOZZO DA FORLI
FORMALDEHYDE **8**:234
aldehyde **1**:268
preservative **8**:234
FORMALISM (art criticism) **2**:207
FORMALISM (literature) **8**:234 *bibliog.*
See also STRUCTURALISM
FORMALISM (mathematics)
mathematics, history of **13**:226
FORMAN (North Dakota)
map (46° 7′N 97° 38′W) **14**:248
FORMAN, MILOS **8**:234
FORMENTERA (Spain)
Balearic Islands **3**:36 *map*
FORMIC ACID **8**:234
nettle **14**:104
FORMIGAS (Portugal)
Azores **2**:381–382 *map*
FORMOSA *see* TAIWAN
FORMOSA (Argentina)
map (26° 11′S 58° 11′W) **2**:149
FORMOSA (province in Argentina)
map (25° 0′S 60° 0′W) **2**:149
FORMOSA ISLAND
map (11° 12′N 16° 15′W) **9**:399
FORMOSA STRAIT
map (24° 0′N 19° 0′E) **19**:13
FORMULA ONE CARS
automobile racing **2**:360 *illus.*
FORMULA TRANSLATION LANGUAGE *see* FORTRAN
FORREST (county in Mississippi)
map (31° 10′N 89° 15′W) **13**:469
FORREST, EDWIN **8**:234 *bibliog.*
as Othello **19**:149 *illus.*
Astor Place Riot **2**:269
Bird, Robert Montgomery **3**:290
FORREST, JOHN, 1st BARON FORREST **8**:235 *bibliog.*
Australia, history of **2**:340 *map*
exploration **7**:336 *map*
FORREST, NATHAN BEDFORD **8**:235 *bibliog.*
FORREST CITY (Arkansas)
map (35° 1′N 90° 47′W) **2**:166
FORRESTAL, JAMES V. **8**:235 *bibliog.*
FORRESTER, JAY WRIGHT **8**:235
computer design and development **8**:235
FORRESTON (Illinois)
map (42° 8′N 89° 35′W) **11**:42
FORSSMANN, WERNER
Cournand, André **5**:314
Richards, Dickinson Woodruff **16**:211
FORST (Germany, East and West)
map (51° 44′N 14° 39′E) **9**:140
FORSTER, E.M. **8**:235 *bibliog.*, *illus.*
FORSTERITE
olivine **14**:380 *table*
FORSYTE SAGA, THE (books) **8**:235
Galsworthy, John **9**:21–22
FORSYTH (Georgia)
map (33° 2′N 83° 56′W) **9**:114
FORSYTH (county in Georgia)
map (34° 15′N 84° 5′W) **9**:114
FORSYTH (Missouri)
map (36° 41′N 93° 6′W) **13**:476
FORSYTH (Montana)
map (46° 16′N 106° 41′W) **13**:547
FORSYTH (county in North Carolina)
map (36° 10′N 80° 15′W) **14**:242
FORSYTH, JOHN **8**:235–236
FORSYTHIA **8**:236 *illus.*; **17**:288 *illus.*
FORT, PAUL **8**:236
FORT ADAMS (Mississippi)
map (31° 5′N 91° 33′W) **13**:469
FORT ALBANY (Ontario)
map (52° 15′N 81° 37′W) **14**:393
FORT ASSINIBOINE (Alberta)
map (54° 20′N 114° 46′W) **1**:256
FORT ATKINSON (Wisconsin)
map (42° 56′N 88° 50′W) **20**:185
FORT BEND (county in Texas)
map (29° 32′N 95° 47′W) **19**:129
FORT BENNING (Georgia) **8**:236
FORT BENTON (Montana)
map (47° 49′N 110° 40′W) **13**:547
FORT BERTHOLD RESERVATION
Hidatsa **10**:158–159
FORT BRAGG (California)
map (39° 26′N 123° 48′W) **4**:31
FORT BRAGG (North Carolina) **8**:236
FORT BRANCH (Indiana)
map (38° 15′N 87° 35′W) **11**:111
FORT BRIDGER (Wyoming)
map (41° 19′N 110° 23′W) **20**:301
FORT CALHOUN (Nebraska)
map (41° 32′N 96° 1′W) **14**:70
FORT CAROLINE (Florida)
Laudonnière, René Goulaine de **12**:236
Ribaut, Jean **16**:205
FORT-CHIMO (Quebec)
map (58° 6′N 68° 25′W) **16**:18
FORT CHIPEWYAN (Alberta)
map (58° 42′N 111° 8′W) **1**:256
FORT COBB (Oklahoma)
map (35° 6′N 98° 26′W) **14**:368
FORT COLLINS (Colorado)
map (40° 35′N 105° 5′W) **5**:116
FORT COVINGTON (New York)
map (44° 59′N 74° 30′W) **14**:149
FORT-DAUPHIN (Madagascar)
map (25° 2′S 47° 0′E) **13**:38
FORT DAVIS (Alabama)
map (32° 15′N 85° 43′W) **1**:234
FORT DAVIS (Texas)
map (30° 35′N 103° 54′W) **19**:129
FORT-DE-FRANCE (Martinique) **8**:236
map (14° 36′N 61° 5′W) **20**:109
FORT DEARBORN (Illinois) **8**:236
War of 1812 **20**:26 *map*
FORT DEFIANCE (Arizona)
map (35° 45′N 109° 5′W) **2**:160
FORT DEPOSIT (Alabama)
map (31° 59′N 86° 35′W) **1**:234
FORT DIX (New Jersey) **8**:236
swine flu **18**:392
FORT DODGE (Iowa)
map (42° 30′N 94° 10′W) **11**:244
FORT DONELSON (Kentucky)
Fort Henry and Fort Donelson **8**:236
FORT DUCHESNE (Utah)
map (40° 17′N 109° 52′W) **19**:492
FORT DUQUESNE (Pennsylvania) **8**:236
Forbes, John **8**:220
French and Indian Wars **8**:313–314 *map*

FORT FAIRFIELD (Maine)
map (46° 46′N 67° 50′W) **13**:70
FORT FITZGERALD (Alberta)
map (59° 53′N 111° 37′W) **1**:256
FORT FRANCES (Ontario)
map (48° 36′N 93° 24′W) **14**:393
FORT FRANKLIN (Northwest Territories)
map (65° 11′N 123° 46′W) **14**:258
FORT FRASER (British Columbia)
map (54° 4′N 124° 33′W) **3**:491
FORT GAINES (Georgia)
map (31° 37′N 85° 3′W) **9**:114
FORT GARLAND (Colorado)
map (37° 26′N 105° 26′W) **5**:116
FORT-GEORGE (Quebec)
map (53° 50′N 79° 0′W) **16**:18
FORT GIBSON (Oklahoma)
map (35° 48′N 95° 15′W) **14**:368
FORT GIBSON LAKE
map (36° 0′N 95° 18′W) **14**:368
FORT GOOD HOPE (Northwest Territories)
map (66° 15′N 128° 38′W) **14**:258
FORT HALL (Idaho)
map (43° 2′N 112° 26′W) **11**:26
FORT HENRY AND FORT DONELSON (Kentucky) **8**:236 *bibliog.*
FORT HOOD (Texas) **8**:237
FORT JEFFERSON (Florida)
Dry Tortugas (Florida) **6**:284
FORT KENT (Maine)
map (47° 15′N 68° 36′W) **13**:70
FORT KLAMATH (Oregon)
map (42° 42′N 122° 0′W) **14**:427
FORT KNOX (Kentucky) **8**:237
FORT-LAMY (Chad) *see* N'DJAMENA (Chad)
FORT-LAMY N'DJAMENA (Chad)
map (12° 7′N 15° 3′E) **4**:266
FORT LARAMIE (Wyoming)
map (42° 13′N 104° 31′W) **20**:301
FORT LARAMIE TREATY
Fitzpatrick, Thomas **8**:132
FORT LAUDERDALE (Florida) **8**:237; **14**:233 *illus.*
map (26° 7′N 80° 8′W) **8**:172
FORT LEE (New Jersey)
map (40° 51′N 73° 58′W) **14**:129
FORT LORAMIE (Ohio)
map (40° 21′N 84° 22′W) **14**:357
FORT LOUDON (Pennsylvania)
map (39° 55′N 77° 54′W) **15**:147
FORT LOUDOUN LAKE RESERVOIR
map (35° 45′N 84° 10′W) **19**:104
FORT LUPTON (Colorado)
map (40° 5′N 104° 49′W) **5**:116
FORT McHENRY (Maryland) **8**:237; **13**:191 *illus.*
McHenry, James **13**:18
War of 1812 **20**:26 *map*
FORT MACLEOD (Alberta)
map (49° 43′N 113° 25′W) **1**:256
FORT McMURRAY (Alberta)
map (56° 44′N 111° 23′W) **1**:256
FORT McPHERSON (Northwest Territories)
map (67° 27′N 134° 53′W) **14**:258
FORT MADISON (Iowa)
map (40° 38′N 91° 27′W) **11**:244
FORT MEADE (Florida)
map (27° 45′N 81° 48′W) **8**:172
FORT MILL (South Carolina)
map (35° 1′N 80° 57′W) **18**:98
FORT MORGAN (Colorado)
map (40° 15′N 103° 48′W) **5**:116
FORT MOULTRIE (South Carolina) **8**:237
FORT MYERS (Florida)
map (26° 37′N 81° 54′W) **8**:172
FORT MYERS BEACH (Florida)
map (26° 27′N 81° 57′W) **8**:172
FORT NELSON (British Columbia)
map (58° 49′N 122° 39′W) **3**:491
FORT NELSON RIVER
map (59° 30′N 124° 0′W) **3**:491
FORT NIAGARA (New York) **8**:237
French and Indian Wars **8**:313 *map*
FORT NORMAN (Northwest Territories)
map (64° 54′N 125° 34′W) **14**:258
FORT PAYNE (Alabama)
map (34° 27′N 85° 43′W) **1**:234
FORT PECK LAKE
map (47° 45′N 106° 50′W) **13**:547
FORT PIERCE (Florida)
map (27° 27′N 80° 20′W) **8**:172
FORT PIERRE (South Dakota)
map (44° 21′N 100° 22′W) **18**:103
FORT PLAIN (New York)
map (42° 56′N 74° 38′W) **14**:149
FORT PORTAL (Uganda)
map (0° 40′N 30° 17′E) **19**:372
FORT PROVIDENCE (Northwest Territories)
map (61° 21′N 117° 39′W) **14**:258
FORT QU'APPELLE (Saskatchewan)
map (50° 56′N 103° 9′W) **17**:81
FORT RELIANCE (Northwest Territories)
map (62° 42′N 109° 8′W) **14**:258
FORT RESOLUTION (Northwest Territories)
map (61° 10′N 113° 40′W) **14**:258
FORT ROUILLÉ
Toronto (Ontario) **19**:242
FORT SAINT JAMES (British Columbia)
map (54° 26′N 124° 15′W) **3**:491
FORT SAINT JOHN (British Columbia)
map (56° 15′N 120° 51′W) **3**:491
FORT SASKATCHEWAN (Alberta)
map (53° 43′N 113° 13′W) **1**:256
FORT SCOTT (Kansas)
map (37° 50′N 94° 42′W) **12**:18
FORT SEVERN (Ontario)
map (56° 0′N 87° 38′W) **14**:393
FORT-SIBUT (Central African Republic)
map (5° 44′N 19° 5′E) **4**:251
FORT SIMPSON (Northwest Territories)
map (61° 52′N 121° 23′W) **14**:258
FORT SMITH (Arkansas) **8**:237
map (35° 23′N 94° 25′W) **2**:166
FORT STANWIX, TREATY OF
Indian treaties **11**:106–107
Johnson, Sir William **11**:437
FORT STOCKTON (Texas)
map (30° 53′N 102° 53′W) **19**:129
FORT SULLIVAN *see* FORT MOULTRIE (South Carolina)
FORT SUMNER (New Mexico)
map (34° 28′N 104° 15′W) **14**:136
FORT SUMTER (South Carolina) **8**:237 *bibliog., illus.*; **18**:99 *illus.*
firing on (1861) **5**:19–20 *illus.*
flag **8**:135 *illus.*
Fort Moultrie **8**:237
Lincoln, Abraham **12**:349
national parks **14**:38–39 *map, table*
Sumter, Thomas **18**:340
FORT THOMPSON (South Dakota)
map (44° 3′N 99° 26′W) **18**:103
FORT TICONDEROGA *see* TICONDEROGA
FORT UNION (New Mexico)
Santa Fe Trail **17**:68
FORT VALLEY (Georgia)
map (32° 33′N 83° 53′W) **9**:114
FORT VERMILION (Alberta)
map (58° 24′N 116° 0′W) **1**:256
FORT WALTON BEACH (Florida)
map (30° 25′N 86° 36′W) **8**:172
FORT WASHAKIE (Wyoming)
map (43° 0′N 108° 53′W) **20**:301
FORT WAYNE (Indiana) **8**:238
map (41° 4′N 85° 9′W) **11**:111
FORT WELLINGTON (Guyana)
map (6° 24′N 57° 36′W) **9**:410
FORT WHITE (Florida)
map (29° 55′N 82° 43′W) **8**:172
FORT WILLIAM (Scotland)
map (56° 49′N 5° 7′W) **19**:403
FORT WORTH (Texas) **8**:238
map (32° 45′N 97° 20′W) **19**:129
FORT YATES (North Dakota)
map (46° 5′N 100° 38′W) **14**:248
FORT YUKON (Alaska)
map (66° 34′N 145° 17′W) **1**:242
FORTALEZA (Brazil) **8**:238
map (3° 43′S 38° 30′W) **3**:460
FORTAS, ABE **8**:238 *bibliog.*
FORTEAU (Newfoundland)
map (51° 28′N 56° 58′W) **14**:166
FORTES, MEYER **8**:238
FORTESCUE RIVER
map (21° 0′S 116° 6′E) **2**:328
FORTH (computer language) **8**:238
computer languages **5**:160p
FORTH, RIVER **8**:238
FORTH RAILWAY BRIDGE (Scotland) **3**:481 *illus.*
FORTIFICATION **8**:238–241 *bibliog., illus.*
ancient and medieval **8**:238–239
Gla **9**:192
Krak des Chevaliers **12**:126–127
Messene **13**:322
Rome, ancient **16**:279 *map*
Tiryns **19**:209
Trelleborg **19**:294
Troy (archaeological site) **19**:313
castle **4**:189–191
China
Great Wall of China **9**:323
city **5**:3
fieldworks **8**:238
France
Maginot Line **13**:51
Great Britain
Antonine Wall **2**:70
Hadrian's Wall **10**:8
Maiden Castle **13**:66
Offa's Dyke **14**:353
Israel
Masada **13**:194
Leonardo da Vinci **12**:291
Mesopotamian art and architecture **13**:321
Peloponnesus
Mistra **13**:482
permanent **8**:238
strategy and tactics, military **18**:289
weapons **20**:74
FORTÍN AYACUCHO (Paraguay)
map (19° 58′S 59° 47′W) **15**:77
FORTÍN CORONEL EUGENIO GARAY (Paraguay)
map (20° 31′S 62° 8′W) **15**:77
FORTÍN FLORIDA (Paraguay)
map (20° 45′S 59° 17′W) **15**:77
FORTÍN GARRAPATAL (Paraguay)
map (21° 27′S 61° 30′W) **15**:77
FORTÍN INGAVI (Paraguay)
map (19° 55′S 60° 47′W) **15**:77
FORTÍN PAREDES (CORONELES SÁNCHEZ) (Paraguay)
map (19° 20′S 59° 58′W) **15**:77
FORTÍN TENIENTE MONTANÍA (Paraguay)
map (22° 4′S 59° 57′W) **15**:77
FORTINE (Montana)
map (48° 46′N 114° 54′W) **13**:547
FORTRAN **8**:241 *bibliog., illus.*
computer languages **5**:160o; **5**:160p
FORTUNA (California)
map (40° 36′N 124° 9′W) **4**:31
FORTUNA (mythology) **8**:241
FORTUNA PRIMIGENIA, SANCTUARY OF
temple **19**:97
FORTUNE (periodical)
Fortune 500 **8**:242
Luce, Henry Robinson **12**:449–450
Silberman, Charles **17**:303
FORTUNE BAY
map (47° 25′N 55° 25′W) **14**:166
FORTUNE 50
corporation **5**:273 *table*
FORTUNE 500 **8**:242
FORTUNE HARBOUR (Newfoundland)
map (49° 31′N 55° 15′W) **14**:166
FORTUNE-TELLING **8**:241 *bibliog., illus.*
divination **6**:202
tarot **19**:38
FORTUNE THEATRE **8**:241–242 *bibliog.*
FORTUNY, MARIANO
stage lighting **18**:210
FORTVILLE (Indiana)
map (39° 56′N 85° 51′W) **11**:111
FORTY-NINERS *see* GOLD RUSH
FORUM **8**:242 *bibliog., illus.*
Rome, ancient **8**:242 *illus.*; **16**:302 *illus.*
FOSBURY, DICK
track and field **19**:260
FOSCOLO, UGO **8**:242 *bibliog.*
FOSDICK, HARRY EMERSON **8**:242
FOSS, LUKAS **8**:242–243 *bibliog.*
FOSSA **8**:243 *illus.*
FOSSE TEMPLES
Lachish **12**:160
FOSSEY, DIAN
Leakey (family) **12**:259
FOSSIL (Oregon)
map (45° 0′N 120° 13′W) **14**:427
FOSSIL FUELS *see* COAL AND COAL MINING; ENERGY SOURCES; FUEL; NATURAL GAS; PETROLEUM
FOSSIL RECORD **8**:243–248 *bibliog., illus.*
See also EXTINCT SPECIES; PREHISTORIC ANIMALS; PREHISTORIC HUMANS
African prehistory **1**:172–173
amber **1**:325
amphibians **1**:378
ancient landscapes, reconstruction **8**:247
Arduino, Giovanni **2**:145
bird **3**:279 *illus.*
falcon **8**:12
hesperornis **10**:151
Ichthyornis **11**:19
moa **13**:486–487
owl **14**:472–473
perching birds **15**:161
Brongniart, Alexandre **3**:503
Cambrian Period **4**:50–52 *illus.*
Carboniferous Period **4**:137–139 *illus.*
carnivore **4**:157
cave dwellers **4**:224
Cenozoic Era **4**:245–246
chalk **4**:271
continental shield **5**:230
coprolite **5**:255
coquina **5**:257
Cretaceous Period **5**:339–341
Darwin, Charles **6**:41
Devonian Period **6**:144–146
Dubois, Eugène **6**:289
Earth, geological history of **7**:12
earth history **8**:244–245
evolution **7**:320–324 *illus.*; **8**:246–247
fish **8**:120
Agassiz, Louis Rodolphe **1**:182
arthrodire **2**:216
Chondrichthyes **4**:404
coelacanth **5**:91
conodont **5**:197
ostracoderm **14**:458
shark **17**:242
forgery, Piltdown man **15**:303
fossil chemistry **8**:247–248
fossil formations **8**:243–244
Füchsel, Georg Christian **8**:352
fungi **8**:365
geologic time **9**:103–105 *table*
geosyncline **9**:119
Gesner, Konrad von **9**:159
Gondwanaland **9**:243
Hooke, Robert **10**:227
ice ages **11**:8–11
insect **11**:193
ant **2**:38
cockroach **5**:88
dragonfly **6**:255
invertebrate **11**:234
Protozoa **15**:580
Jurassic Period **11**:475–477
kinds of fossils **8**:243–244
La Brea Tar Pit **12**:144
Leakey (family) **12**:258–259
limestone **12**:345
mammal **13**:99–101
deer **6**:79
eohippus **7**:215
Irish elk **11**:266
marsupial **13**:174
mastodon **13**:217
monkey **13**:535
perissodactyl **15**:171
primate **15**:539–541 *illus.*
rodent **16**:266
saber-toothed cats **17**:5
titanothere **19**:211
marine invertebrates
archaeocyathid **2**:115
blastoid **3**:328
brachiopod **3**:435
bryozoan **3**:530
chiton **4**:399
conodont **5**:197
crinoid **5**:350
cystoid **5**:411
echinoderm **7**:37
eurypterid **7**:310
foraminifera **8**:219–220
graptolite **9**:294
horseshoe crab **10**:252
mollusk **13**:511
ostracod **14**:458
trilobite **4**:51–52; **19**:299
marl **13**:160
Marsh, Othniel Charles **13**:171
Mesozoic Era **13**:322
micropaleontology **13**:386
Murchison, Roderick Impey **13**:647
Olduvai Gorge **14**:377
Oppel, Albert **14**:407
Orbigny, Alcide Dessalines D' **14**:416
Ordovician Period **14**:420–422
overview **8**:248
paleobotany **15**:30–32
paleoclimatology **15**:32–34 *map*
paleoecology **15**:34–35
paleogeography **8**:248
paleomagnetism **15**:41–42
paleontology **15**:42
Paleozoic Era **15**:42–43
Permian Period **15**:174–176
Petrified Forest National Park **15**:204
petrified wood **15**:204–205
phylogeny **15**:279
plants **15**:333–335
conifer **5**:190–191
cycad **5**:402
fern **8**:57–58
flower **8**:178
ginkgo **9**:184
grass **9**:295
horsetail **10**:253 *illus.*

FOSSIL RECORD (cont.)
orchid 14:420
redwood 16:117
plate tectonics 15:354
Pleistocene Epoch 15:366
pollen stratigraphy 15:407
Precambrian time 15:491–493
prehistoric life, evidence 8:245–246
prehistory 15:517
Quaternary Period 16:15
Recent Epoch 16:106–107
reptile
dinosaur 6:179–182
Edaphosaurus 7:54
Ichthyosaurus 11:19–20
lizard 12:382
mosasaur 13:596
Plesiosaur 15:367–368
Pterodactyl 15:606
Rhamphorhynchus 16:192
snake 17:382
tuatara 19:326
turtle 19:352
seamount 17:174
Sedgwick, Adam 17:183
sediment, marine 17:183–184
Silurian Period 17:310
Simpson, George Gaylord 17:317
stratigraphy 18:292–293
stromatolite 18:302
Suess, Eduard 18:323
swamp, marsh, and bog 18:378
Tertiary Period 19:122–125
Triassic Period 19:292–295
FOSSORIAL WASP *see* DIGGER WASP
FOSSTON (Minnesota)
map (47° 35′N 95° 45′W) 13:453
FOSTER (county in North Dakota)
map (47° 25′N 98° 50′W) 14:248
FOSTER, ABIGAIL 8:248
FOSTER, STEPHEN 8:248 *bibliog.*
American music 1:349–350 *illus.*
minstrel shows
Christy, Edwin P. 4:416–417
FOSTER, WILLIAM Z. 8:248
FOSTER CARE *see* ADOPTION AND FOSTER CARE
FOSTER GRANDPARENT PROGRAM
ACTION (federal agency) 1:89
FOSTER VILLAGE (Hawaii)
map (21° 22′N 157° 56′W) 10:72
FOSTERS (Alabama)
map (33° 6′N 87° 41′W) 1:234
FOSTORIA (Ohio)
map (41° 9′N 83° 25′W) 14:357
FOTHERGILL, JOHN 8:248 *bibliog.*
FOUCAULD, CHARLES DE 8:248–249 *bibliog.*
FOUCAULT, JEAN 8:249
Foucault pendulum 8:249
gyroscope 9:416
FOUCAULT, MICHEL 8:249
FOUCAULT PENDULUM 8:249
FOUCHÉ, JOSEPH 8:249 *bibliog.*
intelligence gathering 11:204
FOUGÈRES (France)
map (48° 21′N 1° 12′W) 8:260
FOUKE (Arkansas)
map (33° 16′N 93° 53′W) 2:166
FOUL BAY
map (23° 30′N 35° 39′E) 7:76
FOULARD 8:249
FOULWIND, CAPE
map (41° 45′S 171° 28′E) 14:158
FOUMBAN (Cameroon)
map (5° 43′N 10° 55′E) 4:61
FOUND ART
Duchamp, Marcel 6:290
Stankiewicz, Richard 18:219
FOUND POEM 8:249
FOUNDATION, BRIDGE
bridge (engineering) 3:481–482
cofferdam 5:94
FOUNDATION, BUILDING 8:249–250 *bibliog., illus.*
caisson 4:19
cofferdam 5:94
house (in Western architecture) 10:271 *illus.*
soil mechanics 18:38
FOUNDATIONS AND ENDOWMENTS 8:250–251 *bibliog.*
Carnegie, Andrew 4:155
Danforth Foundation 6:31
Duke Endowment 6:295
Ford Foundation 8:223
fund raising 8:360
government regulation 8:251
Guggenheim (family) 9:392
Guggenheim Memorial Foundation 9:393
Hershey, Milton Snaveley 10:148
Hopkins, Johns 10:232
Juilliard, Augustus D. 11:465
Kellogg, W. K. 12:38
Kresge Foundation 12:129
MacArthur Foundation 13:6
McGill, James 13:16
Mellon Foundation 13:287
National Foundation on the Arts and the Humanities 14:32
Nuffield Foundation 14:291
Peabody, George 15:123
Robert Wood Johnson Foundation 16:241
Rockefeller (family) 16:250
Rockefeller Foundation 16:251
Rosenwald, Julius 16:316
Russell Sage Foundation 16:351
Sage, Russell 17:12
Sloan Foundation 17:363
FOUNDRY 8:251
zinc overingestion
vitamins and minerals 19:621
FOUNTAIN (Florida)
map (30° 30′N 85° 25′W) 8:172
FOUNTAIN (county in Indiana)
map (40° 7′N 87° 13′W) 11:111
FOUNTAIN CITY (Wisconsin)
map (44° 8′N 91° 43′W) 20:185
FOUNTAIN INN (South Carolina)
map (34° 42′N 82° 12′W) 18:98
FOUNTAIN OF YOUTH *see* PONCE DE LEÓN, JUAN
FOUNTAIN PEN 15:140; 15:141 *illus.*
FOUNTAINHEAD, THE (book)
Rand, Ayn 16:82
FOUNTAINS 8:251–252 *bibliog.*
FOUNTAINS ABBEY 13:518 *illus.*
FOUQUET, JEAN 8:252 *bibliog.*
Charlemagne's coronation 11:328 *illus.*; 15:63 *illus.*
Les Heures d'Étienne Chevalier 13:274 *illus.*; 13:519 *illus.*; 19:145 *illus.*
trial of Jean II 13:393 *illus.*
FOUQUET, NICOLAS 8:252
Le Brun, Charles 12:253
Vaux-le-Vicomte, Château de 19:529
FOUR BEARS (Mandan chief) 13:111 *illus.*
FOUR-COLOR THEOREM (mathematics) 8:252 *bibliog.*
FOUR CROSS ROADS (Barbados)
map (13° 10′N 59° 32′W) 3:75
FOUR-EYED FISH 8:252–253 *illus.*
FOUR FREEDOMS 8:253
human rights 10:298
4-H PROGRAM 8:253 *bibliog.*
Smith-Lever Act of 1914 17:372
FOUR HORSEMEN OF THE APOCALYPSE, THE (book) 8:253
Blasco-Ibáñez, Vicente 3:328
Dürer, Albrecht 3:387 *illus.*; 6:304; 16:155 *illus.*
442nd REGIMENTAL COMBAT TEAM
Japanese Americans 14:442
Oriental Americans 14:442
FOUR-O'CLOCK (botany) 8:253
flower 9:87 *illus.*
FOUR POWER TREATY (1921)
Washington Conference 20:44
FOUR QUARTETS (poems) 8:253 *bibliog.*
Eliot, T. S. 7:140
FOURCHE LAFAVE RIVER
map (34° 58′N 92° 35′W) 2:166
FOURCHE MOUNTAIN
map (34° 50′N 93° 20′W) 2:166
FOURCHU (Nova Scotia)
map (45° 43′N 60° 15′W) 14:269
FOURCROY, ANTOINE FRANÇOIS, COMTE DE 8:253 *bibliog.*
FOURIER, CHARLES 8:253 *bibliog.*
Considerant, Victor Prosper 5:206
Marxism 13:183
Meeker, Nathan Cook 13:278
right-to-work laws 16:222
socialism 18:19
utopias 19:498
FOURIER, JOSEPH 8:253 *bibliog.*
Fourier analysis 8:253–254
mathematics, history of 13:226
FOURIER ANALYSIS 8:253–254 *bibliog.*
harmonics 10:51
Jordan, Camille 11:450
mathematics, history of 13:226
motion, harmonic 13:608–609
periodic function 15:166
X-ray diffraction 20:308
FOURNEYRON, BENOÎT
technology, history of 19:66
FOURNIER, HENRI ALAIN *see* ALAIN-FOURNIER
FOURTEEN POINTS 8:254 *bibliog.*
Paris Peace Conference 15:88
United States, history of the 19:453
Wilson, Woodrow 20:167
World War I 20:241
14TH AMENDMENT 8:254 *bibliog.*
Baker v. *Carr* 3:28
black codes 3:313–314
Civil Rights Cases 5:13–14
due process 6:293
Escobedo v. *Illinois* 7:237
Gideon v. *Wainwright* 9:177
Gitlow v. *New York* 9:191
Griswold v. *Connecticut* 9:367–368
juvenile delinquency 11:480
equal protection of the laws 7:223–224
5th Amendment 8:74
freedom of religion 8:298
freedom of speech 8:298
Furman v. *Georgia* 8:371–372
Hurtado v. *California* 10:319
jury 11:477
law, history of 12:246
Mapp v. *Ohio* 13:138
Munn v. *Illinois* 13:643
naturalization 14:50
Plessy v. *Ferguson* 15:368
Reconstruction 16:109
Reynolds v. *Sims* 16:191
Roth v. *United States* 16:321–322
Shelley v. *Kraemer* 17:253–254
6th Amendment 17:331
Slaughterhouse Cases 17:351
text 5:221–222
trial 19:292
Twining v. *New Jersey* 19:360
United States, history of the 19:449
University of California v. *Bakke* 19:470
4th AMENDMENT 8:254–255 *bibliog.*
evidence 7:317–318
Griswold v. *Connecticut* 9:368
Mapp v. *Ohio* 13:138
search warrant 17:175
self-incrimination 17:191
text 5:220
warrant 20:30
wiretapping 20:183
writ of assistance 20:291
FOURTH DIMENSION
relativity 16:135 *illus.*
space-time continuum 18:137
world line 20:219
FOURTH ESTATE 8:255
FOURTH OF JULY *see* INDEPENDENCE DAY
FOURTH REPUBLIC *see* FRANCE, HISTORY OF
FOUTA DJALLON HIGHLANDS
map (11° 30′N 12° 30′W) 9:397
FOVEA
eye 7:348 *illus.*
FOVEAUX STRAIT
map (46° 35′S 168° 0′E) 14:158
FOWL *see* POULTRY
FOWLER (Colorado)
map (38° 8′N 104° 1′W) 5:116
FOWLER (Indiana)
map (40° 37′N 87° 19′W) 11:111
FOWLER (Kansas)
map (37° 23′N 100° 12′W) 12:18
FOWLER (Michigan)
map (43° 0′N 84° 44′W) 13:377
FOWLER, FRANCIS GEORGE
Fowler, H.W. 8:255
FOWLER, H.W. 8:255 *bibliog.*
FOWLES, JOHN 8:255
FOX (American Indians) 8:255 *bibliog.*
Black Hawk War 3:315
Chief Keokuk 11:121 *illus.*
Iowa 11:247
Sauk 17:96
Wananikwe 20:21
FOX (animal) 4:283 *illus.*; 8:255–256 *bibliog., illus.*
Arctic 2:141 *illus.*
fur 8:370 *table*
FOX, CAROL
Chicago, Lyric Opera of 4:342
FOX, CHARLES JAMES 8:256 *bibliog., illus.*
FOX, GEORGE 8:256 *bibliog.*
Friends, Society of 8:332–333
FOX, MARGARET 8:256
FOX, VIRGIL 8:256
FOX, WILLIAM
film, history of 8:82
FOX HARBOUR (Newfoundland)
map (52° 22′N 55° 41′W) 14:166
FOX HUNT 10:313 *illus.*
FOX ISLAND (Washington)
map (47° 16′N 122° 37′W) 20:35
FOX ISLANDS (Alaska)
map (54° 0′N 168° 0′W) 1:242
FOX LAKE (Illinois)
map (42° 25′N 88° 9′W) 11:42
map (42° 25′N 88° 9′W) 11:42
FOX RIVER (Illinois)
map (41° 21′N 88° 50′W) 11:42
FOX RIVER (Wisconsin)
map (44° 32′N 88° 1′W) 20:185
FOX TERRIER 6:220 *illus.*; 8:256–257 *bibliog., illus.*
FOX-TROT 8:257
FOX VALLEY (Saskatchewan)
map (50° 29′N 109° 28′W) 17:81
FOXE, JOHN 8:257 *bibliog.*
FOXE BASIN
map (68° 25′N 77° 0′W) 14:258
FOXE PENINSULA
map (65° 0′N 76° 0′W) 14:258
FOXGLOVE (botany) 5:121 *illus.*; 8:257 *illus.*
digitalis 6:175
folk medicine 8:201
medicinal plants 13:266
poisonous plants and animals 15:383
FOXHOUND *see* AMERICAN FOXHOUND; ENGLISH FOXHOUND
FOXPARK (Wyoming)
map (41° 5′N 106° 9′W) 20:301
FOXTAIL (botany) 8:257
FOXWORTH (Mississippi)
map (31° 14′N 89° 52′W) 13:469
FOXX, JIMMIE 8:257
FOY, EDDIE 8:257
FOYLE, LAKE
map (55° 7′N 7° 8′W) 11:258
FOYT, A. J. 8:257 *bibliog.*
FOZZIE BEAR *see* MUPPETS
FRACASTORO, GIROLAMO 8:257
bacteria 3:16
syphilis
medicine 13:269
FRACCI, CARLA 8:257–258 *bibliog.*
FRACTAL 8:258 *bibliog.*
computer graphics 5:160n
FRACTION 8:258 *bibliog., illus.*
arithmetic 2:158
Brouncker, William 3:512
decimal 6:73 *illus.*
mathematics, history of 13:223
rational number 16:92
FRACTIONATION 8:258
See also CHROMATOGRAPHY; ION EXCHANGE
distillation 6:200
phase equilibrium 15:223
FRACTURE 8:258–259 *bibliog.*
bone diseases 3:377
Chinese medicine 4:391
orthopedics 14:450
FRACTURE (geology)
fault 8:36–38
joint (geology) 11:440
oceanic fracture zones 14:339
FRACTURE ZONES, OCEANIC *see* OCEANIC FRACTURE ZONES
FRAGONARD, JEAN HONORÉ 8:259 *bibliog., illus.*
Bathers 8:259 *illus.*
The Swing 16:265 *illus.*
FRAGRANCES *see* FLAVORS AND FRAGRANCES; PERFUME
FRAGRANT SNOWBALL (botany) 19:568 *illus.*
FRAHM, KARL HERBERT *see* BRANDT, WILLY
FRAILE MUERTO (Uruguay)
map (32° 31′S 54° 32′W) 19:488
FRAKTUR
folk art 8:197 *illus.*
FRAMINGHAM (Massachusetts)
map (42° 17′N 71° 25′W) 13:206
FRAMPTON, HOLLIS
film, history of 8:87
FRANC-TIREUR 8:278 *illus.*
FRANCE 8:259–265 *bibliog., illus., map, table*
agriculture and fishing 8:264
aircraft, military *see* AIRCRAFT, MILITARY
archaeology
Carnac 4:154
cave dwellers 4:224
Combe Grenal 5:130
Cro-Magnon man 5:353–354
Font de Gaume 8:205
lake dwelling 12:171
Lartet, Édouard Armand 12:208
Lascaux 12:210
Les Combarelles 12:296
Levalloisian 12:301–302
megalith 13:278–279
menhir 13:297
Niaux Cave 14:177
Terra Amata 15:39 *illus.*; 19:119
Trois Frères, Les 19:305

Vallonet Cave **19**:508
Vix **19**:623
army
French foreign legion **8**:310
rank, military **16**:86 *table*
regiment **16**:128
art *see* FRENCH ART AND ARCHITECTURE
cities
Aix-en-Provence **1**:228–229
Ajaccio **1**:229
Amiens **1**:369
Angers **1**:414
Angoulême **2**:6
Argenteuil **2**:146
Arras **2**:188
Aubusson **2**:316
Avignon **2**:376
Bayonne **3**:134
Besançon **3**:227
Béziers **3**:233
Biarritz **3**:237
Bordeaux **3**:396
Boulogne-sur-Mer **3**:422
Brest **3**:474
Caen **4**:12–13
Calais **4**:21
Cambrai **4**:50
Cannes **4**:109
Carcassonne **4**:141
Chartres **4**:300
Cherbourg **4**:331
Clermont-Ferrand **2**:368; **5**:52
Clichy **5**:54
Colmar **5**:105
Dieppe **6**:162
Dijon **6**:175
Douai **6**:245
Dunkerque **6**:300
Foix **8**:193
Fontainebleau **8**:205
Grenoble **9**:359
La Rochelle **12**:148
Le Havre **12**:254
Le Mans **12**:254
Lille **12**:341
Limoges **12**:345–346
Lourdes **12**:436
Lyon **12**:477–478 *illus.*
Marseille **13**:170–171 *illus.*
Metz **13**:350
Montbéliard **13**:551
Montpellier **13**:557–558
Mulhouse **13**:636
Nancy **14**:12
Nantes **14**:13
Narbonne **14**:21
Nice **14**:180 *illus.*
Nîmes **14**:198
Orléans **14**:446
Paris **15**:84–87 *illus., map*
Pau **15**:116
Périgueux **15**:166
Perpignan **15**:178
Poitiers **15**:385–386
Reims **16**:131
Rennes **16**:157
Rouen **16**:324
Saint-Denis **17**:17
Saint-Étienne **17**:18
Saint-Nazaire **17**:24
Strasbourg **18**:289
Toulon **19**:249–250
Toulouse **19**:250
Tours **19**:253–254
Troyes **19**:313
Verdun **19**:550
Versailles **19**:561
Vichy **19**:571
climate **8**:261 *table*
mistral **13**:482
Communism *see* COMMUNISM
cosmetics **5**:281–282
dance
Académie Royale de Danse **1**:69
gavotte **9**:63
minuet **13**:461
defense, national **6**:82 *table*
neutron bomb **14**:109
demography **8**:262–263
economic activity **8**:263–265
banking systems **3**:68
consumer price index **11**:170 *table*
Monnet, Jean **13**:536
Rothschild (family) **16**:322
unemployment rate **7**:160
value-added tax **19**:509
education **7**:61; **8**:263
academy **1**:70–71
Buisson, Ferdinand Édouard **3**:552–553
European universities **7**:307 *table*
Ferry, Jules François Camille **8**:60
Guizot, François **9**:401
lycée **12**:474
Paris, Universities of **15**:88
St. Cyr **17**:17
Thénard, Louis Jacques, Baron **19**:155
energy and power **8**:264
breeder reactor **3**:472
solar energy **18**:42 *illus.*
tidal energy power station **19**:192 *illus.*
flag **8**:259 *illus.*
foreign policy **8**:226
government **8**:265
French Community **8**:309
medals and decorations **13**:262–263 *illus.*
municipal government **13**:642
police **15**:396
republic **16**:172
health **8**:263
psychopathology, treatment of **15**:599
history *see* FRANCE, HISTORY OF
house (in Western architecture) **10**:268 *illus.*
Institut de France **11**:195
land and resources **8**:261–262 *table*
languages
Basque language **3**:116
Celtic languages **4**:241
French language **16**:280–281
Provençal language **16**:280–281
Romance languages **16**:280
libraries
Bibliothèque Nationale **3**:243
literature *see* FRENCH LITERATURE
manufacturing **8**:263–264 *illus.*
automotive industry **2**:366–367 *table*
silk **17**:307
map (46° 0′N 2° 0′E) **7**:268
mining **8**:264 *illus.*
Monaco **13**:515–517
national anthem
"Marseillaise, La" **13**:170
navy
Darlan, Jean **6**:39
Gloire (battleship) **3**:127 *illus.*
man-of-war **8**:333 *illus.*
rank, military **16**:87 *table*
newspapers
Figaro, Le **8**:75
Philipon, Charles **15**:235
overseas departments and territories
French Guiana **8**:310–311 *illus., map, table*
French Polynesia **8**:321–322
French Southern and Antarctic Territories **8**:326
Guadeloupe **9**:385
Martinique **13**:181
Mayotte **13**:248
New Caledonia **14**:119 *map*
Réunion **16**:184
Saint Martin **17**:24
Saint Pierre and Miquelon **17**:26
Wallis and Futuna Islands **20**:16
patron saint
Denis, Saint **6**:108
people **8**:262–263
Basques **3**:116
women in society **20**:204 *table*
physical features
Belfort Gap **3**:174
Blanc, Mont **3**:326
Gris-Nez, Cape **9**:367
Guettard, Jean Étienne **9**:392
Massif Central **13**:213
Mer de Glace **13**:303
Mont-Saint-Michel **13**:544
Riviera **16**:234
stalactite and stalagmite **18**:213 *illus.*
Vosges **19**:635
Pic du Midi Observatory **14**:318 *illus., illus.*
pistol **15**:318
postage stamp **15**:230 *illus.*
regions
Alsace-Lorraine **1**:310 *map*
Angoumois **2**:6
Anjou **2**:30 *map*
Argonne **2**:152
Artois **2**:224
Aunis **2**:324
Auvergne **2**:368–369
Béarn **3**:144
Belleau Wood **3**:187
Berry **3**:225
Bourbonnais **3**:423
Brittany **3**:498 *map*
Burgundy **3**:570–571 *map*
Champagne **4**:276 *map*
Comtat **5**:167
Corsica **5**:277 *illus.*
Côte d'Azur **5**:304
Dauphiné **6**:46
Flanders **8**:152 *map*
Franche-Comté **8**:273
Gascony **9**:54
Guiènne **9**:394
Île-de-France **11**:40 *map*
Languedoc **12**:199
Limousin **12**:346–347 *map*
Lyonnais **12**:478
Maine **13**:74
Marche **13**:146
Nivernais **14**:204
Normandy **14**:220 *map*
Orléanais **14**:445–446 *map*
Picardy **15**:290
Poitou **15**:386
Provence **15**:583 *map*
Roussillon **16**:327
Saintonge **17**:28
Touraine **19**:251
rivers, lakes, and waterways **8**:261
Aisne River **1**:228
Dordogne River **7**:270 *illus.*
Garonne River **9**:50
Gavarnie Falls **9**:62
Isère River **11**:286
Loire River **12**:398
Marne River **13**:162
Rhône River **16**:203
Saône River **17**:72
Seine River **17**:189
Somme River **18**:62
social security **18**:14
socialism *see* SOCIALISM
space exploration
Centre Nationale d'Études Spatiales **4**:255
tennis **19**:108
theater
Antoine, André **2**:69
Barrault, Jean Louis **3**:93
Bernhardt, Sarah **3**:221–222
boulevard theater **3**:421
Comédie Française, La **5**:131
Comédie Italienne, La **5**:132
Copeau, Jacques **5**:248–249
drame bourgeois **6**:262
Dullin, Charles **6**:296
Folies-Bergère **8**:195
Guignol, Grand **9**:394–395
Jouvet, Louis **11**:456
Talma, François Joseph **19**:17
theater, history of the **19**:147; **19**:149
theater of the absurd **19**:154
Théâtre National Populaire (TNP) **19**:154
Vilar, Jean **19**:596
well-made play **20**:99
titles of nobility **19**:214 *table*
trade and tourism **8**:264–265
transportation **8**:264
locomotive **12**:390 *illus.*
railroad **16**:73; **16**:75 *illus.*
roads and highways **16**:237
urban planning *see* URBAN PLANNING
vegetation and animal life **8**:261–262
wine **20**:175
FRANCE, ANATOLE **8**:273 *bibliog.*
FRANCE, HISTORY OF **8**:265–273 *bibliog., illus., maps, table*
Algeria **1**:289
Aquitaine **2**:95–96
Burgundy **3**:570–571 *map*
colonialism **5**:111–112
exploration and settlement in colonial America **19**:437 *map*
French Empire **8**:309–310
French Equatorial Africa **8**:310
French West Africa **8**:326
Gabon **9**:5
Guiènne **9**:394
historians *see* HISTORY—French historians
Kampuchea (Cambodia) **12**:12
Laos **12**:204
liberalism **12**:312
Louisiana **12**:434
Madagascar **13**:39
mathematics, history of **13**:226
metric system **13**:345
Morocco **13**:586–587
Paris **15**:87
political parties **15**:403
rulers **8**:270 *table*
socialism **18**:19–23
125 BC–751 AD Roman and early Frankish period
Clovis **5**:70
Gaul **8**:265–266; **9**:60–61
Goths **9**:263
Merovingians (dynasty) **13**:312
Neustria **14**:107
751–987 Carolingian kingdom **8**:270 *table*
Carolingians **4**:162
Charlemagne **4**:289–290 *map*
Charles II, Frankish emperor (Charles the Bald) **4**:292
Charles III, Frankish emperor (Charles the Fat) **4**:292
Charles III, King (Charles the Simple) **4**:292
Charles Martel **4**:291
Frankish kingdom **8**:266–267
Louis IV, King (Louis d'Outremer) **12**:423–424
987–1328 Capetian kingdom **8**:270 *table*
Blanche of Castile **3**:327
Bouvines, Battle of **3**:426
Capetians (dynasty) **4**:122–123; **8**:267–268
Charles IV, King (Charles the Fair) **4**:292
Eleanor of Aquitaine **7**:103
English land holdings (12th century) **8**:267 *map*
feudalism **8**:64–65
Henry I, King **10**:127
Hugh Capet, King **10**:292
Louis IX, King **12**:424–425
Louis VI, King (Louis the Fat) **12**:424
Louis VII, King **12**:424
Louis VIII, King **12**:424
Philip I, King **15**:232
Philip II, King (Philip Augustus) **15**:232
Philip III, King (Philip the Bold) **15**:232
Philip IV, King (Philip the Fair) **15**:232–233
Philip V, King (Philip the Tall) **15**:233
1328–1589 Valois rule **8**:270 *table*
Anne of Brittany **2**:32
Armagnacs and Burgundians **2**:171
Bourbon, Charles de Bourbon, Duc de **3**:423
Catherine de Médicis **4**:209
Charles V, Holy Roman Emperor **4**:295
Charles V, King (Charles the Wise) **4**:292–293
Charles VI, King (Charles the Mad or Well-Beloved) **4**:293
Charles VII, King (Charles the Well-Served) **4**:293
Charles VIII, King **4**:293
consolidation of royal power **8**:268
dauphin **6**:46
Edward, the Black Prince **7**:67
Europe, history of **7**:286
Francis I, King of France **8**:275–276
Francis II, King of France **8**:276
Guise (family) **9**:400
Henry II, King **10**:127
Henry III, King of France **10**:127
Henry VIII, King of England **10**:127
Hundred Years' War *see* HUNDRED YEARS' WAR
Italian Wars **11**:319–320
John II, King (John the Good) **11**:427
Louis XI, King **12**:425
Louis XII, King **12**:425
Margaret of Valois **13**:149
Orléans (family) **14**:446
Philip the Bold, Duke of Burgundy **15**:231
Philip VI, King **15**:233
Religion, Wars of **16**:141
Saint Bartholomew's Day Massacre **17**:16
Valois (dynasty) **19**:508
Viète, François **19**:580
1589–1789 Bourbons and First Republic **8**:270 *table*
American Revolution **1**:359 *map*; **1**:360–361
Anne of Austria **2**:32
Bourbon (dynasty) **3**:423
Bourbon, Louis Henri de Bourbon-Condé, Duc de **3**:423
Camisards **4**:62
Choiseul, Étienne François, Duc de **4**:403
civil wars, insurrections, and annexations **8**:270 *map*
Colbert, Jean Baptiste **5**:97

FRANCE, HISTORY OF (cont.)
Condé (family) **5**:172
costume **5**:299–301 *illus.*
Devolution, War of **6**:143
Diamond Necklace, Affair of the **6**:152
Europe, history of **7**:290–291
European possessions *c.*1648 **7**:289 *map*
Franche-Comté **8**:273
Fronde **8**:339
Gallicanism **9**:19
German acquisitions in 1648 **9**:151 *map*
Grand Alliance, War of the **9**:284
Great Britain, history of **9**:315
Henry IV, King **10**:128
Huguenots **10**:294–295
intendant **11**:206
Louis XIII, King **12**:425–426
Louis XIV, King **12**:426–427
Louis XV, King **12**:427
Louis XVI, king **12**:427–428
Louis XVII, King **12**:428
Marie Antoinette **13**:151
Marie de Médicis **13**:151–152
Mazarin, Jules **13**:249–250
Mississippi Scheme **13**:474
Nantes, Edict of **14**:13
Necker, Jacques **14**:75
old regime and the Enlightenment **8**:269
Orléans, Philippe II, Duc d' **14**:446
parlement **15**:92
Pompadour, Jeanne Antoinette Poisson, Marquise de **15**:423
Quebec (province in Canada) **16**:20
Richelieu, Armand Jean du Plessis, Cardinal et Duc de **16**:213
Savoy (region) **17**:102
Seven Years' War *see* SEVEN YEARS' WAR
Spanish Succession, War of the *see* SPANISH SUCCESSION, WAR OF THE
States-General **18**:234
Thirty Years' War *see* THIRTY YEARS' WAR
Turgot, Anne Robert Jacques **19**:341–342
1789–1815 French Revolutionary and Napoleonic era
Austerlitz, Battle of **2**:326
Beauharnais (family) **3**:146
Berthier, Louis Alexandre **3**:226
Bonaparte (family) **3**:375–376
Concordat of 1801 **5**:171
Consulate **5**:225
Continental System **5**:230
Declaration of the Rights of Man and of the Citizen (1789) **3**:253–254
Directory **6**:187–188
European possessions 1815 **7**:291 *map*
extent of the Empire **14**:18 *map*
French Empire **8**:309
French Revolution *see* FRENCH REVOLUTION
French Revolutionary Wars **8**:325–326
Haiti **10**:16
Italy, history of **11**:329
Josephine **11**:452
LaPlace, Pierre Simon de **12**:205
Latin American territory *c.*1790 **12**:219 *map*
Murat, Joachim **13**:647
Napoleon I, Emperor of the French (Napoléon Bonaparte) **14**:15–18
Napoleonic Wars *see* NAPOLEONIC WARS
Netherlands **14**:102–103
Talleyrand-Périgord, Charles Maurice de **19**:16–17
1815–1848 Bourbon Restoration and Orleans monarchy **8**:272 *table*
Blanc, Louis **3**:326
Charles X, King **4**:293
Guizot, François **9**:401–402
July Revolution **11**:466
LaPlace, Pierre Simon de **12**:205
Louis Philippe, King **12**:423
Louis XVIII, King **12**:428
Revolutions of 1848 **16**:188 *illus.*
Talleyrand-Périgord, Charles Maurice de **19**:16–17
1848–1870 Second Republic and Empire **8**:271–272
Crimean War *see* CRIMEAN WAR
Indochina **11**:146
Nadar **14**:4
Napoleon III, Emperor (Louis Napoléon Bonaparte) **14**:18–19
Offenbach, Jacques **14**:353–354
1870–1940 Third Republic **8**:272
Action Française **1**:89
Bloch, Marc **3**:334
Blum, Léon **3**:346
Boulanger, Georges **3**:421
Briand, Aristide **3**:476
Commune of Paris **5**:142
Daladier, Édouard **6**:11
Doumergue, Gaston **6**:249
Dreyfus affair **6**:271–272
Franco-Prussian War *see* FRANCO-PRUSSIAN WAR
French Empire **8**:309–310 *map*
Gambetta, Léon **9**:24–25
Hitler, Adolf **10**:188
Laval, Pierre **12**:240–241
Lebanon **12**:267
MacMahon, Marie Edme Patrice Maurice de **13**:33
Millerand, Alexandre **13**:429
Moroccan crises **13**:583
Panama Canal **15**:56–57
Poincaré, Raymond **15**:380
presidents **8**:270 *table*
Simon, Jules François **17**:315
Stavisky affair **18**:239
Syria **18**:414
Thiers, Adolphe **19**:168–169
Triple Entente **19**:302
Vietnam **19**:583
World War I *see* WORLD WAR I
1940–1945 World War II
Darlan, Jean François **6**:39
de Gaulle, Charles **6**:59
Laval, Pierre **12**:240–241
Pétain, Henri Philippe **15**:199
Vichy Government **19**:571
World War II *see* WORLD WAR II
1946–1958 Fourth Republic **8**:272–273
Algerian War **1**:290
Auriol, Vincent **2**:324
Dien Bien Phu, Battle of **6**:162
French Union **8**:326
Indochina holdings **19**:585 *map*
Mollet, Guy **13**:510
Monnet, Jean **13**:536
presidents **8**:270 *table*
Suez Crisis **18**:325
Vietnam War *see* VIETNAM WAR
1958–Present Fifth Republic **8**:273
Chirac, Jacques **4**:397
de Gaulle, Charles **6**:59
Debré, Michel **6**:70
Giscard d'Estaing, Valéry **9**:190
Greenpeace **9**:354
Mauroy, Pierre **13**:237
Mitterrand, François **13**:485–486
Pompidou, Georges **15**:425
presidents **8**:270 *table*
FRANCESCA, PIERO DELLA *see* PIERO DELLA FRANCESCA
FRANCESVILLE (Indiana)
map (40° 59'N 86° 53'W) **11**:111
FRANCEVILLE (Gabon)
map (1° 38'S 13° 35'E) **9**:5
FRANCHE-COMTÉ (France) **8**:273
Besançon **3**:227
Burgundy **3**:570
FRANCHÈRE, JOSEPH
Canadian art and architecture **4**:89
FRANCHET D'ESPEREY, LOUIS
World War I **20**:223–224; **20**:243
FRANCHISE (business) **8**:273 *bibliog.*
hotel **10**:262
retailing **16**:183
FRANCHISE (political) *see* SUFFRAGE
FRANCIA (Uruguay)
map (32° 33'S 56° 37'W) **19**:488
FRANCIA, JOSÉ GASPAR RODRÍGUEZ DE **8**:273–274
FRANCIS, LAKE
map (45° 2'N 71° 20'W) **14**:123
FRANCIS, LYDIA MARIA *see* CHILD, LYDIA MARIA
FRANCIS, SAM **8**:274 *bibliog., illus.*
Composition **8**:274 *illus.*
FRANCIS I, EMPEROR OF AUSTRIA *see* FRANCIS II, HOLY ROMAN EMPEROR
FRANCIS I, HOLY ROMAN EMPEROR **8**:276
Polish Succession, War of the **15**:398
FRANCIS I, KING OF FRANCE **5**:69 *illus.*; **8**:275–276 *bibliog., illus.*; **16**:155 *illus.*
Fontainebleau (France) **8**:205
Fontainebleau, Château de **8**:205
Fontainebleau, school of **8**:205–206
Louvre **12**:437
meeting with Henry VIII on the Field of the Cloth of Gold **9**:312 *illus.*
Montmorency, Anne, Duc de **13**:557
FRANCIS II, HOLY ROMAN EMPEROR **8**:276 *bibliog.*
Holy Alliance **10**:209
FRANCIS II, KING OF FRANCE **8**:276
FRANCIS OF ASSISI, SAINT **8**:274 *bibliog., illus.*
stigmata **18**:268
FRANCIS JOSEPH, EMPEROR OF AUSTRIA **8**:274–275 *bibliog., illus.*
Elizabeth, Empress of Austria **7**:141
FRANCIS DE SALES, SAINT **8**:274 *bibliog.*
FRANCIS XAVIER, SAINT **8**:275 *bibliog., illus.*
Goa, Daman, and Diu **9**:214
FRANCISCANS **8**:276–277 *bibliog.*
Alexander of Hales **1**:275
Anthony of Padua, Saint **2**:50
Bonaventure, Saint **3**:376
Francis of Assisi, Saint **8**:274
Gregory IX, Pope **9**:357
Honorius III, Pope **10**:224
John XXII, Pope **11**:428
Mexico, history of **13**:363
Middle Ages **14**:394–396 *illus.*
missions
California **4**:36
missions, Christian **13**:467–468
Spanish missions **18**:160–161
monastic art and architecture **13**:518
FRANCISCO DE ORELLANA (Ecuador)
map (0° 28'S 76° 58'W) **7**:52
FRANCISCO LISBOA, ANTONIO *see* ALEIJADINHO
FRANCISTOWN (Botswana)
climate **3**:417 *table*
map (21° 11'S 27° 32'E) **3**:416
FRANCIUM **8**:277
alkali metals **1**:295
element **7**:130 *table*
Group IA periodic table **15**:167
metal, metallic element **13**:328
FRANCK, CÉSAR **8**:277 *bibliog.*
Chausson, Ernest **4**:305
Indy, Vincent d' **11**:160
FRANCK, JAMES **8**:277
FRANCK, JOHANN
music, history of Western **13**:666
FRANCO, FRANCISCO **8**:277–278 *bibliog., illus.*
caudillo **4**:219
Juan Carlos I, King of Spain **11**:457
Santa Cruz de Tenerife (Canary Islands) **17**:68
Spain, history of **18**:149 *illus.*
Spanish Civil War **18**:156–157
FRANCO-PRUSSIAN WAR **8**:278–279 *bibliog., illus., map*
balloon **3**:52
causes **8**:278–279
French soldiers **8**:278 *illus.*
Gambetta, Léon **9**:24
Germany, history of **9**:152–153
Krupp (family) **12**:132
major battles **8**:278 *map*
Napoleon III, Emperor of the French (Louis Napoléon Bonaparte) **14**:19
Prussian soliders **8**:279 *illus.*
World War I **20**:219
FRANCO-SARDINIAN WAR
Victor Emmanuel II, King of Italy **19**:573
FRANÇOIS (Newfoundland)
map (47° 35'N 56° 45'W) **14**:166
FRANÇOIS, CLAUDE *see* LUC, FRÈRE (Claude François)
FRANÇOIS, HERMANN K. VON
World War I **20**:224–226
FRANCONI (family) **8**:279
FRANCONIA **8**:279
German territories *c.*1176 **9**:149 *map*
FRANCONIA NOTCH **14**:125 *illus.*
map (44° 8'N 71° 41'W) **14**:123
FRANCONIAN DYNASTY *see* SALIAN (dynasty)
FRANJU, GEORGES
Feuillade, Louis **8**:66
FRANK, ANNE **8**:279 *bibliog.*
FRANK, ILYA MIKHAILOVICH **8**:279
FRANK, JACOB **8**:279
FRANK, JEROME
legal realism **12**:243
FRANK, ROBERT **8**:280
photography, history and art of **15**:272
FRANKEL, ZACHARIAS **8**:280 *bibliog.*
FRANKENMUTH (Michigan)
map (43° 20'N 83° 44'W) **13**:377
FRANKENSTEIN (book) **8**:280 *bibliog.*
frontispiece to 1831 edition **17**:143 *illus.*
Shelley, Mary Wollstonecraft **17**:253
FRANKENTHALER, HELEN **8**:280 *bibliog., illus.*
Blue Territory **8**:280 *illus.*
FRANKFIELD (Jamaica)
map (18° 9'N 77° 22'W) **11**:351
FRANKFORT (Indiana)
map (40° 17'N 86° 31'W) **11**:111
FRANKFORT (Kansas)
map (39° 42'N 96° 25'W) **12**:18
FRANKFORT (Kentucky) **8**:280
map (38° 12'N 84° 52'W) **12**:47
FRANKFORT (Maine)
map (44° 36'N 68° 53'W) **13**:70
FRANKFORT (Michigan)
map (44° 38'N 86° 14'W) **13**:377
FRANKFORT (Ohio)
map (39° 24'N 83° 11'W) **14**:357
FRANKFORT (South Dakota)
map (44° 53'N 98° 18'W) **18**:103
FRANKFURT (Germany, East and West)
map (52° 20'N 14° 33'E) **9**:140
FRANKFURT, TREATY OF (1871)
Franco-Prussian War **8**:279
FRANKFURT AM MAIN (West Germany) **8**:280–281 *illus.*
map (50° 7'N 8° 40'E) **9**:140
FRANKFURT PARLIAMENT **8**:281 *bibliog.*
Revolutions of 1848 **16**:189
FRANKFURTER (meat) *see* SAUSAGE
FRANKFURTER, FELIX **8**:281 *bibliog., illus.*; **12**:246 *illus.*
American Civil Liberties Union **8**:281
Supreme Court of the United States **8**:281; **18**:357
FRANKINCENSE **8**:282
FRANKISH EMPIRE *see* FRANKS
FRANKISTS
Frank, Jacob **8**:279
FRANKL, PAUL **8**:282 *bibliog.*
FRANKL, VIKTOR **8**:282 *bibliog.*
FRANKLAND, SIR EDWARD **8**:282
FRANKLIN (county in Alabama)
map (34° 25'N 87° 50'W) **1**:234
FRANKLIN (Arizona)
map (32° 42'N 109° 5'W) **2**:160
FRANKLIN (county in Arkansas)
map (35° 35'N 93° 55'W) **2**:166
FRANKLIN (county in Florida)
map (29° 45'N 84° 50'W) **8**:172
FRANKLIN (Georgia)
map (33° 17'N 85° 8'W) **9**:114
FRANKLIN (county in Georgia)
map (34° 20'N 83° 15'W) **9**:114
FRANKLIN (county in Idaho)
map (42° 10'N 111° 50'W) **11**:26
FRANKLIN (county in Illinois)
map (38° 0'N 88° 55'W) **11**:42
FRANKLIN (Indiana)
map (39° 29'N 86° 3'W) **11**:111
FRANKLIN (county in Indiana)
map (39° 25'N 85° 1'W) **11**:111
FRANKLIN (county in Iowa)
map (42° 43'N 93° 15'W) **11**:244
FRANKLIN (county in Kansas)
map (38° 35'N 95° 15'W) **12**:18
FRANKLIN (Kentucky)
map (36° 43'N 86° 35'W) **12**:47
FRANKLIN (county in Kentucky)
map (38° 14'N 84° 52'W) **12**:47
FRANKLIN (Louisiana)
map (29° 48'N 91° 30'W) **12**:430
FRANKLIN (county in Louisiana)
map (32° 8'N 91° 40'W) **12**:430
FRANKLIN (Maine)
map (44° 32'N 68° 9'W) **13**:70
FRANKLIN (county in Maine)
map (44° 55'N 70° 25'W) **13**:70
FRANKLIN (Massachusetts)
map (42° 5'N 71° 24'W) **13**:206
FRANKLIN (county in Massachusetts)
map (42° 36'N 72° 36'W) **13**:206
FRANKLIN (county in Mississippi)
map (31° 30'N 90° 55'W) **13**:469
FRANKLIN (county in Missouri)
map (38° 25'N 91° 3'W) **13**:476
FRANKLIN (Nebraska)
map (40° 6'N 98° 57'W) **14**:70
FRANKLIN (county in Nebraska)
map (40° 10'N 98° 55'W) **14**:70
FRANKLIN (New Hampshire)
map (43° 27'N 71° 39'W) **14**:123
FRANKLIN (New Jersey)
franklinite **8**:285
map (41° 7'N 74° 35'W) **14**:129

FRANKLIN (county in New York)
map (44° 35′N 74° 15′W) **14**:149
FRANKLIN (North Carolina)
map (35° 11′N 83° 23′W) **14**:242
FRANKLIN (county in North Carolina)
map (36° 10′N 78° 15′W) **14**:242
FRANKLIN (Ohio)
map (39° 34′N 84° 18′W) **14**:357
FRANKLIN (county in Ohio)
map (40° 0′N 83° 0′W) **14**:357
FRANKLIN (Pennsylvania)
map (41° 24′N 79° 50′W) **15**:147
FRANKLIN (county in Pennsylvania)
map (39° 55′N 77° 43′W) **15**:147
FRANKLIN (Tennessee)
map (35° 55′N 86° 52′W) **19**:104
FRANKLIN (county in Tennessee)
map (35° 10′N 86° 5′W) **19**:104
FRANKLIN (Texas)
map (31° 2′N 96° 29′W) **19**:129
FRANKLIN (county in Texas)
map (33° 10′N 95° 15′W) **19**:129
FRANKLIN (county in Vermont)
map (44° 52′N 72° 55′W) **19**:554
FRANKLIN (Virginia)
map (36° 41′N 76° 55′W) **19**:607
FRANKLIN (county in Virginia)
map (37° 0′N 79° 50′W) **19**:607
FRANKLIN (county in Washington)
map (46° 30′N 119° 0′W) **20**:35
FRANKLIN (West Virginia)
map (38° 39′N 79° 20′W) **20**:111
FRANKLIN (Wisconsin)
map (42° 54′N 88° 3′W) **20**:185
FRANKLIN, ARETHA **8**:282
soul music **18**:71 *illus.*
FRANKLIN, BENJAMIN **8**:282–284 *bibliog., illus.*
Albany Congress **1**:251–252
bookman and printer **8**:282–283
civic leader and scientist **8**:283
defender of American rights **8**:283–284
diplomat **8**:284
electricity **7**:107–108 *illus.*; **7**:120
Fothergill, John **8**:248
glass harmonica **9**:201–202
Hutchinson, Thomas **10**:323
"JOIN or DIE" cartoon **1**:355 *illus.*
lightning rods **12**:340
Pennsylvania, University of **15**:152
physics, history of **15**:284 *illus.*
politician and provincial agent **8**:283
Poor Richard's Almanack **15**:429
postal services **15**:459–460 *illus.*
FRANKLIN, FREDERIC **8**:284
Ballets Russes de Monte Carlo **3**:48
FRANKLIN, JAMES
Franklin, Benjamin **8**:282–283
FRANKLIN, SIR JOHN **8**:284–285 *bibliog., illus.*
Arctic **2**:142 *map*
Great Bear Lake **9**:309
Hall, Charles Francis **10**:21
Mackenzie River **13**:29
Northwest Passage **14**:256–257 *map*
Prudhoe Bay **15**:585
FRANKLIN, JOHN HOPE **8**:285
FRANKLIN, MILES **2**:343 *illus.*; **8**:285 *bibliog.*
FRANKLIN, ROSALIND **8**:285 *bibliog.*
Watson, James D. **20**:67
Wilkins, Maurice **20**:152
FRANKLIN, STATE OF **8**:285 *bibliog.*
Sevier, John **17**:220
FRANKLIN, WILLIAM
Franklin, Benjamin **8**:283
Loyalists **12**:445
FRANKLIN DELANO ROOSEVELT LAKE
map (48° 20′N 118° 10′W) **20**:35
FRANKLIN FALLS RESERVOIR
map (43° 31′N 71° 41′W) **14**:123
FRANKLIN GROVE (Illinois)
map (41° 50′N 89° 18′W) **11**:42
FRANKLIN INSTITUTE **8**:285
Philadelphia (Pennsylvania) **15**:228 *map*
vocational education **19**:624
FRANKLIN AND MARSHALL COLLEGE **8**:285
FRANKLIN PARK (Illinois)
map (41° 56′N 87° 49′W) **11**:42
FRANKLIN STOVE **18**:286 *illus.*
Franklin, Benjamin **8**:283
FRANKLINITE **8**:285
FRANKLINTON (Louisiana)
map (30° 51′N 90° 9′W) **12**:430
FRANKLINTON (North Carolina)
map (36° 6′N 78° 27′W) **14**:242
FRANKLINVILLE (New York)
map (42° 20′N 78° 28′W) **14**:149
FRANKS **8**:285–286 *bibliog., illus., map*
Arnulf, Frankish Emperor **2**:186
Austrasia **2**:346
Carolingians (dynasty) **4**:162
Charlemagne **4**:289–290 *map*
Charles Martel **4**:291
Clovis **5**:70
Europe, history of **7**:283–284
feudalism **8**:64
France, history of **8**:266–267
Germany, history of **9**:148
Invasion of Europe **7**:282 *map*
Italy, history of **11**:327–328
Lombards **12**:399
Lothair I, Frankish Emperor **12**:419
Louis I, Frankish Emperor (Louis the Pious) **12**:429
Louis II, Frankish Emperor **12**:429
Low Countries, history of the **12**:439
Merovingians (dynasty) **13**:312
Netherlands **14**:102
Neustria **14**:107
Pepin the Short, King of the Franks **15**:156
Saxons **17**:104–105
FRANKS PEAK
map (43° 58′N 109° 20′W) **20**:301
FRANKTON (Indiana)
map (40° 13′N 85° 46′W) **11**:111
FRANNY AND ZOOEY (book) **8**:286 *bibliog.*
FRANZ FERDINAND, AUSTRIAN ARCHDUKE **8**:286 *illus.*
World War I **20**:219; **20**:222 *illus.*
FRANZ JOSEF II, PRINCE OF LIECHTENSTEIN
Liechtenstein **12**:325–326 *illus.*
FRANZ JOSEF LAND (USSR) **8**:286
map (81° 0′N 55° 0′E) **19**:388
FRANZ JOSEPH *see* FRANCIS JOSEPH, EMPEROR OF AUSTRIA
FRASCATI NATIONAL LABORATORY **8**:286
FRASCH, HERMAN **8**:286–287
sulfur **18**:334
FRASER, DAWN **8**:287
FRASER, J. MALCOLM **8**:287 *illus.*
Liberal parties **12**:311
FRASER, JAMES EARLE **8**:287 *bibliog.*
FRASER, PETER **8**:287 *bibliog.*
FRASER, SIMON **8**:287 *bibliog.*
Canada, exploration of **4**:80 *map*
FRASER ISLAND
map (25° 15′S 153° 10′E) **2**:328
FRASER RIVER **8**:287
British Columbia **3**:489–490
Fraser, Simon **8**:287
map (49° 9′N 123° 12′W) **3**:491
FRATERNAL SOCIETIES **8**:287–288 *bibliog.*
FRATERNITIES AND SORORITIES **8**:288 *bibliog.*
FRAUD (art) *see* FORGERY IN ART
FRAUD (legal) **8**:288 *bibliog.*
collusion **5**:105
confidence game **5**:178
embezzlement **7**:151
forgery **8**:233
misrepresentation **13**:467
FRAUD, LITERARY *see* LITERARY FRAUD
FRAUENFOLD (Switzerland)
map (47° 34′N 8° 54′E) **18**:394
FRAUNHOFER, JOSEPH VON **8**:288
Fraunhofer lines **8**:288–289
FRAUNHOFER LINES **8**:288–289 *table*
stellar spectrum **18**:252
FRAUNKOFER, JOSEPH VON
diffraction **6**:169
FRAY BENTOS (Uruguay)
map (33° 8′S 58° 18′W) **19**:488
FRAY MARCOS (Uruguay)
map (34° 11′S 55° 44′W) **19**:488
FRAZEE (Minnesota)
map (46° 44′N 95° 42′W) **13**:453
FRAZER (Montana)
map (48° 3′N 106° 2′W) **13**:547
FRAZER, SIR JAMES **8**:289 *bibliog.*
Golden Bough, The **9**:231
magic **13**:50
FRAZIER, EDWARD FRANKLIN **8**:289 *bibliog.*
FRAZIER, JOE **3**:431 *illus.*; **8**:289 *bibliog.*
FREAKE LIMNER **8**:289 *bibliog.*
Mrs. Elizabeth Freake and Baby Mary **5**:110–111 *illus.*
FRÉCHET, MAURICE RENÉ **8**:289
FRÉCHETTE, LOUIS HONORÉ **8**:289 *bibliog.*
Canadian literature **4**:93
FRECKLE **8**:289
FRED LAWRENCE WHIPPLE OBSERVATORY *see* SMITHSONIAN ASTROPHYSICAL OBSERVATORY
FREDERICA (Delaware)
map (39° 1′N 75° 28′W) **6**:88
FREDERICA (Denmark)
map (55° 35′N 9° 46′E) **6**:109
FREDERICK (Maryland) **8**:289
map (39° 25′N 77° 25′W) **13**:188
FREDERICK (county in Maryland)
map (39° 30′N 77° 25′W) **13**:188
FREDERICK (Oklahoma)
map (34° 23′N 99° 1′W) **14**:368
FREDERICK (county in Virginia)
map (39° 15′N 78° 15′W) **19**:607
FREDERICK I, KING OF GERMANY AND HOLY ROMAN EMPEROR (Frederick Barbarossa) **8**:290 *bibliog., illus.*; **9**:149 *illus.*; **15**:65 *illus.*
Germany, history of **9**:149
Hohenstaufen (dynasty) **10**:199
Middle Ages **13**:392
Saxony **17**:105
Welf (family) **20**:97
FREDERICK I, KING OF PRUSSIA **8**:291
Hohenzollern (dynasty) **10**:199
Prussia **15**:586
FREDERICK II, KING OF GERMANY AND HOLY ROMAN EMPEROR **8**:290–291 *bibliog.*
Gela (Italy) **9**:69
Germany, history of **9**:149
Gregory IX, Pope **9**:357
Italy, history of **11**:329
Naples (Italy) **14**:14
Otto IV, King of Germany and Holy Roman Emperor **14**:463
pharmacy **15**:221
Sicily (Italy) **17**:293
FREDERICK II, KING OF PRUSSIA (Frederick the Great) **8**:291–292 *bibliog., illus.*; **9**:152 *illus.*
Austrian Succession, War of the **2**:354
Germany, history of **9**:152
Hohenzollern (dynasty) **10**:199
Potsdam (East Germany) **15**:467
Prussia **15**:586
Sans Souci **17**:65
Seven Years' War **17**:218–219 *illus.*
FREDERICK III, ELECTOR OF SAXONY (Frederick the Wise) **8**:292
Saxony **17**:105 *illus.*
Wittenberg (East Germany) **20**:193
FREDERICK III, EMPEROR OF GERMANY **8**:292
FREDERICK III, KING OF DENMARK **8**:289
Scandinavia, history of **17**:109
FREDERICK III, KING OF GERMANY AND HOLY ROMAN EMPEROR **8**:291 *bibliog.*
FREDERICK IV, ELECTOR PALATINE
Mannheim (West Germany) **13**:125
FREDERICK IV, KING OF DENMARK **8**:289–290
FREDERICK V, ELECTOR PALATINE (the Winter King) **8**:292 *bibliog.*
Palatinate **15**:30
Thirty Years' War **19**:170–171
FREDERICK VI, KING OF DENMARK **8**:290
FREDERICK VII, KING OF DENMARK **8**:290
Denmark **6**:113
FREDERICK AUGUSTUS I, ELECTOR OF SAXONY *see* AUGUSTUS II, KING OF POLAND
FREDERICK AUGUSTUS II, ELECTOR OF SAXONY *see* AUGUSTUS III, KING OF POLAND
FREDERICK BARBAROSSA *see* FREDERICK I, KING OF GERMANY AND HOLY ROMAN EMPEROR (Frederick Barbarossa)
FREDERICK THE GREAT *see* FREDERICK II, KING OF PRUSSIA (Frederick the Great)
FREDERICK HENRY, PRINCE OF ORANGE **8**:292
FREDERICK WILLIAM, ELECTOR OF BRANDENBURG (the Great Elector) **8**:292–293 *bibliog., illus.*
bronze equestrian monument **17**:127 *illus.*
Hohenzollern (dynasty) **10**:199
Potsdam (East Germany) **15**:467
Prussia **15**:586
FREDERICK WILLIAM I, KING OF PRUSSIA **8**:293 *bibliog.*
Frederick II, King of Prussia (Frederick the Great) **8**:291
Hohenzollern (dynasty) **10**:199
Prussia **15**:586
FREDERICK WILLIAM II, KING OF PRUSSIA **8**:293
Prussia **15**:586
FREDERICK WILLIAM III, KING OF PRUSSIA **8**:293 *bibliog.*
Holy Alliance **10**:209
Tilsit, Treaties of **19**:200
FREDERICK WILLIAM IV, KING OF PRUSSIA **8**:293 *bibliog., illus.*
Frankfurt Parliament **8**:281
Revolutions of 1848 **16**:189
FREDERICK THE WISE *see* FREDERICK III, ELECTOR OF SAXONY (Frederick the Wise)
FREDERICKSBURG (Iowa)
map (42° 58′N 92° 12′W) **11**:244
FREDERICKSBURG (Texas)
map (30° 17′N 98° 52′W) **19**:129
FREDERICKSBURG (Virginia) **8**:293
map (38° 18′N 77° 29′W) **19**:607
FREDERICKSBURG, BATTLE OF **5**:26 *illus.*; **8**:293–294 *bibliog.*
FREDERICKTOWN (Missouri)
map (37° 33′N 90° 18′W) **13**:476
FREDERICTON (New Brunswick) **8**:294
map (45° 58′N 66° 39′W) **14**:117
FREDERICTON JUNCTION (New Brunswick)
map (45° 40′N 66° 37′W) **14**:117
FREDERIK WILLEM IV FALLS
map (3° 28′N 57° 37′W) **18**:364
FREDERIKSBORG CASTLE (Denmark)
17:112 *illus.*
FREDERIKSHÅB (Greenland)
map (62° 0′N 49° 43′W) **9**:353
FREDERIKSHAVN (Denmark)
map (57° 26′N 10° 32′E) **6**:109
FREDERIKSSUND (Denmark)
map (55° 50′N 12° 4′E) **6**:109
FREDERIKSTAD (Norway)
map (59° 13′N 10° 57′E) **14**:261
FREDERIKSTED (Virgin Islands)
map (17° 43′N 64° 53′W) **19**:605
FREDHOLM, ERIK IVAR **8**:294
FREDERICK I, ELECTOR OF BRANDENBURG **8**:289
FREDONIA (Arizona)
map (36° 57′N 112° 32′W) **2**:160
FREDONIA (Kansas)
map (37° 32′N 95° 49′W) **12**:18
FREDONIA (New York)
map (42° 27′N 79° 20′W) **14**:149
FREDONIA, REPUBLIC OF *see* FREDONIAN REBELLION
FREDONIAN REBELLION **8**:294 *bibliog.*
FREDRO, ALEXANDER, COUNT **8**:294 *bibliog.*
FREE AND ACCEPTED MASONS, FRATERNAL ORDERS OF THE *see* FREEMASONRY
FREE ASSOCIATION *see* ASSOCIATIONISM
FREE ON BOARD *see* FOB
FREE COUNTRY OF BURGUNDY *see* FRANCHE-COMTÉ (France)
FREE ENTERPRISE SYSTEM *see* CAPITALISM; LAISSEZ-FAIRE
FREE FALL **8**:294 *bibliog.*
differential equations **6**:168
motion, planar **13**:609–610
parachute **15**:75
FREE FRENCH
de Gaulle, Charles **6**:59
Leclerc, Jacques Philippe **12**:268
FREE PORT **8**:294 *bibliog.*
duty free trading **8**:294
FREE RADICAL **8**:294
FREE SCHOOLS **8**:294–295 *bibliog.*
alternative schools **1**:313
Summerhill **18**:339
FREE SILVER **8**:295 *bibliog., illus.*
Bland-Allison Act **3**:327
Bryan, William Jennings **3**:528
Populist party **15**:440
FREE-SOIL PARTY **8**:295 *bibliog.*
Dana, Richard Henry **6**:21
Homestead Act **10**:214
Liberty party **12**:314
United States, history of the **19**:447
Worcester (city in Massachusetts) **20**:216
FREE SPEECH MOVEMENT
California **4**:37
FREE TRADE **8**:295 *bibliog.*
See also CUSTOMS UNION; INTERNATIONAL TRADE; LAISSEZ-FAIRE
Cobden, Richard **5**:84
Corn Laws **5**:267
European Economic Community **7**:299–300
European Free Trade Association **7**:300–301
Great Britain, history of **9**:317

FREE TRADE (cont.)
- Latin American Integration Association 12:228
- Liberal parties 12:311
- Manchester (England) 13:108
- quota 16:28
- Ricardo, David 16:206
- Smith, Adam 17:367
- smuggling 17:374
- tariff 19:36
- Zollverein 20:372

FREE VERSE
- Apollinaire, Guillaume 2:79
- cummings, e. e. 5:387–388
- Eliot, T. S. 7:139–140
- Fletcher, John Gould 8:163
- haiku 10:12
- imagism 11:53
- Laforgue, Jules 12:164
- Mayakovsky, Vladimir Vladimirovich 13:245–246
- Rimbaud, Arthur 16:224
- versification 19:562
- Whitman, Walt 20:140–141

FREE WILL *see* WILL (philosophy)

FREE-WILLERS *see* INDENTURED SERVICE

FREE WRITING *see* AUTOMATIC WRITING

FREEBOOTER *see* PIRACY

FREEBORN (county in Minnesota)
- map (43° 38′N 93° 20′W) 13:453

FREEBURG (Illinois)
- map (38° 26′N 89° 55′W) 11:42

FREEBURG (Missouri)
- map (38° 19′N 91° 55′W) 13:476

FREED, ALAN
- rock music 16:248

FREED, ARTHUR
- film, history of 8:85

FREED, DONALD
- theater of fact 19:153

FREEDMEN'S BUREAU 5:33 *illus.*; 8:295–296 *bibliog.*
- Howard, Oliver O. 10:283
- United States, education in the 19:434

FREEDOM, ACADEMIC *see* ACADEMIC FREEDOM

FREEDOM OF INFORMATION ACT 8:296 *bibliog.*

FREEDOM OF RELIGION 8:297–298 *bibliog.*
- *See also* 1st AMENDMENT
- Catholic Emancipation 4:211
- church and state 4:424–425
- Covenanters 5:319
- *Engel* v. *Vitale* 7:176
- 1st Amendment 8:109
- human rights 10:298
- Hutchinson, Anne 10:322
- Maryland 13:192
- Nantes, Edict of 14:13
- Pledge of Allegiance 15:364
- United States, history of the 19:436

FREEDOM RIDES
- Congress of Racial Equality 5:184

FREEDOM OF SPEECH 8:298–299 *bibliog.*
- *Bridges* v. *California* 3:485
- *Dennis* v. *United States* 6:113
- 1st Amendment 8:109
- *Gitlow* v. *New York* 9:191
- human rights 10:298
- pornography 15:441
- *Roth* v. *United States* 16:321–322
- *Schenck* v. *United States* 17:119
- sedition 17:186
- Smith Act 17:371

FREEDOM OF THE PRESS 8:296–297 *bibliog.*
- *Areopagitica* (book) 2:145
- *Bridges* v. *California* 3:485
- 1st Amendment 8:109
- Graham, Katharine 9:280
- human rights 10:298
- journalism 11:454
- *Miller* v. *California* 13:428–429
- *New York Times Company* v. *Sullivan* 14:156
- *New York Times Company* v. *United States* 14:156
- newspaper 14:171–172
- Pentagon Papers 15:154
- press agencies and syndicates 15:533
- privacy, invasion of 15:556
- *Roth* v. *United States* 16:321–322
- Wilkes, John 20:151–152
- Zenger, John Peter 20:359

FREEDOM OF THE SEAS *see* SEAS, FREEDOM OF THE

FREEDOM TRAIN
- Bicentennial, U.S. 3:243

FREEHOLD (New Jersey)
- map (40° 16′N 74° 17′W) 14:129

FREEHOLDER 8:299

FREELAND (Michigan)
- map (43° 32′N 84° 7′W) 13:377

FREELAND (Pennsylvania)
- map (41° 1′N 75° 47′W) 15:147

FREELING, NICOLAS 8:299

FREELS, CAPE
- map (46° 37′N 53° 33′W) 14:166

FREEMAN (South Dakota)
- map (43° 21′N 97° 26′W) 18:103

FREEMAN, DOUGLAS SOUTHALL 8:299

FREEMAN, LAKE
- map (40° 42′N 86° 45′W) 11:111

FREEMAN, MARY E. WILKINS 8:299

FREEMAN, ORVILLE L. 15:526 *illus.*
- Minnesota 13:456

FREEMAN'S FARM, BATTLES OF
- Saratoga, Battles of 17:75

FREEMASONRY 8:299–300 *bibliog.*, *illus.*
- Anti-Masonic party 2:63
- initiation ceremony 8:299 *illus.*
- *Magic Flute, The* 13:51
- Masonic Temple Building (Chicago) skyscraper 17:350
- secret societies 17:181

FREEPORT (Bahama Islands)
- map (26° 30′N 78° 45′W) 3:23

FREEPORT (Florida)
- map (30° 30′N 86° 8′W) 8:172

FREEPORT (Illinois)
- map (42° 17′N 89° 36′W) 11:42

FREEPORT (Maine)
- map (43° 51′N 70° 6′W) 13:70

FREEPORT (New York)
- map (43° 9′N 73° 35′W) 14:149

FREEPORT (Nova Scotia)
- map (44° 17′N 66° 19′W) 14:269

FREEPORT (Texas)
- map (28° 58′N 95° 22′W) 19:129

FREER (Texas)
- map (27° 53′N 98° 37′W) 19:129

FREER, CHARLES LANG 8:300 *bibliog.*

FREER GALLERY OF ART
- Freer, Charles Lang 8:300

FREESIA 8:170 *illus.*; 8:300 *illus.*

FREESTONE (county in Texas)
- map (31° 44′N 96° 10′W) 19:129

FREETHINKER *see* DEISM

FREETOWN (Sierra Leone) 8:300; 17:297 *illus.*, *table*
- map (8° 30′N 13° 15′W) 17:296

FREEWAY *see* ROADS AND HIGHWAYS

FREEWILL BAPTIST CHURCH
- Bates College 3:121

FREEZE-DRYING 8:300

FREEZING (food) *see* FROZEN FOOD

FREEZING POINT 8:300–301
- antifreeze 2:61
- water 20:48

FREGE, GOTTLOB 8:301 *bibliog.*
- logic 12:396
- mathematics, history of 13:226
- semantics (linguistics) 17:194

FREI MONTALVA, EDUARDO 8:301 *bibliog.*
- Chile 4:357

FREIBERG (Germany, East and West)
- map (50° 54′N 13° 20′E) 9:140

FREIBURG IM BREISGAU (West Germany) 8:301
- map (47° 59′N 7° 51′E) 9:140

FREIE BÜHNE, DIE 8:301 *bibliog.*
- Deutsches Theater 6:136–137

FREIGHT TRANSPORTATION *see* CARGO TRANSPORTATION; RAILROAD

FREIGHTER 8:301 *bibliog.*; 11:113 *illus.*

FREILIGRATH, FERDINAND 8:301

FREISING (Germany, East and West)
- map (48° 23′N 11° 44′E) 9:140

FRÉJUS (France) 8:301 *bibliog.*
- flood and dam failure 8:301

FRELINGHUYSEN, FREDERICK THEODORE 8:301–302 *bibliog.*

FREMANTLE (Australia)
- map (32° 3′S 115° 45′E) 2:328

FREMONT (California)
- map (37° 34′N 122° 1′W) 4:31

FREMONT (county in Colorado)
- map (38° 30′N 105° 30′W) 5:116

FREMONT (county in Idaho)
- map (44° 15′N 111° 30′W) 11:26

FREMONT (Indiana)
- map (41° 44′N 84° 56′W) 11:111

FREMONT (Iowa)
- map (41° 13′N 92° 26′W) 11:244

FREMONT (county in Iowa)
- map (40° 45′N 95° 35′W) 11:244

FREMONT (Michigan)
- map (43° 28′N 85° 57′W) 13:377

FREMONT (Nebraska)
- map (41° 26′N 96° 30′W) 14:70

FREMONT (North Carolina)
- map (35° 33′N 77° 58′W) 14:242

FREMONT (Ohio)
- map (41° 21′N 83° 7′W) 14:357

FREMONT (county in Wyoming)
- map (42° 55′N 108° 30′W) 20:301

FRÉMONT, JOHN C. 8:302 *bibliog.*, *illus.*
- California 4:37
- Civil War, U.S. 5:23 *map*
- exploration of the American west 19:445 *map*
- Great Basin 9:308–309
- Mexican War 13:352 *map*; 13:355
- Nevada 14:113
- Republican party 16:172 *illus.*
- Tahoe, Lake 19:10

FREMONT PEAK
- map (43° 7′N 109° 36′W) 20:301

FREMSTAD, OLIVE 8:302

FRENCH, DANIEL CHESTER 8:302 *bibliog.*, *illus.*
- *Minute Man* 8:302 *illus.*

FRENCH, SIR JOHN
- World War I 20:223; 20:229

FRENCH, JOHN, 1st EARL OF YPRES 8:302

FRENCH ACADEMY *see* ACADÉMIE FRANÇAISE

FRENCH ART AND ARCHITECTURE 8:303–308 *bibliog.*, *illus.*
- *See also* the subheading France under specific art forms, movements, and historic periods, e.g., DECORATIVE ARTS; MODERN ARCHITECTURE; BAROQUE ART AND ARCHITECTURE; etc.; names of specific artists, e.g., FRAGONARD, JEAN HONORÉ; LE CORBUSIER; etc.
- Art Nouveau 2:211–212
- Aubusson (France) 2:316
- Barbizon school 3:79 *illus.*
- baroque art and architecture 3:91
- Beaubourg 3:145
- calligraphy 4:43
- cast-iron architecture 4:185–186
- château 4:302
- costume 5:300–302 *illus.*
- cubism 5:380–381
- Directoire style 6:187
- École des Beaux-Arts 7:42
- Empire style 7:158–159
- Fauvism 8:38–39
- Flamboyant Gothic style 8:150
- folk art 8:196
- Fontainebleau, school of 8:205–206
- gold and silver work 9:229
- Gothic art and architecture 9:255–262
- house (in Western architecture) 10:268 *illus.*
- illuminated manuscripts 11:48
- impressionism 11:62–68
- influence on Canadian art
  - Canadian art and architecture 4:89
- interior design 11:212–214 *illus.*
- ironwork, ornamental 11:279
- jewelry 11:410
- landscape architecture 12:185–187 *illus.*
  - garden 9:40 *illus.*
- landscape painting 12:190–192
- Louis XIV, King of France 12:426
- mannerism 13:124–125
- Merovingian art and architecture 13:311
- museums, art 13:658
- Nabis 14:3
- neoclassicism (art) 14:81–82
- Norman architecture 14:219–220 *illus.*
- postimpressionism 15:462–463
- prehistoric art 15:507–509 *illus.*
- Rayonnant style 16:98
- realism (art) 16:103
- Renaissance 16:154–155
- rococo style 16:263–265 *illus.*
- Romanesque art and architecture 16:282–286 *illus.*
- rugs and carpets 16:342–343 *illus.*
- Salon (art) 17:36
- social realism 18:13
- still-life painting 18:269–270 *illus.*
- styles of Louis XIII-XVI 18:311
- surrealism (art) 18:364–365
- symbolism (art) 18:402
- tapestry 19:31–33

FRENCH BULLDOG 6:219 *illus.*; 8:308–309 *bibliog.*, *illus.*

FRENCH CAMEROONS 4:62

FRENCH-CANADIANS
- Canada 4:75
- literature
  - Blais, Marie Claire 3:324
  - Charbonneau, Robert 4:286
  - Crémazie, Octave 5:338
  - Fréchette, Louis Honoré 8:289
  - Garneau, F. X. 9:48
  - Garneau, Hector de Saint-Denys 9:48
  - Giroux, André 9:190
  - Hébert, Anne 10:101
  - Hémon, Louis 10:119
  - Langevin, André 12:195
  - Martin, Claire 13:179
  - Morin, Paul 13:580
  - Nelligan, Émile 14:79
  - Roy, Gabrielle 16:329
  - Thériault, Yves 19:160–161
- North America 14:232

FRENCH CODE CIVIL *see* NAPOLEONIC CODE

FRENCH COLONIAL EMPIRE 8:309–310 *bibliog.*, *map*
- civil law 5:11–12
- Cochin China 5:85
- colonialism 5:111–112
- East India Company, French 7:32
- Europe, history of 7:293; 7:298
- Fashoda Incident 8:33
- French Union 8:326
- Gallieni, Joseph Simon 9:19
- India, history of 11:92

FRENCH COMMUNITY 8:310
- governor general 9:272

FRENCH CREEK
- map (41° 25′N 79° 50′W) 15:147

FRENCH EAST INDIA COMPANY *see* EAST INDIA COMPANY, FRENCH

FRENCH ENDIVE *see* CHICORY

FRENCH EQUATORIAL AFRICA 8:310
- Brazza, Pierre Paul François Camille Savorgnan de 3:465
- Central African Republic 4:251
- Chad 4:266
- Congo 5:182

FRENCH FOREIGN LEGION 8:310 *bibliog.*
- Corsica (France) 5:277

FRENCH GUIANA 8:310–311 *illus.*, *map*, *table*
- Cayenne 4:227
- climate 8:310–311 *table*
- Devil's Island 6:143
- economy 8:310–311
- flag 8:310 *illus.*
- history 8:311
- land 8:310
- map (4° 0′N 53° 0′W) 18:85
- people 8:311

FRENCH HORN 8:311–312 *bibliog.*, *illus.*; 13:676 *illus.*
- performers
  - Brain, Dennis 3:448
- wind instruments 20:170 *illus.*

FRENCH AND INDIAN WARS 8:312–314 *bibliog.*, *illus.*, *map*, *table*
- Albany Congress 1:251–252
- Amherst, Jeffrey, Baron Amherst 1:369
- Braddock, Edward 3:436
- British Empire 3:496
- Canada, history of 4:81
- Forbes, John 8:220
- Fort Duquesne 8:236
- fur trade 8:371
- Indian Wars 11:109 *map*
- infantry 11:163
- Johnson, Sir William 11:437
- Langlade, Charles Michel de 12:195–196
- Montcalm, Louis Joseph, Marquis de 13:551–552
- New York (state) 14:153
- Pennsylvania 15:150
- Rogers, Robert 16:269
- Shirley, William 17:278
- Ticonderoga 19:192
- United States, history of the 19:439 *illus.*
- Washington, George 20:42–43
- Wolfe, James 20:197

FRENCH LANGUAGE *see* ROMANCE LANGUAGES

FRENCH LICK (Indiana)
- map (38° 33′N 86° 37′W) 11:111

FRENCH LITERATURE 8:314–320 *bibliog.*, *illus.*
- *See also* BELGIAN LITERATURE; FRENCH-CANADIANS—literature; the subheading

French literature under CRITICISM, LITERARY; DRAMA; NOVEL; POETRY; etc.; names of specific authors, e.g., HUGO, VICTOR; PROUST, MARCEL; etc.; titles of specific literary works, e.g., *COMÉDIE HUMAINE, LA* (literary series); *REMEMBRANCE OF THINGS PAST* (book); etc.
Académie Française **1**:69
aestheticism **1**:130
Breton literature **3**:475
chansons de geste **4**:282
courtly love **5**:317
decadence **6**:72
essay **7**:243–244
existentialism **7**:332
fabliau **8**:5
Nabis **14**:3
naturalism (literature) **14**:49–50
new novel **14**:140
Parnassians (literary group) **15**:96
philosophes (intellectual group) **15**:240
Provençal literature **15**:583
realism (literature) **16**:104
romanticism **16**:293
symbolism (literature) **18**:403
FRENCH MUSIC **8**:320–321 *bibliog., illus.*
See also names of specific composers, e.g., BERLIOZ, HECTOR; RAVEL, MAURICE; etc.
bagpipe **3**:22–23
chanson **4**:282
Fauré, Gabriel Urbain **8**:38
impressionism (music) **11**:68
influence on English music **7**:202–203
Jolivet, André **11**:441
"Marseillaise, La" **13**:170
medieval music **13**:274–275
minstrels, minnesingers, and troubadours **13**:460
motet **13**:606
music, history of Western **13**:662; **13**:665–667
opera **14**:400–401 *illus.*
Renaissance music **16**:156
rococo music **16**:263
song **18**:64
FRENCH POLYNESIA **8**:321–322 *bibliog.*
history and government **8**:322
land, people, and economy **8**:321–322
map (15° 0′S 140° 0′W) **14**:334
Marquesas Islands **13**:162–163
Papeete **15**:68
Society Islands **18**:26
Tahiti **19**:10 *map*
FRENCH QUARTER (New Orleans) **12**:432 *illus.*; **14**:141 *illus., map*
FRENCH REVOLUTION **8**:322–325 *bibliog., illus.*
Babeuf, François Noël **3**:6
Barras, Paul François, Vicomte de **3**:93
Bastille **3**:119
Bastille, storming of the **16**:187 *illus.*
Billaud-Varenne, Jean Nicolas **3**:254
Brissot de Warville, Jacques Pierre **3**:487
Carnot, Lazare Nicolas Marguerite **4**:158
causes **8**:322
Condorcet, Marie Jean Antoine Nicolas Caritat, Marquis de **5**:173
consequences **8**:324–325
conservatism **5**:205
Consulate **8**:324
Corday, Charlotte **5**:261
Cordeliers **5**:261
costume **5**:299
Danton, Georges Jacques **6**:34–35
Declaration of the Rights of Man and of the Citizen (1789) **3**:253–254
Directory **6**:187–188; **8**:324
du Barry, Jeanne Bécu, Comtesse **6**:285
émigrés **7**:156
Europe, history of **7**:290–291
Feuillants **8**:66
foundation of the First Republic **8**:323
France, history of **8**:270–271 *map*
Genêt, Edmond **9**:78–79
Girondists **9**:190
guillotine **9**:396
Hébert, Jacques René **10**:101
Jacobins **11**:345
Lafayette, Marie Joseph Paul Yves Roch Gilbert du Motier, Marquis de **12**:163–164
Lavoisier, Antoine Laurent **12**:241–242
Loménie de Brienne, Étienne Charles de **12**:399
Louis XVI, King of France **12**:427–428
Marat, Jean Paul **13**:143
Marie Antoinette **13**:151
"Marseillaise, La" **13**:170
Mirabeau, Honoré Gabriel Riqueti, Comte de **13**:462
Napoleon I, Emperor of the French (Napoléon Bonaparte) **14**:15–16
nationalism **14**:46
Necker, Jacques **14**:75
Orléans, Louis Philippe Joseph, Duc d' (Philippe Égalité) **14**:446
Parisians carrying heads of royal guards on pikes **7**:290 *illus.*
period of reconstruction **8**:323
provinces of France prior to **8**:269 *map*
radicalism **16**:43
Reign of Terror **8**:323
Revolution of 1789 **8**:322–323
Revolution of 1792 **8**:323
Robespierre, Maximilien **16**:242–243
Roland de la Platière, Jeanne Manon Philipon **16**:271
Sieyès, Emmanuel Joseph **17**:298
socialism **18**:19
States-General **18**:234
terrorism **19**:122
Thermidorian reaction **8**:323–324
Tussaud, Madame **19**:355
FRENCH REVOLUTIONARY WARS **8**:325–326 *bibliog., map*
Amiens, Treaty of **1**:369
Campo Formio, Treaty of **4**:67
Dumouriez, Charles François du Perier **6**:298
Europe, history of **7**:291
French Revolution **8**:323
Howe, Richard Howe, Earl **10**:284
Masséna, André **13**:213
Moreau, Jean Victor Marie **13**:576
Napoleon I, Emperor of the French (Napoléon Bonaparte) **14**:16
Napoleonic Wars **14**:19–20
Nelson, Horatio Nelson, Viscount **14**:79–80
Spain, history of **18**:147
strategy and tactics, military **18**:291
Suvorov, Aleksandr Vasilievich **18**:374
FRENCH SETTLEMENT (Louisiana) map (30° 18′N 90° 48′W) **12**:430
FRENCH SOMALILAND *see* DJIBOUTI (country)
FRENCH SOUTHERN AND ANTARCTIC TERRITORIES **8**:326
FRENCH SUDAN *see* MALI
FRENCH TERRITORY OF THE AFARS AND THE ISSAS *see* DJIBOUTI (country)
FRENCH UNION **8**:326
French Community **8**:309
FRENCH WEST AFRICA **8**:326
Ivory Coast **11**:336
FRENCH WEST INDIES **8**:326
FRENCHBURG (Kentucky) map (37° 57′N 83° 37′W) **12**:47
FRENCHMAN BAY map (44° 25′N 68° 10′W) **13**:70
FRENCHMAN BUTTE (Saskatchewan) map (53° 35′N 109° 38′W) **17**:81
FRENCHMAN CREEK map (40° 13′N 100° 50′W) **14**:70
FRENCHMAN RIVER **17**:83 *illus.*
FRENEAU, PHILIP **8**:326 *bibliog.*
FREON **8**:326
fluorine **8**:187
fluorocarbon **8**:188
Midgley, Thomas, Jr. **13**:413
refrigeration **16**:125
FREQUENCY (physics) **8**:326
bridge circuit **3**:484
electromagnetic **7**:117 *table*
microwaves **13**:389
radio
hertz **10**:148
Hertz, Heinrich Rudolph **10**:149
sideband frequency
radio **16**:47
sound and acoustics **18**:73
unit of measurement
units, physical **19**:466
waves and wave motion **20**:72
FREQUENCY ALLOCATION **8**:326–327 *table*
communication transmission **8**:326
ham radio **10**:26
radio **16**:45 *table*
radio and television broadcasting **16**:54; **16**:56–57
television **19**:84
FREQUENCY MODULATION **8**:327 *bibliog.*
Armstrong, Edwin **2**:179
FM radio **8**:192
modulation **13**:500 *illus.*
radio **16**:46–47
radio and television broadcasting **16**:56
television **19**:85
FRERE, SIR JOHN **8**:327 *bibliog.*
FRESCO PAINTING **8**:327–328 *bibliog., illus.*
Ajanta **1**:229
Andrea del Sarto **1**:407
Angelico, Fra **1**:413 *illus.*
baroque art and architecture **3**:89 *illus.*
Byzantine art and architecture **3**:605
Campagnola, Domenico **4**:63
Carracci (family) **4**:166–167 *illus.*
cartoon (art) **4**:175–176
catacombs **4**:197 *illus.*
Cavallini, Pietro **4**:220–221
Cimabue **4**:430–431
Correggio **5**:275–276 *illus.*
Domenichino **6**:230–231
Duccio di Buoninsegna **6**:289–290
Early Christian art and architecture **7**:9–10
Farnese Palace (Rome) **4**:167 *illus.*
Gaddi (family) **9**:6–7
Gaulli, Giovanni Battista **9**:61
Ghirlandaio, Domenico **9**:169
Giordano, Luca **9**:186
Giotto di Bondone **9**:187
Gozzoli, Benozzo **9**:275
Italian art and architecture **11**:312–314 *illus.*
Knossos **1**:116 *illus.*
Lanfranco, Giovanni **12**:194
Latin American art and architecture **12**:224
Leonardo da Vinci **12**:291
Lippi, Filippino **12**:362
Lorenzetti brothers **12**:415
Mantegna, Andrea **13**:129
Martini, Simone **13**:180
Masaccio **13**:193–194
Masolino da Panicale **13**:198
Michelangelo **13**:373–375 *illus.*
Mignard, Pierre **13**:416–417
Minoan art **13**:459
Mogul art and architecture **13**:501
mural painting **13**:645–646
Nazarenes (art group) **14**:66
Orozco, Jose Clemente **14**:447–448
Overbeck, Johann Friedrich **14**:470
painting **15**:19
painting techniques **15**:23
Parmigianino **15**:95
Perugino **15**:196
Piero della Francesca **15**:297
Pintoricchio **15**:308
Pompeii **5**:281 *illus.*
Portuguese art and architecture **15**:456
Raphael **16**:89
Renaissance art and architecture **16**:152
Reni, Guido **16**:157
Rivera, Diego **16**:233 *illus.*
Romanesque art and architecture **16**:284
Signorelli, Luca **17**:302
Sistine Chapel **17**:329
Sodoma, Il **18**:34
Spanish art and architecture **18**:153
tempera **19**:92
Thera **1**:116 *illus.*
Tiepolo (family) **19**:195–196
Tura, Cosimo **19**:339
Uccello, Paolo **19**:370
Vatican museums and galleries **19**:527–528
Veronese, Paolo **19**:559–560
Zuccaro (family) **20**:381
FRESCOBALDI, GIROLAMO **8**:328 *bibliog.*
toccata **19**:220
FRESH WATER **8**:328 *bibliog.*
brackish water **8**:328
iceberg **11**:15
infestation
schistosomiasis **17**:123
limnology **12**:345
Spirogyra **18**:189
Spirostomum **18**:190
storage, glaciers and glaciation **9**:193
swamp, marsh, and bog **18**:376–378
Ulothrix **19**:377
Volvox **19**:633
Vorticella **19**:635
FRESNAY, PIERRE **16**:158 *illus.*
FRESNAYE, ROGER DE LA *see* LA FRESNAYE, ROGER DE
FRESNEL, AUGUSTIN JEAN **8**:328
diffraction **6**:169
interference **11**:208–209
physics, history of **15**:285
FRESNILLO (Mexico) map (23° 10′N 102° 53′W) **13**:357
FRESNO (California) **8**:328
average weather conditions **20**:82 *table*
map (36° 45′N 119° 45′W) **4**:31
FRESNO (county in California) map (36° 45′N 119° 45′W) **4**:31
FRESNO (Montana) map (48° 41′N 109° 57′W) **13**:547
FRETELIN
Timor (Indonesia) **19**:203
FREUD, ANNA **8**:328 *bibliog.*
ego **7**:73
Erikson, Erik **7**:230
FREUD, SIGMUND **8**:329–330 *bibliog., illus.*
abstract expressionism (art) **1**:66
Adler, Alfred **1**:103
atheism **2**:289
Charcot, Jean Martin **4**:287
child development **4**:348; **4**:349
Civilization and Its Discontents **5**:34
comedy **5**:132
complex (psychology) **5**:157
consciousness, states of **5**:200
consulting room **15**:589 *illus.*
crime **5**:347
developmental psychology **6**:142
dreams and dreaming **6**:267
ego **7**:73–74
emotion **7**:157
Fassbinder, Rainer Werner **8**:33
folklore **8**:203
Interpretation of Dreams, The **11**:225
Jung, Carl **11**:467
learning theory **12**:260
libido **12**:314
medicine **13**:271 *illus.*
memory **13**:291
mental health **13**:302
motivation **13**:610
neurosis **14**:107
paranoia **15**:80
personality **15**:189
psychiatry **15**:588
psychoanalysis **15**:588–590
psychohistory **15**:591
psychology, history of **15**:598 *illus.*
psychopathology, treatment of **15**:599
psychotherapy **15**:603
Rank, Otto **16**:87
reasoning **16**:104
schizophrenia **17**:123
stimulant **18**:271
totem **19**:249
unconscious **19**:382
Vienna (Austria) **19**:578
FREUDENTHAL, HANS
languages, artificial **12**:197
FREUND, AUGUST
cyclic compounds **5**:403
FREY **8**:330
FREYA **8**:330
FREYRE, GILBERTO **8**:330 *bibliog.*
Brazilian literature **3**:464
FREYSSINET, EUGÈNE
bridge (engineering) **3**:482
FREYTAG, GUSTAV **8**:330
FRIANT (California) map (36° 59′N 119° 43′W) **4**:31
FRIBURG (Switzerland) map (46° 48′N 7° 9′E) **18**:394
FRICK, FORD **8**:330
FRICK, HENRY CLAY **8**:330 *bibliog., illus.*
Homestead strike **10**:214
FRICK COLLECTION **8**:330 *bibliog.*
Fragonard, Jean Honoré **8**:259
New York (city) **14**:145 *map*
FRICTION **8**:330–331 *bibliog.*
bearing **3**:143–144
fire ignition **8**:100–101 *illus.*
lubrication **12**:447–448
perpetual motion machine **15**:178
FRIDAY
calendar **4**:28
FRIDAY HARBOR (Washington) map (48° 32′N 123° 1′W) **20**:35

FRIDTJOF NANSEN LAND *see* FRANZ JOSEF LAND (USSR)
FRIEDAN, BETTY 8:331 *illus.*
feminism 8:49
FRIEDEL, GEORGES 8:331
FRIEDLAENDER, WALTER 8:331 *bibliog.*
FRIEDLANDER, LEE
photography, history and art of 15:272
FRIEDLÄNDER, MAX J. 8:331 *bibliog.*
FRIEDMAN, ANDRÉ *see* CAPA, ROBERT
FRIEDMAN, BRUCE JAY 8:331 *bibliog.*
FRIEDMAN, HERBERT 8:331
X-ray astronomy 20:306
FRIEDMAN, MILTON 8:331–332 *bibliog., illus.*
economy, national 7:50–51
monetary theory 13:525
FRIEDMAN TEST *see* PREGNANCY TEST
FRIEDMANN, ALEKSANDR 8:332
FRIEDRICH, CARL J. 8:332
FRIEDRICH, CASPAR DAVID 8:332 *bibliog., illus.*
Landscape on the Island of Rügen 9:127 *illus.*
Moonrise over the Sea 16:291 *illus.*
Oak Tree in the Snow 12:191 *illus.*
The Polar Sea 8:332 *illus.*
FRIEDRICH, WALTER
X-ray diffraction discoverer
mineral 13:439
FRIEDRICH WILHELM UNIVERSITY
Berlin, Free University of 3:217
FRIEDRICHSHAFEN (Germany, East and West)
map (47° 39′N 9° 28′E) 9:140
FRIEL, BRIAN 8:332
FRIEND (Nebraska)
map (40° 38′N 97° 17′W) 14:70
FRIENDS, SOCIETY OF 8:332–333 *bibliog.*
American Friends Service Committee 1:340
Dyer, Mary 6:318–319
education
Haverford College 10:71
Swarthmore College 18:379
Fox, George 8:256
Hicks, Elias 10:158
Jones, Rufus Matthew 11:444
pacifism and nonviolent movements 15:9 *illus.*
Penn, William 15:144–145
Shakers 17:235–236
slavery, opposition to 17:355
Susquehanna (Indian tribe) 18:372
United States, history of the 19:437; 19:440
Woolman, John 20:215–216
FRIENDSHIP (New York)
map (42° 12′N 78° 8′W) 14:149
FRIENDSHIP (Tennessee)
map (35° 55′N 89° 14′W) 19:104
FRIENDSHIP (Wisconsin)
map (43° 58′N 89° 49′W) 20:185
FRIENDSHIP OF THE NATIONS (poster) 7:295 *illus.*
FRIENDSHIP TRAIN
Pearson, Drew 15:128
FRIES (Virginia)
map (36° 43′N 80° 59′W) 19:607
FRIESE-GREENE, WILLIAM 8:333 *bibliog.*
FRIEZE 8:333
FRIGATE 8:333 *illus.*
naval vessels 14:55–57 *illus.*
navy 14:63
U.S. modern 14:57 *illus.*
FRIGATE BIRD 3:281 *illus.*; 8:333–334 *illus.*
courtship and mating 3:286 *illus.*
FRIGG 8:334
FRIGIDITY (psychology) 8:334 *bibliog.*
FRIML, RUDOLF 8:334
FRINGE TREE 8:334
FRIO (county in Texas)
map (28° 52′N 99° 5′W) 19:129
FRIONA (Texas)
map (34° 38′N 102° 43′W) 19:129
FRISBEE 8:334
FRISCH, KARL VON 2:11 *illus.*; 8:334 *bibliog.*
animal behavior 2:12
bee 3:159
ethology 7:257
Lorenz, Konrad 12:414
FRISCH, MAX 8:334 *bibliog.*
FRISCH, RAGNAR 8:334
FRISCO CITY (Alabama)
map (31° 26′N 87° 24′W) 1:234
FRISIA
Germanic peoples 9:138
language
Germanic languages 9:135–137 *table*
Low Countries, history of the 12:438
FRISIAN ISLANDS 8:334
map (53° 35′N 6° 40′E) 7:268
FRITCHIE, BARBARA
Frederick (Maryland) 8:289
FRITH, FRANCIS 8:334–335 *bibliog.*
FRITH, WILLIAM 8:335 *bibliog.*
FRITILLARY (botany) 8:335
FRITILLARY (butterfly) *see* CHECKERSPOTS FRITILLARY BUTTERFLY; REGAL FRITILLARY BUTTERFLY
FRIULI-VENEZIA GIULIA (Italy) 8:335
cities
Trieste 19:297
Udine 19:370–371
FRIULIAN LANGUAGE *see* RHETO-ROMANCE LANGUAGES
FROBENIUS, FERDINAND GEORG 8:335
FROBERGER, JOHANN JACOB 8:335 *bibliog.*
FROBISHER, SIR MARTIN 8:335 *bibliog.*
Hall, Charles Francis 10:21
FROBISHER BAY (Northwest Territories) 14:257 *illus.*
map (63° 44′N 68° 28′W) 14:258
FRÖDING, GUSTAF 8:335
FROEBEL, FRIEDRICH WILHELM AUGUST 8:335–336 *bibliog.*
paper folding 15:70
preschool education 15:520
primary education 15:537
FROG 8:336–337 *bibliog., illus.*; 11:469 *illus.*
amphibians 1:377–380 *illus.*
anatomy 8:336
brain 3:443 *illus.*
circulatory system 4:439 *illus.*
respiratory system 16:179–180 *illus.*
skin 17:340 *illus.*
barking frog 3:83
bullfrog 3:560
chirping frog 4:398
chorus frog 4:409
classification, biological 8:336
cricket frog 5:344
Cuban tree frog 5:380
development 6:138 *illus.*
goliath frog 9:240–241
green frog 9:348
green tree frog 18:377 *illus.*
habitat 8:336
importance 8:336–337
leg contraction experiments 7:108 *illus.*; 20:377 *illus.*
leopard frog 12:293
life cycle 8:336–337 *illus.*
development 6:138–139 *illus.*
fertilization 8:60–61 *illus.*
metamorphosis 13:333
little grass frog 12:373
regeneration 16:127
Surinam toad 18:363
toad 19:217
tree frog 19:289
FROGFISH 8:338
anglerfish 1:415
FROGHOPPER
spittlebug 18:190
FROGMAN 8:338 *illus.*
FROGMOUTH (bird) 8:338
FROHMAN, CHARLES AND DANIEL 8:338
FROISSART, JEAN 8:338 *bibliog.*
Chronicles of Froissart 7:285 *illus.*
France, history of 8:268 *illus.*
FROM HERE TO ETERNITY (book)
Jones, James 11:443
FROMBERG (Montana)
map (45° 23′N 108° 54′W) 13:547
FROME, LAKE
map (30° 48′S 139° 48′E) 2:328
FROMENT, NICOLAS 8:338 *bibliog.*
FROMM, ERICH 8:338–339 *bibliog., illus.*
FRONDE 8:339 *bibliog.*
Louis XIV, King of France 12:426
Montpensier, Anne Marie Louise d'Orléans Duchesse de 13:558
parlement 15:92
Turenne, Henri de La Tour d'Auvergne, Vicomte de 19:341
FRONDIZI, ARTURO 8:339 *bibliog.*
FRONT 8:339–340 *bibliog., illus.*
air-mass division 8:340 *illus.*
frost front 8:345
high-pressure region 10:162
tornado 19:240
weather change 8:339–340
weather forecasting 20:76
FRONT RANGE
map (39° 45′N 105° 45′W) 5:116
FRONT ROYAL (Virginia)
map (38° 55′N 78° 11′W) 19:607
FRONTAL LOBE
brain 3:443 *illus.*; 3:446 *illus.*
FRONTENAC (Kansas)
map (37° 29′N 94° 44′W) 12:18
FRONTENAC, LOUIS DE BUADE, COMTE DE 8:340 *bibliog., illus.*
Kingston (Ontario) 12:84
FRONTIER (county in Nebraska)
map (40° 30′N 100° 25′W) 14:70
FRONTIER, U.S. 8:340–345 *bibliog., illus., map*
See also WILD WEST SHOW
Boone, Daniel 3:393–394
Buffalo Bill 3:546–547
camp meetings 4:63
cattlemen's frontier 8:342
Chisholm Trail 4:398
Chouteau (family) 4:410
Conestoga 5:175–176
cowboy 5:320–321
Crockett, Davy 5:355–356
Donner Party 6:240
Earp, Wyatt 7:11
exploration 7:335
farming 8:343
Fink, Mike 8:94
Fort Dearborn 8:236
French and Indian Wars 8:312–314
fur trade 8:341–342 *map*; 8:371
ghost towns 9:169–170
Girty, Simon 9:190
Gist, Christopher 9:191
gold rush 9:228
Hickok, Wild Bill 10:157
historians
Parkman, Francis 15:91–92
Roosevelt, Theodore 16:310
Homestead Act 10:214
hunting 10:313
Indian Wars 11:108
Jefferson, Territory of 11:391
Leatherstocking Tales, The 12:263
life on the frontier 8:344
lure of the frontier 8:343–344
McCoy, Joseph 13:10
Manifest Destiny 13:117
Masterson, Bat 13:216
Meeker, Nathan Cook 13:278
mining 8:342–343
Missouri 13:479
Mountain Meadows Massacre 13:623
mountain men 13:623–624
Nebraska 14:74
Oregon Trail 14:431
origins of the Civil War 5:15–16
outlaws 14:468–469
peasant 15:129
photography
Jackson, William Henry 11:344
Muybridge, Eadweard 13:687
O'Sullivan, Timothy H. 14:459
photography, history and art of 15:269
Preemption Act 15:502
Robertson, James 16:242
Santa Fe Trail 17:68
Smith, Jedediah Strong 17:369
stagecoach 18:210–211 *illus.*
transportation routes 19:445 *map*
Turner, Frederick Jackson 19:349
Turner's theory of 8:344–345
vigilantes 19:592
Watauga Association 20:47
Wells, Fargo and Company 20:101
westward movement 8:340–343 *illus., map*
Wyoming 20:303–304
Zane, Ebenezer 20:355
FRONTIER LITERATURE *see* WESTERNS
FRONTINUS, SEXTUS JULIUS 8:345
FROSCH, PAUL
virus 19:614
FROST 8:345
hoarfrost 10:191
patterned ground 15:115
FROST, ROBERT 1:346 *illus.*; 8:345–346 *bibliog., illus.*
FROST ACTION 8:346 *bibliog.*
erosion and sedimentation 7:232–234
felsenmeer 8:346
frost 8:345
patterned ground 15:115
permafrost 15:173–174
talus 19:18
FROST FLOWER *see* ASTER
FROSTBITE 8:346
thawing of tissue 8:346
FROSTBURG (Maryland)
map (39° 39′N 78° 56′W) 13:188
FROSTPROOF (Florida)
map (27° 44′N 81° 32′W) 8:172
FROTTAGE *see* RUBBING (art)
FROUDE, RICHARD HURRELL
Oxford movement 14:475
FROUDE, WILLIAM 8:346
FROZEN FOOD 8:346–347 *bibliog.*
Birdseye, Clarence 3:291
food preservation 8:212
FRUCTOSE 8:347
carbohydrate 4:133
sugar 18:327
FRUIT FLY 8:347 *bibliog., illus.*
genetics 9:87 *illus.*
Beadle, George W. 3:137
chromosome 9:86 *illus.*
Dobzhansky, Theodosius 6:209
Morgan, Thomas Hunt 13:579
hybrid 10:328 *illus.*
life cycle 8:347 *illus.*
FRUITA (Colorado)
map (39° 9′N 108° 44′W) 5:116
FRUITDALE (Alabama)
map (31° 20′N 88° 25′W) 1:234
FRUITING BODY (slime mold) 17:362 *illus.*
FRUITLAND (Idaho)
map (44° 0′N 116° 55′W) 11:26
FRUITLAND (Maryland)
map (38° 19′N 75° 37′W) 13:188
FRUITS AND FRUIT CULTIVATION 8:347–350 *bibliog., illus.*
See also names of specific fruits, e.g., APPLE; PEAR; LOQUAT; etc.
citrus fruits 4:447–448
espalier 7:242–243
jam and jelly 12:351
nutrition, human 14:305
tropical fruit 19:308–309
FRUITVALE (Washington)
map (46° 37′N 120° 33′W) 20:35
FRUITVILLE (Florida)
map (27° 20′N 82° 30′W) 8:172
FRUM, JOHN
cargo cults 4:147
FRUMENTIUS, SAINT 8:350
FRUNZE (USSR) 8:350
map (42° 54′N 74° 36′E) 19:388
FRUSTRATION (psychology) 8:350 *bibliog.*
FRY, CHRISTOPHER 8:350 *bibliog.*
FRY, EDWIN MAXWELL 8:350 *bibliog.*
FRY, ELIZABETH 8:350–351 *bibliog., illus.*
FRY, FRANKLIN CLARK 8:351
FRY, ROGER 8:351 *bibliog.*
postimpressionism 15:462
FRYE, NORTHROP 8:351 *bibliog.*
genre (literature) 9:93
FRYEBURG (Maine)
map (44° 1′N 70° 59′W) 13:70
FSH *see* FOLLICLE-STIMULATING HORMONE (FSH)
FTC *see* FEDERAL TRADE COMMISSION
FU (prose)
Chinese literature 4:389
FU BAOSHI *see* FU PAO-SHIH (Fu Baoshi)
FU PAO-SHIH (Fu Baoshi) 8:351
FU-SHOU-LU (Fushoulu) 8:351
FU-SHUN (Fushun) (China) 8:351
map (41° 52′N 123° 53′E) 4:362
FUAD I, KING OF EGYPT 8:351
FUCHS, DANIEL 8:351
FUCHS, KLAUS
intelligence gathering 11:204
FUCHS, SIR VIVIAN 8:351–352 *bibliog.*
Antarctica 2:44 *map*
FÜCHSEL, GEORG CHRISTIAN 8:352 *bibliog.*
FUCHSIA 8:352 *illus.*
FUCUS 1:282 *illus.*; 8:352
life cycle 17:177 *illus.*
FUEL 8:352–354 *bibliog., table*
automotive industry 2:367
butane 3:591
charcoal 4:286–287
coal and coal mining 5:75–79
coal gasification 5:79
coke 5:96
consumption
history 8:352–353
trucking industry 19:315–316
United States 8:353 *table*
energy 7:172–173
energy sources 7:173–175
fluidized bed combustion 8:185
furnace 8:372

gas
natural gas **14**:48
oil gas **14**:363
producer gas **15**:561
gasohol **9**:55
gasoline **9**:55
heat content of various fuels **8**:353 *table*
hydrazine **10**:331
hydrocarbon **10**:331
hydrogen **10**:339
hydrogenation **10**:341
kerosene **12**:59
lamp **12**:175–176
liquefied petroleum gas **12**:364
peat **15**:129
petroleum **15**:207–209
power, generation and transmission of **15**:484
propane **15**:569
rockets and missiles **16**:259–260
lithium **12**:370–371
synthetic fuels **18**:409–410
transportation **19**:282
FUEL CELL **8**:354 *bibliog., illus.*
electric car **7**:105
electrolysis **7**:114
power, generation and transmission of **15**:483
types **8**:354
FUEL INJECTION
carburetor **4**:141
FUEL SYSTEM, AUTOMOTIVE *see* CARBURETOR
FUENTES, CARLOS **8**:354–355 *bibliog., illus.*; **12**:230 *illus.*
FUERTE OLIMPO (Paraguay)
map (21° 2′S 57° 54′W) **15**:77
FUGARD, ATHOL **8**:355
FUGGER (family) **8**:355 *bibliog.*
FUGING TUNE **8**:355 *bibliog.*
FUGITIVE SLAVE LAWS **8**:355 *bibliog.*
Civil War, U.S. **5**:16
Fillmore, Millard **8**:80
Underground Railroad **19**:383
FUGITIVES AND AGRARIANS (literary group) **8**:355 *bibliog.*
Ransom, John Crowe **16**:88
Tate, Allen **19**:44
Warren, Robert Penn **20**:31
FUGUE **8**:355 *bibliog.*
absolute music **1**:62
Bach, Johann Sebastian **3**:11
capriccio **4**:128
counterpoint **5**:312
FUGUE IN RED AND BLUE (František Kupka) **12**:138 *illus.*
FÜHRER, DER *see* HITLER, ADOLF
FUJAIRAH (United Arab Emirates)
postage stamp **15**:230 *illus.*
United Arab Emirates **19**:400
FUJI, MOUNT (volcano) **8**:355–356; **11**:360 *illus.*
map (35° 22′N 138° 44′E) **11**:361
FUJIAN (China) *see* FUKIEN (Fujian) (China)
FUJITA, TSUGUHARU **8**:356
FUJIWARA (family)
Japan, history of **11**:367
women in society **20**:203
FUJIYAMA *see* FUJI, MOUNT (volcano)
FUKIEN (Fujian) (China) **8**:356
Amoy **1**:376
Foochow **8**:207–208
FUKUDA TAKEO **8**:356
FUKUI (Japan)
map (36° 4′N 136° 13′E) **11**:361
FUKUOKA (Japan) **8**:356
map (33° 35′N 130° 24′E) **11**:361
FULANI **8**:356 *bibliog.*
Cameroon **4**:61
Hausa **10**:69
Kanuri **12**:24
Maçina **13**:26
Usman dan Fodio **19**:491
FULBE *see* FULANI
FULBRIGHT, J. WILLIAM **8**:356–357 *bibliog., illus.*
Fulbright Exchange Program **8**:357
FULBRIGHT EXCHANGE PROGRAM **8**:357
FULCRUM
lever **12**:302
FULDA (Germany, East and West)
map (50° 33′N 9° 41′E) **9**:140
FULGENS AND LUCRES (play)
Medwall, Henry **13**:278
FULGURITE **8**:357
FULLER, ALFRED CARL **8**:357
FULLER, LOIE **8**:357 *bibliog.*
FULLER, LON
legal realism **12**:243
FULLER, MARGARET **8**:357 *bibliog., illus.*
FULLER, MELVILLE WESTON **8**:357 *bibliog.*
Pollock v. *Farmers' Loan and Trust Co.* **15**:410
United States v. *E. C. Knight Company* **19**:465
FULLER, R. BUCKMINSTER **8**:357–358 *bibliog., illus.*
geodesic dome **9**:97–98
industrial design **11**:156
U.S. pavilion at Montreal's Expo '67 **9**:97 *illus.*
FULLER, THOMAS **8**:358 *bibliog.*
FULLER BRUSH COMPANY
Fuller, Alfred Carl **8**:357
FULLER'S EARTH **8**:358
industrial adsorbant, uses **8**:358
FULLERTON (California)
map (33° 52′N 117° 55′W) **4**:31
FULLERTON (Nebraska)
map (41° 22′N 97° 58′W) **14**:70
FULTON (Alabama)
map (31° 47′N 87° 43′W) **1**:234
FULTON (Arkansas)
map (33° 37′N 93° 49′W) **2**:166
FULTON (county in Arkansas)
map (36° 22′N 91° 42′W) **2**:166
FULTON (county in Georgia)
map (33° 45′N 84° 25′W) **9**:114
FULTON (Illinois)
map (41° 52′N 90° 11′W) **11**:42
FULTON (county in Illinois)
map (40° 30′N 90° 12′W) **11**:42
FULTON (county in Indiana)
map (41° 4′N 86° 13′W) **11**:111
FULTON (Kansas)
map (38° 1′N 94° 43′W) **12**:18
FULTON (county in Kentucky)
map (36° 35′N 89° 5′W) **12**:47
FULTON (Mississippi)
map (34° 16′N 88° 31′W) **13**:469
FULTON (Missouri) **8**:358
map (38° 52′N 91° 57′W) **13**:476
FULTON (New York)
map (43° 19′N 76° 25′W) **14**:149
FULTON (county in New York)
map (43° 0′N 74° 22′W) **14**:149
FULTON (Ohio)
map (40° 28′N 82° 50′W) **14**:357
FULTON (county in Ohio)
map (41° 33′N 84° 9′W) **14**:357
FULTON (county in Pennsylvania)
map (39° 55′N 78° 5′W) **15**:147
FULTON, ROBERT **8**:358 *bibliog.*
Clermont (steamboat) **5**:51–52
Nautilus (submarine) **14**:52
ship **17**:272
steamboat **18**:242
submarine **18**:315
FULTONDALE (Alabama)
map (33° 36′N 86° 48′W) **1**:234
FUMARIC ACID
Rhizopus **16**:197
FUMAROLE **8**:358 *bibliog.*
FUMIGATION **8**:359 *bibliog.*
frankincense **8**:282
FUMITORY (botany) **8**:359
FUNAN (ancient kingdom)
Kampuchea (Cambodia) **12**:12
Oceo **14**:346
FUNANESE
Asia, history of **2**:253
FUNCHAL (Portugal) **8**:359
map (32° 38′N 16° 54′W) **15**:449
FUNCTION (mathematics) **8**:359 *bibliog., illus.*
Alembert, Jean Le Rond d' **1**:271
analytic function
Poincaré, Henri **15**:380
Baire, René **3**:27
Betti, Enrico **3**:232
calculus **4**:24
calculus of variations **4**:24
Carathéodory, Constantin **4**:131
complex function
Cauchy, Augustin Louis **4**:219
Gelfond, Aleksandr Osipovich **9**:69
continuity **5**:230–231
convergence **5**:233
determinant **6**:134
differential calculus **6**:167–168
differential equations **6**:168
elliptic function
Jacobi, Carl Gustav Jacob **11**:345
Euler, Leonhard **7**:264–265
expansion of
Taylor series **19**:51
exponential functions **7**:339–340
Fourier analysis **8**:254
graph **9**:291
infinity **11**:168
integral calculus **11**:200–201
interpolation **11**:225
limit **12**:345
mathematical tables **13**:221
mathematics, history of **13**:226
maxima and minima **13**:239
periodic function **15**:166
potential function
LaPlace, Pierre Simon de **12**:205
quadratic function **16**:5
set theory **17**:213
sine **17**:319
tangent **19**:22
transcendental function **19**:268
trigonometric function
trigonometry **19**:298–299
variables
Borel, Émile **3**:398
FUNCTIONALISM (design) **8**:359–360 *bibliog.*
Beaubourg **3**:145
Greenough, Horatio **9**:353
Mies van der Rohe, Ludwig **13**:415
modern architecture **13**:492–493
FUNCTIONALISM (social science) **8**:360 *bibliog.*
Malinowski, Bronislaw **13**:91
social anthropology **18**:11
FUND RAISING **8**:360 *bibliog.*
Hanna, Mark **10**:38
United Negro College Fund **19**:415
FUND FOR THE REPUBLIC *see* CENTER FOR THE STUDY OF DEMOCRATIC INSTITUTIONS
FUNDAMENTAL CONSTANTS *see* ATOMIC CONSTANTS
FUNDAMENTAL INTERACTIONS **8**:360–361 *bibliog.*
beta decay **3**:229
electroweak theory **7**:128
fundamental particles **8**:362–363
grand unification theories **9**:285–286
gravitation **9**:304–305
hadron **10**:8–9
lepton **12**:295
neutrino **14**:108
nuclear physics **14**:287
parity (physics) **15**:89
physics **15**:280
quark **16**:12–13
reversible and irreversible processes **16**:186
time reversal invariance **19**:202
unified field theory **19**:386
Weinberg, Steven **20**:95
world line **20**:219
xi-hyperon **20**:313
FUNDAMENTAL ORDERS **8**:361
Ludlow, Roger **12**:451–452
FUNDAMENTAL PARTICLES **8**:361–363 *bibliog., table*
accelerator, particle **1**:72–76
alpha particle **1**:308
antimatter **2**:63
baryon **3**:99
Bell's theorem **3**:192
classification of
Gell-Mann, Murray **9**:69–70
collision: Mott, Nevill **13**:616
conversion electron **5**:233
detection
detector, particle **6**:133–134
Glaser's bubble chamber **9**:197
Wilson, Charles Thomson Rees **20**:164
deuteron **6**:136
Dirac, Paul **6**:186–187
electron **7**:119–120
energy level **7**:173
exoelectron **7**:333
fermion **8**:56
gamma rays **9**:34
gluon **9**:212
grand unification theories **9**:285–286
hadron **10**:8–9
integral spin, boson **3**:407
J/psi
Richter, Burton **16**:214
kaon **12**:25
lepton **12**:295
matter **13**:230
meson **13**:315
monopole, magnetic **13**:537
motion, world line **20**:219
muon **13**:644
neutrino **14**:108
neutron **14**:108–109
nuclear physics **14**:287
physics **15**:281
positron **15**:458
proton **15**:578
quark **16**:12–13
photon **15**:274
Rubbia, Carlo **16**:335
stochastic process **18**:273
superstring theories **18**:353
tachyon **19**:6
time reversal invariance **19**:202
Ting, Samuel Chao Chung **19**:206
xi-hyperon **20**:313
FUNDAMENTALISM **8**:363 *bibliog.*
creationism **5**:335–336
evangelicalism **7**:312
folk medicine **8**:201
Graham, Billy **9**:279
Moral Majority **13**:573
Pentecostalism **15**:155
revivalism **16**:186–187
Roberts, Oral **16**:242
Scopes Trial **17**:148
FUNDY, BAY OF **8**:363
map (45° 0′N 66° 0′W) **4**:70
tidal energy **19**:193
FUNERAL CUSTOMS **8**:363–365 *bibliog., illus.*
See also BURIAL; DEATH AND DYING; TOMB
Aegean civilization **1**:117 *illus.*
cemetery **4**:244–245
Chinese archaeology **4**:379 *illus.*
Chiusi **4**:399
cremation **5**:338
Egypt, ancient **7**:84
Egyptian art and architecture **7**:85–90
Etruscans **7**:259–260
jazz **11**:387
mastaba **13**:214
megalith **13**:278–279
modes of disposition **8**:364
mourning **8**:364
mummy **13**:639
passage rites **15**:104
pre-Columbian art and architecture **15**:497
prehistoric evidence **8**:364–365
rites of separation and transition **8**:363–364
sarcophagus **17**:75–76
Southeast Asian art and architecture **18**:107–108
stele **18**:250
suttee **18**:373
wake **20**:7–8
FUNERAL INDUSTRY **8**:365 *bibliog.*
embalming **7**:151
FUNGI **8**:365–368 *bibliog., illus.*
bioluminescence **3**:272
bird's nest fungus **3**:290
boletus **3**:364
bracket fungus **3**:436
classification, biological **5**:43; **8**:365–368
cup fungus **5**:390
earthstar **7**:28
fairy ring mushroom **8**:10
fly agaric **15**:384 *illus.*
hypha **8**:365 *illus.*
hyphochytrid **10**:349
industrial uses **8**:365
jack-o'-lantern **11**:339
lichen **12**:322
life cycle **8**:365–368
microbiology **13**:384
mildew **13**:419
molds **13**:506
slime mold **17**:362 *illus.*
water mold **20**:49
morel **13**:577
mushrooms **13**:659–661 *illus.*
mycology **13**:690
Neurospora **14**:107
nitrogen cycle **14**:203 *illus.*
plant **15**:333–335 *illus.*
poisonous plants and animals **15**:384–385
reproduction **16**:162
Rhizopus **16**:197
soil organisms **18**:39 *illus.*
spore **18**:195
stinkhorn **18**:272
symbiosis
mycorrhiza **13**:690
toadstool **19**:218
truffle **19**:317
yeast **20**:320
FUNGUS DISEASES **8**:369 *bibliog.*
aspergillosis **2**:262
coccidioidomycosis **5**:85
diseases, animal **6**:192
diseases, plant **6**:195
ergot **7**:228
histoplasmosis **10**:181
infectious diseases **11**:165
jewelweed **11**:411
mildew **13**:419
mycology **13**:690
respiratory system disorders **16**:181
ringworm **16**:226
skin diseases **17**:342
systemic **8**:369

FUNICULAR
cable car **4**:6
FUNK, CASIMIR **8**:369
FUNNEL-BEAKER CULTURE
European prehistory **7**:302–303
FUNNEL CLOUD *see* TORNADO; WATERSPOUT
FUNSTON, FREDERICK **8**:369 *bibliog.*
FUQUAY-VARINA (North Carolina)
map (35° 35′N 78° 48′W) **14**:242
FUR **8**:369–371 *bibliog., table*
chinchilla **4**:377
desman **6**:132
ermine **7**:231
fur farming **8**:370
fur industry **8**:371
garment making **8**:370–371
hair **10**:14
important commercial furs **8**:370 *table*
lynx **12**:477
manufacturing **8**:370–371
marketing **8**:370
marten **13**:175–176
mink **13**:451
muskrat **13**:683
nutria **14**:302
rodent **16**:265
sable **17**:5–6
sea otter **17**:169
sources of furs **8**:370
viscacha **19**:616
FUR (people) **8**:369 *bibliog.*
FUR SEAL *see* SEAL (zoology)
FUR SEAL ISLANDS *see* PRIBILOF ISLANDS (Alaska)
FUR TRADE **8**:371 *bibliog.*
Canada
Canada, history of **4**:81–82 *illus., map*
Champlain, Samuel de **4**:277–278
coureur de bois **4**:81 *illus.*
Fraser, Simon **8**:287
Frontenac, Louis de Buade, Comte de **8**:340
Henry, Alexander **10**:122
Hudson's Bay Company **10**:290–291
La Salle, Robert Cavelier, Sieur de **12**:149
La Vérendrye, Pierre Gaultier de Varennes, Sieur de **12**:151
McGill, James **13**:16
Micmac **13**:384
Monts, Pierre du Gua, Sieur de **13**:560
North West Company **14**:252–253
Ottawa (American Indians) **14**:460
Radisson, Pierre Esprit **16**:67–68
Ross, Alexander **16**:318
Selkirk, Thomas Douglas, 5th Earl of **17**:192
western Canada (l821–l870) **10**:291 *map*
trappers **8**:342 *illus.*
United States
American Fur Company **1**:340
Ashley, William Henry **2**:231
Astor, John Jacob **2**:268
Bridges, James **3**:484
Chouteau (family) **4**:410
Fitzpatrick, Thomas **8**:131–132
frontier **8**:341–342 *map*
Idaho **11**:28–29
Michigan **13**:381–382
mountain men **13**:623–624
Potawatomi **15**:466
Russian-American Company **16**:360–361
Smith, Jedediah Strong **17**:369
Washington **20**:38–39
Wyoming **20**:303
FURIES **8**:371
FURMAN UNIVERSITY **8**:371
FURMAN V. GEORGIA **8**:371–372
capital punishment **4**:124
FURNACE **8**:372 *illus.*
arc, electric **2**:112
electric furnace **7**:106
firebrick **8**:106
foundry **8**:251
heat exchanger **10**:98
metallurgy **13**:330–331
open-hearth process **14**:398
Siemens (family) **17**:296
tantalum **19**:25
FURNAS (county in Nebraska)
map (40° 10′N 100° 0′W) **14**:70
FURNEAUX GROUP ISLANDS
map (40° 10′S 148° 5′E) **2**:328
FURNESS, FRANK **8**:372–373 *bibliog.*
Pennsylvania Academy of the Fine Arts **15**:152
FURNISS, HARRY **8**:373
FURNITURE **8**:373–380 *bibliog., illus.*
antique collecting **2**:66–67 *illus.*
Art Nouveau **2**:209 *illus.*
baroque furniture **8**:376
bed **3**:153
Byzantine furniture **8**:374–375
chair **4**:269
Chinese furniture **8**:374
colonial styles in North America **5**:111 *illus.*
contemporary furniture **8**:379
decorative furniture **8**:373
do-it-yourself furniture **8**:380
Egypt
Egyptian art and architecture **7**:89–90
Egyptian furniture **8**:373 *illus.*
folk art **8**:195–197 *illus.*
France
Boulle, André Charles **3**:422
Empire furniture **8**:377
Jacob, Georges **11**:345
Oeben Jean François **14**:351
Riesener, Jean Henri **16**:219
styles of Louis XIII-XVI **18**:311
furniture manufacture **8**:380
Germany
Breuer, Marcel **3**:475
Germany and Austria
Belter, John Henry **3**:193
Biedermeier **3**:247
Mies van der Rohe, Ludwig **13**:415
Gothic furniture **8**:375
Great Britain
Chippendale, Thomas **4**:396
Hepplewhite, George **10**:131
Morris, William **13**:589
Regency style **16**:126
Sheraton, Thomas **17**:256
Greek and Roman furniture **8**:374
influence of technology **8**:380
interior design **11**:210–214
Italy
Bertoia, Harry **3**:226
Brustolon, Andrea **3**:528
Bugatti, Carlo **3**:547
lumber **12**:455–457
mahogany **13**:66
maple **13**:137
marquetry **13**:163
medieval European furniture **8**:375
misericord **13**:466
neoclassic furniture **8**:377
Netherlands
Rietveld, Gerrit Thomas **16**:219
new materials **8**:380
Renaissance furniture **8**:375–376
rococo furniture **8**:376–377
satinwood **17**:88
Scandinavian **8**:379
teak **19**:57
United States
Eames, Charles **7**:5
Goddard, John **9**:219
Grand Rapids (Michigan) **9**:285
Hitchcock, Lambert **10**:186–187
Phyfe, Duncan **15**:278
upholstery **8**:380
veneer **19**:538
Victorian furniture **8**:377
walnut **20**:17
FURTENBACH, JOSEF
stage lighting **18**:210
FÜRTH (Germany, East and West)
map (49° 28′N 10° 59′E) **9**:140
FURTWÄNGLER, WILHELM **8**:380–381 *bibliog.*
Berlin Philharmonic Orchestra **3**:217
FURUNCLE *see* BOIL (skin infection)
FURZE **8**:381
FUSE **8**:381
circuit breaker **4**:438
electrical wiring **7**:107
FUSELI, HENRY **8**:381 *bibliog.*
Titania, Bottom and the Fairies **8**:10
FUSHOULU *see* FU-SHOU-LU (Fushoulu)
FUSHUN (China) *see* FU-SHUN (Fushun) (China)
FUSION, NUCLEAR **8**:381 *bibliog., illus.*
accelerator, particle **1**:72–76
Bethe, Hans **3**:230
binding energy **3**:258
hydrogen **10**:337
hydrogen bomb **10**:339–340
Kapitza, Peter **12**:25
nuclear physics **14**:286–287
plasma physics **15**:346
thermonuclear fusion
laser and maser **12**:212
Thomson, Sir George Paget **19**:175
tokamak **19**:223
FUSION ENERGY **8**:381–383 *bibliog., illus.*
energy sources **7**:175
fuel **8**:352
magnetic bottle **13**:55
research institutions
Frascati National Laboratory **8**:286
Lawrence Berkeley and Lawrence Livermore laboratories **12**:251
Los Alamos National Scientific Laboratory **12**:416
Spitzer, Lyman, Jr. **18**:191
tokamak **19**:223
FUST, JOHANN **8**:383
FUSTEL DE COULANGES, NUMA DENIS **8**:383 *bibliog.*
FUTUNA ISLANDS *see* WALLIS AND FUTUNA ISLANDS
FUTURE FARMERS OF AMERICA **8**:383
FUTURE HOMEMAKERS OF AMERICA **8**:383
FUTURES **8**:383
FUTURISM (art and literature) **8**:383–384 *bibliog., illus.*
Apollinaire, Guillaume **2**:79
Balla, Giacomo **3**:40
Boccioni, Umberto **3**:354
Carrà, Carlo **4**:166
constructivist literature **5**:224
Gabo, Naum **9**:4
Italian art and architecture **11**:311
kinetic art **12**:78
Marinetti, Filippo Tommaso **13**:156
painting **15**:22
Pasternak, Boris **15**:107
Sant'Elia, Antonio **17**:69
sculpture **17**:165
Severini, Gino **17**:219
FUTUROLOGY **8**:384 *bibliog.*
FUX, JOHANN JOSEPH **8**:384 *bibliog.*
fugue **8**:355
FUZZY LOGIC
computer graphics **5**:160n
expert system **7**:334
FYN ISLAND (Denmark) **6**:112 *illus.*
map (55° 20′N 10° 30′E) **6**:109
FYODOR I, GRAND DUKE OF MOSCOW
Rurik (dynasty) **16**:347
FYODOR I, TSAR OF RUSSIA
Russia/Union of Soviet Socialist Republics, history of **16**:353
Time of Troubles **19**:202
FYODOR III, TSAR OF RUSSIA
Sophia **18**:67

G

G (letter) **9**:3 *illus.*
Z (letter) **20**:347
γ RAY *see* GAMMA-RAY ASTRONOMY; GAMMA RAYS
GA **9**:3 *bibliog.*
GABARUS (Nova Scotia)
map (45° 50′N 60° 9′W) **14**:269
GABBRO **9**:3 *bibliog.*
dunite **6**:300
Earth, structure and composition of **7**:22
igneous rock **11**:34
GABBS (Nevada)
map (38° 52′N 117° 55′W) **14**:111
GABERONES *see* GABORONE (Botswana)
GABÈS (Tunisia)
map (33° 53′N 10° 7′E) **19**:335
GABIN, JEAN **9**:3; **16**:158 *illus.*
GABLE **9**:3
GABLE, CLARK **9**:3 *bibliog., illus.*
GABO, NAUM **9**:3–4 *bibliog., illus.*
constructivism **5**:224
Linear Construction Number 2 **9**:4 *illus.*; **17**:166 *illus.*
Pevsner, Antoine **15**:216
GABON **9**:4–5 *bibliog., illus., map, table*
climate **9**:4–5 *table*
economic activity **9**:5 *illus.*
flag **9**:4 *illus.*
history and government **9**:5
land and resources **9**:4–5 *map, table*
Libreville **12**:319
map (1° 0′S 11° 45′E) **1**:136
people **9**:4–5
Fang **8**:20
Schweitzer, Albert **17**:140
GABOR, DENNIS **9**:5–6 *bibliog.*
GABORONE (Botswana) **3**:416 *illus.*; **9**:6
map (24° 45′S 25° 55′E) **3**:416
GABRIEL (angel) **9**:6
GABRIEL (family) **9**:6 *bibliog.*
Petit Trianon **15**:203
GABRIEL (slave) **9**:6
GABRIELI (family) **9**:6 *bibliog.*
Gabrieli, Giovanni
orchestra and orchestration **14**:417
GABROVO (Bulgaria)
map (42° 52′N 25° 19′E) **3**:555
GACKLE (North Dakota)
map (46° 38′N 99° 9′W) **14**:248
GADDA, CARLO EMILIO **9**:6
GADDAFI, MUAMMAR AL- *see* QADDAFI, MUAMMAR AL-
GADDI (family) **9**:6–7 *bibliog.*
GADDIS, WILLIAM **9**:7
GADE, NIELS **9**:7
GADOLIN, JOHAN **9**:7
GADOLINIUM **9**:7
element **7**:130 *table*
lanthanide series **12**:200–201
Marignac, Jean Charles Galissard de, discoverer **13**:152
metal, metallic element **13**:328
GADSDEN (Alabama) **9**:7
map (34° 2′N 86° 2′W) **1**:234
GADSDEN (Arizona)
map (32° 33′N 108° 47′W) **2**:160
GADSDEN (county in Florida)
map (30° 35′N 84° 35′W) **8**:172
GADSDEN, JAMES
Gadsden Purchase **9**:7
GADSDEN PURCHASE **9**:7 *bibliog.*; **19**:446 *map*
Civil War, U.S. **5**:16
Pierce, Franklin **15**:296
GAEA **9**:7
GAEDE, WOLFGANG
vacuum **19**:502
GAELIC ATHLETIC ASSOCIATION
hurling **10**:316
GAELIC LANGUAGES *see* CELTIC LANGUAGES
GAELS **9**:7 *bibliog.*
Ireland, history of **11**:261–263
GAFFNEY (South Carolina)
map (35° 5′N 81° 39′W) **18**:98
GAFORI, FRANCHINO
Renaissance music **16**:156
GAFSA (Tunisia)
map (34° 25′N 8° 48′E) **19**:335
GAG RULES **9**:7 *bibliog.*
GAGAKU *see* BUGAKU
GAGARIN, YURI **9**:8 *bibliog., illus.*; **18**:127 *illus.*
Vostok **19**:636–637
GAGE (county in Nebraska)
map (40° 15′N 96° 40′W) **14**:70
GAGE, N. L.
educational psychology **7**:66
GAGE, THOMAS **9**:8 *bibliog.*
United States, history of the **19**:440
GAGETOWN (New Brunswick)
map (45° 47′N 66° 9′W) **14**:117
GAGNAN, EMIL
skin diving **17**:342
GAGNOA (Ivory Coast)
map (6° 8′N 5° 56′W) **11**:335
GAGNON (Quebec)
map (51° 53′N 68° 10′W) **16**:18
GAHANNA (Ohio)
map (40° 1′N 82° 53′W) **14**:357
GAIL (Texas)
map (32° 46′N 101° 27′W) **19**:129
GAILLARD LAKE
map (41° 21′N 72° 46′W) **5**:193
GAILLIMH *see* GALWAY (city in Ireland)
GAILTALER ALPS (Mountains)
map (46° 42′N 13° 0′E) **2**:348
GAIN (electronics)
amplifier **1**:382
GAINES (county in Texas)
map (32° 45′N 102° 37′W) **19**:129
GAINES, EDMUND PENDLETON **9**:8
GAINES, ERNEST J. **9**:8
GAINESBORO (Tennessee)
map (36° 21′N 85° 39′W) **19**:104
GAINESVILLE (Florida)
map (29° 40′N 82° 20′W) **8**:172
GAINESVILLE (Georgia)
map (34° 18′N 83° 50′W) **9**:114
GAINESVILLE (Missouri)
map (36° 36′N 92° 26′W) **13**:476
GAINESVILLE (Texas)
map (33° 37′N 97° 8′W) **19**:129
GAINSBOROUGH, THOMAS **9**:8–9 *bibliog., illus.*
The Blue Boy **7**:186 *illus.*; **15**:447 *illus.*
The Morning Walk **9**:8 *illus.*

Robert Andrews and Wife 2:199 *illus.*
GAIRDNER, LAKE
map (31° 35′S 136° 0′E) 2:328
GAIRY, SIR ERIC M.
Grenada 9:358
GAISERIC, KING OF THE VANDALS 9:9 *bibliog.*
Vandals 19:518
GAIT (horse) *see* RIDING
GAITÁN, JORGE
Bogotá 3:360
GAITED HORSE *see* AMERICAN SADDLE HORSE
GAITHERSBURG (Maryland)
map (39° 9′N 77° 12′W) 13:188
GAITSKELL, HUGH 9:9 *bibliog.*
GAJAH MADA
Majapahit Empire 13:76
GAKONA (Alaska)
map (62° 18′N 145° 18′W) 1:242
GALACTIC COORDINATES
coordinate systems (astronomy) 5:246
photometry, astronomical 15:274
GALACTOSE
carbohydrate 4:133
sugar 18:327
GALACTOSEMIA 9:9
genetic diseases 9:83
GALAGO 9:9 *illus.*; 15:540 *illus.*
GALAHAD, SIR 9:9–10
Arthur and Arthurian legend 2:219
GALÁN, MOUNT
map (25° 55′S 66° 52′W) 2:149
GALANOS, JAMES
fashion design 8:32
GALÁPAGOS ISLANDS 9:10 *bibliog., map*
cacti and other succulents 4:10
Darwin's finches 6:42–43
Heyerdahl, Thor 10:155
map (0° 30′S 90° 30′W) 7:52
GALATEA 9:10
GALAȚI (Romania) 9:10
map (45° 26′N 28° 3′E) 16:288
GALATIA 9:10 *bibliog.*
La Tène 12:150
GALATIANS, EPISTLE TO THE 9:10 *bibliog.*
GALAUP, JEAN FRANÇOIS DE, COMTE, DE LA PÉROUSE *see* LA PÉROUSE, JEAN FRANÇOIS DE GALAUP, COMTE DE
GALAX (Virginia)
map (36° 40′N 80° 56′W) 19:607
GALAXIES
Andromeda galaxy 1:409 *illus.*
BL Lacertae objects 3:303
clusters of galaxies 4:72; 5:72
Coma cluster 5:129
distance, astronomical 6:199–200
extragalactic systems 7:341–342
Galaxy, The 9:10–13
Local Group of galaxies 12:385
Magellanic Clouds 13:48–49
magnitude 13:60–61
mass of galaxies 7:346
population, stellar 15:437
radio galaxies 16:53–54
Seyfert galaxies 17:232–233
star 18:221–226
steady-state theory 18:240
Virgo cluster of galaxies 19:613
X-ray galaxies 20:309
GALAXY (periodical)
Gold, H. L. 9:227
science fiction 17:144
GALAXY, THE 9:10–13 *bibliog., illus., map*
astronomy, history of 2:280
astronomy and astrophysics 2:284–285
Bok, Bart Jan 3:363
cluster, star 5:72
clusters of galaxies 5:72
cosmology (astronomy) 5:284
Crux 5:370
Curtis, Heber Doust 5:395
halo, galactic 10:25
interstellar matter 11:225–228
Kapteyn, Jacobus Cornelius 12:25–26
life, extraterrestrial 12:328
Local Group of galaxies 12:385
mass 9:10
Olbers's paradox 14:373
Oort, Jan Hendrik 14:396
population, stellar 15:437
radio astronomy 16:48–50
red shift 16:114
Sagittarius 17:12
Scorpius 17:149
Shapley, Harlow 17:241
Shklovsky, Iosif Samuilovich 17:278
stellar evolution 18:250–252
X-ray galaxies 20:309
GALBA, ROMAN EMPEROR 9:13 *bibliog.*
GALBRAITH, JOHN KENNETH 9:13 *bibliog., illus.*
capitalism 4:125
GALDÓS, BENITO PÉREZ *see* PÉREZ GALDÓS, BENITO
GALE, ZONA 9:13 *bibliog.*
GALEN 9:13 *bibliog.*
anatomy 1:395–396
headache 10:85
medicine 13:268 *illus.*
pharmacy 15:221
scoliosis 17:147
soap and detergent 18:7
GALENA 9:13–14 *illus.*
sulfide minerals 18:333
GALENA (Illinois)
map (42° 25′N 90° 26′W) 11:42
GALENA (Kansas)
map (37° 4′N 94° 38′W) 12:18
GALENA (Missouri)
map (36° 48′N 93° 28′W) 13:476
GALEOTTI, VINCENZO
Royal Danish Ballet 16:330
GALERA POINT
map (10° 49′N 60° 55′W) 19:300
GALERIUS, ROMAN EMPEROR 9:14 *bibliog.*
GALESBURG (Illinois)
map (40° 57′N 90° 22′W) 11:42
GALESVILLE (Wisconsin)
map (44° 5′N 91° 21′W) 20:185
GALETON (Pennsylvania)
map (41° 44′N 77° 39′W) 15:147
GALIB, ŞEYH 9:14
GALICIA (historic region of Central Europe) 9:14 *bibliog.*
GALICIA (Spain) 9:14
Santiago de Compostela 4:205 *illus.*; 16:282 *illus.*
GALICIANS
Spain 18:142
GALILEE 9:14 *bibliog.*
GALILEE, SEA OF 9:14
map (32° 48′N 35° 35′E) 11:302
GALILEI, GALILEO *see* GALILEO GALILEI
GALILEI, VINCENZO
Renaissance music 16:156
GALILEO (spacecraft) 9:15 *bibliog.*
GALILEO GALILEI 9:15 *bibliog., illus.*
astronomy, history of 2:279
Dialogue (book) 9:15
Florence (Italy) 8:168
gravitation 9:304
mathematics, history of 13:225
physics, history of 15:282–283 *illus.*
relativity 16:133
Saturn (astronomy) 17:89
solar system 18:45
sound and acoustics 18:71
telescope 19:80–81
Torricelli, Evangelista 19:244
GALINDO, BLAS
Latin American music and dance 12:232
GALION (Ohio)
map (40° 44′N 82° 47′W) 14:357
GALKA'YO (Somalia)
map (6° 49′N 47° 23′E) 18:60
GALL (biology) *see* BILE
GALL (botany) *see* DISEASES, PLANT
GALL (Sioux warrior) 9:16 *bibliog.*
Sitting Bull 17:330
GALL, FRANZ JOSEPH 9:16
phrenology 15:278
GALLA 9:16 *bibliog.*
GALLA PLACIDIA, MAUSOLEUM OF 9:16 *bibliog.*
mosaic 13:595
GALLANT, MAVIS 9:16
GALLATIN (county in Illinois)
map (37° 45′N 88° 13′W) 11:42
GALLATIN (county in Kentucky)
map (38° 45′N 84° 51′W) 12:47
GALLATIN (Missouri)
map (39° 55′N 93° 58′W) 13:476
GALLATIN (county in Montana)
map (45° 30′N 111° 0′W) 13:547
GALLATIN (Tennessee)
map (36° 24′N 86° 27′W) 19:104
GALLATIN, A. E.
Philadelphia Museum of Art 15:229
GALLATIN, ALBERT 9:16–17 *bibliog., illus.*
GALLATIN RANGE
map (45° 15′N 111° 5′W) 13:547
GALLATIN RIVER
map (45° 56′N 111° 29′W) 13:547
GALLAUDET (family) 9:17 *bibliog.*
deaf, education of the 6:65–66
GALLAUDET COLLEGE 9:17
Gallaudet (family) 9:17
GALLBLADDER 1:54 *illus.*; 9:17
digestion, human 6:171–172
disease 9:56 *illus.*
intestine 11:230
liver 12:374–375 *illus.*
GALLE (Sri Lanka)
map (6° 2′N 80° 13′E) 18:206
GALLÉ, ÉMILE 9:17 *bibliog.*
Art Nouveau 2:212
ash table 2:209 *illus.*
enameled glass bottle 2:211 *illus.*
firescreen 2:209 *illus.*
glassware, decorative 9:204
GALLE, JOHANN GOTTFRIED 9:17
GALLEGOS, RÓMULO 9:17 *bibliog.*
GALLEN-KALLELA, AKSELI
Finland 8:97
GALLEON 9:17–18 *bibliog., illus.*
naval vessels 14:55
ship 17:268–269 *illus.*
GALLERIES, ART *see* MUSEUMS, ART
GALLERY GRAVE
tomb 19:230
GALLEY (ship) 9:18 *bibliog., illus.*
naval vessels 14:54 *illus.*
outrigger 14:469
Phoenician galley 15:249 *illus.*
ship 17:265 *illus.*
GALLEY WARFARE 9:18
galleon 9:17–18
galley 9:18
GALLI-CURCI, AMELITA 9:18 *bibliog.*
GALLI DA BIBIENA (family) 9:18–19 *bibliog.*
GALLIA (county in Ohio)
map (38° 50′N 82° 20′W) 14:357
GALLIANO (Louisiana)
map (29° 26′N 90° 20′W) 12:430
GALLIARD
dance 6:24
GALLIC WARS 9:19 *bibliog.*
France, history of 8:266
Vercingetorix 19:549
GALLICANISM 9:19
Innocent XI, Pope 11:181
Louis XIV, King of France 12:427
Pragmatic Sanction 15:487
GALLICO, PAUL 9:19
GALLIENI, JOSEPH SIMON 9:19 *bibliog.*
World War I 20:224
GALLIENUS, ROMAN EMPEROR 9:19
Valerian, Roman Emperor 19:505
GALLINULE 9:19–20 *illus.*
See also RAIL (bird)
purple gallinule 18:377 *illus.*
rail (bird) 16:70 *illus.*
GALLIPOLI CAMPAIGN 9:20 *bibliog., map*
World War I 20:227 *map*; 20:231 *illus.*
GALLIPOLI PENINSULA 9:20
GALLIPOLIS (Ohio)
map (38° 49′N 82° 12′W) 14:357
GALLITIZIN, DEMETRIUS AUGUSTINE 9:20 *bibliog.*
GALLIUM 9:21 *bibliog.*
element 7:130 *table*
Group IIIA periodic table 15:167
Mendeleyev, Dmitry Ivanovich 13:295
metal, metallic element 13:328
transition elements 19:273 *table*
GÄLLIVARE (Sweden)
climate 18:382 *table*
GALLODIER, LOUIS
Royal Swedish Ballet 16:331
GALLON
weights and measures 20:93 *table*
GALLOWAY (Scotland) *see* DUMFRIES AND GALLOWAY (Scotland)
GALLOWAY, JOSEPH 9:21 *bibliog.*
GALLSTONE 9:21 *bibliog.*; 9:56 *illus.*
jaundice 11:385
liver 12:374
surgery 18:361
GALLUP (New Mexico) 9:21
map (35° 32′N 108° 44′W) 14:136
GALLUP, GEORGE 9:21
Gallup Poll 9:21
opinion polls 14:405–406
GALOIS, EVARISTE 9:21 *bibliog.*
mathematics, history of 13:226
GALOSH MISSILE 2:56
GALSWORTHY, JOHN 9:21–22 *bibliog., illus.*
Forsyte Saga, The 8:235
GALT (California)
map (38° 15′N 121° 18′W) 4:31
GALT, SIR ALEXANDER TILLOCH 9:22 *bibliog., illus.*
GALT, JOHN 9:22 *bibliog.*
Canada Company 4:87
GALTIERI, LEOPOLDO FORTUNATO 9:22
GALTON, SIR FRANCIS 9:22–23 *bibliog., illus.*
behavioral genetics 3:170
Darwin, Charles 6:42
eugenics 7:263
heredity 10:140
psychology, history of 15:597
GALUPPI, BALDASSARE 9:23 *bibliog.*
GALVA (Illinois)
map (41° 10′N 90° 3′W) 11:42
GALVA (Iowa)
map (42° 30′N 95° 25′W) 11:244
GALVANI, LUIGI 7:108 *illus.*; 9:23 *bibliog.*
electrochemistry 7:112
frogs' legs experiments 20:377 *illus.*
GALVANIC SKIN RESPONSE 9:23
GALVANIZING *see* ELECTROPLATING
GALVANOMETER 9:23 *bibliog.*
bridge circuit 3:484
Kelvin, William Thomson, 1st Baron, inventor 12:40
measurement 13:256 *illus.*
voltmeter 19:632
Wheatstone bridge 20:127
GALVESTON (Indiana)
map (40° 35′N 86° 11′W) 11:111
GALVESTON (Texas) 9:23; 19:131 *illus.*
map (29° 18′N 94° 48′W) 19:129
GALVESTON (county in Texas)
map (29° 20′N 94° 53′W) 19:129
GALVESTON BAY (Texas)
map (29° 36′N 94° 57′W) 19:129
subsidence 18:316
GALVESTON ISLAND
map (29° 13′N 94° 55′W) 19:129
GÁLVEZ (Argentina)
map (32° 2′S 61° 13′W) 2:149
GALVEZ, BERNARDO DE
Mobile (Alabama) 13:487
GALVEZ, JOSÉ DE
Latin America, history of 12:219
GALWAY (city in Ireland) 9:23
map (53° 16′N 9° 3′W) 11:258
GALWAY (county in Ireland) 9:23
GALWAY, JAMES 9:23–24
GAMA, VASCO DA 9:24 *bibliog., illus.*
Africa 1:157 *map*
Cochin (city) 5:85
exploration 7:334; 7:337 *map*
GAMALIEL 9:24
GAMALIEL (Kentucky)
map (36° 38′N 85° 48′W) 12:47
GAMALIEL OF JABNEH 9:24
GAMBERT, NICHOLAS
Renaissance music 16:156
GAMBETTA, LÉON 9:24–25 *bibliog.*
Franco-Prussian War 8:278–270
liberalism 12:312
GAMBIA 9:25–26 *bibliog., illus., map, table*
cities
Banjul 3:67
climate 9:25 *table*
economy 9:26 *illus.*
flag 9:25 *illus.*
government 9:26
history 9:26
Land 9:25 *map, table*
map (13° 30′N 15° 30′W) 1:136
people 9:25–26
Serer 17:208
Wolof 20:199
GAMBIA RIVER 9:26
map (13° 28′N 16° 34′W) 17:202
GAMBIER (Ohio)
map (40° 23′N 82° 24′W) 14:357
GAMBIER ISLANDS
French Polynesia 8:321–322
GAMBLE HOUSE, DAVID B.
Greene and Greene 9:351
GAMBLING 9:26 *bibliog.*
See also CASINO
Atlantic City (New Jersey) 2:294
baccarat 3:9
bingo 3:259
blackjack 3:321
chemin de fer 4:323
dice games 6:155
dog racing 6:222
gambler's ruin problem, random walk 16:83
games, mathematical 9:31–32
horse racing 10:248; 10:250
Las Vegas (Nevada) 12:210
lottery 12:420
Monte Carlo 13:552
Nevada 14:113
poker 15:386
random variable 16:83
roulette 16:324

GAMBLING (cont.)
Scarne, John **17**:116
GAMBOGE **9**:26–27
GAME BIRDS **9**:27 *bibliog.*
tinamou **19**:205–206
turkey **19**:346 *illus.*
waterfowl **20**:63
woodcock **20**:210
GAME FISH
marlin **13**:160–161
porgy **15**:441
sailfish **17**:15
salmon **17**:34–35
sea bass **17**:168
spot **18**:198
tarpon **19**:38
trout **19**:311–312
walleye **20**:16
weakfish **20**:74
GAME LAWS **9**:27 *bibliog.*
U.S. Fish and Wildlife Service **9**:27
GAME PRESERVE *see* WILDLIFE REFUGE
GAME THEORY **9**:27–29 *bibliog., illus.*
Borel, Émile **3**:398
decision theory **6**:73–74
games **9**:31
games, mathematical **9**:32–33
probability **9**:28; **15**:558
von Neumann, John **19**:634
GAMELAN **9**:29 *bibliog.*
music, non-Western **13**:668
GAMELIN, MAURICE GUSTAVE **9**:29
GAMES **9**:29–31 *bibliog., illus.*
See also CARD GAMES; names of specific games
computer games **5**:160g
game theory **9**:27–29
games, mathematical **9**:31–32
Hoyle, Edmond **10**:286
play **15**:362–363
teaching methods **19**:57
video game **19**:577
word games **9**:30–31
acrostic **1**:85
anagram **1**:388
crossword puzzle **5**:362
rebus **16**:106
riddles **16**:216
Scrabble **17**:156
GAMES, MATHEMATICAL **9**:31–32 *bibliog., illus.*
Gardner, Martin **9**:45
mathematics **13**:221–222
GAMETE
egg **7**:72
embryology **7**:154
meiosis **13**:282
pollination **15**:408
reproduction **16**:161–162
GAMETOPHYTE
alternation of generations **1**:313
moss **13**:605
plant **15**:339
pollen **15**:406
pollination **15**:408
seed cone **17**:187
tracheophyte **19**:258
GAMMA
C (letter) **4**:3
GAMMA GLOBULIN *see* GLOBULIN
GAMMA-RAY ASTRONOMY **9**:33–34 *bibliog.*
astronomy and astrophysics **2**:281–282
High Energy Astronomical Observatory **10**:161
GAMMA RAYS **9**:34 *bibliog.*
electromagnetic radiation **7**:116
fission, nuclear **8**:129
frequency, electromagnetic **7**:117 *table*
periodic table **15**:168
radioactivity **16**:61–62 *illus.*
wavelength, electromagnetic **7**:117 *table*
GAMOW, GEORGE **9**:34 *bibliog., illus.*
big bang theory **3**:248
GAMSON, ANNABELLE
Duncan, Isadora **6**:299
GAN LANGUAGE *see* KAN LANGUAGE
GANADO (Arizona)
map (35° 43′N 109° 33′W) **2**:160
GANADO (Texas)
map (29° 2′N 96° 31′W) **19**:129
GANCE, ABEL **9**:34 *bibliog.*
GAND (Belgium) *see* GHENT (Belgium)
GANDA **9**:34–35 *bibliog.*
African music **1**:168–171
Uganda **19**:373
GANDAK RIVER
map (25° 39′N 85° 13′E) **9**:37
GANDER (Newfoundland) **9**:35
map (48° 57′N 54° 37′W) **14**:166
GANDER (zoology) *see* GOOSE
GANDER LAKE
map (48° 55′N 54° 40′W) **14**:166
GANDERSHEIM, HROSWITHA VON *see* HROSWITHA VON GANDERSHEIM
GANDHARA **9**:35
Taxila **19**:48
GANDHI, INDIRA **9**:35 *bibliog., illus.*
Desai, Morarji Randchhadji **6**:124
India **11**:87 *illus.*; **11**:88
Indian National Congress **11**:104
Narayan, Jayaprakash **14**:20
Nehru, Jawaharlal **14**:78
GANDHI, MAHATMA **2**:258 *illus.*; **9**:36 *bibliog., illus.*; **11**:93 *illus.*
civil disobedience **5**:10
Gujarat (India) **9**:402
India, history of **11**:93
Jinnah, Muhammad Ali **11**:419
Narayan, Jayaprakash **14**:20
Nehru, Jawaharlal **14**:78
New Delhi (India) **14**:120
pacifism and nonviolent movements **15**:8–10 *illus.*
Patel, Vallabhbhai Jhaverbhai **15**:109–110
personality
Erikson, Erik **7**:230–231
GANDHI, RAJIV **9**:35 *illus.*
GANDHINAGAR (India)
map (23° 13′N 72° 41′E) **11**:80
GANDÍA (Spain)
map (38° 58′N 0° 11′W) **18**:140
GANESHA **9**:36
GANG OF FOUR **9**:36
Chiang Ch'ing (Jiang Qing) **4**:339
GANG RANCH (British Columbia)
map (51° 33′N 122° 20′W) **3**:491
GANGES, MOUTHS OF THE
map (22° 0′N 89° 0′E) **3**:64
GANGES CANAL
map (29° 46′N 78° 12′E) **9**:37
GANGES RIVER **9**:36–37 *bibliog., map*; **11**:81 *illus.*
bathing **10**:172 *illus.*
irrigation **11**:283
map (23° 22′N 90° 32′E) **9**:37
GANGRENE **9**:37
frostbite **8**:346
gas gangrene, *Clostridium* **5**:65
hernia **10**:144
Raynaud's disease **16**:97
GANGSTERS *see* ORGANIZED CRIME
GANGTOK (India) **9**:37
map (27° 20′N 88° 37′E) **11**:80
GANIODAIO *see* HANDSOME LAKE
GANN VALLEY (South Dakota)
map (44° 2′N 98° 59′W) **18**:103
GANNET **9**:37 *illus.*
Eocene Epoch **19**:124 *illus.*
GANNET v. *DePASQUALE*
freedom of the press **8**:297
GANNETT, FRANK E. **9**:37
GANNETT PEAK
map (43° 11′N 109° 39′W) **20**:301
GANSO AZUL (Peru)
map (8° 51′S 74° 44′W) **15**:193
GANTT (Alabama)
map (31° 25′N 86° 29′W) **1**:234
GANYMEDE (satellite) **9**:38
Jupiter (planet) **11**:472–474 *illus., table*
Voyager **19**:638
GAO (Mali)
map (16° 16′N 0° 3′W) **13**:89
GAOXIONG (Taiwan) *see* KAOHSIUNG (Gaoxiong) (Taiwan)
GAPOSCHKIN, CECILIA PAYNE- *see* PAYNE-GAPOSCHKIN, CECILIA
GAR **8**:116 *illus.*; **9**:38 *illus.*
GARACHINÉ (Panama)
map (8° 4′N 78° 22′W) **15**:55
GARAND, JOHN CANTIUS **9**:38
rifle, inventor **9**:38
GARBAGE
dump **15**:412 *illus.*
waste disposal systems **20**:46–47
GARBANZO *see* CHICK-PEA
GARBER (Oklahoma)
map (36° 26′N 97° 35′W) **14**:368
GARBERVILLE (California)
map (40° 6′N 123° 48′W) **4**:31
GARBO, GRETA **9**:38 *bibliog., illus.*
GARBORG, ARNE **9**:38 *bibliog.*
GARCÉS, FRANCISCO
Nevada **14**:113
GARCÍ, PAULINE VIARDOT- *see* VIARDOT-GARCÍA, PAULINE
GARCIA, ANASTASIA SOMOZA *see* SOMOZA (family)
GARCIA, JERRY
Grateful Dead, The **9**:301
GARCÍA, MANUEL RODRIGUEZ
voice, singing **19**:626
GARCIA, POLICARPO PAZ *see* PAZ GARCIA, POLICARPO
GARCÍA, ROMEO LUCAS *see* LUCAS GARCÍA, ROMEO
GARCÍA GUTIÉRREZ, ANTONIO
Trovatore, Il **19**:312
GARCÍA LORCA, FEDERICO **9**:38–39 *bibliog., illus.*
House of Bernarda Alba, The **10**:272
Spanish literature **18**:159–160 *illus.*
GARCÍA MÁRQUEZ, GABRIEL **9**:39 *bibliog.*; **12**:230 *illus.*
GARCÍA MORENO, GABRIEL **9**:39
GARCILASO DE LA VEGA **9**:39–40 *bibliog.*
GARDA, LAKE **9**:40
map (45° 40′N 10° 41′E) **11**:321
GARDEN **9**:40–41 *bibliog., illus.*
See also GARDENING; LANDSCAPE ARCHITECTURE
fountains **8**:251–252
gazebo **9**:64
Hanging Gardens of Babylon **17**:216–217 *illus.*
Le Nôtre, André **12**:255
Middleton Place Gardens (South Carolina) **18**:101 *illus.*
Tuileries **19**:329
GARDEN (county in Nebraska)
map (41° 40′N 102° 20′W) **14**:70
GARDEN, MARY **9**:41 *bibliog.*
GARDEN CITY (Kansas)
map (37° 58′N 100° 53′W) **12**:18
GARDEN CITY (Michigan)
map (42° 20′N 83° 20′W) **13**:377
GARDEN CITY (Missouri)
map (38° 34′N 94° 12′W) **13**:476
GARDEN CITY (movement) **9**:41–42 *bibliog., illus.*
Garnier, Tony **9**:50
greenbelt **9**:349
Howard, Ebenezer **10**:283
new towns **14**:143
plan for **9**:42 *illus.*
Wright, Henry **20**:290
GARDEN CITY (New York)
Stewart, Alexander Turney **18**:265
GARDEN CITY (Texas)
map (31° 52′N 101° 29′W) **19**:129
GARDEN OF EARTHLY DELIGHTS, THE (Hieronymus Bosch) **3**:405–406 *illus.*
GARDEN OF EDEN *see* EDEN, GARDEN OF
GARDEN GROVE (California)
map (33° 46′N 117° 57′W) **4**:31
GARDEN GROVE (Iowa)
map (40° 50′N 93° 36′W) **11**:244
GARDEN HELIOTROPE **9**:42
GARDEN ISLAND
map (45° 49′N 85° 30′W) **13**:377
GARDEN PARTY, THE (short story)
Mansfield, Katherine **13**:128
GARDEN PLAIN (Kansas)
map (37° 39′N 97° 41′W) **12**:18
GARDEN OF THE GODS (Colorado) **5**:118 *illus.*
GARDENDALE (Alabama)
map (33° 39′N 86° 49′W) **1**:234
GARDENIA **9**:42 *illus.*
GARDENING **9**:42–44 *bibliog., illus.*
See also GARDEN
annuals and perennials **9**:43
botanical garden **3**:412
compost **5**:157–158
horticulture **10**:254–255
organic gardening **9**:44
pH **15**:218
plant cultivation **9**:43–44
plant pests and diseases **9**:44
seeds and seedlings **9**:43
soil **9**:42–43
vegetable **19**:531–534
GARDENTON (Manitoba)
map (49° 5′N 96° 40′W) **13**:119
GARDEZ (Afghanistan)
map (33° 37′N 69° 7′E) **1**:133
GARDINER (Maine)
map (44° 14′N 69° 46′W) **13**:70
GARDINER (Montana)
map (45° 2′N 110° 42′W) **13**:547
GARDINER, SAMUEL RAWSON **9**:44
GARDINER, STEPHEN **9**:44 *bibliog.*
GARDINERS BAY
map (41° 8′N 72° 10′W) **5**:193
GARDINERS ISLAND
map (41° 5′N 72° 7′W) **14**:149
GARDNER (Kansas)
map (38° 49′N 94° 56′W) **12**:18
GARDNER (Massachusetts)
map (42° 34′N 71° 60′W) **13**:206
GARDNER, ALEXANDER **9**:44
O'Sullivan, Timothy H. **14**:459
GARDNER, ERLE STANLEY **9**:44–45 *bibliog., illus.*
GARDNER, JOHN **9**:45 *illus.*
GARDNER, JOHN W. (educator) **9**:45
Common Cause **5**:138
GARDNER, MARTIN **9**:45
GARDNER LAKE
map (41° 31′N 72° 13′W) **5**:193
GARDNER MUSEUM **9**:45 *bibliog.*
GARDNERVILLE (Nevada)
map (38° 56′N 119° 45′W) **14**:111
GARFIELD (county in Colorado)
map (39° 35′N 108° 0′W) **5**:116
GARFIELD (Kansas)
map (38° 5′N 99° 14′W) **12**:18
GARFIELD (county in Montana)
map (47° 15′N 107° 0′W) **13**:547
GARFIELD (county in Nebraska)
map (41° 55′N 99° 0′W) **14**:70
GARFIELD (New Jersey)
map (40° 53′N 74° 7′W) **14**:129
GARFIELD (New Mexico)
map (32° 46′N 107° 16′W) **14**:136
GARFIELD (county in Oklahoma)
map (36° 25′N 97° 45′W) **14**:368
GARFIELD (county in Utah)
map (37° 45′N 111° 30′W) **19**:492
GARFIELD (Washington)
map (47° 1′N 117° 9′W) **20**:35
GARFIELD (county in Washington)
map (46° 25′N 117° 30′W) **20**:35
GARFIELD, JAMES A. **9**:45–46 *bibliog., illus.*
as president **9**:46
early life **9**:46
Guiteau, Charles Julius **9**:401
GARFIELD, JOHN **9**:46–47 *bibliog.*
GARFIELD HEIGHTS (Ohio)
map (41° 26′N 81° 37′W) **14**:357
GARFUNKEL, ART *see* SIMON AND GARFUNKEL
GARGALLO, PABLO **9**:47 *bibliog.*
GARGANTUA AND PANTAGRUEL (book) **9**:47
French literature **8**:315
Rabelais, François **16**:31–32
GARGOYLE **9**:47
GARIBALDI (British Columbia)
map (49° 58′N 123° 9′W) **3**:491
GARIBALDI (fish) *see* DAMSELFISH
GARIBALDI (Oregon)
map (45° 34′N 123° 55′W) **14**:427
GARIBALDI, GIUSEPPE **9**:47 *bibliog., illus.*; **11**:330 *illus.*
entering Naples in triumph **7**:293 *illus.*
Italy, history of **11**:330
GARIES (South Africa)
climate **18**:80 *table*
GARITA PALMERA (El Salvador)
map (13° 44′N 90° 5′W) **7**:100
GARLAND (Alabama)
map (31° 33′N 86° 49′W) **1**:234
GARLAND (county in Arkansas)
map (34° 35′N 93° 10′W) **2**:166
GARLAND (Texas)
map (32° 54′N 96° 39′W) **19**:129
GARLAND (Utah)
map (41° 45′N 112° 10′W) **19**:492
GARLAND, AUGUSTUS HILL **9**:47–48
GARLAND, HAMLIN **9**:48 *bibliog.*
GARLAND, JUDY **9**:48 *bibliog., illus.*
GARLIC **9**:48 *illus.*
GARMENDÍA, SALVADOR
Venezuela **19**:543
GARMENT TRADE *see* CLOTHING INDUSTRY
GARMENT WORKERS' UNION *see* INTERNATIONAL LADIES' GARMENT WORKERS' UNION
GARNAVILLO (Iowa)
map (42° 52′N 91° 14′W) **11**:244
GARNEAU, F. X. **9**:48
Canadian literature **4**:93
GARNEAU, HECTOR DE SAINT-DENYS **9**:48 *bibliog.*
GARNER (Iowa)
map (43° 6′N 93° 36′W) **11**:244
GARNER (North Carolina)
map (35° 43′N 78° 37′W) **14**:242
GARNER, JOHN NANCE **9**:48–49
GARNERIN, ANDRÉ J. **9**:49
GARNET **3**:296 *illus., table*; **9**:49 *bibliog., illus., table*; **9**:74 *illus.*
divisions **9**:49
eclogite **7**:41
jewelry **9**:49
silicate minerals **17**:305
staurolite **18**:239
GARNET, HENRY HIGHLAND **9**:49 *bibliog.*

GARNETT (Kansas)
  map (38° 17′N 95° 14′W) 12:18
GARNIER, CHARLES
  Jesuit Martyrs of North America 11:402
  Paris Opéra 8:307 *illus.*
GARNIER, JEAN LOUIS CHARLES 9:49 *bibliog.*
GARNIER, ROBERT 9:49
GARNIER, TONY 9:50 *bibliog.*
GARNIERITE 9:50
GARNISH (Newfoundland)
  map (47° 14′N 55° 22′W) 14:166
GARNISHMENT
  attachment (law) 2:313
GARO 9:50 *bibliog.*
GARONNE RIVER 9:50
  map (45° 2′N 0° 36′W) 8:260
GARRARD (county in Kentucky)
  map (37° 40′N 84° 30′W) 12:47
GARRETT (Indiana)
  map (41° 21′N 85° 8′W) 11:111
GARRETT (Kentucky)
  map (37° 29′N 82° 50′W) 12:47
GARRETT (county in Maryland)
  map (39° 30′N 79° 15′W) 13:188
GARRETT, JOÃO BAPTISTA DE ALMEIDA 9:50
GARRETT, JOHN WORK 9:50 *bibliog.*
GARRETT, PAT 9:50 *bibliog.*
GARRETT, W. R.
  secondary education 17:179
GARRICK, DAVID 9:50–51 *bibliog., illus.*
  Cumberland, Richard 5:387
  theater, history of the 19:147–148 *illus.*
GARRIOT, OWEN 9:51
GARRISON (Montana)
  map (46° 31′N 112° 57′W) 13:547
GARRISON (North Dakota)
  map (47° 40′N 101° 25′W) 14:248
GARRISON (Texas)
  map (31° 49′N 94° 29′W) 19:129
GARRISON, WILLIAM LLOYD 9:51 *bibliog., illus.*
  Civil War, U.S. 5:16
  Lundy, Benjamin 12:462
GARRISON DAM
  Hidatsa 10:158
GARROTE 9:51
GARSHIN, VSEVOLOD MIKHAILOVICH 9:51 *bibliog.*
GARSTANG, JOHN 9:52
GARTER, ORDER OF THE
  chivalry 4:399
  Edward III, King of England 7:68
GARTER SNAKE 5:124 *illus.*; 9:52 *illus.*
  colubrid 5:124–125
GÄRTNER, FRIEDRICH VON 9:52 *bibliog.*
GARUDA 9:52
GARUT (Indonesia)
  map (7° 13′S 107° 54′E) 11:147
GARVEY, MARCUS 3:309 *illus.*; 9:52 *bibliog., illus.*
  black nationalism 3:318
GARVIN (county in Oklahoma)
  map (34° 40′N 97° 20′W) 14:368
GARY (Indiana) 9:52; 11:113 *illus.*
  Gary, Elbert Henry 9:52–53
  map (41° 36′N 87° 20′W) 11:111
GARY (West Virginia)
  map (37° 21′N 81° 38′W) 20:111
GARY, ELBERT HENRY 9:52–53
GARY, ROMAIN 9:53
GARYVILLE (Louisiana)
  map (30° 3′N 90° 37′W) 12:430
GARZA (county in Texas)
  map (33° 8′N 101° 15′W) 19:129
GAS 9:53
  See also GASEOUS STATE; GASOLINE
GAS CHAMBER 9:53
GAS CITY (Indiana)
  map (40° 29′N 85° 37′W) 11:111
GAS-FILLED TUBES
  electron tube 7:123–124
  light 12:335
GAS GANGRENE
  Clostridium 5:65
GAS LAWS 9:53 *bibliog.*
  Boyle, Robert 3:434
  Charles, Jacques 4:290
  Dalton's law 6:15
  gaseous state 9:54
  Gay-Lussac, Joseph Louis 9:64
  Graham, Thomas 9:280–281
  Guldberg, Cato Maximilian 9:402
  ideal gas 11:30
  kinetic theory of matter 12:78–79 *illus.*
  thermodynamics 19:164
  van der Waals equation 19:512–513
GAS LIGHTING
  stage lighting 18:210
GAS MASK 9:53 *illus.*
  chemical and biological warfare 4:313
  poison gas 15:382
GAS WARFARE
  weapons 20:75
GASCOIGNE, GEORGE 7:144 *illus.*; 9:53–54 *bibliog.*
GASCONADE (county in Missouri)
  map (38° 25′N 91° 30′W) 13:476
GASCONADE RIVER
  map (38° 40′N 91° 33′W) 13:476
GASCONY (France) 9:54 *map*
  Bayonne 3:134
  Edward I, King of England 7:67–68
GASCOYNE RIVER
  map (24° 52′S 113° 37′E) 2:328
GASEOUS MATTER
  spicule 18:181
GASEOUS STATE 9:54 *bibliog.*
  absolute zero 1:63
  adiabatic process 1:102–103
  chemistry, history of 4:325
  coal gasification 5:79
  cohesion 5:96
  convection 5:232
  density current 6:114
  distillation 6:200
  electroluminescence 7:114
  evaporation 7:313–314
  flowmeter 8:184
  fluid mechanics 8:184–185
  fluorine 8:187–188
  gas laws 9:53
  Graham, Thomas 9:280–281
  Henry, William 10:123
  hydrogen 10:337–339
  ideal gas 11:30
  inert gases 11:161
  interstellar matter 11:225–228
  Joule-Thomson effect 11:453
  kinetic theory 12:78–79 *illus.*
    Boltzmann, Ludwig 3:372
    Maxwell, James Clerk 13:241
  laser and maser 12:213 *table*
  liquefied petroleum gas 12:364
  MACE 13:14
  manometer 13:126
  molecule 13:507–508
  natural gas 14:47–48
  nitrogen 14:202–203
  oil gas 14:363
  phase equilibrium 15:222–223 *illus.*
  plasma physics 15:345–346
  poison gas 15:382
  producer gas 15:561
  pump 15:622–623
  spectrum 18:172
  sublimation (chemistry) 18:313
  suspension 18:371
  temperature 19:93
  thermodynamics 19:164
  triple point 19:302
  valve 19:509
  van der Waals equation 19:512–513
  vapor pressure 19:521
  viscosity 19:616–617
GASKELL, ELIZABETH CLEGHORN 9:54–55 *bibliog., illus.*
GASOHOL 9:55
  agriculture and the food supply 1:197–198
GASOLINE 9:55 *bibliog.*
  additives 9:55
    bromine 3:502
    lead 12:256
  alkane 1:296
  heat content 8:353 *table*
  Kettering, Charles Franklin 12:61
  Midgley, Thomas, Jr. 13:413
  naphtha 14:14
  octane number 14:347
  petroleum 15:207
GASPARRI, PIETRO 9:55
GASPÉ (Quebec)
  map (48° 50′N 64° 29′W) 16:18
GASPÉ, CAPE OF
  map (48° 45′N 64° 10′W) 16:18
GASPÉ PENINSULA (Quebec) 4:72 *illus.*; 9:55–56; 16:19 *illus.*
  map (48° 30′N 65° 0′W) 16:18
GASPEE (British revenue cutter) 9:56
GASPERI, ALCIDE DE *see* DE GASPERI, ALCIDE
GASS, WILLIAM H. 9:56
GASSAWAY (West Virginia)
  map (38° 40′N 80° 47′W) 20:111
GASSEL, LUCAS
  Working the Mine 13:447 *illus.*
GASSENDI, PIERRE 9:56
  materialism 13:219
GASSET, JOSÉ ORTEGA Y *see* ORTEGA Y GASSET, JOSÉ
GASTER, MOSES 9:56
GASTON (North Carolina)
  map (36° 30′N 77° 38′W) 14:242
GASTON (county in North Carolina)
  map (35° 15′N 81° 10′W) 14:242
GASTON, LAKE
  map (36° 35′N 78° 0′W) 14:242
GASTONIA (North Carolina)
  map (35° 16′N 81° 11′W) 14:242
GASTRIN
  hormone, animal 10:236 *table*
GASTRITIS 9:56
GASTROINTESTINAL TRACT *see* DIGESTIVE SYSTEM
GASTROINTESTINAL TRACT DISEASE 9:56–57 *bibliog., illus.*
  anthelmintic drugs 2:49
  cimetidine 4:431
  Giardia 9:172
  ileus 11:40
  immunological disease 9:57
  indigestion 11:144
  infections 9:56–57
  infectious diseases 11:166–167
  intravenous hyperalimentation 9:57
  lesions 9:56–57
  motor function abnormalities 9:56–57
  mucosa 9:57
  neoplastic disease 9:57
  peritonitis 15:172
  surgery 18:361
  ulcer 19:376
GASTRONOMY *see* COOKING
GASTROPOD 9:57–58 *illus.*
  abalone 1:51
  conch 5:170
  cowrie 5:322
  limpet 12:347
  mollusk 13:510–512 *illus.*
  slug 17:364
  snail 17:375–376
  whelk 20:130
GASTROSCOPE 9:58
  photography 15:266
GASTROTRICH
  invertebrate 11:235
GASTRULATION
  development 6:138–139; 6:140–141 *illus.*
  embryo 7:153
  embryology 7:154
GATA, CAPE OF
  map (34° 34′N 33° 2′E) 5:409
GATE (electronics)
  computer 5:160d; 5:160h
  gating circuit 9:58
GATE (Oklahoma)
  map (36° 51′N 100° 4′W) 14:368
GATE, SIMON
  Scandinavian art and architecture 17:114
GATE CITY (Virginia)
  map (36° 38′N 82° 35′W) 19:607
GATERE (Solomon Islands)
  map (7° 55′S 159° 6′E) 18:56
GATES (county in North Carolina)
  map (36° 25′N 76° 40′W) 14:242
GATES, HORATIO 9:58 *bibliog., illus.*
  American Revolution 1:359 *map*
  Conway Cabal
    Washington, George 20:43
  at Saratoga 1:361 *illus.*
  Saratoga, Battles of 17:75
  Schuyler, Philip John 17:138
GATES, SIR THOMAS 9:58 *bibliog.*
GATESHEAD (England) 9:58
  map (54° 58′N 1° 37′W) 19:403
GATESVILLE (North Carolina)
  map (36° 19′N 76° 45′W) 14:242
GATESVILLE (Texas)
  map (31° 26′N 97° 45′W) 19:129
GATEWAY (Colorado)
  map (38° 41′N 108° 59′W) 5:116
GATEWAY ARCH (St. Louis) 13:477 *illus.*; 17:22 *illus.*
GATHERING *see* HUNTER-GATHERERS
GATING CIRCUIT 9:58
  pulse (electronics) 15:621
GATLINBURG (Tennessee)
  map (35° 43′N 83° 31′W) 19:104
GATLING, RICHARD JORDAN 9:58 *bibliog.*
  Gatling gun 9:58
  machine gun 13:21–23 *illus.*
GATOPHOBIA
  phobia 15:248
GATT *see* GENERAL AGREEMENT ON TARIFFS AND TRADE
GATTI-CASAZZA, GIULIO 9:58–59 *bibliog.*
GATUN LAKE
  map (9° 12′N 79° 55′W) 15:56
GAUCHO 2:150 *illus.*; 18:94 *illus.*; 19:489 *illus.*
GAUDENS, AUGUSTUS SAINT- *see* SAINT-GAUDENS, AUGUSTUS
GAUDÍ, ANTONIO 9:59 *bibliog., illus.*
  Art Nouveau 2:211
  Casa Milá 9:59 *illus.*; 18:155 *illus.*
  Spanish art and architecture 18:154–156 *illus.*
  stained-glass window 2:211 *illus.*
GAUDIER-BRZESKA, HENRI 9:59 *bibliog.*
GAUGE (railroad) 16:72–74
GAUGE PARTICLE *see* BOSON
GAUGUIN, PAUL 9:59–60 *bibliog.*
  Marquesas Islands 13:163
  Parau Parau 15:463 *illus.*
  postimpressionism 15:462–463
  Rocks by the Sea 11:66 *illus.*
  Tahitian Women 9:60 *illus.*
  van Gogh, Vincent 19:515
  Van Gogh Painting Sunflowers 11:66 *illus.*
  Vision after the Sermon, or *Jacob Wrestling with the Angel* 18:402 *illus.*
GAUKHUNI MARSH
  map (32° 6′N 52° 52′E) 11:250
GAUL 7:282 *map*; 9:60–61 *bibliog.*
  Burgundy 3:570
  Celts 4:241–243
  Etruscans 7:259
  France, history of 8:265–266
  Gallic Wars 9:19
  La Tène 12:150
  Low Countries, history of the 12:439
  Rome, ancient 16:298
GAULEY BRIDGE (West Virginia)
  map (38° 10′N 81° 11′W) 20:111
GAULEY RIVER
  map (38° 10′N 81° 12′W) 20:111
GAULISH LANGUAGE *see* CELTIC LANGUAGES
GAULLE, CHARLES DE *see* DE GAULLE, CHARLES
GAULLI, GIOVANNI BATTISTA 9:61 *bibliog.*
  The Adoration of the Name of Jesus 9:61
  Bernini, Giovanni Lorenzo 3:222
GAULTIER, PIERRE *see* LA VÉRENDRYE, PIERRE GAULTIER DE VARENNES, SIEUR DE
GAUME, FONT DE *see* FONT DE GAUME (France)
GAUR 9:61 *illus.*
GAUSS, CARL FRIEDRICH 9:61–62 *bibliog., illus.*
  Göttingen Observatory 9:61
  least-squares method 12:262
  mathematics, history of 13:225
  Maxwell's equations 13:242
  number theory 9:61; 14:293
  telegraph, construction 9:62
  Weber, Wilhelm Eduard 20:88
GAUSSIAN DISTRIBUTION
  normal distribution 14:219
GAUSSIAN UNITS
  units, physical 19:466
GAUSTA MOUNTAIN
  map (59° 50′N 8° 39′E) 14:261
GAUTAMA, SIDDHARTHA *see* BUDDHA
GAUTHIER D'AGOTY, JACOB FABIAN
  embryo 10:139 *illus.*
GAUTIER, THÉOPHILE 9:62 *bibliog., illus.*
  decadence 6:72
GAVARNI, PAUL 9:62
  lithograph 12:371
GAVARNIE FALLS 9:62
GAVESTON, PIERS
  Edward II, King of England 7:68
GAVIAL 5:356 *illus.*; 9:62–63 *illus.*
GAVIÓN, JUAN BOSCH *see* BOSCH, JUAN
GÄVLE (Sweden)
  map (60° 40′N 17° 10′E) 18:382
GAVOTTE 9:63
GAVRAS, HENRI COSTA- *see* COSTA-GAVRAS, HENRI
GAWAIN, SIR 9:63
  Arthur and Arthurian legend 2:219
  Sir Gawain and the Green Knight 17:327
GAY, JOHN 9:63 *bibliog., illus.*
  Beggar's Opera, The 3:168
  Threepenny Opera, The 19:182
GAY ACTIVISM 9:63
  homosexuality 10:217
GAY DUTCH *see* PENNSYLVANIA DUTCH
GAY-LUSSAC, JOSEPH LOUIS 9:64 *bibliog.*
  gas laws 9:53

GAYA (India)
map (24° 47′N 85° 0′E) **11**:80
GAYLORD (Michigan)
map (45° 2′N 84° 40′W) **13**:377
GAYLORD (Minnesota)
map (44° 33′N 94° 13′W) **13**:453
GAYOOM, MAUMOON ABDUL
Maldives, Republic of **13**:87
GAYS MILLS (Wisconsin)
map (43° 19′N 90° 51′W) **20**:185
GAZA (Palestine) **9**:64
map (31° 30′N 34° 28′E) **11**:302
World War I **20**:239 *map*, *map*
GAZA STRIP **9**:64
Arab-Israeli Wars **2**:96–97 *map*
cities
Gaza **9**:64
map (31° 25′N 34° 20′E) **11**:302
GAZEBO **9**:64
GAZELLE **9**:64–65 *illus.*
Grant's gazelle **13**:101 *illus.*
GAZELLE BOY *see* FERAL CHILDREN
GAZIANTEP (Turkey)
map (37° 5′N 37° 22′E) **19**:343
GBARNGA (Kenya)
map (7° 0′N 9° 29′W) **12**:313
GBONGAN (Nigeria)
map (7° 29′N 4° 21′E) **14**:190
GDANSK (Poland) **9**:65; **15**:389 *illus.*
map (54° 23′N 18° 40′E) **15**:388
Polish Corridor **15**:397
shipyard strikes **15**:391
GDANSK, GULF OF
map (54° 40′N 19° 15′E) **15**:388
GDP *see* GROSS DOMESTIC PRODUCT
GDYNIA (Poland) **9**:65
map (54° 32′N 18° 33′E) **15**:388
Polish Corridor **15**:397
GEAR **9**:65–66 *bibliog.*, *illus.*
bicycle **3**:245 *illus.*
machine **13**:20 *illus.*
steering system **18**:244–245 *illus.*
transmission, automotive **19**:275–276 *illus.*
GEARHART MOUNTAIN
map (42° 30′N 120° 53′W) **14**:427
GEARY (county in Kansas)
map (39° 0′N 96° 45′W) **12**:18
GEARY (New Brunswick)
map (45° 46′N 66° 29′W) **14**:117
GEARY (Oklahoma)
map (35° 38′N 98° 19′W) **14**:368
GEAUGA (county in Ohio)
map (41° 35′N 81° 12′W) **14**:357
GEB
mythology **13**:697–698
GEBER **9**:66 *bibliog.*
GECKO **9**:66–67 *bibliog.*, *illus.*; **12**:379 *illus.*; **12**:381 *illus.*
dwarf gecko **6**:317
molting **13**:513 *illus.*
GEDDA, NICOLAI **9**:67
GEDDES (South Dakota)
map (43° 15′N 98° 42′W) **18**:103
GEDDES, NORMAN BEL *see* BEL GEDDES, NORMAN
GEDDES, SIR PATRICK **9**:67 *bibliog.*
GEDDES, ROBERT L. **9**:67
GEDERA (Israel)
map (31° 49′N 34° 46′E) **11**:302
GEDROSIA
Persia, ancient **15**:182 *map*
GEEL (Belgium)
map (51° 10′N 5° 0′E) **3**:177
GEER, GERARD JACOB, BARON DE
archaeology **2**:121
GEERTGEN TOT SINT JANS **9**:67 *bibliog.*
GEERTZ, CLIFFORD **9**:67
GEGENSCHEIN **9**:67
OGO **14**:355
GEHENNA *see* HELL
GEHRIG, LOU **9**:67 *bibliog.*
GEIGER, ABRAHAM **9**:67 *bibliog.*
GEIGER, HANS WILHELM **9**:67–68
Geiger counter **9**:68
GEIGER, RUDOLF OSKAR ROBERT WILLIAMS **9**:68
GEIGER COUNTER **9**:68 *bibliog.*, *illus.*
alpha particle
atomic nucleus **2**:309
Blackett, Patrick Maynard Stuart, Baron Blackett **3**:321
Geiger, Hans Wilhelm, inventor **9**:67–68
IMP **11**:60
radioactivity **16**:62 *illus.*
X-ray astronomy **20**:307
GEIGER TREE *see* SEBESTEN
GEIJER, ERIK GUSTAF **9**:68
GEIKIE, SIR ARCHIBALD **9**:68
GEISEL, ERNESTO **9**:68
GEISEL, THEODORE SEUSS *see* SEUSS, DR.
GEISHA **9**:68–69 *bibliog.*
GEISSLER, HEINRICH **9**:69
GEIST
Hegel, Georg Wilhelm Friedrich **10**:105
GEIST RESERVOIR
map (39° 56′N 85° 56′W) **11**:111
GEISTOWN (Pennsylvania)
map (40° 17′N 78° 52′W) **15**:147
GEL **9**:69
napalm **14**:14
GELA (Italy) **9**:69
map (37° 3′N 14° 15′E) **11**:321
GELATIN **9**:69
gum **9**:404–405
gum arabic **9**:405
GELBER, JACK **9**:69
Living Theatre **12**:376
GELDERN, ROBERT FREIHERR VON HEINE- *see* HEINE-GELDERN, ROBERT
GELDING (process) *see* CASTRATION
GELÉE, CLAUDE *see* LORRAIN, CLAUDE
GELEEN (Netherlands)
map (50° 58′N 5° 52′E) **14**:99
GELFOND, ALEKSANDR OSIPOVICH **9**:69
GELIDONYA, CAPE
map (36° 13′N 30° 25′E) **19**:343
GELL-MANN, MURRAY **7**:111 *illus.*; **9**:69–70 *bibliog.*, *illus.*
GELON, TYRANT OF GELA **9**:70
Syracuse (Sicily) **18**:410
GELSENKIRCHEN (West Germany) **9**:70
map (51° 31′N 7° 7′E) **9**:140
GEM (county in Idaho)
map (44° 5′N 116° 20′W) **11**:26
GEM CUTTING **9**:70–71 *bibliog.*, *illus.*
See also GEMS
cabochon cut **9**:70 *illus.*
facet cut **9**:70 *illus.*
jewelry **11**:409–410
tools **9**:70 *illus.*
GEMARA *see* TALMUD
GEMATRIA *see* KABBALAH
GEMAYEL, AMIN **9**:71
Lebanon **12**:267
GEMEENTE MUSEUM (The Hague)
Berlage, Hendrik Petrus **3**:214
GÉMIER, FIRMIN **9**:71
Théâtre National Populaire (TNP) **19**:154
GEMINI (constellation) **9**:71
Castor and Pollux **9**:71
GEMINI (mythology)
Castor and Pollux **4**:191
GEMINI PROGRAM **9**:71–72 *bibliog.*, *illus.*
Agena (rocket) **1**:183
Aldrin, Edwin E. **1**:269–270
Borman, Frank **3**:401
Collins, Michael **5**:104
Conrad, Pete **5**:198
Cooper, Leroy Gordon, Jr. **5**:244
Gordon, Richard F., Jr. **9**:249
Grissom, Virgil I. **9**:367
Johnson Space Center **11**:437
life-support systems **12**:331–333
Lovell, James **12**:438
McDivitt, James **13**:11–12
National Aeronautics and Space Administration **14**:28
Schirra, Walter M., Jr. **17**:122
Scott, David R. **17**:153
space exploration **18**:128 *illus.*
Stafford, Thomas P. **18**:209
Titan (rocket) **19**:211
White, Edward H., II **20**:135
Young, John W. **20**:333
GEMINIANI, FRANCESCO **9**:72 *bibliog.*
GEMISTUS PLETHO, GIORGIUS
Plato **15**:361
GEMMA AUGUSTEA **16**:275 *illus.*
GEMPEI WAR
Japan, history of **11**:367
GEMS **9**:73–75 *bibliog.*, *illus.*
basalt **3**:101
birthstones **3**:296
bloodstone **3**:340
carat **4**:131
cat's-eye **4**:213
chalcedony **4**:270
chrysoberyl **4**:420–421
commercial **9**:75
counterfeit gems **9**:75
desirability factors **9**:73–75
diamond **6**:151–152
emerald **7**:154
garnet **9**:49
gem cutting **9**:70–71
identification tests **9**:73
idocrase **11**:31
intaglio (art) **11**:199
jade **11**:347
jasper **11**:384
jet **11**:406
jewelry **11**:408–411
lapis lazuli **12**:204–205
malachite **13**:78
mineral **13**:438
moonstone **13**:567
onyx **14**:396
opal **14**:397
pearls and pearling **15**:126–128
pegmatite **15**:133
peridot **15**:166
ruby **16**:337
sapphire **17**:73
silicate minerals **17**:304
sphene **18**:180
spinel **18**:185
synthetic **9**:75
tiger's-eye **19**:197
topaz **19**:236–237
tourmaline **19**:253
turquoise **19**:352
zircon **20**:370
zoisite **20**:371
GEMSBOK **9**:75 *illus.*
Kalahari Desert **12**:7
GENE *see* GENETIC CODE; GENETIC ENGINEERING; GENETICS
GENE BANK **9**:75–76 *bibliog.*
agriculture and the food supply **1**:198
plant breeding **15**:343
GENE FLOW
population dynamics
race **16**:33–35
population genetics
evolution **7**:319
GENE SPLICING *see* GENETIC ENGINEERING
GENEALOGY **9**:76 *bibliog.*
kinship **12**:85–86
GENERAL (locomotive) **12**:389 *illus.*
GENERAL, THE (film) **12**:35 *illus.*
GENERAL ACCOUNTING OFFICE **9**:76
GENERAL AGREEMENT ON TARIFFS AND TRADE **9**:76
most-favored-nation status **13**:605
quota **16**:28
tariff **19**:36
tariff acts **19**:37
GENERAL ALLOTMENT ACT *see* DAWES ACT
GENERAL ASSEMBLY (UN)
Pandit, Vijaya Lakshmi **15**:58
United Nations **19**:412–413
GENERAL AVIATION *see* AVIATION
GENERAL DYNAMICS CORPORATION **1**:128 *table*
supersonic transport **18**:353
GENERAL ELECTRIC COMPANY **1**:128 *table*
Langmuir, Irving **12**:196
radio and television broadcasting **16**:54–55
Steinmetz, Charles Proteus **18**:249
GENERAL JUAN MADARIAGA (Argentina)
map (37° 0′S 57° 9′W) **2**:149
GENERAL LAVALLE (Argentina)
map (36° 24′S 56° 58′W) **2**:149
GENERAL MOTORS CORPORATION
automotive industry **2**:363–368
Durant, William Crapo **6**:303
electric car **7**:105
Kettering, Charles Franklin **12**:61
Michigan **13**:382
Oshawa (Canada) **14**:453
GENERAL NATIONAL MORTGAGE ASSOCIATION
Federal National Mortgage Association **8**:41
GENERAL PAZ (Argentina)
map (35° 31′S 58° 19′W) **2**:149
GENERAL PICO (Argentina)
map (35° 40′S 63° 44′W) **2**:149
GENERAL PLAZA (LIMÓN) (Ecuador)
map (2° 58′S 78° 25′W) **7**:52
GENERAL ROCA (Argentina)
map (39° 2′S 67° 35′W) **2**:149
GENERAL SANTOS (Philippines)
map (6° 7′N 125° 11′E) **15**:237
GENERAL SERVICES ADMINISTRATION **9**:77
GENERAL STAFF **9**:77 *bibliog.*
GENERAL STRIKE **9**:77 *bibliog.*
syndicalism **18**:407
GENERAL-SYSTEMS THEORY
bionics **3**:274
GENERAL THEOLOGICAL SEMINARY **9**:77
GENERAL WEATHER SERVICE *see* NATIONAL WEATHER SERVICE
GENERALIFE PALACES
Court of the Pool **12**:186 *illus.*
GENERATION GAP (sociology)
adolescence **1**:107
GENERATION OF '98 (literary group)
Ruiz, José Martínez **16**:344
GENERATIVE GRAMMAR *see* GRAMMAR
GENERATOR **9**:77–78 *bibliog.*, *illus.*
armature **2**:171
circuit, electric **4**:436–438
electromagnet **7**:115
electrostatic
Van de Graaff, Robert Jemison **19**:512
first direct-current generator **15**:481 *illus.*
hydroelectric power **10**:332–335 *illus.*
magnetohydrodynamics **13**:59 *illus.*
power, generation and transmission of **15**:482–484
Siemens (family) **17**:296
stator **18**:238
GENERIC DRUG
pharmaceutical industry **15**:220
GENESEE (Idaho)
map (46° 33′N 116° 56′W) **11**:26
GENESEE (county in Michigan)
map (43° 5′N 83° 40′W) **13**:377
GENESEE (county in New York)
map (43° 0′N 78° 11′W) **14**:149
GENESEE RIVER
map (43° 16′N 77° 36′W) **14**:149
GENESEO (Illinois)
map (41° 27′N 90° 9′W) **11**:42
GENESEO (New York)
map (42° 48′N 77° 49′W) **14**:149
GENESIS, BOOK OF **9**:78 *bibliog.*
Ebla **7**:36
GENÊT, EDMOND (Citizen Genêt) **9**:78 *bibliog.*
GENET, JEAN **9**:78–79 *bibliog.*, *illus.*
GENETIC CODE **9**:79–82 *bibliog.*, *illus.*, *table*
See also DNA; NUCLEIC ACID; RNA
Crick, Francis **5**:343
Franklin, Rosalind **8**:285
genetic engineering **9**:84–85
Khorana, Har Gobind **12**:68
mutation **13**:686–687
Nirenberg, M. W. **14**:201
operon **14**:403–404
protein synthesis **15**:574–576
Watson, James D. **20**:67–68
Wilkins, Maurice **20**:152
GENETIC COUNSELING *see* GENETIC DISEASES
GENETIC DISEASES **9**:82–84 *bibliog.*, *illus.*
albinism **1**:260
amniocentesis **1**:375
behavioral genetics **3**:169–170
birth defects **3**:295
bone diseases **3**:377
chromosome abnormalities **9**:82–84
color blindness **5**:114
congenital pyloric stenosis
gastrointestinal tract disease **9**:56
Cooley's anemia **5**:240
cystic fibrosis **5**:411
cystinuria **5**:411
diagnosis **9**:84
diseases, human **6**:193
Down's syndrome **6**:252
enzyme **7**:214
galactosemia **9**:9
gastrointestinal tract disease **9**:56
gene transmission in families **9**:82
genetic engineering **9**:84–85
genetics **9**:88–90
gout **9**:266–267
headache **10**:86
heart diseases **10**:95
hemophilia **10**:119–120
Huntington's chorea **10**:315
hydrocephaly **10**:331
hyperactive children **10**:347
hypertension **10**:349
immunodeficiency disease **11**:59
kidney disease **12**:71
Klinefelter's syndrome **12**:98
manic-depressive psychosis **13**:116
mental retardation **13**:302
methemoglobinemia **13**:343
multifactorial inheritance **9**:83
muscular dystrophy **13**:656
mutation **13**:686
myositis **13**:691
nervous system, diseases of the **14**:96
obesity **14**:315
operon **14**:403–404
papilloma **15**:71

phenylketonuria **15**:226
population genetics **15**:439–440
race **16**:35
schizophrenia **17**:124
sickle-cell anemia **17**:293
single-gene disorders **9**:82–83
skin diseases **17**:341
spondylitis **18**:192
Tay-Sachs disease **19**:48
varicose vein **19**:523
xeroderma **20**:312
GENETIC DRIFT
population genetics
evolution **7**:319
GENETIC ENGINEERING **9**:84–85 *bibliog., illus.*
agriculture and the food supply **1**:198
animal husbandry **2**:23; **2**:25
artificial insemination **2**:220–221
biopharmaceuticals **3**:275
cloning **5**:64–65
eugenics **7**:263–264
green revolution **9**:348–349
growth hormone **9**:381
hepatitis **10**:130
insulin **11**:198
interferon **11**:210
Khorana, Har Gobind **12**:68
malaria **13**:80
medical ethics **13**:264
medicine **13**:272
patent **15**:110
plant breeding **15**:342–343
plasmid **15**:347
vaccinia **19**:502
GENETIC SCREENING *see* GENETIC DISEASES
GENETICS **9**:85–90 *bibliog., illus., map*
aging **1**:186
antibiotics, resistance to **2**:58
bacteria **3**:18
behavioral genetics **3**:169–170
binomial distribution **3**:260
cat **4**:196
chromosome **5**:412 *illus.*
cell **4**:233–235 *illus.*
development **6**:139–140
Difflugia **6**:169
eugenics **7**:263–264
evolution **7**:318–320
gene bank **9**:76
genetic code **9**:79–82
genetic diseases **9**:82–84 *illus.*
genetic engineering **9**:84–85
heredity **10**:139–141
history **9**:85–86
Avery, Oswald T. **2**:370
Beadle, George W. **3**:137
biology **3**:271
Darwin, Charles **6**:41
Dobzhansky, Theodosius **6**:209–210
Haldane, J. B. S. **10**:17
Lamarck, Jean Baptiste **12**:173
Lederberg, Joshua **12**:268
Luria, Salvador **12**:467
Lwoff, André **12**:473
Lysenko, Trofim Denisovich **12**:480
Mendel, Gregor Johann **9**:85–87; **13**:294
Monod, Jacques Lucien **13**:536
Morgan, Thomas Hunt **13**:579
Sonneborn, Tracy Morton **18**:65
Sutton, Walter S. **18**:373
Tatum, Edward L. **19**:44–45
Temin, Howard Martin **19**:91
Vries, Hugo De **19**:639
Weismann, August **20**:95
Wilson, Edmund B. **20**:164
hybrid **10**:328
life **12**:326–327
meiosis **13**:282
microbiology **13**:384
mimicry **13**:436
mitosis **13**:485
mutation **13**:686–687
operon **14**:403–404
plant **15**:338–339
population genetics **9**:90; **15**:439–440
Protozoa **15**:581
race **16**:33–35
racism **16**:37
sex **17**:224
virus **19**:613–616
zoology **20**:377–378
GENEVA (Alabama)
map (31° 2′N 85° 52′W) **1**:234
GENEVA (county in Alabama)
map (31° 7′N 85° 45′W) **1**:234
GENEVA (Illinois)
map (41° 53′N 88° 18′W) **11**:42
GENEVA (Nebraska)
map (40° 32′N 97° 36′W) **14**:70
GENEVA (New York)
map (42° 52′N 77° 0′W) **14**:149
GENEVA (Switzerland) **9**:90–91 *illus.*; **18**:395 *illus.*
history **9**:91
map (46° 12′N 6° 9′E) **18**:394
GENEVA, LAKE **9**:91; **18**:395 *illus.*
map (46° 25′N 6° 30′E) **18**:394
GENEVA, UNIVERSITY OF **9**:91
GENEVA ACCORDS *see* GENEVA CONFERENCES
GENEVA CONFERENCES **9**:91 *bibliog.*
Vietnam **19**:583–584
Vietnam War **19**:585
GENEVA CONVENTIONS **9**:91
protections under **9**:91
Red Cross **16**:112
war crimes **20**:25
GENÈVE (Switzerland) *see* GENEVA (Switzerland)
GENEVIA (Arkansas)
map (34° 43′N 92° 13′W) **2**:166
GENEVIEVE, SAINT **9**:92
GENF (Switzerland) *see* GENEVA (Switzerland)
GENFERSEE *see* GENEVA, LAKE
GENGHIS KHAN, MONGOL EMPEROR **2**:254 *illus.*; **9**:92 *bibliog., illus.*; **13**:530 *illus.*
flag **8**:135 *illus.*
Kalmyk **12**:8
Khalkhas **12**:65
Mongols **13**:530
GENITAL DISEASES *see* UROGENITAL DISEASES
GENITAL HERPES **10**:145; **10**:146
GENITAL ORGANS *see* SEX ORGANS
GENITOURINARY DISEASES *see* UROGENITAL DISEASES
GENIUS *see* INTELLIGENCE
GENIUS (mythology) **9**:92
GENIUS OF UNIVERSAL EMANCIPATION, THE (periodical)
Lundy, Benjamin **12**:462
GENJI *see TALE OF GENJI, THE* (book)
GENK (Belgium)
map (50° 58′N 5° 30′E) **3**:177
GENNARGENTU MOUNTAINS
map (39° 59′N 9° 19′E) **11**:321
GENNEP, ARNOLD VAN **9**:92
passage rites **15**:103
GENOA (Illinois)
map (42° 6′N 88° 42′W) **11**:42
GENOA (Italy) **9**:92–93 *illus.*
harbor and port **10**:42
history **9**:92–93
boundaries *c.*1360 **7**:285 *map*
boundaries *c.*1560 **7**:288 *map*
doge **6**:222
Doria, Andrea **6**:242
Italian city-state **11**:328 *map*
lighthouse **12**:336
map (44° 25′N 8° 57′E) **11**:321
16th century painting of **11**:328 *illus.*
GENOA (Nebraska)
map (41° 27′N 97° 44′W) **14**:70
GENOA, GULF OF
map (44° 10′N 8° 55′E) **11**:321
GENOCIDE **9**:93 *bibliog.*
Convention on the Prevention and Punishment of the Crime of Genocide **9**:93
Erie **7**:229
historic examples **9**:93
war crimes **20**:25
GENOTYPE
genetics **9**:87–90
GENOVA (Italy) *see* GENOA (Italy)
GENRE (literature) **9**:93
GENRE PAINTING **9**:93 *bibliog.*
American art and architecture **1**:332
Bamboccianti **3**:58
Beham (family) **3**:168–169
Blythe, David Gilmour **3**:348
Boilly, Louis Léopold **3**:363
Bourdon, Sébastien **3**:423–424
Brouwer, Adriaen **3**:512–513
Bruegel (family) **3**:522
Chardin, Jean Baptiste **4**:287–288
Chodowiecki, Daniel Nikolaus **4**:403
Courbet, Gustave **5**:314
Dutch art and architecture **6**:311–313
Géricault, Théodore **9**:122–123
Greuze, Jean Baptiste **9**:359–360
Hooch, Pieter de **10**:224–225
Israëls, Jozef **11**:306
Japanese art and architecture **11**:377–378
Johnson, Eastman **11**:431
Korean art **12**:118
Krieghoff, Cornelius **12**:129
Lancret, Nicolas **12**:178
Le Nain brothers **12**:254–255
Longhi, Pietro **12**:408
Masanobu (1686–1764) **13**:195
Meissonier, Jean Louis Ernest **13**:283
Metsu, Gabriel **13**:349
Millais, Sir John Everett **13**:426
Morland, George **13**:580
Mount, William Sidney **13**:618
Murillo, Bartolomé Esteban **13**:648
painting **15**:21
Steen, Jan **18**:243
Suzor-Côté, M. A. de Foy **18**:374
Tanner, Henry **19**:24
Teniers, David, the Younger **19**:102
Ter Borch, Gerard **19**:114
Waldmüller, Ferdinand Georg **20**:10
Wilkie, Sir David **20**:152
Witte, Emanuel de **20**:193
Woodville, Richard **20**:213
GENROKU ERA (Japan)
Japanese art and architecture **11**:377–378
GENSERIC, KING OF THE VANDALS *see* GAISERIC, KING OF THE VANDALS
GENT (Belgium) *see* GHENT (Belgium)
GENT-BRUGES CANAL
map (51° 3′N 3° 43′E) **3**:177
GENTBRUGGE (Belgium)
map (51° 3′N 3° 45′E) **3**:177
GENTELE, GOERAN
Metropolitan Opera **13**:348
GENTIAN **9**:94 *illus.*
See also FEVERWORT
GENTIAN VIOLET **9**:94
GENTILE, GIOVANNI **9**:94 *bibliog.*
fascism **8**:30
GENTILE DA FABRIANO **9**:94 *bibliog., illus.*
Adoration of the Magi **9**:94 *illus.*
GENTILESCHI (family) **9**:95 *bibliog., illus.*
The Lute Player **9**:95 *illus.*
GENTILI, ALBERICO
international law **11**:221
GENTRY (Arkansas)
map (36° 16′N 94° 29′W) **2**:166
GENTRY (county in Missouri)
map (40° 10′N 94° 25′W) **13**:476
GENTZ, FRIEDRICH VON **9**:95 *bibliog.*
GENUS
See also NOMENCLATURE
classification, biological **5**:43
GEOBALLISTICS *see* BALLISTICS
GEOCENTRIC WORLD SYSTEM **5**:285 *illus.*; **9**:95 *bibliog.*
Battani, al- **3**:125
celestial sphere **4**:230
Copernicus, Nicolaus **5**:250
heliocentric world system **10**:112
Heracleides Ponticus **10**:131
Hipparchus **10**:173
Peurbach, Georg von **15**:216
Ptolemy **15**:606–607
Sacrobosco, Johannes **17**:8
GEOCHEMISTRY **9**:95–97 *bibliog.*
applications **9**:97
chemical changes **9**:95
earth materials, differentiation **9**:96
elements, distribution and migration of **9**:95
evaporite **7**:314
geology **9**:105–106
geology, dynamical **9**:105
history and use of term **9**:95–96
mineral **13**:444
ore deposits **14**:425
research
isotopes **9**:97
rock cycle **9**:96
seas, air, and life **9**:97
solid solution **18**:54
GEODE **9**:97 *bibliog., illus.*
amethyst **1**:368 *illus.*
mineral bodies **9**:97
GEODESIC (mathematics)
spherical trigonometry **18**:180
GEODESIC DOME **3**:552 *illus.*; **9**:97–98 *bibliog., illus.*
Fuller, R. Buckminster **8**:358
GEODESY *see* EARTH, SIZE AND SHAPE OF
GEODUCK **9**:98
GEOFFREY OF MONMOUTH **9**:98
Arthur and Arthurian legend **2**:219
GEOFFROY DE SAINT-HILAIRE, ÉTIENNE
monkey **13**:532
GEOGRAPHICAL LINGUISTICS **9**:98–100 *bibliog., maps*
See also HISTORICAL LINGUISTICS; SOCIOLINGUISTICS
bilingualism **9**:100
dialects **9**:98
ideolects **9**:98
isoglosses **9**:98–99 *maps*
linguistic atlases **9**:98
linguistics **12**:358
sociological factors **9**:100
word geography of the Eastern United States **9**:99 *maps*
GEOGRAPHICAL SOCIETIES **9**:100
GEOGRAPHY **9**:100–103 *bibliog., illus.*
See also GEOGRAPHICAL LINGUISTICS
branches **9**:103
Ratzel, Friedrich **16**:94
central place theory **4**:254–255
culture area **5**:385–386
diffusion, cultural **6**:170
elevation **7**:136
history and evolution **9**:100–101 *illus.*
Davis, William Morris **6**:53
Eratosthenes of Cyrene **7**:227–228
Hakluyt, Richard **10**:17
Idrisi, al- **11**:32
Mackinder, Sir Halford John **13**:29
Morse, Jedidiah **13**:590
Ptolemy **15**:606–607
Richtofen, Ferdinand von **16**:215
Strabo **18**:287
maps and mapmaking **13**:139
professional and educational organizations
geographical societies **9**:100
National Geographic Society **14**:33
remote sensing **16**:147
GEOGRAPHY III (poetry)
Bishop, Elizabeth **3**:297
GEOID *see* EARTH, GRAVITATIONAL FIELD OF
GEOLOGIC SURVEY
De La Beche, Sir Henry Thomas **6**:60
Smith, William **17**:371
United States Geological Survey **19**:462
GEOLOGIC TIME **9**:103–105 *bibliog., table*
age-dating **9**:104–105
carbon-14 radiodating, half-life **10**:19–20
dendrochronology **6**:106–107
radiometric age-dating **16**:65–67
Cenozoic Era **4**:245–246
Eocene Epoch **9**:104
Miocene Epoch **9**:104
Oligocene Epoch **9**:104
Paleocene Epoch **9**:104
Pleistocene Epoch **15**:364–366
Pliocene Epoch **9**:104
Quaternary Period **16**:15
Recent Epoch **16**:106–107
Tertiary Period **19**:122–125
dinosaur **6**:179–182
Earth, structure and composition of **7**:20–23
endangered species **7**:165–168
fossil record **8**:243–248
geophysics **9**:108
history **9**:103–104
ice ages **11**:7–11
invertebrate **11**:234
Lyell, Sir Charles **12**:475
major intervals **9**:103–104
Mesozoic Era **13**:322
Cretaceous Period **9**:104
Jurassic Period **11**:474–477
Triassic Period **19**:292
Olduvai Gorge **14**:377 *illus.*
paleobotany **15**:30–32
paleoclimatology **15**:32
paleogeography **15**:35–38
paleontology **15**:42
Paleozoic Era **15**:42–43
Cambrian Period **4**:50–52
Carboniferous Period **4**:137–139
Devonian Period **6**:144–146
Ordovician Period **14**:420–422
Permian Period **15**:174–175
Silurian Period **17**:310–312
petroleum **15**:208
Phillips, John **15**:239
Precambrian time **15**:491–493
scale **9**:104 *table*
sea level **17**:169
sediment deposit
stage **18**:210
span
Holmes, Arthur **10**:205
GEOLOGICAL INSTRUMENTATION

GEOLOGICAL INSTRUMENTATION (cont.)
alidade **1**:293
electron microprobe
mineral **13**:440
petrography **15**:207
goniometer **9**:244
gravimeter **9**:303
gravity pendulum
Vening Meinesz, Felix **19**:545
inclinometer **11**:74
Joly, John **11**:441
magnetometer **13**:59
petrographic microscope
optical mineralogy **14**:408
scale
Richter scale **16**:215
sand **17**:59
seismometer **17**:189–190
surveying **18**:366–369
theodolite **19**:155–156
transit, surveying **19**:273
GEOLOGICAL OCEANOGRAPHY
oceanography **14**:344–346
GEOLOGICAL SOCIETY
Sorby, Henry Clifton **18**:68
GEOLOGY **9**:105–106 *bibliog., illus.*
Africa **1**:140 *map*
Arduino, Giovanni **2**:144–145
Asia **2**:236 *map*
assay of ores **2**:264
Australia **2**:331 *map*
basalt **3**:101
baselevel **3**:108
basement rock **3**:108
basin and range province **3**:110
batholith **3**:122
beach and coast **3**:135–136
berm **3**:219
birthstones **3**:296
branches
astrogeology **2**:270
dynamical geology **9**:105
economic geology **9**:105
engineering geology **9**:105
environmental geology **9**:105
field geology **8**:48
field geology: felsite **8**:48
geochemistry **9**:95–97
geological oceanography **14**:344–345
geophysics **9**:107–108
historical geology **9**:105
marine geology **13**:231
military geology **9**:105
physical geology **9**:105
structural geology **18**:303
structural geology: Suess, Eduard **18**:323
breccia **3**:470
butte **3**:592
carbon-14 radiodating **10**:19–20
cave **4**:222
Cenozoic Era **4**:245–246
cirque **4**:444–445
conglomerate **5**:181
continental drift **5**:228–229
continental shelf and slope **5**:230
continental shield **5**:230
convection cell **5**:232
coral reef **5**:258
development
geologic time **9**:103–105
Earth, geological history of **7**:11–15
Earth, geomagnetic field of **7**:15–17
Earth, gravitational field of **7**:17
Earth, heat flow in **7**:17–18
Earth, structure and composition of **7**:19–23
Earth sciences **7**:24
earthquakes **7**:25–28
East African Rift System **7**:30–31
erosion and sedimentation **7**:232–234
escarpment **7**:237
Europe **7**:270 *map*
fall line **8**:13 *map*
flume studies **8**:186
geologic map
Strachey, John **18**:287
geologic time **9**:103–105
geomorphology **9**:107
geosyncline **9**:119–120
glaciers and glaciation **9**:192–195
ground temperature **9**:373
groundwater **9**:374–375 *illus.*
ice ages **11**:7–11
International Geophysical Year **11**:220
island arc **11**:297–298
joint (geology) **11**:440
landform evolution **12**:181–183
landslide and avalanche **12**:193
limnology **12**:345
magma **13**:51–52
maps and mapmaking **13**:141
Meteor Crater **13**:337
meteorite craters **13**:337
microseism **13**:388
mid-oceanic ridge **13**:389–390
mineral **13**:438–444
mountain **13**:619–620
mudflow **13**:631
nappe **14**:20
North America **14**:227 *map*
oceanography **14**:344–345
ore deposits **14**:422–426
orogeny **14**:447
paleoecology **15**:34–35
paleogeography **15**:35–38
paleomagnetism **15**:41–42
paleontology **15**:42
pediment **15**:131
petroleum **15**:207–209
petrology **15**:215
physiography **15**:287
plate tectonics **15**:351–357
playa **15**:363
Pleistocene Epoch **15**:364–366
polar wandering **15**:393
pollen stratigraphy **15**:407–408
prehistoric humans **15**:511–512
prehistory **15**:517
radiometric age-dating **16**:65–67
radiometric age-dating, half-life **10**:19–20
regression, marine **16**:129
remote sensing **16**:147
research institutions
JOIDES **11**:438
Lamont-Doherty Geological Observatory **12**:175
rift valleys **16**:221
Ring of Fire **16**:225
salt dome **17**:37–38
seamount **17**:174
soil **18**:36–38
soil mechanics **18**:38
South America **18**:87 *map*
speleology **18**:177
stratigraphy **18**:292–293
subfields **9**:105
subsidence **18**:316–317
tar sands **19**:34
till and tillite **19**:199
uniformitarianism **19**:386
volcano **19**:626–628
weathering **20**:82–83
GEOLOGY, HISTORY OF
Agassiz, Louis Rodolphe **1**:182
Agricola, Georgius **1**:188
Arduino, Giovanni **2**:144–145
Becquerel, Antoine Henri **3**:153
Berzelius, Jöns Jakob **3**:227
Biot, Jean Baptiste **3**:277
Bjerknes, Jacob **3**:302
Boltwood, Bertram Borden **3**:372
Boyle, Robert **3**:434
Brewster, Sir David **3**:476
Brongniart, Alexandre **3**:503
Buckland, William **3**:536
Buddington, Arthur Francis **3**:543
Buffon, Georges, Comte de **3**:547
Chamberlin, Thomas Chrowder **4**:274
Conybeare, W. D. **5**:234
Cuvier, Georges, Baron **5**:399
Dalton, John **6**:14–15
Dana, James Dwight **6**:20
Darwin, Charles **6**:41–42
De La Beche, Sir Henry Thomas **6**:60
development
catastrophism **4**:201
continental drift theory **5**:228–229
crystal **5**:373–374
Earth sciences **7**:24
fossil record **8**:243–248
geologic time **9**:103–105
mineral **13**:438–439
plate tectonics **15**:357
radiometric age-dating **16**:65–67
seismic instruments **12**:175
stratigraphy **18**:292–293
uniformitarianism **19**:386
Dutton, Clarence Edward **6**:315–316
Franklin, Benjamin **8**:282–284
Füchsel, Georg Christian **8**:352
Galileo Galilei **9**:15
Gassendi, Pierre **9**:56
Geikie, Sir Archibald **9**:68
Gilbert, Grove Karl **9**:178–179
Gressley, Amanz **9**:359
Guettard, Jean Étienne **9**:392
Hall, Sir James **10**:22
Halley, Edmond **10**:22–23
Haüy, René-Just **10**:69–70
Hayden, Ferdinand **10**:80–81
Herodotus **10**:144–145
Hess, H. H. **10**:151–152
history **9**:105–106
Holmes, Arthur **10**:205
Hooke, Robert **10**:226–227
Humboldt, Alexander von **10**:301
Hutton, James **10**:323–324
Joly, John **11**:441
Kelvin, William Thomson, 1st Baron **12**:40
Laue, Max **12**:236
Lehmann, Johann Gottlob **12**:276
Leonardo da Vinci **12**:289–291
Lugeon, Maurice **12**:452–453
Lyell, Sir Charles **12**:474–475
Matthews, D. H. **13**:231
Maury, Matthew Fontaine **13**:238
Moore, Raymond Cecil **13**:570
Murchison, Roderick Impey **13**:647
Newton, Sir Isaac **14**:173–175
Oppel, Albert **14**:407
Penck, Walther **15**:142
Phillips, John **15**:239
Playfair, John **15**:363
Pliny the Elder **15**:368
Rosenbusch, Harry **16**:315
Schmitt, Harrison H. **17**:128
Sedgwick, Adam **17**:183
Simpson, George Gaylord **17**:317
Smith, William **17**:371
Sorby, Henry Clifton **18**:68
Steno, Nicolaus **18**:253
Strabo **18**:287
Strachey, John **18**:287
Suess, Eduard **18**:323
Theophrastus **19**:158
Ussher, James **19**:491
Vening Meinesz, Felix **19**:545
Vine, F. J. **19**:600
Wallace, Alfred Russel **20**:13
Wegener, Alfred Lothar **20**:91
Werner, Abraham Gottlob **20**:104
Wollaston, William Hyde **20**:199
GEOMAGNETISM *see* EARTH, GEOMAGNETIC FIELD OF
GEOMETRIC ART *see* OP ART; VORTICISM
GEOMETRIC ISOMER
cis-trans isomerism **4**:445
configuration **5**:178
isomer **11**:299
stereochemistry **18**:258
GEOMETRIC PROGRESSION
progression **15**:563–564
GEOMETRICAL OPTICS
optics **14**:410
GEOMETRY **9**:106–107 *bibliog., illus.*
angle **1**:415
Apollonius of Perga **2**:84
arc **2**:112
arca (mathematics) **2**:145
Archimedes **2**:128
asymptote **2**:286
axiom **2**:377–378
axis (mathematics) **2**:378
Barrow, Isaac **3**:95
branches **9**:106–107 *table*
affine geometry **9**:107
algebraic geometry **1**:285
analytic geometry **1**:390–391
descriptive geometry **6**:126
differential calculus **6**:167–168
differential geometry **6**:169
elliptic geometry **9**:107
equiareal geometry **9**:107
Euclidean geometry **7**:263
hyperbolic geometry **9**:107
non-Euclidean geometry **14**:215–216
projective geometry **15**:565
similarity geometry **9**:107
spherical geometry **9**:106
spherical trigonometry **18**:180
trigonometry **19**:298–299
catenary **4**:202
Cavalieri, Bonaventura **4**:220
centroid **4**:256
circle **4**:435–436 *illus.*
cone **5**:174–175 *illus.*
congruent figures **5**:188
conic sections **5**:188–189
coordinate systems (mathematics) **5**:246–247
cube **5**:380
curvature (mathematics) **5**:396
curve (mathematics) **5**:396
cycloid **5**:404–405
cylinder **5**:406
eccentricity **7**:37
ellipse **7**:147
ellipsoid **7**:148
Euclid **7**:262–263
fractal **8**:258
golden section **9**:232–233
Greece, ancient **9**:106
hexagon **10**:154
Hilbert, David **10**:163
historical development **9**:106
Hyades **10**:327
hyperbola **10**:347–348
line (mathematics) **12**:352–353
logical structure **9**:107
mathematics **13**:222
mathematics, education in **13**:222–223 *bibliog.*
mathematics, history of **13**:223–224; **13**:226
Minkowski, Hermann **13**:451
Monge, Gaspard **13**:527–528
number **14**:293
Pappus **15**:72
parabola **15**:74
parallel **15**:79
parallelogram **15**:79
plane (mathematics) **15**:327
point **15**:381
polygon **15**:419 *illus.*
polyhedron **15**:419–420 *illus.*
prism **15**:553–554
pyramid **15**:634
Pythagoras, theorem of **15**:639
Pythagoras of Samos **15**:639–640
quadrilateral **16**:5
radian **16**:42
rectangle **16**:110
secant **17**:178
slope **17**:363
sphere **18**:180
spiral **18**:188
square **18**:202
symmetry (mathematics) **18**:403–404
tangent **19**:22
topology (mathematics) **19**:237–238
torus **19**:247
transformation **19**:270
trapezoid **19**:283–284
triangle (mathematics) **19**:292
Veblen, Oswald **19**:529
vector analysis **19**:530
volume **19**:632
GEOMORPHOLOGY **9**:107 *bibliog.*
coastal plain **5**:80–81
Earth, structure and composition of **7**:19–23
geography **9**:103
geology **9**:105–106
glaciers and glaciation **9**:192–195
Humboldt, Alexander von **10**:301
Hutton, James **10**:323–324
ice ages **11**:7–11
kame **12**:9
lake, glacial **12**:170
landform evolution **12**:183
littoral zone **12**:373
meander, river **13**:253
patterned ground **15**:115
Penck, Walter **15**:142
physiography **15**:287
playa **15**:363
sand dune **17**:60
GEOPHYSICS **9**:107–108 *bibliog.*
Darwin, Sir George Howard **6**:42
dynamo theory **6**:319
Earth, geomagnetic field of **7**:15–17
Earth, gravitational field of **7**:17
Earth, heat flow in **7**:17–18
Earth, motions of **7**:19
Earth, size and shape of **7**:19
Earth, structure and composition of **7**:19–23
Earth sciences **7**:24
El Niño (ocean current) **7**:99
Elsasser, Walter Maurice **7**:150
European Space Agency **7**:306
Ewing, Maurice **7**:325
geology **9**:105–106
geology, dynamical **9**:105
geomagnetism **9**:108
Gutenberg, Beno **9**:408
Hess, H. H. **10**:151–152
Hurley, Patrick Mason **10**:316
international cooperation **9**:108
International Geophysical Year **11**:220
Jeffreys, Sir Harold **11**:394
Libby, Willard Frank **12**:311
microseism **13**:388
Mohorovičić discontinuity **13**:503
Munk, Walter **13**:643
oceans and atmosphere **9**:108
OGO **14**:354
outer atmosphere **9**:108
plate tectonics **15**:351–357
professional and educational organizations
American Geophysical Union **1**:340; **9**:108
International Union of Geodesy and Geophysics **9**:108
research
Fletcher's Ice Island **8**:163
ore deposits **14**:425

research institutions
JOIDES **11**:438
Lamont-Doherty Geological Observatory **12**:175
solar system **9**:108
solid-earth geophysics **9**:108
subfields **9**:108
Vine, F. J. **19**:600
volcano **9**:108
Wegener, Alfred Lothar **20**:91
GEOPOLITICS **9**:108–109 *bibliog.*
Mackinder, Sir Halford John **13**:29
North America **14**:236
GEORGE (Iowa)
map (43° 21′N 96° 0′W) **11**:244
GEORGE (county in Mississippi)
map (30° 50′N 88° 40′W) **13**:469
GEORGE, DAVID LLOYD *see* LLOYD GEORGE, DAVID, 1st EARL LLOYD-GEORGE OF DWYFOR
GEORGE, HENRY **9**:109 *bibliog., illus.*
single tax **17**:322
socialism **18**:23
GEORGE, JEAN CRAIGHEAD **9**:109
GEORGE, LAKE (Florida)
map (29° 17′N 81° 36′W) **8**:172
GEORGE, LAKE (Michigan)
map (46° 28′N 84° 10′W) **13**:377
GEORGE, LAKE (New York) **9**:109
map (43° 35′N 73° 35′W) **14**:149
GEORGE, LAKE (Uganda)
map (0° 2′N 30° 12′E) **19**:372
GEORGE, SAINT **9**:109 *bibliog.*
GEORGE, STEFAN **9**:109 *bibliog.*
GEORGE I, KING OF ENGLAND, SCOTLAND, AND IRELAND **9**:110 *bibliog., illus.*
Walpole, Sir Robert **20**:18
GEORGE I, KING OF GREECE **9**:112
GEORGE II, DUKE OF SAXE-MEININGEN *see* SAXE-MEININGEN, GEORGE II, DUKE OF
GEORGE II, KING OF ENGLAND, SCOTLAND, AND IRELAND **9**:110 *bibliog.*
theater, history of the **19**:149
Walpole, Sir Robert **20**:18
GEORGE II, KING OF GREECE **9**:112
GEORGE III, KING OF ENGLAND, SCOTLAND, AND IRELAND **9**:110–111 *bibliog., illus.*
American Revolution **1**:357
Declaration of Independence **6**:74
George, Lake **9**:109
Regency **16**:126
toppling of his statue in New York (1776) **9**:315 *illus.*
Vermont **19**:558
GEORGE IV, KING OF ENGLAND, SCOTLAND, AND IRELAND **9**:111 *bibliog., illus.*
Regency **16**:126
regent **16**:128
Royal Pavilion at Brighton **16**:330–331
GEORGE V, KING OF ENGLAND, SCOTLAND, AND IRELAND **9**:111–112 *bibliog., illus.*
GEORGE VI, KING OF ENGLAND, SCOTLAND, AND IRELAND **9**:112 *bibliog., illus.*
GEORGE B. STEVENSON RESERVOIR
map (41° 25′N 78° 5′W) **15**:147
GEORGE CROSS
George VI, King of England, Scotland, and Ireland **9**:112
GEORGE EASTMAN HOUSE **9**:109–110
GEORGE OF PODĚBRADY, KING OF BOHEMIA **9**:110 *bibliog.*
GEORGE TOWN (Bahama Islands)
map (23° 30′N 75° 46′W) **3**:23
GEORGE TOWN (Malaysia) **13**:85 *Illus.*
GEORGE TUPOU I, KING OF TONGA
Tonga **19**:234
GEORGE WASHINGTON BRIDGE **9**:110 *bibliog.*
Ammann, Othmar Hermann **1**:372
Gilbert, Cass **9**:178
GEORGE WASHINGTON BRIDGE
New York (city) **14**:144 *map*
GEORGE WASHINGTON UNIVERSITY, THE **9**:110
GEORGE WEST (Texas)
map (28° 20′N 98° 7′W) **19**:129
GEORGETOWN (Cayman Islands) **9**:112
GEORGETOWN (Colorado)
map (39° 42′N 105° 42′W) **5**:116
GEORGETOWN (Delaware)
map (38° 42′N 75° 23′W) **6**:88
GEORGETOWN (Gambia)
map (13° 30′N 14° 47′W) **9**:25
GEORGETOWN (Georgia)
map (31° 53′N 85° 6′W) **9**:114
GEORGETOWN (Guyana) **9**:112; **9**:411 *illus., table*
map (6° 48′N 58° 10′W) **9**:410
GEORGETOWN (Illinois)
map (39° 59′N 87° 38′W) **11**:42
GEORGETOWN (Kentucky)
map (38° 13′N 84° 33′W) **12**:47
GEORGETOWN (Massachusetts)
map (42° 43′N 71° 0′W) **13**:206
GEORGETOWN (Mississippi)
map (31° 52′N 90° 10′W) **13**:469
GEORGETOWN (Ohio)
map (38° 52′N 83° 54′W) **14**:357
GEORGETOWN (Prince Edward Island)
map (46° 11′N 62° 32′W) **15**:548
GEORGETOWN (South Carolina)
map (33° 23′N 79° 17′W) **18**:98
GEORGETOWN (county in South Carolina)
map (33° 25′N 79° 15′W) **18**:98
GEORGETOWN (Texas)
map (30° 38′N 97° 41′W) **19**:129
GEORGETOWN UNIVERSITY **9**:112
founder
Carroll, John **4**:169
GEORGIA **9**:112–118 *bibliog., illus., map*
archaeology
Etowah Mounds **7**:258
cities
Albany **1**:251
Athens **2**:289
Atlanta **2**:292–293 *illus., map*
Augusta **2**:320
Columbus **5**:126–127
Macon **13**:35
Savannah **17**:99
Warm Springs **20**:30
climate **9**:113
economy **9**:116–117 *illus.*
education **9**:116
Emory University **7**:157
Georgia, state universities and colleges of **9**:118
Mercer University **13**:304
Morehouse College **13**:577
Spelman College **18**:177
flag **9**:113 *illus.*
Fort Benning **8**:236
government and politics **9**:117
history **9**:117–118
Civil War, U.S. **5**:30–31
Felton, William Harrell **8**:48
French and Indian Wars **8**:313
Gordon, John Brown **9**:249
Oglethorpe, James **14**:354
Stephens, Alexander Hamilton **18**:254
Talmadge (family) **19**:17
United States, history of the **19**:438
land and resources **9**:113–115 *illus., map*
map (32° 50′N 83° 15′W) **19**:419
people **9**:115–116
physical features
Okefenokee Swamp **14**:366
Stone Mountain **18**:282
rivers, lakes, and waterways **9**:115 *illus.*
Chattahoochee River **4**:303
seal, state **9**:113 *illus.*
tourism and recreation **9**:116
vegetation and animal life **9**:113
GEORGIA, STATE UNIVERSITIES AND COLLEGES OF **9**:118
GEORGIA, STRAIT OF
map (49° 20′N 124° 0′W) **3**:491
GEORGIAN BAY **9**:118
map (45° 15′N 80° 50′W) **14**:393
map (45° 15′N 80° 50′W) **9**:320
GEORGIAN LANGUAGE (USSR)
Caucasian languages and literature **4**:218
GEORGIAN POETRY **9**:118 *bibliog.*
Brooke, Rupert **3**:509
de la Mare, Walter **6**:60
Drinkwater, John **6**:273
Graves, Robert **9**:302–303
Masefield, John **13**:196
Owen, Wilfrid **14**:471
GEORGIAN SOVIET SOCIALIST REPUBLIC (USSR) **9**:118–119 *bibliog.*
cities
Batumi **3**:128
Tbilisi **19**:51
Elbrus, Mount **7**:102
house **10**:269 *illus.*
GEORGIAN STYLE **9**:119 *bibliog.*
colonial styles in North America **5**:109–110
house (in Western architecture) **10**:267; **10**:270
Independence Hall **11**:78
interior design **11**:213–214 *illus.*
residences
Charleston (South Carolina) **4**:298 *illus.*
Mount Vernon (Washington's home) **13**:618; **19**:610 *illus.*
GEORGIANA (Alabama)
map (31° 33′N 86° 44′W) **1**:234
GEORGICS (poem)
Vergil **19**:551
GEORGINA RIVER
map (23° 30′S 139° 47′E) **2**:328
GEOS (artificial satellite) **9**:119
Molniya **13**:512
study, Earth's shape, magnetic field **9**:119
GEOSYNCLINE **9**:119–120 *bibliog., illus.*
Carboniferous Period **4**:138
Dana, James Dwight **6**:20
Early Permian time
paleogeography **15**:37 *map*
Earth, geological history of **7**:12–13
geochemistry **9**:96
mountain **13**:620
ophiolite **14**:404
orogeny **14**:447
paleogeography **15**:36
plate tectonics **15**:356
syncline and anticline **18**:406
Triassic Period **19**:292–393
GEOTHERMAL ENERGY **9**:120–121 *bibliog.*
energy sources **7**:174–175
geyser **9**:162
hot springs **10**:259
igneous rock **11**:36
New Zealand **14**:160 *illus.*
power, generation and transmission of **9**:120–121; **15**:483
Valley of Ten Thousand Smokes (Alaska) **19**:508
volcano **19**:628
Yellowstone National Park **20**:322
GEOTROPISM
tropism **19**:310 *illus.*
GERA (East Germany) **9**:121
map (50° 52′N 12° 4′E) **9**:140
GERALD (Missouri)
map (38° 24′N 91° 20′W) **13**:476
GERALDINE (Montana)
map (47° 36′N 110° 16′W) **13**:547
GERALDTON (Australia)
map (28° 46′S 114° 36′E) **2**:328
GERALDTON (Ontario)
map (49° 44′N 86° 57′W) **14**:393
GERANIUM **9**:121 *bibliog., illus.*
GÉRARD, FRANÇOIS PASCAL SIMON, BARON **9**:121 *bibliog.*
GÉRARD, JEAN IGNACE ISIDOR *see* GRANDVILLE
GERASA (Jordan) **9**:121 *bibliog.*
GERBASI, VICENTE
Venezuela **19**:543
GERBIL **9**:122 *illus.*; **10**:5 *illus.*
GERBNER, GEORGE
radio and television broadcasting **16**:60
GERELA, ROY **8**:217 *illus.*
GERENUK
antelope **2**:46 *illus.*
ecological adaptation **13**:100 *illus.*
GERESHK (Afghanistan)
map (31° 48′N 64° 34′E) **1**:133
GERGONNE, JOSEPH DIEZ
mathematics, history of **13**:226
GERHARDT, CHARLES FRÉDÉRIC **9**:122
organic chemistry **14**:434–435
GERIATRICS **9**:122 *bibliog.*
aging **1**:185–186
middle age **13**:391
old age **14**:373–374
senility **17**:203
GÉRICAULT, THÉODORE **9**:122–123 *bibliog., illus.*
Officer of the Imperial Guard **8**:307 *illus.*
The Raft of the Medusa **9**:123 *illus.*
GERING (Nebraska)
map (41° 50′N 103° 40′W) **14**:70
GERLACH PEAK
map (49° 12′N 20° 8′E) **5**:413
GERLACHE DE GOMERY, ADRIEN DE, BARON **9**:123
GERM THEORY OF DISEASE
medicine **13**:270–271
Pasteur, Louis **15**:107–108
Protozoa **15**:580
GERM WARFARE *see* CHEMICAL AND BIOLOGICAL WARFARE
GERMAIN, LORD GEORGE **9**:123 *bibliog.*
American Revolution **1**:357
GERMAN ACADEMY OF SCIENCES AT BERLIN (East Germany) *see* AKADEMIE DER WISSENSCHAFTEN DER DDR
GERMAN ART AND ARCHITECTURE **9**:123–127 *bibliog., illus.*
See also AUSTRIAN ART AND ARCHITECTURE; the subheading Germany under names of specific art forms, e.g., ARCHITECTURE; DECORATIVE ARTS; PAINTING; SCULPTURE; etc.; names of specific artists, e.g., DÜRER, ALBRECHT; MIES VAN DER ROHE, LUDWIG; etc.
art history
Mander, Carel van **13**:111
baroque art and architecture **3**:88–91 *illus.*
Bauhaus **3**:129–130
Biedermeier **3**:247
Blaue Reiter, Der **3**:328
Brücke, Die **3**:520–521
caricature **4**:150
Carolingian art and architecture **4**:160–161 *illus.*
Celtic art **4**:239
costume **5**:294–301 *illus.*
Danube school **6**:36
Dresden State Art Collections **6**:270–271
expressionism (art) **7**:340
folk art **8**:196
Germany, history of **9**:148; **9**:152; **9**:155
Glyptothek (museum) **9**:212–213
Gothic art and architecture **9**:258; **9**:260–262
Gothic Revival **9**:262
Greek Revival **9**:346
jewelry **11**:410
Munich (West Germany) **13**:641 *illus.*
museums, art **13**:658
Nazarenes **14**:66
neoclassicism (art) **14**:81–82
Ottonian art and architecture **14**:466–467
pottery and porcelain **15**:471
Renaissance art and architecture **16**:154
rococo style **16**:264 *illus.*
Romanesque art and architecture **16**:283–283
Secession movement **17**:178
suprematism **18**:354
tapestry **19**:31–32
20th century **9**:128
GERMAN AND AUSTRIAN MUSIC **9**:128–131 *bibliog., illus.*
See also names of specific composers, e.g., HANDEL, GEORGE FRIDERIC; MAHLER, GUSTAV; etc.
chorale **4**:407
Germany, history of **9**:152–153
hymn **10**:346
Mannheim school **13**:125
meistersinger **13**:283
minstrels, minnesingers, and troubadours **13**:460
music, history of Western **13**:665–667
opera **14**:400–401
rococo music **16**:263
Salzburg Festival **17**:44–45
serial music **17**:208
song **18**:64
Strauss (family) **18**:293–294
symphony **18**:405
Vienna Philharmonic Orchestra **19**:579
GERMAN CONFEDERATION **9**:132
Carlsbad Decrees **4**:152
Germany, history of **9**:152–153 *map*
Liechtenstein **12**:326
Metternich, Klemens, Fürst von **13**:349
Prussia **15**:585–586 *map*
GERMAN DEMOCRATIC REPUBLIC (East Germany) *see* GERMANY, EAST AND WEST
GERMAN EAST AFRICA **9**:132
Ruanda-Urundi **16**:332
Tanzania **19**:28
GERMAN EAST AFRICA COMPANY *see* EAST AFRICA COMPANY, GERMAN
GERMAN LITERATURE **9**:132–134 *bibliog., illus.*

GERMAN LITERATURE (cont.)
See also AUSTRIAN LITERATURE; the subheading German literature under CRITICISM, LITERARY; DRAMA; NOVEL; POETRY; etc.; names of specific authors, e.g., HESSE, HERMANN; REMARQUE, ERICH MARIA; etc.; titles of specific literary works, e.g., *FAUST*; *MAGIC MOUNTAIN, THE*; etc.
Biedermeier **3**:247
Germany, history of **9**:148–155
Gruppe 47 (literary group) **9**:384
Middle Ages **9**:132
romanticism **16**:292–293
Sturm und Drang **18**:309
GERMAN LONGHAIRED POINTER **9**:134
GERMAN MEASLES **9**:134
blindness **3**:332
heart diseases, congenital **10**:95
measles **13**:253
pregnancy and birth **15**:504
GERMAN SHEPHERD (dog) **6**:214 *illus.*; **9**:135 *bibliog., illus.*
guide dog **9**:394
GERMAN SHORTHAIRED POINTER **6**:218 *illus.*; **9**:135 *bibliog., illus.*
GERMAN WIREHAIRED POINTER **6**:218 *illus.*; **9**:135 *bibliog., illus.*
GERMANDER **9**:135
GERMANIA MUSICAL SOCIETY
American music **1**:349
GERMANIC LANGUAGES **9**:135–137 *bibliog., tables*
Afrikaners **1**:177–178
alphabet, German-Gothic **20**:294 *table*
dictionaries **6**:159
distribution **9**:136 *table*
East Germanic **9**:136 *table*
English language **7**:191–193
Grimm, Jacob and Wilhelm **9**:365–366
Grimm's law **9**:136 *table*; **9**:366
High German Sound Shift **9**:136 *table*
Low Countries, history of the **12**:438
morphology **9**:137
North Germanic **9**:136 *table*
Norway **14**:262
runes **16**:346
separation from Indo-European **9**:136
Slavic languages **17**:358
sound changes **9**:136 *tables*
Verner's Law **9**:136 *table*
Verner, Karl Adolf **19**:559
vocabulary **9**:137
West Germanic **9**:136 *table*
writing and spelling **9**:136–137
GERMANIC LAW **9**:137–138 *bibliog.*
Gierke, Otto Friedrich von **9**:177
history **9**:137–138
law, history of **12**:244
Salic law **17**:32
written record **9**:137–138
GERMANIC MYTHOLOGY *see* NORSE MYTHOLOGY
GERMANIC PEOPLES **9**:138 *bibliog.*
Europe, history of **7**:281
Franks **8**:285–286
Gallic Wars **9**:19
Gaul **9**:60–61
Germany, history of **9**:147
Goths **9**:263
Great Britain, history of **9**:309
Lombards **12**:399
Low Countries, history of the **12**:438–439
Odoacer **14**:350
Portugal, history of **15**:453
Rome, ancient **16**:304
Saxons **17**:104–105
Scandinavia, history of **17**:108
Spain, history of **18**:144
Swabia **18**:375
Vandals **19**:518
women in society **20**:202
GERMANICUS, GAIUS JULIUS CAESAR *see* CALIGULA, ROMAN EMPEROR
GERMANICUS, TIBERIUS CLAUDIUS DRUSUS NERO *see* CLAUDIUS I, ROMAN EMPEROR
GERMANICUS CAESAR **9**:138
GERMANIUM **9**:138 *bibliog.*
element **7**:130 *table*
Group IVA periodic table **15**:167
Mendeleyev, Dmitry Ivanovich **13**:295
semimetal chemical element **9**:138
transition elements **19**:273 *table*
GERMANTOWN (Illinois)
map (38° 33′N 89° 32′W) **11**:42
GERMANTOWN (Tennessee)
map (35° 5′N 89° 49′W) **19**:104
GERMANTOWN (Wisconsin)
map (43° 14′N 88° 6′W) **20**:185
GERMANTOWN, BATTLE OF **1**:361 *illus.*
GERMANUS OF AUXERRE, SAINT **9**:138–139
GERMANY, EAST AND WEST **9**:139–147 *bibliog., illus., map, table*
agriculture **9**:143; **9**:145 *illus.*
aircraft, military *see* AIRCRAFT, MILITARY
army
armored vehicle **20**:268 *illus.*
Groener, Wilhelm **9**:368
art *see* GERMAN ART AND ARCHITECTURE
Berlin Wall **3**:217
cities
Aachen **1**:49
Augsburg **2**:319–320
Baden-Baden **3**:19
Bayreuth **3**:134
Berchtesgaden **3**:208
Berlin **3**:214–217 *illus., map*
Bochum **3**:355
Bonn **3**:380–381 *illus.*
Braunschweig **3**:458
Bremen **3**:472
Bremerhaven **3**:473
Cologne **5**:105
Dachau **6**:4
Darmstadt **6**:39
Dessau **6**:132
Dortmund **6**:243
Dresden **6**:270 *illus.*
Duisburg **6**:294–295
Düsseldorf **6**:308
Erfurt **7**:228
Essen **7**:244
Frankfurt am Main **8**:280–281 *illus.*
Freiburg im Breisgau **8**:301
Gelsenkirchen **9**:70
Gera **9**:121
Gotha **9**:254
Göttingen **9**:264
Halle **10**:22
Hamburg **10**:26–27
Hannover **10**:38–39
Heidelberg **10**:107
Jena **11**:395
Karl-Marx-Stadt **12**:27
Karlsruhe **12**:28
Kassel **12**:30
Kiel **12**:74
Koblenz **12**:104
Krefeld **12**:128
Leipzig **12**:278 *illus.*
Lübeck **12**:446–447
Magdeburg **13**:46–47
Mainz **13**:75
Mannheim **13**:125
Mülheim an der Ruhr **13**:636
Munich **13**:641 *illus.*
Münster **13**:643–644
Neuss **14**:107
Nuremberg **14**:297
Oberammergau **14**:315
Oldenburg **14**:375–376
Osnabrück **14**:455–456
Potsdam **15**:467
Regensburg **16**:128
Rostock **16**:320–321
Saarbrücken **17**:3
Schwerin **17**:140
Solingen **18**:55
Stuttgart **18**:310
Trier **19**:297
Weimar **20**:94
Wiesbaden **20**:146
Wittenberg **20**:193
Worms **20**:284
Wuppertal **20**:297
Würzburg **20**:297
Zweibrücken **20**:383
Zwickau **20**:384
climate **9**:141–142 *table*
communications **9**:142–143
communism *see* COMMUNISM
crime **5**:346 *table*
dance
Jooss, Kurt **11**:446
Wigman, Mary **20**:147
demography **9**:141–142
economic activity **9**:143–145 *illus.*
banking systems **3**:69
consumer price index **11**:170 *table*
unemployment rate **7**:160
education **7**:61; **9**:142; **9**:143
academic freedom **1**:68
European universities **7**:307 *table*
Froebel, Friedrich Wilhelm August **8**:335–336
Gymnasium **9**:412
Heidelberg, University of **10**:107
Herbart, Johann Friedrich **10**:134–135
Jahn, Friedrich Ludwig **11**:349
energy **9**:144; **9**:145
synthetic fuels **18**:410
fishing industry
herring **10**:147
flags **8**:134; **8**:140 *illus.*; **9**:139 *illus.*
Fokker, Anthony Hermann Gerard **8**:193
government and politics **9**:145–146
civil law **5**:12
defense, national **6**:82 *table*
medals and decorations **13**:262 *illus.*
Ulbricht, Walter **19**:376
health **9**:142; **9**:143
history *see* GERMANY, HISTORY OF
land and resources **9**:139–141 *illus., map, table*
languages *see* GERMANIC LANGUAGES
literature *see* GERMAN LITERATURE
manufacturing **9**:144; **9**:145–146 *illus.*
automotive industry **2**:366 *table*
map (50° 59′N 10° 19′E) **7**:268
mining **9**:143–144; **9**:145
music *see* GERMAN AND AUSTRIAN MUSIC
navy
Doenitz, Karl **6**:212–213
Tirpitz, Alfred von **19**:209
newspapers and periodicals
Stern, Der **18**:260
Welt, Die **20**:102
Zeit, Die **20**:358
people **9**:141–144 *illus.*
See also GERMANIC PEOPLES
migration to the United States **11**:55 *map*
women in society **20**:204 *table*
physical features
Black Forest **3**:315
Frisian Islands **8**:334
Harz **10**:65
Helgoland **10**:111
pistol **15**:318 *illus.*
poison gas **15**:382
regions
Baden **3**:19
Bavaria **3**:131 *map*
Brandenburg **3**:453
Brunswick **3**:525–526
Hanover **10**:39–40 *map*
Hesse **10**:152
Mecklenburg **13**:260
Pomerania **15**:422
Rhineland **16**:196
Ruhr Valley **16**:343
Saar **17**:3 *map*
Saxony **17**:105
Schleswig-Holstein **17**:126 *map*
Silesia **17**:304
Thuringia **19**:186
Westphalia **20**:118
Württemberg **20**:297
rifle **16**:220 *illus.*
rivers, lakes, and waterways **9**:139; **9**:141; **9**:146 *illus.*
Elbe River **7**:102
Main River **13**:68
Spree River **18**:199
Weser River **3**:472; **20**:105
rockets and missiles **16**:253–254
service sector and tourism **9**:144; **9**:145
social security **18**:14
socialism *see* SOCIALISM
sociocultural patterns **9**:143
theater
Berliner Ensemble **3**:218
Brahm, Otto **3**:440
Deutsches Theater **6**:136–137
freie Bühne, die **8**:301
Jessner, Leopold **11**:402
Neuber, Carolina and Johann **14**:104
Piscator, Erwin **15**:316
Reinhardt, Max **16**:132
Saxe-Meiningen, George II, Duke of **17**:104
theater, history of the **19**:147–148
titles of nobility **19**:214 *table*
trade **9**:144
transportation **9**:144–145
Autobahn **2**:355
railroad **16**:73; **16**:75 *illus.*
roads and highways **16**:238
vegetation and animal life **9**:141
Warsaw Treaty Organization **20**:32
wine **20**:175–176
GERMANY, HISTORY OF **9**:147–156 *bibliog., illus., maps*
See also HOLY ROMAN EMPIRE; PRUSSIA
Bavaria **3**:131
Berlin **3**:216–217
Brandenburg (East Germany) **3**:453
Burgundy **3**:570–571
civil law **5**:12
colonialism
Herero **10**:141
feudalism **8**:64
Franconia **8**:279
Germanic law **9**:137–138
Hesse (West Germany) **10**:152
historians *see* HISTORY—German historians
Hohenstaufen (dynasty) **10**:199
Hohenzollern (dynasty) **10**:199
Latvian Soviet Socialist Republic (USSR) **12**:236
Mecklenburg **13**:260
Nassau (historical region) **14**:25
navy **14**:63
Palatinate Saxony **15**:30
socialism **18**:20–22
Thuringia **19**:186
Welf (family) **20**:97
Wittelsbach (family) **20**:193
prior to 751 AD
ancient period **9**:147–148
Arminius **2**:173
Austrasia **2**:346
Frankish kingdom **9**:148
Franks **8**:285–286 *map*
Gaul **9**:60–61
Germanic peoples **9**:138
Merovingians **13**:312
751–911 Carolingian dynasty
Arnulf, Frankish Emperor **2**:186
Carolingians **4**:162
Charlemagne **4**:289–290 *map*
Charles III, Frankish Emperor **4**:292
Lothair I, Frankish Emperor **12**:419
Lothair I, King of Lotharingia **12**:419
Lotharingia **12**:419–420
Louis the German, East Frankish King **12**:422
Louis I, Frankish Emperor **12**:429
911–1250 Medieval period **9**:148–151
Conrad I, King **5**:199
Conrad II, King and Holy Roman Emperor **5**:199
Conrad III, King and Holy Roman Emperor **5**:199
Conrad IV, King **5**:199
c.1176 **9**:149 *map*
Drang nach Osten **6**:262
Frederick I, King and Holy Roman Emperor **8**:290
Frederick II, King and Holy Roman Emperor **8**:290–291
Henry I, King of Germany **10**:128
Henry II, King and Holy Roman Emperor **10**:128
Henry III, King of Germany and Holy Roman Emperor **10**:128–129
Henry IV, King of Germany and Holy Roman Emperor **10**:129
Henry V, King and Holy Roman Emperor **10**:129
Henry VI, King and Holy Roman Emperor **10**:129
Henry The Lion, Duke of Saxony and Bavaria **10**:123
Lothair II, King and Holy Roman Emperor **12**:419
Otto I, King and Holy Roman Emperor **14**:462–463
Otto II, King and Holy Roman Emperor **14**:463
Otto III, King and Holy Roman Emperor **14**:463
Otto IV, King **14**:463
Philip of Swabia **15**:232
Saxony **17**:105
Swabia **18**:375
1250-1519 decline of imperial authority
Charles IV, King **4**:293

costume **5**:297 *illus.*
Frederick III, King and Holy Roman Emperor **8**:291
Habsburg (dynasty) **10**:6
Hanseatic League **10**:40–41
Henry VII, King and Holy Roman Emperor **10**:130
Louis IV, King and Holy Roman Emperor **12**:428
Maximilian I, King and Holy Roman Emperor **13**:240
Ottokar II, King of Bohemia (Přemysl Ottokar) **14**:464
Rudolf I, King **16**:338
Sigismund, King and Holy Roman Emperor **17**:299
sword **18**:398 *illus.*
Wenceslas, King of Germany and Bohemia **20**:103
1519–1648 Reformation
Berlichingen, Götz von **3**:214
Charles V, Holy Roman Emperor **4**:294–295
Ferdinand I, Holy Roman Emperor **8**:52–53
Ferdinand II, Holy Roman Emperor **8**:53
Ferdinand III, Holy Roman Emperor **8**:53
Frederick III, Elector of Saxony **8**:292
Frederick V, Elector Palatine (the Winter King) **8**:292
Frederick William, Elector of Brandenburg (the Great Elector) **8**:292–293
Fugger (family) **8**:355
Reformation **9**:151
sword **18**:398 *illus.*
Thirty Years' War *see* THIRTY YEARS' WAR
1648-1789 absolutism
Charles VII, Holy Roman Emperor **4**:295–296
Frederick II, King of Prussia **8**:291–292
Joseph II, Holy Roman Emperor **11**:452
Maria Theresa, Austrian Archduchess, Queen of Hungary and Bohemia **13**:150
Seven Years' War *see* SEVEN YEARS' WAR
War of the Austrian Succession *see* AUSTRIAN SUCCESSION, WAR OF THE
1815–1871 Confederation and Unification
Bismarck, Otto von **3**:298–299
Carlsbad Decrees **4**:152
Europe, history of **7**:292–294 *map*
Franco-Prussian War *see* FRANCO-PRUSSIAN WAR
Frankfurt Parliament **8**:281
Frederick William IV, King of Prussia **8**:293
German Confederation **9**:132; **9**:152
Revolutions of 1848 **16**:189 *illus.*
Seven Weeks' War **17**:216
turnverein **19**:351
unification **9**:152–153
Zollverein **20**:372
1871–1918 Second Reich
Bebel, August **3**:149–150
Bethmann-Hollweg, Theodore **3**:231
Bülow, Bernhard Heinrich Martin, Fürst von **3**:561
Caprivi, Georg Leo, Graf von **4**:128
Frederick III, Emperor **8**:292
Imperial state **9**:153–155
Junkers **11**:471
Kulturkampf **12**:136
Lasalle, Ferdinand **12**:214
Moroccan crises **13**:583
Reichstag **16**:130
Triple Alliance **19**:302
William I, Emperor **20**:156–157
William II, Emperor of Germany **20**:157
World War I *see* WORLD WAR I
1918–1933 Revolution and Weimar Republic
Brüning, Heinrich **3**:525
Ebert, Friedrich **7**:35
Einstein, Albert **7**:93–94
Gierke, Otto Friedrich von **9**:177
Hindenburg, Paul von **10**:169
Meinecke, Friedrich **13**:282
money **13**:527 *illus.*
Müller, Hermann **13**:636
Munich Putsch **13**:641–642
Scapa Flow **17**:115
Stresemann, Gustav **18**:297
Weimar Republic **9**:155; **20**:94–95
1933–1945 Third Reich
Bormann, Martin **3**:401
Braun, Eva **3**:458
concentration camp **5**:169
expansion **9**:156 *map*; **20**:251 *map*
Gdańsk (Poland) **9**:65
Gestapo **9**:159
Goebbels, Joseph **9**:221–222
Goering, Hermann **9**:222
Himmler, Heinrich **10**:167–168
Hitler, Adolf **10**:187–188
Jews **11**:416
League of Nations **12**:258
Lidice (Czechoslovakia) **12**:323
Louis, Joe **12**:422
Nazi-Soviet Pact **14**:67
Nazism **9**:155–156; **14**:67–68
Niemöller, Martin **14**:185
Olympic Games **14**:383
Papen, Franz von **15**:68
Reichstag **16**:130
Ribbentrop, Joachim von **16**:205
Schacht, Hjalmar **17**:116
Speer, Albert **18**:176
Stark, Johannes **18**:227
swastika **18**:379
Third Reich **19**:170
World War II *see* WORLD WAR II
1945–1949 occupation **20**:281 *map*
Berlin Airlift **3**:217
cold war **5**:98
Oder-Neisse line **14**:349 *map*
1949-present **9**:156
Adenauer, Konrad **1**:102
Berlin Wall **3**:217
Brandt, Willy **3**:454–455
Erhard, Ludwig **7**:228
Germany, East and West **9**:146–147
Honecker, Erich **10**:220
Kohl, Helmut **12**:106
Scheel, Walter **17**:118
Schmidt, Helmut **17**:127
Stoph, Willi **18**:284
Strauss, Franz Josef **18**:294
GERMER, LESTER H.
chemistry, history of **4**:328
quantum mechanics **16**:10
GERMINAL (book) **9**:157 *bibliog.*
GERMINATION **9**:157 *bibliog.*
gardening **9**:43
seed **17**:186–187
GERMISTON (South Africa) **9**:157
map (26° 15′S 28° 5′E) **18**:79
GERNRICH, RUDI
fashion design **8**:32
GERNSBACK, HUGO **9**:157
Hugo Award **10**:294
GÉRÔME, JEAN LÉON **9**:157 *bibliog.*
GERONA (Spain)
cathedral
Spanish art and architecture **18**:153
map (41° 59′N 2° 49′E) **18**:140
GERONIMO **2**:73 *illus.*; **9**:157–158 *bibliog., illus.*; **19**:451 *illus.*
Crook, George **5**:359
GERONIMO (Oklahoma)
map (34° 28′N 98° 23′W) **14**:368
GERONTOLOGY *see* AGING; GERIATRICS; OLD AGE
GERRHOSAURID **9**:158
GERRY, ELBRIDGE **9**:158 *bibliog.*
GERRYMANDER **9**:158 *bibliog., illus.*
Baker v. *Carr* **3**:28
Gerry, Elbridge **9**:158
GERSHWIN, GEORGE AND IRA **1**:351 *illus.*; **9**:158–159 *bibliog., illus.*
Porgy and Bess **13**:673 *illus.*; **15**:441
GERSON, JEAN LE CHARLIER DE **9**:159 *bibliog.*
GERSONIDES *see* LEVI BEN GERSHON
GERUSALEMME LIBERATA (poem)
Tasso, Torquato **19**:43
GERVAIS, PAUL
Oreopithecus **14**:432
GESELL, ARNOLD **9**:159
GESNER, KONRAD VON **9**:159 *bibliog.*
GESTALT PSYCHOLOGY **9**:159 *bibliog.*
Brentano, Franz **3**:473
Koffka, Kurt **12**:105–106
Köhler, Wolfgang **12**:106
perception **9**:159; **15**:158–159
Perls, Friedrich S. **15**:173
problem solving **15**:559 *illus.*
psychotherapies **9**:159
reasoning **16**:105
Wertheimer, Max, founder **20**:104
GESTAPO **9**:159 *bibliog.*
Goering, Hermann **9**:222
Himmler, Heinrich **10**:167–168
police state **15**:397
GESTATION **9**:160 *bibliog.*
development **6**:142
horse **10**:241
GESTE DU ROI *see* CHARLEMAGNE CYCLE
GESTURAL PAINTING
modern art **13**:494
GESÙ, IL (church)
Vignola, Giacomo Barozzida **19**:592
GESUALDO, CARLO **9**:160 *bibliog.*
GETAFE (Spain)
map (40° 18′N 3° 43′W) **18**:140
GETHSEMANE **9**:160
Jerusalem **11**:400 *map*
GETIC LANGUAGE *see* DACIAN LANGUAGE
GETTY, J. PAUL **9**:160 *bibliog.*
GETTY MUSEUM **9**:160 *bibliog.*
Los Angeles County Museum of Art **12**:418
GETTYSBURG (Pennsylvania) **9**:160
map (39° 50′N 77° 14′W) **15**:147
GETTYSBURG (South Dakota)
map (45° 1′N 99° 57′W) **18**:103
GETTYSBURG, BATTLE OF **5**:28 *illus.*; **9**:160–161 *bibliog., map*
Ewell, Richard S. **7**:325
Hancock, Winfield Scott **10**:35
Meade, George Gordon **13**:252
Pickett, George E. **15**:293
strategy and tactics, military **18**:291
Stuart, J. E. B. **18**:306
GETTYSBURG ADDRESS **9**:161–162 *bibliog., illus.*
GEULINCX, ARNOLD **9**:162
GEVERS, MARIE *see* TOUSSEUL, JEAN (pseudonym)
GEYERSITE
silica minerals **17**:304
GEYL, PIETER **9**:162
GEYSER **9**:162–163 *bibliog., illus.*
hot springs **10**:259
Old Faithful **14**:375
sinter **17**:325
water **9**:162–163
GEYSER (Montana)
map (47° 16′N 110° 30′W) **13**:547
GEYSERITE *see* SILICA MINERALS
GEZELLE, GUIDO **9**:163 *bibliog.*
GEZER (Israel) **9**:163
GHAGHRA RIVER
map (25° 47′N 84° 37′E) **9**:37
GHANA **9**:163–166 *bibliog., illus., map, table*
art
African art **1**:160–164
cities
Accra **1**:79
Kumasi **9**:164 *table*
Sekondi-Takoradi **17**:190
climate **9**:163–164 *table*
economic activity **9**:164–165 *illus.*
education **9**:164
African universities **1**:176 *table*
flag **9**:163 *illus.*
government **9**:165
history **9**:165–166
Africa, history of **1**:152
Nkrumah, Kwame **14**:206–207
Thirty Years' War **19**:171
land and resources **9**:163 *map, table*
literature
Awoonor, Kofi **2**:377
map (8° 0′N 2° 0′W) **1**:136
people **9**:164
Ewe **8**:325
Fanti **8**:21
Ga **9**:3
rivers, lakes, and waterways **9**:163
Volta, Lake **19**:631
Volta River **19**:631
vegetation and animal life **9**:164
GHANI, ABD AL-AZIZ ABD AL-
Yemen (Sana) **20**:326
GHARAPURI *see* ELEPHANTA (India)
GHARDAÏA (Algeria) **1**:288 *illus.*
map (32° 31′N 3° 37′E) **1**:287
GHARIAL *see* GAVIAL
GHARYAN (Libya)
map (32° 10′N 13° 1′E) **12**:320
GHAT (Libya)
map (24° 58′N 10° 11′E) **12**:320
GHATS **9**:166
GHAZALI, AL- **9**:166 *bibliog.*
GHAZIR (Lebanon)
map (34° 1′N 35° 40′E) **12**:265
GHAZNAVID (dynasty)
Mahmud of Ghazni **13**:65–66
GHAZNI (Afghanistan)
map (33° 33′N 68° 26′E) **1**:133
GHELDERODE, MICHEL DE **9**:166 *bibliog.*
GHENT (Belgium) **9**:166
Artevelde (family) **2**:214
map (51° 3′N 3° 43′E) **3**:177
GHENT, JOOS VAN *see* JOOS VAN GHENT
GHENT, TREATY OF **9**:166 *bibliog.*
War of 1812 **20**:27
GHEORGHE GHEORGHIU DEJ (Romania)
map (46° 14′N 26° 44′E) **16**:288
GHEORGHIU-DEJ, GHEORGHE (statesman) **9**:166–167
Romania **16**:290
GHETTO **9**:167 *bibliog.*
city **5**:6–8
Harlem **10**:49–50
Jews **11**:415
Judaism **11**:462
Warsaw (Poland) **20**:32
GHIBELLINES *see* GUELPHS AND GHIBELLINES
GHIBERTI, LORENZO **9**:167–168 *bibliog., illus.*
The Adoration of the Magi **11**:311 *illus.*
Florence (Italy) **8**:168
Gates of Paradise **3**:101 *illus.*; **9**:167–168 *illus.*
Italian art and architecture **11**:310
GHIN, MOUNT
map (32° 39′N 36° 43′E) **18**:412
GHIORSO, A.
element 104 **7**:132
GHIRLANDAIO, DOMENICO **9**:168–169 *bibliog., illus.*
Goes, Hugo van der **9**:223
Old Man and His Grandson **9**:168 *illus.*; **15**:447 *illus.*
Sistine Chapel **17**:329
GHISLANZONI, ANTONIO
Aïda **1**:201
GHOSE, AUROBINDO *see* AUROBINDO, SRI
GHOST **9**:169 *bibliog.*
GHOST DANCE **9**:169 *bibliog.*
Sitting Bull **17**:330
Smohalla **17**:373
Wovoka **20**:285
GHOST SONATA, THE (play) **9**:169 *bibliog.*
GHOST STORY *see* SUPERNATURAL LITERATURE
GHOST TOWNS **9**:169–170 *bibliog.*
Virginia City (Nevada) **14**:112 *illus.*
GHOSTS (play) **9**:170 *bibliog.*
Ibsen, Henrik **11**:6–7
naturalism **14**:50
GHURIAN (Afghanistan)
map (34° 21′N 61° 30′E) **1**:133
GHUZ *see* TURKMEN
G.I. BILL OF RIGHTS **9**:170 *bibliog.*
GIA DINH (Vietnam)
map (10° 48′N 106° 42′E) **19**:580
GIA LONG
Vietnam **19**:583
GIACOMETTI, ALBERTO **9**:170–171 *bibliog., illus.*
Walking Man II **9**:170 *illus.*
GIACOMO DE VIO *see* CAJETAN
GIACONDA, LA (Leonardo da Vinci) *see* MONA LISA
GIACOSA, GIUSEPPE
Madama Butterfly **13**:39
Tosca **19**:247
GIAEVER, IVAR **9**:171
GIAMBOLOGNA *see* BOLOGNA, GIOVANNI DA
GIANNINI, AMADEO PETER **9**:171 *bibliog.*
GIANT LONGHORN BEETLE **3**:167 *illus.*
GIANT SCHNAUZER *see* SCHNAUZER
GIANT TOAD **9**:171 *illus.*
GIANTS (folklore) **9**:171
GIANT'S CAUSEWAY **9**:171–172 *illus.*; **14**:254 *illus.*
GIAP, VO NGUYEN *see* VO NGUYEN GIAP
GIARDIA **9**:172
protozoal diseases **15**:581
GIAUQUE, WILLIAM FRANCIS **9**:172
GIBBERD, FREDERICK
Liverpool (England) **12**:376
GIBBERELLINS **9**:172
GIBBON **2**:75; **9**:172 *illus.*; **15**:540 *illus.*
ape **2**:74–75 *illus.*
siamang **17**:290
GIBBON (Minnesota)
map (44° 32′N 94° 31′W) **13**:453
GIBBON (Nebraska)
map (40° 45′N 98° 51′W) **14**:70

GIBBON, EDWARD 9:172–173 *bibliog., illus.*
Decline and Fall of the Roman Empire, The History of the 6:76
GIBBON, JOHN
heart-lung machine 10:97
GIBBONS, GRINLING 9:173 *bibliog.*
furniture 8:377
wood carving 20:208
GIBBONS, JAMES 9:173 *bibliog., illus.*
GIBBONS, ORLANDO 9:173 *bibliog.*
GIBBONS* v. *OGDEN 9:173–174
Marshall, John 13:172
navigation, constitutional interpretation 9:173–174
Vanderbilt (family) 19:518–519
GIBBS, JAMES 9:174 *bibliog., illus.*
Radcliffe Camera (Oxford University) 9:174 *illus.*
GIBBS, JOSIAH WILLARD 9:174 *bibliog.*
chemistry, history of 4:328
kinetic theory of matter 12:79
thermochemistry 19:162
GIBBSITE
bauxite 3:131
GIBBSTOWN (New Jersey)
map (39° 50′N 75° 17′W) 14:129
GIBRALTAR 9:174–175 *bibliog., illus., map*
government 9:174–175
history 9:175
map (36° 11′N 5° 22′W) 7:268
GIBRALTAR (Gibraltar)
map (36° 9′N 5° 21′W) 9:174
GIBRALTAR, BAY OF
map (36° 9′N 5° 22′W) 9:174
GIBRALTAR, ROCK OF
Gibraltar 9:174–175 *illus.*
GIBRALTAR, STRAIT OF 9:175
map (35° 57′N 5° 36′W) 18:140
GIBRAN, KAHLIL 9:175 *bibliog.*
GIBSLAND (Louisiana)
map (32° 33′N 93° 3′W) 12:430
GIBSON (Georgia)
map (33° 14′N 82° 36′W) 9:114
GIBSON (county in Indiana)
map (38° 20′N 87° 35′W) 11:111
GIBSON (Louisiana)
map (29° 41′N 90° 59′W) 12:430
GIBSON (county in Tennessee)
map (36° 0′N 89° 55′W) 19:104
GIBSON, ALTHEA 9:175 *bibliog.*
GIBSON, BOB 9:175 *bibliog.*
GIBSON, CHARLES DANA 9:175–176 *bibliog.*
GIBSON, EDWARD 9:176
Skylab 17:348
GIBSON, ELEANOR
cognitive psychology 5:95
GIBSON, JAMES
cognitive psychology 5:95
GIBSON, JOSH 9:176
GIBSON, KENNETH
Newark (New Jersey) 14:164
GIBSON CITY (Illinois)
map (40° 28′N 88° 22′W) 11:42
GIBSON DESERT 9:176
map (24° 30′S 126° 0′E) 2:328
GIBSON GIRL
clothing industry 5:65
Gibson, Charles Dana 9:175–176
GIBSONBURG (Ohio)
map (41° 23′N 83° 19′W) 14:357
GIDDENS, ANTHONY
sociology 18:30
GIDDINGS (Texas)
map (30° 11′N 96° 56′W) 19:129
GIDDINGS, J. LOUIS 9:176
Cape Krusenstern 4:120
GIDE, ANDRÉ 9:176 *bibliog., illus.*
Immoralist, The 11:56
GIDEON 9:177
GIDEON* v. *WAINWRIGHT 9:177 *bibliog.*
Escobedo v. *Illinois* 7:237
Fortas, Abe 8:238
legal aid 12:272
GIDEON'S FIRE (book)
Creasey, John 5:334
GIDEONS INTERNATIONAL
Bible societies 3:241
GIEDION, SIGFRIED 9:177
GIELGUD, SIR JOHN 9:177 *bibliog., illus.*
GIEREK, EDWARD 9:177
Poland 15:390–391
GIERKE, OTTO FRIEDRICH VON 9:177 *bibliog.*
Germanic law 9:177
GIESEKING, WALTER 9:177 *bibliog.*
GIFFARD, HENRI
airship 1:228
GIFFORD (Florida)
map (27° 41′N 80° 25′W) 8:172
GIFFORD, WILLIAM 9:177
GIFTED, EDUCATION OF THE *see* SPECIAL EDUCATION
GIFU (Japan)
map (35° 25′N 136° 45′E) 11:361
GIG
coach and carriage 5:73
GIGAKU 9:178
GIGANTISM
endocrine system, diseases of the 7:170
GIGANTOPITHECUS 9:178
GIGLI, BENIAMINO 9:178 *bibliog.*
GIGOLO
prostitution 15:573
GIICHI, TANAKA *see* TANAKA GIICHI
GIJÓN (Spain) 9:178
map (43° 32′N 5° 40′W) 18:140
GIJSEN, MARNIX 9:178
GIKONGORO (Rwanda)
map (2° 29′S 29° 34′E) 16:378
GIKUYU *see* KIKUYU
GILA (county in Arizona)
map (33° 35′N 110° 45′W) 2:160
GILA BEND (Arizona)
map (32° 57′N 112° 43′W) 2:160
GILA MONSTER 9:178 *bibliog., illus.*
GILA RIVER 9:178
map (32° 43′N 114° 33′W) 5:120
GILBERT (Arizona)
map (33° 21′N 111° 47′W) 2:160
GILBERT (Minnesota)
map (47° 29′N 92° 28′W) 13:453
GILBERT, CASS 9:178 *bibliog.*
Minnesota state capitol 13:454 *illus.*
Waterbury (Connecticut) 20:61
Woolworth Building 20:216
GILBERT, GROVE KARL 9:178–179 *bibliog.*
GILBERT, SIR HUMPHREY 9:179 *bibliog.*
Newfoundland (Canada) 14:168
GILBERT, JOHN
film, history of 8:82
GILBERT, MARIE D. E. R. *see* MONTEZ, LOLA
GILBERT, WILLIAM (physician) 9:179 *bibliog.*
physics, history of 15:282; 15:283
GILBERT, SIR WILLIAM SCHWENK *see* GILBERT AND SULLIVAN
GILBERT ISLANDS *see* KIRIBATI
GILBERT PEAK
map (46° 30′N 121° 25′W) 20:35
GILBERT AND SULLIVAN 9:179 *bibliog., illus.*
D'Oyly Carte, Richard 6:253
GILBERTVILLE (Massachusetts)
map (42° 19′N 72° 12′W) 13:206
GILBRETH, FRANK AND LILLIAN 9:180
time and motion study 19:202
GILCHRIST (county in Florida)
map (29° 45′N 82° 50′W) 8:172
GILDED AGE 9:180
United States, history of the 19:450–452 *illus.*
GILDED AGE, THE (book)
Gilded Age 9:180
GILDFORD (Montana)
map (48° 34′N 110° 18′W) 13:547
GILDING 9:180 *bibliog.*
furniture 8:376
GILDS *see* GUILDS
GILEAD 9:180
GILELS, EMIL 9:180
GILES (county in Tennessee)
map (35° 10′N 87° 0′W) 19:104
GILES (county in Virginia)
map (37° 15′N 80° 40′W) 19:607
GILES, ERNEST
Gibson Desert 9:176
Great Victoria Desert 9:323
GILGAMESH, EPIC OF 7:217 *illus.*; 9:180 *bibliog.*
Anu 2:71
ark 2:164
Deluge 6:96
mythology 13:697
Smith, George 17:368
Uruk 19:490
GILL 9:180–181 *illus.*
fish 8:114 *illus.*
respiratory system 16:178
GILL, SIR DAVID 9:181
astronomy, history of 2:280
GILL, DE LANCEY
Wolf Robe 4:338 *illus.*
GILL, IRVING 9:181–182 *bibliog.*
GILLAM (Manitoba)
map (56° 21′N 94° 43′W) 13:119
GILLESPIE (Illinois)
map (39° 7′N 89° 49′W) 11:42
GILLESPIE (county in Texas)
map (30° 17′N 98° 52′W) 19:129
GILLESPIE, DIZZY 9:182 *bibliog.*
jazz 11:389 *illus.*
GILLETT (Arkansas)
map (34° 7′N 91° 22′W) 2:166
GILLETT (Wisconsin)
map (44° 54′N 88° 18′W) 20:185
GILLETTE (Wyoming)
map (44° 18′N 105° 30′W) 20:301
GILLETTE, WILLIAM H. 9:182
GILLIAM (county in Oregon)
map (45° 20′N 120° 15′W) 14:427
GILLIAM, TERRY
"Monty Python's Flying Circus" 13:560
GILLIATT, PENELOPE 9:182
GILLIÉRON, JULES
linguistic atlases 9:98
GILLOT, CLAUDE 9:182 *bibliog.*
GILLRAY, JAMES 9:182 *bibliog.*
cartoon (art)
wig 20:146 *illus.*
GILLY, FRIEDRICH 9:182
GILLYFLOWER 9:182
GILMAN (Illinois)
map (40° 46′N 87° 60′W) 11:42
GILMAN (Iowa)
map (41° 53′N 92° 47′W) 11:244
GILMAN (Wisconsin)
map (45° 10′N 90° 48′W) 20:185
GILMAN, CHARLOTTE PERKINS 9:182 *bibliog.*
GILMAN, DANIEL COIT 9:182 *bibliog.*
GILMAN, LAWRENCE 9:182–183 *bibliog.*
GILMER (county in Georgia)
map (34° 45′N 84° 25′W) 9:114
GILMER (Texas)
map (32° 44′N 94° 57′W) 19:129
GILMER (county in West Virginia)
map (38° 55′N 80° 50′W) 20:111
GILMER, ELIZABETH MERIWETHER *see* DIX, DOROTHY
GILMORE, GARY MARK
suicide 18:330
GILMORE, DAME MARY 9:183
GILMORE, PATRICK SARSFIELD
American music 1:350
band 3:61
GILMORE CITY (Iowa)
map (42° 44′N 94° 27′W) 11:244
GILPIN (county in Colorado)
map (39° 50′N 105° 35′W) 5:116
GILPIN, WILLIAM
Colorado 5:115
GILROY (California)
map (37° 0′N 121° 43′W) 4:31
GILROY, NORMAN THOMAS 9:183
GILSON, ÉTIENNE 9:183 *bibliog.*
scholasticism 17:132
GILTNER (Nebraska)
map (40° 47′N 98° 9′W) 14:70
GILUWE, MOUNT
map (6° 5′S 143° 50′E) 15:72
GILYAK *see* NIVKH
GIMEL
C (letter) 4:3
GIMLI (Manitoba)
map (50° 38′N 96° 59′W) 13:119
GIN 9:183
juniper 11:470
GIN RUMMY
rummy 16:345
GINASTERA, ALBERTO 9:183 *bibliog.*
GINGER 9:183–184 *bibliog., illus.*
cardamon 4:143
ginger lily 9:184
turmeric 19:349
GINGER LILY 9:184
GINGER MAN, THE (book)
Donleavy, J. P. 6:238–239
GINGHAM 9:184
muslin 13:683
GINGIVITIS 9:184
periodontics 15:170
GINGRICH, ARNOLD
Esquire 7:243
GINKGO 9:184 *illus.*; 11:475 *illus.*
gymnosperm 9:414
GINNIE MAE *see* GENERAL NATIONAL MORTGAGE ASSOCIATION
GINSBERG, ALLEN 9:184–185 *bibliog., illus.*
"Howl" 10:285
GINSENG 9:185 *bibliog., illus.*
angelica tree 1:413
spikenard 18:183
GINZBERG, ASHER *see* ACHAD HA-AM
GINZBERG, LOUIS 9:185 *bibliog.*
GINZBURG, MOISEI
Russian art and architecture 16:364
GINZBURG, NATALIA 9:185
GINZBURG, VITALY LAZAREVICH 9:185
GIOBERTI, VINCENZO 9:185
GIOCONDA, LA see MONA LISA
GIOCONDO, FRA GIOVANNI 9:186 *bibliog.*
GIOLITTI, GIOVANNI 9:186 *bibliog.*
GIONO, JEAN 9:186 *bibliog.*
Pagnol, Marcel 15:14
GIORDANO, LUCA 9:186 *bibliog.*
GIORDANO, UMBERTO 9:186
GIORGIONE 9:186–187 *bibliog., illus.*
Cesare Borgia 3:399 *illus.*
Fête Champêtre 15:20 *illus.*
The Tempest 9:186 *illus.*; 12:189 *illus.*
Titian 19:212
GIOTTO DI BONDONE 9:187 *bibliog., illus.*
abstract art 1:64
Betrayal, The 9:187 *illus.*; 11:312 *illus.*
Cennini, Cennino 4:245
Florence (Italy) 8:168
grisaille 9:367
International Style (Gothic art) 11:223
Italian art and architecture 11:312
Padua (Italy) 15:12
Saint Francis of Assisi 8:274 *illus.*
GIOVANNI, NIKKI 9:188 *bibliog.*
GIOVANNI DA MONTECORVINO 9:188 *bibliog.*
GIOVANNI DI PAOLO 9:188 *bibliog.*
GIPARU *see* UR (Iraq)
GIPPIUS, ZINAIDA NIKOLAYEVNA *see* HIPPIUS, ZINAIDA NIKOLAYEVNA
GIRAFFE 9:188 *bibliog., illus.*; 17:98 *illus.*
blood pressure 3:339
deer 6:79
evolution 7:318
horn (biology) 10:238
okapi 14:365
GIRALDA (tower) 9:188
Moorish art and architecture 13:571
Spanish art and architecture 18:152
GIRARD (Illinois)
map (39° 27′N 89° 47′W) 11:42
GIRARD (Kansas)
map (37° 31′N 94° 51′W) 12:18
GIRARD (Texas)
map (33° 22′N 100° 40′W) 19:129
GIRARD, STEPHEN 9:188 *bibliog.*
GIRARDON, FRANÇOIS 9:188–189 *bibliog.*
GIRARDOT (Colombia)
map (4° 18′N 74° 48′W) 5:107
GIRAUD, HENRI HONORÉ 9:189
GIRAUDOUX, JEAN 9:189 *bibliog., illus.*
GIRDLE-TAILED LIZARD 9:189 *illus.*
GIRL SCOUTS OF THE U.S.A. *see* SCOUTING
GIRNE (Cyprus) *see* KYRENIA (Cyprus)
GIRODET-TRIOSON, ANNE LOUIS 9:189–190 *bibliog.*
GIRÓN (Ecuador)
map (3° 10′S 79° 8′W) 7:52
GIRONDINS *see* GIRONDISTS
GIRONDISTS 9:190 *bibliog.*
Brissot de Warville, Jacques Pierre 3:487
Corday, Charlotte 5:261
Cordeliers 5:261
Dumouriez, Charles François du Perier 6:298
French Revolution 8:323
Roland de la Platière, Jeanne Manon Philipon 16:271
GIROUX, ANDRÉ 9:190
GIRSU
Lagash 12:165
GIRTIN, THOMAS 9:190 *bibliog.*
GIRTON COLLEGE (Cambridge University) 4:53
GIRTY, SIMON 9:190 *bibliog.*
GIRWA RIVER
map (28° 15′N 81° 5′E) 14:86
GISANT
tomb 19:231
GISBORNE (New Zealand)
map (38° 40′S 178° 1′E) 14:158
GISCARD D'ESTAING, VALÉRY 9:190 *bibliog., illus.*
Chirac, Jacques 4:397
GISENYI (Rwanda)
map (1° 42′S 29° 15′E) 16:378
GISH, DOROTHY AND LILLIAN 9:190–191 *bibliog., illus.*
GISLEBERTUS 9:191 *bibliog.*
Romanesque art and architecture 16:284 *illus.*

GISSING, GEORGE ROBERT 9:191 *bibliog.*
realism (literature) 16:104
GIST, CHRISTOPHER 9:191
GITEGA (Burundi)
map (3° 26′S 29° 56′E) 3:582
GITKSAN (American Indians)
Tsimshian 19:323
GITLOW v. NEW YORK 9:191
"bad tendency test" 9:191
freedom of speech 8:298; 9:191
GIULINI, CARLO MARIA 9:191
GIULIO PIPPI *see* GIULIO ROMANO
GIULIO ROMANO 9:191–192 *bibliog., illus.*
architecture 2:135
The Bath of Cupid and Psyche 9:192 *illus.*
Veronese, Paolo 19:559
GIUNTA PISANO 9:192 *bibliog.*
GIURGIU (Romania)
map (43° 53′N 25° 57′E) 16:288
GIURGOLA, ROMALDO 9:192
GIURLANI, ALDO *see* PALAZZESCHI, ALDO
GIVHANS (South Carolina)
map (33° 1′N 80° 21′W) 18:98
GIZA (Egypt) 9:192
Egypt, ancient 7:81 *map*
map (30° 1′N 31° 13′E) 7:76
pyramids 15:635 *illus.*
Great Pyramid of Khufu 15:635 *illus.*
Khafre, Pyramid of 2:130 *illus.*
Menkaure, King of Egypt 13:298
sphinx 18:180
temple 19:94
GIZO (Solomon Islands)
map (8° 6′S 156° 51′E) 18:56
GIZZARD 9:192
GJELLERUP, KARL ADOLPH 9:192
GJIROKASTËR (Albania)
map (40° 5′N 20° 10′E) 1:250
GJOA HAVEN (Northwest Territories)
map (68° 38′N 95° 57′W) 14:258
GLA (Greece) 9:192 *bibliog.*
Aegean civilization 1:115 *map*
GLACE BAY (Nova Scotia)
map (46° 12′N 59° 57′W) 14:269
GLACIER (county in Montana)
map (48° 40′N 112° 55′W) 13:547
GLACIER NATIONAL PARK 9:195 *bibliog.*; 13:549 *illus.*; 14:38 *map, table*
GLACIERS AND GLACIATION 9:192–195 *bibliog., illus.*
Cenozoic Era 4:246
cirque 4:444–445
coral reef 5:258
Driftless Area 6:272
drumlin 6:282
Earth, geological history of 7:15
erosion and sedimentation 7:232–234
erratic, glacial 7:234–235
esker 7:238
Europe 7:269–270 *map*
firn 8:108
fjord 8:133
Fletcher's Ice Island 8:163
Flint, Richard Foster 8:165
fossil record 8:244 *illus.*
glacial features, location indicating Permian climates 15:33 *map*
glacier
Aletsch Glacier 1:272
contemporary, Northern Hemisphere 15:11 *map*
Malaspina Glacier (Alaska) 13:80
Mer de Glace (France) 13:303
hydrosphere 10:344
ice ages 11:7–11 *map*
ice sheets
Antarctica 9:193–194
Columbia Icefield 5:125–126
Greenland 9:193–194
iceberg 11:15 *illus.*
isostasy 11:300
kame 12:9
lake, glacial 12:169–170
landform evolution 12:182–183 *illus.*
mammoth 13:106–107
Milankovitch theory 13:418–419
moraine 13:572
paleoclimatology 15:32–34 *map*
paleogeography 15:38
permafrost 15:173–174
Pleistocene Epoch 15:365–366 *map*
Quaternary Period 16:15
quick clay 16:25
Ross Ice Shelf (Antarctica) 16:318
sand and gravel 9:194–195
till and tillite 19:199
Tyndall, John 19:363
varved deposit 19:524
GLACKENS, WILLIAM 9:195 *bibliog., illus.*
Chez Mouquin 9:195 *illus.*
GLADBROOK (Iowa)
map (42° 11′N 92° 43′W) 11:244
GLADDEN, WASHINGTON 9:195 *bibliog.*
Social Gospel 18:12
GLADE SPRING (Virginia)
map (36° 47′N 81° 47′W) 19:607
GLADES (county in Florida)
map (26° 59′N 81° 12′W) 8:172
GLADESVILLE BRIDGE (Australia) 3:482 *illus.*
GLADEWATER (Texas)
map (32° 33′N 94° 56′W) 19:129
GLADIATORS 9:195 *bibliog.*; 16:303 *illus.*
Spartacus 18:165
stadium 18:208
GLADIOLUS 9:195–196 *illus.*
GLADSTONE (Australia)
map (23° 51′S 151° 16′E) 2:328
GLADSTONE (Manitoba)
map (50° 13′N 98° 57′W) 13:119
GLADSTONE (Michigan)
map (45° 50′N 87° 3′W) 13:377
GLADSTONE (Missouri)
map (39° 13′N 94° 34′W) 13:476
GLADSTONE, WILLIAM EWART 9:196 *bibliog., illus.*; 9:317 *illus.*
Disraeli, Benjamin, 1st Earl of Beaconsfield 6:197–198
Great Britain, history of 9:317
Liberal parties 12:311
liberalism 12:312
Parnell, Charles Stewart 15:96
Victoria, Queen of England, Scotland, and Ireland 19:574
GLADWIN (Michigan)
map (43° 59′N 84° 29′W) 13:377
GLADWIN (county in Michigan)
map (44° 0′N 84° 25′W) 13:377
GLÅMA RIVER
map (59° 12′N 10° 57′E) 14:261
GLAMORGAN (Wales) 9:196
cities
Cardiff 4:143
Swansea 18:379
GLAMORGANSHIRE (Wales) *see* GLAMORGAN (Wales)
GLAND 9:196–197
adenoma 1:102
adrenal gland 1:108
cystic fibrosis 5:411
digestive system 6:174
endocrine system 7:168–169 *illus.*
endocrine system, diseases of the 7:169–171
hormone, animal 10:234–237
lachrymal, tears 19:58
liver 12:374
lizard 12:379–380
pancreas 15:57–58
papilloma 15:71
parathyroid gland 15:83
pineal gland 15:306
pituitary gland 15:322
prostate gland 15:573
salivary glands 17:34
snake 17:379
surgery 18:361
thymus gland 19:187
thyroid gland 19:188
GLANDERS 9:197
GLANDULAR FEVER *see* MONONUCLEOSIS
GLANVILL, RANULF DE
development of common law 5:139
GLAREANUS, HEINRICH
Renaissance music 16:156
GLARNER ALPS
map (46° 55′N 9° 0′E) 18:394
GLASCO (Kansas)
map (39° 22′N 97° 50′W) 12:18
GLASCOCK (county in Georgia)
map (33° 15′N 82° 35′W) 9:114
GLASER, DONALD 9:197
GLASGOW (Kentucky)
map (37° 0′N 85° 55′W) 12:47
GLASGOW (Missouri)
map (39° 14′N 92° 50′W) 13:476
GLASGOW (Montana)
map (48° 12′N 106° 38′W) 13:547
GLASGOW (Scotland) 9:197; 19:409 *illus.*
map (55° 53′N 4° 15′W) 19:403
photojournalism 15:273
GLASGOW, ELLEN 9:197 *bibliog.*
GLASGOW, UNIVERSITY OF 9:197
GLASGOW SCHOOL OF ART 13:31 *illus.*
GLASHOW, SHELDON 9:197
GLASPELL, SUSAN 9:197 *bibliog.*
Provincetown Players 15:584
GLASS 9:197–201 *bibliog., illus.*
borosilicate, boron 3:403
bottle 3:418–419
calcium oxide 4:22
etching, caustic chemicals 4:219
fiberglass 8:69
firebrick 8:106
furnace 9:198 *illus.*
glass ceramics 9:201
glassblowing 3:418–419 *illus.*; 9:202
glassware, decorative 9:202–204
glassy state 9:205
laser 12:213
manufacturing
plate glass 9:198–199 *illus.*
tools 9:200 *illus.*
materials technology 13:219–221
optical glass
lens 12:286–287
telescope 19:81–82
Zeiss, Carl 20:358
packaging 15:11–12
safety glass, cellulose 4:238
silica, fulgurite 8:357
soda 18:31
sodium in 18:33
stained glass 18:211–213
Stiegel, Henry William 18:267
tektites 19:74–75
tempering 19:93
water glass 20:48
window 20:173
GLASS, CARTER 9:201 *bibliog.*
GLASS, PHILIP 9:201
GLASS, STAINED *see* STAINED GLASS
GLASS, VOLCANIC *see* OBSIDIAN
GLASS CERAMICS 9:201 *bibliog.*
quartz 16:14
GLASS HARMONICA 9:201–202 *bibliog.*
GLASS HOUSE 11:435 *illus.*
Johnson, Philip 11:434–435
GLASS MENAGERIE, THE (play) 9:202 *bibliog.*
Williams, Tennessee 20:160–161
GLASS MOUNTAINS 14:367 *illus.*
GLASS SNAKE 9:202; 12:381 *illus.*
GLASS-STEAGALL ACTS 9:202
GLASSBLOWING 3:418–419 *illus.*; 9:202 *bibliog., illus.*
Geissler, Heinrich 9:69
glass 9:197–198
tools 9:200 *illus.*
GLASSBORO (New Jersey)
map (49° 32′N 99° 15′W) 14:129
GLASSCOCK (county in Texas)
map (31° 48′N 101° 30′W) 19:129
GLASSFISH 9:202
icefish 11:16
GLASSWARE, DECORATIVE 9:202–204 *bibliog., illus.*
American glass 9:204
ancient glass 9:202–203
antique collecting 2:66 *illus.*
Art Deco 2:208 *illus.*
Art Nouveau 2:211 *illus.*
beads and beadwork 3:138
cameo 4:54
chandelier 4:279
colonial styles in North America 5:111 *illus.*
craft 5:327 *illus.*
English and Irish glass 9:203–204
French glass 9:204
Gallé, Émile 9:17
glass 9:197
Islamic glass 9:203
Lalique, René 12:171–172
medieval European glass 9:203
northern Renaissance glass 9:203
Orrefors 14:448–449
Roman art and architecture 16:276
stained glass 18:211–213
Steuben glass 18:262
Stiegel, Henry William 18:267
Swedish glass 9:204
Tiffany, Louis Comfort 19:196
Waterford (city in Ireland) 20:63
Waterford glass 20:63
GLASSY STATE 9:205 *bibliog.*
See also LIQUID
GLASTONBURY (Connecticut)
map (41° 43′N 72° 37′W) 5:193
GLAUBER, JOHANN RUDOLF 9:205 *bibliog.*
Glauber's salt 9:205
GLAUBERITE 9:205
saline lake evaporite 9:205
GLAUBER'S SALT 9:205
Glauber, Johann Rudolf 9:205
sulfur 18:336
GLAUCHAU (Germany, East and West)
map (50° 49′N 12° 32′E) 9:140
GLAUCOMA 9:205 *bibliog., illus.*
blindness 3:332–333
poppy 15:432
treatment
marijuana 13:153
GLAUCOPHANE
facies, metamorphic rock 13:332 *table*
GLAUCUS 9:205
GLAZE 9:206 *bibliog., illus.*
faïence 8:8
lithium 12:370
majolica 13:76
pottery and porcelain 15:468–469
GLAZER, NATHAN 9:206
GLAZKOV, YURY NIKOLAYEVICH 9:206
GLAZUNOV, ALEKSANDR KONSTANTINOVICH 9:206 *bibliog.*
GLEASON (Tennessee)
map (36° 13′N 88° 37′W) 19:104
GLEASON, JACKIE 9:206–207 *bibliog.*
GLEE 9:207
GLEE CLUB *see* GLEE
GLEICHEN (Alberta)
map (50° 52′N 113° 3′W) 1:256
GLEINALPE MOUNTAINS
map (47° 15′N 15° 3′E) 2:348
GLEIZES, ALBERT 9:207 *bibliog.*
GLEN ALPINE (North Carolina)
map (35° 44′N 81° 47′W) 14:242
GLEN BURNIE (Maryland)
map (39° 10′N 76° 37′W) 13:188
GLEN CANYON
map (37° 10′N 110° 50′W) 19:492
GLEN CANYON DAM 2:163 *illus.*; 6:17 *illus.*
GLEN ELLYN (Illinois)
map (41° 52′N 88° 3′W) 11:42
GLEN FLORA (Texas)
map (29° 21′N 96° 12′W) 19:129
GLEN LYON (Pennsylvania)
map (41° 10′N 76° 5′W) 15:147
GLEN ROCK (New Jersey)
map (40° 58′N 74° 8′W) 14:129
GLEN ROSE (Texas)
map (32° 14′N 97° 45′W) 19:129
GLEN ULLIN (North Dakota)
map (46° 49′N 101° 50′W) 14:248
GLEN WHITE (West Virginia)
map (37° 44′N 81° 17′W) 20:111
GLENBORO (Manitoba)
map (49° 32′N 99° 15′W) 13:119
GLENBURN (North Dakota)
map (48° 31′N 101° 13′W) 14:248
GLENCOE (Alabama)
map (33° 57′N 85° 56′W) 1:234
GLENCOE (Illinois)
map (42° 8′N 87° 45′W) 11:42
GLENCOE (Minnesota)
map (44° 46′N 94° 9′W) 13:453
GLENCOE, MASSACRE OF 9:207 *bibliog.*
GLENDALE (Arizona)
map (33° 32′N 112° 11′W) 2:160
GLENDALE (California) 9:207
map (34° 10′N 118° 17′W) 4:31
GLENDALE (Ohio)
map (39° 16′N 84° 28′W) 14:357
GLENDALE (Oregon)
map (42° 44′N 123° 26′W) 14:427
GLENDALE (Utah)
map (37° 19′N 112° 36′W) 19:492
GLENDALE (Wisconsin)
map (43° 7′N 87° 57′W) 20:185
GLENDIVE (Montana)
map (47° 6′N 104° 43′W) 13:547
GLENDO (Wyoming)
map (42° 30′N 105° 2′W) 20:301
GLENDO RESERVOIR
map (42° 31′N 104° 58′W) 20:301
GLENDON (Alberta)
map (54° 15′N 111° 10′W) 1:256
GLENDORA (California)
map (34° 8′N 117° 52′W) 4:31
GLENDOWER, OWEN 9:207
GLENMORA (Louisiana)
map (30° 59′N 92° 35′W) 12:430
GLENN (county in California)
map (39° 25′N 122° 25′W) 4:31
GLENN, JOHN H., JR. 9:207 *bibliog., illus.*; 18:127 *illus.*
Mercury program 13:308 *illus.*
GLENNALLEN (Alaska)
map (62° 7′N 145° 33′W) 1:242
GLENNS FERRY (Idaho)
map (42° 57′N 115° 18′W) 11:26
GLENNVILLE (Georgia)
map (31° 56′N 81° 56′W) 9:114
GLENORCHY (New Zealand)
map (44° 51′S 168° 23′E) 14:158
GLENROCK (Wyoming)
map (42° 52′N 105° 52′W) 20:301

GLENS FALLS (New York)
map (43° 19′N 73° 39′W) **14**:149
GLENSHAW (Pennsylvania)
map (40° 31′N 79° 57′W) **15**:147
GLENSIDE (Pennsylvania)
map (40° 6′N 75° 9′W) **15**:147
GLENVIEW (Illinois)
map (42° 4′N 87° 48′W) **11**:42
GLENVILLE (Minnesota)
map (43° 34′N 93° 17′W) **13**:453
GLENVILLE (West Virginia)
map (38° 56′N 80° 50′W) **20**:111
GLENWOOD (Arkansas)
map (34° 20′N 93° 33′W) **2**:166
GLENWOOD (Iowa)
map (41° 3′N 95° 45′W) **11**:244
GLENWOOD (Minnesota)
map (45° 39′N 95° 23′W) **13**:453
GLENWOOD (New Mexico)
map (33° 19′N 108° 53′W) **14**:136
GLENWOOD (Utah)
map (38° 46′N 111° 59′W) **19**:492
GLENWOOD CITY (Wisconsin)
map (45° 4′N 92° 10′W) **20**:185
GLENWOOD SPRINGS (Colorado)
map (39° 33′N 107° 19′W) **5**:116
GLENWOODVILLE (Alberta)
map (49° 22′N 113° 21′W) **1**:256
GLIADIN
celiac disease **4**:231
sprue **18**:201
GLIDDEN (Wisconsin)
map (46° 9′N 90° 34′W) **20**:185
GLIDDEN, JOSEPH FARWELL **9**:207
GLIDE (Oregon)
map (43° 18′N 123° 6′W) **14**:427
GLIDER **1**:211 *illus.*; **9**:207–208 *bibliog.*, *illus.*
aerial sports **1**:121–122 *illus.*
airborne troops **1**:210
Chanute, Octave **4**:282
competition glides **9**:208
Lilienthal, Otto **12**:341
GLIDING *see* GLIDER
GLIDING FISH *see* FLYING FISH
GLIDING LEMUR *see* COLUGO
GLIDING SQUIRREL *see* FLYING SQUIRREL
GLIÈRE, REINHOLD MORITZOVICH **9**:208 *bibliog.*
GLINKA, MIKHAIL IVANOVICH **9**:208 *bibliog.*
Russian music **16**:367 *illus.*
GLINSKAYA, YELENA
Ivan IV, Grand Duke of Moscow and Tsar of Russia **11**:332
GLITTER ROCK
rock music **16**:249
GLITTERTINDEN MOUNTAIN
map (61° 39′N 8° 33′E) **14**:261
GLOBE **9**:208
See also MAPS AND MAPMAKING
equator **7**:225
GLOBE (Arizona)
map (33° 24′N 110° 47′W) **2**:160
GLOBE THEATRE **9**:208–209
Burbage, Richard **3**:566
Chamberlain's Men **4**:274
GLOBEFISH *see* PUFFER
GLOBULE **9**:209
Barnard, E. E. **9**:209
GLOBULIN **9**:209
antibody **2**:60; **11**:57–58
antitoxin **2**:69
blood **3**:337
gamma globulin
immunity **11**:57
inflammation **11**:169
immunoglobulins **11**:57–58
lymphatic system **12**:475
serum **17**:210
serum globulin **9**:209
GLOCKENSPIEL **9**:209 *bibliog.*, *illus.*
GLOEOCAPSA **9**:209
GLOMAR CHALLENGER *see* DEEP SEA DRILLING PROJECT
GLORIOUS REVOLUTION **9**:209 *bibliog.*
English Bill of Rights **3**:253
Great Britain, history of **9**:314–315
Ireland, history of **11**:263
Stuart, James Francis Edward **18**:305
William III, King of England, Scotland, and Ireland **20**:156
GLORY-BOWER **9**:209
GLOSSARY
dictionary **6**:159–160
specific subjects
ballet terms **3**:45-57
computer terms **5**:160h–160i
narrative and dramatic devices **14**:22-23
video terms **19**:576d–576f
GLOSSOLALIA *see* TONGUES, SPEAKING IN
GLOSSY SNAKE
colubrid **5**:125
GLOSTER (Mississippi)
map (31° 12′N 91° 1′W) **13**:469
GLOUCESTER (England) **9**:209
map (51° 53′N 2° 14′W) **19**:403
GLOUCESTER (Massachusetts) **9**:209; **13**:210 *illus.*
map (42° 41′N 70° 39′W) **13**:206
GLOUCESTER (county in New Jersey)
map (39° 50′N 75° 10′W) **14**:129
GLOUCESTER (Virginia)
map (37° 25′N 76° 32′W) **19**:607
GLOUCESTER (county in Virginia)
map (37° 25′N 76° 30′W) **19**:607
GLOUCESTER, HUMPHREY, DUKE OF **9**:210 *bibliog.*
Duke Humphrey's Library, Oxford **12**:316 *illus.*
GLOUCESTERSHIRE (England) **9**:210
cities
Gloucester **9**:209
GLOUSTER (Ohio)
map (39° 30′N 82° 5′W) **14**:357
GLOVER, REVEREND JESSE
Day, Stephen **6**:55
GLOVER ISLAND
map (48° 44′N 57° 45′W) **14**:166
GLOVERSVILLE (New York)
map (43° 3′N 74° 20′W) **14**:149
GLOVERTOWN (Newfoundland)
map (48° 41′N 54° 2′W) **14**:166
GLOVES **9**:210 *bibliog.*
GLOWWORM **9**:210 *illus.*
bioluminescence **3**:272
firefly **8**:106
GLOXINIA **9**:210 *illus.*
GLUBB, SIR JOHN BAGOT **9**:210
GLUCAGON **9**:210–211 *bibliog.*
hormones **10**:236
metabolism **13**:327
GLUCK, ALMA **9**:211
GLUCK, CHRISTOPH WILLIBALD **9**:211 *bibliog.*, *illus.*
Armide **5**:41 *illus.*
music, history of Western **13**:666
opera **14**:400 *illus.*
overture **14**:470
GLUCOCORTICOID **9**:211
adrenal gland **1**:108
adrenocorticotropic hormone **1**:109
corticoid **5**:278
eczema **7**:54
endocrine system **7**:169
endocrine system, diseases of the **7**:170
hormone, animal **10**:237
inflammation **11**:169
Kendall, Edward **12**:41
Rhizopus **16**:197
steroid **18**:261
GLUCOSE **9**:211
carbohydrate **4**:132–133
diabetes **6**:148–149
hypoglycemia **10**:351
metabolism **13**:327
nutrition, human **14**:306 *illus.*
sugar **18**:327
GLUCOSE TOLERANCE TEST **9**:211
diabetes **6**:148–149
GLUE *see* ADHESIVE
GLUEBALLS
gluon **9**:212
GLUON **9**:212 *bibliog.*
fundamental particles **8**:361; **8**:362–363 *table*
physics **15**:281
GLUTEN
celiac disease **4**:231
sprue **18**:201
wheat **20**:126
GLYCERALDEHYDE
carbohydrate **4**:133
GLYCERIN *see* GLYCEROL
GLYCEROL **9**:212
fat **8**:33
polyhydric alcohol **15**:420
stearin **18**:242
whaling **20**:123
GLYCINE
zwitterion **20**:384
GLYCOGEN **9**:212
carbohydrate **4**:132
Cori, Carl Ferdinand and Gerty Teresa **5**:262
glucagon **9**:211
lactic acid **12**:161
liver **12**:374
metabolism **13**:325; **13**:327
hypoglycemia **10**:351
GLYCOL **9**:212
GLYCOLYSIS
metabolism **13**:326
pyruvic acid **15**:639
GLYCON
Farnese Heracles **8**:28
GLYCOSIDE **9**:212 *illus.*
GLYNDEBOURNE OPERA FESTIVAL **9**:212 *bibliog.*
GLYNDON (Minnesota)
map (46° 52′N 96° 35′W) **13**:453
GLYNN (county in Georgia)
map (31° 15′N 81° 35′W) **9**:114
GLYPTODONT
edentates **7**:56
GLYPTOTHEK (museum) **9**:212–213
GMELIN, LEOPOLD **9**:213
Handbuch der inorganischen Chemie **9**:213
GMUNDEN (Austria)
map (47° 55′N 13° 48′E) **2**:348
GNAEUS NAEVIUS *see* NAEVIUS, GNAEUS
GNAT *see* MIDGE
GNATCATCHER **9**:213 *illus.*
GNATHOSTOMATA **9**:213
invertebrate **11**:235
GNATWREN **9**:213
GNEISENAU, AUGUST WILHELM ANTON, GRAF NEITHARDT VON **9**:213
GNEISS **9**:213; **13**:331 *illus.*
kyanite **12**:143
GNETID
Ephedra **7**:215–216
Gnetum **9**:213
gymnosperm **9**:414
GNETUM **9**:213
GNIEZNO (Poland)
map (52° 31′N 17° 37′E) **15**:388
GNJILANE (Yugoslavia)
map (42° 28′N 21° 29′E) **20**:340
GNOME *see* FAIRY
GNOSTICISM **9**:213–214 *bibliog.*, *illus.*
antinomianism **2**:64
apocalyptic literature **2**:79
Apocryphal New Testament **2**:79
Aurobindo, Sri **2**:325
Basilides **3**:110
Cerinthus **4**:260
Clement of Alexandria, Saint **5**:49
Docetism **6**:210
Hermetic literature **10**:142
Irenaeus, Saint **11**:265
Mandaeans **13**:110
Manichaeism **13**:116–117
Nag Hammadi Papyri **14**:5
Ophites **14**:404
Valentinus **19**:505
GNOTOBIOTICS **9**:214
GNP *see* GROSS NATIONAL PRODUCT
GNU *see* WILDEBEEST
GO (game) **9**:30 *illus.*; **9**:214 *bibliog.*
GO-BANG (game) *see* GO (game)
GO-DAIGO, EMPEROR
Japan, history of **11**:368
GOA, DAMAN, AND DIU **9**:214–215 *map*
map (14° 20′N 74° 0′E) **11**:80
map (20° 10′N 73° 0′E) **11**:80
map (20° 42′N 70° 59′E) **11**:80
GOASCORAN RIVER
map (13° 36′N 87° 45′W) **7**:100
GOAT **9**:215 *bibliog.*, *illus.*
See also MOUNTAIN GOAT
angora **9**:215
animal husbandry **2**:24
ibex **11**:4
mountain life **13**:622
ruminant **16**:345
wool **20**:213
GOAT GRASS **20**:126 *illus.*
GOATFISH **9**:215–216 *illus.*
GOATSUCKER (bird) **9**:216
GOBBI, TITO **9**:216
GOBELINS **9**:216 *bibliog.*
Le Brun, Charles **12**:252
tapestry **19**:33
GOBI **2**:235 *illus.*; **9**:216–217 *bibliog.*, *illus.*, *map*
desert **6**:127
map (43° 0′N 106° 0′E) **13**:529
GOBINEAU, JOSEPH ARTHUR, COMTE DE **9**:217 *bibliog.*
racism **16**:37
GOBLIN *see* FAIRY
GOBY **9**:217 *illus.*
GOD **9**:217–219 *bibliog.*, *illus.*
Allah **1**:298
Anselm, Saint **2**:35
Bible **3**:238
biblical concepts **9**:218
Christianity **4**:412–414
deism **6**:86
Descartes, René **6**:126
Hinduism **10**:170
Holy Spirit **10**:211
immanence, divine **11**:54
incarnation **11**:73
Islam **11**:290–292
Jesus Christ **11**:403–406
Judaism **11**:458–463
monotheism **9**:208
pantheism **15**:61
polytheism **9**:217–218; **15**:422
primitive religion **15**:544–545
religion **16**:137–141
Spinoza, Baruch **18**:187
theism **19**:155
theology **19**:157–158
theosophy **19**:159–160
transcendence, divine **19**:268
Trinity **19**:300–301
Zoroastrianism **20**:379
GODARD, JEAN LUC **9**:219 *bibliog.*, *illus.*
film, history of **8**:86
GODAVARI RIVER
map (17° 0′N 81° 45′E) **11**:80
GODDARD (Kansas)
map (37° 39′N 97° 34′W) **12**:18
GODDARD, JOHN **9**:219
GODDARD, ROBERT **9**:219–220 *bibliog.*, *illus.*
Goddard Space Flight Center **9**:220
jet propulsion **11**:407
Jet Propulsion Laboratory **11**:407
rockets and missiles **16**:253 *illus.*
GODDARD COLLEGE **9**:220
GODDARD SPACE FLIGHT CENTER **9**:220
Goddard, Robert **9**:220
National Aeronautics and Space Administration **14**:28
GODDEN, RUMER **9**:220 *bibliog.*
GODE, ALEXANDER
languages, artificial **12**:197–198
GÖDEL, KURT **9**:220
logical positivism **12**:397
mathematics, history of **13**:226
GODERICH (Ontario)
map (43° 45′N 81° 43′W) **14**:393
GODESCALC GOSPELS **11**:47 *illus.*
GODEY, LOUIS ANTOINE **9**:220 *bibliog.*
GODEY'S LADY'S BOOK (periodical)
Godey, Louis Antoine **9**:220
Hale, Sarah Josepha **10**:19
periodical **15**:169
GODFREY (Illinois)
map (38° 57′N 90° 11′W) **11**:42
GODFREY, ARTHUR **9**:220 *bibliog.*
GODFREY OF BOUILLON **9**:220–221 *bibliog.*
Jerusalem, Latin Kingdom of **11**:401
GODHAVN (Greenland)
map (69° 15′N 53° 33′W) **9**:353
GODIVA, LADY **9**:221
Coventry (England) **5**:319
GODKIN, EDWIN LAWRENCE **9**:221 *bibliog.*
GODOY, MANUEL DE **9**:221 *bibliog.*
Charles IV, King of Spain **4**:297
Ferdinand VII, King of Spain **8**:54
Spain, history of **18**:147
GODOY CRUZ (Argentina)
map (32° 55′S 68° 50′W) **2**:149
GODS LAKE
map (54° 40′N 94° 20′W) **13**:119
GODS LAKE (Manitoba)
map (54° 40′N 94° 9′W) **13**:119
GODS THEMSELVES, THE (book)
Asimov, Isaac **2**:260
GODTHÅB (Greenland) **9**:221
map (64° 11′N 51° 44′W) **9**:353
GODUNOV, ALEKSANDR **9**:221
GODUNOV, BORIS *see* BORIS GODUNOV, TSAR OF RUSSIA
GODWIN, MARY WOLLSTONECRAFT *see* WOLLSTONECRAFT, MARY
GODWIN, WILLIAM **9**:221 *bibliog.*
anarchism **1**:392
Wollstonecraft, Mary **20**:199
GODWIN AUSTEN **9**:221
map (35° 53′N 76° 30′E) **15**:27
mountain climbing **13**:621
GODWIN-AUSTEN, HENRY HAVERSHAM
Godwin Austen **9**:221
GOEBBELS, JOSEPH **9**:221–222 *bibliog.*, *illus.*
nazism **14**:68
GOEHR, ALEXANDER
English music **7**:203–204
GOEPPERT MAYER, MARIE *see* MAYER, MARIE GOEPPERT
GOERDELER, KARL FRIEDRICH **9**:222 *bibliog.*
GOERING, HERMANN **9**:222 *bibliog.*, *illus.*
Nuremberg Trials **14**:297 *illus.*
GOERITZ, MATHIAS **9**:222 *bibliog.*

GOES (artificial satellite) **9**:222
meteorology **13**:342
weather patterns supply **9**:222
GOES (Netherlands)
map (51° 30′N 3° 54′E) **14**:99
GOES, HUGO VAN DER **9**:223 *bibliog., illus.*
Portinari Altarpiece **9**:223 *illus.*
GOETHALS, GEORGE WASHINGTON **9**:223 *bibliog.*
Panama Canal **15**:57
GOETHE, JOHANN WOLFGANG VON **9**:133 *illus.*; **9**:223–224 *bibliog., illus.*
Eckermann, Johann Peter **7**:39
Faust **8**:38
Herder, Johann Gottfried von **10**:138
Humboldt, Wilhelm von, Freiherr **10**:301
Schiller, Johann Christoph Friedrich von **17**:120–121
Sorrows of Young Werther, The **18**:70
theater, history of the **19**:148 *illus.*
Weimar (East Germany) **20**:94
GOETHE PRIZE FOR LITERATURE
Freud, Sigmund **8**:329
GOETHITE **9**:224
limonite **12**:346
GOFF (Kansas)
map (39° 40′N 95° 56′W) **12**:18
GOFF, BRUCE ALONZO **9**:224 *bibliog.*
GOFFMAN, ERVING **9**:225
GOFFSTOWN (New Hampshire)
map (43° 1′N 71° 36′W) **14**:123
GOG AND MAGOG **9**:225
GOGAMA (Ontario)
map (47° 40′N 81° 43′W) **14**:393
GOGARTEN, FRIEDRICH **9**:225
GOGEBIC (county in Michigan)
map (46° 25′N 89° 40′W) **13**:377
GOGEBIC, LAKE
map (46° 30′N 89° 35′W) **13**:377
GOGOL, NIKOLAI **9**:225 *bibliog., illus.*
Dead Souls **6**:65
Inspector General, The **11**:194
GOIÂNIA (Brazil)
map (16° 40′S 49° 16′W) **3**:460
GOIÁS (Brazil)
map (15° 0′S 49° 0′W) **3**:460
GOIDELIC LANGUAGES
Celtic languages **4**:241
GOITER **9**:225 *bibliog.*
endocrine system, diseases of the **7**:170
iodine **11**:238–239
iodine deficiency
vitamins and minerals **19**:620
nutritional-deficiency diseases **14**:307
surgery
Kocher, Emil **12**:105
thyroid function test **19**:188
thyroid gland **19**:188
GOJUNOTO, THE (pagoda) **11**:373 *illus.*; **15**:14 *illus.*
GÖK TÜRK
Turks **19**:347
GOKSTAD SHIP BURIAL **9**:225–226
Vikings **19**:594
GOLAN HEIGHTS **11**:303 *illus.*
Israel **11**:306
map (32° 55′N 35° 42′E) **18**:412
GOLCONDA (Illinois)
map (37° 22′N 88° 29′W) **11**:42
GOLCONDA (Nevada)
map (40° 57′N 117° 30′W) **14**:111
GOLD **9**:226–227 *bibliog., illus.*
See also GOLD RUSH
abundances of common elements **7**:131 *table*
alchemy **1**:262–263
dentistry **6**:116
element **7**:130 *table*
extraction and refining **9**:227
cyanide process **5**:400
Fort Knox (Kentucky) **8**:237
Group IB periodic table **15**:167
Inca **11**:73
metal **13**:328
money **13**:526
mythology and legends
El Dorado **7**:98
Midas **13**:390
native elements **14**:47
ore deposits **9**:226
Africa **1**:149 *map*
Australia **2**:340 *map*
calaverite **4**:21
Johannesburg (South Africa) **11**:422–423 *illus.*
Kalgoorlie (Australia) **12**:8
major ore deposits **14**:424–425 *table*
placer deposit **15**:325
South Africa **18**:82
South Dakota **18**:105
Witwatersrand (South Africa) **20**:194
world distribution **14**:423 *map*
qualitative chemical analysis **16**:6
transition elements **19**:273
GOLD, H. L. **9**:227
GOLD, HERBERT **9**:228 *bibliog.*
GOLD, MICHAEL **9**:228
GOLD, THOMAS **9**:228
GOLD BEACH (Oregon)
map (42° 25′N 124° 25′W) **14**:427
GOLD COAST *see* GHANA
GOLD GLOVE AWARD (baseball)
Parker, Dave **15**:90
GOLD MEDAL WINNERS
Olympic Games **14**:383–385 *illus.*
GOLD RUSH **8**:343 *illus.*; **9**:228 *bibliog., illus.*
Australia, history of **2**:340
British Columbia, history of **3**:492
California **4**:37; **19**:444 *illus.*
Chinese Americans **14**:441
Colorado **5**:119
Conestoga **5**:175–176
Death Valley **6**:70 *illus.*
frontier **8**:341–342 *map*
Idaho **11**:29
Klondike (Yukon Territory) **12**:98
Marshall, James Wilson **13**:172
Montana **13**:550
Nevada **14**:114
Nome (Alaska) **14**:215
prospecting equipment **9**:228 *illus.*
Sacramento (California) **17**:7
Sacramento River **17**:8
Sutter, John Augustus **18**:373
Tabor, Horace W. **19**:5
Vanderbilt, Cornelius **19**:518
Victoria (Australia) **19**:573
Virginia City (Nevada) **14**:112 *illus.*
GOLD AND SILVER WORK **9**:228–230 *bibliog., illus.*
antique collecting **2**:66 *illus.*
Cellini, Benvenuto **4**:236–237
Celtic art **4**:239–240 *illus.*
craft **5**:327 *illus.*
Etruscans **7**:261
Fabergé, Peter Carl **8**:4
gilding **9**:180
Jamnitzer (family) **11**:357–358
jewelry **11**:408–411
Korean art **12**:117
Meissonnier, Juste Aurèle **13**:283
Minoan art **13**:458–459
Mycenaean gold death mask **13**:689 *illus.*
Navajo **14**:54
Nazca **14**:67
Nicholas of Verdun **14**:181
Persian art and architecture **15**:186–187
Pollaiuolo (family) **15**:405
pre-Columbian art and architecture **15**:499
Roman art and architecture **16**:277
steppe art **18**:255–256 *illus.*
Vicús **19**:576
GOLD STANDARD **9**:230 *bibliog.*
exchange rate **7**:326–327
inflation **11**:171
money **13**:526
GOLDBACH CONJECTURE **9**:230–231 *bibliog.*
GOLDBERG, ARTHUR J. **9**:231 *bibliog.*; **15**:526 *illus.*
labor law **9**:231
United States Supreme Court **9**:231
GOLDBERG, BERTRAND **9**:231 *bibliog.*
GOLDBERG, RUBE **9**:231 *bibliog.*
comic strip **5**:135–136
GOLDBORO (Nova Scotia)
map (45° 11′N 61° 39′W) **14**:269
GOLDEN (Colorado)
map (39° 46′N 105° 13′W) **5**:116
GOLDEN (Illinois)
map (40° 7′N 91° 1′W) **11**:42
GOLDEN ALGAE *see* ALGAE, GOLDEN ALGAE
GOLDEN ASS, THE (book) **9**:231 *bibliog.*
Apuleius **2**:92
GOLDEN BOUGH, THE (book) **9**:231 *bibliog.*
Frazer, Sir James **8**:289
GOLDEN BOWL, THE (book) **9**:231
GOLDEN BOY (play)
Odets, Clifford **14**:350
GOLDEN BULL **9**:231
Germany, history of **9**:150
Holy Roman Empire **10**:210
GOLDEN BUTTONS (botany) *see* TANSY
GOLDEN CALF **9**:231
GOLDEN CHAIN (botany) **9**:231
GOLDEN CITY (Missouri)
map (37° 24′N 94° 5′W) **13**:476
GOLDEN CUP (botany) **9**:231
GOLDEN EAGLE *see* EAGLE
GOLDEN FLEECE (mythology) **9**:232
Jason **11**:384
GOLDEN FLEECE, BURGUNDIAN ORDER OF THE
chivalry **4**:399
GOLDEN FLEECE AWARD
Proxmire, William **15**:584
GOLDEN GATE (waterway) **9**:232; **17**:53 *illus.*
GOLDEN GATE BRIDGE **4**:32; **9**:232 *bibliog.*; **17**:53 *illus.*
Ammann, Othmar Hermann **1**:372
GOLDEN HIND (ship) **17**:267 *illus.*
Drake, Sir Francis **6**:256
GOLDEN HINDE MOUNTAIN
map (49° 40′N 125° 45′W) **3**:491
GOLDEN HORDE, KHANATE OF THE **9**:232 *bibliog.*
Batu Khan **3**:128
Mongol rule **13**:530 *map*
Russia/Union of Soviet Socialist Republics, history of **16**:352–353
GOLDEN MEADOW (Louisiana)
map (29° 23′N 90° 16′W) **12**:430
GOLDEN-MOUTH TURBAN SHELL **17**:251 *illus.*
GOLDEN NOTEBOOK, THE (book) **9**:232
GOLDEN PALM (award)
Cannes Film Festival **4**:109
GOLDEN RATIO *see* GOLDEN SECTION
GOLDEN RECTANGLE **9**:233 *illus.*
GOLDEN RETRIEVER **6**:218 *illus.*; **9**:232 *bibliog., illus.*
guide dog **9**:394
GOLDEN SECTION **9**:232–233 *bibliog., illus.*
Fibonacci sequence **8**:69
form divided **9**:232
GOLDEN SPIDER BEETLE **3**:167 *illus.*
GOLDEN TREASURY OF ENGLISH SONGS AND LYRICS (book)
Palgrave, Francis Turner **15**:47
GOLDEN VALLEY (county in Montana)
map (46° 20′N 109° 8′W) **13**:547
GOLDEN VALLEY (county in North Dakota)
map (46° 55′N 103° 45′W) **14**:248
GOLDENBERG, EMANUEL *see* ROBINSON, EDWARD G.
GOLDENDALE (Washington)
map (45° 49′N 120° 50′W) **20**:35
GOLDENEYE (bird)
foot **3**:288 *illus.*
GOLDENRAIN TREE **9**:233 *illus.*
GOLDENROD **9**:233 *illus.*
GOLDENSON, LEONARD
radio and television broadcasting **16**:57
GOLDFADEN, ABRAHAM **9**:233
Yiddish theater **20**:328
GOLDFIELD (Iowa)
map (42° 44′N 93° 55′W) **11**:244
GOLDFIELD (Nevada)
map (37° 42′N 117° 14′W) **14**:111
GOLDFINCH **9**:233–234 *bibliog., illus.*
finch **8**:93
GOLDFISCH, SAMUEL *see* GOLDWYN, SAMUEL
GOLDFISH **8**:117 *illus.*; **9**:234 *bibliog., illus.*
GOLDIE, SIR GEORGE **9**:234 *bibliog.*
GOLDING, WILLIAM **9**:234–235 *bibliog., illus.*
Lord of the Flies **12**:413
GOLDMAN, EDWIN FRANKO **9**:235
GOLDMAN, EMMA **9**:235 *bibliog., illus.*
GOLDMANN, MAX *see* REINHARDT, MAX
GOLDMARK, KARL **9**:235 *bibliog.*
GOLDMARK, PETER CARL **9**:235 *bibliog.*
radio and television broadcasting **16**:59
GOLDONI, CARLO **9**:235–236 *bibliog.*
GOLDSBORO (North Carolina)
map (35° 23′N 77° 59′W) **14**:242
GOLDSCHMIDT, MEYER ARON **9**:236 *bibliog.*
GOLDSMITH, MYRON **9**:236
GOLDSMITH, OLIVER **9**:236 *bibliog., illus.*
She Stoops to Conquer **17**:247
Vicar of Wakefield, The **19**:568
GOLDSTEIN, JOSEPH L. **9**:236
GOLDSTONE TRACKING STATION **9**:236
GOLDTHWAITE (Texas)
map (31° 27′N 98° 34′W) **19**:129
GOLDWATER, BARRY M. **9**:236–237 *bibliog., illus.*
Johnson, Lyndon B. **11**:434
presidential elections **15**:531
Republican party **16**:175
Vietnam War **19**:586
GOLDWYN, SAMUEL **9**:237 *bibliog., illus.*
GOLEM **9**:237
GOLETA (California)
map (34° 27′N 119° 50′W) **4**:31
GOLF **9**:237–240 *bibliog., illus., tables*
Bradley, Pat **3**:438
British Open Champions **9**:238 *table*
Carner, JoAnne **4**:155
Casper, Billy **4**:182
equipment **9**:237 *illus.*
Hagen, Walter **10**:9
history **9**:237–240
Hogan, Ben **10**:197
international play **9**:239–240
Jones, Bobby **11**:442
Lopez, Nancy **12**:412
Masters Champions **9**:238–239 *illus., table*
Nelson, Byron **14**:79
Nicklaus, Jack **14**:183
Palmer, Arnold **15**:50
Palmer, Sandra **15**:51
Player, Gary **15**:363
Professional Golfers Association (PGA) Champions **9**:238–239 *illus., table*
rules **9**:240
Saint Andrews (Scotland) **17**:16
Sarazen, Gene **17**:75
Snead, Sam **17**:384
Stacy, Hollis **18**:208
Trevino, Lee **19**:291
U.S. Open Champions **9**:238–239 *illus., table*
Vardon, Harry **19**:521
Watson, Tom **20**:68
Whitworth, Kathy **20**:143
Wright, Mickey **20**:290
Zaharias, Babe Didrikson **20**:348
GOLFITO (Costa Rica)
map (8° 38′N 83° 11′W) **5**:291
GOLGI, CAMILLO **9**:240
Ramón y Cajal, Santiago **16**:81
GOLGI APPARATUS **9**:240 *bibliog.*
cell **4**:232 *illus.*; **4**:233
GOLIAD (Texas)
map (28° 40′N 97° 23′W) **19**:129
Texas **19**:134
GOLIAD (county in Texas)
map (28° 37′N 97° 25′W) **19**:129
GOLIATH **9**:240
GOLIATH BEETLE **3**:167 *illus.*
GOLIATH FROG **9**:240–241 *illus.*
GOLTZIUS, HENDRIK **9**:241 *bibliog.*
Spranger, Bartholomäus **18**:199
GOMATI RIVER
map (25° 32′N 83° 10′E) **9**:37
GOMBE STREAM RESEARCH CENTER
Goodall, Jane **9**:245
GOMBERT, NICOLAS
mass (musical setting) **13**:201
GOMBRICH, SIR ERNST H. **9**:241 *bibliog.*
GOMBROWICZ, WITOLD **9**:241
GOMEL (USSR)
map (52° 25′N 31° 0′E) **19**:388
GÓMEZ, JUAN VICENTE **9**:241 *bibliog.*
GOMORRAH *see* SODOM AND GOMORRAH
GOMPERS, SAMUEL **9**:241 *bibliog., illus.*; **12**:155 *illus.*
Socialist party **18**:25
GOMUŁKA, WŁADYSŁAW **9**:241–242 *bibliog.*
Poland **15**:391
GONADOTROPIN **9**:242 *bibliog.*
endocrine system **7**:169
menstruation **13**:301
pituitary gland **15**:322
pregnancy and birth **15**:503
pregnancy test **15**:506
GONADS *see* SEX ORGANS
GONAÏVES (Haiti)
map (19° 27′N 72° 41′W) **10**:15
GONÂVE GULF
map (19° 0′N 73° 30′W) **10**:15
GONÂVE ISLAND
map (18° 51′N 73° 3′W) **10**:15
GONBAD-E QABUS (Iran)
map (37° 17′N 55° 17′E) **11**:250
GONÇALVES, NUNO **9**:242 *bibliog.*
Panel of the High Constables **15**:455 *illus.*

GONÇALVES DIAS, ANTÔNIO 9:242
GONCHAROV, IVAN ALEKSANDROVICH 9:242
GONCHAROVA, NATALIA SERGEYEVNA 9:242 *bibliog.*
Larionov, Mikhail Fyodorovich 12:207
GONCOURT, EDMOND DE AND JULES DE 9:242–243 *bibliog.*
GOND 9:243 *bibliog.*
GONDER (Ethiopia) 9:243
map (12° 40′N 37° 30′E) 7:253
GONDOLA 9:243
GONDWANALAND 9:243 *bibliog.*; 15:354 *map*
Cambrian Period 4:50
Carboniferous Period 4:138
continental drift 5:228
earth, geological history of 7:13–14 *illus.*
ice ages 11:9
Jurassic Period 11:474
lungfish 12:463
marsupial 13:174
Mesozoic Era 13:322
ocean and sea 14:327
Ordovician Period 14:420
paleogeography 15:36–37
Paleozoic Era 15:42
Permian Period 15:176
plate tectonics 15:357
Silurian Period 17:310–311
***GONE WITH THE WIND* (book)** 9:243 *bibliog.*
Mitchell, Margaret 13:483
GONE WITH THE WIND (film) 9:3 *illus.*
GONG 9:243 *bibliog., illus.*; 13:675 *illus.*
African 1:169
Japanese music 11:381 *illus.*
music, non-Western 13:668
percussion instruments 15:162 *illus.*
GONGOLA RIVER
map (9° 30′N 12° 4′E) 14:190
GÓNGORA Y ARGOTE, LUIS DE 9:243–244 *bibliog., illus.*
Alonso, Dámaso 1:307–308
Gongorism 9:244
GONGORISM 9:244 *bibliog.*
Góngora y Argote, Luis de 9:243–244
GOÑI (Uruguay)
map (33° 31′S 56° 24′W) 19:488
GONIOMETER 9:244
external morphology
mineral 13:439
GONIUM 9:244
GONOCOCCUS *see NEISSERIA*
GONORRHEA 9:244 *bibliog.*
arthritis 2:214
baby, newborn
antiseptic 2:68
cervicitis 4:261–262
conjunctivitis 5:191
infectious diseases 11:167
Neisseria 14:79
treatment
pregnancy and birth 15:506
urogenital diseases 19:487
GONVILLE AND CAIUS COLLEGE (Cambridge University) 4:53
GONZAGA (family) 9:244 *bibliog.*
Mantegna, Andrea 13:129
Pisanello, Antonio 15:316
GONZALES (Louisiana)
map (30° 14′N 90° 55′W) 12:430
GONZALES (Texas)
map (29° 30′N 97° 27′W) 19:129
GONZALES (county in Texas)
map (29° 28′N 97° 30′W) 19:129
GONZÁLES, JUAN JOSÉ TORRES *see* TORRES GONZÁLES, JUAN JOSÉ
GONZALES, PANCHO 9:244–245 *bibliog., illus.*
GONZALES, RODOLFO "CORKY"
Chicano 4:343
GONZÁLEZ, ADOLFO SUÁREZ *see* SUÁREZ GONZÁLEZ, ADOLFO
GONZÁLEZ, FELIPE
Spain 18:143
Spain, history of 18:149
GONZALEZ, JOSÉ VICTORIANO *see* GRIS, JUAN
GONZÁLEZ, JULIO 9:245 *bibliog.*
GONZÁLEZ MARQUEZ, FELIPE 9:245
GONZALO DE CÓRDOBA *see* FERNÁNDEZ DE CÓRDOBA, GONZALO
GOOBER *see* PEANUT
GOOCHLAND (Virginia)
map (37° 41′N 77° 53′W) 19:607
GOOCHLAND (county in Virginia)
map (37° 45′N 78° 0′W) 19:607
GOOD, THOMAS
educational psychology 7:66
GOOD EARTH, THE (book)
Buck, Pearl S. 3:535
GOOD FRIDAY 9:245
GOOD HOPE, CAPE OF 9:245
Dias, Bartolomeu 6:153
map (34° 24′S 18° 30′E) 18:79
GOOD NEIGHBOR POLICY 9:245 *bibliog.*
Roosevelt, Franklin Delano 16:309
GOOD SAMARITAN LAW
United States
first aid 8:109
GOOD SHEPHERD, THE (mosaic) 7:9 *illus.*
GOOD SOLDIER SCHWEIK, THE (book) 9:245
Hašek, Jaroslav 10:66
GOODALL, JANE 2:53 *illus.*; 9:245 *bibliog.*
Leakey (family) 12:259
GOODBYE, MR. CHIPS (book) 9:245–246
Hilton, James 10:165
GOODENOUGH, WARD 9:246
GOODERHAM (Ontario)
map (44° 54′N 78° 23′W) 14:393; 14:461
GOODHEART, GEORGE J.
chiropractic 4:398
GOODHUE (county in Minnesota)
map (44° 22′N 92° 42′W) 13:453
GOODHUE, BERTRAM GROSVENOR 9:246 *bibliog.*
Cram, Ralph Adams 5:328
GOODING (Idaho)
map (42° 56′N 114° 43′W) 11:26
GOODING (county in Idaho)
map (42° 55′N 114° 50′W) 11:26
GOODLAND (Kansas)
map (39° 21′N 101° 43′W) 12:18
GOODLANDS (Mauritius)
map (20° 2′S 57° 38′E) 13:237
GOODMAN (Mississippi)
map (32° 58′N 89° 55′W) 13:469
GOODMAN (Wisconsin)
map (45° 38′N 88° 21′W) 20:185
GOODMAN, BENNY 9:246 *bibliog.*
Christian, Charlie 4:411
Krupa, Gene 12:132
swing 18:393
GOODMAN, NELSON 9:246
GOODMAN, THEODOSIA *see* BARA, THEDA
GOODNEWS BAY (Alaska)
map (59° 7′N 161° 35′W) 1:242
GOODNIGHT, CHARLES 9:246 *bibliog.*
GOODRICH (North Dakota)
map (47° 28′N 100° 8′W) 14:248
GOODRICH, BENJAMIN F. 9:246
GOODRICH, WILLIAM *see* ARBUCKLE, FATTY
GOODRICKE, JOHN
binary stars 3:256–257
GOODWATER (Alabama)
map (33° 4′N 86° 3′W) 1:234
GOODWIN, PHILIP
Museum of Modern Art 13:657
GOODYEAR (Arizona)
map (33° 26′N 112° 21′W) 2:160
GOODYEAR, CHARLES 9:246 *bibliog.*; 19:450 *illus.*
rubber 16:333
GOODYEAR BLIMP
airship 1:228
GOOLAGONG, EVONNE 9:246
GOONEY BIRD *see* ALBATROSS
GOOSE 9:246–247 *bibliog., illus.*
Canada goose 19:332 *illus.*
duck 6:290–291
imprinting 11:68
poultry 15:474–475 *illus.*
GOOSE, SOLAN *see* GANNET
GOOSE BAY 9:247
GOOSE CREEK (South Carolina)
map (33° 0′N 80° 1′W) 18:98
GOOSE CREEK RESERVOIR
map (32° 58′N 80° 3′W) 18:98
GOOSE LAKE
map (41° 57′N 120° 25′W) 4:31
GOOSEBERRY 9:247
GOOSEFISH 1:415–416 *illus.*; 8:117 *illus.*; 9:247
GOOSEFOOT (botany) 9:247
saltbush 17:38
GOOSSENS, SIR EUGENE 9:247 *bibliog.*
GOP *see* REPUBLICAN PARTY
GOPHER 9:247–248 *illus.*
pocket gopher 15:376–377
GÖPPINGEN (Germany, East and West)
map (48° 42′N 9° 40′E) 9:140
GORAKHPUR (India)
map (26° 45′N 83° 22′E) 11:80
GORBACHEV, MIKHAIL 9:248 *illus.*
GORDA PLATE
plate tectonics 15:351 *map*
GORDIAN KNOT 9:248
GORDIAN WORM 9:248
GORDIGIANI, MICHELE
Elizabeth Barrett Browning 3:518 *illus.*
GORDILLO, FRANCISCO
South Carolina 18:100
GORDIMER, NADINE 9:248 *bibliog.*
GORDIN, JACOB 9:248 *bibliog.*
GORDION (Turkey) 9:248–249 *bibliog.*
GORDIUM (Turkey) *see* GORDION (Turkey)
GORDON (Georgia)
map (32° 53′N 83° 20′W) 9:114
GORDON (county in Georgia)
map (34° 30′N 84° 50′W) 9:114
GORDON (Nebraska)
map (42° 48′N 102° 12′W) 14:70
GORDON (Wisconsin)
map (46° 15′N 91° 48′W) 20:185
GORDON, ADAM LINDSAY 9:249 *bibliog.*
GORDON, CAROLINE 9:249 *bibliog.*
GORDON, CHARLES GEORGE 9:249 *bibliog., illus.*
Ward, Frederick Townsend 20:29
GORDON, CYRUS H. 9:249
GORDON, LORD GEORGE
Gordon, Riots 9:249–250
GORDON, GEORGE HAMILTON-, 4TH EARL OF ABERDEEN *see* ABERDEEN, GEORGE HAMILTON-GORDON, 4TH EARL OF
GORDON, JOHN BROWN 9:249 *bibliog.*
GORDON, JUDAH LEIB 9:249 *bibliog.*
GORDON, RICHARD F., JR. 2:82 *illus.*; 9:249
Apollo program 2:82 *illus.*
Gemini program 9:73
GORDON, RUTH 9:249
GORDON RIOTS 9:249–250 *bibliog.*
Erskine, Thomas, 1st Baron Erskine 7:235
GORDON SETTER 6:218 *illus.*; 9:250 *bibliog., illus.*
GORDONSVILLE (Virginia)
map (38° 8′N 78° 11′W) 19:607
GORDY, BERRY, JR.
Motown 13:616
GORE (Ethiopia)
map (8° 8′N 35° 33′E) 7:253
GORE (Nova Scotia)
map (45° 7′N 63° 43′W) 14:269
GORE, CHARLES 9:250 *bibliog.*
GORE, THOMAS P. 9:250 *bibliog.*
GORE BAY (Ontario)
map (45° 55′N 82° 28′W) 14:393
GOREE (Texas)
map (33° 28′N 99° 31′W) 19:129
GOREN, CHARLES H. 9:250 *bibliog.*
GORENKO, ANNA ANDREYEVNA *see* AKHMATOVA, ANNA
GOREVILLE (Illinois)
map (37° 33′N 88° 58′W) 11:42
GOREY, EDWARD 9:250 *bibliog.*
ballet poster 3:44 *illus.*
GORGAN (Iran)
map (36° 50′N 54° 29′E) 11:250
GORGAS, WILLIAM C.
Panama Canal 15:57
GORGES, SIR FERDINANDO 9:250 *bibliog.*
Maine 13:74
GORGIAS 9:251 *bibliog.*
GORGON 9:251
Medusa 13:278
GORGOSAURUS 9:251 *bibliog.*
GORHAM (New Hampshire)
map (44° 23′N 71° 10′W) 14:123
GORHAM, JABEZ
Rhode Island 16:201
GORILLA 2:75 *illus.*; 9:251 *bibliog., illus.*
animal communication 2:20
ape 2:74–76
brain 3:443 *illus.*
GORINCHEM (Netherlands)
map (51° 50′N 5° 0′E) 14:99
GÖRING, HERMANN *see* GOERING, HERMANN
GORIS, JAN ALBERT *see* GIJSEN, MARNIX
GORKHA
Gurkha 9:406
GORKY (USSR) 9:251–252
map (56° 20′N 44° 0′E) 19:388
GORKY, ARSHILE 9:252 *bibliog., illus.*
The Liver Is the Cock's Comb 9:252 *illus.*
GORKY, MAKSIM 9:252–253 *bibliog., illus.*
The Lower Depths 1:87 *illus.*
Russian literature 16:366 *illus.*
GORKY RESERVOIR
map (57° 0′N 43° 10′E) 19:629
GÖRLITZ (Germany, East and West)
map (51° 9′N 14° 59′E) 9:140
GORMAN, ARTHUR P.
Maryland 13:192
GORRIE, JOHN
refrigeration 16:124
GORSE
flower 8:179 *illus.*
furze 8:381
pollination 15:408 *illus.*
GORSHKOV, SERGEI
navy 14:65
GORSKY, ALEKSANDR
Bolshoi Ballet 3:372
GORTER, C. J.
two-fluid model
superconductivity 18:350
GORTON, JOHN GREY 9:253 *bibliog., illus.*
GORTON, SAMUEL 9:253 *bibliog.*
Warwick (Rhode Island) 20:33
GORTONITES
Gorton, Samuel 9:253
GOSAINTHAN MOUNTAIN
map (28° 22′N 85° 50′E) 14:86
GOSDEN, FREEMAN FISHER *see* AMOS 'N' ANDY (radio comedy team)
GOSFORD, ARCHIBALD ACHESON, 2d EARL OF 9:253
GOSHAWK 8:229 *illus.*
hawk 10:76
GOSHEN (Indiana)
map (41° 35′N 85° 50′W) 11:111
GOSHEN (Kentucky)
map (38° 24′N 85° 34′W) 12:47
GOSHEN (New York)
map (41° 24′N 74° 20′W) 14:149
GOSHEN (Nova Scotia)
map (45° 23′N 61° 59′W) 14:269
GOSHEN (county in Wyoming)
map (42° 5′N 104° 15′W) 20:301
GOSLAR (Germany, East and West)
map (51° 54′N 10° 25′E) 9:140
GOSNOLD, BARTHOLOMEW 9:253
Cape Cod 4:120
Massachusetts 13:210
GOSPEL BOOK OF SAINT MÉDARD OF SOISSONS
miniature from 13:520 *illus.*
GOSPEL MUSIC 9:253–254 *bibliog.*
See also SPIRITUALS
Franklin, Aretha 8:282
Jackson, Mahalia 11:343
soul music 18:71
GOSPELS *see* BIBLE; names of specific Gospels, e.g., LUKE, GOSPEL ACCORDING TO; MATTHEW, GOSPEL ACCORDING TO; etc.
GOSPER (county in Nebraska)
map (40° 30′N 99° 50′W) 14:70
GOSSAERT, JAN 9:254 *bibliog.*
GOSSAGE, WILLIAM 9:254
GOSSAMER ALBATROSS (aircraft) 8:165 *illus.*
GOSSAMER CONDOR (aircraft)
flight, human-powered 8:164–165
GOSSANS *see* OXIDE MINERALS
GOSSEC, FRANÇOIS JOSEPH 9:254
GOSSIP COLUMNIST
Hopper, Hedda 10:233
Winchell, Walter 20:167–168
GOSTIVAR (Yugoslavia)
map (41° 47′N 20° 54′E) 20:340
GÖTEBORG (Sweden) 9:254; 18:383 *illus.*
map (57° 43′N 11° 58′E) 18:382
GOTHA (aircraft) 1:216 *illus.*; 9:254 *illus.*; 20:246
GOTHA (city in East Germany) 9:254
map (50° 57′N 10° 41′E) 9:140
GOTHART, MATHIS *see* GRÜNEWALD, MATTHIAS
GOTHENBURG (Nebraska)
map (40° 56′N 100° 9′W) 14:70
GOTHIC ART AND ARCHITECTURE 2:193–194; 9:255–262 *bibliog., illus.*
arch and vault 2:113–114
architecture 2:133–134 *illus.*
Arnolfo di Cambio 2:186
buttress 3:600–601
cathedrals and churches 4:205–207 *illus.*
Amiens Cathedral 1:370
Canterbury Cathedral 4:116

Chartres Cathedral **4**:300–301 *illus.*
Cologne Cathedral **5**:105 *illus.*
Notre Dame de Paris (cathedral) **14**:267 *illus.*
Reims Cathedral **16**:131
Saint-Denis (church) **17**:17
Sainte-Chapelle **17**:28
Salisbury Cathedral **17**:34
Strasbourg Cathedral **18**:289
Westminster Abbey **20**:117–118 *illus.*
choir stall **8**:375 *illus.*
clerestory **5**:51
costume **5**:294–297 *illus.*
decorative arts **9**:260–261
Doge's Palace **6**:222
English art and architecture **7**:183–184
Flamboyant Gothic style **8**:150
Flemish art and architecture **8**:162
French art and architecture **8**:304–305
furniture **8**:375
gargoyle **9**:47
Gentile da Fabriano **9**:94
German art and architecture **9**:124–125
Goes, Hugo van der **9**:223
Gothic Revival **9**:262–263
iconography **11**:22
illuminated manuscripts **11**:48
International style (art) **9**:261
Italian art and architecture **11**:309–310
jewelry **11**:410
Kraft, Adam **12**:126
Latin American art and architecture **12**:223
Limbourg brothers **12**:343
monastic art and architecture **13**:519
painting **15**:19
Perpendicular Gothic style **15**:177
Pisano, Andrea **15**:316
Pisano, Nicola and Giovanni **15**:316
Portuguese art and architecture **15**:456
Rayonnant style **16**:98
Riemenschneider, Tilman **16**:218–219
rose window **16**:314
Scandinavian art and architecture **17**:111–112
sculpture **17**:162–163 *illus.*
Sluter, Claus **17**:364–365
Spanish art and architecture **18**:153; **18**:155 *illus.*
stained glass **18**:211–213
Stoss, Veit **18**:285
triforium **19**:297
Tudor style **19**:329
tympanum **19**:362
Villard de Honnecourt **19**:598
Vischer (family) **19**:616
William of Sens **20**:155
GOTHIC REVIVAL **2**:136 *illus.*; **9**:262–263 *bibliog., illus.*
American art and architecture **1**:328; **1**:329
architecture **2**:136
Barry, Sir Charles **3**:95–96
Butterfield, William **3**:593
Cram, Ralph Adams **5**:328
Davis, Alexander Jackson **6**:50
Gilbert, Cass **9**:178
Goodhue, Bertram Grosvenor **9**:246
Gothic art and architecture **9**:262
house (in Western architecture) **10**:270
jewelry **11**:411
Latrobe, Benjamin Henry **12**:235
mosaic **13**:596
Pugin, Augustus **15**:617
Renwick, James **16**:159
Saint John the Divine, Cathedral of **17**:19
Saint Patrick's Cathedral **16**:159 *illus.*; **17**:24
Scott, Sir George Gilbert **17**:153
stained glass **18**:212
Trinity Church **1**:328 *illus.*
Upjohn, Richard **19**:471
Victorian style **19**:576 *illus.*
Westminster Palace **20**:118
Wyatt, James **20**:297
GOTHIC ROMANCE **9**:263 *bibliog.*
Beckford, William **3**:152
Dinesen, Isak **6**:178
du Maurier, Daphne **6**:286
"Fall of the House of Usher, The" **8**:13
Godwin, William **9**:221
Hawkes, John **10**:77
Hawthorne, Nathaniel **10**:79
Holt, Victoria **10**:208–209
James, Henry **11**:353–354
Lewis, Matthew Gregory **12**:306
Michaels, Barbara **13**:372
"Pit and the Pendulum, The" **15**:319
Poe, Edgar Allan **15**:377–378
Radcliffe, Ann **16**:41
Scott, Sir Walter **17**:154
Shelley, Mary Wollstonecraft **17**:252–253
supernatural literature **18**:352
Walpole, Horace, 4th Earl of Orford **20**:18
GOTHS **9**:263 *bibliog.*
Alaric I, King of the Visigoths **1**:240
Germanic languages **9**:136–137
Greece, ancient **9**:334
invasions of Europe **7**:282 *map*
Moorish art and architecture **13**:570
Spain, history of **18**:144 *illus.*
Theodoric the Great, King of the Ostrogoths **19**:156
Theodosius I, Roman Emperor (Theodosius the Great) **19**:156
GOTLAND (Sweden) **9**:263
map (57° 30′N 18° 33′E) **18**:382
GOTOVAC, JAKOV
Yugoslavia **20**:342
GÖTTERDÄMMERUNG see RING OF THE NIBELUNG, THE (opera cycle)
GOTTFRIED VON STRASSBURG **9**:263–264 *bibliog.*
GOTTHEIL, GUSTAV **9**:264
GOTTHELF, JEREMIAS **9**:264 *bibliog.*
GÖTTINGEN (West Germany) **9**:264
map (51° 32′N 9° 55′E) **9**:140
GOTTLIEB, ADOLPH **9**:264 *bibliog., illus.*
Etendue Rouge **9**:264 *illus.*
GOTTMAN, JEAN
megalopolis **13**:280
GOTTSCHALK, LOUIS MOREAU **9**:264 *bibliog.*
American music **1**:349
GOTTWALD, KLEMENT **9**:264
GOTTWALDOV (Czechoslovakia)
map (49° 13′N 17° 41′E) **5**:413
GÖTZEN, COUNT ADOLF VON
Kivu, Lake **12**:94
GOUACHE **9**:265 *bibliog.*
painting techniques **15**:25
watercolor **20**:61
GOUDA (Netherlands)
map (52° 1′N 4° 43′E) **14**:99
GOUDIMEL, CLAUDE
Renaissance music **16**:156
GOUDSMIT, SAMUEL A.
chemistry, history of **4**:328
GOUIN RESERVOIR
map (48° 38′N 74° 54′W) **16**:18
GOUJON, JEAN **9**:265 *bibliog.*
GOULART, JOÃO **9**:265 *bibliog.*
GOULBURN (Australia)
map (34° 45′S 149° 43′E) **2**:328
GOULD (Arkansas)
map (33° 59′N 91° 34′W) **2**:166
GOULD, BENJAMIN APTHORP **9**:265
Argentine National Observatory **9**:265
Astronomical Journal **9**:265
GOULD, CHESTER **9**:265
GOULD, GLENN **9**:265 *bibliog.*
GOULD, JAY **9**:265 *bibliog.*
Fisk, James **8**:128
New York (state) **14**:150
GOULD, MORTON **9**:265
GOULD, STEPHEN JAY **9**:266
evolution **7**:324
GOULD CITY (Michigan)
map (46° 6′N 85° 42′W) **13**:377
GOULDS (Florida)
map (25° 33′N 80° 23′W) **8**:172
GOULED APTIDON, HASSAN
Djibouti (country) **6**:208
GOUNDAM (Mali)
map (16° 25′N 3° 40′W) **13**:89
GOUNOD, CHARLES **9**:266 *bibliog., illus.*
GOURD **9**:266 *illus.*
cassabanana **4**:183
Indians of North America, music and dance of the **11**:142–143 *illus.*
pumpkin **15**:623
squash **18**:203
vegetable **19**:532 *illus.*
GOURMONT, REMY DE **9**:266 *bibliog.*
GOUT **9**:266–267 *bibliog.*
arthritis **2**:214–215
kidney stone **12**:72
uric acid **19**:486
GOUTHIÈRE, PIERRE JOSEPH DÉSIRÉ **9**:267
GOUVERNEUR (New York)
map (44° 20′N 75° 28′W) **14**:149
GOUYAVE (Grenada)
map (12° 10′N 61° 44′W) **9**:358
GOVE (Kansas)
map (38° 58′N 100° 29′W) **12**:18
GOVE (county in Kansas)
map (38° 55′N 100° 30′W) **12**:18
GOVENLOCK (Saskatchewan)
map (49° 15′N 109° 48′W) **17**:81
GOVERNADOR VALADARES (Brazil)
map (18° 51′S 41° 56′W) **3**:460
GOVERNMENT **9**:267–269 *bibliog.*
See also CONGRESS OF THE UNITED STATES; CONSTITUTION OF THE UNITED STATES; EXECUTIVE BRANCH; SUPREME COURT OF THE UNITED STATES; UNITED STATES, DEPARTMENTS, AGENCIES AND COMMISSIONS; the subheading government under names of specific countries, e.g., BRAZIL; UNITED STATES; etc.; specific branches of the U.S. government, e.g., EXECUTIVE BRANCH; CONGRESS OF THE UNITED STATES; etc.
bureaucracy **3**:568
city-state **5**:9
civil service **5**:14
commune **5**:142
conservatism **5**:205
constitution **5**:212
economic planning **7**:47
eminent domain **7**:156
finance
bond **3**:376
budget **3**:543–544
cost-benefit analysis **5**:290
income tax **11**:75–77
national debt **14**:31–32 *table*
revenue sharing **16**:185
savings bond **17**:100–101
taxation **19**:46–47
zero-based budgeting **20**:361
flag **8**:133
fraud, prevention **8**:288
game theory **9**:27–28
income, national **11**:74–75
information storage and retrieval **11**:173
legislature **12**:274–275
liberalism **12**:312
Machiavelli, Nicolò **13**:18–19
municipal government **13**:642–643
officials
alderman **1**:269
chancellor **4**:278
coroner **5**:271
governor general **9**:272
intendant **11**:206
justice of the peace **11**:478
king **12**:80
mayor **13**:248
notary public **14**:267
ombudsman **14**:387
police **15**:396–397
president **15**:522
prime minister **15**:542
prosecuting attorney **15**:572
sheriff **17**:257
viceroy **19**:571
Parliament **15**:92–93
passport **15**:106
political science **15**:403–404
proportional representation **15**:572
recall **16**:106
referendum and initiative **16**:118–119
representation **16**:160–161
revolution **16**:187–188
Senate, Roman **17**:199–200
separation of powers **17**:206
social contract **18**:11
sovereignty **18**:113
special-interest groups **18**:167–168
state (in political philosophy) **18**:228
Aristotle **2**:158
subdivisions
borough **3**:404
canton **4**:118
county **5**:313
state (political unit) **18**:228
territory **19**:122
township **19**:256
sunset laws **18**:348–349
systems
absolutism **1**:63
aristocracy **2**:155
authoritarianism **2**:354–355
communism **5**:146–150
democracy **6**:97–98
despotism **6**:132
dictatorship **6**:159
fascism **8**:30
federalism **8**:43
feudalism **8**:64–65
junta **11**:471
Marxism **13**:183–184
monarchy **13**:517
nazism **14**:67–68
oligarchy **14**:377
police state **15**:397
republic **16**:172
socialism **18**:19–24
totalitarianism **19**:248
town meeting **19**:255
treason **19**:285
veto **19**:567
welfare state **20**:97–98
GOVERNMENT OF INDIA ACT
Linlithgow, Victor Alexander John Hope, 2d Marquess of **12**:358–359
GOVERNMENT PRINTING OFFICE, UNITED STATES **9**:270
Washington, D.C. **20**:41 *map*
GOVERNMENT REGULATION **9**:270–272 *bibliog.*
See also names of specific agencies, e.g., FEDERAL COMMUNICATIONS COMMISSION; INTERSTATE COMMERCE COMMISSION; etc.
administrative law **1**:104–105
advertising **1**:113
affirmative action **1**:132
antiregulatory trends **9**:271–272
aviation **2**:374
censorship **4**:246–248
child labor **4**:350
coal and coal mining **5**:79
common carrier **5**:138
conservation **5**:202–203
consumer protection **5**:226
Depression of the 1930s **6**:120
diseases, occupational **6**:194
economy, national **7**:50–51
employment and unemployment **7**:160
environmental impact statement **7**:212
Environmental Protection Agency **7**:212
equal opportunity **7**:223
Equal Rights Amendment **7**:224
fiscal policy **8**:109–110
fishing industry **8**:127–128
fur **8**:370–371
genetic engineering **9**:85
housing **10**:276; **10**:279
hunting **10**:313–314
inflation **11**:170–171
international trade, quotas **16**:28
laissez-faire **12**:167
Lochner v. *New York* **12**:386
meat and meat packing **13**:258
milk **13**:423
minimum wage **13**:446
West Coast Hotel Company v. *Parrish* **20**:108
mixed economy **13**:486
monopoly and competition **13**:537–540
motorcycle **13**:614
Munn v. *Illinois* **13**:643
Nader, Ralph **14**:5 *illus.*
nursing home **14**:299–300
nutrition, human **14**:306–307
open shop **14**:398
packaging **15**:12
pesticides **15**:198
petroleum industry **15**:214
pharmaceutical industry **15**:220
pharmacy **15**:221
pollutants, chemical **15**:410–411
pollution control **15**:415–416
poverty **15**:478–480
public health **15**:608
public utility **15**:610–611
pure food and drug laws **15**:628–629
radio and television broadcasting **16**:54–56
railroad **16**:72–73; **16**:76
right-to-work laws **16**:222
Robinson-Patman Act **16**:246
safety, automotive **17**:10–11
shellfish **17**:255
Sherman Anti-Trust Act **17**:258–259
socialist law **18**:25
toxicology **19**:256
transportation **19**:280
trucking industry **19**:314–315

GOVERNMENT REGULATION (cont.)
unemployment insurance **19**:383–384
whaling **20**:123
wildlife refuge **20**:150
wine **20**:175–176
workers' compensation **20**:217
zoning **20**:373–374
GOVERNMENT WORKERS *see* CIVIL SERVICE
GOVERNOR **9**:272 *bibliog.*
presidential elections **15**:529
GOVERNOR GENERAL **9**:272 *bibliog.*
viceroy **19**:571
GOVERNOR GENERAL'S AWARD
Atwood, Margaret **2**:316
Avison, Margaret **2**:376
Giroux, André **9**:190
Grove, Frederick Philip **9**:378
MacLennan, Hugh **13**:32
Raddall, Thomas H. **16**:41–42
Wiseman, Adele **20**:189
GOVERNORS ISLAND (New York City) **9**:272
GOWANDA (New York)
map (42° 28′N 78° 56′W) **14**:149
GOWER, JOHN **9**:272–273 *bibliog.*
GOWON, YAKUBU **9**:273 *bibliog.*
GOYA (Argentina)
map (29° 8′S 59° 16′W) **2**:149
GOYA, FRANCISCO DE **9**:273–274 *bibliog., illus.*
bichon frise **3**:244 *illus.*
Ferdinand II, King of Aragon **8**:52 *illus.*
Ferdinand VII, King of Spain **8**:54 *illus.*
Granados, Enrique **9**:283
Il y a beaucoup à sucer **7**:249 *illus.*
Los Caprichos **7**:249 *illus.*; **9**:274 *illus.*; **9**:293 *illus.*
The Nude Maja **18**:154 *illus.*
Spanish art and architecture **18**:154
The Third of May, 1808 **2**:198–199 *illus.*; **9**:273 *illus.*; **18**:147 *illus.*
Wellington, Arthur Wellesley, 1st Duke of **20**:100 *illus.*
witchcraft **20**:192 *illus.*
GOYATHLAY *see* GERONIMO
GOYEN, JAN VAN **9**:274 *bibliog.*
GOYEN, WILLIAM **9**:274 *bibliog.*
GOYIGAMA
Sinhalese **17**:323
GOYTISOLO, JUAN **9**:274 *bibliog.*
Spanish literature **18**:160
GOZO ISLAND
map (36° 3′N 14° 15′E) **13**:94
GOZZI, CARLO, CONTE **9**:274–275 *bibliog.*
GOZZOLI, BENOZZO **9**:275 *bibliog.*
Procession of the Magi **13**:265 *illus.*; **16**:148 *illus.*
GRAAFF, ROBERT JEMISON VAN DE *see* VAN DE GRAAFF, ROBERT JEMISON
GRABAR
Armenian language **2**:173
GRABAU, A. W.
catastrophism **4**:201
GRABBE, CHRISTIAN DIETRICH **9**:275 *bibliog.*
GRABEN *see* HORST AND GRABEN
GRACCHUS (family) **9**:275 *bibliog.*
Rome, ancient **16**:300
GRACE (Idaho)
map (42° 35′N 111° 44′W) **11**:26
GRACE (theology) **9**:275 *bibliog.*
Molina, Luis de **13**:509
predestination **15**:501–502
GRACE, W. R. **9**:275–276 *bibliog.*
GRACE CHURCH (New York City)
cathedrals and churches **4**:208
GRACES **9**:276
GRACEVILLE (Florida)
map (30° 58′N 85° 31′W) **8**:172
GRACEVILLE (Minnesota)
map (45° 34′N 96° 26′W) **13**:453
GRACIÁN Y MORALES, BALTASAR
Spanish literature **18**:159
GRACIOSA (Portugal)
Azores **2**:381–382 *map*
GRACKLE **9**:276 *bibliog., illus.*
GRADAÚS (Brazil)
map (7° 43′S 51° 11′W) **3**:460
GRADE (score) *see* EDUCATIONAL MEASUREMENT
GRADER
earth-moving machinery **7**:24
GRADIENT *see* VECTOR ANALYSIS
GRADUATE EDUCATION **9**:276–277 *bibliog.*
See also names of specific institutions, e.g., JOHNS HOPKINS UNIVERSITY, THE; SORBONNE; etc.
Fulbright Exchange Program **8**:357
Gilman, Daniel Coit **9**:182
Graduate Record Examination **9**:277
Rhodes scholarships **16**:202
scholarships, fellowships, and loans **17**:130
university **19**:468–469
GRADUATE RECORD EXAMINATION **9**:277
GRADY (Arkansas)
map (34° 5′N 91° 42′W) **2**:166
GRADY (county in Georgia)
map (30° 55′N 84° 15′W) **9**:114
GRADY (New Mexico)
map (34° 49′N 103° 19′W) **14**:136
GRADY (county in Oklahoma)
map (35° 5′N 97° 55′W) **14**:368
GRADY, HENRY WOODFIN **9**:277–278 *bibliog.*
GRAEBNER, FRITZ **9**:278
GRAETTINGER (Iowa)
map (43° 14′N 94° 45′W) **11**:244
GRAF, URS **9**:278 *bibliog.*
GRAF ZEPPELIN (airship) **1**:227; **9**:278
GRAFFITI **9**:278 *bibliog.*
inscription **11**:186
modern art **13**:496
neoexpressionism **13**:496
GRAFT **9**:278 *bibliog.*
GRAFTING (botany) **9**:278–279 *bibliog., illus.*
cloning **5**:64
plant propagation **15**:345
principles and methods **9**:278–279
purposes **9**:278
GRAFTING OF ORGANS AND TISSUES *see* TRANSPLANTATION, ORGAN
GRAFTON (Australia)
map (29° 41′S 152° 56′E) **2**:328
GRAFTON (Massachusetts)
map (42° 12′N 71° 41′W) **13**:206
GRAFTON (county in New Hampshire)
map (43° 55′N 71° 50′W) **14**:123
GRAFTON (North Dakota)
map (48° 25′N 97° 25′W) **14**:248
GRAFTON (Ohio)
map (41° 16′N 82° 4′W) **14**:357
GRAFTON (West Virginia)
map (39° 20′N 80° 1′W) **20**:111
GRAHAM (county in Arizona)
map (33° 15′N 109° 50′W) **2**:160
GRAHAM (county in Kansas)
map (41° 20′N 99° 55′W) **12**:18
GRAHAM (North Carolina)
map (36° 5′N 79° 25′W) **14**:242
GRAHAM (county in North Carolina)
map (35° 20′N 83° 50′W) **14**:242
GRAHAM (Texas)
map (33° 6′N 98° 35′W) **19**:129
GRAHAM, BILLY **9**:279 *bibliog., illus.*
GRAHAM, BRUCE
skyscraper **17**:350
GRAHAM, GEORGE **9**:279
clocks and watches **5**:63
planetarium **15**:328
GRAHAM, JAMES, 1ST MARQUESS OF MONTROSE *see* MONTROSE, JAMES GRAHAM, 1ST MARQUESS OF
GRAHAM, JOHN
abstract expressionism **1**:65–66
GRAHAM, KATHARINE **9**:280 *bibliog., illus.*
GRAHAM, MARTHA **9**:280 *bibliog., illus.*; **13**:496 *illus.*
dance **6**:28
Hawkins, Erick **10**:77
Noguchi, Isamu **14**:213
GRAHAM, MOUNT
map (32° 42′N 109° 52′W) **2**:160
GRAHAM, OTTO **9**:280 *bibliog.*
GRAHAM, PETER *see* ABRAHAMS, PETER
GRAHAM, THOMAS **9**:280–281
GRAHAM OF CLAVERHOUSE, JOHN *see* DUNDEE, JOHN GRAHAM OF CLAVERHOUSE, 1ST VISCOUNT
GRAHAM ISLAND
map (53° 40′N 132° 30′W) **3**:491
GRAHAM LAND (Antarctica) *see* ANTARCTIC PENINSULA
GRAHAME, KENNETH **9**:281 *bibliog.*
illustrated
Shepard, Ernest Howard **17**:256
Wind in the Willows, The **20**:172
GRAHN, LUCILE **9**:281 *bibliog.*
GRAIL, HOLY **9**:281 *bibliog.*
Arthur and Arthurian legend **2**:219
Galahad, Sir **9**:9–10
gold and silver work **9**:229
Montserrat (mountain) **13**:560
GRAIN (agriculture) **9**:281–282 *bibliog., illus.*
agriculture, history of **1**:189–190
agriculture and the food supply **1**:194–199 *map*
barley **3**:84
Borlaug, Norman Ernest **3**:401
bran **3**:452
corn **5**:265–267
diet, human **6**:164
ergot **7**:228
futures **8**:383
grass **9**:295
green revolution **9**:348–349
marketing **9**:281
millet **13**:429
nutrition, human **14**:305–306
nutritional analysis **9**:281–282
oats **14**:314
production **9**:281
rice **16**:207–208
rye **16**:379
sorghum **18**:69
steppe life **18**:257
storage **9**:281
grain elevator **9**:282
uses **9**:281–282
gin **9**:183
whiskey **20**:132–133
wheat **20**:124–126
GRAIN (measure)
weights and measures **20**:92–94
GRAIN, WOOD *see* WOOD (botany)
GRAIN ALCOHOL *see* ETHYL ALCOHOL
GRAIN ELEVATOR **9**:282; **14**:235 *illus.*
Kansas **12**:20 *illus.*
GRAIN SORGHUM *see* SORGHUM
GRAINFIELD (Kansas)
map (39° 7′N 100° 28′W) **12**:18
GRAINGER (county in Tennessee)
map (36° 20′N 83° 30′W) **19**:104
GRAINGER, PERCY **9**:282 *bibliog.*
GRAM (legume) *see* CHICK-PEA
GRAM (measurement)
units, physical **19**:466
weights and measures **20**:93 *table*
GRAM, HANS CHRISTIAN
bacteria **3**:15–16
GRAMBLING (Louisiana)
map (32° 32′N 92° 43′W) **12**:430
GRAMERCY (Louisiana)
map (30° 3′N 90° 41′W) **12**:430
GRAMICIDIN *see* ANTIBIOTICS
GRAMMAR **9**:282–283 *bibliog.*
Chomsky, Noam **4**:404
Dionysius Thrax **6**:184
linguistics **12**:354–356
Panini **15**:59
parts of speech **15**:100–101
phonology and morphology **15**:254–255
pidgin **15**:294
transformational grammar **12**:356–357
applied linguistics **2**:90
psycholinguistics **15**:591
semantics (linguistics) **17**:193
syntax **18**:408–409
GRAMMAR SCHOOLS *see* PRIMARY EDUCATION
GRAMMY AWARD **9**:283
Cash, Johnny **4**:181
Cosby, Bill **5**:280
Horowitz, Vladimir **10**:241
Midler, Bette **13**:414
Mitchell, Joni **13**:483
GRAMPIAN (Scotland) **9**:283
Aberdeen (county) **1**:56
Banff **3**:62
GRAMPIAN MOUNTAINS
map (56° 45′N 4° 0′W) **19**:403
GRAM'S STAIN *see* GRAM, HANS CHRISTIAN
GRAMSCI, ANTONIO **9**:283 *bibliog.*
socialism **18**:23
GRAN CAPITÁN, EL *see* FERNÁNDEZ DE CÓRDOBA, GONZALO
GRAN CHACO *see* CHACO
map (23° 0′S 60° 0′W) **2**:149
GRAN COLOMBIA
Bolívar, Simón **3**:365
Latin America, history of **12**:220
GRAN PARADISO MOUNTAIN
map (45° 32′N 7° 16′E) **11**:321
GRAN QUIVIRA
Coronado, Francisco Vázquez de **5**:270
Wichita (Indian tribe) **20**:144
GRAN SASSO D'ITALIA MOUNTAINS
map (42° 27′N 13° 42′E) **11**:321
GRANADA (city in Nicaragua) **9**:283
León (Nicaragua) **12**:289
map (11° 56′N 85° 57′W) **14**:179
GRANADA (city in Spain) **9**:283 *bibliog.*
Alhambra **1**:291–292 *illus.*
cathedral
Cano, Alonso **4**:112
garden **9**:40
map (37° 13′N 3° 41′W) **18**:140
GRANADA (Colorado)
map (38° 4′N 102° 19′W) **5**:116
GRANADA (Minnesota)
map (43° 42′N 94° 21′W) **13**:453
GRANADA (region in Spain) **9**:283
cities
Granada **9**:283
history
Boabdil **3**:349
Moriscos **13**:580
Spain, history of **18**:145–146 *map*
GRANADOS, ENRIQUE **9**:283 *bibliog.*
Spanish music **18**:161 *illus.*
GRANBURY (Texas)
map (32° 27′N 97° 47′W) **19**:129
GRANBY (Massachusetts)
map (42° 15′N 72° 31′W) **13**:206
GRANBY (Missouri)
map (36° 55′N 94° 15′W) **13**:476
GRANBY (Quebec)
map (45° 24′N 72° 44′W) **16**:18
GRANBY, LAKE
map (40° 9′N 105° 50′W) **5**:116
GRAND (county in Colorado)
map (40° 10′N 106° 10′W) **5**:116
GRAND (county in Utah)
map (38° 55′N 109° 35′W) **19**:492
GRAND ALLIANCE, WAR OF THE **9**:284 *bibliog.*
French and Indian Wars **8**:312
Louis XIV, King of France **12**:427
Palatinate **15**:30
William III, King of England, Scotland, and Ireland **20**:156
GRAND ANSE BAY
map (12° 2′N 61° 46′W) **9**:358
GRAND ARMY OF THE REPUBLIC **9**:284 *bibliog.*
GRAND BAHAMA ISLAND
Bahama Islands **3**:23
map (26° 38′N 78° 25′W) **3**:23
GRAND BALLON MOUNTAIN
map (47° 55′N 7° 8′E) **8**:260
GRAND BANK (city in Newfoundland)
map (47° 6′N 55° 46′W) **14**:166
GRAND BANKS **9**:284 *map*
Gulf Stream **9**:403
GRAND-BASSAM (Ivory Coast)
map (5° 12′N 3° 44′W) **11**:335
GRAND BAY
map (50° 45′S 68° 45′W) **2**:149
GRAND BAY (Alabama)
map (30° 29′N 88° 21′W) **1**:234
GRAND BAY (Grenada)
map (12° 28′N 61° 25′W) **9**:358
GRAND BAY (New Brunswick)
map (45° 18′N 66° 12′W) **14**:117
GRAND BEACH (Manitoba)
map (50° 35′N 96° 40′W) **13**:119
GRAND BRUIT (Newfoundland)
map (47° 41′N 58° 13′W) **14**:166
GRAND CANAL (China)
map (32° 12′N 119° 31′E) **10**:326
GRAND CANAL (Ireland)
map (53° 21′N 6° 14′W) **11**:258
GRAND CANAL (Italy) **9**:284
Venice (Italy) **19**:544
GRAND CANE (Louisiana)
map (32° 5′N 93° 49′W) **12**:430
GRAND CANYON (Arizona) **2**:161 *illus.*; **9**:284–285 *illus.*; **18**:316 *illus.*
limestone **12**:344 *illus.*
map (36° 10′N 112° 45′W) **2**:160
national parks **14**:37–38 *illus., map, table*
GRAND CANYON OF THE TENNESSEE
Chattanooga **4**:303
GRAND CANYON OF THE YELLOWSTONE, THE (painting)
Moran, Thomas **13**:573
GRAND CENTRAL TERMINAL **9**:285 *bibliog.*
New York (city) **14**:145 *map*
GRAND CENTRE (Alberta)
map (54° 25′N 110° 13′W) **1**:256
GRAND COULEE (Washington)
map (47° 56′N 119° 0′W) **20**:35
GRAND COULEE DAM **6**:17 *illus.*; **9**:285 *bibliog.*; **20**:36 *illus.*
GRAND COULEE HYDROELECTRIC STATION
power, generation and transmission of **15**:482
GRAND DUCHY OF LITHUANIA *see* LITHUANIAN SOVIET SOCIALIST REPUBLIC (USSR)

GRAND DUCHY OF LUXEMBOURG *see* LUXEMBOURG (country)
GRAND FALLS (city in Newfoundland)
map (48° 56′N 55° 40′W) **14**:166
GRAND FALLS (New Brunswick)
map (47° 3′N 67° 44′W) **14**:117
GRAND FALLS (waterfall in Newfoundland) *see* CHURCHILL FALLS (Newfoundland)
GRAND FORKS (British Columbia)
map (49° 2′N 118° 27′W) **3**:491
GRAND FORKS (North Dakota) **9**:285
map (47° 55′N 97° 3′W) **14**:248
GRAND FORKS (county in North Dakota)
map (47° 55′N 97° 30′W) **14**:248
GRAND GUIGNOL *see* GUIGNOL, GRAND
GRAND HARBOR
map (35° 53′N 14° 31′E) **13**:94
GRAND HAVEN (Michigan)
average weather conditions **20**:82 *table*
map (43° 4′N 86° 13′W) **13**:377
GRAND HILLS
map (33° 15′S 55° 7′W) **19**:488
GRAND ILLUSION (film) **8**:85 *illus.*; **16**:158 *illus.*
GRAND ISLAND (Nebraska) **9**:285
map (40° 55′N 98° 21′W) **14**:70
map (46° 30′N 30′N 86° 40′W) **13**:377
GRAND ISLE (Louisiana)
map (29° 14′N 90° 0′W) **12**:430
GRAND ISLE (county in Vermont)
map (44° 48′N 73° 17′W) **19**:554
GRAND JUNCTION (Colorado)
map (39° 5′N 108° 33′W) **5**:116
GRAND JUNCTION (Iowa)
map (42° 2′N 94° 14′W) **11**:244
GRAND JURY **9**:285 *bibliog.*
See also 5th AMENDMENT
indictment **11**:144
Hurtado v. *California* **10**:319
inquest **11**:183
investigations **9**:285
jury **11**:478
GRAND LAKE (Louisiana)
map (29° 55′N 92° 47′W) **12**:430
GRAND LAKE (Maine)
map (45° 15′N 67° 50′W) **13**:70
GRAND LAKE (Michigan)
map (45° 18′N 83° 30′W) **13**:377
GRAND LAKE (Newfoundland)
map (49° 0′N 57° 25′W) **14**:166
GRAND LAKE (Ohio)
map (40° 30′N 84° 32′W) **14**:357
GRAND LEDGE (Michigan)
map (42° 45′N 84° 45′W) **13**:377
GRAND MAL SEIZURE
epilepsy **7**:219–220 *table*
GRAND MANAN CHANNEL
map (44° 45′N 66° 52′W) **13**:70
GRAND MARAIS (Michigan)
map (46° 40′N 85° 59′W) **13**:377
GRAND MARAIS (Minnesota)
map (47° 45′N 90° 20′W) **13**:453
GRAND NATIONAL (horse race)
steeplechase **18**:243–244 *illus.*
GRAND OLD PARTY *see* REPUBLICAN PARTY
GRAND OLE OPRY **9**:285 *bibliog.*
country and western music **5**:312–313 *illus.*
Williams, Hank **20**:159
GRAND PORTAGE (Minnesota)
map (47° 58′N 89° 41′W) **13**:453
GRAND PRAIRIE (Texas)
map (32° 45′N 96° 59′W) **19**:129
GRAND PRIX
automobile racing **2**:360
world champions **2**:361 *table*
GRAND RAPIDS (Manitoba)
map (53° 8′N 99° 20′W) **13**:119
GRAND RAPIDS (Michigan) **9**:285
map (42° 58′N 85° 40′W) **13**:377
GRAND RAPIDS (Minnesota)
map (47° 14′N 93° 31′W) **13**:453
GRAND RIVER (Michigan)
map (43° 4′N 86° 15′W) **13**:377
GRAND RIVER (Missouri)
map (39° 23′N 93° 6′W) **13**:476
GRAND RIVER (Ohio)
map (41° 46′N 81° 17′W) **14**:357
GRAND ROY (Grenada)
map (12° 8′N 61° 45′W) **9**:358
GRAND SANUSI *see* SANUSI, AL-
GRAND TETON MOUNTAIN
map (43° 44′N 110° 48′W) **20**:301
GRAND TETON NATIONAL PARK **9**:285 *bibliog.*; **14**:37–39 *illus., map, table*
Jackson Hole (Wyoming) **11**:344
GRAND TRAVERSE (county in Michigan)
map (44° 50′N 85° 35′W) **13**:377
GRAND TRAVERSE BAY
map (45° 2′N 85° 30′W) **13**:377
GRAND TRUNK RAILWAY
Canada, history of **4**:83
GRAND UNIFICATION THEORIES **9**:285–286 *bibliog.*
See also UNIFIED FIELD THEORY
superstring theories **18**:353
GRAND VALLEY (Colorado)
map (39° 27′N 108° 3′W) **5**:116
GRAND WASH CLIFFS
map (35° 40′N 113° 50′W) **2**:160
GRANDE-ANSE (New Brunswick)
map (47° 48′N 65° 11′W) **14**:117
GRANDE CASE NOYALE (Mauritius)
map (20° 1′S 57° 39′E) **13**:237
GRANDE COMORE ISLAND
Comoros **5**:153–154 *map*
map (11° 35′S 43° 20′E) **5**:153
GRANDE DE AÑASCO RIVER
map (18° 16′N 67° 11′W) **15**:614
GRANDE DE ARECIBO RIVER
map (18° 29′N 66° 42′W) **15**:614
GRANDE DE MARATI RIVER
map (18° 29′N 66° 32′W) **15**:614
GRANDE DE MATAGALPA RIVER
map (12° 54′N 83° 32′W) **14**:179
GRANDE MOUNTAIN
map (42° 28′N 13° 34′E) **11**:321
GRANDE PEUR ("Great Fear")
French Revolution **8**:322
GRANDE-PRAIRIE (Alberta)
map (55° 10′N 118° 48′W) **1**:256
GRANDE RIVER
map (15° 51′S 64° 39′W) **3**:366
GRANDE RIVIÈRE SUD-EST (Mauritius)
map (20° 17′S 57° 46′E) **13**:237
GRANDE-TERRE
Guadeloupe **9**:385
GRANDFALLS (Texas)
map (31° 20′N 102° 51′W) **19**:129
GRANDFATHER CLAUSE **9**:286
GRANDFATHER CLOCK **5**:62 *illus.*
GRANDFATHER MOUNTAIN
map (36° 7′N 81° 48′W) **14**:242
GRANDFIELD (Oklahoma)
map (34° 13′N 98° 41′W) **14**:368
GRANDMA MOSES *see* MOSES, GRANDMA
GRAND'MERE (Quebec)
map (46° 37′N 72° 41′W) **16**:18
GRANDVIEW (Manitoba)
map (51° 10′N 100° 45′W) **13**:119
GRANDVIEW (Washington)
map (46° 15′N 119° 54′W) **20**:35
GRANDVIEW HEIGHTS (Ohio)
map (40° 1′N 83° 3′W) **14**:357
GRANDVILLE **9**:286 *bibliog.*
GRANGE, HOWARD EDWARD *see* GRANGE, RED
GRANGE, NATIONAL **9**:286 *bibliog.*
GRANGE, RED **9**:286–287 *bibliog., illus.*
football **8**:217
GRANGER (Iowa)
map (41° 46′N 93° 49′W) **11**:244
GRANGER (Washington)
map (46° 21′N 120° 11′W) **20**:35
GRANGER (Wyoming)
map (41° 35′N 109° 58′W) **20**:301
GRANGER MOVEMENT
government regulation **9**:270
Grange, National **9**:286
Munn v. *Illinois* **13**:643
railroad **16**:72
GRANGEVILLE (Idaho)
map (45° 56′N 116° 7′W) **11**:26
GRANITE **9**:287 *bibliog.*
alteration, mineral **1**:312
gneiss **9**:213
igneous rock **11**:34
magma **13**:52
mineral occurrence **13**:442
mining and quarrying **13**:449 *illus.*
origin, debate **9**:287
ornamental stone **9**:287
rock **16**:247
silica minerals **17**:304
Vermont **19**:557 *illus.*
wolframite **20**:199
GRANITE (county in Montana)
map (46° 20′N 113° 25′W) **13**:547
GRANITE (Oklahoma)
map (34° 58′N 99° 23′W) **14**:368
GRANITE CITY (Illinois)
map (38° 42′N 90° 9′W) **11**:42
GRANITE FALLS (Minnesota)
map (44° 49′N 95° 33′W) **13**:453
GRANITE FALLS (North Carolina)
map (35° 48′N 81° 26′W) **14**:242
GRANITE LAKE
map (48° 8′N 57° 5′W) **14**:166
GRANITE PEAK (Montana)
map (45° 10′N 109° 48′W) **13**:547
GRANITE PEAK (Nevada)
map (41° 40′N 117° 35′W) **14**:111
GRANITEVILLE (South Carolina)
map (33° 34′N 81° 48′W) **18**:98
GRANITEVILLE (Vermont)
map (44° 8′N 72° 29′W) **19**:554
GRANODIORITE **9**:287 *bibliog.*
silica minerals **17**:304
GRANT (county in Arkansas)
map (34° 15′N 92° 30′W) **2**:166
GRANT (county in Indiana)
map (40° 33′N 85° 40′W) **11**:111
GRANT (county in Kansas)
map (37° 35′N 101° 15′W) **12**:18
GRANT (county in Kentucky)
map (38° 39′N 84° 39′W) **12**:47
GRANT (county in Louisiana)
map (31° 37′N 92° 32′W) **12**:430
GRANT (Michigan)
map (43° 20′N 85° 49′W) **13**:377
GRANT (county in Minnesota)
map (45° 55′N 96° 0′W) **13**:453
GRANT (Nebraska)
map (40° 50′N 101° 56′W) **14**:70
GRANT (county in Nebraska)
map (41° 55′N 101° 40′W) **14**:70
GRANT (county in New Mexico)
map (32° 50′N 108° 20′W) **14**:136
GRANT (county in North Dakota)
map (46° 20′N 101° 40′W) **14**:248
GRANT (county in Oklahoma)
map (36° 50′N 97° 50′W) **14**:368
GRANT (county in Oregon)
map (44° 30′N 119° 0′W) **14**:427
GRANT (county in South Dakota)
map (45° 10′N 96° 45′W) **18**:103
GRANT (county in Washington)
map (47° 10′N 119° 30′W) **20**:35
GRANT (county in West Virginia)
map (39° 5′N 79° 15′W) **20**:111
GRANT (county in Wisconsin)
map (42° 52′N 90° 43′W) **20**:185
GRANT, CARY **5**:383 *illus.*; **9**:287 *bibliog., illus.*
GRANT, ULYSSES S. **3**:438 *illus.*; **9**:287–289 *bibliog., illus.*; **15**:269 *illus.*
cartoon depicting **16**:110 *illus.*
Civil War, U.S. **5**:21–30 *illus., map*
Indian Wars **11**:108
Lee, Robert E. **12**:270
Parker, Ely S. **15**:90
Petersburg campaign **15**:202
president **9**:289
Republican party **16**:173 *illus.*
Richmond (Virginia) **16**:214
Sherman, William Tecumseh **17**:258
tomb (New York City) **19**:231
United States, history of the **19**:448 *illus.*
Vicksburg Campaign **19**:571–572 *map*
Whiskey Ring **20**:133
Wilderness Campaign **20**:150
GRANT CITY (Missouri)
map (40° 29′N 94° 25′W) **13**:476
GRANT PARK (California)
average weather conditions **20**:82 *table*
GRANT PARK (Illinois)
map (41° 14′N 87° 39′W) **11**:42
GRANTS
Agency for International Development **1**:183
finance, state and local **8**:92
foreign aid **8**:224–225
foundations and endowments **8**:250–251
revenue sharing **16**:185
GRANTS (New Mexico)
map (35° 9′N 107° 52′W) **14**:136
GRANTS PASS (Oregon)
map (42° 26′N 123° 19′W) **14**:427
GRANTSBURG (Wisconsin)
map (45° 47′N 92° 41′W) **20**:185
GRANTSVILLE (Utah)
map (40° 36′N 112° 28′W) **19**:492
GRANTSVILLE (West Virginia)
map (38° 55′N 81° 6′W) **20**:111
GRANTVILLE (Georgia)
map (33° 14′N 84° 50′W) **9**:114
GRANULATION, SOLAR **9**:289
supergranules **9**:289
GRANULITE
facies, metamorphic rock **13**:332 *table*
GRANULOPOIETIN (hormone)
hormone, animal **10**:236 *table*
GRANUM (Alberta)
map (49° 52′N 113° 30′W) **1**:256
GRANVILLE (New York)
map (43° 24′N 73° 16′W) **14**:149
GRANVILLE (county in North Carolina)
map (36° 20′N 78° 40′W) **14**:242
GRANVILLE (North Dakota)
map (48° 16′N 100° 47′W) **14**:248
GRANVILLE, JOHN CARTERET, 1ST EARL *see* CARTERET, JOHN, 1ST EARL OF GRANVILLE
GRANVILLE-BARKER, HARLEY **9**:289 *bibliog.*
GRANVILLE LAKE
map (56° 18′N 100° 30′W) **13**:119
GRAPE **8**:348 *illus.*; **9**:289–290 *bibliog., illus.*
cissus **4**:445
rafflesia **16**:69
raisin **16**:78
sea grapes **11**:229 *illus.*
wine **20**:175 *illus.*
GRAPE HYACINTH **9**:290
GRAPEFRUIT **9**:290 *bibliog., illus.*
citrus fruits **4**:447 *illus.*
GRAPELAND (Texas)
map (31° 29′N 95° 29′W) **19**:129
GRAPES OF WRATH, THE (book) **9**:290 *bibliog.*
Dust Bowl **6**:308 *illus.*
Steinbeck, John **18**:248
GRAPEVINE LAKE
map (32° 59′N 97° 6′W) **19**:129
GRAPH **9**:290–291 *bibliog., illus.*
algebra **1**:284
histogram **10**:180
isogram **11**:299
topology **19**:237
GRAPHIC ARTS **9**:291–294 *bibliog., illus.*
aquatint **2**:93
Austria
Bartsch, Adam von **3**:98–99
Kubin, Alfred **12**:134
Belgium
Bry, Théodore de **3**:528
Rops, Félicien **16**:312
block printing **3**:334
computer graphics **5**:160L–160n
Czechoslovakia
Hollar, Wenceslaus **10**:203
drawing **6**:263–265
drypoint **6**:285
engraving **7**:205–206
etching **7**:248–249
Finiguerra, Maso **8**:94
France
Bonnard, Pierre **3**:381
Bracquemond, Félix **3**:436
Callot, Jacques **4**:47
Daumier, Honoré **6**:45–46
Doré, Gustave **6**:241–242
Gavarni, Paul **9**:62
Grandville **9**:286
Gravelot, Hubert François **9**:302
Meryon, Charles **13**:313
Moreau (family) **13**:576
Nanteuil, Robert **14**:13
Picasso, Pablo **15**:290–292
Saint-Aubin (family) **17**:16
Toulouse-Lautrec, Henri de **19**:250–251
Vallotton, Félix **19**:508
Villon, Jacques **19**:599
Vuillard, Édouard **19**:640
Germany
Dürer, Albrecht **6**:304
Kirchner, Ernst Ludwig **12**:87
Kollwitz, Käthe **12**:107
Master E. S. **13**:215
Master of the Housebook **13**:215
Schongauer, Martin **17**:133
Slevogt, Max **17**:361
Wolgemut, Michael **20**:199
Great Britain
Beardsley, Aubrey **3**:142–143
Cruikshank, George **5**:365
Hayter, Stanley William **10**:84
Hogarth, William **10**:198
Italy
Bartolozzi, Francesco **3**:98
Piranesi, Giovanni Battista **15**:314–315
Japan
Harunobu **10**:64
Hiroshige **10**:175
Hokusai **10**:199–200
Kaigetsudo (art movement) **12**:6
Kiyomasu **12**:94
Kiyonaga **12**:94
Kiyonobu I **12**:94
Kuniyoshi **12**:137
Masanobu (1686–1764) **13**:195
Moronobu **13**:587
Sharaku **17**:241
Ukiyo-e **19**:375
Utamaro **19**:496
lithograph **12**:371
mechanical drawing **13**:259

GRAPHIC ARTS (cont.)
Mexico
Posada, José Guadalupe **15**:457
museums
Albertina **1**:259
Netherlands
Escher, Maurits Corneille **7**:237
Goltzius, Hendrik **9**:241
Lucas van Leyden **12**:448
Rembrandt **16**:145
Seghers, Hercules **17**:188
Norway
Munch, Edvard **13**:640
poster **15**:461–462
Russia
Grosman, Tatyana **9**:370
silk-screen printing **17**:308
Spain
Goya, Francisco de **9**:273–274
Switzerland
Graf, Urs **9**:278
Merian (family) **13**:310
United States
Baskin, Leonard **3**:116
Currier and Ives **5**:394
Gropper, William **9**:369
Hassam, Childe **10**:66–67
Kent, Rockwell **12**:45
Motherwell, Robert **13**:607
Pennell, Joseph **15**:145
Shahn, Ben **17**:235
West, Benjamin **20**:106
woodcuts and wood engravings **20**:210–211
GRAPHIC TABLET (computer term) **5**:160h
GRAPHITE
carbon **4**:134 *illus.*
Dixon, Joseph **6**:207
drawing **6**:263
pencil **15**:141
refractory materials **16**:124
GRAPPA (beverage)
rue **16**:339
GRAPTOLITE **9**:294 *bibliog., illus.*
Ordovician Period **14**:421
Paleozoic Era **15**:43
GRASONVILLE (Maryland)
map (38° 57′N 76° 13′W) **13**:188
GRASS (botany) **9**:295–297 *bibliog., illus.*
bamboo **3**:58–59
bluegrass **3**:345
bluestem **3**:346; **9**:299 *illus.*
buffalo grass **9**:299 *illus.*
cotton grass **19**:332 *illus.*
fescue **8**:62
foxtail **8**:257
grama **9**:299 *illus.*
grasslands **9**:299–301
ironwood **9**:299 *illus.*
millet **13**:429
needlegrass **9**:299 *illus.*
oats **14**:314
ragweed **9**:299 *illus.*
reed (botany) **16**:117
rice **16**:207–208
rye **16**:379
savanna life **17**:97–99
saw grass **18**:377 *illus.*
sedge **17**:183 *illus.*
short grass **9**:299 *illus.*
solidago **9**:299 *illus.*
sorghum **18**:69 *illus.*
steppe life **18**:257 *illus.*
structure **9**:297
tallgrass **9**:299 *illus.*
timothy **19**:203
uses
animal feed **9**:295
hay **10**:80
human consumption **9**:295
pasture **15**:109
turf **9**:295; **18**:257 *illus.*
weeds **9**:297
western wheat grass **9**:299 *illus.*
wheat **20**:124–126
wormwood **18**:257 *illus.*
GRASS, GÜNTER **9**:297–298 *bibliog., illus.*
Tin Drum, The **19**:205
GRASS CREEK (Wyoming)
map (43° 56′N 108° 39′W) **20**:301
GRASS FINCH **9**:298
GRASS LODGES (American Indians) *see* SHOSHONI (American Indians)
GRASS NUT *see* PEANUT
GRASS TREE **9**:298
GRASS VALLEY (California)
map (39° 13′N 121° 4′W) **4**:31
GRASSE, FRANÇOIS JOSEPH PAUL, COMTE DE **9**:298 *bibliog.*
American Revolution **1**:359 *map*
Yorktown Campaign **20**:331
GRASSELLI (Alabama)
map (33° 27′N 86° 54′W) **1**:234
GRASSFLAT (Pennsylvania)
map (41° 0′N 78° 7′W) **15**:147
GRASSHOPPER **2**:217 *illus.*; **9**:298–299 *bibliog., illus.*
anatomy **11**:187 *illus.*
katydid **12**:31
locust **12**:392
metamorphosis **11**:190 *illus.*; **13**:333–334 *illus.*
mouth **11**:188 *illus.*
sound frequencies produced **18**:73 *table*
sound receptors **11**:189 *illus.*
GRASSI, CRISTOFARD
painting of Genoa **11**:328 *illus.*
GRASSLANDS **9**:299–301 *bibliog., illus.*
See also PRAIRIE
climax community **5**:59
ecology **7**:42; **7**:46 *illus.*; **9**:299–301
grass **9**:295–297; **9**:299–301
habitat **10**:5
human influence **9**:301
Miocene flora and fauna **19**:125 *illus.*
National Forest System, U.S. **14**:32
savanna life **17**:97–99
steppe life **18**:256–257 *illus.*
temperate climate **9**:299–300
tropical climate **9**:300–301
tundra **9**:301
world distribution **3**:273 *map*; **15**:344 *map*
GRASSMAN, HERMANN
mathematics, history of **13**:226
GRASSO, ELLA T. **9**:301
Connecticut **5**:196
GRASSRANGE (Montana)
map (47° 1′N 108° 48′W) **13**:547
GRATEFUL DEAD, THE **9**:301
GRATIAN **9**:301 *bibliog.*
GRATIAN, ROMAN EMPEROR IN THE WEST **9**:301 *bibliog.*
Valentinian II, Roman Emperor in the West **19**:505
GRATIOT (county in Michigan)
map (43° 20′N 84° 35′W) **13**:377
GRATTAN, HENRY **9**:301 *bibliog.*
GRAU, MAURICE
Metropolitan Opera **13**:348
GRAU, SHIRLEY ANN **9**:301
GRAU SAN MARTÍN, RAMÓN **9**:301–302 *bibliog.*
GRAUN, KARL HEINRICH **9**:302 *bibliog.*
GRAUPNER, CHRISTOPH **9**:302 *bibliog.*
GRAVE *see* BURIAL
GRAVEL **9**:302
conglomerate (geology) **5**:181
glaciers and glaciation **9**:194–195
littoral zone **12**:373
roads and highways **16**:236 *illus.*; **16**:238 *illus.*
GRAVELOT, HUBERT FRANÇOIS **9**:302 *bibliog.*
GRAVES (county in Kentucky)
map (36° 45′N 88° 40′W) **12**:47
GRAVES, MICHAEL **9**:302 *bibliog., illus.*
Portland Building **9**:302 *illus.*
GRAVES, MORRIS **9**:302 *bibliog.*
GRAVES, NANCY **9**:302 *bibliog.*
GRAVES, ROBERT **9**:303 *bibliog.*
GRAVES, THOMAS
American Revolution **1**:359 *map*
GRAVE'S DISEASE
endocrine system, diseases of the **7**:170
GRAVETTIAN **9**:303 *bibliog.*
camp, Kostenki **12**:124–125
Dolní Věstonice **6**:226
Mousterian **13**:626
Perigordian **15**:166
prehistoric art **15**:508
Venus figurines **15**:40 *illus.*
GRAVIMETER **9**:303 *bibliog., illus.*
Earth, gravitational field of **7**:17
GRAVIMETRIC ANALYSIS
quantitative chemical analysis **16**:8
GRAVISCA *see* TARQUINIA
GRAVITATION **9**:304–305 *bibliog., illus.*
aerodynamics **1**:123
air **1**:203
black hole **3**:315–316
celestial mechanics **4**:230
center of gravity **4**:250
centrifuge **4**:256
characteristics **9**:304
cosmology (astronomy) **5**:284
dynamics **6**:319
Earth, gravitational field of **7**:17
Earth, size and shape of **7**:19
Earth tide **7**:25
EötvöS, Lóránt, Baron von Vásárosnemény **7**:215
erosion and sedimentation **7**:232–233
escape velocity **7**:236–237 *table*
force **8**:220
free fall **8**:294
fundamental interactions **8**:360–361
geotaxis
taxis **19**:48
law of gravitation **14**:174
mass (physics) **13**:201
measurement
gravimeter **9**:303
units, physical **19**:466
Vening Meinesz, Felix **19**:545
moon
mascon **13**:196
motion, planar **13**:609–610
perturbation **15**:191
relativity **16**:133–137 *illus.*
solar system **18**:45
space medicine **18**:133
theory **9**:304–305
Dicke, Robert **6**:156
Einstein, Albert **7**:93–94
Hooke, Robert **10**:226–227
Newton, Sir Isaac **14**:174
three-body problem **19**:181–182
tide **19**:194
time reversal invariance **19**:202
two-body problem **19**:360
unified field theory **19**:385–386
universal, Newton's law **9**:304 *illus.*
water wave **20**:57; **20**:59
weight (physics) **20**:92
weightlessness **20**:92
GRAVITATIONAL COLLAPSE **9**:305 *bibliog.*
black hole **3**:315–316
degenerate matter **6**:85
gravitational waves **9**:306
Schwarzschild radius **17**:139
GRAVITATIONAL CONSTANT
atomic constants **2**:308–309
Cavendish, Henry **4**:226
free fall **8**:294
GRAVITATIONAL LENS **9**:305–306 *bibliog.*
GRAVITATIONAL RADIATION
relativity **16**:136–137 *illus.*
GRAVITATIONAL WAVES **9**:306 *bibliog.*
gravitational collapse **9**:305
GRAVITON
fundamental particle **8**:362 *table*
GRAVITY *see* GRAVITATION
GRAVITY, CENTER OF *see* CENTER OF GRAVITY
GRAVITY'S RAINBOW (book) **9**:306 *bibliog.*
Pynchon, Thomas **15**:634
GRAVURE *see* INTAGLIO (printing); ROTOGRAVURE
GRAY (Georgia)
map (33° 1′N 83° 32′W) **9**:114
GRAY (county in Kansas)
map (37° 45′N 100° 25′W) **12**:18
GRAY (Kentucky)
map (36° 57′N 84° 0′W) **12**:47
GRAY (county in Texas)
map (35° 23′N 100° 50′W) **19**:129
GRAY, ASA **9**:306 *bibliog.*
GRAY, ELISHA **9**:306 *bibliog.*
GRAY, FRANCINE DU PLESSIX **9**:306
GRAY, ROBERT **9**:306
GRAY, SIMON **9**:307
GRAY, STEPHEN
physics, history of **15**:283
GRAY, THOMAS **9**:307 *bibliog., illus.*
"Elegy Written in a Country Churchyard" (poem) **7**:129
GRAY PANTHERS **9**:307
GRAYBEARD *see* SPANISH MOSS
GRAYLING (fish) **9**:307
GRAYLING (Michigan)
map (44° 40′N 84° 43′W) **13**:377
GRAYLYN CREST (Delaware)
map (39° 48′N 75° 31′W) **6**:88
GRAY'S ANATOMY (book) **9**:307
GRAYS HARBOR
map (46° 56′N 124° 5′W) **20**:35
GRAYS HARBOR (county in Washington)
map (47° 9′N 123° 45′W) **20**:35
GRAY'S MANUAL OF BOTANY (book)
Gray, Asa **9**:306
GRAYSON (Kentucky)
map (38° 20′N 82° 57′W) **12**:47
GRAYSON (county in Kentucky)
map (37° 30′N 86° 20′W) **12**:47
GRAYSON (county in Texas)
map (33° 38′N 96° 42′W) **19**:129
GRAYSON (county in Virginia)
map (36° 40′N 81° 5′W) **19**:607
GRAYSON, DAVID *see* BAKER, RAY STANNARD
GRAYSVILLE (Alabama)
map (33° 38′N 85° 9′W) **1**:234
GRAYSVILLE (Tennessee)
map (35° 27′N 85° 5′W) **19**:104
GRAYVILLE (Illinois)
map (38° 16′N 87° 59′W) **11**:42
GRAYWACKE **9**:307 *bibliog.*
beds, formation **9**:307
sandstone **9**:307
Triassic Period **19**:293
GRAZ (Austria) **9**:307
map (47° 5′N 15° 27′E) **2**:348
GRAZIANI, RODOLFO **9**:307–308
GRAZING
grass **9**:295
pasture **15**:109
GREASE *see* FATS AND OILS; LUBRICATION
GREASEWOOD **9**:308
GREAT ABACO ISLAND
Bahama Islands **3**:23
map (26° 28′N 77° 5′W) **3**:23
GREAT AGNOSTIC *see* INGERSOLL, ROBERT GREEN
GREAT ARTESIAN BASIN **9**:308
Australia **2**:331
map (25° 0′S 143° 0′E) **2**:328
GREAT ATLANTIC AND PACIFIC TEA COMPANY
Hartford, Huntington **10**:62
GREAT AUSTRALIAN BASIN *see* GREAT ARTESIAN BASIN
GREAT AUSTRALIAN BIGHT **9**:308
map (35° 0′S 130° 0′E) **2**:328
GREAT AWAKENING **9**:308 *bibliog.*
Davies, Samuel **6**:50
Dickinson, Jonathan **6**:158
Edwards, Jonathan **7**:69–70
evangelicalism **7**:312
Methodism **13**:344
Tennent, Gilbert **19**:102
Tennent, William **19**:102
United States, history of the **19**:438 *illus.*
Whitefield, George **20**:138
GREAT BARRIER ISLAND
map (36° 10′S 175° 25′E) **14**:158
New Zealand **14**:156
GREAT BARRIER REEF **2**:330 *illus.*; **9**:308 *bibliog., illus.*
map (18° 0′S 145° 50′E) **2**:328
GREAT BARRINGTON (Massachusetts)
map (42° 12′N 73° 22′W) **13**:206
GREAT BASIN **9**:308–309 *bibliog.*
map (40° 0′N 117° 0′W) **19**:419
Mojave Desert **13**:505
Nevada **14**:109–110 *illus.*
GREAT BAY
map (39° 30′N 74° 23′W) **14**:129
GREAT BEAR LAKE **9**:309
map (66° 0′N 120° 0′W) **14**:258
GREAT BELT, STRAIT OF THE
map (55° 30′N 11° 0′E) **6**:109
GREAT BEND (Kansas)
map (38° 22′N 98° 46′W) **12**:18
GREAT BILMA ERG DESERT
map (18° 30′N 14° 0′E) **14**:187
GREAT BITTER LAKE
map (30° 20′N 32° 23′E) **18**:324
GREAT BOOKS PROGRAM **9**:309
Adler, Mortimer J. **1**:104
Erskine, John **7**:235
St. John's College **17**:20
GREAT BRITAIN **9**:309
See also ENGLAND; ENGLISH ART AND ARCHITECTURE; ENGLISH LANGUAGE; ENGLISH LITERATURE; ENGLISH MUSIC; GREAT BRITAIN, HISTORY OF; NORTHERN IRELAND; SCOTLAND; UNITED KINGDOM; WALES
GREAT BRITAIN (ship)
navel vessels **14**:54–57
GREAT BRITAIN, HISTORY OF **9**:309–318 *bibliog., illus., maps, tables*
See also IRELAND, HISTORY OF; SCOTLAND—history; WALES—history
attainder, bill of **2**:313
British Empire *see* BRITISH EMPIRE
common law **5**:139–140
Commonwealth of Nations **5**:141
Conservative parties **5**:205
coronation **5**:271
duel **6**:293

exploration and settlement in colonial America **19**:437 *map*
historians *see* HISTORY—British historians
house (in Western architecture) **10**:265–267 *illus.*
liberalism **12**:312
London **12**:402
mathematics, history of **13**:226
monarchs **9**:312 *table*
navy **14**:62
Parliament **15**:92–93
political parties **15**:400–402
prime ministers **9**:316 *table*
privy council **15**:558
radicalism **16**:43–44
slavery **17**:353–355
smuggling **17**:374
socialism **18**:19–23
territories ceded to the United States, 1818–1846 **19**:446 *map*
weights and measures **20**:94
55 BC–449 AD Roman period
Agricola, Gnaeus Julius **1**:188
Antonine Wall **2**:70
Boadicea **3**:349
Caledonia **4**:27
Hadrian's Wall **10**:8
Rome, ancient **9**:309
449–1066 Anglo-Saxon rule
Æthelbert, King of Kent **1**:131
Æthelred II, King **1**:131
Alfred, King of England **1**:280
Anglo-Saxon Chronicle, The **2**:3
Anglo-Saxons **2**:3
Athelstan, King of Wessex **2**:289
Augustine of Canterbury, Saint **2**:321
Bede, Saint **3**:153
Canute, King **4**:118
Danelaw **6**:31
East Anglia **7**:31
Edgar, King of England **7**:56
Edward the Confessor, King of England **7**:67
Edward the Elder, King of Wessex **7**:67
Egbert, King of Wessex **7**:71–72
Germanic peoples **9**:309–310
Harold II, King **10**:53–54
Mercia **13**:304
Northumbria **14**:256
Offa, King of Mercia **14**:353
Offa's Dyke **14**:353
Oswald, Saint **14**:459
Sweyn, King of Denmark **18**:388
Vikings **19**:595
Wessex **20**:106
1066–1154 Norman Conquest
Anselm, Saint **2**:35
Domesday Book **6**:231
feudalism **8**:64–65
Hastings, Battle of **10**:67
Henry I, King **10**:124
heraldry **10**:132–134
Lanfranc **12**:194
Matilda **13**:228
Normandy (France) **14**:221
Normans **9**:310–311; **14**:221
Stephen, King **18**:254
William I, King (William the Conqueror) **20**:155
William II, King (William Rufus) **20**:155–156
1154–1399 Plantagenets
Angevins (dynasties) **1**:414
Baliol, John de **3**:38
Bannockburn, Battle of **3**:71
Barons' War **3**:88
Becket, Saint Thomas **3**:151
Bouvines, Battle of **3**:426
Burgh, Hubert de **3**:569
Cinque Ports **4**:435
Edward, the Black Prince **7**:67
Edward I, King of England **7**:67–68
Edward II, King of England **7**:68
Edward III, King of England **7**:68
Eleanor of Aquitaine **7**:103
Henry II, King **10**:124–125
Henry III, King of England **10**:125
Hundred Years' War *see* HUNDRED YEARS' WAR
John, King **11**:426–427
Magna Carta **13**:52–53
Middle Ages **9**:310–313
Montfort, Simon de, Earl of Leicester **13**:555–556
Mortimer (family) **13**:592
Peasants' Revolt **15**:129
Richard I, King of England **16**:209–210
Richard II, King of England **16**:210
1399–1485 Lancaster and York
Beaufort (family) **3**:146
Edward IV, King **7**:68
Edward V, King **7**:68
Europe, history of **7**:286
Henry IV, King **10**:125
Henry V, King **10**:125–126
Henry VI, King **10**:126
John of Gaunt, Duke of Lancaster **11**:425
Lancaster (dynasty) **9**:312–313; **12**:177
Margaret of Anjou **13**:148–149
Richard III, King **16**:210–211
Roses, Wars of the **16**:316 *map*
Warwick, Richard Neville, Earl of **20**:33
York (dynasty) **20**:330
1485-1603 House of Tudor
Anne of Cleves **2**:32
Boleyn, Anne **3**:364
Burghley, William Cecil, 1st Baron **3**:569
Catherine of Aragon **4**:209
coin **14**:296 *illus.*
Cranmer, Thomas **5**:331–332
Cromwell, Thomas, 1st Earl of Essex **5**:358
Darnley, Henry Stewart, Lord **6**:39
Drake, Sir Francis **6**:256–257
Edward VI, King of England **7**:68
Elizabeth I, Queen of England **7**:141–142
Elizabethan Age **7**:143–144
Essex, Robert Devereux 2nd Earl of **7**:245
Grey, Lady Jane **9**:360
Hawkins, Sir John **10**:77–78
Henry VII, King **10**:126
Henry VIII, King **10**:126–127
Howard (family) **10**:282
Howard, Catherine **10**:282–283
Leicester, Robert Dudley, Earl of **12**:277
Mary I, Queen **13**:185–186
More, Saint Thomas **13**:575
Northumberland, John Dudley, Duke of **14**:256
Parker, Matthew **15**:90
Parr, Catherine **15**:97
Percy (family) **15**:163
Pole, Reginald **15**:395
Raleigh, Sir Walter **16**:79
Reformation **9**:313; **16**:123
Renaissance **16**:149
Salisbury, Robert Cecil, 1st Earl of **17**:33
Somerset, Edward Seymour, 1st Duke of **18**:61
Spanish Armada **18**:150–151
Tudor (dynasty) **19**:328
Walsingham, Sir Francis **20**:19
Whitgift, John **20**:139
Wolsey, Thomas **20**:200
1603–1649 House of Stuart
Bishops' Wars **3**:298
Buckingham, George Villiers, 1st Duke of **3**:535–536
Cavaliers **4**:220
Charles I, King **4**:291
costume **5**:299 *illus.*
Covenanters **5**:319
English Civil War **7**:189–190
Fawkes, Guy **8**:39
James I, King **11**:355
Laud, William **12**:236
Roundheads **16**:325
Salisbury, Robert Cecil, 1st Earl of **17**:33
Star Chamber **18**:226
Strafford, Thomas Wentworth, 1st Earl of **18**:287–288
Stuart (family) **18**:304
Wallis, John **20**:16
1649–1660 Commonwealth and Protectorate
Blake, Robert **3**:325
Cromwell, Oliver **5**:357–358
First Anglo-Dutch War **2**:3
Puritanism **15**:630
1660–1714 Stuart Restoration
Anglo-Dutch Wars *see* ANGLO-DUTCH WARS
Anne, Queen of England, Scotland, and Ireland **2**:32
Berwick, James Fitzjames, Duke of **3**:227
Boyne, Battle of the **3**:434
Charles II, King **4**:291–292
Clarendon, Edward Hyde, 1st Earl of **5**:36–37
Clarendon Code **5**:37
English Bill of Rights **3**:253
Glorious Revolution **9**:209
Grand Alliance, War of the **9**:284
Jacobites **11**:346
James II, King **11**:356
Marlborough, John Churchill, 1st Duke of **13**:160
Mary II, Queen **13**:186
Monck, George, 1st Duke of Albemarle **13**:522
Monmouth, James Scott, Duke of **13**:536
Oates, Titus **14**:313
Pepys, Samuel **15**:157–158
Restoration **16**:182
Settlement, Act of **17**:214
Shaftesbury, Anthony Ashley Cooper, 1st Earl of **17**:234
Stuart, James Francis Edward **18**:305–306
Test Acts **19**:126
Tory party **19**:247
War of the Spanish Succession *see* SPANISH SUCCESSION, WAR OF THE
Whig party (England) **20**:130
William III, King **20**:156
1714–1837 House of Hanover
American Revolution *see* AMERICAN REVOLUTION
Bentinck (family) **3**:205
Bolingbroke, Henry St. John **3**:364
Burke, Edmund **3**:571
Canning, George **4**:111
Carteret, John, 1st Earl of Granville **4**:173
Castlereagh, Robert Stewart, Viscount **4**:191
Catholic Emancipation **4**:211
Chartism **4**:300
Cobbett, William **5**:83–84
Corn Laws **5**:267
enclosure **7**:163
French Revolutionary Wars *see* FRENCH REVOLUTIONARY WARS
George I, King **9**:110
George II, King **9**:110
George III, King **9**:110–111
George IV, King **9**:111
Gordon Riots **9**:249–250
Hanover (dynasty) **10**:39
Industrial Revolution **9**:315–316; **11**:158–159
Jay's Treaty **11**:387
Kitchener, Herbert Kitchener, 1st Earl **12**:91
Liverpool, Robert Banks Jenkinson, 2d Earl of **12**:376
Napoleonic Wars *see* NAPOLEONIC WARS
Newcastle, Thomas Pelham-Holles, 1st Duke of **14**:164
Peel, Sir Robert **15**:132
Pelham, Henry **15**:137–138
Pitt, William (the Elder) **15**:320
Pitt, William (the Younger) **15**:320–321
poor laws **15**:429
Reform Acts **16**:120–121
Regency **16**:126
Rockingham, Charles Watson-Wentworth, 2d Marquess of **16**:260
Seven Years' War *see* SEVEN YEARS' WAR
South African War *see* SOUTH AFRICAN WAR
South Sea Bubble **18**:106
Stuart, Charles Edward (Bonnie Prince Charlie) **18**:304–305
Tory party **19**:247
Venezuela Boundary Dispute **19**:544
Victoria, Queen of England, Scotland, and Ireland **9**:317; **19**:574
Walpole, Sir Robert **20**:18
War of 1812 *see* WAR OF 1812
Wellington, Arthur Wellesley, 1st Duke of **20**:100
Wilkes, John **20**:151–152
William IV, King **20**:156
1837–1910 Victorian and Edwardian periods
Aberdeen, George Hamilton-Gordon, 4th Earl of **1**:56
Acton, Lord **1**:90
Balfour, Arthur **3**:37
Bright, John **3**:486
Campbell-Bannerman, Sir Henry **4**:66
Chamberlain, Joseph **4**:273–274
Churchill, Lord Randolph **4**:425
Crimean War *see* CRIMEAN WAR
Derby, Edward Stanley, 14th Earl of **6**:121
Disraeli, Benjamin, 1st Earl of Beaconsfield **6**:197–198
Eastern Question **7**:34
Edward VII, King **7**:69
Gladstone, William Ewart **9**:196
Hay-Pauncefote Treaty **10**:80
Melbourne, William Lamb, 2d Viscount **13**:286
Palmerston, Henry John Temple, 3d Viscount **15**:51
Rhodes, Cecil John **16**:202
Rosebery, Archibald Philip Primrose, 5th Earl of **16**:314
Salisbury, Robert Cecil, 3d Marquess of **17**:33
Shaftesbury, Anthony Ashley Cooper, 7th Earl of **17**:234–235
sword **18**:398 *illus.*
Triple Entente **19**:302
1910-present
Asquith, Herbert Henry, 1st Earl of Oxford and Asquith **2**:263
Attlee, Clement, 1st Earl Attlee **2**:315–316
Baldwin, Stanley **3**:35–36
Beaverbrook, Max Aitken, 1st Baron **3**:149
Bevan, Aneurin **3**:232
Bevin, Ernest **3**:233
Birkenhead, F. E. Smith, 1st Earl of **3**:292
Callaghan, James **4**:40
Chamberlain, Neville **4**:274
Chanak Crisis **4**:278
Charles, Prince of Wales **4**:290
Churchill, Sir Winston **4**:426–427
Cripps, Sir Stafford **5**:350–351
Douglas-Home, Sir Alec **6**:248
Eden, Sir Anthony **7**:55–56
Edward VIII, King **7**:69
Elizabeth II, Queen **7**:142
Falkland Islands **8**:13
George V, King **9**:111–112
George VI, King of England, Scotland, and Ireland **9**:112
Healey, Denis **10**:86
Heath, Edward **10**:99
Jenkins, Roy **11**:395–396
Kinnock, Neil **12**:84
Labour party **12**:156–157
Law, Andrew Bonar **12**:247
Lloyd George, David, 1st Earl Lloyd-George of Dwyfor **12**:383–384
MacDonald, Ramsay **13**:12–13
Macmillan, Harold **13**:34
modern era **9**:317–318
Mountbatten of Burma, Louis Mountbatten, 1st Earl **13**:624–625
Northern Ireland **14**:255
Powell, Enoch **15**:480–481
Profumo scandal **15**:562
Steel, David Martin Scott **18**:243
Suez Crisis **18**:325
suffrage, women's **18**:326
Thatcher, Margaret **19**:143
Thorpe, Jeremy **19**:179–180
Titanic **19**:211
Wilson, Sir Harold **20**:164–165
Windsor (dynasty) **20**:174
World War I *see* WORLD WAR I
World War II *see* WORLD WAR II
Zimbabwe (Rhodesia) **20**:365–366
GREAT CANADIAN *see* IBERVILLE, PIERRE LE MOYNE, SIEUR D'
GREAT CIRCLE **9**:318
spherical trigonometry **18**:180
GREAT COMMONER *see* PITT, WILLIAM (the Elder)
GREAT DANE **6**:215 *illus.*; **9**:318–319 *bibliog.*, *illus.*
GREAT DISMAL SWAMP
map (36° 30′N 76° 30′W) **14**:242
GREAT DIVIDE *see* CONTINENTAL DIVIDE
GREAT DIVIDE BASIN
map (42° 0′N 108° 10′W) **20**:301
GREAT DIVIDING RANGE **2**:330 *illus.*; **9**:319
map (25° 0′S 147° 0′E) **2**:328
GREAT DUKE, THE *see* WELLINGTON, ARTHUR WELLESLEY, 1ST DUKE OF
GREAT EASTERN (ship) **9**:319 *bibliog.*, *illus.*
ship **17**:272–273 *illus.*
GREAT EASTERN ERG DESERT
map (30° 30′N 7° 0′E) **1**:287
GREAT EGG HARBOR
map (39° 18′N 74° 40′W) **14**:129

GREAT ELECTOR, THE *see* FREDERICK WILLIAM, ELECTOR OF BRANDENBURG (the Great Elector)
GREAT EXHIBITION OF 1851 (London) *see* CRYSTAL PALACE
GREAT EXPECTATIONS (book) **9**:319 *bibliog.*
GREAT EXUMA ISLAND
map (23° 32′N 75° 50′W) **3**:23
GREAT FALLS (Manitoba)
map (50° 27′N 96° 2′W) **13**:119
GREAT FALLS (Montana) **9**:319
map (47° 30′N 111° 17′W) **13**:547
GREAT FALLS (South Carolina)
map (34° 34′N 80° 54′W) **18**:98
GREAT GATSBY, THE (book) **9**:319 *bibliog.*
Fitzgerald, F. Scott **8**:130–131
GREAT GEOMETER *see* APOLLONIUS OF PERGA
GREAT GLEN (Scotland) **17**:149 *illus.*
GREAT HUNGARIAN PLAIN
map (46° 45′N 19° 45′E) **10**:307
GREAT INAGUA ISLAND
Bahama Islands **3**:23
map (21° 5′N 73° 18′W) **3**:23
GREAT INDIAN DESERT *see* THAR DESERT
GREAT ISLAND
map (41° 55′N 70° 4′W) **13**:206
GREAT KARROO (plateau)
map (32° 25′S 22° 40′E) **18**:79
GREAT LAKES **9**:319–320 *bibliog., map*
art subject
Moran, Thomas **13**:573
bays and waterways
Georgian Bay **9**:118
Green Bay **9**:347
Erie, Lake **7**:229–230 *map*
history
Allouez, Claude Jean **1**:303
Brûlé, Étienne **3**:523
Duluth, Daniel Greysolon, Sieur **6**:296
Huron, Lake **10**:317 *map*
lake, glacial **12**:170
Michigan, Lake **13**:382–383 *map*
Ontario, Lake **14**:395–396 *map*
St. Lawrence Seaway **17**:21–22
Superior, Lake **18**:351–352 *map*
GREAT LAKES NAVAL TRAINING CENTER **9**:320
GREAT LEAP FORWARD **9**:320 *bibliog.*
China **4**:367
China, history of **4**:376
Mao Tse-tung (Mao Zedong) **13**:135
GREAT MAHELE
Kamehameha (dynasty) **12**:9
GREAT MIAMI RIVER
map (39° 6′N 84° 49′W) **14**:357
GREAT MOSQUE
Mecca (Saudi Arabia) **13**:258–259
GREAT NORTH MOUNTAIN
map (39° 0′N 78° 45′W) **19**:607
GREAT NORTHERN RAILWAY (England)
locomotive **12**:390 *illus.*
GREAT PECONIC BAY
map (40° 56′N 72° 30′W) **5**:193
GREAT PLAINS **9**:320–321 *bibliog.*
Colorado **5**:115
frontier **8**:341–344
Indian Wars **11**:108
Indians, American **11**:124–125 *maps*; **11**:129–130
Kansas **12**:17
map (40° 0′N 100° 0′W) **14**:225
Montana **13**:546
Nebraska **14**:74
North America **14**:227
pioneers **8**:343 *illus.*
South Dakota **18**:102
United States, history of the **19**:450–451
GREAT PURGE **9**:321 *bibliog.*
Europe, history of **7**:295
Russia/Union of Soviet Socialist Republics, history of **16**:359
Stalin, Joseph **18**:214
Stalinism **5**:147
Vyshinsky, Andrei Yanuarievich **19**:640
GREAT PYRENEES **6**:214 *illus.*; **9**:321 *bibliog., illus.*
GREAT RED SPOT **9**:321
Jupiter (planet) **11**:473 *illus.*
GREAT RIFT VALLEY **9**:321–322 *bibliog., illus.*
Dead Sea **6**:64
East African Rift System **7**:30–31
Ethiopia **7**:252
Kenya **12**:52
Kivu, Lake **12**:94
map (5° 0′S 30° 0′E) **1**:136
Rudolf, Lake **16**:338
Tanganyika, Lake **19**:22
GREAT RUAHA RIVER
map (7° 56′S 37° 52′E) **19**:27
GREAT SACANDAGA LAKE
map (43° 8′N 74° 10′W) **14**:149
GREAT SALT LAKE **9**:322 *bibliog.*; **19**:495 *illus.*
evaporite **7**:314
lake, glacial **12**:170
map (41° 10′N 112° 30′W) **19**:492
GREAT SALT LAKE DESERT
map (40° 40′N 113° 30′W) **19**:492
GREAT SALT POND
map (41° 10′N 71° 35′W) **16**:198
GREAT SAND HILLS
map (50° 35′N 109° 5′W) **17**:81
GREAT SANDY DESERT **9**:322
map (21° 30′S 125° 0′E) **2**:328
GREAT SCARCIES RIVER
map (8° 55′N 13° 8′W) **17**:296
GREAT SCHISM *see* SCHISM, GREAT
GREAT SEAL OF THE UNITED STATES **9**:322 *bibliog., illus.*
GREAT SERPENT MOUND (Ohio) *see* MOUND BUILDERS
GREAT SLAVE LAKE **9**:322
map (61° 30′N 114° 0′W) **14**:258
GREAT SMOKY MOUNTAINS **9**:322; **19**:104 *illus.*
national parks **14**:37–39 *illus., map, table*
Tennessee **19**:102
GREAT SOCIALIST CULTURAL REVOLUTION *see* CULTURAL REVOLUTION
GREAT SOCIETY, THE *see* JOHNSON, LYNDON B.
GREAT SOUND
map (32° 17′N 64° 51′W) **3**:219
GREAT SOUTH BAY
map (40° 40′N 73° 17′W) **5**:193
GREAT TREK **9**:322–323 *bibliog.*
GREAT TSAU MOUNTAIN
map (21° 14′S 22° 45′E) **3**:416
GREAT VICTORIA DESERT **9**:323
map (28° 30′S 127° 45′E) **2**:328
GREAT WALL OF CHINA **2**:252 *illus.*; **4**:361 *illus.*; **9**:323 *bibliog., illus.*; **19**:460 *illus.*
Chinese archaeology **4**:378
fortification **8**:238–239
Hopei (Hebei) **10**:230–231
GREAT WESTERN
ship **17**:273
GREAT WESTERN ERG DESERT
map (30° 30′N 0° 30′E) **1**:287
GREAT WHITE FLEET **19**:452 *illus.*
GREAT WHITE SHARK
shark **17**:242–243 *illus.*
GREAT WHITE WAY, THE *see* BROADWAY
GREAT YARMOUTH (England)
map (52° 37′N 1° 44′E) **19**:403
GREAT ZAB RIVER
map (36° 0′N 43° 21′E) **11**:255
GREATBATCH, WILLIAM
pacemaker, artificial **15**:4
GREATER ANTILLES *see* ANTILLES, GREATER AND LESSER
GREATER KHINGAN RANGE
map (49° 40′N 122° 0′E) **4**:362
GREATER KUDU *see* ANTELOPE
GREATER SUNDA ISLANDS *see* SUNDA ISLANDS (Indonesia)
GREATHEAD, JAMES HENRY
tunnel **19**:338
GREBE **3**:281 *illus.*; **9**:323–324 *bibliog., illus.*
courtship and mating **2**:21 *illus.*; **3**:286 *illus.*
finfoot **8**:93
GRÉBOUN, MOUNT
map (20° 0′N 8° 35′E) **14**:187
GRECHKO, GEORGY MIKHAILOVICH **9**:324
GRECO, CAPE OF
map (34° 56′N 34° 5′E) **5**:409
GRECO, EL *see* EL GRECO
GRECO, JOSÉ **9**:324
GRECO-ROMAN WRESTLING **20**:287 *illus.*
GREECE **9**:324–329 *bibliog., illus., map, table*
See also GREECE, ANCIENT
agriculture and fishing **9**:326–327
archaeology *see* AEGEAN CIVILIZATION; GREECE, ANCIENT
architecture *see* GREEK ARCHITECTURE
art *see* GREEK ART
cities
Athens **2**:289–291 *illus., map*
Corinth **5**:263
Iráklion **11**:249
Kalámai **12**:7
Patras **15**:112–113
Piraeus **15**:314
Salonika **17**:36
climate **9**:324–325 *table*
economic activity **9**:326–327 *illus.*
education **9**:326
European universities **7**:308 *table*
flag **9**:324 *illus.*
folk dance
hasapikos **10**:66
government **9**:327
history prior to 4th century *see* GREECE, ANCIENT
history since 4th century **9**:327–329
Balkan Wars **3**:38
Byzantine Empire **3**:607–608
Capo d'Istria, Giovanni Antonio, Count **4**:126–127
Constantine I, King **5**:208
Constantine II, King **5**:208
Cyprus **5**:409
Damaskinós **6**:19
EAM-ELAS **7**:5
EOKA **7**:215
George I, King **9**:112
George II, King **9**:112
Izmir **11**:338
Karamanlis, Konstantinos G. **12**:27
Mavrokordátos, Aléxandros **13**:238
Metaxás, Ioánnis **13**:335
Navarino, Battle of **14**:58
Otto, King of Greece **14**:463
Papagos, Alexandros **15**:67
Papandréou, Andreas **15**:67
Papandréou, Georgios **15**:67
Paul, King **15**:117
Turkey **19**:345–346
Venizélos, Eleuthérios **19**:546
World War I **20**:230; **20**:238–239
World War II *see* WORLD WAR II
islands
Aegina **1**:118
Corfu **5**:262
Crete **5**:342 *illus.*
Cyclades **5**:402
Delos **6**:94–95
Dodecanese **6**:212
Euboea **7**:261
Ithaca **11**:331
Lesbos **12**:296
Melos **13**:288
Naxos **14**:66
Rhodes **16**:201–202
Salamis **17**:30
Samos **17**:47
land and resources **9**:324–326 *map, table*
language *see* GREEK LANGUAGE
literature *see* GREEK LITERATURE, MODERN
map (39° 0′N 22° 0′E) **7**:268
music
Theodorakis, Mikis **19**:156
national anthem
Solomos, Dionysios **18**:57
newspaper **14**:172
people **7**:275 *illus.*; **9**:326; **9**:328 *illus.*
Cyprus **5**:407
physical features
Athos, Mount **2**:292
Corinth, Isthmus of **5**:263
Olympus, Mount **14**:385
Parnassus **15**:96
regions
Peloponnesus **15**:139
Thessaly **19**:168
resources **9**:326
rivers, lakes, and waterways **9**:325–326
urban planning *see* URBAN PLANNING
vegetation **9**:326
GREECE (New York)
map (43° 14′N 77° 38′W) **14**:149
GREECE, ANCIENT **9**:329–334 *bibliog., illus., maps*
agriculture, history of **1**:190
archaeology
Curtius, Ernst Robert **5**:396
Messene **13**:323
Orchomenos **14**:420
architecture *see* GREEK ARCHITECTURE
army
hoplite **10**:232
art *see* GREEK ART
astronomy
Aristarchus of Samos **2**:155
astronomy, history of **2**:277
constellation **5**:211
Eratosthenes of Cyrene **7**:227–228
Heracleides Ponticus **10**:131
Hipparchus **10**:173
Meton **13**:345
Ptolemy **15**:606–607
cities
Athens **2**:289–291 *illus.*
Chaeronea **4**:267
Cnidus **5**:73
Corinth **5**:263
Epidaurus **7**:218–219
Megalopolis **13**:280
Messene **13**:322
Olynthus **14**:385
Orchomenos **14**:420
Plataea **15**:351
Pylos **15**:634
Sicyon **17**:294
Sparta **18**:164–165
Thebes (Greece) **19**:155
Thermopylae **19**:167
coin **14**:296 *illus.*
colonies
Agrigento **1**:199
Cumae **5**:386
Cyrene **5**:410
Doura-Europos **6**:249
Paestum **15**:13
Syracuse (Sicily) **18**:410–411
cooking **5**:238 *illus.*
costume **5**:293 *illus.*
cosmetics **5**:281
jewelry **11**:408–409 *illus.*
dance **6**:22–23 *illus.*
drama *see* DRAMA; THEATER, HISTORY OF THE
education **7**:59–60
humanities, education in the **10**:300
literacy and illiteracy **12**:368
element **7**:129 *illus.*
engineering **7**:177
Eupalinus **7**:265
pump **15**:622
technology, history of **19**:62
tunnel **19**:337
games, mathematical **9**:32
geography **9**:100–101 *illus.*
Pausanias (geographer) **15**:119
Strabo (geographer) **18**:287
Greek fire **9**:342
Greek music **5**:344–345 *illus.*
greyhound, dog **9**:361
historians *see* HISTORY—Greek historians
history
Aegean civilization **1**:114–118 *illus.*
Alexander the Great **1**:273–275
archaic period **9**:329–331
Athens **2**:289
city-state **5**:9
colonization (6th century) **9**:330 *map*
Delian League **6**:92–93
Demosthenes **6**:104–105
Dorians **6**:242
Europe, history of **7**:280
exploration **7**:334
Greece **9**:327–328
Hellenistic Age **10**:114
Macedonia, Kingdom of **13**:15
Pelopidas **15**:138–139
Peloponnesian War **15**:139
Pericles **15**:165
Persian Wars **15**:187–188
Rome, ancient **16**:298–300
Sparta **18**:164–165
Thebes (Greece) **19**:155
Timoleon **19**:203
5th century **9**:331–333 *map*
holy sites
Delos **6**:94–95
Delphi **6**:95
Eleusis **7**:135
Nemea **14**:80
Olympia **14**:381
house (in Western architecture) **10**:264–266 *illus.*
ideals
aretê **2**:146
Ionia **11**:241
Ephesus **7**:216
Miletus **13**:419
Priene **15**:536
language *see* GREEK LANGUAGE
law **12**:242
inheritance **11**:177
literature *see* GREEK LITERATURE, ANCIENT
logic **12**:395
magnetism **13**:56

maps and mapmaking 13:138–139 *illus.*
mathematics
Archimedes 2:128
Diophantus 6:185
Euclid 7:262–263
Eudoxus of Cnidus 7:263
Hero of Alexandria 10:144
mathematics, history of 13:223
Pappus 15:72
Pythagoras of Samos 15:639–640
medicine 13:268
Aristotle 13:268
biology 3:268
Hippocrates 10:174; 13:268
music *see* GREEK MUSIC
mythology *see* GREEK MYTHOLOGY
naval vessels 14:54 *illus.*
galley 9:18
officials
archons 2:137
ephors 7:216
philosophy *see* GREEK PHILOSOPHY
regions
Achaea 1:80
Aetolia 1:131
Arcadia 2:112
Argos 2:152–153
Attica 2:314
Boeotia 3:358
Epirus 7:220–221
Euboea 7:261
Messenia 13:323
Peloponnesus 15:139
Phocis 15:249
Pontus 15:428
riddles 16:216
semaphore 17:194
Seven Wonders of the World 17:216–218
slavery 17:352
solar energy 18:42
sports
boxing 3:431
gymnasium 9:412
gymnastics 9:412
history 18:195
Isthmian Games 11:308
Olympic Games 14:382
Pythian Games 15:640
stadium 18:208
wrestling 20:287
state (in political philosophy) 18:229
technology, history of 19:62
textile industry 19:136 *illus.*
theater *see* THEATER, HISTORY OF THE
tomb 19:230
weights and measures 20:93
women in society 20:201
GREEK ARCHITECTURE 9:334–337 *bibliog., illus.*
acanthus 1:71–72
Acropolis 1:84–85
Aegean civilization 1:115–117 *illus.*
agora 1:187
Archaic period 9:335–337
architecture 2:131–132 *illus.*
architrave 2:137
Athens 2:289–291 *illus.*
building types 9:334–335
Byzantine art and architecture 3:604
Callicrates 4:41
Callimachus (sculptor) 4:46
capital 4:123
cella 4:236
classical period 9:337
colonnade 5:112
column 5:129
crypt 5:371
entablature 7:208
Epidaurus 7:218
Greek art 9:337–338; 9:340
Greek Revival 9:345–346
Hellenistic period 9:337
Hippodamus of Miletus 10:174
house (in Western architecture) 10:264–266
Ictinus 11:24
interior design 11:211
Messene 13:323
Mnesicles 13:486
music and concert halls 13:669
naos 14:14
Olympia 14:381
Orchomenos 14:420
ornaments and moldings 9:336 *illus.*
Paestum 15:13
Parthenon 2:291 *illus.*
Pausanias (geographer) 15:119
Pella 15:138
post and lintel 15:459
Priene 15:536
Pylos 15:634
Samothrace 17:47
Seven Wonders of the World 17:216–218
stoa 18:273
Stuart, James 18:305
technology, history of 19:62–63 *illus.*
Tegea 19:72
temple 19:95–97 *illus.*
Temple of Poseidon 19:63 *illus.*
tympanum 19:362
GREEK ART 2:192–193 *illus.*; 9:337–342 *bibliog., illus.*
See also the subheading Greece under specific art forms, e.g., ARCHITECTURE; PAINTING; SCULPTURE; etc.
Apelles 2:76
archaic period 9:338–339
art criticism 2:207
bas-relief 3:100 *illus.*
bronzes 3:507–508 *illus.*
classical period 9:340–342
costume 5:293 *illus.*
Elgin Marbles 7:137
encaustic painting 7:162
Etruscans 7:259–260
furniture 8:374
geometric period 9:338
Getty Museum 9:160
Hellenistic period 9:342
iconography 11:21
illuminated manuscripts 11:46
jewelry 11:408–409 *illus.*
Metropolitan Museum of Art, The 13:348
Minoan art 13:458–459
mosaic 13:593
mural painting 13:646
museums, art 13:658
neoclassicism (art) 14:81–82
Oltos 14:381
Olympia 14:381
Onesimos 14:390
Pergamum 15:165
perspective 15:190
Phidias 15:226–227
Pompeii 15:424
portraiture 15:446
pottery and porcelain 15:470 *illus.*
Olympic Games 14:382 *illus.*
Pylos 15:634
red-figure pottery 4:257 *illus.*
Samothrace 17:47
sarcophagus 17:75–76
Selinus 17:192
Seven Wonders of the World 17:216–218
Sicyon 17:294
Spina 18:183
stele 18:250
steppe art 18:255 *illus.*
still-life painting 18:268
terra-cotta figures 19:29 *illus.*; 19:119 *illus.*
Vatican museums and galleries 19:527–528
Villanovans 19:597
Vix 19:623
Winckelmann, Johann 20:168
GREEK CROSS 5:360; 5:361 *illus.*
GREEK CROSS CHURCHES
Byzantine art and architecture 3:604
GREEK DRAMA *see* DRAMA; THEATER, HISTORY OF THE
GREEK FIRE 9:342 *illus.*
fortification 8:238
weapons 20:74
GREEK LANGUAGE 9:342–343 *bibliog.*
alphabet 20:293–294 *illus.*
ancient Greek
dictionary 6:159
Linear B 12:353–354
linguistics 12:354
inscription 11:185–186
modern Greek
Greek literature, modern 9:344
Renaissance 16:149
Rosetta Stone 16:317
secondary education 17:179
GREEK LITERATURE, ANCIENT 9:343–344 *bibliog., illus.*
archaic period 9:343
authors
Aeschylus 1:128–129
Aesop 1:130
Alcaeus 1:262
Alcman 1:264
Anacreon 1:387
Apollonius of Rhodes 2:84–85
Archilochus 2:128
Aristophanes 2:155–156
Bacchylides 3:9–10
Callimachus (poet) 4:46
Corinna 5:262
Cratinus 5:333
Eupolis 7:265
Euripides 7:266
Heliodorus of Emesa 10:112
Herodotus 10:144
Hesiod 10:151
Homer 10:213
Ibycus 11:7
Isocrates 11:298–299
Longinus 12:409
Longus 12:410
Lucian 12:450
Lysias 12:480
Menander 13:292–293
Mimnermus 13:436
Philemon 15:231
Pindar 15:304–305
Plutarch 15:372
Sappho 17:73
Simonides of Ceos 17:316
Sophocles 18:67–68
Stesichorus 18:262
Theocritus 19:155
Theognis 19:157
Thucydides 19:183–184
Tyrtaeus 19:368
Xenophon 20:312
Bacchae, The (play) 3:9
biography 3:263
book 3:383
classical period 9:343–344
classicism 5:42
Clouds, The 5:68
comedy 5:132
criticism
Murray, Gilbert 13:650
dithyramb 6:202
Electra 7:105
Hellenistic period 9:344
History of the Peloponnesian War 10:185–186
History of the Persian Wars, The 10:186
Iliad 11:40
Latin literature 12:234
Lysistrata 12:480
Medea 13:263
Odyssey 14:351
Oedipus Rex 14:351
Oresteia 14:432
Poetics of Aristotle 15:378
Renaissance 16:149
satire 17:88
satyr play 17:92
tragedy 19:265
Trojan Woman, The 19:305
GREEK LITERATURE, MODERN 9:344 *bibliog.*
authors
Cavafy, C. P. 4:220
Elytis, Odysseus 7:150
Kazantzakis, Nikos 12:34
Palamas, Kostis 15:29
Ritsos, Yannis 16:229
Seferis, George 17:187
Sikelianos, Angelos 17:302
Solomos, Dionysios 18:57
Xenopoulos, Gregorios 20:312
GREEK MUSIC 9:344–345 *bibliog., illus.*
Byzantine music 3:608
instruments 5:345 *illus.*
aulos 2:323
kithara 12:93
lyre 12:479
GREEK MYTHOLOGY
Adonis 1:107
Antaeus 2:38
Antigone 2:62
Antiope 2:64
Aphrodite 2:78
Apollo 2:80
Arachne 2:106
Ares 2:146
Arethusa 2:146
Argus 2:153
Ariadne 2:153
Aristaeus 2:155
Artemis 2:213
Asclepius 2:228
Atalanta 2:287
Athena 2:289
Atlantis 2:296
Atlas 2:297
Atreus 2:312
Augeas 2:319
basilisk 3:110
Bellerophon 3:187
Boreas 3:398
Cadmus 4:12
caduceus 4:12
Calypso 4:49
Cassandra 4:183
Castor and Pollux 4:191
Cecrops 4:228
centaur 4:249
Cephalus 4:257
Cerberus 4:259
Chaos 4:283
Charon 4:299
Chiron 4:397
Circe 4:435
Clytemnestra 5:73
Colchis 5:97
cornucopia 5:269
Cronus 5:359
Cyclops 5:406
Daedalus 6:5–6
Danaë 6:21
Danaus 6:21
Daphne 6:36
Daphnis 6:36
Dardanus 6:37
Delos (Greece) 6:94
Demeter 6:96
Deucalion 6:136
Diomedes 6:184
Dionysus 6:184–185
Dodona 6:212
Echo 7:39
Electra 7:105
Elysian Fields 7:150
Endymion 7:171
Eos 7:215
Erebus 7:228
Erechtheus 7:228
Eris 7:231
Eros 7:232
Europa 7:267
Eurynome 7:309–310
Fates 8:34
Furies 8:371
Gaea 9:7
Galatea 9:10
Glaucus 9:205
Golden Fleece 9:232
Gordian knot 9:248
Gorgon 9:251
graces 9:276
griffin 9:362
Hades 10:7–8
Halcyone 10:17
Hanging Gardens of Babylon 17:216
harpy 10:56
Hecate 10:103
Hector 10:104
Hecuba 10:104
Helen of Troy 10:110
Helenus 10:111
Helios 10:113
Hephaestus 10:131
Hera 10:131
Hercules 10:138
Hermaphroditus 10:142
Hermes 10:142
Hermione 10:142–143
Hero and Leander 10:144
Hesperides 10:151
Hestia 10:153
Hippolyte 10:174
Hippolytus 10:174
Hyacinthus 10:327
Hydra 10:329
Hygeia 10:345
Hymen 10:345
Iphigenia 11:248
Iris 11:266
Ixion 11:338
Jason 11:384
labyrinth and maze 12:158
Lamia 12:175
Laomedon 12:202
Leda 12:268
Lethe 12:299
Leto 12:299
Lotus-Eaters 12:421
maenads 13:45
Marsyas 13:175
Medea 13:263
Medusa 13:278
Memnon 13:290
Menelaus 13:297
Messina, Strait of 13:324
Midas 13:390
Milo 13:432
Minos 13:459
Minotaur 13:460
Mnemosyne 13:486
Morpheus 13:587
muses 13:656
mythology 13:700–701
Narcissus 14:21
Nemesis 14:81
Neoptolemus 14:85
Nereus 14:89
Nestor 14:97

GREEK MYTHOLOGY (cont.)
Nike **14**:195
Niobe **14**:200
nymphs **14**:309–310
Odysseus **14**:350–351
Oedipus **14**:351
Olympus, Mount **14**:385
oracle **14**:413
Orestes **14**:432
Orion **14**:444
Orpheus **14**:448
Palamedes **15**:29–30
Palladium **15**:48
Pan **15**:53
Pandora **15**:59
Paris (mythology) **15**:87
Parnassus **15**:96
Pegasus **15**:132
Pelops **15**:139
Penelope **15**:142–143
Persephone **15**:180
Perseus **15**:180
Phaethon **15**:218
Philoctetes **15**:240
Philomela and Procne **15**:240
Phoenix **15**:251
Pirithous **15**:315
Pleiades **15**:364
Pluto **15**:372
Polyphemus **15**:421
Poseidon **15**:458
Priam **15**:534
Priapus **15**:534
Prometheus **15**:567
Proteus **15**:577
Psyche **15**:588
Pygmalion **15**:633
Python **15**:640
Rhadamanthus **16**:192
Sarpedon **17**:79
satyr **17**:92
Scylla and Charybdis **17**:167
Selene **17**:190
Semele **17**:195
Seven against Thebes **17**:215
Silenus **17**:304
Sireus **17**:328
Sisyphus **17**:329
Styx **18**:312
Tantalus **19**:25
Tartarus **19**:41
Thanatos **19**:142
Theseus **19**:167–168
Thetis **19**:168
Tiresias **19**:208
Titans **19**:211
Trojan War **19**:305
Uranus **19**:479
women in society **20**:201
Zeus **20**:362 *illus.*
GREEK ORTHODOX CHURCH *see* ORTHODOX CHURCH
GREEK PHILOSOPHY
Anaxagoras **1**:398
Anaximander **1**:398
Anaximenes **1**:398
aretê **2**:146
Aristotle **2**:156–158
Cynics **5**:406–407
Democritus **6**:103
Diogenes of Apollonia **6**:183–184
Eleatic School **7**:103
element **7**:129
Empedocles **7**:157–158
Epicurus **7**:218
epistemology **7**:221
Gorgias **9**:251
Heraclitus **10**:131–132
Milesian school **13**:419
natural law **14**:48
philosophy **15**:243–244
Plato **15**:360–361
pre-Socratic philosophy **15**:532–533
Socrates **18**:31
Sophists **18**:67
stoicism **18**:278
Thales of Miletus **19**:142
Xenocrates **20**:311–312
GREEK REVIVAL **9**:345–346 *bibliog., illus.*
American art and architecture **1**:328
architecture **2**:136
Barry, Sir Charles **3**:95–96
Benjamin, Asher **3**:201
British Museum **3**:497 *illus.*
Capitol of the United States **4**:126
Cockerell, Charles Robert **5**:87
Davis, Alexander Jackson **6**:50
Gilly, Friedrich **9**:182
house (in Western architecture) **10**:270
Illinois state capitol **11**:43 *illus.*
Latrobe, Benjamin Henry **12**:235
Mills, Robert **13**:430–431
Monticello **19**:610 *illus.*
neoclassicism (art) **14**:82
plantation **12**:433 *illus.*
Regency style **16**:126
Smirke, Sir Robert **17**:366
Strickland, William **18**:298
Stuart, James **18**:305
Walter, Thomas U. **20**:19
GREELEY (Colorado)
map (40° 25′N 104° 42′W) **5**:116
GREELEY (Kansas)
map (38° 22′N 95° 8′W) **12**:18
GREELEY (county in Kansas)
map (38° 30′N 101° 50′W) **12**:18
GREELEY (Nebraska)
map (41° 33′N 98° 32′W) **14**:70
GREELEY (county in Nebraska)
map (41° 35′N 98° 30′W) **14**:70
GREELEY, HORACE **9**:346–347 *bibliog., illus.*
Grinnell, Josiah Bushnell **9**:366
Liberal Republican party **12**:312
GREELEYVILLE (South Carolina)
map (33° 35′N 79° 58′W) **18**:98
GREELY, ADOLPHUS WASHINGTON **9**:347
GREEN (county in Kentucky)
map (37° 15′N 85° 35′W) **12**:47
GREEN (county in Wisconsin)
map (42° 43′N 89° 38′W) **20**:185
GREEN, ADOLPHE **5**:131
GREEN, HENRY **9**:347 *bibliog.*
GREEN, HETTY **9**:347
GREEN, JULIAN **9**:347 *bibliog.*
GREEN, PAUL **9**:347 *bibliog.*
GREEN, THEODORE FRANCIS **9**:347 *bibliog.*
GREEN, THOMAS HILL **9**:347 *bibliog.*
GREEN, WILLIAM **9**:347
GREEN ALGAE *see* ALGAE, GREEN ALGAE
GREEN BANK OBSERVATORY *see* NATIONAL RADIO ASTRONOMY OBSERVATORY
GREEN BAY (city in Wisconsin) **9**:347–348
map (44° 30′N 88° 1′W) **20**:185
Nicolet, Jean **14**:184
GREEN BAY (inlet) **9**:347
GREEN BEAN *see* BEAN
GREEN BERETS
Vietnam War **19**:586
GREEN BRIER (Tennessee)
map (36° 27′N 86° 49′W) **19**:104
GREEN CITY (Missouri)
map (40° 16′N 92° 57′W) **13**:476
GREEN COLLEGE (Oxford University) **14**:474
GREEN COVE SPRINGS (Florida)
map (30° 0′N 81° 41′W) **8**:172
GREEN FOREST (Arkansas)
map (36° 20′N 93° 26′W) **2**:166
GREEN FROG **9**:348 *bibliog., illus.*
GREEN JAY **11**:386 *illus.*
GREEN KNOB MOUNTAIN
map (38° 57′N 79° 28′W) **20**:111
GREEN LAKE (Saskatchewan)
map (54° 17′N 107° 47′W) **17**:81
GREEN LAKE (Wisconsin)
map (43° 51′N 88° 57′W) **20**:185
GREEN LAKE (county in Wisconsin)
map (43° 48′N 89° 0′W) **20**:185
GREEN MANSIONS (book) **9**:348 *bibliog.*
Hudson, William Henry **10**:289
GREEN MARCH
Western Sahara **20**:116
GREEN MOUNTAIN BOYS **9**:348
Allen, Ethan **1**:299
Bennington (Vermont) **3**:204
Vermont **19**:558
Warner, Seth **20**:30
GREEN MOUNTAIN RESERVOIR
map (39° 52′N 106° 17′W) **5**:116
GREEN MOUNTAINS **9**:348
Berkshire Hills **3**:214
map (43° 45′N 72° 45′W) **19**:554
GREEN PASTURES, THE (play)
Connelly, Marc **5**:197
GREEN PEPPER (vegetable) *see* PEPPER (vegetable)
GREEN PETER RESERVOIR
map (44° 28′N 122° 30′W) **14**:427
GREEN PLOVER *see* LAPWING
GREEN REVOLUTION **9**:348–349 *bibliog., illus.*
agriculture and the food supply **1**:198
Borlaug, Norman Ernest **3**:401
Indonesia **11**:149
Pakistan **15**:28
plant breeding **15**:343
GREEN RIVER **9**:349
map (38° 11′N 109° 53′W) **5**:120
Powell, John Wesley **15**:481
GREEN RIVER (Kentucky)
map (37° 55′N 87° 30′W) **12**:47
GREEN RIVER (Utah)
map (38° 59′N 110° 10′W) **19**:492
GREEN RIVER (Washington)
map (47° 33′N 122° 20′W) **20**:35
GREEN RIVER (Wyoming)
map (41° 32′N 109° 28′W) **20**:301
GREEN RIVER LAKE
map (37° 15′N 85° 15′W) **12**:47
GREEN RIVER RESERVOIR
map (44° 37′N 72° 31′W) **19**:554
GREEN SNAKE **5**:124 *illus.*
GREEN SPRINGS (Ohio)
map (41° 15′N 83° 3′W) **14**:357
GREEN SWAMP
map (34° 10′N 78° 20′W) **14**:242
GREEN TURTLE *see* SEA TURTLE
GREEN v. *NEW KENT COUNTY SCHOOL BOARD*
busing, school **3**:589
GREEN VALLEY (Arizona)
map (31° 50′N 111° 0′W) **2**:160
GREEN VALLEY (Illinois)
map (40° 24′N 89° 38′W) **11**:42
GREENACRES (Washington)
map (47° 39′N 117° 6′W) **20**:35
GREENAWAY, KATE **9**:349 *bibliog.*
GREENBACK **9**:349 *bibliog.*
GREENBACK PARTY **9**:349 *bibliog.*
Butler, Benjamin Franklin **3**:591
Socialist Labor party **18**:24
Weaver, James B. **20**:83
GREENBELT **9**:349 *bibliog.*
garden city **9**:41–42
GREENBERG, CLEMENT **9**:349
GREENBERG, JOSEPH H. **9**:350
African languages **1**:165
Indian languages, American **11**:99
GREENBOTTLE *see* BLOWFLY
GREENBRIER (Arkansas)
map (35° 14′N 92° 23′W) **2**:166
GREENBRIER (botany) **9**:350
GREENBRIER (county in West Virginia)
map (37° 55′N 80° 25′W) **20**:111
GREENBRIER RIVER
map (37° 39′N 80° 53′W) **20**:111
GREENBURG (Louisiana)
map (30° 51′N 90° 40′W) **12**:430
GREENCASTLE (Indiana)
map (39° 38′N 86° 52′W) **11**:111
GREENCASTLE (Pennsylvania)
map (39° 47′N 77° 44′W) **15**:147
GREENDALE (Indiana)
map (39° 7′N 84° 52′W) **11**:111
GREENDALE (Wisconsin)
map (42° 57′N 88° 0′W) **20**:185
GREENE (county in Alabama)
map (32° 55′N 88° 0′W) **1**:234
GREENE (county in Arkansas)
map (36° 8′N 90° 32′W) **2**:166
GREENE (county in Georgia)
map (33° 35′N 83° 10′W) **9**:114
GREENE (county in Illinois)
map (39° 18′N 90° 24′W) **11**:42
GREENE (county in Indiana)
map (39° 5′N 87° 0′W) **11**:111
GREENE (county in Iowa)
map (42° 2′N 94° 22′W) **11**:244
GREENE (county in Mississippi)
map (31° 15′N 88° 40′W) **13**:469
GREENE (county in Missouri)
map (37° 15′N 93° 20′W) **13**:476
GREENE (New York)
map (42° 20′N 75° 46′W) **14**:149
GREENE (county in New York)
map (42° 13′N 73° 52′W) **14**:149
GREENE (county in North Carolina)
map (35° 30′N 77° 40′W) **14**:242
GREENE (county in Ohio)
map (39° 41′N 83° 56′W) **14**:357
GREENE (county in Pennsylvania)
map (39° 55′N 80° 15′W) **15**:147
GREENE (county in Tennessee)
map (36° 15′N 82° 50′W) **19**:104
GREENE (county in Virginia)
map (38° 18′N 78° 28′W) **19**:607
GREENE, CHARLES SUMNER AND HENRY MATHER *see* GREENE AND GREENE (architectural firm)
GREENE, GRAHAM **7**:202 *illus.*; **9**:350 *bibliog., illus.*
Power and the Glory, The **15**:486
GREENE, MAURICE
English music **7**:203
GREENE, NATHANAEL **9**:350–351 *bibliog., illus.*
American Revolution **1**:359 *map*; **1**:363
Greensboro (North Carolina) **9**:354
GREENE, ROBERT **9**:351 *bibliog.*
Shakespeare, William **17**:237
GREENE, WILLIAM FRIESE- *see* FRIESE-GREENE, WILLIAM
GREENE AND GREENE (architectural firm) **9**:351 *bibliog.*
GREENEVILLE (Tennessee)
map (36° 10′N 82° 50′W) **19**:104
GREENFIELD (Illinois)
map (39° 21′N 90° 12′W) **11**:42
GREENFIELD (Indiana)
map (39° 21′N 90° 12′W) **11**:111
GREENFIELD (Iowa)
map (41° 18′N 94° 28′W) **11**:244
GREENFIELD (Massachusetts)
map (42° 36′N 72° 36′W) **13**:206
GREENFIELD (Missouri)
map (37° 25′N 93° 51′W) **13**:476
GREENFIELD (Ohio)
map (39° 21′N 83° 23′W) **14**:357
GREENFIELD (Tennessee)
map (36° 9′N 88° 48′W) **19**:104
GREENFIELD (Wisconsin)
map (42° 58′N 88° 2′W) **20**:185
GREENFIELD HILL (Connecticut)
map (41° 11′N 73° 17′W) **5**:193
GREENFIELD VILLAGE (Michigan)
Dearborn (Michigan) **6**:68
Ford (family) **8**:221
GREENHOUSE **9**:351 *bibliog., illus.*
floriculture **8**:169–170
horticulture **10**:255 *illus.*
hydroponics **10**:343
GREENHOUSE EFFECT **9**:351–352 *bibliog., illus.*
carbon cycle (atmosphere) **4**:136
climate **5**:57
energy sources **7**:175
long-wave radiation
air **1**:203
paleoclimatology **15**:34
radio astronomy **16**:49
Sagan, Carl Edward **17**:11
solar radiation **9**:351–352
Venus (planet) **19**:547; **19**:548
GREENLAND **9**:352–353 *bibliog., illus., map*
cities
Godthôb **9**:221
climate **9**:352
weather variation and extremes **20**:80 *table*
economic activity **9**:352–353
fjord **8**:133
flag **9**:352 *illus.*
geology
cryolite **5**:371
halide minerals **10**:21
Ordovician Period **14**:421 *map*
Precambrian rock formations **15**:492 *map*
Tertiary Period **19**:123 *map*
Wegener, Alfred Lothar **20**:91
government **9**:353
history **9**:353
Eric the Red **7**:229
Leif Eriksson **12**:277–278
Nansen, Fridtjof **14**:13
Nordenskjöld, Adolf Erik, Baron **14**:218
land **9**:352
glaciers and glaciation **9**:193
iceberg **11**:15
languages
Indian languages, American **11**:101
map (70° 0′N 40° 0′W) **14**:225
people **9**:352
Eskimo **7**:238–242
GREENLAND (Arkansas)
map (36° 0′N 94° 10′W) **2**:166
GREENLAND SEA
map (77° 0′N 1° 0′W) **14**:225
GREENLEAF (Kansas)
map (39° 44′N 96° 59′W) **12**:18
GREENLEE (county in Arizona)
map (33° 15′N 109° 25′W) **2**:160
GREENLING **9**:353
GREENOCK (Scotland) **9**:353
GREENOUGH, HORATIO **9**:353–354 *bibliog., illus.*
functionalism (design) **8**:360
George Washington (statue) **1**:330 *illus.*; **9**:354 *illus.*; **17**:164 *illus.*
GREENPEACE (environmental organization) **9**:354 *bibliog.*
GREENPORT (New York)
map (41° 6′N 72° 22′W) **14**:149
GREENSAND **9**:354
GREENSBORO (Alabama)
map (32° 42′N 87° 36′W) **1**:234
GREENSBORO (Florida)
map (30° 34′N 84° 45′W) **8**:172
GREENSBORO (Georgia)
map (33° 35′N 83° 11′W) **9**:114
GREENSBORO (Maryland)
map (38° 59′N 75° 48′W) **13**:188
GREENSBORO (North Carolina) **9**:354

map (36° 4′N 79° 47′W) **14**:242
SNCC **17**:384
GREENSBURG (Indiana)
map (39° 20′N 85° 29′W) **11**:111
GREENSBURG (Kansas)
map (37° 36′N 99° 18′W) **12**:18
GREENSBURG (Kentucky)
map (37° 16′N 85° 30′W) **12**:47
GREENSBURG (Pennsylvania)
map (40° 18′N 79° 33′W) **15**:147
GREENSPOND (Newfoundland)
map (49° 4′N 53° 34′W) **14**:166
GREENSVILLE (county in Virginia)
map (36° 40′N 77° 30′W) **19**:607
GREENTOWN (Indiana)
map (40° 29′N 85° 58′W) **11**:111
GREENUP (Illinois)
map (39° 15′N 88° 10′W) **11**:42
GREENUP (Kentucky)
map (38° 34′N 82° 50′W) **12**:47
GREENUP (county in Kentucky)
map (38° 30′N 82° 55′W) **12**:47
GREENVIEW (Illinois)
map (40° 5′N 89° 44′W) **11**:42
GREENVILLE (Alabama)
map (31° 50′N 86° 38′W) **1**:234
GREENVILLE (California)
map (40° 8′N 120° 57′W) **4**:31
GREENVILLE (Florida)
map (30° 28′N 83° 38′W) **8**:172
GREENVILLE (Georgia)
map (33° 2′N 84° 43′W) **9**:114
GREENVILLE (Illinois)
map (38° 53′N 89° 25′W) **11**:42
GREENVILLE (Kentucky)
map (37° 12′N 87° 11′W) **12**:47
GREENVILLE (Liberia)
map (5° 1′N 9° 3′W) **12**:313
GREENVILLE (Michigan)
map (43° 11′N 85° 15′W) **13**:377
GREENVILLE (Mississippi)
map (33° 25′N 91° 5′W) **13**:469
GREENVILLE (Missouri)
map (37° 8′N 90° 27′W) **13**:476
GREENVILLE (New Hampshire)
map (42° 46′N 71° 49′W) **14**:123
GREENVILLE (North Carolina)
map (35° 37′N 77° 23′W) **14**:242
GREENVILLE (Ohio)
map (40° 6′N 84° 38′W) **14**:357
GREENVILLE (Pennsylvania)
map (41° 24′N 80° 23′W) **15**:147
GREENVILLE (Rhode Island)
map (41° 52′N 71° 33′W) **16**:198
GREENVILLE (South Carolina) **9**:354
map (34° 51′N 82° 23′W) **18**:98
GREENVILLE (county in South Carolina)
map (34° 50′N 82° 20′W) **18**:98
GREENVILLE (Texas)
map (33° 8′N 96° 7′W) **19**:129
GREENVILLE, TREATY OF (1795)
Delaware (American Indians) **6**:91
Fallen Timbers, Battle of **8**:14
Indian treaties **11**:106
Little Turtle **12**:373
GREENWAY, FRANCIS
Sydney (Australia) **18**:401
GREENWICH (Connecticut) **9**:354
map (41° 1′N 73° 38′W) **5**:193
GREENWICH (England) **9**:354
Naval Hospital (now the Royal Naval College) **20**:286 *illus.*
GREENWICH (Ohio)
map (41° 2′N 82° 31′W) **14**:357
GREENWICH BAY
map (41° 40′N 71° 25′W) **16**:198
GREENWICH MEAN TIME **9**:354
time (physics) **19**:201
GREENWICH MERIDIAN *see* PRIME MERIDIAN
GREENWICH OBSERVATORY *see* ROYAL GREENWICH OBSERVATORY
GREENWICH POINT
map (41° 0′N 73° 34′E) **5**:193
GREENWICH VILLAGE **9**:354–355 *bibliog.*
New York (city) **14**:145 *map*
GREENWOOD (Arkansas)
map (35° 13′N 94° 15′W) **2**:166
GREENWOOD (Indiana)
map (39° 37′N 86° 7′W) **11**:111
GREENWOOD (county in Kansas)
map (37° 50′N 96° 15′W) **12**:18
GREENWOOD (Mississippi)
map (33° 31′N 90° 11′W) **13**:469
GREENWOOD (Nebraska)
map (40° 58′N 96° 27′W) **14**:70
GREENWOOD (South Carolina)
map (34° 12′N 82° 10′W) **18**:98
GREENWOOD (county in South Carolina)
map (34° 10′N 82° 5′W) **18**:98
GREENWOOD (Wisconsin)
map (44° 46′N 90° 36′W) **20**:185
GREENWOOD, JOHN
dentistry **6**:115
GREENWOOD, LAKE
map (34° 15′N 82° 2′W) **18**:98
GREENWOOD LAKE (New York)
map (41° 11′N 74° 19′W) **14**:129
GREER (county in Oklahoma)
map (34° 55′N 99° 35′W) **14**:368
GREER (South Carolina)
map (34° 56′N 82° 14′W) **18**:98
GREER, GERMAINE **9**:355
GREERS FERRY LAKE
map (35° 30′N 92° 10′W) **2**:166
GREESON, LAKE
map (34° 10′N 93° 45′W) **2**:166
GREGG (county in Texas)
map (32° 30′N 94° 50′W) **19**:129
GREGG, JOHN ROBERT
shorthand **17**:284
GREGG, WILLIAM **9**:355 *bibliog.*
GREGG v. *GEORGIA*
capital punishment **4**:124
GREGOR, WILLIAM
titanium **19**:211
GREGORIAN CALENDAR
calendar **4**:28
GREGORIAN CHANT *see* PLAINSONG
GREGORIAN CHURCH *see* ARMENIAN CHURCH
GREGORY (South Dakota)
map (43° 14′N 99° 26′W) **18**:103
GREGORY (county in South Dakota)
map (43° 12′N 99° 10′W) **18**:103
GREGORY, ANDRE
acting **1**:88
GREGORY, SIR AUGUSTUS CHARLES
Australia, history of **2**:340 *map*
GREGORY, CYNTHIA **9**:355
GREGORY, DICK **9**:355 *bibliog.*
GREGORY, HORACE **9**:355
GREGORY, ISABELLA AUGUSTA, LADY **9**:355 *bibliog.*; **11**:267 *illus.*
Abbey Theatre **1**:52–53
GREGORY, JAMES **9**:355
ballistics **3**:50
GREGORY I, POPE **9**:356 *bibliog., illus.*
Italian music **11**:317
Italy, history of **11**:327
medieval music **13**:274 *illus.*
GREGORY II, POPE **9**:356
GREGORY V (Patriarch of Constantinople) **9**:356–357
GREGORY VII, POPE **9**:357 *bibliog.*
Europe, history of **7**:284
Henry IV, King of Germany and Holy Roman Emperor **10**:129
investiture controversy **11**:238; **13**:393 *illus.*
Salerno (Italy) **17**:31
GREGORY IX, POPE **9**:357
GREGORY XI, POPE **9**:357
Catherine of Siena, Saint **4**:209
GREGORY XIII, POPE **9**:357
calendar **4**:27–28
GREGORY XV, POPE
propaganda **15**:568
GREGORY THE GREAT *see* GREGORY I, POPE
GREGORY OF NAZIANZUS, SAINT **9**:355–356 *bibliog.*
GREGORY OF NYSSA, SAINT **9**:356
GREGORY THAUMATURGUS, SAINT **9**:356
GREGORY OF TOURS, SAINT **9**:356
GREIFSWALD (Germany, East and West)
map (54° 5′N 13° 23′E) **9**:140
GREIN, J. T. **9**:357 *bibliog.*
GREIZ (Germany, East and West)
map (50° 39′N 12° 12′E) **9**:140
GRENÅ (Denmark)
map (56° 25′N 10° 53′E) **6**:109
GRENADA **9**:357–358 *bibliog., illus., map*
cities
Saint George's **17**:18
flag **8**:142 *illus.*; **9**:358 *illus.*
history and government **9**:357–358
land, people, and economy **9**:357
map (12° 7′N 61° 40′W) **20**:109
GRENADA (Mississippi)
map (33° 47′N 89° 55′W) **13**:469
GRENADA (county in Mississippi)
map (33° 45′N 89° 50′W) **13**:469
GRENADA, TREATY OF (1500)
Fernández de Córdoba, Gonzalo **8**:58
GRENADE **9**:358 *bibliog., illus.*
shrapnel **17**:286
whaling **20**:123 *illus.*
GRENADIER (military) **9**:358
France-Prussian War **8**:278 *illus.*
GRENADIER (zoology) **9**:358–359
GRENADINE *see* POMEGRANATE
GRENADINE ISLANDS **9**:359
map (12° 25′N 61° 35′W) **9**:358
GRENFELL, SIR WILFRED **9**:359 *bibliog.*
GRENIER, PASQUIER
tapestry **19**:33
GRENOBLE (France) **9**:359
GRENORA (North Dakota)
map (48° 37′N 103° 56′W) **14**:248
GRENVILLE (Grenada)
map (12° 7′N 61° 37′W) **9**:358
GRENVILLE, GEORGE **9**:359
American Revolution **1**:354
GRENVILLE, SIR RICHARD **9**:359
Roanoke Colony **16**:239
GRESHAM (Oregon)
map (45° 30′N 122° 26′W) **14**:427
GRESHAM'S LAW **9**:359
GRESIK (Indonesia)
map (7° 9′S 112° 38′E) **11**:147
GRESSLEY, AMANZ **9**:359
GRETNA (Louisiana)
map (29° 55′N 90° 3′W) **12**:430
GRETNA (Nebraska)
map (41° 8′N 96° 15′W) **14**:70
GRETNA (Virginia)
map (36° 57′N 79° 22′W) **19**:607
GRÉTRY, ANDRÉ **9**:359
GRETZKY, WAYNE **9**:359
GREUZE, JEAN BAPTISTE **9**:359–360 *bibliog.*
GREVELINGEN
map (51° 45′N 4° 0′E) **14**:99
GREVILLE, FULKE, 1st BARON BROOKE **9**:360 *bibliog.*
GREW, NEHEMIAH **9**:360
biology **3**:269
GREY, ALBERT HENRY GEORGE GREY, 4th EARL **9**:360
GREY, CHARLES GREY, 2d EARL **9**:360 *bibliog.*
GREY, SIR EDWARD **9**:360 *bibliog.*
GREY, SIR GEORGE **9**:360 *bibliog.*
GREY, LADY JANE **9**:360 *bibliog., illus.*
Northumberland, John Dudley, Duke of **14**:256
GREY, ZANE **9**:360–361 *bibliog., illus.*
Zanesville (Ohio) **20**:355
GREY CUP (football)
football **8**:218
Grey, Albert Henry George Grey, 4th Earl **9**:360
GREY EAGLE (Minnesota)
map (45° 50′N 94° 45′W) **13**:453
GREY ISLANDS
map (50° 50′N 55° 37′W) **14**:166
GREYBULL (Wyoming)
map (44° 30′N 108° 3′W) **20**:301
GREYFRIARS (Oxford University) **14**:474
GREYHOUND **6**:216 *illus.*; **9**:361 *bibliog., illus.*
dog racing **6**:222
Italian greyhound **11**:314
saluki **17**:39
GREYHOUND RACING *see* DOG RACING
GREYLOCK, MOUNT
map (42° 38′N 73° 10′W) **13**:206
GREYMOUTH (New Zealand)
map (42° 28′S 171° 12′E) **14**:158
GRIBBLE **9**:361
GRIBOYEDOV, ALEKSANDR SERGEYEVICH **9**:361
GRID **9**:361
electron tube **7**:122–123
telephone and electric power systems **9**:361
GRID PLAN *see* URBAN PLANNING
GRIDLEY (California)
map (39° 22′N 121° 42′W) **4**:31
GRIDLEY (Illinois)
map (40° 45′N 88° 53′W) **11**:42
GRIEF
funeral customs **8**:364
GRIEG, EDVARD **9**:361–362 *bibliog., illus.*
GRIEG, NINA HAGERUP **9**:362 *illus.*
GRIEG, NORDAHL BRUN **9**:362
GRIEN, HANS BALDUNG- *see* BALDUNG-GRIEN, HANS
GRIERSON, JOHN
documentary **6**:211
film, history of **8**:84
GRIESE, BOB **9**:362
GRIEVANCE PROCEDURE **9**:362 *bibliog.*
arbitration **9**:362
GRIFFES, CHARLES TOMLINSON **9**:362 *bibliog.*
GRIFFIN (Georgia)
map (33° 15′N 84° 16′W) **9**:114
GRIFFIN (mythology) **9**:362
GRIFFIN, DONALD R.
echolocation **7**:39
GRIFFIN, MARION MAHONY **9**:362 *bibliog.*
GRIFFIN, WALTER BURLEY **9**:362–363 *bibliog.*
Canberra **4**:99–100
GRIFFITH (Indiana)
map (41° 32′N 87° 25′W) **11**:111
GRIFFITH, ARTHUR **9**:363
Sinn Fein **17**:323
GRIFFITH, D. W. **9**:363 *bibliog., illus.*
film, history of **8**:82 *illus.*
GRIFFITHS, PHILIP JONES
photojournalism **15**:273
GRIGGS (county in North Dakota)
map (47° 30′N 98° 15′W) **14**:248
GRIGGS v. *DUKE POWER COMPANY*
equal opportunity **7**:223
GRIGGSVILLE (Illinois)
map (39° 42′N 90° 43′W) **11**:42
GRIGNARD, VICTOR **9**:363
Grignard reagents **9**:363–364
GRIGNARD REAGENTS **9**:363–364 *bibliog., illus.*
Grignard, Victor **9**:363
GRIGOROVICH, DMITRY VASILIEVICH **9**:364
GRIGOROVICH, YURY NIKOLAYEVICH **9**:364
Bolshoi Ballet **3**:372
GRIJALVA, JUAN DE
Mexico, history of **13**:362
Tabasco (Mexico) **19**:3
GRIJALVA RIVER
map (18° 36′N 92° 39′W) **13**:357
GRIKES **12**:182 *illus.*; **12**:344 *illus.*
GRILLET, ALAIN ROBBE- *see* ROBBE-GRILLET, ALAIN
GRILLPARZER, FRANZ **9**:364 *bibliog.*
GRIMALDI (family)
Monaco **13**:516–517
GRIMALDI, FRANCESCO MARIA **9**:364
diffraction **6**:169 *illus.*
GRIMALDI, JOSEPH **9**:364 *bibliog.*
biography
Dickens, Charles **6**:156
GRIMALDI MAN **9**:364 *bibliog.*
GRIMBALD GOSPELS **11**:47 *illus.*
GRIMES (county in Texas)
map (30° 35′N 96° 0′W) **19**:129
GRIMES GRAVES **9**:364–365
GRIMKÉ, SARAH MOORE AND ANGELINA EMILY **9**:365 *bibliog., illus.*
Weld, Theodore Dwight **20**:96
GRIMM, JACOB AND WILHELM **9**:365–366 *bibliog., illus.*
Hansel and Gretel **10**:41
linguistics
Grimm's law **9**:366
GRIMM, MELCHIOR, BARON VON **9**:366
GRIMMELSHAUSEN, HANS JAKOB CHRISTOFFEL VON **9**:366 *bibliog.*
GRIMM'S FAIRY TALES (book) **9**:366 *bibliog.*
folklore **8**:203
Grimm, Jacob and Wilhelm **9**:365–366
GRIMM'S LAW **9**:366 *bibliog.*
Germanic languages **9**:136 *table*
Grimm, Jacob and Wilhelm **9**:365–366
historical linguistics **10**:182
GRIMSBY (England) **9**:366
map (53° 35′N 0° 5′W) **19**:403
GRIMSEL PASS
map (46° 34′N 8° 21′E) **18**:394
GRIMSEY ISLAND
map (66° 34′N 18° 0′W) **11**:17
GRIMSHAW (Alberta)
map (56° 11′N 117° 36′W) **1**:256
GRINDAL, EDMUND **9**:366 *bibliog.*
GRINDALL CREEK (Virginia)
map (37° 27′N 77° 27′W) **19**:607
GRINDEL, EUGÈNE *see* ÉLUARD, PAUL
GRINDING AND POLISHING
abrasive **1**:61
machine tools **13**:25 *illus.*
GRINNELL (Iowa)
map (41° 45′N 92° 43′W) **11**:244
GRINNELL, JOSIAH BUSHNELL **9**:366
GRINNELL COLLEGE **9**:366
GRIS, JUAN **9**:366–367 *bibliog., illus.*
The Dice **9**:367 *illus.*
Spanish art and architecture **18**:156
GRIS-NEZ, CAPE **9**:367
map (50° 52′N 1° 35′E) **8**:260
GRISAILLE **9**:367
enamel **7**:162
GRISEOFULVIN
antibiotics **2**:57
fungus diseases **8**:369

GRISI, CARLOTTA 9:367 *bibliog.*
Perrot, Jules **15**:178
GRISI, GIULIA 9:367
GRISON 9:367 *illus.*
GRISSOM, VIRGIL I. 9:367 *bibliog.*
Mercury program **13**:308
GRISWOLD (Iowa)
map (41° 14′N 95° 8′W) **11**:244
GRISWOLD v. CONNECTICUT 9:367–368
birth control 9:367–368
privacy, invasion of **15**:556
GRIVAS, GEORGIOS
EOKA 7:215
GRIZZLY BEAR *see* BEAR
GROCERY CHAINS *see* SUPERMARKET
GROCK 9:368 *bibliog.*
GROENENDAEL *see* BELGIAN SHEEPDOG
GROENER, WILHELM 9:368 *bibliog.*
Hindenburg, Paul von **10**:169
GROESBECK (Texas)
map (31° 31′N 96° 32′W) **19**:129
GROFÉ, FERDE 9:368
GROG *see* VERNON, EDWARD
GROIN (anatomy)
hernia **10**:143
ringworm **16**:226
GROIN (shore structure) *see* GROYNE
GROLIER, JEAN 9:368 *bibliog.*
GROMYKO, ANDREI ANDREYEVICH 9:368; **15**:525 *illus.*
GRONINGEN (horse) *see* COACH HORSE
GRONINGEN (Netherlands) 9:368
map (53° 13′N 6° 33′E) **14**:99
GRONINGEN (Suriname)
map (5° 48′N 55° 28′W) **18**:364
GROOM *see* MARRIAGE
GROOM (Texas)
map (35° 12′N 101° 6′W) **19**:129
GROOMING (horse) *see* RIDING
GROOMS, RED 9:368 *bibliog.*
happenings **10**:41
GROOTE, GERHARD 9:369 *bibliog.*
GROOTE EYLANDT ISLAND
map (14° 0′S 136° 40′E) **2**:328
GROPIUS, WALTER 9:369 *bibliog., illus.*
Bauhaus **2**:136 *illus.*; **3**:129–130 *illus.*; **11**:222 *illus.*
Breuer, Marcel **3**:475
Harvard University Graduate Center 9:369 *illus.*
modern architecture **13**:490
GROPPER, WILLIAM 9:369 *bibliog.*
GROS, ANTOINE JEAN, BARON 9:369–370 *bibliog.*
Joachim Murat (painting) **13**:647 *illus.*
Napoleon I at Battle of Eylau (painting) **16**:356 *illus.*
GROS MORNE (peak)
map (49° 36′N 57° 48′W) **14**:166
GROS MORNE NATIONAL PARK (Newfoundland) **14**:167 *illus.*
GROS VENTRES (American Indians) 9:370 *bibliog.*
GROSBEAK 9:370 *bibliog., illus.*
GROSEILLIERS, MÉDARD CHOUART DES
Radisson, Pierre Esprit **16**:67
Wisconsin **20**:188
GROSHOLTZ, MARIE *see* TUSSAUD, MADAME
GROSMAN, TATYANA 9:370 *bibliog.*
GROSS, CHAIM 9:370–371 *bibliog.*
GROSS, MILT
comic strip **5**:135–136
GROSS DOMESTIC PRODUCT 9:371
GROSS NATIONAL PRODUCT 9:371 *bibliog.*
defense, national **6**:82 *table*
economics **7**:48
foreign aid **8**:224
income, national **11**:74–75
Kuznets, Simon S. **12**:142
national debt **14**:31–32 *table*
GROSSE, HANS
aerial sports **1**:122
GROSSER FELDBERG MOUNTAIN
map (50° 14′N 8° 26′E) 9:140
GROSSETESTE, ROBERT 9:371 *bibliog.*
GROSSETO (Italy)
map (42° 46′N 11° 8′E) **11**:321
GROSSGLOCKNER MOUNTAIN
map (47° 4′N 12° 42′E) **2**:348
GROSSULAR
garnet 9:49
GROSSVENEDIGER MOUNTAIN
map (47° 6′N 12° 21′E) **2**:348
GROSVENOR, GILBERT HOVEY 9:371
National Geographic Magazine **14**:33
GROSWATER BAY
map (54° 20′N 57° 30′W) **14**:166
GROSZ, GEORGE 9:371–372 *bibliog., illus.*
Beauty, I Cherish You 9:371 *illus.*
GROTE, GEORGE 9:372 *bibliog.*
GROTEFEND, GEORG FRIEDRICH 9:372
GROTESQUE (literature) 9:372 *bibliog.*
Bierce, Ambrose **3**:248
GROTIUS, HUGO 9:372 *bibliog., illus.*
international law **11**:221
law, history of **12**:245 *illus.*
natural law **14**:48
seas, freedom of the **17**:175
GROTON (Connecticut) 9:372
map (41° 19′N 72° 12′W) **5**:193
GROTON (Massachusetts)
map (42° 37′N 71° 34′W) **13**:206
GROTON (New York)
map (42° 35′N 76° 22′W) **14**:149
GROTON (South Dakota)
map (45° 27′N 98° 6′W) **18**:103
GROTOWSKI, JERZY 9:372–373 *illus.*
improvisational and experimental theater **11**:69
Polish Laboratory Theater **15**:397
theory of acting **1**:86
GROTTHUS, THEODOR
photochemistry **15**:257
GROTTOES (Virginia)
map (38° 16′N 78° 56′W) **19**:607
GROUARD MISSION (Alberta)
map (55° 31′N 116° 9′W) **1**:256
GROUND, ELECTRICAL 9:373
electrical wiring **7**:106–107
GROUND BASS 9:373
GROUND CHERRY *see* CHINESE LANTERN PLANT
GROUND-EFFECT MACHINE *see* AIR-CUSHION VEHICLE
GROUND HEMLOCK *see* YEW
GROUND NUT *see* PEANUT
GROUND PINE *see* CLUB MOSS
GROUND SLOTH *see* SLOTH
GROUND SNAKE **17**:377 *illus.*
See also EARTH SNAKE
GROUND SQUIRREL
biological clock **3**:264
GROUND TEMPERATURE 9:373 *bibliog.*
monsoon **13**:543–544
GROUND WAVE 9:373
broadcasting wave 9:373
components 9:373
GROUNDHOG 9:373–374 *illus.*
Groundhog Day 9:374
GROUNDHOG DAY 9:374
GROUNDSEL 9:374
cineraria **4**:434
GROUNDWATER 9:374–376 *bibliog., illus., table*
aquifer **2**:94
artesian well **2**:214
composition, potable 9:374 *table*
desert **6**:127
discharge and recharge 9:374
fault **8**:38
flow: Darcy, Henry Philibert Gaspard **6**:37
frost action **8**:346
geothermal energy 9:120–121
geyser 9:162–163
glaciers and glaciation 9:194
hot springs **10**:259
hydrologic cycle **10**:341
hydrosphere **10**:344
landslide and avalanche **12**:193
movement 9:374
Nebraska **14**:71–72
origin 9:374
pollution 9:374–375
quality 9:374
Recent Epoch **16**:107
river and stream **16**:230
speleology **18**:177
spring (water) **18**:199
stalactite and stalagmite **18**:213
supply development 9:375–376
water resources **20**:50
water supply **20**:53
water table **20**:57
GROUP DYNAMICS 9:376 *bibliog.*
conformity **5**:179
deviance **6**:143
group functioning 9:376
Lewin, Kurt **12**:305
prison **15**:555
psychology **15**:595
size factor 9:376
social psychology **18**:12–13
GROUP f/64 (photography group)
Cunningham, Imogen **5**:390
Weston, Edward **20**:118
GROUP OF SEVEN 9:376 *bibliog., illus.*
Canadian art and architecture **4**:90
Carmichael, Frank **4**:153
Fitzgerald, Lionel LeMoine 9:376
Harris, Lawren **10**:57–58
Jackson, Alexander Young **11**:340; **11**:342
Johnston, Franz **11**:437
Lismer, Arthur **12**:366
MacDonald, J. E. H. **13**:12
Varley, Frederick **19**:523
GROUP OF THE SIXTIES, THE (literary group)
Roberts, Sir Charles G. D. **16**:241
GROUP THEATRE, THE 9:376–377 *bibliog.*
acting **1**:88
Adler, Jacob, Stella, and Luther **1**:104
Carnovsky, Morris **4**:159
Clurman, Harold **5**:71
Crawford, Cheryl, founder **5**:333
method acting **13**:343
Odets, Clifford **14**:350
Strasberg, Lee **18**:289
Tamiris, Helen **19**:19
GROUP THEORY 9:377 *bibliog.*
See also SET THEORY
algebra **1**:284–285
basic axioms 9:377
category **4**:202
classification of groups 9:377
Dickson, Leonard **6**:159
field **8**:71
Frobenius, Ferdinand Georg **8**:335
Galois, Evariste 9:21
isomorphism **11**:300
Jordan, Camille **11**:450
mathematics, history of **13**:226
ring (mathematics) **16**:225
Wigner, Eugene Paul **20**:147
GROUP THERAPY 9:377 *bibliog.*
Gestalt psychology 9:159
humanistic psychology **10**:299
psychotherapy **15**:603
sex therapy **17**:227
transactional analysis **19**:267–268
GROUPE DES GRIOTS, LE
Duvalier, François **6**:316
GROUPER 9:377–378 *illus.*
jewfish **11**:412
GROUSE 9:378 *bibliog., illus.*
capercaillie **8**:229 *illus.*
game birds 9:27
ptarmigan **15**:605–606
sand grouse **17**:61
GROUSE CREEK (Utah)
map (41° 42′N 113° 53′W) **19**:492
GROVE, FREDERICK PHILIP 9:378
GROVE, SIR GEORGE 9:378 *bibliog.*
GROVE CITY (Ohio)
map (39° 53′N 83° 6′W) **14**:357
GROVE CITY (Pennsylvania)
map (41° 10′N 80° 5′W) **15**:147
GROVE HILL (Alabama)
map (31° 42′N 87° 47′W) **1**:234
GROVEPORT (Ohio)
map (39° 51′N 82° 53′W) **14**:357
GROVES, LESLIE
Manhattan Project **13**:116
GROVETON (New Hampshire)
map (44° 36′N 71° 31′W) **14**:123
GROVETON (Texas)
map (31° 3′N 95° 8′W) **19**:129
GROVEVILLE (New Jersey)
map (40° 11′N 74° 40′W) **14**:129
GROWTH 9:378–381 *bibliog.*
See also DEVELOPMENT
allometric growth 9:379
cell **4**:234–235 *illus.*
development **6**:137
differentiation 9:379
embryo **7**:152–153 *illus.*
embryology **7**:154
growth hormone 9:381
hormone, animal **10**:234
human body 9:380
adolescence **1**:106
child development **4**:348–350 *illus.*
infancy **11**:162–163
insect **11**:188–189
molting **13**:513
mushrooms **13**:661
plant **15**:339–340 *illus.*
regeneration **16**:126–128 *illus.*
GROWTH HORMONE 9:381
auxin **2**:369
endocrine system, diseases of the **7**:169; **7**:170
genetic engineering 9:84
hormone, animal **10**:236; **10**:237
medicine **13**:271
pituitary gland **15**:322
thyroid gland **19**:188
GROYNE
coastal protection **5**:81 *illus.*
GROZA, LOU 9:381
GROZNYY (USSR)
map (43° 20′N 45° 42′E) **19**:388
GRUB 9:381–382
GRUB STREET 9:382
GRUDZIĄDZ (Poland)
map (53° 29′N 18° 45′E) **15**:388
GRUEN, VICTOR 9:382 *bibliog.*
GRUENBERG, LOUIS 9:382
GRUENTHER, ALFRED MAXIMILIAN 9:382
GRUMIAUX, ARTHUR 9:382
GRUMMAN, LEROY 9:382
GRUMMAN AIRCRAFT ENGINEERING CORPORATION
Grumman, Leroy 9:382
Lunar Excursion Module **12**:460–461
GRUMMAN TBF-1 AVENGER 9:382
GRUNDTVIG, NICOLAI FREDERIK SEVERIN 9:382 *bibliog.*
GRUNDY (county in Illinois)
map (41° 22′N 88° 26′W) **11**:42
GRUNDY (county in Iowa)
map (42° 22′N 92° 45′W) **11**:244
GRUNDY (county in Missouri)
map (40° 5′N 93° 35′W) **13**:476
GRUNDY (county in Tennessee)
map (35° 25′N 85° 45′W) **19**:104
GRUNDY (Virginia)
map (37° 17′N 82° 6′W) **19**:607
GRUNDY CENTER (Iowa)
map (42° 22′N 92° 47′W) **11**:244
GRÜNEWALD, MATTHIAS 9:382–383 *bibliog., illus.*
Danube school **6**:36
German art and architecture 9:126
Isenheim Altarpiece 9:383 *illus.*; **16**:155 *illus.*
Colmar (France) **5**:105
GRUNION 9:383–384
GRUNITZY, NICOLAS
Togo **19**:222
GRUNT 9:384 *illus.*
GRUNWALD, BATTLE OF *see* TANNENBERG, BATTLES OF
GRUPPE 47 (literary group) 9:384
GRUVER (Texas)
map (36° 16′N 101° 24′W) **19**:129
GRYPHIUS, ANDREAS 9:384 *bibliog.*
GSR *see* GALVANIC SKIN RESPONSE
GU KAIZHI *see* KU K'AI-CHIH
GUABITO (Panama)
map (9° 30′N 82° 37′W) **15**:55
GUACANAYABO ,GULF OF
map (20° 28′N 77° 30′W) **5**:377
GUADALAJARA (Mexico) 9:384; **13**:359 *illus.*
map (20° 40′N 103° 20′W) **13**:357
GUADALAJARA (Spain)
map (40° 38′N 3° 10′W) **18**:140
GUADALCANAL 9:384–385 *bibliog., map*
map (9° 32′S 160° 12′E) **18**:56
World War II **20**:267
GUADALQUIVIR RIVER 9:385
map (36° 47′N 6° 22′W) **18**:140
GUADALUPE (county in New Mexico)
map (34° 50′N 104° 45′W) **14**:136
GUADALUPE (county in Texas)
map (29° 32′N 98° 0′W) **19**:129
GUADALUPE HIDALGO, TREATY OF 9:385 *bibliog.*
Mexican War **13**:352 *map*; **13**:355
Polk, James K. **15**:405
United States, history of the **19**:444
GUADALUPE MOUNTAINS
map (32° 20′N 105° 0′W) **14**:136
GUADALUPE MOUNTAINS NATIONAL PARK **19**:133 *illus.*
GUADALUPE PEAK
map (31° 50′N 104° 52′W) **19**:129
GUADALUPE VICTORIA (Mexico)
map (24° 27′N 104° 7′W) **13**:357
GUADALUPITA (New Mexico)
map (36° 8′N 105° 14′W) **14**:136
GUADELOUPE 9:385
Basse-Terre **3**:118
map (16° 15′N 61° 35′W) **20**:109
GUADIANA RIVER
map (37° 14′N 7° 22′W) **18**:140
GUAJARÁ MIRIM (Brazil)
map (10° 48′S 65° 22′W) **3**:460
GUAJIRA PENINSULA
map (12° 0′N 71° 40′W) **5**:107
GUALACEO (Ecuador)
map (2° 54′S 78° 47′W) **7**:52
GUALAQUIZA (Ecuador)
map (3° 24′S 78° 33′W) **7**:52
GUALEGUAY (Argentina)
map (33° 9′S 59° 20′W) **2**:149

GUALEGUAYCHÚ (Argentina)
map (33° 1′S 58° 31′W) **2**:149
GUAM (U.S.) **9**:385
Agana **1**:182
flag **8**:144 *illus.*
Guam, University of **9**:385
history
Spanish-American War **18**:150
World War II **20**:260
map (13° 28′N 144° 47′E) **14**:334
people
Chamorro **4**:276
Micronesians **13**:386
GUAM, UNIVERSITY OF **9**:385
GUAMOTE (Ecuador)
map (1° 56′S 78° 43′W) **7**:52
GUAN HANQING *see* KUAN HAN-CH'ING (Guan Hanqing)
GUANABACOA (Cuba)
map (23° 7′N 82° 18′W) **5**:377
GUANABANA *see* CUSTARD APPLE
GUANACO **9**:385 *illus.*
llama **12**:382
GUANAJA (Honduras)
map (16° 27′N 85° 54′W) **10**:218
GUANAJUATO (city in Mexico) **9**:385
map (21° 1′N 101° 15′W) **13**:357
GUANAJUATO (state in Mexico) **9**:385–386
cities
Guanajuato **9**:385
León **12**:289
San Cayetano **12**:225 *illus.*
GUANARE (Venezuela)
map (9° 3′N 69° 45′W) **19**:542
GUANGDONG (China) *see* KWANGTUNG (Guangdong) (China)
GUANGXI (China) *see* KWANGSI (Guangxi) (China)
GUANGZHOU (China) *see* CANTON (Guangzhou) (China)
GUÁNICA (Puerto Rico)
map (17° 58′N 66° 55′W) **15**:614
GUANINE
genetic code **9**:79–81 *illus.*
mutation **13**:686
nucleic acid **14**:289 *illus.*
protein synthesis **15**:575
GUANO **9**:386
cave **4**:222
phosphorite **15**:256
GUANO (Ecuador)
map (1° 35′S 78° 38′W) **7**:52
GUANO ISLANDS ACT
United States outlying territories **19**:464
GUANPATA (Honduras)
map (15° 1′N 85° 2′W) **10**:218
GUANTÁNAMO (Cuba) **9**:386
map (20° 8′N 75° 12′W) **5**:377
GUANTÁNAMO BAY **9**:386
Platt Amendment **15**:362
GUAPI (Colombia)
map (2° 36′N 77° 54′W) **5**:107
GUÁPILES (Costa Rica)
map (10° 13′N 83° 46′W) **5**:291
GUAPORÉ RIVER
map (11° 54′S 65° 1′W) **3**:460
GUAQUI (Bolivia)
map (16° 35′S 68° 51′W) **3**:366
GUARANDA (Ecuador)
map (1° 36′S 79° 0′W) **7**:52
GUARANI (American Indians) **9**:386 *bibliog.*
GUARANTEED STUDENT LOANS
scholarships, fellowships, and loans **17**:130–131
GUARANTY **9**:386
surety **18**:358
GUARARÉ (Panama)
map (7° 49′N 80° 17′W) **15**:55
GUARD CELLS (botany)
stomata **18**:280
GUARD OF HONOR (book)
Cozzens, James Gould **5**:324
GUARDA (Portugal)
map (40° 32′N 7° 16′W) **15**:449
GUARDAFUI, CAPE *see* ASIR, CAPE
GUARDI, FRANCESCO **9**:386–387 *bibliog., illus.*
Ascension Day at Venice **9**:386 *illus.*
GUARDIA, FIORELLO LA *see* LA GUARDIA, FIORELLO
GUARDIAN **9**:387
appointment **9**:387
incompetence **11**:77
natural guardians **9**:387
parent **15**:84
special guardian **9**:387
GUARDIAN (periodical) *see MANCHESTER GUARDIAN*
GUARE, JOHN **9**:387
GUAREIM RIVER
map (30° 12′S 57° 36′W) **19**:488
GUÁRICO RESERVOIR
map (9° 5′N 67° 25′W) **19**:542
GUARINI, GIOVANNI BATTISTA **9**:387
GUARINI, GUARINO **9**:387 *bibliog.*
dome **6**:230 *illus.*
GUARNERI (family) **9**:387 *bibliog.*
GUARNIERI, CAMARGO
Latin American music and dance **12**:232
GUASAVE (Mexico)
map (25° 34′N 108° 27′W) **13**:357
GUATAJIAGUA (El Salvador)
map (13° 40′N 88° 13′W) **7**:100
GUATEMALA **9**:388–389 *bibliog., illus., map, table*
archaeology
Kaminaljuyú **12**:10
Piedras Negras **15**:295
Quiriguá **16**:27
Tikal **19**:198
Uaxactún **19**:369
art
See also the subheading Guatemala under ARCHITECTURE
Latin American art and architecture **12**:225 *illus.*
pre-Columbian art and architecture **15**:495
cities
Antigua **2**:62
Guatemala City **9**:389
economic activity **9**:388
education
Latin American universities **12**:233
flag **8**:134; **9**:388 *illus.*
government **9**:388
history **9**:388–389
Barrios, Justo Rufino **3**:95
Belize **3**:184
Carrera, José Rafael **4**:167
Estrada Cabrera, Manuel **7**:247
land **9**:388–389 *map, table*
literature
Asturias, Miguel Ángel **2**:285–286
map (15° 30′N 90° 15′W) **14**:225
national parks **14**:41 *map*; **14**:43 *table*
people **9**:388
GUATEMALA CITY (Guatemala) **9**:389
climate **9**:389 *table*
map (14° 38′N 90° 31′W) **9**:389
GUAUGURINA (Papua New Guinea)
map (10° 37′S 150° 28′E) **15**:72
GUAVA **9**:390
GUAVIARE RIVER
map (4° 3′N 67° 44′W) **5**:107
GUAYAGUAYARE (Trinidad and Tobago)
map (10° 8′N 61° 2′W) **19**:300
GUAYAMA (Puerto Rico)
map (17° 59′N 66° 7′W) **15**:614
GUAYAQUIL (Ecuador) **9**:390
climate **7**:52 *table*; **18**:86 *table*
map (2° 10′S 79° 50′W) **7**:52
GUAYAQUIL ,GULF OF
map (3° 0′S 80° 30′W) **7**:52
GUAYAS RIVER
map (2° 36′S 79° 52′W) **7**:52
GUAYMAS (Mexico)
climate **13**:356 *table*
map (27° 56′N 110° 54′W) **13**:357
GUAYULE **9**:390
GUBAREV, ALEKSEI **9**:390
GUDE, HANS
Scandinavian art and architecture **17**:113
GUDEA, GOVERNOR OF LAGASH **13**:319 *illus.*
Lagash **12**:165
GUDENA RIVER
map (56° 29′N 10° 13′E) **6**:109
GUDERIAN, HEINZ **9**:390 *bibliog.*
GUDRUN **9**:390
GÜELL, EUSEBIO
Gaudí, Antonio **9**:59
GUELPH (Ontario)
map (43° 33′N 80° 15′W) **14**:393
GUELPHS AND GHIBELLINES **9**:390 *bibliog.*
See also HOHENSTAUFFEN (dynasty); WELF (family)
Dante Alighieri **6**:34
Henry VII, King of Germany and Holy Roman Emperor (Henry of Luxemburg) **10**:130
Malatesta (family) **13**:80
Scala (family) **17**:106
GUENON **9**:390–391 *illus.*
GUERCINO **9**:391 *bibliog.*
GUERICKE, OTTO VON **9**:391
GUÉRIN, PIERRE NARCISSE, BARON **9**:391 *bibliog.*
GUERNICA
Picasso, Pablo **15**:291
GUERNSEY (Channel Islands) **4**:281 *illus., map*; **9**:391
map (49° 28′N 2° 35′W) **19**:403
GUERNSEY (county in Ohio)
map (40° 3′N 81° 30′W) **14**:357
GUERNSEY (Wyoming)
map (42° 16′N 104° 45′W) **20**:301
GUERNSEY CATTLE
dairying **6**:7
GUERRERO (Mexico) **9**:391
Acapulco **1**:72
Chilpancingo **4**:357–358
GUERRERO, FRANCISCO
Spanish music **18**:162
GUERRERO, JACINTO
zarzuela **20**:356
GUERRILLA THEATER **9**:392 *bibliog. bibliog.*
GUERRILLAS **9**:391–392
commando **5**:137
Fort Bragg (North Carolina) **8**:236
franc-tireur **8**:278 *illus.*
Mau Mau **13**:232
minutemen **13**:462
Mosy, John Singleton **13**:596
Namibia **14**:12
Nkomo, Joshua **14**:206
Palestine Liberation Organization **15**:46
Quantrill, William C. **16**:9
rangers **16**:85
revolution **16**:188
terrorism **19**:122
Viet Cong **19**:579
Vietnam War **19**:586–587
Vo Nguyen Giap **19**:624
war **20**:25
GUESCLIN, BERTRAND DU *see* DU GUESCLIN, BERTRAND
GUESDE, JULES
Jaurès, Jules **11**:385
socialism **18**:21
GUESS, GEORGE *see* SEQUOYA (Cherokee Indian)
GUETTARD, JEAN ÉTIENNE **9**:392
GUEVARA, CHE **9**:392 *bibliog., illus.*
GUEYDAN (Louisiana)
map (30° 2′N 92° 30′W) **12**:430
GUGGENHEIM (family) **9**:392 *bibliog.*
Guggenheim Memorial Foundation **9**:393
GUGGENHEIM, ALICIA PATTERSON
Patterson (family) **15**:115
GUGGENHEIM, PEGGY **9**:392–393 *bibliog.*
GUGGENHEIM FUND FOR THE PROMOTION OF AERONAUTICS
aviation **2**:372
GUGGENHEIM MEMORIAL FOUNDATION **9**:393
GUGGENHEIM MUSEUM **1**:329 *illus.*; **9**:393 *bibliog., illus.*; **13**:493 *illus.*; **20**:288 *illus.*
Guggenheim (family) **9**:392
modern art **13**:494
New York (city) **14**:145 *map*
GUIANA BASIN
Atlantic Ocean bottom **2**:295 *map*
GUIANA HIGHLANDS
map (5° 0′N 64° 0′W) **19**:542
GUIANA SHIELD
South America **18**:87
GUIARD, ADÉLAIDE LABILLE *see* LABILLE-GUIARD, ADÉLAIDE
GUICCIARDINI, FRANCESCO **9**:393 *bibliog.*
GUICHÓN (Uruguay)
map (32° 21′S 57° 12′W) **19**:488
GUIDANCE, EDUCATIONAL *see* CAREER EDUCATION; SECONDARY EDUCATION
GUIDANCE AND CONTROL SYSTEMS **9**:393–394 *bibliog.*
astronautics **2**:274–276
ballistic missile **3**:349
cruise missile **5**:365
gyroscope **9**:416
rockets and missiles **16**:254
space exploration **18**:121
submarine **18**:315
surface-to-air missile **18**:359
torpedo (projectile) **19**:242–243
GUIDE DOG **9**:394 *bibliog.*
German shepherd **9**:135
GUIDED MISSILE *see* ROCKETS AND MISSILES
GUIDO D'AREZZO **9**:394 *bibliog.*
GUIÉNNE (France) **9**:394
Hundred Years' War **10**:304
GUIERS, LAKE
map (16° 12′N 15° 50′W) **17**:202
GUIGNOL, GRAND **9**:394–395
GUIJA LAKE
map (14° 17′N 89° 31′W) **7**:100
GUILARTE, MOUNT
map (18° 9′N 66° 46′W) **15**:614
GUILDFORD (England)
map (51° 14′N 0° 35′W) **19**:403
GUILDHALL (Vermont)
map (44° 34′N 71° 34′W) **19**:554
GUILDS **9**:395 *bibliog., illus.*
academies of art **1**:70
apprenticeship **2**:91
labor union **12**:154
meistersinger **13**:283
Middle Ages **13**:394
secret societies **17**:181
Twelve Great Companies
coats of arms **9**:395 *illus.*
GUILFORD (Maine)
map (45° 14′N 69° 29′W) **13**:70
GUILFORD (county in North Carolina)
map (36° 5′N 79° 45′W) **14**:242
GUILFORD, FREDERICK NORTH, 2d EARL OF *see* NORTH, LORD
GUILLAIN-BARRÉ SYNDROME
influenza **11**:172
GUILLAUME, CHARLES ÉDOUARD **9**:395
GUILLAUME, LOUIS
Lee's surrender at Appomattox **5**:30 *illus.*
GUILLAUME DE LORRIS **9**:395
Roman de la Rose, Le **16**:278
GUILLAUME IX, DUKE OF AQUITAINE
Provençal literature **15**:583
GUILLAUMIN, ARMAND **9**:395–396 *bibliog.*
GUILLEMIN, ROGER
Schally, Andrew Victor **17**:117
GUILLEMOT **9**:396 *illus.*
GUILLÉN, JORGE **9**:396
GUILLÉN, NICOLÁS **9**:396 *bibliog.*
GUILLERM, NELLY *see* VERDY, VIOLETTE
GUILLOTINE **9**:396 *illus.*
GUILTY PLEA (law)
criminal justice **5**:349; **5**:350
GUIMARD, HECTOR **9**:396–397 *bibliog.*
Art Nouveau **2**:210–212
Paris Métro subway stations **2**:212 *illus.*
side table **8**:378 *illus.*
wrought-iron gate **2**:211 *illus.*
GUINEA **9**:397–398 *bibliog., illus., map, table*
African art **1**:162
cities
Conakry **5**:168
economic activity **9**:397
flag **9**:397 *illus.*
government **9**:398
history **9**:397–398
Touré, Sékou **19**:251
land **9**:397 *map, table*
literature
Laye, Camara **12**:252
map (11° 0′N 10° 0′W) **1**:136
people **9**:397
GUINEA, GULF OF **9**:398
map (2° 0′N 2° 30′E) **1**:136
GUINEA-BISSAU **9**:398–399 *bibliog., map, table*
cities
Bissau **3**:299
Bolama **9**:399 *table*
economy **9**:398
flag **9**:399 *illus.*
government **9**:399
history **9**:398–399
land **9**:398–399 *map, table*
map (12° 0′N 15° 0′W) **1**:136
people **9**:398
GUINEA FOWL **9**:399
helmeted guinea fowl **17**:98 *illus.*
GUINEA PIG **9**:399–400 *illus.*
genetic code **10**:140 *illus.*
GÜINES (Cuba)
map (22° 50′N 82° 2′W) **5**:377
GUINEVERE **9**:400
GUINICELLI, GUIDO **9**:400 *bibliog.*
GUINNESS, SIR ALEC **9**:400 *bibliog.*
GUINNESS BOOK OF WORLD RECORDS, THE **9**:400
GÜIRA DE MELENA (Cuba)
map (22° 48′N 82° 30′W) **5**:377
GÜIRALDES, RICARDO **9**:400
GUIRATINGA (Brazil)
map (16° 21′S 53° 45′W) **3**:460
GÜIRIA (Venezuela)
map (10° 34′N 62° 18′W) **19**:542
GUISANBOURG (French Guiana)
map (4° 25′N 51° 56′W) **8**:311
GUISCARD, ROBERT *see* ROBERT GUISCARD
GUISE (family) **9**:400 *bibliog.*

GUISE (cont.)
Francis II, King of France **8**:276
Henry II, King of France **10**:127
Henry III, King of France **10**:127
GUITAR **9**:400–401 *bibliog.*, *illus.*; **13**:677 *illus.*; **18**:300–301 *illus.*
balalaika **3**:30
electric **7**:125 *illus.*
Christian, Charlie **4**:411
performers
Bream, Julian **3**:468
Reinhardt, Django **16**:132
Segovia, Andrés **17**:188
Spanish music **18**:161
GUITARFISH **9**:401 *illus.*
GUITEAU, CHARLES JULIUS **9**:401 *bibliog.*
GUITRY, SACHA **9**:401 *bibliog.*
GUIZHON (China) *see* KWEICHOW (Guizhon) (China)
GUIZOT, FRANÇOIS **9**:401–402 *bibliog.*
GUJARAT (India) **9**:402
cities
Ahmadabad **1**:200
Baroda **3**:87
Indian art and architecture **11**:97
map (22° 0′N 72° 0′E) **11**:80
GUJRANWALA (Pakistan) **9**:402
map (32° 26′N 74° 33′E) **15**:27
GUJRAT
map (32° 34′N 74° 5′E) **15**:27
GULAG **9**:402 *bibliog.*
Stalinism **5**:147
GULAG ARCHIPELAGO, THE (book) **9**:402
Solzhenitsyn, Aleksandr **18**:59
GULBENKIAN, CALOUSTE SARKIS **9**:402 *bibliog.*
GULDBERG, CATO MAXIMILIAN **9**:402
Waage, Peter **20**:3
GULF (county in Florida)
map (30° 0′N 85° 10′W) **8**:172
GULF AND BAY **9**:402–403 *bibliog.*
See also OCEAN AND SEAS; names of specific bodies of water, e.g., FUNDY, BAY OF; MEXICO, GULF OF; etc.
circulation, types **9**:402–403
coastal plain **5**:81
depth factor **9**:403
environment **9**:402–403
fjord **8**:133
harbor and port **10**:42; **10**:43 *illus.*
intertidal life **11**:229–230
lagoon **12**:165–166
major gulfs and bays **9**:403
Moon, near side **13**:564 *map*
ocean and sea **14**:325–332
photic zone **15**:257
tidal energy **19**:192–193
GULF HAMMOCK (Florida)
map (29° 15′N 82° 43′W) **8**:172
GULF OF MEXICO *see* MEXICO, GULF OF
GULF SHORES (Alabama)
map (30° 17′N 87° 41′W) **1**:234
GULF STREAM **9**:403 *bibliog.*, *illus.*
Iselin, Columbus O'Donnell **11**:286
ocean-atmosphere interaction **14**:321
ocean currents **14**:324
ocean currents and wind systems, worldwide **14**:322–323 *maps*
Sargasso Sea **17**:77
GULFPORT (Florida)
map (27° 44′N 82° 43′W) **8**:172
GULFPORT (Mississippi) **9**:403–404
map (30° 22′N 89° 6′W) **13**:469
GULICK, LUTHER HALSEY **9**:404 *bibliog.*
GULKANA (Alaska)
map (62° 16′N 145° 23′W) **1**:242
GULL **9**:404 *bibliog.*, *illus.*
animal behavior **2**:12 *illus.*
kittiwake **12**:93
Utah **19**:493
GULL FALLS (Waterfall)
map (64° 24′N 20° 8′W) **11**:17
GULLAH (black culture)
creole **5**:338
Georgia **9**:118
GULLIVER'S TRAVELS (book) **9**:404 *bibliog.*
Swift, Jonathan **18**:389
GULU (Uganda)
map (2° 47′N 32° 18′E) **19**:372
GUM **9**:404
carob **4**:159–160
chicle **4**:346
gum arabic **9**:405
resins
Pelletier, Pierre Joseph **15**:138
tragacanth **19**:264–265
GUM ARABIC **9**:404–405
tree **19**:288
GUMA, ALEX LA *see* LA GUMA, ALEX
GUMBO *see* OKRA
GUMBO-LIMBO (botany) **9**:405
GUMILEV, NIKOLAI STEPANOVICH **9**:405 *bibliog.*
GUMM, FRANCES *see* GARLAND, JUDY
GUMPLANT *see* GUMWEED
GUMPLOWICZ, LUDWIG
Social Darwinism **18**:12
GUMS (mouth)
dentistry **6**:116
gingivitis **9**:184
periodontics **15**:170
pyorrhea **15**:634
GUMWEED **9**:405 *bibliog.*
GUN *see* FIREARMS; WEAPONS
GUN CONTROL **9**:405 *bibliog.*
National Rifle Association of America **14**:45
right to bear arms **16**:222
GUN DOG *see* SPORTING DOG
GUNCOTTON **9**:405
explosives **7**:339
GUNDESTRUP (Denmark)
European prehistory **7**:306
GUNDOBAD, KING OF THE BURGUNDIANS
duel **6**:293
GUNDULIĆ, IVAN
Yugoslavia **20**:342
GUNJUR (Gambia)
map (13° 11′N 16° 46′W) **9**:25
GUNNARSSON, GUNNAR **9**:405
GUNNBJORNS MOUNTAIN
map (68° 55′N 29° 53′W) **9**:353
GUNNEL **9**:405
GUNNISON (Colorado)
map (38° 33′N 106° 56′W) **5**:116
GUNNISON (county in Colorado)
map (38° 45′N 107° 0′W) **5**:116
GUNNISON (Utah)
map (39° 9′N 111° 49′W) **19**:492
GUNNISON RIVER
map (39° 3′N 108° 35′W) **5**:116
GUNPOWDER **9**:405–406
ammunition **1**:373
du Pont (family) **6**:286–287
explosives **7**:339
firearms **8**:105–106
strategy and tactics, military **18**:290
weapons **20**:74
GUNPOWDER FALLS RIVER
map (39° 24′N 76° 22′W) **13**:188
GUNPOWDER PLOT (1605)
Fawkes, Guy **8**:39
GUNTER, EDMUND
slide rule **17**:361
GUNTERSVILLE (Alabama)
map (34° 21′N 86° 18′W) **1**:234
GUNTERSVILLE LAKE
map (34° 45′N 86° 3′W) **1**:234
GÜNTHER, IGNAZ **9**:406 *bibliog.*
GÜNTHER, JOHANN CHRISTIAN **9**:406
GUNTHER, JOHN **9**:406
GUNTUR (India)
map (16° 18′N 80° 27′E) **11**:80
GUO MORUO *see* KUO MO-JO (Guo Moruo)
GUO XI *see* KUO HSI (Guo Xi)
GUOMINDANG *see* KUOMINTANG (Guomingdang)
GUPPY **9**:406 *illus.*
molly **13**:512
tropical fish **19**:307–308 *illus.*
GUPTA (dynasty) **9**:406 *bibliog.*
Asia, history of **2**:251 *illus.*
India, history of **11**:89 *map*
Indian art and architecture **11**:94–96
Pataliputra **15**:109
GURDON (Arkansas)
map (33° 55′N 93° 9′W) **2**:166
GUREVICH, MIKHAIL I.
MiG **13**:416
GURI RESERVOIR
map (7° 30′N 62° 50′W) **19**:542
GURKHA **9**:406 *bibliog.*
knife **18**:399 *illus.*
Nepal **14**:87
GURLEY, JOHN
monetary theory **13**:525
GURNARD, FLYING **9**:406–407 *illus.*
sea robin **17**:170
GURNEY, DAN **9**:407
GURU **9**:407
GURUPÁ (Brazil)
map (1° 25′S 51° 39′W) **3**:460
GURYEV (USSR)
map (47° 7′N 51° 56′E) **19**:388
GUSAU (Nigeria)
map (12° 12′N 6° 40′E) **14**:190
GUSTAFSSON, GRETA LOVISA *see* GARBO, GRETA
GUSTAV HOLM, CAPE
map (67° 0′N 34° 0′W) **9**:353
GUSTAV I, KING OF SWEDEN **9**:407 *bibliog.*
Scandinavia, history of **17**:109
Vasa (dynasty) **19**:525
GUSTAV II ADOLF, KING OF SWEDEN (Gustavus Adolphus) **9**:407 *bibliog.*, *illus.*
acquisitions 1611–1632 **17**:109 *map*
artillery **2**:223–224
Battle of Lützen **17**:109 *illus.*
Göteborg **9**:254
strategy and tactics, military **18**:290
Thirty Years' War **19**:171 *map*
Wallenstein, Albrecht Wenzel von **20**:15
weapons **20**:75
GUSTAV III, KING OF SWEDEN **9**:407–408 *bibliog.*
coronation **17**:112 *illus.*
Scandinavia, history of **17**:110
GUSTAV IV ADOLF, KING OF SWEDEN **9**:408 *bibliog.*
Scandinavia, history of **17**:110
GUSTAV VI ADOLF, KING OF SWEDEN **9**:408
GUSTAVUS ADOLPHUS *see* GUSTAV II ADOLF, KING OF SWEDEN (Gustavus Adolphus)
GUSTINE (California)
map (37° 16′N 120° 60′W) **4**:31
GUSTON, PHILIP **9**:408 *bibliog.*, *illus.*
Cadran **9**:408 *illus.*
GÜSTROW (Germany, East and West)
map (53° 48′N 12° 10′E) **9**:140
GUT *see* INTESTINE
GUTENBERG, BENO **9**:408
GUTENBERG, JOHANN **9**:408–409 *bibliog.*, *illus.*
book **3**:384
Fust, Johann **8**:383
Germany, history of **9**:151
Mainz (West Germany) **13**:75
printing **15**:551
type, printing **19**:363
GUTENBERG BIBLE **3**:384 *illus.*; **9**:409 *bibliog.*; **15**:550 *illus.*
book **3**:384
GÜTERSLOH (Germany, East and West)
map (51° 54′N 8° 23′E) **9**:140
GUTHRIE (county in Iowa)
map (41° 38′N 94° 30′W) **11**:244
GUTHRIE (Kentucky)
map (36° 39′N 87° 10′W) **12**:47
GUTHRIE (Oklahoma)
map (35° 53′N 97° 25′W) **14**:368
GUTHRIE (Texas)
map (33° 37′N 100° 19′W) **19**:129
GUTHRIE, A. B., JR. **9**:409
GUTHRIE, EDWIN RAY **9**:409
psychology, history of **15**:597
GUTHRIE, JANET **9**:409
GUTHRIE, SAMUEL **9**:409
GUTHRIE, SIR TYRONE **9**:409 *bibliog.*
GUTHRIE, WOODY AND ARLO **9**:409 *bibliog.*
Seeger, Pete **17**:187
GUTHRIE CENTER (Iowa)
map (41° 41′N 94° 30′W) **11**:244
GUTI
Mesopotamian art and architecture **13**:319
GUTIÉRREZ, ANTONIO GARCÍA *see* GARCÍA GUTIÉRREZ, ANTONIO
GUTIÉRREZ, BERNARDO
Texas **19**:133
GUTIÉRREZ NÁJERA, MANUEL
Mexico **13**:360
GUTIRREZ, JOSÉ ÁNGEL
Chicano **4**:343
GUTLAND
Luxembourg (country) **12**:471
GUTS see GRAND UNIFICATION THEORIES
GUTTA-PERCHA **9**:409
Siemens (family) **17**:296
GUTTATION **9**:410
GUTTE, B.
zoology **20**:377
GUTTENBERG (Iowa)
map (42° 47′N 91° 6′W) **11**:244
GUY DE LUSIGNAN
Cyprus **5**:409
GUYANA **9**:410–411 *bibliog.*, *illus.*, *map*, *table*
cities
Georgetown **9**:112
economy **9**:410
flag **9**:410 *illus.*
history and government **9**:411
Burnham, Forbes **3**:578
Jagan, Cheddi **11**:348
Jonestown **11**:444
land and resources **9**:410–411 *map*, *table*
map (5° 0′N 59° 0′W) **18**:85
people **9**:410
Carib **4**:147
Warrau **20**:30–31
philately **15**:230 *illus.*
GUYANDOTTE RIVER
map (38° 25′N 82° 23′W) **20**:111
GUYENNE *see* GUIÈNNE (France)
GUYMON (Oklahoma)
map (36° 41′N 101° 29′W) **14**:368
GUYOT (marine geology)
Hess, H. H. **10**:151–152
Seamount **17**:174
GUYOT, ARNOLD
Great Smoky Mountains **9**:322
GUYOT, MOUNT
map (35° 42′N 83° 15′W) **19**:104
GUYS, CONSTANTIN **9**:411 *bibliog.*
GUYS AND DOLLS (book)
Runyon, Damon **16**:346
GUYTON (Georgia)
map (32° 20′N 81° 24′W) **9**:114
GUZMÁN, ANTONIO
Dominican Republic **6**:234
GUZMÁN, GASPAR DE *see* OLIVARES, GASPAR DE GUZMÁN, CONDE-DUQUE DE
GUZMÁN, GASPAR DE, CONDE-DUQUE DE OLIVARES *see* OLIVARES, GASPAR DE GUZMÁN, CONDE-DUQUE DE
GUZMÁN, JACOBO ARBENZ *see* ARBENZ GUZMÁN, JACOBO
GUZMÁN, MARTIN LUIS
Mexico **13**:360
GUZMÁN BLANCO, ANTONIO **9**:411 *bibliog.*
GWADABAWA (Nigeria)
map (13° 20′N 5° 15′E) **14**:190
GWAI RIVER
map (17° 59′S 26° 52′E) **20**:365
GWALIOR (India)
map (26° 13′N 78° 10′E) **11**:80
GWANDA (Zimbabwe)
map (20° 57′S 29° 1′E) **20**:365
GWATAR BAY
map (25° 4′N 61° 36′E) **15**:27
GWATHMEY, CHARLES **9**:411 *bibliog.*
GWATHMEY, ROBERT **9**:411
GWDA RIVER
map (53° 4′N 16° 44′E) **15**:388
GWENT (Wales) **9**:411–412
GWERU (Zimbabwe)
map (19° 27′S 29° 49′E) **20**:365
GWINN (Michigan)
map (46° 17′N 87° 26′W) **13**:377
GWINNER (North Dakota)
map (46° 14′N 97° 40′W) **14**:248
GWINNETT (county in Georgia)
map (34° 0′N 84° 0′W) **9**:114
GWYNEDD (Wales) **9**:412
cities
Caernarvon **4**:13
GWYNNE, NELL **9**:412 *bibliog.*
GYMNASIUM (exercise building) **9**:412
GYMNASIUM (school) **9**:412
GYMNASTICS **9**:412–414 *bibliog.*, *illus.*
apparatus **9**:413 *illus.*
Comaneci, Nadia **5**:130
history **9**:412
Jahn, Friedrich Ludwig **11**:349
Korbut, Olga **12**:111
Latynina, Larisa **12**:236
Olympic Games **14**:383 *illus.*
Rome, anicent **18**:196 *illus.*
scoring **9**:413–414
GYMNOPHIONA (Apoda)
amphibians **1**:378–379 *illus.*
GYMNOSPERM **9**:414 *bibliog.*
conifer **5**:189–191
cycad **5**:402
Ephedra **7**:215–216
evergreen **7**:316
flower **8**:178
ginkgo **9**:184
Gnetum **9**:213
Jurassic Period **11**:475 *illus.*
plant **15**:334–335 *illus.*
pollination **15**:408
reproduction **16**:162
spermatophyte **18**:179
tracheophyte **19**:258
tree **19**:286–287 *illus.*
Triassic Period **19**:294
GYMNOTID **9**:414
knife fish **12**:99
GYMNURE **9**:414
GYNECOLOGY **9**:414 *bibliog.*
abortion **1**:60

anorexia nervosa **2**:34
DES **6**:123
frigidity **8**:334
lumbago **12**:454–455
obstetrics **14**:319
pregnancy and birth **15**:502–506
surgery **18**:361
toxic shock syndrome **19**:256
urogenital diseases **19**:487
GYOKUDO **9**:414–415 *bibliog.*
GYÖNGYÖS (Hungary)
map (47° 47′N 19° 56′E) **10**:307
GYÖR (Hungary) **9**:415
map (47° 42′N 17° 38′E) **10**:307
GYÖRGYI, ALBERT VON SZENT- *see* SZENT-GYÖRGYI, ALBERT VON
GYPSIES **9**:415 *bibliog., illus.*
nomad **14**:215
wake **20**:8
GYPSUM **9**:415–416 *illus.*
calcium **4**:22
commercial uses **9**:416
monoclinic system **13**:536
Oklahoma **14**:367 *illus.*
sulfate minerals **18**:333
GYPSUM (Colorado)
map (39° 39′N 106° 57′W) **5**:116
GYPSUMVILLE (Manitoba)
map (51° 45′N 98° 35′W) **13**:119
GYPSY MOTH **9**:416 *bibliog., illus.*
GYROCOMPASS **5**:156
GYROSCOPE **9**:416 *bibliog., illus.*
compass, navigational **5**:155–156
guidance and control systems **9**:393–394
inventor: Sperry, Elmer Ambrose **18**:179
rockets and missiles **16**:254
space exploration **18**:122

H

H (letter) **10**:3 *illus.*
H. D. *see* DOOLITTLE, HILDA (H. D.)
HA-ARAVA RIVER
map (31° 4′N 35° 7′E) **11**:302
HA GIANG (Vietnam)
map (22° 50′N 104° 59′E) **19**:580
HAAKON (county in South Dakota)
map (44° 18′N 101° 33′W) **18**:103
HAAKON IV, KING OF NORWAY **10**:3 *bibliog.*
HAAKON VII, KING OF NORWAY **10**:3
Trondheim (Norway) **19**:306
HAANPÄÄ, PENTTI
Finnish literature **8**:99
HAAPAI GROUP
map (19° 42′S 174° 29′W) **19**:233
HAARLEM (Netherlands) **10**:3
map (52° 23′N 4° 38′E) **14**:99
HAARLEM, GHERRIT VAN *see* GEERTGEN TOT SINT JANS
HAAVIKKO, PAAVO **10**:3
HAAVIO, MARTTI *see* MUSTRAPÄÄ, P. (pseudonym)
HABAKKUK, BOOK OF **10**:3
HABANA, LA (Cuba) *see* HAVANA (Cuba)
HABASESTI (Romania) **7**:303 *illus.*; **14**:83–84 *illus.*
HABBAN
map (14° 21′N 47° 5′E) **20**:324
HABEAS CORPUS **10**:3–4
Constitution of the United States **5**:217
writ **20**:291
HABELER, PETER
mountain climbing **13**:622
HABER, FRITZ **10**:4 *bibliog.*
HABER-BOSCH PROCESS
Bosch, Carl **3**:405
HABERDASHERS, WORSHIPFUL COMPANY OF
coat of arms **10**:134 *illus.*
HABERLE, JOHN **10**:4 *bibliog.*
HABERMAS, JÜRGEN
sociology **18**:30
HABERSHAM (county in Georgia)
map (34° 40′N 83° 30′W) **9**:114
HABEUS CORPUS
prisoners' rights **15**:555
HABIGANJ (Bangladesh)
map (24° 23′N 91° 25′E) **3**:64
HABIT **10**:4 *bibliog.*
behavior, influences **10**:4
learning theory **12**:261
HABITAT **10**:4–6 *bibliog., illus.*
beaver **3**:149 *illus.*
bee **3**:156–158 *illus.*
biome **3**:274; **10**:4
biosphere **3**:276–277
chaparral **4**:283–284
conservation **5**:203
deep-sea life **6**:77–79
desert **10**:4–6
destruction
endangered species **7**:167 *illus.*
national parks **14**:44
snowmobile **18**:5
forest **8**:227–230
freshwater lakes **10**:4
grasslands **9**:299–301
intertidal life **11**:229–230
invertebrate **11**:234
jungle and rain forest **11**:468–470
lizard **12**:378–379
mountain life **13**:622–623
North American lake **12**:168 *illus.*
ocean **10**:4–5
ocean and sea **14**:331
plant **15**:340–341 *illus.*
savanna life **17**:97–99
steppe life **18**:256–257
swamp forest, Carboniferous Period **15**:31 *illus.*
terrestrial **10**:5–6
Triassic Period **19**:294 *illus.*
HABITAT (Montreal)
Safdie, Moshe **17**:10
HABITUAL OFFENDER LAWS
crime **5**:347
HABRÉ, HISSÈNE
Chad **4**:266
HABSBURG (dynasty) **2**:350 *illus.*; **10**:6 *bibliog., illus.*
Albert I, King of Germany **1**:254
Albert II, King of Germany **1**:254
Austria-Hungary **2**:351–352
Brabant, Duchy of **3**:435
Charles II, King of Spain **4**:296
Charles V, Holy Roman Emperor **4**:294–295
Charles VI **4**:295
Czechoslovakia **5**:416
European holdings c.1360 **7**:285 *map*
European holdings c.1560 **7**:288 *map*
European holdings c.1648 **7**:289 *map*
Ferdinand I, Holy Roman Emperor **8**:52–53
Ferdinand II, Holy Roman Emperor **8**:53
Flemish art and architecture **8**:160–163
Francis II, Holy Roman Emperor **8**:276
Francis Joseph, Emperor of Austria **8**:274–275
Frederick III, Holy Roman Emperor **8**:291
Fugger (family) **8**:355
Germany, history of **9**:149–152 *map*
Holy Roman Empire **10**:211
Hungary **10**:310
Italian Wars **11**:319
Joseph I, Holy Roman Emperor **11**:451
Joseph II, Holy Roman Emperor **11**:452
Leopold II, Holy Roman Emperor **12**:294–295
Low Countries, history of the **12**:439–440; **12**:441
Maria Theresa, Austrian Archduchess, Queen of Hungary and Bohemia **13**:150
Mary of Burgundy **13**:185
Matthias, Holy Roman Emperor **13**:231–232
Maximilian I, Holy Roman Emperor **13**:240
Philip I, King of Castile (Philip the Handsome) **15**:234
Philip II, King of Spain **15**:234
Philip III, King of Spain **15**:234–235
Philip IV, King of Spain **15**:235
portraits
Leoni (family) **12**:292
Moro, Antonio **13**:583
Pragmatic Sanction **15**:487
Rudolf I, King of Germany **16**:338
Rudolf II, Holy Roman Emperor **16**:338
Spain, history of **18**:145–147
Thirty Years' War **19**:171–172
HABU **10**:6
HABYARIMANA, JUVENAL
Rwanda **16**:378
HACHETTE, JEAN NICOLAS PIERRE
mathematics, history of **13**:226
HACHIJO ISLAND
map (33° 5′N 139° 48′E) **11**:361
HACHINOHE (Japan)
map (40° 30′N 141° 29′E) **11**:361
HACILAR (Turkey) **10**:6–7 *bibliog.*
HACKBERRY (Arizona)
map (35° 22′N 113° 44′W) **2**:160
HACKBERRY (botany) **10**:7 *illus.*
HACKBERRY (Louisiana)
map (29° 59′N 93° 21′W) **12**:430
HACKENSACK (New Jersey) **10**:7
map (40° 53′N 74° 3′W) **14**:129
HACKENSACK RIVER
map (40° 43′N 74° 6′W) **14**:129
HACKETT (Arkansas)
map (35° 11′N 94° 25′W) **2**:166
HACKETTSTOWN (New Jersey)
map (40° 51′N 74° 50′W) **14**:129
HACKMATACK *see* POPLAR; TAMARACK
HACKNEY (horse) **10**:243 *illus.*
HACKNEY CARRIAGE
coach and carriage **5**:73; **5**:75
HADAL ZONE **10**:7
ocean and sea **14**:331
oceanic trenches **14**:341
HADAMARD, JACQUES SALOMON **10**:7
mathematics, history of **13**:226
HADASSAH **10**:7 *bibliog.*
Szold, Henrietta **18**:416
HADDAM (Kansas)
map (39° 51′N 97° 18′W) **12**:18
HADDEN, BRITON
Luce, Henry Robinson **12**:449–450
HADDOCK **5**:89–90 *illus.*; **8**:124 *illus.*; **10**:7 *illus.*
fishing industry **8**:127
HADDONFIELD (New Jersey)
map (39° 54′N 75° 2′W) **14**:129
HADDUMMATI ATOLL
map (1° 55′N 73° 25′E) **13**:87
HADERSLEV (Denmark)
map (55° 15′N 9° 30′E) **6**:109
HADES (mythology) **10**:7–8
Cerberus **4**:259
Charon **4**:299
HADHR, AL- *see* HATRA (Iraq)
HADLEY, HENRY K.
Berkshire Music Festival **3**:214
HADLEY, JOHN
meteorology **13**:342
navigation **14**:60
HADLEY CELL **10**:8
cyclone and anticyclone **5**:405
high-pressure region **10**:162
jet stream **11**:407
HADLOCK (Washington)
map (48° 2′N 122° 46′W) **20**:35
HADRIAN, MAUSOLEUM OF *see* CASTEL SANT'ANGELO
HADRIAN, ROMAN EMPEROR **10**:8 *bibliog., illus.*
caesar **4**:13
Edirne (Turkey) **7**:57
Hadrian's Wall **10**:8
Juvenal **11**:480
Naples (Italy) **14**:15
Pantheon (Rome) **15**:61–62 *illus.*
Roman law **16**:278
Rome, ancient **16**:303
HADRIAN'S VILLA **10**:8 *bibliog.*
HADRIAN'S WALL **10**:8 *bibliog.*; **17**:151 *illus.*
fortification **8**:238–239
Hadrian, Roman Emperor **10**:8
HADRON **10**:8–9
fundamental particles **8**:362 *table*; **8**:363
quark **16**:12
HADUR SHU'AYB MOUNTAIN
map (15° 18′N 43° 59′E) **20**:325
HAECKEL, ERNST HEINRICH **10**:9
anatomy **1**:397–398
ecology **7**:42
Java man **11**:385
Monera **13**:523
ontogeny **14**:396
phylogeny **15**:279
Protista **15**:577
zoology **20**:377 *illus.*
HAEJU (Korea)
map (38° 2′N 125° 42′E) **12**:113
HAFEZ, MOHAMMED SHAMSODDIN **10**:9 *bibliog.*
Shiraz (Iran) **17**:277
HAFNARFJÖRDUR (Iceland)
map (64° 3′N 21° 56′W) **11**:17
HAFNER, DOROTHY
porcelain **5**:327 *illus.*
HAFNIUM **10**:9
element **7**:130 *table*
Group IVB periodic table **15**:167
metal, metallic element **13**:328
transition elements **19**:273
HAFUN, CAPE OF
map (10° 27′N 51° 26′E) **18**:60
HAGAN (Georgia)
map (32° 9′N 81° 56′W) **9**:114
HAGANAH
Jabotinsky, Vladimir **11**:339
Palestine **15**:45
HAGAR **10**:9
Ishmael **11**:287
HAGEN (Germany, East and West)
map (51° 22′N 7° 28′E) **9**:140
HAGEN, WALTER **10**:9 *bibliog.*
HAGERMAN (Idaho)
map (42° 49′N 114° 54′W) **11**:26
HAGERMAN (New Mexico)
map (33° 7′N 104° 20′W) **14**:136
HAGERSTOWN (Indiana)
map (39° 55′N 85° 10′W) **11**:111
HAGERSTOWN (Maryland) **10**:9
map (39° 39′N 77° 43′W) **13**:188
HAGFISH **8**:117 *illus.*; **10**:9 *illus.*
lamprey **12**:176
HAGGADAH **11**:461 *illus.*
halachah **10**:17
Passover **15**:106; **17**:182
seder **17**:182
HAGGAI, BOOK OF **10**:9
HAGGARD, H. RIDER **10**:10 *bibliog.*
HAGIA SOPHIA **2**:133 *illus.*; **10**:10 *bibliog., illus.*
Anthemius of Tralles **2**:49
Byzantine art and architecture **3**:604–605 *illus.*
cathedrals and churches **4**:204–205 *illus.*
dome **6**:229
Isidorus of Miletus **11**:288
Islamic art and architecture **11**:297
Istanbul (Turkey) **11**:307
Justinian I, Byzantine Emperor (Justinian the Great) **11**:479
mosaic **13**:595
HAGIOGRAPHY **10**:10 *bibliog.*
Attar, Farid al-Din Abu Hamid **2**:314
saint **17**:15
HAGIWARA SAKUTARO **10**:10
HAGMAN, LARRY
Martin, Mary **13**:179
HAGUE (Saskatchewan)
map (52° 30′N 106° 25′W) **17**:81
HAGUE, FRANK **10**:11 *bibliog.*
HAGUE, THE (Netherlands) **10**:10–11 *illus.*
map (52° 6′N 4° 18′E) **14**:99
HAGUE, TREATY OF THE
Quadruple Alliance **16**:5
HAGUE CONFERENCES **10**:11 *bibliog.*
privateering **15**:557
war crimes **20**:25
HAGUE COURT *see* HAGUE TRIBUNAL
HAGUE TRIBUNAL
Hague conferences **10**:11
International Court of Justice **11**:219
HAGUES PEAK (peak)
map (40° 29′N 105° 38′W) **5**:116
HAHIRA (Georgia)
map (30° 57′N 83° 22′W) **9**:114
HAHN, OTTO **10**:11 *illus.*
element 105 **7**:132
Meitner, Lise **13**:283
uranium **19**:477
HAHNEMANN, SAMUEL
homeopathy **10**:212
medicine **13**:270
HAHNIUM
element 105 **7**:132
superheavy elements **18**:351
HAHNVILLE (Louisiana)
map (29° 58′N 90° 24′W) **12**:430
HAI DUONG (Vietnam)
map (20° 56′N 106° 19′E) **19**:580
HAI-K'OU (China)
map (20° 6′N 110° 21′E) **4**:362
HAIDA (American Indians) **10**:12 *bibliog.*
art
Indians of North America, art of the **11**:139
wood sculpture **11**:127 *illus.*
money **13**:525 *illus.*
passage rites **15**:103
potlatch **15**:467
Queen Charlotte Islands **16**:21–22
totem **19**:249
Tsimshian **19**:323
HAIDALLA, MUHAMMAD OULD
Mauritania **13**:237
HAIFA (Israel) **10**:12
climate **11**:303 *table*
map (32° 50′N 35° 0′E) **11**:302
HAIG, ALEXANDER **10**:12
HAIG, DOUGLAS HAIG, 1ST EARL **10**:12 *bibliog., illus.*
Somme, Battles of the **18**:61–62

World War I **20**:229 *illus.*; **20**:236–237; **20**:242
HAIGHT-ASHBURY (California)
Jefferson Airplane **11**:393
San Francisco (California) **17**:53
HAIKU **10**:12 *bibliog.*
Basho **3**:108
Buson **3**:590
Japanese literature **11**:380
HAIL AND HAILSTONES **10**:12–13 *bibliog., illus.*
meteorology **13**:341–343
precipitation **15**:493
radar meteorology **16**:41
weather modification **20**:80
HAIL MARY PRAYER *see* AVE MARIA
HAILE SELASSIE, EMPEROR OF ETHIOPIA **10**:13–14 *bibliog., illus.*
Ethiopia **7**:254
HAILEY (Idaho)
map (43° 31′N 114° 19′W) **11**:26
HAILEYVILLE (Oklahoma)
map (34° 52′N 95° 36′W) **14**:368
HAINAN (China) **10**:14
map (19° 0′N 109° 30′E) **4**:362
HAINES (Alaska)
map (59° 15′N 135° 25′W) **1**:242
HAINES (Oregon)
map (44° 55′N 117° 56′W) **14**:427
HAINES CITY (Florida)
map (28° 7′N 81° 37′W) **8**:172
HAINES JUNCTION (Yukon Territory)
map (60° 45′N 137° 30′W) **20**:345
HAIPHONG (Vietnam) **10**:14
map (20° 52′N 106° 41′E) **19**:580
HAIR **10**:14 *bibliog., illus.*
baldness **3**:34
cosmetics **5**:280–283 *table*
depilatory **6**:118
follicle
skin **17**:341 *illus.*
hirsutism **10**:176
molting **13**:513
radiation injury **16**:42
wig **20**:146–147
HAIRDRESSING
barber **3**:77
sideburns
Burnside, Ambrose E. **3**:579
HAIRPIECE *see* WIG
HAIRWORM *see* GORDIAN WORM
HAIRY APE, THE (play) **10**:14–15
HAISE, FRED W. **10**:15
Apollo program **2**:83
HAITI **10**:15–16 *bibliog., illus., map, table*
cities
Cap-Haïtien **4**:119
Port-au-Prince **15**:442–443
economic activity **10**:15–16
flag **10**:15 *illus.*
government **10**:16
history **10**:16
Boyer, Jean Pierre **3**:434
Christophe, Henri **4**:416
Dessalines, Jean Jacques **6**:132
Duvalier, François **6**:316
Duvalier, Jean Claude **6**:316
Latin America, history of **12**:221
Louisiana Purchase **12**:435
Pétion, Alexandre Sabès **15**:202
Toussaint L'Ouverture, François **19**:254
land **10**:15 *map, table*
Latin American music and dance **12**:231 *illus.*
map (19° 0′N 72° 25′W) **20**:109
people **10**:15
voodoo **19**:634–635
HAITINK, BERNARD **10**:16–17
HAJJ **2**:101 *illus.*
Arabs **2**:106
Islam **11**:292
HAJJ ABDULLAH *see* PHILBY, H. ST. JOHN
HAJJ UMAR *see* UMAR, AL-HAJJ
HAKE **5**:89 *illus.*; **8**:117 *illus.*; **10**:17 *illus.*
cod **5**:89–90
HAKIM, TAWFIQ AL- **10**:17
HAKLUYT, RICHARD **10**:17 *bibliog.*
Bry, Théodore de **3**:528
HAKODATE (Japan) **10**:17
map (41° 45′N 140° 43′E) **11**:361
HALACHAH **10**:17 *bibliog.*
Judaism **11**:459
midrash **13**:414
HALAS, GEORGE **10**:17
HALASZ, GYULA *see* BRASSAÏ
HALAULA (Hawaii)
map (20° 14′N 155° 46′W) **10**:72
HALAWA, CAPE OF
map (21° 10′N 156° 43′W) **10**:72
HALBA (Lebanon)
map (34° 33′N 36° 5′E) **12**:265
HALBERSTADT (Germany, East and West)
map (51° 54′N 11° 2′E) **9**:140
HALCYONE **10**:17
HALD, EDWARD
Scandinavian art and architecture **17**:114
HALDANE, J. B. S. **10**:17 *bibliog.*
life **12**:327
HALDEMAN, H. R.
Watergate **20**:64
HALDIMAND, SIR FREDERICK **10**:18 *bibliog.*
HALE (county in Alabama)
map (32° 45′N 87° 40′W) **1**:234
HALE (Missouri)
map (39° 36′N 93° 20′W) **13**:476
HALE (county in Texas)
map (34° 2′N 101° 47′W) **19**:129
HALE, EDWARD EVERETT **10**:18 *bibliog.*
HALE, GEORGE ELLERY **10**:18 *bibliog., illus.*
Mount Wilson Observatory **13**:618
Palomar Observatory **15**:52
Yerkes Observatory **20**:326
HALE, JOHN PARKER
New Hampshire **14**:125
HALE, NATHAN **10**:18 *bibliog., illus.*
HALE, SARAH JOSEPHA **10**:19 *bibliog.*
HALE OBSERVATORIES *see* MOUNT WILSON OBSERVATORY; PALOMAR OBSERVATORY
HALEAKALA CRATER **10**:19; **10**:73 *illus.*; **19**:420 *illus.*
map (20° 43′N 156° 13′W) **10**:72
national parks **14**:38–39 *map, table*
HALEIWA (Hawaii)
map (21° 35′N 158° 7′W) **10**:72
HALES, STEPHEN **10**:19
biology **3**:270
photosynthesis **15**:275
HALETHORPE (Maryland)
map (39° 15′N 76° 41′W) **13**:188
HALÉVY, JACQUES **10**:19
HALÉVY, LUDOVIC
Carmen **4**:153
HALEY, ALEX **10**:19 *illus.*
Roots **16**:312
HALEY, BILL
rock music **16**:248
HALEYVILLE (Alabama)
map (34° 14′N 87° 37′W) **1**:234
HALF-LIFE **10**:19–20 *bibliog., illus., table*
beta decay **3**:229
Boltwood, Bertram Borden **3**:372
geologic time **9**:104–105
radiometric age-dating **16**:65
radium isotope **16**:68
Rutherford, Sir Ernest **16**:376
of some naturally occurring atoms **16**:65 *table*
transuranium elements **19**:282
uranium **19**:477
HALF-MOON (fish) *see* CHUB
HALF MOON (ship) *see* HUDSON, HENRY
HALFBEAK **10**:20
HALFTONE **10**:20
photoengraving **15**:260
HALFWAY (Maryland)
map (39° 37′N 77° 46′W) **13**:188
HALFWAY (Oregon)
map (44° 53′N 117° 7′W) **14**:427
HALFWAY COVENANT **10**:20 *bibliog.*
HALFWAY HOUSE
handicapped persons **10**:36
prison **15**:555
psychopathology, treatment of **15**:601
HALIBURTON (Ontario)
map (45° 3′N 78° 3′W) **14**:393; **14**:461
HALIBURTON, T. C. **10**:20 *bibliog.*
Canadian literature **4**:93
HALIBUT **8**:155 *illus.*; **10**:20 *illus.*
HALICARNASSUS (Turkey) **10**:20
mausoleum
Scopas **17**:147
Seven Wonders of the World **17**:217 *illus.*
tomb **19**:230
HALIDE **10**:20
carbon **4**:135
HALIDE EDIB ADIVAR **10**:20–21
HALIDE MINERALS **10**:21
cryolite **5**:370
fluorite **8**:188
mineral **13**:443 *table*
sylvite **18**:402
HALIFAX (North Carolina)
map (36° 20′N 77° 35′W) **14**:242
HALIFAX (county in North Carolina)
map (36° 20′N 77° 40′W) **14**:242
HALIFAX (Nova Scotia) **10**:21; **14**:270 *illus.*
map (44° 39′N 63° 36′W) **14**:269
HALIFAX (Virginia)
map (36° 46′N 78° 56′W) **19**:607
HALIFAX (county in Virginia)
map (36° 45′N 79° 0′W) **19**:607
HALIFAX, CHARLES MONTAGU, 1ST EARL OF **10**:21 *bibliog.*
HALIFAX, EDWARD FREDERICK LINDLEY WOOD, 1ST EARL OF **10**:21 *bibliog.*
HALIL *see* AULOS
HALITE **10**:21
crystallography **5**:374 *illus.*; **13**:439 *illus.*
oceanic mineral resources **14**:340
salt dome **17**:37
HALL (county in Georgia)
map (34° 20′N 83° 50′W) **9**:114
HALL (county in Nebraska)
map (40° 50′N 98° 30′W) **14**:70
HALL (county in Texas)
map (34° 30′N 100° 43′W) **19**:129
HALL, ASAPH
Deimos **6**:85
Phobos **15**:249
United States Naval Observatory **19**:464
HALL, CHARLES FRANCIS **10**:21 *bibliog.*
HALL, CHARLES MARTIN
aluminum **1**:317
HALL, G. STANLEY **10**:21 *bibliog.*
primary education **15**:538
psychology, history of **15**:596; **15**:598 *illus.*
HALL, SIR JAMES **10**:21–22 *bibliog.*
geosyncline **9**:119
HALL, JAMES NORMAN
Mutiny on the Bounty **13**:687
HALL, JOSEPH
satire **17**:88
HALL, MARSHALL
zoology **20**:377
HALL, SIR PETER **10**:22
Waiting for Godot **19**:154 *illus.*
HALL, RICHARD
Zimbabwe Ruins **20**:367
HALL EFFECT **10**:22
HALL-HÉROULT PROCESS
aluminum **1**:317
metallurgy **13**:330
HALL MEADOW BROOK RESERVOIR
map (41° 52′N 73° 10′W) **5**:193
HALLA, MOUNT
map (33° 22′N 126° 32′E) **12**:113
HALLAJ, AL- **10**:22 *bibliog.*
HALLAM, LEWIS
acting **1**:87
HALLANDALE (Florida)
map (25° 59′N 80° 9′W) **8**:172
HALLE (Belgium)
map (50° 44′N 4° 13′E) **3**:177
HALLE (East Germany) **10**:22
map (51° 29′N 11° 58′E) **9**:140
HALLE, ADAM DE LA *see* ADAM DE LA HALLE
HALLÉ, SIR CHARLES **10**:22 *bibliog.*
HALLE DES MACHINES **4**:185 *illus.*
HALLECK, FITZ-GREENE **10**:22 *bibliog.*
HALLECK, HENRY W. **10**:22 *bibliog.*
Civil War, U.S. **5**:25; **5**:27 *illus.*
HALLEIN (Austria)
map (47° 41′N 13° 6′E) **2**:348
HALLETTSVILLE (Texas)
map (29° 27′N 96° 56′W) **19**:129
HALLEY, EDMOND **10**:22–23 *bibliog., illus.*
astronomy, history of **2**:278
HALLEY'S COMET **5**:133–134 *illus.*; **10**:23 *bibliog., illus.*; **18**:51 *illus.*
Clairaut, Alexis Claude **5**:35
Halley, Edmond **10**:23
HALLIDAY (North Dakota)
map (47° 21′N 102° 20′W) **14**:248
HALLIDIE, ANDREW S.
cable car **4**:6
HALLOCK (Minnesota)
map (48° 47′N 96° 57′W) **13**:453
HALLOWEEN **10**:23
HALLOWELL (Maine)
map (44° 17′N 69° 48′W) **13**:70
HALLS (Tennessee)
map (35° 53′N 89° 24′W) **19**:104
HALLSTATT (Austria) **10**:23–24 *bibliog.*
bronze warrior **7**:304 *illus.*
burial **7**:304 *illus.*
Celtic art **4**:239
Celts **4**:241–242 *map*
European prehistory **7**:305
Urnfield culture **19**:487
Vix **19**:623
HALLSTEAD (Pennsylvania)
map (41° 58′N 75° 45′W) **15**:147
HALLSVILLE (Missouri)
map (39° 7′N 92° 13′W) **13**:476
HALLUCINATION **10**:24 *bibliog.*
consciousness, states of **5**:200
fantasy **8**:21
schizophrenia **17**:123
sensory deprivation **17**:205
vertigo **19**:563
HALLUCINOGENS **10**:24 *bibliog.*
alkaloid **1**:296
angel dust **1**:412
consciousness, states of **5**:200
counterculture **5**:311
drug abuse **6**:279
Indians, American **11**:119
LSD **12**:445
marijuana **13**:152–153
mushrooms **13**:661
nutmeg **14**:302
peyote **15**:217
psilocybin **15**:587
psychopathology, treatment of **15**:600 *illus.*
psychotropic drugs **15**:603; **15**:605
synesthesia **18**:407
HALMSTAD (Sweden)
map (56° 39′N 12° 50′E) **18**:382
HALO (art) *see* MANDORLA
HALO (atmosphere) **10**:24 *bibliog.*
HALO, GALACTIC **10**:25
HALOGENS **10**:25
astatine **2**:267
Balard, Antoine Jérôme **3**:33
bromine **3**:502
chlorine **4**:400–401
compounds
halide **10**:20
nitrogen **14**:202
pollutants, chemical **15**:410
fluorine **8**:187–188
Group VIIA periodic table **10**:25
iodine **11**:238–239
ion and ionization **11**:240
reactions
calcium **4**:22
refrigeration **16**:125
salts
halide minerals **10**:21
HALOGETON **10**:25
HALOID COMPANY *see* XEROX CORPORATION
HALON
fire prevention and control **8**:104
HALOTHANE
anesthetics **1**:410
HALPRIN, LAWRENCE **10**:25 *bibliog.*
landscape architecture **12**:188
HALS, FRANS **10**:25 *bibliog., illus.*
Dutch art and architecture **6**:309
impasto **11**:60
Mother and Child **6**:309 *illus.*
Women Regents of the Old Men's Home At Haarlem, The **10**:25 *illus.*
HALSEY (Nebraska)
map (41° 54′N 100° 16′W) **14**:70
HALSEY, WILLIAM F. **10**:25–26 *bibliog.*
HALSTAD (Minnesota)
map (47° 21′N 96° 50′W) **13**:453
HALSTEAD (Kansas)
map (38° 0′N 97° 30′W) **12**:18
HALSTON
fashion design **8**:32
HALTIA MOUNTAIN
map (69° 18′N 21° 16′E) **8**:95
HAM (chimpanzee)
space medicine **18**:132 *illus.*
HAM (meat) *see* MEAT AND MEAT PACKING; PIG
HAM RADIO **10**:26 *bibliog.*
ionosphere **11**:242
Maxim (family) **13**:239
radio **16**:47
HAMA (Syria) **10**:26
map (35° 8′N 36° 45′E) **18**:412
HAMADAN (Iran) **10**:26
map (34° 48′N 48° 30′E) **11**:250
Persian art and architecture **15**:184
HAMADRYAD *see* COBRA
HAMAMATSU (Japan)
map (34° 42′N 137° 44′E) **11**:361
HAMAN **10**:26
HAMAR (Norway)
map (60° 48′N 11° 6′E) **14**:261
HAMBLEN (county in Tennessee)
map (36° 15′N 83° 15′W) **19**:104
HAMBURG (Arkansas)
map (33° 14′N 91° 48′W) **2**:166
HAMBURG (Iowa)
map (40° 36′N 95° 39′W) **11**:244

HAMBURG (New Jersey)
map (41° 9′N 74° 35′W) **14**:129
HAMBURG (New York)
map (42° 43′N 78° 50′W) **14**:149
HAMBURG (Pennsylvania)
map (40° 34′N 75° 59′W) **15**:147
HAMBURG (West Germany) **10**:26–27 *illus.*
fishing industry
herring **10**:147
map (53° 33′N 9° 59′E) **9**:140
medieval times **9**:150 *illus.*
HAMBURGER (meat) *see* FOOD SERVICE SYSTEMS; MEAT AND MEAT PACKING
HAMBURGIAN **10**:27 *bibliog.*
HAMDEN (Connecticut)
map (41° 21′N 72° 56′W) **5**:193
HAMDEN (Ohio)
map (39° 10′N 82° 32′W) **14**:357
HAMDI, IBRAHIM AL-
Yemen (Sana) **20**:326
HAMEAU
landscape architecture **12**:186
HÄMEENLINNA (Finland)
map (61° 0′N 24° 27′E) **8**:95
HAMEL, MARTINE VAN *see* VAN HAMEL, MARTINE
HAMEL, THÉOPILE
Canadian art and architecture **4**:89
HAMELN (Germany, East and West)
map (52° 6′N 9° 21′E) **9**:140
HAMERSLEY RANGE
map (21° 53′S 116° 46′E) **2**:328
HAMGYONG MOUNTAINS
map (41° 50′N 128° 30′E) **12**:113
HAMHUNG (North Korea) **10**:27
map (39° 54′N 127° 32′E) **12**:113
HAMILCAR BARCA **10**:27 *bibliog.*
HAMILL, DOROTHY **10**:27; **11**:14 *illus.*
HAMILTON (Alabama)
map (34° 9′N 88° 6′W) **1**:234
HAMILTON (Bermuda) **10**:27
map (32° 17′N 64° 46′W) **3**:219
HAMILTON (county in Florida)
map (30° 30′N 83° 0′W) **8**:172
HAMILTON (Georgia)
map (32° 45′N 84° 53′W) **9**:114
HAMILTON (county in Illinois)
map (38° 5′N 88° 30′W) **11**:42
HAMILTON (county in Indiana)
map (40° 5′N 86° 3′W) **11**:111
HAMILTON (county in Iowa)
map (42° 23′N 93° 40′W) **11**:244
HAMILTON (Kansas)
map (37° 59′N 96° 10′W) **12**:18
HAMILTON (county in Kansas)
map (38° 0′N 101° 45′W) **12**:18
HAMILTON (Michigan)
map (42° 41′N 86° 0′W) **13**:377
HAMILTON (Missouri)
map (39° 45′N 94° 1′W) **13**:476
HAMILTON (Montana)
map (46° 15′N 114° 9′W) **13**:547
HAMILTON (county in Nebraska)
map (40° 50′N 98° 0′W) **14**:70
HAMILTON (New York)
map (42° 50′N 75° 33′W) **14**:149
HAMILTON (county in New York)
map (43° 40′N 74° 30′W) **14**:149
HAMILTON (New Zealand)
map (37° 47′S 175° 17′E) **14**:158
HAMILTON (North Carolina)
map (35° 57′N 77° 12′W) **14**:242
HAMILTON (Ohio)
map (39° 26′N 84° 30′W) **14**:357
HAMILTON (county in Ohio)
map (39° 6′N 84° 31′W) **14**:357
HAMILTON (Ontario) **10**:27
map (43° 15′N 79° 51′W) **14**:393
HAMILTON (Scotland)
map (55° 47′N 4° 3′W) **19**:403
HAMILTON (county in Tennessee)
map (35° 15′N 85° 5′W) **19**:104
HAMILTON (Texas)
map (31° 42′N 98° 7′W) **19**:129
HAMILTON (county in Texas)
map (31° 40′N 98° 10′W) **19**:129
HAMILTON, ALEXANDER **6**:293 *illus.*; **8**:43 *illus.*; **10**:27–28 *bibliog.*, *illus.*
Bank of the United States **3**:67
Burr, Aaron **3**:579
Coast Guard, U.S. **5**:80
Constitution of the United States **5**:213–214
Coxe, Tench **5**:323
Federalist, The **8**:43
Federalist party **8**:43
Jefferson, Thomas **11**:392–393
Madison, James **13**:41–42
New York (city) **14**:147
Paterson (New Jersey) **15**:111
Schuyler, Philip John **17**:138
state rights **18**:233
United States, history of the **19**:442–443 *illus.*
Washington, George **20**:43
Whiskey Rebellion **20**:133
HAMILTON, ALICE **10**:28–29 *bibliog.*, *illus.*
diseases, occupational **6**:193
HAMILTON, EMMA, LADY **10**:29 *bibliog.*
HAMILTON, GEORGE HEARD **10**:29
HAMILTON, HENRY
American Revolution **1**:359 *map*
Clark, George Rogers **5**:38
HAMILTON, IAN
Gallipoli campaign **9**:20
World War I **20**:231
HAMILTON, LAKE
map (34° 30′N 93° 5′W) **2**:166
HAMILTON, MOUNT
map (37° 21′N 121° 38′W) **4**:31
map (39° 14′N 115° 32′W) **14**:111
HAMILTON, RICHARD **10**:29
HAMILTON, SCOTT **10**:29
HAMILTON, VIRGINIA **10**:29
HAMILTON, W. D.
sociobiology **18**:26
HAMILTON, SIR WILLIAM **10**:29
neoclassicism (art) **14**:81
HAMILTON, SIR WILLIAM ROWAN **10**:29 *bibliog.*
HAMILTON RIVER *see* CHURCHILL RIVER (Newfoundland)
HAMILTON SOUND
map (49° 30′N 54° 30′W) **14**:166
HAMILTON SQUARE (New Jersey)
map (40° 14′N 74° 40′W) **14**:129
HAMITES **1**:145 *map*; **10**:29 *bibliog.*
Galla **9**:16
HAMITIC LANGUAGES
African languages **1**:166 *map*
Asia **2**:244 *map*
Hamites **10**:29
HAMITO-SEMITIC LANGUAGES *see* HAMITIC LANGUAGES; SEMITIC LANGUAGES
HAMLET (North Carolina)
map (34° 53′N 79° 42′W) **14**:242
HAMLET (play) **10**:30 *bibliog.*
dumb show **6**:297
Zealand (Denmark) **20**:357
HAMLIN (county in South Dakota)
map (44° 40′N 97° 12′W) **18**:103
HAMLIN (Texas)
map (32° 53′N 100° 8′W) **19**:129
HAMLIN (West Virginia)
map (38° 17′N 82° 6′W) **20**:111
HAMLIN, HANNIBAL **10**:30 *bibliog.*
HAMM (Germany, East and West)
map (51° 41′N 7° 49′E) **9**:140
HAMMAMET (Tunisia)
map (36° 24′N 10° 37′E) **19**:335
HAMMAN LIT (Tunisia)
map (36° 44′N 10° 20′E) **19**:335
HAMMARSKJÖLD, DAG **10**:30 *bibliog.*, *illus.*
HAMMER (ear bone)
ear **7**:6 *illus.*
HAMMER (tool)
pneumatic **15**:375 *illus.*
HAMMER (weapon)
knight **12**:100 *illus.*
HAMMER, MIKE (fictional character)
Spillane, Mickey **18**:183
HAMMER THROW
track and field **19**:261
HAMMER v. DAGENHART **10**:30
child labor case **10**:30
United States v. *Darby* **19**:465
HAMMERFEST (Norway) **10**:30–31; **14**:262 *illus.*
HAMMERHEAD SHARK **17**:243 *illus.*
HAMMERJAW FISH **6**:78 *illus.*
HÄMMERLING, JOACHIM
Acetabularia **1**:79
HAMMERSTEIN, OSCAR, II **10**:31 *bibliog.*
HAMMETT, DASHIELL **10**:31 *bibliog.*
Maltese Falcon, The **13**:96
HAMMON (Oklahoma)
map (35° 38′N 99° 23′W) **14**:368
HAMMOND (Indiana) **10**:31
map (41° 36′N 87° 30′W) **11**:111
HAMMOND (Louisiana)
map (30° 30′N 90° 28′W) **12**:430
HAMMOND, JAMES HENRY **10**:31
HAMMOND, JAY
Alaska **1**:245
HAMMOND, JOHN **10**:31 *bibliog.*
boogie-woogie **3**:383
HAMMOND, JOHN HAYS, JR. **10**:31
HAMMONDSPORT (New York)
map (42° 25′N 77° 13′W) **14**:149
HAMMONTON (New Jersey)
map (39° 38′N 74° 48′W) **14**:129
HAMMURABI, CODE OF **10**:31 *bibliog.*
Asia, history of **2**:249–250 *illus.*
Babylonian law, Near East influence **10**:31
Hammurabi, King of Babylonia **10**:32
law, history of **12**:244
medicine **13**:267
Mesopotamian art and architecture **13**:320 *illus.*
slavery **17**:352
women in society **20**:201
HAMMURABI, KING OF BABYLONIA **10**:32 *bibliog.*, *illus.*
Hammurabi, Code of **10**:31
Mari **13**:149–150
sculptured head of **13**:317 *illus.*
Stele depicting Hammurabi and Shamash **2**:249 *illus.*; **13**:320 *illus.*
HAMPDEN (county in Massachusetts)
map (42° 7′N 72° 36′W) **13**:206
HAMPDEN (Newfoundland)
map (49° 33′N 56° 51′W) **14**:166
HAMPDEN (North Dakota)
map (48° 32′N 98° 40′W) **14**:248
HAMPDEN, JOHN **10**:32 *bibliog.*
HAMPEL, ANTON JOSEPH
French horn **8**:311–312
HAMPSHIRE (England) **10**:32 *bibliog.*
cities
Portsmouth **15**:448
Southampton **18**:107
Winchester **20**:168
HAMPSHIRE (county in Massachusetts)
map (42° 19′N 72° 38′W) **13**:206
HAMPSHIRE (county in West Virginia)
map (39° 20′N 78° 37′W) **20**:111
HAMPSHIRE, STUART NEWTON **10**:32
HAMPSTEAD (North Carolina)
map (34° 22′N 77° 49′W) **14**:242
HAMPTON (Arkansas)
map (33° 32′N 92° 28′W) **2**:166
HAMPTON (Georgia)
map (33° 23′N 84° 17′W) **9**:114
HAMPTON (Iowa)
map (42° 45′N 93° 12′W) **11**:244
HAMPTON (New Brunswick)
map (45° 32′N 65° 51′W) **14**:117
HAMPTON (New Hampshire)
map (42° 56′N 70° 50′W) **14**:123
HAMPTON (New Jersey)
map (40° 42′N 74° 58′W) **14**:129
HAMPTON (South Carolina)
map (32° 52′N 81° 7′W) **18**:98
HAMPTON (county in South Carolina)
map (32° 45′N 81° 5′W) **18**:98
HAMPTON (Virginia) **10**:32
map (37° 1′N 76° 22′W) **19**:607
HAMPTON, FRED
Black Panther party **3**:318
HAMPTON, LIONEL **10**:32
vibraphone **19**:567
HAMPTON, WADE (1752–1835) **10**:32
HAMPTON, WADE (1818–1902) **10**:32–33 *bibliog.*
HAMPTON BAYS (New York)
map (40° 53′N 72° 31′W) **14**:149
HAMPTON COURT **10**:33 *bibliog.*; **11**:212 *illus.*
HAMPTON ROADS **10**:33
map (36° 58′N 76° 20′W) **19**:607
Norfolk (Virginia) **14**:218
HAMPTON UNIVERSITY **10**:33
HAMRUN (Malta)
map (35° 53′N 14° 29′E) **13**:94
HAMSTER **10**:33 *illus.*
animal experimentation **2**:22
HAMSUN, KNUT **10**:33–34 *bibliog.*, *illus.*; **14**:265 *illus.*
HAMTRAMCK (Michigan)
map (42° 24′N 83° 3′W) **13**:377
HAN (dynasty) **10**:34 *bibliog.*
Asia, history of **2**:253
China, history of **4**:371 *map*
Chinese archaeology **4**:378
Chinese art and architecture **4**:380; **4**:381; **4**:386
Chinese calendar **4**:388
Chinese literature **4**:389
Chow Chow **4**:410 *illus.*
Confucianism **5**:180
funeral customs **4**:379 *illus.*
Han Wu Ti **10**:34
Korean art **12**:117 *illus.*
mounted horseman (statue) **4**:371 *illus.*
temple **19**:98
Wang Mang, Emperor of China **20**:22
HAN-CHUNG (China)
map (32° 59′N 107° 11′E) **4**:362
HAN GAN *see* HAN KAN (Han Gan)
HAN KAN (Han Gan) **10**:34 *bibliog.*
HAN RIVER
map (37° 45′N 126° 11′E) **12**:113
HAN-SHUI RIVER
map (30° 35′N 114° 17′E) **4**:362
HAN-TAN (China)
map (36° 37′N 114° 29′E) **4**:362
HAN WU-TI (Han Wudi) **2**:252 *illus.*; **10**:34
China, history of **4**:371
Han **10**:34
HAN WUDI *see* HAN WU TI (Han Wudi)
HAN-YANG (China) *see* WU-HAN (Wuhan) (China)
HANA (Hawaii)
map (20° 45′N 155° 59′W) **10**:72
HANAHAN (South Carolina)
map (32° 55′N 80° 0′W) **18**:98
HANALEI BAY
map (22° 13′N 159° 31′W) **10**:72
HANAMAULU (Hawaii)
map (21° 59′N 159° 22′W) **10**:72
HANAPEPE (Hawaii)
map (21° 55′N 159° 35′W) **10**:72
HANCEVILLE (British Columbia)
map (51° 55′N 123° 3′W) **3**:491
HANCOCK (county in Georgia)
map (33° 20′N 83° 5′W) **9**:114
HANCOCK (county in Illinois)
map (40° 25′N 91° 5′W) **11**:42
HANCOCK (county in Indiana)
map (39° 47′N 85° 46′W) **11**:111
HANCOCK (county in Iowa)
map (43° 7′N 93° 45′W) **11**:244
HANCOCK (county in Kentucky)
map (37° 50′N 86° 45′W) **12**:47
HANCOCK (county in Maine)
map (44° 40′N 68° 20′W) **13**:70
HANCOCK (Maryland)
map (39° 42′N 78° 11′W) **13**:188
HANCOCK (Michigan)
map (47° 7′N 88° 35′W) **13**:377
HANCOCK (Minnesota)
map (45° 30′N 95° 48′W) **13**:453
HANCOCK (county in Mississippi)
map (30° 35′N 89° 30′W) **13**:469
HANCOCK (New York)
map (41° 57′N 75° 17′W) **14**:149
HANCOCK (county in Ohio)
map (41° 2′N 83° 39′W) **14**:357
HANCOCK (county in Tennessee)
map (36° 35′N 83° 15′W) **19**:104
HANCOCK (county in West Virginia)
map (40° 30′N 80° 33′W) **20**:111
HANCOCK (Wisconsin)
map (44° 8′N 89° 31′W) **20**:185
HANCOCK, JOHN **10**:34 *bibliog.*, *illus.*
Quincy (Massachusetts) **16**:27
HANCOCK, THOMAS
rubber **16**:332
HANCOCK, WALTER KIRTLAND
Stone Mountain **18**:282
HANCOCK, WINFIELD SCOTT **10**:35 *bibliog.*
HAND
artificial hand **2**:221 *illus.*
folk dance **8**:200
human body **10**:296e *illus.*
metal hand **3**:274 *illus.*
muscle **13**:654
primate **15**:539 *illus.*
HAND (county in South Dakota)
map (44° 30′N 99° 0′W) **18**:103
HAND, LEARNED **10**:35 *bibliog.*, *illus.*
HAND AX
Paleolithic Period **15**:38–40 *illus.*
HAND TOOLS **10**:35
adz **1**:114
blowtorch **3**:341
carpentry **4**:164
drill **6**:272–273
knife **18**:397
plane (carpentry) **15**:327
saw **17**:102–103 *illus.*
technology, history of **19**:61 *illus.*
HANDBALL **10**:35 *bibliog.*
See also JAI ALAI
racquetball **16**:38
squash (game) **18**:202
HANDEDNESS **10**:35 *bibliog.*
animal **10**:35
humans **10**:35
preference, theories **10**:35
HANDEL, GEORGE FRIDERIC **10**:36 *bibliog.*, *illus.*
opera **14**:399–400 *illus.*
Oratorio **14**:416
Roubiliac, Louis François **16**:324
Water Music **3**:91 *illus.*
HANDICAPPED PERSONS **10**:36–37 *bibliog.*
architectural barriers **10**:36
birth defects **3**:295
blindness **3**:332–333

HANDICAPPED PERSONS (cont.)
deafness 6:66–67
education 10:36
Head Start 10:85
special education 18:166–167
equal protection of the laws 7:224
institutionalization 11:196–197
Keller, Helen 12:37–38
learning disabilities 12:259–260
marriage and sterilization 10:36
eugenics 7:263
mental health 13:302
mental retardation 13:302
occupational therapy 14:321
physical therapy 15:280
rehabilitation medicine 16:129–130
social and welfare services 18:17–18
Special Olympics 18:168
HANDICRAFTS *see* CRAFT
HANDKE, PETER 10:37 *bibliog., illus.*
HANDLIN, OSCAR 10:37 *bibliog.*
HANDSOME LAKE 10:37 *bibliog.*
HANDWRITING *see* CALLIGRAPHY
HANDY, W. C. 3:312 *illus.*; 10:37 *bibliog., illus.*
Memphis (Tennessee) 13:292
HANEY (British Columbia)
map (49° 13′N 122° 36′W) 3:491
HANFORD (California)
map (36° 20′N 119° 39′W) 4:31
HANFORD, BEN
campaign poster (1904) 18:23 *illus.*
HANG GLIDING 1:122 *illus.*
HANGAYN MOUNTAINS
map (47° 30′N 100° 0′E) 13:529
HANGCHOW (Hangzhou) (China) 10:38
map (30° 15′N 120° 10′E) 4:362
HANGCHOW BAY
map (30° 20′N 121° 0′E) 4:362
HANGING 10:38
lynching 12:476–477
HANGING GARDENS OF BABYLON
Nebuchadnezzar II, King of Babylonia 14:74
Seven Wonders of the World 17:216–217
HANGING VALLEY
glaciers and glaciation 9:193 *illus.*
landform evolution 12:182 *illus.*
HANGZHOU (China) *see* HANGCHOW (Hangzhou) (China)
HANISH ISLANDS
map (13° 45′N 42° 45′E) 20:325
HANKINSON (North Dakota)
map (46° 4′N 96° 54′W) 14:248
HANKOW (China) *see* WU-HAN (Wuhan) (China)
HANMER SPRINGS (New Zealand)
map (42° 31′S 172° 49′E) 14:158
HANNA (Alberta)
map (51° 38′N 111° 54′W) 1:256
HANNA (Oklahoma)
map (35° 12′N 95° 53′W) 14:368
HANNA (Wyoming)
map (41° 52′N 106° 34′W) 20:301
HANNA, MARK 10:38 *bibliog.*
cartoon 4:176 *illus.*; 19:569 *illus.*
McKinley, William 13:30
Republican party 16:174
HANNA CITY (Illinois)
map (40° 42′N 89° 48′W) 11:42
HANNAFORD (North Dakota)
map (47° 19′N 98° 11′W) 14:248
HANNAH (North Dakota)
map (48° 58′N 98° 42′W) 14:248
HANNIBAL (Carthaginian general) 10:38 *bibliog., illus.*
Carthage 4:173
Fabius (family) 8:4
Punic Wars 15:624–625 *illus.*
Rome, ancient 16:298
Salamanca (Spain) 17:29
Scipio Africanus Major 17:147
HANNIBAL (city in Missouri) 10:38
map (39° 42′N 91° 22′W) 13:476
HANNOVER (West Germany) 10:38–39
map (52° 24′N 9° 44′E) 9:140
Seven Years' War 17:218 *map*
HANOI (Vietnam) 10:39 *illus.*
climate 19:581 *table*
map (21° 2′N 105° 51′) 19:580
HANOVER (city in Germany) *see* HANNOVER (West Germany)
HANOVER (dynasty) 10:39 *bibliog.*
George I, King 9:110
George III 9:110–111
George III, King of England, Scotland, and Ireland 9:110–111
George IV, King of England, Scotland, and Ireland 9:111
Salic law 17:32
Settlement, Act of 17:214
Welf (family) 20:97
William IV, King of England, Scotland, and Ireland 20:156
HANOVER (Illinois)
map (42° 15′N 90° 17′W) 11:42
HANOVER (Indiana)
map (38° 43′N 85° 28′W) 11:111
HANOVER (Kansas)
map (39° 54′N 96° 53′W) 12:18
HANOVER (Massachusetts)
map (42° 7′N 70° 49′W) 3:409
HANOVER (New Mexico)
map (32° 48′N 108° 4′W) 14:136
HANOVER (Pennsylvania)
map (39° 48′N 76° 59′W) 15:147
HANOVER (region in Germany) 10:39–40 *map*
Saxony 17:105
HANOVER (town in New Hampshire) 10:39
map (43° 42′N 72° 18′W) 14:123
HANOVER (Virginia)
map (37° 46′N 77° 22′W) 19:607
HANOVER (county in Virginia)
map (37° 42′N 77° 20′W) 19:607
HANOVER PARK (Illinois)
map (42° 0′N 88° 9′W) 11:42
HANS BRINKER, OR THE SILVER SKATES (book)
Dodge, Mary Mapes 6:212
HANSARD (British Columbia)
map (54° 5′N 121° 52′W) 3:491
HANSBERRY, LORRAINE 10:40 *illus.*
Raisin in the Sun, A 16:78
HANSEATIC LEAGUE 10:40–41 *bibliog., map*
centers 13:395 *map*
city-state 5:9
herring 10:147
Lübeck (West Germany) 12:446–447
piracy 15:312
HANSEL AND GRETEL (fairy tale) 10:41
HANSEN, C.F.
Scandinavian art and architecture 17:113
HANSEN, EMIL *see* NOLDE, EMIL
HANSEN'S DISEASE *see* LEPROSY
HANSFORD (county in Texas)
map (36° 15′N 101° 20′W) 19:129
HANSKA (Minnesota)
map (44° 9′N 94° 30′W) 13:453
HANSLICK, EDUARD 10:41 *bibliog.*
music criticism 13:670
Wolf, Hugo 20:196
HANSOM CAB
Central Park (New York City) 14:147 *illus.*
coach and carriage 5:75
HANSON (county in South Dakota)
map (43° 40′N 97° 50′W) 18:103
HANSON, DUANE 10:41 *bibliog.*
photorealism 15:275
HANSON, HOWARD
Eastman School of Music 7:34
HANSON, JOHN 10:41
HANUKKAH *see* CHANUKAH
HAP HAWKINS LAKE
map (44° 58′N 112° 51′W) 13:547
HAPPENINGS 10:41 *bibliog.*
Dine, Jim 6:178
environmental art 7:209–210
Grooms, Red 9:368
Kaprow, Allan 12:25
Klein, Yves 12:96
modern art 13:494–495
Oldenburg, Claes 14:376
Paik, Nam June 15:14–15
Rauschenberg, Robert 16:94
HAPPY (Texas)
map (34° 45′N 101° 52′W) 19:129
HAPPY CAMP (California)
map (41° 48′N 123° 22′W) 4:31
HAPPY VALLEY-GOOSE BAY (Newfoundland)
map (53° 20′N 60° 25′W) 14:166
HAPPY WARRIOR *see* SMITH, ALFRED E.
HAPSBURG (dynasty) *see* HABSBURG (dynasty)
HAR TAVOR *see* TABOR, MOUNT
HARA KEI *see* HARA TAKASHI
HARA-KIRI 10:41 *bibliog.*
suicide 18:330
HARA TAKASHI 10:41
HARAHAN (Louisiana)
map (29° 56′N 90° 12′W) 12:430
HARALSON (county in Georgia)
map (33° 50′N 85° 10′W) 9:114
HARAPPA
Asia, history of 2:250
Indus civilization 11:152–153 *map*
HARAR (Ethiopia) 10:42
HARARE (Zimbabwe) 10:42; 20:365 *illus., table*
map (17° 50′S 31° 3′E) 20:365
HARBIN (China) 4:364 *table*; 10:42
map (45° 45′N 126° 41′E) 4:362
HARBINGER, THE (periodical)
Ripley, George 16:228
HARBOR AND PORT 10:42–44 *bibliog., illus.*
dredging 6:268–269
free port 8:294
major seaports worldwide 19:281 *map*
Rotterdam (Netherlands) 16:323
HARBOR BEACH (Michigan)
map (43° 51′N 82° 39′W) 13:377
HARBOR OF REFUGE
map (38° 19′N 75° 9′W) 6:88
HARBOR SPRINGS (Michigan)
map (45° 26′N 85° 0′W) 13:377
HARBOUR DEEP (Newfoundland)
map (50° 22′N 56° 31′W) 14:166
HARBOUR GRACE (Newfoundland)
map (47° 42′N 53° 13′W) 14:166
HARBOURVILLE (Nova Scotia)
map (45° 9′N 64° 49′W) 14:269
HARCOURT, WILLIAM 10:44
HARD DISK (computer term) 5:160h
HARD-EDGE PAINTING 10:45 *bibliog.*
Albers, Josef 1:253
Anuszkiewicz, Richard 2:72
Hélion, Jean 10:112
Kelly, Ellsworth 12:38–39
minimal art 13:446
modern art 13:494
Moholy-Nagy, László 13:503
Noland, Kenneth 14:213–214
HARD TIMES (book) 10:45
HARDANGER FJORD
map (60° 10′N 6° 0′E) 14:261
HARDAWAY, STEVELAND MORRIS *see* WONDER, STEVIE
HARDBACK, GOLDEN *see* CINQUEFOIL
HARDEE (county in Florida)
map (27° 29′N 81° 48′W) 8:172
HARDEE, WILLIAM J. 10:45
HARDEEVILLE (South Carolina)
map (32° 17′N 81° 5′W) 18:98
HARDEMAN (county in Tennessee)
map (35° 15′N 89° 0′W) 19:104
HARDEMAN (county in Texas)
map (34° 15′N 99° 42′W) 19:129
HARDEN, SIR ARTHUR 10:45
Euler-Chelpin, Hans von 7:265
HARDENBERG, FRIEDRICH BARON VON *see* NOVALIS
HARDENBERG, KARL AUGUST, FÜRST VON 10:45 *bibliog.*
HARDENING 10:45
metallurgy 13:330
HARDERWIJK (Netherlands)
map (52° 21′N 5° 36′E) 14:99
HARDESTY (Oklahoma)
map (36° 37′N 101° 12′W) 14:368
HARDIE, KEIR 10:45 *bibliog.*
HARDIN (Illinois)
map (39° 9′N 90° 37′W) 11:42
HARDIN (county in Illinois)
map (37° 22′N 88° 17′W) 11:42
HARDIN (county in Iowa)
map (42° 23′N 93° 15′W) 11:244
HARDIN (county in Kentucky)
map (37° 40′N 85° 55′W) 12:47
HARDIN (Montana)
map (45° 44′N 107° 37′W) 13:547
HARDIN (county in Ohio)
map (40° 39′N 83° 36′W) 14:357
HARDIN (county in Tennessee)
map (35° 10′N 88° 10′W) 19:104
HARDIN (county in Texas)
map (30° 15′N 94° 22′W) 19:129
HARDIN, JOHN WESLEY
outlaws 14:468
HARDING (county in New Mexico)
map (35° 50′N 103° 50′W) 14:136
HARDING (county in South Dakota)
map (45° 30′N 103° 30′W) 18:103
HARDING, CHESTER 10:45–46 *bibliog.*
HARDING, LAKE
map (32° 45′N 85° 10′W) 1:234
HARDING, LORD
1913 attempt on life of 11:93 *illus.*
HARDING, SAINT STEPHEN 10:46
HARDING, WARREN G. 10:46–47 *bibliog., illus.*
early life 10:46
political convention 15:399
president 10:46–47
Republican party 16:174
Teapot Dome 19:58
United States, history of the 19:454
HARDINSBURG (Kentucky)
map (37° 47′N 86° 28′W) 12:47
HARDISTY (Alberta)
map (52° 40′N 111° 18′W) 1:256
HARDNESS, MINERAL 10:47 *bibliog.*
gems 9:73 *illus.*
mineral identification 13:442
Mohs' scale of hardness 10:47
test materials 10:47
HARDNESS, WATER *see* WATER SOFTENER
HARDOUIN-MANSART, JULES 10:47 *bibliog.*
Grand Trianon bedroom (Versailles) 18:311 *illus.*
HARDTNER (Kansas)
map (37° 1′N 98° 39′W) 12:18
HARDTOP (automobile)
body design 2:359
HARDWARE, COMPUTER *see* COMPUTER HARDWARE
HARDWICK (Georgia)
map (33° 9′N 83° 13′W) 9:114
HARDWICK (Vermont)
map (44° 30′N 72° 22′W) 19:554
HARDWICK, ELIZABETH 10:47
HARDWICK HALL
house (in Western architecture) 10:266
HARDWOOD *see* WOOD (botany)
HARDY (Arkansas)
map (36° 19′N 91° 29′W) 2:166
HARDY (county in West Virginia)
map (39° 5′N 78° 50′W) 20:111
HARDY, ALEXANDRE 10:47
HARDY, GODFREY H.
biology 3:271
evolution 7:319
population genetics 15:439
HARDY, HUGH
Hardy Holzman Pfeiffer Associates 10:48
HARDY, OLIVER *see* LAUREL AND HARDY
HARDY, THOMAS 7:201 *illus.*; 10:47–48 *bibliog., illus.*
Dorset (England) 6:243
Far from the Madding Crowd 8:21
Jude the Obscure 11:464
Return of the Native, The 16:184
Tess of the D'Urbervilles 19:126
HARDY BOYS (fictional characters) 10:48
HARDY HOLZMAN PFEIFFER ASSOCIATES 10:48 *bibliog.*
HARDY-WEINBERG LAW
evolution 7:319
genetics 9:90
population genetics 15:439
HARE (zoology) 2:140–141 *illus.*; 10:48–49 *illus.*
arctic hare 13:104 *illus.*
pika 15:301
rabbit 16:30
HARE, DAVID 10:49 *bibliog.*
HARE, THOMAS
proportional representation 15:572
HARE BAY
map (51° 18′N 55° 50′W) 14:166
HARE BAY (Newfoundland)
map (48° 51′N 54° 1′W) 14:166
HARE-HAWES-CUTTING ACT
Quezon, Manuel Luis 16:25
HARE KRISHNA 10:49 *bibliog.*; 16:142 *illus.*
HARELBEKE (Belgium)
map (50° 51′N 3° 18′E) 3:177
HARELIP *see* CLEFT LIP AND PALATE
HAREM 10:49 *bibliog.*
HARER *see* HARAR (Ethiopia)
HARFORD (county in Maryland)
map (39° 32′N 76° 21′W) 13:188
HARGEISA (Somalia)
map (9° 30′N 44° 3′E) 18:60
HARGRAVE, LAWRENCE
kite (object) 12:92
HARGREAVES, JAMES 10:49
spinning 18:186
HARI, MATA *see* MATA HARI
HARIJANS *see* UNTOUCHABLES
HARINGVLIET
map (51° 47′N 4° 10′E) 14:99
HARIRI, TELL *see* MARI (Syria)
HARIRUD (TEDZHEN) RIVER
map (37° 24′N 60° 38′E) 1:133
HARKARVY, BENJAMIN
Netherlands Dance Theater 14:103
HARKNESS, GEORGIA ELMA 10:49
HARKNESS, REBEKAH
Harkness Ballet 10:49
Joffrey Ballet 11:422
HARKNESS BALLET 10:49 *bibliog.*
HARLAN (family) 10:49 *bibliog.*
HARLAN (Iowa)
map (41° 39′N 95° 19′W) 11:244
HARLAN (Kentucky)
map (36° 51′N 83° 19′W) 12:47

HARLAN (county in Kentucky)
map (36° 55′N 83° 10′W) **12**:47
HARLAN (county in Nebraska)
map (40° 10′N 99° 25′W) **14**:70
HARLAN, JOHN MARSHALL (1833–1911)
Civil Rights Cases **5**:14
Harlan (family) **10**:49
HARLAN, JOHN MARSHALL (1899–1971) **12**:246 *illus.*
Harlan (family) **10**:49
HARLAN COUNTY LAKE
map (40° 4′N 99° 16′W) **14**:70
HARLECH CASTLE (Wales) **20**:11 *illus.*
HARLEM (Georgia)
map (33° 25′N 82° 19′W) **9**:114
HARLEM (Montana)
map (48° 32′N 108° 47′W) **13**:547
HARLEM (New York)
history
Powell, Adam Clayton, Jr. **15**:480
New York (city) **14**:145 *map*
HARLEM (New York City) **10**:49–50
HARLEM GLOBETROTTERS **10**:50 *bibliog.*
basketball **3**:112
HARLEM RENAISSANCE **10**:50 *bibliog.*
black American literature **3**:304
Cullen, Countee **5**:384
Fisher, Rudolph **8**:123
Hughes, Langston **10**:293
Johnson, James Weldon **11**:432
Locke, Alain **11**:387
McKay, Claude **13**:27
Toomer, Jean **19**:236
HARLEM RIVER
map (40° 48′N 73° 56′W) **14**:129
HARLEQUIN **3**:43 *illus.*; **5**:137 *illus.*; **10**:50 *bibliog., illus.*
HARLEQUIN BUG
stinkbug **18**:272
HARLEQUINADE **5**:137 *illus.*
HARLEY, ROBERT, 1st EARL OF OXFORD **10**:50 *bibliog.*
HARLINGEN (Netherlands)
map (53° 10′N 5° 24′E) **14**:99
HARLINGEN (Texas)
map (26° 11′N 97° 42′W) **19**:129
HARLOW, HARRY F. **10**:50–51
emotion
depression **7**:157
HARLOW, JEAN **10**:51 *bibliog.*
HARLOWTON (Montana)
map (46° 26′N 109° 50′W) **13**:547
HARMENSEN, JAKOB *see* ARMINIUS, JACOBUS
HARMODIUS AND ARISTOGITON **10**:51
HARMON (county in Oklahoma)
map (34° 45′N 99° 50′W) **14**:368
HARMONIC MOTION *see* HARMONICS; MOTION, HARMONIC
HARMONICA **10**:51 *bibliog., illus.*
Japanese music **11**:381 *illus.*
sheng **17**:255
HARMONICS (physics) **10**:51 *bibliog.*
harmonic law
Kepler's laws **12**:58
motion, circular **13**:608
musical tone components **10**:51
waves and wave motion **20**:71–72
HARMONIUM
reed organ **16**:118
HARMONY (Indiana)
map (39° 32′N 87° 4′W) **11**:111
HARMONY (Maine)
map (44° 58′N 69° 33′W) **13**:70
HARMONY (music) **10**:51–52 *bibliog., illus.*
See also COUNTERPOINT
Arensky, Anton Stepanovich **2**:145
bass (music) **3**:117
chord **4**:407
figured bass **8**:75
Holst, Gustav **10**:208
madrigal **13**:45
melody **13**:288
music, acoustics of **13**:661–662
music, history of Western **13**:662
HARMONY SOCIETY
New Harmony (Indiana) **14**:126
HARMOSE, HIGH PRIEST OF NEKHEN
Hierakonpolis **10**:159
HARMSWORTH, ALFRED, VISCOUNT NORTHCLIFFE *see* NORTHCLIFFE, ALFRED HARMSWORTH, VISCOUNT
HARMSWORTH, ALFRED SIDNEY *see* ROTHERMERE, HAROLD SIDNEY HARMSWORTH, VISCOUNT
HARNACK, ADOLF VON **10**:52 *bibliog., illus.*
HARNESS **10**:52–53 *illus.*
yoke **20**:329
HARNESS HORSE **10**:53
horse racing **10**:247–248 *illus.*
HARNESS RACING *see* HORSE RACING
HARNETT (county in North Carolina)
map (35° 25′N 78° 50′W) **14**:242
HARNETT, WILLIAM **10**:53 *bibliog., illus.*
illusionism **11**:49–50
My Gems **10**:53 *illus.*
HARNEY (county in Oregon)
map (43° 0′N 117° 0′W) **14**:427
HARNEY LAKE
map (43° 14′N 119° 7′W) **14**:427
HARNEY PEAK
map (44° 0′N 103° 30′W) **18**:103
HARNICK, SHELDON *see* BOCK, JERRY, AND HARNICK, SHELDON
HÄRNÖSAND (Sweden)
map (62° 38′N 17° 56′E) **18**:382
HARO, DON LUIS DE
Philip IV, King of Spain **15**:235
HARO STRAIT
map (48° 30′N 123° 15′W) **20**:35
HAROLD I, KING OF NORWAY (Harold Fairhair) **10**:54 *bibliog.*; **19**:594 *illus.*
HAROLD II, KING OF ENGLAND **10**:53–54 *bibliog.*
Edward the Confessor, King of England **7**:67
William I, King of England (William the Conqueror) **20**:155
HAROLD III, KING OF NORWAY (Harold Hardrada) **10**:54
HARP **10**:54–55 *bibliog., illus.*; **18**:300–301 *illus.*
aeolian harp **1**:119
African **1**:169 *illus.*
musical instruments **13**:677–678 *illus.*
sound frequencies produced **18**:73 *table*
HARPE BROTHERS
outlaws **14**:468
HARPER (Kansas)
map (37° 17′N 98° 1′W) **12**:18
HARPER (county in Kansas)
map (37° 10′N 98° 5′W) **12**:18
HARPER (Liberia)
map (4° 25′N 7° 43′W) **12**:313
HARPER (county in Oklahoma)
map (36° 50′N 99° 40′W) **14**:368
HARPER (Texas)
map (30° 18′N 99° 15′W) **19**:129
HARPER, WILLIAM RAINEY **10**:55 *bibliog.*
Chicago, University of **4**:342
community and junior colleges **5**:151
HARPER'S (periodical) **10**:55 *bibliog.*
Harvey, George **10**:65
HARPERS FERRY (West Virginia) **10**:55 *bibliog.*; **20**:110 *illus.*
raid on federal arsenal (1859)
Brown, John **3**:515
HARPER'S WEEKLY (periodical)
Curtis, George William **5**:395
firing on Fort Sumter **8**:237 *illus.*
Nast, Thomas **14**:25–26
HARPIGNIES, HENRI **10**:55 *bibliog.*
HARPOCRATES *see* HORUS
HARPOON **10**:55
Eskimo **7**:240
whaling **20**:122–123 *illus.*
HARPSICHORD **10**:55–56 *bibliog., illus.*; **13**:678 *illus.*
Chambonnières, Jacques Champion de **4**:275
composers
Bach, Johann Sebastian **3**:11
Couperin (family) **5**:313–314
Frescobaldi, Girolamo **8**:328
Galuppi, Baldassare **9**:23
Graupner, Christoph **9**:302
French music **8**:320–321
keyboard instruments **12**:63 *illus.*
performers
Landowska, Wanda **12**:184
piano **15**:288
spinet **18**:185
HARPY **10**:56
HARPY TOMB
Xanthus **20**:311
HARRAR (Ethiopia) *see* HARAR (Ethiopia)
HARRIER (dog) **6**:216 *illus.*; **10**:56 *illus.*
HARRIER (hawk) *see* HAWK
HARRIMAN (family) **10**:56–57 *bibliog.*
Hill, James Jerome **10**:164
HARRIMAN (Tennessee)
map (35° 56′N 84° 33′W) **19**:104
HARRIMAN RESERVOIR
map (42° 50′N 72° 53′W) **19**:554
HARRINGTON (Delaware)
map (38° 56′N 75° 35′W) **6**:88
HARRINGTON (Washington)
map (47° 29′N 118° 15′W) **20**:35
HARRINGTON, GORDON
behavioral genetics **3**:170
HARRINGTON, JAMES **10**:57 *bibliog.*
HARRINGTON PARK (New Jersey)
map (40° 59′N 73° 59′W) **14**:129
HARRINGTON SOUND
map (32° 19′N 64° 43′W) **3**:219
HARRIOT, THOMAS **10**:57 *bibliog.*
HARRIS (county in Georgia)
map (32° 45′N 84° 55′W) **9**:114
HARRIS (Minnesota)
map (45° 35′N 92° 59′W) **13**:453
HARRIS (county in Texas)
map (29° 50′N 95° 22′W) **19**:129
HARRIS, BENJAMIN **10**:57 *bibliog.*
HARRIS, FRANK **10**:57 *bibliog., illus.*
HARRIS, JOEL CHANDLER **10**:57 *bibliog.*
Emory University **7**:157
Uncle Remus **19**:381
HARRIS, JOHN
encyclopedia **7**:163
HARRIS, JOHN BEYNON *see* WYNDHAM, JOHN
HARRIS, JULIE **10**:57
HARRIS, LAWREN **10**:57–58 *bibliog.*
Maligne Lake, Jasper Park **4**:89 *illus:*
HARRIS, PATRICIA ROBERTS **10**:58
HARRIS, ROBERT
Canadian art and architecture **4**:89
HARRIS, ROY **10**:58 *bibliog.*
Schuman, William Howard **17**:136
HARRIS, THOMAS A.
transactional analysis **19**:267
HARRIS, THOMAS LAKE **10**:58
HARRIS, TOWNSEND **10**:58 *bibliog.*
HARRIS, WILLIAM TORREY **10**:58 *bibliog.*
HARRIS, ZELLIG
linguistics **12**:356–357
HARRIS POLL *see* OPINION POLLS
HARRISBURG (Arkansas)
map (35° 34′N 90° 43′W) **2**:166
HARRISBURG (Illinois)
map (37° 44′N 88° 33′W) **11**:42
HARRISBURG (Nebraska)
map (41° 33′N 103° 44′W) **14**:70
HARRISBURG (Pennsylvania) **10**:58
map (40° 16′N 76° 52′W) **15**:147
HARRISON (Arkansas)
map (36° 14′N 93° 7′W) **2**:166
HARRISON (Idaho)
map (47° 27′N 116° 47′W) **11**:26
HARRISON (county in Indiana)
map (38° 13′N 86° 7′W) **11**:111
HARRISON (county in Iowa)
map (41° 38′N 93° 45′W) **11**:244
HARRISON (county in Kentucky)
map (38° 25′N 84° 19′W) **12**:47
HARRISON (Michigan)
map (44° 1′N 84° 48′W) **13**:377
HARRISON (county in Mississippi)
map (31° 30′N 89° 5′W) **13**:469
HARRISON (county in Missouri)
map (40° 20′N 94° 0′W) **13**:476
HARRISON (Nebraska)
map (42° 41′N 103° 53′W) **14**:70
HARRISON (county in Ohio)
map (40° 16′N 81° 5′W) **14**:357
HARRISON (county in Texas)
map (32° 30′N 94° 25′W) **19**:129
HARRISON (county in West Virginia)
map (39° 18′N 80° 20′W) **20**:111
HARRISON, BENJAMIN **10**:58–59 *bibliog., illus.*
early career **10**:58–59
Indianapolis (Indiana) **11**:115
president **10**:59
Republican party **16**:173
HARRISON, GEORGE **16**:58 *illus.*
Beatles, The **3**:144–145 *illus.*
rock music **16**:248 *illus.*
Shankar, Ravi **17**:240
HARRISON, JOHN **10**:59–60
navigation **14**:60
HARRISON, PETER **10**:60 *bibliog.*
HARRISON, REX **10**:60 *bibliog.*
musical comedy **13**:673 *illus.*
HARRISON, WALLACE K. **10**:60
Metropolitan Opera **13**:348
stained glass **18**:212
United Nations Headquarters **13**:492 *illus.*
HARRISON, WILLIAM HENRY **10**:60–61 *bibliog., illus.*
early life **10**:60–61
Log Cabin Almanac **20**:130 *illus.*
political career **10**:61
Tippecanoe, Battle of **19**:207
Whig party (United States) **20**:130 *illus.*
HARRISON LAKE
map (49° 30′N 121° 50′W) **3**:491
HARRISONBURG (Louisiana)
map (31° 46′N 91° 49′W) **12**:430
HARRISONBURG (Virginia)
map (36° 34′N 78° 58′W) **19**:607
HARRISONVILLE (Missouri)
map (38° 39′N 94° 21′W) **13**:476
HARRISVILLE (Michigan)
map (44° 39′N 83° 17′W) **13**:377
HARRISVILLE (New York)
map (44° 9′N 75° 19′W) **14**:149
HARRISVILLE (West Virginia)
map (39° 13′N 81° 3′W) **20**:111
HARRODSBURG (Kentucky)
map (37° 46′N 84° 51′W) **12**:47
HARROGATE (England) **10**:61
map (54° 0′N 1° 33′W) **19**:403
HARROW (farm machinery) **10**:61 *bibliog.*
HARROW SCHOOL **10**:61
HARRY S TRUMAN RESERVOIR
map (38° 10′N 93° 45′W) **13**:476
HARRY STRUNK LAKE
map (40° 23′N 100° 13′W) **14**:70
HARSHA, INDIAN KING
Gupta (dynasty) **9**:406
HART (county in Georgia)
map (34° 20′N 83° 0′W) **9**:114
HART (county in Kentucky)
map (37° 20′N 85° 55′W) **12**:47
HART (Michigan)
map (43° 42′N 86° 22′W) **13**:377
HART (Texas)
map (34° 23′N 102° 7′W) **19**:129
HART, SIR BASIL LIDDELL *see* LIDDELL HART, SIR BASIL
HART, GARY **10**:61
HART, H. L. A. **10**:61–62
law **12**:242–243
state (in political philosophy) **18**:233
HART, LORENZ **10**:62 *bibliog.*
HART, MOSS **10**:62
HART, WILLIAM S. **10**:62
HART MEMORIAL TROPHY
Howe, Gordie **10**:283
Hull, Bobby **10**:296
Orr, Bobby **14**:448
Richard, Maurice **16**:209
HART MOUNTAIN
map (52° 29′N 101° 25′W) **13**:119
HARTACK, BILL **10**:62
HARTE, BRET **10**:62 *bibliog.*
HARTEBEEST **2**:46 *illus.*
HARTFORD (Alabama)
map (31° 6′N 85° 42′W) **1**:234
HARTFORD (Arkansas)
map (35° 1′N 94° 23′W) **2**:166
HARTFORD (Connecticut) **5**:194 *illus.*; **10**:62
map (41° 46′N 72° 41′W) **5**:193
HARTFORD (county in Connecticut)
map (41° 46′N 72° 41′W) **5**:193
HARTFORD (Kansas)
map (38° 18′N 95° 58′W) **12**:18
HARTFORD (Kentucky)
map (37° 27′N 86° 55′W) **12**:47
HARTFORD (Michigan)
map (42° 12′N 86° 10′W) **13**:377
HARTFORD (Wisconsin)
map (43° 19′N 88° 22′W) **20**:185
HARTFORD, HUNTINGTON **10**:62
HARTFORD CITY (Indiana)
map (40° 27′N 85° 22′W) **11**:111
HARTFORD CONVENTION **10**:62 *bibliog.*
United States, history of the **19**:444
War of 1812 **20**:27
HARTFORD WITS *see* CONNECTICUT WITS
HARTIGAN, GRACE **10**:62
HARTINGTON (Nebraska)
map (42° 37′N 97° 16′W) **14**:70
HARTLAND (Maine)
map (44° 53′N 69° 27′W) **13**:70
HARTLAND (New Brunswick)
map (46° 18′N 67° 32′W) **14**:117
HARTLAND (Wisconsin)
map (43° 6′N 88° 21′W) **20**:185
HARTLEPOOL (England) **10**:62
map (54° 42′N 1° 11′W) **19**:403
HARTLEY (Iowa)
map (43° 11′N 95° 29′W) **11**:244
HARTLEY (Texas)
map (35° 53′N 102° 24′W) **19**:129
HARTLEY (county in Texas)
map (35° 50′N 102° 38′W) **19**:129
HARTLEY, DAVID
associationism **2**:265–266

HARTLEY, MARSDEN **10**:63 *bibliog., illus.*
Painting Number 5 **10**:63 *illus.*
HARTMANN, EDUARD VON **10**:63 *bibliog.*
HARTMANN, HEINZ
moral awareness **13**:573
psychoanalysis **15**:590
HARTMANN, NICOLAI **10**:63 *bibliog.*
HARTMANN VON AUE **10**:63
HARTOG, JAN DE **10**:63
HARTSELLE (Alabama)
map (34° 27′N 86° 56′W) **1**:234
HARTSHORNE (Oklahoma)
map (34° 51′N 95° 34′W) **14**:368
HARTSHORNE, CHARLES **10**:63 *bibliog.*
HARTSVILLE (South Carolina)
map (34° 23′N 80° 4′W) **18**:98
HARTSVILLE (Tennessee)
map (36° 24′N 86° 10′W) **19**:104
HARTT, FREDERICK **10**:63
HARTUNG, HANS **10**:64 *bibliog.*
HARTVILLE (Missouri)
map (37° 15′N 92° 31′W) **13**:476
HARTWELL (Georgia)
map (34° 21′N 82° 56′W) **9**:114
HARTWELL LAKE
map (34° 30′N 82° 55′W) **18**:98
HARUN AL-RASHID **10**:64 *bibliog.*
Arabian Nights **2**:100
Arabs **2**:102
Mashhad (Iran) **13**:196
HARUNOBU **10**:64 *bibliog.*
Courtesan **19**:375 *illus.*
HARVARD (Illinois)
map (42° 25′N 88° 37′W) **11**:42
HARVARD (Nebraska)
map (40° 37′N 98° 6′W) **14**:70
HARVARD CENTER FOR COGNITIVE STUDIES
Bruner, Jerome Seymour **3**:525
HARVARD CLASSIFICATION OF STARS **10**:64
Cannon, Annie Jump **4**:112
distance, astronomical **6**:199
Harvard College Observatory **10**:64
Henry Draper Catalogue **10**:123
star spectra **18**:223 *illus.*
HARVARD COLLEGE OBSERVATORY **10**:64 *bibliog.*
Bond, William Cranch **3**:376
Menzel, Donald Howard **13**:303
Payne-Gaposchkin, Cecilia **15**:122
Pickering, Edward Charles **15**:293
Shapley, Harlow **17**:241
HARVARD MOUNT
map (38° 55′N 106° 19′W) **5**:116
HARVARD MUSEUM FOR COMPARATIVE ZOOLOGY
Simpson, George Gaylord **17**:317
HARVARD UNIVERSITY **10**:64 *bibliog.*; **13**:209 *illus.*
architecture
Sert, José Luis **17**:210
Conant, James Bryant **5**:168
Dumbarton Oaks **6**:297–298
Eliot, Charles William **7**:138
football **8**:216
Graduate Center **9**:369 *illus.*
Hamilton, Alice **10**:28–29
humanities, education in the **10**:300
Jencks, Christopher **11**:395
Keppel, Francis **12**:58
Law School
Langdell, Christopher Columbus **12**:195
Lowell, Abbott Lawrence **12**:443
Putnam, Frederic Ward **15**:632
Quincy, Josiah **16**:27
Radcliffe College **16**:41
Rumford, Benjamin Thomson, Count **16**:344–345
HARVEST FISH *see* BUTTERFISH
HARVEST FLY *see* CICADA
HARVEST MITE *see* CHIGGER
HARVESTER (farm machinery) **1**:192–193 *illus.*; **10**:65 *bibliog.*; **13**:457 *illus.*
combine **5**:130–131 *illus.*
cotton **1**:237 *illus.*
reaper **16**:104 *illus.*
HARVESTMAN *see* DADDY LONGLEGS
HARVEY (film) **18**:266 *illus.*
HARVEY (Illinois)
map (41° 37′N 87° 39′W) **11**:42
HARVEY (county in Kansas)
map (38° 0′N 97° 25′W) **12**:18
HARVEY (Louisiana)
map (29° 54′N 90° 5′W) **12**:430
HARVEY (New Brunswick)
map (45° 43′N 64° 43′W) **14**:117
HARVEY (North Dakota)
map (47° 47′N 99° 56′W) **14**:248
HARVEY, GEORGE **10**:65 *bibliog.*
HARVEY, WILLIAM **1**:396 *illus.*; **10**:65 *bibliog., illus.*
biology **3**:268
blood circulation and heart function **10**:65
Fabricius ab Aquapendente, Hieronymus **8**:5
Galen **9**:13
Malpighi, Marcello **13**:93
medicine **13**:269–270 *illus.*
physiology **15**:287
On the Motion of the Heart **13**:270 *illus.*
HARVEY MUDD COLLEGE
Claremont Colleges **5**:36
HARVEY'S WEEKLY (periodical)
Harvey, George **10**:65
HARWICH (England) **10**:65
HARWICH (Massachusetts)
map (41° 41′N 70° 1′W) **13**:206
HARWICH PORT (Massachusetts)
map (41° 40′N 70° 5′W) **13**:206
HARYANA (India) **10**:65
cities
Chandigarh **4**:279
map (29° 20′N 76° 20′E) **11**:80
HARZ **10**:65
HASAN ALI SHAH
Aga Khan **1**:181
HASANLU (Iran) **10**:65
Persian art and architecture **15**:184
HASAPIKOS **10**:66
HASBAYYA (Lebanon)
map (33° 24′N 35° 41′E) **12**:265
HASBROUCK HEIGHTS (New Jersey)
map (40° 52′N 74° 4′W) **14**:129
HASDRUBAL **10**:66
Punic Wars **15**:624
HASEGAWA TOHAKU *see* TOHAKU
HAŠEK, JAROSLAV **10**:66 *bibliog.*
Good Soldier Schweik, The **9**:245
HASHEMITE KINGDOM OF JORDAN *see* JORDAN
HASHIMOTO, TEIZO
kite (object) **12**:92 *illus.*
HASHISH (drug)
hemp **10**:120
marijuana **13**:152
HASIDEANS **10**:66 *bibliog.*
HASIDISM **10**:66 *bibliog.*
See also HASIDEANS
Baal Shem Tov **3**:5
Judaism **11**:462
Kabbalah **12**:3
HAŞIM, AHMET *see* AHMET HAŞIM
HASKELL (county in Kansas)
map (37° 35′N 100° 50′W) **12**:18
HASKELL (Oklahoma)
map (35° 50′N 95° 40′W) **14**:368
HASKELL (county in Oklahoma)
map (35° 15′N 95° 5′W) **14**:368
HASKELL (Texas)
map (33° 10′N 99° 44′W) **19**:129
HASKELL (county in Texas)
map (33° 8′N 99° 42′W) **19**:129
HASKINS, DE WITT
tunnel **19**:338
HASMONEANS *see* MACCABEES (family)
HASSAM, CHILDE **10**:66–67 *bibliog., illus.*
Boston Common at Dusk **10**:66 *illus.*
HASSAN II, KING OF MOROCCO **10**:67
HASSANI, ALI NASSER MUHAMMAD AL-
Yemen (Aden) **20**:324
HASSE, JOHANN ADOLPH **10**:67 *bibliog.*
HASSEL, ODD **10**:67
HASSELT (Belgium)
map (50° 56′N 5° 20′E) **3**:177
HÄSSLEHOLM (Sweden)
map (56° 9′N 13° 46′E) **18**:382
HASSLER, HANS LEO **10**:67 *bibliog.*
HASSON, TOM
musical comedy **13**:674 *illus.*
HASTINGS (Barbados)
map (13° 4′N 59° 35′W) **3**:75
HASTINGS (England) **10**:67
map (50° 51′N 0° 36′E) **19**:403
HASTINGS (Florida)
map (29° 40′N 81° 30′W) **8**:172
HASTINGS (Michigan)
map (42° 39′N 85° 17′W) **13**:377
HASTINGS (Minnesota)
map (44° 44′N 92° 51′W) **13**:453
HASTINGS (Nebraska)
map (40° 35′N 98° 23′W) **14**:70
HASTINGS (New Zealand)
map (39° 38′S 176° 51′E) **14**:158
HASTINGS, BATTLE OF **9**:310 *illus.*; **10**:67 *bibliog.*
armor **2**:174
Bayeux Tapestry **3**:133; **14**:222 *illus.*
William I, King of England (William the Conqueror) **20**:155
HASTINGS, LANSFORD W.
Donner Party **6**:240
HASTINGS, THOMAS
Carrère and Hastings **4**:168
hymn **10**:347
HASTINGS, WARREN **10**:67 *bibliog., illus.*
India, history of **11**:92
HASTY (Colorado)
map (38° 7′N 102° 58′W) **5**:116
HASWELL (Colorado)
map (38° 27′N 103° 9′W) **5**:116
HAT
bowler **7**:275 *illus.*
costume **5**:293–302 *illus.*
HAT YAI (Thailand)
map (7° 1′N 100° 28′E) **19**:139
HATCH (New Mexico)
map (32° 40′N 107° 9′W) **14**:136
HATCH (Utah)
map (37° 39′N 112° 26′W) **19**:492
HATCH, CARL
Hatch Acts **10**:68
HATCH, WILLIAM H.
Hatch Acts **10**:68
HATCH ACTS **10**:68
1887 act
agriculture, history of **1**:192
HATCHBACK (automobile)
body design **2**:359
HATCHET LAKE (Nova Scotia)
map (44° 35′N 63° 40′W) **14**:269
HATCHETFISH **10**:68 *illus.*
HATCHING SNAKE **17**:381 *illus.*
HATFIELD (Arkansas)
map (34° 29′N 94° 23′W) **2**:166
HATFIELD (Massachusetts)
map (42° 22′N 72° 36′W) **13**:206
HATFIELDS AND McCOYS
feud **8**:63
HATHA YOGA
yoga **20**:329
HATHAWAY, ANNE
Shakespeare, William **17**:236
HATHAWEKELA (American Indians)
Shawnee **17**:246
HATHOR (Egyptian deity) **7**:87 *illus.*; **10**:68
Dendera **6**:106
Edfu **7**:56
HATO MAYOR (Dominican Republic)
map (18° 46′N 69° 15′W) **6**:233
HATOYAMA ICHIRO **10**:68
HATRA (Iraq) **10**:68
HATSHEPSUT, QUEEN OF EGYPT **10**:68
Deir el-Bahri **6**:86
Senmut **17**:203
HATTERAS, CAPE **10**:68; **14**:245 *illus.*
Gulf Stream **9**:403
map (35° 13′N 75° 32′W) **14**:242
HATTERSLEY, MARTIN
Canada **4**:79
HATTI
Hittite art and architecture **10**:188
languages, extinct **12**:198
HATTIESBURG (Mississippi)
map (31° 19′N 89° 16′W) **13**:469
HATTON (North Dakota)
map (47° 38′N 97° 27′W) **14**:248
HATTUSA *see* BOĞAZKÖY (Turkey)
HAUCH, JOHANNES CARSTEN **10**:68
HAUGESUND (Norway)
map (59° 25′N 5° 18′E) **14**:261
HAUGHEY, CHARLES JAMES **10**:68–69
Ireland, history of **11**:265
HAUKSBEE, FRANCIS
physics, history of **15**:283
HAUPT v. UNITED STATES
treason **19**:285
HAUPTMANN, BRUNO RICHARD **10**:69 *bibliog.*
HAUPTMANN, GERHART **10**:69 *bibliog., illus.*
HAURAKI GULF
map (36° 20′S 175° 5′E) **14**:158
HAUSA **10**:69 *bibliog.*
African music **1**:168–171 *illus.*
Afroasiatic languages **1**:180
Nigeria **14**:192
Usman dan Fodio **19**:491
HAUSA (Morocco)
map (27° 6′N 10° 55′W) **13**:585
HAUSHOFER, KARL
geopolitics **9**:109
HAUSSMANN, GEORGES EUGÈNE, BARON **10**:69 *bibliog.*
Paris **15**:86
HAUT SÛRE, LAKE
map (49° 54′N 5° 53′E) **12**:472
HAUTECLOQUE, PHILIPPE, VICOMTE DE *see* LECLERC, JACQUES PHILIPPE
HAUULA (Hawaii)
map (21° 37′N 157° 55′W) **10**:72
HAÜY, RENÉ-JUST **10**:69–70 *bibliog.*
crystal **5**:374
mineral **13**:439
HAVANA (Arkansas)
map (35° 7′N 93° 32′W) **2**:166
HAVANA (Cuba) **5**:378 *illus.*; **5**:379 *illus.*; **10**:70 *map*
climate **5**:378 table; **14**:228 *table*
history
street scene (c.1515) **12**:218 *illus.*
Velázquez de Cuéllar, Diego **19**:537
map (23° 8′N 82° 22′W) **5**:377
HAVANA (Illinois)
map (40° 18′N 90° 4′W) **11**:42
HAVANA (North Dakota)
map (45° 57′N 97° 37′W) **14**:248
HAVANA BROWN CAT **4**:195 *illus.*; **10**:71 *illus.*
HAVASU, LAKE
map (34° 30′N 114° 20′W) **2**:160
HAVEL, VÁCLAV **10**:71
HAVELL, E. B.
Indian art and architecture **11**:98
HAVELOCK (North Carolina)
map (34° 53′N 76° 54′W) **14**:242
HAVELOCK (Ontario)
map (55° 26′N 77° 53′W) **14**:393; **14**:461
HAVELOCK (Swaziland)
map (25° 56′S 31° 6′E) **18**:380
HAVEN (Kansas)
map (37° 54′N 97° 47′W) **12**:18
HAVERFORD COLLEGE **10**:71
HAVERHILL (Massachusetts)
map (42° 47′N 71° 5′W) **13**:206
HAVERMAN, MARGARETA
Huysum, Jan van **10**:326
HAVERSIAN SYSTEMS (anatomy)
bone **3**:377 *illus.*
HAVERSTRAW (New York)
map (41° 12′N 73° 58′W) **14**:149
HAVILAND (Kansas)
map (37° 37′N 99° 6′W) **12**:18
HAVILAND, WILLIAM
French and Indian Wars **8**:313 *map*
HAVILAND CHINA *see* LIMOGES WARE
HAVILLAND, OLIVIA DE *see* DE HAVILLAND, OLIVIA
HAVLICEK, JOHN **10**:71 *bibliog.*
HAVRE (Montana)
map (48° 33′N 109° 41′W) **13**:547
HAVRE DE GRACE (Maryland)
map (39° 33′N 76° 6′W) **13**:188
HAVRE-SAINT-PIERRE (Quebec)
map (50° 14′N 63° 36′W) **16**:18
HAW KNOB MOUNTAIN
map (35° 19′N 84° 2′W) **19**:104
HAWAII (island) **10**:71
Hawaii (state) **10**:73
Hilo **10**:165
Liliuokalani, Queen of Hawaii **12**:341
map (19° 30′N 155° 30′W) **10**:72
HAWAII (state) **10**:71–76 *bibliog., illus., map*
agriculture **10**:74–75 *illus.*
art
Oceanic art **14**:336–339
cities
Hilo **10**:165
Honolulu **10**:223
climate **10**:73–74
cultural institutions **10**:74
economy **10**:74–76 *illus.*
education **10**:74
Hawaii, University of **10**:76
flag **10**:71 *illus.*
government and politics **10**:74
historic sites **10**:74
history **10**:76
Cook, James **5**:236
Dole, Sanford Ballard **6**:224
Kamehameha (dynasty) **12**:9
Liliuokalani, Queen of Hawaii **12**:341
incest **11**:74
islands
Hawaii (island) **10**:71
Maui **13**:233
Oahu **14**:311
land and resources **10**:71–74 *illus., map*
lava **12**:240
mountain **13**:619
physiographic regions **10**:73
volcano **19**:627
map (20° 0′N 157° 45′W) **10**:72
music and dance

hula **10**:295
ukulele **19**:376
people **10**:74
Oriental Americans **14**:442 *illus.*
race **16**:34 *illus.*
physical features
Haleakla Crater **10**:19
Kilauea **12**:76
Mauna Kea **13**:233
Mauna Loa **13**:233–234
sampan **17**:48
seal, state **10**:71 *illus.*
surfing **18**:359
tourism **10**:75
vegetation and animal life **10**:74
HAWAII, UNIVERSITY OF 10:76
Mauna Kea Observatory **13**:233
HAWAII VOLCANOES NATIONAL PARK
Mauna Loa **13**:233–234
HAWAIIAN GOOD LUCK PLANT *see* TI
HAWAIIAN HONEYCREEPER 10:76
HAWALLI (Kuwait)
map (29° 19′N 48° 2′E) **12**:141
HAWAR ISLAND
map (25° 40′N 50° 45′E) **3**:24
HAWARDEN (Iowa)
map (43° 0′N 96° 29′W) **11**:244
HAWES, JOSIAH JOHNSON
photography, history and art of **15**:269
Southworth, Albert Sands, and Hawes, Josiah Johnson **18**:112–113
HAWESVILLE (Kentucky)
map (37° 54′N 86° 45′W) **12**:47
HAWI (Hawaii)
map (20° 14′N 155° 50′W) **10**:72
HAWICK (Scotland)
map (55° 25′N 2° 47′W) **19**:403
HAWK 10:76–77 *bibliog., illus.*
birds of prey **3**:290–291
eagle **7**:3–4
eye **3**:285 *illus.*
falcon **8**:12
falconry **8**:12–13
kite (bird) **12**:91–92
red-tailed hawk **9**:300 *illus.*
HAWKE, ROBERT 10:77
HAWKE BAY
map (39° 20′S 177° 30′E) **14**:158
HAWKER HARRIER JET HELICOPTER **19**:639 *illus.*
HAWKES, JOHN 10:77 *bibliog.*
HAWKESBURY (Ontario)
map location (45° 36′N 74° 37′W) **14**:393; **14**:461
HAWKFISH 10:77
HAWKING *see* FALCONRY
HAWKING, STEPHEN WILLIAM 10:77 *bibliog.*
HAWKINS (county in Tennessee)
map (36° 30′N 83° 0′W) **19**:104
HAWKINS (Wisconsin)
map (45° 31′N 90° 43′W) **20**:185
HAWKINS, ANTHONY HOPE *see* HOPE, ANTHONY (pseudonym)
HAWKINS, COLEMAN 10:77 *bibliog.*
HAWKINS, ERICK 10:77 *bibliog.*
HAWKINS, SIR JOHN 10:77–78 *bibliog.*
Drake, Sir Francis **6**:256
HAWKINS, JOHN ISAAC
piano **15**:289 *illus.*
HAWKINSVILLE (Georgia)
map (32° 17′N 83° 28′W) **9**:114
HAWKS, HOWARD 10:78 *bibliog.*
HAWKSBILL MOUNTAIN
map (38° 33′N 78° 23′W) **19**:607
HAWKSMOOR, NICHOLAS 10:78 *bibliog.*
Blenheim Palace **3**:330
HAWKWEED 10:78
HAWKWOOD, SIR JOHN 10:78
Uccello, Paolo **19**:370
HAWLEY (Pennsylvania)
map (41° 28′N 75° 11′W) **15**:147
HAWLEY-SMOOT TARIFF ACT
Smoot, Reed **17**:374
tariff acts **19**:36–37
HAWORTH (New Jersey)
map (40° 58′N 73° 59′W) **14**:129
HAWORTH, SIR WALTER NORMAN 10:78
HAWTHORN 8:228 *illus.*; **10**:78–79 *illus.*
HAWTHORNE (California)
map (33° 55′N 118° 21′W) **4**:31
HAWTHORNE (Florida)
map (29° 36′N 82° 5′W) **8**:172
HAWTHORNE (Nevada)
map (38° 32′N 118° 38′W) **14**:111
HAWTHORNE (New Jersey)
map (40° 57′N 74° 9′W) **14**:129
HAWTHORNE, NATHANIEL 10:79 *bibliog., illus.*
House of the Seven Gables, The **10**:274
Lathrop, Rose Hawthorne **12**:216
Salem (Massachusetts) **17**:31
Scarlett Letter, The **17**:116
HAWTHORNE EFFECT
Hawthorne studies **10**:79
HAWTHORNE STUDIES 10:79 *bibliog.*
Mayo, Elton **13**:248
HAXTUN (Colorado)
map (40° 39′N 102° 38′W) **5**:116
HAY 10:80
sorghum **18**:69
timothy **19**:203
HAY, JOHN M. 10:80 *bibliog.*
McKinley, William **13**:30–31
Open Door Policy **14**:398
HAY-BUNAU-VARILLA TREATY
Panama Canal Zone **15**:57
HAY FEVER
antihistamine **2**:63
HAY-PAUNCEFOTE TREATY 10:80
Hay, John M. **10**:80
HAY RIVER
map (60° 52′N 115° 44′W) **4**:70
HAY RIVER (Northwest Territories)
map (60° 51′N 115° 40′W) **14**:258
HAY SPRINGS (Nebraska)
map (42° 41′N 102° 41′W) **14**:70
HAY TREATIES *see* HAY-PAUNCEFOTE TREATY
HAYAKAWA, S. I. 10:80 *bibliog.*
HAYASHI EVOLUTIONARY TRACK 10:80
HAYDÉE, MARCIA 10:80 *bibliog.*
Stuttgart Ballet **18**:310
HAYDEN (Arizona)
map (33° 0′N 110° 47′W) **2**:160
HAYDEN (Colorado)
map (40° 30′N 107° 16′W) **5**:116
HAYDEN, CARL 10:80
HAYDEN, FERDINAND 10:80–81 *bibliog.*
United States Geological Survey **19**:462
HAYDEN, MELISSA 10:81
HAYDEN, ROBERT 10:81
HAYDEN, TOM
counterculture **5**:311
HAYDN, FRANZ JOSEF 4:272 *illus.*; **5**:41–42 *illus.*; **10**:81 *bibliog., illus.*
music, history of Western **13**:665–666 *illus.*
scherzo **17**:119
string quartet **18**:300 *illus.*
symphony **18**:405
HAYDN, MICHAEL 10:81–82 *bibliog.*
HAYDON, BENJAMIN ROBERT 10:82 *bibliog.*
HAYEK, FRIEDRICH AUGUST VON 10:82 *bibliog.*
HAYES (Louisiana)
map (30° 6′N 92° 56′W) **12**:430
HAYES (county in Nebraska)
map (40° 30′N 101° 5′W) **14**:70
HAYES, HELEN 10:82 *bibliog.*
HAYES, MOUNT
map (63° 37′N 146° 43′W) **1**:242
HAYES, RUTHERFORD B. 10:82–83 *bibliog., illus.*
Reconstruction **16**:110
Republican party **16**:173
HAYES CENTER (Nebraska)
map (40° 31′N 101° 1′W) **14**:70
HAYES RIVER
map (57° 3′N 92° 9′W) **13**:119
HAYESVILLE (North Carolina)
map (35° 3′N 83° 49′W) **14**:242
HAYFIELD (Minnesota)
map (43° 53′N 92° 51′W) **13**:453
HAYFORK (California)
map (40° 33′N 123° 11′W) **4**:31
HAYKAL, MUHAMMED HUSAYN
Egypt **7**:77
HAYMARKET RIOT 10:83 *bibliog., illus.*
HAYMARKET THEATRE 10:83
Foote, Samuel **8**:219
Tree, Sir Herbert Beerbohm **19**:288
HAYNE, ROBERT YOUNG 10:83–84 *bibliog.*
HAYNES (Arkansas)
map (34° 53′N 90° 47′W) **2**:166
HAYNESVILLE (Louisiana)
map (32° 58′N 93° 8′W) **12**:430
HAYNEVILLE (Alabama)
map (32° 6′N 86° 35′W) **1**:234
HAYS (Kansas)
map (38° 53′N 99° 20′W) **12**:18
HAYS (Montana)
map (48° 3′N 108° 43′W) **13**:547
HAYS (county in Texas)
map (30° 0′N 98° 0′W) **19**:129
HAYS, MARY LUDWIG *see* MOLLY PITCHER
HAYS, WILL 10:84
film, history of **8**:82; **8**:84
HAYS CODE *see* HAYS, WILL
HAYSVILLE (Kansas)
map (37° 34′N 97° 21′W) **12**:18
HAYTER, STANLEY WILLIAM 10:84 *bibliog.*
graphic arts **9**:293
HAYTI (Missouri)
map (36° 14′N 89° 44′W) **13**:476
HAYTI (South Dakota)
map (44° 40′N 97° 12′W) **18**:103
HAYWARD (California)
map (37° 40′N 122° 5′W) **4**:31
HAYWARD (Wisconsin)
map (46° 1′N 91° 29′W) **20**:185
HAYWOOD (county in North Carolina)
map (35° 35′N 83° 0′W) **14**:242
HAYWOOD (county in Tennessee)
map (35° 35′N 89° 20′W) **19**:104
HAYWOOD, WILLIAM DUDLEY 10:84
Industrial Workers of the World **11**:160
Socialist party **18**:25
HAZARD (Kentucky)
map (37° 15′N 83° 12′W) **12**:47
HAZE
mist **13**:481
HAZEL **8**:179
See also FILBERT
pollination **15**:408 *illus.*
HAZEL GREEN (Wisconsin)
map (42° 32′N 90° 26′W) **20**:185
HAZELTON (Idaho)
map (42° 41′N 114° 8′W) **11**:26
HAZELTON (North Dakota)
map (46° 29′N 100° 17′W) **14**:248
HAZELWOOD (North Carolina)
map (35° 28′N 83° 0′W) **14**:242
HAZEN (North Dakota)
map (47° 18′N 101° 38′W) **14**:248
HAZLEHURST (Georgia)
map (31° 52′N 82° 36′W) **9**:114
HAZLEHURST (Mississippi)
map (31° 52′N 90° 24′W) **13**:469
HAZLET (New Jersey)
map (40° 26′N 74° 13′W) **14**:129
HAZLETON (Iowa)
map (42° 37′N 91° 54′W) **11**:244
HAZLETON (Pennsylvania)
map (40° 58′N 75° 59′W) **15**:147
HAZLITT, WILLIAM 10:84 *bibliog., illus.*
Charles Lamb **12**:174 *illus.*
HAZM, IBN
Ring of the Dove
courtly love **5**:317
HAZOR (Israel) **10**:84–85 *bibliog.*
HEAD
microcephaly **13**:384
skull **17**:345 *illus.*
HEAD BAY D'ESPOIR (Newfoundland)
map (47° 56′N 55° 45′W) **14**:166
HEAD-HUNTING 10:85 *bibliog.*
magic **13**:49 *illus.*
Mundurucú **13**:640
Naga (people) **14**:6
scalping **17**:107
HEAD START 10:85 *bibliog.*
compensatory education **5**:156
day-care center **6**:55
primary education **15**:538
HEADACHE 10:85–86 *bibliog.*
famous sufferers **10**:86
menopause **13**:300
HEADE, MARTIN 10:86 *bibliog.*
HEADFISH *see* OCEAN SUNFISH
HEADLAND (Alabama)
map (31° 21′N 85° 20′W) **1**:234
HEADLEY (British Columbia)
map (49° 21′N 120° 4′W) **3**:491
HEALDSBURG (California)
map (38° 37′N 122° 52′W) **4**:31
HEALDTON (Oklahoma)
map (34° 14′N 97° 29′W) **14**:368
HEALER
folk medicine **8**:201
shaman **17**:238–239 *illus.*
HEALEY, DENIS 10:86
HEALTH
animal experimentation **2**:22
assembly line **2**:265
environmental health **7**:210–212
health-care systems **10**:87–89
mental health **13**:302
pollution, environmental **15**:411–415
public health **15**:608
research institutions
National Institutes of Health **14**:34
HEALTH, EDUCATION, AND WELFARE, U.S. DEPARTMENT OF *see* EDUCATION, U.S. DEPARTMENT OF; HEALTH AND HUMAN SERVICES, U.S. DEPARTMENT OF
HEALTH-CARE SYSTEMS 10:87–89 *bibliog.*
American Medical Association **1**:348
Blue Cross **3**:342
Blue Shield **3**:343
Europe **10**:88
fund raising **8**:360
Great Britain **19**:408
Bevan, Aneurin **3**:232
Head Start **10**:85
Health and Human Services, U.S. Department of **10**:86
hospice **10**:256
hospital **10**:256–258
institutionalization **11**:196–197
Medicaid **13**:264
Medicare **13**:265
nursing home **14**:299–300
occupational therapy **14**:321
old age **14**:374
paramedic **15**:80
pharmacy **15**:221–222
physical therapy **15**:280
Robert Wood Johnson Foundation **16**:241
HEALTH FOODS 10:89 *bibliog.*
HEALTH AND HUMAN SERVICES, U.S. DEPARTMENT OF 10:86–87 *bibliog.*
National Institutes of Health **14**:34
nutrition guidelines **14**:306–307
public health **15**:608
social security **18**:15–16
HEALTH INSURANCE
Blue Cross **3**:342
Blue Shield **3**:343
health-care systems **10**:87–88
hospital **10**:257; **10**:258
Medicaid **13**:264
Medicare **13**:265
social security **18**:14
welfare state **20**:98
HEALTH-MAINTENANCE ORGANIZATION
health-care systems **10**:88
hospital **10**:258
HEALTH RESORTS, WATERING-PLACES, AND SPAS
Baden-Baden (West Germany) **3**:19
bath **3**:122
Epidaurus **7**:218
Hot Springs (Arkansas) **10**:259
Saratoga Springs (New York) **17**:75
Vichy (France) **19**:571
Warm Springs (Georgia) **20**:30
White Sulphur Springs (West Virginia) **20**:138
Wiesbaden (West Germany) **20**:146
HEALTH AND SAFETY LAWS *see* CONSUMER PROTECTION; PURE FOOD AND DRUG LAWS
HEALY (Kansas)
map (38° 36′N 100° 37′W) **12**:18
HEALY, G. P. A. 10:89 *bibliog.*
John Calhoun **4**:29 *illus.*
The Peacemakers **19**:448 *illus.*
HEANEY, SEAMUS 10:89 *bibliog.*
HEARD (county in Georgia)
map (33° 20′N 85° 10′W) **9**:114
HEARD ISLAND AND THE McDONALD ISLANDS (Australia) **10**:89
HEARING *see* EAR
HEARING (law) *see* DUE PROCESS; TRIAL (law)
HEARING AID 10:89–90 *bibliog.*
HEARING LOSS *see* DEAFNESS
HEARN, LAFCADIO 10:90 *bibliog.*
HEARNE (Texas)
map (30° 53′N 96° 36′W) **19**:129
HEARNE, SAMUEL 10:90 *bibliog., illus.*
Canada, exploration of **4**:80 *map*
Great Slave Lake **9**:322
Slave River **17**:351
HEARSAY *see* EVIDENCE
HEARST (Ontario)
map (49° 41′N 83° 40′W) **14**:393
HEARST, WILLIAM RANDOLPH 10:90–91 *bibliog., illus.*
journalism **11**:455
San Simeon palace
Morgan, Julia **13**:578
Spanish-American War **18**:149
HEART 10:91–94 *bibliog., illus.*

HEART (cont.)
See also CARDIOVASCULAR SYSTEM; HEART DISEASES
anatomy **10**:91–92 *illus.*
atria **10**:91–92 *illus.*
blood flow **10**:92
circulatory system **4**:441–442
coronary artery **5**:271
electrocardiograph **7**:111–112
embryo **10**:92
evolution **10**:94
examination, medical **10**:94
Harvey, William **10**:65
heart, artificial **10**:94–95
muscle
biopotential **3**:276
cardiac muscle **13**:653 *illus.*
cell **4**:235 *illus.*
muscle contraction **13**:654–655
physiology **10**:91 *illus.*
reptile **16**:168–169
space medicine **18**:133
structure and function **10**:91–92
His (family) **10**:177
Purkinje, Jan Evangelista **15**:630
valves **10**:91–92 *illus.*; **10**:94; **19**:509 *illus.*
artificial organs **2**:222 *illus.*
ventricles **10**:91–92 *illus.*
HEART, ARTIFICIAL **10**:94–95 *bibliog.*
Cooley, Denton A. **5**:240
HEART OF ATLANTA MOTEL, INC. v. UNITED STATES **10**:95
HEART ATTACK **10**:95
cardiopulmonary resuscitation **4**:144
HEART CATHETERIZATION *see* CARDIAC CATHETERIZATION
HEART CLAM *see* COCKLE
HEART OF DARKNESS (book) **10**:95 *bibliog.*
HEART DISEASES **10**:95–96 *bibliog.*
See also ARTERY
American Heart Association **1**:340
cholesterol **4**:404
coronary, exercise **7**:330 *table*
diseases and disorders
aneurysm **1**:411
blue baby **3**:342
cor pulmonale **5**:257
endocarditis **7**:168
heart attack **10**:95
heart failure **10**:96
heartburn **10**:97
hypertension **10**:349
infarction **11**:164
pericarditis **15**:165
pulmonary embolism **15**:619
rheumatic fever **16**:194
thrombosis **19**:183
Einthoven, Willem **7**:94
heart **10**:94
menopause **13**:299
palpitation **15**:52
Richards, Dickinson Woodruff **16**:211
shock, physiologic **17**:278
stress, biological **18**:297
surgery **18**:362
artificial organs **2**:222 *illus.*
Barnard, Christiaan **3**:85
Cooley, Denton A. **5**:240
heart, artificial **10**:94–95
heart-lung machine **10**:97
medicine **13**:272
open-heart **18**:361 *illus.*
Shumway, Norman Edward **17**:289
transplantation, organ **19**:277
treatment
foxglove **8**:257
nitroglycerin **14**:203
pacemaker, artificial **15**:4
HEART FAILURE **10**:96 *bibliog.*
cardiopulmonary resuscitation **4**:144
cardiovascular diseases **4**:144
digitalis **6**:175
first aid **8**:108–109
hypertension **10**:349
shock, physiologic **17**:278
HEART LAKE
map (44° 16′N 110° 29′W) **20**:301
HEART-LUNG MACHINE **10**:97 *bibliog., illus.*
DeBakey, Michael **6**:70
surgery **18**:362
HEART MASSAGE *see* CARDIOPULMONARY RESUSCITATION
HEART MUSCLE *see* MYOCARDIUM
HEART RIVER
map (46° 47′N 100° 51′W) **14**:248
HEARTBEAT
antiarrhythmic drugs
lidocaine **12**:323
procainamide **15**:559
quinidine **16**:27
quinine **16**:27
circulatory system **4**:442
fetus **15**:503; **15**:505
heart **10**:93–94 *illus.*
heart diseases **10**:96
hyperventilation **10**:349
palpitation **15**:52
pulse (biology) **15**:621
HEARTBREAK HOUSE (play)
Shaw, George Bernard **17**:245
HEARTBURN **10**:97
HEARTWOOD
tree **19**:286–287 *illus.*
wood **20**:205
HEAT, BODY *see* BODY TEMPERATURE
HEAT CAPACITY **10**:97 *bibliog.*
chemical energy **4**:315
HEAT ENGINE **10**:97
Carnot cycle **4**:159
engine **7**:177
heat pump **10**:98–99
internal-combustion engine **11**:215
ocean thermal energy conversion **14**:333
Rankine, William John Macquorn **16**:88
thermodynamics **19**:164
HEAT EXCHANGER **10**:97–98 *bibliog.*
condenser **5**:172
incinerator **11**:74
HEAT EXHAUSTION *see* HEATSTROKE
HEAT AND HEAT TRANSFER **10**:98 *bibliog., illus.*
alarm systems **1**:240
aluminum **1**:316
annealing **2**:33
Black, Joseph **3**:303
ceramics **4**:257–259
chimney **4**:358
Clausius, Rudolf **5**:45
combustion **5**:131
convection **5**:232
cryogenics **5**:370–371
Earth, heat flow in **7**:17–18
flame **8**:150
Fourier, Joseph **8**:253
furnace **8**:372
ground temperature **9**:373
heat capacity **10**:97
heat engine **10**:97
heat exchanger **10**:97–98
heat pump **10**:98–99
heating systems **10**:99–100
Hess's law **10**:151
infrared radiation **11**:175
insulating materials **11**:197
insulator **11**:197
isothermal process **11**:301
Joule, James Prescott **11**:453
kerosene **12**:59
light **12**:335
materials technology **13**:220–221
measurement **10**:98
British thermal unit **3**:497
calorie **4**:47
calorimeter **4**:47
thermometer **19**:166–167
units, physical **19**:467
mechanical equivalent of heat
energy **7**:172
medicinal use
hyperthermia **10**:349
phonon **15**:255
physics, history of **15**:285–286
plumbing **15**:371
refractory materials **16**:124
Rossby waves **16**:318–319
Rumford, Benjamin Thomson, Count **16**:344–345
solar collectors **18**:40–41
solar energy **18**:41–42
specific heat
heat capacity **10**:97
stove **18**:286
superfluidity **18**:351
temperature **19**:92–93
thermal pollution
pollution, environmental **15**:412
thermodynamics **19**:162–165
thermoelectricity **19**:165
thermostat **19**:167
Tyndall, John **19**:363
HEAT PUMP **10**:98–99 *bibliog.*
HEAT RASH *see* PRICKLY HEAT
HEATH (botany) **10**:99 *bibliog.*
arbutus **2**:111–112
azalea **2**:380
bearberry **3**:142
blueberry **3**:344
cranberry **5**:329
heather **10**:99
huckleberry **10**:289
leucothoe **12**:300
mountain laurel **13**:622
rhododendron **16**:203
rosemary **16**:314
HEATH, EDWARD **10**:99 *bibliog., illus.*
Thatcher, Margaret **19**:143
HEATH, PERCY
Modern Jazz Quartet **13**:498
HEATH SPRINGS (South Carolina)
map (34° 36′N 80° 40′W) **18**:98
HEATHER **10**:99 *bibliog., illus.*
heath **10**:99
HEATHSVILLE (Virginia)
map (37° 55′N 76° 28′W) **19**:607
HEATING SYSTEMS **10**:99–100 *bibliog.*
heat pump **10**:98–99
HEATSTROKE **10**:100
HEAVEN **10**:100 *bibliog.*
China, history of **4**:370
HEAVENER (Oklahoma)
map (34° 53′N 94° 36′W) **14**:368
HEAVISIDE, OLIVER
ionosphere **11**:241
HEAVY METAL ROCK
rock music **16**:249
HEAVY WATER **10**:100
HEBBEL, CHRISTIAN FRIEDRICH **10**:100 *bibliog.*
HEBBRONVILLE (Texas)
map (27° 18′N 98° 41′W) **19**:129
HEBE **17**:113 *illus.*
HEBEI (China) *see* HOPEI (Hebei) (China)
HEBER (Arizona)
map (34° 26′N 110° 36′W) **2**:160
HEBER CITY (Utah)
map (40° 30′N 111° 25′W) **19**:492
HEBER SPRINGS (Arkansas)
map (35° 30′N 92° 2′W) **2**:166
HEBERDEN'S NODES *see* OSTEOARTHRITIS
HÉBERT, ANNE **10**:101
HÉBERT, JACQUES RENÉ **10**:101
HÉBERT, LOUIS PHILIPPE **10**:101 *bibliog.*
HEBGEN LAKE
map (44° 47′N 111° 14′W) **13**:547
HEBREW LANGUAGE **10**:101 *bibliog.*
alphabet **20**:294 *table*
Ben-Yehudah, Eliezer **3**:195
Canaanite **1**:179
Israel **11**:305
HEBREW NUMERAL
numeral **14**:294
HEBREW UNION COLLEGE **10**:101–102
HEBREW AND YIDDISH LITERATURE **10**:102 *bibliog., illus.*
See also YIDDISH THEATER
authors
Agnon, S. Y. **1**:187
Aleichem, Sholem **1**:270–271
Amichai, Yehuda **1**:369
Ansky, Shloime **2**:35
Asch, Sholem **2**:228
Bialik, Hayyim Nahman **3**:236
Goldfaden, Abraham **9**:233
Gordin, Jacob **9**:248
Gordon, Judah Leib **9**:249
Judah ha-Levi **11**:458
Luzzatto, Moses Hayyim **12**:473
Manasseh ben Israel **13**:108
Mendele Mokher Sefarim **13**:294
Oz, Amos **14**:480
Peretz, Y. L. **15**:163
Shlonsky, Abraham **17**:278
Singer, Isaac Bashevis **17**:322
Tchernichowsky, Saul **19**:52–53
Zunz, Leopold **20**:382
Jewish Daily Forward **11**:412
HEBREWS, EPISTLE TO THE **10**:102 *bibliog.*
HEBRIDES (Scotland) **10**:102–103 *bibliog.*
Magnus VI, King of Norway (Magnus the Law-Mender) **13**:61
map (57° 0′N 6° 30′W) **7**:268
Skye **17**:346
HEBRON (Illinois)
map (42° 28′N 88° 26′W) **11**:42
HEBRON (Indiana)
map (41° 19′N 87° 12′W) **11**:111
HEBRON (Jordan) **10**:103
map (31° 32′N 35° 6′E) **11**:447
HEBRON (Maryland)
map (38° 25′N 75° 41′W) **13**:188
HEBRON (Nebraska)
map (40° 10′N 97° 35′W) **14**:70
HEBRON (Newfoundland)
map (58° 12′N 62° 38′W) **14**:166
HEBRON (North Dakota)
map (46° 54′N 102° 3′W) **14**:248
HECATAEUS
Herodotus **10**:144
HECATE **10**:103
HECATE STRAIT
map (53° 0′N 131° 0′W) **3**:491
HECETA, BRUNO
Washington **20**:38
HECHT, BEN **10**:103
HECKEL, ERICH **3**:520 *illus.*; **10**:103 *bibliog., illus.*
Glassy Day **10**:103 *illus.*
Portrait of a Man **9**:292 *illus.*
HECKER, ISAAC THOMAS **10**:103 *bibliog.*
HECKEWELDER, JOHN GOTTLIEB ERNESTUS **10**:103–104 *bibliog.*
HECLA (South Dakota)
map (45° 53′N 98° 9′W) **18**:103
HECTANOOGA (Nova Scotia)
map (44° 6′N 66° 2′W) **14**:269
HECTARE
weights and measures **20**:93 *table*
HECTOLITER
weights and measures **20**:93 *table*
HECTOR **10**:104
Iliad **11**:40
HECTOR (Minnesota)
map (44° 45′N 94° 43′W) **13**:453
HECUBA **10**:104
HEDA, WILLEM CLAESZ **10**:104 *bibliog.*
HEDAYAT, SADEQ **10**:104 *bibliog.*
HEDDA GABLER (play) **10**:104 *bibliog.*
Ibsen, Henrik **11**:6–7
HEDENBERGITE
pyroxene **15**:638
HEDGE MUSTARD *see* TUMBLEWEED
HEDGE SPARROW **10**:104
HEDGEHOG **10**:104 *illus.*; **13**:104 *illus.*
gymnure **9**:414
HEDGING *see* FUTURES
HEDIN, SVEN ANDERS **10**:104
Gobi **9**:217
Lop Nor (China) **12**:412
HEDJAZ (Saudi Arabia) *see* HEJAZ (Saudi Arabia)
HEDLEY (Texas)
map (34° 52′N 100° 39′W) **19**:129
HEDONISM **10**:105 *bibliog.*
Cyrenaics **5**:409
Epicureanism **7**:218
ethics **7**:251
HEDRICK (Iowa)
map (41° 11′N 92° 19′W) **11**:244
HEEMSKERCK, JACOB VAN
Svalbard (Norway) **18**:374
HEEMSKERCK, MAARTEN VAN **10**:105 *bibliog.*
HEERENVEEN (Netherlands)
map (52° 57′N 5° 55′E) **14**:99
HEERLEN (Netherlands)
map (50° 54′N 5° 59′E) **14**:99
HEEZEN, BRUCE
mid-oceanic ridge **13**:389
HEFEI (China) *see* HOFEI (Heifei) (China)
HEFLIN (Alabama)
map (33° 39′N 85° 35′W) **1**:234
HEFNER, HUGH **10**:105
HEGEL, GEORG WILHELM FRIEDRICH **10**:105–106 *bibliog., illus.*
absolute **1**:62
alienation **1**:294
art criticism **2**:207
dialectic **6**:150
dialectical materialism **6**:150
economics **7**:48
idealism **11**:30
Marx, Karl **13**:181–182
Marxism **13**:183
philosophy **15**:243 *illus.*; **15**:245
state (in political philosophy) **18**:231–232 *illus.*
HEGIRA **10**:106
Muhammad **10**:106
HEIAN (Japan)
Japan, history of **11**:367
Japanese art and architecture **11**:374
Kyoto (Japan) **12**:143
HEIBERG, JOHAN LUDVIG **10**:106 *bibliog.*
HEIDEGGER, MARTIN **10**:106–107 *bibliog., illus.*
existentialism **7**:332
phenomenology **15**:225
HEIDELBERG (Mississippi)
map (31° 53′N 88° 59′W) **13**:469
HEIDELBERG (West Germany) **10**:107
map (49° 25′N 8° 43′E) **9**:140
HEIDELBERG, UNIVERSITY OF **10**:107
HEIDELBERG MAN **10**:107 *bibliog.*
HEIDEN, ERIC **10**:107; **14**:385 *illus.*
HEIDENSTAM, VERNER VON **10**:107 *bibliog.*

HEIDI (book) **10**:108
Spyri, Johanna **18**:201
HEIFETZ, JASCHA **10**:108 *bibliog.*
HEIJERMANS, HERMAN **10**:108 *bibliog.*
HEIJI WARS
Burning of Sanjo Palace **11**:368 *illus.*
HEILBRON, SIR IAN MORRIS **10**:108
HEILBROUN (Germany, East and West)
map (49° 8′N 9° 13′E) **9**:140
HEILUNG-KIANG *see* MANCHURIA (China)
HEIMDALL **10**:108
HEIMLICH MANEUVER
first aid **8**:109 *illus.*
HEIMSKRINGLA (book) **10**:108
HEINE, HEINRICH **10**:108–109 *bibliog.*, *illus.*
HEINE-GELDERN, ROBERT **10**:109
HEINKEL, ERNST
jet propulsion **11**:407
HEINLEIN, ROBERT **10**:109 *bibliog.*
Stranger in a Strange Land **18**:288–289
HEINROTH, O.
animal behavior **2**:11
ethology **7**:257
HEINZ, HENRY JOHN **10**:109 *bibliog.*
HEINZE, F. ("FRITZ") AUGUSTUS
Montana **13**:550
HEIR **10**:109
Roman law **16**:279
will (law) **20**:153
HEISENBERG, WERNER KARL **10**:109–110 *bibliog.*, *illus.*; **15**:286 *illus.*
chemistry, history of **4**:328
determinism **6**:134
quantum mechanics **16**:10
Schrödinger, Erwin **17**:135
uncertainty principle **19**:381
HEISMAN TROPHY **10**:110
Blanchard, Doc **3**:326–327
Davis, Glenn **6**:51
Hornung, Paul **10**:240
Simpson, O. J. **17**:317
Staubach, Roger **18**:239
HEITLER, WALTER
chemistry, history of **4**:328
HEJAZ (Saudi Arabia) **10**:110
cities
Jidda **11**:417
Mecca **13**:258–259 *illus.*
Medina **13**:275
Husayn ibn Ali **10**:319–320
map (24° 30′N 38° 30′E) **17**:94
HEJDUK, JOHN **10**:110 *bibliog.*
HEKLA **10**:110
HEL **10**:110
HELD, AL **10**:110 *bibliog.*
HELEN OF TROY **10**:110 *bibliog.*
HELENA, SAINT **10**:111
Constantius I, Roman Emperor **5**:210
Sinai **17**:318
HELENA (Arkansas)
map (34° 32′N 90° 35′W) **2**:166
HELENA (Montana) **10**:110–111; **13**:550 *illus.*
map (46° 36′N 112° 1′W) **13**:547
HELENA (Oklahoma)
map (36° 33′N 98° 16′W) **14**:368
HELENUS **10**:111
HELGOLAND **10**:111
map (54° 12′N 7° 53′E) **9**:140
HELICOPTER **10**:111–112 *bibliog.*, *illus.*
aircraft, military **1**:217
aviation **2**:217
night sights **14**:193
Sikorsky, Igor **17**:303
vertical takeoff and landing (VTOL) **19**:639
HELIGOLAND *see* HELGOLAND
HELIOCENTRIC WORLD SYSTEM **10**:112
Copernicus, Nicolaus **5**:250
cosmology (astronomy) **5**:284–289
geocentric world system **9**:95
HELIODORUS OF EMESA **10**:112
HELIOGABALUS, ROMAN EMPEROR **10**:112 *bibliog.*
Homs (Syria) **10**:217
HELIOGRAPHY
Niepce, Joseph Nicéphore **14**:185 *illus.*
HÉLION, JEAN **10**:112 *bibliog.*
HELIOPOLIS (Egypt) **7**:81 *map*; **10**:112–113
Cleopatra's Needles **5**:51
HELIOS **10**:113
Colossus of Rhodes **17**:217–218 *illus.*
HELIOSTAT *see* COELOSTAT
HELIOTROPE (botany) **10**:113 *illus.*
See also GARDEN HELIOTROPE
HELIOTROPE (gem) **9**:74 *illus.*
See also BLOODSTONE
HELIOZOAN **10**:113
actinosphaerium **1**:89
HELIUM **10**:113 *bibliog.*
abundances of common elements **7**:131 *table*
commercial uses **10**:113
element **7**:130 *table*
fusion, nuclear **8**:381–382 *illus.*
Group 0 periodic table **15**:167
inert gases **11**:161
laser and maser **12**:213 *table*
liquid helium
cryogenics **5**:371
Landau, Lev **12**:181
Lockyer, Sir Joseph Norman **12**:388
occurrence **10**:113
proton-proton reaction **15**:578–579
spectrum **18**:169 *illus.*
stellar evolution **18**:251
superfluidity **18**:351
HELIX
spiral **18**:188
HELL **10**:113 *bibliog.*
HELL-VILLE (Madagascar)
map (13° 25′S 48° 16′E) **13**:38
HELLAAKOSKI, AARO
Finnish literature **8**:99
HELLBENDER **10**:114
HELLEBORE **10**:114
HELLENIC PLATE
plate tectonics **15**:351 *map*
HELLENIC REPUBLIC *see* GREECE
HELLENISM **10**:114
Farnese Heracles **8**:28
Greek art **9**:342
Greek Revival **9**:345–346
Laocoön **12**:202
Lysippus **12**:480
mosaic **13**:593
mural painting **13**:646
Nike of Samothrace **14**:195
Pella **15**:138
Priene **15**:536
Vatican museums and galleries **19**:527
HELLENISTIC AGE **10**:114 *bibliog.*
Alexander the Great **1**:273–275 *illus.*, *map*
Greece, ancient **9**:333
Greek architecture **9**:337
Greek art **9**:342
Middle East, history of the **13**:401
Pergamum **15**:164–165
temple **19**:97
HELLER, JOSEPH **1**:347–348 *illus.*; **10**:114–115 *bibliog.*, *illus.*
Catch-22 **4**:202
HELLER, WALTER **10**:115
Council of Economic Advisers **5**:310
HELLERTOWN (Pennsylvania)
map (40° 35′N 75° 21′W) **15**:147
HELLESPONT *see* DARDANELLES
HELLGRAMMITE *see* DOBSONFLY
HELLMAN, LILLIAN **10**:115 *bibliog.*, *illus.*
HELLS CANYON
map (45° 20′N 116° 45′W) **14**:427
HELMAND RIVER
map (31° 12′N 61° 34′E) **1**:133
HELMET
armor **2**:174–175
heraldry **10**:134
HELMET DIVING *see* DIVING, DEEP-SEA
HELMETED LIZARD **10**:115
HELMHOLTZ, HERMANN LUDWIG FERDINAND VON **10**:115–116 *bibliog.*, *illus.*
color **5**:113
color perception **5**:114
mathematics, history of **13**:226
ophthalmoscope
surgery **18**:362
psychology, history of **15**:596
HELMINTH
parasitic diseases **15**:82
worm **20**:284
HELMOND (Netherlands)
map (51° 29′N 5° 40′E) **14**:99
HELMONT, JOHANNES BAPTISTA VAN **10**:116 *bibliog.*
biology **3**:270
photosynthesis **15**:275
HELMSTEDT (Germany, East and West)
map (52° 13′N 11° 0′E) **9**:140
HÉLOISE
Abelard, Peter **1**:55
HELPER (Utah)
map (39° 41′N 110° 51′W) **19**:492
HELPER, HINTON ROWAN **10**:116 *bibliog.*
HELPMANN, SIR ROBERT **10**:116 *bibliog.*
HELSINGBORG (Sweden)
map (56° 3′N 12° 42′E) **18**:382
HELSINGFORS (Finland) *see* HELSINKI (Finland)
HELSINGØR (Denmark)
map (56° 2′N 12° 37′E) **6**:109
HELSINKI (Finland) **8**:95–96 *illus.*, *table*; **10**:116–117 *illus.*
history **10**:117
map (60° 10′N 24° 58′E) **8**:95
HELSINKI DECLARATION
Brezhnev, Leonid Ilich **3**:476
human rights **10**:298
HELST, BARTHOLOMEUS VAN DER **10**:117 *bibliog.*
HELVETIC REPUBLIC **10**:117
HELVETII
Gallic Wars **9**:19
HELVÉTIUS, CLAUDE ADRIEN **10**:117
HEMANGIOMA
birthmark **3**:296
HEMATITE **10**:117 *illus.*
ocher **14**:346
oxide minerals **14**:476
HEMATOLOGY **10**:117 *bibliog.*
blood tests **3**:339
diagnostic tests **6**:149
HEMICHORDATE **10**:117–118 *bibliog.*
HEMIMORPHITE **10**:118
orthorhombic system **14**:451
HEMINGFORD (Nebraska)
map (42° 19′N 103° 4′W) **14**:70
HEMINGWAY, ERNEST **1**:347 *illus.*; **10**:118–119 *bibliog.*, *illus.*
Farewell to Arms, A **8**:23
For Whom the Bell Tolls **8**:219
Old Man and the Sea, The **14**:375
Sun Also Rises, The **18**:345–346
HEMIPLEGIA **10**:119
HEMIPODE **10**:119
HEMIPTERA **10**:119 *bibliog.*
assassin bug **2**:264
backswimmer **3**:13
bedbug **3**:153
chinch bug **4**:377
pill bug **15**:303
stinkbug **18**:272
water boatman **20**:48
water bug **20**:48
water strider **20**:52
HEMISPHERE *see* NORTHERN HEMISPHERE; SOUTHERN HEMISPHERE
HEMLOCK (botany) **10**:119 *illus.*
See also POISON HEMLOCK
HEMLOCK LAKE
Finger Lakes **8**:93
HEMODIALYSIS *see* KIDNEY, ARTIFICIAL
HEMOGLOBIN **10**:119 *bibliog.*
anemia **1**:409–410
blood **3**:337–338; **9**:89 *illus.*
Cooley's anemia **5**:240
coordination compounds **5**:248
deficiency diseases **10**:119
Fischer, Hans **8**:110
Hemophilus **10**:120
heterocyclic compound **10**:153
Hoppe-Seyler, Felix **10**:232
iron **11**:270–271
malaria **13**:80
methemoglobinemia **13**:343
operon **14**:403
Perutz, Max Ferdinand **15**:196
pigment, skin **15**:300
protein **15**:574
replacement **10**:119
sickle-cell anemia **17**:293
Svedberg, Theodor **18**:374
HÉMON, LOUIS **10**:119
Canadian literature **4**:93
HEMOPHILIA **10**:119–120 *bibliog.*, *illus.*
blood **3**:338
genetic diseases **9**:83
HEMOPHILUS **10**:120
chancroid **4**:279
respiratory system disorders **16**:181
HEMORRHAGE **10**:120 *bibliog.*
first aid **8**:108 *illus.*
hemophilia **10**:120
purpura **15**:630
sickle-cell anemia **17**:293
stress, biological **18**:298
stroke **18**:302
nervous system, diseases of the **14**:96
treatment
astringent **2**:270
surgery **10**:120
venom **19**:546
Vitamin K **19**:619
HEMORRHOIDS **10**:120 *bibliog.*
HEMP **10**:120
See also SISAL
hallucinogens **10**:24
hibiscus **10**:157
hops **10**:233
marijuana **13**:152–153 *illus.*
principal growing areas **8**:68 *map*
HEMPEL, CARL GUSTAV **10**:120
HEMPHILL (Texas)
map (31° 20′N 93° 51′W) **19**:129
HEMPHILL (county in Texas)
map (35° 50′N 100° 15′W) **19**:129
HEMPSTEAD (county in Arkansas)
map (33° 45′N 93° 40′W) **2**:166
HEMPSTEAD (New York)
map (40° 42′N 73° 37′W) **14**:149
HEMPSTEAD (Texas)
map (30° 6′N 96° 5′W) **19**:129
HENAN (China) *see* HONAN (Henan) (China)
HENBANE **10**:120–121
HENCH, PHILIP SHOWALTER **10**:121
Kendall, Edward **12**:41
HENDERSON (county in Illinois)
map (40° 48′N 90° 50′W) **11**:42
HENDERSON (Kentucky)
map (37° 50′N 87° 35′W) **12**:47
HENDERSON (county in Kentucky)
map (37° 45′N 87° 35′W) **12**:47
HENDERSON (Nevada)
map (36° 2′N 114° 59′W) **14**:111
HENDERSON (North Carolina)
map (36° 20′N 78° 25′W) **14**:242
HENDERSON (county in North Carolina)
map (35° 25′N 82° 30′W) **14**:242
HENDERSON (Tennessee)
map (35° 27′N 88° 38′W) **19**:104
HENDERSON (county in Tennessee)
map (35° 40′N 88° 28′W) **19**:104
HENDERSON (Texas)
map (32° 9′N 94° 48′W) **19**:129
HENDERSON (county in Texas)
map (32° 13′N 95° 50′W) **19**:129
HENDERSON, ALEXANDER **10**:121 *bibliog.*
HENDERSON, ARTHUR **10**:121 *bibliog.*
HENDERSON, FLETCHER
Armstrong, Louis **2**:179
HENDERSON, RICHARD **10**:121
Transylvania Company **19**:283
HENDERSON, THOMAS
astronomy, history of **2**:280
HENDERSON ISLAND
Pitcairn Island **15**:319
HENDERSONVILLE (North Carolina)
map (35° 19′N 82° 28′W) **14**:242
HENDERSONVILLE (Tennessee)
map (36° 18′N 86° 37′W) **19**:104
HENDRICK, BURTON J.
Sims, William Sowden **17**:317
HENDRICKS (county in Indiana)
map (39° 45′N 86° 30′W) **11**:111
HENDRICKS, THOMAS A. **10**:121
HENDRIX, JIMI **10**:121 *bibliog.*
HENDRY (county in Florida)
map (26° 36′N 81° 13′W) **8**:172
HENG O *see* CH'ANG-O (Chang E)
HENG SAMRIN **10**:121
HENG-YANG (China)
map (26° 51′N 112° 30′E) **4**:362
HENGE MONUMENTS *see* MEGALITH; STONE ALIGNMENTS
HENGELO (Netherlands)
map (52° 15′N 6° 45′E) **14**:99
HENIE, SONJA **10**:121 *bibliog.*
HENLE, FRIEDRICH **10**:121
Henle's loop **12**:73 *illus.*
medicine **13**:270
HENLEY, WILLIAM ERNEST **10**:121–122 *bibliog.*
HENLOPEN, CAPE OF
map (38° 48′N 75° 5′W) **6**:88
HENNA **10**:121–122
cosmetics **5**:281
HENNEBIQUE, FRANÇOIS
bridge (engineering) **3**:482
HENNEPIN (Illinois)
map (41° 15′N 89° 21′W) **11**:42
HENNEPIN (county in Minnesota)
map (45° 3′N 93° 30′W) **13**:453
HENNEPIN, LOUIS **10**:122 *bibliog.*
exploration of colonial America **19**:437 *map*
Minneapolis (Minnesota) **13**:451
Niagara Falls **14**:177 *illus.*
HENNESSEY (Oklahoma)
map (36° 6′N 97° 54′W) **14**:368
HENNIKER (New Hampshire)
map (43° 11′N 71° 49′W) **14**:123
HENNING (Minnesota)
map (46° 19′N 95° 27′W) **13**:453
HENNING (Tennessee)
map (35° 41′N 89° 34′W) **19**:104

HENRI, ROBERT **10**:122 *bibliog., illus.*
Eva Green **10**:122 *illus.*
HENRICO (county in Virginia)
map (37° 30′N 77° 20′W) **19**:607
HENRIETTA (Texas)
map (33° 49′N 98° 12′W) **19**:129
HENRIETTA MARIA **10**:122 *bibliog.*
HENRIETTA MARIA, CAPE
map (55° 9′N 82° 20′W) **14**:393
HENRY (county in Alabama)
map (31° 33′N 85° 15′W) **1**:234
HENRY (county in Georgia)
map (33° 30′N 84° 10′W) **9**:114
HENRY (Illinois)
map (41° 47′N 89° 41′W) **11**:42
HENRY (county in Illinois)
map (41° 22′N 90° 10′W) **11**:42
HENRY (county in Indiana)
map (39° 55′N 85° 22′W) **11**:111
HENRY (inductance) **10**:122
units, physical **19**:467 *table*
HENRY (county in Iowa)
map (41° 0′N 91° 30′W) **11**:244
HENRY (county in Kentucky)
map (38° 26′N 85° 9′W) **12**:47
HENRY (county in Missouri)
map (38° 25′N 93° 50′W) **13**:476
HENRY (county in Ohio)
map (41° 20′N 84° 4′W) **14**:357
HENRY (county in Tennessee)
map (35° 20′N 88° 15′W) **19**:104
HENRY (county in Virginia)
map (36° 40′N 79° 50′W) **19**:607
HENRY, ALEXANDER **10**:122 *bibliog.*
HENRY, ANDREW
Ashley, William Henry **2**:231
fur trade **8**:371
HENRY, SIR EDWARD
fingerprinting **8**:93
HENRY, FORT *see* FORT HENRY AND FORT DONELSON (Kentucky)
HENRY, JOSEPH **10**:122 *bibliog.*; **19**:450 *illus.*
electromagnetic induction **7**:115
inductance
henry **10**:122
HENRY, O. *see* O. HENRY
HENRY, PATRICK **10**:122–123 *bibliog., illus.*
Richmond (Virginia) **16**:214
HENRY, WILLIAM **10**:123
Henry's law
phase equilibrium **15**:223
HENRY I, KING OF ENGLAND **10**:124 *bibliog.*
HENRY I, KING OF FRANCE **10**:127
HENRY I, KING OF GERMANY (Henry the Fowler) **10**:128 *bibliog.*
Germany, history of **9**:149
Leipzig (East Germany) **12**:278
HENRY II, KING OF CASTILE
Peter I, King of Castile (Peter the Cruel) **15**:200
HENRY II, KING OF ENGLAND **10**:124–125 *bibliog., illus.*
common law **5**:139
Eleanor of Aquitaine **7**:103
Great Britain, history of **9**:311
Ireland, history of **11**:262
Louis VII, King of France **12**:424
manor house from reign of **13**:126 *illus.*
HENRY II, KING OF FRANCE **10**:127 *bibliog.*
Diane de Poitiers **6**:153
tomb **19**:231
HENRY II, KING OF GERMANY AND HOLY ROMAN EMPEROR **10**:128 *bibliog.*
HENRY III, KING OF ENGLAND **10**:125 *bibliog., illus.*
Montfort, Simon de, Earl of Leicester **13**:555–556
HENRY III, KING OF FRANCE **10**:127 *bibliog., illus.*
Religion, Wars of **16**:141
York (dynasty) **20**:330
HENRY III, KING OF GERMANY AND HOLY ROMAN EMPEROR **10**:128–129 *bibliog.*
Germany, history of **9**:149
HENRY IV, KING OF ENGLAND **10**:125 *bibliog.*
Henry IV, Parts 1 and 2 (play) **10**:124
Lancaster (dynasty) **12**:177
Richard II (play) **16**:209
Richard II, King of England **16**:210
HENRY IV, KING OF FRANCE **10**:128 *bibliog., illus.*
Bourbon (dynasty) **3**:423
Europe, history of **7**:287
France, history of **8**:268
French art and architecture **8**:305
Henry III, King of France **10**:127
Margaret of Valois **13**:149
Marie de Médicis **13**:151–152
Mornay, Philippe de **13**:582
Nantes, Edict of **14**:13
Pau (France) **15**:116
Religion, Wars of **16**:141
Sully, Maximilien de Béthune, Duc de **18**:338
HENRY IV, KING OF GERMANY AND HOLY ROMAN EMPEROR **10**:129 *bibliog., illus.*
Europe, history of **7**:284
Germany, history of **9**:149
investiture controversy **11**:237; **13**:393 *illus.*
Reggio nell'Emilia (Italy) **16**:128
HENRY IV, PARTS 1 AND 2 (play) **10**:124
Falstaff **8**:15
HENRY V, KING OF ENGLAND **10**:125–126 *bibliog., illus.*
Henry IV, Parts 1 and 2 (play) **10**:124
Henry V (play) **10**:124
Hundred Years' War **10**:305
Lancaster (dynasty) **12**:177
HENRY V, KING OF GERMANY AND HOLY ROMAN EMPEROR **10**:129 *bibliog.*
HENRY V (play) **10**:124 *bibliog.*
HENRY VI, KING OF ENGLAND **10**:126 *bibliog.*
Edward IV, King of England **7**:68
Lancaster (dynasty) **12**:177
Margaret of Anjou **13**:148–149
Northampton (England) **14**:253
Roses, Wars of the **16**:316
Warwick, Richard Neville, Earl of **20**:33
York (dynasty) **20**:330
HENRY VI, KING OF GERMANY AND HOLY ROMAN EMPEROR **10**:129 *bibliog.*
HENRY VII, KING OF ENGLAND **10**:126 *bibliog.*
coin **14**:296 *illus.*
Great Britain, history of **9**:313
Richard III (play) **16**:209
Roses, Wars of the **16**:316
Tudor (dynasty) **19**:328
HENRY VII, KING OF GERMANY AND HOLY ROMAN EMPEROR (Henry of Luxemburg) **10**:130
HENRY VIII, KING OF ENGLAND **10**:126–127 *bibliog., illus.*
Cromwell, Thomas, 1st Earl of Essex **5**:358
Elizabeth I, Queen of England **7**:141
Europe, history of **7**:287
Great Britain, history of **9**:313
Holbein, Hans, the Younger **10**:201
meeting with Francis I on the Field of the Cloth of Gold **9**:312 *illus.*
More, Saint Thomas **13**:575
Reformation **16**:123
wives
Anne of Cleves **2**:32
Boleyn, Anne **3**:364
Catherine of Aragon **4**:209
Howard, Catherine **10**:282–283
Parr, Catherine **15**:97
Seymour, Jane **17**:233
Wolsey, Thomas **20**:200
Yorkshire (England) **20**:331
HENRY DRAPER CATALOGUE
astronomical catalogs and atlases **2**:276
Cannon, Annie Jump **4**:112
Harvard classification of stars **10**:64
Harvard College Observatory **10**:64
Pickering, Edward Charles **15**:293
HENRY THE FOWLER *see* HENRY I, KING OF GERMANY (Henry the Fowler)
HENRY THE LION, DUKE OF SAXONY AND BAVARIA **10**:123 *bibliog.*
Braunschweig **3**:458
Frederick I, King of Germany and Holy Roman Emperor (Frederick Barbarossa) **8**:290
Saxony **17**:105
Welf (family) **20**:97
HENRY OF LUXEMBURG *see* HENRY VII, KING OF GERMANY AND HOLY ROMAN EMPEROR (Henry of Luxemburg)
HENRY THE NAVIGATOR **10**:123–124 *bibliog., illus.*; **15**:453 *illus.*
exploration **7**:334
Madeira Islands **13**:40
Portugal, history of **15**:454
HENRY THE PROUD, DUKE OF BAVARIA
Welf (family) **20**:97
HENRY STREET SETTLEMENT (New York City)
Wald, Lillian D. **20**:9
HENRYETTA (Oklahoma)
map (35° 27′N 95° 59′W) **14**:368
HENRY'S LAW
phase equilibrium **15**:223
HENRYSON, ROBERT **10**:130 *bibliog.*
HENSCHEL, SIR GEORGE **10**:130 *bibliog.*
HENSLOW, JOHN STEVENS
Darwin, Charles **6**:41
HENSON, JIM
Muppets **13**:644–645 *illus.*
HENSON, MATTHEW A. **2**:143 *illus.*
Peary, Robert Edwin **15**:128
HENTSCH, RICHARD
Marne, Battles of the **13**:162
HENZADA (Burma)
map (17° 38′N 95° 28′E) **3**:573
HENZE, HANS WERNER **10**:130 *bibliog.*
HEPARIN **10**:130
anticoagulant **2**:60
pulmonary embolism **15**:619
HEPATIC ARTERY
liver **12**:374
HEPATITIS **10**:130 *bibliog.*
Blumberg, Baruch S. **3**:346
cirrhosis **4**:445
diseases, animal **6**:191
infectious diseases **11**:167
jaundice **11**:385
liver **12**:374
HEPATOPANCREATIC DUCT **11**:231 *illus.*
HEPBURN, JAMES, 4TH EARL OF BOTHWELL *see* BOTHWELL, JAMES HEPBURN, 4TH EARL OF
HEPBURN, JAMES CURTIS
Yokohama (Japan) **20**:329
HEPBURN, KATHARINE **5**:383 *illus.*; **10**:131 *bibliog., illus.*
Bogart, Humphrey **3**:359
Tracy, Spencer **19**:262
HEPBURN ACT
Roosevelt, Theodore **16**:310
HEPHAESTUS **10**:131
HEPHTHALITES
Asia, history of **2**:251
Taxila **19**:48
HEPHZIBAH (Georgia)
map (33° 19′N 82° 6′W) **9**:114
HEPPLEWHITE, GEORGE **10**:131 *bibliog.*
HEPPNER (Oregon)
map (45° 21′N 119° 33′W) **14**:427
HEPTAGON
polygon **15**:419 *illus.*
HEPWORTH, DAME BARBARA **10**:131 *bibliog.*
HEPWORTH, CECIL
film, history of **8**:81
HERA **10**:131
mythology **13**:700
HERACLEIDES PONTICUS **10**:131 *bibliog.*
HERACLES *see* HERCULES
HERACLITUS **10**:131–132 *bibliog.*
logos **12**:397
pre-Socratic philosophy **15**:532
HERACLIUS, BYZANTINE EMPEROR **10**:132 *bibliog.*
HERALDRY **10**:132–134 *bibliog., illus.*
cross **5**:361
flag **8**:134
fleur-de-lis **8**:163
guilds **9**:395 *illus.*
Indus civilization **11**:154
tartan **19**:40–41
HERAT (Afghanistan) **10**:134
map (34° 20′N 62° 12′E) **1**:133
HERB OF GRACE *see* RUE
HERB LAKE (Manitoba)
map (54° 47′N 99° 47′W) **13**:119
HERB MEDICINE
Chinese medicine **4**:391
medicinal plants **13**:266
HERBACEOUS PLANT **10**:134
HERBART, JOHANN FRIEDRICH **10**:134–135 *bibliog., illus.*
primary education **15**:537
HERBERT, GEORGE **10**:135 *bibliog.*
HERBERT, VICTOR **10**:135 *bibliog.*
Pittsburgh Symphony Orchestra **15**:322
HERBERT, WALLY **2**:142–143 *illus., map*
HERBICIDE **10**:135–136 *bibliog., illus.*
chemical and biological warfare **4**:312
environmental health **7**:212
gardening **9**:44
hazardous herbicides **10**:136
pesticides **15**:197–198
pollutants, chemical **15**:410
properties and use **10**:136
types **10**:135–136
HERBIVORE **10**:136 *bibliog.*
appendix **2**:88
HERBLOCK **10**:136
cartoon (editorial and political) **4**:177 *illus.*
HERBNORE
dinosaur **6**:179–182 *table*
HERBS AND SPICES **10**:136–137 *bibliog., illus.*
See also FLAVORS AND FRAGRANCES; names of specific herbs and spices, e.g., ANISE; BASIL (botany); CUMIN; etc.
early uses **10**:137
essential oils **7**:244–245
medicinal plants **13**:266–267
modern uses **10**:137
spice trade **18**:180–181
synthetic flavorings **10**:137
HERCEGOVINA (Yugoslavia) **3**:407 *map*
HERCULANEUM (Italy) **10**:137–138 *bibliog., illus.*
Getty Museum **9**:160
mural painting **13**:646; **19**:144 *illus.*
Pompeii **15**:423–424
Roman art and architecture **16**:276
HERCULANEUM (Missouri)
map (38° 16′N 90° 23′W) **13**:476
HERCULES **10**:138 *bibliog., illus.*
Cerberus **4**:259
Hydra (mythology) **10**:329
Nemea **14**:80
theft of the apples of the Hesperides **17**:160 *illus.*
HERCULES' CLUB (botany) **10**:138
angelica tree **1**:413
HERDER, JOHANN GOTTFRIED VON **10**:138 *bibliog.*
HÉRÉ, EMMANUEL
Nancy (France) **14**:12
HEREDIA, JOSÉ MARÍA
Latin American literature **12**:229
HEREDIA, JOSÉ MARIA DE **10**:138–139
HEREDITY **10**:139–141 *bibliog., illus.*
Avery, Oswald T. **2**:370
behavioral genetics **3**:169–170
birth defects **3**:295
cancer **4**:103
development **6**:139–140
eugenics **7**:263–264
fruit fly **8**:347
Galton, Sir Francis **9**:22–23
genetic code **9**:79–82
genetic diseases **9**:82–84
genetic engineering **9**:84–85
genetics **9**:85–90
intelligence **11**:203–204
Lamarck, Jean Baptiste **12**:173–174
life **12**:326–327
Mendel, Gregor Johann **13**:294
mimicry **13**:436
Morgan, Thomas Hunt **13**:579
plant engineering **15**:342–343
population genetics **15**:439–440
race **16**:33–35
racism **16**:37
Sutton, Walter S. **18**:373
Weismann, August **20**:95
Wilson, Edmund B. **20**:164
HEREFORD (Arizona)
map (31° 26′N 110° 6′W) **2**:160
HEREFORD (Texas)
map (34° 49′N 102° 24′W) **19**:129
HEREFORD CATTLE **4**:216 *illus.*; **12**:20 *illus.*
HEREFORD AND WORCESTER (England) **10**:141
cities
Worcester **20**:216
HERERO **10**:141 *bibliog.*
HERESY **10**:141–142 *bibliog.*
adoptionism **1**:107
Albigenses **1**:260
antinomianism **2**:64
Apollinarianism **2**:79
Arianism **2**:153–154
Arnauld, Antoine **2**:183
Bogomils **3**:360
Docetism **6**:210
Donatists **6**:237
dualism **6**:287
Ebionites **7**:35–36
Eunomius **7**:265
Eutyches **7**:311
Galileo Galilei **9**:15
gnosticism **9**:213–214
Honorius I, Pope **10**:224
Hussites **10**:321
Inquisition **11**:183–185

torture **19**:247
Lollards **12**:398
Manichaeism **13**:116–117
Marcion **13**:147
Monophysitism **13**:537
Monothelitism **13**:540
Montanism **13**:551
Nestorianism **14**:97
Ophites **14**:404
Paulicians **15**:119
Pelagianism **15**:137
Priscillian **15**:553
quietism **16**:26
Sabellianism **17**:5
Spinoza, Baruch **18**:187 *illus.*
Waldenses **20**:9
HEREWARD THE WAKE **10**:142
HERFORD (Germany, East and West)
map (52° 6′N 8° 40′E) **9**:140
HERGESHEIMER, JOSEPH **10**:142
HERING, EWALD
color perception **5**:114
HERINGTON (Kansas)
map (38° 40′N 96° 57′W) **12**:18
HERISAU (Switzerland)
map (47° 23′N 9° 17′E) **18**:394
HERITAGE CANADA
historic preservation **10**:182
HERJULFSON, BJARNE
exploration **7**:337 *map*
HERKIMER (New York)
map (43° 2′N 74° 59′W) **14**:149
HERKIMER (county in New York)
map (43° 25′N 75° 0′W) **14**:149
HERKIMER, NICHOLAS **10**:142
HERKOMER, HUBERT
social realism **18**:13
HERMAN, JERRY
musical comedy **13**:675
HERMANN (Missouri)
map (38° 42′N 91° 27′W) **13**:476
HERMANSVILLE (Michigan)
map (45° 42′N 87° 37′W) **13**:377
HERMANVILLE (Mississippi)
map (31° 58′N 90° 50′W) **13**:469
HERMAPHRODITE **10**:142 *bibliog.*
barnacle **3**:85
earthworm **7**:30
occurrence **10**:142
pseudohermaphrodite **10**:142
reproduction **16**:162
HERMAPHRODITUS **10**:142
HERMAS **10**:142
Apostolic Fathers **2**:85
HERMES **10**:142
caduceus **4**:12
HERMETIC LITERATURE **10**:142
HERMIONE **10**:142–143
HERMISTON (Oregon)
map (45° 51′N 119° 17′W) **14**:427
HERMIT **10**:143 *bibliog.*
Carthusians **4**:174
monasticism **13**:521 *illus.*
Simeon Stylites, Saint **17**:314
HERMIT CRAB **10**:143 *illus.*
HERMITAGE (Arkansas)
map (33° 27′N 92° 10′W) **2**:166
HERMITAGE (Missouri)
map (37° 56′N 93° 19′W) **13**:476
HERMITAGE (Newfoundland)
map (47° 33′N 55° 56′W) **14**:166
HERMITAGE BAY
map (47° 35′N 56° 5′W) **14**:166
HERMITAGE MUSEUM **10**:143 *bibliog.*
Winter Palace **20**:181
HERMITE, CHARLES **10**:143
mathematics, history of **13**:226
HERMOGENES OF PRIENE
Greek architecture **9**:337
Magnesia **13**:53
HERMON, MOUNT **10**:143
map (33° 26′N 35° 51′E) **12**:265
HERMOSILLO (Mexico) **10**:143
map (29° 4′N 110° 58′W) **13**:357
HERNAD RIVER
map (47° 56′N 21° 8′E) **10**:307
HERNÁNDEZ, GREGORIO *see* FERNÁNDEZ, GREGORIO
HERNÁNDEZ DE CÓRDOBA, FRANCISCO
León (Nicaragua) **12**:289
Mexico, history of **13**:362
HERNANDO (county in Florida)
map (28° 34′N 82° 22′W) **8**:172
HERNANDO (Mississippi)
map (34° 49′N 89° 59′W) **13**:469
HERNDON, WILLIAM HENRY **10**:143 *bibliog.*
Lincoln, Mary Todd **12**:350
Rutledge, Ann **16**:376
HERNIA **10**:143–144 *bibliog.*
hiatus hernia **10**:144
heartburn **10**:97
inguinal hernia **10**:143
strangulated **10**:144
surgery causing **10**:143–144
HERNING (Denmark)
map (56° 8′N 8° 59′E) **6**:109
HERO (literature)
narrative and dramatic devices **14**:22
HERO OF ALEXANDRIA **10**:144
automaton **2**:358
boiler **3**:362
engineering **7**:177
jet propulsion **11**:407
pump **15**:622
turbine **19**:340
vending machine **19**:538
HERO AND LEANDER **10**:144
Dardanelles **6**:37 *map*
HERO LONGHORN BEETLE **3**:167 *illus.*
HEROD (dynasty) **10**:144 *bibliog.*
HEROD ANTIPAS
Herod (dynasty) **10**:144
HEROD THE GREAT
Herod (dynasty) **10**:144
Jews **11**:413–414
Masada **13**:194
temple **19**:96 *illus.*
HERODOTUS **10**:144–145 *bibliog.*, *illus.*
geography **9**:100
history **10**:183; **10**:184
History of the Persian Wars, The **10**:186
Persian Wars **15**:188
Seven Wonders of the World **17**:216
Thucydides **19**:184
HEROD'S TEMPLE **19**:96 *illus.*
HEROIC COUPLET
Dryden, John **6**:284–285
Pope, Alexander **15**:430
versification **19**:562
HEROIN **10**:145 *bibliog.*
drug abuse **6**:280; **6**:281
drug trafficking **6**:281
methadone **13**:343
morphine **13**:487
opium **14**:406
respiratory system disorders **16**:181
HERON **3**:281 *illus.*; **3**:289; *illus.*; **10**:145 *bibliog.*, *illus.*
egret **7**:74
HERON LAKE (Minnesota)
map (43° 47′N 95° 19′W) **13**:453
HEROPHILUS
anatomy **1**:395
HÉROULT, PAUL L. T.
aluminum **1**:317
HERPES **10**:145–146 *bibliog.*
chicken pox **4**:345
encephalitis **7**:162
mononucleosis **13**:537
shingles **17**:262
skin diseases **17**:342
venereal disease **19**:540
virus particle **19**:613 *illus.*
HERPES ZOSTER *see* CHICKEN POX; SHINGLES
HERPETOLOGY **10**:146 *bibliog.*
HERREID (South Dakota)
map (45° 50′N 100° 4′W) **18**:103
HERRENCHIEMSEE, SCHLOSS
Louis II's Bavarian palaces **12**:423
HERRERA, FERNANDO DE
Spanish literature **18**:158
HERRERA, FRANCISCO DE **10**:146 *bibliog.*
HERRERA, JOSÉ JOAQUÍN
Mexican War **13**:351–352
HERRERA, JUAN DE **10**:146 *bibliog.*
Spanish art and architecture **18**:153
HERRERA, OMAR TORRIJOS *see* TORRIJOS HERRERA, OMAR
HERRERA CAMPINS, LUIS **10**:146
HERRICK, ROBERT **10**:146 *bibliog.*
HERRICK, SAMUEL
Institute of Navigation **11**:195
HERRIMAN, GEORGE
comic strip **5**:135
HERRIN (Illinois)
map (37° 48′N 89° 2′W) **11**:42
HERRING **8**:124 *illus.*; **10**:146–147 *bibliog.*, *illus.*
menhaden **13**:297
sardine **17**:76
world fishing grounds **8**:125 *map*
HERRING, AUGUSTUS M.
Chanute, Octave **4**:282
HERRING COVE (Nova Scotia)
map (44° 34′N 63° 34′W) **14**:269
HERRIOT, ÉDOUARD **10**:147 *bibliog.*
HERSCHEL, SIR JOHN **10**:147 *bibliog.*, *illus.*; **15**:268 *illus.*
mathematics, history of **13**:226
HERSCHEL, SIR WILLIAM **10**:147–148 *bibliog.*, *illus.*
astronomy, history of **2**:279
binary stars **3**:256–257
galaxy **2**:280 *illus.*
solar system **18**:45
telescope **10**:147
Uranus **10**:147
HERSCHER (Illinois)
map (41° 3′N 88° 6′W) **11**:42
HERSEY, JOHN **10**:148 *bibliog.*, *illus.*
HERSHEY (Nebraska)
map (41° 10′N 101° 0′W) **14**:70
HERSHEY (Pennsylvania)
map (40° 17′N 76° 39′W) **15**:147
HERSHEY, ALFRED DAY **10**:148
Luria, Salvador **12**:467
virus **19**:614
HERSHEY, MILTON SNAVELEY **10**:148 *bibliog.*
HERSTAL (Belgium)
map (50° 40′N 5° 38′E) **3**:177
HERSTMONCEUX ROYAL OBSERVATORY *see* ROYAL GREENWICH OBSERVATORY
HERTFORD (North Carolina)
map (36° 11′N 76° 28′W) **14**:242
HERTFORD (county in North Carolina)
map (36° 20′N 76° 57′W) **14**:242
HERTFORD COLLEGE (Oxford University) **14**:474
HERTFORDSHIRE (England) **10**:148
cities
Saint Albans **17**:15–16
HERTS AND TALLANT
music and concert halls **13**:670
HERTWIG, OSCAR **10**:148
HERTZ **7**:117 *table*; **10**:148
frequency allocations **8**:326–327 *table*
Hertzian resonance
Kastler, Alfred **12**:30
units, physical **19**:466 *table*
HERTZ, GUSTAV **10**:148–149
Franck, James **10**:148
Nobel Prize **10**:149
quantum mechanics **10**:148
HERTZ, HEINRICH RUDOLPH **10**:149 *bibliog.*
hertz **10**:148
Maxwell's equations **13**:242
optics **14**:410
radio **16**:44
HERTZ, JOSEPH HERMAN **10**:149
HERTZLIYYA (Israel)
map (32° 11′N 34° 50′E) **11**:302
HERTZOG, JAMES BARRY MUNNIK **10**:149 *bibliog.*
Smuts, Jan **17**:375
South Africa **18**:83
HERTZSPRUNG, EJNAR **10**:149
HERTZSPRUNG-RUSSELL DIAGRAM **10**:149–150 *bibliog.*, *illus.*
astronomy and astrophysics **2**:284
Harvard classification of stars **10**:64
Hayashi evolutionary track **10**:80
Hertzsprung, Ejnar **10**:149
main sequence **10**:149; **13**:68
pulsating stars **15**:621
Russell, Henry Norris **16**:350
star **18**:225–226
stars, magnitude and spectral types **10**:149–150
stellar evolution **18**:250–251 *illus.*
stellar spectrum **18**:252 *illus.*
subdwarf **18**:313
subgiant **18**:313
variable star **19**:522–523
HERULI
Germanic peoples **9**:138
HERUT (political party)
Begin, Menachem **3**:168
HERZBERG, GERHARD **10**:150
HERZEGOVINA *see* BOSNIA AND HERCEGOVINA (Yugoslavia)
HERZEN, ALEKSANDR IVANOVICH **10**:150 *bibliog.*
HERZL, THEODOR **10**:150 *bibliog.*, *illus.*; **11**:416 *illus.*
Zionism **20**:369
HERZOG (book)
Bellow, Saul **3**:190–191
HERZOG, ÉMILE *see* MAUROIS, ANDRÉ
HERZOG, MAURICE
Annapurna **2**:32
HERZOG, WERNER **10**:150 *bibliog.*
The Mystery of Kaspar Hauser (film)
feral children **8**:51
HESBURGH, THEODORE M. **10**:150–151 *bibliog.*
HESCHEL, ABRAHAM JOSHUA **10**:151 *bibliog.*
HESDIN, JACQUEMART DE **10**:151 *bibliog.*
HESIOD **10**:151 *bibliog.*
aretê **2**:146
Theogony **19**:157
HESPERIA (California)
map (34° 25′N 117° 18′W) **4**:31
HESPERIA (Michigan)
map (43° 34′N 86° 4′W) **13**:377
HESPERIDES **10**:151
HESPERORNIS **3**:279 *illus.*; **10**:151 *bibliog.*
HESS, GERMAIN HENRI
chemistry, history of **4**:327
Hess's law **10**:151
HESS, H. H. **10**:151
HESS, DAME MYRA **10**:151–152 *bibliog.*
HESS, RUDOLF **10**:152 *bibliog.*, *illus.*
Nuremberg Trials **14**:297
HESS, VICTOR **10**:152
cosmic rays **5**:283
HESS, WALTER RUDOLF **10**:152
HESSE (West Germany) **10**:152
cities
Darmstadt **6**:39
Frankfurt am Main **8**:280–281 *illus.*
Kassel **12**:30
Wiesbaden **20**:146
history
Germany in 1648 **9**:151 *map*
Germany 1815–1871 **9**:153 *map*
Nassau (historical region) **14**:25
Philip of Hesse **15**:232
HESSE, HERMANN **9**:134 *illus.*; **10**:152–153 *bibliog.*, *illus.*
Steppenwolf **18**:257
HESSE-DARMSTADT
Hesse (West Germany) **10**:152
HESSE-KASSEL
Hesse (West Germany) **10**:152
HESSE-NASSAU
Hesse (West Germany) **10**:152
HESSEL, JOHANN F. C.
mineral **13**:439
HESSEN (West Germany) *see* HESSE (West Germany)
HESSIANS **10**:153 *bibliog.*
Hesse (West Germany) **10**:152
Knyphausen, Wilhelm, Baron von **12**:103
Trenton, Battle of **19**:291
HESSITE
telluride minerals **19**:91
HESS'S LAW **10**:151
chemical energy **4**:315
endothermic and exothermic reactions **7**:171
HESSTON (Kansas)
map (38° 8′N 97° 26′W) **12**:18
HESTIA **10**:153
HESTON, LEONARD
behavioral genetics **3**:170
HET NEDERLANDS BALLET *see* DUTCH NATIONAL BALLET
HETEROCYCLE *see* HETEROCYCLIC COMPOUND
HETEROCYCLIC COMPOUND **10**:153 *bibliog.*
aromatic compounds **2**:186
chemical nomenclature **4**:321 *illus.*
pyrrole **15**:639
rings, types **10**:153
HETEROCYCLIC COMPOUNDS
alicyclic compounds **1**:293
HETERODYNE PRINCIPLE **10**:153–154 *bibliog.*, *illus.*
radio **16**:45; **16**:46
radio frequency
conversion **10**:153–154
unknown, calibration **10**:154
superheterodyne circuit
Armstrong, Edwin **2**:179
HETH (letter)
H (letter) **10**:3
HETTINGER (North Dakota)
map (46° 0′N 102° 39′W) **14**:248
HETTINGER (county in North Dakota)
map (46° 30′N 102° 20′W) **14**:248
HEULANDITE *see* ZEOLITE
HEUNEBURG (Germany)
European prehistory **7**:305
HEURISTICS
cybernetics **5**:401
problem solving **15**:559
HEUVELTON (New York)
map (44° 37′N 75° 25′W) **14**:149
HEVELIUS, JOHANNES
astronomy, history of **2**:279
HEVESY, GEORG VON **10**:154 *bibliog.*
HEWISH, ANTONY **10**:154
Mullard Radio AStronomy Observatory **13**:636
pulsar **15**:620
HEWITT, ABRAM STEVENS **10**:154 *bibliog.*

HEWITT, JOHN H.
American music **1**:349
HEXACHLOROPHENE **10**:154
antiseptic **2**:68
HEXAGON **10**:154
polygon **15**:419 *illus.*
HEXAGONAL SYSTEM **10**:154–155
common minerals **10**:155
crystal **5**:375 *illus.*
emerald **7**:154
symmetry classes **10**:154
HEXOKINASE
metabolism **13**:327
HEYDEN, JAN VAN DER **10**:155 *bibliog.*
HEYDRICH, REINHARD
Holocaust **10**:206
Lidice (Czechoslovakia) **12**:323
HEYERDAHL, THOR **10**:155 *bibliog., illus.*
balsa **3**:54
Easter Island **7**:33
Kon-Tiki **12**:108
Ra II **16**:29 *illus.*
HEYROVSKÝ, JAROSLAV **10**:155
HEYSE, PAUL VON **10**:155 *bibliog.*
HEYWARD, DUBOSE **10**:155 *bibliog.*
Porgy and Bess **15**:441
HEYWOOD, JOHN **10**:155–156 *bibliog.*
HEYWOOD, THOMAS **10**:156 *bibliog.*
HEYWORTH (Illinois)
map (40° 19′N 88° 59′W) **11**:42
HEZEKIAH, KING OF JUDAH **10**:156
HI-FI *see* HIGH FIDELITY
HIALEAH (Florida) **10**:156
map (25° 49′N 80° 17′W) **8**:172
HIATUS HERNIA *see* HERNIA
HIAWASSEE (Georgia)
map (34° 58′N 83° 46′W) **9**:114
HIAWATHA **10**:156 *bibliog.*
Iroquois League **11**:280
Mohawk **13**:502
HIAWATHA (Kansas)
map (39° 51′N 95° 32′W) **12**:18
HIAWATHA (Utah)
map (39° 29′N 111° 1′W) **19**:492
HIBA, AL- *see* LAGASH (Iraq)
HIBBERT, ELEANOR BURFORD *see* HOLT, VICTORIA
HIBBING (Minnesota)
map (47° 25′N 92° 56′W) **13**:453
HIBERNATION **10**:156 *bibliog.*
bear **3**:140
body temperature **3**:358
lungfish **12**:463
pika **15**:301
turtle **19**:353
HIBISCUS **8**:179 *illus.*; **10**:156–157 *illus.*; **13**:92 *illus.*
pollination **15**:408 *illus.*
HICKMAN (Kentucky)
map (36° 34′N 89° 11′W) **12**:47
HICKMAN (county in Kentucky)
map (36° 40′N 89° 0′W) **12**:47
HICKMAN (county in Tennessee)
map (35° 50′N 87° 25′W) **19**:104
HICKOCK BELT (trophy)
Mantle, Mickey **13**:131
Robinson, Brooks **16**:243
HICKOK, WILD BILL **10**:157 *bibliog., illus.*
Deadwood (South Dakota) **6**:65
HICKORY **10**:157 *bibliog., illus.*
pecan **15**:129–130
HICKORY (Mississippi)
map (32° 19′N 89° 1′W) **13**:469
HICKORY (county in Missouri)
map (37° 55′N 93° 20′W) **13**:476
HICKORY (North Carolina)
map (35° 44′N 81° 21′W) **14**:242
HICKORY BARK BEETLE **3**:167 *illus.*
HICKS, EDWARD **10**:157–158 *bibliog., illus.*
The Peaceable Kingdom **10**:157 *illus.*
HICKS, ELIAS **10**:158 *bibliog.*
HICKS, SIR JOHN RICHARD **10**:158
HICKSVILLE (New York)
map (40° 46′N 73° 32′W) **14**:149
HICKSVILLE (Ohio)
map (41° 18′N 84° 46′W) **14**:357
HIDA MOUNTAINS
map (36° 25′N 137° 40′E) **11**:361
HIDAKA RANGE
map (42° 35′N 142° 45′E) **11**:361
HIDALGO (Mexico) **10**:158
cities
Pachuca **15**:4–5
map (24° 15′N 99° 26′W) **13**:357
HIDALGO (county in New Mexico)
map (32° 0′N 108° 40′W) **14**.136
HIDALGO (county in Texas)
map (26° 25′N 98° 10′W) **19**:129
HIDALGO, JUAN
Spanish music **18**:162
HIDALGO DEL PARRAL (Mexico)
map (26° 56′N 105° 40′W) **13**:357
HIDALGO Y COSTILLA, MIGUEL **10**:158 *bibliog., illus.*; **12**:220 *illus.*
Guadalajara (Mexico) **9**:384
Latin America, history of **12**:219
Mexico, history of **13**:363–364 *illus.*
HIDATSA (American Indians) **10**:158–159 *bibliog.*
buffalo hunt **11**:129 *illus.*
Crow **5**:363
Gros Ventres **9**:370
Mississippian culture **14**:239
Sacagawea **17**:6
HIDES *see* LEATHER AND HIDES
HIDETADA, SHOGUN OF JAPAN
Tokugawa (family) **19**:223
HIDEYORI, TOYOTOMI
Ieyasu, Shogun of Japan **11**:32
HIDEYOSHI **10**:159 *bibliog.*
castle **4**:190
Ieyasu, Shogun of Japan **11**:32
Japan, history of **11**:368–369
Osaka (Japan) **14**:452
shogun **17**:281
HIERAKONPOLIS (Egypt) **7**:81 *map*; **10**:159
HIERO I, TYRANT OF SYRACUSE **10**:159
HIERO II, TYRANT OF SYRACUSE **10**:159
Punic Wars **15**:624
HIEROGLYPHICS **10**:159–161 *bibliog., illus.*
Book of the Dead **3**:386 *illus.*
Champollion, Jean François **4**:278
Dresden Codex **13**:244 *illus.*
Egyptology **7**:90
Hittites **10**:189 *illus.*
hoopoe **10**:228
inscription **11**:186
languages, extinct **12**:198–199
Palermo Stone **15**:43
pre-Columbian art and architecture **15**:497
Rosetta Stone **16**:317 *illus.*
shorthand **17**:284
syllabaries **20**:293
Tanis **19**:23
Ugarit **19**:374
writing systems, evolution of **20**:292 *illus.*
Zapotec writing **20**:356
HIGBEE (Missouri)
map (39° 19′N 92° 31′W) **13**:476
HIGGINS, MARGUERITE **10**:161
HIGGINS, WILLIAM **10**:161
HIGGINS LAKE
map (44° 30′N 84° 45′W) **13**:377
HIGGINSON, HENRY LEE
Boston Symphony Orchestra **3**:410
HIGGINSON, THOMAS WENTWORTH **10**:161 *bibliog.*
Dickinson, Emily **6**:158
HIGGINSVILLE (Missouri)
map (39° 4′N 93° 43′W) **13**:476
HIGGS PARTICLE **10**:161
HIGH ALTITUDE OBSERVATORY **10**:161
HIGH ATLAS MOUNTAINS
map (31° 30′N 6° 0′W) **13**:585
HIGH BLOOD PRESSURE *see* HYPERTENSION
HIGH BRIDGE (New Jersey)
map (40° 40′N 74° 54′W) **14**:129
HIGH DAN LAKE *see* NASSER, LAKE
HIGH ENERGY ASTRONOMICAL OBSERVATORY (artificial satellite) **10**:161
space exploration **18**:123
X-ray astronomy **20**:306–307
HIGH FIDELITY **10**:161 *bibliog.*
HIGH JUMP
track and field **19**:260 *illus.*
HIGH-LEVEL LANGUAGES
computer **5**:160f; **5**:160h
computer languages **5**:160o–160p
computer programming **5**:163–164
HIGH POINT (Bermuda)
map (32° 15′N 64° 50′W) **3**:219
HIGH POINT (New Jersey)
map (41° 19′N 74° 40′W) **14**:129
HIGH POINT (North Carolina)
map (35° 58′N 80° 1′W) **14**:242
HIGH PRAIRIE (Alberta)
map (55° 26′N 116° 29′W) **1**:256
HIGH-PRESSURE REGION **10**:162 *bibliog.*
desert **6**:126
Hadley cell **10**:8
HIGH RIVER (Alberta)
map (50° 35′N 113° 52′W) **1**:256
HIGH SCHOOL *see* SECONDARY EDUCATION
HIGH SEAS
maritime law **13**:158
right of search **16**:222
seas, freedom of the **17**:175–176
HIGH SPRINGS (Florida)
map (29° 50′N 82° 36′W) **8**:172
HIGH TECHNOLOGY **10**:162
HIGH WIND OVER JAMAICA, A (book)
Hughes, Richard **10**:293
HIGH-WIRE WALKING (circus act)
Wallenda (family) **20**:15
HIGH WYCOMBE (England)
map (51° 38′N 0° 46′W) **19**:403
HIGHER EDUCATION *see* UNIVERSITY
HIGHFIELD (Zimbabwe)
map (17° 50′S 31° 0′E) **20**:365
HIGHLAND (Illinois)
map (38° 44′N 89° 41′W) **11**:42
HIGHLAND (Indiana)
map (41° 33′N 87° 27′W) **11**:111
HIGHLAND (New York)
map (41° 43′N 73° 58′W) **14**:149
HIGHLAND (county in Ohio)
map (39° 12′N 83° 37′W) **14**:357
HIGHLAND (Scotland) **10**:162
cities
Inverness **11**:233
counties (former)
Caithness **4**:19
HIGHLAND (county in Virginia)
map (38° 20′N 79° 38′W) **19**:607
HIGHLAND CATTLE **4**:216 *illus.*
HIGHLAND GAMES **10**:162 *bibliog.*; **17**:149 *illus.*
HIGHLAND MOCCASIN *see* COPPERHEAD (snake)
HIGHLAND PARK (Illinois)
map (42° 11′N 87° 48′W) **11**:42
HIGHLAND PARK (Michigan)
map (42° 24′N 83° 6′W) **13**:377
HIGHLAND PONY
pony **15**:428
HIGHLAND SPRINGS (Virginia)
map (37° 33′N 77° 20′W) **19**:607
HIGHLANDS (county in Florida)
map (27° 20′N 81° 16′W) **8**:172
HIGHLANDS (New Jersey)
map (40° 24′N 73° 59′W) **14**:129
HIGHLANDS (North Carolina)
map (35° 3′N 83° 12′W) **14**:242
HIGHLANDS, THE (Scotland) **10**:162 *bibliog.*
Argyll (Scotland) **2**:153
Ross and Cromarty **16**:318
tartan **19**:40
United Kingdom **19**:405
HIGHMORE (South Dakota)
map (44° 31′N 99° 27′W) **18**:103
HIGHTSTOWN (New Jersey)
map (40° 16′N 74° 31′W) **14**:129
HIGHWAY SAFETY ACTS
transportation **19**:282
"HIGHWAYMAN, THE" (poem)
Noyes, Alfred **14**:277
HIGHWAYS *see* ROADS AND HIGHWAYS
HIGUCHI ICHIYO **10**:162
HIIUMAA
Estonian Soviet Socialist Republic **7**:247
HIJACKING *see* AIRPLANE HIJACKING
HIKING **10**:162–163 *bibliog.*
See also MOUNTAIN CLIMBING
Appalachian Trail **2**:86
backpacker **14**:37 *illus.*
hypothermia **10**:351
youth hostel **20**:337
HIKMET RAN, NAZIM *see* NAZIM HIKMET
HILALI
Berbers **3**:207
HILARY OF POITIERS, SAINT **10**:163 *bibliog.*
HILBERT (Wisconsin)
map (44° 9′N 88° 10′W) **20**:185
HILBERT, DAVID **10**:163 *bibliog.*
Euclidean geometry **7**:263
mathematics, history of **13**:226
von Neumann, John **19**:634
HILDEBRAND (literature) *see* BEETS, NICOLAAS
HILDEBRAND (pope) *see* GREGORY VII, POPE
HILDEBRAND, ADOLF VON (sculptor) **10**:163 *bibliog.*
HILDEBRAND BROTHERS (inventors)
motorcycle **13**:614
HILDEBRANDT, JOHANN LUCAS VON **10**:163 *bibliog.*
belvedere **3**:193
Upper Belvedere, The **2**:352 *illus.*
HILDESHEIM (Germany, East and West)
map (52° 9′N 9° 57′E) **9**:140
HILDRETH (Nebraska)
map (40° 20′N 99° 3′W) **14**:70
HILL (geology) *see* KAME
HILL (county in Montana)
map (48° 40′N 110° 5′W) **13**:547
HILL (county in Texas)
map (32° 2′N 97° 10′W) **19**:129
HILL, A. P. **10**:163 *bibliog.*
HILL, ARCHIBALD V.
Meyerhof, Otto **14**:369
HILL, D. H. **10**:163–164 *bibliog.*
HILL, D. O., AND ADAMSON, ROBERT **10**:164 *bibliog.*
photography, history and art of **15**:268 *illus.*
HILL, GEORGE WILLIAM
three-body problem **19**:181
HILL, JAMES JEROME **10**:164 *bibliog.*
Harriman (family) **10**:56–57
HILL, JOE **10**:164 *bibliog.*
Industrial Workers of the World **11**:160
HILL, ROBERT
photosynthesis **15**:275
HILL, SIR ROWLAND **10**:164 *bibliog.*
postal services **15**:460
HILL, URELI CORELLI
New York Philharmonic **14**:155
HILL BANK (Belize)
map (17° 35′N 88° 42′W) **3**:183
HILL CITY (Kansas)
map (39° 22′N 99° 51′W) **12**:18
HILL TIPPERA (India) *see* TRIPURA (India)
HILLABY, MOUNT
map (13° 12′N 59° 35′W) **3**:75
HILLARY, SIR EDMUND **10**:164 *bibliog., illus.*
Ross Dependency (Antarctica) **16**:318
HILLCREST HEIGHTS (Maryland)
map (38° 52′N 76° 57′W) **13**:188
HILLEL **10**:164–165 *bibliog.*
HILLER, JOHANN ADAM
German and Austrian music **9**:130
singspiel **17**:322
HILLERØD (Denmark)
Frederiksborg Castle **17**:112 *illus.*
map (55° 56′N 12° 19′E) **6**:109
HILLIARD (Florida)
map (30° 41′N 81° 55′W) **8**:172
HILLIARD, NICHOLAS **10**:165 *bibliog., illus.*
Elizabeth I of England **7**:184 *illus.*; **9**:312 *illus.*
miniature painting **13**:445
Oliver, Isaac **14**:379
Portrait of a Youth **7**:143 *illus.*; **10**:165 *illus.*
Treatise on the Art of Limning, A
limners **12**:345
HILLMAN, SIDNEY **10**:165 *bibliog.*
HILLMAN MOTOR CAR COMPANY
automotive industry **2**:364
HILLQUIT, MORRIS
Socialist party **18**:25
HILLS (Minnesota)
map (43° 32′N 96° 21′W) **13**:453
HILLS CREEK RESERVOIR
map (43° 40′N 122° 26′W) **14**:427
HILLS-OF-SNOW (botany) *see* HYDRANGEA
HILLSBORO (Illinois)
map (39° 9′N 89° 29′W) **11**:42
HILLSBORO (Kansas)
map (38° 21′N 97° 12′W) **12**:18
HILLSBORO (Missouri)
map (38° 14′N 90° 34′W) **13**:476
HILLSBORO (New Hampshire)
map (43° 7′N 71° 54′W) **14**:123
HILLSBORO (New Mexico)
map (32° 55′N 107° 34′W) **14**:136
HILLSBORO (North Dakota)
map (47° 26′N 97° 3′W) **14**:248
HILLSBORO (Ohio)
map (39° 12′N 83° 37′W) **14**:357
HILLSBORO (Oregon)
map (45° 31′N 122° 59′W) **14**:427
HILLSBORO (Texas)
map (32° 1′N 97° 8′W) **19**:129
HILLSBORO (Wisconsin)
map (43° 39′N 90° 21′W) **20**:185
HILLSBOROUGH (county in Florida)
map (27° 55′N 82° 15′W) **8**:172
HILLSBOROUGH (Grenada)
map (12° 28′N 61° 28′W) **9**:358
HILLSBOROUGH (New Brunswick)
map (45° 56′N 64° 39′W) **14**:117
HILLSBOROUGH (county in New Hampshire)
map (42° 58′N 71° 45′W) **14**:123

HILLSBOROUGH (North Carolina)
map (36° 5′N 79° 7′W) **14**:242
HILLSBOROUGH BAY (Florida)
map (27° 52′N 82° 27′W) **8**:172
HILLSBOROUGH BAY (Prince Edward Island)
map (46° 10′N 63° 5′W) **15**:548
HILLSBOROUGH RIVER
map (46° 13′N 62° 7′W) **15**:548
HILLSDALE (Michigan)
map (41° 55′N 84° 38′W) **13**:377
HILLSDALE (county in Michigan)
map (41° 53′N 84° 36′W) **13**:377
HILLSDALE (New Jersey)
map (41° 0′N 74° 2′W) **14**:129
HILLSIDE (New Jersey)
map (40° 42′N 74° 13′W) **14**:129
HILLSVILLE (Virginia)
map (36° 46′N 80° 44′W) **19**:607
HILO (Hawaii) **10**:165
map (19° 43′N 155° 5′W) **10**:72
HILO BAY
map (19° 44′N 155° 5′W) **10**:72
HILTNER, WILLIAM A.
Yerkes Observatory **20**:327
HILTON (New York)
map (43° 17′N 77° 48′W) **14**:149
HILTON, CONRAD **10**:165 *bibliog.*
HILTON, JAMES **10**:165
Goodbye, Mr. Chips **9**:245–246
HILTON HEAD ISLAND (South Carolina)
map (32° 13′N 80° 45′W) **18**:98
HILTON HOTELS
hotel **10**:261–262 *illus.*
HILVERDING, FRANZ
Kirov Ballet **12**:89
HILVERSUM (Netherlands)
map (52° 14′N 5° 10′E) **14**:99
HIMACHAL PRADESH (India) **10**:165
map (32° 0′N 77° 0′E) **11**:80
HIMALAYAN CAT **4**:195 *illus.*; **10**:165–166 *illus.*
longhaired cats **12**:408
HIMALAYAS **2**:234 *illus.*; **10**:166–167 *bibliog., illus., map*
art and architecture
Ellora **7**:149
Lamaist art and architecture **12**:172
Bhutan **3**:235
climate **10**:167
geology **10**:166
Himachal Pradesh **10**:165
India **11**:81
map (28° 0′N 84° 0′E) **10**:167
mountain climbing **13**:621
mountain life **13**:623 *illus.*
Nepal **14**:87 *illus.*
ranges and peaks **10**:166–167 *illus., map*
Annapurna **2**:32
Everest, Mount **7**:315
Godwin Austen **9**:221
Kanchenjunga **12**:13
Karakoram Range **12**:27
Sherpa **17**:259
Tibet **19**:189–190
vegetation and animal life **10**:167
HIMEJI (Japan)
castle **4**:190–191
map (34° 49′N 134° 42′E) **11**:361
HIMMLER, HEINRICH **10**:167–168 *bibliog., illus.*
HIMYARITIC LANGUAGE
Ma'rib **13**:151
HINCHE (Haiti)
map (19° 9′N 72° 1′W) **10**:15
HINCHINBROOK ISLAND
map (60° 22′N 146° 30′W) **1**:242
HINCKLEY (Illinois)
map (41° 46′N 88° 38′W) **11**:42
HINCKLEY (Minnesota)
map (46° 1′N 92° 56′W) **13**:453
HINCKLEY (Utah)
map (39° 20′N 112° 40′W) **19**:492
HINCKLEY, JOHN W., JR.
crime **5**:345
Reagan, Ronald **16**:102
HINCKS, SIR FRANCIS **10**:168 *bibliog.*
HINDEMITH, PAUL **10**:168 *bibliog., illus.*
HINDENBURG (airship)
airship **1**:226–227 *bibliog., illus.*; **20**:360–361 *illus.*
HINDENBURG, PAUL VON **10**:169 *bibliog., illus.*
Hitler, Adolf **10**:187
Ludendorff, Erich **12**:451
Tannenberg, Battles of **19**:24
World War I **20**:226 *illus.*; **20**:233
HINDI LANGUAGE
India **11**:83–84
Indo-Iranian languages **11**:145–146
HINDMAN (Kentucky)
map (37° 20′N 82° 59′W) **12**:47
HINDS (county in Mississippi)
map (32° 15′N 90° 25′W) **13**:469
HINDU *see* HINDUISM
HINDU-ARABIC SYSTEM
decimal **6**:73
numeral **14**:294
HINDU KUSH **10**:169
map (36° 0′N 71° 30′E) **1**:133
people
Indo-Iranian languages **11**:145–146
Kafir **12**:5
HINDUISM **10**:169–173 *bibliog., illus.*; **16**:140 *map*
art and architecture
folk art **8**:198
Indian art and architecture **11**:96–97 *illus.*
Mahabilipuram Shore Temple **13**:63 *illus.*
Southeast Asian art and architecture **18**:107–110
Asia, history of **2**:254; **2**:256
avatars **2**:369
Balinese **3**:37
beliefs and practices **10**:169–170
bhakti **3**:233–234
Brahmo Samaj **3**:440
caste **4**:186–187; **4**:187 *illus.*
Dayananda Sarasvati **6**:56
deities **10**:170
Brahma and Brahman **3**:440
Durga **6**:305
Ganesha **9**:36
Garuda **9**:52
Kali **12**:8
Krishna **12**:130
Lakshmi **12**:171
Shakti **17**:237
Shiva **17**:278
Vishnu **19**:617
dharma **6**:148
dietary laws **6**:165
fakir **8**:11
forms of worship **10**:170–171
funeral customs **11**:149 *illus.*
cremation **8**:364 *illus.*
Ganges River **11**:81 *illus.*
bathing **10**:172 *illus.*
guru **9**:407
Hare Krishna **10**:49; **16**:142 *illus.*
history **10**:172–173
Asia, history of **2**:250
India, history of **11**:89–90
migration to India **11**:87
Vijayanagar (India) **19**:593
Holst, Gustav **10**:208
incarnation **11**:73
Indian music **11**:103
karma **12**:28
Kashmir **12**:30
Krishnamurti, Jiddu **12**:130
literature **10**:172–173
Bhagavad Gita **3**:233
Indian literature **11**:101
Kamasutra **12**:9
Mahabharata, The **13**:64
Ramayana **16**:80
Upanishads **19**:471
Vedas **19**:530–531
Madhva **13**:41
mantra **13**:131
Manu **13**:131
Muslim League **13**:683
mythology **13**:695 *illus.*; **13**:699
Naga (mythological character) **14**:6
Narmada River **14**:21
nirvana **14**:201
om (symbol) **10**:170 *illus.*
Pahari **15**:14
Pakistan **15**:29
pantheism **15**:61
philosophy **10**:170; **15**:246
Vedanta **19**:530
Radhakrishnan, Sir Sarvepalli **16**:42
Rajput **16**:78
Ramakrishna **16**:79
Roy, Rammohun **16**:329
sacred cities and festivals **10**:171–172
shadow play **17**:234
sin **17**:317–318
soul **18**:70
suttee **18**:373
Tantra **19**:25
temple **10**:171–172 *illus.*; **19**:98
Bhubaneswar **3**:234
Elephanta **7**:134
Ellora **7**:148
Khajuraho **12**:65
Konarak **12**:108
Mahabalipuram **13**:63–64 *illus.*
Prambanan **15**:489
transmigration of souls **19**:274
Untouchables **19**:470–471
Varanasi **19**:521
Vivekananda **19**:622
wedding ceremony
marriage **13**:164 *illus.*
passage, rites of **15**:104 *illus.*
women in society **20**:203
Yamuna River **20**:317
yoga **20**:328–329
HINDUSTAN **10**:173
HINE, LEWIS
photography, history and art of **15**:269 *illus.*
photojournalism **15**:273
HINES (Oregon)
map (43° 34′N 119° 5′W) **14**:427
HINES, EARL **10**:173 *bibliog.*
HINES CREEK (Alberta)
map (56° 15′N 118° 36′W) **1**:256
HINESVILLE (Georgia)
map (31° 51′N 81° 36′W) **9**:114
HINGHAM (Massachusetts)
map (42° 14′N 70° 53′W) **13**:206
HINGHAM BAY
map (42° 17′N 70° 55′W) **3**:409
HINGOL RIVER
map (25° 23′N 65° 28′E) **15**:27
HINN ISLAND
map (68° 30′N 16° 0′E) **14**:261
HINNY
hybrid **10**:328
mule **13**:636
HINSDALE (county in Colorado)
map (37° 50′N 107° 20′W) **5**:116
HINSDALE (Illinois)
map (41° 48′N 87° 56′W) **11**:42
HINSDALE (Montana)
map (48° 24′N 107° 5′W) **13**:547
HINSDALE (New Hampshire)
map (42° 47′N 72° 29′W) **14**:123
HINSHELWOOD, SIR CYRIL NORMAN **10**:173 *bibliog.*
HINT AMM SEFIAN
Hierakonpolis **10**:159
HINTON (Alberta)
map (53° 25′N 117° 34′W) **1**:256
HINTON (Oklahoma)
map (35° 28′N 98° 21′W) **14**:368
HINTON (West Virginia)
map (37° 41′N 80° 53′W) **20**:111
HIP
joint (anatomy) **11**:439 *illus.*
muscle **13**:654
HIPPARCHUS (astronomer) **10**:173 *bibliog.*
astronomy, history of **2**:277
geography **9**:101
Greece, ancient **9**:331
mathematics, history of **13**:224
planetary motion **2**:278 *illus.*
HIPPARCHUS (Athenian tyrant)
Harmodius and Aristogiton **10**:51
Peisistratus **15**:134
HIPPER, FRANZ VON
World War I **20**:232; **20**:235
HIPPIAS
Greece, ancient **9**:331
Harmodius and Aristogiton **10**:51
Peisistratus **15**:134
HIPPIES
counterculture **5**:311
HIPPIUS, ZINAIDA NIKOLAYEVNA **10**:173–174 *bibliog.*
HIPPOCRATES **10**:174 *bibliog., illus.*
examination, medical **7**:326
medicine **13**:268 *illus.*
zoology **20**:376
HIPPOCRATIC OATH **10**:174
medical ethics **13**:264
medicine **13**:268
HIPPODAMUS OF MILETUS **10**:174 *bibliog.*
HIPPODROME *see* STADIUM
HIPPOLYTE **10**:174
HIPPOLYTUS **10**:174
HIPPOLYTUS OF ROME, SAINT **10**:175
Callistus I, Pope **4**:46
HIPPOPOTAMUS **10**:175 *bibliog., illus.*; **13**:105 *illus.*
Eocene Epoch **19**:124 *illus.*
ivory and ivory carving **11**:336
HIQÜEY (Dominican Republic)
map (18° 37′N 68° 42′W) **6**:233
HIRAM OF TYRE
Phoenicia **15**:250
HIRE, LAURENT DE LA *see* LA HIRE, LAURENT DE
HIRE PURCHASE *see* INSTALLMENT PLAN
HIRMAND, LAKE
map (30° 45′N 61° 10′E) **11**:250
HIRO (Yeshuhiro Wakabayashi)
fashion photography **8**:33
HIROHITO, EMPEROR OF JAPAN **10**:175 *bibliog., illus.*
Japan, history of **11**:370–371
HIROSHIGE **10**:175 *bibliog.*
Kaigetsudo **12**:6
HIROSHIMA (Japan) **10**:175–176 *bibliog., illus.*
map (34° 24′N 132° 27′E) **11**:361
World War II **20**:279 *illus.*
HIRSCH, SAMSON RAPHAEL **10**:176 *bibliog.*
HIRSCHBEIN, PERETZ
Yiddish theater **20**:328
HIRSCHSPRUNG'S DISEASE
gastrointestinal tract disease **9**:56
HIRSHFIELD, MORRIS **10**:176 *bibliog.*
HIRSHHORN, JOSEPH
Hirshhorn Museum and Sculpture Garden **10**:176
HIRSHHORN MUSEUM AND SCULPTURE GARDEN **10**:176 *bibliog.*
Bunshaft, Gordon **3**:564
Washington, D.C. **20**:41 *map*
HIRST, EDMUND L.
chemistry, history of **4**:329
HIRSUTISM **10**:176 *bibliog.*
HIS (family) **10**:176–177
HISHIKAWA MORONOBU *see* MORONOBU
HISINGER, W.
cerium **4**:260
HISPANIC AMERICANS **10**:177–180 *bibliog., illus., map*
Chicano **4**:343
Colombians **10**:179
Cubans **10**:177; **10**:179
Dominicans **10**:179
ethnic minorities **7**:255
immigration to the United States **11**:55 *map*
Mexican-Americans **10**:177–178
North America **14**:232
Puerto Ricans **10**:177; **10**:178–179
salsa (music) **17**:36
HISPANIOLA **10**:180
Dominican Republic **6**:233–234 *illus., map, table*
Latin America, history of **12**:218 *illus.*
Louisiana Purchase **12**:435
map (19° 0′N 71° 0′W) **20**:109
HISS, ALGER **10**:180 *bibliog.*
Nixon, Richard M. **14**:204
United States, history of the **19**:457
HISSARLIK (Turkey)
Troy (archaeological site) **19**:312–313
HISTAMINE
headache **10**:86
HISTIDINE
operon **14**:404
HISTIOCYTE
lymphatic system **12**:475
HISTOCHEMISTRY
histology **10**:180
HISTOCOMPATIBILITY ANTIGENS
antigen **2**:62
HISTOGRAM **10**:180 *bibliog., illus.*
graph **9**:290–291 *illus.*
statistics **18**:236
statistics, nonparametric **18**:237
HISTOLOGY **10**:180–181 *bibliog.*
anatomy **1**:396
artery **2**:213 *illus.*
cell **4**:232
circulatory system **4**:442 *illus.*
cytology **5**:411–412
Golgi, Camillo **9**:240
histologic examinations **10**:180
Malpighi, Marcello **13**:93
zoology **20**:376–377
HISTOPATHOLOGY
histology **10**:180–181
HISTOPLASMOSIS **10**:181
fungus diseases, pneumonia **8**:369
respiratory system disorders **16**:181
HISTORIC PRESERVATION **10**:181–182 *bibliog.*
antique collecting **2**:65–68
costume **5**:292
Esherick, Joseph **7**:238
international **10**:182
Noël Hume, Ivor **14**:212
Philae **15**:229
salvage archaeology **17**:40
Savannah (Georgia) **17**:99
Viollet-le-Duc, Eugène Emmanuel **19**:603
Weese, Harry **20**:90
Williamsburg (Virginia) **20**:162 *illus.*
HISTORIC SITES ACT OF 1935 **10**:181
HISTORICAL GEOGRAPHY **9**:103
HISTORICAL LINGUISTICS **10**:182–183 *bibliog.*

HISTORICAL LINGUISTICS (cont.)
See also GEOGRAPHICAL LINGUISTICS
applied linguistics **2**:90
Berbers **3**:207
Bopp, Franz **3**:395
dictionary **6**:159–160
Grimm's law **9**:366
Indian languages, American **11**:98
Jones, Sir William **11**:444
linguistics **12**:354–358
methods
comparative **10**:182–183
internal reconstruction **10**:183
names, personal **14**:9–10
Sapir, Edward **17**:72
Verner, Karl Adolf **19**:559
HISTORICISM
criticism, literary **5**:351
history **10**:185
Vico, Giambattista **19**:572
HISTORIOGRAPHY *see* HISTORY
HISTORY **10**:183–185 *bibliog., illus.*
See also the subheading history under the names of specific countries, e.g., BELGIUM; PERU; etc.
American historians
Adams, Brooks **1**:93
Adams, Charles Francis **1**:93
Adams, Henry **1**:94
Adams, Herbert Baxter **1**:94
Adams, James Truslow **1**:94
Allen, Frederick Lewis **1**:299
Andrews, Charles McLean **1**:408
Bancroft, George **3**:60
Bancroft, Hubert Howe **3**:61
Beard, Charles A. **3**:142
Becker, Carl L. **3**:151
Bemis, Samuel Flagg **3**:194
Bolton, Herbert Eugene **3**:372
Catton, Bruce **4**:217
Channing, Edward **4**:281
Commager, Henry Steele **5**:136–137
Dodd, William Edward **6**:211
Dunning, William Archibald **6**:301
Durant, Will and Ariel **6**:303
Fiske, John **8**:129
Franklin, John Hope **8**:285
Freeman, Douglas Southall **8**:299
Handlin, Oscar **10**:37
Hofstadter, Richard **10**:197
Langer, William L. **12**:195
McMaster, John Bach **13**:33
Miller, Perry **13**:428
Morison, Samuel Eliot **13**:580
Motley, John Lothrop **13**:611
Nevins, Allan **14**:115
Parkman, Francis **15**:91–92
Prescott, William Hickling **15**:522
Ryan, Cornelius **16**:378
Sandburg, Carl **17**:61
Schlesinger, Arthur M. **17**:125
Schlesinger, Arthur M., Jr. **17**:125
Sparks, Jared **18**:163
Turner, Frederick Jackson **19**:349
Webb, Walter Prescott **20**:86
Woodward, C. Vann **20**:213
Arab historians
Ibn Battuta **11**:5
Ibn Khaldun **11**:5
Masudi, al- **13**:218
Tabari, al- **19**:3
archaeology **2**:116–126
Belgian historians
Pirenne, Henri **15**:315
black American historians
Du Bois, W. E. B. **6**:285
Franklin, John Hope **8**:285
Woodson, Carter Godwin **20**:213
British historians
Acton, John Emerich Edward Dalberg Acton, 1st Baron **1**:90
Bede, Saint **3**:153
Bryce, James Bryce, 1st Viscount **3**:529
Buckle, Henry Thomas **3**:536
Burnet, Gilbert **3**:577
Clarendon, Edward Hyde, 1st Earl of **5**:36–37
Gardiner, Samuel Rawson **9**:44
Geoffrey of Monmouth **9**:98
Gibbon, Edward **9**:172–173
Grote, George **9**:372
Holinshed, Raphael **10**:202–203
Liddell Hart, Sir Basil Henry **12**:323
Macaulay, Thomas Babington **13**:6
Maitland, Frederick William **12**:76
Rymer, Thomas **16**:380
Stubbs, William **18**:307
Symonds, John Addington **18**:404
Tawney, Richard Henry **19**:45
Toynbee, Arnold **19**:257
Trevelyan, G. M. **19**:291
Byzantine historians
Anna Comnena **2**:31
Procopius of Caesarea **15**:561
Canadian historians
Garneau, F. X. **9**:48
Chinese historians
Chinese literature **4**:389
Ssu-ma Ch'ien (Sima Qian) **18**:207
Ssu-ma Kuang (Sima Guang) **18**:207
chronology **4**:419–420
classical **10**:184
Danish historians
Saxo Grammaticus **17**:104
Dutch historians
Geyl, Pieter **9**:162
Huizinga, Johan **10**:295
Egyptian historians *see* EGYPTOLOGY
folk history *see* ETHNOHISTORY
French historians
Aulard, Alphonse **2**:323
Bloch, Marc **3**:334
Braudel, Fernand **3**:458
Duchesne, André **6**:290
Froissart, Jean **8**:338
Fustel de Coulanges, Numa Denis **8**:383
Joinville, Jean, Sire de **11**:440
Michelet, Jules **13**:375
Saint-Simon, Louis de Rouvroy, Duc de **17**:27
Taine, Hippolyte Adolphe **19**:11
Villehardouin, Geoffroi de **19**:598
Voltaire **19**:632
frontier **8**:345
genealogy **9**:76
German historians
Droysen, Johann Gustav **6**:274
Meinecke, Friedrich **13**:282
Mommsen, Theodor **13**:515
Ranke, Leopold von **16**:87
Spengler, Oswald **18**:178
Treitschke, Heinrich von **19**:290
Greek historians
Arrian **2**:188
Grote, George **9**:372
Herodotus **10**:144–145
Polybius **15**:418
Thucydides **19**:183–184
Xenophon **20**:312
Icelandic historians
Snorri Sturluson **18**:3
Italian historians
Baronius, Caesar **3**:88
Croce, Benedetto **5**:355
Guicciardini, Francesco **9**:393
Machiavelli, Niccolò **13**:18–19
Vergil, Polydore **19**:551
Vico, Giambattista **19**:572
Jewish historians
Josephus, Flavius **11**:452
Marxist laws of history
communism **5**:146
Marxism **13**:184
medieval historians **10**:184
Huizinga, Johan **10**:295
Pirenne, Henri **15**:315
non-Western **10**:184
oral history **14**:414
prehistory **15**:517
professional and educational organizations
American Historical Association **1**:340
psychohistory **15**:591
Pulitzer Prize *see* LITERATURE—Pulitzer Prize
Roman historians
Caesar, Gaius Julius **4**:13–15
Gibbon, Edward **9**:172–173
Livy **12**:378
Mommsen, Theodor **13**:515
Pliny the Younger **15**:368
Polybius **15**:418
Sallust **17**:34
Suetonius **18**:323
Tacitus, Cornelius **19**:6
Varro **19**:524
scope of **10**:183–184
Spanish historians
Prescott, William H. **15**:522
Swedish historians
Dalin, Olof von **6**:13
Swiss historians
Burckhardt, Jakob **3**:567
Sismondi, Jean Charles Léonard Simonde de **17**:329
technology, history of **19**:61–69
Western **10**:184–185
HISTORY, LITERARY *see* CRITICISM, LITERARY
HISTORY OF EMILY MONTAGUE (book)
Canadian literature **4**:93
HISTORY OF ENGLAND FROM THE ACCESSION OF JAMES THE SECOND
Macaulay, Thomas Babington **13**:6
HISTORY OF ROME (book)
Livy **12**:378
Mommsen, Theodor **13**:515
HISTORY OF THE PELOPONNESIAN WAR (book) **10**:185–186 *bibliog.*
history **10**:183 *illus.*; **10**:184
Thucydides **19**:183–184
HISTORY OF THE PEOPLE OF THE UNITED STATES
McMaster, John Bach **13**:33
HISTORY OF THE PERSIAN WARS, THE (book) **10**:186
HITACHI (Japan)
map (36° 36′N 140° 39′E) **11**:361
HITCHCOCK (county in Nebraska)
map (40° 10′N 101° 10′W) **14**:70
HITCHCOCK (Texas)
map (29° 21′N 95° 1′W) **19**:129
HITCHCOCK, ALFRED **10**:186 *bibliog., illus.*
Chabrol, Claude **4**:264
HITCHCOCK, HENRY-RUSSELL **10**:186
modern architecture **13**:490
HITCHCOCK, LAMBERT **10**:186–187 *bibliog.*
furniture **8**:377
HITE REPORT, THE (book)
sexual intercourse **17**:231
HITLER, ADOLF **8**:30 *illus.*; **9**:156 *illus.*; **10**:187–188 *bibliog., illus.*
Berchtesgaden **3**:208
Braun, Eva **3**:458
cartoon lampooning Nazi-Soviet Pact **16**:359 *illus.*
Doenitz, Karl **6**:212–213
economic policy **10**:187–188
Europe, history of **7**:296–298
foreign policy and war plans **10**:188
Germany, history of **9**:155–156
Goebbels, Joseph **9**:221–222
Goerdeler, Karl Friedrich **9**:222
Goering, Hermann **9**:222
Himmler, Heinrich **10**:168
Hindenburg, Paul von **10**:169
Mein Kampf **13**:282
Munich Putsch **13**:641–642
nazism **14**:67–68
Papen, Franz von **15**:68
Polish Corridor **15**:397
political philosophy **10**:187
propaganda poster **15**:568 *illus.*
Reichstag **16**:130
roads and highways **16**:238
Roehm, Ernst **16**:268
Schacht, Hjalmar **17**:116
Third Reich **19**:170
World War II **10**:188; **20**:249–275 *illus.*
HITRA ISLAND
map (63° 33′N 8° 45′E) **14**:261
HITTITE ART AND ARCHITECTURE **10**:188–189 *bibliog., illus.*
Alaca Hüyük **1**:239
Boğazköy **3**:359–360
Carchemish **4**:141
relief carving **10**:188 *illus.*
Sphinx Gate (at Alaca Hüyük) **10**:189 *illus.*
temple **19**:95
HITTITES **10**:189–190 *bibliog., illus., map*
cities
Alalakh **1**:239
Boğazköy **3**:359–360
Ugarit **19**:374
inscription **11**:185
Iron Age **11**:271
language **10**:190
hieroglyphics **10**:159–161; **10**:189 *illus.*
languages, extinct **12**:198
writing systems, evolution of **20**:292; **20**:295
Mitanni **13**:482
Ramses II, King of Egypt **16**:82
slavery **17**:352
Winckler, Hugo **20**:168
HIVA OA
Marquesas Islands **13**:163
HIVES **10**:190 *bibliog.*
HIWANNEE (Mississippi)
map (31° 43′N 88° 48′W) **13**:469
HJØRRING (Denmark)
map (57° 28′N 9° 59′E) **6**:109
HJORTH, SØREN
technology, history of **19**:67
HKAKABO, MOUNT
map (28° 20′N 97° 32′E) **3**:573
HLA ANTIGENS *see* HISTOCOMPATIBILITY ANTIGENS
HLATIKULU (Swaziland)
map (27° 0′S 31° 25′E) **18**:380
HMONG
Meo **13**:303
HO **10**:190 *bibliog.*
Mundari **13**:640
HO (Ghana)
map (6° 35′N 0° 30′E) **9**:164
HO CHI MINH **10**:190 *bibliog., illus.*
Viet Minh **19**:579
Vietnam **19**:583–584
Vietnam War **19**:584–585 *illus.*
HO CHI MINH CITY (Vietnam) **10**:190–191 *illus.*; **19**:583 *illus.*
climate **2**:237 *table*; **19**:581 *table*
map (10° 45′N 106° 40′E) **19**:580
HO-FEI (China)
map (31° 51′N 117° 17′E) **4**:362
HO-HO-KUS (New Jersey)
map (41° 0′N 74° 7′W) **14**:129
HO-KANG (China)
map (47° 24′N 130° 17′E) **4**:362
HOA BINH (Vietnam)
map (20° 50′N 105° 20′E) **19**:580
HOAR, EBENEZER ROCKWOOD **10**:191 *bibliog.*
HOAR, GEORGE FRISBIE
Hoar, Ebenezer Rockwood **10**:191
HOARE, HENRY
landscape architecture **12**:187
HOARFROST **10**:191
black frost **10**:191
dew point **10**:191
frost **8**:345
HOARHOUND *see* HOREHOUND (botany)
HOATZIN **10**:191 *illus.*
HOBAN, JAMES **10**:191
Capitol of the United States **4**:126
White House **20**:137
HOBART (Australia) **10**:192 *bibliog.*
education
Tasmania University **2**:345 *table*
map (42° 53′S 147° 19′E) **2**:328
HOBART (Indiana)
map (41° 32′N 87° 15′W) **11**:111
HOBART (Oklahoma)
map (35° 1′N 99° 6′W) **14**:368
HOBART, GARRET A. **10**:192
HOBBEMA, MEINDERT **10**:192 *bibliog.*
Watermill with a Red Roof **12**:191 *illus.*
HOBBES, THOMAS **10**:192 *bibliog., illus.*
educational psychology **7**:66
egoism **7**:74
law **12**:242
Leviathan **12**:304
materialism **13**:219
natural law **14**:48
political parties **15**:400
primitive societies **15**:546
representation **16**:161
social contract **18**:11
state (in political philosophy) **18**:231 *illus.*
HOBBIT, THE (book)
Tolkien, J. R. R. **19**:226
HOBBLEBUSH *see* VIBURNUM
HOBBS (New Mexico)
map (32° 42′N 103° 8′W) **14**:136
HOBBY, OVETA CULP **10**:192
Health and Human Services, U.S. Department of **10**:86
HOBBYHORSE
toy **19**:257
HOBGOOD (North Carolina)
map (36° 2′N 77° 24′W) **14**:242
HOBHOUSE, LEONARD TRELAWNY **10**:193 *bibliog.*
HOBOKEN (Belgium)
map (51° 10′N 4° 21′E) **3**:177
HOBOKEN (New Jersey) **10**:193
map (40° 45′N 74° 3′W) **14**:129
HOBSON, JOHN A. **10**:193 *bibliog.*
imperialism **11**:62
HOBSON, LAURA Z. **10**:193
HOBSON, WILLIAM
New Zealand, history of **14**:161
HOCCLEVE, THOMAS **10**:193 *bibliog.*
HOCHALMSPITZE (peak)
map (47° 1′N 13° 19′E) **2**:348
HOCHGOLLING MOUNTAIN
map (47° 16′N 13° 45′E) **2**:348

HOCHHUTH, ROLF 10:193 *bibliog.*
HOCHKÖNIG MOUNTAIN
map (47° 25′N 13° 4′E) 2:348
HOCHSCHWAB MOUNTAIN
map (47° 37′N 15° 9′E) 2:348
HOCKEY *see* FIELD HOCKEY; ICE HOCKEY
HOCKING (county in Ohio)
map (39° 30′N 82° 28′W) 14:357
HOCKING, WILLIAM ERNEST 10:193 *bibliog.*
HOCKING RIVER
map (39° 12′N 81° 45′W) 14:357
HOCKLEY (county in Texas)
map (33° 38′N 102° 17′W) 19:129
HOCKNEY, DAVID 10:193–194 *bibliog., illus.*
Two Boys in a Swimming Pool 7:188 *illus.*; 10:193 *illus.*
HODEIR, ANDRÉ
Barraqué, Jean 3:93
HODGE (Louisiana)
map (32° 17′N 92° 43′W) 12:430
HODGE, CHARLES
fundamentalism 8:363
HODGEMAN (county in Kansas)
map (38° 5′N 99° 55′W) 12:18
HODGENVILLE (Kentucky)
map (37° 34′N 85° 44′W) 12:47
HODGES, LUTHUR 15:526 *illus.*
HODGKIN, ALAN LLOYD 10:194
Huxley, Andrew Fielding 10:324
HODGKIN, DOROTHY CROWFOOT 10:194
HODGKIN'S DISEASE 10:194
alkaloid 1:296
lymphatic system 12:476
HODGSON (Manitoba)
map (51° 13′N 97° 34′W) 13:119
HODLER, FERDINAND 10:194 *bibliog., illus.*
The Inspiration 10:194 *illus.*
HÓDMEZŐVÁSÁRHELY (Hungary)
map (46° 25′N 20° 20′E) 10:307
HODNA SHATT
map (35° 25′N 4° 45′E) 1:287
HOE (farm implement)
Egypt, ancient 1:189 *illus.*
HOE, RICHARD MARCH 10:194
HOE, RICHARD MARSH 19:450 *illus.*
HOF (Germany, East and West)
map (50° 18′N 11° 55′E) 9:140
HOFEI (Hefei) (China) 10:194
HOFF, MARCIAN E., JR.
computer industry 5:160o
HOFFA, JAMES R. 10:194–195 *bibliog.*
Teamsters, Chauffeurs, Warehousemen, and Helpers of America, International Brotherhood of 19:58
HOFFER, ABRAM
megavitamin therapy 13:280
HOFFER, ERIC 10:195 *bibliog.*
HOFFMAN, ABBIE
counterculture 5:311
HOFFMAN, DUSTIN 10:195
HOFFMAN, JOHN T.
Tweed, William M. 19:358
HOFFMAN, MALVINA 10:195 *bibliog.*
HOFFMANN, BANESH
Einstein, Albert 7:94
HOFFMANN, ERNST THEODOR AMADEUS 10:195 *bibliog., illus.*
HOFFMANN, FRIEDRICH 10:195 *bibliog.*
HOFFMANN, JOSEF 10:195 *bibliog.*
Art Deco 2:207
Art Nouveau 2:212
HOFHAIMER, PAUL
Renaissance music 16:156
HOFMANN, ALBERT
LSD 12:445
HOFMANN, AUGUST WILHELM VON 10:196 *bibliog.*
HOFMANN, HANS 10:196 *bibliog., illus.*
modern art 13:493
Orchestral Dominance in Green 10:196 *illus.*
HOFMANN, JOSEF CASIMIR 10:196 *bibliog.*
HOFMANNSTHAL, HUGO VON 10:196–197 *bibliog., illus.*
Rosenkavalier, Der 16:315
Salzburg Festival 17:44–45
Strauss, Richard 18:294–295
HOFSTADTER, RICHARD 10:197
HOFSTADTER, ROBERT 10:197
HOFSTRA UNIVERSITY 10:197
HOFUF (Saudi Arabia) 10:197
map (25° 22′N 49° 34′E) 17:94
HOG *see* PIG
HOG ISLAND (Prince Edward Island)
map (46° 36′N 63° 48′W) 15:548
HOG ISLAND (Virginia)
map (37° 25′N 75° 41′W) 19:607
HOG-NOSED SKUNK *see* SKUNK
HOGAN 10:197 *bibliog.*
HOGAN, BEN 10:197 *bibliog., illus.*
HOGANSVILLE (Georgia)
map (33° 11′N 84° 55′W) 9:114
HOGARTH, WILLIAM 10:198 *bibliog., illus.*
graphic arts 9:292
Gravelot, Hubert François 9:302
Marriage à la Mode 7:186 *illus.*; 10:198 *illus.*
Shortly After the Marriage 7:186 *illus.*
HOGARTH PRESS
Woolf, Virginia 20:215
HOGBACK MOUNTAIN (Montana)
map (44° 54′N 112° 7′W) 13:547
HOGBACK MOUNTAIN (Nebraska)
map (41° 40′N 103° 44′W) 14:70
HOGELAND (Montana)
map (48° 51′N 108° 40′W) 13:547
HOGG, JAMES 10:198
Selkirk (Scotland) 17:192
HOGNOSE SNAKE 10:199
colubrid 5:125
HOH (American Indians)
Quileute-Hoh and Chemakum 16:26
HOHE ACHT, MOUNT
map (50° 23′N 7° 0′E) 9:140
HOHENSTAUFEN (dynasty) 10:199 *bibliog.*
Conrad III, King of Germany and Holy Roman Emperor 5:199
Conrad IV, King of Germany 5:199
Frederick I, King of Germany and Holy Roman Emperor (Frederick Barbarossa) 8:290
Frederick II, King of Germany and Holy Roman Emperor 8:290–291
Germany, history of 9:149 *map*
Guelphs and Ghibellines 9:390
Henry VI, King of Germany and Holy Roman Emperor 10:129
Holy Roman Empire 10:210
Naples, Kingdom of 14:15
Swabia 18:375
Welf (family) 20:97
HOHENWALD (Tennessee)
map (35° 33′N 87° 33′W) 19:104
HOHENZOLLERN (dynasty) 10:199
Albert, First Duke of Prussia 1:254
Europe, history of 7:290
Frederick I, Elector of Brandenburg 8:289
Frederick I, King of Prussia 8:291
Frederick II, Emperor of Germany 8:292
Frederick II, King of Prussia (Frederick the Great) 8:291–292
Frederick William, Elector of Brandenburg (the Great Elector) 8:292–293
Frederick William I, King of Prussia 8:293
Frederick William II, King of Prussia 8:293
Frederick William III, King of Prussia 8:293
Frederick William IV, King of Prussia 8:293
Germany, history of 9:151–152 *map*
Prussia 15:585–586 *map*
William I, Emperor of Germany 20:156–157
William II, Emperor of Germany 20:157
HOHOE (Ghana)
map (7° 9′N 0° 28′E) 9:164
HOHOKAM CULTURE 10:199 *bibliog.*
Arizona 2:163
Indians of North America, art of the 11:140
North American archaeology 14:239 *illus.*
Phoenix (Arizona) 15:251
Pima 15:303
HOISINGTON (Kansas)
map (38° 31′N 98° 47′W) 12:18
HOJO CLAN
Japan, history of 11:368
HOKAH (Minnesota)
map (43° 45′N 91° 21′W) 13:453
HOKAN LANGUAGES
Indian languages, American 11:100 *table*
HOKE (county in North Carolina)
map (35° 0′N 79° 15′W) 14:242
HOKKAIDO (Japan) 10:199; 11:362 *illus.*
cities
Sapporo 17:73
map (44° 0′N 143° 0′E) 11:361
people
Ainu 1:203
HOKUSAI 10:199–200 *bibliog., illus.*
Mount Fuji on a Clear Day 10:200 *illus.*; 11:378 *illus.*
HOLABIRD, WILLIAM 10:200 *bibliog.*
HOLBACH, PAUL HENRI DIETRICH, BARON D' 10:200 *bibliog.*
materialism 13:219
HOLBEIN, HANS, THE ELDER 10:200 *bibliog.*
HOLBEIN, HANS, THE YOUNGER 10:200–201 *bibliog., illus.*
The Ambassadors 10:201 *illus.*
anamorphosis 1:391
caravel drawing 19:278 *illus.*
Death, Dance of 6:68
Desiderius Erasmus 7:227 *illus.*; 16:149 *illus.*
drawing 6:264 *illus.*
Freiburg im Breisgau (West Germany) 8:301
Henry VIII, King of England 10:126 *illus.*
Renaissance art and architecture 16:154
Saint Thomas More 9:126 *illus.*; 13:576 *illus.*; 16:149 *illus.*
HOLBERG, LUDVIG, BARON 10:202 *bibliog.*
Norwegian literature 14:265
HOLBROOK (Arizona)
map (34° 54′N 110° 10′W) 2:160
HOLBROOK (Massachusetts)
map (42° 9′N 71° 1′W) 13:206
HOLBROOK, JOSIAH
lyceum 12:474
HOLDEN (Alberta)
map (53° 14′N 112° 14′W) 1:256
HOLDEN (Massachusetts)
map (42° 21′N 71° 52′W) 13:206
HOLDEN (Missouri)
map (38° 43′N 94° 1′W) 13:476
HOLDEN (West Virginia)
map (37° 50′N 82° 4′W) 20:111
HOLDEN, OLIVER
fuging tune 8:355
HOLDEN, WILLIAM 10:202 *bibliog.*
HOLDENVILLE (Oklahoma)
map (35° 5′N 96° 24′W) 14:368
HOLDER (Florida)
map (28° 58′N 82° 25′W) 8:172
HÖLDERLIN, FRIEDRICH 10:202 *bibliog.*
HOLDHEIM, SAMUEL 10:202
HOLDICH (Argentina)
map (45° 57′S 68° 13′W) 2:149
HOLDING COMPANY 10:202
HOLDREGE (Nebraska)
map (40° 26′N 99° 22′W) 14:70
HOLE IN THE MOUNTAIN PEAK
map (40° 55′N 115° 5′W) 14:111
HOLETOWN (Barbados)
map (13° 11′N 59° 39′W) 3:75
HOLGATE (Ohio)
map (41° 15′N 84° 8′W) 14:357
HOLGATE, EDWIN H.
Canadian art and architecture 4:90
HOLGUÍN (Cuba)
map (20° 53′N 76° 15′W) 5:377
HOLIDAY 10:202 *bibliog.*
See also names of holidays
HOLIDAY, BILLIE 10:202–203 *bibliog., illus.*
HOLIDAY INNS
hotel 10:262 *table*
HOLINSHED, RAPHAEL 10:203
HOLISTIC MEDICINE 10:203
HOLL, FRANK
social realism 18:13
HOLLADAY (Utah)
map (40° 40′N 111° 49′W) 19:492
HOLLAND (country) *see* NETHERLANDS
HOLLAND (historic region) 10:203
costume 5:298 *illus.*
HOLLAND (Michigan) 13:380 *illus.*
map (42° 47′N 86° 7′W) 13:377
HOLLAND, CLIFFORD M.
Holland Tunnel 10:203
HOLLAND, HENRY 10:203 *bibliog.*
Brown, Capability 3:513
HOLLAND, JOHN PHILIP 10:203 *bibliog.*
submarine 18:315
HOLLAND, SIR SIDNEY 9:203–204
HOLLAND TUNNEL 10:204
New York (city) 14:145 *maps*
tunnel 19:337 *table*
HOLLANDALE (Mississippi)
map (33° 10′N 90° 58′W) 13:469
HOLLANDER MACHINE
paper 15:69
HOLLAR, WENCESLAUS 10:204 *bibliog.*
HOLLEIN, HANS 10:204 *bibliog.*
HOLLERITH, HERMAN 10:204
computer 5:160–160a
computer industry 5:160n
punched card 15:623
HOLLES, THOMAS PELHAM-, 1ST DUKE OF NEWCASTLE *see* NEWCASTLE, THOMAS PELHAM-HOLLES, 1ST DUKE OF
HOLLEY, ROBERT
Khorana, Har Gobind 12:68
Nirenberg, M. W. 14:201
HOLLIDAY, CYRUS
Topeka (Kansas) 19:237
HOLLIDAY, JOHN "DOC"
Earp, Wyatt 7:11
HOLLIDAYSBURG (Pennsylvania)
map (40° 26′N 78° 23′W) 15:147
HOLLINS (Virginia)
map (37° 21′N 79° 56′W) 19:607
HOLLIS (Oklahoma)
map (34° 41′N 99° 55′W) 14:368
HOLLISTER (California)
map (36° 51′N 121° 24′W) 4:31
HOLLISTON (Massachusetts)
map (42° 12′N 71° 26′W) 13:206
HOLLWEG, THEOBALD VON BETHMANN- *see* BETHMANN-HOLLWEG, THEOBALD VON
HOLLY 10:204 *bibliog., illus.*
winterberry 20:181
HOLLY (Colorado)
map (38° 3′N 102° 7′W) 5:116
HOLLY, BUDDY 10:204 *bibliog.*
HOLLY GROVE (Arkansas)
map (34° 36′N 91° 12′W) 2:166
HOLLY HILL (Florida)
map (29° 14′N 81° 2′W) 8:172
HOLLY SHELTER SWAMP
map (34° 15′N 77° 51′W) 14:242
HOLLY SPRINGS (Mississippi)
map (34° 41′N 89° 26′W) 13:469
HOLLYHOCK 10:204–205 *illus.*; 13:92 *illus.*
HOLLYWOOD (California) 10:205 *bibliog.*
See also FILM, HISTORY OF
Los Angeles (California) 12:417 *map*
HOLLYWOOD (Florida)
map (26° 0′N 80° 9′W) 8:172
HOLLYWOOD TEN, THE 10:205 *bibliog.*
Un-American Activities, House Committee on 19:380
HOLM, CELESTE 6:50 *illus.*
musical comedy 13:674 *illus.*
HOLM, HANYA 10:205 *bibliog.*
HOLMEN (Wisconsin)
map (43° 58′N 91° 15′W) 20:185
HOLMES (county in Florida)
map (30° 55′N 85° 45′W) 8:172
HOLMES (county in Mississippi)
map (33° 5′N 90° 10′W) 13:469
HOLMES (county in Ohio)
map (40° 33′N 81° 55′W) 14:357
HOLMES, ARTHUR 10:205 *bibliog.*
HOLMES, LARRY 10:205
Ali, Muhammad 1:292
HOLMES, ODETTA *see* ODETTA
HOLMES, OLIVER WENDELL 10:205–206 *bibliog., illus.*
HOLMES, OLIVER WENDELL, JR. 10:206 *bibliog., illus.*
law 12:243
legal realism 12:243
Lochner v. *New York* 12:386
Olmstead v. *United States*
wiretapping 20:183
Schenck v. *United States* 17:119
Swift and Company v. *United States* 18:390
HOLMES, SHERLOCK (fictional character) 10:206 *bibliog.*
Doyle, Sir Arthur Conan 6:253
Hound of the Baskervilles, The 10:264
HOLMIA (Guyana)
map (4° 58′N 59° 35′W) 9:410
HOLMIUM 10:206
element 7:130 *table*
lanthanide series 12:200–201
metal, metallic element 13:328
HOLOCAUST 10:206–207 *bibliog., illus.*
Jews 11:416–417
nazism 14:68
Pius XII, Pope 15:324
HOLOCENE EPOCH *see* RECENT EPOCH
HOLOGRAPHY 10:207–208 *bibliog., illus.*

HOLOGRAPHY (cont.)
Gabor, Dennis **9**:5–6; **10**:207
laser and maser **12**:213
lensless photography **10**:208
light **10**:207–208
microfilm **13**:385
perspective **10**:207
ultrasonics **19**:378 *illus.*
HOLOPLANKTON *see* ZOOPLANKTON
HOLST, GUSTAV **10**:208 *bibliog., illus.*
HOLSTEBRO (Denmark)
map (56° 21′N 8° 38′E) **6**:109
HOLSTEIN (Germany) *see* SCHLESWIG-HOLSTEIN (West Germany)
HOLSTEIN (Iowa)
map (42° 29′N 95° 33′W) **11**:244
HOLSTEIN, FRIEDRICH VON **10**:208 *bibliog.*
HOLSTEIN-FRIESIAN CATTLE **4**:216 *illus.*; **6**:9 *illus.*; **13**:380 *illus.*
dairying **6**:7
HOLSTEINSBORG (Greenland)
map (66° 55′N 53° 40′W) **9**:353
HOLSTON RIVER
map (35° 57′N 83° 51′W) **19**:104
HOLT (Alabama)
map (33° 15′N 87° 29′W) **1**:234
HOLT (Michigan)
map (42° 39′N 84° 31′W) **13**:377
HOLT (county in Missouri)
map (40° 5′N 95° 15′W) **13**:476
HOLT (county in Nebraska)
map (42° 30′N 98° 50′W) **14**:70
HOLT, HAROLD **10**:208
HOLT, JOSEPH **10**:208
HOLT, VICTORIA **10**:208–209
HOLT RESERVOIR
map (33° 20′N 87° 25′W) **1**:234
HOLTON (Kansas)
map (39° 28′N 95° 44′W) **12**:18
HOLTON, A. LINWOOD, JR.
Virginia **19**:612
HOLTVILLE (California)
map (32° 49′N 115° 23′W) **4**:31
HOLY ALLIANCE **10**:209
HOLY CROSS (Alaska)
map (62° 12′N 159° 47′W) **1**:242
HOLY CROSS, COLLEGE OF THE **10**:209
HOLY FAMILY **10**:209
HOLY FAMILY, EXPIATORY TEMPLE OF THE
Gaudí, Antonio **9**:59
HOLY GHOST *see* HOLY SPIRIT
HOLY GRAIL *see* GRAIL, HOLY
HOLY INNOCENTS **10**:209
HOLY LAND *see* CANAAN; PALESTINE
HOLY LEAGUE
Religion, Wars of **16**:141
HOLY ORDERS **10**:209 *bibliog.*
HOLY ROMAN EMPIRE **10**:209–211 *bibliog., illus., maps, table*
Albert I, Margrave of Brandenburg **1**:254
Austria **2**:349–350
boundaries c.1560 **7**:288 *map*
boundaries c.1648 **7**:289 *map*
Burgundy **3**:570–571 *map*
Charlemagne **4**:289–290
crown **11**:460 *illus.*
emperors **10**:211 *table*
Europe, history of **7**:284–285 *map*
Germany, history of **9**:149–151 *maps*
Habsburg (dynasty) **10**:6
history **10**:210–211
imperialism **11**:62
Luxembourg (country) **12**:471–472
Middle Ages **13**:392 *map*
state (in political philosophy) **18**:230
theory of the empire **10**:209–210
Worms (West Germany) **20**:284
962–1138 Saxon and Salian dynasties
Conrad II, King of Germany and Holy Roman Emperor **5**:199
Henry II, King of Germany and Holy Roman Emperor **10**:128
Henry III, King of Germany and Holy Roman Emperor **10**:128–129
Henry IV, King of Germany and Holy Roman Emperor **10**:129
Henry V, King of Germany and Holy Roman Emperor **10**:129
Lothair II, King of Germany and Holy Roman Emperor **12**:419
Otto I, King of Germany and Holy Roman Emperor (Otto the Great) **14**:462–463
Otto II, King of Germany and Holy Roman Emperor **14**:463
Otto III, King of Germany and Holy Roman Emperor **14**:463
1138–1273 Hohenstaufens
Alfonso X, King of Castile **1**:279
Conrad III, King of Germany and Holy Roman Emperor **5**:199
Frederick I, King of Germany and Holy Roman Emperor (Frederick Barbarossa) **8**:290
Frederick II, King of Germany and Holy Roman Emperor **8**:290–291
Henry VI, King of Germany and Holy Roman Emperor **10**:129
Hohenstaufen (dynasty) **10**:199
Otto IV, King of Germany and Holy Roman Emperor **14**:463
Palatinate **15**:30
Philip of Swabia **15**:232
Welf (family) **20**:97
1273-1438 mixed dynasties
Albert I, King of Germany **1**:254
Albert II, King of Germany **1**:254
Charles IV, Emperor **4**:293
Henry VII, King (Henry of Luxemburg) **10**:130
Louis IV, King of Germany and Holy Roman Emperor (Louis the Bavarian) **12**:428
Rudolf I, King of Germany **16**:338
Sigismund, King of Germany and Holy Roman Emperor **17**:299
Wenceslas, King of Germany and Bohemia **20**:103
1438–1806 Habsburgs
Charles V, Holy Roman Emperor **4**:294–295
Charles VI, Holy Roman Emperor **4**:295
Charles VII, Holy Roman Emperor **4**:295–296
Ferdinand I, Holy Roman Emperor **8**:52–53
Ferdinand II, Holy Roman Emperor **8**:53
Ferdinand III, Holy Roman Emperor **8**:53
Francis I, Holy Roman Emperor **8**:276
Francis II, Holy Roman Emperor **8**:276
Frederick III, King of Germany and Holy Roman Emperor **8**:291
Italian Wars **11**:319–320
Joseph I, Emperor **11**:451
Joseph II, Emperor **11**:452
Leopold I, Emperor **12**:294
Leopold II, Emperor **12**:294–295
Matthias, Emperor **13**:231–232
Maximilian I, Emperor **13**:240
Maximilian II, Emperor **13**:240–241
Rudolf II, Emperor **16**:338
Suleiman I, Sultan of the Ottoman Empire (Suleiman the Magnificent) **18**:332–333
Thirty Years' War *see* THIRTY YEARS' WAR
Westphalia, Peace of **20**:119
HOLY SPIRIT **10**:211
charismatic movement **4**:288–289
Pentecost **15**:155
Trinity **19**:300–301
HOLY WEEK
Easter **7**:32
Good Friday **9**:245
Passion cycle **15**:105
HOLYOAKE, KEITH
New Zealand, history of **14**:163
HOLYOKE (Colorado)
map (40° 35′N 102° 18′W) **5**:116
HOLYOKE (Massachusetts) **10**:211
map (42° 12′N 72° 37′W) **13**:206
HOLYROOD (Kansas)
map (38° 35′N 98° 25′W) **12**:18
HOLZ, ARNO **10**:211
HOLZMAN, MALCOLM
Hardy Holzman Pfeiffer Associates **10**:48
HOMANS, GEORGE CASPAR **10**:212 *bibliog.*
HOMAYUN *see* HUMAYUN, MOGUL EMPEROR OF INDIA
HOMBORI TONDO MOUNTAIN
map (15° 16′N 1° 40′W) **13**:89
HOME, SIR ALEC DOUGLAS- *see* DOUGLAS-HOME, SIR ALEC
"HOME, SWEET HOME" (song)
Payne, John Howard **15**:122
HOME BOX OFFICE
cable TV **4**:7
HOME ENERGY ASSISTANCE PROGRAM
social and welfare services **18**:17
HOME INSURANCE BUILDING (Chicago)
Jenney, William LeBaron **11**:396
skyscraper **17**:348
HOME OWNERS LOAN CORPORATION
housing **10**:277
HOME PLACE (Indiana)
map (39° 55′N 86° 7′W) **11**:111
HOME RULE BILLS **10**:212 *bibliog.*
Carson, Sir Edward **4**:169–170
Gladstone, William Ewart **9**:196
Ireland, history of **11**:264
Liberal parties **12**:311
Northern Ireland **14**:255
Parnell, Charles Stewart **15**:96
Redmond, John **16**:115
HOMECOMING, THE (play)
Pinter, Harold **15**:308
HOMEDALE (Idaho)
map (43° 37′N 116° 56′W) **11**:26
HOMEOMORPHISM
topology **19**:238
HOMEOPATHY **10**:212 *bibliog.*
Hahnemann, Samuel **13**:270
HOMEOSAURUS **11**:476 *illus.*
HOMEOSTASIS **10**:212–213 *bibliog.*
Cannon, Walter B. **10**:212
cybernetics **5**:401
hormone, animal **10**:234
hunger and thirst **10**:310–311
motivation **13**:610
thyroid gland **19**:188
HOMEOWNERS INSURANCE
fire insurance **8**:102
HOMER **9**:343–344 *illus.*; **10**:213 *bibliog., illus.*
aretê **2**:146
Iliad **11**:40
Odysseus **14**:350–351
Odyssey **14**:351
Trojan War **19**:305
HOMER (Alaska)
map (59° 39′N 151° 33′W) **1**:242
HOMER (Georgia)
map (34° 20′N 83° 30′W) **9**:114
HOMER (Louisiana)
map (32° 48′N 93° 4′W) **12**:430
HOMER (Michigan)
map (42° 9′N 84° 49′W) **13**:377
HOMER (New York)
map (42° 38′N 76° 11′W) **14**:149
HOMER, LOUISE **10**:213 *bibliog.*
HOMER, WINSLOW **10**:213–214 *bibliog., illus.*
American art and architecture **1**:333
Northeaster **1**:333 *illus.*; **10**:214 *illus.*
Woodcutter and the Fallen Tree **20**:62 *illus.*
HOMER CITY (Pennsylvania)
map (40° 32′N 79° 10′W) **15**:147
HOMER YOUNGS PEAK
map (45° 19′N 113° 41′W) **13**:547
HOMERIC EPITHET **10**:214
HOMERIC HYMNS **10**:214
HOMERTON COLLEGE (Cambridge University) **4**:53
HOMERVILLE (Georgia)
map (31° 2′N 82° 45′W) **9**:114
HOMESTAKE MINE
South Dakota **18**:105
HOMESTEAD (Florida)
map (25° 29′N 80° 29′W) **8**:172
HOMESTEAD ACT **10**:214 *bibliog.*
frontier **8**:343
Preemption Act **15**:502
public domain **15**:608
HOMESTEAD STRIKE **10**:214 *bibliog.*
Frick, Henry Clay **8**:330
Goldman, Emma **9**:235
Schwab, Charles Michael **17**:138
HOMEWOOD (Alabama)
map (33° 29′N 86° 48′W) **1**:234
HOMEWOOD (Illinois)
map (41° 34′N 87° 40′W) **11**:42
HOMICIDE **10**:214–215
criminal homicide, distinctions **10**:214–215
manslaughter **13**:128
murder **13**:647–648
suicide **18**:330–331
HOMING PIGEON *see* PIGEON; PIGEON RACING
HOMINIDS *see* PREHISTORIC HUMANS
HOMINY (Oklahoma)
map (36° 25′N 96° 24′W) **14**:368
HOMO ERECTUS **10**:215–216 *illus. bibliog., illus.*
African prehistory **1**:173
Chinese archaeology **4**:378
Chou-k'ou-tien (Zhoukoudian) **4**:409–410
Coon, Carleton **5**:243
cultural evidence **10**:216
Dubois, Eugène **6**:289
fossil record **10**:215–216
Heidelberg man **10**:107
Homo habilis **10**:216
Java man **11**:385
Lantian man **12**:201
Leakey (family) **12**:259
Lumley, Henry de **12**:459
Neanderthalers **14**:69
Oldowan **14**:376
Olduvai Gorge **14**:377
Peking man **15**:136
Pleistocene epoch **12**:201
prehistoric humans **15**:513–515 *map*
Solo man **18**:56
stone-tool culture **10**:215 *illus.*
Ternifine man **19**:118
HOMO HABILIS **10**:216 *bibliog., illus.*
African prehistory **1**:172–173
Australopithecus **2**:346
Leaky (family) **12**:259
Olduvai Gorge **14**:377
prehistoric humans **15**:513–514 *map*
Skull 1470 **17**:346
HOMO SAPIENS
classification, biological **5**:43 *table*
Cro-Magnon man **5**:353–354 *illus.*
Neanderthalers **14**:68–69 *illus.*
prehistoric humans **15**:514–515 *illus., map*
HOMOGENIZATION **10**:216
milk **13**:423
HOMOLOGOUS SERIES **10**:216
HOMOLOGY (comparative anatomy) **5**:155
HOMOLOPSINE
colubrid **5**:125
HOMOMORPHISM
group theory **9**:377
HOMONCULUS **10**:139 *illus.*
HOMOPOLYMER **10**:216
HOMOPTERA **10**:216–217 *illus.*
aphid **2**:77
cicada **4**:428
jumping plant louse **11**:466
Kermes **12**:59
leafhopper **12**:257
mealybug **13**:252
scale insect **17**:107
spittlebug **18**:190
treehopper **19**:289–290
whitefly **20**:139
HOMOSEXUALITY **10**:217 *bibliog.*
AIDS **1**:201
Ellis, Havelock **7**:148
gay activism **9**:63
Masters and Johnson reports **13**:216
prison **15**:555
prostitution **15**:573
sexual development **17**:229–230
venereal disease **19**:540
HOMS (Syria) **10**:217
map (34° 44′N 36° 43′E) **18**:412
HON GAY (Vietnam)
map (20° 57′N 107° 5′E) **19**:580
HONAN (Henan) (China) **10**:217
cities
Cheng-chou (Zhengzhou) **4**:330
K'ai-feng (Kaifeng) **12**:6
HONDA MOTOR COMPANY
automotive industry **2**:367
HONDECOETER, MELCHIOR D' **10**:217
HONDIUS, JADOCUS **13**:139 *illus.*
HONDO (New Mexico)
map (33° 23′N 105° 16′W) **14**:136
HONDO (Texas)
map (29° 21′N 99° 9′W) **19**:129
HONDO RIVER
map (18° 29′N 88° 19′W) **3**:183
HONDURAS **10**:218–220 *bibliog., illus., map, table*
art and archaeology
Copán **5**:248
pre-Columbian art and architecture **15**:495–501
cities
Tegucigalpa **19**:72
economic activity **10**:219
education
Latin American universities **12**:233
flag **10**:218 *illus.*
government **10**:219
history **10**:219–220
El Salvador **7**:101
land and resources **10**:218–219 *map, table*
map (15° 0′N 86° 30′W) **14**:225
Mosquito Coast **13**:603
people **10**:219

Carib **4**:147
Lenca **12**:281
Miskito **13**:466
HONDURAS, CAPE OF
map (16° 1′N 86° 2′W) **10**:218
HONDURAS, GULF OF
map (16° 10′N 87° 50′W) **4**:148
HONEA PATH (South Carolina)
map (34° 27′N 82° 24′W) **18**:98
HONECKER, ERICH **10**:220 *bibliog.*
HØNEFOSS (Norway)
map (60° 10′N 10° 18′E) **14**:261
HONEGGER, ARTHUR **10**:220 *bibliog.*
HONEOYE LAKE
Finger Lakes **8**:93
HONESDALE (Pennsylvania)
map (41° 34′N 75° 16′W) **15**:147
HONESTY (botany) **10**:220
HONEY **10**:220 *bibliog.*
beekeeping **3**:161 *illus.*
mead **13**:251
wasp **20**:46
HONEY BEAR *see* KINKAJOU
HONEY BUSH **10**:220
HONEY EATER (bird) **10**:220
HONEY GLIDER POSSUM **13**:175 *illus.*
HONEY GUIDE (bird) **10**:220
ratel **16**:92
HONEY LAKE
map (40° 16′N 120° 19′W) **4**:31
HONEY LOCUST (botany) **10**:220–221 *illus.*
HONEYBEE
anatomy **3**:155 *illus.*
mouth **11**:188 *illus.*
wings **11**:191 *illus.*
bee **3**:154–159 *illus.*
beekeeping **3**:161–162 *illus.*
behavior **2**:11 *illus.*
animal communication **2**:18
dance language **3**:158 *illus.*; **3**:159
Frisch, Karl von **8**:334
hive **3**:156 *illus.*
honey **10**:220
HONEYCREEPER (bird) **10**:221
Hawaiian honeycreeper **10**:76
HONEYDEW (insect secretion)
aphid **2**:77
leafhopper **12**:257
HONEYDEW MELON *see* MELON
HONEYMOON BAY (British Columbia)
map (48° 49′N 124° 10′W) **3**:491
HONEYSUCKLE **10**:221 *illus.*
beauty bush **3**:147
feverwort **8**:66
viburnum **19**:567–568
weigela **20**:92
HONG KONG **10**:221–223 *bibliog., illus., map, table*
cities
Kowloon **12**:126
Victoria **19**:573
climate **10**:221–222 *table*
economy and trade **10**:221–223 *illus.*
education
Chinese universities **4**:394 *table*
Chinese University of Hong Kong **4**:394–395
Hong Kong, University of **10**:223
history **10**:223
map (22° 15′N 114° 10′E) **2**:232
subway **18**:318 *table*
HONG KONG, UNIVERSITY OF **10**:223
HONGUEDO, STRAIT OF
map (49° 15′N 64° 0′W) **16**:18
HONIARA (Solomon Islands)
map (9° 26′S 159° 57′E) **18**:56
HONNECOURT, VILLARD DE *see* VILLARD DE HONNECOURT
HONNINGSVÅG (Norway) **14**:263 *illus.*
HONOKAA (Hawaii)
map (20° 5′N 155° 28′W) **10**:72
HONOLULU (Hawaii) **10**:73 *illus.*; **10**:223
climate **19**:421 *table*
map (21° 19′N 157° 52′W) **10**:72
HONOLULU (county in Hawaii)
map (21° 30′N 158° 0′W) **10**:72
HONOMU (Hawaii)
map (19° 52′N 155° 7′W) **10**:72
HONOR SYSTEM **10**:223–224
HONORIUS, ROMAN EMPEROR IN THE WEST **10**:224 *bibliog.*
Stilicho, Flavius **18**:268
HONORIUS I, POPE **10**:224
HONORIUS III, POPE **10**:224
HONSHU (Japan) **10**:224; **11**:362 *illus.*
cities
Hiroshima **10**:175–176 *illus.*
Kobe **12**:104
Kyoto **12**:143
Nagoya **14**:6
Osaka **14**:452
Sendai **17**:200
Tokyo **19**:223–225 *illus., map*
Yokohama **20**:329
Japanese giant salamander **11**:379
map (36° 0′N 138° 0′E) **11**:361
HONTHORST, GERRIT VAN **10**:224 *bibliog.*
HOOCH, PIETER DE **10**:224–225 *bibliog., illus.*
Interior with Woman Holding a Glass **10**:225 *illus.*
HOOD (county in Texas)
map (32° 27′N 97° 48′W) **19**:129
HOOD, FORT (Texas) *see* FORT HOOD (Texas)
HOOD, HUGH JOHN BLAGDON **10**:225
HOOD, JOHN B. **10**:225 *bibliog.*
Civil War, U.S. **5**:23 *map*; **5**:30
HOOD, MOUNT **10**:225; **14**:428 *illus.*
map (45° 23′N 121° 41′W) **14**:427
HOOD, RAYMOND **10**:225 *bibliog.*
HOOD, ROBIN *see* ROBIN HOOD
HOOD, THOMAS **10**:225 *bibliog.*
HOOD COLLEGE **10**:225
HOOD RIVER (Oregon)
map (45° 43′N 121° 31′W) **14**:427
HOOD RIVER (county in Oregon)
map (45° 30′N 121° 40′W) **14**:427
HOODED SKUNK *see* SKUNK
HOOF, NAIL, AND CLAW **10**:225–226 *illus.*
cat **4**:194 *illus.*
horse **10**:242 *illus.*; **10**:245 *illus.*
human nail **10**:225–226
cosmetics **5**:281–282 *table*
HOOFT, PIETER CORNELISZOON **10**:226 *bibliog.*
HOOGEVEEN (Netherlands)
map (52° 43′N 6° 29′E) **14**:99
HOOK, SIDNEY **10**:226 *bibliog.*
HOOKE, ROBERT **1**:396–397 *illus.*; **10**:226–227 *bibliog.*
anatomy **1**:396–397 *illus.*
biology **3**:269
interference **11**:208
microbiology **13**:384
Micrographia (book) **20**:376 *illus.*
motion, harmonic **13**:608
Newton, Sir Isaac **14**:174
HOOKED RUGS
rugs and carpets **16**:341
HOOKER (family) **10**:227 *bibliog.*
HOOKER (county in Nebraska)
map (41° 55′N 101° 5′W) **14**:70
HOOKER (Oklahoma)
map (36° 52′N 101° 13′W) **14**:368
HOOKER, JOSEPH **5**:29 *illus.*; **10**:227 *bibliog.*
Civil War, U.S. **5**:23 *map*; **5**:27
HOOKER, RICHARD **10**:227 *bibliog.*
HOOKER, THOMAS **10**:227 *bibliog.*
Fundamental Orders **8**:361
HOOKER CHEMICAL AND PLASTICS CORPORATION
pollutants, chemical **15**:411
HOOKE'S LAW *see* MOTION, HARMONIC
HOOKHAM, MARGARET *see* FONTEYN, DAME MARGOT
HOOKSETT (New Hampshire)
map (43° 6′N 71° 28′W) **14**:123
HOOKWORM **10**:227
diseases, animal **6**:192
life cycle **15**:82 *illus.*
HOOLEHUA (Hawaii)
map (21° 10′N 157° 6′W) **10**:72
HOONAH (Alaska)
map (58° 7′N 135° 26′W) **1**:242
HOOPA *see* HUPA (American Indians)
HOOPER (Nebraska)
map (41° 37′N 96° 33′W) **14**:70
HOOPER BAY (Alaska)
map (61° 31′N 166° 6′W) **1**:242
HOOPESTON (Illinois)
map (40° 28′N 87° 40′W) **11**:42
HOOPLE (North Dakota)
map (48° 32′N 97° 38′W) **14**:248
HOOPOE **10**:228 *illus.*
HOORN (Netherlands)
map (52° 38′N 5° 4′E) **14**:99
HOOSAC RANGE
map (42° 45′N 73° 2′W) **13**:206
HOOSAC TUNNEL *see* TUNNEL
HOOSIC RIVER
map (42° 54′N 73° 39′W) **14**:149
HOOSICK FALLS (New York)
map (42° 54′N 73° 21′W) **14**:149
HOOSIER SCHOOLMASTER, THE (book)
Eggleston, Edward **7**:73
HOOTCHY-KOOTCHY (dance) *see* BELLY DANCE
HOOVER, HERBERT **10**:228–229 *bibliog., illus.*
Curtis, Charles **5**:395
De re metallica **6**:62
Iowa **11**:246
Republican party **16**:174–175 *illus.*
United States, history of the **19**:454
HOOVER, J. EDGAR **10**:229–230 *bibliog., illus.*
Federal Bureau of Investigation **8**:40–41
HOOVER, WILLIAM HENRY
vacuum cleaner **19**:502
HOOVER COMMISSIONS *see* HOOVER, HERBERT
HOOVER DAM **6**:15 *illus.*; **10**:230 *bibliog.*; **14**:113 *illus.*
HOOVER RESERVOIR
map (40° 8′N 82° 53′W) **14**:357
HOP HORNBEAM (botany) **10**:230 *illus.*
HOP TREE **10**:230
HOPATCONG (New Jersey)
map (40° 56′N 74° 39′W) **14**:129
HOPATCONG, LAKE **14**:131 *illus.*
map (40° 57′N 74° 38′W) **14**:129
HOPE (Alaska)
map (60° 55′N 149° 38′W) **1**:242
HOPE (Arkansas)
map (33° 40′N 93° 36′W) **2**:166
HOPE (British Columbia)
map (49° 23′N 121° 26′W) **3**:491
HOPE (Indiana)
map (39° 18′N 85° 46′W) **11**:111
HOPE, ANTHONY **10**:230 *bibliog.*
HOPE, BOB **10**:230 *bibliog., illus.*
HOPE, VICTOR ALEXANDER JOHN, 2D MARQUESS OF LINLITHGOW *see* LINLITHGOW, VICTOR ALEXANDER JOHN HOPE, 2D MARQUESS OF
HOPE DIAMOND
diamond **6**:151–152 *illus.*
HOPE MILLS (North Carolina)
map (34° 59′N 78° 57′W) **14**:242
HOPE VALLEY (Rhode Island)
map (41° 30′N 71° 43′W) **16**:198
HOPEDALE (Louisiana)
map (29° 51′N 89° 41′W) **12**:430
HOPEDALE (Massachusetts)
map (42° 8′N 71° 33′W) **13**:206
HOPEDALE (Newfoundland)
map (55° 28′N 60° 13′W) **14**:166
HOPEI (Hebei) (China) **10**:230–231
cities
Tientsin (Tianjin) **19**:195
temple to Kuan-yin **19**:98 *illus.*
HOPELAWN (New Jersey)
map (40° 32′N 74° 18′W) **14**:129
HOPELCHÉN (Mexico)
map (19° 46′N 89° 51′W) **13**:357
HOPES ADVANCE, CAPE OF
map (61° 4′N 69° 34′W) **16**:18
HOPEWELL (Virginia)
map (37° 18′N 77° 17′W) **19**:607
HOPEWELL CULTURE
Mound Builders **13**:617
North American archaeology **14**:238–239 *illus.*
HOPI (American Indians) **10**:231 *bibliog., illus.*
Indians of North America, music and dance of the **11**:143
kachina **12**:4
North American archaeology **14**:240
Oraibi **14**:413–414
snake dance **11**:131 *illus.*; **17**:382
HOPKINS (county in Kentucky)
map (37° 20′N 87° 30′W) **12**:47
HOPKINS (Missouri)
map (40° 33′N 94° 49′W) **13**:476
HOPKINS (county in Texas)
map (32° 8′N 95° 35′W) **19**:129
HOPKINS, ESEK **10**:231
flag **8**:135 *illus.*
HOPKINS, SIR FREDERICK GOWLAND **10**:231
growth-stimulating vitamins **10**:231
tryptophane, amino acid **10**:231
HOPKINS, GERARD MANLEY **10**:231 *bibliog., illus.*
HOPKINS, HARRY L. **10**:231–232 *bibliog.*
HOPKINS, JOHNS **10**:232
HOPKINS, MARK **10**:232 *bibliog.*
California **4**:37
HOPKINS, SAMUEL **10**:232 *bibliog.*
HOPKINS, STEPHEN **10**:232
HOPKINSON, FRANCIS **10**:232
HOPKINSVILLE (Kentucky)
map (36° 52′N 87° 29′W) **12**:47
HOPKINTON (Iowa)
map (42° 21′N 91° 15′W) **11**:244
HOPKINTON (Massachusetts)
map (42° 13′N 71° 31′W) **13**:206
HOPLAND (California)
map (38° 58′N 123° 7′W) **4**:31
HOPLITE **10**:232
armor **2**:174
HOPPE, WILLIE **10**:232 *bibliog.*
HOPPE-SEYLER, FELIX **10**:232
HOPPER, DEWOLF **10**:232 *bibliog.*
HOPPER, EDWARD **10**:232–233 *bibliog., illus.*
From Williamsburg Bridge **10**:233 *illus.*
Whitney Museum of American Art **20**:142
HOPPER, HEDDA **10**:233 *bibliog.*
HOPPNER, JOHN **10**:233 *bibliog.*
HOPS **10**:233 *illus.*
beer **3**:162–163
hop tree **10**:230
HOPSCOTCH (book)
Cortázar, Julio **5**:278
HOQUIAM (Washington)
map (46° 59′N 123° 53′W) **20**:35
HORA **10**:233
HORACE **10**:233–234 *bibliog.*
Art of Poetry
criticism, literary **5**:351
carpe diem **4**:163
satire **17**:88
HORATII **10**:234
HORATIO (Arkansas)
map (33° 56′N 94° 21′W) **2**:166
HORATIUS **10**:234
HOREHOUND (botany) **10**:234
HORGEN (Switzerland)
map (47° 15′N 8° 36′E) **18**:394
HORICON (Wisconsin)
map (43° 27′N 88° 38′W) **20**:185
HORIZONTAL SYSTEM (astronomy)
coordinate systems **5**:245–246
HORMONE, ANIMAL **10**:234–237 *bibliog., illus., table*
adrenal gland **1**:108
Addison's disease **1**:101
adrenaline **1**:108
aldosterone **1**:269
corticoid **5**:278
glucocorticoid **9**:211
noradrenaline **14**:218
aging **1**:185
biochemistry **3**:262
birth control **3**:294
cancer **4**:105 *illus.*
cholesterol **4**:404
cyclic AMP **5**:403
endocrine system **7**:168–169
endocrine system, diseases of the **7**:169–171
estrous cycle **7**:248
gallbladder **9**:17
genetic engineering **9**:84
gland **9**:196–197
Golgi apparatus **9**:240
growth **9**:380
homeostasis **10**:212
juvenile hormone **11**:480
Kendall, Edward **12**:41
lipid hormones **12**:362
medicine **13**:271
menopause **13**:299
menstruation **13**:301
metabolism **13**:327
molting **13**:513
pancreas **15**:58
glucagon **9**:210–211
insulin **11**:197–198
parathyroid **15**:83
pituitary gland **15**:322
adrenocorticotropic hormone **1**:109
antidiuretic hormone **2**:61
gonadotropin **9**:242
growth hormone **9**:381
oxytocin **14**:479
prolactin **15**:567
prostaglandins **15**:572–573
radioimmunoassay **16**:64
serotonin **17**:209–210
sex change **17**:224
sex hormones **17**:226–227
sleep **17**:360
Starling, Ernest Henry **18**:227
steroids **18**:261
Sutherland, Earl W., Jr. **18**:372
thyroid gland **19**:188
goiter **9**:225
thyroxine **19**:188
HORMONE, PLANT **10**:237 *bibliog.*
abscisic acid **1**:62
auxin **2**:369
cytokinin **5**:411
gibberellins **9**:172
plant **15**:339
HORMUZ, STRAIT OF **10**:238
map (26° 34′N 56° 15′E) **11**:250

HORN (biology) **10**:238
antelope **2**:47
HORN (music)
African music **1**:169–170 *illus.*
cornet **5**:268–269 *illus.*
French horn **8**:311–312
musical instruments **13**:676–677 *illus.*
HORN, CAPE 10:238
map (55° 59′S 67° 16′W) **4**:355
HORN, PHILIP DE MONTMORENCY, COMTE DE 10:238
HORN ISLAND
map (30° 13′N 88° 38′W) **13**:469
HORNA LAGOON
map (64° 17′N 15° 16′W) **11**:17
HORNBEAK (Tennessee)
map (36° 20′N 89° 18′W) **19**:104
HORNBEAM (botany) **10**:238 *illus.*
hop hornbeam **10**:230
ironwood **11**:279
HORNBECK (Louisiana)
map (31° 20′N 93° 24′W) **12**:430
HORNBILL 10:238–239 *illus.*
HORNBLENDE
amphibole **1**:381 *illus.*
HORNBLOWER, HORATIO (fictional character)
Forester, C. S. **8**:230
HORNBOSTEL, ERICH M. VON
musical instruments **13**:676
HORNE, LENA 10:239 *bibliog., illus.*
HORNE, MARILYN 10:239 *bibliog.*
HORNED LIVERWORT *see* HORNWORT
HORNED LIZARD *see* HORNED TOAD
HORNED RATTLESNAKE *see* SIDEWINDER (snake)
HORNED TOAD 10:239 *illus.*; **12**:379 *illus.*
HORNELL (New York)
map (42° 19′N 77° 40′W) **14**:149
HORNET (aircraft carrier)
World War II **20**:265–266 *illus.*
HORNET (insect) *see* WASP (zoology)
HORNEY, KAREN 10:239–240 *bibliog.*
HORNFELS 10:240
facies, metamorphic rock **13**:332 *table*
formation, temperature range **10**:240
metamorphic rock **13**:332
HORNIMAN, ANNIE ELIZABETH FREDERICKA 10:240 *bibliog.*
HORNSBY, ROGERS 10:240 *bibliog., illus.*
HORNUNG, PAUL 10:240 *bibliog.*
HORNWORT 10:240 *bibliog.*
bryophyte **3**:530
pollination **15**:409
HOROSCOPE
astrology **2**:272
HOROVITZ, ISRAEL 10:241
HOROWITZ, VLADIMIR 10:241 *bibliog., illus.*
HORROR FILMS AND SHOWS
Browning, Tod **3**:519
Guignol, Grand **9**:394–395
Karloff, Boris **12**:28
Lugosi, Bela **12**:453 *illus.*
HORROR NOVELS AND STORIES
King, Stephen **12**:81
HORRY (county in South Carolina)
map (33° 55′N 79° 0′W) **18**:98
HORSE 10:241–246 *bibliog., illus.*
agriculture, history of **1**:191–192 *illus.*
anatomy **10**:241–242 *illus.*
feet **13**:102 *illus.*
hoof **10**:226 *illus.*
animal husbandry **2**:23
armor **2**:174 *illus.*
ass **2**:263
biological locomotion **3**:266 *illus.*
breeding
horse racing **10**:246–247
Hungary **10**:308 *illus.*
Kentucky **12**:51 *illus.*
Lexington (Kentucky) **12**:309
breeds **10**:243–244 *illus.*
American saddle horse **1**:366 *illus.*
Appaloosa **2**:86–87 *illus.*
Arabian horse **2**:99 *illus.*
Belgian horse **3**:174 *illus.*
Cleveland Bay horse **5**:75 *illus.*
Clydesdale **5**:72–73 *illus.*
draft horse **6**:254
hackney **10**:243 *illus.*
light horses **12**:336
Lippizaner **12**:363 *illus.*
Morgan (horse) **13**:578
Percheron **15**:161 *illus.*
pinto **15**:308 *illus.*
pony **15**:428 *illus.*
quarter horse **16**:13 *illus.*
Shetland pony **17**:260 *illus.*
Shire **17**:277
Standardbred **18**:216–217 *illus.*
Suffolk (horse) **18**:325 *illus.*
Tennessee walking horse **19**:108 *illus.*
Thoroughbred **19**:179 *illus.*
Welsh pony **20**:102 *illus.*
coach horse **5**:75
colors **10**:244
palomino **15**:52 *illus.*
pinto **15**:308 *illus.*
diseases **10**:241; **10**:244
distemper **6**:200
glanders **9**:197
donkey **6**:238
evolution **10**:245 *illus.*
eohippus **7**:215 *illus.*
Pleistocene Epoch **15**:366–367 *illus.*
quagga **16**:5 *illus.*
tarpan **19**:38 *illus.*
Tertiary Period **19**:124–125 *illus.*
titanothere **19**:211 *illus.*
gaits **10**:241
harness **10**:52–53 *illus.*
harness horse **10**:53
history **10**:245–246
horse racing *see* HORSE RACING
horseshoe **10**:251–252
hybrids **10**:245
lack of, Incan Empire **11**:70
mule **13**:636
mustang **13**:685–686
Muybridge, Eadweard **13**:687–688 *illus.*
perissodactyl **15**:171
polo **15**:416–417
Przewalski's horse **15**:586
reproduction **10**:241
riding **16**:216–217
saddle horse **17**:9
size **10**:244
steppe life **18**:257
trotter **19**:311
wild horse **10**:245–246
HORSE CHESTNUT 8:348 *illus.*; **10**:246 *illus.*
buckeye **3**:535
leaf **15**:336 *illus.*
HORSE CREEK (Wyoming)
map (41° 25′N 105° 11′W) **20**:301
HORSE DISTEMPER **6**:200
HORSE GENTIAN *see* FEVERWORT
HORSE LATITUDES 10:246 *bibliog.*
climate **10**:246
Sargasso Sea **17**:77
HORSE RACING 10:246–250 *bibliog., illus., tables*
betting **10**:248
Derby, The **6**:121
handicapping **10**:248
harness horse **10**:53
harness racing **10**:248 *illus.*
history **10**:246–247
information theory **11**:174
jockeys **10**:248; **10**:250
Arcaro, Eddie **2**:112–113
Cauthen, Steve **4**:220
Cordero, Angel **5**:261
Hartack, Bill **10**:62
Murphy, Isaac **13**:649–650
Richards, Gordon **16**:211
Sande, Earl **17**:62
Shoemaker, Willie **17**:280–281
Kentucky **12**:50 *illus.*
Kentucky Derby **12**:52
pari-mutuel betting **10**:250
quarter horse **16**:13
racehorses **10**:247; **10**:249–250 *table*
regulation and organization **10**:250
sprinting **10**:248
Standardbred **18**:216–217
steeplechase **10**:248; **18**:243
Thoroughbred **19**:179
Thoroughbred racing **10**:247–249 *table*
trotter **19**:311
HORSE SHOW 10:250 *bibliog., illus.*
See also RODEO
Lippizaner **12**:363
riding **16**:217
HORSEBACK RIDING *see* RIDING
HORSEFLY 10:250–251 *illus.*
deerfly **6**:81
HORSEHAIR **8**:67 *illus.*
HORSEHEAD LAKE
map (47° 2′N 99° 47′W) **14**:248
HORSEHEADS (New York)
map (42° 10′N 76° 50′W) **14**:149
HORSEMANSHIP *see* RIDING
HORSEMINT *see* MINT (botany)
HORSENS (Denmark)
map (55° 52′N 9° 52′E) **6**:109
HORSEPOWER 10:251
dynamometer **6**:319–320
power **15**:481
HORSERADISH 10:251 *illus.*
HORSESHOE 10:251–252 *bibliog., illus.*
magnet **13**:54
HORSESHOE CRAB 10:252 *bibliog., illus.*
HORSESHOE FALLS *see* NIAGARA FALLS
HORSESHOE PITCHING 10:252
HORSESHOE RESERVOIR
map (34° 0′N 111° 40′W) **2**:160
HORSETAIL (botany) **10**:252–253 *bibliog., illus.*; **15**:334 *illus.*
Jurassic Period **11**:475 *illus.*
Permian Period **15**:174 *illus.*
pteridophyte **15**:606
Triassic Period **19**:294 *illus.*
HØRSHOLM (Denmark)
map (55° 53′N 12° 30′E) **6**:109
HORSLEY, VICTOR
surgery **18**:361
HORST, LOUIS
modern dance **13**:497
HORST AND GRABEN 10:253–254 *bibliog., illus.*
East African Rift System **7**:30–31
examples **10**:254
fault **8**:36–38; **10**:253
mountain **13**:620
plate tectonics **15**:352–353
rift valleys **16**:221
HORTA, MARIA TERESA
Three Marias, The (Portuguese literary trio) **19**:182
HORTA, VICTOR 10:254 *bibliog.*
Art Nouveau **2**:210
HORTHY DE NAGYBÁNYA, MIKLÓS 10:254 *bibliog., illus.*
HORTICULTURE 10:254–255 *bibliog., illus.*
See also BOTANY
arboriculture **2**:110–111
Bailey, Liberty Hyde **3**:26
Burbank, Luther **3**:566
espalier **7**:242–243
gardening **9**:42–44
greenhouse **9**:351
hydroponics **10**:343
terrarium **19**:120–121
vegetable **19**:531–534
HORTON (Kansas)
map (39° 40′N 95° 32′W) **12**:18
HORTON, ALONZO E.
San Diego (California) **17**:52
HORTON, LESTER 10:255 *bibliog.*
HORTONVILLE (Wisconsin)
map (44° 20′N 88° 38′W) **20**:185
HORTUS CAVE **15**:515 *illus.*
HORUS 7:84 *illus.*; **10**:255; **13**:400 *illus.*
mythology **13**:697–698
pharaoh **15**:219
temple
Edfu **7**:56
HORVÁTH, ÖDÖN VON 10:255 *bibliog.*
HOSEA, BOOK OF 10:255 *bibliog.*
HOSMER (South Dakota)
map (45° 34′N 99° 28′W) **18**:103
HOSMER, HARRIET 10:255–256 *bibliog.*
HOSPERS (Iowa)
map (43° 4′N 95° 54′W) **11**:244
HOSPICE 10:256
death and dying **6**:69
HOSPITAL 10:256–258 *bibliog., illus.*
See also names of specific hospitals, e.g., BEDLAM; MAYO CLINIC; etc.
costs **10**:258
health-care systems **10**:87–89
history **10**:256
Mansur Hospital **13**:269
medicine **13**:268–269 *illus.*
institutionalization **11**:196
Mayo (family) **13**:248
nosocomial **14**:266
nursing (profession) **14**:298–299
Osler, Sir William **14**:454
psychopathology, treatment of **15**:599–600
Reed, Walter **16**:118
Schweitzer, Albert **17**:139–140
HOSPITAL INSURANCE
Blue Cross **3**:342
Blue Shield **3**:343
health-care systems **10**:87–88
hospital **10**:257; **10**:258
Medicaid **13**:264
Medicare **13**:265
HOSPITALERS 10:258–259 *bibliog.*
Krak des Chevaliers **12**:127
Malta **13**:95
Rhodes (Greece) **16**:201–202
HOSSTON (Louisiana)
map (32° 53′N 93° 53′W) **12**:430
HOSTAGE
airplane hijacking **1**:222
Iranian hostage crisis **11**:253–254
HOSTEL *see* YOUTH HOSTEL
HOSTILE TAKEOVER
conglomerate **5**:180
HOSTILITY
social psychology **18**:13
HOT DOG (meat) *see* SAUSAGE
HOT PRESSING *see* PRESSING
HOT SPRING (county in Arkansas)
map (34° 18′N 92° 55′W) **2**:166
HOT SPRINGS
erosion and sedimentation **7**:233
fumarole **8**:357
geothermal energy **9**:120–121
geyser **9**:162–163
Hot Springs (Arkansas) **10**:259
Iceland **11**:17
medicinal waters **10**:259
sinter **17**:325
HOT SPRINGS (Arkansas) **2**:169 *illus.*; **10**:259
map (34° 30′N 93° 3′W) **2**:166
national parks **14**:38–39 *map, table*
HOT SPRINGS (North Carolina)
map (35° 54′N 82° 50′W) **14**:242
HOT SPRINGS (South Dakota)
map location (43° 26′N 103° 29′W) **18**:103
HOT SPRINGS (county in Wyoming)
map (43° 45′N 108° 32′W) **20**:301
HOT SULPHUR SPRINGS (Colorado)
map (40° 4′N 106° 6′W) **5**:116
HOTCHKISS (Colorado)
map (38° 48′N 107° 43′W) **5**:116
HOTEL 10:259–262 *bibliog., illus., table*
See also YOUTH HOSTEL
disasters **10**:262
Kansas City (Missouri) **12**:22
Las Vegas (Nevada) **12**:210
franchise (business) **8**:273
Hilton, Conrad **10**:165
inn (19th century) **10**:259 *illus.*
labor union
Hotel and Restaurant Employees and Bartenders International Union **10**:262
Statler, Ellsworth Milton **18**:238
HÔTEL DE BOURGOGNE, THÉÂTRE DE L' 10:262 *bibliog.*
HOTEL AND RESTAURANT EMPLOYEES AND BARTENDERS INTERNATIONAL UNION 10:262
HOTEVILLA (Arizona)
map (35° 56′N 110° 41′W) **2**:160
HOTSPUR *see* PERCY, HENRY
HOTTENTOT (South Africa) *see* KHOIKHOI
HOTTETERRE, JEAN
oboe **14**:316
HOUDINI, HARRY 10:263 *bibliog., illus.*
HOUDON, JEAN ANTOINE 10:263–264 *bibliog., illus.*
HOUGH, EMERSON 10:264
HOUGHTON (Michigan)
map (47° 6′N 88° 34′W) **13**:377
HOUGHTON (county in Michigan)
map (46° 50′N 88° 45′W) **13**:377
HOUGHTON (New York)
map (42° 25′N 78° 10′W) **14**:149
HOUGHTON, ARTHUR AMORY
Steuben glass **18**:262
HOUGHTON LAKE (Michigan)
map (44° 18′N 84° 45′W) **13**:377
HOULKA (Mississippi)
map (34° 2′N 89° 1′W) **13**:469
HOULTON (Maine)
map (46° 8′N 67° 51′W) **13**:70
HOUMA (Louisiana)
map (29° 36′N 90° 43′W) **12**:430
HOUMT ESSOUK (Tunisia)
map (33° 59′N 10° 51′E) **19**:335
HOUND **6**:216–217 *illus.*
Afghan hound **1**:132
American foxhound **1**:339–340
basenji **3**:108
basset hound **3**:118
beagle **3**:138
black-and-tan coonhound **3**:319
bloodhound **3**:339
borzoi **3**:405
dachshund **6**:4
English foxhound **7**:190
greyhound **9**:361
harrier (dog) **10**:56
Irish wolfhound **11**:269–270

Norwegian elkhound **14**:265
otter hound **14**:462
Pharaoh hound **15**:219
Rhodesian ridgeback **16**:202
saluki **17**:39
Scottish deerhound **17**:155
whippet **20**:131
HOUND OF THE BASKERVILLES, THE (book) **10**:264
HOUND'S TONGUE (botany) **10**:264
HOUPHOUËT-BOIGNY, FÉLIX **10**:264 *bibliog.*
Ivory Coast **11**:336
HOUR ANGLE **10**:264
HOUSATONIC (Massachusetts)
map (42° 16'N 73° 22'W) **13**:206
HOUSATONIC RIVER **10**:264
map (41° 10'N 73° 7'W) **5**:193
HOUSE (in Western architecture) **10**:264–272 *bibliog., illus.*
See also BUILDING CONSTRUCTION; HOUSING; PLANTATION
architecture **2**:130
atrium **2**:312–313
brownstone **3**:519
chalet **4**:271
château **4**:302
chimney **4**:358
contemporary construction **10**:217
cornice **5**:269
Davis, Alexander Jackson **6**:50
decorative arts **6**:76
early forms and materials **10**:264
Egyptian art and architecture **7**:86 *illus.*
Elizabethan style **7**:146
English art and architecture **7**:184
Esherick, Joseph **7**:238
European prehistory
broch **3**:500
Iron Age **7**:305 *illus.*
Neolithic Period **7**:303 *illus.*
folk art **8**:196–198
furniture **8**:373–380 *illus., illus.*
gable **9**:3
Gill, Irving **9**:181–182
Greek and Roman **10**:264–266
Greene and Greene **9**:351
Gwathmey, Charles **9**:411
heating systems **10**:99–100
igloo, Eskimo **11**:126 *illus.*
Indians, American **11**:120–121 *illus.*
cliff dwellers **5**:54–55 *illus.*
earth lodge **11**:120 *illus.*
hogan **10**:197
Nootka dwelling **14**:217 *illus.*
tepee **19**:114
wickiup **20**:145
wigwam **20**:147
interior design **11**:210–214
Johnson, Philip **11**:434–435
Latin American art and architecture **12**:226
Le Corbusier **12**:254 *illus.*
lumber **12**:455 *illus.*
manorialism **13**:126 *illus.*
Maybeck, Bernard **13**:246
Mesolithic Period **13**:315 *illus.*
Neolithic Period **7**:303 *illus.*; **14**:83 *illus.*
Paleolithic Period **15**:39 *illus.*
plumbing **15**:371 *illus.*
prairie school **15**:489
Robie House **16**:243
Roman art and architecture **16**:274
roof and roofing **16**:306 *illus.*
Safdie, Moshe **17**:10
saltbox house **5**:110 *illus.*
Schindler, Rudolf M. **17**:121
Shaw, Richard Norman **17**:246
sod house **8**:343 *illus.*
solar energy **18**:41–42 *illus.*
Soleri, Paolo **18**:53
Taliesin West **19**:16
Van de Velde, Henry **19**:512
villa **19**:596
Voysey, Charles Francis Annesley **19**:638
Wright, Frank Lloyd **20**:288–289
HOUSE (New Mexico)
map (34° 39'N 103° 54'W) **14**:136
HOUSE, COLONEL *see* HOUSE, EDWARD M.
HOUSE, EDWARD M. **10**:272 *bibliog.*
HOUSE OF BERNARDA ALBA, THE (play) **10**:272
HOUSE OF BURGESSES *see* BURGESSES, HOUSE OF
HOUSE OF COMMONS
Parliament **15**:92–93
HOUSE OF DAVID **10**:272
HOUSE OF LORDS
Parliament **15**:92–93
HOUSE OF REPRESENTATIVES OF THE UNITED STATES **10**:272–274 *bibliog., illus.*
Cannon, Joseph Gurney **4**:112
Congress of the United States **5**:184–187 *illus.*
Congressional Record **5**:188
Constitution of the United States **5**:216
gag rules **9**:7
genesis and framework of the Constitution **5**:213–214
Rankin, Jeannette **16**:87–88
speakers
Albert, Carl **1**:253
McCormack, John W. **13**:10
O'Neill, Thomas P. **14**:390
Rayburn, Sam **16**:96–97
Reed, Thomas B. **16**:118
Un-American Activities, House Committee on **19**:380–381
Washington, D.C. **20**:41 *map*
whip **20**:131
HOUSE OF THE FAUN *see* FAUN, HOUSE OF THE
HOUSE OF THE SEVEN GABLES, THE (book) **10**:274 *bibliog.*
Hawthorne, Nathaniel **10**:79
HOUSEBOAT **3**:351 *illus.*; **10**:274 *bibliog.*
HOUSEFLY **10**:274 *bibliog., illus.*; **11**:192 *illus.*
anatomy **8**:190 *illus.*
life cycle **8**:190 *illus.*
mouth **11**:188 *illus.*
HOUSELEEK *see SEMPERVIVUM*
HOUSEMAN, A. E. **10**:280 *illus.*
HOUSEMAN, JOHN **10**:274
Mercury Theatre **13**:308
HOUSEPLANTS **10**:274–276 *bibliog., illus.*
See also names of specific plants, e.g., APHELANDRA; DIEFFENBACHIA; etc.
HOUSING **10**:276–280 *bibliog., illus.*
See also URBAN PLANNING
civil rights, *Shelley* v. *Kraemer* **17**:253–254
condominium **5**:172–173
equal opportunity **7**:223
Federal Housing Administration **8**:41
Federal National Mortgage Association **8**:41
hotel **10**:259–262
house (in Western architecture) **10**:271
Housing and Urban Development, U.S. Department of **10**:280
inner city **11**:179
integration, racial **11**:203
Levitt, William Jaird **12**:304
mobile home **13**:487–488
mortgage **13**:591–592
old age **14**:373–374
poverty **15**:479
rent control **16**:159
socialist law **18**:25
suburbs **18**:317
tenant **19**:101
HOUSING AND URBAN DEVELOPMENT, U.S. DEPARTMENT OF **10**:280 *bibliog.*
Federal Housing Administration **8**:41
flag **8**:148 *illus.*
housing **10**:277
Washington, D.C. **20**:41 *map*
HOUSMAN, LAURENCE **10**:280
HOUSTON (county in Alabama)
map (31° 10'N 85° 20'W) **1**:234
HOUSTON (British Columbia)
map (54° 24'N 126° 38'W) **3**:491
HOUSTON (county in Georgia)
map (32° 30'N 83° 40'W) **9**:114
HOUSTON (county in Minnesota)
map (43° 38'N 91° 28'W) **13**:453
HOUSTON (Mississippi)
map (33° 54'N 89° 0'W) **13**:469
HOUSTON (Missouri)
map (37° 22'N 91° 58'W) **13**:476
HOUSTON (county in Tennessee)
map (36° 20'N 87° 45'W) **19**:104
HOUSTON (Texas) **10**:280–281 *bibliog., map*; **19**:131 *illus.*
climate **14**:228 *table*; **19**:421 *table*
harbor and port **10**:42
history **10**:281
map (29° 46'N 95° 22'W) **19**:129
HOUSTON (county in Texas)
map (31° 20'N 95° 20'W) **19**:129
HOUSTON, LAKE
map (29° 58'N 95° 7'W) **19**:129
HOUSTON, SAM **10**:282 *bibliog., illus.*
Texas **19**:134
Texas Revolution **19**:135
HOVE (England)
map (50° 49'N 0° 10'W) **19**:403
HOVELL, WILLIAM H.
Murray River **13**:650
HOVER FLY **8**:189 *illus.*
HOVERCRAFT *see* AIR-CUSHION VEHICLE
HOVHANESS, ALAN **10**:282
HOWARD (county in Arkansas)
map (34° 7'N 94° 0'W) **2**:166
HOWARD (family) **10**:282 *bibliog.*
HOWARD (county in Indiana)
map (40° 29'N 86° 8'W) **11**:111
HOWARD (county in Iowa)
map (43° 20'N 92° 18'W) **11**:244
HOWARD (Kansas)
map (37° 28'N 96° 16'W) **12**:18
HOWARD (county in Maryland)
map (39° 16'N 76° 48'W) **13**:188
HOWARD (county in Missouri)
map (39° 10'N 92° 40'W) **13**:476
HOWARD (county in Nebraska)
map (41° 15'N 98° 30'W) **14**:70
HOWARD (South Dakota)
map (44° 1'N 97° 32'W) **18**:103
HOWARD (county in Texas)
map (32° 22'N 101° 25'W) **19**:129
HOWARD (Wisconsin)
map (44° 33'N 88° 4'W) **20**:185
HOWARD, ALAN **19**:151 *illus.*
HOWARD, BRONSON **10**:282
HOWARD, CATHERINE **10**:282–283 *bibliog.*
HOWARD, EBENEZER **10**:283 *bibliog.*
garden city **9**:41–42
greenbelt **9**:349
new towns **14**:143
urban planning **19**:484
HOWARD, HENRY, EARL OF SURREY *see* SURREY, HENRY HOWARD, EARL OF
HOWARD, JOHN **5**:383 *illus.*
HOWARD, LESLIE **10**:283
HOWARD, LUKE
meteorology **13**:342
HOWARD, MAY
music hall, vaudeville, and burlesque **13**:671
HOWARD, OLIVER O. **10**:283 *bibliog.*
HOWARD, ROY WILSON **10**:283 *bibliog.*
HOWARD, SIDNEY COE **10**:283 *bibliog.*
HOWARD, THOMAS
Cromwell, Thomas, 1st Earl of Essex **5**:358
HOWARD CITY (Michigan)
map (43° 24'N 85° 28'W) **13**:377
HOWARD LAKE (Minnesota)
map (45° 4'N 94° 4'W) **13**:453
HOWARD UNIVERSITY **10**:283
HOWDY DOODY
radio and television broadcasting **16**:58 *illus.*
HOWE (Indiana)
map (41° 43'N 85° 25'W) **11**:111
HOWE, CAPE
map (37° 31'S 149° 59'E) **2**:328
HOWE, EDGAR WATSON **10**:283
HOWE, ELIAS **10**:283 *bibliog.*
sewing machine **11**:155 *illus.*; **17**:224
HOWE, GORDIE **10**:283–284 *bibliog., illus.*
HOWE, IRVING **10**:284
HOWE, JAMES WONG **10**:284
HOWE, JOSEPH **10**:284 *bibliog.*
HOWE, JULIA WARD **10**:284 *bibliog.*
suffrage, women's **18**:326
HOWE, RICHARD HOWE, EARL **10**:284
American Revolution **1**:358–359 *map*
HOWE, WILLIAM HOWE, 5TH VISCOUNT **10**:284 *bibliog.*
American Revolution **1**:358–359 *map*; **1**:360
Long Island, Battle of **12**:406
HOWELL (Michigan)
map (42° 36'N 83° 55'W) **13**:377
HOWELL (county in Missouri)
map (36° 50'N 91° 55'W) **13**:476
HOWELL, DOUGLASS
sketchbook **5**:327 *illus.*
HOWELL, F. CLARK **10**:284
Torralba and Ambrona (Spain) **19**:243
HOWELLS, WILLIAM DEAN **10**:285 *bibliog., illus.*
realism (literature) **16**:104
HOWELLS, WILLIAM WHITE **10**:285
HOWICK (New Zealand)
map (36° 54'S 174° 56'E) **14**:158
HOWITZER **2**:223–224 *illus.*; **10**:285 *bibliog., illus.*
"HOWL" (poem) **10**:285
HOWLAND (Maine)
map (45° 14'N 68° 40'W) **13**:70
HOWLAND ISLAND
map (0° 48'N 176° 38'W) **14**:334
United States outlying territories **19**:464
HOWLEY (Newfoundland)
map (49° 10'N 57° 7'W) **14**:166
HOWRAH (India) **10**:285
map (22° 35'N 88° 20'E) **11**:80
HOXHA, ENVER **10**:285–286 *bibliog.*
HOXIE (Arkansas)
map (36° 3'N 90° 58'W) **2**:166
HOXIE (Kansas)
map (39° 21'N 100° 26'W) **12**:18
HOYERSWERDA (Germany, East and West)
map (51° 26'N 14° 14'E) **9**:140
HOYLE, EDMOND **10**:286
HOYLE, SIR FRED **10**:286 *illus.*
HOYLETON (Illinois)
map (38° 27'N 89° 16'W) **11**:42
HOYT LAKES (Minnesota)
map (47° 31'N 92° 8'W) **13**:453
HOYTE, DESMOND
Guyana **9**:411
HR DIAGRAM *see* HERTZSPRUNG-RUSSELL DIAGRAM
HRABANUS MAURUS *see* RABANUS MAURUS
HRABOVSKY, LEONID
Russian music **16**:369
HRADČANY CASTLE
Prague (Czechoslovakia) **15**:488 *illus.*
HRADEC KRÁLOVÉ (Czechoslovakia)
map (50° 12'N 15° 50'E) **5**:413
HRDLIČKA, ALEŠ **10**:286
HRON RIVER
map (47° 49'N 18° 45'E) **5**:413
HROSWITHA VON GANDERSHEIM **10**:286 *bibliog.*
HROZNÝ, BEDŘICH
languages, extinct **12**:198
HSI-AN *see* SIAN (Xi'an) (China)
HSI CHIANG (Xi Jiang)(China) **10**:286
HSI-CHIANG (Xi Jiang) RIVER
map (22° 25'N 113° 23'E) **4**:362
HSI K'ANG *see* CHI K'ANG (Ji Kang)
HSI-NING (China)
map (36° 38'N 101° 55'E) **4**:362
HSIA (Xia) (dynasty) **10**:286 *bibliog.*
Asia, history of **2**:251
HSIA KUEI (Xia Gui) **10**:287 *bibliog.*
HSIA-MEN (Xiamen) *see* AMOY (China)
HSIANG LANGUAGE
Sino-Tibetan languages **17**:324
HSIANG-T'AN (China)
map (27° 51'N 112° 54'E) **4**:362
HSIEH LING-YÜN (Xie Lingyun)
Chinese literature **4**:389
HSIEN-MING, LEE
Tcherepnin, Alexsandr Nikolayevich **19**:52
HSIN (dynasty)
Wang Mang, Emperor of China **20**:22
HSIN-CHU (Taiwan)
map (24° 48'N 120° 58'E) **19**:13
HSIN-KAO PEAK
map (23° 28'N 120° 57'E) **19**:13
HSINCHING (China) *see* CH'ANG-CH'UN (Changchun) (China)
HSOIUEH PEAK
map (24° 24'N 121° 12'E) **19**:13
HSÜAN-TSANG (Xuanzang) **10**:287 *bibliog.*
HSÜAN T'UNG, EMPEROR OF CHINA *see* PU-YI, HENRY, EMPEROR OF CHINA
HSÜN TZU
Confucianism **5**:180
philosophy **15**:247
HTLV VIRUSES
retrovirus **16**:184
HU HAN-MIN (Hu Hanmin) **10**:287
HU HANMIN *see* HU HAN-MIN (Hu Hanmin)
HU-HO-HAO-T'E (China)
map (40° 51'N 111° 40'E) **4**:362
HU-LUN, LAKE
map (49° 1'N 117° 32'E) **13**:529
HU SHI *see* HU SHIH (Hu Shi)
HU SHIH (Hu Shi) **10**:287 *bibliog.*
HU YAO-PANG (Hu Yaobang) **10**:287
China **4**:369
HUA GUOFENG *see* HUA KUO-FENG (Hua Guofeng)

HUA KUO-FENG (Hua Guofeng) **10**:287
China **4**:369
Gang of Four **9**:36
HUA-LIEN (Taiwan)
map (23° 58′N 121° 36′E) **19**:13
HUACARAJE (Bolivia)
map (13° 33′S 63° 45′W) **3**:366
HUACHO (Peru)
map (11° 7′S 77° 37′W) **15**:193
HUACHUCA CITY (Arizona)
map (31° 34′N 110° 21′W) **2**:160
HUAI RIVER
map (32° 58′N 118° 17′E) **4**:362
HUAJUAPAN DE LEÓN (Mexico)
map (17° 48′N 97° 46′W) **13**:357
HUALALAI (volcano)
map (19° 42′N 155° 52′W) **10**:72
HUALAPAI PEAK
map (35° 4′N 113° 54′W) **2**:160
HUALLAGA RIVER
map (5° 10′S 75° 32′W) **15**:193
HUALLANCA (Peru)
map (8° 49′S 77° 52′W) **15**:193
HUAMACHUCO (Peru)
map (7° 48′S 78° 4′W) **15**:193
HUAMBO (Angola) **10**:287
map (12° 30′S 15° 40′E) **2**:5
HUAMBO (Peru)
map (15° 44′S 72° 7′W) **15**:193
HUANCAVELICA (Peru)
map (12° 46′S 75° 2′W) **15**:193
HUANCAYO (Peru)
map (12° 4′S 75° 14′W) **15**:193
HUANCHACA (Bolivia)
map (20° 20′S 66° 39′W) **3**:366
HUANDO (Peru)
map (12° 29′S 74° 58′W) **15**:193
HUANG GONGWANG *see* HUANG KUNG-WANG (Huang Gongwang)
HUANG HE *see* HWANG HO (Hwang He)
HUANG KUNG-WANG (Huang Gongwang) **10**:287
HUANG TI *see* YELLOW EMPEROR
HUANG-TI NEI-CHING see NEI-CHING
HUANG T'ING-CHIEN (Huang Tingjian)
Chinese literature **4**:390
HUANGUELÉN (Argentina)
map (37° 2′S 61° 57′W) **2**:149
HUÁNUCO (Peru)
map (9° 55′S 76° 14′W) **15**:193
HUANUCO VIEJO
Inca **11**:72
HUANUNI (Bolivia)
map (18° 16′S 66° 51′W) **3**:366
HUARAL (Peru)
map (11° 30′S 77° 12′W) **15**:193
HUARAZ (Peru)
map (9° 32′S 77° 32′W) **15**:193
HUARI (Peru) **10**:287 *bibliog.*
Inca **11**:70
Nazca **14**:67
pre-Columbian art and architecture **15**:495; **15**:500–501
HUARMEY (Peru)
map (10° 4′S 78° 10′W) **15**:193
HUÁSCAR **11**:70–71 *illus.*
Atahualpa **2**:287
Huayna Capac **10**:288
HUASCARÁN **10**:287
map (9° 7′S 77° 37′W) **15**:193
HUASTEC (American Indians) **10**:287–288 *bibliog.*
HUATABAMPO (Mexico)
map (26° 50′N 109° 38′W) **13**:357
HUAYNA CAPAC **10**:288 *bibliog.*
Inca empire **11**:70 *map*
HUBBARD (Iowa)
map (42° 18′N 93° 18′W) **11**:244
HUBBARD (county in Minnesota)
map (47° 7′N 94° 55′W) **13**:453
HUBBARD (Texas)
map (31° 51′N 96° 48′W) **19**:129
HUBBARD, ELBERT **10**:288
furniture **8**:379
HUBBARD, KIN **10**:288
HUBBARD, L. RONALD
Scientology **17**:146
HUBBARD LAKE
map (44° 49′N 83° 34′W) **13**:377
HUBBARDS (Nova Scotia)
map (44° 38′N 64° 4′W) **14**:269
HUBBELL, CARL **10**:288
HUBBLE, EDWIN **2**:281 *illus.*; **10**:288 *bibliog., illus.*
astronomy and astrophysics **2**:284–285
extragalactic systems **7**:343–344
HUBBLE'S CONSTANT **10**:288 *bibliog.*
cosmology (astronomy) **5**:284
distance, astronomical **6**:200
extragalactic systems **7**:344
Hubble, Edwin **10**:288
Hubble time **10**:288
Humason, Milton La Salle **10**:300
quasar **16**:14–15 *illus.*
red shift **16**:114
steady-state theory **18**:240
HUBEI (China) *see* HUPEI (Hubei) (China)
HUBER, EUGEN
Swiss code of civil law **5**:12
HUBER, WOLF **10**:288 *bibliog.*
Danube school **6**:36
HUBLI (India)
map (15° 21′N 75° 10′E) **11**:80
HÜCKEL, ERICH
Debye, Peter **6**:72
ion and ionization **11**:240
HUCKEL, ERICH
chemistry, history of **4**:328
HUCKLEBERRY **10**:289
HUCKLEBERRY FINN (book) **10**:289 *bibliog.*
Twain, Mark **19**:357
HUDDERSFIELD (England)
map (53° 39′N 1° 47′W) **19**:403
HUDDINGE (Sweden)
map (59° 14′N 17° 59′E) **18**:382
HUDIKSVALL (Sweden)
map (61° 44′N 17° 7′E) **18**:382
HUDSON (Florida)
map (28° 22′N 82° 42′W) **8**:172
HUDSON (Iowa)
map (42° 24′N 92° 28′W) **11**:244
HUDSON (Massachusetts)
map (42° 24′N 71° 35′W) **13**:206
HUDSON (Michigan)
map (41° 51′N 84° 21′W) **13**:377
HUDSON (New Hampshire)
map (42° 46′N 71° 26′W) **14**:123
HUDSON (county in New Jersey)
map (40° 45′N 74° 5′W) **14**:129
HUDSON (New York)
map (42° 15′N 73° 47′W) **14**:149
HUDSON (Ohio)
map (41° 15′N 81° 26′W) **14**:357
HUDSON (South Dakota)
map (43° 8′N 96° 27′W) **18**:103
HUDSON (Wisconsin)
map (44° 53′N 92° 45′W) **20**:185
HUDSON, HENRY **10**:289 *bibliog., illus.*
Arctic **2**:142 *map*
Catskill Mountains **4**:213
Delaware **6**:87
exploration **7**:336–337 *map*
flag **8**:135 *illus.*
Hudson Bay **10**:289
Hudson River **10**:289
New York (state) **14**:153
Northwest Passage **14**:256
HUDSON, MANLEY OTTMER **10**:289
HUDSON, WILLIAM HENRY **10**:289 *bibliog.*
Green Mansions **9**:348
HUDSON BAY **4**:75 *illus.*; **10**:289
James Bay **11**:355
map (60° 0′N 86° 0′W) **4**:70
HUDSON BAY (Saskatchewan)
map (52° 52′N 102° 25′W) **17**:81
HUDSON CANYON *see* SUBMARINE CANYON
HUDSON FALLS (New York)
map (43° 18′N 73° 35′W) **14**:149
HUDSON HOPE (British Columbia)
map (56° 2′N 121° 55′W) **3**:491
HUDSON MOTOR CAR COMPANY
automotive industry **2**:363–366
HUDSON RIVER **10**:289–290 *bibliog.*; **14**:152 *illus.*
Holland Tunnel **10**:203
Hudson, Henry **10**:289
map (40° 42′N 74° 2′W) **14**:149
New York (state) **14**:148; **14**:153
tunnel **19**:338
HUDSON RIVER SCHOOL **10**:290 *bibliog.*
American art and architecture **1**:332
Church, Frederick Edwin **4**:423
Cole, Thomas **5**:99–100
Cropsey, Jaspar **5**:359
Doughty, Thomas **6**:246
Durand, Asher Brown **6**:302–303
Heade, Martin **10**:86
Kensett, John Frederick **12**:45
landscape painting **12**:192
Luminism **12**:459
painting **15**:23
Whittredge, Worthington **20**:143
HUDSON STRAIT
map (62° 30′N 72° 0′W) **14**:258
HUDSON'S BAY COMPANY **10**:290–291 *bibliog., illus., map*
Canada, history of **4**:82–83 *map*
Chinook (Indian tribe) **4**:395
Douglas, Sir James **6**:247
Edmonton (Alberta) **7**:58
flag **8**:135 *illus.*
Hearne, Samuel **10**:90
Idaho **11**:29
Indian trappers **10**:290 *illus.*
Manitoba **13**:122
mountain men **13**:624
North West Company **14**:252–253
Oregon Question **14**:431
Radisson, Pierre Esprit **16**:67–68
Red River Rebellion **16**:113
Red River Settlement **16**:113
Rupert's Land **16**:347
Thompson, David **19**:174
HUDSONVILLE (Michigan)
map (42° 52′N 85° 52′W) **13**:377
HUDSPETH (county in Texas)
map (31° 25′N 105° 22′W) **19**:129
HUE (Vietnam) **10**:291
map (16° 28′N 107° 36′E) **19**:580
HUEFFER, FORD HERMAN *see* FORD, FORD MADOX
HUEHUETENANGO (Guatemala)
map (15° 20′N 91° 28′W) **9**:389
HUELVA (Spain)
map (37° 16′N 6° 57′W) **18**:140
HUERFANO (county in Colorado)
map (37° 45′N 105° 10′W) **5**:116
HUERTA, VICTORIANO **10**:291 *bibliog., illus.*
Mexico, history of **13**:365
Villa, Pancho **19**:596
Wilson, Woodrow **20**:167
Zapata, Emiliano **20**:356
HUETAMO DE NÚÑEZ (Mexico)
map (18° 35′N 100° 53′W) **13**:357
HUEYTOWN (Alabama)
map (33° 27′N 86° 59′W) **1**:234
HUFUF, AL- (Saudi Arabia) *see* HOFUF (Saudi Arabia)
HÜGEL, FRIEDRICH, BARON VON **10**:291–292
HUGENBERG, ALFRED
Hitler, Adolf **10**:187
HUGENSZ, LUCAS *see* LUCAS VAN LEYDEN
HUGGINS, SIR GODFREY *see* MALVERN, GODFREY HUGGINS, 1ST VISCOUNT
HUGGINS, SIR WILLIAM **10**:292
astronomy, history of **2**:279
HUGH BUTLER LAKE
map (40° 22′N 100° 42′W) **14**:70
HUGH CAPET, KING OF FRANCE **10**:292 *bibliog.*
Capetians (dynasty) **4**:122–123
France, history of **8**:267
HUGH THE GREAT, COUNT OF PARIS
Louis IV, King of France (Louis d'Outremer) **12**:424
HUGH OF SAINT VICTOR **10**:292
HUGHES (Alaska)
map (66° 3′N 154° 16′W) **1**:242
HUGHES (Arkansas)
map (34° 57′N 90° 28′W) **2**:166
HUGHES (county in Oklahoma)
map (35° 5′N 96° 15′W) **14**:368
HUGHES (county in South Dakota)
map (44° 22′N 98° 57′W) **18**:103
HUGHES, CHARLES EVANS **10**:292 *bibliog., illus.*
Johnson, Hiram Warren **11**:432
navy **14**:64
Schechter Poultry Corporation v. *United States* **17**:117
Supreme Court of the United States **18**:357
West Coast Hotel Company v. *Parrish* **20**:108
HUGHES, HOWARD **10**:292 *bibliog.*
HUGHES, JOHN JOSEPH **10**:292–293 *bibliog.*
HUGHES, LANGSTON **10**:293 *bibliog., illus.*
HUGHES, RICHARD **10**:293 *bibliog.*
HUGHES, RUPERT **10**:293
HUGHES, RUSSELL MERIWETHER *see* LA MERI
HUGHES, TED **10**:293 *bibliog.*
HUGHES, THOMAS **10**:293 *bibliog.*
Rugby School **16**:340
HUGHES, WILLIAM MORRIS **10**:293–294 *bibliog.*
HUGHES AIRCRAFT COMPANY **1**:128 *table*
HUGHES HALL (Cambridge University) **4**:53
HUGHESVILLE (Pennsylvania)
map (41° 14′N 76° 44′W) **15**:147
HUGO (Colorado)
map (39° 8′N 103° 28′W) **5**:116
HUGO (Oklahoma)
map (34° 1′N 95° 31′W) **14**:368
HUGO, VICTOR **8**:317 *illus.*; **10**:294 *bibliog., illus.*; **16**:293 *illus.*
Hernani **10**:294 *illus.*
Hunchback of Notre Dame, The **10**:304
Misérables, Les **13**:466
HUGO AWARD **10**:294
Asimov, Isaac **2**:260
Blish, James **3**:333
Dickson, Gordon R. **6**:158–159
Le Guin, Ursula **12**:254
Pohl, Frederik **15**:380
Sturgeon, Theodore **18**:309
HUGOTON (Kansas)
map (37° 11′N 101° 21′W) **12**:18
HUGUENOT CONSPIRACY OF AMBOISE
Francis II, King of France **8**:276
HUGUENOTS **8**:268 *illus.*; **10**:294–295 *bibliog., illus.*
Camisards **4**:62
France, history of **8**:268
Henry III, King of France **10**:127
Louis XIV, King of France **12**:427
Mornay, Philippe de **13**:582–583
Nantes, Edict of **14**:13
Religion, Wars of **16**:141
Ribaut, Jean **16**:205
Richelieu, Armand Jean du Plessis, Cardinal et Duc de **16**:213
Saint Bartholomew's Day Massacre **17**:16
HUI **10**:295 *bibliog.*
HUI-TSUNG *see* SUNG HUI-TSUNG (Song Huizong)
HUIARAU RANGE
map (38° 45′S 177° 0′E) **14**:158
HUIDOBRO, VICENTE **10**:295 *bibliog.*
HUILA, MOUNT
map (3° 0′N 76° 0′W) **5**:107
HUILLICHE
Araucanians **2**:109–110
HUITZILOPOCHTLI (Aztec deity) **2**:384 *illus.*; **10**:295 *bibliog.*
Aztec **2**:384
temple **2**:383 *illus.*
HUIXTLA (Mexico)
map (15° 9′N 92° 28′W) **13**:357
HUIZINGA, JOHAN **10**:295
HUKBALAHAP (HUK) MOVEMENT
Magsaysay, Ramón **13**:62
Philippines **15**:238
Quirino, Elpidio **16**:28
HULA **10**:295
HULA VALLEY
map (33° 8′N 35° 37′E) **11**:302
HULAGÜ
Turks **19**:348
HULBERT (Michigan)
map (46° 21′N 85° 9′W) **13**:377
HULBERT (Oklahoma)
map (35° 56′N 95° 9′W) **14**:368
HULDANGE
map (50° 10′N 6° 1′E) **12**:472
HULELE ISLAND
map (4° 11′N 73° 32′E) **13**:87
HULL (England) **10**:295
map (53° 45′N 0° 20′W) **19**:403
HULL (Illinois)
map (39° 43′N 91° 13′W) **11**:42
HULL (Iowa)
map (43° 11′N 96° 8′W) **11**:244
HULL (Massachusetts)
map (42° 17′N 70° 53′W) **13**:206
HULL (Quebec)
map (45° 26′N 75° 43′W) **16**:18
HULL, BOBBY **10**:295–296 *bibliog.*
HULL, CLARK **10**:296 *bibliog.*; **15**:597 *illus.*
concept formation and attainment **5**:169
habit **10**:4
learning theory **12**:261
motivation **13**:610
HULL, CORDELL **10**:296 *bibliog.*
World War II **20**:259
HULL, ISAAC **10**:296
HULL, WILLIAM **10**:296
HULL HOUSE **10**:296 *bibliog.*
HULME, ETTA
cartoon (editorial and political) **4**:176
HULME, T. E. **10**:296 *bibliog.*
HÜLSHOFF, ANNETTE ELISABETH VON DROSTE- *see* DROSTE-HÜLSHOFF, ANNETTE ELISABETH VON
HULST, HENDRIK CHRISTOFFELL VAN DE **10**:296
HULWAN (Egypt)
map (29° 51′N 31° 20′E) **7**:76
HUMACAO (Puerto Rico)
map (18° 9′N 65° 50′W) **15**:614
HUMAHUACA (Argentina)
map (23° 12′S 65° 21′W) **2**:149
HUMAN BEHAVIOR *see* BEHAVIOR, HUMAN

HUMAN BODY **10**:296–297 *bibliog., illus.*
See also specific parts of the human body, e.g., BRAIN; BREAST; EAR; etc.
acupuncture **1**:91 *illus.*
aging **1**:185–186
anthropometry **2**:55
biological equilibrium **3**:265
blood group distribution **9**:89 *map*
child development **4**:349 *illus.*
circulatory system **4**:440 *illus.*
classification, biological **5**:43 *table*
cloning **5**:64–65
cremation **5**:338
cryobiology **5**:370
death and dying **6**:68–69
dehydration **6**:85
development **6**:140–142 *illus.*
digestive system **6**:171 *illus.*
embryo **7**:153 *illus.*
endocrine system **7**:168–169
excretory system **7**:327–328
exercise **7**:329–331
fluids *see* BODY FLUIDS
frostbite **8**:346
function
diagnostic tests **6**:149–150
examination, medical **7**:326
fever, temperature **8**:66
telemetry **19**:78
genetics **9**:90
growth **9**:380
handedness **10**:35
hermaphrodite **10**:142
infancy **11**:162–163
lymphatic system **12**:475
metabolism **13**:325; **13**:327
muscle **13**:651–654
nervous system **14**:91–95
nutrition, human **14**:304–307
obesity **14**:315–316
poison gas **15**:382
premature aging **1**:186
race **16**:33–35
reproductive system, human **16**:163–166 *illus.*
respiratory system **16**:178–181 *illus.*
senses **17**:204–205
sex chromosomes **9**:88 *illus.*
skeleton, human **17**:334–337 *illus.*
skin **17**:340
sleep **6**:267 *illus.*
tissue, animal **19**:210
HUMAN CHORIONIC GONADOTROPIN *see* GONADOTROPIN
HUMAN DISEASES *see* DISEASES; DISEASES, HUMAN
HUMAN ECOLOGY **10**:297 *bibliog.*
city **5**:4–8
culture area **5**:386
desert life **6**:131
geography **9**:103
inner city **11**:179
population dynamics **15**:438–439
Sauer, Carl **17**:96
urban planning **19**:481–485 *illus.*
HUMAN EVOLUTION *see* PREHISTORIC HUMANS
HUMAN FACTORS ENGINEERING **10**:297 *bibliog.*
assembly line **2**:265
HUMAN GEOGRAPHY *see* HUMAN ECOLOGY
HUMAN LIFE
early years mortality **12**:331 *table*
life span **12**:330–331
maximum life span for some **12**:330 *table*
HUMAN POTENTIAL MOVEMENT *see* HUMANISTIC PSYCHOLOGY
HUMAN-POWERED FLIGHT *see* FLIGHT, HUMAN-POWERED
HUMAN RELATIONS AREA FILES
Murdock, George Peter **13**:648
HUMAN RIGHTS **10**:297–298 *bibliog., illus.*
Carter, Jimmy **4**:172
Chicano **4**:343
civil rights **5**:12–13
Czechoslovakia **5**:416
feminism **8**:48–49
Four Freedoms **8**:253
gay activism **9**:63
Geneva conventions **9**:91
handicapped persons **10**:36–37
natural law **14**:48
9th Amendment **14**:200
Pérez Esquivel, Adolfo **15**:164
Robeson, Paul **16**:242
slavery **17**:357
socialist law **18**:25
women in society **20**:202; **20**:203–204
HUMAN RIGHTS ORGANIZATIONS
American Civil Liberties Union **1**:337–338
Amnesty International **1**:375
B'nai B'rith **3**:348
Congress of Racial Equality **5**:184
Council of Europe **5**:310
Gray Panthers **9**:307
Hadassah **10**:7
National Association for the Advancement of Colored People **14**:29
National Congress of American Indians **14**:31
National Organization for Women **14**:35–36
HUMAN T-CELL LYMPHOTROPIC VIRUSES *see* HTLV VIRUSES
HUMANE SOCIETY *see* SOCIETY FOR THE PREVENTION OF CRUELTY TO ANIMALS
HUMANISM **10**:298–299 *bibliog.*
Arnold, Matthew **2**:185
Ascham, Roger **2**:228
atheism **2**:289
Babbitt, Irving **3**:5
Calvin, John **4**:48–49
educational philosophy **7**:63–64
Erasmus, Desiderius **7**:227
French literature **8**:315
humanities, education in the **10**:300
Italian literature **11**:315
Middle Ages **13**:396
Montaigne, Michel de **13**:545
More, Saint Thomas **13**:575–576
political science **15**:403–404
Red Cross **16**:112
Renaissance **16**:149
Renaissance music **16**:155–156
HUMANISTIC PSYCHOLOGY **10**:299–300 *bibliog.*
creative arts and peer therapies **10**:299
educational psychology **7**:66
Esalen Institute **7**:236
Maslow, Abraham H. **13**:196–198
personality **15**:189
Rogers, Carl **16**:269
Szasz, Thomas **18**:415
HUMANITÉ, L' (periodical) **10**:300
HUMANITIES, EDUCATION IN THE **10**:300 *bibliog.*
definition **10**:300
Great Books Program **9**:309
Hutchins, Robert M. **10**:322
professional and educational organizations
American Academy of Arts and Sciences **1**:327
American Council of Learned Societies **1**:338
American Philosophical Society **1**:352
HUMANSVILLE (Missouri)
map (37° 48′N 93° 35′W) **13**:476
HUMASON, MILTON LA SALLE **10**:300
HUMAYUN, MOGUL EMPEROR OF INDIA **10**:300 *bibliog.*
Mogul art and architecture **13**:500
New Delhi (India) **14**:120
Taj Mahal **19**:14
HUMBE MOUNTAINS
map (12° 13′S 15° 25′E) **2**:5
HUMBER, RIVER **10**:300
map (53° 40′N 0° 10′W) **19**:403
HUMBERSIDE (England) **10**:300
cities
Beverley **3**:233
Grimsby **9**:366
HUMBERT I, COUNT OF SAVOY
Savoy (dynasty) **17**:102
HUMBERT I, KING OF ITALY **10**:300 *bibliog.*
Monza (Italy) **13**:560
HUMBERT II, KING OF ITALY **10**:300–301
HUMBERTO ROMERO, CARLOS
El Salvador **7**:101
HUMBIRD (Wisconsin)
map (44° 32′N 90° 53′W) **20**:185
HUMBOLDT (Arizona)
map (34° 30′N 112° 14′W) **2**:160
HUMBOLDT (county in California)
map (41° 45′N 123° 50′W) **4**:31
HUMBOLDT (Illinois)
map (39° 36′N 88° 19′W) **11**:42
HUMBOLDT (Iowa)
map (42° 44′N 94° 13′W) **11**:244
HUMBOLDT (county in Iowa)
map (42° 45′N 94° 15′W) **11**:244
HUMBOLDT (Kansas)
map (37° 49′N 95° 26′W) **12**:18
HUMBOLDT (Nebraska)
map (40° 10′N 95° 57′W) **14**:70
HUMBOLDT (county in Nevada)
map (41° 30′N 118° 0′W) **14**:111
HUMBOLDT (Saskatchewan)
map (52° 12′N 105° 7′W) **17**:81
HUMBOLDT (South Dakota)
map (43° 39′N 97° 4′W) **18**:103
HUMBOLDT (Tennessee)
map (35° 49′N 88° 55′W) **19**:104
HUMBOLDT, ALEXANDER VON **10**:301 *bibliog., illus.*
geography **9**:102–103
Orinoco River **14**:444
HUMBOLDT, WILHELM VON **10**:301 *bibliog.*
HUMBOLDT CURRENT (Peru Current)
ocean currents and wind systems, worldwide **14**:322–323 *maps*
HUMBOLDT RIVER
map (40° 2′N 118° 31′W) **14**:111
HUME, BASIL **10**:301
HUME, DAVID **10**:301–302 *bibliog., illus.*
associationism **2**:265–266
causality **4**:219
empiricism **7**:159
induction **11**:151
miracle **13**:462
philosophy **15**:245
HUME, HAMILTON H.
Murray River **13**:650
HUME, IVOR NOËL *see* NOËL HUME, IVOR
HUMESTON (Iowa)
map (40° 52′N 93° 30′W) **11**:244
HUMIDIFIER **10**:302
HUMIDITY **10**:302 *bibliog.*
calculation **10**:302
cloud **5**:66–67
evapotranspiration **7**:315
landform evolution **12**:182–183
measurement
hygrometer **10**:345
psychrometer **13**:341 *illus.*
meteorology **13**:342
HUMMEL, JOHANN NEPOMUK **10**:302 *bibliog.*
HUMMINGBIRD **10**:302–303 *bibliog., illus.*; **11**:469 *illus.*
pollination **15**:408–409 *illus.*
ruby-throated hummingbird **3**:280 *illus.*
chick **3**:287 *illus.*
nest **3**:287 *illus.*
HUMOR *see* COMEDY; SATIRE; WIT
HUMPBACK WHALE *see* WHALE
HUMPERDINCK, ENGELBERT **10**:303
HUMPHREY (Arkansas)
map (34° 25′N 91° 42′W) **2**:166
HUMPHREY (Nebraska)
map (41° 41′N 97° 29′W) **14**:70
HUMPHREY, DORIS **10**:303 *bibliog.*
Limón, José **12**:346
Weidman, Charles **20**:91
HUMPHREY, HUBERT H., JR. **10**:303–304 *bibliog., illus.*; **15**:524 *illus.*
Mondale, Walter F. **13**:522
Vietnam War **19**:587
HUMPHREYS (county in Mississippi)
map (33° 10′N 90° 30′W) **13**:469
HUMPHREYS (county in Tennessee)
map (36° 10′N 87° 50′W) **19**:104
HUMPHREYS, MOUNT
map (37° 17′N 118° 40′W) **4**:31
HUMPHREY'S EXECUTOR v. *UNITED STATES*
president of the United States **15**:527
HUMPHREYS PEAK
map (35° 20′N 111° 40′W) **2**:160
HUMULIN
insulin **11**:198
HUMUS **10**:304
compost **5**:157–158
gardening **9**:43
manure **13**:133
HÚNA BAY
map (65° 50′N 20° 50′W) **11**:17
HUNAN (China) **10**:304
HUNCHBACK
Pott's disease **15**:473
HUNCHBACK OF NOTRE DAME, THE (book) **10**:304
Hugo, Victor **10**:294
HUNDERTWASSER **10**:304 *bibliog.*
HUNDRED FLOWERS MOVEMENT
Mao Tse-tung (Mao Zedong) **13**:135
HUNDRED YEARS' WAR **8**:268 *illus.*; **10**:304–305 *bibliog., illus.*
Agincourt, Battle of **1**:185
Artevelde (family) **2**:214
Brétigny, Treaty of **3**:474
Crécy, Battle of **5**:336; **9**:312 *illus.*
du Guesclin, Bertrand **6**:286
Dunois, Jean, Comte de (the Bastard of Orléans) **6**:301
Edward, the Black Prince **7**:67
Edward III, King of England **7**:68
Europe, history of **7**:286
France, history of **8**:268
Hawkwood, Sir John **10**:78
Henry V, King of England **10**:125–126
Jacquerie **11**:347
Joan of Arc, Saint **11**:420
Mont-Saint-Michel **13**:544
Suffolk, William de la Pole, 4th Earl and 1st Duke of **18**:325
Valois (dynasty) **19**:508
HUNEDOARA (Romania)
map (45° 45′N 22° 54′E) **16**:288
HUNEKER, JAMES GIBBONS **10**:305 *bibliog.*
HUNG HSIU-CH'ÜAN
Taiping Rebellion **19**:12
HUNG LOU MENG see DREAM OF THE RED CHAMBER, THE
HUNG-SHUI RIVER
map (23° 45′N 109° 30′E) **4**:362
HUNG-WU
Ming (dynasty) **13**:444
money **13**:526 *illus.*
HUNGARIAN LITERATURE **10**:305–306 *bibliog.*
authors
Ady, Endre **1**:114
Arany, János **2**:109
Déry, Tibor **6**:123
Eötvös, Jozsef, Baron von Vásárosnemény **7**:215
Jókai, Maurus **11**:440
József, Attila **11**:457
Madách, Imre **13**:37
Molnár, Ferenc **13**:512
Móricz, Zsigmond **13**:579–580
Orkeny, Istvan **14**:445
Petőfi, Sándor **15**:203
HUNGARIAN MUSIC **10**:306 *bibliog.*
Dohnányi, Ernst von **6**:224
Kodály, Zoltán **12**:105
Ligeti, György **12**:334
Liszt, Franz **12**:367
HUNGARIAN POINTER *see* VIZSLA
HUNGARIAN REVOLUTION **5**:148 *illus.*; **10**:306 *bibliog.*
communism **5**:148
Kádár, János **12**:4
Nagy, Imre **14**:7
refugee **16**:125
HUNGARIAN RHAPSODIES, THE (musical compositions)
Liszt, Franz **12**:367
HUNGARY **10**:306–310 *bibliog., illus., map, table*
agriculture **10**:309
archaeology
European prehistory **7**:301–302 *map*
Vértesszöllös **19**:563
art **10**:309
Vasarely, Victor **19**:525
cities
Budapest **3**:538 *map*
Debrecen **6**:70
Esztergom **7**:248
Györ **9**:415
Miskolc **13**:466–467
Pécs **15**:130–131
Szeged **18**:416
climate **10**:307 *table*
communism *see* COMMUNISM
culture **10**:309
dog
komondor **12**:108
kuvasz **12**:140
economic activities **10**:309
education **10**:308
European universities **7**:308 *table*
flag **10**:306 *illus.*
government **10**:309
health **10**:308–309
history **10**:309–310
Andrássy, Gyula **1**:406
Andrew II, King **1**:407
Austria-Hungary **2**:351–352
Báthory (family) **3**:122–123
Bethlen, Gábor, Prince of Transylvania **3**:231
Bethlen, István, Count **3**:231
Bocskay, István, Prince of Transylvania **3**:355
Charles I, Emperor of Austria-Hungary **4**:291
Charles I, King (Charles Robert) **4**:296
communist crisis of 1956 **5**:148
Horthy de Nagybánya, Miklós **10**:254
Hungarian Revolution **10**:306

HUNGARY (cont.)
Hunyadi, János **10**:315
Jagello (dynasty) **11**:348
John I, King (John Zápolya) **11**:427
John II, King (John Sigismund Zápolya) **11**:427
Joseph I, Holy Roman Emperor **11**:451
Kádár, János **12**:4
Kossuth, Lajos **12**:124
Kun, Béla **12**:136
Ladislas I, King **12**:162
Louis I, King (Louis the Great) **12**:428
Louis II, King **12**:428–429
Magyars **13**:62–63
Maria Theresa, Austrian Archduchess, Queen of Hungary and Bohemia **13**:150
Matthias, Holy Roman Emperor **13**:231–232
Matthias Corvinus, King **13**:232
Nagy, Imre **14**:7
Rákosi, Mátyás **16**:79
Revolutions of 1848 **16**:188
Stephen I, King (Saint Stephen) **18**:254
Suleiman I, Sultan of the Ottoman Empire (Suleiman the Magnificent) **18**:332–333
Tisza, István, Count **19**:210
Transylvania (Romania) **19**:283
industry, mining, and energy **10**:309
land and resources **10**:307–308
language
Ural-Altaic languages **19**:475
literature *see* HUNGARIAN LITERATURE
map (47° 0′N 20° 0′E) **7**:268
music *see* HUNGARIAN MUSIC
Olympic Games **14**:383
people **10**:308–309
physical features **7**:271 *illus.*
rivers, lakes, and waterways **10**:307–308
Balaton, Lake **3**:33
Tisza River **19**:210
trade **10**:309
Warsaw Treaty Organization **20**:32
HUNGER AND THIRST **10**:310–311 *bibliog.*
homeostasis **10**:212
HUNGNAM (Korea)
map (39° 50′N 127° 38′E) **12**:113
HUNGRY HORSE RESERVOIR
map (48° 15′N 113° 50′W) **13**:547
HUNKERS AND BARNBURNERS **10**:311 *bibliog.*
HUNKPAPA (American Indians) *see* SIOUX (American Indians)
HUNLEY, H. L. (ship)
Civil War, U.S. **5**:32
HUNS **10**:311 *bibliog.*
Asia, history of **2**:251
Attila **2**:315
invasion of Europe **7**:282 *map*
Mongolia **13**:530
HUNSBERGE MOUNTAINS
map (27° 45′S 17° 12′E) **14**:10
HUNT (county in Texas)
map (33° 7′N 96° 5′W) **19**:129
HUNT, E. HOWARD
Watergate **20**:64
HUNT, GEORGE
Kwakiutl **12**:142
HUNT, H. L. **10**:311
HUNT, HELEN *see* JACKSON, HELEN HUNT
HUNT, HOLMAN **10**:311 *bibliog., illus.*
Claudio and Isabella **7**:187 *illus.*; **10**:311 *illus.*
Millais, Sir John Everett **13**:426
Rossetti, Dante Gabriel **16**:319
HUNT, IRENE **10**:311
HUNT, JOHN WESLEY
Lexington (Kentucky) **12**:309
HUNT, LEIGH **10**:311–312 *bibliog.*
HUNT, RICHARD MORRIS **10**:312 *bibliog.*
Hunt, William Morris **10**:312
Metropolitan Museum of Art, The **13**:348
HUNT, WALTER
sewing machine **17**:223
HUNT, WILLIAM MORRIS **10**:312 *bibliog., illus.*
The Bathers **10**:312 *illus.*
HUNT, WILSON PRICE
Wyoming **20**:303
HUNTER (North Dakota)
map (47° 12′N 97° 13′W) **14**:248
HUNTER (Utah)
map (40° 42′N 112° 1′W) **19**:492
HUNTER, EVAN **10**:312
HUNTER, JOHN
dentistry **6**:115
medicine **13**:270
HUNTER, KRISTIN **10**:312
HUNTER COLLEGE *see* NEW YORK, CITY UNIVERSITY OF
HUNTER-GATHERERS **10**:313 *bibliog., illus.*
Aborigines, Australian **1**:59
blowgun **3**:341
boomerang **3**:393
Cro-Magnon man **5**:353
Eskimo **7**:238–241 *illus.*
Indians, American **11**:118–119; **11**:126 *illus.*; **11**:128–131; **11**:135 *illus.*
North America c.1500 **11**:125 *map*
South America c.1500 **11**:133 *map*
Mesolithic Period **13**:314–315 *illus.*
monogamy **13**:536
Neolithic Period **14**:84
nomad **14**:214
Paleolithic Period **15**:39 *illus.*
prehistoric humans **15**:513–517
primitive societies **15**:546
Pygmy **15**:633
San **17**:49 *illus.*
Tasaday **19**:41
urban anthropology **19**:480
women in society **20**:201
HUNTERDON (county in New Jersey)
map (40° 33′N 74° 55′W) **14**:129
HUNTERS (Washington)
map (48° 7′N 118° 12′W) **20**:35
HUNTERS RIVER (Prince Edward Island)
map (46° 21′N 63° 21′W) **15**:548
HUNTERS IN THE SNOW (Pieter Bruegel) **3**:522 *illus.*
HUNTING **10**:313–314 *bibliog., illus.*
cheetah **4**:309
duck **6**:292
endangered species **7**:167 *illus., illus.*
falconry **8**:12–13
game birds **9**:27
game laws **9**:27
history **10**:313
Homo erectus **10**:216
hunter-gatherers **10**:313
Indians, American **11**:119–120
Mesolithic Period **13**:314
sport hunting **10**:313–314
tartan **19**:40 *illus.*
HUNTING DOG *see* SPORTING DOG
HUNTING HORN
French horn **8**:311
HUNTING ISLAND
map (32° 20′N 80° 30′W) **18**:98
HUNTINGBURG (Indiana)
map (38° 18′N 86° 57′W) **11**:111
HUNTINGDON (Pennsylvania)
map (40° 29′N 78° 1′W) **15**:147
HUNTINGDON (county in Pennsylvania)
map (40° 29′N 78° 1′W) **15**:147
HUNTINGDON (Quebec)
map (45° 5′N 74° 10′W) **16**:18
HUNTINGDON (Tennessee)
map (36° 0′N 88° 26′W) **19**:104
HUNTINGTON (family) **10**:314 *bibliog.*
HUNTINGTON (Indiana)
map (40° 53′N 85° 30′W) **11**:111
HUNTINGTON (county in Indiana)
map (40° 53′N 85° 30′W) **11**:111
HUNTINGTON (Oregon)
map (44° 21′N 117° 16′W) **14**:427
HUNTINGTON (West Virginia) **10**:314
map (38° 25′N 82° 26′W) **20**:111
HUNTINGTON, ANNA HYATT **10**:314 *bibliog.*
HUNTINGTON, COLLIS P.
Stanford, Leland **18**:217
HUNTINGTON, ELLSWORTH **10**:314
climate **5**:58
geography **9**:102
HUNTINGTON, HENRY EDWARDS
Huntington Library **10**:314–315
HUNTINGTON BAY
map (40° 55′N 73° 25′W) **5**:193
HUNTINGTON BEACH (California) **10**:314
map (33° 39′N 117° 60′W) **4**:31
HUNTINGTON LAKE
map (40° 50′N 85° 25′W) **11**:111
HUNTINGTON LIBRARY **10**:314–315 *bibliog.*
Huntington (family) **10**:314
HUNTINGTON'S CHOREA **10**:315
chorea **4**:408
genetic diseases **9**:83–84
nervous system, diseases of the **14**:96
HUNTLAND (Tennessee)
map (35° 3′N 86° 17′W) **19**:104
HUNTLEY (Montana)
map (45° 54′N 108° 19′W) **13**:547
HUNTSVILLE (Alabama) **1**:238 *illus.*; **10**:315
map (34° 44′N 86° 35′W) **1**:234
HUNTSVILLE (Arkansas)
map (36° 5′N 93° 44′W) **2**:166
HUNTSVILLE (Missouri)
map (39° 26′N 92° 33′W) **13**:476
HUNTSVILLE (Ontario)
map (45° 20′N 79° 13′W) **14**:393
HUNTSVILLE (Tennessee)
map (36° 25′N 84° 29′W) **19**:104
HUNTSVILLE (Texas)
map (30° 43′N 95° 33′W) **19**:129
HUNTSVILLE (Utah)
map (41° 16′N 111° 46′W) **19**:492
HUNYADI, JÁNOS **10**:315 *bibliog.*
HUON GULF
map (7° 10′S 147° 25′E) **15**:72
HUON ISLANDS
New Caledonia **14**:119
HUOT, CHARLES
Canadian art and architecture **4**:89
HUPA (American Indians) **10**:315 *bibliog.*
Indians of North America, art of the **11**:139
Yurok **20**:347
HUPEI (Hubei) (China) **10**:315
cities
Wu-han (Wuhan) **20**:296
HURD, CAPE
map (45° 13′N 81° 44′W) **14**:393; **19**:241
HURD, PETER **10**:315 *bibliog.*
HURDLE RACES
steeplechase **18**:243–244
track and field **19**:260
HURDY-GURDY **10**:315–316 *bibliog., illus.*
vielle **19**:578
HURLEY (Mississippi)
map (30° 40′N 88° 30′W) **13**:469
HURLEY (New Mexico)
map (32° 42′N 108° 8′W) **14**:136
HURLEY (South Dakota)
map (43° 17′N 97° 5′W) **18**:103
HURLEY (Wisconsin)
map (46° 28′N 90° 8′W) **20**:185
HURLEY, PATRICK MASON **10**:316
HURLING **10**:316
HURLOCK (Maryland)
map (38° 38′N 75° 52′W) **13**:188
HUROK, SOL **10**:316 *bibliog.*
HURON (American Indians) **10**:316–317 *bibliog.*
Delaware **6**:91
Erie **7**:229
Indians of North America, art of the **11**:141
Ottawa **14**:460
Zacherie Vincent **11**:130 *illus.*
HURON (county in Michigan)
map (43° 50′N 83° 0′W) **13**:377
HURON (Ohio)
map (41° 24′N 82° 33′W) **14**:357
HURON (county in Ohio)
map (41° 15′N 82° 37′W) **14**:357
HURON (South Dakota)
map (44° 22′N 98° 13′W) **18**:103
HURON, LAKE **10**:317 *map*
Manitoulin Islands **13**:122
map (44° 30′N 82° 15′W) **9**:320
waterways
Mackinac, Straits of **13**:29
Sault Sainte Marie Canals **17**:96
HURON MOUNTAINS
map (46° 45′N 87° 45′W) **13**:377
HURONIAN ERA
ice ages **11**:7–11
HURRIAN LANGUAGE
languages, extinct **12**:198
HURRICANE (aircraft) **10**:317 *illus.*
HURRICANE (Utah)
map (37° 11′N 113° 17′W) **19**:492
HURRICANE (West Virginia)
map (38° 26′N 82° 1′W) **20**:111
HURRICANE CLIFFS (Arizona)
map (39° 25′N 113° 0′W) **2**:160
HURRICANE CLIFFS (Utah)
map (37° 11′N 113° 11′W) **19**:492
HURRICANE AND TYPHOON **10**:317–319 *bibliog., illus.*
Beaufort scale **3**:146
cirrus clouds **4**:445
cyclone and anticyclone **5**:405–406
energy source **10**:317
floods and flood control **8**:167
Great Red Spot, Jupiter **11**:473 *illus.*
low-pressure region **12**:443
Pacific Ocean **15**:7
structure of storm **10**:317–318
surveillance systems **10**:319
National Hurricane Center **20**:79
radar meteorology **16**:41
weather forecasting **20**:78–79 *illus.*
tropical cyclone **10**:318 *illus.*
weather modification **20**:80
wind, rotation speed **10**:318
HURSAGKALAMA *see* KISH (Iraq)
HURST, FANNIE **10**:319
HURSTON, ZORA NEALE **10**:319 *bibliog.*
HURTADO, MIGUEL DE LA MADRID *see* DE LA MADRID HURTADO, MIGUEL
HURTADO v. CALIFORNIA **10**:319
HURTER, FERDINAND, AND DRIFFIELD, VERO C. **10**:319
actinometer **1**:89
HURTSBORO (Alabama)
map (32° 14′N 85° 25′W) **1**:234
HUS, JAN *see* HUSS, JOHN
HUSÁK, GUSTAV **10**:319
Czechoslovakia **5**:416
HÚSAVÍK (Iceland)
map (66° 4′N 17° 18′W) **11**:17
HUSAYN, TAHA *see* TAHA HUSAYN
HUSAYN HAYKAL, MUHAMMED *see* HAYKAL, MUHAMMED HUSAYN
HUSAYN IBN ALI **10**:319–320
Middle East, history of the **13**:407
HUSAYNI, AMIN AL- **10**:320
HUSBAND *see* FAMILY; MARRIAGE
HUSS, JOHN **10**:320 *bibliog.*
Czech literature **5**:412
Czechoslovakia **5**:416
Hussites **10**:321
Prague (Czechoslovakia) **15**:488
Sigismund, King of Germany and Holy Roman Emperor **17**:299
HUSSAR **10**:320
uniform **4**:221 *illus.*
HUSSEIN, SADDAM **10**:320
Iraq **11**:256
HUSSEIN I, KING OF JORDAN **10**:320–321 *bibliog., illus.*
Middle East, history of the **13**:409
HUSSERL, EDMUND **10**:321 *bibliog., illus.*
phenomenology **15**:225
HUSSEY, OBED
McCormick, Cyrus Hall **13**:10
reaper **16**:104
HUSSEY, RUTH **5**:383 *illus.*
HUSSITES **10**:321 *bibliog.*
Basel, Council of **3**:108
Czech music **5**:413
George of Poděbrady, King of Bohemia **9**:110
Huss, John **10**:320
Martin V, Pope **13**:180
Procopius the Great **15**:561
Wenceslas, King of Germany and Bohemia **20**:103
Žižka, Jan **20**:371
HUSTISFORD (Wisconsin)
map (43° 21′N 88° 36′W) **20**:185
HUSTLE (dance) **10**:321
HUSTON, JOHN **10**:322 *bibliog.*
documentary **6**:211
HUSUM (Germany, East and West)
map (54° 28′N 9° 3′E) **9**:140
HUTCHESON, FRANCIS **10**:322 *bibliog.*
HUTCHINS, ROBERT M. **10**:322 *bibliog.*
Center for the Study of Democratic Institutions **4**:250
Chicago, University of **4**:342
Great Books Program **9**:309
HUTCHINSON (family)
American music **1**:349
HUTCHINSON (Kansas) **10**:322
map (38° 5′N 97° 56′W) **12**:18
HUTCHINSON (Minnesota)
map (44° 54′N 94° 22′W) **13**:453
HUTCHINSON (county in South Dakota)
map (43° 20′N 97° 45′W) **18**:103
HUTCHINSON (county in Texas)
map (35° 50′N 101° 20′W) **19**:129
HUTCHINSON, ANNE **10**:322 *bibliog., illus.*
antinomianism **2**:64
HUTCHINSON, EDITH *see* ASHCROFT, DAME PEGGY
HUTCHINSON, GEORGE EVELYN **10**:322–323 *bibliog.*
HUTCHINSON, THOMAS **10**:323 *bibliog.*
Franklin, Benjamin **8**:284

HUTSON, DON **10**:323 *bibliog.*
HUTSONVILLE (Illinois)
map (39° 7′N 87° 39′W) **11**:42
HUTTEN, ULRICH VON **10**:323 *bibliog.*
HUTTERIAN BRETHREN **10**:323 *bibliog.*
HUTTERITES *see* HUTTERIAN BRETHREN
HUTTIG (Arkansas)
map (33° 2′N 92° 11′W) **2**:166
HUTTO (Texas)
map (30° 33′N 97° 33′W) **19**:129
HUTTON, JAMES **10**:323–324 *bibliog., illus.*
archaeology **2**:123
Theory of the Earth **9**:105 *illus.*
unconformity **19**:382
HUTU
Burundi **3**:582–583
Rwanda **16**:378
Tutsi **19**:356
HUXFORD (Alabama)
map (31° 13′N 87° 28′W) **1**:234
HUXLEY, ALDOUS **10**:324 *bibliog., illus.*
Brave New World (book) **3**:458
HUXLEY, ANDREW FIELDING **10**:324
Hodgkin, Alan Lloyd **10**:194
HUXLEY, SIR JULIAN **10**:324–325 *bibliog., illus.*
HUXLEY, THOMAS HENRY **10**:325
Darwin, Charles **6**:42
Neanderthalers **14**:69
HUXTABLE, ADA LOUISE **10**:325
HUY (Belgium)
map (50° 31′N 5° 14′E) **3**:177
HUYGENS, CHRISTIAAN **10**:325 *bibliog., illus.*
astronomy, history of **2**:279
clock pendulum **10**:325; **15**:142
Huygens's principle **10**:325–326
light **12**:335
mathematics, history of **13**:225
optics **14**:410
physics, history of **18**:285 *illus.*
Saturn (astronomy) **17**:89
Saturn, rings **10**:325
Titan (astronomy) **19**:210
wave theory of light **10**:325
HUYGENS, CONSTANTIJN **10**:325 *bibliog.*
HUYGENS'S PRINCIPLE **10**:325–326
HUYSMANS, JORIS KARL **10**:326 *bibliog.*
decadence **6**:72
HUYSUM, JAN VAN **10**:326 *bibliog.*
HVANNADALSHNÚKUR MOUNTAIN
map (64° 1′N 16° 41′W) **11**:17
HVAR ISLAND
map (43° 9′N 16° 45′E) **20**:340
HWANG HAI *see* YELLOW SEA
HWANG HO (Huang He) **10**:326–327 *map*
Asia, history of **2**:251
China **4**:365
Chinese archaeology **4**:378
irrigation **11**:282–283
map (32° 19′N 115° 2′E) **10**:326
HYACINTH **8**:170 *illus.*; **10**:327 *illus.*
HYACINTHUS **10**:327
HYADES **10**:327
Taurus **19**:45
HYALINE MEMBRANE DISEASE **10**:327
respiratory system disorders **16**:182
HYANNIS (Massachusetts) **10**:327
map (41° 39′N 70° 17′W) **13**:206
HYANNIS (Nebraska)
map (41° 59′N 101° 44′W) **14**:70
HYATT, ALPHEUS **10**:327
Woods Hole Marine Biological Laboratory **20**:212
HYATT, JOHN WESLEY **10**:327–328
celluloid **4**:238
HYATTSVILLE (Maryland)
map (38° 56′N 76° 56′W) **13**:188
HYATTVILLE (Wyoming)
map (44° 15′N 107° 36′W) **20**:301
HYBRID **10**:328 *bibliog., illus.*
crossbreeding **10**:328
gene bank **9**:76
grape **9**:290
grass **9**:295
green revolution **9**:348 *illus.*
iris **11**:266
lily **12**:342
pear **15**:125–126
pineapple **15**:306
plant breeding **15**:342–343
plant propagation **15**:345
rice **16**:208
rose **16**:313
soybean **18**:115
sterility **10**:328
tangerine **19**:22
wheat **20**:125
HYBRID COMPUTER **10**:328–329 *bibliog.*
computer **5**:159
differential analyzer **6**:166
HYCO LAKE
map (36° 30′N 79° 5′W) **14**:242
HYDABURG (Alaska)
map (55° 12′N 132° 49′W) **1**:242
HYDE (county in North Carolina)
map (35° 30′N 76° 15′W) **14**:242
HYDE (county in South Dakota)
map (44° 30′N 99° 30′W) **18**:103
HYDE, DOUGLAS **10**:329 *bibliog.*
HYDE, EDWARD, 1ST EARL OF CLARENDON *see* CLARENDON, EDWARD HYDE, 1ST EARL OF
HYDE AMENDMENT
abortion **1**:60
HYDE PARK (Guyana)
map (6° 30′N 58° 16′W) **9**:410
HYDE PARK (New York state) **10**:329
map (41° 47′N 73° 56′W) **14**:149
HYDE PARK (Vermont)
map (44° 36′N 72° 37′W) **19**:554
HYDEN (Kentucky)
map (37° 10′N 83° 22′W) **12**:47
HYDER (Alaska)
map (55° 55′N 130° 1′W) **1**:242
HYDER ALI **10**:329 *bibliog.*
HYDERABAD (India) **10**:329
map (17° 23′N 78° 29′E) **11**:80
HYDERABAD (Pakistan) **10**:329
map (25° 22′N 68° 22′E) **15**:27
HYDRA (mythology) **10**:329
HYDRA (zoology) **10**:329–330 *bibliog., illus.*
early years mortality **12**:331 *table*
regeneration **16**:127 *illus.*
HYDRANGEA **10**:330 *illus.*
HYDRATE **10**:330
hygroscopicity **10**:345
salt (chemistry) **17**:37
HYDRAULIC (British Columbia)
map (52° 36′N 121° 42′W) **3**:491
HYDRAULIC PRESS
Bramah, Joseph **3**:451
hydraulic systems **10**:330
HYDRAULIC SYSTEMS **10**:330–331 *bibliog., illus.*
brake **3**:449
flume studies **8**:186
hydrologic sciences **10**:342
Pascal, Blaise **15**:102
Pascal's law **15**:102
HYDRAZINE **10**:331
HYDRIDE **10**:331
chemical nomenclature **4**:320
hydrogen **10**:338
HYDRO (Oklahoma)
map (35° 33′N 98° 35′W) **14**:368
HYDROBIOLOGY
limnology **12**:345
HYDROCARBON **10**:331 *bibliog., illus.*
aliphatic compounds **1**:295
carbon **4**:135
chemical nomenclature **4**:321 *illus.*
coal tar **5**:79–80
cracking process
petroleum industry **15**:214 *illus.*
pyrolysis **15**:637
cyclic compounds **5**:403–404
derivatives
alcohol **1**:264
amide **1**:369
amine **1**:370
carbonyl group **4**:139
carboxylic acid **4**:139–140 *table*
ester **7**:246
ether (chemistry) **7**:249–250
hydroxyl group **10**:344
nitrile **14**:202
radical (chemistry) **16**:43
gases
Freon **8**:326
Henry, William **10**:123
natural gas **14**:47
hydrogen **10**:337–339
hydrophilic and hydrophobic substances **10**:343
nitration **14**:202
Topchiyev, Aleksandr Vasilievich **19**:237
organic chemistry **14**:436
petroleum **15**:207
gasoline **9**:55
naphtha **14**:14
pentane **15**:155
solvent **18**:59
turpentine **19**:351
Wurtz, Charles Adolphe **20**:297
Ziegler, Karl **20**:363
HYDROCEPHALY **10**:331
nervous system, diseases of the **14**:95
HYDROCHEMISTRY
limnology **12**:345
HYDROCHLORIC ACID **10**:331–332
Gossage, William **9**:254
stomach **18**:279–280 *illus.*
antacid **2**:38
HYDRODYNAMICS
Bernoulli's law **3**:223
fluid mechanics **8**:184–185
Froude, William **8**:346
Kármán vortex street
Kármán, Theodore von **12**:28
magnetohydrodynamics **13**:58–59
Reynolds, Osborne **16**:191
Stokes, Sir George Gabriel **18**:278
HYDROELECTRIC POWER **10**:332–335 *bibliog., illus., tables*
Columbia River **5**:126
Congo River **5**:184
consumption
fuel **8**:353 *table*
dam **6**:15–18
electrical energy production **10**:335 *table*
North America **14**:229
plants
Canada **4**:75 *illus.*
Grand Coulee Dam **9**:285
major generating stations (U.S.) **15**:482 *map*
Oregon **14**:429–430 *illus.*
South America **18**:95
Tennessee Valley Authority **19**:107–108
tidal energy **19**:192–193
waterwheel **20**:66–67
HYDROFOIL **10**:335–337 *bibliog., illus.*
Bell, Alexander Graham **3**:185
Muncey, Bill **13**:639
ship **17**:275
HYDROGEN **10**:337–339 *bibliog., table*
absorption
platinum **15**:360
astrochemistry **2**:270
Galaxy, The **9**:12
halo, galactic **10**:25
Herzberg, Gerhard **10**:150
interstellar matter **11**:226–228
nebula **14**:74–75
proton-proton reaction **15**:578–579
radio astronomy **16**:49–50 *illus.*
stellar evolution **18**:250
atomic clock **2**:308
borines
Lipscomb, William Nunn, Jr. **12**:364
Cavendish, Henry **4**:225–226
compounds **10**:338
acetyl group **1**:80
aldehyde **1**:267
alkyl group **1**:297
aryl group **2**:226
carboxylic acid **4**:139–140 *table*
ethyl group **7**:257
hydride **10**:331
hydrocarbon **10**:331
hydroxyl group **10**:344
methyl group **13**:344–345
nitrogen **14**:202
peroxide **15**:177
phenyl group **15**:226
fuel cell **8**:354 *illus.*
fusion, nuclear **8**:381
Group IA periodic table **15**:167
heat content **8**:353 *table*
isotope
deuterium **6**:136
tritium **19**:304
laser and maser **12**:213 *table*
liquid hydrogen **10**:339
cryogenics **5**:370
Dewar, Sir James **6**:146
molecule
chemical bond **4**:313
electron configuration **7**:120
hydrogen bond **10**:340
occurrence **7**:131 *table*; **10**:337
origin of life **12**:327 *illus.*
pH **15**:217
photodissociation
photochemistry **15**:258
preparation and manufacture **10**:338
properties **10**:337–338 *table*
quantum mechanics **16**:11
spectrum
hydrogen spectrum **10**:340–341
triple point **19**:302
uses **10**:338–339
hydrogen bomb **10**:339–340
HYDROGEN BOMB **10**:339–340 *bibliog., illus.*
Bethe, Hans **3**:230
development **10**:339
fallout **8**:14
lithium **12**:371
Los Alamos National Scientific Laboratory **12**:416
neutron bomb **14**:109
Oppenheimer, J. Robert **14**:407–408
Teller, Edward **19**:90
tests
Bikini (Marshall Islands) **3**:250
Eniwetok (Marshall Islands) **7**:206
Lop Nor (China) **12**:412
testing **10**:340
types **10**:339–340
HYDROGEN BOND **10**:340
chemical bond **4**:313
intermolecular forces **11**:215
water **20**:47–48
HYDROGEN CYANIDE
laetrile **12**:163
HYDROGEN PEROXIDE
peroxide **15**:177
Thénard, Louis Jacques, Baron, discoverer **19**:155
HYDROGEN SPECTRUM **10**:340–341 *bibliog., illus., table*
Balmer, Johann Jakob **3**:53
Balmer series **10**:340 *table*
lines **10**:340–341
Lyman, Theodore **12**:475
quantum mechanics **16**:11
spectrum **18**:169 *illus.*
HYDROGENATION **10**:341
fats and oils **8**:35
metabolism **13**:326
synthetic fuels **18**:409
HYDROGRAPHY **10**:341 *illus.*
hydrologic sciences **10**:342
littoral zone **12**:373
HYDROLOGIC CYCLE **10**:341–342 *bibliog., illus., table*
evaporation **7**:314
evapotranspiration **7**:314–315
forest **8**:227–230
global cycle **10**:341 *table*
greenhouse effect **9**:352
groundwater **9**:374
history **10**:341
human activity, influence on **10**:342
hydrosphere **10**:344
land phase **10**:341–342
ocean-atmosphere interaction **10**:341
thunderstorm **19**:185
HYDROLOGIC INSTRUMENTATION
bathyscaphe **3**:123
hydrometer **10**:343
hydrophone **10**:343
oceanographic instrumentation **14**:342–344
salinometer **17**:33
Stevin, Simon **18**:265
turbidimeter **19**:339
HYDROLOGIC SCIENCES **10**:342
aquifer **2**:94
artesian well **2**:214
bed load **3**:153
Darcy, Henry Philibert Gaspard **6**:37
Earth sciences **7**:24
geophysics **9**:108
hydrography **10**:342
hydrologic cycle **10**:341–342
hydrology **10**:342
lake (body of water) **12**:167–169
limnology **10**:342; **12**:345
meander, river **13**:253
oceanic mineral resources **14**:340–341
oceanography **10**:342; **14**:344–345
remote sensing **16**:147
river and stream **16**:229–232
SEASAT **17**:176
spring (water) **18**:199
Stevin, Simon **18**:265
swamp, marsh, and bog **18**:376–378
wake (water) **20**:8
water resources **20**:50–51
water table **20**:57
waterfall **20**:63
HYDROLOGY
baselevel **3**:108
braided stream **3**:441
evapotranspiration **7**:314–315
firn **8**:108
flash flood **8**:153
flume studies **8**:186
fresh water **8**:328
frost action **8**:346
geochemistry **9**:95–97
geyser **9**:162–163
Gilbert, Grove Karl **9**:178–179
glaciers and glaciation **9**:192–195
groundwater **9**:374–376

HYDROLOGY (cont.)
hot springs **10**:259
hydrologic cycle **10**:341–342
International Association of Hydrology
snow and snowflake **18**:4
International Hydrological Decade **11**:220
lake, glacial **12**:169–170
landslide and avalanche **12**:192–193
river delta **16**:232–233
sea level **17**:169
water table **20**:57
HYDROLYSIS **10**:342–343 *illus.*
salt (chemistry) **17**:37
weathering **20**:82–83
HYDROMETEORS *see* METEOROLOGY
HYDROMETER **10**:343
HYDROPHILIC AND HYDROPHOBIC SUBSTANCES **10**:343
soap and detergent **18**:6–7 *illus.*
HYDROPHOBIA *see* RABIES
HYDROPHONE **10**:343; **14**:344 *illus.*
HYDROPHYSICS
limnology **12**:345
HYDROPLANE *see* HYDROFOIL
HYDROPONICS **10**:343 *illus.*
HYDROQUINONE **10**:344 *illus.*
HYDROSCOPICITY
absorption **10**:345
deliquescent materials **10**:345
HYDROSPHERE **10**:344
See also OCEAN AND SEA
Earth, structure and composition of **7**:23
Earth sciences **7**:24
hydrologic cycle **10**:341–342
HYDROSTATICS
Archimedes' principle **2**:128
fish, swim bladder **18**:390
fluid mechanics **8**:185
Pascal, Blaise **15**:102
Pascal's law **15**:102
Stevin, Simon **18**:265
HYDROTHERAPY **10**:344 *bibliog.*
HYDROTHERMAL VENT **10**:344
deep-sea life **6**:79
HYDROXYL GROUP **10**:344
alcohol **1**:264
organic chemistry **14**:437
pH **15**:217
sterol **18**:262
HYENA **10**:344 *illus.*
aardwolf **1**:50
HYÈRES ISLANDS
map (43° 0′N 6° 20′E) **8**:260
HYESAN (Korea)
map (41° 23′N 128° 12′E) **12**:113
HYGEIA **10**:345
HYGROMETER **10**:345 *illus.*
humidity **10**:302
inventors
Daniell, John Frederic **6**:32
Fahrenheit, Gabriel Daniel **8**:8
meteorology **13**:341
HYGROSCOPICITY **10**:345
HYKSOS **10**:345 *bibliog., illus.*
Egypt, ancient **7**:82
HYMEN (mythology) **10**:345
HYMENOPTERA **10**:346
ant **2**:35–38
bee **3**:154–159
digger wasp **6**:174 *illus.*
ichneumon fly **11**:19 *illus.*
sawfly **17**:104 *illus.*
wasp **20**:45–46
HYMERA (Indiana)
map (39° 11′N 87° 18′W) **11**:111
HYMES, DELL
ethnography of speaking **18**:28
HYMN **10**:346–347 *bibliog.*
American music **1**:348–349
Ansky, Shloime **2**:35
Billings, William **3**:255–256
Byzantine music **3**:608
canticle **4**:117
cantus firmus **4**:118
carol **4**:160
chorale **4**:407
Cowper, William **5**:322
dithyramb **6**:202
gospel music **9**:254
Grundtvig, Nicolai Frederik Severin **9**:382
Homeric hymns **10**:214
Mason (family) **13**:198
meter (music) **13**:343
Te Deum laudamus **19**:53
Watts, Isaac **20**:69
Wesley, Charles **20**:105
HYNDMAN (Pennsylvania)
map (39° 49′N 78° 44′W) **15**:147
HYNDMAN PEAK
map (43° 50′N 114° 10′W) **11**:26
HYPERACTIVE CHILDREN **10**:347
predisposing factors **10**:347
treatment **10**:347
HYPERBARIC CHAMBER **10**:347 *bibliog.*
HYPERBOLA **10**:347–348 *bibliog., illus.*
applications **10**:348
navigation **14**:60
conic section **5**:188 *illus.*
construction **10**:347–348
eccentricity **7**:37
hyperbolic functions **10**:348
spiral **18**:188
HYPERBOLE
figures of speech **8**:76
HYPERBOLIC FUNCTIONS **10**:348 *bibliog.*
HYPERBOLIC GEOMETRY
geometry **9**:107
non-Euclidean geometry **14**:215–216
HYPERBOLOID
hyperbola **10**:348
HYPERCALCEMIA
endocrine system, diseases of the **7**:170
HYPERGAMY
Maratha **13**:143
HYPERINSULINISM *see* INSULIN
HYPERION (astronomy)
Saturn (astronomy) **17**:90–91 *table*
HYPERKINETIC IMPULSE DISORDER *see* HYPERACTIVE CHILDREN
HYPERON
baryon **3**:99
HYPEROPIA **10**:348
eyeglasses **7**:351
HYPERPARATHYROIDISM
endocrine system, diseases of the **7**:170
HYPERPLASIA *see* GROWTH
HYPERSENSITIVITY *see* ALLERGY
HYPERSTHENE *see* PYROXENE
HYPERTENSION **10**:348–349 *bibliog., table*
arteriosclerosis **2**:213
cardiovascular diseases **4**:145
heart diseases **10**:96
nervous system, diseases of the **14**:96
pregnancy and birth **15**:504–505
reserpine **16**:176
stroke **18**:302
upper limits, normal **10**:349 *table*
HYPERTHERMIA **10**:349 *bibliog.*
body temperature **3**:357–358
cancer **4**:105 *illus.*
HYPERTHYROIDISM
endocrine system, diseases of the **7**:170
thyroid gland **19**:188
HYPERTRICHOSIS *see* HIRSUTISM
HYPERTROPHIC CARDIOMYOPATHY (heart disease) **10**:95
HYPERTROPHY *see* GROWTH
HYPERVENTILATION **10**:349
vertigo **19**:563
HYPNOS *see* SOMNUS
HYPNOSIS **10**:350–351 *bibliog.*
analgesic **1**:388
anesthetics **1**:411
Charcot, Jean Martin **4**:287
consciousness, states of **5**:200; **10**:350
Hull, Clark **10**:296
medical, psychological applications **10**:350
memory, sensory modalties after **10**:350
Mesmer, Franz Anton **13**:314
posthypnotic response **10**:350
psychopathology, treatment of **15**:599
trance **19**:266
HYPNOTIC DRUGS
barbiturate **3**:78
chloral hydrate **4**:400
meprobamate **13**:303
paraldehyde **15**:78
phenobarbital **15**:225
sedative **17**:181–182
HYPOADRENOCORTICISM
endocrine system, diseases of the **7**:170
HYPOCHLOROUS ACID
chlorine **4**:400
HYPOCHONDRIA **10**:351
HYPOCOLIUS **10**:351
HYPOGLYCEMIA **10**:351 *bibliog.*
glucagon **9**:210–211
glucose tolerance test **9**:211
HYPOGONADISM
endocrine system, diseases of the **7**:171
HYPOLIMNION *see* LAKE (body of water)
HYPOPHYSIS *see* PITUITARY GLAND
HYPOPITUITARISM
endocrine system, diseases of the **7**:170
HYPOTHALAMUS **3**:444 *illus.*
anorexia nervosa **2**:34
brain **3**:446
emotion **7**:157
endocrine system **7**:169
endocrine system, diseases of the **7**:169–170
fever **8**:66
hormones
antidiuretic hormone **2**:61
oxytocin **14**:479
reproduction **16**:161
sex change **17**:225
hunger and thirst **10**:310–311
obesity **14**:315
pituitary gland **15**:322
Schally, Andrew Victor **17**:117
sex hormones **17**:226
suprachiasmatic nuclei
biological clock **3**:265
HYPOTHECATION **10**:351
HYPOTHERMIA **10**:351
body temperature **3**:357–358
HYPOTHYROIDISM
endocrine system, diseases of the **7**:170
hormone, animal **10**:237
thyroid gland **19**:188
HYPOXIA **10**:351
HYPSOGRAPHIC CURVE **10**:351
land elevation distribution **10**:351
HYRACOIDEA
mammal **13**:105–106 *illus.*
HYRACOTHERIUM *see* EOHIPPUS
HYRAX **10**:351–352 *illus.*; **13**:105 *illus.*
HYRUM (Utah)
map (41° 38′N 111° 51′W) **19**:492
HYRY, ANTTI
Finnish literature **8**:99
HYSHAM (Montana)
map (46° 18′N 107° 14′W) **13**:547
HYSSOP **10**:352
HYSTERECTOMY **10**:352 *bibliog.*
sex change **17**:224
HYSTERESIS **10**:352
curve
magnetism **13**:56–57 *illus.*
electret **7**:105
ferromagnet magnetization **10**:352
loop **10**:352
Steinmetz, Charles Proteus **18**:249
HYSTERIA **10**:352
Charcot, Jean Martin **4**:287
Freud, Sigmund **8**:329
Janet, Pierre **11**:358
neurosis **14**:107
trance **19**:266
HYTHE (Alberta)
map (55° 20′N 119° 33′W) **1**:256
HYVINKÄÄ (Finland)
map (60° 38′N 24° 52′E) **8**:95

I

I (letter) **11**:3 *illus.*
I (psychology)
ego **7**:73
I-CH'ANG (China)
map (30° 42′N 111° 11′E) **4**:362
I CHING (*Yijing*) **11**:3 *bibliog.*
I. F. STONE'S WEEKLY (periodical)
Stone, I. F. **18**:280
I-GO (game) *see* GO (game)
I-LAN (Taiwan)
map (24° 45′N 121° 44′E) **19**:13
"I LOVE LUCY" (television series)
Ball, Lucille **3**:40
radio and television broadcasting **16**:59 *illus.*
I-PIN (China)
map (28° 50′N 104° 40′E) **4**:362
I WANT YOU (James Montgomery Flagg) **15**:462 *illus.*
IACOCCA, LEE **11**:3
IAEGER (West Virginia)
map (37° 28′N 81° 49′W) **20**:111
IAMBIC METER
Archilochus **2**:128
versification **19**:562
IAMBLICHUS **11**:3 *bibliog.*
IAPETUS (astronomy)
Saturn (astronomy) **17**:90–91 *table*
IAPETUS OCEAN
Cambrian Period **4**:50–51
IAŞI (Romania) **11**:3
map (47° 10′N 27° 35′E) **16**:288
IBADAN (Nigeria) **11**:3
map (7° 17′N 3° 30′E) **14**:190
IBAGUÉ (Colombia)
map (4° 27′N 75° 14′W) **5**:107
IBALOI
Igorot **11**:38
IBÁÑEZ, VICENTE BLASCO- *see* BLASCO-IBÁÑEZ, VICENTE
IBARBOUROU, JUANA DE
Uruguay **19**:489
IBARRA (Ecuador)
map (0° 21′N 78° 7′W) **7**:52
IBB (Yemen) (Sana)
map (14° 1′N 44° 10′E) **20**:325
IBERIA *see* GEORGIAN SOVIET SOCIALIST REPUBLIC
IBERIA (county in Louisiana)
map (30° 50′N 91° 52′W) **12**:430
IBERIA (Missouri)
map (38° 5′N 92° 18′W) **13**:476
IBERIAN MOUNTAINS
map (41° 0′N 2° 30′W) **18**:140
IBERIAN PENINSULA **11**:3–4
See also PORTUGAL, HISTORY OF; SPAIN, HISTORY OF
map (40° 0′N 5° 0′W) **18**:140
Tagus River **19**:10
IBERT, JACQUES **11**:4
IBERVILLE (Louisiana)
map (30° 18′N 91° 7′W) **12**:430
IBERVILLE (county in Louisiana)
map (30° 15′N 91° 20′W) **12**:430
IBERVILLE, PIERRE LE MOYNE, SIEUR D' **11**:4 *bibliog.*
Mississippi **13**:471
IBEX **11**:4
Himalayan **13**:623 *illus.*
IBIBIO **11**:4 *bibliog.*
IBICUY (Argentina)
map (33° 44′S 59° 10′W) **2**:149
IBIS **11**:4–5 *illus.*; **11**:469 *illus.*
IBIZA (Spain) **11**:5
Balearic Islands **3**:36
map (38° 54′N 1° 26′E) **18**:140
IBIZA ISLAND
map (39° 0′N 1° 25′E) **18**:140
IBIZAN HOUND **11**:5 *bibliog.*
IBM *see* INTERNATIONAL BUSINESS MACHINES
IBN *see under the second element of the name for Arabic names beginning with IBN not listed below*
IBN ABD AL-RAHMAN, ABD AL-AZIZ *see* IBN SAUD, KING OF SAUDI ARABIA
IBN AL-MUQAFFA **11**:5 *bibliog.*
IBN BATTUTA **11**:5 *bibliog.*
Africa **1**:157 *map*
geography **9**:101
IBN EZRA, ABRAHAM BEN MEIR **11**:5 *bibliog.*
IBN GABIROL, SOLOMON BEN JUDAH **11**:5 *bibliog.*
IBN KHALDUN **11**:5 *bibliog.*
geography **9**:101
IBN SAUD, KING OF SAUDI ARABIA **11**:5–6
IBO (ethnic group) **11**:6 *bibliog.*
Biafra **3**:236
Hausa **10**:69
Nigeria **14**:192
IBO (Mozambique)
map (12° 20′S 40° 35′E) **13**:627
IBOUNDJI, MOUNT
map (1° 8′S 11° 48′E) **9**:5
IBSAMBUL *see* ABU SIMBEL
IBSEN, HENRIK **11**:6–7 *bibliog., illus.*; **14**:265 *illus.*
Doll's House, A **6**:226
drama **6**:260–261
Enemy of the People, An **7**:171–172
Ghosts **9**:170
Hedda Gabler **10**:104
Wild Duck, The **20**:148
IBUPROFEN **11**:7
IBUSE MASUJI **11**:7
IBYCUS **11**:7 *bibliog.*
ICA (Perù)
map (14° 4′S 75° 42′W) **15**:193
IÇÁ (PUTUMAYO) RIVER
map (3° 7′S 67° 58′W) **5**:107
ICARUS **18**:51 *illus.*
See also DAEDALUS (mythology)
ICAZA, JORGE **11**:7
ICBM *see* BALLISTIC MISSILE
ICE
hail and hailstones **10**:12–13
refrigeration **16**:124–125
salt-ice-brine system **15**:224 *illus.*
ICE, OCEANIC *see* ICEBERG; PACK ICE
ICE, RIVER AND LAKE **11**:7 *bibliog.*
floods and flood control **8**:167
lake, glacial **12**:169–170
moraine **13**:572

patterned ground **15**:115
varved deposit **19**:524
ICE AGES **11**:7–11 *bibliog., illus., map, table*
Agassiz, Louis Rodolphe **1**:182
ancient ice ages **11**:8
duration **11**:7–8
Earth, geological history of **7**:15
evidence **11**:7–10
fossil record **8**:247
geologic time
Jurassic Period **11**:477 *map*
Ordovician Period **14**:421 *map*
Paleozoic Era **15**:43
Permian Period **15**:175 *map*
Pleistocene Epoch **15**:364–366 *map*
Precambrian time **15**:492 *map*
Quaternary Period **16**:15
Silurian Period **17**:311 *map*
Tertiary Period **19**:123 *map*
Triassic Period **19**:295 *map*
glaciers and glaciation **9**:193–194
loess **12**:393
mammoth **13**:106–107
Milankovitch theory **13**:418–419
ocean and sea **14**:327
paleoclimatology **15**:32–34
paleoecology **15**:34
paleotemperature **15**:42
radiometric age-dating **16**:66
Scandinavia, history of **17**:107
till and tillite **19**:199
ICE CAPS **12**:182 *illus.*
ICE CREAM **11**:11 *bibliog.*
ICE FOG *see* FOG
ICE HOCKEY **11**:11–13 *bibliog., illus., table*
Beliveau, Jean **3**:183
Blake, Toe **3**:325
Bossy, Mike **3**:408
Campbell, Clarence **4**:65
Clarke, Bobby **5**:40
equipment and the rink **11**:12–13 *illus.*
Esposito, Phil **7**:243
Gretzky, Wayne **9**:359
history **11**:11
Howe, Gordie **10**:283
Hull, Bobby **10**:295–296
Lafleur, Guy **12**:164
Olympic Games **14**:385 *illus.*
Orr, Bobby **14**:448
play of the game **11**:12–13
Richard, Maurice **16**:209
Stanley Cup **11**:11–12 *table*
ICE MILK *see* ICE CREAM
ICE PLANT (botany) **11**:13
ICE SKATING **11**:13–15 *bibliog., illus.*
See also ICE HOCKEY
Button, Dick **3**:600
figure skating **11**:14–15
Fleming, Peggy **8**:159
Hamill, Dorothy **10**:27
Hamilton, Scott **10**:29
Henie, Sonja **10**:121
history **11**:13–14
skate design **11**:14
speed skating **11**:15
Heiden, Eric **10**:107
Olympic Games **14**:385 *illus.*
ICEBERG **11**:15 *bibliog., illus.*
glaciers and glaciation **9**:194
International Ice Patrol **11**:220
Northern Hemisphere drift limits **15**:11 *map*
research stations **11**:15
size and movement **11**:15
sources **11**:15
ICEBOATING **11**:15–16 *bibliog., illus.*; **20**:186 *illus.*
ICEBOX *see* REFRIGERATION
ICEBREAKER **2**:41 *illus.*; **2**:144 *illus.*; **11**:16
Coast Guard, U.S. **5**:80
Glacier **11**:15
nuclear-powered ship **17**:275
ICEFIELD *see* GLACIERS AND GLACIATION
ICEFISH **11**:16
ICELAND **11**:16–18 *bibliog., illus., map, table*
arts **11**:17–18
cities
Reykjavik **16**:190
climate **11**:17 *table*
polar easterlies **15**:393
economic activity **11**:18
education **11**:17
European universities **7**:308 *table*
farmhouses **10**:268 *illus.*
flag **11**:16 *illus.*
geothermal energy **9**:120–121
government **11**:18
health **11**:17
historians *see* HISTORY—Icelandic historians
history **11**:18
Scandinavia, history of **17**:111
Sigurdsson, Jón **17**:302
hurdy-gurdy **10**:315–316 *illus.*
land **11**:17 *map, table*
language
Germanic languages **9**:135–137 *table*
map (65° 0′N 18° 0′W) **7**:268
people **11**:17–18
physical features
Hekla **10**:110
ICELAND SPAR *see* CALCITE; **4**:21–22 *illus.*
ICELANDIC LITERATURE **11**:18–19 *bibliog.*
authors
Gunnarsson, Gunnar **9**:405
Laxness, Halldór Kiljan **12**:252
Sigurjónsson, Jóhann **17**:302
Snorri Sturluson **18**:3
Thórdarson, Agnar **19**:177–178
Thoroddsen, Jón **19**:179
collector
Magnússon, Árni **13**:61
Edda **7**:54–55
saga **17**:11
Skaldic literature **17**:331–332
ICHIKAWA (family) **11**:19 *bibliog.*
ICHNEUMON *see* MONGOOSE
ICHNEUMON FLY **11**:19 *illus.*
ICHTHYOLOGY **11**:19 *bibliog.*
ICHTHYORNIS **11**:19; **3**:279 *illus.*; **11**:19 *bibliog.*
ICHTHYOSAURUS **11**:19–20 *bibliog., illus.*
ICHTHYOSIS
xeroderma **20**:312
ICKES, HAROLD **11**:20 *bibliog.*
Public Works Administration **15**:611
ICON **11**:20 *bibliog., illus.*
Byzantine art and architecture **3**:604
monastic art and architecture **13**:520 *illus.*
mosaic **13**:595
Rublev, Andrei **16**:337
Russian art and architecture **16**:361–362
ICONIUM *see* KONYA (Turkey)
ICONNU *see* WHITEFISH
ICONOCLASM **11**:20–21 *bibliog.*
Byzantine art and architecture **3**:605
Byzantine Empire **3**:608
icon **11**:20
iconostasis **11**:24
John Damascene, Saint **11**:424
Leo III, Byzantine Emperor (Leo the Isaurian) **12**:287–288
mosaic **13**:595
Nicaea, councils of **14**:178
Nicephorus, Saint **14**:180
Orthodox church **14**:450
ICONOGRAPHY **11**:21–24 *bibliog., illus.*
cross **5**:360–361
Early Christian art and architecture **7**:9
iconology
Panofsky, Erwin **15**:60
symbolism (art) **18**:402–403
Islamic art and architecture **11**:294
mandorla **13**:112
painting **15**:19
studies **11**:23–24
symbolism (art) **18**:402–403
Theophanes the Greek **19**:158
tombstone **19**:232 *illus.*
ICONOSTASIS **11**:24 *bibliog.*
cathedrals and churches **4**:204 *illus.*
icon **11**:20
Russian art and architecture **16**:361–362
ICOSAHEDRON **15**:419 *illus.*
ICSH (interstitial cell-stimulating hormone)
sex hormones **17**:226
ICSU *see* INTERNATIONAL COUNCIL OF SCIENTIFIC UNIONS (ICSU)
ICTINUS **11**:24 *bibliog.*
Parthenon **2**:193 *illus.*
ID
psychoanalysis **15**:589
IDA (county in Iowa)
map (42° 23′N 93° 28′W) **11**:244
IDA GROVE (Iowa)
map (42° 21′N 95° 28′W) **11**:244
IDABEL (Oklahoma)
map (33° 54′N 94° 50′W) **14**:368
IDAH (Nigeria)
map (7° 7′N 6° 43′E) **14**:190
IDAHO **11**:24–30 *bibliog., illus., map*
agriculture **11**:27–28 *illus.*
cities
Boise **3**:363
Idaho Falls **11**:30
Pocatello **15**:376
Sun Valley **18**:346
climate **11**:25
economic activity **11**:27–28
education **11**:27
Idaho, state universities and colleges of **11**:30
flag **11**:25 *illus.*
government **11**:28
history **11**:28–30
land and resources **11**:24–26 *map*; **11**:29 *illus.*
map (45° 0′N 115° 0′W) **19**:419
mining **11**:28; **11**:29
people **11**:25; **11**:27
Bannock **3**:71
Cayuse **4**:227
Kutenai **12**:139–140
Nez Percé **14**:175–176
Shoshoni **17**:284–285
physical features
Craters of the Moon National Monument **5**:333
Sawtooth Mountains **11**:29 *illus.*
rivers, lakes, and waterways **11**:25; **11**:27 *illus.*
Snake River **17**:383
seal, state **11**:25 *illus.*
Teton Dam **19**:127
vegetation and animal life **11**:25
IDAHO (county in Idaho)
map (45° 50′N 115° 30′W) **11**:26
IDAHO, STATE UNIVERSITIES AND COLLEGES OF **11**:30
IDAHO CITY (Idaho)
map (43° 50′N 115° 50′W) **11**:26
IDAHO FALLS (Idaho) **11**:30
map (43° 30′N 112° 2′W) **11**:26
IDAHO SPRINGS (Colorado)
map (39° 45′N 105° 31′W) **5**:116
IDEAL GAS **11**:30
gas laws **9**:53
IDEALISM **11**:30 *bibliog.*
Arnold, Matthew **2**:185
Bradley, Francis Herbert **3**:437
Creighton, James Edwin **5**:337–338
epistemology **7**:222
Fichte, Johann Gottlieb **8**:69–70
Gentile, Giovanni **9**:94
Green, Thomas Hill **9**:347
Hegel, Georg Wilhelm Friedrich **10**:105–106
metaphysics **13**:334
Moore, G. E. **13**:568
Royce, Josiah **16**:331
Schelling, Friedrich Wilhelm Joseph von **17**:119
IDENTIFICATION (psychology)
defense mechanisms (psychology) **6**:83
IDENTITY, TRIGONOMETRIC
trigonometry **19**:298–299
IDENTITY CRISIS
Erikson, Erik **7**:230
IDENTITY FORMATION
adolescence **1**:106
IDEOGRAM
hieroglyphics **10**:160
IDEOGRAPHY
writing systems, evolution of **20**:291
IDEOLECT
geographical linguistics **9**:98
IDEOLOGISTS (philosophy)
Destutt de Tracy, Antoine Louis Claude, Comte **6**:133
IDEOLOGY **11**:30–31 *bibliog.*
See also names of specific ideologies, e.g., ANARCHISM; NAZISM; SOCIALISM; etc.
IDFU *see* EDFU (Egypt)
ÍDHI, MOUNT
map (35° 18′N 24° 43′E) **9**:325
IDI AMIN DADA *see* AMIN DADA, IDI
IDIOPHONES
musical instruments **13**:676
IDIOT, THE (book) **11**:31 *bibliog.*
Dostoyevsky, Fyodor Mikhailovich **6**:245
IDLE, ERIC
"Monty Python's Flying Circus" (television series) **13**:560
IDLIB (Syria)
map (35° 55′N 36° 38′E) **18**:412
IDOCRASE **11**:31
californite, variety **11**:31
gemstone **11**:31
tetragonal system **19**:127
IDOL **11**:31 *bibliog.*
IDOMENEUS **11**:31–32
IDRIS, KING OF LIBYA **11**:32 *bibliog.*
IDRIS, YUSUF
Egypt **7**:77
IDRIS II
Fez (Morocco) **8**:66
IDRISI, AL- **11**:32
geography **9**:101
IDYLL (literature) **11**:32
IDYLLS OF THE KING (poem) **11**:32 *bibliog.*
Tennyson, Alfred, Lord **19**:112
IEMITSU, SHOGUN OF JAPAN
Tokugawa (family) **19**:223
IEPER (Belgium) *see* YPRES (Belgium)
IESI (Italy)
map (43° 31′N 13° 14′E) **11**:321
IEYASU, SHOGUN OF JAPAN **11**:32 *bibliog.*
Japan, history of **11**:368–369
Tokugawa (family) **19**:223
IFE (Africa) **11**:32 *bibliog.*
map (7° 30′N 4° 30′E) **14**:190
prehistoric art **1**:174 *illus.*
Yoruba **20**:331
IFFLAND, AUGUST WILHELM
theater, history of the **19**:148
IFNI (Morocco) **11**:32
IFORAS MOUNTAINS
map (20° 0′N 2° 0′E) **13**:89
IFUAGO
rice terraces **1**:194 *illus.*
IFUGAO
Igorot **11**:38
IGBO *see* IBO (ethnic group)
IGLESIAS (Italy)
map (39° 19′N 8° 32′E) **11**:321
IGLOO **11**:126 *illus.*
Eskimo **7**:239
IGLOOLIK (Northwest Territories)
map (69° 24′N 81° 49′W) **14**:258
IGNACIO (Colorado)
map (37° 7′N 107° 38′W) **5**:116
IGNATIUS OF ANTIOCH, SAINT **11**:33 *bibliog.*
Apostolic Fathers **2**:85
catholic **4**:211
IGNATIUS OF ANTIOCH, SAINT
Docetism **6**:210
IGNATIUS OF LOYOLA, SAINT **5**:310 *illus.*; **11**:32–33 *bibliog., illus.*
Jesuits **11**:402–403
meditation **13**:275–276
Montserrat (mountain) **13**:560
IGNEOUS ROCK **11**:33–36 *bibliog., illus.*
alteration, mineral **1**:312
andesite **1**:404
basalt **3**:101
basement rock **3**:108
batholith **3**:122
chalcopyrite **4**:270
chemical formation **11**:35 *illus.*
chlorite **4**:401
dacite **6**:4
deposits, Triassic Period **19**:295 *map*
diabase **6**:148
dike (geology) **6**:176
diorite **6**:185
dunite **6**:300
eclogite **7**:41–42
economic deposits **11**:36
feldspar **8**:46–47
feldspathoid **8**:47
felsite **8**:48
foliation **8**:195
fossil record **8**:244 *illus.*
gabbro **9**:3
garnet **9**:49
gneiss **9**:213
granite **9**:287
granodiorite **9**:287
Johannsen, Albert **11**:423
kimberlite **12**:77
laccolith **12**:158
lamprophyre **12**:176
latite **12**:234
lava **12**:240
magma **13**:51–52
metamorphic rock **13**:331–333
mineral occurrence **13**:442
molybdenite **13**:514
monzonite **13**:560
niccolite **14**:180
obsidian **14**:319
ophiolite **14**:404
ore deposits **14**:424–425 *table*
oxide minerals **14**:476
paleomagnetism **15**:41
pegmatite **15**:133
pentlandite **15**:155
peridotite **15**:166
perovskite **15**:177
petrography **15**:206–207
petrology **15**:215
phenocryst **15**:225

IGNEOUS ROCK (cont.)
phosphorite **15**:256
pluton **15**:373
porphyry **15**:442
pyroxene **15**:638
pyrrhotite **15**:638
quartz **16**:13–14
quartz monzonite **16**:14
rhyolite **16**:204
rock **16**:247
Rosenbusch, Harry **16**:315
silica minerals **17**:304
sill **17**:309
sodalite **18**:32
sphene **18**:180
stibnite **18**:266
syenite **18**:401
sylvanite **18**:402
tuff **19**:329
IGNITION SYSTEM **11**:36–38 *bibliog., illus.*
Bosch, Robert **3**:406–407
breaker-point ignition system **11**:36–38
electronic ignition **11**:38
internal-combustion engine **11**:215
Kettering, Charles Franklin **12**:61
relay (control device) **16**:137
IGOR, GRAND DUKE OF RUSSIA
Rurik (dynasty) **16**:347
IGOROT **11**:38 *bibliog.*
IGRISH KHALAM, KING
Ebla **7**:36
IGUAÇU FALLS **3**:461 *illus.*; **11**:38; **18**:89 *illus.*
map (25° 41′S 54° 26′W) **3**:460
IGUALA (Mexico)
map (18° 21′N 99° 32′W) **13**:357
IGUANA **11**:38–39 *bibliog., illus.*
Galápagos Islands **9**:10
land iguana **14**:167 *illus.*
marine iguana **12**:381 *illus.*
IGUANODON **11**:39 *bibliog., illus.*
IGUATU (Brazil)
climate **3**:461 *table*
IGUIDI ERG
map (26° 35′N 5° 40′W) **1**:287
IGY *see* INTERNATIONAL GEOPHYSICAL YEAR
IHA-YARDEN *see* JORDAN RIVER
IHARA SAIKAKU **11**:39 *bibliog.*
IHEMA, LAKE
map (1° 52′S 30° 47′E) **16**:378
IHIALA (Nigeria)
map (5° 51′N 6° 51′E) **14**:190
IJEBU-IGBO (Nigeria)
map (6° 56′N 4° 1′E) **14**:190
IJEBU-ODE (Nigeria)
map (6° 50′N 3° 56′E) **14**:190
IJILL, MOUNT
map (22° 38′N 12° 33′W) **13**:236
IJMUIDEN (Netherlands)
map (52° 27′N 4° 36′E) **14**:99
IJSSEL RIVER
map (52° 30′N 6° 0′E) **14**:99
IJSSELMEER **11**:39
map (52° 45′N 5° 25′E) **14**:99
IJUW (Nauru)
map (0° 30′S 166° 57′E) **14**:51
IK **11**:39 *bibliog.*
IKARE (Nigeria)
map (7° 32′N 5° 45′E) **14**:190
IKARÍA ISLAND
map (37° 41′N 26° 20′E) **9**:325
IKEDA HAYATO **11**:40
IKERRE (Nigeria)
map (7° 31′N 5° 14′E) **14**:190
IKHANATON *see* AKHENATEN
IKIRE (Nigeria)
map (7° 23′N 4° 12′E) **14**:190
IKON *see* ICON
IKORODU (Nigeria)
map (6° 37′N 3° 31′E) **14**:190
IKOT EKPENE (Nigeria)
map (5° 12′N 7° 40′E) **14**:190
IL GESÙ, CHURCH OF (Rome) **4**:207 *illus.*
cathedrals and churches **4**:207
ÎLE-DE-FRANCE (France) **11**:40 *map*
ÎLE DE LA CITÉ (Paris) **15**:87 *map*
ÎLE DU DIABLE *see* DEVIL'S ISLAND (French Guiana)
ILEITIS *see* ENTERITIS
ILESHA (Nigeria)
map (7° 38′N 4° 45′E) **14**:190
ILEUS **11**:40
digestion, human **6**:172
enteritis **7**:208
intestine **11**:230
paralytic ileus **11**:40
ILF, ILYA
Union of Soviet Socialist Republics **19**:395
ILFORD (Manitoba)
map (56° 4′N 95° 35′W) **13**:119
ILI RIVER
map (45° 24′N 74° 2′E) **19**:388
ILIAD (epic) **11**:40 *bibliog.*; **13**:76 *illus.*
Achilles **1**:82
Agamemnon **1**:181–182
Gla **9**:192
Homer **10**:213
Troy (archaeological site) **19**:312
ILIAMNA (Alaska)
map (59° 45′N 154° 54′W) **1**:242
ILIFF (Colorado)
map (40° 45′N 103° 4′W) **5**:116
ILINI
Illinois (American Indians) **11**:45
ILIO POINT
map (21° 13′N 157° 15′W) **10**:72
ILION *see* TROY (archaeological site)
ILION (New York)
map (43° 1′N 75° 2′W) **14**:149
ILIOS *see* TROY (archaeological site)
ILKHANS
Turks **19**:348
ILLAPEL (Chile)
map (31° 38′S 71° 10′W) **4**:355
ILLEGAL ALIEN *see* ALIEN, ILLEGAL
ILLICA, LUIGI
Madama Butterfly **13**:39
Tosca **19**:247
ILLICH, IVAN **11**:40 *bibliog.*
ILLIMANI, MOUNT
map (16° 39′S 67° 48′W) **3**:366
ILLINOIS **11**:40–45 *bibliog., illus., map*
agriculture **11**:43–44 *illus.*
cities
Bloomington **3**:340
Cairo **4**:19
Champaign-Urbana **4**:276–277
Chicago **4**:340–342 *illus., map*
Decatur **6**:72
Evanston **7**:313
Peoria **15**:156
Rockford **16**:260
Springfield **18**:200
Waukegan **20**:70
climate **11**:41
culture **11**:43
economy **11**:43–44 *illus.*
education **11**:43
Chicago, University of **4**:342
Illinois, state universities of **11**:45
Loyola University **12**:445
Northwestern University **14**:260
Winnetka Plan **20**:180
flag **11**:41 *illus.*
government and politics **11**:44
Great Lakes Naval Training Center **9**:320
historical sites **11**:43
history **11**:44–45
Altgeld, John Peter **1**:313
Chicago **4**:340–342
Lincoln, Abraham **12**:348
Tonty, Henri de **19**:235
land and resources **11**:41–43 *illus., map*
map (40° 0′N 89° 0′W) **19**:419
people **11**:43
rivers, lakes, and waterways **11**:41
Illinois River **11**:46
seal, state **11**:41 *illus.*
transportation and trade **11**:44
vegetation and animal life **11**:41
ILLINOIS (American Indians) **11**:45 *bibliog.*
Winnebago **20**:180
ILLINOIS, STATE UNIVERSITIES OF **11**:45
Committee for School Mathematics
mathematics, new **13**:227
ILLINOIS RIVER (Arkansas)
map (35° 30′N 95° 6′W) **2**:166
ILLINOIS RIVER (Illinois) **11**:46
map (38° 58′N 90° 27′W) **11**:42
ILLIOPOLIS (Illinois)
map (39° 51′N 89° 15′W) **11**:42
ILLITE
clay minerals **5**:47
ILLITERACY *see* LITERACY AND ILLITERACY
ILLUMINATED MANUSCRIPTS **11**:46–48 *bibliog., illus.*
Bible Moralisée **12**:316 *illus.*
book **3**:384
Book of Hours **3**:386
book illustration **3**:386–388
Book of Kells **3**:388
Breviary of the Duchess of Burgundy **4**:27 *illus.*
Byzantine art and architecture **3**:606
calligraphy **4**:42 *illus.*
Carolingian art and architecture **4**:161 *illus.*
Celtic art **4**:240 *illus.*
Clovio, Giulio **5**:70
Codex Borbonicus (Aztec) **12**:223 *illus.*
Codex Mendoza (Aztec) **2**:382 *illus.*
Codex Zouche-Nuttall (Mixtec) **15**:498 *illus.*
Colombe (family) **5**:106
Commentary on the Apocalypse **16**:286 *illus.*
Dresden Codex (Maya) **13**:244 *illus.*
Early Christian art and architecture **7**:10
Ebbo Gospels **12**:316 *illus.*
English art and architecture **7**:182–184
Exeter Book **7**:331
Flemish art and architecture **8**:160
Giovanni di Paolo **9**:188
Gothic art and architecture **9**:260
Hesdin, Jacquemart de **10**:151
Ireland, history of **11**:261
Islamic art and architecture **11**:293
Levnî, Ressam **12**:304–305
Limbourg brothers **12**:343
Master Honoré **13**:215
Merovingian art and architecture **13**:311
miniature painting **13**:445
monastic art and architecture **13**:520 *illus.*
Ottonian art and architecture **14**:467
painting **15**:19
Persian art and architecture **15**:186 *illus.*
Romanesque art and architecture **16**:286 *illus.*
Spanish art and architecture **18**:152
Theophanes the Greek **19**:158
Trés Riches Heures du Duc de Berry **3**:384 *illus.*; **7**:284 *illus.*; **11**:48 *illus.*; **12**:343 *illus.*
Utrecht Psalter **15**:587 *illus.*
Winchester Pontifical **7**:184 *illus.*
ILLUMINATION *see* LIGHTING DEVICES
ILLUSIONISM **11**:49–50 *bibliog.*
Gothic art and architecture **9**:260–261
Guercino **9**:391
Haberle, John **10**:4
Hanson, Duane **10**:41
Harnett, William **10**:53
Holbein, Hans, the Younger **10**:201
Lanfranco, Giovanni **12**:194
Mantegna, Andrea **13**:129
Maulpertsch, Franz Anton **13**:233
Melozzo da Forli **13**:288–289
Mural painting **13**:646
perspective **15**:190–191
Piranesi, Giovanni Battista **15**:315
Veronese, Paolo **19**:559–560
ILLUSIONS **11**:48–49 *bibliog., illus.*
optical illusion **15**:159 *illus.*
perception **11**:48–49; **15**:158–160
susceptibility, cultural differences **11**:49
theories **11**:49
ILLUSTRATED LONDON NEWS, THE **11**:50
ILLUSTRE-THÉÂTRE
Béjart, Madeleine **3**:172
ILLYRIA **7**:282 *map*; **11**:50 *bibliog.*
languages, extinct **12**:198
ILLYRICUM *see* ILLYRIA
ILMEN, LAKE **11**:50
ILMENITE **11**:50
oxide minerals **14**:476
titanium ore **11**:50
ILO *see* INTERNATIONAL LABOR ORGANIZATION
ILO (Peru)
map (17° 38′S 71° 20′W) **15**:193
ILOBASCO (El Salvador)
map (13° 51′N 88° 51′W) **7**:100
ILOILO (Philippines) **11**:50
map (10° 42′N 122° 34′E) **15**:237
ILOPANGO LAKE
map (13° 40′N 89° 3′W) **7**:100
ILORIN (Nigeria)
map (8° 30′N 4° 32′E) **14**:190
ILWU *see* INTERNATIONAL LONGSHOREMEN'S UNIONS
IMAGE, OPTICAL **11**:50–51 *bibliog., illus.*
lens **12**:285–286
mirage **13**:463
mirror **13**:464–465 *illus.*
IMAGE AND IMAGERY (literature) **11**:51 *bibliog.*
IMAGE AND IMAGERY (sensation)
perception **15**:159–160
IMAGE PROCESSING **11**:51–53 *bibliog., illus.*
compression **11**:51–52 *illus.*
enhancement **11**:52 *illus.*
pattern recognition **15**:114–115
recognition **11**:53 *illus.*
restoration **11**:53 *illus.*
types **11**:51–53
use **11**:51–53
IMAGINARY NUMBER
complex number **5**:157
IMAGISM **11**:53 *bibliog.*
Aldington, Richard **1**:269
Doolittle, Hilda (H. D.) **6**:240
haiku **10**:12
Hulme, T. E. **10**:296
Lowell, Amy **11**:443–444
Pound, Ezra **15**:475–476
IMAM **11**:53–54
IMATRA (Finland)
map (61° 10′N 28° 46′E) **8**:95
IMBODEN (Arkansas)
map (36° 12′N 91° 10′W) **2**:166
IMEWS SERIES
military warning and detection systems **13**:422
IMHOTEP **11**:54 *bibliog.*
Ṣaqqara **17**:74
IMÍAS (Cuba)
map (20° 4′N 74° 38′W) **5**:377
IMIDAZOLE
purine **15**:630
IMIPRAMINE *see* TRICYCLICS
IMITATION FOODS
food technology **8**:213
IMJIM RIVER
map (37° 47′N 126° 40′E) **12**:113
IMLAY (Nevada)
map (40° 39′N 118° 9′W) **14**:111
IMLAY CITY (Michigan)
map (43° 2′N 83° 5′W) **13**:377
IMMACULATE CONCEPTION **11**:54
Bernadette, Saint **3**:220
Duns Scotus, John **6**:301
Mary **13**:184
Pius IX, Pope **15**:323
IMMANENCE, DIVINE **11**:54
Lotze, Rudolf Hermann **12**:421
IMMIGRATION **11**:54–56 *bibliog., illus., map*
alien **1**:293
Chinese Exclusion Acts **4**:388–389
Ellis Island (New York City) **7**:148
ethnic minorities **7**:255–256
Great Britain, history of **9**:318
Hispanic Americans **10**:177–180 *map*
historians
Handlin, Oscar **10**:37
housing **10**:276
indentured service **11**:78
naturalization **14**:51
North America **14**:231–232; **14**:236
Oriental Americans **14**:441–443
United States, history of the **19**:451 *illus.*
IMMIGRATION AND NATURALIZATION SERVICE, U.S.
immigration **11**:54
IMMOKALEE (Florida)
map (26° 25′N 81° 25′W) **8**:172
IMMORALIST, THE (book) **11**:56
Gide, André **9**:176
IMMORTALITY **11**:56 *bibliog.*
Gilgamesh, Epic of **9**:180
IMMORTELLE *see* CORAL TREE
IMMUNITY (biology) **11**:56–59 *bibliog., illus.*
aging **1**:185–186
AIDS **1**:201
antibiotics **2**:58
antibodies **2**:59–60; **11**:57–58
antigen **2**:61–62
antitoxin **2**:69
autoimmune diseases **2**:356
autoimmunity **11**:58
Behring, Emil Adolf von **3**:171
cancer (disease) **11**:59
Ehrlich, Paul (1854–1915) **7**:90
genetic engineering **9**:84; **9**:85
history **11**:57
immune system **11**:57–58 *illus.*
immunodeficiency disease **11**:59–60
immunology **11**:60
immunosuppression
transplantation, organ **19**:277
immunotherapy **11**:59
cancer **4**:105 *illus.*
infectious diseases **11**:164; **11**:166; **11**:167
inflammation **11**:169
influenza **11**:171–172
interferon **11**:210
lupus erythematosus **12**:466

lymphatic system **12**:475–476
Metchnikoff, Elie **13**:335
parasitic diseases **15**:83
public health **15**:608
Rh factor **16**:192
Roux, Pierre Paul Émile **17**:327
Schick test **17**:120
serum **17**:210
serum sickness **17**:210
spleen **18**:191
stress, biological **18**:298
swine flu **18**:392
thymus **19**:187
transplantation **11**:59
vaccination **19**:501
IMMUNITY (law) **11**:59
extraterritoriality **7**:346
self-incrimination **17**:191
IMMUNIZATION *see* IMMUNITY (biology)
IMMUNODEFICIENCY DISEASE **11**:59–60 *bibliog.*
agammaglobulinemia **11**:59
gastrointestinal tract disease **9**:57
immunity **11**:57
immunology **11**:60
lupus erythematosus **12**:466
major immunity systems
B and T lymphocytes deficiencies **11**:59–60
multiple myeloma **13**:638
myasthenia gravis **13**:689
primary and secondary **11**:59
tissue transplantation treatment **11**:60
IMMUNOGLOBULIN *see* GLOBULIN
IMMUNOLOGY **11**:60 *bibliog.*
allergy **11**:60
bacteria **3**:18
Behring, Emil Adolf von **3**:171
blood tests **3**:339
Bordet, Jules **3**:398
Burnet, Sir Macfarlane **3**:577
genetic engineering **9**:84
immunity **11**:57
Jerne, Niels K. **11**:397
Medawar, Peter Brian **13**:263
Pasteur, Louis **15**:108
Roux, Pierre Paul Émile **16**:327
Wassermann, August von **20**:46
IMOLA (Italy)
map (44° 21′N 11° 42′E) **11**:321
IMP (artificial satellite) **11**:60
scientific satellite **11**:60
space exploration **11**:60
IMPACT CRATER *see* METEORITE CRATERS
IMPACT ENERGY TESTS
materials technology **13**:219 *illus.*
IMPALA **11**:60 *illus.*; **17**:98 *illus.*
IMPARTIAL ADMINISTRATION OF JUSTICE ACT
Intolerable Acts **11**:231
IMPASTO **11**:60
Monticelli, Adolphe **13**:557
Ryder, Albert Pinkham **16**:379
IMPEACHMENT **11**:60–61 *bibliog., illus.*
Chase, Samuel **4**:301
Constitution of the United States **5**:216
framework of the Constitution **5**:214
House of Representatives of the United States **10**:273
Johnson, Andrew **11**:431
Nixon, Richard M. **14**:206
president of the United States **15**:527
Senate of the United States **17**:199
Supreme Court of the United States **18**:355
IMPEDANCE **11**:61
capacitance **4**:119
circuit, electric **4**:437
electronic components **11**:61
ohm **14**:363
IMPERATIVISM
ethics **7**:250–251
IMPERIA (Italy)
map (43° 53′N 8° 3′E) **11**:321
IMPERIAL (county in California)
map (33° 5′N 115° 20′W) **4**:31
IMPERIAL (Missouri)
map (38° 22′N 90° 23′W) **13**:476
IMPERIAL (Nebraska)
map (40° 31′N 101° 39′W) **14**:70
IMPERIAL ACADEMY
Chinese universities **4**:394
IMPERIAL COLLEGE OF SCIENCE AND TECHNOLOGY
royal college of science
Shaw, Sir Napier **17**:246
IMPERIAL PALACE (Tokyo) **19**:224–225 *illus., map*
IMPERIAL VALLEY (California) **4**:34 *illus.*; **11**:61
map (32° 50′N 115° 30′W) **4**:31
Salton Sea **17**:39
IMPERIALISM **11**:61–62 *bibliog., illus.*
Africa, history of **1**:156–159
colonialism **5**:111–112
Europe, history of **7**:293
Hobson, John A. **10**:193
Lenin, Vladimir Ilich **12**:282–283
Manifest Destiny **13**:117
Social Darwinism **18**:12
Spanish-American War **18**:150
IMPETIGO **11**:62
skin diseases **17**:342
IMPHAL (India)
map (24° 49′N 93° 57′E) **11**:80
IMPORT AND EXPORT TRADE *see* INTERNATIONAL TRADE
IMPORTANCE OF BEING EARNEST, THE (play) **11**:62 *bibliog.*
Wilde, Oscar **20**:148–149
IMPOTENCE **11**:62 *bibliog.*
IMPREGNATION *see* FERTILIZATION
IMPRESSED WARE CULTURE
European prehistory **7**:302
IMPRESSIONISM (art) **11**:62–68 *bibliog., illus.*
American art and architecture **1**:334
Bazille, Frédéric **3**:135
Caillebotte, Gustave **4**:16–17
Canadian art and architecture **4**:89
Cassatt, Mary **4**:183
Cézanne, Paul **4**:263–264
Corinth, Lovis **5**:263
Couture, Thomas **5**:318
Degas, Edgar **6**:84
drawing **6**:265
French art and architecture **8**:306–307
Guillaumin, Armand **9**:395
Hassam, Childe **10**:66–67
Jongkind, Johan Barthold **11**:445
landscape painting **12**:192
Liebermann, Max **12**:324
Monet, Claude **13**:523–524
Morisot, Berthe **13**:580
painting **15**:22
Pissarro, Camille **15**:317
Renoir, Pierre Auguste **16**:158–159
Rosso, Medardo **16**:320
Sisley, Alfred **17**:328–329
Slevogt, Max **17**:361
Suzor-Côté, M. A. de Foy **18**:374
Weir, Julian Alden **20**:95
Zorn, Anders **20**:371
IMPRESSIONISM (music) **11**:68 *bibliog.*
Afternoon of a Faun, The **1**:181
Chausson, Ernest **4**:305
Debussy, Claude **6**:71–72
French music **8**:321
Gieseking, Walter **9**:177
Griffes, Charles Tomlinson **9**:362
Ravel, Maurice **16**:94–95
IMPRESSMENT OF SEAMEN (U.S. history)
Jay's Treaty **11**:387
War of 1812 **20**:26
IMPRINTING **11**:68–69 *bibliog., illus.*
animal behavior **2**:11 *illus.*; **2**:13
duck **6**:292
Lorenz, Konrad **12**:414
IMPRISONMENT *see* PRISON
IMPRISONMENT, FALSE
tort **19**:245
IMPROVISATION (music)
cadenza **4**:11
jazz **11**:388–389
IMPROVISATIONAL AND EXPERIMENTAL THEATER **11**:69 *bibliog.*
Artaud, Antonin **2**:213
Chaikin, Joseph **4**:268
Foreman, Richard **2**:227
Grotowski, Jerzy **9**:372–373
guerrilla theater **9**:392
Off-Broadway theater **14**:352–353
Off-Off Broadway theater **14**:353
Polish Laboratory Theater **15**:397
Provincetown Players **15**:584
Reinhardt, Max **16**:132
IMRU' AL-QAIS **11**:69 *bibliog.*
IN MEDIAS RES
narrative and dramatic devices **14**:22
IN THE NIGHT KITCHEN (book) **4**:353 *illus.*
IN-VITRO FERTILIZATION
artificial insemination **2**:221
INA (Illinois)
map (38° 9′N 88° 54′W) **11**:42
INANNA (Iraq)
Uruk **19**:490
INARI LAKE
map (69° 0′N 28° 0′E) **8**:95
INBOARD ENGINE
motorboat **13**:612
INBOARD/OUTBOARD ENGINE UNIT
motorboat **13**:612
INBORN ERRORS OF METABOLISM *see* METABOLISM
INCA (American Indians) **11**:69–73 *bibliog., illus., map*
aftermath of Spanish conquest **11**:73
agricultural production **11**:72
ancient farming methods **1**:190 *illus.*
art and architecture **11**:72
ceremonial knife **11**:121 *illus.*
Latin American art and architecture **12**:222–223
masonry **11**:72 *illus.*
pre-Columbian art and architecture **15**:501 *illus.*
Aymara **2**:379
bureaucracy **11**:71 *illus.*
colonialism **11**:71
culture **11**:71–73
Cuzco **5**:399–400
empire **11**:69–71 *map*
headache, treatment **10**:85
incest **11**:74
Indians, American **11**:118
labor force **11**:72
Latin America, history of **12**:217; **12**:218
Machu Picchu **2**:125 *illus.*; **12**:223 *illus.*; **13**:25–26 *illus.*; **15**:501 *illus.*
mummy **13**:639
Pachacamac **15**:4
Pizarro, Francisco **15**:324
Quechua **16**:21
Quito **16**:28
religion **11**:73
Sun worship **11**:73
road system **11**:72
roads and highways **16**:235
royal roads **11**:70 *map*
rulers
Atahualpa **2**:287
Huayna Capac **10**:288
Manco Capac **13**:110
Pachacuti **15**:4
Sacsahuaman **17**:8
state organization **11**:71–72
storage and record keeping **11**:72–73
Toledo, Francisco de **19**:226
INCANDESCENT LAMP **11**:73 *bibliog.*
Edison, Thomas Alva, inventor **7**:57–58
lighting devices **12**:338 *illus.*
stage lighting **18**:210
Swan, Sir Joseph Wilson **18**:379
tungsten-filament
Langmuir, Irving **12**:196
vacuum **19**:502
INCARNATION **11**:73 *bibliog.*
Docetism **6**:210
Dodd, C. H. **6**:211
icon **11**:20
pharaoh **15**:219
INCENSE
sandalwood **17**:61
INCENSE CEDAR **11**:73
INCEST **11**:73–74 *bibliog.*
exogamy **7**:333
family **8**:15–16
INCH
weights and measures **20**:93 *table*
INCHELIUM (Washington)
map (48° 18′N 118° 12′W) **20**:35
INCHON (South Korea) **11**:74
Korean War **12**:120–121 *map*
map (37° 28′N 126° 38′E) **12**:113
INCHWORM **11**:74
INCINERATOR **11**:74
electric and steam generation **11**:74
INCISORS
teeth **19**:70–72 *illus.*
INCLINE VILLAGE (Nevada)
map (39° 16′N 119° 56′W) **14**:111
INCLINED PLANE
simple machines **17**:316
INCLINOMETER **11**:74
INCOME, NATIONAL **11**:74–75 *bibliog., tables*
balance of payments **3**:31–32
distribution (economics) **6**:200
economics **7**:48
fiscal policy **8**:109–110
gross national product **9**:371; **11**:74–75
multiplier effect **13**:638
personal income account **11**:75
saving and investment **17**:100
INCOME, PERSONAL
annual income by sex **17**:227 *table*
monetary theory **13**:525
personal income tax **11**:76–77
population **15**:437
INCOME TAX **11**:75–77 *bibliog.*
corporation **11**:76–77
double taxation **11**:76–77
economy, national **7**:49–51
Internal Revenue Service **11**:218
negative income tax **11**:77
Friedman, Milton **8**:332
personal income tax **11**:76–77
Pollock v. Farmers' Loan and Trust Co. **15**:409–410
Reagan, Ronald **16**:102
16th Amendment **5**:222; **17**:331
tax loopholes **11**:76
taxation **19**:46–47
INCOMES POLICY **11**:77 *bibliog.*
INCOMPETENCE (law) **11**:77
INCUBUS **11**:77
INCUNABULA **11**:77–78 *bibliog.*
book **3**:385
INDEFINITE INTEGRAL *see* INTEGRAL CALCULUS
INDENTURED SERVICE **11**:78
INDEPENDENCE (county in Arkansas)
map (35° 45′N 91° 35′W) **2**:166
INDEPENDENCE (California)
map (36° 48′N 118° 12′W) **4**:31
INDEPENDENCE (Iowa)
map (42° 28′N 91° 54′W) **11**:244
INDEPENDENCE (Kansas)
map (37° 13′N 95° 42′W) **12**:18
INDEPENDENCE (Kentucky)
map (38° 57′N 84° 32′W) **12**:47
INDEPENDENCE (Louisiana)
map (30° 38′N 90° 30′W) **12**:430
INDEPENDENCE (Missouri) **11**:78
map (39° 5′N 94° 24′W) **13**:476
INDEPENDENCE (Oregon)
map (44° 51′N 123° 11′W) **14**:427
INDEPENDENCE (Virginia)
map (36° 37′N 81° 9′W) **19**:607
INDEPENDENCE (Wisconsin)
map (44° 21′N 91° 25′W) **20**:185
INDEPENDENCE DAY **11**:78 *bibliog.*
Liberty Bell **12**:314
INDEPENDENCE FJORD
map (82° 8′N 25° 15′W) **9**:353
INDEPENDENCE HALL **11**:78 *bibliog.*; **15**:146 *illus.*
Liberty Bell **12**:314
Philadelphia (Pennsylvania) **15**:228 *map*
INDEPENDENCE MOUNTAINS
map (41° 15′N 116° 5′W) **14**:111
INDEPENDENT CANDIDATE (U.S.)
Anderson, John **1**:402
INDEPENDENT SCHOOLS
Great Britain
British education **3**:495
Eton College **7**:258
Harrow School **10**:61
Rugby School **16**:340
United States
private schools **15**:557
INDEPENDENT THEATER MOVEMENT
theater, history of the **19**:149–150
INDEPENDENT TREASURY SYSTEM **11**:78 *bibliog.*
Polk, James K. **15**:405
Van Buren, Martin **19**:511
INDETERMINATE ANALYSIS
Leonardo Pisano **12**:291
INDETERMINATE SENTENCE
criminal justice **5**:350
prison **15**:554; **15**:555
INDEX (list) **11**:78–79 *bibliog.*
information science **11**:172
INDEX (of Forbidden Books) **11**:78
INDEX FOSSIL *see* FOSSIL RECORD
INDEX OFFENSES *see* FEDERAL BUREAU OF INVESTIGATION
INDEX OF REFRACTION **11**:79
dispersion (physics) **6**:197
interaction with matter
electromagnetic radiation **7**:117
isometric system **11**:299
light measures **11**:79
mineral **13**:442
optical mineralogy **14**:408
optics **14**:410–411
prism (physics) **15**:554
refraction **16**:123
Snell, Willebrord van Roijen **18**:3
INDIA **11**:79–88 *bibliog., illus., map, table*
agriculture **11**:85–86 *illus.*
irrigation **11**:283
lumber **12**:455
tea **19**:53–54 *illus.*
archaeology and historic sites
Ajanta **1**:229

INDIA (cont.)
Amaravati 1:321
Bharhut 3:234
Bhubaneswar 3:234
Bodh Gaya 3:356
Cunningham, Sir Alexander 5:389
Elephanta 7:134
Ellora 7:148–149
Fatehpur Sikri 8:34
Foote, Robert Bruce 8:219
Indus civilization 11:153–154 *map*
Khajuraho 12:65
Konarak 12:108
Mahabalipuram 13:63–64
New Delhi 14:120
Pataliputra 15:109
Sarnath 17:78
Taj Mahal 19:14–15
army
Gurkha 9:406
art 11:85
See also INDIAN ART AND ARCHITECTURE
birth control 3:295
cities
Agra 1:187–188
Ahmadabad 1:200
Ajanta 1:229
Allahabad 1:298
Amritsar 1:383
Bangalore 3:63
Baroda 3:87
Bhopal 3:234
Bikaner 11:82 *table*
Bombay 3:374–375 *map*
Calcutta 4:24–25 *illus.*
Chandigarh 4:279
Cochin 5:85
Darjeeling 6:38
Gangtok 9:37
Howrah 10:285
Hyderabad 10:329
Indore 11:150
Jaipur 11:350
Kanpur 12:16
Lucknow 12:450–451
Madras 13:43
Mysore 13:692
Nagpur 14:6
New Delhi 14:120
Pataliputra 15:109
Poona 15:429
Srinagar 18:207
Trivandrum 11:83 *illus.*
Varanasi 19:521
climate 11:82–83 *table*
monsoon 13:544 *illus.*
communism *see* COMMUNISM
cosmetics 5:281
dance 6:26 *illus.*
bharata natyam 3:234
demography 11:84–85
economic activity 11:85–87 *illus.*; 11:88
education 7:59–62; 11:85
South Asian universities 18:95 *table*
family 8:17
famine 8:18–19
flag 11:79 *illus.*
forestry and fishing 11:86–87
government 11:87
caste 4:187
defense, national 6:82 *table*
health 11:85
Hindustan 10:173
history *see* INDIA, HISTORY OF
land 11:80–83 *illus.*, *map*, *table*
continental drift 15:354 *map*
languages 11:83–84
Aryan 2:226
Dravidian languages 6:263
Indo-Iranian languages 11:145–146
Pahari 15:14
literature *see* INDIAN LITERATURE
manufacturing and mining 11:85–86 *illus.*
map (20° 0′N 77° 0′E) 2:232
marriage 13:164
moonstone 13:567
music *see* INDIAN MUSIC
mythology 13:695 *illus.*; 13:699–700 *illus.*
nuclear energy
Bhabha, Homi Jehangir 3:233
people 2:242 *illus.*; 11:83–85 *illus.*
Andamanese 1:400
Badaga 3:18
Bhil 3:234
caste 4:186–187
Garo 9:50
Gond 9:243
Ho 10:190
Khasi 12:66
Khond 12:68
Lushai 12:467
Maratha 13:143
Mundari 13:640
Naga (people) 14:6
Oraon 14:416
Pahari 15:14
population 15:434
race 16:33–34 *illus.*, *map*
Rajput 16:78
Santal 17:68–69
Tamil 19:19
Thugs 19:184
women in society 20:204 *table*
philosophy 15:246–247
Buddhism 3:539–540
Hinduism 10:169–170
physical features
Deccan Plateau 6:73
Ghats 9:166
Kanchenjunga 12:13
Thar Desert 19:143
political parties 11:87
Indian National Congress 11:104
railroad 16:74
religion 11:84
Bene Israel 3:196
Buddhism *see* BUDDHISM
Hinduism *see* HINDUISM
India, history of 11:88–93
Jainism 11:349–350
karma 12:28
Malabar Christians 13:78
Parsis 15:98
philosophy 15:246–247
Sikhs 17:302
South India, Church of 18:106
Teresa, Mother 19:115
Vedas (sacred books) 19:530–531
Wali Allah, Shah 20:11
Zoroastrianism 20:379
Republic Day celebration 11:84 *illus.*
resources 11:83
power 11:85
rivers, lakes, and waterways 11:83
Brahmaputra River 3:440
Ganges River 9:36–37 *map*
Indus 11:152 *map*
Narmada River 14:21
Yamuna River 20:317
silk 17:307–308
soils 11:82
states and territories
Andaman Islands 1:400
Andhra Pradesh 1:405
Assam 2:264
Bengal 3:198–199
Bihar 3:250
Goa, Daman, and Diu 9:214–215 *map*
Gujarat 9:402
Haryana 10:65
Himachal Pradesh 10:165
Karnataka 12:28–29
Kashmir 12:29–30 *map*
Kerala 12:58
Laccadive Islands 12:158
Madhya Pradesh 13:41
Maharashtra 13:64
Manipur 13:118
Meghalaya 13:280
Mizoram 13:486
Nagaland 14:6
Nicobar Islands 14:183
Orissa 14:445
Pondicherry 15:426
Punjab 15:626
Rajasthan 16:78
Sikkim 17:303 *map*
Tamil Nadu 19:19
Tripura 19:303
Uttar Pradesh 19:499
theater, history of the 19:148
trade 11:87
vegetation and animal life 11:83
women in society 20:203
yoga 20:328–329
INDIA, HISTORY OF 11:88–93 *bibliog.*, *illus.*, *maps*
Bangladesh *see* BANGLADESH
caste 4:186–187
Gond 9:243
Hinduism 10:169–173
Hyderabad 10:329
Islamic influence 11:90–91
Pakistan *see* PAKISTAN
refugee 16:125
socialism 18:24
prior to 1526
ancient period 11:88–89 *maps*
Asia, history of 2:250–251
Asoka, Emperor 2:261
Chandragupta Maurya, Emperor 4:279–280
Cunha, Tristao da 5:389
Delhi Sultanate 6:92
Gupta (dynasty) 9:406
herbs and spices 10:136–137 *illus.*
Indus civilization 11:152–154
Maurya (dynasty) 13:238
medicine 13:268
medieval period 11:89–90
Muslim invasions 2:255–256
Oceo 14:346
Pataliputra 15:109
slavery 17:352
Vijayanagar 19:593
1526–1707 Mogul Empire
Akbar 1:229–230
Aurangzeb, Mogul Emperor of India 2:324
Babur, Mogul Emperor 3:7
Humayun, Mogul Emperor of India 10:300
Jahangir, Mogul Emperor 11:349
Moguls (dynasty) 11:91 *map*; 13:502
Shah Jahan, Mogul Emperor 17:235
Sher Shah 17:256
1707-1947 colonial era
Almeida, Francisco de 1:306
Black Hole of Calcutta 3:316
British Empire 3:495–496 *illus.*
Clive, Robert 5:61
Cornwallis, Charles Cornwallis, 1st Marquess 5:270
Curzon, George Nathaniel Curzon, 1st Marquess 5:396
Dalhousie, James Andrew Broun Ramsay, 1st Marquess of 6:12
Duff, Alexander 6:293
Dupleix, Joseph François 6:302
East India Company, British 7:31
East India Company, French 7:32
European influence 11:91–92
Gandhi, Mahatma 9:36
Great Britain, history of 9:315
Hastings, Warren 10:67
Hyder Ali 10:329
Indian Mutiny 11:103–104
Indian National Congress 11:104
Maratha 13:143
Minto, Gilbert Elliot, 4th Earl of 13:461
Muslim League 13:683
nationalist movement 11:93 *illus.*
Nepal 14:87–88
Pakistan 15:29
Patel, Vallabhbhai Jhaverbhai 15:109–110
Roy, Rammohun 16:329
Tilak, Bal Gangadhar 19:198
Tippu Sultan, Sultan of Mysore 19:207
Wellesley, Richard Colley Wellesley, Marquess 20:99–100
1947-present 11:87–88
Bhave, Acharya Vinoba 3:234
Desai, Morarji Randchhadji 6:124
Gandhi, Indira 9:35
Gandhi, Rajiv 9:35
India-Pakistan Wars 11:93–94
Krishna Menon, Venegalil Krishnan 12:130
Narayan, Jayaprakesh 14:20
Nehru, Jawaharlal 14:78
Pandit, Vijaya Lakshmi 15:58–59
Radhakrishnan, Sir Sarvepalli 16:42
Singh, Charan 17:322
INDIA ACT OF 1784
East India Company, British 7:31
INDIA-PAKISTAN WARS 11:93–94 *bibliog.*
INDIAN ACT (1951) (Canada)
Indians, American 11:138
INDIAN AFFAIRS, BUREAU OF 11:94 *bibliog.*
Indians, American 11:137; 11:138
Parker, Ely S. 15:90
INDIAN AFFAIRS AND NORTHERN DEVELOPMENT, DEPARTMENT OF (Canada)
Indians, American 11:138
INDIAN ARCHAEOLOGICAL SURVEY
Cunningham, Sir Alexander 5:389
INDIAN ART AND ARCHITECTURE 11:94–98 *bibliog.*, *illus.*
See also INDIA—archaeology and historic sites
Ajanta 1:229
Basawan 3:101
Bharhut 3:234
Buddhist 11:95
Buddhist shrine at Sanchi 11:89 *illus.*
Coomaraswamy, Ananda Kentish 5:242–243
Fatehpur Sikri 8:34
folk art 8:198
Gupta (dynasty) 9:406
Hindu medieval art 11:96–97
Indus civilization 11:153–154 *illus.*
Islamic art and architecture 11:293–297
jewelry 11:408
Mahabalipuram 13:63–64
Mansur 13:129
miniature painting 11:97–98
modern period 11:98
Mogul art and architecture 13:500
Mohenjo-daro 11:154 *illus.*
museums, art 13:658
Pataliputra 15:109
Qutb Minar 16:28
Royal Ontario Museum 16:330
rugs and carpets 16:341 *illus.*
Sanchi 17:58
Sarnath 17:78
Southeast Asian art and architecture 18:107–108
stamp found at Mohenjo-daro 11:88 *illus.*
stupa 18:308
Taj Mahal 19:14–15
Taxila 19:48
temple 19:97–98 *illus.*
Bhubaneswar 3:234
Elephanta 7:134
Ellora 7:148–149
Khajuraho 12:65
Konarak 12:108
terra-cotta bodhisattva 19:120
INDIAN BEAN *see* CATALPA
INDIAN BROOK (Nova Scotia)
map (46° 23′N 60° 32′W) 14:269
INDIAN CLAIMS COMMISSION
Indian treaties 11:107
Indians, American 11:137
INDIAN DEPARTMENT *see* INDIAN AFFAIRS, BUREAU OF
INDIAN ELEPHANT 7:133–134 *illus.*
INDIAN FIG *see* PRICKLY PEAR
INDIAN FLYING FOX *see* BAT
INDIAN GRAVE MOUNTAIN
map (32° 59′N 84° 21′W) 9:114
INDIAN HEAD (Saskatchewan)
map (50° 32′N 103° 40′W) 17:81
INDIAN INTERCOURSE ACT *see* INDIAN TERRITORY
INDIAN LAKE (Michigan)
map (45° 59′N 86° 20′W) 13:377
INDIAN LAKE (New York)
map (43° 47′N 74° 16′W) 14:149
INDIAN LANGUAGES, AMERICAN 11:98–101 *bibliog.*, *tables*; 12:355 *map*
Central America 11:99–100 *table*
future 11:101
grammatical structure 11:99
Indians, American 11:123–125
language contact 11:99–101
language names 11:98
North America 11:98–100 *table*; 14:234 *map*
Gros Ventres 9:370
Kwakiutl 12:142
Mojave 13:504
Nootka 14:217
Quileute-Hoh and Chemakum 16:26
Sequoya 17:207
sign language 17:300
writing systems, evolution of 20:293
Yamasee 20:316–317
origins and classification 11:98–99
scientific study 11:98
anthropological linguistics 2:50
Boas, Franz 3:349
Powell, John Wesley 15:481
Sapir, Edward 17:72
Whorf, Benjamin Lee 20:144
South America 11:99–100 *table*; 18:93 *map*
Tupí 19:339
Yanamamo 20:318
unclassified languages 11:100 *table*
INDIAN LITERATURE 11:101–102 *bibliog.*
authors
Bhartrihari 3:234
Bhavabhuti 3:234
Candidas 4:107
Chatterjee, Bankim Chandra 4:303–304
Iqbal, Muhammad 11:249
Jhabvala, R. Prawer 11:417

Kalidasa **12**:8
Naidu, Sarojini **14**:7
Narayan, R. K. **14**:20
Rao, Raja **16**:88
Tagore, Sir Rabindranath **19**:9–10
Bhagavad Gita **3**:233
Kamasutra **12**:9
Mahabarata, The **13**:64
Ramayana **16**:80
Upanishads **19**:471
INDIAN MUSIC **11**:102–103 *bibliog., illus.*; **13**:668 *illus.*
instruments **11**:102–103 *illus.*
sitar **17**:330 *illus.*
vina **19**:599
raga **16**:69
Shankar, Ravi **17**:240
INDIAN MUTINY **11**:103–104 *bibliog.*
Dalhousie, James Andrew Broun Ramsay, 1st Marquess of **6**:12
India, history of **11**:92
Kanpur (India) **12**:16
Lawrence, John Laird Mair Lawrence, 1st Baron **12**:250
Lucknow (India) **12**:451
mutiny **13**:687
INDIAN MYTHOLOGY
mythology **13**:699–700
INDIAN NATIONAL CONGRESS **11**:104 *bibliog.*
Gandhi, Mahatma **9**:36
India, history of **11**:92–93
Muslim League **13**:683
Patel, Vallabhbhai Jhaverbhai **15**:109–110
INDIAN OCEAN **11**:104–106 *bibliog., map*
Agulhas Current **1**:200
climate **11**:104
economy **11**:104
history **11**:104–106
islands and island groups
Andaman Islands **1**:400
British Indian Ocean Territory (Chagos Archipelago) **3**:496–497
Christmas Island **4**:415
Cocos Islands **5**:89
French Southern and Antarctic Territories **8**:326
Heard Island and the McDonald Islands **10**:89
Kerguelen Islands **11**:105 *map*
Madagascar **13**:37–39 *illus., map, table*
Maldives, Republic of **13**:86–87
Male (Republic of Maldives) **13**:87
Mauritius **13**:237 *map*
Pemba (Tanzania) **15**:140
Réunion **16**:184
Seychelles **17**:232 *illus., map*
Socotra **18**:30
Sri Lanka **18**:205–207 *illus., map, table*
Zanzibar (Tanzania) **20**:355
mid-oceanic ridge **13**:389–390
Ninetyeast Ridge **14**:199
oceanic trenches **14**:342
plate tectonics **15**:351 *map*; **15**:353
seas, gulfs, and bays
Arabian Sea **2**:100
Bass Strait **3**:117
Bengal, Bay of **3**:199
Great Australian Bight **9**:308
Malacca, Strait of **13**:78
Sunda Strait **18**:347
tributaries and ocean, dimensions **14**:326 *table*
water characteristics **11**:104
INDIAN PAINTBRUSH (botany) **11**:106
INDIAN PIPE (botany) **11**:106
INDIAN REMOVAL ACT (1830)
Five Civilized Tribes **8**:132
INDIAN REORGANIZATION ACT **11**:106
Indians, American **11**:137
INDIAN RICE *see* WILD RICE
INDIAN RIVER (county in Florida)
map (27° 43′N 80° 36′W) **8**:172
INDIAN RIVER (Michigan)
map (45° 25′N 84° 37′W) **13**:377
INDIAN RIVER BAY
map (38° 36′N 75° 5′W) **6**:88
INDIAN SCHOOLS, AMERICAN **11**:106 *bibliog.*
INDIAN SERVICE *see* INDIAN AFFAIRS, BUREAU OF
INDIAN SPRINGS (Nevada)
map (36° 34′N 115° 40′W) **14**:111
INDIAN TERRITORY **11**:106 *bibliog.*
Creek (people) **5**:337
Dawes Act **6**:54
Five Civilized Tribes **8**:132
Indians, American **11**:137
Oklahoma **14**:371
Spotted Tail **18**:198
Wichita (Indian tribe) **20**:144
INDIAN TRADE AND INTERCOURSE ACT (1790)
Indians, American **11**:138
INDIAN TREATIES **11**:106–107 *bibliog., illus.*
Indians, American **11**:137
Laramie Treaty
Spotted Tail **18**:198
New Echota, Treaty of
Watie, Stand **20**:67
INDIAN TUNA *see* PRICKLY PEAR
INDIAN WARS **11**:107–110 *bibliog., illus., maps*
See also names of specific Indian tribes, e.g., CHEYENNE (American Indians); PUEBLO (American Indians); etc.
colonial period **11**:107
Crook, George **5**:359
Custer, George Armstrong **5**:397–398
Eastern United States **11**:107–109 *map*
Kintpuash **12**:86
Little Turtle **12**:373
Logan, John **12**:393
Miles, Nelson A. **13**:419
original lands and reservations **11**:108–110 *maps*
United States, history of the **19**:437–439 *illus.*
wars and conflicts
Bacon's Rebellion **3**:14
Black Hawk War **3**:315
Fallen Timbers, Battle of **8**:14
French and Indian Wars **8**:312–314
King Philip's War **12**:82
Little Bighorn, Battle of the **12**:372
Pequot War **15**:158
Pontiac's Rebellion **15**:427
Sand Creek Massacre **17**:59–60
Seminole Wars **17**:197
Tippecanoe, Battle of **19**:207
War of 1812 **20**:25–28
Wounded Knee **20**:284–285
Weatherford, William **20**:82
Western United States **11**:108–110 *map*
INDIANA **11**:110–115 *bibliog., illus., map*
agriculture **11**:113 *illus.*
cities
Bloomington **3**:340
Columbus **11**:112
Evansville **7**:313
Fort Wayne **8**:238
Gary **9**:52
Hammond **10**:31
Indianapolis **11**:115
Lafayette **12**:163
Madison **11**:112 *illus.*
New Harmony **14**:126
South Bend **18**:96
Terre Haute **19**:121
Vincennes **19**:599
climate **11**:110
economy **11**:112–114 *illus.*
education **11**:112
Butler University **3**:592
De Pauw University **6**:62
Indiana, state universities of **11**:115
Notre Dame University **14**:267
Saint Mary's College **17**:24
flag **11**:110 *illus.*
government and politics **11**:114
history **11**:114–115
Morton, Oliver **13**:592
Vincennes, François Marie Bissot, Sieur de **19**:599
land and resources **11**:110–112 *map*
map (40° 0′N 86° 15′W) **19**:419
people **11**:112
rivers, lakes, and waterways **11**:110
Wabash River **20**:3
seal, state **11**:110 *illus.*
tourism **11**:113–114 *illus.*
wildlife **11**:112
writers **11**:112
INDIANA (Pennsylvania)
map (40° 37′N 79° 9′W) **15**:147
INDIANA (county in Pennsylvania)
map (40° 37′N 79° 9′W) **15**:147
INDIANA, ROBERT **11**:115 *bibliog., illus.*
Eight **11**:115 *illus.*
INDIANA, STATE UNIVERSITIES OF **11**:115
INDIANA DUNES NATIONAL LAKESHORE **11**:114 *illus.*
INDIANAPOLIS (Indiana) **11**:112 *illus.*; **11**:115
busing, school **3**:590
map (39° 46′N 86° 9′W) **11**:111
INDIANAPOLIS 500 RACE
automobile racing **2**:360
winners **2**:361 *table*
INDIANOLA (Iowa)
map (41° 22′N 93° 34′W) **11**:244
INDIANOLA (Mississippi)
map (33° 27′N 90° 39′W) **13**:469
INDIANOLA (Nebraska)
map (40° 14′N 100° 25′W) **14**:70
INDIANS, AMERICAN **11**:115–138 *bibliog., illus., maps*
See also NORTH AMERICAN ARCHAEOLOGY
American Indian Movement **1**:340–341
art *see* INDIANS OF NORTH AMERICA, ART OF THE; PRE-COLUMBIAN ART AND ARCHITECTURE
astronomy in the New World **2**:115
blood type **11**:116
Cahokia Mounds **4**:16
cannibalism **4**:109
canoe **4**:113
ceremonies **11**:122–123 *illus.*; **11**:131 *illus.*
cliff dwellers **5**:54–55
clothing and personal adornment **11**:121 *illus.*; **11**:123 *illus.*; **11**:135 *illus.*
moccasin **13**:488
wampum **20**:21 *illus.*
contributions to world culture **11**:117
cooking techniques
pemmican **15**:140
culture areas, Middle and South American **11**:124 *map*; **11**:132 *map*
Central and South Andean **11**:134
Circumcaribbean and North Andean **11**:133–134
Marginal Nomadic **11**:135–136
Mesoamerican **11**:133
Tropical Forest **11**:134–135
culture areas, North American **11**:124 *map*
Arctic **11**:126
California **11**:128–129
Eastern Woodlands **11**:130–131
Great Basin **11**:128
Northwest Coast **11**:126–127
Plains-Prairie **11**:129–130
Plateau **11**:128
Southeast **11**:131
Southwest **11**:131–133
Subarctic **11**:126
dance *see* INDIANS OF NORTH AMERICA, MUSIC AND DANCE OF THE; LATIN AMERICAN MUSIC AND DANCE
diet and subsistence methods **11**:118–119 *illus.*; **11**:127–128 *illus.*
North America c.1500 **11**:125 *map*
South America c.1500 **11**:133 *map*
education *see* INDIAN SCHOOLS, AMERICAN
ethnographers
Boas, Franz **3**:349
Catlin, George **4**:212
Gallatin, Albert **9**:16
Hrdlička, Aleš **10**:286
Morgan, Lewis Henry **13**:578–579
Powell, John Wesley **15**:481
Schoolcraft, Henry Rowe **17**:134
Wissler, Clark **20**:190
Folsom culture **8**:204
hallucinogens and stimulants **11**:119
head-hunting **10**:85
historic sites
Acoma **1**:83–84
Arizona **2**:162
Canyon de Chelly National Monument **4**:119
Chaco Canyon **4**:264–265
Mesa Verde National Park **13**:313–314 *illus.*
Oraibi **14**:413–414
Taos Pueblo **14**:139 *illus.*
history
Acoma **1**:83–84
Atahualpa **2**:287
Black Hawk War **3**:315
Black Kettle **3**:316–317
Brant, Joseph **3**:455
Caldwell, Billy **4**:26
California history **4**:36
Cibola, Seven Golden Cities of **4**:428
Cochise **5**:85–86
Colorado history **5**:119
conquistadors **5**:197
Cornplanter **5**:269
Cornstalk **5**:269
Cortés, Hernán **5**:278
Crazy Horse **5**:334
Crook, George **5**:359
Crowfoot **5**:363
Custer, George Armstrong **5**:397–398
Dawes Act **6**:54
De Smet, Pierre Jean **6**:63
Eliot, John **7**:139
European contact, early impact of **11**:136–137 *illus.*
Five Civilized Tribes **8**:132
Fletcher, Alice **8**:163
French and Indian Wars **8**:312–314
frontier **8**:342
fur trade **8**:371
Gall **9**:16
Geronimo **9**:157–158
Handsome Lake **10**:37
Hiawatha **10**:156
Huayna Capac **10**:288
Indian Affairs, Bureau of **11**:94
Indian Reorganization Act **11**:106
Indian Territory **11**:106
Indian treaties **11**:106–107; **19**:286
Indian Wars **11**:107–110
Iroquois League **11**:279–280
Jogues, Saint Isaac **11**:422
Johnson, Emily Pauline **11**:432
Kansas history **12**:21
King Philip's War **12**:82
Kino, Eusebio Francisco **12**:84–85
Kintpuash **12**:86
Little Bighorn, Battle of the **12**:372
Little Turtle **12**:373
Logan, John **12**:393
Louisiana history **12**:433–434
McGillivray, Alexander **13**:16
Manco Capac **13**:110
Mangas Coloradas **13**:114–115
Manuelito **13**:131
Massasoit **13**:212–213
Miantonomo **13**:370
Michigan history **13**:381–382
Miles, Nelson A. **13**:419
Montana history **13**:549–550
Montezuma II **13**:555
National Congress of American Indians **14**:31
Nebraska history **14**:73–74
Ohio history **14**:361
Oklahoma history **14**:371
Osceola **14**:452–453
Parker, Ely S. **15**:90
Parker, Quanah **15**:90–91
Pequot War **15**:158
Pocahontas **15**:376
politics and warfare **11**:122
Pontiac's Rebellion **15**:427
Popé **15**:430
Poundmaker **15**:476
Red Cloud **16**:112
Red Jacket **16**:112
Ross, John **16**:318
Sacagawea **17**:6
Sand Creek Massacre **17**:59–60
Seminole Wars **17**:197
Sequoya **17**:207
Sitting Bull **17**:330
slavery **17**:353–354 *illus.*
Smohalla **17**:373
South Dakota **18**:105–106
Spanish missions **11**:128 *illus.*; **18**:160–161
Squanto **18**:202
Tecumseh (Shawnee Indian) **19**:69
Tekakwitha, Kateri **19**:74
Tippecanoe, Battle of **19**:207
Uncas **19**:381
Wananikwe **20**:21
Washakie **20**:34
Washington history **20**:38
Watie, Stand **20**:67
Wounded Knee **20**:284–285
Wovoka **20**:285
Wyoming history **20**:303–304
20th century **11**:137–138 *illus.*
Hohokam culture **10**:199
housing and architecture **11**:117 *illus.*; **11**:120–121 *illus.*
hogan **10**:197
tepee **19**:114

INDIANS, AMERICAN (cont.)
wickiup **20**:145
wigwam **20**:147
hunting **10**:313; **11**:118–120 *illus.*; **11**:135 *illus.*
curare **5**:390
kin groups **11**:118
lands and reservations
Indian Territory **11**:106
lands ceded **11**:108–110 *maps*
national parks **14**:44
languages *see* INDIAN LANGUAGES, AMERICAN
literature *see* INDIANS OF NORTH AMERICA, LITERATURE OF THE
marriage **13**:165
medicine
spikenard **18**:183
mestizo **13**:324
metallurgy **11**:121–122
Mogollon culture **1**:392–393
Mound Builders **11**:130 *illus.*; **13**:617
music *see* INDIANS OF NORTH AMERICA, MUSIC AND DANCE OF THE; LATIN AMERICAN MUSIC AND DANCE
Nuclear America, defined **11**:118
origins **11**:116
peace pipe **15**:123
physical characteristics **11**:116 *illus.*
population estimates **11**:116–117
potlatch **15**:467
powwow **15**:486
primitive societies **15**:546
race **16**:33–34 *illus.*, *map*
religion **11**:122–123 *illus.*
corn dance **5**:267
Delaware Prophet **6**:91
ghost dance **9**:169
Handsome Lake **10**:37
initiation rites **15**:103–104
kachina **12**:4
kiva **12**:93–94
Native American Church **14**:47
peyote **15**:217
powwow **15**:486
shaman **17**:238–239
Shawnee Prophet **17**:247
Smohalla **17**:373
snake dance **17**:382
Sun dance **18**:346
totem **19**:249
Wananikwe **20**:21
Wovoka **20**:285
Yaqui **20**:319
Zuñi **20**:382
scalping **11**:129 *illus.*; **17**:107
social and political units **11**:118
Spiro Mound **18**:189
sports
lacrosse **12**:161
Thorpe, Jim **19**:180
tobogganing **19**:220
tomahawk **19**:229
totem **19**:249
travois **19**:285
tribes, Middle and South American **18**:91–92
Araucanians **2**:109–110
Arawak **2**:110
Aymara **2**:379
Aztec **2**:382–384
Bororo **3**:403–404
Carib **4**:147
Chibcha **4**:340
Chimu **4**:359
Colorado **5**:120
Cuna **5**:388
Guaraní **9**:386
Huastec **10**:287–288
Inca **11**:69–73
Jívaro **11**:419
Lenca **12**:281
Maya **13**:243–245
Mesoamerica **13**:314
Miskito **13**:466
Mixtec **13**:486
Mochica **13**:488
Mundurucú **13**:640–641
Olmec **14**:380
Peru **2**:55 *illus.*
Quechua **16**:21
Tarascan **19**:35
Tehuelche **19**:73
Tlaxcalan **19**:216
Toltec **19**:228–229
Tupí **19**:339
Warrau **20**:31
Yanomamo **20**:318
Zapotec **20**:356
tribes, North American
Abnaki **1**:57
Alabama **1**:238
Aleut **1**:272
Algonquin **1**:291
Anasazi **1**:392–394; **2**:163
Apache **2**:73
Apalachee **2**:74
Arapaho **2**:109
Arikara **2**:154
Assiniboin **2**:265
Bannock **3**:71
Bella Coola **3**:186
Blackfoot **3**:321
Caddo **4**:11
Carrier Indians **4**:168
Catawba **4**:201
Cayuga **4**:227
Cayuse **4**:227
Chemakum **16**:26
Cherokee **4**:332
Cheyenne **4**:338
Chickasaw **4**:345
Chinook **4**:395–396
Choctaw **4**:402–403
Comanche **5**:129–130
Cree **5**:336–337
Creek **5**:337
Crow **5**:363
Delaware **6**:91
Eskimo **7**:238–242
Five Civilized Tribes **8**:132
Flathead **8**:155
Fox **8**:255
Gros Ventres **9**:370
Haida **10**:12
Hidatsa **10**:158–159
Hohokam culture **2**:163; **10**:199
Hopi **10**:231
Hupa **10**:315
Huron **10**:316–317
Illinois **11**:45
Ingalik **11**:175–176
Iroquois League **11**:279–280
Kansa **12**:16
Kickapoo **12**:70
Kiowa **12**:86
Klamath **12**:94–95
Kutenai **12**:139–140
Kwakiutl **12**:142
Mahican **13**:64–65
Mandan **13**:110–111
Massachuset **13**:204–205
Menominee **13**:299
Miami **13**:370
Micmac **13**:384
Missouri **13**:480
Modoc **13**:499
Mohawk **13**:502
Mohegan **13**:503
Mojave **13**:504–505
Montauk **13**:551
Narragansett **14**:21–22
Natchez **14**:26
Navajo **2**:163 *illus.*; **14**:53–54
Nez Percé **14**:175–176
Nisqually **14**:201
Nootka **14**:217–218
Ojibwa **14**:364
Okanogan **14**:365
Omaha **14**:385
Oneida **14**:389
Onondaga **14**:391
Osage **14**:451–452
Oto **14**:460
Ottawa **14**:460
Paiute **15**:25
Papago **15**:66
Passamaquoddy **15**:104–105
Pawnee **15**:121
Pennacook **15**:145
Penobscot **15**:153
Pequot **15**:158
Pima **15**:303–304
Pomo **15**:423
Potawatomi **15**:466
Pueblo **15**:613–614
Puyallup **15**:633
Quapaw **16**:12
Quileute-Hoh **16**:26
Salish **17**:34
Seminole **17**:197
Seneca **17**:200
Shawnee **17**:246
Shoshoni **17**:284–285
Shuswap **17**:289–290
Sioux **17**:326
Spokan **18**:192
Susquehanna **18**:372
Tillamook **19**:199
Tlingit **19**:216
Tsimshian **19**:323–324
Tuscarora **19**:355
Ute **19**:496
Wampanoag **20**:21
Washo **20**:45
Wenatchee **20**:103
Wichita **20**:144
Winnebago **20**:179–180
Yakima **20**:314
Yamasee **20**:316–317
Yana **20**:317
Yaqui **20**:319
Yuma **20**:346
Yurok **20**:347
Zuñi **20**:382
wampum **20**:21 *illus.*
INDIANS OF MIDDLE AND SOUTH AMERICA, ART OF THE *see* PRE-COLUMBIAN ART AND ARCHITECTURE
INDIANS OF MIDDLE AND SOUTH AMERICA, MUSIC AND DANCE OF THE *see* LATIN AMERICAN MUSIC AND DANCE
INDIANS OF NORTH AMERICA, ART OF THE **11**:138–141 *bibliog.*, *illus.*; **14**:238–240 *illus.*
See also ARCHITECTURE—Indians of North America
Arctic **11**:138
basketry **3**:115–116
Anasazi **1**:393–394 *illus.*
beads and beadwork **3**:137–138
California and Basin-Plateau **11**:139
Copán **5**:248
Eskimo **7**:241
Indians, American **11**:121–122 *illus.*
Navajo **14**:53–54
Northeast, Southeast, and Subarctic **11**:140
Northwest Coast **11**:139
Plains **11**:140
pottery
Anasazi **1**:393–394 *illus.*
Zuñi jug **11**:121 *illus.*
powwow **15**:486
prehistoric art **15**:510
present-day **11**:141
rugs and carpets **16**:343
sandpainting **14**:53 *illus.*
Scholder, Fritz **17**:132
Southwest **11**:140
totem **19**:249 *illus.*
wood carving **20**:207–208
Haida sculpture **11**:127
INDIANS OF NORTH AMERICA, LITERATURE OF THE
Brown, Dee **3**:513
Castaneda, Carlos **4**:186
Johnson, Emily Pauline **11**:432
McNickle, D'Arcy **13**:35
Momaday, N. Scott **13**:514
Welch, James **20**:96
INDIANS OF NORTH AMERICA, MUSIC AND DANCE OF THE **11**:141–144 *bibliog.*, *illus.*
Cadman, Charles Wakefield **4**:12
dance **6**:21
corn dance **5**:267; **11**:143 *illus.*
dance paraphernalia and attire **11**:144; **18**:106 *illus.*
dance styles **11**:143
ghost dance **9**:169
ghost dance, Wovoka **20**:285
masked dances **11**:143–144
rain dance, Hopi **11**:131 *illus.*
snake dance **17**:382
snake dance, Hopi **11**:131 *illus.*
snowshoe dance **11**:142 *illus.*
South Dakota **18**:106 *illus.*
Sun dance **18**:346
Indians, American **11**:122–123 *illus.*
Pascola ceremony
Yaqui **20**:319
powwow **15**:486
Shalako Festival
Zuñi **20**:382
INDIANTOWN (Florida)
map (27° 1′N 80° 28′W) **8**:172
INDIC LANGUAGES
Indo-Iranian languages **11**:145
INDICATING TUBE
electron tube **7**:124
INDICATOR (chemistry) **11**:144 *bibliog.*, *table*
pH **15**:217
titration **19**:215
INDICTMENT **11**:144
5th Amendment **8**:74
grand jury **9**:285
INDIGESTION **11**:144
INDIGO **11**:144 *bibliog.*
INDIJA (Yugoslavia)
map (45° 3′N 20° 5′E) **20**:340
INDIO *see* MESTIZO
INDIO (California)
map (33° 43′N 116° 13′W) **4**:31
INDIRECT TAXES *see* TAXATION
INDISPENSABLE STRAIT
map (9° 0′S 160° 30′E) **18**:56
INDIUM **11**:144–145 *bibliog.*
cost **11**:144–145
element **7**:130 *table*
Group IIIA periodic table **11**:144; **15**:167
metal, metallic element **13**:328
native elements **14**:47
superconductivity **18**:350 *table*
INDIVIDUAL PSYCHOLOGY
Adler, Alfred **1**:103
INDIVIDUAL THERAPY
sex therapy **17**:227
INDO-ARYAN LANGUAGES
Indo-Iranian languages **11**:145
INDO-ARYANS *see* PAHARI
INDO-EUROPEAN LANGUAGES **11**:145 *bibliog.*; **12**:355 *map*
Armenian language **2**:173
Aryan **2**:226
Asia **2**:244 *map*
Baltic languages **3**:54–55
Basque language **3**:116
Celtic languages **4**:241
English language **7**:191–193
Europe **7**:274 *map*
Germanic languages **9**:135–137 *table*
Greek language **9**:342–343
Grimm's law **9**:136 *table*; **9**:366
historical linguistics **10**:182–183
Indo-Iranian languages **11**:145–146
Indo-Uralic hypothesis
Ural-Altaic languages **19**:476
Jones, Sir William **11**:444
languages, extinct **12**:198–199
Latin language **12**:233–234
North America **14**:234 *map*
Romance languages **16**:280–281
Slavic languages **17**:357–358
South America **18**:93 *map*
INDO-IRANIAN LANGUAGES **11**:145–146 *bibliog.*
India **11**:83–84
India, history of **11**:89
Indian literature **11**:101–102
Khond **12**:68
INDOCHINA **11**:146
See also KAMPUCHEA (Cambodia); LAOS; SOUTHEAST ASIA; VIETNAM
Annam **2**:31
Asia, history of **2**:259
Cochin China **5**:85
Tonkin (Vietnam) **19**:234
Vietnam War **19**:584–591
INDOCHINA WAR *see* VIETNAM WAR
INDONESIA **11**:146–150 *bibliog.*, *illus.*, *map*, *table*
agriculture **11**:148–149 *illus.*
art and architecture **11**:148
batik **3**:123–124 *illus.*
Borobudur **3**:402–403
folk art **8**:198 *illus.*
Southeast Asian art and architecture **18**:110
temple **19**:97–98 *illus.*
Toradja house **18**:107 *illus.*
cities
Bandung **3**:62
Banjarmasin **3**:67
Jakarta **11**:350–351 *illus.*
Medan **13**:263
Palembang **15**:30
Semarang **17**:195
Surabaya **18**:358
climate **11**:146; **11**:148 *table*
communications satellite **5**:145
economic activity and planning **11**:148–149 *illus.*; **11**:150
education **11**:148
Southeast Asian universities **18**:111–112 *table*
flag **11**:146 *illus.*
government **11**:149
history **11**:149–150
East India Company, Dutch **7**:31–32
Majapahit Empire **13**:76
spice trade **18**:180–181
Srivijaya Empire **18**:207
Suharto **18**:330
Sukarno **18**:332
World War II **20**:260–261 *map*
island groups and territories **11**:146–147 *map*
Bali **3**:37
Borneo **3**:402
Irian Jaya **11**:266
Java **11**:385
Moluccas **13**:514
Sulawesi **18**:332
Sumatra **18**:338–339
Sunda Islands **18**:347

Timor **19**:203
Komodo dragon **12**:107–108
land and resources **11**:146–148 *map, table*
languages
Malayo-Polynesian languages **13**:83
map (5° 0'S 120° 0'E) **2**:232
mining and manufacturing **11**:148–149
tin **19**:205
people **2**:243 *illus.*; **11**:148
Alorese **1**:308
Ambonese **1**:325
Balinese **3**:37
Batak **3**:121
Bugis **3**:548
Dayak **6**:56
Javanese **11**:386
Minangkabau **13**:436–437
physical features
Krakatoa **12**:127
religion
Batak **3**:121
Islam **11**:290
rivers, lakes, and waterways **11**:146; **11**:150 *illus.*
vegetation and animal life **11**:146
INDORE (India) **11**:150
map (22° 43'N 75° 50'E) **11**:80
INDRA
fertility rites **8**:60
INDRAMAYU (Indonesia)
map (6° 20'S 108° 19'E) **11**:147
INDRI **11**:150–151 *illus.*; **15**:540 *illus.*
INDUCTANCE **11**:151
electromagnetic units **7**:118
henry **10**:122
Henry, Joseph **10**:122
inductor **11**:151–152
Lenz's law **12**:287
magnetic field interaction **11**:151
INDUCTION (embryology)
development **6**:138
INDUCTION (reasoning process) **11**:151 *bibliog.*
deduction **6**:77
educational psychology **7**:66
inductive reasoning **11**:151
logic **12**:396
problem of induction **11**:151
reasoning **16**:104
INDUCTION, ELECTROMAGNETIC *see* ELECTROMAGNETIC INDUCTION
INDUCTION, MATHEMATICAL **11**:151 *bibliog.*
See also INDUCTION (reasoning process)
proof, mathematical **15**:568
INDUCTOR **11**:151–152 *bibliog.*
automobile **11**:151
circuit, electric **4**:437
fluctuation reduction **11**:151
induction coil **11**:151
Lenz's law **12**:287
INDULGENCES **11**:152
Crusades **5**:368
Luther, Martin **12**:468–469
simony **17**:316
Tetzel, Johann **19**:127
INDUS **11**:152 *map*
irrigation **11**:283
map (24° 20'N 67° 47'E) **11**:152
INDUS CIVILIZATION **11**:152–154 *bibliog., illus., map*
agriculture, history of **1**:190
Asia, history of **2**:250
culture **11**:153–154
decline **11**:154
Fairservis, Walter **8**:9
hieroglyphics **10**:159–161
India, history of **11**:88
Indian art and architecture **11**:94–95 *illus.*
major centers **11**:153 *map*
Marshall, Sir John Hubert **13**:173
Mohenjo-daro **2**:250 *illus.*
origins **11**:153
roads and highways **16**:235
slavery **17**:352
stamp found at Mohenjo-daro **11**:88 *illus.*
Tepe Yahya **19**:114
Wheeler, Sir Mortimer **20**:129
writing systems, evolution of **20**:292
INDUSTRIAL ARCHAEOLOGY **11**:154 *bibliog.*
Chellean **4**:311
INDUSTRIAL ARTS PROGRAMS **11**:154–155 *bibliog.*
See also APPRENTICESHIP; TECHNICAL EDUCATION; VOCATIONAL EDUCATION
Smith-Hughes Act **17**:372
INDUSTRIAL CHEMISTRY *see* CHEMICAL INDUSTRY
INDUSTRIAL DESIGN **11**:155–156 *bibliog.*
Bauhaus **3**:130
Beaubourg **3**:145
Behrens, Peter **3**:171
computer-aided design and computer-aided manufacturing **5**:160j-160L
Dreyfuss, Henry **6**:272
Eames, Charles **7**:5
furniture **8**:380
Gropius, Walter **9**:369
Hollein, Hans **10**:204
Loewy, Raymond **12**:393
Morris, William **13**:589
Nelson, George **14**:79
Roche, Kevin **16**:246–247
Teague, Walter D. **19**:57
INDUSTRIAL DISEASES *see* DISEASES, OCCUPATIONAL
INDUSTRIAL ENGINEERING **11**:156 *bibliog.*
computer-aided design and computer-aided manufacturing **5**:160j-160L
furniture **8**:380
genetic engineering **9**:85
industrial relations **11**:157–158
pollution control **15**:415–416
time and motion study **19**:202
INDUSTRIAL MANAGEMENT **11**:156–157 *bibliog.*
bureaucracy **3**:568
Gilbreth, Frank and Lillian **9**:180
industrial engineering **11**:156
industrial psychology **11**:157
operations research **14**:403
process control **15**:560–561
systems engineering **18**:414–415
Taylor, Frederick Winslow **19**:49
time and motion study **19**:202
INDUSTRIAL PARK **11**:157
INDUSTRIAL POLLUTION *see* POLLUTION, ENVIRONMENTAL
INDUSTRIAL PSYCHOLOGY **11**:157 *bibliog.*
assembly line **2**:265
Hawthorne studies **10**:79
human factors engineering **10**:297
Mayo, Elton **13**:248
psychology **15**:595
Taylor, Frederick Winslow **19**:49
time and motion study **19**:202
INDUSTRIAL RELATIONS **11**:157–158 *bibliog.*
See also LABOR UNION
arbitration (labor-management and commercial) **2**:110
boycott **3**:433
closed shop **5**:65
Federal Mediation and Conciliation Service **8**:41
general strike **9**:77
industrial management **11**:156
industrial psychology **11**:157
injunction **11**:178
Jones, Samuel Milton **11**:444
Labor-Management Relations Act **12**:152
Labor-Management Reporting and Disclosure Act **12**:152
Lever, William Hesketh, 1st Viscount Leverhulme **12**:303
Lochner v. *New York* **12**:386
lockout **12**:388
mediation **13**:264
minimum wage
West Coast Hotel Company v. *Parrish* **20**:108
National Labor Relations Act **14**:34
National Labor Relations Board **14**:34–35
National Mediation Board **14**:35
open shop **14**:398
right-to-work laws **16**:222
sabotage **17**:6
socialist law **18**:25
strike **18**:298–299
underemployment **19**:383
workers' compensation **20**:217
INDUSTRIAL REVOLUTION **11**:158–160 *bibliog., illus.*
Chartism **4**:300
city **5**:3–4
Cobbett, William **5**:83–84
diseases, occupational **6**:193
engineering **7**:178
Europe, history of **7**:292 *illus.*
factory system **8**:7
family **8**:17
food industry **8**:209
fuel **8**:353
Germany, history of **9**:153 *illus.*; **9**:154
Great Britain, history of **9**:316 *illus.*
industrial archaeology **11**:154
loom **12**:410–411
Luddites **12**:451
machine tools **13**:23–24
Malthus, Thomas Robert **13**:96
Manchester (England) **13**:108
manufacturing **13**:132
mass production **13**:203
Massachusetts **13**:209
mechanical engineering **13**:259–260
metallurgy **13**:330
navy **14**:63
process control **15**:560
social effects **11**:160
socialism **18**:19
spinning **18**:186
spread of industrialization **11**:159–160
steam engine **18**:240–241
technical education **19**:59
technology **19**:60
technology, history of **19**:65–68
textile industry **19**:137
tourism **19**:252
United Kingdom **19**:409 *illus.*
urban planning **19**:482–484
Young Women's Christian Association **20**:336
INDUSTRIAL SAFETY *see* SAFETY, INDUSTRIAL
INDUSTRIAL SOCIOLOGY
Hawthorne studies **10**:79
INDUSTRIAL TRAINING PROGRAMS *see* VOCATIONAL EDUCATION
INDUSTRIAL UNION **11**:160 *bibliog.*
International Ladies' Garment Workers' Union **11**:221
Lewis, John L. **12**:306
United Mine Workers of America **19**:411–412
INDUSTRIAL WASTES
waste disposal systems **20**:47
INDUSTRIAL WORKERS OF THE WORLD **11**:160 *bibliog.*
Debs, Eugene V. **6**:70–71
Haywood, William Dudley **10**:84
Hill, Joe **10**:164
Lawrence (Massachusetts) **12**:249
Paterson (New Jersey) **15**:111
sabotage **17**:6
Socialist party **18**:25
syndicalism
socialism **18**:21
INDUSTRY
aerospace industry **1**:125–128
assembly line **2**:264–265
automotive industry **2**:363–368
bookbinding **3**:389–390
building construction **3**:548–552
carpet industry **4**:165
chemical industry **4**:317
clothing industry **5**:65–66
computer industry **5**:160n-160o
cosmetics **5**:280–283
dry cleaning **6**:283–284
electronics industry **7**:126
employment and unemployment **7**:159
factory system **8**:6–7
food industry **8**:208–211
funeral industry **8**:365
industrial design **11**:155–156
industrial management **11**:156–157
industrial park **11**:157
input-output analysis **11**:182
iron and steel industries **11**:272–278
labor union **12**:152–156
manufacturing **13**:131–133
mass production **13**:203–204
metallurgy **13**:330–331
mining and quarrying **13**:446
organic chemistry **14**:439–440
petroleum industry **15**:209–215
pharmaceutical industry **15**:219–220
power, generation and transmission of **15**:481–482
printing **15**:552–553
publishing **15**:611–612
radio **16**:45–47
radio and television broadcasting **16**:54–60
refining, metal **16**:119
soap and detergent **18**:7–8
technology, history of **19**:65–69
telephone industry **19**:80
television **19**:83–89
textile industry **19**:135–137
toxicology **19**:256
trade associations **19**:262–263
transportation **19**:278–282
INDUSTRY (Illinois)
map (40° 20'N 90° 36'W) **11**:42
INDY, VINCENT D' **11**:160 *bibliog.*
INE, KING
Wessex **20**:106
INEQUALITY (mathematics) **11**:161 *bibliog., illus.*
conditional **11**:161
graph **9**:291
real numbers **11**:161
INERT GASES **11**:161 *bibliog.*
argon **2**:152
chemical and physical properties **11**:161
commercial uses **11**:161
gaseous elements **11**:161
Group 0 periodic table **15**:167
helium **10**:113
ion and ionization **11**:240 *illus.*
krypton **12**:132–133
neon **14**:84–85
radon **16**:68–69
Ramsay, Sir William **16**:81
Rayleigh, Lord **16**:97
Travers, Morris William, discoverer **19**:284
xenon **20**:312
INERTIA **11**:161 *bibliog.*
law of
laws of motion **12**:251
mass (physics) **13**:201
moment of inertia **13**:515
motion, harmonic **13**:608
INERTIAL GUIDANCE SYSTEM *see* GUIDANCE AND CONTROL SYSTEMS
INEZ (Kentucky)
map (37° 52'N 82° 32'W) **12**:47
INFALLIBILITY **11**:161–162 *bibliog.*
Döllinger, Ignaz von **6**:226
ultramontanism **19**:377
Vatican Council, First **19**:527
INFANCY **11**:162–163 *bibliog.*
breast-feeding **3**:469
cognitive development **11**:162
crib death **5**:342
gastrointestinal tract disease **9**:56
genetic diseases **9**:82
heart diseases **10**:95
hyaline membrane disease **10**:327
hydrocephaly **10**:331
immunodeficiency disease **11**:60
importance of **11**:162
isolation effect
Harlow, Harry F. **10**:50–51
jaundice **11**:385
learning during **11**:162–163
marasmus **13**:143
pediatrics **15**:131
phenylketonuria **15**:226
physical and motor development **11**:162
premature baby **15**:518
sexual development **17**:228–229
social behavior **11**:162–163
speech development **18**:175
whooping cough **20**:143
INFANT (law) *see* MINOR (law)
INFANTICIDE **11**:163 *bibliog.*
women in society **20**:203
INFANTILE PARALYSIS *see* POLIOMYELITIS
INFANTRY **11**:163–164 *bibliog., illus.*
airborne troops **1**:210
battalion **3**:124
English Civil War **7**:190 *illus.*
Garand, John Cantius **9**:38
history **11**:163
infantrymen **11**:164 *illus.*
Janissaries **11**:358
machine gun **13**:21–23
mortar **13**:591
musket **13**:682–683
rangers **16**:85
recoilless rifle **16**:108
strategy and tactics, military **18**:290
weapons **11**:164 *illus.*
INFARCTION **11**:164
aneurysm **1**:411
enzyme **7**:214
heart attack **10**:95
pulmonary infarction **11**:164
respiratory system disorders **16**:182
stroke **11**:164
INFECTIOUS DISEASES **11**:164–168 *bibliog.*
AIDS **1**:201
amebiasis **1**:326
anthrax **2**:50
antibiotics **2**:57–59
antibody **2**:59–60
arthritis **2**:214
bites and stings **3**:300
bone diseases **3**:377
bronchitis **3**:503

INFECTIOUS DISEASES (cont.)
brucellosis **3**:520
bubonic plague **3**:532
candidiasis **4**:107
carbuncle **4**:141
chancroid **4**:279
chicken pox **4**:345–346
cholera **4**:403
coccidioidomycosis **5**:85
coccidiosis **5**:85
cold, common **5**:97
colitis **5**:102
Colorado tick fever **5**:121
control, results of **7**:210
diphtheria **6**:185
diseases, animal **6**:191–192
diseases, childhood **6**:192–193
diseases, occupational **6**:193
ear disease **7**:7
encephalitis **7**:162
environmental health **7**:210
epidemiology **7**:219
Escherichia, E. Coli **7**:237
eye diseases **7**:350–351
fifth disease **8**:74
filariasis **8**:78
food poisoning and infection **8**:211
Fracastoro, Girolamo **8**:257
fungus diseases **8**:369
gastrointestinal tract infections **11**:167
genetic diseases **9**:82
German measles **9**:134
glanders **9**:197
gonorrhea **9**:244
Hemophilus **10**:120
hepatitis **10**:130
herpes **10**:145–146
histoplasmosis **10**:181
history
control of disease **7**:210–212
environmental health **7**:210
Hodgkin's disease **10**:194
immunity **11**:58
impetigo **11**:62
inflammation **11**:169
influenza **11**:171–172
interferon **11**:210
kidney disease **12**:72
Klebsiella **12**:95
Koch, Robert
medicine **13**:271
leprosy **12**:295
leptospirosis **12**:296
mastoiditis **13**:217
measles **13**:253
meningitis **13**:298
mononucleosis **13**:537
multiple sclerosis **13**:638
mycoplasmal penumonia **13**:690
nervous system, diseases of the **14**:96
Nocardia **14**:212
nocardiosis **14**:212
orchitis **14**:420
osteomyelitis **14**:457
pediatrics **15**:131
penicillin **15**:143
peritonitis **15**:172
preventive medicine **11**:167–168
protozoal diseases **15**:581
quarantine **16**:12
rabies **16**:32
relapsing fever **16**:132
respiratory system disorders **16**:181
ringworm **16**:226
scarlet fever **17**:115
serum **17**:210
sinusitis **17**:326
skin diseases **17**:342
splenomegaly **18**:191
Staphylococcus **18**:220
Streptococcus **18**:297
sty **18**:311
sulfa drugs **18**:333
syphilis **18**:410
tetanus **19**:126
thrush **4**:107
tonsillitis **19**:235
tonsils **19**:235
toxic shock syndrome **19**:256
trachoma **19**:258
trench fever **19**:290
trichomoniasis **19**:296
tuberculosis **19**:327
tularemia **19**:330
typhus **19**:366–367
urogenital diseases **19**:487
vaccination **19**:501
venereal disease **19**:539–541
virus **19**:613–616
whooping cough **20**:143
yaws **20**:320
yellow fever **20**:322

INFECTIOUS ENTERITIS *see* DISTEMPER
INFELD, LEOPOLD
Einstein, Albert **7**:94
INFERENCE (mathematics) **11**:168 *bibliog.*
null hypothesis **14**:292
probability distribution **11**:168
proof, mathematical **15**:568
random variable **16**:83
theoretical physics **19**:159
INFERIORITY COMPLEX (psychology) **5**:157
INFERTILITY
artificial insemination **2**:220–221
fertility, human **8**:60
INFIERNILLO RESERVOIR
map (18° 35′N 101° 45′W) **13**:357
INFINITESIMAL (mathematics) **11**:168
Cavalieri, Bonaventura **4**:220
INFINITY (mathematics) **11**:168–169 *bibliog., illus.*
comparison of infinities **11**:168–169
study of limit **11**:168
INFLAMMATION **11**:169 *bibliog.*
abscess **1**:62
aspirin **2**:262
bronchitis **3**:503
chemical mediators **11**:169
chronic or long term **11**:169
drug administration **11**:169
erythema **7**:236
gallbladder **9**:17
gastritis **9**:56
gastrointestinal tract disease **9**:56–57
infectious diseases **11**:165
liver, hepatitis **10**:130
meningitis **13**:298
mononucleosis **13**:537
orchitis **14**:420
pericarditis **15**:165
peritonitis **15**:172
pharyngitis **15**:222
phlebitis **15**:248
physical characteristics **11**:169
pleurisy **15**:368
pneumonia **15**:376
process **11**:169
rheumatic fever **16**:194
rheumatism **16**:194–195
rhinitis **16**:196
sinus **17**:325
sinusitis **17**:326
strep throat **18**:297
tendonitis **19**:101
tic **19**:191
tonsillitis **19**:235
tonsils **19**:235
INFLATION **11**:169–171 *bibliog.*
consumer price index **5**:225
cost-push inflation **11**:170
economics **7**:49
economy, national **7**:50–51
fiscal policy **8**:109–110
income tax **11**:77
incomes policy **11**:77
monetary theory **13**:525
solutions **11**:171
stagflation **18**:211
INFLATIONARY THEORY **11**:171
INFLUENZA **11**:171–172 *bibliog.*
pandemic **11**:171–172
prevention **11**:171
respiratory system disorders **16**:181
swine flu **18**:392
vaccination **11**:172; **19**:501
virus particle **19**:613 *illus.*
virus strains **11**:171
INFORMATION OVERLOAD
human factors engineering **10**:297
INFORMATION SCIENCE **11**:172–173 *bibliog.*
information storage and retrieval **11**:173–174
information theory **11**:174–175
professional and educational organizations
American Library Association **1**:341–342
reasoning **16**:104–105
INFORMATION SERVICES, ELECTRONIC *see* ELECTRONIC INFORMATION SYSTEMS
INFORMATION STORAGE AND RETRIEVAL **11**:173–174 *bibliog.*
brain bilateralism **3**:448
compact disc **5**:154–155
computer **5**:159–160i
computer memory **5**:160p–161
computer networking **5**:163
computer software **5**:164–165
computers and privacy **5**:166–167
database **6**:43–44
electrical and electronic engineering **7**:106
ERIC Clearinghouses **7**:228–229
holography **10**:207–208
Inca **11**:72–73
information science **11**:172–173
information theory **11**:174
input-output devices **11**:182–183
microfilm **13**:385
minicomputer **13**:446
on-line computer **14**:388
pattern recognition **15**:114
punched card **15**:623–624
tape recorder **19**:30
videotext **19**:577
INFORMATION SYSTEMS, ELECTRONIC *see* ELECTRONIC INFORMATION SYSTEMS
INFORMATION THEORY **11**:174 *bibliog.*
artificial intelligence **2**:221
cybernetics **5**:401
entropy **7**:209
noise **14**:213
Shannon, Claude Elwood **17**:240
INFRARED ASTRONOMICAL SATELLITE
space exploration **18**:123
INFRARED ASTRONOMY **11**:175 *bibliog.*
astronomy and astrophysics **2**:281
history **11**:175
instrumentation **11**:175
night sights **14**:193
PbS detector **11**:175
INFRARED PHOTOCHEMISTRY
photochemistry **15**:259
INFRARED RADIATION **11**:175 *bibliog.*
faint object detection **11**:175
frequency, electromagnetic **7**:117 *table*
heat-sensing applications **11**:175
Herschel, Sir William **11**:175
photochemistry **15**:259
photography **15**:266 *illus.*
spectroscopy **18**:170–171 *illus.*
wavelength, electromagnetic **7**:117 *table*
INGALIK (American Indians) **11**:175–176 *bibliog.*
INGE, WILLIAM **11**:176 *bibliog.*
INGE, WILLIAM RALPH **11**:176 *bibliog.*
INGEGNARI, ANGELO
stage lighting **18**:210
INGEN-HOUSZ, JAN
photosynthesis **15**:275
INGERSOLL, ROBERT GREEN **11**:176 *bibliog.*
INGERSOLL, SIMON
Stamford (Connecticut) **18**:215
INGHAM (county in Michigan)
map (42° 37′N 84° 22′W) **13**:377
INGHARRA *see* KISH (Iraq)
INGLEWOOD (California)
map (33° 58′N 118° 21′W) **4**:31
INGLIS (Manitoba)
map location (50° 57′N 101° 15′W) **13**:119
INGOLDSBY, THOMAS *see* BARHAM, RICHARD HARRIS
INGOLSTADT (Germany, East and West)
map (48° 46′N 11° 27′E) **9**:140
INGONISH (Nova Scotia)
map (46° 42′N 60° 22′W) **14**:269
INGRES, JEAN AUGUSTE DOMINIQUE **11**:176–177 *bibliog., illus.*
Jupiter and Thetis **14**:82 *illus.*
Mademoiselle Rivière **15**:447 *illus.*
Napoleon I, Emperor of the French **14**:16 *illus.*
Saint Joan of Arc **11**:420 *illus.*
Turkish Bath **8**:307 *illus.*
Woman Bathing **11**:176 *illus.*
INGVAEONIC LANGUAGES
Germanic languages **9**:136
INHACA ISLAND
map (26° 3′S 32° 57′E) **13**:627
INHALATION
drug **6**:275 *illus.*
respiratory system **16**:180 *illus.*
respiratory system disorders **16**:181
INHAMBANE (Mozambique)
map (23° 51′S 35° 29′E) **13**:627
INHARRIME (Mozambique)
map (24° 29′S 35° 1′E) **13**:627
INHERITANCE (biology) *see* HEREDITY
INHERITANCE (law) **11**:177 *bibliog.*
escheat **7**:237
estate **7**:246
genealogy **9**:76
heir **10**:109
inheritance tax **11**:177–178
kinship **12**:85–86
primogeniture **15**:547
will **20**:153
INHERITANCE TAX **11**:177–178 *bibliog.*
INHIBITOR (chemistry) **11**:178
See also CATALYST
INITIAL TEACHING ALPHABET **11**:178 *bibliog.*
INITIATION RITES
passage rites **15**:103–104 *illus.*
INITIATIVE (government) *see* REFERENDUM AND INITIATIVE
INJASUTI MOUNTAIN
map (29° 9′S 29° 23′E) **18**:79
INJECTION
drug **6**:275 *illus.*
lethal injection **12**:299
vaccination **19**:501
INJECTION MOLDING
plastics **15**:349 *illus.*
INJUNCTION **11**:178
mandatory injunction **11**:178
prohibitory injunction **11**:178
writ **20**:291
INJURIES *see* WOUNDS AND INJURIES
INK **11**:178 *bibliog.*
Gutenberg, Johann **9**:408–409
lampblack **12**:176
linseed oil **12**:359
printing **11**:178
thermography **19**:166
writing **11**:178
INKERMAN, BATTLE OF
Crimean War **5**:348
INKSTER (North Dakota)
map (48° 9′N 97° 39′W) **14**:248
INLAND SEA **11**:178–179
map (34° 20′N 133° 30′E) **11**:361
INMAN (Kansas)
map (38° 14′N 97° 47′W) **12**:18
INMAN (South Carolina)
map (35° 3′N 82° 5′W) **18**:98
INN RIVER **11**:179
map (48° 35′N 13° 28′E) **6**:35
INNATE IDEAS **11**:179 *bibliog.*
INNER CITY **11**:179
city **5**:6
ghetto **9**:167
housing **10**:278; **10**:279
social work **18**:19
squatter **18**:203
INNER MONGOLIA (China) **11**:179
Ordos Desert **14**:420
INNER PRODUCT *see* VECTOR ANALYSIS
INNER SPEECH **11**:179 *bibliog.*
INNES, MICHAEL **11**:179
INNESS, GEORGE **11**:179–180 *bibliog., illus.*
The Lackawanna Valley **11**:180 *illus.*
INNINA *see* ISHTAR (Mesopotamian deity)
INNISFAIL (Alberta)
map (52° 2′N 113° 57′W) **1**:256
INNOCENT III, POPE **11**:180–181 *bibliog., illus.*
Crusades **5**:369
Europe, history of **7**:285
Frederick II, King of Germany and Holy Roman Emperor **8**:290
Italy, history of **11**:329
Middle Ages **13**:393
Otto IV, King of Germany and Holy Roman Emperor **14**:463
Sverre, King of Norway **18**:375
INNOCENT IV, POPE **11**:181 *bibliog.*
INNOCENT XI, POPE **11**:181
INNOCENT XII, POPE **11**:181
INNS OF COURT **11**:181 *bibliog.*
common law records **5**:139
expansion of the common law **5**:140
law, history of **12**:246
INNSBRUCK (Austria) **11**:181
map (47° 16′N 11° 24′E) **2**:348
INNVIERTEL (region in Austria)
map (48° 10′N 13° 15′E) **2**:348
INOCULATION *see* VACCINATION
INOLA (Oklahoma)
map (36° 9′N 95° 31′W) **14**:368
İWNÖNÜ, İWSMET **11**:181
Turkey **19**:346
INORGANIC CHEMISTRY **11**:181–182 *bibliog.*
chemical industry production **4**:319 *table*
chemical nomenclature **4**:320–321
compounds **11**:181–182
amphoteric compounds **1**:382
azide **2**:381
beryllium **3**:227
boron **3**:403
bromine **3**:502
calcium **4**:22

carbon **4**:134–135
carbonate minerals **4**:137
chalcogens **4**:270
chlorine **4**:400–401
chromium **4**:419
cobalt **5**:83
copper **5**:253–254
fluorine **8**:187–188
gallium **9**:21
germanium **9**:138
hydrate **10**:330
hydrochloric acid **10**:331–332
hydrogen **10**:338–339
hydrophilic and hydrophobic substances **10**:343
iodine **11**:239
lead **12**:256
lime **12**:343
lithium **12**:370–371
magnesium **13**:54
manganese **13**:114
mercury **13**:306
mineral acid **13**:444
nitric acid **14**:202
nitrogen **14**:202–203
oxygen **14**:477–478
phosphorus **15**:256–257
plutonium **15**:373
potassium **15**:465
radium **16**:68
rubidium **16**:336
salt (chemistry) **17**:37
selenium **17**:190
sodium **18**:33–34
sulfur **18**:335–336
sulfuric acid **18**:336
thallium **19**:142
tin **19**:204–205
titanium **19**:210
tungsten **19**:333–334
uranium **19**:477
zinc **20**:368
Gay-Lussac, Joseph Louis **9**:64
glassy state **9**:205
Gmelin, Leopold **9**:213
history **4**:328
macromolecule **13**:37
INOSITOL
vitamins and minerals **19**:620
INOUCDJOUAC (Quebec)
map (58° 27′N 78° 6′W) **16**:18
INOWROCLAW (Poland)
map (52° 48′N 18° 15′E) **15**:388
INPUT-OUTPUT ANALYSIS **11**:182 *bibliog.*
economy, national **7**:49–51
Leontief, Wassily **12**:292
multiplier effect **13**:638
physiocrats **15**:286–287
INPUT-OUTPUT DEVICES **11**:182–183 *bibliog.*
central processing unit **4**:255
computer **5**:160d; **5**:160e; **5**:160h
computer, personal **5**:160i
computer graphics **5**:160m
computer terminal **5**:165
punched card **15**:623–624
INQUEST **11**:183
INQUISITION **11**:183–185 *bibliog., illus.*
brainwashing **3**:449
heresy **10**:141–142 *illus.*
Index **11**:78
Jiménez de Cisneros, Francisco **11**:418–419
procedures **11**:184
Spain, history of **18**:145
Torquemada, Tomás de **19**:243
wheel **19**:247 *illus.*
INQUISITORIAL PROCEDURE (law)
adversary procedure **1**:111
INSANITY, LEGAL **11**:185 *bibliog.*
Bazelon, David L. **3**:134–135
crime **5**:345
forensic science **8**:227
incompetence **11**:77
Sickles, Daniel Edgar **17**:293
INSCRIPTION **11**:185–186 *bibliog., illus.*
Behistun **3**:171
Egyptology **7**:90
Tanis **19**:23
tombstone **19**:232 *illus.*
writing systems, evolution of **20**:292
INSECT **11**:186–193 *bibliog., illus.*
See also names of specific insects, e.g., CICADA; DAMSELFLY; etc.
anatomy **11**:186–188 *illus.*
antenna **2**:47
eye **7**:348
hormone, animal **10**:237 *table*
juvenile hormone **11**:480
skeletal system **17**:333
animal behavior **11**:191–193
animal migration **2**:25–27 *illus.*
Fabre, Jean Henri **8**:5
Frisch, Karl von **8**:334
Réaumur, René Antoine Ferchault de **16**:105
territoriality **19**:121
biological locomotion **3**:266
coloration, biological **5**:122
communication *see* ANIMAL COMMUNICATION
evolution **11**:193
forest **8**:227–228
fossil record **8**:244 *illus.*
infectious diseases **11**:166
insect repellents
bugbane **3**:547
citronella **4**:447
feverfew **8**:66
life cycle **11**:189–191 *illus.*
cocoon **5**:89
larva **12**:208
metamorphosis **13**:333
parthenogenesis **15**:100
pupa **15**:626
orders of insects **11**:193
Anoplura **2**:34
Coleoptera *see* BEETLE
Collembola *see* SPRINGTAIL
Dermaptera *see* EARWIG
Diplura **6**:186
Diptera *see* FLY
Embioptera **7**:151–152
Ephemoptera *see* MAYFLY
Hemiptera **10**:119
Homoptera **10**:216–217 *illus.*
Hymenoptera **10**:346
Isoptera **11**:300
Lepidoptera **12**:295 *bibliog.*
Mallophaga **13**:92
Mecoptera **13**:260
Neuroptera **14**:107
Odonata **14**:350
Orthoptera **14**:450 *bibliog.*
Plecoptera *see* STONE FLY
Protura **15**:582
Siphonaptera **17**:326
Strepsiptera **18**:297
Thysanoptera *see* THRIPS
Thysanura *see* BRISTLETAIL
Trichoptera *see* CADDIS FLY
Zoraptera **20**:379
pesticide **15**:196–198 *illus.*
pheromone **15**:226
pollination **15**:408–409 *illus.*
steppe life **18**:257
stinging, venom **19**:546
Swammerdam, Jan **18**:376
swamp, marsh, and bog **18**:376
INSECTICIDE
pesticide **15**:196–198 *illus.*
INSECTIVORE **11**:193 *bibliog.*
mammal **13**:102; **13**:104 *illus.*
INSELBERG **11**:194
INSEMINATION, ARTIFICIAL *see* ARTIFICIAL INSEMINATION
INSIDE PASSAGE (Canada)
British Columbia **3**:489
INSOLATION **11**:194 *bibliog.*
climate **5**:57
evapotranspiration **7**:314–315
INSOMNIA *see* SLEEP
INSPECTOR GENERAL, THE (play) **11**:194
Gogol, Nikolai **9**:225
INSTALLMENT PLAN **11**:194 *bibliog.*
consumer credit **5**:225
finance company **8**:92
INSTAMATIC CAMERA **4**:56 *illus.*
INSTANT CAMERA *see* POLAROID CAMERA
INSTANT FOODS
food technology **8**:213
INSTANT REPLAY *see* VIDEO RECORDING
INSTINCT **11**:194–195 *bibliog., illus.*
animal behavior **2**:13
animal courtship and mating **2**:20–22
imprinting **11**:68–69
insect **11**:191
Lorenz, Konrad **12**:414
McDougall, William (psychologist) **13**:14
motivation **13**:610
INSTITUT DE FRANCE **11**:195
Académie des Sciences **1**:69
INSTITUT PASTEUR *see* PASTEUR INSTITUTE
INSTITUTE FOR ADVANCED STUDY **11**:195
Flexner, Abraham **8**:163–164
Strömgren, Bengt Georg Daniel **18**:302
Veblin, Oswald **19**:529
von Neumann, John **19**:634
Yang, Chen Ning **20**:317
INSTITUTE FOR ARCHITECTURE AND URBAN STUDIES
Eisenman, Peter **7**:96
INSTITUTE OF ELECTRICAL AND ELECTRONIC ENGINEERS
electrical and electronic engineering **7**:106
INSTITUTE OF JOURNALISTS (Great Britain) **11**:195
INSTITUTE OF MANAGEMENT SCIENCES
management science **13**:107
INSTITUTE OF NAVIGATION **11**:195
INSTITUTION, SOCIAL **11**:196
functionalism (social science) **8**:360
marriage **13**:163–166
norm, social **14**:219
social structure and organization **18**:16–17
INSTITUTIONAL FEEDING *see* FOOD SERVICE SYSTEMS
INSTITUTIONAL STOCKHOLDERS *see* CORPORATION, OWNERSHIP
INSTITUTIONALIZATION **11**:196–197 *bibliog.*
INSTRUCTION OF PTAH HOTEP, THE
etiquette **7**:258
INSTRUCTION SET (computer term) **5**:160f
INSTRUCTIONAL AIDS *see* TEACHING AIDS, AUDIOVISUAL; TEACHING MACHINES
INSTRUMENTATION *see* AIRCRAFT INSTRUMENTATION; ASTRONOMICAL INSTRUMENTATION; AUTOMOTIVE INSTRUMENTATION; CHEMICAL INSTRUMENTATION; GEOLOGICAL INSTRUMENTATION; MATHEMATICAL INSTRUMENTATION; MEDICAL INSTRUMENTATION; METEOROLOGICAL INSTRUMENTATION; OCEANOGRAPHIC INSTRUMENTATION; OPTICAL INSTRUMENTATION
INSTRUMENTS, MUSICAL *see* MUSICAL INSTRUMENTS
INSULATING MATERIALS **11**:197
aluminum **1**:319
kapok **12**:25
perlite **15**:172
INSULATOR, ELECTRICAL **11**:197 *bibliog., table*
See also CONDUCTION, ELECTRIC; SEMICONDUCTOR
dielectric **6**:161
INSULIN **11**:197–198 *bibliog.*
Abel, John J. **1**:55
Banting, Sir Frederick G. **3**:71
Best, Charles **3**:228
diabetes **6**:148–149
diabetes mellitus **11**:198
genetic engineering **9**:84–85; **9**:85
glucagon **9**:211
glucose tolerance test **9**:211
growth **9**:379
hormone, animal **10**:235; **10**:236 *table;* **10**:237
hypoglycemia **10**:351
Jerusalem artichoke **11**:402
MacLeod, John James Rickard **13**:33
metabolism **13**:327
pancreas **15**:58
shock therapy **17**:279
structure
Sanger, Frederick **17**:64
synthesis **11**:198
INSULL, SAMUEL **11**:198 *bibliog.*
INSURANCE **11**:198–199 *bibliog.*
actuary **1**:91
Blue Cross **3**:342
Blue Shield **3**:343
fire insurance **8**:102
floods and flood control **8**:168
health-care systems **10**:87–88
history **11**:199
life insurance **12**:329–330
Lloyd's of London **12**:384
no-fault insurance **14**:207
savings and loan association **17**:100
social security **18**:14–16
unemployment insurance **19**:383–384
INTAGLIO (art) **11**:199 *bibliog.*
cameo **4**:54
etching **7**:248–249
graphic arts **9**:291
Hayter, Stanley William **10**:84
onyx **14**:396
INTAGLIO (printing) **11**:199–200 *bibliog.*
engraving **7**:205–206
gravure **11**:199
line intaglio **11**:199
platemaking **15**:357
printing **15**:551
INTEGER **11**:200
arithmetic **2**:158
induction, mathematical **11**:151
magic square **13**:51
number **14**:292–293
number theory **14**:293–294
prime number **15**:542–543
rational number **16**:92
zero **20**:361
INTEGRAL CALCULUS **11**:200–201 *bibliog., illus.*
calculus **4**:24
Cavalieri, Bonaventura **4**:220
Eudoxus of Cnidus **7**:263
Fourier analysis **8**:254
Fredholm, Erik Ivar **8**:294
infinitesimal (mathematics) **11**:168
Lebesgue, Henri Léon **12**:267
Leibniz, Gottfried Wilhelm von **12**:276
mathematics, history of **13**:225
Newton, Sir Isaac **14**:173
INTEGRALISM
Sorokin, Pitirim A. **18**:69
INTEGRATED CIRCUIT **11**:201–202 *bibliog., illus.*
calculator, electronic **4**:23
computer **5**:160b–160c; **5**:160d; **5**:160g; **5**:160h
computer-aided design and computer-aided manufacturing **5**:160k–160L
computer industry **5**:160o
computer memory **5**:161
electromagnetic pulse **7**:116
microelectronics **13**:385
Noyce, Robert **14**:277
printed circuit **15**:550
rectifier **16**:110–111
semiconductor **17**:196–197
transistor **19**:271–272
INTEGRATION, RACIAL **11**:202–203 *bibliog.*
Alexander v. *Holmes County (Miss.) Board of Education* **1**:275
Anderson, Marian **1**:402
apartheid **2**:74
black Americans **3**:309–311
Black Muslims **3**:317
Brown v. *Board of Education of Topeka, Kansas* **3**:517
busing, school **3**:589–590
civil rights **5**:13
Civil Rights Acts **5**:13
Clark, Kenneth B. **5**:39
Coleman Report **5**:100
Coloureds **5**:123
Congress of Racial Equality **5**:184
Heart of Atlanta Motel, Inc. v. *United States* **10**:95
Jackson, Jesse L. **11**:343
Jim Crow laws **11**:418
land-grant colleges **12**:178
Little Rock (Arkansas) **12**:373
Maryland **13**:193
Mississippi **13**:473
Montgomery (Alabama) **13**:556
Morgan v. *Virginia* **13**:579
pacifism and nonviolent movements **15**:10
Plessy v. *Ferguson* **15**:368
SNCC **17**:384
South Carolina **18**:101
Southern Christian Leadership Conference **18**:112
Texas **19**:134
United States, history of the **19**:452; **19**:457; **19**:459 *illus.*
Wallace, George **20**:14
Washington, Booker T. **20**:39
INTELLIGENCE **11**:203–204 *bibliog.*
ape **2**:76
artificial intelligence **2**:221
behavioral genetics **3**:170
blenny **3**:330
carnivore **4**:157
cat **4**:196
child development **4**:348–349
chimpanzee **4**:359
cognitive psychology **5**:94–95
dolphin **6**:228
educational psychology **7**:66
Galton, Sir Francis **9**:23
infancy **11**:163

INTELLIGENCE (cont.)
Jensen, Arthur **11**:396
mental retardation **13**:302
occupational success factors **11**:203
psychosis **15**:602
schizophrenia **17**:123
Shockley, William Bradford **17**:279
tests **11**:203–204
Binet, Alfred **3**:258
Burt, Sir Cyril **3**:581
controversy **11**:203–204
psychological measurement **15**:592–593
psychology, history of **15**:597–598
range **11**:203
Stanford-Binet test **18**:217–218
Terman, Lewis **19**:116
Thorndike, Edward L. **19**:179
twins, identical **11**:204
viewpoints **11**:203–204
INTELLIGENCE OPERATIONS **11**:204–205 *bibliog.*
balloon **3**:52
Central Intelligence Agency **4**:254
counterintelligence **11**:204–205
cryptology **5**:371–373
espionage **7**:243–244
Federal Bureau of Investigation **8**:40–41
KGB **12**:64
military warning and detection systems **13**:421–422
National Security Agency **14**:45–46
organizations **11**:205
SAMOS **17**:47
Secret Service **17**:181
U-2 **19**:369
wiretapping **20**:183
World War II **20**:266; **20**:272
INTELSAT (International Telecommunications Satellite Organization) **11**:205 *bibliog.*
communications satellite **5**:144–145 *illus.*
Early Bird **7**:8–9
satellite, artificial **17**:87 *illus.*
space exploration **18**:123
INTENDANT **11**:206 *bibliog.*
INTER-AMERICAN HIGHWAY
Ciudad Juárez **5**:9
INTER-AMERICAN UNIVERSITY OF PUERTO RICO **11**:206
INTER-PARLIAMENTARY UNION **11**:206
INTERACTIONS, FUNDAMENTAL *see* FUNDAMENTAL INTERACTIONS
INTERCALATION COMPOUNDS **11**:206
INTERCONTINENTAL BALLISTIC MISSILE see BALLISTIC MISSILE
INTERCONTINENTAL HOTEL (Paris) **10**:261 *illus.*
INTEREST **11**:206–207 *bibliog.*, *illus.*
banking systems **3**:69
compound interest **11**:206–207 *illus.*
discount rate **6**:189
exponential functions **7**:339
Federal Reserve System **8**:42
government regulation **11**:207
mathematical tables **13**:221
monetary policy **13**:524
monetary theory **13**:525
usury **19**:491
INTEREST TEST *see* PSYCHOLOGICAL MEASUREMENT
INTERFACE (computer term) **5**:160h
INTERFERENCE (physics) **11**:207–209 *bibliog.*, *illus.*
light **12**:334 *illus.*
optics **14**:411–412
Young, Thomas **20**:334
INTERFEROMETER **11**:209–210 *bibliog.*, *illus.*
Michelson, Albert Abraham, inventor **13**:375–376
Michelson-Morley experiment **13**:376
radio astronomy **16**:52–53
star **18**:222
tracking station **19**:262
INTERFERON **11**:210 *bibliog.*
AIDS **1**:201
biopharmaceuticals **3**:275
genetic engineering **9**:84–85
virus **19**:615
INTERIOR, UNITED STATES DEPARTMENT OF THE **11**:210
flag **8**:148 *illus.*
Indian Affairs, Bureau of **11**:94
National Forest System **14**:32
national parks system
national parks **14**:36–39
secretary of the interior
see articles of specific presidents, e.g., COOLIDGE, CALVIN; ROOSEVELT, THEODORE; etc.; names of specific secretaries of the interior
United States Geological Survey **19**:462
INTERIOR DECORATION
See also DECORATIVE ARTS
interior design **11**:210
INTERIOR DESIGN **11**:210–214 *bibliog.*, *illus.*
See also DECORATIVE ARTS
Adam, Robert **1**:92
aesthetic elements **11**:210–211
ancient interior design **11**:211
antique collecting **2**:65–68
Art Deco **2**:207–208; **11**:214
Art Nouveau **11**:214
Arts and Crafts movement **2**:225
baroque art and architecture **2**:88–91; **11**:212–213
Biedermeier style **3**:247
Cameron, Charles **4**:59
Clérisseau, Charles Louis **5**:51
colonial styles in North America **5**:109–111
cornice **5**:269
Cuvilliés, François **5**:399
design process **11**:211
Empire style **7**:158–159
functional considerations **11**:210
furniture **8**:373–380
Georgian style **11**:213–214
Hagia Sophia **10**:10
Lalique, René **12**:171–172
medieval interior design **11**:211 212
modern architecture **13**:490–493
modern design **11**:214
Morris, William **13**:589
mosaic **13**:593
neoclassicism **11**:213–214
Poiret, Paul **15**:381
postmodern architecture **15**:463–464
Primaticcio, Francesco **15**:542
Regency style **16**:126
Renaissance design **11**:212
rococo style **11**:212–214; **16**:263–265
styles of Louis XIII-XVI **18**:311
Tiffany, Louis Comfort **19**:196
Urban, Joseph **19**:480
Versailles, Palace of **19**:561
White House **20**:137–138
INTERIOR MONOLOGUE *see* STREAM OF CONSCIOUSNESS
INTERJECTION
parts of speech **15**:101
INTERLAKEN (Switzerland) **11**:214
map (46° 41′N 7° 51′E) **18**:394
INTERLEAVED MEMORY
computer memory **5**:161
INTERLINGUA *see* LANGUAGES, ARTIFICIAL
INTERLUDE **11**:214 *bibliog.*
INTERMEDIATE RANGE NUCLEAR FORCE TALKS **2**:178
INTERMEDIN
endocrine system **7**:169
hormones **10**:236 *table*
pigment, skin **15**:300
pituitary gland **15**:322
INTERMENT *see* BURIAL
INTERMEZZO **11**:214
interlude **11**:214
INTERMOLECULAR ATTRACTION
aggregation **1**:184
INTERMOLECULAR FORCES **11**:215 *bibliog.*
dispersion forces **11**:215
hydrogen bond **10**:340; **11**:215
intermolecular interactions **11**:215
molecule **13**:508
INTERNAL AUDIT *see* AUDIT
INTERNAL-COMBUSTION ENGINE **11**:215–218 *bibliog.*, *illus.*
Benz, Karl **3**:206
carburetor **4**:140–141
Daimler, Gottlieb **6**:7
Diesel, Rudolf, inventor **6**:163
diesel engine **6**:163 *illus.*
engine **7**:177
flywheel **8**:191–192
heat engine **11**:215
history **11**:215
Lenoir, Jean Joseph Étienne **12**:285
lubrication **12**:448 *illus.*
Maybach, Wilhelm **13**:246
moped **13**:572
motorboat **13**:612 *illus.*
motorcycle **13**:612–614 *illus.*
Niepce, Joseph Nicéphore **14**:185
octane number **14**:347
operation **11**:215–218
Otto, Nikolaus August, inventor **14**:462
Papin, Denis **15**:71
piston engine **8**:191–192
systems **11**:215–218
cooling **5**:241–242
exhaust **7**:331–332
ignition **11**:36–38
transmission **19**:275–276
technology, history of **19**:66–67
trucking industry **19**:314
Wankel engine **20**:23–24 *illus.*
INTERNAL MEDICINE
medicine **13**:272
medicine, education in **13**:273
INTERNAL REVENUE SERVICE **11**:218 *bibliog.*
See also INCOME TAX
Tax Court, U.S. **19**:45
Treasury, U.S. Department of the **19**:285
Washington, D.C. **20**:41 *map*
INTERNAL SECURITY ACT OF 1950 *see* McCARRAN ACT
INTERNATIONAL, SOCIALIST **11**:218 *bibliog.*
Bebel, August **3**:149–150
Jaurès, Jean **11**:385
Liebknecht (family) **12**:324
Marx, Karl **13**:182
socialism **18**:21–22
INTERNATIONAL AMATEUR ATHLETIC FEDERATION
Pan-American Games **15**:53
track and field **19**:259
INTERNATIONAL ANTI-SLAVERY SOCIETY
slavery **17**:357
INTERNATIONAL ASSOCIATION OF ACADEMIES
scientific associations **17**:146
INTERNATIONAL ASSOCIATION OF AUTOMOBILE CLUBS
roads and highways **16**:238
INTERNATIONAL ASSOCIATION OF GEODESY
Vening Meinesz, Felix **19**:545
INTERNATIONAL ASSOCIATION OF MACHINISTS AND AEROSPACE WORKERS **11**:218 *bibliog.*
INTERNATIONAL ATOMIC ENERGY AGENCY **11**:218–219 *bibliog.*
INTERNATIONAL BANK FOR RECONSTRUCTION AND DEVELOPMENT *see* WORLD BANK
INTERNATIONAL BOWLING BOARD
lawn bowls **12**:248
INTERNATIONAL BROTHERHOOD OF ELECTRICAL WORKERS *see* ELECTRICAL WORKERS, INTERNATIONAL BROTHERHOOD OF
INTERNATIONAL BROTHERHOOD OF TEAMSTERS, CHAUFFEURS, WAREHOUSEMEN, AND HELPERS OF AMERICA *see* TEAMSTERS, CHAUFFEURS, WAREHOUSEMEN, AND HELPERS OF AMERICA, INTERNATIONAL BROTHERHOOD OF
INTERNATIONAL BUREAU OF WEIGHTS AND MEASURES **11**:219
INTERNATIONAL BUSINESS MACHINES CORPORATION
computer **5**:160a
computer industry **5**:160n–160o
Hollerith, Herman **10**:204
Watson (family) **20**:67
INTERNATIONAL CANOE FEDERATION
canoeing and kayaking **4**:114
INTERNATIONAL CENTER FOR THEATER RESEARCH
Brook, Peter **3**:509
INTERNATIONAL CHIROPRACTOR'S ASSOCIATION
chiropractic **4**:397
INTERNATIONAL CIVIL AVIATION ORGANIZATION **11**:219
air law **1**:209
aviation **2**:375
INTERNATIONAL COMMUNICATIONS AGENCY see UNITED STATES INFORMATION AGENCY
INTERNATIONAL CONFEDERATION OF FREE TRADE UNIONS **11**:219
World Federation of Trade Unions **20**:218
INTERNATIONAL CONGRESS OF PHYSICS, 1900
physics, history of **15**:283
INTERNATIONAL COUNCIL OF SCIENTIFIC UNIONS (ICSU)
scientific associations **17**:146
INTERNATIONAL COURT OF JUSTICE **11**:219 *bibliog.*
Hague conferences **10**:11
international law **11**:221
jurisdiction **11**:219
members **11**:219
United Nations **19**:412–413
INTERNATIONAL CRIMINAL POLICE ORGANIZATION *see* INTERPOL
INTERNATIONAL DATE LINE **11**:220 *map*
longitude **12**:409
INTERNATIONAL DEVELOPMENT ASSOCIATION **11**:220
World Bank **20**:218
INTERNATIONAL ENVIRONMENTAL PROTECTION ACT OF 1983
conservation **5**:203
INTERNATIONAL FALLS (Minnesota) **11**:220
map (48° 36′N 93° 25′W) **13**:453
INTERNATIONAL FINANCE CORPORATION **11**:220
World Bank **20**:218
INTERNATIONAL FLAG CODE **17**:300–301 *illus.*
INTERNATIONAL GEOGRAPHICAL UNION
geographical societies **9**:100
INTERNATIONAL GEOPHYSICAL YEAR **11**:220 *bibliog.*
Antarctica **2**:45
Fuchs, Sir Vivian **8**:351–352
geophysics **9**:108
International Council of Scientific Unions **11**:220
National Aeronautics and Space Administration **14**:28
Ross Dependency (Antarctica) **16**:318
satellite, artificial **17**:85
scientific Earth exploration **11**:220
space exploration **18**:119
INTERNATIONAL GOVERNMENT
government **9**:269
League of Nations **12**:257–258
United Nations **19**:412–415
INTERNATIONAL GREYHOUND RACING ASSOCIATION
dog racing **6**:222
INTERNATIONAL HYDROLOGICAL DECADE **11**:220 *bibliog.*
INTERNATIONAL ICE HOCKEY FEDERATION
ice hockey **11**:12
INTERNATIONAL ICE PATROL **11**:220
Coast Guard, U.S. **5**:80
iceberg **11**:15
iceberg position prediction **11**:220
INTERNATIONAL INSTITUTE FOR CONSERVATION OF HISTORIC AND ARTISTIC WORKS
art conservation and restoration **2**:205
INTERNATIONAL LABOR ORGANIZATION **11**:220 *bibliog.*
INTERNATIONAL LADIES' GARMENT WORKERS' UNION **11**:221 *bibliog.*
clothing industry **5**:65
Dubinsky, David **6**:287
INTERNATIONAL LANGUAGE *see* LANGUAGES, ARTIFICIAL
INTERNATIONAL LAW **11**:221–222 *bibliog.*
annexation **2**:33
arbitration **2**:110
blockade **3**:334
Bluntschli, Johann Kaspar **3**:347
Calvo Doctrine
Calvo, Carlos **4**:49
citizenship **4**:447
conservation **5**:203
contraband **5**:231
embargo **7**:151
extraterritoriality **7**:346
foreign policy **8**:225–226
genocide **9**:93
Grotius, Hugo **9**:372
Hague conferences **10**:11
Hudson, Manley Ottmer **10**:289
human rights **10**:298
immunity **11**:59
International Court of Justice **11**:219
intervention **11**:230

law **12**:243
mediation **13**:264
neutrality **14**:108
piracy **15**:312
political science **15**:403
pollutants, chemical **15**:411
Pueblo Incident **15**:614
Pufendorf, Samuel, Baron von **15**:616
right of asylum **16**:222
right of search **16**:222
sanctions **17**:58
sanctuary **17**:59
Sea, Law of the **17**:167–168
seas, freedom of the **17**:175–176
sovereignty **18**:113
space law **18**:132
territorial waters **19**:121
treaty **19**:285–286
United Nations **19**:412–413
war **20**:25
Geneva conventions **9**:91
prisoner of war **15**:555–556
war crimes **20**:25
INTERNATIONAL LONGSHOREMEN'S UNIONS **11**:222 *bibliog.*
Bridges, Harry **3**:484–485
containerization **5**:227
INTERNATIONAL MAIZE AND WHEAT IMPROVEMENT CENTER
green revolution **9**:348
INTERNATIONAL MONETARY FUND **11**:222 *bibliog.*
balance of payments **3**:31–32
Bretton Woods Conference **3**:475
exchange rate **7**:327
INTERNATIONAL NUCLEAR FUEL CYCLE EVALUATION
breeder reactor **3**:472
INTERNATIONAL OLYMPIC COMMITTEE (IOC)
Olympic Games **14**:384
INTERNATIONAL PHONETIC ALPHABET
phonetics **15**:252
INTERNATIONAL PLANNED PARENTHOOD FEDERATION
birth control **3**:295
Sanger, Margaret **17**:65
INTERNATIONAL PRACTICAL TEMPERATURE SCALE
measurement **13**:255 *illus.*
INTERNATIONAL PRESS INSTITUTE **11**:222
INTERNATIONAL PSYCHO-ANALYTICAL ASSOCIATION
Freud, Sigmund **8**:329
Jung, Carl **11**:467
INTERNATIONAL RELATIONS *see* FOREIGN POLICY
INTERNATIONAL RESEARCH COUNCIL (IRC)
scientific associations **17**:146
INTERNATIONAL RICE RESEARCH INSTITUTE (IRRI)
green revolution **9**:349
INTERNATIONAL ROAD FEDERATION
roads and highways **16**:238
INTERNATIONAL SHOOTING UNION (ISU)
shooting **17**:282
INTERNATIONAL SKATEBOARD ASSOCIATION
skateboarding **17**:332–333
INTERNATIONAL STYLE (Bauhaus art) **2**:136 *illus.*; **11**:222–223 *bibliog.*, *illus.*
architecture **2**:136
Art Deco **2**:207
Asplund, Erik Gunnar **2**:263
Bauhaus **3**:129–130
Belluschi, Pietro **3**:192
Blake, Peter **3**:325
Breuer, Marcel **3**:475
Fry, Edwin Maxwell **8**:350
German art and architecture **9**:128
Hitchcock, Henry-Russell **10**:186
Hood, Raymond **10**:225
interior design **11**:214
Johnson, Philip **11**:434–435
Lake Shore Drive Apartments (Mies van der Rohe) **2**:200 *illus.*
Markelius, Sven Gottfrid **13**:159
Mendelsohn, Eric **13**:295
Mies van der Rohe, Ludwig **13**:415
modern architecture **13**:491–493
Neutra, Richard **14**:107–108
Niemeyer, Oscar **14**:185
O'Gorman, Juan **14**:355
Saarinen, Eero **17**:4
Scharoun, Hans **17**:117
Smithson, Alison and Peter **17**:372
Stone, Edward Durell **18**:280
Stubbins, Hugh **18**:306
INTERNATIONAL STYLE (Gothic art) **11**:223 *bibliog.*
Broederlam, Melchior **3**:501
Gentile da Fabriano **9**:94
Gothic art and architecture **9**:261
Limbourg Brothers **12**:343
Lorenzo Monaco **12**:415
Master Francke **13**:215
painting **15**:19
Pisanello, Antonio **15**:316
Reims Cathedral **16**:131
Renaissance art and architecture **16**:154
Sassetta **17**:84
INTERNATIONAL SYSTEM OF UNITS
measurement **13**:254
metric system **13**:347
units, physical **19**:465–467 *tables*
weights and measures **20**:94
INTERNATIONAL TELECOMMUNICATIONS SATELLITE ORGANIZATION *see* INTELSAT (International Telecommunications Satellite) (artificial satellite)
INTERNATIONAL TENNIS FEDERATION
tennis **19**:109
INTERNATIONAL TRADE **11**:223–224 *bibliog.*
See also FREE TRADE
balance of payments **3**:31–32
bill of exchange **3**:251
C.I.F. **4**:430
consul (modern government official) **5**:225
contraband **5**:231
customs union **5**:398
dumping **11**:223
embargo **7**:151
Europe **7**:279–280
factor endowments **11**:223
foreign policy **8**:225–226
free port **8**:294
General Agreement on Tariffs and Trade **9**:77
government regulation **11**:223–224
history **11**:224
clipper ship **5**:60–61
Dilmun **6**:176
East India Company, British **7**:31
East India Company, Dutch **7**:31–32
East India Company, French **7**:32
Harris, Townsend **10**:58
Industrial Revolution **11**:159
Jay's Treaty **11**:387
mercantilism **13**:303
Middle Ages **13**:394–395 *map*
Open Door Policy **14**:398
piracy **15**:312–313
Silk Road **17**:308
spice trade **18**:180–181
tariff acts **19**:36–37
Indian Ocean **11**:104–106
international law **11**:221–222
letter of credit **12**:299
Massachusetts **13**:211
Middle East **13**:400
most-favored-nation status **13**:605
neutrality **14**:108
Ohlin, Bertil **14**:363
organizations
Council for Mutual Economic Assistance **5**:310
European Economic Community **7**:299–300
European Free Trade Association **7**:300–301
Export-Import Bank **7**:340
International Trade Commission, U.S. **11**:224
Latin American Integration Association **12**:228
Organization for Economic Cooperation and Development **14**:440
Organization of Petroleum Exporting Countries **14**:440
World Bank **20**:218
quota **16**:28
rice **16**:207–208
ship **17**:269
shipping route **17**:277
tariff **19**:36
wheat **20**:126
INTERNATIONAL TRADE COMMISSION, U.S. **11**:224 *bibliog.*
INTERNATIONAL TYPOGRAPHICAL UNION **11**:224–225 *bibliog.*
INTERNATIONAL ULTRAVIOLET EXPLORER (artificial satellite)
space exploration **18**:123
ultraviolet astronomy **19**:379
INTERNATIONAL UNION OF ELECTRICAL, RADIO AND MACHINE WORKERS *see* ELECTRICAL, RADIO AND MACHINE WORKERS, INTERNATIONAL UNION OF
INTERNATIONAL UNION OF GEODESY AND GEOPHYSICS
geophysics **9**:108
Vening Meinesz, Felix **19**:545
INTERNATIONAL UNION OF PURE AND APPLIED CHEMISTRY *see* CHEMICAL NOMENCLATURE
INTERNATIONAL UNION FOR THE CONSERVATION OF NATURE AND NATURAL RESOURCES
endangered species
Red Data Book **16**:113
INTERNATIONAL WHALING COMMISSION
whale **20**:122
whaling **20**:123
INTERNATIONAL WORKERS' DAY *see* MAY DAY
INTERNATIONAL WORKINGMEN'S ASSOCIATION
International, Socialist **11**:218
socialism **18**:21 *illus.*
INTERNATIONAL YEARS OF THE QUIET SUN **11**:225
INTERNATIONAL YOUTH HOSTEL FEDERATION
youth hostel **20**:337
INTERPLANETARY MONITORING PLATFORM *see* IMP (artificial satellite)
INTERPOL **11**:225 *bibliog.*
INTERPOLATION **11**:225 *illus.*
Hermite, Charles **10**:143
mathematical tables **13**:221
numerical analysis **14**:294–295
theory
Gelfond, Aleksandr Osipovich **9**:69
INTERPRETATION OF DREAMS, THE (book) **11**:225; **15**:590 *illus.*
Freud, Sigmund **8**:329
INTERPRETER (computer program) **11**:225
compiler **5**:157
computer **5**:160h
computer languages **5**:160o
computer software **5**:164
INTERSTATE COMMERCE
common carrier **5**:138
Constitution of the United States **5**:216–217
Cooley v. *Board of Port Wardens* **5**:240
government regulation **9**:270–271
integration, racial
Heart of Atlanta Motel, Inc. v. *United States* **10**:95
Morgan v. *Virginia* **13**:579
Interstate Commerce Commission **11**:225
Leisy v. *Hardin* **12**:279
Mann Act **13**:124
Munn v. *Illinois* **13**:643
National Labor Relations Board v. *Jones & Laughlin Steel Corporation* **14**:35
Parker v. *Brown* **15**:91
pure food and drug laws **15**:628–629
Swift and Company v. *United States* **18**:390
United States v. *Darby* **19**:465
United States v. *E. C. Knight Company* **19**:465
INTERSTATE COMMERCE COMMISSION **11**:225 *bibliog.*
common carrier **5**:138
government regulation **9**:270–271
railroad **16**:72; **16**:73; **16**:76
trucking industry **19**:314–315
United States, history of the **19**:451
INTERSTATE HIGHWAY SYSTEM **11**:225
roads and highways **16**:238
transportation **19**:282
turnpike **19**:351
weight limits
trucking industry **19**:315
INTERSTELLAR DUST *see* INTERSTELLAR MATTER
INTERSTELLAR GAS
gas **11**:225–228
Struve, Otto **18**:304
INTERSTELLAR MATTER **11**:225–228 *bibliog.*, *illus.*
astrochemistry **2**:270
cosmology (astronomy) **5**:284–289
extinction **7**:341
Galaxy, The **9**:10
gegenschein **9**:67
globule **9**:209
halo, galactic **10**:25
interstellar reddening **11**:229
nebula **14**:74–75
neutron star **14**:109
Olbers, Heinrich **14**:373
Olbers's paradox **14**:373
origin of life **12**:327
radio astronomy **16**:50
stellar evolution **18**:250–252
stellar spectrum **18**:252
Strömgren spheres
Strömgren, Bengt Georg Daniel **18**:302
supernova **18**:352
Trumpler, Robert Julius **19**:320
INTERSTELLAR REDDENING **11**:229
extinction **7**:341
interstellar matter **11**:229
Trumpler, Robert Julius **19**:320
INTERSTITIAL CELL-STIMULATING HORMONE
sex hormones **17**:226
INTERTIDAL LIFE **11**:229–230 *bibliog.*, *illus.*
animal life **11**:229–230
Atlantic Coast **11**:230
ecology **11**:229–230
littoral zone **11**:130
marine biology **11**:229–230
ocean and sea **11**:229–230
Pacific Coast **11**:229–230
plant life **11**:229–230
swamp, marsh, and bog **18**:377–378
Ulothrix **19**:377
zones **11**:230
INTERVENTION **11**:230
civil law **11**:230
foreign policy **8**:226
international law **11**:230
INTESTACY (law)
escheat **7**:237
heir **10**:109
inheritance **11**:177
next of kin **14**:175
will **20**:153
INTESTINE **1**:54 *illus.*; **7**:328 *illus.*; **11**:230–231 *bibliog.*, *illus.*
appendix **2**:87–88
bacteria
Escherichia **7**:237
circulatory system **4**:440 *illus.*
defecation **11**:231
digestion, human **6**:171–172
digestive system **6**:174
diseases and disorders
celiac disease **4**:231
coccidiosis **5**:85
colitis **5**:102
constipation **5**:212
diarrhea **6**:153
diverticulosis **6**:202
dysentery **6**:320
enteritis **7**:208
indigestion **11**:144
drug **6**:275
drug absorption **6**:275 *illus.*
duodenum **6**:302
gallbladder **9**:17
ileus **11**:40
large intestine **11**:230–231
lymphatic system **12**:475
small intestine **11**:230
INTHANON MOUNTAIN
map (18° 35′N 98° 29′E) **19**:139
INTOLERABLE ACTS **11**:231–232 *bibliog.*
North, Lord **14**:223–224
United States, history of the **19**:440
INTOLERANCE (film) **9**:363 *illus.*
INTRACOASTAL WATERWAY **11**:232
INTRAUTERINE DEVICE
birth control **3**:293–294
INTROJECTION (psychology)
defense mechanisms **6**:83
INTROSPECTION **11**:232
human behavior investigations **11**:232
Titchener, Edward B. **19**:212
INTROVERSION *see* EXTRAVERSION-INTROVERSION (psychology)
INTRUSIVE ROCK *see* IGNEOUS ROCK
INTUITION **11**:232
Bergson, Henri **3**:211
ethics **7**:250
logic **12**:396
mathematics, history of **13**:226
INTUTU (Peru)
map (3° 39′S 74° 44′W) **15**:193
INUIT CIRCUMPOLAR CONFERENCE **2**:144

INUPIK LANGUAGE
  Eskimo **7**:239
INUVIK (Northwest Territories) **11**:259 *illus.*
  map (68° 25′N 133° 30′W) **14**:258
INVALIDES, LES
  Hardouin-Mansart, Jules **10**:47
INVARIANT (mathematics)
  Noether, Emmy **14**:212
INVENTION **11**:232–233 *bibliog.*
  See also names of individual inventors, e.g., EDISON, THOMAS ALVA; WHITNEY, ELI; etc.
  patent **15**:110
  research and development **19**:60
INVERCARGILL (New Zealand) **11**:233
  map (46° 24′S 168° 21′E) **14**:158
INVERNESS (Scotland) **11**:233
  map (57° 27′N 4° 15′W) **19**:403
INVERNESS (county in Scotland) **11**:233
INVERNESS (Florida)
  map (28° 51′N 82° 20′W) **8**:172
INVERNESS (Nova Scotia)
  map (46° 14′N 61° 18′W) **14**:269
INVERSE SQUARE LAW **11**:233
INVERSION (meteorology) **11**:233–234 *bibliog.*
  cyclone and anticyclone **5**:405
  frontal inversion **11**:234
  lapse rate **12**:206
  nocturnal inversions **11**:233–234
  pollution, environmental **15**:415
INVERTEBRATE **11**:234–237 *bibliog.*
  See also names of specific invertebrates, e.g., SEA ANEMONE; SNAIL; etc.
  aging **1**:185–186
  animal **2**:11
  biological locomotion **3**:266
  body covering **11**:236
  classification, biological **11**:234–235
    arthropod **2**:216–218 *illus.*
    brachiopod **3**:435 *illus.*
    bryozoan **3**:530
    Cephalochordata **4**:256
    coelenterate **5**:91–92 *illus.*
    comb jelly **5**:130 *illus.*
    echinoderm **7**:37–39 *illus.*
    entoproct **7**:208
    hemichordate **10**:117–118
    mesozoan **13**:322
    metazoan **13**:335
    mollusk **13**:510–512 *illus.*
    onychophoran **14**:396
    phoronid **15**:255
    Protista **15**:577–578
    Protozoa **15**:579–581 *illus.*
    rotifer **16**:323 *illus.*
    sponge **18**:193–194 *illus.*
    tunicate **19**:334
    worm **20**:283–284 *illus.*
  fossil record **8**:243–248; **11**:234
  growth **9**:380
  hormone, animal **10**:237 *table*
  life cycle **11**:237
  maximum life span for some **12**:330 *table*
  regeneration **11**:237
  structure **11**:235–236
    circulatory system **4**:438–439 *illus.*
    ear **7**:6–7
    endocrine system **7**:168
    eye **7**:348
    skeletal system **17**:333
INVESTITURE CONTROVERSY **11**:237–238 *bibliog., illus.*; **13**:393 *illus.*
  Anselm, Saint **2**:35
  Callistus II, Pope **4**:46
  church and state **4**:424–425
  Europe, history of **7**:284
  Germany, history of **9**:149
  Gregory VII, Pope **9**:357
  Henry I, King of England **10**:124
  Henry IV, King of Germany and Holy Roman Emperor **10**:129
  Henry V, King of Germany and Holy Roman Emperor **10**:129
  Lateran councils **12**:215
  Matilda of Tuscany **13**:228
  Paschal II, Pope **15**:102
INVESTMENT *see* SAVING AND INVESTMENT
INVESTMENT BANKING **11**:238 *bibliog.*
  banking systems **3**:69
  Law, John **12**:247
INVESTMENT CASTING PROCESS *see* LOST-WAX PROCESS
INVISIBLE MAN (book) **11**:238 *bibliog.*
  Ellison, Ralph **7**:148
INYANGA MOUNTAINS
  map (18° 0′S 33° 0′E) **20**:365
INYANGANI MOUNTAIN
  map (18° 20′S 32° 50′E) **20**:365
INYO (county in California)
  map (36° 35′N 117° 25′W) **4**:31
INYOKERN (California)
  map (35° 39′N 117° 49′W) **4**:31
IO (satellite) **11**:238 *bibliog., illus.*
  Jupiter (planet) **11**:472 *illus., table*
  satellite **17**:85
  solar system **18**:49
  Voyager **19**:638
I/O DEVICES *see* INPUT-OUTPUT DEVICES
IO MOTH **3**:598–599 *illus.*
IOÁNNINA (Greece)
  map (39° 40′N 20° 50′E) **9**:325
IODINE **11**:238–239 *bibliog., illus.*
  abundances of common elements **7**:131 *table*
  element **7**:130 *table*
  endocrine system, diseases of the **7**:170
  goiter **9**:225
  Group VIIA periodic table **15**:167
  halogen, element **11**:238
  halogens **10**:25
  health science use **11**:239
  history **11**:238–239
  kelp **12**:40
  occurrence **11**:239
  properties **11**:239
  radioactive isotope medicine **13**:272
  salt (sodium chloride) **17**:37
  vitamins and minerals **19**:620–621
    Recommended Daily Allowances **19**:619 *table*
IOL (Algeria) **11**:239 *bibliog.*
IOLA (Kansas)
  map (37° 55′N 95° 24′W) **12**:18
IOLITE *see* CORDIERITE
ION EXCHANGE **11**:240
ION AND IONIZATION **11**:239–240 *bibliog., illus.*
  active transport **1**:89–90
  anion **2**:29
  carbanion **4**:132
  carbonium ion **4**:139
  cation **4**:212
  chemical nomenclature **4**:319–321
  chemical symbolism and notation **4**:322
  conduction, electric **5**:174
  dissociation **6**:198
  electrochemical equivalent **7**:112
  interstellar matter **11**:226
  ion exchange **11**:240
  ionization **11**:240 *illus.*
    Arrhenius, Svante August **2**:188
    detector, particle **6**:133–134
    discharge, electrical **6**:188
    gas, radioactivity **16**:62
    hydrogen **10**:338
    smoke detector **17**:373
  mass spectrometry **13**:204
  Nernst, Walther **14**:89
  pH **15**:217
  plasma physics **15**:345–346
  potential, electric
    biopotential **3**:275 *illus.*
    neurophysiology **14**:105–106
  salt (chemistry) **17**:37
  scintillation **17**:146
  substitution
    solid solution **18**:54
  Thomson, Sir Joseph John **19**:176
  valence **19**:503
  zwitterion **20**:384
ION PROPULSION
  rockets and missiles **16**:260
ION PUMP
  active transport **1**:89–90
IONA (Nova Scotia)
  map (45° 58′N 60° 48′W) **14**:269
IONE (Oregon)
  map (45° 30′N 119° 50′W) **14**:427
IONE (Washington)
  map (48° 45′N 117° 25′W) **20**:35
IONESCO, EUGÈNE **11**:240–241 *bibliog., illus.*
  Bald Soprano, The
    comedy **5**:132
  theater of the absurd **19**:154
IONIA (Greece) **11**:241 *bibliog.*
  cities
    Magnesia **13**:53
  Greece, ancient **9**:330–331 *map*; **9**:331
IONIA (Michigan)
  map (42° 59′N 85° 4′W) **13**:377
IONIA (county in Michigan)
  map (43° 0′N 85° 5′W) **13**:377
IONIAN ISLANDS
  map (38° 30′N 20° 30′E) **9**:325
IONIAN SEA **11**:241
  islands and island groups
    Corfu (Greece) **5**:262
    Ithaca (Greece) **11**:331
  map (39° 0′N 19° 0′E) **13**:277
  seas, gulfs, and bays
    Messina, Strait of **13**:324
IONIAN STYLE
  Greek art **9**:337–342
IONIC BOND *see* CHEMICAL BOND
IONIC ORDER **2**:131 *illus.*; **9**:335 *illus.*
  Greek architecture **9**:337
  temple **19**:96–97
IONIUM-THORIUM DATING
  radiometric age-dating **16**:66–67
IONIZATION *see* ION AND IONIZATION
IONOSPHERE **11**:241–243 *bibliog., illus.*
  Appleton, Sir Edward Victor **2**:89
  chemosphere **4**:329
  Earth, geomagnetic field of **7**:16
  National Space Development Agency **14**:46
  observational evidence **11**:242
  origin and description **11**:241–242
  plasma physics **15**:345–346
  radio broadcasting **11**:242
  Van Allen radiation belts **19**:510
IORA **11**:243
IORGA, NICOLAE **11**:243 *bibliog.*
IOSCO (county in Michigan)
  map (44° 20′N 83° 35′W) **13**:377
IOTA (letter)
  I (letter) **11**:3
IOWA **11**:243–248 *bibliog., illus., map*
  agriculture **11**:246; **11**:247–248
  cities
    Cedar Rapids **4**:229
    Council Bluffs **5**:310
    Davenport **6**:46
    Des Moines **6**:123–124
    Dubuque **6**:289
    Iowa City **11**:248
    Sioux City **17**:326
  climate **11**:243; **11**:245
  economic activity **11**:246–247 *illus.*
  education **11**:245–246
    Drake University **6**:257
    Grinnell College **9**:366
    Iowa, state universities of **11**:248
  flag **11**:243 *illus.*
  government and politics **11**:247
  history **11**:247–248
    Dubuque, Julien **6**:289
  land and topography **11**:243–244 *map*; **11**:247–248
  map (42° 15′N 93° 15′W) **19**:419
  people **11**:245–246
    Omaha **14**:385
    Sauk **17**:96
  resources **11**:245
  rivers, lakes, and waterways **11**:243
  seal, state **11**:243 *illus.*
  vegetation and animal life **11**:245
IOWA (American Indians) **11**:116 *illus.*; **11**:248 *bibliog.*
IOWA (county in Iowa)
  map (41° 38′N 92° 5′W) **11**:244
IOWA (county in Wisconsin)
  map (43° 0′N 90° 8′W) **20**:185
IOWA, STATE UNIVERSITIES OF **11**:248
IOWA CITY (Iowa) **11**:248
  map (41° 40′N 91° 32′W) **11**:244
IOWA FALLS (Iowa)
  map (42° 31′N 93° 16′W) **11**:244
IOWA PARK (Texas)
  map (33° 57′N 98° 40′W) **19**:129
IOWA RIVER
  map (41° 10′N 91° 2′W) **11**:244
IPANEMA (Brazi) **18**:91 *illus.*
IPECAC **11**:248
IPHIGENIA **11**:248
IPITÁ (Bolivia)
  map (19° 20′S 63° 32′W) **3**:366
IPIUTAK **11**:248 *bibliog.*
IPOH (Malaysia)
  map (4° 35′N 101° 5′E) **13**:84
IPOLY RIVER
  map (47° 49′N 18° 52′E) **10**:307
IPSWICH (Australia)
  map (27° 36′S 152° 46′E) **2**:328
IPSWICH (England)
  map (52° 4′N 1° 10′E) **19**:403
IPSWICH (Massachusetts)
  map (42° 41′N 70° 50′W) **13**:206
IPSWICH (South Dakota)
  map (45° 27′N 99° 2′W) **18**:103
IPSWICH RIVER
  map (42° 42′N 70° 48′W) **13**:206
IQ (intelligence quotient) *see* INTELLIGENCE
IQBAL, MUHAMMAD **11**:249 *bibliog.*
IQUIQUE (Chile)
  map (20° 13′S 70° 10′W) **4**:355
IQUITOS (Peru)
  climate **15**:193 *table*
  map (3° 46′S 73° 15′W) **15**:193
IRA *see* IRISH REPUBLICAN ARMY
IRA (Texas)
  map (32° 35′N 101° 0′W) **19**:129
IRAAN (Texas)
  map (30° 54′N 101° 54′W) **19**:129
IRACOUBO (French Guiana)
  map (5° 29′N 53° 13′W) **8**:311
IRÁKLION (Greece) **11**:249
  map (35° 20′N 25° 9′E) **9**:325
IRAN **11**:249–253 *bibliog., illus., map, table*
  agriculture and fishing **11**:252
  archaeology
    Behistun **3**:171
    Dur-Untash **6**:302
    Ecbatana **7**:37
    Fertile Crescent **8**:60
    Hasanlu **10**:65
    Luristan **12**:467
    Pasargadae **14**:101
    Persepolis **15**:180
    Susa **18**:370
    Tepe Yahya **19**:114
  art
    Islamic art and architecture **11**:297
    mosque **13**:601–602 *illus.*
    museums, art **13**:658
    Persian art and architecture **15**:183–187 *illus.*
  cities
    Abadan **1**:51
    Hamadan **10**:26
    Isfahan **11**:287
    Mashhad **13**:196
    Qum **16**:28
    Shiraz **17**:277
    Tabriz **19**:5
    Tehran **19**:72–73
  climate **11**:250–251 *table*
  economic activity **11**:252–253 *illus.*
  education **11**:251
    Middle Eastern universities **13**:410–412 *table*
  flag **11**:249 *illus.*
  history **11**:252–253
    See also PERSIA, ANCIENT
    Abbas I **1**:52
    Bani-Sadr, Abolhassan **3**:66
    Central Treaty Organization **4**:255
    Cyrus the Great, King of Persia **5**:410
    Elam **7**:101–102
    Iranian hostage crisis **11**:253–254
    Iraq **11**:256
    Khomeini, Ayatollah Ruhollah **12**:67–68
    Middle East, history of the **13**:402–408; **13**:403–410
    Mosaddeq, Muhammad **13**:593
    Muhammad Reza Shah Pahlavi (1919–80) **13**:634
    Nadir Shah **14**:5
    Nasr al-Din Shah **14**:24
    Reza Shah Pahlavi (1878–1944) **16**:192
    Sassanians **17**:83–84
    Seljuks **17**:192
    Shapur I, King of Persia **17**:241
    Shapur II, King of Persia **17**:241
    sword (18th century) **18**:398 *illus.*
    Tehran Conference **19**:73
    Timur **19**:204
    Timurids (dynasty) **19**:204
    World War II **20**:256
  Kurdistan **12**:138–139
  land and resources **11**:249–251 *map, table*
    Iranian plate **15**:351 *map*
  languages
    Indo-Iranian languages **11**:145–146
  literature *see* PERSIAN LITERATURE
  manufacturing **11**:252–253 *illus.*
  map (32° 0′N 53° 0′E) **2**:232
  nuclear energy **14**:284 *table*
  people **11**:251–252 *illus.*
    Bakhtiari **3**:28
    Baluch **3**:57
    Khamseh **12**:65
    Kurds **12**:139
    Qashqai **16**:3
    Turkmen **19**:347
  physical features
    Demavend, Mount **6**:96
    Elburz Mountains **7**:102–103

Zagros Mountains 20:348
religion
Babism 3:7
Zoroastrianism 20:379–380
resources 11:251
petroleum industry 15:210
rivers, lakes, and waterways 11:250
Urmia, Lake 19:487
vegetation and animal life 11:250–251
IRAN MOUNTAINS
map (2° 5′N 114° 55′E) 13:84
IRANIAN HOSTAGE CRISIS 11:253–254
Carter, Jimmy 4:172
Central Intelligence Agency 3:254
IRAQ 11:254–256 *bibliog., illus., map, table*
agriculture 11:256 *illus.*
archaeology
Babylon 3:8
Ctesiphon 5:377
Doura-Europos 6:249
Eridu 7:229
Fertile Crescent 8:60
Hatra 10:68
Jarmo 11:383
Khorsabad 12:68
Kish 12:90
Lagash 12:165
Mari 13:149–150
Nimrud 14:199
Nineveh 14:199–200
Nippur 14:201
Samarra 17:46
Seleucia 17:190
Shanidar 17:240
Sippar 17:326–327
Tepe Gawra 19:114
Ur 19:474
Uruk 19:490
cities
Baghdad 3:21–22 *illus.*
Basra 3:116
Mosul 13:606
climate 11:254–255 *table*
cultural institutions 11:254
economic activity 11:254–256 *illus.*
education 11:254
Middle Eastern universities 13:410–412 *table*
flag 11:254 *illus.*
government 11:256
history 11:256
See also MESOPOTAMIA
Bell, Gertrude 3:186
Faisal I, King 8:11
Hussein, Saddam 10:320
Middle East, history of the 13:402–410
Sumer 18:339
Islamic art and architecture 11:294
land and resources 11:254–255 *map, table*
Saudi Arabia border 17:93
languages 11:254
Indo-Iranian languages 11:145–146
map (33° 0′N 44° 0′E) 2:232
mining and manufacturing 11:255
people 11:254
Kurds 12:139
Turkmen 19:347
religion 11:254
rivers, lakes, and waterways 11:256 *illus.*
Euphrates River 7:265
Shatt-al-Arab 17:245
Tigris River 19:197–198 *map*
transportation and trade 11:256
IRAS *see* INFRARED ASTRONOMY
IRAZÚ VOLCANO
map (9° 58′N 83° 53′W) 5:291
IRBIL (Iraq)
map (36° 11′N 44° 1′E) 11:255
IRC *see* INTERNATIONAL RESEARCH COUNCIL (IRC)
IREDELL (county in North Carolina)
map (35° 50′N 80° 55′W) 14:242
IREDELL, JAMES 11:257 *bibliog.*
IRELAND 11:257–261 *bibliog., illus., map, table*
See also NORTHERN IRELAND
Abbey Theatre 1:52–53
agriculture 11:259–260 *illus.*
potato 15:466
archaeology
lake dwelling 12:171
Newgrange 14:168
architecture 11:260
art 11:260
See also CELTIC ART
Yeats, Jack Butler 20:320
Blarney stone 3:328
Celtic languages 4:241
cities
Cork 5:263–264
Dublin 6:287–288 *illus.*
Dún Laoghaire 6:298
Galway 9:23
Kilkenny 12:76
Killarney 12:77
Limerick 12:344
Londonderry 12:405
Sligo 17:361
Tipperary 19:207
Waterford 20:63
clan 5:36
climate 11:257–259 *table*
counties
Carlow 4:151
Cavan 4:222
Clare 5:36
Cork 5:264
Donegal 6:237
Dublin 6:288
Galway 9:23
Kerry 12:60
Kildare 12:76
Kilkenny 12:76
Laoighis 12:202
Leitrim 12:279
Limerick 12:344
Longford 12:407
Louth 12:436–437
Mayo 13:248
Meath 13:258
Monaghan 13:517
Offaly 14:353
Roscommon 16:313
Sligo 17:361–362
Tipperary 19:207
Waterford 20:63
Westmeath 20:117
Wexford 20:119
Wicklow 20:145
economic activities 11:259–261 *illus.*
education 11:260
European universities 7:308 *table*
Trinity College, Dublin 19:301
famine
dulse 6:296
potato famine 8:18
flag 11:257 *illus.*
government 11:261
history *see* IRELAND, HISTORY OF
hurling 10:316
jig 11:417
Kerry blue terrier 12:60
land and resources 11:257–259 *illus., map, table*
language
Celtic languages 4:241
literature *see* IRISH LITERATURE
map (53° 0′N 8° 0′W) 7:268
music
bagpipe 3:22–23
Stanford, Sir Charles Villiers 18:217
Patrick, Saint 15:113
people 11:259–260
Celts 4:241–243
Gaels 9:7
migration to the United States 11:55 *map*
political parties
Fianna Fáil 8:67
Fine Gael 8:93
Sinn Fein 17:323
regions
Connacht 5:191
Leinster 12:278
Munster 13:644
Ulster 19:377
religion 11:259
rivers, lakes, and waterways 11:259
Shannon, River 17:240
shamrock 17:239
transportation 11:261
vegetation and animal life 11:259
IRELAND, HISTORY OF 11:261–265 *bibliog., illus., maps*
See also NORTHERN IRELAND
Great Britain, history of 9:309–318
prior to 1170
Brian Boru 3:476
Connacht 5:191
Dowth 6:253
early Gaelic period 11:261
Knowth 12:102
Leinster 12:278
Malachy, Saint 13:79
medieval period 11:261–263
Munster 13:644
Palladius, Saint 15:48
Patrick, Saint 15:113
Tara 19:34–35
Ulster 19:377
Viking invasions 11:262
1170–1600 early English rule
Anglo-Norman conquest 11:262–263
Elizabeth I, Queen of England 7:142
English plantations 11:262 *map*
Pale 15:30
principal clans and Norman families (1170) 11:262 *map*
Spenser, Edmund 18:178–179
Tyrone, Hugh O'Neill, 2d Earl of 19:368
1600–1921 English domination and rise of nationalism
Black and Tans 3:319
Boyne, Battle of the 3:434
Carson, Sir Edward 4:169–170
Catholic Emancipation 4:211
Cornwallis, Charles Cornwallis, 1st Marquess 5:270
Davitt, Michael 6:53
Easter Rising 7:33
emigrants 11:54 *illus.*
Emmet, Robert 7:156
Fenians 8:50
Grattan, Henry 9:301
growth of Irish nationalism 11:264
Home Rule Bills 10:212
home-rule movement 11:264
Jacobites 11:346
modern period 11:263–265
O'Connell, Daniel 14:346
Orangemen 14:415
Parnell, Charles Stewart 15:96
Peel, Sir Robert 15:132
Protestant ascendancy 11:263
Redmond, John 16:115
revolutionary era 11:263–264
Sinn Fein 17:323
Strafford, Thomas Wentworth, 1st Earl of 18:288
Swift, Jonathan 18:389
Test Acts 19:126
United Irishmen, Society of 19:401
1921–1949 Irish Free State
Belfast 3:174
Birkenhead, F. E. Smith, 1st Earl of 3:292
Collins, Michael 5:104
Cosgrave (family) 5:280
de Valera, Eamon 6:64
Eire 11:265
Griffith, Arthur 9:363
Irish Free State 11:264–265
Northern Ireland 14:255
Sinn Fein 17:323
1949-present
Cosgrave (family) 5:280
Fianna Fáil (political party) 8:67
Fine Gael (political party) 8:93
FitzGerald, Garret 8:131
Haughey, Charles James 10:68–69
Irish Republican Army 11:269
Londonderry (city in Northern Ireland) 12:405
Lynch, John 12:476
Northern Ireland 11:265
O'Brien, Conor Cruise 14:317
Paisley, Ian 15:25
Republic 11:265
IRELAND, JOHN (clergyman) 11:265–266 *bibliog.*
IRELAND, JOHN (composer) 11:266 *bibliog.*
IRELAND, NORTHERN *see* NORTHERN IRELAND
IRELAND, WILLIAM H. V.
literary fraud 12:370
IRELAND ISLAND
map (32° 19′N 64° 50′W) 3:219
IRENAEUS, SAINT 11:266 *bibliog.*
IRENAEUS, SAINT
Docetism 6:210
IRENE (South Dakota)
map (43° 5′N 97° 10′W) 18:103
IRENE, BYZANTINE EMPRESS 11:266 *bibliog.*
IRENG RIVER
map (3° 33′N 59° 51′W) 9:410
IRETON, HENRY
Waterford (city in Ireland) 20:63
IRGUN ZVAI LEUMI
Begin, Menachem 3:168
Jabotinsky, Vladimir 11:339
IRIAN BARAT *see* IRIAN JAYA (Indonesia)
IRIAN JAYA (Indonesia) 11:266
IRIDIUM 11:266
corrosion resistant 11:266
dinosaur 6:182
element 7:130 *table*
Group VIII periodic table 15:167
metal, metallic element 13:328
Tennant, Smithson, discoverer 19:102
transition elements 19:273
IRINGA (Tanzania)
map (7° 46′S 35° 42′E) 19:27
IRION (county in Texas)
map (31° 15′N 101° 0′W) 19:129
IRIONA (Honduras)
map (15° 57′N 85° 11′W) 10:218
IRIS (botany) 8:170 *illus.*; 11:266–267 *bibliog., illus.*
blue-eyed grass 3:342
crocus 5:356
Freesia 8:300
gladiolus 9:195
structure 11:266
varieties and uses 11:266
IRIS (eye)
eye 7:348–349 *illus.*
IRIS (mythology) 11:266
IRISH ART *see* CELTIC ART
IRISH ELK 11:266
IRISH FREE STATE *see* IRELAND, HISTORY OF
IRISH LITERARY RENAISSANCE 11:267 *bibliog., illus.*
Abbey Theatre 1:52–53
Colum, Padraic 5:125
Gregory, Isabella Augusta, Lady 9:355
Hyde, Douglas 10:329
Ireland, history of 11:264
Irish literature 11:267–268
Moore, George 13:567
O'Casey, Sean 14:319–320
Robinson, Lennox 16:245
Russell, George W. 16:350
Synge, John Millington 18:407
Yeats, William Butler 20:321
IRISH LITERATURE 11:268 *bibliog., illus.*
See also titles of specific literary works, e.g., *FINNEGANS WAKE*; *PLAYBOY OF THE WESTERN WORLD, THE* (play); etc.
Abbey Theatre 1:52–53
authors
Beckett, Samuel 3:151–152
Behan, Brendan 3:169
Clarke, Austin 5:40
Colum, Padraic 5:125
Croker, Thomas Crofton 5:357
Dunsany, Lord 6:301
Edgeworth, Maria 7:57
Ervine, St. John Greer 7:235
Fitzmaurice, George 8:131
Friel, Brian 8:332
Gregory, Isabella Augusta, Lady 9:355
Heaney, Seamus 10:89
Hyde, Douglas 10:329
Johnston, Denis 11:437
Joyce, James 11:456–457
MacNeice, Louis 13:35
Moore, Brian 13:567
Moore, George 13:568
Moore, Thomas 13:570
O'Brien, Edna 14:317
O'Casey, Sean 14:319–320
O'Connor, Frank 14:347
O'Faolain, Sean 14:352
O'Flaherty, Liam 14:354
Russell, George W. 16:350
Stephens, James 18:254–255
Synge, John Millington 18:407
Yeats, William Butler 20:321
epic
Cuchulain 5:381
Fenian cycle (tales) 8:50
Ireland 11:260
Irish Literary Renaissance 11:267
IRISH MOSS 11:269
IRISH REPUBLICAN ARMY 11:269 *bibliog.*
Ireland, history of 11:264; 11:265
IRISH REPUBLICAN BROTHERHOOD *see* FENIANS
IRISH SEA 11:269
islands and island groups
Isle of Man 11:298
map (53° 30′N 5° 20′W) 19:403
IRISH SETTER 6:219 *illus.*; 11:269 *bibliog., illus.*
IRISH TERRIER 6:220 *illus.*; 11:269–270 *bibliog., illus.*
IRISH VOLUNTEERS
Easter Rising 7:33
IRISH WATER SPANIEL 6:218 *illus.*; 11:270 *bibliog., illus.*
IRISH WOLFHOUND 6:217 *illus.*; 11:270 *bibliog., illus.*
IRITIS
eye diseases 7:351
IRKUTSK (USSR) 11:270; 19:393 *illus.*

IRKUTSK (cont.)
climate **19**:390 *table*
map (52° 16′N 104° 20′E) **19**:388
IRMA (Alberta)
map (52° 55′N 111° 14′W) **1**:256
IRON **11**:270–272 *bibliog.*
See also IRON AND STEEL INDUSTRY
abundances of common elements **7**:131 *table*
aqueous solutions **11**:270
biological
digestion, human **6**:172
hemoglobin **10**:119
methemoglobinemia **13**:343
starvation, nutritional-deficiency disease **18**:228
vitamins and minerals **19**:619 *table*; **19**:621
carbonate minerals **4**:137
chemical properties **11**:270
coils
inductor **11**:152
corrosion **5**:276–277; **11**:270
Cort, Henry **5**:277–278
element **7**:130 *table*
ferrocene
Fischer, Ernst Otto **8**:110
goethite **9**:224
Group VIII periodic table **15**:167
hematite **10**:117
laterite **12**:215
limonite **12**:346
magnetism **13**:56
magnetite **13**:58
metal, metallic element **13**:328
metallurgy **13**:330
mica **13**:370
native elements **14**:47
occurrence **11**:270
oceanic mineral resources **14**:340
ore
weathering **20**:83
ore deposits
Mesabi Range **13**:314
world distribution **14**:423 *map*
worldwide **11**:273 *map*
organometallic compounds **11**:271
oxide minerals **14**:476
physical properties **11**:270
phytoplankton
plankton **15**:332
principal producing and consuming nations **11**:273 *map*
pyrite **15**:637
silicate minerals **17**:304–305
sulfide minerals **18**:333
transition elements **19**:273 *table*
uranium minerals **19**:478
wrought iron **20**:295
IRON (county in Michigan)
map (46° 15′N 88° 25′W) **13**:377
IRON (county in Missouri)
map (37° 35′N 90° 40′W) **13**:476
IRON (county in Utah)
map (37° 45′N 113° 20′W) **19**:492
IRON (county in Wisconsin)
map (46° 15′N 90° 15′W) **20**:185
IRON AGE **11**:272 *bibliog., illus.*
African prehistory **1**:172 *map*; **1**:174–175
broch **3**:500
Celtic art **4**:238–241
Celtic house **10**:265 *illus.*
Celts **4**:241–243 *map*
European prehistory **7**:301 *map*; **7**:305–306
Greek art **9**:338
Hallstatt **10**:23
housing **7**:305 *illus.*
La Tène **12**:150
lake dwelling **12**:171
metallurgy **13**:330
prehistoric art **15**:509–510
Scandinavia, history of **17**:108
technology, history of **19**:62
Tollund man **19**:227
Villanovans **19**:597
Vix **19**:623
IRON BELT (Wisconsin)
map (46° 25′N 90° 19′W) **20**:185
IRON BUTTERFLY (rock group)
rock music **16**:249
IRON CITY (Tennessee)
map (35° 1′N 87° 35′W) **19**:104
IRON CROSS (Germany)
medals and decorations **13**:262 *illus.*
IRON CURTAIN **7**:297 *map*; **11**:272
cold war **5**:98
IRON DEFICIENCY ANEMIA *see* ANEMIA
IRON-EXCHANGE RESIN *see* WATER SOFTENER
IRON-FRONT BUILDINGS *see* CAST-IRON ARCHITECTURE
IRON GATE **11**:272
map (44° 30′N 22° 0′E) **20**:340
IRON GUARD **11**:272
IRON LUNG **11**:272
respirator **16**:178
IRON MOUNTAIN (Michigan)
map (45° 49′N 88° 4′W) **13**:377
IRON MOUNTAINS (Virginia)
map (36° 30′N 81° 50′W) **19**:607
IRON RIVER (Michigan)
map (46° 5′N 88° 39′W) **13**:377
IRON RIVER (Wisconsin)
map (46° 34′N 91° 24′W) **20**:185
IRON AND STEEL INDUSTRY **11**:272–278 *bibliog., illus., map*
additives, boron **3**:403
Bessemer, Sir Henry **3**:228
blacksmith **3**:322
blast furnace **3**:328
bonderizing **3**:376
Bramah, Joseph **3**:451
bridge (engineering) **3**:483 *table*
building construction **11**:272–278
Carnegie, Andrew **4**:155
cast-iron architecture **4**:185–186
casting **4**:188–189
Darby (family) **6**:37
electric furnace **7**:106
Fairbairn, Sir William **8**:9
Fairless, Benjamin **8**:9
fluorite **8**:188
forge **8**:232–233
foundry **8**:251
Frick, Henry Clay **8**:330
Gary, Elbert Henry **9**:52–53
hardening **10**:45
Hewitt, Abram Stevens **10**:154
Homestead strike **10**:214
India **11**:85–86 *illus.*
Industrial Revolution **11**:159 *illus.*
iron **11**:272–274
Johnstown (Pennsylvania) **11**:438
Kelly, William **12**:39
Krupp (family) **12**:132
labor union
Murray, Philip **13**:650
United Steelworkers of America **19**:465
manganese **13**:114
metallurgy **13**:330–331
molybdenum **13**:514
Morgan (family) **13**:577
open-hearth process **14**:398
Pennsylvania **15**:151
pipe and pipeline **15**:310–311
Pittsburgh (Pennsylvania) **15**:321
Réaumur, René Antoine Ferchault de **16**:105
Ruhr Valley (West Germany) **16**:343
Salop (England) **17**:36
Schwab, Charles Michael **17**:138
shipbuilding **17**:276
smelting **17**:366
stainless steel **18**:213
steel making, firebrick **8**:106
steel processing **11**:277–278
continuous casting **11**:277 *illus.*
steel production **11**:273–275 *illus., map*
basic oxygen process **11**:276
Bessemer process **11**:274–276 *illus.*
electric furnace **11**:276–277
open-hearth process **11**:276; **14**:398
steel mills **11**:277–278
technology, history of **19**:65–67
Thomas, Sidney Gilchrist **19**:174
Wilkinson, John **20**:153
wrought iron **20**:295
IRON TSAR *see* NICHOLAS I, EMPEROR OF RUSSIA
IRONCLAD (ship)
Monitor and *Merrimack* **13**:531–532
IRONDALE (Alabama)
map (33° 32′N 86° 42′W) **1**:234
IRONDEQUOIT (New York)
map (43° 12′N 77° 36′W) **14**:149
IRONTON (Missouri)
map (37° 36′N 90° 38′W) **13**:476
IRONTON (Ohio)
map (38° 31′N 82° 40′W) **14**:357
IRONWEED **11**:278
IRONWOOD **11**:278–279
bumelia **3**:562
IRONWOOD (Michigan)
map (46° 27′N 90° 10′W) **13**:377
IRONWORK, ORNAMENTAL **11**:279 *bibliog., illus.*
Gargallo, Pablo **9**:47
Tijou, Jean **19**:198
IRONY **11**:279 *bibliog.*
See also SATIRE
dramatic irony **14**:22
Erasmus, Desiderius
Praise of Folly, The **15**:489
figures of speech **8**:76
saga **17**:11
IROQUOIS (American Indians) *see* IROQUOIS LEAGUE
IROQUOIS (county in Illinois)
map (40° 47′N 87° 44′W) **11**:42
IROQUOIS (South Dakota)
map (44° 22′N 97° 51′W) **18**:103
IROQUOIS LEAGUE **11**:279–280 *bibliog., illus.*
Cayuga **4**:227
Champlain, Samuel de **4**:277–278
Delaware **6**:91
French and Indian Wars **8**:312; **8**:314
Handsome Lake **10**:37
Hiawatha **10**:156
Huron **10**:316
Indians, American **11**:130
Indians of North America, art of the **11**:140 *illus.*
Indians of North America, music and dance of the **11**:143
Johnson, Sir William **11**:437
Miami **13**:370
Mohawk **13**:502
Oneida **14**:389
Onondaga **14**:391
Pennsylvania **15**:150
Red Jacket **16**:112
Seneca **17**:200
Susquehanna **18**:372
Tonty, Henri de **19**:235
tribal council **11**:117 *illus.*
Tuscarora **19**:355
United States, history of the **19**:437–438
women in society **20**:201
IROQUOIS RIVER
map (41° 5′N 87° 49′W) **11**:42
IRRADIATION *see* RADIATION THERAPY; RADIOLOGY
IRRATIONAL NUMBER **11**:280 *bibliog.*
See also RATIONAL NUMBER
algebra **1**:284
arithmetic **2**:158
classes **11**:280
e **7**:3
Euclid **7**:262
mathematics, history of **13**:226
Pythagoras of Samos **15**:639–640
real number **16**:103
square root **18**:202
transcendental number **19**:268
IRRAWADDY RIVER **3**:572 *illus.*; **11**:280
map (15° 50′N 95° 6′E) **3**:573
IRREDENTISM **11**:280
IRRESISTIBLE IMPULSE
insanity, legal **11**:185
IRREVERSIBLE PROCESSES *see* REVERSIBLE AND IRREVERSIBLE PROCESSES
IRRICANA (Alberta)
map (51° 19′N 113° 37′W) **1**:256
IRRIGATION **11**:280–283 *bibliog., illus., table*
aqueduct **2**:93–94
Archimedes' screw **2**:128–129
closed-conduit irrigation **11**:281–282
desert **1**:197 *illus.*
evapotranspiration **7**:314–315
Imperial Valley (California) **4**:34 *illus.*
Inca **11**:72
land reclamation **12**:179
major systems, worldwide **11**:282–283 *table*
Nebraska **14**:74
problems **11**:282
sprinkler system **11**:282 *illus.*
surface irrigation **11**:281
vegetable **19**:532
water-lifting machines **11**:281
windmills and wind power **20**:172–173
IRTYSH RIVER **11**:283
map (61° 4′N 68° 52′E) **19**:388
IRÚN (Spain)
map (43° 21′N 1° 47′W) **18**:140
IRVINE (Alberta)
map (49° 57′N 110° 16′W) **1**:256
IRVINE (Kentucky)
map (37° 42′N 83° 58′W) **12**:47
IRVINES LANDING (British Columbia)
map (49° 38′N 124° 3′W) **3**:491
IRVING (Illinois)
map (39° 12′N 89° 24′W) **11**:42
IRVING (Texas)
map (32° 49′N 96° 56′W) **19**:129
IRVING, EDWARD **11**:283 *bibliog.*
IRVING, SIR HENRY **1**:87 *illus.*; **11**:284 *bibliog., illus.*
IRVING, JOHN **11**:284
IRVING, ROBERT **11**:284
IRVING, WASHINGTON **1**:343 *illus.*; **11**:284–285 *bibliog., illus.*
New York (state) **14**:150
Rip Van Winkle **16**:228
IRVINGTON (Kentucky)
map (37° 53′N 86° 17′W) **12**:47
IRVINGTON (New Jersey)
map (40° 44′N 74° 14′W) **14**:129
IRWIN (county in Georgia)
map (31° 35′N 83° 15′W) **9**:114
IRWIN (Pennsylvania)
map (40° 20′N 79° 42′W) **15**:147
IRWIN, JAMES **11**:285
Apollo program **2**:83–84
IRWIN, LORD *see* HALIFAX, EDWARD FREDERICK LINDLEY WOOD, 1ST EARL OF
IRWINTON (Georgia)
map (32° 49′N 83° 10′W) **9**:114
IS FJORD
map (78° 15′N 15° 0′E) **14**:261
ISAAC **11**:285
ISAAC, HEINRICH **11**:285 *bibliog.*
ISAAC I COMNENUS, BYZANTINE EMPEROR **11**:285
ISAAC II ANGELUS, BYZANTINE EMPEROR **11**:285 *bibliog.*
ISAACS, RUFUS DANIEL, 1ST MARQUESS OF READING *see* READING, RUFUS DANIEL ISAACS, 1ST MARQUESS OF
ISABEL (South Dakota)
map (45° 24′N 101° 26′W) **18**:103
ISABELA ISLAND
map (0° 30′S 91° 6′W) **7**:52
ISABELLA (county in Michigan)
map (43° 35′N 84° 50′W) **13**:377
ISABELLA I, QUEEN OF CASTILE (Isabella the Catholic) **11**:285–286 *bibliog., illus.*
Ferdinand II, King of Aragon **8**:52
Ferdinand and Isabella **18**:146 *illus.*
Spain, history of **18**:145
Spanish art and architecture **18**:153
ISABELLA II, QUEEN OF SPAIN **11**:286 *bibliog.*
Prim, Juan **15**:537
Spain, history of **18**:148
ISABELLA TIGER MOTH **3**:598–599 *illus.*
ISABEY, JEAN BAPTISTE **11**:286 *bibliog.*
ISACKS, BRYAN L.
plate tectonics **15**:357
ÍSAFJÖRDUR (Iceland)
map (66° 8′N 23° 13′W) **11**:17
ISAIAH (prophet) **11**:460 *illus.*; **17**:162 *illus.*
ISAIAH, BOOK OF **11**:286 *bibliog.*
Dead Sea Scrolls **6**:65
ISALO MASSIF MOUNTAINS
map (22° 45′S 45° 15′E) **13**:38
ISANTI (Minnesota)
map (45° 29′N 93° 15′W) **13**:453
ISANTI (county in Minnesota)
map (45° 35′N 93° 15′W) **13**:453
ISAR RIVER
map (48° 49′N 12° 58′E) **9**:140
ISCA DUNNONIORUM *see* EXETER (England)
ISCARIOT, JUDAS *see* JUDAS ISCARIOT
ISCHEMIA
artery blockage
stroke **18**:302
ISCHIA ISLAND
map (40° 43′N 13° 54′E) **11**:321
ISE BAY
map (52° 30′N 10° 33′E) **6**:109
ISELIN (New Jersey)
map (40° 34′N 74° 19′W) **14**:129
ISELIN, COLUMBUS O'DONNELL **11**:286
ocean circulation **11**:286
Woods Hole Oceanographic Institution **11**:286
ISÈRE RIVER **11**:286
ISEYIN (Nigeria)
map (7° 58′N 3° 36′E) **14**:190
ISFAHAN (Iran) **11**:252 *illus.*; **11**:287
congregational mosque **13**:601 *illus.*
map (32° 40′N 51° 38′E) **11**:250
Royal Mosque **2**:241 *illus.*; **15**:185 *illus.*
ISHERTON (Guyana)
map (2° 19′N 59° 22′W) **9**:410
ISHERWOOD, CHRISTOPHER **11**:287 *bibliog., illus.*
ISHI
Yana **20**:317

ISHIKAWA TAKUBOKU **11**:287
ISHIM RIVER
map (57° 45′N 71° 12′E) **19**:388
ISHIWARA, JUN
quantum mechanics **16**:10
ISHMAEL **11**:287
ISHPEMING (Michigan)
map (46° 30′N 87° 40′W) **13**:377
ISHTAR (Mesopotamian deity) **11**:287
fertility rites **8**:60
mother goddess **13**:607
mythology **13**:696 *illus.*
temple
Mari **13**:150
Uruk **19**:490
ISHTAR GATE
Mesopotamian art and architecture **13**:321 *illus.*
ISIDORE OF SEVILLE, SAINT **11**:287 *bibliog.*
León (Spanish city) **12**:289
ISIDORUS OF MILETUS **11**:288 *bibliog.*
Hagia Sophia **2**:133 *illus.*; **4**:204 *illus.*; **10**:10
ISINGLASS
sturgeon **18**:309
ISIRO (Zaire)
map (2° 47′N 27° 37′E) **20**:350
ISIS (Egyptian deity) **5**:51 *illus.*; **7**:87 *illus.*; **11**:288 *bibliog.*
fertility rites **8**:60
mother goddess **13**:606–607
ISKANDER BEY *see* SKANDERBEG
ISKENDERUN (Turkey)
map (36° 37′N 36° 7′E) **19**:343
ISKER RIVER
map (43° 44′N 24° 27′E) **3**:555
ISKOWITZ, EDWARD ISRAEL *see* CANTOR, EDDIE
ISKRA
Lenin, Vladimir Ilich **12**:282
ISLA DE PASCUA *see* EASTER ISLAND
ISLA MUJERES (Mexico)
Quintana Roo **16**:27
ISLAM **2**:102 *map*; **11**:288–293 *bibliog., illus., map*; **16**:140 *map*
See also DRUZES; SHIITES; SUNNITES
Abbasids **1**:52
Abu Bakr **1**:66
Africa, history of **1**:155–156
Aga Khan **1**:181
Aisha **1**:228
Ali **1**:292
Allah **1**:298
Almohads **1**:306
Almoravids **1**:307
Arabian music **2**:99–100
Arabs **2**:101–106
art *see* ISLAMIC ART AND ARCHITECTURE
Asia, history of **2**:254–256
Babism **3**:7
baths **3**:122
Berbers **3**:207
Bukhari, al- **3**:553
caliphate **4**:39; **11**:289–290
Circassians **4**:435
circumcision **4**:442–443
Crusades **5**:366–369
Damascus (Syria) **6**:18–19 *illus.*
dervish **6**:123
dietary laws **6**:165
distribution **11**:293 *map*
doctrines **11**:290–292
education **7**:60
Middle Eastern universities **13**:410–412
emir **7**:156
Europe, history of **7**:283
Fakhr al-Din **8**:11
fakir **8**:11
family **8**:16
Farabi, al- **8**:21
Fatima (daughter of Muhammad) **8**:34
Fulani **8**:356
Fur **8**:369
Ghazali, al- **9**:166
harem **10**:49
Hausa **10**:69
Hejaz (Saudi Arabia) **10**:110
historic sites **11**:293 *map*
Hui **10**:295
imam **11**:53–54
India, history of **11**:90
inheritance **11**:177
Ismailis **11**:298
Javanese **11**:386
Jerusalem (Israel) **11**:399–401 *illus., map*; **11**:400–401
jihad (holy war) **11**:290; **11**:418
Kaaba **12**:3
Kashmir **12**:30
Khomeini, Ayatollah Ruhollah **12**:67–68
koran **11**:288–291; **12**:110
Saudi Arabia **17**:95
Last Day **11**:290
Lilith **12**:341
mahdi **13**:64
Mahmud of Ghazni **13**:65–66
Malays **13**:84
mathematics, history of **13**:224
Mecca (Saudi Arabia) **11**:289 *illus.*; **13**:258–259 *illus.*
medicine **13**:268–269 *illus.*
Medina (Saudi Arabia) **13**:275
Middle East **13**:398
Middle East, history of the **13**:402–403
migration from India **11**:87
Moguls **11**:290
Moor **13**:567
Moriscos **13**:580
mosque **11**:291–292 *illus.*; **13**:601–602 *illus.*
Muawiyah I, Umayyad Caliph **13**:630
Muhammad **11**:288–289 *illus.*; **13**:632–633
Muhasibi, al- **13**:634
mullah **13**:636
Muslim League **13**:683
obligatory journey to Mecca *see* HAJJ
Ottoman Empire **11**:290
Pakistan **15**:29
Palestine **15**:44
Pan-Islamism
Jamal al-Din al-Afghani **11**:352–353
Philippines **15**:238
philosophy *see* ISLAMIC PHILOSOPHY
polygamy **15**:419
predestination **11**:290–291
Ramadan **16**:79
Saladin **17**:29
Samarra (Iraq) **17**:46
Sanusi, al- **17**:71
Seljuks **17**:192
Sharia **17**:241–242
sin **17**:318
slavery **17**:353
Somali **18**:59
Songhai (people) **18**:65
Spain, history of **18**:144–146 *illus., maps*
Sufism **18**:327
sultan **18**:338
Ten Commandments **19**:100
Tuareg **19**:326
Turks **19**:347–348
Umar I **19**:379
Umayyads **19**:380
Union of Soviet Socialist Republics **19**:393
usury **19**:491
Wahhabism **20**:7
women in society **20**:203
15th century manuscript (detail) **13**:530 *illus.*
ISLAM, NATION OF *see* BLACK MUSLIMS
ISLAM IN THE WEST, WORLD COMMUNITY OF *see* BLACK MUSLIMS
ISLAMABAD (Pakistan) **11**:293
map (33° 42′N 73° 10′E) **15**:27
ISLAMIC ART AND ARCHITECTURE **11**:293–297 *bibliog., illus.*
calligraphy **4**:45 *illus.*
Egypt **7**:78 *illus.*
garden **9**:40
Indian art and architecture **11**:97
landscape painting **12**:188
Metropolitan Museum of Art, The **13**:348
minaret **13**:437
Mogul art and architecture **13**:500–502
Moorish art and architecture **13**:570–571
mosaic **13**:595–596 *illus.*
mosque **13**:601–602 *illus.*
Persian art and architecture **15**:183–187
Riza-i-Abbasi **16**:234
Royal Mosque (Isfahan) **2**:241 *illus.*
Royal Ontario Museum **16**:330
Samarra **17**:46
Sinan **17**:318
stained glass **18**:211
Sultan Muhammad **18**:338
Taj Mahal **19**:14–15
tomb **19**:231
Topkapi Palace Museum **19**:237
ISLAMIC PHILOSOPHY
Farabi, al- **8**:21
Ghazali, al- **9**:166
Kindi, al- **12**:78
Muhasibi, al- **13**:634
philosophy **15**:244
ISLAMIC REPUBLIC OF IRAN *see* IRAN
ISLAMIC REPUBLIC AT MAURITANIA *see* MAURITANIA
ISLAND (county in Washington)
map (48° 7′N 122° 36′W) **20**:35
ISLAND ARC **11**:297–298 *bibliog.*
ocean and sea **14**:327
orogeny **14**:447
plate tectonics **15**:354–356; **15**:356
remnants, mountain ranges **11**:298
Ring of Fire **16**:225
structural geology **18**:303
subduction zone **18**:312–313
volcanic islands **11**:297–298
ISLAND BEACH
map (39° 50′N 74° 5′W) **14**:129
ISLAND FALLS (Maine)
map (46° 0′N 68° 16′W) **13**:70
ISLAND FALLS (Saskatchewan)
map (55° 32′N 102° 21′W) **17**:81
ISLAND LAKE (Manitoba)
map (53° 58′N 94° 47′W) **13**:119
ISLAND PARK (Idaho)
map (44° 24′N 111° 19′W) **11**:26
ISLAND POND (Vermont)
map (44° 49′N 71° 53′W) **19**:554
ISLANDS, BAY OF
map (49° 10′N 58° 15′W) **14**:166
ISLAS MALVINAS *see* FALKLAND ISLANDS
ISLAY ISLAND
map (55° 46′N 6° 10′W) **19**:403
ISLE AU HAUT
map (44° 3′N 68° 38′W) **13**:70
ISLE OF MAN **11**:298 *bibliog.*
Celtic languages **4**:241
flag **8**:144 *illus.*
Magnus VI, King of Norway (Magnus the Law-Mender) **13**:61
Manx cat **13**:134
map (54° 15′N 4° 30′W) **19**:403
people
Gaels **9**:7
ISLE OF PALMS (South Carolina)
map (32° 47′N 79° 48′W) **18**:98
ISLE OF PINES **11**:298
map (21° 40′N 82° 50′W) **5**:377
ISLE ROYALE
map (48° 0′N 89° 0′W) **13**:377
ISLE OF WIGHT (England) **11**:298 *bibliog.*
map (50° 40′N 1° 20′W) **19**:403
ISLE OF WIGHT (Virginia)
map (36° 54′N 76° 43′W) **19**:607
ISLE OF WIGHT (county in Virginia)
map (36° 50′N 76° 42′W) **19**:607
ISLES DERNIERES
map (29° 2′N 90° 47′W) **12**:430
ISLETON (California)
map (38° 10′N 121° 37′W) **4**:31
ISLETS OF LANGERHANS
hormone, animal **10**:235 *illus.*
pancreas **15**:58 *illus.*
ISLINGTON (Massachusetts)
map (42° 13′N 71° 11′W) **3**:409
ISLIP (New York)
demolition derby **6**:104
ISMAIL, MOULAY *see* MOULAY ISMAIL
ISMAIL I, SHAH OF PERSIA
Middle East, history of the **13**:405
ISMAIL PASHA **11**:298 *bibliog.*
Egypt **7**:80
Middle East, history of the **13**:406
ISMAILIA (Egypt)
map (30° 35′N 32° 16′E) **7**:76
ISMAILIS **11**:298 *bibliog.*
Aga Khan **1**:181
Assassins **2**:264
Druzes **6**:283
Fatimids **8**:34
ISNA (Egypt)
map (25° 18′N 32° 33′E) **7**:76
ISNEG
Igorot **11**:38
ISOBAR (isogram) **11**:299
ISOCHRON (isogram) **11**:299
ISOCRATES **11**:298–299 *bibliog.*
ISOELECTRIC POINT **11**:299
ISOGLOSS
geographical linguistics **9**:98–99 *maps*
ISOGRAM **11**:299
ISOHYET (isogram) **11**:299
radar meteorology **16**:41
ISOLA FARNESE *see* VEII (Italy)
ISOLATION OF AFFECT (psychology)
defense mechanisms **6**:83
ISOLATIONISM **11**:299 *bibliog.*
Langer, William **12**:195
United States, history of the **19**:455
World War II **20**:257
ISOMER **11**:299
cis-trans isomerism **4**:445
configuration **5**:178
coordination compounds **5**:247–248
gasoline
octane number **14**:347
molecule **13**:508
monosaccharide **13**:540
optical activity **14**:408
photoisomerization
photochemistry **15**:258
stereochemistry **18**:258–259
structural isomers
organic chemistry **14**:436
ISOMETRIC CRYSTAL SYSTEM *see* ISOMETRIC SYSTEM; names of specific types of rocks and minerals, e.g., GARNET; IRON; etc.
ISOMETRIC DRAWING **13**:259 *illus.*
ISOMETRIC SYSTEM **11**:299
common minerals **11**:299
crystal **5**:374 *illus.*; **11**:299
isotropic minerals **11**:299
ISOMETRICS (exercise) **11**:299–300
ISOMORPH **11**:300
Mitscherlich, Eilhard **13**:485
ISOMORPHISM **11**:300 *bibliog.*
elements of two systems **11**:300
structure **11**:300
ISONZO, BATTLES OF THE
World War I **20**:229–230 *illus.*; **20**:233; **20**:238 *map*
ISONZO, 12th BATTLE OF *see* CAPORETTO, BATTLE OF
ISOPOD **11**:300 *bibliog., illus.*
freshwater isopod **12**:168 *illus.*
ISOPRENE **11**:300 *illus.*
diene, compound **11**:300
elastomer **11**:300
rubber **11**:300; **16**:334
terpene **19**:118–119
Wallach, Otto **20**:15
ISOPROPYL ALCOHOL
alcohol **1**:264 *table*
ISOPTERA **11**:300
termite **19**:116–117
ISOSTASY **11**:300
Dutton, Clarence Edward **6**:316
Earth, structure and composition of **7**:21
geosyncline **9**:119
ISOSTATIC PRESSING *see* PRESSING
ISOTHERM **11**:300–301 *bibliog.*
Humboldt, Alexander von **10**:301
polar climate **15**:392
ISOTHERMAL PROCESS **11**:301
ISOTHERMAL REMANENT MAGNETISM (IRM)
paleomagnetism **15**:41–42
ISOTONICS
isometrics **11**:299
ISOTOPE **11**:301 *bibliog.*
Aston, Francis William **2**:268
atomic bomb **2**:307
atomic weight **2**:311–312
carbon **4**:133
cesium **4**:262
chemical symbolism and notation **4**:322
cobalt **5**:82
copper **5**:252
deuterium **6**:136
element **7**:131
element 104 **7**:132
element 105 **7**:132
element 106 **7**:132
erbium **7**:228
geochemistry, research **9**:97
half-life **10**:19–20 *table*
hydrogen **10**:337
tritium **19**:304
industrial and scientific use **11**:301
lanthanum **12**:201
mass number **13**:203
medicine **13**:272
neptunium **14**:89
nuclear energy **14**:278–284
nuclear physics **14**:285–286
oxygen **14**:477
paleoclimatology **15**:34
periodic table **15**:168
plutonium **15**:373
radioactivity **16**:61
radiochemistry **16**:63
radiometric age-dating **16**:65–67
radium **16**:68
radon **16**:68–69
rhenium **16**:193
rubidium **16**:336
samarium **17**:45

ISOTOPE (cont.)
separation and spectrography
laser and maser 12:213
Soddy, Frederick 18:32
stable isotopes 11:301
sulfur 18:335
superheavy elements 18:351
synthesis 11:301
transmutation of elements 19:277
transuranium elements 19:282
types 11:301
uranium 19:477
vanadium 19:516
ISOTOPIC TRACER *see* NUCLEAR MEDICINE
ISOZAKI, ARATA 11:301 *bibliog.*
ISPARTA (Turkey)
map (37° 46′N 30° 33′E) 19:343
ISRAEL 11:301–306 *bibliog., illus., map, table*
See also ISRAEL, KINGDOM OF
agriculture 11:304 *illus.*; 11:305
arts 11:305
Safdie, Moshe 17:10
cities
Acre 1:84
Beersheba 3:163
Bethlehem 3:230–231
Elat 7:102
Haifa 10:12
Jaffa 11:348
Jerusalem 11:399–401 *illus., map*
Nazareth 14:67
Tel Aviv 19:75 *illus.*
Tiberias 19:189
climate 11:303–304 *table*
crime 5:346 *table*
economic activity 11:305–306
education 11:305
Middle Eastern universities 13:410–412 *table*
Tel Aviv University 19:75
flag 11:302 *illus.*
foreign relations
Egypt 7:79–81
government 11:306
defense, national 6:82 *table*
intelligence gathering 11:205
medals and decorations 13:262 *illus.*
welfare spending 20:98 *table*
Hadassah 10:7
Hebrew language 10:101
historic sites
Beth-shan 3:230
Caesarea 4:15
Ezion-Geber 7:352
Gezer 9:163
Hazor 10:84–85
Jericho 11:397
Lachish 12:160
Masada 13:194
Megiddo 13:280
history 11:306
Arab-Israeli Wars 2:96–98 *map*
Begin, Menachem 3:168
Ben-Gurion, David 3:195
Ben-Zvi, Itzhak 3:195
Dayan, Moshe 6:56
Eban, Abba 7:35
Entebbe 7:208
Eshkol, Levi 7:238
Fertile crescent 8:60
Gaza Strip 9:64
Iraq 11:256
Kibbutz 12:70
Lebanon 12:267
Meir, Golda 13:282–283
Middle East, history of the 13:408–409
Palestine 15:45–46 *maps*
Palestine Liberation Organization 15:46
Rabin, Yitzhak 16:32
Shamir, Yitzhak 17:239
Sharett, Moshe 17:241
Sharon, Ariel 17:244
socialism 18:23–24
Suez Crisis 18:325
Weizmann, Chaim 20:96
hora (dance) 10:233
irrigation 11:283
Jews 11:416–417
Kibbutz 12:70
land and resources 11:302–304 *illus., map, table*
land reclamation 12:179
literature
Hebrew and Yiddish literature 10:102
map (31° 30′N 35° 0′E) 2:232
Olympic Games 14:383
people 11:304–305
Jews 11:412
women in society 20:204 *table*
physical features
Carmel, Mount 4:153
Negev 14:77
Sharon, Plain of 17:244
Tabor, Mount 19:5
political parties 11:306
postage stamp 15:230 *illus.*
religion 11:304
Judaism 11:458–463
rivers, lakes, and waterways 11:303–304 *illus.*
Galilee, Sea of 9:14
Suez Canal 18:324
West Bank 20:108
Zionism 20:369–370
ISRAEL, KINGDOM OF 3:238 *map*; 11:306 *bibliog.*
cities
Ezion-geber 7:352
Gezer 9:163
Hazor 10:84–85
history
Ahab, King of Israel 1:200
David, King of Israel 6:48
Galilee 9:14
Herod (dynasty) 10:144
Jehu, King of Israel 11:394
Jeroboam I, King of Israel 11:397–398
Judah, Kingdom of 11:458
Palestine 15:45–46 *maps*
Phoenicia 15:250
Rehoboam, King of Israel 16:130
Samaria 17:45
Sargon II, King of Assyria 17:78
Saul, King 17:96
Solomon, King of Israel 18:56
Jews 11:412–413
Palestine 15:43–44
ISRAEL, MANASSEH BEN *see* MANASSEH BEN ISRAEL
ISRAELI, ISAAC BEN SOLOMON 11:306 *bibliog.*
ISRAELI, ISAAC D′ *see* D'ISRAELI, ISAAC
ISRAELI-ARAB WARS *see* ARAB-ISRAELI WARS
ISRAËLS, JOZEF 11:306 *bibliog.*
ISSANO (Guyana)
map (5° 49′N 59° 25′W) 9:410
ISSAQUENA (county in Mississippi)
map (32° 40′N 91° 0′W) 13:469
ISSAS
Djibouti (country) 6:208
ISSEI *see* NISEI
ISSYK-KUL, LAKE
map (42° 25′N 77° 15′E) 19:388
ISTANBUL (Turkey) 11:307–308 *bibliog., illus., map*; 19:345 *illus.*
art and architecture
Hagia Sophia 2:133 *illus.*; 10:10
Islamic art and architecture 11:293
mosaic 13:594
Saint Savior in the Chora 17:26
Theophanes the Greek 19:158
Topkapi Palace Museum 19:237
Byzantium 3:608
climate 19:343 *table*
history 11:307–308
map (41° 1′N 28° 58′E) 19:343
silk 17:307
ISTHMIAN GAMES 11:308 *bibliog.*
ISTHMUS OF PANAMA *see* PANAMA
ISTOKPOGA, LAKE
map (27° 22′N 81° 17′W) 8:172
ISTRIA 11:308
map (45° 15′N 14° 0′E) 20:340
ITA *see* INITIAL TEACHING ALPHABET
ITABUNA (Brazil)
map (14° 48′S 39° 16′W) 3:460
ITAGAKI TAISUKE 11:308
ITAITUBA (Brazil)
map (4° 17′S 55° 59′W) 3:460
ITALIAN ART AND ARCHITECTURE 11:308–314 *bibliog., illus.*
See also the subheading Italy under names of specific art forms, movements, and historic periods, e.g., ARCHITECTURE; GRAPHIC ARTS; NEOCLASSICISM (art); BAROQUE ART AND ARCHITECTURE; etc.; names of specific artists, e.g., CANOVA, ANTONIO; TITIAN; etc.
Berenson, Bernard 3:208
calligraphy 4:42–43 *illus.*
campanile 4:64–65
costume 5:295–298 *illus.*
Fascist art 8:30–31
Florence 8:168–169 *illus., map*
folk art 8:196 *illus.*
fresco painting 8:327
futurism 8:383–384
Genoa 9:92
house (in Western architecture) 10:269 *illus.*
interior design 11:212
landscape architecture 12:185; 12:186 *illus.*
garden 9:40
landscape painting 12:188
Macchiaioli 13:9
Mannerism 13:124–125
Milan 13:418 *illus.*
mosaic 13:596
museums, art 13:658
Naples 14:14–15
opera houses 14:401–402
painting 15:19–20
Palermo 15:43
Parma 15:95
Perugia 15:195
Piacenza 15:287
pottery and porcelain 15:471
Prato 15:490
Rome 16:296
sculpture 17:163–164 *illus.*
still-life painting 18:268–269 *illus.*
Uffizi 19:371
Vatican museums and galleries 19:528
Venice 19:544–545 *illus.*
ITALIAN GREYHOUND 6:217 *illus.*; 11:314 *bibliog., illus.*
ITALIAN LITERATURE 11:315–317 *bibliog., illus.*
See also the subheading Italian literature under DRAMA; EPIC; NOVEL; POETRY; etc.; names of specific authors, e.g., LAMPEDUSA, GIUSEPPE DI; PIRANDELLO, LUIGI; etc.; titles of specific literary works, e.g., *DECAMERON* (book); *ORLANDO FURIOSO* (poem); etc.
humanism 10:299
neorealism 14:85–86
pastoral literature 15:108–109
sonnet 18:65
ITALIAN MUSIC 11:317–319 *bibliog., illus.*
See also names of specific composers, e.g., FRESCOBALDI, GIROLAMO; MONTEVERDI, CLAUDIO; etc.
bagpipe 3:22–23
harpsichord 10:56
madrigal 13:45
medieval music 13:274–275
music, history of Western 13:665–666
musical notation and terms 13:680–681
Naples 14:14–15
opera 14:399–401
oratorio 14:416
Renaissance music 16:156
symphony 18:405
ITALIAN SOMALILAND *see* SOMALIA
ITALIAN WARS 11:319–320 *bibliog.*
Cateau-Cambrésis, Treaty of 4:202
condottieri 5:173
Julius II, Pope 11:466
Louis XII, King of France 12:425
ITALIANO, ANNA MARIA *see* BANCROFT, ANNE
ITALLIE, JEAN CLAUDE VAN *see* VAN ITALLIE, JEAN CLAUDE
ITALO-TURKISH WAR 11:320 *bibliog.*
ITALY 11:320–326 *bibliog., illus., map, table*
agriculture 11:325
silk 17:307–308
wine 20:176
aircraft, military *see* AIRCRAFT, MILITARY
archaeology
See also AEGEAN CIVILIZATION; ETRUSCANS; ROME, ANCIENT
Herculaneum 10:138
art *see* ITALIAN ART AND ARCHITECTURE
cities
Alessandria 1:272
Amalfi 1:320
Ancona 1:400
Anzio 2:73
Assisi 2:265
Bari 3:81
Bergamo 3:209
Bologna 3:370
Bolzano 3:373
Brescia 3:473
Cagliari 4:16
Cassino 4:184
Catania 4:200
Como 5:153
Cosenza 5:280
Cremona 5:338
Ferrara 8:58
Florence 8:168–169 *illus., map*
Foggia 8:193
Forlì 8:234
Gela 9:69
Genoa 9:92–93 *illus.*
La Spezia 12:149–150
Livorno 12:378
Lucca 12:449
Messina 13:324
Milan 13:418 *illus.*
Modena 13:490
Monza 13:560
Naples 14:14–15 *illus.*
Novara 14:272
Padua 15:12–13
Palermo 15:43
Parma 15:95
Pavia 15:120
Perugia 15:195
Piacenza 15:287
Pisa 15:315
Pistoia 15:317
Prato 15:490
Ravenna 16:95
Reggio di Calabria 16:128
Reggio nell'Emilia 16:128
Rimini 16:224
Rome 16:294–297 *illus., map*
Salerno 17:31
San Remo 17:57
Sassari 17:84
Siena 17:296
Taormina 19:29
Taranto 19:35
Terni 19:118
Trieste 19:297
Turin 19:342
Udine 19:370–371
Venice 19:544–545 *illus.*
Verona 19:559
Vicenza 19:571
climate 11:322–323 *table*
communism *see* COMMUNISM
cosmetics 5:281
cultural institutions 11:324–325
dance
Ebreo, Guglielmo 7:36
tarantella 19:35
demography 11:323–324 *illus.*
economic activity 11:325–326
unemployment rate 7:160
education 11:324
academy 1:70
Bologna, University of 3:371
European universities 7:308 *table*
Montessori, Maria 13:553
Padua, University of 15:13
Parma, University of 15:95
Rome, University of 16:304
flag 11:320 *illus.*
government 11:326
republic 16:172
history *see* ITALY, HISTORY OF
house (in Western architecture) 10:269 *illus.*
kidnapping 12:71
land and resources 11:320–323 *illus., map, table*
languages
Romance languages 16:280–281
law
civil law 5:11
literature *see* ITALIAN LITERATURE
Mafia 13:46
manufacturing and mining 11:325
map (42° 50′N 12° 50′E) 7:268
music *see* ITALIAN MUSIC
naval vessels 14:57 *illus.*
people 7:275 *illus.*; 11:323–325 *illus.*
migration to the United States 11:55 *map*
physical features
Apennines 2:76
Blue Grotto 3:343
Capri 4:128
Dolomites 6:226
Elba 7:102
Etna, Mount 7:258
Monte Cassino 13:552
Pontine Marshes 15:427
Riviera 16:234
Sardinia 17:76
Sicily 17:292–293 *illus.*
Stromboli 18:302
Vesuvius 19:565
regions
Abruzzi 1:61
Apulia 2:92
Basilicata 3:110

Calabria 4:21
Campania 4:64
Emilia-Romagna 7:156
Friuli-Venezia Giulia 8:335
Latium 12:235
Liguria 12:340
Lombardy 12:399
Marche 13:146
Molise 13:509
Piedmont 15:295
Trentino-Alto Adige 19:291
Tuscany 19:354–355
Tyrol 19:367–368 *map*
Umbria 19:380
Valle d'Aosta 19:507
Veneto 19:541
rivers, lakes, and waterways 11:323
Adige River 1:103
Albano, Lake 1:251
Arno River 2:184
Avernus, Lake 2:370
Como, Lake 5:153
Garda, Lake 9:40
Lugano, Lake 12:452
Maggiore, Lake 13:49
Nemi, Lake 14:81
Po River 15:376
Rubicon River 16:336
Tiber River 19:189
Volturno River 19:632
roads and highways 16:238
Spoleto Festival 18:192
theater
Comédie Italienne, La 5:132
commedia dell'arte 5:137–138
Fo, Dario 8:192
Galli da Bibiena (family) 9:18–19
stage lighting 18:210
theater, history of the 19:146–147
theater architecture and staging 19:152
titles of nobility 19:214 *table*
trade 11:326
urban planning *see* URBAN PLANNING
Vaiont Dam 19:503
vegetation and animal life 11:323
ITALY, HISTORY OF 11:326–331 *bibliog., illus., maps;* 11:327
historians *see* HISTORY—Italian historians
prehistory *see* AEGEAN CIVILIZATION; ETRUSCANS; ROME, ANCIENT
Rome 16:296–297
San Marino 17:56
Sicily 17:292–293
Somalia 18:61
476–1350 barbarian invasions 4:289 *map*
Charles II, King of Naples (Charles the Lame) 4:296
commune 5:142
Guelphs and Ghibellines 9:390
Lombards 12:399
Louis II, Frankish Emperor 12:429
Middle Ages 11:327–328
Normans 14:221
Papal States 15:67
rise of city-states 11:328
Robert Guiscard 16:241
Theodoric the Great, King of the Ostrogoths 19:156
1350–1600 Renaissance 11:329
Borgia (family) 3:399–400
Charles III, King of Naples 4:296
city-state 5:9
coin 14:296 *illus.*
condottieri 5:173
costume 5:295–297 *illus.*
Este (family) 7:246
Hawkwood, Sir John 10:78
Italian Wars 11:319–320
Machiavelli, Nicolò 13:18
Medici (family) 13:265
Naples, Kingdom of 14:15
Renaissance 16:148–149
sword 18:398 *illus.*
1600–1815 Spanish domination and Napoleonic Era
Napoleon I, Emperor of the French (Napoléon Bonaparte) 14:16
Napoleonic Empire in 1812 14:18 *map*
Risorgimento 16:228
1815–1870 Restoration and unification 11:329–330 *map*
Camorra 4:62
Carbonari 4:137
Cavour, Camillo Benso, Conte di 4:226
Europe, history of 7:292
Ferrari, Giuseppe 8:58–59
Garibaldi, Giuseppe 9:47
Mazzini, Giuseppe 13:250
Revolutions of 1848 16:188
Risorgimento 11:329; 16:228
Sardinia, Kingdom of 17:76–77
Seven Weeks' War 17:216
Victor Emmanuel II, King of Italy 19:572–573
1870–1922 kingdom
Humbert I, King 10:300
irredentism 11:280
Marconi, Guglielmo 13:147
Savoy (dynasty) 17:101
Savoy (region) 17:102
Triple Alliance 19:302
World War I *see* WORLD WAR I
1922–1946 rise of Fascism 11:330–331
Balbo, Italo 3:33
Blackshirts 3:322
de Gasperi, Alcide 6:59
fascism 8:30
Gentile, Giovanni 9:94
Humbert II, King 10:300–301
Lateran Treaty 12:215
League of Nations 12:258
Libya 12:321
Mussolini, Benito 13:684
Victor Emmanuel III, King of Italy 19:573
World War II *see* WORLD WAR II
1946-present 11:331
Craxi, Bettino 5:333
Einaudi, Luigi 7:92
Fanfani, Amintore 8:20
Moro, Aldo 13:583
socialism 18:23
ITANAGAR (India)
map (27° 20′N 93° 50′E) 11:80
ITANY RIVER
map (3° 40′N 54° 0′W) 8:311
ITASCA (county in Minnesota)
map (47° 30′N 93° 37′W) 13:453
ITASCA (Texas)
map (32° 10′N 97° 9′W) 19:129
ITASCA, LAKE 13:455 *illus.*
map (47° 18′N 95° 18′W) 13:453
ITAWAMBA (county in Mississippi)
map (34° 20′N 88° 20′W) 13:469
ITCHING PARROT, THE (book)
Fernández de Lizardi, José Joaquín 8:58
ITÉNEZ RIVER
map (11° 54′S 65° 1′W) 3:366
ITHACA (Greece) 11:331
ITHACA (Michigan)
map (43° 18′N 84° 36′W) 13:377
ITHACA (New York) 11:331
ITHÁKI (Greece) *see* ITHACA (Greece)
ITHOME *see* MESSENE (Greece)
ITO HIROBUMI 11:331–332 *bibliog.*
ITTA BENA (Mississippi)
map (33° 30′N 90° 20′W) 13:469
ITTEN, JOHANNES
Bauhaus 3:130
ITURBI, JOSÉ 11:332
ITURBIDE, AGUSTÍN DE 11:332 *bibliog., illus.*
Latin America, history of 12:219–220
Mexico, history of 13:364
ITZÁ
Chichén Itzá 4:344
Maya 13:243–244
ITZEHOE (Germany, East and West)
map (53° 55′N 9° 31′E) 9:140
IUD *see* INTRAUTERINE DEVICE
IUKA (Mississippi)
map (34° 49′N 88° 11′W) 13:469
IVA (South Carolina)
map (34° 19′N 82° 40′W) 18:98
IVA (Western Samoa)
map (13° 41′S 172° 10′W) 20:117
IVAN I, GRAND DUKE OF MOSCOW
Rurik (dynasty) 16:347
Russia/Union of Soviet Socialist Republics, history of 16:352
IVAN III, GRAND DUKE OF MOSCOW (Ivan the Great) 11:332 *bibliog.*
Europe, history of 7:286
Russia/Union of Soviet Socialist Republics, history of 16:353
IVAN IV, GRAND DUKE OF MOSCOW AND TSAR OF RUSSIA (Ivan the Terrible) 11:332–333 *bibliog., illus.*
Russia/Union of Soviet Socialist Republics, history of 16:353 *illus.*
IVAN V, TSAR OF RUSSIA
Sophia 18:66
IVAN THE GREAT *see* IVAN III, GRAND DUKE OF MOSCOW (Ivan the Great)
IVAN THE TERRIBLE *see* IVAN IV, GRAND DUKE OF MOSCOW AND TSAR OF RUSSIA (Ivan the Terrible)
IVANCHENKOV, ALEKSANDR 11:333 *bibliog.*
IVANGRAD (Yugoslavia)
map (42° 50′N 19° 52′E) 20:340
IVANHOE (book) 11:333
Scott, Sir Walter 17:154
IVANHOE (Minnesota)
map (44° 28′N 96° 15′W) 13:453
IVANOV, ALEKSANDR
Russian art and architecture 16:362
IVANOV, GEORGY 11:333
IVANOV, LEV IVANOVICH 11:333 *bibliog.*
ballet 3:43
IVANOV, VSEVOLOD VYACHESLAVOVICH 11:333 *bibliog.*
IVANOVO (USSR)
map (57° 0′N 40° 59′E) 19:388
IVANOVSKY, DIMITRI
virus 19:613–614
IVES, BURL 11:333
IVES, CHARLES EDWARD 11:334 *bibliog., illus.*
American music 1:351
IVES, JAMES MERRITT *see* CURRIER AND IVES
IVO (Bolivia)
map (20° 27′S 63° 26′W) 3:366
IVORY COAST 11:334–336 *bibliog., illus., map, table*
cities
Abidjan 1:57
climate 11:335 *table*
economic activity 11:335–336
education
African universities 1:176 *table;* 1:177 *illus.*
flag 11:334 *illus.*
government 11:336
history 11:336
Houphouët-Boigny, Félix 10:264
land and people 11:334–335 *map, table*
map (8° 0′N 5° 0′W) 1:136
IVORY AND IVORY CARVING 11:336–337 *bibliog., illus.*
Byzantine art and architecture 3:606 *illus.*
Carolingian art and architecture 4:160
Coptic art and architecture 5:255 *illus.*
Diptych of Anastasius 17:161 *illus.*
Moorish art and architecture 13:570 *illus.*
Paleolithic Period
Venus figurines 15:40 *illus.*
scrimshaw 17:158
sculpture techniques 17:166
types of ivory 11:336
IVREA (Italy)
map (45° 28′N 7° 52′E) 11:321
IVUJIVIK (Quebec)
map (62° 24′N 77° 55′W) 16:18
IVY 11:337 *bibliog., illus.*
IVY LEAGUE 11:337 *bibliog.*
Brown University 3:517
Columbia University 5:126
Cornell University 5:268
Dartmouth College 6:40
Harvard University 10:64
Pennsylvania, University of 15:152
Princeton University 15:549 *bibliog.*
Yale University 20:315
IWAKI (Japan)
map (37° 3′N 140° 55′E) 11:361
IWO (Nigeria)
map (7° 38′N 4° 11′E) 14:190
IWO JIMA 11:337–338 *bibliog.*
navy 14:64
World War II 20:277–278 *illus., map*
IWW *see* INDUSTRIAL WORKERS OF THE WORLD
IXIAMAS (Bolivia)
map (13° 45′S 68° 9′W) 3:366
IXION 11:338
IXTACIHUATL 11:338
IYAWADI-NMAI *see* IRRAWADDY RIVER
IZABAL, LAKE
map (15° 30′N 89° 10′W) 9:389
IZALCO (El Salvador)
map (13° 45′N 89° 40′W) 7:100
IZAPA (Mexico) 11:338 *bibliog.*
Kaminaljuyú 12:10
Maya 13:243
pre-Columbian art and architecture 15:496
Tikal 19:198
Uaxactún 19:369
IZARD (county in Arkansas)
map (36° 7′N 91° 53′W) 2:166
IZHEVSK (USSR)
map (56° 51′N 53° 14′E) 19:388
IZMIR (Turkey) 11:338
Magnesia 13:53
map (38° 25′N 27° 9′E) 19:343
IZMIT (Turkey)
map (40° 46′N 29° 55′E) 19:343
IZU ISLANDS
map (34° 30′N 139° 30′E) 11:361
IZVESTIA (periodical) 11:338

J

J (letter) 11:338 *illus.*
G (letter) 9:3
J. PERCY PRIEST LAKE
map (36° 5′N 86° 30′W) 19:104
JABALPUR (India)
map (23° 10′N 79° 57′E) 11:80
JABBAR, KAREEM ABDUL *see* ABDUL-JABBAR, KAREEM
"JABBERWOCKY" (poem)
Carroll, Lewis 4:169
JABIER AL-AHMAD AL-SABAH, SHEIKH
Kuwait (country) 12:142
JABILURA
major ore deposits 14:424–425 *table*
JABLA (Syria)
map (35° 21′N 35° 55′E) 18:412
JABLONEC NAD NISOU (Czechoslovakia)
map (50° 44′N 15° 10′E) 5:413
JABŁONSKI, HENRYK
Poland 15:390
JABOTINSKY, VLADIMIR 11:339 *bibliog.*
JACALTENANGO (Guatemala)
map (15° 40′N 91° 44′W) 9:389
JACAMAR 11:339
JACANA 11:339 *illus.*
shorebirds 17:283
JACARANDA 11:339
J'ACCUSE (letter)
Zola, Émile 20:372
JÁCHAL (Argentina)
map (30° 14′S 68° 45′W) 2:149
JACK (fish) 8:115 *illus.*
pilot fish 15:303
pompano 15:423
JACK (mechanism) 11:339
hydraulic systems 10:330–331 *illus.*
JACK (county in Texas)
map (33° 15′N 98° 10′W) 19:129
JACK-IN-THE-PULPIT (botany) 11:339 *illus.*
JACK MOUNTAIN
map (48° 47′N 120° 57′W) 20:35
JACK-O'-LANTERN (fungus) 11:339
JACK THE RIPPER 11:339–340 *bibliog.*
JACKAL 11:340 *bibliog., illus.*
JACKASS *see* ASS
JACKASS, LAUGHING *see* KOOKABURRA
JACKDAW 11:340
imprinting 11:69
JACKHAMMER
pneumatic systems 15:375
JACKHEAD HARBOUR (Manitoba)
map (51° 52′N 97° 16′W) 13:119
JACKPOTS (card game) *see* POKER (card game)
JACKS (card game) *see* POKER (card game)
JACKS (children's game) 11:340 *bibliog. bibliog.*
JACKSBORO (Tennessee)
map (36° 20′N 84° 11′W) 19:104
JACKSBORO (Texas)
map (33° 13′N 98° 10′W) 19:129
JACKSON (Alabama)
map (31° 31′N 87° 53′W) 1:234
JACKSON (county in Alabama)
map (34° 45′N 86° 0′W) 1:234
JACKSON (county in Arkansas)
map (35° 38′N 91° 15′W) 2:166
JACKSON (California)
map (38° 21′N 120° 46′W) 4:31
JACKSON (county in Colorado)
map (40° 40′N 106° 20′W) 5:116
JACKSON (county in Florida)
map (30° 50′N 85° 10′W) 8:172
JACKSON (Georgia)
map (33° 18′N 83° 58′W) 9:114
JACKSON (county in Georgia)
map (34° 10′N 83° 35′W) 9:114

JACKSON (county in Illinois)
map (37° 45′N 89° 20′W) **11**:42
JACKSON (county in Indiana)
map (38° 53′N 86° 3′W) **11**:111
JACKSON (county in Iowa)
map (42° 10′N 90° 35′W) **11**:244
JACKSON (county in Kansas)
map (39° 25′N 95° 50′W) **12**:18
JACKSON (Kentucky)
map (37° 33′N 83° 23′W) **12**:47
JACKSON (county in Kentucky)
map (37° 25′N 84° 0′W) **12**:47
JACKSON (Louisiana)
map (30° 50′N 91° 13′W) **12**:430
JACKSON (county in Louisiana)
map (32° 18′N 92° 35′W) **12**:430
JACKSON (Michigan) **11**:340
map (42° 15′N 84° 24′W) **13**:377
JACKSON (county in Michigan)
map (42° 15′N 84° 24′W) **13**:377
JACKSON (Minnesota)
map (43° 37′N 95° 1′W) **13**:453
JACKSON (county in Minnesota)
map (43° 38′N 95° 10′W) **13**:453
JACKSON (Mississippi) **11**:340; **13**:471 *illus.*
map (32° 18′N 90° 12′W) **13**:469
JACKSON (county in Mississippi)
map (30° 30′N 88° 40′W) **13**:469
JACKSON (Missouri)
map (37° 23′N 89° 40′W) **13**:476
JACKSON (county in Missouri)
map (39° 0′N 94° 20′W) **13**:476
JACKSON (North Carolina)
map (36° 23′N 77° 25′W) **14**:242
JACKSON (county in North Carolina)
map (35° 20′N 83° 10′W) **14**:242
JACKSON (Ohio)
map (39° 3′N 82° 39′W) **14**:357
JACKSON (county in Ohio)
map (39° 0′N 82° 37′W) **14**:357
JACKSON (county in Oklahoma)
map (34° 35′N 99° 20′W) **14**:368
JACKSON (county in Oregon)
map (42° 25′N 122° 40′W) **14**:427
JACKSON (South Carolina)
map (33° 20′N 81° 47′W) **18**:98
JACKSON (county in South Dakota)
map (43° 30′N 101° 40′W) **18**:103
JACKSON (Tennessee)
map (35° 37′N 88° 49′W) **19**:104
JACKSON (county in Tennessee)
map (36° 25′N 85° 40′W) **19**:104
JACKSON (county in Texas)
map (29° 0′N 96° 35′W) **19**:129
JACKSON (county in West Virginia)
map (38° 50′N 81° 40′W) **20**:111
JACKSON (county in Wisconsin)
map (44° 17′N 90° 45′W) **20**:185
JACKSON (Wyoming)
map (43° 29′N 110° 38′W) **20**:301
JACKSON, ALEXANDER YOUNG **11**:340 *bibliog.*
JACKSON, ANDREW **11**:340–342 *bibliog., illus.*
as president **11**:341–342; **15**:526
Bank of the United States **3**:67
at Battle of New Orleans **20**:27 *illus.*
Calhoun, John C. **4**:29
cartoon **19**:570 *illus.*
Civil War, U.S. **5**:15
Clay, Henry **5**:46
Crockett, Davy **5**:355–356
Democratic party **6**:99–100 *illus.*
Eaton, John Henry **7**:35
Kitchen Cabinet **12**:91
Memphis (Tennessee) **13**:292
Nashville (Tennessee) **14**:24
nullification **14**:292
patronage **15**:114
Polk, James K. **15**:404
United States, history of the **19**:444–446
Van Buren, Martin **19**:511
War of 1812 **20**:28
Weatherford, William **20**:82
Whig party (United States) **20**:130
JACKSON, CHARLES **11**:342
JACKSON, CHARLES T.
Morton, William **13**:593
JACKSON, GLENDA **11**:342
JACKSON, HELEN HUNT **11**:342–343 *bibliog.*
JACKSON, HENRY M. **11**:343 *bibliog.*
JACKSON, JESSE L. **11**:343 *bibliog., illus.*
JACKSON, MAHALIA **11**:343 *bibliog.*
JACKSON, MICHAEL **11**:343 *illus.*
JACKSON, MILT
Modern Jazz Quartet **13**:498
JACKSON, REGGIE **3**:107 *illus.*; **11**:343 *bibliog.*
JACKSON, ROBERT HOUGHWOUT **11**:343–344 *bibliog.*
JACKSON, SHELDON **11**:344 *bibliog.*
JACKSON, SHIRLEY **11**:344
JACKSON, STONEWALL **11**:344 *bibliog., illus.*
Bull Run, Battles of **19**:448 *illus.*
Chancellorsville, Battle of **4**:279
Civil War, U.S. **5**:21–24 *illus., map*; **5**:27
Lee, Robert E. **12**:270
Stone Mountain **18**:282
JACKSON, THOMAS J. *see* JACKSON, STONEWALL
JACKSON, WILLIAM HENRY **11**:344 *bibliog.*
JACKSON HOLE (Wyoming) **11**:344; **20**:300 *illus.*
JACKSON LABORATORY **11**:344
JACKSON LAKE (Georgia)
map (33° 22′N 83° 52′W) **9**:114
JACKSON LAKE (Wyoming)
map (43° 55′N 110° 40′W) **20**:301
JACKSON PURCHASE
Kentucky **12**:46
JACKSONBORO (South Carolina)
map (32° 46′N 80° 27′W) **18**:98
JACKSON'S ARM (Newfoundland)
map (49° 52′N 56° 47′W) **14**:166
JACKSONVILLE (Alabama)
map (33° 49′N 85° 46′W) **1**:234
JACKSONVILLE (Arkansas)
map (34° 52′N 92° 7′W) **2**:166
JACKSONVILLE (Florida) **11**:344–345
map (30° 20′N 81° 40′W) **8**:172
JACKSONVILLE (Illinois)
map (39° 44′N 90° 14′W) **11**:42
JACKSONVILLE (North Carolina)
map (34° 45′N 77° 26′W) **14**:242
JACKSONVILLE (Oregon)
map (42° 19′N 122° 57′W) **14**:427
JACKSONVILLE (Texas)
map (31° 58′N 95° 17′W) **19**:129
JACKSONVILLE BEACH (Florida)
map (30° 18′N 81° 24′W) **8**:172
JACMEL (Haiti)
map (18° 14′N 72° 32′W) **10**:15
JACOB **11**:345 *bibliog.*
JACOB, FRANÇOIS **11**:345
biology **3**:271
genetics **9**:89
Lwoff, André **12**:473
Monod, Jacques Lucien **13**:536
operon **14**:403
JACOB, GEORGES **11**:345
Empire style **7**:158–159
JACOBABAD
map (28° 17′N 68° 26′E) **15**:27
JACOBEAN LITERATURE **11**:345
Bacon, Francis **3**:13–14
Beaumont, Francis, and Fletcher, John **3**:147
Donne, John **6**:239
Jonson, Ben **11**:445–446
masque **13**:200
Middleton, Thomas **13**:413
Shakespeare, William **17**:236–237
JACOBEAN THEATER
Beaumont, Francis, and Fletcher, John **3**:147
Chamberlain's Men **4**:274
Dekker, Thomas **6**:86
drama **6**:258–259
Globe Theatre **9**:208–209
JACOBI, CARL GUSTAV JACOB **11**:345 *bibliog.*
JACOBI, FRIEDRICH HEINRICH **11**:345 *bibliog.*
JACOBI, LOTTE **11**:345
JACOBINA (Brazil)
map (11° 11′S 40° 31′W) **3**:460
JACOBINS **11**:345 *bibliog.*
Fouché, Joseph **8**:249
radicalism **16**:43
Robespierre, Maximilien **16**:242
JACOBITE CHURCH **11**:346 *bibliog.*
Malabar Christians **13**:78
Monophysitism **13**:537
JACOBITES **11**:346 *bibliog.*
Battle of Culloden Moor **17**:152 *illus.*
Stuart, Charles Edward (Bonnie Prince Charlie) **18**:304–305
Stuart, James Francis Edward **18**:305–306
tartan **19**:40 *illus.*
Tory party **19**:247
JACOBS, CHARLES M.
tunnel **19**:338
JACOBS, GEORGE
trial of **17**:31 *illus.*
JACOBS, KLAUS J. **16**:217 *illus.*
JACOBS, SALLY
A Midsummer Night's Dream set **19**:151 *illus.*
JACOBS, W. W. **11**:346
JACOB'S LADDER (botany) **11**:346
JACOB'S PILLOW DANCE FESTIVAL **11**:346 *bibliog.*
JACOB'S STAFF **11**:346 *bibliog.*
Levi ben Gershon **12**:303
navigation **14**:59
JACOBSEN, ARNE **11**:346 *bibliog.*
JACOBSEN, JENS PETER **11**:346–347 *bibliog.*
JACOBSEN, ROBERT
Scandinavian art and architecture **17**:114
JACOBSON'S ORGAN **11**:347
lizard **12**:380
reptile **16**:171
snake **17**:378–379 *illus.*
JACOBY, LEE *see* COBB, LEE J.
JACOPONE DA TODI **11**:347
JACQUARD, JOSEPH MARIE **11**:347
loom **19**:136–137 *illus.*
JACQUELINE OF HAINAUT **11**:347
JACQUERIE **11**:347 *bibliog.*
JACQUES-CARTIER, MOUNT
map (48° 59′N 65° 57′W) **16**:18
JACQUES-CARTIER, STRAIT OF
map (50° 0′N 63° 30′W) **16**:18
JACQUET RIVER (New Brunswick)
map (47° 55′N 66° 0′W) **14**:117
JADE **9**:70 *illus.*; **11**:347 *bibliog., illus.*
Chinese archaeology **4**:379 *illus.*
Chinese art and architecture **4**:384 *illus.*
human virtues **11**:347
jewelry **11**:408
ornaments and tools **11**:347 *illus.*
peoples using **11**:347
JADEITE
jade **11**:347
pyroxene **15**:638
JADWIGA, QUEEN OF POLAND **11**:348 *bibliog.*
JAEGER **11**:348
JAÉN (Peru)
map (5° 42′S 78° 47′W) **15**:193
JAÉN (Spain)
map (37° 46′N 3° 47′W) **18**:140
JAFFA (Israel) **11**:304 *illus.*; **11**:348
map (32° 4′N 35° 46′E **11**:302
JAFFNA (Sri Lanka)
map (9° 40′N 80° 0′E) **18**:206
JAFFNA LAGOON
map (9° 35′N 80° 15′E) **18**:206
JAFFREY (New Hampshire)
map (42° 50′N 72° 4′W) **14**:123
JAGAN, CHEDDI **11**:348 *bibliog.*
Burnham, Forbes **3**:577
Guyana **9**:411
JAGELLO (dynasty) **11**:348 *bibliog.*
Jadwiga, Queen **11**:348
Poland **15**:391
JAGGER, MICK
Rolling Stones, The **16**:272
JAGIELLO *see* JAGELLO (dynasty)
JAGUAR **11**:348–349 *bibliog., illus.*; **11**:469 *illus.*
JAGUARUNDI **11**:349
JAGÜEY GRANDE (Cuba)
map (22° 32′N 81° 8′W) **5**:377
JAHAN, SHAH, MOGUL EMPEROR OF INDIA *see* SHAH JAHAN, MOGUL EMPEROR OF INDIA
JAHANGIR, MOGUL EMPEROR OF INDIA **11**:90 *illus.*; **11**:349 *bibliog.*
Fatehpur Sikri **8**:34
Lahore (Pakistan) **12**:167
Mogul art and architecture **13**:501–502 *illus.*
JAHIZ, ABU UTHMAN AMR AL- **11**:349
JAHN, FRIEDRICH LUDWIG **11**:349
gymnastics **9**:413
JÄHN, SIGMUND **11**:349
JAHNN, HANS HENNY **11**:349
JAHROM (Iran)
map (28° 31′N 53° 33′E) **11**:250
JAI ALAI **11**:349 *bibliog.*
JAIL *see* PRISON
JAINISM **11**:349–350 *bibliog.*; **16**:140 *map*
Asia, history of **2**:250
Ellora **7**:148
India, history of **11**:89
Indian art and architecture **11**:94
nirvana **14**:201
philosophy **15**:246
yoga **20**:328–329
JAIPUR (India) **11**:350
map (26° 55′N 75° 49′E) **11**:80
JAKARTA (Indonesia) **11**:150 *illus.*; **11**:350–351 *illus.*
climate **2**:237 *table*; **11**:148 *table*
map (6° 10′S 106° 48′E) **11**:147
JAKOBSON, ROMAN **11**:351
language and literature **12**:197
JAKOBSTAD (Finland)
map (63° 40′N 22° 42′E) **8**:95
JAL (New Mexico)
map (32° 7′N 103° 12′W) **14**:136
JALALABAD (Afghanistan)
map (34° 26′N 70° 28′E) **1**:133
JALÁN RIVER
map (14° 39′N 86° 12′W) **10**:218
JALAPA (Guatemala)
map (14° 38′N 89° 59′W) **9**:389
JALAPA (Mexico) **11**:351
map (17° 43′N 92° 49′W) **13**:357
JALAPA (Nicaragua)
map (13° 55′N 86° 8′W) **14**:179
JALISCO (Mexico) **11**:351
cities
Guadalajara **9**:384
JALLABA
Darfur **6**:37
JALPAN (Mexico)
map (21° 14′N 99° 29′W) **13**:357
JAM AND JELLY **12**:351 *bibliog.*
pectin **15**:131
JAMAARE RIVER
map (12° 6′N 10° 14′E) **14**:190
JAMAICA **11**:351–352 *bibliog., illus., map, table*
Afro-American cults **1**:178
cities
Kingston **12**:84
economic activity **11**:352
flag **11**:351 *illus.*
government **11**:352
history **11**:352
Bustamante, Sir Alexander **3**:590
Eyre, Edward John **7**:352
Manley (family) **13**:122
Seaga, Edward **17**:172
land **11**:351–352 *illus., map, table*
map (18° 15′N 77° 30′W) **20**:109
people **11**:352
Rastafarians **16**:91
reggae **16**:128
JAMAICA BAY
map (40° 36′N 73° 51′W) **14**:129
JAMAIS VU PHENOMENON
consciousness, states of **5**:200
JAMAL AL-DIN AL-AFGHANI **11**:352–353 *bibliog.*
JAMALPUR (Bangladesh)
map (24° 55′N 89° 56′E) **3**:64
JAMALZADE, MOHAMMED ALI **11**:353
JAMAME (Somalia)
map (0° 4′N 42° 46′E) **18**:60
JAMBELI CHANNEL
map (3° 0′S 80° 0′W) **7**:52
JAMBES (Belgium)
map (50° 28′N 4° 52′E) **3**:177
JAMBI (Indonesia)
map (1° 36′S 103° 37′E) **11**:147
JAMBIYA **18**:399 *illus.*
JAMES, CHARLES
fashion design **8**:32
JAMES, EARL OF DOUGLAS *see* DOUGLAS (family)
JAMES, EDWIN
Pikes Peak **15**:301
JAMES, EPISTLE OF **11**:353
JAMES, HENRY **1**:345 *illus.*; **11**:353–354 *bibliog., illus.*
Ambassadors, The **1**:324–325
American, The **1**:326–327
Bostonians, The **3**:411
Daisy Miller **6**:10
Golden Bowl, The **9**:231
novel **14**:275
realism (literature) **16**:104
The Turn of the Screw **14**:275 *illus.*
JAMES, JESSE **11**:354 *bibliog.*
outlaws **14**:468 *illus.*
Younger brothers **20**:336
JAMES, LAKE
map (35° 45′N 81° 55′W) **14**:242
JAMES, P. D. **11**:354
JAMES, SAINT (the "brother" of Jesus Christ) **11**:353
JAMES, SAINT (James the Great) **11**:353
Santiago (Spain) **17**:70
JAMES, SAINT (James the Lesser) **11**:353
JAMES, THOMAS **11**:354 *bibliog.*
JAMES, WILLIAM **11**:354–355 *bibliog., illus.*
emotion **7**:157
pragmatism **15**:487
psychology, history of **15**:596 *illus.*
JAMES I, KING OF ARAGON (James the Conqueror) **11**:355 *bibliog.*
JAMES I, KING OF ENGLAND **11**:355–356 *bibliog., illus.*
Coke, Sir Edward **5**:96
coronation **17**:152 *illus.*
Irish settlements **11**:262 *map*

London Company **12**:405
Salisbury, Robert Cecil, 1st Earl of **17**:33
tobacco **19**:218
Tudor (dynasty) **19**:328
JAMES I, KING OF SCOTLAND **11**:356–357 *bibliog.*
JAMES II, KING OF ARAGON **11**:355 *bibliog.*
JAMES II, KING OF ENGLAND, SCOTLAND, AND IRELAND **11**:356 *bibliog., illus.*
Danby, Thomas Osborne, 1st Earl of **6**:21
English Bill of Rights **3**:253
Glorious Revolution **9**:209
Great Britain, history of **9**:314
Jacobites **11**:346
Jeffreys, George Jeffreys, 1st Baron **11**:394
Londonderry (city in Northern Ireland) **12**:405
Monmouth, James Scott, Duke of **13**:536
Oates, Titus **14**:313
Shaftesbury, Anthony Ashley Cooper, 1st Earl of **17**:234
Stuart, James Francis Edward **18**:305–306
Test Acts **19**:126
William III, King of England, Scotland, and Ireland **20**:156
JAMES IV, KING OF SCOTLAND **11**:357 *bibliog.*
JAMES V, KING OF SCOTLAND **11**:357 *bibliog.*
JAMES VI, KING OF SCOTLAND *see* JAMES I, KING OF ENGLAND
JAMES BAY
map (53° 30′N 80° 30′W) **14**:393
JAMES CITY (county in Virginia)
map (37° 17′N 76° 48′W) **19**:607
JAMES ISLAND (South Carolina)
map (32° 42′N 79° 58′W) **18**:98
JAMES NORRIS TROPHY
Orr, Bobby **14**:448
JAMES RIVER (Missouri)
map (36° 45′N 93° 30′W) **13**:476
JAMES RIVER (South Dakota)
map (42° 52′N 97° 18′W) **18**:103
JAMES RIVER (Virginia) **11**:355
map (36° 57′N 76° 26′W) **19**:607
JAMES WATT (steamship)
ship **17**:273
JAMESBURG (New Jersey)
map (40° 21′N 74° 26′W) **14**:129
JAMES BAY **11**:355
JAMESON, SIR LEANDER STARR **11**:357 *bibliog.*
Harare (Zimbabwe) **10**:42
JAMESON RAID
Jameson, Sir Leander Starr **11**:357–358
JAMESPORT (Missouri)
map (39° 58′N 93° 48′W) **13**:476
JAMESTOWN (Kentucky)
map (36° 59′N 85° 4′W) **12**:47
JAMESTOWN (New York)
map (42° 6′N 79° 14′W) **14**:149
JAMESTOWN (North Dakota)
map (46° 54′N 98° 42′W) **14**:248
JAMESTOWN (Tennessee)
map (36° 26′N 84° 57′W) **19**:104
JAMESTOWN (Virginia) **11**:357 *bibliog., illus.*
De La Warr, Thomas West, 12th Baron **6**:61
Gates, Sir Thomas **9**:58
London Company **12**:405
massacre of 1622 **11**:107 *illus.*
Pocahontas **15**:376
Powhatan **15**:486
Rolfe, John **16**:271
slavery **17**:354
Smith, John **17**:369
United States, history of the **19**:436
Virginia **19**:611
JAMESTOWN RESERVOIR
map (47° 15′N 98° 40′W) **14**:248
JAMESTOWN WEED *see* JIMSONWEED
JAMITTEPEC (Mexico)
map (16° 17′N 97° 49′W) **13**:357
JAMMU (India)
Kashmir (India) **12**:29–30
map (32° 42′N 74° 52′E) **11**:80
JAMNAGAR (India)
map (22° 28′N 70° 4′E) **11**:80
JAMNITZER (family) **11**:357–358 *bibliog.*
gold and silver work **9**:230
JAMSHEDPUR (India)
map (22° 48′N 86° 11′E) **11**:80
JAMUNA RIVER
Brahmaputra River **3**:440
map (23° 51′N 89° 45′E) **3**:64
JANÁČEK, LEOŠ **11**:358 *bibliog.*
Brno **3**:499
Czech music **5**:413
JANATA PARTY
India **11**:88
JANE EYRE (book) **11**:358 *bibliog.*
Brontë, Charlotte **3**:504
JANEQUIN, CLÉMENT **11**:358 *bibliog.*
music, history of Western **13**:665
JANESVILLE (California)
map (40° 18′N 120° 32′W) **4**:31
JANESVILLE (Minnesota)
map (44° 7′N 93° 42′W) **13**:453
JANESVILLE (Wisconsin)
map (42° 41′N 89° 1′W) **20**:185
JANET, PIERRE **11**:358 *bibliog.*
JANEWAY, ELIZABETH **11**:358
JANISSARIES **11**:358 *bibliog.*; **14**:465 *illus.*
Mahmud II, Sultan of the Ottoman Empire **13**:65
Mehmed II, Sultan of the Ottoman Empire **13**:281
Murad II, Sultan of the Ottoman Empire **13**:645
Ottoman Empire **14**:464
Selim III, Sultan of the Ottoman Empire **17**:192
JANNINGS, EMIL **11**:359
JANSEN (Saskatchewan)
map (51° 47′N 104° 43′W) **17**:81
JANSENISM **11**:359 *bibliog., illus.*
Arnauld, Antoine **2**:183
Arnauld, Jacqueline Marie Angélique **2**:183
Pascal, Blaise **15**:102
Saint-Cyran, Abbé de **17**:17
JANSKY, KARL **11**:359 *bibliog.*
radio astronomy **16**:47 *illus.*
radio telescope **16**:50
JANSON, H. W. **11**:359 *bibliog.*
JANSSEN, CÉSAR
astronomy, history of **2**:279
JANSSEN, HANS AND ZACHARIAS
microscope **13**:387
JANSSEN, JULES **11**:359
JANSZOON, WILLEM
exploration **7**:335
JANUARY
birthstones **3**:296 *illus., table*
calendar **4**:28
JANUS **11**:360
JAPAN **11**:360–367 *bibliog., illus., map, table*
agriculture **11**:365–366 *illus.*
lumber **12**:455
rice **16**:207–208
silk **17**:307
soybean **18**:114–115
tea **19**:53–54
aircraft, military *see* AIRCRAFT, MILITARY
akita (dog) **1**:231
art *see* JAPANESE ART AND ARCHITECTURE
bonsai **3**:382
cities
Fukuoka **8**:356
Hakodate **10**:17
Hiroshima **10**:175–176 *illus.*
Kawasaki **12**:32
Kitakyushu **12**:91
Kobe **12**:104
Kyoto **12**:143
Nagasaki **14**:6
Nagoya **14**:6
Nara **14**:20
Osaka **14**:452
Sapporo **17**:73
Sendai **17**:200
Tokyo **19**:223–225 *illus., map*
Yokohama **20**:329
climate **11**:362–363 *table*
cooking **5**:240
crime **5**:346 *table*
culture
Benedict, Ruth **3**:197
dance **6**:26–27 *illus.*
Bugaku **3**:547
Dengaku **6**:107
demography **11**:363–364
disputed island claims **11**:362
Kuril Islands **12**:139
economic activity **11**:365–366 *illus.*
ore deposits **14**:426
robot **16**:246
unemployment rate **7**:160
education **7**:62; **11**:364
Japanese universities **11**:382–383 *table*
Tokyo, University of **19**:225–226
energy and power **11**:366
fishing **11**:366 *illus.*
greenling **9**:353
flag **11**:360 *illus.*
folklore
oni **14**:390
geisha **9**:68–69
government **11**:366–367
defense, national **6**:82 *table*
foreign policy **8**:225
hara-kiri **10**:41
health **11**:364
history *see* JAPAN, HISTORY OF
housing **10**:279
land and resources **11**:360–363 *illus., map, table*
language *see* JAPANESE LANGUAGE
literature *see* JAPANESE LITERATURE
manufacturing **2**:246–247 *illus.*; **11**:365 *illus.*; **13**:133
automotive industry **2**:364; **2**:366 *table*; **2**:367
map (36° 0′N 138° 0′E) **2**:232
martial arts **13**:176–178
medicine **13**:268
music *see* JAPANESE MUSIC
mythology
Amaterasu **1**:322
National Hero Honors Order
Oh, Sadaharu **14**:355
navy
Togo Heihachiro **19**:222
Yamato (battleship) **3**:127–128 *illus.*
Yukikase (destroyer) **6**:133
Zero (aircraft) **20**:361
newspaper **14**:172
people **2**:242 *illus.*; **11**:363–365 *illus.*
Ainu **1**:203
migration to the United States **11**:55 *map*
race **16**:34 *illus.*
women in society **20**:204 *table*
physical features
Fuji, Mount **8**:355–356
Iwo Jima **11**:337–338
Ring of Fire **16**:225
political parties **11**:366
Katsura Taro **12**:31
postage stamp **15**:230 *illus.*
prostitution **15**:573
regions
Bonin Islands **3**:379–380
Hokkaido **10**:199
Honshu **10**:224
Kyushu **12**:143
Ryukyu Islands **16**:380
Shikoku **17**:261
religion **11**:363
Buddhism **3**:541–542
Nichiren **14**:180
Pure Land Buddhism **15**:629
Shinto **17**:262–263
Soka-gakkai **18**:39
Zen Buddhism **20**:358–359
rivers, lakes, and waterways **11**:363
Inland Sea **11**:178–179
sake **17**:28
space technology
National Space Development Agency **14**:46
sports
Oh, Sadaharu **14**:355
wrestling **20**:287 *illus.*
theater
Bunraku **3**:563
Dengaku **6**:107
gigaku **9**:178
Japanese music **11**:382
Kabuki **12**:4 *illus.*
Kyogen **12**:143
No drama **14**:207
theater, history of the **19**:148–149
trade **11**:366
Harris, Townsend **10**:58
transportation **11**:366
locomotive **12**:390 *illus.*
railroad **16**:74; **16**:76 *illus.*
roads and highways **16**:238
sampan **17**:48
tunnel **19**:339
urban planning *see* URBAN PLANNING
vegetation and animal life **11**:363
wedding ceremony **13**:163 *illus.*
women pearl divers **15**:127 *illus.*
JAPAN, HISTORY OF **11**:367–372 *bibliog., illus., map*
Asia, history of **2**:254
Korea, history of **12**:116–117
Sino-Japanese Wars **17**:323
women in society **20**:203
prior to 1180
Heian period **11**:367
Japanese music **11**:381 *illus.*
Jingo **11**:419
Jomon culture **11**:367
Kammu **11**:367
Nara period **11**:367
Shotoku Taishi **17**:286
Yamato period **11**:367
1180–1867 shogunates
American warships in Tokyo Bay (1854) **2**:256 *illus.*
Ashikaga period **11**:368
feudalism **8**:64
Francis Xavier, Saint **8**:275
Hideyoshi **10**:159
Ieyasu, Shogun **11**:32
Kamakura period **11**:367–368
Nobunaga **14**:211–212
Period of Unification **11**:368–369
Perry, Matthew Calbraith **15**:179
samurai **17**:49
shogun **17**:281
Tokugawa (family) **11**:369; **19**:223
1868–1926 Meiji and Taisho periods
coin **14**:296 *illus.*
Hara Takashi **10**:41
Itagaki Taisuke **11**:308
Ito Hirobumi **11**:331
Kato Takaaki **12**:31
Katsura Taro **12**:31
Manchuria (China) **13**:109
Matsukata Masayoshi **13**:230
Meiji Restoration **13**:281–282
Okuma Shigenobu **14**:372
Ozaki Yukio **14**:479–480
Russo-Japanese War *see* RUSSO-JAPANESE WAR
Saigo Takamori **17**:15
Saionji Kimmochi **17**:28
World War I *see* WORLD WAR I
Yamagata Aritomo **20**:316
1926-present **11**:370–372
Akihito **1**:231
expansion 1875–1942 **11**:371 *map*
expansion 1931–1941 **20**:259 *map*
Fukuda Takeo **8**:356
Hatoyama Ichiro **10**:68
Hirohito, Emperor **10**:175
Ikeda Hayato **11**:40
Konoe Fumimaro **12**:109
Miki Takeo **13**:417
Nakasone Yasuhiro **14**:8
Ohira Masayoshi **14**:363
Sato Eisaku **17**:88
Shidehara Kijuro **17**:260
Suzuki Zenko **18**:374
Taiwan **19**:14
Tanaka Giichi **19**:21
Tanaka Kakuei **19**:21
Tojo Hideki **19**:222
Vietnam **19**:583
World War II *see* WORLD WAR II
Yoshida Shigeru **20**:332
JAPAN, SEA OF **11**:372
map (40° 0′N 135° 0′E) **11**:361
JAPAN PLATE
plate tectonics **15**:351 *map*
JAPAN TRENCH *see* OCEANIC TRENCHES
JAPANESE-AMERICAN CITIZENS LEAGUE
Oriental Americans **14**:442
JAPANESE-AMERICANS *see* NISEI; ORIENTAL AMERICANS
JAPANESE ART AND ARCHITECTURE **11**:365; **11**:372–379 *bibliog., illus.*
See also the subheading Japan under specific art forms, e.g., ARCHITECTURE; DECORATIVE ARTS; PAINTING; etc.; names of specific artists, e.g., HOKUSAI; UNKEI; etc.
calligraphy **4**:45
castle **4**:190–191
celadon **4**:229
craft **5**:326
Daibutsu (Great Buddha) **2**:241 *illus.*; **11**:375 *illus.*
Fenollosa, Ernest Francisco **8**:50–51
folk art **8**:198 *illus.*
Freer, Charles Lang **8**:300
garden **9**:41 *illus.*
graphic arts **9**:291
Hoodo (Phoenix Hall) **19**:99 *illus.*
Hoodo, Byodoin temple (Kyoto) **11**:374 *illus.*
interior design **11**:211
ivory and ivory carving **11**:336–337
jewelry **11**:408
Kaigetsudo **12**:6
Kano school *see* KANO SCHOOL
kite (object) **12**:92 *illus.*
Korean art **12**:117
Kyoto **12**:143
museums, art **13**:658
Nanga school *see* NANGA SCHOOL

JAPANESE ART AND ARCHITECTURE (cont.)
netsuke **14**:104
paper folding **15**:70–71 *illus.*
Pine Trees and Eagle **11**:376 *illus.*
Portrait of Jion Daishi **11**:375 *illus.*
Royal Ontario Museum **16**:330
Secession movement **17**:178
Soami **18**:6
temple **19**:98–99 *illus.*
tomb **19**:231
Ukiyo-e **19**:375
JAPANESE BEETLE **3**:166–167 *illus.*; **11**:379
life cycle **3**:166 *illus.*
JAPANESE BOBTAIL CAT **4**:195 *illus.*; **11**:379 *illus.*
JAPANESE CHIN **11**:379 *illus.*
JAPANESE DOLL THEATER *see* BUNRAKU
JAPANESE GIANT SALAMANDER **11**:379
JAPANESE LANGUAGE **11**:379 *bibliog.*; **12**:355 *map*
Asia **2**:244 *map*
Japan **11**:363
Ural-Altaic languages **19**:475
writing systems, evolution of
Kana syllabary **20**:293
JAPANESE LITERATURE **11**:380 *bibliog.*
authors
Abe Kobo **1**:55
Akutagawa Ryunosuke **1**:232
Basho **3**:108
Buson **3**:590
Chikamatsu Monzaemon **4**:347
Dazai Osamu **6**:57
Enchi Fumiko **7**:162
Endo Shusaku **7**:168
Hagiwara, Sakutaro **10**:10
Higuchi Ichiyo **10**:162
Ibuse Masuji **11**:7
Ihara Saikaku **11**:39
Ishikawa Takuboku **11**:287
Kawabata Yasunari **12**:32
Mishima Yukio **13**:466
Mori Ogai **13**:579
Murasaki Shikibu **13**:645
Nagai Kafu **14**:6
Natsume Soseki **14**:47
Oe Kenzaburo **14**:351
Ooka Shohei **14**:396
Sei Shonagon **17**:189
Shiga Naoya **17**:260
Shimazaki, Toson **17**:261–262
Tanizaki Junichiro **19**:23
Tsubouchi Shoyo **19**:325
Ueda Akinari **19**:371
Yokomitsu Riichi **20**:329
Zeami Motokiyo **20**:357
JAPANESE MUSIC **11**:380–382 *bibliog.*, *illus.*; **13**:668 *illus.*
Bugaku **3**:547
Bunraku **3**:563
characteristics **11**:380
Dengaku **6**:107
instruments **11**:380–382 *illus.*
Kabuki **12**:4
koto **12**:125
JAPANESE PAGODA TREE **11**:382 *illus.*
JAPANESE RICE WINE *see* SAKE
JAPANESE SNOWBALL (botany) *see* VIBURNUM
JAPANESE SPANIEL **6**:217 *illus.*
JAPANESE SPIDER CRAB **5**:324 *illus.*
JAPANESE UNIVERSITIES **11**:382–383 *bibliog.*, *table*
JAPURÁ RIVER
map (3° 8′S 64° 46′W) **3**:460
JAQUÉ (Panama)
map (7° 31′N 78° 10′W) **15**:55
JAQUES-DALCROZE, ÉMILE *see* DALCROZE, ÉMILE JAQUES
JARAI *see* MONTAGNARDS
JARDINES DE LA REINA ISLANDS
map (20° 50′N 78° 55′W) **5**:377
JARI RIVER
map (1° 9′S 51° 54′W) **3**:460
JARMO (Iraq) **11**:383 *bibliog.*
JAROSŁAW (Poland)
map (50° 2′N 22° 42′E) **15**:388
JARRATT (Virginia)
map (36° 48′N 77° 28′W) **19**:607
JARRELL, RANDALL **11**:383 *bibliog.*
JARRY, ALFRED **11**:383 *bibliog.*
JARUZELSKI, WOJCIECH **11**:383
Poland **15**:391
JARVES, DEMING
glassware, decorative **9**:204
JARVIE (Alberta)
map (54° 27′N 113° 59′W) **1**:256
JARVIS, GREGORY **11**:383
JARVIK-7 (artificial heart) **10**:94-95
JARVIS, JOHN W.
DeWitt Clinton **5**:60 *illus.*
JARVIS ISLAND
map (0° 23′S 160° 2′W) **14**:334
United States outlying territories **19**:464
JARVISBURG (North Carolina)
map (36° 9′N 75° 52′W) **14**:242
JASMINE **11**:384 *illus.*
See also CAPE JASMINE
JASON **11**:384
JASONVILLE (Indiana)
map (39° 10′N 87° 12′W) **11**:111
JASPER **11**:384
gem colors **11**:384
quartz **16**:14
JASPER (Alabama)
map (33° 50′N 87° 17′W) **1**:234
JASPER (Alberta)
map (52° 53′N 118° 5′W) **1**:256
JASPER (Arkansas)
map (36° 0′N 93° 11′W) **2**:166
JASPER (Florida)
map (30° 31′N 82° 57′W) **8**:172
JASPER (Georgia)
map (34° 28′N 84° 26′W) **9**:114
JASPER (county in Georgia)
map (33° 20′N 83° 40′W) **9**:114
JASPER (county in Illinois)
map (39° 0′N 88° 10′W) **11**:42
JASPER (Indiana)
map (38° 24′N 86° 56′W) **11**:111
JASPER (county in Indiana)
map (40° 57′N 87° 9′W) **11**:111
JASPER (county in Iowa)
map (41° 38′N 91° 0′W) **11**:244
JASPER (county in Mississippi)
map (32° 0′N 89° 5′W) **13**:469
JASPER (Missouri)
map (37° 20′N 94° 18′W) **13**:476
JASPER (county in Missouri)
map (37° 15′N 94° 20′W) **13**:476
JASPER (county in South Carolina)
map (32° 30′N 81° 0′W) **18**:98
JASPER (Tennessee)
map (35° 4′N 85° 38′W) **19**:104
JASPER (Texas)
map (30° 55′N 94° 1′W) **19**:129
JASPER (county in Texas)
map (30° 40′N 94° 0′W) **19**:129
JASPER NATIONAL PARK (Canada) **14**:226 *illus.*
JASPER WARE
Wedgwood, Josiah **20**:89–90
JASPERS, KARL **11**:384–385 *bibliog.*, *illus.*
existentialism **7**:332
phenomenology **15**:225
JASSY (Romania) *see* IAŞI (Romania)
JASSY, TREATY OF
Russo-Turkish Wars **16**:374
JAT
caste **4**:186
JAUJA (Peru)
map (11° 48′S 75° 30′W) **15**:193
JAUNDICE **11**:385 *bibliog.*
blood and liver diseases **11**:385
hepatitis **10**:130
infancy, Rh factor **11**:385
liver **12**:374
mononucleosis **13**:537
spirochete **18**:189
yellow fever **20**:322
yellowing, skin and eye **11**:385
JAURÈS, JEAN **11**:385 *bibliog.*
JAVA (Indonesia) **11**:149 *illus.*; **11**:385
archaeology
Borobudur **3**:402–403 *illus.*
Prambanan **15**:489
art
batik **3**:123–124 *illus.*
cities
Bandung **3**:62
Jakarta **11**:350–351 *illus.*
Semarang **17**:195
Surabaya **18**:358
map (7° 30′S 110° 0′E) **11**:147
money **13**:525 *illus.*
music
gamelan **9**:29
music, non-Western **13**:668
Raffles, Sir Thomas Stamford **16**:69
Southeast Asian art and architecture **18**:110
theater
puppet **15**:627 *illus.*
shadow play **17**:234
JAVA MAN **11**:385 *bibliog.*
Dubois, Eugène **6**:289
Homo erectus **10**:215
JAVA SEA **11**:385–386
map (5° 0′S 110° 0′E) **11**:147
Sunda Strait **18**:347
JAVA TRENCH
plate tectonics **15**:351 *map*
JAVACHEFF, CHRISTO *see* CHRISTO
JAVANESE **11**:386 *bibliog.*
JAVELIN FISH **6**:78 *illus.*
JAVELIN THROW
track and field **19**:260–262 *illus.*
JAVELINA *see* PECCARY
JAVITS, JACOB K. **11**:386 *bibliog.*
JAVORIE MOUNTAIN
map (48° 27′N 19° 18′E) **5**:413
JAW
alligator **13**:99 *illus.*
dog **4**:157 *illus.*; **13**:99 *illus.*
gulper eel **7**:71 *illus.*
joint (anatomy) **11**:439 *illus.*
muscles **13**:653
orthodontics **14**:449
rodent **16**:265 *illus.*
snake **17**:380 *illus.*
JAWARA, DAWDA K.
Gambia **9**:26
JAWFISH **11**:386
JAWLENSKY, ALEXEY VON **11**:386 *bibliog.*
JAWLESS FISH *see* HAGFISH; LAMPREY
JAWORSKI, LEON **11**:386
Nixon, Richard M. **14**:206
Watergate **20**:64
JAXARTES RIVER *see* SYR DARYA
JAY **4**:283 *illus.*; **8**:228–229 *illus.*; **11**:386 *bibliog.*, *illus.*
blue jay **3**:343
JAY (Florida)
map (30° 57′N 87° 9′W) **8**:172
JAY (county in Indiana)
map (40° 26′N 84° 59′W) **11**:111
JAY (Oklahoma)
map (36° 25′N 94° 48′W) **14**:368
JAY, JOHN **11**:387 *bibliog.*, *illus.*
Jay's Treaty **11**:387
JAY PEAK
map (44° 55′N 72° 32′W) **19**:554
JAYA PEAK
map (4° 5′S 137° 11′E) **11**:147
JAYAWARDENE, J. R. **11**:387
Sri Lanka **18**:206
JAYCEES INTERNATIONAL **11**:387
JAY'S TREATY **11**:387 *bibliog.*
Detroit **6**:135
Jay, John **11**:387
Rutledge, John **16**:377
United States, history of the **19**:443
Washington, George **20**:44
Wayne, Anthony **20**:73
JAYTON (Texas)
map (33° 15′N 100° 34′W) **19**:129
JAZ MURIAN LAKE
map (27° 20′N 58° 55′E) **11**:250
JAZZ **11**:387–390 *bibliog.*, *illus.*
Ailey, Alvin **1**:202–203
American music **1**:351 *illus.*
Armstrong, Louis **2**:179
Baker, Josephine **3**:28
Basie, Count **3**:109
Basin Street **3**:110
bebop **3**:150
Bechet, Sidney **3**:150
Beiderbecke, Bix **3**:171–172
Belafonte, Harry **3**:173
Blake, Eubie **3**:324
bluegrass music **3**:345
blues **3**:345–346
boogie-woogie **3**:383
Brubeck (family) **3**:519
Christian, Charlie **4**:411
Cole, Nat King **5**:99
Coltrane, John **5**:124
Davis, Miles **6**:52
Ellington, Duke **7**:147
Fitzgerald, Ella **8**:130
Gillespie, Dizzy **9**:182
Hammond, John **10**:31
Hampton, Lionel **10**:32
Hawkins, Coleman **10**:77
Hines, Earl **10**:173
Holiday, Billie **10**:202
Krupa, Gene **12**:132
Mingus, Charles **13**:444
Modern Jazz Quartet **13**:498
Monk, Thelonious **13**:532
Morton, Jelly Roll **13**:592
Newport (Rhode Island) **14**:170
Newport Jazz Festival **14**:171
Oliver, King **14**:379
Parker, Charlie **15**:89–90
Peterson, Oscar **15**:202
Reinhardt, Django **16**:132
Schuller, Gunther **17**:136
styles **11**:387–388 *illus.*
swing **18**:392–393
Tatum, Art **19**:44
Taylor, Cecil **19**:48
Vaughan, Sarah **19**:528
Waller, Fats **20**:16
Whiteman, Paul **20**:139
Young, Lester **20**:334
JAZZ PATTERN *see* ART DECO
JAZZ-ROCK
rock music **16**:249
JAZZIN (Lebanon)
map (33° 32′N 35° 34′E) **12**:265
JDL *see* JEWISH DEFENSE LEAGUE
JEAN, GRAND DUKE OF LUXEMBOURG
Luxembourg (country) **12**:472
JEAN-CHRISTOPHE (book)
Rolland, Romain **16**:271
JEANERETTE (Louisiana)
map (29° 55′N 91° 40′W) **12**:430
JEANNERET, CHARLES ÉDOUARD *see* LE CORBUSIER
JEANNETTE (Pennsylvania)
map (40° 20′N 79° 35′W) **15**:147
JEANS (clothing)
denim **6**:108
JEANS, SIR JAMES **11**:390 *bibliog.*
blackbody radiation **3**:321
Rayleigh-Jeans law **11**:390
JEBEL SAWDA MOUNTAIN
map (18° 18′N 42° 22′E) **17**:94
JEDDORE LAKE
map (48° 3′N 55° 55′W) **14**:166
JEDLITZKA, MARIA *see* JERITZA, MARIA
JEEP **11**:390–391 *bibliog.*, *illus.*
JEFF DAVIS (county in Georgia)
map (31° 50′N 82° 40′W) **9**:114
JEFF DAVIS (county in Texas)
map (30° 42′N 104° 5′W) **19**:129
JEFFERS (Minnesota)
map (44° 3′N 95° 12′W) **13**:453
JEFFERS, ROBINSON **11**:391 *bibliog.*
JEFFERSON (county in Alabama)
map (33° 40′N 87° 0′W) **1**:234
JEFFERSON (county in Arkansas)
map (34° 17′N 91° 55′W) **2**:166
JEFFERSON (county in Colorado)
map (39° 30′N 105° 15′W) **5**:116
JEFFERSON (county in Florida)
map (30° 25′N 83° 50′W) **8**:172
JEFFERSON (Georgia)
map (34° 7′N 83° 35′W) **9**:114
JEFFERSON (county in Georgia)
map (33° 5′N 82° 25′W) **9**:114
JEFFERSON (county in Idaho)
map (43° 50′N 112° 20′W) **11**:26
JEFFERSON (county in Illinois)
map (38° 25′N 88° 57′W) **11**:42
JEFFERSON (county in Indiana)
map (38° 44′N 85° 23′W) **11**:111
JEFFERSON (Iowa)
map (42° 1′N 94° 23′W) **11**:244
JEFFERSON (county in Iowa)
map (41° 0′N 91° 57′W) **11**:244
JEFFERSON (county in Kansas)
map (39° 15′N 95° 25′W) **12**:18
JEFFERSON (county in Kentucky)
map (38° 10′N 85° 40′W) **12**:47
JEFFERSON (Louisiana)
map (29° 58′N 90° 10′W) **12**:430
JEFFERSON (county in Louisiana)
map (29° 40′N 90° 5′W) **12**:430
JEFFERSON (county in Mississippi)
map (31° 45′N 91° 0′W) **13**:469
JEFFERSON (county in Missouri)
map (38° 18′N 90° 35′W) **13**:476
JEFFERSON (county in Montana)
map (46° 7′N 112° 3′W) **13**:547
JEFFERSON (county in Nebraska)
map (40° 10′N 97° 5′W) **14**:70
JEFFERSON (county in New York)
map (44° 0′N 76° 0′W) **14**:149
JEFFERSON (North Carolina)
map (36° 26′N 81° 28′W) **14**:242
JEFFERSON (Ohio)
map (41° 44′N 80° 46′W) **14**:357
JEFFERSON (county in Ohio)
map (40° 22′N 80° 37′W) **14**:357
JEFFERSON (county in Oklahoma)
map (34° 5′N 97° 50′W) **14**:368
JEFFERSON (Oregon)
map (44° 43′N 123° 1′W) **14**:427
JEFFERSON (county in Oregon)
map (44° 40′N 121° 10′W) **14**:427
JEFFERSON (county in Pennsylvania)
map (41° 9′N 79° 5′W) **15**:147
JEFFERSON (county in Tennessee)
map (36° 5′N 83° 25′W) **19**:104
JEFFERSON (Texas)
map (32° 46′N 94° 21′W) **19**:129
JEFFERSON (county in Texas)
map (29° 55′N 94° 10′W) **19**:129
JEFFERSON (county in Washington)
map (47° 50′N 122° 36′W) **20**:35
JEFFERSON (county in West Virginia)
map (39° 20′N 77° 52′W) **20**:111
JEFFERSON (Wisconsin)
map (43° 1′N 88° 48′W) **20**:185

JEFFERSON (county in Wisconsin)
map (43° 2′N 88° 46′W) **20**:185
JEFFERSON, ARTHUR STANLEY *see* LAUREL AND HARDY
JEFFERSON, BLIND LEMON
blues **3**:346
JEFFERSON, JOSEPH **11**:391
JEFFERSON, MOUNT (Nevada)
map (38° 46′N 116° 55′W) **14**:111
JEFFERSON, MOUNT (Oregon)
map (44° 40′N 121° 47′W) **14**:427
JEFFERSON, TERRITORY OF **11**:391
JEFFERSON, THOMAS **6**:99 *illus.*; **11**:391–393 *bibliog.*, *illus.*
American art and architecture **1**:327
archaeology **2**:124
as governor of Virginia **11**:391–392
as minister to France **11**:392
as president **11**:393
as Secretary of State **11**:392–393
Charlottesville (Virginia) **4**:299
civil rights **5**:12
Civil War, U.S. **5**:15
Constitution of the United States **5**:213
Declaration of Independence **6**:74–76
Democratic party **6**:99
Embargo Act **7**:151
Hamilton, Alexander **10**:28
Kentucky and Virginia Resolutions **12**:51
Kościuszko, Tadeusz **12**:123
Lewis and Clark Expedition **12**:307
Library of Congress **12**:319
Louisiana Purchase **12**:435–436
Madison, James **13**:42
Marbury v. *Madison* **13**:144
Monroe, James **13**:541–542
Monticello **13**:557; **19**:610 *illus.*
Natural Bridge (Virginia) **19**:610 *illus.*
Rushmore, Mount **16**:348
state rights **18**:233
12th Amendment **19**:358
United States, history of **19**:442–443 *illus.*
University of Virginia's Rotunda **2**:136 *illus.*; **19**:609 *illus.*
Virginia, state universities and colleges of **19**:612
JEFFERSON AIRPLANE **11**:393
JEFFERSON CITY (Missouri) **11**:393; **13**:480 *illus.*
map (38° 34′N 92° 10′W) **13**:476
JEFFERSON CITY (Tennessee)
map (36° 7′N 83° 30′W) **19**:104
JEFFERSON DAVIS (county in Louisiana)
map (30° 15′N 92° 45′W) **12**:430
JEFFERSON DAVIS (county in Mississippi)
map (31° 35′N 89° 50′W) **13**:469
JEFFERSON MEMORIAL
Washington, D.C. **20**:40 *illus.*, *map*
JEFFERSON RIVER
map (45° 56′N 111° 30′W) **13**:547
JEFFERSONTOWN (Kentucky)
map (38° 12′N 85° 35′W) **12**:47
JEFFERSONVILLE (Georgia)
map (32° 41′N 83° 20′W) **9**:114
JEFFERSONVILLE (Indiana)
map (38° 17′N 85° 44′W) **11**:111
JEFFORDS, THOMAS **11**:394
JEFFREY, FRANCIS **11**:394 *bibliog.*
JEFFREYS, GEORGE JEFFREYS, 1st BARON **11**:394 *bibliog.*
JEFFREYS, SIR HAROLD **11**:394 *bibliog.*
JEFFRIES, JAMES J. **11**:394
JEHANGIR *see* JAHANGIR, MOGUL EMPEROR OF INDIA
JEHOIAKIM, KING OF JUDAH **11**:394
JEHOSHAPHAT, KING OF JUDAH **11**:394
JEHOVAH *see* GOD
JEHOVAH'S WITNESSES **11**:394 *bibliog.*
Russell, Charles Taze **16**:350
Rutherford, Joseph Franklin **16**:376
JEHU, KING OF ISRAEL **11**:394; **15**:44 *illus.*
JEJUNUM
digestion, human **6**:171
intestine **11**:230
JEKYLL ISLAND
map (31° 4′N 81° 25′W) **9**:114
JELENIA GÓRA (Poland)
map (50° 55′N 15° 46′E) **15**:388
JELLICO (Tennessee)
map (36° 35′N 84° 8′W) **19**:104
JELLICOE, ANN **11**:394–395 *bibliog.*
JELLICOE, SIR JOHN
World War I **20**:235
JELLY *see* JAM AND JELLY
JELLYFISH **5**:91 *illus.*; **11**:395 *bibliog.*, *illus.*
bioluminescence **3**:272
coelenterate **5**:91–92
Huxley, Thomas Henry **10**:325
plankton **15**:332
poisonous plants and animals **15**:385
Precambrian time **15**:491 *illus.*
JEMAL PASHA
Young Turks **20**:336
JEMBER (Indonesia)
map (8° 10′S 113° 42′E) **11**:147
JEMEZ PUEBLO (New Mexico)
map (35° 37′N 106° 43′W) **14**:136
JEMEZ SPRINGS (New Mexico)
map (35° 46′N 106° 42′W) **14**:136
JEMISON, MARY **11**:395
JENA (East Germany) **11**:395
JENA (Louisiana)
map (31° 41′N 92° 8′W) **12**:430
JENA MILK GLASS
Zsigmondy, Richard Adolf **20**:380
JENCKS, CHRISTOPHER **11**:395
JENCKS, JOSEPH, JR.
Pawtucket (Rhode Island) **15**:121
JENGHIZ KHAN *see* GENGHIS KHAN, MONGOL EMPEROR
JENKINS (county in Georgia)
map (32° 45′N 82° 0′W) **9**:114
JENKINS (Kentucky)
map (37° 10′N 82° 38′W) **12**:47
JENKINS, CHARLES FRANCIS **11**:395 *bibliog.*
JENKINS, RICHARD *see* BURTON, RICHARD (actor)
JENKINS, ROY **11**:395–396
JENKINS' EAR, WAR OF
French and Indian Wars **8**:313
Vernon, Edward **19**:559
JENKINSON, ROBERT BANKS, 2D EARL OF LIVERPOOL *see* LIVERPOOL, ROBERT BANKS JENKINSON, 2D EARL OF
JENKINSVILLE (South Carolina)
map (34° 16′N 81° 17′W) **18**:98
JENKINTOWN (Pennsylvania)
map (40° 6′N 75° 8′W) **15**:147
JENNER, BRUCE **11**:396 *bibliog.*
decathlon **6**:72
JENNER, EDWARD **11**:396 *bibliog.*
biology **3**:269
cowpox **5**:322
immunity **11**:57
medicine **13**:270
smallpox **17**:365
vaccination **19**:501
vaccinia **19**:502
JENNEY, WILLIAM LEBARON **11**:396 *bibliog.*
skyscraper **17**:348
JENNINGS (Florida)
map (30° 36′N 83° 6′W) **8**:172
JENNINGS (county in Indiana)
map (38° 59′N 85° 36′W) **11**:111
JENNINGS (Louisiana)
map (30° 13′N 92° 39′W) **12**:430
JENNINGS (Missouri)
map (38° 44′N 90° 17′W) **13**:476
JENNINGS, ISAIAH **19**:450 *illus.*
JENNY (ass) *see* ASS
JENRETTE, JOHN
ABSCAM **1**:62
JENSEN (Utah)
map (40° 22′N 109° 17′W) **19**:492
JENSEN, ARTHUR **11**:396 *bibliog.*
JENSEN, GEORG
jewelry **11**:411
JENSEN, HANS **11**:396
Wigner, Eugene Paul **20**:147
JENSEN, JOHANNES VILHELM **11**:396 *bibliog.*
JENSEN BEACH (Florida)
map (27° 15′N 80° 14′W) **8**:172
JEQUIÉ (Brazil)
map (13° 51′S 40° 5′W) **3**:460
JERASH *see* GERASA (Jordan)
JERAULD (county in South Dakota)
map (44° 3′N 98° 37′W) **18**:103
JERBOA **11**:396 *illus.*
JEREMIAH (prophet) **17**:162 *illus.*
JEREMIAH, BOOK OF **11**:397 *bibliog.*
JÉRÉMIE (Haiti)
map (18° 39′N 74° 7′W) **10**:15
JEREZ DE LA FRONTERA (Spain) **11**:397
map (36° 41′N 6° 8′W) **18**:140
JERICHO (Jordan) **11**:397 *bibliog.*
Kenyon, Dame Kathleen **12**:57
JERIMOTH HILL
map (41° 52′N 71° 47′W) **16**:198
JERITZA, MARIA **11**:397 *bibliog.*
JERKY *see* PEMMICAN
JERNE, NIELS K. **11**:397
JEROBOAM I, KING OF ISRAEL **11**:397–398 *bibliog.*
JEROME, SAINT **11**:398 *bibliog.*, *illus.*
JEROME (Idaho)
map (42° 43′N 114° 31′W) **11**:26
JEROME (county in Idaho)
map (42° 40′N 114° 20′W) **11**:26
JEROME, JENNIE
Churchill, Lord Randolph **4**:425
JEROME OF PRAGUE **11**:398
JERROLD, DOUGLAS WILLIAM **11**:398 *bibliog.*
JERSEY (Channel Islands) **4**:281 *map*; **11**:398
map (49° 15′N 2° 10′W) **19**:403
JERSEY (county in Illinois)
map (39° 7′N 90° 20′W) **11**:42
JERSEY (textile) **11**:398
JERSEY CATTLE **4**:216 *illus.*
JERSEY CITY (New Jersey) **11**:398–399
Hague, Frank **10**:11
map (40° 44′N 74° 2′W) **14**:129
JERSEY SHORE (Pennsylvania)
map (41° 12′N 77° 16′W) **15**:147
JERSEYVILLE (Illinois)
map (39° 7′N 90° 20′W) **11**:42
JERUSALEM (Israel) **11**:305 *illus.*; **11**:399–401 *bibliog.*, *illus.*, *map*
history **11**:400–401
Egypt **7**:81
Palestine **15**:44
in 16th century **15**:44 *illus.*
map (31° 46′N 35° 14′E) **11**:302
religious landmarks **11**:399–401 *illus.*, *map*
Dome of the Rock (detail) **13**:595 *illus.*
Zion **20**:369
JERUSALEM, LATIN KINGDOM OF **11**:401–402 *bibliog.*, *map*
Angevins (dynasties) **1**:414
Crusades
siege **5**:367–368 *illus.*
Godfrey of Bouillon **9**:220–221
Palestine **15**:44
JERUSALEM ARTICHOKE **11**:402 *illus.*; **19**:533 *illus.*
sunflower **18**:348
JERUSALEM THORN *see* CRUCIFIXION THORN
JERVAS, CHARLES
Alexander Pope **15**:430 *illus.*
JERVIS, JOHN (admiral)
Saint Vincent, Cape **17**:27
JERVIS, JOHN B. (civil engineer)
locomotive **12**:389
JERWAN
Nineveh **14**:200
JESENICE (Yugoslavia)
map (46° 27′N 14° 4′E) **20**:340
JESPERSEN, OTTO **11**:402
JESSAMINE (county in Kentucky)
map (37° 55′N 84° 35′W) **12**:47
JESSNER, LEOPOLD **11**:402 *bibliog.*
JESSORE (Bangladesh)
map (23° 10′N 89° 13′E) **3**:64
JESTER *see* FOOL
JESUIT ESTATES ACT **11**:402 *bibliog.*
JESUIT MARTYRS OF NORTH AMERICA **11**:402 *bibliog.*
Brébeuf, Saint Jean de **3**:470
Jogues, Saint Isaac **11**:422
JESUITS **11**:402–403 *bibliog.*
Borgia, Saint Francis **3**:400
Campion, Saint Edmund **4**:67
cathedrals and churches **4**:207
Charles III, King of Spain **4**:296
education
Detroit, University of **6**:136
Fordham University **8**:224
Georgetown University **9**:112
Holy Cross, College of the **10**:209
Loyola University **12**:445
Marquette University **13**:163
Saint Louis University **17**:23
San Francisco, University of **17**:54
Francis Xavier, Saint **8**:275
Ignatius Loyola, Saint **11**:32–33
Jesuit Estates Act **11**:402
Latin America, history of **12**:219
missions, Christian **13**:467–468
Paul III, Pope **15**:118
scholasticism **17**:132
JESUITS' BARK *see* CINCHONA
JESUP (Georgia)
map (31° 36′N 81° 53′W) **9**:114
JESUP (Iowa)
map (42° 29′N 92° 4′W) **11**:244
JESUS CHRIST **11**:403–406 *bibliog.*, *illus.*, *map*
baptism **3**:73 *illus.*; **11**:403 *illus.*
beatitude **3**:144
Calvary **4**:48
Christ **4**:411
Christianity **4**:412–414
Christology **11**:405–406
Arianism **2**:153–154
Chalcedon, Council of **4**:270
Docetism **6**:210; **11**:406
Monophysitism **13**:537
Nicaea, Councils of **11**:406
Christopher, Saint **4**:416
crucifixion **5**:364
detail from the sarcophagus of Junius Bassus **17**:161 *illus.*
Easter **7**:32
Ecce Homo **11**:405 *illus.*
Europe, history of **7**:281–282
Galilee, Sea of **9**:14
Gethsemane **9**:160
Good Friday **9**:245
Gospels **11**:403
John, Gospel According to **11**:423–424
Luke, Gospel According to **12**:453–454
Mark, Gospel According to **13**:159
Matthew, Gospel According to **13**:231
Hermon, Mount **10**:143
Holy Family **10**:209
incarnation **11**:73
James, Saint (the "brother" of Jesus Christ) **11**:353
Joseph of Arimathea **11**:451
journeys and historic sites **3**:239 *map*
Judas Iscariot **11**:463
Last Supper **12**:214
Logos **11**:405–406
Lord's Prayer **11**:404; **12**:413
Mary **13**:184–185
Mary Magdalene **13**:185
messiah **13**:324
Mount of Olives **13**:618
Nazareth (Israel) **14**:67
Palestine in the time of Jesus **11**:404 *map*
passion play **15**:105
Pilate, Pontius **15**:301–302
resurrection **16**:183
Second Coming of Christ **17**:178
Shroud of Turin **17**:288
stations of the cross **18**:235
stigmata **18**:268
Tabor, Mount **19**:5
Teilhard de Chardin **19**:73–74
Transfiguration **19**:269
Trinity **19**:300–301
virgin birth **19**:605
JESUS COLLEGE (Cambridge University) **4**:53
JESUS COLLEGE (Oxford University) **14**:474
JET (gemstone) **11**:406
JET (Oklahoma)
map (36° 40′N 98° 11′W) **14**:368
JET AIRCRAFT **2**:372–375 *illus.*
B-1 bomber **3**:3–4
Concorde **5**:171
engine
jet propulsion **11**:406–407
ramjet **16**:80–81 *illus.*
Rolls-Royce **16**:272
turbojet **11**:406 *illus.*
F-15 Eagle **8**:3
F-16 Fighting Falcon **8**:3
F-86 Sabre **8**:3
MiG **13**:416
Mirage **13**:462–463
supersonic transport **18**:353
U-2 **19**:369
V-1 **19**:500
VTOL **19**:639
Whittle, Sir Frank **20**:142
X-15 **20**:311
JET ENGINE *see* ENGINE; JET AIRCRAFT
JET LAG *see* BIOLOGICAL CLOCK
JET PROPULSION **11**:406–407 *bibliog.*, *illus.*
compressor **5**:158
hydrofoil **10**:336 *illus.*
ramjet **16**:80–81
research institutions
Jet Propulsion Laboratory **11**:407
rockets and missiles **16**:251–260
Rolls-Royce **16**:272
JET PROPULSION LABORATORY **11**:407
Goldstone Tracking Station **9**:236
Kármán, Theodore von **12**:28
National Aeronautics and Space Aministration **14**:28
radar astronomy **16**:40
JET STREAM **11**:407–408 *bibliog.*
balloon **3**:52

JET STREAM (cont.)
Rossby waves **16**:318–319
weather forecasting **20**:76
westerlies **20**:115
wind **20**:168
JETA ISLAND
map (11° 53′N 16° 15′W) **9**:399
JETFOIL *see* HYDROFOIL
JETHRO TULL **11**:408
JETMORE (Kansas)
map (38° 3′N 99° 54′W) **12**:18
JETSAM *see* FLOTSAM, JETSAM, AND LAGAN
JETTY
coastal protection **5**:81 *illus.*
harbor and port **10**:44 *illus.*
JEUNE FRANCE
Jolivet, André **11**:441
JEWELED LIZARD *see* LACERTID
JEWELL (Iowa)
map (42° 20′N 93° 39′W) **11**:244
JEWELL (county in Kansas)
map (39° 50′N 98° 15′W) **12**:18
JEWELL RIDGE (Virginia)
map (37° 11′N 81° 48′W) **19**:607
JEWELRY **11**:408–411 *bibliog., illus.*
ancient **11**:408–409
Art Deco **2**:208
Art Nouveau **2**:210 *illus.*
Aztec gold pectoral **15**:499 *illus.*
birthstones **3**:296
cameo **4**:54 *illus.*
costume **5**:292–303 *illus.*
crowns and coronets **5**:364
Egyptian art and architecture **7**:89 *illus.*
Etruscans **7**:261
Fabergé, Peter Carl **8**:4
garnet **9**:49
gem cutting **9**:70–71
gold **9**:227 *illus.*
gold and silver work **9**:228–230
Greek jewelry **11**:408 *illus.*
Indians of North America, art of the **11**:139–140
Lalique, René **12**:171–172
Lamaist art and architecture **12**:173
Mesopotamian art and architecture **13**:317
Middle Ages **11**:409–410 *illus.*
miniature painting **13**:445
Minoan art **13**:458–459
pearls and pearling **15**:127 *illus.*
Persian art and architecture **15**:186–187
platinum **15**:359
Renaissance jewelry **11**:409–410 *illus.*
Roman art and architecture **16**:277
Spanish art and architecture **18**:151
steppe art **18**:255–256
Tiffany, Charles Lewis **19**:196
Topkapi Palace Museum **19**:237
Victorian jewelry **11**:411 *illus.*
Vikings **19**:595 *illus.*
17th century to the present day **11**:410–411
18th century European jewelry **11**:410 *illus.*
JEWELWEED **11**:411
JEWETT, SARAH ORNE **11**:412 *bibliog.*
JEWETT CITY (Connecticut)
map (41° 36′N 71° 59′W) **5**:193
JEWFISH **11**:412
JEWISH COMMUNITY CENTERS *see* YOUNG MEN'S HEBREW ASSOCIATION; YOUNG WOMEN'S HEBREW ASSOCIATION
JEWISH DAILY FORWARD (periodical) **11**:412 *bibliog.*
JEWISH DEFENSE LEAGUE **11**:412 *bibliog.*
JEWISH RECONSTRUCTIONIST FOUNDATION
Kaplan, Mordecai Menahem **12**:25
JEWISH THEOLOGICAL SEMINARY OF AMERICA **11**:412
JEWS **11**:412–417 *bibliog., illus., map*
See also JUDAISM
anti-Semitism **2**:68; **11**:414–416
Arabs **11**:414; **11**:416
Ashkenazim **2**:230–231; **11**:414–415
Bene Israel **3**:196
birthstones **3**:296
B'nai B'rith **3**:348
circumcision **4**:442–443
ghetto **9**:167
Hebrew and Yiddish literature **10**:102
historians *see* HISTORY—Jewish historians
history
Asia, history of **2**:250
Babylonia **11**:414
Babylonian Captivity **3**:9
Balfour Declaration **3**:37; **11**:416
Bar Kochba **3**:74
Biblical period **11**:412–413
concentration camp **5**:169
Cromwell, Oliver **5**:358
Dead Sea **6**:64–65
diaspora **11**:413; **11**:414; **11**:417
Dubnow, Simon **6**:288–289
Essenes **7**:244
Frank, Anne **8**:279
ghetto **11**:415
Hadrian, Roman Emperor **10**:8
Hellenistic period **11**:413
Herod (dynasty) **10**:144
Hitler, Adolf **10**:187–188
Holocaust **10**:206; **11**:416–417
Israel, Kingdom of **11**:412–413
Judah, Kingdom of **11**:413
Khazars **12**:66
Levites **12**:304
Maccabees **11**:413
Manuel I, King of Portugal **13**:131
Masada **11**:414
Middle Ages **11**:414–415
Middle East, history of the **13**:401; **13**:407–409
Nebuchadnezzar II, King of Babylonia **14**:74
Pale **15**:30
Palestine **15**:44–46
Pharisees **15**:219
Philip IV, King of France (Philip the Fair) **15**:232
pogrom **15**:380
Portugal, history of **15**:453
Roman period **11**:413–414
Sanhedrin **17**:65
Sigismund I, King of Poland **17**:299
slavery **17**:352
Spain, history of **18**:145
Warsaw (Poland) **20**:32
Warsaw Uprising **20**:33
women in society **20**:201
Zealots **20**:357
Israel **11**:304; **11**:416–417
Jerusalem (Israel) **11**:399–401
Jesus Christ **11**:403–406
Jewish Defense League **11**:412
languages
Germanic languages **9**:135–137 *table*
Hebrew language **10**:101
Romance languages **16**:280
Russia **11**:416
Semites **17**:197–198
Sephardim **11**:414; **17**:206
shofar **17**:281
Tay-Sachs disease **19**:48
Yiddish theater **20**:328
Young Men's Hebrew Association **20**:334–335
Young Women's Hebrew Association **20**:336
Zionism **11**:416–417; **20**:369–370
JEW'S HARP **11**:417
JEZEBEL **11**:417
JEZREEL, VALLEY OF *see* ESDRAELION, PLAIN OF
JFET *see* TRANSISTOR
JHABVALA, R. PRAWER **11**:417
JHELUM
map (32° 56′N 73° 44′E) **15**:27
JHELUM RIVER
map (31° 12′N 72° 8′E) **11**:152
JHERING, RUDOLF VON
law **12**:242–243
JI KANG *see* CHI K'ANG (Ji Kang)
JIANG JINGGUO *see* CHIANG CHING-KUO (Jiang Jingguo)
JIANG QING *see* CHIANG CHI'ING (Jiang Qing)
JIANGSU *see* KIANGSU (Jiangsu) (China)
JIANGXI (China) *see* KIANGSI (Jiangxi) (China)
JICARILLA INDIANS
Apache **2**:73
JIDD HAFS (Bahrain)
map (26° 13′N 50° 32′E) **3**:24
JIDDA (Saudi Arabia) **11**:417; **17**:95 *illus.*
map (21° 30′N 39° 12′E) **17**:94
JIG **11**:417
JIGSAW PUZZLE **11**:417–418 *bibliog.*
JIH-K'A-TSE (China)
map (29° 17′N 88° 53′E) **19**:190
JIHAD (holy war) **11**:418
Islam **11**:290
Saladin **17**:29
JIHLAVA (Czechoslovakia)
map (49° 24′N 15° 36′E) **5**:413
JIHLAVA RIVER
map (48° 55′N 16° 37′E) **5**:413
JIM CROW **3**:307 *illus.*
black Americans **3**:308–309
JIM CROW LAWS **11**:418 *bibliog., illus.*
cartoon about **11**:418 *illus.*
United States, history of the **19**:452
JIM HOGG (county in Texas)
map (27° 0′N 98° 45′W) **19**:129
JIM THORPE (Pennsylvania)
map (40° 52′N 75° 45′W) **15**:147
JIM WELLS (county in Texas)
map (27° 45′N 98° 5′W) **19**:129
JIMÉNEZ, JUAN RAMÓN **11**:418 *bibliog.*
Spanish literature **18**:159
JIMÉNEZ DE CISNEROS, FRANCISCO **11**:418–419
JIMÉNEZ DE QUESADA, GONZALO **11**:419 *bibliog.*
Latin American art and architecture **12**:227
JIMSONWEED **11**:419
Indians, American **11**:119
medicinal plants **13**:266
JIN (dynasties) *see* CHIN (Jin)
JINAN (China) *see* TSINAN (Jinan) (China)
JINGDE ZHEN *see* CHING-TE-CHEN (Jingde Zhen)
JINGO **11**:419
JINGU KOGO *see* JINGO
JINJA (Uganda)
map (0° 26′N 33° 12′E) **19**:372
JINNAH, MUHAMMAD ALI **11**:419 *bibliog.*
India, history of **11**:93
Muslim League **13**:683
JINNI **11**:419
Lilith **12**:341
JINOTEGA (Nicaragua)
map (13° 6′N 86° 0′W) **14**:179
JINOTEPE (Nicaragua)
map (11° 51′N 86° 12′W) **14**:179
JIPIJAPA (Ecuador)
map (1° 20′S 80° 35′W) **7**:52
JIQUILISCO BAY
map (13° 10′N 88° 28′W) **7**:100
JIRÁSEK, ALOIS
Czech literature **5**:412
JIRD *see* GERBIL
JIRJA (Egypt)
map (26° 20′N 31° 53′E) **7**:76
JITTERBUG (dance) **11**:419
JIU RIVER
map (43° 47′N 23° 48′E) **16**:288
JÍVARO (American Indians) **11**:419 *bibliog.*
head-hunting **10**:85
wake **20**:8
JIVE (music) *see* JITTERBUG (dance)
JO DAVIESS (county in Illinois)
map (42° 22′N 90° 8′W) **11**:42
JOACHIM, SAINT **11**:420
JOACHIM, JOSEPH **11**:419–420 *bibliog.*
JOAN, POPE **11**:420
Callistus III, Pope **4**:47
JOAN I, QUEEN OF NAPLES **11**:420
Charles III, King of Naples **4**:296
JOAN OF ARC, SAINT **11**:420 *bibliog., illus.*
Charles VII, King of France (Charles the Well-Served) **4**:293
France, history of **8**:268
Hundred Years' War **10**:304–305
Rouen (France) **16**:324
Saint Joan (play) **17**:19
JOAN THE MAD, QUEEN OF CASTILE **11**:420
Philip I, King of Castile (Philip the Handsome) **15**:234
JOÃO PESSOA (Brazil)
map (7° 7′S 34° 52′W) **3**:460
JOAQUIN Y. GONZÁLEZ (Argentina)
map (25° 5′S 64° 11′W) **2**:149
JOB, BOOK OF **11**:420–421 *bibliog.*
JOB CORPS **11**:421 *bibliog.*
JOBBERS *see* WHOLESALING
JOBS *see* EMPLOYMENT AND UNEMPLOYMENT
JOBST OF MORAVIA
Wenceslas, King of Germany and Bohemia **20**:103
JOCASEE, LAKE
map (35° 0′N 82° 55′W) **18**:98
JOCHO **11**:421
JOCHUM, EUGEN **11**:421
JOCK ITCH
ringworm **16**:226
skin diseases **17**:342
JOCKEY CLUB
horse racing **10**:250
JOCKEYS *see* HORSE RACING
JOCORO (El Salvador)
map (13° 37′N 88° 1′W) **7**:100
JODHPUR (India)
map (26° 17′N 73° 2′E) **11**:80
JODRELL BANK EXPERIMENTAL STATION *see* NUFFIELD RADIO ASTRONOMY LABORATORIES
JOE-PYE WEED **11**:421
JOEL, BOOK OF **11**:421
JOENSUU (Finland)
map (62° 36′N 29° 46′E) **8**:95
JOFFRE, JOSEPH JACQUES CÉSAIRE **11**:421 *bibliog.*
Marne, Battles of the **13**:162
Verdun, Battle of **19**:550
World War I **20**:222–224 *illus.*; **20**:232–233
JOFFREY, ROBERT *see* JOFFREY BALLET
JOFFREY BALLET **11**:421–422
Arpino, Gerald **2**:187
JOGAILLO *see* JAGELLO (dynasty)
JOGAILLO, GRAND DUKE OF LITHUANIA *see* WLADYSLAW II (or V), KING OF POLAND
JOGGING *see* RUNNING AND JOGGING
JOGUES, SAINT ISAAC **11**:422 *bibliog.*
Jesuit Martyrs of North America **11**:402
JOHANAN BEN ZAKKAI **11**:422 *bibliog.*
JOHANNES VON TEPL **11**:422
JOHANNESBURG (California)
map (35° 22′N 117° 38′W) **4**:31
JOHANNESBURG (South Africa) **11**:422–423 *illus.*; **18**:80–81 *illus., table*
gold refining **9**:226 *illus.*
map (26° 15′S 28° 0′E) **18**:79
JOHANNSEN, ALBERT **11**:423
JOHANNSEN, WILHELM
genetics **9**:87
JOHANSON, DONALD
Australopithecus **2**:346
JOHN, AUGUSTUS **11**:423 *bibliog.*
JOHN, ELTON **11**:423 *bibliog.*
JOHN, EPISTLES OF **11**:423 *bibliog.*
JOHN, GOSPEL ACCORDING TO **11**:423–424 *bibliog.*
Jesus Christ **11**:403–404
JOHN, KING OF ENGLAND **11**:426–427 *bibliog., illus.*
Magna Carta **13**:52–53
Philip II, King of France (Philip Augustus) **15**:232
JOHN, SAINT **11**:423
logos **12**:397
Revelation, Book of **16**:185
JOHN I, KING OF HUNGARY (John Zápolya) **11**:427 *bibliog.*
Suleiman I, Sultan of the Ottoman Empire (Suleiman the Magnificent) **18**:332–333
JOHN I, KING OF PORTUGAL (John the Great) **11**:428 *bibliog.*
Pereira, Nuno Álvares **15**:163
Portugal, history of **15**:453
JOHN I TZIMISCES, BYZANTINE EMPEROR **11**:426
JOHN II, KING OF FRANCE (John the Good) **11**:427 *bibliog.*
Hundred Years' War **10**:305
JOHN II, KING OF HUNGARY (John Sigismund Zápolya) **11**:427 *bibliog.*
JOHN II, KING OF POLAND (John Casimir) **11**:427 *bibliog.*
Vasa (dynasty) **19**:525
JOHN II, KING OF PORTUGAL (John the Perfect) **11**:428 *bibliog.*
Portugal, history of **15**:453
Tordesillas, Treaty of **19**:239
JOHN II COMNENUS, BYZANTINE EMPEROR **11**:426
JOHN III, KING OF POLAND (John Sobieski) **11**:427–428 *bibliog.*
JOHN III, KING OF PORTUGAL (John the Pious) **11**:428
Portugal, history of **15**:453
JOHN IV, KING OF PORTUGAL **11**:428
Brazilian history **3**:463
JOHN V, KING OF PORTUGAL (John the Magnanimous) **11**:428
JOHN V PALAEOLOGUS, BYZANTINE EMPEROR **11**:426
JOHN VI, KING OF PORTUGAL **11**:428
Portugal, history of **15**:454
JOHN VI CANTACUZENUS, BYZANTINE EMPEROR **11**:426
JOHN XII, POPE
Holy Roman Empire **10**:209
JOHN XXII, POPE **11**:428 *bibliog.*
church music **4**:424

Louis IV, King of Germany and Holy Roman Emperor (Louis the Bavarian) 12:428
JOHN XXIII, "ANTIPOPE" 11:429 *bibliog.*
JOHN XXIII, POPE 11:429 *bibliog., illus.*
JOHN OF AUSTRIA, DON 11:424 *bibliog.*
JOHN THE BAPTIST, SAINT 11:424 *bibliog.;* 17:162 *illus.*
JOHN BAPTIST DE LA SALLE, SAINT 11:424
JOHN BIRCH SOCIETY 11:424 *bibliog.*
JOHN BROWN'S BODY (poem)
Benét, Stephen Vincent 3:198
JOHN BULL (locomotive) 11:424 *bibliog.*
locomotive 12:389
JOHN BULL (personification) *see* BULL, JOHN (personification)
JOHN OF THE CROSS, SAINT 11:424 *bibliog.*
JOHN DAMASCENE, SAINT 11:424 *bibliog.*
icon 11:20
JOHN DAY (Oregon)
map (44° 25′N 118° 57′W) 14:427
JOHN DAY RIVER
map (45° 44′N 120° 39′W) 14:427
JOHN DORY (fish) 8:117 *illus.;* 11:425 *illus.*
JOHN F. KENNEDY CENTER FOR THE PERFORMING ARTS *see* KENNEDY CENTER FOR THE PERFORMING ARTS
JOHN F. KENNEDY INTERNATIONAL AIRPORT 1:223 *illus.*
JOHN THE FEARLESS, DUKE OF BURGUNDY 11:425 *bibliog.*
Philip the Good, Duke of Burgundy 15:231
JOHN FREDERICK, ELECTOR OF SAXONY
Saxony 17:105
JOHN OF GAUNT, DUKE OF LANCASTER 11:425 *bibliog.*
Lancaster (dynasty) 12:177
Richard II, King of England 16:210
Wycliffe, John 20:298 *illus.*
JOHN THE GOOD *see* JOHN II, KING OF FRANCE (John the Good)
JOHN THE GREAT see JOHN I, KING OF PORTUGAL (John the Great)
JOHN H. KERR RESERVOIR
map (36° 35′N 78° 30′W) 19:607
JOHN HANCOCK CENTER (Chicago) 4:342 *illus.;* 19:428 *illus.*
skyscraper 17:349–350 *illus.*
JOHN HENRY 11:425
JOHN JAY COLLEGE OF CRIMINAL JUSTICE
New York, City University of 14:154
JOHN THE MAGNANIMOUS *see* JOHN V, KING OF PORTUGAL (John the Magnanimous)
JOHN MARTIN RESERVOIR
map (38° 5′N 103° 2′W) 5:116
JOHN MAURICE OF NASSAU 11:425 *bibliog.*
JOHN NEPOMUCENE, SAINT 11:425
JOHN PAUL I, POPE 11:425 *bibliog.*
JOHN PAUL II, POPE 11:425–426 *bibliog., illus.;* 15:66 *illus.*
Kraków (Poland) 12:127
JOHN THE PERFECT *see* JOHN II, KING OF PORTUGAL (John the Perfect)
JOHN THE PIOUS *see* JOHN III, KING OF PORTUGAL (John the Pious)
JOHN REDMOND RESERVOIR
map (38° 18′N 95° 55′W) 12:18
JOHN OF SALISBURY 11:426 *bibliog.*
JOHNNY APPLESEED *see* CHAPMAN, JOHN (Johnny Appleseed)
JOHNNY CARP *see* GOLDFISH
JOHNNY-JUMP-UP *see* PANSY; VIOLET (botany)
JOHNS, ADELA ROGERS ST. *see* ST. JOHNS, ADELA ROGERS
JOHNS, JASPER 11:429–430 *bibliog., illus.*
encaustic painting 7:162
Flag on an Orange Field 1:336 *illus.;* 11:429 *illus.*
Three Flags 13:495 *illus.*
JOHNS HOPKINS HOSPITAL
Hopkins, Johns 10:232
JOHNS HOPKINS UNIVERSITY, THE 11:430 *bibliog.*
Adams, Herbert Baxter 1:94
Applied Physics Laboratory
Uhuru 19:374
Gilman, Daniel Coit 9:182
graduate education 9:276
Hall, G. Stanley 10:21
Hopkins, Johns 10:232
Osler, Sir William 14:454
JOHNS ISLAND
map (32° 40′N 80° 5′W) 18:98
JOHNSON (county in Arkansas)
map (35° 35′N 93° 25′W) 2:166
JOHNSON (county in Georgia)
map (32° 40′N 82° 40′W) 9:114
JOHNSON (county in Illinois)
map (37° 25′N 88° 52′W) 11:42
JOHNSON (county in Indiana)
map (39° 29′N 86° 3′W) 11:111
JOHNSON (county in Iowa)
map (41° 38′N 91° 32′W) 11:244
JOHNSON (Kansas)
map (37° 34′N 101° 45′W) 12:18
JOHNSON (county in Kansas)
map (38° 50′N 94° 50′W) 12:18
JOHNSON (county in Kentucky)
map (37° 50′N 82° 50′W) 12:47
JOHNSON (county in Missouri)
map (38° 45′N 93° 50′W) 13:476
JOHNSON (county in Nebraska)
map (40° 25′N 96° 15′W) 14:70
JOHNSON (county in Tennessee)
map (36° 30′N 81° 50′W) 19:104
JOHNSON (county in Texas)
map (32° 20′N 97° 20′W) 19:129
JOHNSON (Vermont)
map (44° 38′N 72° 41′W) 19:554
JOHNSON (county in Wyoming)
map (44° 0′N 106° 30′W) 20:301
JOHNSON, ANDREW 11:430–431 *bibliog., illus.*
as president 11:431
cartoon depicting 16:109 *illus.*
early life 11:430–431
impeachment 11:61 *illus.*
Curtis, Benjamin Robbins 5:395
Raleigh (North Carolina) 16:79
Reconstruction 16:109
Stanton, Edwin M. 18:220
Stevens, Thaddeus 18:263
Tenure of Office Act 19:113
Trumbull, Lyman 19:319
United States, history of the 19:449
JOHNSON, C. PHILIP
modern architecture 13:490
JOHNSON, CHARLES SPURGEON 11:431 *bibliog.*
JOHNSON, EASTMAN 11:431 *bibliog., illus.*
In the Fields 11:431 *illus.*
JOHNSON, EDWARD 11:431–432 *bibliog.*
JOHNSON, EMILY PAULINE 11:432 *bibliog.*
JOHNSON, EYVIND 11:432 *bibliog.;* 18:387 *illus.*
JOHNSON, FENTON 11:432
JOHNSON, HIRAM WARREN 11:432 *bibliog.*
California 4:37
JOHNSON, JACK 3:432 *illus.;* 11:432 *bibliog.*
JOHNSON, JAMES WELDON 11:432 *bibliog., illus.*
JOHNSON, JOHN G.
Philadelphia Museum of Art 15:229
JOHNSON, JOHN HAROLD 11:432–433 *bibliog.*
JOHNSON, JOHN ROSAMOND 11:433
JOHNSON, LYNDON B. 11:433–434 *bibliog., illus.;* 15:526 *illus.;* 15:527 *illus.;* 19:457 *illus.;* 19:568 *illus.*
as president 11:434
early life 11:433–434
Fair Deal 8:9
Fortas, Abe 8:238
Memorial Library
Bunshaft, Gordon 3:564
portrait
Hurd, Peter 10:315
signing the 1964 Civil Rights Act 15:524 *illus.*
Tonkin Gulf Resolution 19:234–235
United States, history of the 19:459–460
Vietnam War 19:587–588
War on Poverty 20:28
Warren Commission 20:31
JOHNSON, PHILIP 11:434–435 *bibliog., illus.*
Glass House 11:435 *illus.;* 13:493 *illus.*
Seagram Building 1:329 *illus.;* 17:173
JOHNSON, PIERRE MARC
Canada 4:79
JOHNSON, RAFER 11:435
JOHNSON, REVERDY 11:435 *bibliog.*
JOHNSON, RICHARD M. 11:435 *bibliog.*
JOHNSON, ROBERT WOOD
Robert Wood Johnson Foundation 16:241
JOHNSON, SAMUEL (philosopher) 11:435 *bibliog.*
JOHNSON, SAMUEL (writer) 11:435–436 *bibliog., illus.*
Boswell, James 3:411–412
Life of Samuel Johnson, The 12:330
doggerel 6:223
English language 7:193
neoclassicism (literature) 14:82
portrait
Reynolds, Sir Joshua 16:191
JOHNSON, TOM LOFTIN 11:436
JOHNSON, UWE 11:436 *bibliog.*
JOHNSON, VIRGINIA ESHELMAN
Masters and Johnson reports 13:216 *illus.*
JOHNSON, WALTER PERRY 11:436 *bibliog.*
JOHNSON, SIR WILLIAM 11:437 *bibliog.*
French and Indian Wars 8:313 *map*
Johnson, Emily Pauline 11:432
Rome (New York) 16:297
JOHNSON, WILLIAM SAMUEL 11:437 *bibliog.*
JOHNSON CITY (New York)
map (42° 7′N 75° 57′W) 14:149
JOHNSON CITY (Tennessee)
map (36° 19′N 82° 21′W) 19:104
JOHNSON CITY (Texas)
map (30° 17′N 98° 25′W) 19:129
JOHNSON-CLARENDON TREATY
Johnson, Reverdy 11:435
JOHNSON FOUNDATION *see* ROBERT WOOD JOHNSON FOUNDATION
JOHNSON SPACE CENTER 11:437; 18:122 *illus.*
National Aeronautics and Space Administration 14:28 *illus.*
JOHNSONBURG (Pennsylvania)
map (41° 29′N 78° 41′W) 15:147
JOHNSONDALE (California)
map (35° 58′N 118° 32′W) 4:31
JOHNSONS CROSSING (Yukon Territory)
map (60° 29′N 133° 16′W) 20:345
JOHNSONVILLE (New Zealand)
map (41° 14′S 174° 47′E) 14:158
JOHNSONVILLE (South Carolina)
map (33° 49′N 79° 27′W) 18:98
JOHNSTON (county in North Carolina)
map (35° 20′N 78° 25′W) 14:242
JOHNSTON (county in Oklahoma)
map (34° 20′N 96° 40′W) 14:368
JOHNSTON (Rhode Island)
map (41° 50′N 71° 30′W) 16:198
JOHNSTON (South Carolina)
map (33° 50′N 81° 48′W) 18:98
JOHNSTON, ALBERT SIDNEY 11:437 *bibliog.*
Civil War, U.S. 5:21–22
Shiloh, Battle of 17:261
JOHNSTON, DENIS 11:437
JOHNSTON, EDWARD
calligraphy 4:43 *illus.*
JOHNSTON, FRANZ 11:437 *bibliog.*
JOHNSTON, JOSEPH E. 11:437–438 *bibliog., illus.*
Civil War, U.S. 5:21; 5:23 *map;* 5:24; 5:27; 5:30
Peninsular Campaign 15:144
JOHNSTON, SAMUEL 11:438
JOHNSTON ATOLL
United States outlying territories 19:464
JOHNSTON CITY (Illinois)
map (37° 49′N 88° 56′W) 11:42
JOHNSTON ISLAND (Hawaii)
map (17° 0′N 168° 30′W) 10:72
JOHNSTON ISLAND (Oceania)
map (16° 45′N 169° 32′W) 14:334
JOHNSTOWN (New York)
map (43° 0′N 74° 22′W) 14:149
JOHNSTOWN (Ohio)
map (40° 9′N 82° 41′W) 14:357
JOHNSTOWN (Pennsylvania) 11:438 *bibliog.*
map (40° 20′N 78° 55′W) 15:147
JOHOR BAHARU (Malaysia)
map (1° 28′N 103° 45′E) 13:84
JOIDES 11:438 *bibliog.*
Woods Hole Oceanographic Institution 20:213
JOINER (Arkansas)
map (35° 31′N 90° 9′W) 2:166
JOINT (anatomy) 11:438–440 *bibliog., illus.*
cartilage 4:175
chiropractic 4:397
diseases and disorders
arthritis 2:214–216
bunions, corns, and calluses 3:563
bursitis 3:581
collagen disease 5:102–103
gout 9:266–267
leukopenia 12:301
lupus erythematosus 12:466
myasthenia gravis 13:689
osteoarthritis 11:457
rheumatism 16:194–195
sprain 18:198–199
tendonitis 19:101
ligament 12:333
muscle 13:651–652
sports medicine 18:197
surgery 18:362
JOINT (geology) 11:440 *bibliog.*
fault 8:36–38
JOINT-CHIEFS OF STAFF
Defense, U.S. Department of 6:82–83
JOINT COMMISSION ON ACCREDITATION ON HOSPITALS 10:257
JOINT FAMILY *see* EXTENDED FAMILY
JOINT-STOCK COMPANY 11:440
corporation 5:272
stock (finance) 18:273
JOINT TENANCY 11:440
JOINVILLE, JEAN, SIRE DE 11:440
JOJOBA 11:440 *bibliog.*
JÓKAI, MAURUS 11:440
JOKWE *see* CHOKWE
JOLAS, BETSY 11:441
JOLIET (Illinois)
map (41° 32′N 88° 5′W) 11:42
JOLIET (Montana)
map (45° 29′N 108° 58′W) 13:547
JOLIET JUNIOR COLLEGE
community and junior colleges 5:151
JOLIETTE (Quebec)
map (46° 1′N 73° 27′W) 16:18
JOLIOT-CURIE, FRÉDÉRIC AND IRÈNE 11:441 *bibliog.*
JOLIVET, ANDRÉ 11:441
JOLLIET, LOUIS 11:441 *bibliog.*
Canada, history of 4:80 *map*
exploration of colonial America 19:437 *map*
Marquette, Jacques 13:163
Missouri River 13:481
Quapaw 16:12
JOLSON, AL 11:441 *bibliog.*
JOLY, JOHN 11:441 *bibliog.*
JOMBANG (Indonesia)
map (7° 33′S 112° 14′E) 11:147
JOMMELLI, NICCOLÒ 11:441 *bibliog.*
JOMON CULTURE
Japan, history of 11:367
Japanese art and architecture 11:372
midden 13:390
terra-cotta figurine 11:372 *illus.*
JONAH (prophet)
Jonah, Book of 11:442
Nineveh 14:200
JONAH, BOOK OF 11:442 *bibliog.*
iconography 11:22
JONATHAN 11:442
JONATHAN, J. LEABUA
Lesotho 12:298
JONES (county in Georgia)
map (33° 5′N 83° 35′W) 9:114
JONES (county in Iowa)
map (42° 5′N 91° 7′W) 11:244
JONES (county in Mississippi)
map (31° 35′N 89° 10′W) 13:469
JONES (county in North Carolina)
map (35° 5′N 77° 20′W) 14:242
JONES (Oklahoma)
map (35° 34′N 97° 17′W) 14:368
JONES (county in South Dakota)
map (43° 58′N 100° 40′W) 18:103
JONES (county in Texas)
map (32° 45′N 97° 52′W) 19:129
JONES, ANSON 11:442
JONES, ANTHONY ARMSTRONG-, 1st EARL OF SNOWDON *see* SNOWDON, ANTHONY ARMSTRONG-JONES, 1st EARL OF
JONES, BOBBY 11:442 *bibliog., illus.*
JONES, BRIAN
Rolling Stones, The 16:272
JONES, CASEY 11:442
JONES, DAVID ROBERT *see* BOWIE, DAVID
JONES, SIR EDWARD BURNE- *see* BURNE-JONES, SIR EDWARD
JONES, ERNEST 15:598 *illus.*
JONES, GEORGE 11:442 *bibliog.*

JONES, HENRY ARTHUR **11**:442 *bibliog.*
JONES, INIGO **11**:442–443 *bibliog.*
The Banqueting House (Whitehall Palace, London) **7**:185 *illus.*
Double Cube Room, Wilton House (Salisbury) **11**:212 *illus.*
English art and architecture **7**:185
masque **13**:200
Wiltshire (England) **20**:167
JONES, JAMES (novelist) **11**:443 *bibliog.*
JONES, JAMES EARL (actor) **11**:443
JONES, JENNIFER
Selznick, David O. **17**:193
JONES, JIM (cult leader)
Jonestown (Guyana) **11**:444
JONES, JOHN LUTHER *see* JONES, CASEY
JONES, JOHN PAUL (musician) **16**:249 *illus.*
JONES, JOHN PAUL (naval officer) **11**:443 *bibliog., illus.*
Bonhomme Richard **1**:357 *illus.*
JONES, LEROI *see* BARAKA, IMAMU AMIRI
JONES, MARGO **11**:443
repertory theater **16**:160
JONES, MARY HARRIS *see* JONES, MOTHER
JONES, MOTHER **11**:443–444
JONES, ROBERT EDMOND **11**:444 *bibliog.*
JONES, RUFUS MATTHEW **11**:444 *bibliog.*
JONES, SAMUEL MILTON **11**:444 *bibliog.*
JONES, SPIKE **11**:444
JONES, TERRY
"Monty Python's Flying Circus" **13**:560
JONES, SIR WILLIAM (linguist and jurist) **11**:444 *bibliog.*
historical linguistics **10**:182
linguistics **12**:356
JONES, WILLIAM (politician)
Bank of the United States **3**:67
JONES ACT OF 1917
Puerto Rico **15**:616
JONES BILL
Muñoz Rivera, Luis **13**:643
JONESBORO (Arkansas)
map (35° 50′N 90° 42′W) **2**:166
JONESBORO (Georgia)
map (33° 32′N 84° 21′W) **9**:114
JONESBORO (Illinois)
map (37° 27′N 89° 16′W) **11**:42
JONESBORO (Louisiana)
map (32° 15′N 92° 43′W) **12**:430
JONESBORO (Maine)
map (44° 40′N 67° 35′W) **13**:70
JONESBORO (Tennessee)
map (36° 18′N 82° 28′W) **19**:104
JONESBURG (Missouri)
map (38° 51′N 91° 18′W) **13**:476
JONESTOWN (Guyana) **11**:444 *bibliog.*
People's Temple mass murder-suicide **16**:142 *illus.*
JONESTOWN (Mississippi)
map (34° 14′N 90° 28′W) **13**:469
JONESVILLE (Louisiana)
map (31° 38′N 91° 49′W) **12**:430
JONESVILLE (Michigan)
map (41° 59′N 84° 40′W) **13**:377
JONESVILLE (North Carolina)
map (36° 15′N 80° 51′W) **14**:242
JONESVILLE (South Carolina)
map (34° 50′N 81° 41′W) **18**:98
JONESVILLE (Virginia)
map (36° 41′N 83° 7′W) **19**:607
JONG, ERICA **11**:444–445 *illus.*
JONGKIND, JOHAN BARTHOLD **11**:445 *bibliog.*
JONKER, INGRID **11**:445
JÖNKÖPING (Sweden)
map (57° 47′N 14° 11′E) **18**:382
JONQUIL **11**:445
narcissus **14**:21
JONSON, BEN **7**:195 *illus.*; **11**:445–446 *bibliog., illus.*
comedy **5**:132
drama **6**:259
masque **13**:200
Pocahontas **15**:376 *illus.*
Volpone **19**:631
JONUTA (Mexico)
map (18° 5′N 92° 8′W) **13**:357
JOOS VAN CLEVE **11**:446 *bibliog.*
JOOS VAN GHENT **11**:446 *bibliog.*
JOOS VAN WASSENHOVE *see* JOOS VAN GHENT
JOOSS, KURT **11**:446 *bibliog.*
JOPLIN (Missouri)
map (37° 6′N 94° 31′W) **13**:476
JOPLIN, JANIS **11**:446 *bibliog.*
JOPLIN, SCOTT **11**:446–447 *bibliog., illus.*
ragtime **16**:70
JOPPA (Illinois)
map (37° 12′N 88° 51′W) **11**:42
JOPPA (Maryland)
map (39° 26′N 76° 22′W) **13**:188
JORDAENS, JACOB **11**:447 *bibliog.*
JORDAN **11**:447–450 *bibliog., illus., map, table*
archaeology
Gerasa **9**:121
Jericho **11**:397
Shechem **18**:248
cities
Amman **1**:372
Bethlehem **3**:230–231
climate **11**:448; **11**:449 *table*
economic activity **11**:448–449
education **11**:448
Middle Eastern universities **13**:410–412 *table*
flag **11**:447 *illus.*
government **11**:449
history **11**:449–450
Abdullah **1**:54–55
Arab-Israeli Wars **2**:96–97 *map*
Fertile Crescent **8**:60
Glubb, Sir John Bagot **9**:210
Hussein I, King **10**:320–321
Jerusalem (Israel) **11**:399
Middle East, history of the **13**:409–410
Palestine **15**:44; **15**:46
West Bank **20**:108
land **11**:448
map (31° 0′N 36° 0′E) **2**:232
people **2**:242 *illus.*; **11**:448
rivers, lakes, and waterways **11**:448
JORDAN (Montana)
map (47° 19′N 106° 55′W) **13**:547
JORDAN, BARBARA **11**:450 *bibliog., illus.*
JORDAN, CAMILLE **11**:450
mathematics, history of **13**:226
JORDAN, JUNE **11**:450
JORDAN, VERNON **11**:450
JORDAN RIVER **11**:448 *illus.*; **11**:450–451
map (31° 46′N 35° 33′E) **11**:302
West Bank **20**:108
JORDAN RIVER (United States)
map (40° 49′N 112° 8′W) **19**:492
JORDAN VALLEY (Oregon)
map (42° 58′N 117° 3′W) **14**:427
JORIS, FRANÇOISE MALLET- *see* MALLET-JORIS, FRANÇOISE
JORN, ASGER
Amoureux dans l'espace **17**:114 *illus.*
JORNADO DEL MUERTO DESERT
map (33° 20′N 106° 50′W) **14**:136
JŌRURI *see* BUNRAKU
JOS (Nigeria)
map (9° 55′N 8° 53′E) **14**:190
JOS PLATEAU
map (9° 30′N 9° 0′E) **14**:190
JOSÉ BATLLE Y ORDÓÑEZ (Uruguay)
map (33° 28′S 55° 7′W) **19**:488
JOSEPH (Biblical figure) **11**:451
JOSEPH (Oregon)
map (45° 21′N 117° 14′W) **14**:427
JOSEPH, CHIEF **11**:451 *bibliog., illus.*
Nez Percé **14**:176 *illus.*
JOSEPH, FATHER **11**:451
JOSEPH, SAINT **11**:451; **17**:162 *illus.*
JOSEPH I, HOLY ROMAN EMPEROR **11**:451
JOSEPH II, HOLY ROMAN EMPEROR **11**:452 *bibliog.*
and Catherine the Great **16**:355 *illus.*
Maria Theresa, Austrian Archduchess, Queen of Hungary and Bohemia **13**:150
JOSEPH ANDREWS (book) **11**:451 *bibliog.*
Fielding, Henry **8**:73
JOSEPH OF ARIMATHEA **11**:451 *bibliog.*
JOSEPH BONAPARTE GULF
map (14° 15′S 128° 30′E) **2**:328
JOSEPH P. KENNEDY, JR. FOUNDATION
Special Olympics **18**:168
JOSEPHINE (Empress) **11**:452 *bibliog.*
Malmaison **13**:93
JOSEPHINE (county in Oregon)
map (42° 20′N 122° 45′W) **14**:427
JOSEPHSON, BRIAN DAVID **11**:452 *bibliog.*
Josephson Effect
superconductivity **18**:350
JOSEPHSON, ERNST
Scandinavian art and architecture **17**:114
JOSEPHUS, FLAVIUS **11**:452 *bibliog.*
Masada **13**:194
JOSETSU **11**:452 *bibliog.*
JOSHUA, BOOK OF **11**:452 *bibliog.*
Jericho **11**:397
JOSHUA TREE (botany) **11**:452–453 *illus.*
Mojave Desert **13**:505
yucca **20**:339
JOSHUA TREE (California)
map (34° 8′N 116° 19′W) **4**:31
JOSIAH, KING OF JUDAH **11**:453
JOSQUIN DES PREZ **11**:453 *bibliog.*
music, history of Western **13**:665
JOST VAN DYKE
Virgin Islands **19**:605
JOTUNHEIMEN **11**:453
JOULE **11**:453
units, physical **19**:466–467 *tables*
work (physics) **20**:217
JOULE, JAMES PRESCOTT **11**:453 *bibliog.*
Joule-Thomson effect **11**:453
physics, history of **15**:285
thermochemistry **19**:161
thermodynamics **19**:163
JOULE-THOMSON EFFECT **11**:453 *bibliog.*
cryogenics **5**:370
gas, throttling process **11**:453
Joule, James Prescott **11**:453
Kelvin, William Thomson, 1st Baron **12**:40
JOURDANTON (Texas)
map (28° 55′N 98° 33′W) **19**:129
JOURNAL *see* PERIODICAL
JOURNAL OF THE AMERICAN MEDICAL ASSOCIATION **11**:453
JOURNALISM **11**:453–456 *bibliog.*
See also NEWSPAPER; PHOTOJOURNALISM; YELLOW JOURNALISM; names of specific journalists, e.g., BERNSTEIN, CARL, and WOODWARD, BOB; BUCHWALD, ART; etc.
advocacy journalism **11**:456
black Americans **3**:313
evidence, sources of **7**:317
forms of journalism **11**:454
Fourth Estate **8**:255
freedom of the press **8**:296–297
Gannett, Frank E. **9**:37
Greeley, Horace **9**:347
group journalism
Time **19**:201
Harris, Benjamin **10**:57
Hearst, William Randolph **10**:90
history **11**:454
investigative reporting **11**:456
new journalism **11**:455; **11**:456
American literature **1**:347
McClure, S. S. **13**:10
Talese, Gay **19**:16
Wolfe, Tom **20**:198
newscasts
Chancellor, John **4**:278
Cronkite, Walter **5**:359
Murrow, Edward R. **13**:651
Pearson, Drew **15**:128
radio and television broadcasting **16**:56
Smith, Howard K. **17**:368
Thomas, Lowell **19**:173
Winchell, Walter **20**:167–168
newsreel **14**:173
Ochs, Adolph Simon **14**:346
Patterson (family) **15**:115
Peabody Award *see* PEABODY AWARD
press agencies and syndicates **15**:533
professional and educational organizations **11**:456
American Newspaper Publishers Association **1**:352
American Society of Newspaper Editors **1**:367
Institute of Journalists (Great Britain) **11**:195
International Press Institute **11**:222
Pulitzer, Joseph **15**:618
Pulitzer Prize **15**:618–619
Atkinson, Brooks **2**:292
Baker, Russell **3**:28
Bernstein, Carl, and Woodward, Bob **3**:223
Boston Globe **3**:410
Childs, Marquis William **4**:354
Conrad, Paul **4**:177 *illus.*; **5**:198
Daley, Arthur **6**:11
Darling, Jay Norwood **6**:39
Goldberg, Rube **9**:231
Herblock **10**:136
Higgins, Marguerite **10**:161
Huxtable, Ada Louise **10**:325
Lippmann, Walter **12**:363
McCutcheon, John T. **13**:11
McGrory, Mary **13**:17
Mauldin, Bill **4**:177 *illus.*; **13**:233
Mott, Frank Luther **13**:616
Oliphant, Patrick **14**:378
Patterson (family) **15**:115
Pegler, Westbrook **15**:132
Pyle, Ernie **15**:633
Reston, James Barrett **16**:182
St. Louis Post-Dispatch **17**:23
Salisbury, Harrison **17**:33
Trudeau, Garry **19**:316
Watterson, Henry **20**:69
Russel, Benjamin **16**:348
sportswriting
Rice, Grantland **16**:209
Sulzberger, Arthur Hays **18**:338
Thomas, Isaiah **19**:173
war reportage
Caesar, Gaius Julius **4**:15
Crane, Stephen **5**:330–331
Pyle, Ernie **15**:633
Reid, Whitelaw **16**:131
Russell, Sir William Howard **16**:351
Salisbury, Harrison **17**:33
JOURNALS (bookkeeping) *see* BOOKKEEPING
JOURNEYMAN *see* GUILDS
JOUVET, LOUIS **11**:456
JOY OF COOKING (book) **11**:456
JOYCE (Louisiana)
map (31° 58′N 92° 37′W) **12**:430
JOYCE, JAMES **7**:201 *illus.*; **11**:268 *illus.*; **11**:456–457 *bibliog., illus.*
Dubliners **6**:288
Dún Laoghaire (Ireland) **6**:298
epiphany **7**:220
Finnegans Wake **8**:99
Portrait of the Artist as a Young Man, A **15**:446
Ulysses **19**:379
JOYCE, WILLIAM *see* LORD HAW-HAW
JOYOUS ENTRY (charter)
Brabant, Duchy of **3**:435
JOYSTICK (computer term) **5**:160h
JÓZSEF, ATTILA **11**:457
JPL *see* JET PROPULSION LABORATORY
JUAB (county in Utah)
map (39° 42′N 112° 38′W) **19**:492
JUAN CARLOS I, KING OF SPAIN **11**:457
JUAN CHI (Ruan Ji) **11**:457 *bibliog.*
JUAN DE FUCA, STRAIT OF **11**:457
map (48° 18′N 124° 0′W) **20**:35
JUAN FERNÁNDEZ ISLAND
map (33° 0′S 80° 0′W) **14**:334
JUAN L. LACAZE (Uruguay)
map (34° 26′S 57° 27′W) **19**:488
JUAN VIÑAS (Costa Rica)
map (9° 54′N 83° 45′W) **5**:291
JUANA INÉS DE LA CRUZ, SOR **11**:457–458 *bibliog.*
JUANA LA LOCA *see* JOAN THE MAD, QUEEN OF CASTILE
JUANJUÍ (Peru)
map (7° 11′S 76° 45′W) **15**:193
JUANTORENA, ALBERTO **19**:260 *illus.*
JUÁREZ (Argentina)
map (37° 40′S 59° 48′W) **2**:149
JUÁREZ (Mexico) *see* CIUDAD JUÁREZ (Mexico)
JUÁREZ, BENITO **11**:458 *bibliog., illus.*
Ciudad Juárez **5**:9
Díaz Porfirio **6**:154
Mexico, history of **13**:364
Oaxaca (city in Mexico) **14**:314
JUÀZEIRO (Brazil)
map (9° 25′S 40° 30′W) **3**:460
JUAZEIRO DO NORTE (Brazil)
map (7° 12′S 39° 20′W) **3**:460
JUBA I, KING OF NUMIDIA
Numidia **14**:295
JUBA II, KING OF NUMIBIA
Iol **11**:239
JUBA RIVER
map (0° 12′S 42° 40′E) **18**:60
JUBAL, STRAIT OF
map (27° 40′N 33° 55′E) **7**:76
JUBAYL (Lebanon)
map (34° 7′N 35° 39′E) **12**:265
JUBY, CAPE
map (27° 58′N 12° 55′W) **13**:585
JUCHEREAU DE SAINT DENIS, LOUIS *see* SAINT DENIS, LOUIS JUCHEREAU DE

JUCHITÁN (DE ZARAGOZA) (Mexico)
map (16° 26′N 95° 1′W) **13**:357
JUD SÜSS (book)
Feuchtwanger, Lion **8**:63
JUDAEA *see* JUDEA
JUDAEO-ROMANCE LANGUAGE *see* LADINO LANGUAGE
JUDAH **11**:458
JUDAH, KINGDOM OF **3**:238 *map*; **11**:458
Ahaz, King of Judah **1**:200
Hezekiah, King of Judah **10**:156
Jehoiakim, King of Judah **11**:394
Jehoshaphat, King of Judah **11**:394
Jews **11**:413
Nebuchadnezzar II, King of Babylonia **14**:74
Palestine **15**:43–44
Rehoboam, King of Israel **16**:130
Zedekiah, King **20**:357
JUDAH, THEODORE D. **11**:458
JUDAH HA-LEVI **11**:458 *bibliog.*
JUDAH HA-NASI **11**:458
JUDAISM **11**:458–463 *bibliog., illus.*; **16**:140 *map*
See also BIBLE—Old Testament; JEWS
Asia, history of **2**:250
Babylonian Captivity **11**:460
beliefs **11**:459
Bene Israel **3**:196
calendar **11**:459
cantor **4**:118
Caro, Joseph ben Ephraim **4**:159
Conservative Judaism **11**:463
Frankel, Zacharias **8**:280
Schechter, Solomon **17**:117
Dead Sea Scrolls **6**:65
diaspora **6**:153
dietary laws **6**:165
kosher **12**:123–124
education
Jewish Theological Seminary of America **11**:412
private schools **15**:557
theological seminaries **19**:157
Yeshiva University **20**:327
Elijah Ben Solomon **7**:138
Essenes **7**:244
Falashas **8**:11–12
Galilee **9**:14
Gamaliel of Jabneh **9**:24
ghetto **11**:462
Ginzberg, Louis **9**:185
God **9**:217–219
halachah **10**:17; **11**:459
Midrash **13**:414
Hasideans **10**:66
Hasidism **10**:66; **11**:462
Baal Shem Tov **3**:5
Hellenistic Judaism **11**:460
Hillel **10**:164
House of David **10**:272
ibn Gabirol, Solomon ben Judah **11**:5
Jerusalem (Israel) **11**:399–401 *illus., map*
Judgment, Last **11**:464
Kabbalah **12**:3
Karaites **12**:26
Luria, Isaac ben Solomon **12**:466–467
Maccabees **11**:460; **13**:7
Maimonides **11**:461; **13**:68
Masorah **13**:199
medicine **13**:267
Middle East **13**:398
midrash **13**:414
mysticism **11**:461–462
National Conference of Christians and Jews **14**:30–31
origins **11**:459–460
Orthodox Judaism **11**:463
Pharisees **11**:460
philosophy **15**:244
practices **11**:459
prophets **11**:460; **15**:572
See also names of specific prophets, e.g., ELIJAH; JONAH; etc.
pseudepigrapha **15**:587
rabbi **16**:30
Reform Judaism **11**:463
Baeck, Leo **3**:20
Einhorn, David **7**:92
Geiger, Abraham **9**:67
Gottheil, Gustav **9**:264
Holdheim, Samuel **10**:202
Kohler, Kaufmann **12**:106
Wise, Isaac Mayer **20**:189
Wise, Stephen Samuel **20**:189
rituals and festivals
bar mitzvah **3**:74
Chanukah **4**:282
liturgy **11**:459
Passover **15**:105–106
Pentecost **15**:155
Purim **15**:629
Rosh Hashanah **16**:317
Sabbath **17**:5
seder **17**:182
Shavuoth **17**:245
Tabernacles, Feast of **19**:4
Yom Kippur **20**:329
Rosenzweig, Franz **16**:316
Sabbatai Zevi **17**:5
Sadducees **11**:460; **17**:9
Samaritans **17**:45
Septuagint **17**:206
sin **17**:318
soul **18**:70
Star of David **18**:226
synagogue **18**:406
synagogue service **11**:462 *illus.*
tabernacle **19**:4
Talmud **19**:17–18
midrash **13**:414
Mishnah **13**:466
Rashi **16**:90
Talmudic Judaism **11**:460–461
Ten Commandments **19**:100
Ten Lost Tribes of Israel **19**:100
Tiberias (Israel) **19**:189
Torah **11**:459; **19**:238
reading of the Torah **16**:139 *illus.*
usury **19**:491
women in society **20**:201
Zionism *see* ZIONISM
JUDAS ISCARIOT **11**:463 *bibliog.*
Gethsemane **9**:160
JUDAS TREE *see* REDBUD
JUDD, DONALD **11**:463 *bibliog.*
JUDE, EPISTLE OF **11**:463
JUDE, SAINT **11**:463
JUDE THE OBSCURE (book) **11**:464 *bibliog.*
JUDEA
Caesarea **4**:15
Herod (dynasty) **10**:144
Jesus Christ **11**:404 *map*
Maccabees (family) **13**:7
JUDENBURG (Austria)
map (47° 10′N 14° 40′E) **2**:348
JUDGE
criminal justice **5**:350
JUDGE, W.Q.
theosophy **19**:159–160
JUDGE ADVOCATE GENERAL *see* MILITARY JUSTICE
JUDGEMENT
legal procedure **12**:273
JUDGES, BOOK OF **11**:464 *bibliog.*
JUDGMENT **11**:464
confessed judgment **11**:464
default judgment **11**:464
JUDGMENT, LAST **11**:464
Second Coming of Christ **17**:178
JUDICIAL DUEL *see* TRIAL BY BATTLE
JUDICIAL REVIEW **11**:464 *bibliog.*
administrative law **1**:105
Constitution of the United States **5**:219
constitutional provisions, worldwide **11**:464
framework of the Constitution **5**:214
law **12**:243
Marbury v. *Madison* **13**:144
Marshall, John **13**:172
separation of powers **17**:206
Story, Joseph **18**:285
Supreme Court of the United States **18**:356
JUDIQUE (Nova Scotia)
map (45° 52′N 61° 30′W) **14**:269
JUDITH, BOOK OF **11**:464
JUDITH BASIN (county in Montana)
map (46° 55′N 110° 10′W) **13**:547
JUDITH PEAK
map (47° 13′N 109° 13′W) **13**:547
JUDO
martial arts **13**:177–178 *illus.*
JUDSON, ADONIRAM **11**:464–465 *bibliog.*
JUDSON, ARTHUR
radio and television broadcasting **16**:55
JUDSON, WHITCOMB L.
zipper **20**:370
JUDSONIA (Arkansas)
map (35° 16′N 91° 38′W) **2**:166
JUGENDSTIL *see* ART NOUVEAU
JUGNAUTH, ANEEROOD
Mauritius **13**:237
JUGURTHA, KING OF NUMIDIA **11**:465
JUH
Geronimo **9**:157–158
JUHÁSZ, GYULA
Hungarian literature **10**:306
JUHL, FINN
Scandinavian art and architecture **17**:114
JUIGALPA (Nicaragua)
map (12° 5′N 85° 24′W) **14**:179
JUILLIARD, AUGUSTUS D. **11**:465
JUILLIARD SCHOOL, THE **11**:465
architecture
Lincoln Center for the Performing Arts **12**:350
Erskine, John **7**:235
Juilliard, Augustus D. **11**:465
Schuman, William Howard **17**:136
JUILLIARD STRING QUARTET
Juilliard School, The **11**:465
JUIZ DE FORA (Brazil)
map (21° 45′S 43° 20′W) **3**:460
JUJITSU
martial arts **13**:177–178
JUJUBE (botany) **11**:465 *illus.*
crucifixion thorn **5**:365
JUJUY (province in Argentina)
map (23° 0′S 66° 0′W) **2**:149
JUKEBOX **11**:465
JULESBURG (Colorado)
map (40° 59′N 102° 16′W) **5**:116
JULIACA (Peru)
map (15° 30′S 70° 8′W) **15**:193
JULIAN , GEORGE WASHINGTON **11**:465 *bibliog.*
JULIAN ALPS
map (46° 0′N 14° 0′E) **20**:340
JULIAN THE APOSTATE, ROMAN EMPEROR **11**:466 *bibliog.*
JULIAN CALENDAR
calendar **4**:28
JULIAN DAY **11**:466
JULIANA, QUEEN OF THE NETHERLANDS **11**:466
JULIANATOP (peak)
map (3° 41′N 56° 32′W) **18**:364
JULIANEHÅB (Greenland)
map (60° 43′N 46° 1′W) **9**:353
JULIUS CAESAR (play) **11**:466 *bibliog.*
JULIUS CAESAR (Roman dictator) *see* CAESAR, GAIUS JULIUS
JULIUS II, POPE **11**:466 *bibliog.*
Bramante, Donato **3**:452
Louis XII, King of France **12**:425
Michelangelo **13**:373
Raphael **16**:89
JULIUS III, POPE **11**:318 *illus.*
JULLIEN, LOUIS
American music **1**:349
JULLUNDUR (India)
map (31° 19′N 75° 34′E) **11**:80
JULY
birthstones **3**:296 *illus., table*
calendar **4**:28
JULY REVOLUTION **11**:466
Charles X, King of France **4**:293
Europe, history of **7**:292
Louis Philippe, King of France **12**:423
JUMBO (elephant) **11**:466
JUMMU (state in India) *see* KASHMIR (India)
JUMNA RIVER *see* YAMUNA RIVER
JUMPING
track and field **19**:260–261 *illus.*
JUMPING PLANT LOUSE **11**:466
JUNCO **11**:466–467 *illus.*
JUNCTION (Texas)
map (30° 29′N 99° 46′W) **19**:129
JUNCTION (Utah)
map (38° 14′N 112° 13′W) **19**:492
JUNCTION CITY (Arkansas)
map (33° 1′N 92° 43′W) **2**:166
JUNCTION CITY (Kansas)
map (39° 2′N 96° 50′W) **12**:18
JUNCTION CITY (Kentucky)
map (37° 35′N 84° 48′W) **12**:47
JUNCTION CITY (Oregon)
map (44° 13′N 123° 12′W) **14**:427
JUNE
birthstones **3**:296 *illus., table*
calendar **4**:28
JUNE BUG **11**:467
JUNEAU (Alaska) **1**:244 *illus.*; **11**:467; **19**:420 *illus.*
map (58° 20′N 134° 27′W) **1**:242
JUNEAU (Wisconsin)
map (43° 24′N 88° 42′W) **20**:185
JUNEAU (county in Wisconsin)
map (43° 57′N 90° 8′W) **20**:185
JUNEAU, SOLOMON
Milwaukee (Wisconsin) **13**:434
JUNEBERRY **11**:467
serviceberry **17**:211
JUNG, CARL **11**:467–468 *bibliog., illus.*; **15**:598 *illus.*
abstract expressionism (art) **1**:66
archetype **14**:22
complex (psychology) **5**:157
dreams and dreaming **6**:267
extraversion-introversion **7**:346; **11**:467
folklore **8**:203
Freud, Sigmund **8**:329
libido **12**:314
mandala **13**:110
middle age **13**:390
motivation and personality **11**:467
psychoanalysis **15**:590
symbols **11**:467
theories **11**:467–468
therapy **11**:467–468
unconscious **19**:382–383
unconscious psyche **11**:467
JUNGFRAU **11**:468
map (46° 32′N 7° 58′E) **18**:394
JUNGLE, THE (book) **11**:468
Sinclair, Upton **17**:319
JUNGLE BOOK, THE (book) **11**:468
feral children **8**:51
Kipling, Rudyard **12**:86–87
mongoose **13**:531 *illus.*
JUNGLE AND RAIN FOREST **2**:330 *illus.*; **11**:468–470 *bibliog., illus., map*
biome **3**:273–274 *map*
climax community **5**:59
deciduous plant **6**:73
ecology **7**:42
forest **8**:228
habitat **10**:5
Olympic National Forest **14**:229 *illus.*
South America **18**:89 *map*
tree **19**:288
world distribution **3**:273 *map*; **15**:344 *map*
JUNGMANN, JOSEF
Czech literature **5**:412
JUNI, JUAN DE **11**:470 *bibliog.*
JUNIATA (county in Pennsylvania)
map (40° 33′N 77° 25′W) **15**:147
JUNIATA RIVER
map (40° 24′N 77° 1′W) **15**:147
JUNÍN (Argentina)
map (34° 35′S 60° 57′W) **2**:149
JUNÍN (Ecuador)
map (0° 56′S 80° 13′W) **7**:52
JUNIOR CHAMBER OF COMMERCE *see* JAYCEES INTERNATIONAL
JUNIOR COLLEGES *see* COMMUNITY AND JUNIOR COLLEGES
JUNIOR HIGH SCHOOLS *see* MIDDLE SCHOOLS AND JUNIOR HIGH SCHOOLS
JUNIPER (botany) **11**:470 *illus.*; **17**:288 *illus.*
North Dakota **14**:249 *illus.*
JUNIPER (New Brunswick)
map (46° 33′N 67° 13′W) **14**:117
JUNIUS **11**:470 *bibliog.*
JUNK (ship) **11**:470–471 *bibliog., illus.*
ship **17**:264 *illus.*
JUNKER, WILHELM
Ubangi River **19**:370
JUNKERS **11**:471
JUNKERS, HUGO
aviation **2**:374
JUNO (mythology) **11**:471
Veii **19**:535
JUNO (rocket) **16**:256 *illus.*
Jupiter (rocket) **11**:474
Redstone **16**:117
JUNO AND THE PAYCOCK (play)
O'Casey, Sean **14**:319–320
JUNOT, ANDOCHE **11**:471
JUNTA **11**:471 *bibliog.*
JUNTO, THE
Franklin, Benjamin **8**:283
JUPITER (Florida)
map (26° 56′N 80° 6′W) **8**:172
JUPITER (mythology) **11**:471
JUPITER (planet) **2**:282 *illus.*; **11**:471–474 *bibliog., illus., table*
atmosphere **11**:472
Great Red Spot **9**:321; **11**:473 *illus.*; **18**:126 *illus.*
hydrogen **10**:337
magnetic field **11**:472
Mayr, Simon **13**:249
planets **15**:329–331
radio astronomy **16**:48
rings **11**:473
satellites **11**:472–474 *illus., table*
Callisto **4**:46
Europa (astronomy) **7**:267
Ganymede **9**:38
Io **11**:238
Kowal, Charles T. **12**:126
solar system **18**:46–49 *illus., table*
space exploration **18**:123; **18**:126
Galileo (spacecraft) **9**:15
Pioneer **15**:309–310
Voyager **19**:637–638
Trojans **19**:305

JUPITER (cont.)
weather **11**:472
winds **11**:472
JUPITER (rocket) **11**:474; **16**:256 *illus.*
von Braun, Wernher **19**:633
JURA (mountain range) **11**:474
Belfort Gap **3**:174
map (46° 45'N 6° 30'E) **18**:394
Switzerland **18**:394–395
JURA ISLAND
map (56° 0'N 5° 50'W) **19**:403
JURASSIC PERIOD **11**:474–477 *bibliog., illus., map*
climate **11**:475
continental drift **5**:228
dinosaurs **6**:179–182; **11**:475–476 *illus.*
Allosaurus **1**:303
Brachiosaurus **3**:435
Brontosaurus **3**:504–505
Camptosaurus **4**:67–68
Compsognathus **5**:158
Diplodocus **6**:185–186
Iguanadon **11**:39
Nanosaurus **14**:13
Ornitholestes **14**:47
Rhamphorhynchus **16**:192
Stegosaurus **18**:246
extinct mammals **13**:102–103 *illus.*
flora **11**:475 *illus.*
fossil record **8**:245–247; **11**:475; **11**:476
geography **11**:474–476
ginkgo **9**:184
Gondwanaland **9**:243
landforms **11**:477 *map*
life **11**:476–477
Mesozoic Era **13**:322
Oppel, Albert **14**:407
paleotectonics **11**:474–476
polar wandering **15**:393 *map*
rock formations **11**:477 *map*
JURCHEN
Altaic languages **19**:476
Chin (Jin) **4**:360
China, history of **4**:372
JURISDICTION
court **5**:315
JURISPRUDENCE *see* LAW
JURUÁ RIVER
map (2° 37'S 65° 44'W) **3**:460
JURY **11**:477–478 *bibliog.*
See also 6th AMENDMENT; 7th AMENDMENT
common law **5**:139
coroner's jury
inquest **11**:183
law, history of **12**:245
legal procedure **12**:273
petit jury **15**:202–203
trial **19**:292
JUS SANGUINES
citizenship **4**:447
JUS SOLI
citizenship **4**:447
JUSTICE, U.S. DEPARTMENT OF **11**:478 *bibliog.*
attorney general **2**:316
See also articles of specific presidents, e.g., GRANT, ULYSSES S.; ROOSEVELT, FRANKLIN DELANO; etc; names of specific attorneys general, e.g., KENNEDY, ROBERT F.; RICHARDSON, ELLIOTT L.; etc.
flag **8**:148 *illus.*
busing, school **3**:590
Federal Bureau of Investigation **8**:40–41
Washington, D.C. **20**:41 *map*
JUSTICE OF THE PEACE **11**:478
marriage **13**:166
Morris, Esther **13**:588
powers and duties **11**:478
JUSTIN I, BYZANTINE EMPEROR
Justinian I, Byzantine Emperor (Justinian the Great) **11**:479
JUSTIN MARTYR, SAINT **11**:478 *bibliog.*
JUSTINE (book) **11**:478 *bibliog.*
Sade, Marquis de **17**:9
JUSTINIAN CODE **11**:478–479 *bibliog.*
civil law **5**:11
law, history of **12**:244–245
Roman law **16**:278
JUSTINIAN I, BYZANTINE EMPEROR (Justinian the Great) **3**:607 *illus.*; **11**:479 *bibliog.*; **12**:244 *illus.*; **17**:58 *illus.*
Egypt, ancient **7**:83
Hagia Sophia **10**:10
mosaic **13**:595
Procopius of Caesarea **15**:561
Roman law **16**:278–279
Theodora, Byzantine Empress **19**:156
JUSTUS VAN GHENT *see* JOOS VAN GHENT
JUTE **8**:67–68 *illus., map*; **11**:479 *bibliog.*
cellulose **4**:238
hibiscus **10**:157
JUTIAPA (Guatemala)
map (14° 17'N 89° 54'W) **9**:389
JUTICALPA (Honduras)
map (14° 42'N 86° 15'W) **10**:218
JUTLAND (Denmark) **11**:479
cities
Ålborg **1**:261
Århus **2**:153
map (56° 0'N 9° 15'E) **6**:109
JUTLAND, BATTLE OF **11**:479 *bibliog.*; **14**:64 *illus.*
World War I **20**:235 *illus.*
JUTRA, CLAUDE **11**:479
JUVARRA, FILIPPO **11**:479–480 *bibliog.*
JUVENAL **11**:480 *bibliog.*
satire **17**:88
JUVENILE DELINQUENCY **11**:480 *bibliog.*
computer crime **5**:160L
crime **5**:347
JUVENILE DIABETES
diabetes **6**:148–149
JUVENILE HORMONE **11**:480 *bibliog.*
hormone, animal **10**:237
JUVENILE RIGHTS
juvenile delinquency **11**:480
JUŽNA MORAVA RIVER
map (43° 42'N 21° 23'E) **20**:340
JYLLAND *see* JUTLAND (Denmark)
JYVÄSKYLÄ (Finland)
map (62° 14'N 25° 44'E) **8**:95

K

K (letter) **12**:3 *illus.*
K (vitamin) *see* VITAMIN K
K-BAR **18**:399 *illus.*
K-MESON *see* KAON
K-2 (mountain) *see* GODWIN AUSTEN
KA LAE
map (18° 55'N 155° 41'W) **10**:72
KA-YA-TEN-NAE
Geronimo **9**:157
KAABA **12**:3; **13**:258 *illus.*
Middle East, history of the **13**:402
KAALA PEAK
map (21° 31'N 158° 9'W) **10**:72
KAAPSTAD *see* CAPE TOWN (South Africa)
KABALE (Uganda)
map (1° 15'S 29° 59'E) **19**:372
KABALEGA FALLS
map (2° 17'N 31° 41'E) **19**:372
KABALEVSKY, DMITRI **12**:3 *bibliog.*
Russian music **16**:369
KABBALAH **11**:415 *illus.*; **12**:3 *bibliog.*
Hasidism **10**:66
Judaism **11**:461 *illus.*
Luria, Isaac ben Solomon **12**:466–467
Luzzatto, Moses Hayyim **12**:473
Scholem, Gershom Gerhard **17**:133
KABUKI **12**:4 *bibliog., illus.*
Bunraku **3**:564
dance **6**:27
Ichikawa (family) **11**:19
theater, history of the **19**:148–149 *illus.*
KABUL (Afghanistan) **1**:134 *illus., table*; **12**:4
map (34° 31'N 69° 12'E) **1**:133
KABUL RIVER
map (33° 55'N 72° 14'E) **15**:27
KABWE (Zambia)
map (14° 27'S 28° 27'E) **20**:354
KABYLE **12**:4 *bibliog.*
KACEW, ROMAIN *see* GARY, ROMAIN
KACHIN LANGUAGE
Sino-Tibetan languages **17**:324
KACHINA **12**:4 *bibliog.*
Indians of North America, art of the **11**:140
Pueblo (American Indians) **15**:613
KÁDÁR, JÁNOS **12**:4 *bibliog.*
Hungary **10**:310
KADOKA (South Dakota)
map (43° 50'N 101° 31'W) **18**:103
KADOMA (Zimbabwe)
map (18° 21'S 29° 55'E) **20**:365
KADUNA (Nigeria)
map (10° 33'N 7° 27'E) **14**:190
KADUNA RIVER
map (8° 45'N 5° 45'E) **14**:190
KAEL, PAULINE **12**:4–5
KAENA POINT
map (21° 35'N 158° 17'W) **10**:72
KAENDLER, JOHANN JOACHIM
rhinoceros **16**:264 *illus.*
KAESONG (Korea) **12**:5
map (37° 59'N 126° 33'E) **12**:113
KAFFIR CAT **12**:5 *illus.*
KAFIR **12**:5 *bibliog.*
KAFIRI LANGUAGE
Indo-Iranian languages **11**:145–146
KAFKA, FRANZ **12**:5–6 *bibliog., illus.*
Brod, Max **3**:501
The Castle **4**:191
The Trial **19**:292
KAFU RIVER
map (1° 8'N 31° 5'E) **19**:372
KAFUE RIVER
map (15° 56'S 28° 55'E) **20**:354
KAGANOVICH, LAZAR
Khrushchev, Nikita Sergeyevich **12**:69
KÅGE, WILHELM
Scandinavian art and architecture **17**:114
KAGEL, MAURICIO
Latin American music and dance **12**:232
KAGERA RIVER
map (0° 57'S 31° 47'E) **19**:27
KAGOSHIMA (Japan)
map (31° 36'N 130° 33'E) **11**:361
KAGU **12**:6
KAHALUU (Hawaii)
map (21° 28'N 157° 50'W) **10**:72
KAHANAMOKU, DUKE
surfing **18**:359
KAHN, ALBERT **12**:6 *bibliog.*
KAHN, HERMAN
futurology **8**:384
KAHN, LOUIS **12**:6 *bibliog.*
Mellon, Paul **13**:287
KAHN, OTTO
Metropolitan Opera **13**:348
KAHOKA (Missouri)
map (40° 25'N 91° 43'W) **13**:476
KAHOOLAWE (Hawaii)
Hawaii (state) **10**:73
map (20° 33'N 156° 37'W) **10**:72
KAHUKU (Hawaii)
map (21° 41'N 157° 57'W) **10**:72
KAHUKU POINT
map (21° 43'N 157° 59'W) **10**:72
KAHULUI (Hawaii)
map (20° 54'N 156° 28'W) **10**:72
K'AI-FENG (Kaifeng) (China) **12**:6
map (34° 51'N 114° 21'E) **4**:362
KAIETEUR FALL (Waterfall)
map (5° 10'N 59° 28'W) **9**:410
KAIGETSUDO **12**:6 *bibliog.*
KAILAS, UUNO
Finnish literature **8**:99
KAILAS MOUNTAINS
map (31° 0'N 82° 0'E) **10**:167
KAILASA TEMPLE
Ellora **7**:148
KAILUA (Hawaii)
map (21° 24'N 157° 44'W) **10**:72
KAILUA BAY
map (21° 25'N 157° 44'W) **10**:72
KAILUA KONA (Hawaii)
map (19° 39'N 155° 59'W) **10**:72
KAIN, KAREN **3**:41 *illus.*; **14**:29 *illus.*
KAINAH (American Indians)
Blackfoot **3**:321
KAINJI LAKE
map (10° 30'N 4° 35'E) **14**:190
KAIPAROWITS PLATEAU
map (37° 20'N 111° 15'W) **19**:492
KAISER (title) *see* CAESAR
KAISER, ERALD
Robert and Clara Schumann **9**:131 *illus.*
KAISER, GEORG **12**:6–7 *bibliog.*
KAISER, HENRY JOHN **12**:7 *bibliog.*
KAISER, RAY
Eames, Charles **7**:5
KAISER-WILHELM-GESELLSCHAFT *see* MAX PLANCK SOCIETY FOR THE ADVANCEMENT OF SCIENCE
KAISERSLAUTERN (Germany, East and West)
map (49° 26'N 7° 46'E) **9**:140
KAIWI:YO:H
Handsome Lake **10**:37
KAIWI CHANNEL
map (21° 15'N 157° 30'W) **10**:72
KAJAANI (Finland)
map (64° 14'N 27° 41'E) **8**:95
KAJAKI, LAKE
map (32° 22'N 65° 16'E) **1**:133
KAKE (Alaska)
map (56° 58'N 133° 46'W) **1**:242
KAKI *see* PERSIMMON
KALA-AZAR **12**:7
assassin bug **2**:264
leishmaniasis **12**:279
midge **13**:413
protozoal diseases **15**:581
KALAHARI DESERT **3**:416–417 *table*; **6**:126; **12**:7 *bibliog.*
map (24° 0'S 21° 30'E) **18**:79
people **2**:52 *illus.*
San **17**:49 *illus.*
KALAHEO (Hawaii)
map (21° 56'N 159° 32'W) **10**:72
KALÁMAI (Greece) **12**:7
map (37° 4'N 22° 7'E) **9**:325
KALAMÁTA (Greece) *see* KALÁMAI (Greece)
KALAMAZOO (Michigan) **12**:7
map (42° 17'N 85° 32'W) **13**:377
KALAMAZOO (county in Michigan)
map (42° 14'N 85° 32'W) **13**:377
KALANCHOE **12**:7
KALASASAYA
Tiahuanaco **19**:188
KALB, BARTON DE *see* KALB, JOHANN
KALB, JOHANN **12**:7
KALE **12**:7 *illus.*; **19**:532 *illus.*
KALEIDOSCOPE
Brewster, Sir David **3**:476
KALEMIE (Zaire)
map (5° 56'S 29° 12'E) **20**:350
KALENJIN (ethnic group)
Kenya **12**:54
KALEVALA (poem) **12**:7–8
KALFF, WILLEM **12**:8 *bibliog.*
KALGAN (China)
map (40° 50'N 114° 53'E) **4**:362
KALGOORLIE (Australia) **12**:8
map (30° 45'S 121° 28'E) **2**:328
KALHU *see* NIMRUD
KALI (Indian deity) **12**:8
mother goddess **13**:607
KALIBANGAN
Indus civilization **11**:153 *map*
KALIDASA **12**:8 *bibliog.*
Shakuntala (play) **17**:237
KALIMANTAN
Indonesia **11**:146–147 *map*
KÁLIMNOS (Greece)
Dodecanese **6**:212
KALINGA
Igorot **11**:38
KALININ (USSR) **12**:8
map (56° 52'N 35° 55'E) **19**:388
KALININGRAD (USSR) **12**:8
KALISPELL (Montana)
map (48° 12'N 114° 19'W) **13**:547
KALISZ (Poland)
map (51° 46'N 18° 6'E) **15**:388
KALKASKA (Michigan)
map (44° 44'N 85° 11'W) **13**:377
KALKASKA (county in Michigan)
map (44° 40'N 85° 5'W) **13**:377
KALLMANN, FRANZ
behavioral genetics **3**:170
KALMAR (Sweden)
map (56° 40'N 16° 22'E) **18**:382
KALMAR, UNION OF
Denmark **6**:112
Scandinavia, history of **17**:108–109 *map*
KALMAR SOUND
map (56° 40'N 16° 25'E) **18**:382
KALMYK **12**:8 *bibliog.*
KALMYK AUTONOMOUS SOVIET SOCIALIST REPUBLIC (USSR)
Kalmyk **12**:8
KALOGEROPOULOS, MARIA *see* CALLAS, MARIA
KALOHI CHANNEL
map (21° 0'N 156° 56'W) **10**:72
KALONA (Iowa)
map (41° 29'N 91° 43'W) **11**:244
KALSKAG (Alaska)
map (61° 30'N 160° 23'W) **1**:242
KALTAG (Alaska)
map (64° 20'N 158° 44'W) **1**:242
KALUNDBORG (Denmark)
map (55° 41'N 11° 6'E) **6**:109
KALUTARA (Sri Lanka)
map (6° 35'N 79° 58'E) **18**:206
KAMA RESERVOIR
map (55° 45'N 52° 0'E) **19**:629
map (58° 52'N 56° 15'E) **19**:388
KAMAKOU (peak)
map (21° 7'N 156° 52'W) **10**:72
KAMAKURA (Japan)
Japan, history of **11**:367–368
Japanese art and architecture **11**:375
shogun **17**:281
Yoritomo **20**:330
KAMALIA
map (30° 44'N 72° 39'E) **15**:27
KAMANANUI RIVER
map (21° 38'N 158° 3'W) **10**:72

KAMASUTRA (book) **12**:9
cosmetics in India **5**:281
KAMBA **12**:9 *bibliog.*
KAMBALDA
major ore deposits **14**:424–425 *table*
KAMCHATKA PENINSULA **12**:9 *map*
map (56° 0′N 160° 0′E) **19**:388
KAMCHIYA RIVER
map (43° 2′N 27° 53′E) **3**:555
KAME **12**:9 *bibliog.*
components **12**:9
glacial debris **12**:9
glaciers and glaciation **9**:192–195
KAMEHAMEHA (dynasty) **12**:9 *bibliog.*
Hawaii (state) **10**:76
KAMEKEHA, LYDIA *see* LILIUOKALANI, QUEEN OF HAWAII
KAMENEV, LEV BORISOVICH **12**:9–10 *bibliog.*
Stalin, Joseph **18**:214
KAMENJAK, CAPE
map (44° 46′N 13° 55′E) **20**:340
KAMERLINGH ONNES, HEIKE **12**:10
cryogenics **5**:371
superconductivity **18**:350
KAMERNY THEATER
Taïrov, Aleksandr Yakovlevich **19**:12
KAMET MOUNTAIN
map (30° 54′N 79° 37′E) **11**:80
KAMI
Shinto **17**:262
KAMIAH (Idaho)
map (46° 14′N 116° 2′W) **11**:26
KAMIKAZE
Japan, history of **11**:371 *illus.*
World War II **20**:278–279 *illus.*
Zero (aircraft) **20**:361
KAMINA (Zaire)
map (8° 44′S 25° 0′E) **20**:350
KAMINALJUYÚ (Guatemala) **12**:10 *bibliog.*; **14**:237 *map*
Kidder, Alfred Vincent **12**:71
Maya **13**:243
Teotihuacán **19**:113
Tikal **19**:198
KAMINSKA, IDA
Yiddish theater **20**:328
KAMINSKY, MELVYN *see* BROOKS, MEL
KAMISHIMO
samurai **17**:49 *illus.*
KAMLOOPS (British Columbia) **12**:10
map (50° 40′N 120° 20′W) **3**:491
KAMP, PETER VAN DE *see* VAN DE KAMP, PETER
KAMPALA (Uganda) **12**:10; **19**:372 *illus.*
climate **19**:372 *table*
Ganda **9**:35
map (0° 19′N 32° 25′E) **19**:372
KAMPEN (Netherlands)
map (52° 33′N 5° 54′E) **14**:99
KAMPESKA, LAKE
map (44° 56′N 97° 14′W) **18**:103
KAMPOT(Kampuchea)
map (10° 37′N 104° 11′E) **12**:11
KAMPSVILLE (Illinois)
map (39° 18′N 90° 37′W) **11**:42
KAMPUCHEA (Cambodia) **12**:10–13 *bibliog., illus., map, table*
art
Southeast Asian art and architecture **18**:108–109 *illus.*
temple **19**:98
cities
Battambang **3**:124
Phnom Penh **15**:248
economy **12**:12
education **12**:11
Southeast Asian universities **18**:111 *table*
flag **12**:10 *illus.*
history **12**:12–13
Angkor **1**:414–415
Heng Samrin **10**:121
Khieu Samphan **12**:66
Khmer Empire **12**:67
Khmer Rouge **12**:67
Lon Nol **12**:400
Norodom Sihanouk **14**:222
Pol Pot **15**:387
refugee **16**:125
Vietnam **19**:584
Vietnam War **19**:584–591 *illus.*
Indochina **11**:146
land and resources **12**:10–11 *map, table*
map (13° 0′N 105° 0′E) **2**:232
people **12**:11
Khmer **12**:66–67
rivers, lakes, and waterways **12**:11
KAMSACK (Saskatchewan)
map (51° 34′N 101° 54′W) **17**:81
KÁMUK MOUNT
map (9° 17′N 83° 4′W) **5**:291
KAN-CHOU (China)
map (25° 54′N 114° 55′E) **4**:362
KAN LANGUAGE
Sino-Tibetan languages **17**:324
KAN RIVER
Kiangsi (Jiangxi) (China) **12**:70
map (29° 12′N 116° 0′E) **20**:318
KANA *see* JAPANESE LANGUAGE
KANAB (Utah)
map (37° 3′N 112° 32′W) **19**:492
KANAB CREEK
map (36° 24′N 112° 38′W) **2**:160
KANABEC (county in Minnesota)
map (45° 55′N 93° 17′W) **13**:453
KANANGA (Zaire)
map (5° 54′S 22° 25′E) **20**:350
KANARRAVILLE (Utah)
map (37° 32′N 113° 11′W) **19**:492
KANAWHA (Iowa)
map (42° 56′N 93° 48′W) **11**:244
KANAWHA (county in West Virginia)
map (38° 20′N 81° 30′W) **20**:111
KANAWHA RIVER
map (38° 50′N 82° 8′W) **20**:111
KANAZAWA (Japan)
map (36° 34′N 136° 39′E) **11**:361
KANCHENJUNGA **12**:13
map (27° 42′N 88° 8′E) **14**:86
KANDAHAR (Afghanistan) **12**:13
map (31° 32′N 65° 30′E) **1**:133
KANDAVU PASSAGE
map (18° 45′S 178° 0′E) **8**:77
KANDH *see* KHOND
KANDINSKY, WASSILY **12**:13–14 *bibliog., illus.*
abstract expressionism **1**:65
Bauhaus **3**:129–130 *illus.*
Blaue Reiter, Der **3**:328
Couple on Horseback **16**:363 *illus.*
First Abstract Watercolor **13**:494 *illus.*
Improvisation 33 **1**:64 *illus.*; **12**:14 *illus.*
Münter, Gabriele **13**:644
KANDIYOHI (county in Minnesota)
map (45° 7′N 95° 0′W) **13**:453
KÄNDLER, JOHANN JOACHIM
pottery and porcelain **15**:471 *illus.*
vase **13**:283 *illus.*
KANDY (Sri Lanka) **12**:14
map (7° 18′N 80° 38′E) **18**:206
KANE (Illinois)
map (39° 11′N 90° 21′W) **11**:42
KANE (county in Illinois)
map (41° 53′N 88° 18′W) **11**:42
KANE (Pennsylvania)
map (41° 40′N 78° 49′W) **15**:147
KANE (county in Utah)
map (37° 15′N 111° 50′W) **19**:492
KANE, PAUL **12**:14 *bibliog.*
Canadian art and architecture **4**:88
Clallam medicine-man mask dance **11**:122 *illus.*; **13**:50 *illus.*
The Man That Always Rides **4**:88 *illus.*
Man Who Gives the War Whoop **11**:126 *illus.*
KANEM-BORNU **12**:14–15 *bibliog.*
Kanuri **12**:24
KANEOHE (Hawaii)
map (21° 25′N 157° 48′W) **10**:72
KANEOHE BAY
map (21° 28′N 157° 49′W) **10**:72
KANESH *see* KÜLTEPE (Turkey)
K'ANG-HSI (Kangxi), **EMPEROR OF CHINA** **12**:15 *bibliog.*
rugs and carpets **16**:342
KANG-TI-SSU MOUNTAIN
map (31° 29′N 80° 45′E) **19**:190
K'ANG-T'O MOUNTAIN
map (27° 52′N 92° 30′E) **19**:190
KANG YOUWEI *see* K'ANG YU-WEI (Kang Youwei)
K'ANG YU-WEI (Kang Youwei) **12**:15 *bibliog.*
KANGAROO **12**:15 *bibliog., illus.*; **13**:104 *illus.*
ecological adaptation **13**:100 *illus.*
feet **13**:102 *illus.*
marsupial **13**:174
KANGAROO ISLAND
map (35° 50′S 137° 6′E) **2**:328
KANGAROO RAT **12**:15–16 *illus.*
KANGAROO THORN **12**:16
KANGGYE (Korea)
map (40° 58′N 126° 34′E) **12**:113
KANGHWA BAY
map (37° 20′N 126° 35′E) **12**:113
KANGHWA ISLAND
map (37° 40′N 126° 27′E) **12**:113
KANGXI, EMPEROR OF CHINA *see* K'ANG-HSI (Kangxi), EMPEROR OF CHINA
KANIA, STANISŁPAW **12**:16
Poland **15**:390–391
KANISHKA
Taxila **19**:48
KANKAKEE (Illinois)
map (41° 7′N 87° 52′W) **11**:42
KANKAKEE (county in Illinois)
map (41° 7′N 87° 52′W) **11**:42
KANKAKEE RIVER
map (41° 23′N 88° 16′W) **11**:42
KANKAN (Guinea)
map (10° 23′N 9° 18′W) **9**:397
KANNADA
Dravidian languages **6**:263
KANNAMI KIYOTSUGU
No drama **14**:207
KANNAPOLIS (North Carolina)
map (35° 30′N 80° 37′W) **14**:242
KANNER'S SYNDROME
autistic children **2**:355
KANO (Nigeria) **1**:144 *illus.*; **12**:16; **14**:191 *illus., table*
map (12° 0′N 8° 30′E) **14**:190
KANO CHRONICLE
Hausa **10**:69
KANO EITOKU *see* EITOKU
KANO MASANOBU *see* MASANOBU (1434–1530)
KANO MOTONOBU *see* MOTONOBU
KANO SANRAKU *see* SANRAKU
KANO SCHOOL
Eitoku **7**:97
Japanese art and architecture **11**:376
Masanobu (1434–1530) **13**:195
Motonobu **13**:611
Okyo **14**:372
Sanraku **17**:65
Tanyu **19**:26
KANO TANYU *see* TANYU
KANOPOLIS (Kansas)
map (38° 43′N 98° 9′W) **12**:18
KANOPOLIS LAKE
map (38° 38′N 98° 0′W) **12**:18
KANPUR (India) **12**:16
map (26° 28′N 80° 21′E) **11**:80
KANSA (American Indians) **12**:16 *bibliog.*
Omaha (American Indians) **14**:385
KANSAS **12**:16–22 *bibliog., illus., map*
agriculture **12**:19–20 *illus.*
cities
Abilene **1**:57
Atchison **2**:288
Dodge City **6**:212
Hutchinson **10**:322
Kansas City **12**:22
Salina **17**:32
Topeka **19**:237
Wichita **20**:144–145
climate **12**:17
economic activity **12**:19–21 *illus.*
education **12**:19
Kansas, state universities and colleges of **12**:22
flag **12**:17 *illus.*
government and politics **12**:21
history **12**:21–22
Emigrant Aid Company **7**:156
Kansas-Nebraska Act **12**:22–23
Lane, James Henry **12**:194
Lecompton Constitution **12**:268
Robinson, Charles **16**:243
land and resources **12**:16–19 *map*
manufacturing and transportation **12**:20 *illus.*
map (38° 30′N 98° 15′W) **19**:419
people **12**:19
Iowa **11**:248
Kickapoo **12**:70
Sauk **17**:96
rivers, lakes, and waterways **12**:17
seal, state **12**:17 *illus.*
vegetation and animal life **12**:17
KANSAS (Illinois)
map (39° 33′N 87° 56′W) **11**:42
KANSAS, STATE UNIVERSITIES AND COLLEGES OF **12**:22
KANSAS CITY (Kansas) **12**:22 *illus.*; **13**:478 *illus.*
map (39° 7′N 94° 39′W) **12**:18
KANSAS CITY (Missouri) **12**:22 *illus.*
history
Pendergast, Thomas Joseph **15**:142
map (39° 5′N 94° 35′W) **13**:476
KANSAS CITY CHIEFS (football team) **8**:217 *illus.*
KANSAS-NEBRASKA ACT **12**:22–23 *bibliog.*
Civil War, U.S. **5**:16 *illus.*
Indian Territory **11**:106
Lecompton Constitution **12**:268
Lincoln, Abraham **12**:348
Pierce, Franklin **15**:296
popular sovereignty **15**:433
Republican party **16**:172
United States, history of the **19**:447
KANSAS PACIFIC RAILROAD **19**:268 *map*
KANSAS RIVER
map (39° 7′N 94° 36′W) **12**:18
KANSU (China) **12**:23
amphora **4**:378 *illus.*
Lan-chou (Lanzhou) **12**:177
Ningsia (Ningxia) **14**:200
KANT, IMMANUEL **12**:23–24 *bibliog., illus.*
aesthetics **1**:131
Cassirer, Ernst **4**:184
categorical imperative **4**:202
Critique of Judgment
criticism, literary **5**:351
Critique of Pure Reason **5**:352
ethics **7**:251
Fichte, Johann Gottlieb **8**:69
idealism **11**:30
innate ideas **11**:179
noumenon **12**:24; **14**:268
phenomenon **12**:24
philosophy **15**:245
Schopenhauer, Arthur **17**:134
state (in political philosophy) **18**:229
substance **18**:317
transcendentalism **19**:268
KANTHAPURA (book)
Rao, Raja **16**:88
KANTNER, PAUL
Jefferson Airplane **11**:393
KANTOROVICH, LEONID V. **12**:24
KANU *see* KENYA AFRICAN NATIONAL UNION (KANU)
KANURI **12**:24 *bibliog.*
KANYE (Botswana)
map (24° 59′S 25° 19′E) **3**:416
KAO HSIAO-SHENG (Gao Xiaosheng)
Chinese literature **4**:390
KAO NGO
Dream of the Red Chamber, The **6**:266
KAO-TSUNG, EMPEROR OF CHINA
T'ang (Tang) (dynasty) **19**:21
KAOHSIUNG (Gaoxiong) (Taiwan) **12**:25
map (22° 38′N 120° 17′E) **19**:13
KAOKOVELD (plateau)
map (21° 0′S 14° 20′E) **14**:10
KAOLACK (Senegal)
map (14° 9′N 16° 4′W) **17**:202
KAOLIN
ceramics **4**:258 *illus.*
clay minerals **5**:46
pottery and porcelain **15**:468
weathering **20**:83
KAON **12**:25
Lee, Tsung Dao **12**:270
KAPAA (Hawaii)
map (22° 5′N 159° 19′W) **10**:72
KAPFENBERG (Austria)
map (47° 26′N 15° 18′E) **2**:348
KAPH (letter)
K(letter) **12**:3
KAPITAL, DAS (book) **12**:25
Marx, Karl **13**:182
socialism **18**:20 *illus.*
KAPITZA, PETER **12**:25 *bibliog.*
KAPLAN (Louisiana)
map (30° 0′N 92° 17′W) **12**:430
KAPLAN, MORDECAI MENAHEM **12**:25 *bibliog.*
KAPODISTRIAS, GIOVANNI ANTONIO, COUNT *see* CAPO D'ISTRIA, GIOVANNI ANTONIO, COUNT
KAPOK **12**:25 *illus.*
KAPOS RIVER
map (46° 44′N 18° 30′E) **10**:307
KAPOSI'S SARCOMA
AIDS **1**:201
KAPOSVÁR (Hungary)
map (46° 22′N 17° 47′E) **10**:307
KAPPA (letter)
K(letter) **12**:3
KAPPELHOFF, DORIS *see* DAY, DORIS
KAPROW, ALLAN **12**:25 *bibliog.*
happenings **10**:41
KAPTAI (Bangladesh)
map (22° 21′N 92° 17′E) **3**:64
KAPTEYN, JACOBUS CORNELIUS **12**:25–26
astronomy, history of **2**:280
KAPUAS RIVER
map (0° 25′S 109° 40′E) **11**:147
KAPUSKASING (Ontario)
map (49° 25′N 82° 26′W) **14**:393
KAPUSTIN YAR **12**:26
KARA-BOGAZ GULF
map (41° 0′N 53° 15′E) **19**:388

KARA-KALPAK AUTONOMOUS SOVIET SOCIALIST REPUBLIC (USSR)
Uzbek Soviet Socialist Republic **19**:499
KARA-KIRGHIZ *see* KIRGHIZ SOVIET SOCIALIST REPUBLIC (USSR)
KARA KUM **12**:26
map (39° 0′N 60° 0′E) **19**:388
KARA SEA
map (76° 0′N 80° 0′E) **19**:388
KARABUK (Turkey)
map (41° 12′N 32° 37′E) **19**:343
KARACHI (Pakistan) **12**:26 *illus.*; **15**:26 *illus.*, *table*
map (24° 52′N 67° 3′E) **15**:27
missions, Christian **13**:467 *illus.*
KARADJORDJEVIĆ (dynasty)
Miloš, Prince of Serbia **13**:432
KARADŽIĆ, VUK STEFANOVIĆ
Yugoslavia **20**:342
KARAGANDA (USSR)
map (49° 50′N 73° 10′E) **19**:388
KARAGEORGEVITCH, BOGDAR
Art Nouveau silverware **2**:210 *illus.*
KARAITES **12**:26 *bibliog.*
KARAJAN, HERBERT VON **12**:26 *bibliog.*
Berlin Philharmonic Orchestra **3**:217
KARAKALPAK **12**:26–27 *bibliog.*
KARAKORAM RANGE **12**:27
Godwin Austen **9**:221
map (35° 30′N 77° 0′E) **15**:27
mountain climbing **13**:622
KARAKUL SHEEP **17**:248–249 *illus.*
KARAMAN (Turkey)
map (37° 11′N 33° 14′E) **19**:343
KARAMANLIS, KONSTANTINOS G. **12**:27
Greece **9**:329
KARAMZIN, NIKOLAI MIKHAILOVICH **12**:27 *bibliog.*
KARANGA *see* SHONA
Zimbabwe Ruins **20**:366
KARATE
martial arts **13**:177 *illus.*
KARAVELOV, LYUBEN
Bulgaria **3**:556
KARAWANKEN MOUNTAINS
map (46° 30′N 14° 25′E) **2**:348
KARBALA (Iraq)
map (32° 36′N 44° 2′E) **11**:255
KARDHITSA (Greece)
map (39° 21′N 21° 55′E) **9**:325
KARDIVA CHANNEL
map (5° 0′N 73° 20′E) **13**:87
KARELIA (USSR) **12**:27
Finland **8**:98
Ural-Altaic languages **19**:475
KAREN (people) **12**:27
KAREN LANGUAGES
Sino-Tibetan languages **17**:324
Southeast Asian languages **18**:110–111
KARHULA (Finland)
map (60° 31′N 26° 57′E) **8**:95
KARIBA (Zimbabwe)
map (16° 30′S 28° 45′E) **20**:365
KARIBA, LAKE
map (17° 0′S 28° 0′E) **20**:365
KARIMATA STRAIT
map (2° 5′S 108° 40′E) **11**:147
KARIMGANJ (Bangladesh)
map (24° 52′N 92° 22′E) **3**:64
KARINSKA, BARBARA **12**:27 *bibliog.*
KARINTHY, FRIGYES
Hungarian literature **10**:306
KARISIMBI, MOUNT
map (1° 30′S 29° 27′E) **16**:378
KARL-MARX-STADT (East Germany) **12**:27
cities
Zwickau **20**:384
map (50° 50′N 12° 55′E) **9**:140
KARLFELDT, ERIK AXEL **12**:27
KARLOFF, BORIS **12**:28 *bibliog.*
KARLOVAC (Yugoslavia)
map (45° 29′N 15° 34′E) **20**:340
KARLOVY VARY (Czechoslovakia) **12**:28
Carlsbad Decrees **4**:152
map (50° 11′N 12° 52′E) **5**:413
KARLOWITZ, TREATY OF
Köprülü (family) **12**:110
Russo-Turkish Wars **16**:374
KARLSEFNI, THORFINN *see* THORFINN KARLSEFNI
KARLSKIRCHE
Fischer von Erlach, Johann Bernhard **8**:111
KARLSKOGA (Sweden)
map (59° 20′N 14° 31′E) **18**:382
KARLSKRONA (Sweden)
map (56° 10′N 15° 35′E) **18**:382
KARLSRUHE (West Germany) **12**:28
map (49° 3′N 8° 24′E) **9**:140
KARLSTAD (Minnesota)
map (48° 35′N 96° 31′W) **13**:453
KARLSTAD (Sweden)
map (59° 22′N 13° 30′E) **18**:382
KARLSTADT **12**:28 *bibliog.*
KARLUK
Turks **19**:347
KARMA **12**:28
Buddhism **3**:539
Hinduism **10**:170
sin **17**:317
transmigration of souls **19**:274
KARMAL, BABRAK **12**:28
Afghanistan **1**:135
KÁRMÁN, THEODORE VON **12**:28 *bibliog.*
Kármán vortex street **12**:28
law of turbulence **12**:28
KARMEL, MOUNT
map (32° 44′N 35° 2′E) **11**:302
KARNAK (Egypt) **12**:28 *bibliog.*
Khons, Temple of **2**:130 *illus.*; **19**:95 *illus.*
Luxor **12**:473
temple **19**:94–95
Thebes **19**:155
KARNAK (Illinois)
map (37° 18′N 88° 58′W) **11**:42
KARNAPHULI RESERVOIR
map (22° 42′N 92° 12′E) **3**:64
KARNATAKA (India) **12**:28–29
cities
Bangalore **3**:63
Mysore **13**:692
map (14° 0′N 76° 0′E) **11**:80
Tippu Sultan, Sultan of Mysore **19**:207
KARNES (county in Texas)
map (28° 52′N 97° 53′W) **19**:129
KARNES CITY (Texas)
map (28° 53′N 97° 54′W) **19**:129
KAROK (American Indians)
Yurok **20**:347
KARPATHOS (Greece)
Dodecanese **6**:212
map (35° 40′N 27° 10′E) **9**:325
KÁRPATHOS STRAIT
map (35° 50′N 27° 30′E) **9**:325
KARPOV, ANATOLY **12**:29 *bibliog.*
KARRE MOUNTAINS
map (6° 33′N 15° 40′E) **4**:251
KARRER, PAUL **12**:29
KARS (Turkey)
map (40° 36′N 43° 5′E) **19**:343
KARSAVINA, TAMARA PLATONOVNA **12**:29 *bibliog.*
Ballets Russes de Serge Diaghilev **3**:48
KARSH, YOUSEF **12**:29 *illus.*
Sir Winston Churchill **4**:426 *illus.*
KARST TOPOGRAPHY
cave **4**:222
China **4**:361 *illus.*
KARTALA MOUNTAIN
map (11° 45′S 43° 22′E) **5**:153
KARTHAUS (Pennsylvania)
map (41° 7′N 78° 7′W) **15**:147
KASAAN (Alaska)
map (55° 32′N 132° 24′W) **1**:242
KASAI RIVER
map (3° 6′S 16° 57′E) **20**:350
KASAR AL KABIR (Morocco)
map (35° 1′N 5° 54′W) **13**:585
KASAVUBU, JOSEPH **12**:29 *bibliog.*
Mobutu Sese Seko **13**:488
KÄSEBIER, GERTRUDE **12**:29 *bibliog.*
KASHAN (Iran)
map (33° 59′N 51° 29′E) **11**:250
KASHEGELOK (Alaska)
map (60° 50′N 157° 50′W) **1**:242
KASHGAR (China) **4**:364 *table*
map (39° 29′N 75° 59′E) **4**:362
KASHMIR (India) **12**:29–30 *map*
cities
Srinagar **18**:207
India-Pakistan Wars **11**:93
Indo-Iranian languages **11**:145
map (34° 0′N 76° 0′E) **11**:80
KASHUBIAN LANGUAGE
Slavic languages **17**:358
KASILOF (Alaska)
map (60° 23′N 151° 18′W) **1**:242
KASKASKIA
Illinois (American Indians) **11**:45
KASKASKIA RIVER
map (37° 59′N 89° 56′W) **11**:42
KASOS STRAIT
map (35° 30′N 26° 30′E) **9**:325
KASPROWICZ, JAN
Polish literature **15**:398
KASSALA (Sudan)
map (15° 28′N 36° 24′E) **18**:320
KASSEBAUM, NANCY LANDON **12**:184
KASSEL (West Germany) **12**:30
map (51° 19′N 9° 29′E) **9**:140
KASSEM, ABDUL KARIM
Iraq **11**:256
KASSITES **12**:30 *bibliog.*
Mesopotamia **13**:316
KASTLER, ALFRED **12**:30
KASTRIOTI, GEORGE *see* SKANDERBEG
KATA
martial arts **13**:177–178
KATABATIC WIND *see* MOUNTAIN AND VALLEY WINDS
KATAHDIN, MOUNT
map (45° 55′N 68° 55′W) **13**:70
KATANGA (Belgian Congo) *see* SHABA (Zaire)
KATANGA PLATEAU
map (10° 0′S 26° 0′W) **20**:350
KATAYEV, VALENTIN PETROVICH **12**:30
KATERINA, MOUNT
map (28° 31′N 33° 57′E) **7**:76
KATERÍNI (Greece)
map (40° 16′N 22° 30′E) **9**:325
KATIOLA (Ivory Coast)
map (8° 8′N 5° 6′W) **11**:335
KATMAI, MOUNT **12**:30
map (58° 17′N 154° 56′W) **1**:242
national parks **14**:38–39 *map*, *table*
Valley of Ten Thousand Smokes **19**:508
KATMANDU (Nepal) **12**:30–31
climate **14**:87 *table*
map (27° 43′N 85° 19′E) **14**:86
KATO KOMEI *see* KATO TAKAAKI
KATO TAKAAKI **12**:31
KATOWICE (Poland) **12**:31
map (50° 16′N 19° 0′E) **15**:388
KATRINEHOLM (Sweden)
map (59° 0′N 16° 12′E) **18**:382
KATSINA ALA RIVER
map (7° 48′N 8° 52′E) **14**:190
KATSOYANNIS, MICHAEL
insulin **11**:198
KATSUKAWA SHUNRO *see* HOKUSAI
KATSURA TARO **12**:31
KATSUSHIKA HOKUSAI *see* HOKUSAI
KATTEGAT **12**:31
map (57° 0′N 11° 0′E) **6**:109
KATTWINKEL, WILHELM
Olduvai Gorge **14**:376
KATWIJK AAN ZEE (Netherlands)
map (52° 13′N 4° 24′E) **14**:99
KATYDID **11**:192 *illus.*; **12**:31 *illus.*
grasshopper **9**:298–299
KATZ, SIR BERNARD **12**:31
KATZ, DAVID
attitude and attitude change **2**:315
KATZ v. UNITED STATES
privacy, invasion of **15**:556
wiretapping **20**:183
KATZENJAMMER KIDS, THE **5**:135 *illus.*
Dirks, Rudolph **6**:188
KAU DESERT
map (19° 21′N 155° 19′W) **10**:72
KAUAI (Hawaii)
Hawaii (state) **10**:73; **10**:75 *illus.*
map location (22° 0′N 159° 30′W) **10**:72
KAUAI CHANNEL
map (21° 45′N 158° 50′W) **10**:72
KAUFBEUREN (Germany, East and West)
map (47° 53′N 10° 37′E) **9**:140
KAUFFMANN, ANGELICA **12**:31 *bibliog.*
KAUFMAN (Texas)
map (32° 35′N 96° 19′W) **19**:129
KAUFMAN (county in Texas)
map (32° 38′N 96° 18′W) **19**:129
KAUFMAN, DENIS *see* VERTOV, DZIGA
KAUFMAN, GEORGE S. **12**:31–32 *bibliog.*, *illus.*
Connelly, Marc **5**:197
Ferber, Edna **8**:52
KAUIKEOULI *see* KAMEHAMEHA (dynasty)
KAUKAUNA (Wisconsin)
map (44° 17′N 88° 17′W) **20**:185
KAUKAUVELD (plateau)
map (20° 0′S 20° 30′E) **14**:10
KAUMAKANI (Hawaii)
map (21° 6′N 157° 2′W) **10**:72
KAUMALAPAU (Hawaii)
map (20° 47′N 156° 59′W) **10**:72
KAUNAKAKAI (Hawaii)
map (21° 6′N 157° 1′W) **10**:72
KAUNAS (USSR) **12**:32
KAUNDA, KENNETH D. **12**:32 *bibliog.*
KAURA NAMODA (Nigeria)
map (12° 35′N 6° 35′E) **14**:190
KAURI PINE **12**:32
Lacandón **12**:158
KAUTSKY, KARL JOHANN **12**:32 *bibliog.*
socialism **18**:21
KAVAD, KING OF PERSIA
Persia, ancient **15**:183
KAVAJË (Albania)
map (41° 11′N 19° 33′E) **1**:250
KAVÁLA (Greece)
map (40° 56′N 24° 25′E) **9**:325
KAVARRATI
Laccadive Islands (India) **12**:158
KAVIENG (Papua New Guinea)
map (2° 35′S 150° 50′E) **15**:72
KAVIR DESERT
map (34° 40′N 54° 30′E) **11**:250
KAVIRONDO *see* LUO
KAW (American Indians) *see* KANSA (American Indians)
KAW (French Guiana)
map (4° 29′N 52° 2′W) **8**:311
KAW (Oklahoma)
map (36° 46′N 96° 50′W) **14**:368
KAWABATA YASUNARI **12**:32 *bibliog.*
KAWAIKINI (peak)
map (22° 5′N 159° 29′W) **10**:72
KAWASAKI (Japan) **12**:32
map (35° 32′N 139° 43′E) **11**:361
KAWASAKI DISEASE **12**:32
KAWATAKE MOKUAMI
Kabuki **12**:4
KAWM UMBU (Egypt)
map (24° 28′N 32° 57′E) **7**:76
KAY (county in Oklahoma)
map (36° 50′N 97° 10′W) **14**:368
KAY, CONNIE
Modern Jazz Quartet **13**:498
KAY, JOHN **12**:32–33
flying shuttle **20**:84 *illus.*
KAY, MARSHALL
paleogeography **15**:36
KAYAK **4**:113 *illus.*
Eskimo **7**:240
KAYAKING *see* CANOEING AND KAYAKING
KAYE, DANNY **12**:33 *bibliog.*
KAYE, NORA
American Ballet Theatre **1**:337
KAYENTA (Arizona)
map (36° 42′N 110° 16′W) **2**:160
KAYES (Mali)
map (14° 27′N 11° 26′W) **13**:89
KAYSERI (Turkey)
map (38° 43′N 35° 30′E) **19**:343
KAZAKH **12**:33 *bibliog.*
KAZAKH SOVIET SOCIALIST REPUBLIC (USSR) **12**:33 *bibliog.*
cities
Alma-Ata **1**:305
Kara Kum **12**:26
people
Kazakh **12**:33
KAZAKH STEPPE
map (49° 0′N 72° 0′E) **19**:388
KAZAKHSTAN *see* KAZAKH SOVIET SOCIALIST REPUBLIC (USSR)
KAZAKHSTANIA (ancient landmass)
plate tectonics **15**:354 *map*
KAZAKOV, MATVEI
Russian art and architecture **16**:362
KAZAN (USSR) **12**:33
map (55° 49′N 49° 8′E) **19**:388
KAZAN, ELIA **12**:33–34 *bibliog.*
Actors Studio **1**:90
KAZANLUK (Bulgaria)
map (42° 37′N 25° 24′E) **3**:555
KAZANTZAKIS, NIKOS **12**:34 *bibliog.*, *illus.*
KAZBEK, MOUNT
map (42° 42′N 44° 31′E) **4**:218
KAZERUN (Iran)
map (29° 37′N 51° 38′E) **11**:250
KAZIN, ALFRED **11**:34
KDKA (broadcasting station)
radio and television broadcasting **16**:54 *illus.*
KEA **12**:34
KEAAU (Hawaii)
map (19° 37′N 155° 2′W) **10**:72
KEAHOLE POINT
map (19° 44′N 156° 3′W) **10**:72
KEAMS CANYON (Arizona)
map (35° 49′N 110° 12′W) **2**:160
KEAN (family) **12**:34–35 *bibliog.*, *illus.*
KEAN, CHARLES
Kean (family) **12**:34–35
theater, history of the **19**:149
KEAN, EDMUND
Kean (family) **12**:34 *illus.*
KEANSBURG (New Jersey)
map (40° 27′N 74° 8′W) **14**:129

KEARNEY (Missouri)
map (39° 22′N 94° 22′W) **13**:476
KEARNEY (Nebraska)
map (40° 42′N 99° 5′W) **14**:70
KEARNEY (county in Nebraska)
map (40° 30′N 98° 50′W) **14**:70
KEARNS (Utah)
map (40° 39′N 111° 59′W) **19**:492
KEARNY (Arizona)
map (33° 3′N 110° 55′W) **2**:160
KEARNY (county in Kansas)
map (38° 0′N 101° 20′W) **12**:18
KEARNY (New Jersey)
map (40° 46′N 74° 9′W) **14**:129
KEARNY, PHILIP **12**:35 *bibliog.*
KEARNY, STEPHEN WATTS **12**:35 *bibliog.*
Mexican War **13**:352 *map*; **13**:354–355
Santa Fe (New Mexico) **17**:68
KEARSARGE (ship) **5**:32 *illus.*
Winslow, John Ancrum **20**:180
KEATING, GEOFFREY
Irish literature **11**:268
KEATON, BUSTER **12**:35 *bibliog., illus.*
film, history of **8**:82–83
KEATON, DIANE **12**:35
KEATS, JOHN **7**:198 *illus.*; **12**:35–36 *bibliog., illus.*
Adonais **1**:107
Endymion **7**:171
Hunt, Holman **10**:311
KEBAN, LAKE
map (38° 50′N 39° 15′E) **19**:343
KEBLE, JOHN **12**:36 *bibliog.*
Oxford movement **14**:475
KEBLE COLLEGE (Oxford University) **14**:474
Butterfield, William **3**:593
KEBNE, MOUNT
map (67° 53′N 18° 33′E) **18**:382
KECHI (Kansas)
map (37° 48′N 97° 17′W) **12**:18
KECSKEMÉT (Hungary)
map (46° 54′N 19° 42′E) **10**:307
KEDAH, TELL EL- *see* HAZOR (Israel)
KEDGWICK (New Brunswick)
map (47° 39′N 67° 21′W) **14**:117
KEDIRI (Indonesia)
map (7° 49′S 112° 1′E) **11**:147
KEELE PEAK
map (63° 26′N 130° 19′W) **20**:345
KEELER, CHRISTINE
Profumo scandal **15**:562
KEELER, LEONARDE
lie detector **12**:323
KEELER, RUBY
Berkeley, Busby **3**:213
KEELING, WILLIAM
Cocos Islands **5**:89
KEELING ISLANDS *see* COCOS ISLANDS (Australia)
KEELS (Newfoundland)
map (48° 36′N 53° 24′W) **14**:166
KEENE (New Hampshire)
map (42° 56′N 72° 17′W) **14**:123
KEENE, CAROLYN
Drew, Nancy **6**:271
KEESEVILLE (New York)
map (44° 30′N 73° 29′W) **14**:149
KEESHOND **6**:219 *illus.*; **12**:36 *bibliog., illus.*
KEETMANSHOOP (Namibia)
climate **14**:11 *table*
map (26° 36′S 18° 8′E) **14**:10
KEFALLINÍA ISLAND
map (38° 15′N 20° 35′E) **9**:325
KEFAR NAHUM (Israel) *see* CAPERNAUM
KEFAR SAVA (Israel)
map (32° 10′N 34° 54′E) **11**:302
KEFAUVER, ESTES **12**:36 *bibliog.*
KEFFI (Nigeria)
map (8° 51′N 7° 52′E) **14**:190
KEFLAVÍK (Iceland)
map (64° 2′N 22° 36′W) **11**:17
KEGALLA (Sri Lanka)
map (7° 15′N 80° 21′E) **18**:206
KEI *see* UNKEI
KEIKI, SHOGUN OF JAPAN *see* YOSHINOBU, SHOGUN OF JAPAN
KEINO, KIPCHOGE **12**:37
KEIR, JAMES **12**:37
KEITA, MODIBO
Mali **13**:91
KEITEL, WILHELM **12**:37
Nuremberg Trials **14**:297 *illus.*
KEITH (county in Nebraska)
map (41° 15′N 101° 40′W) **14**:70
KEITH, BENJAMIN FRANKLIN
music hall, vaudeville, and burlesque **13**:672
KEIYASI (Fiji)
map (17° 54′S 177° 45′E) **8**:77
KEJIA LANGUAGE
Sino-Tibetan languages **17**:324
KEKAHA (Hawaii)
map (21° 58′N 159° 43′W) **10**:72
KÉKES MOUNTAIN
map (47° 55′N 20° 2′E) **10**:307
KEKKONEN, URHO K. **12**:37 *illus.*
KEKULÉ VON STRADONITZ, FRIEDRICH AUGUST **12**:37 *bibliog., illus.*
organic chemistry **14**:435
KELANG (Malaysia)
map (3° 2′N 101° 27′E) **13**:84
KELANI RIVER
map (6° 58′N 79° 52′E) **18**:206
KELKIT RIVER
map (40° 46′N 36° 32′E) **19**:343
KELL, JOSEPH *see* BURGESS, ANTHONY
KELLER, GOTTFRIED **12**:37 *bibliog.*
KELLER, HELEN **12**:37–38 *bibliog., illus.*
KELLEY, EDGAR STILLMAN **12**:38
KELLEY, FLORENCE **12**:38 *bibliog.*
KELLEY, OLIVER HUDSON
Grange, National **9**:286
KELLEY, WILLIAM MELVIN **11**:38
KELLEYS ISLAND
map (41° 36′N 82° 42′W) **14**:357
KELLIHER (Saskatchewan)
map (51° 15′N 103° 44′W) **17**:81
KELLNER, SÁNDOR *see* KORDA, SIR ALEXANDER
KELLOGG (Idaho)
map (47° 32′N 116° 7′W) **11**:26
KELLOGG (Iowa)
map (41° 43′N 92° 54′W) **11**:244
KELLOGG (Minnesota)
map (44° 18′N 91° 59′W) **13**:453
KELLOGG, FRANK B. **12**:38 *bibliog.*
Kellogg-Briand Pact **12**:38
Tacna-Arica Dispute **19**:6
KELLOGG, JOHN HARVEY
meat imitations **13**:257
KELLOGG, W. K. **12**:38 *bibliog.*
KELLOGG-BRIAND PACT **12**:38 *bibliog.*
Kellogg, Frank B. **12**:38
KELLY, ELLSWORTH **12**:38–39 *bibliog., illus.*
Yellow-Blue **12**:39 *illus.*
KELLY, EMMETT **12**:39
KELLY, GENE **12**:39 *bibliog., illus.*
KELLY, GEORGE
personality **15**:190
KELLY, GRACE **12**:39 *bibliog.*
Rainier III, Prince of Monaco **16**:78
KELLY, NED **12**:39 *bibliog.*
Nolan, Sidney **14**:213
KELLY, RICHARD
ABSCAM **1**:62
KELLY, WALT
comic strip **5**:136
KELLY, WILLIAM **12**:39 *bibliog.*
iron and steel industry **11**:275
KELLYVILLE (Oklahoma)
map (35° 57′N 96° 13′W) **14**:368
KELMSCOTT PRESS **12**:39–40 *bibliog.*
book **3**:385
calligraphy **4**:43
Kelmscott Chaucer **13**:589 *illus.*
Morris, William **13**:589
KELOWNA (British Columbia)
map (49° 53′N 119° 29′W) **3**:491
KELP **1**:282 *illus.*; **12**:40 *bibliog.*
bromine **3**:502
commercial uses **12**:40
food **12**:40
intertidal life **11**:230
iodine **11**:239
Laminaria **11**:229 *illus.*
seaweed **17**:177
KELPIE (dog) **12**:40 *bibliog., illus.*
KELPIE (Scottish folklore)
Loch Ness monster **12**:386
KELSEN, HANS
law **12**:242
KELSEY, HENRY **12**:40
Saskatchewan River **17**:83
KELSEY BAY (British Columbia)
map (50° 24′N 125° 57′W) **3**:491
KELSEYVILLE (California)
map (38° 59′N 122° 50′W) **4**:31
KELSO (Washington)
map (46° 9′N 122° 54′W) **20**:35
KELUANG (Malaysia)
map (2° 2′N 103° 19′E) **13**:84
KELVIN, WILLIAM THOMSON, 1ST BARON **12**:40 *bibliog., illus.*
geologic time **9**:104
Kelvin scale **12**:40
KELVIN SCALE **12**:40 *bibliog.*
absolute zero **1**:63
Celsius scale **4**:238
gas laws **9**:53
Kelvin, William Thomson, 1st Baron **12**:40
temperature **19**:93
units, physical **19**:466–467 *table*
KEMAL, YAŞHAR *see* YAŞAR KEMAL
KEMANO (British Columbia)
map (53° 34′N 127° 56′W) **3**:491
KEMBLE (family) **12**:41 *bibliog.*
KEMBLE, FANNY
Kemble (family) **12**:41
KEMENY, JOHN
nuclear energy **14**:283
KEMEROVO (USSR)
map (55° 20′N 86° 5′E) **19**:388
KEMI (Finland)
map (65° 49′N 24° 32′E) **8**:95
KEMI RIVER
map (65° 47′N 24° 30′E) **8**:95
KEMIJÄRVI (Finland)
map (66° 40′N 27° 25′E) **8**:95
KEMIJÄRVI LAKE
map (66° 36′N 27° 24′E) **8**:95
KEMMERER (Wyoming)
map (41° 48′N 110° 32′W) **20**:301
KEMP, JACK **12**:41
KEMP, WILL
acting **1**:87
KEMPER (county in Mississippi)
map (32° 45′N 88° 40′W) **13**:469
KEMPIS, THOMAS À *see* THOMAS À KEMPIS
KEMPS BAY (Bahama Islands)
map (24° 2′N 77° 33′W) **3**:23
KEMPTEN (Germany, East and West)
map (47° 43′N 10° 19′E) **9**:140
KENAI (Alaska)
map (60° 33′N 151° 15′W) **1**:242
KENAI MOUNTAINS
map (60° 0′N 150° 0′W) **1**:242
KENAI PENINSULA
map (60° 10′N 150° 0′W) **1**:242
KENANSVILLE (Florida)
map (27° 53′N 80° 59′W) **8**:172
KENANSVILLE (North Carolina)
map (34° 58′N 77° 58′W) **14**:242
KENDAL (Saskatchewan)
map (50° 15′N 103° 37′W) **17**:81
KENDALL (Florida)
map (25° 41′N 80° 19′W) **8**:172
KENDALL (county in Illinois)
map (41° 38′N 88° 27′W) **11**:42
KENDALL (county in Texas)
map (29° 55′N 98° 40′W) **19**:129
KENDALL, AMOS **12**:41 *bibliog.*
KENDALL, EDWARD **12**:41
Hench, Philip Showalter **10**:121
KENDALL, GEORGE WILKINS **12**:41
KENDALL PARK (New Jersey)
map (40° 25′N 74° 34′W) **14**:129
KENDALLVILLE (Indiana)
map (41° 27′N 85° 16′W) **11**:111
KENDO
martial arts **13**:178
KENDREW, JOHN COWDERY **12**:41
KENEALLY, THOMAS
Australian literature **2**:344
KENEDY (Texas)
map (28° 49′N 97° 51′W) **19**:129
KENEDY (county in Texas)
map (26° 52′N 97° 45′W) **19**:129
KENEMA (Sierra Leone)
map (7° 52′N 11° 12′W) **17**:296
KENESAW (Nebraska)
map (40° 37′N 98° 39′W) **14**:70
KENILOREA, PETER
Solomon Islands **18**:57
KENILWORTH (Utah)
map (39° 42′N 110° 47′W) **19**:492
KENITRA (Morocco)
map (34° 16′N 6° 40′W) **13**:585
KENLY (North Carolina)
map (35° 36′N 78° 7′W) **14**:242
KENMARE (North Dakota)
map (48° 40′N 102° 5′W) **14**:248
KENNAN, GEORGE F. **12**:41 *bibliog.*
cold war **5**:98
KENNARD (Nebraska)
map (41° 28′N 96° 12′W) **14**:70
KENNEBEC (county in Maine)
map (44° 25′N 69° 45′W) **13**:70
KENNEBEC (South Dakota)
map (43° 54′N 99° 52′W) **18**:103
KENNEBEC RIVER
map (44° 0′N 69° 50′W) **13**:70
KENNEBUNK (Maine)
map (43° 23′N 70° 33′W) **13**:70
KENNEDY (Alabama)
map (33° 35′N 87° 59′W) **1**:234
KENNEDY (family) **12**:41–42 *bibliog., illus.*
Hyannis (Massachusetts) **10**:327
Kennedy, Edward M. **12**:42
Kennedy, John F. **12**:42
Kennedy, Robert F. **12**:44
Shriver, Sargent **17**:287
KENNEDY, ARTHUR
Death of a Salesman **19**:150 *illus.*
KENNEDY, CAPE *see* CAPE CANAVERAL (Florida)
KENNEDY, EDWARD M. **12**:42 *illus.*
Kennedy (family) **12**:41–42
KENNEDY, JACQUELINE *see* ONASSIS, JACQUELINE BOUVIER KENNEDY
KENNEDY, JOHN F. **12**:42–44 *bibliog., illus.*
cabinet **15**:526 *illus.*
Cuban Missile Crisis **5**:380; **15**:525 *illus.*
Democratic party **6**:102 *illus.*
John F. Kennedy Library **12**:317 *illus.*
Kennedy (family) **12**:41–42
Kennedy Center for the Performing Arts **12**:44
Onassis, Jacqueline Bouvier Kennedy **14**:388–389
Oswald, Lee Harvey **14**:459
presidential debate **15**:531 *illus.*
radio and television broadcasting **16**:59 *illus.*
United States, history of the **19**:457–460 *illus.*
vocational education **19**:625
Warren Commission **20**:31–32
KENNEDY, JOSEPH PATRICK
Kennedy (family) **12**:41–42
Kennedy, John F. **12**:42
KENNEDY, ROBERT F. **12**:44 *bibliog., illus.*; **15**:526 *illus.*
Kennedy (family) **12**:41–42
Luthuli, Albert John **12**:470 *illus.*
Vietnam War **19**:587
KENNEDY, WILLIAM **12**:44
KENNEDY CENTER FOR THE PERFORMING ARTS **12**:44 *bibliog.*
Bernstein, Leonard **3**:224
Washington, D.C. **20**:41 *map*
KENNEDY CHANNEL
map (81° 0′N 65° 0′W) **4**:70
KENNEDY INTERNATIONAL AIRPORT
Trans World Airlines terminal **17**:4 *illus.*
KENNEDY SPACE CENTER **12**:44–45
astronautics **2**:275
National Aeronautics and Space Administration **14**:28 *illus.*
KENNELLY, ARTHUR EDWIN
ionosphere **11**:241
KENNELLY-HEAVISIDE LAYER
ionosphere **11**:242
KENNER (Louisiana)
map (29° 59′N 90° 15′W) **12**:430
KENNESAW MOUNTAIN
map (33° 58′N 84° 34′W) **9**:114
KENNETH I, KING OF SCOTLAND
Clackmannan **5**:35
Picts **15**:294
Scotland **17**:151
KENNETT (Missouri)
map (36° 14′N 90° 3′W) **13**:476
KENNETT SQUARE (Pennsylvania)
map (39° 51′N 75° 43′W) **15**:147
KENNEWICK (Washington)
map (46° 12′N 119° 7′W) **20**:35
KENO HILL (Yukon Territory)
map (63° 55′N 135° 18′W) **20**:345
KENORA (Ontario)
map (49° 47′N 94° 29′W) **14**:393
KENOSHA (Wisconsin) **12**:45
map (42° 35′N 87° 49′W) **20**:185
KENOSHA (county in Wisconsin)
map (42° 6′N 88° 4′W) **20**:185
KENSAL (North Dakota)
map (47° 18′N 98° 44′W) **14**:248
KENSETT, JOHN FREDERICK **12**:45 *bibliog.*
KENSICO RESERVOIR
map (41° 5′N 73° 46′W) **5**:193
KENSINGTON (Connecticut)
map (41° 38′N 72° 46′W) **5**:193
KENSINGTON (Kansas)
map (39° 46′N 99° 2′W) **12**:18
KENSINGTON (Maryland)
map (39° 2′N 77° 3′W) **13**:188
KENSINGTON (Prince Edward Island)
map (46° 26′N 63° 38′W) **15**:548
KENSINGTON PALACE
sunken gardens of **12**:187 *illus.*
KENSINGTON RUNE STONE **12**:45 *bibliog.*
KENT (county in Delaware)
map (39° 10′N 75° 32′W) **6**:88
KENT (England) **2**:3 *map*; **12**:45
cities
Canterbury **4**:116
Dover **6**:250
Maidstone **13**:66–67

KENT (county in Maryland)
map (39° 13′N 76° 4′W) **13**:188
KENT (county in Michigan)
map (43° 5′N 85° 35′W) **13**:377
KENT (Ohio)
map (41° 9′N 81° 22′W) **14**:357
KENT (county in Rhode Island)
map (41° 40′N 71° 38′W) **16**:198
KENT (county in Texas)
map (33° 8′N 100° 47′W) **19**:129
KENT (Washington)
map (47° 23′N 122° 14′W) **20**:35
KENT, JAMES 12:45
common law **5**:140
English music **7**:203
KENT, ROCKWELL 12:45 *bibliog.*
KENT, WILLIAM 12:45 *bibliog.*
Burlington, Richard Boyle, 3d Earl of **3**:572
KENT ISLAND
map (38° 55′N 76° 20′W) **13**:188
KENT STATE UNIVERSITY
Vietnam War **19**:588
KENTIGERN, SAINT
Glasgow (Scotland) **9**:197
KENTLAND (Indiana)
map (40° 46′N 87° 27′W) **11**:111
KENTON (county in Kentucky)
map (38° 56′N 84° 33′W) **12**:47
KENTON (Michigan)
map (46° 28′N 88° 54′W) **13**:377
KENTON (Ohio)
map (40° 39′N 83° 36′W) **14**:357
KENTON (Tennessee)
map (36° 12′N 89° 1′W) **19**:104
KENTUCKY 12:45–51 *bibliog., illus., map*
cities
Frankfort **8**:280
Lexington **12**:309
Louisville **12**:436
Owensboro **14**:472
Paducah **15**:13
climate **12**:46
culture **12**:48
economy **12**:48–51 *illus.*
education **12**:48
Berea College **3**:208
Kentucky, state universities of **12**:51
flag **12**:46 *illus.*
Fort Knox **8**:237
government and politics **12**:50
history **12**:50–51
Boone, Daniel **3**:393–394
historical sites **12**:48
Shelby, Isaac **17**:250
land **12**:46–48 *map*
map (37° 30′N 85° 15′W) **19**:419
mining **12**:48–49 *illus.*
people **12**:48
physical features
Mammoth Cave **13**:107
rivers, lakes, and waterways **12**:46–48
Cumberland River **5**:387
seal, state **12**:46 *illus.*
tourism **12**:49–50 *illus.*
vegetation and wildlife **12**:48
yodel **20**:328
KENTUCKY, STATE UNIVERSITIES OF 12:51
KENTUCKY COFFEE TREE 12:52 *illus.*
KENTUCKY DERBY 10:246 *illus.*; **12**:50 *illus.*; **12**:52 *bibliog.*
winners **10**:249 *table*
KENTUCKY LAKE
map (36° 25′N 88° 5′W) **12**:47
KENTUCKY RIVER
map (38° 41′N 85° 11′W) **12**:47
KENTUCKY SADDLE HORSE *see* AMERICAN SADDLE HORSE
KENTUCKY AND VIRGINIA RESOLUTIONS 12:51–52 *bibliog.*
Civil War, U.S. **5**:15
Madison, James **13**:42; **13**:43
KENTVILLE (Nova Scotia)
map (45° 5′N 64° 30′W) **14**:269
KENTWOOD (Louisiana)
map (30° 56′N 90° 31′W) **12**:430
KENYA 12:52–56 *bibliog., illus., map, table*
agriculture **12**:55 *illus.*
animal life **12**:54 *illus.*
archaeology
Leakey (family) **12**:258–259
Olorgesailie **14**:381
arts **12**:54
African art **1**:160–164
cities
Mombasa **13**:514–515
Nairobi **14**:8
Wajir **12**:53 *table*
climate **12**:53 *table*
economy **12**:55–56 *illus.*
education **12**:54
African universities **1**:176 *table*
flag **12**:52 *illus.*
foreign trade **12**:55–56
government **12**:56
history **12**:56
Kenyatta, Jomo **12**:56–57
Mau Mau **13**:232
Mboya, Tom **13**:251
Moi, Daniel arap **13**:504
land and resources **12**:52–54 *map, table*
language **12**:54
literature
African literature **1**:167–168
Ngugi wa Thiong'o **14**:176
manufacturing and energy **12**:55
map (1° 0′N 38° 0′E) **1**:136
people **12**:54
Galla **9**:16
Kamba **12**:9
Kikuyu **12**:76
Luo **12**:465
Masai **13**:194–195
Turkana **19**:342
physical features
Kenya, Mount **12**:56
Kilimanjaro **1**:138 *illus.*
religion **12**:54
rivers, lakes, and waterways **12**:53
Rudolf, Lake **16**:338
sports
Keino, Kipchoge **12**:37
tourism **12**:55
vegetation **12**:53–54
KENYA, MOUNT 12:56
map (0° 10′S 37° 20′E) **12**:53
KENYA AFRICAN NATIONAL UNION (KANU)
Mboya, Tom **13**:251
KENYATTA, JOMO 12:56–57 *bibliog., illus.*
Kenya **12**:56
KENYON (Minnesota)
map (44° 16′N 92° 59′W) **13**:453
KENYON, DAME KATHLEEN 12:57
KENYON REVIEW (periodical)
Ramsom, John Crowe **16**:88
KENZAN 12:57 *bibliog.*
plate **11**:377 *illus.*
KEOGH PLAN
pension **15**:154
KEOKEA (Hawaii)
map (20° 24′N 156° 21′W) **10**:72
KEOKUK (Iowa)
map (40° 24′N 91° 24′W) **11**:244
KEOKUK (county in Iowa)
map (41° 17′N 92° 10′W) **11**:244
KEOSAUQUA (Iowa)
map (40° 44′N 91° 58′W) **11**:244
KEOTA (Iowa)
map (41° 21′N 91° 57′W) **11**:244
KEOWEE, LAKE
map (34° 45′N 82° 55′W) **18**:98
KEPES, GYORGY 12:57 *bibliog.*
KEPLER, JOHANNES 2:278 *illus.*; **12**:57–58 *bibliog., illus.*
astronautics **2**:274
astronomy, history of **2**:278
Kepler's laws **12**:58
solar system **18**:44–45
KEPLERIAN MOTION
perturbation **15**:191
KEPLER'S LAWS 12:58 *bibliog., illus.*
Kepler, Johannes **12**:57–58
law, physical **12**:248
law of areas **12**:58
orbital elements **14**:417
physics, history of **15**:283
solar system **18**:45
KEPONE
pollutants, chemical **15**:410
KEPPEL, FRANCIS 12:58
KEPPLER, JOSEPH
The Bosses of the Senate **19**:451 *illus.*
The Pygmies Attack **16**:174 *illus.*
KERALA (India) **12**:58
cities
Cochin **5**:85
map (10° 0′N 76° 30′E) **11**:80
KERATIN 12:58
feather **8**:39
hair **10**:14
hoof, nail, and claw **10**:225
horn (biology) **10**:238
skin **17**:341 *illus.*
wool **20**:214
KERATITIS
eye diseases **7**:351
KERBALA (Iraq)
Islam **11**:293 *map*
KERBY (Oregon)
map (42° 12′N 123° 39′W) **14**:427
KERCH (USSR)
map (45° 22′N 36° 27′E) **19**:388
KEREKOU, MATHIEU
Benin **3**:200–201
KEREMA (Papua New Guinea)
map (8° 0′S 145° 45′E) **15**:72
KERENSKY, ALEKSANDR FYODOROVICH 12:58–59 *bibliog.*
World War I **20**:238
KERENSKY, ALEXSANDR FYODOROVICH
Russian Revolutions of 1917 **16**:371 *illus.*
KERGUELEN CABBAGE 12:59
KERGUELEN ISLANDS
French Southern and Antarctic Territories **8**:326
Indian Ocean bottoms **11**:105 *map*
KERINCI, MOUNT
map (1° 42′S 101° 16′E) **11**:147
KÉRKIRA (Greece)
map (39° 36′N 19° 56′E) **9**:325
KERKRADE (Netherlands)
map (50° 52′N 6° 4′E) **14**:99
KERKYRA *see* CORFU (Greece)
KERLE, JACOBUS DE
Renaissance music **16**:156
KERLL, JOHANN KASPAR
music, history of Western **13**:666
KERMADEC ISLANDS
map (29° 16′S 177° 55′W) **14**:334
New Zealand **14**:159
KERMADEC-TONGA TRENCH
plate tectonics **15**:351 *map*
KERMADEC TRENCH
Pacific Ocean bottom **15**:6–7 *map*
KERMAN (Iran)
map (30° 17′N 57° 5′E) **11**:250
KERMANSHAH (Iran)
map (34° 19′N 47° 4′E) **11**:250
***KERMES* 12**:59
KERMIT (Texas)
map (31° 51′N 103° 6′W) **19**:129
KERMIT THE FROG *see* MUPPETS
KERN (county in California)
map (35° 20′N 119° 55′W) **4**:31
KERN, JEROME 12:59 *bibliog.*
Fields, Dorothy **8**:73
KERN RIVER
map (35° 13′N 119° 17′W) **4**:31
KERNER COMMISSION
race riots **16**:35
KERNERSVILLE (North Carolina)
map (36° 7′N 80° 4′W) **14**:242
KERNITE
borate minerals **3**:396
KERO **11**:72 *illus.*
KEROSENE 12:59
heat content **8**:353 *table*
lamp **12**:175–176 *illus.*
original and current uses **12**:59
petroleum **15**:207
KEROUAC, JACK 12:59 *bibliog., illus.*
Frank, Robert **8**:280
On the Road **14**:388
KERR (county in Texas)
map (30° 0′N 99° 18′W) **19**:129
KERR, CLARK 12:59–60 *illus.*
KERR, SIR JOHN ROBERT 12:60
KERR, R.
relativity **16**:136
KERROBERT (Saskatchewan)
map (51° 55′N 109° 8′W) **17**:81
KERRVILLE (Texas)
map (30° 3′N 99° 8′W) **19**:129
KERRY (Ireland) **12**:60
cities
Killarney **12**:77
KERRY BLUE TERRIER 6:220 *illus.*; **12**:60 *bibliog., illus.*
KERSHAW (South Carolina)
map (34° 33′N 80° 35′W) **18**:98
KERSHAW (county in South Carolina)
map (34° 20′N 80° 40′W) **18**:98
KERTÉSZ, ANDRÉ 12:60 *bibliog., illus.*
Broken Bench **12**:60 *illus.*
photography, history and art of **15**:271
KERWIN, JOSEPH 12:60
KERWIN, PATRICK 12:60–61
KESEY, KEN 12:61 *illus.*
One Flew Over the Cuckoo's Nest **14**:389
KESHENA (Wisconsin)
map (44° 52′N 88° 38′W) **20**:185
KESSELRING, ALBERT 12:61 *bibliog.*
World War II **20**:271
KESTELMAN, SARA **19**:151 *illus.*
KESTREL *see* FALCON
KETCHIKAN (Alaska)
map (55° 21′N 131° 35′W) **1**:242
KETCHUM (Idaho)
map (43° 41′N 114° 22′W) **11**:26
KETO-ACIDOSIS
diabetes **6**:148
KETOACIDOSIS (ketosis)
metabolism **13**:327
KETONE 12:61 *bibliog.*
acetone **1**:80
carbonyl group **4**:139
Claisen, Ludwig **5**:35
diabetes **6**:148
lactone **12**:161–162
metabolism **13**:327
nutrition, human **14**:306 *illus.*
quinone **16**:27
KETOSIS
dieting **6**:165
ketone **12**:61
KETOU (Benin)
map (7° 22′N 2° 36′E) **3**:200
KETTERING (England)
map (52° 24′N 0° 44′W) **19**:403
KETTERING (Ohio)
map (39° 41′N 84° 10′W) **14**:357
KETTERING, CHARLES FRANKLIN 12:61 *bibliog.*
Midgley, Thomas, Jr. **13**:413
KETTLE (geology)
glaciers and glaciation **9**:194
lake, glacial **12**:170
KETTLE, TILLIE
Warren Hastings **10**:67 *illus.*
KETTLE FALLS (Washington)
map (48° 36′N 118° 3′W) **20**:35
KETTLE RIVER
map (45° 52′N 92° 45′W) **13**:453
KETTLEDRUM 12:61–62 *bibliog., illus.*; **13**:675 *illus.*
percussion instruments **15**:162 *illus.*
KETT'S REBELLION
Somerset, Edward Seymour, 1st Duke of **18**:61
KEUKA LAKE
Finger Lakes **8**:93
map (42° 27′N 77° 10′W) **14**:149
KEVIN (Montana)
map (48° 45′N 111° 58′W) **13**:547
KEW GARDENS (England) **3**:412 *illus.*; **12**:62
Hooker (family) **10**:227
KEWANEE (Illinois)
map (41° 14′N 89° 56′W) **11**:42
KEWANNA (Indiana)
map (41° 1′N 86° 25′W) **11**:111
KEWAUNEE (Wisconsin)
map (44° 27′N 87° 30′W) **20**:185
KEWAUNEE (county in Wisconsin)
map (44° 30′N 87° 38′W) **20**:185
KEWEENAW (county in Michigan)
map (46° 5′N 88° 5′W) **13**:377
KEWEENAW BAY
map (46° 56′N 88° 23′W) **13**:377
KEWEENAW POINT
map (47° 30′N 87° 50′W) **13**:377
KEY *see* LOCK AND KEY
KEY (music) **12**:62
tonality **19**:232–233
KEY, FRANCIS SCOTT 12:62 *illus.*
flag **8**:134
Frederick (Maryland) **8**:289
"Star-Spangled Banner, The" **18**:226
KEY BISCAYNE
map (25° 42′N 80° 10′W) **8**:172
KEY DEER
deer **6**:79
KEY LARGO (Florida)
map (25° 4′N 80° 28′W) **8**:172
KEY LARGO ISLAND
map (25° 16′N 80° 19′W) **8**:172
KEY WEST (Florida) **12**:62
map (24° 33′N 81° 48′W) **8**:172
KEYA PAHA (county in Nebraska)
map (42° 50′N 99° 45′W) **14**:70
KEYBOARD, COMPUTER 12:62
computer **5**:160e; **5**:160h
KEYBOARD INSTRUMENTS 12:62–63 *bibliog., illus.*; **13**:678 *illus.*
celesta **4**:229–230 *illus.*
clavichord **5**:45
figured bass **8**:75
harpsichord **10**:55–56 *illus.*
key **12**:62
organ (musical instrument) **14**:432–434
piano **15**:288–289
player piano **15**:363
portative organ **15**:443–444
spinet **18**:185
tablature **19**:4
toccata **19**:220
virginal **19**:606 *illus.*
KEYES (Oklahoma)
map (36° 49′N 102° 15′W) **14**:368

KEYHOLE RESERVOIR
map (44° 21'N 104° 51'W) **20**:301
KEYNES, JOHN MAYNARD **12**:63–64 *bibliog., illus.*
capitalism **4**:125
economics **7**:49
economy, national **7**:50–51
inflation **11**:170
monetary theory **13**:525
KEYS, FLORIDA *see* FLORIDA KEYS (islands); KEY WEST (Florida)
KEYSER (West Virginia)
map (39° 26'N 78° 59'W) **20**:111
KEYSER, HENDRIK DE **12**:64
cathedrals and churches **4**:208
KEYSTONE (Iowa)
map (42° 0'N 92° 12'W) **11**:244
KEYSTONE (South Dakota)
map (43° 54'N 103° 25'W) **18**:103
KEYSTONE KOPS **12**:64 *bibliog.*
KEYSTONE LAKE
map (36° 15'N 96° 25'W) **14**:368
KEYSVILLE (Virginia)
map (37° 4'N 78° 29'W) **19**:607
KEYTESVILLE (Missouri)
map (39° 26'N 92° 56'W) **13**:476
KEYWORD IN CONTEXT (KWIC) INDEXING
information science **11**:172
KGB **12**:64 *bibliog.*
intelligence gathering **11**:205
police **15**:396
police state **15**:397
KHABAROVSK (USSR)
map (48° 27'N 135° 6'E) **19**:388
KHADAFY, MUAMMAR AL- *see* QADDAFI, MUAMMAR AL-
KHAFRE, KING OF EGYPT **2**:192 *illus.*; **12**:64
pyramid of **2**:130 *illus.*
KHAIRPUR
map (27° 32'N 68° 46'E) **15**:27
KHAJURAHO (India) **12**:65 *bibliog.*
Indian art and architecture **11**:97
KHAKI **12**:65
KHALDUN, IBN *see* IBN KHALDUN
KHALID, KING OF SAUDI ARABIA **12**:65
Saudi Arabia **17**:96
KHALIL, EL *see* HEBRON (Jordan)
KHALKHAS **12**:65 *bibliog.*
Ural-Altaic languages **19**:476
KHALKIS (Greece)
map (38° 28'N 23° 36'E) **9**:325
KHAM, FAZLAR
skyscraper **17**:350
KHAMA, SIR SERETSE
Botswana **3**:417
KHAMBHAT, GULF OF
map (21° 0'N 72° 30'E) **11**:80
KHAMEMEI, HOJATOLISLAM ALI
Iran **11**:253
KHAMSEH **12**:65 *bibliog.*; **15**:186 *illus.*
KHAN *see* the first element of the name for names ending with the title khan
KHAN YUNIS (Palestine)
map (31° 21'N 34° 19'E) **11**:302
KHANABAD (Afghanistan)
map (36° 41'N 69° 7'E) **1**:133
KHANDALLAH (New Zealand)
map (41° 15'S 174° 47'E) **14**:158
KHANEWAL
map (30° 18'N 71° 56'E) **15**:27
KHANIÁ (Greece)
map (35° 31'N 24° 2'E) **9**:325
KHANKA, LAKE
map (45° 0'N 132° 24'E) **4**:362
KHANTS **12**:65 *bibliog.*
Ostyak language
Ural-Altaic languages **19**:475
KHARIJISM (religion)
Berbers **3**:207
KHARIJITES (dissident group)
Ali **1**:292
Middle East, history of the **13**:402
KHARKOV (USSR) **12**:65–66
map (50° 0'N 36° 15'E) **19**:388
KHARTOUM (Sudan) **12**:66; **18**:321 *illus.*
climate **18**:320 *table*
fall of **1**:156 *illus.*
Mahdi Seige (1884–85)
Gordon, Charles George **9**:249
map (15° 36'N 32° 32'E) **18**:320
KHASA *see* PAHARI
KHASI **12**:66 *bibliog.*
KHASKOVO (Bulgaria)
map (41° 56'N 25° 33'E) **3**:555
KHATCHATURIAN, ARAM **12**:66 *bibliog.*
KHAYYAM, OMAR *see* OMAR KHAYYAM
KHAZARS **12**:66 *bibliog.*
Asia, history of **2**:254 *map*
KHETH (letter) *see* HETH (letter)
KHIEU SAMPHAN **12**:66
KHIVA (USSR)
Uzbek Soviet Socialist Republic **19**:499
KHLYNOV (USSR) *see* KIROV (USSR)
KHMELNYTSKY, BOHDAN *see* CHMIELNICKI, BOHDAN
KHMER **12**:66–67 *bibliog.*
Asia, history of **2**:253
Khmer Empire **12**:67
KHMER EMPIRE **12**:67 *bibliog.*
Angkor **1**:414–415
Asia, history of **2**:255 *map*
Kampuchea (Cambodia) **12**:12
Lopburi **12**:412
Southeast Asian art and architecture **18**:108–109
KHMER LANGUAGE *see* MON-KHMER LANGUAGES
KHMER ROUGE **12**:67
Kampuchea (Cambodia) **12**:12–13
Khieu Samphan **12**:66
Pol Pot **15**:387
religious repression **12**:12 *illus.*
KHNOPFF, FERNAND
The Sphinx **18**:403 *illus.*
KHOIKHOI **12**:67 *bibliog.*; **16**:34 *illus.*
steatopygia **18**:242
KHOISAN LANGUAGES **12**:355 *map*
African languages **1**:167
KHOLM (Afghanistan)
map (36° 42'N 67° 41'E) **1**:133
KHOMEINI, AYATOLLAH RUHOLLAH **12**:67–68 *illus.*; **13**:408 *illus.*
Iran **11**:253
Iranian hostage crisis **11**:253–254
Kurds **12**:139
Muhammad Reza Shah Pahlavi **13**:634
Qum (Iran) **16**:28
Tabriz (Iran) **19**:5
KHON KAEN (Thailand)
map (16° 26'N 102° 50'E) **19**:139
KHOND **12**:68 *bibliog.*
KHONS, TEMPLE OF **2**:130 *illus.*; **19**:95 *illus.*
KHORANA, HAR GOBIND **12**:68
genetics **9**:88
Nirenberg, M. W. **14**:201
KHORMAKSAR (Yemen) (Aden)
climate **20**:324 *table*
KHORRAMABAD (Iran)
map (33° 30'N 48° 20'E) **11**:250
KHORRAMSHAHR (Iran)
map (30° 25'N 48° 11'E) **11**:250
KHORSABAD (Iraq) **12**:68 *bibliog.*
Botta, Paul Emile **3**:417
Mesopotamian art and architecture **13**:321
Nimrud **14**:199
KHOSRU I, KING OF PERSIA **12**:68 *bibliog.*
Ctesiphon **5**:377
KHOSRU II, KING OF PERSIA
Persia, ancient **15**:183
KHOURIBGA (Morocco)
map (32° 54'N 6° 57'W) **13**:585
KHOWST (Afghanistan)
map (33° 22'N 69° 57'E) **1**:133
KHRUNOV, YEVGENY **12**:68
KHRUSHCHEV, NIKITA SERGEYEVICH **5**:98 *illus.*; **12**:68–69 *bibliog., illus.*
communism **5**:147–149 *illus.*
Cuban Missile Crisis **5**:380
Eisenhower, Dwight D. **7**:96
Kennedy, John F. **12**:43
Russia/Union of Soviet Socialist Republics, history of **16**:360
KHRYSOKHOU BAY
map (35° 6'N 32° 25'E) **5**:409
KHUFU, KING OF EGYPT **12**:69
funeral ship **17**:263
Great Pyramid (Cheops) **7**:85 *illus.*; **15**:635 *illus.*
KHULNA (Bangladesh)
map (22° 48'N 89° 33'E) **3**:64
KHUSROU, AMIR
Indian literature **11**:101
KHVOY (Iran)
map (38° 33'N 44° 58'E) **11**:250
KHYBER PASS **12**:69
map (34° 5'N 71° 10'E) **1**:133
KI (cosmic power)
martial arts **13**:178
KI NO TSURAYUKI
Japanese literature **11**:380
KIA (Solomon Islands)
map (7° 33'S 158° 26'E) **18**:56
KIANA (Alaska)
map (66° 59'N 160° 25'W) **1**:242
KIANG **12**:69–70 *illus.*
KIANGSI (Jiangxi) (China) **12**:70
KIANGSU (Jiangsu) (China) **12**:70
cities
Nanking (Nanjing) **14**:12
Soochow (Suzhou) **18**:66
KIAOCHOW (China)
Japan, history of **11**:370
KIAWAH ISLAND
map (32° 35'N 80° 5'W) **18**:98
KIBBUTZ **12**:70 *bibliog.*
socialism **18**:24
KIBERI (Papua New Guinea)
map (7° 25'S 143° 48'E) **15**:72
KIBUMBU (Burundi)
map (3° 32'S 29° 45'E) **3**:582
KIBUNGO (Rwanda)
map (2° 10'S 30° 32'E) **16**:378
KIBUYE (Rwanda)
map (2° 3'S 29° 21'E) **16**:378
KIČEVO (Yugoslavia)
map (41° 31'N 20° 57'E) **20**:340
KICHBEI MORONOBU *see* MORONOBU
KICHEN
symbiosis **18**:402
KICKAPOO (American Indians) **12**:70 *bibliog.*
Wananikwe **20**:21
KICKAPOO RIVER
map (43° 5'N 90° 53'W) **20**:185
KICKING BEAR (Sioux Indian)
Battle of the Little Bighorn **11**:108 *illus.*
KICKING HORSE PASS
map (51° 27'N 116° 18'W) **1**:256
KID, THOMAS *see* KYD, THOMAS
KIDD, CAPTAIN **12**:70 *bibliog.*
piracy **15**:313 *illus.*
KIDD, WILLIAM *see* KIDD, CAPTAIN
KIDDER (county in North Dakota)
map (47° 0'N 99° 45'W) **14**:248
KIDDER, ALFRED VINCENT **12**:70–71 *bibliog.*
KIDNAPPING **12**:71 *bibliog.*
Hauptmann, Bruno Richard **10**:69
Lindbergh, Charles A. **12**:351
KIDNEY, ARTIFICIAL **12**:71 *bibliog.*
dialysis **6**:151
kidney disease **12**:72
KIDNEY BEAN
bean **3**:139–140
KIDNEY DISEASE **12**:71–72 *bibliog.*
albumin **1**:261
Bright, Richard **3**:486
Bright's disease **3**:486
cystinuria **5**:411
dialysis **6**:151
enzyme **7**:214–215
fungus diseases **8**:369
heredity abnormalities **12**:71
hypertension **10**:349
joe-pye weed **11**:421
kidney, artificial **12**:71
kidney stone **12**:72
magnesium, imbalance **13**:54
nephritis **12**:71–72
disorders damaging nephrons **12**:71
Streptococcus **18**:297
urogenital diseases **19**:487
renal blood flow disorders **12**:71
toxicity **12**:72
transplantation, organ **19**:277
tumors **12**:72
uremia **19**:485
Wilms's tumor *see* WILMS'S TUMOR
KIDNEY STONE **12**:72
phosphate minerals **15**:256
uric acid **19**:486
KIDNEYS **1**:54 *illus.*; **12**:72–74 *bibliog., illus.*
aldosterone **1**:269
anatomy **12**:72–73 *illus.*
circulatory system **4**:440 *illus.*
Henle, Friedrich **10**:121
antidiuretic hormone **2**:61
Bowman, Sir William **3**:430
diuretic drugs **6**:202
electrolytes in **7**:115
evolution **12**:74
excretory system **7**:327–328 *illus.*
National Kidney Foundation **14**:34
reptile **16**:169
transplantation, organ **19**:277
urea **19**:485
urine **19**:486
urine production **12**:73–74
KIEL (West Germany) **12**:74
map (54° 20'N 10° 8'E) **9**:140
KIEL (Wisconsin)
map (43° 55'N 88° 2'W) **20**:185
KIEL CANAL **4**:96
Baltic Sea **3**:55
KIELCE (Poland)
map (50° 52'N 20° 37'E) **15**:388
KIELER BAY
map (54° 35'N 10° 35'E) **9**:140
KIELLAND, ALEXANDER LANGE **12**:74 *bibliog.*
KIENHOLZ, EDWARD **12**:74–75 *bibliog.*
KIERKEGAARD, SØREN **12**:75 *bibliog., illus.*
existentialism **7**:332
philosophy **15**:245
KIESLER, FREDERICK JOHN **12**:75 *bibliog.*
KIESTER (Minnesota)
map (43° 32'N 93° 42'W) **13**:453
KIEV (USSR) **12**:75–76; **19**:394 *illus.*
history **12**:76
Rurik (dynasty) **16**:347
Russia/Union of Soviet Socialist Republics, history of **16**:351–352 *map*
Slavs **17**:359
Svyatoslav I, Duke **18**:375
Vladimir I, Grand Duke of Kiev **19**:623
Yaroslav I, Grand Duke of Kiev **20**:319
map (50° 26'N 30° 31'E) **19**:388
KIEVAN RUS' *see* KIEV (USSR), HISTORY
KIGALI (Rwanda) **12**:76
map (1° 57'S 30° 4'E) **16**:378
KIHEI (Hawaii)
map (20° 47'N 156° 28'W) **10**:72
KII CHANNEL
map (33° 55'N 134° 55'E) **11**:361
KIKINDA (Yugoslavia)
map (45° 50'N 20° 28'E) **20**:340
KIKUYU **12**:76 *bibliog.*
Kenya **12**:56
Mau Mau **13**:232
KIKWIT (Zaire)
map (5° 2'S 18° 49'E) **20**:350
KILARNEY (Manitoba)
map (49° 12'N 99° 42'W) **13**:119
KILAUEA **12**:76
map (22° 13'N 159° 25'W) **10**:72
national parks **14**:38–39 *map, table*
KILAUEA CRATER
map (19° 25'N 155° 17'W) **10**:72
KILAUEA POINT
map (22° 14'N 159° 24'W) **10**:72
KILDARE (Ireland) **12**:76
KILGORE (Texas)
map (32° 23'N 94° 53'W) **19**:129
KILIMANJARO **1**:138 *illus.*; **12**:76; **19**:28 *illus.*
map (3° 4'S 37° 22'E) **19**:27
KILIMS
folk art **8**:196; **8**:199
KILKENNY (city in Ireland) **12**:76
KILKENNY (county in Ireland) **12**:76
cities
Kilkenny **12**:76
map (52° 39'N 7° 15'W) **11**:258
KILKENNY, STATUTES OF
Ireland, history of **11**:263
KILL VAN KULL
map (40° 39'N 74° 5'W) **14**:129
KILLAM (Alberta)
map (52° 47'N 111° 51'W) **1**:256
KILLARNEY (Ireland) **12**:76
KILLARNEY, LAKE
map (25° 3'N 77° 27'W) **3**:23
KILLBUCK (Ohio)
map (40° 30'N 81° 59'W) **14**:357
KILLDEER **9**:300 *illus.*
chick **3**:287 *illus.*
nest **3**:287 *illus.*
plover **15**:369
KILLDEER (North Dakota)
map (47° 22'N 102° 45'W) **14**:248
KILLEEN (Texas)
map (31° 8'N 97° 44'W) **19**:129
KILLER BEE **3**:158; **3**:161–162
KILLER WHALE *see* WHALE
KILLIFISH **12**:77
molly **13**:512
platy **15**:362
KILLINEK ISLAND
map (60° 24'N 64° 40'W) **14**:166
KILLINGTON PEAK
map (43° 36'N 72° 49'W) **19**:554
KILLY, JEAN CLAUDE **12**:77
KILMARNOCK (Scotland)
map (55° 36'N 4° 30'W) **19**:403
KILMARNOCK (Virginia)
map (37° 43'N 76° 23'W) **19**:607
KILMER, JOYCE **12**:77
KILMICHAEL (Mississippi)
map (33° 27'N 89° 34'W) **13**:469
KILN **4**:259 *illus.*; **12**:77 *illus.*
brick and bricklaying **3**:477–478
continuous kiln **12**:77 *illus.*

KILN (cont.)
intermittent kiln 12:77
lime (chemical compound)
furnace 8:372
KILOGRAM (measurement)
units, physical 19:466
weights and measures 20:93 *table*
KILOMETER (measurement)
weights and measures 20:93 *table*
KILPATRICK, WILLIAM HEARD 12:77 *bibliog.*
Montessori method 13:554
KILRAIN, JAKE 3:431 *illus.*
KILT
tartan 19:40
KIM (book)
Kipling, Rudyard 12:86–87
KIM (Colorado)
map (37° 15′N 103° 21′W) 5:116
KIM IL SUNG 12:77 *bibliog.*
communism 5:149
Korea 12:116
KIM JUNG IL
Korea 12:116
KIMBALL (Minnesota)
map (45° 19′N 94° 18′W) 13:453
KIMBALL (Nebraska)
map (41° 14′N 103° 40′W) 14:70
KIMBALL (county in Nebraska)
map (41° 15′N 103° 40′W) 14:70
KIMBALL (South Dakota)
map (43° 45′N 98° 57′W) 18:103
KIMBERLEY (South Africa) 12:77
map (28° 43′S 24° 46′E) 18:79
KIMBERLEY PLATEAU
map (17° 0′S 127° 0′E) 2:328
KIMBERLITE 12:77 *bibliog.*
mantle 13:130
notable pipes 12:77
ore deposits
major ore deposits 14:424–425 *table*
pipe fissures 12:77
ultramafic rock 12:77
KIMBERLY (Idaho)
map (42° 32′N 114° 22′W) 11:26
KIMBLE (county in Texas)
map (30° 30′N 99° 45′W) 19:129
KIMBUNDU *see* MBUNDU
KIMCHAEK (Korea)
map (40° 41′N 129° 12′E) 12:113
KIMCHON (Korea)
map (36° 7′N 128° 5′E) 12:113
KINABALU MOUNTAIN
map (6° 5′N 116° 33′E) 13:84
KINCAID (Illinois)
map (39° 35′N 89° 25′W) 11:42
KINCAID (Saskatchewan)
map (49° 39′N 107° 0′W) 17:81
KINCAID LAKE
map (37° 48′N 89° 26′W) 11:42
KINCARDINE (Ontario)
map (44° 11′N 81° 38′W) 14:393; 19:241
KINCARDINE (Scotland) 12:78
KINDE (Michigan)
map (43° 56′N 83° 0′W) 13:377
KINDERGARTEN *see* PRESCHOOL EDUCATION
KINDERSLEY (Saskatchewan)
map (51° 27′N 109° 10′W) 17:81
KINDI, AL- 12:78 *bibliog.*
KINDIA (Guinea)
map (10° 4′N 12° 51′W) 9:397
KINDRED (North Dakota)
map (46° 39′N 97° 1′W) 14:248
KINDU (Zaire)
map (2° 57′S 25° 56′E) 20:350
KINEMATICS 12:78
See also MOTION, CIRCULAR; MOTION, PARTICLE; MOTION, PLANAR
force 8:220
Milne, Edward Arthur 13:431
KINESIOLOGY
chiropractic 4:397–398
KINETIC ART 12:78 *bibliog.*
Calder, Alexander 4:25
Gabo, Naum 9:4
mobile 13:487
op art 14:397
Richter, Hans 16:214
Rickey, George W. 16:216
sculpture techniques 17:167
Tinguely, Jean 19:206
KINETIC ENERGY 12:78
Boltzmann constant 3:372
conservation, laws of 5:204 *illus.*
energy 7:172
KINETIC THEORY OF MATTER 12:78–79 *bibliog., illus.*
Boltzmann constant 3:372
Brownian motion 3:517–518
development 12:78
gases 12:78–79
Boltzmann, Ludwig 3:372
Maxwell, James Clerk 13:241
heat and heat transfer 10:98
liquid 12:364–365
liquids and solids 12:79
physical chemistry 15:279
reversible and irreversible processes 16:186
transport, molecular scale 12:79
mean free path 12:79
KINETICS *see* CHEMICAL KINETICS AND EQUILIBRIUM
KINETIN
cytokinin 5:411
KINETOGRAPH
film, history of 8:81
KINETOSCOPE
film, history of 8:81 *illus.*
KING 12:80 *bibliog.*
divine right 6:203
pharaoh 15:219
titles of nobility and honor 19:213
KING (North Carolina)
map (36° 17′N 80° 22′W) 14:242
KING (county in Texas)
map (33° 38′N 100° 15′W) 19:129
KING (county in Washington)
map (47° 26′N 121° 48′W) 20:35
KING, B. B. 12:80; 16:204 *illus.*
KING, BILLIE JEAN 12:80 *bibliog., illus.*
KING, BRUCE
New Mexico 14:138
KING, CLARENCE
O'Sullivan, Timothy H. 14:459
United States Geological Survey 19:462
KING, CORETTA SCOTT *see* KING, MARTIN LUTHER, JR.
KING, ERNEST JOSEPH 12:80
KING, MARTIN LUTHER, JR. 3:310 *illus.*; 5:13 *illus.*; 12:80–81 *bibliog., illus.*; 15:524 *illus.*; 19:459 *illus.*
civil disobedience 5:10
Montgomery (Alabama) 13:556
pacifism and nonviolent movements 15:10 *illus.*
Selma (Alabama) 17:192
SNCC 17:384
Southern Christian Leadership Conference 18:112
KING, RUFUS 12:81 *bibliog.*
KING, STEPHEN 12:81
KING, W. L. MACKENZIE 4:87 *illus.*; 12:81–82 *bibliog., illus.*
Canada, history of 4:86
Liberal parties 12:311
KING, WILLIAM RUFUS DE VANE 12:82
KING CITY (California)
map (36° 13′N 121° 8′W) 4:31
KING CITY (Missouri)
map (40° 3′N 94° 31′W) 13:476
KING CRAB *see* HORSESHOE CRAB
KING FEATURES SYNDICATE
press agencies and syndicates 15:533
KING GEORGE (Virginia)
map (38° 16′N 77° 11′W) 19:607
KING GEORGE (county in Virginia)
map (38° 15′N 77° 10′W) 19:607
KING GEORGE'S WAR
French and Indian Wars 8:313
Shirley, William 17:278
KING HILL (Idaho)
map (43° 0′N 115° 12′W) 11:26
KING AND I, THE (musical)
Mongkut, King of Siam 13:528
KING ISLAND
map (39° 50′S 144° 0′E) 2:328
KING LEAR (play) 12:82
KING MUST DIE, THE (book)
Renault, Mary 16:157
KING OLIVER'S JAZZ BAND 1:351 *illus.*
KING PENGUIN 2:42–43 *illus.*; 3:281 *illus.*
KING PHILIP'S WAR 11:109 *map*; 12:82 *bibliog.*
Indian Wars 11:107
Narragansett 14:21–22
Springfield (Massachusetts) 18:200
Uncas 19:381
United States, history of the 19:437
Wampanoag 20:21
KING OF PRUSSIA (Pennsylvania)
map (40° 5′N 75° 23′W) 15:147
KING AND QUEEN (county in Virginia)
map (37° 42′N 76° 50′W) 19:607
KING AND QUEEN COURT HOUSE (Virginia)
map (37° 40′N 76° 53′W) 19:607
KING SNAKE 5:124 *illus.*; 12:82 *bibliog., illus.*
colubrid 5:125
mimicry 13:435 *illus.*
KING WILLIAM (Virginia)
map (37° 41′N 77° 1′W) 19:607
KING WILLIAM (county in Virginia)
map (37° 42′N 77° 5′W) 19:607
KING WILLIAM ISLAND
map (69° 0′N 97° 30′W) 14:258
KING WILLIAM'S TOWN (South Africa)
map (32° 51′S 27° 22′E) 18:79
KING WILLIAM'S WAR 11:109 *map*
French and Indian Wars 8:312
KINGBIRD 12:83 *illus.*
flycatcher (bird) 8:191
KINGFISH *see* LONG, HUEY PIERCE, JR.
KINGFISHER (bird) 12:83 *bibliog., illus.*
courtship and mating 3:286 *illus.*
Tertiary Period 19:124 *illus.*
KINGFISHER (Oklahoma)
map (35° 52′N 97° 56′W) 14:368
KINGFISHER (county in Oklahoma)
map (35° 55′N 97° 55′W) 14:368
KINGFISHER(bird)
kookaburra 12:110
KINGIS QUAIR, THE
James I, King of Scotland 11:357
KINGLET 12:83 *illus.*
KINGMAN (Arizona)
map (35° 12′N 114° 4′W) 2:160
KINGMAN (Kansas)
map (37° 39′N 98° 7′W) 12:18
KINGMAN (county in Kansas)
map (37° 35′N 98° 5′W) 12:18
KINGMAN (Maine)
map (45° 33′N 68° 12′W) 13:70
KINGMAN REEF
map (6° 24′N 162° 22′W) 14:334
United States outlying territories 19:464
KINGS (county in California)
map (36° 20′N 119° 39′W) 4:31
KINGS (county in New York)
map (40° 42′N 74° 0′W) 14:149
KINGS, BOOKS OF 12:83–84 *bibliog.*
KINGS, VALLEY OF THE *see* VALLEY OF THE KINGS (Egypt)
KING'S BENCH *see* KING'S COURT
KING'S COLLEGE (Cambridge University) 4:53
chapel 7:183 *illus.*
Perpendicular Gothic style 15:177
KING'S COURT
common law 5:139
KING'S LAW *see* KING'S COURT
KINGS MOUNTAIN (North Carolina)
map (35° 15′N 81° 20′W) 14:242
KINGS PEAK
map (40° 46′N 110° 22′W) 19:492
KINGS RIVER
map (35° 29′N 93° 35′W) 2:166
KINGSBURY (county in South Dakota)
map (44° 20′N 97° 30′W) 18:103
KINGSFORD (Michigan)
map (45° 48′N 88° 4′W) 13:377
KINGSHILL (Virgin Islands)
map (17° 44′N 64° 48′W) 19:605
KINGSLAND (Arkansas)
map (33° 52′N 92° 18′W) 2:166
KINGSLAND (Georgia)
map (30° 48′N 81° 41′W) 9:114
KINGSLEY (Iowa)
map (42° 35′N 95° 58′W) 11:244
KINGSLEY (Michigan)
map (44° 35′N 85° 32′W) 13:377
KINGSLEY, CHARLES 12:84 *bibliog.*
socialism 18:20
KINGSLEY, HENRY
Australian literature 2:343
KINGSPORT (Tennessee)
map (36° 32′N 82° 33′W) 19:104
KINGSTON (Jamaica) 12:84
climate 11:352 *table*
map (18° 0′N 76° 48′W) 11:351
KINGSTON (Massachusetts)
map (41° 59′N 70° 43′W) 13:206
KINGSTON (Missouri)
map (39° 39′N 94° 2′W) 13:476
KINGSTON (New York) 12:84
map (41° 56′N 74° 0′W) 14:149
KINGSTON (Nova Scotia)
map (44° 59′N 64° 57′W) 14:269
KINGSTON (Oklahoma)
map (34° 0′N 96° 43′W) 14:368
KINGSTON (Ontario) 12:84
map (44° 18′N 76° 34′W) 14:393
KINGSTON (Pennsylvania)
map (41° 16′N 75° 54′W) 15:147
KINGSTON (Rhode Island)
map (41° 29′N 71° 31′W) 16:198
Narragansett 14:21–22
KINGSTON (Tennessee)
map (35° 52′N 84° 31′W) 19:104
KINGSTON UPON HULL (England) *see* HULL (England)
KINGSTOWN (Ireland) *see* DÚN LAOGHAIRE (Ireland)
KINGSTREE (South Carolina)
map (33° 40′N 79° 50′W) 18:98
KINGSVILLE (Texas)
map (27° 31′N 97° 52′W) 19:129
KINGWOOD (West Virginia)
map (39° 28′N 79° 41′W) 20:111
KINKAJOU 12:84 *illus.*
KINKONY, LAKE
map (16° 8′S 45° 50′E) 13:38
KINMUNDY (Illinois)
map (38° 46′N 88° 51′W) 11:42
KINNAIRDS HEAD
map (57° 42′N 2° 0′W) 19:403
KINNERET, YAM *see* GALILEE, SEA OF
KINNEY (county in Texas)
map (29° 22′N 100° 25′W) 19:129
KINNOCK, NEIL 12:84
KINO, EUSEBIO FRANCISCO 12:84–85 *bibliog.*
Arizona 2:164
Spanish missions 18:160
Tucson (Arizona) 19:328
Yuma (Indian tribe) 20:346
KINORHYNCH
invertebrate 11:235
KINROSS (Scotland) 12:85
KINSEY REPORTS 12:85 *bibliog.*
Ellis, Havelock 7:148
Lashley, Karl S. 12:213
Masters and Johnson reports 13:216
sexual intercourse 17:231
KINSHASA (Zaire) 12:85; 20:349 *illus.*
climate 20:351 *table*
map (4° 18′S 15° 18′E) 20:350
KINSHIP 12:85–86 *bibliog.*
Arabs 2:104–105
clan 5:36
extended family 7:341
family 8:16–17
incest 11:73–74
lineage 12:353
matriarchy 13:229
Murdock, George Peter 13:648
primitive societies 15:546
totem 19:249
tribe 19:295
women in society 20:201
KINSLEY (Kansas)
map (37° 55′N 99° 25′W) 12:18
KINSMAN (Ohio)
map (41° 27′N 80° 36′W) 14:357
KINSTON (North Carolina)
map (35° 16′N 77° 35′W) 14:242
KINTPUASH 12:86
KINUSO (Alberta)
map (55° 20′N 115° 25′W) 1:256
KINYETI MOUNTAIN
map (3° 57′N 32° 54′E) 18:320
KINZUA (Oregon)
map (44° 59′N 120° 3′W) 14:427
KIOWA (American Indians) 12:86 *bibliog.*
Apache 2:73
Indians of North America, art of the 11:141
Indians of North America, music and dance of the 11:143
KIOWA (Colorado)
map (39° 21′N 104° 28′W) 5:116
KIOWA (county in Colorado)
map (38° 25′N 102° 50′W) 5:116
KIOWA (Kansas)
map (37° 1′N 98° 29′W) 12:18
KIOWA (county in Kansas)
map (37° 35′N 99° 15′W) 12:18
KIOWA (Oklahoma)
map (34° 43′N 95° 54′W) 14:368
KIOWA (county in Oklahoma)
map (34° 55′N 99° 0′W) 14:368
KIPCHAK KHANATE *see* GOLDEN HORDE, KHANATE OF THE
KIPCHAKS
Golden Horde, Khanate of the 9:232
Ural-Altaic languages 19:476
KIPLING, RUDYARD 7:201 *illus.*; 12:86–87 *bibliog., illus.*
Captains Courageous 4:129
Jungle Book, The 11:468
KIPNUK (Alaska)
map (59° 56′N 164° 3′W) 1:242
KIPPHARDT, HEINAR
theater of fact 19:153
KIPRENSKY, OREST
Russian art and architecture 16:362
KIPUSHI (Zaire)
map (11° 46′N 27° 14′E) 20:350
KIRA KIRA (Solomon Islands)
map (10° 27′S 161° 56′E) 18:56
KIRBY, ROLLIN

cartoon (editorial and political) **4**:178 *illus.*
censorship (cartoon) **4**:247 *illus.*
"Mr. Dry" (cartoon) **4**:176 *illus.*
KIRBY, WILLIAM
Canadian literature **4**:93
KIRCHHOFF, GUSTAV ROBERT **12**:87
cesium **4**:262
Kirchhoff's laws **12**:87
KIRCHHOFF'S LAWS **12**:87 *bibliog.*
circuit, electric **4**:436
electrical values, circuits and networks **12**:87
KIRCHNER, ERNST LUDWIG **3**:520 *illus.*; **12**:87 *bibliog., illus.*
A Group of Artists **3**:520 *illus.*
Nude in a Room: Fränzi **9**:128 *illus.*
Self-portrait with Model **12**:87 *illus.*
KIRGHIZ **12**:87–88 *bibliog.*
Turks **19**:347; **19**:348
Uighur **19**:374
KIRGHIZ SOVIET SOCIALIST REPUBLIC (USSR) **12**:88
cities
Frunze **8**:350
people
Kirghiz **12**:87–88
KIRGHIZ STEPPE
map (49° 0′N 81° 0′E) **19**:388
KIRGHIZIA *see* KIRGHIZ SOVIET SOCIALIST REPUBLIC (USSR)
KIRIBATI **12**:88 *bibliog., illus., map*
Christmas Island (Pacific Ocean) **4**:415
cities
Tarawa **19**:35
economy **12**:88
flag **8**:143 *illus.*; **12**:88 *illus.*
history and government **12**:88
land and people **12**:88
map (4° 0′S 175° 0′E) **14**:334
Phoenix Islands **15**:251
KIRIKKALE (Turkey)
map (39° 50′N 33° 31′E) **19**:343
KIRIN (China)
Manchuria **13**:109
map (43° 51′N 126° 33′E) **4**:362
KIRK, CLAUDE R., JR.
Florida **8**:175
KIRK, NORMAN ERIC **12**:88–89 *bibliog.*
KIRKCALDY (Scotland) **12**:89
map (56° 7′N 3° 10′W) **19**:403
KIRKCUDBRIGHT (Scotland) **12**:89
KIRKE, SIR DAVID **12**:89 *bibliog.*
KIRKLAND (Illinois)
map (42° 6′N 88° 51′W) **11**:42
KIRKLAND (Texas)
map (34° 23′N 100° 4′W) **19**:129
KIRKLAND (Washington)
map (47° 41′N 122° 12′W) **20**:35
KIRKLAND, GELSEY **12**:89
KIRKLAND, LANE **12**:89
KIRKLAND, SAMUEL
Oneida **14**:389
KIRKLAND LAKE (Ontario)
map (48° 9′N 80° 2′W) **14**:393
KIRKLIN (Indiana)
map (40° 12′N 86° 22′W) **11**:111
KIRKPATRICK, JEANE **12**:89
KIRKSVILLE (Missouri)
map (40° 12′N 92° 35′W) **13**:476
osteopathic medicine **14**:457
KIRKUK (Iraq)
map (35° 28′N 44° 28′E) **11**:255
KIRKWALL (Scotland)
map (58° 59′N 2° 58′W) **19**:403
KIRKWOOD (Missouri)
map (38° 35′N 90° 24′W) **13**:476
KIRLIAN PHOTOGRAPHY **12**:89 *bibliog.*
KIROV (USSR) **12**:89
map (58° 38′N 49° 42′E) **19**:388
KIROV, SERGEI
Great Purge **9**:321
Stalin, Joseph **18**:214
KIROV BALLET **12**:89–90 *bibliog.*
Balanchine, George **3**:32–33
Baryshnikov, Mikhail **3**:99
Sergeyev, Konstantin **17**:208
KIRSEHIR (Turkey)
map (39° 9′N 34° 10′E) **19**:343
KIRSTEIN, LINCOLN **12**:90 *bibliog.*
New York City Ballet **14**:154
KIRTHAR RANGE
map (27° 0′N 67° 10′E) **15**:27
KIRTLAND (New Mexico)
map (36° 44′N 108° 21′W) **14**:136
KIRUNA (Sweden)
map (67° 51′N 20° 16′E) **18**:382
ore deposits
major ore deposits **14**:424–425 *table*
KIRWIN RESERVOIR
map (39° 39′N 99° 50′W) **12**:18
KIRYATH GATH (Israel)
map (31° 37′N 34° 46′E) **11**:302
KIRYATH MALACHI (Israel)
map (31° 42′N 34° 38′E) **11**:302
KIRYATH SHEMONA (Israel)
map (33° 12′N 35° 35′E) **11**:302
KIRYATH TIVON (Israel)
map (32° 43′N 35° 8′E) **11**:302
KISANGANI (Zaire) **12**:90
climate **20**:351 *table*
map (0° 30′S 25° 12′E) **20**:350
KISH (Iraq) **12**:90 *bibliog.*
Mesopotamian art and architecture **13**:318
wheel **20**:127–128
KISHINEV (USSR) **12**:90
map (47° 0′N 28° 50′E) **19**:388
KISHON RIVER
map (32° 49′N 35° 2′E) **11**:302
KISHORGANJ (Bangladesh)
map (24° 26′N 90° 46′E) **3**:64
KISKÖREI RESERVOIR
map (47° 35′N 20° 40′E) **10**:307
KISMAYU (Somalia)
map (0° 23′S 42° 30′E) **18**:60
KISPOKOTHA
Shawnee (American Indians) **17**:246
KISRA *see* KHOSRU I, KING OF PERSIA
KISS (rock group)
rock music **16**:249
KISS OF THE SPIDER WOMAN (book)
Puig, Manuel **15**:617
KISSIMMEE (Florida)
map (28° 18′N 81° 24′W) **8**:172
KISSIMMEE, LAKE
map (27° 55′N 81° 16′W) **8**:172
KISSIMMEE RIVER
map (27° 10′N 80° 53′W) **8**:172
KISSING BUG *see* ASSASSIN BUG
KISSINGER, HENRY A. **12**:90–91 *bibliog., illus.*
Egypt **7**:80
Nixon, Richard M. **14**:205
president of the United States **15**:524
Vietnam War **19**:588 *illus.*; **19**:590
KISSISSING LAKE
map (55° 10′N 101° 20′W) **13**:119
KISUMU (Kenya)
map (0° 6′S 34° 45′E) **12**:53
KIT CARSON (Colorado)
map (38° 46′N 102° 48′W) **5**:116
KIT CARSON (county in Colorado)
map (39° 15′N 102° 35′W) **5**:116
KITAB AL- 'IBAR
Ibn Khaldun **11**:5
KITAGAWA UTAMARO *see* UTAMARO
KITAKAMI RIVER
map (38° 25′N 141° 19′E) **11**:361
KITAKYUSHU (Japan) **12**:91
map (33° 53′N 130° 50′E) **11**:361
KITCHEN CABINET **12**:91
cabinet **4**:5
Kendall, Amos **12**:41
KITCHEN GODS **12**:91
KITCHEN MIDDEN *see* MIDDEN
KITCHENER (Ontario) **12**:91
map (43° 27′N 80° 29′W) **14**:393
KITCHENER, HERBERT KITCHENER, 1ST EARL **12**:91 *bibliog.*
concentration camp **5**:169
Khartoum (Sudan) **12**:66
Omdurman (Sudan) **14**:387
World War I **20**:228
KITE (bird) **12**:91–92 *illus.*
everglade lite **18**:377 *illus.*
KITE (object) **12**:92–93 *bibliog., illus.*
tetrahedral
Bell, Alexander Graham **3**:185
KITE SWALLOWTAIL BUTTERFLY **3**:597 *illus.*
butterflies and moths **3**:595
KITHARA **9**:345 *illus.*; **12**:93 *bibliog., illus.*
KITIKITISH *see* WICHITA (American Indians)
KITIMAT (British Columbia)
map (54° 3′N 128° 33′W) **3**:491
KITIMAT RANGES
map (53° 30′N 128° 50′W) **3**:491
KITRIDGE POINT
map (13° 10′N 59° 25′W) **3**:75
KITSAP (county in Washington)
map (47° 41′N 122° 44′W) **20**:35
KITT PEAK NATIONAL OBSERVATORY **12**:93
Goldsmith, Myron **9**:236
KITTANNING (Pennsylvania)
map (40° 49′N 79° 32′W) **15**:147
KITTATINNY MOUNTAINS
map (41° 00′N 75° 00′W) **14**:129
KITTERY (Maine)
map (43° 5′N 70° 45′W) **13**:70
KITTINGER, JOSEPH
aerial sports **1**:122
parachute **15**:75
KITTITAS (Washington)
map (46° 59′N 120° 25′W) **20**:35
KITTITAS (county in Washington)
map (47° 13′N 121° 1′W) **20**:35
KITTIWAKE **12**:93
KITTSON (county in Minnesota)
map (48° 45′N 96° 43′W) **13**:453
KITTY HAWK (airplane)
Wright, Orville and Wilbur **20**:290
KITWANGA (British Columbia)
map (55° 6′N 128° 3′W) **3**:491
KITWE (Zambia) **12**:93
map (12° 49′S 28° 13′E) **20**:354
KITZBÜHEL (Austria) **2**:348 *illus.*
KIVA **12**:93–94 *bibliog.*
Chaco Canyon **4**:264–265
Indians of North America, art of the **11**:140
Indians of North America, music and dance of the **11**:143
Mesa Verde National Park (Colorado) **13**:314
snake dance **17**:382
KIVALINA (Alaska)
map (67° 59′N 164° 33′W) **1**:242
KIVI, ALEKSIS
Finnish literature **8**:99
KIVU, LAKE **12**:94
map (2° 0′S 29° 10′E) **16**:378
KIWI (bird) **3**:280 *illus.*; **12**:94 *bibliog., illus.*
KIWI (fruit) **12**:94
KIYOMASU **12**:94 *bibliog.*
KIYONAGA **12**:94 *bibliog.*
KIYONOBU I **12**:94 *bibliog.*
KIZIL RIVER
map (41° 44′N 35° 58′E) **19**:343
KJELLÉN, RUDOLF
geopolitics **9**:109
KJÖLLEN MOUNTAINS **18**:383 *illus.*
KKK *see* KU KLUX KLAN
KLADNO (Czechoslovakia)
map (50° 8′N 14° 5′E) **5**:413
KLAGENFURT (Austria)
map (46° 38′N 14° 18′E) **2**:348
KLAKAH (Indonesia)
map (7° 59′S 113° 15′E) **11**:147
KLAMATH (American Indians) **12**:94–95 *bibliog.*
Indians of North America, art of the **11**:140
Modoc **13**:499
KLAMATH (county in Oregon)
map (42° 40′N 121° 30′W) **14**:427
KLAMATH FALLS (Oregon)
map (42° 13′N 121° 46′W) **14**:427
KLAMATH MOUNTAINS
map (41° 40′N 123° 20′W) **4**:31
Oregon **14**:428
KLAMATH RIVER
map (41° 33′N 124° 4′W) **4**:31
KLAMI, UUNO
Finland **8**:96
KLAPROTH, MARTIN HEINRICH **12**:95
cerium **4**:260
KLARA RIVER
map (59° 23′N 13° 32′E) **18**:382
KLASEN, GERTRUDE *see* LAWRENCE, GERTRUDE
KLAWOCK (Alaska)
map (55° 33′N 133° 6′W) **1**:242
KLEBERG (county in Texas)
map (27° 18′N 97° 43′W) **19**:129
KLEBSIELLA **12**:95
KLEE, PAUL **12**:95 *bibliog., illus.*
Abstraction **20**:62 *illus.*
Bauhaus **3**:129–130 *illus.*
Fish Magic **12**:95 *illus.*
KLEIN, CALVIN
fashion design **8**:32
KLEIN, FELIX **12**:95
Klein bottle **12**:96
non-Euclidean geometry **14**:216
transformation **19**:270
KLEIN, MELANIE **12**:96 *bibliog.*
KLEIN, YVES **12**:96
KLEIN BOTTLE **12**:96 *bibliog., illus.*
topology **19**:237
KLEIST, HEINRICH VON **12**:96 *bibliog.*
KLEIST PRIZE
Brecht, Bertolt **3**:470
KLEMME (Iowa)
map (43° 1′N 93° 36′W) **11**:244
KLEMPERER, OTTO **12**:96 *bibliog.*
Pittsburgh Symphony Orchestra **15**:322
KLENZE, LEO VON **12**:96–97 *bibliog.*
Glyptothek **9**:212–213
KLEPTOMANIA **12**:97
KLERKSDORP (South Africa)
map (26° 58′S 26° 39′E) **18**:79
KLET' MOUNTAIN
map (48° 52′N 14° 17′E) **5**:413
KLEVE (Germany, East and West)
map (51° 48′N 6° 9′E) **9**:140
KLICKITAT (county in Washington)
map (45° 50′N 121° 7′W) **20**:35
KLIMT, GUSTAV **12**:97 *bibliog., illus.*
Fulfillment (The Kiss) **2**:353 *illus.*; **12**:97 *illus.*
Hoffmann, Josef **10**:195
KLIMUK, P. I. **12**:97
KLINE, FRANZ **12**:97–98 *bibliog., illus.*
Copper and Red **12**:98 *illus.*
KLINEFELTER'S SYNDROME **12**:98
mental retardation **13**:302
KLINT, KAARE
Scandinavian art and architecture **17**:114
KLONDIKE (card game)
solitaire (card game) **18**:56
KLONDIKE (Yukon Territory) **12**:98 *bibliog.*
KLOPSTOCK, FRIEDRICH GOTTLIEB **12**:98 *bibliog.*
KLOSTERNEUBURG (Austria)
map (48° 18′N 16° 20′E) **2**:348
KLUCK, ALEXANDER VON
Marne, Battles of the **13**:162
World War I **20**:222–224
KLUCKHOHN, CLYDE **12**:98 *bibliog.*
KLYSTRON **12**:98–99 *bibliog., illus.*
KLYUCHEVSKAYA SOPKA VOLCANO
map (56° 4′N 160° 38′E) **19**:388
KMT *see* KUOMINTANG (Guomindang)
KNABSTRUP *see* COACH HORSE
KNAPP (Wisconsin)
map (44° 57′N 92° 5′W) **20**:185
KNAUS, LUDWIG
Hermann Ludwig Ferdinand von Helmholtz **10**:115–116 *illus.*
KNEE
joint (anatomy) **11**:439 *illus.*
reflex **16**:120
sports medicine **18**:198
KNEE LAKE
map (55° 3′N 94° 40′W) **13**:119
KNELLER, SIR GODFREY **12**:99 *bibliog.*
KNESSET (parliament)
Israel **11**:306
KNICKERBOCKER GROUP **12**:99 *bibliog.*
Cooper, James Fenimore **5**:243
Drake, Joseph Rodman **6**:257
KNIDOS *see* CNIDUS
KNIEVEL, EVEL **12**:99 *bibliog.*
KNIFE **18**:399 *illus.*
KNIFE FISH **12**:99 *illus.*
gymnotid **9**:414
KNIFE RIVER
map (47° 20′N 101° 23′W) **14**:248
KNIGHT **4**:221 *illus.*; **12**:99–100 *bibliog., illus.*
See also HOSPITALERS; TEMPLARS; TEUTONIC KNIGHTS
armor **2**:174 *illus.*
Aztec **2**:382 *illus.*
chivalry **4**:399
courtly love **5**:317
draft horse **6**:254
duel **6**:293
feudalism **8**:64
heraldry **10**:132–134
Middle Ages **13**:393
Shire (horse) **17**:277
titles of nobility and honor **19**:214
KNIGHT, BOBBY **12**:100
KNIGHT, ETHERIDGE **12**:100
KNIGHT, JOSEPH P.
American music **1**:349
KNIGHT, WILLIAM J. (PETE)
X-15 **20**:311
KNIGHTS OF COLUMBUS **12**:100
KNIGHTS HOSPITALERS *see* HOSPITALERS
KNIGHTS OF LABOR **12**:100–101 *bibliog.*
Gibbons, James **9**:173
Labor Day **12**:152
labor union **12**:154–155
United States, history of the **19**:451
KNIGHTS OF SAINT JOHN
nursing (profession) **14**:2
KNIGHTS OF THE GOLDEN CIRCLE
copperheads **5**:254
KNIGHTSTOWN (Indiana)
map (39° 48′N 85° 32′W) **11**:111
KNILLER, GOTTFRIED *see* KNELLER, SIR GODFREY
KNIPPING, PAUL
x-ray diffraction discoverer
mineral **13**:439
KNITTELFELD (Austria)
map (47° 14′N 14° 50′E) **2**:348
KNITTING **12**:101 *bibliog., illus.*
jersey **11**:398

KNJAŽEVAC (Yugoslavia)
map (43° 34′N 22° 16′E) **20**:340
KNOB NOSTER (Missouri)
map (38° 46′N 93° 33′W) **13**:476
KNOBELSDORFF, GEORG WENZESLAUS VON
Sans Souci **17**:65
KNOPF, ALFRED A. **11**:101
KNOSSOS (Crete) **12**:101–102 *bibliog., illus.*
architecture **1**:115 *illus.*; **2**:131; **5**:342 *illus.*
Evans, Sir Arthur **7**:312
fresco painting **1**:116 *illus.*
Great Palace **12**:101 *illus.*
Greece, ancient **9**:329
labyrinth and maze **12**:158
Linear B **12**:353
Minoan art **13**:458–459 *illus.*
KNOT (unit of speed)
Beaufort scale **3**:146
KNOTS AND HITCHES
macrame **13**:36
KNOTT (county in Kentucky)
map (37° 20′N 83° 0′W) **12**:47
KNOTWEED *see* SMARTWEED
KNOW-NOTHING PARTY **12**:102 *bibliog., illus.*
United States, history of the **19**:447
KNOWLEDGE *see* EPISTEMOLOGY
KNOWLTON, CHARLES
birth control **3**:294
KNOWTH (Ireland) **12**:102 *bibliog.*
Newgrange **14**:168
KNOX (county in Illinois)
map (40° 52′N 90° 13′W) **11**:42
KNOX (Indiana)
map (41° 18′N 86° 37′W) **11**:111
KNOX (county in Indiana)
map (38° 45′N 87° 25′W) **11**:111
KNOX (county in Kentucky)
map (36° 55′N 83° 50′W) **12**:47
KNOX (county in Maine)
map (44° 10′N 69° 12′W) **13**:70
KNOX (county in Missouri)
map (40° 10′N 92° 10′W) **13**:476
KNOX (county in Nebraska)
map (42° 40′N 97° 50′W) **14**:70
KNOX (county in Ohio)
map (40° 23′N 82° 29′W) **14**:357
KNOX (Pennsylvania)
map (41° 14′N 79° 32′W) **15**:147
KNOX (county in Tennessee)
map (36° 0′N 83° 55′W) **19**:104
KNOX (county in Texas)
map (33° 38′N 99° 42′W) **19**:129
KNOX, FORT (Kentucky) *see* FORT KNOX (Kentucky)
KNOX, HENRY **12**:102 *bibliog.*; **19**:442 *illus.*
KNOX, JOHN **12**:102–103 *bibliog., illus.*
Perth (city in Scotland) **15**:191
Presbyterianism **15**:519
Scotland, Church of **17**:152
KNOX, PHILANDER CHASE **12**:103 *bibliog.*
KNOX CITY (Texas)
map (33° 25′N 99° 49′W) **19**:129
KNOXVILLE (Georgia)
map (32° 44′N 84° 1′W) **9**:114
KNOXVILLE (Illinois)
map (40° 55′N 90° 17′W) **11**:42
KNOXVILLE (Iowa)
map (41° 19′N 93° 6′W) **11**:244
KNOXVILLE (Tennessee) **12**:103; **19**:105 *map*
map (35° 58′N 83° 56′W) **19**:104
KNYPHAUSEN, WILHELM, BARON VON **12**:103
KO-CHIU (China)
map (23° 22′N 103° 6′E) **4**:362
KO-HEMP *see* KUDZU
KOALA **12**:103–104 *bibliog., illus.*; **13**:104 *illus.*; **13**:175 *illus.*
phalanger **15**:218
KOAN **12**:104 *bibliog.*
Zen Buddhism **20**:358–359
KOB **12**:104 *illus.*
KOBAR SINK
map (14° 0′N 40° 30′E) **7**:253
KOBE (Japan) **12**:104
map (34° 41′N 135° 10′E) **11**:361
KØBENHAVN (Denmark) *see* COPENHAGEN (Denmark)
KOBER, LEOPOLD
mid-oceanic ridge **13**:389
KOBLENZ (West Germany) **12**:104
map (50° 21′N 7° 35′E) **9**:140
KOBRIN, LEON
Yiddish theater **20**:328
KOBYLA, ANDREI IVANOVICH
Romanov (dynasty) **16**:290
KOČANI (Yugoslavia)
map (41° 55′N 22° 25′E) **20**:340
KOCH, EDWARD I. **12**:104 *bibliog.*
KOCH, ROBERT **3**:17 *illus.*; **12**:104–105 *bibliog.*
bacteria **3**:17–18
biology **3**:269
Koch's Postulates **12**:105
medicine **13**:271
microbiology **13**:384
KOCHANOWSKI, JAN
Polish literature **15**:398
KOCHER, EMIL **12**:105 *bibliog.*
KOCHI (Japan)
map (33° 33′N 133° 33′E) **11**:361
KODAK CAMERAS **4**:55
disc camera **4**:59
KODAK COMPANY *see* EASTMAN KODAK COMPANY
KODÁLY, ZOLTÁN **12**:105 *bibliog.*
Hungarian music **10**:306
KODIAK (Alaska)
map (57° 48′N 152° 23′W) **1**:242
KODIAK ISLAND (Alaska) **12**:105
map (57° 30′N 153° 30′W) **1**:242
KODOK *see* FASHODA INCIDENT
KOELREUTER, JOSEPH G.
plant breeding **15**:342
KOEN, FANNY BLANKERS- *see* BLANKERS-KOEN, FANNY
KOEN, J. S.
influenza **11**:172
KOENIGSWALD, G. H. R. VON
Gigantopithecus **9**:178
KOESTLER, ARTHUR **11**:105 *bibliog., illus.*
Darkness at Noon **6**:38–39
KOETSU **12**:105 *bibliog.*
Japanese art and architecture **11**:377
Sotatsu **18**:70
KOFFKA, KURT **12**:105–106
Gestalt psychology **9**:159
Köhler, Wolfgang **12**:106
Wertheimer, Max **20**:104
KOFORIDUA (Ghana)
map (6° 3′N 0° 17′W) **9**:164
KOFU (Japan)
map (35° 39′N 138° 35′E) **11**:361
KOGAN, LEONID
Russian music **16**:369
KØGE (Denmark)
map (55° 27′N 12° 11′E) **6**:109
KØGE BAY
map (55° 30′N 12° 20′E) **6**:109
KOGON RIVER
map (11° 9′N 14° 42′W) **9**:397
KOGURYO KINGDOM
Korea, history of **12**:116
Korean art **12**:117–118 *illus.*
KOHALA MOUNTAINS
map (20° 5′N 155° 45′W) **10**:72
KOHAT
map (33° 35′N 71° 26′E) **15**:27
KOHIMA (India)
map (25° 40′N 94° 7′E) **11**:80
KOHL, HELMUT **12**:106
KOHLBERG, LAWRENCE
moral awareness **13**:572
KOHLER, KAUFMANN **12**:106 *bibliog.*
KÖHLER, WOLFGANG **12**:106 *bibliog.*
Gestalt psychology **9**:159
Koffka, Kurt **12**:105
learning theory **12**:261
Pavlov, Ivan Petrovich **15**:120
Wertheimer, Max **20**:104
KOHOUTEK (comet) **5**:134 *illus.*
KOHUT, HEINZ
psychoanalysis **15**:590
KOIDERN (Yukon Territory)
map (61° 58′N 140° 25′W) **20**:345
KOIVISTO, MAUNO
Finland **8**:98
KOKAND (USSR)
Uzbek Soviet Socialist Republic **19**:499
KOKKOLA (Finland)
map (63° 50′N 23° 7′E) **8**:95
KOKO (gorilla)
animal communication **2**:20
KOKO CRATER
map (21° 16′N 157° 41′W) **10**:72
KOKO HEAD
map (21° 16′N 157° 42′W) **10**:72
KOKO NOR **12**:106
map (36° 50′N 100° 20′E) **4**:362
KOKOMO (Indiana)
map (40° 29′N 86° 8′W) **11**:111
KOKOMO (Mississippi)
map (31° 12′N 90° 0′W) **13**:469
KOKOPO (Papua New Guinea)
map (4° 20′S 152° 15′E) **15**:72
KOKOSCHKA, OSKAR **12**:106 *bibliog., illus.*
Vienna, State Opera **12**:106 *illus.*
KOKOSING RIVER
map (40° 22′N 82° 12′W) **14**:357
KOKRINES (Alaska)
map (64° 56′N 154° 42′W) **1**:242
KOKSOAK RIVER
map (58° 32′N 68° 10′W) **16**:18
KOLA NUT **12**:106–107
KOLA PENINSULA
map (67° 30′N 37° 0′E) **19**:388
KOLBE, GEORG **12**:107 *bibliog.*
KOLDA (Senegal)
map (12° 53′N 14° 57′W) **17**:202
KOLDEWEY, ROBERT
Hanging Gardens of Babylon **17**:216
KOLDING (Denmark)
map (55° 31′N 9° 29′E) **6**:109
KOLFF, WILLEM
kidney, artificial **12**:71
KOLHAPUR (India)
map (16° 42′N 74° 13′E) **11**:80
KOLIGANEK (Alaska)
map (59° 48′N 157° 25′W) **1**:242
KOLINGBA, ANDRÉ
Central African Republic **4**:252
KOLLANTAI, ALEKSANDRA **12**:107 *bibliog.*
KOLLÁR, JAN
Czech literature **5**:412
KOLLER, CARL
cocaine **5**:85
KOLLWITZ, KÄTHE **12**:107 *bibliog., illus.*
Woman with a Blue Shawl **12**:107 *illus.*
KOLMOGOROV, A. N.
probability **15**:558
KÖLN (West Germany) *see* COLOGNE (West Germany)
KÖLN-LINDENTHAL *see* COLOGNE (West Germany)
KOLOA (Hawaii)
map (21° 55′N 159° 28′W) **10**:72
KOLUMADULU ATOLL
map (2° 25′N 73° 10′E) **13**:87
KOLWEZI (Zaire)
map (10° 43′S 25° 28′E) **20**:350
KOLYMA RIVER
map (69° 30′N 161° 0′E) **19**:388
KOM EL-AHMAR *see* HIERAKONPOLIS (Egypt)
KOM OMBO *see* OMBOS
KOMADUGU GANA RIVER
map (13° 5′N 12° 24′E) **14**:190
KOMADUGU YOBE RIVER
map (13° 43′N 13° 20′E) **14**:190
KOMANDORSKIYE ISLANDS *see* COMMANDER ISLANDS (USSR)
map (55° 0′N 167° 0′E) **19**:388
KOMAR, CHRIS **3**:44 *illus.*
KOMÁRNO (Czechoslovakia)
map (47° 45′N 18° 9′E) **5**:413
KOMAROV, VLADIMIR **12**:107 *bibliog.*
KOMENSKÝ, JAN ÁMOS *see* COMENIUS, JOHN AMOS
KOMODO DRAGON **12**:107–108 *bibliog., illus.*; **12**:381 *illus.*
monitor **13**:531
KOMOÉ RIVER
map (5° 12′N 3° 44′W) **11**:335
KOMONDOR **6**:214 *illus.*; **12**:108 *illus.*
KOMOTINI (Greece)
map (41° 8′N 25° 25′E) **9**:325
KOMPONG CHAM (Kampuchea)
map (12° 0′N 105° 27′E) **12**:11
KOMPONG CHNANG (Kampuchea)
map (12° 15′N 104° 40′E) **12**:11
KOMPONG KLEANG (Kampuchea)
map (13° 6′N 104° 8′E) **12**:11
KOMPONG SOM (Kampuchea)
map (10° 38′N 103° 30′E) **12**:11
KOMPONG SOM BAY
map (10° 50′N 103° 32′E) **12**:11
KOMPONG SPEU (Kampuchea)
map (11° 27′N 104° 32′E) **12**:11
KOMPONG THOM (Kampuchea)
map (12° 42′N 104° 54′E) **12**:11
KOMSOMOLSK (USSR)
map (50° 35′N 137° 2′E) **19**:388
KON-TIKI (expedition) **12**:108
Heyerdahl, Thor **10**:155
Kon-Tiki (raft) **10**:155 *illus.*
KON-TIKI (raft) **10**:155 *illus.*
Polynesians **15**:421
ship **17**:263
KONARAK **12**:108 *bibliog.*
Indian art and architecture **11**:97
KONAWA (Oklahoma)
map (34° 58′N 96° 45′W) **14**:368
KONDO *see* TEMPLE
KONDRATYEVA, MARINA **3**:371 *illus.*
KONG ISLAND
map (11° 20′N 103° 0′E) **12**:11
KONG RIVER
map (13° 32′N 105° 58′E) **12**:203
KONGO, KINGDOM OF **12**:108 *bibliog.*
Congo **5**:182
KÖNIG, FRIEDRICH
printing **15**:551
KÖNIGSBERG (Germany) *see* KALININGRAD (USSR)
KONIGSBERG, ALLEN S. *see* ALLEN, WOODY
KÖNIGSBERG BRIDGE PROBLEM **12**:108–109 *bibliog., illus.*
KONIN (Poland)
map (52° 13′N 18° 16′E) **15**:388
KÖNKÄMÄ RIVER
map (68° 29′N 22° 17′E) **8**:95
KONKANI LANGUAGE
Indo-Iranian languages **11**:145
KONKOURÉ RIVER
map (9° 58′N 13° 42′W) **9**:397
KONOE FUMIMARO **12**:109 *bibliog.*
World War II **20**:259
KONONGO (Ghana)
map (6° 37′N 1° 11′W) **9**:164
KONSTANZ (Germany, East and West)
map (47° 40′N 9° 10′E) **9**:140
KONTUM PLATEAU
map (13° 55′N 108° 5′E) **19**:580
KONVERSATIONS-LEXICON
encyclopedia **7**:165
KONYA (Turkey) **12**:109
map (37° 52′N 32° 31′E) **19**:343
KOOCANUSA, LAKE
map (49° 0′N 115° 10′W) **13**:547
KOOCHICHING (county in Minnesota)
map (48° 15′N 93° 45′W) **13**:453
KOOK, ABRAHAM ISAAC **12**:109 *bibliog.*
KOOKABURRA **12**:109–110 *illus.*
kingfisher **12**:83
KOOLAU RANGE
map (21° 35′N 158° 0′W) **10**:72
KOONING, WILLEM DE *see* DE KOONING, WILLEM
KOONTZ LAKE (Indiana)
map (41° 25′N 86° 29′W) **11**:111
KOOPMANS, TJALLING C. **12**:110
KOOSHAREM (Utah)
map (38° 31′N 111° 53′W) **19**:492
KOOSKIA (Idaho)
map (46° 9′N 115° 59′W) **11**:26
KOOTENAI (county in Idaho)
map (47° 40′N 116° 40′W) **11**:26
KOOTENAY LAKE
map (49° 35′N 116° 50′W) **3**:491
KOPER (Yugoslavia)
map (45° 33′N 13° 44′E) **20**:340
KÖPING (Sweden)
map (59° 31′N 16° 0′E) **18**:382
KOPIT, ARTHUR
theater of fact **19**:153
KOPPA (letter)
Q (letter) **16**:3
KOPPEH MOUNTAINS
map (37° 50′N 58° 0′E) **11**:250
KÖPPEN, WLADIMIR PETER **12**:110 *bibliog.*
climatic change **5**:55–58
KOPRIVNICA (Yugoslavia)
map (46° 10′N 16° 50′E) **20**:340
KÖPRÜLÜ (family) **12**:110 *bibliog.*
KORAB MOUNTAINS
map (41° 47′N 20° 34′E) **1**:250
KORALPE MOUNTAINS
map (46° 50′N 14° 58′E) **2**:348
KORAN **12**:110 *bibliog.*
calligraphy **4**:45
Fakhr al-Din **8**:11
imam **11**:53–54
Islam **11**:288–291
Middle East, history of the **13**:402
Muhammad **13**:632
revelation **16**:184
Sharia **17**:241–242
slavery **17**:353
Tabari, Al- **19**:3
KORAT (cat) **4**:195 *illus.*; **12**:110–111 *illus.*
KORBUT, OLGA **12**:111 *illus.*; **14**:383 *illus.*
gymnastics **9**:413
KORÇË (Albania)
map (40° 37′N 20° 46′E) **1**:250
KORČULA ISLAND
map (42° 57′N 16° 50′E) **20**:340
KORDA, SIR ALEXANDER **12**:111 *bibliog.*
KORDESTAN (Iran) *see* KURDISTAN
KORDOFAN
African languages **1**:166–167 *map*
Darfur **6**:37
KORE *see* PERSEPHONE
KOREA **12**:111–116 *bibliog., illus., map, table*
agriculture, fishing, and forestry **12**:114

arts **12**:114
See also KOREAN ART
cities
Hamhung **10**:27
Inchon **11**:74
Kaesong **12**:5
Pusan **15**:631
Pyongyang **15**:634
Seoul **17**:205–206
Taegu **19**:7
Taejon **19**:7
Wonsan **20**:205
climate **12**:111–113 *table*
communism *see* COMMUNISM
demography **12**:112–113
economic activity **12**:113–114 *illus.*
education
Korean universities **12**:113–114; **12**:118–119
flags **12**:112 *illus.*
government **12**:115
health **12**:113
history *see* KOREA, HISTORY OF
land and resources **12**:111–113 *map*
language *see* KOREAN LANGUAGE
manufacturing and power **12**:114 *illus.*
Ko-Ri nuclear power station **14**:280–281 *illus.*
map (36° 30′N 128° 0′E) (South Korea) **2**:232
map (40° 0′N 127° 0′E) (North Korea) **2**:232
music **12**:115 *illus.*
people **12**:112
printing **15**:551
religion **12**:112
resources **12**:112
rivers, lakes, and waterways **12**:112
trade **12**:114; **12**:115
vegetation and animal life **12**:112
KOREA, HISTORY OF **12**:116–117 *bibliog.*
See also KOREAN WAR
Asia, history of **2**:253–254
Chun Doo Hwan **4**:422
communism **5**:149
contact with the West and Japan **12**:116–117
Japan, history of **11**:367
Kim Il Sung **12**:77
Koryo (dynasty) **12**:116
Park Chung Hee **15**:89
Pueblo Incident **15**:614
Rhee, Syngman **16**:193
Sino-Japanese Wars **17**:323
Three Kingdoms period **12**:116
Yi (dynasty) **12**:116
KOREA, NORTH *see* KOREA
KOREA, REPUBLIC OF *see* KOREA, HISTORY OF
KOREA, SOUTH *see* KOREA
KOREA BAY
map (39° 0′N 124° 0′E) **4**:362
KOREA STRAIT
map (34° 0′N 129° 0′E) **11**:361
KOREAN AMERICANS *see* ORIENTAL AMERICANS
KOREAN ART **12**:117–118 *bibliog., illus.*
celadon **4**:229
Chong Son **4**:405
folk art **8**:198
Japanese art and architecture **11**:373
lacquer basket (Han dynasty) **12**:117 *illus.*
pottery and porcelain **15**:469
Silla stoneware **12**:117 *illus.*
Tomb of the Dancing Figures (Koguryo dynasty) **12**:118 *illus.*
water bowl (Koryo period) **12**:118 *illus.*
KOREAN LANGUAGE **12**:118 *bibliog.*; **12**:355 *map*
Asia **2**:244 *map*
Ural-Altaic languages **19**:475
KOREAN UNIVERSITIES **12**:118–119 *bibliog., table*
KOREAN WAR **12**:119–122 *bibliog., illus., maps*
airborne troops **1**:210
armistice line and demilitarized zone **12**:120 *map*
Asia, history of **2**:260
Chinese intervention **12**:121
cold war **5**:98
Eisenhower, Dwight D. **7**:96
grenade **9**:358
Inchon (South Korea) **11**:74
Inchon landing **12**:120–121 *map*
infantry **11**:163
invasion of South Korea **12**:119–121
Kim Il Sung **12**:77
MacArthur, Douglas **13**:5
MacArthur's dismissal **12**:121–122
navy **14**:64–65
Ridgway, Matthew B. **16**:216
Seoul (South Korea) **17**:206
38th parallel **12**:120–121 *map*
Truman, Harry S. **19**:318
uniform **1**:207 *illus.*; **2**:182 *illus.*
United Nations **19**:413
United States, history of the **19**:456 *illus.*
Van Fleet, James Alward **19**:514
KOREKORE *see* SHONA
KOREMATSU v. UNITED STATES **12**:122
Nisei **14**:201
KORHOGO (Ivory Coast)
map (9° 27′N 5° 38′W) **11**:335
KORIN **12**:122–123 *bibliog.*
Irises **11**:377 *illus.*
KORMAKITI, CAPE OF
map (35° 24′N 32° 56′E) **5**:409
KORNBERG, ARTHUR **12**:123 *bibliog.*
Ochoa, Severo **14**:346
KORNILOV, LAVR GEORGIYEVICH **12**:123
Russian Revolutions of 1917 **16**:371; **16**:372
KORO SEA
map (18° 0′S 179° 50′E) **8**:77
KOROLEV, SERGEI **12**:123 *bibliog.*
KOROLEVU (Fiji)
map (18° 13′S 177° 44′E) **8**:77
KÖRÖS RIVER
map (46° 43′N 20° 12′E) **10**:307
KOROVIN, KONSTANTIN
Russian art and architecture **16**:363
KOROVOU (Fiji)
map (17° 57′S 178° 21′E) **8**:77
KORSAKOV, NIKOLAI ANDREYEVICH RIMSKY- *see* RIMSKY-KORSAKOV, NIKOLAI ANDREYEVICH
KORSØR (Denmark) **6**:110 *illus.*
map (55° 20′N 11° 9′E) **6**:109
KORTRIJK (Belgium)
map (50° 50′N 3° 16′E) **3**:177
KORYAK *see* CHUKCHI
KORYO (dynasty)
Korea, history of **12**:116
Korean art **12**:117–118 *illus.*
KORZENIOWSKI, JÓSEF TEODOR KONRAD *see* CONRAD, JOSEPH
KÓS (Greece) *see* COS (Greece)
KOSCIUSKO (county in Indiana)
map (41° 14′N 85° 51′W) **11**:111
KOSCIUSKO (Mississippi)
map (32° 58′N 89° 35′W) **13**:469
KOSCIUSKO, MOUNT **12**:123
map (36° 27′S 148° 16′E) **2**:328
KOŚCIUSZKO, TADEUSZ **12**:123 *bibliog.*
Kosciusko, Mount **12**:123
KOSHER **12**:123–124 *bibliog.*
dietary laws **6**:165
KOSHKONONG, LAKE
map (42° 52′N 88° 58′W) **20**:185
KOŠICE (Czechoslovakia) **12**:124
map (48° 43′N 21° 15′E) **5**:413
KOSINSKI, JERZY **12**:124 *bibliog., illus.*
KOSKENNIEMI, VEIKKO ANTERO
Finnish literature **8**:99
KOSMOS *see* COSMOS (satellite program)
KOSOVO AND METOHIJA (province in Yugoslavia)
map (42° 30′N 21° 0′E) **20**:340
KOSOVSKA MITROVICA (Yugoslavia)
map (42° 53′N 20° 52′E) **20**:340
KOSRAE ISLAND
United States outlying territories **19**:464
KOSSEL, ALBRECHT **12**:124
KOSSEL, WALTER
chemistry, history of **4**:328
KOSSUTH (county in Iowa)
map (43° 12′N 94° 15′W) **11**:244
KOSSUTH, LAJOS **12**:124 *bibliog., illus.*
Debrecen (Hungary) **6**:70
KOSTENKI (USSR) **12**:124–125 *bibliog.*
KOSYGIN, ALEKSEI N. **12**:125 *bibliog.*
KOSZALIN (Poland)
map (54° 12′N 16° 9′E) **15**:388
KOSZTOLÁNYI, DEZSŐ
Hungarian literature **10**:306
KOT DIJI (India)
Indus civilization **11**:153
KOTA BAHARU (Malaysia)
map (6° 8′N 102° 15′E) **13**:84
KOTA KINABALU (Malaysia)
map (5° 59′N 116° 4′E) **13**:84
KOTKA (Finland)
map (60° 28′N 26° 55′E) **8**:95
KOTLIK (Alaska)
map (63° 2′N 163° 33′W) **1**:242
KOTO **12**:125 *bibliog., illus.*
KOTOR BAY **20**:343 *illus.*
map (42° 25′N 18° 35′E) **20**:340
KOTTO RIVER
map (4° 14′N 22° 2′E) **4**:251
KOTZEBUE (Alaska)
map (66° 53′N 162° 39′W) **1**:242
KOTZEBUE, OTTO VON **12**:125 *bibliog.*
KOUFAX, SANDY **3**:107 *illus.*; **12**:125 *bibliog., illus.*
KOULA-MOUTOU (Gabon)
map (1° 8′S 12° 29′E) **9**:5
KOUNDOUGOU
map (11° 44′N 4° 31′W) **19**:472
KOUNTCHÉ, SEYNI
Niger **14**:188
KOUNTZE (Texas)
map (30° 23′N 94° 19′W) **19**:129
KOUPREY **14**:473 *illus.*
KOUROS **3**:507 *illus.*; **17**:160 *illus.*
KOUROU (French Guiana)
map (5° 9′N 52° 39′W) **8**:311
KOUROUSSA (Guinea)
map (10° 39′N 9° 53′W) **9**:397
KOUSSEVITZKY, SERGE **12**:125–126 *bibliog.*
Berkshire Music Festival **3**:214
KOUTS (Indiana)
map (41° 19′N 87° 2′W) **11**:111
KOVALENOK, VLADIMIR **12**:126 *bibliog.*
KOVICH, ROBERT **3**:44 *illus.*
KOVNO (USSR) *see* KAUNAS (USSR)
KOWAL, CHARLES T. **12**:126
Chiron (astronomy) **4**:397
KOWLOON (Hong Kong) **10**:222 *map*; **12**:126
KOWT-E ASHROW (Afghanistan)
map (34° 27′N 68° 48′E) **1**:133
KOYUK (Alaska)
map (64° 56′N 161° 8′W) **1**:242
KOYUKUK (Alaska)
map (64° 53′N 157° 43′W) **1**:242
KOYUKUK RIVER
map (64° 56′N 157° 30′W) **1**:242
KOZAN (Turkey)
map (37° 27′N 35° 49′E) **19**:343
KOZINTSEV, GRIGORY **12**:126
KRA, ISTHMUS OF
map (10° 20′N 99° 0′E) **19**:139
KRAAL
Masai **13**:195
KRACAUER, SIEGFRIED **12**:126
film, history of **8**:80
KRAEPELIN, EMIL **12**:126
abnormal psychology **1**:57
psychopathology, treatment of **15**:599
schizophrenia **17**:124
KRAFFT, DAVID VON
Charles XII, King of Sweden **4**:297 *illus.*
KRAFT, ADAM **12**:126 *bibliog.*
KRAGUJEVAC (Yugoslavia)
map (44° 1′N 20° 55′E) **20**:340
KRAIT **12**:126 *illus.*; **17**:377 *illus.*
KRAK DES CHEVALIERS (Syria) **12**:126–127 *bibliog.*
KRAKATOA **12**:127 *bibliog.*
map (6° 7′S 105° 24′E) **11**:147
KRAKÓW (Poland) **12**:127; **15**:389 *illus.*
map (50° 3′N 19° 58′E) **15**:388
KRALICE BIBLE
Czech literature **5**:412
KRALJEVICA (Yugoslavia)
map (45° 16′N 14° 34′E) **20**:340
KRALJEVO (Yugoslavia)
map (43° 43′N 20° 41′E) **20**:340
KRAMER, JACK **12**:127
KRAMSKOI, IVAN
Russian art and architecture **16**:362
KRANJ (Yugoslavia)
map (46° 15′N 14° 21′E) **20**:340
KRAPF, LUDWIG
Kilimanjaro **12**:76
KRASICKI, IGNACY
Polish literature **15**:398
KRASNADAR (USSR)
map (45° 2′N 39° 0′E) **19**:388
KRASNER, LEE **12**:127 *bibliog.*
KRASNODAR (USSR) **12**:127
KRASNOYARSK (USSR) **12**:127
map (56° 1′N 92° 50′E) **19**:388
KRATIE (Kampuchea)
map (12° 29′N 106° 1′E) **12**:11
KRAUS, KARL **12**:127 *bibliog.*
KRAWANG (Indonesia)
map (6° 19′S 107° 17′E) **11**:147
KRAWANG, CAPE
map (5° 56′S 107° 0′E) **11**:147
KREBS, ERNEST T., JR.
laetrile **12**:163
KREBS, ERNEST T., SR.
laetrile **12**:163
KREBS, SIR HANS ADOLF **12**:128
Krebs cycle **12**:128
KREBS CYCLE **12**:128
coenzyme **5**:92
fermentation **8**:55
lipid **12**:362
metabolism **13**:325–326
KREFELD (West Germany) **12**:128
KREISKY, BRUNO **12**:128
KREISLER, FRITZ **12**:128 *bibliog.*
KREMER, HENRY
flight, human-powered **8**:164
KREMLIN **12**:128–129 *bibliog., illus.*
Moscow **13**:597 *map*
KREMMLING (Colorado)
map (40° 3′N 106° 24′W) **5**:116
KREMS (Austria)
map (48° 25′N 15° 36′E) **2**:348
KREMS, BALTASAR
sewing machine **17**:223
KRENEK, ERNST **12**:129 *bibliog.*
KRENIVERITE
telluride minerals **19**:91
KRENNERITE **12**:129
telluride mineral **12**:129
KRESGE FOUNDATION **12**:129
KRESS, SAMUEL H. **12**:129
National Gallery of Art **14**:33
KRESSENSTEIN, KRESS VON
World War I **20**:235
KREUTZBERG, HARALD
modern dance **13**:497
KREUTZER, RODOLPHE **12**:129 *bibliog.*
KREUTZMANN, BILL
Grateful Dead, The **9**:301
KRIANGSAK CHOMANAN
Thailand **19**:141
KRIEGHOFF, CORNELIUS **12**:129 *bibliog.*
KRIGE, UYS
South Africa **18**:81
KRILL **12**:129–130 *bibliog., illus.*
fishing industry **8**:128
zooplankton **20**:378
KRIPKE, SAUL **12**:130
KRISCH, KARL VON
Tinbergen, Nikolaas **19**:206
KRISHNA (Hindu deity) **11**:97 *illus.*; **12**:130 *bibliog., illus.*
Bhagavad Gita **3**:233
KRISHNA I, RASHTRAKUTAN KING
Ellora **7**:148
KRISHNA MENON, VENEGALIL KRISHNAN **12**:130 *bibliog.*
KRISHNA RIVER
map (15° 57′N 80° 59′E) **11**:80
KRISHNAMURTI, JIDDU **12**:130 *bibliog.*
theosophy **19**:160
KRISTIANSAND (Norway) **12**:130
map (58° 10′N 8° 0′E) **14**:261
KRISTIANSTAD (Sweden)
map (56° 2′N 14° 8′E) **18**:382
KRISTIANSUND (Norway)
map (63° 7′N 7° 45′E) **14**:261
KRIVOI ROG (USSR) **12**:130
map (47° 55′N 33° 21′E) **19**:388
KRIZA, JOHN
American Ballet Theatre **1**:337
KRK ISLAND
map (45° 5′N 14° 35′E) **20**:340
KRLEŽA, MIROSLAV
Yugoslavia **20**:342
KROEBER, ALFRED L. **12**:130–131 *bibliog.*
Sauer, Carl **17**:96
KROKODIL RIVER *see* LIMPOPO RIVER
KROMDRAAI *see* STERKFONTEIN (South Africa)
KRONECKER, LEOPOLD
mathematics, history of **13**:226
KRONOS *see* CRONUS
KRONSTAD *see* BRAŞOV (Romania)
KROOMDRAAI *see* STERKFONTEIN
KROONSTAD (South Africa)
map (27° 46′S 27° 12′E) **18**:79
KROPOTKIN, PYOTR ALEKSEYEVICH **12**:131 *bibliog., illus.*
socialism **18**:20–21
KROTZ SPRINGS (Louisiana)
map (30° 32′N 91° 45′W) **12**:430
KRU **12**:131 *bibliog.*
KRUGER, PAUL **12**:131 *bibliog.*
Pretoria (South Africa) **15**:533
South African War **18**:84
KRUIF, PAUL DE *see* DE KRUIF, PAUL
KRUJË (Albania)
map (41° 30′N 19° 48′E) **1**:250
KRUMMHORN **12**:131–132 *bibliog., illus.*

KRUNG KOH KONG (Kampuchea)
map (11° 37′N 102° 59′E) **12**:11
KRUNG THEP *see* BANGKOK (Thailand)
KRUPA, GENE **12**:132
KRUPP (family) **12**:132 *bibliog.*
Essen (West Germany) **7**:244
KRUPSKAYA, NADEZHDA KONSTANTINOVNA **12**:132 *bibliog.*
KRUSEMAN, JAN ADAM
Biedermeier-style painting **3**:247 *illus.*
KRUSENSTERN, ADAM JOHANN **12**:132
Cape Krusenstern **4**:120
KRUSTEVA, OLGA
Bulgarian literature **3**:557
KRUŠVAC (Yugoslavia)
map (43° 35′N 21° 20′E) **20**:340
KRUTCH, JOSEPH WOOD **11**:132
KRYLOV, IVAN ANDREYEVICH **12**:132 *bibliog.*
KRYPTON **12**:132–133 *bibliog.*
abundances of common elements **7**:131 *table*
element **7**:130 *table*
Group O periodic table **15**:167
inert gas **11**:161
transition elements **19**:273 *table*
Travers, Morris William **19**:284
KSHATRIYA
caste **4**:186
Maratha **13**:143
Rajput **16**:78
KSHESSINSKA, MATILDE
Kirov Ballet **12**:90
KSOUR ESSAF (Tunisia)
map (35° 25′N 11° 0′E) **19**:335
KU K'AI-CHIH (Gu Kaizhi) **12**:133 *bibliog.*
Chinese art and architecture **4**:381 *illus.*
KU KLUX KLAN **12**:133 *bibliog., illus.*
radicalism **16**:44
secret societies **17**:181
Watson, Thomas E. **20**:68
KUALA LUMPUR (Malaysia) **12**:133
climate **13**:85 *table*
map (3° 10′N 101° 42′E) **13**:84
KUALA TERENGGANU (Malaysia)
map (5° 20′N 103° 8′E) **13**:84
KUAN HAN-CH'ING (Guan Hanqing) **12**:133–134 *bibliog.*
KUAN-TIN (Buddhist deity)
temple **19**:98 *illus.*
KUAN-YIN (Buddhist deity) **4**:387 *illus.*; **20**:208–209 *illus.*
KUANG-CHOU *see* CANTON (China)
KUANG-HSÜ, EMPEROR OF CHINA
Tz'u-hsi, Dowager Empress of China (Cixi) **19**:368
KUBASOV, VALERY N. **12**:134
Apollo-Soyuz Test Project **2**:84
KUBELSKY, BENJAMIN *see* BENNY, JACK
KUBIN, ALFRED **12**:134 *bibliog.*
KUBITSCHEK, JUSCELINO **12**:134 *bibliog.*
Brasília **3**:457
Niemeyer, Oscar **14**:185
KUBLAI KHAN, MONGOL EMPEROR **12**:134 *bibliog., illus.*; **15**:417 *illus.*
Asia, history of **2**:256
China, history of **4**:372
money **13**:526 *illus.*
Yüan (Yuan) (dynasty) **20**:338
KÜBLER-ROSS, ELISABETH
death and dying **6**:69
KUBRICK, STANLEY **12**:134–135 *bibliog., illus.*
KUCHING (Malaysia)
map (1° 33′N 110° 20′E) **13**:84
KUCHUK KAINARJI, TREATY OF *see* KÜCÜK KAINARJI, TREATY OF
KUCINICH, DENNIS
Cleveland (Ohio) **5**:52
KÜCÜK KAINARJI, TREATY OF
Crimean War **5**:348
Russia/Union of Soviet Socialist Republics, history of **16**:355
Russo-Turkish Wars **16**:374
KUDU **2**:46 *illus.*
KUDUS (Indonesia)
map (6° 48′S 110° 50′E) **11**:147
KUDZU **12**:135
KUEI CHIANG RIVER **4**:361 *illus.*
KUEI-LIN (China)
map (25° 11′N 110° 9′E) **4**:362
KUEI-YANG (China)
map (26° 35′N 106° 43′E) **4**:362
KUFSTEIN (Austria)
map (47° 35′N 12° 10′E) **2**:348
KUHLAU, JOHANN
Denmark **6**:111
KUHN, HANS GEORG
Moosbrugger, Caspar **13**:571
KUHN, HEINRICH **15**:257 *illus.*
photography, history and art of **15**:270
KUHN, RICHARD **12**:135
vitamins and minerals **12**:135
KUHNAU, JOHANN
German and Austrian music **9**:130
KUIBYSHEV (USSR) **12**:135
map (53° 12′N 50° 9′E) **19**:388
KUIBYSHEV RESERVOIR
map (53° 40′N 49° 0′E) **19**:629
KUINDZHI, ARKHIP
Russian art and architecture **16**:362
KUIPER, GERARD **12**:135 *bibliog.*
Lunar and Planetary Laboratory, U. of Arizona **12**:135
planets **12**:135
Saturn (astronomy) **17**:90
Yerkes Observatory **20**:327
KUIU ISLAND
map (57° 45′N 134° 10′W) **1**:242
KUJU, MOUNT
map (33° 5′N 131° 15′E) **11**:361
KUKENAAM FALLS **12**:135
KUKRI **18**:399 *illus.*
KUKRIT PRAMOJ
Thailand **19**:141
KUKULCÁN *see* QUETZALCÓATL
KULA (Yugoslavia)
map (45° 36′N 19° 32′E) **20**:340
KULA KANGRI MOUNTAIN
map (28° 3′N 90° 27′E) **3**:235
KULA RING **12**:135 *bibliog.*
Trobriand Islanders **19**:304
KULAKS **12**:135–136
Stalin, Joseph **18**:214
KULAN *see* ONAGER (animal)
KULDJA (China)
map (43° 55′N 81° 14′E) **4**:362
KULESHOV, LEV
film, history of **8**:83
KULLAB
Uruk **19**:490
KULM (North Dakota)
map (46° 24′N 98° 57′W) **14**:248
KULMBACH, HANS VON **12**:136 *bibliog.*
KULP, JOHN LAURENCE
stratigraphy **18**:293
KÜLTEPE (Turkey) **12**:136 *bibliog.*
KULTURKAMPF **12**:136
Germany, history of **9**:154
KUM (Iran) *see* QUM (Iran)
KUM RIVER
map (36° 0′N 126° 40′E) **12**:113
KUMAMOTO (Japan)
map (32° 48′N 130° 43′E) **11**:361
KUMANOVO (Yugoslavia)
map (42° 8′N 21° 43′E) **20**:340
KUMANS *see* CUMANS
KUMASI (Ghana)
climate **9**:164 *table*
map (6° 41′N 1° 35′W) **9**:164
KUMIN, MAXINE **12**:136
KUMON RANGE
map (26° 30′N 97° 15′E) **3**:573
KUMQUAT **12**:136 *illus.*
citrus fruits **4**:448
KUN, BÉLA **12**:136 *bibliog.*
K'UN-LUN SHAN *see* KUNLUN MOUNTAINS
K'UN-MING (Kunming) (China) **12**:136
map (25° 5′N 102° 40′E) **4**:362
KUNDERA, MILAN **12**:136–137
!KUNG *see* SAN
KUNG, H. H.
Soong (family) **18**:66
KÜNG, HANS **12**:137
KUNG FU
martial arts **13**:177 *illus.*
K'UNG SHANG-JEN (Kong Shangren)
Chinese literature **4**:390
KUNITZ, STANLEY J. **11**:137
KUNIYOSHI (Utagawa) **12**:137 *bibliog.*
KUNIYOSHI, YASUO **12**:137 *bibliog.*
KUNLUN MOUNTAINS **12**:137
map (36° 30′N 88° 0′W) **4**:362
KUNMING (China) *see* K'UN-MING (Kunming) (China)
KUNSAN (Korea)
map (35° 58′N 126° 41′E) **12**:113
KUNSTLER, WILLIAM **12**:137
KUO HSI (Guo Xi) **12**:137 *bibliog.*
KUO MO-JO (Guo Moruo) **12**:137 *bibliog.*
KUOMINTANG (Guomindang) **12**:137–138 *bibliog., illus.*
Asia, history of **2**:259
Chiang Kai-shek **4**:339
China, history **4**:375–376
communism in China **5**:148
Mao Tse-tung (Mao Zedong) **13**:135
Northern Expedition **14**:254
Sun Yat-sen **18**:346
Wang Ching-wei (Wang Jingwei) **20**:22
warlords **20**:30
KUOPIO (Finland)
map (62° 54′N 27° 41′E) **8**:95
KUPANG (Indonesia)
map (10° 10′S 123° 35′E) **11**:147
KUPFFER CELL
liver **12**:374
KUPKA, FRANTIŠEK **12**:138 *bibliog., illus.*
Fugue in Red and Blue **12**:138 *illus.*
KUPPER, CHRISTIAN CURIL MARIE *see* DOESBURG, THEO VAN
KUPREANOF ISLAND
map (56° 50′N 133° 30′W) **1**:242
KUPRIN, ALEKSANDR IVANOVICH **12**:138 *bibliog.*
KURASHIKI (Japan)
map (34° 35′N 133° 46′E) **11**:361
KURCHATOV, IGOR
element 104 **7**:132
KURCHATOVIUM
superheavy elements **18**:351
KURDISTAN **12**:138–139 *bibliog., map*
Kurds **12**:139
KURDS **12**:139 *bibliog.*
Iraq **11**:254
Kurdistan **12**:138–139 *illus.*
Persia, ancient **15**:181
Qashqai **16**:3
KURDUFAN (region in Sudan)
map (12° 0′N 27° 0′E) **18**:320
KURDZHALI (Bulgaria)
map (41° 39′N 25° 22′E) **3**:555
KURGAN (USSR)
map (55° 26′N 65° 18′E) **19**:388
KURIL ISLANDS **12**:139
map (46° 10′N 152° 0′E) **19**:388
Ring of Fire **16**:225
KURIL TRENCH
oceanic trenches **14**:341–342
Pacific Ocean bottom **15**:6–7 *map*
plate tectonics **15**:351 *map*
KURILE ISLANDS *see* KURIL ISLANDS
KUROSAWA, AKIRA **12**:139 *bibliog.*
film, history of **8**:86 *illus.*
KUROSHIO CURRENT
ocean-atmosphere interaction **14**:321
KURSK (USSR)
map (51° 42′N 36° 12′E) **19**:388
KURTISTOWN (Hawaii)
map (19° 36′N 155° 4′W) **10**:72
KURU
diseases, animal **6**:191
nervous system, diseases of the **14**:96
psychosomatic disorders **15**:602
KURUKH
Dravidian languages **6**:263
KURUME (Japan)
map (33° 19′N 130° 31′E) **11**:361
KURUNEGALA (Sri Lanka)
map (7° 29′N 80° 22′E) **18**:206
KURZHAAR *see* GERMAN SHORTHAIRED POINTER
KUSCH, POLYKARP **12**:139
KUSH *see* CUSH
KUSKOKWIM BAY
map (59° 45′N 162° 25′W) **1**:242
KUSKOKWIM MOUNTAINS
map (62° 30′N 156° 0′W) **1**:242
KUSNASOSRO *see* SUKARNO
KUSTI (Sudan)
map (13° 10′N 32° 40′E) **18**:320
KUTAHYA (Turkey)
map (39° 25′N 29° 59′E) **19**:343
KUTCH, GULF OF
map (22° 36′N 69° 30′E) **11**:80
KUTCH, RANN OF
India-Pakistan Wars **11**:93
KUTENAI (American Indians) **12**:139–140 *bibliog.*
Flathead **8**:155
KUTNO (Poland)
map (52° 15′N 19° 23′E) **15**:388
KUTUZOV, MIKHAIL ILLARIONOVICH **12**:140 *bibliog.*
Napoleonic Wars **14**:19
KUTZTOWN (Pennsylvania)
map (40° 31′N 75° 47′W) **15**:147
KUVASZ **6**:215 *illus.*; **12**:140 *bibliog., illus.*
KUWAIT (city) **12**:141 *illus.*
climate **12**:141 *table*
map (29° 20′N 47° 59′E) **12**:141
KUWAIT (country) **12**:140–142 *bibliog., illus., map, table*
desalination **6**:125 *illus.*
economic activity **12**:141
education **2**:104 *illus.*
Middle Eastern universities **13**:410–412 *table*
flag **12**:140 *illus.*
government **12**:141
history **12**:141–142
map (29° 30′N 47° 45′E) **2**:232
people **12**:140–141
women in society **20**:204 *table*
Saudi Arabia border **17**:93
KUWAIT BAY
map (29° 30′N 48° 0′E) **12**:141
KUYBYSHEV (USSR) *see* KUIBYSHEV (USSR)
KUYUNJIK *see* NINEVEH (Iraq)
KUZBAS *see* KUZNETSK BASIN
KUZNETS, SIMON S. **12**:142
KUZNETSK BASIN **12**:142
KVARNER, GULF OF
map (44° 45′N 14° 15′E) **20**:340
KVASS (beer) **3**:163
KVERK MOUNTAIN
map (64° 43′N 16° 38′W) **11**:17
KWAHU PLATEAU
map (6° 30′N 0° 30′W) **9**:164
KWAJALEIN (Marshall Islands)
World War II **20**:276
KWAKIUTL (American Indians) **11**:127 *illus.*; **12**:142 *bibliog.*
Boas, Franz **3**:349 *illus.*
cannibalism **4**:109 *illus.*
Indians of North America, art of the **11**:139
mask **11**:139 *illus.*; **13**:197 *illus.*
Nootka **14**:217
potlatch **15**:467
primitive societies **15**:546
Tsimshian **19**:324
KWAKOEGRON (Suriname)
map (5° 15′N 55° 20′W) **18**:364
KWANG HSU, EMPEROR OF CHINA *see* KUANG-HSÜ, EMPEROR OF CHINA
KWANGCHOW *see* CANTON (China)
KWANGJU (Korea)
map (35° 9′N 126° 54′E) **12**:113
KWANGO RIVER
map (3° 14′S 17° 23′E) **20**:350
KWANGSI (Guangxi) (China) **4**:361 *illus.*; **12**:142
KWANGTUNG (Guangdong) (China) **12**:142
Canton (Guangzhou) **4**:117–118 *illus.*
Hainan **10**:14
KWANMO, MOUNT
map (41° 42′N 129° 13′E) **12**:113
KWASHIORKOR **12**:142–143
marasmus **13**:143
nutritional-deficiency diseases **14**:307
protein **15**:574
starvation **18**:228
KWEICHOW (Guizhon) (China) **2**:143
KWEICHOW PLATEAU
map (27° 0′N 107° 0′E) **4**:362
KWEKWE (Zimbabwe)
map (18° 55′S 29° 49′E) **20**:365
KWIC (Keyword in Context) INDEXING
information science **11**:172
KWILU RIVER
map (3° 22′S 17° 22′E) **20**:350
KYAIKTO (Burma)
map (17° 18′N 97° 1′E) **3**:573
KYANITE **12**:143 *illus.*
facies
metamorphic rock **13**:332 *table*
occurrence **12**:143
optical mineralogy **14**:408 *illus.*
refractory products manufacture **12**:143
sillimanite **17**:309
staurolite **18**:239
KYD, THOMAS **12**:143 *bibliog.*
Spanish Tragedy, The (play)
drama **6**:259 *illus.*
KYLE (Saskatchewan)
map (50° 50′N 108° 2′W) **17**:81
KYMOGRAPH
zoology **20**:377
KYOGA, LAKE
map (1° 30′N 33° 0′E) **19**:372
KYOGEN **12**:143 *bibliog.*
Kabuki **12**:4
KYONGGI BAY
map (37° 25′N 126° 0′E) **12**:113
KYOTO (Japan) **11**:364 *illus.*; **12**:143
See also HEIAN
Byodoin temple **19**:99 *illus.*
garden **9**:41 *illus.*
Japan, history of **11**:369
Japanese art and architecture **11**:374
map (35° 0′N 135° 45′E) **11**:361
KYPRIANOU, SPYRAS
Cyprus **5**:409

KYRENIA (Cyprus) **5**:408 *illus.*
map (35° 20′N 33° 19′E) **5**:409
KYSICA MOUNTAIN
map (50° 54′N 20° 55′E) **15**:388
KYUSHU (Japan) **12**:143
cities
Fukuoka **8**:356
Kitakyushu **12**:91
Nagasaki **14**:6
KYUSHU ISLAND
map (33° 0′N 131° 0′E) **11**:361
KYUSTENDIL (Bulgaria)
map (42° 17′N 22° 41′E) **3**:555
KYZYL KUM **12**:143
map (42° 0′N 64° 0′E) **19**:388
people
Karakalpak **12**:26

L

L (letter) **12**:144 *illus.*
L-DOPA *see* LEVODOPA
l-TRYPTOPHAN
sedative **17**:182
L-1011 TRISTAR AIRCRAFT **1**:127 *illus.*
LA *see* under the element of the name following LA, except for entries listed below
LA BANDA (Argentina)
map (27° 44′S 64° 15′W) **2**:149
LA BARGE (Wyoming)
map (42° 16′N 110° 12′W) **20**:301
LA BELLE (Florida)
map (26° 46′N 81° 26′W) **8**:172
LA BREA (Trinidad and Tobago)
map (10° 15′N 61° 37′W) **19**:300
LA BREA TAR PIT **12**:144–145 *bibliog., illus.*
fossil record **8**:244; **12**:144–145
Los Angeles (California) **12**:417 *map*
Pleistocene Epoch **15**:366–367 *illus.*
LA BROA BAY
map (22° 35′N 82° 0′W) **5**:377
LA BRUYÈRE, JEAN DE **12**:145 *bibliog.*
LA CALERA (Chile)
map (32° 47′S 71° 12′W) **4**:355
LA CEIBA (Honduras)
map (15° 47′N 86° 50′W) **10**:218
LA-CHAUX-DE-FONDS (Switzerland)
map (47° 6′N 6° 50′E) **18**:394
LA CHORRERA (Colombia)
map (0° 44′S 73° 1′W) **5**:107
LA CHORRERA (Panama)
map (8° 53′N 79° 47′W) **15**:55
LA COLORADO (Mexico)
map (28° 41′N 110° 25′W) **13**:357
LA CONCEPCIÓN (Venezuela)
map (10° 38′N 71° 50′W) **19**:542
LA CORUÑA (Spain) **12**:145
map (43° 22′N 8° 23′W) **18**:140
LA CRESCENT (Minnesota)
map (43° 50′N 91° 19′W) **13**:453
LA CROSSE (Indiana)
map (41° 19′N 86° 53′W) **11**:111
LA CROSSE (Kansas)
map (38° 32′N 99° 18′W) **12**:18
LA CROSSE (Virginia)
map (36° 42′N 78° 6′W) **19**:607
LA CROSSE (Wisconsin) **12**:145
map (43° 49′N 91° 15′W) **20**:185
LA CROSSE (county in Wisconsin)
map (43° 53′N 91° 7′W) **20**:185
LA CRUZ (Costa Rica)
map (11° 4′N 85° 39′W) **5**:291
LA CRUZ (Uruguay)
map (33° 58′S 56° 15′W) **19**:488
LA DIGUE ISLAND
map (4° 21′S 55° 50′E) **19**:574
LA DORADA (Colombia)
map (5° 27′N 74° 40′W) **5**:107
LA ENCANTADA, MOUNT
map (31° 0′N 115° 24′W) **13**:357
LA ESMERALDA (Mexico)
map (27° 17′N 103° 39′W) **13**:357
LA ESMERALDA (Paraguay)
map (22° 13′S 62° 38′W) **15**:77
LA ESPERANZA (Honduras)
map (14° 20′N 88° 10′W) **10**:218
LA ESTRELLA (Bolivia)
map (16° 30′S 63° 45′W) **3**:366
LA FARGE (Wisconsin)
map (43° 35′N 90° 38′W) **20**:185
LA FARGE, JOHN **12**:195 *bibliog.*
stained glass **18**:212
LA FARGE, OLIVER HAZARD PERRY **12**:145 *bibliog.*
LA FAYETTE, COMTESSE DE **12**:145 *bibliog.*
LA FERASSIE (France)
funeral customs **8**:365
LA FLESCHE, CHIEF JOSEPH
Omaha (American Indians) **14**:385
LA FLESCHE, FRANCIS
Fletcher, Alice **8**:163
LA FLORIDA (Guatemala)
map (16° 33′N 90° 27′W) **9**:389
LA FOLLETTE (Tennessee)
map (36° 23′N 84° 7′W) **19**:104
LA FOLLETTE, ROBERT M. **12**:145–146 *bibliog., illus.*
Progressive party **15**:564
LA FONTAINE (Indiana)
map (40° 40′N 85° 43′W) **11**:111
LA FONTAINE, JEAN DE **12**:146 *bibliog., illus.*
fable **8**:4–5
LA FRESNAYE, ROGER DE **12**:146 *bibliog.*
LA GALITE ISLAND
map (37° 32′N 8° 56′E) **19**:335
LA GOULETTE (Tunisia)
map (36° 49′N 10° 18′E) **19**:335
LA GRANDE (Oregon)
map (45° 20′N 118° 5′W) **14**:427
LA GRANGE (Georgia)
map (33° 2′N 85° 2′W) **9**:114
LA GRANGE (Illinois)
map (41° 49′N 87° 55′W) **11**:42
LA GRANGE (Kentucky)
map (38° 24′N 85° 23′W) **12**:47
LA GRANGE (Maine)
map (45° 10′N 68° 51′W) **13**:70
LA GRANGE (North Carolina)
map (35° 19′N 77° 47′W) **14**:242
LA GRANGE (Texas)
map (29° 54′N 96° 52′W) **19**:129
LA GRAVETTE *see* GRAVETTIAN
LA GUAIRA (Venezuela) **12**:146–147
map (10° 36′N 66° 56′W) **19**:542
LA GUARDIA (Bolivia)
map (17° 54′S 63° 20′W) **3**:366
LA GUARDIA, FIORELLO **12**:147 *bibliog., illus.*
Tammany Hall **19**:20
LA GUARDIA-NORRIS ACT *see* NORRIS-LA GUARDIA ACT
LA GUMA, ALEX **12**:147
LA HABRA (California)
map (33° 56′N 117° 57′W) **4**:31
LA HAGUE, CAPE
map (49° 43′N 1° 57′W) **8**:260
LA HARPE (Kansas)
map (37° 55′N 95° 18′W) **12**:18
LA HAVE RIVER
map (44° 14′N 64° 20′W) **14**:269
LA HIRE, LAURENT DE **12**:147 *bibliog.*
LA ISABELA (Cuba)
map (22° 57′N 80° 1′W) **5**:377
LA JARA (Colorado)
map (37° 16′N 105° 58′W) **5**:116
LA JUNTA (Colorado)
map (37° 59′N 103° 33′W) **5**:116
LA LECHE LEAGUE
breast feeding **3**:469
LA LIBERTAD (El Salvador)
map (13° 29′N 89° 19′W) **7**:100
LA LOCHE (Saskatchewan)
map (56° 29′N 109° 27′W) **17**:81
LA LOUVIÈRE (Belgium)
map (50° 28′N 4° 11′E) **3**:177
LA MADELEINE (France) *see* MAGDALENIAN
LA MALBAIE (Quebec)
map (47° 39′N 70° 10′W) **16**:18
LA MAMA EXPERIMENTAL THEATRE CLUB
Serban, André **17**:207
LA MARMORA PEAK
map (39° 59′N 9° 19′E) **11**:321
LA MARQUE (Texas)
map (29° 22′N 94° 58′W) **19**:129
LA MASSANA (Andorra)
map (42° 32′N 1° 31′E) **1**:405
LA MERCED (Peru)
map (11° 3′S 75° 19′W) **15**:193
LA MERI **12**:147 *bibliog.*
LA MESA (New Mexico)
map (32° 7′N 106° 42′W) **14**:136
LA MOILLE (Illinois)
map (41° 32′N 89° 17′W) **11**:42
LA MOINE RIVER
map (39° 59′N 90° 31′W) **11**:42
LA MOTTE, PIERRE DE ST. PAUL, SIEUR DE
Vermont **19**:553
LA MOURE (North Dakota)
map (46° 21′N 98° 18′W) **14**:248
LA MOURE (county in North Dakota)
map (46° 30′N 98° 30′W) **14**:248
LA OROYA (Peru)
map (11° 32′S 75° 54′W) **15**:193
LA PALMA (El Salvador)
map (14° 19′N 89° 11′W) **7**:100
LA PALMA (Panama)
map (7° 42′N 80° 12′W) **15**:55
LA PAMPA (province in Argentina)
map (38° 30′S 65° 0′W) **2**:149
LA PARAGUA (Venezuela)
map (6° 50′N 63° 20′W) **19**:542
LA PAZ (Argentina)
map (30° 45′S 59° 39′W) **2**:149
LA PAZ (Bolivia) **3**:367–368 *illus., table*; **12**:147–148 *illus.*
map (16° 30′S 68° 9′W) **3**:366
LA PAZ (Mexico) **12**:148
climate **13**:356 *table*
map (24° 10′N 110° 18′W) **13**:357
LA PAZ (Uruguay)
map (34° 46′S 56° 15′W) **19**:488
LA PÉROUSE, JEAN FRANÇOIS DE GALAUP, COMTE DE **8**:271 *illus.*; **12**:148 *bibliog.*
LA PEROUSE STRAIT
map (45° 45′N 142° 0′E) **11**:361
LA PINE (Oregon)
map (43° 40′N 121° 30′W) **14**:427
LA PLACE (Louisiana)
map (30° 4′N 90° 29′W) **12**:430
LA PLATA (Argentina) **12**:148
map (34° 55′S 57° 57′W) **2**:149
LA PLATA (county in Colorado)
map (37° 20′N 107° 50′W) **5**:116
LA PLATA (Maryland)
map (38° 32′N 76° 59′W) **13**:188
LA PLATA (Missouri)
map (40° 2′N 92° 29′W) **13**:476
LA PORTE (Indiana)
map (41° 36′N 86° 43′W) **11**:111
LA PORTE (county in Indiana)
map (41° 36′N 86° 43′W) **11**:111
LA PORTE CITY (Iowa)
map (42° 19′N 92° 12′W) **11**:244
LA PRYOR (Texas)
map (28° 57′N 99° 51′W) **19**:129
LA RIOJA (Argentina)
map (29° 26′S 66° 51′W) **2**:149
LA RIOJA (province in Argentina)
map (30° 0′S 67° 30′W) **2**:149
LA ROCHEFOUCAULD, FRANÇOIS, DUC DE **12**:148 *bibliog.*
La Fayette, Comtesse de **12**:145
LA ROCHELLE (France) **12**:148
map (46° 10′N 1° 10′W) **8**:260
LA ROMANA (Dominican Republic)
map (18° 25′N 68° 58′W) **6**:233
LA RONGE (Saskatchewan)
map (55° 6′N 105° 17′W) **17**:81
LA RONGE, LAKE
map (55° 10′N 105° 0′W) **17**:81
LA RUE (Ohio)
map (40° 35′N 83° 23′W) **14**:357
LA RUE, PIERRE DE
mass (musical setting) **13**:201
LA SAL (Utah)
map (38° 19′N 109° 15′W) **19**:492
LA SALLE (Colorado)
map (40° 21′N 104° 42′W) **5**:116
LA SALLE (Illinois)
map (41° 20′N 89° 6′W) **11**:42
LA SALLE (county in Illinois)
map (41° 25′N 88° 55′W) **11**:42
LA SALLE (county in Louisiana)
map (31° 40′N 92° 10′W) **12**:430
LA SALLE (county in Texas)
map (28° 20′N 99° 5′W) **19**:129
LA SALLE, JOHN BAPTIST DE, SAINT *see* JOHN BAPTIST DE LA SALLE, SAINT
LA SALLE, ROBERT CAVELIER, SIEUR DE **12**:149 *bibliog., illus., map*
Canada, exploration of **4**:80 *map*
exploration **7**:336–337 *map*
exploration of colonial America **19**:437 *map*
Mississippi River **13**:473
Ohio **14**:361
Ohio River **14**:363
Peoria (Illinois) **15**:156
South Bend (Indiana) **18**:96
Tonty, Henri de **19**:235
LA SARRE (Quebec)
map (48° 48′N 79° 12′W) **16**:18
LA SCALA **12**:149 *bibliog.*
Abbado, Claudio **1**:52
Gatti-Casazza, Giulio **9**:58–59
Giulini, Carlo Maria **9**:191
LA SCIE (Newfoundland)
map (49° 57′N 55° 36′W) **14**:166
LA SELLE PEAK
map (18° 22′N 71° 59′W) **10**:15
LA SERENA (Chile)
map (29° 54′S 71° 16′W) **4**:355
LA SOULE (sport)
sports, history of **18**:196
LA SPEZIA (Italy) **12**:149–150
map (44° 7′N 9° 50′E) **11**:321
LA TASAJERA (El Salvador)
map (13° 16′N 88° 52′W) **7**:100
LA TÈNE (Switzerland) **12**:150 *bibliog.*
Celtic art **4**:238–240
Celts **4**:241; **4**:242 *illus.*
European prehistory **7**:305–306
LA TOUR, CHARLES
Saint John (New Brunswick) **17**:19
LA TOUR, GEORGES DE **12**:150 *bibliog., illus.*
The New Born **12**:150 *illus.*
LA TOUR, MAURICE QUENTIN DE **12**:150–151 *bibliog.*
Pompadour, Jeanne Antoinette Poisson, Marquise de **15**:423 *illus.*
LA TOUR D'AUVERGNE, HENRI DE, VICOMTE DE TURENNE *see* TURENNE, HENRI DE LA TOUR D'AUVERGNE, VICOMTE DE
LA TRINITÉ (Caen, France)
Norman architecture **14**:220
LA TUQUE (Quebec)
map (47° 26′N 72° 47′W) **16**:18
LA UNIÓN (El Salvador)
map (13° 20′N 87° 51′W) **7**:100
LA URBANA (Venezuela)
map (7° 8′N 66° 56′W) **19**:542
LA VALE (Maryland)
map (39° 39′N 78° 49′W) **13**:188
LA VALLEY (Colorado)
map (37° 6′N 105° 22′W) **5**:116
LA VEGA (Dominican Republic)
map (19° 13′N 70° 31′W) **6**:233
LA VENTA (Mexico) **12**:151 *bibliog.*; **14**:237 *map*
Olmec **14**:380
pre-Columbian art and architecture **15**:496 *illus.*
LA VÉRENDRYE, PIERRE GAULTIER DE VARENNES, SIEUR DE **12**:151 *bibliog.*
Missouri River **13**:481
North Dakota **14**:251
Red River of the North **16**:113
Saskatchewan River **17**:83
Winnipeg (Manitoba) **20**:180
LA VERGNE (Tennessee)
map (36° 2′N 86° 39′W) **19**:104
LA VETA (Colorado)
map (37° 31′N 105° 0′W) **5**:116
LA VISTA (Nebraska)
map (41° 10′N 96° 3′W) **14**:70
LA ZARCA (Mexico)
map (25° 50′N 104° 44′W) **13**:357
LAAU POINT
map (21° 6′N 157° 19′W) **10**:72
LABADIEVILLE (Louisiana)
map (29° 50′N 90° 57′W) **12**:430
LABAN, RUDOLF VON **12**:151 *bibliog.*
LABÉ (Guinea)
map (11° 19′N 12° 17′W) **9**:397
LABE RIVER *see* ELBE RIVER
LABETTE (county in Kansas)
map (37° 10′N 95° 15′W) **12**:18
LABICHE, EUGÈNE MARIN **12**:151 *bibliog.*
LABILLE-GUIARD, ADÉLAIDE **12**:151 *bibliog.*
LABOR (childbirth) *see* PREGNANCY AND BIRTH
LABOR, U.S. DEPARTMENT OF **12**:151–152
diseases, occupational **6**:194
flag **8**:148 *illus.*
government regulation **9**:271
Occupational Safety and Health Administration **14**:320
public health **15**:608
secretary of labor *see* articles of specific presidents, e.g., HOOVER, HERBERT; JOHNSON, LYNDON B.; etc.; names of specific secretaries of labor, e.g., PERKINS, FRANCES; WILSON, W. B.; etc.
Washington, D.C. **20**:41 *map*
LABOR CAMP *see* CONCENTRATION CAMP
LABOR DAY **12**:152
LABOR FORCE **12**:152 *bibliog.*
See also EMPLOYMENT AND UNEMPLOYMENT
Bagley, Sarah G. **3**:22
child labor **4**:350
civilization **5**:34
domestic service **6**:231–232
Fair Labor Standards Act of 1938
Hammer v. *Dagenhart* **10**:30
Hawthorne studies **10**:79
Incan state organization **11**:72
indentured service **11**:78
industrial psychology **11**:157
Kelley, Florence **12**:38
Lochner v. *New York* **12**:386
Marxism **13**:183–184
migrant labor **13**:417
slavery **17**:351–357

LABOR FORCE (cont.)
women in society **20**:202; **20**:203–204 *table*
young people **20**:335–336
LABOR-MANAGEMENT RELATIONS ACT **12**:152 *bibliog.*
boycott **3**:433
closed shop **5**:65
injunction **11**:178
Labor-Management Reporting and Disclosure Act **12**:152
National Labor Relations Act **14**:34
National Labor Relations Board **14**:35
right-to-work laws **16**:222
Taft, Robert A. **19**:7
Truman, Harry S. **19**:318
LABOR-MANAGEMENT REPORTING AND DISCLOSURE ACT **12**:152
injunction **11**:178
Labor-Management Relations Act **12**:152
National Labor Relations Act **14**:34
LABOR AND SOCIALIST INTERNATIONAL *see* INTERNATIONAL, SOCIALIST
LABOR STATISTICS, U.S. BUREAU OF
consumer price index **5**:225
employment and unemployment **7**:160
labor force **12**:152
LABOR THEORY OF VALUE
Marxism **13**:183–184
Ricardo, David **16**:206
Smith, Alan **17**:366–367
LABOR UNION **12**:152–156 *bibliog., illus., table*
See also INDUSTRIAL RELATIONS
Actors' Equity Association **1**:90
Amalgamated Clothing and Textile Workers Union **1**:321
American Federation of Labor and Congress of Industrial Organizations **1**:338–339
American Federation of Musicians **1**:339
American Federation of State, County, and Municipal Employees **1**:339
American Federation of Teachers **1**:339
apprenticeship **2**:91
arbitration (labor-management and commercial) **2**:110
Carpenters and Joiners of America, United Brotherhood of **4**:164
closed shop **5**:65
clothing industry **5**:65–66
collective bargaining **12**:153–154
game theory **9**:27–29
Communication Workers of America **5**:142
community and junior colleges **5**:152
Depression of the 1930s **6**:120
Electrical, Radio and Machine Workers, International Union of **7**:106
Electrical Workers, International Brotherhood of **7**:107
featherbedding **8**:40
Great Britain
Trades Union Congress **19**:264
Transport and General Workers' Union **19**:277
grievance procedure **9**:362
Haymarket Riot **10**:83
Homestead strike **10**:214
Hotel and Restaurant Employees and Bartenders International Union **10**:262
industrial relations **11**:157–158
industrial union **11**:160
Industrial Workers of the World **11**:160
integration, racial **11**:202
International Association of Machinists and Aerospace Workers **11**:218
International Confederation of Free Trade Unions **11**:219
International Ladies' Garment Workers' Union **11**:221
international longshoremen's unions **11**:222
International Typographical Union **11**:224–225
Knights of Labor **12**:101
Labor-Management Relations Act **12**:152
Labor-Management Reporting and Disclosure Act **12**:152
largest unions in U.S. **12**:156 *table*
leaders
Abel, I. W. **1**:55
Bagley, Sarah G. **3**:22
Bevin, Ernest **3**:233
Bridges, Harry **3**:484–485
Bustamante, Sir Alexander **3**:590
Chavez, Cesar **4**:305
Chicano **4**:343
Debs, Eugene V. **6**:70–71
Dubinsky, David **6**:287
Fitzsimmons, Frank Edward **8**:132
Flynn, Elizabeth Gurley **8**:191
Gierek, Edward **9**:177
Gompers, Samuel **9**:241
Green, William **9**:347
Haywood, William Dudley **10**:84
Hill, Joe **10**:164
Hillman, Sidney **10**:165
Hoffa, James R. **10**:194–195
Jones, Mother **11**:443–444
Kirkland, Lane **12**:89
Lewis, John L. **12**:306
Meany, George **13**:253
Murray, Philip **13**:650
Owen, Robert **14**:471
Randolph, A. Philip **16**:83
Reuther, Walter P. **16**:184
Wałesa, Lech **20**:11
Wilson, W. B. **20**:165
Woodcock, Leonard **20**:210
legislation **12**:156
May Day **13**:242
membership in U.S. **12**:156 *table*
National Education Association **14**:32
National Labor Relations Act **14**:34
National Labor Relations Board **14**:35
National Labor Relations Board v. *Jones & Laughlin Steel Corporation* **14**:35
New Deal era **12**:155–156
Newspaper Guild **14**:173
open shop **14**:398
pension **15**:154
Pinkerton, Allan **15**:307
Poland **15**:391
political action **12**:154
Railway Brotherhoods **16**:77
right-to-work laws **16**:222
Roosevelt, Theodore **16**:310
sabotage **17**:6
socialism **18**:21
special-interest groups **18**:167–168
statistics **12**:156 *tables*
strike **18**:298
syndicalism **18**:407
Teamsters, Chauffeurs, Warehousemen, and Helpers of America, International Brotherhood of **19**:58 *bibliog.*
union label **19**:387
union shop **19**:387
United Auto Workers **19**:401
United Farm Workers
migrant labor **13**:417
United Mine Workers of America **19**:411–412
United States, history of the **19**:451; **19**:457
United Steelworkers of America **19**:465
Wagner, Robert F., Sr. **20**:6
West Virginia **20**:114
World Federation of Trade Unions **20**:218
yellow-dog contract **20**:322
LABORATORY, ASTRONOMICAL *see* ASTRONOMY AND ASTROPHYSICS—research institutions
LABORATORY, CLINICAL
diagnostic tests **6**:149–150
LABORATORY, SCIENTIFIC *see* SCIENTIFIC RESEARCH
LABORATORY ANIMAL ACT (United States)
vivisection **19**:623
LABOUR PARTY (New Zealand)
Savage, Michael Joseph **17**:97
socialism **18**:22–23
LABOUR PARTY (United Kingdom) **12**:156–157 *bibliog.*
Attlee, Clement, 1st Earl Attlee **2**:315–316
Benn, Anthony Wedgwood **3**:202
Bevan, Aneurin **3**:232
Bevin, Ernest **3**:233
Callaghan, James **4**:40
Cripps, Sir Stafford **5**:350–351
Fabian Society **8**:4
Foot, Michael **8**:214
Gaitskell, Hugh **9**:9
Great Britain, history of **9**:317–318
Healey, Denis **10**:86
Henderson, Arthur **10**:121
Kinnock, Neil **12**:84
Laski, Harold **12**:214
MacDonald, Ramsay **13**:12–13
socialism **18**:22–23 *illus.*
Wilson, Sir Harold **20**:164–165
LABOV, WILLIAM
sociolinguistic variation **18**:27–28
LABRADOR (Canada) **12**:157
Churchill Falls **4**:427
Churchill River (Newfoundland) **4**:427
Goose Bay **9**:247
LABRADOR CURRENT
ocean currents and wind systems, worldwide **14**:322–323 *maps*
LABRADOR RETRIEVER **6**:213 *illus.*; **6**:218 *illus.*; **12**:157 *bibliog., illus.*
guide dog **9**:394
LABRADOR SEA
map (57° 0′N 53° 0′W) **4**:70
LABRADORITE **13**:440 *illus.*
feldspar **8**:46
LABROUSTE, HENRI **12**:157 *bibliog.*
LABRUNIE, GÉRARD *see* NERVAL, GÉRARD DE
LABUAN (Malaysia)
Straits Settlements **18**:288
LABUTTA (Burma)
map (16° 9′N 94° 46′E) **3**:573
LABYRINTH FISH
Betta **3**:232
Siamese fighting fish **17**:291
LABYRINTH AND MAZE **12**:157–158 *bibliog.*
architecture **2**:129
LAC *see* LACQUER
LAC DES ALLEMANDS RIVER
map (29° 55′N 90° 35′W) **12**:430
LAC DU FLAMBEAU (Wisconsin)
map (45° 58′N 89° 53′W) **20**:185
LAC GIAO (Vietnam)
map (12° 40′N 108° 3′E) **19**:580
LAC LA BICHE (Alberta)
map (54° 46′N 111° 58′W) **1**:256
LAC LA CROIX
map (48° 21′N 92° 5′W) **13**:453
LAC QUI PARLE (county in Minnesota)
map (45° 0′N 96° 8′W) **13**:453
LAC SEUL
map (50° 20′N 92° 30′W) **14**:393
LACAILLE, NICOLAS LOUIS DE **12**:158
LACAN, JACQUES **12**:158
LACANDÓN (American Indians) **12**:158 *bibliog.*
LACANTUM RIVER
map (16° 36′N 90° 39′W) **9**:389
LACCADIVE ISLANDS (India) **12**:158
map (10° 0′N 73° 0′E) **11**:80
LACCOLITH **12**:158
LACE **12**:158–160 *bibliog., illus.*
Chantilly lace **12**:159 *illus.*
needlework **14**:76 *illus.*
LACERTID **12**:160
LACEWING **11**:192 *illus.*; **12**:160 *illus.*
aphid **2**:77
LACEY (Washington)
map (47° 7′N 122° 49′W) **20**:35
LACHAISE, GASTON **12**:160 *bibliog.*
LACHISH (Israel) **12**:160 *bibliog.*
LACHLAN RIVER
map (34° 21′S 143° 57′E) **2**:328
LACHRYMAL GLAND
tear gas **19**:58
tears **19**:58
LACHUTE (Quebec)
map (45° 38′N 74° 20′W) **16**:18
LACKAWANNA (New York)
map (42° 49′N 78° 50′W) **14**:149
LACKAWANNA (county in Pennsylvania)
map (41° 24′N 75° 40′W) **15**:147
LACKAWANNA RIVER **12**:160
LACLEDE (county in Missouri)
map (37° 40′N 92° 35′W) **13**:476
LACLÈDE, PIERRE
St. Louis (Missouri) **17**:22
LACOMBE (Alberta)
map (52° 28′N 113° 44′W) **1**:256
LACON (Illinois)
map (41° 2′N 89° 24′W) **11**:42
LACONA (Iowa)
map (41° 12′N 93° 23′W) **11**:244
LACONIA (New Hampshire)
map (43° 31′N 71° 29′W) **14**:123
LACOOCHEE (Florida)
map (28° 28′N 82° 10′W) **8**:172
LACQUER **12**:160–161 *bibliog., illus.*
Chinese art and architecture **4**:383–384 *illus.*
paint **15**:16
shellac **17**:252
LACROIX, SYLVESTRE FRANÇOIS
mathematics, history of **13**:226
LACROSSE (sport) **12**:161 *bibliog., illus.*
LACROSSE (Washington)
map (46° 49′N 117° 53′W) **20**:35
LACTANTIUS, LUCIUS CAECILIUS FIRMIANUS **12**:161 *bibliog.*
LACTEAL
lymphatic system **12**:475
LACTIC ACID **12**:161
fermentation **8**:55
fermentation product **12**:161
industrial uses **12**:161
Lactobacillus **12**:161
Meyerhof, Otto **14**:369
shock, physiologic **17**:279
LACTOBACILLUS **12**:161
LACTOGENIC HORMONE *see* SEX HORMONES
LACTONE **12**:161–162
organic compound **12**:161–162
LACTOSE
milk **13**:423
sugar **18**:327
LADAKH RANGE
map (34° 0′N 78° 0′E) **10**:167
LADD (Illinois)
map (41° 23′N 89° 13′W) **11**:42
LADDONIA (Missouri)
map (39° 15′N 91° 39′W) **13**:476
LADEWIG, MARION **12**:162
LADIES' CHRISTIAN ASSOCIATION *see* YOUNG WOMEN'S CHRISTIAN ASSOCIATION
LADIES HOME JOURNAL (periodical)
Bok, Edward William **3**:363–364
Curtis, Cyrus H. K. **5**:395
periodical **15**:169
LADIES ISLAND
map (32° 30′N 80° 45′W) **18**:98
LADIES PEACE *see* CAMBRAI, TREATY OF
LADIES' TRESSES (botany) **12**:162
LADINO LANGUAGE
Romance languages **16**:280
LADISLAS I, SAINT *see* LADISLAS I, KING OF HUNGARY
LADISLAS I, KING OF HUNGARY **12**:162 *bibliog.*
LADOGA (Indiana)
map (39° 55′N 86° 48′W) **11**:111
LADOGA, LAKE **12**:162
map (61° 0′N 31° 30′E) **19**:388
LADRONE ISLANDS *see* MARIANA ISLANDS
LADSON (South Carolina)
map (32° 59′N 80° 9′W) **18**:98
"LADY BIRD" JOHNSON *see* JOHNSON, LYNDON B.
LADY BYNG MEMORIAL TROPHY
Hull, Bobby **10**:296
LADY CHATTERLEY'S LOVER (book) **12**:162 *bibliog.*
Lawrence, D. H. **11**:249–250
LADY MARGARET HALL (Oxford University) **14**:474
LADYBIRD BEETLE *see* LADYBUG
LADYBUG **12**:162 *bibliog., illus.*
shell **17**:252 *illus.*
two-spotted ladybug **3**:167 *illus.*
LADY'S-EARDROPS (botany) **8**:352 *illus.*
LADY'S SLIPPER (botany) **12**:162 *illus.*; **14**:419 *illus.*
LADY'S SORREL *see* WOOD SORREL
LADYSMITH (British Columbia)
map (48° 58′N 123° 49′W) **3**:491
LADYSMITH (South Africa)
map (28° 34′S 29° 45′E) **18**:79
LADYSMITH (Wisconsin)
map (45° 28′N 91° 12′W) **20**:185
LAE (Papua New Guinea)
map (6° 45′S 147° 0′E) **15**:72
LÆAESØ ISLAND
map (57° 16′N 11° 1′E) **6**:109
LAËNNEC, RENÉ THÉOPHILE HYACINTHE **12**:162–163
examination, medical **7**:326
LAER, PIETER VAN **12**:163 *bibliog.*
Bamboccianti **3**:58
LAETOLIL (Tanzania) **12**:163
Leakey (family) **12**:259
LAETRILE **12**:163 *bibliog.*
LAFARGUE, PAUL
socialism **18**:21
LAFAYETTE (Alabama)
map (32° 54′N 85° 24′W) **1**:234
LAFAYETTE (county in Arkansas)
map (33° 12′N 93° 35′W) **2**:166
LAFAYETTE (Colorado)
map (40° 0′N 105° 5′W) **5**:116
LAFAYETTE (county in Florida)
map (30° 0′N 83° 10′W) **8**:172
LAFAYETTE (Georgia)
map (34° 42′N 85° 17′W) **9**:114

LAFAYETTE (Indiana) **12**:163
map (40° 25′N 86° 53′W) **11**:111
LAFAYETTE (Louisiana) **12**:163
map (30° 14′N 92° 1′W) **12**:430
LAFAYETTE (county in Louisiana)
map (30° 13′N 92° 3′W) **12**:430
LAFAYETTE (county in Mississippi)
map (34° 20′N 89° 30′W) **13**:469
LAFAYETTE (county in Missouri)
map (39° 5′N 93° 45′W) **13**:476
LAFAYETTE (Tennessee)
map (36° 32′N 86° 1′W) **19**:104
LAFAYETTE (county in Wisconsin)
map (42° 42′N 90° 8′W) **20**:185
LAFAYETTE, MARIE JOSEPH PAUL YVES ROCH GILBERT DU MOTIER, MARQUIS DE **12**:163–164 *bibliog., illus.*
Great Pyrenees **9**:321
LAFAYETTE, MOUNT
map (44° 10′N 71° 38′W) **14**:123
LAFFITTE, JEAN *see* LAFITTE, JEAN
LAFIAGI (Nigeria)
map (8° 52′N 5° 25′E) **14**:190
LAFITAU, JOSEPH
Iroquois League **11**:280 *illus.*
LAFITTE, JEAN **12**:164 *bibliog.*; **19**:131 *illus.*
LAFLEUR, GUY **12**:164
LAFONTAINE, SIR LOUIS HIPPOLYTE **12**:164 *bibliog., illus.*
LAFORGUE, JULES **12**:164 *bibliog.*
LAFOSSE, CHARLES DE **12**:164–165 *bibliog.*
LAFOURCHE (county in Louisiana)
map (29° 35′N 90° 20′W) **12**:430
LAFOURCHE, BAYOU
map (29° 5′N 90° 14′W) **12**:430
LAGAN *see* FLOTSAM, JETSAM, AND LAGAN
LAGASH (Iraq) **12**:165 *bibliog.*
Mesopotamian art and architecture **13**:318–319 *illus.*
LÅGEN RIVER
map (61° 8′N 10° 25′E) **14**:261
LAGER (beer) **3**:163
LAGERFELD, KARL
fashion design **8**:32
LAGERKVIST, PÄR **12**:165 *bibliog.*
LAGERLÖF, SELMA **12**:165 *bibliog.*
LAGHOUAT (Algeria)
map (33° 50′N 2° 59′E) **1**:287
LAGOMORPH **12**:165
mammal **13**:103–104 *illus.*
LAGOON **12**:165–166 *bibliog., illus.*
LAGOS (Nigeria) **12**:166 *bibliog.*; **14**:189 *illus.*; **14**:191 *illus., table*
map (6° 27′N 3° 24′E) **14**:190
LAGOS DE MORENO (Mexico)
map (21° 21′N 101° 55′W) **13**:357
LAGOZZA CULTURE
lake dwelling **12**:171
LAGRANGE (Indiana)
map (41° 39′N 85° 25′W) **11**:111
LAGRANGE (county in Indiana)
map (41° 39′N 85° 25′W) **11**:111
LAGRANGE (Wyoming)
map (41° 38′N 104° 10′W) **20**:301
LAGRANGE, JOSEPH LOUIS DE **12**:166 *bibliog., illus.*
astronomy, history of **2**:278
École Polytechnique **12**:166
mathematics, history of **13**:225
three-body problem **19**:181
LAGUNA (New Mexico)
map (35° 2′N 107° 23′W) **14**:136
LAGUNA BEACH (California)
map (33° 33′N 117° 51′W) **4**:31
LAGUNA DEL PERRO
map (34° 40′N 105° 57′W) **14**:136
LAGUNA MADRE LAGOON
map (27° 0′N 97° 35′W) **19**:129
LAGUNAS (Peru)
map (5° 14′S 75° 38′W) **15**:193
LAGUNILLAS (Bolivia)
map (19° 38′S 63° 43′W) **3**:366
LAHAINA (Hawaii)
map (20° 52′N 156° 41′W) **10**:72
LAHAR *see* MUDFLOW
LAHIJ
map (13° 2′N 44° 54′E) **20**:324
LAHIJAN (Iran)
map (37° 12′N 50° 1′E) **11**:250
LAHONTAN RESERVOIR
map (39° 24′N 119° 7′W) **14**:111
LAHORE (Pakistan) **12**:166–167
Badshahi Mosque **13**:601 *illus.*
map (31° 35′N 74° 18′E) **15**:27
LAHTI (Finland)
map (60° 58′N 25° 40′E) **8**:95
LAIBACH, CONGRESS OF
congress system **5**:187–188
LAIE (Hawaii)
map (21° 39′N 157° 56′W) **10**:72
LAIKA **12**:167
space medicine **18**:132
Sputnik **18**:201
LAING (EDWARD) STORE (New York)
cast-iron architecture **4**:186
LAING, HUGH
Tudor, Antony **19**:329
LAING, R. D. **12**:167 *bibliog.*
humanistic psychology **10**:299
mental health **13**:302
Szasz, Thomas **18**:415
LAINGSBURG (Michigan)
map (42° 54′N 84° 21′W) **13**:377
LÁIRGE, PORT (Ireland) *see* WATERFORD (city in Ireland)
LAISSEZ-FAIRE **12**:167 *bibliog.*
economics **7**:48
free trade **8**:295
government regulation **9**:270
physiocrats **15**:286–287
Say, Jean Baptiste **17**:106
Smith, Adam **17**:366
LAJOS *see* LOUIS for Hungarian kings named LAJOS
LAKE (for lakes whose names begin with the word Lake) *see* under the second element of the name, e.g., COMO, LAKE; LOUISE, LAKE (Alberta); etc.
LAKE (body of water) **12**:167–169 *bibliog., illus., table*
See also LAKE, GLACIAL; names of specific lakes, e.g., BRAS D'OR LAKE; GREAT SALT LAKE; etc.
classification factors **12**:167–169
composition **12**:168–169
environmental problems **12**:169
Euglena **7**:264
eutrophication **7**:311
habitat **10**:5
North America **12**:168 *illus.*
hydrologic cycle **10**:341
hydrosphere **10**:344
ice, river and lake **11**:7
limnology **12**:345
hydrologic sciences **10**:342
major lakes, worldwide **12**:169 *table*
Moon, near side **13**:564 *map*
origin **12**:167
oxbow lake **14**:473
photic zone **15**:257
plankton **15**:331–333
river delta **16**:232–233
saline **12**:168–169
glauberite **9**:205
thermocline **19**:162
varved deposit **19**:524
water circulation **12**:167–168
water resources **20**:50
LAKE (county in California)
map (39° 0′N 122° 45′W) **4**:31
LAKE (county in Colorado)
map (39° 15′N 106° 20′W) **5**:116
LAKE (dye) **12**:169
LAKE (county in Florida)
map (28° 50′N 81° 45′W) **8**:172
LAKE (county in Illinois)
map (42° 22′N 87° 50′W) **11**:42
LAKE (county in Indiana)
map (41° 25′N 87° 22′W) **11**:111
LAKE (county in Michigan)
map (44° 0′N 85° 50′W) **13**:377
LAKE (county in Minnesota)
map (47° 42′N 91° 25′W) **13**:453
LAKE (county in Montana)
map (47° 35′N 114° 5′W) **13**:547
LAKE (county in Ohio)
map (41° 43′N 81° 15′W) **14**:357
LAKE (county in Oregon)
map (42° 45′N 120° 20′W) **14**:427
LAKE (county in South Dakota)
map (44° 0′N 97° 5′W) **18**:103
LAKE (county in Tennessee)
map (36° 20′N 89° 30′W) **19**:104
LAKE, GLACIAL **9**:193 *illus.*; **12**:169–170 *bibliog.*
Finger Lakes **8**:93
Gilbert, Grove Karl **9**:178–179
glaciogenic lakes **12**:169–170
landform evolution **12**:183
pluvial lakes **12**:170
playa **15**:363
strandline **18**:288
varved deposit **19**:524
LAKE ANDES (South Dakota)
map (43° 9′N 98° 32′W) **18**:103
LAKE ARGENTINO
map (50° 13′S 72° 25′W) **2**:149
LAKE ARTHUR (Louisiana)
map (30° 5′N 92° 41′W) **12**:430
LAKE ARTHUR (New Mexico)
map (33° 0′N 104° 22′W) **14**:136
LAKE BAIKAL RIFT VALLEY
plate tectonics **15**:351 *map*
LAKE BUTLER (Florida)
map (30° 1′N 82° 20′W) **8**:172
LAKE CALUMET RIVER
map (41° 41′N 87° 35′W) **11**:42
LAKE CHAMPLAIN, BATTLE OF
Macdonough, Thomas **13**:14
LAKE CHARLES (Louisiana) **12**:170
map (30° 13′N 93° 12′W) **12**:430
LAKE CITY (Arkansas)
map (35° 49′N 90° 26′W) **2**:166
LAKE CITY (Colorado)
map (38° 2′N 107° 19′W) **5**:116
LAKE CITY (Florida)
map (30° 12′N 82° 38′W) **8**:172
LAKE CITY (Iowa)
map (42° 16′N 94° 44′W) **11**:244
LAKE CITY (Michigan)
map (44° 20′N 85° 13′W) **13**:377
LAKE CITY (Minnesota)
map (44° 27′N 92° 16′W) **13**:453
LAKE CITY (Pennsylvania)
map (42° 1′N 80° 21′W) **15**:147
LAKE CITY (South Carolina)
map (33° 52′N 79° 45′W) **18**:98
LAKE CITY (Tennessee)
map (36° 13′N 84° 9′W) **19**:104
LAKE CRYSTAL (Minnesota)
map (44° 6′N 94° 13′W) **13**:453
LAKE DELTON (Wisconsin)
map (43° 35′N 89° 47′W) **20**:185
LAKE DISTRICT (England) **12**:170–171 *bibliog.*; **19**:406 *illus.*
LAKE DWELLING **12**:171 *bibliog.*
European prehistory **7**:302
La Tène **12**:171
LAKE EFFECT
climate **5**:58
LAKE ERIE, BATTLE OF
Perry, Oliver Hazard **15**:179
War of 1812 **20**:26 *map*
LAKE FOREST (Illinois)
map (42° 15′N 87° 50′W) **11**:42
LAKE GENEVA (Wisconsin)
map (42° 36′N 88° 26′W) **20**:185
LAKE GEORGE (New York)
map (43° 26′N 73° 43′W) **14**:149
LAKE HARBOUR (Northwest Territories)
map (62° 51′N 69° 53′W) **14**:258
LAKE HAVASU CITY (Arizona)
London Bridge **12**:405
map (34° 27′N 114° 22′W) **2**:160
LAKE HIAWATHA (New Jersey)
map (40° 53′N 74° 23′W) **14**:129
LAKE JACKSON (Texas)
map (29° 2′N 95° 27′W) **19**:129
LAKE LINDEN (Michigan)
map (47° 11′N 88° 26′W) **13**:377
LAKE MILLS (Iowa)
map (43° 25′N 93° 32′W) **11**:244
LAKE MILLS (Wisconsin)
map (43° 5′N 88° 55′W) **20**:185
LAKE MINCHUMINA (Alaska)
map (63° 53′N 152° 19′W) **1**:242
LAKE ODESSA (Michigan)
map (42° 47′N 85° 8′W) **13**:377
LAKE PARK (Minnesota)
map (46° 53′N 96° 6′W) **13**:453
LAKE PLACID (Florida)
map (27° 18′N 81° 22′W) **8**:172
LAKE PLEASANT (New York)
map (43° 28′N 74° 25′W) **14**:149
LAKE POETS
Lake District (England) **12**:171
LAKE PROVIDENCE (Louisiana)
map (32° 48′N 91° 11′W) **12**:430
LAKE PUKAKI (New Zealand)
map (44° 11′S 170° 9′E) **14**:158
LAKE SAINT CLAIR RIVER
map (42° 25′N 82° 41′W) **13**:377
LAKE SUPERIOR IRON
ore deposits
major ore deposits **14**:424–425 *table*
LAKE OF THE WOODS **12**:171
LAKE OF THE WOODS (county in Minnesota)
map (48° 15′N 94° 50′W) **13**:453
LAKE VILLAGE (Arkansas)
map (33° 20′N 91° 17′W) **2**:166
LAKE WALES (Florida)
map (27° 54′N 81° 35′W) **8**:172
LAKE WHATCOM RIVER
map (48° 43′N 122° 20′W) **20**:35
LAKE WORTH (Florida)
map (26° 37′N 80° 3′W) **8**:172
LAKEDAIMONIA
Mistra **13**:482
LAKEFIELD (Minnesota)
map (43° 41′N 95° 10′W) **13**:453
LAKEHURST (New Jersey)
map (40° 1′N 74° 19′W) **14**:129
LAKELAND (Florida)
map (28° 3′N 81° 57′W) **8**:172
LAKELAND (Georgia)
map (31° 2′N 83° 4′W) **9**:114
LAKELAND TERRIER **6**:220 *illus.*; **12**:171 *bibliog., illus.*
LAKEMONT (Pennsylvania)
map (40° 31′N 78° 23′W) **15**:147
LAKEMORE (Ohio)
map (41° 1′N 81° 25′W) **14**:357
LAKEPORT (California)
map (39° 3′N 122° 55′W) **4**:31
LAKESIDE (Arizona)
map (34° 9′N 109° 58′W) **2**:160
LAKESIDE (Oregon)
map (43° 34′N 124° 11′W) **14**:427
LAKETOWN (Utah)
map (41° 49′N 111° 19′W) **19**:492
LAKEVIEW (Michigan)
map (42° 18′N 85° 12′W) **13**:377
LAKEVIEW (Oregon)
map (42° 11′N 120° 21′W) **14**:427
LAKEVILLE (Massachusetts)
map (41° 58′N 73° 27′W) **13**:206
LAKEVILLE (Minnesota)
map (44° 39′N 93° 14′W) **13**:453
LAKEWOOD (California)
map (33° 50′N 118° 8′W) **4**:31
LAKEWOOD (Colorado)
map (39° 44′N 105° 6′W) **5**:116
LAKEWOOD (New Jersey)
map (40° 6′N 74° 13′W) **14**:129
LAKEWOOD (New York)
map (42° 6′N 79° 20′W) **14**:149
LAKEWOOD (Ohio)
map (41° 29′N 81° 48′W) **14**:357
LAKEWOOD (Wisconsin)
map (45° 18′N 88° 31′W) **20**:185
LAKEWOOD CENTER (Washington)
map (47° 10′N 122° 31′W) **20**:35
LAKIN (Kansas)
map (37° 56′N 101° 15′W) **12**:18
LAKOTA (American Indians) *see* SIOUX
LAKOTA (North Dakota)
map (48° 2′N 98° 21′W) **14**:248
LAKSHADWEEP *see* LACCADIVE ISLANDS (India)
LAKSHMI **12**:171
LALANDE, JOSEPH JÉRÔME LE FRANÇAIS DE **12**:171
LALEH ZAR, MOUNT
map (29° 24′N 56° 46′E) **11**:250
LALEMONT, GABRIEL
Jesuit Martyrs of North America **11**:402
LALIBELA (Ethiopia) **12**:171 *bibliog.*
LALIQUE, RENÉ **12**:171–172 *bibliog.*
Art Deco **2**:207
corsage ornaments **2**:210 *illus.*
glassware, decorative **9**:204
jewelry **11**:411
smoked glass vase **2**:208 *illus.*
LALO, ÉDOUARD **12**:172
LAMA-KARA (Togo)
map (9° 33′N 1° 12′E) **19**:222
LAMAISM *see* TIBETAN BUDDHISM
LAMAIST ART AND ARCHITECTURE **12**:172–173 *bibliog., illus.*
LAMALINE (Newfoundland)
map (46° 52′N 55° 49′W) **14**:166
LAMAR (county in Alabama)
map (33° 50′N 88° 5′W) **1**:234
LAMAR (Colorado)
map (38° 5′N 102° 37′W) **5**:116
LAMAR (county in Georgia)
map (33° 5′N 84° 7′W) **9**:114
LAMAR (county in Mississippi)
map (31° 15′N 89° 30′W) **13**:469
LAMAR (Missouri)
map (37° 29′N 94° 17′W) **13**:476
LAMAR (county in Texas)
map (33° 32′N 93° 33′W) **19**:129
LAMAR, LUCIUS Q. C. **12**:173 *bibliog.*
LAMAR, MIRABEAU BUONAPARTE **12**:173 *bibliog.*
LAMARCK, JEAN BAPTISTE **12**:173–174 *bibliog., illus.*
animal classification **12**:173–174
biology **3**:269
evolution **7**:318; **12**:173–174
heredity **10**:139–140
Lysenko, Trofim Denisovich **12**:480
LAMARCKISM
evolution **7**:318
LAMARTINE, ALPHONSE DE **12**:174 *bibliog.*
LAMAS (Peru)
map (6° 25′S 76° 35′W) **15**:193
LAMAZE, FERNAND
pregnancy and birth **15**:506
LAMB (county in Texas)
map (34° 2′N 102° 17′W) **19**:129
LAMB (zoology) *see* SHEEP; WOOL

LAMB, LADY CAROLINE *see* PONSONBY, LADY CAROLINE
LAMB, CHARLES **12**:174 *bibliog., illus.*
LAMB, WILLIAM, 2D VISCOUNT MELBOURNE *see* MELBOURNE, WILLIAM LAMB, 2D VISCOUNT
LAMB, WILLIS EUGENE, JR. **12**:174
Lamb Shift **12**:174
LAMB AND MUTTON
meat and meat packing **13**:257 *table*
sheep **17**:248–249
LAMBARÉNÉ (Gabon)
map (0° 42′S 10° 13′E) **9**:5
Schweitzer, Albert **17**:140 *illus.*
LAMBASA (Fiji)
map (16° 26′S 179° 24′E) **8**:77
LAMBAYEQUE (Peru)
map (6° 42′S 79° 55′W) **15**:193
LAMBDA (letter)
L **12**:144
LAMBERT (Montana)
map (47° 41′N 104° 37′W) **13**:547
LAMBERT GLACIER
map (71° 0′S 70° 0′E) **2**:40
LAMBERTON (Minnesota)
map (44° 14′N 95° 16′W) **13**:453
LAMBERTVILLE (New Jersey)
map (40° 22′N 74° 57′W) **14**:129
LAMB'S-QUARTERS (botany) *see* GOOSEFOOT (botany)
LAMBTON, JOHN GEORGE, 1st EARL OF DURHAM *see* DURHAM, JOHN GEORGE LAMBTON, 1st EARL OF
LAME DEER (Montana)
map (45° 37′N 106° 40′W) **13**:547
LAME DUCK (politics) **12**:174
20th Amendment **19**:359
LAMEDH (letter)
L **12**:144
LAMENNAIS, FÉLICITÉ ROBERT DE **12**:175 *bibliog.*
LAMENT FOR THE MAKARIS (poem)
Dunbar, William **6**:298
LAMENTATIONS, BOOK OF **12**:175
LAMÈQUE (New Brunswick)
map (47° 47′N 64° 38′W) **14**:117
LAMESA (Texas)
map (32° 44′N 101° 57′W) **19**:129
LAMÍA (Greece)
map (38° 54′N 22° 26′E) **9**:325
LAMIA (mythology) **12**:175
LAMIZANA, SANGOULÉ
Upper Volta **19**:473
LAMOILLE (county in Vermont)
map (44° 35′N 72° 37′W) **19**:554
LAMOILLE RIVER
map (44° 35′N 73° 10′W) **19**:554
LAMONI (Iowa)
map (40° 37′N 93° 56′W) **11**:244
LAMONT (California)
map (35° 15′N 118° 55′W) **4**:31
LAMONT (Iowa)
map (42° 36′N 91° 39′W) **11**:244
LAMONT (Oklahoma)
map (36° 41′N 97° 33′W) **14**:368
LAMONT-DOHERTY GEOLOGICAL OBSERVATORY **12**:175
Deep-Sea Drilling Project **6**:77
JOIDES **11**:438
mid-oceanic ridge **13**:389
oceanography **14**:346
LAMOUR, DOROTHY
Hope, Bob **10**:230
L'AMOUR, LOUIS **12**:144
LAMP **12**:175–176 *bibliog., illus.*
arc, electric **2**:112
diode **6**:183
fluorescent light **8**:186–187
incandescent lamp **11**:73
Lalique, René **12**:171–172
lighting devices **12**:338 *illus.*
mercury **13**:306
mercury-vapor
ultraviolet light **19**:379
safety lamp
Davy, Sir Humphry **6**:53
vapor lamp
inert gases **11**:161
xenon **20**:312
LAMP SHELL *see* BRACHIOPOD
LAMPASAS (Texas)
map (31° 4′N 98° 11′W) **19**:129
LAMPASAS (county in Texas)
map (31° 20′N 98° 15′W) **19**:129
LAMPAZOS DE NARANJO (Mexico)
map (27° 1′N 100° 31′W) **13**:357
LAMPBLACK **12**:176
carbon **4**:134
LAMPEDUSA, GIUSEPPE DI **12**:176
LAMPI, VILHO
Finland **8**:97
LAMPREY **8**:112 *illus.*; **8**:117 *illus.*; **12**:176 *bibliog., illus.*
hagfish **10**:9
LAMPROPHYRE **12**:176
composition **12**:176
LAMY, JEAN BAPTISTE **12**:176–177 *bibliog.*
LAN-CHOU (Lanzhou) (China) **12**:177
LAN-T'IEN MAN *see* LANTIAN MAN
LAN XANG
Lao **12**:201
LANAI (Hawaii)
Hawaii (state) **10**:73
map (20° 50′N 156° 55′W) **10**:72
LANAI CITY (Hawaii)
map (20° 50′N 156° 55′W) **10**:72
LANARK (Illinois)
map (42° 6′N 89° 50′W) **11**:42
LANARK (Scotland) **12**:177
LANCASHIRE (England) **12**:177; **19**:407 *illus.*
CITIES
Blackpool **3**:322
Bolton **3**:372
LANCASTER (California)
map (34° 42′N 118° 8′W) **4**:31
LANCASTER (dynasty) **12**:177 *bibliog.*
Great Britain, history of **9**:312–313
Henry IV, King of England **10**:125
Henry V, King of England **10**:125–126
Henry VI, King of England **10**:126
Henry VII, King of England **10**:126
John of Gaunt, Duke **11**:425
Margaret of Anjou **13**:148–149
Roses, Wars of the **16**:316 *map*
York (dynasty) **20**:330
LANCASTER (England)
map (54° 3′N 2° 48′W) **19**:403
LANCASTER (Kentucky)
map (37° 37′N 84° 35′W) **12**:47
LANCASTER (Missouri)
map (40° 31′N 92° 32′W) **13**:476
LANCASTER (county in Nebraska)
map (40° 45′N 96° 45′W) **14**:70
LANCASTER (New Hampshire)
map (44° 29′N 71° 34′W) **14**:123
LANCASTER (Ohio)
map (39° 43′N 82° 36′W) **14**:357
LANCASTER (Pennsylvania) **12**:177; **15**:149 *illus.*
map (40° 2′N 76° 19′W) **15**:147
LANCASTER (county in Pennsylvania)
map (40° 2′N 76° 19′W) **15**:147
LANCASTER (South Carolina)
map (34° 43′N 80° 46′W) **18**:98
LANCASTER (county in South Carolina)
map (34° 40′N 80° 45′W) **18**:98
LANCASTER (Texas)
map (32° 36′N 96° 46′W) **19**:129
LANCASTER (Virginia)
map (37° 46′N 76° 28′W) **19**:607
LANCASTER (county in Virginia)
map (37° 45′N 76° 30′W) **19**:607
LANCASTER (Wisconsin)
map (42° 51′N 90° 43′W) **20**:185
LANCASTER, BURT **12**:177
LANCASTER, HENRY, EARL OF
Lancaster (dynasty) **12**:177
LANCASTER, HENRY OF GROSMONT, DUKE OF
Lancaster (dynasty) **12**:177
LANCASTER, JOSEPH **12**:177 *bibliog.*
LANCASTER, THOMAS, EARL OF
Lancaster (dynasty) **12**:177
LANCASTER SOUND
map (74° 13′N 84° 0′W) **14**:258
LANCE CREEK (Wyoming)
map (43° 2′N 104° 39′W) **20**:301
LANCELET *see* AMPHIOXUS; CEPHALOCHORDATA
LANCELOT, SIR **12**:178 *bibliog.*
LANCET (periodical) **12**:178
LANCET FISH **12**:178 *illus.*
LANCEY, DE (family) *see* DE LANCEY (family)
LANCRET, NICOLAS **12**:178 *bibliog.*
Marie Camargo **3**:43 *illus.*
LAND, EDWIN **12**:178 *bibliog.*
color perception theory **12**:178
polarized light **12**:178; **15**:394
Polaroid Land camera **12**:178
LAND ACT (1881)
Davitt, Michael **6**:53
LAND-GRANT COLLEGES **12**:178 *bibliog.*
See also PUBLIC DOMAIN
agriculture, history of **1**:192
Alabama, state universities of **1**:238
Alaska, University of **1**:247
Arizona, state universities **2**:164
Arkansas, state universities and colleges of **2**:170
California, state universities and colleges of **4**:38
Colorado, state universities and colleges of **5**:120
Cornell University **5**:268
Delaware, state university and college **6**:91
District of Columbia, University of the **6**:201
Florida, state universities of **8**:176
Georgia, state universities and colleges of **9**:118
Guam, University of **9**:385
Hawaii, University of **10**:76
Idaho, state universities and colleges of **11**:30
Illinois, state universities of **11**:45
Indiana, state universities of **11**:115
Iowa, state universities of **11**:248
Kansas, state universities and colleges of **12**:22
Kentucky, state universities of **12**:51
Louisiana, state universities of **12**:435
Maine, state universities of **13**:75
Maryland, state universities and colleges of **13**:193
Massachusetts, state universities and colleges of **13**:212
Morrill, Justin S. **13**:588
Morrill Acts **13**:588
Nebraska, state university and colleges of **14**:74
Nevada, University of **14**:114
New Hampshire, state university and colleges of **14**:126
New Jersey, state university and colleges of **14**:133–134
New Mexico, state universities of **14**:140
North Carolina, state universities of **14**:246–247
North Dakota, state universities and colleges of **14**:252
Ohio, state universities of **14**:362
Oklahoma, state universities of **14**:371
Oregon, state universities and colleges of **14**:430–431
Pennsylvania, state universities and colleges of **15**:151–152
Puerto Rico, University of **15**:616
Reserve Officers Training Corps **16**:176
Rhode Island, state university and college of **16**:201
Smith-Lever Act of 1914 **17**:372
South Carolina, state universities and colleges of **18**:101–102
South Dakota, state universities and colleges of **18**:106
Tennessee, state universities of **19**:107
Texas, state universities of **19**:135
United States, education in the **19**:434–435
Utah, state universities and colleges of **19**:496
Vermont, state university and colleges of **19**:558
Washington, state universities and college of **20**:44
West Virginia, state universities and colleges of **20**:115
Wisconsin, University of **20**:188–189
Wyoming, University of **20**:304
LAND MANAGEMENT, BUREAU OF (U.S.)
Interior, United States Department of the **11**:210
LAND O'LAKES (Wisconsin)
map (46° 10′N 89° 13′W) **20**:185
LAND ORDINANCE OF 1785
Northwest Territory (U.S. history) **14**:259
LAND RECLAMATION **12**:178–181 *bibliog., illus., map*
Delta Plan **6**:95–96
drainage systems **6**:255
irrigation **11**:280–283
landfill **12**:181
Netherlands **14**:98–99 *illus.*
polder **15**:395
LAND REFORM
agriculture and the food supply **1**:198
LAND TRANSPORTATION *see* RAILROAD; ROADS AND HIGHWAYS; TRANSPORTATION
LAND USE *see* CONSERVATION; HUMAN ECOLOGY; URBAN PLANNING; ZONING
LANDAU (carriage)
coach and carriage **5**:75
LANDAU, LEV **12**:181 *bibliog., illus.*
liquid helium **12**:181
physics **12**:181
LANDAU, MARK ALEKSANDROVICH *see* ALDANOV, M. A.
LANDAU-ALDANOV *see* ALDANOV, M.A.
LANDER (county in Nevada)
map (40° 0′N 117° 0′W) **14**:111
LANDER (Wyoming)
map (42° 50′N 108° 44′W) **20**:301
LANDER, HARALD
Royal Danish Ballet **16**:330
LANDER, JOHN AND RICHARD
exploration **7**:335
LANDFILL **12**:181 *bibliog.*
land reclamation **12**:180–181
pollutants, chemical **15**:411
pollution control **15**:415
sanitary landfill, usage **12**:181
LANDFORM EVOLUTION **12**:181–183 *bibliog., illus.*
climatic effects
arid climate **12**:183
climatic change **12**:183
humid climate **12**:182
coastal landform **12**:183
crustal movements and volcanism effects **12**:183
desert **6**:128–129
erosion **12**:182–183
erosion and sedimentation **7**:232–234
glaciation effect **12**:183
horst and graben **10**:253–254 *illus.*
Jurassic Period **11**:477 *map*
landforms **12**:182 *illus.*
landslide and avalanche **12**:192
limestone **12**:345 *illus.*
plate tectonics **15**:351
Precambrian time **15**:492
LANDFORMS **12**:182 *illus.*
Bryan, Kirk **3**:528
cliff (escarpment) **7**:237
drumlin **6**:282
Dutton, Clarence Edward **6**:315–316
floodplain **8**:165–166
France **8**:261
geomorphology **9**:107
geosyncline **9**:119–120
hypsographic curve **10**:351
inselberg **11**:194
moraine **13**:572
mountain **13**:619
pediment (geology) **15**:131
Penck, Walther **15**:142
peneplain **15**:143
physiography **15**:287
plateau **15**:358
Playfair, John **15**:363
river and stream **16**:229–232
topography **19**:237
valley and ridge province **19**:507–508
wind action **20**:170
LANDI, STEFANO
opera **14**:399
LANDINI, FRANCESCO **12**:183 *bibliog.*; **13**:663 *illus.*
LANDIS (North Carolina)
map (35° 33′N 80° 37′W) **14**:242
LANDIS, KENESAW MOUNTAIN **12**:183–184 *bibliog.*
LANDLORD *see* LEASE; TENANT
LANDMARK ARCHITECTURE
historic preservation **10**:181–182
LANDON, ALF **12**:184 *bibliog.*
LANDOR, WALTER SAVAGE **12**:184 *bibliog.*
LANDOWSKA, WANDA **12**:184 *bibliog.*
LANDRUM (South Carolina)
map (35° 11′N 82° 11′W) **18**:98
LANDRUM-GRIFFIN ACT *see* LABOR-MANAGEMENT REPORTING AND DISCLOSURE ACT
LAND'S END (England) **12**:184
map (50° 3′N 5° 44′W) **19**:403
LANDSAT (artificial satellite) **12**:184–185 *bibliog., illus.*
photographs **12**:184–185 *illus.*; **18**:123 *illus.*
satellite, artificial **17**:87 *illus.*
LANDSCAPE ARCHITECTURE **12**:185–188 *bibliog., illus.*
Brown, Capability **3**:513
Central Park **4**:254
Downing, Andrew Jackson **6**:252
England **12**:186–187
fountains **8**:251–252
France **12**:185–186
garden **9**:40–41
gazebo **9**:64
Halprin, Lawrence **10**:25
Hooker (family) **10**:227

Italy 12:185
Kent, William 12:45
labyrinth and maze 12:158
Le Nôtre, André 12:255
Marot (family) 13:162
Noguchi, Isamu 14:213
Olmsted, Frederick Law 14:380
Price, Sir Uvedale 15:535
Repton, Humphry 16:171–172
Robert, Hubert 16:241
Roman art and architecture 16:274
Tuileries 19:329
Vanbrugh, Sir John 19:517
Versailles, Palace of 19:561
Winterthur Museum 20:181
LANDSCAPE PAINTING 12:188–192 *bibliog.*, *illus.*
Austria
Waldmüller, Ferdinand Georg 20:10
Belgium
Brouwer, Adriaen 3:512
Bruegel (family) 3:522 *illus.*
Patinir, Joachim 15:112
Rubens, Peter Paul 16:336
Canada
Canadian art and architecture 4:89
Group of Seven 9:376
Morrice, James W. 13:587
Suzor-Côté, M. A. de Foy 18:374
China
Chao Meng-fu (Zhao Mengfu) 4:282
Chinese art and architecture 4:381 *illus.*
Fan K'uan 8:20
Hsia Kuei (Xia Gui) 10:286
Huang Kung-wang (Huang Gongwang) 10:287
Kuo Hsi (Guo Xi) 12:137
Ma Yüan (Ma Yuan) 13:3
Mi Fei 13:369
Tai Chin (Dai Jin) 19:11
Wang Meng 20:22
Wang Wei 20:22
France
Barbizon school 3:79 *illus.*
Boudin, Eugène Louis 3:420
Corot, Jean Baptiste Camille 5:271–272
Daubigny, Charles François 6:45
Diaz de la Peña, Narcisse Virgile 6:155
Guillaumin, Armand 9:395–396
Harpignies, Henri 10:55
Lorrain, Claude 12:415–416
Michel, Georges 13:372
Moreau (family) 13:576
Poussin, Nicolas 15:477
Rousseau, Théodore 16:327
Sisley, Alfred 17:328–329
Vernet (family) 19:559
Germany
Altdorfer, Albrecht 1:311–312
Corinth, Lovis 5:263
Cranach, Lucas, the Elder 5:329
Danube school 6:36
Friedrich, Caspar David 8:332
German art and architecture 9:126
Loutherbourg, Philippe Jacques de 12:437
Richter, Adrian Ludwig 16:214
Runge, Philipp Otto 16:346
Great Britain
Bonington, Richard Parkes 3:380
Cole, Thomas 5:99–100
Constable, John 5:206–207
Cotman, John Sell 5:304
Cozens (family) 5:323–324
Crome, John 5:357
English art and architecture 7:187
Gainsborough, Thomas 9:9
Girtin, Thomas 9:190
Palmer, Samuel 15:51
Robert Andrews and Wife (Gainsborough) 2:199 *illus.*
Sutherland, Graham 18:373
Turner, Joseph Mallord William 19:350
Ward, James 20:29
Wilson, Richard 20:165
Wright, Joseph 20:290
iconography 11:22–23
India
Mogul art and architecture 13:501
Italy
Baldovinetti, Alesso 3:34
Canaletto 4:98
Domenichino 6:230–231
Perugino 15:195
Ricci (family) 16:206
Rosa, Salvator 16:312
Zuccarelli, Francesco 20:381
Japan
Gyokudo 9:414–415
Hokusai 10:199–200
Japanese art and architecture 11:374–376
Josetsu 11:452
Sesshu 17:212–213
Shubun 17:289
Taiga 19:11
Korea
Chong Son 4:405
Mexico
Velasco, José María 19:536
Netherlands
Avercamp, Hendrik van 2:369–370
Berchem, Nicolaes Pieterszoon 3:208
Cuyp, Aelbert 5:399
Dutch art and architecture 6:311
Goyen, Jan van 9:274
Heyden, Jan van der 10:155
Hobbema, Meindert 10:192
Jongkind, Johan Barthold 11:445
Mauve, Anton 13:238
Neer, Aert van der 14:76–77
Ruisdael, Jacob van 16:343
Ruisdael, Salomon van 16:344
Seghers, Hercules 17:188
painting 15:21–22
Renaissance art and architecture 16:154
Russia
Russian art and architecture 16:362–363
Switzerland
Witz, Konrad 20:194–195
United States
Allston, Washington 1:304–305
American art and architecture 1:332–333
Berman, Eugene 3:219
Bierstadt, Albert 3:248
Blakelock, Ralph Albert 3:326
Carmichael, Frank 4:153
Chase, William Merritt 4:301
Church, Frederick Edwin 4:423
Cropsey, Jaspar 5:359
Doughty, Thomas 6:246
Durand, Asher Brown 6:302–303
Hartley, Marsden 10:62–63
Homer, Winslow 10:213–214
Hudson River school 10:290
Inness, George 11:179–180
Luminism 12:459
Martin, Homer Dodge 13:179
Moran, Thomas 13:573
Moses, Grandma 13:600
Vanderlyn, John 19:519
Whittredge, Worthington 20:143
LANDSEER (dog) *see* NEWFOUNDLAND (dog)
LANDSEER, SIR EDWIN 12:192 *bibliog.*
LANDSHUT (Germany, East and West)
map (48° 33′N 12° 9′E) 9:140
LANDSLIDE AND AVALANCHE 12:192–193 *bibliog.*, *illus.*
catastrophic events 12:193
classification 12:192–193
earthquakes 7:27
erosion and sedimentation 7:233
landform evolution 12:181–183
Moon, rockfalls 12:193
mudflows 12:193; 13:631
prevention and damage limitation 12:193
LANDSMÅL (language)
Norway 14:262
LANDSTEINER, KARL 12:193
surgery 18:362
LANDY, JOHN
Bannister, Roger 3:71
LANE (county in Kansas)
map (38° 30′N 100° 30′W) 12:18
LANE (county in Oregon)
map (44° 0′N 122° 40′W) 14:427
LANE, FITZ HUGH 12:193 *bibliog.*
Luminism 12:459
LANE, HUGH
Tate Gallery, The 19:44
LANE, JAMES HENRY 12:194 *bibliog.*
LANE-FOX PITT RIVERS, AUGUSTUS HENRY *see* PITT RIVERS, AUGUSTUS HENRY LANE-FOX
LANESBORO (Minnesota)
map (43° 43′N 91° 59′W) 13:453
LANETT (Alabama)
map (32° 57′N 85° 12′W) 1:234
LANFRANC 12:194 *bibliog.*
William I, King of England (William the Conqueror) 20:155
LANFRANCO, GIOVANNI 12:194 *bibliog.*
LANG, ANDREW 12:194 *bibliog.*
LANG, FRITZ 8:83 *illus.*; 12:194–195 *bibliog.*, *illus.*
Metropolis 8:83 *illus.*; 12:194 *illus.*
LANG BAY (British Columbia)
map (49° 47′N 124° 21′W) 3:491
LANG ISLAND
map (68° 44′N 14° 50′E) 14:261
LANGDALE (Alabama)
map (32° 44′N 85° 11′W) 1:234
LANGDELL, CHRISTOPHER COLUMBUS 12:195
LANGDON (North Dakota)
map (48° 46′N 98° 22′W) 14:248
LANGDON, HARRY
film, history of 8:83
LANGDON, JOHN 12:195 *bibliog.*
LANGE, ALEXIS
community and junior colleges 5:151–152
LANGE, DAVID 12:195
LANGE, DOROTHEA 12:195 *bibliog.*, *illus.*
Migrant Mother, Nipomo, California 12:195 *illus.*
LANGELAND ISLAND
map (54° 50′N 10° 50′E) 6:109
LANGENTHAL (Switzerland)
map (47° 13′N 7° 47′E) 18:394
LANGER, SUZANNE K. 12:195 *bibliog.*
LANGER, WILLIAM 12:195 *bibliog.*
North Dakota 14:251
LANGERHAGEN (Germany, East and West)
map (52° 27′N 9° 44′E) 9:140
LANGERHANS, ISLETS OF *see* PANCREAS
LANGEVIN, ANDRÉ 12:195
LANGFORD (South Dakota)
map (45° 36′N 97° 50′W) 18:103
LANGFORD, NATHANIEL P.
Teton Range 19:127
LANGGAARD, RUED 12:195
LANGHANKE, LUCILLE VASCONCELLS *see* ASTOR, MARY
LANGHANS, CARL GOTTHARD 12:195–196 *bibliog.*
Brandenburg Gate 3:453
LANGIA MOUNTAINS
map (3° 35′N 33° 40′E) 19:372
LANGLADE (county in Wisconsin)
map (45° 15′N 89° 2′W) 20:185
LANGLADE, CHARLES MICHEL DE 12:196
LANGLAND, WILLIAM 12:196 *bibliog.*
Piers Plowman 15:297
LANGLEY (Oklahoma)
map (36° 30′N 95° 4′W) 14:368
LANGLEY (South Carolina)
map (33° 31′N 81° 50′W) 18:98
LANGLEY, SAMUEL PIERPONT 12:196 *bibliog.*
bolometer 3:371
LANGLEY PARK (Maryland)
map (38° 59′N 76° 59′W) 13:188
LANGLOIS (Oregon)
map (42° 56′N 124° 27′W) 14:427
LANGMUIR, IRVING 12:196 *bibliog.*, *illus.*
plasma physics 15:345
LANGRUTH (Manitoba)
map (50° 24′N 98° 38′W) 13:119
LANGSTROTH BEEHIVE 3:161 *illus.*
LANGTON, STEPHEN 12:196 *bibliog.*
LANGTRY, LILLIE 12:196 *bibliog.*
LANGUAGE
See also LINGUISTICS; NONVERBAL COMMUNICATION; WRITING SYSTEMS, EVOLUTION OF
animal communication 2:18–20
Asia 2:244 *map*
citizens band radio 4:446
cockney 5:87
communication 5:143–144
computer languages 5:160o–160p
creole (linguistics) 5:338
Esperanto 7:243
Europe 7:274 *map*
foreign languages, teaching of 8:225
language groups
African languages 1:165–167 *map*
Afroasiatic languages 1:178–181 *map*
Arabic language 2:100
Armenian language 2:173
Baltic languages 3:54–55
Basque language 3:116
Caucasian language and literature 4:218
Celtic languages 4:241
Dravidian languages 6:263
English language 7:191–193
Germanic languages 9:135–137 *table*
Greek language 9:342–343
Indian languages, American 11:98–101 *table*
Indo-European languages 11:145
Indo-Iranian languages 11:145–146
Japanese language 11:379
Korean language 12:118
Latin language 12:233–234
Malayo-Polynesian languages 13:82–84
Oceanic languages 14:339
Romance languages 16:280–281
Sino-Tibetan languages 17:324–325
Slavic languages 17:357–358
Southeast Asian languages 18:110–111
Swahili 18:375
Ural-Altaic languages 19:474–476
language and literature 12:196–197
languages, artificial 12:197–198
languages, extinct 12:198–199
languages of the world 12:355 *map*
lingua franca 12:354
North America 14:234 *map*
pidgin 15:294
sign language 17:299–300
slang 17:350
South America 18:93 *map*
LANGUAGE AND LITERATURE 12:196–197 *bibliog.*
analysis
information theory 11:174
Carnap, Rudolf 4:154
communication 5:144
concept formation and attainment 5:169
culture 5:384
education
applied linguistics 2:90–91
foreign languages, teaching of 8:225
language laboratory 19:55 *illus.*
reading education 16:100–101
secondary education 17:179–180
humanities, education in the 10:300
infancy 11:162–163
inner speech 11:179
names, personal 14:9–10
LANGUAGES, ARTIFICIAL 12:197–198 *bibliog.*
See also COMPUTER LANGUAGES
communication 5:143
Esperanto 7:243
Interlingua 12:197–198
Peano, Giuseppe 15:125
mathematics 13:221
sign language 17:299–300
symbolic logic
Carnap, Rudolf 4:154
LANGUAGES, EXTINCT 12:198–199 *bibliog.*
Akkadian 12:198
Cornish 4:241; 12:198
Curonian language 3:55
Dacian 12:198
Dalmatian 12:198
Romance languages 16:280
Elamite 12:198
Etruscan 12:198
Germanic languages 9:136 *table*
Hattic 12:198
Hittite 10:190; 12:198
Hurrian 12:198
Illyrian 12:198
Indian languages, American 11:100 *tables*
Jurchen
Altaic languages 19:476
Latin language 12:233–234
Luwian 12:198–199
Lycian 12:199
Lydian 12:198
Manx 4:241
Oceanic languages 14:339
Palaic 12:198
Phrygian 12:198
Prussian language 3:55
Slavic languages 17:358
Sumerian 12:198
Thracian 12:198
Ugaritic 19:374
Urartian 12:198
writing systems, evolution of 20:292
syllabaries 20:293
LANGUE D'OC LITERATURE *see* PROVENÇAL LITERATURE
LANGUEDOC (France) 12:199 *bibliog.*, *map*
cities

LANGUEDOC (cont.)
Béziers **3**:233
Montpellier **13**:557–558
L'ANGUILLE RIVER
map (34° 44'N 90° 40'W) **2**:166
LANGUR **12**:199 *illus.*; **13**:533 *illus.*; **15**:540 *illus.*
animal behavior **2**:15–16
animal communication **2**:20 *illus.*
LANHAM (Maryland)
map (38° 58'N 76° 52'W) **13**:188
LANIER (county in Georgia)
map (31° 3'N 83° 2'W) **9**:114
LANIER, SIDNEY **12**:199 *bibliog.*
Macon (Georgia) **13**:35
L'ANNÉE PSYCHOLOGIQUE (periodical)
Binet, Alfred **3**:258
LANOLIN **12**:199
LANREZAC, CHARLES
World War I **20**:223
LANSDOWNE, HENRY CHARLES KEITH PETTY-FITZMAURICE, 5TH MARQUESS OF **12**:199–200 *bibliog.*
L'ANSE (Michigan)
map (46° 45'N 88° 27'W) **13**:377
L'ANSE AUX MEADOWS **12**:144 *bibliog.*; **14**:237 *map*
Thorfinn Karlsefni **19**:178
LANSFORD (North Dakota)
map (48° 38'N 101° 23'W) **14**:248
LANSFORD (Pennsylvania)
map (40° 50'N 75° 53'W) **15**:147
LANSING (Illinois)
map (41° 35'N 87° 32'W) **11**:42
LANSING (Iowa)
map (43° 22'N 91° 13'W) **11**:244
LANSING (Kansas)
map (39° 14'N 94° 55'W) **12**:18
LANSING (Michigan) **12**:200
map (42° 43'N 84° 34'W) **13**:377
LANSING, ROBERT **12**:200 *bibliog., illus.*
LANSTON, TOLBERT
Monotype, inventor **13**:541
LANTANA **12**:200
LANTERN FISH **6**:79 *illus.*; **8**:117 *illus.*; **12**:200 *illus.*
LANTHANIDE SERIES **12**:200–201 *bibliog., table*
cerium **4**:260
dysprosium **6**:320
erbium **7**:228
europium **7**:309
gadolinium **9**:7
holmium **10**:206
lanthanum **12**:201
lutetium **12**:468
Marignac, Jean Charles Galissard de **13**:152
metal **13**:328
metallic elements **13**:328
neodymium **14**:83
praseodymium **15**:489
promethium **15**:567
samarium **17**:45
terbium **19**:115
thulium **19**:184
Welsbach, Carl Auer, Baron von **20**:101
ytterbium **20**:337
yttrium **20**:337–338
LANTHANUM **12**:201
element **7**:130 *table*
lanthanide series **12**:200–201
metal, metallic element **13**:328
Mosander, Carl G. **12**:201
phosphate minerals **15**:255–256
uses **12**:201
LANTIAN MAN **12**:201
Heidelberg man **10**:107
LANVIN, JEANNE **12**:201 *bibliog.*
fashion design **8**:31
LANZHOU (China) *see* LAN-CHOU (Lanzhou) (China)
LAO **12**:201–202 *bibliog.*; **12**:204 *illus.*
LAO-TZU (Laozi) **2**:252 *illus.*; **12**:202 *bibliog.*
Tao Te Ching (Daode Jing) **19**:28
Taoism **19**:28–29
LAOCOÖN **9**:341 *illus., illus.*; **9**:341 *illus.*; **12**:202 *bibliog., illus.*; **17**:160 *illus.*
El Greco painting **15**:20 *illus.*
Vatican museums and galleries **19**:527
LAOIGHIS (Ireland) **12**:202
LAOMEDON **12**:202
LAON (France)
cathedral **9**:257–258 *illus.*
Villard de Honnecourt **19**:598
map (49° 34'N 3° 40'E) **8**:260
LAONA (Wisconsin)
map (45° 34'N 88° 40'W) **20**:185
LAOS **12**:202–204 *bibliog., illus., map, table*
art
Southeast Asian art and architecture **18**:107–108
cities
Luang Prabang **12**:446
Vientiane **19**:579
climate **12**:203 *table*
Dooley, Thomas **6**:240
economic activities **12**:204
education
Southeast Asian universities **18**:111 *table*
flag **12**:202 *illus.*
government **12**:204
history **12**:204
Pathet Lao **15**:111–112
Souphanouvong **18**:77
Souvanna Phouma **18**:113
Vietnam War **19**:584–590 *maps*
Indochina **11**:146
land **12**:203 *map, table*
map (18° 0'N 105° 0'E) **2**:232
people **12**:203–204 *illus.*
Lao **12**:201
Meo **13**:303
LAOZI *see* LAO-TZU (Laozi)
LAPEER (Michigan)
map (43° 3'N 83° 19'W) **13**:377
LAPEER (county in Michigan)
map (43° 10'N 83° 15'W) **13**:377
LAPIDARY *see* GEM CUTTING
LAPIS LAZULI **9**:74 *illus.*; **12**:204–205 *bibliog., illus.*
composition **12**:204–205
feldspathoid **8**:47
metamorphic rock **12**:204–205
sodalite **18**:32
sources **12**:205
ultramarine **19**:377
LAPLACE, PIERRE SIMON DE **12**:205 *bibliog., illus.*
astronomy, history of **2**:278
Houdon, Jean Antoine **10**:263
mathematics, history of **13**:225
LAPLAND **12**:205 *bibliog.*
Finland **8**:95
Lapps **12**:205
LAPLAND LONGSPUR *see* LONGSPUR
LAPORTE (Colorado)
map (40° 38'N 105° 8'W) **5**:116
LAPORTE (Pennsylvania)
map (41° 25'N 76° 30'W) **15**:147
LAPPEENRANTA (Finland)
map (61° 4'N 28° 11'E) **8**:95
LAPPI *see* LAPLAND
LAPPLAND *see* LAPLAND
LAPPS **7**:275 *illus.*; **8**:98 *illus.*; **12**:205–206 *bibliog., illus.*; **14**:262 *illus.*; **16**:34 *illus.*
Arctic **2**:143
Lapland **12**:205
Ural-Altaic languages **19**:475
LAPSE RATE **12**:206
LAPTEV SEA
map (76° 0'N 126° 0'E) **19**:388
LAPWAI (Idaho)
map (46° 24'N 116° 48'W) **11**:26
LAPWING **12**:206
L'AQUILA (Italy)
map (42° 22'N 13° 22'E) **11**:321
LAR RAMIE, JACQUES
Wyoming **20**:303
LARACHE (Morocco)
map (35° 12'N 6° 10'W) **13**:585
LARAMIE (Wyoming) **12**:206
map (41° 19'N 105° 35'W) **20**:301
LARAMIE (county in Wyoming)
map (41° 15'N 104° 40'W) **20**:301
LARAMIE MOUNTAINS
map (42° 0'N 105° 40'W) **20**:301
LARAMIE RIVER
map (42° 12'N 104° 32'W) **20**:301
LARC (computer) **5**:160b
LARCENY **12**:206 *bibliog.*
kleptomania **12**:97
robbery **16**:240
LARCH **12**:206–207 *illus.*
LARD *see* FATS AND OILS
LARDNER, RING **12**:207 *bibliog.*
LARDNER, RING, JR.
Hollywood Ten, The **10**:204
LAREDO (Texas) **12**:207
map (27° 31'N 99° 30'W) **19**:129
LARES **12**:207
LARGE NUMBERS, LAW OF **12**:207 *bibliog.*
expected value **7**:333–334
LARGE-SCALE INTEGRATION *see* LSI
L'ARGENT, BAY (Newfoundland)
map (47° 33'N 54° 54'W) **14**:166
LARGILLIÈRE, NICOLAS DE **12**:207 *bibliog.*
Rigaud, Hyacinthe **16**:222
LARGO (Florida)
map (27° 55'N 82° 47'W) **8**:172
LARIMER (county in Colorado)
map (40° 40'N 105° 30'W) **5**:116
LARIMORE (North Dakota)
map (47° 54'N 97° 38'W) **14**:248
LARIONOV, MIKHAIL FYODOROVICH **12**:207
LÁRISA (Greece)
map (39° 38'N 22° 25'E) **9**:325
LARK **12**:207–208 *illus.*
LARK HARBOUR (Newfoundland)
map (49° 6'N 58° 23'W) **14**:166
LARKANA
map (27° 33'N 68° 13'E) **15**:27
LARKIN, PHILIP **12**:208 *bibliog.*
LARKIN, THOMAS OLIVER **12**:208 *bibliog.*
LARKSPUR **12**:208
locoweed **12**:392
LARNACA (Cyprus)
map (34° 55'N 33° 38'E) **5**:409
LARNED (Kansas)
map (38° 11'N 99° 6'W) **12**:18
LAROCQUE, FRANÇOIS ANTOINE
Wyoming **20**:303
LAROSE (Louisiana)
map (29° 35'N 90° 23'W) **12**:430
LAROUSSE, PIERRE **12**:208
Grand dictionnaire universel du XIXe siècle
encyclopedia **7**:165
LARRYS RIVER (Nova Scotia)
map (45° 13'N 61° 23'W) **14**:269
LARS PORSENA, KING OF CLUSIUM **12**:208
LARSEN BAY (Alaska)
map (57° 33'N 154° 4'W) **1**:242
LARSEN ICE SHELF
map (68° 30'S 62° 30'W) **2**:40
LARSON, JOHN A.
lie detector **12**:323
LARSSON, CARL
Scandinavian art and architecture **17**:114
LARTET, ÉDOUARD ARMAND **12**:208
Dryopithecus **6**:285
LARTIGUE, JACQUES HENRI **12**:208
LARUE (county in Kentucky)
map (37° 35'N 85° 40'W) **12**:47
LARVA **12**:208 *bibliog.*
butterflies and moths **3**:595
caddis fly **4**:11 *illus.*
caterpillar **4**:202–203
chordate **4**:407
cocoon **5**:89
coelenterate **5**:92
cutworm **5**:398
flea **8**:158
glowworm **9**:210
grub **9**:381–382
gypsy moth **9**:416 *illus.*
inchworm **11**:74
insect **11**:190 *illus.*
juvenile hormone **11**:480
Lepidoptera **12**:295
Mexican jumping bean **13**:351
myiasis **13**:690
nematode
filariasis **8**:78
neoteny **14**:86
regeneration **16**:127
snake fly **17**:383 *illus.*
soil organisms **18**:39 *illus.*
tent caterpillar **19**:113
LARYNGITIS **12**:208
LARYNGOLOGY
surgery **18**:362
LARYNX **12**:209 *bibliog., illus.*
artificial organs **2**:222
laryngitis **12**:208
monkey **13**:534
phonetics **15**:251
respiratory system disorders **16**:181–182
speech **18**:174 *illus.*
LAS *see under the element of the name following* LAS, *except for those entries listed below*
LAS ANIMAS (Colorado)
map (38° 4'N 103° 13'W) **5**:116
LAS ANIMAS (county in Colorado)
map (37° 20'N 104° 0'W) **5**:116
LAS CAMPANAS OBSERVATORY **12**:209
LAS CASAS, BARTOLOMÉ DE **12**:209 *bibliog., illus.*
Latin American literature **12**:229
Mexico, history of **13**:363
slavery **17**:353
LAS CRUCES (New Mexico) **12**:209–210
map (32° 23'N 106° 29'W) **14**:136
LAS FLORES (Argentina)
map (36° 3'S 59° 7'W) **2**:149
LAS LAJAS (Argentina)
map (38° 31'S 70° 22'W) **2**:149
LAS LAJAS (Panama)
map (8° 15'N 81° 52'W) **15**:55
LAS LOMITAS (Argentina)
map (24° 42'S 60° 36'W) **2**:149
LAS MINAS MOUNTAIN
map (14° 33'N 88° 39'W) **10**:218
LAS OVEJAS (Argentina)
map (37° 1'S 70° 45'W) **2**:149
LAS PALMAS (Spain) **12**:210
Canary Islands **4**:99
LAS PIEDRAS (Bolivia)
map (11° 6'S 66° 10'W) **3**:366
LAS PIEDRAS (Puerto Rico)
map (18° 11'N 65° 52'W) **15**:614
LAS PIEDRAS (Uruguay)
map (34° 44'S 56° 13'W) **19**:488
LAS PLUMAS (Argentina)
map (43° 43'S 67° 15'W) **2**:149
LAS RAMAS (Ecuador)
map (1° 50'S 79° 48'W) **7**:52
LAS ROSAS (Argentina)
map (32° 28'S 61° 34'W) **2**:149
LAS TABLAS (Panama)
map (7° 46'N 80° 17'W) **15**:55
LAS VEGAS (Honduras)
map (14° 49'N 88° 6'W) **10**:218
LAS VEGAS (Nevada) **12**:210; **14**:114 *illus.*
Hilton Hotel **10**:261 *illus.*
Hughes, Howard **10**:292
map (36° 11'N 115° 8'W) **14**:111
LAS VEGAS (New Mexico)
map (35° 36'N 105° 13'W) **14**:136
LASAGNE **15**:106 *illus.*
LASCANO (Uruguay)
map (33° 40'S 54° 12'W) **19**:488
LASCAUX (France) **12**:210 *bibliog., illus.*
cave dwellers **4**:224 *illus.*
cave painting **13**:646; **15**:508 *illus.*
LASDUN, DENYS
National Theatre **14**:46
LASER **12**:210–213 *bibliog., illus., table*
applications **12**:212–213
cathode ray **4**:211
compact disc **5**:154–155 *illus.*
holography **10**:208
information storage and retrieval **11**:173
metallurgy **13**:331
optical computing **5**:160g
printing **15**:553
scanning **17**:114
sound recording and reproduction **18**:76
surgery **18**:362 *illus.*
videodisk **19**:577
Basov, Nikolai Gennadiyevich **3**:116
distance, astronomical **6**:199
fluorescence **8**:186
gallium **9**:21
infrared photochemistry
photochemistry **15**:259
infrared radiation **11**:175
light **12**:335
coherent light **5**:96
Maiman, Theodore Harold **13**:68
optics **14**:412–413
LASER DISC *see* COMPACT DISC
LASHIO (Burma)
map (22° 56'N 97° 45'E) **3**:573
LASHLEY, KARL S. **12**:213 *bibliog., illus.*
LASKE, OSKAR
Austrians defeat Russians in Galicia, World War I **20**:230 *illus.*
LASKI, HAROLD **12**:214 *bibliog.*
LASKIN, BORA **12**:214
LASKY, JESSE L.
Zukor, Adolph **20**:381
LASSALLE, FERDINAND **12**:214 *bibliog.*
socialism **18**:20
LASSELL, WILLIAM **12**:214
LASSEN (county in California)
map (40° 40'N 120° 40'W) **4**:31
LASSEN PEAK (volcano) **12**:214
map (40° 29'N 121° 31'W) **4**:31
national parks **4**:35 *illus.*; **14**:38–39 *map, table*
LASSO, ORLANDO DI
music, history of Western **13**:664 *illus.*
LASSUS, ROLAND DE **12**:214 *bibliog.*
LASSWELL, HAROLD D. **12**:214 *bibliog.*
LAST JUDGEMENT
hell **10**:113
LAST MOUNTAIN LAKE
map (51° 5'N 105° 10'W) **17**:81
LAST SUPPER **12**:214 *bibliog.*

Eucharist **7**:262
Grail, Holy **9**:281
Mass **13**:200
LAST SUPPER, THE (painting)
Leonardo da Vinci **12**:289; **12**:291
mural painting **13**:645–646 *illus.*
LAST OF THE MOHICANS, THE (book)
see LEATHERSTOCKING TALES, THE (books)
LAST YEAR AT MARIENBAD (film)
Robbe-Grillet, Alain **16**:240
LASTMAN, PIETER
Altar Scene **4**:424 *illus.*
LATACUNGA (Ecuador)
map (0° 56′S 78° 37′W) **7**:52
LATAH (county in Idaho)
map (46° 50′N 116° 40′W) **11**:26
LATAKIA (Syria) **12**:214–215
map (35° 31′N 35° 47′E) **18**:412
LATE BRONZE AGE *see* BRONZE AGE
LATE GEORGE APLEY, THE (book)
Marquand, J. P. **13**:162
LATE ISLAND
map (18° 48′S 174° 39′W) **19**:233
LATEEN SAIL
caravel **4**:132
cutter **5**:398
ship **17**:266 *illus.*
LATERAN COUNCILS **12**:215
Arnold of Brescia **2**:186
Callistus II, Pope **4**:46
Innocent III, Pope **11**:180–181
LATERAN TREATY **12**:215
Gasparri, Pietro **9**:55
Italy, history of **11**:330
Pius XI, Pope **15**:323
LATERITE **12**:215 *bibliog.*
bauxite **3**:131
ore **12**:215
pedalfer **15**:131
tropical weathering **12**:215
LATEX **12**:215
gutta-percha **9**:409
resin **16**:177
rubber **16**:333–334
LATHE **12**:215–216 *bibliog., illus.*
machine tools **13**:23–25 *illus.*
LATHROP (Missouri)
map (39° 33′N 94° 20′W) **13**:476
LATHROP, ROSE HAWTHORNE **12**:216 *bibliog.*
LATIMER (county in Oklahoma)
map (34° 55′N 95° 15′W) **14**:368
LATIMER, HUGH **12**:216 *bibliog.*
Oxford (England) **14**:474
LATIN AMERICA *see* CENTRAL AMERICA; EXPLORATION; LATIN AMERICA, HISTORY OF; LATIN AMERICAN ART AND ARCHITECTURE; LATIN AMERICAN LITERATURE; LATIN AMERICAN MUSIC AND DANCE; LATIN AMERICAN UNIVERSITIES
LATIN AMERICA, HISTORY OF **12**:216–222 *bibliog., illus., maps*
See also MEXICO, HISTORY OF; the subheading history under names of specific countries, e.g., GUATEMALA; PANAMA; etc.
caudillo **4**:219
Central America **4**:253
Peru **15**:194–195
pre-Columbian art and architecture **15**:495–501
prior to 1492 pre-Columbian period
Aztec **2**:382–384
Inca **11**:69–73
Indian civilizations **12**:216–217
Maya **13**:243–245
1492–1808 discovery and colonization
colonial era **12**:217–219 *illus., map*
conquistadors **5**:197
El Dorado **7**:98
encomienda **7**:163
Las Casas, Bartolomé de **12**:209
New Granada **14**:121
New Spain **14**:142
1808–1825 rise of nationalism
Bolivár, Simón **3**:365
San Martin, José de **17**:57
wars for independence **12**:219–220; **12**:220 *map*
1825-present
Alliance for Progress **1**:302
Central American Federation **4**:253
Chaco War **4**:265
Good Neighbor Policy **9**:245
Latin American Integration Association **12**:228
migration to the United States **11**:55 *map*
national period **12**:220–222
Organization of American States **14**:440
Pacific, War of the **15**:5
political and socioeconomic development **12**:221–222
suffrage, women's **18**:326
Tacna-Arica Dispute **19**:6
Triple Alliance, War of the **19**:302
Walker, William **20**:12
Zelaya, José Santos **20**:358
LATIN AMERICAN ART AND ARCHITECTURE **12**:222–228 *bibliog., illus.*
See also the specific art forms subdivided by Latin American countries, e.g., ARCHITECTURE—Brazil; PAINTING—Mexico; etc.
jewelry **11**:408
pre-Columbian art and architecture **15**:495–501
LATIN AMERICAN FREE TRADE ASSOCIATION *see* LATIN AMERICAN INTEGRATION ASSOCIATION
LATIN AMERICAN INTEGRATION ASSOCIATION **12**:228
customs union **5**:398
LATIN AMERICAN LITERATURE **12**:228–231 *bibliog., illus.*
See also specific literary forms subdivided by Latin American countries, e.g., NOVEL—Argentine literature; POETRY—Brazilian literature; etc.; names of specific authors, e.g., FUENTES, CARLO; VALLEJO, CÉSAR; etc.
exile literature **12**:230–231
literature of independence **12**:229
Mexican Revolution **12**:229–230
modernism **12**:229
native and early colonial writings **12**:228–229
LATIN AMERICAN MUSIC AND DANCE **12**:231–232 *bibliog., illus.*
Alonso, Alicia **1**:307
cha cha **4**:264
Chávez, Carlos **4**:305
Ginastera, Alberto **9**:183
hustle **10**:321
tango **19**:23
LATIN AMERICAN UNIVERSITIES **12**:232–233 *bibliog., table*
LATIN CROSS **5**:360; **5**:361 *illus.*
LATIN LANGUAGE **12**:233–234 *bibliog.*
See also names of specific letters of the English language, e.g., U (letter); W (letter); etc.
alphabet, evolution of **20**:294 *table*
dictionaries **6**:159
grammar
Donatus, Aelius **6**:237
Varro **19**:524
inscription **11**:186
linguistics **12**:356
Romance languages **16**:280–281
secondary education **17**:179
Vulgar Latin
Romance languages **16**:280–281
writing systems, evolution of **20**:293–294
LATIN LITERATURE **12**:234 *bibliog.*
authors
Apuleius **2**:92
Ausonius **2**:325
Caesar, Gaius Julius **4**:15
Cato, Marcus Porcius (Cato the Elder) **4**:212–213
Catullus **4**:217
Cicero, Marcus Tullius **4**:428–429
Donatus, Aelius **6**:237
Ennius, Quintus **7**:207
Horace **10**:233–234
Juvenal **11**:480
Livius Andronicus **12**:378
Livy **12**:378
Lucan **12**:448
Lucilius **12**:450
Lucretius **12**:451
Martial **13**:176
Naevius, Gnaeus **14**:5
Ovid **14**:470–471
Persius **15**:188
Petronius Arbiter **15**:215
Plautus **15**:362
Pliny the Elder **15**:368
Pliny the Younger **15**:368
Propertius, Sextus **15**:570
Quintilian **16**:27
Sallust **17**:34
Seneca, Lucius Annaeus **17**:200
Statius **18**:238
Suetonius **18**:323
Tacitus, Cornelius **19**:6
Terence **19**:115
Tibullus **19**:191
Varro **19**:524
Vergil **19**:551
comedy **5**:132
De rerum natura **6**:62
LATIN QUARTER (Paris) **15**:86 *map*
LATIN SQUARE *see* MAGIC SQUARE
LATINA (Italy)
map (41° 28′N 12° 52′E) **11**:321
LATINI, BRUNETTO
encyclopedia **7**:163
LATINS **12**:234
Alba Longa **1**:248
Rome, ancient **16**:297
LATITE **12**:234
LATITUDE **12**:234–235
biome **3**:274
geography **9**:101
horse latitudes **10**:246
navigation **14**:59
tropic of Cancer (zone) **19**:307
tropic of Capricorn **19**:307
zones, reconstructed indicating Permian climates **15**:33 *map*
LATIUM (Italy) **12**:235
cities
Anzio **2**:73
Cassino **4**:184
Rome **16**:294–297 *illus., map*
history
Italy, history of **11**:327
Rome, ancient **16**:297–298
Latins **12**:234
Pontine Marshes **15**:427
LATOUR, HENRI FANTIN- *see* FANTIN-LATOUR, HENRI
LATROBE (Pennsylvania)
map (40° 19′N 79° 23′W) **15**:147
LATROBE, BENJAMIN HENRY **12**:235 *bibliog., illus.*
Capitol of the United States **4**:126
cathedrals and churches **4**:208
Greek Revival **9**:346
White House **20**:137
LATTANY, MRS. JOHN *see* HUNTER, KRISTIN
LATTER DAY SAINTS, CHURCH OF JESUS CHRIST OF *see* MORMONISM
LATVIAN SOVIET SOCIALIST REPUBLIC (USSR) **12**:235–236 *bibliog., map*
Baltic languages **3**:54–55
cities
Riga **16**:221
economy **12**:236
history **12**:236
Livonia **12**:378
land and people **12**:235–236
LATYNINA, LARISA **12**:236
LAU GROUP (Islands)
map (18° 20′S 178° 30′E) **8**:77
LAUCHHAMMER (Germany, East and West)
map (51° 30′N 13° 47′E) **9**:140
LAUD, WILLIAM **12**:236 *bibliog.*
LAUDA, NIKI **12**:236
LAUDER, HARRY
music hall, vaudeville, and burlesque **13**:672
LAUDERDALE (county in Alabama)
map (34° 53′N 87° 40′W) **1**:234
LAUDERDALE (Mississippi)
map (32° 31′N 88° 31′W) **13**:469
LAUDERDALE (county in Mississippi)
map (32° 25′N 88° 40′W) **13**:469
LAUDERDALE (county in Tennessee)
map (35° 45′N 89° 40′W) **19**:104
LAUDONNIÈRE, RENÉ GOULAINE DE **12**:236 *bibliog.*
LAUE, MAX VON **12**:236
crystal **5**:376
mineral **13**:439
X-ray diffraction **20**:308
LAUGHING GAS
anesthetics **1**:410
dentistry **6**:115
nitrous oxide, nitrogen **14**:202
LAUGHING JACKASS *see* KOOKABURRA
LAUGHLIN PEAK
map (36° 38′N 104° 12′W) **14**:136
LAUGHTON, CHARLES **12**:236–237 *bibliog., illus.*
LAUNCESTON (Australia)
map (41° 26′S 147° 8′E) **2**:328
LAUNCH VEHICLE *see* ROCKETS AND MISSILES, ROCKETS, SPACE
LAURANA, FRANCESCO **12**:237 *bibliog.*
LAURASIA
paleography **15**:37 *map*
plate tectonics **15**:354 *map*
LAUREL **12**:237 *bibliog., illus.*
avocado **2**:376
bay leaf **3**:132
California laurel **4**:38
mountain laurel **13**:622
Pythian Games **15**:640
sassafras **17**:83
LAUREL (Delaware)
map (38° 33′N 75° 34′W) **6**:88
LAUREL (Indiana)
map (39° 30′N 85° 11′W) **11**:111
LAUREL (county in Kentucky)
map (37° 10′N 84° 10′W) **12**:47
LAUREL (Maryland)
map (39° 6′N 76° 51′W) **13**:188
LAUREL (Mississippi)
map (31° 42′N 89° 8′W) **13**:469
LAUREL (Montana)
map (45° 40′N 108° 46′W) **13**:547
LAUREL (Nebraska)
map (42° 26′N 97° 6′W) **14**:70
LAUREL, SALVADOR **2**:95 *illus.*
LAUREL, STAN *see* LAUREL AND HARDY
LAUREL BAY (South Carolina)
map (32° 27′N 80° 48′W) **18**:98
LAUREL AND HARDY **12**:238 *bibliog., illus.*
LAUREL LEAF (stone tool)
Solutrean **18**:58
LAUREL MOUNTAIN
map (39° 10′N 79° 50′W) **20**:111
LAUREL RIVER LAKE
map (36° 50′N 84° 20′W) **12**:47
LAURELDALE (Pennsylvania)
map (40° 23′N 75° 55′W) **15**:147
LAURELVILLE (Ohio)
map (39° 28′N 82° 44′W) **14**:357
LAUREN, RALPH
fashion design **8**:32
LAURENCE, MARGARET **12**:238 *bibliog.*
LAURENS (county in Georgia)
map (32° 30′N 8° 30′W) **9**:114
LAURENS (Iowa)
map (42° 51′N 94° 51′W) **11**:244
LAURENS (South Carolina)
map (34° 30′N 82° 1′W) **18**:98
LAURENS (county in South Carolina)
map (34° 30′N 82° 0′W) **18**:98
LAURENS, HENRI **12**:238 *bibliog.*
LAURENS, HENRY **12**:238 *bibliog., illus.*
LAURENT, AUGUSTE **12**:238–239
organic chemistry **14**:434–435
LAURENT, LOUIS STEPHEN ST. *see* ST. LAURENT, LOUIS STEPHEN
LAURENT, YVES SAINT *see* SAINT LAURENT, YVES
LAURENTIA (ancient landmass)
plate tectonics **15**:354 *map*
LAURENTIAN LIBRARY **12**:239
LAURENTIAN MOUNTAINS **12**:239
map (48° 0′N 71° 0′W) **16**:18
LAURENTIAN SHIELD *see* CANADIAN SHIELD
LAURENTIDES *see* LAURENTIAN MOUNTAINS
LAURIER, SIR WILFRID **12**:239 *bibliog., illus.*
Canada, history of **4**:85; **4**:86
Liberal parties **12**:311
LAURINBURG (North Carolina)
map (34° 47′N 79° 27′W) **14**:242
LAURIUM (Michigan)
map (47° 14′N 88° 26′W) **13**:377
LAUSANNE (Switzerland) **12**:239
map (46° 31′N 6° 38′E) **18**:394
LAUSANNE, TREATY OF (1912) *see* OUCHY, TREATY OF
LAUSANNE, TREATY OF (1923) **12**:239–240 *bibliog.*
Chanak Crisis **4**:278
Curzon, George Nathaniel Curzon, 1st Marquess **5**:396
Kurds **12**:139
Middle East **13**:407 *map*
World War I **20**:246
LAUSSEL, VENUS OF see VENUS OF LAUSSEL
LAUTARO **12**:240 *bibliog.*
LAUTARO (Chile)
map (38° 31′S 72° 27′W) **4**:355
LAUTI, TOALIPI
Tuvalu **19**:356
LAUTOKA (Fiji)
map (17° 37′S 177° 27′E) **8**:77
LAUTREC, HENRI DE TOULOUSE- *see* TOULOUSE-LAUTREC, HENRI DE

LAUZUN, DUC DE
Montpensier, Anne Marie Louise d'Orléans, Duchesse de **13**:558
LAVA **12**:240 *bibliog., illus.*
basalt **3**:101
cave **4**:222
composition **12**:240
fumarole **8**:358
flows **12**:240
igneous rock **11**:33
magma **13**:51–52
obsidian **14**:319
olivine **14**:380
pitchstone **15**:320
rille **16**:224
rock **16**:247
scoria **17**:148
seafloor spreading **17**:172
silicate minerals **17**:305
trachyte **19**:258
volcano **19**:626–628
LAVA HOT SPRINGS (Idaho)
map (42° 37′N 112° 1′W) **11**:26
LAVACA (county in Texas)
map (29° 22′N 96° 55′W) **19**:129
LAVAL (France)
map (48° 4′N 0° 46′W) **8**:260
LAVAL (Quebec) **12**:240
map (45° 33′N 73° 44′W) **16**:18
LAVAL, CARL GUSTAF DE *see* DE LAVAL, CARL GUSTAF
LAVAL, FRANÇOIS DE **12**:240 *bibliog.*
LAVAL, PIERRE **12**:240–241 *bibliog.*
Vichy Government **19**:571
LAVAL UNIVERSITY **12**:241
Montreal, University of **13**:558–560
LAVALLEJA, JUAN ANTONIO **12**:241
LAVENDER **12**:241 *illus.*
LAVER, ROD **12**:241 *bibliog.*
LAVERAN, CHARLES **12**:241 *bibliog.*
malaria **13**:80
LAVILLETTE (New Brunswick)
map (47° 16′N 65° 18′W) **14**:117
LAVINA (Montana)
map (46° 18′N 108° 56′W) **13**:547
LAVOISIER, ANTOINE LAURENT **4**:325 *illus.*; **12**:241–242 *bibliog., illus.*
calcium **4**:22
element **7**:129
organic chemistry **14**:434
oxygen **14**:476
phlogiston theory **14**:248
photosynthesis **15**:275
sulfur **18**:334
thermodynamics **19**:162
LAVONIA (Georgia)
map (34° 26′N 83° 6′W) **9**:114
LAVROVSKY, LEONID
Kirov Ballet **12**:89
LAW **12**:242–244 *bibliog.*
See also ADMINISTRATIVE LAW; AIR LAW; BUSINESS LAW; CIVIL LAW; CONTRACT (law); CRIMINAL JUSTICE; ESTATE; MARITIME LAW; MILITARY JUSTICE; PROPERTY; WILL (law); etc.; headings beginning with the word LEGAL; the subheading law under the names of specific countries
abstract **1**:63
act of God **1**:86
adoption and foster care **1**:107
adversary procedure **1**:111
advocate **1**:114
affidavit **1**:132
alias **1**:292
animal experimentation **2**:22
artificial insemination **2**:220–221
assault and battery **2**:264
attainder, bill of **2**:313
attorney **2**:316
bigamy **3**:249
blackmail **3**:321
body snatching **3**:357
bona fide **3**:375
breach of the peace **3**:465
bribery **3**:477
burglary **3**:569–570
casuistry **4**:193
civil disobedience **5**:10
civil law **5**:11–12
collusion **5**:105
common law **5**:138–141
community property **5**:153
conspiracy **5**:206
consumer protection
Nader, Ralph **14**:5 *illus.*
contempt **5**:227
court **5**:314–316
damages **6**:18
death and dying **6**:69
defamation **6**:81
defense counsel **6**:83
demurrer **6**:105
deposition **6**:118
diseases, occupational **6**:194
double jeopardy **6**:246
education **12**:243
equity (law) **7**:226–227
ethics **7**:251
ex post facto law **7**:326
freeholder **8**:299
game laws **9**:27
Good Samaritan Law
first aid **8**:109
gun control **9**:405
habeas corpus **10**:3–4
handicapped persons **10**:36–37
history *see* LAW, HISTORY OF
incompetence **11**:77
injunction **11**:178
international law **11**:221–222
joint tenancy **11**:440
jury **11**:477–478
Justice, U.S. Department of **11**:478
justice of the peace **11**:478
larceny **12**:206
liability **12**:311
malice **13**:91
malpractice **13**:93
mandamus **13**:110
marriage **13**:165–166
minor **13**:459
misrepresentation **13**:467
mortmain **13**:592
natural law **14**:48
negligence **14**:77
next of kin **14**:175
nuisance **14**:291–292
osteopathic medicine **14**:457
paralegal services **15**:78
pardon **15**:83
parent **15**:84
perjury **15**:172
pharmacy **15**:221
political science **15**:403
pollutants, chemical **15**:411
pollution control **15**:415–416
probation **15**:559
professional and educational organizations
American Bar Association **1**:337
Inns of Court **11**:181
prosecuting attorney **15**:572
prostitution **15**:573–574
public domain **15**:608
receiver **16**:106
riot **16**:228
sex change **17**:224
squatter **18**:203
sumptuary laws **18**:340
tear gas **19**:58
treason **19**:285
trespass **19**:291
trial **19**:291–292
usury **19**:491
vagrancy **19**:502–503
women in society **20**:204
writ **20**:291
LAW, ANDREW BONAR **12**:247 *bibliog.*
LAW, HISTORY OF **12**:244–247 *bibliog., illus.*
Blackstone, Sir William **3**:322
civil law **5**:11–12
common law **5**:138–141
Draco **6**:254
Fortas, Abe **8**:238
Germanic law **9**:137–138
Grotius, Hugo **9**:372
Hammurabi, Code of **10**:31
Hand, Learned **10**:35
Justinian Code **11**:478–479
Kent, James **12**:45
Maine, Sir Henry **13**:75
Manu **13**:131
maritime law **13**:158
Napoleonic Code **14**:19
Roman law **16**:278–279
Savigny, Friedrich Karl von **17**:99
state (in political philosophy) **18**:229–232
Supreme Court of the United States **18**:355–358
LAW, JOHN **12**:247 *bibliog.*
Mississippi Scheme **13**:474
LAW, PHYSICAL **12**:248 *bibliog.*
gravitation **9**:304–305
inverse square law **11**:233
Kepler's laws **12**:58
laws of motion **12**:251
Maxwell's equations **13**:241–242
properties **12**:248
quantum mechanics **16**:9–11
relativity **16**:132–137
theoretical physics **19**:159
uncertainty principle **19**:381
LAW, WILLIAM **12**:248 *bibliog.*
LAW OF AVERAGES *see* LARGE NUMBERS, LAW OF
LAW SCHOOL ADMISSION TEST (LSAT)
Educational Testing Service **7**:66
LAW OF THE SEA *see* SEA, LAW OF THE
LAWANG (Indonesia)
map (7° 49′S 112° 42′E) **11**:147
LAWANGAN *see* DAYAK
LAWES, HENRY **12**:248 *bibliog.*
music, history of Western **13**:666
LAWES, SIR JOHN BENNETT **12**:248
LAWES, WILLIAM
Lawes, Henry **12**:248
LAWLER, RAY
Australian literature **2**:344
LAWN *see* GRASS (botany)
LAWN BOWLS (sport) **12**:248–249 *bibliog., illus.*; **14**:159 *illus.*
LAWN TENNIS *see* TENNIS
LAWNLEAF **12**:249
LAWRENCE (county in Alabama)
map (34° 30′N 87° 20′W) **1**:234
LAWRENCE (county in Arkansas)
map (36° 5′N 91° 5′W) **2**:166
LAWRENCE (county in Illinois)
map (38° 43′N 87° 43′W) **11**:42
LAWRENCE (county in Indiana)
map (38° 50′N 86° 28′W) **11**:111
LAWRENCE (Kansas)
map (38° 58′N 95° 14′W) **12**:18
LAWRENCE (county in Kentucky)
map (38° 5′N 82° 45′W) **12**:47
LAWRENCE (Massachusetts) **12**:249 *bibliog.*
map (42° 42′N 71° 9′W) **13**:206
LAWRENCE (county in Mississippi)
map (31° 35′N 90° 5′W) **13**:469
LAWRENCE (county in Missouri)
map (37° 5′N 93° 50′W) **13**:476
LAWRENCE (county in Ohio)
map (38° 40′N 82° 35′W) **14**:357
LAWRENCE (county in Pennsylvania)
map (41° 0′N 80° 20′W) **15**:147
LAWRENCE (ship)
Perry, Oliver Hazard **15**:179
LAWRENCE (county in South Dakota)
map (44° 22′N 103° 45′W) **18**:103
LAWRENCE (county in Tennessee)
map (35° 15′N 87° 25′W) **19**:104
LAWRENCE, ABBOTT **12**:249
LAWRENCE, D. H. **7**:201 *illus.*; **12**:249–250 *bibliog., illus.*
Lady Chatterley's Lover **12**:162
Rainbow, The **16**:77–78
Sons and Lovers **18**:66
Women in Love **20**:200–201
LAWRENCE, DAVID
U.S. News and World Report **19**:490
LAWRENCE, ERNEST ORLANDO **12**:250 *bibliog.*
accelerator, particle **1**:74–75
lawrencium **12**:251
LAWRENCE, GERTRUDE **12**:250 *bibliog.*
LAWRENCE, SIR HENRY
Lucknow (India) **12**:451
LAWRENCE, JACOB **12**:250 *bibliog.*
LAWRENCE, JOHN LAIRD MAIR LAWRENCE, 1st BARON **12**:250 *bibliog.*
LAWRENCE, T. E. **12**:250–251 *bibliog., illus.*
Seven Pillars of Wisdom **17**:215–216
World War I **20**:234–235; **20**:243–244
LAWRENCE, SIR THOMAS **12**:251 *bibliog., illus.*
Charles William Lambton **12**:251 *illus.*
LAWRENCE OF ARABIA *see* LAWRENCE, T. E.
LAWRENCE BERKELEY AND LAWRENCE LIVERMORE LABORATORIES **12**:251
LAWRENCE LIVERMORE LABORATORY *see* LAWRENCE BERKELEY AND LAWRENCE LIVERMORE LABORATORIES
LAWRENCEBURG (Indiana)
map (39° 6′N 84° 51′W) **11**:111
LAWRENCEBURG (Kentucky)
map (38° 2′N 84° 54′W) **12**:47
LAWRENCEBURG (Tennessee)
map (35° 15′N 87° 20′W) **19**:104
LAWRENCEVILLE (Georgia)
map (33° 57′N 84° 0′W) **9**:114
LAWRENCEVILLE (Illinois)
map (38° 44′N 87° 41′W) **11**:42
LAWRENCEVILLE (New Jersey)
map (40° 18′N 74° 44′W) **14**:129
LAWRENCEVILLE (Virginia)
map (36° 45′N 77° 51′W) **19**:607
LAWRENCIUM **12**:251
actinide series **1**:88
element **7**:130 *table*
Lawrence, Ernest Orlando **12**:251
metal, metallic element **13**:328
transuranium elements **19**:286
LAWS OF MOTION **12**:251 *bibliog.*
aerodynamicss **1**:123
celestial mechanics **4**:230
dynamics **6**:319
force **8**:220
friction **8**:330–331
Galileo Galilei **9**:15
inertia **11**:161
Kepler's laws **12**:58
kinematics **12**:78
law, physical **12**:248
motion, circular **13**:607–608
motion, planar **13**:609
Newton, Sir Isaac **14**:174
physics **15**:280
relativity **16**:133 *illus.*
three-body problem **19**:181
time-reversed motion
time reversal invariance **19**:202
wind **20**:168
LAWSON, HENRY **12**:251–252
LAWSON, H. J.
bicycle **3**:244
LAWSON, JOHN HOWARD
Hollywood Ten, The **10**:204
LAWSON, WILLIAM
Great Dividing Range **9**:319
LAWSON'S CRITERION
fusion energy **8**:383
LAWSUIT
legal procedure **12**:272–273
LAWTON (Michigan)
map (42° 10′N 85° 50′W) **13**:377
LAWTON (North Dakota)
map (48° 18′N 98° 22′W) **14**:248
LAWTON (Oklahoma) **12**:252
map (34° 37′N 98° 25′W) **14**:368
LAWU, MOUNT
map (7° 38′S 111° 11′E) **11**:147
LAWYER *see* ATTORNEY
LAXATIVE *see* CATHARTIC
LAXNESS, HALLDÓR KILJAN **12**:252 *bibliog.*
LAY LAKE
map (33° 5′N 86° 30′W) **1**:234
LAYAMON **12**:252
LAYARD, SIR AUSTEN **12**:252 *bibliog.*
Mesopotamian art and architecture **2**:123 *illus.*
Nimrud **14**:199
Nippur **14**:201
Tepe Gawra **19**:114
LAYE, CAMARA **12**:252 *bibliog.*
LAYTON (Utah)
map (41° 4′N 111° 58′W) **19**:492
LAYTONVILLE (California)
map (39° 41′N 123° 29′W) **4**:31
LAZAREV, V. G. **12**:252
LAZARSFELD, PAUL F.
sociology **18**:30
LAZARUS **12**:252
LAZARUS, EMMA **12**:252 *bibliog.*
LAZIO (Italy) *see* LATIUM (Italy)
LAZURITE *see* LAPIS LAZULI
LE *see the element of the name following* LE *for names not listed below*
LE BEL, JOSEPH ACHILLE
chemistry, history of **4**:327
organic chemistry **14**:435
stereochemistry **18**:258
LE BLOND, J. B. A.
Summer Palace (Peterhof) **16**:362 *illus.*
LE BRUN, CHARLES **12**:252–253 *bibliog., illus.*
The Chancellor Séuier in the Procession of Marie Thérèe's Entrance into Paris, 26 August 1660 **12**:253 *illus.*
Girardon, François **9**:189
Gobelins **9**:216
The Life of Louis XIV **19**:32 *illus.*
Mignard, Pierre **13**:416–417
tapestry **19**:33
Vaux-le-Vicomte, Château de **19**:529
Versailles, Palace of **19**:561
LE CARRÉ, JOHN **12**:253 *bibliog.*
LE CENTER (Minnesota)
map (44° 24′N 93° 44′W) **13**:453
LE CHÂTELIER, HENRI LOUIS **12**:253
LE CLAIRE (Iowa)
map (41° 36′N 90° 21′W) **11**:244

LE CONTE, MOUNT
map (35° 38′N 83° 29′W) **19**:104
LE CORBUSIER **12**:253–254 *bibliog., illus.*
Chandigarh (India) **4**:279
modern architecture **13**:491
monastic art and architecture **13**:521
Notre Dame du Haut, Church of **4**:208 *illus.*; **12**:253 *illus.*; **13**:492 *illus.*
Xenakis, Yannis **20**:311
LE DUAN
Vietnam **19**:583
LE DUC THO
Vietnam War **19**:588 *illus.*; **19**:590
LE FIGARO see FIGARO, LE (newspaper)
LE FLORE (county in Oklahoma)
map (34° 55′N 94° 45′W) **14**:368
LE GONIDEC, JEAN FRANÇOIS
Breton literature **3**:475
LE GRAND (California)
map (37° 14′N 120° 15′W) **4**:31
LE GRAND SAINT BERNARD HOSPICE
hotel **10**:260
LE GUIN, URSULA **12**:254
LE HAVRE (France) **12**:254
map (49° 30′N 0° 8′E) **8**:260
LE JEUNE, CLAUDE
Renaissance music **16**:156
LE MANS (France) **12**:254
map (48° 0′N 0° 12′E) **8**:260
LE MARS (Iowa)
map (42° 47′N 96° 10′W) **11**:244
LE MONDE see MONDE, LE
LE MOUSTIER (France) *see* MOUSTERIAN
LE MOYNE, CHARLES, SIEUR DE LONGUEUIL *see* LONGUEUIL, CHARLES LE MOYNE, SIEUR DE
LE MOYNE, JACQUES
scalping **17**:107
LE MOYNE, JEAN BAPTISTE, SIEUR DE BIENVILLE *see* BIENVILLE, JEAN BAPTISTE LE MOYNE, SIEUR DE
LE MOYNE, PIERRE, SIEUR D'IBERVILLE *see* IBERVILLE, PIERRE LE MOYNE, SIEUR D'
LE NAIN BROTHERS **12**:254–255 *bibliog., illus.*
The Traveller's Rest **12**:255 *illus.*
LE NÔTRE, ANDRÉ **12**:255 *bibliog.*
garden **9**:40 *illus.*
landscape architecture **12**:186–187 *illus.*
Tuileries **19**:329
Vaux-le-Vicomte, Château de **19**:529
Versailles, Palace of **12**:187 *illus.*; **19**:561
LE PAON, J. B.
Marquis de Lafayette **12**:163 *illus.*
LE PICHON, XAVIER
plate tectonics **15**:357
LE PUY (France)
map (45° 2′N 3° 53′E) **8**:260
LE ROY (Minnesota)
map (43° 31′N 92° 30′W) **13**:453
LE ROY (New York)
map (42° 59′N 77° 59′W) **14**:149
LE SACRE DU PRINTEMPS (ballet)
Ballets Russes de Serge Diaghilev **3**:48–49
LE SECQ, HENRI
photography, history and art of **15**:268
LE SEIG, THEO (pseudonym) *see* SEUSS, DR.
LE SUEUR (Minnesota)
map (44° 27′N 93° 54′W) **13**:453
LE SUEUR (county in Minnesota)
map (44° 22′N 93° 45′W) **13**:453
LE SUEUR, EUSTACHE **12**:255 *bibliog.*
LE SUEUR, LUCILLE *see* CRAWFORD, JOAN
LE TELLIER, FRANÇOIS MICHEL, MARQUIS DE LOUVOIS *see* LOUVOIS, FRANÇOIS MICHEL LE TELLIER, MARQUIS DE
LE VAU, LOUIS **12**:255 *bibliog.*
Vaux-le-Vicomte, Château de **19**:529
Versailles, Palace of **19**:561
LEA (county in New Mexico)
map (32° 45′N 103° 20′W) **14**:136
LEACH, ALEXANDER ARCHIBALD *see* GRANT, CARY
LEACH, SIR EDMUND **12**:256
LEACHVILLE (Arkansas)
map (35° 56′N 90° 15′W) **2**:166
LEACOCK, RICHARD
documentary **6**:211
LEACOCK, STEPHEN **12**:256 *bibliog.*
LEAD **12**:256 *bibliog.*
cerussite **4**:261
compounds **12**:256
photoelectric cell **15**:259
element **7**:130 *table*
galena **9**:13–14
Group IVA periodic table **15**:167
metal, metallic element **13**:328
native elements **14**:47
occurrence **12**:256
Driftless Area **6**:272
world distribution **14**:423 *map*
ore
wulfenite **20**:296
pollutants, chemical **15**:410
production **12**:256
pyromorphite **15**:638
radiometric age-dating **16**:66
roof and roofing **16**:306
sulfide minerals **18**:333
superconductivity **18**:350 *table*
toxicity **12**:256
uranium minerals **19**:478
uses **12**:256
vanadinite **19**:516
LEAD (South Dakota)
map (44° 21′N 103° 46′W) **18**:103
LEADBELLY **12**:256 *bibliog.*
LEADER (Saskatchewan)
map (50° 53′N 109° 31′W) **17**:81
LEADERSHIP
chief **4**:346
group dynamics **9**:376
LEADORE (Idaho)
map (44° 41′N 113° 21′W) **11**:26
LEADVILLE (Colorado)
map (39° 15′N 106° 20′W) **5**:116
LEADWORT **12**:257 *illus.*
sea lavender **17**:169
LEAF
deciduous plant **6**:73
photosynthesis **15**:276 *illus.*
plant **15**:336–337 *illus.*
tree **19**:287 *illus.*
LEAF-EATING MONKEY *see* LANGUR
LEAF RIVER (Mississippi)
map (31° 0′N 88° 45′W) **13**:469
LEAF RIVER (Quebec)
map (58° 47′N 70° 4′W) **16**:18
LEAFBIRD **12**:257
LEAFHOPPER **12**:257
LEAGUE OF ARAB STATES *see* ARAB LEAGUE
LEAGUE OF AUGSBURG *see* AUGSBURG, LEAGUE OF
LEAGUE OF COMMUNISTS IN YUGOSLAVIA
Yugoslavia **20**:343
LEAGUE OF NATIONS **12**:257–258 *bibliog.*
Europe, history of **7**:294–295
Fourteen Points **8**:254
Geneva (Switzerland) **9**:91
Geneva conferences **9**:91
Hitler, Adolf **10**:188
International Court of Justice **11**:219
mandate system **13**:111
Namibia **14**:12
Nansen, Fridtjof **14**:13 *illus.*
Palestine **15**:44
Paris Peace Conference **15**:88
sanctions **17**:58
United Nations **19**:412
Wilson, Woodrow **20**:167
World War I **20**:245
World War II **20**:248–249
LEAGUE FOR THE INDEPENDENCE OF VIETNAM *see* VIET MINH
LEAGUE OF THE PUBLIC WEAL
Louis XI, King of France **12**:425
LEAGUE OF UNITED LATIN AMERICAN CITIZENS
Chicano **4**:343
LEAGUE OF WOMEN VOTERS **12**:258
Catt, Carrie Chapman **4**:213
LEAHY, WILLIAM DANIEL **12**:258 *bibliog.*
LEAKE (county in Mississippi)
map (32° 45′N 89° 30′W) **13**:469
LEAKESVILLE (Mississippi)
map (31° 9′N 88° 33′W) **13**:469
LEAKEY (Texas)
map (29° 44′N 99° 46′W) **19**:129
LEAKEY (family) **1**:172 *illus.*; **12**:258–259 *bibliog., illus.*
Homo erectus **10**:215
Laetolil **12**:163
LEAKEY, LOUIS S. B. **1**:172 *illus.*
Homo habilis **10**:216
Leakey (family) **12**:258–259
Oldowan **14**:376
Olduvai Gorge **14**:376–377
Olorgesailie **14**:381
Omo **14**:388
Proconsul **15**:561
LEAKEY, MARY **1**:172 *illus.*
Australopithecus **2**:346
Leakey (family) **12**:258–259 *illus.*
Oldowan **14**:376
Olduvai Gorge **14**:376–377
Olorgesailie **14**:381
Proconsul **15**:561
LEAKEY, RICHARD
Leakey (family) **12**:258–259 *illus.*
Skull 1470 **17**:346
LEALMAN (Florida)
map (27° 50′N 82° 41′W) **8**:172
LEAMINGTON
map (42° 3′N 82° 36′W) **14**:393
LEAMINGTON (England)
map (52° 18′N 1° 31′W) **19**:403
LEAMINGTON (Ontario)
map (42° 3′N 82° 36′W) **19**:241
LEAN, DAVID **12**:259 *bibliog.*
LEANDER *see* HERO AND LEANDER
LEANING TOWER, THE (Pisa) **11**:308 *illus.*
LEAP YEAR
calendar **4**:28
LEAR, EDWARD **12**:259 *bibliog.*
nonsense verse **14**:217
LEAR, NORMAN **12**:259
LEARNED SOCIETIES *see* SCIENTIFIC ASSOCIATIONS
LEARNING IN ANIMALS
animal behavior **2**:12 *illus.*; **2**:13 *illus.*
animal communication **2**:20
ape **2**:76
culture **5**:384
dolphin **6**:227 *illus.*
fear **8**:39
imprinting **11**:68–69
Köhler, Wolfgang **12**:106
primate **15**:541
Thorndike, Edward L. **19**:179
LEARNING DISABILITIES **12**:259–260 *bibliog.*
dyslexia **6**:320
hyperactive children **10**:347
special education **18**:166–167
LEARNING LABORATORY *see* TEACHING AIDS, AUDIOVISUAL
LEARNING THEORY **12**:260–261 *bibliog.*
anxiety **2**:72
behavior modification **3**:169
Bettelheim, Bruno **3**:232
biofeedback **3**:263
child development **4**:348–350
concept formation and attainment **5**:169
conditioning **5**:172
culture **5**:384
developmental psychology **6**:142
Ebbinghaus, Hermann **7**:35
educational psychology **7**:66
Estes, William Kaye **7**:246
experimental psychology **7**:334
fear **8**:39
habit **10**:4
Harlow, Harry F. **10**:50–51
Hull, Clark **10**:296
illusions **11**:49
infancy **11**:162–163
information theory **11**:174
insight **12**:261
latent learning **12**:261
memory **13**:290–292
Miller, Neal E. **13**:428
Montessori method **13**:554
Mowrer, O. Hobart **13**:626
Pavlov, Ivan Petrovich **15**:120
personality **15**:189–190
phobia **15**:249
Piaget, Jean **15**:287–288
preschool education **15**:521
programmed learning **15**:562–563
psycholinguistics **15**:592
psychology **15**:594
psychology, history of **15**:597
psychopathology, treatment of **15**:600
reasoning **16**:104–105
reinforcement **12**:260
Guthrie, Edwin Ray **9**:409
"Sesame Street" **17**:212
skill learning **17**:339
Skinner, B. F. **17**:343–344
social psychology **18**:13
socialization **18**:26
speech development **18**:175–176
Thorndike, Edward L. **19**:179
Tolman, Edward C. **19**:227
trial-and-error learning **12**:261
two-factor learning **12**:261
Watson, John B. **20**:68
LEARY, TIMOTHY
counterculture **5**:311
LEASE **12**:261 *bibliog.*
encumbrance **7**:163
tenant **19**:101
LEASE, MARY ELIZABETH (Mary Ellen Lease) **12**:261–262
LEASOWES, THE
landscape architecture **12**:187
LEAST-SQUARES METHOD **12**:262 *bibliog.*
mathematics, history of **13**:225
LEATHER AND HIDES **12**:262–263 *bibliog., table*
catechu **4**:202
depilatory **6**:118
arsenic **2**:189
finishing **12**:262–263
fur **8**:369–371
shoes **17**:279–280 *illus.*
sources **12**:263
suede **18**:323
synthetic substitutes **12**:263
tanning **12**:262
types and uses **12**:262 *table*
LEATHER JACKET (zoology) *see* CRANE FLY
LEATHERBACK TURTLE **12**:263 *bibliog., illus.*
LEATHERNECKS *see* MARINE CORPS, U.S.
LEATHERSTOCKING TALES, THE (books) **12**:263
Bumppo, Natty **3**:562
Cooper, James Fenimore **5**:243
Deerslayer, The **6**:81
LEATHERWOOD **12**:263
LEAVENWORTH (Kansas)
map (39° 19′N 94° 55′W) **12**:18
LEAVENWORTH (county in Kansas)
map (39° 15′N 95° 0′W) **12**:18
LEAVES OF GRASS (book) **12**:263 *bibliog.*
Whitman, Walt **20**:140–141
LEAVIS, F. R. **12**:263 *bibliog.*
Snow, C. P., Baron Snow **18**:3
LEAVITT, HENRIETTA SWAN **12**:263–264 *bibliog.*
Magellanic Clouds **13**:49
LEAWOOD (Kansas)
map (38° 58′N 94° 37′W) **12**:18
LEBANON **12**:264–267 *bibliog., illus., map, table*
agriculture **12**:265
cities
Baalbek **3**:5
Beirut **3**:172
Tripoli **19**:302
climate **12**:264; **12**:265 *table*
economic activity **12**:265–266
education **12**:265
American University of Beirut **1**:367
Middle Eastern universities **13**:410–412 *table*
flag **12**:264 *illus.*
government **12**:266
history **12**:266–267
Middle East, history of the **13**:409–410
United Nations **19**:414
land and resources **12**:264
literature
Abu Madi, Iliya **1**:66
map (33° 50′N 35° 50′E) **2**:232
people **12**:264–265
religion **12**:264
Druzes **6**:283
Maronites **13**:162
trade **12**:266
LEBANON (Indiana)
map (40° 3′N 86° 28′W) **11**:111
LEBANON (Kansas)
map (39° 49′N 98° 33′W) **12**:18
LEBANON (Kentucky)
map (37° 34′N 85° 15′W) **12**:47
LEBANON (Missouri)
map (37° 41′N 92° 40′W) **13**:476
LEBANON (New Hampshire)
map (43° 38′N 72° 15′W) **14**:123
LEBANON (Ohio)
map (39° 26′N 84° 13′W) **14**:357
LEBANON (Oregon)
map (44° 32′N 122° 54′W) **14**:427
LEBANON (Pennsylvania)
map (40° 20′N 76° 25′W) **15**:147
LEBANON (county in Pennsylvania)
map (40° 20′N 76° 25′W) **15**:147
LEBANON (South Dakota)
map (45° 4′N 99° 46′W) **18**:103
LEBANON (Tennessee)
map (36° 12′N 86° 18′W) **19**:104
LEBANON (Virginia)
map (36° 54′N 82° 5′W) **19**:607

LEBANON JUNCTION (Kentucky)
map (37° 50′N 85° 44′W) **12**:47
LEBANON MOUNTAINS
Lebanon **12**:264
map (33° 50′N 35° 40′E) **12**:265
LEBEDEV, VALENTIN **12**:267
LEBENSRAUM
Germany, history of **9**:155
Ratzel, Friedrich **16**:94
LEBESGUE, HENRI LÉON **12**:267
mathematics, history of **13**:226
LEBLANC, NICOLAS
chemical industry **4**:317
Leblanc process **4**:318 *illus.*
soap and detergent **18**:7
LEBLANC PROCESS **4**:318 *illus.*
Solvay process **18**:58
LEBOMBO MOUNTAINS
map (26° 30′S 32° 0′E) **18**:380
LEBOYER, FREDERICK
pregnancy and birth **15**:506
LEBRUN, CHARLES FRANÇOIS **8**:324 *illus.*
LEBRUN, LOUISE ÉLISABETH VIGÉE- *see* VIGÉE-LEBRUN, LOUISE ÉLISABETH
LEBU (Chile)
map (37° 37′S 73° 39′W) **4**:355
LECCE (Italy)
map (40° 23′N 18° 11′E) **11**:321
LECCO (Italy)
map (45° 51′N 9° 23′E) **11**:321
LECHTALER ALPS (Mountains)
map (47° 15′N 10° 30′E) **2**:348
LECITHIN **12**:267–268
chocolate **4**:402
Hoppe-Seyler, Felix **10**:232
lipid **12**:361–362
LECLERC, JACQUES PHILIPPE **12**:268 *bibliog.*
LeCLERCQ, TANAQUIL
New York City Ballet **14**:155
LECOMPTE (Louisiana)
map (31° 5′N 92° 24′W) **12**:430
LECOMPTON CONSTITUTION **12**:268
LECONTE DE LISLE, CHARLES MARIE **12**:268 *bibliog.*
LED ZEPPELIN
rock music **16**:249 *illus.*
LEDA **12**:268
LEDBETTER, HUDDIE *see* LEADBELLY
LEDERBERG, JOSHUA **12**:268
Tatum, Edward L. **19**:44
LEDERER, JOHN
West Virginia **20**:114
LEDERER, RAYMOND
ABSCAM **1**:62
LEDGERS (bookkeeping) *see* BOOKKEEPING
LEDO ROAD *see* BURMA ROAD
LEDOUX, CLAUDE NICOLAS **12**:268 *bibliog.*
boudoir **11**:213 *illus.*
visionary architecture **19**:617
LEDUC (Alberta)
map (53° 16′N 113° 33′W) **1**:256
LEDUC, OZIAS
Canadian art and architecture **4**:89
LEDUC, RENÉ
jet propulsion **11**:407
LEE (county in Alabama)
map (32° 35′N 85° 20′W) **1**:234
LEE (county in Arkansas)
map (34° 45′N 90° 45′W) **2**:166
LEE (family) **12**:268–269 *bibliog., illus.*
Lee, Robert E. **12**:269
LEE (county in Florida)
map (26° 34′N 81° 55′W) **8**:172
LEE (county in Georgia)
map (31° 45′N 84° 10′W) **9**:114
LEE (county in Illinois)
map (41° 45′N 89° 18′W) **11**:42
LEE (county in Iowa)
map (40° 40′N 91° 30′W) **11**:244
LEE (county in Kentucky)
map (37° 35′N 83° 45′W) **12**:47
LEE (Massachusetts)
map (42° 19′N 73° 15′W) **13**:206
LEE (county in Mississippi)
map (34° 15′N 88° 40′W) **13**:469
LEE (county in North Carolina)
map (35° 30′N 79° 10′W) **14**:242
LEE (county in South Carolina)
map (34° 10′N 80° 20′W) **18**:98
LEE (county in Texas)
map (30° 20′N 96° 55′W) **19**:129
LEE (county in Virginia)
map (36° 42′N 83° 0′W) **19**:607
LEE, ANN **12**:269 *bibliog.*
Shakers **17**:236
LEE, ARTHUR
Deane, Silas **6**:68
LEE, CHARLES **12**:269 *bibliog.*
Monmouth, Battle of **13**:535
LEE, FRANCIS LIGHTFOOT
Lee (family) **12**:269
LEE, GYPSY ROSE
music hall, vaudeville, and burlesque **13**:673
LEE, HARPER
To Kill a Mockingbird **19**:216–217
LEE, HENRY
Lee, Robert E. **12**:269
LEE, HENRY "LIGHT HORSE HARRY"
Lee (family) **12**:269
LEE, IVY
public relations **15**:610
LEE, JESSE **12**:269 *bibliog.*
LEE, JOHN DOYLE **12**:269 *bibliog.*
Mountain Meadows Massacre **13**:623
LEE, MANFRED BENNINGTON *see* QUEEN, ELLERY
LEE, RICHARD (anthropologist) **2**:52 *illus.*
LEE, RICHARD HENRY (political leader)
Lee (family) **12**:268–269 *illus.*
LEE, ROBERT E. **12**:269–270 *bibliog., illus.*
Antietam, Battle of **2**:61
Bull Run, Battles of **3**:558–559
Chancellorsville, Battle of **4**:279
Civil War, U.S. **5**:20–30 *map*
Fredericksburg, Battle of **8**:293–294
Gettysburg, Battle of **9**:161
Grant, Ulysses S. **9**:288–289
Harpers Ferry (West Virginia) **10**:55
Peninsular Campaign **15**:144
Petersburg campaign **15**:202
portrait
Stone Mountain **18**:282
surrender at Appomattox **5**:30 *illus.*
Washington and Lee University **20**:45
Wilderness Campaign **20**:150
LEE, RUSSELL
photography, history and art of **15**:272
LEE, TSUNG DAO **12**:270
LEE, WILLIAM
knitting **12**:101
LEE KUAN YEW **12**:270
LEECH **12**:271 *bibliog., illus.*
biological locomotion **3**:266
dog leech **12**:168 *illus.*
LEECH LAKE
map (47° 9′N 94° 23′W) **13**:453
LEECHBURG (Pennsylvania)
map (40° 38′N 79° 36′W) **15**:147
LEEDEY (Oklahoma)
map (35° 52′N 99° 21′W) **14**:368
LEEDS (Alabama)
map (33° 33′N 86° 33′W) **1**:234
LEEDS (England) **5**:4 *illus.*; **12**:271
map (53° 50′N 1° 35′W) **19**:403
LEEDS (North Dakota)
map (48° 17′N 99° 27′W) **14**:248
LEEDS, THOMAS OSBORNE, 1ST DUKE OF *see* DANBY, THOMAS OSBORNE, 1ST EARL OF
LEEK **12**:271 *illus.*; **19**:534 *illus.*
LEELANAU (county in Michigan)
map (44° 55′N 85° 50′W) **13**:377
LEER (Germany, East and West)
map (53° 14′N 7° 26′E) **9**:140
LEES SUMMIT (Missouri)
map (38° 55′N 94° 23′W) **13**:476
LEESBURG (Florida)
map (28° 49′N 81° 53′W) **8**:172
LEESBURG (Georgia)
map (31° 44′N 84° 10′W) **9**:114
LEESBURG (Virginia)
map (39° 7′N 77° 34′W) **19**:607
LEESVILLE (Louisiana)
map (31° 8′N 93° 16′W) **12**:430
LEESVILLE LAKE
map (37° 5′N 79° 25′W) **19**:607
LEETONIA (Ohio)
map (40° 53′N 80° 45′W) **14**:357
LEEUWENHOEK, ANTONI VAN **12**:271–272 *bibliog., illus.*
anatomy **1**:396
bacteria **3**:16
biology **3**:269 *illus.*
heredity **10**:139
medicine **13**:269
microbiology **13**:384
microscope **13**:387
sperm cells **20**:376 *illus.*
LEEUWIN, CAPE
map (34° 22′S 115° 8′E) **2**:328
LEEWARD ISLANDS **12**:272
Anguilla **2**:7
Antigua and Barbuda **2**:62
map (17° 0′N 63° 0′W) **20**:109
Montserrat (island) **13**:560
Netherland Antilles **14**:103
Saint Martin (France) **17**:24
LEEWARDEN (Netherlands)
map (53° 12′N 5° 46′E) **14**:99
LEFEBVRE, MARCEL **12**:272 *bibliog.*
LEFÈVRE D'ÉTAPLES, JACQUES **12**:272 *bibliog.*
LEFLORE (county in Mississippi)
map (33° 35′N 90° 20′W) **13**:469
LEFORS (Texas)
map (35° 26′N 100° 48′W) **19**:129
LEFSCHETZ, SOLOMON **12**:272
LEFT, THE (politics) *see* LIBERAL PARTIES; LIBERALISM; NEW LEFT
LEFT BANK (Paris) **15**:86 *map*
LEFT-HANDEDNESS *see* HANDEDNESS
LEG
biological locomotion **3**:266 *illus.*
bird **3**:283
muscle **13**:654
pain
sciatica **17**:141
skeleton, human **17**:336
varicose vein **19**:523
LEGAL AID **12**:272 *bibliog.*
See also RIGHT TO COUNSEL (law)
LEGAL CODES
Field, David Dudley, Jr. **8**:71
Field, Stephen Johnson **8**:72
Hammurabi, Code of **10**:31
LEGAL POSITIVISM *see* POSITIVISM
LEGAL PROCEDURE **12**:272–273 *bibliog.*
appeal **2**:87
arrest **2**:188
attachment **2**:313
brief **3**:485
common law **5**:138–141
complaint **5**:157
death and dying **6**:69
defense counsel **6**:83
equity (law) **7**:226–227
evidence **7**:316–318
indictment **11**:144
judgment **11**:464
jury **11**:477–478
law **12**:243
plea bargaining **15**:363–364
prosecuting attorney **15**:572
search warrant **17**:175
sentence **17**:205
subpoena **18**:316
summons **18**:339
Supreme Court of the United States **18**:356–357
trial **19**:292
warrant **20**:30
witness **20**:192–193
LEGAL SERVICES CORPORATION
legal aid **12**:272
LEGALISM (Chinese philosophy)
China, history of **4**:371
philosophy **15**:247
LEGALISM (political science)
political science **15**:403
LEGARÉ, JOSEPH
Canadian art and architecture **4**:89
LEGAZPI, MIGUEL LÓPEZ DE
Philippines **15**:238
LEGEND **12**:273 *bibliog.*
See also FOLKTALE; names of specific legendary characters, e.g., LUCRETIA; PRESTER JOHN; etc.; names of specific legendary places, e.g., ATLANTIS; EL DORADO; etc.
Arthur and Arthurian legend **2**:219
folklore **8**:203
LEGENDRE, ADRIEN MARIE
mathematics, history of **13**:226
LEGER, ALEXIS SAINT-LEGER *see* PERSE, SAINT-JOHN
LEGER, BARRY ST. *see* ST. LEGER, BARRY
LÉGER, FERNAND **12**:274 *bibliog., illus.*
film, history of **8**:84
The Great Parade **12**:274 *illus.*
LÉGER, JULES **12**:274
LÉGER, PAUL ÉMILE **12**:274 *bibliog.*
LEGGETT (California)
map (39° 52′N 123° 43′W) **4**:31
LEGHORN (fowl) *see* CHICKEN
LEGHORN (Italy) *see* LIVORNO (Italy)
LEGION, FRENCH FOREIGN *see* FRENCH FOREIGN LEGION
LEGION, ROMAN **7**:281 *illus.*; **12**:274 *bibliog.*
uniform **11**:164 *illus.*
LEGION OF DECENCY (Catholic) *see* NATIONAL CATHOLIC OFFICE FOR MOTION PICTURES
LEGION OF HONOR
medals and decorations **13**:263
Napoleon I, Emperor of the French (Napoléon Bonaparte) **14**:17
LEGIONNAIRES' DISEASE **12**:274
environmental health **7**:210
LEGISLATURE **12**:274–275 *bibliog.*
administrative law **1**:105
apportionment
Baker v. *Carr* **3**:28
proportional representation **15**:572
Reynolds v. *Sims* **16**:191
Congress of the United States **5**:184–187
House of Representatives of the United States **10**:272–274
Senate of the United States **17**:198–199
democracy **6**:97
Inter-Parliamentary Union **11**:206
Parliament **15**:92–93
parliamentary procedure **15**:93–95
representation **16**:160–161
States-General **18**:234
LEGLESS LIZARD **12**:275
LEGNAGO (Italy)
map (45° 11′N 11° 18′E) **11**:321
LEGNANI, PIERINA
Kirov Ballet **12**:90
LEGNICA (Poland)
map (51° 13′N 16° 9′E) **15**:388
LEGUÍA Y SALCEDO, AUGUSTO BERNARDINO **12**:275
Peru **15**:195
LEGUME **12**:275
acacia **1**:68
alfalfa **1**:278
bean **3**:139–140
cowpea **5**:321
diet, human **6**:164
hay **10**:80
lentil **12**:287
licorice **12**:323
lima bean **12**:342
pea **15**:122
peanut **15**:125
savanna life **17**:98
soybean **18**:114–115
vetch **19**:565
LEHÁR, FRANZ **12**:275 *bibliog.*
LEHI (Utah)
map (40° 24′N 111° 51′W) **19**:492
LEHIGH (Oklahoma)
map (34° 28′N 96° 13′W) **14**:368
LEHIGH (county in Pennsylvania)
map (40° 36′N 75° 29′W) **15**:147
LEHIGH ACRES (Florida)
map (26° 36′N 81° 39′W) **8**:172
LEHIGH RIVER
map (40° 41′N 75° 12′W) **15**:147
LEHIGH UNIVERSITY **12**:275
LEHIGHTON (Pennsylvania)
map (40° 49′N 75° 45′W) **15**:147
LEHMAN, HERBERT H. **12**:275–276 *bibliog.*
LEHMAN, ROBERT
Metropolitan Museum of Art, The **13**:348
LEHMANN, JOHANN GOTTLOB **12**:276 *bibliog.*
LEHMANN, LILLI
Tristan and Isolde (opera) **19**:303
LEHMANN, LOTTE **12**:276
LEHMANN-HAUPT, C. F.
Urartu **19**:480
LEHMBRUCK, WILHELM **12**:276 *bibliog.*
Duisburg (West Germany) **6**:294–295
LEHR (North Dakota)
map (46° 17′N 99° 21′W) **14**:248
LEIBL, WILHELM **12**:276 *bibliog.*
LEIBNITZ, GOTTFRIED WILHELM VON
philosophy **15**:245
LEIBNIZ, GOTTFRIED WILHELM VON **12**:276–277 *bibliog., illus.*
Clarke, Samuel **5**:40
computer **5**:160
Hannover (West Germany) **10**:39
logic **12**:396
mathematics, history of **13**:225 *illus.*
rationalism **16**:92; **16**:93
LEICESTER (England) **12**:277
map (52° 38′N 1° 5′W) **19**:403
LEICESTER, ROBERT DUDLEY, EARL OF **12**:277 *bibliog.*
Elizabeth I, Queen of England **7**:142
LEICESTER, SIMON DE MONTFORT, EARL OF *see* MONTFORT, SIMON DE, EARL OF LEICESTER
LEICESTERSHIRE (England) **12**:277
Leicester **12**:277
LEICHHARDT, LUDWIG
Australia, history of **2**:340 *map*
exploration **7**:338

Forrest, John, 1st Baron Forrest **8**:235
LEIDEN (Netherlands) **12**:277
library of University of Leiden **12**:315 *illus.*
map (52° 9′N 4° 30′E) **14**:99
medicine **13**:270
LEIF ERIKSSON **12**:277–278 *bibliog.*
exploration **7**:337 *map*
L'Anse aux Meadows **12**:144
Vinland **19**:601
LEIGH, VIVIEN **9**:3 *illus.*
LEIGHTON, FREDERICK, BARON LEIGHTON OF STRETTON **12**:278 *bibliog.*
LEINE RIVER
map (52° 43′N 9° 32′E) **9**:140
LEINO, EINO
Finnish literature **8**:99
LEINSDORF, ERICH **12**:278
LEINSTER (Ireland) **12**:278
LEIPSIC (Ohio)
map (41° 6′N 83° 59′W) **14**:357
LEIPZIG (East Germany) **12**:278 *illus.*
map (51° 19′N 12° 20′E) **9**:140
LEIPZIG, BATTLE OF
Schwarzenberg (family) **17**:139
LEIRIA (Portugal)
map (39° 45′N 8° 48′W) **15**:449
LEISHMANIASIS **12**:279
kala-azar **12**:7
protozoal diseases **15**:581
rhinitis **16**:196
LEISLER, JACOB **12**:279 *bibliog.*
LEISY* v. *HARDIN **12**:279
LEITCHFIELD (Kentucky)
map (37° 29′N 86° 18′W) **12**:47
LEITHA RIVER
map (47° 54′N 17° 17′E) **10**:307
LEITRIM (Ireland) **12**:279
LEIVICK, H.
Yiddish theater **20**:328
LEIX *see* LAOIGHIS (Ireland)
LEK RIVER
map (52° 0′N 6° 0′E) **14**:99
LELAND (Illinois)
map (41° 37′N 88° 48′W) **11**:42
LELAND (Michigan)
map (45° 1′N 85° 45′W) **13**:377
LELAND (Mississippi)
map (33° 24′N 90° 54′W) **13**:469
LELOIR, LUIS FREDERICO **12**:279
LELONG, LUCIEN
fashion design **8**:32
LELY, SIR PETER **12**:279 *bibliog.*
LEM *see* LUNAR EXCURSION MODULE
LEM, STANISŁAW **12**:279–280 *bibliog.*
LEMAÎTRE, GEORGES ÉDOUARD **12**:280
LÉMAN, LAC *see* GENEVA, LAKE
LEMASS, SEAN
Ireland, history of **11**:265
LEMBERG (Austria) *see* LVOV (USSR)
LEMERCIER, JACQUES **12**:280 *bibliog.*
Louvre **12**:437
LEMHI (county in Idaho)
map (44° 55′N 113° 50′W) **11**:26
LEMHI PASS
map (44° 58′N 113° 27′W) **11**:26
LEMHI RANGE
map (44° 30′N 113° 25′W) **11**:26
LEMIEUX, JEAN-PAUL
Canadian art and architecture **4**:91
LEMITAR (New Mexico)
map (34° 9′N 106° 55′W) **14**:136
LEMMING **12**:280 *illus.*
LEMMON (South Dakota)
map (45° 56′N 102° 10′W) **18**:103
LEMMON, MOUNT
map (32° 26′N 110° 47′W) **2**:160
LEMNOS
map (39° 54′N 25° 21′E) **9**:325
LEMON **12**:280 *bibliog., illus.*
citrus fruits **4**:447 *illus.*
LEMON BALM *see* BALM
LEMON GROVE (California)
map (32° 44′N 117° 2′W) **4**:31
LEMOORE (California)
map (36° 18′N 119° 47′W) **4**:31
LEMOVICES (tribe)
Limousin (France) **12**:346
LEMOYNE, JEAN BAPTISTE **12**:280–281 *bibliog.*
LEMOYNE, PIERRE *see* IBERVILLE, PIERRE LE MOYNE, SIEUR D'
LEMPA RIVER
map (13° 14′N 88° 49′W) **7**:100
LEMUR **12**:281 *bibliog., illus.*; **13**:104 *illus.*; **15**:540 *illus.*
aye-aye **2**:378
colugo **5**:125
forelimb **13**:102 *illus.*
pollination **15**:409
LENA (Illinois)
map (42° 23′N 89° 50′W) **11**:42
LENA (Wisconsin)
map (44° 57′N 88° 3′W) **20**:185
LENA RIVER **12**:281
map (72° 25′N 126° 40′E) **19**:388
LENARD, PHILIPP EDUARD ANTON **12**:281
Einstein, Albert **7**:94
LENAWEE (county in Michigan)
map (41° 53′N 84° 4′W) **13**:377
LENCA (American Indians) **12**:281 *bibliog.*
LEND-LEASE **12**:281 *bibliog.*
Roosevelt, Franklin Delano **16**:309
World War II **20**:257
LENDL, IVAN **12**:281
LENEXA (Kansas)
map (38° 58′N 94° 44′W) **12**:18
L'ENFANT, PIERRE CHARLES **12**:281–282 *bibliog.*
Washington, D.C. **20**:40
LENGLEN, SUZANNE **12**:282
LENGTH
measurement **13**:254
units, physical **19**:466
weights and measures **20**:93 *table*
LENHERT, P. GALEN
Hodgkin, Dorothy Crowfoot **10**:194
LENIN, VLADIMIR ILICH **12**:282–283 *bibliog., illus.*
Bolsheviks and Mensheviks **3**:371
communism **5**:146–147 *illus.*
Krupskaya, Nadezhda Konstantinovna **12**:132
New Economic Policy **14**:121
Polish-Soviet War **15**:398
Russian Revolutions of 1917 **12**:282–283; **16**:188 *illus.*; **16**:371–373 *illus.*
Russia/Union of Soviet Socialist Republics, history of **16**:359 *illus.*
socialism **18**:21–22 *illus.*
Stalin, Joseph **18**:213–214
tomb **19**:231
Trotsky, Leon **19**:310–311
World War I **20**:238
Zinoviev, Grigory Yevseyevich **20**:369
LENIN PRIZE
Landau, Lev **12**:181
LENINGRAD (USSR) **12**:283–285 *bibliog., illus., map*
art and architecture
Hermitage Museum **10**:143
Winter Palace **20**:181
Five, The **8**:132
history
Centennial anniversary (1803) **16**:355 *illus.*
Peter I, Emperor of Russia (Peter the Great) **15**:201
World War II **20**:271
Kirov Ballet **12**:89–90
map (59° 55′N 30° 15′E) **19**:388
subway **18**:318 *table*
LENINGRAD STATE UNIVERSITY **12**:285
Union of Soviet Socialist Republics, universities of the **19**:399 *table*
LENKORAN (USSR)
climate **19**:390 *table*
LENNI-LENAPE *see* DELAWARE (American Indians)
LENNOA **12**:285
LENNON, JOHN
Beatles, The **3**:144–145 *illus.*
LENNOX (South Dakota)
map (43° 21′N 96° 53′W) **18**:103
LENNOX, EARLS AND DUKES OF
Stuart (family) **18**:304
LENOIR (North Carolina)
map (35° 55′N 81° 32′W) **14**:242
LENOIR (county in North Carolina)
map (35° 15′N 77° 40′W) **14**:242
LENOIR, JEAN JOSEPH ÉTIENNE **12**:285 *bibliog.*
LENOIR CITY (Tennessee)
map (35° 48′N 84° 16′W) **19**:104
LENOX (Georgia)
map (31° 16′N 83° 28′W) **9**:114
LENOX (Iowa)
map (40° 53′N 94° 34′W) **11**:244
LENOX (Massachusetts)
map (42° 22′N 73° 17′W) **13**:206
LENOX, JAMES
New York Public Library **14**:155
LENS (eye) **7**:348–349 *illus.*
LENS (France)
map (50° 26′N 2° 50′E) **8**:260
LENS (optics) **12**:285–287 *bibliog., illus.*
See also OPTICAL INSTRUMENTATION
aperture **2**:76
camera **4**:54; **4**:55–56
cinematography **4**:433
coma (optics) **5**:129
concave **7**:351 *illus.*
contact lens **5**:226–227
convex **7**:351 *illus.*
Dollond, John **6**:226
focal point **8**:192
image, optical **11**:50–51 *illus.*
interference **11**:209
lanthanum **12**:201
Leeuwenhoek, Antoni van **12**:271
microscope **13**:387–388
optics **14**:410–411 *illus.*
telescope **19**:80–83
LENS, GRAVITATIONAL *see* GRAVITATIONAL LENS
LENT **12**:287
Ash Wednesday **2**:229
fasting **8**:33
Palm Sunday **15**:49
LENTIL **12**:287 *bibliog., illus.*; **19**:533 *illus.*
LENYA, LOTTE
musical comedy **13**:674 *illus.*
Weill, Kurt **20**:94
LENZ'S LAW **12**:287
inductance **11**:151
LEO (constellation) **12**:287
LEO I, POPE **12**:288 *bibliog.*
Chalcedon, Council of **4**:270
Charlemagne's coronation **15**:63 *illus.*
LEO III, BYZANTINE EMPEROR (Leo the Isaurian) **12**:287–288
LEO III, POPE **12**:288
Charlemagne's coronation **11**:328 *illus.*
LEO VI, BYZANTINE EMPEROR (Leo the Wise) **12**:288 *bibliog.*
LEO IX, POPE **12**:288
Schism, Great **17**:122
LEO X, POPE **12**:288 *bibliog.*
Medici (family) **13**:265
LEO XIII, POPE **12**:288–289 *bibliog., illus.*
LEO BELGICUS **12**:438 *map*
LEOBEN (Austria)
map (47° 23′N 15° 6′E) **2**:348
LÉOGÂNE (Haiti)
map (18° 31′N 72° 38′W) **10**:15
LEOLA (Arkansas)
map (34° 10′N 92° 35′W) **2**:166
LEOLA (South Dakota)
map (45° 43′N 98° 56′W) **18**:103
LEOMINSTER (Massachusetts)
map (42° 32′N 71° 45′W) **13**:206
LEON (county in Florida)
map (30° 30′N 84° 15′W) **8**:172
LEON (Iowa)
map (40° 44′N 93° 45′W) **11**:244
LEON (Kansas)
map (37° 42′N 96° 46′W) **12**:18
LEÓN (Mexico) **12**:289
map (21° 7′N 101° 40′W) **13**:357
LEÓN (Nicaragua) **12**:289
map (12° 26′N 86° 53′W) **14**:179
LEÓN (region in Spain) **12**:289
Alfonso X, King of Castile **1**:279
cities
León **12**:289
Ferdinand III, Spanish King of Castile **8**:53
HISTORY
Alfonso VI, King **1**:279
Portugal, history of, **15**:453
Spain, history of **18**:145–146 *maps*
LEÓN (Spain) **12**:289
cathedral
rose window **16**:314
map (42° 36′N 5° 34′W) **18**:140
LEON (county in Texas)
map (31° 18′N 95° 55′W) **19**:129
LEÓN, ARTHUR SAINT- *see* SAINT-LEÓN, ARTHUR
LEON, DANIEL DE *see* DE LEON, DANIEL
LEÓN, JUAN PONCE DE *see* PONCE DE LEÓN, JUAN
LÉON, LUIS DE
Spanish literature **18**:158
LEÓN, MOUNT
map (20° 53′S 60° 19′W) **15**:77
LEONARD (North Dakota)
map (46° 39′N 97° 15′W) **14**:248
LEONARD, BENNY
boxing **3**:432
LEONARD, ELMORE **12**:289
LEONARD, HELEN LOUISE *see* RUSSELL, LILLIAN
LEONARDO DA VINCI **12**:289–291 *bibliog., illus.*
bridge (engineering) **3**:480
camera obscura **4**:59
drawing **6**:263 *illus.*; **6**:264
drawing of a Vitruvian man **7**:286 *illus.*
The Last Supper **13**:645 *illus.*
Madonna of the Rocks **12**:290 *illus.*
mathematics, history of **13**:225
mechanical drawing **13**:259
Mona Lisa **11**:312 *illus.*; **12**:291 *illus.*; **13**:515
National Gallery of Art **14**:33
Renaissance art and architecture **16**:152
scientific investigations **12**:291
self-portrait **12**:290 *illus.*
The Virgin and Child with Saint Anne **16**:152 *illus.*
LEONARDO PISANO **12**:291 *bibliog.*
Fibonacci sequence **8**:69
mathematics, history of **13**:224
LEONARDTOWN (Maryland)
map (38° 17′N 76° 38′W) **13**:188
LEONCAVALLO, RUGGERO **12**:291–292
LEONE, MONTE
Simplon Pass **17**:316
LEONI (family) **12**:292
LEONI, RAÚL
Venezuela **19**:544
LEONIDAS, KING OF SPARTA **12**:292; **14**:81 *illus.*
LEONIDOV, IVAN
Russian art and architecture **16**:364
LEONIDS *see* METEOR AND METEORITE
LEONIN
organum **14**:441
LEONINUS *see* LEONIN
LEONORA (Australia)
map (28° 53′S 121° 20′E) **2**:328
LEONOV, ALEKSEI **12**:292
Apollo-Soyuz Test Project **2**:84
LEONOV, LEONID MAKSIMOVICH **12**:292 *bibliog.*
LEONTIEF, WASSILY **12**:292 *bibliog., illus.*
input-output analysis **11**:182
LEONVILLE (Louisiana)
map (30° 29′N 91° 59′W) **12**:430
LEOPARD **4**:196 *illus.*; **12**:292–293 *bibliog., illus.*
snow leopard **13**:623 *illus.*
LEOPARD FROG **12**:293 *illus.*
life cycle **1**:379 *illus.*
LEOPARD SEAL **2**:42–43 *illus.*
LEOPARD SOCIETY *see* NGBE (Leopard Society)
LEOPARDI, GIACOMO, CONTE **11**:293 *bibliog.*
LEOPOLD, ALDO **12**:293 *bibliog.*
wilderness conservation **12**:293
LEOPOLD, DUKE OF AUSTRIA
Richard I, King of England **16**:209
LEOPOLD, NATHAN
Darrow, Clarence S. **6**:39
LEOPOLD I, HOLY ROMAN EMPEROR **12**:294 *bibliog.*
LEOPOLD I, KING OF THE BELGIANS **12**:293–294 *bibliog., illus.*
inauguration of **12**:442 *illus.*
LEOPOLD II, HOLY ROMAN EMPEROR **12**:294–295 *bibliog.*
LEOPOLD II, KING OF THE BELGIANS **12**:294 *bibliog.*
Zaire **20**:352
LEOPOLD II, LAKE *see* MAI-NDOMBE, LAKE
LEOPOLD III, KING OF THE BELGIANS **12**:294 *bibliog., illus.*
demonstrations against return of **12**:442 *illus.*
LEOPOLDVILLE (Belgian Congo) *see* KINSHASA (Zaire)
LEOTARD (clothing)
circus **4**:444
LEOTI (Kansas)
map (38° 29′N 101° 21′W) **12**:18
LEOVIGILD, KING OF THE VISIGOTHS
Spain, history of **18**:144
LEPAGE, JULES BASTIEN- *see* BASTIEN-LEPAGE, JULES
LEPANTO (Arkansas)
map (35° 36′N 90° 20′W) **2**:166
LEPANTO, BATTLE OF **12**:295 *bibliog.*; **14**:465 *illus.*
LEPAUTRE, PIERRE
rococo style **16**:263
LEPENSKI VER
Mesolithic settlement **13**:315 *illus.*
LEPIDOPTERA *see* BUTTERFLIES AND MOTHS

LEPIDUS, MARCUS AEMILIUS 12:295
Rome, ancient 16:302
LEPRECHAUN *see* FAIRY
LEPROSY 12:295 *bibliog.*
Damien, Father 6:19
Mycobacterium 13:690
LEPSIUS, KARL
Tanis 19:23
LEPTIS MAGNA (Libya) 12:295 *bibliog.*
LEPTOCEPHALUS
eel 7:70–71 *illus.*, *illus.*
LEPTON 12:295
antimatter 2:63
electron 7:119–120
fermion 8:56
fundamental particles 8:361; 8:362 *table*
grand unification theories 9:286
muon 13:644
neutrino 14:108
quark 16:12
LEPTOSPIROSIS 12:296
diseases, animal 6:191
hepatitis 10:130
LERBERGHE, CHARLES VAN *see* VAN LERBERGHE, CHARLES
LÉRIDA (Spain)
map (41° 37′N 0° 37′E) 18:140
LERMA, DUQUE DE
Philip III, King of Spain 15:234–235
LERMONTOV, MIKHAIL 12:296 *illus.*
LERNER, ALAN JAY, AND LOEWE, FREDERICK 12:296 *bibliog.*
LERWICK (Scotland)
map (60° 9′N 1° 9′W) 19:403
LÉRY, JOSEPH GASPARD CHAUSSE-GROS DE
French and Indian Wars 8:313 *map*
LES CAYES (Haiti)
map (18° 12′N 73° 45′W) 10:15
LES COMBARELLES (France) 12:296
LES EYZIES (France)
Font de Gaume 8:205
LES SIX (composers of music)
Auric, Georges 2:324
Honegger, Arthur 10:220
Milhaud, Darius 13:419–420
Poulenc, Francis 15:473
Satie, Erik 17:88
LESAGE, ALAIN RENÉ 12:296 *bibliog.*
LESAGE, JEAN
Canada, history of 4:87
LESATIMA MOUNTAIN
map (0° 19′S 36° 37′E) 12:53
LESBIANISM 12:296
homosexuality 10:217
LESBOS (Greece) 12:296
map (39° 10′N 26° 20′E) 9:325
LESCARBOT, MARC
Canadian literature 4:93
LESCH-NYHAN SYNDROME
gout 9:266
LESCOT, PIERRE 12:296
Louvre 12:437
LESH, PHIL
Grateful Dead, The 9:301
LESION
skin diseases 17:341
stress, biological 18:297–298
LESKOVAC (Yugoslavia)
map (42° 59′N 21° 57′E) 20:340
LESLIE (Arkansas)
map (35° 50′N 92° 34′W) 2:166
LESLIE (Georgia)
map (31° 57′N 84° 5′W) 9:114
LESLIE (county in Kentucky)
map (37° 5′N 83° 25′W) 12:47
LESLIE (Michigan)
map (42° 27′N 84° 26′W) 13:377
LESLIE (West Virginia)
map (38° 3′N 80° 43′W) 20:111
LESLIE, P. H.
demography 6:103
LESOTHO 12:296–298 *bibliog.*, *illus.*, *map*
cities
Maseru 13:196
economic activity 12:297–298 *illus.*
flag 12:297 *illus.*
history 12:298
Mosheshwe, King of the Sotho 13:600–601
land 12:297 *map*
map (29° 30′S 28° 30′E) 1:136
people 12:297
Sotho 18:70
LESS-DEVELOPED COUNTRIES *see* THIRD WORLD
LESSEPS, FERDINAND MARIE, VICOMTE DE 12:298 *bibliog.*, *illus.*
LESSER ANTILLES *see* ANTILLES, GREATER AND LESSER
LESSER CAUCASUS MOUNTAINS
map (41° 0′N 44° 35′E) 4:218
LESSER KHINGAN RANGE
map (50° 0′N 126° 25′E) 4:362
LESSER SHEATHBILL *see* SHEATHBILL
LESSER SLAVE LAKE
map (55° 25′N 115° 30′W) 1:256
LESSER SUNDA ISLANDS *see* SUNDA ISLANDS (Indonesia)
LESSING, DORIS 12:298 *bibliog.*
Golden Notebook, The 9:232
LESSING, GOTTHOLD 12:298–299 *bibliog.*, *illus.*
fable 8:4–5
German literature 9:132–133
LESUR, DANIEL
Jolivet, André 11:441
LESZNO (Poland)
map (51° 51′N 16° 35′E) 15:388
LETCHER (county in Kentucky)
map (37° 10′N 82° 50′W) 12:47
LETCHER (South Dakota)
map (43° 54′N 98° 8′W) 18:103
LETHAL INJECTION 12:299
LETHBRIDGE (Alberta) 12:299
map (49° 42′N 112° 50′W) 1:256
LETHE 12:299
LETHEM (Guyana)
map (3° 23′N 59° 48′W) 9:410
LETO 12:299
LETOÖN
Xanthus 20:311
LETTER OF CREDIT 12:299
LETTERPRESS 12:299–300 *bibliog.*, *illus.*
flatbed cylinder press 8:154
Gutenberg, Johann 9:408–409
photography 15:265
platemaking 15:357–358
stereotype 18:260
thermography 19:166
web-fed press 20:85
LETTOW-VORBECK, PAUL VON
World War I 20:244
LETTS (people) *see* LATVIAN SOVIET SOCIALIST REPUBLIC (USSR)
LETTUCE 12:300 *illus.*
romaine 19:532 *illus.*
sea lettuce
seaweed 17:177
LEUCIPPUS 12:300
pre-Socratic philosophy 15:533
LEUCITE
feldspathoid 8:47
LEUCON 18:193 *illus.*
LEUCOTHOE 12:300
LEUCTRA, BATTLE OF
Epaminondas 7:215
LEUKEMIA 12:300–301 *bibliog.*
alkaloid 1:296
benzene 3:206
blood 3:338
cancer 4:101
chemotherapy 12:301
diagnosis 12:300–301
environmental health 7:212
fungus diseases 8:369
leukocytosis 12:301
lymphatic system 12:476
polycythemia 15:418
splenomegaly 18:191
LEUKOCYTE (white blood cell)
blood 3:336
LEUKOCYTOSIS 12:301
LEUKODERMA 12:301
skin diseases 17:341
LEUKOPENIA 12:301
lymphatic system 12:476
LEUKORRHEA 12:301 *bibliog.*
LEUTZE, EMANUEL 12:301 *bibliog.*
Düsseldorf Akademie 6:308
Washington Crossing the Delaware 1:333 *illus.*
LEUVEN (Belgium)
map (50° 53′N 4° 42′E) 3:177
LEV (USSR) *see* LVOV (USSR)
LEVALLOISIAN 12:301–302 *bibliog.*
Mousterian 13:626
Paleolithic Period 15:39
prehistoric humans 15:515
LEVAN (Utah)
map (39° 33′N 111° 52′W) 19:492
LEVANT 12:302
LEVEE 12:302
floods and flood control 8:167
LEVELERS (England) 12:302 *bibliog.*
suffrage
democracy 6:97
LEVELLAND (Texas)
map (33° 35′N 102° 23′W) 19:129
LEVER 12:302 *illus.*
ancient use 12:302
forms of machine 12:302
muscle 13:651–652
simple machines 17:316
technology, history of 19:63 *illus.*
LEVER, WILLIAM HESKETH, 1ST VISCOUNT LEVERHULME 12:303 *bibliog.*
LEVER HOUSE (New York) 2:137 *illus.*
Bunshaft, Gordon 3:564
LEVER-WOOD *see* HOP HORNBEAM (botany)
LEVERHULME, WILLIAM HESKETH LEVER, 1ST VISCOUNT *see* LEVER, WILLIAM HESKETH, 1ST VISCOUNT LEVERHULME
LEVERING (Michigan)
map (45° 38′N 84° 47′W) 13:377
LEVERRIER, URBAIN JEAN JOSEPH 12:303 *bibliog.*
astronomy, history of 2:279
LEVERTOV, DENISE 12:303 *bibliog.*
LÉVESQUE, RENÉ 12:303 *bibliog.*
LEVI BEN GERSHON 12:303 *bibliog.*
LÉVI-STRAUSS, CLAUDE 2:54 *illus.*; 12:303–304 *bibliog.*, *illus.*
Mauss, Marcel 13:238
primitive religion 15:543
Savage Mind, The 17:97
totem 19:249
LEVIATHAN (treatise) 12:304 *bibliog.*
Hobbes, Thomas 10:192
title page (1651 ed.) 18:231 *illus.*
LEVINE, DAVID
caricature of Leo Tolstoi 4:150
LEVINE, JACK 12:304 *bibliog.*
LEVINE, JAMES 12:304
LEVIRATE
marriage 13:165
LÉVIS (Quebec)
map (46° 48′N 71° 11′W) 16:18
LÉVIS, FRANÇOIS GASTON, DUQUE DE
French and Indian Wars 8:313 *map*
LEVISA FORK RIVER
map (38° 6′N 82° 36′W) 12:47
LEVITAN, ISAAK
Russian art and architecture 16:363
LEVITES 12:304 *bibliog.*
Aaron 1:50
LEVITICUS, BOOK OF 12:304 *bibliog.*
LEVITSKY, DMITRI
Russian art and architecture 16:362
LEVITT, HELEN
photography, history and art of 15:272
LEVITT, WILLIAM JAIRD 12:304 *bibliog.*
housing 10:277
LEVITTOWN (New York)
map (40° 41′N 73° 31′W) 14:149
LEVITTOWN (Pennsylvania)
map (40° 9′N 74° 50′W) 15:147
LEVITTOWNS (suburban development)
housing 10:277 *illus.*
Levitt, William Jaird 12:304
LEVKÁS ISLAND
map (38° 39′N 20° 27′E) 9:325
LEVNI, RESSAM 12:304–305 *bibliog.*
LEVODOPA 12:305
LEVUKA (Fiji)
map (17° 41′S 178° 50′E) 8:77
LEVY (county in Florida)
map (29° 20′N 82° 45′W) 8:172
LEVY, DAVID
chess 4:336
LEVY, WALTER J.
parapsychology 15:81
LEWES (Delaware)
map (38° 47′N 75° 8′W) 6:88
LEWES, GEORGE HENRY 12:305 *bibliog.*
LEWIN, KURT 12:305 *bibliog.*
group dynamics 9:376
motivation 13:610
psychology, history of 15:597
LEWIS (county in Idaho)
map (46° 15′N 116° 25′W) 11:26
LEWIS (county in Kentucky)
map (38° 32′N 83° 21′W) 12:47
LEWIS (county in Missouri)
map (40° 7′N 91° 45′W) 13:476
LEWIS (county in New York)
map (43° 50′N 75° 30′W) 14:149
LEWIS (county in Tennessee)
map (35° 30′N 87° 30′W) 19:104
LEWIS (county in Washington)
map (46° 35′N 122° 22′W) 20:35
LEWIS (county in West Virginia)
map (39° 0′N 80° 30′W) 20:111
LEWIS, SIR ARTHUR 12:305
LEWIS, C. DAY *see* DAY-LEWIS, CECIL
Spender, Stephen 18:177–178
LEWIS, C. S. 12:305 *bibliog.*, *illus.*
LEWIS, CARL 12:305
LEWIS, CLARENCE IRVING 12:306 *bibliog.*
LEWIS, G. E.
Ramapithecus 16:80
LEWIS, GILBERT NEWTON 12:306 *bibliog.*
acids and bases 1:83
activity 1:90
chemistry, history of 4:328
organic chemistry 14:435
LEWIS, JERRY LEE
rock music 16:248
LEWIS, JOHN (musician)
Modern Jazz Quartet 13:498
LEWIS, JOHN L. 12:306 *bibliog.*
industrial union 11:160
United Mine Workers of America 19:411–412
LEWIS, MATTHEW GREGORY 12:306 *bibliog.*
LEWIS, MEADE LUX
boogie-woogie 3:383
LEWIS, MERIWETHER 12:306 *bibliog.*
Lewis and Clark Expedition 12:307–308 *illus.*
LEWIS, ROBERT
Actors Studio 1:90
LEWIS, SINCLAIR 12:306–307 *bibliog.*, *illus.*
Arrowsmith (book) 2:188–189
Babbitt 3:5
Elmer Gantry 7:149
Main Street 13:69
LEWIS, WYNDHAM 12:307 *bibliog.*
vorticism 19:635
LEWIS AND CLARK (county in Montana)
map (47° 15′N 112° 25′W) 13:547
LEWIS AND CLARK EXPEDITION 12:307–308 *bibliog.*, *illus.*, *map*; 19:445 *map*
Clark, William 5:39
exploration 7:335–336 *map*
Hidatsa 10:158
Lewis, Meriwether 12:306
Montana 13:550
Nebraska 14:74
Oregon 14:430
Sacagawea 17:6
Sioux City 17:326
Snake River 17:383
Yakima (Indian tribe) 20:314
LEWIS AND CLARK LAKE
map (42° 50′N 97° 45′W) 18:103
LEWIS ISLAND
map (58° 10′N 6° 40′W) 19:403
LEWIS RANGE (Mountain Range)J
map (48° 30′N 113° 15′W) 16:262
LEWIS RIVER
map (44° 8′N 110° 40′W) 20:301
LEWIS RUN (Pennsylvania)
map (41° 52′N 78° 40′W) 15:147
LEWIS SMITH LAKE
map (34° 5′N 87° 7′W) 1:234
LEWISBURG (Kentucky)
map (36° 59′N 86° 57′W) 12:47
LEWISBURG (Pennsylvania)
map (40° 58′N 76° 53′W) 15:147
LEWISBURG (Tennessee)
map (35° 27′N 86° 48′W) 19:104
LEWISBURG (West Virginia)
map (37° 48′N 80° 27′W) 20:111
LEWISITE
chemical and biological warfare 4:312
LEWISPORTE (Newfoundland)
map (49° 15′N 55° 3′W) 14:166
LEWISTON (Idaho)
map (46° 25′N 117° 1′W) 11:26
LEWISTON (Maine) 12:308
map (44° 6′N 70° 13′W) 13:70
LEWISTON (Michigan)
map (44° 53′N 84° 18′W) 13:377
LEWISTON (Minnesota)
map (44° 0′N 91° 49′W) 13:453
LEWISTON (Utah)
map (41° 58′N 111° 51′W) 19:492
LEWISTOWN (Illinois)
map (40° 24′N 90° 9′W) 11:42
LEWISTOWN (Montana)
map (47° 4′N 109° 26′W) 13:547
LEWISTOWN (Pennsylvania)
map (40° 36′N 77° 31′W) 15:147
LEWISVILLE (Arkansas)
map (33° 22′N 93° 35′W) 2:166
LEWISVILLE (Texas)
map (33° 3′N 96° 60′W) 19:129
LeWITT, SOL 12:308 *bibliog.*
conceptual art 5:170
LEXICOLOGY AND LEXICOGRAPHY 12:308–309 *bibliog.*
See also DICTIONARY
applied linguistics 2:90
linguistics 12:358
parts of speech 15:100–101
LEXINGTON (Georgia)
map (33° 52′N 83° 7′W) 9:114
LEXINGTON (Illinois)
map (40° 39′N 88° 47′W) 11:42

LEXINGTON (Kentucky) **12**:309
map (38° 3′N 84° 30′W) **12**:47
LEXINGTON (Massachusetts) **13**:211 *illus.*
map (42° 27′N 71° 14′W) **13**:206
LEXINGTON (Michigan)
map (43° 16′N 82° 32′W) **13**:377
LEXINGTON (Mississippi)
map (33° 7′N 90° 3′W) **13**:469
LEXINGTON (Missouri)
map (39° 11′N 93° 52′W) **13**:476
LEXINGTON (Nebraska)
map (40° 47′N 99° 45′W) **14**:70
LEXINGTON (North Carolina)
map (35° 49′N 80° 15′W) **14**:242
LEXINGTON (Oregon)
map (45° 27′N 119° 41′W) **14**:427
LEXINGTON (South Carolina)
map (34° 0′N 81° 14′W) **18**:98
LEXINGTON (county in South Carolina)
map (33° 50′N 81° 20′W) **18**:98
LEXINGTON (Tennessee)
map (35° 39′N 88° 24′W) **19**:104
LEXINGTON (Virginia)
map (37° 47′N 79° 27′W) **19**:607
LEXINGTON AND CONCORD, BATTLES OF **12**:309 *bibliog.*
American Revolution **1**:355 *illus.*
Concord (Massachusetts) **5**:171
minutemen **13**:462
LEXINGTON PARK (Maryland)
map (38° 16′N 76° 27′W) **13**:188
LEYDEN (Netherlands) *see* LEIDEN (Netherlands)
LEYDEN, LUCAS VAN *see* LUCAS VAN LEYDEN
LEYDEN JAR **12**:309
capacitor **4**:119
physics, history of **15**:284
LEYLAND MOTORS
automotive industry **2**:366
LEYSTER, JUDITH **12**:309 *bibliog.*
LEYTE ISLAND
MacArthur, Douglas **13**:5 *illus.*
map (10° 50′N 124° 50′E) **15**:237
World War II **20**:278 *illus.*
LH *see* LUTEINIZING HORMONE
LHASA (Tibet/China) **12**:309–310 *bibliog.*
climate **2**:237 *table*
Forbidden City **8**:220
map (29° 40′N 91° 9′E) **19**:190
Potala palace **19**:190 *illus.*
LHASA APSO **6**:219 *illus.*; **12**:310 *bibliog., illus.*
LHOTE, HENRI
Tassili n'Ajjer **19**:43
L'HUMANITÉ see HUMANITÉ, L'
LI BO *see* LI PO (Li Bo)
LI CH'ING-CHAO (Li Quingzhao)
Chinese literature **4**:390
LI FEI-KAN *see* PA CHIN (Ba Jin)
LI GONGLIN *see* LI KUNG-LIN (Li Gonglin)
LI HONGZHANG *see* LI HUNG-CHANG (Li Hongzhang)
LI HUNG-CHANG (Li Hongzhang) **12**:310 *bibliog.*
LI KUNG-LIN (Li Gonglin) **12**:310 *bibliog.*
LI LUNG-MIEN *see* LI KUNG-LIN (Li Gonglin)
LI PAI *see* LI PO (Li Bo)
LI PO (Li Bo) **12**:310 *bibliog.*
LI SHIH-CHEN
Chinese medicine **4**:391
LI SIXUN *see* LI SSU-HSÜN (Li Sixun)
LI SSU (political figure)
Ch'in (Qin) **4**:359
LI SSU-HSÜN (Li Sixun) (artist) **12**:310 *bibliog.*
LI TANG *see* LI T'ANG (Li Tang)
LI T'ANG (Li Tang) **12**:310
LI TZU-CH'ENG (Li Zicheng) **12**:310
LI YÜ (Li Yu) **12**:310–311
LI YÜAN, EMPEROR OF CHINA
T'ang (Tang) (dynasty) **19**:21
LI ZICHENG *see* LI TZU-CH'ENG (Li Zicheng)
LIABILITIES (accounting) *see* BOOKKEEPING
LIABILITY **12**:311
workers' compensation **20**:217
LIABILITY INSURANCE
insurance **11**:198–199
LIANG KAI *see* LIANG K'AI
LIANG K'AI (Liang Kai) **12**:311 *bibliog.*
LIAO-YÜAN (China)
map (42° 54′N 125° 7′E) **4**:362
LIAR DICE (game)
dice games **6**:155
LIARD RIVER
map (61° 52′N 121° 18′W) **20**:345
LIBAVIUS, ANDREAS
chemistry, history of **4**:325
LIBBY (Montana)
map (48° 23′N 115° 33′W) **13**:547
LIBBY, WILLARD FRANK **12**:311 *bibliog.*
radiometric age-dating **16**:67
LIBEL *see* DEFAMATION
LIBERAL (Kansas)
map (37° 2′N 100° 55′W) **12**:18
LIBERAL (Missouri)
map (37° 34′N 94° 31′W) **13**:476
LIBERAL ARTS *see* HUMANITIES, EDUCATION IN THE
LIBERAL PARTIES **12**:311–312 *bibliog.*
Canada
Canada, history of **4**:87
King, W.L. Mackenzie **12**:81–82
Laurier, Sir Wilfred **12**:239
Mackenzie, Alexander (1822–92) **13**:28
Pearson, Lester **15**:128
Trudeau, Pierre Elliot **19**:316
Great Britain
Asquith, Herbert Henry, 1st Earl of Oxford and Asquith **2**:263
Gladstone, William Ewart **9**:196
Great Britain, history of **9**:317
Lloyd George, David 1st Earl Lloyd-George of Dwyfor **12**:383–384
Whig party **20**:130
liberalism **12**:312
LIBERAL REPUBLICAN PARTY **12**:312 *bibliog.*
Greeley, Horace **9**:347
Republican party **16**:173
LIBERALISM **12**:312 *bibliog.*
Group Theatre, The **9**:376–377
Locke, John **12**:388
Manchester (England) **13**:108
Scandinavia, history of **17**:110
socialism **18**:20
totalitarianism **19**:248
LIBERATION THEOLOGY **12**:312
LIBERATOR, THE (periodical)
Garrison, William Lloyd **9**:51
LIBEREC (Czechoslovakia)
map (50° 46′N 15° 3′E) **5**:413
LIBERIA **12**:312–314 *bibliog., illus., map, table*
art
African art **1**:160–164
cities
Monrovia **13**:543
economic activity **12**:313–314 *illus.*
education **12**:313
African universities **1**:176 *table*
flag **12**:313 *illus.*
flag of convenience **8**:149
government **12**:313
history **12**:313–314
American Colonization Society **1**:338
Doe, Samuel K. **6**:212
Tolbert, William R., Jr. **19**:226
Tubman, William V.S. **19**:328
land and resources **12**:312–314 *map, table*
map (6° 30′N 9° 30′W) **1**:136
people **12**:313
Kru **12**:131
Mende **13**:293–294
LIBERIA (Costa Rica)
map (10° 38′N 85° 27′W) **5**:291
LIBERTARIANISM
newspaper **14**:171–172
LIBERTY (county in Florida)
map (30° 20′N 84° 50′W) **8**:172
LIBERTY (county in Georgia)
map (31° 50′N 81° 30′W) **9**:114
LIBERTY (Indiana)
map (39° 38′N 84° 56′W) **11**:111
LIBERTY (Kentucky)
map (37° 19′N 84° 56′W) **12**:47
LIBERTY (Mississippi)
map (31° 9′N 90° 48′W) **13**:469
LIBERTY (Missouri)
map (39° 15′N 94° 25′W) **13**:476
LIBERTY (county in Montana)
map (48° 30′N 111° 0′W) **13**:547
LIBERTY (New York)
map (41° 48′N 74° 45′W) **14**:149
LIBERTY (North Carolina)
map (35° 51′N 79° 34′W) **14**:242
LIBERTY (South Carolina)
map (34° 48′N 82° 42′W) **18**:98
LIBERTY (Texas)
map (30° 3′N 94° 47′W) **19**:129
LIBERTY (county in Texas)
map (30° 7′N 94° 48′W) **19**:129
LIBERTY, STATUE OF *see* STATUE OF LIBERTY
LIBERTY BELL **12**:314 *bibliog.*
Allentown **1**:301
LIBERTY CENTER (Ohio)
map (41° 27′N 84° 7′W) **14**:357
LIBERTY ENLIGHTENING THE WORLD (statue) *see* STATUE OF LIBERTY
LIBERTY FEDERATION *see* MORAL MAJORITY
LIBERTY LAKE
map (39° 25′N 76° 53′W) **13**:188
LIBERTY PARTY **12**:314 *bibliog.*
Birney, James Gillespie **3**:293
LIBERTYVILLE (Illinois)
map (42° 17′N 87° 57′W) **11**:42
LIBIDO **12**:314
extraversion-introversion **7**:346
psychoanalysis **15**:589
LIBIN, SOLOMON
Yiddish theater **20**:328
LIBON OF ELIS
Olympia (Greece) **14**:381
LIBRA (constellation) **12**:314
LIBRARY **12**:314–318 *bibliog., illus.*
Ambrosian Library **1**:325
Arab library c.1237 **13**:403 *illus.*
Bibliothèque Nationale **3**:243
British Museum **3**:497
Carnegie, Andrew **4**:155
catalog **12**:315 *illus.*
classification systems **12**:315
cuneiform **5**:389
Dewey, Melvil **6**:147
Folger Shakespeare Library **8**:195
Grolier, Jean **9**:368
history **12**:315–318
Huntington Library **10**:314–315
information science **11**:172
interlibrary cooperation **12**:318
Laurentian Library **12**:239
Library of Congress **12**:318–319
microfilm **13**:385
Morgan Library **13**:579
National Portrait Gallery **14**:45
New York Public Library **14**:155
Newberry Library **14**:164
Nineveh **14**:200
private **12**:315–318 *illus.*
professional and educational organizations
American Library Association **1**:341–342
Canadian Library Association **4**:92–93
Library Association **12**:318
Library Association of Australia **12**:318
public **12**:315–318 *illus.*
Vatican Library
Nicholas V, Pope **14**:182
LIBRARY ASSOCIATION **12**:318 *bibliog.*
LIBRARY ASSOCIATION OF AUSTRALIA **12**:318
LIBRARY COMPANY OF PHILADELPHIA
Logan, James **12**:393
LIBRARY OF CONGRESS **12**:318–319 *bibliog., illus.*
MacLeish, Archibald **13**:32
Performing Arts Library
Kennedy Center for the Performing Arts **12**:44
Putnam, Herbert **15**:632
Washington, D.C. **20**:41 *map*
LIBRATION **12**:319
moon **13**:561 *illus.*
Trojans **19**:305
LIBRETTO **12**:319 *bibliog.*
See also MUSICAL COMEDY; OPERA
LIBREVILLE (Gabon) **12**:319
climate **9**:5 *table*
map (0° 23′N 9° 27′E) **9**:5
LIBRIUM **12**:319
psychotropic drugs **15**:604
sedative **17**:182
tranquilizer **19**:266
LIBYA **12**:319–321 *bibliog., illus., map, table*
art
African art **1**:160–164
cities
Al-Kufra **12**:320 *table*
Beida **3**:171
Benghazi **3**:199
Tobruk **19**:220
Tripoli **19**:302
economic activity **12**:321 *illus.*
education **12**:321
African universities **1**:176 *table*
flag **8**:134; **12**:319 *illus.*
government **12**:321
history **12**:321
Chad **4**:266
Cyrenaica **5**:409
Cyrene **5**:410
Idris, King **11**:32
Italo-Turkish War **11**:320
Leptis Magna **12**:295
Qaddafi, Muammar al- **16**:3
World War II **20**:256; **20**:263 *map*
land and resources **12**:320–321 *map, table*
map (27° 0′N 17° 0′E) **1**:136
people **12**:321; **13**:399 *illus.*
Tuareg **19**:325–326
LIBYAN DESERT **12**:321–322
Egypt **7**:74
map (24° 0′N 25° 0′E) **1**:136
Qattara Depression **16**:4
LICATA (Italy)
map (37° 5′N 13° 56′E) **11**:321
LICE *see* LOUSE
LICHEN **12**:322 *bibliog., illus.*
commercial product use **12**:322
growth rate **12**:322
habitat **12**:322
lungwort **12**:465
physiology **12**:322
reindeer moss **12**:322
reproduction **12**:322
tundra **19**:332 *illus.*
types **12**:322
LICHTENSTEIN, ROY **12**:322 *bibliog., illus.*
Maybe **15**:429 *illus.*
Okay, Hot Shot **12**:322 *illus.*
LICINIUS, ROMAN EMPEROR **12**:323
Constantine I, Roman Emperor **5**:208
LICK, JAMES
Lick Observatory **12**:323
LICK OBSERVATORY **12**:323 *bibliog.*
crab nebula
pulsar **15**:621
LICKING (Missouri)
map (37° 30′N 91° 51′W) **13**:476
LICKING (county in Ohio)
map (40° 5′N 82° 30′W) **14**:357
LICKING RIVER
map (39° 6′N 84° 30′W) **12**:47
LICORICE **12**:323 *illus.*
anise **2**:29–30
LIDDELL, ALICE
Carroll, Lewis **4**:169
LIDDELL HART, SIR BASIL **12**:323
LIDDY, G. GORDON
Watergate **20**:64
LIDGERWOOD (North Dakota)
map (46° 5′N 97° 9′W) **14**:248
LIDICE (Czechoslovakia) **12**:323
LIDKÖPING (Sweden)
map (58° 30′N 13° 10′E) **18**:382
LIDOCAINE **12**:323
dentistry **6**:116
LIE, SOPHUS
mathematics, history of **13**:226
LIE, TRYGVE HALVDAN **12**:323 *bibliog.*
LIE DETECTOR **12**:323–324 *bibliog.*
galvanic skin response **9**:23
LIEBERMANN, MAX **12**:324 *bibliog.*
LIEBIG, JUSTUS, BARON VON **12**:324 *bibliog., illus.*
biochemistry **3**:261 *illus.*
Hofmann, August Wilhelm von **10**:196
organic chemistry **12**:324
physiological chemistry **12**:324
soil fertility **12**:324
stereochemistry **18**:258
Wöhler, Friedrich **20**:195
LIEBIG'S LAW OF THE MINIMUM
plant distribution **15**:343
LIEBKNECHT (family) **12**:324 *bibliog.*
LIEBKNECHT, KARL
Liebknecht (family) **12**:324
Luxemburg, Rosa **12**:473
LIEBKNECHT, WILHELM
Liebknecht (family) **12**:324
socialism **18**:21
LIEBL, WILHELM
Trübner, Wilhelm **19**:313
LIEBLING, A.J. **12**:324 *bibliog.*
LIECHTENSTEIN **12**:324–326 *bibliog., illus., map*
cities
Vaduz **19**:502
economic activity **12**:325
flag **12**:325 *illus.*
history and government **12**:326
land and people **12**:325 *map*
map (47° 9′N 9° 35′E) **7**:268
LIEDER *see* SONG
LIÈGE (Belgium) **12**:326
history
World War I **20**:222–223

LIÈGE (cont.)
map (50° 38′N 5° 34′E) **3**:177
Walloons **20**:16
LIEN 12:326
encumbrance **7**:163
title **19**:213
LIENZ (Austria)
map (46° 50′N 12° 47′E) **2**:348
LIEPA, MARIS **3**:371 *illus.*
LIESTAL (Switzerland)
map (47° 29′N 7° 44′E) **18**:394
LIFAR, SERGE 12:326 *bibliog.*
Ballets Russes de Monte Carlo **3**:48
LIFE 12:326–327 *bibliog., illus.*
death and dying **6**:68–69
development **6**:137–142
life, extraterrestrial **12**:328
middle age **13**:391
origin of life **12**:327
creation accounts **5**:334–335
creationism **5**:335–336
evolution **7**:318–325
Miller, Stanley Lloyd **13**:428
Oparin, Aleksandr Ivanovich **14**:397
Prigogine, Ilya **15**:537
spontaneous generation **18**:194
virus **19**:616
properties of life **12**:326–327
anaerobe **1**:387
chemical energy **4**:315
nucleic acid **14**:288–291
oxygen **14**:477
LIFE (periodical) **12**:326 *bibliog.*
Bourke-White, Margaret **3**:424
Burrows, Larry **3**:580–581
Capa, Robert **4**:119
Eisenstaedt, Alfred **7**:96
Luce, Henry Robinson **12**:449
photography, history and art of **15**:271
Smith, W. Eugene **17**:371
LIFE, EXTRATERRESTRIAL 12:327–329 *bibliog., illus.*
conditions required **12**:328
debate, history **12**:327–328
life **12**:327
planetary systems **15**:329
radio astronomy **16**:50
Sagan, Carl Edward **17**:11
search for, programs **12**:328–329
Von Däniken, Erich **19**:633
Voyager message **19**:638
LIFE-CRISIS RITES *see* PASSAGE RITES
LIFE CYCLE
fruit fly **8**:347 *illus.*
housefly **8**:190 *illus.*
insect **11**:189–191 *illus.*
larva **12**:208
ontogeny **14**:396
seaweed **17**:177 *illus.*
Sporozoa **18**:195
LIFE EXPECTANCY *see* LIFE SPAN
LIFE WITH FATHER (play)
Day, Clarence **6**:55
Lindsay, Howard, and Crouse, Russel **12**:352
LIFE INSURANCE 12:329–330 *bibliog.*
annuity **2**:33–34
endowment insurance **12**:329
group insurance **12**:330
insurance **11**:198–199
mutual life insurance **12**:330
obesity **14**:315–316
term insurance **12**:329
whole life insurance **12**:329
LIFE IS A DREAM (play)
Calderón de la Barca, Pedro **4**:26
LIFE PLANT *see* KALANCHOE
LIFE OF RILEY, THE (film and TV series)
Bendix, William **3**:196
LIFE OF SAMUEL JOHNSON, THE (book) **12**:330 *bibliog.*
biography **3**:263
Boswell, James **3**:411–412
LIFE SPAN 12:330–331 *bibliog., tables*
aging **1**:185–186
environmental health **7**:210
gastrointestinal tract disease **9**:56
horse **10**:241
hypertension **10**:349
limiting factors **12**:331
maximum, animals and plants **12**:330 *table*
plants **12**:330
public health **15**:608
radiation injury **16**:42–43
LIFE-SUPPORT SYSTEMS (space) **12**:331–333 *bibliog., illus.*
spacecraft **12**:331
spacesuit **12**:332 *illus.*; **12**:333
LIFE-SUPPORT SYSTEMS (submarine) *see* BATHYSCAPHE; OCEANOGRAPHY; SCUBA; SUBMARINE
LIFE TRANSITIONS *see* PASSAGE RITES
LIFE ZONE
plant distribution **15**:343
LIFESAVING AND WATER SAFETY 12:333 *bibliog.*
first aid **8**:108–109
LIFFEY RIVER
map (53° 22′N 6° 14′W) **11**:258
LIFT
aerodynamics **1**:123
LIFT BRIDGE **3**:483 *table*
bridge (engineering) **3**:481
LIFUKA ISLAND
map (19° 48′S 174° 21′W) **19**:233
LIGAMENT 12:333
collagen **5**:102
connective tissue **5**:196
dislocation **6**:196
joint (anatomy) **11**:438
tissue, animal **19**:210
LIGAND 12:333–334 *illus., table*
chelating agent **12**:334
chemical nomenclature **4**:320
coordination compounds **12**:333–334
Van Vleck, J. H. **19**:516
LIGETI, GYÖRGY 12:334
LIGHT 12:334–336 *bibliog., illus.*
absorption **1**:63
qualitative chemical analysis **16**:7
abstract photography
Kepes, Gyorgy **12**:57
alarm systems **1**:240
bending of rays
mirage **13**:463
binary stars **3**:257
bioluminescence **3**:272
characterization **12**:334 *illus.*
charge-coupled device **4**:288
coherent light **5**:96
color **5**:112–113
color perception **5**:114
pigment **15**:300
cosmology (astronomy) **5**:287
detection
eye **7**:348–350
diffraction **6**:169 *illus.*
dimming switches
resistor **16**:177
dispersion (physics) **6**:197
Doppler effect **6**:240–241
dualistic **12**:335–336
electric light
circuit, electric **4**:436 *illus.*
electric light bulb
vacuum **19**:502
electroluminescence **7**:114
emission
qualitative chemical analysis **16**:7
ether (physics) **7**:250
fiber optics **8**:68–69
Fizeau, Armand Hippolyte Louis **8**:133
flash photography **8**:153
fluorescence **8**:186
fluorometer **8**:188
mineral **8**:186
focal point **8**:192
gegenschein **9**:67
halo **10**:24
holography **10**:207–208
hydrogen spectrum **10**:340–341
index of refraction **11**:79
infrared radiation **11**:175
intensity
candela **4**:106
candlepower **4**:107
measurement **13**:255
interference (physics) **11**:207–209
lens **12**:285–286
lumen **12**:458
luminescence **12**:458
luminescence, mineral **12**:458
measurement **13**:255
angstrom **2**:7
diffraction grating **6**:169–170
Fitzgerald-Lorentz contraction **8**:131
fluorometer **8**:188
footcandle **12**:339
photometer **15**:273–274
Newton, Sir Isaac **14**:173–174
optical computing **5**:160g
optics **14**:409–413 *illus.*
particle theory **12**:334 *illus.*
phosphor **15**:256
phosphorescence **15**:256
photochemistry **15**:257–259
photoelectric cell **15**:259–260
photoelectric effect **15**:260
photometry, astronomical **15**:274
photon **15**:274
phototaxis
taxis **19**:48
physics, history of **15**:284–285
plant (botany)
growth **9**:381
polarized light **15**:394–395
optical mineralogy **14**:409 *illus.*
prism (physics) **15**:553–554 *illus.*
production **12**:334–335
incandescent lamp **11**:73
quantum mechanics **16**:9–11 *illus.*
reduction
extinction **7**:341
reflection **16**:119
luster, mineral **12**:468
parabola **15**:74
refraction **16**:123–124
atmospheric refraction **2**:304
rainbow **16**:77 *illus.*
Rømer, Ole **16**:304–305
scattering
liquid crystal **12**:365
Tyndall, John **19**:363
semaphore **17**:194–195
sky **17**:346
sources **12**:334–335
magnesium **13**:54
tritium **19**:304
spectroscope **18**:169 *illus.*
spectrum **18**:172–173 *illus.*
speed **12**:335 *illus.*
Einstein, Albert **7**:93
Michelson, Albert Abraham **13**:375–376
stroboscope **18**:301
theory, development **12**:335–336
transformation
absorption, light **1**:63
trapping
photosynthesis **15**:276–277
tropism **19**:309–310 *illus.*
twilight **19**:360
ultraviolet light **19**:379
velocity
atomic constants **2**:308
wave theory **12**:334 *illus.*
Arago, François **2**:107
Euler, Leonhard **7**:264–265
Huygens, Christiaan **10**:325
Huygens's principle **10**:325–326
waves
frequency **8**:326
X rays **20**:309–311
zodiacal light **20**:371
LIGHT AMPLIFICATION BY STIMULATED EMISSION OF RADIATION *see* LASER
LIGHT IN AUGUST (book)
Faulkner, William **8**:36
LIGHT HORSE HARRY *see* LEE, HENRY "LIGHT HORSE HARRY"
LIGHT HORSES 10:243 *illus.*; **12**:336
horse **10**:244
LIGHT METER *see* ACTINOMETER
LIGHT PEN (computer term) **5**:160h
LIGHT RAPID TRANSIT *see* STREETCAR
LIGHT-YEAR 12:336
LIGHTFOOT, JOSEPH BARBER
prehistory **15**:517
LIGHTHOUSE 12:336–337 *bibliog., illus.*
Barnegat Lighthouse **14**:128 *illus.*
Cape Hatteras **14**:245
construction **12**:336–337 *illus.*
Eddystone Lighthouse
Smeaton, John **17**:365
history **12**:336–337
illumination **12**:336–337
Fresnel, Augustin Jean **8**:328
modern developments **12**:337
Montauk Point (New York) **14**:152 *illus.*
Nubble Lighthouse (Maine) **19**:417 *illus.*
optical systems **12**:337
Pharos of Alexandria **17**:218 *illus.*
LIGHTING, CINEMATOGRAPHIC **4**:433
LIGHTING, STAGE *see* STAGE LIGHTING
LIGHTING DEVICES 12:337–339 *bibliog., illus.*
black light, scheelite **17**:118
candle **4**:107
chandelier **4**:279
coal gas
Murdock, William **13**:648
Farmer, Moses **8**:24
fluorescent light **8**:186–187
houseplants **10**:276
incandescent lamp **11**:73
krypton **12**:133
lamp **12**:175–176
lighthouse **12**:336–337
limelight
Drummond, Thomas **6**:282
neon **14**:85
searchlight **17**:175
stage lighting **18**:210
stroboscope **18**:301
technology, history of **19**:67 *illus.*
Tiffany lamp **2**:211 *illus.*; **9**:204 *illus.*; **19**:196 *illus.*
Welsbach, Carl Auer, Baron von **20**:101
LIGHTNING 12:339–340 *bibliog., illus.*
ball lightning **12**:340
cause **12**:339
death and injury, U.S. **12**:339
discharge, electrical **6**:188
electricity **7**:108–109 *illus.*
forest fires **12**:340
formation **12**:339–340
Franklin, Benjamin **8**:283
lightning rods **12**:340
shock wave **17**:279
static electricity **18**:234
thunderstorms **12**:339
weather modification **20**:80
whistler **20**:134
LIGHTNING BUG *see* FIREFLY
LIGHTNING ROD
Franklin, Benjamin **8**:283
lightning **12**:340
LIGHTSHIP *see* LIGHTHOUSE
LIGNIN 12:340 *bibliog.*
white rot fungus **20**:138
LIGNITE 12:340
coal and coal mining **5**:76–77 *map*
sedimentary rock **17**:185
LIGNITE (North Dakota)
map (48° 53′N 102° 34′W) **14**:248
LIGONIER (Indiana)
map (41° 28′N 85° 35′W) **11**:111
LIGONIER (Pennsylvania)
map (40° 15′N 79° 14′W) **15**:147
LIGURIA (Italy) **12**:340
cities
Genoa **9**:92–93 *illus.*
La Spezia **12**:149–150
LIGURIAN SEA
map (43° 30′N 9° 0′E) **11**:321
LIHOLINO, ALEXANDER *see* KAMEHAMEHA (dynasty)
LIHUE (Hawaii)
map (21° 59′N 159° 22′W) **10**:72
LIJ YASU
Haile Selassie, Emperor **10**:13
LIK RIVER
map (18° 31′N 102° 31′E) **12**:203
LIKASI (Zaire)
map (10° 59′S 26° 44′E) **20**:350
LIKOUALA RIVER
map (1° 13′S 16° 48′E) **5**:182
LIKUD (political party)
Begin, Menachem **3**:168
Israel **11**:306
LI'L ABNER (comic strip)
Capp, Al **4**:127
LILAC 8:170 *illus.*; **12**:340 *illus.*
LILBOURN (Missouri)
map (36° 35′N 89° 37′W) **13**:476
LILBURNE, JOHN
Levelers **12**:302
LILIENTHAL, DAVID 12:340–341 *bibliog.*
LILIENTHAL, OTTO 1:211 *illus.*; **12**:341 *bibliog.*
glider **9**:208
LILIOM (play)
Molnár, Ferenc **13**:512
LILITH 12:341
LILIUOKALANI, QUEEN OF HAWAII 12:341 *bibliog.*
LILLE (France) **12**:341
map (50° 38′N 3° 4′E) **8**:260
LILLINGTON (North Carolina)
map (35° 24′N 78° 49′W) **14**:242
LILLO, GEORGE 12:341
LILLOOET (British Columbia)
map (50° 42′N 121° 56′W) **3**:491
LILLOOET RIVER
map (49° 45′N 122° 8′W) **3**:491
LILONGWE (Malawi) **12**:341
map (13° 59′S 33° 44′E) **13**:81
LILY
water lily **20**:49
LILY (botany) **8**:170 *illus.*; **12**:341–342 *bibliog., illus.*
adder's-tongue **1**:99
aloe **1**:307
Amaryllis **1**:322
asparagus fern **2**:261–262
aspidistra **2**:262
bear grass **3**:141–142
carrion flower **4**:168
fritillary **8**:335
grape hyacinth **9**:290
grass tree **9**:298

greenbrier **9**:350
lily of the valley **12**:342
meadow saffron **13**:252
sarsaparilla **17**:79
sego lily **17**:188
Solomon's seal **18**:57
spikenard **18**:183
squill **18**:204
star-of-Bethlehem **18**:226
Sternbergia **18**:261
tulip **19**:330
LILY (periodical)
Bloomer, Amelia Jenks **3**:340
LILY-OF-THE-FIELD *see STERNBERGIA*
LILY PAD see WATER LILY
LILY OF THE VALLEY **12**:342 *illus.*
LIM BAY CHANNEL
map (56° 55′N 9° 10′E) **6**:109
LIMA (Montana)
map (44° 38′N 112° 36′W) **13**:547
LIMA (Ohio)
map (40° 46′N 84° 6′W) **14**:357
LIMA (Peru) **12**:342 *illus.*; **15**:192–194 *illus., table*
Latin American art and architecture **12**:224 *illus.*
map (12° 3′S 77° 3′W) **15**:193
Pizarro, Francisco **15**:324
LIMA, ALMEIDA
schizophrenia **17**:124
LIMA BEAN **12**:342–343 *illus.*
LIMA NUEVA (Honduras)
map (15° 23′N 87° 56′W) **10**:218
LIMANN, HILLA
Ghana **9**:166
LIMASSOL (Cyprus)
map (34° 40′N 33° 2′E) **5**:409
LIMBE (Malawi)
Blantyre **3**:328
LIMBOURG, POL
Limbourg brothers **12**:343
LIMBOURG BROTHERS **12**:343 *bibliog., illus.*
Flemish art and architecture **8**:160
International Style (Gothic art) **11**:223
medieval feast **5**:238 *illus.*
Très Riches Heures du Duc de Berry (book) **3**:384 *illus.*; **7**:284 *illus.*; **11**:48 *illus.*; **12**:343 *illus.*; **13**:394 *illus.*
LIME (chemical compound) **12**:343
calcium **4**:22
compost **5**:158
LIME (fruit) **12**:343–344 *illus.*
citrus fruits **4**:447
lumber **12**:456 *illus.*
LIME VILLAGE (Alaska)
map (61° 21′N 155° 28′W) **1**:242
LIMELIGHT
Drummond, Thomas **6**:282
stage lighting **18**:210
LIMEN *see* CONSCIOUSNESS, STATES OF
LIMERICK (city in Ireland) **12**:344
map (52° 40′N 8° 38′W) **11**:258
LIMERICK (comic verse) **12**:344
Lear, Edward **12**:259
LIMERICK (county in Ireland) **12**:344
cities
Limerick **12**:344
LIMESTONE **12**:344–345 *bibliog., illus.*
calcite **4**:21–22
calcium **4**:22
calcium carbonate **4**:22–23
chalk **4**:271
composition **12**:344–345
coquina **5**:257
Devonian Period **6**:145
Earth, geological history of **7**:12
emery **7**:155
evaporite **7**:314
formations
cave **4**:222
coral reef **5**:258
karst landscape **4**:361 *illus.*
stalactite and stalagmite **18**:213
geochemistry **9**:96
geode **9**:97
Grand Canyon **12**:344 *illus.*
Greek architecture **9**:336
idocrase **11**:31
Illinois **11**:44 *illus.*
Indiana **11**:113 *illus.*
lapis lazuli **12**:205
lithograph **12**:371
marble **13**:144
mineral and ore host **12**:345
mining and quarrying **13**:449
oolite **14**:396
organic and inorganic **12**:345
petroleum **15**:208
sedimentary rock **12**:344–345; **17**:184–185 *illus.*
siderite **17**:294
smithsonite **17**:372
speleology **18**:177
sphalerite **18**:180
stonewort **18**:284
stratigraphy **18**:292 *illus.*
stromatolite **18**:302
willemite **20**:154
LIMESTONE (county in Alabama)
map (34° 50′N 87° 0′W) **1**:234
LIMESTONE (Maine)
map (46° 55′N 67° 50′W) **13**:70
LIMESTONE (county in Texas)
map (31° 35′N 96° 35′W) **19**:129
LIMIT (mathematics) **12**:345 *bibliog.*
convergence **5**:233
differential calculus **6**:167–168
function **12**:345
infinity **11**:168–169
integral calculus **11**:200–201
mathematics **13**:222
sequence **17**:207
LIMITATIONS, STATUTE OF *see* STATUTE OF LIMITATIONS
LIMNERS **12**:345 *bibliog.*
folk art **8**:197–198 *illus.*
Freake limner **8**:289
Oliver, Isaac **14**:379
portraiture **15**:446
LIMNOLOGY **12**:345
ecology **7**:42–46
fresh water environments **12**:345
Hutchinson, George Evelyn **10**:322–323
hydrologic sciences **10**:342
lake (body of water) **12**:167–169
LIMOGES (France) **12**:345–346
Hundred Years' War **10**:305 *illus.*
Limoges ware **12**:346
map (45° 50′N 1° 16′E) **8**:260
LIMOGES WARE **12**:346 *bibliog.*
LIMON (Colorado)
map (39° 16′N 103° 41′W) **5**:116
LIMÓN (Costa Rica)
map (10° 0′N 83° 2′W) **5**:291
LIMÓN, JOSÉ **12**:346 *bibliog.*
LIMONITE **12**:346 *illus.*
ocher **14**:346
source **12**:346
LIMOSIN, LÉONARD **12**:346 *bibliog.*
LIMOUSIN (France) **12**:346–347 *map*
cattle and cattle raising **4**:216
LIMPET **12**:347; **13**:510 *illus.*
Atlantic plate limpet **11**:229 *illus.*
gastropod **9**:57–58 *illus.*
intertidal life **11**:230
Lister's keyhole limpet **11**:229 *illus.*
rough limpet **11**:229 *illus.*
LIMPKIN **12**:347
LIMPOPO RIVER **12**:347
map (25° 15′S 33° 30′E) **18**:79
LIN BIAO *see* LIN PAIO (Lin Biao)
LIN PIAO (Lin Biao) **12**:347 *bibliog.*
Mao Tse-tung (Mao Zedong) **13**:135
LINACRE COLLEGE (Oxford University) **14**:474
LINARES (Chile)
map (35° 51′S 71° 36′W) **4**:355
LINARES (Mexico)
map (24° 52′N 99° 34′W) **13**:357
LINARES (Spain)
map (38° 5′N 3° 38′W) **18**:140
LINCH (Wyoming)
map (43° 37′N 106° 12′W) **20**:301
LINCOLN (Argentina)
map (34° 52′S 61° 32′W) **2**:149
LINCOLN (Arkansas)
map (35° 57′N 94° 25′W) **2**:166
LINCOLN (county in Arkansas)
map (33° 57′N 91° 47′W) **2**:166
LINCOLN (California)
map (38° 54′N 121° 17′W) **4**:31
LINCOLN (county in Colorado)
map (39° 0′N 103° 30′W) **5**:116
LINCOLN (England) **12**:347
map (53° 14′N 0° 33′W) **19**:403
LINCOLN (county in Georgia)
map (33° 50′N 82° 30′W) **9**:114
LINCOLN (county in Idaho)
map (43° 0′N 114° 10′W) **11**:26
LINCOLN (Illinois)
map (40° 9′N 89° 22′W) **11**:42
LINCOLN (Kansas)
map (39° 2′N 98° 9′W) **12**:18
LINCOLN (county in Kansas)
map (39° 5′N 98° 10′W) **12**:18
LINCOLN (county in Kentucky)
map (37° 30′N 84° 40′W) **12**:47
LINCOLN (county in Louisiana)
map (32° 37′N 92° 40′W) **12**:430
LINCOLN (Maine)
map (45° 22′N 68° 30′W) **13**:70
LINCOLN (county in Maine)
map (44° 5′N 69° 30′W) **13**:70
LINCOLN (Michigan)
map (44° 41′N 83° 25′W) **13**:377
LINCOLN (county in Minnesota)
map (44° 22′N 96° 13′W) **13**:453
LINCOLN (county in Mississippi)
map (31° 30′N 90° 25′W) **13**:469
LINCOLN (county in Missouri)
map (39° 5′N 90° 57′W) **13**:476
LINCOLN (Montana)
map (46° 58′N 112° 41′W) **13**:547
LINCOLN (county in Montana)
map (48° 25′N 115° 15′W) **13**:547
LINCOLN (Nebraska) **12**:347
map (40° 48′N 96° 42′W) **14**:70
LINCOLN (county in Nebraska)
map (41° 0′N 100° 15′W) **14**:70
LINCOLN (county in Nevada)
map (37° 40′N 115° 0′W) **14**:111
LINCOLN (New Hampshire)
map (44° 3′N 71° 40′W) **14**:123
LINCOLN (county in New Mexico)
map (33° 45′N 105° 30′W) **14**:136
LINCOLN (county in North Carolina)
map (35° 30′N 81° 15′W) **14**:242
LINCOLN (county in Oklahoma)
map (35° 40′N 96° 50′W) **14**:368
LINCOLN (county in Oregon)
map (44° 59′N 123° 52′W) **14**:427
LINCOLN (county in South Dakota)
map (43° 15′N 96° 42′W) **18**:103
LINCOLN (county in Tennessee)
map (35° 15′N 87° 25′W) **19**:104
LINCOLN (county in Washington)
map (47° 35′N 118° 25′W) **20**:35
LINCOLN (county in West Virginia)
map (38° 10′N 82° 5′W) **20**:111
LINCOLN (county in Wisconsin)
map (45° 20′N 89° 45′W) **20**:185
LINCOLN (county in Wyoming)
map (42° 15′N 110° 45′W) **20**:301
LINCOLN, ABRAHAM **12**:347–349 *bibliog., illus.*; **19**:448 *illus.*
assassination
Booth (family) **3**:394
Ford's Theatre **8**:224
biographers
Hay, John M. **10**:80
Herndon, William Henry **10**:143
Sandburg, Carl **17**:61
caricature **4**:150 *illus.*
Civil War, U.S. **5**:17–30
Davis, David **6**:51
Davis, Henry Winter **6**:51
death of **5**:31 *illus.*
Decatur (Illinois) **6**:72
election of 1860 **5**:17 *illus., map*
Emancipation Proclamation **5**:29 *illus.*; **7**:151 *illus.*
Gettysburg Address **9**:161–162 *illus.*
Greeley, Horace **9**:346
Hamlin, Hannibal **10**:30
Illinois **11**:43
inaugural address **5**:19 *illus.*
Lincoln, Mary Todd **12**:350
Lincoln-Douglas debates **12**:348–349
portrait
French, Daniel Chester **8**:302
Rushmore, Mount **16**:348
president of the United States **15**:526; **15**:527
Reconstruction **16**:108–109
Republican party **16**:172–173 *illus.*
Rutledge, Ann **16**:376
slavery **12**:348–349; **17**:357
Springfield (Illinois) **18**:200
United States, history of the **19**:448–449
LINCOLN, BENJAMIN **12**:349–350 *bibliog.*
American Revolution **1**:359 *map*
LINCOLN, MARY TODD **12**:350 *bibliog., illus.*
Lexington (Kentucky) **12**:309
Lincoln, Abraham **12**:348
LINCOLN, MOUNT
map (39° 21′N 106° 7′W) **5**:116
LINCOLN, ROBERT TODD
Lincoln, Mary Todd **12**:350
LINCOLN CENTER FOR THE PERFORMING ARTS **12**:350
architecture
Harrison, Wallace K. **10**:60
Juilliard School, The **11**:465
Metropolitan Opera **13**:348
New York (city) **14**:145 *map*
New York City Ballet **14**:154
Schuman, William Howard **17**:136
LINCOLN CITY (Oregon)
map (44° 59′N 123° 59′W) **14**:427
LINCOLN COLLEGE (Oxford University) **14**:474
LINCOLN-DOUGLAS DEBATES **5**:17 *illus.*
Douglas, Stephen A. **6**:248
Lincoln, Abraham **12**:348–349
presidential elections **15**:531
LINCOLN LABORATORY **12**:350
LINCOLN PARK (Colorado)
map (37° 35′N 104° 12′W) **5**:116
LINCOLN PARK (Michigan)
map (42° 14′N 83° 9′W) **13**:377
LINCOLN TUNNEL **19**:337 *table*
Ammann, Othmar Hermann **1**:372
New York (city) **14**:145 *maps*
LINCOLN UNIVERSITY **12**:350
LINCOLNSHIRE (England) **12**:350
Fens, The **8**:51
Lincoln **12**:347
LINCOLNTON (Georgia)
map (33° 48′N 82° 28′W) **9**:114
LINCOLNTON (North Carolina)
map (35° 29′N 81° 14′W) **14**:242
LINCOS
languages, artificial **12**:197
LIND (Washington)
map (46° 58′N 118° 37′W) **20**:35
LIND, JAMES
scurvy: medicine **13**:270
LIND, JENNY **12**:350–351 *bibliog.*
American music **1**:349 *illus.*
LINDALE (Georgia)
map (34° 11′N 85° 11′W) **9**:114
LINDAU (Germany, East and West)
map (47° 33′N 9° 41′E) **9**:140
LINDBERGH, ANNE MORROW **12**:351
Lindbergh, Charles A. **12**:351
Morrow, Dwight **13**:590
LINDBERGH, CHARLES A. **12**:351 *bibliog., illus.*
Hauptmann, Bruno Richard **10**:69
kidnapping **12**:71
LINDBLAD, BERTIL
astronomy, history of **2**:280
LINDEMANN, FERDINAND VON
mathematics, history of **13**:226
LINDEMANN, FREDERICK ALEXANDER **12**:351 *bibliog.*
LINDEN (Alabama)
map (32° 18′N 87° 47′W) **1**:234
LINDEN (botany) **12**:351–352 *illus.*
wood **20**:205 *illus.*
LINDEN (Indiana)
map (40° 11′N 86° 55′W) **11**:111
LINDEN (New Jersey)
map (40° 38′N 74° 15′W) **14**:129
LINDEN (Tennessee)
map (35° 37′N 87° 50′W) **19**:104
LINDEN (Texas)
map (33° 1′N 94° 22′W) **19**:129
LINDENHURST (New York)
map (40° 41′N 73° 22′W) **14**:149
LINDENOWS FJORD
map (60° 45′N 43° 30′W) **9**:353
LINDENWOLD (New Jersey)
map (39° 49′N 74° 59′W) **14**:129
LINDERHOF, SCHLOSS
Louis II's Bavarian palaces **12**:423
LINDGREN, WALDEMAR
ore deposits
classification **14**:422–423
LINDI (Tanzania)
map (10° 0′S 39° 43′E) **19**:27
LINDISFARNE GOSPELS
illuminated manuscripts **11**:46 *illus.*; **11**:47
LINDNER, RICHARD **12**:352 *bibliog., illus.*
Leopard Lilly **12**:352 *illus.*
LINDON (Colorado)
map (39° 44′N 103° 24′W) **5**:116
LINDSAY (California)
map (36° 12′N 119° 5′W) **4**:31
LINDSAY (Nebraska)
map (41° 42′N 97° 42′W) **14**:70
LINDSAY (Oklahoma)
map (34° 50′N 97° 38′W) **14**:368
LINDSAY, SIR DAVID **12**:352 *bibliog.*
LINDSAY, HOWARD, AND CROUSE, RUSSEL **12**:352
LINDSAY, JOHN V. **12**:352 *bibliog.*
Liberal parties **12**:312
LINDSAY, VACHEL **12**:352 *bibliog.*
Springfield (Illinois) **18**:200
LINDSBORG (Kansas)
map (38° 35′N 97° 40′W) **12**:18
LINE (mathematics) **12**:352–353 *bibliog., illus.*
axis (mathematics) **2**:378
centroid **4**:256
golden section **9**:232–233
linear equation **12**:354
parallel **15**:79
projective geometry **15**:565
slope **17**:363
LINE ISLANDS
Kiribati **12**:88
map (0° 5′N 157° 0′W) **14**:334
LINEAGE **12**:353
clan **5**:36
genealogy **9**:76

LINEAGE (cont.)
kinship **12**:85
polygamy **15**:419
LINEAR A
Linear B **12**:354
LINEAR ACCELERATOR *see* ACCELERATOR, PARTICLE
LINEAR ALGEBRA **12**:353 *bibliog.*
matrix **13**:230
vector analysis **19**:530
LINEAR B **12**:353–354 *bibliog., illus.*
inscription **11**:186
Pylos **15**:634
Ventris, Michael **19**:546
LINEAR EQUATION **12**:354 *bibliog., illus.*
algebra **1**:284
Cramer's rule **5**:328
matrix **13**:230
numerical analysis **14**:295
polynomial **15**:421
LINEAR POTTERY CULTURE *see* DANUBIAN CULTURE
LINEAR PROGRAMMING
industrial management **11**:157
numerical analysis **14**:295
operations research **14**:403
LINEAR REGRESSION ANALYSIS
correlation and regression **5**:276
LINECUT
photoengraving **15**:260
LINEN **12**:354 *bibliog.*
flax **8**:157–158
"LINES COMPOSED A FEW MILES ABOVE TINTERN ABBEY" (poem)
Lyrical Ballads **12**:479
LINESVILLE (Pennsylvania)
map (41° 39′N 80° 26′W) **15**:147
LINEVILLE (Iowa)
map (40° 35′N 93° 32′W) **11**:244
LINGAYEN GULF
map (16° 15′N 120° 14′E) **15**:237
LINGUA COSMICA *see* LINCOS
LINGUA FRANCA **12**:354 *bibliog.*
See also CREOLE (linguistics); PIDGIN
Swahili **18**:375
LINGUISTIC AND ANALYTIC PHILOSOPHY *see* ANALYTIC AND LINGUISTIC PHILOSOPHY
LINGUISTICS **12**:354–358 *bibliog., map*
See also LANGUAGE
animal communication **2**:20
anthropological linguistics **2**:50–51
applied linguistics **2**:90–91
Bloomfield, Leonard **3**:340
Chomsky, Noam **4**:404
cryptology **5**:371–373
geographical linguistics **9**:98–100
grammar **9**:282–283
historical linguistics **10**:182–183
Humboldt, Wilhelm von, Freiherr **10**:301
Jakobson, Roman **11**:351
Jespersen, Otto **11**:402
major branches **12**:357–358
lexicology and lexicography **12**:308–309
phonetics **15**:251–253
phonology and morphology **15**:254–255
semantics **17**:193–194
syntax **18**:408–409
names, personal **14**:9–10
Prague school **15**:488
psycholinguistics **15**:591–592
reading education **16**:100–101 *bibliog.*
Saussure, Ferdinand de **17**:97
sociolinguistics **18**:27–28
speech **18**:175
synchronic linguistics **12**:356
Whorf, Benjamin Lee **20**:144
LINH PEAK
map (15° 4′N 107° 59′E) **19**:580
LINKED RING BROTHERHOOD **12**:358 *bibliog.*
Coburn, Alvin Langdon **5**:84
Evans, Frederick Henry **7**:312
LINKÖPING (Sweden)
map (58° 25′N 15° 37′E) **18**:382
LINLITHGOW, VICTOR ALEXANDER JOHN HOPE, 2d MARQUESS OF **12**:358–359
LINN (county in Iowa)
map (42° 5′N 91° 32′W) **11**:244
LINN (county in Kansas)
map (38° 15′N 94° 50′W) **12**:18
LINN (Missouri)
map (38° 29′N 91° 51′W) **13**:476
LINN (county in Missouri)
map (39° 50′N 93° 5′W) **13**:476
LINN (county in Oregon)
map (44° 30′N 122° 30′W) **14**:427
LINNA, VÄINÖ
Finnish literature **8**:99
LINNAEUS, CAROLUS **12**:359 *bibliog., illus.*
biology **3**:269
botany **3**:413–414 *illus.*
Celsius scale **4**:238
classification, biological **5**:42
evolution **7**:318
Indians, American **11**:115
Ray, John **16**:96
twinflower **19**:360
Uppsala (Sweden) **19**:473
LINNE, CARL VON *see* LINNAEUS, CAROLUS
LINNEAN SOCIETY
scientific associations **17**:145
LINNEBACH, ADOLF
stage lighting **18**:210
LINNEUS (Missouri)
map (39° 53′N 93° 11′W) **13**:476
LINOTYPE **12**:359 *bibliog., illus.*
Mergenthaler, Ottmar **13**:310
typesetting **19**:365 *illus.*
LINSEED OIL **12**:359–360
fats and oils source **8**:35
flax **8**:157–158
LINTEL *see* POST AND LINTEL
LINTHICUM HEIGHTS (Maryland)
map (39° 12′N 76° 39′W) **13**:188
LINTON (Indiana)
map (39° 2′N 87° 10′W) **11**:111
LINTON (North Dakota)
map (46° 16′N 100° 14′W) **14**:248
LINWOOD (New Jersey)
map (39° 21′N 74° 34′W) **14**:129
LINZ (Austria) **12**:360
map (48° 18′N 14° 18′E) **2**:348
LION **12**:360 *bibliog., illus.*
anatomy **13**:98–99 *illus.*
animal behavior **2**:14 *illus.*
LION OF THE NORTH *see* GUSTAV II ADOLF, KING OF SWEDEN (Gustavus Adolphus)
LIONEL TOWN (Jamaica)
map (17° 48′N 77° 14′W) **11**:351
LIONFISH **12**:360
scorpion fish **17**:148
LIONHEAD (goldfish) **9**:234 *illus.*
LIONS, GULF OF
map (43° 0′N 4° 0′E) **8**:260
LIOTARD, JEAN ÉTIENNE
Turkish woman and her servant **19**:348 *illus.*
LIP *see* MOUTH AND THROAT
LIPAN INDIANS
Apache **2**:73
LIPARI ISLANDS (Italy)
map (38° 30′N 14° 57′E) **11**:321
Stromboli **18**:302
LIPCHITZ, CHAIM JACOB *see* LIPCHITZ, JACQUES
LIPCHITZ, JACQUES **12**:360–361 *bibliog., illus.*
Song of the Vowels **12**:361 *illus.*
LIPID **12**:361–362 *bibliog., illus.*
cerebroside glycolipid **12**:361
cholesterol **4**:403–404
complex lipids **12**:361–362
distribution and function **12**:361–362
fat **8**:33–34
glyceride compounds **12**:362
hormone, animal **10**:235
lecithin **12**:267–268
liver **12**:374
metabolism **12**:362
Lynen, Feodor **12**:477
phosphosphingolipids **12**:361
simple lipids **12**:361
sphingosine **12**:361
steroid **18**:261–262
triglycerides **12**:361–362
LIPMANN, FRITZ ALBERT **12**:362
LIPOIC ACID
coenzyme **5**:92
LIPOLYSIS
noradrenaline **14**:218
LIPOPROTEIN
cholesterol **4**:404
lipid **12**:362
LIPPERSHEY, HANS
telescope **19**:80
LIPPI, FILIPPINO **12**:362 *bibliog.*
Botticelli, Sandro **3**:418
LIPPI, FRA FILIPPO **12**:362–363 *bibliog., illus.*
Botticelli, Sandro **3**:417–418
Madonna and Child **12**:362 *illus.*
LIPPI, LIPPINO *see* LIPPI, FILIPPINO
LIPPI, LIPPO *see* LIPPI, FRA FILIPPO
LIPPIZANER **10**:243 *illus.*; **12**:363 *bibliog., illus.*
LIPPMANN, GABRIEL **12**:363 *bibliog.*
LIPPMANN, O.
clinical psychology **5**:59
LIPPMANN, WALTER **12**:363 *bibliog., illus.*
LIPPOLD, RICHARD **12**:363–364 *bibliog., illus.*
Variation No. 7:Full Moon **12**:363 *illus.*
LIPPSTADT (Germany, East and West)
map (51° 40′N 8° 19′E) **9**:140
LIPS **18**:174 *illus.*
LIPSCOMB (Alabama)
map (33° 25′N 86° 56′W) **1**:234
LIPSCOMB (Texas)
map (36° 14′N 100° 16′W) **19**:129
LIPSCOMB (county in Texas)
map (36° 15′N 100° 15′W) **19**:129
LIPSCOMB, WILLIAM NUNN, JR. **12**:364
borines **12**:364
LIPSET, SEYMOUR MARTIN **12**:364
LIPSTICK
cosmetics **5**:282–283 *table*
LIPSTICK TREE *see* ANNATTO TREE
LIPTON, SIR THOMAS **12**:364 *bibliog.*
LIQUEFIED NATURAL GAS
heat content **8**:353 *table*
petroleum industry **15**:210; **15**:212–213
LIQUEFIED PETROLEUM GAS **12**:364
butane **3**:591
commercial use **12**:364
heat content **8**:353 *table*
petroleum industry **15**:210
propane **15**:569
LIQUID **12**:364–365 *bibliog.*
capillarity **4**:123
cohesion **5**:96
conduction, electric **12**:365
convection **5**:232
density **6**:113 *table*
density current **6**:114
distillation **6**:200 *illus.*
emulsion **7**:161
enthalpy **7**:208
evaporation **7**:313–314
fluid mechanics **8**:184–185
heat exchanger **10**:97–98
hydraulic systems **10**:330–331
kinetic theory of matter **12**:79
laser **12**:213 *table*
liquid crystal **12**:365
measurement
flowmeter **8**:184
hydrometer **10**:343
manometer **13**:126
osmosis **14**:455
phase equilibrium **15**:222–224 *illus.*
pressure, siphon **17**:326
properties of **8**:185
pump **15**:622–623
solutions **12**:365
solvent **18**:58–59
statics **18**:235
superfluidity **18**:351
surface tension **12**:364–365; **18**:358
suspension **18**:371
triple point **19**:302
valve **19**:509
van der Waals equation **19**:512–513
vapor pressure **19**:521
viscosity **19**:616–617
LIQUID CRYSTAL **12**:365 *bibliog.*
LIQUID DROP MODEL
nuclear physics **14**:286
LIQUID HYDROGEN *see* HYDROGEN
LIQUORS *see* names of specific kinds of liquors, e.g., BRANDY; WHISKEY; etc.
LISA, MANUEL
Montana **13**:550
LISBOA (Portugal) *see* LISBON (Portugal)
LISBOA, ANTÔNIO FRANCISCO *see* ALEIJADINHO
LISBON (Maine)
map (44° 2′N 70° 6′W) **13**:70
LISBON (New Hampshire)
map (44° 13′N 71° 55′W) **14**:123
LISBON (North Dakota)
map (46° 27′N 97° 41′W) **14**:248
LISBON (Ohio)
map (40° 47′N 80° 46′W) **14**:357
LISBON (Portugal) **12**:365–366 *bibliog., illus.*; **15**:450 *illus., table*; **15**:454 *illus.*
history **12**:365–366
map (38° 43′N 9° 8′W) **15**:449
LISBURNE, CAPE
map (68° 52′N 166° 14′W) **1**:242
LISCANO, JUAN
Venezuela **19**:543
LISLE, ALICE
Jeffreys, George Jeffreys, 1st Baron **11**:394
LISLE, CLAUDE JOSEPH ROUGET DE *see* ROUGET DE LISLE, CLAUDE JOSEPH
L'ISLE, JEAN BAPTISTE ROMÉ DE
mineral **13**:439
LISMAN (Alabama)
map (32° 5′N 88° 17′W) **1**:234
LISMER, ARTHUR **12**:366 *bibliog.*
LISMORE (Australia)
map (28° 48′S 153° 17′E) **2**:328
LISMORE (Nova Scotia)
map (45° 42′N 62° 16′W) **14**:269
LISP (computer language) **12**:366
computer languages **5**:160p
LISPING
speech **18**:175
LISS, JOHANN *see* LYS, JAN
LISSAJOUS FIGURE **12**:366
LISSITZKY, EL **12**:366 *bibliog., illus.*
Story of Two Squares **12**:366 *illus.*
LISTER, JOSEPH **12**:366 *bibliog., illus.*
bacteria **3**:18
surgery **18**:361 *illus.*
LISTON, SONNY
Ali, Muhammad **1**:292
LISZT, FRANZ **12**:367 *bibliog., illus.*; **16**:293 *illus.*
Hungarian music **10**:306
Montez, Lola **13**:555
music, history of Western **13**:666 *illus.*
symphonic poem **18**:404–405
Weimar (East Germany) **20**:94
LISZT CONTEST
Berman, Lazar **3**:219
LITANI RIVER
map (3° 40′N 54° 0′W) **18**:364
LITANY **12**:367
LITCHFIELD (Connecticut)
map (41° 45′N 73° 11′W) **5**:193
LITCHFIELD (county in Connecticut)
map (41° 45′N 73° 11′W) **5**:193
LITCHFIELD (Illinois)
map (39° 11′N 89° 39′W) **11**:42
LITCHFIELD (Michigan)
map (42° 3′N 84° 46′W) **13**:377
LITCHFIELD (Minnesota)
map (45° 8′N 94° 31′W) **13**:453
LITCHFIELD LAW SCHOOL
Reeve, Tapping **16**:118
LITCHFIELD PARK (Arizona)
map (33° 30′N 112° 22′W) **2**:160
LITCHI **12**:367–368 *illus.*
LITCHVILLE (North Dakota)
map (46° 39′N 98° 11′W) **14**:248
LITER
weights and measures **20**:93 *table*
LITERACY AND ILLITERACY **12**:368–370 *bibliog., map*
adult education **1**:110
reading education **16**:100–101 *bibliog.*
Right-to-Read Program **16**:222
world distribution of illiteracy **12**:369 *map*
LITERARY CRITICISM *see* CRITICISM, LITERARY
LITERARY FRAUD **12**:370 *bibliog.*
Macpherson, James **13**:36
LITERARY GUILD
book club **3**:386
LITERARY HISTORY *see* CRITICISM, LITERARY
LITERARY MODERNISM **12**:370 *bibliog.*
American literature **1**:345
Brazilian literature **3**:464
Dada **6**:4–5
futurism **8**:383–384
surrealism (film, literature, theater) **18**:366
vorticism **19**:635
LITERARY SYMBOL
figures of speech **8**:76
LITERARY THEORY *see* CRITICISM, LITERARY
LITERATURE **12**:370
See also names of specific literary forms, e.g., NOVEL; POETRY; etc.; names of specific literary periods, e.g., ELIZABETHAN AGE; MEDIEVAL DRAMA; etc.; names of specific authors, e.g., MILTON, JOHN; TOLSTOI, COUNT LEO; etc.; names of specific works of literature, e.g., *PARADISE LOST* (poem); *TOM SAWYER* (book); etc.
African literature **1**:167–168
American literature **1**:343–348
black American literature **3**:303–304

Arabic literature 2:101
Augustan age 2:320
Australian literature 2:343–344
Austrian literature 2:354
Belgian literature 3:175
best-seller 3:228–229
Bollingen Prize in Poetry *see* BOLLINGEN PRIZE IN POETRY
Brazilian literature 3:464
Breton literature 3:475
Bulgarian literature 3:557
Caldecott Medal *see* CALDECOTT MEDAL
Canadian literature 4:93–94
Catalan literature 4:198
children's literature 4:351–354
Chinese literature 4:389
confessional literature 5:177
Cornish literature 5:269
criticism, literary *see* CRITICISM, LITERARY
Czech literature 5:412–413
Danish literature 6:32–33
Dutch and Flemish literature 6:313–314
Edgar Allan Poe Award *see* EDGAR ALLAN POE AWARD
English literature 7:193–202
Finnish literature 8:99
folk literature *see* FOLKLORE; FOLKTALE
forms
allegory 1:298–299
annals 2:31
anthology 2:49
autobiography 2:355–356
belles lettres 3:187
bestiary 3:229
biography 3:263–264
blank verse 3:327
comedy 5:132
diary 6:153
drama 6:257–262
eclogues 7:42
elegy 7:129
epic 7:217
epigram 7:219
epistle 7:222
epitaph 7:222
essay 7:243
fable 8:4–5
fairy tale 8:10–11
farce 8:22–23
folktale 8:204
haiku 10:12
legend 12:273
limerick 12:344
lyric 12:479
novel 14:272–276
novella and novelette 14:276
ode 14:348
oral literature 14:414
parable 15:73
parody 15:96
pastiche 15:108
poetry 15:378–379
prose 15:572
saga 17:11
short story 17:283
sonnet 18:55
tragedy 19:265
French literature 8:315
genre 9:93
Gothic romance 9:263
mystery, suspense and detective fiction 13:692–693
pastoral literature 15:108–109
romance 16:280
science fiction 17:143–144
Westerns 20:117
German literature 9:132–134
Governor General's Award *see* GOVERNOR GENERAL'S AWARD
Great Books Program 9:309
Greek literature, ancient 9:343–344
Greek literature, modern 9:344
Hebrew and Yiddish literature 10:102
Hugo Award *see* HUGO AWARD
Hungarian literature 10:305–306
Icelandic literature 11:18–19
Indian literature 11:101–102
Irish literature 11:267–268
Italian literature 11:315–317
Japanese literature 11:380
language and literature 12:196–197
Latin American literature 12:228–231
Latin literature 12:234
Lenin Peace Prize
Neruda, Pablo 14:90
Zweig, Arnold 20:383
Lorne Pierce Medal *see* LORNE PIERCE MEDAL
Middle Ages
courtly love 5:317
medieval drama 13:273–274
movements
avant-garde 2:369
beat generation 3:144
classicism 5:42
Dada 6:4–5
decadence 6:72
formalism 8:234
literary modernism 12:370
naturalism 14:49–50
realism (literature) 16:104
romanticism 16:292–293
socialist realism 18:25
Sturm und Drang 18:309
surrealism (film, literature, theater) 18:366
symbolism 18:403
National Book Awards *see* NATIONAL BOOK AWARDS
Newbery Medal *see* NEWBERY MEDAL
Nobel Prize 14:208–211 *table*
Asturias, Miguel Ángel 2:285–286
Beckett, Samuel 3:151–152
Bellow, Saul 3:190
Benavente y Martínez, Jacinto 3:195
Bergson, Henri 3:211
Bjørnson, Bjørnstjerne 3:303
Böll, Heinrich 3:369
Buck, Pearl S. 3:535
Bunin, Ivan Alekseyevich 3:563
Camus, Albert 4:68
Canetti, Elias 4:108
Carducci, Giosuè 4:145
Deledda, Grazia 6:92
Echegaray y Eizaguirre, José 7:37
Eliot, T. S. 7:139–140
Eucken, Rudolf Christoph 7:262
Faulkner, William 8:36
France, Anatole 8:273
Galsworthy, John 9:21–22
García Márquez, Gabriel 9:39
Gide, André 9:176
Gjellerup, Karl Adolph 9:192
Golding, William 9:234–235
Hamsun, Knut 10:33–34
Hauptmann, Gerhart 10:69
Heidenstam, Verner von 10:107
Hemingway, Ernest 10:118–119
Hesse, Hermann 10:152–153
Heyse, Paul von 10:155
Jensen, Johannes Vilhelm 11:396
Jiménez, Juan Ramón 11:418
Johnson, Eyvind 11:432
Karlfeldt, Erik Axel 12:27
Kawabata Yasunari 12:32
Kipling, Rudyard 12:86–87
Lagerkvist, Pär 12:165
Lagerlöf, Selma 12:165
Laxness, Halldór Kiljan 12:252
Lewis, Sinclair 12:306–307
Maeterlinck, Maurice 3:175 *illus.*; 13:45–46
Mann, Thomas 13:123–124
Martin du Gard, Roger 13:179
Martinson, Harry Edmund 13:181
Mauriac, François 13:234
Mistral, Frédéric 13:482
Mistral, Gabriela 13:482
Mommsen, Theodor 13:515
Montale, Eugenio 13:545
Neruda, Pablo 14:90
Noel-Baker, Philip John, Baron Noel-Baker 14:212
O'Neill, Eugene 14:389–390
Pasternak, Boris 15:107
Perse, Saint-John 15:179–180
Pirandello, Luigi 15:314
Pontoppidan, Henrik 15:427
Quasimodo, Salvatore 16:15
Reymont, Władysław Stanisław 16:190–191
Rolland, Romain 16:271
Romains, Jules 16:272–273
Russell, Bertrand 16:349
Sachs, Nelly 17:7
Sartre, Jean Paul 17:79–80
Seferis, George 17:187
Shaw, George Bernard 17:245
Sholokhov, Mikhail Aleksandrovich 17:281
Sillanpää, Frans Eemil 17:309
Simon, Claude 17:314–315
Singer, Isaac Bashevis 17:322
Solzhenitsyn, Aleksandr 18:59
Soyinka, Wole 18:115
Spitteler, Carl 18:190
Steinbeck, John 18:248
Suttner, Bertha von 18:373
Tagore, Sir Rabindranath 19:9–10
Undset, Sigrid 19:383
White, Patrick 2:344; 20:135–136
Yeats, William Butler 20:321
Norwegian literature 14:265–266
O. Henry Award *see* O. HENRY AWARD
Persian literature 15:187
Polish literature 15:398
Portuguese literature 15:456–457
Provençal literature 15:583
Pulitzer Prize 15:618–619
Abbott, George 1:53
Andrews, Charles McLean 1:408
Ashbery, John 2:229
Auden, W. H. 2:318
Bemis, Samuel Flagg 3:194
Benét, Stephen Vincent 3:198
Benét, William Rose 3:198
Bennett, Michael 3:203
Berryman, John 3:225
Bishop, Elizabeth 3:297
Bock, Jerry, and Harnick, Sheldon 3:355
Bok, Edward William 3:363–364
Bromfield, Louis 3:502
Brooks, Gwendolyn 3:511
Brooks, Van Wyck 3:511
Buck, Pearl S. 3:535
Cather, Willa 4:208–209
Catton, Bruce 4:217
Channing, Edward 4:281
Cheever, John 4:310
Connelly, Marc 5:197
Cozzens, James Gould 5:324
Cushing, Harvey W. 5:397
De Voto, Bernard 6:64
Dillard, Annie 6:176
Drury, Allen 6:283
Dubos, Rene 6:289
Durant, Will and Ariel 6:303
Faulkner, William 8:36
Ferber, Edna 8:52
Fletcher, John Gould 8:163
Freeman, Douglas Southall 8:299
Frost, Robert 8:345–346
Garland, Hamlin 9:48
Gershwin, George and Ira 9:158–159
Glasgow, Ellen 9:197
Glaspell, Susan 9:197
Goldberg, Rube 9:231
Grau, Shirley Ann 9:301
Green, Paul 9:347
Guthrie, A. B., Jr. 9:409
Haley, Alex 10:19
Hart, Moss 10:61
Hemingway, Ernest 10:118–119
Hersey, John 10:148
Hofstadter, Richard 10:197
Howard, Sidney Coe 10:283
Inge, William 11:176
Kaufman, George S. 12:31–32
Kennan, George F. 12:41
Kennedy, John F. 12:42
Kennedy, William 12:44
Kumin, Maxine 12:136
Kunitz, Stanley J. 11:137
La Farge, Oliver Hazard Perry 12:145
Lewis, Sinclair 11:306–307
Lindsay, Howard, and Crouse, Russel 12:352
Lowell, Amy 11:443–444
Lowell, Robert, Jr. 12:444–445
McGinley, Phyllis 13:16
MacLeish, Archibald 13:32
Mailer, Norman 13:67
Malamud, Bernard 13:79
Marquand, J. P. 13:162
Millay, Edna St. Vincent 13:426
Miller, Arthur 6:69–70; 13:427
Miller, Perry 13:428
Mitchell, Margaret 13:483
Momaday, N. Scott 13:514
Moore, Marianne 13:569
Morison, Samuel Eliot 13:580
Nemerov, Howard 14:80–81
Nevins, Allan 14:115
O'Connor, Edwin 14:347
O'Neill, Eugene 14:389–390
Parrington, Vernon L. 15:97
Perry, Ralph Barton 15:179
Pershing, John J. 15:180–181
Pupin, Michael Idvorsky 15:626
Rawlings, Marjorie Kinnan 16:95
Richter, Conrad 16:214
Robinson, Edwin Arlington 16:244
Roethke, Theodore 16:268
Sagan, Carl Edward 17:11
Sandburg, Carl 17:61
Saroyan, William 17:78–79
Schlesinger, Arthur M., Jr. 17:125
Sexton, Anna 17:228
Shapiro, Karl 17:241
Shepard, Sam 17:256
Sherwood, Robert E. 17:259
Simpson, Louis 17:317
Sims, William Sowden 17:317
Sinclair, Upton 17:319
Snodgrass, W. D. 18:3
Snyder, Gary 18:5–6
Stafford, Jean 18:209
Stegner, Wallace 18:245
Stevens, Wallace 18:264
Styron, William 18:312
Tarkington, Booth 19:37
Turner, Frederick Jackson 19:349
Van Doren, Carl 19:513
Walker, Alice 20:12
Warren, Charles 20:32
Warren, Robert Penn 20:31
Welty, Eudora 20:102
Wharton, Edith 20:124
White, Theodore 20:136
White, William Allen 20:136
Wilbur, Richard 20:147–148
Wilder, Thornton 20:149–150
Williams, Tennessee 20:160–161
Williams, William Carlos 20:161
Wouk, Herman 20:284
Renaissance 16:149
Romanian literature 16:290
Russian literature 16:364–367
Spanish literature 18:157–160
Stalin Prize
Fast, Howard 8:33
Seghers, Anna 17:188
Sholokhov, Mikhail Aleksandrovich 17:281
Simonov, Konstantin Kirill Mikhailovich 17:316
Swedish literature 18:386–387
Welsh literature 20:101–102
LITHIUM (drug) 12:370
drug 6:278
manic depressive psychosis 13:116
psychotropic drugs 15:604
LITHIUM (element) 12:370–371 *bibliog.*
abundances of common elements 7:131 *table*
alkali metals 1:295
element 7:130 *table*
energy sources 7:175
Group IA periodic table 15:167
silicate minerals 17:304–305
solid-state physics 18:54
transmutation of elements 19:276
LITHOGRAPH 12:371 *bibliog., illus.* *See also* OFFSET LITHOGRAPHY
Bonnard, Pierre 3:381
book illustration 3:388
Currier and Ives 5:394
Daumier, Honoré 6:45–46
Gavarni, Paul 9:62
Goya, Francisco de 9:273–274
graphic arts 9:293–294
Grosman, Tatyana 9:370
Kollwitz, Käthe 12:107
Munch, Edvard 13:640
printing 15:551–552
Senefelder, Aloys, inventor 17:201
Toulouse-Lautrec, Henri de 19:250–251
Vuillard, Édouard 19:640
West, Benjamin 20:106–107
LITHOLOGY *see* PETROGRAPHY
LITHONIA (Georgia)
map (33° 43′N 84° 6′W) 2:292
LITHOSPHERE 12:371 *bibliog.*
barysphere element 12:371
Earth, gravitational field of 7:17
Earth, structure and composition of 7:20–23
Earth sciences 7:24
oceanic mineral resources 14:340–341
oceanic trenches 14:341–342
plate tectonics 15:351–357
LITHOTHAMNION 12:371
LITHOTOMY
surgery 18:360
LITHUANIAN SOVIET SOCIALIST REPUBLIC (USSR) 12:371–372 *bibliog., map*
Baltic languages 3:54–55
cities
Kaunas 12:32
Vilna 19:599
economic activities 12:372
history 12:372
Cossacks 5:290
Europe, history of 7:286
Vytautas, Grand Duke of Lithuania 19:640
Jagello (dynasty) 11:348
land and people 12:372
LITITZ (Pennsylvania)
map (40° 9′N 76° 18′W) 15:147

LITOTES
figures of speech **8**:76
LITTLE, MALCOLM *see* MALCOLM X
LITTLE AMERICA (Antarctica)
Ross Ice Shelf **16**:318
LITTLE ARKANSAS RIVER
map (37° 43′N 97° 22′W) **12**:18
LITTLE BELT, STRAIT OF THE
map (55° 20′N 9° 45′E) **6**:109
LITTLE BELT MOUNTAINS
map (46° 45′N 110° 35′W) **13**:547
LITTLE BIGHORN, BATTLE OF THE **11**:108 *illus.*; **12**:372 *bibliog.*
Cheyenne (American Indians) **4**:338
Crazy Horse **5**:334
Custer, George Armstrong **5**:397–398
Gall **9**:16
Indian Wars **11**:109–110 *map*
Rain-in-the-Face, Chief **11**:129 *illus.*
Sitting Bull **17**:330
LITTLE BITTER LAKE
map (30° 13′N 32° 33′E) **18**:324
LITTLE BLUE RIVER
map (39° 41′N 96° 40′W) **12**:18
LITTLE BOW RIVER
map (49° 53′N 112° 29′W) **1**:256
LITTLE BULLHEAD (Manitoba)
map (51° 40′N 96° 51′W) **13**:119
LITTLE CATALINA (Newfoundland)
map (48° 33′N 53° 2′W) **14**:166
LITTLE COLORADO RIVER
map (36° 11′N 111° 48′W) **2**:160
LITTLE DIPPER **12**:372
constellation **5**:212
Polaris **15**:393
LITTLE EGG HARBOR
map (39° 35′N 74° 18′W) **14**:129
LITTLE EGYPT (dancer)
belly dance **3**:192
LITTLE ENTENTE **12**:372–373 *bibliog.*
LITTLE FALLS (Minnesota)
map (45° 59′N 94° 21′W) **13**:453
LITTLE FALLS (New York)
map (43° 3′N 74° 52′W) **14**:149
LITTLE FLOWER, THE *see* LA GUARDIA, FIORELLO
LITTLE FORK RIVER
map (48° 31′N 93° 35′W) **13**:453
LITTLE FORT (British Columbia)
map (51° 25′N 120° 12′W) **3**:491
LITTLE GIDDING
Ferrar, Nicholas **8**:58
LITTLE GRASS FROG **12**:373
LITTLE HOUSE ON THE PRAIRIE (book)
Wilder, Laura Ingalls **20**:149
LITTLE HUMBOLDT RIVER
map (41° 0′N 117° 43′W) **14**:111
LITTLE JULIANA (steamboat)
Stevens (family) **18**:263
LITTLE KANAWHA RIVER
map (39° 16′N 81° 34′W) **20**:111
LITTLE LEAGUE BASEBALL **12**:373
Williamsport (Pennsylvania) **20**:162
LITTLE LONDON (Jamaica)
map (18° 15′N 78° 13′W) **11**:351
LITTLE MECATINA RIVER
map (50° 28′N 59° 35′W) **14**:166
LITTLE MERMAID (statue) **6**:110 *illus.*
LITTLE MIAMI RIVER
map (39° 5′N 84° 26′W) **14**:357
LITTLE MISSOURI RIVER
map (33° 49′N 92° 54′W) **2**:166
map (47° 30′N 102° 25′W) **19**:419
LITTLE PECONIC BAY
map (40° 59′N 72° 24′W) **5**:193
LITTLE PEE DEE RIVER
map (33° 42′N 79° 11′W) **18**:98
LITTLE PRINCE, THE (book)
Saint-Exupéry, Antoine de **17**:18
LITTLE RED RIDING HOOD (fairy tale) **8**:10 *illus.*
LITTLE RED RIVER
map (35° 11′N 91° 27′W) **2**:166
LITTLE REVIEW, THE (periodical)
Anderson, Margaret **1**:402
LITTLE RICHARD
rock music **16**:248
LITTLE RIVER (county in Arkansas)
map (33° 42′N 94° 15′W) **2**:166
LITTLE RIVER (Kansas)
map (38° 24′N 98° 1′W) **12**:18
LITTLE ROCK (Arkansas) **2**:168 *illus.*; **12**:373
integration, racial
Central High School **3**:310 *illus.*; **12**:247 *illus.*
map (34° 44′N 92° 15′W) **2**:166
LITTLE ROCK (Iowa)
map (43° 26′N 95° 55′W) **11**:244
LITTLE SANDY RIVER
map (38° 35′N 82° 51′W) **12**:47
LITTLE SCARCIES RIVER
map (8° 51′N 13° 9′W) **17**:296
LITTLE SIOUX RIVER
map (41° 49′N 96° 4′W) **11**:244
LITTLE SNAKE RIVER
map (40° 27′N 108° 26′W) **5**:116
LITTLE TRAMP
Chaplin, Charlie **4**:284–285 *illus.*
LITTLE TURTLE (Miami chief) **12**:373 *bibliog.*
Indian Wars **11**:107
LITTLE VALLEY (New York)
map (42° 15′N 78° 48′W) **14**:149
LITTLE WABASH RIVER
map (37° 54′N 88° 5′W) **11**:42
LITTLE WHITE RIVER
map (43° 44′N 100° 40′W) **18**:103
LITTLE WOOD RIVER
map (42° 57′N 114° 21′W) **11**:26
LITTLE ZAB RIVER
map (35° 12′N 43° 25′E) **11**:255
LITTLEFIELD (Texas)
map (33° 55′N 102° 20′W) **19**:129
LITTLEFORK (Minnesota)
map (48° 24′N 93° 33′W) **13**:453
LITTLESTOWN (Pennsylvania)
map (39° 45′N 77° 5′W) **15**:147
LITTLETON (Colorado)
map (39° 37′N 105° 1′W) **5**:116
LITTLETON (Massachusetts)
map (42° 32′N 71° 31′W) **13**:206
LITTLETON (New Hampshire)
map (44° 18′N 71° 46′W) **14**:123
LITTLETON (North Carolina)
map (36° 26′N 77° 54′W) **14**:242
LITTLETON (West Virginia)
map (39° 42′N 80° 31′W) **20**:111
LITTLETON, HARVEY
studio glass **5**:327 *illus.*
LITTLETON, THOMAS
common law treatises **5**:140
LITTON INDUSTRIES, INC. **1**:128 *table*
LITTORAL ZONE **12**:373
benthonic zone **3**:205
bottom, materials **12**:373
habitat **10**:4–5
intertidal life **11**:229–230
ocean and sea **14**:331
seaward from shoreline, distance **12**:373
subdivisions **12**:373
LITTRÉ, ÉMILE
dictionary **6**:159
LITURGY **12**:373–374 *bibliog.*
See also CHURCH MUSIC
Black Mass **3**:317
Book of Common Prayer **3**:386
breviary **3**:475
canticle **4**:117
Christmas **4**:415
Divine Office **6**:203
doxology **6**:253
Easter **7**:32
Epiphany **7**:220
Good Friday **9**:245
Hinduism **10**:170
Holy Family **10**:209
litany **12**:367
Lord's Prayer **12**:413
Mass **13**:200
Pentecost **15**:155
prayer **15**:490
purification, rites of **15**:629
vestments **19**:565
LITVINOV, MAKSIM MAKSIMOVICH **12**:374 *bibliog.*
LIU CH'E *see* HAN WU TI (Han Wudi)
LIU CHI, EMPEROR OF CHINA *see* LIU PANG, EMPEROR OF CHINA
LIU-CHOU (China)
map (24° 22′N 109° 32′E) **4**:362
LIU PANG, EMPEROR OF CHINA
Han **10**:34
LIU SHAO-CH'I (Liu Shaoqi) **12**:374 *bibliog.*
LIU SHAOQI *see* LIU SHAO-CH'I (Li Shaoqi)
LIU TSUNG-YUAN (Liu Zongyuan)
Chinese literature **4**:390
LIUTPRAND
Lombards **12**:399
LIVE-FOREVER PLANT (botany) *see* STONECROP (botany)
LIVE OAK (Florida)
map (30° 18′N 82° 59′W) **8**:172
LIVE OAK (county in Texas)
map (28° 20′N 98° 5′W) **19**:129
LIVENGOOD (Alaska)
map (65° 32′N 148° 33′W) **1**:242
LIVER **1**:54 *illus.*; **7**:328 *illus.*; **12**:374–375 *bibliog.*, *illus.*
anatomy **12**:375 *illus.*
circulatory system **4**:440 *illus.*
diseases and disorders **12**:374
cirrhosis **4**:445
fungus diseases **8**:369
hepatitis **10**:130
jaundice **11**:385
leukopenia **12**:301
malaria **13**:80
splenomegaly **18**:191
drug **6**:275–276
drug administration **6**:275 *illus.*
function **12**:374–375 *illus.*
function test, enzyme **7**:215
metabolism **12**:374–375
cholesterol **4**:404
lipid **12**:362
Minot, George **13**:460
regeneration **12**:374
transplantation, organ **19**:277
urea **19**:485
Whipple, George Hoyt **20**:131
LIVER FLUKE *see* FLUKE (flatworm)
LIVERMORE (California)
map (37° 41′N 121° 46′W) **4**:31
LIVERMORE (Iowa)
map (42° 52′N 94° 11′W) **11**:244
LIVERMORE (Kentucky)
map (37° 29′N 87° 8′W) **12**:47
LIVERMORE, MOUNT
map (30° 38′N 104° 10′W) **19**:129
LIVERMORE FALLS (Maine)
map (44° 28′N 70° 11′W) **13**:70
LIVERPOOL (England) **12**:375–376; **19**:410 *illus.*
map (53° 25′N 2° 55′W) **19**:403
LIVERPOOL (Nova Scotia)
map (44° 2′N 64° 43′W) **14**:269
LIVERPOOL, ROBERT BANKS JENKINSON, 2d EARL OF **12**:376 *bibliog.*
LIVERWORT **12**:376 *bibliog.*, *illus.*; **15**:333–334 *illus.*
bryophyte **3**:530
moss **13**:603–605
LIVERY COMPANIES *see* GUILDS
LIVES OF EMINENT PHILOSOPHERS
Diogenes Laërtius **6**:184
LIVES OF THE MOST EMINENT PAINTERS, SCULPTORS, AND ARCHITECTS (book)
Vasari, Giorgio **19**:525
LIVESTOCK *see* ANIMAL HUSBANDRY; CATTLE AND CATTLE RAISING
LIVIA DRUSILLA **12**:376
Drusus (family) **6**:283
LIVING THEATRE **12**:376–377 *bibliog.*, *illus.*
Chaikin, Joseph **4**:268
LIVING WILL
death and dying **6**:69
euthanasia **7**:311
LIVINGSTON (Alabama)
map (32° 35′N 88° 11′W) **1**:234
LIVINGSTON (family) **12**:377 *bibliog.*
LIVINGSTON (Illinois)
map (38° 58′N 89° 46′W) **11**:42
LIVINGSTON (county in Illinois)
map (40° 53′N 88° 38′W) **11**:42
LIVINGSTON (Kentucky)
map (37° 18′N 84° 13′W) **12**:47
LIVINGSTON (county in Kentucky)
map (37° 15′N 88° 20′W) **12**:47
LIVINGSTON (Louisiana)
map (30° 30′N 90° 45′W) **12**:430
LIVINGSTON (county in Louisiana)
map (30° 25′N 90° 45′W) **12**:430
LIVINGSTON (county in Michigan)
map (42° 38′N 83° 50′W) **13**:377
LIVINGSTON (county in Missouri)
map (39° 45′N 93° 35′W) **13**:476
LIVINGSTON (Montana)
map (45° 40′N 110° 34′W) **13**:547
LIVINGSTON (New Jersey)
map (40° 48′N 74° 19′W) **14**:129
LIVINGSTON (county in New York)
map (42° 48′N 77° 49′W) **14**:149
LIVINGSTON (Tennessee)
map (36° 23′N 85° 19′W) **19**:104
LIVINGSTON (Texas)
map (30° 43′N 94° 56′W) **19**:129
LIVINGSTON, ROBERT R.
Livingston (family) **12**:377
Louisiana Purchase **12**:435
LIVINGSTON MANOR (New York)
map (41° 54′N 74° 50′W) **14**:149
LIVINGSTONE (Zambia)
map (17° 50′S 25° 53′E) **20**:354
LIVINGSTONE, DAVID **12**:377–378 *bibliog.*, *illus.*
Africa **1**:157 *illus.*, *map*
exploration **7**:335–338 *map*
Stanley, Sir Henry Morton **18**:219
Tanganyika, Lake **19**:22
Victoria Falls **19**:575
Zambezi River **20**:352
Zambia **20**:353
LIVINGSTONE FALLS
map (4° 50′S 14° 30′E) **20**:350
LIVINGSTONE MOUNTAINS
map (9° 45′S 34° 20′E) **13**:81
LIVIUS ANDRONICUS **12**:378
LIVO RIVER
map (65° 24′N 26° 48′E) **8**:95
LIVONIA (Louisiana)
map (30° 33′N 91° 33′W) **12**:430
LIVONIA (Michigan)
map (42° 25′N 83° 23′W) **13**:377
LIVONIA (New York)
map (42° 49′N 77° 40′W) **14**:149
LIVONIA (USSR) **12**:378 *bibliog.*
Ural-Altaic languages **19**:475
LIVONIAN KNIGHTS
Livonia **12**:378
Teutonic Knights **19**:128
LIVORNO (Italy) **12**:378
map (43° 33′N 10° 19′E) **11**:321
LIVRE DE PEINTRE
book illustration **3**:388
LIVS
Livonia **12**:378
LIVY **10**:184 *illus.*; **12**:378 *bibliog.*
Padua (Italy) **15**:13
LIZARD **12**:378–382 *bibliog.*, *illus.*
agama **1**:181–182
anatomy **12**:379–382 *illus.*
skeletal system **12**:381 *illus.*; **17**:334 *illus.*
skin **17**:340 *illus.*
animal behavior **12**:379–382 *illus.*
anole **12**:381 *illus.*
Australian frilled lizard **2**:342–343
basilisk **12**:381 *illus.*
chameleon **4**:275
classification, biological **12**:382
distribution and habitat **12**:378–379
dwarf gecko **6**:317
earless monitor **7**:8
evolution **12**:382
flap-footed lizard **8**:153
flying dragon **12**:381 *illus.*
gecko **9**:66–67
gerrhosaurid **9**:158
Gila monster **9**:178
girdle-tailed lizard **9**:189
glass snake **9**:202
helmeted lizard **10**:115
horned toad **10**:239
iguana **11**:38
Komodo dragon **12**:107–108
lacertid **12**:160
legless lizard **12**:275
Mexican beaded lizard **13**:350
molting **13**:513 *illus.*
monitor **13**:531
mosasaur **13**:596
night lizard **14**:192
parthenogenesis **15**:100
race runner **16**:36
regeneration **16**:127 *illus.*
growth **9**:379
skink **17**:343
teiid **19**:73
teju **19**:74
Triassic Period **19**:294 *illus.*
LIZARD HEAD PEAK
map (42° 47′N 109° 11′W) **20**:301
LIZARDFISH **12**:382
LIZARDI, JOSÉ JOAQUÍN FERNÁNDEZ DE *see* FERNÁNDEZ DE LIZARDI, JOSÉ JOAQUÍN
LIZARD'S TAIL (botany) **12**:382
LJUBLJANA (Yugoslavia) **12**:382
map (46° 3′N 14° 31′E) **20**:340
LJUNGAN RIVER
map (62° 19′N 17° 23′E) **18**:382
LJUSNAN RIVER
map (61° 12′N 17° 8′E) **18**:382
LLAMA **12**:382 *illus.*
alpaca **1**:308
animal husbandry **2**:23
ruminant **16**:345
LLANETTI (Wales)
map (51° 42′N 4° 10′W) **19**:403
LLANO (Texas)
map (30° 45′N 98° 41′W) **19**:129
LLANO (county in Texas)
map (30° 43′N 98° 40′W) **19**:129
LLANO ESTACADO
map (33° 30′N 102° 40′W) **19**:129
LLANOS
map (5° 0′N 70° 0′W) **19**:542
LLERA (Mexico)
map (23° 19′N 99° 1′W) **13**:357
LLEWELLYN, KARL
legal realism **12**:243
LLEYN PENINSULA
map (52° 54′N 4° 30′W) **19**:403
LLOSA, MARIO VARGAS *see* VARGAS LLOSA, MARIO
LLOYD, CHRIS EVERT **12**:382–383 *bibliog.*, *illus.*; **19**:110 *illus.*
LLOYD, HAROLD **12**:383 *bibliog.*
film, history of **8**:82

LLOYD, HENRY DEMAREST **12**:383 *bibliog.*
LLOYD, MARGARET
modern dance **13**:497
LLOYD GEORGE, DAVID, 1st EARL LLOYD-GEORGE OF DWYFOR **12**:383–384 *bibliog., illus.*
Liberal parties **12**:311
Paris Peace Conference **15**:88
World War I **20**:236
LLOYD GEORGE, DAVID 1ST EARL LLOYD-GEORGE OF DWYFOR
Paris Peace Conference **20**:244 *illus.*
LLOYD'S OF LONDON **12**:384 *bibliog.*
LNG *see* LIQUIFIED NATURAL GAS
LOA (Utah)
map (38° 24′N 111° 38′W) **19**:492
LOA RIVER
map (21° 26′S 70° 4′W) **4**:355
LOACH **12**:384 *illus.*
LOAM *see* SOIL
LOANS
Agency for International Development **1**:183
banking systems **3**:68–69
consumer
credit union **5**:336
finance company **8**:92
consumer credit **5**:225
foreign aid **8**:224–225
savings and loan association **17**:100
scholarships, fellowships, and loans **17**:130–131
LOBACHEVSKY, NIKOLAI IVANOVICH **12**:384 *bibliog.*
mathematics, history of **13**:226
non-Euclidean geometry **14**:216
LOBAMBA (Swaziland)
map (26° 27′S 31° 12′E) **18**:380
LOBBYIST **12**:384 *bibliog.*
American Medical Association **1**:348
National Rifle Association of America **14**:45
special-interest groups **18**:167–168
LOBELIA **12**:384–385
water lobelia **12**:168 *illus.*
LOBELVILLE (Tennessee)
map (35° 47′N 87° 49′W) **19**:104
LOBENGULA, KING OF THE NDEBELE **12**:385 *bibliog.*
LOBERÍA (Argentina)
map (38° 9′S 58° 47′W) **2**:149
LOBITO (Angola)
map (12° 20′S 13° 34′E) **2**:5
LOBO, FRANCISCO RODRIGUES
Portuguese literature **15**:457
LOBOLA *see* BRIDE-PRICE
LOBOS, HEITOR VILLA- *see* VILLA-LOBOS, HEITOR
LOBOTOMY
psychopathology, treatment of **15**:600
LOBSTER **12**:385 *bibliog., illus.*
Jurassic Period **11**:476
Maine **13**:71 *illus.*
shellfish **17**:254–255 *illus.*
LOBSTICK LAKE
map (54° 0′N 64° 50′W) **14**:166
LOCAL ANESTHETICS *see* ANESTHETICS
LOCAL EDUCATION AUTHORITIES
British education **3**:493–494
LOCAL GOVERNMENT *see* MUNICIPAL GOVERNMENT (local government)
LOCAL GROUP OF GALAXIES **7**:342 *illus.*; **12**:385 *bibliog.*
clusters of galaxies **5**:72
Galaxy, The **9**:10
Magellanic Clouds **13**:48–49
LOCAL-REALITY CONDITION (physics)
Bell's theorem **3**:192
LOCARNO (Switzerland) **12**:385
map (46° 10′N 8° 48′E) **18**:394
LOCARNO PACT **12**:385–386 *bibliog.*
LOCH LOMOND *see* LOMOND, LOCH
LOCH NESS *see* NESS, LOCH
LOCH NESS MONSTER **12**:386 *bibliog.*
Ness, Loch **14**:97
LOCHNER* v. *NEW YORK **12**:386
Holmes, Oliver Wendell, Jr. **10**:206
LOCHSA RIVER
map (46° 8′N 115° 36′W) **11**:26
LOCK (waterways) **4**:95 *illus.*
canal **4**:94–97 *illus.*
harbor and port **10**:43
Panama Canal **15**:57 *illus.*
St. Lawrence Seaway **17**:21–22
Sault Sainte Marie Canals **17**:96–97
LOCK HAVEN (Pennsylvania)
map (41° 8′N 77° 27′W) **15**:147
LOCK AND KEY **12**:386–387 *bibliog., illus.*
frontier, U.S. **8**:344
hotel **10**:262
Yale, Linus, Jr. **20**:315
LOCKE, ALAIN **11**:387 *bibliog.*
LOCKE, DAVID ROSS *see* NASBY, PETROLEUM V.
LOCKE, JOHN **12**:387–388 *bibliog., illus.*; **15**:242 *illus.*
civil rights **5**:12
Declaration of Independence **6**:74
democracy **6**:97
educational psychology **7**:66
law **12**:242
liberalism **12**:312
natural law **14**:48
philosophy **15**:245
political parties **15**:400
psychology, history of **15**:596
social contract **18**:11
state (in political philosophy) **18**:229; **18**:232
Whig party (England) **20**:130
LOCKEPORT (Nova Scotia)
map (43° 42′N 65° 7′W) **14**:269
LOCKHART (Texas)
map (29° 53′N 97° 41′W) **19**:129
LOCKHEED AIRCRAFT CORPORATION **1**:128 *table*
LOCKHEED P-38 LIGHTNING AIRCRAFT *see* P-38 LIGHTNING
LOCKJAW *see* TETANUS
LOCKNEY (Texas)
map (34° 7′N 101° 27′W) **19**:129
LOCKOUT **12**:388
LOCKPORT (Illinois)
map (41° 36′N 88° 3′W) **11**:42
LOCKPORT (Louisiana)
map (29° 39′N 90° 32′W) **12**:430
LOCKPORT (New York)
map (43° 10′N 78° 42′W) **14**:149
LOCKWOOD (Missouri)
map (37° 23′N 93° 57′W) **13**:476
LOCKWOOD, BELVA ANN BENNETT **12**:388 *bibliog.*
LOCKYER, SIR JOSEPH NORMAN **12**:388 *bibliog.*
archaeoastronomy **2**:115
astronomy, history of **2**:279
LOCOMOTION, BIOLOGICAL *see* BIOLOGICAL LOCOMOTION
LOCOMOTIVE **12**:388–392 *bibliog., illus., table*
Baldwin, Matthias W. **3**:35
railroad **16**:74–75 *illus.*
steam engine **18**:240–241 *illus.*
Best Friend of Charleston **3**:228
Big Boy **12**:389 *illus.*; **12**:391
Experiment **12**:389
General **12**:389 *illus.*
John Bull **11**:424
Mallard **12**:390 *illus.*
Rocket **12**:388–389 *illus.*; **16**:251 *illus.*; **19**:67 *illus.*
Tom Thumb **19**:229
Stephenson, George and Robert **18**:255
Stevens, John **18**:263
Trevithick, Richard **19**:291
types **12**:391 *table*
diesel locomotive **12**:390–391 *illus.*
electric locomotive **12**:390–391 *illus.*
steam locomotive **12**:388–391 *illus.*
wheel arrangement **12**:389 *illus.*; **12**:391 *table*
Whyte classification of locomotives **12**:391 *table*
LOCOWEED **12**:392
LOCUS (mathematics)
curve **5**:396
ellipse **7**:147
LOCUST (insect) **12**:392 *bibliog., illus.*
animal migration **2**:25
cicada **4**:428
grasshopper **9**:298–299
LOCUST (plant) **12**:392
LOCUST BIRDS
pratincole **15**:490
LOCUST FORK RIVER
map (33° 33′N 87° 11′W) **1**:234
LOCUST GROVE (Oklahoma)
map (36° 12′N 95° 10′W) **14**:368
LOCUST RIVER
map (39° 40′N 93° 17′W) **13**:476
LOD (Israel)
map (31° 58′N 34° 54′E) **11**:302
LODE DEPOSIT
vein deposit **19**:536
LODESTONE *see* MAGNETITE
LODGE (family) **12**:392 *bibliog.*
LODGE, HENRY CABOT
Lodge (family) **12**:392
LODGE, HENRY CABOT, JR.
Lodge (family) **12**:392
LODGE, JOHN DAVIS
Lodge (family) **12**:392
LODGE, THOMAS **12**:392–393 *bibliog.*
LODGE GRASS (Montana)
map (45° 19′N 107° 22′W) **13**:547
LODGEPOLE (Alberta)
map (53° 6′N 115° 19′W) **1**:256
LODGEPOLE CREEK
map (41° 13′N 103° 20′W) **20**:301
LODI (California)
map (38° 8′N 121° 16′W) **4**:31
LODI (Italy)
map (45° 19′N 9° 30′E) **11**:321
LODI (New Jersey)
map (40° 53′N 74° 5′W) **14**:129
LODI (Ohio)
map (41° 3′N 82° 1′W) **14**:357
LODI (Wisconsin)
map (43° 19′N 89° 32′W) **20**:185
LODI, PEACE OF
Italian Wars **11**:319
LODOMERIA, KINGDOM OF GALICIA AND *see* GALICIA (historic region of Central Europe)
ŁÓDŹ (Poland) **12**:393
map (51° 46′N 19° 30′E) **15**:388
World War I **20**:226–227 *map*
LOEB, RICHARD
Darrow, Clarence S. **6**:39
LOEFFLER, FRIEDRICH
virus **19**:614
LOESS **12**:393 *bibliog., illus.*
cliffs **12**:393 *illus.*
composition **12**:393
deposits **12**:393
Driftless Area **6**:272
formation **12**:393
fossil record **8**:247
ice ages **11**:8–10
Pleistocene Epoch **15**:365–366
surface sediment **12**:393
wind action **20**:170
LOESS PLATEAU
map (37° 0′N 106° 0′E) **4**:362
LOEW, MARCUS
film, history of **8**:82
Zukor, Adolph **20**:381
LOEWE, FREDERICK
Lerner, Alan Jay, and Loewe, Frederick **12**:296
LOEWI, OTTO
Dale, Sir Henry Hallett **6**:11
LOEWY, RAYMOND **12**:393
LOFOTEN ISLANDS
map (68° 30′N 15° 0′E) **14**:261
Norway **14**:260
LOG (navigation)
speed measurement
navigation **14**:58–59 *illus.*
LOG CABIN BILL *see* PREEMPTION ACT
LOGAN (county in Arkansas)
map (35° 15′N 93° 45′W) **2**:166
LOGAN (county in Colorado)
map (41° 40′N 103° 5′W) **5**:116
LOGAN (county in Illinois)
map (40° 10′N 89° 18′W) **11**:42
LOGAN (Iowa)
map (41° 39′N 95° 47′W) **11**:244
LOGAN (Kansas)
map (39° 40′N 99° 34′W) **12**:18
LOGAN (county in Kansas)
map (38° 55′N 101° 10′W) **12**:18
LOGAN (county in Kentucky)
map (36° 50′N 86° 55′W) **12**:47
LOGAN (county in Nebraska)
map (41° 35′N 100° 30′W) **14**:70
LOGAN (New Mexico)
map (35° 22′N 103° 25′W) **14**:136
LOGAN (county in North Dakota)
map (46° 25′N 99° 25′W) **14**:248
LOGAN (Ohio)
map (39° 32′N 82° 25′W) **14**:357
LOGAN (county in Ohio)
map (40° 22′N 83° 46′W) **14**:357
LOGAN (county in Oklahoma)
map (35° 55′N 97° 25′W) **14**:368
LOGAN (Utah)
map (41° 44′N 111° 50′W) **19**:492
LOGAN (West Virginia)
map (37° 51′N 81° 59′W) **20**:111
LOGAN (county in West Virginia)
map (37° 52′N 81° 57′W) **20**:111
LOGAN, JAMES (Mingo Indian) *see* LOGAN, JOHN (Mingo Indian)
LOGAN, JAMES (public official) **12**:393 *bibliog.*
LOGAN, JOHN (Mingo Indian) **12**:393
LOGAN, JOHN ALEXANDER **12**:393–394 *bibliog.*
LOGAN, MOUNT **12**:394
LOGAN, MOUNT (Washington)
map (48° 32′N 120° 57′W) **20**:35
LOGAN, MOUNT (Yukon Territory)
map (60° 34′N 140° 24′W) **20**:345
LOGAN MOUNTAINS
map (61° 30′N 129° 0′W) **20**:345
LOGANBERRY *see* BLACKBERRY
LOGANSPORT (Indiana)
map (40° 45′N 86° 21′W) **11**:111
LOGANSPORT (Louisiana)
map (31° 58′N 93° 58′W) **12**:430
LOGANVILLE (Georgia)
map (33° 50′N 83° 54′W) **9**:114
LOGARITHM **12**:394 *bibliog.*
Briggs, Henry **3**:486
Brouncker, William **3**:512
e **7**:3
exponent **7**:339
hyperbolic functions **10**:348
interpolation **11**:225
mathematical tables **13**:221
Napier, John **14**:14
slide rule **17**:361
LOGGERHEAD TURTLE **12**:394 *illus.*
LOGGING **12**:394–395 *bibliog., illus.*
forestry **8**:231
lumber **12**:455 *illus.*; **12**:457–458
Ontario **14**:394 *illus.*
Washington **20**:37 *illus.*
LOGIC **12**:395–397 *bibliog., table*
artificial intelligence **2**:221
axiom **2**:377–378
computer **5**:160e; **5**:160f
deduction **6**:77
dialectic **6**:150
fallacy **8**:14
geometry, logical structure **9**:107
history **12**:395–396
Aristotle **2**:157
mathematics, history of **13**:226
induction **11**:151
intuitionist logic **12**:396
mathematical logic **12**:396
Boole, George **3**:392–393
Boolean algebra **3**:393
Carnap, Rudolf **4**:154
Frege, Gottlob **8**:301
games, mathematical **9**:32
history of theories **12**:395–396
Leibniz, Gottfried Wilhelm von **12**:276–277
Lewis, Clarence Irving **12**:306
mathematics **13**:221
Peano, Giuseppe **15**:125
Quine, Willard Van Orman **16**:27
symbols **12**:396
modal logic **12**:397
Occam's razor **14**:320
paradox (mathematics) **15**:75–76
Russell's paradox **16**:351
Zeno's paradoxes **20**:360
philosophy **15**:242
pragmatics **12**:397
reasoning **16**:104
Russell, Bertrand **16**:349
science, philosophy of **17**:142
set theory **17**:213
syllogism **18**:401–402
symbolic logic *see* LOGIC—mathematical logic
traditional logic **12**:375
Venn diagram **19**:546
LOGICAL POSITIVISM **12**:397 *bibliog.*
analytic and linguistic philosophy **1**:389–390
atheism **2**:289
Bergmann, Gustav **3**:210
Carnap, Rudolf **4**:154
Hempel, Carl Gustav **10**:120
philosophy **15**:245
Wittgenstein, Ludwig **20**:193–194
LOGLAN
languages, artificial **12**:197
LOGO (computer language) **12**:397
computer languages **5**:160p
computers in education **5**:165
LOGOGRAPHIC WRITING *see* WRITING SYSTEMS, EVOLUTION OF
LOGONE RIVER
map (12° 6′N 15° 2′E) **4**:251
LOGOS **12**:397–398 *bibliog.*
Heraclitus **10**:131–132
Jesus Christ **11**:405–406
natural law **14**:48
Plato **15**:361
LOGOTHERAPY (psychotherapy)
Frankl, Viktor **8**:282
LOGROLLING *see* BIRLING
LOGROÑO (Spain)
map (42° 28′N 2° 27′W) **18**:140
LOGWOOD **12**:398
LOHRVILLE (Iowa)
map (42° 17′N 94° 33′W) **11**:244
LOIASIS *see* EYE WORM

LOIRE RIVER 12:398 *bibliog.*
map (47° 16′N 2° 11′W) 8:260
LOISY, ALFRED FIRMIN 12:398 *bibliog.*
modernism 13:498
LOÍZA (Puerto Rico)
map (18° 23′N 65° 54′W) 15:614
LOIZA RESERVOIR
map (18° 17′N 66° 0′W) 15:614
LOJA (Ecuador)
map (4° 0′S 79° 13′W) 7:52
LOK, MICHAEL
Frobisher, Sir Martin 8:335
LOKEN TEKOJÄRVI RESERVOIR
map (67° 55′N 27° 40′E) 8:95
LOKEREN (Belgium)
map (51° 6′N 4° 0′E) 3:177
LOKI 12:398
Balder 3:33
mythology 13:702
LOKOJA (Nigeria)
map (7° 47′N 6° 45′E) 14:190
LOKORO RIVER
map (1° 43′S 18° 23′E) 20:350
LOLITA (book)
Nabokov, Vladimir 14:3–4
LOLLAND ISLAND
map (54° 46′N 11° 30′E) 6:109
LOLLARDS 12:398 *bibliog.*
LOLO (Montana)
map (46° 45′N 114° 5′W) 13:547
LOLO PASS
map (46° 38′N 114° 35′W) 11:26
LOLOTIQUE (El Salvador)
map (13° 33′N 88° 21′W) 7:100
LOMA, MOUNT
map (9° 13′N 11° 7′W) 17:296
LOMA MOUNTAINS
map (9° 10′N 11° 7′W) 17:296
LOMAX (family) 12:398 *bibliog.*
Seeger, Pete 17:187
LOMAX, ALAN
Lomax (family) 12:398
LOMAX, JOHN AVERY
Leadbelly 12:256
Lomax (family) 12:398
LOMBARD (Illinois)
map (41° 53′N 88° 1′W) 11:42
LOMBARD, PETER *see* PETER LOMBARD
LOMBARDI, VINCE 12:398–399 *bibliog., illus.*
LOMBARDIA (Italy) *see* LOMBARDY (Italy)
LOMBARDO (family) 12:399 *bibliog.*
LOMBARDS 12:399 *bibliog.*
invasion of Europe 7:282 *map*
Italy, history of 11:327
LOMBARDY (Italy) 12:399
cities
Bergamo 3:209
Brescia 3:473
Como 5:153
Cremona 5:338
Milan 13:418 *illus.*
Monza 13:560
Pavia 15:120
history
Frederick I, King of Germany and Holy Roman Emperor (Frederick Barbarossa) 8:290
Italian unification 11:330 *map*
Sforza (family) 17:233
Visconti (family) 19:616
Romanesque art and architecture 16:284
LOMBROSO, CESARE 12:399 *bibliog.*
crime 5:346
LOMÉ (Togo) 12:399
climate 19:222 *table*
map (6° 8′N 1° 13′E) 19:222
LOMÉNIE DE BRIENNE, ÉTIENNE CHARLES DE 12:399 *bibliog.*
LOMMEL (Belgium)
map (51° 14′N 5° 18′E) 3:177
LOMOND, LOCH 12:400
map (56° 8′N 4° 38′W) 19:403
LOMONOSOV, MIKHAIL VASILEVICH 12:400
Moscow State University 13:599
LOMONOSOV MEDAL
Heyerdahl, Thor 10:155
LOMONOSOV RIDGE 12:400
map (88° 0′N 140° 0′E) 2:139
LOMPOC (California)
map (34° 38′N 120° 27′W) 4:31
LOMZA (Poland)
map (53° 11′N 22° 5′E) 15:388
LON NOL 12:400
LONACONING (Maryland)
map (39° 34′N 78° 59′W) 13:188
LONDON (Arkansas)
map (35° 20′N 93° 15′W) 2:166
LONDON (England) 7:276 *illus.*; 12:400–402 *bibliog., illus., map*
architecture and historic sites 12:401–402 *map*
Buckingham Palace 3:536 *illus.*
Cleopatra's Needles 5:51
Gibbs, James 9:174
Holland, Henry 10:203
London Bridge 12:404–405
Nash, John 14:23–24
Piccadilly Circus 12:402
Royal Naval College (formerly the Greenwich Naval Hospital) 20:286 *illus.*
St. James's Palace 17:19
Saint Pancras Station 19:576 *illus.*
Saint Paul's Cathedral 17:25
Tower of London 19:254
Westminster Abbey 20:117–118
Westminster Palace 20:118
Whitehall Palace 20:139
Wren, Sir Christopher 20:286
art
National Gallery, London 14:33
Tate Gallery, The 19:44
Victoria and Albert Museum 19:575
Wallace Collection, The 20:15
climate 19:404 *table*
cockney 5:87
education 12:400–402
Lancaster, Joseph 12:177
London, University of 12:403–404
government 12:400
Greenwich 9:354
guilds 9:395 *illus.*
harbor and port 10:43
history 12:402
London, treaties and conferences of 12:403
World War II 20:255 *illus.*; 20:275
map (51° 30′N 0° 10′W) 19:403
police 15:396
Scotland Yard 17:153
pollution, environmental 15:414
theater
Covent Garden 5:319
Drury Lane Theatre 6:283
Globe Theatre 9:208–209
Haymarket Theatre 10:83
Old Vic Theatre 14:375
transportation 12:400
Euston Station 19:402 *illus.*
subway 18:318–319 *illus., table*
Twelve Great Companies of London (guilds) 9:395 *illus.*
water supply 20:56 *illus.*
waterwheel 20:66 *illus.*
zoological gardens 20:374–375 *illus.*
LONDON (Kentucky)
map (37° 8′N 84° 5′W) 12:47
LONDON (Ohio)
map (39° 53′N 83° 27′W) 14:357
LONDON (Ontario) 12:402
map (42° 59′N 81° 14′W) 14:393
LONDON (Texas)
map (30° 41′N 99° 35′W) 19:129
LONDON, FRITZ
chemistry, history of 4:328
LONDON, JACK 12:402–403 *bibliog., illus.*
Call of the Wild, The (book) 4:39
LONDON, TREATIES AND CONFERENCES OF 12:403
Balkan Wars 3:38
World War I 20:222
LONDON, UNIVERSITY OF 12:403–404 *table*
London School of Economics and Political Science
Wallas, Graham 20:15
Webb, Sidney and Beatrice 20:86
LONDON BRIDGE 12:401 *map*; 12:404–405 *illus.*
bridge (engineering) 3:480
LONDON COMPANY 12:405 *bibliog.*
colonial America land grants 19:437 *map*
Gates, Sir Thomas 9:58
Pilgrims 15:302
LONDON MARATHON
running and jogging 16:346
LONDON NAVAL CONFERENCE (1930)
London, treaties and conferences of 12:403
Washington Conference 20:45
LONDON AND NORTH EASTERN RAILWAY
locomotive 12:390 *illus.*
LONDONDERRY (city in Northern Ireland) 12:405
LONDONDERRY (county in Northern Ireland) 12:405
cities
Londonderry 12:405
LONDONDERRY (Northern Ireland)
map (55° 0′N 7° 19′W) 19:403
LONDONTOWNE (Maryland)
map (38° 55′N 76° 33′W) 13:188
LONE MOUNTAIN
map (45° 23′N 103° 44′W) 18:103
LONE OAK (Kentucky)
map (37° 2′N 88° 40′W) 12:47
LONE PINE (California)
map (36° 36′N 118° 4′W) 4:31
LONE TREE (Iowa)
map (41° 29′N 91° 26′W) 11:244
LONE WOLF (Oklahoma)
map (34° 59′N 99° 15′W) 14:368
LONELY CROWD, THE (book) 12:405
conformity 5:179
LONG (family) 12:405–406 *bibliog., illus.*
LONG (county in Georgia)
map (31° 42′N 81° 40′W) 9:114
LONG, CRAWFORD
anesthetics 1:410
LONG, EARL KEMP
Long (family) 12:405–406
LONG, GEORGE WASHINGTON DE *see* DE LONG, GEORGE WASHINGTON
LONG, HUEY PIERCE, JR. 12:405 *illus.*
Long (family) 12:405–406
Louisiana 12:434–435
populism 15:440
LONG, JAMES
Texas 19:133
LONG, JEFFERSON F. 16:185
LONG, RUSSELL B.
Long (family) 12:405–406
LONG, STEPHEN H. 12:406 *bibliog.*
exploration of the American west 19:445 *map*
Nebraska 14:74
LONG BEACH (California) 12:406
map (33° 46′N 118° 11′W) 4:31
subsidence 18:317
LONG BEACH (Mississippi)
map (30° 22′N 89° 7′W) 13:469
LONG BEACH (New York)
map (40° 35′N 73° 41′W) 14:149
LONG BRANCH (New Jersey)
map (40° 18′N 74° 0′W) 14:129
LONG CREEK (Oregon)
map (44° 43′N 119° 6′W) 14:427
LONG DAY'S JOURNEY INTO NIGHT (play)
O'Neill, Eugene 14:389–390
LONG HARBOUR (Newfoundland)
map (47° 26′N 53° 48′W) 14:166
LONG ISLAND (Massachusetts)
map (42° 19′N 70° 58′W) 13:206
LONG ISLAND (New York) 12:406
map (40° 50′N 73° 0′W) 14:149
Montauk Point 13:551
Queens 16:22
LONG ISLAND, BATTLE OF 12:406
Washington, George 20:43
LONG ISLAND SOUND 12:406
map (41° 5′N 72° 58′W) 5:193
LONG ISLAND (New York)
Long Island, Battle of 12:406
LONG LAKE (Michigan)
map (45° 12′N 83° 30′W) 13:377
LONG LAKE (New York)
map (43° 58′N 74° 25′W) 14:149
LONG LAKE (North Dakota)
map (46° 43′N 100° 7′W) 14:248
LONG MARCH 4:376 *map*; 12:406
China, history of 4:375–376 *map*
Mao Tse-tung (Mao Zedong) 13:135
LONG PARLIAMENT 12:407 *bibliog.*
Charles I, King of England, Scotland, and Ireland 4:291
Cromwell, Oliver 5:358
English Civil War 7:189–190
Pym, John 15:634
LONG POINT
map (42° 34′N 80° 15′W) 19:241
LONG POINT (Manitoba)
map (53° 2′N 98° 40′W) 13:119
LONG POINT (Ontario)
map (42° 34′N 80° 15′W) 14:393
LONG POINT BAY
map (42° 40′N 80° 14′W) 19:241
LONG POINT BAY (Ontario)
map (42° 40′N 80° 14′W) 14:393
LONG PRAIRIE (Minnesota)
map (45° 59′N 94° 52′W) 13:453
LONG RANGE MOUNTAINS
map (49° 20′N 57° 30′W) 14:166
LONG-TAILED TIT 12:407
LONG WALLS, THE
Callicrates 4:41
LONG XUYEN (Vietnam)
map (10° 23′N 105° 25′E) 19:580
LONGA RIVER
map (10° 15′S 13° 30′E) 2:5
LONGAN 12:407
LONGBAUGH, HARRY *see* SUNDANCE KID
LONGBILL SPEAR *see* SPEARFISH
LONGBOAT KEY (Florida)
map (27° 24′N 82° 39′W) 8:172
LONGEVITY *see* LIFE SPAN
LONGFELLOW, HENRY WADSWORTH 12:407 *bibliog., illus.*; 13:210 *illus.*
Gloucester (Massachusetts) 9:209
Portland (Maine) 15:445
Song of Hiawatha, The 18:64
LONGFORD (Ireland) 12:407
map (53° 44′N 7° 47′W) 11:258
LONGHAIRED CATS 12:407–408 *bibliog., illus.*
LONGHENA, BALDASSARRE 12:408 *bibliog.*
Venice (Italy) 19:544
LONGHI, PIETRO 12:408 *bibliog., illus.*
Viewing the Rhinoceros 12:408 *illus.*
LONGHORN CATTLE
cattle and cattle raising 4:215
LONGINUS 12:409 *bibliog.*
on the sublime
criticism, literary 5:351
LONGITUDE 12:409
geography 9:101
Greenwich mean time 9:354
international date line 11:220 *map*
navigation 14:59–60
prime meridian 15:542
time zones 19:203
LONGITUDE, CELESTIAL
conjunction 5:191
great circle 9:318
LONGITUDINAL VALLEY
map (36° 0′S 72° 0′W) 4:355
LONGITUDINAL WAVES *see* WAVES AND WAVE MOTION
LONGMEADOW (Massachusetts)
map (42° 3′N 72° 34′W) 13:206
LONGMEN *see* LUNG-MEN (Longmen) (China)
LONGMONT (Colorado)
map (40° 10′N 105° 6′W) 5:116
LONGREACH (Australia)
map (23° 26′S 144° 15′E) 2:328
LONGS PEAK
Long, Stephen H. 12:406
map (40° 15′N 105° 37′W) 5:116
LONGSHIP *see* VIKINGS
LONGSHORE CURRENT
longshore drift 12:409
LONGSHORE DRIFT 12:409 *bibliog.*
beach and coast 3:136
coastal protection 5:81
estuary 7:248
rip current 12:409
sand and sediment deposit 12:409
LONGSHOREMEN'S UNIONS *see* INTERNATIONAL LONGSHOREMEN'S UNIONS
LONGSPUR 12:409 *illus.*
bunting 3:564
LONGSTREET, JAMES 12:409 *bibliog., illus.*
LONGSWORD, WILLIAM
Normans 14:221
LONGUEUIL (Quebec)
map (45° 32′N 73° 30′W) 16:18
LONGUEUIL, CHARLES LE MOYNE, SIEUR DE 12:410
LONGUS 12:410 *bibliog.*
LONGVIEW (Texas)
map (32° 30′N 94° 44′W) 19:129
LONGVIEW (Washington)
map (46° 8′N 122° 57′W) 20:35
LONIGAN, STUDS (fictional character)
Farrell, James T. 8:29
LÖNNROT, ELIAS
Finland 8:96
Kalevala 12:7–8
LONOKE (Arkansas)
map (34° 47′N 91° 54′W) 2:166
LONOKE (county in Arkansas)
map (34° 45′N 91° 52′W) 2:166
LONSDALE (Minnesota)
map (44° 29′N 93° 25′W) 13:453
LOO, CHARLES ANDRÉ VAN *see* VAN LOO, CHARLES ANDRÉ
LOOGOOTEE (Indiana)
map (38° 41′N 86° 55′W) 11:111
LOOK (periodical)
Cowles, Gardner 5:321
LOOK BACK IN ANGER (play)
Osborne, John 14:452
LOOK HOMEWARD, ANGEL (book)
Wolfe, Thomas 20:197–198

LOOKING GLASS, CHIEF
  Nez Percé 14:176
LOOKOUT, CAPE
  map (34° 35′N 76° 32′W) 14:242
LOOKOUT MOUNTAIN 5:29 *illus.*
  Chattanooga 4:303
  map (34° 25′N 85° 40′W) 1:234
LOOKOUT PASS
  map (47° 27′N 115° 42′W) 11:26
LOOKOUT POINT RESERVOIR
  map (43° 52′N 122° 40′W) 14:427
LOOM 12:410–411 *bibliog., illus.*
  Cartwright, Edmund 4:178
  draw loom 12:410
  flying shuttle 12:410; 20:84 *illus.*
  Jacquard, Joseph Marie 11:347
  Lowell, Francis Cabot 12:444
  power loom 12:411; 20:84 *illus.*
  rugs and carpets 16:340–343
  tapestry 19:31
  textile industry 19:136
  treadle loom 12:410 *illus.*
  weaving 20:83–85 *illus.*
LOOMIS (Nebraska)
  map (40° 29′N 99° 31′W) 14:70
LOOMIS (Washington)
  map (48° 49′N 119° 38′W) 20:35
LOON (bird) 3:280–281 *illus.*; 12:411 *bibliog., illus.*
LOOP HEAD
  map (52° 34′N 9° 56′W) 11:258
LOOS, ADOLF 12:411 *bibliog.*
LOOS, ANITA 12:411
LOOSESTRIFE (botany) 12:411–412 *illus.*
LOP NOR (China) 12:412 *bibliog.*
LOP NOR LAKE
  map (40° 20′N 90° 15′E) 4:362
LOPATKA, CAPE
  map (50° 52′N 156° 40′E) 19:388
LOPBURI (Thailand) 12:412
LOPE DE RUEDA *see* RUEDA, LOPE DE
LOPE DE VEGA CARPIO, FELIX *see* VEGA, LOPE DE
LOPES, FERNÃO
  Portuguese literature 15:456
LÓPEZ, FRANCISCO SOLANO 12:412 *bibliog.*
  Triple Alliance, War of the 19:302
LÓPEZ DE CÁRDENAS, GARCÍA
  Coronado, Francisco Vázquez de 5:270
  Grand Canyon 9:285
LÓPEZ DE MENDOZA, ÍÑIGO
  Spanish literature 18:157
LOPEZ ISLAND
  map (48° 30′N 122° 54′W) 20:35
LOPEZ, NANCY 12:412
LÓPEZ PORTILLO Y PACHECO, JOSÉ 12:412 *illus.*
  Mexico, history of 13:366
LÓPEZ VELARDE, RAMÓN 12:412–413
LOPHOPHORATE 12:413
LOQUAT 12:413 *illus.*
LORA, LAKE
  map (29° 20′N 64° 50′E) 1:133
LORAIN (Ohio)
  map (41° 28′N 82° 10′W) 14:357
LORAIN (county in Ohio)
  map (41° 22′N 82° 6′W) 14:357
LORCA (Spain)
  map (37° 40′N 1° 42′W) 18:140
LORCA, FEDERICO GARCÍA *see* GARCÍA LORCA, FEDERICO
LORD, DANIEL
  film, history of 8:84
LORD HAW-HAW 12:413
LORD HOWE ISLAND
  map (31° 33′S 159° 5′E) 2:328
LORD LYON, COURT OF THE
  heraldry 10:134
LORD OF THE FLIES (book) 12:413 *bibliog.*
  Golding, William 9:234–235
LORD OF THE RINGS, THE (book)
  Tolkien, J. R. R. 19:226
LORDS, HOUSE OF
  Parliament 15:92–93
LORDS APPELLANT
  Richard II, King of England 16:210
LORD'S PRAYER 12:413 *bibliog.*
LORD'S SUPPER *see* EUCHARIST
LORDSBURG (New Mexico)
  map (32° 21′N 108° 43′W) 14:136
LOREAUVILLE (Louisiana)
  map (30° 3′N 91° 44′W) 12:430
LOREN, SOPHIA 12:413 *bibliog., illus.*
LORENGAU (Papua New Guinea)
  map (2° 0′S 147° 15′E) 15:72
LORENTZ, HENDRIK ANTOON 12:413–414 *bibliog., illus.*
  Einstein, Albert 7:93
  Fitzgerald-Lorentz contraction 8:131
  physics, history of 15:284–286 *illus.*
  relativity 16:134
LORENTZ, PARE
  documentary 6:211
LORENTZEN, C. A.
  naval battle of Copenhagen 17:110 *illus.*
LORENZ, KONRAD 12:414 *bibliog., illus.*
  On Agression 14:388
  aggressive behavior 12:414
  animal behavior 2:11–12 *illus.*
  comparative behavior 12:414
  ethology 7:257; 12:414
  imprinting 11:69
  Tinbergen, Nikolaas 19:206
LORENZETTI BROTHERS 12:414–415 *bibliog., illus.*
  Allegories of Good and Bad Government (Ambrogio Lorenzetti) 12:189 *illus.*; 12:414 *illus.*
LORENZINI, CARLO *see* COLLODI, CARLO
LORENZO DI CREDI 12:415 *bibliog.*
LORENZO MONACO 12:415 *bibliog.*
LORETO (Bolivia)
  map (15° 13′S 64° 40′W) 3:366
LORETO (Mexico)
  map (26° 1′N 111° 21′W) 13:357
LORETTO (Kentucky)
  map (37° 38′N 85° 25′W) 12:47
LORETTO (Tennessee)
  map (35° 5′N 87° 26′W) 19:104
LORIAN SWAMP
  map (0° 40′N 39° 35′E) 12:53
LORICIFERA 12:415
LORIKEET 15:97–98 *illus.*
LORIMOR (Iowa)
  map (41° 7′N 94° 3′W) 11:244
LORIS 12:415 *illus.*
  galago 9:9
LORIS (South Carolina)
  map (34° 4′N 78° 53′W) 18:98
LORMAN (Mississippi)
  map (31° 49′N 91° 3′W) 13:469
LORNA DOONE (book)
  Blackmore, Richard Doddridge 3:321
LORNE (New Brunswick)
  map (47° 53′N 66° 8′W) 14:117
LORNE PIERCE MEDAL
  Carman, Bliss 4:153
LORRAIN, CLAUDE 12:415–416 *bibliog., illus.*
  The Embarkation of Odysseus 12:190 *illus.*
  Odysseus Restoring Chryseis to Her Father 12:415 *illus.*
LORRAINE *see* ALSACE-LORRAINE (France)
LORRAINE, CROSS OF 5:360; 5:361 *illus.*
LOS *see* under the element of the name following LOS, except for those entries listed below
LOS ALAMOS (Mexico)
  map (28° 40′N 103° 30′W) 13:357
LOS ALAMOS (New Mexico) 12:416
  map (35° 53′N 106° 19′W) 14:136
LOS ALAMOS (county in New Mexico)
  map (35° 50′N 106° 20′W) 14:136
LOS ALAMOS NATIONAL SCIENTIFIC LABORATORY 12:416
  accelerator, particle 1:73–74
  atomic bomb 2:307
  Manhattan Project 13:116
  Oppenheimer, J. Robert 14:408
LOS AMATES (Guatemala)
  map (15° 16′N 89° 6′W) 9:389
LOS ANGELES (California) 4:32 *illus.* 5:7 *illus.*; 12:416–418 *bibliog., illus., map*; 14:233 *illus.*
  Bonaventure Hotel 10:261 *illus.*
  Bradley, Tom 3:438
  busing, school 3:590
  climate 14:228 *table*
  history 12:418
  Hollywood 10:204
  La Brea Tar Pit 12:144–145 *illus.*
  Los Angeles County Museum of Art 12:418
  map (34° 3′N 118° 15′W) 4:31
  population mix 12:416
  recall 16:106
  Watts Towers 20:69–70
LOS ANGELES (county in California)
  map (34° 20′N 118° 10′W) 4:31
LOS ANGELES (Chile)
  map (37° 28′S 72° 21′W) 4:355
LOS ANGELES AQUEDUCT
  map (35° 22′N 118° 5′W) 4:31
LOS ANGELES COUNTY MUSEUM OF ART 12:418
LOS ANGELES TIMES/WASHINGTON POST SYNDICATE
  press agencies and syndicates 15:533
LOS ANTIGUOS (Argentina)
  map (46° 33′S 71° 37′W) 2:149
LOS BANOS (California)
  map (37° 4′N 120° 51′W) 4:31
LOS BLANCOS (Argentina)
  map (23° 36′S 62° 36′W) 2:149
LOS CHACOS (Bolivia)
  map (14° 33′S 62° 11′W) 3:366
LOS CHILES (Costa Rica)
  map (11° 2′N 84° 43′W) 5:291
LOS CHONOS ARCHIPELAGO
  map (45° 0′S 74° 0′W) 4:355
LOS FRENTONES (Argentina)
  map (26° 25′S 61° 25′W) 2:149
LOS GATOS (California)
  map (37° 14′N 121° 59′W) 4:31
LOS LUNAS (New Mexico)
  map (34° 48′N 106° 44′W) 14:136
LOS MILLARES (Spain) 12:418 *bibliog.*
LOS MOCHIS (Mexico)
  map (25° 45′N 108° 57′W) 13:357
LOS PALACIOS (Cuba)
  map (22° 35′N 83° 15′W) 5:377
LOS PINOS RIVER
  map (36° 56′N 107° 36′W) 5:116
LOS TEQUES (Venezuela)
  map (10° 21′N 67° 2′W) 19:542
LÖSCH, AUGUST
  central place theory 4:254–255
LOSEY, JOSEPH 12:418 *bibliog., illus.*
LOST COLONY OF ROANOKE *see* ROANOKE, LOST COLONY OF
LOST GENERATION (literature)
  All Quiet on the Western Front 1:297
  Dos Passos, John 6:243
  Hemingway, Ernest 10:118–119
  Stein, Gertrude 18:247
LOST HORIZON (book)
  Hilton, James 10:165
LOST NATION (Iowa)
  map (41° 58′N 90° 49′W) 11:244
LOST RIVER RANGE
  map (44° 10′N 113° 35′W) 11:26
LOST TRAIL PASS
  map (45° 41′N 113° 57′W) 11:26
LOST-WAX PROCESS 12:418–419 *bibliog., illus.*
  bronzes 3:506
  casting 4:189
  sculpture techniques 17:167 *illus.*
LOT (biblical character) 12:419
LOT RIVER
  map (44° 18′N 0° 20′E) 8:260
LOTA (Chile)
  map (37° 5′S 73° 10′W) 4:355
LOTHAIR, KING OF LOTHARINGIA 12:419
LOTHAIR I, FRANKISH EMPEROR 12:419
  holdings 4:289 *map*
  Verdun, Treaty of 19:550
LOTHAIR II, KING OF GERMANY AND HOLY ROMAN EMPEROR 12:419
LOTHARINGIA 12:419–420 *bibliog.*
  Lothair, King 12:419
LOTHIAN (Scotland) 12:420
LOTIKIPI PLAIN
  map (4° 36′N 34° 55′E) 12:53
LOTKA, ALFRED J.
  demography 6:103
LOTOFAGA (Western Samoa)
  map (13° 59′S 171° 50′W) 20:117
LOTT (Texas)
  map (31° 12′N 97° 2′W) 19:129
LOTTERY 12:420 *bibliog.*
  gambling 9:26
"LOTTERY, THE" (short story)
  Jackson, Shirley 11:343
LOTTI, ANTONIO
  mass (musical setting) 13:201
LOTTO, LORENZO 12:420 *bibliog.*
LOTUS 12:420–421 *illus.*
  water lily 20:49
LOTUS-EATERS 12:421
LOTZE, RUDOLF HERMANN 12:421 *bibliog.*
LOU GEHRIG'S DISEASE *see* AMYOTROPHIC LATERAL SCLEROSIS
LOUBOMO (Congo)
  map (4° 12′S 12° 41′E) 5:182
LOUCHHEIM, JEROME
  radio and television broadcasting 16:55
LOUD, JOHN H.
  pen 15:140
LOUDON (Tennessee)
  map (35° 44′N 84° 20′W) 19:104
LOUDON (county in Tennessee)
  map (35° 45′N 84° 20′W) 19:104
LOUDONVILLE (Ohio)
  map (40° 38′N 82° 14′W) 14:357
LOUDOUN (county in Virginia)
  map (39° 5′N 77° 30′W) 19:607
LOUDSPEAKER 12:421 *bibliog., illus.*
  impedance 11:61
  operation 12:421
  parabola 15:74
  types and systems 12:421
LOUGA (Senegal)
  map (15° 37′N 16° 13′W) 17:202
LOUGANIS, GREG 12:421; 18:391 *illus.*
LOUGH NEAGH *see* NEAGH, LOUGH
LOUGHBOROUGH (England)
  map (52° 47′N 1° 11′W) 19:403
LOUGHEED, PETER
  Alberta 1:257
LOUIN (Mississippi)
  map (31° 59′N 89° 16′W) 13:469
LOUIS, GILBERT NEWTON
  heavy water 10:100
LOUIS, JOE 3:432 *illus.*; 12:422 *bibliog., illus.*
LOUIS, MORRIS 12:422 *bibliog., illus.*
  Pillars of Dawn 12:422 *illus.*
LOUIS, SAINT *see* LOUIS IX, KING OF FRANCE (Saint Louis)
LOUIS, VICTOR 12:422
LOUIS I, FRANKISH EMPEROR (Louis the Pious) 12:429 *bibliog.*
LOUIS I, KING OF BAVARIA 12:423
  Montez, Lola 13:555
LOUIS I, KING OF FRANCE *see* LOUIS I, FRANKISH EMPEROR (Louis the Pious)
LOUIS I, KING OF HUNGARY (Louis the Great) 12:428 *bibliog.*
LOUIS II, FRANKISH EMPEROR 12:429
LOUIS II, KING OF BAVARIA 12:423 *bibliog.*
  Bayreuth Wagner Festival 3:134
  Louis II's Bavarian Palaces 12:423
  Wagner, Richard 20:5
LOUIS II'S BAVARIAN PALACES 12:423
LOUIS II, KING OF HUNGARY 12:428–429
LOUIS IV, KING OF FRANCE (Louis D'Outremer) 12:423–424
LOUIS IV, KING OF GERMANY AND HOLY ROMAN EMPEROR (Louis the Bavarian) 12:428
  Marsilius of Padua 13:173
  Wittelsbach (family) 20:193
LOUIS VI, KING OF FRANCE (Louis the Fat) 12:424 *bibliog.*
  Suger, Abbot of Saint-Denis 18:330
LOUIS VII, KING OF FRANCE (Louis The Young) 12:424 *bibliog.*
  Eleanor of Aquitaine 7:103
  Suger, Abbot of Saint-Denis 18:330
LOUIS VIII, KING OF FRANCE 12:424
LOUIS IX, KING OF FRANCE (Saint Louis) 7:284 *illus.*; 8:267 *illus.*; 12:424–425 *bibliog., illus.*
  Crusades 5:369
  historians
    Joinville, Jean, Sire de 11:440
  Rayonnant style 16:98
LOUIS XI, KING OF FRANCE 12:425 *bibliog., illus.*
  Spanish Succession, War of the 18:162–163
LOUIS XII, KING OF FRANCE 12:425 *bibliog.*
LOUIS XIII, KING OF FRANCE 12:425–426 *bibliog.*
  Anne of Austria 2:32
  art
    interior design styles 18:311
    Vouet, Simon 19:637
  Marie de Médicis 13:152
  Richelieu, Armand Jean du Plessis, Cardinal et Duc de 16:213
  Thirty Years' War 19:171
LOUIS XIV, KING OF FRANCE 7:289 *illus.*; 8:269 *illus.*; 12:426–427 *bibliog., illus.*
  Aix-la-Chapelle, Treaties of 1:229
  ballet 3:42 *illus.*
  Colbert, Jean Baptiste 5:97
  costume 5:299 *illus.*
    shoes 17:280 *illus.*
  dance 6:25
  Devolution, War of 6:143
  etiquette 7:258
  Europe, history of 7:288–289
  Flanders 8:152 *map*
  Fouquet, Nicolas 8:252
  France, history of 8:268–269
  French art and architecture 8:305–306
  Fronde 8:339
  Gobelins 9:216

LOUIS XIV, KING OF FRANCE (cont.)
Grand Alliance, War of the **9**:284
Great Pyrenees **9**:321
interior design styles **18**:311 *illus.*
The Life of Louis XIV **19**:32 *illus.*
Louisiana **12**:429
Louvois, François Michel Le Tellier, Marquis de **12**:437
Lully, Jean Baptiste **12**:454
Maintenon, Françoise d'Aubigné, Marquise de **13**:75
Mazarin, Jules **13**:249–250
Montespan, Françoise Athénaïs de Rochechouart, Marquise de **13**:553
Montpensier, Anne Marie Louise d'Orléans, Duchesse de **13**:558
Philip V, King of Spain **15**:235
portrait
Nanteuil, Robert **14**:13
Rigaud, Hyacinthe **16**:222
Spanish Succession, War of the **18**:162–163
tapestry **19**:32 *illus.*
territorial expansion under **8**:269 *map*
William III, King of England, Scotland, and Ireland **20**:156
LOUIS XV, KING OF FRANCE **12**:427 *bibliog.*
du Barry, Jeanne Bécu, Comtesse **6**:285
Fleury, André Hercule de **8**:163
interior design styles **18**:311
Orléans, Philippe II, Duc d' **14**:446
Pompadour, Jeanne Antoinette Poisson, Marquise de **15**:423
Stanisław I, King of Poland **18**:218
LOUIS XVI, KING OF FRANCE **8**:31 *illus.*; **8**:271 *illus.*; **8**:322 *illus.*; **12**:427–428 *bibliog.*, *illus.*
Diamond Necklace, Affair of the **6**:152
Europe, history of **7**:290–291
French Revolution **8**:322–323
interior design styles **18**:311
Marie Antoinette **13**:151
Mirabeau, Honoré Gabriel Riqueti, Comte de **13**:462
LOUIS XVII, KING OF FRANCE **12**:428 *bibliog.*
LOUIS XVIII, KING OF FRANCE **12**:428 *bibliog.*
Napoleon I, Emperor of the French (Napoléon Bonaparte) **14**:18
Talleyrand-Périgord, Charles Maurice de **19**:17
LOUIS ANTOINE
dauphin **6**:46
LOUIS THE BAVARIAN *see* LOUIS IV, KING OF GERMANY AND HOLY ROMAN EMPEROR (Louis the Bavarian)
LOUIS D'OUTREMER *see* LOUIS IV, KING OF FRANCE (Louis D'Outremer)
LOUIS THE FAT *see* LOUIS VI, KING OF FRANCE (Louis the Fat)
LOUIS THE GERMAN, EAST FRANKISH KING **12**:422
duel **6**:293
holdings **4**:289 *map*
Verdun, Treaty of **19**:550
LOUIS THE GREAT *see* LOUIS I, KING OF HUNGARY (Louis the Great)
LOUIS NAPOLÉON *see* NAPOLEON III, EMPEROR OF THE FRENCH (Louis Napoléon Bonaparte)
LOUIS PHILIPPE, KING OF FRANCE **12**:423 *bibliog.*, *illus.*
caricature **4**:150 *illus.*
Guizot, François **9**:401–402
Orléans (family) **14**:446
Orléans, Louis Philippe Joseph, Duc d' **14**:446
Revolutions of 1848 **16**:188
LOUIS THE PIOUS *see* LOUIS I, FRANKISH EMPEROR (Louis the Pious)
LOUIS THE YOUNG *see* LOUIS VII, KING OF FRANCE (Louis the Young)
LOUISA (county in Iowa)
map (41° 12′N 91° 15′W) **11**:244
LOUISA (Kentucky)
map (38° 7′N 82° 36′W) **12**:47
LOUISA (Virginia)
map (38° 1′N 78° 1′W) **19**:607
LOUISA (county in Virginia)
map (38° 0′N 78° 0′W) **19**:607
LOUISBOURG (Nova Scotia) **12**:429
Canada, history of **4**:81
French and Indian Wars **8**:313 *map*
map (45° 55′N 59° 58′W) **14**:269
LOUISBURG (Kansas)
map (38° 37′N 94° 41′W) **12**:18
LOUISBURG (North Carolina)
map (36° 6′N 78° 18′W) **14**:242
LOUISE, LAKE (Alberta) **4**:72 *illus.*; **12**:429
map (51° 26′N 116° 11′W) **1**:256
LOUISIADE ARCHIPELAGO
map (11° 0′S 153° 0′E) **15**:72
LOUISIANA **12**:429–435 *bibliog.*, *illus.*, *map*
agriculture and forestry **12**:433
cities
Alexandria **1**:277–278
Baton Rouge **3**:124
Bogalusa **3**:359
Lafayette **12**:163
Lake Charles **12**:170
Monroe **13**:541
Natchitoches **14**:26–27
New Orleans **14**:140–141 *illus.*, *map*
Shreveport **17**:286
climate **12**:431
culture **12**:432
economic activities **12**:431–433 *illus.*
education **12**:432
Louisiana, state universities of **12**:435
Tulane University **19**:330
fishing industry **12**:431 *illus.*; **12**:433
flag **12**:429 *illus.*
government and politics **12**:433
health **12**:432
historic sites **12**:432
history **12**:433–435
Bienville, Jean Baptiste Le Moyne, Sieur de **3**:247
La Salle, Robert Cavelier, Sieur de **12**:149
Long (family) **12**:405–406
Mississippi Scheme **13**:474
land **12**:429–432 *map*
map (31° 15′N 92° 15′W) **19**:419
Napoleonic Code **14**:19
people **12**:432
Cajuns **4**:19
Creoles **5**:338–339
resources **12**:432
rivers, lakes, and waterways **12**:431 *illus.*
Pontchartrain, Lake **15**:427
Red River **16**:113
seal, state **12**:429 *illus.*
vegetation and animal life **12**:431–432; **12**:434 *illus.*
LOUISIANA (Missouri)
map (39° 27′N 91° 3′W) **13**:476
LOUISIANA, STATE UNIVERSITIES OF **12**:435
LOUISIANA PURCHASE **12**:435–436 *bibliog.*, *illus.*, *map*; **19**:446 *map*
Jefferson, Thomas **11**:393
Monroe, James **13**:541
Oklahoma **14**:370
West Florida Controversy **20**:108
LOUISVILLE (Georgia)
map (33° 0′N 82° 24′W) **9**:114
LOUISVILLE (Illinois)
map (38° 46′N 88° 30′W) **11**:42
LOUISVILLE (Kentucky) **12**:48 *illus.*; **12**:436
Kentucky Derby **10**:246 *illus.*
map (38° 16′N 85° 45′W) **12**:47
LOUISVILLE (Mississippi)
map (33° 7′N 89° 3′W) **13**:469
LOUISVILLE (Nebraska)
map (41° 0′N 96° 10′W) **14**:70
LOUISVILLE (Ohio)
map (40° 50′N 81° 16′W) **14**:357
LOUISVILLE (Tennessee)
map (35° 49′N 84° 3′W) **19**:104
LOUISVILLE COURIER-JOURNAL
Watterson, Henry **20**:69
LOUISY, ALLAN
Saint Lucia **17**:23
LOUP (county in Nebraska)
map (41° 55′N 99° 30′W) **14**:70
LOUP CITY (Nebraska)
map (41° 17′N 98° 58′W) **14**:70
LOUP RIVER
map (41° 24′N 97° 19′W) **14**:70
LOURDES (France) **12**:436
faith healing **8**:11
LOURENÇO MARQUES (Mozambique) *see* MAPUTO (Mozambique)
LOUSE **12**:436 *bibliog.*, *illus.*
See also WOOD LOUSE
Anoplura **2**:34
egg **12**:436 *illus.*
relapsing fever **16**:132
skin diseases **17**:342
trench fever **19**:290
typhus **19**:366–367
LOUSMA, JACK **12**:436 *bibliog.*
Skylab **17**:348
LOUTH (Ireland) **12**:436–437
LOUTHERBOURG, PHILIPPE JACQUES DE **12**:437
L'OUVERTURE, FRANÇOIS DOMINIQUE TOUSSAINT *see* TOUSSAINT L'OUVERTURE, FRANÇOIS DOMINIQUE
LOUVIERS (Colorado)
map (39° 28′N 105° 1′W) **5**:116
LOUVOIS, FRANÇOIS MICHEL LE TELLIER, MARQUIS DE **12**:437 *bibliog.*
LOUVRE **12**:437 *bibliog.*, *illus.*
architecture
Lescot, Pierre **12**:296
Perrault, Claude **15**:178
Egyptology **7**:90
interior design
Le Brun, Charles **12**:253
Percier, Charles **15**:162
LOVAGE **12**:437
LOVE (county in Oklahoma)
map (34° 0′N 97° 15′W) **14**:368
LOVE CANAL (Niagara Falls, N.Y.)
pollutants, chemical **15**:411
LOVEBIRD **15**:97 *illus.*
LOVECH (Bulgaria)
map (43° 8′N 24° 43′E) **3**:555
LOVECRAFT, H. P. **12**:438 *bibliog.*
Derleth, August **6**:121
LOVEJOY, ARTHUR O.
Essays in the History of Ideas
criticism, literary **5**:352
LOVELACE, ADA
Ada (computer language) **1**:91
computer languages **5**:160p
LOVELACE, RICHARD **11**:438
LOVELAND (Colorado)
map (40° 24′N 105° 5′W) **5**:116
LOVELAND PASS
map (39° 40′N 105° 53′W) **5**:116
LOVELL (Wyoming)
map (44° 50′N 108° 24′W) **20**:301
LOVELL, SIR BERNARD **12**:438
Nuffield Radio Astronomy Laboratories **14**:291
LOVELL, JAMES **12**:438 *bibliog.*
Apollo program **2**:81–83
Gemini program **9**:72–73
LOVELL, TOM
painting of Republican convention **15**:399 *illus.*
LOVELL HEALTH HOUSE
Neutra, Richard **14**:107–108
LOVELOCK (Nevada)
map (40° 11′N 118° 28′W) **14**:111
LOVES PARK (Illinois)
map (42° 19′N 89° 3′W) **11**:42
LOVESTONE, JAY
Communist party, U.S.A. **5**:151
LOVILIA (Iowa)
map (41° 8′N 92° 55′W) **11**:244
LOVING (New Mexico)
map (32° 17′N 104° 6′W) **14**:136
LOVING (county in Texas)
map (31° 47′N 103° 30′W) **19**:129
LOVINGSTON (Virginia)
map (37° 46′N 78° 52′W) **19**:607
LOVINGTON (Illinois)
map (39° 43′N 88° 38′W) **11**:42
LOVINGTON (New Mexico)
map (32° 57′N 103° 21′W) **14**:136
LOW, SETH **12**:438 *bibliog.*
LOW COUNTRIES *see* BELGIUM; LUXEMBOURG (country); NETHERLANDS
LOW COUNTRIES, HISTORY OF THE **12**:438–443 *bibliog.*, *illus.*, *map*
See also BELGIUM—history; LUXEMBOURG (country)—history and government; NETHERLANDS—history
Brabant, Duchy of **3**:435
Flanders **8**:152
Flemish art and architecture **8**:159–163
Holland (historic region) **10**:203
Leo Belgicus **12**:438 *map*
Nassau (historical region) **14**:25
prior to 925
early history **12**:438–439
Lotharingia **12**:419–420
925–1579
Burgundian and Habsburg rule **12**:439–440
Charles the Bold, Duke of Burgundy **4**:290–291
Dutch Revolt **6**:314–315
Horn, Philip de Montmorency, Comte de **10**:238
Hundred Years' War *see* HUNDRED YEARS' WAR
Jacqueline of Hainaut **11**:347
Philip the Bold, Duke of Burgundy **15**:231
Philip the Good, Duke of Burgundy **15**:231
William I, Prince of Orange (William the Silent) **20**:158
1579–1815
Anglo-Dutch Wars *see* ANGLO-DUTCH WARS
Dutch West India Company **6**:315
East India Company, Dutch **7**:31–32
Frederick Henry, Prince of Orange **8**:292
French domination and liberation **12**:441–442
French Revolutionary Wars *see* FRENCH REVOLUTIONARY WARS
John Maurice of Nassau **11**:425
Maurice of Nassau, Prince of Orange **13**:235
Oldenbarnevelt, Johan van **14**:375
Spanish Armada **18**:150–151
Spanish and Austrian Netherlands **12**:441
United Provinces **12**:440–441 *map*
War of the Grand Alliance *see* GRAND ALLIANCE, WAR OF THE
War of the Spanish Succession *see* SPANISH SUCCESSION, WAR OF THE
William III, King of England, Scotland, and Ireland **20**:156
Witt, Johan de **20**:193
1815–present
World War I *see* WORLD WAR I
World War II *see* WORLD WAR II
LOW-PRESSURE REGION **12**:443
cloud **5**:67 *illus.*; **20**:76 *illus.*
polar easterlies **15**:393
semipermanent lows **12**:443
LOWELL (Arkansas)
map (36° 15′N 94° 8′W) **2**:166
LOWELL (Indiana)
map (41° 18′N 87° 25′W) **11**:111
LOWELL (Massachusetts) **12**:443
Bagley, Sarah G. **3**:22
map (42° 39′N 71° 18′W) **13**:206
LOWELL (Michigan)
map (42° 56′N 85° 20′W) **13**:377
LOWELL (Oregon)
map (43° 55′N 122° 47′W) **14**:427
LOWELL, ABBOTT LAWRENCE **12**:443 *bibliog.*
LOWELL, AMY **11**:443–444 *bibliog.*, *illus.*
LOWELL, FRANCIS CABOT **12**:444
Appleton, Nathan **2**:89
LOWELL, JAMES RUSSELL **11**:444 *bibliog.*
LOWELL, PERCIVAL **12**:444 *bibliog.*
life, extraterrestrial **12**:328
Mars (planet) **13**:167
Pluto (planet) **15**:372
LOWELL, ROBERT, JR. **1**:347 *illus.*; **12**:444–445 *bibliog.*, *illus.*
LOWELLVILLE (Ohio)
map (41° 2′N 80° 32′W) **14**:357
LOWER ARROW LAKE
map (49° 40′N 118° 8′W) **3**:491
LOWER CALIFORNIA *see* BAJA CALIFORNIA (Mexico)
LOWER CLASS *see* CLASS, SOCIAL
LOWER EAST SIDE
New York (city) **14**:145 *map*
LOWER HUTT (New Zealand)
map (41° 13′S 174° 55′E) **14**:158
LOWER LAKE ERNE
map (54° 26′N 7° 46′W) **11**:258
LOWER MONUMENTAL LAKE
map (46° 36′N 118° 20′W) **20**:35
LOWER NEW YORK BAY
map (40° 33′N 74° 2′W) **14**:129
LOWER PAIA (Hawaii)
map (20° 55′N 156° 23′W) **10**:72
LOWER POST (British Columbia)
map (59° 55′N 128° 30′W) **3**:491
LOWER RED LAKE
map (48° 0′N 94° 50′W) **13**:453
LOWER SAXONY (West Germany)
Braunschweig **3**:458
LOWER SILESIA *see* SILESIA

LOWER WEST PUBNICO (Nova Scotia)
map (43° 38′N 65° 48′W) **14**:269
LOWESTOFT (England)
map (52° 29′N 1° 45′E) **19**:403
LOWNDES (county in Alabama)
map (32° 10′N 86° 40′W) **1**:234
LOWNDES (county in Georgia)
map (30° 50′N 83° 15′W) **9**:114
LOWNDES (county in Mississippi)
map (33° 30′N 88° 30′W) **13**:469
LOWRY, MALCOLM **11**:445 *bibliog.*
LOWTH, ROBERT
grammar **9**:283
mythology **13**:694 *illus.*
LOWVILLE (New York)
map (43° 47′N 75° 29′W) **14**:149
LOXLEY (Alabama)
map (30° 37′N 87° 45′W) **1**:234
LOXODROME *see* CHART
LOYAL (Wisconsin)
map (44° 44′N 90° 30′W) **20**:185
LOYAL ORANGE ORDER *see* ORANGEMEN
LOYALISTS **12**:445 *bibliog., illus.*
Canada, history of **4**:81
De Lancey (family) **6**:61
Lynch, Charles **12**:476
United States, history of the **19**:440–441
LOYALTON (California)
map (39° 41′N 120° 14′W) **4**:31
LOYALTY ISLANDS
New Caledonia **14**:119
LOYOLA, IGNATIUS, SAINT *see* IGNATIUS LOYOLA, SAINT
LOYOLA UNIVERSITY **12**:445
LOZNICA (Yugoslavia)
map (44° 32′N 19° 13′E) **20**:340
LPG *see* LIQUEFIED PETROLEUM GAS
LSD **12**:445 *bibliog.*
ergot **7**:228
hallucinogens **10**:24
medicinal plants **13**:266
psilocybin **15**:587
psychotropic drugs **15**:605
LSI (LARGE-SCALE INTEGRATION) (electronics)
computer **5**:160b–160c
LU-CHOU (China)
map (28° 58′N 105° 25′E) **4**:362
LU HSÜN (Lu Xun) **12**:445–446 *bibliog.*
LÜ-SHUN (Lüshun) (China) **12**:446
map (38° 48′N 121° 16′E) **4**:362
Russo-Japanese War **16**:373
LÜ-TA (Lüda) (China) **12**:446
Ta-lien (Dalian) **19**:3
LU VERNE (Iowa)
map (42° 55′N 94° 5′W) **11**:244
LU XUN *see* LU HSÜN (Lu Xun)
LUALABA RIVER
map (0° 26′N 25° 20′E) **20**:350
LUANDA (Angola) **2**:5 *illus.*; **12**:446
map (8° 48′S 13° 14′E) **2**:5
LUANG NAM THA (Laos)
map (20° 57′N 101° 25′E) **12**:203
LUANG PRABANG (Laos) **12**:446
Laos **12**:204
map (19° 52′N 102° 8′E) **12**:203
LUANG PRABANG RANGE
map (18° 30′N 101° 15′E) **12**:203
LUANGUE RIVER
map (4° 17′S 20° 2′E) **2**:5
LUANSHYA (Zambia)
map (13° 8′S 28° 24′E) **20**:354
LUAPULA (people)
Lunda **12**:462
LUAPULA RIVER
map (9° 26′S 28° 33′E) **20**:350
LUBA **12**:446 *bibliog.*
LUBANGO (Angola)
map (14° 55′S 13° 30′E) **2**:5
LUBBERS, RUUD
Netherlands **14**:103
LUBBOCK (Texas) **12**:446
"Lubbock Lights" **19**:385 *illus.*
map (33° 35′N 101° 51′W) **19**:129
LUBBOCK (county in Texas)
map (33° 38′N 100° 43′W) **19**:129
LUBBOCK, JOHN, 1ST BARON AVEBURY **12**:446 *bibliog.*
Neolithic Period **14**:84
Paleolithic Period **15**:38
LUBCKE, HARRY
Emmy Awards **7**:157
LUBEC (Maine)
map (44° 52′N 66° 59′W) **13**:70
LÜBECK (West Germany) **12**:446–447
Hanseatic League **10**:40–41
map (53° 52′N 10° 40′E) **9**:140
LUBIN (Poland)
map (51° 24′N 16° 13′E) **15**:388
LUBITSCH, ERNST **12**:447 *bibliog.*
film, history of **8**:83; **8**:84
LUBLIN (Poland) **12**:447
Jagello (dynasty) **11**:348
map (51° 15′N 22° 35′E) **15**:388
LUBOVITCH, LAR **12**:447 *bibliog.*
LUBRICANT *see* FATS AND OILS; LUBRICATION
LUBRICATION **12**:447–448 *bibliog., illus.*
application systems **12**:447–448
functions **12**:447
molybdenite **13**:514
petroleum **15**:207
types **12**:447
LUBUDI (Zaire)
map (9° 57′S 25° 58′E) **20**:350
LUBUMBASHI (Zaire) **12**:448
map (11° 40′S 27° 28′E) **20**:350
LUC, FRÈRE (Claude François)
Canadian art and architecture **4**:88
LUCALOX
new ceramics applications **4**:258
LUCAN **12**:448 *bibliog.*
LUCAS (county in Iowa)
map (41° 0′N 93° 15′W) **11**:244
LUCAS (Kansas)
map (39° 4′N 98° 32′W) **12**:18
LUCAS (county in Ohio)
map (41° 38′N 83° 37′W) **14**:357
LUCAS, GEORGE **12**:448
film, history of **8**:87 *illus.*
LUCAS, JERRY **3**:113 *illus.*
LUCAS VAN LEYDEN **12**:448–449 *bibliog., illus.*
Lot and His Daughters **12**:449 *illus.*
LUCASVILLE (Ohio)
map (38° 53′N 82° 60′W) **14**:357
LUCCA (Italy) **12**:449
map (43° 50′N 10° 29′E) **11**:321
LUCE (county in Michigan)
map (46° 30′N 85° 35′W) **13**:377
LUCE, CLARE BOOTHE **12**:449 *bibliog., illus.*
LUCE, HENRY ROBINSON **12**:449–450 *bibliog., illus.*
documentary **6**:211
Time **19**:201
LUCE, STEPHEN B. **12**:450 *bibliog.*
LUCEDALE (Mississippi)
map (30° 55′N 88° 35′W) **13**:469
LUCERNE (Switzerland) **12**:450
map (47° 3′N 8° 18′E) **18**:394
LUCERNE, LAKE **12**:450
map (47° 0′N 8° 28′E) **18**:394
LUCHOU (China) *see* HOFEI (Hefei) (China)
LUCHU ISLANDS *see* RYUKYU ISLANDS
LUCIA DI LAMMERMOOR **12**:450 *bibliog.*
LUCIAN **12**:450 *bibliog.*
LUCIFER *see* SATAN
LUCIFERIANS *see* SATANISM
LUCILIUS **12**:450
LUCITE *see* PLASTICS
LUCK (Wisconsin)
map (45° 34′N 92° 28′W) **20**:185
LUCKENWALDE (Germany, East and West)
map (52° 5′N 13° 10′E) **9**:140
LUCKNOW (India) **12**:450–451
map (26° 51′N 80° 55′E) **11**:80
LUCKNOW PACT
Muslim League **13**:683
LUCKY PEAK LAKE
map (43° 33′N 116° 0′W) **11**:26
LUCRETIA **12**:451
Rome, ancient **16**:297
LUCRETIUS **12**:451 *bibliog.*
De rerum natura **6**:62
LUCULLUS, LUCIUS LICINIUS **12**:451 *bibliog.*
LUCY (Tennessee)
map (18° 0′N 56° 0′W) **19**:104
LUCY, SAINT **12**:451
LUCY CAVENDISH COLLEGIATE SOCIETY (Cambridge University) **4**:53
LÜDA (China) *see* LÜ-TA (China)
LUDDITES **12**:451 *bibliog.*
radicalism **16**:44
LUDENDORF, ERICH
World War I **20**:241–243
LUDENDORFF, ERICH **12**:451 *bibliog.*
Hindenburg, Paul von **10**:169
Munich Putsch **13**:642
Somme, Battles of the **18**:61
Tannenberg, Battles of **19**:24
World War I **20**:222; **20**:226 *illus.*
LÜDENSCHEID (Germany, East and West)
map (51° 13′N 7° 38′E) **9**:140
LUDHIANA (India)
map (30° 54′N 75° 51′E) **11**:80
LUDINGTON (Michigan)
map (43° 57′N 86° 27′W) **13**:377
LUDLOW (Massachusetts)
map (42° 10′N 72° 29′W) **13**:206
LUDLOW (Vermont)
map (43° 24′N 72° 42′W) **19**:554
LUDLOW, JOHN MALCOLM FORBES
socialism **18**:20
LUDLOW, ROGER **12**:451–452
LUDLOW'S CODE *see* LUDLOW, ROGER
LUDOVICE, JOÃO PEDRO FREDERICO **12**:452 *bibliog.*
LUDOWICI (Georgia)
map (31° 43′N 81° 45′W) **9**:114
LUDVIKA (Sweden)
map (60° 9′N 15° 11′E) **18**:382
LUDWIG *see* LOUIS for German kings named Ludwig
LUDWIG, CARL F. W.
zoology **20**:377
LUDWIG, CHRISTA **12**:452 *bibliog.*
LUDWIG, EMIL **12**:452
LUDWIG, JACK **12**:452
LUDWIG, JOHANN PETER FRIEDRICH *see* LUDOVICE, JOÃO PEDRO FREDERICO
LUDWIG, OTTO **12**:452 *bibliog.*
LUDWIGSBURG (Germany, East and West)
map (48° 53′N 9° 11′E) **9**:140
LUDWIGSHAFEN (Germany, East and West)
map (49° 29′N 8° 26′E) **9**:140
LUEPA (Venezuela)
map (5° 43′N 61° 31′W) **19**:542
LUFKIN (Texas)
map (31° 20′N 94° 44′W) **19**:129
LUFTWAFFE
Goering, Hermann **9**:222
World War II **20**:254–255; **20**:264; **20**:273; **20**:275
LUG (mythology) **12**:452
LUGANO (Switzerland)
map (46° 1′N 8° 58′E) **18**:394
LUGANO, LAKE **12**:452
LUGARD, FREDERICK JOHN DEALTRY LUGARD, 1st BARON **12**:452 *bibliog.*
LUGE **12**:452
LUGENDA RIVER
map (11° 25′S 38° 33′E) **13**:627
LUGEON, MAURICE **12**:452–453
LUGER (pistol) **15**:318 *illus.*
LUGNÉ-POË, AURÉLIEN-MARIE
Nabis **14**:3
LUGO (Spain)
map (43° 0′N 7° 34′W) **18**:140
LUGOJ (Romania)
map (45° 41′N 21° 54′E) **16**:288
LUGONES, LEOPOLDO **12**:453
LUGOSI, BELA **12**:453 *bibliog., illus.*
LUGWIG *see* LOUIS for German kings named LUDWIG
LUGWORM **12**:453 *bibliog.*
gill **9**:181 *illus.*
LUIK (Belgium) *see* LIÈGE (Belgium)
LUISETTI, HANK **12**:453
LUKÁCS, GYÖRGY **12**:453 *bibliog., illus.*
socialism **18**:24
LUKANGA SWAMP
map (14° 25′S 27° 45′E) **20**:354
LUKE, SAINT **12**:454 *bibliog.*; **13**:520 *illus.*
LUKE, GOSPEL ACCORDING TO **12**:453–454 *bibliog.*
Jesus Christ **11**:403–404
LUKEMAN, AUGUSTUS
Stone Mountain **18**:282
LUKES, STEVEN
sociology **18**:30
LUKEVILLE (Arizona)
map (31° 53′N 112° 49′W) **2**:160
LUKS, GEORGE **12**:454 *bibliog.*
comic strip **5**:135
LULAC *see* LEAGUE OF UNITED LATIN AMERICAN CITIZENS
LULEÅ (Sweden)
map (65° 34′N 22° 10′E) **18**:382
LULEÅ RIVER
map (65° 35′N 22° 3′E) **18**:382
LULING (Texas)
map (29° 41′N 97° 39′W) **19**:129
LULL, RAYMOND **12**:454 *bibliog.*
LULLY, JEAN BAPTISTE **12**:454 *bibliog., illus.*
Alceste **14**:400 *illus.*
kettledrum **12**:61
minuet **13**:461
music, history of Western **13**:666
overture **14**:470
LULUA RIVER
map (5° 2′S 21° 7′E) **20**:350
LULY, MUHAMMAD OULD
Mauritania **13**:237
LUMBAGO **12**:454–455
LUMBER **12**:455–458 *bibliog., illus.*
forestry **8**:230–231
history **12**:457
Idaho **11**:28
important U.S. timber species **12**:456–457 *illus.*
logging **12**:394
lumber-making process **12**:457–458
Norway **14**:263 *illus.*
Oregon **14**:429–430
pencil **15**:141
plywood **15**:374–375
veneer **19**:538
wood **20**:205–206 *illus.*
ash **2**:228–229
Douglas fir **6**:248
elm **7**:149
fir **8**:99–100
linden **12**:351–352
mahogany **13**:66
maple **13**:137
oak **14**:311
pine **15**:305
redwood **16**:117
rosewood **16**:317
satinwood **17**:88
southern white cedar **18**:112
spruce **18**:201
teak **19**:57
tulip tree **19**:330
turpentine tree **19**:352
walnut **20**:17
yellowwood **20**:323
LUMBER CITY (Georgia)
map (31° 56′N 82° 41′W) **9**:114
LUMBER RIVER
map (34° 12′N 79° 10′W) **18**:98
LUMBERJACK *see* BIRLING; LOGGING
LUMBERTON (Mississippi)
map (31° 0′N 89° 27′W) **13**:469
LUMBERTON (North Carolina)
map (34° 37′N 79° 0′W) **14**:242
LUMBY (British Columbia)
map (50° 15′N 118° 58′W) **3**:491
LUMEN **12**:458
units, physical **19**:467 *table*
LUMET, SIDNEY **12**:458
LUMIÈRE, LOUIS AND AUGUSTE **12**:458 *bibliog.*
film, history of **8**:81
Lumière, Louis
documentary **6**:211
LUMINAL *see* PHENOBARBITAL
LUMINANCE
television **19**:87–88
LUMINESCENCE **12**:458 *bibliog.*
auroras **2**:325
bioluminescence **3**:272
chemiluminescence **12**:458
fluorescence **8**:186
lighting devices **12**:337–338
luminous intensity
measurement **13**:255
units, physical **19**:466–467 *table*
phosphorescence **15**:256
quasar **16**:14–15
LUMINESCENCE, MINERAL **12**:458
fluorescence **8**:186
LUMINISM **12**:459 *bibliog.*
Church, Frederick Edwin **4**:423
Heade, Martin **10**:86
Hudson River school **10**:290
Kensett, John Frederick **12**:45
Lane, Fitz Hugh **12**:193
painting **15**:23
LUMLEY, HENRY DE **12**:459
Terra Amata (France) **19**:119
Vallonet Cave (France) **19**:508
LUMMER, OTTO **12**:459
LUMPFISH **12**:459
LUMPKIN (Georgia)
map (32° 3′N 84° 48′W) **9**:114
LUMPKIN (county in Georgia)
map (34° 35′N 84° 0′W) **9**:114
LUMPY JAW
fungus diseases **8**:369
respiratory system disorders **16**:181
LUMUMBA, PATRICE **12**:459 *bibliog., illus.*
Kisangani **12**:90
LUNA (mythology) **12**:459
LUNA (county in New Mexico)
map (32° 15′N 107° 45′W) **14**:136
LUNA (spacecraft) **12**:459–460 *bibliog., illus., table*
flights **12**:460 *table*
Lunokhod **12**:465 *illus.*
space exploration **18**:124 *illus.*
LUNA, TRISTÁN DE
Florida **8**:175
LUNA MOTH **3**:598–599 *illus.*
LUNA PIER (Michigan)
map (41° 48′N 83° 27′W) **13**:377
LUNAR *see* MOON

LUNAR CALENDAR
calendar 4:27–28
LUNAR EXCURSION MODULE 2:80 *illus.*; 12:460–461 *bibliog.*, *illus.*
Anders, William Alison 1:401
Apollo Program 12:460–461
Cernan, Eugene 4:260
Duke, Charles, Jr. 6:295
space exploration 18:128
testing apparatus 18:121 *illus.*
LUNAR ORBITER 12:461 *bibliog.*, *illus.*, *illus.*
Ranger (space probe) 16:84
space exploration 18:124
LUNAR RHYTHM
biological clock 3:264
LUNAR ROVER 12:461–462 *illus.*
Apollo program 2:83–84 *illus.*
Duke, Charles, Jr. 6:295
Irwin, James 11:285
Scott, David R. 17:153
space exploration 18:129 *illus.*, *illus.*
LUNAR SOCIETY
Birmingham (England) 3:292–293
LUND (Nevada)
map (38° 52′N 115° 0′W) 14:111
LUNDA 12:462 *bibliog.*
Chokwe 4:403
LUNDAR (Manitoba)
map (50° 42′N 98° 2′W) 13:119
LUNDI RIVER
map (21° 43′S 32° 34′E) 20:365
LUNDMARK, KNUT 12:462
LUNDY, BENJAMIN 12:462 *bibliog.*
LÜNEBURG (Germany, East and West)
map (53° 15′N 10° 23′E) 9:140
LUNENBURG (Massachusetts)
map (42° 36′N 71° 44′W) 13:206
LUNENBURG (Nova Scotia)
map (44° 23′N 64° 19′W) 14:269
LUNENBURG (Virginia)
map (36° 58′N 78° 16′W) 19:607
LUNENBURG (county in Virginia)
map (37° 0′N 78° 15′W) 19:607
LUNÉVILLE, TREATY OF
Napoléon I, Emperor of the French (Napoléon Bonaparte) 14:17
LUNG, ARTIFICIAL *see* HEART-LUNG MACHINE; IRON LUNG
LUNG-MEN (Longmen) (China) 12:462 *bibliog.*
LUNG-SHAN CULTURE
Chinese archaeology 4:378
LUNGFISH 8:117 *illus.*; 12:462–463 *illus.*
LUNGS 12:463–465 *bibliog.*, *illus.*
alveoli 12:463–464 *illus.*
bronchial tube 3:502–503
circulatory system 4:440 *illus.*
diseases and disorders
aspergillosis 2:262
asthma 2:268
black lung 3:317
bronchitis 3:503
brown lung 3:516–517
cancer 4:101; 4:102; 4:104
cor pulmonale 5:257
cystic fibrosis 5:411
diseases, occupational 6:193–194
dust, atmospheric 6:308
emphysema 7:158
environmental health 7:211
fungus diseases 8:369
histoplasmosis 10:181
hyaline membrane disease 10:327
infarction 11:164
Legionnaires' disease 12:274
mycoplasmal pneumonia 13:690
pleurisy 15:368
pneumonia 15:375–376
psittacosis 15:588
pulmonary embolism 15:619
respiratory system disorders 16:181–182
smoke 17:373
smoking 17:373–374
suffocation 18:325
tuberculosis 19:327 *illus.*
drug, inhalation 6:275 *illus.*
evolution 12:464
heart-lung machine 10:97
iron lung 11:272
pulmonary function test 15:620
respiratory system 16:178; 16:180 *illus.*
LUNGUÉ-BUNGO RIVER
map (14° 19′S 23° 14′E) 2:5
LUNGWORT 12:322 *illus.*; 12:465
LUNOKHOD 12:465 *bibliog.*, *illus.*
Luna (spacecraft) 12:460
space exploration 18:124 *illus.*
LUNSAR (Sierra Leone)
map (8° 41′N 12° 32′W) 17:296
LUNT, ALFRED, AND FONTANNE, LYNN 12:465 *bibliog.*, *illus.*
LUNT, PAUL S.
status 18:239
LUNULE
hoof, nail, and claw 10:225–226
LUO 12:465 *bibliog.*
Mboya, Tom 13:251
LUORAWETLAN LANGUAGE
Ural-Altaic languages 19:476
LUPENI (Romania)
map (45° 22′N 23° 13′E) 16:288
LUPERCALIA 12:465–466
LUPINE 12:466 *illus.*
germination 9:157
LUPUS ERYTHEMATOSUS 12:466 *bibliog.*
arthritis 2:215
collagen disease 5:102–103
myasthenia gravis 13:689
LUQUE, HERNÁN DE
Pizarro, Francisco 15:324
LURAY (Virginia)
map (38° 40′N 78° 28′W) 19:607
LURAY CAVERNS (Virginia) 12:466
cave 4:222
LURÇAT, JEAN 12:466
Song of the World 19:33 *illus.*
tapestry 19:33
LURIA, ALEKSANDR ROMANOVICH 12:466 *bibliog.*
LURIA, ISAAC BEN SOLOMON 12:466–467 *bibliog.*
Kabbalah 12:3
LURIA, SALVADOR 12:467
Hershey, Alfred Day 10:148
LURIE, ALISON 12:467
LÚRIO RIVER
map (13° 35′S 40° 32′E) 13:627
LURISTAN (Iran) 12:467 *bibliog.*
Persian art and architecture 15:183
LURS
Qashqai 16:3
LUSAKA (Zambia) 12:467; 20:353–354 *illus.*, *table*
climate 1:142 *table*
map (15° 25′S 28° 17′E) 20:354
LUSATIANS *see* WENDS
LUSHAI 12:467
LUSHNJE (Albania)
map (40° 56′N 19° 42′E) 1:250
LÜSHUN (China) *see* LÜ-SHUN (Lüshun) (China)
LUSIADS, THE (epic)
Camões, Luis Vaz de 4:62
LUSIGNAN, GUY DE *see* GUY DE LUSIGNAN
LUSITAN *see* LUSITANIA (Roman province)
LUSITANIA (Roman province) 12:467
Portugal, history of 15:452–453
LUSITANIA (ship) 12:467 *bibliog.*, *illus.*
ship 17:272 *illus.*
Wilson, Woodrow 20:167
World War I 20:232 *illus.*; 20:236
LUSK (Wyoming)
map (42° 46′N 104° 27′W) 20:301
LUSO (Angola)
map (11° 47′S 19° 52′E) 2:5
LUSTER 12:468
light reflection
mineral surface 12:468
LUSTERWARE
pottery and porcelain 15:470–471
LUT DESERT
map (33° 0′N 57° 0′E) 11:250
LÜTA (DAIREN) (China)
map (38° 53′N 121° 35′E) 4:362
LUTE 12:468 *bibliog.*, *illus.*
African music 1:169–170 *illus.*
Amati (family) 1:322
Bream, Julian 3:468
chitarrone 4:398
Dowland, John 6:251–252
guitar 9:400–401
Indian music 11:102–103 *illus.*
Japanese music 11:381 *illus.*
mandolin 13:111–112 *illus.*
musical instruments 13:677–679 *illus.*
sitar 17:330 *illus.*
stringed instruments 18:300–301 *illus.*
theorbo 19:158
ud 2:99–100 *illus.*
vina 19:599
LUTEINIZING HORMONE (LH)
endocrine system, diseases of the 7:171
gonadotropin 9:242
hormones 10:236
pituitary gland 15:322
LUTEOTROPIC HORMONE
hormones 10:236 *table*
LUTETIUM 12:468
element 7:130 *table*
lanthanide series 12:200–201; 12:468
metal, metallic element 13:328
LUTHER (Michigan)
map (44° 2′N 85° 41′W) 13:377
LUTHER (Oklahoma)
map (35° 40′N 97° 12′W) 14:368
LUTHER, MARTIN 12:468–469 *bibliog.*, *illus.*
church music 4:424
Europe, history of 7:287
Frederick III, Elector of Saxony (Frederick the Wise) 8:292
Germany, history of 9:151
Leipzig (East Germany) 12:278
Lutheranism 12:469
marriage 13:166
Melanchthon, Philipp 13:284
Peasants' War 15:129
psychohistory 15:591
Reformation 16:122 *illus.*
Tetzel, Johann 19:127
Wittenberg (East Germany) 20:193
Worms (West Germany) 20:284
LUTHER* v. *BORDEN 12:469
LUTHERANISM 12:469–470 *bibliog.*
Augsburg Confession 2:320
Book of Concord 3:386
cantata 4:116
cantor 4:118
Chemnitz, Martin 4:329
chorale 4:407
departure for the New World 19:438 *illus.*
education
Concordia colleges 5:171
St. Olaf College 17:24
Europe, history of 7:287
Flacius Illyricus, Matthias 8:133
Fry, Franklin Clark 8:351
Germany, history of 9:151
hymn 10:346
Luther, Martin 12:468–469
mass (musical setting) 13:201
Muhlenberg (family) 13:634
Philip of Hesse 15:232
Reformation 16:121 *map*
Schmucker, Samuel Simon 17:128
Small Catechism 4:202
Sweden 18:383
Thirty Years' War 19:171 *map*
Walther, Carl Ferdinand Wilhelm 20:20
LUTHERVILLE-TIMONIUM (Maryland)
map (39° 25′N 76° 37′W) 13:188
LUTHULI, ALBERT JOHN 12:470 *bibliog.*, *illus.*
LUTI (Solomon Islands)
map (7° 14′S 156° 59′E) 18:56
LUTON (England)
map (51° 53′N 0° 25′W) 19:403
LUTOSŁAWSKI, WITOLD 12:470
LUTULI, ALBERT JOHN *see* LUTHULI, ALBERT JOHN
LUTYENS, SIR EDWIN LANDSEER 12:471 *bibliog.*
Liverpool (England) 12:375–376
LUTYENS, ELISABETH 12:471
LÜTZEN, BATTLE OF 17:109 *illus.*
Wallenstein, Albrecht Wenzel von 20:15
LUVERNE (Alabama)
map (31° 43′N 86° 16′W) 1:234
LUVERNE (Minnesota)
map (43° 39′N 96° 13′W) 13:453
LUWIAN LANGUAGES
languages, extinct 12:198–199
LUX (measurement)
units, physical 19:467 *table*
LUXEMBOURG (city in Luxembourg) 12:471; 12:472 *illus.*, *table*
map (49° 54′N 6° 5′E) 7:268
LUXEMBOURG (country) 12:471–472 *bibliog.*, *illus.*, *map*, *table*
cities
Luxembourg 12:471
economic activity 12:471
flag 12:471 *illus.*
history and government 12:471–472
boundaries c.1360 7:285 *map*
Low Countries, history of the 12:438–443 *map*
Thorn, Gaston 19:178
World War II 20:252–253 *map*
land and people 12:471–472 *map*, *table*
map (49° 36′N 6° 9′E) 12:472
LUXEMBOURG PALACE 12:472 *bibliog.*
Brosse, Salomon de 3:512
château 4:302
LUXEMBURG (Wisconsin)
map (44° 32′N 87° 42′W) 20:185
LUXEMBURG, HENRY OF *see* HENRY VII, KING OF GERMANY AND HOLY ROMAN EMPEROR (Henry of Luxemburg)
LUXEMBURG, ROSA 12:473 *bibliog.*
socialism 18:22
LUXOR (Egypt) 12:473 *bibliog.*
temple 19:94–95
Thebes 19:155
LUXORA (Arkansas)
map (35° 45′N 89° 56′W) 2:166
LUZERN (Switzerland) *see* LUCERNE (Switzerland)
LUZERNE (county in Pennsylvania)
map (41° 14′N 75° 53′W) 15:147
LUZON (Philippines) 12:473
cities
Baguio 3:23
Manila 13:117–118 *illus.*
Quezon City 16:25
map (16° 0′N 121° 0′E) 15:237
people
Igorot 11:38
LUZON STRAIT
map (20° 30′N 121° 0′E) 15:237
LUZZATTO, MOSES HAYYIM 12:473 *bibliog.*
LVOV (USSR) 12:473
map (49° 50′N 24° 0′E) 19:388
LVOV, GEORGY
Russia/Union of Soviet Socialist Republics, history of 16:359
LWOFF, ANDRÉ 12:473
Jacob, François 11:345
Monod, Jacques Lucien 13:536
LWÓW (Poland) *see* LVOV (USSR)
LYAKHOV, VLADIMIR 12:473
LYALLPUR (Pakistan) 12:473
map (31° 25′N 73° 5′E) 15:27
LYAUTEY, LOUIS HUBERT 12:474 *bibliog.*
LYCÉE 12:474
LYCEUM (adult education programs) 12:474
LYCEUM SCHOOL OF ACTING *see* AMERICAN ACADEMY OF DRAMATIC ART
LYCEUM THEATRE
Irving, Sir Henry 11:284
LYCHEE *see* LITCHI
LYCIA 12:474
languages, extinct 12:199
Xanthus 20:311
LYCOMING (county in Pennsylvania)
map (41° 14′N 77° 0′W) 15:147
LYCOPHYTINA
plant 15:334
LYCOPOD *see* CLUB MOSS
LYCURCTUS CUP 9:203 *illus.*
LYCURGUS 12:474
LYDGATE, JOHN 11:474 *bibliog.*
LYDIA 12:474
Croesus, King 5:357
languages, extinct 12:198
money 13:526 *illus.*; 14:296 *illus.*
Persia, ancient 15:182 *map*
Sardis 17:77
LYE
caustic chemicals 4:219–220
LYE, LEN
animation 2:29
LYELL, SIR CHARLES 12:474–475 *bibliog.*, *illus.*
Agassiz, Louis Rodolphe 1:182
archaeology 2:123
paleogeography 15:35
Pleistocene Epoch 15:364
prehistory 15:517
uniformitarianism 19:386
LYKENS (Pennsylvania)
map (40° 34′N 76° 43′W) 15:147
LYLE (Minnesota)
map (43° 30′N 92° 57′W) 13:453
LYLES (Tennessee)
map (35° 55′N 87° 21′W) 19:104
LYLY, JOHN 12:475 *bibliog.*
LYMAN (county in South Dakota)
map (43° 55′N 99° 52′W) 18:103
LYMAN (Wyoming)
map (41° 20′N 110° 18′W) 20:301
LYMAN, JOHN
Canadian art and architecture 4:90
LYMAN, THEODORE 12:475
ultraviolet research 12:475
LYMPH
lymphatic system 12:475
tissue, animal 19:210
LYMPHATIC SYSTEM 12:475–476 *bibliog.*, *illus.*
adenoids 1:102
cell types 12:475
diseases and disorders 12:476
cancer 4:102 *illus.*

filariasis **8**:78
Hodgkin's disease **10**:194
leukemia **12**:300–301
leukopenia **12**:301
lymphoma **12**:476
mononucleosis **13**:537
myasthenia gravis **13**:689
immunity **12**:475–476
lipid **12**:361–362
lymph nodes **12**:475–476 *illus.*
spleen **18**:191
thymus **19**:187
tonsils **19**:235
LYMPHOCYTES
blood **3**:336
cloning **5**:64
immunity **11**:57
immunodeficiency disease **11**:59
lymphatic system **12**:475
thymus **19**:187
LYMPHOMA **12**:476
Hodgkin's disease **12**:476
lymphatic system **12**:476
splenomegaly **18**:191
LYNCH (Kentucky)
map (36° 58′N 82° 55′W) **12**:47
LYNCH, BENITO **12**:476
LYNCH, CHARLES **12**:476
lynching **12**:477
LYNCH, JOHN **12**:476
Ireland, history of **11**:265
LYNCHBURG (Ohio)
map (39° 14′N 83° 48′W) **14**:357
LYNCHBURG (South Carolina)
map (34° 4′N 80° 4′W) **18**:98
LYNCHBURG (Tennessee)
map (35° 17′N 86° 22′W) **19**:104
LYNCHBURG (Virginia) **12**:476
map (37° 24′N 79° 10′W) **19**:607
LYNCHING **12**:476–477 *bibliog.*
LYND, ROBERT S. **12**:477
LYNDEN (Washington)
map (48° 57′N 122° 27′W) **20**:35
LYNDHURST (Ohio)
map (41° 31′N 81° 30′W) **14**:357
LYNDON (Kansas)
map (38° 36′N 95° 41′W) **12**:18
LYNDONVILLE (Vermont)
map (44° 32′N 72° 1′W) **19**:554
LYNDORA (Pennsylvania)
map (40° 51′N 79° 55′W) **15**:147
LYNEN, FEODOR **12**:477
LYNN (Indiana)
map (40° 3′N 84° 56′W) **11**:111
LYNN (Massachusetts) **12**:477
map (42° 28′N 70° 57′W) **13**:206
LYNN (county in Texas)
map (33° 8′N 100° 43′W) **19**:129
LYNN HAVEN (Florida)
map (30° 15′N 85° 39′W) **8**:172
LYNN LAKE (Manitoba)
map (56° 51′N 101° 3′W) **13**:119
LYNNDYL (Utah)
map (39° 31′N 112° 22′W) **19**:492
LYNNFIELD (Massachusetts)
map (42° 32′N 71° 3′W) **13**:206
LYNNWOOD (Washington)
map (47° 49′N 122° 19′W) **20**:35
LYNWOOD (California)
map (33° 55′N 118° 12′W) **4**:31
LYNX **12**:477 *illus.*
caracal **4**:129
LYNX-POINT *see* COLORPOINT SHORTHAIR CAT
LYON (France) **8**:263 *illus.*; **12**:477–478 *illus.*
map (45° 45′N 4° 51′E) **8**:260
LYON (county in Iowa)
map (43° 23′N 96° 10′W) **11**:244
LYON (county in Kansas)
map (38° 25′N 96° 10′W) **12**:18
LYON (county in Kentucky)
map (37° 0′N 88° 5′W) **12**:47
LYON (county in Minnesota)
map (44° 22′N 95° 50′W) **13**:453
LYON (county in Nevada)
map (39° 0′N 119° 10′W) **14**:111
LYON, COUNCILS OF **12**:478
LYON, GEORGE
sandstorm and dust storm **17**:63 *illus.*
LYON, MARY **12**:478 *bibliog.*
LYON, MATTHEW **12**:478
LYON, NATHANIEL **12**:478 *bibliog.*
LYON MOUNTAIN (New York)
map (44° 43′N 73° 55′W) **14**:149
LYONNAIS (France) **12**:478
LYONS (Colorado)
map (40° 13′N 105° 16′W) **5**:116
LYONS (Georgia)
map (32° 12′N 82° 19′W) **9**:114
LYONS (Indiana)
map (38° 59′N 87° 5′W) **11**:111
LYONS (Kansas)
map (38° 21′N 98° 12′W) **12**:18
LYONS (Michigan)
map (42° 59′N 84° 57′W) **13**:377
LYONS (Nebraska)
map (41° 56′N 96° 28′W) **14**:70
LYONS (New York)
map (43° 4′N 77° 0′W) **14**:149
LYONS, JOSEPH ALOYSIUS **12**:478
LYONS, LEONARD **12**:478
LYOT, BERNARD FERDINAND **12**:479
coronagraph **5**:270–271
LYRA **12**:479
LYRE **9**:345 *illus.*; **12**:479 *bibliog., illus.*
African **1**:169
kithara **12**:93
musical instruments **13**:678
LYREBIRD **12**:479
LYRIC **12**:479 *bibliog.*
canzone **4**:119
ode **14**:348
Persian literature **15**:187
Wordsworth, William **20**:216–217
LYRICAL BALLADS (book) **12**:479 *bibliog.*
Wordsworth, William **20**:216–217
LYS, JAN **12**:479 *bibliog.*
LYSANDER **12**:479–480 *bibliog.*
LYSENKO, TROFIM DENISOVICH **12**:480 *bibliog.*
Lamarck, Jean Baptiste **12**:173
LYSERGIC ACID
alkaloid **1**:296
Woodward, Robert Burns **20**:213
LYSERGIC ACID DIETHYLAMIDE *see* LSD
LYSIAS **12**:480 *bibliog.*
LYSIMACHUS, MACEDONIAN KING **12**:480
loosestrife (botany) **12**:411
LYSIPPUS **12**:480 *bibliog.*
Farnese Heracles **8**:28
LYSISTRATA (play) **12**:480 *bibliog.*
LYSOSOME **12**:480
cell **4**:232 *illus.*
LYSOZYME
Fleming, Sir Alexander **8**:159
lysosome **12**:480
LYTTON (British Columbia)
map (50° 14′N 121° 34′W) **3**:491
LYTTON, EDWARD BULWER-, 1ST BARON LYTTON *see* BULWER-LYTTON, EDWARD, 1ST BARON LYTTON
LYTTON, EDWARD ROBERT BULWER-LYTTON, 1ST EARL OF *see* BULWER-LYTTON, EDWARD ROBERT, 1ST EARL OF LYTTON

M

M (letter) **13**:3 *illus.*
M. GORKY MOSCOW ART ACADEMIC THEATER *see* MOSCOW ART THEATER
MA RIVER
map (19° 47′N 105° 56′E) **19**:580
MA-TSU ISLAND
map (26° 9′N 119° 56′E) **19**:13
MA YUAN (Ma Yuan) **13**:3 *bibliog.*
MAALAEA BAY
map (20° 47′N 156° 29′W) **10**:72
MAAN (Jordan)
map (30° 20′N 36° 30′E) **11**:447
MAANYAN *see* DAYAK
MAAS, NICOLAES *see* MAES, NICOLAES
MAAS RIVER *see* MEUSE RIVER
MAASTRICHT (Netherlands) **13**:3
map (50° 52′N 5° 43′E) **14**:99
MAAT (Egyptian goddess) **12**:244 *illus.*
MAAZEL, LORIN **13**:5
MABABE DEPRESSION
map (18° 50′S 24° 15′E) **3**:416
MABADUAN (Papua New Guinea)
map (9° 16′S 142° 44′E) **15**:72
MABARUMA (Guyana)
map (8° 12′N 59° 47′W) **9**:410
MABILLON, JEAN
history **10**:185
MABLETON (Georgia)
map (33° 49′N 84° 35′W) **2**:292
MABUSE, JAN *see* GOSSAERT, JAN
M′ *see* MAC for names beginning with the prefix M′
Mc *see* Mac for names beginning with the prefix Mc
MACADAM **13**:3
roads and highways **16**:237
McADAM (New Brunswick)
map (45° 36′N 67° 20′W) **14**:117
MACADAM, JOHN LOUDON
macadam **13**:3
roads and highways **16**:237
MACADAMIA NUT **13**:3
McADOO (Pennsylvania)
map (40° 54′N 76° 1′W) **15**:147
McADOO, WILLIAM G. **13**:3 *bibliog.*
McALESTER (Oklahoma)
map (34° 56′N 95° 46′W) **14**:368
McALLEN (Texas)
map (26° 12′N 98° 15′W) **19**:129
MacALPIN, KENNETH *see* KENNETH I, KING OF SCOTLAND
MACAO (Portugal) **13**:4 *map*
map (22° 14′N 113° 35′E) **4**:362
MACAPÁ (Brazil)
map (0° 2′N 51° 3′W) **3**:460
MACAQUE **13**:4 *illus.*
Barbary ape **3**:76
brain **3**:443 *illus.*
hand **15**:539 *illus.*
rhesus monkey **16**:193
MACARÁ (Ecuador)
map (4° 23′S 79° 57′W) **7**:52
McARDLE'S DISEASE
enzyme **7**:214
MACARIUS THE EGYPTIAN, SAINT **13**:5 *bibliog.*
MACARONI **15**:106 *illus.*
McARTHUR (Ohio)
map (39° 15′N 82° 29′W) **14**:357
McARTHUR, CHARLES
Hecht, Ben **10**:103
MacARTHUR, DOUGLAS **13**:5 *bibliog., illus.*
Eisenhower, Dwight D. **7**:94
Korean War **12**:120–122
Roxas y Acuna, Manuel **16**:328
Truman, Harry S. **15**:523 *illus.*; **19**:318
World War II **20**:260–261; **20**:267; **20**:278 *illus.*; **20**:280–281
MacARTHUR FOUNDATION **13**:5–6
MACAS (Ecuador)
map (2° 19′S 78° 7′W) **7**:52
MACAU (Brazil)
map (5° 7′S 36° 38′W) **3**:460
MACAU (Portugal) *see* MACAO (Portugal)
MACAULAY, THOMAS BABINGTON **13**:6 *bibliog., illus.*
Indian literature **11**:101–102
McAULIFFE, CHRISTA **13**:6
MACAW **11**:469 *illus.*; **13**:6 *illus.*; **15**:97 *illus.*
MACAYA PEAK
map (18° 25′N 74° 0′W) **10**:15
M'BA, LEON
Gabon **9**:5
McBAIN (Michigan)
map (44° 12′N 85° 13′W) **13**:377
McBAIN, ED *see* HUNTER, EVAN
McBEE (South Carolina)
map (34° 28′N 80° 15′W) **18**:98
MACBETH (play) **13**:6–7 *bibliog.*
Macbeth, King of Scotland **13**:7
MACBETH, ANN
Art Nouveau cushion **2**:209 *illus.*
MACBETH, KING OF SCOTLAND **13**:7 *bibliog.*
Moray (Scotland) **13**:575
Nairn (Scotland) **14**:8
McBRIDE (British Columbia)
map (53° 18′N 120° 10′W) **3**:491
McBRIDE, PATRICIA **13**:7
M'BRIDGE RIVER
map (7° 14′S 12° 52′E) **2**:5
MACCABEES (family) **13**:7 *bibliog.*
Chanukah **4**:282
Jews **11**:413
MACCABEES, BOOKS OF **13**:7 *bibliog.*
McCALL (Idaho)
map (44° 55′N 116° 6′W) **11**:26
McCALL'S (periodical) **13**:7
McCALLUM (Newfoundland)
map (47° 38′N 56° 15′W) **14**:166
McCAMEY (Texas)
map (31° 8′N 102° 13′W) **19**:129
McCARDELL, CLAIRE **8**:32 *illus.*; **13**:7 *bibliog.*
fashion design **8**:32 *illus.*
McCARRAN, PATRICK A. *see* McCARRAN ACT
McCARRAN ACT **13**:7–8 *bibliog.*
Communist party, U.S.A. **5**:151
immigration **11**:56
subversion **18**:317
Truman, Harry S. **19**:318
Un-American Activities, House Committee on **19**:381
McCARTHY (Alaska)
map (61° 26′N 142° 55′W) **1**:242
MacCARTHY, A. H.
Logan, Mount **12**:394
McCARTHY, CHARLIE
Bergen, Edgar, and McCarthy, Charlie **3**:209
McCARTHY, EUGENE **13**:8 *bibliog.*
Vietnam War **19**:587
McCARTHY, JOE **13**:8
McCARTHY, JOSEPH R. **13**:8 *bibliog., illus.*
Communist party, U.S.A. **5**:151
Kennedy, Robert F. **12**:44
Lehman, Herbert H. **12**:276
Murrow, Edward R. **13**:651
radicalism **16**:44
radio and television broadcasting **16**:57
Truman, Harry S. **19**:318
Un-American Activities, House Committee on **19**:380–381
United States, history of the **19**:457 *illus.*
McCARTHY, MARY **13**:8–9 *bibliog., illus.*
McCARTHYISM *see* McCARTHY, JOSEPH R.
McCARTNEY, PAUL
Beatles, The **3**:144–145 *illus.*
McCARTY, MACLYN **13**:9
MacLeod, Colin M. **13**:32
nucleic acid **14**:289
McCARVER, MORTON MATTHEW
Tacoma (Washington) **19**:6
McCAULEY, MARY LUDWIG *see* MOLLY PITCHER
McCAY, WINSOR
animation **2**:28
comic strip **5**:135
McCAYSVILLE (Georgia)
map (34° 59′N 84° 23′W) **9**:114
MACCHIAIOLI (art group) **13**:9 *bibliog.*
McCLAIN (county in Oklahoma)
map (35° 0′N 97° 30′W) **14**:368
McCLELLAN, GEORGE B. **5**:21–29 *illus., map*; **13**:9 *bibliog., illus.*
Peninsular Campaign **15**:144
McCLELLANVILLE (South Carolina)
map (33° 5′N 79° 28′W) **18**:98
MACCLENNY (Florida)
map (30° 18′N 82° 7′W) **8**:172
McCLERNAND, JOHN ALEXANDER **13**:9
MACCLESFIELD (England)
map (53° 16′N 2° 7′W) **19**:403
McCLINTIC, GUTHRIE
Cornell, Katharine **5**:268
McCLINTOCK, BARBARA **13**:9
McCLINTOCK, LEOPOLD
Franklin, Sir John **8**:285
McCLOSKEY, JOHN **13**:9 *bibliog.*
McCLUNG, NELLIE **13**:9
McCLURE (Illinois)
map (37° 19′N 89° 26′W) **11**:42
McCLURE (Pennsylvania)
map (40° 42′N 77° 19′W) **15**:147
McCLURE, ROBERT
Northwest Passage **14**:256
McCLURE, S. S. **13**:9–10 *bibliog.*
journalism **11**:455
M'CLURE STRAIT
map (74° 30′N 116° 0′W) **14**:258
McCLURE'S MAGAZINE
McClure, S. S. **13**:10
muckrakers **13**:630–631
Steffens, Lincoln **18**:245
McCLUSKY (North Dakota)
map (47° 29′N 100° 27′W) **14**:248
McCOLL (South Carolina)
map (34° 40′N 79° 33′W) **18**:98
McCOMAS (West Virginia)
map (37° 23′N 81° 17′W) **20**:111
McCOMB (Mississippi)
map (31° 14′N 90° 27′W) **13**:469
McCONAUGHY, LAKE
map (41° 15′N 101° 50′W) **14**:70
McCONE (county in Montana)
map (47° 35′N 105° 45′W) **13**:547
McCONNELLSBURG (Pennsylvania)
map (39° 56′N 77° 59′W) **15**:147
McCONNELSVILLE (Ohio)
map (39° 39′N 81° 51′W) **14**:357
McCOOK (Nebraska)
map (40° 12′N 100° 38′W) **14**:70
McCOOK (county in South Dakota)
map (43° 40′N 97° 20′W) **18**:103
McCOOL, FINN (fictional character)
Fenian cycle (tales) **8**:50
McCORMACK, JOHN (singer) **13**:10 *bibliog.*
McCORMACK, JOHN W. (politician) **13**:10
McCORMICK (South Carolina)
map (33° 55′N 82° 17′W) **18**:98
McCORMICK (county in South Carolina)
map (33° 55′N 82° 20′W) **18**:98

McCORMICK, CYRUS HALL 13:10 *bibliog.*; 19:450 *illus.*
reaper 16:104 *illus.*
McCORMICK, PATRICIA 13:10
McCORMICK, ROBERT RUTHERFORD 13:10 *bibliog.*
Patterson (family) 15:115
McCOSH, JAMES 13:10 *bibliog.*
McCOY (family) *see* HATFIELDS AND McCOYS
McCOY, JOSEPH 13:10
McCRACKEN (county in Kentucky)
map (37° 5′N 88° 45′W) 12:47
McCRAY V. UNITED STATES 13:10–11
MacCREADY, PAUL B.
flight, human-powered 8:164
McCREARY (county in Kentucky)
map (36° 45′N 84° 30′W) 12:47
McCREARY (Manitoba)
map (50° 46′N 99° 30′W) 13:119
McCULLERS, CARSON 13:11 *bibliog.*
McCULLOCH (county in Texas)
map (31° 10′N 99° 20′W) 19:129
McCULLOCH, HUGH 13:11 *bibliog.*
McCULLOCH, WARREN
automata, theory of 2:357
McCULLOCH* v. *MARYLAND 13:11
Marshall, John 13:172
McCULLOUGH MOUNTAIN
map (35° 36′N 115° 11′W) 14:111
McCUNE (Kansas)
map (37° 21′N 95° 1′W) 12:18
McCURTAIN (Oklahoma)
map (35° 9′N 94° 58′W) 14:368
McCURTAIN (county in Oklahoma)
map (34° 10′N 94° 45′W) 14:368
McCUTCHEON, JOHN T. 13:11
McDERMITT (Nevada)
map (41° 59′N 117° 36′W) 14:111
MacDIARMID, HUGH 13:11 *bibliog.*
McDIVITT, JAMES 13:11–12
Apollo program 2:81
Gemini program 9:72
MacDONALD (clan)
Glencoe, Massacre of 9:207
McDONALD (Kansas)
map (39° 47′N 101° 22′W) 12:18
McDONALD (county in Missouri)
map (36° 40′N 94° 20′W) 13:476
MACDONALD, DWIGHT 13:12 *bibliog.*
MacDONALD, J. E. H. 13:12 *bibliog.*
The Solemn Land 4:89 *illus.*; 9:376 *illus.*
MacDONALD, JEANETTE
Eddy, Nelson, and MacDonald, Jeanette 7:55
Lubitsch, Ernst 12:447
MACDONALD, SIR JOHN A. 13:12 *bibliog., illus.*
Canada, history of 4:84
Pacific Scandal 15:8
Whiskey Ring 20:133
MACDONALD, JOHN D. 13:12
MACDONALD, JOHN SANDFIELD 13:12
MacDONALD, RAMSAY 13:12–13 *bibliog., illus.*
Labour party 12:156
poster depicting 9:317 *illus.*; 18:23 *illus.*
MACDONALD, ROSS 13:13 *bibliog., illus.*
McDONALD ISLANDS *see* HEARD ISLAND AND THE McDONALD ISLANDS (Australia)
McDONALD OBSERVATORY 13:13 *bibliog.*
Kuiper, Gerard 12:135
Strömgren, Bengt Georg Daniel 18:302
MACDONALD-WRIGHT, STANTON 13:13 *bibliog.*
synchromism 18:406
McDONNELL-DOUGLAS CORPORATION 1:128 *table*
aviation 2:372
Douglas, Donald Wills 6:247
MACDONNELL RANGES (Australia) 2:330 *illus.*; 13:13
map (23° 45′S 133° 20′E) 2:328
McDONOUGH (Georgia)
map (33° 27′N 84° 9′W) 9:114
McDONOUGH (county in Illinois)
map (40° 27′N 90° 43′W) 11:42
MACDONOUGH, THOMAS 13:14 *bibliog.*
McDOUGALL, WILLIAM (political leader) 13:14
McDOUGALL, WILLIAM (psychologist) 13:14 *bibliog.*
McDOWELL (county in North Carolina)
map (35° 40′N 82° 5′W) 14:242
McDOWELL (county in West Virginia)
map (37° 22′N 81° 40′W) 20:111
MacDOWELL, EDWARD 13:14 *bibliog., illus.*
American music 1:350–351 *illus.*
McDOWELL, EPHRAIM 18:361 *illus.*
McDOWELL, IRVIN 5:20 *illus.*; 13:14 *bibliog.*
Civil War, U.S. 5:23 *map*
MacDOWELL RESERVOIR
map (42° 55′N 72° 0′W) 14:123
McDUFFIE (county in Georgia)
map (33° 30′N 82° 30′W) 9:114
MACE (spice) 13:14–15
nutmeg 14:302
MACE (weapon) 13:14
knight 12:100 *illus.*
riot control weapon 13:14
use, legal controls 13:14
MacEACHEN, ALLAN J. 13:15
MACEDONIA 9:327 *illus.*; 13:15 *bibliog., map*
Balkan Wars 3:38
cities
Salonika 17:36
Skopje 17:344
map (41° 50′N 22° 0′E) 20:340
Slavic languages 17:358
MACEDONIA, KINGDOM OF 13:15 *bibliog.*
Alexander the Great 1:273–275 *map*
Antigonus I Monophthalmus 2:62
Antigonus II Gonatas 2:62
Antigonus III Doson 2:62
Antipater 2:65
armor 2:174
Byzantine art and architecture 3:605
Cassander, King 4:183
cities
Pella 15:138
Demetrius I Poliorcetes, King 6:96–97
Eumenes II, King of Pergamum 7:265
Greece, ancient 9:332–334
Lysimachus, King 12:480
Olympias 14:382
Perdiccas 15:163
Perseus, King 15:180
Philip II, King 15:233
Philip V, King 15:234
Philippi 15:235
Rome, ancient 16:298–300 *illus.*
Seleucids (dynasty) 17:190–191
Seleucus I Nicator, Macedonian King 17:191
MACEIÓ (Brazil)
map (9° 40′S 35° 43′W) 3:460
McENROE, JOHN 13:15–16 *bibliog., illus.*
MACERATA (Italy)
map (43° 18′N 13° 27′E) 11:321
McEWEN (Tennessee)
map (36° 6′N 87° 38′W) 19:104
McEWEN, SIR JOHN 13:16 *bibliog.*
McFADDEN (Wyoming)
map (41° 39′N 106° 8′W) 20:301
McFARLAND (Wisconsin)
map (43° 1′N 89° 17′W) 20:185
McGEE, THOMAS D'ARCY 13:16 *bibliog.*
McGEHEE (Arkansas)
map (33° 38′N 91° 24′W) 2:166
McGILL (Nevada)
map (39° 23′N 114° 47′W) 14:111
McGILL, JAMES 13:16
McGILL UNIVERSITY 13:16
McGill, James 13:16
MACGILLICUDDY'S REEKS
Kerry (Ireland) 12:60
McGILLIVRAY, ALEXANDER 13:16 *bibliog.*
McGINLEY, PHYLLIS 13:16 *bibliog.*
McGOVERN, GEORGE S. 13:16 *bibliog.*
Eagleton, Thomas F. 7:4
presidential elections 15:531
MACGOWAN, KENNETH
Jones, Robert Edmond 11:444
McGRATH (Alaska)
map (62° 58′N 155° 38′W) 1:242
McGRAW, JOHN 13:16 *bibliog.*
McGREGOR (Iowa)
map (43° 1′N 91° 11′W) 11:244
MacGREGOR (Manitoba)
map (49° 57′N 98° 49′W) 13:119
McGREGOR (Texas)
map (31° 26′N 97° 24′W) 19:129
McGREGOR, JOHN
canoe 4:113
MacGREGOR, ROBERT *see* ROB ROY
McGRORY, MARY 13:17
McGUFFEY, WILLIAM HOLMES 13:17 *bibliog.*
primary education 15:537
McGUILLICUDDY, CORNELIUS ALEXANDER *see* MACK, CONNIE
MACH, ERNST 13:17 *bibliog., illus.*
Mach number 13:17
positivism 15:458
scientific philosophy 13:17
MACH NUMBER 13:17
F-15 Eagle 8:3 *illus.*
Mach, Ernst 13:17
sound barrier 18:74
supersonic transport 18:353
X-15 20:311
MÁCHA, KAREL HYNEK 13:17 *bibliog.*
Czech literature 5:412
MACHACHI (Ecuador)
map (0° 30′S 78° 34′W) 7:52
MACHADO, ANTONIO 13:17–18 *bibliog.*
MACHADO DE ASSIS, JOAQUIM MARIA 13:17 *bibliog.*
Brazilian literature 3:464
MACHADO DE CASTRO, JOAQUIM
Portuguese art and architecture 15:456
MACHADO Y MORALES, GERARDO 13:18 *bibliog.*
MACHALA (Ecuador)
map (3° 16′S 79° 58′W) 7:52
MACHAULT, JEAN BAPTISTE DE
Louis XV, King of France 12:427
MACHAUT, GUILLAUME DE 13:18 *bibliog.*
ballade 3:40–41
medieval music 13:275 *illus.*
music, history of Western 13:665
MACHEL, SAMORA
Mozambique 13:628
McHENRY (Illinois)
map (42° 21′N 88° 16′W) 11:42
McHENRY (county in Illinois)
map (42° 19′N 88° 27′W) 11:42
McHENRY (county in North Dakota)
map (48° 10′N 100° 40′W) 14:248
McHENRY, FORT *see* FORT McHENRY (Maryland)
McHENRY, JAMES 13:18
MACHIAS (Maine)
map (44° 43′N 67° 28′W) 13:70
MACHIAS BAY
map (44° 40′N 67° 20′W) 13:70
MACHIAS RIVER
map (44° 43′N 67° 22′W) 13:70
MACHIAVELLI, NICOLÒ 13:18–19 *bibliog., illus.*
Florence (Italy) 8:168
Prince, The 15:547
Renaissance 16:149
state (in political philosophy) 18:231 *illus.*
state (political unit) 18:228
MACHINE 13:19–21 *bibliog., illus.*
See also ELECTRICAL AND ELECTRONIC TECHNOLOGY; ENERGY TECHNOLOGY; ENGINEERING TECHNOLOGY; FARMS AND FARMING; MACHINES AND IMPLEMENTS; names of specific machines, e.g., PERPETUAL MOTION MACHINE; ROBOT; WINDMILL; etc.
business machines 3:589
design
engineering 7:177–178
human factors engineering 10:297
mechanical engineering 13:259–260
earth-moving machinery 7:23–24 *illus.*
machine tools 13:23–25 *illus.*
simple machines 17:316
teaching machines 19:55–56
vending machine 19:538
MACHINE GUN 8:105 *illus.*; 13:21–23 *bibliog., illus.*
aircraft machine guns 13:23
Browning, John Moses 3:518
development 13:21–23
firearms arms 8:106
fully automatic guns 13:23
Garand, John Cantius 9:38
Gatling, Richard Jordan 9:58
Maxim (family) 13:239
World War I 20:247 *illus.*
MACHINE LANGUAGE (computer term) 5:160f, 5:160h
computer languages 5:160o
MACHINE TOOLS 13:23–25 *bibliog., illus.*
Allis, Edward Phelps 1:303
Bramah, Joseph 3:451
comparator 5:155
drilling machine 13:24 *illus.*
grinding machine 13:25 *illus.*
lathe 12:215–216
lubrication 12:447–448
manufacturing 13:132–133
mass production 13:204
Maudslay, Henry 13:232
mill 13:424–425
milling machines 13:23–24 *illus.*
Nasmyth, James 14:24
shaper 13:23 *illus.*
MACHINES, SIMPLE *see* SIMPLE MACHINES
MACHINISTS AND AEROSPACE WORKERS *see* INTERNATIONAL ASSOCIATION OF MACHINISTS AND AEROSPACE WORKERS
MACHU PICCHU (Peru) 2:125 *illus.*; 12:223 *illus.*; 13:25–26 *bibliog., illus.*
map (13° 7′S 72° 34′W) 15:193
pre-Columbian art and architecture 15:501 *illus.*
solar energy 18:43
MACHUCA, PEDRO 13:26 *bibliog.*
McHUGH, JIMMY
Fields, Dorothy 8:73
MACÍAS NGUEMA, FRANCISCO
Equatorial Guinea 7:225–226
MACÍAS NGUEMA BIYOGO *see* BIOKO (Equatorial Guinea)
MAÇINA (region in Mali) 13:26
map (14° 30′N 5° 0′W) 13:89
MacINNES, HELEN 13:26
McINTOSH (county in Georgia)
map (31° 30′N 81° 25′W) 9:114
McINTOSH (county in North Dakota)
map (46° 10′N 99° 25′W) 14:248
McINTOSH (county in Oklahoma)
map (35° 25′N 95° 40′W) 14:368
McINTOSH (South Dakota)
map (45° 55′N 101° 21′W) 18:103
MACINTOSH, CHARLES 13:26
MacIVER, LOREN 13:26 *bibliog.*
MacIVER, ROBERT MORRISON 13:26
MACK, CONNIE 13:26–27 *bibliog.*
MACK, KARL
Napoleonic Wars 14:19
MACKAY (Australia)
map (21° 9′S 149° 11′E) 2:328
MacKAY (family) 13:27 *bibliog.*
MACKAY (Idaho)
map (43° 55′N 113° 37′W) 11:26
McKAY, CLAUDE 13:27 *bibliog.*
McKAY, DONALD 13:27 *bibliog.*
clipper ship 5:60
MacKAYE, STEELE 13:27
Delsarte, François 6:95
MACKE, AUGUST 13:27 *bibliog.*
Blaue Reiter, Der 3:328
McKEAN (county in Pennsylvania)
map (41° 49′N 78° 27′W) 15:147
McKEAN, THOMAS 13:27 *bibliog.*
McKECHNIE, FLORENCE *see* ELDRIDGE, FLORENCE
McKEE (Kentucky)
map (37° 25′N 84° 1′W) 12:47
McKEES ROCKS (Pennsylvania)
map (40° 28′N 80° 10′W) 15:147
McKEESPORT (Pennsylvania)
map (40° 21′N 79° 52′W) 15:147
MACKENSEN, AUGUST VON
WORLD WAR I 20:230; 20:234
MACKENZIE (Guyana)
map (6° 0′N 58° 17′W) 9:410
McKENZIE (county in North Dakota)
map (47° 45′N 103° 25′W) 14:248
McKENZIE (Tennessee)
map (36° 8′N 88° 31′W) 19:104
MACKENZIE, SIR ALEXANDER (1764–1820) 13:27 *bibliog.*
Canada, exploration of 4:80 *map*
exploration 7:335–336 *map*
Mackenzie River 13:29
Peace River 15:123
MACKENZIE, ALEXANDER (1822–92) 13:28 *bibliog., illus.*
Canada, history of 4:84
MCKENZIE, DAN PETER
plate tectonics 15:357
MACKENZIE, SIR WILLIAM 13:28
MACKENZIE, WILLIAM LYON 13:28 *bibliog., illus.*
Canada, history of 4:82
Rebellions of 1837 16:105
MACKENZIE BAY
map (69° 0′N 136° 30′W) 20:345
McKENZIE BRIDGE (Oregon)
map (44° 5′N 123° 4′W) 14:427
MACKENZIE MOUNTAINS
map (64° 0′N 130° 0′W) 20:345

MACKENZIE RIVER 13:28–29 *map*; 14:259 *illus.*
map (69° 15′N 134° 8′W) 14:258
MACKEREL 13:29 *bibliog., illus.*
bonito 3:380
world fishing grounds 8:125 *map*
McKIM, CHARLES FOLLEN *see* McKIM, MEAD, AND WHITE
McKIM, JAMES
slavery 17:357 *illus.*
McKIM, MEAD, AND WHITE 13:29 *bibliog.*
American art and architecture 1:330
Carrère and Hastings 4:168
White, Stanford 20:136
MACKINAC (county in Michigan)
map (46° 10′N 85° 20′W) 13:377
MACKINAC, STRAITS OF 13:29; 13:379 *illus.*
MACKINAC BRIDGE 13:379 *illus.*
MACKINAC ISLAND (Michigan) 13:379 *illus.*
Mackinac, Straits of 13:29
map (45° 51′N 84° 37′W) 13:377
MACKINAW (Illinois)
map (40° 32′N 89° 21′W) 11:42
MACKINAW CITY (Michigan)
map (45° 47′N 84° 44′W) 13:377
MACKINDER, SIR HALFORD JOHN 13:29 *bibliog.*
geopolitics 9:109
Kenya, Mount 12:56
McKINLEY (county in New Mexico)
map (35° 40′N 108° 15′W) 14:136
McKINLEY, MOUNT 13:30; 13:620 *illus.*
map (63° 30′N 151° 0′W) 1:242
national parks 14:38–39 *map, table*
McKINLEY, WILLIAM 13:30–31 *bibliog., illus.*
Hanna, Mark 10:38
presidential elections cartoon 15:530 *illus.*; 19:569 *illus.*
Republican party 16:174 *illus.*
Spanish-American War 18:149–150
McKINLEY TARIFF *see* TARIFF ACTS
McKINLEYVILLE (California)
map (40° 57′N 124° 6′W) 4:31
McKINNEY (Texas)
map (33° 12′N 96° 37′W) 19:129
MACKINTOSH, CHARLES RENNIE 13:31 *bibliog., illus.*
Art Deco 2:207
Glasgow School of Art 13:31 *illus.*
Secession movement 17:178
stained-glass doors 2:211 *illus.*
MACKINTOSH, ELIZABETH *see* TEY, JOSEPHINE
McKISSICK, FLOYD B.
Congress of Racial Equality 5:184
MACKLIN (Saskatchewan)
map (52° 20′N 109° 56′W) 17:81
MACKSVILLE (Kansas)
map (37° 58′N 98° 58′W) 12:18
MacLAINE, SHIRLEY 13:31
McLAREN, NORMAN 13:31–32 *illus.*
animation 2:29
Blinkety Blank 13:32 *illus.*
McLAUGHLIN PLANETARIUM
Royal Ontario Museum 16:330
McLAURIN (Mississippi)
map (31° 10′N 89° 13′W) 13:469
MACLAURIN, COLIN 13:32
Taylor series 19:51
McLEAN (Illinois)
map (40° 19′N 89° 10′W) 11:42
McLEAN (county in Illinois)
map (40° 40′N 88° 50′W) 11:42
McLEAN (county in Kentucky)
map (37° 30′N 87° 15′W) 12:47
McLEAN (county in North Dakota)
map (47° 40′N 101° 10′W) 14:248
McLEAN (Texas)
map (35° 14′N 100° 36′W) 19:129
MACLEAN, DONALD
intelligence gathering 11:205
Philby, H. St. John 15:231
MACLEAN'S (periodical) 13:32
McLEANSBORO (Illinois)
map (38° 6′N 88° 32′W) 11:42
MacLEISH, ARCHIBALD 13:32 *bibliog.*
Library of Congress 12:319
McLENNAN (county in Texas)
map (31° 35′N 97° 13′W) 19:129
MacLENNAN, HUGH 13:32 *bibliog., illus.*
Canadian literature 4:93–94 *illus.*
McLEOD (county in Minnesota)
map (44° 50′N 94° 15′W) 13:453
McLEOD, ANNE 14:297 *illus.*
MacLEOD, COLIN M. 13:32
McCarty, Maclyn 13:9
nucleic acid 14:289
MacLEOD, FIONA (pseudonym) *see* SHARP, WILLIAM
MacLEOD, JOHN JAMES RICKARD 13:33
MACLEOD, LAKE
map (24° 0′S 113° 35′E) 2:328
McLEOD LAKE (British Columbia)
map (54° 59′N 123° 2′W) 3:491
McLEVY, JASPER
Bridgeport 3:484
McLOUGHLIN, JOHN 13:33 *bibliog.*
McLOUGHLIN, MOUNT
map (42° 27′N 122° 19′W) 14:427
McLUHAN, MARSHALL 13:33 *bibliog.*
McLURE (British Columbia)
map (51° 3′N 120° 14′W) 3:491
MacMAHON, MARIE EDME PATRICE MAURICE DE 13:33 *bibliog.*
Simon, Jules François 17:315
McMAHON, WILLIAM 13:33 *bibliog.*
McMANUS, GEORGE
comic strip 5:136
McMANUS, LOUIS
Emmy Awards 7:157
McMASTER, JOHN BACH 13:33 *bibliog.*
McMASTER UNIVERSITY 13:33
MacMILLAN, DONALD BAXTER 13:33 *bibliog.*
McMILLAN, EDWIN
Seaborg, Glenn T. 17:171
MACMILLAN, HAROLD 13:34 *bibliog., illus.*
Profumo scandal 15:562
MacMILLAN, KENNETH 13:34 *bibliog.*
Royal Ballet, The 16:329
MacMILLAN, KIRKPATRICK
bicycle 3:244 *illus.*
McMILLAN LAKE
map (32° 40′N 104° 20′W) 14:136
McMINN (county in Tennessee)
map (35° 25′N 84° 40′W) 19:104
McMINNVILLE (Oregon)
map (45° 13′N 123° 12′W) 14:427
McMINNVILLE (Tennessee)
map (35° 41′N 85° 46′W) 19:104
MacMONNIES, FREDERICK WILLIAM 13:34 *bibliog.*
McMULLEN (county in Texas)
map (28° 20′N 98° 38′W) 19:129
McMURDO SOUND
map (77° 30′S 165° 0′E) 2:40
McMURTRY, LARRY 13:34–35 *bibliog.*
MacNAB, SIR ALLAN NAPIER 13:35 *bibliog.*
M'NAGHTEN RULE
crime 5:345
insanity, legal 11:185
McNAIR, RONALD E. 13:35
McNAIRY (county in Tennessee)
map (35° 10′N 88° 35′W) 19:104
McNAMARA, ROBERT S. 13:35 *bibliog.*; 15:526 *illus.*
McNARY (Arizona)
map (34° 4′N 109° 51′W) 2:160
McNARY-HAUGEN BILL
Coolidge, Calvin 5:241
McNAUGHTON, ANDREW GEORGE LATTA 13:35 *bibliog.*
MacNEICE, LOUIS 13:35 *bibliog.*
Spender, Stephen 18:177–178
McNEIL ISLAND
map (47° 13′N 122° 41′E) 20:35
McNEILL (Mississippi)
map (30° 40′N 89° 38′W) 13:469
MACNEISH, RICHARD S. 13:35
McNICKLE, D'ARCY 13:35
MACOMB (Illinois)
map (40° 27′N 90° 40′W) 11:42
MACOMB (county in Michigan)
map (42° 40′N 82° 54′W) 13:377
MACON (airship)
airship 1:228
Akron and *Macon* 1:232
MACON (county in Alabama)
map (32° 20′N 85° 40′W) 1:234
MACON (Georgia) 13:35
map (32° 50′N 83° 38′W) 9:114
MACON (county in Georgia)
map (32° 20′N 84° 0′W) 9:114
MACON (county in Illinois)
map (39° 51′N 89° 32′W) 11:42
MACON (Mississippi)
map (33° 7′N 88° 34′W) 13:469
MACON (Missouri)
map (39° 44′N 92° 28′W) 13:476
MACON (county in Missouri)
map (39° 48′N 92° 35′W) 13:476
MACON (county in North Carolina)
map (35° 10′N 83° 25′W) 14:242
MACON (county in Tennessee)
map (36° 30′N 86° 0′W) 19:104
MACON, DAVE
Grand Ole Opry 9:285
MACON, NATHANIEL 13:35 *bibliog.*
MACONCHY, ELIZABETH 13:35–36 *bibliog.*
MACON'S BILL NO. 2
Macon, Nathaniel 13:35
MACOUPIN (county in Illinois)
map (39° 17′N 89° 53′W) 11:42
MacPHAIL, AGNES CAMPBELL 13:36
McPHATTER, CLYDE
soul music 18:71
McPHEE, JOHN 13:36
McPHERSON (Kansas)
map (38° 22′N 97° 40′W) 12:18
McPHERSON (county in Kansas)
map (38° 25′N 97° 40′W) 12:18
McPHERSON (county in Nebraska)
map (41° 35′N 101° 0′W) 14:70
McPHERSON (county in South Dakota)
map (45° 45′N 99° 15′W) 18:103
McPHERSON, AIMEE SEMPLE 13:36 *bibliog., illus.*
MACPHERSON, JAMES 13:36 *bibliog.*
literary fraud 12:370
Ossian 14:456
MACQUARIE RIDGE
plate tectonics 15:351 *map*
MACQUARIE RIVER
map (30° 7′S 147° 24′E) 2:328
McRAE (Arkansas)
map (35° 7′N 91° 49′W) 2:166
McRAE (Georgia)
map (32° 4′N 82° 53′W) 9:114
MACRAME 5:327 *illus.*; 13:36 *bibliog.*
MACREADY, WILLIAM CHARLES 13:36 *bibliog.*
Astor Place Riot 2:269
McROBERTS (Kentucky)
map (37° 12′N 82° 40′W) 12:47
MACROBIOTA
soil organisms 18:39 *illus.*
MACROCHEIR *see* ARTAXERXES I, KING OF PERSIA
MACROECONOMICS
economics 7:47–49
monetary theory 13:524
MACROLIDES
antibiotics 2:57; 2:59
MACROMOLECULE 13:36–37 *bibliog.*
isoelectric point 11:299
molecular weight 13:37
Staudinger, Hermann 18:239
osmosis 14:455
purification and study techniques 13:37
MACRONUCLEUS *see* NUCLEUS
MACROPHAGE (biology) *see* PHAGOCYTOSIS
McSHERRYSTOWN (Pennsylvania)
map (39° 48′N 77° 2′W) 15:147
McTAVISH, SIMON
North West Company 14:252
McTEAGUE (book)
Norris, Frank 14:222–223
McVEIGH (Kentucky)
map (37° 32′N 82° 15′W) 12:47
McVILLE (North Dakota)
map (47° 46′N 98° 11′W) 14:248
McWILLIAMS (Alabama)
map (31° 50′N 87° 6′W) 1:234
MACY'S (department store) 6:118
MAD (periodical) 13:37
MAD ANTHONY WAYNE *see* WAYNE, ANTHONY
MAD-DOG WEED *see* WATER PLANTAIN
MADABA (Jordan)
map (31° 43′N 35° 48′E) 11:447
MADÁCH, IMRE 13:37
MADAGASCAN GIRDLED LIZARD *see* GERRHOSAURID
MADAGASCAR 13:37–39 *bibliog., illus., map, table*
African art 1:163–164
animal life
false sunbird 8:15
fossa 8:243
lemur 12:281
cities
Antananarivo 2:39
climate 13:37; 13:39 *table*
economic activity 13:38–39
flag 13:37 *illus.*
history and government 13:39
land and resources 13:37–39 *illus., map, table*
language
Malayo-Polynesian languages 13:83
map (19° 0′S 46° 0′E) 1:136
people 13:37–38
MADAGASCAR HEDGEHOG *see* TENREC
MADAMA BUTTERFLY (opera) 13:39 *bibliog.*
MADAME BOVARY (book) 13:39 *bibliog.*; 14:274 *illus.*
Flaubert, Gustave 8:156–157
MADANG (Papua New Guinea)
map (5° 15′S 145° 50′E) 15:72
MADARIPUR (Bangladesh)
map (23° 10′N 90° 12′E) 3:64
MADAWASKA (Maine)
map (47° 21′N 68° 20′W) 13:70
MADAWASKA RIVER
map (45° 27′N 76° 21′W) 14:393; 14:461
MADDEN LAKE
map (9° 15′N 79° 35′W) 15:56
MADDER (botany) 13:39
bedstraw 3:154
buttonbush 3:600
Cape jasmine 4:120
woodruff 20:212
MADDER (dye)
glycoside 9:212
MADDOCK (North Dakota)
map (47° 58′N 99° 32′W) 14:248
MADDOX, LESTER G. 13:39 *bibliog.*
MADDOX, RICHARD LEACH 13:39–40
MADEIRA ISLANDS 13:40 *map*
cities
Funchal 8:359
map (32° 40′N 16° 45′W) 15:449
wine 20:176
MADEIRA RIVER 13:40
map (3° 22′S 58° 45′W) 1:323
MADELEGABEL MOUNTAIN
map (47° 18′N 10° 18′E) 2:348
MADELIA (Minnesota)
map (44° 3′N 94° 25′W) 13:453
MADEMOISELLE *see* MONTPENSIER, ANNE MARIE LOUISE D'ORLÉANS, DUCHESSE DE
MADEMOISELLE O'MURPHY (*Nude Lying on a Sofa*)
Boucher, François 3:419–420 *illus.*
MADERA (California)
map (36° 57′N 120° 3′W) 4:31
MADERA (county in California)
map (37° 15′N 119° 45′W) 4:31
MADERA (Mexico)
map (29° 12′N 108° 7′W) 13:357
MADERNA, BRUNO 13:40 *bibliog.*
MADERNO, CARLO 13:40 *bibliog.*
Saint Peter's Basilica 17:25
MADERNO, STEFANO 13:40 *bibliog.*
MADERO, FRANCISCO I. 13:40–41 *bibliog., illus.*
Díaz, Porfirio 6:154
Mexico, history of 13:365
San Luis Potosí (city in Mexico) 17:56
Villa, Pancho 19:596
Zapata, Emiliano 20:355–356
MADERSPERGER, JOSEPH
sewing machine 17:223
MADETOJA, LEEVI
Finland 8:96
MADHVA 13:41
MADHYA PRADESH (India) 13:41
cities
Bhopal 3:234
Indore 11:150
Khajuraho 12:65
map (23° 0′N 79° 0′E) 11:80
MADILL (Oklahoma)
map (34° 6′N 96° 46′W) 14:368
MADINAH, AL- (Saudi Arabia) *see* MEDINA (Saudi Arabia)
MADINAT AL-SHAB
map (12° 50′N 44° 56′E) 20:324
MADINAT ISA (Bahrain)
map (26° 10′N 50° 33′E) 3:24
MADISON (Alabama)
map (34° 42′N 86° 45′W) 1:234
MADISON (county in Alabama)
map (34° 45′N 86° 30′W) 1:234
MADISON (county in Arkansas)
map (36° 5′N 93° 45′W) 2:166
MADISON (Florida)
map (30° 28′N 83° 25′W) 8:172
MADISON (county in Florida)
map (30° 30′N 83° 30′W) 8:172
MADISON (Georgia)
map (33° 36′N 83° 28′W) 9:114
MADISON (county in Georgia)
map (34° 10′N 83° 15′W) 9:114
MADISON (county in Idaho)
map (43° 45′N 111° 40′W) 11:26
MADISON (county in Illinois)
map (38° 49′N 89° 58′W) 11:42
MADISON (Indiana) 11:112 *illus.*
map (38° 44′N 85° 23′W) 11:111
MADISON (county in Indiana)
map (40° 7′N 85° 43′W) 11:111
MADISON (county in Iowa)
map (41° 17′N 94° 0′W) 11:244
MADISON (Kansas)
map (38° 8′N 96° 8′W) 12:18
MADISON (county in Kentucky)
map (37° 45′N 84° 15′W) 12:47

MADISON (county in Louisiana)
map (32° 22′N 91° 15′W) **12**:430
MADISON (Maine)
map (44° 48′N 69° 53′W) **13**:70
MADISON (Minnesota)
map (45° 1′N 96° 11′W) **13**:453
MADISON (county in Mississippi)
map (32° 40′N 90° 0′W) **13**:469
MADISON (county in Missouri)
map (37° 30′N 90° 20′W) **13**:476
MADISON (county in Montana)
map (45° 20′N 111° 55′W) **13**:547
MADISON (Nebraska)
map (41° 50′N 97° 27′W) **14**:70
MADISON (county in Nebraska)
map (41° 55′N 97° 35′W) **14**:70
MADISON (New Jersey)
map (40° 46′N 74° 25′W) **14**:129
MADISON (county in New York)
map (43° 5′N 75° 42′W) **14**:149
MADISON (North Carolina)
map (36° 23′N 79° 58′W) **14**:242
MADISON (county in North Carolina)
map (35° 55′N 82° 40′W) **14**:242
MADISON (county in Ohio)
map (39° 53′N 83° 27′W) **14**:357
MADISON (South Dakota)
map (44° 0′N 97° 7′W) **18**:103
MADISON (county in Tennessee)
map (35° 35′N 88° 50′W) **19**:104
MADISON (county in Texas)
map (30° 58′N 95° 55′W) **19**:129
MADISON (Virginia)
map (38° 23′N 78° 15′W) **19**:607
MADISON (county in Virginia)
map (38° 25′N 78° 15′W) **19**:607
MADISON (West Virginia)
map (38° 4′N 81° 49′W) **20**:111
MADISON (Wisconsin) **13**:41
map (43° 5′N 89° 22′W) **20**:185
MADISON, DOLLEY **13**:41 *bibliog.*
MADISON, JAMES **13**:41–43 *bibliog., illus.*
Bill of Rights **3**:252–253
Constitution of the United States **5**:213–214
Kentucky and Virginia Resolutions **12**:52
Madison, Dolley **13**:41
Marbury v. *Madison* **13**:144
Monroe, James **13**:541–542
Virginia **19**:611
MADISON HEIGHTS (Virginia)
map (37° 25′N 79° 8′W) **19**:607
MADISON RANGE
map (45° 15′N 111° 20′W) **13**:547
MADISON RIVER
map (45° 56′N 111° 30′W) **20**:301
MADISON SQUARE GARDEN (New York City)
basketball **3**:111–112 *illus.*
MADISON SQUARE THEATER
Belasco, David **3**:174
MADISONVILLE (Kentucky)
map (37° 20′N 87° 30′W) **12**:47
MADISONVILLE (Louisiana)
map (30° 24′N 90° 9′W) **12**:430
MADISONVILLE (Tennessee)
map (35° 31′N 84° 22′W) **19**:104
MADISONVILLE (Texas)
map (30° 57′N 95° 55′W) **19**:129
MADIUN (Indonesia)
map (7° 37′S 111° 31′E) **11**:147
MADONNA DELLA CARCERI (Prato)
cathedrals and churches **4**:206
MADRAS (city in India) **13**:43
climate **11**:82 *table*
map (13° 4′N 80° 16′E) **11**:80
MADRAS (Oregon)
map (44° 38′N 121° 8′W) **14**:427
MADRAS (state in India) *see* TAMIL NADU (India)
MADRAS (textile) **13**:43
MADRASAH
Turks **19**:347–348
MADRE DE DIOS RIVER
map (10° 59′S 66° 8′W) **3**:366
MADRE LAGOON
map (25° 0′N 97° 40′W) **13**:357
MADRID (Alabama)
map (31° 1′N 85° 24′W) **1**:234
MADRID (Iowa)
map (41° 53′N 93° 49′W) **11**:244
MADRID (Nebraska)
map (40° 51′N 101° 33′W) **14**:70
MADRID (Spain) **13**:43–45 *bibliog., illus., map*; **18**:142 *illus.*
climate **18**:141 *table*
history **13**:44–45
map (40° 24′N 3° 41′W) **18**:140
Prado **15**:487
subway **18**:318 *table*
MADRID HURTADO, MIGUEL DE LA *see* DE LA MADRID HURTADO, MIGUEL
MADRIGAL **13**:45 *bibliog.*
baroque music **3**:91–92
Byrd, William **3**:602
collections and editions
Morley, Thomas **13**:581
Deller, Alfred **6**:94
English music **7**:203
Gesualdo, Carlo **9**:160
Gibbons, Orlando **9**:173
Italian music **11**:317
Marenzio, Luca **13**:148
Monteverdi, Claudio **13**:554
music, history of Western **13**:663 *illus.*
Renaissance music **16**:156
Weelkes, Thomas **20**:90
Wilbye, John **20**:148
MADRONE TREE
arbutus **2**:111–112 *illus.*
MADSEN, EGON **13**:45
MADURA ISLAND
map (7° 0′S 113° 20′E) **11**:147
MADURAI (India)
map (9° 56′N 78° 7′E) **11**:80
MADWOMAN OF CHAILLOT, THE (play)
Giraudoux, Jean **9**:189
MAEBASHI (Japan)
map (36° 23′N 139° 4′E) **11**:361
MAECENAS, GAIUS **13**:45
Horace **10**:233–234
Vergil **19**:551
MAELSTROM *see* WHIRLPOOL
MAELZEL, JOHANN
metronome **13**:347
MAENADS **13**:45
MAES, NICOLAES **13**:45 *bibliog.*
MAES RIVER *see* MEUSE RIVER
MAESA, JULIA
Heliogabalus, Roman Emperor **10**:112
MAETERLINCK, MAURICE **3**:175 *illus.*; **13**:45–46 *bibliog., illus.*
MAFALDE **15**:106 *illus.*
MAFEKING (Manitoba)
map (52° 41′N 101° 6′W) **13**:119
MAFEKING (South Africa) **13**:46 *bibliog.*
map (25° 53′S 25° 39′E) **18**:79
MAFIA **13**:46 *bibliog.*
secret societies **17**:181
Sicily (Italy) **17**:293
syndicate **18**:407
MAFIA ISLAND
map (7° 50′S 39° 50′E) **19**:27
MAFINGA HILLS
map (10° 0′S 33° 30′E) **20**:354
MAGADAN (USSR)
map (59° 34′N 150° 48′E) **19**:388
MAGADI, LAKE
map (1° 52′S 36° 17′E) **12**:53
MAGAN
Dilmun **6**:176
MAGANGUE (Colombia)
map (9° 14′N 74° 45′W) **5**:107
MAGAZINE *see* PERIODICAL; PULP MAGAZINES; names of specific magazines, e.g., *FOREIGN AFFAIRS* (journal); *HARPER'S* (periodical); *LOOK* (periodical); etc.
MAGAZINE MOUNTAIN
map (35° 10′N 93° 38′W) **2**:166
MAGDALEN COLLEGE (Oxford University) **14**:474
MAGDALEN ISLANDS **13**:46
MAGDALENA (Bolivia)
map (13° 20′S 64° 8′W) **3**:366
MAGDALENA (New Mexico)
map (34° 7′N 107° 14′W) **14**:136
MAGDALENA RIVER **13**:46
map (11° 6′N 74° 51′W) **5**:107
MAGDALENE COLLEGE (Cambridge University) **4**:53
MAGDALENIAN **13**:46 *bibliog.*
Font de Gaume **8**:205
Hamburgian **10**:27
Lascaux **12**:210
Les Combarelles **12**:296
Niaux Cave **14**:177
Perigordian **15**:166
prehistoric art **15**:507 *illus.*
Trois Frères, Les **19**:305
MAGDEBURG (East Germany) **13**:46–47
map (52° 7′N 11° 38′E) **9**:140
MAGDELENA (Mexico)
map (20° 55′N 103° 57′W) **13**:357
MAGEE (Mississippi)
map (31° 52′N 89° 44′W) **13**:469
MAGEE, AUGUSTUS
Texas **19**:133
MAGELANG (Indonesia)
map (7° 28′S 110° 13′E) **11**:147
MAGELLAN, FERDINAND **13**:47–48 *bibliog., illus., map*
exploration **7**:335–337 *map*
Guam (U.S.) **9**:385
Magellan, Strait of **13**:48
Mariana Islands (U.S.) **13**:151
Moluccas (Indonesia) **13**:514
Philippines **15**:238
route of **13**:47 *map*
Saipan (Mariana Islands) **17**:28
Tierra del Fuego **19**:196
MAGELLAN, STRAIT OF **13**:48
map (54° 0′S 71° 0′W) **4**:355
MAGELLANIC CLOUDS (astronomy) **13**:48–49 *bibliog., illus.*
Cepheids **4**:257
Galaxy, The **9**:11
Local Group of galaxies **12**:385
supergiant **18**:351
MAGEN DAVID *see* STAR OF DAVID
MAGENDIE, FRANÇOIS
pharmacology **15**:220
MAGETAN (Indonesia)
map (7° 39′S 111° 20′E) **11**:147
MAGGIE: A GIRL OF THE STREETS (book)
Crane, Stephen **5**:330
MAGGIORE, LAKE **13**:49
MAGGOT
myiasis **13**:690
MAGHAGHA (Egypt)
map (28° 39′N 30° 50′E) **7**:76
MAGHREB *see* MAGHRIB
MAGHREE
North Africa **14**:224
MAGHRIB **13**:49
MAGI **13**:49
Epiphany **7**:220
MAGIC (primitive religion) **13**:49–50 *bibliog., illus.*
cannibalism **4**:109
dance **6**:21–22 *illus.*
fertility rites **8**:60
Frazer, Sir James **8**:289
Golden Bough, The **9**:231
herbs and spices **10**:137
mistletoe **13**:481–482
shaman **17**:238 *illus.*
superstition **18**:353
witchcraft **20**:191–192
MAGIC ACTS **13**:50–51
Houdini, Harry **10**:263 *illus.*
Scarne, John **17**:116
MAGIC FLUTE, THE (opera) **13**:51 *bibliog.*
Metropolitan Opera **13**:348 *illus.*
MAGIC MOUNTAIN, THE (book) **13**:51 *bibliog.*
Mann, Thomas **13**:123–124
MAGIC REALISM **13**:51 *bibliog.*
Albright, Ivan Le Lorraine **1**:261
Blume, Peter **3**:347
Evergood, Philip **7**:316
Tooker, George **19**:238
MAGIC RESERVOIR
map (43° 17′N 114° 23′W) **11**:26
MAGIC SQUARE **13**:51 *bibliog., illus.*
Latin square **13**:51
MAGINOT, ANDRÉ *see* MAGINOT LINE (France)
MAGINOT LINE (France) **13**:51 *bibliog.*
fortification **8**:240
World War II **20**:252–253 *map*
MAGLEMOSIAN *see* MESOLITHIC PERIOD
MAGLOIRE, PAUL E.
Duvalier, François **6**:316
MAGMA **13**:52 *bibliog., illus.*
basalt **3**:101
chemistry **13**:52
composition **13**:52 *illus.*
Earth, geological history of **7**:11
formation **13**:51–52
geothermal energy **9**:120
granite **9**:287
igneous rock **11**:33–36
lamprophyre **12**:176
petrography **15**:206–207
petrology **15**:215
phenocryst **15**:225
plate tectonics **15**:354–355
rock **16**:247
seafloor spreading **17**:172
silicate compounds **13**:52 *illus.*
volcano **19**:626–628
MAGNA (Utah)
map (40° 42′N 112° 6′W) **19**:492
MAGNA CARTA **13**:52–53 *bibliog.*
due process **6**:292
Great Britain, history of **9**:311
John, King of England **11**:426–427 *illus.*
Langton, Stephen **12**:196
law, history of **12**:245
MAGNASCO, ALESSANDRO **13**:53 *bibliog.*
MAGNESIA (Turkey) **13**:53 *bibliog.*
MAGNESIA ALBA
laxative
magnesium **13**:54
MAGNESITE **13**:53
refractory materials **16**:124
MAGNESIUM **13**:53–54 *bibliog., illus.*
abundances of common elements **7**:131 *table*
alkaline earth metals **1**:295
biological significance **13**:54
carbonate minerals **4**:137
compounds **13**:54
corrosion prevention **13**:53
dolomite **6**:226
element **7**:130 *table*
Grignard reagents **9**:363–364
Group IIA periodic table **15**:167
metal, metallic element **13**:328
occurrence **13**:53
olivine **14**:379–380
production **13**:53–54 *illus.*
pyroxene **15**:638
silicate minerals **17**:304–305
talc **19**:15
uranium minerals **19**:478
vitamins and minerals **19**:621
Recommended Daily Allowances **19**:619 *table*
MAGNESIUM CARBONATE **13**:54
antacid **2**:38
MAGNESIUM SULFATE *see* EPSOM SALTS
MAGNET **13**:54–55 *bibliog., illus.*
MAGNETIC BOTTLE **13**:55 *bibliog.*
fusion energy **8**:382
MAGNETIC COMPASS **5**:155–156 *illus.*
MAGNETIC DISK
camera **4**:59
computer **5**:160b; **5**:160e; **5**:160f
computer memory **5**:161
information storage and retrieval **11**:173
MAGNETIC DRUM
information storage and retrieval **11**:173
MAGNETIC FLUX (unit of measurement) **19**:467
MAGNETIC MOMENT **13**:55
dipole moment **13**:55
electric current flow **13**:55
electron
Bohr magnetron **3**:362; **13**:55
Kusch, Polykarp **12**:139
Lamb, Willis Eugene, Jr. **12**:174
neutron
Bloch, Felix **3**:334
proton
Stern, Otto **18**:260
Rabi, Isidor Isaac **16**:32
MAGNETIC MONOPOLE *see* MONOPOLE, MAGNETIC
MAGNETIC POLE *see* EARTH, GEOMAGNETIC FIELD OF
MAGNETIC RECORDING
information storage and retrieval **11**:173
tape recorder **19**:30 *illus.*
video recording **19**:577 *illus.*
MAGNETIC STAR **13**:55 *bibliog.*
MAGNETIC STORM **13**:55 *bibliog.*
Earth, geomagnetic field of **7**:16–17
electric current disturbances **13**:55
phases **13**:55
radio-communication and navigational problems **13**:55
Van Allen radiation belts **19**:510
MAGNETIC TAPE
See also MAGNETIC RECORDING
computer **5**:160b; **5**:160e–160f
computer memory **5**:161
information storage and retrieval **11**:173
sound recording and reproduction **18**:74–75 *illus.*
MAGNETISM **13**:55–58 *bibliog., illus.*
Ampère, André Marie **1**:377
Anderson, Philip Warren **1**:402
antiferromagnetism **13**:57
Bullard, Sir Edward **3**:559
cobalt **5**:82
compass, navigational **5**:155–156
Coulomb, Charles Augustin de **5**:308
Curie temperature **5**:392
diamagnetism **13**:57–58
Oersted, Hans Christian **14**:352
Earth, geomagnetic field of **7**:15–17
electricity **7**:109
electromagnet **7**:115
electromagnetic units **7**:118–119
electromagnetism
Cherenkov radiation **4**:331

dipole 6:186
electromagnetic induction 7:115–116
electroweak theory 7:128
fundamental interactions 8:361
fundamental particles 8:362
Gilbert, William (physician) 9:179
grand unification theories 9:286
Lenz's law 12:287
magnetohydrodynamics 13:58–59
permeability, magnetic 13:55–58
railgun 16:70–71
solid-state physics 18:55
electronic structure
Mott, Nevill 13:616
electrostatics 7:128
Faraday, Michael 8:21–22
Fermi-Dirac principle
solid-state physics 18:55
ferrimagnetism 13:57
ferrite 8:59
ferromagnetism 13:56–57 illus.
antiferromagnetism 13:57
solid-state physics 18:55
Fitzgerald, George Francis 8:131
generator 9:78
history 13:56
hysteresis 10:352
inclinometer 11:74
iron 11:270
Landau, Lev 12:181
Laplace, Pierre Simon de 12:205
loudspeaker 12:421
magnet 13:54–55 illus.
function 13:54 illus.
types 13:54
zirconium 20:370
magnetic materials, applications 13:58
magnetic moment 13:55
Maxwell, James Clerk 13:241
Maxwell's equations 13:241–242
measurement 13:255–256
magnetometer 13:59
Mesmer, Franz Anton 13:314
metal 13:329
Néel, Louis Eugène Félix 14:76
oxide minerals 14:476
paleomagnetism 15:41–42
paramagnetism 13:57
parity (physics) 15:89
physics 15:281
physics, history of 15:283–284
plasma physics 15:346
solenoid 18:53
superconductivity 18:350
terbium 19:115
time reversal invariance 19:202
unified field theory 19:385–386
Van Vleck, J. H. 19:516
Weber, Wilhelm Eduard 20:88
MAGNETITE 13:58
emery 7:155
igneous rock 11:36
magnet 13:54–55
magnetism 13:56–57
major ore deposits 14:424–425 table
occurrence 13:58
oxide minerals 14:476
MAGNETOHYDRODYNAMICS 13:58–59 bibliog., illus.
development 13:58–59
plasma physics 15:346
power, generation and transmission of 15:483
power generators 13:59
Sun 18:342
MAGNETOMETER 13:59
archaeology 2:119
IMP 11:60
MAGNETOSPHERE 13:59–60 bibliog., illus.
divisions 13:59–60
Earth, geomagnetic field of 7:16–17
Elsasser, Walter 7:150
formation, theory 13:60
geophysics 9:108
IMP 11:60
magnetic storm 13:55
OGO 14:355
Van Allen radiation belts 19:510
MAGNETRON 13:60 bibliog.
Bohr magnetron 3:362
electron tube 7:123–124
radar 16:39
MAGNIFICAT 13:60 bibliog.
cantus firmus 4:118
MAGNITOGORSK (USSR) 13:60; 19:393 illus., illus.
map (53° 27′N 59° 4′E) 19:388
MAGNITUDE (astronomy) 13:60–61 bibliog.
Hyades 10:327
star 18:221
distance, astronomical 6:199
Hertzsprung-Russell diagram 10:149
Payne-Gaposchkin, Cecilia 15:122
Pickering, Edward Charles 15:293
MAGNOLIA 13:61 illus.; 15:337 illus.
Tertiary Period 19:124 illus.
tulip tree 19:330
MAGNOLIA (Arkansas)
map (33° 16′N 93° 14′W) 2:166
MAGNOLIA (Minnesota)
map (43° 39′N 96° 5′W) 13:453
MAGNOLIA (Mississippi)
map (31° 9′N 90° 28′W) 13:469
MAGNUM (photograph news agency)
Capa, Robert 4:119
Cartier-Bresson, Henri 4:175
photojournalism 15:273
MAGNUS VI, KING OF NORWAY (Magnus the Law-Mender) 13:61
MAGNUS VII, KING OF NORWAY (Magnus Eriksson) 13:61
Scandinavia, history of 17:108
MAGNÚSSON, ÁRNI 13:61 bibliog.
MAGOFFIN (county in Kentucky)
map (37° 40′N 83° 5′W) 12:47
MAGOG (Quebec)
map (45° 16′N 72° 9′W) 16:18
MAGPIE 13:61–62 illus.
bell magpie 3:186
MAGPIE LARK see AUSTRALIAN MUDNEST BUILDER
MAGPIE ROBIN 13:62
MAGRATH (Alberta)
map (49° 25′N 112° 52′W) 1:256
MAGRITTE, RENÉ 13:62 bibliog., illus.
The Human Condition I 18:365 illus.
The Red Model 13:62 illus.
surrealism (art) 18:364
MAGSAYSAY, RAMÓN 13:62 bibliog.
Quirino, Elpidio 16:28
MAGWE (Burma)
map (20° 9′N 94° 55′E) 3:573
MAGYARS 13:62–63 bibliog.
Henry I, King of Germany 10:128
Hungary 10:309
Szeklers 18:416
MAH-JONGG 13:63 bibliog., illus.
MAHABALIPURAM (India) 13:63–64 bibliog., illus.
temple 13:63 illus.
MAHABHARAT RANGE
map (27° 40′N 84° 30′E) 14:86
MAHABHARATA, THE (poem) 13:64 bibliog.
Bhagavad Gita 3:233
Hinduism 10:173
puppet 15:627 illus.
MAHAICONY (Guyana)
map (6° 36′N 57° 48′W) 9:410
MAHAKAM RIVER
map (0° 35′S 117° 17′W) 11:147
MAHAN, ALFRED THAYER 13:64 bibliog.
Luce, Stephen B. 12:450
navy 14:63–64
MAHANOY CITY (Pennsylvania)
map (40° 49′N 76° 8′W) 15:147
MAHARAJAH see RAJAH
MAHARASHTRA (India) 13:64
cities
Bombay 3:374–375 map
Nagpur 14:6
Poona 15:429
map (19° 0′N 76° 0′E) 11:80
people
Maratha 13:143
temple
Elephanta 7:134
Ellora 7:148
MAHASKA (county in Iowa)
map (41° 17′N 92° 35′W) 11:244
MAHAVIRA see JAINISM
MAHAWELI RIVER
map (8° 27′N 81° 13′E) 18:206
MAHAYANA
Buddhism 3:539–543
philosophy 15:247
MAHDI 13:64 bibliog.
Africa, history of 1:156
Omdurman (Sudan) 14:387
Sudan 18:322
MAHÉ (island)
Seychelles 17:232 map
MAHÉBOURG (Mauritius)
map (20° 24′S 57° 42′E) 13:237
MAHENDRA, KING
Nepal 14:88
MAHFUZ, NAJIB 13:64
Egypt 7:77
MAHI-MAHI see DORADO
MAHICAN (American Indians) 13:64–65 bibliog.
Narragansett 14:21–22
MAHILLON, VICTOR-CHARLES
musical instruments 13:675–676
MAHLER, GUSTAV 9:131 illus.; 13:65 bibliog., illus.; 13:666 illus.
orchestra and orchestration 14:418
Walter, Bruno 20:19
MAHMUD-E ERAGI (Afghanistan)
map (35° 1′N 69° 20′E) 1:133
MAHMUD OF GHAZNI 13:65–66 bibliog.
Firdawsi 8:100
India, history of 11:91
Multan (Pakistan) 13:637
sultan 18:338
MAHMUD II, SULTAN OF THE OTTOMAN EMPIRE 13:65 bibliog.
Janissaries 11:358
Ottoman Empire 14:465
MAHNOMEN (Minnesota)
map (47° 19′N 96° 1′W) 13:453
MAHNOMEN (county in Minnesota)
map (47° 17′N 95° 47′W) 13:453
MAHOGANY 13:66 illus.
chinaberry 4:377
lumber 12:457 illus.
red lauan 16:112
wood 20:205 illus.
MAHOMET (Illinois)
map (40° 12′N 88° 24′W) 11:42
MAHONE, WILLIAM
Virginia 19:612
MAHONING (county in Ohio)
map (41° 6′N 80° 39′W) 14:357
MAHONING RIVER
map (40° 58′N 80° 23′W) 14:357
MAHONY, MARION see GRIFFIN, MARION MAHONY
MAHOPAC (New York)
map (41° 22′N 73° 45′W) 14:149
MAHRATTA see MARATHA
MAHRE (brothers) 13:66
MAHSEER
minnow 13:458
MAI-NDOMBE, LAKE
map (2° 0′S 18° 20′E) 20:350
MAIANO (family) 13:66 bibliog.
MAID OF ORLÉANS see JOAN OF ARC, SAINT
MAIDEN (North Carolina)
map (35° 35′N 81° 13′W) 14:242
MAIDEN CASTLE (England) 13:66 bibliog.
European prehistory 7:306
MAIDENHAIR TREE see GINKGO
MAIDSTONE (England) 13:66–67
map (51° 17′N 0° 32′E) 19:403
MAIDUGURI (Nigeria)
map (11° 51′N 13° 10′E) 14:190
MAIGRET, INSPECTOR JULES (fictional character)
Simenon, Georges 17:314
MAIKO RIVER
map (0° 14′N 25° 33′E) 20:350
MAIL, ELECTRONIC see ELECTRONIC MAIL
MAIL DELIVERY see POSTAL SERVICES
MAIL-ORDER BUSINESS 13:67 bibliog.
book club 3:386
direct mail 6:187
publishing 15:611
retailing 16:183
Ward, Montgomery 20:29
Wond, Robert E. 20:207
MAILER, NORMAN 13:67 bibliog., illus.
American Dream, An 1:338
Monroe, Marilyn 13:542
Naked and the Dead, The 14:9
MAILI (Hawaii)
map (21° 25′N 158° 11′W) 10:72
MAILLART, ROBERT 13:67 bibliog.
bridge (engineering) 3:482
MAILLOL, ARISTIDE 13:67–68 bibliog., illus.
Pomona 13:68 illus.
MAIMAN, THEODORE HAROLD 13:68 bibliog.
MAIMON, SOLOMON 13:68 bibliog.
MAIMONIDES 13:68 bibliog.
Judaism 11:461
medicine 13:268
Tiberias (Israel) 19:189
MAIN RIVER 13:68
map (50° 0′N 8° 18′E) 9:140
MAIN SEQUENCE (astronomy) 13:68–69 bibliog.
astronomy and astrophysics 2:284
carbon cycle (astronomy) 4:135–136
Hayashi evolutionary track 10:80
Hertzsprung-Russell diagram 10:149
mass-luminosity relation 13:203
stellar evolution 18:250
subdwarf 18:313
subgiant 18:313
T Tauri stars 19:3
MAIN STREET (book) 13:69 bibliog.
Lewis, Sinclair 11:306–307
MAINBOCHER 13:69 bibliog.
fashion design 8:32
MAINE 13:69–74 bibliog., illus., map
agriculture 13:71 illus.; 13:72–73
cities
Augusta 2:320
Bangor 3:66
Bar Harbor 3:74
Bath 3:122
Lewiston 12:308
Portland 15:445
climate 13:71
economy 13:72–73
education 13:72
Bates College 3:121
Bowdoin College 3:427
Maine, state universities of 13:75
flag 13:69 illus.
forestry and fishing 13:72–73 illus.
government and politics 13:73–74
historical sites 13:72
history 13:74
Gorges, Sir Ferdinando 9:250
Missouri Compromise 13:480–481
land and resources 13:69–71 illus., map
manufacturing 13:73
map (45° 15′N 69° 15′W) 19:419
parks and reserves
Acadia National Park 1:71
people 13:71–72
Abnaki 1:57
Passamaquoddy 15:104–105
Penobscot 15:153
rivers, lakes, and waterways 13:71
Penobscot River 15:153
seal, state 13:69 illus.
tourism 13:73
vegetation and animal life 13:71
MAINE (region in France) 13:74
MAINE (ship) 13:74 bibliog.
Spanish-American War 18:150 illus.
MAINE, SIR HENRY 13:75 bibliog.
MAINE, STATE UNIVERSITIES OF 13:75
MAINE COON CAT 4:195 illus.; 13:75 illus.
longhaired cats 12:408
MAINE DE BIRAN 13:75 bibliog.
MAINFRAME COMPUTER 5:160d illus.; 5:160h
central processing unit 4:255
computer languages 5:160o
MAINLAND ISLAND (Orkney Islands)
map (59° 0′N 3° 10′W) 19:403
MAINLAND ISLAND (Shetland Islands)
map (60° 20′N 1° 22′W) 19:403
MAINSTREAMING
handicapped persons 10:36–37
MAINTENON, FRANÇOISE D'AUBIGNÉ, MARQUISE DE 13:75 bibliog.
MAINZ (West Germany) 13:75
map (50° 1′N 8° 16′E) 9:140
MAIO ISLAND
map (15° 15′N 23° 10′W) 4:122
MAIORESCU, TITU
Romanian literature 16:290
MAIPÚ (Argentina)
map (36° 52′S 57° 52′W) 2:149
MAIPÚ (Chile)
map (33° 31′S 70° 46′W) 4:355
MAIRET, JEAN 13:76 bibliog.
MAISÍ, CAPE OF
map (20° 15′N 74° 9′W) 5:377
MAISON CARRÉE 2:132 illus.; 13:76
MAISONNEUVE, PAUL DE CHOMEDEY, SIEUR DE 13:76 bibliog.
MAISONS, CHÂTEAU DE
château 4:302
MAITLAND (Australia)
map (32° 44′S 151° 33′E) 2:328
MAITLAND (Nova Scotia)
map (45° 19′N 63° 30′W) 14:269
MAITLAND, FREDERIC WILLIAM 13:76 bibliog.
MAITREYA see BUDDHA
MAIZE see CORN (botany)
MAJAPAHIT EMPIRE 13:76 bibliog.
MAJDANEK CONCENTRATION CAMP
Lublin (Poland) 12:447
MAJI MAJI REBELLION
Tanzania 19:28
MAJOLICA 13:76–77 bibliog., illus.
Minton ware 13:461
pottery and porcelain 15:470 illus.
terra-cotta 19:120

MAJOR (county in Oklahoma)
map (36° 20′N 98° 30′W) **14**:368
MAJOR, CLARENCE **13**:77 *bibliog.*
MAJOR BARBARA (play) **13**:77 *bibliog.*
Shaw, George Bernard **17**:245
MAJOR INDOOR SOCCER LEAGUE (MISL)
soccer **18**:11
MAJOR SCALE
scale (music) **17**:107
MAJORCA (Spain) **13**:77 *bibliog.*
Balearic Islands **3**:36
map (39° 30′N 3° 0′E) **18**:140
Palma **15**:49–50
MAJORELLE, LOUIS
Art Nouveau designs **2**:209 *illus.*; **2**:211 *illus.*
MAJRIT *see* MADRID (Spain)
MAJUNGA (Madagascar)
map (15° 43′S 46° 19′E) **13**:38
MAKAHA (Hawaii)
map (21° 28′N 158° 13′W) **10**:72
MAKAHUENA POINT
map (21° 52′N 159° 27′W) **10**:72
MAKAPANSGAT (South Africa) **13**:77 *bibliog.*
Dart, Raymond **6**:39
prehistoric humans **15**:512–513
MAKAPUU HEAD
map (21° 19′N 157° 39′W) **10**:72
MAKARIOS III **13**:77 *bibliog.*
MAKAROV, OLEG **13**:77
MAKAROVA, NATALIA **13**:77–78 *bibliog.*, *illus.*
MAKASARESE *see* BUGIS
MAKASSAR STRAIT
map (2° 0′S 117° 30′E) **11**:147
MAKEMIE, FRANCIS **13**:78 *bibliog.*
MAKENI (Sierra Leone)
map (8° 53′N 12° 3′W) **17**:296
MAKEUP *see* COSMETICS
MAKEUP, THEATRICAL *see* COSTUME AND MAKEUP, THEATRICAL
MAKGADIKGADI SALT PANS
map (20° 45′S 25° 30′E) **3**:416
MAKHACHKALA (USSR)
map (42° 58′N 47° 30′E) **19**:388
MAKHPIYA LUTA *see* RED CLOUD (Indian chief)
MAKIN ISLAND
World War II **20**:267
MAKINS, JAMES
porcelain **5**:327 *illus.*
MAKKAH (Saudi Arabia) *see* MECCA (Saudi Arabia)
MAKÓ (Hungary)
map (46° 13′N 20° 29′E) **10**:307
MAKOKOU (Gabon)
map (0° 34′N 12° 52′E) **9**:5
MAKURDI (Nigeria)
map (7° 45′N 8° 32′E) **14**:190
MAL-I TOMORRIT MOUNTAIN
map (40° 40′N 20° 9′E) **1**:250
MALABAR CHRISTIANS **13**:78 *bibliog.*
MALABO (Equatorial Guinea) **13**:78
map (3° 45′N 8° 47′E) **7**:226
MALACCA (Malaysia) *see* MELAKA (Malaysia)
MALACCA, STRAIT OF **13**:78
map (2° 30′N 101° 20′E) **13**:84
Srivijaya Empire **18**:207
MALACHI, BOOK OF **13**:78
MALACHITE **9**:74 *illus.*; **13**:78–79 *illus.*
MALACHY, SAINT **13**:79 *bibliog.*
MALAD CITY (Idaho)
map (42° 12′N 112° 15′W) **11**:26
MÁLAGA (Colombia)
map (6° 42′N 72° 44′W) **5**:107
MALAGA (New Mexico)
map (32° 14′N 104° 4′W) **14**:136
MÁLAGA (Spain) **13**:79
map (36° 43′N 4° 25′W) **18**:140
MALAGASH (Nova Scotia)
map (45° 46′N 63° 23′W) **14**:269
MALAGASY REPUBLIC *see* MADAGASCAR
MALAITA ISLAND
map (9° 0′S 161° 0′E) **18**:56
MALAKAL (Sudan)
map (9° 31′N 31° 39′E) **18**:320
MALAKOFF (Texas)
map (32° 10′N 96° 1′W) **19**:129
MALAMUD, BERNARD **1**:347 *illus.*; **13**:79 *bibliog.*, *illus.*
MALAMUTE *see* ALASKAN MALAMUTE
MALAN, DANIEL F. **13**:79 *bibliog.*
MALANG (Indonesia)
map (7° 59′S 112° 37′E) **11**:147
MALANJE (Angola)
map (9° 32′S 16° 20′E) **2**:5
MALAPROPISM
sheridan, richard brinsley
Rivals, The **16**:229
MÄLAREN LAKE
map (59° 30′N 17° 12′E) **18**:382
MALARGÜE (Argentina)
map (35° 28′S 69° 35′W) **2**:149
MALARIA **13**:79–80 *bibliog.*, *illus.*
DDT **6**:57
medicine **13**:271
parasite life cycle **13**:80 *illus.*
Plasmodium **15**:347
protozoal diseases **15**:581
quinidine **16**:27
quinine **16**:27
race **16**:35
relapse theories **13**:80
splenomegaly **18**:191
Sporozoa **18**:195
MALASPINA GLACIER **13**:80
MALATESTA (family) **13**:80 *bibliog.*
Rimini (Italy) **16**:224
MALAWI **13**:80–82 *bibliog.*, *illus.*, *map*, *table*
cities
Blantyre **3**:328
Lilongwe **12**:341
climate **13**:81 *table*
economic activity **13**:82
education **13**:81–82
African universities **1**:176 *table*
flag **13**:81 *illus.*
history and government **13**:82
Banda, H. Kamuzu **3**:61
Chilembwe, John **4**:357
houses and villages **13**:82 *illus.*
land **13**:80–81 *map*, *table*
map (13° 30′S 34° 0′E) **1**:136
Nyasa, Lake **14**:308
people **13**:81–82 *illus.*
Nguni **14**:176
Yao **20**:318
MALAWI, LAKE *see* NYASA, LAKE
MALAY ARCHIPELAGO **13**:82
Borneo **3**:402
Wallace, Alfred Russel **20**:13
MALAY PENINSULA **13**:82
map (6° 0′N 101° 0′E) **13**:84
MALAYA *see* MALAYSIA
MALAYALAM
Dravidian languages **6**:263
MALAYANS *see* MALAYS
MALAYER (Iran)
map (34° 17′N 48° 50′E) **11**:250
MALAYO-POLYNESIAN LANGUAGES **12**:355 *map*; **13**:82–84 *bibliog.*
Asia **2**:244 *map*
Indonesian **13**:83
Melanesian **13**:83
Micronesian **13**:83
Oceanic languages **14**:339
Polynesian **13**:83
South America **18**:93 *map*
Southeast Asian languages **18**:110–111
MALAYS **13**:84 *bibliog.*
Asia, history of **2**:253
Malaysia **13**:86
MALAYSIA **13**:84–86 *bibliog.*, *illus.*, *map*, *table*
art
Southeast Asian art and architecture **18**:107–108
Borneo **3**:402
cities
Kuala Lumpur **12**:133
Melaka **13**:284
climate **13**:85 *table*
economic activity **13**:85
education **13**:85
Southeast Asian universities **18**:111–112 *table*
flag **13**:84 *illus.*
government **13**:85
welfare spending **20**:98 *table*
history **13**:85–86
Abdul Rahman, Tunku **1**:54
Lee Kuan Yew **12**:270
Straits Settlements **18**:288
World War II **20**:260–261 *map*
land and resources **13**:84–85 *map*, *table*
languages
Malayo-Polynesian languages **13**:83
map (2° 30′N 112° 30′E) **2**:232
people **13**:85
Malays **13**:84
Minangkabau **13**:436–437
states
Sabah **17**:4
Sarawak **17**:75
tin **19**:205
MALAZGRIT (Turkey) *see* MANZIKERT, BATTLE OF
MALBONE, EDWARD GREENE **13**:86 *bibliog.*
MALBORK (Poland)
map (54° 2′N 19° 1′E) **15**:388
MALCOLM X **3**:311 *illus.*; **13**:86 *bibliog.*, *illus.*
MALCOLM III, KING OF SCOTLAND (Malcolm Canmore) **13**:86 *bibliog.*
Edinburgh (Scotland) **7**:57
Highland Games **10**:162
MALCOM (Iowa)
map (41° 43′N 92° 33′W) **11**:244
MALDEN (Massachusetts)
map (42° 26′N 71° 4′W) **13**:206
MALDEN (Missouri)
map (36° 34′N 89° 57′W) **13**:476
MALDIVE ISLANDS *see* MALDIVES, REPUBLIC OF
MALDIVES, REPUBLIC OF **13**:86–87 *bibliog.*, *illus.*
cities
Male **13**:87
flag **13**:87 *illus.*
map (3° 15′N 73° 0′E) **2**:232
MALDONADO (Uruguay)
map (34° 54′S 54° 57′W) **19**:488
MALE *see* MEN (biology)
MALE (Republic of Maldives) **13**:87
map (4° 10′N 73° 31′E) **13**:87
MALE ATOLL
map (4° 25′N 73° 30′E) **13**:87
MALEBRANCHE, NICHOLAS **13**:87 *bibliog.*
MALEIC ACID **13**:87
industrial uses **13**:87
MALEKULA
Vanuatu **19**:520
MALENKOV, GEORGY M. **13**:87–88
Khrushchev, Nikita Sergeyevich **12**:69
MALEVICH, KASIMIR **13**:88 *bibliog.*, *illus.*
Eight Red Rectangles **13**:88 *illus.*
Pevsner, Antoine **15**:216
suprematism **18**:354
Suprematist Composition **16**:364 *illus.*
MALFORMATIONS, CONGENITAL *see* BIRTH DEFECTS
MALHERBE, FRANÇOIS DE **13**:88 *bibliog.*
MALHEUR (county in Oregon)
map (43° 15′N 117° 40′W) **14**:427
MALHEUR LAKE
map (43° 20′N 118° 45′W) **14**:427
MALHEUREUX, CAPE
map (4° 48′S 55° 32′E) **19**:574
MALI **13**:88–91 *bibliog.*, *illus.*, *map*, *table*
art
African art **1**:160–164
cities
Bamako **3**:58
Timbuktu **19**:201
climate **13**:89 *table*
economic activity **13**:90
flag **13**:88 *illus.*
government **13**:90–91
history **13**:90–91
Africa, history of **1**:152
Bambara kingdoms **3**:58
Maçina **13**:26
Mansa Musa, Emperor of Mali **13**:127
Senegal **17**:202
Umar, al-Hajj **19**:379
land and resources **13**:88–90 *illus.*, *map*, *table*
map (17° 0′N 4° 0′W) **1**:136
people **13**:90
Dogon **6**:223
Songhai (people) **18**:65
Tuareg **19**:325–326
postage stamp **15**:230 *illus.*
MALICE **13**:91
murder **13**:647
MALINA, JUDITH
Living Theatre **12**:376
MALINOWSKI, BRONISLAW **13**:91 *bibliog.*
Kula Ring **12**:135
magic **13**:50
MALIPIERO, GIAN FRANCESCO **13**:91
MALJAMAR (New Mexico)
map (32° 51′N 103° 46′W) **14**:136
MALLARD **6**:291–292 *illus.*; **13**:91 *illus.*
flight **3**:282–283 *illus.*
MALLARMÉ, STÉPHANE **13**:91 *bibliog.*
Afternoon of a Faun, The **1**:181
Debussy, Claude **6**:71
MALLAWI (Egypt)
map (27° 44′N 30° 50′E) **7**:76
MALLE, LOUIS **13**:91–92
MALLEA, EDUARDO **13**:92 *bibliog.*
MALLEMUCK *see* ALBATROSS
MALLET, PAUL AND PIERRE
Nebraska **14**:73
MALLET-JORIS, FRANÇOISE **13**:92
MALLETTS BAY
map (44° 34′N 73° 14′W) **19**:554
MALLOPHAGA **13**:92
louse **12**:436
MALLORCA (Spain) *see* MAJORCA (Spain)
MALLORY, STEPHEN RUSSELL **13**:92 *bibliog.*
Civil War, U.S. **5**:32
MALLOW **13**:92 *illus.*
Althaea **1**:313
cotton **5**:305
hibiscus **10**:156–157
hollyhock **10**:204
okra **14**:372
velvetleaf **19**:538
MALLOWAN, SIR MAX **13**:92–93
Nimrud **14**:199
MALLOY v. HOGAN
Twining v. *New Jersey* **19**:360
MALMAISON **13**:93
Percier, Charles **15**:162
MALMBERGET (Sweden)
map (67° 10′N 20° 40′E) **18**:382
MALMÖ (Sweden) **13**:93
map (55° 36′N 13° 0′E) **18**:382
MALNUTRITION
diet, human **6**:164
famine **8**:18–19
gastrointestinal tract disease **9**:56–57
kwashiorkor **12**:143
marasmus **13**:143
nutritional-deficiency diseases **14**:307–308
starvation **18**:228
MALONE (New York)
map (44° 51′N 74° 17′W) **14**:149
MALORY, SIR THOMAS **13**:93 *bibliog.*
Morte Darthur **13**:591
MALOTI MOUNTAINS
map (29° 5′S 28° 20′E) **12**:297
MALPASO RESERVOIR
map (17° 10′N 93° 40′W) **13**:357
MALPASSET DAM
Fréjus **8**:301
MALPEQUE BAY
map (46° 30′N 63° 47′W) **15**:548
MALPIGHI, MARCELLO **1**:396–397 *illus.*; **13**:93 *bibliog.*
biology **3**:269
MALPRACTICE **13**:93 *bibliog.*
negligence **14**:77
MALRAUX, ANDRÉ **13**:93–94 *bibliog.*, *illus.*
MALT **13**:94 *bibliog.*
beer **3**:162–163
whiskey **20**:133
MALT LIQUOR (beer) **3**:163
MALTA (island) **13**:94–95 *bibliog.*, *illus.*, *map*, *table*
archaeology
Tarxien **19**:41
temple **19**:94 *illus.*
cities
Valletta **19**:507
economic activity **13**:95
flag **13**:94 *illus.*
government **13**:95
history **13**:95
Mintoff, Dominic **13**:461
land **13**:94
map (35° 53′N 14° 27′E) **13**:94
people **13**:94
postage stamp **15**:230 *illus.*
MALTA (Montana)
map (48° 21′N 107° 52′W) **13**:547
MALTA, KNIGHTS OF *see* HOSPITALERS
MALTA CHANNEL
map (56° 44′N 26° 53′E) **11**:321
MALTA FEVER *see* BRUCELLOSIS
MALTESE (cat) **4**:195 *illus.*
MALTESE (dog) **6**:217 *illus.*; **13**:95–96 *bibliog.*, *illus.*
bichon frise **3**:244
MALTESE CROSS **5**:360; **5**:361 *illus.*
MALTESE FALCON, THE (book) **13**:96
Hammett, Dashiell **10**:31
MALTHUS, THOMAS ROBERT **13**:96 *bibliog.*
evolution **7**:318
population **15**:433
birth control **3**:294
population dynamics **15**:438
Ricardo, David **16**:206
MALTO
Dravidian languages **6**:263
MALTOSE
sugar **18**:327
MALTZ, ALBERT
Hollywood Ten, The **10**:204

MALUKU *see* MOLUCCAS (Indonesia)
MALVERN (Arkansas)
map (34° 22′N 92° 49′W) **2**:166
MALVERN (Iowa)
map (41° 0′N 95° 35′W) **11**:244
MALVERN, GODFREY HUGGINS, 1ST VISCOUNT **13**:96 *bibliog.*
MALVINAS, ISLAS *see* FALKLAND ISLANDS
MALY THEATER **13**:96
Moscow **13**:597 *map*
MAMALA BAY
map (21° 18′N 157° 57′W) **10**:72
MAMALLAPURAM *see* MAHABALIPURAM (India)
MAMARA (Peru)
map (14° 14′S 72° 35′W) **15**:193
MAMAS AND THE PAPAS, THE
rock music **16**:249
MAMBA **13**:96 *illus.*
black mamba **15**:384 *illus.*
MAMELUCO *see* MESTIZO
MAMELUKES **13**:96–97 *bibliog.*
Asia, history of **2**:255 *map*
defeat by Napoleon **13**:406 *illus.*
Islamic art and architecture **11**:296–297
Middle East, history of the **13**:404
Turks **19**:348
MAMET, DAVID **13**:97
MAMMAL **13**:97–106 *bibliog., illus.*
See also names of specific mammals, e.g., BAT; WALRUS; etc.
aging **1**:185–186
behavior, social **13**:98–99
animal behavior **2**:14–17 *illus.*
animal communication **2**:20 *illus.*
animal courtship and mating **2**:21–22
animal migration **2**:27
territoriality **19**:121
biological characteristics **13**:97–99
anatomy **13**:97–98 *illus.*
brain **3**:443 *illus.*
coloration, biological **5**:122
estrous cycle **7**:248
feet **13**:102 *illus.*
gestation **9**:160
hair **10**:14
hoof, nail, and claw **10**:225–226 *illus.*
horn (biology) **10**:238
intestine **11**:230
molting **13**:513
parthenogenesis **15**:100
reproduction **16**:163
respiratory system **16**:179–181 *illus.*
biological locomotion **3**:266 *illus.*
ecological adaptation **13**:98; **13**:100 *illus.*
evolution **7**:323–324; **13**:103 *illus.*
Matthew, William Diller **13**:231
Simpson, Chatles Gaylord **17**:317
fossil record **13**:99–101
Jurassic Period **11**:475 *illus.*
Tertiary Period **19**:124 *illus.*
herbivore **10**:136
leather and hides **12**:262–263
life span **12**:330 *table*
mountain life **13**:622
orders of mammals **13**:101–106 *illus.*
Artiodactyla **2**:224; **13**:105–106 *illus.*
Carnivora **4**:156–157; **13**:103; **13**:105 *illus.*
Chiroptera **13**:102; **13**:104 *illus., illus.*
Dermoptera **13**:102; **13**:104 *illus., illus.*
Edentata **7**:56; **13**:103–104 *illus.*
Hyracoidea **13**:105–106 *illus., illus.*
Insectivora **11**:193 *illus.*; **13**:102; **13**:104 *illus.*
Lagomorpha **12**:165; **13**:103–104 *illus.*
Marsupialia **13**:102; **13**:104 *illus.*; **13**:174–175 *illus.*
Monotretata **13**:101; **13**:104 *illus.*; **13**:540–541 *illus.*
Mysticeti **13**:103; **13**:105 *illus., illus.*
Odontoceti **13**:103; **13**:105 *illus., illus.*
Perissodactyla **13**:105–106 *illus.*; **15**:171
Pholidota **13**:103–104 *illus., illus.*
primate **13**:103–106 *illus.*; **15**:539–542 *illus.*
Proboscidea **13**:103–106 *illus.*; **15**:559
Rodentia **13**:103–104 *illus.*; **16**:265–266 *illus.*
Sirenia **13**:105–106 *illus.*; **17**:327–328 *illus.*
Tubulidentata **13**:103–104 *illus.*; **19**:328
savanna life **17**:98
steppe life **18**:257
ungulate **19**:384
MAMMARY GLAND *see* BREAST
MAMMOGRAPHY **13**:106 *bibliog.*
cancer **4**:104 *illus.*
MAMMOTH (animal) **13**:102 *illus.*; **13**:106–107 *bibliog., illus.*
Dolní Věstonice **6**:226
emperor mammoth **15**:367 *illus.*
ivory and ivory carving **11**:336
La Brea Tar Pit **12**:144
Pleistocene Epoch **15**:366–367 *illus.*
proboscidean **15**:559
woolly mammoth **13**:106–107
MAMMOTH (Arizona)
map (32° 43′N 110° 38′W) **2**:160
MAMMOTH (West Virginia)
map (38° 16′N 81° 22′W) **20**:111
MAMMOTH CAVE **12**:50 *illus.*; **13**:107 *bibliog.*
cave **4**:222
national parks **14**:38–39 *map, table*
MAMMOTH LAKES (California)
map (37° 38′N 118° 58′W) **4**:31
MAMMOTH SPRING (Arkansas)
map (36° 30′N 91° 33′W) **2**:166
MAMORÉ RIVER
map (10° 23′S 65° 53′W) **3**:366
MAMOU (Louisiana)
map (30° 38′N 92° 25′W) **12**:430
MAMPONG (Ghana)
map (7° 4′N 1° 24′W) **9**:164
MAMRY, LAKE
map (54° 8′N 21° 42′E) **15**:388
MAMUSHI **17**:380 *illus.*
MAN
See also HOMO SAPIENS; HUMAN BODY
animal behavior **2**:17–18
anthropology **2**:51–55 *illus.*
ethnography **7**:256–257
prehistoric humans **15**:511–517 *illus.*
race **16**:33–35 *illus.*
MAN (Ivory Coast)
map (7° 24′N 7° 33′W) **11**:335
MAN (West Virginia)
map (37° 45′N 81° 53′W) **20**:111
MAN, EARLY *see* PREHISTORIC HUMANS
MAN, FELIX H.
photography, history and art of **15**:271
MAN, ISLE OF *see* ISLE OF MAN
MAN OF LA MANCHA (musical)
Don Quixote **6**:236
MAN LANGUAGE *see* MIAO-YAO LANGUAGES
MAN AND SUPERMAN (play)
comedy **5**:132
Shaw, George Bernard **17**:245
MAN WITHOUT A COUNTRY (short story)
Hale, Edward Everett **10**:18
MANA **13**:107 *bibliog.*
Indians, American **11**:123
Maori **13**:136
Polynesians **15**:421
MANA (Hawaii)
map (22° 2′N 159° 46′W) **10**:72
MANA RIVER
map (5° 44′N 53° 54′W) **8**:311
MANADO (Indonesia)
map (1° 29′N 124° 51′E) **11**:147
MANAGEMENT AND BUDGET, U.S. OFFICE OF **13**:107
government regulation **9**:272
president of the United States **15**:525
MANAGEMENT SCIENCE **13**:107 *bibliog.*
See also BUSINESS ADMINISTRATION; INDUSTRIAL MANAGEMENT
accounting **1**:77–78
industrial psychology **11**:157
industrial relations **11**:157–158
operations research **14**:403
systems engineering **18**:414–415
Taylor, Frederick Winslow **19**:49
MANAGUA (Nicaragua) **13**:108; **14**:179 *illus., table*
map (12° 9′N 86° 17′W) **14**:179
MANAGUA, LAKE
map (12° 20′N 86° 20′W) **14**:179
MANAHAWKIN (New Jersey)
map (39° 42′N 74° 16′W) **14**:129
MANAKARA (Madagascar)
map (22° 8′S 48° 1′E) **13**:38
MANAKIN **13**:108
MANAMA (Bahrain) **13**:108
climate **3**:25 *table*
map (26° 13′N 50° 35′E) **3**:24
MANANJARY (Madagascar)
map (21° 13′S 48° 20′E) **13**:38
MANAOS (Brazil) *see* MANAUS (Brazil)
MANASLU MOUNTAIN
map (28° 33′N 84° 33′E) **14**:86
MANASQUAN (New Jersey)
map (40° 7′N 74° 3′W) **14**:129
MANASSA (Colorado)
map (37° 11′N 105° 56′W) **5**:116
MANASSAS (Virginia)
Bull Run, Battles of **3**:558–559 *map*
map (38° 45′N 77° 28′W) **19**:607
MANASSAS PARK (Virginia)
map (38° 47′N 77° 28′W) **19**:607
MANASSEH BEN ISRAEL **13**:108 *bibliog.*
MANATEE **13**:105 *illus.*
sirenia **17**:327–328 *illus.*
MANATEE (county in Florida)
map (27° 26′N 82° 25′W) **8**:172
MANATÍ (Puerto Rico)
map (18° 26′N 66° 29′W) **15**:614
MANAUS (Brazil) **1**:323 *illus.*; **13**:108
climate **3**:461 *table*; **18**:86 *table*
harbor and port **10**:42
map (3° 8′S 60° 1′W) **3**:460
MANCALA (game) **9**:30
MANCELONA (Michigan)
map (44° 54′N 85° 4′W) **13**:377
MANCHAUG (Massachusetts)
map (42° 6′N 71° 45′W) **13**:206
MANCHE, LA *see* ENGLISH CHANNEL
MANCHESTER (Connecticut)
map (41° 47′N 72° 31′W) **5**:193
MANCHESTER (England) **13**:108
harbor and port **10**:42
Manchester, Victoria University of **13**:108–109
map (53° 30′N 2° 15′W) **19**:403
spinning factories in mid-19th century **11**:158 *illus.*
urban planning **19**:482
MANCHESTER (Georgia)
map (32° 51′N 84° 37′W) **9**:114
MANCHESTER (Iowa)
map (42° 29′N 91° 27′W) **11**:244
MANCHESTER (Kentucky)
map (37° 9′N 83° 46′W) **12**:47
MANCHESTER (Massachusetts)
map (42° 34′N 70° 46′W) **13**:206
MANCHESTER (Michigan)
map (42° 9′N 84° 2′W) **13**:377
MANCHESTER (New Hampshire) **13**:108; **14**:126 *illus.*
map (42° 59′N 71° 28′W) **14**:123
MANCHESTER (Ohio)
map (38° 41′N 83° 36′W) **14**:357
MANCHESTER (Tennessee)
map (35° 29′N 86° 5′W) **19**:104
MANCHESTER (Vermont)
map (43° 10′N 73° 5′W) **19**:554
MANCHESTER, VICTORIA UNIVERSITY OF **13**:108–109
Nuffield Radio Astronomy Laboratories **14**:291
MANCHESTER CENTER (Vermont)
map (43° 11′N 73° 3′W) **19**:554
MANCHESTER GUARDIAN **13**:109 *bibliog.*
Manchester (England) **13**:108
MANCHESTER SCHOOL
Manchester (England) **13**:108
MANCHESTER TERRIER **6**:217 *illus.*; **6**:220 *illus.*; **13**:109 *illus.*
MANCHING (Germany)
European prehistory **7**:306
MANCHIONEAL (Jamaica)
map (18° 2′N 76° 17′W) **11**:351
MANCHU (dynasty) *see* CH'ING (Qing) (dynasty)
MANCHU LANGUAGE
Altaic languages **19**:476
MANCHUKUO **13**:109
Sino-Japanese Wars **17**:323
World War II **20**:249
MANCHURIA (China) **13**:109 *bibliog., map*
Chinese Eastern Railway **4**:388
cities
An-shan (Anshan) **1**:387
Fu-shun (Fushun) **8**:351
Harbin (Haerbin) **10**:42
Lü-shun (Lüshun) **12**:446
Lü-ta (Lüda) **12**:446
Shen-yang (Shenyang) **17**:255
history
Chang Tso-lin (Zhang Zuolin) **4**:281
Manchukuo **13**:109
Sino-Japanese Wars **17**:323
MANCHURIAN CANDIDATE, THE (book)
Condon, Richard **5**:173
MANCO CAPAC **13**:110 *bibliog.*
Cuzco **5**:400
Pizarro, Francisco **15**:324
MANCO INCA
Inca **11**:73
MANCOS (Colorado)
map (37° 21′N 108° 18′W) **5**:116
MAND RIVER
map (28° 11′N 51° 17′E) **11**:250
MANDAEANS **13**:110 *bibliog.*
gnosticism **9**:214
MANDALA **13**:110 *bibliog., illus.*
Japanese art and architecture **11**:374
Lamaist art and architecture **12**:172 *illus.*
Southeast Asian art and architecture **18**:110
MANDALAY (Burma) **13**:110
map (22° 0′N 96° 5′E) **3**:573
MANDAMUS **13**:110
prisoners' rights **15**:555
writ **20**:291
MANDAN (American Indians) **13**:110–111 *bibliog., illus.*
earth lodge **11**:120 *illus.*
Hidatsa **10**:158
Mississippian culture **14**:239
scalping **11**:129 *illus.*
shaman **17**:238 *illus.*
MANDAN (North Dakota)
map (46° 50′N 100° 54′W) **14**:248
MANDARA MOUNTAINS
map (10° 45′N 13° 40′E) **14**:190
MANDARIN (bird) *see* WATERFOWL
MANDARIN (fruit) *see* TANGERINE
MANDARIN LANGUAGE
China **4**:365
Sino-Tibetan languages **17**:324
MANDATE SYSTEM **13**:111
MANDE **1**:147 *illus.*; **13**:111 *bibliog.*
Sierra Leone **17**:297; **17**:298
MANDEL, MARVIN
Maryland **13**:193
MANDELA, NELSON
African National Congress **1**:171; **1**:172
MANDELSTAM, OSIP EMILIEVICH **13**:111 *bibliog.*
MANDER, CAREL VAN **13**:111 *bibliog.*
MANDERSON (Wyoming)
map (44° 16′N 107° 58′W) **20**:301
MANDEVILLE (Jamaica)
map (18° 2′N 77° 30′W) **11**:351
MANDEVILLE (Louisiana)
map (30° 22′N 90° 4′W) **12**:430
MANDEVILLE, BERNARD **13**:111 *bibliog.*
MANDINKA DRUM RHYTHM
African music **1**:171 *illus.*
MANDINKA SONG
African music **1**:171 *illus.*
MANDOLIN **13**:111–112 *bibliog., illus.*
MANDRAKE (botany) **13**:112
MANDRILL **13**:112 *illus.*; **13**:533 *illus.*
MANET, ÉDOUARD **13**:112–113 *bibliog., illus.*
The Balcony **11**:67 *illus.*
Bar at the Folies Bergère **11**:67 *illus.*; **13**:113 *illus.*
Déjeuner sur l'herbe **15**:22 *illus.*
Émile Zola **20**:372 *illus.*
The Execution of the Emperor Maximilian **13**:364 *illus.*
The Fifer **13**:112 *illus.*
Morisot, Berthe **13**:580
MANFREDONIA (Italy)
map (41° 38′N 15° 55′E) **11**:321
MANFREDONIA ,GULF OF
map (41° 35′N 16° 5′E) **11**:321
MANGANESE **13**:114 *bibliog.*
abundances of common elements **7**:131 *table*
alloys **13**:114
compounds **13**:114
element **7**:130 *table*
fertilizer component **13**:114
Group VIIB periodic table **15**:167
manganite **13**:114
metal, metallic element **13**:328
occurrence **13**:114
ore
deposits, world distribution **14**:423 *map*
weathering **20**:83
oxide minerals **14**:476
psilomelane **15**:588
pyrolusite **15**:637
rhodochrosite **16**:203
rhodonite **16**:203

MANGANESE (cont.)
Scheele, Carl Wilhelm, discoverer **17**:115
transition elements **19**:273–274 *table*
uranium minerals **19**:478
uses **13**:114
vitamins and minerals **19**:621
MANGANESE NODULE **13**:114 *bibliog.*
formation and discovery **13**:114
Manganese Nodule Project **13**:114
ocean and sea **14**:332
oceanic mineral resources **14**:340–341 *illus.*
oceanography **14**:346
sediment, marine **17**:184
world distribution **14**:423 *map*
MANGANITE **13**:114
garnet **9**:49
pyrolusite **15**:637
MANGAS COLORADAS **13**:114 *bibliog.*
Cochise **5**:86
MANGBETU **13**:114–115
MANGE **13**:115
MANGHAM (Louisiana)
map (32° 19′N 91° 47′W) **12**:430
MANGIN, ALPHONSE
searchlight **17**:175
MANGIN, CHARLES
Verdun, Battle of **19**:550
MANGO **13**:115 *bibliog., illus.*
MANGO CREEK (Belize)
map (16° 32′N 88° 29′W) **3**:183
MANGOPE, LUCAS
Bophuthatswana **3**:395
MANGOSTEEN **13**:115 *illus.*
MANGROVE **13**:115–116 *bibliog., illus.*
distribution **11**:468 *map*
swamp, marsh, and bog **18**:378 *illus.*
MANGROVE SNAKE
colubrid **5**:124
MANGUM (Oklahoma)
map (34° 53′N 99° 30′W) **14**:368
MANHATTAN (Kansas)
map (39° 11′N 96° 35′W) **12**:18
MANHATTAN (New York City) **13**:116 *bibliog.*; **14**:145 *map*
Bowery, The **3**:428
Central Park **4**:254
Greenwich Village **9**:354–355
Harlem **10**:49–50
Minuit, Peter **13**:461
MANHATTAN (ship) **2**:144 *illus.*; **19**:24 *illus.*
Arctic **2**:142 *map*
Northwest Passage **14**:257 *map*
MANHATTAN PROJECT **13**:116 *bibliog.*
atomic bomb **2**:307
chain reaction, nuclear **4**:269
Chamberlain, Owen **4**:274
Einstein, Albert **7**:94
Fermi, Enrico **8**:55–56
Franck, James **8**:277
nuclear energy **14**:279
Oak Ridge National Laboratory **14**:312
Oppenheimer, J. Robert **14**:407–408
Teller, Edward **19**:90
Urey, Harold Clayton **19**:486
Wigner, Eugene Paul **20**:147
MANHATTAN TRANSFER (book)
Dos Passos, John **6**:243
MANHEIM (Pennsylvania)
map (40° 10′N 76° 24′W) **15**:147
MANI-KONGOS (African Kings) *see* KONGO, KINGDOM OF
MANIC-DEPRESSIVE PSYCHOSIS **13**:116 *bibliog.*
Kraepelin, Emil **12**:126
lithium (drug) **12**:370
psychotropic drugs **15**:604
MANICHAEISM **13**:116–117 *bibliog.*
Bogomils **3**:360
gnosticism **9**:214
MANICORÉ (Brazil)
map (5° 49′S 61° 17′W) **3**:460
MANICOTTI **15**:106 *illus.*
MANICOUAGAN RESERVOIR
map (51° 30′N 68° 19′W) **16**:18
MANIERA *see* MANNERISM (art)
MANIFEST DESTINY **13**:117 *bibliog.*
Mexican War **13**:351
Spanish-American War **18**:149
United States, history of the **19**:444
MANIGOTAGAN (Manitoba)
map (51° 6′N 96° 18′W) **13**:119
MANILA (Arkansas)
map (35° 53′N 90° 10′W) **2**:166
MANILA (Philippines) **13**:117–118 *illus.*; **15**:236–237 *illus., table*
map (14° 35′N 121° 0′E) **15**:237
World War II **20**:278
MANILA (Utah)
map (40° 59′N 109° 43′W) **19**:492
MANILA BAY **13**:118
MANILA BAY, BATTLE OF (1898) **14**:63 *illus.*
Dewey, George **6**:146
Spanish-American War **18**:150
MANILLA (Iowa)
map (41° 53′N 95° 14′W) **11**:244
MANIOC **13**:118 *illus.*
MANIPUR (India) **13**:118 *bibliog.*
map (25° 0′N 94° 0′E) **11**:80
MANISA (Turkey)
map (38° 36′N 27° 26′E) **19**:343
MANISTEE (Michigan)
map (44° 15′N 86° 19′W) **13**:377
MANISTEE (county in Michigan)
map (44° 20′N 86° 0′W) **13**:377
MANISTEE RIVER
map (44° 15′N 86° 21′W) **13**:377
MANISTIQUE (Michigan)
map (45° 57′N 86° 15′W) **13**:377
MANISTIQUE LAKE
map (46° 15′N 85° 45′W) **13**:377
MANISTIQUE RIVER
map (45° 57′N 86° 15′W) **13**:377
MANITO (Illinois)
map (40° 25′N 89° 47′W) **11**:42
MANITOBA (Canada) **13**:118–122 *bibliog., illus., map*
cities
Brandon **3**:454
Churchill **4**:425
Winnipeg **20**:180
climate **13**:120
economic activities **13**:121
education
Brandon University **4**:92 *table*
Manitoba, University of **13**:122
Winnipeg, University of **4**:92 *table*; **20**:180
Winnipeg University **4**:92 *table*
flag **13**:118 *illus.*
government **13**:121–122
history **13**:122
Manitoba Schools Question **13**:122
Red River Rebellion **16**:113
Red River Settlement **16**:113
Schreyer, Edward Richard **17**:135
land and resources **13**:118–120 *map*
map (54° 0′N 97° 0′W) **4**:70
people **13**:120
Sioux **17**:326
rivers, lakes, and waterways **13**:120
Assiniboine River **2**:265
Nelson River **14**:80
Winnipeg, Lake **20**:180
MANITOBA, LAKE
map (51° 0′N 98° 45′W) **13**:119
MANITOBA, UNIVERSITY OF **13**:122
MANITOBA SCHOOLS QUESTION **13**:122 *bibliog.*
Canada, history of **4**:85
MANITOU ISLAND
map (47° 25′N 87° 37′W) **13**:377
MANITOU SPRINGS (Colorado)
map (38° 52′N 104° 55′W) **5**:116
MANITOULIN ISLANDS **13**:122
map (45° 45′N 82° 30′W) **14**:393
MANITOWOC (Wisconsin)
map (44° 6′N 87° 40′W) **20**:185
MANITOWOC (county in Wisconsin)
map (44° 5′N 87° 50′W) **20**:185
MANIWAKI (Quebec)
map (46° 23′N 75° 58′W) **16**:18
MANIZALES (Colombia)
map (5° 5′N 75° 32′W) **5**:107
MANKATO (Kansas)
map (39° 47′N 98° 12′W) **12**:18
MANKATO (Minnesota)
map (44° 10′N 94° 1′W) **13**:453
MANKAYANA (Swaziland)
map (26° 42′S 31° 0′E) **18**:380
MANLEY (family) **13**:122 *bibliog.*
Jamaica **11**:352
Seaga, Edward **17**:172
MANLY (Iowa)
map (43° 17′N 93° 12′W) **11**:244
MANMAN
Latin American music and dance **12**:231 *illus.*
MANN, SIR DONALD
Mackenzie, Sir William **13**:28
MANN, HEINRICH **13**:122 *bibliog.*
MANN, HORACE **13**:122–123 *bibliog.*
Antioch College **2**:64
MANN, JAMES
Mann Act **13**:124
MANN, MURRAY GELL- *see* GELL-MANN, MURRAY
MANN, THEODORE
Circle in the Square **4**:436
MANN, THOMAS **9**:134 *illus.*; **13**:123–124 *bibliog., illus.*
Death in Venice **6**:70
Magic Mountain, The **13**:51
MANN ACT **13**:124
MANNA **13**:124
sego lily **17**:188
MANNAEANS
Hasanlu **10**:65
MANNAR, GULF OF
map (8° 30′N 79° 0′E) **11**:80
MANNAR ISLAND
map (9° 3′N 79° 50′E) **18**:206
MANNER, EEVA-LIISA
Finnish literature **8**:99
MANNERHEIM, CARL GUSTAF EMIL **13**:124 *bibliog.*
MANNERHEIM LINE *see* MANNERHEIM, CARL GUSTAF EMIL
MANNERISM (art) **13**:124–125 *bibliog., illus.*
Andrea del Sarto **1**:407
architecture **2**:135
Arcimboldo, Giuseppe **2**:137
Bandinelli, Baccio **3**:62
Bassano (family) **3**:117–118
Beccafumi, Domenico **3**:150
Bronzino **3**:508–509
Carracci (family) **4**:166–167
Cellini, Benvenuto **4**:237
costume **5**:297
El Greco **7**:99
Flemish art and architecture **8**:162
Fontainebleau, school of **8**:205–206
Friedlaender, Walter **8**:331
Giulio Romano **9**:191–192
Goltzius, Hendrik **9**:241
Jamnitzer (family) **11**:357–358
Latin American art and architecture **12**:224
Leoni (family) **12**:292
Machuca, Pedro **13**:26
Michelangelo **13**:372–375
Morales, Luís de **13**:573
mural painting **13**:646
painting **15**:20
Parmigianino **15**:95
Peruzzi, Baldassare **15**:196
Pontormo, Jacopo Carucci da **15**:427
Porta, Giacomo della **15**:443
Primaticcio, Francesco **15**:542
Renaissance art and architecture **16**:152; **16**:155
Rosso Fiorentino **16**:320
Sanmicheli, Michele **17**:65
sculpture **17**:163–164
Serlio, Sebastiano **17**:209
Spanish art and architecture **18**:153
Spranger, Bartholomäus **18**:199
styles of Louis XIII-XVI **18**:311
Tacca, Pietro **19**:5–6
Vasari, Giorgio **19**:525
Vittoria, Alessandro **19**:621
Volterra, Daniele da **19**:632
Vries, Adriaen de **19**:639
Zuccaro (family) **20**:381
MANNERS *see* ETIQUETTE
MANNFORD (Oklahoma)
map (36° 9′N 96° 21′W) **14**:368
MANNHEIM (West Germany) **13**:125
Mannheim school **13**:125
map (49° 29′N 8° 29′E) **9**:140
MANNHEIM, AMÉDÉE
slide rule **17**:361
MANNHEIM SCHOOL **13**:125 *bibliog.*
orchestra and orchestration **14**:418
Stamitz (family) **18**:216
MANNIKIN **13**:125
ricebird **16**:209
MANNING (Iowa)
map (41° 55′N 95° 3′W) **11**:244
MANNING (North Dakota)
map (47° 14′N 102° 47′W) **14**:248
MANNING (South Carolina)
map (33° 42′N 80° 13′W) **18**:98
MANNING, HENRY EDWARD **13**:125 *bibliog.*
MANNINGTON (West Virginia)
map (39° 32′N 80° 20′W) **20**:111
MANNOSE
carbohydrate **4**:133
MANNVILLE (Alberta)
map (53° 20′N 111° 10′W) **1**:256
MANO RIVER
map (6° 56′N 11° 31′W) **17**:296
MANOLETE **13**:126 *bibliog.*
MANOMETER **13**:126
measurement **13**:254–255 *illus.*
MANON LESCAUT (book)
Prévost, Abbé **15**:534
MANONO (Zaire)
map (7° 18′S 27° 25′E) **20**:350
MANOR (Saskatchewan)
map (49° 36′N 102° 5′W) **17**:81
MANORIALISM **13**:126–127 *bibliog., illus.*
agriculture, history of **1**:190
enclosure **7**:163
Europe, history of **7**:284
feudalism **8**:64
France, history of **8**:267
interior design **11**:211–212
manor house **13**:126 *illus.*
Marxism **13**:184
Middle Ages **13**:394
peasant **15**:129
Peasants' Revolt **15**:129
Peasants' War **15**:129
slavery **17**:353
MANOUCHES
gypsies **9**:415
MANRESA (Spain)
map (41° 44′N 1° 50′E) **18**:140
MANRIQUE, JORGE
Spanish literature **18**:157
MANSA MUSA, EMPEROR OF MALI **13**:127 *bibliog.*
MANSARD ROOF
Mansart, François **13**:127
MANSART, FRANÇOIS **13**:127 *bibliog.*
MANSART, JULES HARDOUIN- *see* HARDOUIN-MANSART, JULES
MANSEL ISLAND
map (62° 0′N 79° 50′W) **16**:18
MANSFELD, ERNST, GRAF VON **13**:127–128 *bibliog.*
Thirty Years' War **19**:171 *map*
MANSFIELD (Arkansas)
map (35° 4′N 94° 13′W) **2**:166
MANSFIELD (England)
map (53° 9′N 1° 11′W) **19**:403
MANSFIELD (Georgia)
map (33° 31′N 83° 44′W) **9**:114
MANSFIELD (Louisiana)
map (32° 2′N 93° 43′W) **12**:430
MANSFIELD (Massachusetts)
map (42° 2′N 71° 13′W) **13**:206
MANSFIELD (Missouri)
map (37° 6′N 92° 35′W) **13**:476
MANSFIELD (Ohio)
map (40° 46′N 82° 31′W) **14**:357
MANSFIELD (Pennsylvania)
map (41° 48′N 77° 5′W) **15**:147
MANSFIELD, KATHERINE **13**:128 *bibliog., illus.*
MANSFIELD, MIKE **13**:128
MANSFIELD, MOUNT
map (44° 33′N 72° 49′W) **19**:554
MANSFIELD COLLEGE (Oxford University) **14**:474
MANSHIP, PAUL **13**:128 *bibliog., illus.*
Actaeon **13**:128 *illus.*
MANSI *see* KHANTS
MANSLAUGHTER **13**:128
homicide **10**:214–215
MANSON (Iowa)
map (42° 32′N 94° 32′W) **11**:244
MANSON (Washington)
map (47° 53′N 120° 9′W) **20**:35
MANSON, CHARLES **13**:128 *bibliog.*
MANSTEIN, ERICH VON
World War II **20**:268
MANSUR **13**:129 *bibliog.*
MANSUR, ABOLQASEM *see* FIRDAWSI
MANSUR, AL- **13**:129
MANSURA (Louisiana)
map (31° 4′N 92° 3′W) **12**:430
MANTA (Ecuador)
map (0° 57′S 80° 44′W) **7**:52
MANTEGNA, ANDREA **13**:129–130 *bibliog., illus.*
The Agony in the Garden **13**:129 *illus.*
Crucifixion **11**:405 *illus.*
The Dead Christ **16**:151 *illus.*
Padua (Italy) **15**:12
MANTELET
fortification **8**:238
MANTENO (Illinois)
map (41° 14′N 88° 12′W) **11**:42
MANTEO (North Carolina)
map (35° 55′N 75° 40′W) **14**:242
MANTI (Utah)
map (39° 16′N 111° 38′W) **19**:492
MANTIS *see* PRAYING MANTIS
MANTISFLY **13**:130 *illus.*
MANTLE (geology) **13**:130 *bibliog., illus.*
batholith **3**:122
Bullard, Sir Edward **3**:559
convection cell **5**:232
Earth, geological history of **7**:11
Earth, heat flow in **7**:18
Earth, structure and composition of **7**:19–20
geochemistry **9**:96–97
Mohole Project **13**:503
ophiolite **14**:404
peridotite **15**:166

plate tectonics **15**:351–357
silicate minerals **17**:304
MANTLE, MICKEY **13**:130–131 *bibliog., illus.*
MANTORVILLE (Minnesota)
map (44° 5′N 92° 45′W) **13**:453
MANTOVA (Italy)
map (45° 9′N 10° 48′E) **11**:321
MANTRA **13**:131
yoga **20**:329
MANTUA (Cuba)
map (22° 17′N 84° 17′W) **5**:377
MANTUA (Italy)
Gonzaga (family) **9**:244
Italian city-state **11**:328 *map*
MANTUAN SUCCESSION, WAR OF THE
Gonzaga (family) **9**:244
MANU (mythology) **13**:131 *bibliog.*
MANU (Peru)
map (12° 15′S 70° 50′W) **15**:193
MANUAL TRAINING *see* INDUSTRIAL ARTS PROGRAMS; VOCATIONAL EDUCATION
MANUEL, JUAN
Spanish literature **18**:157
MANUEL I, COMNENUS, BYZANTINE EMPEROR **13**:131 *bibliog.*
MANUEL I, KING OF PORTUGAL (Manuel the Fortunate) **13**:131 *bibliog.*
Portugal, history of **15**:453
MANUEL II, KING OF PORTUGAL
Portugal, history of **15**:455
MANUEL II PALAEOLOGUS, BYZANTINE EMPEROR **13**:131 *bibliog.*
Sicilian Vespers **17**:292
MANUELINE STYLE
Manuel I, King of Portugal **13**:131
Portuguese art and architecture **15**:456
MANUELITO **13**:131 *bibliog.*
MANUFACTURING **13**:131–133 *bibliog., table*
See also INDUSTRY; TECHNOLOGY, HISTORY OF
assembly line **2**:264–265; **13**:133
automation **2**:357; **13**:133
computer-aided design and computer-aided manufacturing **5**:160j–160L
Consumer Product Safety Commission **5**:225
consumer protection **5**:226
employment and unemployment **7**:159
women in society **20**:204 *table*
factory system **8**:6–7; **13**:132
flowchart **8**:178
industrial archaeology **11**:154
industrial design **11**:155–156
industrial engineering **11**:156
industrial management **11**:156–157
interchangeable parts **13**:132
mass production **13**:203
process control **15**:560–561
Revolution to Civil War **13**:132
robot **16**:246
trademark **19**:263
wholesaling **20**:143
MANUKAU (New Zealand)
map (37° 2′S 174° 54′E) **14**:158
MANUKAU HARBOR
map (37° 1′S 174° 44′E) **14**:158
MANUMISSION *see* SLAVERY
MANURE **13**:133–134 *bibliog.*
dung beetle **6**:300
fertilizer **8**:61–62
MANUREWA (New Zealand)
map (37° 2′S 174° 54′E) **14**:158
MANUSCRIPTS, ILLUMINATED *see* CODEX; ILLUMINATED MANUSCRIPTS
MANUTIUS, ALDUS **13**:134
book **3**:384–385
MANVEL (North Dakota)
map (48° 4′N 97° 10′W) **14**:248
MANVILLE (New Jersey)
map (40° 32′N 74° 36′W) **14**:129
MANX CAT **4**:195 *illus.*; **13**:134 *illus.*
MANX LANGUAGE
Celtic languages **4**:241
MANY (Louisiana)
map (31° 34′N 93° 29′W) **12**:430
MANY-HORNED ADDER *see* VIPER
MANYIKA *see* SHONA
MANZANILLO (Cuba)
map (20° 21′N 77° 7′W) **5**:377
MANZANILLO (Mexico)
map (19° 3′N 104° 20′W) **13**:357
MANZANILLO BAY
map (19° 45′N 71° 46′W) **10**:15
MANZANITA **4**:283 *illus.*
MANZANO (New Mexico)
map (34° 39′N 106° 21′W) **14**:136
MANZANO PEAK
map (34° 35′N 106° 26′W) **14**:136
MANZANOLA (Colorado)
map (38° 6′N 103° 52′W) **5**:116
MANZIKERT, BATTLE OF **13**:134
MANZINI (Swaziland)
map (26° 30′S 31° 25′E) **18**:380
MANZONI, ALESSANDRO **13**:134 *bibliog.*
MANZÙ, GIACOMO **13**:134 *bibliog.*
MAO *see* MONOAMINE OXIDASE INHIBITORS
MAO TSE-TUNG (Mao Zedong) **13**:134–136 *bibliog., illus.*
Chiang Ch'ing (Jiang Qing) **4**:339
China, history of **4**:375–377 *illus.*
communism **5**:147–148
Cultural Revolution **5**:384
early life **13**:134–135
Great Leap Forward **9**:320
Lin Piao (Lin Biao) **12**:347
Long March **12**:406
mausoleum (Peking) **15**:134 *illus.*
socialism **18**:22
MAO TUN (Mao Dun)
Chinese literature **4**:390
MAO ZEDONG *see* MAO TSE-TUNG (Mao Zedong)
MAOKE MOUNTAINS
map (4° 0′S 138° 0′E) **11**:147
MAORI **13**:136 *bibliog., illus.*
body marking **3**:357 *illus.*
carved canoe prow **14**:337 *illus.*
chief **13**:136 *illus.*
head-hunting **10**:85
house post **14**:336 *illus.*
magic **13**:49
Maori Wars **13**:136
New Zealand **14**:159
New Zealand, history of **14**:161 *illus.*
taboo **19**:5
Waitangi, Treaty of **20**:7
MAORI WARS **13**:136 *bibliog.*
Maori **13**:136
New Zealand, history of **14**:161–162
MAP TURTLE **13**:136–137 *illus.*
MAPA *see* MEXICAN AMERICAN POLITICAL ASSOCIATION
MAPAI PARTY
Ben-Gurion, David **3**:195
MAPIRE (Venezuela)
map (7° 45′N 64° 42′W) **19**:542
MAPLE **13**:137–138 *bibliog., illus.*
box elder **3**:430
maple syrup and sugar **13**:138
MAPLE CREEK (Saskatchewan)
map (49° 55′N 109° 27′W) **17**:81
MAPLE LAKE (Minnesota)
map (45° 14′N 94° 0′W) **13**:453
MAPLE RIVER
map (42° 0′N 95° 59′W) **11**:244
MAPLE SHADE (New Jersey)
map (39° 57′N 75° 0′W) **14**:129
MAPLE SYRUP AND SUGAR **13**:138 *bibliog.*
maple **13**:137–138
Vermont **19**:555 *illus.*
MAPLESVILLE (Alabama)
map (32° 47′N 86° 52′W) **1**:234
MAPLETON (Iowa)
map (42° 10′N 95° 47′W) **11**:244
MAPLETON (Oregon)
map (44° 2′N 123° 52′W) **14**:427
MAPLEWOOD (Missouri)
map (38° 37′N 90° 19′W) **13**:476
MAPP v. OHIO **13**:138
MAPS AND MAPMAKING **13**:138–142 *bibliog., illus.*
aerial photography **1**:119–120
atlas **2**:297
chart **4**:300
elevation **7**:136
four-color theorem **8**:252
geography **9**:101–102 *illus.*
history **13**:139–140 *illus.*
Block, Adriaen **3**:334
Champlain, Samuel de **4**:277
Cook, James **5**:234–236
Cosa, Juan de la **5**:280
Flint, Richard Foster **8**:165
Lacaille, Nicolas Louis de **12**:158
Mercator, Gerardus **13**:304
Murray, Sir John (oceanographer) **13**:650
Rowland, Henry Augustus **16**:328
Strachey, John **18**:287
hypsographic curve **10**:351
isogram **11**:299
isotherm **11**:300–301
Leo Belgicus **12**:438 *map*
Lunar Orbiter **12**:461
map projection **13**:141–142 *illus.*
map scale **13**:140
radar meteorology **16**:41
surveying **18**:369
topography **19**:237
types of maps **13**:140–142 *illus.*
water table **20**:57
weather map **20**:77 *illus.*
MAPUCHE
Araucanians **2**:109–110
MAPUNGUBWE (South Africa) **13**:142 *bibliog.*
MAPUTO (Mozambique) **13**:142–143; **13**:628 *illus.*
map (25° 58′S 32° 35′E) **13**:627
MAQUILLAGE *see* COSMETICS
MAQUOKETA (Iowa)
map (42° 4′N 90° 40′W) **11**:244
MAQUOKETA RIVER
map (42° 11′N 90° 19′W) **11**:244
MAR CHIQUITA, LAKE
map (30° 42′S 62° 36′W) **2**:149
MAR DEL PLATA (Argentina) **2**:150 *illus.*
map (38° 0′S 57° 33′W) **2**:149
MARA (rodent)
cavy **4**:226–227 *illus.*
MARAÃ (Brazil)
map (1° 50′S 65° 22′W) **3**:460
MARABÁ (Brazil)
map (5° 21′S 49° 7′W) **3**:460
MARACAIBO (Venezuela) **13**:143
map (10° 40′N 71° 37′W) **19**:542
MARACAIBO, LAKE **13**:143; **19**:543 *illus.*
map (9° 50′N 71° 30′W) **19**:542
MARACAY (Venezuela)
map (10° 15′N 67° 36′W) **19**:542
MARADI (Niger)
map (13° 29′N 7° 6′E) **14**:187
MARADONA, DIEGO
soccer **18**:10
MARAGHEH (Iran)
map (37° 23′N 46° 13′E) **11**:250
MARAIS, MARIN
program music **15**:562
MARAIS DES CYGNES RIVER
map (38° 12′N 94° 25′W) **12**:18
MARAJÓ (Brazil) **13**:143
map (1° 0′S 49° 30′W) **3**:460
MARANA (Arizona)
map (32° 27′N 111° 13′W) **2**:160
MARANHÃO (Brazil)
map (5° 0′S 45° 0′W) **3**:460
MARAÑÓN RIVER
map (4° 42′S 74° 40′W) **15**:193
MARAS (Turkey)
map (37° 36′N 36° 55′E) **19**:343
MARASMUS **13**:143
kwashiorkor **12**:143
nutritional-deficiency diseases **14**:307
starvation **18**:228
MARAT, JEAN PAUL **13**:143 *bibliog., illus.*
Corday, Charlotte **5**:261
MARATHA **13**:143 *bibliog.*
caste **4**:186
Gond **9**:243
Indo-Iranian languages **11**:145
Poona **15**:429
Rajput **16**:78
MARATHON **13**:143–144 *bibliog.*
Benoit, Joan **3**:204
Bikila, Abebe **3**:250
Rodgers, Bill **16**:267
running and jogging **16**:346
Shorter, Frank **17**:284
Switzer, Kathy **18**:393
MARATHON (Florida)
map (24° 43′N 81° 5′W) **8**:172
MARATHON (New York)
map (42° 26′N 76° 2′W) **14**:149
MARATHON (Ontario)
map (48° 40′N 86° 25′W) **14**:393
MARATHON (Texas)
map (30° 12′N 103° 15′W) **19**:129
MARATHON (Wisconsin)
map (44° 56′N 89° 50′W) **20**:185
MARATHON (county in Wisconsin)
map (44° 53′N 89° 45′W) **20**:185
MARATHON, BATTLE OF **9**:331 *illus.*; **13**:144
marathon **13**:143–144
Miltiades **13**:432
MARAT/SADE (play)
Weiss, Peter **20**:95–96
MARAVAN (Solomon Islands)
map (7° 51′S 156° 42′E) **18**:56
MARAVICH, PETE **13**:144 *bibliog.*
MARAVOVO (Solomon Islands)
map (9° 17′S 159° 38′E) **18**:56
MARAWI (Philippines)
map (8° 1′N 124° 18′E) **15**:237
MARBLE **13**:144
calcite **4**:21–22
calcium carbonate **4**:22–23
composition **13**:144
metamorphic rock **13**:331 *illus.*
mining and quarrying **13**:449
Roman art and architecture **16**:275
sculptures **13**:144
MARBLE (Minnesota)
map (47° 19′N 93° 18′W) **13**:453
MARBLE FALLS (Texas)
map (30° 34′N 98° 17′W) **19**:129
MARBLE HILL (Missouri)
map (37° 18′N 89° 58′W) **13**:476
MARBLE ROCK (Iowa)
map (42° 58′N 92° 52′W) **11**:244
MARBLEBOROUGH'S WAR *see* SPANISH SUCCESSION, WAR OF THE
MARBLED CONE **17**:251 *illus.*
MARBLEHEAD (Massachusetts)
map (42° 30′N 70° 51′W) **13**:206
MARBLES (game) **13**:144 *bibliog.*
MARBURG (Germany, East and West)
map (50° 49′N 8° 46′E) **9**:140
MARBURY v. MADISON **13**:144 *bibliog.*
judicial review **11**:464
Marshall, John **13**:172
MARC, FRANZ **13**:144–145 *bibliog., illus.*
Blaue Reiter, Der **3**:328–329
The Blue Horse **3**:328 *illus.*
Yellow Horses **13**:145 *illus.*
MARCA POINT
map (16° 31′S 11° 42′E) **2**:5
MARCA-RELLI, CONRAD **13**:145 *bibliog.*
MARCABRU (Marcabrun) (Provençal troubadour)
minstrels, minnesingers, and troubadours **13**:460
Provençal literature **15**:583
MARCAL RIVER
map (47° 41′N 17° 32′E) **10**:307
MARCANTONIO, VITO **13**:145 *bibliog.*
MARCASITE **13**:145
pyrite **13**:145
sulfide mineral **13**:145
MARCEAU, MARCEL **13**:145 *bibliog., illus.*
mime and pantomime **13**:434 *illus.*
MARCEL, GABRIEL **13**:145–146 *bibliog.*
existentialism **7**:332
MARCELINE (Missouri)
map (39° 43′N 92° 57′W) **13**:476
MARCELLO, BENEDETTO **13**:146 *bibliog.*
MARCELLUS, MARCUS CLAUDIUS **13**:146 *bibliog.*
MARCH (month of the year)
birthstones **3**:296 *illus., table*
calendar **4**:28
MARCH (music) **13**:146
band **3**:61
composers
Elgar, Sir Edward **7**:137
Sousa, John Philip **18**:77–78
MARCH REVOLUTION *see* RUSSIAN REVOLUTIONS OF 1917
MARCH RIVER
map (48° 10′N 16° 59′E) **2**:348
MARCH OF THE WOMEN (Oct. 5, 1789)
French Revolution **8**:323
MARCH ON WASHINGTON (1963)
King, Martin Luther, Jr. **12**:80
Southern Christian Leadership Conference **18**:112
MARCHE (France) **13**:146
MARCHE (Italy) **13**:146
MARCHE, JACQUES DE LA
Bourbon (dynasty) **3**:423
MARCHEGIANO, ROCCO FRANCIS *see* MARCIANO, ROCKY
MARCHFELD, BATTLE OF (1278)
Rudolf I, King of Germany **16**:338
MARCIAN, ROMAN EMPEROR IN THE EAST
Chalcedon, Council of **4**:270
MARCIANO, ROCKY **3**:432 *illus.*; **13**:146 *bibliog., illus.*
MARCION **13**:147 *bibliog.*
MARCO POLO (ship)
clipper ship **5**:60
MARCOLA (Oregon)
map (44° 10′N 122° 52′W) **14**:427
MARCOMANNI
Germanic peoples **9**:138
MARCONI, GUGLIELMO **13**:147 *bibliog., illus.*
radio **16**:44–45 *illus.*
radio and television broadcasting **16**:55 *illus.*
St. John's (Newfoundland) **17**:19
MARCOS, FERDINAND E. **13**:147 *bibliog.*

MARCOS, FERDINAND E. (cont.)
Aquino, Corazon C. **2**:95
Philippines **15**:238
MARCOS JUÁREZ (Argentina)
map (32° 42′S 62° 6′W) **2**:149
MARCOS PAZ (Argentina)
map (34° 46′S 58° 50′W) **2**:149
MARCUS (Iowa)
map (42° 50′N 95° 48′W) **11**:244
MARCUS AURELIUS, ROMAN EMPEROR **3**:507 *illus.*; **13**:147–148 *bibliog., illus.*
equestrian statue **16**:275 *illus.*
Naples (Italy) **14**:15
Roman expansion under **16**:299 *map*
Rome, ancient **16**:303 *illus.*
MARCUSE, HERBERT **13**:148 *bibliog.*; **18**:24 *illus.*
MARCY, GEORGE
musical comedy **13**:674 *illus.*
MARCY, MOUNT
map (44° 7′N 73° 56′W) **14**:149
MARCY, WILLIAM L. **13**:148 *bibliog.*
Ostend Manifesto **14**:457
MARDAN
map (34° 21′N 72° 2′E) **15**:27
MARDI GRAS **13**:148; **19**:430 *illus.*
Rio de Janeiro **4**:156 *illus.*
MARDUK (Mesopotamian deity) **13**:148
Etemenaki **19**:95 *illus.*
Mesopotamian art and architecture **13**:321
mythology **13**:696–697 *illus.*
Nippur **14**:201
MARE, WALTER DE LA *see* DE LA MARE, WALTER
MARE TRANQUILITATIS (sea)
moon **13**:563–564 *illus., map*
MAREK'S DISEASE
diseases, animal **6**:192
MARENGO (county in Alabama)
map (32° 15′N 87° 50′W) **1**:234
MARENGO (Illinois)
map (42° 15′N 88° 37′W) **11**:42
MARENGO (Iowa)
map (41° 48′N 92° 4′W) **11**:244
MARENISCO (Michigan)
map (46° 23′N 90° 30′W) **13**:377
MARENZIO, LUCA **13**:148 *bibliog.*
MARE'S TAIL (cloud) **13**:148
MARE'S TAIL (plant) **13**:148
MARETT, ROBERT R.
primitive religion **15**:543
MAREY, ÉTIENNE JULES **13**:148 *bibliog.*
film, history of **8**:81
MARFA (Texas)
map (30° 18′N 104° 1′W) **19**:129
MARGAI, SIR MILTON **13**:148 *bibliog.*
MARGAREE (Nova Scotia)
map (46° 24′N 61° 5′W) **14**:269
MARGARET, MAID OF NORWAY
Scotland **17**:151
MARGARET I, QUEEN OF DENMARK, NORWAY, AND SWEDEN **13**:149 *bibliog.*
Scandinavia, history of **17**:108–109
MARGARET II, QUEEN OF DENMARK **13**:149
MARGARET OF ANGOULÊME *see* MARGARET OF NAVARRE
MARGARET OF ANJOU **13**:148–149 *bibliog.*
Roses, Wars of the **16**:316
MARGARET OF AUSTRIA **13**:149 *bibliog.*
MARGARET OF NAVARRE **13**:149 *bibliog.*
MARGARET ROSE, PRINCESS
Snowdon, Antony Armstrong-Jones, 1st Earl of **18**:5
MARGARET OF SCOTLAND, SAINT **13**:149
Malcolm III, King of Scotland (Malcolm Canmore) **13**:86
MARGARET OF VALOIS **13**:149 *bibliog.*
MARGARETVILLE (New York)
map (42° 9′N 74° 39′W) **14**:149
MARGARINE **13**:149
coconut **5**:88
McCray v. *United States* **13**:10–11
safflower **17**:11
soybean **18**:115
sunflower **18**:348
MARGARITA ISLAND
map (11° 0′N 64° 0′W) **19**:542
MARGATE (England)
map (51° 24′N 1° 24′E) **19**:403
MARGATE (Florida)
map (26° 18′N 80° 12′W) **8**:172
MARGATE CITY (New Jersey)
map (39° 20′N 74° 31′W) **14**:129
MARGAY **13**:105 *illus.*
MARGHERITA PEAK
map (0° 22′N 29° 51′E) **20**:350
MARGIN BUYING (stock) *see* STOCK MARKET
MARGOW DESERT
map (30° 45′N 63° 10′E) **1**:133
MARI (Syria) **13**:149–150 *bibliog.*
Mesopotamian art and architecture **13**:318; **13**:320 *illus.*
MARIA I, QUEEN OF PORTUGAL
Portugal, history of **15**:454
MARIA II, QUEEN OF PORTUGAL (Maria da Glória) **13**:150
Pedro I, Emperor of Brazil **15**:131
Portugal, history of **15**:454
MARÍA CRISTINA DE BOURBON, QUEEN OF SPAIN
Spain, history of **18**:148
MARÍA GRANDE (Argentina)
map (31° 39′S 59° 54′W):149
MARIA THERESA, AUSTRIAN ARCHDUCHESS, QUEEN OF HUNGARY AND BOHEMIA **13**:150 *bibliog., illus.*
Austrian Succession, War of the **2**:354
Francis I, Holy Roman Emperor **8**:276
Polish Succession, War of the **15**:398
Pragmatic Sanction **15**:487
MARIACHI
Guadalajara (Mexico) **9**:384
MARIANA ISLANDS **13**:150–151
flag **8**:144 *illus.*
Guam (U.S.) **9**:385
map (16° 0′N 145° 30′E) **14**:334
Pacific Islands, Trust Territory of the **15**:5
Saipan **17**:28
subduction zone **18**:313
World War II **20**:277
MARIANA TROUGHS *see* MARIANAS TRENCH
MARIANAO (Cuba)
map (23° 5′N 82° 26′W) **5**:377
MARIANAS TRENCH **13**:151
exploration
Piccard, Auguste **15**:292
map (16° 0′N 148° 0′E) **14**:334
oceanic trenches **14**:341
Pacific Ocean bottom **15**:6–7 *map*
plate tectonics **15**:351 *map*
MARIANNA (Arkansas)
map (34° 46′N 90° 46′W) **2**:166
MARIANNA (Florida)
map (30° 47′N 85° 14′W) **8**:172
MARIAS ISLANDS
Nayarit (Mexico) **14**:66
MA'RIB (Yemen) **13**:151 *bibliog.*
Sheba **17**:247–248
MARIBOR (Yugoslavia)
map (46° 33′N 15° 39′E) **20**:340
MARICOPA (county in Arizona)
map (33° 30′N 112° 20′W) **2**:160
MARICOURT (Quebec)
map (61° 36′N 71° 58′W) **16**:18
MARICULTURE
plankton **15**:332
MARIE (Queen consort of Ferdinand, King of Romania) **13**:151
MARIE ANTOINETTE **8**:31 *illus.*; **13**:151 *bibliog., illus.*
Diamond Necklace, Affair of the **6**:152
Joseph II, Holy Roman Emperor **11**:452
Louis XVI, King of France **12**:427–428
portrait
Vigée-Lebrun, Louise Élisabeth **19**:591 *illus.*
MARIE BYRD LAND (region in Antarctica)
map (80° 0′S 120° 0′W) **2**:40
MARIE DE FRANCE **13**:151
MARIE DE L'INCARNATION **13**:151 *bibliog.*
MARIE DE MÉDICIS **13**:151–152 *bibliog.*
Richelieu, Armand Jean du Plessis, Cardinal et Duc de **16**:213
MARIENVILLE (Pennsylvania)
map (41° 28′N 79° 7′W) **15**:147
MARIES (county in Missouri)
map (38° 10′N 91° 55′W) **13**:476
MARIETTA (Georgia)
map (33° 57′N 84° 33′W) **9**:114
MARIETTA (Minnesota)
map (45° 1′N 96° 25′W) **13**:453
MARIETTA (OHIO) **13**:152
map (39° 25′N 81° 27′W) **14**:357
Ohio Company of Associates **14**:362
Putnam, Rufus **15**:632
MARIETTA (Oklahoma)
map (33° 56′N 97° 7′W) **14**:368
MARIETTE, AUGUSTE **13**:152
Aïda **1**:201
MARIEVILLE (Quebec)
map (45° 26′N 73° 10′W) **16**:18
MARIGNAC, JEAN CHARLES GALISSARD DE **13**:152
ytterbium **20**:337
MARIGOLD **13**:152 *illus.*
MARIINSK WATERWAY *see* VOLGA-BALTIC WATERWAY
MARIJUANA **13**:152–153 *bibliog., illus.*
drug abuse **6**:279; **6**:280
hallucinogens **10**:24
hemp **10**:120
psychotropic drugs **15**:603
MARÍLIA (Brazil)
map (22° 13′S 49° 56′W) **3**:460
MARIMBA **13**:153
Latin American music and dance **12**:231 *illus.*
vibraphone **19**:567
MARIN (county in California)
civic center **20**:289 *illus.*
map (38° 5′N 122° 45′W) **4**:31
MARIN, JOHN **13**:153 *bibliog., illus.*
Variations on Brooklyn **13**:153 *illus.*
MARÍN, LUIS MUÑOZ *see* MUÑOZ MARÍN, LUIS
MARINE BIOLOGY **13**:153 *bibliog.*
See also ALGAE; PROTOZOA
albatross **1**:252
animal migration **2**:27
aquarium **2**:93
beardworm **3**:143
blastoid **3**:328
booby (bird) **3**:382–383
brachiopod **3**:435
bryozoan **3**:530
cephalopod **4**:256
cetacean **4**:262
chiton **4**:398–399
coastal plain **5**:80–81
conodont **5**:197
coquina **5**:257
coral reef **5**:258–260
Cousteau, Jacques-Yves **5**:317–318
crinoid **2**:350
cystoid **5**:411
deep-sea life **6**:77–79
echinoderm **7**:37
ecology **7**:42–46
Eskimo **7**:238
fossil record **8**:243–248
archaeocyathid **2**:115
Cambrian Period **4**:50–52 *illus.*
Carboniferous Period **4**:138–139
Devonian Period **6**:145–146 *illus.*
eurypterid **7**:310 *illus.*
graptolite **9**:294 *illus.*
Mesozoic Era **13**:322
Ordovician Period **14**:422 *illus.*
Paleozoic Era **15**:43
Silurian Period **17**:310–312 *illus.*
Tertiary Period **19**:124
Triassic Period **19**:293 *illus.*
trilobite **19**:299 *illus.*
geochemistry **9**:96
gulf and bay **9**:403
habitat **10**:4–5
hemichordate **10**:117–118
Hyatt, Alpheus **10**:327
intertidal life **11**:230
Mediterranean Sea **13**:277
metamorphosis **13**:334
nekton **14**:79
ocean and sea **14**:331
oil spills **14**:363–364
ooze, deep-sea **14**:396–397
ostracod **14**:458
plankton **15**:331–333
red tide **16**:114–115
research institutions
Scripps Institution of Oceanography **17**:158
Woods Hole Marine Biological Laboratory **20**:212
Sargasso Sea **17**:77
seaweed **17**:177
stromatolite **18**:302
Woods Hole Oceanographic Institution **20**:213
zooplankton **20**:378
MARINE CITY (Michigan)
map (42° 43′N 82° 30′W) **13**:377
MARINE CORPS, U.S. **13**:153–155 *bibliog., illus.*
flag **8**:148 *illus.*
history of **13**:153–154
rank, military **16**:86 *table*
uniforms and insignia **13**:154–155 *illus.*
United States Armed Forces Institute **19**:462
World War II **20**:267
MARINE INSURANCE
Lloyd's of London **12**:384
MARINE PROTECTION RESEARCH AND SANCTUARY ACT
pollution control **15**:416
MARINE SEDIMENTATION *see* SEDIMENT, MARINE
MARINE TRANSGRESSION *see* TRANSGRESSION, MARINE
MARINER **13**:155–156 *bibliog., illus.*
missions
Deimos **6**:85
Mars **13**:156; **13**:168
Mercury **13**:156; **13**:305–306 *illus.*
outer planets **13**:156
Phobos **15**:249
Venus **13**:155
Venus (planet) **19**:547
relativity **16**:135
Sagan, Carl Edward **17**:11
space exploration **18**:125 *illus.*
MARINETTE (Wisconsin)
map (45° 6′N 87° 38′W) **20**:185
MARINETTE (county in Wisconsin)
map (45° 20′N 88° 0′W) **20**:185
MARINETTI, FILIPPO TOMMASO **13**:156 *bibliog.*
Boccioni, Umberto **3**:354
Fascist art **8**:30–31
futurism **8**:383–384
MARINGÁ (Brazil)
map (23° 25′S 51° 55′W) **3**:460
MARINGOUIN (Louisiana)
map (30° 29′N 91° 31′W) **12**:430
MARINI, MARINO **13**:156 *bibliog.*
MARINIDS
Fez (Morocco) **8**:66
MARINISM (poetry)
Marino, Giambattista **13**:156–157
MARINO, GIAMBATTISTA **13**:156–157 *bibliog.*
MARIO-MARENO *see* CANTINFLAS
MARION (Alabama)
map (32° 32′N 87° 26′W) **1**:234
MARION (county in Alabama)
map (34° 5′N 87° 55′W) **1**:234
MARION (Arkansas)
map (35° 13′N 90° 12′W) **2**:166
MARION (county in Arkansas)
map (36° 20′N 92° 45′W) **2**:166
MARION (county in Florida)
map (29° 10′N 82° 0′W) **8**:172
MARION (county in Georgia)
map (32° 25′N 84° 30′W) **9**:114
MARION (Illinois)
map (37° 44′N 88° 56′W) **11**:42
MARION (county in Illinois)
map (38° 38′N 88° 57′W) **11**:42
MARION (Indiana)
map (40° 33′N 85° 40′W) **11**:111
MARION (county in Indiana)
map (39° 46′N 86° 9′W) **11**:111
MARION (Iowa)
map (42° 2′N 91° 36′W) **11**:244
MARION (county in Iowa)
map (41° 17′N 93° 3′W) **11**:244
MARION (Kansas)
map (38° 21′N 97° 1′W) **12**:18
MARION (county in Kansas)
map (38° 25′N 97° 5′W) **12**:18
MARION (Kentucky)
map (37° 20′N 88° 5′W) **12**:47
MARION (county in Kentucky)
map (37° 35′N 85° 15′W) **12**:47
MARION (Louisiana)
map (32° 54′N 92° 15′W) **12**:430
MARION (Michigan)
map (44° 6′N 85° 9′W) **13**:377
MARION (county in Mississippi)
map (31° 15′N 89° 50′W) **13**:469
MARION (county in Missouri)
map (39° 50′N 91° 37′W) **13**:476
MARION (North Carolina)
map (35° 41′N 82° 1′W) **14**:242
MARION (North Dakota)
map (46° 37′N 98° 20′W) **14**:248
MARION (Ohio)
map (40° 35′N 83° 8′W) **14**:357
MARION (county in Ohio)
map (40° 35′N 83° 8′W) **14**:357
MARION (county in Oregon)
map (45° 6′N 122° 47′W) **14**:427
MARION (South Carolina)
map (34° 11′N 79° 24′W) **18**:98
MARION (county in South Carolina)
map (34° 5′N 79° 25′W) **18**:98
MARION (South Dakota)
map (43° 25′N 97° 16′W) **18**:103

MARION (county in Tennessee)
map (35° 10′N 85° 40′W) **19**:104
MARION (county in Texas)
map (32° 47′N 94° 25′W) **19**:129
MARION (Virginia)
map (36° 50′N 81° 31′W) **19**:607
MARION (county in West Virginia)
map (39° 30′N 80° 15′W) **20**:111
MARION (Wisconsin)
map (44° 21′N 89° 5′W) **20**:185
MARION, FRANCIS **13**:157 *bibliog.*
American Revolution **1**:359 *map*
MARION, LAKE
map (33° 30′N 80° 25′W) **18**:98
MARION JUNCTION (Alabama)
map (32° 26′N 87° 14′W) **1**:234
MARIONETTE *see* PUPPET
MARIONVILLE (Missouri)
map (37° 0′N 93° 38′W) **13**:476
MARIPOSA (California)
map (37° 29′N 119° 58′W) **4**:31
MARIPOSA (county in California)
map (37° 29′N 119° 58′W) **4**:31
MARIPOSA LILY see SEGO LILY
MARIS, ROGER **13**:157
MARISCAL ESTIGARRIBIA (Paraguay)
map (22° 2′S 60° 38′W) **15**:77
MARISOL **13**:157 *bibliog., illus.*
Women and Dog **13**:157 *illus.*
MARISSA (Illinois)
map (38° 15′N 89° 45′W) **11**:42
MARITAIN, JACQUES **13**:157 *bibliog.*
scholasticism **17**:132
MARITIME ADMINISTRATION
Commerce, U.S. Department of **5**:138
United States Merchant Marine Academy **19**:462
MARITIME CLIMATE **13**:157 *bibliog.*
ocean-atmosphere interaction **14**:321
MARITIME COMMUNICATIONS
frequency allocation **8**:326–327
semaphore **17**:194–195
MARITIME LAW **13**:158 *bibliog.*
barratry **3**:93
flat of convenience **8**:149
flotsam, jetsam, and lagan **8**:177
hypothecation **10**:351
neutrality **14**:108
oceanography **14**:344–345
MARITIME PROVINCES **13**:158
New Brunswick (Canada) **14**:115–118 *illus.*
Nova Scotia (Canada) **14**:269–271 *illus.*
Prince Edward Island (Canada) **15**:547–549 *illus.*
MARITSA RIVER
map (41° 42′N 26° 19′E) **3**:555
MARITZ, GERRIT
Pietermaritzburg (South Africa) **15**:297
MARIUS, GAIUS **13**:158 *bibliog.*
Catulus, Quintus Lutatius **4**:217
Rome, ancient **16**:301
Sulla, Lucius Cornelius **18**:336
MARIVAUX, PIERRE CARLET DE CHAMBLAIN DE **13**:158 *bibliog.*
Harlequin **10**:50
MARJ UYUN (Lebanon)
map (33° 22′N 35° 35′E) **12**:265
MARJORAM **13**:158
MARJORIBANKS, SIR DUDLEY
golden retriever **9**:232
MARK, GOSPEL ACCORDING TO **13**:159 *bibliog.*
Jesus Christ **11**:403–404
MARK, SAINT **13**:158–159 *bibliog.*
MARK ANTONY
Octavia **14**:347
MARK I (computer) **5**:160a
computer industry **5**:160n
MARKA (Somalia)
map (1° 47′N 44° 52′E) **18**:60
MARKED TREE (Arkansas)
map (35° 32′N 90° 25′W) **2**:166
MARKELIUS, SVEN GOTTFRID **13**:159
MARKER, CHRIS
documentary **6**:211
MARKERWAARD (region in Netherlands)
map (52° 33′N 5° 15′E) **14**:99
MARKESAN (Wisconsin)
map (43° 42′N 88° 59′W) **20**:185
MARKET ECONOMY *see* LAISSEZ-FAIRE
MARKET POWER *see* MONOPOLY AND COMPETITION (economics)
MARKET RESEARCH
census **4**:249
public opinion **15**:609
MARKET SYSTEM *see* CAPITALISM
MARKETING **13**:159 *bibliog.*
advertising **1**:111–114
direct mail **6**:187
grain **9**:281
mail-order business **13**:67
management science **13**:107
opinion polls **14**:405
propaganda **15**:568–569
public opinion **15**:609
retailing **16**:183
sales **17**:32
trademark **19**:263
trading stamps **19**:264
wholesaling **20**:143
MARKHAM (Illinois)
map (41° 36′N 87° 41′W) **11**:42
MARKHAM, EDWIN **13**:159 *bibliog.*
MARKHAM, MOUNT
map (82° 51′S 161° 21′E) **2**:40
MARKLE (Indiana)
map (40° 50′N 85° 20′W) **11**:111
MARKLEEVILLE (California)
map (38° 41′N 119° 47′W) **4**:31
MARKOV, ANDREI ANDREYEVICH **13**:159–160
MARKOV PROCESS
Markov, Andrei Andreyevich **13**:159–160
stochastic process **18**:273
MARKOVA, DAME ALICIA **13**:160 *bibliog.*
Ballets Russes de Monte Carlo **3**:48
MARKS (Mississippi)
map (34° 16′N 90° 16′W) **13**:469
MARKS, LILLIAN ALICIA *see* MARKOVA, DAME ALICIA
MARKSMANSHIP *see* SHOOTING (sport)
MARKSVILLE (Louisiana)
map (31° 8′N 92° 4′W) **12**:430
MARL **13**:160
commercial use **13**:160
MARLBORO (county in South Carolina)
map (34° 35′N 79° 40′W) **18**:98
MARLBORO MUSIC SCHOOL AND FESTIVAL
Busch, Adolf **3**:585
MARLBOROUGH (Guyana)
map (7° 29′N 58° 38′W) **9**:410
MARLBOROUGH (Massachusetts)
map (42° 21′N 71° 33′W) **13**:206
MARLBOROUGH (New Hampshire)
map (42° 54′N 72° 13′W) **14**:123
MARLBOROUGH, JOHN CHURCHILL, 1ST DUKE OF **13**:160 *bibliog., illus.*
Great Britain, history of **9**:315
Spanish Succession, War of the **18**:162–163
MARLBOROUGH, SARAH CHURCHILL, DUCHESS OF **13**:160 *bibliog.*
Anne, Queen of England, Scotland, and Ireland **2**:32
Marlborough, John Churchill, 1st Duke of **13**:160
MARLETTE (Michigan)
map (43° 20′N 83° 5′W) **13**:377
MARLEY, BOB
reggae **16**:128
MARLIN (fish) **8**:117 *illus.*; **13**:160–161 *illus.*
MARLIN (Texas)
map (31° 18′N 96° 53′W) **19**:129
MARLINTON (West Virginia)
map (38° 13′N 80° 6′W) **20**:111
MARLOW (Oklahoma)
map (34° 39′N 97° 57′W) **14**:368
MARLOWE, CHRISTOPHER **7**:194 *illus.*; **13**:161 *bibliog.*
Doctor Faustus **6**:210; **13**:50 *illus.*
Tamburlaine the Great **19**:19
MARLOWE, PHILIP (fictional character)
Farewell, My Lovely **8**:23
MARMADUKE (Arkansas)
map (36° 11′N 90° 23′W) **2**:166
MARMALADE *see* JAM AND JELLY
MARMARA, SEA OF **3**:318 *map*; **13**:161
map (40° 40′N 28° 15′E) **19**:343
seas, gulfs, and bays
Bosporus **3**:407 *map*
MARMARTH (North Dakota)
map (46° 18′N 103° 54′W) **14**:248
MARMET (West Virginia)
map (38° 15′N 81° 4′W) **20**:111
MARMOSET **13**:104 *illus.*; **13**:161 *illus.*; **15**:540 *illus.*
monkey **13**:534
tamarin **19**:18
MARMOT
groundhog **9**:373–374
steppe life **18**:257 *illus.*
MARNE, BATTLES OF THE **13**:161–162 *bibliog.*
Joffre, Joseph Jacques Césaire **11**:421
World War I **20**:224–225 *illus., map*; **20**:241–242
MARNE RIVER **13**:162
map (48° 49′N 2° 24′E) **8**:260
MAROA (Illinois)
map (40° 2′N 88° 57′W) **11**:42
MAROA (Venezuela)
map (2° 43′N 67° 33′W) **19**:542
MAROMOKOTRO MOUNTAIN
map (14° 1′S 48° 59′E) **13**:38
MARONDERA (Zimbabwe)
map (18° 10′S 31° 36′E) **20**:365
MARONI RIVER
map (5° 45′N 53° 58′W) **8**:311
MARONITES **13**:162 *bibliog.*
MAROS RIVER
map (46° 15′N 20° 13′E) **10**:307
MAROT (family) **13**:162 *bibliog.*
MAROT, CLÉMENT **13**:162 *bibliog.*
MAROVOAY (Madagascar)
map (16° 6′S 46° 39′E) **13**:38
MAROWIJNE RIVER
map (5° 45′N 53° 58′W) **18**:364
MARQUAND (Missouri)
map (37° 26′N 90° 10′W) **13**:476
MARQUAND, J. P. **13**:162 *bibliog.*
MARQUE AND REPRISAL, LETTER OF *see* PRIVATEERING
MARQUÉS, RENÉ
Latin American literature **12**:230
MARQUESAS ISLANDS **13**:162–163
map (9° 0′S 139° 30′W) **14**:334
MARQUESS (title)
titles of nobility and honor **19**:213–214
MARQUETRY **13**:163 *bibliog.*
Oeben, Jean François **14**:351
Riesener, Jean Henri **16**:219
MARQUETTE (Kansas)
map (38° 33′N 97° 50′W) **12**:18
MARQUETTE (Michigan)
map (46° 33′N 87° 24′W) **13**:377
MARQUETTE (county in Michigan)
map (46° 30′N 87° 40′W) **13**:377
MARQUETTE (county in Wisconsin)
map (43° 48′N 89° 25′W) **20**:185
MARQUETTE, JACQUES **13**:163 *bibliog.*
Canada, history of **4**:80 *map*
exploration of colonial America **19**:437 *map*
Michigan **13**:381
Missouri River **13**:481
Quapaw **16**:12
Sault Sainte Marie (Michigan) **17**:96
MARQUETTE UNIVERSITY **13**:163
MÁRQUEZ, GABRIEL GARCÍA *see* GARCÍA MÁRQUEZ, GABRIEL
MARQUIS (Grenada)
map (12° 6′N 61° 37′W) **9**:358
MARQUIS, DON **13**:163 *bibliog.*
MARRAH, MOUNT
map (13° 4′N 24° 21′E) **18**:320
MARRAKECH (Morocco) **13**:163; **13**:587 *illus.*
map (31° 38′N 8° 0′W) **13**:585
MARRERO (Louisiana)
map (29° 54′N 90° 7′W) **12**:430
MARRIAGE **13**:163–166 *bibliog., illus.*
adultery **1**:110
alienation of affections **1**:294
Arabs **2**:105–106
arranged marriages **13**:164
bigamy **3**:249
bride-price **3**:479
common law **5**:140; **13**:165
community property **5**:153
concubinage **5**:172
concubine **5**:171
courtly love **5**:317
divorce **6**:205–206
dowry **6**:252
endogamy **7**:171
exogamy **7**:333
family **8**:18
fertility rites **8**:60
heraldry **10**:134
incest **11**:73–74
kinship **12**:86
legal marriage
definition **13**:165
history **13**:165–166
marriage broker **13**:164
marriage contract **13**:165–166
monogamy **13**:536
Nevada **14**:113
partner selection **13**:164
passage rites **15**:104
polygamy **15**:419
psychotherapy **15**:603
remarriage **13**:165
sexual intercourse **17**:231
spouses
expectations and demands **13**:164
obligations and rights **13**:164
stages **13**:164–165
wedding **13**:163–164 *illus.*; **13**:166 *illus.*
women in society **20**:201; **20**:202; **20**:203
MARRIAGE OF FIGARO, THE (opera) **13**:166 *bibliog.*
MARRIAGE OF FIGARO, THE (play) **13**:166 *bibliog.*
Beaumarchais, Pierre Caron de **3**:146
MARRIAGE ITALIAN STYLE (book)
De Filippo, Eduardo **6**:58
MARRIC, J. J. *see* CREASEY, JOHN
MARRIED WOMEN'S PROPERTY ACT (1875)
common law **5**:140
MARROTTE, EDME
meteorology **13**:342
MARROW (vegetable) **19**:532 *illus.*
MARRYAT, FREDERICK **13**:166
MARS (mythology) **13**:166; **13**:701 *illus.*
MARS (Pennsylvania)
map (40° 42′N 80° 6′W) **15**:147
MARS (planet) **13**:166–169 *bibliog., illus., table*
atmosphere **13**:167–168
canals
Lowell, Percival **12**:444
Schiaparelli, Giovanni Virginio **17**:120
characteristics **13**:167 *table, table*; **18**:46 *table*
Olympus Mons **13**:167 *illus.*
Eros (astronomy) **7**:232
origin of life **12**:327
Pickering, William Henry **15**:293
planets **15**:329–331
satellites **13**:167
Deimos **6**:85
Phobos **15**:249
solar system **18**:46–49 *illus., table*
space exploration **18**:125–126 *illus.*
Mariner **13**:156
Mars (spacecraft) **13**:169–170
Viking (spacecraft) **19**:593–594
Viking Lander Photographs **13**:168 *illus.*
Zond **20**:373
surface appearance **13**:167
MARS (spacecraft) **13**:169–170 *bibliog., illus.*
Mars probes **13**:169
MARS HILL (Maine)
map (46° 31′N 67° 52′W) **13**:70
MARS HILL (North Carolina)
map (35° 47′N 82° 29′W) **14**:242
MARSALA (Italy)
map (37° 48′N 12° 26′E) **11**:321
MARSAXLOKK BAY
map (35° 49′N 14° 33′E) **13**:94
MARSDEN, SAMUEL
New Zealand, history of **14**:161
"MARSEILLAISE, LA" (anthem) **13**:170
Strasbourg (France) **18**:289
MARSEILLE (France) **13**:170–171 *illus.*
climate **8**:261 *table*
map (43° 18′N 5° 24′E) **8**:260
Unité d'Habitation **12**:254 *illus.*
MARSEILLE, FOLQUET DE
minstrels, minnesingers, and troubadours **13**:460
MARSEILLES (Illinois)
map (41° 20′N 88° 43′W) **11**:42
MARSH *see* SWAMP, MARSH, AND BOG
MARSH, GEORGE PERKINS **13**:171
MARSH, DAME NGAIO **13**:171 *bibliog.*
MARSH, OTHNIEL CHARLES **13**:171 *bibliog.*
vertebrate paleontology **13**:171
MARSH, REGINALD **13**:171 *bibliog., illus.*
Why Not Use the "L"? **13**:171 *illus.*
MARSH HARBOUR (Bahama Islands)
map (26° 33′N 77° 3′W) **3**:23
MARSH ISLAND
map (29° 35′N 91° 53′W) **12**:430
MARSH MALLOW
mallow **13**:92
MARSH MARIGOLD
cowslip (botany) **5**:322
MARSH TEST
arsenic **2**:189
MARSHALL (county in Alabama)
map (34° 20′N 86° 20′W) **1**:234
MARSHALL (Arkansas)
map (35° 55′N 92° 38′W) **2**:166
MARSHALL (Illinois)
map (39° 23′N 87° 42′W) **11**:42

MARSHALL (county in Illinois)
map (41° 0′N 89° 25′W) **11**:42
MARSHALL (county in Indiana)
map (41° 21′N 86° 19′W) **11**:111
MARSHALL (county in Iowa)
map (42° 2′N 92° 55′W) **11**:244
MARSHALL (county in Kansas)
map (39° 50′N 96° 30′W) **12**:18
MARSHALL (county in Kentucky)
map (36° 55′N 88° 20′W) **12**:47
MARSHALL (Michigan)
map (42° 16′N 84° 58′W) **13**:377
MARSHALL (Minnesota)
map (44° 27′N 95° 47′W) **13**:453
MARSHALL (county in Minnesota)
map (48° 20′N 96° 15′W) **13**:453
MARSHALL (county in Mississippi)
map (34° 50′N 89° 30′W) **13**:469
MARSHALL (Missouri)
map (39° 7′N 93° 12′W) **13**:476
MARSHALL (North Carolina)
map (35° 48′N 82° 41′W) **14**:242
MARSHALL (county in Oklahoma)
map (34° 0′N 96° 45′W) **14**:368
MARSHALL (county in South Dakota)
map (45° 40′N 97° 38′W) **18**:103
MARSHALL (county in Tennessee)
map (35° 25′N 86° 50′W) **19**:104
MARSHALL (Texas)
map (32° 33′N 94° 23′W) **19**:129
MARSHALL (county in West Virginia)
map (39° 52′N 80° 40′W) **20**:111
MARSHALL, ALFRED **13**:171 *bibliog.*
economics **7**:49
MARSHALL, GEORGE C. **13**:171–172 *bibliog., illus.*
MARSHALL, JAMES WILSON **13**:172 *bibliog.*
MARSHALL, JOHN **13**:172 *bibliog., illus.*
Brown v. *Maryland* **3**:517
Cohens v. *Virginia* **5**:95–96
Constitution of the United States **5**:212; **5**:216–217
Dartmouth College v. *Woodward* **6**:40
law, history of **12**:246 *illus.*
McCulloch v. *Maryland* **13**:11
Marbury v. *Madison* **13**:144
Supreme Court of the United States **18**:357–358
United States, history of the **19**:445
MARSHALL, SIR JOHN HUBERT **13**:172–173
civilization **5**:34
Taxila **19**:48
MARSHALL, PAULE **13**:173
MARSHALL, SAMUEL LYMAN ATWOOD **13**:173
MARSHALL, THOMAS R. **13**:173 *bibliog.*
MARSHALL, THURGOOD **13**:173 *bibliog.*; **15**:524 *illus.*; **18**:355 *illus.*
MARSHALL FIELD WHOLESALE STORE **1**:328 *illus.*; **16**:212 *illus.*
Field (family) **8**:71
MARSHALL FORD DAM
Colorado River (Texas) **5**:121
MARSHALL ISLANDS (U.S.) **13**:173
Bikini **3**:250
Eniwetok **7**:206
flag **8**:144 *illus.*
map (9° 0′N 168° 0′E) **14**:334
Pacific Islands, Trust Territory of the **15**:5
World War II **20**:276–277 *map*
MARSHALL PLAN **13**:173 *bibliog.*
cold war **5**:98
foreign aid **8**:224
Marshall, George C. **13**:172
Organization for Economic Cooperation and Development **14**:440
Truman, Harry S. **19**:317
United States, history of the **19**:456
MARSHALL SPACE FLIGHT CENTER
von Braun, Wernher **19**:633
MARSHALLBERG (North Carolina)
map (34° 44′N 76° 31′W) **14**:242
MARSHALLTON (Delaware)
map (39° 45′N 75° 39′W) **6**:88
MARSHALLTOWN (Iowa)
map (42° 3′N 92° 55′W) **11**:244
MARSHFIELD (Massachusetts)
map (42° 7′N 70° 43′W) **3**:409
MARSHFIELD (Missouri)
map (37° 15′N 92° 54′W) **13**:476
MARSHFIELD (Wisconsin)
map (44° 40′N 90° 10′W) **20**:185
MARSHFIELD HILLS (Massachusetts)
map (42° 9′N 70° 44′W) **13**:206
MARSHVILLE (North Carolina)
map (34° 59′N 80° 26′W) **14**:242
MARSILIUS OF PADUA **13**:173 *bibliog.*
state (in political philosophy) **18**:230
MARSING (Idaho)
map (43° 33′N 116° 48′W) **11**:26
MARSTON, JOHN **13**:174 *bibliog.*
MARSUPIAL **11**:469 *illus.*; **13**:174–175 *bibliog., illus.*
bandicoot **3**:62
cuscus **5**:396–397
gestation **9**:160
kangaroo **12**:15
koala **12**:103–104
mammal **13**:102; **13**:104 *illus.*
mole **13**:174; **13**:175 *illus.*; **13**:507
mouse **13**:174; **13**:175 *illus.*
numbat **14**:292
opossum **14**:407
phalanger **15**:218
Tasmanian devil **19**:42
Tasmanian wolf **19**:42–43
wallaby **20**:13
wombat **20**:200
MARSYAS **13**:175
MARTABAN, GULF OF
map (16° 30′N 97° 0′E) **3**:573
MARTEL, CHARLES *see* CHARLES MARTEL
MARTEN (weasel) **13**:175–176 *illus.*
MARTHA'S VINEYARD
Wampanoag **20**:21
MARTHA'S VINEYARD (Massachusetts) **13**:176 *bibliog.*
map (41° 25′N 70° 40′W) **13**:206
Wampanoag **20**:21
MARTÍ, JOSÉ **13**:176 *bibliog.*
MARTIAL **13**:176 *bibliog.*
Juvenal **11**:480
MARTIAL ARTS **13**:176–178 *bibliog., illus.*
basic techniques **13**:176–178
colored belts **13**:176–177
hand conditioning **13**:178
history **13**:176
MARTIAL LAW **13**:178 *bibliog.*
military justice **13**:421
MARTIAN CHRONICLES, THE (book) **13**:178
MARTIGNY (Switzerland)
map (46° 6′N 7° 4′E) **18**:394
MARTIN (bird) **13**:178–179 *illus.*
MARTIN (county in Florida)
map (27° 7′N 80° 31′W) **8**:172
MARTIN (county in Indiana)
map (38° 45′N 86° 50′W) **11**:111
MARTIN (county in Kentucky)
map (37° 50′N 82° 30′W) **12**:47
MARTIN (county in Minnesota)
map (43° 38′N 94° 30′W) **13**:453
MARTIN (county in North Carolina)
map (35° 50′N 77° 5′W) **14**:242
MARTIN (South Dakota)
map (43° 10′N 101° 44′W) **18**:103
MARTIN (Tennessee)
map (36° 21′N 88° 51′W) **19**:104
MARTIN (county in Texas)
map (32° 22′N 101° 58′W) **19**:129
MARTIN, AGNES BERNICE **13**:179 *bibliog.*
MARTIN, ARCHER **13**:179
MARTIN, CLAIRE **13**:179
MARTIN, FRANK **13**:179 *bibliog.*
MARTIN, HOMER DODGE **13**:179
MARTIN, JOHN **13**:179 *bibliog.*
modern dance **13**:497
MARTIN, JOSEPH WILLIAM, JR. **13**:179
MARTIN, JOSIAH
North Carolina **14**:246
MARTIN, LUTHER **13**:179 *bibliog.*
MARTIN, MARY **13**:179
MARTIN, PIERRE DENIS
Louis XIV, King of France **7**:289 *illus.*
MARTIN IV, POPE
Peter III, King of Aragon (Peter the Great) **15**:200
MARTIN V, POPE **13**:180 *bibliog.*
MARTIN DU GARD, ROGER **13**:179 *bibliog.*
MARTIN LAKE
map (32° 50′N 85° 55′W) **1**:234
MARTIN OF TOURS, SAINT **13**:179–180 *bibliog.*
relics
chapel **4**:284
MARTINEAU, HARRIET **13**:180 *bibliog.*
MARTINEZ (California)
map (37° 55′N 121° 55′W) **4**:31
MARTÍNEZ, JACINTO BENAVENTE Y *see* BENAVENTE Y MARTÍNEZ, JACINTO
MARTINEZ, RAUL
Latin American art and architecture **12**:228
MARTÍNEZ DE LA TORRE (Mexico)
map (20° 4′N 97° 3′W) **13**:357
MARTÍNEZ ESPINEL, VICENTE *see* ESPINEL, VICENTE MARTÍNEZ
MARTÍNEZ SIERRA, GREGORIO **13**:180 *bibliog.*
MARTINI, SIMONE **13**:180 *bibliog., illus.*
Guidoriccio da Fogliano **13**:180 *illus.*
MARTINIQUE **13**:181 *bibliog.*
cities
Fort-de-France **8**:236
map (14° 40′N 61° 0′W) **20**:109
Pelée, Mount **15**:137
MARTINS, PETER **13**:181 *bibliog.*; **14**:154 *illus.*
New York City Ballet **14**:155
MARTINS FERRY (Ohio)
map (40° 6′N 80° 44′W) **14**:357
MARTINSBURG (Pennsylvania)
map (40° 19′N 78° 20′W) **15**:147
MARTINSBURG (West Virginia)
map (39° 27′N 77° 58′W) **20**:111
MARTINSON, HARRY EDMUND **13**:181 *bibliog.*
MARTINSVILLE (Illinois)
map (39° 20′N 87° 53′W) **11**:42
MARTINSVILLE (Indiana)
map (39° 26′N 86° 25′W) **11**:111
MARTINSVILLE (Virginia)
map (36° 41′N 79° 52′W) **19**:607
MARTINŮ, BOHUSLAV **13**:181 *bibliog.*
MARTON (New Zealand)
map (40° 5′S 175° 23′E) **14**:158
MARTORELL, JOHANOT
Catalan literature **4**:198
MARUYAMA OKYO *see* OKYO
MARV DASHT (Iran)
map (29° 50′N 52° 40′E) **11**:250
MARVELL (Arkansas)
map (34° 33′N 90° 55′W) **2**:166
MARVELL, ANDREW **13**:181 *bibliog.*
MARVIN v. *MARVIN*
marriage **13**:165
MARVINE, MOUNT
map (38° 40′N 111° 39′W) **19**:492
MARWAYNE (Alberta)
map (53° 32′N 110° 20′W) **1**:256
MARX, CHICO *see* MARX BROTHERS
MARX, GROUCHO *see* MARX BROTHERS
MARX, HARPO *see* MARX BROTHERS
MARX, KARL **13**:181–182 *bibliog., illus.*
alienation **1**:294
communism **5**:146 *illus.*
Communist Manifesto **5**:151
determinism **6**:134
dialectical materialism **6**:150
economics **7**:48
elites **7**:141
Engels, Friedrich **7**:176–177
Europe, history of **7**:293
Greeley, Horace **9**:346
Hegel, Georg Wilhelm Friedrich **10**:106
International, Socialist **11**:218
Kapital, Das **12**:25
law **12**:242–243
Marxism **13**:183–184
materialism **13**:219
Ricardo, David **16**:206
socialism **18**:19–20
state (in political philosophy) **18**:232
Trier (West Germany) **19**:297
MARX BROTHERS **13**:182–183 *bibliog., illus.*
Marx, Harpo
fool **8**:213
MARXISM **13**:183–184 *bibliog.*
art criticism **2**:207
Bernstein, Eduard **3**:223–224
Bolsheviks and Mensheviks **3**:371
bourgeoisie **3**:424
class, social **5**:40
communism **5**:146
criticism **13**:184
dialectical materialism **6**:150
dictatorship of the proletariat **6**:159
educational philosophy **7**:63
Engels, Friedrich **7**:176–177
Ethiopia **7**:254–255
Gramsci, Antonio **9**:283
imperialism **11**:62
influences **13**:184
Kautsky, Karl Johann **12**:32
Lassalle, Ferdinand **12**:214
law **12**:243
Lenin, Vladimir Ilich **12**:282–283
Lukács, György **12**:453
Luxemburg, Rosa **12**:473
Mao Tse-tung (Mao Zedong) **13**:136
Marx, Karl **13**:181
Plekhanov, Georgy Valentinovich **15**:366–367
profit **15**:561–562
proletariat **15**:567
property **15**:570–571
publications
Communist Manifesto **5**:151
Kapital, Das **12**:25
socialism **18**:19–24
sociology **18**:30
Soviet education **18**:113–114
state (in political philosophy) **18**:232
theory **13**:183–184
MARY **13**:184–185 *bibliog., illus.*
Anne, Saint **2**:32
Bernadette, Saint **3**:220
Carmelites **4**:153
courtly love **5**:317
Ephesus, Council of **7**:216
Fátima (Portugal) **8**:34
iconography **11**:21–24
Immaculate Conception **11**:54
Joachim, Saint **11**:420
Joseph, Saint **11**:451
virgin birth **19**:605
MARY (city in Russia) *see* MERV
MARY, QUEEN OF SCOTS **13**:186–187 *bibliog., illus.*
battle between her supporters and the Protestant Lords **17**:152 *illus.*
Elizabeth I, Queen of England **7**:141
husbands
Bothwell, James Hepburn, 4th Earl of **3**:415
Darnley, Henry Stewart, Lord **6**:39
Francis II, King of France **8**:276
Kinross (Scotland) **12**:85
MARY I, QUEEN OF ENGLAND **13**:185–186 *bibliog., illus.*
Grey, Lady Jane **9**:360
MARY II, QUEEN OF ENGLAND, SCOTLAND, AND IRELAND **13**:186 *bibliog.*
English Bill of Rights **3**:253
Glorious Revolution **9**:209
William III, King of England, Scotland, and Ireland **20**:156
MARY OF BURGUNDY **13**:185
Habsburg (dynasty) **10**:6 *illus.*
"MARY HAD A LITTLE LAMB" (nursery rhyme)
Hale, Sarah Josepha **10**:19
MARY MAGDALENE **13**:185
MARY AND MARTHA **13**:185
MARYINSKY THEATRE *see* KIROV BALLET
MARYKNOLL MISSIONERS **13**:187 *bibliog.*
MARYLAND **13**:187–193 *bibliog., illus., map*
Camp David **4**:63
cities
Annapolis **2**:31–32 *illus.*
Baltimore **3**:55–56 *map*
Bethesda **3**:230
Frederick **8**:289
Hagerstown **10**:9
Salisbury **17**:33
climate **13**:189
cultural institutions **13**:190
economic activity **13**:191
education **13**:190
Hood College **10**:225
Johns Hopkins University, The **11**:430
Maryland, state universities and colleges of **13**:193
St. John's College **17**:20
fishing and forestry **13**:191
flag **13**:187 *illus.*
flower, state
black-eyed Susan **3**:314–315
geographical linguistics **9**:99 *map*
government and politics **13**:191
historical sites and recreation **13**:190
history **13**:191–192
Brent, Margaret **3**:473
Calvert (family) **4**:48
Martin, Luther **13**:179
United States, history of the **19**:436
land and resources **13**:187–189 *illus., map*
map (39° 0′N 76° 45′W) **19**:419
people **13**:190
resources **13**:189
rivers, lakes, and waterways **13**:189
seal, state **13**:187 *illus.*
transportation and shipping **13**:191
vegetation and animal life **13**:189 *illus.*
MARYLAND, STATE UNIVERSITIES AND COLLEGES OF **13**:193

MARYLAND CITY (Maryland)
map (39° 6′N 76° 50′W) **13**:188
MARYLAND HEIGHTS (Missouri)
map (38° 44′N 90° 27′W) **13**:476
MARYMOUNT COLLEGE **13**:193
MARY'S IGLOO (Alaska)
map (65° 9′N 165° 4′W) **1**:242
MARYSTOWN (Newfoundland)
map (47° 10′N 55° 9′W) **14**:166
MARYSVALE (Utah)
map (38° 27′N 112° 11′W) **19**:492
MARYSVILLE (California)
map (39° 9′N 121° 35′W) **4**:31
MARYSVILLE (Kansas)
map (39° 51′N 96° 39′W) **12**:18
MARYSVILLE (Michigan)
map (42° 54′N 82° 29′W) **13**:377
MARYSVILLE (Ohio)
map (40° 14′N 83° 22′W) **14**:357
MARYSVILLE (Pennsylvania)
map (40° 20′N 76° 56′W) **15**:147
MARYSVILLE (Washington)
map (48° 3′N 122° 11′W) **20**:35
MARYVILLE (Missouri)
map (40° 21′N 94° 52′W) **13**:476
MARYVILLE (Tennessee)
map (35° 46′N 83° 58′W) **19**:104
MASACCIO **13**:193–194 *bibliog., illus.*
Italian art and architecture **11**:312
Lippi, Filippino **12**:362
Madonna and Child Enthroned **13**:193 *illus.*
The Tribute Money **16**:151 *illus.*
MASADA (Israel) **3**:242 *illus.*; **13**:194 *bibliog., illus.*
Zealots **20**:357
MASAI **1**:144 *illus.*; **13**:194–195 *bibliog., illus.*
cattle and cattle raising **4**:214 *illus.*
MASAKA (Uganda)
map (0° 20′S 31° 44′E) **19**:372
MASAN (Korea)
map (35° 11′N 128° 32′E) **12**:113
MASANOBU (1434–1530) **13**:195 *bibliog.*
MASANOBU (1686–1764) **13**:195 *bibliog.*
MASARYK, JAN **13**:195 *bibliog.*
MASARYK, TOMÁŠ **13**:195 *bibliog., illus.*
Czechoslovakia **5**:416
MASAYA (Nicaragua)
map (11° 58′N 86° 6′W) **14**:179
MASBATE ISLAND
map (12° 15′N 123° 30′E) **15**:237
MASCAGNI, PIETRO **13**:195
MASCARENE ISLANDS
dodo bird **6**:212
MASCON **13**:196
Lunar Orbiter **12**:461
MASCOT (Tennessee)
map (36° 4′N 83° 44′W) **19**:104
MASCOUTAH (Illinois)
map (38° 29′N 89° 48′W) **11**:42
MASCULINITY *see* MEN (biology)
MASEFIELD, JOHN **13**:196 *bibliog.*
MASER **13**:196
Townes, Charles Hard **19**:255
MASERU (Lesotho) **13**:196
map (29° 28′S 27° 30′E) **12**:297
MASHABA MOUNTAINS
map (18° 45′S 30° 32′E) **20**:365
MASHHAD (Iran) **13**:196
map (36° 18′N 59° 36′E) **11**:250
MASINA, GIULIETTA **8**:48 *illus.*
MASINISSA **13**:196
Numidia **14**:295
Punic Wars **15**:625
Sophonisba **18**:68
MASISEA (Peru)
map (8° 36′S 74° 19′W) **15**:193
MASJED SOLEYMAN (Iran)
map (31° 58′N 49° 18′E) **11**:250
MASK (electronics)
computer **5**:160h
computer-aided design and computer-aided manufacturing **5**:160L
MASK, LAKE
map (53° 35′N 9° 20′W) **11**:258
MASKS **11**:139–140; **13**:196–197 *bibliog., illus.*
African art **1**:160–164 *illus.*
African ivory mask **11**:337 *illus.*
African witch doctor mask **15**:544 *illus.*
Amenhotep III's death mask **15**:447 *illus.*
Chimu gold funerary mask **15**:501 *illus.*
folk art **8**:196
gigaku **9**:178
Indians of North America, art of the **11**:139–141 *illus.*
Indians of North America, music and dance of the **11**:143–144
Lamaist art and architecture **12**:173
Mycenaean gold death mask **13**:689 *illus.*
New Hebrides **14**:336 *illus.*
Phoenician gold mask **15**:250 *illus.*
pre-Columbian art and architecture **15**:501
Roman art and architecture **16**:275
Tutankhamen's gold funerary mask **19**:355 *illus.*
MASLOW, ABRAHAM H. **13**:198 *bibliog.*
humanistic psychology **10**:299
motivation **13**:610
personality **15**:189
MASOCH, LEOPOLD VON SACHER *see* SACHER-MASOCH, LEOPOLD VON
MASOCHISM **13**:198 *bibliog.*
sadism **17**:10
MASOLINO DA PANICALE **13**:198 *bibliog.*
MASON (family) **13**:198 *bibliog.*
MASON (county in Illinois)
map (40° 15′N 89° 55′W) **11**:42
MASON (county in Kentucky)
map (38° 35′N 83° 48′W) **12**:47
MASON (Michigan)
map (42° 35′N 84° 26′W) **13**:377
MASON (county in Michigan)
map (44° 0′N 86° 15′W) **13**:377
MASON (Ohio)
map (39° 17′N 84° 19′W) **14**:357
MASON (Tennessee)
map (35° 25′N 89° 33′W) **19**:104
MASON (Texas)
map (30° 45′N 99° 14′W) **19**:129
MASON (county in Texas)
map (30° 43′N 99° 15′W) **19**:129
MASON (county in Washington)
map (47° 20′N 123° 9′W) **20**:35
MASON (county in West Virginia)
map (38° 45′N 82° 0′W) **20**:111
MASON, CHARLES
Mason-Dixon line **13**:199
MASON, GEORGE **13**:198–199 *bibliog.*
Bill of Rights **3**:252
MASON, JAMES **13**:199 *bibliog.*
MASON, JAMES MURRAY **13**:199
Trent Affair **19**:290
MASON, JOHN (1586–1635) **13**:199 *bibliog.*
Gorges, Sir Ferdinando **9**:250
New Hampshire **14**:125
MASON, JOHN (1600?–1672)
Pequot War **15**:158
MASON, JOHN Y.
Ostend Manifesto **14**:457
MASON, LOWELL **1**:349 *illus.*
MASON, PERRY (fictional character)
Gardner, Erle Stanley **9**:44–45
MASON CITY (Illinois)
map (40° 12′N 89° 42′W) **11**:42
MASON CITY (Iowa)
map (43° 9′N 93° 12′W) **11**:244
MASON CITY (Nebraska)
map (41° 13′N 99° 18′W) **14**:70
MASON-DIXON LINE **13**:199 *bibliog., map*
geographical linguistics **9**:98–99 *map*
MASONIC ORDERS *see* FREEMASONRY
MASONRY (stonework)
brick and bricklaying **3**:477–478
Inca **11**:72 *illus.*
lighthouse **12**:336
stonemasonry **18**:283
MASONS *see* FREEMASONRY
MASONTOWN (Pennsylvania)
map (39° 51′N 79° 54′W) **15**:147
MASORAH **13**:199 *bibliog.*
MASPERO, SIR GASTON **13**:199
MASPERO, HENRI
Maspero, Sir Gaston **13**:199
MASQAT *see* MUSCAT
MASQUE **13**:200 *bibliog., illus.*
"MASQUE OF THE RED DEATH, THE" (short story) **13**:200
MASS (liturgy) **13**:200–201 *bibliog.*
Eucharist **7**:262
MASS (musical setting) **13**:201 *bibliog.*
antiphon **2**:65
Byzantine music **3**:608
cantus firmus **4**:118
composers **13**:201
Bernstein, Leonard **3**:224
Bruckner, Anton **3**:521
Byrd, William **3**:602
Caldara, Antonio **4**:25
Dufay, Guillaume **6**:293
Obrecht, Jacob **14**:316
Okeghem, Jean d' **14**:366
Palestrina, Giovanni Pierluigi da **15**:46–47
Italian music **11**:318 *illus.*
music, history of Western **13**:665
plainsong **15**:326
Renaissance music **16**:156
requiem **16**:176
sequence **17**:207
Stabat Mater **18**:207
MASS (physics) **13**:201 *bibliog.*
conservation, laws of **5**:204
electron
atomic constants **2**:309
energy **7**:172
energy relationship
Einstein, Albert **7**:93
fundamental particles **8**:361; **8**:362 *table*
gravitational force **13**:201
inertia **11**:161; **13**:201
law of mass action
Guldberg, Cato Maximilian **9**:402
Waage, Peter **20**:3
matter **13**:230–231
measurement **13**:254–255
units, physical **19**:466 *illus.*
neutrino **14**:108
pound **15**:475
proton
atomic constants **2**:309
star **18**:224
theory of relativity **13**:201
weight (physics) **20**:92
MASS, CENTER OF *see* CENTER OF GRAVITY
MASS, LAW OF CONSERVATION OF *see* CONSERVATION, LAWS OF
MASS COMMUNICATION **13**:201–203 *bibliog.*
advertising **1**:111–114
communications satellite **5**:144–145 *illus.*
future **13**:202–203
McLuhan, Marshall **13**:33
newspaper **14**:172–173 *illus., table*
periodical **13**:169–170 *illus.*
presidential elections **15**:529–531
primitive methods **13**:201
propaganda **15**:568–569
publishing **15**:611–612
radio and television broadcasting **16**:54–60
telecommunications **19**:75–76
MASS DEFECT (physics) **13**:203 *bibliog.*
MASS-LUMINOSITY RELATION **13**:203
Eddington, Sir Arthur **7**:55
star **18**:224
MASS MEDIA *see* MASS COMMUNICATION
MASS NUMBER **13**:203
MASS PRODUCTION **13**:203–204 *bibliog.*
assembly line **2**:264–265
automation **2**:357–358
automotive industry **2**:363–368
Ford (family) **8**:221
Model T **13**:490
technology, history of **19**:67–68 *illus.*
clocks and watches
Thomas, Seth **19**:174
furniture
Eames, Charles **7**:5
industrial design **11**:155–156
industrial engineering **11**:156
industrial management **11**:156–157
industrial psychology **11**:157
manufacturing **13**:133
shipbuilding
Kaiser, Henry John **12**:7
textile industry
Whitney, Eli **20**:141
MASS SPECTROMETRY **13**:204 *bibliog.*
Aston, Francis William **2**:268
Dempster, Arthur Jeffrey **6**:105
mass defect **13**:203
mass spectrometers **13**:204
uses **13**:204
MASS TRANSIT *see* BUS; ELEVATED RAILROAD; STREETCAR; SUBWAY; TRANSPORTATION
MASSABESIC LAKE
map (42° 58′N 71° 23′W) **14**:123
MASSAC (county in Illinois)
map (37° 15′N 88° 40′W) **11**:42
MASSACHUSET (American Indians) **13**:204–205 *bibliog.*
MASSACHUSETTS **13**:205–212 *bibliog., illus., map*
agriculture, forestry, and fishing **13**:209
cities
Amherst **1**:369
Boston **3**:408–410 *illus., map*
Brockton **3**:501
Brookline **3**:510
Cambridge **4**:52
Concord **5**:171
Fall River **8**:13
Gloucester **9**:209
Holyoke **10**:211
Hyannis **10**:327
Lawrence **12**:249
Lowell **12**:443
Lynn **12**:477
New Bedford **14**:115
Northampton **14**:253
Pittsfield **15**:322
Plymouth **15**:374
Provincetown **15**:584
Quincy **16**:26–27
Salem **17**:31
Somerville **18**:61
Springfield **18**:200
Worcester **20**:216
climate **13**:205; **13**:207
culture **13**:208
economic activity **13**:209; **13**:211
education **13**:208–209 *illus.*
Amherst College **1**:369
Andover Newton Theological School **1**:406
Boston College **3**:410
Boston Latin School **3**:410
Boston University **3**:411
Brandeis University **3**:453
Clark University **5**:40
Harvard University **10**:64
Holy Cross, College of the **10**:209
Lyon, Mary **12**:478
Mann, Horace **13**:122–123 *bibliog.*
Massachusetts, state universities and colleges of **13**:212
Massachusetts Institute of Technology **13**:212
Mount Holyoke College **13**:618
Northeastern University **14**:254
Palmer, Alice Freeman **15**:50
Parker, Francis Wayland **15**:90
Peabody, Elizabeth **15**:122–123
Radcliffe College **16**:41
Simmons College **17**:314
Smith College **17**:371–372
Tufts University **19**:329
Wellesley College **20**:100
Wheaton College **20**:126
Wheelock College **20**:129
Williams College **20**:161
flag **13**:205 *illus.*
flower, state
trailing arbutus **19**:265
government and politics **13**:209–210
gerrymander **9**:158 *illus.*
historic sites **13**:208
history **13**:210–211
American Revolution **1**:355
Bunker Hill, Battle of **3**:563
coin **14**:296 *illus.*
Eliot, John **7**:139
Hutchinson, Thomas **10**:323
Intolerable Acts **11**:231–232
Lexington and Concord, Battles of **12**:309
Lodge (family) **12**:392
Maine **13**:74
Massachusetts Bay Company **13**:212
Otis, James **14**:460
Pynchon, William **15**:634
Revere, Paul **16**:185–186
Sacco and Vanzetti case **17**:6
Salem Witch Trials **17**:31
Shays's Rebellion **17**:247
Shirley, William **17**:277–278
land and resources **13**:205–207 *map*
manufacturing **13**:209
map (42° 20′N 71° 50′W) **19**:419
people **13**:207–208
Massachuset **13**:204
recreation and sports **13**:208–209
regions
Berkshire Hills **3**:214
Cape Cod **4**:120
Martha's Vineyard **13**:176
Nantucket Island **14**:14
rivers, lakes, and waterways **13**:207
Buzzards Bay **3**:601
seal, state **13**:205 *illus.*
vegetation and animal life **13**:207
MASSACHUSETTS, STATE UNIVERSITIES AND COLLEGES OF **13**:212
MASSACHUSETTS BAY
map (42° 20′N 70° 50′W) **13**:206

MASSACHUSETTS BAY COLONY *see* MASSACHUSETTS BAY COMPANY
MASSACHUSETTS BAY COMPANY **13**:212 *bibliog.*
Endecott, John **7**:168
Gorges, Sir Ferdinando **9**:250
Hutchinson, Anne **10**:322
Massachusetts **13**:210
Phips, Sir William **15**:248
Plymouth Colony **15**:374
primary education **15**:537
town meeting **19**:255
United States, history of the **19**:436
Winthrop (family) **20**:181
MASSACHUSETTS CENTINEL AND THE REPUBLICAN JOURNAL, THE
Russel, Benjamin **16**:348
MASSACHUSETTS COLORED REGIMENT, 54TH *see* 54TH MASSACHUSETTS COLORED REGIMENT
MASSACHUSETTS EMIGRANT AID COMPANY *see* EMIGRANT AID COMPANY
MASSACHUSETTS GOVERNMENT ACT *see* INTOLERABLE ACTS
MASSACHUSETTS INSTITUTE OF TECHNOLOGY **13**:212
Lincoln Laboratory **12**:350
Samuelson, Paul A. **17**:49
vocational education **19**:624
Wiener, Norbert **20**:146
MASSAGE, CARDIAC *see* CARDIOPULMONARY RESUSCITATION
MASSASAUGA **13**:212 *illus.*
MASSASOIT **13**:212–213 *bibliog.*
Samoset **17**:47
Squanto **18**:202
Wampanoag **20**:21
MASSENA (New York)
map (44° 56′N 74° 54′W) **14**:149
MASSÉNA, ANDRÉ **13**:213 *bibliog.*
MASSENET, JULES **13**:213 *bibliog.*
MASSEY (New Zealand)
map (36° 51′S 174° 36′E) **14**:158
MASSEY, VINCENT **13**:213
MASSEY, WILLIAM **13**:213 *bibliog.*
MASSIF CENTRAL (France) **13**:213
Limousin **12**:346–347 *map*
map (45° 0′N 3° 10′E) **8**:260
MASSILLON (Ohio)
map (40° 48′N 81° 32′W) **14**:357
MASSINE, LEONID **13**:213 *bibliog.*
Ballets Russes de Monte Carlo **3**:48
MASSINGER, PHILIP **13**:213–214 *bibliog.*
MASSIVE MOUNT
map (39° 12′N 106° 28′W) **5**:116
MASSON, ANDRÉ **13**:214 *bibliog.*
surrealism (art) **18**:364–365
MASSYS, QUENTIN **13**:214 *bibliog.*, *illus.*
moneychanger **3**:69 *illus.*
portrait of Paracelsus **13**:214 *illus.*
MASTABA **13**:214 *bibliog.*
Egyptian art and architecture **7**:86
pyramids **15**:635
MASTARNA *see* LARS PORSENA, KING OF CLUSIUM
MASTECTOMY **13**:215 *bibliog.*
cancer **4**:105–106
sex change **17**:224
MASTER E. S. **13**:215 *bibliog.*
MASTER OF FLÉMALLE *see* CAMPIN, ROBERT
MASTER FRANCKE **13**:215 *bibliog.*
MASTER HONORÉ **13**:215 *bibliog.*
MASTER OF MOULINS **13**:215 *bibliog.*
MASTER OF TAHULL
Maiestas Christi fresco **16**:285 *illus.*
MASTER OF THE AMSTERDAM CABINET *see* MASTER OF THE HOUSEBOOK
MASTER OF THE HOUSEBOOK **13**:215 *bibliog.*
MASTER OF THE KING'S MUSIC (Great Britain)
Bax, Sir Arnold **3**:131–132
MASTER OF THE PLAYING CARDS **13**:215 *bibliog.*
MASTER OF THE QUEEN'S MUSIC (Great Britain)
Bliss, Sir Arthur **3**:333
MASTERS, EDGAR LEE **13**:215–216 *bibliog.*
Spoon River Anthology **18**:194
MASTERS, WILLIAM HOWELL
Masters and Johnson reports **13**:216 *illus.*
MASTERS AND JOHNSON REPORTS **13**:216 *bibliog.*, *illus.*
sex therapy **13**:216
sexual intercourse **17**:231
sexual preference **13**:216
MASTERSINGER *see* MEISTERSINGER
MASTERSON, BAT **13**:216 *bibliog.*
MASTERTON (New Zealand)
map (40° 57′S 175° 40′E) **14**:158
MASTIC **13**:216
MASTICATION
muscle **13**:653
MASTIFF **6**:214 *illus.*; **13**:216 *bibliog.*, *illus.*
bull mastiff **3**:558
MASTIGOPHORA **13**:217
See also FLAGELLATA
Chilomonas **4**:357
Euglena **7**:264
Protozoa **15**:579 *illus.*
MASTITIS **13**:217
MASTODON **13**:217 *bibliog.*, *illus.*
Pleistocene Epoch **15**:366–367 *illus.*
MASTOIDITIS **13**:217
MASTROIANNI, MARCELLO **13**:217
MASTURBATION **13**:217–218 *bibliog.*
fetishism **8**:63
sexual development **17**:229–230
MASUDI, AL- **13**:218
MASURIA (Poland) *see* MASURIAN LAKES (Poland)
MASURIAN LAKES (POLAND) **13**:218
map (53° 45′N 21° 0′E) **15**:388
World War I **20**:226–227 *map*; **20**:230
MAT RIVER
map (41° 39′N 19° 34′E) **1**:250
MATA HARI **13**:218 *bibliog.*, *illus.*
MATABELELAND
Ndebele **14**:68
MATADI (Zaire)
map (5° 49′S 13° 27′E) **20**:350
MATADOR (Texas)
map (34° 1′N 100° 49′W) **19**:129
MATAGALPA (Nicaragua)
map (12° 55′N 85° 55′W) **14**:179
MATAGORDA (county in Texas)
map (28° 53′N 96° 0′W) **19**:129
MATALAYA (Turkey)
map (38° 21′N 38° 19′E) **19**:343
MATALE (Sri Lanka)
map (7° 28′N 80° 37′E) **18**:206
MATAMOROS (Mexico)
map (25° 53′N 97° 30′W) **13**:357
MATANE (Quebec)
map (48° 51′N 67° 32′W) **16**:18
MATANZAS (Cuba)
map (23° 3′N 81° 35′W) **5**:377
MATANZAS (Mexico)
map (21° 37′N 101° 38′W) **13**:357
MATANZIMA, KAISER DALIWONGA
Transkei **19**:274
MATARA (Sri Lanka)
map (5° 56′N 80° 33′E) **18**:206
MATARÓ (Spain)
map (41° 32′N 2° 27′E) **18**:140
MATAS, RUDOLPH
surgery **18**:361
MATAUTU (Western Samoa)
map (13° 57′S 171° 56′W) **20**:117
MATAVAI (Western Samoa)
map (13° 28′S 172° 35′W) **20**:117
MATAWAN (New Jersey)
map (40° 25′N 74° 14′W) **14**:129
MATCH **13**:218 *bibliog.*
MATÉ **13**:218
MATEHUALA (Mexico)
map (23° 39′N 100° 39′W) **13**:357
MATERA (Italy)
map (40° 40′N 16° 37′E) **11**:321
MATERIA MEDICA, DE
Dioscorides, Pedanius **6**:185
MATERIALISM **13**:218–219 *bibliog.*
dialectical materialism **6**:150
Feuerbach, Ludwig **8**:65–66
Holbach, Paul Henri Dietrich, Baron d' **10**:200
metaphysics **13**:334
MATERIALS TECHNOLOGY **13**:219–221 *bibliog.*, *illus.*, *table*
laser **12**:212–213 *illus.*
mechanical properties **13**:220 *table*
plastics **15**:347–351
recycling of materials **16**:111
rubber **16**:332–335
ultrasonics **18**:74 *illus.*; **19**:378 *illus.*
MATEUR (Tunisia)
map (37° 3′N 9° 40′E) **19**:335
MATEWAN (West Virginia)
map (37° 37′N 82° 10′W) **20**:111
MATHEMATICAL GAMES *see* GAMES, MATHEMATICAL
MATHEMATICAL INSTRUMENTATION
abacus **1**:51
caliper **4**:39
compass, mathematical **5**:155
digital technology **6**:175
goniometer **9**:244
measurement **13**:253–257
slide rule **17**:361
vernier **19**:559
weights and measures **20**:92–94
MATHEMATICAL LOGIC
logic **12**:396
MATHEMATICAL PRINCIPLES OF NATURAL PHILOSOPHY (book) *see PRINCIPIA* (book)
MATHEMATICAL TABLES **13**:221
accuracy **13**:221
interpolation **11**:225
logarithm **12**:394
MATHEMATICS **13**:221–222 *bibliog.*
See also MATHEMATICAL INSTRUMENTATION
algebra **1**:283–285
applied mathematics **13**:222
area **2**:145
arithmetic **2**:158–159
axiom **2**:377–378
biomathematics **3**:272
calculus **4**:24
catastrophe theory **4**:200
category **4**:202
celestial mechanics **4**:230
centroid **4**:256
chain **4**:268
chi-square distribution **4**:339
circle **4**:435–436 *illus.*
complex number **5**:157
computer **5**:160f
constant **5**:207
convergence **5**:233
decision theory **6**:73–74
deduction **6**:77
differential calculus **6**:167–168
e **7**:3
eccentricity **7**:37
equation **7**:224–225
error **7**:235
factor analysis **8**:6
Fibonacci sequence **8**:69
field **8**:71
Fourier analysis **8**:253–254
fractal **8**:258
fraction **8**:258
function **8**:359
game theory **9**:27–29
games, mathematical **9**:31–33
geometry **9**:106–107
golden section **9**:232–233
graph **9**:290–291
group theory **9**:377
hyperbola **10**:347–348
induction, mathematical **11**:151
industrial management **11**:156–157
infinitesimal (mathematics) **11**:168
infinity **11**:168–169
integer **11**:200
integral calculus **11**:200–201
inverse square law **11**:233
least-squares method **12**:262
limit **12**:345
line **12**:352–353
linear algebra **12**:353
logarithm **12**:394
logic **12**:395–397
magic square **13**:51
mathematical tables **13**:221
mathematics, education in **13**:222–223
mathematics, history of **13**:223–227
mathematics, new **13**:227
matrix **13**:230
maxima and minima **13**:239
Maxwell's equations **13**:241–242
mean **13**:252–253
median **13**:264
metamathematics
Tarski, Alfred **19**:39
Möbius strip **13**:488
mode (mathematics) **13**:489
non-Euclidean geometry **14**:215–216
normal distribution **14**:219
number **14**:292–293
number theory **14**:293–294
numeral **14**:294
numerical analysis **14**:294–295
operations research **14**:403
parabola **15**:74
paradox (mathematics) **15**:75
parameter **15**:80
periodic function **15**:166
permutation and combination **15**:176
philosophy **15**:241–243
pi **15**:287
plane **15**:327
point **15**:381
Poisson distribution **15**:385
polynomial **15**:421
population genetics **15**:439–440
prime number **15**:542–543
probability **15**:558
professional and educational organizations **17**:145 *table*
progression **15**:563–564
proof, mathematical **15**:568
pure mathematics **13**:222
Pythagoras, theorem of **15**:639
queuing theory **16**:24–25
radical (mathematics) **16**:43
random variable **16**:83
random walk **16**:83
rationalism **16**:92
regiomontanus **16**:129
Rheticus **16**:194
ring **16**:225
Roche's limit **16**:247
root (mathematics) **16**:311
scalar **17**:106
scientific notation **17**:146
sequence (mathematics) **17**:206–207
series **17**:209
set theory **17**:213
sine **17**:319
spiral **18**:188
square root **18**:202
statistics **18**:235–237
statistics, nonparametric **18**:237–238
stochastic process **18**:273
syllogism **18**:401–402
symmetry (mathematics) **18**:403–404
tangent **19**:22
Taylor series **19**:51
theoretical physics **19**:158–159
topology **19**:237–238
torus **19**:247
transformation **19**:270
translation (mathematics) **19**:274
trigonometry **19**:298–299
variable **19**:522
vector analysis **19**:530
volume **19**:632
Zeno's paradoxes **20**:360
MATHEMATICS, EDUCATION IN **13**:222–223 *bibliog.*
Cuisenaire method **5**:383
mathematics, history of **13**:226
mathematics, new **13**:227
secondary education **17**:180
MATHEMATICS, HISTORY OF **13**:223–227 *bibliog.*, *illus.*
Abel, Niels Henrik **1**:55
Alembert, Jean Le Rond d' **1**:271
Apollonius of Perga **2**:84
Archimedes **2**:128
Babbage, Charles **3**:5
Baire, René **3**:27
Banach, Stefan **3**:59
Barrow, Isaac **3**:95
Bernoulli, Daniel **3**:223
Bernoulli, Jacques **3**:223; **13**:225
Betti, Enrico **3**:232
Birkhoff, George David **3**:292
Bolyai, János **3**:372
Boole, George **3**:392
Borel, Émile **3**:398
Bourbaki, Nicolas **3**:422–423
Bowditch, Nathaniel **3**:426–427
Briggs, Henry **3**:486
Brouncker, William **3**:512
Brouwer, L. E. J. **3**:513
Cantor, Georg **4**:118; **13**:226
Cardano, Gerolamo **4**:143
Cauchy, Augustin Louis **4**:219; **13**:226
Cavalieri, Bonaventura **4**:220
Cayley, Arthur **4**:227
Chebyshev, Pafnuty Lvovich **4**:306
Christoffel, Elwin Bruno **4**:416
Clairaut, Alexis Claude **3**:35
Darwin, Sir George Howard **6**:42
de Moivre, Abraham **6**:62
Dedekind, Richard **6**:76–77
Dee, John **6**:77
Desargues, Gérard **6**:125
Descartes, René **13**:225
Dickson, Leonard **6**:159
Digges, Thomas **6**:174
Diophantus **6**:185
Dirichlet, Peter Gustav Lejeune **6**:188; **13**:226
Duhamel, Jean **6**:294
Eratosthenes of Cyrene **7**:227–228
Euclid **7**:262–263; **13**:223
Eudoxus of Cnidus **7**:263
Euler, Leonhard **7**:264–265
Fermat, Pierre de **8**:55; **13**:225
Ferrari, Lodovico **8**:59
Fisher, Sir Ronald Aylmer **8**:122–123
Fourier, Joseph **8**:253; **13**:226
Fréchet, Maurice René **8**:289
Fredholm, Erik Ivar **8**:294
Frege, Gottlob **8**:301
Frobenius, Ferdinand Georg **8**:335
Galileo Galilei **13**:225
Galois, Evariste **9**:21

Gauss, Carl Friedrich 9:61–62; 13:225
Gelfond, Aleksandr Osipovich 9:69
Gödel, Kurt 9:220; 13:226
Gregory, James 9:356
Hadamard, Jacques Salomon 10:7
Halley, Edmond 10:22
Hamilton, Sir William Rowan 10:29
Harriot, Thomas 10:57
Hermite, Charles 10:143; 13:226
Hero of Alexandria 10:144
Hertz, Heinrich Rudolph 10:149
Hilbert, David 10:163; 13:226
Hooke, Robert 10:226–227
Jacobi, Carl Gustav Jacob 11:345
Jordan, Camille 11:450
Kelvin, William Thomson, 1st Baron 12:40
Klein, Felix 12:95
Kronecker, Leopold 13:226
Lagrange, Joseph Louis de 12:166; 13:225–226
Laplace, Pierre Simon de 12:205; 13:225
Lebesque, Henri Léon 12:267
Lefschetz, Solomon 12:272
Leibniz, Gottfried Wilhelm von 12:276–277; 13:225
Leonardo Pisano 12:291
Lie, Sophus 13:226
Lobachevsky, Nikolai Ivanovich 12:384
Maclaurin, Colin 13:32
Markov, Andrei Andreyevich 13:159–160
Maupertuis, Pierre Louis Moreau de 13:234
Mersenne, Marin 13:312
Minkowski, Hermann 13:451
Möbius, August Ferdinand 13:226; 13:488
Monge, Gaspard 13:527–528
Napier, John 13:224; 14:14
Newton, Sir Isaac 13:225
Neyman, Jerzy 14:175
Noether, Emmy 14:212
Nyquist, Harry 14:310
Pappus 13:224; 15:72
Pascal, Blaise 15:102
Peano, Giuseppe 15:125
Plato 13:223
Playfair, John 15:363
Plücker, Julius 15:370
Poincaré, Henri 15:380
Ptolemy 13:224
Pythagoras of Samos 13:223; 15:639–640
Quételet, Lambert Adolphe 16:23
Riemann, Georg Friedrich Bernhard 16:218
Riemann,Georg Friedrich Bernhard 13:226
Russell, Bertrand 13:226; 16:349
Shannon, Claude Elwood 17:240
Spinoza, Baruch 18:187–188
Stevin, Simon 18:265
Talbot, William Henry 19:15
Tarski, Alfred 19:39
Tartaglia, Niccolò 19:40
Taylor, Brook 19:48
Thom, René 19:172
Veblen, Oswald 19:529
Viète, François 13:224; 19:579–580
von Neumann, John 19:634
Wallis, John 20:16
Waring, Edward 20:30
Weierstrass, Karl Theodor 13:226; 20:91–92
Whitehead, Alfred 13:226; 20:139
Wiener, Norbert 20:146
MATHEMATICS, NEW 13:227 *bibliog.*
history 13:227
isomorphism 11:300
mathematics, education in 13:222
reaction 13:227
MATHER (family) 13:227–228 *bibliog., illus.*
MATHER (Pennsylvania)
map (39° 56′N 80° 5′W) 15:147
MATHER, COTTON 1:342 *illus.*
Mather (family) 13:227–228 *illus.*
Salem Witch Trials 17:31
MATHER, INCREASE
Mather (family) 13:227
MATHER, RICHARD
Mather (family) 13:227
MATHESIUS, VILÉM
Prague school 15:488
MATHESON, SCOTT M.
Utah 19:495
MATHEWS (Louisiana)
map (29° 42′N 90° 33′W) 12:430
MATHEWS (Virginia)
map (37° 26′N 76° 19′W) 19:607
MATHEWS (county in Virginia)
map (37° 25′N 76° 20′W) 19:607
MATHEWS, CHARLES AND CHARLES JAMES 13:228
MATHEWS, MAX V.
computer music 5:162
MATHEWS, SHAILER 13:228 *bibliog.*
MATHEWSON, CHRISTY 13:228 *bibliog.*
MATHIAS, BOB 13:228 *bibliog.*
decathlon 6:72
MATHIEU, GEORGES 13:228
MATHIS (Texas)
map (28° 6′N 97° 50′W) 19:129
MATÍAS ROMERO (Mexico)
map (16° 53′N 95° 2′W) 13:357
MATILDA 13:228 *bibliog.*
Stephen, King of England 18:254
MATILDA OF TUSCANY 13:228 *bibliog.*
MATING, ANIMAL *see* ANIMAL COURTSHIP AND MATING
MATINICUS ISLAND
map (43° 54′N 68° 55′W) 13:70
MATINS *see* DIVINE OFFICE
MATISSE, HENRI 13:228–229 *bibliog., illus.*
Dance 8:308 *illus.*
Fauvism 8:38–39
Flowering Ivy 13:229 *illus.*
stained glass 18:212
Ulysses (book) 14:276 *illus.*
MATO GROSSO (Brazil) 13:229
MATO GROSSO (city in Brazil)
map (15° 0′S 59° 57′W) 3:460
MATO GROSSO (state in Brazil)
map (11° 0′S 55° 0′W) 3:460
MATO GROSSO DO SUL (Brazil)
map (20° 30′S 53° 30′W) 3:460
MATO GROSSO PLATEAU
map (15° 30′S 56° 0′W) 3:460
MATOŠ, A. G.
Yugoslavia 20:342
MATOS GUERRA, GREGÓRIO DE 13:229
MATRA (Oman)
map (23° 38′N 58° 34′E) 14:386
MATRIARCHY 13:229–230 *bibliog.*
Bachofen, Johann Jakob 3:12
Elam 7:102
women in society 20:201
MATRILINEAGE
See also names of specific peoples, e.g., CARIB (American Indians); ONONDAGA (American Indians); etc.
clan 5:36
kinship 12:85
lineage 12:353
matriarchy 13:229–230
polygamy 15:419
women in society 20:201
MATRIX (geology) 13:230
MATRIX (mathematics) 13:230 *bibliog.*
algebra 1:284–285
Cayley, Arthur 4:227
determinant 6:134
equation 7:224
Hermite, Charles 10:143
linear algebra 12:353
MATRUH (Egypt)
map (31° 21′N 27° 14′E) 7:76
MATSAPHA (Swaziland)
map (26° 29′S 31° 23′E) 18:380
MATSU ISLAND GROUP (Taiwan)
Quemoy (Taiwan) 16:23
MATSUKATA MASAYOSHI 13:230
MATSUMOTO (Japan) 13:230
MATSUO MUNEFUSA *see* BASHO
MATSUOKA YOSUKE 13:230 *bibliog.*
MATSUYAMA (Japan) 13:230
map (33° 50′N 132° 45′E) 11:361
MATTA ECHAURREN, ROBERTO SEBASTIÁN 13:230 *bibliog.*
Latin American art and architecture 12:228
MATTAPOISETT (Massachusetts)
map (41° 40′N 70° 49′W) 13:206
MATTAPONI RIVER
map (37° 31′N 76° 47′W) 19:607
MATTAWAMKEAG (Maine)
map (45° 31′N 68° 21′W) 13:70
MATTAWAMKEAG RIVER
map (45° 30′N 68° 24′W) 13:70
MATTEOTTI CRISIS 13:230
MATTER 13:230–231 *bibliog.*
See also SOLID
absolute zero 1:62–63
antimatter 2:63
Aristotle 2:157
electricity 7:110
electromagnetic radiation 7:117–118
enthalpy 7:208
fundamental interactions 8:360–361
fundamental particles 8:361–363
gaseous state 9:54
Graham, Thomas 9:280
kinetic theory of matter 12:79
liquid 12:364–365
Lorentz, Hendrik Antoon 12:413–414
mass (physics) 13:201
phase equilibrium 15:222–224
physical chemistry 15:279
plasma physics 15:345–346
quantum mechanics 16:9–11
Rutherford, Sir Ernest 16:375
statics 18:234–235
superconductivity 18:350
superfluidity 18:351
theoretical physics 19:158–159
thermodynamics 19:164
MATTERHORN 1:309 *illus.*; 13:231; 18:395 *illus.*
map (45° 59′N 7° 43′E) 18:394
MATTESON, TOMPKINS H.
Trial of George Jacobs (painting) 17:31 *illus.*
MATTHES, ROLAND 14:384 *illus.*
MATTHEW, GOSPEL ACCORDING TO 13:231 *bibliog.*
Jesus Christ 11:403–404
MATTHEW, SAINT 3:239 *illus.*; 13:231
Salerno (Italy) 17:31
stained glass 18:212 *illus.*
MATTHEW, WILLIAM DILLER 13:231
MATTHEW TOWN (Bahama Islands)
map (20° 57′N 73° 40′W) 3:23
MATTHEWS, D. H. 13:231 *bibliog.*
MATTHEWS, SIR STANLEY 13:231
MATTHEWS RIDGE (Guyana)
map (7° 30′N 60° 10′W) 9:410
MATTHIAS, HOLY ROMAN EMPEROR 13:231–232 *bibliog.*
MATTHIAS, JOSEPH BEN *see* JOSEPHUS, FLAVIUS
MATTHIAS, SAINT 13:231
MATTHIAS I HUNYADI *see* MATTHIAS CORVINUS, KING OF HUNGARY
MATTHIAS CORVINUS, KING OF HUNGARY 13:232 *bibliog.*
Hungary 10:310
MATTHIESSEN, F. O. 13:232 *bibliog.*
MATTINGLY, THOMAS 13:232
MATTOON (Illinois)
map (39° 29′N 88° 22′W) 11:42
MATTOON (Wisconsin)
map (45° 1′N 89° 2′W) 20:185
MATTYDALE (New York)
map (43° 6′N 76° 9′W) 14:149
MATURÍN (Venezuela)
map (9° 45′N 63° 11′W) 19:542
MATZO
Passover 17:182
MAU ESCARPMENT
map (0° 40′S 36° 2′E) 12:53
MAU MAU 13:232 *bibliog.*
Kenyatta, Jomo 12:57
MAUCHLY, JOHN WILLIAM 13:232 *bibliog.*
computer 5:160a *illus.*
computer industry 5:160n
Eckert, John Presper 7:39
UNIVAC 19:467
MAUD (Oklahoma)
map (35° 8′N 96° 46′W) 14:368
MAUDE, SIR FREDERICK S.
World War I 20:234; 20:240
MAUDSLAY, HENRY 13:232
machine tools 13:23
Nasmyth, James 14:24
MAUER FOSSIL *see* HEIDELBERG MAN
MAUÉS (Brazil)
map (3° 24′S 57° 42′W) 3:460
MAUGA SILISILI MOUNTAIN
map (13° 35′S 172° 27′W) 20:117
MAUGHAM, W. SOMERSET 13:233 *bibliog., illus.*
Of Human Bondage 14:352
MAUI (Hawaii) 13:233
Haleakala Crater 10:19
Hawaii (state) 10:73 *illus.*
map (20° 45′N 156° 15′W) 10:72
MAULDIN (South Carolina)
map (34° 47′N 82° 19′W) 18:98
MAULDIN, BILL 13:233
cartoon (editorial and political) 4:176; 4:177 *illus.*
MAULPERTSCH, FRANZ ANTON 13:233 *bibliog.*
MAUMEE (Ohio)
map (41° 34′N 83° 39′W) 14:357
MAUMELIE, LAKE
map (34° 55′N 92° 40′W) 2:166
MAUNA KEA (Hawaii) 13:233
map (19° 50′N 155° 28′W) 10:72
radio astronomy 16:53
MAUNA KEA OBSERVATORY 13:233
MAUNA LOA (Hawaii) 13:233–234
map (19° 29′N 155° 36′W) 10:72
national parks 14:38–39 *map, table*
MAUNALUA BAY
map (21° 17′N 157° 44′W) 10:72
MAUNGATUROTO (New Zealand)
map (36° 6′S 174° 22′E) 14:158
MAUNOIR, JULIEN
Breton literature 3:475
MAUNOURY, MICHEL J.
World War I 20:223–224
MAUPASSANT, GUY DE 13:234 *bibliog.*
MAUPEOU, RENÉ DE
Louis XV, King of France 12:427
MAUPERTUIS, PIERRE LOUIS MOREAU DE 13:234 *bibliog.*
Clairaut, Alexis Claude 5:35
evolution 7:318
MAUREPAS, LAKE
map (30° 15′N 90° 30′W) 12:430
map (30° 15′N 90° 30′W) 12:430
MAURER, ALFRED HENRY 13:234
MAURETANIA (ancient Africa) 4:173 *map*
lol 11:239
MAURIAC, FRANÇOIS 13:234 *bibliog., illus.*
MAURICE, DUKE OF SAXONY
Saxony 17:105
MAURICE, FREDERICK DENISON 13:234–235 *bibliog.*
socialism 18:20
MAURICE, HERMANN *see* SAXE, MAURICE, COMTE DE
MAURICE, SAINT 13:234
MAURICE OF NASSAU, PRINCE OF ORANGE 13:235 *bibliog.*
Oldenbarnevelt, Johan van 14:375
MAURICE RIVER
map (39° 13′N 75° 2′W) 14:129
MAURIER, DAPHNE DU *see* DU MAURIER, DAPHNE
MAURIER, GEORGE DU *see* DE MAURIER, GEORGE
MAURITANIA 13:235–237 *bibliog., illus., map, table*
cities
Nouakchott 14:268
climate 13:235–236 *table*
economic activity 13:236
flag 13:235 *illus.*
government 13:236
history 13:236–237
Daddah, Moktar Ould 6:5
Western Sahara 20:116
land and resources 13:235–236 *map, table*
meteorite craters 13:339
map (20° 0′N 12° 0′W) 1:136
people 13:235–236 *illus.*
MAURITIUS 13:237 *bibliog., map*
cities
Port Louis 15:443
dodo bird 6:212
flag 8:137 *illus.*
map (20° 17′S 57° 33′E) 1:136
MAURITSHUIS PALACE (The Hague)
Campen, Jacob van 4:66
MAUROIS, ANDRÉ 13:237 *bibliog.*
MAUROY, PIERRE 13:237
MAURRAS, CHARLES
Action Française 1:89
MAURY (county in Tennessee)
map (35° 35′N 87° 0′W) 19:104
MAURY, MATTHEW FONTAINE 13:238 *bibliog., illus.*; 14:344 *illus.*
MAURY ISLAND
map (47° 20′N 122° 24′W) 20:35
MAURY RIVER
map (37° 37′N 79° 27′W) 19:607
MAURYA (dynasty) 13:238 *bibliog.*
Asia, history of 2:251
Asoka, Emperor of India 2:261
Chandragupta Maurya, Emperor 4:279–280
India, history of 11:89 *map*
Pataliputra 15:109
MAUSOLEUM *see* TOMB
MAUSOLEUM AT HALICARNASSUS *see* HALICARNASSUS
MAUSOLUS 13:238
Mausoleum at Halicarnassus 17:217 *illus.*
tomb 19:230
MAUSS, MARCEL 13:238
MAUSTON (Wisconsin)
map (43° 48′N 90° 5′W) 20:185
MAUVE, ANTON 13:238
MAVERICK (Arizona)
map (33° 43′N 109° 32′W) 2:160
MAVERICK (county in Texas)
map (28° 45′N 100° 18′W) 19:129
MAVROKORDÁTOS, ALÉXANDROS 13:238

MAWLAIK (Burma)
map (23° 38′N 94° 24′E) **3**:573
MAWSIL, AL- (Iraq) *see* MOSUL (Iraq)
MAWSON, SIR DOUGLAS **13**:238 *bibliog.*
Antarctica **2**:44 *map*
MAX (North Dakota)
map (47° 49′N 101° 18′W) **14**:248
MAX-PLANCK-GESELLSCHAFT ZUR FÖRDERUNG DER WISSENSCHAFTEN *see* MAX PLANCK SOCIETY FOR THE ADVANCEMENT OF SCIENCE
MAX PLANCK SOCIETY FOR THE ADVANCEMENT OF SCIENCE **13**:238–239
Bothe, Walther Wilhelm **3**:415
Göttingen (West Germany) **9**:264
Hahn, Otto **10**:11
MAXENTIUS
basilica **16**:274 *illus.*
Constantine I, Roman Emperor **5**:208
Maximian, Roman Emperor **13**:239
MAXIM *see* APHORISM, MAXIM, AND PROVERB
MAXIM (family) **13**:239 *bibliog.*
inventions **13**:239
machine gun **13**:23
MAXIM, HIRAM PERCY
Maxim (family) **13**:239
MAXIM, HIRAM STEVENS
Maxim (family) **13**:239
MAXIM, HUDSON
Maxim (family) **13**:239
MAXIMA AND MINIMA **13**:239 *bibliog., illus.*
calculus of variations **4**:24
differential calculus **6**:167
in operations research **14**:403
MAXIMIAN, ROMAN EMPEROR **13**:239
MAXIMILIAN, ELECTOR AND DUKE OF BAVARIA **13**:239–240 *bibliog.*
Thirty Years' War **19**:170–171
MAXIMILIAN, EMPEROR OF MEXICO **13**:240 *bibliog., illus.*
Carlota **4**:151
Mexico, history of **13**:364 *illus.*
Querétaro (city in Mexico) **16**:23
MAXIMILIAN I, HOLY ROMAN EMPEROR **9**:150 *illus.*; **13**:240 *bibliog., illus.*
Germany, history of **9**:150
Habsburg (dynasty) **10**:6 *illus.*
Mary of Burgundy **13**:185
MAXIMILIAN I, KING OF BAVARIA **13**:240
MAXIMILIAN II, HOLY ROMAN EMPEROR **13**:240–241 *bibliog.*
MAXIMS, THE (book)
La Rochefoucauld, François, Duc de **12**:148
MAXIMUS, SAINT **13**:241
MAXIXE
Castle, Vernon and Irene **4**:191
MAXWELL (California)
map (39° 17′N 122° 11′W) **4**:31
MAXWELL (Iowa)
map (41° 53′N 93° 24′W) **11**:244
MAXWELL (Nebraska)
map (41° 5′N 100° 31′W) **14**:70
MAXWELL (New Mexico)
map (36° 32′N 104° 33′W) **14**:136
MAXWELL, JAMES CLERK **13**:241 *bibliog., illus.*
Boltzmann, Ludwig **3**:372
electromagnetic radiation **7**:116–117 *illus.*
Faraday, Michael **8**:22
kinetic theory of matter **12**:79
Maxwell-Boltzmann kinetic theory of gases **13**:241
Maxwell's equations **13**:241–242
optics **14**:410
radio **16**:44
Saturn (astronomy) **17**:89
MAXWELL MOTOR CORPORATION
automotive industry **2**:363
MAXWELL'S EQUATIONS **13**:241–242 *bibliog.*
blackbody radiation **3**:321
Einstein, Albert **7**:93
electromagnetic induction **7**:115–116
electromagnetic radiation **7**:116–117
electrostatics **7**:128
law, physical **12**:248
magnetism **13**:56
parity (physics) **15**:89
physics **15**:281
plasma physics **15**:346
quantum mechanics **16**:11
unified field theory **19**:385–386
MAY (botany) *see* HAWTHORN
MAY (month of the year)
birthstones **3**:296 *illus., table*
calendar **4**:28
MAY (Texas)
map (31° 59′N 98° 55′W) **19**:129
MAY, ELAINE
Nichols, Mike **14**:182
MAY DAY **13**:242
Maypole dance **13**:248–249
morris dance **13**:589
MAY FOURTH MOVEMENT
China, history of **4**:375
MAY PEN (Jamaica)
map (17° 58′N 77° 14′W) **11**:351
MAYA **13**:243–245 *bibliog., illus.*
agriculture, history of **1**:190
archaeological sites
archaeology **2**:125 *illus.*
Bonampak **3**:375; **15**:497 *illus.*
Chichén Itzá **4**:343–344
Copán **5**:248
Izapa **11**:338
Kaminaljuyú **12**:10
Mayapán **13**:246
Mérida (Mexico) **13**:310
Palenque **15**:30
Piedras Negras **15**:295
Quiriguá **16**:27
Tikal **19**:198
Tula **19**:329–330
Uaxactún **19**:369
Uxmal **19**:499
art
Latin American art and architecture **12**:222; **12**:227
pre-Columbian art and architecture **15**:496–499 *illus.*
astronomy in the New World **2**:115
Catherwood, Frederick **4**:210
ceremonial-civic centers **13**:244–245 *illus.*
economy **13**:244
Huastec **10**:287
impact of European contact **13**:245
Indians, American **11**:118; **11**:133
Kidder, Alfred Vincent **12**:71
Lacandón **12**:158
Latin America, history of **12**:216
Mexico, history of **13**:361–362 *illus.*
pyramid **15**:636 *illus.*
religion **13**:245
maize god **11**:134 *illus.*
quetzal **16**:24 *illus.*
Quetzalcóatl/Kukulkán **16**:24
stele **14**:231 *illus.*; **18**:250
Stephens, John Lloyd **18**:255
Teotihuacán, relations with **19**:113
Thompson, J. Eric **19**:175
tobacco **19**:218
Toltec **19**:229
writing systems, evolution of **20**:292
Yucatán Peninsula **20**:338 *map*
MAYA MOUNTAINS
map (16° 40′N 88° 50′W) **3**:183
MAYAGÜEZ (Puerto Rico)
map (18° 12′N 67° 9′W) **15**:614
MAYAKOVSKY, VLADIMIR VLADIMIROVICH **13**:245–246 *bibliog., illus.*
MAYAPÁN (Mexico) **13**:246 *bibliog.*
Chichén Itzá **4**:344
Maya **13**:243–244
MAYAPPLE *see* MANDRAKE (botany)
MAYBACH, WILHELM **13**:246 *bibliog.*
MAYBECK, BERNARD **13**:246 *bibliog.*
Morgan, Julia **13**:578
MAYER (Arizona)
map (34° 24′N 112° 14′W) **2**:160
MAYER, JOHANN TOBIAS **13**:246 *bibliog.*
MAYER, JULIUS ROBERT
photosynthesis **15**:275
MAYER, LOUIS B. **13**:246 *bibliog.*
MAYER, MARIA GOEPPERT **13**:246
MAYERSVILLE (Mississippi)
map (32° 54′N 91° 3′W) **13**:469
MAYERTHORPE (Alberta)
map (53° 57′N 115° 8′W) **1**:256
MAYES (county in Oklahoma)
map (36° 20′N 95° 15′W) **14**:368
MAYFIELD (Kentucky)
map (36° 44′N 88° 38′W) **12**:47
MAYFIELD, JULIAN **13**:246
MAYFIELD HEIGHTS (Ohio)
map (41° 31′N 81° 27′W) **14**:357
MAYFLOWER (botany)
hawthorn **10**:79
MAYFLOWER (ship) **13**:247 *bibliog., illus.*
Pilgrims **15**:302
White, Peregrine **20**:136
MAYFLOWER COMPACT
Mayflower (ship) **13**:247
Pilgrims **15**:302
Plymouth Colony **15**:374
MAYFLY **13**:247–248 *bibliog., illus.*
MAYHEM **13**:248
MAYNARD (Iowa)
map (42° 46′N 91° 53′W) **11**:244
MAYNARD (Massachusetts)
map (42° 30′N 71° 33′W) **13**:206
MAYNARD, ROBERT
piracy **15**:313 *illus.*
MAYNARDVILLE (Tennessee)
map (36° 15′N 83° 48′W) **19**:104
MAYO (family) **13**:248 *bibliog.*
Mayo Clinic **13**:248
MAYO (Florida)
map (30° 3′N 83° 10′W) **8**:172
MAYO (Ireland) **13**:248
MAYO (Yukon Territory)
map (63° 35′N 135° 54′W) **20**:345
MAYO, ELTON **13**:248
Hawthorne studies **10**:79
MAYO CLINIC **13**:248
Mayo (family) **13**:248
Rochester (Minnesota) **16**:247
MAYODAN (North Carolina)
map (36° 25′N 79° 58′W) **14**:242
MAYON, MOUNT **15**:237 *illus.*
MAYOR **13**:248
municipal government **13**:642
MAYOTTE (France) **13**:248
Comoros **5**:154
map (12° 50′S 45° 10′E) **1**:136
MAYPOLE DANCE **13**:248–249
fertility rites **8**:60
MAYR, ERNST **13**:249
MAYR, JOHANN SIMON **13**:249 *bibliog.*
MAYR, SIMON **13**:249
MAYS, WILLIE **3**:107 *illus.*; **13**:249 *bibliog., illus.*
MAYS LANDING (New Jersey)
map (39° 27′N 74° 44′W) **14**:129
MAYSLES, AL
documentary **6**:211
MAYSVILLE (Kentucky)
map (38° 39′N 83° 46′W) **12**:47
MAYSVILLE (Missouri)
map (39° 48′N 94° 35′W) **13**:476
MAYSVILLE (Oklahoma)
map (34° 49′N 97° 24′W) **14**:368
MAYTAG, FREDERICK LOUIS **13**:249
MAYUMBA (Gabon)
map (3° 25′S 10° 39′E) **9**:5
MAYVILLE (New York)
map (42° 15′N 79° 30′W) **14**:149
MAYVILLE (North Dakota)
map (47° 30′N 97° 19′W) **14**:248
MAYVILLE (Wisconsin)
map (43° 30′N 88° 33′W) **20**:185
MAYWOOD (Illinois)
map (41° 53′N 87° 51′W) **11**:42
MAYWOOD (New Jersey)
map (40° 56′N 74° 4′W) **14**:129
MAZABUKA (Zambia)
map (15° 51′S 27° 46′E) **20**:354
MAZAMA, MOUNT
Crater Lake **5**:332–333
MAZAR-E SHARIF (Afghanistan)
map (36° 42′N 67° 6′E) **1**:133
MAZARA DEL VALLO (Italy)
map (37° 39′N 12° 36′E) **11**:321
MAZARIN, JULES **13**:249–250 *bibliog., illus.*
Anne of Austria **2**:32
Fronde **8**:339
Louis XIV, King of France **12**:426
MAZARINI, GIULIO *see* MAZARIN, JULES
MAZATENANGO (Guatemala)
map (14° 32′N 91° 30′W) **9**:389
MAZATLÁN (Mexico) **13**:250; **13**:359 *illus.*
map (23° 13′N 106° 25′W) **13**:357
MAZATZAL MOUNTAINS
map (34° 0′N 111° 55′W) **2**:160
MAZATZAL PEAK
map (34° 3′N 111° 28′W) **2**:160
MAZE *see* LABYRINTH AND MAZE
MAZEPA, IVAN STEPANOVICH **13**:250 *bibliog.*
MAZEPPA (Minnesota)
map (44° 17′N 92° 32′W) **13**:453
MAZOMANIE (Wisconsin)
map (43° 11′N 89° 48′W) **20**:185
MAZON (Illinois)
map (41° 14′N 88° 25′W) **11**:42
MAZURKA **13**:250
Chopin, Frédéric **4**:405
MAZZINI, GIUSEPPE **13**:250 *bibliog., illus.*
Italy, history of **11**:329
Risorgimento **16**:228
MAZZOLA, FRANCESCO *see* PARMIGIANINO
MBABANE (Swaziland) **13**:250–251; **18**:380–381 *illus., table*
map (26° 18′S 31° 6′E) **18**:380
MBABO, MOUNT
map (7° 16′N 12° 9′E) **4**:61
MBAÏKI (Central African Republic)
map (3° 53′N 18° 0′E) **4**:251
MBALE (Uganda)
map (1° 5′N 34° 10′E) **19**:372
MBANDAKA (Zaire)
map (0° 4′N 18° 16′E) **20**:350
MBANZA-NGUNGU (Zaire)
map (5° 15′S 14° 52′E) **20**:350
MBD (minimal brain dysfunction) *see* HYPERACTIVE CHILDREN
MBINI (Equatorial Guinea) **13**:251
Equatorial Guinea **7**:225
MBOMOU RIVER
map (4° 8′N 22° 26′E) **4**:251
MBOUR (Senegal)
map (14° 24′N 16° 58′W) **17**:202
MBOYA, TOM **13**:251 *bibliog.*
MBUA (Fiji)
map (16° 48′S 178° 37′E) **8**:77
MBUJI-MAYI (Zaire)
map (6° 9′S 23° 38′E) **20**:350
MBUNDU **13**:251 *bibliog.*
MBUTHA (Fiji)
map (16° 39′S 179° 50′E) **8**:77
MBUTI
Pygmy **15**:633
MEAD (beverage) **13**:251
beer **3**:162
honey **10**:220
MEAD (Nebraska)
map (41° 14′N 96° 29′W) **14**:70
MEAD, GEORGE HERBERT **13**:251 *bibliog.*
pragmatism **15**:487
role **16**:271
sociology **18**:30
MEAD, JAMES R.
Wichita (Kansas) **20**:144
MEAD, LAKE **13**:251
map (36° 5′N 114° 25′W) **14**:111
national parks **14**:38–39 *map, table*
MEAD, MARGARET **2**:54 *illus.*; **13**:251–252 *bibliog., illus.*
adolescence **1**:107
Bateson, Gregory **3**:121
MEAD, WILLIAM RUTHERFORD *see* McKIM, MEAD, AND WHITE
MEADE (Kansas)
map (37° 17′N 100° 20′W) **12**:18
MEADE (county in Kansas)
map (37° 15′N 100° 20′W) **12**:18
MEADE (county in Kentucky)
map (38° 0′N 86° 10′W) **12**:47
MEADE (county in South Dakota)
map (44° 35′N 102° 40′W) **18**:103
MEADE, GEORGE GORDON **5**:28 *illus.*; **13**:252 *bibliog.*
Barnegat Lighthouse **14**:128 *illus.*
Civil War, U.S. **5**:23 *map*
Gettysburg, Battle of **9**:161
Wilderness Campaign **20**:150
MEADOW (Texas)
map (33° 20′N 102° 12′W) **19**:129
MEADOW LAKE (Saskatchewan)
map (54° 8′N 108° 26′W) **17**:81
MEADOW RUE **13**:252
MEADOW SAFFRON **13**:252
colchicine **5**:97
MEADOW VALLEY WASH
map (36° 39′N 114° 35′W) **14**:111
MEADOWCROFT ROCKSHELTER (Pennsylvania) **13**:252 *bibliog.*; **14**:237 *map*
MEADOWLARK **13**:252 *illus.*
foot **3**:288 *illus.*
MEADVILLE (Mississippi)
map (31° 28′N 90° 54′W) **13**:469
MEADVILLE (Missouri)
map (39° 47′N 93° 18′W) **13**:476
MEADVILLE (Pennsylvania)
map (41° 38′N 80° 9′W) **15**:147
MEAFORD (Ontario)
map (44° 36′N 80° 35′W) **14**:393; **19**:241
MEAGHER (county in Montana)
map (46° 40′N 111° 5′W) **13**:547
MEAKERVILLE (Alaska)
map (60° 32′N 145° 0′W) **1**:242
MEALYBUG **13**:252
MEAN **13**:252–253
median **13**:264
psychological measurement **15**:593
weight (mathematics) **20**:92
MEANDER, RIVER **13**:253 *bibliog.*
floodplain **8**:165; **13**:253
flume studies **8**:186
oxbow lake **14**:473
river and stream **16**:231
MEANY, GEORGE **12**:155 *illus.*; **13**:253 *bibliog., illus.*
MEARES, JOHN **13**:253 *bibliog.*
MEARNS, THE (Scotland) *see* KINCARDINE (Scotland)

MEASLES **13**:253
mastoiditis **13**:217
MEASUREMENT **13**:253–257 *bibliog., illus.*
See also the subheading measurement under appropriate main headings, e.g., LIGHT; RADIATION; etc.; names of specific instruments or units of measurement, e.g., ANGSTROM; ALTIMETER; etc.
area **2**:145
Celsius scale **4**:238
distance, astronomical **6**:199–200
electromagnetic units **7**:118–119
errors **7**:235
Fahrenheit scale **8**:8
International Bureau of Weights and Measures **11**:219
length **13**:254
mass **13**:254–255
metric system **13**:345–347
National Bureau of Standards **14**:30
standard deviation **18**:216
temperature **19**:92–93
time (physics) **19**:201
uncertainty principle **19**:381
units of measurement
units, physical **19**:465–467
weights and measures **20**:92–94
MEASUREMENT, EDUCATIONAL *see* EDUCATIONAL MEASUREMENT
MEASUREMENT, PSYCHOLOGICAL *see* PSYCHOLOGICAL MEASUREMENT
MEASURING WORM *see* INCHWORM
MEAT ANALOGS *see* MEAT IMITATIONS
MEAT IMITATIONS **13**:257 *bibliog.*
MEAT AND MEAT PACKING **13**:257–258 *bibliog., table*
Armour, Philip Danforth **2**:177–178
artificial insemination **2**:220
cattle and cattle raising **4**:214–217
cooking **5**:237–240
diseases, animal **6**:190
factory farming **8**:6
inspection and grading system **13**:258
meat imitations **13**:257
nutrition, human **14**:305
production, consumption, and cost **13**:257 *table*
slaughtering and processing procedures **13**:257–258
smoked meat
food preservation **8**:212
hickory **10**:157
types of meat
bacon **3**:13
pig **15**:299
poultry **15**:473–475
sausage **17**:97
sheep **17**:248–249
veal **19**:529
venison **19**:546
United States **13**:257–258 *table*
whaling **20**:123 *illus.*
MEAT TENDERIZERS
herbs and spices **10**:137
MEATH (Ireland) **13**:258
neolithic period
Knowth **12**:102
MEBANE (North Carolina)
map (36° 6′N 79° 16′W) **14**:242
MECCA (Indiana)
map (39° 44′N 87° 20′W) **11**:111
MECCA (Saudi Arabia) **13**:258–259 *bibliog., illus.*
Arabs **2**:101–102
hajj to Mecca *see* HAJJ
Kaaba **12**:3
map (21° 27′N 39° 49′E) **17**:94
Middle East, history of the **13**:402
Muhammad **13**:632–633
MECHANIC FALLS (Maine)
map (44° 7′N 70° 24′W) **13**:70
MECHANICAL DRAWING **13**:259 *bibliog., illus.*
descriptive geometry **6**:126
Monge, Gaspard **13**:527
MECHANICAL ENGINEERING **13**:259–260 *bibliog., illus.*
bionics **3**:274–275
computer-aided design and computer-aided manufacturing **5**:160j–160L
development **13**:259–260
engineering **7**:178
Hooke, Robert **10**:226–227
hydraulic systems **10**:330–331
internal-combustion engine **11**:215–218
Lagrange, Joseph Louis de **12**:166
pneumatic systems **15**:375
printing **15**:550–553
professional and educational organizations
American Society of Mechanical Engineers **13**:260
British Institute of Mechanical Engineers **13**:260
pulley **15**:619 *illus.*
pump **15**:622–623
rolamite **16**:270
statics **18**:234–235
statistical thermodynamics **18**:235
stator **18**:238
MECHANICS (mathematics)
translation (mathematics) **19**:274
MECHANICS (physics)
acceleration **1**:72
adhesion **1**:102
aerodynamics **1**:123–124
angular momentum **2**:7
ballistics **3**:49–51
celestial mechanics **4**:230
Center of Gravity **4**:250
centrifugal and centripetal forces **4**:255
cohesion **5**:96
Coriolis effect **5**:263
damping **6**:19
dynamics **6**:319
Euler, Leonhard **7**:264–265
fluid mechanics **8**:184–185
force **8**:220
Foucault pendulum **8**:249
free fall **8**:294
friction **8**:330–331
inertia **11**:161
kinematics **12**:78
laws of motion **12**:251
Lissajous figure **12**:366
mass (physics) **13**:201
moment of inertia **13**:515
momentum **13**:515
motion, circular **13**:608
motion, harmonic **13**:608–609
motion, planar **13**:609–610
pendulum **15**:142
physics **15**:280
physics, history of **15**:283
potential energy **15**:466
power **15**:481
precession **15**:493
quantum mechanics **16**:9–11
resonance (physics) **16**:178
simple machines **17**:316
speed **18**:176
statics **18**:234
statistical mechanics **15**:280–281
Boltzmann, Ludwig **3**:372
Einstein, Albert **7**:93
Gibbs, Josiah Willard **9**:174
telescope **19**:82–83
torque **19**:243
velocity **19**:538
watt **20**:68
waves and wave motion **20**:71–72
weight (physics) **20**:92
MECHANICS, RELATIVISTIC *see* RELATIVITY
MECHANICSBURG (Ohio)
map (40° 4′N 83° 34′W) **14**:357
MECHANICSVILLE (Virginia)
map (37° 36′N 77° 22′W) **19**:607
MECHANICVILLE (New York)
map (42° 54′N 73° 42′W) **14**:149
MECHELEN (Belgium)
map (51° 2′N 4° 28′E) **3**:177
MECK, NADEZHDA VON
Tchaikovsky, Peter Ilich **19**:51–52
MECKLENBURG (county in North Carolina)
Mecklenburg Declaration of Independence **13**:260
MECKLENBURG (county in North Carolina)
map (35° 15′N 80° 50′W) **14**:242
MECKLENBURG (region in East Germany) **13**:260
Germany in 1648 **9**:151 *map*
MECKLENBURG (county in Virginia)
map (36° 45′N 78° 25′W) **19**:607
MECKLENBURG DECLARATION OF INDEPENDENCE **13**:260 *bibliog.*
MECKLENBURG RESOLVES *see* MECKLENBURG DECLARATION OF INDEPENDENCE
MECKLENBURGER BAY
map (54° 20′N 11° 40′E) **9**:140
MECOPTERA **13**:260
scorpion fly **17**:148–149
MECOSTA (county in Michigan)
map (43° 35′N 85° 20′W) **13**:377
MECSEK MOUNTAINS
map (46° 15′N 18° 5′E) **10**:307
MEDAL OF FREEDOM
Copland, Aaron **5**:250–251
MEDAL OF MERIT
Bacher, Robert Fox **3**:11
MEDALS AND DECORATIONS **13**:260–263 *bibliog., illus.*
American awards **13**:260–263
campaign and gallantry awards **13**:260
cross **5**:361
European awards **13**:263
history **13**:260
numismatics **14**:295–296
Pisanello, Antonio **15**:316
MEDAN (Indonesia) **13**:263
map (3° 35′N 98° 40′E) **11**:147
MÉDANOS (Argentina)
map (38° 50′S 62° 41′W) **2**:149
MEDARYVILLE (Indiana)
map (41° 5′N 86° 55′W) **11**:111
MEDAWAR, PETER BRIAN **13**:263
transplantation, organ **19**:277
MEDEA (mythology) **13**:263
MEDEA (play) **13**:263 *bibliog.*
Euripides **7**:266
MEDELLÍN (Colombia) **13**:263
map (6° 15′N 75° 35′W) **5**:107
MEDES *see* MEDIA (Mesopotamia)
MEDFIELD (Massachusetts)
map (42° 11′N 71° 18′W) **3**:409
MEDFLY *see* MEDITERRANEAN FRUIT FLY
MEDFORD (Massachusetts)
map (42° 25′N 71° 7′W) **3**:409
MEDFORD (New Jersey)
map (39° 54′N 74° 49′W) **14**:129
MEDFORD (Oklahoma)
map (36° 48′N 97° 44′W) **14**:368
MEDFORD (Oregon) **13**:263
map (42° 19′N 122° 52′W) **14**:427
MEDFORD (Wisconsin)
map (45° 9′N 90° 20′W) **20**:185
MEDFORD LAKES (New Jersey)
map (39° 52′N 74° 49′W) **14**:129
MEDGIDIA (Romania)
map (44° 15′N 28° 16′E) **16**:288
MEDIA (Mesopotamia) **13**:263–264 *bibliog.*
Cyaxares, King **5**:400
Ecbatana **7**:37
Nimrud **14**:199
Nineveh **14**:200
Persia, ancient **15**:181–182 *illus., map*
Persian art and architecture **15**:184
MEDIA (Pennsylvania)
map (39° 54′N 75° 23′W) **15**:147
MEDIA NEWS CORPORATION
press agencies and syndicates **15**:533
MEDIAN **13**:264
mean **13**:264
numbers, set **13**:264
triangle (mathematics) **19**:292
MEDIAPOLIS (Iowa)
map (41° 0′N 91° 10′W) **11**:244
MEDIAŞ (Romania)
map (46° 10′N 24° 21′E) **16**:288
MEDIATION **13**:264 *bibliog.*
See also ARBITRATION
Federal Mediation and Conciliation Service **8**:41
National Mediation Board **14**:35
MEDICAID **13**:264 *bibliog.*
health-care systems **10**:87
hospital **10**:258
nursing home **14**:299
MEDICAL ETHICS **13**:264 *bibliog.*
death and dying **6**:69
euthanasia **7**:310–311
genetic engineering **9**:85
Hippocratic oath **10**:174
MEDICAL EXAMINATION *see* EXAMINATION, MEDICAL
MEDICAL EXAMINER
coroner **5**:271
MEDICAL INSTRUMENTATION
biosensor **3**:276
bronchoscope **3**:503
diathermy **6**:153–154
dosimeter **6**:244
electrocardiograph **7**:111–112
electroencephalograph **7**:113–114
electron microscope **7**:120–122
electrophoresis **7**:126
endoscope **7**:171
examination, medical **7**:326
fluoroscope **8**:188
gastroscope **9**:58
heart diseases **10**:96
heart-lung machine **10**:97
hyperbaric chamber **10**:347
iron lung **11**:272
mammography **13**:106
microscope **13**:387–388
nuclear magnetic resonance imaging **14**:284
ophthalmoscope **14**:404–405
oxygen tent **14**:478
PETT **15**:215–216
radiation therapy **16**:43
radiography **16**:63
radiology **16**:64–65
respirator **16**:178
scintillation counter **17**:146–147
spirometer, pulmonary function test **15**:620
stethoscope **18**:262
sunlamp **18**:348
surgery **18**:360–363
thermometer **19**:166
MEDICAL INSURANCE *see* HEALTH INSURANCE
MEDICAL LAKE (Washington)
map (47° 34′N 117° 41′W) **20**:35
MEDICARE **13**:265 *bibliog.*
health-care systems **10**:87
hospital **10**:258
social security **18**:14–15
MEDICI (family) **13**:265; **16**:148 *illus.*
academies of art **1**:70
Bandinelli, Baccio **3**:62
Botticelli, Sandro **3**:418
Catherine de Médicis **4**:209
Florence (Italy) **8**:168–169
Italy, history of **11**:329
landscape architecture **12**:185
Laurentian Library **12**:239
Livorno (Italy) **12**:378
Machiavelli, Nicolò **13**:18
Marie de Médicis **13**:151–152
Medici Chapel **13**:265–266
Michelangelo **13**:372–373
museums, art **13**:657
pawnbroker **15**:121
Piero di Cosimo **15**:297
Verrocchio, Andrea del **19**:560
MEDICI, COSIMO DE′ (1389–1464)
Medici (family) **13**:265
MEDICI, COSIMO I, DE′ (1519–1574)
Medici (family) **13**:265
MEDICI, LORENZO DE′ (the Magnificent)
Medici (family) **13**:265 *illus.*
MEDICI, LORENZO DE′ (1492–1519)
Medici (family) **13**:265
MEDICI CHAPEL **13**:265–266 *bibliog.*
Michelangelo **13**:373–375
MEDICINAL LEECH **12**:271 *illus.*
MEDICINAL PLANTS **13**:266–267 *bibliog., illus.*
agrimony **1**:199
alkaloid **1**:296
aloe **1**:307
arum **2**:226
belladonna **3**:187
betel **3**:230
betony **3**:232
bindweed **3**:258
botanical garden **3**:412
butterfly weed **3**:600
calendula **4**:28
celery **4**:229
chamomile **4**:276
coca **5**:84–85
comfrey **5**:135
croton **5**:363
Datura **6**:45
Ephedra **7**:215–216
eucalyptus **7**:261–262
fenugreek **8**:51
feverfew **8**:66
figwort **8**:76
foxglove **8**:257
garlic **9**:48
gentian **9**:94
ginseng **9**:185
goldenrain tree **9**:233
henbane **10**:121
hollyhock **10**:204
honey bush **10**:220
hops **10**:233
horehound **10**:234
horsetail **10**:253
hyssop **10**:352
Indian pipe **11**:106
jacaranda **11**:339
jack-in-the-pulpit **11**:339
jasmine **11**:384
Jerusalem artichoke **11**:402
jewelweed **11**:411
jimsonweed **11**:419
joe-pye weed **11**:421
juniper **11**:470
lungwort **12**:465
mandrake **13**:112
meadow saffron **13**:252
mistletoe **13**:481

MEDICINAL PLANTS (cont.)
morning glory **13**:583
mustard **13**:686
nightshade **14**:194
orchid **14**:420
paperbark **15**:71
parsley **15**:99
peony **15**:155 *illus.*
poppy **15**:432
potato **15**:465
prickly ash **15**:535
Queen Anne's lace **16**:21
rauwolfia **16**:94
rhubarb **16**:203
roles **15**:340–341
active ingredients **13**:266
drug **6**:274
folk medicine **8**:201
herbs and spices **10**:137
in history **13**:266
rue **16**:339
saffron **17**:11
saltbush **17**:38
sarsaparilla **17**:79
sassafras **17**:83
sausage tree **17**:97
senna **17**:203
speedwell **18**:176
spikenard **18**:183
strophanthus **18**:303
sweet gum **18**:387
tamarind **19**:18
tansy **19**:25
tea **19**:53
teasel **19**:58
witch hazel **20**:191
MEDICINE **13**:267–272 *bibliog., illus.*
acupuncture **1**:91
ambulance **1**:326
animal experimentation **2**:22
caduceus **4**:12
child development **4**:348
child psychiatry **4**:350–351
Chinese medicine **4**:390–391
chiropractic **4**:397–398
computer modeling **5**:162
current advances **13**:272
dermatology **6**:122
diagnostic tests **6**:149–150
drug **6**:274–279
education *see* MEDICINE, EDUCATION IN
engineering
biomedical engineering **3**:274
biotechnology **3**:277
genetic engineering **9**:84–85
epidemiology **7**:219
ethics **7**:252
medical ethics **13**:264
examination, medical **7**:326
folk medicine **8**:201
foundations and endowments
Duke Endowment **6**:295
Kresge Foundation **12**:129
Nuffield Foundation **14**:291
genetic counseling **9**:83–84
geriatrics **9**:122
gynecology **9**:414
hallucinogens **10**:24
health-care systems **10**:87–89
hematology **10**:117
history *see* MEDICINE, HISTORY OF
holistic medicine **10**:203
homeopathy **10**:212
hospice **10**:256
hospital **10**:256–258
hypnosis **10**:350
immunology **11**:60
laser **12**:212–213
magic **13**:49–50
malpractice **13**:93
medical statistics
biomathematics **3**:272
medicinal plants **13**:266–267
naturopathy **14**:51
neurology **14**:105
Nobel Prize in Physiology or Medicine *see* PHYSIOLOGY—Nobel Prize in Physiology or Medicine
nuclear medicine **14**:284–285
nursing (profession) **14**:298–299
obstetrics **14**:319
ophthalmology **14**:404
orthomolecular medicine **14**:450
orthopedics **14**:450
osteopathic medicine **14**:457
paramedic **15**:80
patent medicine **15**:110
pathology **15**:112
pediatrics **15**:131
periodicals
Journal of the American Medical Association **11**:453
Lancet **12**:178
petrochemicals **15**:205
pharmaceutical industry **15**:219–220
pharmacology **15**:220
photography, scientific **15**:271–272
physical therapy **15**:280
plastic surgery **15**:347
podiatry **15**:377
professional and educational organizations **17**:145 *table*
Académie des Sciences **13**:269
Akademie der Wissenschaften der DDR **1**:229
American Medical Association **1**:348
Collegium Naturae Curiosorum **13**:269
Royal Society of London **13**:269
psychiatry **15**:588
public health **15**:608
quarantine **16**:12
radioimmunoassay **16**:63–64
radiology **16**:64–65
rehabilitation medicine **16**:129–130
research institutions
National Institutes of Health **14**:34
Pasteur Institute **15**:108
Rockefeller University **16**:251
Sloan-Kettering Institute for Cancer Research **17**:363
shaman **17**:238–239
space medicine **18**:132–134
specialties **13**:272; **13**:273
sports medicine **18**:197–198
surgery **18**:360–363
transplantation, organ **13**:272
veterinary medicine **19**:566–567
MEDICINE, EDUCATION IN **13**:272–273 *bibliog.*
American Medical Association **1**:348
Blackwell, Elizabeth **3**:322–323
Boerhaave, Hermann **3**:358
chiropractic **4**:397
dentistry **6**:116
education **7**:60
Flexner, Abraham **8**:163–164
Fothergill, John **8**:248
geriatrics **9**:122
graduate **13**:273
Hamilton, Alice **10**:28–29
Hippocratic oath **10**:174
hospital **10**:256
medicine **13**:272
19th century **13**:270
Osler, Sir William **14**:454
osteopathic medicine **14**:457
physiology **15**:287
postgraduate **13**:273
undergraduate **13**:272
veterinary medicine **19**:566
MEDICINE, HISTORY OF
anatomy **1**:395–398
apothecary **2**:85
Aristotle **13**:268
Boerhaave, Hermann **3**:358
Bright, Richard **3**:486
cardiovascular diseases **4**:145
Celsus, Aulus Cornelius **4**:238
Chinese medicine **4**:390–391
Code of Hammurabi **13**:267
Cosmas and Damian, Saints **5**:280
Dooley, Thomas **6**:240
drug **6**:274–275
Egyptian medicine **13**:267
environmental health **7**:210–211
Fabricius ab Aquapendente, Hieronymus **8**:5
Freud, Sigmund **13**:271
Greece, ancient **13**:268
headache **10**:85
Hippocrates **10**:174; **13**:268
Hippocratic oath **10**:174
Hoffmann, Friedrich **10**:195
India, medicine in **13**:268
Islamic Empire medicine **13**:268–269
Israeli, Isaac ben Solomon **11**:306
Japanese medicine **13**:268
Malpighi, Marcello **13**:93
Mayo (family) **13**:248
medicinal plants **13**:266
medicine **13**:269–272 *illus.*
Medieval period **13**:269
Middle Eastern medicine **13**:267–268
Mosaic Code **13**:267
Nostradamus **14**:266–267
Oriental medicine **13**:267–268
Osler, Sir William **14**:454
Paracelsus **15**:74
Pasteur, Louis **15**:107–108
pharmacy **15**:221
primitive medicine **13**:267
psychopathology, treatment of **15**:599–601
Reed, Walter **16**:118
Renaissance period **13**:269
Rome, ancient **13**:268
Rush, Benjamin **16**:347
Schweitzer, Albert **17**:139–140
Shumway, Norman Edward **17**:289
space medicine **18**:132
Spock, Benjamin **18**:191–192
surgery **18**:360–363
Sydenham, Thomas **18**:400
technology, history of **19**:69
Vesalius, Andreas **19**:564
Virchow, Rudolf **19**:604
Yegorov, Boris B. **20**:322
MEDICINE BOW (Wyoming)
map (41° 54′N 106° 12′W) **20**:301
MEDICINE BOW MOUNTAINS
map (41° 30′N 106° 30′W) **20**:301
MEDICINE BOW PEAK
map (41° 21′N 106° 19′W) **20**:301
MEDICINE BOW RIVER
map (42° 0′N 106° 40′W) **20**:301
MEDICINE CREEK
map (39° 43′N 93° 24′W) **13**:476
MEDICINE CREEK TREATY
Puyallup **15**:633
MEDICINE HAT (Alberta)
map (50° 3′N 110° 40′W) **1**:256
MEDICINE LAKE (Montana)
map (48° 30′N 104° 30′W) **13**:547
MEDICINE LODGE (Kansas)
map (37° 17′N 98° 35′W) **12**:18
MEDICINE LODGE TREATY OF 1867
Comanche **5**:129–130
MEDICINE MAN *see* SHAMAN
MEDICINE WHEEL *see* ARCHAEOASTRONOMY
MEDIEVAL ART *see* CAROLINGIAN ART AND ARCHITECTURE; GOTHIC ART AND ARCHITECTURE; MEROVINGIAN ART AND ARCHITECTURE; MIDDLE AGES, ART; OTTONIAN ART AND ARCHITECTURE; ROMANESQUE ART AND ARCHITECTURE
MEDIEVAL DRAMA **13**:273–274 *bibliog., illus.*
allegory **1**:299
Bale, John **3**:36
Coventry (England) **5**:319
drama **6**:258
Dutch and Flemish literature **6**:314
Everyman **7**:316
interlude **11**:214
mystery play **19**:145 *illus.*
passion play **15**:105
puppet **15**:627
theater, history of the **19**:145 *illus.*
theater architecture and staging **19**:152
MEDIEVAL MUSIC **13**:274–275 *bibliog., illus.*
Binchois, Gilles **3**:257
English music **7**:202–203
French music **8**:320 *illus.*
German and Austrian music **9**:129
instruments
keyboard instruments **12**:63
mandolin **13**:111–112
portative organ **15**:443–444
rebec **16**:105
sackbut **17**:7
shawm **17**:246
vielle **19**:578
Italian music **11**:317
Landini, Francesco **12**:183
Machaut, Guillaume de **13**:18
madrigal **13**:45
minstrels, minnesingers, and troubadours **13**:460
motet **13**:606
music, history of Western **13**:662–663 *illus.*
organum **14**:441
plainsong **15**:325–326
polyphony **15**:421
song **18**:64
Vitry, Philippe de **19**:621
MEDIEVAL PERIOD *see* MIDDLE AGES
MEDILL, JOSEPH
Patterson (family) **15**:115
MEDINA (New York)
map (43° 13′N 78° 23′W) **14**:149
MEDINA (North Dakota)
map (46° 54′N 99° 18′W) **14**:248
MEDINA (Ohio)
map (41° 8′N 81° 52′W) **14**:357
MEDINA (county in Ohio)
map (41° 8′N 81° 52′W) **14**:357
MEDINA (Saudi Arabia) **13**:275
Arabs **2**:101
history
Middle East, history of the **13**:402
map (24° 28′N 39° 36′E) **17**:94
Muhammad **13**:632
MEDINA (county in Texas)
map (29° 20′N 99° 5′W) **19**:129
MEDINA-SIDONIA, 7TH DUKE OF
Spanish Armada **18**:150–151
MEDITATION **13**:275–276 *bibliog., illus.*
consciousness, states of **5**:200
mandala **13**:110
mantra **13**:131
prayer **15**:490
Zen Buddhism **20**:358–359
MEDITATIONS (book)
Marcus Aurelius, Roman Emperor **13**:148
MEDITERRANEAN CLIMATE **13**:276 *bibliog.*
characteristics **13**:276
mistral **13**:482
occurrence, world areas **13**:276
plant distribution **15**:344 *map*
tree **19**:288
MEDITERRANEAN FEVER *see* BRUCELLOSIS
MEDITERRANEAN FRUIT FLY
fruit fly **8**:347
MEDITERRANEAN SEA **13**:276–278 *bibliog., map*
climate **13**:276–277
Mediterranean climate **13**:276
mistral **13**:482
economy **13**:277
geology **13**:276
hydrology and marine life **13**:277
islands and island groups
Balearic Islands **3**:36 *map*
Corsica (France) **5**:277 *illus.*
Crete **5**:342 *illus.*
Cyclades **5**:402
Cyprus **5**:407–409 *illus., map, table*
Ibiza **11**:5
Majorca (Spain) **13**:77
Malta **13**:94–95 *illus., map, table*
Minorca (Spain) **13**:459
Sardinia (Italy) **17**:76
Sicily (Italy) **17**:292–293 *illus.*
Levant **12**:302
map (35° 0′N 20° 0′E) **13**:277
seas, gulfs, and bays
Bosporus **3**:407 *map*
Dardanelles **6**:37 *map*
Gibraltar, Strait of **9**:175
Ionian Sea **11**:241
Tyrrhenian Sea **19**:368
MEDLAR **13**:278
MEDNY
Commander Islands (USSR) **5**:137
MEDORA (Indiana)
map (38° 49′N 86° 10′W) **11**:111
MEDORA (North Dakota)
map (46° 55′N 103° 31′W) **14**:248
MEDTNER, NIKOLAI
Russian music **16**:369
MEDUCTIC (New Brunswick)
map (46° 0′N 67° 29′W) **14**:117
MEDUSA (mythology) **3**:576 *illus.*; **13**:278; **20**:202 *illus.*
cameo **4**:54 *illus.*
Cellini, Benvenuto **4**:237 *illus.*
Gorgon **9**:251
Pegasus **15**:132
Perseus **15**:180
MEDUSA (zoology) *see* JELLYFISH
MEDVEDEV, ROY A. and ZHORES A. **13**:278
MEDWALL, HENRY **13**:278
MEDWAY (Massachusetts)
map (42° 8′N 71° 24′W) **13**:206
MEDWAY RIVER
map (44° 8′N 64° 36′W) **14**:269
MEEGEREN, HANS VAN
forgery in art **8**:233
The Young Christ **8**:233 *illus.*
MEEKATHARRA (Australia)
map (26° 36′S 118° 29′E) **2**:328
MEEKER (Colorado)
map (40° 2′N 107° 55′W) **5**:116
MEEKER (county in Minnesota)
map (45° 5′N 94° 30′W) **13**:453
MEEKER, NATHAN COOK **13**:278
MEELPAEG LAKE RESERVOIR
map (48° 16′N 56° 35′W) **14**:166
MEERKAT *see* MONGOOSE; SURICATE
MEERSCHAUM **13**:278
clay minerals **5**:47
MEERUT (India)
map (28° 59′N 77° 42′E) **11**:80
MEES, CHARLES EDWARD KENNETH **13**:278
MEESE, EDWIN **13**:278

MEETEETSE (Wyoming)
map (44° 9′N 108° 52′W) 20:301
MEGALITH 13:278–279 *bibliog., illus.*
archaeoastronomy 2:114–115
cairn 4:17
Carnac (France) 4:154
Cotswold-Severn (Great Britain) 5:304
Dowth (Ireland) 6:253
European prehistory 7:302
Knowth (Ireland) 12:102
Los Millares (Spain) 12:418
menhir 13:297
Mnajdra (Malta) 19:94 *illus.*
Newgrange (Ireland) 14:168
prehistoric art 15:510
Southeast Asian art and architecture 18:108
stone alignments 18:281–282
Stonehenge (England) 18:283 *illus.*
Tarxien (Malta) 19:41
Woodhenge (England) 20:211
MEGALOPOLIS
metropolitan area 13:347
MEGALOPOLIS (city in ancient Greece) 13:280 *bibliog.*
MEGALOPOLIS (urban area) 13:280
city 5:6
MEGANTHROPUS 13:280 *bibliog.*
MEGANTIC MOUNTAIN
map (45° 28′N 71° 9′W) 16:18
MEGAPODE 13:280
MEGARON
house (in Western architecture) 10:264
MEGASPORANGIUM *see* SPORANGIUM
MEGAVITAMIN THERAPY 13:280
orthomolecular medicine 14:450
Pauling, Linus Carl 15:119
vitamins and minerals 19:619
MEGHALAYA (India) 13:280
Khasi 12:66
map (25° 30′N 91° 15′E) 11:80
MEGIDDO (Israel) 13:280 *bibliog.*
MEHEMET ALI (Egyptian viceroy) *see* MUHAMMED ALI PASHA
MEHERRIN RIVER
map (36° 26′N 76° 57′W) 19:607
MEHMED II, SULTAN OF THE OTTOMAN EMPIRE 13:281 *bibliog., illus.*
Middle East, history of the 13:404–405 *illus.*
Ottoman Empire 14:464
MEHMED V RASHID, SULTAN OF THE OTTOMAN EMPIRE
Ottoman Empire 14:466
MEHRGARH
Indus civilization 11:153
MEHTA, ZUBIN 13:281 *bibliog.*
MEHTAR LAM (Afghanistan)
map (34° 39′N 70° 10′E) 1:133
MEI LAN-FANG 13:281 *bibliog.*
theater, history of the 19:148
MEIER, RICHARD 13:281 *bibliog.*
MEIGHEN, ARTHUR 13:281 *bibliog.*
MEIGS (Georgia)
map (31° 4′N 83° 6′W) 9:114
MEIGS (county in Ohio)
map (39° 5′N 82° 0′W) 14:357
MEIGS (county in Tennessee)
map (35° 30′N 84° 50′W) 19:104
MEIJI (emperor)
Japan, history of 11:370 *illus.*
Meiji Restoration 13:281–282
MEIJI RESTORATION 13:281–282 *bibliog., illus.*
constitution
Okuma Shigenobu 14:372
Ito Hirobumi 11:331
Japan, history of 11:370
Saigo Takamori 17:15
MEIKTILA (Burma)
map (20° 52′N 95° 52′E) 3:573
MEILHAC, HENRI
Carmen 4:153
MEIN KAMPF (book) 13:282
Hitler, Adolf 10:187
nazism 14:67–68
MEINECKE, FRIEDRICH 13:282 *bibliog.*
MEINESZ, FELIX VENING *see* VENING MEINESZ, FELIX
MEININGEN PLAYERS
Saxe-Meiningen, George II, Duke of 17:104
MEINONG, ALEXIUS 13:282 *bibliog.*
MEIOSIS 13:282
cell 4:234–235 *illus.*
development 6:137
fern 8:57
genetics 9:86–87
growth 9:378
parthenogenesis 15:99–100
reproduction 16:162
seed cone 17:187
sex 17:224
MEIR, GOLDA 13:282–283 *bibliog., illus.*
MEISSEN (Germany, East and West)
map (51° 10′N 13° 28′E) 9:140
MEISSEN WARE 13:283 *bibliog., illus.*
chinoiserie 4:395
Nymphenburg ware 14:309
pottery and porcelain 15:471 *illus.*
rhinoceros 16:264 *illus.*
MEISSNER, W.
Meissner effect
superconductivity 18:350
MEISSONIER, JEAN LOUIS ERNEST 13:283
MEISSONNIER, JUSTE AURÈLE 13:283 *bibliog.*
furniture 8:373
gold and silver work 9:230
MEISTERSINGER (poet-musician) 13:283 *bibliog.*
MEISTERSINGER, DIE (opera) 14:401 *illus.*
MEITNER, LISE 13:283 *bibliog.*
MEJIA, PAUL
Farrell, Suzanne 8:30
MEKERRHANE SABKHA
map (26° 19′N 1° 20′E) 1:287
MEKNÈS (Morocco) 13:283–284
map (33° 53′N 5° 37′W) 13:585
MEKONG RIVER 2:235 *illus.*; 12:13 *illus.*; 13:284 *map*
Kampuchea (Cambodia) 12:11
map (10° 33′N 105° 24′E) 2:232
MEKORYUK (Alaska)
map (60° 23′N 166° 12′W) 1:242
MÉKROU RIVER
map (12° 24′N 2° 49′E) 3:200
MELA 10:172 *illus.*
MELAKA (Malaysia) 13:284
history
spice trade 18:181
Straits Settlements 18:288
map (2° 12′N 102° 15′E) 13:84
MELANCHOLIA (depression) 6:118
MELANCHTHON, PHILIPP 13:284 *bibliog.*
Augsburg Confession 2:320
Wittenberg (East Germany) 20:193
MELANESIA 13:284
art
Oceanic art 14:337
Southeast Asian art and architecture 18:107
languages
creole 5:338
Malayo-Polynesian languages 13:83
map (13° 0′S 164° 0′E) 14:334
money 13:525 *illus.*
Oceania 14:334–335 *maps*
people
Melanesians 13:284–285
Papuans 15:73
race 16:33–34 *illus., map*
Trobriand Islanders 19:304
primitive religion 15:544 *illus.*
cargo cults 4:147
mana 13:107
MELANESIANS 13:284–285 *bibliog.*
Trobriand Islanders 19:304
MELANIN
freckle 8:289
hair 10:14
leukoderma 12:301
pigment, skin 15:300–301
skin 17:341 *illus.*
MELANOPHLOGITE
silica minerals 17:304
MELATONIN
hormone, animal 10:236 *table*
pineal gland 15:306
MELBA, DAME NELLIE 13:285 *bibliog.*
MELBOURNE (Arkansas)
map (36° 4′N 91° 54′W) 2:166
MELBOURNE (Australia) 13:285–286 *illus., map*
climate 2:332 *table*
education
La Trobe University 2:345 *table*
Melbourne University 2:345 *table*
Monash University 2:345 *table*
map (37° 49′S 144° 58′E) 2:328
MELBOURNE (Florida)
map (28° 5′N 80° 37′W) 8:172
MELBOURNE (Iowa)
map (41° 57′N 93° 6′W) 11:244
MELBOURNE, WILLIAM LAMB, 2D VISCOUNT 13:286 *bibliog.*
Victoria, Queen of England, Scotland, and Ireland 19:574
MELCHIOR, LAURITZ 13:286 *bibliog.*
MELCHIZEDEK 13:286
MELETIUS OF ANTIOCH, SAINT 13:286
MELFI, CONSTITUTIONS OF
Frederick II, King of Germany and Holy Roman Emperor 8:290
MELFORT (Saskatchewan)
map (52° 52′N 104° 36′W) 17:81
MÉLIÈS, GEORGES 13:286–287 *bibliog.*
film, history of 8:81
MELILLA (Spain) 13:287
map (35° 19′N 2° 58′W) 13:585
MELINCUE (Argentina)
map (33° 39′S 61° 27′W):149
MELIPILLO (Chile)
map (33° 42′S 71° 13′W) 4:355
MELITA (Manitoba)
map (49° 16′N 101° 0′W) 13:119
MELK, ABBEY OF
Prandtauer, Jakob 15:489
MELLAART, JAMES
Çatal Hüyük 4:198
Hacilar 10:7
MELLEN (Wisconsin)
map (46° 20′N 90° 40′W) 20:185
MELLETTE (South Dakota)
map (45° 9′N 98° 30′W) 18:103
MELLETTE (county in South Dakota)
map (43° 35′N 100° 45′W) 18:103
MELLON, ANDREW P.
National Portrait Gallery 14:45
MELLON, ANDREW W. 13:287 *bibliog., illus.*
National Gallery of Art 14:33
MELLON, PAUL 13:287
National Gallery of Art 14:33
MELLON FOUNDATION 13:287
National Gallery of Art 14:33
MELNIKOV, KONSTANTIN
Russian art and architecture 16:364
MELO (Uruguay)
map (32° 22′S 54° 11′W) 19:488
MELODRAMA 13:287 *bibliog.*
Benda, Jiří Antonín 3:196
Crébillon 5:336
drama 6:260
Dumas, Alexandre (1802–70) 6:296–297
film series 8:91
Kabuki 12:4 *illus.*
MacKaye, Steele 13:27
MELODY 13:287–288 *bibliog.*
cantus firmus 4:118
classical period in music 5:41
Indian music 11:103
Indians of North America, music and dance of the 11:142
sequence 17:207
Webern, Anton von 20:88
MELON 13:288 *illus.*
MELON SHELL 17:251 *illus.*
MELON TREE *see* PAPAYA
MELONITE
telluride minerals 19:91
MELOS (Greece) 13:288
Cyclades (Greece) 5:402
MELOZZO DA FORLÌ 13:288 *bibliog.*
MELPOMENE
muses 13:656
MELRHIR SHATT
map (34° 20′N 6° 20′E) 1:287
MELROSE (Massachusetts)
map (42° 27′N 71° 4′W) 13:206
MELROSE (Minnesota)
map (45° 40′N 94° 49′W) 13:453
MELROSE (New Mexico)
map (34° 26′N 103° 38′W) 14:136
MELROSE (Wisconsin)
map (44° 8′N 91° 1′W) 20:185
MELSTONE (Montana)
map (46° 36′N 107° 52′W) 13:547
MELTING POINT 13:288 *bibliog.*
eutectic point 7:310
sample purity 13:289
MELTWATER
esker 7:238
glaciers and glaciation 9:194
mudflow 13:631
MELTZER, ALLAN
monetary theory 13:525
MELUHHA
Dilmun 6:176
MELUN (France)
map (48° 32′N 2° 40′E) 8:260
MELVERN (Kansas)
map (38° 30′N 95° 38′W) 12:18
MELVILLE (Louisiana)
map (30° 42′N 91° 45′W) 12:430
MELVILLE (Saskatchewan)
map (50° 55′N 102° 48′W) 17:81
MELVILLE, ANDREW 13:288–289 *bibliog.*
MELVILLE, HERMAN 1:344 *illus.*; 13:289 *bibliog., illus.*
Billy Budd 3:256
Marquesas Islands 13:163
Moby-Dick 13:488
MELVILLE, LAKE
map (53° 45′N 59° 30′W) 14:166
MELVILLE BAY
map (75° 30′N 63° 0′W) 9:353
MELVILLE ISLAND (Australia)
map (11° 40′S 131° 0′E) 2:328
MELVILLE ISLAND (Northwest Territories)
map (75° 15′N 110° 0′W) 14:258
MELVILLE PENINSULA
map (68° 0′N 84° 0′W) 14:258
MELVIN (Illinois)
map (40° 34′N 88° 15′W) 11:42
MELVIN (Texas)
map (31° 13′N 99° 35′W) 19:129
MEM (letter)
M (letter) 13:3
MEMBRANE (biology)
active transport 1:89–90
cell 4:233
lipid 12:361–362
development 6:140
egg 7:72 *illus.*
endoplasmic reticulum 7:171
eucaryote 7:262
membrane chemistry 13:289–290
muscle contraction 13:655
mutation 13:686
neurophysiology 14:106
osmosis 14:455 *illus.*
MEMBRANE CHEMISTRY 13:289–290 *bibliog.*
MEMBRANOPHONES
musical instruments 13:676
MEMEL RIVER *see* NEMAN RIVER
MEMLING, HANS 13:290 *bibliog., illus.*
Saint Ursula reliquary panel 8:160 *illus.*
vase of flowers 18:269 *illus.*
Virgin and Child 13:290 *illus.*
MEMMINGEN (Germany, East and West)
map (47° 59′N 10° 11′E) 9:140
MEMMINGER, CHRISTOPHER GUSTAVUS 12:290
MEMNON 13:290
MEMORIAL DAY 13:290
Logan, John Alexander 12:394
MEMORY 13:290–292 *bibliog.*
amnesia 1:375
dreams and dreaming 6:267
Ebbinghaus, Hermann 7:35
hypnosis 10:350
information storage and retrieval 11:173–174
perception 15:160
speech development 18:175
MEMORY, COMPUTER *see* COMPUTER MEMORY
MEMPHIS (Egypt) 7:81 *map*; 13:292 *bibliog.*
mythology 13:697
Saqqara 17:74
MEMPHIS (Missouri)
map (40° 28′N 92° 10′W) 13:476
MEMPHIS (Tennessee) 13:292 *illus.*; 19:105 *map*
map (35° 8′N 90° 3′W) 19:104
MEMPHIS (Texas)
map (34° 44′N 100° 32′W) 19:129
MEMPHREMAGOG, LAKE
map (45° 5′N 72° 15′W) 19:554
MEN (biology)
baldness 3:34
castration 4:192
endocrine system, diseases of the 7:170–171
homosexuality 10:217
orchitis 14:420
prostate gland 15:573
reproductive system, human 16:163–164 *illus.*
semen 17:195
sex change 17:224–225
sex hormones 17:226
sexual development 17:228–230
sperm 18:179
vasectomy 19:525
MENA (Arkansas)
map (34° 35′N 94° 15′W) 2:166
MENA, JUAN DE
Spanish literature 18:157
MENAHGA (Minnesota)
map (46° 45′N 95° 6′W) 13:453
MENAI STRAITS (Wales)
bridge (engineering) 3:480–481 *illus.*
MENANDER 13:292–293 *bibliog.*
comedy 5:132
MENARCHE
menstruation 13:301

MENARD (county in Illinois)
map (40° 1′N 89° 51′W) **11**:42
MENARD (Texas)
map (30° 55′N 99° 47′W) **19**:129
MENARD (county in Texas)
map (30° 52′N 99° 50′W) **19**:129
MENARD, MICHEL B.
Galveston (Texas) **9**:23
MENASHA (Wisconsin)
map (44° 13′N 88° 26′W) **20**:185
MENCIUS **13**:293 *bibliog.*
Confucianism **5**:180
philosophy **15**:247
MENCKEN, H. L. **13**:293 *bibliog., illus.*
MENDAÑA DE NEYRA, ÁLVARO DE
Marquesas Islands **13**:162
Solomon Islands **18**:57
MENDE **13**:293–294 *bibliog.*
African music **1**:168–171
polygamy **15**:419
MENDEL, GREGOR JOHANN **13**:294 *bibliog., illus.*
biology **3**:271
Brno **3**:499
evolution **7**:318
genetics **9**:85–87 *illus.*; **13**:294
heredity **10**:140–141
Mendel's laws of heredity **13**:294
segregation (genetics) **10**:139 *illus.*
MENDELE MOKHER SEFARIM **13**:294
MENDELEVIUM **13**:294
actinide series **1**:88
element **6**:130 *table*
metal, metallic element **13**:328
Seaborg, Glenn T. **17**:171–172
transuranium elements **19**:286
MENDELEYEV, DMITRY IVANOVICH **4**:326 *illus.*; **13**:294–295 *bibliog., illus.*
critical temperature concept **13**:295
mendelevium **13**:294
periodic law **13**:295
periodic table **13**:294–295; **15**:166–167
element **7**:130
Principles of Chemistry **13**:295
Russian Chemical Society **13**:295
MENDELSOHN, ERIC **13**:295 *bibliog., illus.*
Einstein Tower **13**:295 *illus.*
MENDELSSOHN, FELIX **13**:295–296 *bibliog., illus.*
MENDELSSOHN, LARRY
demolition derby **6**:104
MENDELSSOHN, MOSES **13**:296 *bibliog.*
Judaism **11**:462
MENDENHALL (Mississippi)
map (31° 58′N 89° 52′W) **13**:469
MENDERES, ADNAN **13**:296
MÉNDEZ (Ecuador)
map (2° 43′S 78° 19′W) **7**:52
MENDEZ, APARICIO
Uruguay **19**:490
MENDHAM (New Jersey)
map (40° 46′N 74° 36′W) **14**:129
MENDIVIL, HILARIO
doll **12**:226 *illus.*
MENDOCINO (California)
map (39° 19′N 123° 48′W) **4**:31
MENDOCINO (county in California)
map (39° 25′N 123° 25′W) **4**:31
MENDOTA (California)
map (36° 45′N 120° 23′W) **4**:31
MENDOTA (Illinois)
map (41° 33′N 89° 7′W) **11**:42
MENDOTA, LAKE
map (43° 5′N 89° 25′W) **20**:185
MENDOZA (Argentina)
map (32° 53′S 68° 49′W) **2**:149
MENDOZA (province in Argentina)
map (34° 30′S 68° 30′W) **2**:149
MENDOZA, ANTONIO DE **13**:296 *bibliog.*
MENDOZA, PEDRO DE **13**:296
MENE DE MAUROA (Venezuela)
map (10° 43′N 71° 1′W) **19**:542
MENELAUS (mathematician)
mathematics, history of **13**:224
MENELAUS (mythology) **13**:297
MENELIK II, EMPEROR OF ETHIOPIA **13**:297 *bibliog.*
Ethiopia **7**:254
MENÉNDEZ DE AVILÉS, PEDRO **13**:297 *bibliog.*
Florida **8**:175
MENENG POINT
map (0° 32′S 166° 57′E) **14**:51
MENES, KING OF EGYPT **13**:297
Egypt, ancient **7**:81
Narmer Palette **7**:82 *illus.*; **17**:159 *illus.*
MENESES, GUILLERMO
Venezuela **19**:543
MENESES, JORGE DE
Papua New Guinea **15**:73
MENGELBERG, WILLEM
Concertgebouw Orchestra **5**:170
MENGES, COPIA DE
Charles III, King of Spain **4**:296 *illus.*
MENGISTU HAILE MARIAM **13**:297
Ethiopia **7**:255
MENGOZZI-COLONNA, GIROLAMO
Tiepolo (family) **19**:195
MENGS, ANTON RAPHAEL **13**:297 *bibliog.*
Johann Winckelmann **20**:168 *illus.*
neoclassicism (art) **14**:81
MENHADEN **13**:297
fishing industry **8**:127
MENHIR **13**:297
megalith **13**:279
stone alignments **18**:281
Stonehenge **18**:283
MENIERE'S DISEASE **13**:297
deafness **6**:67
ear disease **7**:7–8
MENIFEE (county in Kentucky)
map (37° 55′N 83° 35′W) **12**:47
MENINGITIS **13**:298
encephalitis **7**:162
epidemic **13**:298
mastoiditis **13**:217
mumps **13**:639
Neisseria **14**:79
nervous system, diseases of the **14**:95; **14**:96
stress, biological **18**:298
tuberculosis **19**:327
MENINGOCOCCUS *see NEISSERIA*
MENIPPUS
satire **17**:88
MENKAURE, KING OF EGYPT **7**:87 *illus.*; **13**:298
MENKEN, ADAH ISAACS **13**:298 *bibliog.*
MENLO PARK (California)
map (37° 28′N 122° 13′W) **4**:31
MENNIN, PETER **13**:298
MENNINGER (family) **13**:298 *bibliog.*
Menninger Clinic **13**:298
Menninger Psychotherapy Research Project
projective tests **15**:566
MENNO (South Dakota)
map (43° 14′N 97° 34′W) **18**:103
MENNO SIMONS **13**:298 *bibliog.*
Mennonites **13**:298–299
MENNONITES **13**:298–299 *bibliog., illus.*
See also ANABAPTISTS
Amish **13**:298–299 *illus.*
Boehm, Martin **3**:358
conscientious objector **5**:200
Kansas **12**:22
Lancaster (Pennsylvania) **12**:177
Ohio **14**:360 *illus.*
MENO (Oklahoma)
map (36° 24′N 98° 11′W) **14**:368
MENOMINEE (American Indians) **13**:299 *bibliog.*
MENOMINEE (Michigan)
map (45° 6′N 87° 37′W) **13**:377
MENOMINEE (county in Michigan)
map (45° 35′N 87° 30′W) **13**:377
MENOMINEE (county in Wisconsin)
map (45° 0′N 88° 40′W) **20**:185
MENOMINEE RIVER
map (45° 5′N 87° 36′W) **20**:185
MENOMONEE FALLS (Wisconsin)
map (43° 11′N 88° 7′W) **20**:185
MENOMONEE RIVER
map (43° 2′N 87° 54′W) **20**:185
MENOMONIE (Wisconsin)
map (44° 53′N 91° 55′W) **20**:185
MENON, VENEGALIL KRISHNAN KRISHNA *see* KRISHNA MENON, VENEGALIL KRISHNAN
MENONGUE (Angola)
map (14° 36′S 17° 48′E) **2**:5
MENOPAUSE **13**:299–300 *bibliog.*
blood vascular symptoms **13**:300
emotional changes **13**:300
estrogen replacement therapy **13**:300
hormonal changes **13**:300
menstruation **13**:301
middle age **13**:390
musculoskeletal changes **13**:300
ovarian function **13**:300
reproduction **16**:163
sex hormones **17**:226–227
sexual activity **13**:299–300
vaginal diseases **13**:299–300
MENORCA (Spain) *see* MINORCA (Spain)
MENOTTI, GIAN CARLO **13**:300 *bibliog., illus.*
Spoleto Festival **18**:192
MENS REA **13**:300
crime **5**:345
MENSES *see* MENSTRUATION
MENSHEVIKS *see* BOLSHEVIKS AND MENSHEVIKS
MENSHIKOV, ALEKSANDR DANILOVICH, PRINCE **13**:300
MENSHIKOV, ALEKSANDR SERGEYEVICH
Menshikov, Aleksandr Danilovich, Prince **13**:300
MENSTRUATION **13**:300–302 *bibliog.*
adolescence **1**:106
amenorrhea **1**:326
anorexia nervosa **2**:34
birth control **3**:294
dysmenorrhea **6**:320
endocrine system, diseases of the **7**:171
gynecology **9**:414
headache **10**:86
hormones **13**:301
estrous cycle **7**:248
sex hormones **17**:226
menopause **13**:299
premenstrual stress **15**:518
reproduction **16**:163
sexual development **17**:229–230
toxic shock syndrome **19**:256
uterus **19**:497
MENTAL FUNCTIONING *see* CONSCIOUSNESS, STATES OF
MENTAL HEALTH **13**:301 *bibliog.*
See also names of specific disorders, e.g., ANXIETY; MANIC-DEPRESSIVE PSYCHOSIS; etc.
Bedlam (London) **3**:154
clinical psychology **5**:59
community mental health **5**:152–153
Dix, Dorothea **6**:206
handicapped persons **10**:36
homosexuality **10**:217
institutionalization **11**:196–197
Menninger (family) **13**:298
National Institute of Mental Health **14**:34
neurosis **14**:107
psychiatry **15**:588
psychoanalysis **15**:588–591
psychopathology, treatment of **15**:599–601
psychopathy **15**:601
psychosis **15**:602
psychosomatic disorders **15**:602
psychotherapy **15**:602–603
psychotropic drugs **15**:603–605
Rush, Benjamin **16**:347
senility **17**:203
Szasz, Thomas **18**:415
MENTAL ILLNESS *see* MENTAL HEALTH
MENTAL RETARDATION **13**:301–302 *bibliog.*
Down's syndrome **6**:252
handicapped persons **10**:36
institutionalization **11**:196
Klinefelter's syndrome **12**:98
phenylketonuria **15**:226
special education **18**:166–167
Special Olympics **18**:168
speech **18**:175
MENTAL TELEPATHY *see* TELEPATHY
MENTAL TESTS *see* EDUCATIONAL MEASUREMENT; INTELLIGENCE, TESTS; PSYCHOLOGICAL MEASUREMENT
MENTAWAI ISLANDS
map (3° 0′S 100° 10′E) **11**:147
MENTONE (Texas)
map (31° 42′N 103° 36′W) **19**:129
MENTOR (Ohio)
map (41° 40′N 81° 20′W) **14**:357
MENTUHOTEP II, KING OF EGYPT
Deir el-Bahri **6**:85–86
MENTZEL, ADOLF VON *see* MENZEL, ADOLF VON
MENTZER (pseudonym) *see* FISCHART, JOHANN BAPTIST
MENU (computer term) **5**:160h
MENUHIN, YEHUDI **13**:302 *bibliog.*
MENZEL, ADOLF VON **13**:302–303 *bibliog.*
realism (art) **16**:103
MENZEL, DONALD HOWARD **13**:303
MENZEL, JIRI
film, history of **8**:87
MENZEL BOURGUIBA (Tunisia)
map (37° 10′N 9° 48′E) **19**:335
MENZIES, SIR ROBERT GORDON **13**:303 *bibliog., illus.*
Liberal parties **12**:311
MEO **13**:303
MEO LANGUAGE *see* MIAO-YAO LANGUAGES
MEPERIDINE *see* DEMEROL
MEPPEL (Netherlands)
map (52° 42′N 6° 11′E) **14**:99
MEPROBAMATE **13**:303
sedative **17**:182
MEQUON (Wisconsin)
map (43° 13′N 87° 58′W) **20**:185
MER DE GLACE **13**:303
MER ROUGE (Louisiana)
map (32° 47′N 91° 48′W) **12**:430
MERAMEC RIVER
map (38° 23′N 90° 21′W) **13**:476
MERANO (Italy)
map (46° 40′N 11° 9′E) **11**:321
MERASHEEN (Newfoundland)
map (47° 25′N 54° 21′W) **14**:166
MERCALLI SCALE
earthquakes **7**:25
MERCANTILISM **13**:303 *bibliog.*
Colbert, Jean Baptiste **5**:97
colonialism **5**:112
Frederick II, King of Prussia (Frederick the Great) **8**:291–292
guilds **9**:395
Hanseatic League **10**:40–41
Navigation Acts **14**:61–62
physiocrats **15**:287
piracy **15**:313
Smith, Adam **17**:367
MERCATOR, GERARDUS **13**:139 *illus.*; **13**:304 *bibliog.*
geography **9**:101
MERCATOR PROJECTION
chart **4**:300
MERCED (California)
map (37° 18′N 120° 29′W) **4**:31
MERCED (county in California)
map (37° 15′N 120° 40′W) **4**:31
MERCED RIVER
map (37° 21′N 120° 58′W) **4**:31
MERCEDES (Corrientes province, Argentina)
map (29° 12′S 58° 5′W) **2**:149
MERCEDES (suburb of Buenos Aires, Argentina)
map (34° 39′S 59° 27′W):149
MERCEDES (Texas)
map (26° 9′N 97° 55′W) **19**:129
MERCEDES (Uruguay)
map (33° 16′S 58° 1′W) **19**:488
MERCEDES-BENZ **2**:367 *illus.*
MERCENARIES **13**:304 *bibliog.*
condottieri **5**:173
Gurkha **9**:406
Hawkwood, Sir John **10**:78
Hessians **10**:153
Wallenstein, Albrecht Wenzel von **20**:15
Ward, Frederick Townsend **20**:29
MERCER (county in Illinois)
map (41° 10′N 90° 43′W) **11**:42
MERCER (county in Kentucky)
map (37° 50′N 84° 50′W) **12**:47
MERCER (county in Missouri)
map (40° 25′N 93° 35′W) **13**:476
MERCER (county in New Jersey)
map (40° 13′N 74° 45′W) **14**:129
MERCER (county in North Dakota)
map (47° 20′N 101° 50′W) **14**:248
MERCER (county in Ohio)
map (40° 33′N 84° 34′W) **14**:357
MERCER (Pennsylvania)
map (41° 14′N 80° 15′W) **15**:147
MERCER (county in Pennsylvania)
map (41° 14′N 80° 15′W) **15**:147
MERCER (county in West Virginia)
map (37° 23′N 81° 8′W) **20**:111
MERCER (Wisconsin)
map (46° 10′N 90° 4′W) **20**:185
MERCER, JOHN **13**:304
MERCER, JOHNNY **13**:304 *bibliog.*
MERCER, MABEL **13**:304
MERCER ISLAND (city in Washington)
map (47° 35′N 122° 15′W) **20**:35
MERCER ISLAND (island in Washington)
map (47° 35′N 122° 15′W) **20**:35
MERCER UNIVERSITY **13**:304
MERCERSBURG (Pennsylvania)
map (39° 50′N 77° 54′W) **15**:147
MERCERSBURG THEOLOGY
Schaff, Philip **17**:116
MERCERVILLE (New Jersey)
map (40° 14′N 74° 41′W) **14**:129
MERCHANDISING *see* RETAILING
MERCHANT MARINE
See also SHIPPING
Coast Guard, U.S. **5**:80

United States Merchant Marine Academy **19**:462
MERCHANT MARINE ACADEMY, UNITED STATES *see* UNITED STATES MERCHANT MARINE ACADEMY
MERCHANT SHIP *see* CARGO TRANSPORTATION
MERCHANT OF VENICE, THE (play) **13**:304
MERCIA **2**:3 *map*; **13**:304 *bibliog.*
Æthelflæd **1**:131
Alfred, King of England **1**:280
Athelstan, King of Wessex **2**:289
Edward the Elder, King of Wessex **7**:67
Offa, King of Mercia **14**:353
MERCIER, DÉSIRÉ JOSEPH **13**:304–305
MERCIER, HONORÉ **13**:305
MERCILESS PARLIAMENT OF 1388
Richard II, King of England **16**:210
MERCIN (Turkey)
map (36° 48′N 34° 38′E) **19**:343
MERCKX, EDDIE **13**:305
MERCOAL (Alberta)
map (53° 10′N 117° 5′W) **1**:256
MERCURY (element) **13**:306–307 *bibliog.*
abundances of common elements **7**:131 *table*
amalgam, metallic **1**:320–321
antiseptic
bacteria **3**:16
cinnabar **4**:434
compounds **13**:306
element **7**:130 *table*
Group IIB periodic table **15**:167
industrial uses **13**:306
thermometer **19**:166
medicinal uses **13**:306
thermometer **19**:166
metal, metallic element **13**:328
native elements **14**:47
occurrence **13**:306
poisoning **13**:307
environmental health **7**:211
Smith, W. Eugene **17**:371
pollutants, chemical **15**:410
pump
vacuum **19**:502
quicksilver **13**:306
sulfide minerals **18**:333
superconductivity **18**:350 *table*
switches **13**:306
transition elements **19**:273
MERCURY (mythology) **3**:370 *illus.*; **13**:305; **16**:153 *illus.*
MERCURY (Nevada)
map (36° 40′N 115° 59′W) **14**:111
MERCURY (planet) **13**:305–306 *bibliog., illus., table*; **18**:48 *illus.*
astronomical data **13**:305–306
characteristics **13**:305–306 *table*
gravitation **9**:305
Mariner **13**:156
discoveries **13**:306
pictures **13**:305 *illus.*
orbit **13**:305–306
Dicke, Robert **6**:156
Einstein, Albert **7**:93
relativity **16**:135 *illus.*
planets **15**:329–331
radio astronomy **16**:48
solar system **18**:46–48 *illus., table*
MERCURY PROGRAM **13**:307–308 *bibliog., illus.*
astronauts **2**:274 *illus.*
Carpenter, Scott **4**:164
Cooper, Leroy Gordon, Jr. **5**:244
Glenn, John H., Jr. **9**:207
Grissom, Virgil I. **9**:367
Schirra, Walter M., Jr. **17**:122
Shepard, Alan B., Jr. **17**:256
Slayton, D. K. **17**:359
Atlas (missile) **2**:297 *illus.*
development **13**:307
life-support systems **12**:331–333
Mercury spacecraft **13**:307–308 *illus.*
missions **13**:308
National Aeronautics and Space Administration **14**:28
Redstone **16**:117
space exploration **18**:126–127 *illus.*
space medicine **18**:132
MERCURY THEATRE **13**:308
MERCY KILLING *see* EUTHANASIA
MÈRE ANGÉLIQUE *see* ARNAULD, JACQUELINE MARIE ANGÉLIQUE
MEREDITH (New Hampshire)
map (43° 39′N 71° 30′W) **14**:123
MEREDITH, GEORGE **13**:308–309 *bibliog., illus.*
MEREDITH, JAMES
Mississippi **13**:473
MEREDITH, OWEN *see* BULWER-LYTTON, EDWARD ROBERT, 1ST EARL OF LYTTON
MEREDITH, WILLIAM **13**:309
MEREDOSIA (Illinois)
map (39° 50′N 90° 34′W) **11**:42
MERENSKY REEF
major ore deposits **14**:424–425 *table*
MEREZHKOVSKY, DMITRY SERGEYEVICH **13**:309 *bibliog.*
MERGANSER **13**:309–310 *illus.*
duck **6**:292
MERGENTHALER, OTTMAR **13**:310 *bibliog.*
Linotype, inventor **12**:359
MERGER (business) **13**:310 *bibliog.*
See also CONGLOMERATE (business)
arbitrage **2**:110
conglomerate **5**:180–181
corporation **5**:273–274
monopoly and competition **13**:538–539
MERGUI (Burma)
map (12° 26′N 98° 36′E) **3**:573
MERGUI ARCHIPELAGO
map (12° 0′N 98° 0′E) **3**:573
MERI, LA *see* LA MERI
MERI, VEIJO
Finnish literature **8**:99
MERIAN (family) **13**:310 *bibliog.*
MÉRIDA (Mexico) **13**:310
map (20° 58′N 89° 37′W) **13**:357
MÉRIDA (Spain)
map (38° 55′N 6° 20′W) **18**:140
MERIDA (Venezuela)
climate **19**:542 *table*
map (8° 36′N 71° 8′W) **19**:542
MÉRIDA CORDILLERA MOUNTAINS
map (8° 40′N 71° 0′W) **19**:542
MERIDEN (Connecticut)
map (41° 32′N 72° 48′W) **5**:193
MERIDIAN (geography)
longitude **12**:409
prime meridian **15**:542
transit circle **19**:273 *illus.*
MERIDIAN (Idaho)
map (43° 37′N 116° 24′W) **11**:26
MERIDIAN (Mississippi) **13**:310
map (32° 22′N 88° 42′W) **13**:469
MERIDIAN (Texas)
map (31° 55′N 97° 39′W) **19**:129
MERIDIANVILLE (Alabama)
map (34° 51′N 86° 35′W) **1**:234
MERIKANTO, AARRE
Finland **8**:96
MERIKANTO, OSKAR
Finland **8**:96
MÉRIMÉE, PROSPER **13**:310 *bibliog.*
Carmen **4**:153
MERINA (tribe)
Madagascar **13**:38; **13**:39
MERINO (Colorado)
map (40° 29′N 103° 21′W) **5**:116
MERINO SHEEP **17**:249 *illus.*
MERINOS (Uruguay)
map (32° 24′S 56° 54′W) **19**:488
MERIONETHSHIRE (Wales) *see* GWYNEDD (Wales)
MERISI, MICHELANGELO *see* CARAVAGGIO, MICHELANGELO MERISI DA
MERIT SYSTEM PROTECTION BOARD *see* CIVIL SERVICE COMMISSION
MERIWETHER (county in Georgia)
map (33° 5′N 84° 40′W) **9**:114
MERKEL, UNA **8**:84 *illus.*
MERLEAU-PONTY, MAURICE **13**:310–311 *bibliog.*
MERLIN (of Arthurian legend) **13**:311
MERLIN (radio astronomy)
Nuffield Radio Astronomy Laboratories **14**:291
MERMAID **13**:311
MERMAN, ETHEL **13**:311 *bibliog.*
MERNA (Nebraska)
map (41° 29′N 99° 46′W) **14**:70
MEROË (Sudan) **13**:311 *bibliog.*
MEROITIC SCRIPT
hieroglyphics **10**:160–161
MEROLA, GAETANO
San Francisco Opera Association **17**:54
MERON, MOUNT
map (32° 58′N 35° 25′E) **11**:302
MEROSTOMATA *see* HORSESHOE CRAB
MEROVECH (Merovingian chief)
Franks **8**:286
MEROVINGIAN ART AND ARCHITECTURE **13**:311 *bibliog.*
French art and architecture **8**:303
MEROVINGIANS (dynasty) **13**:312 *bibliog.*
Carolingians (dynasty) **4**:162
Clichy (France) **5**:54
France, history of **8**:266
Franks **8**:286
Germany, history of **9**:148
Neustria **14**:107
MEROWEN *see* MEROVECH
MERREDIN (Australia)
map (31° 29′S 118° 16′E) **2**:328
MERRIAM, CHARLES E. **13**:312 *bibliog.*
MERRICK (county in Nebraska)
map (41° 10′N 98° 5′W) **14**:70
MERRICK, DAVID **13**:312
MERRIFIELD, R. BRUCE **13**:312
MERRILL (Iowa)
map (42° 43′N 96° 15′W) **11**:244
MERRILL (Oregon)
map (42° 1′N 121° 36′W) **14**:427
MERRILL (Wisconsin)
map (45° 11′N 89° 41′W) **20**:185
MERRILL, FRANK D.
World War II **20**:266–267
MERRILL, JAMES **13**:312 *bibliog.*
MERRILL, LEWIS
Stanford-Binet test **18**:217
MERRILL, ROBERT **13**:312
MERRILL, SCOTT
musical comedy **13**:674 *illus.*
MERRILLAN (Wisconsin)
map (44° 27′N 90° 50′W) **20**:185
MERRILLVILLE (Indiana)
map (41° 29′N 87° 20′W) **11**:111
MERRIMAC (American Indians) *see* PENNACOOK (American Indians)
MERRIMACK (county in New Hampshire)
map (43° 20′N 71° 40′W) **14**:123
MERRIMACK (ship) *see MONITOR* AND *MERRIMACK* (ships)
MERRIMACK RIVER
map (42° 49′N 70° 49′W) **14**:123
MERRIMAN (Nebraska)
map (42° 55′N 101° 42′W) **14**:70
MERRIMAN, BRIAN
Irish literature **11**:268
MERRITT (British Columbia)
map (50° 7′N 120° 47′W) **3**:491
MERRITT ISLAND (Florida)
map (28° 21′N 80° 42′W) **8**:172
MERRITT RESERVOIR
map (42° 35′N 100° 55′W) **14**:70
MERRY-GO-ROUND (play)
Schnitzler, Arthur **17**:129
MERRY MONARCH *see* CHARLES II, KING OF ENGLAND, SCOTLAND, AND IRELAND
MERRY PRANKSTERS
Kesey, Ken **11**:61
MERRY WIDOW, THE (operetta)
Lehár, Franz **12**:275
MERRY WIVES OF WINDSOR, THE (play) **13**:312 *bibliog.*
Falstaff **8**:15
MERRYVILLE (Louisiana)
map (30° 45′N 93° 33′W) **12**:430
MERSE, PÁL SZINYEI *see* SZINYEI MERSE, PÁL
MERSEBURG (Germany, East and West)
map (51° 21′N 11° 59′E) **9**:140
MERSEN, TREATY OF **4**:289 *map*
Carolingians (dynasty) **4**:162
Charles II, Frankish emperor (Charles the Bald) **4**:292
Lothair, King of Lotharingia **12**:419
MERSENNE, MARIN **13**:312
MERSEY, RIVER (England) **13**:312
MERSEY RIVER (Nova Scotia)
map (44° 2′N 64° 43′W) **14**:269
MERTHIOLATE
antiseptic **2**:68
MERTHYR TYDFIL (Wales)
map (51° 46′N 3° 23′W) **19**:403
MERTON, ROBERT **13**:313
role **16**:271
MERTON, THOMAS **13**:313 *bibliog.*
MERTON COLLEGE (Oxford University) **14**:474
MERTZON (Texas)
map (31° 16′N 100° 49′W) **19**:129
MERU, MOUNT
map (3° 14′S 36° 40′E) **19**:27
MERULO, CLAUDIO
Renaissance music **16**:156
MERV **13**:313
MERVIN (Saskatchewan)
map (53° 20′N 108° 53′W) **17**:81
MERWIN, LAKE
map (45° 59′N 122° 26′W) **20**:35
MERWIN, W. S. **13**:313 *bibliog.*
MERYON, CHARLES **13**:313 *bibliog.*
MERZ ART
Schwitters, Kurt **17**:141
MERZIFON (Turkey)
map (40° 53′N 35° 29′E) **19**:343
MESA (Arizona) **13**:313
map (33° 25′N 111° 50′W) **2**:160
MESA (county in Colorado)
map (39° 0′N 108° 30′W) **5**:116
MESA (landform)
plateau **15**:358
MESA VERDE NATIONAL PARK (Colorado) **5**:118 *illus.*; **13**:313–314 *illus.*; **14**:38–39 *map, table*
Anasazi **1**:393 *illus.*
Cliff Palace **14**:239 *illus.*; **15**:613 *illus.*
North American archaeology **14**:237 *map*
MESABI RANGE **13**:314; **13**:456 *illus.*
iron and steel industry **11**:273
map (47° 30′N 92° 50′W) **13**:453
MESAYITONIA (Cyprus)
map (34° 42′N 33° 3′E) **5**:409
MESCAL *see* TEQUILA
MESCALERO (New Mexico)
map (33° 9′N 105° 46′W) **14**:136
MESCALERO INDIANS
Apache **2**:73
MESCALINE *see* PEYOTE
MESELSON, MATTHEW STANLEY
biology **3**:271
MESETA
Portugal **15**:448
MESEWA (Ethiopia)
climate **7**:254 *table*
map (15° 38′N 39° 28′E) **7**:253
MESHED (Iran) *see* MASHHAD (Iran)
MESILIM, KING OF KISH
Kish **12**:90
MESILLA (New Mexico)
map (32° 16′N 106° 48′W) **14**:136
MESKWAKIHUK *see* FOX (American Indians)
MESMER, FRANZ ANTON **13**:314
MESOAMERICA **13**:314 *bibliog.*
agriculture, history of **1**:190
archaeology
sites **14**:237 *map*
Indians, American **11**:115–138 *illus., maps*
Aztec **2**:382–384
Maya **13**:243–245
Mixtec **13**:486
Olmec **14**:380
Teotihuacán **19**:113–114
Toltec **19**:228–229
Zapotec **20**:356
Kidder, Alfred Vincent **12**:70–71
Latin America, history of **12**:216
Mexico, history of **13**:361–362
pre-Columbian art and architecture **15**:495–499
pyramids **15**:636
MESOBIOTA
soil organisms **18**:39 *illus.*
MESODERM
development **6**:138; **6**:141 *illus.*
growth **9**:379
MESODINIUM RUBRUM
red tide **16**:114
MESOLITHIC PERIOD **13**:314–315 *bibliog., illus.*
agriculture, history of **1**:189–190
Cape Denbigh **4**:120
Creswellian **5**:339
Ertebølle culture **7**:235
fishing industry **8**:125
Maglemosian art **7**:302 *illus.*
midden **13**:390
prehistoric art **15**:509
prehistoric humans **15**:515–516
Star Carr **18**:226
MESON **3**:531 *illus.*; **13**:315
annihilation **2**:33
Bethe, Hans **3**:230
fundamental particles **8**:362
hadron **10**:8
K-meson
Yang, Chen Ning **20**:317
pi meson **13**:315
nuclear physics **14**:287
Powell, Cecil Frank, discoverer **15**:480
quark **16**:12
Yukawa, Hideki **20**:344
MESOPOTAMIA **1**:231 *map*; **13**:315–317 *bibliog., illus., map*
agriculture, history of **1**:190
archaeology
Woolley, Sir Leonard **20**:215
art *see* MESOPOTAMIAN ART AND ARCHITECTURE

MESOPOTAMIA (cont.)
Ashurbanipal, King of Assyria **2**:231
Ashurnasirpal II, King of Assyria **2**:232
Asia, history of **2**:249–250
Assyria **2**:266
Babylonia **3**:8–9
costume **5**:293
cuneiform
Smith, George **17**:368
Elam **7**:101
Fertile Crescent **8**:60
Hammurabi, King of Babylonia **10**:32
hieroglyphics **10**:159–161
Kassites **12**:30
languages, extinct **12**:198
Middle East, history of the **13**:400–401
Mitanni **13**:482
mythology *see* NEAR EASTERN MYTHOLOGY
Rawlinson, Sir Henry Creswicke **16**:95
roads and highways **16**:235
Sargon, King of Akkad **17**:78
slavery **17**:352
Suleiman I, Sultan of the Ottoman Empire (Suleiman the Magnificent) **18**:332–333
Sumer **18**:339
wagon **20**:6
World War I **20**:232; **20**:234; **20**:239–240 *map*; **20**:244
writing systems, evolution of **20**:292
MESOPOTAMIAN ART AND ARCHITECTURE **3**:8 *illus.*; **13**:317–322 *bibliog., illus.*
archaeology **2**:117 *illus.*; **2**:123 *illus.*
architecture **2**:130 *illus.*
Asia, history of **2**:240
Assyrian winged bull **13**:320 *illus.*
Babylon **3**:8
bas-relief **3**:100 *illus.*; **7**:217 *illus.*
costume **5**:293
Ctesiphon **5**:377
cylinder seal **13**:317 *illus.*
Doura-Europos **6**:249
glassware, decorative **9**:202
gold and silver work **9**:228
gypsum figurines **13**:318 *illus.*
Hanging Gardens of Babylon **17**:216–217
Hittite art and architecture **10**:188–189; **10**:189
house (in Western architecture) **10**:264
inscription **11**:185
jewelry **11**:408
Khorsabad **12**:68
Kish **12**:90
Lagash **12**:165
Mari **13**:149–150
Nimrud **14**:199
Nineveh **14**:200
Nippur **14**:201
painting **15**:18
Palmyra **15**:51–52
Phoenician art **15**:250–251
pottery and porcelain **15**:470
Standard of Ur **13**:316 *illus.*
Sumerian harp **13**:318 *illus.*
temple **19**:94
Tepe Gawra **19**:114
Ur **19**:474 *illus.*
Uruk **19**:490
ziggurat **19**:95 *illus.*; **20**:363
MESOSCAPHE
Piccard, Auguste **15**:292
MESOSPHERE **13**:322 *bibliog.*
jet stream **11**:407–408
noctilucent cloud **14**:212
MESOZOAN **13**:322
invertebrate **11**:234–235
MESOZOIC ERA **13**:322 *bibliog.*
Africa **1**:140 *map*
Asia **2**:236 *map*
Australia **2**:331 *map*
continental drift **5**:228
Cretaceous Period **5**:339–341; **13**:322
cycad **5**:402
dinosaur **6**:179–182
Earth, geological history of **7**:11–14 *illus., map*
Europe **7**:270 *map*
fossil record **8**:245–248
geologic time **9**:104–105 *table*; **13**:322
Gondwanaland **9**:243
Jurassic Period **11**:474–477; **13**:322
life **13**:322
North America **14**:227 *map*
paleoclimatology **15**:32
paleogeography **13**:322
plate tectonics **13**:322
reptiles **16**:170 *illus., table*
South America **18**:87 *map*
Triassic Period **13**:322; **19**:292–295
United States **19**:422 *map*
MESQUAKIE *see* FOX (American Indians)
MESQUITE (botany) **13**:322
desert life **6**:130
MESQUITE (Nevada)
map (36° 48′N 114° 4′W) **14**:111
MESQUITE (Texas)
map (32° 46′N 96° 36′W) **19**:129
"MESSAGE TO GARCIA, A" (essay)
Hubbard, Elbert **10**:288
MESSALINA **13**:322
Rome, ancient **16**:302
MESSENE (Greece) **13**:322 *bibliog.*
MESSENGER RNA
genetic code **9**:80–82 *illus.*
nucleic acid **14**:290–291 *illus.*
virus **19**:614–615 *illus.*
MESSENIA **13**:323
MESSERSCHMIDT, FRANZ XAVIER **13**:323 *bibliog.*
MESSERSCHMITT, WILLY **13**:323 *bibliog.*
MESSERSCHMITT BF 109 **13**:323 *bibliog., illus.*
MESSERSCHMITT ME 262A AIRCRAFT **2**:372–373 *illus.*
MESSIAEN, OLIVIER **13**:323 *bibliog.*
Jolivet, André **11**:441
MESSIAH **13**:323–324 *bibliog.*
cargo cults **4**:147
Christ **4**:411
Europe, history of **7**:281–282
Jesus Christ **11**:403–406
Judaism **11**:461–462
Sabbatai Zevi **17**:5
MESSIAH, THE (epic)
Klopstock, Friedrich Gottlieb **12**:98
MESSIER, CHARLES **13**:324 *bibliog.*
Messier catalog **13**:324
MESSIER OBJECTS
Virgo **19**:613
MESSINA (Italy) **13**:324
map (38° 11′N 15° 33′E) **11**:321
Richard I, King of England **16**:209–210
MESSINA, ANTONELLO DA *see* ANTONELLO DA MESSINA
MESSINA, STRAIT OF **13**:324
map (38° 15′N 15° 35′E) **11**:321
MESSNER, REINHOLD
mountain climbing **13**:622
MESTIZO **13**:324 *bibliog.*
Guaraní **9**:386
Indians, American **11**:137
mulatto **13**:635
South America **18**:91–92
MEŠTROVIĆ, IVAN **13**:324 *bibliog.*
META RIVER
map (6° 12′N 67° 28′W) **19**:542
METABASITE ROCK
metamorphic rock **13**:332
METABOLISM **13**:324–327 *bibliog.*
acidosis **1**:82
aging **1**:185–186
alkalosis **1**:296
animal migration **2**:27
ATP **2**:312
biochemistry **3**:261
body temperature **3**:357–358
bone diseases **3**:377
camel **4**:54
carbohydrate **4**:133
diabetes **6**:148–149
celiac disease **4**:231
cholesterol **4**:404
citric acid **4**:447
coenzyme **5**:92
copper, inborn errors **14**:96
corticoid **5**:278
cyclic AMP **5**:403
cytochrome **5**:411
dehydration **6**:85
digestion, human **6**:170–173
digestive system **6**:173–174
diseases, animal **6**:192
drug **6**:276
endocrine system **7**:168–169
endocrine system, diseases of the **7**:169–171
enzyme **7**:214
excretory system **7**:327–328
exercise **7**:329–330
fat **8**:33
fermentation **8**:55
galactosemia **9**:9
genetic diseases **9**:82
behavioral genetics **3**:170
glucocorticoid **9**:211
glucose
glucose tolerance test **9**:211
hypoglycemia **10**:351
goiter **9**:225
growth **9**:380
growth hormone **9**:381
hibernation **10**:156
hormone, animal **10**:234–237
insulin **11**:197
Krebs cycle **12**:128
lactic acid **12**:161
lipid **12**:362
Lipmann, Fritz Albert **12**:362
liver **12**:374–375
Lynen, Feodor **12**:477
Mitchell, Peter **13**:483
mitochondrion **13**:485
nervous system, diseases of the **14**:96
nucleic acid **14**:288–291
nutrition, human **14**:304–307
nutritional-deficiency diseases **14**:307
obesity **14**:315
operon **14**:403–404
oxygen **14**:477
pancreatitis **15**:58
phosphorus **15**:257
photosynthesis **15**:277
physiology **15**:287
protein **15**:574
purine
gout **9**:266
uric acid **19**:486
pyruvic acid **15**:639
starvation **18**:228
steroid **18**:261
stress, biological **18**:298
sugar
Krebs, Sir Hans Adolf **12**:128
thyroid
thyroid function test **19**:187–188
thyroid gland **19**:188
METABOLISTS (architectural group)
postmodern architecture **15**:464
METACOMET (Indian chief)
King Philip's War **12**:82
Massasoit **13**:213
Wampanoag **20**:21
METAIRIE (Louisiana)
map (29° 59′N 90° 9′W) **12**:430
METAL **13**:327–329 *bibliog., illus., table*
alloys **1**:303–304; **13**:328
atomic properties **13**:328
band theory **13**:329
Mott, Nevill **13**:616
bonding **13**:328
chelation **4**:311
chemical properties **13**:328
conduction, electric **5**:174
contact potential **5**:227
corrosion **5**:276–277
dowsing **6**:252
element **7**:131–132
actinide elements **13**:328 *table*
lanthanide elements **13**:328 *table*
metallic elements **13**:328–329
native elements **14**:47
representative elements **13**:328 *table*
transition elements **13**:328 *table*; **19**:273
exoelectron **7**:333
extraction, metallurgy **13**:330–331
Faraday's laws of electrolysis **8**:22
food poisoning and infection **8**:211
gadolinium **9**:7
gold **9**:266–267
hardness tests **13**:219 *illus.*
heavy metals
pollutants, chemical **15**:410
holmium **10**:206
hydride **10**:331
iridium **11**:266
iron **11**:270–271
isolation
electrolysis **7**:114–115
radium **16**:68
laser **12**:212–213
lead **12**:256
lutetium **12**:468
machine tools **13**:23–25
magnesium **13**:53–54
magnet **13**:54–55
manganese **13**:114
mercury **13**:306–307
metalloids **13**:328
metallurgy **13**:329–331
mining and quarrying **13**:446; **13**:449
mirror **13**:464
molybdenum **13**:514
native elements **14**:47
neodymium **14**:82
neptunium **14**:89
nickel **14**:183
nobelium **14**:211
ore
oxide minerals **14**:476
packaging **15**:11–12
periodic table **15**:166–169
photoelectric effect **15**:260
physical characteristics **13**:327–328
platinum **15**:359–360
plutonium **15**:373
polonium **15**:417
praseodymium **15**:489–490
products
nail **14**:7–8
wire **20**:182
qualitative chemical analysis **16**:6–7 *illus.*
radiation injury **16**:42
recycling of materials **16**:111
refining **16**:119
roof and roofing **16**:306
shrapnel **17**:286
solid-state physics **18**:54–55
structure **13**:328
X-ray diffraction **20**:309
thermionic emission **19**:161
tool and die making **19**:236
transition elements **19**:273
weapons **20**:74–75
welding and soldering **20**:96–97
METAL DETECTOR **13**:329
METAL FATIGUE **13**:329
METALINE FALLS (Washington)
map (48° 52′N 117° 22′W) **20**:35
METALLIC BOND *see* CHEMICAL BOND
METALLIC CHEMISTRY
inorganic chemistry **11**:182
METALLOGRAPHY
metallurgy **13**:330
photography **15**:266
METALLOID
metal **13**:328
METALLURGY **13**:329–331 *bibliog., illus.*
Agricola, Georgius **1**:188
De re metallica **6**:62
alloy **1**:303–304
amalgam, metallic **1**:320–321
annealing **2**:33
Beaker culture **3**:139
blacksmith **3**:322
blast furnace **3**:328
brazing **3**:465
Bronze Age **7**:302–303
casting **4**:188–189
foundry **8**:251
lost-wax process **12**:418–419 *illus.*
electroplating **7**:126–127
extrusion **7**:346–347
flotation process **8**:177
flux **8**:189
forge **8**:232–233
hardening **10**:45
Iron Age **11**:271–272
iron and steel industry **11**:277–278
materials technology **13**:219–221
metal fatigue **13**:329
open-hearth process **14**:398
powder metallurgy **15**:480
refining, metal **16**:119
sintering **17**:325
smelting **17**:366
technology, history of **19**:62
tempering **19**:93
welding and soldering **20**:96–97
METALPOINT (drawing technique) **6**:263
METALWORK, DECORATIVE
antique collecting **2**:66 *illus.*
Byzantine art and architecture **3**:606
Celtic art **4**:239–241
chalice **4**:271
chandelier **4**:279
craft **5**:327 *illus.*
enamel **7**:161–162
Etruscans **7**:260–261 *illus.*
German art and architecture **9**:123–124
gilding **9**:180
gold and silver work **9**:228–230
Hittite art and architecture **10**:189
ironwork, ornamental **11**:279
jewelry **11**:408–411
Persian art and architecture **15**:186
pewter **15**:217
pre-Columbian art and architecture **15**:499–501
METAMORPHIC ROCK **13**:331–333 *bibliog., illus.*
basement rock **3**:108
bornite **3**:402
chalcopyrite **4**:270

chlorite **4**:401
chrysoberyl **4**:420–421
classification basis **13**:331
composition **13**:331–333
contact metamorphism **13**:332
continental shield **5**:230
facies **13**:332 *table*
feldspar **8**:46–47
feldspathoid **8**:47
foliation **8**:195
formation **13**:331–332
pressure **13**:331; **13**:332–333
temperature **13**:331; **13**:332–333
galena **9**:13–14
garnet **9**:49
geochemistry **9**:96
gneiss **9**:213
hornfels **10**:240
ice ages **11**:8
igneous rock **13**:332
index minerals **13**:332
lapis lazuli **12**:204–205
mafic rocks **13**:332; **13**:333
marble **13**:144
metabasites **13**:332
mica **13**:370–371
mineral occurrence **13**:442
major ore deposits **14**:424–425 *table*
mylonite **13**:690
occurrence **13**:331–333
oxide minerals **14**:476
peridotite **15**:166
petrography **15**:206–207
petrology **15**:215
phyllite **15**:278
pluton **15**:373
polymetamorphism **13**:333
quartz **16**:13–14
quartzite **16**:14
recrystallization of minerals **13**:331; **13**:333
rhodochrosite **16**:203
rock **16**:247
scapolite **17**:115
schist **17**:123
slate **17**:351
sphalerite **18**:180
METAMORPHOSES (book by Apuleius) *see GOLDEN ASS, THE* (book)
METAMORPHOSES (poem) **13**:333 *bibliog.*
METAMORPHOSIS **13**:333–334 *bibliog., illus.*
butterflies and moths **3**:595
chordate **4**:407
development **6**:137
frog **8**:336
insect **11**:189–191 *illus.*
juvenile hormone (insect) **11**:480
larva **12**:208
Lepidoptera **12**:295
naiad (insect) **14**:7
nymph (insect) **14**:309
salamander and newt **17**:30
stages **13**:333–334
METAMORPHOSIS (book)
Kafka, Franz **12**:5–6
METÁN (Argentina)
map (25° 29′S 64° 57′W) **2**:149
METAPAN (El Salvador)
map (14° 20′N 89° 27′W) **7**:100
METAPHOR **13**:334 *bibliog.*
allegory **1**:298–299
bestiary **3**:229
fable **8**:4–5
figures of speech **8**:76
Homeric epithet **10**:214
image and imagery **11**:51
parable **15**:73
METAPHYSICAL POETRY **13**:334 *bibliog.*
conceit **5**:168
Cowley, Abraham **5**:321
Crashaw, Richard **5**:332
Donne, John **6**:239
English literature **7**:196
Herbert, George **10**:135
METAPHYSICS **13**:334–335 *bibliog.*
Anselm, Saint **2**:35
Aquinas, Saint Thomas **2**:94–95
Aristotle **2**:157
Bradley, Francis Herbert **3**:437
Critique of Pure Reason **5**:352
dualism **6**:287
Gioberti, Vincenzo **9**:185
Hartmann, Nicolai **10**:63
Heidegger, Martin **10**:106–107
monism **13**:531
nominalism **14**:215
Nostradamus **14**:266–267
ontology **13**:334–335
philosophy **15**:243
Spinoza, Baruch **18**:187–188
Strawson, Peter Frederick **18**:296
substance **18**:317
universals **19**:467
Whitehead, Alfred North **20**:139
METASTASIO, PIETRO **13**:335 *bibliog.*
libretto **12**:319
METASTASIS **13**:335
cancer **4**:102–103 *illus.*
nervous system, diseases of the **14**:96
METATHERIAN *see* MARSUPIAL
METAXÁS, IOÁNNIS **13**:335 *bibliog.*
METAZOAN **13**:335
METCALF, JOHN
roads and highways **16**:237
METCALF, RALPH
New Hampshire **14**:125
METCALFE (county in Kentucky)
map (37° 0′N 85° 40′W) **12**:47
METCALFE, CHARLES THEOPHILUS METCALFE, BARON **13**:335 *bibliog.*
METCHNIKOFF, ELIE **13**:335 *bibliog.*
immunity **11**:57
yogurt **20**:329
METELLUS NUMIDICUS, QUINTUS CAECILIUS **13**:336
METELLUS PIUS, QUINTUS CAECILIUS **13**:336
METEMPSYCHOSIS *see* TRANSMIGRATION OF SOULS
METEOR CRATER (Arizona) **13**:337 *bibliog., illus.*; **13**:338 *illus.*; **18**:51 *illus.*
METEOR AND METEORITE **13**:336–337 *bibliog., illus., table*
achondrite **1**:82
chondrite **4**:404–405
classification **13**:336–337
Earth, structure and composition of **7**:20
meteor showers **13**:336
Northern Hemisphere **13**:336 *table*
meteorite craters **13**:337–339
nickel **14**:183
notable meteorites
Hoba West **13**:337
Tunguska fireball **19**:334
Willamette Meteorite **13**:336 *illus.*
olivine **14**:380
oxide minerals **14**:476
shooting or falling star **13**:336
solar system **18**:50
METEORITE CRATERS **13**:337–339 *bibliog., illus.*
astroblemes **13**:338–339
coesite **5**:93
Earth, structure and composition of **7**:23
giant meteorites, explosive power **13**:337
location, worldwide **13**:339
Meteor Crater (Arizona) **13**:337
Odessa (Texas) **14**:349
shock-wave damage **13**:338–339
stishovite **18**:273
structure **13**:338
METEOROID
meteor and meteorite **13**:336–337 *illus.*
METEOROLOGICAL COUNCIL
Shaw, Sir Napier **17**:246
METEOROLOGICAL INSTRUMENTATION **13**:339–341 *bibliog., illus.*
anemometer **1**:410
balloon **3**:53
barometer **3**:87–88
chart
Halley, Edmond **10**:22
climate **5**:55
cosmic rays **5**:283–284
history
meteorology **13**:341–342
hygrometer **10**:345
paleoclimatology **15**:34
radar **16**:40
radar meteorology **16**:41
radiosonde **16**:67
remote sensing **16**:147 *illus.*
satellites and rockets
Applications Technology Satellite **2**:89–90
GOES (artificial satellite) **9**:222
Nimbus (artificial satellite) **14**:198
OGO (artificial satellite) **14**:355
satellite, artificial **17**:86–87 *illus.*
sounding rocket **18**:77
space exploration **18**:123
Synchronous Meteorological Satellite **18**:406
TIROS (artificial satellite) **19**:208–209
Shaw, Sir Napier **17**:246
thermometer **19**:166
types **13**:340 *illus.*
weather variation and extremes **20**:80–82
METEOROLOGY **13**:341–343 *bibliog., illus.*
air **1**:203–204
air mass **1**:209
atmosphere **2**:298
atmospheric meteorology **13**:341
atmospheric sciences **2**:304
balloon **3**:53
categorization, basis **13**:341
physical laws **13**:341
climate **5**:55–58
cloud **5**:66–68
cyclone and anticyclone **5**:405–406
doldrums **6**:224
drought **6**:273–274
dust devil **6**:308–309
dynamic meteorology **13**:341
Earth sciences **7**:24
Earth tide **7**:25
European Space Agency **7**:306
evapotranspiration **7**:314–315
Ferrel cell **8**:59
foehn **8**:193
fog **8**:193
front **8**:339–340
frost **8**:345
geophysics **9**:108
glaciers and glaciation **9**:192–195
government agencies **13**:342
greenhouse effect **9**:351–352
hail and hailstones **10**:12–13
halo **10**:24
high-pressure region **10**:162
historic development **13**:341–342
Bjerknes, Vilhelm and Jacob **3**:302
Buys Ballot, Christoph Hendrik Diederik **3**:601
Friedmann, Aleksandr **8**:332
Geiger, Rudolf Oskar Robert Williams **9**:68
Helmholtz, Hermann Ludwig Ferdinand von **10**:115–116
Köppen, Wladimir Peter **12**:110
Maury, Matthew Fontaine **13**:238
Schaefer, Vincent Joseph **17**:116
Shaw, Sir Napier **17**:246
Sverdrup, Harald Ulrik **18**:375
von Neumann, John **19**:634
Wegener, Alfred Lothar **20**:91
Willett, Hurd Curtis **20**:154
hoarfrost **10**:191
horse latitudes **10**:246
humidity **10**:302
hurricane and typhoon **10**:317–319
hydrologic cycle **10**:341–342
hydrologic sciences **10**:342
ice ages **11**:7–11
International Geophysical Year **11**:220
International Hydrological Decade **11**:220
International Years of the Quiet Sun **11**:225
inversion **11**:233–234
jet stream **11**:407–408
Rossby waves **16**:318
lightning **12**:339–340
limnology **12**:345
low-pressure region **12**:443
magnetic storm **13**:55
maps and mapmaking **13**:141
mare's tail (cloud) **13**:148
maritime climate **13**:157
Mediterranean climate **13**:276
mesosphere **13**:322
meteorological instrumention **13**:339–341
micrometeorology **13**:341
mirage **13**:463
mist **13**:481
mistral **13**:482
modern meteorology **13**:342–343
mountain and valley winds **13**:624
nacreous cloud **14**:4
Namias, Jerome **14**:10
National Meteorological Center **14**:35
Nimbus **14**:198
noctilucent cloud **14**:212
ocean-atmosphere interaction **14**:321–322
orographic precipitation **14**:447
paleoclimatology **15**:32–34
physical meteorology **13**:341
polar easterlies **15**:393
precipitation **15**:493–495
professional and educational organizations
World Meteorological Organization **20**:219
radar meteorology **13**:341–342; **16**:41
rain shadow effect **16**:77
scope **13**:341
semiarid climate **17**:195–196
sirocco **17**:328
sky **17**:346
snow and snowflake **18**:4
squall and squall line **18**:201–202
stratosphere **18**:293
stratus clouds **18**:293
synoptic meteorology **13**:341–342
telemetry **19**:78
thermocline **19**:162
thermosphere **19**:167
thunderstorm **19**:185
tornado **19**:239–240
trade winds **19**:263
troposphere **19**:310
twilight **19**:360
urban climate **19**:480
waterspout **20**:66
weather forecasting **20**:78–79
weather modification **20**:79–80
weather variation and extremes **20**:80–82
weathering **20**:82–83
westerlies **20**:115
whirlwind **20**:132
whistler **20**:134
wind **20**:168
wind action **20**:170
wind chill **20**:170
wind rose diagram **20**:171
World Weather Watch **20**:281
zonda **20**:373
METER (electrical)
Stanley, William **18**:219
METER (literature)
versification **19**:562
METER (measurement)
Earth, size and shape of **7**:19
measurement **13**:253–254
units, physical **19**:466 *table*
weights and measures **20**:93–94 *table*
METER (music) **13**:343
hymn **10**:346
Indians of North America, music and dance of the **11**:142
rhythm **16**:204
METER-KILOGRAM-SECOND (MKS) UNITS
units, physical **19**:466–467 *table*
METHADONE **13**:343 *bibliog.*
Darvon **6**:40
detoxification drug **13**:343
development **13**:343
drug abuse **6**:281
heroin **10**:145
maintenance **13**:343
morphine **13**:587
respiratory system disorders **16**:182
METHANAL
aldehyde **1**:268
METHANE **13**:343
coal and coal mining **5**:79
fuel **8**:353
graphic formula **14**:435 *illus.*
methanogen **13**:343
natural gas **14**:47
origin of life **12**:327 *illus.*
Saturn (astronomy) **17**:90
septic tank **17**:206
waste disposal systems **20**:47
METHANOGEN **13**:343
METHANOL *see* METHYL ALCOHOL
METHEDRINE
amphetamine **1**:377
METHEMOGLOBINEMIA **13**:343
METHICILLIN
antibiotics **2**:59
penicillin **15**:143–144
METHIONINE
genetic code **9**:80–81 *illus.*
METHOD ACTING **1**:88; **13**:343 *bibliog.*
Actors Studio **1**:90
Adler, Jacob, Stella, and Luther **1**:104
Group Theatre, The **9**:376–377
Stanislavsky, Konstantin **18**:218
Strasberg, Lee **18**:289
METHODISM **13**:344 *bibliog., illus.*
Allen, Richard **1**:299–300
Asbury, Francis **2**:227
camp meetings **4**:63
circuit rider **4**:438
Coke, Thomas **5**:96–97
Duke Endowment **6**:295
education
Denver, University of **6**:117
Northwestern University **14**:260
Syracuse University **18**:411
Embury, Philip **7**:154

METHODISM (cont.)
Evangelical United Brethren Church **7**:312
Great Awakening **9**:308
Great Britain, history of **9**:317
Harkness, Georgia Elma **10**:49
Lee, Jesse **12**:269
Wesley (family) **20**:105
Whitefield, George **20**:138
METHODIUS, SAINT *see* CYRIL AND METHODIUS, SAINTS
METHOW (Washington)
map (48° 8′N 120° 0′W) **20**:35
METHUEN (Massachusetts)
map (42° 44′N 71° 11′W) **13**:206
METHUEN, TREATY OF
Portugal, history of **15**:454
METHUSELAH **13**:344
METHYL ALCOHOL **13**:344
antifreeze **2**:61
Dumas, Jean Baptiste André, discoverer **6**:297
heat content **8**:353 *table*
nuclear magnetic resonance spectrum **18**:171 *illus.*
METHYL FLUORIDE
laser **12**:213 *table*
METHYL GROUP **13**:344–345
acetone **1**:80
methyl alcohol **13**:344
METHYL ISOCYANATE
Bhopal **3**:234
METHYLENE **13**:345
METHYLENE BLUE
methemoglobinemia **13**:343
MÉTIS
Red River Rebellion **16**:113
Riel, Louis **16**:218
METLAKATLA (Alaska)
map (55° 8′N 131° 35′W) **1**:242
Tsimshian **19**:324
METOAC
Montauk **13**:551
METON **13**:345
METONYMY
figures of speech **8**:76
METOPE
architecture **2**:131 *illus.*
Greek architecture **9**:335–336
MÉTREAUX, ALFRED
Easter Island **7**:33
METRIC SYSTEM **13**:345–347 *bibliog., table*
International Bureau of Weights and Measures **11**:219
LaPlace, Pierre Simon de **12**:205
Lavoisier, Antoine Laurent **12**:241–242
Michelson, Albert Abraham **13**:375–376
units, physical **19**:465–466 *table*
weights and measures **20**:94
METRO-GOLDWYN-MAYER
film, history of **8**:87
Goldwyn, Samuel **9**:237
Mayer, Louis B. **13**:246
METROLINER **13**:347 *bibliog.*
METROLOGY
weights and measures **20**:92–94
METRONOME **13**:347
METROPOLIS (film) **8**:83 *illus.*; **12**:194 *illus.*
METROPOLIS (Illinois)
map (37° 9′N 88° 44′W) **11**:42
METROPOLITAN AREA **13**:347
METROPOLITAN MUSEUM OF ART, THE **13**:347–348 *bibliog., illus.*
Cloisters, The **5**:64
New York (city) **14**:145 *map*
METROPOLITAN OPERA **13**:348–349 *bibliog., illus.*
art and architecture
Chagall, Marc **4**:268
Lincoln Center for the Performing Arts **12**:350
Bing, Sir Rudolf **3**:258
Converse, Frederick Shepherd **5**:233
Gatti-Casazza, Giulio **9**:58–59
Johnson, Edward **11**:431–432
Levine, James **12**:304
New York (city) **14**:145 *map*
singers
Albanese, Licia **1**:248–249
Anderson, Marian **1**:402
Baccaloni, Salvatore **3**:9
Bori, Lucrezia **3**:400
Caballé, Montserrat **4**:3
Caruso, Enrico **4**:178
Farrar, Geraldine **8**:29
Gigli, Beniamino **9**:178
Gobbi, Tito **9**:216
Homer, Louise **10**:213
Horne, Marilyn **10**:239
Lehmann, Lotte **12**:276
Ludwig, Christa **12**:452
Melchior, Lauritz **13**:286
Merrill, Robert **13**:312
Milnes, Sherrill **13**:432
Moore, Grace **13**:568
Pinza, Ezio **15**:308
Ponselle, Rosa **15**:426
Traubel, Helen **19**:284
Tucker, Richard **19**:328
Warren, Leonard **20**:31
METSU, GABRIEL **13**:349 *bibliog., illus.*
The Sick Child **13**:349 *illus.*
METSYS, QUENTIN *see* MASSYS, QUENTIN
METTER (Georgia)
map (32° 24′N 82° 3′W) **9**:114
METTERNICH, KLEMENS, FÜRST VON **2**:350 *illus.*; **13**:349–350 *bibliog., illus.*
Europe, history of **7**:292
Vienna, Congress of **19**:579
METZ (France) **13**:350
map (49° 8′N 6° 10′E) **8**:260
METZGER, HENRI
Xanthus **20**:311
MEUDON OBSERVATORY *see* PARIS OBSERVATORY
MEULEBEKE (Belgium)
map (50° 57′N 3° 17′E) **3**:177
MEULNER, PIETER
Gustav II Adolf, King of Sweden **17**:109 *illus.*
MEUN, JEAN DE
Roman de la Rose, Le **16**:278
MEUNIER, CONSTANTIN **13**:350
Battle for Brussels **12**:442 *illus.*
MEUSE RIVER **13**:350
Delta Plan **6**:95–96
map (51° 49′N 5° 1′E) **16**:195
Romanesque art and architecture **16**:285 *illus.*
MEXIA (Texas)
map (31° 41′N 96° 29′W) **19**:129
MEXICA (tribe) *see* AZTEC
MEXICALI (Mexico) **13**:350
map (32° 40′N 115° 29′W) **13**:357
MEXICAN AMERICAN POLITICAL ASSOCIATION
Chicano **4**:343
MEXICAN-AMERICANS *see* CHICANO
MEXICAN BEADED LIZARD **13**:350
MEXICAN CLIFF FROG *see* CHIRPING FROG
MEXICAN HAIRLESS DOG **13**:350–351 *bibliog., illus.*
MEXICAN HAT (Utah)
map (37° 9′N 109° 52′W) **19**:492
MEXICAN JUMPING BEAN **13**:351
MEXICAN REVOLUTION *see* MEXICO, HISTORY OF
MEXICAN SALAMANDER **13**:351
MEXICAN WAR **13**:351–355 *bibliog., illus., map*; **19**:445 *illus.*
American Southwest campaigns **13**:354–355
Bear Flag Republic **3**:141
central campaign **13**:353–354
Cerro Gordo and Puebla **13**:352–354 *map*
Contreras, Battle of **5**:232
Contreras, Churubusco, and Chapultepec **13**:354
Davis, Jefferson **6**:51
Guadalupe Hidalgo, Treaty of **9**:385
Kearny, Stephen Watts **12**:35
Lee, Robert E. **12**:270
Lincoln, Abraham **12**:348
Marine Corps, U.S. **13**:154
Monterrey (Mexico) **13**:553
Monterrey and Buena Vista **13**:352–353 *map*
navy **14**:63
northern campaign **13**:352–353
Polk, James K. **15**:405
Santa Anna, Antonio López de **17**:66
Santa Fe (New Mexico) **17**:68
Scott, Winfield **17**:154–155
Slidell, John **17**:361
Slidell mission **13**:351–352
Stockton, Robert Field **18**:276
Taylor, Zachary **19**:50
Texas Rangers **19**:135
uniform **2**:182 *illus.*
U.S. policy **13**:351
Wilmot Proviso **20**:163
MEXICO **13**:355–361 *bibliog., illus., map, table*
agriculture **13**:361
green revolution **9**:348
archaeology **2**:125 *illus.*
Bonampak **3**:375
Caso, Alfonso **4**:182
Catherwood, Frederick **4**:210
Chichén Itzá **4**:343–344
Choiula **4**:404
El Tajín **7**:101
Izapa **11**:338
La Venta **12**:151
Mayapán **13**:246
Mérida **13**:310
Mitla **13**:485
Monte Albán **13**:552
Palenque **15**:30
Puebla (state in Mexico) **15**:613
Remojadas **16**:146
San Lorenzo **17**:55–56
Tehuacán Valley **19**:73
Tenochtitlán **19**:112
Teotihuacán **19**:113–114
Tula **19**:329–330
Uxmal **19**:499
Xochicalco **20**:313
art **13**:360
See also the subheading Mexico under specific art forms, e.g., ARCHITECTURE; PAINTING; etc.
Latin American art and architecture **12**:222–228 *illus.*
museums, art **13**:658
pre-Columbian art and architecture **15**:495
cities
Acapulco **1**:72
Aguascalientes **1**:199
Campeche **4**:66
Chetumal **4**:337
Chihuahua **4**:347
Chilpancingo **4**:357–358
Ciudad Juárez **5**:9
Ciudad Victoria **5**:9
Colima **5**:102
Cuernavaca **5**:382–383
Culiacán **5**:383
Durango **6**:303
Guadalajara **9**:384
Guanajuato **9**:385
Hermosillo **10**:143
Jalapa **11**:351
La Paz **12**:148; **13**:356 *table*
León **12**:289
Mazatlán **13**:250
Mérida **13**:310
Mexicali **13**:350
Mexico City **13**:366–368 *illus., map*
Monterrey **13**:553
Morelia **13**:577
Oaxaca **14**:314
Pachuca **15**:4–5
Puebla **15**:613
Querétaro **16**:23
Saltillo **17**:38–39
San Luis Potosí **17**:56
Tampico **19**:20
Tepic **19**:114
Tijuana **19**:198
Tlaxcala **19**:216
Toluca **19**:229
Torreón **19**:244
Tuxtla Gutiérrez **19**:356–357
Veracruz **19**:548–549
Villahermosa **19**:597
Xochimilco **20**:313
Zacatecas **20**:347
climate **13**:356 *table*; **13**:358
dance
Ballet Folklórica of Mexico **12**:232 *illus.*
demography **13**:359
economic activity **13**:360–361
North America **14**:234–236
education **13**:359
Latin American universities **12**:233 *table*
Mexico, National Autonomous University of **13**:366
ethnography
Redfield, Robert **16**:115
flag **13**:356 *illus.*
government **13**:361
defense, national **6**:82 *table*
Morrow, Dwight **13**:590
political parties **15**:402
republic **16**:172
health **13**:359
history *see* MEXICO, HISTORY OF
independence day
Hidalgo y Costilla, Miguel **10**:158
land and resources **13**:355–359 *map, table*
language **13**:359
literature
Altamirano, Ignacio Manuel **1**:311
Azuela, Mariano **2**:384
Díaz Mirón, Salvador **6**:155
Fernández de Lizardi, José Joaquín **8**:58
Fuentes, Carlos **8**:354–355
Juana Inés de la Cruz, Sor **11**:457–458
Latin American literature **12**:229–230
López Velarde, Ramón **12**:412–413
Nervo, Amado **14**:91
Paz, Octavio **15**:122
Torres Bodet, Jaime **19**:244
Usigli, Rodolfo **19**:490
Villaurrutia, Xavier **19**:598
Yáñez, Augustín **20**:317
manufacturing **13**:360
chemical industry **4**:319
map (23° 0′N 102° 0′W) **14**:225
migration to the United States **11**:55 *map*
mining **13**:360–361
silver **17**:312
money **13**:525 *illus.*
music
Chávez, Carlos **4**:305
national parks **14**:43 *table*
nuclear energy **14**:284
people **13**:359–360
Creoles **5**:338–339
Huastec **10**:287–288
Kickapoo **12**:70
Lacandón **12**:158
Maya **13**:243–245
Mixtec **13**:486
North America **14**:232
settlement in the United States **10**:177–178 *map*
Tarascan **17**:35
Tlaxcalan **19**:217
Yaqui **20**:319
Zapotec **20**:356
physical features
Ixtachihuatl **11**:338
Parícutin **15**:84
Popocatépetl **15**:431
Sierra Madre **17**:298
Tehuantepec, Isthmus of **19**:73
religion **13**:359
Quetzalcóatl **16**:24
Tezcatlipoca **19**:138
resources **13**:358–359
rivers, lakes, and waterways **13**:358
soils **13**:356
states
Aguascalientes **1**:199
Baja California **3**:27
Campeche **4**:66
Chiapas **4**:340
Chihuahua **4**:347
Coahuila **5**:75
Colima **5**:102
Durango **6**:303
Guanajuato **9**:385–386
Guerrero **9**:391
Hidalgo **10**:158
Jalisco **11**:351
México **13**:366
Michoacán **13**:383
Morelos **13**:577
Nayarit **14**:66
Nuevo León **14**:291
Oaxaca **14**:314
Puebla **15**:613
Querétaro **16**:23
Quintana Roo **16**:27
San Luis Potosí **17**:56
Sinaloa **17**:318
Sonora **18**:66
Tabasco **19**:3
Tamaulipas **19**:18
Tlaxcala **19**:216
Veracruz **19**:549
Yucatán **20**:338
Zacatecas **20**:347
trade **13**:361
transportation **13**:361
railroad **16**:73
vegetation and animal life **13**:358
MEXICO (Maine)
map (44° 34′N 70° 33′W) **13**:70
MEXICO (Missouri)
map (39° 10′N 91° 53′W) **13**:476
MEXICO (New York)
map (43° 28′N 76° 14′W) **14**:149
MÉXICO (state in Mexico) **13**:366
cities
Toluca **19**:229
MEXICO, GULF OF **13**:366
Gulf Stream **9**:403
islands and island groups
Dry Tortugas **6**:284
Florida Keys **8**:176
map (25° 0′N 90° 0′W) **14**:225
seas, gulfs, and bays
Florida, Straits of **8**:176
Intracoastal Waterway **11**:232

MEXICO, HISTORY OF 13:361–366 *bibliog., illus.*
See also LATIN AMERICA, HISTORY OF
pre-Columbian period
Aztec 13:362
Chichén Itzá 4:343–344
Cholula 4:404
Maya 13:243–245; 13:245
Mayan and central highland civilizations 13:361–362
Montezuma II 13:555
Toltec 13:362; 19:228–229
Zapotec 20:356
1517–1810 Spanish conquest and colonization
Chapultepec 4:285
Cortés, Hernán 5:278
Cuauhtémoc 5:377
Mendoza, Antonio de 13:296
New Spain 13:362–363
Spanish conquest 13:362–363
Velasco, Luis de 19:536
Velázquez de Cuéllar, Diego 19:537
Villa de Valladolid (early Spanish settlement) 12:217 *illus.*
1810–1910 republic
Arista, Mariano 2:154–155
California 4:36–37
Carlota 4:151
Díaz, Porfirio 6:154
Guadalupe Hidalgo, Treaty of 9:385
Hidalgo y Costilla, Miguel 10:158
independence to 1910 13:363–365
Iturbide, Agustín de 11:332
Juárez, Benito 11:458
Maximilian, Emperor of Mexico 13:240
Mexican War *see* MEXICAN WAR
Morelos y Pavón, José María 13:577
Santa Anna, Antonio López de 17:66
territory ceded to the United States, 1848 19:446 *map*
Texas 19:134
Texas Revolution 19:135
1910–1915 Mexican Revolution
Calles, Plutarco Elías 4:41
Cárdenas, Lázaro 4:143
Carranza, Venustiano 4:167
Huerta, Victoriano 10:291
Madero, Francisco I. 13:40–41
Mexican Revolution 13:365
Villa, Pancho 19:596
Zapata, Emiliano 20:355–356
1915-present
Alemán Valdés, Miguel 1:271
Ávila Camacho, Manuel 2:376
Cárdenas, Lázaro 4:143
Carranza, Venustiano 4:167
de la Madrid Hurtado, Miguel 6:60
Diaz Ordaz, Gustavo 6:155
Echeverría, Álvarez, Luis 7:37
López Portillo y Pacheco, José 12:412
Northern Dynasty 13:365–366
Obregón, Álvaro 14:316–317
MEXICO, NATIONAL AUTONOMOUS UNIVERSITY OF 13:366; 13:368 *illus.*
MEXICO CITY (Mexico) 13:366–368 *illus., map*
art
Cathedral 12:224 *illus.*
Latin American art and architecture 12:223–228
mosaic 13:596
Orozco, José Clemente 14:448
Palacio Nacional 12:227 *illus.*
Plaza de las Tres Culturas 13:360 *illus.*
Rivera, Diego 16:233
climate 13:356 *table*
history 13:368
Mexico, history of 13:363
Tenochtitlán 19:112
map (19° 24′N 99° 9′W) 13:357
subsidence 18:317
subway 18:318 *table*
MEXICO TRENCH
plate tectonics 15:351 *map*
MEYER, ADOLF 13:368 *bibliog.*
MEYER, BARON DE
Photo-Secession 15:257
MEYER, CONRAD FERDINAND 13:368 *bibliog.*
MEYER, LOTHAR 13:368 *bibliog.*
periodic table 15:166–167
MEYERBEER, GIACOMO 13:369 *bibliog.*
MEYERHOF, OTTO 14:369
MEYERHOLD, VSEVOLOD EMILIEVICH 13:369 *bibliog.*
constructivist theater 5:224–225
improvisational and experimental theater 11:69
theater, history of the 19:150
MEYERS CHUCK (Alaska)
map (55° 44′N 132° 12′W) 1:242
MEYERSDALE (Pennsylvania)
map (39° 45′N 79° 5′W) 15:147
MEYMANEH (Afghanistan)
map (35° 55′N 64° 47′E) 1:133
MEZEE, PHOEBE ANNE OAKLEY *see* OAKLEY, ANNIE
MEZEREON (botany)
daphne 6:36
MEZZO-SOPRANO 13:369 *bibliog.*
MHLUME (Swaziland)
map (26° 2′S 31° 50′E) 18:380
MHO
Ohm's law 14:363
MI FEI 13:369 *bibliog.*
MIAMI (American Indians) 13:370 *bibliog.*
Fort Wayne (Indiana) 8:238
Little Turtle 12:373
MIAMI (Arizona)
map (33° 24′N 110° 52′W) 2:160
MIAMI (Florida) 13:369–370 *illus.*
climate 19:421 *table*
Hispanic Americans 10:179
jai alai 11:349
map (25° 46′N 80° 12′W) 8:172
1980 riots 13:370
Florida 8:176
MIAMI (county in Indiana)
map (40° 45′N 86° 4′W) 11:111
MIAMI (county in Kansas)
map (38° 35′N 94° 50′W) 12:18
MIAMI (county in Ohio)
map (40° 2′N 84° 13′W) 14:357
MIAMI (Oklahoma)
map (36° 53′N 94° 53′W) 14:368
MIAMI (Texas)
map (35° 42′N 100° 38′W) 19:129
MIAMI BEACH (Florida) 8:173 *illus.*; 13:370 *illus.*; 19:429 *illus.*
map (25° 47′N 80° 8′W) 8:172
MIAMI CANAL
map (25° 47′N 80° 15′W) 8:172
MIAMI SPRINGS (Florida)
map (25° 49′N 80° 17′W) 8:172
MIAMISBURG (Ohio)
map (39° 38′N 84° 17′W) 14:357
MIANEH (Iran)
map (37° 26′N 47° 42′E) 11:250
MIANTONOMO 13:370 *bibliog.*
Uncas 19:381
MIANWALI
map (32° 35′N 71° 33′E) 15:27
MIAO *see* MEO
MIAO-YAO LANGUAGES
Southeast Asian languages 18:110–111
MIASKOVSKY, NICOLAI 13:370 *bibliog.*
Russian music 16:369
MICA 13:370–371 *bibliog., illus.*
alteration, mineral 1:312
chlorite 4:401
color 13:370
deposits 13:370–371
diorite 6:185
flake mica 13:370–371
granite 9:287
granodiorite 9:287
muscovite mica 13:370
phlogopite mica 13:370–371
quartzite 16:14
rock 16:247
silicate minerals 13:370–371; 17:305
uses 13:370–371
MICAH, BOOK OF 13:371
MICHAEL (archangel) 13:371; 16:361 *illus.*
MICHAEL, KING OF ROMANIA
Romania 16:290
MICHAEL, TSAR OF RUSSIA 13:372 *bibliog.*
Romanov (dynasty) 16:290
Time of Troubles 19:202
MICHAEL VIII, PALAEOLOGUS, BYZANTINE EMPEROR 13:371–372 *bibliog.*
MICHAEL THE BRAVE 13:372
MICHAEL CERULARIUS 13:371
Isaac I Comnenus, Byzantine Emperor 11:285
Schism, Great 17:122
MICHAELIS-MENTEN EQUATION
enzyme 7:213
MICHAELMAS DAISY *see* ASTER
MICHEL, CLAUDE *see* CLODION
MICHEL, GEORGES 13:372 *bibliog.*
MICHEL, ROBERT H. 13:372
MICHELANGELO 13:372–375 *bibliog., illus.*
architecture 2:135
Creation of Adam 2:190 *illus.*
David (sculpture) 6:47; 11:311 *illus.*; 17:163 *illus.*
early Florentine years 13:372–373
Farnese Palace 8:28
Florence (Italy) 8:168
forgery in art 8:233
The Holy Family 13:372 *illus.*
Italian art and architecture 11:309
Julius II, Pope, tomb 13:373
Libyan Sibyl 15:24 *illus.*
Marcus Aurelius, equestrian statue 16:275 *illus.*
Medici Chapel 13:265–266; 13:373–374
Moses 13:373 *illus.*
Pietà 13:373; 13:375; 16:153 *illus.*
portrait
Volterra, Daniele da 19:632
Renaissance art and architecture 16:151
Saint Peter's Basilica 17:25
sculpture 17:163
Sistine Chapel 11:313 *illus.*; 13:374 *illus.*; 15:24 *illus.*; 17:329
zoology 20:376
MICHELET, JULES 13:375 *bibliog.*
MICHELI, PIER ANTONIO
fungi 8:365
MICHELIN, ANDRÉ AND ÉDOUARD 13:375 *bibliog.*
MICHELOZZO 13:375 *bibliog.*
Florence (Italy) 8:168
MICHELS, ROBERT
oligarchy 14:377
MICHELSBERG CULTURE
European prehistory 7:302–303
MICHELSON, ALBERT ABRAHAM 13:375–376 *bibliog., illus.*
interferometer 11:209
measuring devices inventor 13:375–376
Michelson-Morley experiment 13:376
range finder 13:375–376
MICHELSON, MOUNT
map (69° 19′N 144° 17′W) 1:242
MICHELSON-MORLEY EXPERIMENT 13:376 *bibliog.*
ether (physics) 7:250; 13:376
light 12:336
Michelson, Albert Abraham 13:375–376
physics, history of 15:284
relativity 16:133 *illus.*
MICHENER, JAMES A. 13:376 *bibliog.*
MICHES (Dominican Republic)
map (18° 59′N 69° 3′W) 6:233
MICHIGAMEA (American Indians)
Illinois 11:45
MICHIGAN 13:376–382 *bibliog., illus., map*
agriculture 13:380 *illus.*
cities
Ann Arbor 2:31
Battle Creek 3:126
Bay City 3:132
Dearborn 6:68
Detroit 6:134–136 *map*
Flint 8:165
Grand Rapids 9:285
Holland 13:380 *illus.*
Jackson 11:340
Kalamazoo 12:7
Lansing 12:200
Muskegon 13:682
Saginaw 17:12
Sault Sainte Marie 17:96
Warren 20:31
climate 13:378
culture 13:379–380
economic activity 13:380–381 *illus.*
education 13:379
Detroit, University of 6:136
state universities and colleges of 13:383
environmental health 7:212
flag 13:376 *illus.*
forestry and fishing 13:380; 13:382
government and politics 13:381
historic sites 13:380
history 13:381–382
Toledo (Ohio) 19:226
land and resources 13:377–379 *illus., map*
Manitoulin Islands 13:122
manufacturing and energy 13:381 *illus.*
map (44° 0′N 85° 0′W) 19:419
mineral resources 13:379
mining 13:380–381
parks and reserves 13:378 *illus.*
people 13:379
Ottawa 14:460
recreation and sports 13:380
rivers, lakes, and waterways 13:378–379 *illus.*
Mackinac, Straits of 13:29
seal, state 13:376 *illus.*
transportation 13:381
vegetation and animal life 13:378–379
MICHIGAN (North Dakota)
map (48° 7′N 98° 7′W) 14:248
MICHIGAN, LAKE 13:378 *illus.*; 13:382–383 *map*
Mackinac, Straits of 13:29
map (44° 0′N 87° 0′W) 9:320
Nicolet, Jean 14:184
MICHIGAN, STATE UNIVERSITIES AND COLLEGES OF 13:383
Vietnam War 19:587
MICHIGAN CENTER (Michigan)
map (42° 14′N 84° 20′W) 13:377
MICHIGAN CITY (Indiana)
map (41° 43′N 86° 54′W) 11:111
MICHIKAMAU LAKE
map (54° 15′N 64° 0′W) 14:166
MICHIPICOTEN ISLAND
map (47° 45′N 85° 45′W) 14:393
MICHOACÁN (Mexico) 13:383
cities
Morelia 13:577
MICKEY MOUSE (fictional character) 13:383
Disney, Walt 6:197
MICKIEWICZ, ADAM 13:383–384 *bibliog.*
MICMAC (American Indians) 11:126 *illus.*; 13:384 *bibliog.*
MICO MOUNTAINS
map (15° 30′N 88° 55′W) 9:389
MICOMBERO, MICHEL
Burundi 3:583
MICON 13:384 *bibliog.*
MICROBIOLOGY 13:384 *bibliog.*
See also MICROORGANISM
blood tests 3:339
diagnostic tests 6:149–150
genetic code 9:79–82
history 13:384
Avery, Oswald T. 2:370
biology 3:269; 3:271
Bruce, Sir David 3:519
Carroll, James 4:168
Crick, Francis 5:343
Dubos, Rene 6:289
Franklin, Rosalind 8:285
Hershey, Alfred Day 10:148
Hooke, Robert 10:226–227
Pasteur, Louis 15:107–108
Waksman, Selman Abraham 20:8
Watson, James D. 20:67–68
Wilkins, Maurice 20:152
micropaleontology 13:386
nutrient cycles 14:303–304
research
Escherichia, E. Coli 7:237
Euglena 7:264
microscope 13:387–388
techniques 13:384
MICROCEPHALY 13:384
skull size 13:384
MICROCLIMATE 13:384–385 *bibliog.*
Geiger, Rudolf Oskar Robert Williams 9:68
insolation 11:194
meteorology 13:341
urban climate 19:480
MICROCLINE
feldspar 8:46 *illus.*
MICROCOCCUS 13:385
MICROCOMPUTER 13:385 *bibliog.*
automation 2:358
automotive instrumentation 2:368
computer 5:160f–160g; 5:160h
computer, personal 5:160i–160j
computers in education 5:165
microprocessor 13:387
MICRODOT
intelligence gathering 11:204
MICROECONOMICS
economics 7:47–49
MICROELECTRONICS 13:385 *bibliog.*
computer 5:160b–160c *illus.*
computer industry 5:160o
gold, use 9:227
integrated circuit 11:201–202 *illus.*; 13:385
microminiaturization 13:385
microprocessor 13:387
printed circuit 13:385; 15:550
semiconducting material 13:385
semiconductor 17:196–197

MICROELECTRONICS (cont.)
solid-state physics **13**:385; **18**:54–55
thin-film circuits **19**:169
MICROFICHE *see* MICROFILM
MICROFILM **13**:385 *bibliog.*
aperture card **13**:385
imput-output devices **11**:183
machines **13**:385
microfiche **13**:385
microfilm reader **12**:318 *illus.*
ultrafiche **13**:385
uses **13**:385
MICROFORMS *see* MICROFILM
MICROLITH *see* MESOLITHIC PERIOD
MICROMETER **13**:254 *illus.*; **13**:385
Maudslay, Henry **13**:232
MICRONESIA **13**:386
education
Guam, University of **9**:385
flag **8**:144 *illus.*
Malayo-Polynesian languages **13**:83
map (11° 0′N 159° 0′E) **14**:334
Oceania **14**:334–335 *map*
Oceanic art **14**:339
Pacific Islands, Trust Territory of the **15**:5
people
Micronesians **13**:386
race **16**:33–34 *illus.*, *map*
United States outlying territories **19**:464
MICRONESIANS **13**:386 *bibliog.*
MICRONUCLEUS *see* NUCLEUS
MICROORGANISM
See also names of specific microorganisms, e.g., *PANDORINA*; PNEUMOCOCCUS; etc.
algae **1**:280–283 *illus.*
bacteria **3**:14–18 *illus.*
food poisoning and infection **8**:211
fungi **8**:365–367 *illus.*
genetics **9**:89–90
gnotobiotics **9**:214
immunology **11**:60
infectious diseases **11**:164–165
microbiology **13**:384
Monera **13**:523
procaryote **15**:560
Protozoa **15**:579–581 *illus.*
soil organisms **18**:39 *illus.*
virus **19**:613–616 *illus.*
MICROPALEONTOLOGY **13**:386 *bibliog.*
conodont **5**:197
fossil record **8**:243–248
paleoecology **15**:34–35
MICROPHONE **13**:386–387 *bibliog.*, *illus.*
directivity **13**:386
modulation **13**:499
operation **13**:386
sound and acoustics **18**:73–74
transducer **19**:269
types **13**:386
MICROPHOTOGRAPHY
mircofilm **13**:385
photography **15**:266 *illus.*
MICROPROCESSOR **13**:387 *bibliog.*
byte **3**:603
computer **5**:160c *illus.*; **5**:160h
computer, personal **5**:160i
computer industry **5**:160o
integrated circuit **11**:201–202
process control **15**:560–561
video game **19**:577
MICROSCOPE **1**:397 *illus.*; **13**:387–388 *bibliog.*, *illus.*
biology **3**:268–269
blink microscope **3**:333
comparator **5**:155
electron microscope **7**:120–122
Hooke, Robert **10**:226–227
Leeuwenhoek, Antoni van **12**:271–272
measurement **13**:254
medicine **13**:269
metallurgy **13**:331
microbiology **13**:384
microsurgery **18**:362
optics **14**:411
petrographic microscope
optical mineralogy **14**:408–409 *illus.*
petrography **15**:207
Zeiss, Carl **20**:358
MICROSCOPY
holography **10**:208
phase contrast
Zernike, Frits **20**:361
MICROSEISM **13**:388
MICROSPORANGIUM *see* ANTHER SAC
MICROSURGERY *see* SURGERY
MICROWAVE OVEN **13**:388 *bibliog.*
MICROWAVES **13**:389 *bibliog.*
amplification
klystron **12**:98–99
application and use **13**:388
dangers **13**:389
frequency, electromagnetic **7**:117 *table*
generation, transmission, and reception **13**:389
holography **10**:208
laser **12**:210–213
microwave tube
electron tube **7**:123–124
magnetron **13**:60
traveling-wave tube **19**:284
radar **16**:39
remote sensing **16**:148
spectroscopy **18**:171
waveguide **20**:70
wavelength, electromagnetic **7**:117 *table*
MICTURATION
bladder, urinary **3**:323
MID-ATLANTIC RIDGE *see* ATLANTIC OCEAN; MID-OCEANIC RIDGE
MID-OCEANIC RIDGE **13**:389–390 *bibliog.*, *illus.*, *map*
Atlantic Ocean **2**:294–296 *map*
Woods Hole Oceanographic Institution **20**:213
description **13**:389
Earth, geological history of **7**:14
Earth, heat flow in **7**:18
Ewing, Maurice **7**:325
formation **13**:390
igneous rock **11**:34
Indian Ocean bottom **11**:105 *map*
mountain **13**:620
mountain range **13**:390
ocean and sea **14**:327
oceanic fracture zones **14**:339
Pacific Ocean **15**:6–8 *map*
plate tectonics **15**:353 *map*
rift valleys **16**:221
seafloor spreading **13**:390; **17**:172
structural geology **18**:303
Tertiary Period **19**:123
transform fault **19**:270
Vine, F. J. **19**:600
volcano **19**:628
worldwide **14**:328–329 *map*; **15**:351 *map*
MIDAS **13**:390
MIDAS TOMB
Gordion **9**:248
MIDDELBURG (Netherlands)
map (51° 30′N 3° 37′E) **14**:99
MIDDELFART (Denmark)
map (55° 30′N 9° 45′E) **6**:109
MIDDEN **13**:390
Ertebølle culture **7**:235
MIDDLE AGE **13**:390–391 *bibliog.*
psychology **13**:391
running and jogging **16**:346
social and physical changes **13**:391
spread
obesity **14**:315
MIDDLE AGES **13**:391–396 *bibliog.*, *illus.*, *map*
See also MEDIEVAL DRAMA; MEDIEVAL MUSIC
agriculture **13**:394
agriculture, history of **1**:190–191 *illus.*
plow **15**:369
alchemy **1**:263
army **2**:180–181
art
Carolingian art and architecture **4**:160–161
cathedrals and churches **4**:205
chair **4**:269 *illus.*
chapel **4**:284
chapter house **4**:285
Cloisters, The **5**:64
drawing **6**:264
English art and architecture **7**:181–184
French art and architecture **8**:303–305
furniture **8**:375
German art and architecture **9**:123–125
Gothic art and architecture **9**:255–262
iconography **11**:22
interior design **11**:211–212
Italian art and architecture **11**:308–314
Merovingian art and architecture **13**:311
Metropolitan Museum of Art, The **13**:348
misericord **13**:466
monastic art and architecture **13**:517–521
Ottonian art and architecture **14**:466–467
painting **15**:19–20
Romanesque art and architecture **16**:282–286 *illus.*
Scandinavian art and architecture **17**:111–112 *illus.*
Spanish art and architecture **18**:152–153
tomb **19**:231
astronomy
Battani, al- **3**:125
Charlemagne, Frankish emperor **4**:289–290
chivalry **4**:399
city **5**:3
towns **13**:393
towns in Europe **13**:395 *map*
urban planning **19**:481
commerce and trade routes **13**:395 *map*
commune **5**:142
cooking **5**:238–239 *illus.*
costume **5**:294–297 *illus.*
chastity belt **4**:301–302
cosmetics **5**:281
jewelry **11**:409–410 *illus.*
shoes **17**:280 *illus.*
court, the **13**:393
courtly love **5**:317
dance **6**:23 *illus.*
dance, social **6**:29–30
Maypole dance **13**:248–249
Dark Ages **6**:38
Death, Dance of **6**:68
Domesday Book **6**:231
draft horse **6**:254
education **7**:60
church and learning **13**:394–396
European universities **7**:306
Paris, Universities of **15**:88
scholasticism **17**:131–132
university **13**:395–396
enclosure **7**:163
engineering **7**:177
Europe, history of **7**:282–286
feudalism **8**:64–65; **13**:392
France, history of **8**:266–268
Franks **8**:285–286
genealogy **9**:76
Germany, history of **9**:148–151
Golden Bull **9**:231
Great Britain, history of **9**:310
guilds **9**:395
Hanseatic League **10**:40–41
heraldry **10**:132
historians *see* HISTORY—medieval historians
Holy Roman Empire **10**:209–211
hospital **10**:256 *illus.*
house **10**:266 *illus.*
castle **4**:189–190 *illus.*
château **4**:302
inquisition **11**:183–185
torture **19**:247 *illus.*
Italy, history of **11**:327–329
Jews **11**:414–415
knight **12**:99–100
law
common law **5**:139
law, history of **12**:244–245
lingua franca **12**:354
literature
See also MIDDLE ENGLISH; OLD ENGLISH
allegory **1**:299
Arthur and Arthurian legend **2**:219
bestiary **3**:229
book **3**:383–384
Canterbury Tales, The **4**:116–117
Decameron **6**:72
fabliau **8**:5
French literature **8**:314–315
German literature **9**:132
Hroswitha von Gandersheim **10**:286
literacy and illiteracy **12**:368
medieval drama **13**:273–274
Roman de la Rose, Le **16**:278
saga **17**:11
logic **12**:395–396
Low Countries, history of the **12**:438
manorialism **13**:126–127; **13**:394
maps and mapmaking **13**:139
mathematics, history of **13**:224
medicine **13**:269
pacifism and nonviolent movements **15**:9
papacy **13**:392–393; **15**:63–65
Papal States **15**:67
Peasants' Revolt **15**:129
philosophy **15**:244
piracy **15**:312
political structure of **13**:392–393
Portugal, history of **15**:453–454
qualitative chemical analysis **16**:6
roads and highways **16**:235
Scandinavia, history of **17**:108–109
slavery **17**:353
society and economy **13**:393–394
Spain, history of **18**:144–146
state (in political philosophy) **18**:230
taxation **19**:46
technology, history of **19**:63–65
towns **13**:393–394
trade and industry **13**:394–395
wagon **20**:6
weapons **2**:180 *illus.*; **20**:74–75
weights and measures **20**:94
women in society **20**:202
MIDDLE AMERICA *see* CARIBBEAN SEA; CENTRAL AMERICA; MESOAMERICA; MEXICO
MIDDLE ATLAS MOUNTAINS
map (33° 30′N 5° 0′W) **13**:585
MIDDLE BRONZE AGE *see* BRONZE AGE
MIDDLE CLASS *see* CLASS, SOCIAL
MIDDLE EAST **13**:396–400 *bibliog.*, *illus.*
See also names of specific countries, e.g., EGYPT; IRAN; etc.
agriculture **13**:398–399 *illus.*
fellahin **8**:47
irrigation **11**:283
art
See also OTTOMAN ART
Cycladic art **5**:402–403
Hittite art and architecture **10**:188–189
Islamic art and architecture **11**:293–297
Mesopotamian art and architecture **13**:317–322
Persian art and architecture **15**:183–187
Phoenician art **15**:250–251
belly dance **3**:192
climate **13**:397–398
cosmetics in the ancient world **5**:281
definitions and boundaries **13**:396–397
demography **13**:399
economy **13**:399–400
education
Middle Eastern universities **13**:410–412
fishing and forestry **13**:399
garden **9**:40
history *see* MIDDLE EAST, HISTORY OF THE
industry **13**:399
land **13**:396–397 *illus.*
languages **13**:398
marriage **13**:164
mining **13**:399
music, non-Western **13**:667–668
people **13**:398
Arabs **2**:103–106
Bakhtiari **3**:28–29
Baluch **3**:57
Bedouin **3**:154
fellahin **8**:47
Jews **11**:412–417
Khamseh **12**:65
Kurds **12**:139
Qashqai **16**:3
Semites **17**:197–198
Turkmen **19**:347
Turks **19**:347–349
physical features
Arabian Desert **2**:98–99
Esdraelon, Plain of **7**:238
Hermon, Mount **10**:143
Syrian Desert **18**:414
regions
Kurdistan **12**:138–139 *illus.*
North Africa **14**:224
Sinai **17**:318
West Bank **20**:108
religion **13**:398
Arabs **2**:103–104
Islam **11**:288–293
resources **13**:398
energy comsumption and production **7**:174 *table*
oil and gas reserves **15**:209 *table*
petroleum industry **15**:210 *table*
rivers, lakes, and waterways **13**:397 *illus.*
Dead Sea **6**:64–65
Euphrates River **7**:265

Jordan River **11**:450–451
Red Sea **16**:113–114 *map*
Tigris River **19**:197–198 *map*
soils **13**:398
tell **19**:90
trade **13**:400
transportation **13**:399–400
vegetation and animal life **13**:398
MIDDLE EAST, HISTORY OF THE **13**:400–410 *bibliog., illus., maps*
See also names of specific Middle Eastern countries, e.g., ARABIA; BAHRAIN; etc.; the subheading history under specific modern countries, e.g., IRAN; ISRAEL; etc.
Asia, history of **2**:249–250; **2**:254–255
Fertile Crescent **8**:60
Gaza **9**:64
Islam **11**:288–293
Jerusalem (Israel) **11**:400–401
Kurds **12**:139
Palestine **15**:44–46 *maps*
refugee **16**:125
slavery **17**:352–353; **17**:357
Turks **19**:347–348
prior to 570
See also EGYPT, ANCIENT; MESOPOTAMIA; PERSIA, ANCIENT
Anatolia and Persia **13**:401
ancient history **13**:400–402
Ebla **7**:36
Egypt and Mesopotamia **13**:400–401
Masada **13**:194
Palmyra **15**:51–52
Phoenicia **15**:249–250
Shechem **17**:248
Syria-Palestine **13**:401
Ugarit **19**:374
Urartu **19**:479–480
570–1500
See also BYZANTINE EMPIRE; OTTOMAN EMPIRE
Abbasids **1**:52; **13**:403–404
Abu Bakr **1**:66
Ali **1**:292
Almohads **1**:306
Almoravids **1**:307
Assassins **2**:264
Ayyubids **2**:380
caliphate **4**:39; **13**:402–404 *map*
Fatimids **8**:34
Ibn Battuta **11**:5
Jerusalem, Latin Kingdom of **11**:401–402
Mamelukes **13**:96–97
Muhammad **13**:632–633
Nur al-Din **14**:297
Saladin **17**:29
Umayyads **19**:380
1500–1900
See also OTTOMAN EMPIRE
Abbas I **1**:52
Qajar rule in Persia **13**:406
19th century **13**:405–406
1900-present
See also ARAB-ISRAELI WARS
Baath party **3**:5
balance of power **13**:409 *map*
boundaries after World War I **13**:407 *map*
Gaza Strip **9**:64
Jordan and Lebanon **13**:409–410
Pahlavi rule in Iran **13**:408
Palestine Liberation Organization **13**:409–410
suffrage, women's **18**:326–327
20th century **13**:406–410
World War I *see* WORLD WAR I
World War II *see* WORLD WAR II
MIDDLE EASTERN UNIVERSITIES **13**:410–412 *bibliog., table*
MIDDLE ENGLISH **13**:412 *bibliog.*
Arthur and Arthurian legend **2**:219
Canterbury Tales, The **4**:116–117
Chaucer, Geoffrey **4**:304
English language **7**:191–192
Hoccleve, Thomas **10**:193
Langland, William **12**:196
Lygate, John **12**:474
Malory, Sir Thomas **13**:93
medieval drama **13**:273–274
Morte Darthur **13**:591
Piers Plowman **15**:297
Sir Gawain and the Green Knight **17**:327
MIDDLE LOUP RIVER
map (41° 17′N 98° 23′W) **14**:70
MIDDLE RACCOON RIVER
map (41° 34′N 94° 12′W) **11**:244
MIDDLE RIVER
map (41° 29′N 93° 24′W) **11**:244
MIDDLE SCHOOLS AND JUNIOR HIGH SCHOOLS **13**:412–413 *bibliog.*
home economics
Future Homemakers of America **8**:383
MIDDLE STEWIACKE (Nova Scotia)
map (45° 13′N 63° 8′W) **14**:269
MIDDLE STONE AGE *see* MESOLITHIC PERIOD
MIDDLEBORO (Massachusetts)
map (41° 49′N 70° 55′W) **13**:206
MIDDLEBOURNE (West Virginia)
map (39° 30′N 80° 54′W) **20**:111
MIDDLEBURG (Pennsylvania)
map (40° 47′N 77° 3′W) **15**:147
MIDDLEBURY (Vermont)
map (44° 1′N 73° 10′W) **19**:554
MIDDLEBURY COLLEGE **13**:413
MIDDLEFIELD (Ohio)
map (41° 28′N 81° 5′W) **14**:357
MIDDLEMARCH (book) **13**:413 *bibliog.*
Eliot, George **7**:138–139
MIDDLEPORT (New York)
map (43° 13′N 78° 29′W) **14**:149
MIDDLEPORT (Ohio)
map (39° 0′N 82° 3′W) **14**:357
MIDDLESBORO (Kentucky)
map (36° 36′N 83° 43′W) **12**:47
MIDDLESBROUGH (England)
map (54° 35′N 1° 14′W) **19**:403
MIDDLESEX (Belize)
map (17° 2′N 88° 31′W) **3**:183
MIDDLESEX (county in Connecticut)
map (41° 33′N 72° 39′W) **5**:193
MIDDLESEX (England) **13**:413
MIDDLESEX (county in Massachusetts)
map (42° 22′N 71° 6′W) **13**:206
MIDDLESEX (county in New Jersey)
map (40° 25′N 74° 25′W) **14**:129
MIDDLESEX (county in Virginia)
map (37° 40′N 76° 35′W) **19**:607
MIDDLESEX, LIONEL CRANFIELD, EARL OF
James I, King of England **11**:356
MIDDLETON (Nova Scotia)
map (44° 57′N 65° 4′W) **14**:269
MIDDLETON (Tennessee)
map (35° 4′N 88° 54′W) **19**:104
MIDDLETON (Wisconsin)
map (43° 6′N 89° 30′W) **20**:185
MIDDLETON, HENRY
Middleton Place Gardens (South Carolina) **18**:101 *illus.*
MIDDLETON, THOMAS **13**:413 *bibliog.*
MIDDLETOWN (Connecticut)
map (41° 33′N 72° 39′W) **5**:193
MIDDLETOWN (Delaware)
map (39° 25′N 75° 47′W) **6**:88
MIDDLETOWN (Illinois)
map (40° 11′N 89° 35′W) **11**:42
MIDDLETOWN (Indiana)
map (40° 3′N 85° 32′W) **11**:111
MIDDLETOWN (Kentucky)
map (38° 15′N 85° 32′W) **12**:47
MIDDLETOWN (Maryland)
map (39° 27′N 77° 33′W) **13**:188
MIDDLETOWN (New Jersey)
map (40° 24′N 74° 7′W) **14**:129
MIDDLETOWN (New York)
map (41° 27′N 74° 25′W) **14**:149
MIDDLETOWN (Ohio)
map (39° 29′N 84° 25′W) **14**:357
MIDDLETOWN (Pennsylvania)
map (40° 12′N 76° 44′W) **15**:147
MIDDLETOWN (Rhode Island)
map (41° 32′N 71° 17′W) **16**:198
MIDGE **13**:413 *bibliog., illus.*
MIDGIC (New Brunswick)
map (45° 59′N 64° 18′W) **14**:117
MIDGLEY, THOMAS, JR. **13**:413 *bibliog.*
refrigeration **16**:125
MIDHOPE, SIR ELIAS DE
harrier (dog) **10**:56
MIDIANITES **13**:413 *bibliog.*
MIDLAND (California)
map (33° 52′N 114° 48′W) **4**:31
MIDLAND (Michigan)
map (43° 37′N 84° 14′W) **13**:377
MIDLAND (county in Michigan)
map (43° 40′N 84° 25′W) **13**:377
MIDLAND (North Carolina)
map (35° 14′N 80° 30′W) **14**:242
MIDLAND (Ontario)
map (44° 45′N 79° 53′W) **14**:393
MIDLAND (South Dakota)
map (44° 4′N 101° 10′W) **18**:103
MIDLAND (Texas) **13**:414
map (32° 0′N 102° 5′W) **19**:129
MIDLAND (county in Texas)
map (31° 48′N 102° 0′W) **19**:129
MIDLAND PARK (Kansas)
map (37° 35′N 97° 20′W) **12**:18
MIDLANDS (England) **13**:414
cities
Birmingham **3**:292–293
counties
Bedfordshire **3**:153–154
Derbyshire **6**:121
Leicestershire **12**:277
Staffordshire **18**:209
Warwickshire **20**:33
Triassic Period **19**:294 *illus.*
MIDLER, BETTE **13**:414
MIDRASH **13**:414 *bibliog.*
A MIDSUMMER NIGHT'S DREAM (play) **13**:414 *bibliog.*; **19**:146 *illus.*; **19**:151 *illus.*
MIDVALE (Idaho)
map (44° 28′N 116° 44′W) **11**:26
MIDVALE (Utah)
map (40° 37′N 111° 54′W) **19**:492
MIDWAY (Alabama)
map (32° 5′N 85° 31′W) **1**:234
MIDWAY (U.S.) **13**:414 *bibliog.*
map (28° 13′N 177° 22′W) **10**:72
map (28° 13′N 177° 22′W) **14**:334
World War II **14**:64 *illus.*; **20**:266 *illus.*
MIDWEST (Wyoming)
map (43° 25′N 106° 16′W) **20**:301
MIDWEST CITY (Oklahoma)
map (35° 27′N 97° 24′W) **14**:368
MIDWIFE **13**:414 *bibliog.*
pregnancy and birth **15**:502 *illus.*
MIDWIFE TOAD **13**:414–415 *illus.*
MIELEC (Poland)
map (50° 18′N 21° 25′E) **15**:388
MIELZINER, JO **13**:415 *bibliog.*
Death of a Salesman set **19**:150 *illus.*
MIES VAN DER ROHE, LUDWIG **13**:415 *bibliog., illus.*
apartment house **9**:129 *illus.*
architecture **2**:136
Bauhaus **3**:130
chair **8**:379 *illus.*
German Pavilion for the 1929 Barcelona Exposition **13**:491 *illus.*
Lake Shore Drive Apartments **2**:200 *illus.*; **13**:415 *illus.*
modern architecture **13**:490–491
Seagram Building **1**:329 *illus.*; **17**:173
Toronto (Ontario) **19**:242
MIESCHER, JOHANN **13**:416
MIESZKO I, KING OF POLAND
Piast (dynasty) **15**:289
MIFFLIN (county in Pennsylvania)
map (40° 37′N 77° 40′W) **15**:147
MIFFLIN, THOMAS **13**:416 *bibliog.*
Conway Cabal **5**:234
MIFFLINBURG (Pennsylvania)
map (40° 55′N 77° 3′W) **15**:147
MIFFLINTOWN (Pennsylvania)
map (40° 34′N 77° 24′W) **15**:147
MIG **13**:416 *bibliog., illus.*
MiG-15 **13**:416 *illus.*
MiG 21 **1**:215 *illus.*
MiG-21MF **13**:416 *illus.*
MiG-25 **13**:416 *illus.*
Soviet aircraft development **13**:416
World War II **13**:416
MIGNARD, PIERRE **13**:416–417 *bibliog.*
MIGRAINE
headache **10**:86
MIGRANT LABOR **13**:417 *bibliog.*
photography
Lange, Dorothea **12**:195 *illus.*
South Africa **18**:82
MIGRATION, ANIMAL *see* ANIMAL MIGRATION
MIGRATION, HUMAN
Basques **3**:116
North America **14**:232
North American archaeology **14**:236
population **15**:434
race **16**:34
refugee **16**:125–126
MIGRATORY BIRD CONSERVATION ACT (United States)
wildlife refuge **20**:150
MIGUEL ALEMÁN RESERVOIR
map (18° 13′N 96° 32′W) **13**:357
MIHAJLOVIĆ, DRAŽA **13**:417 *bibliog.*
MIKAN, GEORGE **3**:112 *illus.*; **13**:417 *bibliog.*
MIKHAYLOVGRAD (Bulgaria)
map (43° 25′N 23° 13′E) **3**:555
MIKI TAKEO **13**:417
MIKKELI (Finland)
map (61° 41′N 27° 15′E) **8**:95
MIKONGO MOUNTAINS
map (0° 15′N 10° 55′E) **9**:5
MIKOYAN, ANASTAS IVANOVICH **13**:417 *bibliog.*
MIKOYAN, ARTEM I.
MiG **13**:416
MILACA (Minnesota)
map (45° 45′N 93° 39′W) **13**:453
MILADUMMADULU ATOLL
map (6° 15′N 73° 15′E) **13**:87
MILAGRO (Ecuador)
map (2° 7′S 79° 36′W) **7**:52
MILAM (county in Texas)
map (30° 47′N 96° 57′W) **19**:129
MILAN (Georgia)
map (32° 1′N 83° 4′W) **9**:114
MILAN (Illinois)
map (41° 27′N 90° 34′W) **11**:42
MILAN (Indiana)
map (39° 7′N 85° 8′W) **11**:111
MILAN (Italy) **11**:325 *illus.*; **13**:418 *illus.*
Ambrosian Library **1**:325
art and architecture
Italian art and architecture **11**:308–314
Milan Cathedral **2**:134 *illus.*
Sant'Ambrogio **17**:69
history **13**:418
Italian city-state **11**:328 *map*
Sforza (family) **17**:233
Visconti (family) **19**:616
La Scala **12**:149
map (45° 28′N 9° 12′E) **11**:321
MILAN (Michigan)
map (42° 5′N 83° 40′W) **13**:377
MILAN (Missouri)
map (40° 12′N 93° 7′W) **13**:476
MILAN (New Mexico)
map (35° 9′N 107° 54′W) **14**:136
MILAN (Tennessee)
map (35° 55′N 88° 46′W) **19**:104
MILAN, KING OF SERBIA
Serbia **17**:207–208
MILÁN, LUIS
Renaissance music **16**:156
MILANKOVITCH THEORY **13**:418–419 *bibliog., illus.*
climate **5**:58
ice ages **11**:11
paleoclimatology **15**:32–34
MILANO (Italy) *see* MILAN (Italy)
MILAREPA **13**:419 *bibliog.*
MILBANK (South Dakota)
map (45° 13′N 96° 38′W) **18**:103
MILBRIDGE (Maine)
map (44° 32′N 67° 53′W) **13**:70
MILDEW **13**:419
diseases, plant **6**:194–195
MILE
weights and measures **20**:93 *table*
MILEKE *see* BAMILEKE
MILES, NELSON A. **13**:419 *bibliog.*
Gall **9**:16
Geronimo **9**:158
MILES CITY (Montana)
map (46° 25′N 105° 51′W) **13**:547
MILESIAN SCHOOL **13**:419 *bibliog.*
pre-Socratic philosophy **15**:532
Thales of Miletus **19**:142
MILESTONE (Saskatchewan)
map (50° 0′N 104° 30′W) **17**:81
MILESTONE, LEWIS **13**:419 *bibliog.*
MILETUS (Greece) **13**:419
Ionia **11**:241
urban planning **19**:481
MILFORD (Connecticut)
map (41° 13′N 73° 4′W) **5**:193
MILFORD (Delaware)
map (38° 55′N 75° 25′W) **6**:88
MILFORD (Illinois)
map (40° 38′N 87° 42′W) **11**:42
MILFORD (Iowa)
map (43° 20′N 95° 9′W) **11**:244
MILFORD (Maine)
map (44° 57′N 68° 39′W) **13**:70
MILFORD (Massachusetts)
map (42° 8′N 71° 32′W) **13**:206
MILFORD (Michigan)
map (42° 35′N 83° 36′W) **13**:377
MILFORD (New Hampshire)
map (42° 50′N 71° 39′W) **14**:123
MILFORD (New Jersey)
map (40° 34′N 75° 6′W) **14**:129
MILFORD (Pennsylvania)
map (41° 19′N 74° 48′W) **15**:147
MILFORD (Utah)
map (38° 24′N 113° 1′W) **19**:492
MILFORD CENTER (Ohio)
map (40° 11′N 83° 26′W) **14**:357
MILFORD LAKE
map (39° 15′N 97° 0′W) **12**:18
MILGRAM, STANLEY **13**:419
conformity **5**:179

MILHAUD, DARIUS 13:419–420 *bibliog., illus.*
harmonica 10:51
MILIARIA
skin diseases 17:341
MILIĆ, JAN 13:420
MILITARY ACADEMIES 13:420–421 *bibliog.*
See also SERVICEMEN'S OPPORTUNITY COLLEGES
St. Cyr 17:17
Sandhurst, Royal Military Academy at 17:62
South Carolina, state universities and colleges of 18:102
United States Air Force Academy 19:462
United States Coast Guard Academy 19:462
United States Merchant Marine Academy 19:462
United States Military Academy 19:462–463
United States Naval Academy 19:463–464
Woolrich (England) technology, history of 19:66
MILITARY AID
foreign aid 8:224–225 *table*
MILITARY AIRCRAFT *see* AIRCRAFT, MILITARY
MILITARY DECORATIONS *see* MEDALS AND DECORATIONS
MILITARY DRESS *see* UNIFORM
MILITARY ENGINEERS
technology, history of 19:66
MILITARY GEOLOGY 9:105
MILITARY HYGIENE
Rush, Benjamin 16:347
MILITARY-INDUSTRIAL COMPLEX 13:422 *bibliog.*
defense, national 6:82
Mills, C. Wright 13:430
MILITARY JUSTICE 13:421 *bibliog.*
court-martial 5:316
desertion 6:131
martial law 13:178
military police 13:421
mutiny 13:687
MILITARY JUSTICE, UNIFORM CODE OF *see* UNIFORM CODE OF MILITARY JUSTICE
MILITARY NURSING
Nightingale, Florence 14:193
MILITARY POLICE 13:421
Shore Patrol 17:283
MILITARY RANK *see* RANK, MILITARY
MILITARY SERVICE *see* CONSCRIPTION
MILITARY STRATEGY AND TACTICS *see* STRATEGY AND TACTICS, MILITARY
MILITARY STRENGTH *see* DEFENSE, NATIONAL
MILITARY TRANSPORTATION
C-47 Skytrain
DC-3 6:57
jeep 11:390–391 *illus.*
MILITARY UNIFORM *see* UNIFORM
MILITARY WARNING AND DETECTION SYSTEMS 13:421–422 *bibliog.*
Airborne Warning and Control System 1:210
BMEWS 3:348
COSMOS 5:289–290
Discoverer (artificial satellite) 6:189
Goose Bay (Labrador) 9:247
radar 16:38–40 *illus.*
SAMOS 17:47
signaling 17:300–301
U-2 19:369
Vela (artificial satellite) 19:536
MILITIA 13:422–423
National Guard 14:34
Reserve Officers Training Corps 16:176
right to bear arms 16:222
2d Amendment 17:178
MILK 13:423 *bibliog., table*
albumin 1:261
Babcock, Stephen Moulton 3:6
breast-feeding 3:469
casein 4:181
composition of the milk of different mammals 13:423 *table*
condensed milk
Borden, Gail 3:396
dairying 6:7
diseases, animal 6:190
diseases, human
galactosemia 9:9
gastrointestinal tract disease 9:57
tuberculosis 19:327
fermentation
Lactobacillus 12:161
goat 9:215
lactic acid
Scheele, Carl Wilhelm 17:115
marketing
dairying 6:9–10
nutrition, human 14:305
nutritional content 13:423
pigeon milk 15:299
processing 13:423
butter 3:592–593
cheese 4:308–309
churn 4:427
equipment 6:8–9 *illus.*
homogenization 10:216
packaging 13:423
pasteurization 15:108
products 13:423
fats and oils source 8:35
ice cream 11:11
uses 13:423 *table*
yogurt 20:329
MILK BANK
breast-feeding 3:469
MILK RIVER
map (48° 5′N 106° 15′W) 13:547
MILK RIVER (city in Alberta)
map (49° 9′N 112° 5′W) 1:256
MILK SNAKE 13:423–424 *illus.*
king snake 12:82
MILKFISH 13:424
MILKWEED 8:348 *illus.*; 13:424
butterfly weed 3:600
MILKWORT 13:424
MILKY WAY *see* GALAXY, THE
MILL 13:424–425 *bibliog., illus.*
energy sources 7:174
windmills and wind power 20:173 *illus.*
MILL, JAMES 13:425 *bibliog.*
associationism 2:266
economics 7:48
MILL, JOHN STUART 13:425 *bibliog., illus.*
associationism 2:266
On Liberty 14:388
Mill, James 13:425
psychology, history of 15:596
socialism 18:20
state (in political philosophy) 18:232
suffrage, women's 18:326
utilitarianism 19:497
MILL CITY (Oregon)
map (44° 45′N 122° 29′W) 14:427
MILL ON THE FLOSS, THE (book) 13:426
MILL VALLEY (California)
map (37° 54′N 122° 32′W) 4:31
MILLAIS, SIR JOHN EVERETT 13:426 *bibliog., illus.*
Christ in the House of His Parents 15:519 *illus.*
Hunt, Holman 10:311
Ophelia 13:426 *illus.*
Rossetti, Dante Gabriel 16:319
MILLAR, KENNETH (pseudonym) *see* MACDONALD, ROSS
MILLAR, MARGARET 13:426
MILLARAN CULTURE *see* LOS MILLARES (Spain)
MILLARD (county in Utah)
map (39° 0′N 113° 0′W) 19:492
MILLAY, EDNA ST. VINCENT 13:426 *bibliog., illus.*
Provincetown Players 15:584
MILLBROOK (New York)
map (41° 47′N 73° 42′W) 14:149
MILLBURY (Massachusetts)
map (42° 11′N 71° 46′W) 13:206
MILLCREEK (Utah)
map (40° 43′N 111° 51′W) 19:492
MILLCREEK TOWNSHIP (Pennsylvania)
map (42° 5′N 80° 10′W) 15:147
MILLE, AGNES DE *see* DE MILLE, AGNES
MILLE, CECIL B. DE *see* DE MILLE, CECIL B.
MILLE LACS (county in Minnesota)
map (45° 55′N 93° 38′W) 13:453
MILLE LACS LAKE
map (46° 15′N 93° 40′W) 13:453
MILLEDGEVILLE (Georgia)
map (33° 4′N 83° 14′W) 9:114
MILLEDGEVILLE (Illinois)
map (41° 58′N 89° 46′W) 11:42
MILLEN (Georgia)
map (32° 48′N 81° 57′W) 9:114
MILLENARIANISM 13:426–427 *bibliog.*
Adventists 1:111
cargo cults 4:147
eschatology 7:237
fundamentalism 8:363
Plymouth Brethren 15:374
Second Coming of Christ 17:178
Shakers 17:235–236
MILLER (county in Arkansas)
map (33° 20′N 93° 55′W) 2:166
MILLER (county in Georgia)
map (31° 10′N 84° 45′W) 9:114
MILLER (county in Missouri)
map (38° 12′N 92° 25′W) 13:476
MILLER (South Dakota)
map (44° 31′N 98° 59′W) 18:103
MILLER, ALFRED JACOB
A Bourgeois and His Squaw 13:624 *illus.*
Migration of the Pawnees 11:136 *illus.*
MILLER, ARTHUR 13:427 *bibliog., illus.*
Death of a Salesman 6:69–70
Kazan, Elia 12:33–34
Monroe, Marilyn 13:542–543
MILLER, CINCINNATUS HINER *see* MILLER, JOAQUIN (pseudonym)
MILLER, G. WILLIAM 13:427
MILLER, GEORGE ARMITAGE 13:427
MILLER, GLENN 13:427
MILLER, HENRY 13:427–428 *bibliog., illus.*
Tropic of Cancer 19:307
MILLER, JAMES AND ELIZABETH
cancer 4:102
MILLER, JOAQUIN 13:428
MILLER, LEWIS
Chautauqua 4:305
MILLER, NEAL E. 13:428
psychology, history of 15:597
MILLER, PERRY 13:428
MILLER, SAMUEL FREEMAN 13:428
Slaughterhouse Cases 17:351
MILLER, STANLEY LLOYD 13:428 *bibliog.*
origin of life 12:327 *illus.*
MILLER, W. D.
dentistry 6:116
MILLER, WILLIAM (religious figure) 13:428 *bibliog.*
Adventists 1:111
MILLER, WILLIAM H. (scientist)
mineral 13:439
MILLER v. CALIFORNIA 13:428–429 *bibliog.*
erotic and pornographic literature 7:234
pornography 15:441
MILLERAND, ALEXANDRE 13:429 *bibliog.*
MILLERITE 13:429
nickel ore 13:429
occurrence 13:429
MILLERITES (religious group)
Adventists 1:111
Miller, William (religious figure) 13:428
MILLERS FALLS (Massachusetts)
map (42° 35′N 72° 30′W) 13:206
MILLERS FERRY (Alabama)
map (32° 6′N 87° 22′W) 1:234
MILLERS RIVER
map (42° 35′N 72° 30′W) 13:206
MILLERSBURG (Ohio)
map (40° 33′N 81° 55′W) 14:357
MILLERSBURG (Pennsylvania)
map (40° 33′N 76° 58′W) 15:147
MILLERTON (New York)
map (41° 57′N 73° 31′W) 14:149
MILLERTOWN (Newfoundland)
map (48° 49′N 56° 33′W) 14:166
MILLES, CARL 13:429 *bibliog.*
MILLET (agriculture) 9:281 *illus.*; 13:429 *bibliog., illus.*
MILLET, JEAN FRANÇOIS 13:429–430 *bibliog., illus.*
The Gleaners 13:429 *illus.*
Rousseau, Théodore 16:327
social realism 18:13
MILLETT, KATE 13:430
MILLIGAN (Florida)
map (30° 45′N 86° 38′W) 8:172
MILLIGAN (Nebraska)
map (40° 30′N 97° 23′W) 14:70
MILLIKAN, ROBERT 7:111 *illus.*; 13:430 *bibliog.*
electricity 7:110–111 *illus.*
Millikan's oil-drop experiment 13:430
quantum mechanics 16:10
MILLIKAN'S OIL-DROP EXPERIMENT 13:430 *bibliog.*
apparatus 13:430
determination of e 13:430
electricity 7:110
Millikan, Robert 13:430
MILLILITER
weights and measures 20:93 *table*
MILLING MACHINES
machine tools 13:23–24 *illus.*
MILLINGTON (Michigan)
map (43° 17′N 83° 32′W) 13:377
MILLINGTON (Tennessee)
map (35° 21′N 89° 54′W) 19:104
MILLINOCKET (Maine)
map (45° 39′N 68° 43′W) 13:70
MILLIPEDE 13:430 *illus.*
myriapod 13:691
soil organisms 18:39 *illus.*
MILLIS (Massachusetts)
map (42° 10′N 71° 22′W) 13:206
MILLS (county in Iowa)
map (41° 0′N 95° 35′W) 11:244
MILLS (county in Texas)
map (31° 30′N 98° 37′W) 19:129
MILLS (Wyoming)
map (42° 50′N 106° 22′W) 20:301
MILLS, BERNARD
radio astronomy 16:52
MILLS, C. WRIGHT 13:430 *bibliog.*
elites 7:140
MILLS, ROBERT 13:430–431 *bibliog.*
MILLS, WILBUR D. 13:431
MILLS COLLEGE 13:431
campanile
Morgan, Julia 13:578
MILLS CROSS RADIO TELESCOPE SYSTEMS
radio astronomy 16:52
MILLSBORO (Delaware)
map (38° 36′N 75° 17′W) 6:88
MILLSTONE RIVER
map (40° 33′N 74° 34′W) 14:129
MILLTOWN MALBAY (Ireland)
map (52° 52′N 9° 23′W) 11:258
MILLVILLE (Massachusetts)
map (42° 2′N 71° 35′W) 13:206
MILLVILLE (New Jersey)
map (39° 24′N 75° 2′W) 14:129
MILNE, A. A. 13:431 *bibliog., illus.*
Winnie-the-Pooh (book) 4:353 *illus.*; 20:180
MILNE, DAVID 13:431 *bibliog.*
MILNE, EDWARD ARTHUR 13:431
MILNER, ALFRED MILNER, VISCOUNT 13:431 *bibliog.*
MILNES, SHERRILL 13:432 *bibliog.*
MILNOR (North Dakota)
map (46° 16′N 97° 27′W) 14:248
MILO (Alberta)
map (50° 34′N 112° 53′W) 1:256
MILO (athlete) 13:432
MILO (botany)
sorghum 18:69
MILO (Iowa)
map (41° 17′N 93° 27′W) 11:244
MILO (Maine)
map (45° 15′N 68° 59′W) 13:70
MILO RIVER
map (11° 4′N 9° 14′W) 9:397
MÍLOS (Greece) *see* MELOS (Greece)
MILOŠ, PRINCE OF SERBIA 13:432
MIŁOSZ, CZESŁAW 13:432
MILROY (Indiana)
map (39° 30′N 85° 28′W) 11:111
MILROY (Pennsylvania)
map (40° 43′N 77° 35′W) 15:147
MILSTEIN, NATHAN 13:432 *bibliog.*
MILTIADES 13:432 *bibliog.*
MILTON (Delaware)
map (38° 47′N 75° 19′W) 6:88
MILTON (Florida)
map (30° 38′N 87° 3′W) 8:172
MILTON (Massachusetts)
map (42° 15′N 71° 5′W) 3:409
MILTON (New Hampshire)
map (43° 25′N 70° 59′W) 14:123
MILTON (North Dakota)
map (48° 38′N 98° 3′W) 14:248
MILTON (Pennsylvania)
map (41° 1′N 76° 51′W) 15:147
MILTON (Vermont)
map (44° 38′N 73° 7′W) 19:554
MILTON (Wisconsin)
map (42° 47′N 88° 56′W) 20:185
MILTON, JOHN 7:196 *illus.*; 13:432–433 *bibliog., illus.*
Areopagitica 2:145
Paradise Lost 15:75
pastoral literature 15:109
Samson Agonistes 17:48
MILTON, LAKE
map (41° 6′N 80° 58′W) 14:357
MILTON-FREEWATER (Oregon)
map (45° 56′N 118° 23′W) 14:427
MILTOWN
meprobamate 13:303
tranquilizer 19:266
MILWAUKEE (Wisconsin) 13:433–434 *bibliog., illus.*; 20:184 *illus.*
average weather condition 20:82 *table*
map (43° 2′N 87° 55′W) 20:185

MILWAUKEE (county in Wisconsin)
map (43° 2′N 87° 58′W) **20**:185
MILWAUKEE RIVER
map (43° 2′N 87° 54′W) **20**:185
MILWAUKIE (Oregon)
map (45° 27′N 122° 38′W) **14**:427
MIMAMSA
philosophy **15**:246
MIMAS (astronomy)
Saturn (astronomy) **17**:90–91 *table*
MIMBRES
Mangas Coloradas **13**:114
pottery **14**:240 *illus.*
MIME AND PANTOMIME **13**:434 *bibliog., illus.*
Barrault, Jean Louis **3**:93
choreography **4**:408
commedia dell'arte **5**:137–138
Deburau, Jean Gaspard **6**:71
dumb show **6**:297
Marceau, Marcel **13**:145
morris dance **13**:589
Pierrot **15**:297
MIMEOGRAPH **13**:434 *bibliog.*
MIMESIS
criticism, literary **5**:351
narrative and dramatic devices **14**:22
MIMETITE **2**:189 *illus.*; **13**:434
MIMICRY **13**:434–436 *bibliog., illus.*
Batesian mimicry **13**:435
coloration, biological **5**:121–122
insect **11**:191 *illus.*
Müllerian mimicry **13**:435–436
MIMIR **13**:436
MIMNERMUS **13**:436 *bibliog.*
MIMOSA **13**:436
See also ACACIA
kangaroo thorn **12**:16
MIMS (Florida)
map (28° 40′N 80° 51′W) **8**:172
MIN LANGUAGE
Sino-Tibetan languages **17**:324
MINA (Nevada)
map (38° 24′N 118° 7′W) **14**:111
MINA AL-AHMADI (Kuwait)
map (29° 4′N 48° 8′E) **12**:141
MINAI
Islamic art and architecture **11**:296
MINAMATA BAY (Japan)
pollutants, chemical **15**:410
MINAMOTO (family)
Japan, history of **11**:367
Yoritomo **20**:330
MINANGKABAU **13**:436–437 *bibliog.*
MINARET **13**:437 *bibliog.*
Islamic art and architecture **11**:293
Persian art and architecture **15**:185–186
Qutb Minar **16**:28
Spanish art and architecture **18**:152
MINAS (Uruguay)
map (34° 23′S 55° 14′W) **19**:488
MINAS BASIN
map (45° 20′N 64° 0′W) **14**:269
MINAS DE ORO (Honduras)
map (14° 46′N 87° 20′W) **10**:218
MINAS GERAIS (Brazil)
map (18° 0′S 44° 0′W) **3**:460
MINATARE (Nebraska)
map (41° 48′N 103° 30′W) **14**:70
MINATITLÁN (Mexico)
map (17° 59′N 94° 31′W) **13**:357
MINCO (Oklahoma)
map (35° 19′N 97° 57′W) **14**:368
MIND *see* CONSCIOUSNESS, STATES OF
MIND CONTROL *see* BRAINWASHING
MINDANAO (Philippines) **13**:437
cities
Davao **6**:46
map (8° 0′N 125° 0′E) **15**:237
people
Tasaday **19**:41
MINDANAO SEA
map (9° 10′N 124° 25′E) **15**:237
MINDEL GLACIATION
Heidelberg man **10**:107
MINDÊLO
Cape Verde Islands **4**:121–122
MINDEN (Germany, East and West)
map (52° 17′N 8° 55′E) **9**:140
MINDEN (Louisiana)
map (32° 37′N 93° 17′W) **12**:430
MINDEN (Nebraska)
map (40° 30′N 98° 57′W) **14**:70
MINDEN (Nevada)
map (38° 57′N 119° 45′W) **14**:111
MINDENMINES (Missouri)
map (37° 28′N 94° 35′W) **13**:476
MINDORO ISLAND
map (12° 50′N 121° 5′E) **15**:237
MINDORO STRAIT
map (12° 20′N 120° 40′E) **15**:237
MINDSZENTY, JOZSEF **13**:437 *bibliog.*
right of asylum **16**:222
MINE (excavation for extraction of ores) *see* MINING AND QUARRYING
MINE (explosive) **13**:437–438 *bibliog., illus.*
Bushnell, David **3**:585
land mine **13**:438 *illus.*
mine sweeping **13**:438
naval vessels **14**:57 *illus.*
naval mine **13**:437–438 *illus.*
sonar **18**:62
weapons **20**:75
MINE HILL (New Jersey)
map (40° 53′N 74° 36′W) **14**:129
MINE WORKERS *see* UNITED MINE WORKERS OF AMERICA
MINEOLA (New York)
map (40° 45′N 73° 38′W) **14**:149
MINER (county in South Dakota)
map (44° 0′N 97° 37′W) **18**:103
MINERAL **13**:438–444 *bibliog., illus., table*
See also names of specific minerals, e.g., IRON; MAGNESIUM; etc.
alteration, mineral **1**:312
vein deposit **19**:536
anisotropic minerals
optical mineralogy **14**:409
biominerals
phosphate minerals **15**:256
uremia **19**:485
birthstones **3**:296
classes
arsenate minerals **2**:189; **13**:443 *table*
borate minerals **3**:396; **13**:443 *table*
carbonate minerals **4**:137; **13**:443 *table*
chromate minerals **4**:417; **13**:443 *table*
halide minerals **10**:21; **13**:443 *table*
molybdate minerals **13**:443 *table*
native elements **13**:443 *table*; **14**:47
nitrate minerals **13**:443 *table*; **14**:201–202
oxide minerals **13**:443 *table*; **14**:476
phosphate minerals **13**:443 *table*; **15**:255–256
silica minerals **13**:443 *table*; **17**:304
silicate minerals **13**:443 *table*; **17**:304–305
sulfate minerals **13**:443 *table*; **18**:333
sulfide minerals **13**:443 *table*; **18**:333–334
synthetic minerals **13**:442
telluride minerals **13**:443 *table*; **19**:91
tungstate minerals **13**:443 *table*
uranium minerals **13**:443 *table*; **19**:478
vanadate minerals **13**:443 *table*
classification **13**:442
Bergman, Sir Torbern **3**:210
Dana, James Dwight **6**:20
Werner, Abraham Gottlob **20**:104
clay minerals **5**:46–47
cleavage **5**:47
copper-bearing **5**:252 *table*
crystallography **13**:439–440 *illus.*
crystal systems **5**:375 *illus.*
dichroism **6**:156
double salt **6**:246
Earth sciences **7**:24
extraterrestrial minerals **13**:444
meteor and meteorite **13**:336–337
Moon **13**:562 *illus.*
foliation **8**:195
gems **9**:73–75
geochemistry **9**:96
geode **9**:97
geology **9**:105–106
groundwater, content **9**:374
hardness, mineral **10**:47
hexagonal system **10**:154–155
identification **13**:441–442
electron microprobe **13**:440
fluorescence, mineral **8**:186
index of refraction **13**:442
Joint Committee on Powder Diffraction Standards **13**:442
radiometric age-dating **16**:65–67
X-ray diffraction **13**:439; **13**:442; **20**:309
igneous rock **11**:33–36; **13**:442
isotropic minerals
isometric system **11**:299
luminescence **12**:458
luster **12**:468
marble **13**:144
metamorphic rock **13**:331–333; **13**:442–443
mineral water **13**:444
mineralogy
Agricola, Georgius **1**:188; **13**:439
chemical mineralogy **13**:440–441
Friedel, Georges **8**:331
history **13**:438–439
Joly, John **11**:441
optical mineralogy **14**:408–409
petrography **15**:206–207
related sciences **13**:444
Rosenbusch, Harry **16**:315
synthetic mineralogy **13**:442
mining and quarrying **13**:446; **13**:449
names **13**:443
International Mineralogical Association **13**:442
native elements **14**:47
occurrence **13**:442
ocean and sea **14**:332
oceanic mineral resources **14**:340–341
oceanic nutrients **14**:341
oceanography **14**:345–346
ore deposits **14**:422–426 *illus., map*
petrified wood **15**:204
petrology **15**:215
placer deposit **15**:325
professional and educational organizations
International Mineralogical Association **13**:442
pseudomorph **15**:587
Recent Epoch **16**:107
regolith **16**:129
salt dome **17**:38
schist **17**:123
Sea, Law of the **17**:167–168
sedimentary rock **13**:443; **17**:184–186
territorial waters **19**:121
variation
solid solution **18**:54
water quality **20**:51
MINERAL (county in Colorado)
map (37° 40′N 106° 55′W) **5**:116
MINERAL (county in Montana)
map (47° 8′N 114° 42′W) **13**:547
MINERAL (county in Nevada)
map (38° 30′N 118° 30′W) **14**:111
MINERAL (nutrition) *see* VITAMINS AND MINERALS
MINERAL (county in West Virginia)
map (39° 22′N 78° 55′W) **20**:111
MINERAL ACID **13**:444
MINERAL DEPOSITS *see* ORE DEPOSITS
MINERAL OIL **13**:444
MINERAL POINT (Wisconsin)
map (42° 52′N 90° 11′W) **20**:185
MINERAL SPRINGS (Arkansas)
map (33° 53′N 93° 55′W) **2**:166
MINERAL WATER **13**:444
epsom salts **7**:222
Vichy (France) **19**:571
MINERAL WELLS (Texas)
map (32° 48′N 98° 7′W) **19**:129
MINERALOCORTICOID *see* ALDOSTERONE
MINER'S LUNG *see* BLACK LUNG
MINERSVILLE (Pennsylvania)
map (40° 41′N 76° 16′W) **15**:147
MINERSVILLE (Utah)
map (38° 13′N 112° 55′W) **19**:492
MINERVA (mythology) **13**:444
MINERVA (Ohio)
map (40° 44′N 81° 6′W) **14**:357
MINES, BUREAU OF (U.S.)
Interior, United States Department of the **11**:210
MINESWEEPER
mine **13**:438
naval vessels **14**:57 *illus.*
MINET-EL-BEIDA *see* UGARIT
MINEVILLE (New York)
map (44° 5′N 73° 31′W) **14**:149
MING (dynasty) **13**:444 *bibliog.*
art
armchair **8**:374 *illus.*
bed **8**:374 *illus.*
Chinese art and architecture **4**:382; **4**:385–386 *illus.*
lacquer **12**:160 *illus.*
pottery and porcelain **15**:468 *illus.*
Tai Chin (Dai Jin) **19**:11
temple **19**:98
Tung Ch'i-ch'ang (Dong Qichang) **19**:333
Asia, history of **2**:256
China, history of **4**:372
Chinese literature **4**:390
Li Tzu-ch'eng (Li Zicheng) **12**:310
money **13**:526 *illus.*
MING HUANG *see* T'ANG HSÜAN-TSUNG (Tang Xuanzong)
MINGEI
folk art **8**:198
MINGO (American Indians)
Logan, John **12**:393
MINGO (county in West Virginia)
map (37° 40′N 82° 7′W) **20**:111
MINGO JUNCTION (Ohio)
map (40° 19′N 80° 37′W) **14**:357
MINGUS, CHARLES **13**:444
MINH MANG
Vietnam **19**:583
MINHO RIVER
map (41° 52′N 8° 51′W) **15**:449
MINIATURE PAINTING **13**:445 *bibliog., illus.*
Basawan **3**:101
Bihzad, Kamal al-Din **3**:250
Callot, Jacques **4**:47
Carriera, Rosalba **4**:168
Clouet (family) **5**:68–69
Cooper, Samuel **5**:244
Cosway, Richard **5**:303–304
English art and architecture **7**:184
Fontana, Lavinia **8**:206
Fouquet, Jean **8**:252
Fragonard, Jean Honoré **8**:259
Hilliard, Nicholas **10**:165
Holbein, Hans, the Younger **10**:200–201
Indian art and architecture **11**:97
Isabey, Jean Baptiste **11**:286
Islamic art and architecture **11**:297
Les Heures d'Étienne Chevalier **13**:274 *illus.*
Levnî, Ressam **12**:304–305
Limbourg brothers **12**:343
limners **12**:345
Lorenzo Monaco **12**:415
Malbone, Edward Greene **13**:86
Master Honoré **13**:215
Mogul art and architecture **13**:501–502 *illus.*
Morse, Samuel F. B. **13**:590
Oliver, Isaac **14**:379
Peale (family) **15**:124
Persian art and architecture **15**:185–186 *illus.*; **15**:186
Portrait of a Youth **7**:143 *illus.*
Sultan Muhammad **18**:338
MINIATURE PINSCHER **6**:217 *illus.*; **13**:445 *bibliog., illus.*
MINIBIKE
motorcycle **13**:612
MINICOMPUTER **13**:446 *bibliog.*
computer **5**:160c; **5**:160h
computer industry **5**:160o
computer languages **5**:160o
MINICOY ISLAND
Laccadive Islands (India) **12**:158
map (8° 17′N 73° 2′E) **11**:80
MINICYCLE *see* MOTORCYCLE
MINIDOKA (county in Idaho)
map (42° 50′N 113° 40′W) **11**:26
MINIER (Illinois)
map (40° 26′N 89° 19′W) **11**:42
MINIMAL ART **13**:446 *bibliog.*
Andre, Carl **1**:406
Anuszkiewicz, Richard **2**:72
Calder, Alexander **4**:25
Caro, Anthony **4**:159
drawing **6**:265
Flavin, Dan **8**:157
Held, Al **10**:110
Judd, Donald **11**:463
LeWitt, Sol **12**:308
Martin, Agnes Bernice **13**:179
modern art **13**:495
Morris, Robert (artist) **13**:588
Smith, Tony **17**:370–371
MINIMAL BRAIN DYSFUNCTION (MBD) *see* HYPERACTIVE CHILDREN
MINIMAX THEOREM
game theory **9**:27
MINIMUM WAGE **13**:446 *bibliog.*
employment and unemployment **7**:160
government regulation **9**:271
West Coast Hotel Company v. *Parrish* **20**:108
MINING AND QUARRYING **13**:446–450 *bibliog., illus.*
American Smelting and Refining Company
Guggenheim (family) **9**:392

MINING AND QUARRYING (cont.)
assay of ores **2**:264
California **4**:35–36
Canada **4**:77; **4**:79 *illus.*
chert and flint
Grimes Graves **9**:364–365
coal and coal mining **5**:75–79 *illus.*
common terms **13**:447
diamond **6**:152; **13**:449 *illus.*
drainage systems **6**:255
dynamite **6**:319
emerald **7**:154
equipment **13**:448–449
drilling **6**:273
earth-moving machinery **7**:23–24
European prehistory tools **7**:302 *illus.*
pump **15**:622–623
exploration
geochemistry **9**:97
felsite **8**:48
future trends **13**:449
geology, economic **9**:105
gold **9**:226–227
history **13**:446–447
Agricola, Georgius **1**:188
Comstock Lode **5**:167
engineering **7**:177
European prehistory **7**:303
frontier **8**:341–343 *map*
gold rush **9**:228
MacKay (family) **13**:27
Tabor, Horace W. **19**:5
technology, history of **19**:65
iron and steel industry **11**:273–274 *map*
marble **13**:144
mining
methods **13**:448
mine supports **13**:447–448
safety regulations **13**:449
surface mining **13**:448 *illus.*
underground mining **13**:447–448 *illus.*
ore deposits **14**:425–426
world distribution **14**:423 *map*
placer deposit **15**:325
quarrying
aggregate quarry mining **13**:449
methods **13**:449
surface mining **13**:449
Vermont **19**:557 *illus.*
safety lamp
Davy, Sir Humphry **6**:53–54
salt (sodium chloride) **17**:37
Hallstatt **10**:23
Sea, Law of the **17**:167–168
silver **17**:312
strip mining *see* STRIP MINING
sulfide minerals **18**:334
sulfur **18**:334–335
tar sands **19**:34
turquoise **19**:352
United Mine Workers of America **19**:411–412
vein deposit **19**:536
waste disposal systems **20**:46
MINIOTA (Manitoba)
map (50° 8′N 101° 0′W) **13**:119
MINISTRY, CHRISTIAN **13**:450 *bibliog., illus.*
apostolic succession **2**:85
bishop **3**:297
Blackwell, Antoinette Louisa Brown **3**:323
holy orders **10**:209
Middle Ages **13**:392–393
priest **15**:536
MINITARI *see* HIDATSA (American Indians)
MINIVET **13**:451
MINK **13**:451 *illus.*
fur **8**:370
MINKOWSKI, HERMANN **13**:451
Geometry of numbers **13**:451
MINKUS, LUDWIG **13**:451
MINNA (Nigeria)
map (9° 37′N 6° 33′E) **14**:190
MINNE, GEORGES **13**:451
MINNEAPOLIS (Kansas)
map (39° 8′N 97° 42′W) **12**:18
MINNEAPOLIS (Minnesota) **13**:451 *bibliog.*; **13**:454 *illus.*
climate **14**:228 *table*
Guthrie, Sir Tyrone **9**:409
map (44° 59′N 93° 13′W) **13**:453
MINNEDOSA (Manitoba)
map (50° 14′N 99° 51′W) **13**:119
MINNEHAHA (county in South Dakota)
map (43° 38′N 96° 47′W) **18**:103
MINNELLI, LIZA **13**:452 *bibliog., illus.*
MINNELLI, VINCENTE **13**:452 *bibliog.*
MINNEOLA (Kansas)
map (37° 26′N 100° 1′W) **12**:18
MINNEOTA (Minnesota)
map (44° 58′N 93° 12′W) **13**:453
MINNESINGERS *see* MINSTRELS, MINNESINGERS, AND TROUBADOURS
MINNESOTA **13**:452–457 *bibliog., illus., map*
agriculture **13**:455; **13**:457 *illus.*
cities
Duluth **6**:296
International Falls **11**:220
Minneapolis **13**:451
Rochester **16**:247
Saint Cloud **17**:17
Saint Paul **17**:24–25
climate **13**:454
economic activity **13**:455–456 *illus.*
education **13**:455
Carleton College **4**:151
St. Olaf College **17**:24
state universities of **13**:457–458
flag **13**:452 *illus.*
government and politics **13**:456
history **13**:456–457
Farmer-Labor party **8**:24
land and resources **13**:452–454 *map*
map (46° 0′N 94° 15′W) **19**:419
mining **13**:455–456 *illus.*
Mesabi Range **13**:314
people **13**:454–455
Sioux **17**:326
rivers, lakes, and waterways **13**:454
seal, state **13**:452 *illus.*
tourism **13**:455
vegetation and animal life **13**:454
MINNESOTA, STATE UNIVERSITIES OF **13**:457–458
mayo clinic **13**:248
Mayo (family) **13**:248
MINNESOTA LAKE (Minnesota)
map (43° 51′N 93° 50′W) **13**:453
MINNESOTA RIVER
map (44° 54′N 93° 10′W) **13**:453
MINNEWAUKAN (North Dakota)
map (48° 4′N 99° 15′W) **14**:248
MINNIE THE MOOCHER (song)
Calloway, Cab **4**:47
MINNOW **13**:458 *bibliog., illus.*
cave fish **4**:225
chub **4**:422
dace **6**:4
MINO DA FIESOLE **13**:458 *bibliog.*
MIÑO RIVER
map (41° 52′N 8° 51′W) **18**:140
MINOAN ART **13**:458–459 *bibliog., illus.*
Aegean civilization **1**:115–117 *illus.*
costume **5**:293 *illus.*
Evans, Sir Arthur **7**:312 *illus.*
gold and silver work **9**:228
jewelry **11**:409
Knossos **12**:101–102 *illus.*
mural painting **13**:646
Phaistos **15**:218
temple **19**:95
Thera **19**:160
MINOAN SCRIPTS *see* LINEAR B
MINOANS *see* AEGEAN CIVILIZATION; MINOAN ART
MINOCQUA (Wisconsin)
map (45° 52′N 89° 43′W) **20**:185
MINONG (Wisconsin)
map (46° 6′N 91° 49′W) **20**:185
MINONK (Illinois)
map (40° 54′N 89° 2′W) **11**:42
MINOR (law) **13**:459 *bibliog.*
children's rights **4**:354
MINOR ARTS *see* DECORATIVE ARTS
MINOR PLANET *see* ASTEROID
MINOR SCALE
scale (music) **17**:107
MINORCA (Spain) **13**:459
Balearic Islands **3**:36
map (40° 0′N 4° 0′E) **18**:140
MINORITIES *see* ETHNIC MINORITIES
MINORITY BUSINESS DEVELOPMENT AGENCY **13**:459
Commerce, U.S. Department of **5**:138
MINOS **13**:459
MINOS, PALACE OF
Knossos **12**:101–102 *illus.*
MINOT (North Dakota) **13**:459
map (48° 14′N 101° 18′W) **14**:248
MINOT, GEORGE **13**:460
MINOTAUR **13**:460
MINOW, NEWTON C.
radio and television broadcasting **16**:60
MINOWSKI, HERMANN
relativity **16**:134
MINQUA (American Indians) *see* SUSQUEHANNA (American Indians)
MINSHULL, ELIZABETH
Milton, John **13**:433
MINSK (USSR) **13**:460
Kurgan Slabi, World War II memorial **19**:392 *illus.*
Kurgan Slabi,World War II memorial **19**:392 *illus.*
map (53° 54′N 27° 34′E) **19**:388
MINSK MAZOWIECKI (Poland)
map (52° 11′N 21° 34′E) **15**:388
MINSTER (Ohio)
map (40° 24′N 84° 23′W) **14**:357
MINSTREL SHOWS
music hall, vaudeville, and burlesque **13**:671 *illus.*
ragtime **16**:70
MINSTRELS, MINNESINGERS, AND TROUBADOURS **13**:460 *bibliog., illus.*
Austrian literature **2**:354
Blondel de Nesle **3**:335
French music **8**:320
German literature **9**:132
Limousin (France) **12**:346–347
medieval music **13**:274–275
meistersinger **13**:283
music, history of Western **13**:662; **13**:665
Provençal literature **15**:583
Sachs, Hans **17**:7
song **18**:64
Tannhäuser **19**:24–25
vielle **19**:578
Walther von der Vogelweide **20**:20
MINT (botany) **13**:460–461 *illus.*
balm **3**:53
basil **3**:109
bee balm **3**:159
bells of Ireland **3**:192
bergamot **3**:209
betony **3**:232
bugleweed **3**:548
catnip **4**:212
coleus **5**:101
dittany **6**:202
germander **9**:135
hyssop **10**:352
lavender **12**:241
marjoram **13**:158
nettle **14**:104
patchouli **15**:109
pennyroyal **15**:153
peppermint **15**:157
rosemary **16**:314
Salvia **17**:40
savory **17**:101
skullcap **17**:346
spearmint **18**:165–166
MINTAGE **13**:461 *bibliog.*
United States
Rush, Benjamin **16**:347
Treasury, U.S. Department of the **19**:285
MINTAKA PASS
map (36° 58′N 74° 54′E) **15**:27
MINTO (Alaska)
map (64° 53′N 149° 11′W) **1**:242
MINTO (North Dakota)
map (48° 17′N 97° 15′W) **14**:248
MINTO (Yukon Territory)
map (62° 34′N 136° 51′W) **20**:345
MINTO, GILBERT ELLIOT, 4TH EARL OF **13**:461 *bibliog.*
Morley, John Morley, Viscount **13**:581
MINTOFF, DOMINIC **13**:461
MINTON WARE **13**:461 *bibliog.*
pottery and porcelain **15**:472
MINTONETTE *see* VOLLEYBALL
MINTURN (Colorado)
map (39° 35′N 106° 26′W) **5**:116
MINUET **6**:29 *illus.*; **13**:461 *bibliog.*
dance **6**:23–24 *illus.*
scherzo **17**:119
MINUF (Egypt)
map (30° 28′N 30° 56′E) **7**:76
MINUIT, PETER **13**:461 *bibliog.*
Manhattan (New York City) **13**:116
MINUTEMAN (statue) **13**:211 *illus.*
French, Daniel Chester **8**:302
MINUTEMAN MISSILE **13**:462
rockets and missiles **16**:254 *illus.*
Strategic Air Command **18**:289
MINUTEMEN **13**:462 *bibliog.*
militia **13**:422
statue **13**:211 *illus.*
MINYAS, TREASURY OF
Orchomenos **14**:420
MIO (Michigan)
map (44° 39′N 84° 8′W) **13**:377
MIOCENE EPOCH
geologic time **9**:104 *table*
Merychippus **10**:245 *illus.*
Tertiary Period **19**:123–125 *illus., table*
MIOGEOSYNCLINE
geosyncline **9**:119–120
MIPS (computer term) **5**:160h
MIQUELON
Saint Pierre and Miquelon (France) **17**:26
MIRABAI
women in society **20**:203
MIRABEAU, HONORÉ GABRIEL RIQUETI, COMTE DE **13**:462 *bibliog.*
MIRACLE **13**:462 *bibliog.*
MIRACLE PLAYS *see* MEDIEVAL DRAMA
MIRAGE (aircraft) **13**:462–463 *bibliog., illus.*
France aircraft development **13**:462–463
MIRAGE (atmospheric phenomenon) **13**:463
displaced image **13**:463
fata morgana **8**:34
light refraction **13**:463
meteorology **13**:341
MIRAMAR (Argentina)
map (38° 16′S 57° 51′W) **2**:149
MIRAMAR (New Zealand)
map (41° 19′S 174° 49′E) **14**:158
MIRANDA (satellite) **13**:463 *bibliog.*
Uranus (astronomy) **19**:478–479
MIRANDA, FRANCISCO DE **13**:463 *bibliog.*
Venezuela **19**:544
MIRANDA, FRANCISCO DE SÁ DE *see* SÁ DE MIRANDA, FRANCISCO DE
MIRANDA DE EBRO (Spain)
map (42° 41′N 2° 57′W) **18**:140
MIRANDA v. ARIZONA **13**:463 *bibliog.*
evidence **7**:317–318
MIRANDOLA, GIOVANNI, CONTE PICO DELLA *see* PICO DELLA MIRANDOLA, GIOVANNI, CONTE
MIRAVAL, RAIMON DE
minstrels, minnesingers, and troubadours **13**:460
MIRAVALLES VOLCANO
map (10° 45′N 85° 10′W) **5**:291
MIRBEAU, OCTAVE **13**:463 *bibliog.*
MIRIM LAGOON
map (32° 45′S 52° 50′W) **19**:488
MIRLITONS
musical instruments **13**:676
MIRÓ, JOAN **13**:463–464 *bibliog., illus.*
Personages and a Dog in Front of the Scene **13**:464 *illus.*
Spanish art and architecture **18**:156
surrealism (art) **18**:364–365
MIRÓN, SALVADOR DÍAZ *see* DÍAZ MIRÓN, SALVADOR
MIRPUR KHAS
map (25° 32′N 69° 0′E) **15**:27
MIRROR **13**:464–465 *bibliog., illus.*
image, optical **11**:50–51
magnetic mirror
magnetic bottle **13**:55
reflection **16**:119
telescope **19**:80–81
types
concave **13**:464–465 *illus.*
convex **13**:464–465 *illus.*
scientific and technical mirrors **13**:464
MIRROR IMAGE
stereochemistry **18**:258 *illus.*
MIRTÖÖN SEA
map (36° 51′N 23° 18′E) **9**:325
MIRV MISSILE **13**:465
MX missile **13**:688
Poseidon **15**:458
rockets and missiles **16**:255
strategic missiles **13**:465
MIRZA TAKI KAHN
Nasr al-Din Shah **14**:24
MISANTHROPE, THE (play) **13**:466
Molière **13**:509
MISCARRIAGE
abortion **1**:60
pregnancy and birth **15**:504
MISCHEL,WALTER
personality **15**:190
MISCOU CENTRE (New Brunswick)
map (47° 57′N 64° 34′W) **14**:117
MISDEMEANOR **13**:466
assault and battery **2**:264
larceny **12**:206
riot **16**:228
solicitation **18**:54
MISENHEIMER (North Carolina)
map (35° 29′N 80° 17′W) **14**:242
MISER, THE (play) **13**:466

MISÉRABLES, LES (book) **13**:466
Hugo, Victor **10**:294
MISERICORD **13**:466
MISHAWAKA (Indiana)
map (41° 40′N 86° 11′W) **11**:111
MISHICOT (Wisconsin)
map (44° 14′N 87° 38′W) **20**:185
MISHIMA YUKIO **13**:466 *bibliog.*
MISHMI HILLS
map (29° 0′N 96° 0′E) **19**:190
MISHNAH **13**:466 *bibliog.*
Akiba ben Joseph **1**:230
halachah **10**:17
Judah ha-Nasi **11**:458
Talmud **19**:17–18
Tiberias (Israel) **19**:189
MISIONES (province in Argentina)
map (27° 0′S 55° 0′W) **2**:149
MISKITO (American Indians) **13**:466 *bibliog.*
Mosquito Coast **13**:603
MISKOLC (Hungary) **13**:466–467
map (48° 6′N 20° 47′E) **10**:307
MISOGYNY
women in society **20**:201
MISPRISION **13**:467
MISRATA (Libya)
map (32° 23′N 15° 6′E) **12**:320
MISREPRESENTATION **13**:467
MISS AMERICA PAGEANT
Atlantic City (New Jersey) **2**:294
MISS JULIE (play) **13**:467
Strindberg, August **18**:299
MISS PIGGY
Muppets **13**:645 *illus.*
MISSAUKEE (county in Michigan)
map (44° 20′N 85° 5′W) **13**:377
MISSILES *see* ROCKETS AND MISSILES
MISSINAIBI RIVER
map (50° 44′N 81° 29′W) **14**:393
MISSION (Kansas)
map (39° 2′N 94° 39′W) **12**:18
MISSION (South Dakota)
map (43° 18′N 100° 40′W) **18**:103
MISSION CITY (British Columbia)
map (49° 8′N 122° 18′W) **3**:491
MISSION INDIANS *see* SPANISH MISSIONS
MISSION RANGE
map (47° 30′N 113° 55′W) **13**:547
MISSIONS, CHRISTIAN **13**:467–468 *bibliog., illus.*
Allouez, Claude Jean **1**:303
Baraga, Frederick **3**:74–75
Boniface, Saint **3**:379
Brainerd, David **3**:449
Bray, Thomas **3**:458–459
Carey, William **4**:147
Claver, Saint Peter **5**:45
Cyril and Methodius, Saints **5**:410
Damien, Father **6**:19
de Nobili, Roberto **6**:62
De Smet, Pierre Jean **6**:63
Flaget, Benedict Joseph **8**:149
Francis Xavier, Saint **8**:275
Franciscans **13**:467–468
Gallitzin, Demetrius Augustine **9**:20
Giovanni da Montecorvino **9**:188
Grenfell, Sir Wilfred **9**:359
Hawaii (state) **10**:76
Heckewelder, John Gottlieb Ernestus **10**:103–104
Jackson, Sheldon **11**:343
Jesuit Martyrs of North America **11**:402
Jesuits **11**:402; **13**:467–468
Judson, Adoniram **11**:464–465
Kenya **12**:56
Léger, Paul Émile **12**:274
Malabar Christians **13**:78
Marie de l'Incarnation **13**:151
Maryknoll Missioners **13**:187
Morrison, Robert **13**:589
Paul, Saint **15**:116–117
Ricci, Matteo **16**:207
Richard, Gabriel **16**:209
Schweitzer, Albert **17**:139–140
Serra, Junípero **17**:210
Spanish missions **18**:160–161 *illus.*
Uganda **19**:373
Williams, Eleazer **20**:159
Zeisberger, David **20**:358
MISSISQUOI BAY
map (45° 5′N 73° 10′W) **19**:554
MISSISQUOI RIVER
map (45° 0′N 73° 8′W) **19**:554
MISSISSAUGA (Ontario)
map (43° 35′N 79° 37′W) **14**:393; **19**:241
MISSISSINEWA LAKE
map (40° 42′N 85° 52′W) **11**:111
MISSISSINEWA RIVER
map (40° 46′N 86° 2′W) **11**:111
MISSISSIPPI **13**:468–473 *bibliog., illus., map*
agriculture **13**:470–472 *illus.*
cities
Biloxi **3**:256
Gulfport **9**:403–404
Jackson **11**:340
Meridian **13**:310
Natchez **14**:26
Vicksburg **19**:571
climate **13**:468
economic activity **13**:470–471 *illus.*
education **13**:470
state universities of **13**:473
fishing **13**:470–471 *illus.*
flag **13**:468 *illus.*
floods and flood control **8**:166 *illus.*
forestry **13**:471–472 *illus.*
government and politics **13**:471
historical sites **13**:470
history **13**:471–473
Davis, Jefferson **6**:51–52
land and resources **13**:468–469 *map*
manufacturing **13**:470
map (32° 50′N 89° 30′W) **19**:419
people **13**:468; **13**:470
rivers, lakes, and waterways **13**:468
Yazoo River **20**:320
seal, state **13**:468 *illus.*
transportation **13**:471
MISSISSIPPI (county in Arkansas)
map (35° 45′N 90° 6′W) **2**:166
MISSISSIPPI (county in Missouri)
map (36° 50′N 89° 15′W) **13**:476
MISSISSIPPI, STATE UNIVERSITIES OF **13**:473
MISSISSIPPI BUBBLE *see* MISSISSIPPI SCHEME
MISSISSIPPI DELTA **16**:233 *illus.*
map (29° 10′N 89° 15′W) **12**:430
MISSISSIPPI RIVER **12**:431 *illus.*; **13**:470 *illus.*; **13**:473–474 *bibliog., map*; **14**:229 *illus.*; **19**:424 *illus.*
exploration and development **13**:473–474
de Soto, Hernando **6**:63
Jolliet, Louis **11**:441
La Salle, Robert Cavelier, Sieur de **12**:149
flood control **13**:473
map (29° 0′N 89° 15′W) **13**:474
navigation and economic use **13**:473
Pontchartrain, Lake **15**:427
steamboat **18**:242 *illus.*
MISSISSIPPI SCHEME **13**:474 *bibliog.*
Law, John **12**:247
MISSISSIPPI SOUND
map (30° 15′N 88° 40′W) **13**:469
MISSISSIPPI SYSTEM OF INLAND WATERWAYS
canal **4**:97
MISSISSIPPI VALLEY
major ore deposits **14**:424–425 *table*
MISSISSIPPIAN CULTURE
Cahokia Mounds **4**:16
Mound Builders **13**:617–618
North American archaeology **14**:239
Spiro Mound **18**:189
MISSISSIPPIAN SYSTEM (geology)
Carboniferous Period **4**:137
MISSOULA (Montana) **13**:474
map (46° 52′N 114° 1′W) **13**:547
MISSOULA (county in Montana)
map (47° 0′N 113° 55′W) **13**:547
MISSOURI **13**:475–480 *bibliog., illus., map*
agriculture **13**:478–479 *illus.*
cities
Cape Girardeau **4**:120
Fulton **8**:358
Hannibal **10**:38
Independence **11**:78
Jefferson City **11**:393
Kansas City **12**:22 *illus.*
Saint Joseph **17**:20
St. Louis **17**:22–23 *illus.*
Springfield **18**:200
climate **13**:477
economic activity **13**:478
education **13**:477
Harris, William Torrey **10**:58
Saint Louis University **17**:23
state universities and colleges of **13**:480
Westminster College **20**:118
flag **13**:475 *illus.*
flower, state
hawthorn **10**:78
government and politics **13**:478–479
history **13**:479–480
Missouri Compromise **13**:480–481
land and resources **13**:475–477 *map*
map (38° 30′N 93° 30′W) **19**:419
mineral resources **13**:477
people **13**:477
rivers, lakes, and waterways **13**:477–478 *illus.*
seal, state **13**:475 *illus.*
vegetation and animal life **13**:477
MISSOURI (American Indians) **13**:480
Iowa (American Indians) **11**:248
MISSOURI (battleship)
World War II **20**:279–280 *illus.*
MISSOURI, STATE UNIVERSITIES AND COLLEGES OF **13**:480
MISSOURI COMPROMISE **13**:480 *bibliog.*
Civil War, U.S. **5**:16
Dred Scott v. *Sandford* **6**:268
Kansas-Nebraska Act **12**:22–23
MISSOURI ENABLING ACT
Missouri Compromise **13**:480–481
MISSOURI RIVER **13**:475 *illus.*; **13**:481 *illus.*; **14**:249 *illus.*
Arikara **2**:154
map (38° 50′N 90° 8′W) **13**:474
Mississippi River **13**:473
MISSOURI VALLEY (Iowa)
map (41° 33′N 95° 53′W) **11**:244
MIST **13**:481
MISTASSINI, LAKE
map (51° 0′N 73° 37′W) **16**:18
MR. SAMMLER'S PLANET (book)
Bellow, Saul **3**:190–191
MISTI VOLCANO
map (16° 18′S 71° 24′W) **15**:193
MISTLETOE **13**:481–482 *bibliog., illus.*
MISTRA (Greece) **13**:482 *bibliog.*
MISTRAL **13**:482
Mediterranean climate **13**:276
MISTRAL, FRÉDÉRIC **13**:482 *bibliog.*
MISTRAL, GABRIELA **13**:482 *bibliog.*
MRS. DALLOWAY (book)
Woolf, Virginia **20**:215
MITANNI **13**:482
Mesopotamia **13**:316
MITCHELL (county in Georgia)
map (31° 15′N 84° 10′W) **9**:114
MITCHELL (Indiana)
map (38° 44′N 86° 28′W) **11**:111
MITCHELL (county in Iowa)
map (43° 20′N 92° 45′W) **11**:244
MITCHELL (county in Kansas)
map (39° 25′N 98° 15′W) **12**:18
MITCHELL (Nebraska)
map (41° 57′N 103° 48′W) **14**:70
MITCHELL (county in North Carolina)
map (36° 0′N 82° 10′W) **14**:242
MITCHELL (Oregon)
map (44° 34′N 120° 9′W) **14**:427
MITCHELL (South Dakota)
map (43° 43′N 104° 1′W) **18**:103
MITCHELL (county in Texas)
map (32° 22′N 100° 52′W) **19**:129
MITCHELL, ARTHUR **13**:482 *bibliog.*
ballet **3**:45
Dance Theatre of Harlem **6**:30
MITCHELL, BILLY **13**:482–483 *bibliog.*
aircraft bombing **3**:373
World War I **20**:242
MITCHELL, CAMERON
Death of a Salesman **19**:150 *illus.*
MITCHELL, EDGAR D. **13**:482–483 *bibliog.*
Apollo program **2**:83
MITCHELL, JOAN **13**:483 *bibliog.*
MITCHELL, JOHN N. **13**:483 *bibliog.*
Watergate **20**:64
MITCHELL, JONI **13**:483 *bibliog.*
MITCHELL, MARGARET **13**:483 *bibliog.*
Gone with the Wind **9**:243
MITCHELL, MARIA **13**:483 *bibliog.*
MITCHELL, MOUNT **13**:483; **14**:243 *illus.*
map (35° 46′N 82° 16′W) **14**:242
MITCHELL, PETER **13**:483
MITCHELL, S. WEIR **13**:483 *bibliog.*
MITCHELL, WESLEY CLAIR **13**:483–484 *bibliog.*
MITCHELLVILLE (Iowa)
map (41° 40′N 93° 22′W) **11**:244
MITE **13**:484 *bibliog., illus.*
arachnid **2**:106–107 *illus.*
chigger **4**:347
diseases, animal **6**:192
skin diseases **17**:342
soil organisms **18**:39 *illus.*
MITFORD (family) **13**:484 *bibliog.*
MITFORD, NANCY
Mitford (family) **13**:484
MITHRA (ancient deity)
Mithraism **13**:484–485
MITHRADATES I
Arsacids **2**:189
MITHRADATES II
Arsacids **2**:189
MITHRADATES VI, KING OF PONTUS (Mithradates the Great) **13**:484 *bibliog.*
MITHRAISM **13**:484–485 *bibliog.*
MITILINI (Greece)
map (39° 6′N 26° 32′E) **9**:325
MITLA (Mexico) **13**:485 *bibliog.*; **14**:237 *map*
Zapotec **20**:356
MITO (Japan)
map (36° 22′N 140° 28′E) **11**:361
MITOCHONDRION **13**:485
cell **4**:232 *illus.*; **4**:233
cytochrome **5**:411 *illus.*
genetics **9**:89–90
MITOSIS **13**:485
cell **4**:234 *illus.*
development **6**:137
genetics **9**:89
growth **9**:378
MITRE, BARTOLOMÉ **13**:485 *bibliog.*
MITROPOULOS, DIMITRI **13**:485 *bibliog.*
MITSCHERLICH, EILHARD **13**:485 *bibliog.*
MITSUBISHI A6M-ZERO-SEN
Zero (aircraft) **20**:361 *illus.*
MITTEN CRAB **5**:324 *illus.*
MITTERRAND, FRANÇOIS **13**:485–486 *bibliog., illus.*
France **8**:265
France, history of **8**:273
socialism **18**:23
MITÚ (Colombia)
map (1° 8′N 70° 3′W) **5**:107
MITUMBA MOUNTAINS
map (6° 0′S 29° 0′E) **20**:350
MIX, TOM **13**:486 *bibliog.*
MIXED ECONOMY **13**:486 *bibliog.*
economic planning **7**:47
MIXED NERVE
peripheral nervous system **15**:171
MIXTEC (American Indians) **13**:486 *bibliog.*
Caso, Alfonso **4**:182
Codex Zouche-Nuttall **15**:498 *illus.*
mask **13**:197 *illus.*
Mitla **13**:485
Monte Albán **13**:552
pre-Columbian art and architecture **15**:499
Zapotec **20**:356
MIXTURE (chemistry)
compound, chemical **5**:158
MIYAKONOJO (Japan)
map (31° 44′N 131° 4′E) **11**:361
MIYAMOTO MUSASHI *see* NITEN
MIZEN HEAD
map (51° 27′N 9° 49′W) **11**:258
MIZOGUCHI, KENJI **13**:486 *bibliog.*
MIZORAM (India) **13**:486
map (23° 30′N 93° 0′E) **11**:80
MIZQUE (Bolivia)
map (17° 56′S 65° 19′W) **3**:366
MJØSA LAKE
map (60° 40′N 11° 0′E) **14**:261
MKS (meter-kilogram-second) UNITS
units, physical **19**:466 *table*
MLADÁ BOLESLAV (Czechoslovakia)
map (50° 23′N 14° 59′E) **5**:413
MLADENOVAC (Yugoslavia)
map (44° 26′N 20° 42′E) **20**:340
MLJET ISLAND
map (42° 45′N 17° 30′E) **20**:340
MMBATHO
Bophuthatswana **3**:395
MMR (vaccine)
diseases, childhood **6**:193
MNAJDRA (temple) **19**:94 *illus.*
MNEMON *see* ARTAXERXES II, KING OF PERSIA
MNEMONICS *see* MEMORY
MNEMOSYNE **13**:486
MNESICLES **13**:486
MO (Norway)
map (66° 15′N 14° 8′E) **14**:261
MO-NO-MA-HA, MOUNT
map (36° 5′N 89° 40′E) **19**:190
MOA (bird) **13**:486–487 *illus.*
MOA RIVER
map (6° 59′N 11° 36′W) **17**:296
MOAB (ancient kingdom) **13**:487 *bibliog.*
MOAB (Utah)
map (38° 35′N 109° 33′W) **19**:492
MOBAYE (Central African Republic)
map (4° 19′N 21° 11′E) **4**:251
MOBERG, VILHELM **13**:487
MOBERLY (Missouri)
map (39° 25′N 92° 26′W) **13**:476
MOBIL OIL CORPORATION
advertising **1**:114
MOBILE (Alabama) **1**:237 *illus.*; **13**:487
map (30° 42′N 88° 5′W) **1**:234
MOBILE (county in Alabama)
map (30° 50′N 88° 15′W) **1**:234
MOBILE (art) **13**:487 *bibliog.*

MOBILE (cont.)
Calder, Alexander **4**:25
kinetic art **12**:78
MOBILE BAY
map (30° 25′N 88° 0′W) **1**:234
MOBILE BAY, BATTLE OF **5**:22 *illus.*
Farragut, David Glasgow **8**:29
MOBILE HOME **13**:487–488 *bibliog.*
camping **4**:67
housing **10**:277–278; **10**:279
prefabrication **15**:502
MOBILE RIVER **13**:488
map (30° 40′N 88° 2′W) **1**:234
MÖBIUS, AUGUST FERDINAND **13**:488
mathematics, history of **13**:226
Möbius strip **13**:488
MÖBIUS STRIP **13**:488 *bibliog., illus.*
topology **19**:237
MOBRIDGE (South Dakota)
map (45° 32′N 100° 26′W) **18**:103
MOBUTU SESE SEKO **13**:488 *bibliog.*
Zaire **20**:352
MOBY-DICK (book) **13**:488 *bibliog.*
Melville, Herman **13**:289–290
MOCAMBIQUE (Mozambique)
map (15° 3′S 40° 42′E) **13**:627
MOCCASIN (foot covering) **13**:488 *bibliog.*
MOCCASIN (zoology)
water moccasin **20**:49
MOCHE *see* MOCHICA
MOCHICA **13**:488 *bibliog.*
pre-Columbian art and architecture **15**:500
Vicús **19**:576
MOCHUDI (Botswana)
map (24° 28′S 26° 5′E) **3**:416
MOCK EPIC **13**:489 *bibliog.*
Fielding, Henry
Tom Jones **19**:229
Heine, Heinrich
Atta Troll **10**:109
Pope, Alexander **15**:430
Rape of the Lock, The **16**:88
MOCK ORANGE **13**:489 *illus.*
Osage orange **14**:452
MOCKEL, ALBERT
Belgian literature **3**:175
MOCKINGBIRD **13**:489 *illus.*
MOCKSVILLE (North Carolina)
map (35° 54′N 80° 34′W) **14**:242
MÔCO, MOUNT
map (12° 28′S 15° 10′E) **2**:5
MOCORITO (Mexico)
map (25° 29′N 107° 55′W) **13**:357
MOCTEZUMA (Mexico)
map (29° 48′N 109° 42′W) **13**:357
MODE (mathematics) **13**:489
MODE (music) **13**:489 *bibliog.*
Arabian music **2**:99–100
music, non-Western **13**:667
MODE 1925, LA *see* ART DECO
MODEL (mathematics)
computer modeling **5**:162
industrial management **11**:156–157
management science **13**:107
operations research **14**:403
systems engineering **18**:415
MODEL (sociology)
social psychology **18**:13
social structure and organization **18**:16
MODEL T (automobile) **2**:365 *illus.*; **13**:490 *bibliog., illus.*
automotive industry **2**:363–364
Ford (family) **8**:220–221
MODELING, COMPUTER *see* COMPUTER MODELING
MODEM **13**:490
computer **5**:160h
MODENA (Italy) **13**:490
Este (family) **7**:246
Italian city-state **11**:328 *map*
Italian unification **11**:330 *map*
map (44° 40′N 10° 55′E) **11**:321
MODERN ARCHITECTURE **13**:490–493 *bibliog., illus.*
architecture **2**:136–137
Art Deco **2**:207–208
Art Nouveau **2**:209–212
Austria
Loos, Adolf **12**:411
Wagner, Otto **20**:4
brutalism **3**:528
cathedrals and churches **4**:208
Finland
Aalto, Alvar **1**:49–50
Saarinen, Eliel **17**:4
fountains **8**:252
France
Beaubourg **3**:145
Le Corbusier **13**:491
functionalism (design) **8**:360
Germany
Bauhaus **3**:129–130; **13**:490–491
Behrens, Peter **3**:171
German art and architecture **9**:128
Gropius, Walter **9**:369
Mies van der Rohe, Ludwig **13**:415
Moholy-Nagy, László **13**:503
Great Britain
Crystal Palace **5**:376
International Style (Bauhaus art) **11**:222–223
Latin American art and architecture **12**:228
Le Corbusier **12**:253–254
neoplasticism and constructivism **13**:491
Netherlands
Berlage, Hendrik Petrus **3**:214
de Stijl (periodical) **6**:63–64
Rietveld, Gerrit Thomas **16**:219
opera houses **14**:402
postmodern architecture **15**:463–464
Russia
constructivism **5**:224
Spain
Gaudí, Antonio **9**:59
Team X **13**:493
United States
American art and architecture **1**:330
Belluschi, Pietro **3**:192
Breuer, Marcel **3**:475
Bunshaft, Gordon **3**:564
Burnham, Daniel Hudson **3**:577
Chicago school of architecture **4**:342–343
Fuller, R. Buckminster **8**:357–358
Giurgola, Romaldo **9**:192
Goff, Bruce Alonzo **9**:224
Hejduk, John **10**:110
Hitchcock, Henry-Russell **10**:186
Johnson, Philip **11**:434–435
Kahn, Louis **12**:6
Moholy-Nagy, László **13**:503
Saarinen, Eero **17**:4
Skidmore, Owings, and Merrill **17**:337
Wright, Frank Lloyd **20**:288–289
MODERN ART **2**:198–202; **13**:493–496 *bibliog., illus.*
See also names of specific artists, e.g., CHRISTO; VASARELY, VICTOR; etc.
abstract art **1**:63–65
abstract expressionism **1**:65–66
Armory Show **2**:177
Art Deco **2**:207–208
Art Nouveau **2**:209–212
Austrian art and architecture **2**:353
Barr, Alfred H., Jr. **3**:92
Bauhaus **3**:129–130
Blaue Reiter, Der **3**:328
Canadian art and architecture **4**:90–91
CoBrA (artists' group) **5**:84
color-field painting **5**:114
conceptual art **5**:170
constructivism **5**:224
cubism **5**:380–381
Dada **6**:4–5
de Stijl (periodical) **6**:63–64
earthworks **7**:28
English art and architecture **7**:188
environmental art **7**:209–210
expressionism (art) **7**:340
French art and architecture **8**:308
futurism **8**:383–384
graphic arts **9**:293–294
Guggenheim Museum **9**:393
happenings **10**:41
hard-edge painting **10**:45
Hirshhorn Museum and Sculpture Garden **10**:176
interior design **11**:214
Japanese art and architecture **11**:378
minimal art **13**:446; **13**:495
Museum of Modern Art **13**:657
museums, art **13**:657
neoexpressionism **14**:83
op art **14**:397
origins of contemporary art **13**:493–494
orphism **14**:448
painting **15**:22–23
photorealism **15**:274–275
pop art **15**:429
Read, Sir Herbert **16**:100
Scandinavian art and architecture **17**:114
sculpture **17**:165–166 *illus.*
Spanish art and architecture **18**:154–156
suprematism **18**:354
surrealism (art) **18**:364–366
Tate Gallery, The **19**:44
vorticism **19**:635
MODERN CLASSICAL MUSIC
See also AVANT-GARDE
aleatory music **1**:270
Antheil, George **2**:48–49
atonality **2**:312
Babbitt, Milton **3**:5–6
Barber, Samuel **3**:77
Bartók, Béla **3**:97–98
Berg, Alban **3**:208–209
Bernstein, Leonard **3**:224
Boulez, Pierre **3**:421–422
Cage, John **4**:15
Copland, Aaron **5**:250–251
Cowell, Henry **5**:321
Crumb, George **5**:366
Dello Joio, Norman **6**:94
English music **7**:203–204
French music **8**:321
German and Austrian music **9**:131
Gershwin, George and Ira **9**:158–159
Glass, Philip **9**:201
Harris, Roy **10**:58
Hindemith, Paul **10**:168
Holst, Gustav **10**:208
Italian music **11**:319
Ives, Charles Edward **11**:334
jazz **11**:389–390
Jolas, Betsy **11**:441
Jolivet, André **11**:441
Krenek, Ernst **12**:129
Lutyens, Elisabeth **12**:471
Maconchy, Elizabeth **13**:35–36
music, history of Western **13**:666–667
Nono, Luigi **14**:216–217
Penderecki, Krzysztof **15**:142
Poulenc, Francis **15**:473
Russian music **16**:369
Satie, Erik **17**:87–88
Schoenberg, Arnold **17**:130
Schuller, Gunther **17**:136
serial music **17**:208
Sessions, Roger **17**:213
Shostakovich, Dmitry **17**:285
sonata **18**:63
Spanish music **18**:162
Stravinsky, Igor **18**:295
symphony **18**:405
Vaughan Williams, Ralph **19**:528–529
Walton, Sir William **20**:20–21
Webern, Anton von **20**:88
Wolpe, Stefan **20**:199
Xenakis, Yannis **20**:311
MODERN DANCE **13**:496–498 *bibliog., illus.*
Ailey, Alvin **1**:202–203
Arpino, Gerald **2**:187
Butler, John **3**:591
Cunningham, Merce **5**:390
dance **6**:28
Denishawn **6**:108
Duncan, Isadora **6**:299
eurhythmics **7**:265–266
Falco, Louis **8**:12
Graham, Martha **9**:280
Hawkins, Erick **10**:77
Holm, Hanya **10**:204–205
Horton, Lester **10**:255
Humphrey, Doris **10**:303
Jacob's Pillow Dance Festival **11**:346
Limón, José **12**:346
Lubovitch, Lar **12**:447
Netherlands Dance Theater **14**:103
Nikolais, Alwin **14**:195
Rainer, Yvonne **16**:78
St. Denis, Ruth **17**:17–18
Shawn, Ted **17**:246
Sokolow, Anna **18**:39
Taylor, Paul **19**:49–50
Weidman, Charles **20**:91
Wigman, Mary **20**:147
MODERN JAZZ QUARTET **13**:498
MODERN MATHEMATICS *see* MATHEMATICS, NEW
MODERN MUSIC *see* COMPUTER MUSIC; DISCO MUSIC; ELECTRONIC MUSIC; MODERN CLASSICAL MUSIC; ROCK MUSIC
MODERNISM (theology) **13**:498 *bibliog.*
Blondel, Maurice **3**:335
Hügel, Friedrich, Baron von **10**:291–292
Loisy, Alfred Firmin **12**:398
Pius X, Pope **15**:323
Tyrrell, George **19**:368
MODERNISM, LITERARY *see* LITERARY MODERNISM
MODERNISM, SPANISH (literature)
Darío, Rubén **6**:37–38
Latin American literature **12**:229
Martí, José **13**:176
Silva, José Asunción **17**:312
Spanish literature **18**:159
MODERSOHN-BECKER, PAULA **13**:498–499 *bibliog., illus.*
Old Peasant Woman in the Garden **13**:498 *illus.*
MODEST PROPOSAL, A (book) **13**:499
MODESTO (California)
map (37° 39′N 120° 60′W) **4**:31
MODICA (Italy)
map (36° 51′N 14° 47′E) **11**:321
MODIGLIANI, AMEDEO **13**:499 *bibliog., illus.*
female nude **13**:499 *illus.*
Seated Nude **11**:314 *illus.*
Soutine, Chaim **18**:113
MÖDLING (Austria)
map (48° 5′N 16° 17′E) **2**:348
MODOC (American Indians) **13**:499 *bibliog.*
Kintpuash **12**:86
MODOC (county in California)
map (41° 35′N 120° 45′W) **4**:31
MODOC WAR **11**:109 *map*
MODULAR CONSTRUCTION
shipbuilding **17**:276
MODULATION **13**:499–500 *bibliog., illus.*
amplitude modulation **1**:383; **13**:500
frequency modulation **8**:327; **13**:500
pulse (electronics) **15**:621
pulse code modulation (PCM)
sound recording and reproduction **18**:76
radio **16**:45
signal variation **13**:500
telecommunications **19**:75–76
transmitter **19**:276
wave variation **13**:500
MOE (Australia)
map (38° 10′S 146° 15′E) **2**:328
MOE, JØRGEN ENGEBRETSEN **13**:500
MOENGO (Suriname)
map (5° 37′N 54° 24′W) **18**:364
MOENKOPI (Arizona)
map (36° 7′N 111° 13′W) **2**:160
MOERITHERIUM **7**:134 *illus.*
MOFFAT (county in Colorado)
map (40° 40′N 108° 10′W) **5**:116
MOFFIT (North Dakota)
map (46° 41′N 100° 18′W) **14**:248
MOFOLO, THOMAS **13**:500 *bibliog.*
MOGADISHU (Somalia) **13**:500; **18**:60–61 *illus., table*
map (2° 1′N 45° 20′E) **18**:60
MOGADON
sedative **17**:182
MOGAUNG (Burma)
map (25° 18′N 96° 56′E) **3**:573
MOGOLLON CULTURE (American Indians) **11**:124 *map*
Anasazi **1**:392–393
MOGOTON, MOUNT
map (13° 45′N 86° 23′W) **14**:179
MOGUL ART AND ARCHITECTURE **13**:500–502 *bibliog., illus.*
architecture **13**:500–501
Basawan **3**:101
Fatehpur Sikri **8**:34
Humayun, Mogul Emperor of India **10**:300
Indian art and architecture **11**:97
Islamic art and architecture **11**:297
Mansur **13**:129
painting **13**:502–503
Qutb Minar **16**:28
Shah Jahan, Mogul Emperor of India **17**:235
Taj Mahal **19**:14–15
tomb **19**:231
MOGULS (dynasty) **13**:502 *bibliog.*
Akbar **1**:229–230
Aurangzeb, Mogul Emperor of India **2**:324
Babur, Mogul Emperor **3**:7
Humayun, Mogul Emperor of India **10**:300
India, history of **11**:90–91 *map*
Islam **11**:290
Mogul art and architecture **13**:500–502 *illus.*
Shah Jahan, Mogul Emperor **17**:235
MOHAIR
angora **2**:6
MOHALL (North Dakota)
map (48° 46′N 101° 31′W) **14**:248
MOHAMMED SHAH, SULTAN SIR
Aga Khan **1**:181
MOHAMMEDANISM *see* ISLAM

MOHAMMEDIA (Morocco)
map (33° 44′N 7° 24′W) **13**:585
MOHAVE (American Indians) *see* MOJAVE (American Indians)
MOHAVE (county in Arizona)
map (35° 30′N 113° 55′W) **2**:160
MOHAVE, LAKE
map (35° 25′N 114° 38′W) **2**:160
MOHAVE DESERT *see* MOJAVE DESERT
MOHAWK (American Indians) **13**:502 *bibliog.*
Brant, Joseph **3**:455
Hiawatha **10**:156
Iroquois League **11**:279–280
Jogues, Saint Isaac **11**:422
Johnson, Emily Pauline **11**:432
Mahican **13**:64
MOHAWK MOUNTAIN
map (41° 49′N 73° 17′W) **5**:193
MOHAWK PRINCESS *see* JOHNSON, EMILY PAULINE
MOHAWK RIVER **13**:502
map (42° 47′N 73° 42′W) **14**:149
MOHEGAN (American Indians) **13**:503 *bibliog.*
Miantonomo **13**:370
Pequot **15**:158
Uncas **19**:381
MOHELI ISLAND
Comoros **5**:153–154 *map*
map (12° 15′S 43° 45′E) **5**:153
MOHENJO-DARO **11**:153–154 *illus., map*
Asia, history of **2**:250
bust found at **2**:250 *illus.*
MOHICAN (American Indians) *see* MAHICAN (American Indians)
MOHICAN RIVER
map (40° 22′N 82° 9′W) **14**:357
MOHICANVILLE RESERVOIR
map (40° 45′N 82° 0′W) **14**:357
MOHL, HUGO VON **13**:503
photosynthesis **15**:276
MOHNS RIDGE
plate tectonics **15**:351 *map*
MOHO DISCONTINUITY *see* MOHOROVIČIĆ DISCONTINUITY
MOHOLE PROJECT **13**:503
Deep-Sea Drilling Project **6**:77
mantle **13**:130
MOHOLY-NAGY, LÁSZLÓ **13**:503 *bibliog., illus.*
Bauhaus **3**:129–130 *illus.*
Construction VII **13**:503 *illus.*
kinetic art **12**:78
MOHOROVIČIĆ DISCONTINUITY **13**:503 *bibliog.*
basement rock **3**:108
Earth, crust and mantle layer **13**:503
Earth, structure and composition of **7**:20–21
mantle **13**:130
Mohole Project **13**:503
MOHS SCALE *see* HARDNESS, MINERAL
MOI (people) *see* MONTAGNARDS
MOI, DANIEL ARAP **13**:504 *illus.*
MOIETY **13**:504
MOILLON, LOUISE **13**:504 *bibliog.*
MOINGWENA (American Indians)
Illinois **11**:45
MOIRAI *see* FATES
MOIRÉ
taffeta **19**:7
MOISEIWITSCH, TANYA **13**:504
MOISEYEV, IGOR ALEKSANDROVICH **13**:504
MOISIE RIVER
map (50° 12′N 66° 4′W) **16**:18
MOISSAN, HENRI **13**:504
MOIVRE, ABRAHAM DE *see* DE MOIVRE, ABRAHAM
MOJARRA **13**:504
MOJAVE (American Indians) **13**:504–505 *bibliog.*
MOJAVE (California)
map (35° 3′N 118° 10′W) **4**:31
MOJAVE DESERT **6**:126; **13**:505 *bibliog.*
map (35° 0′N 117° 0′W) **4**:31
MOKAPU PENINSULA
map (21° 27′N 157° 45′W) **10**:72
MOKAPU POINT
map (21° 28′N 157° 43′W) **10**:72
MOKPO (Korea)
map (34° 48′N 126° 22′E) **12**:113
MOL (Belgium)
map (51° 11′N 5° 6′E) **3**:177
MOLA (fish)
ocean sunfish **14**:332
MOLA, EMILIO **18**:149 *illus.*
MOLALITY (chemistry)
concentration **5**:168
MOLALLA (Oregon)
map (45° 9′N 122° 35′W) **14**:427
MOLARITY (chemistry)
concentration **5**:168
MOLARS
teeth **19**:70–71 *illus.*
MOLASSE **13**:505 *bibliog.*
MOLASSES **13**:505
rum **16**:344
sugar production **18**:328–330
MOLASSES ACT **13**:505
MOLAY, JACQUES DE **19**:93 *illus.*
MOLDAVIA **13**:505
Cuza, Alexandru Ion **5**:399
history
Michael the Brave **13**:372
Stephen the Great, Prince **18**:254
Romania **16**:290
MOLDAVIAN SOVIET SOCIALIST REPUBLIC (USSR) **13**:505–506
Bessarabia **3**:228
cities
Kishinev **12**:90
MOLDING
injection molding **15**:349 *illus.*
MOLDOVEANU, MOUNT
map (45° 36′N 24° 44′E) **16**:288
MOLDS **13**:506 *bibliog., illus.*
antibiotics **2**:57
bread mold **13**:506
Rhizopus **16**:197
conditions for growth **13**:506
fermentation **8**:55
fungi **8**:366; **13**:506
green mold **13**:506 *illus.*
mildew **13**:419
Neurospora **14**:107
penicillin **15**:144 *illus.*
slime mold **17**:362
water mold **20**:49
MOLE (animal) **13**:506–507 *bibliog., illus.*
burrow **13**:506–507 *illus.*
classification, biological **13**:506–507
desman **6**:132
feet **13**:102 *illus.*
marsupial mole **13**:174; **13**:175 *illus.*; **13**:507
soil organisms **18**:39 *illus.*
star-nosed mole **13**:100 *illus.*
MOLE (birthmark) **13**:507
MOLE (unit of substance) **13**:507
concentration **5**:168–169
stoichiometry **18**:277
units, physical **19**:466–467 *table*
MOLE SNAKE *see* KING SNAKE
MOLECH **13**:507
MOLECULAR BIOLOGY
biology **3**:268; **3**:271
genetic code **9**:79–82
MOLECULAR WEIGHT **13**:507
See also ATOMIC WEIGHT
Avogadro, Amedeo **2**:377
Avogadro number **2**:377
determination
osmosis **14**:455
molecule **13**:508
Staudinger, Hermann **18**:239
ultracentrifuge
Svedberg, Theodor **18**:374
Wurtz, Charles Adolphe **20**:297
MOLECULE **13**:507–508 *bibliog., illus.*
angstrom **2**:7
anion **2**:29
arrangement
liquid crystal **12**:365
stereochemistry **18**:258–259
chemical bond **4**:313–315
chemical compound **13**:507
chemical symbolism and notation **4**:321–322
colloidal particle
Perrin, Jean Baptiste **15**:178
compound, chemical **5**:158
configuration **5**:178
conformational analysis
Hassel, Odd **10**:67
diffusion **6**:170
electrochemical equivalent **7**:112
force
cohesion **5**:96
intermolecular forces **11**:215; **13**:508
free radical **8**:294
interstellar matter **11**:226
ion and ionization **11**:239–240
isomers **13**:508
stereoisomer **13**:508
structural isomer **13**:508
kinetic theory of matter **12**:78–79 *illus.*
macromolecule **13**:36–37
measurement
mass spectrometry **13**:204
molecular structure **13**:508
chemical symbolism and notation **4**:322
Debye, Peter **6**:72
exclusion principle **7**:250
organic chemistry **14**:438
spectroscopy **18**:170–172
molecular weight **13**:507
monomer **13**:537
nucleic acid **14**:288–291
virus **19**:613–616
optical activity **14**:408
photochemistry **15**:257–259
protein
enzyme **7**:213–214 *illus.*
protein molecule
enzyme **7**:212–215
quantitative chemical analysis **13**:508
resonance (chemistry) **16**:177–178
synthesis
stereochemistry **18**:259
Woodward, Robert Burns **20**:213
MOLENAER, JAN
Leyster, Judith **12**:309
MOLEPOLOLE (Botswana)
map (24° 25′S 25° 30′E) **3**:416
MOLEY, RAYMOND
Roosevelt, Franklin Delano **16**:308
MOLIÈRE **1**:86–87 *illus.*; **8**:316 *illus.*; **13**:508–509 *bibliog., illus.*
Béjart, Madeleine **3**:172
Bourgeois Gentleman, The **3**:424
Charpentier, Marc Antoine **4**:299
comedy **5**:132
drama **6**:259
Lully, Jean Baptiste **12**:454
Misanthrope, The **13**:466
Miser, The **13**:466
Tartuffe **19**:41
theater, history of the **19**:147 *illus.*
MOLINA, LUIS DE **13**:509 *bibliog.*
MOLINA, TIRSO DE *see* TIRSO DE MOLINA
MOLINE (Illinois)
map (41° 30′N 90° 31′W) **11**:42
MOLINE (Kansas)
map (37° 22′N 96° 18′W) **12**:18
MOLINO (Florida)
map (30° 43′N 87° 20′W) **8**:172
MOLINOS, MIGUEL DE **13**:509 *bibliog.*
quietism **16**:26
MOLISE (Italy) **13**:509
MOLL FLANDERS (book) **13**:509–510 *bibliog.*
Defoe, Daniel **6**:83–84
MOLLENDO (Peru)
map (17° 2′S 72° 1′W) **15**:193
MOLLET, GUY **13**:510
MOLLUSK **13**:510–512 *bibliog., illus.*; **15**:35 *illus.*
anatomy **13**:510–511
bivalve **3**:301; **13**:510–511 *illus.*; **17**:252 *illus.*
Cephalopoda **4**:256; **13**:511–512 *illus.*
chiton **4**:398–399; **13**:511 *illus.*
clam **5**:35–36
classification, biological **13**:511–512
cockle **5**:87
conch **5**:170
cowrie **5**:322
cuttlefish **5**:398
fossil record
ammonite **1**:372–373
Deshayes, Gerard Paul **6**:131
Ordovician Period **14**:422 *illus.*
Silurian Period **17**:310 *illus.*
Triassic Period **19**:293 *illus.*
gastropod **9**:57–58 *illus.*
Gastropoda **13**:510–512 *illus.*
intertidal life **11**:229 *illus.*
invertebrate **11**:235
limpet **12**:347
mother-of-pearl **13**:607
mussel **13**:683–684
nautiloid **14**:52
nautilus **14**:52–53
octopus **14**:348
oyster **14**:479
pearls and pearling **15**:126–128
piddock **15**:294
scallop **17**:107
shell **13**:510–512 *illus.*; **17**:250–252 *illus.*
shellfish **17**:254–255 *illus.*
shipworm **17**:277
slug **17**:364
snail **17**:375–376
squid **18**:203–204
territoriality **19**:121
tusk shell **13**:511–512 *illus.*; **19**:355
univalve **17**:252 *illus.*
whelk **20**:130
MOLLY (fish) **13**:512
guppy **9**:406
MOLLY MAGUIRES **13**:512 *bibliog.*
MOLLY PITCHER **13**:512
MOLNÁR, FERENC **13**:512 *bibliog.*
MOLNIYA **13**:512
communications satellite **5**:145
MOLOCH *see* MOLECH
MOLOKAI (Hawaii)
Hawaii (state) **10**:73
map (21° 7′N 157° 0′W) **10**:72
MOLOPO RIVER
map (28° 30′S 20° 13′E) **18**:79
MOLOTOV (USSR) *see* PERM (USSR)
MOLOTOV, VYACHESLAV MIKHAILOVICH **13**:513 *bibliog.*
Khrushchev, Nikita Sergeyevich **12**:69
Nazi-Soviet Pact **14**:67
MOLSON LAKE
map (54° 12′N 96° 45′W) **13**:119
MOLTING **13**:513 *bibliog., illus.*
amphibians **13**:513
bird **13**:513
feather **8**:40
developmental molts **13**:513
hormone, animal **10**:237 *table*
lizard **12**:379; **13**:513 *illus.*
mammal **13**:513
mayfly **13**:247
rattlesnake **16**:93
reptile **13**:513; **16**:168
snake **17**:379 *illus.*
MOLTKE, HELMUTH JOHANNES LUDWIG, GRAF VON **13**:513 *bibliog.*
Schlieffen, Alfred, Graf von **17**:126
World War I **20**:222–224 *illus.*
MOLTKE, HELMUTH KARL BERNHARD, GRAF VON **13**:514 *bibliog.*
general staff **9**:77
MOLTMANN, JÜRGEN **13**:514 *bibliog.*
MOLUCCA BALM *see* BELLS OF IRELAND
MOLUCCA SEA
map (0° 0′S 125° 0′E) **11**:147
MOLUCCAS (Indonesia) **13**:514 *bibliog.*
Ambonese **1**:325
map (5° 0′S 130° 0′E) **11**:147
spice trade **18**:180–181
MOLYBDATE MINERALS
mineral **13**:443 *table*
sulfate minerals **18**:333
wulfenite **20**:296
MOLYBDENITE **13**:514
sulfide minerals **18**:333–334
MOLYBDENUM **13**:514 *bibliog.*
abundances of common elements **7**:131 *table*
element **7**:130 *table*
Group IVB periodic table **15**:167
metal, metallic element **13**:328
molybdenite **13**:514
ore
major ore deposits **14**:423–425 *map, table*
wulfenite **20**:296
sulfide minerals **18**:333
transition elements **19**:273
uses **13**:514
vitamins and minerals **19**:621
MOLYNEUX, EDWARD
fashion design **8**:32
MOMADAY, N. SCOTT **13**:514
Kiowa **12**:86
MOMBASA (Kenya) **13**:514–515
climate **12**:53 *table*
map (4° 3′S 39° 40′E) **12**:53
MOMENCE (Illinois)
map (41° 10′N 87° 40′W) **11**:42
MOMENT OF INERTIA **13**:515 *bibliog.*
angular momentum **2**:7
distribution of mass **13**:515
energy of **7**:172
equation **13**:515
motion, circular **13**:608
MOMENTUM **13**:515 *bibliog.*
angular momentum **2**:7
conservation, laws of **5**:204
inertia **11**:161
laws of motion **13**:515
MOMI (Fiji)
map (17° 55′S 177° 17′E) **8**:77
MOMMSEN, THEODOR **13**:515 *bibliog.*
MOMOYAMA PERIOD (Japan)
castle **4**:190–191
Eitoku **7**:97
Japanese art and architecture **11**:376
MON **13**:515 *bibliog.*
Asia, history of **2**:253–254 *map*
Burma **3**:575

MON (cont.)
Lopburi **12**:412
Pegu (Burma) **15**:133
Southeast Asian art and architecture **18**:109
Thailand **19**:141
MØN ISLAND (Denmark)
map (55° 0′N 12° 20′E) **6**:109
MON-KHMER LANGUAGES
Asia **2**:244 *map*
Southeast Asian languages **18**:110–111
MONA (Utah)
map (39° 49′N 111° 51′W) **19**:492
MONA LISA **11**:312 *illus.*; **12**:291 *illus.*; **13**:515 *bibliog.*
Dada **6**:5
Louvre **12**:437
MONA PASSAGE
map (18° 30′N 67° 45′W) **4**:148
MONACA (Pennsylvania)
map (40° 41′N 80° 17′W) **15**:147
MONACHISM *see* MONASTICISM
MONACO **7**:271 *illus.*; **13**:515–517 *bibliog., illus., map*
cities
Monte Carlo **13**:552
economic activity **13**:516
flag **13**:516 *illus.*
government **13**:517
history **13**:516–517
land **13**:515–516
map (43° 45′N 7° 25′E) **7**:268
people **13**:516
postage stamp **15**:230 *illus.*
Rainier III, Prince of Monaco **16**:78
MONACO, LORENZO *see* LORENZO MONACO
MONADNOCK **13**:517
MONADNOCK, MOUNT (New Hampshire)
map (42° 52′N 72° 7′W) **14**:123
monadnock **13**:517
MONADNOCK BUILDING
skyscraper **17**:350
MONAGAS, JOSÉ TADEO
Páez, José Antonio **15**:13
MONAGHAN (Ireland) **13**:517
map (54° 15′N 6° 58′W) **11**:258
MONAHANS (Texas)
map (31° 36′N 102° 54′W) **19**:129
MONAMINE OXIDASE INHIBITOR (antidepressant) **6**:119
MONANGO (North Dakota)
map (46° 10′N 98° 43′W) **14**:248
MONARCH BUTTERFLY **3**:597 *illus.*; **5**:121 *illus.*
animal migration **2**:25–27 *illus.*
butterflies and moths **3**:595
coloration, biological **5**:122
mimicry **13**:434–435 *illus.*
MONARCH MOUNTAIN
map (51° 54′N 125° 53′W) **3**:491
MONARCH PASS
map (38° 30′N 106° 19′W) **5**:116
MONARCHIANISM **13**:517 *bibliog.*
Paul of Samosata **15**:117–118
Sabellianism **17**:5
MONARCHY **13**:517 *bibliog.*
absolutism **1**:63
coronation **5**:271
government **9**:267; **9**:269
king **12**:80
Middle Ages **13**:392
queen **16**:21
regent **16**:128
titles of nobility and honor **19**:213
MONASTERY *see* MONASTIC ART AND ARCHITECTURE; MONASTICISM
MONASTIC ART AND ARCHITECTURE **13**:517–521 *bibliog., illus.*
abbey **1**:52
Ajanta **1**:229
Amaravati **1**:321
Carolingian art and architecture **4**:160–161
Certosa di Pavia **4**:261
chapel **4**:284
chapter house **4**:285
cloister **5**:64
Cluny **5**:71
convent **5**:232–233
English art and architecture **7**:182
Hieronymites monastery **15**:455–456 *illus.*
iconography **11**:22
Ireland, history of **11**:261
Merovingian art and architecture **13**:311
Norman architecture **14**:220
patronage **13**:520
Romanesque art and architecture **16**:283 *illus.*
Salisbury Cathedral **17**:34
Southeast Asian art and architecture **18**:109–110
Spanish art and architecture **18**:153
MONASTICISM **13**:521 *bibliog., illus.*; **16**:138 *illus.*
abbey **1**:52
Anthony, Saint **2**:49
asceticism **2**:228
Athanasius, Saint **2**:288
Augustinians **2**:321
Basil the Great, Saint **3**:109
Benedict, Saint **3**:197
Benedictines **3**:197–198
Bernard of Clairvaux, Saint **3**:220–221
Carmelites **4**:153
Carthusians **4**:174
Cassian, Saint John **4**:184
Cassiodorus **4**:184
Cistercians **4**:445–446
Cluny **5**:71
convent **5**:232–233
Dominicans **6**:234
Franciscans **8**:276–277
Gregory I, Pope **9**:356
Harding, Saint Stephen **10**:46
herbs and spices **10**:137
hermit **10**:143
Hospitalers **10**:258–259
Jesuits **11**:402–403
Merton, Thomas **13**:313
Middle Ages **13**:394–396
monastic art and architecture **13**:517–521
Montserrat (mountain) **13**:560
nun **14**:296
Orthodox church **14**:450
religious orders **16**:143
Templars **19**:93–94
Teutonic Knights **19**:127–128
tonsure **19**:235
Trappists **19**:284
Zen Buddhism **20**:358–359 *illus.*
MONAZITE **13**:522
phosphate minerals **15**:256
MONBUTTU *see* MANGBETU
MONCH CHAJRCHAN, MOUNT
map (46° 45′N 91° 30′E) **13**:529
MÖNCHENGLADBACH (Germany, East and West)
map (51° 12′N 6° 28′E) **9**:140
MONCK, CHARLES STANLEY MONCK, 4th VISCOUNT **13**:522
MONCK, GEORGE, 1st DUKE OF ALBEMARLE **13**:522 *bibliog.*
MÖNCKEBERG'S SCLEROSIS
arteriosclerosis **2**:213
MONCKS CORNER (South Carolina)
map (33° 12′N 80° 1′W) **18**:98
MONCKTON, ROBERT
French and Indian Wars **8**:313 *map*
MONCLOVA (Mexico)
map (26° 54′N 101° 25′W) **13**:357
MONCTON (New Brunswick) **13**:522
map (46° 6′N 64° 47′W) **14**:117
MOND (family) **13**:522 *bibliog.*
MONDALE, WALTER F. **13**:522 *bibliog., illus.*
Senate of the United States **17**:199
MONDAY
calendar **4**:28
MONDAY FEVER *see* BROWN LUNG
MONDE, LE **13**:522
MONDEGO, CAPE OF
map (40° 11′N 8° 55′W) **15**:449
MONDEGO RIVER
map (40° 9′N 8° 52′W) **15**:449
MONDOVI (Wisconsin)
map (44° 34′N 91° 40′W) **20**:185
MONDRIAN, PIET **13**:523 *bibliog., illus.*
Broadway Boogie Woogie **2**:202 *illus.*
Composition in Color B **6**:313 *illus.*
Composition with Red, Yellow, and Blue **1**:64 *illus.*; **6**:63 *illus.*, *illus.*; **13**:523 *illus.*
de Stijl (periodical) **6**:63–64
Doesburg, Theo van **6**:213
Dutch art and architecture **6**:313
MONERA (bacteria) **3**:14; **13**:523
classification, biological **5**:43
organisms in class **13**:523
MONESSEN (Pennsylvania)
map (40° 9′N 79° 53′W) **15**:147
MONET, CLAUDE **13**:523–524 *bibliog., illus.*
The Houses of Parliament **13**:524 *illus.*
Impression: Sunrise **11**:63 *illus.*
impressionism **11**:68
Regatta at Argenteuil **15**:22 *illus.*
Renoir, Pierre Auguste **16**:158
Rouen Cathedral **11**:64 *illus.*
Sargent, John Singer **17**:77
Water Lilies **2**:201 *illus.*
MONETARY POLICY **13**:524 *bibliog.*
See also FISCAL POLICY
central bank **4**:253–254
economics **7**:49
economy, national **7**:50–51
Eurodollar **7**:267
European Economic Community **7**:300
Federal Reserve System **8**:41–42
Friedman, Milton **8**:331–332
gold **9**:227
gold standard **9**:230
Great Britain
Thatcher, Margaret **19**:143
incomes policy **11**:77
inflation **11**:169–171
money **13**:527
recession **16**:107
stagflation **18**:211
United States
free silver **8**:295
Greenback party **9**:349
Jefferson, Thomas **11**:392
MONETARY THEORY **13**:524–525 *bibliog.*
Fisher, Irving **8**:122
Friedman, Milton **8**:331–332
Keynesian model **13**:525
money **13**:527
quantity theory **13**:525
MONETT (Missouri)
map (36° 55′N 93° 55′W) **13**:476
MONETTE (Arkansas)
MAP LOCATION 3553N09021W)map (35° 53′N 90° 21′W) **2**:166
MONEY **13**:524–527 *bibliog., illus.*
See also INTEREST
ancient **13**:527
coin depicting Philip II **15**:233 *illus.*
denarius **6**:106
Syracuse decadrachm **18**:410 *illus.*
banking systems **3**:68–69
Civil War, U.S. **5**:33
counterfeiting **5**:312
definitions **13**:527
demand deposit **6**:96
devaluation **6**:137
dollar **6**:225
Eurodollar **7**:267
exchange rate **7**:326
free silver **8**:295
Friedman, Milton **8**:331–332
functions **13**:526
gold **9**:227 *illus.*
gold standard **9**:230
greenback **9**:349
Gresham's law **9**:359
history **13**:525–526
inflation **11**:169–171
Law, John **12**:247
mintage **13**:461
monetary policy **13**:524
monetary theory **13**:524–525
negotiable instrument **14**:77–78
numismatics **14**:295–296 *illus.*
pound sterling **15**:476
silver **17**:312
traveler's check **19**:284
usury **19**:491
Veblen, Thorstein B. **19**:529
wampum **20**:21
watermark **20**:65
MONEY (botany) *see* HONESTY (botany)
MONEY-CHANGER **3**:69 *illus.*
MONEY MARKET FUNDS
banking systems **3**:68–69
money **13**:527
MONEY SUPPLY
monetary theory **13**:524–525
money **13**:527
MONEYWORT **13**:527
MONFALCONE (Italy)
map (45° 49′N 13° 32′E) **11**:321
MONFERRATO (Italy)
map (45° 8′N 8° 27′E) **11**:321
MONGE, GASPARD **13**:527–528 *bibliog.*
differential geometry **6**:169
mathematics, history of **13**:226
mechanical drawing **13**:259
MONGE, LUIS ALBERTO
Costa Rica **5**:292
MONGKUT, KING OF SIAM **13**:528 *bibliog.*
MONGOLIA **13**:528–530 *bibliog., illus., map, table*
cities
Ulan Bator **19**:376
climate **13**:528–529 *table*
economic activity **13**:528–529 *illus.*
education **13**:528
exploration **7**:338
flag **13**:528 *illus.*
government **13**:529
history **13**:530
Tsedenbal, Yumzhagiyen **19**:322
Lamaist art and architecture **12**:172–173
land and resources **13**:528–529 *map, table*
languages
Ural-Altaic languages **19**:476
map (46° 0′N 105° 0′E) **2**:232
people **2**:243 *illus.*; **13**:528–529 *illus.*
Buryat **3**:583
Khalkhas **12**:65
nomads **2**:240 *illus.*
race **16**:34 *illus.*
Tungus **19**:334
Tuvan **19**:356
religion **13**:528
MONGOLIAN LAMAISM *see* KUBLAI KHAN, MONGOL EMPEROR
MONGOLISM *see* DOWN'S SYNDROME
MONGOLS **2**:240 *illus.*; **13**:530 *bibliog., illus., map*
Asia, history of **2**:254; **2**:255–256 *map*
Carpini, Giovanni da Pian del **4**:166
cavalry **4**:221
China, history of **4**:372
Delhi Sultanate **6**:92
Genghis Khan **9**:92
Golden Horde, Khanate of the **9**:232
Huns **10**:311
Kalmyk **12**:8
Kazakh **12**:33
Khalkhas **12**:65
Kirghiz **12**:87
Korea, history of **12**:116
Kublai Khan, Emperor **12**:134
Mongolia **13**:528; **13**:530
Russia/Union of Soviet Socialist Republics, history of **16**:352 *map*
Samarkand (USSR) **17**:45–46
Tatar **19**:43
Timur **19**:204
Turks **19**:347–348
Uighur **19**:374
Yakut **20**:314
Yüan (Yuan) (dynasty) **20**:338
MONGOOSE **13**:530–531 *illus.*
banded mongoose **17**:98 *illus.*
MONGOS RANGE (mountain range)
map (8° 45′N 23° 0′E) **4**:251
MONGUOR LANGUAGE
Ural-Altaic languages **19**:476
MONIDA PASS
map (44° 33′N 112° 18′W) **11**:26
MONILIASIS *see* CANDIDIASIS
MONISM **13**:531
metaphysics **13**:334
MONITEAU (county in Missouri)
map (38° 35′N 92° 35′W) **13**:476
MONITOR (lizard) **13**:531 *illus.*
Komodo dragon **12**:107
MONITOR AND MERRIMACK (ships)
Civil War, U.S. **5**:22; **7**:229 *illus.*, *bibliog., illus.*
Civil War, U.S. **5**:22; **5**:32 *illus.*
Ericsson, John **7**:229
naval vessels **14**:55 *illus.*
MONITOR RANGE
map (38° 45′N 116° 30′W) **14**:111
MONIZ, ANTÓNIO CAETANO DE ABREU FREIRE EGAS *see* EGAS MONIZ, ANTÓNIO
MONK (religion) *see* MONASTICISM
MONK, THE (book)
Lewis, Matthew Gregory **12**:306
MONK, MEREDITH **13**:532
MONK, THELONIOUS **13**:532
MONKEY **11**:469 *illus.*; **13**:532–535 *bibliog., illus.*
animal behavior **2**:16 *illus.*
baboon **3**:7
Barbary ape **3**:76
capuchin **4**:129
drill **6**:272
gorilla **9**:251
guenon **9**:390–391
howler monkey **13**:533–534 *illus.*; **15**:540 *illus.*
langur **12**:199
macaque **13**:4
mandrill **13**:112
marmoset **13**:161
New World monkeys **13**:534–535
anatomy **13**:534
classification, biological **13**:534
Old World monkeys **13**:532–534

anatomy **13**:532–534
classification, biological **13**:532
patas monkey **13**:104 *illus.*
primate **15**:539–542
rhesus monkey **16**:193
space medicine **18**:132
tamarin **19**:18
teeth **19**:70
vervet monkey **15**:540 *illus.*
yellow fever **20**:322
MONKEY DOG *see* AFFENPINSCHER
MONKEY FLOWER **13**:535
MONKEY PUZZLE TREE **13**:535 *illus.*
pine nut **15**:306
MONKEY SPIDER *see* TARANTULA
MONKEY TRIAL *see* SCOPES TRIAL
"MONKEY'S PAW, THE" (short story)
Jacobs, W. W. **11**:346
MONMOUTH (Illinois)
map (40° 55′N 90° 39′W) **11**:42
MONMOUTH (county in New Jersey)
map (40° 16′N 74° 17′W) **14**:129
MONMOUTH (Oregon)
map (44° 51′N 123° 14′W) **14**:427
MONMOUTH, BATTLE OF **1**:362 *illus.*; **13**:535–536 *bibliog.*
American Revolution **1**:361–362
Molly Pitcher **13**:512
Washington, George **20**:43
MONMOUTH, JAMES SCOTT, DUKE OF **13**:536 *bibliog.*
Jeffreys, George Jeffreys, 1st Baron **11**:394
MONMOUTHSHIRE (Wales) *see* GWENT (Wales)
MONNET, JEAN **13**:536 *bibliog.*
European Community **7**:299
MONO (county in California)
map (38° 0′N 118° 55′W) **4**:31
MONO LAKE
map (38° 0′N 119° 0′W) **4**:31
MONO RIVER
map (6° 17′N 1° 51′E) **19**:222
MONOAMINE OXIDASE INHIBITORS
antidepressants **2**:60–61
psychotropic drugs **15**:604
MONOCACY RIVER
map (39° 13′N 77° 27′W) **13**:188
MONOCHROMATOR **13**:536
MONOCLINIC SYSTEM **13**:536
crystal **5**:375 *illus.*
MONOCOT
flower **8**:183 *illus.*
plant **15**:335 *illus.*
MONOCOTYLEDON *see* MONOCOT
MONOD, JACQUES LUCIEN **13**:536
biology **3**:271
genetics **9**:89
Jacob, François **11**:345
Lwoff, André **12**:473
operon **14**:403
MONODRAMA
Draper, Ruth **6**:263
MONOGAMY **13**:536 *bibliog.*
polygamy **15**:419
MONOHYDRIC ALCOHOL **13**:536
ethyl alcohol **7**:257
methyl alcohol **13**:344
MONOLOGUE
dramatic monologue **14**:22
MONOMER **13**:537 *illus.*
MONOMOY ISLAND
map (41° 35′N 69° 59′W) **13**:206
MONON (Indiana)
map (40° 52′N 86° 53′W) **11**:111
MONONA (county in Iowa)
map (42° 0′N 95° 55′W) **11**:244
MONONA (Wisconsin)
map (43° 4′N 89° 20′W) **20**:185
MONONGAHELA RIVER **13**:537
map (40° 27′N 80° 0′W) **20**:111
MONONGALIA (county in West Virginia)
map (39° 38′N 80° 0′W) **20**:111
MONONUCLEOSIS **13**:537 *bibliog.*
hepatitis **10**:130
herpes **10**:145
MONOPHYSITISM **13**:537 *bibliog.*
Armenian church **2**:172
Chalcedon, Council of **4**:270
Coptic art and architecture **5**:255
Coptic church **5**:255
Cyril of Alexandria, Saint **5**:410
Eutyches **7**:311
Jacobite church **11**:346
Malabar Christians **13**:78
Monothelitism **13**:540
Tigré **19**:197
MONOPLACOPHORA
mollusk **13**:511
MONOPOLE, MAGNETIC **13**:537
MONOPOLY (game) **13**:537 *bibliog.*
MONOPOLY AND COMPETITION (economics) **13**:537–540 *bibliog.*, *tables*
cartel **4**:171
cartoon (*c.*1890) **19**:451 *illus.*
Clayton Anti-Trust Act **5**:47
Federal Trade Commission **8**:42
film, history of **8**:85
government regulation **9**:270
guilds **9**:395
merger **13**:310
newspaper **14**:171
petroleum industry **15**:214
public utility **15**:610–611
radio and television broadcasting **16**:57
Robinson-Patman Act **16**:246
Rockefeller (family) **16**:250
Roosevelt, Theodore **16**:310
Sherman Anti-Trust Act **17**:258–259
supply and demand **18**:353–354
trade associations **19**:263
trustee **19**:321–322
United States v. *E. C. Knight Company* **19**:465
MONORAIL
elevated railroad **7**:135
MONOSACCHARIDE **13**:540
See also POLYSACCHARIDE
carbohydrate **4**:133
sugar **18**:327
MONOSODIUM GLUTAMATE **13**:540
MONOTHEISM **13**:540 *bibliog.*
Akhenaten **1**:230
Asia, history of **2**:250
atheism **2**:288–289
God **9**:218
Judaism **11**:458–463
Unitarianism **19**:399–400
MONOTHELITISM **13**:540
Maronites **13**:162
Maximus, Saint **13**:241
Monophysitism **13**:537
MONOTREMATA (zoology) *see* MONOTREME
MONOTREME **13**:540–541 *illus.*
classification, biological **13**:540–541
mammal **13**:101; **13**:104 *illus.*
MONOTYPE **13**:541 *bibliog.*
Lanston, Tolbert, inventor **13**:541
typesetting **19**:365
MONRO, SIR CHARLES
World War I **20**:231
MONROE (county in Alabama)
map (31° 55′N 87° 20′W) **1**:234
MONROE (county in Arkansas)
map (34° 40′N 91° 15′W) **2**:166
MONROE (county in Florida)
map (25° 10′N 81° 10′W) **8**:172
MONROE (Georgia)
map (33° 47′N 83° 43′W) **9**:114
MONROE (county in Georgia)
map (33° 5′N 83° 55′W) **9**:114
MONROE (county in Illinois)
map (38° 25′N 90° 12′W) **11**:42
MONROE (county in Indiana)
map (39° 7′N 86° 30′W) **11**:111
MONROE (county in Iowa)
map (41° 0′N 92° 52′W) **11**:244
MONROE (county in Kentucky)
map (36° 45′N 85° 45′W) **12**:47
MONROE (Louisiana) **13**:541
map (32° 33′N 92° 7′W) **12**:430
MONROE (Michigan)
map (41° 55′N 83° 24′W) **13**:377
MONROE (county in Michigan)
map (41° 55′N 83° 26′W) **13**:377
MONROE (county in Mississippi)
map (33° 55′N 88° 30′W) **13**:469
MONROE (county in Missouri)
map (39° 30′N 92° 0′W) **13**:476
MONROE (Nebraska)
map (41° 28′N 97° 36′W) **14**:70
MONROE (New York)
map (41° 20′N 74° 11′W) **14**:149
MONROE (county in New York)
map (43° 10′N 77° 36′W) **14**:149
MONROE (North Carolina)
map (34° 59′N 80° 33′W) **14**:242
MONROE (county in Ohio)
map (39° 40′N 81° 5′W) **14**:357
MONROE (Oregon)
map (44° 19′N 123° 18′W) **14**:427
MONROE (county in Pennsylvania)
map (40° 59′N 75° 12′W) **15**:147
MONROE (county in Tennessee)
map (35° 25′N 84° 15′W) **19**:104
MONROE (Utah)
map (38° 38′N 112° 7′W) **19**:492
MONROE (county in West Virginia)
map (37° 35′N 80° 30′W) **20**:111
MONROE (Wisconsin)
map (42° 36′N 89° 38′W) **20**:185
MONROE (county in Wisconsin)
map (43° 55′N 90° 38′W) **20**:185
MONROE, BILL
bluegrass music **3**:345
MONROE, HARRIET **13**:541 *bibliog.*
MONROE, JAMES **13**:541–542 *bibliog.*, *illus.*
as president **13**:542
early life **13**:541–542
Gabriel (slave) **9**:6
Monroe Doctrine **13**:543
Richmond (Virginia) **16**:214
MONROE, MARILYN **13**:542–543 *illus.*
suicide **18**:331
MONROE CITY (Missouri)
map (39° 39′N 91° 44′W) **13**:476
MONROE DOCTRINE **13**:543 *bibliog.*
Canning, George **4**:111
Drago, Luis Mariá **6**:254–255
isolationism **11**:299
Monroe, James **13**:541; **13**:542
Olney, Richard **14**:381
Roosevelt, Theodore **16**:311
Roosevelt Corollary
United States, history of the **19**:452
United States, history of the **19**:445
Venezuela Boundary Dispute **19**:544
MONROE LAKE
map (39° 5′N 86° 25′W) **11**:111
MONROEVILLE (Alabama)
map (31° 31′N 87° 20′W) **1**:234
MONROEVILLE (Indiana)
map (40° 58′N 84° 52′W) **11**:111
MONROEVILLE (Pennsylvania)
map (40° 26′N 79° 47′W) **15**:147
MONROVIA (California)
map (34° 9′N 118° 3′W) **4**:31
MONROVIA (Liberia) **13**:543
climate **12**:314 *table*
map (6° 18′N 10° 47′W) **12**:313
MONS (Belgium) **13**:543
map (50° 27′N 3° 56′E) **3**:177
World War I **20**:223–225 *map*
MONSON (Maine)
map (45° 17′N 69° 30′W) **13**:70
MONSON (Massachusetts)
map (42° 6′N 72° 19′W) **13**:206
MONSOON **13**:543–544 *bibliog.*, *illus.*
Asia **13**:543–544
climate **2**:236–238 *map*
India **11**:82–83
occurrence, areas worldwide **13**:543–544
Pacific Ocean **15**:7
social and economic implications **13**:544
tropical climate **19**:307
MONSTERA **13**:544
MONT BELVIEU (Texas)
map (29° 51′N 94° 54′W) **19**:129
MONT BLANC *see* BLANC, MONT
MONT BLANC TUNNEL *see* TUNNEL
MONT CENIS TUNNEL *see* TUNNEL
MONT D' IBERVILLE
map (58° 53′N 63° 43′W) **16**:18
MONT-LAURIER (Quebec)
map (46° 33′N 75° 30′W) **16**:18
MONT-SAINT-MICHEL (France) **13**:544
MONTAGE
Cornell, Joseph **5**:268
Eisenstein, Sergei Mikhailovich **7**:97
film, history of **8**:83
MONTAGNARDS **13**:544 *bibliog.*
French Revolution **8**:323
MONTAGU, ASHLEY **13**:544
MONTAGU, CHARLES, 1ST EARL OF HALIFAX *see* HALIFAX, CHARLES MONTAGU, 1ST EARL OF
MONTAGU, JOHN, 4TH EARL OF SANDWICH *see* SANDWICH, JOHN MONTAGU, 4TH EARL OF
MONTAGU-CHELMSFORD REPORT
Chelmsford, Frederic, 1st Viscount **4**:311
MONTAGUE (California)
map (41° 44′N 122° 32′W) **4**:31
MONTAGUE (Michigan)
map (43° 25′N 86° 22′W) **13**:377
MONTAGUE (Prince Edward Island)
map (46° 10′N 62° 39′W) **15**:548
MONTAGUE (Texas)
map (33° 40′N 97° 43′W) **19**:129
MONTAGUE (county in Texas)
map (33° 37′N 97° 45′W) **19**:129
MONTAGUE, WILLIAM PEPPERELL **13**:544–545
MONTAGUE ISLAND (Alaska)
map (60° 0′N 147° 30′W) **1**:242
MONTAIGNE, MICHEL DE **13**:545 *bibliog.*, *illus.*
essay **7**:243
Essays of Montaigne **7**:244
French literature **8**:315
noble savage **14**:211
MONTALE, EUGENIO **13**:545 *bibliog.*
MONTALVA, EDUARDO FREI *see* FREI MONTALVA, EDUARDO
MONTALVO, JUAN **13**:545–546
MONTANA **13**:546–551 *bibliog.*, *illus.*, *map*
agriculture **13**:548–550 *illus.*
cities
Anaconda **1**:387
Billings **3**:255
Butte **3**:592
Great Falls **9**:319
Helena **10**:110–111
Missoula **13**:474
climate **13**:546
economic activities **13**:548–549 *illus.*
education **13**:548
state universities and colleges of **13**:551
flag **13**:546 *illus.*
flower, state
bitterroot **3**:301
Glacier National Park **9**:195
government **13**:549
historic sites **13**:548
history **13**:549–551
Bozeman Trail **3**:434
Clark, William Andrews **5**:39
Daly, Marcus **6**:15
land and resources **13**:546–548 *map*
map (47° 0′N 110° 0′W) **19**:419
mineral resources **13**:548
mining **13**:548; **13**:550 *illus.*
people **13**:548
Assiniboin **2**:265
Cheyenne **4**:338
Crow **5**:363
Flathead **8**:155
Gros Ventres **9**:370
Sioux **17**:326
rivers, lakes, and waterways **13**:546
Yellowstone River **20**:323
seal, state **13**:546 *illus.*
vegetation and animal life **13**:546; **13**:548
MONTANA (region in Peru) **15**:192
MONTANA, STATE UNIVERSITIES AND COLLEGES OF **13**:551
MONTANISM **13**:551 *bibliog.*
MONTAUBAN (France)
map (44° 1′N 1° 21′E) **8**:260
MONTAUK (American Indians) **13**:551 *bibliog.*
MONTAUK HARBOR
map (41° 4′N 71° 55′W) **5**:193
MONTAUK POINT (New York) **13**:551; **14**:152 *illus.*
map (41° 4′N 71° 57′W) **14**:149
MONTBÉLIARD (France) **13**:551
MONTCALM (county in Michigan)
map (43° 20′N 85° 10′W) **13**:377
MONTCALM, LOUIS JOSEPH, MARQUIS DE **13**:551–552 *bibliog.*, *illus.*
French and Indian Wars **8**:313–314 *map*
MONTCLAIR (California)
map (34° 6′N 117° 41′W) **4**:31
MONTCLAIR (New Jersey)
map (40° 49′N 74° 13′W) **14**:129
MONTE, PHILIPPE DE
Renaissance music **16**:156
MONTE ALBÁN (Mexico) **13**:552 *bibliog.*; **14**:237 *map*
Mexico, history of **13**:361–362
tomb 7
Mixtec **13**:486
Zapotec **20**:356
MONTE ALEGRE (Brazil)
map (2° 1′S 54° 4′W) **3**:460
MONTE CARLO (Monaco) **13**:552
Monaco **13**:516 *map*
MONTE CASEROS (Argentina)
map (30° 15′S 57° 39′W) **2**:149
MONTE CASSINO **13**:552 *bibliog.*
MONTE CREEK (British Columbia)
map (50° 39′N 119° 57′W) **3**:491
MONTE CRISTI (Dominican Republic)
map (19° 52′N 71° 39′W) **6**:233
MONTE CRISTO (Bolivia)
map (14° 43′S 61° 14′W) **3**:366
MONTE CRISTO MOUNTAIN
map (14° 25′N 89° 21′W) **7**:100
MONTE LINDO RIVER
map (23° 56′S 57° 12′W) **15**:77
MONTE PERDIDO
map (42° 40′N 0° 5′E) **18**:140
MONTE ROSA
map (45° 55′N 7° 52′E) **18**:394
MONTE VISTA (Colorado)
map (37° 35′N 106° 9′W) **5**:116
MONTEAGLE (Tennessee)
map (35° 15′N 85° 50′W) **19**:104
MONTEAGUDO (Bolivia)
map (19° 49′S 63° 59′W) **3**:366

MONTECRISTI (Ecuador)
map (1° 3′S 80° 40′W) **7**:52
MONTECRISTO ISLAND
map (42° 20′N 10° 19′E) **11**:321
MONTEFIORE, SIR MOSES **13**:552 *bibliog.*
MONTEGO BAY (Jamaica)
map (18° 28′N 77° 55′W) **11**:351
MONTEGUT (Louisiana)
map (29° 29′N 90° 33′W) **12**:430
MONTEJO, FRANCISCO DE
Tabasco (Mexico) **19**:3
MONTELIUS, OSCAR
prehistory **15**:517
MONTELLO (Nevada)
map (41° 16′N 114° 12′W) **14**:111
MONTELLO (Wisconsin)
map (43° 48′N 89° 20′W) **20**:185
MONTEMEZZI, ITALO **13**:552 *bibliog.*
MONTEMORELOS (Mexico)
map (25° 12′N 99° 49′W) **13**:357
MONTENEGRO (Yugoslavia) **13**:552–553 *map*
cities
Titograd **19**:215
map (42° 30′N 19° 18′E) **20**:340
MONTEREY (California) **13**:553
map (36° 37′N 121° 55′W) **4**:31
MONTEREY (county in California)
map (36° 40′N 121° 38′W) **4**:31
MONTEREY (Tennessee)
map (36° 9′N 85° 16′W) **19**:104
MONTEREY (Virginia)
map (38° 25′N 79° 35′W) **19**:607
MONTEREY BAY (California) **4**:33 *illus.*
map (36° 45′N 121° 55′W) **4**:31
MONTEREY PARK (California)
map (34° 4′N 118° 7′W) **4**:31
MONTERÍA (Colombia)
map (8° 46′N 75° 53′W) **5**:107
MONTERREY (Mexico) **13**:553
climate **13**:356 *table*; **14**:228 *table*
map (25° 40′N 100° 19′W) **13**:357
Mexican War **13**:352–353 *map*
MONTES CLAROS (Brazil)
map (16° 43′S 43° 52′W) **3**:460
MONTESANO (Washington)
map (46° 59′N 123° 36′W) **20**:35
MONTESPAN (France) CAVE ART **15**:509 *illus.*
MONTESPAN, FRANÇOISE ATHÉNAÏS DE ROCHECHOUART, MARQUISE DE **13**:553 *bibliog.*
MONTESQUIEU, CHARLES LOUIS DE SECONDAT, BARON DE LA BRÈDE ET DE **8**:317 *illus.*; **13**:553 *illus.*
government **9**:267–268
separation of powers **17**:206
Spirit of the Laws, The **18**:188
state (in political philosophy) **18**:232
MONTESSORI, MARIA **13**:553 *bibliog.*
Montessori method **13**:554
MONTESSORI METHOD **13**:554 *bibliog.*
MONTEUX, PIERRE **13**:554 *bibliog.*
MONTEVALLO (Alabama)
map (33° 6′N 86° 52′W) **1**:234
MONTEVERDI, CLAUDIO **13**:554 *bibliog., illus.*
Italian music **11**:318 *illus.*
music, history of Western **13**:666
opera **14**:399 *illus.*
orchestra and orchestration **14**:417
scherzo **17**:119
MONTEVIDEO (Minnesota)
map (44° 57′N 95° 43′W) **13**:453
MONTEVIDEO (Uruguay) **13**:555; **19**:489 *illus., table*
map (34° 53′S 56° 11′W) **19**:488
MONTEZ, LOLA **13**:555 *bibliog.*
MONTEZUMA (county in Colorado)
map (37° 20′N 108° 30′W) **5**:116
MONTEZUMA (Georgia)
map (32° 18′N 84° 2′W) **9**:114
MONTEZUMA (Indiana)
map (39° 48′N 87° 22′W) **11**:111
MONTEZUMA (Iowa)
map (41° 35′N 92° 32′W) **11**:244
MONTEZUMA (Kansas)
map (37° 36′N 100° 27′W) **12**:18
MONTEZUMA CASTLE NATIONAL MONUMENT **11**:120 *illus.*, *illus.*; **13**:555 *bibliog.*
MONTEZUMA I
Aztec **2**:382
MONTEZUMA II **13**:363 *illus.*; **13**:555 *bibliog., illus.*
Latin America, history of **12**:216
MONTFERRAND (France) *see* CLERMONT-FERRAND (France)
MONTFERRAT (Italy) **11**:326 *illus.*
MONTFORT (Wisconsin)
map (42° 58′N 90° 26′W) **20**:185
MONTFORT, SIMON DE, EARL OF LEICESTER **13**:555–556 *bibliog.*
Barons' War **3**:88
MONTGOLFIER BROTHERS **13**:556 *bibliog.*
balloon **3**:51
MONTGOMERY (Alabama) **1**:236 *illus.*; **13**:556
King, Martin Luther, Jr. **12**:80
map (32° 23′N 86° 18′W) **1**:234
MONTGOMERY (county in Alabama)
map (32° 10′N 86° 10′W) **1**:234
MONTGOMERY (county in Arkansas)
map (34° 35′N 93° 40′W) **2**:166
MONTGOMERY (county in Georgia)
map (32° 10′N 82° 35′W) **9**:114
MONTGOMERY (county in Illinois)
map (39° 9′N 89° 29′W) **11**:42
MONTGOMERY (county in Indiana)
map (40° 5′N 86° 50′W) **11**:111
MONTGOMERY (county in Iowa)
map (41° 0′N 95° 8′W) **11**:244
MONTGOMERY (county in Kansas)
map (37° 10′N 95° 45′W) **12**:18
MONTGOMERY (county in Kentucky)
map (38° 5′N 83° 55′W) **12**:47
MONTGOMERY (Louisiana)
map (31° 40′N 92° 53′W) **12**:430
MONTGOMERY (county in Maryland)
map (39° 5′N 77° 9′W) **13**:188
MONTGOMERY (Minnesota)
map (44° 26′N 93° 35′W) **13**:453
MONTGOMERY (county in Mississippi)
map (33° 30′N 89° 45′W) **13**:469
MONTGOMERY (county in Missouri)
map (38° 57′N 91° 27′W) **13**:476
MONTGOMERY (county in New York)
map (42° 57′N 74° 22′W) **14**:149
MONTGOMERY (county in North Carolina)
map (35° 20′N 79° 50′W) **14**:242
MONTGOMERY (county in Ohio)
map (39° 54′N 84° 15′W) **14**:357
MONTGOMERY (Pennsylvania)
map (41° 10′N 76° 52′W) **15**:147
MONTGOMERY (county in Pennsylvania)
map (40° 7′N 75° 21′W) **15**:147
MONTGOMERY (county in Tennessee)
map (36° 30′N 87° 25′W) **19**:104
MONTGOMERY (county in Texas)
map (30° 18′N 95° 30′W) **19**:129
MONTGOMERY (county in Virginia)
map (37° 10′N 80° 20′W) **19**:607
MONTGOMERY (West Virginia)
map (38° 11′N 81° 19′W) **20**:111
MONTGOMERY, L. M. **13**:556 *bibliog.*
Canadian literature **4**:93
MONTGOMERY, RICHARD **13**:556
American Revolution **1**:358–359 *map*
MONTGOMERY OF ALAMEIN, BERNARD LAW MONTGOMERY, 1ST VISCOUNT **13**:556–557 *bibliog., illus.*
Alamein, El **1**:239
World War II **20**:258 *illus.*; **20**:262–263; **20**:273
MONTGOMERY CITY (Missouri)
map (38° 59′N 91° 30′W) **13**:476
MONTGOMERYSHIRE (Wales) *see* POWYS (Wales)
MONTH
calendar **4**:27–28
MONTH IN THE COUNTRY, A (play)
Turgenev, Ivan **19**:341
MONTHERLANT, HENRY DE **13**:557 *bibliog.*
MONTI, EUGENIO
bobsledding **3**:353
MONTICELLI, ADOLPHE **13**:557 *bibliog.*
MONTICELLITE
olivine **14**:380 *table*
MONTICELLO (Arkansas)
map (33° 38′N 91° 47′W) **2**:166
MONTICELLO (Florida)
map (30° 33′N 83° 52′W) **8**:172
MONTICELLO (Georgia)
map (33° 18′N 83° 40′W) **9**:114
MONTICELLO (Illinois)
map (40° 1′N 88° 34′W) **11**:42
MONTICELLO (Indiana)
map (40° 45′N 86° 46′W) **11**:111
MONTICELLO (Iowa)
map (42° 15′N 91° 12′W) **11**:244
MONTICELLO (Kentucky)
map (36° 50′N 84° 51′W) **12**:47
MONTICELLO (Mississippi)
map (31° 33′N 90° 7′W) **13**:469
MONTICELLO (Missouri)
map (40° 7′N 91° 43′W) **13**:476
MONTICELLO (New York)
map (41° 39′N 74° 42′W) **14**:149
MONTICELLO (Thomas Jefferson's home) **13**:557 *bibliog., illus.*; **19**:610 *illus.*
Jefferson, Thomas **11**:391; **11**:393
MONTICELLO (Utah)
map (37° 52′N 109° 21′W) **19**:492
MONTICELLO (Wisconsin)
map (42° 45′N 89° 35′W) **20**:185
MONTICELLO JUNIOR COLLEGE
community and junior colleges **5**:151
MONTIJO (Portugal)
map (38° 42′N 8° 58′W) **15**:449
MONTIJO DE GUZMÁN, EUGENIA MARIA DE *see* EUGÉNIE
MONTINI, GIOVANNI BATTISTA *see* PAUL VI, POPE
MONTMAGNY (Quebec)
map (46° 59′N 70° 33′W) **16**:18
MONTMORENCY (county in Michigan)
map (45° 0′N 84° 10′W) **13**:377
MONTMORENCY (Quebec)
map (46° 52′N 71° 9′W) **16**:18
MONTMORENCY, ANNE, DUC DE **13**:557 *bibliog.*
MONTMORENCY, PHILIP DE, COMTE DE HORN *see* HORN, PHILIP DE MONTMORENCY, COMTE DE
MONTOUR (county in Pennsylvania)
map (40° 58′N 76° 37′W) **15**:147
MONTOURSVILLE (Pennsylvania)
map (41° 15′N 76° 55′W) **15**:147
MONTPARNASSE (Paris) **15**:86–87 *map*
MONTPELIER (Idaho)
map (42° 19′N 111° 18′W) **11**:26
MONTPELIER (Indiana)
map (40° 33′N 85° 17′W) **11**:111
MONTPELIER (Ohio)
map (41° 35′N 84° 36′W) **14**:357
MONTPELIER (Vermont) **13**:557
map (44° 16′N 72° 35′W) **19**:554
MONTPELLIER (France) **13**:557–558
map (43° 36′N 3° 53′E) **8**:260
MONTPENSIER, ANNE MARIE LOUISE D'ORLÉANS, DUCHESSE DE **13**:558 *bibliog.*
MONTREAL (Quebec) **4**:77 *illus.*; **13**:558–559 *bibliog., illus., map*
climate **4**:74 *table*
Expo '67 **4**:156 *illus.*; **16**:17 *illus.*
harbor and port **10**:42
history **13**:558
Maisonneuve, Paul de Chomedey, Sieur de **13**:76
McGill University **13**:16
map (45° 31′N 73° 34′W) **16**:18
Olympic Games **14**:383 *illus.*
subway **18**:318 *illus., table*
MONTREAL, UNIVERSITY OF **13**:558–560
MONTREAL LAKE (city in Saskatchewan)
map (54° 3′N 105° 46′W) **17**:81
MONTREAL LAKE (lake in Saskatchewan)
map (54° 20′N 105° 40′W) **17**:81
MONTREUX (Switzerland)
map (46° 26′N 6° 55′E) **18**:394
MONTROSE (Colorado)
map (38° 29′N 107° 53′W) **5**:116
MONTROSE (county in Colorado)
map (38° 20′N 108° 20′W) **5**:116
MONTROSE (Iowa)
map (40° 31′N 91° 25′W) **11**:244
MONTROSE (Michigan)
map (43° 11′N 83° 54′W) **13**:377
MONTROSE (Pennsylvania)
map (41° 50′N 75° 53′W) **15**:147
MONTROSE, JAMES GRAHAM, 1ST MARQUESS OF **13**:560 *bibliog.*
MONTROSS (Virginia)
map (38° 6′N 76° 50′W) **19**:607
MONTS, PIERRE DU GUA, SIEUR DE **13**:560 *bibliog.*
MONTSERRAT (island) **13**:560
map (16° 45′N 62° 12′W) **20**:109
MONTSERRAT (mountain) **13**:560
MONTSINÉRY (French Guiana)
map (4° 54′N 52° 30′W) **8**:311
MONTT, EFRAÍN RÍOS *see* RÍOS MONTT, EFRAÍN
MONTVALE (New Jersey)
map (41° 3′N 74° 2′W) **14**:129
"MONTY PYTHON'S FLYING CIRCUS" **13**:560
MONUMENT (Oregon)
map (44° 49′N 119° 25′W) **14**:427
MONUMENT VALLEY **2**:161 *illus.*; **2**:163 *illus.*; **13**:560; **19**:494 *illus.*
sandstone pillars **17**:63 *illus.*
MONUMENTS, PUBLIC *see* PUBLIC MONUMENTS
MONYWA (Burma)
map (22° 5′N 95° 8′E) **3**:573
MONZA (Italy) **13**:560
MONZONITE **13**:560 *bibliog.*
latite **12**:234
MOODUS RESERVOIR
map (41° 30′N 72° 24′W) **5**:193
MOODY (county in South Dakota)
map (44° 0′N 96° 40′W) **18**:103
MOODY, DEBORAH **13**:560–561 *bibliog.*
MOODY, DWIGHT L. **13**:561 *bibliog.*
MOODY, HELEN WILLS *see* WILLS, HELEN NEWINGTON
MOODY, WILLIAM H.
Twining v. *New Jersey* **19**:360
MOODY, WILLIAM VAUGHN **13**:561 *bibliog.*
MOODY BIBLE INSTITUTE
Moody, Dwight L. **13**:561
MOON **13**:561–566 *bibliog., illus., maps*
astronomical data **13**:561–562 *illus.*
distance, astronomical **6**:199
Earth, motions of **7**:18 *illus.*
Earth tide **7**:25
earthshine **7**:28
eclipse **7**:40–41 *illus.*
ephemeris time **7**:216
halo **10**:24
libration **12**:319
Mayer, Johann Tobias **13**:246
nutation **14**:301
occultation **14**:320
perturbation **15**:191
phases **13**:561 *illus.*
solar system **18**:46; **18**:50 *illus.*
tide **19**:193–194 *illus., table*
chemical composition **13**:562
evolution **13**:566
exploration
Apollo landing sites **13**:564 *map*
Apollo program **2**:80–84 *illus., table*
bootprint, Neil Armstrong **13**:563 *illus.*
first men on the moon **18**:129 *illus.*
Kennedy Space Center **12**:44–45
Luna (spacecraft) **12**:459–460 *illus., table*
Lunar Excursion Module **12**:460–461 *illus.*
Lunar Orbiter **12**:461 *illus.*
Lunar Rover **12**:461–462 *illus.*
Lunokhod **12**:465 *illus.*
Pioneer (spacecraft) **15**:309 *illus.*
Ranger (space probe) **16**:84 *illus.*
Soyuz **18**:115–118 *illus., table*
space exploration **18**:123–124 *illus.*
space law **18**:132
Surveyor **18**:369–370 *illus.*
Zond **20**:372–373 *illus., table*
formation **13**:566
surface features **13**:562–565 *illus., maps*
craters **13**:563–565 *maps*
drawing by Galileo **2**:279 *illus.*
Far Side **13**:565 *map*
Grimaldi, Francesco Maria **9**:364
Kuiper, Gerard **12**:135
lunar rock **13**:562–563 *illus.*
mascon **13**:196
Near Side **13**:564 *map*
rille **16**:224
temperature **13**:563; **13**:566
MOON, KEITH
Who, The **20**:143
MOON, SUN MYUNG **13**:566 *bibliog.*
religious cults **16**:143 *illus.*
MOON RAT *see* GYMNURE
MOON TREATY
space law **18**:132
MOONEYE **13**:566
MOONFISH **13**:566 *illus.*
MOONSEED **13**:566–567
MOONSTONE **9**:74 *illus.*; **13**:567 *illus.*
June birthstone **13**:567
Sri Lanka **13**:567
MOONWORT **8**:57 *illus.*
See also HONESTY (botany)
MOOR **13**:567 *bibliog.*
Granada (region in Spain) **9**:283
Portugal, history of **15**:453
Spain, history of **18**:144–146 *map*
Spanish music **18**:161
MOORCROFT (Wyoming)
map (44° 16′N 104° 57′W) **20**:301
MOORE (Montana)
map (46° 59′N 109° 42′W) **13**:547
MOORE (county in North Carolina)
map (35° 20′N 79° 30′W) **14**:242
MOORE (Oklahoma)
map (35° 20′N 97° 29′W) **14**:368

MOORE (county in Tennessee)
map (35° 20′N 86° 20′W) **19**:104
MOORE (Texas)
map (29° 3′N 99° 1′W) **19**:129
MOORE (county in Texas)
map (35° 50′N 101° 52′W) **19**:129
MOORE, BRIAN **13**:567 *bibliog.*
MOORE, CHARLES WILLARD **13**:567 *bibliog.*
fountains **8**:252
Saint Joseph's Fountain **15**:464 *illus.*
MOORE, CLEMENT CLARKE **13**:567
MOORE, DOUGLAS STUART **13**:567 *bibliog.*
MOORE, G. E. **13**:567–568 *bibliog.*
ethics **7**:250–251
MOORE, GEORGE **13**:568 *bibliog.*, *illus.*
realism (literature) **16**:104
MOORE, GERALD **13**:568
MOORE, GORDON
Noyce, Robert **14**:277
MOORE, GRACE **13**:568 *bibliog.*
MOORE, HENRY **13**:568–569 *bibliog.*, *illus.*
King and Queen **3**:508 *illus.*; **17**:165 *illus.*
Locking Piece **7**:188 *illus.*; **13**:569 *illus.*
Reclining Woman **13**:495 *illus.*
MOORE, SIR JOHN
La Coruña (Spain) **12**:145
MOORE, MARIANNE **13**:569 *bibliog.*, *illus.*
MOORE, MARY TYLER **13**:569
MOORE, PAUL, JR. **13**:569
MOORE, RAYMOND CECIL **13**:570
MOORE, STANFORD **13**:570
MOORE, THOMAS **13**:570
MOORE COLLEGE OF ART **13**:570
MOORE HAVEN (Florida)
map (26° 50′N 81° 5′W) **8**:172
MOORE RESERVOIR
map (44° 25′N 71° 50′W) **14**:123
MOOREA ISLAND
Society Islands **18**:26
MOOREFIELD (West Virginia)
map (39° 4′N 78° 58′W) **20**:111
MOORELAND (Oklahoma)
map (36° 26′N 99° 12′W) **14**:368
MOORESVILLE (Indiana)
map (39° 37′N 86° 22′W) **11**:111
MOORESVILLE (North Carolina)
map (35° 35′N 80° 48′W) **14**:242
MOORHEAD (Minnesota)
map (46° 53′N 96° 45′W) **13**:453
MOORHEAD (Mississippi)
map (33° 27′N 90° 30′W) **13**:469
MOORHEN *see* GALLINULE
MOORISH ART AND ARCHITECTURE **13**:570–571 *bibliog.*, *illus.*
Alhambra **1**:291–292 *illus.*
Giralda (tower) **9**:188
Granada (city in Spain) **9**:283
Indian art and architecture **11**:97
Islamic art and architecture **11**:294–297
ivory casket **13**:570 *illus.*
landscape architecture **12**:186 *illus.*
Latin American art and architecture **12**:223–224
Seville (Spain) **17**:220 *illus.*
Spanish art and architecture **18**:152–153 *illus.*
MOORISH IDOL **13**:571
MOOSBRUGGER, CASPAR **13**:571 *bibliog.*
MOOSE **8**:229 *illus.*; **13**:105 *illus.*; **13**:571–572 *bibliog.*, *illus.*
deer **6**:79
elk **7**:146
tundra **19**:332 *illus.*
MOOSE JAW (Saskatchewan) **13**:572
map (50° 23′N 105° 32′W) **17**:81
MOOSE LAKE (Manitoba)
map (53° 43′N 100° 20′W) **13**:119
MOOSE LAKE (Minnesota)
map (46° 26′N 92° 45′W) **13**:453
MOOSE MOUNTAIN
map (49° 45′N 102° 37′W) **17**:81
MOOSE PASS (Alaska)
map (60° 29′N 149° 22′W) **1**:242
MOOSEHEAD LAKE
map (45° 40′N 69° 40′W) **13**:70
MOOSOMIN (Saskatchewan)
map (50° 7′N 101° 40′W) **17**:81
MOOSONEE (Ontario)
map (51° 17′N 80° 39′W) **14**:393
MOOSUP (Connecticut)
map (41° 43′N 71° 53′W) **5**:193
MOPED **13**:572 *bibliog.*
motorcycle **13**:612
MOPTI (Mali)
map (14° 30′N 4° 12′W) **13**:89
MOQUEGUA (Peru)
map (17° 12′S 70° 56′W) **15**:193
MORA (Minnesota)
map (45° 53′N 93° 18′W) **13**:453
MORA (New Mexico)
map (35° 58′N 105° 20′W) **14**:136
MORA (county in New Mexico)
map (36° 0′N 105° 0′W) **14**:136
MORADABAD (India)
map (28° 50′N 78° 47′E) **11**:80
MORAINE **13**:572 *bibliog.*
erosion and sedimentation **7**:232
glaciers and glaciation **9**:193 *illus.*
lake, glacial **12**:170
till and tillite **19**:199
types **13**:572
MORAL AWARENESS **13**:572–573 *bibliog.*
conscience **5**:199
ethics **7**:250–251
folklore **8**:203
hypnosis **10**:350
McGuffey, William Holmes **13**:17
natural law **14**:48
MORAL MAJORITY **13**:573
censorship **4**:248
evangelicalism **7**:312
Falwell, Jerry **8**:15
Republican party **16**:176
MORAL RE-ARMAMENT **13**:573 *bibliog.*
Buchman, Frank **3**:534
MORALES, CRISTÓBAL DE
mass (musical setting) **13**:201
Renaissance music **16**:156
Spanish music **18**:161–162
MORALES, LUÍS DE **13**:573 *bibliog.*
MORALES BERMÚDEZ, FRANCISCO **13**:573
Peru **15**:195
MORALITY PLAY *see* MEDIEVAL DRAMA
MORAN (Kansas)
map (37° 55′N 95° 10′W) **12**:18
MORAN (Michigan)
map (46° 0′N 84° 50′W) **13**:377
MORAN (Texas)
map (32° 33′N 99° 10′W) **19**:129
MORAN, THOMAS **13**:573 *bibliog.*
escaping slaves **19**:447 *illus.*
MORANDI, GIORGIO **13**:573 *bibliog.*
MORANT BAY (Jamaica)
map (17° 53′N 76° 25′W) **11**:351
MORANT POINT
map (17° 55′N 76° 10′W) **11**:351
MORANTE, ELSA **13**:574
MORATIN, LEANDRO FERNÁNDEZ DE
Spanish literature **18**:159
MORATORIUM **13**:574
MORATUWA (Sri Lanka)
map (6° 46′N 79° 53′E) **18**:206
MORAVA RIVER
map (48° 10′N 16° 59′E) **5**:413
MORAVIA (Czechoslovakia) **13**:574 *map*
cities
Brno **3**:499
Ostrava **14**:458
Germany in 1648 **9**:151 *map*
Paleolithic Period **2**:126 *illus.*
MORAVIA (Iowa)
map (40° 53′N 92° 49′W) **11**:244
MORAVIA (New York)
map (42° 43′N 76° 25′W) **14**:149
MORAVIA, ALBERTO **11**:316 *illus.*; **13**:574 *bibliog.*, *illus.*
neorealism **14**:85–86
MORAVIAN CHURCH **13**:574–575 *bibliog.*
American music **1**:349
Bethlehem (Pennsylvania) **3**:231
Boehler, Peter **3**:358
Chelcicky, Peter **4**:311
Ettwein, John **7**:261
Heckewelder, John Gottlieb Ernestus **10**:103–104
Moravian College **13**:575
Spangenberg, Augustus Gottlieb **18**:149
Zinzendorf, Nikolaus Ludwig, Graf von **20**:369
MORAVIAN COLLEGE **13**:575
MORAWHANNA (Guyana)
map (8° 16′N 59° 45′W) **9**:410
MORAY (Scotland) **13**:575
MORAY EEL **8**:117 *illus.*; **13**:575 *illus.*
eel **7**:70
MORAY FIRTH
map (57° 50′N 3° 30′W) **19**:403
MORAZÁN, FRANCISCO **13**:575 *bibliog.*
MORDANT
dye **6**:317
MORDECAI *see* ESTHER, BOOK OF
MORDEN (Manitoba)
map (49° 11′N 98° 5′W) **13**:119
MORDVINIAN LANGUAGE
Uralic languages **19**:475
MORE, HENRY **13**:575 *bibliog.*
MORE, SAINT THOMAS **9**:126 *illus.*; **13**:575–576 *bibliog.*, *illus.*
Renaissance **16**:149 *illus.*
Utopia **19**:497
MOREA *see* PELOPONNESUS (Greece)
MOREAU (family) **13**:576
MOREAU, GUSTAVE **13**:576 *bibliog.*, *illus.*
Galatea **13**:576 *illus.*
MOREAU, JEAN VICTOR MARIE **13**:576
MOREAU, JEANNE **13**:576–577
MOREAU RIVER
map (45° 18′N 100° 43′W) **18**:103
MOREAUVILLE (Louisiana)
map (31° 2′N 91° 58′W) **12**:430
MOREHEAD (Kentucky)
map (38° 11′N 83° 25′W) **12**:47
MOREHEAD CITY (North Carolina)
map (34° 43′N 76° 43′W) **14**:242
MOREHEAD PLANETARIUM
Chapel Hill **4**:284
MOREHOUSE (county in Louisiana)
map (32° 47′N 91° 47′W) **12**:430
MOREHOUSE (Missouri)
map (36° 51′N 89° 41′W) **13**:476
MOREHOUSE COLLEGE **13**:577
MOREL **13**:577
fungi **8**:368
mushrooms **13**:660
MORELAND (Kentucky)
map (37° 30′N 84° 49′W) **12**:47
MORELIA (Mexico) **13**:577
map (19° 42′N 101° 7′W) **13**:357
MORELL (Prince Edward Island)
map (46° 25′N 62° 42′W) **15**:548
MORELOS (Mexico) **13**:577
cities
Cuernavaca **5**:382–383
map (26° 42′N 107° 40′W) **13**:357
pre-Columbian period
Xochicalco **20**:313
MORELOS Y PAVÓN, JOSÉ MARÍA **13**:577 *bibliog.*
Latin America, history of **12**:219
Mexico, history of **13**:364
Morelia (Mexico) **13**:577
MORENCI (Arizona)
map (33° 5′N 109° 22′W) **2**:160
MORENCI (Michigan)
map (41° 43′N 84° 13′W) **13**:377
MORENO, J. L.
role **16**:271
MORÉRI, LOUIS
Grand Dictionnaire Historique, Le
encyclopedia **7**:163
MORES *see* FOLKWAYS
MORESBY, JOHN
Port Moresby (Papua New Guinea) **15**:443
MORESBY ISLAND
map (52° 50′N 131° 55′W) **3**:491
MOREY PEAK
map (38° 37′N 116° 17′W) **14**:111
MORGAGNI, GIOVANNI B.
pathologic anatomy
medicine **13**:270
MORGAN (county in Alabama)
map (34° 25′N 86° 50′W) **1**:234
MORGAN (county in Colorado)
map (40° 15′N 103° 45′W) **5**:116
MORGAN (family) **13**:577 *bibliog.*, *illus.*
MORGAN (Georgia)
map (31° 32′N 84° 36′W) **9**:114
MORGAN (county in Georgia)
map (33° 35′N 83° 30′W) **9**:114
MORGAN (horse) **10**:243 *illus.*; **13**:578 *illus.*
American saddle horse **1**:366
MORGAN (county in Illinois)
map (39° 44′N 90° 14′W) **11**:42
MORGAN (county in Indiana)
map (39° 27′N 86° 25′W) **11**:111
MORGAN (county in Kentucky)
map (37° 55′N 83° 15′W) **12**:47
MORGAN (Minnesota)
map (44° 25′N 94° 56′W) **13**:453
MORGAN (county in Missouri)
map (38° 25′N 92° 55′W) **13**:476
MORGAN (Montana)
map (49° 0′N 107° 50′W) **13**:547
MORGAN (county in Ohio)
map (39° 38′N 81° 48′W) **14**:357
MORGAN (county in Tennessee)
map (36° 8′N 84° 40′W) **19**:104
MORGAN (Utah)
map (41° 2′N 111° 41′W) **19**:492
MORGAN (county in Utah)
map (41° 5′N 111° 37′W) **19**:492
MORGAN (county in West Virginia)
map (39° 38′N 78° 15′W) **20**:111
MORGAN, CONWAY LLOYD **13**:578
MORGAN, DANIEL **13**:578 *bibliog.*
American Revolution **1**:359 *map*
Cowpens, Battle of **5**:322
MORGAN, SIR HENRY **13**:578 *bibliog.*
Panama City (Panama) **15**:57
piracy **15**:313
MORGAN, JOHN HUNT **13**:578 *bibliog.*
MORGAN, JOHN PIERPONT (J. P.)
Morgan (family) **13**:577
Morgan Library **13**:579
Pennsylvania **15**:151
MORGAN, JOHN PIERPONT, JR.
Morgan (family) **13**:577 *illus.*
MORGAN, JULIA **13**:578 *bibliog.*
MORGAN, JUNIUS SPENCER
Morgan (family) **13**:577
MORGAN, LEWIS HENRY **13**:578–579 *bibliog.*
culture **5**:385
Parker, Ely S. **15**:90
MORGAN, MORGAN
West Virginia **20**:114
MORGAN, THOMAS HUNT **13**:579 *bibliog.*
genetics **9**:87
Mendel, Gregor Johann **13**:294
zoology **20**:378
MORGAN, WILLIAM G.
volleyball **19**:630
MORGAN, WILLIAM JASON
plate tectonics **15**:357
MORGAN, WILLIAM WILSON
Yerkes Observatory **20**:327
MORGAN CITY (Louisiana)
map (29° 42′N 91° 12′W) **12**:430
MORGAN LIBRARY **13**:579
architecture
McKim, Mead, and White **13**:29
East Room **12**:317 *illus.*
Morgan (family) **13**:577
MORGAN v. VIRGINIA **13**:579
MORGANFIELD (Kentucky)
map (37° 41′N 87° 55′W) **12**:47
MORGANFIELD, McKINLEY *see* WATERS, MUDDY
MORGANITO (Venezuela)
map (5° 4′N 67° 44′W) **19**:542
MORGANTON (North Carolina)
map (35° 45′N 81° 41′W) **14**:242
MORGANTOWN (Indiana)
map (39° 22′N 86° 16′W) **11**:111
MORGANTOWN (Kentucky)
map (37° 14′N 86° 41′W) **12**:47
MORGANTOWN (Mississippi)
map (31° 34′N 91° 20′W) **13**:469
MORGANTOWN (West Virginia) **13**:579
map (39° 38′N 79° 57′W) **20**:111
MORGENTHAU (family) **13**:579 *bibliog.*
MORGENTHAU, HANS **13**:579 *bibliog.*
MORGHAB (MURGAB) RIVER
map (38° 18′N 61° 12′E) **1**:133
MORI OGAI **13**:579
MORIAH (Trinidad and Tobago)
map (11° 15′N 60° 43′W) **19**:300
MORIAH, MOUNT
map (39° 17′N 114° 12′W) **14**:111
MORIARTY (New Mexico)
map (34° 59′N 106° 3′W) **14**:136
MÓRICZ, ZSIGMOND **13**:579–580 *bibliog.*
MÖRIKE, EDUARD **13**:580 *bibliog.*
MORIN, PAUL **13**:580
MORINVILLE (Alberta)
map (53° 48′N 113° 39′W) **1**:256
MORIOKA (Japan)
map (39° 42′N 141° 9′E) **11**:361
MORISCOS **13**:580 *bibliog.*
MORISON, SAMUEL ELIOT **13**:580
MORISOT, BERTHE **13**:580 *bibliog.*, *illus.*
The Butterfly Chase **11**:66 *illus.*
The Cradle **13**:580 *illus.*
MORITZ, JOHANN GOTTFRIED
tuba **19**:326
MORIYAMA, RAYMOND
Canadian art and architecture **4**:91
MORLAND, GEORGE **13**:580 *bibliog.*
MORLEY, CHRISTOPHER **13**:581 *bibliog.*
MORLEY, EDWARD W.
Michelson-Morley experiment **13**:376
MORLEY, JOHN MORLEY, VISCOUNT **13**:581
Minto, Gilbert Eliot, 4th Earl of **13**:461
MORLEY, LAWRENCE WHITAKER
plate tectonics **15**:357
MORLEY, THOMAS **13**:581 *bibliog.*

MORMON PEAK
map (36° 57′N 114° 30′W) **14**:111
MORMON TEMPLE (Salt Lake City) **13**:582 *illus.*
MORMON TRAIL **14**:431 *map*; **19**:445 *map*
MORMONISM **13**:581–582 *bibliog., illus., map*
Brigham Young University **3**:486
genealogy **9**:76
gull **9**:404
history **13**:581–582
Illinois **11**:45
Mormon migrations **13**:581 *map*
Mountain Meadows Massacre **13**:623
organization and beliefs **13**:582
polygamy **13**:165 *illus.*; **15**:419
saint **17**:15
Salt Lake City **17**:38
sego lily **17**:188
Smith, Joseph **13**:581–582; **17**:369–370 *illus.*
Strang, James Jesse **18**:288
Taylor, John **19**:49
Temple at Salt Lake City **13**:582 *illus.*
tithe **19**:212
Utah **19**:496
Utah War **19**:496
Young, Brigham **13**:582; **20**:332–333
MORMYRID **13**:582
MORNAY, PHILIPPE DE **13**:582–583 *bibliog.*
MORNING GLORY **13**:583 *illus.*
bindweed **3**:258
hallucinogens **10**:24
lawnleaf **12**:249
sweet potato **18**:388
MORNING STAR
Castor and Pollux **4**:191
MORNING SUN (Iowa)
map (41° 5′N 91° 15′W) **11**:244
MORO (people)
Mindanao (Philippines) **13**:437
MORO, ALDO **13**:583 *bibliog.*
MORO, ANTONIO **13**:583 *bibliog.*
MORO, IL *see* SFORZA, LUDOVICO
MORO GULF
map (6° 51′N 123° 0′E) **15**:237
MOROBE (Papua New Guinea)
map (7° 45′S 147° 35′E) **15**:72
MOROCCAN CRISES **13**:583 *bibliog.*
Algeciras Conference **1**:285
Europe, history of **7**:293
World War I **20**:220
MOROCCO **13**:583–587 *bibliog., illus., map, table*
agriculture **13**:585–586
cities
Agadir **1**:181
Casablanca **4**:179–180 *illus.*
Ceuta **4**:263
Fez **8**:66
Marrakech **13**:163
Meknès **13**:283–284
Melilla (Spain) **13**:287
Rabat **16**:30
Tangier **19**:22–23 *illus.*
Tinerhir **13**:586 *illus.*
climate **13**:584 *table*
economic activity **13**:585–586
education **13**:585
African universities **1**:176 *table*
flag **13**:584 *illus.*
government **13**:586
history **13**:586–587
Abd el-Krim **1**:54
Algeciras Conference **1**:285
Hassan II, King **10**:67
Lyautey, Louis Hubert **12**:474
Moroccan crises **13**:583
Muhammad V, King of Morocco **13**:634
World War II **20**:262 *map*
industry, mining, and power **13**:586
land and resources **13**:583–585 *map, table*
map (30° 0′N 9° 0′W) **1**:136
Moorish art and architecture **13**:570–571
people **13**:584–585
physical features
Atlas Mountains **2**:297
Rif **16**:219
regions
Ifni **11**:32
Western Sahara **20**:116
rivers, lakes, and waterways **13**:584
trade **13**:586
MOROCCO (Indiana)
map (40° 57′N 87° 27′W) **11**:111
MOROGORO (Tanzania)
map (6° 49′S 37° 40′E) **19**:27
MORÓN (Argentina)
map (34° 39′S 58° 37′W) **2**:149
MORÓN (Cuba)
map (22° 6′N 78° 38′W) **5**:377
MORÓN DE LA FRONTERA (Spain)
map (37° 8′N 5° 27′W) **18**:140
MORONDAVA (Madagascar)
map (20° 17′S 44° 17′E) **13**:38
MORONI (Republic of the Comoros) **13**:587
map (11° 41′S 43° 16′E) **5**:153
MORONI (Utah)
map (39° 32′N 111° 35′W) **19**:492
MORONI, GIOVANNI BATTISTA **13**:587
MORONOBU **13**:587 *bibliog.*
Kiyonobu I **12**:94
MOROTO MOUNTAIN
map (2° 32′N 34° 46′E) **19**:372
MORPHEUS **13**:587
MORPHINE **13**:587
Demerol **6**:96
drug trafficking **6**:281
heroin **10**:145
methadone **13**:343
nalorphine **14**:9
opiate receptor **14**:405
opium **14**:406
psychotropic drugs **15**:603; **15**:605
MORPHOGENESIS
cell **4**:233
development **6**:137
growth **9**:379
hormone, animal **10**:234
MORPHOLOGY (biology) *see* ANATOMY
MORPHOLOGY (geology)
meander, river **13**:253
mineral **13**:441
pegmatite **15**:133
river delta **16**:233
MORPHOLOGY (linguistics) *see* PHONOLOGY AND MORPHOLOGY
MORPHOU (Cyprus)
map (35° 12′N 32° 59′E) **5**:409
MORPHOU BAY
map (35° 10′N 32° 50′E) **5**:409
MORPHY, PAUL
chess **4**:336
MORRICE, JAMES W. **13**:587 *bibliog.*
Canadian art and architecture **4**:89
MORRICE, NORMAN **13**:587–588
MORRILL (Nebraska)
map (41° 58′N 103° 56′W) **14**:70
MORRILL (county in Nebraska)
map (41° 40′N 103° 0′W) **14**:70
MORRILL, JUSTIN S. **13**:588 *bibliog.*
Morrill Acts **13**:588
MORRILL ACTS **13**:588
land-grant colleges **12**:178
Morrill, Justin S. **13**:588
Reserve Officers Training Corps **16**:176
technical education **19**:59
United States, education in the **19**:434
United States, history of the **19**:449
university **19**:468
MORRILL TARIFF (1861)
tariff acts **19**:37
MORRILTON (Arkansas)
map (35° 9′N 92° 45′W) **2**:166
MORRIS (family) **13**:588 *bibliog.*
MORRIS (Illinois)
map (41° 22′N 88° 26′W) **11**:42
MORRIS (county in Kansas)
map (38° 40′N 96° 35′W) **12**:18
MORRIS (Manitoba)
map (49° 21′N 97° 22′W) **13**:119
MORRIS (Minnesota)
map (45° 35′N 95° 55′W) **13**:453
MORRIS (county in New Jersey)
map (40° 55′N 74° 30′W) **14**:129
MORRIS (Oklahoma)
map (35° 36′N 95° 51′W) **14**:368
MORRIS (county in Texas)
map (33° 5′N 94° 45′W) **19**:129
MORRIS, ESTHER **13**:588
MORRIS, GOUVERNEUR
Morris (family) **13**:588
MORRIS, ROBERT (artist) **13**:588 *bibliog.*
MORRIS, ROBERT (merchant) **13**:588 *bibliog.*
MORRIS, WILLIAM **13**:588–589 *bibliog., illus.*
Art Nouveau **2**:209–210
Blackthorn wallpaper **2**:225 *illus.*; **20**:17 *illus.*
book **3**:385
Burne-Jones, Sir Edward **3**:576–577
calligraphy **4**:43–44
Kelmscott Press **12**:39–40
stained glass **18**:212 *illus.*
Wiener Werkstätte **20**:146
MORRIS, WRIGHT **13**:589 *bibliog.*
MORRIS DANCE **13**:589
MORRIS MOTORS
automotive industry **2**:364–366
MORRIS PLAINS (New Jersey)
map (40° 49′N 74° 29′W) **14**:129
MORRISBURG (Ontario)
map (44° 54′N 75° 11′W) **14**:393
MORRISON (Illinois)
map (41° 49′N 89° 58′W) **11**:42
MORRISON (county in Minnesota)
map (46° 0′N 94° 19′W) **13**:453
MORRISON, MARION MICHAEL *see* WAYNE, JOHN
MORRISON, ROBERT **13**:589 *bibliog.*
MORRISON, TONI **13**:589
MORRISONVILLE (Illinois)
map (39° 25′N 89° 27′W) **11**:42
MORRISTOWN (Arizona)
map (33° 51′N 112° 37′W) **2**:160
MORRISTOWN (Indiana)
map (39° 40′N 85° 42′W) **11**:111
MORRISTOWN (New Jersey) **13**:590
map (40° 48′N 74° 29′W) **14**:129
MORRISTOWN (Tennessee)
map (36° 13′N 83° 18′W) **19**:104
MORRISVILLE (Pennsylvania)
map (40° 13′N 74° 47′W) **15**:147
MORRISVILLE (Vermont)
map (44° 34′N 72° 44′W) **19**:554
MORRO (Ecuador)
map (2° 39′S 80° 19′W) **7**:52
MORROW (Louisiana)
map (30° 50′N 92° 5′W) **12**:430
MORROW (county in Ohio)
map (40° 33′N 82° 50′W) **14**:357
MORROW (county in Oregon)
map (45° 25′N 119° 35′W) **14**:427
MORROW, DWIGHT **13**:590 *bibliog.*
MORS ISLAND
map (56° 50′N 8° 45′E) **6**:109
MORSE (Saskatchewan)
map (50° 25′N 107° 3′W) **17**:81
MORSE, JEDIDIAH **13**:590
MORSE, SAMUEL F. B. **13**:590 *bibliog., illus.*; **19**:450 *illus.*
Morristown (New Jersey) **13**:590
Morse code **13**:590
National Academy of Design **13**:590
telegraph **19**:77
MORSE, WAYNE LYMAN **13**:590 *bibliog.*
MORSE CODE **13**:590–591 *bibliog., table*
early forms **13**:590
ham radio **10**:26
Morse, Samuel F. B. **13**:590
signaling **17**:300–301 *illus.*
telegraph **19**:76–77 *illus.*
MORSE RESERVOIR
map (40° 6′N 86° 2′W) **11**:111
MORSZTYN, JAN ANDRZEJ
Polish literature **15**:398
MORSZTYN, ZBIGNIEW
Polish literature **15**:398
MORTALITY *see* DEATH AND DYING; DEMOGRAPHY; LIFE SPAN; POPULATION; POPULATION DYNAMICS
MORTAR **13**:591 *bibliog., illus.*
ammunition **1**:373
weapon use **13**:591
MORTE DARTHUR (book) **13**:591 *bibliog.*
Malory, Sir Thomas **13**:93
MORTGAGE **13**:591–592 *bibliog.*
banking systems **3**:68
deed **6**:77
encumbrance **7**:163
Federal Home Loan Bank Board **8**:41
Federal Housing Administration **8**:41
Federal National Mortgage Association **8**:41
housing **10**:277; **10**:279
hypothecation **10**:351
installment plan **11**:194
negotiable instrument **14**:77–78
savings bank **17**:100
savings and loan association **17**:100
title **19**:213
MORTICIAN *see* FUNERAL INDUSTRY
MORTIMER (family) **13**:592
MORTIMER, JOHN **13**:592
MORTMAIN **13**:592
MORTON (Illinois)
map (40° 37′N 89° 28′W) **11**:42
MORTON (county in Kansas)
map (37° 10′N 101° 45′W) **12**:18
MORTON (Mississippi)
map (32° 21′N 89° 40′W) **13**:469
MORTON (county in North Dakota)
map (46° 35′N 101° 10′W) **14**:248
MORTON (Texas)
map (33° 44′N 102° 46′W) **19**:129
MORTON, ANTHONY *see* CREASEY, JOHN
MORTON, JELLY ROLL **13**:592 *bibliog.*
blues **3**:346
MORTON, LEVI P. **13**:592 *bibliog.*
MORTON, OLIVER **13**:592 *bibliog.*
MORTON, THOMAS **13**:593 *bibliog.*
Quincy (Massachusetts) **16**:27
MORTON, WILLIAM **13**:593; **19**:450 *illus.*
anesthetics **1**:410
dentistry **6**:116
medicine **13**:271 *illus.*
surgery **18**:361 *illus.*
MORULA
development **6**:137; **6**:140
MORVEN (North Carolina)
map (34° 52′N 80° 1′W) **14**:242
MOSADDEQ, MUHAMMAD **13**:593 *bibliog.*
Iran **11**:253
Middle East, history of the **13**:408
MOSAIC **13**:593–596 *bibliog., illus.*
Aztec snake mosaic **15**:498 *illus.*
Byzantine art and architecture **3**:604–606 *illus.*
classical and Hellenistic mosaics **13**:593
Early Christian art and architecture **7**:9–10
The Empress Theodora and Her Retinue **13**:594 *illus.*
Galla Placidia, Mausoleum of **9**:16
medieval mosaics **13**:595–596
modern era **13**:596
Pechstein, Max **15**:130
Piazza Armerina **15**:289–290
Pompeii **15**:424 *illus.*
pre-Columbian art and architecture **11**:121–122 *illus.*
Roman art and architecture **16**:276–277
Saint Mark's Basilica **17**:24
San Vitale **17**:58 *illus.*
Santa Costanza **17**:67
Sumer wheel mosaic **20**:127 *illus.*
The Unswept Floor **13**:594 *illus.*
MOSAIC CODE
medicine **13**:267
MOSAIC DISEASE *see* TOBACCO
MOSAN STYLE
Romanesque art and architecture **16**:284–286
MOSASAUR **13**:596 *illus.*
MOSBRUGGER, CASPAR *see* MOOSBRUGGER, CASPAR
MOSBY, JOHN SINGLETON **13**:596
MOSBY'S CONFEDERACY
Mosby, John Singleton **13**:596
MOSCA, GAETANO **13**:596 *bibliog.*
elites **7**:140
MOSCHELES, IGNAZ **13**:596 *bibliog.*
MOSCONI, WILLIE **13**:596 *bibliog.*
MOSCOW (Idaho)
map (46° 44′N 117° 0′W) **11**:26
MOSCOW (USSR) **13**:596–599 *bibliog., illus., map*
climate **7**:272 *table*; **19**:390 *table*
cultural life **13**:598
economy **13**:598
history **13**:598–599
Dimitry Donskoi Grand Duke **6**:177
Europe, history of **7**:286
Ivan III, Grand Duke (Ivan the Great) **11**:332
Ivan IV, Grand Duke and Tsar of Russia (Ivan the Terrible) **11**:332–333
medieval plan of **16**:353 *illus.*
Napoleonic Wars **14**:19
Rurik (dynasty) **16**:347
Russia/Union of Soviet Socialist Republics, history of **16**:352–353 *map*
Vasily III, Grand Duke of Moscow **19**:526
Kremlin **12**:128–129 *illus.*
map (55° 45′N 41° 49′E) **19**:388
October Revolution anniversary parade **19**:394 *illus., illus.*
Red Square **19**:394 *illus.*
Saint Basil's Cathedral **16**:361 *illus.*
subway **18**:318 *table*
MOSCOW, TREATY OF
Russo-Finnish War **16**:373
MOSCOW ART THEATER **13**:599 *bibliog.*; **19**:150 *illus.*
acting **1**:88
Moscow **13**:597 *map*

Nemirovich-Danchenko, Vladimir Ivanovich **14**:81
Stanislavsky, Konstantin **18**:218
MOSCOW STATE UNIVERSITY **13**:599
Lomonosov, Mikhail Vasilevich **12**:400
Union of Soviet Socialist Republics, universities of the **19**:399 *table*
MOSELEY, HENRY GWYN JEFFREYS **13**:599 *bibliog.*
chemistry, history of **4**:328
periodic table **15**:168
MOSELLE (Mississippi)
map (31° 30′N 89° 17′W) **13**:469
MOSELLE RIVER **13**:599
map (50° 22′N 7° 36′E) **16**:195
MOSES 3:237 *illus.*; **13**:599–600 *bibliog., illus.*
Jews **11**:412–413 *illus.*
Judaism **11**:459 *illus.*
Suez (Egypt) **18**:323
Ten Commandments **19**:100
MOSES (sculpture)
Michelangelo **13**:373 *illus.*
MOSES, EDWIN **13**:600
MOSES, GRANDMA **13**:600 *bibliog., illus.*
Look, It's a New Little Colt **13**:600 *illus.*
MOSES, ROBERT **13**:600 *bibliog.*
MOSES LAKE (Washington)
map (47° 8′N 119° 17′W) **20**:35
MOSFET *see* TRANSISTOR
MOSHEIM (Tennessee)
map (36° 11′N 82° 57′W) **19**:104
MOSHESHWE, KING OF THE SOTHO **13**:600–601 *bibliog.*
Lesotho **12**:298
Maseru (Lesotho) **13**:196
Sotho **18**:70
MOSHI (Tanzania)
map (3° 21′S 37° 20′E) **19**:27
MOSHOESHOE *see* MOSHESHWE, KING OF THE SOTHO
MOSHTAQUE AHMED, KHONDAKER
Bangladesh **3**:66
MOSINEE (Wisconsin)
map (44° 47′N 89° 43′W) **20**:185
MOSKVA (USSR) *see* MOSCOW (USSR)
MOSLEM *see* ISLAM
MOSLEY, SIR OSWALD **13**:601 *bibliog.*
MOSQUE **13**:601–602 *bibliog., illus.*
Arab type **13**:601
Damascus (Syria) **6**:18 *illus.*
Iranian type **13**:601
Islam **11**:291–292 *illus.*
Islamic art and architecture **11**:293–297
minaret **13**:437
Moorish art and architecture **13**:570–571
Mosque of Sultan Hasan (Cairo) **7**:78 *illus.*
Persian art and architecture **15**:185–186 *illus.*
Royal Mosque (Isfahan) **2**:241 *illus.*; **11**:252 *illus.*
Sinan **17**:318
Spanish art and architecture **18**:152
Turkish type **13**:602
MOSQUERA (Colombia)
map (2° 30′N 78° 29′W) **5**:107
MOSQUERO (New Mexico)
map (35° 47′N 103° 58′W) **14**:136
MOSQUITIA (region in Honduras)
map (15° 0′N 84° 0′W) **10**:218
MOSQUITO (aircraft) **13**:602 *bibliog., illus.*
MOSQUITO (zoology) **8**:189 *illus.*; **13**:602–603 *bibliog., illus.*
botfly **3**:415
control
guppy **9**:406
dengue fever **6**:108
filariasis **8**:78
life cycle **13**:602 *illus.*
malaria life cycle **13**:80 *illus.*
mosquito fish **13**:603
Plasmodium **15**:347
protozoal diseases **15**:581
Reed, Walter **16**:118
sound receptors **11**:189 *illus.*
yellow fever **20**:322
MOSQUITO COAST **13**:603 *bibliog.*
Miskito **13**:466
MOSQUITO CREEK
map (41° 22′N 80° 45′W) **14**:357
MOSQUITO FISH **12**:168 *illus.*; **13**:603 *illus.*
MOSQUITOS, GULF OF
map (9° 0′N 81° 15′W) **15**:55
MOSS **13**:603–605 *bibliog., illus.*
See also CLUB MOSS; SPANISH MOSS
bryophyte **3**:530
classification, biological **13**:603
importance **13**:605
Irish moss **11**:229 *illus.*
life cycle **13**:604–605 *illus.*
peat **15**:129
Permian Period **15**:174 *illus.*
plant **15**:333–334 *illus.*
reproduction **16**:162
structure **13**:603
tundra **19**:332 *illus.*
MOSS, REINDEER
lichen **12**:322
MOSS, STIRLING **13**:605 *bibliog.*
MOSS ANIMAL *see* BRYOZOAN
MOSS POINT (Mississippi)
map (30° 25′N 88° 29′W) **13**:469
MÖSSBAUER, RUDOLF LUDWIG **13**:605
gamma rays **13**:605
Mössbauer effect **13**:605
MOSSELBAAI (South Africa)
map (34° 11′S 22° 8′E) **18**:79
MOSSENDJO (Congo)
map (2° 57′S 12° 44′E) **5**:182
MOSSI **13**:605 *bibliog.*
Ouagadougou (Upper Volta) **14**:467
MOSSLEIGH (Alberta)
map (50° 43′N 113° 20′W) **1**:256
MOSSOLOV, ALEXANDER
Russian music **16**:369
MOSSORÓ (Brazil)
map (5° 11′S 37° 20′W) **3**:460
MOST (Czechoslovakia)
map (50° 32′N 13° 39′E) **5**:413
MOST-FAVORED-NATION STATUS **13**:605
MOSTAR (Yugoslavia)
map (43° 20′N 17° 49′E) **20**:340
MOSTEL, SAMUEL JOEL *see* MOSTEL, ZERO
MOSTEL, ZERO **13**:605 *bibliog.*
MOSTIŞTEA RIVER
map (44° 15′N 27° 10′E) **16**:288
MOSUL (Iraq) **13**:606
map (36° 20′N 43° 8′E) **11**:255
MOSZKOWSKI, MORITZ **13**:606
MOTAGUA RIVER
map (15° 44′N 88° 14′W) **9**:389
MOTALA (Sweden)
map (58° 33′N 15° 3′E) **18**:382
MOTEL *see* HOTEL
MOTET **13**:606 *bibliog.*
cantus firmus **4**:118
composers
Byrd, William **3**:602
Lassus, Roland de **12**:214
Machaut, Guillaume de **13**:18
Obrecht, Jacob **14**:316
Tallis, Thomas **19**:17
French music **8**:320
medieval music **13**:275
Renaissance music **16**:156
MOTH *see* BUTTERFLIES AND MOTHS
MOTH FLY **8**:189 *illus.*
MOTHBALLS
naphthalene **14**:14
MOTHER COURAGE (play) **13**:606
Berliner Ensemble **3**:218 *illus.*
drama **6**:261 *illus.*
MOTHER GODDESS **13**:606–607 *bibliog., illus.*
Ceres (mythology) **4**:260
Cybele **5**:400
Demeter **6**:96
Eleusinian mysteries **7**:134–135
Ishtar **11**:287
Isis **11**:288
Kali **12**:8
Lakshmi **12**:171
Shakti **17**:237
temples
Tarxien (Malta) **19**:41
Venus of Willendorf **19**:548 *illus.*
MOTHER GOOSE **13**:607 *bibliog.*
Greenaway, Kate **9**:349
Perrault, Charles **15**:178
MOTHER-OF-PEARL **13**:607
aragonite **2**:107–108
interference (physics) **11**:207
pearls and pearling **15**:126–127
MOTHER-OF-THOUSANDS (botany) *see* SAXIFRAGE
MOTHERS OF INVENTION, THE (rock group)
Zappa, Frank **20**:356
MOTHERWELL (Scotland) **13**:607
map (55° 48′N 4° 0′W) **19**:403
MOTHERWELL, ROBERT **13**:607 *bibliog., illus.*
Summertime in Italy **13**:607 *illus.*
MOTIER, MARIE JOSEPH PAUL YVES ROCH GILBERT DU *see* LAFAYETTE, MARIE JOSEPH PAUL YVES ROCH GILBERT DU MOTIER, MARQUIS DE
MOTION (animal) *see* BIOLOGICAL LOCOMOTION; CHOREOGRAPHY; EURHYTHMICS; MUYBRIDGE, EADWEARD
MOTION, CIRCULAR **13**:607–608
angular momentum **2**:7
astronomy, history of **2**:277
Coriolis effect **5**:263
definitions and formulas **13**:608
Foucault pendulum **8**:249
moment of inertia **13**:515
momentum **13**:515
motion, harmonic **13**:608–609
Newton, Sir Isaac **14**:174
precession **15**:493
torque **19**:243
two-body problem **19**:360
velocity **19**:538
MOTION, HARMONIC **13**:608–609 *bibliog., illus.*
damping **6**:19
elliptical motion **13**:609
Galileo Galilei **9**:15
Hooke, Robert **10**:226–227
Lissajous figure **12**:366
pendulum **15**:142
waves and wave motion **20**:72
MOTION, LAWS OF *see* LAWS OF MOTION
MOTION, PARTICLE
Brownian motion **3**:517–518
kinetic theory of matter **12**:78–79 *illus.*
MOTION, PLANAR **13**:609–610 *bibliog.*
acceleration **1**:72; **13**:609
calculating position **13**:609
definitions and formulas **13**:609–610
free fall **8**:294
Galileo Galilei **9**:15
inertia **11**:161
momentum **13**:515
speed **18**:176
two-body problem **19**:360
velocity **13**:609–610; **19**:538
Zeno's paradoxes **20**:360
MOTION, PLANETARY *see* CELESTIAL MECHANICS
MOTION, WAVE *see* WATER WAVE; WAVES AND WAVE MOTION
MOTION PICTURE ARTS AND SCIENCES, ACADEMY OF *see* ACADEMY AWARDS
MOTION PICTURE ASSOCIATION OF AMERICA
censorship **4**:248
film, history of **8**:82
MOTION PICTURE ENGINEERS, SOCIETY OF
Jenkins, Charles Francis **11**:395
MOTION PICTURE PRODUCERS AND DISTRIBUTORS OF AMERICA *see* MOTION PICTURE ASSOCIATION OF AMERICA
MOTION PICTURE TECHNOLOGY *see* CINEMATOGRAPHY
MOTION PICTURES *see* ANIMATION; CINEMATOGRAPHY; COMEDY; DOCUMENTARY; FILM, HISTORY OF; FILM PRODUCTION; HORROR SHOWS; NEWSREEL; WESTERNS
MOTION SICKNESS **13**:610
Dramamine **6**:262
inner ear disturbance **13**:610
shipboard **13**:610
space medicine **18**:133–134
vertigo **19**:563
MOTIVATION **13**:610–611 *bibliog.*
achievement motivation **1**:81–82
emotion **7**:157
homeostasis **13**:610
Jung, Carl **11**:467
Maslow, Abraham H. **13**:196–198
psychology **15**:594
social psychology **18**:13
theories and sources **13**:610–611
MOTLEY (county in Texas)
map (34° 2′N 100° 47′W) **19**:129
MOTLEY, JOHN LOTHROP **13**:611 *bibliog.*
MOTMOT **13**:611
MOTOCROSS
motorcycling **13**:615–616 *illus.*
MOTON, ROBERT RUSSA **13**:611 *bibliog.*
MOTONOBU **13**:611 *bibliog.*
MOTOR **13**:611–612 *bibliog., illus.*
alternating-current motor **13**:611–612
Tesla, Nikola **19**:126
armature **2**:171
direct-current motor **13**:611–612
electric car **7**:105
electromagnet **7**:115
hydraulic systems **10**:331
outboard motor **13**:612 *illus.*
Stanley, William **18**:219
stator **18**:238
MOTOR NERVE
amyotrophic lateral sclerosis **1**:386
muscle **13**:651
peripheral nervous system **15**:171
MOTOR VEHICLE *see* AUTOMOBILE; AUTOMOTIVE INDUSTRY; BUS; MOTORCYCLE; TRUCKING INDUSTRY
MOTOR VEHICLE INDUSTRY *see* AUTOMOTIVE INDUSTRY
MOTORBIKE *see* MOPED; MOTORCYCLE
MOTORBOAT **13**:612 *bibliog., illus.*; **20**:66 *illus.*
boat and boating **3**:351 *illus.*
MOTORCYCLE **13**:612–614 *bibliog., illus.*
See also MOTORCYCLING
Daimler, Gottlieb **6**:7
history **13**:612–614
moped **13**:572
present trends **13**:614
MOTORCYCLING **13**:614–616 *bibliog., illus., table*
Knievel, Evel **12**:99
racing **13**:614–615 *illus., table*
MOTORWAY *see* ROADS AND HIGHWAYS
MOTOWN **13**:616 *bibliog.*
rhythm and blues **16**:205
soul music **18**:71
Wonder, Stevie **20**:204–205
MOTT (North Dakota)
map (46° 22′N 102° 20′W) **14**:248
MOTT, FRANK LUTHER **13**:616
best-seller **3**:229
MOTT, JOHN R. **13**:616 *bibliog.*
MOTT, JORDAN **19**:450 *illus.*
MOTT, LUCRETIA COFFIN **13**:616 *bibliog., illus.*
Seneca Falls Convention **17**:200–201
MOTT, NEVILL **13**:616
MOTTE, COMTESSE DE LA
Diamond Necklace, Affair of the **6**:152
MOTTELSON, BEN ROY **13**:616
MOUFLON (sheep) **13**:624 *illus.*
MOUILA (Gabon)
map (1° 52′S 11° 1′E) **9**:5
MOULAY ISMAIL
Meknès (Morocco) **13**:284
MOULINS (France)
map (46° 34′N 3° 20′E) **8**:260
MOULMEIN (Burma) **13**:616
map (16° 30′N 97° 38′E) **3**:573
MOULMEINGYUN (Burma)
map (16° 23′N 95° 16′E) **3**:573
MOULTON (Alabama)
map (34° 29′N 87° 18′W) **1**:234
MOULTON (Iowa)
map (40° 41′N 92° 41′W) **11**:244
MOULTON, ALEXANDER
bicycle **3**:244 *illus;* **3**:246
MOULTRIE (Georgia)
map (31° 11′N 83° 47′W) **9**:114
MOULTRIE (county in Illinois)
map (39° 35′N 88° 40′W) **11**:42
MOULTRIE, FORT *see* FORT MOULTRIE (South Carolina)
MOULTRIE, LAKE
map (33° 20′N 80° 5′W) **18**:98
MOULTRIE, WILLIAM *see* FORT MOULTRIE (South Carolina)
MOUND (geology) *see* KAME
MOUND BAYOU (Mississippi)
map (33° 54′N 90° 44′W) **13**:469
MOUND BUILDERS **13**:617–618 *bibliog., illus.*
Cahokia Mounds **4**:16
Etowah Mounds **7**:258
Great Serpent Mound (Ohio) **11**:130 *illus.*; **13**:617 *illus.*; **14**:358 *illus.*
Indiana **11**:114
Indians, American **11**:130 *illus.*
Indians of North America, art of the **11**:140–141
Iowa **11**:247
Mississippian tradition **13**:617–618; **14**:239–240 *illus.*
Ohio **14**:358 *illus.*
Spiro Mound **18**:189
West Virginia **20**:114
Wisconsin **20**:188

Woodland tradition **13**:617; **14**:238–239 *illus.*
MOUND CITY (Illinois)
map (37° 5′N 89° 10′W) **11**:42
MOUND CITY (Kansas)
map (38° 8′N 94° 49′W) **12**:18
MOUND CITY (South Dakota)
map (45° 44′N 100° 4′W) **18**:103
MOUNDBUILDER (bird) *see* MEGAPODE
MOUNDOU (Chad)
map (8° 34′N 16° 5′E) **4**:266
MOUNDRIDGE (Kansas)
map (38° 12′N 97° 31′W) **12**:18
MOUNDS (Illinois)
map (37° 7′N 89° 12′W) **11**:42
MOUNDS (Oklahoma)
map (35° 53′N 96° 4′W) **14**:368
MOUNDSVILLE (West Virginia)
map (39° 55′N 80° 44′W) **20**:111
MOUNDVILLE (Alabama)
map (32° 59′N 87° 38′W) **1**:234
MOUNT (for mountains whose names begin with the word Mount) *see* under the second element of the name, e.g., HOOD, MOUNT; McKINLEY, MOUNT; etc.
MOUNT, WILLIAM SIDNEY **13**:618 *bibliog., illus.*
Rabbit Trapping **13**:618 *illus.*
MOUNT AIRY (Maryland)
map (39° 23′N 77° 9′W) **13**:188
MOUNT AIRY (North Carolina)
map (36° 31′N 80° 37′W) **14**:242
MOUNT ALBERT (New Zealand)
map (36° 53′S 174° 44′E) **14**:158
MOUNT ALLISON UNIVERSITY **13**:618
MOUNT ANGEL (Oregon)
map (45° 4′N 122° 48′W) **14**:427
MOUNT ARLINGTON (New Jersey)
map (40° 56′N 74° 38′W) **14**:129
MOUNT AYR (Iowa)
map (40° 43′N 94° 14′W) **11**:244
MOUNT CARMEL (Illinois)
map (38° 25′N 87° 46′W) **11**:42
MOUNT CARMEL (Newfoundland)
map (47° 9′N 53° 29′W) **14**:166
MOUNT CARMEL (Pennsylvania)
map (40° 48′N 76° 25′W) **15**:147
MOUNT CARROLL (Illinois)
map (42° 6′N 89° 58′W) **11**:42
MOUNT CLEMENS (Michigan)
map (42° 36′N 82° 53′W) **13**:377
MOUNT DESERT ISLAND
map (44° 20′N 68° 20′W) **13**:70
MOUNT DORA (Florida)
map (28° 48′N 81° 38′W) **8**:172
MOUNT EDEN (New Zealand)
map (36° 53′S 174° 45′E) **14**:158
MOUNT ENTERPRISE (Texas)
map (31° 55′N 94° 41′W) **19**:129
MOUNT FOREST (Ontario)
map (43° 59′N 80° 44′W) **14**:393; **19**:241
MOUNT GAMBIER (Australia)
map (37° 50′S 140° 46′E) **2**:328
MOUNT GILEAD (North Carolina)
map (35° 10′N 79° 56′W) **14**:242
MOUNT GILEAD (Ohio)
map (40° 33′N 82° 50′W) **14**:357
MOUNT HAGEN (Papua New Guinea)
map (5° 50′S 144° 15′E) **15**:72
MOUNT HOLLY (New Jersey)
map (39° 59′N 74° 47′W) **14**:129
MOUNT HOLLY (North Carolina)
map (35° 18′N 81° 1′W) **14**:242
MOUNT HOLLY SPRINGS (Pennsylvania)
map (40° 7′N 77° 11′W) **15**:147
MOUNT HOLYOKE COLLEGE **13**:618
Lyon, Mary **12**:478
Seven Sisters Colleges **17**:216
MOUNT HOPE (Kansas)
map (37° 52′N 97° 40′W) **12**:18
MOUNT HOPE (West Virginia)
map (37° 54′N 81° 10′W) **20**:111
MOUNT HOPE BAY
map (41° 42′N 71° 15′W) **16**:198
MOUNT HOREB (Wisconsin)
map (43° 0′N 89° 44′W) **20**:185
MOUNT IDA (Arkansas)
map (34° 34′N 93° 38′W) **2**:166
MOUNT ISA (Australia)
map (20° 44′S 139° 30′E) **2**:328
MOUNT JACKSON (Virginia)
map (38° 45′N 78° 39′W) **19**:607
MOUNT JEWETT (Pennsylvania)
map (41° 44′N 78° 38′W) **15**:147
MOUNT JOY (Pennsylvania)
map (40° 7′N 76° 31′W) **15**:147
MOUNT JULIET (Tennessee)
map (36° 12′N 86° 31′W) **19**:104
MOUNT KISCO (New York)
map (41° 12′N 73° 44′W) **14**:149
MOUNT LEBANON (Pennsylvania)
map (40° 23′N 80° 3′W) **15**:147
MOUNT MORRIS (Illinois)
map (42° 3′N 89° 26′W) **11**:42
MOUNT MORRIS (Michigan)
map (43° 7′N 83° 42′W) **13**:377
MOUNT MORRIS (New York)
map (42° 44′N 77° 53′W) **14**:149
MOUNT OLIVE (Alabama)
map (33° 41′N 86° 52′W) **1**:234
MOUNT OLIVE (Illinois)
map (39° 4′N 89° 43′W) **11**:42
MOUNT OLIVE (North Carolina)
map (35° 12′N 78° 4′W) **14**:242
MOUNT OF OLIVES **13**:618
Jerusalem **11**:400 *map*
MOUNT OLIVET (Kentucky)
map (38° 32′N 84° 2′W) **12**:47
MOUNT PLEASANT (Iowa)
map (40° 58′N 91° 33′W) **11**:244
MOUNT PLEASANT (Michigan)
map (43° 35′N 84° 47′W) **13**:377
MOUNT PLEASANT (Pennsylvania)
map (40° 9′N 79° 33′W) **15**:147
MOUNT PLEASANT (South Carolina)
map (32° 47′N 79° 52′W) **18**:98
MOUNT PLEASANT (Tennessee)
map (35° 32′N 87° 13′W) **19**:104
MOUNT PLEASANT (Texas)
map (33° 9′N 94° 58′W) **19**:129
MOUNT PLEASANT (Utah)
map (39° 33′N 111° 27′W) **19**:492
MOUNT POCONO (Pennsylvania)
map (41° 8′N 75° 22′W) **15**:147
MOUNT PROSPECT (Illinois)
map (42° 4′N 87° 56′W) **11**:42
MOUNT PULASKI (Illinois)
map (40° 1′N 89° 17′W) **11**:42
MOUNT RAINIER (Maryland)
map (38° 56′N 76° 58′W) **13**:188
MOUNT ROSKILL (New Zealand)
map (36° 55′S 174° 45′E) **14**:158
MOUNT SHASTA (California)
map (41° 19′N 122° 19′W) **4**:31
MOUNT SINAI SCHOOL OF MEDICINE
New York, City University of **14**:154
MOUNT STERLING (Illinois)
map (39° 59′N 90° 45′W) **11**:42
MOUNT STERLING (Kentucky)
map (38° 4′N 83° 56′W) **12**:47
MOUNT STERLING (Ohio)
map (39° 43′N 83° 16′W) **14**:357
MOUNT STEWART (Prince Edward Island)
map (46° 22′N 62° 52′W) **15**:548
MOUNT UNIACKE (Nova Scotia)
map (44° 54′N 63° 50′W) **14**:269
MOUNT UNION (Pennsylvania)
map (40° 23′N 77° 53′W) **15**:147
MOUNT VERNON (Georgia)
map (32° 11′N 82° 36′W) **9**:114
MOUNT VERNON (Illinois)
map (38° 19′N 88° 55′W) **11**:42
MOUNT VERNON (Indiana)
map (37° 56′N 87° 54′W) **11**:111
MOUNT VERNON (Kentucky)
map (37° 21′N 84° 20′W) **12**:47
MOUNT VERNON (Missouri)
map (37° 6′N 93° 49′W) **13**:476
MOUNT VERNON (New York) **13**:618
MOUNT VERNON (Ohio)
map (40° 23′N 82° 29′W) **14**:357
MOUNT VERNON (Texas)
map (33° 11′N 95° 13′W) **19**:129
MOUNT VERNON (Washington)
map (48° 25′N 122° 20′W) **20**:35
MOUNT VERNON (Washington's home) **13**:618 *bibliog.*; **19**:610 *illus.*
historic preservation **10**:181
Vernon, Edward **19**:559
Washington, George **20**:42–43
MOUNT WASHINGTON (Kentucky)
map (38° 3′N 85° 32′W) **12**:47
MOUNT WELLINGTON (New Zealand)
map (36° 54′S 174° 51′E) **14**:158
MOUNT WILSON OBSERVATORY **13**:618–619
Babcock, Horace Welcome **3**:6
Bowen, Ira Sprague **3**:428
Hale, George Ellery **10**:18
Humason, Milton La Salle **10**:300
Los Angeles (California) **12**:417 *map*
observatory, astronomical **14**:317
Shapley, Harlow **17**:241
MOUNTAIN **13**:619–620 *bibliog., illus., table*
arête **2**:146
basin and range province **3**:110
chain, formation
island arc **11**:297
orogeny **14**:447
Paleozoic Era **15**:43
classes
Lehmann, Johann Gottlob **12**:276
continental drift **5**:228
dome mountains **13**:619 *illus.*
Earth, geological history of **7**:13
escarpment **7**:237
esker **7**:238
fault **8**:37
fault-block mountains **13**:619 *illus.*
fold **8**:194–195 *illus.*
folded mountains **13**:619–620 *illus.*
geographic distribution **13**:619
geosyncline **9**:119-120
highest mountains on each continent **13**:620 *table*
igneous rock **11**:35
inselberg **11**:194
landform evolution **12**:183
Moon **13**:564–565 *maps*
mountain climates **13**:620–621
mountain climbing **13**:621–622
mountain life **13**:622–623
plate tectonics **15**:354–356 *illus.*
river and stream **16**:231 *illus.*
structural geology **18**:303
subduction zone **18**:312–313
submarine mountain
mid-oceanic ridge **13**:389 *illus.*
seamount **17**:174
MOUNTAIN (Wisconsin)
map (45° 11′N 88° 28′W) **20**:185
MOUNTAIN ASH (botany) **13**:620
MOUNTAIN BROOK (Alabama)
map (33° 29′N 86° 46′W) **1**:234
MOUNTAIN CHINCHILLA *see* VISCACHA
MOUNTAIN CITY (Georgia)
map (34° 55′N 83° 23′W) **9**:114
MOUNTAIN CITY (Nevada)
map (41° 50′N 115° 58′W) **14**:111
MOUNTAIN CITY (Tennessee)
map (36° 28′N 81° 48′W) **19**:104
MOUNTAIN CLIMATES **13**:620–621 *bibliog.*
landform evolution **12**:183
mountain and valley winds **13**:624
orographic precipitation **14**:447
rain shadow effect **16**:77
MOUNTAIN CLIMBING **13**:621–622 *bibliog., illus.*
changing techniques **13**:622
conservation of mountains **13**:621–622
equipment **13**:621–622 *illus.*
Himalayas
Everest, Mount **7**:315
Sherpa **17**:259
history **13**:621
Matterhorn **13**:231
types of climbing **13**:621
MOUNTAIN CREEK (Alabama)
map (32° 43′N 86° 29′W) **1**:234
MOUNTAIN GOAT **13**:105 *illus.*; **13**:622 *illus.*
MOUNTAIN GROVE (Missouri)
map (37° 8′N 92° 16′W) **13**:476
MOUNTAIN HOME (Arkansas)
map (36° 20′N 92° 23′W) **2**:166
MOUNTAIN HOME (Idaho)
map (43° 8′N 115° 41′W) **11**:26
MOUNTAIN LAKE PARK (Maryland)
map (39° 24′N 79° 23′W) **13**:188
MOUNTAIN LAUREL **13**:622; **17**:288 *illus.*
laurel **12**:237
MOUNTAIN LIFE **13**:622–623 *bibliog., illus.*
See also names of specific plants and animals, e.g., BITTERROOT; MUSK-OX; etc.
tundra **19**:332–333 *illus.*
MOUNTAIN LION *see* PUMA
MOUNTAIN MEADOWS MASSACRE **13**:623 *bibliog.*
Lee, John Doyle **12**:269
Utah War **19**:497
MOUNTAIN MEN **13**:623–624 *bibliog., illus.*
Bridger, James **3**:484
Colorado **5**:119
Fitzpatrick, Thomas **8**:131
frontier **8**:342
fur trade **8**:371
Smith, Jedediah Strong **17**:369
Williams, William Sherley **20**:161
MOUNTAIN NILE RIVER
map (9° 30′N 30° 30′E) **18**:320
MOUNTAIN SHEEP **13**:624 *bibliog., illus.*
MOUNTAIN AND VALLEY WINDS **13**:624 *bibliog.*
chinook **4**:396
foehn **8**:193
mountain climates **13**:621
mountain winds **13**:624
polar climate **15**:392
valley winds **13**:624
zonda **20**:373
MOUNTAIN VIEW (Arkansas)
map (35° 52′N 92° 7′W) **2**:166
MOUNTAIN VIEW (Missouri)
map (36° 59′N 91° 42′W) **13**:476
MOUNTAIN VIEW (Oklahoma)
map (35° 6′N 98° 45′W) **14**:368
MOUNTAIN VILLAGE (Alaska)
map (62° 5′N 163° 44′W) **1**:242
MOUNTAINAIR (New Mexico)
map (34° 31′N 106° 15′W) **14**:136
MOUNTAINAIRE (Arizona)
map (35° 8′N 111° 39′W) **2**:160
MOUNTAINEERING *see* MOUNTAIN CLIMBING
MOUNTBATTEN, PHILIP, DUKE OF EDINBURGH *see* EDINBURGH, PHILIP MOUNTBATTEN, DUKE OF
MOUNTBATTEN OF BURMA, LOUIS MOUNTBATTEN, 1ST EARL **13**:624–625 *bibliog., illus.*
MOUNTIES *see* ROYAL CANADIAN MOUNTED POLICE
MOUNTRAIL (county in North Dakota)
map (48° 10′N 102° 20′W) **14**:248
MOURA (Brazil)
MOUSE (computer term) **5**:160h
map (1° 27′S 61° 38′W) **3**:460
MOURNE MOUNTAINS
map (54° 10′N 6° 5′W) **11**:258
MOURNING *see* DEATH AND DYING; FUNERAL CUSTOMS
MOURNING BECOMES ELECTRA (plays)
O'Neill, Eugene **14**:389–390
MOUSE (animal) **13**:625–626 *bibliog., illus.*
animal experimentation **2**:22
cloning **5**:64
Jackson Laboratory **11**:344
circulatory system **4**:439 *illus.*
deer mouse **6**:81; **9**:300 *illus.*
marsupial mouse **13**:174; **13**:175 *illus.*
pygmy mouse **13**:105 *illus.*
Rauscher mouse leukemia **12**:301
skin **17**:340 *illus.*
wood mouse **8**:228 *illus.*
MOUSE (computer term) **5**:160h
MOUSE, FAT-TAILED *see* GERBIL
MOUSE DEER *see* CHEVROTAIN
MOUSEBIRD **3**:280 *illus.*; **13**:626
coly **5**:129
MOUSSA ALI MOUNTAIN
map (12° 28′N 42° 24′E) **6**:208
MOUSTERIAN **13**:626 *bibliog.*
Châtelperronian **4**:303
Combe Grenal **5**:130
Levalloisian **12**:301–302
Neanderthalers **14**:69 *illus.*
Paleolithic Period **15**:40
Perigordian **15**:166
points **15**:40 *illus.*
prehistoric humans **15**:515 *illus.*
Solutrean **18**:58
MOUTH ORGAN *see* HARMONICA
MOUTH AND THROAT **18**:174 *illus.*
canker **4**:108
cleft lip and palate **5**:48
dentistry **6**:116
drug **6**:275 *illus.*
eustachian tube **7**:310
examination, medical **7**:326
inflammation
canker **4**:109
gingivitis **9**:184
pharyngitis **15**:222
strep throat **18**:297
insect **11**:186; **11**:188 *illus.*
laryngitis **12**:208
larynx **12**:209
lizard **12**:380
mosquito **13**:603
muscles **13**:653
phonetics **15**:251
respiratory system disorders **16**:181–182
tongue **19**:234
tonsils **19**:235 *illus.*
worm **20**:283
MOUTON, JEAN
mass (musical setting) **13**:201
Renaissance music **16**:156
MOVIES *see* ANIMATION; CINEMATOGRAPHY; COMEDY; DOCUMENTARY; FILM, HISTORY OF; FILM PRODUCTION; HORROR SHOWS; NEWSREEL; WESTERNS
MOVILLE (Iowa)
map (42° 29′N 96° 4′W) **11**:244

MOVIMIENTO NACIONALISTA REVOLUCIONARIO (MNR)
Bolivia 3:369
MOWAT, FARLEY 13:626
MOWAT, SIR OLIVER 13:626 *bibliog.*
MOWER (county in Minnesota)
map (43° 40′N 92° 45′W) **13**:453
MOWRER, O. HOBART 13:626 *bibliog.*
MOXIBUSTION
Chinese medicine **4**:391
MOXOS PLAIN
map (15° 0′S 65° 0′W) **3**:366
MOYLE (British Columbia)
map (49° 17′N 115° 50′W) **3**:491
MOYNIHAN, DANIEL PATRICK 13:626 *bibliog.*
MOYOBAMBA (Peru)
map (6° 3′S 76° 58′W) **15**:193
MOZAMBIQUE 13:626–628 *bibliog., illus., map, table*
African music **1**:168–171
cities
Maputo **13**:142–143
Sofala **18**:34
climate **13**:627–628 *table*
economic activity **13**:627–628
education **13**:627
flag **13**:627 *illus.*
government **13**:628
history **13**:628
Zimbabwe (Rhodesia) **20**:366
land and resources **13**:626–627 *map*
map (18° 15′S 35° 0′E) **1**:136
people **13**:627
Shona **17**:281
Thonga **19**:177
Yao **20**:318
MOZAMBIQUE CHANNEL
map (19° 0′S 41° 0′E) **1**:136
MOZAMBIQUE RIDGE
Indian Ocean bottom **11**:105 *map*
MOZARABIC ART *see* SPANISH ART AND ARCHITECTURE
MOZARABS 13:628
MOZART, WOLFGANG AMADEUS 9:130 *illus.*; 13:628–629 *bibliog., illus.*
aleatory music **1**:270
classical period in music **5**:42
concerto **5**:170
Da Ponte, Lorenzo **6**:3
Don Giovanni **6**:235
Grumiaux, Arthur **9**:382
Magic Flute, The **13**:50–51
Marriage of Figaro, The **13**:166
music, history of Western **13**:666 *illus.*
opera **14**:400 *illus.*
overture **14**:470
Salieri, Antonio **17**:32
Salzburg Festival **17**:44
serenade **17**:208
string quartet **18**:300 *illus.*
symphony **18**:405
MRIDANGA
Indian music **11**:102–103
MROŻWEK, SŁAWOMIR 13:629
MS. (periodical) 13:629
Steinem, Gloria **18**:248–249
MSAKON (Tunisia)
map (35° 44′N 10° 35′E) **19**:335
MSG *see* MONOSODIUM GLUTAMATE
MSHESHWE *see* MOSHESHWE, KING OF THE SOTHO
MSIDA (Malta)
map (35° 54′N 14° 29′E) **13**:94
MTV (television channel)
cinematography **4**:434
video, music **19**:576f
MTWARA (Tanzania)
map (10° 16′S 40° 11′E) **19**:27
MU (letter)
M (letter) **13**:3
MU CH'I (Muqi) 13:630 *bibliog.*
MU GIA PASS
map (17° 40′N 105° 47′E) **12**:203
MU-TAN-CHIANG (China)
map (44° 35′N 129° 36′E) **4**:362
MUANG KHAMMOUAN (Laos)
map (17° 24′N 104° 48′E) **12**:203
MUANG KHONG (Laos)
map (14° 7′N 105° 51′E) **12**:203
MUANG KHONGXEDON (Laos)
map (15° 34′N 105° 49′E) **12**:203
MUANG PAKXAN (Laos)
map (18° 22′N 103° 39′E) **12**:203
MUANG SING (Laos)
map (21° 11′N 101° 9′E) **12**:203
MUARA ISLAND
map (5° 0′N 115° 6′E) **3**:524
MUAWIYAH I, UMAYYAD CALIPH 13:630 *bibliog.*
Ali **1**:292
Middle East, history of the **13**:402–403
Umayyads **19**:380
MUBARAK, HOSNI
Egypt **7**:81
MUBI (Nigeria)
map (10° 18′N 13° 20′E) **14**:190
MUCH ADO ABOUT NOTHING (play) 13:630 *bibliog.*
MUCHA, ALFONS 13:630 *bibliog., illus.*
Job poster **2**:209 *illus.*
railroad poster **15**:461 *illus.*
Slavia **13**:630 *illus.*
MUCHE, GEORG
Bauhaus **3**:129–130 *illus.*
MUCHINGA MOUNTAINS
map (12° 0′S 31° 45′E) **20**:354
MUCKRAKERS 13:630–631 *bibliog.*
Adams, Samuel Hopkins **1**:98
Jungle, The **11**:468
Lloyd, Henry Demarest **12**:383
Phillips, David Graham **15**:239
Sinclair, Upton **17**:319
Steffens, Lincoln **18**:245
Tarbell, Ida M. **19**:35
MUCOSA
gastrointestinal tract disease **9**:57
stomach **18**:280
MUCOUS MEMBRANE
decongestant drugs **6**:76
infectious diseases **11**:166–167
inflammation, sinusitis **17**:326
nose, rhinitis **16**:196
polyp **15**:421
purpura **15**:630
sinus **17**:325
tear gas **19**:58
tongue **19**:234 *illus.*
MUD CRACKS 13:631 *bibliog.*
clay minerals **13**:631
MUD DAUBER **20**:45 *illus.*
MUD PLANTAIN *see* WATER PLANTAIN
MUD PUPPY 13:631 *illus.*
MUD TURTLE 13:631 *illus.*
MUDDY WATERS (singer) *see* WATERS, MUDDY
MUDÉJAR ART *see* SPANISH ART AND ARCHITECTURE
MUDFLOW 13:631 *bibliog.*
debris **13**:631
erosion and sedimentation **7**:232
landslide and avalanche **12**:193
types **13**:631
MUDLARK *see* AUSTRALIAN MUDNEST BUILDER
MUDMEN (Papua New Guinea) **15**:103 *illus.*
MUDMINNOW 13:632
minnow **13**:458
MUDSKIPPER *see* GOBY; WALKING FISH
MUELLER, GERD
soccer **18**:11
MUFFLER (automotive) *see* EXHAUST SYSTEM
MUFULIRA (Zambia)
map (12° 33′S 28° 14′E) **20**:354
MUGABE, ROBERT 13:632 *illus.*
Nkomo, Joshua **14**:206
Smith, Ian D. **17**:369
Zimbabwe (Rhodesia) **20**:365; **20**:366
MUGGERIDGE, EDWARD JAMES *see* MUYBRIDGE, EADWEARD
MUGHAL ART AND ARCHITECTURE *see* MOGUL ART AND ARCHITECTURE
MUGWUMPS 13:632 *bibliog.*
MUH SABKHA (Salt Lake)
map (34° 30′N 38° 20′E) **18**:412
MUHAMMAD 13:402 *illus.*; 13:632–633 *bibliog.*
Ali **1**:292
Arabs **2**:101–102
daughter
Fatima **8**:34
emir **7**:156
Europe, history of **7**:283
Hegira **10**:106
Islam **11**:288–289
Mecca (Saudi Arabia) **13**:258–259
Medina (Saudi Arabia) **13**:275
Middle East, history of the **13**:402
wife
Aisha **1**:228
MUHAMMAD, ABU ABDALLAH *see* BOABDIL
MUHAMMAD, CAPE OF
map (27° 44′N 34° 15′E) **7**:76
MUHAMMAD, ELIJAH 3:317 *illus.*; 13:633 *bibliog., illus.*
Black Muslims **3**:317–318
Malcolm X **13**:86
MUHAMMAD, JALAL UD-DIN *see* AKBAR, MOGUL EMPEROR OF INDIA
MUHAMMAD, WALLACE D.
Black Muslims **3**:317
MUHAMMAD AHMAD
mahdi **13**:64
MUHAMMAD ALI (boxer) *see* ALI, MUHAMMAD (boxer)
MUHAMMAD ALI PASHA 13:633 *bibliog., illus.*
Egypt **7**:80
Khartoum (Sudan) **12**:66
Mamelukes **13**:97
Middle East, history of the **13**:406
MUHAMMAD OF GHOR
Delhi Sultanate **6**:92
MUHAMMAD II *see* MEHMED II, SULTAN OF THE OTTOMAN EMPIRE
MUHAMMAD REZA SHAH PAHLAVI (1919–80) 13:634 *bibliog., illus.*
Iran **11**:253
Iranian hostage crisis **11**:253–254
Khomeini, Ayatollah Ruhollah **12**:67–68
MUHAMMAD SAID
Middle East, history of the **13**:406
MUHAMMAD TUGHLUQ
Delhi Sultanate **6**:92
MUHAMMAD V, KING OF MOROCCO 13:634
MUHAMMAD VI, OTTOMAN SULTAN
Middle East, history of the **13**:408
MUHAMMED *see under* MUHAMMAD except for names listed below
MUHARRAQ ISLAND, AL-
map (26° 16′N 50° 37′E) **3**:24
MUHASIBI, AL- 13:634 *bibliog.*
MUHAVURA **16**:378 *illus.*
MUHLENBERG (family) 13:634 *bibliog.*
MUHLENBERG (county in Kentucky)
map (37° 15′N 87° 10′W) **12**:47
MUHLENBERG COLLEGE
Allentown **1**:301
MUHLENBERG'S TURTLE *see* BOG TURTLE
MÜHLHAUSEN (Germany, East and West)
map (51° 12′N 10° 27′E) **9**:140
MUIR, EDWIN 13:634 *bibliog.*
MUIR, JOHN 13:635 *bibliog.*
John Muir National Historic Site (California) **4**:34
Sierra Club **17**:296
MUISNE (Ecuador)
map (0° 36′N 80° 2′W) **7**:52
MUJIBUR RAHMAN 13:635 *bibliog., illus.*
Bangladesh **3**:66
Pakistan **15**:29
MUKDEN (China) *see* SHEN-YANG (Shenyang) (China)
MUKDEN INCIDENT
Sino-Japanese Wars **17**:323
MUKWONAGO (Wisconsin)
map (42° 52′N 88° 20′W) **20**:185
MULANJE MOUNTAINS
map (15° 58′S 35° 38′E) **13**:81
MULATTO 13:635
Creoles **5**:338
South America **18**:91–92
MULATUPO (Panama)
map (8° 57′N 77° 45′W) **15**:55
MULBERRY (Arkansas)
map (35° 30′N 94° 3′W) **2**:166
MULBERRY (botany) 8:348 *illus.*; 13:635 *illus.*
banyan **3**:72
breadfruit **3**:467–468
fig **8**:74
Osage orange **14**:452
silk **17**:306–307
MULBERRY (Florida)
map (27° 54′N 81° 59′W) **8**:172
MULBERRY (Indiana)
map (40° 21′N 86° 40′W) **11**:111
MULBERRY FORK RIVER
map (33° 33′N 87° 11′W) **1**:234
MULBERRY RIVER
map (35° 28′N 94° 3′W) **2**:166
MULCASTER, RICHARD 13:635
MULCH
gardening **9**:43
MULCHÉN (Chile)
map (37° 43′S 72° 14′W) **4**:355
MULDER, GERARDUS JOHANNES
protein **15**:574
MULDOON, ROBERT DAVID 13:635–636
MULDRAUGH (Kentucky)
map (37° 56′N 85° 59′W) **12**:47
MULDROW (Oklahoma)
map (35° 24′N 94° 36′W) **14**:368
MULE 13:636 *illus.*
donkey **6**:238
glanders **9**:197
horse **10**:245
hybrid **10**:328 *illus.*
MULE DEER **4**:283 *illus.*
MULESHOE (Texas)
map (34° 13′N 102° 43′W) **19**:129
MULHACÉN
map (37° 3′N 3° 19′W) **18**:140
MULHALL (Oklahoma)
map (36° 4′N 97° 24′W) **14**:368
MÜLHEIM AN DER RUHR (West Germany) 13:636
MULHOUSE (France) 13:636
map (47° 45′N 7° 20′E) **8**:260
MULL ISLAND
map (56° 27′N 6° 0′W) **19**:403
MULLAH **13**:636
MULLAN (Idaho)
map (47° 28′N 115° 48′W) **11**:26
MULLARD RADIO ASTRONOMY OBSERVATORY 13:636 *bibliog.*
observatory, astronomical **14**:318
MULLEIN 13:636 *illus.*
MULLEN (Nebraska)
map (42° 3′N 101° 1′W) **14**:70
MULLENS (West Virginia)
map (37° 35′N 81° 23′W) **20**:111
MÜLLER, FRANZ HEINRICH
Royal Copenhagen ware **16**:330
MÜLLER, FREDERIK PALUDIN- *see* PALUDIN-MÜLLER, FREDERIK
MÜLLER, FRITZ
mimicry **13**:435
MÜLLER, HERMANN 13:636
MÜLLER, JOHANN *see* REGIOMONTANUS
MÜLLER, MAX ADOLF
jet propulsion **11**:407
MÜLLER, OTTO **3**:520 *illus.*
MÜLLER, PAUL 13:637
DDT **6**:57
MÜLLER, WILHELM
Geiger counter **9**:68
MULLET 13:637 *illus.*
MULLET, RED *see* GOATFISH
MULLETT LAKE
map (45° 30′N 84° 30′W) **13**:377
MULLICA RIVER
map (39° 33′N 74° 25′W) **14**:129
MULLIKEN, ROBERT SANDERSON 13:637
MULLINGAR (Ireland)
map (53° 32′N 7° 20′W) **11**:258
MULLINS (South Carolina)
map (34° 12′N 79° 15′W) **18**:98
MULLINVILLE (Kansas)
map (37° 35′N 99° 29′W) **12**:18
MULRONEY, BRIAN 13:637 *illus.*
MULTAN (Pakistan) 13:637
map (30° 11′N 71° 29′E) **15**:27
MULTATULI (pseudonym)
Dutch and Flemish literature **6**:314
MULTIELECTRODE TUBE
electron tube **7**:123
MULTILINGUALISM *see* BILINGUALISM
MULTINATIONAL CORPORATION *see* CORPORATION
MULTIPLE BIRTH 13:637–638 *bibliog.*
Siamese twins **17**:291
MULTIPLE INDEPENDENTLY (TARGETED) REENTRY VEHICLE *see* MIRV MISSILE
MULTIPLE MIRROR TELESCOPE *see* SMITHSONIAN ASTROPHYSICAL OBSERVATORY
MULTIPLE MYELOMA 13:638
MULTIPLE PERSONALITIES
neurosis **14**:107
schizophrenia **17**:124
MULTIPLE PROPORTIONS, LAW OF
chemical combination, laws of **4**:315
MULTIPLE SCLEROSIS 13:638 *bibliog.*
nervous system, diseases of the **14**:95–96
MULTIPLEXER 13:638
Farmer, Moses **8**:24
telegraph **19**:77
MULTIPLICATION
arithmetic **2**:158
associative law **2**:266
commutative law **5**:153
distributive law **6**:201
MULTIPLIER EFFECT 13:638
MULTITASKING (computer term) **5**:160h
MULTIVIBRATOR 13:638
MULTNONAH (county in Oregon)
map (45° 30′N 122° 22′W) **14**:427

MULVANE (Kansas)
  map (37° 29′N 97° 14′W) 12:18
MUM *see* CHRYSANTHEMUM
MUMFORD, LEWIS 13:638 *bibliog.*
MUMMING PLAY 13:638–639 *bibliog.*
MUMMY 13:639 *bibliog., illus.*
  embalming 7:151
MUMPS 13:639
MUN RIVER
  map (15° 19′N 105° 30′E) 19:139
MUNCEY, BILL 13:639
MUNCH, CHARLES 13:639–640 *bibliog.*
  Berkshire Music Festival 3:214
MUNCH, EDVARD 13:640 *bibliog., illus.*
  Clair de lune 20:211 *illus.*
  Friedrich Wilhelm Nietzsche 14:185 *illus.*
  Puberty 17:113 *illus.*
  The Scream 13:640 *illus.*
MÜNCHEN (West Germany) *see* MUNICH (West Germany)
MUNCIE (Indiana)
  Lynd, Robert S. 12:477
  map (40° 11′N 85° 23′W) 11:111
MUNCK, JENS
  Churchill River (Saskatchewan-Manitoba) 4:427
MUNCY (Pennsylvania)
  map (41° 12′N 76° 47′W) 15:147
MUNDARI 13:640 *bibliog.*
  Ho 10:190
  language 2:244 *map*
MUNDELEIN (Illinois)
  map (42° 16′N 88° 0′W) 11:42
MUNDURUCÚ (American Indians) 13:640–641 *bibliog.*
MUNFORD (Tennessee)
  map (35° 27′N 89° 47′W) 19:104
MUNFORDVILLE (Kentucky)
  map (37° 16′N 85° 54′W) 12:47
MUNGO, SAINT *see* KENTIGERN, SAINT
MUNI, PAUL 13:641
MUNICH (West Germany) 9:144 *illus.*; 13:641 *illus.*
  climate 9:142 *table*
  Glyptothek 9:212–213
  history 13:641
  Klenze, Leo von 12:97
  map (48° 8′N 11° 34′E) 9:140
  Puppet Theater 15:627 *illus.*
MUNICH CONFERENCE 13:641 *bibliog.*
  Chamberlain, Neville 4:274
  Daladier, Édouard 6:11
  Europe, history of 7:297
  World War II 20:250 *illus.*
MUNICH PUTSCH 13:641–642 *bibliog.*
  Hitler, Adolf 10:187
MUNICIPAL GOVERNMENT (local government) 13:642–643 *bibliog.*
  alderman 1:269
  bond 3:376
  boss, political 3:407–408
  city manager 5:8
  finance, state and local 8:92
  franchise (business) 8:273
  housing 10:279
  Johnson, Tom Loftin 11:436
  mayor 13:248
  patronage 15:114
  police 15:396
  recall 16:106
  revenue sharing 16:185
  sales tax 17:32
  sheriff 17:257
  town meeting 19:255
  township 19:256
  zoning 20:373–374
MUNIONG RANGE *see* SNOWY MOUNTAINS
MUNISING (Michigan)
  map (46° 25′N 86° 40′W) 13:377
MUNK, KAJ 13:643
MUNK, WALTER 13:643
MUNKÁCSY, MIHÁLY
  Hungary 10:309
MUNKU-SARDYK, MOUNT
  map (51° 45′N 100° 32′E) 19:388
MUNN v. ILLINOIS 13:643
  government regulation 9:270
  Waite, Morrison Remick 20:7
MUÑOZ MARÍN, LUIS 13:643 *bibliog.*
MUÑOZ RIVERA, LUIS 13:643 *bibliog.*
MUNRO, HECTOR HUGH *see* SAKI (writer)
MUNSEE *see* DELAWARE (American Indians)
MUNSELL COLOR SYSTEM 5:113 *illus.*
MUNSEY, FRANK ANDREW 13:643 *bibliog.*
MUNSTER (Indiana)
  map (41° 34′N 87° 30′W) 11:111
MUNSTER (Ireland) 13:644
MÜNSTER (West Germany) 13:643–644
  map (51° 57′N 7° 37′E) 9:140
MÜNTER, GABRIELE 13:644 *bibliog.*
MUNTJAC 13:644 *illus.*
MUNUSCONG LAKE
  map (46° 10′N 84° 8′W) 13:377
MÜNZER, THOMAS 13:644 *bibliog.*
  Zwickau (East Germany) 20:384
MUON 13:644
  fundamental particles 8:362 *table*
MUONG LANGUAGES *see* VIET-MUONG LANGUAGES
MUPPETS 13:644–645 *illus.*
  "Sesame Street" 17:212 *illus.*
MUQADDIMAH
  Ibn Khaldun 11:5
MUQAFFA, IBN AL- *see* IBN AL-MUQAFFA
MUQARNAS
  Islamic art and architecture 11:295
MUQAYSHIT ISLAND
  map (24° 12′N 53° 42′E) 19:401
MUQAYYAR *see* UR (Iraq)
MUQDISHO (Somalia) *see* MOGADISHU (Somalia)
MUQI *see* MU-CH'I (Muqi)
MUR RIVER
  map (46° 18′N 16° 53′E) 2:348
MURAD I, SULTAN OF THE OTTOMAN EMPIRE 13:645
  Janissaries 11:358
MURAD II, SULTAN OF THE OTTOMAN EMPIRE 13:645
  Mehmed II, Sultan of the Ottoman Empire 13:281
  Ottoman Empire 14:464
MURAD IV, SULTAN OF THE OTTOMAN EMPIRE
  Ottoman Empire 14:465
MURAL PAINTING 13:645–647 *bibliog., illus.*
  African art 1:164 *illus.*
  Benton, Thomas Hart (painter) 3:205–206
  Blashfield, Edwin Howland 3:328
  Egypt, ancient 7:84 *illus.*
  Egyptian art and architecture 7:88–89 *illus.*
  Eitoku 7:97
  Etruscans 7:259
  fresco painting 8:327
  Hunt, William Morris 10:312
  La Farge, John 12:145
  Latin American art and architecture 12:227–228 *illus.*
  Leonardo da Vinci 12:289–291
  Martini, Simone 13:180
  Orozco, José Clemente 14:447–448
  painting techniques 15:23
  Parrish, Maxfield 15:97
  Portinari, Cândido 15:445
  Puvis de Chavannes, Pierre 15:632
  Rivera, Diego 16:233
  Shahn, Ben 17:235
  Signorelli, Luca 17:302
  Siqueiros, David Alfaro 17:327
  Tamayo, Rufino 19:18–19
  Watts, George Frederic 20:69
MURAMUYA (Burundi)
  map (3° 16′S 29° 37′E) 3:582
MURASAKI SHIKIBU 13:647
  Tale of Genji, The 19:15
MURAT, JOACHIM 13:647 *bibliog., illus.*
  Bonaparte (family) 3:375
MURAT RIVER
  map (38° 39′N 39° 50′E) 19:343
MURCHISON, RODERICK IMPEY 13:647 *bibliog.*
  Permian Period 15:174
  Sedgwick, Adam 17:183
MURCHISON MOUNTAINS
  map (20° 11′S 134° 26′E) 14:158
MURCHISON RIVER
  map (27° 42′S 114° 9′E) 2:328
MURCIA (city in Spain) 13:647
  map (37° 59′N 1° 7′W) 18:140
MURCIA (region in Spain) 13:647
  cities
    Murcia 13:647
MURDER 13:647–648 *bibliog.*
  capital punishment 4:124
  crime 5:345; 5:346 *table*
  genocide 9:93
  homicide 10:214–215
  lynching 12:476–477
MURDER, INC. 13:648 *bibliog.*
MURDER IN THE CATHEDRAL (play)
  Eliot, T. S. 7:140
MURDERKILL RIVER
  map (39° 3′N 75° 24′W) 6:88
"MURDERS IN THE RUE MORGUE, THE" (short story)
  Poe, Edgar Allan 15:378
MURDO (South Dakota)
  map (43° 53′N 100° 43′W) 18:103
MURDOCH, IRIS 13:648 *bibliog., illus.*
MURDOCH, RUPERT 13:648 *bibliog.*
  journalism 11:455–456
MURDOCK, GEORGE PETER 13:648
MURDOCK, WILLIAM 13:648
  coal gas illumination 13:648
  sun-and-planet gear 13:648
MUREŞ RIVER
  map (46° 15′N 20° 13′E) 16:288
MURFREESBORO (Arkansas)
  map (34° 4′N 93° 41′W) 2:166
MURFREESBORO (North Carolina)
  map (36° 27′N 77° 6′W) 14:242
MURFREESBORO (Tennessee)
  map (35° 51′N 86° 23′W) 19:104
MURFREESBORO, BATTLE OF 5:26 *illus.*
MURGAB (MORGHAB) RIVER
  map (38° 18′N 61° 12′E) 1:133
MURIATIC ACID *see* HYDROCHLORIC ACID
MURILLO, BARTOLOMÉ ESTEBAN 13:648–649 *bibliog., illus.*
  Herrera, Francisco de 10:146
  A Peasant Boy 15:358 *illus.*
  The Young Begger 13:649 *illus.*
MURMANSK (USSR) 13:649
MURMEAN SEA *see* BARENTS SEA
MURNAU, F. W. 13:649 *bibliog.*
MUROMACHI (Japan)
  Japan, history of 11:368
  Japanese art and architecture 11:375–376
MURORAN (Japan)
  map (42° 18′N 140° 59′E) 11:361
MURPHY (Idaho)
  map (43° 13′N 116° 33′W) 11:26
MURPHY (North Carolina)
  map (35° 5′N 84° 1′W) 14:242
MURPHY, AUDIE 13:649 *bibliog.*
MURPHY, CHARLES
  Tammany Hall 19:20
MURPHY, FRANK 13:649 *bibliog.*
MURPHY, GARDNER 13:649 *bibliog.*
MURPHY, GEORGE 13:649 *bibliog.*
MURPHY, ISAAC 13:649–650
MURPHY, JOHN
  ABSCAM 1:62
MURPHY, MICHAEL
  Esalen Institute 7:236
MURPHY, WILLIAM PARRY
  Minot, George 13:460
  Whipple, George Hoyt 20:131
MURPHYSBORO (Illinois)
  map (37° 46′N 89° 20′W) 11:42
MURRAY (county in Georgia)
  map (34° 50′N 84° 45′W) 9:114
MURRAY (Iowa)
  map (41° 3′N 93° 57′W) 11:244
MURRAY (Kentucky)
  map (36° 37′N 88° 19′W) 12:47
MURRAY (county in Minnesota)
  map (44° 0′N 95° 45′W) 13:453
MURRAY (Nebraska)
  map (40° 55′N 95° 55′W) 14:70
MURRAY (county in Oklahoma)
  map (34° 30′N 97° 5′W) 14:368
MURRAY (Utah)
  map (40° 40′N 111° 53′W) 19:492
MURRAY, SIR ARCHIBALD
  World War I 20:239
MURRAY, GILBERT 13:650 *bibliog.*
MURRAY, HENRY A.
  motivation 13:610
  psychological measurement 15:593
MURRAY, SIR JAMES (lexicographer) 13:650 *bibliog.*
  Oxford English Dictionary, The 14:474–475
MURRAY, JAMES (soldier) 13:650 *bibliog.*
  French and Indian Wars 8:313 *map*
MURRAY, JOHN (clergyman) 13:650 *bibliog.*
MURRAY, SIR JOHN (oceanographer) 13:650 *bibliog.*
MURRAY, JOHN 4TH EARL OF DUNMORE *see* DUNMORE, JOHN MURRAY, 4TH EARL OF
MURRAY, LAKE
  map (34° 4′N 97° 4′W) 14:368
MURRAY, PAULI 13:650
MURRAY, PHILIP 13:650 *bibliog.*
  United Steelworkers of America 19:465
MURRAY HEAD (Prince Edward Island)]
  map (46° 0′N 62° 28′W) 15:548
MURRAY RIVER 2:333 *illus.*; 13:650
  map (35° 22′S 139° 22′E) 2:328
MURRAYVILLE (Illinois)
  map (39° 35′N 90° 15′W) 11:42
MURRIETA, JOAQUÍN 13:650–651 *bibliog.*
  outlaws 14:468–469
MURROW, EDWARD R. 13:651 *bibliog., illus.*
  radio and television broadcasting 16:56–57 *illus.*
MURRUMBIDGEE RIVER 13:651
  map (34° 43′S 143° 12′E) 2:328
MURUD MOUNTAIN
  map (3° 52′N 115° 30′E) 13:84
MÜRZZUSCHLAG (Austria)
  map (47° 36′N 15° 41′E) 2:348
MUSALA MOUNTAIN
  map (42° 11′N 23° 34′E) 3:555
MUSAYID (Qatar)
  map (24° 59′N 51° 32′E) 16:4
MUSCAT (Oman) 13:651
  climate 14:386 *table*
  map (23° 37′N 58° 35′E) 14:386
MUSCATATUCK RIVER
  map (38° 46′N 86° 10′W) 11:111
MUSCATINE (Iowa)
  map (41° 25′N 91° 3′W) 11:244
MUSCATINE (county in Iowa)
  map (41° 28′N 91° 10′W) 11:244
MUSCLE 13:651–654 *bibliog., illus.*
  biological locomotion 3:265–266
  cardiac muscle 13:653 *illus.*
  chiropractic 4:397
  classification 13:653
  diseases and disorders
    amyotrophic lateral sclerosis 1:386–387
    apraxia 2:91–92
    ataxia 2:287
    atrophy 2:313
    hyperactive children 10:347
    menopause 13:299
    multiple sclerosis 13:638
    muscular dystrophy 13:656
    myasthenia gravis 13:689
    myositis 13:691
    nervous system, diseases of the 14:95–96
    palsy 15:52
    paralysis 15:79
    Parkinson's disease 15:91
    rheumatism 16:194–195
    tetanus 19:126
    tetany 19:126–127
    tic 19:191
    trichinosis 19:296
  exercise 7:331
  eye 7:349 *illus.*
  invertebrate 11:237
  major muscles and muscle groups 13:652–654 *illus.*
  mechanics 13:651
  muscle contraction 13:654–656
  muscle relaxant
    curare 5:390–391
    nitroglycerin 14:203
    Valium 19:506
  orthopedics 14:450
  skeletal muscle 13:652–654 *illus.*
  smooth muscle 13:653 *illus.*
  space medicine 18:133
  speech 18:173–175
  sports medicine 18:197
  structure and function 13:651
    bursa 13:653
    cell 4:235 *illus.*; 4:236
    fibers 13:654 *illus.*
    myoglobin 13:691
    retinacula 13:653
    sheaths 13:653
  tissue, animal 19:210
MUSCLE CONTRACTION 13:654–656 *bibliog., illus.*
  active transport 1:89–90
  ATP 13:656
  biopotential 3:276
  convulsion 5:234
  exercise 7:329
  headache 10:85
  intestine 11:230
  isometrics 11:299
  Meyerhof, Otto 14:369
  peristalsis 15:171–172
  skeletal muscle 13:655 *illus.*
  smooth muscle 13:655
  Swammerdam, Jan 18:376
  uterus, pregnancy and birth 15:503; 15:505
MUSCLE SHOALS (Alabama)
  map (34° 45′N 87° 40′W) 1:234
MUSCODA (Wisconsin)
  map (43° 11′N 90° 27′W) 20:185
MUSCONETCONG RIVER
  map (40° 36′N 75° 11′W) 14:129
MUSCOVITE

facies, metamorphic rock **13**:332 *table*
mica **13**:370–371
MUSCOVY *see* MOSCOW (USSR)
MUSCOVY COMPANY
Cabot, Sebastian **4**:7
Chancellor, Richard **4**:278–279
MUSCULAR DYSTROPHY **13**:656 *bibliog.*
genetic diseases **9**:83
myositis **13**:691
nervous system, diseases of the **14**:96
MUSEO CHIARAMONTE
Vatican museums and galleries **19**:527
MUSEO GREGORIANO EGIZIANO
Vatican museums and galleries **19**:528
MUSEO GREGORIANO ETRUSCO
Vatican museums and galleries **19**:528
MUSEO PIO-CLEMENTINO
Vatican museums and galleries **19**:527
MUSEO SACRO
Vatican museums and galleries **19**:528
MUSES **13**:656 *bibliog.*
Delphi **6**:95
MUSEUM OF FINE ARTS, BOSTON **13**:656 *bibliog.*
MUSEUM OF MODERN ART, THE **13**:657 *bibliog.*
Barr, Alfred H., Jr. **3**:92
industrial design **11**:156
Kracauer, Siegfried **12**:126
modern art **13**:494
New York (city) **14**:145 *map*
Steichen, Edward **18**:246
Stone, Edward Durell **18**:280
Szarkowski, John **18**:415
MUSEUM OF NON-OBJECTIVE ART *see* GUGGENHEIM MUSEUM
MUSEUMS, ART **13**:657–659 *bibliog.*
antique collecting **2**:65–68
art collectors and patrons **2**:204
art conservation and restoration **2**:205
Bargello (museum) **3**:81
Barr, Alfred H., Jr. **3**:92
British Museum **3**:497
Brooklyn Museum, The **3**:510
Chicago, Art Institute of **4**:342
Cleveland Museum of Art **5**:54
Cloisters, The **5**:64
Cooper-Hewitt Museum **5**:245
Corcoran Gallery of Art **5**:261
Courtauld Institute of Art **5**:316
Detroit Institute of Arts, The **6**:136
Escorial **7**:238
Fitzwilliam Museum **8**:132
Freer Gallery of Art
Freer, Charles Lang **8**:300
Frick Collection **8**:330
Gardner Museum **9**:45
Getty Museum **9**:160
Guggenheim Museum **9**:393
Harvard University **10**:64
Hermitage Museum **10**:143
Hirshhorn Museum and Sculpture Garden **10**:176
historic preservation **10**:181–182
historical development **13**:657
Kremlin **12**:128–129
Los Angeles County Museum of Art **12**:418
Louvre **12**:437
major museums of the world **13**:658
Metropolitan Museum of Art, The **13**:347–348
Museum of Fine Arts, Boston **13**:656
Museum of Modern Art, The **13**:657
National Collection of Fine Arts **14**:30
National Gallery, London **14**:33
National Gallery of Art **14**:33
National Portrait Gallery **14**:44–45
Pennsylvania Academy of the Fine Arts **15**:152
Philadelphia Museum of Art **15**:229
Pitti Palace **15**:321
Prado **15**:487
Rijksmuseum **16**:223
Royal Ontario Museum **16**:330
San Francisco art museums **17**:54
Smithsonian Institution **17**:372
Tate Gallery, The **19**:44
Topkapi Palace Museum **19**:237
Uffizi **19**:371
Vatican museums and galleries **19**:527–528
Victoria and Albert Museum **19**:575
Wallace Collection, The **20**:15
Walters Art Gallery **20**:20
Whitney Museum of American Art **20**:142
Winterthur Museum **20**:181
Yale University Art Gallery
Hamilton, George Heard **10**:29
MUSEUMS OF SCIENCE AND INDUSTRY **13**:659 *bibliog.*
important science museums **13**:659
American Museum of Natural History **1**:348
British Museum **3**:497
Field Museum of Natural History **8**:72
Franklin Institute **8**:285
National Air and Space Museum **14**:28–29
Smithsonian Institution **17**:372
origin and development **13**:659
Peabody, George **15**:123
Putnam, Frederic Ward **15**:632
Rosenwald, Julius **16**:316
MUSGRAVE, THEA **13**:659 *bibliog.*
MUSHIN (Nigeria)
map (6° 32'N 3° 22'E) **14**:190
MUSHROOMS **8**:228 *illus.*; **13**:659–661 *bibliog., illus.*
anatomy **13**:661 *illus.*
classification **13**:660–661
fairy ring mushroom **8**:10
food poisoning and infection **8**:211
food source **13**:661
fungi **8**:368 *illus.*
morel **13**:577
poisonous plants and animals **15**:384–385
reproduction and growth **13**:661
toadstool **19**:218
MUSI RIVER
map (2° 20'S 104° 56'E) **11**:147
MUSIAL, STAN **13**:661 *bibliog., illus.*
MUSIC
See also names of specific composers, e.g., GRIEG, EDVARD; STRAVINSKY, IGOR; etc.; names of specific musical instruments, e.g., TRUMPET; VIOLIN; etc.; names of specific national music, e.g., HUNGARIAN MUSIC; INDIAN MUSIC; etc.
absolute music **1**:62
aleatory music **1**:270
Baroque music **3**:91–92
black Americans **3**:311
bluegrass music **3**:345
blues **3**:345–346
boogie-woogie **3**:383
calypso **4**:49
chamber music **4**:272–273
choral music **4**:405–407
church music **4**:424
classical period in music **5**:41–42
computer music **5**:162–163
consort music **5**:206
counterpoint **5**:312
country and western music **5**:312–313
disco music **6**:189
education
American music **1**:350–351
arts, education in the **2**:224–225
Auer, Leopold **2**:319
Boulanger, Nadia **3**:421
Curtis Institute of Music, The **5**:395
Czerny, Carl **5**:416
Dalcroze, Émile Jaques **6**:11
Eastman School of Music **7**:34
eurhythmics **7**:265–266
Juilliard School, The **11**:465
Kelley, Edgar Stillman **12**:38
Mason (family) **13**:198
Mennin, Peter **13**:298
Menuhin, Yehudi **13**:302
Moore, Douglas Stuart **13**:567
New England Conservatory of Music **14**:121
Orff, Carl **14**:432
Paine, John Knowles **15**:15
Piston, Walter **15**:319
Sessions, Roger **17**:213
Westminster Choir College **20**:118
electronic music **7**:124–126
folk music **8**:202–203
forms
ballade **3**:40–41
cadenza **4**:11
concerto **5**:170
étude **7**:261
fugue **8**:355
intermezzo **11**:214
march **13**:146
nocturne **14**:212
oratorio **14**:416
overture **14**:470
polonaise **15**:417
prelude **15**:518
program music **15**:562
requiem **16**:176
rondo **16**:305
scherzo **17**:119
serenade **17**:208
sonata **18**:63
string quartet **18**:300
suite **18**:331–332
swing **18**:392–393
symphonic poem **18**:404–405
symphony **18**:405
toccata **19**:220
foundations and endowments
Julliard, Augustus D. **11**:465
Gospel music **9**:253–254
Grammy Award **9**:283
harmony **10**:51–52
high fidelity
frequency modulation (FM) **8**:327
historians and scholars
See also MUSIC CRITICISM
Ansermet, Ernest **2**:35
Burney, Charles **3**:577
Dent, Edward Joseph **6**:114
Fétis, François Joseph **8**:63
Grove, Sir George **9**:378
Newman, Ernest **14**:169–170
Pizzetti, Ildebrando **15**:325
Sachs, Curt **17**:7
Tovey, Sir Donald Francis **19**:254
impressionism (music) **11**:68
Indians of North America, music and dance of the **11**:141–143 *illus.*
influence on non-Western music **13**:668
jazz **11**:387–390
labor union
American Federation of Musicians **1**:339
Medieval music **13**:274–275
melody **13**:288
meter **13**:343
metronome **13**:347
mode **13**:489
patron saint
Cecilia, Saint **4**:228
polyphony **15**:421
printing and publishing
choral music **4**:406–407
Italian music **11**:318
madrigal **13**:45
Renaissance music **16**:156
Pulitzer Prize **15**:618–619
Argento, Dominick **2**:152
Barber, Samuel **3**:77
Carter, Elliott **4**:171
Colgrass, Michael **5**:101
Crumb, George **5**:366
Davidovsky, Mario **6**:49
Dello Joio, Norman **6**:94
Joplin, Scott **11**:446–447
Moore, Douglas Stuart **13**:567
Piston, Walter **15**:319
Wuorinen, Charles **20**:296
ragtime **16**:70
recitative **16**:107–108
reggae **16**:128
Renaissance music **16**:155–156
rhythm **16**:204
rhythm and blues **16**:204–205
rock music **16**:247–250
Rococo music **16**:263
romanticism **16**:293–294
scale (music) **17**:106–107
serial music **17**:208
song **18**:64
soul music **18**:71
tempo **19**:100
theory
Arensky, Anton Stepanovich **2**:145
Busoni, Ferruccio **3**:590
Campion, Thomas **4**:67
Chinese music **4**:391–392
Guido d'Arezzo **9**:394
Hindemith, Paul **10**:168
Pythagoras of Samos **15**:639–640
Rameau, Jean Philippe **16**:80
Vitry, Philippe de **19**:621
tonality **19**:232–233
tone **19**:233
twelve-tone system **19**:358–359
variations **19**:523
Voyager **19**:638
MUSIC, ACOUSTICS OF **13**:661–662 *bibliog.*
Greek music **9**:345
harmonics **10**:51
Helmholtz, Hermann Ludwig Ferdinand von **10**:115–116
keyboard instruments **12**:62–63
organ (musical instrument) **14**:432–433
pitch **15**:320
sound and acoustics **18**:73
tuning fork **19**:334
voice, singing **19**:625–626
MUSIC, HISTORY OF WESTERN **13**:662–667 *bibliog., illus.*
English music **7**:202
French music **8**:320–321
Italian music **11**:317–319
jazz **11**:387–390 *illus.*
Latin American music and dance **12**:231–232
medieval music **13**:274–275
musical notation and terms **13**:679–681
opera **14**:399–401
orchestra and orchestration **14**:417–419
Renaissance music **16**:155–157
rock music **16**:247–250
Spanish music **18**:161–162
symphony **18**:405
MUSIC, NON-WESTERN **13**:667–669 *bibliog., illus.*
Arabian music **2**:99–100
Byzantine music **3**:608
Chinese music **4**:391–393
gong **9**:243 *illus.*
Hovhaness, Alan **10**:282
Indian music **11**:102–103 *illus.*
influences by Western music **13**:668
Japanese music **11**:380–382
MUSIC BOX **13**:669 *bibliog.*
MUSIC COMPETITIONS **13**:669 *bibliog.*
MUSIC AND CONCERT HALLS **13**:669–670 *bibliog.*
Carnegie Hall **4**:155
Festspielhaus (Richard Wagner) **13**:666 *illus.*; **14**:402 *illus., illus.*
Kennedy Center for the Performing Arts **12**:44
La Scala **12**:149
Lincoln Center for the Performing Arts **12**:350
music hall, vaudeville, and burlesque **13**:672
opera houses **14**:401–402 *illus., illus.*
Radio City Music Hall **16**:53
reverberation time **18**:73 *illus.*
Teatro Colón (Buenos Aires) **18**:92 *illus.*
MUSIC CRITICISM **13**:670 *bibliog.*
Cui, César **5**:383
Gilman, Lawrence **9**:182–183
Hanslick, Eduard **10**:41
Huneker, James Gibbons **10**:305
Kelley, Edgar Stillman **12**:38
Mason (family) **13**:198
Newman, Ernest **14**:169–170
Schumann, Robert **17**:137
Shaw, George Bernard **17**:245–246
Thomson, Virgil **19**:177
Wolf, Hugo **20**:196
MUSIC FESTIVALS **13**:670–671 *bibliog.*
Berkshire Music Festival **3**:214
Salzburg Festival **17**:44–45
Spoleto Festival **18**:192
MUSIC HALL, VAUDEVILLE, AND BURLESQUE **13**:671–673 *bibliog., illus.*
See also REVUE
American music **1**:349–350 *illus.*
Cantor, Eddie **4**:118
Christy, Edwin P. **4**:416–417
Cohan, George M. **5**:95
Foy, Eddie **8**:257
Heiberg, Johan Ludvig **10**:106
Jolson, Al **11**:441
Russell, Lillian **16**:351
Weber, Joseph, and Fields, Lew **20**:87
MUSIC VIDEO *see* VIDEO, MUSIC
MUSICAL BOW
musical instruments **13**:677–678
MUSICAL COMEDY **13**:673–675 *bibliog., illus.*
See also COMEDY; OPERETTA; REVUE
American music **1**:351
Astaire, Fred **2**:267
burletta **3**:572
choreography
Bennett, Michael **3**:203
Holm, Hanya **10**:204–205
Robbins, Jerome **16**:240

MUSICAL COMEDY (cont.)
classification **13**:673–674
composers
Berlin, Irving **3**:217
Bernstein, Leonard **3**:224
Bock, Jerry **3**:355
Gershwin, George and Ira **9**:158–159
Kern, Jerome **12**:59
Lerner, Alan Jay, and Loewe, Frederick **12**:296
Porter, Cole **15**:444
Romberg, Sigmund **16**:294
Sondheim, Stephen **18**:63–64
Styne, Jules **18**:311
Weill, Kurt **20**:94
Willson, Meredith **20**:163
directors and producers
Abbott, George **1**:53
Bennett, Michael **3**:203
Merrick, David **13**:312
White, George **20**:135
Foy, Eddie **8**:257
history **13**:674–675
Kelly, Gene **12**:39
Merman, Ethel **13**:311
Rodgers, Richard, and Hart, Lorenz **16**:267
Rogers, Ginger **16**:269
stage and set design
Aronson, Boris **2**:186–187
writers
Abbott, George **1**:53
Comden, Betty, and Green, Adolphe **5**:131
Fields, Dorothy **8**:73
Hammerstein, Oscar, II **10**:31
Harnick, Sheldon **3**:355
Lindsay, Howard, and Crouse, Russel **12**:352
MUSICAL INSTRUMENTS **13**:675–679 *bibliog., illus.*
See also MEDIEVAL MUSIC; names of specific instruments, e.g., ACCORDION; VIOLIN; etc.
African **1**:168–170 *illus.*
ancient
aulos **2**:323
Greek music **9**:345
kithara **12**:93
lyre **12**:479
Southeast Asian art and architecture **18**:108
Arabian music **2**:99–100
baritone **3**:81
Chinese music **4**:392–393 *illus.*
classification **13**:675–676
collections **13**:679
electronic music **7**:124–126
theremin **19**:160
folk music **8**:203
Indian music **11**:102–103 *illus.*
Japanese music **11**:381–382
keyboard instruments **12**:62–63 *illus.*
Korea **12**:115 *illus.*
Latin American music and dance **12**:231
music, acoustics of **13**:661–662
music, non-Western **13**:667–668
music box **13**:669
orchestra and orchestration **14**:417–419
percussion instruments **15**:162–163
16th to 18th centuries
barrel organ **3**:94
chitarrone **4**:398
cittern **4**:448
clavichord **5**:45
flageolet **8**:149
glass harmonica **9**:201–202
hurdy-gurdy **10**:315–316 *illus.*
krummhorn **12**:131–132
lute **12**:468
ophicleide **14**:404
recorder **16**:110 *illus.*
spinet **18**:185
theorbo **19**:158
viol **19**:601–602
virginal **19**:606
sound and acoustics **18**:72–73 *illus., table*
stringed instruments **18**:300–301
tablature **19**:4
tenor **19**:112
treble **19**:286
wind instruments **20**:170–171
MUSICAL NOTATION AND TERMS **13**:679–681 *bibliog., illus., table*
clef **5**:48 *illus.*
electronic music **7**:125
glossary of musical terms **13**:680 *table*
Indians of North America, music and dance of the **11**:142
meter (music) **13**:343
plainsong **15**:326
staff **18**:209
tablature **19**:4
tempo **19**:100
trill **19**:299
Vitry, Philippe de **19**:621
MUSICAL REVUE *see* REVUE
MUSICALS *see* MUSICAL COMEDY; REVUE; OPERETTA
MUSIL, ROBERT **13**:681 *bibliog.*
MUSK **13**:681
civet **5**:9
hibiscus **10**:157
mud turtle **13**:631
musk deer **13**:681
MUSK DEER **13**:681 *illus.*
MUSK-OX **2**:140–141 *illus.*; **13**:681–682 *illus.*
animal behavior **2**:15 *illus.*
MUSK TURTLE **13**:682 *illus.*
MUSKEG BAY
map (48° 55′N 95° 15′W) **13**:453
MUSKEGET CHANNEL
map (41° 25′N 70° 20′W) **13**:206
MUSKEGO (Wisconsin)
map (42° 54′N 88° 8′W) **20**:185
MUSKEGON (Michigan) **13**:682
map (43° 14′N 86° 16′W) **13**:377
MUSKEGON (county in Michigan)
map (43° 20′N 86° 10′W) **13**:377
MUSKEGON HEIGHTS (Michigan)
map (43° 12′N 86° 12′W) **13**:377
MUSKEGON RIVER
map (43° 14′N 86° 20′W) **13**:377
MUSKELLUNGE **13**:682 *illus.*
MUSKET **13**:682–683 *bibliog., illus.*
Brown Bess **13**:682–683
firearms **8**:105
firing devices **13**:683 *illus.*
history **13**:682–683
MUSKETEER **7**:190 *illus.*
MUSKIE, EDMUND S. **13**:683
Carter, Jimmy **4**:172
MUSKINGUM RIVER
map (40° 3′N 81° 59′W) **14**:357
MUSKINGUN (county in Ohio)
map (39° 57′N 81° 57′W) **14**:357
MUSKMELON **13**:288 *illus.*
MUSKOGEE (Oklahoma) **13**:683
map (35° 45′N 95° 22′W) **14**:368
MUSKOGEE (county in Oklahoma)
map (35° 40′N 95° 25′W) **14**:368
MUSKRAT **13**:683 *bibliog., illus.*
MUSLIM *see* ISLAM
MUSLIM LEAGUE **13**:683 *bibliog.*
Jinnah, Muhammad Ali **11**:419
MUSLIN **13**:683
MUSSADEGH, MOHAMMAD *see* MOSADDEQ, MUHAMMAD
MUSSAU ISLANDS
money **13**:525 *illus.*
MUSSEL **13**:510 *illus.*; **13**:683–684 *bibliog.*
blue mussel **11**:229 *illus.*
shellfish **17**:254 *illus.*
gill **9**:181 *illus.*
intertidal life **11**:230
MUSSELSHELL (county in Montana)
map (46° 30′N 108° 20′W) **13**:547
MUSSELSHELL RIVER
map (47° 21′N 107° 58′W) **13**:547
MUSSEN, PAUL
moral awareness **13**:573
MUSSET, ALFRED DE **13**:684 *bibliog.*
MUSSOLINI, BENITO **13**:684 *bibliog., illus.*
Europe, history of **7**:295; **7**:297
fascism **8**:30 *illus.*
Haile Selassie, Emperor of Ethiopia **10**:13
Italy, history of **11**:330–331 *illus.*
Milan (Italy) **13**:418
roads and highways **16**:238
Victor Emmanuel III, King of Italy **19**:573
World War II **20**:249–271 *illus.*
Zog I, King of Albania **20**:371
MUSSORGSKY, MODEST **13**:685 *bibliog., illus.*
Boris Godunov (opera) **3**:400–401
Five, The **8**:132
Russian music **16**:367–368 *illus.*
MUSTAFA IV, SULTAN OF THE OTTOMAN EMPIRE
Selim III, Sultan of the Ottoman Empire **17**:192
MUSTANG (aircraft) **1**:215 *illus.*; **13**:685 *bibliog., illus.*
MUSTANG (horse) **13**:685–686 *illus.*
MUSTAPÄÄ, P. (pseudonym)
Finnish literature **8**:99
MUSTARD (botany) **13**:686 *illus.*
Alyssum **1**:320
candytuft **4**:108
charlock **4**:298
cress **5**:339
Dijon (France) **6**:175
gillyflower **9**:182
honesty (botany) **10**:220
horseradish **10**:251
Kerguelen cabbage **12**:59
radish **16**:67
roquette **16**:312
rose of Jericho **16**:314
rutabaga **16**:374
seed, glycoside **9**:212
shepherd's purse **17**:256
stocks **18**:276
toothwort **19**:236
turnip **19**:351
watercress **20**:62
MUSTARD GAS
chemical and biological warfare **4**:311; **4**:312
Haber, Fritz **10**:4
poison gas **15**:382
MUSTEL, AUGUSTE
celesta **4**:229–230
MUTA NZIGE *see* EDWARD, LAKE
MUTAMID, CALIPH AL-
Samarra (Iraq) **17**:46
MUTANABBI, AL- **13**:686
MUTARE (Zimbabwe)
map (18° 58′S 32° 40′E) **20**:365
MUTASIM, AL-
Middle East, history of the **13**:404
Samarra (Iraq) **17**:46
MUTATION **13**:686–687 *bibliog.*
antibiotics **2**:58
bacteria **3**:18
cancer **4**:103 *illus.*
evolution **7**:319–320
genetic code **9**:81
genetic diseases **9**:82–84
genetics **9**:88–90
heredity **10**:140
natural selection **14**:49
new species **7**:320
nucleic acid **14**:290
population genetics **15**:439
Tatum, Edward L. **19**:44
MUTESA I, KABAKA OF BUGANDA
Uganda **19**:373
MUTHESIUS, HERMANN
industrial design **11**:155
MUTHMANNITE
telluride minerals **19**:91
MUTI, RICCARDO **13**:687
MUTINY **13**:687 *bibliog.*
MUTINY ON THE BOUNTY (book) **13**:687
Nordhoff, Charles **14**:218
MUTINY ON THE BOUNTY (event)
Bligh, William **3**:331
Bounty **3**:422
MUTSUHITO, EMPEROR OF JAPAN **13**:282 *illus.*
MUTT AND JEFF (comic strip) **5**:135 *illus.*
MUTTON *see* LAMB AND MUTTON
MUTUAL FUND **13**:687 *bibliog.*
MUTUAL LIFE INSURANCE
life insurance **12**:330
MUTUAL SAVINGS BANK *see* SAVINGS BANK
MUYBRIDGE, EADWEARD **13**:687–688 *bibliog., illus.*
Eakins, Thomas **7**:4
film, history of **8**:80–81 *illus.*
human motion studies **15**:270 *illus.*
Isadora Duncan **6**:28 *illus.*
Marey, Étienne Jules **13**:148
MUYINGA (Burundi)
map (2° 51′S 30° 20′E) **3**:582
MUZIO, CLAUDIA **13**:688 *bibliog.*
MUZOREWA, ABEL T. **13**:688 *bibliog.*
Nkomo, Joshua **14**:206
Zimbabwe (Rhodesia) **20**:366
MVOUNG RIVER
map (0° 4′N 12° 18′E) **9**:5
MWAMBUTSA IV, KING OF BURUNDI
Burundi **3**:583
MWANGA, KABAKA OF BUGANDA
Uganda **19**:373
MWANZA (Tanzania)
map (2° 31′S 32° 54′E) **19**:27
MWATA YAMVO (royal line)
Lunda **12**:462
MWERU, LAKE
map (8° 45′S 29° 40′E) **20**:354
MX MISSILE **13**:688 *bibliog., illus.*; **16**:255
MY ÁNTONIA (book) **13**:688–689 *bibliog.*
MY FAIR LADY (musical)
Lerner, Alan Jay, and Loewe, Frederick **12**:296
musical comedy **13**:673 *illus.*
MY LAI INCIDENT **13**:689 *bibliog.*
Vietnam War **19**:587; **19**:589 *map*
MY LITTLE CHICKADEE (film) **8**:73 *illus.*
MY THO (Vietnam)
map (10° 21′N 106° 21′E) **19**:580
MYASSINE, LEONID *see* MASSINE, LEONID
MYASTHENIA GRAVIS **13**:689 *bibliog.*
neostigmine **14**:86
MYCENAE (Greece) **13**:689–690 *bibliog., illus.*
Aegean civilization **1**:114–118 *illus.*
Agamemnon (mythology) **1**:182
art
gold and silver work **9**:228
Minoan art **13**:459
Atreus (mythology) **2**:312
burial
domed tomb of Atreus **19**:230 *illus.*
grave sites **13**:689 *illus.*
Greece, ancient **9**:329
Linear B **12**:353–354
Orchomenos **14**:420
Schliemann, Heinrich **17**:126–127
Tiryns **19**:209
MYCERINUS, KING OF EGYPT *see* MENKAURE, KING OF EGYPT
MYCIN (expert system) **7**:334
MYCOBACTERIUM **13**:690
respiratory system disorders **16**:181
tuberculosis **19**:327
Koch, Robert **12**:104
MYCOLOGY **13**:690 *bibliog.*
MYCOPLASMA **13**:690 *bibliog.*
diseases, animal **6**:192
infectious diseases **11**:164–165
pneumonia **15**:375–376
respiratory system disorders **16**:181
urethritis **11**:167
MYCOPLASMAL PNEUMONIA **13**:690
MYCORRHIZA **13**:690
mushrooms **13**:660
MYCOSES *see* FUNGUS DISEASES
MYCOSTATIN
antibiotics **2**:57
MYELIN
cholesterol **4**:403
multiple sclerosis **13**:638
nervous system **14**:92
neurophysiology **14**:106
MYELOMA
leukemia **12**:300
multiple myeloma **13**:638
MYELOMATOSIS *see* MULTIPLE MYELOMA
MYERS, MICHAEL
ABSCAM **1**:62
MYERS, RONALD
brain bilateralism **3**:448
MYERSTOWN (Pennsylvania)
map (40° 22′N 76° 19′W) **15**:147
MYIASIS **13**:690
MYINGYAN (Burma)
map (21° 28′N 95° 23′E) **3**:573
MYITKYINA (Burma)
map (25° 23′N 97° 24′E) **3**:573
World War II **20**:276
MYLONITE **13**:690
MYMENSINGH (Bangladesh)
map (24° 45′N 90° 24′E) **3**:64
MYNAH **13**:690–691 *illus.*
MYOCARDIAL INFARCTION *see* HEART ATTACK
MYOCARDIUM **10**:91–92 *illus.*
fibers **13**:653 *illus.*
heart diseases **10**:95; **10**:96
muscle contraction **13**:654–655
MYOGLOBIN **13**:691
MYOPIA **13**:691
eye diseases **7**:351
eyeglasses **7**:351–352
MYOSIN
biological locomotion **3**:265
muscle contraction **13**:654–656
MYOSITIS **13**:691
myositis ossificans **13**:691
MYRDAL, GUNNAR AND ALVA **13**:691 *bibliog.*
MYRDALS GLACIER
map (63° 40′N 19° 5′W) **11**:17
MYRIAPOD **13**:691
MYRIVILIS, STRATIS
Greek literature, modern **9**:344
MYRNAM (Alberta)
map (53° 40′N 111° 14′W) **1**:256
MYRON **13**:691 *bibliog.*
MYRRH (botany) **13**:691
MYRTLE (botany) **13**:691–692 *illus.*
allspice **1**:304
bottlebrush **3**:419

clove 5:69
guava 9:390
paperbark 15:71
periwinkle 15:172
sweet gale 18:387
turpentine tree 19:352
MYRTLE BEACH (South Carolina) 18:100 *illus.*
map (33° 42′N 78° 52′W) 18:98
MYRTLE CREEK (Oregon)
map (43° 1′N 123° 17′W) 14:427
MYRTLE GROVE (Florida)
map (30° 25′N 87° 18′W) 8:172
MYRTLE POINT (Oregon)
map (43° 4′N 124° 8′W) 14:427
MYSORE (city in India) 13:692
MYSORE (state in India) *see* KARNATAKA (India)
MYSTERIES, VILLA OF THE 13:692 *bibliog.*
fresco 15:424 *illus.*
mural painting 13:645
MYSTERY, SUSPENSE, AND DETECTIVE FICTION 13:692–693 *bibliog.*
authors
Allingham, Margery 1:303
Ambler, Eric 1:325
Biggers, Earl Derr 3:249
Buchan, John, 1st Baron Tweedsmuir 3:532
Cain, James M. 4:17
Carr, John Dickson 4:166
Chandler, Raymond T. 4:279
Charteris, Leslie 4:300
Chesterton, G. K. 4:337
Christie, Dame Agatha 4:414–415
Collins, Wilkie 5:104
Creasey, John 5:334
Crichton, Michael 5:343
Day-Lewis, C. 6:55
Derleth, August 6:121
Doyle, Sir Arthur Conan 6:253
Dürrenmatt, Friedrich 6:307
Fearing, Kenneth 8:39
Fish, Robert L. 8:121
Fisher, Rudolph 8:123
Fleming, Ian 8:159
Freeling, Nicolas 8:299
Gardner, Erle Stanley 9:44–45
Hammett, Dashiell 10:31
Innes, Michael 11:179
James, P. D. 11:354
Le Carré, John 12:253
Leonard, Elmore 12:289
Macdonald, John D. 13:12
Macdonald, Ross 13:13
MacInnis, Helen 13:26
Marsh, Dame Ngaio 13:171
Michaels, Barbara 13:372
Millar, Margaret 13:426
Poe, Edgar Allan 15:377–378
Queen, Ellery 16:21
Rohmer, Sax 16:270
Sayers, Dorothy L. 17:106
Simenon, Georges 17:314
Spillane, Mickey 18:183
Stoker, Bram 18:278
Stout, Rex 18:285
Symons, Julian 18:404
Tey, Josephine 19:138
Thomas, Ross 19:174
Van Dine, S. S. 19:513
Waugh, Hillary 20:70
Westlake, Donald E. 20:117
Woods, Sara 20:212
Edgar Allan Poe Award *see* EDGAR ALLAN POE AWARD
pulp magazines 15:620
MYSTERY, SUSPENSE, AND DETECTIVE SHOWS
film noir 8:89
Hitchcock, Alfred 10:186
Serling, Rod 17:209
MYSTERY CULTS 13:693 *bibliog.*
Eleusinian mysteries 7:134–135
Orpheus 14:448
secret societies 17:181
MYSTERY OF KASPAR HAUSER, THE (film)
feral children 8:51
MYSTERY PLAY *see* MEDIEVAL DRAMA
MYSTIC (Connecticut)
Connecticut 5:194
map (41° 21′N 71° 58′W) 5:193
MYSTICETI
mammal 13:103; 13:105 *illus.*
MYSTICISM 13:693 *bibliog.*
Bernard of Clairvaux, Saint 3:220–221
Böhme, Jakob 3:361
Bonaventure, Saint 3:376
Bourignon, Antoinette 3:424
Catherine of Siena, Saint 4:209
dervish 6:123
Eckhart, Meister 7:39
Friedrich, Caspar David 8:332
Gerson, Jean le Charlier de 9:159
Ghazali, al- 9:166
Groote, Gerhard 9:369
Hallaj, al- 10:22
Hugh of Saint Victor 10:292
John of the Cross, Saint 11:424
Judaism 11:461–462
Law, William 12:248
Lull, Raymond 12:454
Luria, Isaac ben Solomon 12:466–467
quietism 16:26
religious cults 16:143
Ruysbroeck, John 16:377
Schwenkfeld von Ossig, Kaspar 17:140
Soloviev, Vladimir Sergeyevich 18:57
Sufism 18:327
Suso, Heinrich 18:370
Swedenborg, Emanuel 18:386
Tauler, Johannes 19:45
Teresa of Ávila, Saint 19:115–116
Underhill, Evelyn 19:383
MYTH OF SISYPHUS, THE 13:693
Camus, Albert 4:68
MYTHOLOGICAL REPRESENTATIONS
Italian art and architecture 11:311
Poussin, Nicolas 15:477
MYTHOLOGY 13:694–704 *bibliog., illus.*
See also names of specific mythological characters, e.g., ADONIS; ZEUS; etc.; names of specific national mythologies, e.g., GREEK MYTHOLOGY; NORSE MYTHOLOGY; etc.
authors
Bulfinch, Thomas 3:553
Frazer, Sir James 8:289
bushmaster 3:585 *illus.*
creation accounts 5:334–335; 13:695
dance 6:22–23 *illus.*
Dogon 6:223
dragon 6:255
fertility rites 8:60
folklore 8:203
genius 9:92
giants 9:171
Greek art 9:339–342
Lug 12:452
mother goddess 13:606–607
origins of deities 13:695
pomegranate 15:422
primitive religion 15:544
renewal and rebirth 13:695–696
riddles 16:216
sibyl 17:292
study of myths 13:694
supernatural literature 18:352
totem 19:249
types of myths 13:695–696
unicorn 19:384
women in society 20:201
MYTILENE *see* LESBOS (Greece)
MYTON (Utah)
map (40° 12′N 110° 4′W) 19:492
MYXEDEMA
endocrine system, diseases of the 7:170
MYXOBACTERIA 13:704
MYXOMYCOTA *see* SLIME MOLD
MZILIKAZI (chief)
Ndebele 14:68
MZIMBA (Malawi)
map (11° 52′S 33° 34′E) 13:81
MZUZU (Malawi)
map (11° 27′S 33° 55′E) 13:81

N

N (letter) 14:3 *illus.*
NA-CH'Ü (China)
map (31° 34′N 92° 0′E) 19:190
NA-MU, LAKE
map (30° 42′N 90° 30′E) 19:190
NAACP *see* NATIONAL ASSOCIATION FOR THE ADVANCEMENT OF COLORED PEOPLE
NAALEHU (Hawaii)
map (19° 4′N 155° 35′W) 10:72
NAAS (Ireland)
map (53° 13′N 6° 39′W) 11:258
NABALOI
Igorot 11:38
NABATAEA, KINGDOM OF
Jordan 11:449
Petra 15:203
NABEUL (Tunisia)
map (36° 27′N 10° 44′E) 19:335
NABIS (art and literary group) 14:3 *bibliog.*
Bonnard, Pierre 3:381
Denis, Maurice 6:108
Gauguin, Paul 9:59–60
Vallotton, Félix 19:508
Vuillard, Édouard 19:640
NABLUS (Jordan)
map (32° 13′N 35° 16′E) 11:447
NABNASSET (Massachusetts)
map (42° 37′N 71° 25′W) 3:409
NABOKOV, VLADIMIR 14:3–4 *bibliog., illus.*
NABONIDUS, KING OF CHALDEA
Nebuchadnezzar II, King of Babylonia 14:74
Ur 19:474
NABOPOLASSAR
Nebuchadnezzar II, King of Babylonia 14:74
NABUCO, JOAQUIM 14:4 *bibliog.*
NACHAL OZ (Israel)
map (31° 28′N 34° 29′E) 11:302
NACHTIGAL, GUSTAV 14:4
Africa 1:157 *map*
Tibesti Massif 19:189
NACOGDOCHES (Texas)
map (31° 36′N 94° 39′W) 19:129
NACOGDOCHES (county in Texas)
map (31° 37′N 94° 40′W) 19:129
NACOZARI [DE GARCÍA] (Mexico)
map (30° 24′N 109° 39′W) 13:357
NACRE *see* MOTHER-OF-PEARL
NACREOUS CLOUD 14:4
NAD *see* NICOTINAMIDE ADENINE DINUCLEOTIDE
NADAR 14:4 *bibliog., illus.*
Gioacchino Rossini 16:320 *illus.*
NADELMAN, ELIE 14:4 *bibliog.*
NADER, RALPH 14:5 *bibliog., illus.*
Educational Testing Service 7:67
NADIR (Virgin Islands)
map (18° 19′N 64° 53′W) 19:605
NADIR SHAH 14:5 *bibliog.*
NADP *see* NICOTINAMIDE ADENINE DINUCLEOTIDE PHOSPHATE
NAE *see* NATIONAL ACADEMY OF ENGINEERING
NÆSTVED (Denmark)
map (55° 14′N 11° 46′E) 6:109
NAEVIUS, GNAEUS 14:5
NAFUD 14:5
map (28° 30′N 41° 0′E) 17:94
NAG HAMMADI PAPYRI 14:5 *bibliog., illus.*
NAGA (mythological character) 14:6
NAGA (people) 14:6 *bibliog.*
Nagaland (India) 14:6
NAGA (Philippines)
map (10° 13′N 123° 45′E) 15:237
NAGA HILLS
map (26° 0′N 95° 0′E) 3:573
NAGA LANGUAGE
Sino-Tibetan languages 17:324
NAGAI KAFU 14:6
NAGALAND (India) 14:6
map (26° 0′N 95° 0′E) 11:80
Naga (people) 14:6
NAGANA
tsetse fly 19:323
NAGANO (Japan)
map (36° 39′N 138° 11′E) 11:361
NAGARA *see* TEMPLE
NAGAROTE (Nicaragua)
map (12° 16′N 86° 34′W) 14:179
NAGASAKI (Japan) 14:6
map (32° 48′N 129° 55′E) 11:361
World War II 20:279 *illus.*
NAGEL, ERNEST 14:6 *bibliog.*
NAGOYA (Japan) 14:6
map (35° 10′N 136° 55′E) 11:361
NAGPUR (India) 14:6
map (21° 9′N 79° 6′E) 11:80
NAGUA (Dominican Republic)
map (19° 23′N 69° 50′W) 6:233
NAGUIB, MUHAMMAD
Nasser, Gamal Abdel 14:25
NAGUMO, CHUICHI
Pearl Harbor 15:126
NAGURSKI, BRONKO 14:6–7 *bibliog.*
NAGY, IMRE 14:7 *bibliog.*
Hungarian Revolution 10:306
NAGY, IVAN AKOS 14:7 *bibliog.*
NAGY, LÁSZLÓ MOHOLY- *see* MOHOLY-NAGY, LÁSZLÓ
NAGY-MILIC MOUNTAIN
map (48° 35′N 21° 28′E) 10:307
NAGYBÁNYA, MIKLÓS HORTHY DE *see* HORTHY DE NAGYBÁNYA, MIKLÓS
NAGYKANIZSA (Hungary)
map (46° 27′N 17° 0′E) 10:307
NAHA (Japan)
map (26° 13′N 127° 40′E) 11:361
NAHANT (Massachusetts)
map (42° 25′N 70° 55′W) 3:409
NAHARIYYA (Israel)
map (33° 0′N 35° 5′E) 11:302
NAHARRO, BARTOLOMÉ DE TORRES
Spanish literature 18:158
NAHUM, BOOK OF 14:7
NAHUNTA (Georgia)
map (31° 12′N 81° 59′W) 9:114
NAIAD (insect) 14:7
nymph (insect) 14:309
NAIDU, SAROJINI 14:7
NAIL (anatomy) *see* HOOF, NAIL, AND CLAW
NAIL (metal) 14:7–8 *bibliog., illus.*
NAIN (Newfoundland)
map (56° 32′N 61° 41′W) 14:166
NAIPAUL, V. S. 14:8 *bibliog.*
NAIRN (Scotland) 14:8
NAIROBI (Kenya) 12:53–54 *illus., table*; 14:8
map (1° 17′S 36° 49′E) 12:53
NAISMITH, JAMES 14:8 *bibliog.*
basketball 3:111–112 *illus.*
NAIVASHA, LAKE
map (0° 46′S 36° 21′E) 12:53
NAIVE ART *see* PRIMITIVISM (art)
NAJAFABAD (Iran)
map (32° 37′N 51° 21′E) 11:250
NAJJER PLATEAU
map (25° 10′N 8° 0′E) 1:287
NAKASONE YASUHIRO 14:8
NAKED AND THE DEAD, THE (book) 14:9
Mailer, Norman 13:67
NAKHODKA (USSR)
map (42° 48′N 132° 52′E) 19:388
NAKHON PATHOM (Thailand)
map (13° 49′N 100° 3′E) 19:139
NAKHON RATCHASIMA (Thailand)
map (14° 58′N 102° 7′E) 19:139
NAKHON SAWAN (Thailand)
map (15° 41′N 100° 7′E) 19:139
NAKHON SI THAMMARAT (Thailand)
map (8° 26′N 99° 58′E) 19:139
NAKIAN, REUBEN 14:9 *bibliog.*
NAKIMA (Ontario)
map (50° 10′N 86° 42′W) 14:393
NAKNEK (Alaska)
map (58° 44′N 157° 2′W) 1:242
NAKOTA (American Indians) *see* ASSINIBOIN (American Indians); SIOUX (American Indians)
NAKSKOV (Denmark)
map (54° 50′N 11° 9′E) 6:109
NAKTONG RIVER
map (35° 7′N 128° 57′E) 12:113
NAKURU (Kenya)
map (0° 17′S 36° 4′E) 12:53
NAKURU, LAKE 12:55 *illus.*
NAKUSP (British Columbia)
map (50° 15′N 117° 48′W) 3:491
NALATALE (Zimbabwe) 14:9 *bibliog.*
NALLY, EDWARD J.
radio and television broadcasting 16:55
NALORPHINE 14:9
NALOXONE
nalorphine 14:9
NAM DINH (Vietnam)
map (20° 25′N 106° 10′E) 19:580
NAMAK, LAKE
map (34° 45′N 51° 36′E) 11:250
NAMATANAI (Papua New Guinea)
map (3° 40′S 152° 25′E) 15:72
NAMATH, JOE 14:9 *bibliog., illus.*
NAMBOUWALU (Fiji)
map (16° 59′S 178° 42′E) 8:77
NAMEKAGON RIVER
map (46° 5′N 92° 6′W) 20:185
NAMES, PERSONAL 14:9–10 *bibliog.*
Indian languages, American 11:98
NAMHAN RIVER
map (37° 31′N 127° 18′E) 12:113
NAMIAS, JEROME 14:10
NAMIB DESERT 6:126; 14:10
map (23° 0′S 15° 0′E) 14:11
NAMIBIA 14:10–12 *bibliog., illus., map, table*
Caprivi Strip 4:128
cities
Keetmanshoop 14:11 *table*
Tsumeb 14:11 *table*
Windhoek 20:172
flag 14:10 *illus.*
government 14:12
history 14:12
mandate system 13:111
Nujoma, Sam 14:292
land, people, and economy 14:11–12
map (22° 0′S 17° 0′E) 1:136

NAMIBIA (cont.)
people
Herero **10**:141
Khoikhoi **12**:67
Ovambo **14**:469
San **17**:49–50
NAMIN (Iran)
map (38° 25′N 48° 30′E) **11**:250
NAMOI RIVER
map (30° 0′S 148° 7′E) **2**:328
NAMOS (Norway)
map (64° 29′N 11° 30′E) **14**:261
NAMPA (Alberta)
map (56° 2′N 117° 8′W) **1**:256
NAMPA (Idaho)
map (43° 34′N 116° 34′W) **11**:26
NAMPO (Korea)
map (38° 45′N 125° 23′E) **12**:113
NAMPULA (Mozambique)
map (15° 7′S 39° 15′E) **13**:627
NAMUR (Belgium) **14**:12
map (50° 28′N 4° 52′E) **3**:177
World War I **20**:223
NAN-CH'ANG (China)
map (28° 34′N 115° 56′E) **4**:362
NAN HAI *see* CHINA SEA, SOUTH
NAN-LING MOUNTAINS
map (25° 0′N 112° 0′E) **4**:362
NAN-NING (China)
map (22° 48′N 108° 20′E) **4**:362
NAN RIVER
map (15° 42′N 100° 9′E) **19**:139
NAN SHAN MOUNTAINS
map (39° 6′N 98° 40′E) **4**:362
NAN-YANG (China)
map (33° 0′N 112° 32′E) **4**:362
NANA (book)
Zola, Émile **20**:372
NANAIMO (British Columbia)
map (49° 10′N 123° 56′W) **3**:491
NANAK, GURU
Sikhs **17**:302
NANAKULI (Hawaii)
map (21° 23′N 158° 9′W) **10**:72
NANCE (county in Nebraska)
map (41° 25′N 98° 0′W) **14**:70
NANCY (France) **14**:12
map (48° 41′N 6° 12′E) **8**:260
NANDA DEVI (India) **11**:81
map (30° 23′N 79° 59′E) **11**:80
NANDI (Fiji)
map (17° 48′S 177° 25′E) **8**:77
NANDURI (Fiji)
map (16° 27′S 179° 9′E) **8**:77
NANGA PARBAT MOUNTAIN
map (35° 15′N 74° 36′E) **15**:27
NANGA SCHOOL
Buncho **3**:562
Gyokudo **9**:414–415
Tessai **19**:126
NANKING (Nanjing) (China) **4**:366 *illus.*; **14**:12
map (32° 3′N 118° 47′E) **4**:362
NANKING, TREATY OF
Ch'ing (Qing) (dynasty) **4**:395
NANNI DI BANCO **14**:12–13 *bibliog.*
NANOSAURUS **14**:13
NANSEN, FRIDTJOF **2**:142 *illus., map*; **14**:13 *bibliog., illus.*
exploration **7**:338
refugee **16**:126
NANTES (France) **14**:13
map (47° 13′N 1° 33′W) **8**:260
NANTES, EDICT OF **14**:13 *bibliog.*
France, history of **8**:268
Huguenots **10**:294–295
Nantes (France) **14**:13
NANTEUIL, ROBERT **14**:13 *bibliog.*
NANTICOKE (Pennsylvania)
map (41° 12′N 76° 0′W) **15**:147
NANTICOKE RIVER
map (38° 16′N 75° 56′W) **13**:188
NANTON (Alberta)
map (50° 21′N 113° 46′W) **1**:256
NANTUCKET (Massachusetts)
map (41° 17′N 70° 6′W) **13**:206
NANTUCKET (county in Massachusetts)
map (41° 17′N 70° 6′W) **13**:206
NANTUCKET ISLAND **14**:14
map (41° 16′N 70° 3′W) **13**:206
Mitchell, Maria **13**:483
NANTUCKET SLEIGHRIDE
whaling **20**:122 *illus.*
NANTUCKET SOUND
map (41° 30′N 70° 15′W) **13**:206
NANTY GLO (Pennsylvania)
map (40° 28′N 78° 50′W) **15**:147
NANUQUE (Brazil)
map (17° 50′S 40° 21′W) **3**:460
NAO, CAPE OF
map (38° 44′N 0° 14′E) **18**:140
NAOGAON (Bangladesh)
map (24° 47′N 88° 56′E) **3**:64
NAOS **14**:14
NAPA (California)
map (38° 18′N 122° 17′W) **4**:31
NAPA (county in California)
map (38° 18′N 122° 17′W) **4**:31
wine **20**:176 *illus.*
NAPALM **14**:14
phosphorus **15**:256
NAPATA
Nubia **14**:277
NAPATREE POINT
map (41° 19′N 71° 50′W) **16**:198
NAPERVILLE (Illinois)
map (41° 47′N 88° 9′W) **11**:42
NAPHTHA **14**:14
NAPHTHALENE **14**:14 *illus.*
coal tar **5**:80
NAPIER (New Zealand)
map (39° 29′S 176° 55′E) **14**:158
NAPIER, JOHN **14**:14 *bibliog.*
logarithm **12**:394
mathematics, history of **13**:224–225 *illus.*
NAPLES (Florida)
map (26° 8′N 81° 48′W) **8**:172
NAPLES (Idaho)
map (48° 34′N 116° 24′W) **11**:26
NAPLES (Italy) **5**:4 *illus.*; **14**:14–15 *illus.*
15th century **11**:328 *illus.*
map (40° 51′N 14° 17′E) **11**:321
NAPLES, KINGDOM OF **14**:15 *bibliog.*
Alfonso V, King of Aragon **1**:279
Angevins (dynasties) **1**:414
Camorra **4**:62
Charles I, King (Charles of Anjou) **4**:296
Charles II, King **4**:296
Charles III, King **4**:296
Ferdinand I, King of Naples **8**:53
Fernández de Córdoba, Gonzalo **8**:58
Foggia (Italy) **8**:193
Garibaldi, Giuseppe **9**:47
Joan I, Queen **11**:420
Murat, Joachim **13**:647
René of Anjou **16**:157
Sicily (Italy) **17**:293
Two Sicilies, Kingdom of the **19**:360
NAPO RIVER
map (3° 20′S 72° 40′W) **15**:193
NAPOLEON (North Dakota)
map (46° 30′N 99° 46′W) **14**:248
NAPOLEON (Ohio)
map (41° 23′N 84° 8′W) **14**:357
NAPOLEON I, EMPEROR OF THE FRENCH (Napoléon Bonaparte) **14**:15–18 *bibliog., illus., map*
Battle of Eylau **16**:356 *illus.*
Bonaparte (family) **3**:375–376
cartoon depicting **14**:17 *illus.*
Consulate **5**:225
Egyptology **7**:90
Elba (Italy) **7**:102
émigrés **7**:156
Empire style **7**:158–159
Europe, history of **7**:291
Ferdinand VII, King of Spain **8**:54
Fouché, Joseph **8**:249
France, history of **8**:271 *illus.*
French Revolution **8**:324–325 *illus.*
French Revolutionary Wars **8**:325–326
Germany, history of **9**:152
Gobelins **9**:216
Gros, Antoine Jean, Baron **9**:369–370
Holy Roman Empire **10**:211
Hundred Days, The **14**:18
Illyria **11**:50
Italian and Egyptian campaigns **14**:16
Josephine **11**:452
Leipzig (East Germany) **12**:278
Louisiana Purchase **12**:435
Louvre **12**:437
Low Countries, history of the **12**:441
Malmaison **13**:93
Metternich, Klemens, Fürst von **13**:349
Naples, Kingdom of **14**:15
Napoleonic Empire c.1812 **14**:18 *map*
Napoleonic Wars **14**:19–20 *map*
Percier, Charles **15**:162
Pichegru, Jean Charles **15**:292
portraiture
David, Jacques Louis **6**:48
Gérard, François Pascal Simon, Baron **9**:121
Ingres, Jean Auguste Dominique **11**:176
Saint Helena **17**:19
Simplon Pass **17**:316
Talleyrand-Périgord, Charles Maurice de **19**:16–17
Tilsit, Treaties of **19**:200–201
tomb **19**:231
Toussaint L'Ouverture, François Dominique **19**:254
victory over Mamelukes **13**:406 *illus.*
Waterloo, Battle of **20**:64–65 *map*
Wellington, Arthur Wellesley, 1st Duke of **20**:100
NAPOLEON III, EMPEROR OF THE FRENCH (Louis Napoléon Bonaparte) **14**:18–19 *bibliog., illus.*
Eugénie **7**:264
France, history of **8**:271–272
Franco-Prussian War **8**:278–279
official photographers
Bisson, Louis and Auguste **3**:299–300
Utrecht (Netherlands) **19**:498
NAPOLEONIC CODE **14**:19 *bibliog.*
civil law **5**:11–12
law, history of **12**:245 *illus.*
women in society **20**:202
NAPOLEONIC WARS **7**:290 *illus.*; **14**:19–20 *bibliog., map*
Austerlitz, Battle of **2**:326
Blücher, Gebhard Leberecht von **3**:341–342
cannon **4**:112 *illus.*
Continental System **5**:230
Copenhagen **5**:250
Frederick William III, King of Prussia **8**:293
hussar **4**:221 *illus.*
Junot, Andoche **11**:471
Kutuzov, Mikhail Illarionovich **12**:140
Lisbon (Portugal) **12**:366
Masséna, André **13**:213
Metternich, Klemens, Fürst von **13**:349
Moreau, Jean Victor Marie **13**:576
Murat, Joachim **13**:647
Napoleon I, Emperor of the French (Napoléon Bonaparte) **14**:18
Ney, Michel **14**:175
Paris, treaties of **15**:87
Portugal, history of **15**:454
Prussia **15**:585–586 *map*
Quadruple Alliance **16**:5
right of search **16**:222
Russia/Union of Soviet Socialist Republics, history of **16**:356
Russo-Turkish Wars **16**:374
Scandinavia, history of **17**:110
Scharnhorst, Gerhard Johann David von **17**:117
Soult, Nicolas Jean de Dieu **18**:71
Spain, history of **18**:147
strategy and tactics, military **18**:291
Tilsit, Treaties of **19**:200–201
Trafalgar, Battle of **19**:264
Waterloo, Battle of **20**:65 *map*
Wellington, Arthur Wellesley, 1st Duke of **20**:100
Yorck von Wartenburg, Ludwig, Graf **20**:330
NAPOLEONVILLE (Louisiana)
map (29° 57′N 91° 1′W) **12**:430
NAPOLI (Italy) *see* NAPLES (Italy)
NAPPANEE (Indiana)
map (41° 27′N 86° 0′W) **11**:111
NAPPE **14**:20
NARA (Japan) **14**:20
Japan, history of **11**:367
Japanese art and architecture **11**:373–374
map (34° 41′N 135° 50′E) **11**:361
Shinto shrine entranceway **17**:262 *illus.*
Unkei **19**:470
NARA VISA (New Mexico)
map (35° 37′N 103° 6′W) **14**:136
NARAM SIN
Ebla **7**:36
NARAMATA (British Columbia)
map (49° 36′N 119° 35′W) **3**:491
NARANJAL (Ecuador)
map (2° 42′S 79° 37′W) **7**:52
NARASIMHADEVA, INDIAN EMPEROR
Konarak **12**:108
NARAYAN, JAYAPRAKASH **14**:20 *bibliog.*
NARAYAN, R. K. **14**:20 *bibliog.*
NARAYANGANJ (Bangladesh)
map (23° 37′N 90° 30′E) **3**:64
NARBONNE (France) **14**:21
map (43° 11′N 3° 0′E) **8**:260
NARCISSISM *see* NARCISSUS (mythology)
NARCISSUS (botany) **14**:21 *illus.*
daffodil **6**:6
jonquil **11**:445
NARCISSUS (mythology) **14**:21
NARCOANALYSIS
sedative **17**:182
NARCOLEPSY
sleep **17**:360
NARCOTIC
analgesic **1**:388
codeine **5**:90
Darvon **6**:40
drug abuse **6**:279
heroin **10**:145
methadone **13**:343
morphine **13**:587
nalorphine **14**:9
opium **14**:406
phenazocine **15**:225
NAREW RIVER
map (52° 26′N 20° 42′E) **15**:388
NARIÑO, ANTONIO **14**:21 *bibliog.*
NARMADA RIVER **14**:21
map (21° 38′N 72° 36′E) **11**:80
NARMER, KING OF EGYPT *see* MENES, KING OF EGYPT
NARODNAYA, MOUNT
map (65° 1′N 60° 1′E) **19**:388
NARODNAYA VOLYA *see* NARODNIKI
NARODNIKI **14**:21 *bibliog.*
Russia/Union of Soviet Socialist Republics, history of **16**:358
NARRAGANSETT (American Indians) **14**:21–22 *bibliog.*
Miantonomo **13**:370
Montauk **13**:551
Pequot **15**:158
NARRAGANSETT BAY **14**:22; **16**:199 *illus.*
map (41° 40′N 71° 20′W) **16**:198
NARRATIVE AND DRAMATIC DEVICES **14**:22–23 *bibliog.*
anti-hero **2**:62–63
Aristophanes **2**:155–156
Browning, Robert **3**:518
Bumppo, Natty **3**:562
Byronic hero **3**:603
carpe diem **4**:163
Carter, Nick **4**:173
Don Juan **6**:236
double **6**:245–246
dumb show **6**:297
Greek drama, ancient **1**:129
novel **14**:272–276
Shakespeare, William **17**:237
NARRATOR
narrative and dramatic devices **14**:22
NARROWS (Virginia)
map (37° 20′N 80° 48′W) **19**:607
NARROWS, THE
map (40° 37′N 74° 3′W) **14**:129
NARSSAG (Greenland)
map (60° 54′N 46° 0′W) **9**:353
NARVA (USSR) **14**:23
NARVÁEZ, PÁNFILO DE **14**:23
exploration of colonial America **19**:437 *map*
Tampa (Florida) **19**:20
Velázquez de Cuéllar, Diego **19**:537
NARVIK (Norway) **14**:23
NARWHAL **14**:23 *illus.*; **20**:120 *illus.*
cetacean **4**:262
ivory and ivory carving **11**:336
NAS *see* NATIONAL ACADEMY OF SCIENCES
NASA *see* NATIONAL AERONAUTICS AND SPACE ADMINISTRATION
NASBY, PETROLEUM V. **14**:23
NASCIMENTO, EDSON ARANTES DO *see* PELÉ (athlete)
NASDA *see* NATIONAL SPACE DEVELOPMENT AGENCY
NASH (county in North Carolina)
map (35° 55′N 78° 0′W) **14**:242
NASH, CHARLES WILLIAM **14**:23
NASH, JOHN **14**:23–24 *bibliog.*
landscape architecture **12**:187
Price, Sir Uvedale **15**:535
Regency Style **16**:126 *illus.*
Repton, Humphry **16**:171–172
Royal Pavilion at Brighton **16**:330–331 *illus.*
NASH, OGDEN **14**:24
Weill, Kurt **20**:94
NASH, PAUL
Battle of Britain **20**:255 *illus.*
NASH MOTOR COMPANY
automotive industry **2**:364; **2**:366
NASHE, THOMAS **14**:24 *bibliog.*
NASHUA (Iowa)
map (42° 57′N 92° 32′W) **11**:244
NASHUA (Montana)
map (48° 8′N 106° 22′W) **13**:547

NASHUA (New Hampshire) **14**:24
map (42° 46′N 71° 27′W) **14**:123
NASHUA RIVER
map (42° 46′N 71° 27′W) **13**:206
NASHVILLE (Arkansas)
map (33° 57′N 93° 51′W) **2**:166
NASHVILLE (Georgia)
map (31° 12′N 83° 15′W) **9**:114
NASHVILLE (Illinois)
map (38° 21′N 89° 23′W) **11**:42
NASHVILLE (Indiana)
map (39° 12′N 86° 15′W) **11**:111
NASHVILLE (North Carolina)
map (35° 58′N 77° 58′W) **14**:242
NASHVILLE (Tennessee) **14**:24; **19**:103 *illus.*; **19**:105 *map*
Grand Ole Opry **9**:285
Henderson, Richard **10**:121
map (36° 9′N 86° 48′W) **19**:104
NASHWAAKSIS (New Brunswick)
map (45° 59′N 66° 39′W) **14**:117
NÄSI LAKE
map (61° 37′N 23° 42′E) **8**:95
NASIK (India)
map (19° 59′N 73° 48′E) **11**:80
NASIR, IBRAHAM
Maldives, Republic of **13**:87
NASMYTH, ALEXANDER
Robert Burns **3**:578 *illus.*
NASMYTH, JAMES **14**:24 *bibliog.*
NASOPHARYNX *see* MOUTH AND THROAT
NASR AL-DIN SHAH **14**:24 *bibliog.*
NASSAU (Bahamas) **3**:24 *illus.*; **14**:25
map (25° 5′N 77° 21′W) **3**:23
NASSAU (county in Florida)
map (30° 40′N 81° 45′W) **8**:172
NASSAU (historical region) **14**:25
Germany 1815–1871 **9**:153 *map*
John Maurice of Nassau **11**:425
NASSAU (New York)
map (42° 31′N 73° 37′W) **14**:149
NASSAU (county in New York)
map (40° 45′N 73° 38′W) **14**:149
NASSAUVILLE (Florida)
map (30° 34′N 81° 31′W) **8**:172
NASSAWADOX (Virginia)
map (37° 28′N 75° 51′W) **19**:607
NASSER, GAMAL ABDEL **14**:25 *bibliog.*, *illus.*
Egypt **7**:80 *illus.*
Middle East, history of the **13**:409
Suez Crisis **18**:325
United Arab Republic **19**:401
NASSER, LAKE **14**:25
map (22° 40′N 32° 0′E) **7**:76
NÄSSJÖ (Sweden)
map (57° 39′N 14° 41′E) **18**:382
NAST, THOMAS **14**:25–26 *bibliog.*, *illus.*
"Boss" Tweed cartoon **4**:176 *illus.*; **19**:358 *illus.*
cartoon (editorial and political) **4**:176
cartoon attacking Andrew Johnson's Reconstruction **16**:109 *illus.*
GOP elephant **16**:173 *illus.*
Man with the (Carpet) Bags, The **4**:164 *illus.*
Santa Claus **17**:67 *illus.*
Tammany Hall **19**:20 *illus.*
Uncle Sam **19**:381–382
NASTURTIUM **14**:26 *illus.*
NATAL (city in Brazil) **14**:26
map (5° 47′S 35° 13′W) **3**:460
NATAL (province in South Africa) **14**:26
cities
Durban **6**:304
Pietermaritzburg **15**:297
history
Pretorius, Andries **15**:534
map (28° 40′S 30° 40′E) **18**:79
people
Zulu **20**:382
NATALIA (Texas)
map (29° 11′N 98° 52′W) **19**:129
NATANSON, MAURICE ALEXANDER **14**:26
NATARAJA *see* SHIVA
NATASHQUAN (Quebec)
map (50° 12′N 61° 49′W) **16**:18
NATCHEZ (American Indians) **14**:26 *bibliog.*
Mississippian culture **14**:239
NATCHEZ (Mississippi) **13**:471–472 *illus.*; **14**:26
map (31° 34′N 91° 23′W) **13**:469
NATCHEZ TRACE **8**:341 *map*
NATCHITOCHES (Louisiana) **14**:26–27
map (31° 46′N 93° 5′W) **12**:430
NATCHITOCHES (county in Louisiana)
map (31° 42′N 93° 8′W) **12**:430
NATEWA BAY
map (16° 35′S 179° 40′E) **8**:77
NATHAN, GEORGE JEAN **14**:27 *bibliog.*
NATHAN, ROBERT **14**:27
NATHANS, DANIEL **14**:27
Smith, Hamilton **17**:368
NATICK (Massachusetts)
map (42° 17′N 71° 21′W) **13**:206
NATICK COBBLER *see* WILSON, HENRY
NATION **14**:27
NATION, CARRY AMELIA **14**:27 *bibliog.*, *illus.*
NATION, THE (periodical) **14**:27
Godkin, Edwin Lawrence **9**:221
Krutch, Joseph Wood **11**:132
Norton, Charles Eliot **14**:260
Villard, Oswald Garrison **19**:598
NATION OF ISLAM *see* BLACK MUSLIMS
NATIONAL ACADEMY OF DESIGN
Durand, Asher Brown **6**:302
Morse, Samuel F. B. **13**:590
NATIONAL ACADEMY OF ENGINEERING
National Academy of Sciences **14**:27
NATIONAL ACADEMY OF RECORDING ARTS AND SCIENCES
Grammy Award **9**:283
NATIONAL ACADEMY OF SCIENCES **14**:27–28 *bibliog.*
Agassiz, Louis Rodolphe **1**:182
Food and Nutrition Board, United States
nutritional-deficiency diseases **14**:308
Washington, D.C. **20**:41 *map*
Wiener, Norbert **20**:146
NATIONAL ACADEMY OF TELEVISION ARTS AND SCIENCES
Emmy Awards **7**:156–157
NATIONAL ACCOUNTING
See also INCOME, NATIONAL
balance of payments **3**:31–32
NATIONAL ADVISORY COMMITTEE FOR AERONAUTICS *see* NATIONAL AERONAUTICS AND SPACE ADMINISTRATION
NATIONAL AERONAUTICS AND SPACE ADMINISTRATION **14**:28 *bibliog.*, *illus.*
Agena (rocket) **1**:183
Apollo program **2**:80–84
astronaut **2**:274
aviation **2**:374
communications satellite **5**:144–145
Explorer **7**:338
Gemini program **9**:71–73
Goddard Space Flight Center **9**:220
history **14**:28
IMP **11**:60
Jet Propulsion Laboratory **11**:407
Johnson Space Center **11**:437
Kennedy Space Center **12**:44–45
OAO **14**:312–313
OGO **14**:354
OSO **14**:456
programs **14**:28
SEASAT **17**:176
space exploration **18**:120
space station **18**:136–137
Space Telescope **18**:137
Synchronous Meteorological Satellite **18**:406
TIROS **19**:208
Uhuru **19**:374
von Braun, Wernher **19**:633
NATIONAL AIR AND SPACE MUSEUM **14**:28–29
NATIONAL AMERICAN WOMAN SUFFRAGE ASSOCIATION
suffrage, women's **18**:326
NATIONAL ANTHEM *see* ANTHEM; the subheading national anthem under names of specific countries, e.g., FRANCE; NORWAY; etc.
NATIONAL ARCHIVES AND RECORDS SERVICE **14**:29
NATIONAL ASSEMBLY (France)
French Revolution **8**:322–323
NATIONAL ASSESSMENT OF EDUCATIONAL PROGRESS (organization) **14**:29 *bibliog.*
Tyler, Ralph Winfred **19**:362
NATIONAL ASSOCIATION OF BROADCASTERS
censorship **4**:248
NATIONAL ASSOCIATION OF MANUFACTURERS **14**:29
NATIONAL ASSOCIATION OF SOCIAL WORKERS
social work **18**:19
NATIONAL ASSOCIATION FOR STOCK CAR RACING
stock car race **2**:361 *illus.*
NATIONAL ASSOCIATION FOR THE ADVANCEMENT OF COLORED PEOPLE **14**:29 *bibliog.*, *illus.*
black Americans **3**:309
Du Bois, W. E. B. **6**:285
Johnson, James Weldon **11**:432
Marshall, Thurgood **13**:173
Wilkins, Roy **20**:152
NATIONAL ASTRONOMY AND IONOSPHERE CENTER
Arecibo Observatory **2**:145
radio astronomy **16**:53
NATIONAL AUDUBON SOCIETY *see* AUDUBON SOCIETY, NATIONAL
NATIONAL BALLET OF CANADA **3**:41 *illus.*; **14**:29–30 *bibliog.*, *illus.*
NATIONAL BALLOON FACILITY
National Center for Atmospheric Research **14**:30
NATIONAL BANK **14**:30 *bibliog.*
See also CENTRAL BANK
banking systems **3**:68
Comptroller of the Currency, Office of the **5**:159
Federal Deposit Insurance Corporation **8**:41
United States see FEDERAL RESERVE SYSTEM
NATIONAL BASEBALL HALL OF FAME AND MUSEUM
Cooperstown (New York) **5**:245
NATIONAL BASKETBALL ASSOCIATION (NBA)
basketball **3**:112–114 *illus.*, *tables*
NATIONAL BIRTH CONTROL LEAGUE
Sanger, Margaret **17**:65
NATIONAL BOOK AWARDS **14**:30
Ashbery, John **2**:229
Barth, John **3**:97
Bellow, Saul **3**:190
Bettelheim, Bruno **3**:232
Bishop, Elizabeth **3**:297
Carson, Rachel **4**:170
Catton, Bruce **4**:217
Cheever, John **4**:310
Dickey, James **6**:157
Ellison, Ralph **7**:148
Ginsberg, Allen **9**:184–185
Hamilton, Virginia **10**:29
Jones, James **11**:443
Kosinski, Jerzy **12**:124
Krutch, Joseph Wood **11**:132
Lowell, Robert, Jr. **12**:444–445
Mailer, Norman **13**:67
Malamud, Bernard **13**:79
Moore, Marianne **13**:569
Morris, Wright **13**:589
Natanson, Maurice Alexander **14**:26
Nemerov, Howard **14**:80–81
Nevins, Allan **14**:115
Oates, Joyce Carol **14**:313
Percy, Walker **15**:163
Pynchon, Thomas **15**:634
Ransom, John Crowe **16**:88
Rich, Adrienne **16**:209
Roethke, Theodore **16**:268
Roth, Philip **16**:321
Stevens, Wallace **18**:264
Thomas, Lewis **19**:173
NATIONAL BROADCASTING COMPANY
radio and television broadcasting **16**:54–59
NATIONAL BUREAU OF STANDARDS **14**:30 *bibliog.*
Commerce, U.S. Department of **5**:138
metric system **13**:346
NATIONAL CANCER INSTITUTE
National Institutes of Health **14**:34
NATIONAL CATHOLIC OFFICE FOR MOTION PICTURES
censorship **4**:248
film, history of **8**:84
NATIONAL CENTER FOR ATMOSPHERIC RESEARCH **14**:30
High Altitude Observatory **10**:161
NATIONAL CENTER FOR SERVICE LEARNING
ACTION (federal agency) **1**:89
NATIONAL CITY (California)
map (32° 40′N 117° 6′W) **4**:31
NATIONAL COLLECTION OF FINE ARTS **14**:30 *bibliog.*
Washington, D.C. **20**:41 *map*
NATIONAL COLLEGIATE ATHLETIC ASSOCIATION **14**:30
basketball **3**:112
basketball champions **3**:114 *table*
golf **9**:239
soccer **18**:10–11
NATIONAL COMMITTEE FOR A SANE NUCLEAR POLICY (SANE)
Spock, Benjamin **18**:192
NATIONAL COMMITTEE FOR AN EFFECTIVE CONGRESS **14**:30
NATIONAL CONFERENCE OF CHRISTIANS AND JEWS **14**:30–31
NATIONAL CONGRESS OF AMERICAN INDIANS **14**:31
Parker, Ely S. **15**:90
NATIONAL CONSERVATIVE POLITICAL ACTION COMMITTEE **14**:31
NATIONAL CONVENTION (France)
French Revolution **8**:323–324
NATIONAL COUNCIL OF CHURCHES **14**:31 *bibliog.*
Blake, Eugene Carson **3**:324
Fry, Franklin Clark **8**:351
NATIONAL COUNCIL OF ENGINEERING EXAMINERS
civil engineering **5**:11
NATIONAL COUNCIL OF NEGRO WOMEN
Bethune, Mary McLeod **3**:231
NATIONAL COVENANT OF 1638
Covenanters **5**:319
NATIONAL CRIME SURVEY
crime **5**:346
NATIONAL DEBT **14**:31–32 *bibliog.*, *table*
Treasury, U.S. Department of the **19**:285
NATIONAL DEFENSE *see* DEFENSE, NATIONAL
NATIONAL DEFENSE ACT
Reserve Officers Training Corps **16**:176
NATIONAL DEFENSE EDUCATION ACT **14**:32
secondary education **17**:180
United States, education in the **19**:435
United States, history of the **19**:458
NATIONAL DEFENSE EDUCATION ACT LOANS *see* NATIONAL DIRECT STUDENT LOANS
NATIONAL DEMOCRATIC PARTY (political party)
Egypt **7**:79
NATIONAL DIRECT STUDENT LOANS
scholarships, fellowships, and loans **17**:130–131
NATIONAL ECONOMY *see* ECONOMY, NATIONAL
NATIONAL EDUCATION ASSOCIATION **14**:32 *bibliog.*
Educational Testing Service **7**:66
primary education **15**:538
secondary education **17**:179
NATIONAL ELECTRIC CODE
electrical wiring **7**:107
NATIONAL ENDOWMENT FOR THE ARTS
repertory theater **16**:160
NATIONAL ENDOWMENT FOR THE HUMANITIES
humanities, education in the **10**:300
NATIONAL ENQUIRER **14**:32
Burnett, Carol **3**:577
NATIONAL ENVIRONMENTAL POLICY ACT OF 1969
conservation **5**:202
NATIONAL FARM WORKERS
Chicano **4**:343
NATIONAL FARMER-LABOR PARTY *see* FARMER-LABOR PARTY
NATIONAL FARMERS ORGANIZATION **14**:32 *bibliog.*
NATIONAL FARMERS UNION **14**:32
NATIONAL FILM BOARD OF CANADA **14**:32
NATIONAL FOOTBALL LEAGUE
football **8**:217–218 *tables*
NATIONAL FOREST SYSTEM (U.S.) **14**:32 *bibliog.*
forestry **8**:230
NATIONAL FORMULARY (NF)
pharmacopoeia **15**:220–221
NATIONAL FOUNDATION ON THE ARTS AND THE HUMANITIES **14**:32
NATIONAL GALLERY, LONDON **12**:401 *map*; **14**:33 *bibliog.*
NATIONAL GALLERY OF ART **14**:33 *bibliog.*, *illus.*; **15**:133 *illus.*
architecture
Pei, I. M. **15**:133–134 *illus.*
Gulbenkian, Calouste Sarkis **9**:402
Kress, Samuel H. **12**:129
Mellon, Andrew W. **13**:287
Mellon, Paul **13**:287
Washington, D.C. **20**:41 *map*

NATIONAL GALLERY OF BRITISH ART
see TATE GALLERY, THE
NATIONAL GAY TASK FORCE
gay activism **9**:63
NATIONAL GEOGRAPHIC MAGAZINE
(periodical) **14**:33 *bibliog.*
Grosvenor, Gilbert Hovey **9**:371
National Geographic Society **14**:33
NATIONAL GEOGRAPHIC SOCIETY
14:33
geographical societies **9**:100
Grosvenor, Gilbert Hovey **9**:371
National Geographic Magazine
14:33
NATIONAL GEOGRAPHIC SOCIETY–PALOMAR OBSERVATORY SKY SURVEY **14**:33–34 *bibliog.*
Anglo-Australian Telescope **1**:416
astronomical catalogs and atlases
2:276
NATIONAL GUARD **14**:34 *bibliog.*
militia **13**:423
2d Amendment **17**:178
NATIONAL HEART, LUNG, AND BLOOD INSTITUTE
National Institutes of Health **14**:34
NATIONAL HIGHWAY SAFETY ADMINISTRATION
ambulance **1**:326
NATIONAL HISTORIC PRESERVATION ACT OF 1966
historic preservation **10**:181
NATIONAL HOME STUDY COUNCIL
correspondence school **5**:276
NATIONAL HONOR SOCIETY **14**:34
NATIONAL INCOME *see* INCOME, NATIONAL
NATIONAL INDIAN YOUTH COUNCIL
National Congress of American Indians **14**:31
NATIONAL INDUSTRIAL INSTITUTE
Spain **18**:142
NATIONAL INDUSTRIAL RECOVERY ACT (United States)
National Recovery Administration
14:45
Public Works Administration **15**:611
NATIONAL INSTITUTE OF ALLERGY AND INFECTIOUS DISEASES
National Institutes of Health **14**:34
NATIONAL INSTITUTE OF ARTS AND LETTERS
National Book Awards **14**:30
NATIONAL INSTITUTE OF CHILD HEALTH AND HUMAN DEVELOPMENT
National Institutes of Health **14**:34
NATIONAL INSTITUTE OF EDUCATION **14**:34
National Assessment of Educational Progress **14**:29
NATIONAL INSTITUTE OF MENTAL HEALTH **14**:34
radio and television broadcasting
16:60
NATIONAL INSTITUTE OF OCCUPATIONAL SAFETY AND HEALTH
diseases, occupational **6**:194
stress, biological **18**:297
NATIONAL INSTITUTES OF HEALTH
14:34
genetic engineering **9**:85
NATIONAL KIDNEY FOUNDATION
14:34
NATIONAL LABOR RELATIONS ACT
14:34 *bibliog.*
grievance procedure **9**:362
Labor-Management Relations Act
12:152
labor union **12**:155
National Labor Relations Board
14:34–35
National Labor Relations Board v. *Jones & Laughlin Steel Corporation* **14**:35
Wagner, Robert F., Sr. **20**:6
NATIONAL LABOR RELATIONS BOARD **14**:34–35 *bibliog.*
NATIONAL LABOR RELATIONS BOARD* v. *JONES & LAUGHLIN STEEL CORPORATION **14**:35 *bibliog.*
NATIONAL LAND LEAGUE
Davitt, Michael **6**:53
NATIONAL LIBERATION FRONT (Greece) *see* EAM-ELAS
NATIONAL LIBERATION FRONT OF SOUTH VIETNAM (NLFSV)
Viet Cong **19**:579
Vietnam War **19**:585–589
NATIONAL LIBRARY OF MEDICINE
National Institutes of Health **14**:34
NATIONAL MEDAL FOR LITERATURE
Aiken, Conrad **1**:201
Auden, W. H. **2**:318
White, E. B. **20**:134–135
NATIONAL MEDAL OF SCIENCE
Eckert, John Presper **7**:39
Wiener, Norbert **20**:146
NATIONAL MEDIATION BOARD **14**:35
NATIONAL MEDICAL ASSOCIATION (China)
Chinese medicine **4**:391
NATIONAL MERIT SCHOLARSHIPS
14:35
scholarships, fellowships, and loans
17:131
NATIONAL METEOROLOGICAL CENTER **14**:35
NATIONAL MONUMENTS, U.S.
national parks **14**:36; **14**:38–39
map, table
NATIONAL MUSEUM OF AMERICAN ART *see* NATIONAL COLLECTION OF FINE ARTS
NATIONAL MUSEUM OF AMERICAN HISTORY **14**:35
NATIONAL MUSEUM OF DESIGN *see* COOPER-HEWITT MUSEUM
NATIONAL MUSEUM OF HISTORY AND TECHNOLOGY *see* NATIONAL MUSEUM OF AMERICAN HISTORY
NATIONAL OCEAN SURVEY (U.S.)
14:35
Seismic Sea Wave Warning System
8:167
NATIONAL OCEANIC AND ATMOSPHERIC ADMINISTRATION **14**:35
GOES (artificial satellite) **9**:222
hydrography **10**:341
meteorology **13**:342–343
National Ocean Survey **14**:35
National Weather Service **14**:46
oceanography **14**:346
NATIONAL ORGANIZATION FOR THE CYPRUS STRUGGLE *see* EOKA
NATIONAL ORGANIZATION FOR WOMEN **14**:35–36 *bibliog., illus.*
Equal Rights Amendment **7**:224
Friedan, Betty **8**:331
Murray, Pauli **13**:560
NATIONAL PANEL ON HIGH SCHOOL AND ADOLESCENT EDUCATION
secondary education **17**:180
NATIONAL PARKS **14**:36–44 *bibliog., illus., maps, tables*
historic preservation **10**:181
NATIONAL PARKS SYSTEM (U.S.)
Acadia National Park **1**:71
badlands **3**:20
Big Bend National Park **3**:249;
19:133 *illus.*
Bryce Canyon National Park **3**:529
Canyon de Chelly National Monument **4**:119
Carlsbad Caverns **4**:151–152
Chaco Canyon **4**:264–265
Crater Lake **5**:332–333
Death Valley **4**:33 *illus.*; **6**:70 *illus.*
Denali National Park **13**:30; **14**:226 *illus.*
Dinosaur National Monument **6**:182
Everglades **7**:316 *illus.*
Glacier National Park **9**:195
Grand Canyon **2**:161 *illus.*; **9**:284–285 *illus.*
Grand Teton National Park **9**:285
Great Smoky Mountains **9**:322
Guadalupe Mountains National Park
19:133 *illus.*
Haleaka Crater **10**:19
Hot Springs (Arkansas) **10**:259
Interior, United States Department of the **11**:210
Lassen Peak **12**:214
Lassen Volcanic National Park **4**:35 *illus.*
Mammoth Cave **13**:107
Mauna Loa **13**:233–234
Mesa Verde National Park **5**:118 *illus.*; **13**:313–314
Moran, Thomas **13**:573
Olmsted, Frederick Law **14**:380
Petrified Forest National Park
15:204
photography
Adams, Ansel **1**:93
Rainier, Mount **16**:78
Redwood National Park **16**:117
Sequoia National Park **4**:35 *illus.*;
17:207
Teton Range **19**:127
tourism **19**:252
Valley of Ten Thousand Smokes
19:508
Yellowstone National Park **20**:322–323
Yosemite National Park **4**:35 *illus.*;
20:332
NATIONAL PARTY (South Africa)
14:44 *bibliog.*
NATIONAL PEOPLE'S CONGRESS
China **4**:369
NATIONAL PORTRAIT GALLERY
14:44–45 *bibliog.*
architecture
Mills, Robert **13**:431
National Collection of Fine Arts
14:30
Washington, D.C. **20**:41 *map*
NATIONAL PRESERVES, U.S.
national parks **14**:38–39 *map, table*
NATIONAL PUBLIC RADIO
radio and television broadcasting
16:60
NATIONAL RADIO ASTRONOMY OBSERVATORY **14**:45 *bibliog.*
radio astronomy **16**:51–53 *illus.*
Reber, Grote **16**:106
Struve, Otto **18**:304
NATIONAL RECOVERY ADMINISTRATION **14**:45 *bibliog.*
Depression of the 1930s **6**:120
New Deal **14**:119–120
Roosevelt, Franklin Delano **16**:309
Schechter Poultry Corporation v. *United States* **17**:117
NATIONAL RECREATION AREAS, U.S.
national parks **14**:38–39 *map, table*
NATIONAL REGISTER OF HISTORIC PLACES
historic preservation **10**:181
NATIONAL REPUBLICAN PARTY
Whig party (United States) **20**:130
NATIONAL RESEARCH COUNCIL, UNITED STATES
Food and Nutrition Board, United States
nutritional-deficiency diseases
14:308
NATIONAL RIFLE ASSOCIATION
gun control **9**:405
NATIONAL RIFLE ASSOCIATION OF AMERICA **14**:45
shooting **17**:282
NATIONAL ROAD **8**:341 *map*; **14**:45 *bibliog.*
roads and highways **16**:237
Springfield (Ohio) **18**:200
NATIONAL SCENIC TRAIL ACT
hiking **10**:162
NATIONAL SCIENCE FOUNDATION
14:45 *bibliog.*
Arecibo Observatory **2**:145
Deep-Sea Drilling Project **6**:77
JOIDES **11**:438
Mohole Project **13**:503
manganese nodule **13**:114
National Radio Astronomy Observatory **14**:45
secondary education **17**:180
NATIONAL SECURITY
censorship **4**:247–248
freedom of the press **8**:296
president of the United States
15:523
NATIONAL SECURITY AGENCY **14**:45–46 *bibliog.*
intelligence gathering **11**:205
NATIONAL SECURITY COUNCIL **14**:46 *bibliog.*
president of the United States
15:525
NATIONAL SOCIALIST GERMAN WORKERS' PARTY (NSDAP)
Hitler, Adolf **10**:187
NATIONAL SOCIETY FOR THE PROMOTION OF INDUSTRIAL EDUCATION
secondary education **17**:179
NATIONAL SPACE DEVELOPMENT AGENCY **14**:46 *bibliog.*
Japan **14**:46
NATIONAL SYSTEM OF INTERSTATE AND DEFENSE HIGHWAYS *see* INTERSTATE HIGHWAY SYSTEM
NATIONAL TAIWAN UNIVERSITY
14:46
Chinese universities **4**:394
NATIONAL TEACHERS ASSOCIATION *see* NATIONAL EDUCATION ASSOCIATION
NATIONAL TELEVISION SYSTEM COMMITTEE
compatible color system
television **19**:89
NATIONAL THEATRE **14**:46 *bibliog.*
Hall, Peter **10**:22
Old Vic Theatre **14**:375
NATIONAL TRUST FOR HISTORIC PRESERVATION
historic preservation **10**:181
NATIONAL UNION CATALOG
Library of Congress **12**:318
NATIONAL UNION OF WOMEN'S SUFFRAGE SOCIETIES
SUFFRAGE, WOMEN'S **18**:326
NATIONAL URBAN LEAGUE *see* URBAN LEAGUE, NATIONAL
NATIONAL VELVET (book)
Bagnold, Enid **3**:22
NATIONAL WEATHER SERVICE **14**:46 *bibliog.*
meteorology **13**:342–343
Namias, Jerome **14**:10
National Meteorological Center
14:35
River and Flood Forecasting Service
8:167
weather forecasting **20**:76
NATIONAL WILDLIFE REFUGE SYSTEM (United States)
wildlife refuge **20**:150
NATIONAL WOMAN SUFFRAGE ASSOCIATION
suffrage, women's **18**:326
NATIONAL WOMEN'S PARTY
suffrage, women's **18**:326
NATIONAL ZOOLOGICAL PARK **14**:46
NATIONALISM **14**:46–47 *bibliog.*
Asia, history of **2**:259–260
Australian literature **2**:343–344
Basques **3**:116
Canadian art and architecture **4**:90–91
China
China, history of **4**:374–375
Kuomintang **12**:137–138
communism **5**:146; **5**:149
Czechoslovakia
Palacký, František **15**:29
education **7**:61
Eurocommunism **5**:150
France
French Revolution **8**:322–325 *illus.*
Germany
Germany, history of **9**:152–153
nazism **14**:67–68
India **11**:79–88
Gandhi, Mahatma **9**:36
India, history of **11**:92–93 *illus.*
Ireland
Home Rule Bills **10**:212
Ireland, history of **11**:264–265
O'Connell, Daniel **14**:346
Italy
fascism **8**:30 *illus.*
Risorgimento **16**:228 *illus.*
Latin America, history of **12**:220–222
Middle East, history of the **13**:406–409
nation **14**:27
Olympic Games **14**:382–384
Russia
Slavophiles and Westernizers
17:358–359
socialism **18**:19–24
Southeast Asia
Khmer Rouge **12**:67
Pathet Lao **15**:111–112
Viet Minh **19**:579
United States
Webster, Daniel **20**:88
World War II **20**:248–249
NATIONALIST CHINA *see* TAIWAN
NATIONALIST PARTY (China) *see* KUOMINTANG (Guomindang)
NATIONALIST PARTY (United States)
Bellamy, Edward **3**:187
NATIVE AMERICAN CHURCH **14**:47 *bibliog.*
Indians of North America, art of the
11:138–141
Kiowa **12**:86
Oto **14**:460
peyote **15**:217
NATIVE AMERICANS *see* INDIANS, AMERICAN
NATIVE ELEMENTS **14**:47 *bibliog.*
arsenic **2**:189
bismuth **3**:299
carbon **4**:133
copper **5**:251–254
diamond **6**:152
gold **9**:226–227
indium **11**:144–145
iron **11**:270–272
lead **12**:256
mercury **13**:306–307
metals **14**:47

mineral **13**:443 *table*
palladium **15**:48
platinum **15**:359–360
selenium **17**:190
silver **17**:312–313
sulfur **18**:334–336
tantalum **19**:25
tellurium **19**:91
tin **19**:204–205
zinc **20**:367–368
NATIVE SON (book) **14**:47
Wright, Richard **20**:290–291
NATO *see* NORTH ATLANTIC TREATY ORGANIZATION
NATOMA (Kansas)
map (39° 11′N 99° 1′W) **12**:18
NATROLITE *see* ZEOLITE
NATRONA (county in Wyoming)
map (43° 0′N 106° 45′W) **20**:301
NATRONA HEIGHTS (Pennsylvania)
map (40° 38′N 79° 44′W) **15**:147
NATSUME SOSEKI **14**:47 *bibliog.*
NATTA, GIULIO **14**:47
NATTAS MOUNTAIN
map (68° 12′N 27° 20′E) **8**:95
NATUFIAN **14**:47 *bibliog.*
Jericho **11**:397
NATURAL BRIDGE (Virginia) **19**:610 *illus.*
NATURAL FOODS *see* HEALTH FOODS
NATURAL GAS **14**:47–48 *bibliog., illus.*
Carboniferous Period **4**:137–139
chemical composition **14**:47–48
consumption **15**:211 *table*
fuel **8**:353 *table*
production and consumption **14**:48
energy sources **7**:174–175 *table*
ethane **7**:249
ethylene **7**:258
fuel **8**:352; **14**:48
government regulation **9**:271
heat content **8**:353 *table*
helium **10**:113
limestone **12**:345
liquefied natural gas
petroleum industry **15**:210; **15**:212–213
methane **13**:343
occurrence **14**:48
gas reserves, worldwide **15**:209 *table*
Louisiana **12**:432
seismometer **17**:189–190 *illus.*
oceanic mineral resources **14**:340
origin **14**:48
petroleum **15**:207
pipe and pipeline **15**:311
production **15**:210–211 *map*
North America **14**:228–229; **14**:236
production and consumption rates **14**:48
products
petrochemicals **15**:205–206
Sea, Law of the **17**:167
transport **14**:48
uses **14**:48
well **20**:302 *illus.*
NATURAL HISTORY (book)
Pliny the Elder **15**:368
NATURAL HISTORY MUSEUM (England)
British Museum **3**:497
NATURAL LAW **14**:48 *bibliog.*
Declaration of Independence **6**:74
Enlightenment **7**:207
Europe, history of **7**:281
Grotius, Hugo **9**:372
law **12**:242
law, history of **12**:245
Pufendorf, Samuel, Baron von **15**:616
state (in political philosophy) **18**:229–232
NATURAL NUMBER *see* NUMBER
NATURAL RESOURCES, CONSERVATION OF *see* CONSERVATION
NATURAL RIGHTS, THEORY OF
Jefferson, Thomas **11**:391
NATURAL SELECTION **14**:49 *bibliog., map*
Darwin, Charles **6**:41–42
animal behavior **2**:11
Origin of Species, On the **14**:443–444
eugenics **7**:263
evolution **7**:318–320
mimicry **13**:435–436
mutation **13**:686
population genetics **15**:439
race **16**:34
sex **17**:224
Wallace, Alfred Russel **20**:13
NATURALISM (art) *see* REALISM (art)
NATURALISM (literature) **14**:49–50 *bibliog., illus.*
American literature **1**:345
Crane, Stephen **5**:330
Dreiser, Theodore **6**:269–270
Farrell, James T. **8**:29
London, Jack **12**:402–403
Norris, Frank **14**:222–223
Sinclair, Upton **17**:319
Sister Carrie **17**:329
Steinbeck, John **18**:248
Danish literature
Jacobsen, Jens Peter **11**:346–347
English literature
Gissing, George Robert **9**:191
Moore, George **13**:568
French literature
Becque, Henry François **3**:152
Zola, Émile **20**:371–372
German literature **9**:133
freie Bühne, die **8**:301
Germinal **9**:157
Hauptmann, Gerhart **10**:69
Holz, Arno **10**:211
Sudermann, Hermann **18**:322–323
German theater
Brahm, Otto **3**:440
realism (literature) **16**:104
Russian literature
Belinsky, Vissarion Grigorievich **3**:182–183
Spanish literature **18**:159
NATURALISM (philosophy) **14**:50 *bibliog.*
ethics **7**:250
Nagel, Ernest **14**:6
Santayana, George **17**:69
NATURALIZATION **14**:50–51 *bibliog.*
Alien and Sedition Acts **1**:293–294
citizenship **4**:447
NATURE (periodical)
Lockyer, Sir Joseph Norman **12**:388
NATURE-NURTURE CONTROVERSY *see* BEHAVIORAL GENETICS
NATURITA (Colorado)
map (38° 14′N 108° 34′W) **5**:116
NATUROPATHY **14**:51
NAUGATUCK (Connecticut)
map (41° 30′N 73° 4′W) **5**:193
NAUGATUCK RIVER
map (41° 19′N 73° 5′W) **5**:193
NAUMBURG (Germany, East and West)
cathedral **17**:162 *illus.*
map (51° 9′N 11° 48′E) **9**:140
NAURU **14**:51 *bibliog., illus., map*
flag **14**:51 *illus.*
map (0° 32′S 166° 55′E) **14**:334
NAUSEA (book) **14**:51 *bibliog.*
Sartre, Jean Paul **17**:80
NAUSEA (medicine) **14**:52
motion sickness **13**:610
NAUSET (American Indians)
Massachuset **13**:204
NAUSHON ISLAND
map (41° 29′N 70° 54′W) **13**:206
NAUSORI (Fiji)
map (18° 2′S 175° 32′E) **8**:77
NAUTICAL ALMANAC **14**:52 *bibliog.*
ephemeris **7**:216
Mayer, Johann Tobias **13**:246
navigation **14**:60
United States Naval Observatory **19**:464
NAUTILOID **14**:52
Ordovician Period **14**:421
Paleozoic Era **15**:43
Silurian Period **17**:310 *illus.*
NAUTILUS (mollusk) **14**:52–53 *illus.*; **15**:35 *illus.*
mollusk **13**:511–512 *illus.*
nautiloid **14**:52
NAUTILUS (submarine) **14**:52 *bibliog., illus.*
Arctic **2**:142 *map*
exploration **7**:338
first (1800) **14**:52
Fulton, Robert **14**:52
nuclear-powered (1954) **14**:52
submarine **18**:315
NAUVOO (Illinois)
Mormonism **13**:582
NAVAJO (American Indians) **2**:163 *illus.*; **14**:53–54 *bibliog., illus.*
art
Indians of North America, art of the **11**:140
rugs and carpets **16**:342–343 *illus.*
sand painting **14**:53 *illus.*
sandpainting **11**:140 *illus.*
Canyon de Chelly National Monument **4**:119
folk medicine **8**:201
hogan **10**:197
Hopi **10**:231
Indians of North America, music and dance of the **11**:144
Kluckhohn, Clyde **12**:98
livestock **11**:131 *illus.*
Manuelito **13**:131
Monument Valley **13**:560
Navajo Indian Reservation **19**:494 *illus.*
North American archaeology **14**:240
social structure and organization **18**:16
NAVAJO (county in Arizona)
map (35° 15′N 110° 20′W) **2**:160
NAVAJO RESERVOIR
map (36° 55′N 107° 30′W) **14**:136
NAVAJO TRIBAL COUNCIL
Navajo **14**:53
NAVAL OBSERVATORY *see* UNITED STATES NAVAL OBSERVATORY
NAVAL STRATEGY AND TACTICS *see* STRATEGY AND TACTICS, NAVAL
NAVAL VESSELS **14**:54–57 *bibliog., illus.*
amphibious warfare **14**:56
designers
Bushnell, David **3**:585
Drebbel, Cornelis **6**:268
Ericsson, John **7**:229
Froude, William **8**:346
Holland, John Philip **10**:203
Rickover, Hyman **16**:216
Great White Fleet **19**:452 *illus.*
specific craft
Dreadnought **6**:266
Monitor and *Merrimack* **13**:531–532
Nautilus **14**:52
Turtle **19**:352
types
aircraft carrier **1**:220–221
battleship **3**:126–128
cruiser **5**:366
destroyer **6**:132–133 *illus.*
frigate **8**:333
galleon **9**:17–18
galley **9**:18; **14**:54
PT boat **15**:605
sailing warships **14**:55
submarine **18**:313–316
weapons **20**:75
NAVAL WAR COLLEGE
Luce, Stephen B. **12**:450
Mahan, Alfred Thayer **13**:64
NAVAN (Ireland)
map (53° 39′N 6° 41′W) **11**:258
NAVARINO, BATTLE OF **14**:58 *bibliog.*
NAVARRE (Ohio)
map (40° 43′N 81° 32′W) **14**:357
NAVARRE (Spain) **14**:58 *bibliog.*
Sancho III, King (Sancho the Great) **17**:58
Spain, history of **18**:145–146 *maps*
NAVARRE, HENRY OF *see* HENRY IV, KING OF FRANCE
NAVARRO (county in Texas)
map (32° 5′N 96° 30′W) **19**:129
NAVASOTA (Texas)
map (30° 23′N 96° 5′W) **19**:129
NAVASSA (North Carolina)
map (34° 16′N 77° 58′W) **14**:242
NAVASSA ISLAND
United States outlying territories **19**:464
NAVE **14**:58
Gothic art and architecture **9**:255–262
Romanesque art and architecture **16**:282
triforium **19**:297
NAVEL
umbilical cord **19**:380
NAVIA (Argentina)
map (34° 47′S 66° 35′W) **2**:149
NAVIGATION **14**:58–61 *bibliog., illus.*
animal migration **2**:27–28
astrolabe, prismatic **2**:271
aviation **2**:374–375
beacon **3**:137
buoy **3**:565–566
canal **4**:94–97
chart **4**:300
compass, navigational **5**:155–156
Cook, James **5**:234–237
Davis, John **6**:52
Doppler effect **6**:241
Gibbons v. *Ogden* **9**:173–174
guidance and control systems **9**:393–394
gyroscope **9**:416
hydrography **10**:341
hydrologic sciences **10**:342
inertial navigation **14**:60–61
Jacob's staff **11**:346
lighthouse **12**:336–337
Mayer, Johann Tobias **13**:246
NAVSTAR **14**:62
professional and educational organizations
Institute of Navigation **11**:195
quadrant **16**:4–5
radar **16**:40
radio techniques **14**:60
Relay **16**:137
research institutions
United States Naval Observatory **19**:464
salvage, marine **17**:39
satellite, artificial **17**:86
sextant **17**:227–228
space exploration **18**:123
Stevin, Simon **18**:265
traffic control **19**:264
Transit (artificial satellite) **19**:272
wind rose diagram **20**:171
NAVIGATION ACTS **14**:61–62 *bibliog.*
mercantilism **13**:303
smuggling **17**:374
United States, history of the **19**:440
NAVOJOA (Mexico)
map (27° 6′N 109° 26′W) **13**:357
NAVON, YITZHAK
Israel **11**:306
NAVRATILOVA, MARTINA **14**:62
NAVSTAR **14**:62 *bibliog.*
space exploration **18**:123
NAVUA (Fiji)
map (18° 14′S 178° 10′E) **8**:77
NAVY **14**:62–66 *bibliog., illus., table*
See also the subheading navy under names of specific countries, e.g., FRANCE; UNITED STATES; JAPAN; etc.
Britannia Royal Naval College **3**:489
defense, national **6**:82 *table*
galley warfare **9**:18
major sea battles of history **14**:63 *table*
military academies **13**:420
mine **13**:437–438 *illus.*
mutiny **13**:687
naval vessels **14**:54–57
rank, military **16**:86–87 *table*
rockets and missiles **16**:255
semaphore **17**:194
signaling **17**:301
sonar **18**:62
strategy and tactics, military **18**:291
torpedo **19**:242
uniforms and insignia (U.S.) **14**:65–66 *illus.*
World War I **20**:220
NAVY, U.S. DEPARTMENT OF THE
Coast Guard, U.S. **5**:80
Defense, U.S. Department of **6**:82–83
United States Naval Observatory **19**:464
NAWABSHAH
map (26° 15′N 68° 25′E) **15**:27
NAXOS (Greece) **14**:66
Cyclades (Greece) **5**:402
NAYAR
polygamy **15**:419
NAYARIT (Mexico) **14**:66
cities
Tepic **19**:114
NAYAYA
philosophy **15**:246
NAZARÉ (Brazil)
map (13° 2′S 39° 0′W) **3**:460
NAZARENES **14**:66 *bibliog.*
Austrian art and architecture **2**:353
Brown, Ford Madox **3**:513–514
Leighton, Frederick, Baron Leighton of Stretton **12**:278
mural painting **13**:646
Overbeck, Johann Friedrich **14**:470
Schnorr von Carolsfeld, Julius **17**:130
NAZARETH (Israel) **14**:67
map (32° 42′N 35° 18′E) **11**:302
NAZARETH (Pennsylvania)
map (40° 44′N 75° 19′W) **15**:147
NAZAS (Mexico)
map (25° 14′N 104° 8′W) **13**:357
NAZCA **14**:67 *bibliog., illus.*
earth drawings **14**:67 *illus.*
Paracas **15**:74
pottery **15**:500 *illus.*
pre-Columbian art and architecture **15**:500
Uhle, Max **19**:374

NAZCA (Peru)
map (14° 50'S 74° 57'W) **15**:193
NAZCA PLATE
plate tectonics **15**:351 *map*
NAZI-SOVIET PACT **9**:156 *map*; **14**:67 *bibliog.*
cartoon **16**:359 *illus.*
Hitler, Adolf **10**:188
Stalin, Joseph **18**:214
World War II **20**:250–251 *illus.*
NAZIM HIKMET **14**:67
NAZIMOVA, ALLA **14**:67
NAZISM **14**:67–68 *bibliog.*
anti-Semitism **2**:68
Austria **2**:351
Blackshirts **3**:322
censorship **4**:246 *illus.*
Drang nach Osten **6**:262
Eichmann, Adolf **7**:91
Europe, history of **7**:296
fascism **8**:30
freedom of speech **8**:298
genocide **9**:93
German literature **9**:134
Germany, history of **9**:155–156
Gestapo **9**:159
ghetto **9**:167
Goebbels, Paul Joseph **9**:221–222
Goering, Hermann **9**:222
Hess, Rudolf **10**:152
Himmler, Heinrich **10**:167–168
Hitler, Adolf **10**:187–188
Holocaust **10**:206
Mein Kampf **13**:282
Munich Putsch **13**:641–642
Niemöller, Martin **14**:185
Nuremberg (West Germany) **14**:297
Nuremberg rallies **7**:295 *illus.*; **9**:156 *illus.*; **18**:232 *illus.*
Nuremberg Trials **14**:297
occupation of Norway (1940) **17**:110 *illus.*
propaganda poster **15**:568 *illus.*
radicalism **16**:44
Ribbentrop, Joachim von **16**:205
Riefenstahl, Leni **16**:218
Roehm, Ernst **16**:268
Rosenberg, Alfred **16**:314–315
Speer, Albert **18**:176
Strasser, Gregor **18**:289
swastika **18**:379
Third Reich **19**:170
totalitarianism **19**:248
Vichy Government **19**:571
World War II **20**:248–258 *illus.*, *map*; **20**:261–265 *illus.*, *map*; **20**:268–275 *illus.*, *map*; **20**:280 *illus.*
resistance movements **20**:271–272 *illus.*
NAZOREANS *see* MANDAEANS
NBC *see* NATIONAL BROADCASTING COMPANY
NC (NUMERICAL CONTROL) TECHNOLOGY **5**:160k
NCAA *see* NATIONAL COLLEGIATE ATHLETIC ASSOCIATION
NCAI *see* NATIONAL CONGRESS OF AMERICAN INDIANS
NCAR *see* NATIONAL CENTER FOR ATMOSPHERIC RESEARCH
NDEBELE **14**:68 *bibliog.*
Lobengula, King of the Ndebele **12**:385
residential art **1**:164 *illus.*; **18**:82 *illus.*
Shona **17**:281
NDEMBU
Lunda **12**:462
N'DJAMENA (Chad) **4**:266 *illus.*, *table*; **14**:68
map (12° 7'N 15° 3'E) **4**:266
NDOLA (Zambia) **14**:68
map (12° 58'S 28° 38'E) **20**:354
NDOTO MOUNTAINS
map (1° 45'N 37° 7'E) **12**:53
NE WIN, U **14**:68 *bibliog.*
Burma **3**:575
Nu, U **14**:277
NEAGH, LOUGH **14**:68
map (54° 37'N 6° 25'W) **11**:258
NEANDERTHALERS **2**:53 *illus.*; **14**:68–69 *bibliog.*, *illus.*
Bordes, François **3**:398
cave dwellers **4**:224 *illus.*
Coon, Carleton **5**:243
Fontéchevade man **8**:207
funeral customs **8**:365
Heidelberg man **10**:107
Lumley, Henry de **12**:459
prehistoric humans **15**:514–515 *illus.*, *map*
Shanidar (Iraq) **17**:240
skull **14**:68 *illus.*
NEAP TIDE
tide **19**:193–194 *illus.*
NEAR EAST **14**:69
See also names of specific countries, e.g., EGYPT; TURKEY (country); etc.
archaeology **2**:122
art
Islamic art and architecture **11**:293–297
Mesopotamian art and architecture **13**:317–321
Persian art and architecture **15**:183–187
Bronze Age **3**:506
Hammurabi, Code of **10**:31
history
Aramaeans **2**:108–109
Hatra **10**:68
Hittites **10**:189–190
Magnesia **13**:53
World War II **20**:256
music
David, Félicien César **6**:47
people
Arabs **2**:103–106
photography
Du Camp, Maxime **6**:286
Frith, Francis **8**:334–335
religion
Arabs **2**:103–104
NEAR EASTERN MYTHOLOGY
Canaanite mythology
Astarte **2**:267
Baal **3**:5
Dagon **6**:6
mythology **13**:698–699
Cybele **5**:400
Egyptian mythology *see* EGYPTIAN MYTHOLOGY
Mesopotamian mythology
Anu **2**:71
Ea **7**:3
Enuma Elish **7**:209
Gilgamesh, Epic of **9**:180
Ishtar **11**:287
Marduk **13**:148
mythology **13**:696–697
Pyramus and Thisbe **15**:636
Semiramis **17**:197
Ugarit **19**:374
Ur **19**:474
Uruk **19**:490
mythology **13**:696–699
NEAR ISLANDS
map (52° 40'N 173° 30'E) **1**:242
NEARSIGHTEDNESS *see* MYOPIA
NEATH (Wales)
map (51° 40'N 3° 48'W) **19**:403
NEBBIA v. *NEW YORK*
government regulation **9**:271
Munn v. *Illinois* **13**:643
NEBLINA PEAK
map (0° 48'N 66° 2'W) **3**:460
NEBO (Illinois)
map (39° 27'N 90° 47'W) **11**:42
NEBO, MOUNT
map (39° 49'N 111° 46'W) **19**:492
NEBRASKA **14**:69–74 *bibliog.*, *illus.*, *map*
agriculture **14**:71 *illus.*; **14**:72 *illus.*; **14**:73 *illus.*
cities
Grand Island **9**:285
Lincoln **12**:347
Omaha **14**:385
climate **14**:71
culture **14**:72
economic activities **14**:73
education **14**:72
state university and colleges of **14**:74
flag **14**:69 *illus.*
government **14**:73
historical sites **14**:72
history **14**:73–74
Kansas-Nebraska Act **12**:22–23
land and resources **14**:70–72 *illus.*, *map*
map (41° 30'N 100° 0'W) **19**:419
people **14**:72–73
Omaha **14**:385
Sioux **17**:326
Winnebago **20**:179–180
rivers, lakes, and waterways **14**:71
Platte River **15**:362
seal, state **14**:69 *illus.*
vegetation and animal life **14**:71
NEBRASKA, STATE UNIVERSITY AND COLLEGES OF **14**:74
NEBRASKA CITY (Nebraska)
map (40° 41'N 95° 52'W) **14**:70
NEBRODI MOUNTAINS
map (37° 55'N 14° 35'E) **11**:321
NEBUCHADNEZZAR II, KING OF BABYLONIA **14**:74 *bibliog.*
Babylon **3**:8
Hanging Gardens of Babylon **17**:216
Ur **19**:474
NEBULA **2**:283 *illus.*; **14**:74–75 *bibliog.*, *illus.*
Crab nebula **5**:325–326
Cygnus **5**:406
Dreyer, J. L. E. **6**:271
energy source **14**:74–75
extragalactic systems **7**:341
globule **9**:209
Hubble, Edwin **10**:288
interstellar matter **11**:225–228 *illus.*
Lundmark, Knut **12**:462
Lyra **12**:479
Messier, Charles **13**:324
Orion nebula **14**:444–445
planetary nebula **15**:329
pulsar **15**:620
radio astronomy **16**:50
solar system **18**:52
stellar evolution **18**:250
supernova **18**:352
theories, solar system **18**:52 *illus.*
ultraviolet radiation **14**:74–75
NEBULA AWARD
Asimov, Isaac **2**:260
Dickson, Gordon R. **6**:158–159
Le Guin, Ursula **12**:254
Sturgeon, Theodore **18**:309
Wilhelm, Kate **20**:151
NECEDAH (Wisconsin)
map (44° 2'N 90° 5'W) **20**:185
NECHAKO RESERVOIR
map (53° 25'N 125° 10'W) **3**:491
NECHE (North Dakota)
map (48° 59'N 97° 33'W) **14**:248
NECHO II, KING OF EGYPT **14**:75 *bibliog.*
NECKER, JACQUES **8**:270 *illus.*; **14**:75 *bibliog.*
NECKLACE *see* JEWELRY
NECOCHEA (Argentina)
map (38° 33'S 58° 45'W) **2**:149
NECROPHOBIA
phobia **15**:248
NECROPOLIS *see* CEMETERY
NECROSIS **14**:75
infarction **11**:164
NECTARINE **14**:75–76
NEDERLAND (Texas)
map (29° 58'N 93° 60'W) **19**:129
NEEDHAM (Massachusetts)
map (42° 17'N 71° 14'W) **3**:409
NEEDLE **14**:76
NEEDLEFISH **14**:76
NEEDLES (California)
map (34° 51'N 114° 37'W) **4**:31
NEEDLEWORK **14**:76 *bibliog.*, *illus.*
appliqué **2**:91
clothing industry **5**:65
crochet **5**:355
embroidery **7**:152
lace **12**:158–160 *illus.*
quilting **16**:26
NEEL, ALICE **14**:76 *bibliog.*
NÉEL, LOUIS EUGÈNE FÉLIX **14**:76
NÉEL TEMPERATURE
magnetism **13**:57
NEENAH (Wisconsin)
map (44° 11'N 88° 28'W) **20**:185
NEEPAWA (Manitoba)
map (50° 13'N 99° 29'W) **13**:119
NEER, AERT VAN DER **14**:76–77 *bibliog.*
NEFERTITI **5**:281 *illus.*; **7**:87 *illus.*; **14**:77 *bibliog.*, *illus.*
NEFTA (Tunisia)
map (33° 52'N 7° 33'E) **19**:335
NEFUD *see* NAFUD
NEGATIVE NUMBER
algebra **1**:284
NEGAUNEE (Michigan)
map (46° 30'N 87° 36'W) **13**:377
NEGEDAL
Tungus **19**:334
NEGELEIN, WARBUS
photosynthesis **15**:275
NEGEV **14**:77
map (30° 30'N 34° 55'E) **11**:302
NEGLIGENCE **14**:77 *bibliog.*
liability **12**:311
malpractice **13**:93
tort **19**:245–246
NEGOMBO (Sri Lanka)
map (7° 13'N 79° 50'E) **18**:206
NEGOTIABLE INSTRUMENT **14**:77–78 *bibliog.*
bond **3**:376
business law **3**:589
NEGOTIABLE ORDER OF WITHDRAWAL (NOW) ACCOUNTS
banking systems **3**:69
money **13**:527
NEGOTIATION
arbitration (labor-management and commercial) **2**:110
game theory **9**:27–29 *illus.*
industrial relations **11**:158
mediation **13**:264
NÈGRE, CHARLES **14**:78 *bibliog.*
NEGRILLO *see* PYGMY
NEGRITO **14**:78 *bibliog.*
Pygmy **15**:633
NEGRITUDE (movement)
African literature **1**:168
Césaire, Aimé **4**:262
Damas, Léon Gontran **6**:18
Senghor, Léopold Sédar **17**:203
NEGRO, AMERICAN *see* BLACK AMERICANS
NEGRO, RIO **14**:78
map (40° 0'S 67° 0'W) **2**:149
NEGRO ENSEMBLE COMPANY
Ward, Douglas Turner **20**:29
NEGRO RIVER (Argentina)
map (41° 2'S 62° 47'W) **2**:149
NEGRO RIVER (Brazil)
map (3° 8'S 59° 55'W) **1**:323
NEGRO RIVER (Uruguay)
map (33° 24'S 58° 22'W) **19**:488
NEGROS ISLAND
map (10° 0'N 123° 0'E) **15**:237
NEGUAC (New Brunswick)
map (47° 15'N 65° 5'W) **14**:117
NEHEMIAH *see* EZRA AND NEHEMIAH, BOOKS OF
NEHER, CASPAR **14**:78
NEHRU, JAWAHARLAL **11**:87–88 *illus.*; **14**:78 *bibliog.*, *illus.*
India, history of **11**:93 *illus.*
NEI-CHING
Yellow Emperor
Chinese medicine **4**:390–391
NEIAFU (Tonga)
map (18° 39'S 173° 59'W) **19**:233
NEIDHART VON REUENTHAL **14**:78–79 *bibliog.*
German and Austrian music **9**:129
NEIHART (Montana)
map (46° 56'N 110° 44'W) **13**:547
NEILL, A. S.
Summerhill **18**:339
NEILLSVILLE (Wisconsin)
map (44° 34'N 90° 36'W) **20**:185
NEILSON, JOHN SHAW **14**:79 *bibliog.*
NEISSE RIVER
map (52° 4'N 14° 46'E) **9**:140
NEISSERIA **14**:79
gonorrhea **9**:244
meningococcus **13**:298
NEITHARDT *see* GRÜNEWALD, MATTHIAS
NEIVA (Colombia)
map (2° 56'N 75° 18'W) **5**:107
NEKHEN *see* HIERAKONPOLIS (Egypt)
NEKOOSA (Wisconsin)
map (44° 19'N 89° 54'W) **20**:185
NEKRASOV, NIKOLAI ALEKSEYEVICH **14**:79 *bibliog.*
NEKTON **14**:79
marine food chain **14**:330 *illus.*
oceanography **14**:345
plankton **15**:331
NELIGH (Nebraska)
map (42° 8'N 98° 2'W) **14**:70
NELLIGAN, ÉMILE **14**:79
NELSON (county in Kentucky)
map (37° 50'N 85° 30'W) **12**:47
NELSON (Nebraska)
map (40° 12'N 98° 4'W) **14**:70
NELSON (New Zealand)
map (41° 17'S 173° 17'E) **14**:158
NELSON (county in North Dakota)
map (47° 55'N 98° 10'W) **14**:248
NELSON (county in Virginia)
map (37° 45'N 78° 55'W) **19**:607
NELSON, BYRON **14**:79
NELSON, GEORGE **14**:79
NELSON, HORATIO NELSON, VISCOUNT **14**:79–80 *bibliog.*, *illus.*
Decatur, Stephen **6**:72
Hamilton, Emma, Lady **10**:29
Napoleonic Wars **14**:19
Trafalgar, Battle of **19**:264
NELSON, ROBERT **14**:80
NELSON HOUSE (Manitoba)
map (55° 47'N 98° 51'W) **13**:119
NELSON RIVER **14**:80
map (57° 4'N 92° 30'W) **13**:119
NELSONVILLE (Ohio)
map (39° 27'N 82° 14'W) **14**:357
NEMAHA (county in Kansas)
map (39° 50'N 96° 0'W) **12**:18

NEMAHA (county in Nebraska)
map (40° 25′N 95° 50′W) **14**:70
NEMAN RIVER 14:80
NEMATODE 14:80 *bibliog.*
cat **4**:194
diseases, animal **6**:192
eye worm **7**:351
filariasis **8**:78
hookworm **10**:227
invertebrate **11**:235
molting **13**:513
parasitic diseases **15**:82–83 *illus.*
pinworm **15**:308
worm **20**:283 *illus.*
NĚMCOVÁ, BOŽENA
Czech literature **5**:412
NEMEA (Greece) **14**:80 *bibliog.*
NEMEROV, HOWARD 14:80–81 *bibliog.*
NEMERTEAN *see* RIBBON WORM
NEMESIS 14:81
NEMI, LAKE 14:81
NEMIROVICH-DANCHENKO, VLADIMIR IVANOVICH 14:81 *bibliog.*
Moscow Art Theater **13**:599
NENAGH (Ireland)
map (52° 52′N 8° 12′W) **11**:258
NENANA (Alaska)
map (64° 34′N 149° 7′W) **1**:242
NENTSY *see* SAMOYED (people)
NEO-CONFUCIANISM
Confucianism **5**:180
Sung (Song) (dynasty) **18**:348
NEOCLASSICISM (architecture)
architecture **2**:135
Austria
Austrian art and architecture **2**:353
cathedrals and churches **4**:208
France
Brosse, Salomon de **3**:512
Chalgrin, Jean François Thérèse **4**:271
Directoire style **6**:187
federal style **8**:42
Louis, Victor **12**:422
Petit Trianon **15**:203
Soufflot, Jacques Germain **18**:70
Germany
Gilly, Friedrich **9**:182
Schinkel, Karl Friedrich **17**:121
Great Britain
Adam, Robert **1**:92
Dance, George **6**:28
Regency style **16**:126
Soane, Sir John **18**:6
Wyatt, James **20**:297
house (in Western architecture) **10**:270
Russia
Cameron, Charles **4**:59
Quarenghi, Giacomo **16**:12
Zakharov, Adrian **20**:352
Spain
Prado **15**:487
United States
American art and architecture **1**:327–330
Baltimore Cathedral **12**:235 *illus.*
federal style **8**:42
Latrobe, Benjamin Henry **12**:235
Monticello **13**:557
White House **20**:137–138
Venezuela
Villanueva, Juan de **19**:598
NEOCLASSICISM (art) **14**:81–82 *bibliog., illus.*
art criticism **2**:207
Denmark
Bindesbøll, Michael Gottlieb Birkner **3**:257
Thorvaldsen, Bertel **19**:180
drawing **6**:265
France
Clérisseau, Charles Louis **5**:51
David, Jacques Louis **6**:47–48
Girardon, François **9**:188–189
Guérin, Pierre Narcisse, Baron **9**:391
Ingres, Jean Auguste Dominique **11**:176–177
Lemercier, Jacques **12**:280
Pauline Borghese as Venus Victrix (Canova) **2**:199 *illus.*
Prud'hon, Pierre Paul **15**:585
styles of Louis XIII-XVI **18**:311
Vien, Joseph Marie **19**:578
furniture **8**:377
Germany
German art and architecture **9**:127–128
Klenze, Leo von **12**:96–97
Mengs, Anton Raphael **13**:297
Great Britain
Chambers, Sir William **4**:274–275
Cockerell, Charles Robert **5**:87
English art and architecture **7**:187
Etty, William **7**:261
Flaxman, John **8**:158
Sheraton, Thomas **17**:256
Wedgwood, Josiah **20**:89–90
iconography **11**:23
interior design **11**:213–214 *illus.*
Italy
Batoni, Pompeo Girolamo **3**:124
Canova, Antonio **4**:115
Italian art and architecture **11**:310; **11**:311; **11**:314
Piranesi, Giovanni Battista **15**:314–315
Pisano, Nicola and Giovanni **15**:316
jewelry **11**:411
painting **15**:21–22
Portuguese art and architecture **15**:456
pyramids **15**:635
Russian art and architecture **16**:362
sculpture **17**:164–165 *illus.*
Spanish art and architecture **18**:154
Switzerland
Kauffmann, Angelica **12**:31
tomb **19**:231 *illus.*
United States
Allston, Washington **1**:304–305
American art and architecture **1**:327
Crawford, Thomas **5**:333
Hosmer, Harriet **10**:255–256
Nadelman, Elie **14**:4
Powers, Hiram **15**:486
Rogers, Randolph **16**:269
Story, William Wetmore **18**:285
Vanderlyn, John **19**:519
West, Benjamin **20**:106–107
NEOCLASSICISM (literature) **14**:82 *bibliog.*
See also CLASSICISM (literature)
authors
Addison, Joseph **1**:100
Clarendon, Edward Hyde, 1st Earl of **5**:36–37
Corneille, Pierre **5**:267–268
Dryden, John **6**:284–285
Gay, John **9**:63
Oldham, John **14**:376
Pope, Alexander **15**:430
Racine, Jean **16**:36–37
criticism, literary **5**:351
drama **6**:259
German literature **9**:132
Johnson, Samuel (writer) **11**:435–436
mock epic **13**:489
narrative and dramatic devices **14**:22
Swift, Jonathan **18**:389
NEOCLASSICISM (music)
Roussel, Albert **16**:327
NEOCOLONIALISM
colonialism **5**:112
NEODESHA (Kansas)
map (37° 25′N 95° 41′W) **12**:18
NEODYMIUM 14:82
element **7**:130 *table*
lanthanide series **12**:200–201
laser **12**:213 *table*
metal **13**:328
Welsbach, Carl Auer, Baron von **20**:101
NEOEXPRESSIONISM 14:83
modern art **13**:496
NEOGA (Illinois)
map (39° 19′N 88° 27′W) **11**:42
NEOIMPRESSIONISM 14:83 *bibliog.*
Guillaumin, Armand **9**:395
painting **15**:22
Seurat, Georges **17**:215
The Models **11**:67 *illus.*
Signac, Paul **17**:300
NEOLITHIC PERIOD 14:83–84 *bibliog., illus.*
agriculture, history of **1**:190
archaeology **2**:118 *illus.*
Çatal Hüyük **4**:197–198
Dowth (Ireland) **6**:253
Jarmo (Iraq) **11**:383
Jericho (Jordan) **11**:397
Shanidar (Iraq) **17**:240
Skara Brae **17**:332
barrow **3**:95
China, history of **4**:370
Chinese archaeology **4**:378
cooking **5**:237
European prehistory **7**:301–302 *map*
Battle-Axe culture **3**:126
Danubian culture **6**:36
lake dwelling **12**:171
megalith **13**:279
pottery **14**:84
Persian art and architecture **15**:183 *illus.*
pottery and porcelain **15**:468 *illus.*
pottery and porcelain **15**:468 *illus.*
Iranian pottery **15**:183 *illus.*
prehistoric art **15**:509–510
stone alignments **18**:281–282
technology, history of **19**:61
NEOLITHIC REVOLUTION
archaeology **2**:125–126
NEON 14:84–85 *bibliog.*
abundances of common elements **7**:131 *table*
electron configuration **7**:120
element **7**:130 *table*
Group 0 periodic table **15**:167
inert gases **11**:161
laser **12**:213 *table*
light **12**:335
sculpture
Flavin, Dan **8**:157
spectrum **18**:169 *illus.*
Travers, Morris William **19**:284
NEON (Kentucky)
map (37° 12′N 82° 43′W) **12**:47
NEOPIT (Wisconsin)
map (44° 59′N 88° 50′W) **20**:185
NEOPLASM
cancer **4**:101–106
tumor **19**:331
NEOPLASTIC DISEASE
gastrointestinal tract disease **9**:57
NEOPLASTICISM
de Stijl (periodical) **6**:63–64
modern architecture **13**:491
Oud, Jacobus Johannes Pieter **14**:467
Rietveld, Gerrit Thomas **16**:219
NEOPLATONISM 14:85 *bibliog.*
Abravanel, Judah **1**:61
Cambridge Platonists **4**:52
chain of being **4**:268–269
Dionysius the Pseudo-Areopagite **6**:184
Erigena, John Scotus **7**:230
Farabi, al- **8**:21
Ficino, Marsilio **8**:70
Iamblichus **11**:3
Israeli, Isaac ben Solomon **11**:306
pantheism **15**:61
Pico della Mirandola, Giovanni, Conte **15**:294
Plotinus **15**:368–369
Porphyry **15**:442
Proclus **15**:561
Schwenkfeld von Ossig, Kaspar **17**:140
Shelley, Percy Bysshe **17**:253
NEOPRENE
Nieuwland, Julius Arthur **14**:186
NEOPTOLEMUS 14:85
NEOREALISM 14:85–86
Antonioni, Michelangelo **2**:70
De Sica, Vittorio **6**:63
Fellini, Federico **8**:48
film, history of **8**:86
Rossellini, Roberto **16**:319
Visconti, Luchino **19**:616
Vittorini, Elio **19**:621–622
NEOSHO (county in Kansas)
map (37° 35′N 95° 15′W) **12**:18
NEOSHO (Missouri)
map (36° 52′N 94° 22′W) **13**:476
NEOSHO RIVER
map (35° 48′N 95° 18′W) **14**:368
NEOSTIGMINE 14:86
NEOTENIN *see* JUVENILE HORMONE
NEOTENY 14:86
larva **12**:208
NEPAL 14:86–88 *bibliog., illus., map, table*
cities
Katmandu **12**:30–31
economic activities **14**:87–88 *illus.*
flag **14**:86 *illus.*
history and government **14**:87–88
Lamaist art and architecture **12**:172–173
land and resources **14**:86–87 *illus., map, table*
languages
Indo-Iranian languages **11**:145–146
map (28° 0′N 84° 0′E) **2**:232
people **2**:243 *illus.*; **14**:87–88 *illus.*
Gurkha **9**:406
Pahari **15**:14
Sherpa **17**:259
physical features
Annapurna **2**:32
NEPALESE ART *see* LAMAIST ART AND ARCHITECTURE
NEPALGANJ (Nepal)
map (28° 3′N 81° 37′E) **14**:86
NEPHELINE
feldspathoid **8**:47
NEPHI (Utah)
map (39° 43′N 111° 50′W) **19**:492
NEPHRITE
jade **11**:347
NEPHRITIS *see* KIDNEY DISEASE
NEPHRON
kidney **12**:72–73 *illus.*
NEPOMUCENE, JOHN, SAINT *see* JOHN NEPOMUCENE, SAINT
NEPONSET RIVER
map (42° 17′N 71° 2′W) **3**:409
NEPTUNE (mythology) **14**:88
NEPTUNE (New Jersey)
map (40° 12′N 74° 2′W) **14**:129
NEPTUNE (planet) **14**:88–89 *bibliog., illus., table*
astronomical data **14**:88
characteristics **14**:88–89 *table*
discovery
Adams, John Couch **1**:96
Galle, Johann Gottfried **9**:17
Kuiper, Gerard **12**:135
Lassell, William **12**:214
Leverrier, Urbain Jean Joseph **12**:303
planets **15**:329–331
radio astronomy **16**:48
satellites **14**:89 *illus.*
Nereid **14**:88–89
Triton **18**:49 *illus.*
solar system **18**:46–47 *illus., table*; **18**:49 *illus.*
Voyager **19**:638
NEPTUNE BEACH (Florida)
map (30° 19′N 81° 24′W) **8**:172
NEPTUNE CITY (New Jersey)
map (40° 12′N 74° 3′W) **14**:129
NEPTUNIUM 14:89
actinide series **1**:88
element **7**:130 *table*
metal, metallic element **13**:328
Seaborg, Glenn T. **17**:171
transmutation of elements **19**:277
transuranium elements **19**:286
NEREID (satellite)
Neptune (planet) **14**:88–89 *illus.*
NEREIDS (mythology)
Andromeda (mythology) **1**:409
monument
Xanthus **20**:311
Nereus **14**:89
NEREUS 14:89
NERI, SAINT PHILIP 14:89 *bibliog.*
NERITIC ZONE 14:89
epipelagic zone **7**:220
ocean and sea **14**:331
pelagic zone **15**:137
NERNST, WALTHER 14:89 *bibliog.*
Nernst lamp **14**:89
thermodynamics **14**:89
NERO, ROMAN EMPEROR 14:90 *bibliog., illus.*
coin **14**:296 *illus.*
Naples (Italy) **14**:15
Rome, ancient **16**:302
NERO, TIBERIUS CLAUDIUS
Livia Drusilla **12**:376
NERO CLAUDIUS DRUSUS GERMANICUS
Drusus (family) **6**:283
NERUDA, JAN
Czech literature **5**:412
NERUDA, PABLO 12:230 *illus.*; **14**:90 *bibliog.*
NERVA, ROMAN EMPEROR
Rome, ancient **16**:303
NERVAL, GÉRARD DE 14:90 *bibliog.*
NERVE, AUDITORY *see* AUDITORY NERVE
NERVE, OPTIC *see* OPTIC NERVE
NERVE AGENTS
chemical and biological warfare **4**:311–313
NERVE CELL **3**:447 *illus.*
acetylcholine **1**:80
aging **1**:185
biopotential **3**:275–276
cell **4**:235 *illus.*; **4**:236
nervous system **14**:91–92 *illus.*
neural function
graded potential **14**:92
hyperpolarization **14**:92
spike discharge **14**:92
neurophysiology **14**:105–106
cell structure **14**:105–106
operation **14**:94–95
polarity **14**:92
potential **14**:106
receptors **14**:92
structure and function **14**:91–92
synapse **14**:106

NERVE CELL (cont.)
types of neurons **14**:95
Purkinje cells
Purkinje, Jan Evangelista **15**:630
reflex
nervous system **14**:94–95
spinal cord **18**:184
NERVE IMPULSE
Eccles, Sir John **7**:37
Hodgkin, Alan Lloyd **10**:194
Huxley, Andrew Fielding **10**:324
Katz, Sir Bernard **12**:31
neurophysiology **14**:106
NERVI, PIER LUIGI **14**:91 *bibliog.*
Italian art and architecture **11**:310
Pallazzo dello Sport (Rome) **4**:244 *illus.*
NERVII
Germanic peoples **9**:138
NERVO, AMADO **14**:91 *bibliog.*
NERVOUS SYSTEM **14**:91–95 *bibliog., illus.*
acetylcholine **1**:80
aging **1**:185
autonomic nervous system **14**:92; **14**:94 *illus.*
biological clock **3**:265
biological locomotion **3**:267–268
bionics **3**:274
biopotential **3**:275–276
brain **3**:442–448; **14**:95
drug **6**:276–277
earthworm **7**:29
endocrine system **7**:168
histology
Golgi, Camillo **9**:240
insect **11**:188–189 *illus.*
integration **14**:95
invertebrate **11**:236–237
lower organism **14**:92
metabolism **13**:327
motor nervous system **14**:94 *illus.*
muscle **13**:651
myelin
nodes of Ranvier **14**:92
structure and function **14**:92
neurology **14**:105
neuropharmacology **14**:105
opiate receptor **14**:405
optic nerve, eye **7**:348; **7**:350
pain **15**:15
peripheral nerve cell **14**:91 *illus.*
peripheral nervous system **15**:171
physiology
Adrian, Edgar Douglas **1**:109
Axelrod, Julius **2**:377
biopotential **3**:276
electrophysiology, sensation **17**:204
muscle contraction **13**:654–656 *illus.*
neurophysiology **14**:105–106
psychopathology, treatment of **15**:599
psychopathy **15**:601
Ramón y Cajal, Santiago **16**:81
reflex **14**:92–95; **16**:119–120
feedback **14**:93–94
nerve cell **14**:94–95
regeneration **16**:127
sciatic **17**:141
sedative **17**:181–182
senses **17**:204–205
skin **17**:341
space medicine **18**:133
spinal cord **14**:92–93; **18**:184 *illus.*
stimulant **18**:271
strychnine **18**:304
surgery **18**:361
Cushing, Harvey W. **5**:397
sympathetic nervous system
biofeedback **3**:263
synapse **14**:92
trigeminal nerve **19**:191
neuralgia **14**:105
vagus nerve
stomach **18**:280
vertebrates **14**:92
spinal cord **14**:92
NERVOUS SYSTEM, DISEASES OF THE **14**:95–96 *bibliog.*
Alzheimer's disease **1**:320
amnesia **1**:375
amyotrophic lateral sclerosis **1**:386–387
aphasia **2**:76–77
apraxia **2**:91–92
ataxia **2**:287
cerebral palsy **4**:259–260
chorea **4**:408
coma (unconscious state) **3**:129
concussion **5**:172
convulsion **5**:234
Cushing's ulcer **19**:376
degenerative diseases **14**:95–96
dementia **6**:96
diagnostic tests **14**:96
Down's syndrome **6**:252
encephalitis **7**:162
environmental health **7**:210–212
epilepsy **7**:219–220
genetic diseases **14**:96
headache **10**:85–86
Huntington's chorea **10**:315
infections **14**:96
leprosy **12**:295
meningitis **13**:298
metabolic disorders **14**:96
multiple sclerosis **13**:638
muscular dystrophy **13**:656
myasthenia gravis **13**:689
neuralgia **14**:105
palsy **15**:52
paralysis **15**:79
Parkinson's disease **15**:91
poisoning **14**:96
poliomyelitis **15**:397
psychosis **15**:602
psychosomatic disorders **15**:602
rabies **16**:32
red tide **16**:114
Reye's syndrome **16**:190
shingles **17**:262
sleep disturbances **17**:360
speech **18**:174
stroke **18**:301–302
Tay-Sachs disease **19**:48
tetanus **19**:126
tic **19**:191
Tourette's syndrome **19**:251
treatment
atropine **2**:313
brain **3**:447
psychotropic drugs **15**:603–605
tumor **14**:96
wounds and injuries **14**:96
NESBIT, E. **14**:96 *bibliog.*
NESCH, ROLF
Scandinavian art and architecture **17**:114
NESHOBA (county in Mississippi)
map (32° 45′N 89° 5′W) **13**:469
NESKAUPSTADUR (Iceland)
map (65° 10′N 13° 43′W) **11**:17
NESPELEM (Washington)
map (48° 10′N 118° 59′W) **20**:35
NESS (county in Kansas)
map (38° 30′N 99° 55′W) **12**:18
NESS, LOCH **14**:96–97; **17**:149 *illus.*
Loch Ness monster **12**:386
map (57° 15′N 4° 30′W) **19**:403
NESS CITY (Kansas)
map (38° 27′N 99° 54′W) **12**:18
NESSELRODE, KARL ROBERT, COUNT **14**:97 *bibliog.*
NESSI, PIO BAROJA Y *see* BAROJA Y NESSI, PIO
NEST
bird **3**:286–287 *illus.*
termite **19**:117
wasp **20**:45
weaver **20**:83
NESTEROV, MIKHAIL
Russian art and architecture **16**:362
NESTOR **14**:97
palace of nestor
Pylos **15**:634
NESTORIAN CHURCH **14**:97 *bibliog.*
Ephraem the Syrian, Saint **7**:216–217
NESTORIANISM **14**:97 *bibliog.*
Cyril of Alexandria, Saint **5**:410
Ephesus, Council of **7**:216
NESTOS RIVER
map (40° 41′N 24° 44′E) **9**:325
NESTROY, JOHANN **14**:97 *bibliog.*
NETANYA (Israel)
map (32° 20′N 34° 51′E) **11**:302
NETCONG (New Jersey)
map (40° 54′N 74° 42′W) **14**:129
NETHERLANDS **14**:97–103 *bibliog., illus., map, table*
agriculture **14**:100–102 *illus.*
ART **14**:100
See also the subheading netherlands under specific art forms, e.g., ARCHITECTURE; PAINTING; SCULPTURE; etc.
Dutch art and architecture **6**:309–313
Flemish art and architecture **8**:159–162
birth control **3**:294–295
cities
Alkmaar **1**:297
Amsterdam **1**:383–385 *illus., map*
Arnhem **2**:184
Breda **3**:471
Delft **6**:92
Dordrecht **6**:241
Edam **7**:54
Eindhoven **7**:92
Groningen **9**:368
Haarlem **10**:3
Hague, The **10**:10–11 *illus.*
Leiden **12**:277
Maastricht **13**:3
Nijmegen **14**:195
Rotterdam **16**:323 *illus.*
's Hertogenbosch **17**:259
Utrecht **19**:498
civil law **5**:11
climate **14**:98 *table*
dance
Dutch National Ballet **6**:314
folk dance **8**:200 *illus.*
economic activity **14**:100–102 *illus.*
education **14**:100
European universities **7**:308 *table*
flag **14**:98 *illus.*
floriculture **8**:170
tulip **19**:330
government **14**:102
health care **14**:100
historians *see* HISTORY—Dutch historians
history **14**:102–103
Beatrice, Queen of the Netherlands **3**:145
Bernhard of Lippe-Biesterfeld **3**:221
colonialism **5**:111–112
costume **5**:298 *illus.*
exploration and settlement in colonial America **19**:437 *map*
Holland **10**:203
Juliana, Queen **11**:466
Latin American territory c.1790 **12**:219 *map*
Low Countries, history of the **12**:438–443 *map*
Margaret of Austria **13**:149
Maurice of Nassau, Prince of Orange **13**:235
Maximilian I, Holy Roman Emperor **13**:240
Orange (dynasty) **14**:414
Remonstrants **16**:146
Spanish Succession, War of the **18**:162–163 *map*
States-General **18**:234
Suriname **18**:364
Wilhelmina, Queen **20**:151
William I, King **20**:157–158
William I, Prince of Orange (William the Silent) **20**:158
William II, King **20**:158
William II, Prince of Orange **20**:158
William III, King **20**:158
Witt, Johan de **20**:193
World War II **20**:252–253 *illus., map*
ice skating **11**:13–14
keeshond (dog) **12**:36
land and resources **14**:98–100 *illus., map*
Delta Plan **6**:95–96
land reclamation **12**:179–180 *illus., map*
language
Germanic languages **9**:135–137 *tables*
literature *see* DUTCH AND FLEMISH LITERATURE
manufacturing and mining **14**:100–101
map (52° 15′N 5° 30′E) **7**:268
music
Ameling, Elly **1**:326
Badings, Henk **3**:19
Concertgebouw Orchestra **5**:170
Obrecht, Jacob **14**:316
people **14**:100
physical features
Frisian Islands **8**:334
polder **15**:395
resources **14**:99–100
rivers, lakes, and waterways **14**:98–99 *illus.*
IJsselmeer **11**:39
North Sea Canal **14**:252
roads and highways **16**:238
trade **14**:101–102
transportation **14**:101
windmills and wind power **20**:172
NETHERLANDS ANTILLES **14**:103 *bibliog.*
Aruba **2**:225–226
cities
Willemstad **20**:154
Curaçao **5**:390
flag **8**:142 *illus.*
map (12° 15′N 69° 0′W) **20**:109
Saint Martin (France) **17**:24
NETHERLANDS DANCE THEATER **14**:103 *bibliog.*
Dantzig, Rudi Van **6**:35
NETHERLANDS EAST INDIES *see* INDONESIA
NETHERLANDS FOUNDATION FOR RADIO ASTRONOMY
Westerbrok Observatory **20**:115
NETO, AGOSTINHO ANTÓNIO **14**:103
Mbundu **13**:251
NETRAKONA (Bangladesh)
map (24° 53′N 90° 43′E) **3**:64
NETSCHER, CASPAR
Christiaan Huygens **10**:325 *illus.*
NETSUKE **14**:104 *bibliog., illus.*
NETTLE **14**:104
artillery plant **2**:224
NETTLETON (Mississippi)
map (34° 5′N 88° 44′W) **13**:469
NETWORKING, COMPUTER *see* COMPUTER NETWORKING
NETWORKS, RADIO AND TELEVISION *see* RADIO BROADCASTING; TELEVISION BROADCASTING; names of specific networks, e.g., BRITISH BROADCASTING CORPORATION; NATIONAL BROADCASTING COMPANY; PUBLIC BROADCASTING SERVICE; etc.
NEUBER, CAROLINA **14**:104
NEUBRANDENBURG (East Germany) **9**:144 *illus.*
map (53° 33′N 13° 15′E) **9**:140
NEUCHÂTEL (Switzerland) **14**:104
map (46° 59′N 6° 56′E) **18**:394
NEUCHÂTEL, LAKE **14**:104
map (46° 52′N 6° 50′E) **18**:394
NEUILLY, TREATY OF
World War I **20**:246
NEUMANN, JOHANN BALTHASAR **14**:104 *bibliog.*
Vierzehnheiligen **3**:90 *illus.*
Würzburg Residenz **20**:297
NEUMANN, SAINT JOHN NEPOMUCENE **14**:104–105 *bibliog.*
NEUMANN, JOHN VON *see* VON NEUMANN, JOHN
NEUMEIER, JOHN **14**:105 *bibliog.*
NEUMÜNSTER (Germany, East and West)
map (54° 4′N 9° 59′E) **9**:140
NEUNKIRCHEN (Austria)
map (47° 43′N 16° 5′E) **2**:348
NEUNKIRCHEN (Germany, East and West)
map (49° 20′N 7° 10′E) **9**:140
NEUQUÉN (Argentina)
map (38° 57′S 68° 4′W) **2**:149
NEUQUÉN (province in Argentina)
map (39° 0′S 70° 0′W) **2**:149
NEURAL NET AUTOMATION
automata, theory of **2**:356
NEURALGIA **14**:105
Fothergill, John **8**:248
glossopharyngeal neuralgia **14**:105
sciatica **17**:141
NEUROLINGUISTICS
linguistics **12**:358
NEUROLOGY **14**:105
Charcot, Jean Martin **4**:287
child psychiatry **4**:350–351
NEUROMA
neuralgia **14**:105
NEURON *see* NERVE CELL; NERVOUS SYSTEM
NEUROPHARMACOLOGY **14**:105
drug **6**:276–277
Katz, Sir Bernard **12**:31
psychotropic drugs **15**:604
NEUROPHYSIOLOGY **14**:105–106 *bibliog.*
biopotential **3**:275–276
neurotransmitter **14**:107
reflex **16**:120
schizophrenia **17**:124
senses **17**:204–205
skin **17**:341
spinal cord **18**:184
tissue, animal **19**:210
NEUROPSYCHOLOGY
Lashley, Karl S. **12**:213
Luria, Aleksandr Romanovich **12**:466
NEUROPTERA **14**:106
alderfly **1**:269
ant lion **2**:38
dobsonfly **6**:209
lacewing **12**:160
Mantisfly **13**:130
snake fly **17**:382–383
NEUROSIS **14**:106–107 *bibliog.*
anorexia nervosa **2**:34

anxiety **2**:72
complex (psychology) **5**:157
compulsive behavior **5**:159
defense mechanisms (psychology) **6**:83
depression **6**:118
dissociation (psychology) **6**:198
fear **8**:39
fixation **8**:132
Freud, Sigmund **8**:329
hypochondria **10**:351
hysteria **10**:352
kleptomania **12**:97
learning theory **12**:260
Narcissus (mythology) **14**:21
phobia **15**:248–249
psychosomatic disorders **15**:602
psychotherapy **15**:602
NEUROSPORA **14**:107
NEUROSURGERY *see* NERVOUS SYSTEM—surgery
NEUROTRANSMITTER **14**:107
acetylcholine **1**:80
Katz, Sir Bernard **12**:31
Alzheimer's disease **1**:320
drug **6**:277
endocrine system **7**:168
endocrine system, diseases of the **7**:169; **7**:170
muscle contraction **13**:655
noradrenaline **14**:218
opiate receptor **14**:405
NEURUPPIN (Germany, East and West)
map (52° 55′N 12° 48′E) **9**:140
NEUSCHWANSTEIN CASTLE **9**:141 *illus.*
Louis II's Bavarian palaces **12**:423
NEUSE RIVER
map (35° 6′N 76° 30′W) **14**:242
NEUSIEDLER LAKE
map (47° 50′N 16° 46′E) **2**:348
NEUSS (West Germany) **14**:107
NEUSTRELITZ (Germany, East and West)
map (53° 21′N 13° 4′E) **9**:140
NEUSTRIA **14**:107
NEUTRA, RICHARD **14**:107–108 *bibliog.*
NEUTRALITY **14**:108 *bibliog.*
Embargo Act **7**:151
right of search **16**:222
Switzerland **18**:394; **18**:397
NEUTRALIZATION **14**:108
acids and bases **1**:83
drug, antacid **2**:38
salt (chemistry) **17**:37
NEUTRINO **14**:108 *bibliog.*
beta decay **3**:229
fundamental particles **8**:362 *table*
parity (physics) **15**:89
Pauli, Wolfgang **15**:118–119
Sun **18**:345
NEUTRON **14**:108–109 *bibliog.*
atom **2**:305
atomic nucleus **2**:310–311
atomic nucleus, detection **2**:311 *illus.*
baryon **3**:99
beryllium **3**:227
binding energy **3**:257–258
Bloch, Felix **3**:334
Bothe, Walther Wilhelm **3**:415
discovery **14**:108–109
Chadwick, Sir James **4**:267
fundamental interactions **8**:361
fundamental particles **8**:361; **8**:362 *table*
neutron bomb **14**:109
slow neutrons **14**:109
structure: Hofstadter, Robert **10**:197
NEUTRON BOMB **14**:109 *bibliog.*
NEUTRON STAR **14**:109 *bibliog.*
Chandrasekhar, Subrahmanyan **4**:280
Chandrasekhar limit **4**:280
degenerate matter **6**:85
Gold, Thomas **9**:228
Landau, Lev **12**:181
pulsar **14**:109; **15**:620
relativity **16**:136
stellar evolution **18**:251
supernova **18**:352
theories **14**:109
Zwicky, Fritz **20**:384
NEUTROPENIA
blood **3**:338
NEUVO MUNDO, MOUNT
map (21° 55′S 66° 53′W) **3**:366
NEVA RIVER **14**:109
Leningrad (USSR) **12**:283–284 *map*
NEVADA **14**:109–114 *bibliog., illus., map*
agriculture **14**:112–113 *illus.*
archaeology **2**:117 *illus.*
cities
Carson City **4**:170
Elko **7**:146
Las Vegas **12**:210
Reno **16**:157
climate **14**:110
culture **14**:112
economic activities **14**:112–114 *illus.*; **14**:114
education **14**:112
Nevada, University of **14**:114
flag **14**:110 *illus.*
government **14**:113
history **14**:113–114
Comstock Lode **5**:167
land and resources **14**:109–112 *illus., map*
mountain **13**:619–620
map (39° 0′N 117° 0′W) **19**:419
mining **14**:113
people **14**:112 *illus.*
Mojave **13**:504–505
Paiute **15**:25
Shoshoni **17**:284–285
Washo **20**:45
rivers, lakes, and waterways **14**:110
seal, state **14**:110 *illus.*
tourism **14**:113
vegetation and animal life **14**:110
NEVADA (county in Arkansas)
map (33° 40′N 93° 15′W) **2**:166
NEVADA (county in California)
map (39° 16′N 121° 1′W) **4**:31
NEVADA (Iowa)
map (42° 1′N 93° 27′W) **11**:244
NEVADA (Missouri)
map (37° 51′N 94° 22′W) **13**:476
NEVADA, UNIVERSITY OF **14**:114
NEVADA CITY (California)
map (36° 16′N 121° 1′W) **4**:31
NÉVÉ *see* FIRN
NEVE, FELIPE DE
Los Angeles (California) **12**:418
NEVE MOUNTAINS
map (13° 52′S 13° 26′E) **2**:5
NEVELSON, LOUISE **14**:114–115 *bibliog., illus.*
Chapel of the Good Shepherd **14**:114 *illus.*
NEVERS (France)
map (47° 0′N 3° 9′E) **8**:260
NEVERS, ERNIE **14**:115
NEVILLE, EMILY **14**:115
NEVILLE, RICHARD, EARL OF WARWICK *see* WARWICK, RICHARD NEVILLE, EARL OF
NEVIN, ETHELBERT WOODBRIDGE **14**:115
NEVINS, ALLAN **14**:115
oral history **14**:414
NEVIS
Saint Kitts-Nevis **17**:20
NEVSEHIR (Turkey)
map (38° 38′N 34° 43′E) **19**:343
NEVSKY, ALEXANDER *see* ALEXANDER NEVSKY
NEW ALBANY (Indiana)
map (38° 18′N 85° 49′W) **11**:111
NEW ALBANY (Mississippi)
map (34° 29′N 89° 0′W) **13**:469
NEW ALBIN (Iowa)
map (43° 30′N 91° 17′W) **11**:244
NEW ALBION
Drake, Sir Francis **6**:256
NEW AMERICAN CYCLOPAEDIA
Dana, Charles Anderson **6**:20
Ripley, George **16**:228
NEW AMSTERDAM *see* NEW YORK (city)
NEW AMSTERDAM (Guyana)
map (6° 15′N 57° 31′W) **9**:410
NEW ATHENS (Illinois)
map (38° 19′N 89° 53′W) **11**:42
NEW AUGUSTA (Mississippi)
map (31° 12′N 89° 2′W) **13**:469
NEW BEDFORD (Massachusetts) **14**:115
map (41° 38′N 70° 56′W) **13**:206
NEW BERLIN (New York)
map (42° 38′N 75° 20′W) **14**:149
NEW BERLIN (Wisconsin)
map (42° 58′N 88° 7′W) **20**:185
NEW BERN (North Carolina) **14**:115; **14**:244 *illus.*
map (35° 7′N 77° 3′W) **14**:242
NEW BETHLEHEM (Pennsylvania)
map (41° 0′N 79° 20′W) **15**:147
NEW BLOOMFIELD (Pennsylvania)
map (40° 25′N 77° 11′W) **15**:147
NEW BOSTON (Ohio)
map (38° 45′N 82° 56′W) **14**:357
NEW BOSTON (Texas)
map (33° 28′N 94° 25′W) **19**:129
NEW BRAUNFELS (Texas)
map (29° 42′N 98° 8′W) **19**:129
NEW BREMEN (Ohio)
map (40° 26′N 84° 23′W) **14**:357
NEW BRITAIN (Connecticut)
map (41° 40′N 72° 47′W) **5**:193
NEW BRITAIN (Papua New Guinea) **14**:115
map (6° 0′S 150° 0′E) **15**:72
NEW BRUNSWICK (province in Canada)
map (46° 30′N 66° 15′W) **4**:70
NEW BRUNSWICK (city in New Jersey) **14**:115
map (40° 29′N 74° 27′W) **14**:129
NEW BRUNSWICK (province in Canada) **14**:115–118 *bibliog., illus., map*
Campobello Island **4**:67
cities
Bathurst **3**:123
Fredericton **8**:294
Moncton **13**:522
Saint John **17**:19
climate **14**:116
economic activity **14**:116 *illus.*; **14**:117–118 *illus.*
education
Fredericton, University of New Brunswick at **4**:92 *table*
Moncton, Université de **4**:92 *table*
Mount Allison University **4**:92 *table*; **13**:618
New Brunswick, University of **14**:118
St. John, University of New Brunswick at **4**:92 *table*
flag **14**:116 *illus.*
government **14**:118
history **14**:118
land and resources **14**:116–117 *map*
people **14**:117
rivers, lakes, and waterways **14**:116
vegetation and animal life **14**:116
NEW BRUNSWICK, UNIVERSITY OF **14**:118
NEW BRUTALISM (architecture)
Le Corbusier **12**:254
NEW BUFFALO (Michigan)
map (41° 47′N 86° 45′W) **13**:377
NEW CALEDONIA **14**:119 *map*
bird
kagu **12**:6
cities
Nouméa **14**:268
map (21° 30′S 165° 30′E) **14**:334
ore mineral
garnierite **9**:50
NEW CANAAN (Connecticut)
map (41° 9′N 73° 30′W) **5**:193
NEW CARLISLE (Ohio)
map (39° 56′N 84° 2′W) **14**:357
NEW CASTLE (Colorado)
map (39° 34′N 107° 32′W) **5**:116
NEW CASTLE (Delaware) **6**:90 *illus.*
map (39° 40′N 75° 34′W) **6**:88
NEW CASTLE (county in Delaware)
map (39° 44′N 75° 33′W) **6**:88
NEW CASTLE (Indiana)
map (39° 55′N 85° 22′W) **11**:111
NEW CASTLE (Kentucky)
map (38° 26′N 85° 10′W) **12**:47
NEW CASTLE (Pennsylvania)
map (41° 0′N 80° 20′W) **15**:147
NEW CASTLE (Virginia)
map (37° 30′N 80° 7′W) **19**:607
NEW CHINA NEWS AGENCY
People's Daily **15**:156
NEW CITY (New York)
map (41° 9′N 73° 59′W) **14**:149
NEW CLASS, THE (book)
Djilas, Milovan **6**:208
NEW COLLEGE (Oxford University) **14**:474
NEW CONCORD (Ohio)
map (40° 0′N 81° 44′W) **14**:357
NEW CONNECTICUT *see* VERMONT
NEW CRITICISM **14**:119 *bibliog.*
Brooks, Cleanth **3**:511
criticism, literary **5**:352
Ransom, John Crowe **16**:88
Tate, Allen **19**:44
Warren, Robert Penn **20**:31
NEW CUMBERLAND (West Virginia)
map (40° 30′N 80° 36′W) **20**:111
NEW DEAL **14**:119–120 *bibliog., illus.*
Agricultural Adjustment Administration **1**:188
agriculture, history of **1**:193
Civilian Conservation Corps **5**:34
Commons, John R. **5**:141
Democratic party **6**:101
Depression of the 1930s **6**:119–120
Farm Security Administration
photography, history and art of **15**:271–272
Hopkins, Harry L. **10**:231–232
housing **10**:277
Hughes, Charles Evans **10**:292
labor union **12**:155
Lend-Lease **12**:281
National Recovery Administration **14**:45
Public Works Administration **15**:611
Roosevelt, Franklin Delano **16**:308–309
social security **18**:14–15
socialism **18**:23
tariff acts **19**:37
Tennessee Valley Authority **19**:107
unemployment insurance **19**:384
United States, history of the **19**:454 *illus.*
United States v. *Butler* **19**:464
Works Progress Administration **20**:217–218
NEW DELHI (India) **11**:84 *illus.*; **14**:120 *illus.*
climate **11**:82 *table*
history **14**:120
map (28° 36′N 77° 12′E) **11**:80
Mogul art and architecture **13**:500–501
Qutb Minar **16**:28
urban planning
Lutyens, Sir Edwin Landseer **12**:471
NEW DEMOCRATIC PARTY **14**:120
NEW ECONOMIC POLICY **14**:121 *bibliog.*
Europe, history of **7**:295
Lenin, Vladimir Ilich **12**:283
Leninism **5**:147
Russian Revolutions of 1917 **16**:373
Russia/Union of Soviet Socialist Republics, history of **16**:359
NEW EDINBURG (Arkansas)
map (33° 46′N 92° 14′W) **2**:166
NEW EGYPT (New Jersey)
map (40° 4′N 74° 32′W) **14**:129
NEW ELLENTON (South Carolina)
map (33° 24′N 81° 42′W) **18**:98
NEW ENGLAND **14**:121
See also names of specific states, e.g., CONNECTICUT; MAINE; etc.
art
limners **12**:345
Luminism **12**:459
colonial styles in North America **5**:110–111
geographical linguistics **9**:98–99 *map*
historians
Miller, Perry **13**:428
history
Adams, James Truslow **1**:94
French and Indian Wars **8**:312–313
Gorges, Sir Ferdinando **9**:250
King Philip's War **12**:82
lumber **12**:457
Massachusetts **13**:210–211
Pequot War **15**:158
Plymouth Colony **15**:374
Randolph, Edward **16**:83
Smith, John **17**:369
United States, history of the **19**:436
Winthrop (family) **20**:181–182
intertidal life **11**:229–230
music
Ives, Charles Edward **11**:334
rivers, lakes, and waterways
Connecticut River **5**:196
Housatonic River **10**:264
saltbox house **10**:270 *illus.*
shellfish **17**:254–255
NEW ENGLAND (North Dakota)
map (46° 32′N 102° 52′W) **14**:248
NEW ENGLAND, COUNCIL OF
colonial America land grants **19**:437 *map*
Gorges, Sir Ferdinando **9**:250
London Company **12**:405
Plymouth Colony **15**:374
NEW ENGLAND COMPANY *see* MASSACHUSETTS BAY COMPANY
NEW ENGLAND CONFEDERATION
Massachusetts **13**:210
NEW ENGLAND CONSERVATORY OF MUSIC **14**:121
American music **1**:350
Converse, Frederick Shepherd **5**:233
NEW ENGLAND EMIGRANT AID COMPANY *see* EMIGRANT AID COMPANY
NEW ENGLAND PRIMER (book)
primary education **15**:537

NEW EXISTENTIALISM
Wilson, Colin **20**:164
NEW FACTUALISM *see* MODERN ARCHITECTURE
NEW FLORENCE (Missouri)
map (38° 54′N 91° 27′W) **13**:476
NEW FOREST **8**:228 *illus.*
NEW FRANCE **14**:121
Acadia **1**:71
Canada, history of **4**:81 *map*
Champlain, Samuel de **4**:277–278
French and Indian Wars **8**:312–314
Frontenac, Louis de Buade, Comte de **8**:340
fur trade **8**:371
governors **4**:85 *table*
intendant **11**:206
La Vérendrye, Pierre Gaultier de Varennes, Sieur de **12**:151
Monts, Pierre du Gua, Sieur de **13**:560
Passamaquoddy **15**:104–105
Talon, Jean **19**:18
NEW FRANKLIN (Missouri)
map (39° 1′N 92° 44′W) **13**:476
NEW FRONTIER
Kennedy, John F. **12**:43
NEW GEORGIA GROUP (Islands)
map (8° 15′S 157° 0′E) **18**:56
NEW GLARUS (Wisconsin)
map (42° 49′N 89° 38′W) **20**:185
NEW GLASGOW (Nova Scotia)
map (45° 35′N 62° 39′W) **14**:269
NEW GRANADA **14**:121 *bibliog.*
colonial Latin America *c.*1790 **12**:219 *map*
Jiménez de Quesada, Gonzalo **11**:419
NEW GUINEA **14**:121–122 *bibliog., map*
art
debating stool **14**:337 *illus.*
Oceanic art **14**:336–339
sculpture **14**:337 *illus.*
Southeast Asian art and architecture **18**:107
bird of paradise **3**:290
bowerbird **3**:428
cannibalism **4**:109–110
flap-footed lizard **8**:153
history **14**:122
World War II **20**:267
Irian Jaya **11**:266
jungle and rain forest **11**:469
languages
Oceanic languages **14**:339
map (5° 0′S 140° 0′E) **14**:334
NEW HALL (Cambridge University) **4**:53
NEW HAMPSHIRE **14**:122–126 *bibliog., illus., map*
cities
Concord **5**:171
Exeter **7**:331
Hanover **10**:39
Manchester **13**:108
Nashua **14**:24
Portsmouth **15**:448
climate **14**:122
economic activity **14**:124–125
education **14**:124
Dartmouth College **6**:40
state university and colleges of **14**:126
flag **14**:122 *illus.*
government and politics **14**:125
history **14**:125–126
Langdon, John **12**:195
Mason, John **13**:199
United States, history of the **19**:436
land and resources **14**:122–124 *map*
map (43° 35′N 71° 40′W) **19**:419
people **14**:124
physical features
Washington, Mount **20**:44
White Mountains **20**:138
rivers, lakes, and waterways **14**:122
Winnipesaukee, Lake **20**:180
seal, state **14**:122 *illus.*
vegetation and animal life **14**:122
NEW HAMPSHIRE, STATE UNIVERSITY AND COLLEGES OF **14**:126
NEW HAMPTON (Iowa)
map (43° 3′N 92° 19′W) **11**:244
NEW HANOVER (county in North Carolina)
map (34° 15′N 77° 50′W) **14**:242
NEW HANOVER ISLAND
map (2° 30′S 150° 15′E) **15**:72
NEW HARMONY (Indiana) **14**:126 *bibliog.*
map (38° 8′N 87° 56′W) **11**:111
Owen, Robert **14**:471
NEW HARTFORD (Connecticut)
map (41° 53′N 72° 59′W) **5**:193
NEW HAVEN (Connecticut) **14**:126–127 *illus.*
history
Davenport, John **6**:47
Eaton, Theophilus **7**:35
map (41° 18′N 72° 56′W) **5**:193
NEW HAVEN (county in Connecticut)
map (41° 18′N 72° 56′W) **5**:193
NEW HAVEN (Illinois)
map (37° 55′N 88° 8′W) **11**:42
NEW HAVEN (Indiana)
map (41° 4′N 85° 1′W) **11**:111
NEW HAVEN (West Virginia)
map (38° 59′N 81° 58′W) **20**:111
NEW HAVEN HARBOR
map (41° 15′N 72° 56′W) **5**:193
NEW HAZELTON (British Columbia)
map (55° 15′N 127° 35′W) **3**:491
NEW HEBRIDES *see* VANUATU
NEW HEBRIDES TRENCH
plate tectonics **15**:351 *map*
NEW HEBRON (Mississippi)
map (31° 44′N 83° 58′W) **13**:469
NEW HOLLAND (Pennsylvania)
map (40° 6′N 76° 5′W) **15**:147
NEW HOLSTEIN (Wisconsin)
map (43° 57′N 88° 5′W) **20**:185
NEW HUMANISM
Babbitt, Irving **3**:5
NEW IBERIA (Louisiana)
map (30° 0′N 91° 49′W) **12**:430
NEW IRELAND (Papua New Guinea) **14**:127
map (3° 20′S 152° 0′E) **15**:72
NEW JERSEY **14**:127–133 *bibliog., illus., map*
agriculture **14**:131 *illus.*
cities
Atlantic City **2**:294
Bayonne **3**:134
Camden **4**:53
Cape May **4**:120–121
Elizabeth **7**:141
Hackensack **10**:7
Hoboken **10**:193
Jersey City **11**:398–399
Morristown **13**:590
New Brunswick **14**:115
Newark **14**:164
Passaic **15**:104
Paterson **15**:111
Princeton **15**:549
Trenton **19**:291
climate **14**:128
culture **14**:131
economy **14**:131–132
education **14**:130
Drew University **6**:271
Fairleigh Dickinson University **8**:9
Institute for Advanced Study **11**:195
Princeton Theological Seminary **15**:549
Princeton University **15**:549 *bibliog.*
state university and colleges of **14**:133–134
Stevens Institute of Technology **18**:264
Thomas Edison College **19**:174
Westminster Choir College **20**:118
flag **14**:127 *illus.*
Fort Dix **8**:236
geographical linguistics **9**:99 *map*
government and politics **14**:130 *illus.*; **14**:132–133
historical sites **14**:128–130 *illus.*; **14**:131
history **14**:133
Carteret, Philip **4**:173
United States, history of the **19**:436
land and resources **14**:127–130 *map*
manufacturing **14**:131
map (40° 15′N 74° 30′W) **19**:419
people **14**:130–131
physical features
Palisades **15**:47
pine barrens **18**:378
resources **14**:130
zincite **20**:368
rivers, lakes, and waterways **14**:128; **14**:131 *illus.*
seal, state **14**:127 *illus.*
shellfish **17**:254
tourism **14**:131–132 *illus.*
transportation **14**:132
vegetation **14**:128
wildlife **14**:130
NEW JERSEY, STATE UNIVERSITY AND COLLEGES OF **14**:133–134
NEW JERSEY TEA (botany) **14**:134
NEW JERUSALEM, CHURCH OF THE **14**:134 *bibliog.*
Swedenborg, Emanuel **18**:386
NEW JOHNSONVILLE (Tennessee)
map (36° 1′N 87° 58′W) **19**:104
NEW JOURNALISM *see* JOURNALISM
NEW KENSINGTON (Pennsylvania)
map (40° 34′N 79° 46′W) **15**:147
NEW KENT (Virginia)
map (37° 31′N 76° 59′W) **19**:607
NEW KENT (county in Virginia)
map (37° 30′N 77° 0′W) **19**:607
NEW LEFT
counterculture **5**:311–312
guerrilla theater **9**:392
Marcuse, Herbert **13**:148
socialism **18**:24
NEW LEIPZIG (North Dakota)
map (46° 22′N 101° 57′W) **14**:248
NEW LEXINGTON (Ohio)
map (39° 43′N 82° 13′W) **14**:357
NEW LISBON (Wisconsin)
map (43° 53′N 90° 10′W) **20**:185
NEW LONDON (Connecticut) **14**:134
map (41° 21′N 72° 7′W) **5**:193
NEW LONDON (county in Connecticut)
map (41° 21′N 72° 7′W) **5**:193
NEW LONDON (Iowa)
map (40° 55′N 91° 24′W) **11**:244
NEW LONDON (Minnesota)
map (45° 18′N 94° 56′W) **13**:453
NEW LONDON (Missouri)
map (39° 35′N 91° 24′W) **13**:476
NEW LONDON (New Hampshire)
map (43° 25′N 71° 59′W) **14**:123
NEW LONDON (Ohio)
map (41° 5′N 82° 24′W) **14**:357
NEW LONDON (Wisconsin)
map (44° 23′N 88° 45′W) **20**:185
NEW MADRID (Missouri)
map (36° 36′N 89° 32′W) **13**:476
NEW MADRID (county in Missouri)
map (36° 35′N 89° 40′W) **13**:476
NEW MARTINSVILLE (West Virginia)
map (39° 39′N 80° 52′W) **20**:111
NEW MATHEMATICS *see* MATHEMATICS, NEW
NEW MEADOWS (Idaho)
map (44° 58′N 116° 32′W) **11**:26
NEW METLAKATLA *see* METLAKATLA (Alaska)
NEW MEXICO **14**:134–140 *bibliog., illus., map*
agriculture **14**:137–138 *illus.*
archaeology and historic sites **14**:137
Acoma **1**:83–84
Anasazi Ruins **1**:394
Zuñi **20**:382
Carlsbad Caverns **4**:151–152
Chaco Canyon **4**:264–265
cities
Alamogordo **1**:240
Albuquerque **1**:261
Gallup **9**:21
Las Cruces **12**:209–210
Los Alamos **12**:416
Santa Fe **17**:68
Taos **19**:29
climate **14**:135
culture **14**:137
economic activity **14**:137–138 *illus.*; **14**:140
education **14**:137
St. John's College **17**:20
state universities of **14**:140
energy sources **14**:138
flag **14**:135 *illus.*
government **14**:138
history **14**:138–140
Mexican War **13**:352 *map*; **13**:354–355
Oñate, Juan de **14**:389
Polk, James K. **15**:405
Schmitt, Harrison H. **17**:128
Spanish missions **18**:160–161
Indians of North America, art of the **11**:140
land and resources **14**:134–137 *illus., map*
Los Alamos National Scientific Laboratory **12**:416
manufacturing **14**:138
map (34° 30′N 106° 0′W) **19**:419
mining **14**:138
people **14**:137
Apache **2**:73
Hispanic Americans **10**:177
Navajo **14**:53–54
Pueblo **15**:613–614
resources **14**:137
rivers, lakes, and waterways **14**:135 *illus.*
Pecos River **15**:130
seal, state **14**:135 *illus.*
tourism **14**:138
vegetation and animal life **14**:135
White Sands Missile Range **20**:138
NEW MEXICO, STATE UNIVERSITIES OF **14**:140
NEW MIAMI (Ohio)
map (39° 26′N 84° 32′W) **14**:357
NEW MILFORD (Connecticut)
map (41° 35′N 73° 25′W) **5**:193
NEW MILFORD (New Jersey)
map (40° 56′N 74° 1′W) **14**:129
NEW NETHERLAND **14**:140
Minuit, Peter **13**:461
New Sweden **14**:142
patroons **15**:114
Stuyvesant, Peter **18**:310
United States, history of the **19**:436
NEW NOVEL **14**:140 *bibliog.*
Beckett, Samuel **3**:151–152
Butor, Michel **3**:592
Duras, Marguerite **6**:304
Robbe-Grillet, Alain **16**:240
Sarraute, Nathalie **17**:79
Simon, Claude **17**:314
NEW OBJECTIVITY
Bordewijk, Ferdinand **3**:398
NEW ORLEANS (Louisiana) **12**:431–432 *illus.*; **14**:140–142 *bibliog., illus., map*
Basin Street **3**:110
history
Bienville, Jean Baptiste Le Moyne, Sieur de **3**:247
jazz **11**:387–388
map (29° 58′N 90° 7′W) **12**:430
Mardi Gras **13**:148
Pontchartrain, Lake **12**:427
NEW ORLEANS, BATTLE OF
Farragut, David Glasgow **8**:29
War of 1812 **20**:26–28 *illus., map*
NEW PALTZ (New York)
map (41° 45′N 74° 5′W) **14**:149
NEW PARIS (Ohio)
map (39° 51′N 84° 48′W) **14**:357
NEW PHILADELPHIA (Ohio)
map (40° 30′N 81° 27′W) **14**:357
NEW PINE CREEK (Oregon)
map (42° 1′N 120° 18′W) **14**:427
NEW PLYMOUTH (Idaho)
map (43° 58′N 116° 49′W) **11**:26
NEW PLYMOUTH (New Zealand)
map (39° 4′S 174° 5′E) **14**:158
NEW POMERANIA
New Britain **14**:115
NEW PORT RICHEY (Florida)
map (28° 16′N 82° 43′W) **8**:172
NEW PRAGUE (Minnesota)
map (44° 32′N 93° 34′W) **13**:453
NEW PROVIDENCE (New Jersey)
map (40° 42′N 74° 24′W) **14**:129
NEW PROVIDENCE ISLAND
Bahama Islands **3**:23
map (25° 2′N 77° 24′W) **3**:23
NEW REALISM
Hanson, Duane **10**:41
Perry, Ralph Barton **15**:179
NEW REPUBLIC (periodical)
Lippmann, Walter **12**:363
NEW RICHMOND (Ohio)
map (38° 57′N 84° 17′W) **14**:357
NEW RICHMOND (Wisconsin)
map (45° 7′N 92° 32′W) **20**:185
NEW RIGHT
Moral Majority **13**:573
National Conservative Political Action Committee **14**:31
O'Connor, Sandra Day **14**:347
NEW RIVER (Belize)
map (18° 22′N 88° 24′W) **3**:183
NEW RIVER (Guyana)
map (3° 23′N 57° 36′W) **9**:410
NEW RIVER (Virginia)
map (38° 10′N 81° 12′W) **19**:607
NEW ROADS (Louisiana)
map (30° 42′N 91° 26′W) **12**:430
NEW ROCHELLE (New York) **14**:142
map (40° 55′N 73° 47′W) **14**:149
NEW ROCKFORD (North Dakota)
map (47° 41′N 99° 15′W) **14**:248
NEW ROSS (Nova Scotia)
map (44° 44′N 64° 27′W) **14**:269
NEW SALEM (North Dakota)
map (46° 51′N 101° 25′W) **14**:248
NEW SARUM (England) *see* SALISBURY (England)
NEW SCHOOL FOR SOCIAL RESEARCH **14**:142
Beard, Charles A. **3**:142
Dewey, John **6**:147
Mitchell, Wesley Clair **13**:483–484
NEW SHARON (Iowa)
map (41° 28′N 92° 39′W) **11**:244

NEW SMYRNA BEACH (Florida)
map (29° 2′N 80° 56′W) **8**:172
NEW SOUTH WALES (Australia) **14**:142 *map*
cities
Broken Hill **3**:501
Newcastle **14**:164
flag **8**:145 *illus.*
history
Australia, history of **2**:340
Parkes, Sir Henry **15**:91
Phillip, Arthur **15**:239
map (33° 0′S 146° 0′E) **2**:328
physical features
Kosciusko, Mount **12**:123
Snowy Mountains **18**:5
NEW SPAIN **14**:142
colonial Latin America *c.*1790 **12**:219 *map*
Mendoza, Antonio de **13**:296
Mexico, history of **13**:362–363
Velasco, Luis de **19**:536
NEW STONE AGE *see* NEOLITHIC PERIOD
NEW SWEDEN **14**:142 *bibliog.*
Delaware **6**:90
NEW TAZWELL (Tennessee)
map (36° 27′N 83° 33′W) **19**:104
NEW TESTAMENT *see* BIBLE
NEW THOUGHT **14**:142–143 *bibliog.*
Quimby, Phineas Parkhurst **16**:26
NEW TOWN (North Dakota)
map (47° 59′N 102° 30′W) **14**:248
NEW TOWNS **14**:143 *bibliog.*
Brasília (Brazil) **3**:457 *illus.*
Chandigarh (India) **4**:279
city **5**:7
garden city **9**:42
greenbelt **9**:349
housing **10**:277
Islamabad (Pakistan) **11**:293
Reston (Virginia) **16**:182
urban planning **19**:484
NEW ULM (Minnesota)
map (44° 19′N 94° 28′W) **13**:453
NEW VIENNA (Ohio)
map (39° 19′N 83° 42′W) **14**:357
NEW WAVE **14**:143 *bibliog.*
Belmondo, Jean Paul **3**:192
Cahiers du Cinéma (periodical) **4**:16
Chabrol, Claude **4**:264
Duras, Marguerite **6**:304
film, history of **8**:86
Godard, Jean Luc **9**:219
Moreau, Jeanne **13**:576–577
Renoir, Jean **16**:158
Resnais, Alain **16**:177
Truffaut, François **19**:316–317
NEW-WAVE ROCK
rock music **16**:249
NEW WESTMINSTER (British Columbia)
map (49° 12′N 122° 55′W) **3**:491
NEW WILMINGTON (Pennsylvania)
map (41° 7′N 80° 20′W) **15**:147
NEW WORLD INFORMATION ORDER
press agencies and syndicates **15**:533
NEW WORLD QUAIL *see* QUAIL
NEW YORK (city) **14**:143–147 *bibliog., illus., maps*
architecture
cast-iron architecture **4**:186
Chrysler Building **4**:420
Empire State Building **7**:158
Flagg, Ernest **8**:149–150
Flatiron Building **8**:156; **18**:246 *illus.*
Gilbert, Cass **9**:178
Gothic Revival **9**:262–263
Grand Central Terminal **9**:285
Guggenheim Museum **1**:329 *illus.*; **20**:288 *illus.*
Hardy Holzman Pfeiffer Associates **10**:48
Harrison, Wallace K. **10**:60
Hood, Raymond **10**:225
hotel **10**:262
Hunt, Richard Morris **10**:312
Lever House **2**:137 *illus.*
Lincoln Center for the Performing Arts **12**:350
Radio City Music Hall **16**:53
Rockefeller Center **16**:250–251
Saint John the Divine, Cathedral of **17**:19
Saint Patrick's Cathedral **16**:159 *illus.*; **17**:24
Seagram Building **17**:173
skyscraper **17**:349 *illus.*
Waldorf-Astoria **10**:260 *illus.*
White, Stanford **20**:136
Whitney Museum of American Art **3**:475 *illus.*
Woolworth Building **20**:216
World Trade Center **20**:219
art
abstract expressionism **1**:65
Cooper-Hewitt Museum **5**:245
Guggenheim Museum **9**:393
Metropolitan Museum of Art, The **13**:348
modern art **13**:493–495
Museum of Modern Art **13**:657
Statue of Liberty **18**:238
Whitney Museum of American Art **20**:142
boroughs
Bronx, the **3**:505
Brooklyn **3**:510
Manhattan **5**:6 *illus.*; **13**:116
Queens **16**:22
Staten Island **18**:234
Bowery, The **3**:428
Bronx Zoo **3**:505
Central Park **4**:254
climate **14**:143; **19**:421 *table*
clothing industry **5**:65–66
economy **14**:146; **14**:147
education **14**:146
Allen, James Edward, Jr. **1**:299
Barnard College **3**:86
Clark, Kenneth B. **5**:39
Columbia University **5**:126
Cooper Union **5**:244
Fordham University **8**:224
Jewish Theological Seminary of America **11**:412
New School for Social Research **14**:142
New York, City University of **14**:154
New York University **14**:156
Parsons School of Design **15**:99
Pratt Institute **15**:490
Rockefeller University **16**:251
Teachers College, Columbia University **19**:54
Union Theological Seminary **19**:399
Yeshiva University **20**:327
Ellis Island **7**:148
ethnic composition **14**:146
government **14**:146
Governors Island **9**:272
Greenwich Village **9**:354–355
growth **5**:5 *maps*
Harlem **10**:49–50
Hispanic Americans **10**:177; **10**:178; **10**:179 *illus.*
history **14**:147
See also NEW NETHERLAND
American Revolution **1**:358
Astor Place Riot **2**:269
British occupation, 1776 **1**:359 *illus.*
De Lancey (family) **6**:61
Draft Riots **6**:254
harbor (18th century) **19**:436 *illus.*
Hewitt, Abram Stevens **10**:154
Koch, Edward I. **12**:104
La Guardia, Fiorello **12**:147
Leisler, Jacob **12**:279
Lindsay, John V. **12**:352
Long Island, Battle of **12**:406
Low, Seth **12**:438
Minuit, Peter **13**:461
skyscraper **17**:349–350 *illus.*
Smith, Alfred E. **17**:367
Tammany Hall **19**:19–20
Tweed, William M. **19**:358
United States, history of the **19**:436
urban planning **19**:482
Walker, Jimmy **20**:12
Washington's triumphal entry, 1783 **1**:364 *illus.*
Whitney, William Collins **20**:142
Wood, Fernando **20**:206
housing **10**:276
linguistics, sociolinguistic variation **18**:27
map (40° 43′N 74° 1′W) **14**:149
music
Carnegie Hall **4**:155
jazz **11**:388–389
Tin Pan Alley **19**:205
photography
Abbott, Berenice **1**:53
Riis, Jacob August **16**:222–223 *illus.*
points of interest **14**:144–146 *maps*
rent control **16**:159
theater
Broadway **3**:499–500; **5**:6 *illus.*
Mercury Theatre **13**:308
Off-Broadway theater **14**:352–353
Off-Off Broadway theater **14**:353
transportation **14**:146
subway **18**:318 *illus., table*
Wall Street **20**:12–13
water supply **20**:54–55 *illus., map*
NEW YORK (county in New York)
map (40° 46′N 73° 55′W) **14**:149
NEW YORK (state) **14**:147–154 *bibliog., illus., map*
agriculture **14**:151
art
Hudson River School **10**:290
limners **12**:345
cities
Albany **1**:251
Binghamton **3**:259
Buffalo **3**:546
Cooperstown **5**:245
Elmira **7**:149
Hyde Park **10**:329
Ithaca **11**:331
Kingston **12**:84
Mount Vernon **13**:618
New Rochelle **14**:142
New York **14**:143–147 *illus., maps*
Newburgh **14**:164
Niagara Falls **14**:177
Rochester **16**:247
Rome **16**:297
Sag Harbor **14**:152 *illus.*
Saratoga Springs **17**:75
Schenectady **17**:119
Syracuse **18**:410
Tarrytown **14**:150
Troy **19**:313
Utica **19**:497
Yonkers **20**:329–330
climate **14**:148
cultural institutions **14**:150
economic activity **14**:151–152
education **14**:150
Bard College **3**:80
Barnard College **3**:86
Colgate University **5**:101
Columbia University **5**:126
Cooper Union **5**:244
Cornell University **5**:268
Elmira College **7**:150
Fordham University **8**:224
Hofstra University **10**:197
Jewish Theological Seminary of America **11**:412
Marymount College **13**:193
New School For Social Research **14**:142
New York, City University of **14**:154
New York, State University of **14**:154
New York University **14**:156
Nott, Eliphalet **14**:268
Parsons School of Design **15**:99
Pratt Institute **15**:490
Rensselaer Polytechnic Institute **16**:159
Rochester Institute of Technology **16**:247
Rockefeller University **16**:251
Russell Sage College **16**:351
St. Lawrence University **17**:22
St. Vladimir's Orthodox Theological Seminary **17**:27
Sarah Lawrence College **17**:74
Skidmore College **17**:337
Syracuse University **18**:411
Teachers College, Columbia University **19**:54
Union College **19**:386–387
United States Merchant Marine Academy **19**:462
United States Military Academy **19**:462–463
Vassar College **19**:526
Wells College **20**:101
White, Andrew Dickson **20**:134
Willard, Emma Hart **20**:154
Yeshiva University **20**:327
flag **14**:148 *illus.*
geographical linguistics **9**:99 *map*
government and politics **14**:152
Harriman (family) **10**:56–57
Liberal parties **12**:311–312
Tilden, Samuel J. **19**:199
historic sites **14**:150
history **14**:152–153
Antirent War **2**:68
Carey, Hugh **4**:146–147
Cleveland, Grover **5**:52
Clinton (family) **5**:59–60
Conkling, Roscoe **5**:191
Crown Point **5**:364
Cuomo, Mario **5**:390
Dewey, Thomas E. **6**:147
Fish (family) **8**:111
Free-Soil party **8**:295
French and Indian Wars **8**:312–314
Hunkers and Barnburners **10**:311
Livingston (family) **12**:377
Morris (family) **13**:588
Moses, Robert **13**:600
New Netherland **14**:140
patroons **15**:114
Rockefeller, Nelson A. **16**:250
Roosevelt, Franklin Delano **16**:307–308
Roosevelt, Theodore **16**:310
Seymour, Horatio **17**:233
Smith, Alfred E. **17**:367
Vermont **19**:558
land and resources **14**:148 *illus., map*
manufacturing **14**:151
map (43° 0′N 106° 0′W) **19**:419
people **14**:150–151
Cayuga **4**:227
Iroquois League **11**:279–280
Mohawk **13**:502
Montauk **13**:551
Oneida **14**:389
Onondaga **14**:391
Seneca **17**:200
Tuscarora **19**:355
physical features
Adirondack Mountains **1**:103
Catskill Mountains **4**:213
Long Island **12**:406
Montauk Point **13**:551
rent control **16**:159
rivers, lakes, and waterways **14**:148
Erie Canal **7**:230 *map*
Finger Lakes **8**:93
George, Lake **9**:109
Hudson River **10**:289–290
Mohawk River **13**:502
New York State Barge Canal **14**:156
Placid, Lake **15**:325
seal, state **14**:148 *illus.*
vegetation and animal life **14**:148; **14**:150
wine **20**:176
NEW YORK, CITY UNIVERSITY OF **14**:154
New York, State University of **14**:154
open admission **14**:398
NEW YORK, STATE UNIVERSITY OF **14**:154
Cornell University **5**:268
NEW YORK BOTANICAL GARDEN
Britton, Nathaniel **3**:499
Bronx, the **3**:505
NEW YORK CITY BALLET **4**:409 *illus.*; **6**:25 *illus.*; **14**:154–155 *bibliog., illus.*
Afternoon of a Faun, The **1**:181
Balanchine, George **3**:32–33
ballet **3**:44–45 *illus.*
Baryshnikov, Mikhail **3**:99
Bolender, Todd **3**:364
Bonnefous, Jean Pierre **3**:381
d'Amboise, Jacques **6**:19
Farrell, Suzanne **8**:30
Hayden, Melissa **10**:81
Irving, Robert **11**:284
Karinska, Barbara **12**:27
Kirkland, Gelsey **12**:89
Kirstein, Lincoln **12**:90
McBride, Patricia **13**:7
Martins, Peter **13**:181
Robbins, Jerome **16**:240
Tallchief, Maria **19**:16
NEW YORK CITY OPERA **14**:155
Sills, Beverly **17**:309–310
NEW YORK DAILY NEWS **14**:155
journalism **11**:455
McCormick, Robert Rutherford **13**:10
Munsey, Frank Andrew **13**:643
Patterson (family) **15**:115
press agencies and syndicates **15**:533
tabloids **19**:5
NEW YORK DRAMA CRITICS CIRCLE AWARD
Bankhead, Tallulah **3**:67–68
Eldridge, Florence **7**:103
Hansberry, Lorraine **10**:40
McCullers, Carson **13**:11
Mamet, David **13**:97
Merman, Ethel **13**:311
Miller, Arthur **13**:427
Page, Geraldine **15**:13
Stoppard, Tom **18**:284
Waters, Ethel **20**:65
Williams, Tennessee **20**:160–161
NEW YORK EVENING POST
Bigelow, John **3**:249
NEW YORK FIVE (architectural group)
Eisenman, Peter **7**:96
Graves, Michael **9**:302

NEW YORK FIVE (cont.)
Gwathmey, Charles **9**:411
Hejduk, John **10**:110
Meier, Richard Alan **13**:281
NEW YORK HERALD
Bennett, James Gordon **3**:202–203
NEW YORK JOURNAL
yellow journalism **20**:322
NEW YORK MAGAZINE (periodical)
Murdoch, Rupert **13**:648
Steinem, Gloria **18**:248
NEW YORK MARATHON
running and jogging **16**:346
NEW YORK MARITIME COLLEGE
New York, State University of **14**:154
NEW YORK MILLS (Minnesota)
map (46° 31′N 95° 22′W) **13**:453
NEW YORK PHILHARMONIC **14**:155 *bibliog.*
American music **1**:350
Bernstein, Leonard **3**:224
Carnegie Hall **4**:155
NEW YORK POETS **14**:155
NEW YORK PUBLIC LIBRARY **14**:155 *bibliog.*
New York (city) **14**:145 *map*
NEW YORK REVIEW OF BOOKS (periodical)
Hardwick, Elizabeth **10**:47
NEW YORK SCHOOL *see* ABSTRACT EXPRESSIONISM
NEW YORK STATE BARGE CANAL **14**:156
NEW YORK STOCK EXCHANGE **18**:274–275 *illus.*
NEW YORK SUN
Dana, Charles Anderson **6**:20
Day, Benjamin Henry **6**:55
journalism **11**:455
NEW YORK TIMES, THE **14**:156 *bibliog.*
Atkinson, Brooks **2**:269
Baker, Russell **3**:28
freedom of the press **8**:296–297
Jones, George **11**:442
New York Times Company v. *Sullivan* **14**:156
New York Times Company v. *United States* **14**:156
newspaper **14**:171 *illus.*
Ochs, Adolph Simon **14**:346
press agencies and syndicates **15**:533
Raymond, Henry Jarvis **16**:97
Reston, James Barrett **16**:182
Sulzberger, Arthur Hays **18**:338
Wicker, Tom **20**:145
NEW YORK TIMES COMPANY* v. *SULLIVAN **14**:156
defamation **6**:81
tort **19**:246
NEW YORK TIMES COMPANY* v. *UNITED STATES **14**:156 *bibliog.*
Pentagon Papers **15**:154
Supreme Court of the United States **18**:357
NEW YORK TRIBUNE
Dana, Charles Anderson **6**:20
Greeley, Horace **9**:346
Reid, Whitelaw **16**:131
NEW YORK UNIVERSITY **14**:156
NEW YORK WEEKLY JOURNAL
Zenger, John Peter **20**:359
NEW YORK WORLD
Pulitzer, Joseph **15**:618
yellow journalism **20**:322
NEW YORK ZOOLOGICAL PARK *see* BRONX ZOO
NEW YORKER, THE (periodical) **14**:156 *bibliog.*; **15**:170 *illus.*
Bogan, Louise **3**:359
Croce, Arlene **5**:355
Gilliatt, Penelope **9**:182
Kael, Pauline **12**:5
Ross, Harold **16**:318
Thurber, James **19**:186
Updike, John **19**:471
White, E. B. **20**:134–135
NEW ZEALAND **14**:156–161 *bibliog., illus., map, table*
agriculture **14**:160 *illus.*
animal life **14**:159
kea **12**:34
kiwi **12**:94
New Zealand Wattlebird **14**:163
New Zealand wren **14**:163–164
art
art **14**:159–160
Oceanic art **14**:338
cities
Auckland **2**:317 *illus.*
Christchurch **4**:411
Dunedin **6**:299
Invercargill **11**:233
Wellington **20**:100
climate **14**:157 *table*
Cook, Mount **5**:237
economic activity **14**:160
education **14**:159
universities **14**:163
exploration *see* EXPLORATION
fjord **8**:133
flag **14**:157 *illus.*
geyser **9**:162
government **14**:160–161
health **14**:159
history *see* NEW ZEALAND, HISTORY OF
islands and territories
Antipodes Islands **2**:65
Auckland Islands **2**:317
Cook Islands **5**:237
Niue **14**:204
Pitcairn Island **15**:319–320 *map*
Ross Dependency (Antarctica) **16**:318
Tokelau **19**:223
land and resources **14**:156–159 *illus., map, table*
literature
Ashton-Warner, Sylvia **2**:231
Marsh, Dame Ngaio **13**:171
map (41° 0′S 174° 0′E) **14**:334
New Zealand, Church of the Province of **14**:161
parks and reserves
Fiordland National Park **14**:157 *illus.*
people **14**:159
Maori **13**:136
resources **14**:159
petroleum **15**:210
rivers, lakes, and waterways
Cook Strait **5**:237
Sutherland Falls **18**:373
trade **14**:160
vegetation **14**:157; **14**:159
NEW ZEALAND, CHURCH OF THE PROVINCE OF **14**:161 *bibliog.*
NEW ZEALAND, HISTORY OF **14**:161–163 *bibliog., illus., map, table*
Maori Wars **13**:136
New Zealand, history of **14**:161–162
prime ministers **14**:162 *table*
Seddon, Richard John **17**:182
Waitangi, Treaty of **20**:7
Wakefield, Edward Gibbon **20**:8
prior to 1900
discovery and settlement **14**:161–162
Grey, Sir George **9**:360
Vogel, Sir Julius **19**:625
1900-present
Anzus Treaty **2**:73
Blundell, Sir Denis **3**:347
foreign affairs **14**:163
Fraser, Peter **8**:287
Holland, Sir Sidney **9**:203
Kirk, Norman Eric **12**:88–89
Lange, David **12**:195
Massey, William **13**:213
modern state **14**:162–163
Muldoon, Robert David **13**:635–636
Savage, Michael Joseph **17**:97
Ward, Sir Joseph **20**:29
NEW ZEALAND COMPANY
New Zealand, history of **14**:161–162 *illus.*
NEW ZEALAND UNIVERSITIES **14**:163 *table*
NEW ZEALAND WATTLEBIRD **14**:163
NEW ZEALAND WREN **14**:163–164
NEWARK (Arkansas)
map (35° 42′N 91° 27′W) **2**:166
NEWARK (Delaware) **14**:164
map (39° 41′N 75° 45′W) **6**:88
NEWARK (New Jersey) **14**:164
map (40° 44′N 74° 10′W) **14**:129
Newark International Airport **14**:132 *illus.*
NEWARK (New York)
map (43° 3′N 77° 6′W) **14**:149
NEWARK (Ohio)
map (40° 4′N 82° 24′W) **14**:357
NEWARK BAY
map (40° 39′N 74° 9′W) **14**:129
NEWARK VALLEY (New York)
map (42° 14′N 76° 11′W) **14**:149
NEWAYGO (Michigan)
map (43° 25′N 85° 48′W) **13**:377
NEWAYGO (county in Michigan)
map (43° 35′N 85° 50′W) **13**:377
NEWBERG (Oregon)
map (45° 18′N 122° 58′W) **14**:427
NEWBERN (Alabama)
map (32° 36′N 87° 38′W) **1**:234
NEWBERN (Tennessee)
map (36° 7′N 89° 16′W) **19**:104
NEWBERRY (Florida)
map (29° 39′N 82° 37′W) **8**:172
NEWBERRY (Michigan)
map (46° 21′N 85° 30′W) **13**:377
NEWBERRY (South Carolina)
map (34° 17′N 81° 37′W) **18**:98
NEWBERRY (county in South Carolina)
map (34° 15′N 81° 40′W) **18**:98
NEWBERRY, WALTER LOOMIS
Newberry Library **14**:164
NEWBERRY LIBRARY **14**:164
NEWBERY, JOHN
Newbery Medal **14**:164
NEWBERY MEDAL **14**:164
Coatsworth, Elizabeth **5**:82
George, Jean Craighead **9**:109
Hamilton, Virginia **10**:29
Hunt, Irene **10**:311
Neville, Emily **14**:115
Speare, Elizabeth **18**:165
NEWBORN *see* INFANCY
NEWBURG (Missouri)
map (37° 55′N 91° 54′W) **13**:476
NEWBURGH (Indiana)
map (37° 57′N 87° 24′W) **11**:111
NEWBURGH (New York) **14**:164
map (41° 30′N 74° 1′W) **14**:149
NEWBURYPORT (Massachusetts)
map (42° 49′N 70° 53′W) **13**:206
NEWCASTLE (Australia) **14**:164
map (32° 56′S 151° 46′E) **2**:328
Newcastle University **2**:345 *table*
NEWCASTLE (Maine)
map (44° 2′N 69° 33′W) **13**:70
NEWCASTLE (Nebraska)
map (42° 39′N 96° 53′W) **14**:70
NEWCASTLE (New Brunswick)
map (47° 0′N 65° 34′W) **14**:117
NEWCASTLE (Wyoming)
map (43° 50′N 104° 11′W) **20**:301
NEWCASTLE, THOMAS PELHAM-HOLLES, 1ST DUKE OF **14**:164 *bibliog.*
NEWCASTLE UPON TYNE (England) **14**:164–165
map (54° 59′N 1° 35′W) **19**:403
NEWCOMB, SIMON **14**:165 *bibliog.*
American Astronomical Society **1**:337
NEWCOMEN, THOMAS **14**:165 *bibliog.*
steam engine **11**:158 *illus.*; **14**:165; **18**:241 *illus.*
NEWCOMERSTOWN (Ohio)
map (40° 16′N 81° 36′W) **14**:357
NEWELL (South Dakota)
map (44° 43′N 103° 25′W) **18**:103
NEWELLTON (Louisiana)
map (32° 10′N 91° 14′W) **12**:430
NEWENHAM, CAPE
map (58° 37′N 162° 12′W) **1**:242
NEWFANE (New York)
map (43° 17′N 78° 43′W) **14**:149
NEWFANE (Vermont)
map (42° 59′N 72° 39′W) **19**:554
NEWFIELD (New Jersey)
map (39° 33′N 75° 1′W) **14**:129
NEWFOUND GAP (pass)
map (35° 37′N 83° 25′W) **19**:104
NEWFOUND LAKE
map (43° 40′N 71° 47′W) **14**:123
NEWFOUNDLAND (Canada) **14**:165–168 *bibliog., illus., map*
cities
Corner Brook **5**:268
Gander **9**:35
St. John's **17**:19
climate **14**:165; **14**:167
economic activity **14**:167–168 *illus.*
education
Newfoundland, Memorial University of **14**:168
fishing industry **14**:165 *illus.*; **14**:167
flag **8**:145 *illus.*; **14**:165 *illus.*
government **14**:168
history **14**:168
L'Anse aux Meadows **12**:144
Labrador **12**:157
land and resources **14**:165–167 *illus., map*
map (52° 0′N 56° 0′W) **4**:70
people **14**:167
rivers, lakes, and waterways **14**:167
Churchill Falls **4**:427
Churchill River **4**:427
vegetation and animal life **14**:167
NEWFOUNDLAND (dog) **6**:214 *illus.*; **14**:168 *bibliog., illus.*
NEWFOUNDLAND, MEMORIAL UNIVERSITY OF **14**:168
NEWGRANGE (Ireland) **14**:168 *bibliog.*
neolithic carving **15**:509 *illus.*
NEWHALEM (Washington)
map (48° 41′N 121° 16′W) **20**:35
NEWHALL, BEAUMONT **14**:169
NEWHOUSE, SAMUEL I. **14**:169 *illus.*
NEWHOUSE FOUNDATION
Newhouse, Samuel I. **14**:169
NEWINGTON (Connecticut)
map (41° 43′N 72° 45′W) **5**:193
NEWKIRK (Oklahoma)
map (36° 53′N 97° 3′W) **14**:368
NEWLAND (North Carolina)
map (36° 5′N 81° 56′W) **14**:242
NEWLANDS, JOHN ALEXANDER REINA **14**:169 *bibliog.*
NEWMAN (Illinois)
map (39° 48′N 87° 59′W) **11**:42
NEWMAN, ARNOLD **14**:169
NEWMAN, BARNETT **14**:169 *bibliog., illus.*
Blue Midnight **14**:169 *illus.*
NEWMAN, EDWIN **14**:169
NEWMAN, ERNEST **14**:169–170 *bibliog.*
NEWMAN, JOHN HENRY **14**:170 *bibliog., illus.*
Oxford movement **14**:475
NEWMAN, LARRY
aerial sports **1**:122
NEWMAN, PAUL **14**:170 *bibliog., illus.*
NEWMAN GROVE (Nebraska)
map (41° 45′N 97° 47′W) **14**:70
NEWMARKET (New Hampshire)
map (43° 5′N 70° 56′W) **14**:123
NEWNAN (Georgia)
map (33° 23′N 84° 48′W) **9**:114
NEWNHAM COLLEGE (Cambridge University) **4**:53
NEWPORT (Arkansas)
map (35° 37′N 91° 17′W) **2**:166
NEWPORT (Indiana)
map (39° 53′N 87° 24′W) **11**:111
NEWPORT (Maine)
map (44° 50′N 69° 17′W) **13**:70
NEWPORT (New Hampshire)
map (43° 21′N 72° 9′W) **14**:123
NEWPORT (North Carolina)
map (34° 48′N 76° 51′W) **14**:242
NEWPORT (Oregon)
map (44° 38′N 124° 3′W) **14**:427
NEWPORT (Pennsylvania)
map (40° 29′N 77° 8′W) **15**:147
NEWPORT (Rhode Island) **14**:170; **16**:199–200 *illus.*
Coddington, William **5**:90
map (41° 13′N 71° 18′W) **16**:198
Newport Jazz Festival **14**:171
NEWPORT (county in Rhode Island)
map (41° 35′N 71° 15′W) **16**:198
NEWPORT (Tennessee)
map (35° 58′N 83° 11′W) **19**:104
NEWPORT (Vermont)
map (44° 57′N 72° 12′W) **19**:554
NEWPORT (Wales)
map (52° 1′N 4° 51′W) **19**:403
NEWPORT (Washington)
map (48° 11′N 117° 3′W) **20**:35
NEWPORT, CHRISTOPHER
Jamestown (Virginia) **11**:357
NEWPORT BEACH (California)
map (33° 37′N 117° 56′W) **4**:31
NEWPORT JAZZ FESTIVAL **14**:171 *bibliog.*
NEWPORT NEWS (Virginia) **14**:171
map (37° 4′N 76° 28′W) **19**:607
NEWRY (South Carolina)
map (34° 43′N 82° 55′W) **18**:98
NEWS AGENCIES *see* PRESS AGENCIES AND SYNDICATES
NEWS OF THE WORLD
darts **6**:40
NEWSCAST *see* JOURNALISM; RADIO BROADCASTING; TELEVISION BROADCASTING
NEWSDAY
Patterson (family) **15**:115
NEWSPAPER **14**:171–173 *bibliog., illus., table*
See also PHOTOJOURNALISM; names of specific newspapers, e.g., *NEW YORK DAILY NEWS; WASHINGTON POST, THE*; etc.
advertising **1**:112–113
authoritarian press **14**:172
cartoon (editorial and political) **4**:176–178
circulation **14**:171 *table*
comic strip **5**:135–136
daily newspapers, worldwide **14**:171 *table*
freedom of the press **8**:296–297
future **14**:172
Great Britain
Northcliffe, Alfred Harmsworth, Viscount **14**:253

Walter (family) **20**:19
Italy **11**:323 *illus.*
journalism **11**:453–456
libertarian press **14**:171–172
mass communication **13**:202
music criticism **13**:670
Newspaper Guild **14**:173
Penny Press **15**:153
press agencies and syndicates **15**:533
printing **15**:552 *illus.*
PROFESSIONAL AND EDUCATIONAL ORGANIZATIONS
American Newspaper Publishers Association **1**:352
public relations **15**:610
South America
Recife **16**:107
stereotype **18**:260
tabloids **19**:5
Third World press **14**:172
United States
Bradford (family) **3**:436–437
Campbell, John **4**:65
Cowles, Gardner **5**:321
Gannett, Frank E. **9**:37
Greeley, Horace **9**:346–347 *illus.*
Harris, Benjamin **10**:57
Hearst, William Randolph **10**:90–91
Howard, Roy Wilson **10**:283
Jones, George **11**:442
Murdoch, Rupert **13**:648
New York Times, The **14**:156
Newhouse, Samuel I. **14**:169
Niles, Hezekiah **14**:197
Ochs, Adolph Simon **14**:346
Patterson (family) **15**:115
Pulitzer, Joseph **15**:618
Raymond, Henry Jarvis **16**:97
Russel, Benjamin **16**:348–349
Scripps, Edward Wyllis **17**:158
Sulzberger, Arthur Hays **18**:338
Villard, Oswald Garrison **19**:598
Watterson, Henry **20**:69
White, William Allen **20**:136
NEWSPAPER GUILD **14**:173
NEWSPRINT
manufacture **14**:167 *illus.*
newspaper **14**:172
production, worldwide **15**:70 *table*
NEWSREEL **14**:173 *bibliog.*
documentary **6**:211
Porter, Edwin S. **15**:444
Vertov, Dziga **19**:563
NEWSWEEK (periodical) **14**:173
NEWT *see* SALAMANDER AND NEWT
NEWTON (county in Arkansas)
map (35° 52′N 93° 15′W) **2**:166
NEWTON (Georgia)
map (31° 19′N 84° 20′W) **9**:114
NEWTON (county in Georgia)
map (33° 35′N 83° 50′W) **9**:114
NEWTON (Illinois)
map (38° 59′N 88° 10′W) **11**:42
NEWTON (county in Indiana)
map (40° 46′N 87° 27′W) **11**:111
NEWTON (Iowa)
map (41° 42′N 93° 3′W) **11**:244
NEWTON (Kansas)
map (38° 3′N 97° 21′W) **12**:18
NEWTON (Massachusetts)
map (42° 21′N 71° 11′W) **13**:206
NEWTON (measurement)
units, physical **19**:466–467 *tables*
NEWTON (Mississippi)
map (32° 19′N 89° 10′W) **13**:469
NEWTON (county in Mississippi)
map (32° 25′N 89° 5′W) **13**:469
NEWTON (county in Missouri)
map (36° 55′N 94° 20′W) **13**:476
NEWTON (New Jersey)
map (41° 3′N 74° 45′W) **14**:129
NEWTON (North Carolina)
map (35° 40′N 81° 13′W) **14**:242
NEWTON (Texas)
map (30° 51′N 93° 46′W) **19**:129
NEWTON (county in Texas)
map (30° 40′N 93° 46′W) **19**:129
NEWTON, HUEY P.
Black Panther party **3**:318
NEWTON, SIR ISAAC **14**:173–175 *bibliog., illus.*
astronautics **2**:274
astronomy, history of **2**:278
biology **3**:269
calculus **14**:173
celestial mechanics **4**:230; **14**:174
Clairaut, Alexis Claude **5**:35
Clarke, Samuel **5**:40
dispersion (physics) **6**:197
gravitation **9**:304–305 *illus.*; **14**:174
Earth, size and shape of **7**:19
Halley, Edmond **10**:22
interference (physics) **11**:207–209
Kepler's laws **12**:58
laws of motion *see* LAWS OF MOTION
mathematics, history of **13**:225
Maupertuis, Pierre Louis Moreau de **13**:234
method of approximation
equation **7**:224
error **7**:235
optics **14**:173–174; **14**:410
physics, history of **15**:282–285 *illus.*
precession of the equinoxes **15**:493
Principia **14**:173–174; **15**:550
relativity **16**:132–133
telescope **19**:81 *illus.*
two-body problem **19**:360
NEWTON FALLS (New York)
map (44° 13′N 74° 59′W) **14**:149
NEWTON SQUARE (Pennsylvania)
map (39° 59′N 75° 24′W) **15**:147
NEWTON'S RINGS *see* INTERFERENCE (physics)
NEWTONTOPPEN MOUNTAIN
map (79° 2′N 17° 30′E) **14**:261
NEWTOWN (Newfoundland)
map (49° 12′N 53° 31′W) **14**:166
NEWVILLE (Pennsylvania)
map (40° 10′N 77° 24′W) **15**:147
NEXØ, MARTIN ANDERSEN- **14**:175
NEXT OF KIN **14**:175
NEY, MICHEL **14**:175 *bibliog., illus.*
Waterloo, Battle of **20**:64
NEYMAN, JERZY **14**:175
NEYRA, ALVARO DE MENDAÑA DE *see* MENDAÑA DE NEYRA, ÁLVARO DE
NEYSHABUR (Iran)
map (36° 12′N 58° 50′E) **11**:250
NEZ PERCÉ (American Indians) **14**:175–176 *bibliog., illus.*
Appaloosa **2**:86–87
Indians of North America, art of the **11**:140
Joseph, Chief **11**:451
Montana **13**:548
NEZ PERCE (county in Idaho)
map (46° 20′N 116° 50′W) **11**:26
NEZAMI, NEZAMODDIN ILYAS **14**:176
NEZPERCE (Idaho)
map (46° 14′N 116° 14′W) **11**:26
NEZVAL, VÍTĚZSLAV
Czech literature **5**:412
NGADJU *see* DAYAK
NGAMI, LAKE
map (20° 37′S 22° 40′E) **3**:416
NGANASAN *see* SAMOYED (people)
NGANGERABELI PLAIN
map (1° 30′S 40° 15′E) **12**:53
NGAU ISLAND
map (18° 2′S 179° 18′E) **8**:77
NGAWI (Indonesia)
map (7° 24′S 111° 26′E) **11**:147
NGBE (Leopard Society)
secret societies **17**:181
NGO DINH DIEM **14**:176 *bibliog.*
flag **8**:149
Vietnam War **19**:584–587
NGOKO RIVER
map (1° 40′N 16° 3′E) **5**:182
NGOUNIÉ RIVER
map (0° 37′S 10° 18′E) **9**:5
NGOZI (Burundi)
map (2° 54′S 29° 50′E) **3**:582
NGUEMA, FRANCISCO MACÍAS *see* MACÍAS NGUEMA, FRANCISCO
NGUGI WA THOING'O **14**:176
NGUNI **14**:176 *bibliog.*
Ndebele **14**:68
Sotho **18**:70
Swazi **18**:379
Thonga **19**:177
Xhosa **20**:312
Zulu **20**:381–382
NGUOI THUONG see MONTAGNARDS
NGURU (Nigeria)
map (12° 52′N 10° 27′E) **14**:190
NGUYEN (dynasty)
Vietnam **19**:583
NGUYEN DU
Vietnam **19**:582
NGUYEN THAT THANH *see* HO CHI MINH
NGUYEN VAN THIEU **14**:177
Vietnam War **19**:584–590 *illus.*
NHA TRANG (Vietnam) **19**:581 *illus.*
map (12° 15′N 109° 11′E) **19**:580
NHLANGANO (Swaziland)
map (27° 6′S 31° 17′W) **18**:380
NI TSAN (Ni Zan) **14**:177 *bibliog.*
NI ZAN *see* NI TSAN (Ni Zan)
NIACIN (Vitamin B_3)
coenzyme **5**:92
megavitamin therapy **13**:280
pellagra **15**:138
vitamins and minerals **19**:619
Recommended Dietary Allowances **19**:618 *table*
NIAGARA (county in New York)
map (43° 10′N 78° 42′W) **14**:149
NIAGARA (ship)
Perry, Oliver Hazard **15**:179
NIAGARA (Wisconsin)
map (45° 46′N 88° 2′W) **20**:185
NIAGARA, FORT *see* FORT NIAGARA (New York)
NIAGARA FALLS **14**:151 *illus.*; **14**:177 *illus.*; **14**:392 *illus.*
map (43° 5′N 79° 4′W) **14**:393; **19**:241
waterfall **20**:62–63 *illus.*
Watson, Elkanah **20**:67
NIAGARA FALLS (city in New York) **14**:177
map (43° 6′N 79° 2′W) **14**:149
NIAGARA FALLS (city in Ontario) **14**:177
map (43° 6′N 79° 4′W) **14**:393
NIAGARA MOVEMENT **14**:29 *illus.*
Du Bois, W. E. B. **6**:285
NIAGARA RIVER **14**:177
map (43° 15′N 79° 4′W) **14**:149
NIAMEY (Niger) **14**:177
map (13° 31′N 2° 7′E) **14**:187
NIAMTOUGOU (Togo)
map (9° 46′N 1° 6′E) **19**:222
NIANGUA RIVER
map (37° 58′N 92° 48′W) **13**:476
NIANTIC (American Indians)
Mohegan **13**:503
Narragansett **14**:21–22
Pequot **15**:158
NIAUX CAVE (France) **14**:177
prehistoric art **15**:508
NIB (pen) **15**:140
NIBBLER *see* CHUB
NIBELUNGENLIED (poem) **14**:177–178 *bibliog.*
Siegfried (mythology) **17**:295
NICAEA **14**:178 *bibliog.*
NICAEA, COUNCILS OF **14**:178 *bibliog.*
Arianism **2**:153–154
Athanasius, Saint **2**:288
Constantine I, Roman Emperor **5**:209
council, ecumenical **5**:309–310
Eusebius of Caesarea **7**:310
Eusebius of Nicomedia **7**:310
iconoclasm **11**:20–21
Jesus Christ **11**:406
Nicaea **14**:178
NICARAGUA **14**:178–179 *bibliog., illus., map, table*
cities
Granada **9**:283
León **12**:289
Managua **13**:108
economic activities **14**:179
education **14**:178
Latin American universities **12**:233 *table*
flag **14**:178 *illus.*
government **14**:179
history **14**:179
Ortega Saavedra, Daniel **14**:449
Sandinistas **17**:62
Somoza (family) **18**:62
Walker, William **20**:12
Zelaya, José Santos **20**:358
land and resources **14**:178 *map, table*
literature
Darío, Rubén **6**:37–38
map (13° 0′N 85° 0′W) **14**:225
Mosquito Coast **13**:603
people **14**:178
Miskito **13**:466
pre-Columbian art and architecture **15**:495–501
NICARAGUA, LAKE **14**:180
map (11° 30′N 85° 30′W) **14**:179
NICCOLITE **14**:180
NICE (France) **14**:180 *illus.*
map (43° 42′N 7° 15′E) **8**:260
Mardi Gras **13**:148
NICENE CREED
creed **5**:337
Nicaea, councils of **14**:178
NICEPHORUS, SAINT **14**:180 *bibliog.*
NICETAS (bishop)
Te Deum laudamus **19**:53
NICEVILLE (Florida)
map (30° 31′N 86° 29′W) **8**:172
NICHIREN **14**:180 *bibliog.*
NICHOLAS, GRAND DUKE OF RUSSIA (1856–1929)
World War I **20**:230–231
NICHOLAS (county in Kentucky)
map (38° 20′N 84° 2′W) **12**:47
NICHOLAS (county in West Virginia)
map (38° 17′N 80° 45′W) **20**:111
NICHOLAS, GRAND DUKE OF RUSSIA (1856–1929)
World War I **20**:226
NICHOLAS, SAINT **14**:180–181 *bibliog.*
Santa Claus **17**:67
NICHOLAS I, EMPEROR OF RUSSIA **14**:181 *bibliog., illus.*
Decembrists **6**:73
Nesselrode, Karl Robert, Count **14**:97
Russia/Union of Soviet Socialist Republics, history of **16**:357
World War I **20**:234 *illus.*
NICHOLAS I, POPE **14**:182 *bibliog.*
NICHOLAS II, EMPEROR OF RUSSIA **14**:181–182 *bibliog., illus.*
Alexandra Fyodorovna, consort of **1**:277
Hague conferences **10**:11
Pskov (USSR) **15**:588
Rasputin, Grigory Yefimovich **16**:91
Romanov (dynasty) **16**:290–291
Russian Revolution of 1905 **16**:370
Russian Revolutions of 1917 **16**:371 *illus.*
Russia/Union of Soviet Socialist Republics, history of **16**:358–359
NICHOLAS V, POPE **14**:182 *bibliog.*
NICHOLAS CHANNEL
map (23° 25′N 80° 5′W) **5**:377
NICHOLAS OF CUSA **14**:181 *bibliog.*
NICHOLAS OF VERDUN **14**:181 *bibliog.*
Flemish art and architecture **8**:161–162
graphic arts **9**:292
NICHOLASVILLE (Kentucky)
map (37° 53′N 84° 34′W) **12**:47
NICHOLLS (Georgia)
map (31° 31′N 82° 38′W) **9**:114
NICHOLS, MARIA LONGWORTH
Rockwood ware **16**:306
NICHOLS, MIKE **14**:182
NICHOLSON (Pennsylvania)
map (41° 38′N 75° 47′W) **15**:147
NICHOLSON, BEN **14**:182 *bibliog.*
NICHOLSON, SIR FRANCIS **14**:182
NICHOLSON, JACK **14**:182 *bibliog.*
NICHOLSON RIVER
map (17° 31′S 139° 36′E) **2**:328
NICHOMACHOS **14**:182–183
NICIAS **14**:183
NICKEL **14**:183 *bibliog.*
abundances of common elements **7**:131 *table*
Cronstedt, Axel Fredrik, Baron **5**:359
element **7**:130 *table*
Group VIII periodic table **15**:167
metal, metallic element **13**:328
Mond (family) **13**:522
ore
garnierite **9**:50
major ore deposits **14**:424–425 *table*
millerite **13**:429
niccolite **14**:180
pentlandite **15**:155
platinum **15**:359
world distribution **14**:423 *map*
transition elements **19**:273 *table*
NICKEL SILVER
copper **5**:252
NICKELODEON
film, history of **8**:81–82
NICKERSON (Kansas)
map (38° 8′N 98° 5′W) **12**:18
NICKLAUS, JACK **14**:183 *bibliog., illus.*
golf **9**:240 *illus.*
NICOBAR ISLANDS (India) **14**:183
map (8° 0′N 93° 30′E) **11**:80
NICOL, WILLIAM
mineral **13**:439
Nicol prism **15**:394 *illus.*
optical activity **14**:408
optical mineralogy **14**:409
NICOLA (British Columbia)
map (50° 10′N 120° 40′W) **3**:491
NICOLAI, OTTO **14**:183
NICOLET (Quebec)
map (46° 13′N 72° 37′W) **16**:18
NICOLET, JEAN **14**:184
Green Bay **9**:347
Mackinac, Straits of **13**:29
Michigan, Lake **13**:383
NICOLET, LAKE
map (46° 23′N 84° 14′W) **13**:377
NICOLLET (county in Minnesota)
map (44° 22′N 94° 13′W) **13**:453

NICOLLS TOWN (Bahama Islands)
map (25° 8′N 78° 0′W) 3:23
NICOLÒ OF VERONA
Romanesque art and architecture 16:284
NICOSIA (Cyprus) 5:408 *table*; 14:184
map (35° 10′N 33° 22′E) 5:409
NICOT, JEAN
nicotine 14:184
NICOTINAMIDE ADENINE DINUCLEOTIDE (NAD)
coenzyme 5:92–93
NICOTINAMIDE ADENINE DINUCLEOTIDE PHOSPHATE (NADP)
photosynthesis 15:275; 15:277
NICOTINE 14:184
smoking 17:374
NICOTINIC ACID
nicotine 14:184
NICOYA ,GULF OF
map (9° 47′N 84° 48′W) 5:291
NICOYA PENINSULA
map (10° 0′N 85° 25′W) 5:291
NIEBHUR, KARSTEN
exploration 7:338
NIEBUHR, H. RICHARD 14:184 *bibliog.*
NIEBUHR, REINHOLD 14:184 *bibliog., illus.*
Liberal parties 12:312
NIEDERE TAUERN MOUNTAINS
map (47° 18′N 14° 0′E) 2:348
NIELSEN, A. C., COMPANY
radio and television broadcasting 16:54
NIELSEN, CARL AUGUST 14:184–185 *bibliog.*
NIEMANN, ALBERT
Tristan and Isolde (opera) 19:303
NIEMEYER, OSCAR 14:185 *bibliog.*
Alvorada Palace 12:228 *illus.*
Belo Horizonte 3:192
Brasília 3:457
Latin American art and architecture 12:228
NIEMÖLLER, MARTIN 14:185 *bibliog.*
NIEN-CH'ING-T'ANG-KU-LA MOUNTAINS
map (30° 0′N 90° 0′E) 19:190
NIENBURG (Germany, East and West)
map (52° 38′N 9° 13′E) 9:140
NIEPCE, JOSEPH NICÉPHORE 14:185 *bibliog., illus.*; 15:267 *illus.*
camera obscura 4:59
Daguerre, Louis J. M. 6:6
NIETZSCHE, FRIEDRICH WILHELM 14:185–186 *bibliog., illus.*
atheism 2:289
Beyond Good and Evil 3:233
Birth of Tragedy, The 3:295
Thus Spake Zarathustra 14:186; 19:186
Weimar (East Germany) 20:94
NIEUW AMSTERDAM (Suriname)
map (5° 53′N 55° 5′W) 18:364
NIEUW NICKERIE (Suriname)
map (5° 57′N 56° 59′W) 18:364
NIEUWLAND, JULIUS ARTHUR 14:186
NIEVO, IPPOLITO 14:186
NIFLHEIM 14:186
NIGDE (Turkey)
map (37° 59′N 34° 42′E) 19:343
NIGER 14:186–188 *bibliog., illus., map, table*
cities
Agadès 14:187 *table*
Niamey 14:177
Zinder 14:187 *table*
climate 14:187 *table*
economic activity 14:188
flag 14:186 *illus.*
history and government 14:188
land and resources 14:186–187 *illus., map, table*
map (16° 0′N 8° 0′E) 1:136
people 14:187–188
Hausa 10:69
Songhai (people) 18:65
NIGER-CONGO LANGUAGES
African languages 1:166–167
NIGER DELTA
map (4° 50′N 6° 0′E) 14:190
NIGER-KORDOFANIAN LANGUAGES 12:355 *map*
African languages 1:166–167
NIGER RIVER 14:188 *bibliog., map*
Maçina 13:26
map (5° 33′N 6° 33′E) 1:136
NIGERIA 14:188–192 *bibliog., illus., map, table*
African music 1:168–171 *illus.*
art 14:191
African art 1:160–164
Biafra 3:236
cities
Abuja 14:192
Ibadan 11:3
Kano 1:144 *illus.*; 12:16
Lagos 12:166
climate 14:189; 14:191 *table*
culture 14:191
economic activity 14:191–192
education 14:190–191
African universities 1:176 *table*
flag 14:189 *illus.*
government 14:192
defense, national 6:82 *table*
history 14:192
Balewa, Sir Abubakar Tafawa 3:36
Fulani 8:356
Goldie, Sir George 9:234
Gowon, Yakubu 9:273
Ife 11:32
Lugard, Frederick John Dealtry Lugard, 1st Baron 12:452
Ojukwu, Chukemeka Odumegwu 14:364–365
Shagari, Shehu 17:235
Usman dan Fodio 19:491
land and resources 14:189–190 *map*
literature
Achebe, Chinua 1:81
African literature 1:167–168
Aluko, Timothy Mofolorunso 1:314
Amadi, Elechi 1:320
Clark, John Pepper 5:38
Ekwensi, Cyprian 7:98
Nzekwu, Onuora 14:310
Okara, Gabriel 14:365
Okigbo, Christopher 14:366
Soyinka, Wole 18:115
Tutuola, Amos 19:356
map (10° 0′N 8° 0′E) 1:136
mining and power 14:191
people 14:189–191
Edo 7:58–59
Fon 8:204
Hausa 10:69
Ibibio 11:4
Ibo 11:6
Kanuri 12:24
Nupe 14:296–297
Tiv 19:217
women in society 20:204 *table*
Yoruba 20:331
rivers, lakes, and waterways 14:189
transportation and trade 14:192
NIGHT ADDER *see* HOGNOSE SNAKE; VIPER
NIGHT BLINDNESS
eye diseases 7:350
Wald, George 20:9
NIGHT LIZARD 14:192 *illus.*
NIGHT MONKEY *see* KINKAJOU
NIGHT SIGHTS 14:193 *bibliog., illus.*
NIGHT AT THE OPERA, A (film) 13:182 *illus.*
NIGHTHAWK 3:281 *illus.*; 14:193 *illus.*
beak 3:289 *illus.*
goatsucker 9:216
NIGHTINGALE 14:193
NIGHTINGALE, FLORENCE 14:193–194 *bibliog., illus.*
nursing 14:298 *illus.*
NIGHTSHADE (botany) 14:194 *bibliog.*; 15:384 *illus.*
bittersweet 3:301
Chinese lantern plant 4:389
datura 6:45
mandrake 13:112
medicinal plants 13:266
pepper (spice) 15:156
petunia 15:216
potato 15:465–466
tomato 19:229
vegetable 19:533 *illus.*
NIH *see* NATIONAL INSTITUTES OF HEALTH
NIHILISM 14:194 *bibliog.*
Benn, Gottfried 3:202
Camus, Albert 4:68
Dada 6:4–5
NIHON *see* JAPAN
NIHON-KAI *see* JAPAN, SEA OF
NIIGATA (Japan)
map (37° 55′N 139° 3′E) 11:361
NIIHAU ISLAND (Hawaii)
Hawaii (state) 10:73
map (21° 55′N 160° 10′W) 10:72
NIJHOFF, MARTINUS 14:194
NIJINSKA, BRONISLAVA 14:194 *bibliog.*
NIJINSKY, VASLAV 3:44 *illus.*; 14:194–195 *bibliog., illus.*
Afternoon of a Faun, The 1:181
Ballets Russes de Serge Diaghilev 3:48 *illus.*
NIJMEGEN (Netherlands) 14:195
map (51° 50′N 5° 50′E) 14:99
NIJMEGEN, PEACE OF
lands acquired 8:269 *map*
Louis XIV, King of France 12:426
NIKE (Greek deity) 14:195
NIKE (rocket)
Nike Apache sounding rocket 18:77 *illus.*
Nike-Hercules 16:255 *illus.*
NIKE (Victory)
Olympia (Greece) 14:381
NIKE OF SAMOTHRACE 14:195 *bibliog.*
Samothrace 17:47
NIKISCH, ARTUR 14:195 *bibliog.*
Berlin Philharmonic Orchestra 3:217
NIKOLAIS, ALWIN 14:195 *bibliog.*
modern dance 13:497 *illus.*
NIKOLAYEV, ANDRIAN 14:195
NIKOLSKI (Alaska)
map (53° 15′N 168° 22′W) 1:242
NIKON 14:195–196 *bibliog.*
NIKŠIĆ (Yugoslavia)
map (42° 46′N 18° 56′E) 20:340
NILE FISH
mormyrid 13:582
NILE RIVER 13:397 *illus.*; 14:196–197 *bibliog., illus., map*; 18:321 *illus.*
Aswan High Dam 2:286
delta 16:233 *illus.*
Egypt 7:74–75 *illus., map*
Egypt, ancient 7:81 *map*
exploration 7:338
floods and flood control 8:166
history and economy 14:197
map (30° 10′N 31° 6′E) 14:196
Nasser, Lake 14:25
NILES (Michigan)
map (41° 50′N 86° 15′W) 13:377
NILES (Ohio)
map (41° 11′N 80° 45′W) 14:357
NILES, HEZEKIAH 14:197
NILES, WILLIAM WHITE
roads and highways 16:238
NILES' WEEKLY REGISTER (periodical)
Niles, Hezekiah 14:197
periodical 15:169
NILGIRI HILLS (India)
people
Badaga 3:18
NILO-SAHARAN LANGUAGES 12:355 *map*
African languages 1:166
NILOTES 1:145 *map*; 14:197 *bibliog.*
Kenya 12:54
Luo 12:465
Nuer 14:291
Sudan 18:321
NILSSON, BIRGIT 14:197–198 *bibliog.*
NIM
games, mathematical 9:33 *illus.*
NIMA *see* NINEVEH (Iraq)
NIMBA, MOUNT
map (7° 35′N 8° 25′W) 11:335
NIMBA MOUNTAINS
map (7° 30′N 8° 30′W) 9:397
NIMBUS (artificial satellite) 14:198 *bibliog., table*; 17:86 *illus.*; 18:123 *illus.*
Landsat 12:184
NIMEIRY, MUHAMMAD GAAFAR AL- 14:198
Sudan 18:322
NÎMES (France) 14:198
Maison Carrée 2:132 *illus.*; 13:76
map (43° 50′N 4° 21′E) 8:260
Pont du Gard 2:94 *illus.*
NIMH *see* NATIONAL INSTITUTE OF MENTAL HEALTH
NIMITZ (aircraft carrier) 14:57 *illus.*
NIMITZ, CHESTER W. 14:198 *bibliog.*
Midway 13:414
World War II 20:267; 20:278
NIMROD LAKE
map (34° 55′N 93° 20′W) 2:166
NIMRUD 14:199 *bibliog.*
black obelisk relief 15:44 *illus.*
Mesopotamian art and architecture 13:321
palaces 13:316 *illus.*; 13:320 *illus.*
NIN, ANAÏS 14:199 *bibliog.*
NIÑA (ship)
Pinzón, Martín Alonso 15:309
NINDISCHGARSTEN MOUNTAIN
map (47° 43′N 14° 4′E) 2:348
"NINE DAYS' QUEEN" *see* GREY, LADY JANE
NINE DEGREE CHANNEL
map (9° 0′N 73° 0′E) 11:80
NINETEEN EIGHTY-FOUR (book) 14:199 *bibliog.*
Orwell, George 14:451
19TH AMENDMENT 14:199 *bibliog.*
suffrage, women's 18:326
text 5:222
NINETY SIX (South Carolina)
map (34° 11′N 82° 1′W) 18:98
NINETYEAST RIDGE 14:199
Indian Ocean 11:104–106
oceanic ridges 14:328–329 *map*
NINEVEH (Iraq) 14:199–200 *bibliog., illus.*
aqueduct 2:94
Botta, Paul Émile 3:417
construction of palace by slaves 19:63 *illus.*
cuneiform library 5:389
Layard, Sir Austen 12:252
Mallowan, Sir Max 13:92–93
Mesopotamian art and architecture 13:321
Sennacherib, King of Assyria 17:203
NING-CHING MOUNTAINS
map (30° 41′N 98° 12′E) 19:190
NING-PO (Ningbo) (China) 14:200
map (29° 52′N 121° 31′E) 4:362
NINGSIA (Ningxia) (China) 14:200
NINGXIA (China) *see* NINGSIA (Ningxia) (China)
NINGYO SHIBAI see BUNRAKU
NINH BINH (Vietnam)
map (20° 15′N 105° 59′E) 19:580
NINIAN, SAINT 14:200 *bibliog.*
NINIGRET POND
map (41° 20′N 71° 40′W) 16:198
NINILCHIK (Alaska)
map (60° 3′N 151° 41′W) 1:242
NINNESCAH RIVER
map (37° 20′N 97° 10′W) 12:18
9th AMENDMENT 14:200
Griswold v. *Connecticut* 9:368
text 5:221
NIOBE 14:200
NIOBIUM 14:200–201 *bibliog.*
alloys
superconductivity 18:350
element 7:130 *table*
Group VB elements 14:200–201
Group VB periodic table 15:167
metal, metallic element 13:328
occurrence 14:200–201
oxide minerals 14:476
transition elements 19:273
Wollaston, William Hyde 20:199
NIOBRARA (Nebraska)
map (42° 45′N 98° 2′W) 14:70
NIOBRARA (county in Wyoming)
map (43° 0′N 104° 30′W) 20:301
NIOBRARA RIVER
map (42° 45′N 98° 0′W) 14:70
NIORT (France)
map (46° 19′N 0° 27′W) 8:260
NIPAWIN (Saskatchewan)
map (53° 22′N 104° 0′W) 17:81
NIPIGON (Ontario)
map (49° 1′N 88° 16′W) 14:393
NIPIGON, LAKE
map (49° 50′N 88° 30′W) 14:393
NIPISSING, LAKE
map (46° 17′N 80° 0′W) 14:393
NIPMUC (American Indians)
Massachuset 13:204
Mohegan 13:503
NIPOMO (California)
map (35° 3′N 120° 29′W) 4:31
NIPPON *see* JAPAN
NIPPUR (Iraq) 14:201 *bibliog.*
archaeology 2:120 *illus.*
NIQMADU II OF UGARIT
Ugarit 19:374
NIRENBERG, M. W. 14:201
genetic code, medicine 13:272
Khorana, Har Gobind 12:68
NIRO, ROBERT DE *see* DE NIRO, ROBERT
NIRVANA 14:201
NIŠ (Yugoslavia)
map (43° 19′N 21° 54′E) 20:340
NISBET, ROBERT ALEXANDER 14:201
NISEI 14:201 *bibliog.*
concentration camp 5:169
Korematsu v. *United States* 12:122
Oriental Americans 14:442
NISKA (American Indians)
Tsimshian 19:323
NISKAYUNA (New York)
map (42° 46′N 73° 50′W) 14:149
NISQUALLY (American Indians) 14:201 *bibliog.*
NISQUALLY RIVER
map (47° 6′N 122° 42′W) 20:35
NISSA TREATY
Russo-Turkish Wars 16:374

NISSAN MOTOR COMPANY
automotive industry **2**:367
NISSANKA MALLA, KING OF LANKA
Polonnaruwa **15**:418
NISSWA (Minnesota)
map (46° 31′N 94° 17′W) **13**:453
NITEN **14**:201 *bibliog.*
NITER **14**:201
nitrate minerals **14**:201
saltpeter **17**:39
NITERÓI (Brazil)
map (22° 53′S 43° 7′W) **3**:460
NITHART *see* GRÜNEWALD, MATTHIAS
NITRA (Czechoslovakia)
map (48° 20′N 18° 5′E) **5**:413
NITRA RIVER
map (47° 46′N 18° 10′E) **5**:413
NITRATE MINERALS **14**:201–202
mineral **13**:443 *table*
niter **14**:201
nitrogen **14**:202
nitrogen cycle **14**:203
rare mineral class **14**:201
soda niter **14**:201–202
uses **14**:201–202
NITRIC ACID **14**:202
caustic chemicals **4**:219
nitrogen **14**:202
production **4**:319 *illus.*
TNT **19**:216
NITRILE **14**:202 *bibliog.*
cyanide **5**:400
NITRITE **14**:202
NITROCELLULOSE
guncotton **9**:405
NITROGEN **14**:202–203 *bibliog.*
abundances of common elements **7**:131 *table*
acid rain **1**:82
chemistry **14**:202
compounds **14**:202
amine **1**:370 *table*
ammonia **1**:372
azide **2**:381
azo group **2**:381
Hofmann, August Wilhelm von **10**:196
hydrazine **10**:331
niter **14**:201
nitric acid **14**:202
nitrides **14**:202
nitrile **14**:202
nitroglycerin **14**:203–204
organic chemistry **14**:437–438
purine **15**:630
pyrimidine **15**:637
diseases
bends **3**:196
element **7**:130 *table*
Group VA periodic table **15**:167
laser **12**:213 *table*
nitrate minerals **14**:201–202
nitrogen cycle **14**:203
occurrence **14**:202
urea **19**:485
uses **14**:202–203
NITROGEN CYCLE **14**:203 *bibliog., illus.*
ammonification **14**:203
biosphere **3**:277
blue-green algae **3**:343; **14**:203
denitrification **14**:203
nitrification **14**:203
nitrogen **14**:202
nitrogen fertilizers **14**:203
nitrogen fixation **14**:203
genetic engineering **9**:84
Haber, Fritz **10**:4
nutrient cycles **14**:303
oceanic nutrients **14**:341
phytoplankton, plankton **15**:332
Rhizobium **16**:196
soil organisms **18**:39
NITROGLYCERIN **14**:203–204
dynamite **6**:319
explosives **7**:339
graphic formula **14**:438 *illus.*
Nobel, Alfred **14**:208
NITROSAMINE
nitrite **14**:202
NITROUS OXIDE *see* LAUGHING GAS
NIUE (New Zealand) **14**:204
flag **8**:143 *illus.*
map (19° 2′S 169° 52′) **14**:334
NIVELLE, ROBERT GEORGES **14**:204 *bibliog.*
World War I **20**:236–237 *illus.*
NIVEN, DAVID **14**:204
NIVERNAIS (France) **14**:204
NIVKH **14**:204 *bibliog.*
NIX **14**:204
NIXON (Texas)
map (29° 16′N 97° 46′W) **19**:129
NIXON, SIR JOHN E.
World War I **20**:232
NIXON, RICHARD M. **14**:204–206 *bibliog., illus.*; **15**:523 *illus.*
Ehrlichman, John **7**:91
executive privilege **7**:328–329
Ford, Gerald R. **8**:221–222
Haig, Alexander **10**:12
impeachment **11**:61
Jordan, Barbara **11**:450
Kissinger, Henry A. **12**:90–91
Mitchell, John N. **13**:483
president of the United States **15**:526–527
presidential debate **15**:531 *illus.*
radio and television broadcasting **16**:59 *illus.*
Republican party **16**:175 *illus.*
revenue sharing **16**:185
Un-American Activities, House Committee on **19**:381 *illus.*
United States, history of the **19**:460–461 *illus.*
United States v. *Richard M. Nixon* **19**:465
Vietnam War **19**:587–590 *illus.*
Watergate **20**:64
NIZA, MARCOS DE
Cibola, Seven Golden Cities of **4**:428
New Mexico **14**:139
NIZER, LOUIS **14**:206
NIZHNI NOVGOROD *see* GORKY (USSR)
NIZHNIY-TAGIL (USSR)
map (57° 55′N 59° 57′E) **19**:388
NIZIP (Turkey)
map (37° 1′N 37° 46′E) **19**:343
NKOMO, JOSHUA **14**:206
Mugabe, Robert **13**:632
Zimbabwe **20**:365; **20**:366
NKRUMAH, KWAME **14**:206–207 *bibliog., illus.*
Africa, history of **1**:159
socialism **18**:24
NKVD *see* KGB
NLRB *see* NATIONAL LABOR RELATIONS BOARD
NMR IMAGING *see* NUCLEAR MAGNETIC RESONANCE IMAGING
NNEWI (Nigeria)
map (6° 0′N 6° 59′E) **14**:190
NO *see* LUXOR (Egypt)
NO DRAMA **14**:207 *bibliog., illus.*
See also DENGAKU
dance **6**:26–27
Japanese literature **11**:380
Japanese music **11**:382
Kabuki **12**:4
theater, history of the **19**:148
Zeami Motokiyo **20**:357
NO EXIT (play) **14**:207 *bibliog.*
Sartre, Jean Paul **17**:80
NO-FAULT INSURANCE **14**:207 *bibliog.*
NO MANS LAND ISLAND
map (41° 15′N 70° 49′W) **13**:206
NOAA *see* NATIONAL OCEANIC AND ATMOSPHERIC ADMINISTRATION
NOAH **14**:207
Ararat, Mount **2**:109
Deluge **6**:96
floods and flood control **8**:166
Semites **17**:197
NOAKHALI (Bangladesh)
map (22° 49′N 91° 6′E) **3**:64
NOATAK (Alaska)
map (67° 34′N 162° 59′W) **1**:242
NOBEL, ALFRED **14**:208 *bibliog., illus.*
dynamite **6**:319
nitroglycerin **14**:203
Nobel Prize **14**:208
nobelium **14**:211
NOBEL FOUNDATION
Nobel Prize **14**:208
NOBEL PRIZE **14**:208–211 *bibliog., tables*
See also the subheading Nobel Prize under the subject disciplines for which the prize is given, e.g., MEDICINE; PEACE; etc.
Nobel, Alfred **14**:208
NOBELIUM **14**:211
actinide series **1**:88
element **6**:130 *table*
metal, metallic element **13**:328
Seaborg, Glenn T. **17**:171–172
transuranium elements **19**:286
NOBILE, UMBERTO **14**:211
Ellsworth, Lincoln **7**:149
NOBILI, ROBERTO DE *see* DE NOBILI, ROBERTO
NOBILITY, TITLES OF *see* TITLES OF NOBILITY AND HONOR
NOBLE (Illinois)
map (38° 42′N 88° 13′W) **11**:42
NOBLE (county in Indiana)
map (41° 24′N 85° 25′W) **11**:111
NOBLE (county in Ohio)
map (39° 45′N 81° 25′W) **14**:357
NOBLE (Oklahoma)
map (35° 8′N 97° 24′W) **14**:368
NOBLE (county in Oklahoma)
map (36° 25′N 97° 15′W) **14**:368
NOBLE, EDWARD J.
radio and television broadcasting **16**:57
NOBLE GASES *see* INERT GASES
NOBLE PIN SHELL **17**:251 *illus.*
NOBLE SAVAGE **14**:212
primitive societies **15**:546
NOBLES (county in Minnesota)
map (43° 38′N 95° 47′W) **13**:453
NOBLESVILLE (Indiana)
map (40° 3′N 86° 1′W) **11**:111
NOBUMORI, SUGIMORI *see* CHIKAMATSU MONZAEMON
NOBUNAGA **14**:212 *bibliog.*
castle **4**:190
Japan, history of **11**:368–369
shogun **17**:281
NOCARDIA **14**:212
NOCARDIOSIS **14**:212
Nocardia **14**:212
respiratory system disorders **16**:181
NOCATEE (Florida)
map (27° 9′N 81° 53′W) **8**:172
NOCICEPTOR
pain **15**:15
NOCONA (Texas)
map (33° 47′N 97° 44′W) **19**:129
NOCTILUCENT CLOUD **14**:212
NOCTURNE **14**:212
Chopin, Frédéric **4**:405
Debussy, Claude **6**:71
Field, John **8**:72
NODAWAY (county in Missouri)
map (40° 20′N 94° 50′W) **13**:476
NODAWAY RIVER
map (39° 54′N 94° 58′W) **13**:476
NODES OF RANVIER
nervous system **14**:92
NODIER, CHARLES **14**:212 *bibliog.*
NOEL (Missouri)
map (36° 33′N 94° 29′W) **13**:476
NOEL-BAKER, PHILIP JOHN, BARON NOEL-BAKER **14**:212
NOËL HUME, IVOR **14**:212
Wolstenholme Towne **20**:200
NOETHER, EMMY **14**:212
NOGALES (Arizona) **14**:212
map (31° 20′N 110° 56′W) **2**:160
NOGALES (Mexico)
map (31° 20′N 110° 56′W) **13**:357
NOGOYÁ (Argentina)
map (32° 24′S 59° 48′W) **2**:149
NOGUCHI, ISAMU **14**:212–213 *bibliog., illus.*
The Sun at Noon **14**:213 *illus.*
NOH DRAMA *see* NO DRAMA
NOISE **14**:213 *bibliog.*
electrical noise **14**:213
filter, electronic **8**:91
noise pollution **15**:414
receiver (communications) **16**:106
sound recording and reproduction **18**:75–76
static **18**:234
NOISE POLLUTION *see* POLLUTION, ENVIRONMENTAL
NOKIA (Finland)
map (61° 28′N 23° 30′E) **8**:95
NOKOMIS (Florida)
map (27° 7′N 82° 27′W) **8**:172
NOKOMIS (Illinois)
map (39° 18′N 89° 18′W) **11**:42
NOLAN (county in Texas)
map (32° 22′N 100° 22′W) **19**:129
NOLAN, SIDNEY **14**:213 *bibliog., illus.*
Ned Kelly in a Landscape **14**:213 *illus.*
NOLAND, KENNETH **14**:213–214 *bibliog., illus.*
Composition **15**:24 *illus.*
Provence **14**:214 *illus.*
NOLDE, EMIL **14**:214 *bibliog., illus.*
Dancers with Candles **7**:340 *illus.*; **14**:214 *illus.*
NOLO CONTENDERE **14**:214
NOLUDAR
sedative **17**:182
NOMAD **14**:214–215 *bibliog., illus.*
Baggara **3**:21
Bakhtiari **3**:28
Bedouin **3**:154
Beja **3**:172
Berbers **3**:207
Buryat **3**:583
gypsies **9**:415
Indians, American **11**:118
Khamseh **12**:65
Khoikhoi **12**:67
Masai **13**:194–195
Mongolia **13**:528–529 *illus.*
Mongolian **2**:240 *illus.*
Pechenegs **15**:130
Pygmy **15**:633
Qashqai **16**:3
rugs and carpets **16**:340–342
Sahara **17**:14 *illus.*
Sahel **13**:236 *illus.*
San **17**:49 *illus.*
Scythians **17**:167
Seljuks **17**:192
Semites **17**:197–198
sled **17**:359
steppe art **18**:255–256
Tuareg **19**:325–326
Turkmen **19**:347
Turks **19**:347–348
Tuvan **19**:356
Yoruk **20**:331
Yukaghir **20**:344
yurt **20**:347
NOMBRE DE DIOS (Panama)
map (9° 35′N 79° 28′W) **15**:55
NOME (Alaska) **14**:215
climate **19**:421 *table*
map (64° 30′N 165° 24′W) **1**:242
NOMENCLATURE
biology **3**:269
chemical nomenclature **4**:319–321
classification, biological **5**:43
Linnaeus, Carolus **12**:359
mineral **13**:442
stratigraphy **18**:292
NOMINALISM **14**:215 *bibliog.*
Goodman, Nelson **9**:246
Hobbes, Thomas **10**:192
Roscellin **16**:312–313
universals **19**:467
William of Occam **20**:155
NOMINATION, POLITICAL
political convention **15**:399–400
presidential elections **15**:529
primary election **15**:538–539
vice-president of the United States **19**:568–570
NOMOGRAM **14**:215
variables, chart **14**:215
NOMOGRAPH *see* NOMOGRAM
NOMUKA GROUP (Islands)
map (20° 13′S 174° 42′W) **19**:233
NON-EUCLIDEAN GEOMETRY **14**:215–216 *bibliog., illus.*
Bolyai, János **3**:372
Cayley, Arthur **4**:227
cosmology (astronomy) **5**:287; **14**:216
elliptic geometry **14**:215
Euclidean geometry **7**:263
geometry **9**:107
historical development **14**:216
hyperbolic geometry **14**:215
Klein, Felix **12**:95
Lobachevsky, Nikolai Ivanovich **12**:384
mathematics, history of **13**:225
parallel **15**:79
Riemann, Georg Friedrich Bernhard **16**:218
NON-INTERCOURSE ACT
Embargo Act **7**:151
NON NOK THA (Thailand) **14**:216 *bibliog.*
Neolithic Period **14**:84
NONAGON **15**:419 *illus.*
NONALIGNED NATIONS MOVEMENT **14**:216
NONCOMMERCIAL TELEVISION *see* TELEVISION, NONCOMMERCIAL
NONCONFORMISTS **14**:216–217 *bibliog.*
church and state **4**:424–425
Puritans **15**:630
NONCONFORMITY (geology) *see* UNCONFORMITY
NONDALTON (Alaska)
map (60° 0′N 154° 49′W) **1**:242
NONDIRECTIVE PSYCHOTHERAPY *see* CLIENT-CENTERED THERAPY; PSYCHOTHERAPY
NONG KHAI (Thailand)
map (17° 52′N 102° 44′E) **19**:139
NONMETALLIC CHEMISTRY
inorganic chemistry **11**:182
NONO, LUIGI **14**:217
NONPARAMETRIC STATISTICS *see* STATISTICS, NONPARAMETRIC

NONPARTISAN LEAGUE 14:217 *bibliog.*
Farmer-Labor party **8**:24
North Dakota **14**:251
NONSENSE VERSE 14:217
Carroll, Lewis **4**:169
Lear, Edward **12**:259
NONSPORTING DOG **6**:219 *illus.*
bichon frise **3**:244 *illus.*
Boston terrier **3**:411
bulldog **3**:559
Chow Chow **4**:410
dalmatian **6**:14
French bulldog **8**:308–309
keeshond **12**:36
Lhasa apso **12**:310
poodle **15**:428–429
schipperke **17**:121–122
Tibetan terrier **19**:191
NONVERBAL COMMUNICATION 14:217 *bibliog.*
animal behavior **2**:11–18 *illus.*
animal communication **2**:18–20 *illus.*
animal courtship and mating **2**:20–22 *illus.*
antenna (biology) **2**:47
ape **2**:76
Bateson, Gregory **3**:121
bee **3**:159
coloration, biological **5**:121–122 *illus.*
communication **5**:143
NONVIOLENCE *see* PACIFISM AND NONVIOLENT MOVEMENTS
NOONAN (North Dakota)
map (48° 54′N 103° 1′W) **14**:248
NOONAN, FREDERICK J.
Earhart, Amelia **7**:8
NOORVIK (Alaska)
map (66° 50′N 161° 12′W) **1**:242
NOOTKA (American Indians) **14**:217–218 *bibliog., illus.*
Indians of North America, art of the **11**:139
NOOTKA SOUND CONVENTION
Meares, John **13**:253
NORA SPRINGS (Iowa)
map (43° 9′N 93° 1′W) **11**:244
NORADRENALINE 14:218
adrenal gland **1**:108
antidepressants **2**:60
drug **6**:277
endocrine system **7**:169
endocrine system, diseases of the **7**:169
fear **8**:39
hormone, animal **10**:236 *table*
neurotransmitter **14**:218
psychotropic drugs **15**:604
sleep **17**:360
NORBECK, PETER
South Dakota **18**:106
NORBORNE (Missouri)
map (39° 18′N 93° 40′W) **13**:476
NORCATUR (Kansas)
map (39° 50′N 100° 11′W) **12**:18
NORCO (Louisiana)
map (30° 0′N 90° 25′W) **12**:430
NORDEGG (Alberta)
map (52° 28′N 116° 4′W) **1**:256
NORDEK
Scandinavia, history of **17**:111
NORDENSKJÖLD, ADOLF ERIK
Arctic **2**:142 *map*
explorations **7**:336 *map*
Northeast Passage **14**:253
Yenisei River **20**:326
NORDHAUSEN (Germany, East and West)
map (51° 30′N 10° 47′E) **9**:140
NORDHOFF, CHARLES 14:218
Mutiny on the Bounty **13**:687
NORDHOFF, HEINZ
Volkswagen **19**:630
NORDHOLLANDS CANAL
map (52° 25′N 4° 50′E) **14**:99
NORDHORN (Germany, East and West)
map (52° 27′N 7° 5′E) **9**:140
NORDIC COUNCIL 14:218 *bibliog.*
NORDIC LANGUAGES
Germanic languages **9**:136
NORDIC SKIING *see* SKIING
NORDICA, LILLIAN 14:218 *bibliog.*
NORDKAPP *see* NORTH CAPE
NORDTVEDT, K., JR.
relativity **16**:135
NORDTVEDT EFFECT
relativity **16**:135
NORELL, NORMAN
fashion design **8**:32
NOREPINEPHRINE *see* NORADRENALINE
NORFOLK (Connecticut)
map (41° 59′N 73° 12′W) **5**:193
NORFOLK (England) **14**:218
NORFOLK (county in Massachusetts)
map (42° 15′N 71° 10′W) **13**:206
NORFOLK (Nebraska)
map (42° 2′N 97° 25′W) **14**:70
NORFOLK (Virginia) **14**:218
map (36° 40′N 76° 14′W) **19**:607
NORFOLK, JOHN HOWARD, 1ST DUKE OF
Howard (family) **10**:282
NORFOLK, THOMAS HOWARD, 2D DUKE OF
Howard (family) **10**:282
NORFOLK, THOMAS HOWARD, 3D DUKE OF
Howard (family) **10**:282
NORFOLK, THOMAS HOWARD, 4TH DUKE OF
Howard (family) **10**:282
NORFOLK ISLAND (Australia) **14**:218
map (29° 2′S 167° 57′E) **14**:334
NORFOLK ISLAND PINE 14:219
NORFOLK NAVAL SHIPYARD
Portsmouth (Virginia) **15**:448
NORFORK LAKE
map (36° 25′N 92° 10′W) **2**:166
NORGE (airship) **1**:226 *illus.*
Nobile, Umberto **14**:211
NORILSK (USSR)
map (69° 20′N 88° 6′E) **19**:388
NORLAND (Florida)
map (25° 57′N 80° 12′W) **8**:172
NORLINA (North Carolina)
map (36° 27′N 78° 12′W) **14**:242
NORM, SOCIAL 14:219
conformity **5**:179
deviance **6**:143
folkways **8**:204
group dynamics **9**:376
institution, social **11**:196
law **12**:242–244
role **16**:271
sociology **18**:28
NORMA (opera) **14**:219 *bibliog.*
Bellini, Vincenzo **3**:190
NORMAL (Illinois)
map (40° 31′N 88° 59′W) **11**:42
NORMAL DISTRIBUTION 14:219 *bibliog., table*
central limit theorem **4**:254; **14**:219
chi-square **4**:339
de Moivre, Abraham **6**:62
educational and psychological tests **14**:219
Quételet, Lambert Adolphe **16**:23
t-test **19**:3
NORMAL FAULT (geology)
fault **8**:37 *illus.*
NORMAL SCHOOL *see* TEACHER EDUCATION
NORMALITY *see* CONCENTRATION (chemistry)
NORMAN (Arkansas)
map (34° 27′N 93° 41′W) **2**:166
NORMAN (county in Minnesota)
map (46° 52′N 96° 30′W) **13**:453
NORMAN (Oklahoma)
map (35° 13′N 97° 26′W) **14**:368
NORMAN, LAKE
map (35° 35′N 80° 55′W) **14**:242
NORMAN ARCHITECTURE 14:219–220 *bibliog., illus.*
architecture **2**:133 *illus., illus.*
cathedrals and churches **4**:205
Durham Cathedral (Great Britain) **6**:306
English art and architecture **7**:182–183
house (in Western architecture) **10**:266; **10**:268 *illus.*
Romanesque art and architecture **16**:283 *illus.*
Tower of London **19**:254
NORMAN CONQUEST
Bayeux Tapestry **3**:133 *illus.*
Great Britain, history of **9**:310
Hastings, Battle of **10**:67
Normans **14**:221–222
William I, King of England (William the Conqueror) **20**:155
NORMAN PARK (Georgia)
map (31° 16′N 83° 38′W) **9**:114
NORMANDIE (France) *see* NORMANDY (France)
NORMANDY (France) **14**:220–221 *map*
cities
Caen **4**:12–13
Cherbourg **4**:331
history
Philip II, King of France (Philip Augustus) **15**:232
William I, King of England **20**:155
Norman architecture **14**:219–220
Normans **14**:221
NORMANDY HILLS
map (48° 35′N 0° 30′W) **8**:260
NORMANDY INVASION 14:221 *bibliog., map*; **15**:273 *illus.*; **19**:455 *illus.*
Allied fleet movements and landing beaches **14**:221 *map*
harbor and port **10**:42
strategy and tactics, military **18**:290
World War II **20**:272 *illus.*; **20**:274 *map*
NORMANS 14:221–222 *bibliog., illus.*
Great Britain, history of **9**:310–311
horseman **14**:222 *illus.*
house (in Western architecture) **10**:268 *illus.*
Irish settlements c.1170 **11**:262 *map*
Italy, history of **11**:328
kingdoms c.1100 **13**:392 *map*
Northampton (England) **14**:253
Sicily (Italy) **17**:293
Vikings **19**:595
NORNS 14:222
NORODOM SIHANOUK 14:222 *bibliog.*
Kampuchea (Cambodia) **12**:12
Lon Nol **12**:400
NØRRESUNDBY (Denmark)
map (57° 4′N 9° 55′E) **6**:109
NORRIS, CHARLES G. 14:222
NORRIS, FRANK 14:222–223 *bibliog.*
NORRIS, GEORGE W. 14:223 *bibliog., illus.*
NORRIS, KATHLEEN 14:223
NORRIS ARM (Newfoundland)
map (49° 5′N 55° 15′W) **14**:166
NORRIS CITY (Illinois)
map (37° 59′N 88° 20′W) **11**:42
NORRIS DAM (TVA) **19**:106 *illus.*
NORRIS-LA GUARDIA ACT
La Guardia, Fiorello **12**:147
labor union **12**:156
National Labor Relations Act **14**:34
Norris, George W. **14**:223
yellow-dog contract **20**:322
NORRIS LAKE
map (36° 20′N 83° 55′W) **19**:104
NORRISH, RONALD GEORGE WREYFORD 14:223
NORRISTOWN (Pennsylvania)
map (40° 7′N 75° 21′W) **15**:147
NORRKÖPING (Sweden) **14**:223
map (58° 36′N 16° 11′E) **18**:382
NORSE LANGUAGES
Germanic languages **9**:136
NORSE MYTHOLOGY
Asgard **2**:228
Balder **3**:33
Bragi **3**:439
Brunhild **3**:525
Edda **7**:54–55
Fafnir **8**:7–8
Fenrir **8**:51
Frey **8**:330
Freya **8**:330
Frigg **8**:334
Gudrun **9**:390
Heindall **10**:108
Hel **10**:110
Loki **12**:398
Mimir **13**:436
mythology **13**:701–702
Nibelungenlied **14**:177–178
Niflheim **14**:186
Norns **14**:222
Odin **14**:350
Ragnarok **16**:69
Thor **19**:177
Valhalla **19**:506
Valkyries **19**:506
ymir **20**:328
NORSEMAN (Australia)
map (32° 12′S 121° 46′E) **2**:328
NORSEMEN *see* VIKINGS
NORTH (South Carolina)
map (33° 37′N 81° 6′W) **18**:98
NORTH, CAPE
map (47° 2′N 60° 25′W) **14**:269
NORTH, FREDERICK *see* NORTH, LORD
NORTH, LORD 14:223–224 *bibliog., illus.*
American Revolution **1**:357
Intolerable Acts **11**:231
NORTH ABINGTON (Massachusetts)
map (42° 8′N 70° 57′W) **3**:409
NORTH ADAMS (Massachusetts)
map (42° 42′N 73° 7′W) **13**:206
NORTH AFRICA 14:224
See also names of specific countries, e.g., LIBYA; MOROCCO; etc.
art
African art **1**:161
Islamic art and architecture **11**:293–297
casbah **4**:180
history
Almohads **1**:306
Almoravids **1**:307
Barbary States **3**:76
Berbers **3**:207
Ibn Khaldun **11**:5
Nubia **14**:277–278
Numidia **14**:295
Vandals **19**:518
World War II **20**:256; **20**:258; **20**:261–263 *illus., maps*
people
Arabs **2**:103–106
Bedouin **3**:154
Berbers **3**:207–208
Hamites **10**:29
religion
Arabs **2**:103–104
NORTH ALBANIAN ALPS
map (42° 30′N 19° 50′E) **1**:250
NORTH AMERICA 14:224–236 *bibliog., illus., maps, tables*
See also names of specific countries, e.g., CANADA; MEXICO; etc.; names of specific provinces and states, e.g., ALBERTA (Canada); CALIFORNIA; SONORA (Mexico); etc.
agriculture **14**:227–228; **14**:231 *map*; **14**:234–235 *illus.*
food production **1**:197 *table*
archaeology **14**:236–240
See also NORTH AMERICAN ARCHAEOLOGY
boundaries and definitions **14**:224
climate **14**:227–228 *map, table*
maritime climate **13**:157
Mediterranean climate **13**:276
precipitation **14**:230 *map*
weather variation and extremes **20**:80–81 *tables*
colonialism **5**:112
demography **14**:232–233 *map*
economy **14**:234–236 *illus.*
education **14**:233
energy and resources **14**:227–230
consumption and production **7**:174 *table*
electrical production **15**:485 *table*
mineral resources **14**:228–230; **14**:231 *map*
petroleum industry **15**:210 *table*
water resources **14**:229–230; **20**:51 *table*
exploration *see* EXPLORATION
fishing **14**:235
forestry **14**:235
geologic time
Ordovician Period **14**:421 *map*
Permian Period **15**:174–175 *map*
Precambrian rock formations **15**:492 *map*
Silurian Period **17**:310–312
Tertiary Period **19**:123 *map*
geology **14**:227 *map*
continental drifting **15**:354 *map*
fit of continents around Mid-Atlantic Ridge **15**:353 *map*
North American plate **15**:351 *map*
health **14**:233
land **14**:226–227 *illus., map*
glaciers and glaciation **9**:193–194
lake, glacial **12**:169–170
mountain **13**:619–620 *table*
languages **14**:234 *map*
anthropological linguistics **2**:50
Indian languages, American **11**:98–101 *table*
people **14**:230–234 *illus., map*
Indians, American **11**:115–138 *illus., maps*
women in society **20**:204 *table*
physical features
Canadian Shield **4**:94
Coast Ranges **5**:80
Great Plains **9**:320–321
Niagara Falls **14**:177 *illus.*
Rocky Mountains **16**:261–263 *illus., map*
Saint Elias, Mount **17**:18
Thousand Islands **19**:180
postal services **15**:459
prehistory *see* NORTH AMERICAN ARCHAEOLOGY
religion **14**:233–234
rivers, lakes, and waterways **14**:229–230 *illus.*

Columbia River **5**:126 *map*
Erie, Lake **7**:229–230 *map*
Great Lakes **9**:319–320 *map*
Huron, Lake **10**:317 *map*
Niagara River **14**:177
Ontario, Lake **14**:395–396 *map*
Red River of the North **16**:113
Saint Clair, Lake **17**:17
St. Lawrence River **17**:21 *map*
St. Lawrence Seaway **17**:21–22
Superior, Lake **18**:351–352 *map*
ten largest rivers **16**:232 *table*
Yukon River **20**:344 *map*
trade **14**:235
truck and bus registration **19**:315 *table*
vegetation **14**:230 *map*
vegetation and animal life
grasslands **9**:300 *illus.*
horse **10**:245–246
intertidal life **11**:229–230
savanna life **17**:97–99
steppe life **18**:256–257
NORTH AMERICA BASIN
Atlantic Ocean bottom **2**:295 *map*
NORTH AMERICAN ARCHAEOLOGY **14**:236–240 *bibliog., illus., map*
See also INDIANS, AMERICAN; MESOAMERICA
Acoma **1**:83–84
Anasazi **1**:392–394
Arctic and subarctic **14**:238 *illus.*
colonial America
Williamsburg **2**:117 *illus.*
Wolstenholme Towne **20**:200
Danger Cave **6**:31
Desert Archaic **14**:238
earliest Americans **14**:236
Eastern Archaic **14**:237–238
Eskimo prehistoric cultures **7**:239 *map*
Folsom culture **8**:204
Hohokam culture **10**:199
Kidder, Alfred Vincent **12**:70–71
L'Anse aux Meadows **12**:144
Meadowcroft Rockshelter **13**:252
Mesa Verde National Park **13**:313–314
Mississippian culture **14**:239
Mound Builders **13**:617–618 *illus.*
Oraibi **14**:413–414
Paleo-Indian culture **14**:236–237 *illus.*
race **16**:34
sites **14**:237 *map*
Southwest **14**:239–240 *illus.*
Woodland culture **14**:238–239
NORTH AMERICAN FALCONERS' ASSOCIATION
falconry **8**:12
NORTH AMERICAN INDIAN ART *see* INDIANS OF NORTH AMERICA, ART OF THE
NORTH AMERICAN PAPAW *see* CUSTARD APPLE
NORTH AMERICAN SOCCER LEAGUE (NASL)
soccer **18**:10–11
NORTH AMHERST (Massachusetts)
map (42° 25′N 72° 32′W) **13**:206
NORTH ANDOVER (Massachusetts)
map (42° 42′N 71° 8′W) **13**:206
NORTH ANSON (Maine)
map (44° 52′N 69° 54′W) **13**:70
NORTH ARLINGTON (New Jersey)
map (40° 47′N 74° 8′W) **14**:129
NORTH ASHEBORO (North Carolina)
map (35° 44′N 79° 49′W) **14**:242
NORTH ATLANTA (Georgia)
map (33° 51′N 84° 21′W) **2**:292
NORTH ATLANTIC TREATY ORGANIZATION **14**:240–241 *bibliog., illus.*
cold war **5**:98
Gruenther, Alfred Maximilian **9**:382
Haig, Alexander **10**:12
headquarters **14**:240 *illus.*
member nations **7**:297 *map*
Truman, Harry S. **19**:317
United States, history of the **19**:456
Warsaw Treaty Organization **20**:32
NORTH ATTLEBORO (Massachusetts)
map (41° 59′N 71° 20′W) **13**:206
NORTH AUGUSTA (South Carolina)
map (33° 30′N 81° 58′W) **18**:98
NORTH BALTIMORE (Ohio)
map (41° 11′N 83° 41′W) **14**:357
NORTH BATTLEFORD (Saskatchewan)
map (52° 47′N 108° 17′W) **17**:81
NORTH BAY (Ontario)
map (46° 19′N 79° 28′W) **14**:393
NORTH BEND (British Columbia)
map (49° 53′N 121° 27′W) **3**:491
NORTH BEND (Nebraska)
map (41° 28′N 96° 47′W) **14**:70
NORTH BENNINGTON (Vermont)
map (42° 56′N 73° 15′W) **19**:554
NORTH BERGEN (New Jersey)
map (40° 48′N 74° 1′W) **14**:129
NORTH BILLERICA (Massachusetts)
map (42° 35′N 71° 17′W) **3**:409
NORTH BORNEO *see* SABAH (Malaysia)
NORTH BRANCH (Minnesota)
map (45° 31′N 92° 58′W) **13**:453
NORTH BRANFORD (Connecticut)
map (41° 20′N 72° 46′W) **5**:193
NORTH BRUNSWICK (New Jersey)
map (40° 28′N 74° 28′W) **14**:129
NORTH CANADIAN RIVER
map (35° 17′N 95° 31′W) **14**:368
NORTH CANTON (Ohio)
map (40° 53′N 81° 24′W) **14**:357
NORTH CAPE **14**:241
map (71° 11′N 25° 48′E) **14**:261
NORTH CAPE MAY (New Jersey)
map (38° 59′N 74° 57′W) **14**:129
NORTH CAROLINA **14**:241–246 *bibliog., illus., map*
agriculture **14**:244–245 *illus.*
cities
Asheville **2**:230
Chapel Hill **4**:284
Charlotte **4**:299
Durham **6**:305
Fayetteville **8**:39
Greensboro **9**:354
New Bern **14**:115
Raleigh **16**:79
Wilmington **20**:163
Winston-Salem **20**:180–181
climate **14**:241; **14**:243
cultural attractions **14**:244
economic activities **14**:244–245 *illus.*
education **14**:243–244
Davidson College **6**:49
Duke University **6**:295
state universities **14**:246–247
Wake Forest University **20**:8
flag **14**:241 *illus.*
Fort Bragg **8**:236
geographical linguistics **9**:98–99 *map*
government **14**:245
historic sites **14**:244
history **14**:245–246
Franklin, State of **8**:285
Iredell, James **11**:257
Johnston, Samuel **11**:438
Regulators **16**:129
Shaftesbury, Anthony Ashley Cooper, 1st Earl of **17**:234
United States, history of the **19**:436
land and resources **14**:241–243 *illus., map*
map (35° 30′N 80° 0′W) **19**:419
people **14**:243
Catawba **4**:201
Cherokee **4**:332
physical features
Black Mountains **3**:317
Dismal Swamp **6**:196
Hatteras, Cape **10**:68
Mitchell, Mount **13**:483
rivers, lakes, and waterways **14**:243
seal, state **14**:241 *illus.*
NORTH CAROLINA, STATE UNIVERSITIES OF **14**:246–247
NORTH CHANNEL (Michigan)
map (46° 2′N 82° 50′W) **13**:377
NORTH CHANNEL (United Kingdom)
map (55° 10′N 5° 40′W) **19**:403
NORTH CHARLESTON (South Carolina)
map (32° 53′N 80° 0′W) **18**:98
NORTH CHICAGO (Illinois)
map (42° 20′N 87° 51′W) **11**:42
NORTH COMINO CHANNEL
map (36° 1′N 14° 20′E) **13**:94
NORTH CONWAY (New Hampshire)
map (44° 3′N 71° 8′W) **14**:123
NORTH CREEK (New York)
map (43° 42′N 73° 59′W) **14**:149
NORTH CROSSETT (Arkansas)
map (33° 11′N 91° 57′W) **2**:166
NORTH DAKOTA **14**:247–252 *bibliog., illus., map*
agriculture **14**:250 *illus.*
cities
Bismarck **3**:298
Fargo **8**:23
Grand Forks **9**:285
Minot **13**:459
climate **14**:247
economic activity **14**:250
education **14**:249
state universities and colleges of **14**:252
flag **14**:247 *illus.*
government and politics **14**:250–251
historic sites **14**:249
history **14**:251–252
Nonpartisan League **14**:217
land and resources **14**:247–249 *illus., map*
badlands **3**:20
map (47° 30′N 100° 15′W) **19**:419
mining **14**:250–251 *illus.*
people **14**:249–250
Arikara **2**:154
Hidatsa **10**:158–159
Mandan **13**:110–111
Sioux **17**:326
rivers, lakes, and waterways **14**:247
seal, state **14**:247 *illus.*
NORTH DAKOTA, STATE UNIVERSITIES AND COLLEGES OF **14**:252
NORTH DARTMOUTH (Massachusetts)
map (41° 38′N 70° 59′W) **13**:206
NORTH EAGLE BUTTE (South Dakota)
map (45° 2′N 101° 15′W) **18**:103
NORTH EAST (Maryland)
map (39° 36′N 75° 56′W) **13**:188
NORTH EAST (Pennsylvania)
map (42° 13′N 79° 50′W) **15**:147
NORTH ENGLISH (Iowa)
map (41° 31′N 92° 5′W) **11**:244
NORTH FALMOUTH (Massachusetts)
map (41° 39′N 70° 37′W) **13**:206
NORTH FORELAND
map (51° 23′N 1° 27′E) **19**:403
NORTH FRISIAN ISLANDS
map (54° 50′N 8° 12′E) **9**:140
NORTH GERMAN CONFEDERATION *see* GERMANY, HISTORY OF
NORTH GRAFTON (Massachusetts)
map (42° 14′N 71° 42′W) **13**:206
NORTH GROSVENORDALE (Connecticut)
map (41° 59′N 71° 54′W) **5**:193
NORTH GULFPORT (Mississippi)
map (30° 25′N 89° 6′W) **13**:469
NORTH HAVEN (Connecticut)
map (41° 23′N 72° 52′W) **5**:193
NORTH HAVRE (Montana)
map (48° 36′N 109° 41′W) **13**:547
NORTH HERO (Vermont)
map (44° 49′N 73° 18′W) **19**:554
NORTH ISLAND (New Zealand)
map (39° 0′S 176° 0′E) **14**:158
NORTH JUDSON (Indiana)
map (41° 13′N 86° 46′W) **11**:111
NORTH KINGSTOWN (Rhode Island)
map (41° 34′N 71° 27′W) **16**:198
NORTH KOREA *see* KOREA; KOREA, HISTORY OF; KOREAN WAR
NORTH LAS VEGAS (Nevada)
map (36° 12′N 115° 7′W) **14**:111
NORTH LITTLE ROCK (Arkansas)
map (34° 46′N 92° 14′W) **2**:166
NORTH LOUP (Nebraska)
map (41° 30′N 98° 46′W) **14**:70
NORTH LOUP RIVER
map (41° 17′N 98° 23′W) **14**:70
NORTH MANCHESTER (Indiana)
map (41° 0′N 85° 46′W) **11**:111
NORTH MANITOU ISLAND
map (45° 6′N 86° 1′W) **13**:377
NORTH MANKATO (Minnesota)
map (44° 10′N 94° 0′W) **13**:453
NORTH MIAMI (Florida)
map (25° 54′N 80° 11′W) **8**:172
NORTH MIAMI BEACH (Florida)
map (25° 56′N 80° 9′W) **8**:172
NORTH MYRTLE BEACH (South Carolina)
map (33° 48′N 78° 42′W) **18**:98
NORTH NAPLES (Florida)
map (26° 12′N 81° 48′W) **8**:172
NORTH OGDEN (Utah)
map (41° 18′N 112° 0′W) **19**:492
NORTH PACIFIC SEALING CONVENTION
Bering Sea controversy **3**:212
NORTH PALISADE MOUNTAIN
map (37° 6′N 118° 31′W) **4**:31
NORTH PARK (Illinois)
map (42° 20′N 89° 2′W) **11**:42
NORTH PEMBROKE (Massachusetts)
map (42° 5′N 70° 47′W) **13**:206
NORTH PLATTE (Nebraska)
map (41° 8′N 100° 46′W) **14**:70
NORTH PLATTE RIVER
map (41° 15′N 100° 45′W) **14**:70
Platte River **15**:362
NORTH POINT (Prince Edward Island)
map (47° 5′N 64° 0′W) **15**:548
NORTH POLE **14**:252
See also EARTH, GEOMAGNETIC FIELD OF; EXPLORATION, ARCTIC
Arctic **2**:142–143 *illus., map*
Boothia Peninsula **3**:395
Earth, motions of **7**:18
exploration **7**:338
icebreaker **11**:16
map location (90° N O° O′) **2**:142
Nautilus **14**:52
Peary, Robert Edwin **15**:128
polar wandering **15**:393 *map*
Silurian Period **17**:310
NORTH POWDER (Oregon)
map (45° 13′N 117° 55′W) **14**:427
NORTH PROVIDENCE (Rhode Island)
map (41° 50′N 71° 25′W) **16**:198
NORTH RACCOON RIVER
map (41° 32′N 93° 58′W) **11**:244
NORTH READING (Massachusetts)
map (42° 34′N 71° 5′W) **3**:409
NORTH RHINE-WESTPHALIA (West Germany)
cities
Aachen **1**:49
Bochum **3**:355
Bonn **3**:380–381 *illus.*
Cologne **5**:105
Dortmund **6**:243
Duisburg **6**:294–295
Düsseldorf **6**:308
Essen **7**:244
Gelsenkirchen **9**:70
Krefeld **12**:128
Mülheim an der Ruhr **13**:636
Münster **13**:643–644
Solingen **18**:55
Wuppertal **20**:297
NORTH RIDGEVILLE (Ohio)
map (41° 23′N 82° 1′W) **14**:357
NORTH RIM (Arizona)
map (36° 12′N 112° 3′W) **2**:160
NORTH RUSTICO (Prince Edward Island)
map (46° 27′N 63° 19′W) **15**:548
NORTH SASKATCHEWAN RIVER
map (53° 15′N 105° 6′W) **4**:70
NORTH SCITUATE (Massachusetts)
map (42° 14′N 70° 47′W) **3**:409
NORTH SEA **14**:252
islands and island groups
Frisian Islands **8**:334
Helgoland **10**:111
Orkney Islands **14**:445
Shetland Islands **17**:259
map (56° 0′N 3° 0′E) **7**:268
seas, gulfs, and bays
Dogger Bank **6**:223
Dover, Strait of **6**:250
Kattegat **12**:31
Skagerrak **17**:331
NORTH SEA CANAL **14**:252
NORTH SHOSHONE PEAK
map (39° 9′N 117° 29′W) **14**:111
NORTH SKUNK RIVER
map (41° 15′N 92° 2′W) **11**:244
NORTH SLOPE (Alaska) *see* PRUDHOE BAY
NORTH STAR (astronomy)
Polaris **15**:393
NORTH STAR (newspaper)
Douglass, Frederick **6**:249
NORTH SUDBURY (Massachusetts)
map (42° 23′N 71° 24′W) **3**:409
NORTH SYDNEY (Nova Scotia)
map (46° 13′N 60° 15′W) **14**:269
NORTH TERRE HAUTE (Indiana)
map (39° 31′N 87° 22′W) **11**:111
NORTH TONAWANDA (New York)
map (43° 2′N 78° 53′W) **14**:149
NORTH TROY (Vermont)
map (45° 0′N 72° 24′W) **19**:554
NORTH UIST ISLAND
map (57° 37′N 7° 22′W) **19**:403
NORTH VANCOUVER (British Columbia)
map (49° 19′N 123° 4′W) **3**:491
NORTH VASSALBORO (Maine)
map (44° 29′N 69° 37′W) **13**:70
NORTH VERNON (Indiana)
map (39° 0′N 85° 38′W) **11**:111
NORTH VIETNAM *see* VIETNAM; VIETNAM WAR
NORTH WEST AMERICA (ship)
Meares, John **13**:253
NORTH WEST CAPE (Australia)
map (21° 45′S 114° 10′E) **2**:328
NORTH WEST COMPANY **14**:252–253 *bibliog.*
Canada, history of **4**:81
Chinook (American Indians) **4**:395
Hudson's Bay Company **10**:290
Mackenzie, Sir Alexander **13**:27
Red River Settlement **16**:113
Selkirk, Thomas Douglas, 5th Earl of **17**:192
Spokane (Washington) **18**:192
Thompson, David **19**:174

NORTH WEST HIGHLANDS
map (57° 30′N 5° 0′W) **19**:403
NORTH-WEST MOUNTED POLICE
Canada, history of **4**:85
NORTH WILKESBORO (North Carolina)
map (36° 10′N 81° 9′W) **14**:242
NORTH WILMINGTON (Massachusetts)
map (42° 34′N 71° 10′W) **3**:409
NORTH WINDHAM (Maine)
map (43° 50′N 70° 26′W) **13**:70
NORTHAMPTON (England) **14**:253
map (52° 14′N 0° 54′W) **19**:403
NORTHAMPTON (Massachusetts) **14**:253
map (42° 19′N 72° 38′W) **13**:206
NORTHAMPTON (county in North Carolina)
map (36° 22′N 77° 20′W) **14**:242
NORTHAMPTON (Pennsylvania)
map (40° 41′N 75° 30′W) **15**:147
NORTHAMPTON (county in Pennsylvania)
map (40° 45′N 75° 18′W) **15**:147
NORTHAMPTON (county in Virginia)
map (37° 20′N 75° 50′W) **19**:607
NORTHAMPTONSHIRE (England) **14**:253
cities
Northampton **14**:253
Peterborough **15**:202
NORTHANTS (England) *see* NORTHAMPTONSHIRE (England)
NORTHBOROUGH (Massachusetts)
map (42° 19′N 71° 39′W) **13**:206
NORTHCLIFFE, ALFRED HARMSWORTH, VISCOUNT **14**:253 *bibliog., illus.*
journalism **11**:455
NORTHEAST CAPE FEAR RIVER
map (34° 11′N 77° 57′W) **14**:242
NORTHEAST LAND ISLAND (Norway)
map (79° 48′N 22° 24′E) **14**:261
NORTHEAST PASSAGE **14**:253 *bibliog.*
Arctic **2**:142 *map*
Borough, Stephen **3**:404
exploration **7**:335; **7**:338
Hudson, Henry **10**:289
Nordenskjöld, Adolf Erik, Baron **14**:218
NORTHEAST POLDER (region in Netherlands)
map (52° 42′N 5° 45′E) **14**:99
NORTHEASTERN UNIVERSITY **14**:254
NORTHERN ACCORD
Panin, Nikita Ivanovich, Count **15**:59
NORTHERN CROSS *see* CYGNUS
NORTHERN DVINA RIVER
map (64° 32′N 40° 30′E) **19**:388
NORTHERN EXPEDITION **14**:254 *bibliog.*
warlords **20**:30
NORTHERN HEMISPHERE
ice conditions, contemporary **15**:11 *map*
meteor and meteorite **13**:336 *table*
permafrost distribution **15**:173 *map*
taiga climate **19**:11
upwelling, oceanic **19**:473–474
weather forecasting **20**:76
westerlies **20**:115
NORTHERN INDIAN LAKE
map (57° 20′N 97° 20′W) **13**:119
NORTHERN IRELAND **14**:254–255 *bibliog., illus., map*
See also IRELAND; IRELAND, HISTORY OF; UNITED KINGDOM
cities
Belfast **3**:174
counties
Antrim **2**:71
Armagh **2**:171
Down **6**:252
Fermanagh **8**:55
Londonderry **12**:405
Tyrone **19**:368
districts **14**:254 *map*
education
British education **3**:493–495
universities **3**:493 *table*
Giant's Causeway **9**:171–172 *illus.*
government and politics **14**:255; **19**:411
history **14**:255
Faulkner, Brian **8**:36
Ireland, history of **11**:265
Irish Republican Army **11**:269
Orangemen **14**:415
Paisley, Ian **15**:25
Protestant-Catholic fighting **11**:265 *illus.*
land **19**:405
map (54° 40′N 6° 45′W) **19**:403
Neagh, Lough **14**:68
people and economy **14**:256
NORTHERN LIGHTS *see* AURORAS (astronomy)
NORTHERN MARIANA ISLANDS *see* MARIANA ISLANDS
NORTHERN PACIFIC RAILROAD **19**:268 *map*
NORTHERN RHODESIA *see* ZAMBIA
NORTHERN SEA ROUTE *see* NORTHEAST PASSAGE
NORTHERN SPORADES ISLANDS
map (39° 17′N 23° 23′E) **9**:325
NORTHERN TERRITORY (Australia) **14**:255–256 *map*
Arnhem Land **2**:184
cities
Alice Springs **1**:293
Darwin **6**:40–41
flag **8**:145 *illus.*
Macdonell Ranges **13**:13
map (20° 0′S 134° 0′E) **2**:328
people
Aranda **2**:109
NORTHERN TUNGUSKA RIVER
map (65° 48′N 88° 4′E) **19**:388
NORTHERN WAR, GREAT **14**:256 *bibliog.*
Charles XII **4**:297
Mazepa, Ivan Stepanovich **13**:250
Peter I, Emperor of Russia (Peter the Great) **15**:200–201
NORTHFIELD (Massachusetts)
map (42° 42′N 72° 27′W) **13**:206
NORTHFIELD (Minnesota)
map (44° 27′N 93° 9′W) **13**:453
NORTHFIELD (New Hampshire)
map (43° 22′N 71° 37′W) **14**:123
NORTHFIELD (New Jersey)
map (39° 22′N 74° 33′W) **14**:129
NORTHFIELD (Vermont)
map (44° 9′N 72° 40′W) **19**:554
NORTHGLENN (Colorado)
map (39° 54′N 104° 58′W) **5**:116
NORTHPORT (Alabama)
map (33° 14′N 87° 35′W) **1**:234
NORTHPORT (Michigan)
map (45° 8′N 85° 37′W) **13**:377
NORTHPORT (Washington)
map (48° 55′N 117° 48′W) **20**:35
NORTHROP, JOHN (inventor)
aviation **2**:374
NORTHROP, JOHN HOWARD (biochemist) **14**:256 *bibliog.*
NORTHROP CORPORATION **1**:128 *table*
NORTHRUP, GEORGE **9**:228 *illus.*
NORTHUMBERLAND (Pennsylvania)
map (40° 54′N 76° 48′W) **15**:147
NORTHUMBERLAND (county in Pennsylvania)
map (40° 49′N 76° 39′W) **15**:147
NORTHUMBERLAND (county in Virginia)
map (37° 50′N 76° 25′W) **19**:607
NORTHUMBERLAND, EARLS (later Dukes) OF *see* PERCY (family)
NORTHUMBERLAND, JOHN DUDLEY, DUKE OF **14**:256 *bibliog.*
Edward VI, King of England **7**:68
expansion of the common law **5**:140
Grey, Lady Jane **9**:360
NORTHUMBERLAND STRAIT
map (46° 0′N 63° 30′W) **14**:269
NORTHUMBRIA **2**:3 *map*; **14**:256
Danelaw **6**:31
Oswald, Saint **14**:459
NORTHVALE RIVER (New Jersey)
map (41° 0′N 73° 57′W) **14**:129
NORTHVILLE (New York)
map (43° 13′N 74° 11′W) **14**:149
NORTHWEST COMPANY
Chinook (Indian tribe) **4**:395
NORTHWEST GANDER RIVER
map (48° 50′N 55° 0′W) **14**:166
NORTHWEST ORDINANCE
Northwest Territory (U.S. history) **14**:259
territory **19**:122
NORTHWEST PASSAGE **14**:256–257 *bibliog., map*
Arctic **2**:142–144 *map*
Baffin, William **3**:21
Cook, James **5**:236
exploration **7**:335; **7**:338
Franklin, Sir John **8**:284–285
Frobisher, Sir Martin **8**:335
Hearne, Samuel **10**:90
Hudson, Henry **10**:289
Lewis and Clark Expedition **12**:307
Parry, Sir William Edward **15**:98
Rasmussen, Knud **16**:90
tanker **19**:24 *illus.*
Vancouver, George **19**:518
NORTHWEST TERRITORIES (Canada) **14**:257–259 *bibliog., illus., map*
cities
Arctic Bay **14**:228 *table*
Yellowknife **20**:322
economic activities **14**:258–259
flag **14**:258 *illus.*
government **14**:259
history **14**:259
land and resources **14**:257
map (70° 0′N 100° 0′W) **4**:70
mining **14**:258
people **14**:257–258 *illus.*
physical features
Baffin Island **3**:21
Boothia Peninsula **3**:395
Ellesmere Island **4**:69 *illus.*; **7**:146–147
Southampton Island **18**:107
Victoria Island **19**:575
rivers, lakes, and waterways
Great Bear Lake **9**:309
Great Slave Lake **9**:322
Mackenzie River **13**:28–29 *map*
NORTHWEST TERRITORY (U.S. history) **14**:259–260 *bibliog., map*; **19**:446 *map*
Harrison, William Henry **10**:60–61
Jay's Treaty **11**:387
Jefferson, Thomas **11**:392
Ohio Company of Associates **14**:362
St. Clair, Arthur **17**:17
United States, history of the **19**:441
NORTHWESTERN UNIVERSITY **14**:260
Evanston (Illinois) **7**:313
NORTHWOOD (Iowa)
map (43° 27′N 93° 13′W) **11**:244
NORTHWOOD (North Dakota)
map (47° 44′N 97° 34′W) **14**:248
NORTON (Kansas)
map (39° 50′N 99° 53′W) **12**:18
NORTON (county in Kansas)
map (39° 50′N 99° 55′W) **12**:18
NORTON (Massachusetts)
map (41° 58′N 71° 11′W) **13**:206
NORTON (New Brunswick)
map (45° 38′N 65° 42′W) **14**:117
NORTON (Ohio)
map (41° 1′N 81° 39′W) **14**:357
NORTON (Virginia)
map (36° 56′N 82° 38′W) **19**:607
NORTON, CHARLES ELIOT **14**:260 *bibliog.*
NORTON, KEN
Ali, Muhammad **1**:292
NORTON, LILLIAN *see* NORDICA, LILLIAN
NORTON SHORES (Michigan)
map (43° 10′N 86° 14′W) **13**:377
NORTON SIMON MUSEUM (Pasadena, California)
Los Angeles County Museum of Art **12**:418
NORTON SOUND
map (63° 50′N 164° 0′W) **1**:242
NORTONVILLE (Kansas)
map (39° 25′N 95° 20′W) **12**:18
NORWALK (California)
map (33° 54′N 118° 5′W) **12**:417
NORWALK (Connecticut) **14**:260
map (41° 7′N 73° 27′W) **5**:193
NORWALK (Iowa)
map (41° 29′N 93° 41′W) **11**:244
NORWALK (Ohio)
map (41° 15′N 82° 37′W) **14**:357
NORWALK RIVER
map (41° 6′N 73° 25′W) **5**:193
NORWAY **14**:260–264 *bibliog., illus., map, table*
agriculture, forestry, and fishing **14**:263 *illus.*
archaeology
Gokstad ship burial **9**:226
arts **14**:262
See also the subheading Norway under specific art forms, e.g., GRAPHIC ARTS; PAINTING; SCULPTURE; etc.
Scandinavian art and architecture **17**:111–114 *illus.*
cities
Bergen **3**:209
Hammerfest **10**:30–31
Kristiansand **12**:130
Narvik **14**:23
Oslo **14**:454 *illus.*
Stavanger **18**:239
Tromsø **14**:261 *table*
Trondheim **19**:306
climate **14**:261 *table*
economic activity **14**:262–263
education **14**:262
European universities **7**:308 *table*
farmhouse **10**:269 *illus.*
fishing industry **8**:126
fjord **8**:133
flag **14**:260 *illus.*
government **14**:263
health **14**:262
history **14**:263–264
Brundtland, Gro Harlem **3**:523
Charles XIV John, King of Sweden **4**:298
Christian I, King of Denmark **4**:412
Christian III, King of Denmark **4**:412
Christian IV, King of Denmark **4**:412
Frederick III, King of Denmark **8**:289
Frederick IV, King of Denmark **8**:289–290
Frederick VI, King of Denmark **8**:290
German occupation of (1940) **17**:110 *illus.*
Haakon IV, King **10**:3
Haakon VII, King **10**:3
Harold I (Harold Fairhair), King **10**:54
Harold III (Harold Hardrada), King **10**:54
Magnus VI, King (Magnus the Law-Mender) **13**:61
Magnus VII, King (Magnus Eriksson) **13**:61
Margaret I, Queen of Denmark, Norway, and Sweden **13**:149
Nansen, Fridtjof **14**:13
Olaf I, King **14**:372–373
Olaf II, King (Saint Olaf) **14**:373
Olaf V, King **14**:373
Scandinavia, history of **17**:107–111 *maps*
Sverre, King **18**:375
World War II **20**:252–253 *illus., map*
land and resources **14**:260–261 *map, table*; **14**:264 *illus.*
language **14**:262
Germanic languages **9**:135–137 *table*
literature see NORWEGIAN LITERATURE
map (62° 0′N 10° 0′E) **7**:268
music
Bull, Ole **3**:558
Flagstad, Kirsten **8**:150
Grieg, Edvard **9**:361–362
national anthem
Bjørnson, Bjørnstjerne **3**:302–303
people **14**:261–262
physical features **7**:271 *illus.*
Jotunheimen **11**:453
North Cape **14**:241
regions
Svalbard **18**:374
NORWAY (Iowa)
map (41° 54′N 91° 55′W) **11**:244
NORWAY (Maine)
map (44° 13′N 70° 32′W) **13**:70
NORWAY (Michigan)
map (45° 47′N 87° 55′W) **13**:377
NORWAY HOUSE (Manitoba)
map (53° 59′N 97° 50′W) **13**:119
NORWEGIAN ELKHOUND **6**:216 *illus.*; **14**:265 *bibliog., illus.*
NORWEGIAN LITERATURE **14**:265–266 *bibliog., illus.*
See also titles of specific literary works, e.g., *DOLL'S HOUSE, A* (play); etc.
authors
Asbjørnsen, Peter Christen **2**:227
Bjørnson, Bjørnstjerne **3**:302–303
Bojer, Johan **3**:363
Bull, Olaf Jacob Martin Luther **3**:557–558
Dass, Petter **6**:43
Duun, Olav **6**:316
Garborg, Arne **9**:38
Grieg, Nordahl Brun **9**:362
Hamsun, Knut **10**:33–34
Ibsen, Henrik **11**:6–7
Kielland, Alexander Lange **12**:74
Moe, Jørgen Engebretsen **13**:500
Øverland, Arnulf **14**:470
Undset, Sigrid **19**:383
Vesaas, Tarjei **19**:564
Vinje, Aasmund Olafsson **19**:601
Wergeland, Henrik Arnold **20**:104
Wildenvey, Herman **20**:149
NORWEGIAN NOBEL COMMITTEE
Nobel Prize **14**:208

NORWEGIAN SEA
map (70° 0′N 2° 0′E) **7**:268
NOR'WESTERS *see* NORTH WEST COMPANY
NORWICH (Connecticut)
map (41° 32′N 72° 5′W) **5**:193
NORWICH (England) **14**:266
map (52° 38′N 1° 18′E) **19**:403
NORWICH (Kansas)
map (37° 27′N 97° 51′W) **12**:18
NORWICH (New York)
map (42° 32′N 75° 31′W) **14**:149
NORWICH (Vermont)
map (43° 43′N 72° 18′W) **19**:554
NORWICH SCHOOL (art)
Cotman, John Sell **5**:304
Crome, John **5**:357
NORWICH TERRIER **6**:220 *illus.*; **14**:266 *bibliog., illus.*
NORWID, KAMIL
Polish literature **15**:398
NORWOOD (Colorado)
map (38° 8′N 108° 20′W) **5**:116
NORWOOD (Massachusetts)
map (42° 11′N 71° 12′W) **13**:206
NORWOOD (Minnesota)
map (44° 46′N 93° 55′W) **13**:453
NORWOOD (New Jersey)
map (40° 60′N 73° 57′W) **14**:129
NORWOOD (North Carolina)
map (35° 14′N 80° 7′W) **14**:242
NORWOOD (Ohio)
map (39° 10′N 84° 28′W) **14**:357
map (39° 10′N 84° 28′W) **14**:357
NORWOODVILLE (Iowa)
map (41° 39′N 93° 33′W) **11**:244
NOSE **14**:266 *bibliog., illus.*
frostbite **8**:346
Jacobson's organ **11**:347
mucous membrane inflammation
rhinitis **16**:196
sinusitis **17**:326
phonetics **15**:252
plastic surgery **15**:347
respiratory system disorders **16**:181–182
senses **17**:204
sinus **17**:325
NOSKOWIAK, SONYA
Weston, Edward **20**:118
NOSOCOMIAL **14**:266
bedsores, ulcer **19**:376
environmental health **7**:210–211
infections
Serratia **17**:210
Staphylococcus **18**:220
NOSSOB RIVER
map (26° 55′S 20° 37′E) **14**:10
NOSTOC **14**:266
NOSTRADAMUS **14**:266–267 *bibliog., illus.*
NOTARY PUBLIC **14**:267
NOTASULGA (Alabama)
map (32° 34′N 85° 40′W) **1**:234
NOTE (business) *see* NEGOTIABLE INSTRUMENT
NOTE (music) *see* TONE (music)
NOTEĆ RIVER
map (52° 44′N 15° 26′E) **15**:388
NOTES FROM THE UNDERGROUND (book) **14**:267
Dostoyevsky, Fyodor Mikhailovich **6**:244–245
NÔTRE, ANDRÉ LE *see* LE NÔTRE, ANDRÉ
NOTRE-DAME (New Brunswick)
map (46° 19′N 64° 43′W) **14**:117
NOTRE DAME BAY
map (49° 45′N 55° 15′W) **14**:166
NOTRE DAME DE CHARTRES *see* CHARTRES CATHEDRAL
NOTRE DAME DE PARIS (book) *see* *HUNCHBACK OF NOTRE DAME, THE* (book)
NOTRE DAME DE PARIS (cathedral) **4**:206 *illus.*; **9**:255–256 *illus.*; **14**:267 *bibliog., illus.*; **15**:85–86 *illus., map*
Gothic art and architecture **9**:260
Paris, Universities of **15**:88
Rayonnant style **16**:98
Virgin of Paris **9**:260 *illus.*
NOTRE DAME DU HAUT, CHURCH OF (Ronchamp, France) **4**:208 *illus.*; **12**:253 *illus.*
NOTRE DAME MOUNTAINS
map (48° 10′N 68° 0′W) **16**:18
NOTRE DAME UNIVERSITY **14**:267
football **8**:216–217
Hesburgh, Theodore M. **10**:150–151
NOTT, ELIPHALET **14**:268 *bibliog.*; **19**:450 *illus.*
NOTTELY LAKE
map (34° 56′N 84° 4′W) **9**:114
NOTTINGHAM (England) **14**:268
map (52° 58′N 1° 10′W) **19**:403
NOTTINGHAMSHIRE (England) **14**:268
NOTTOWAY (Virginia)
map (37° 8′N 78° 5′W) **19**:607
NOTTOWAY (county in Virginia)
map (37° 15′N 77° 55′W) **19**:607
NOTTOWAY RIVER
map (36° 33′N 76° 55′W) **19**:607
NOUA LISBOA (Angola) *see* HUAMBO (Angola)
NOUADHIBOU (Mauritania)
map (20° 54′N 17° 4′W) **13**:236
NOUAKCHOTT (Mauritania) **14**:268
climate **13**:236 *table*
map (18° 6′N 15° 57′W) **13**:236
NOUMÉA (New Caledonia) **14**:268
NOUMENON **14**:268
Kant, Immanuel **12**:24
phenomenon **15**:225–226
NOUN
parts of speech **15**:101
NOUVEAU NOUVEAU ROMAIN
new novel **14**:140
NOUVEAU ROMAN
new novel **14**:140
NOUVELLE-AMSTERDAM *see* AMSTERDAM ISLAND
NOUVELLE FRANCE, CAPE OF
map (62° 27′N 73° 42′W) **16**:18
NOUVELLE REVUE FRANÇAISE (periodical)
Gide, André **9**:176
NOVA **14**:268 *bibliog., illus.*
creation **14**:268
theories **14**:268
variable star **19**:522
NOVA SCOTIA (Canada) **14**:269–271 *bibliog., illus., map*
cities
Amherst **1**:369
Annapolis Royal **2**:32
Dartmouth **6**:40
Halifax **10**:21
Louisbourg **12**:429
Sydney **18**:401
climate **14**:269–270
economic activity **14**:270–271 *illus.*
education
Acadia University **4**:92 *table*
Dalhousie University **4**:92 *table*; **6**:12
Halifax, Nova Scotia College of Art and Design at **4**:92 *table*
Halifax, Nova Scotia Technological College at **4**:92 *table*
King's College, University of **4**:92 *table*
Mount Saint Vincent University **4**:92 *table*
Saint Francis Xavier University **4**:92 *table*
Saint Mary's University **4**:92 *table*
Truro, Nova Scotia Agricultural College at **4**:92 *table*
flag **14**:269 *illus.*
government **14**:271
history **14**:271
Howe, Joseph **10**:284
Tupper, Sir Charles **19**:339
land and resources **14**:269–270 *map*
Bras d'Or Lake **3**:456
Cape Breton Island **4**:120
Sable, Cape **17**:6
Sable Island **17**:6
map (45° 0′N 63° 0′W) **4**:70
people **14**:270
NOVA SCOTIA DUCK TOLLING RETRIEVER **14**:271
NOVAK, JOSEPH (pseudonym) *see* KOSINSKI, JERZY
NOVAK, ROBERT
Evans, Rowland, Jr., and Novak, Robert **7**:313
NOVALIS **14**:271–272 *bibliog.*
NOVARA (Italy) **14**:272
map (45° 28′N 8° 38′E) **11**:321
NOVATIAN **14**:272
NOVATO (California)
map (38° 6′N 122° 34′W) **4**:31
NOVAYA ZEMLYA (USSR) **14**:272
Borough, Stephen **3**:404
map (74° 0′N 57° 0′E) **19**:388
NOVÉ ZÁMKY (Czechoslovakia)
map (47° 59′N 18° 11′E) **5**:413
NOVEL **14**:272–276 *bibliog., illus.*
See also GOTHIC ROMANCE; MYSTERY, SUSPENSE, AND DETECTIVE FICTION; PICARESQUE NOVEL; SCIENCE FICTION; SUPERNATURAL LITERATURE
African literature **1**:167–168
See also national subheadings under NOVEL, e.g., NOVEL—Nigerian literature; NOVEL—South African literature; etc.
American literature **1**:343–348; **14**:274–276
Adamic, Louis **1**:93
Adams, Samuel Hopkins **1**:98
Adler, Renata **1**:104
Agee, James **1**:183
Aiken, Joan **1**:202
Alcott, Louisa May **1**:267
Aldrich, Thomas Bailey **1**:269
Alexander, Lloyd **1**:273
Alger, Horatio **1**:284–285
Algren, Nelson **1**:291
Allen Hervey **1**:299
Anderson, Sherwood **1**:402
Atherton, Gertrude Franklin **2**:292
Auchincloss, Louis **2**:316
Baldwin, James **3**:35
Barnes, Djuna **3**:86
Barth, John **3**:96–97
Barthelme, Donald **3**:97
Baum, L. Frank **3**:130
Beattie, Ann **3**:145
Bellamy, Edward **3**:187
Bellow, Saul **3**:190
Bemelmans, Ludwig **3**:194
Benét, Stephen Vincent **3**:198
Berger, Thomas **3**:209
Berryman, John **3**:225
Bester, Alfred **3**:229
Bird, Robert Montgomery **3**:290
Bishop, John Peale **3**:297
black American literature **3**:304
Blish, James **3**:333
Blume, Judy **3**:346–347
Bodenheim, Maxwell **3**:356
Bontemps, Arna **3**:382
Bourjaily, Vance **3**:424
Boyle, Kay **3**:434
Bradbury, Ray **3**:436
Bradford, Gamaliel **3**:437
Brand, Max **3**:453
Brautigan, Richard **3**:458
Breslin, Jimmy **3**:474
Bromfield, Louis **3**:502
Brown, Charles Brockden **3**:513
Brown, Claude **3**:513
Buck, Pearl S. **3**:535
Bukowski, Charles **3**:553
Buntline, Ned **3**:565
Burnett, Frances Hodgson **3**:577
Burns, John Horne **3**:578
Burroughs, Edgar Rice **3**:580
Burroughs, William S. **3**:580
Cabell, James B. **4**:4
Cable, George Washington **4**:6
Cahan, Abraham **4**:16
Cain, James M. **4**:17
Caldwell, Erskine **4**:26
Caldwell, Taylor **4**:27
Calisher, Hortense **4**:39
Capote, Truman **4**:127
Carter, Lin **4**:173
Cassill, R. V. **4**:184
Cather, Willa **4**:208–209
Chase, Mary Ellen **4**:301
Cheever, John **4**:309–310
Chesnutt, Charles Waddell **4**:334
Child, Lydia Maria **4**:348
Chopin, Kate O'Flaherty **4**:405
Churchill, Winston **4**:425
Clark, Walter van Tilburg **5**:39
Condon, Richard **5**:173
Connell, Evan S., Jr. **5**:196–197
Conroy, Jack **5**:199
Cooper, James Fenimore **5**:243–244
Coover, Robert **5**:248
Corso, Gregory **5**:277
Cozzens, James Gould **5**:324
Crane, Stephen **5**:330
Crawford, Francis Marion **5**:333
Creeley, Robert **5**:337
Crichton, Michael **5**:343
Cullen, Countee **5**:384
cummings, e. e. **5**:387–388
Dahlberg, Edward **6**:7
De Forest, John William **6**:58
Didion, Joan **6**:160–161
Doctorow, E. L. **6**:210
Donleavy, J. P. **6**:238–239
Dos Passos, John **6**:243–244
Dreiser, Theodore **6**:269–270
Ellison, Ralph **7**:148
Erskine, John **7**:235
Farrell, James T. **8**:29
Fast, Howard **8**:33
Faulkner, William **8**:36
Ferber, Edna **8**:52
Fisher, Dorothy Canfield **8**:122
Fisher, Vardis **8**:123
Fitzgerald, F. Scott **8**:130–131
Ford, Paul Leicester **8**:223
Friedan, Betty **8**:331
Fuchs, Daniel **8**:351
Gaddis, William **9**:7
Gaines, Ernest J. **9**:8
Gale, Zona **9**:13
Gallico, Paul **9**:19
Gardner, John **9**:45
Glasgow, Ellen **9**:197
Gold, Herbert **9**:228
Gold, Michael **9**:228
Gordon, Caroline **9**:249
Goyen, William **9**:274
Grau, Shirley Ann **9**:301
Hawkes, John **10**:77
Hawthorne, Nathaniel **10**:79
Heller, Joseph **10**:114–115
Hemingway, Ernest **10**:118–119
Hergesheimer, Joseph **10**:142
Hersey, John **10**:148
Hobson, Laura Z. **10**:193
Howells, William Dean **10**:285
Hudson, William Henry **10**:289
Hunter, Evan **10**:312
Hurst, Fannie **10**:319
Irving, John **11**:284
Jackson, Charles **11**:342
Jackson, Helen Hunt **11**:342–343
James, Henry **11**:353–354
Jones, James **11**:443
Jong, Erica **11**:444–445
Kelley, William Melvin **11**:38
Kennedy, William **12**:44
Kerouac, Jack **12**:59
Kesey, Ken **12**:61
King, Stephen **12**:81
Kosinski, Jerzy **12**:124
Le Guin, Ursula **12**:254
Leonard, Elmore **12**:289
Lewis, Sinclair **12**:306–307
London, Jack **12**:402–403
Loos, Anita **12**:411
Lurie, Alison **12**:467
McCarthy, Mary **13**:8–9
McCullers, Carson **13**:11
McMurtry, Larry **13**:34–35
Mailer, Norman **13**:67
Malamud, Bernard **13**:79
Marquand, J. P. **13**:162
Marshall, Paule **13**:173
Mayfield, Julian **13**:246
Melville, Herman **13**:289–290
Michener, James A. **13**:376
Miller, Arthur **13**:427–428
Mitchell, Margaret **13**:483
Mitchell, S. Weir **13**:483
Morris, Wright **13**:589
Morrison, Toni **13**:589
Nathan, Robert **14**:27
Nordhoff, Charles **14**:218
Norris, Charles G. **14**:222
Norris, Frank **14**:222–223
Norris, Kathleen **14**:223
Oates, Joyce Carol **14**:313
O'Connor, Edwin **14**:347
O'Connor, Flannery **14**:347
O'Hara, John **14**:355–356
Olsen, Tillie **14**:381
Ozick, Cynthia **14**:480
Paulding, James Kirke **15**:118
Percy, Walker **15**:163
Phillips, David Graham **15**:239
Pynchon, Thomas **15**:634
Rand, Ayn **16**:82
Rawlings, Marjorie Kinnan **16**:95
realism (literature) **16**:104
Reed, Ishmael **16**:118
Richter, Conrad **16**:214
Robbins, Harold **16**:240
Roberts, Elizabeth Madox **16**:241
Rölvaag, Ole Edvart **16**:272
Roth, Philip **16**:321
Salinger, J. D. **17**:32
Sarton, May **17**:79
Schulberg, Budd **17**:136
Shaw, Irwin **17**:246
Simms, William Gilmore **17**:314
Sinclair, Upton **17**:319
Southern, Terry **18**:112
Stegner, Wallace **18**:245
Steinbeck, John **18**:248
Stone, Irving **18**:280–281
Stowe, Harriet Beecher **18**:286
Stuart, Jesse **18**:306
Styron, William **18**:312
Susann, Jacqueline **18**:370
Tarkington, Booth **19**:37
Terhune, Albert Payson **19**:116
Twain, Mark **19**:357
Tyler, Anne **19**:361
Updike, John **19**:471
Uris, Leon **19**:487
Van Slyke, Helen **19**:516
Van Vechten, Carl **19**:516

NOVEL (cont.)
Vidal, Gore **19**:576–577
Vonnegut, Kurt, Jr. **19**:634
Walker, Alice **20**:12
Wallace, Edgar **20**:13–14
Wallace, Irving **20**:14
Wambaugh, Joseph **20**:21
Warner, Sylvia Townsend **20**:30
Waters, Frank **20**:65
Welty, Eudora **20**:102–103
West, Jessamyn **20**:107
West, Nathanael **20**:107
Westcott, Glenway **20**:105
Wharton, Edith **20**:124
Whitney, Phyllis **20**:142
Wilder, Thornton **20**:149–150
Williams, John A. **20**:159
Wister, Owen **20**:190
Wolfe, Thomas **20**:197–198
Wouk, Herman **20**:284
Wright, Harold Bell **20**:289
Wright, Richard **20**:290–291
Yerby, Frank **20**:326
Arabic literature **2**:101
Mahfuz, Najib **13**:64
Argentine literature
Cortázar, Julio **5**:278
Güiraldes, Ricardo **9**:400
Lynch, Benito **12**:476
Mallea, Eduardo **13**:92
Puig, Manuel **15**:617
Sábato, Ernesto **17**:4
Australian literature **2**:343–344
Browne, Thomas Alexander **3**:517
Franklin, Miles **8**:285
Richardson, Henry Handel **16**:211–212
Stead, Christina **18**:239–240
West, Morris L. **20**:107
White, Patrick **20**:135–136
Austrian literature **2**:354
Bernhard, Thomas **3**:221
Broch, Hermann **3**:500
Brod, Max **3**:501
Doderer, Heimito von **6**:212
Handke, Peter **10**:37
Kafka, Franz **12**:5–6
Musil, Robert **13**:681
Stifter, Adalbert **18**:267–268
Suttner, Bertha von **18**:373
Werfel, Franz **20**:104
Belgian literature **3**:175
Mallet-Joris, Françoise **13**:92
Simenon, Georges **17**:314
bildungsroman **3**:251
Bolivian literature
Arguedas, Alcides **2**:153
Brazilian literature **3**:464
Amado, Jorge **1**:320
Machado de Assis, Joaquim Maria **13**:17
Rosa, João Guimarães **16**:312
Veríssimo, Érico **19**:551
Bulgarian literature **3**:557
Canetti, Elias **4**:108
Dimov, Dimitur **6**:177
Vazov, Ivan **19**:529
Cameroonian literature
Bebey, Francis **3**:150
Beti, Mongo **3**:231
Canadian literature **4**:93–94
Atwood, Margaret **2**:316
Birney, Earle **3**:293
Blais, Marie Claire **3**:324
Buell, John **3**:544
Callaghan, Morley **4**:40
Charbonneau, Robert **4**:286
Costain, Thomas B. **5**:292
Davies, Robertson **6**:50
de la Roche, Mazo **6**:61
Engel, Marian **7**:176
Giroux, André **9**:190
Grove, Frederick Philip **9**:378
Hébert, Anne **10**:101
Hémon, Louis **10**:119
Langevin, André **12**:195
Laurence, Margaret **12**:238
MacLennan, Hugh **13**:32
Martin, Claire **13**:179
Millar, Margaret **13**:426
Montgomery, L.M. **13**:556
Parker, Sir Gilbert **15**:90
Raddall, Thomas H. **16**:41–42
Richardson, John **16**:212
Richler, Mordecai **16**:214
Ross, Sinclair **16**:318
Roy, Gabrielle **16**:329
Stringer, Arthur **18**:301
Thériault, Yves **19**:160–161
Wilson, Ethel **20**:164
Wiseman, Adele **20**:189
children's literature **4**:351–354
Chilean literature
Barrios, Eduardo **3**:95
Donoso, José **6**:240
Huidobro, Vicente **10**:295
Chinese literature **4**:390
Dream of the Red Chamber, The **6**:266
Pa Chin (Ba Jin) **15**:3
Ts'ao Hsüeh-Ch'in (Cao Xueqin) **19**:322
Wu Ching-Tzu (Wu Jingzi) **20**:296
Colombian literature
García Márquez, Gabriel **9**:39
Cuban literature
Carpentier, Alejo **4**:164
Czech literature **5**:412–413
Čapek, Karel **4**:122
Hašek, Jaroslav **10**:66
Kafka, Franz **12**:5–6
Danish literature **6**:33
Aakjaer, Jeppe **1**:49
Andersen, Hans Christian **1**:401
Bang, Herman **3**:62–63
Branner, Hans Christian **3**:455
Drachmann, Holger Henrik Herholdt **6**:253–254
Gjellerup, Karl Adolph **9**:192
Goldschmidt, Meyer Aron **9**:236
Hauch, Johannes Carsten **10**:68
Jacobsen, Jens Peter **11**:346–347
Jensen, Johannes Vilhelm **11**:396
Nexø, Martin Andersen- **14**:175
Pontoppidan, Henrik **15**:427
Wied, Gustav **20**:145
Dutch and Flemish literature **6**:314
Bordewijk, Ferdinand **3**:398
Bosboom-Toussaint, Anna Louisa Geertruide **3**:405
Conscience, Hendrik **5**:199
Gijsen, Marnix **9**:178
Streuvels, Stijn **18**:298
Teirlinck, Hermes **19**:74
Timmermans, Felix **19**:203
Vestdijk, Simon **19**:565
Vrught, Johanna Petronella **19**:639
Wolff, Elizabeth **20**:198
Wolkers, Jan **20**:199
Ecuadorean literature
Icaza, Jorge **11**:7
English literature **7**:197–202; **14**:273–276
Aldington, Richard **1**:269
Allingham, Margery **1**:303
Ambler, Eric **1**:325
Amis, Kingsley **1**:372
Austen, Jane **2**:326
Bagnold, Enid **3**:22
Ballard, J. G. **3**:41
Beerbohm, Sir Max **3**:163
Behn, Aphra **3**:171
Bennett, Arnold **3**:202
Blackmore, Richard Doddridge **3**:321
Brontë (family) **3**:504
Brophy, Brigid **3**:512
Bunyan, John **3**:565
Burgess, Anthony **3**:569
Burney, Fanny **3**:577
Butler, Samuel (1835–1902) **3**:592
Caine, Sir Hall **4**:17
Carroll, Lewis **4**:169
Carter, Angela **4**:171
Cartland, Barbara **4**:175
Cary, Joyce **4**:179
Chesterton, G. K. **4**:337
Cleland, John **5**:48
Collins, Wilkie **5**:104
Compton-Burnett, Ivy **5**:159
Connolly, Cyril **5**:197
Conrad, Joseph **5**:198
Defoe, Daniel **6**:83–84
Dickens, Charles **6**:156–157
Doyle, Sir Arthur Conan **6**:253
Drabble, Margaret **6**:253
Durrell, Lawrence **6**:306–307
Eliot, George **7**:138–139
Fielding, Henry **8**:73
Firbank, Ronald **8**:100
Ford, Ford Madox **8**:221
Forester, C. S. **8**:230
Forster, E.M. **8**:235
Fowles, John **8**:255
Galsworthy, John **9**:21–22
Gaskell, Elizabeth Cleghorn **9**:54–55
Gissing, George Robert **9**:191
Godden, Rumer **9**:220
Golding, William **9**:234–235
Graves, Robert **9**:302–303
Green, Henry **9**:347
Greene, Graham **9**:350
Haggard, H. Rider **10**:10
Hardy, Thomas **10**:47–48
Hilton, James **10**:165
Holt, Victoria **10**:208–209
Hope, Anthony **10**:230
Hughes, Richard **10**:293
Hughes, Thomas **10**:293
Huxley, Aldous **10**:324
Isherwood, Christopher **11**:287
Kingsley, Charles **12**:84
Kipling, Rudyard **12**:86–87
Koestler, Arthur **11**:105
Lawrence, D. H. **12**:249–250
Lessing, Doris **12**:298
Lewis, Matthew Gregory **11**:306
Lowry, Malcolm **11**:445
Marryat, Frederick **13**:166
Maugham, W. Somerset **13**:233
Meredith, George **13**:308–309
Murdoch, Iris **13**:648
Orwell, George **14**:451
Ouida **14**:467
Peacock, Thomas Love **15**:124
Peake, Mervyn **15**:124
Powell, Anthony **15**:480
Priestly, J. B. **15**:536
Pritchett, V. S. **15**:556
Pym, Barbara **15**:634
Radcliffe, Ann **16**:41
Reade, Charles **16**:100
realism (literature) **16**:104
Renault, Mary **16**:157
Rhys, Jean **16**:204
Richardson, Dorothy M. **16**:211
Richardson, Samuel **16**:212–213
Sackville-West, Victoria **17**:7
Sillitoe, Alan **17**:309
Smollett, Tobias **17**:374
Snow, C.P., Baron Snow **18**:3–4
Spark, Muriel **18**:163
Sterne, Laurence **18**:261
Stevenson, Robert Louis **18**:265
Stewart, Mary **18**:266
Storey, David **18**:284
Taylor, Elizabeth (novelist) **19**:49
Thackeray, William Makepeace **19**:138
Trollope, Anthony **19**:305–306
Trollope, Frances **19**:306
Victorian literature **19**:575
Walpole, Sir Hugh Seymour **20**:18
Waugh, Evelyn **20**:70
Weldon, Fay **20**:97
Wells, H. G. **20**:101
West, Rebecca **20**:107
White, T. H. **20**:136
Williams, Charles **20**:159
Wilson, Angus **20**:164
Wilson, Colin **20**:164
Wodehouse, Sir P. G. **20**:195
Woolf, Virginia **20**:214–215
Zangwill, Israel **20**:355
erotic and pornographic literature **7**:234
Finnish literature **8**:99
Sillanpää, Frans Eemil **17**:309
Waltari, Mika **20**:19
French literature **8**:315–319; **14**:273–276
Alain-Fournier **1**:239
Apollinaire, Guillaume **2**:79
Aragon, Louis **2**:107
Audiberti, Jacques **2**:318
Aymé, Marcel **2**:379
Balzac, Honoré de **3**:57–58
Barbey d'Aurevilly, Jules Amédée **3**:78
Barbusse, Henri **3**:79
Barrès, Maurice **3**:94
Beauvoir, Simone de **3**:148
Bernanos, Georges **3**:220
Bourget, Paul **3**:424
Butor, Michel **3**:592
Camus, Albert **4**:68
Céline, Louis Ferdinand **4**:231
Cendrars, Blaise **4**:245
Chateaubriand, François René, Vicomte de **4**:303
Cocteau, Jean **5**:89
Colette **5**:101
Comédie humaine, La (literary series) **5**:131–132
Constant, Benjamin **5**:207–208
Daudet, Alphonse **6**:45
Duhamel, Georges **6**:294
Dumas, Alexandre (1802–70) **6**:296–297
Flaubert, Gustave **8**:156–157
France, Anatole **8**:273
Gary, Romain **9**:53
Gautier, Théophile **9**:62
Genet, Jean **9**:79
Gide, André **9**:176
Giono, Jean **9**:186
Goncourt, Edmond de and Jules de **9**:242–243
Hugo, Victor **10**:294
Huysmans, Joris Karl **10**:326
La Fayette, Comtesse de **12**:145
Lesage, Alain René **12**:296
Malraux, André **13**:93–94
Martin du Gard, Roger **13**:179
Mauriac, François **13**:234
Mirbeau, Octave **13**:463
Montherlant, Henry de **13**:557
new novel **14**:140
Nin, Anaïs **14**:199
Prévost, Abbé **15**:534
Proust, Marcel **15**:582–583
Queneau, Raymond **16**:23
Rabelais, François **16**:31–32
realism (literature) **16**:104
Robbe-Grillet, Alain **16**:240
Rolland, Romain **16**:271
Romains, Jules **16**:272–273
Sade, Marquis de **17**:9
Sagan, Françoise **17**:11
Saint-Exupéry, Antoine de **17**:18
Sand, George **17**:59
Sarraute, Nathalie **17**:79
Scarron, Paul **17**:116
Scudéry, Madeleine de **17**:158
Simon, Claude **17**:314
Stendhal **18**:252–253
Sue, Eugène **18**:323
Verne, Jules **19**:559
Vian, Boris **19**:567
Yourcenar, Marguerite **20**:337
Zola, Émile **20**:371–372
German literature **9**:132–134
Arnim, Achim **2**:184
Averbach, Berthold **2**:319
Böll, Heinrich **3**:369–370
Bouterwek, Friedrich **3**:425
Brecht, Bertolt **3**:470–471
Feuchtwanger, Lion **8**:63
Fontane, Theodor **8**:206–207
Freytag, Gustav **8**:330
Goethe, Johann Wolfgang von **9**:223–224
Grass, Günter **9**:297–298
Grimmelshausen, Hans Jakob Christoffel von **9**:366
Hesse, Hermann **10**:152–153
Heyse, Paul von **10**:155
Johnson, Uwe **11**:436
Ludwig, Otto **12**:452
Mann, Heinrich **13**:122
Mann, Thomas **13**:123–124
Raabe, Wilhelm **16**:30
Remarque, Erich Maria **16**:144
Richter, Johann Paul Friedrich **16**:214
Seghers, Anna **17**:188
Unruh, Fritz von **19**:470
Wassermann, Jakob **20**:46
Wieland, Christoph Martin **20**:145
Zweig, Arnold **20**:383
Greek literature, modern **9**:344
Kazantzakis, Nikos **12**:34
Xenopoulos, Gregorios **20**:312
Guatemalan literature
Asturias, Miguel Ángel **2**:285–286
Guinean literature
Laye, Camara **12**:252
Hebrew and Yiddish literature **10**:102
Agnon, S. Y. **1**:187
Aleichem, Sholem **1**:270–271
Asch, Sholem **2**:228
Mendele Mokher Sefarim **13**:294
Oz, Amos **14**:479
Singer, Isaac Bashevis **17**:322
Hungarian literature **10**:305–306
Déry, Tibor **6**:123
Eötvös, Jozsef, Baron von Vásárosnemény **7**:215
Jókai, Maurus **11**:440
Móricz, Zsigmond **13**:579–580
Orkeny, Istvan **14**:445
Icelandic literature **11**:19
Gunnarsson, Gunnar **9**:405
Laxness, Halldór Kiljan **12**:252
Thórdarson, Agnar **19**:177–178
Thoroddsen, Jón **19**:179
Indian literature **11**:101–102
Chatterjee, Bankim Chandra **4**:303–304
Jhabvala, R. Prawer **11**:417
Narayan, R. K. **14**:20
Rao, Raja **16**:88
Tagore, Sir Rabindranath **19**:10
Irish literature **11**:268
Beckett, Samuel **3**:151–52
Behan, Brendan **3**:169
Bowen, Elizabeth **3**:427
Edgeworth, Maria **7**:57
Joyce, James **11**:456–457
Moore, Brian **13**:567
Moore, George **13**:568
O'Brien, Edna **14**:317
O'Flaherty, Liam **14**:354

Stephens, James **18**:254–255
Israeli literature
Oz, Amos **14**:479
Italian literature **11**:315–317
Alvaro, Corrado **1**:320
Bassani, Giorgio **3**:117
Boccaccio, Giovanni **3**:353
Bontempelli, Massino **3**:382
Borgese, Giuseppe Antonio **3**:399
Brancati, Vitaliano **3**:452
Buzzati, Dino **3**:601
Calvino, Italo **4**:49
Deledda, Grazia **6**:92
Fogazzaro, Antonio **8**:193
Foscolo, Ugo **8**:242
Ginzburg, Natalia **9**:185
Lampedusa, Giuseppe di **12**:176
Manzoni, Alessandro **13**:134
Morante, Elsa **13**:574
Moravia, Alberto **13**:574
Nievo, Ippolito **14**:186
Palazzeschi, Aldo **15**:30
Pavese, Cesare **15**:120
Silone, Ignazio **17**:310
Svevo, Italo **18**:375
Tozzi, Federigo **19**:257
Verga, Giovanni **19**:550
Vittorini, Elio **19**:621–622
Japanese literature **11**:380
Abe Kobo **1**:55
Dazai Osamu **6**:57
Enchi Fumiko **7**:162
Endo Shusaku **7**:168
Ibuse Masuji **11**:7
Ihara Saikaku **11**:39
Kawabata Yasunari **12**:32
Mishima Yukio **13**:466
Mori Ogai **13**:579
Murasaki Shikibu **13**:647
Nagai Kafu **14**:6
Natsume Soseki **14**:47
Oe Kenzaburo **14**:351
Ooka Shohei **14**:396
Shiga Naoya **17**:260
Shimazaki, Toson **17**:261–262
Tanizaki Junichiro **19**:23
Yokomitsu Riichi **20**:329
Kenyan literature
Ngugi wa Thoing'o **14**:176
Latin American literature **12**:228–231
See also national subdivisions under NOVEL, e.g., NOVEL—Argentine literature; NOVEL—Mexican literature; etc.
Latin literature **12**:234
Apuleius **2**:92
Mexican literature
Altamirano, Ignacio Manuel **1**:311
Azuela, Mariano **2**:384
Fernández de Lizardi, José Joaquín **8**:58
Fuentes, Carlos **8**:354–355
Yáñez, Augustín **20**:317
modern **14**:275–276
naturalism **14**:49–50
new novel *see* NEW NOVEL
Nigerian literature
Achebe, Chinua **1**:81
Aluko, Timothy Mofolorunso **1**:314
Amadi, Elechi **1**:320
Ekwensi, Cyprian **7**:98
Nzekwu, Onuora **14**:310
Tutuola, Amos **19**:356
Norwegian literature
Bjørnson, Bjørnstjerne **3**:302–303
Bojer, Johan **3**:363
Duun, Olav **6**:316
Grieg, Nordahl Brun **9**:362
Hamsun, Knut **10**:33–34
Kielland, Alexander Lange **12**:74
Undset, Sigrid **19**:383
Vesaas, Tarjei **19**:564
origins **14**:272–273
Persian literature
Alavi, Bozorg **1**:248
Peruvian literature
Alegría, Ciro **1**:270
Vargas Llosa, Mario **19**:522
picaresque novel **15**:290
Polish literature **15**:398
Gombrowicz, Witold **9**:241
Lem, Stanisław **12**:279–280
Reymont, Władysław Stanisław **16**:190–191
Sienkiewicz, Henryk **17**:296
Wittlin, Józef **20**:194
Żeromski, Stefan **20**:361
Portuguese literature **15**:457
Castello-Branco, Camillo **4**:187
Eça de Queiroz, José Maria **7**:36
Ribeiro, Aquilino **16**:205
Ribeiro, Bernardim **16**:205
realism (literature) **16**:104
romance **16**:280
Romanian literature **16**:290
Russian literature **14**:273–276; **16**:364–367
Aksakov, Sergei Timofeyevich **1**:232
Aksenov, Vasily Pavlovich **1**:232
Aldanov, M. A. **1**:267
Andreyev, Leonid Nikolayevich **1**:408
Artsybashev, Mikhail Petrovich **2**:225
Bely, Andrei **3**:193–194
Bryusov, Valery Yakovlevich **3**:530
Bulgakov, Mikhail Afanasievich **3**:553–554
Bunin, Ivan Alekseyevich **3**:563
Chernyshevsky, Nikolai Gavrilovich **4**:331–332
Dostoyevsky, Fyodor Mikhailovich **6**:244–245
Ehrenberg, Ilya Grigorievich **7**:90
Fadeyev, Aleksandr Aleksandrovich **8**:7
Fedin, Konstantin Aleksandrovich **8**:44
Gogol, Nikolai **9**:225
Goncharov, Ivan Aleksandrovich **9**:242
Gorky, Maksim **9**:252–253
Ivanov, Vsevolod Vyacheslavovich **11**:333
Katayev, Valentin Petrovich **12**:30
Kuprin, Aleksandr Ivanovich **12**:138
Leonov, Leonid Maksimovich **12**:292
Merezhkovsky, Dmitry Sergeyevich **13**:309
Nabokov, Vladimir **14**:3–4
Olesha, Yury **14**:377
Pasternak, Boris **15**:107
Pilnyak, Boris **15**:303
Saltykov Shchedrin, Mikhail Yevgrafovich **17**:39
Sholokhov, Mikhail Aleksandrovich **17**:281
Simonov, Konstantin Kirill Mikhailovich **17**:316
Sinyavsky, Andrei **17**:326
Solzhenitsyn, Aleksandr **18**:59
Tolstoi, Aleksei Nikolayevich **19**:228
Tolstoi, Count Leo **19**:228
Turgenev, Ivan **19**:341
Voinovich, Vladimir **19**:626
Zamyatin, Yevgeny **20**:355
scope **14**:272
Scottish literature
Barrie, Sir James **3**:94
Scott, Sir Walter **17**:154
Senegalese literature
Sembene, Ousmane **17**:195
South African literature
Abrahams, Peter **1**:61
Cloete, Stuart **5**:64
Coetzee, J. M. **5**:93
Gordimer, Nadine **9**:248
La Guma, Alex **12**:147
Mofolo, Thomas **13**:500
Paton, Alan **15**:112
Schreiner, Olive **17**:134–135
Spanish literature **18**:157–160
Alarcón, Pedro Antonio de **1**:240
Alas, Leopoldo **1**:240
Alemán, Mateo **1**:271
Baroja y Nessi, Pio **3**:87
Blasco-Ibáñez, Vicente **3**:328
Caballero, Fernán **4**:3
Cela, Camilo José **4**:229
Cervantes Saavedra, Miguel de **4**:261
El Caballero Cifar **18**:157
Espinel, Vicente Martínez **7**:243
Goytisolo, Juan **9**:274
Pérez Galdós, Benito **15**:164
Quevedo y Villegas, Francisco Gómez de **16**:25
Ruiz, José Martínez **16**:344
Unamuno, Miguel de **19**:381
Valera y Alcalá Galiano, Juan **19**:505
Valle Inclán, Ramón del **19**:507
Swedish literature **18**:386–387
Ahlin, Lars **1**:200
Almqvist, Carl Jonas Love **1**:307
Bergman, Hjalmar Fredrik Elgérus **3**:210
Bremer, Fredrika **3**:472
Johnson, Eyvind **11**:432
Lagerlöf, Selma **12**:165
Moberg, Vilhelm **13**:487
Rydberg, Abraham Viktor **16**:379
Söderberg, Hjalmar **18**:32
Swiss literature
Frisch, Max **8**:334
Gotthelf, Jeremias **9**:264
Trinidadian literature
Naipaul, V. S. **14**:8
Turkish literature
Halide Edib Adivar **10**:20–21
Yaşar Kemal **20**:319
Uruguayan literature
Benedetti, Mario **3**:196
Venezuelan literature
Gallegos, Rómulo **9**:17
Welsh literature
Owen, Daniel **14**:471
Powys, John Cowper **15**:486
Yugoslav literature
Andrić, Ivo **1**:408
Cankar, Ivan **4**:108
NOVELLA AND NOVELETTE 14:276 *bibliog.*
Boccaccio, Giovanni **3**:353
Droste-Hülshoff, Annette Elisabeth von **6**:273
Higuchi Ichiyo **10**:162
Keller, Gottfried **12**:37
Meyer, Conrad Ferdinand **13**:368
NOVEMBER
birthstones **3**:296 *illus., table*
calendar **4**:28
NOVEMBER REVOLUTION *see* RUSSIAN REVOLUTIONS OF 1917
NOVERRE, JEAN GEORGES 4:408 *illus.*; **14**:276 *bibliog.*
ballet **3**:42
dance **6**:25
NOVGOROD (USSR) **14**:276
Russia/Union of Soviet Socialist Republics, history of **16**:351–353
Theophanes the Greek **19**:158
NOVI LIGURE (Italy)
map (44° 46′N 8° 47′E) **11**:321
NOVI PAZAR (Bulgaria)
map (43° 21′N 27° 12′E) **3**:555
NOVI PAZAR (Yugoslavia)
map (43° 8′N 20° 31′E) **20**:340
NOVI SAD (Yugoslavia) **14**:277
map (45° 15′N 19° 50′E) **20**:340
NOVINGER (Missouri)
map (40° 19′N 92° 42′W) **13**:476
NOVO-KUZNETSK (USSR)
map (53° 45′N 87° 6′E) **19**:388
NOVOCAINE *see* PROCAINE
NOVONIKOLAYEVSK (USSR) *see* NOVOSIBIRSK (USSR)
NOVOSIBIRSK (USSR) **14**:277
map (55° 2′N 82° 55′E) **19**:388
NOVOSIBIRSK RESERVOIR
map (54° 35′N 82° 35′E) **19**:388
NOVOSIBIRSKIYE ISLANDS
map (75° 0′N 142° 0′E) **19**:388
NOVOTNÝ, ANTONÍN
Czechoslovakia **5**:416
NOW *see* NATIONAL ORGANIZATION OF WOMEN
NOW (Negotiable Order of Withdrawal) ACCOUNTS *see* NEGOTIABLE ORDER OF WITHDRAWAL (NOW) ACCOUNTS
NOWA SÓL (Poland)
map (51° 48′N 15° 44′E) **15**:388
NOWATA (Oklahoma)
map (36° 42′N 95° 38′W) **14**:368
NOWATA (county in Oklahoma)
map (36° 45′N 95° 35′W) **14**:368
NOWICKI, MATTHEW 14:277 *bibliog.*
NOWSHAK MOUNTAIN
map (36° 26′N 71° 50′E) **1**:133
NOWSHERA
map (34° 1′N 71° 59′E) **15**:27
NOWY SĄCZ (Poland)
map (49° 38′N 20° 42′E) **15**:388
NOXAPATER (Mississippi)
map (33° 0′N 89° 4′W) **13**:469
NOXEN (Pennsylvania)
map (41° 25′N 76° 3′W) **15**:147
NOXON (Montana)
map (48° 1′N 115° 47′W) **13**:547
NOXON RESERVOIR
map (47° 54′N 115° 40′W) **13**:547
NOXUBEE (county in Mississippi)
map (33° 5′N 88° 35′W) **13**:469
NOYCE, ROBERT 14:277
NOYES, ALFRED 14:277 *bibliog.*
NOYES, JOHN HUMPHREY 14:277 *bibliog.*
Oneida Community **14**:389
NOYON, TREATY OF
Italian Wars **11**:320
NRA *see* NATIONAL RECOVERY ADMINISTRATION; NATIONAL RIFLE ASSOCIATION
NRAO *see* NATIONAL RADIO ASTRONOMY OBSERVATORY
NSAWAM (Ghana)
map (5° 50′N 0° 20′W) **9**:164
NTARE V, KING OF BURUNDI
Burundi **3**:583
NTEM RIVER
map (2° 15′N 9° 45′E) **7**:226
NU (letter)
N **14**:3
NU, U 14:277 *bibliog.*
Burma **3**:575
NUBA 14:277 *bibliog.*
Riefenstahl, Leni **16**:218
NUBIA 14:277–278 *bibliog.*
Cush **5**:397
NUBIA, LAKE *see* NASSER, LAKE
NUBIAN DESERT 14:278
map (20° 30′N 33° 0′E) **18**:320
NUCKOLLS (county in Nebraska)
map (40° 10′N 98° 0′W) **14**:70
NUCLA (Colorado)
map (38° 16′N 108° 33′W) **5**:116
NUCLEAR CHEMISTRY
chemistry **4**:323
NUCLEAR ENERGY 14:278–284 *bibliog., illus., table*
atomic bomb **2**:307–308
Bacher, Robert Fox **3**:11
Bhabha, Homi Jehangir **3**:233
consumption
fuel **8**:353 *table*
energy sources **7**:175 *table*
environmental health **7**:212
fallout **8**:14
fission, nuclear **8**:129
fuel **8**:352; **14**:278
fusion, nuclear **8**:381–382
fusion energy **8**:382–383
history **14**:279
hydrogen bomb **10**:339–340
International Atomic Energy Agency **11**:218–219
isotope **11**:301
major generating stations, U.S. **15**:482 *map*
Nuclear Regulatory Commission **14**:287–288
plutonium **15**:373
pollution, environmental **15**:413–414
proton-proton reaction **15**:578–579
research institutions
Lawrence Berkeley and Lawrence Livermore laboratories **12**:251
Los Alamos National Scientific Laboratory **12**:416
rockets and missiles **16**:260
role of **14**:283–284
scientific basis **14**:278–279
ship **17**:275
icebreaker **11**:16
Nautilus **14**:52
submarine **18**:314–316 *illus.*
SNAP **17**:383–384
technology, history of **19**:68–69
tokamak **19**:223
uranium **19**:477
uranium minerals **19**:478
waste disposal
Nevada **14**:113
nuclear waste disposal **14**:282
NUCLEAR ENERGY REACTOR *see* NUCLEAR REACTOR
NUCLEAR FAMILY 14:284 *bibliog.*
adolescence **1**:107
extended family **7**:341
family **8**:15–18 *illus.*
monogamy **13**:536
NUCLEAR FISSION *see* FISSION, NUCLEAR
NUCLEAR FORCE
fundamental interactions **8**:360–361
fundamental particles **8**:362
nuclear physics **14**:287
NUCLEAR FUSION *see* FUSION, NUCLEAR
NUCLEAR MAGNETIC RESONANCE IMAGING 14:284 *bibliog.*
NUCLEAR MAGNETIC RESONANCE SPECTROSCOPY **18**:171 *illus.*
Bloch, Felix **3**:334
NUCLEAR MEDICINE 14:284 *bibliog.*
radiology **16**:65
tracer
Hevesy, Georg von **10**:154
iodine **11**:239
tritium **19**:304
NUCLEAR NON-PROLIFERATION TREATY
arms control **2**:178

NUCLEAR NON-PROLIFERATION TREATY (cont.)
atomic bomb **2**:308
International Atomic Energy Agency **11**:219
NUCLEAR PHYSICS **14**:284–286 *bibliog., illus.*
atomic nucleus **2**:311
Bethe, Hans **3**:230
Chadwick, Sir James **4**:267
cross-section **5**:361
fission, nuclear **8**:129
fundamental particles **8**:361–363
fusion energy **8**:382–383
gamma rays **9**:34
Geiger, Hans Wilhelm **9**:67–68
Gell-Mann, Murray **9**:69–70
grand unification theories **9**:285–286
instrumentation
accelerator, particle **1**:72–76
betatron **3**:229
cloud chamber **5**:68
detector, particle **6**:133–134
Van de Graaff generator **19**:512
Joliot-Curie, Frédéric and Irène **11**:441
Landau, Lev **12**:181
Manhattan Project **13**:116
physics **15**:281
quark **16**:12–13
radiochemistry **16**:63
reactions
chemical symbolism and notation **4**:322
fusion, nuclear **8**:381–382
nuclear energy **14**:278 *illus.*
research institutions
Brookhaven National Laboratory **3**:510
Lawrence Berkeley and Lawrence Livermore laboratories **12**:251
Rutherford, Sir Ernest **16**:376
Seaborg, Glenn T. **17**:171–172
transmutation of elements **19**:276–277
unified field theory **19**:385–386
von Neumann, John **19**:634
Wigner, Eugene Paul **20**:147
NUCLEAR POLICY
breeder reactor **3**:472
NUCLEAR PROPULSION
Rickover, Hyman **16**:216
rockets and missiles **16**:258–260 *illus., table*
NUCLEAR REACTION
fusion, nuclear **8**:381–382
nuclear energy **14**:278 *illus.*
nuclear physics **14**:284–286
NUCLEAR REACTOR **14**:278–284 *illus., table*
Chernobyl (USSR) **4**:331
components **14**:279
control rods
boron **3**:403
cadmium **4**:12
dysprosium **6**:320
erbium **7**:228
gadolinium **9**:7
hafnium **10**:9
samarium **17**:45
coolant
heavy water **10**:100
helium **10**:113
fission, nuclear **8**:129
fuels
plutonium **15**:373
uranium **19**:477
uranium dioxide pellets **4**:259 *illus.*
Ko-Ri power station, South Korea **14**:280–281 *illus.*
moderator
beryllium **3**:227
heavy water **10**:100
safety **14**:282–283
strontium **18**:303
thorium **19**:178
Three Mile Island power plant **14**:282–283 *illus.*
types **14**:279–282
breeder reactor **3**:471–472
SNAP **11**:383
waste disposal *see* NUCLEAR ENERGY
NUCLEAR REGULATORY COMMISSION **14**:286
hydrogen bomb **10**:339–340
nuclear energy **14**:283
NUCLEAR STRATEGY **14**:286–288 *bibliog.*
See also ARMS CONTROL
antiballistic missile **2**:56–57
atomic bomb **2**:307–308
ballistic missile **3**:49
civil defense **5**:9–10
cruise missile **5**:365–366
cruiser **5**:366
defense, national **6**:82
hydrogen bomb **10**:339
Minuteman Missile **13**:462
MIRV missile **13**:465
MX missile **13**:688
navy **14**:64–65
neutron bomb **14**:109
North Atlantic Treaty Organization **14**:241
Polaris (missile) **15**:393
Poseidon (missile) **15**:458
Rickover, Hyman **16**:216
rockets and missiles **16**:255
strategy and tactics, military **18**:291
submarine **18**:313–316
NUCLEAR SUBMARINE **18**:314–315 *illus.*
naval vessels **14**:56–57 *illus.*
Polaris (missile) **15**:393
Poseidon (missile) **15**:458
Rickover, Hyman **16**:216
submarine **18**:315–316
NUCLEAR TRANSFORMATION
radioactivity **16**:61 *illus.*
NUCLEAR-WASTE DISPOSAL *see* NUCLEAR ENERGY
NUCLEAR WEAPONS
antiballistic missile **2**:56–57
arms control **2**:178
atomic bomb **2**:307–308
ballistic missile **3**:49
cruise missile **5**:365–366
electromagnetic pulse **7**:116
hydrogen bomb **10**:339–340
International Atomic Energy Agency **11**:219
Minuteman missiles **13**:462
MIRV missile **13**:465
MX missile **13**:688
neutron bomb **14**:109
nuclear strategy **14**:288
plutonium **15**:373
Polaris (missile) **15**:393
Poseidon (missile) **15**:458
rockets and missiles **16**:254–256 *illus.*
surface-to-air missile **18**:359
tests
Pauling, Linus Carl **15**:119
salt dome **17**:38
seismogram **17**:189
Vela (artificial satellite) **19**:536
Trident **19**:296–297
weapons **20**:75
NUCLEIC ACID **14**:288–291 *bibliog., illus.*
See also DNA; RNA
Baltimore, David **3**:56
biology **3**:271 *illus.*
cell **4**:232 *illus.*; **4**:233
diseases, animal **6**:191
genetic code **9**:79–82 *illus.*
genetics **9**:87–90
insulin **11**:197–198
Jacob, François **11**:345
Kossel, Albrecht **12**:124
life **12**:326–327
metabolism **13**:326
microbiology **13**:384
nutrient cycles **14**:303–304
protein synthesis **15**:574–576 *illus.*
purine **15**:630
pyrimidine **15**:637
sugar **18**:327
uric acid **19**:486
virus **19**:613–616 *illus.*
X-ray diffraction **20**:308
NUCLEOTIDE
genetic code **9**:79–82 *illus.*
mutation **13**:686–687
nucleic acid **14**:289–291
protein synthesis **15**:575 *illus.*
Sanger, Frederick **17**:64
Todd, Lord Alexander **19**:220
NUCLEUS **14**:291
cell **4**:232–233 *illus.*
Ciliata **4**:430
cloning **5**:64
genetics **9**:86 *illus.*
meiosis **13**:282
mitosis **13**:485
nucleoli **14**:291
NUCLEUS, ATOMIC *see* ATOMIC NUCLEUS
NUDE DESCENDING A STAIRCASE (painting) *see* DUCHAMP, MARCEL
NUDE LYING ON A SOFA (Mademoiselle O'Murphy)
Boucher, François **3**:419–420 *illus.*
NUECES (county in Texas)
map (27° 45′N 97° 40′W) **19**:129
NUECES RIVER
map (27° 50′N 97° 30′W) **19**:129
NUELTIN LAKE
map (60° 20′N 99° 50′W) **13**:119
NUER **14**:291 *bibliog.*
polygamy **15**:419
NUEVA CASAS GRANDES (Mexico)
map (30° 25′N 107° 55′W) **13**:357
NUEVA GERONA (Cuba)
map (21° 53′N 82° 48′W) **5**:377
NUEVA PALMIRA (Uruguay)
map (33° 53′S 58° 25′W) **19**:488
NUEVA ROSITA (Mexico)
map (27° 57′N 101° 13′W) **13**:357
NUEVA SAN SALVADOR (El Salvador)
map (13° 41′N 89° 17′W) **7**:100
NUEVE DE JULIO (Argentina)
map (35° 27′S 60° 52′W) **2**:149
NUEVITAS (Cuba)
map (21° 33′N 77° 16′W) **5**:377
NUEVO BAZTÁN (new town)
Churriguera (family) **4**:427
NUEVO LAREDO (Mexico)
map (27° 30′N 99° 31′W) **13**:357
NUEVO LEÓN (Mexico) **14**:291
cities
Monterrey **13**:553
NUEVO ROCAFUERTE (Ecuador)
map (0° 56′S 75° 24′W) **7**:52
NUFFIELD COLLEGE (Oxford University) **14**:474
NUFFIELD FOUNDATION **14**:291
NUFFIELD RADIO ASTRONOMY LABORATORIES **14**:291 *bibliog.*
Lovell, Sir Bernard **12**:438
NUISANCE **14**:291–292
NUJOMA, SAM **14**:292
NUKU HIVA
Marquesas Islands **13**:162
NUKUALOFA (Tonga) **14**:292
map (21° 8′S 175° 12′W) **19**:233
NUKUNONO
Tokelau **19**:223
NULL HYPOTHESIS **14**:292 *bibliog.*
scientific research use **14**:292
statistical significance **14**:292
statistics **18**:236
t-test **19**:3
NULL SET **14**:292 *bibliog.*
NULLARBOR PLAIN **14**:292
map (31° 0′S 129° 0′E) **2**:328
NULLIFICATION **14**:292 *bibliog.*
Calhoun, John C. **4**:29
Civil War, U.S. **5**:15
Jackson, Andrew **11**:342
Madison, James **13**:43
United States, history of the **19**:446
Webster, Daniel **20**:88
NUMA POMPILIUS
Rome, ancient **16**:297
NUMAZU (Japan)
map (35° 6′N 138° 52′E) **11**:361
NUMBAT **13**:175 *illus.*; **14**:292 *illus.*
NUMBER **14**:292–293 *bibliog.*
algebra **1**:283–284
arithmetic **2**:158–159
base **3**:102
binary number **3**:256
cardinal number **14**:292
complex number **5**:157
decimal **6**:73
development of concept **14**:293
distribution (statistics) **6**:201
duodecimal system **6**:301–302
factor **8**:6
fraction **8**:258
Incan record keeping **11**:72
inequality **11**:161
integer **11**:200
irrational number **11**:280
Minkowski, Hermann **13**:451
natural number: Peano, Giuseppe **15**:125
negative number **14**:293
numeral **14**:294
octane number **14**:347
ordinal number **14**:293
von Neumann, John **19**:634
prime number **15**:542–543
progression **15**:563–564
rational number **16**:92
real number **16**:103
root (mathematics) **16**:311
sequence (mathematics) **17**:206–207
set
mean **13**:252–253
median **13**:264
specific number
e **7**:3
pi **15**:287
zero **20**:361
square root **18**:202
transcendental number **19**:268
transfinite number: Cantor, Georg **4**:118
NUMBER THEORY **14**:293–294 *bibliog.*
Chebyshev, Pafnuty Lvovich **4**:306
Dedekind, Richard **6**:76–77
Dickson, Leonard **6**:159
Diophantine equations **6**:185
Diophantus **6**:185
Euclid **7**:262
Euler, Leonhard **7**:264–265
Fermat, Pierre de **8**:55
Fermat's last theorem **14**:293
Galois, Evariste **9**:21
Gauss, Carl Friedrich **9**:61–62
Gelfond, Aleksandr Osipovich **9**:69
Goldbach conjecture **9**:230–231
Lagrange, Joseph Louis de **12**:166
Leonardo Pisano **12**:291
mathematics **13**:222
mathematics history of **13**:225–226
prime number **15**:542–543
Pythagoras, theorem of **15**:639
transcendental number **19**:268
Waring, Edward **20**:30
NUMBERS, BOOK OF **14**:294 *bibliog.*
NUMERAL **14**:294 *bibliog.*
number **14**:293
NUMERATOR *see* FRACTION
NUMERICAL ANALYSIS **14**:294–295 *bibliog.*
calculus **4**:24
differential calculus **6**:167–168
differential equations **6**:168
golden section **9**:232–233
integral calculus **11**:200–201
interpolation **11**:225
linear equation **12**:354
Newton's method of approximation **7**:224; **7**:235
nomogram **14**:215
NUMERICAL CONTROL TECHNOLOGY *see* NC TECHNOLOGY
NUMEROLOGY
Pythagoras of Samos **15**:639–640
NUMIDIA **4**:173 *map*; **14**:295 *bibliog.*
Jugurtha, King **11**:465
Masinissa **13**:196
NUMISMATICS **14**:295–296 *bibliog., illus.*
denarius **6**:106
Fraser, James Earle **8**:287
mintage **13**:461
Roman art and architecture **16**:277
NUN **14**:296 *bibliog.*
NÚÑEZ CABEZA DE VACA, ÁLVAR *see* CABEZA DE VACA, ÁLVAR NÚÑEZ
NÚÑEZ DE BALBOA, VASCO *see* BALBOA, VASCO NÚÑEZ DE
NUNIVAK ISLAND
Bering Sea **3**:212
map (60° 0′N 166° 30′W) **1**:242
NUNNELLY (Tennessee)
map (35° 52′N 87° 28′W) **19**:104
NUORO (Italy)
map (40° 19′N 9° 20′E) **11**:321
NUPE **14**:296–297 *bibliog.*
polygamy **15**:419
NUR AL-DIN **14**:297
NUR JAHAN
Jahangir, Mogul Emperor **11**:349
NUREMBERG (West Germany) **14**:297
art
Flötner, Peter **8**:177
Gothic art and architecture **9**:261
Jamnitzer (family) **11**:357–358
Stoss, Veit **18**:285
map (49° 27′N 11° 4′E) **9**:140
National Socialist rallies at **9**:156 *illus.*
NUREMBERG LAWS
Europe, history of **7**:296
Germany, history of **9**:155
NUREMBERG TRIALS **14**:297 *bibliog., illus.*
Doenitz, Karl **6**:212–213
Goering, Hermann **9**:222
Hess, Rudolf **10**:152
Jackson, Robert Houghwout **11**:343
Keitel, Wilhelm **12**:37
Krupp (family) **12**:132
Papen, Franz von **15**:68
Ribbentrop, Joachim von **16**:205
Rosenberg, Alfred **16**:314–315
Schacht, Hjalmar **17**:116
Speer, Albert **18**:176
war crimes **20**:25
World War II **20**:280 *illus.*
NUREYEV, RUDOLF **8**:207 *illus.*; **14**:297–298 *bibliog., illus.*
NURHACHI **14**:298 *bibliog.*
China, history of **4**:373
Manchuria **13**:109
NURI *see* KAFIR

NURI ES-SAID
Iraq 11:256
NURISTANI LANGUAGES
Indo-Iranian languages 11:145–146
NURMI, PAAVO 14:298 *bibliog.*
NÜRNBERG (West Germany) *see* NUREMBERG (West Germany)
NURSERY RHYMES 14:298 *bibliog.*
Field, Eugene 8:71
Greenaway, Kate 9:349
Mother Goose 13:607
NURSERY SCHOOL *see* PRESCHOOL EDUCATION
NURSING (breast-feeding) *see* BREAST-FEEDING
NURSING (profession) 14:298–299 *bibliog.*
history 14:298
Dix, Dorothea 6:206
Nightingale, Florence 14:193
midwife 13:414
Robert Wood Johnson Foundation 16:241
NURSING HOME 14:299–300 *bibliog.*
institutionalization 11:196
NUSA TENGGARA *see* LESSER SUNDA ISLANDS
NUT 14:300–301 *bibliog., illus., table*
See also names of specific nuts, e.g., ALMOND (tree); PECAN; etc.
NUT OF PERSIA *see* NECTARINE
NUTATION 14:301 *illus.*
Bradley, James 3:437–438
Earth, motions of 7:18–19
NUTCRACKER (bird) 14:301–302 *illus.*
NUTHATCH 14:302 *illus.*
NUTLEY (New Jersey)
map (40° 49′N 74° 10′W) 14:129
NUTMEG 14:302 *illus.*; 15:337 *illus.*
mace 13:14–15
NUTRIA 14:302 *illus.*
NUTRIENT CYCLES 14:302–304 *bibliog., illus.*
calcium 14:303
carbon cycle (atmosphere) 4:136; 14:303
DDT 14:304
forest 8:227–230
nitrogen cycle 14:203 *illus.*
phosphates 14:303
phosphorus 14:303
sulfur 14:303
NUTRIOSO (Arizona)
map (33° 57′N 109° 13′W) 2:160
NUTRITION, ANIMAL
bird 3:287–288
carnivore 4:156–157
coral 5:257
diseases, animal 6:192
factory farming 8:6
farms and farming 8:25
fish meal 8:122
fodder 8:192–193
grain 9:281–282
hay 10:80
hunger and thirst 10:310
oats 14:314
pasture 15:109
peanut 15:125
NUTRITION, HUMAN 14:304–307 *bibliog., illus.*
bread 3:467
breast feeding 3:469
cannibalism 4:109 *illus.*
carbohydrate 4:132–133; 14:305
chiropractic 4:398
cholesterol 4:404; 14:307
constipation 5:212
consumer education 14:307
diet, human 6:163–164
dietary standards 14:306
dieting 6:165
digestion, human 6:170–173
egg 7:72
energy 14:304–305 *illus.*
essential nutrients 14:305
famine 8:18–19
fat 8:33–34; 14:305
federal guidelines 14:306–307
food groups 14:305–306 *illus.*
food labeling 14:307
grain 9:281–282
headache 10:86
health foods 10:89
hunger and thirst 10:310
kelp 12:40
milk 13:423
nut 14:301
nutritional-deficiency diseases 14:307–308
oats 14:314
orthomolecular medicine 14:450
potato 15:465
protein 14:305; 14:306; 15:574
Recommended Dietary Allowances 14:306
starvation 18:228
sugar 18:327
United Nations Children's Fund 19:415
vitamins and minerals 14:305 *illus.*; 19:618–621
NUTRITION FOUNDATION
hyperactive children 10:347
NUTRITIONAL-DEFICIENCY DISEASES 14:307–308 *bibliog.*
anemia 1:410
beriberi 3:211
diet, human 6:164
goiter 9:225
kwashiorkor 12:142–143
magnesium, imbalance 13:54
marasmus 13:143
megavitamin therapy 13:280
night blindness
Wald, George 20:9
osteoporosis 14:458
pellagra 15:138
protein 15:574
rickets 16:215
scurvy 17:167
sprue 18:201
vitamins and minerals 14:307–308
world health problem 14:308
NUTRITIONIST
nutrition, human 14:304
NUTS AND BOLTS 14:308 *bibliog., illus.*
screw 17:156
NUTTBY MOUNTAIN
map (45° 33′N 63° 13′W) 14:269
NUTTING LAKE (Massachusetts)
map (42° 32′N 71° 16′W) 3:409
NYABARONGO RIVER
map (2° 21′S 30° 22′E) 16:378
NYAKROM (Ghana)
map (5° 37′N 0° 48′W) 9:164
NYALA (Sudan)
map (12° 3′N 24° 53′E) 18:320
NYAMISANA MOUNTAIN
map (3° 3′S 30° 33′E) 3:582
NYANDA (Zimbabwe)
map (20° 5′S 30° 50′E) 20:365
NYANZA-LAC (Burundi)
map (4° 21′S 29° 36′E) 3:582
NYASA, LAKE 13:82 *illus.*; 14:308
map (12° 0′S 34° 30′E) 13:81
NYASALAND *see* ZIMBABWE (Rhodesia)
NYAUNGLEBIN (Burma)
map (17° 57′N 96° 44′E) 3:573
NYBORG (Denmark)
map (55° 19′N 10° 48′E) 6:109
NYCTOPHOBIA
phobia 15:248
NYE (county in Nevada)
map (38° 0′N 116° 30′W) 14:111
NYERERE, JULIUS K. 1:159 *illus.*; 14:308 *bibliog.*; 18:24 *illus.*
Tanzania 19:28
NYÍREGYHÁZA (Hungary)
map (47° 59′N 21° 43′E) 10:307
NYKØBING (Denmark)
map (54° 46′N 11° 53′E) 6:109
map (56° 48′N 8° 52′E) 6:109
NYKÖPING (Sweden)
map (58° 45′N 17° 0′E) 18:382
NYLON 14:308–309 *bibliog., illus.*
Carothers, W. H. 4:162
fiber, textile 8:67
manufacturing 14:309 *illus.*
molecular structure 15:350 *illus.*
plastics 15:349–350
synthetic fibers 18:409
NYMPH (insect) 14:309
cricket 5:344
dragonfly 6:255
mayfly 13:247–248 *illus.*
naiad 14:7
NYMPHAEUM
fountains 8:252
NYMPHENBURG PALACE 14:309 *bibliog.*
Amalienburg Pavilion 1:321
NYMPHENBURG WARE 14:309 *bibliog.*
chinoiserie 4:395
NYMPHOMANIA 14:309 *bibliog.*
satyriasis 17:93
NYMPHS (mythology) 14:309–310
NYNORSK (language) *see* LANDSMÅL (language)
NYONG RIVER
map (3° 17′N 9° 54′E) 4:61
NYQUIST, HARRY 14:310
Nyquist criterion, feedback 14:310
Nyquist interval, sampling 14:310
telecommunications 14:310
NYSA (Poland)
map (50° 29′N 17° 20′E) 15:388
NYSA KLODSKA RIVER
map (50° 49′N 17° 50′E) 15:388
NYSA LUZICKA RIVER
map (52° 4′N 14° 46′E) 15:388
NYSSA (Oregon)
map (43° 53′N 117° 0′W) 14:427
NYSTAD, TREATY OF (1721)
Northern War, Great 14:256
Peter I, Emperor of Russia (Peter the Great) 15:201
Russia/Union of Soviet Socialist Republics, history of 16:354
NYSTAGMUS 14:310
NZEKWU, ONUORA 14:310 *bibliog.*
NZÉRÉKORÉ (Guinea)
map (7° 45′N 8° 49′W) 9:397

O

O (letter) 14:310 *illus.*
O. HENRY 14:310–311 *bibliog., illus.*
O. HENRY AWARD 14:311
Ludwig, Jack 12:452
O. Henry 14:311
Olsen, Tillie 14:381
Parker, Dorothy 15:90
Stafford, Jean 18:209
Yerby, Frank 20:326
OAHE, LAKE
map (45° 30′N 100° 25′W) 18:103
OAHU (Hawaii) 14:311
cities
Honolulu 10:223
Hawaii (state) 10:73
map (21° 30′N 158° 0′W) 10:72
OAK 4:283 *illus.*; 14:311–312 *bibliog., illus.*
English Oak 8:228 *illus.*
Kermes 12:59
leaf 15:336 *illus.*
Louisiana 12:433–434 *illus.*
lumber 12:456 *illus.*
white oak 19:286 *illus.*
wood 20:205 *illus.*
OAK BLUFFS (Massachusetts)
map (41° 27′N 70° 34′W) 13:206
OAK CREEK (Colorado)
map (40° 16′N 106° 57′W) 5:116
OAK GROVE (Louisiana)
map (32° 52′N 91° 23′W) 12:430
OAK HARBOR (Washington)
map (48° 18′N 122° 39′W) 20:35
OAK HILL (Florida)
map (28° 52′N 80° 51′W) 8:172
OAK HILL (Michigan)
map (44° 13′N 86° 19′W) 13:377
OAK HILL (West Virginia)
map (37° 59′N 81° 9′W) 20:111
OAK LAWN (Illinois)
map (41° 43′N 87° 45′W) 11:42
OAK PARK (Illinois)
map (41° 53′N 87° 48′W) 11:42
OAK PARK (Michigan)
map (42° 28′N 83° 11′W) 13:377
OAK RIDGE (Tennessee)
map (36° 1′N 84° 16′W) 19:104
OAK RIDGE NATIONAL LABORATORY 14:312
atomic bomb 2:307
Manhattan Project 13:116
OAK VALLEY (New Jersey)
map (39° 49′N 75° 10′W) 14:129
OAKBORO (North Carolina)
map (35° 13′N 80° 20′W) 14:242
OAKDALE (California)
map (37° 46′N 120° 51′W) 4:31
OAKDALE (Louisiana)
map (30° 49′N 92° 40′W) 12:430
OAKES (North Dakota)
map (46° 8′N 98° 6′W) 14:248
OAKESDALE (Washington)
map (47° 8′N 117° 15′W) 20:35
OAKFIELD (Maine)
map (46° 6′N 68° 10′W) 13:70
OAKFIELD (New York)
map (43° 4′N 78° 16′W) 14:149
OAKHARBOR (Ohio)
map (41° 30′N 83° 9′W) 14:357
OAKHURST (New Jersey)
map (40° 16′N 74° 1′W) 14:129
OAKLAND (California) 14:312
map (37° 47′N 122° 13′W) 4:31
OAKLAND (Iowa)
map (41° 19′N 95° 23′W) 11:244
OAKLAND (Maine)
map (44° 33′N 69° 43′W) 13:70
OAKLAND (Maryland)
map (39° 25′N 79° 24′W) 13:188
OAKLAND (county in Michigan)
map (42° 40′N 83° 25′W) 13:377
OAKLAND (Nebraska)
map (41° 50′N 96° 28′W) 14:70
OAKLAND (Oregon)
map (43° 25′N 123° 18′W) 14:427
OAKLAND CITY (Indiana)
map (38° 20′N 87° 21′W) 11:111
OAKLAND PARK (Florida)
map (26° 12′N 80° 7′W) 8:172
OAKLAWN (Kansas)
map (37° 36′N 97° 18′W) 12:18
OAKLEY (Idaho)
map (42° 15′N 113° 53′W) 11:26
OAKLEY (Kansas)
map (39° 8′N 100° 51′W) 12:18
OAKLEY, ANNIE 14:312 *bibliog.*
OAKLEY, KENNETH 14:312
OAKRIDGE (Oregon)
map (43° 45′N 122° 28′W) 14:427
OAKTOWN (Indiana)
map (38° 52′N 87° 26′W) 11:111
OAKVILLE (Connecticut)
map (41° 36′N 73° 5′W) 5:193
OAKVILLE (Ontario)
map (43° 27′N 79° 41′W) 14:393
OAKWOOD (Ohio)
map (41° 6′N 84° 23′W) 14:357
OAMARU (New Zealand)
map (45° 6′S 170° 58′E) 14:158
OAO (artificial satellite) 14:312–313 *bibliog., illus.*
infrared astronomy 11:175
space exploration 18:123
ultraviolet astronomy 19:379
X-ray astronomy 20:306
OARFISH 14:313 *illus.*
ribbonfish 16:205
OAS *see* ORGANIZATION OF AMERICAN STATES
OATBALOGAN (Philippines)
map (11° 46′N 124° 53′E) 15:237
OATES, JOYCE CAROL 1:347 *illus.*; 14:313 *bibliog., illus.*
OATES, TITUS 14:313 *bibliog.*
OATH 14:313–314
OATS 9:281 *illus.*; 14:314 *bibliog., illus.*
herbicide 10:136 *illus.*
OAU *see* ORGANIZATION OF AFRICAN UNITY
OAXACA (city in Mexico) 14:314
map (17° 3′N 96° 43′W) 13:357
Santo Domingo vault (c.1600) 12:225 *illus.*
OAXACA (state in Mexico) 14:314
history
Mitla 13:485
Monte Albán 13:552
people
Mixtec 13:486
Zapotec 20:356
OB BAY
map (69° 0′N 73° 0′E) 19:388
OB RIVER 14:314
map (66° 45′N 69° 30′E) 19:388
OB TRENCH
Indian Ocean bottom 11:105 *map*
OB-UGRIC LANGUAGES
Ural-Altaic languages 19:475
OBADIAH, BOOK OF 14:314
OBAN (Scotland)
map (56° 25′N 5° 29′W) 19:403
OBANIAN CULTURE (Scotland)
midden 13:390
O'BANNON (Kentucky)
map (38° 17′N 85° 30′W) 12:47
OBASANJO, OLUSEGUN
Nigeria 14:192
OBELISK 14:314–315
Cleopatra's Needles 5:51
OBERÁ (Argentina)
map (27° 29′S 55° 8′W) 2:149
OBERAMMERGAU (West Germany) 14:315
passion play 15:105
OBERLIN (Kansas)
map (39° 49′N 100° 32′W) 12:18
OBERLIN (Louisiana)
map (30° 37′N 92° 46′W) 12:430
OBERLIN (Ohio)
map (41° 18′N 82° 13′W) 14:357
OBERLIN, JOHANN FRIEDRICH 14:315 *bibliog.*
OBERLIN COLLEGE 14:315
American music 1:350
coeducation 5:90
OBERON (satellite)
Uranus (astronomy) 19:478–479
OBERTH, HERMANN 14:315 *bibliog., illus.*
rockets and missiles 16:253 *illus.*
OBESITY 14:315–316 *bibliog.*
dieting 6:165–166
fat 8:34
surgery 18:362

ÓBIDOS (Brazil)
map (1° 55′S 55° 31′W) **3**:460
OBIE AWARDS 14:316
Baraka, Imamu Amiri **3**:75
Cronyn, Hume **5**:359
Mamet, David **13**:97
Monk, Meredith **13**:532
Mostel, Zero **13**:605
Pacino, Al **15**:10
Rabe, David **16**:31
OBION (Tennessee)
map (36° 16′N 89° 12′W) **19**:104
OBION (county in Tennessee)
map (36° 20′N 89° 10′W) **19**:104
OBJECTIVE CORRELATIVE
Eliot, T. S. **7**:140
OBJECTIVISM
Rand, Ayn **16**:82
Zukofsky, Louis **20**:381
OBLONG (Illinois)
map (39° 0′N 87° 55′W) **11**:42
OBOE 13:676 *illus.*; **14**:316 *bibliog., illus.*
bassoon **3**:118–119 *illus.*
English horn **7**:190–191
Japanese music **11**:381–382 *illus.*
shawm **17**:246
sound waves **18**:72 *illus.*
wind instruments **20**:171 *illus.*
OBOTE, MILTON 14:316
Uganda **19**:373
OBRECHT, JACOB 14:316 *bibliog.*
OBREGÓN, ÁLVARO 14:316–317 *bibliog., illus.*
Mexico, history of **13**:365
OBRENOVIĆ (dynasty) *see* ALEXANDER, KING OF SERBIA; MILAN, KING OF SERBIA; MILOŠ, PRINCE OF SERBIA
O'BRIEN (county in Iowa)
map (43° 7′N 95° 35′W) **11**:244
O'BRIEN (Oregon)
map (42° 4′N 123° 42′W) **14**:427
O'BRIEN, CONOR CRUISE 14:317
theater of fact **19**:153
O'BRIEN, EDNA 14:317 *bibliog., illus.*
O'BRIEN, LUCIUS
Canadian art and architecture **4**:89
O'BRIEN, PARRY 14:317
OBSCENITY *see* PORNOGRAPHY
OBSERVATION (test) *see* PSYCHOLOGICAL MEASUREMENT
OBSERVATOIRE DE PARIS *see* PARIS OBSERVATORY
OBSERVATORY, ASTROLOGICAL
Smithsonian Astrological Observatory
Langley, Samuel Pierpont **12**:196
OBSERVATORY, ASTRONOMICAL 14:317–319 *bibliog., illus.*
Allegheny Observatory
Langley, Samuel Pierpont **12**:196
Anglo-Australian Observatory **1**:416
Arecibo Observatory **2**:145
Argentine National Observatory
Gould, Benjamin Apthorp **9**:265
Australian National Radio Astronomy Observatory **2**:344
Byurakan Astrophysical Observatory **3**:604
Cerro Tololo Inter-American Observatory **4**:260–261
Crimean Astrophysical Observatory **5**:348
Dearborn Observatory **6**:68
Dudley Observatory
Gould, Benjamin Apthorp **9**:265
Dunsink Observatory
Hamilton, Sir William Rowan **10**:29
Einstein Tower **13**:295 *illus.*
European Southern Observatory **7**:306
Göttingen Observatory
Gauss, Carl Friedrich **9**:61–62
Mayer, Johann Tobias **13**:246
Hale, George Ellery **10**:18
Harvard College Observatory **10**:64
High Altitude Observatory **10**:161
infrared astronomy **11**:175
Jantar Mantar Observatory **14**:120 *illus.*
Kitt Peak National Observatory **12**:93
Las Campanas Observatory **12**:209
Lick Observatory **12**:323
Lowell Observatory
Lowell, Percival **12**:444
Pluto (planet) **15**:372
Lund Observatory
Galaxy, The **9**:11 *map*
McDonald Observatory **13**:13
Mauna Kea Observatory **13**:233
Meudon Observatory *see* PARIS OBSERVATORY
Mount Wilson Observatory **13**:618
Mullard Radio Astronomy Observatory **13**:636
National Center for Atmospheric Research **14**:30
National Radio Astronomy Observatory **14**:45
Nuffield Radio Astronomy Laboratories **12**:438; **14**:291
optical observatories **14**:317–318
Palomar Observatory **14**:318 *illus., illus.*; **15**:52
Paris Observatory **15**:88
Pic du Midi Observatory **14**:318 *illus., illus.*
Pulkovo Observatory **15**:619
radar astronomy **16**:40
radio astronomy **16**:50–53 *illus.*
radio observatories **14**:318
Royal Greenwich Observatory **16**:330
Royal Observatory, Cape of Good Hope
Gill, Sir David **9**:181
Siding Spring Observatory
Anglo-Australian Telescope **1**:416
Smithsonian Astrophysical Observatory **17**:372
space observatories **14**:318–319
High Energy Astronomical Observatory **10**:161
OAO **14**:312–313 *illus.*
OGO **14**:354–355
OSO **14**:456
Space Telescope **18**:137 *illus.*
Special Astrophysical Observatory **18**:166
United States Naval Observatory **19**:464
University of Leiden
Hertzsprung, Ejnar **10**:149
Uraniborg Observatory **19**:471
Westerbork Observatory **20**:115
Yerkes Observatory **20**:326–327
OBSERVATORY, GEOLOGICAL
Lamont-Doherty Geological Observatory **12**:175
OBSERVATORY, GEOPHYSICAL
OGO **14**:354
Weber, Wilhelm Eduard **20**:88
OBSERVATORY, RADAR
radar astronomy **16**:40
OBSESSIVE BEHAVIOR *see* COMPULSIVE BEHAVIOR
OBSIDIAN 14:319 *illus.*
igneous rock **11**:33
lava **12**:240
Paleolithic Period **15**:38
OBSTETRICS 14:319 *bibliog.*
anthropometry **2**:55
childbirth **14**:319
gynecology **9**:414
midwife **13**:414
pregnancy and birth **15**:504 *illus.*
OBUASI (Ghana)
map (6° 14′N 1° 39′W) **9**:164
OC-EO *see* OCEO (Vietnam)
OCA *see* WOOD SORREL
OCALA (Florida)
map (29° 11′N 82° 7′W) **8**:172
OCAMPO (Mexico)
map (28° 11′N 108° 23′W) **13**:357
OCAMPO, MELCHOR
Mexico, history of **13**:364
OCAÑA (Colombia)
map (8° 15′N 73° 20′W) **5**:107
O'CASEY, SEAN 11:268 *illus.*; **14**:319–320 *bibliog., illus.*
OCCAM, WILLIAM OF *see* WILLIAM OF OCCAM
OCCAM'S RAZOR 14:320
principle of parsimony **14**:320
William of Occam **20**:155
OCCASIONALISM 14:320 *bibliog.*
Geulincx, Arnold **9**:162
Malebranche, Nicholas **13**:87
OCCIPITAL LOBE
brain **3**:443 *illus.*
OCCITAN LANGUAGE *see* PROVENÇAL LANGUAGE
OCCLEVE, THOMAS *see* HOCCLEVE, THOMAS
OCCLUDED FRONT *see* FRONT
OCCULTATION 14:320
OCCUPATIONAL DISEASES *see* DISEASES, OCCUPATIONAL
OCCUPATIONAL SAFETY AND HEALTH, NATIONAL INSTITUTE OF *see* NATIONAL INSTITUTE OF OCCUPATIONAL SAFETY AND HEALTH
OCCUPATIONAL SAFETY AND HEALTH ADMINISTRATION 14:320–321
diseases, occupational **6**:194
environmental health **7**:210
government regulation **9**:271
grain elevator **9**:282
Labor, U.S. Department of **12**:152
OCCUPATIONAL THERAPY 14:321 *bibliog.*
OCCUPATIONS
See also CAREER EDUCATION; VOCATIONAL EDUCATION; names of specific occupations, e.g., JOURNALISM; MEDICINE; etc.
caste **4**:186–187
class, social **5**:40
guilds **9**:395
hunter-gatherers **10**:313
OCEAN (county in New Jersey)
map (39° 58′N 74° 12′W) **14**:129
OCEAN-ATMOSPHERE INTERACTION 14:321–322 *bibliog.*
Atlantic Ocean **2**:296
climate **5**:57
Earth sciences **7**:24
exchange, energy and chemical materials **14**:321
fog **8**:193
geophysics **9**:108
hydrologic cycle **10**:341
ice ages **11**:10
inversion **11**:233–234
maritime climate **13**:157
monsoon **13**:543–544
ocean currents **14**:321; **14**:322–324
ocean and sea **14**:331
ocean waves **14**:321
paleoclimatology **15**:32–34
paleotemperature **15**:42
stratus clouds **18**:293
thermocline **19**:162
trade winds **19**:263
water wave **20**:57–60
waterspout **20**:66
wind **20**:170
OCEAN BLUFF (Massachusetts)
map (42° 6′N 70° 39′W) **13**:206
OCEAN CITY (Maryland)
map (38° 20′N 75° 5′W) **13**:188
OCEAN CITY (New Jersey)
map (39° 16′N 74° 36′W) **14**:129
OCEAN CURRENTS 14:322–324 *bibliog., illus., maps*
advection **1**:110
Aqualhas current **14**:323 *illus.*
Atlantic Ocean **2**:296
Australia, West Australian current **14**:323 *illus.*
Benguela current **14**:323 *illus.*
Brazil Current **3**:464
Canaries Current **4**:98
Caribbean Current **4**:147
Caribbean Sea **4**:148–149
convection currents, plate tectonics **15**:357
density current **6**:114
doldrums **6**:224
Ekman, Vagn Walfrid **7**:98
El Niño (Peru) **7**:99
gulf and bay **9**:402–403
Gulf Stream **9**:403
Humboldt, Alexander von **10**:301
Humboldt Current **10**:301
iceberg **11**:15
Indian Ocean **11**:104
International Ice Patrol **11**:220
Iselin, Columbus O'Donnell **11**:286
Japan **11**:363
longshore drift **12**:409
Maury, Matthew Fontaine **13**:238
Mediterranean Sea **13**:277
Mexico, Gulf of **13**:366
Munk, Walter **13**:643
Nansen, Fridtjof **14**:13
ocean-atmosphere interaction **14**:321–322
oceanographic instrumentation **14**:343 *illus.*
oceanography **14**:345
Pacific Ocean **15**:7
Peruvian Current **14**:323 *illus.*
Pleistocene Epoch **15**:365
rip current **12**:409
river delta **16**:232–233
Southern Current **14**:323 *illus.*
Stommel, Henry Melson **18**:280
submarine canyon **18**:316
trade winds **19**:263
upwelling, oceanic **19**:473–474
Von Arx, William S. **19**:633
warm and cold currents **14**:322–323 *maps*
west wind drift, ocean and sea **14**:327
whirlpool **20**:132
wind **20**:170
wind systems and ocean currents
January conditions **14**:323 *map*
July conditions **14**:323 *map*
OCEAN FALLS (British Columbia)
map (52° 21′N 127° 40′W) **3**:491
OCEAN LINER 14:324–325 *bibliog., illus.*
City of Paris **14**:325 *illus.*
Great Eastern **9**:319
Queen Elizabeth **16**:22 *illus.*
Queen Mary **16**:22
Savannah **17**:99
United States **14**:325 *illus.*
OCEAN PERCH *see* ROCKFISH
OCEAN AND SEA 14:325–332 *bibliog., illus., map, table*
See also names of specific bodies of water, e.g., ATLANTIC OCEAN; BLACK SEA; etc.
amphidromic point **1**:381
bar, offshore **3**:74
basins, oceanic **14**:327
beach and coast **3**:135–137
bed load **3**:153
breaker **3**:468
chalk deposition, fossil record **8**:245
Challenger Expedition **4**:271–272
continental shelf and slope **5**:230; **14**:331
coral reef **5**:258–260
deep-sea life **6**:77–79 *illus.*
density current **6**:114
dimensions, ocean and marginal seas worldwide **14**:326 *table*
drilling-rig platform **15**:212 *illus.*
epeiric seas, Paleozoic Era **15**:42
epicontinental seas
paleogeography **15**:37 *map*
estuary **7**:248
fishing industry **8**:124–128 *map*
food **14**:331
fresh water source **14**:331
gulf and bay **9**:402–403
habitat **10**:4–5
hydrofoil **10**:335–337
hydrography **10**:341
hydrosphere **10**:344
importance **14**:331–332
lagoon **12**:165–166
lapse rate **12**:206
mid-oceanic ridge **13**:389–390; **14**:327
worldwide **14**:328–329 *map*
Mohorovičić discontinuity **13**:503
navigation **14**:58–61
ocean-atmosphere interaction **14**:321–322
ocean currents **14**:322–324
ocean delta
river delta **16**:232
ocean thermal energy conversion **14**:331–332; **14**:333
oceanic fracture zones **14**:327–331; **14**:339
oceanic mineral resources **14**:332; **14**:340–341
oceanic nutrients **14**:341
oceanic trenches **14**:341–342
oceanographic instrumentation **14**:342–344
oceanography **14**:332; **14**:344–346
ooze, deep-sea **14**:397
origin **14**:327
origin of life **12**:327 *illus.*
pack ice **15**:10–11 *map*
paleoclimatology **15**:32–34
paleogeography **15**:35
petroleum **14**:332
plains **14**:327
worldwide **14**:328–329 *map*
plankton **15**:330–331
plate tectonics **15**:352–356 *illus., map*
Pleistocene Epoch **15**:365
pollution control **15**:416
Precambrian time **15**:492
red tide **16**:114
Sea, Law of the **17**:167–168
sea level **17**:169
seafloor, physiography **14**:327–331
seafloor spreading **14**:331; **17**:172 *illus.*
seamount **17**:174
SEASAT **17**:176
seawater **14**:331–332; **17**:177
seaweed **17**:177
sediment, marine **17**:183–184
shipping route **17**:277
shock wave **17**:279
structural geology **18**:303

submarine canyon **18**:316
Sverdrup, Harald Ulrik **18**:375
swell **18**:388
territorial waters **19**:121
thermocline **19**:162
tide **19**:193–194
transgression, marine **19**:271
Triassic Period **19**:292–293
tsunami **19**:325
tunnel **19**:339
Ulothrix **19**:377
upwelling, oceanic **19**:473–474
water mass **20**:49
water wave **20**:57–60 *illus.*
waterspout **20**:66
whirlpool **20**:132
zones
abyssal zone **1**:67
bathyal zone **3**:123
benthonic zone **3**:205
epipelagic zone **7**:220
hadal zone **10**:7
intertidal life **11**:229–230
littoral zone **12**:373
neritic zone **14**:89
pelagic zone **15**:137
photic zone **15**:257
zooplankton **20**:378
OCEAN SPRINGS (Mississippi)
map (30° 25′N 88° 50′W) **13**:469
OCEAN SUNFISH **8**:116 *illus.*; **14**:332 *illus.*
OCEAN THERMAL ENERGY CONVERSION **14**:333 *bibliog.*
ocean currents **14**:322–324
ocean and sea **14**:331–332
OCEANA (county in Michigan)
map (43° 40′N 86° 20′W) **13**:377
OCEANARIUM *see* AQUARIUM
OCEANIA **14**:333–336 *bibliog., illus., map*
art *see* OCEANIC ART
flora and fauna **14**:335
history **14**:335–336
Bougainville, Louis Antoine de **3**:420
island arc **11**:297–298
islands and island groups
Admiralty Islands **1**:105
American Samoa **1**:366 *map*
Antipodes Islands **2**:65
Auckland Islands **2**:317
Bali **3**:37
Bikini (Marshall Islands) **3**:250
Bismarck Archipelago **3**:299
Bonin Islands **3**:379–380
Bora-Bora **3**:395
Borneo **3**:402
Bougainville **3**:402
Caroline Islands (U.S.) **4**:160
Cebu **4**:228
Christmas Island **4**:415
Cook Islands **5**:237
Easter Island **7**:32–33 *illus., map*
Eniwetok (Marshall Islands) **7**:206
Fiji **8**:76–78
French Polynesia **8**:321–322
Guadalcanal **9**:384–385 *map*
Guam (U.S.) **9**:385
Hawaii (state) **10**:71–76 *illus., map*
Hess, H. H. **10**:151–152
Kiribati **12**:88 *illus., map*
Mariana Islands (U.S.) **13**:150–151
Marquesas Islands **13**:162–163
Marshall Islands (U.S.) **13**:173
Melanesia **13**:284
Micronesia **13**:386
Midway (U.S.) **13**:414
Nauru **14**:51 *illus., map*
New Britain **14**:115
New Caledonia **14**:119 *map*
New Guinea **14**:121–122 *map*
New Ireland **14**:127
New Zealand **14**:156–161 *illus., map, table*
Niue (New Zealand) **14**:204
Okinawa **14**:366
Pacific Islands, Trust Territory of the **15**:5
Papua New Guinea **15**:72–73 *illus., map, table*
Phoenix Islands **15**:251
Pitcairn Island **15**:319–320 *map*
Polynesia **15**:421
Saipan (Mariana Islands) **17**:28
Samoa **17**:46 *maps*
Society Islands **18**:26
Solomon Islands **18**:56–57 *map*
Tahiti (French Polynesia) **19**:10 *map*
Tasmania (Australia) **19**:42 *map*
Tonga **19**:233–234 *illus., map*
Tuvalu **19**:356 *map*
Vanuatu **19**:520–521
Wake Island **20**:8
Wallis and Futuna Islands **20**:16
Western Samoa **20**:116–117 *map*
Yap **20**:319
Kon-Tiki **12**:108
languages *see* OCEANIC LANGUAGES
national parks **14**:41–42 *map, table*
people
Melanesians **13**:284–285
Micronesians **13**:386
Negrito **14**:78
Polynesians **15**:421
race **16**:34 *illus.*
Trobriand Islanders **19**:304
primitive religion
cargo cults **4**:147
mana **13**:107
primitive societies
Mead, Margaret **13**:251–252
resources
energy consumption and production **7**:174 *table*
truck and bus registration **19**:315 *table*
weather variation and extremes **20**:80–81 *tables*
OCEANIC ART **14**:336–339 *bibliog., illus.*
Aborigines, Australian **1**:59
Australia **14**:339
Melanesia **14**:337
Micronesia **14**:339
Polynesia **14**:337–339
Southeast Asian art and architecture **18**:107
OCEANIC BANK
seamount **17**:174
OCEANIC BASINS **14**:327
Indian Ocean bottom **11**:105 *map*
Pacific Ocean bottom **15**:6–7 *map*
worldwide **14**:328–329 *map*
OCEANIC FRACTURE ZONES **14**:339
Indian Ocean bottom **11**:105 *map*
ocean and sea **14**:327–331 *map*
Pacific Ocean bottom **15**:6–7 *map*
plate tectonics **15**:351–355 *illus.*
OCEANIC ISLANDS
mid-oceanic ridge **13**:390
OCEANIC LANGUAGES **12**:355 *map*; **14**:339 *bibliog.*
Asia **2**:244 *map*
Malayo-Polynesian languages **13**:82–83
Melanesians **13**:284–285
Southeast Asian languages **18**:110; **18**:111
OCEANIC MINERAL RESOURCES **14**:340–341 *bibliog., illus.*
continental shelf **14**:340
geochemistry **9**:96–97
manganese nodule **13**:114
ocean basin **14**:340
ocean and sea **14**:332
oceanography **14**:345–346
seawater **17**:177
sediment, marine **17**:184
OCEANIC NUTRIENTS **14**:341 *bibliog.*
ocean and sea **14**:327
seawater **17**:177
seaweed **17**:177
OCEANIC PLAINS
Indian Ocean bottoms **11**:105 *map*
ocean and sea **14**:327
Pacific Ocean bottom **15**:6–7 *map*
worldwide **14**:328–329 *map*
OCEANIC RIDGES
Atlantic Ocean bottom **2**:295 *map*
Indian Ocean **11**:105 *map*
Lomonosov Ridge **12**:400
mid-oceanic ridge **13**:389–390
Ninetyeast Ridge **14**:199
Pacific Ocean bottom **15**:6–7 *map*
OCEANIC RISE
Pacific Ocean bottom **15**:6–7 *map*
OCEANIC TRENCHES **14**:341–342 *bibliog., illus., table*
Atlantic Ocean **2**:294–296 *map*
Caribbean Sea **4**:148
deepest in each ocean **14**:342 *table*
Earth, geological history of **7**:14
hadal zone **10**:7
Indian Ocean **11**:104–105 *map*
landform evolution **12**:183
Marianas Trench **13**:151
marine biology **13**:153
mid-oceanic ridge **13**:389–390
ocean and sea **14**:327
Pacific Ocean **15**:5–7 *map*
Piccard, Auguste **15**:292
plate tectonics **15**:351–355 *illus., map*
seamount **17**:174
structural geology **18**:303
subduction zone **14**:341; **18**:312–313
submarine canyon **18**:316
unconformity **19**:382
worldwide **14**:328–329 *map*
OCEANIC UPWELLING *see* UPWELLING, OCEANIC
OCEANOGRAPHIC INSTRUMENTATION **14**:342–344 *bibliog., illus.*
bathyscaphe **3**:123
hydrophone **10**:343
remote sensing **16**:147
salinometer **17**:33
turbidimeter **19**:339
Von Arx, William S. **19**:633
OCEANOGRAPHY **14**:344–346 *bibliog., illus.*
bathyscaphe **3**:123
biological oceanography **14**:344
Challenger Expedition **4**:271–272
oceanographic survey **14**:345
chemical oceanography **14**:344–345
Deep-Sea Drilling Project **6**:77
geological oceanography **14**:344–346
geophysics **9**:107–108
history
Beebe, Charles W. **3**:159
Cousteau, Jacques-Yves **5**:317–318
Ekman, Vagn Walfrid **7**:98
Hess, H. H. **10**:151–152
Iselin, Columbus O'Donnell **11**:286
Maury, Matthew Fontaine **13**:238
Munk, Walter **13**:643
Murray, Sir John (oceanographer) **13**:650
Nansen, Fridtjof **14**:13
Piccard, Auguste **15**:292
Stommel, Henry Melson **18**:280
Sverdrup, Harald Ulrik **18**:375
Thomson, Sir Charles Wyville **19**:175
Von Arx, William S. **19**:633
marine biology **13**:153
marine geology **14**:345
National Ocean Survey, U.S. **14**:35
National Oceanic and Atmospheric Administration **14**:346
ocean and sea **14**:332
physical oceanography **14**:344–345
research and educational institutions and laboratories **14**:346
JOIDES **11**:438
Lamont-Doherty Geological Observatory **12**:175
Scripps Institution of Oceanography **17**:158
Woods Hole Oceanographic Institution **20**:212–213
telemetry **19**:78
OCEANSIDE (California)
map (33° 12′N 117° 23′W) **4**:31
OCELOT **14**:346 *illus.*
OCEO (Vietnam) **14**:346 *bibliog.*
OCHER **14**:346
limonite, pigment **12**:346
OCHILTREE (county in Texas)
map (36° 15′N 100° 50′W) **19**:129
OCHLOCKNEE (Georgia)
map (30° 59′N 84° 5′W) **9**:114
OCHO RIOS (Jamaica)
map (18° 25′N 77° 7′W) **11**:351
OCHOA, SEVERO **14**:346
Kornberg, Arthur **12**:123
OCHRE RIVER (Manitoba)
map (51° 3′N 99° 47′W) **13**:119
OCHS, ADOLPH SIMON **14**:346 *bibliog.*
OCHSENFELD, R.
superconductivity **18**:350
OCILLA (Georgia)
map (31° 36′N 83° 15′W) **9**:114
OCKHAM, WILLIAM OF *see* WILLIAM OF OCCAM
OCMULGEE RIVER
map (31° 58′N 82° 32′W) **9**:114
OCOEE (Florida)
map (28° 35′N 81° 33′W) **8**:172
OCONA (Peru)
map (16° 26′S 73° 7′W) **15**:193
OCONEE (county in Georgia)
map (33° 50′N 83° 25′W) **9**:114
OCONEE (county in South Carolina)
map (34° 50′N 83° 5′W) **18**:98
OCONEE RIVER
map (31° 58′N 82° 32′W) **9**:114
O'CONNELL, DANIEL **14**:346 *bibliog.*
Ireland, history of **11**:263–264 *illus.*
O'CONNOR, CARROLL
radio and television broadcasting **16**:59
O'CONNOR, EDWIN **14**:347
O'CONNOR, FLANNERY **14**:347 *bibliog., illus.*
O'CONNOR, FRANK (pseudonym) **14**:347 *bibliog.*
O'CONNOR, JOHN J. **14**:347
O'CONNOR, SANDRA DAY **14**:347
OCONOMOWOC (Wisconsin)
map (43° 7′N 88° 30′W) **20**:185
OCONTO (Wisconsin)
map (44° 43′N 87° 52′W) **20**:185
OCONTO (county in Wisconsin)
map (44° 57′N 88° 15′W) **20**:185
OCONTO FALLS (Wisconsin)
map (44° 42′N 88° 8′W) **20**:185
OCOTLÁN (Mexico)
map (20° 21′N 102° 46′W) **13**:357
OCOZINGO (Mexico)
map (16° 54′N 92° 7′W) **13**:357
OCRACOKE (North Carolina)
map (35° 7′N 75° 58′W) **14**:242
OCTAGON (building)
American Institute of Architects **1**:341
OCTAGON (figure) **15**:419 *illus.*
OCTAGON (geometry)
polygon **15**:419 *illus.*
OCTAHEDRON **15**:419 *illus.*
OCTAL SYSTEM
base **2**:102
OCTANE NUMBER **14**:347
gasoline **9**:55
OCTAVE **14**:347
scale (music) **17**:106–107
OCTAVIA **14**:347
OCTAVIAN *see* AUGUSTUS, ROMAN EMPEROR
OCTOBER
birthstones **3**:296 *illus., table*
calendar **4**:28
OCTOBER MANIFESTO
Nicholas II, Emperor of Russia **14**:181
Russian Revolution of 1905 **16**:370
OCTOBER WAR (1973)
Arab-Israeli Wars **2**:97–98 *map*
OCTOPUS **14**:348 *bibliog., illus.*
intertidal life **11**:230
mollusk **13**:510–512 *illus.*
OCUCAJE STYLE
Paracas **15**:74
OCUMARE DEL TUY (Venezuela)
map (10° 7′N 66° 46′W) **19**:542
ODA (Ghana)
map (5° 55′N 0° 59′W) **9**:164
ODA NOBUNAGA *see* NOBUNAGA
ODAENATHUS, PRINCE OF PALMYRA
Palmyra **15**:51
ODD COUPLE, THE (play)
Simon, Neil **17**:315
ODE **14**:348 *bibliog.*
Gray, Thomas **9**:307
hymn **10**:346
Keats, John **12**:35–36
Parini, Giuseppe **15**:84
Persian literature **15**:187
Pindar **15**:304–305
"ODE: INTIMATIONS OF IMMORTALITY FROM RECOLLECTIONS OF EARLY CHILDHOOD" (poem) **14**:348
ODELL (Nebraska)
map (40° 3′N 96° 48′W) **14**:70
ODENSE (Denmark) **14**:348–349
map (55° 24′N 10° 23′E) **6**:109
ODENTON (Maryland)
map (39° 5′N 76° 42′W) **13**:188
ODÉON THEATER
Antoine, André **2**:69
ODER-NEISSE LINE **14**:349 *map*
Germany, East and West **9**:146–147
ODER RIVER **14**:349
map (53° 32′N 14° 38′E) **15**:388
ODESSA (Missouri)
map (39° 0′N 93° 57′W) **13**:476
ODESSA (Texas) **14**:349
map (31° 51′N 102° 22′W) **19**:129
ODESSA (USSR) **14**:349 *illus.*
map (46° 28′N 30° 44′E) **19**:388
ODESSA (Washington)
map (47° 20′N 118° 41′W) **20**:35
ODETS, CLIFFORD **14**:350 *bibliog.*
Group Theatre, The **9**:377
ODETTA **14**:350
ODEX AUREUS **3**:389 *illus.*
ODIENNE (Ivory Coast)
map (9° 30′N 7° 34′W) **11**:335
ODIN **14**:350
mythology **13**:702
ODO OF METZ
Charlemagne's Palace Chapel **8**:303 *illus.*
ODOACER **14**:350

ODON (Indiana)
map (38° 51′N 86° 59′W) **11**:111
ODONATA 14:350
damselfly **6**:20
dragonfly **6**:255
O'DONOVAN, MICHAEL *see* O'CONNOR, FRANK (pseudonym)
ODONTOCETI
mammal **13**:103; **13**:105 *illus.*
ODORIC OF PORDENONE 14:350 *bibliog.*
ODOVACAR *see* ODOACER
ODUDUWA
Ife **11**:32
ODUM (Georgia)
map (31° 40′N 82° 2′W) **9**:114
ODUM, EUGENE P. 14:350
ODYSSEUS 14:350–351 *bibliog.*
Calypso **4**:49
Circe **4**:435
Ithaca (Greece) **11**:331
Odyssey **14**:351
Penelope **15**:142–143
Polyphemus **15**:421
Trojan War **14**:350–351; **19**:305
ODYSSEY (epic) **14**:351 *bibliog.*
Homer **10**:213
OE KENZABURO 14:351
OEBEN, JEAN FRANÇOIS 14:351
dressing table **8**:376 *illus.*
furniture **8**:376
Riesener, Jean Henri **16**:219
OECD *see* ORGANIZATION FOR ECONOMIC COOPERATION AND DEVELOPMENT
OECOLAMPADIUS, JOHANNES 14:351 *bibliog.*
OED see OXFORD ENGLISH DICTIONARY, THE
OEDIPUS 14:351 *bibliog.*
riddles **16**:216
OEDIPUS COMPLEX (psychology) **5**:157
OEDIPUS REX (play) **14**:351 *bibliog.*
Sophocles **18**:67
OEDOGONIUM **14**:352
OEHLENSCHLÄGER, ADAM GOTTLOB 14:352
OELWEIN (Iowa)
map (42° 41′N 91° 55′W) **11**:244
OENO ISLAND
Pitcairn Island **15**:319
OERSTED, HANS CHRISTIAN 14:352 *bibliog.*
aluminum **1**:317
OERTER, AL 14:352
OESLING
Luxembourg (country) **12**:471
OF HUMAN BONDAGE (book) **14**:352 *bibliog.*
Maugham, W. Somerset **13**:233
OF MICE AND MEN (book) **14**:352
Steinbeck, John **18**:248
OFAKIM (Israel)
map (31° 17′N 34° 37′E) **11**:302
O'FALLON (Missouri)
map (38° 49′N 90° 42′W) **13**:476
O'FAOLAIN, SEAN 14:352 *bibliog.*
O'FEENY, SEAN ALOYSIUS *see* FORD, JOHN (film director)
OFF-BROADWAY THEATER 14:352–353 *bibliog.*
See also names of specific theaters, e.g., CIRCLE IN THE SQUARE; LIVING THEATER; etc.
Obie Awards **14**:316
OFF-OFF BROADWAY THEATER 14:353 *bibliog.*
OFF-ROAD BIKE *see* MOTORCYCLE
OFFA (Nigeria)
map (8° 9′N 4° 44′E) **14**:190
OFFA, KING OF MERCIA 14:353
OFFALY (Ireland) **14**:353
OFFA'S DYKE (Wales) **14**:353 *bibliog.*
Offa, King of Mercia **14**:353
OFFENBACH (Germany, East and West)
map (50° 8′N 8° 47′E) **9**:140
OFFENBACH, JACQUES 14:353–354 *bibliog., illus.*
OFFENBURG (Germany, East and West)
map (48° 28′N 7° 57′E) **9**:140
OFFICE MACHINES *see* BUSINESS MACHINES
OFFICE OF PERSONNEL MANAGEMENT *see* CIVIL SERVICE COMMISSION
OFFICE OF STRATEGIC SERVICES
Central Intelligence Agency **4**:254
OFFICE OF TECHNOLOGY ASSESSMENT, U.S.
technology **19**:60
OFFSET LITHOGRAPHY 14:354 *bibliog.*
collotype **5**:105
lithograph **12**:371
platemaking **15**:357–358 *illus.*
Senefelder, Aloys, inventor **17**:201
thermography **19**:166
OFFSHORE DRILLING *see* PETROLEUM INDUSTRY
O'FLAHERTY, LIAM 14:354 *bibliog.*
OFU (American Samoa) **1**:366 *map*
OFULA (Israel)
map (32° 38′N 35° 20′E) **11**:302
OGADEN (region in Ethiopia)
map (7° 0′N 46° 0′E) **7**:253
OGADEN (region in Ethiopia)
Somalia **18**:61
OGALLALA (Nebraska)
map (41° 8′N 101° 43′W) **14**:70
OGATA KENZAN *see* KENZAN
OGATA KORIN *see* KORIN
OGBOMOSHO (Nigeria)
map (8° 8′N 4° 15′E) **14**:190
OGBURN, WILLIAM FIELDING 14:354
culture lag **5**:386
OGDEN (Iowa)
map (42° 2′N 94° 2′W) **11**:244
OGDEN (Kansas)
map (39° 7′N 96° 43′W) **12**:18
OGDEN (Utah) **14**:354
map (41° 14′N 111° 58′W) **19**:492
OGDEN, C. K.
languages, artificial **12**:197
OGDEN, PETER SKENE
Nevada **14**:113
Utah **19**:495
OGDENSBURG (New Jersey)
map (41° 5′N 74° 36′W) **14**:129
OGDENSBURG (New York)
map (44° 42′N 75° 29′W) **14**:149
OGEECHEE RIVER
map (31° 51′N 81° 6′W) **9**:114
OGEMAW (county in Michigan)
map (44° 20′N 84° 5′W) **13**:377
OGHUZ *see* TURKMEN
OGHUZ LANGUAGES
Ural-Altaic languages **19**:476
OGILVIE MOUNTAINS
map (65° 0′N 139° 30′W) **20**:345
OGLALA (American Indians) *see* SIOUX
OGLE (county in Illinois)
map (42° 5′N 89° 20′W) **11**:42
OGLESBY (Illinois)
map (41° 18′N 89° 4′W) **11**:42
OGLETHORPE (Georgia)
map (32° 18′N 84° 4′W) **9**:114
OGLETHORPE (county in Georgia)
map (33° 50′N 83° 5′W) **9**:114
OGLETHORPE, JAMES 14:354 *bibliog.*
French and Indian Wars **8**:313
Georgia **9**:117
Savannah (Georgia) **17**:99
OGO (artificial satellite) **14**:354–355 *bibliog., table*
Cunningham, R. Walter **5**:390
scientific contributions **14**:355
OGOOUÉ RIVER
map (0° 49′S 9° 0′E) **9**:5
O'GORMAN, JUAN 14:355 *bibliog.*
OGUZ
Turkmen **19**:347
OH, SADAHARU 14:355 *bibliog.*
OHAIN, HANS VON
jet propulsion **11**:407
O'HAIR, MADALYN MURRAY
freedom of religion **8**:298
O'HARA, FRANK 14:355 *bibliog.*
O'HARA, JOHN 14:355–356 *bibliog.*
O'HIGGINS, BERNARDO 14:356 *bibliog., illus.*
Chile **4**:357
OHIO 14:356–362 *bibliog., illus., map*
agriculture **14**:359–360 *illus.*
cities
Akron **1**:231–232
Canton **4**:118
Chillocothe **4**:357
Cincinnati **4**:431–432 *illus.*
Cleveland **5**:52
Columbus **5**:127
Dayton **6**:57
Marietta **13**:152
Springfield **18**:200
Toledo **19**:226
Youngstown **20**:337
Zanesville **20**:355
climate **14**:358
cultural activity **14**:359
economic activities **14**:359–361 *illus.*
education **14**:359
Antioch College **2**:64
Case Western Reserve University **4**:180
Denison University **6**:108
Hebrew Union College **10**:101–102
McGuffey, William Holmes **13**:17
Oberlin College **14**:315
state universities of **14**:362
flag **14**:356 *illus.*
government **14**:361
Great Serpent Mound **13**:617 *illus.*
history **14**:361–362
Harding, Warren G. **10**:46
Northwest Territory **14**:259–260
Ohio Company of Associates **14**:362
Putnam, Rufus **15**:632
Zane, Ebenezer **20**:355
Indians of North America, art of the **11**:140
land and resources **14**:356–359 *map*
manufacturing **14**:360–361 *illus.*; **14**:362
map (40° 15′N 82° 45′W) **19**:419
mining **14**:360–361; **14**:362
people **14**:359–360 *illus.*
recreation **14**:360
rivers, lakes, and waterways **14**:358
seal, state **14**:356 *illus.*
transportation **14**:360–361 *illus.*; **14**:361–362
tree, state
buckeye **3**:535
vegetation and animal life **14**:358–359
OHIO (Illinois)
map (41° 34′N 89° 28′W) **11**:42
OHIO (county in Indiana)
map (38° 57′N 84° 51′W) **11**:111
OHIO (county in Kentucky)
map (37° 30′N 86° 50′W) **12**:47
OHIO (nuclear submarine) **14**:57 *illus.*
OHIO (county in West Virginia)
map (40° 7′N 80° 38′W) **20**:111
OHIO, STATE UNIVERSITIES OF 14:362
OHIO CITY (Ohio)
map (40° 46′N 84° 37′W) **14**:357
OHIO COMPANY 14:362 *bibliog.*
French and Indian Wars **8**:314
OHIO COMPANY OF ASSOCIATES 14:362 *bibliog.*
Cutler, Manasseh **5**:398
Ohio **14**:361
OHIO COMPANY OF VIRGINIA *see* OHIO COMPANY
OHIO RIVER 14:362–363
map (36° 59′N 89° 8′W) **13**:474
OHIRA MASAYOSHI 14:363
OHLIN, BERTIL 14:363
OHM 14:363
international ohm **14**:363
Ohm, Georg Simon **14**:363
units, physical **19**:466 *table*
OHM, GEORG SIMON 14:363 *bibliog.*
electricity **7**:109–110 *illus.*
Ohm's law **14**:363
OHM'S LAW 14:363 *bibliog.*
Cavendish, Henry **4**:226
circuit, electric **4**:436
Kirchhoff's laws **12**:87
Ohm, Georg Simon **14**:363
resistance, electrical **16**:177
OHŘE RIVER
map (50° 32′N 14° 8′E) **5**:413
OHRID (Yugoslavia)
map (41° 7′N 20° 47′E) **20**:340
OHRID, LAKE
map (41° 2′N 20° 43′E) **1**:250
OIAPOQUE (Brazil)
map (3° 50′N 51° 50′W) **3**:460
OIAPOQUE RIVER
map (4° 8′N 51° 40′W) **3**:460
OIL *see* FATS AND OILS; PETROLEUM; PETROLEUM INDUSTRY
OIL CENTER (New Mexico)
map (32° 30′N 103° 16′W) **14**:136
OIL CITY (Louisiana)
map (32° 45′N 93° 58′W) **12**:430
OIL CITY (Pennsylvania)
map (41° 26′N 79° 42′W) **15**:147
OIL-DROP EXPERIMENT *see* MILLIKAN'S OIL-DROP EXPERIMENT
OIL GAS 14:363
petroleum **15**:207–209
OIL LAMP
lamp **12**:175–176 *illus.*
OIL PAINTING
painting techniques **15**:24
OIL PALM *see* PALM (botany)
OIL SHALE *see* SHALE, OIL
OIL SPILLS 14:363–364 *bibliog.*
cleanup, prevention, and control **14**:364
ecological impact **14**:364
genetic engineering **9**:85
ocean and sea **14**:332
oil-soaked bird **15**:412 *illus.*
OIL TROUGH (Arkansas)
map (35° 38′N 91° 29′W) **2**:166
OILBIRD 14:364
OILDALE (California)
map (35° 25′N 119° 1′W) **4**:31
OILMONT (Montana)
map (48° 44′N 111° 51′W) **13**:547
OILTON (Oklahoma)
map (36° 5′N 96° 35′W) **14**:368
OILTON (Texas)
map (27° 33′N 98° 59′W) **19**:129
OISIN *see* OSSIAN
OISTRAKH, DAVID 14:364
OITA (Japan)
map (33° 14′N 131° 36′E) **11**:361
OJAI (California)
map (34° 27′N 119° 15′W) **4**:31
OJIBWA (American Indians) **14**:364 *bibliog., illus.*
Indians of North America, art of the **11**:141
Indians of North America, music and dance of the **11**:142 *illus.*
Ottawa (American Indians) **14**:460
Potawatomi **15**:466
Schoolcraft, Henry Rowe **17**:134
totem **19**:249
OJINAGA (Mexico)
map (29° 34′N 104° 25′W) **13**:357
OJOS DEL SALADO, MOUNT
map (27° 6′S 68° 32′W) **4**:355
OJUKWU, CHUKEMEKA ODUMEGWU 14:364–365 *bibliog.*
Biafra **3**:236
OK CORRAL, GUNFIGHT AT THE
Earp, Wyatt **7**:11
OKA RIVER
map (56° 20′N 43° 59′E) **19**:388
OKAIHAU (New Zealand)
map (35° 19′S 173° 47′E) **14**:158
OKALOOSA (county in Florida)
map (31° 45′N 86° 35′W) **8**:172
OKANAGAN CENTRE (British Columbia)
map (50° 3′N 119° 27′W) **3**:491
OKANAGAN LAKE
map (50° 0′N 119° 28′W) **3**:491
OKANAGAN LANDING (British Columbia)
map (50° 14′N 119° 22′W) **3**:491
OKANOGAN (American Indians) **14**:365 *bibliog.*
Spokan **18**:192
OKANOGAN (Washington)
map (48° 22′N 119° 35′W) **20**:35
OKANOGAN (county in Washington)
map (48° 39′N 120° 41′W) **20**:35
OKANOGAN RIVER
map (48° 6′N 119° 43′W) **20**:35
OKAPI 14:365 *illus.*
horn (biology) **10**:238
OKARA
map (30° 49′N 73° 27′E) **15**:27
OKARA, GABRIEL 14:365 *bibliog.*
OKARCHE (Oklahoma)
map (35° 44′N 97° 58′W) **14**:368
OKAVANGO RIVER
Botswana **3**:416
OKAVANGO SWAMP 14:365
Botswana **3**:416
map (18° 45′S 22° 45′E) **3**:416
OKAWVILLE (Illinois)
map (38° 26′N 89° 33′W) **11**:42
OKAYAMA (Japan)
map (34° 39′N 133° 55′E) **11**:361
OKE, J. BEVERLEY
quasar **16**:15
OKEECHOBEE (Florida)
map (27° 15′N 80° 50′W) **8**:172
OKEECHOBEE (county in Florida)
map (27° 25′N 80° 52′W) **8**:172
OKEECHOBEE, LAKE 14:365
Florida **8**:171
map (26° 55′N 80° 45′W) **8**:172
O'KEEFFE, GEORGIA 12:29 *illus.*; **14**:365–366 *bibliog., illus.*
Black Iris **14**:365 *illus.*
Stieglitz, Alfred **18**:267
OKEENE (Oklahoma)
map (36° 7′N 98° 19′W) **14**:368
OKEFENOKEE SWAMP 9:115 *illus.*; **14**:366
map (30° 42′N 82° 20′W) **9**:114
OKEGHEM, JEAN D' 14:366 *bibliog.*
mass (musical setting) **13**:201
music, history of Western **13**:663–664 *illus.*
OKEMAH (Oklahoma)
map (35° 26′N 96° 19′W) **14**:368
OKEN, LORENZ
cell **4**:231

OKENE (Nigeria)
map (7° 33′N 6° 15′E) **14**:190
OKFUSKEE (county in Oklahoma)
map (35° 30′N 96° 20′W) **14**:368
OKHOTSK, SEA OF **14**:366
map (53° 0′N 150° 0′E) **19**:388
OKI ISLANDS
map (36° 15′N 133° 15′E) **11**:361
OKIGBO, CHRISTOPHER **14**:366 *bibliog.*
OKINAGAN *see* OKANOGAN (American Indians)
OKINAWA **14**:366
map (26° 30′N 128° 0′E) **11**:361
navy **14**:64
Ryukyu Islands **16**:380
World War II **20**:277–278 *illus., map*
OKINAWA TROUGH
China Sea, East **4**:377
OKLAHOMA **14**:366–371 *bibliog., illus., map*
agriculture **14**:369 *illus.*
cities
Enid **7**:206
Lawton **12**:252
Muskogee **13**:683
Oklahoma City **14**:371–372
Tulsa **19**:331
climate **14**:367
cultural and historic sites **14**:369
Spiro Mound **18**:189
economic activities **14**:369–370 *illus.*
education **14**:369
state universities of **14**:371
flag **14**:367 *illus.*
government **14**:370
history **14**:370
Gore, Thomas P. **9**:250
Indian Territory **11**:106
land and resources **14**:366–368 *illus., map*
manufacturing **14**:369
map (35° 30′N 98° 0′W) **19**:419
mining **14**:369
musical comedy **13**:674 *illus.*
natural resources **14**:367
people **14**:367; **14**:369
Apache **2**:73
Caddo **4**:11
Cayuga **4**:227
Cherokee **4**:332
Cheyenne **4**:338
Chickasaw **4**:345
Choctaw **4**:402–403
Comanche **5**:129–130
Creek **5**:337
Delaware **6**:91
Huron **10**:316–317
Illinois **11**:45
Iowa **11**:248
Kansa **12**:16
Kickapoo **12**:70
Kiowa **12**:86
Miami **13**:370
Missouri **13**:480
Osage **14**:451–452
Oto **14**:460
Ottawa **14**:460
Pawnee **15**:121
Quapaw **16**:12
Sauk **17**:96
Seminole **14**:197; **17**:197
Shawnee **14**:246–247
Wichita **20**:144
rivers, lakes, and waterways **14**:367
seal, state **14**:367 *illus.*
vegetation and animal life **14**:367
OKLAHOMA! (musical) **13**:674 *illus.*
OKLAHOMA (county in Oklahoma)
map (35° 35′N 97° 25′W) **14**:368
OKLAHOMA, STATE UNIVERSITIES OF **14**:371
OKLAHOMA CITY (Oklahoma) **14**:370 *illus.*; **14**:371–372
map (35° 28′N 97° 32′W) **14**:368
rodeo **16**:266
OKLAWAHA (Florida)
map (29° 3′N 81° 56′W) **8**:172
OKMULGEE (Oklahoma)
map (35° 37′N 95° 58′W) **14**:368
OKMULGEE (county in Oklahoma)
map (35° 40′N 95° 55′W) **14**:368
OKOLONA (Arkansas)
map (34° 0′N 93° 20′W) **2**:166
OKOLONA (Kentucky)
map (38° 8′N 85° 41′W) **12**:47
OKOLONA (Mississippi)
map (34° 0′N 88° 45′W) **13**:469
OKOT P'BITEK
African literature **1**:168
OKRA **14**:372 *illus.*
OKTIBBEHA (county in Mississippi)
map (33° 25′N 88° 55′W) **13**:469
OKUMA SHIGENOBU **14**:372 *bibliog.*
Hiroshige **10**:175
OKUMURA MASANOBU *see* MASANOBU (1686–1764)
OKVIK (Alaska) **7**:239 *map*; **14**:372 *bibliog.*
Eskimo **7**:241
OKYO **14**:372 *bibliog.*
OLA (Arkansas)
map (35° 2′N 93° 13′W) **2**:166
OLAF I, KING OF NORWAY **14**:372–373
Sweyn, King of Denmark **18**:388
Trondheim (Norway) **19**:306
OLAF II, KING OF NORWAY (Saint Olaf) **14**:373
Trondheim (Norway) **19**:306
OLAF V, KING OF NORWAY **14**:373
ÓLAFSFJÖRDUR (Iceland)
map (66° 6′N 18° 38′W) **11**:17
OLANCHA (California)
map (36° 17′N 118° 1′W) **4**:31
ÖLAND (Sweden) **18**:384 *illus.*
map (56° 45′N 16° 38′E) **18**:382
OLAR (South Carolina)
map (33° 11′N 81° 11′W) **18**:98
OLATHE (Colorado)
map (38° 36′N 107° 59′W) **5**:116
OLATHE (Kansas)
map (38° 53′N 94° 49′W) **12**:18
OLAVARRÍA (Argentina)
map (36° 54′S 60° 17′W) **2**:149
OLBERS, HEINRICH **14**:373
Olbers's paradox **14**:373
OLBERS'S PARADOX **14**:373
OLBRICH, JOSEPH MARIA **14**:373 *bibliog.*
OLCOTT (New York)
map (43° 20′N 78° 43′W) **14**:149
OLD AGE **14**:373–374 *bibliog.*
See also GERIATRICS
ACTION (federal agency) **1**:89
adult education **1**:110
aging **1**:185–186
American Association of Retired Persons **1**:336–337
discrimination **6**:190
Gray Panthers **9**:307
hospital **10**:258
life span **12**:330–331
Medicare **13**:265
nursing home **14**:299–300
senility **17**:203
social security **18**:14–16
social and welfare services **18**:17
United States, poverty **15**:478
OLD AGE, SURVIVORS, AND DISABILITY INSURANCE (OASDI)
social security **18**:14–15
OLD BAHAMA CHANNEL
map (22° 30′N 78° 50′W) **5**:377
OLD BELIEVERS **14**:374 *bibliog.*
Nikon **14**:195–196
Russia/Union of Soviet Socialist Republics, history of **16**:354
OLD BERING SEA CULTURE **7**:239 *map*
Eskimo **7**:241
Okvik **14**:372
OLD BUDDHA *see* TZ'U-HSI (Cixi), DOWAGER EMPEROR OF CHINA
OLD CATHOLICS **14**:374 *bibliog.*
OLD CHURCH SLAVONIC *see* SLAVIC LANGUAGES
OLD CROW (Yukon Territory)
map (67° 35′N 139° 50′W) **20**:345
OLD CURIOSITY SHOP, THE (book) **14**:274 *illus.*
OLD ENGLISH **14**:374–375 *bibliog.*
Ælfric **1**:118
Anglo-Saxon Chronicle, The **2**:3
Beowulf **3**:207
English language **7**:191
Exeter Book **7**:331
literature **7**:193
Tolkien, J. R. R. **19**:226–227
OLD ENGLISH LITERATURE *see* ENGLISH LITERATURE
OLD ENGLISH SHEEPDOG **6**:214 *illus.*; **14**:375 *bibliog., illus.*
bearded collie **3**:142
OLD FAITHFUL **14**:375; **20**:302 *illus.*
geyser **9**:162–163 *illus.*
OLD FORGE (New York)
map (43° 43′N 74° 58′W) **14**:149
OLD FORGE (Pennsylvania)
map (41° 22′N 75° 44′W) **15**:147
OLD FRITZ *see* FREDERICK II, KING OF PRUSSIA (Frederick the Great)
OLD FUSS AND FEATHERS *see* SCOTT, WINFIELD
OLD HICKORY *see* JACKSON, ANDREW
OLD HICKORY LAKE
map (36° 18′N 86° 30′W) **19**:104
OLD IRONSIDES (locomotive)
Baldwin, Matthias W. **3**:35
OLD IRONSIDES (ship) *see* *CONSTITUTION* (ship)
OLD LONDON BRIDGE *see* LONDON BRIDGE
OLD MAN AND THE SEA, THE (book) **14**:375 *bibliog.*
OLD NORSE *see* ICELANDIC LITERATURE
"OLD OAKEN BUCKET, THE" (song)
Woodworth, Samuel **20**:213
OLD ORCHARD BEACH (Maine)
map (43° 31′N 70° 23′W) **13**:70
OLD PEOPLE *see* OLD AGE
OLD PRETENDER *see* STUART, JAMES FRANCIS EDWARD
OLD PRUSSIAN LANGUAGE *see* BALTIC LANGUAGES
OLD RED SANDSTONE
Devonian Period **6**:144–146
Sedgwick, Adam **17**:183
OLD REGIME *see* FRANCE, HISTORY OF
OLD ROUGH AND READY *see* TAYLOR, ZACHARY
OLD SAYBROOK (Connecticut)
map (41° 18′N 72° 23′W) **5**:193
OLD SPECK MOUNTAIN
map (44° 34′N 70° 57′W) **13**:70
OLD STONE AGE *see* PALEOLITHIC PERIOD
OLD TESTAMENT *see* BIBLE
OLD TIP *see* HARRISON, WILLIAM HENRY
OLD TOWN (Maine)
map (44° 56′N 68° 39′W) **13**:70
OLD VIC THEATRE **14**:375 *bibliog.*
Guthrie, Sir Tyrone **9**:409
OLD WHALING CULTURE **7**:239 *map*
Eskimo **7**:241
OLD WIVES LAKE
map (50° 6′N 106° 0′W) **17**:81
OLDENBARNEVELT, JOHAN VAN **14**:375 *bibliog.*
Maurice of Nassau, Prince of Orange **13**:235
OLDENBURG (West Germany) **14**:375–376
map (53° 8′N 8° 13′E) **9**:140
OLDENBURG, CLAES **14**:376 *bibliog., illus.*
happenings **10**:41
Saw **14**:376 *illus.*
OLDENBURG DYNASTY
Christian I, King of Denmark **4**:412
OLDENZAAL (Netherlands)
map (52° 19′N 6° 56′E) **14**:99
OLDFIELD, BARNEY **14**:376 *bibliog.*
OLDHAM (England)
map (53° 33′N 2° 7′W) **19**:403
OLDHAM (county in Kentucky)
map (38° 23′N 85° 27′W) **12**:47
OLDHAM (South Dakota)
map (44° 14′N 97° 19′W) **18**:103
OLDHAM (county in Texas)
map (35° 23′N 102° 38′W) **19**:129
OLDHAM, JOHN **14**:376
OLDOWAN **14**:376 *bibliog.*
African prehistory **1**:173
Australopithecus **2**:346
Chellean **4**:311
Homo erectus **10**:216
Olduvai Gorge **14**:377
Paleolithic Period **15**:39
prehistoric humans **15**:513
OLDS (Alberta)
map (51° 47′N 114° 6′W) **1**:256
OLDS, JAMES **14**:376
OLDS, RANSOM E.
automotive industry **2**:363
Lansing (Michigan) **12**:200
OLDUVAI GORGE (Tanzania) **14**:376–377 *bibliog., illus.*
African prehistory **1**:173
archaeology **2**:117 *illus.*
Australopithecus **2**:346 *illus.*
Homo habilis **10**:216
Leakey (family) **12**:258–259
map (2° 58′S 35° 22′E) **19**:27
Oldowan **14**:376
Paleolithic Period **15**:38; **15**:39
OLEAN (New York)
map (42° 5′N 78° 26′W) **14**:149
OLEANDER **13**:377 *illus.*
O'LEARY (Prince Edward Island)
map (46° 42′N 64° 13′W) **15**:548
OLEASTER **13**:377
buffalo berry **3**:546
OLEFIN *see* ALKENE
OLENTANGY RIVER
map (39° 58′N 83° 6′W) **14**:357
OLEOMARGARINE *see* MARGARINE
OLEORESINS
fir **8**:100
OLÉRON ISLAND
map (45° 56′N 1° 15′W) **8**:260
OLESHA, YURY **14**:377 *bibliog.*
OLHÃO (Portugal)
map (37° 2′N 7° 50′W) **15**:449
OLIFANTS RIVER
map (24° 10′S 32° 40′E) **18**:79
OLIGARCHY **14**:377
OLIGOCENE EPOCH
extinct mammals **13**:102–103 *illus.*
geologic time **9**:104 *table*
Mesohippus **10**:245 *illus.*
Tertiary Period **19**:123
OLIGOSACCHARIDE **14**:378
ÓLIMBOS *see* OLYMPUS, MOUNT (Greece)
OLIN (Iowa)
map (42° 0′N 91° 9′W) **11**:244
OLINGO **14**:378 *illus.*
OLIPHANT, PATRICK **14**:378
OLITSKI, JULES **14**:378 *bibliog.*
OLIVA, PEACE OF
Thirty Years' War **19**:171
OLIVARES, GASPAR DE GUZMÁN, CONDE-DUQUE DE **14**:378 *bibliog.*
Philip IV, King of Spain **15**:235
Spain, history of **18**:147
OLIVE **7**:270 *illus.*; **8**:348 *illus.*; **14**:378–379 *bibliog., illus.*
ash **2**:228
forsythia **8**:236
fringe tree **8**:334
jasmine **11**:304
lilac **12**:340
Spain **18**:141 *illus.*
OLIVE HILL (Kentucky)
map (38° 16′N 83° 10′W) **12**:47
OLIVER (British Columbia)
map (49° 11′N 119° 33′W) **3**:491
OLIVER (county in North Dakota)
map (47° 10′N 101° 20′W) **14**:248
OLIVER, ISAAC **13**:445 *illus.*; **14**:379 *bibliog.*
OLIVER, JACK ERTLE
plate tectonics **15**:357
OLIVER, JAMES
plow **15**:369
OLIVER, KING **14**:379
jazz **11**:388 *illus.*
King Oliver's Jazz Band **1**:351 *illus.*
Armstrong, Louis **2**:179
OLIVER SPRINGS (Tennessee)
map (36° 3′N 84° 20′W) **19**:104
OLIVER TWIST (book) **14**:379 *bibliog.*
Dickens, Charles **6**:156–157
poor laws **15**:429
OLIVES, MOUNT OF *see* MOUNT OF OLIVES
OLIVET (South Dakota)
map (43° 14′N 97° 40′W) **18**:103
OLIVIA (Minnesota)
map (44° 46′N 94° 59′W) **13**:453
OLIVIER, LAURENCE KERR, BARON OLIVIER OF BRIGHTON **14**:379 *bibliog., illus.*
as Richard III **1**:87 *illus.*
National Theatre **14**:46
OLIVINE **14**:379–380 *bibliog., illus., table*
diabase **6**:148
formation **14**:379
occurrence **14**:380
peridot **15**:166
silicate minerals **14**:379; **17**:305
solid solution **18**:54
types **14**:380 *table*
volcanic bombs **14**:380
OLLA (Louisiana)
map (31° 54′N 92° 14′W) **12**:430
OLLAGÜE (Chile)
map (21° 14′S 68° 16′W) **4**:355
OLLANTAITAMBO (Peru)
map (13° 16′S 72° 16′W) **15**:193
OLLIVIER, EMILE
Liszt, Franz **12**:367
OLLIVIER, MICHEL
Wolfgang Amadeus Mozart **13**:665 *illus.*
OLMEC **14**:380 *bibliog., illus.*
art **2**:125 *illus.*
pre-Columbian art and architecture **15**:496 *illus.*
Izapa **11**:338
La Venta **12**:151
Latin America, history of **12**:216
San Lorenzo **17**:55
OLMEDO, JOSÉ JOAQUIN
Latin American literature **12**:229

OLMOS (Peru)
map (5° 59′S 79° 46′W) **15**:193
OLMSTEAD v. UNITED STATES
wiretapping **20**:183
OLMSTED (county in Minnesota)
map (44° 0′N 92° 23′W) **13**:453
OLMSTED, FREDERICK LAW **14**:380 *bibliog.*
Burnham, Daniel Hudson **3**:577
landscape architecture **12**:188
OLNEY (Illinois)
map (38° 44′N 88° 5′W) **11**:42
OLNEY (Montana)
map (48° 33′N 114° 35′W) **13**:547
OLNEY (Texas)
map (33° 22′N 98° 45′W) **19**:129
OLNEY, RICHARD **14**:381 *bibliog.*
Pullman Strike **15**:619
Venezuela Boundary Dispute **19**:544
OLOMOUC (Czechoslovakia)
map (49° 36′N 17° 16′E) **5**:413
OLORGESAILIE (Kenya) **14**:381 *bibliog.*
OLOSEGA (American Samoa) **1**:366 *map*
OLSEN, TILLIE **14**:381 *bibliog.*
OLSON, CHARLES **14**:381 *bibliog.*
happenings **10**:41
OLSON, FLOYD B.
Farmer-Labor party **8**:24
Minnesota **13**:456
OLSZEWSKI, KAROL S.
cryogenics **5**:370
OLSZTYN (Poland)
map (53° 48′N 20° 29′E) **15**:388
OLT RIVER
map (43° 43′N 24° 51′E) **16**:288
OLTEN (Switzerland)
map (47° 21′N 7° 54′E) **18**:394
OLTON (Texas)
map (34° 11′N 102° 8′W) **19**:129
OLTOS **14**:381 *bibliog.*
OLUSTEE (Oklahoma)
map (34° 33′N 99° 25′W) **14**:368
OLYMPIA (Greece) **14**:381 *bibliog.*
Curtius, Ernst Robert **5**:396
Greek art **9**:337; **9**:340
Olympic Games **14**:382
Statue of Zeus at Olympia **17**:217 *illus.*
OLYMPIA (Washington) **14**:382
map (47° 3′N 122° 53′W) **20**:35
OLYMPIAS **14**:382
Roxana **16**:328
OLYMPIC GAMES **14**:382–385 *bibliog., illus.*
basketball
Bradley, Bill **3**:437
Knight, Bobby **12**:100
Rupp, Adolph **16**:347
Russell, Bill **16**:350
biathlon **3**:237
bobsledding **3**:353
boxing **3**:431–432
boycott **3**:433
Brundage, Avery **3**:523
canoeing and kayaking **4**:114
decathlon **6**:72
Jenner, Bruce **11**:396
Johnson, Rafer **11**:435
Mathias, Bob **13**:228
Thompson, Daley **19**:174
diving **6**:203 *illus.*
Louganis, Greg **12**:421
documentary
Riefenstahl, Leni **16**:218
fencing **8**:49
figure skating
Button, Dick **3**:600
Fleming, Peggy **8**:159
Hamill, Dorothy **10**:27
Hamilton, Scott **10**:29
gold medal winners **14**:383–385 *illus.*
gymnastics **9**:413–414 *illus.*
Comaneci, Nadia **5**:130
Korbut, Olga **12**:111
Latynina, Larisa **12**:236
horse show **10**:250
Steinkraus, Bill **18**:249
ice skating **11**:14
Los Angeles, 1984 **14**:383 *illus.*
Ueberroth, Peter **19**:371
lottery **12**:420
marathon **13**:143–144
Benoit, Joan **3**:204
Bikila, Abebe **3**:250
Shorter, Frank **17**:284
Moscow **13**:599
Munich (West Germany) **13**:641
Olympia (Greece) **14**:381
Pan-American Games **15**:53
pentathlon **15**:155
political overtones **14**:383–384
shooting **17**:282 *illus.*
skiing **17**:339 *illus.*
Killy, Jean Claude **12**:77
Mahre (brothers) **13**:66
Sailer, Toni **17**:15
soccer
Yashin, Lev **20**:319
Special Olympics **18**:168
speed skating
Heiden, Eric **10**:107
sports, history of **18**:195–196
stadium **18**:208
swimming **18**:390–391 *illus.*
Fraser, Dawn **8**:287
McCormick, Patricia **13**:10
Schollander, Don **17**:133
Spitz, Mark **18**:190
Weissmuller, Johnny **20**:96
track and field **19**:259–262 *illus.*
Beamon, Bob **3**:139
Blankers-Koen, Fanny **3**:327
Coe, Sebastian **5**:90
Elliott, Herb **7**:147
Keino, Kipchoge **12**:37
Lewis, Carl **12**:305
Moses, Edwin **13**:600
Nurmi, Paavo **14**:298
O'Brien, Parry **14**:317
Oerter, Al **14**:352
Owens, Jesse **14**:472
Richards, Bob **16**:211
Rudolph, Wilma **16**:339
Ryun, Jim **16**:380
Snell, Peter **18**:3
Thorpe, Jim **19**:180
Viren, Lasse **19**:604–605
Zaharias, Babe Didrikson **20**:348
Zatopek, Emil **20**:356–357
weight lifting
Alexeyev, Vasily **1**:278
wrestling **20**:287 *illus.*
OLYMPIC NATIONAL FOREST **14**:229 *illus.*
OLYMPIC NATIONAL PARK **19**:424 *illus.*; **20**:37 *illus.*
OLYMPIO, SYLVANUS
Togo **19**:222
OLYMPUS, MOUNT (Greece) **14**:385
map (40° 5′N 22° 21′E) **9**:325
Olympic Games **14**:383 *illus.*
OLYMPUS, MOUNT (Washington)
map (47° 48′N 123° 43′W) **20**:35
OLYMPUS MONS (Mars) **13**:167 *illus.*
OLYMPUS MOUNTAIN (Cyprus)
map (34° 56′N 32° 52′E) **5**:409
OLYNTHUS (Greece) **14**:385 *bibliog.*
OMAGUAS (Peru)
map (4° 8′S 73° 15′W) **15**:193
OMAHA (American Indians) **14**:385 *bibliog.*
Fletcher, Alice **8**:163
Mississippian culture **14**:239
Quapaw **16**:12
Sun dance **18**:346
OMAHA (Nebraska) **14**:73 *illus.*; **14**:385
map (41° 16′N 95° 57′W) **14**:70
OMAK (Washington)
map (48° 24′N 119° 31′W) **20**:35
OMAN **2**:103 *illus.*; **14**:385–387 *bibliog., illus., map, table*
cities
Muscat **13**:651
flag **14**:386 *illus.*
government **14**:387
history **14**:387
land, people, and economy **14**:385–387 *illus.*
map (22° 0′N 58° 0′E) **2**:232
OMAN, GULF OF **14**:387
Hormuz, Strait of **10**:238
map (24° 30′N 58° 30′E) **2**:232
OMAR (West Virginia)
map (37° 46′N 82° 0′W) **20**:111
OMAR KHAYYAM **14**:387 *bibliog.*
Rubaiyat of Omar Khayyam **16**:332
OMBALANTU
Ovambo **14**:469
OMBOS **14**:387
OMBU **13**:387
OMBUDSMAN **14**:387 *bibliog.*
Denmark **6**:112
OMDURMAN (Sudan) **14**:387
map (15° 38′N 32° 30′E) **18**:320
OMEGA (Georgia)
map (31° 21′N 83° 36′W) **9**:114
OMEN **14**:387 *bibliog.*
OMETEPE ISLAND
map (11° 30′N 85° 35′W) **14**:179
OMETEPEC (Mexico)
map (16° 41′N 98° 25′W) **13**:357
OMICRON
O (letter) **14**:310
OMNIBUS *see* BUS
OMO (Ethiopia) **14**:387–388 *bibliog.*
Afroasiatic languages **1**:179–180 *map*
Leakey (family) **12**:259
OMO RIVER
map (4° 51′N 36° 55′E) **7**:253
OMPHACTIE
pyroxene **15**:638
OMPHALOS
Apollo **2**:80
OMRIDE (dynasty)
Samaria **17**:45
OMRO (Wisconsin)
map (44° 2′N 88° 44′W) **20**:185
OMSK (USSR) **14**:388
map (55° 0′N 73° 24′E) **19**:388
OMULEW RIVER
map (53° 5′N 21° 32′E) **15**:388
OMUTA (Japan)
map (33° 2′N 130° 27′E) **11**:361
ON AGGRESSION (book) **14**:388
ON LIBERTY (book) **14**:388
ON THE NATURE OF THINGS (poem) *see DE RERUM NATURA*
ON-LINE COMPUTER **5**:160h; **14**:388 *bibliog.*
ON-THE-JOB TRAINING *see* CAREER EDUCATION
ON THE ROAD (book) **14**:388
Kerouac, Jack **12**:59
ON WAR (book)
Clausewitz, Carl Philipp Gottfried von **5**:44–45
ONAGA (Kansas)
map (39° 29′N 96° 10′W) **12**:18
ONAGER (animal)
ass **2**:263
ONAGER (military device)
fortification **8**:238
ONALASKA (Wisconsin)
map (43° 53′N 91° 14′W) **20**:185
ONANCOCK (Virginia)
map (37° 43′N 75° 45′W) **19**:607
ONANGUZZE, LAKE
map (0° 57′S 10° 4′E) **9**:5
ONARGA (Illinois)
map (40° 43′N 88° 1′W) **11**:42
ONASSIS, ARISTOTLE **14**:388 *bibliog.*
Onassis, Jacqueline Bouvier Kennedy **14**:388
ONASSIS, JACQUELINE BOUVIER KENNEDY **14**:388 *bibliog.*; **19**:568 *illus.*
Kennedy, John F. **12**:42
OÑATE, JUAN DE **14**:388–389
exploration of colonial America **19**:437 *map*
ONAWA (Iowa)
map (42° 2′N 96° 6′W) **11**:244
ONCHOCERCIASIS *see* RIVER BLINDNESS
ONCOGENE **14**:389 *bibliog.*
cancer **4**:102
retrovirus **16**:184
ONCOLOGY *see* CANCER
ONDONGA
Ovambo **14**:469
ONE DAY IN THE LIFE OF IVAN DENISOVICH (book) **14**:389 *bibliog.*
ONE FLEW OVER THE CUCKOO'S NEST (book) **14**:389 *bibliog.*
Kesey, Ken **12**:61
ONE FLEW OVER THE CUCKOO'S NEST (film)
Forman, Milos **8**:234
ONE HUNDRED YEARS OF SOLITUDE (book)
García Márquez, Gabriel **9**:39
ONE OF OURS (book)
Cather, Willa **4**:208–209
O'NEALE, MARGARET *see* EATON, MARGARET (Peggy) O'NEALE
ONECO (Florida)
map (27° 27′N 82° 33′W) **8**:172
ONEGA, LAKE **14**:389
map (61° 30′N 35° 45′E) **19**:388
ONEHUNGA (New Zealand)
map (36° 56′S 174° 47′E) **14**:158
ONEIDA (American Indians) **14**:389 *bibliog.*
Iroquois League **11**:279–280
Mahican **13**:65
Susquehanna (American Indians) **18**:372
Williams, Eleazer **20**:159
ONEIDA (county in Idaho)
map (42° 10′N 112° 35′W) **11**:26
ONEIDA (Illinois)
map (41° 4′N 90° 13′W) **11**:42
ONEIDA (Kentucky)
map (37° 16′N 83° 39′W) **12**:47
ONEIDA (New York)
map (43° 6′N 75° 39′W) **14**:149
ONEIDA (county in New York)
map (43° 15′N 75° 30′W) **14**:149
ONEIDA (Tennessee)
map (36° 30′N 84° 31′W) **19**:104
ONEIDA (county in Wisconsin)
map (45° 42′N 89° 30′W) **20**:185
ONEIDA COMMUNITY **14**:389 *bibliog.*
Noyes, John Humphrey **14**:277
utopias **19**:498
ONEIDA LAKE
map (43° 13′N 76° 0′W) **14**:149
O'NEILL (Nebraska)
map (42° 27′N 98° 39′W) **14**:70
O'NEILL, EUGENE **1**:346 *illus.*; **14**:389–390 *bibliog., illus.*
Baker, George Pierce **3**:27
drama **6**:261
Emperor Jones, The **7**:158
Hairy Ape, The **10**:14–15
Jones, Robert Edmond **11**:444
masks **13**:196
New London (Connecticut) **14**:134
Provincetown Players **15**:584
O'NEILL, HENRY NELSON
Eastward Ho **5**:349 *illus.*
O'NEILL, HUGH, 2D EARL OF TYRONE *see* TYRONE, HUGH O'NEILL, 2D EARL OF
O'NEILL, JAMES **14**:390
O'NEILL, TERENCE
Ireland, history of **11**:265
O'NEILL, THOMAS P. **14**:390
ONEKAMA (Michigan)
map (44° 22′N 86° 12′W) **13**:377
ONEONTA (Alabama)
map (33° 57′N 86° 29′W) **1**:234
ONEONTA (New York)
map (42° 27′N 75° 4′W) **14**:149
ONESIMOS **14**:390 *bibliog.*
ONEZHSKOYE OZERO *see* ONEGA, LAKE
ONGANDJERA
Ovambo **14**:469
ONGARUE (New Zealand)
map (38° 43′S 175° 17′E) **14**:158
ONIDA (South Dakota)
map (44° 42′N 100° 4′W) **18**:103
ONIN WAR
Japan, history of **11**:368
ONION **14**:390–391 *bibliog., illus.*; **19**:534 *illus.*
chive **4**:399
leek **12**:271
shallot **17**:238
ONITSHA (Nigeria)
map (6° 9′N 6° 47′E) **14**:190
ONIZUKA, ELLISON **14**:391
ONNES, HEIKE KAMERLINGH *see* KAMERLINGH ONNES, HEIKE
ONOMATOPOEIA
versification **19**:562
ONON RIVER
map (51° 42′N 115° 50′E) **13**:529
ONONDAGA (American Indians) **14**:391 *bibliog.*
Iroquois League **11**:279–280
Syracuse (New York) **18**:410
ONONDAGA (county in New York)
map (43° 3′N 76° 9′W) **14**:149
ONSAGER, LARS **14**:391
ONSET (Massachusetts)
map (41° 45′N 70° 39′W) **13**:206
ONSLOW (county in North Carolina)
map (34° 45′N 77° 20′W) **14**:242
ONSLOW BAY
map (34° 20′N 77° 20′W) **14**:242
ONTARIO (California)
map (34° 4′N 117° 39′W) **4**:31
ONTARIO (Canada) **14**:391–395 *bibliog., illus., map*
cities
Brantford **3**:456
Hamilton **10**:27
Kingston **12**:84
Kitchener **12**:91
London **12**:402
Niagara Falls **14**:177
Oshawa **14**:453
Ottawa **4**:76 *illus.*; **14**:460–461 *illus., map*
Saint Catharines **17**:17
Sault Saint Marie **17**:96
Sudbury **18**:322
Thunder Bay **19**:184
Toronto **4**:69 *illus.*; **19**:240–242 *illus., map*
Windsor **20**:174
climate **14**:391
cultural attractions **14**:394
economic activity **14**:394 *illus.*
education **14**:394
Brock University **4**:92 *table*
Canadian education **4**:91
Carleton University **4**:92 *table*; **4**:151
Guelph, University of **4**:92 *table*
Kingston, Queen's University at **4**:92 *table*
Lakehead University **4**:92 *table*
McMaster University **4**:92 *table*; **13**:33

Ottawa, University of 4:92 *table*; 14:461
Queen's 16:22
Royal Military College of Canada 4:92 *table*
Ryerson Polytechnical Institute 4:92 *table*
Sudbury, Laurentian University of 4:92 *table*
Toronto, University of 4:92 *table*; 19:242
Trent University 4:92 *table*
Waterloo, University of 4:92 *table*
Western Ontario, University of 4:92 *table*; 20:116
Wilfrid Laurier University 4:92 *table*
Windsor, University of 4:92 *table*; 20:174
York University 4:92 *table*; 20:331
flag 14:392 *illus.*
government 14:395
history 14:395
historic sites 14:395
Macdonald, John Sandfield 13:12
Mackenzie, William Lyon 13:28
Mowat, Sir Oliver 13:626
Rebellions of 1837 16:105
Simcoe, John Graves 17:313
land and resources 14:391–393 *map*
Manitoulin Islands 13:122
manufacturing 4:77
map (51° 0′N 85° 0′W) 4:70
people 14:392–394
Cayuga 4:227
Delaware 6:91
Huron 10:316–317
Oneida 14:389
Onondaga 14:391
Seneca 17:200
rivers, lakes, and waterways 14:391–392
Georgian Bay 9:118
Welland Ship Canal 20:99
ONTARIO (county in New York)
map (42° 54′N 77° 17′W) 14:149
ONTARIO (Ohio)
map (40° 46′N 82° 39′W) 14:357
ONTARIO (Oregon)
map (44° 2′N 116° 58′W) 14:427
ONTARIO, LAKE 14:395–396 *map*; 20:66 *illus.*
map (43° 45′N 78° 0′W) 9:320
ONTOGENY 14:396
phylogeny 15:278–279
ONTOLOGY
metaphysics 13:334–335
ONTONAGON (Michigan)
map (46° 52′N 89° 19′W) 13:377
ONTONAGON (county in Michigan)
map (46° 40′N 89° 20′W) 13:377
ONVERWACHT (Suriname)
map (5° 36′N 55° 12′W) 18:364
ONYCHOPHORAN 14:396
invertebrate 11:235
Peripatus 15:171
ONYX 14:396 *illus.*
quartz 16:14
OOGENESIS
egg 7:72
OOKA SHOHEI 14:396
OOLITE 14:396
limestone 12:345
OOLITIC (Indiana)
map (38° 54′N 86° 31′W) 11:111
OOLOGAH (Oklahoma)
map (36° 28′N 95° 42′W) 14:368
OOLOGAH LAKE
map (36° 33′N 95° 36′W) 14:368
OOLTEWAH (Tennessee)
map (35° 4′N 85° 4′W) 19:104
OOPHORECTOMY
sex change 17:224
OOPHORITIS
mumps 13:639
OORT, JAN HENDRIK 2:281 *illus.*; 14:396 *bibliog.*
astronomy, history of 2:280
comet, solar system 18:51
OOS-LONDEN *see* EAST LONDON (South Africa)
OOSTBURG (Wisconsin)
map (43° 37′N 87° 48′W) 20:185
OOSTENDE (Belgium) *see* OSTEND (Belgium)
OOSTERHOUT (Netherlands)
map (51° 38′N 4° 51′E) 14:99
OOSTERSCHELDE
map (51° 30′N 4° 0′E) 14:99
OOZE, DEEP-SEA 14:396–397
deep-sea life 6:79
ocean and sea 14:332
Recent Epoch 16:106
sediment, marine 17:184
OP ART 14:397 *bibliog., illus.*
Anuszkiewicz, Richard 2:72
graphic arts 9:294
illusionism 11:49–50
painting 15:23
Vasarely, Victor 19:525
OPA LOCKA (Florida)
map (25° 54′N 80° 15′W) 8:172
OPAH 8:116 *illus.*; 13:566 *illus.*; 14:397
OPAL 3:296 *illus., table*; 9:74 *illus.*; 14:397 *illus.*
Querétaro (state in Mexico) 16:23
silica minerals 17:304
OPARIN, ALEKSANDR IVANOVICH 14:397
OPAVA (Czechoslovakia)
map (49° 56′N 17° 54′E) 5:413
OPEC *see* ORGANIZATION OF PETROLEUM EXPORTING COUNTRIES
OPECHANCANOUGH
Virginia 19:611
OPEL
automotive industry 2:364
OPELIKA (Alabama)
map (32° 39′N 85° 23′W) 1:234
OPELOUSAS (Louisiana)
map (30° 32′N 92° 5′W) 12:430
OPEN ADMISSION 14:398 *bibliog.*
OPEN CLASSROOM 14:398 *bibliog.*
free schools 8:294–295
OPEN DOOR POLICY 14:398 *bibliog.*
OPEN-HEARTH PROCESS 14:398
furnace 8:372
iron and steel industry 11:276
OPEN-PIT MINING *see* STRIP MINING
OPEN SHOP 14:398 *bibliog.*
OPEN THEATRE
Chaikin, Joseph 4:268
Van Itallie, Jean Claude 19:515
OPEN UNIVERSITY 14:399 *bibliog.*
British education 3:495
OPEQUON CREEK
map (39° 35′N 77° 52′W) 13:188
OPERA 14:399–401 *bibliog., illus.*
See also COMIC OPERA; METROPOLITAN OPERA; OPERETTA
aria 2:153
baroque music 3:91–92
bel canto 3:173
Bing, Sir Rudolf 3:258
China
Peking Opera 15:136
classical period in music 5:42
conductors
Böhm, Karl 3:361
Caldwell, Sarah 4:27
Mahler, Gustav 13:65
Czechoslovakia
Janáček, Leoš 11:358
Smetana, Bedřich 17:366
Weinberger, Jaromír 20:95
Denmark
Langgaard, Rued 12:195
England
Balfe, Michael William 3:37
Bishop, Sir Henry Rowley 3:297
Blow, John 3:341
Britten, Benjamin 3:498–499
Covent Garden 5:319
Davenant, Sir William 6:46
Davies, Peter Maxwell 6:50
Glyndebourne Opera Festival 9:212
Holst, Gustav 10:208
Tippett, Michael 19:207
Vaughan Williams, Ralph 19:528–529
France
Auber, Daniel François Esprit 2:316
Bizet, Georges 3:301–302
Charpentier, Gustave 4:299
Cherubini, Luigi 4:333
Delibes, Léo 6:93
French music 8:320
Gluck, Christoph Willibald 9:211
Gounod, Charles 9:266
Grétry, André 9:359
Halévy, Jacques 10:19
Lully, Jean Baptiste 12:454
Massenet, Jules 13:213
Meyerbeer, Giacomo 13:369
Milhaud, Darius 13:419–420
Mussorgsky, Modest 13:685
Offenbach, Jacques 14:353–354
Poulenc, Francis 15:473
Rameau, Jean Philippe 16:80
Saint-Saëns, Camille 17:26
Spontini, Gaspare 18:194
Thomas, Ambroise 19:172
Germany and Austria
Bayreuth Wagner Festival 3:134
Benda, Jiří Antonín 3:196
Berg, Alban 3:208–209
Busoni, Ferruccio 3:590
Cornelius, Peter 5:268
Egk, Werner 7:73
Einem, Gottfried von 7:92
Flotow, Friedrich von 8:177
German and Austrian music 9:131
Henze, Hans Werner 10:130
Humperdinck, Engelbert 10:303
Krenek, Ernst 12:129
Mozart, Wolfgang Amadeus 13:628–629
Orff, Carl 14:432
Pfitzner, Hans 15:217
singspiel 17:322
Smyth, Dame Ethel 17:375
Strauss, Richard 18:294–295
Wagner, Richard 20:4–5
Weber, Carl Maria von 20:86–87
Weill, Kurt 20:94
Wolf-Ferrari, Ermanno 20:197
intermezzo 11:214
Italy
Bellini, Vincenzo 3:189–190
Boito, Arrigo 3:363
Bononcini, Antonio Maria 3:382
Bononcini, Giovanni 3:381–382
Caccini, Giulio 4:8
cadenza 4:11
Caldara, Antonio 4:25
Cavalli, Pier Francesco 4:220
Cesti, Marc Antonio 4:262
Cherubini, Luigi 4:333
Cilèa, Francesco 4:430
Donizetti, Gaetano 6:238
Giordano, Umberto 9:186
Gluck, Christoph Willibald 9:211
Handel, George Frideric 10:36
Hasse, Johann Adolph 10:67
Italian music 11:318–319
Jommelli, Niccolò 11:441
La Scala 12:149
Leoncavallo, Ruggero 12:291–292
Malipiero, Gian Francesco 13:91
Marcello, Benedetto 13:146
Mascagni, Pietro 13:195
Mayr, Johann Simon 13:249
Montemezzi, Italo 13:552
Monteverdi, Claudio 13:554
Paisiello, Giovanni 15:25
Peri, Jacopo 15:165
Pizzetti, Ildebrando 15:325
Ponchielli, Amilcare 15:426
Puccini, Giacomo 15:612
Rossini, Gioacchino 16:319–320
Salieri, Antonio 17:32
Scarlatti (family) 17:115
Verdi, Giuseppe 19:549–550
verismo 19:551
Zandonai, Riccardo 20:355
Juilliard, Augustus D. 11:465
Latin America
Ginastera, Alberto 9:183
libretto 12:319
Da Ponte, Lorenzo 6:3
Metastasio, Pietro 13:335
Neher, Caspar 14:78
music, history of Western 13:666
music festivals 13:671
musical comedy 13:673
opera houses 14:401–402
operas
Aïda 1:201
Beggar's Opera, The 3:168
Bohème, La 3:360
Boris Godunov 3:400–401
Don Giovanni 6:235
Lucia di Lammermoor 12:450
Madama Butterfly 13:39
Norma 14:219
Porgy and Bess 15:441
Ring of the Nibelung, The 16:225
Rosenkavalier, Der 16:315
Tosca 11:319 *illus.*; 19:247
Traviata, La 19:284–285
Tristan and Isolde 19:303
Trovatore, Il 19:312
William Tell 19:90
overture 14:470
passacaglia and chaconne 15:103
recitative 16:107–108
Russia
Cui, César 5:383
Dargomyzhsky, Aleksandr Sergeyevich 6:37
Glinka, Mikhail Ivanovich 9:208
Mussorgsky, Modest 13:685
Prokofiev, Sergei 15:566–567
Rimsky-Korsakov, Nikolai Andreyevich 16:224–225
Russian music 16:367–369 *illus.*
Shostakovitch, Dmitry 17:285
Tchaikovsky, Peter Ilich 19:51–52
Scotland
Musgrave, Thea 13:659
singers
Ameling, Elly 1:326
Baccaloni, Salvatore 3:9
Baker, Janet 3:28
Berganza, Teresa 3:209
Bergonzi, Carlo 3:210
Björling, Jussi 3:302
Bumbry, Grace 3:562
Caballé, Montserrat 4:3
Callas, Maria 4:41
Carreras, José 4:167–168
Caruso, Enrico 4:178
Chaliapin, Fyodor Ivanovich 4:271
Christoff, Boris 4:416
Corelli, Franco 5:262
De Los Angeles, Victoria 6:61
Domingo, Placido 6:232
Eames, Emma 7:5–6
Farinelli 8:23
Flagstad, Kirsten 8:150
Fremstad, Olive 8:302
Galli-Curci, Amelita 9:18
Garden, Mary 9:41
Gedda, Nicolai 9:67
Gigli, Beniamino 9:178
Gluck, Alma 9:211
Gobbi, Tito 9:216
Grisi, Giulia 9:367
Jeritza, Maria 11:397
Johnson, Edward 11:431–432
Lehmann, Lotte 12:276
McCormack, John 13:10
Melba, Dame Nellie 13:285
Muzio, Claudia 13:688
Nilsson, Birgit 14:197–198
Nordica, Lillian 14:218
Patti, Adelina 15:115–116
Pavarotti, Luciano 15:120
Pons, Lily 15:426
Price, Leontyne 15:534
Schwarzkopf, Elisabeth 17:139
Sills, Beverly 17:309–310
Slezak, Leo 17:361
Sutherland, Joan 18:373
Tebaldi, Renata 19:59
Tetrazzini, Luisa 19:127
Tibbett, Lawrence 19:189
Traubel, Helen 19:284
Tucker, Richard 19:328
Viardot-García, Pauline 19:567
Vickers, Jon 19:571
Spanish music 18:162
stage and set design
Berman, Eugene 3:219
Galli da Bibiena (family) 9:18–19
Zeffirelli, Franco 20:358
United States
American music 1:350
Barber, Samuel 3:77
Bernstein, Leonard 3:224
Cadman, Charles Wakefield 4:12
Chicago, Lyric Opera of 4:342
Copland, Aaron 5:250–251
Floyd, Carlisle 8:184
Gershwin, George and Ira 9:158–159
Glass, Philip 9:201
Menotti, Gian Carlo 13:300
Metropolitan Opera 13:348
Moore, Douglas Stuart 13:567
New York City Opera 14:155
San Francisco Opera Association 17:54
Santa Fe Opera 17:68
Sessions, Roger 17:213
Thomson, Virgil 19:177
voice, singing 19:626
OPERA HOUSES 14:401–402 *bibliog., illus.*
See also names of specific opera houses, e.g., LA SCALA; METROPOLITAN OPERA; etc.
OPERATING SYSTEM 14:402
computer 5:160e–160f; 5:160h
computer programming 5:163
computer software 5:164
OPERATION, SURGICAL *see* SURGERY
OPERATION ANVIL
World War II 20:271
OPERATION BARBAROSSA
World War II 20:256–257 *illus.*
OPERATION BOOTSTRAP
Puerto Rico 15:616
OPERATION BREADBASKET
Jackson, Jesse L. 11:343
OPERATION HUSKY
World War II 20:268
OPERATION OVERLORD *see* NORMANDY INVASION

OPERATION SEA LION *see* BRITAIN, BATTLE OF
OPERATION TORCH
World War II 20:262
OPERATIONAL AMPLIFIER 14:402–403 *bibliog.*
filter, electronic 8:91
integrated circuit 11:201–202
OPERATIONS RESEARCH 14:403 *bibliog.*
Babbage, Charles 3:5
cybernetics 5:401
decision theory 6:73–74
game theory 9:27–29
industrial management 11:157
management science 13:107
maxima and minima 13:239
queuing theory 16:24–25
OPERETTA 14:403 *bibliog.*
See also COMIC OPERA; SINGSPIEL
American music 1:351
composers
Friml, Rudolf 8:334
Gilbert and Sullivan 9:179
Herbert, Victor 10:135
Lehár, Franz 12:275
Offenbach, Jacques 14:353–354
Romberg, Sigmund 16:294
Strauss (family) 18:293–294
Suppé, Franz von 18:353
English music 7:203
libretto 12:319
musical comedy 13:673
OPERON 14:403–404 *bibliog.*
OPHEIM (Montana)
map (48° 51′N 106° 24′W) 13:547
OPHICLEIDE 14:404
bugle 3:548
OPHIOLITE 14:404
plate tectonics 15:356
OPHIR (Oregon)
map (42° 34′N 124° 23′W) 14:427
OPHITES 14:404 *bibliog.*
OPHTHALMOLOGY 14:404
OPHTHALMOMETER
contact lens 5:226–227
OPHTHALMOSCOPE 14:404–405
surgery 18:362
OPHULS, MARCEL 14:405 *bibliog.*
documentary 6:211
OPHULS, MAX 14:405 *bibliog.*
OPIATE RECEPTOR 14:405 *bibliog.*
heroin 10:145
pain 15:15
OPIHIKAO (Hawaii)
map (19° 26′N 154° 53′W) 10:72
OPINION POLLS 14:405–406 *bibliog.*
Gallup, George 9:21
public opinion 15:608
OPITZ, MARTIN
German literature 9:132
OPIUM 14:406 *bibliog., illus.*
addiction 14:406
codeine 5:90
drug abuse 6:279
drug trafficking 6:281
Forbes, Robert Bennet 8:220
heroin 10:145
methadone 13:343
morphine 13:587
narcotic drug 14:406
paregoric 15:84
poppy 14:406 *illus.*; 15:432
psychotropic drugs 15:603
use 14:406
medical use 14:406
OPIUM WARS 2:258 *illus.*; 14:407 *bibliog.*
China, history of 4:373
opium 14:406
OPOBO (Nigeria)
map (4° 34′N 7° 27′E) 14:190
OPÓLE (Poland)
map (50° 41′N 17° 55′E) 15:388
OPORTO (Portugal) *see* PORTO (Portugal)
OPOSSUM 11:469 *illus.*; 13:104 *illus.*; 14:407 *bibliog., illus.*
honey-glider possum 13:175 *illus.*
marsupial 13:174
regeneration 16:127
South American woolly opossum 13:175 *illus.*
OPP (Alabama)
map (31° 17′N 86° 22′W) 1:234
OPPEL, ALBERT 14:407
OPPENHEIMER, J. ROBERT 14:407–408 *bibliog., illus.*
Manhattan Project 13:116
OPPENHEIMER, MAX *see* OPHULS, MAX
OPPORTUNITY (Washington)
map (47° 39′N 117° 15′W) 20:35
OPRICHNINA
Ivan IV, Grand Duke of Moscow and Tsar of Russia (Ivan the Terrible) 11:333
OPS 14:408
OPTIC NERVE
eye 7:350
eye structure 7:348
OPTICAL ACTIVITY 14:408 *bibliog.*
polarimeter 15:393
stereochemistry 18:258
OPTICAL ART *see* OP ART
OPTICAL CHARACTER READER
pattern recognition 15:114–115
OPTICAL COMPUTING 5:160g; 5:160i
OPTICAL DISC *see* COMPACT DISC
OPTICAL FIBERS *see* FIBER OPTICS
OPTICAL ILLUSIONS *see* ILLUSIONS
OPTICAL INSTRUMENTATION
alidade 1:293
binoculars 3:259–260
camera 4:54–62
comparator 5:155
electron microscope 7:120–122
lens 2:76; 12:286
lighthouse 12:337
manufacture, Jena (East Germany) 11:395
microscope 13:387–388
monochromator 13:536
observatory, astronomical 14:317–318
optics 14:411
photometer 15:273–274
polarimeter 15:393
polariscope 15:394
projector 15:566
range finder 16:84
Schmidt telescope 17:128
sextant 17:227–228
spectroheliograph 18:168
spectrophotometer 18:168–169
spectroscope 18:169–170
stereoscope 18:259–260
telescope 19:80–83
theodolite 19:155–156
transit, surveying 19:273
OPTICAL ISOMER *see* STEREOCHEMISTRY
OPTICAL MINERALOGY 14:408–409 *bibliog., illus.*
mineral identification 13:442
petrography 15:207
OPTICAL RECORDING
sound recording and reproduction 18:75 *illus.*
OPTICAL SCANNING
input-output devices 11:183
scanning 17:114
OPTICS 14:409–413 *bibliog., illus.*
aberration, chromatic 1:57
aberration, spherical 1:57
absorption, light 1:63
angstrom 2:7
Biot, Jean Baptiste 3:277
Brewster, Sir David 3:476
candela 4:106
candlepower 4:107
color 5:112–113
coma 5:129
dichroism 6:156
dispersion (physics) 6:197
Doppler effect 6:241
electron optics 7:122
Fermat, Pierre de 8:55
fiber optics 8:68–69
Fizeau, Armand Hippolyte Louis 8:133
focal point 8:192
Foucault, Jean 8:249
Fresnel, Augustin Jean 8:328
geometrical optics 14:410–411
Carathéodory, Constantin 4:131
germanium 9:138
glass 9:198–201
Hamilton, Sir William Rowan 10:29
Helmholtz, Hermann Ludwig Ferdinand von 10:115–116
history 14:409–410
holography 10:207–208
Huygens's principle 10:325–326
hyperopia 10:348
image, optical 11:50–51
index of refraction 11:79
Kepler, Johannes 12:57–58
Laplace, Pierre Simon de 12:205
lens 12:285–287
light 12:334–335
lumen 12:458
microscopy
Zernike, Frits 20:361
mineral identification 13:442
mirror 13:464–465
Newton, Sir Isaac 14:173–174
night sights 14:193
optical activity 14:408
optical illusion 15:159 *illus.*
optical instrumentation 14:411
optical maser, laser 14:412
phonon 15:255
physical optics 14:411–413
diffraction 6:169; 14:412
interference 11:207–209; 14:411
polarized light 14:412; 15:394–395
Wood, Robert Williams 20:207
physics, history of 15:284–285
prism (physics) 15:554
qualitative chemical analysis 16:7
quantum optics 14:412
rainbow 16:77
Raman, Sir Chandrasekhara Venkata 16:79–80
reflection 16:119
refraction 16:123–124
scanning 17:114
stroboscope 18:301
surveillance systems 18:366
telescope 19:82–83
tracking station 19:262
ultraviolet light 19:379
X-ray diffraction 20:308–309
X rays 20:310–311
Young, Thomas 20:334
OPTION TRADING 14:413 *bibliog.*
OPTOMETRIST
eye diseases 7:351
OR FUNCTION (computer term) 5:160d
ORACHE *see* SALTBUSH
ORACLE 14:413
Delphi 6:95
divination 6:202
Dodona 6:212
riddles 16:216
sibyl 17:292
ORACLE (Arizona)
map (32° 37′N 110° 46′W) 2:160
ORACLE BONES 14:413 *bibliog.*
Anyang (China) 4:379 *illus.*
Asia, history of 2:251
Chinese archaeology 4:378; 4:379 *illus.*
Chinese art and architecture 4:380
ORADEA (Romania)
map (47° 3′N 21° 57′E) 16:288
ORAIBI (Arizona) 14:413–414 *bibliog.*
ORAL CONTRACEPTIVES 3:294
ORAL HISTORY 14:414 *bibliog.*
folk music 8:202–203
folklore 8:203
history 10:184
Indians of North America, music and dance of the 11:142–143
Nevins, Allan 14:115
Terkel, Studs 19:116
ORAL LITERATURE 14:414 *bibliog.*
epic 7:217
folklore 8:203
Homer 10:213
Lindsay, Vachel 12:352
Russian literature 16:364
ORAL ROBERTS UNIVERSITY
Roberts, Oral 16:242
ORAN (Algeria) 1:289 *illus.*; 14:414
map (35° 43′N 0° 43′W) 1:287
ORANGE (Australia)
map (33° 17′S 149° 6′E) 2:328
ORANGE (botany) 8:348 *illus.*; 14:414–415 *bibliog., illus.*; 15:337 *illus.*
citrus fruits 4:447 *illus.*
grapefruit 9:290
ORANGE (California)
map (33° 47′N 117° 51′W) 12:417
ORANGE (county in California)
map (33° 43′N 117° 54′W) 4:31
ORANGE (Connecticut)
map (41° 17′N 73° 2′W) 5:193
ORANGE (dynasty) 14:414 *bibliog.*
Frederick Henry, Prince of Orange 8:292
Juliana, Queen of the Netherlands 11:466
Low Countries, history of the 12:441
Maurice of Nassau 13:235
Wilhelmina, Queen of the Netherlands 20:151
William I, King of the Netherlands 20:157–158
William I, Prince of Orange 20:158
William II, King of the Netherlands 20:158
William II, Prince of Orange 20:158
William III, King of England, Scotland, and Ireland 20:156
William III, King of the Netherlands 20:158
ORANGE (county in Florida)
map (28° 32′N 81° 16′W) 8:172
ORANGE (county in Indiana)
map (38° 30′N 86° 30′W) 11:111
ORANGE (Massachusetts)
map (42° 35′N 72° 19′W) 13:206
ORANGE (county in New York)
map (41° 24′N 74° 20′W) 14:149
ORANGE (county in North Carolina)
map (36° 5′N 79° 5′W) 14:242
ORANGE (Texas)
map (30° 1′N 93° 44′W) 19:129
ORANGE (county in Texas)
map (30° 7′N 93° 52′W) 19:129
ORANGE (county in Vermont)
map (44° 0′N 72° 21′W) 19:554
ORANGE (Virginia)
map (38° 15′N 78° 7′W) 19:607
ORANGE (county in Virginia)
map (38° 15′N 78° 0′W) 19:607
ORANGE CITY (Florida)
map (28° 57′N 81° 17′W) 8:172
ORANGE CITY (Iowa)
map (43° 0′N 96° 3′W) 11:244
ORANGE FREE STATE (South Africa) 14:415
cities
Bloemfontein 3:334–335
history
Pretorius, Marthinus Wessel 15:534
map (28° 30′S 27° 0′E) 18:79
people
South Africa 18:81
South African War 18:83–84 *map*
ORANGE GROVE (Texas)
map (27° 58′N 97° 56′W) 19:129
ORANGE PARK (Florida)
map (30° 10′N 81° 42′W) 8:172
ORANGE RIVER 14:415
map (28° 41′S 16° 28′E) 18:79
South Africa 18:79
ORANGE WALK (Belize)
map (18° 6′N 88° 33′W) 3:183
ORANGEBURG (South Carolina)
map (33° 30′N 80° 52′W) 18:98
ORANGEBURG (county in South Carolina)
map (33° 30′N 80° 55′W) 18:98
ORANGEMEN 14:415 *bibliog.*
ORANGEVILLE (Ontario)
map (43° 55′N 80° 6′W) 14:393; 19:241
ORANGEVILLE (Utah)
map (39° 13′N 111° 3′W) 19:492
ORANGO ISLAND
map (11° 10′N 16° 8′W) 9:399
ORANGUTAN 14:415–416 *bibliog., illus.*
ape 2:74–76 *illus.*
ORAON 14:416 *bibliog.*
ORATORIO 14:416 *bibliog.*
See also OPERA
aria 2:153
baroque music 3:91–92
composers
Beethoven, Ludwig van 3:164–165
Caldara, Antonio 4:25
Carissimi, Giacomo 4:150
Charpentier, Marc Antoine 4:299
Handel, George Frideric 10:36
Haydn, Franz Josef 10:81
Honegger, Arthur 10:220
Marcello, Benedetto 13:146
English music 7:203
libretto 12:319
music, history of Western 13:666
ORATORY *see* RHETORIC AND ORATORY
ORBIGNY, ALCIDE DESSALINES D' 14:416
ORBISONIA (Pennsylvania)
map (40° 15′N 77° 54′W) 15:147
ORBIT (astronomy)
astronautics 2:274–275 *illus.*
celestial mechanics 4:230 *illus.*
ellipse 7:147
orbital elements 14:417
planets 15:329–330 *illus.*
satellite, artificial 17:85 *illus.*
ORBITAL 14:416–417 *bibliog.*
electron configuration 7:120
ORBITAL ELEMENTS 14:417 *bibliog., illus.*
comet 5:133
ephemeris time 7:216
Kepler's laws 12:58 *illus.*
ORBITING ASTRONOMICAL OBSERVATORIES *see* OAO (artificial satellite)
ORBITING GEOPHYSICAL OBSERVATORY *see* OGO (artificial satellite)
ORBITING SOLAR OBSERVATORIES *see* OSO (artificial satellite)

ORCAS ISLAND
map (48° 39′N 122° 55′W) **20**:35
ORCHARD (Nebraska)
map (42° 20′N 98° 14′W) **14**:70
ORCHARD HOMES (Montana)
map (46° 55′N 114° 4′W) **13**:547
ORCHARD VALLEY (Wyoming)
map (41° 6′N 104° 19′W) **20**:301
ORCHESTRA AND ORCHESTRATION **14**:417–419 *bibliog., illus.*
baton **3**:124
Berlioz, Hector **3**:218–219
Boston Pops Orchestra **3**:410
Boston Symphony Orchestra **3**:410
Chicago Symphony Orchestra **4**:343
Chinese music **4**:392
classical period in music **5**:41
Cleveland Orchestra, The **5**:54
Concertgebouw Orchestra **5**:170
concerto **5**:170
conducting **5**:173–174
drum (musical instrument) **6**:282
French horn **8**:311–312
Italian music **11**:318–319
Japanese music **11**:381–382 *illus.*
Mannheim school **13**:125
music, non-Western **13**:667–668
New York Philharmonic **14**:155
Philadelphia Orchestra, The **15**:229
Pittsburgh Symphony Orchestra **15**:322
seating arrangement **14**:418 *illus.*
Vienna Philharmonic Orchestra **19**:579
ORCHESTRE DE LA SUISSE ROMANDE
Ansermet, Ernest **2**:35
ORCHID **11**:469 *illus.*; **14**:419–420 *bibliog., illus.*
classification, biological **14**:420
coralroot **5**:261
fairy slipper **8**:10
flowers **14**:419
ladies' tresses **12**:162
lady's slipper **12**:162
pollination **14**:419
seeds **14**:419
twayblade **19**:358
uses
economic use **14**:419–420
floriculture **8**:170
houseplants **10**:274
vanilla **19**:519–520
ORCHITIS **14**:420
mumps **13**:639
ORCHOMENOS (Greece) **14**:420
ORCHON RIVER
map (50° 21′N 106° 5′E) **13**:529
ORCUS, TOMB OF **7**:259 *illus.*
ORD (Nebraska)
map (41° 36′N 98° 56′W) **14**:70
ORD RIVER
map (15° 30′S 128° 21′E) **2**:328
ORDAZ, DIEGO DE
Popocatépetl **15**:431
ORDAZ, GUSTAVO DIAZ *see* DIAZ ORDAZ, GUSTAVO
ORDELAFFI (family)
Forlì (Italy) **8**:234
ORDER OF PATRONS OF HUSBANDRY *see* GRANGE, NATIONAL
ORDINANCE OF 1784
Jefferson, Thomas **11**:392
ORDINANCE OF 1787 *see* NORTHWEST TERRITORY
ORDINATION *see* MINISTRY, CHRISTIAN
ORDINO (Andorra)
map (42° 33′N 1° 32′E) **1**:405
ORDNANCE *see* AMMUNITION; ARTILLERY
ORDÓÑEZ, BARTOLOMÉ **14**:420 *bibliog.*
ORDÓÑEZ, JOSÉ BATLLE Y *see* BATLLE Y ORDÓÑEZ, JOSÉ
ORDOS (China)
Chinese archaeology **4**:378–379
steppe art **18**:256 *illus.*
ORDOS DESERT **14**:420
map (39° 0′N 108° 0′E) **4**:362
ORDOVICIAN PERIOD **14**:420–422 *bibliog., illus., map*
continents **14**:420–421
estimated positions **14**:421 *map*
flooding **14**:421
crinoid **5**:350
economic resources **14**:422
fossil record **8**:245–247
geologic time **9**:103–105
ice ages **11**:8
life **14**:420–422 *illus.*; **15**:35 *illus.*
Paleozoic Era **15**:43
rock formations **14**:421 *map*
ORDWAY (Colorado)
map (38° 13′N 103° 46′W) **5**:116
ORE DEPOSITS **14**:422–426 *bibliog., map, table*
Africa **1**:149 *map*
agate **1**:182–183
amethyst **1**:368
arsenate minerals **2**:189
Asia **2**:247 *map*
assay of ores **2**:264
Australia **2**:335 *map*
bauxite **3**:130–131 *illus.*
beryl **3**:227
borate minerals **3**:396
Buddington, Arthur Francis **3**:543
carbonate minerals **4**:137
classification **14**:422–423
clay minerals **5**:46–47
coal and coal mining **5**:76–77 *map*
cobaltite **5**:83
copper **5**:252
definition **14**:422
diamond **6**:151–152
distribution **14**:423 *map*
emerald **7**:154
Europe **7**:278 *map*
extraction
cyanide process **5**:400
flotation process **8**:177
feldspar **8**:47
garnet **9**:49
geochemistry **9**:97
geode **9**:97
geologic time
Carboniferous Period **4**:137–139
Cenozoic Era **4**:245
Cretaceous Period **5**:339–340
Devonian Period **6**:145
Jurassic Period **11**:476
Permian Period **15**:174
Silurian Period **17**:311
Tertiary Period **19**:125
Triassic Period **19**:292
geology **9**:105–106
gold **9**:226
granite **9**:287
gypsum **9**:415–416 *illus.*
halide minerals **10**:21
igneous rock **11**:33–36
iron and steel industry **11**:272–274 *map*
jade **11**:347
kimberlite **12**:77
laterite **12**:215
lead **12**:256
location
dowsing **6**:252
Landsat **12**:185
seismometer **17**:189–190 *illus.*
magnetite **13**:58
manganese **13**:114
mercury (element) **13**:306
cinnabar **4**:434
mica **13**:370–371 *illus.*
mining and quarrying **14**:425–426
molasse **13**:505
molybdenite **13**:514
niccolite **14**:180
nitrate minerals **14**:201–202
North America **14**:230–231 *map*
oceanic mineral resources **14**:340–341
ore genesis **14**:422
oxide minerals **14**:476
phosphate minerals **15**:255–256
phosphorite **15**:256
placer deposit **15**:325
plate tectonics **15**:356
platinum **15**:359
political and economic importance **14**:426
potassium **15**:464–465
pyrite **15**:637
pyroxene **15**:638
pyrrhotite **15**:638
quartz **16**:13–14
research **14**:425
ruby **16**:337
sand **17**:59
sapphire **17**:73
siderite **17**:294
silica minerals **17**:304
silicate minerals **17**:304–305
silver **17**:312
sodium **18**:32–33
South America **18**:90 *map*
sulfate minerals **18**:333
sulfide minerals **18**:333–334
sulfur **18**:334
talc **19**:15 *illus.*
telluride minerals **19**:91
tin **19**:204–205
topaz **19**:236–237 *illus.*
tungsten **19**:333
turquoise **19**:352 *illus.*
uranium minerals **19**:478
vein deposit **19**:536
wulfenite **20**:296 *illus.*
zinc **20**:367
zircon **20**:370
ORE MOUNTAINS
map (50° 30′N 13° 10′E) **9**:140
ÖREBRO (Sweden)
map (59° 17′N 15° 13′E) **18**:382
OREGANO **14**:426
OREGON **14**:426–430 *bibliog., illus., map*
cities
Astoria **2**:269
Eugene **7**:263
Medford **13**:263
Portland **15**:445
Salem **17**:31
climate **14**:428–429
economy **14**:429
education **14**:429
state universities and colleges of **14**:430–431
flag **14**:426 *illus.*
forestry and fishing **14**:429–430
government and politics **14**:430
history **14**:430
Duniway, Abigail Scott **6**:300
Gray, Robert **9**:306
McLoughlin, John **13**:33
Oregon Question **14**:431
Oregon Trail **14**:431
recall **16**:106
Whitman, Marcus **20**:140
Hood, Mount **10**:225
manufacturing and energy **14**:430
map (44° 0′N 121° 0′W) **19**:419
mineral resources **14**:429
people **14**:429
Cayuse **4**:227
Klamath **12**:94–95
Modoc **13**:499
Paiute **15**:25
Yurok **20**:347
physiographic regions **14**:428–429 *illus., map*
rivers, lakes, and waterways **14**:428
Crater Lake **5**:332–333
Willamette River **20**:154
seal, state **14**:426 *illus.*
vegetation and animal life **14**:429
OREGON (Illinois)
map (42° 1′N 89° 20′W) **11**:42
OREGON (Missouri)
map (39° 59′N 95° 9′W) **13**:476
OREGON (county in Missouri)
map (36° 40′N 91° 25′W) **13**:476
OREGON (Ohio)
map (41° 38′N 83° 28′W) **14**:357
OREGON, STATE UNIVERSITIES AND COLLEGES OF **14**:430–431
OREGON CITY (Oregon)
map (45° 21′N 122° 36′W) **14**:427
OREGON GRAPE *see* BARBERRY
OREGON MYRTLE *see* CALIFORNIA LAUREL
OREGON QUESTION **14**:431 *bibliog.*
Hudson's Bay Company **10**:290
Polk, James K. **15**:405
San Juan Boundary Dispute **17**:55
OREGON TRAIL **8**:341 *map*; **14**:431 *bibliog., map*; **19**:445 *map*
Casper (Wyoming) **4**:182
Chimney Rock National Historic Site **14**:72 *illus.*
historians
Parkman, Francis **15**:91–92
Nebraska **14**:74
Scotts Bluff National Monument **14**:71 *illus.*
OREL (USSR)
map (52° 59′N 36° 5′E) **19**:388
ORELLANA (Peru)
map (6° 54′S 75° 4′W) **15**:193
ORELLANA, FRANCISCO DE **14**:432 *bibliog.*
exploration **7**:337 *map*
OREM (Utah)
map (40° 19′N 111° 42′W) **19**:492
ORENBURG (USSR)
map (51° 54′N 55° 6′E) **19**:388
ORENSE (Argentina)
map (38° 40′S 59° 47′W) **2**:149
ORENSE (Spain)
map (42° 20′N 7° 51′W) **18**:140
OREOPITHECUS **14**:432 *bibliog.*; **15**:541 *illus.*
prehistoric human origins **15**:512
ORESTEIA (plays) **14**:432; **1**:129 *illus.*; **14**:432 *bibliog.*
Agamemnon **1**:181–182
ORESTES **14**:432
ØRESUND, STRAIT OF
map (55° 50′N 12° 40′E) **6**:109
ORFF, CARL **14**:432 *bibliog.*
ORFORD, HORACE WALPOLE, 4TH EARL OF *see* WALPOLE, HORACE, 4TH EARL OF ORFORD
ORFORDVILLE (Wisconsin)
map (42° 38′N 89° 16′W) **20**:185
ORGAN (biology)
See also names of specific organs, e.g., EYE; HEART; PANCREAS; etc.
aplasia **2**:78
artificial organs **2**:222
atrophy **2**:313
cryobiology **5**:370
development
embryo **7**:153 *illus.*
diseases, human **6**:193
embryology **7**:154
gland **9**:196–197
histology **10**:180–181
immunology **11**:60
organ generation
angiogenin **1**:414
ORGAN (musical instrument) **13**:678 *illus.*; **14**:432–434 *bibliog., illus.*
barrel organ **3**:94
church music **4**:424
composers
Bach, Johann Sebastian **3**:10–11
Couperin (family) **5**:313–314
Franck, César **8**:277
Frescobaldi, Girolamo **8**:328
Gabrieli (family) **9**:6
electric organ **7**:125 *illus.*
Hammond **7**:125 *illus.*
history **14**:432–433
keyboard instruments **12**:62–63
mechanics **14**:432–433 *illus.*
organists
Bach, Wilhelm Friedemann **3**:11
Biggs, E. Power **3**:249
Boyce, William **3**:433
Buxtehude, Dietrich **3**:601
Fox, Virgil **8**:256
Hassler, Hans Leo **10**:67
Sweelinck, Jan Pieterszoon **18**:387
Widor, Charles Marie **20**:145
portative organ **15**:443–444
ORGAN, AMERICAN *see* AMERICAN ORGAN
ORGAN OF CORTI
ear **7**:6–7 *illus.*
ORGAN TRANSPLANT *see* TRANSPLANTATION, ORGAN
ORGANELLES, CELL **4**:232–233 *illus.*; **4**:236
active transport **1**:89
cytoplasm **5**:412
mitochondrion **13**:485
ribosomes **16**:206
ORGANETTO *see* PORTATIVE ORGAN
ORGANIC ARCHITECTURE *see* SULLIVAN, LOUIS
ORGANIC CHEMISTRY **14**:434–440 *bibliog., illus.*
biochemistry **3**:260–262; **14**:438
carbanion **4**:132
catalyst **4**:198–199
chemical industry **4**:318–319 *table*; **14**:439–440
chemical nomenclature **4**:321
cis-trans isomerism **4**:445
compounds **14**:436–438
acetaldehyde **1**:79
acetate **1**:80
acetic acid **1**:80
acetone **1**:80
acetyl group **1**:80
acetylene **1**:80
alcohol **1**:264
aldehyde **1**:267–268
alicyclic compounds **1**:293
aliphatic compounds **1**:295
alkane **1**:296
alkene **1**:296–297
alkyl group **1**:297
alkyne **1**:297
amide **1**:369
amine **1**:370 *table*
amino acid **1**:370–371
aniline **2**:8
aromatic compounds **2**:186
aryl group **2**:226
ascorbic acid **2**:228
azide **2**:381
azo group **2**:381
benzaldehyde **3**:206
benzene **3**:206
benzoic acid **3**:207
bromine **3**:502
butane **3**:591
cancer **4**:102
carbon **4**:134–135

ORGANIC CHEMISTRY (cont.)
carbonyl group 4:139
carboxylic acid 4:139–141
chlorine 4:400–401
chloroform 4:401
chlorohydrin 4:401
copolymer 5:251
cyclic compounds 5:403–404
diene 6:162
ester 7:246
ethane 7:249
ether (chemistry) 7:249–250
ethyl alcohol 7:257
ethyl ether 7:257
ethyl group 7:257
ethylene 7:258
fatty acid 8:35
fluorine 8:187–188
fluorocarbon 8:188
formaldehyde 8:234
formic acid 8:234
glycerol 9:212
glycol 9:212
glycoside 9:212
heterocyclic compound 10:153
homologous series 10:216
hydrocarbon 10:331
hydrogen 10:337–338
hydrophilic and hydrophobic substances 10:343
hydroquinone 10:344
hydroxyl group 10:344
isoprene 11:300
ketone 12:61
lactic acid 12:161
lactone 12:161–162
lactose 12:162
lead 12:256
magnesium 13:54
maleic acid 13:87
mercury 13:306
methane 13:343
methyl alcohol 13:344
methyl group 13:344–345
methylene 13:345
monohydric alcohol 13:536
naphtha 14:14
naphthalene 14:14
nitrile 14:202
nitrogen 14:202–203; 14:437–438
palmitic acid 15:51
pentane 15:155
phenol 15:225
phenyl group 15:226
phosphorus 15:256–257
polyester 15:418–419
polyhydric alcohol 15:420
potassium 15:465
propane 15:569
pyrrole 15:639
pyruvic acid 15:639
quinone 16:27
silicones 17:306
terpene 19:118–119
conjugation 5:191
definition 14:434
DES (pharmaceutical) 6:123; 14:438
environment and 14:438–439
extraction 7:341
Grignard reagents 9:363–364
history 4:329; 14:434–436
Barton, Derek 3:98
Berthelot, Marcelin 3:225
Dumas, Jean Baptiste André 6:297; 14:434–435
Erlenmeyer, Richard 7:231
Fischer, Emil Hermann 8:110
Gerhardt, Charles Frédéric 9:122; 14:434–435
Grignard, Victor 9:363
Kekulé von Stradonitz, Friedrich August 12:37; 14:435
Laurent, Auguste 12:238–239; 14:434–435
Lavoisier, Antoine Laurent 14:434
Liebig, Justus, Baron von 12:324
Wöhler, Friedrich 14:434; 20:195
hydrogenation 10:341
isomer 11:299; 14:436
mass spectrometry 13:204
molecular structure 14:436–438
carbonium ion 4:139
monomer 13:537
optical activity 14:408
origin of life 12:327
pesticides 14:438–439; 15:197–198
petrochemicals 15:205–206
polymerization 15:420
pyrolysis 15:637
qualitative chemical analysis 16:7
radical 16:43
reaction, chemical 14:436; 14:438
research 14:438
saponification 17:73
spectroscopy 18:170–172 *illus., table*
stereochemistry 18:258–259
sugar 18:327
ORGANIC FOODS *see* HEALTH FOODS
ORGANIZATION OF AFRICAN UNITY 1:160 *illus.*; 7:253 *illus.*; 14:440 *bibliog.*
ORGANIZATION FOR AFRO-AMERICAN UNITY
Malcolm X 13:86
ORGANIZATION OF AMERICAN STATES 14:440 *bibliog.*
Barbados 3:75–76 *map*
ORGANIZATION FOR ECONOMIC COOPERATION AND DEVELOPMENT 14:440 *bibliog.*
ORGANIZATION FOR EUROPEAN ECONOMIC COOPERATION
Marshall Plan 13:173
ORGANIZATION OF PETROLEUM EXPORTING COUNTRIES 2:105 *illus.*; 14:440 *bibliog.*
Arabs 2:103
balance of payments 3:33
energy sources 7:174–175
Middle East, history of the 13:409–410 *map*
petroleum industry 15:215
solar energy and 18:43
Yamani, Ahmed Zaki 20:316
ORGANIZATIONAL PSYCHOLOGY *see* INDUSTRIAL PSYCHOLOGY
ORGANIZED CRIME 14:441 *bibliog.*
Camorra 4:62
computer crime 5:160L
crime 5:345
drug trafficking 6:281
kidnapping 12:71
Mafia 13:46
Murder, Inc. 13:648
ORGANUM 14:441 *bibliog.*
medieval music 13:275
music, history of Western 13:662; 13:665
ORGASM
sexual intercourse 17:230–231
ORGONE ENERGY
Reich, Wilhelm 16:130
ORGUN (Afghanistan)
map (32° 51′N 69° 7′E) 1:133
ORIBE, MANUEL
Rivera, Fructuoso 16:233
Uruguay 19:490
ORICK (California)
map (41° 17′N 124° 4′W) 4:31
ORIEL COLLEGE (Oxford University) 14:474
ORIENT (Iowa)
map (41° 12′N 94° 25′W) 11:244
ORIENT, THE *see* FAR EAST
ORIENT EXPRESS (train) 14:441 *bibliog.*
ORIENTAL (North Carolina)
map (35° 2′N 76° 42′W) 14:242
ORIENTAL AMERICANS 14:441–443 *bibliog., illus.*
Chinese Americans 14:441–442
California 4:37
Chinese Exclusion Acts 4:388–389
tong 19:233
Filipino Americans 14:442
Japanese Americans 14:442
Nisei 14:201
Korean Americans 14:442
Pacific-Islander Americans 14:442–443
Southeast-Asian Americans 14:443
ORIENTAL POPPY 14:406 *illus.*
ORIENTAL REPUBLIC OF URUGUAY *see* URUGUAY
ORIENTAL SORE
leishmaniasis 12:279
ORIENTATION (botany) *see* TROPISM
ORIENTEERING 14:443 *bibliog.*
ORIGAMI *see* PAPER FOLDING
ORIGEN 14:443 *bibliog.*
Celsus 4:238
ORIGIN OF LIFE *see* LIFE
ORIGIN OF SPECIES, ON THE (book) 7:319 *illus.*; 14:443–444 *bibliog.*
Darwin, Charles 6:41–42
natural selection 14:49
ORIGINAL PACKAGE DOCTRINE
Brown v. *Maryland* 3:517
Leisy v. *Hardin* 12:279
ORIGINAL SIN 14:444
sin 17:318
ORILLIA (Ontario)
map (44° 37′N 79° 25′W) 14:393
ORINDUIK (Guyana)
map (4° 42′N 60° 1′W) 9:410
ORINOCO DELTA
map (9° 15′N 61° 30′W) 19:542
ORINOCO PLAIN
South America 18:87
ORINOCO RIVER 14:444
map (8° 37′N 62° 15′W) 19:542
ORIOLE 14:444 *bibliog., illus.*
blackbird 3:320
ORION (astronomy) 14:444
constellation 5:212
Horsehead Nebula 11:227 *illus., illus.*
ORION (mythology) 14:444
Canis Major and Canis Minor 4:108
ORION NEBULA 14:444–445
nebula 14:75 *illus.*
ORISSA (India) 14:445
cities
Bhubaneswar 3:234
map (20° 0′N 84° 0′E) 11:80
people
Khond 12:68
ORIYA LANGUAGE
Indo-Iranian languages 11:145
ORIZABA (Mexico)
map (18° 51′N 97° 6′W) 13:357
ORIZABA (volcano)
map (19° 1′N 97° 16′W) 13:357
ORKENY, ISTVAN 14:445 *bibliog.*
ORKNEY ISLANDS 14:445 *bibliog.*
map (59° 0′N 3° 0′W) 19:403
Neolithic Period
Skara Brae 17:332
Scapa Flow 17:114–115
ORLAND (California)
map (39° 45′N 122° 11′W) 4:31
ORLANDO (Florida) 8:174 *illus.*; 14:445
map (28° 32′N 81° 23′W) 8:172
Walt Disney World 6:197
ORLANDO, VITTORIO EMANUELE 14:445 *bibliog.*
Paris Peace Conference 15:88
ORLANDO FURIOSO (poem) 14:445 *bibliog.*
Ariosto, Ludovico 2:154
puppet 15:627 *illus.*
ORLANDOS, ANASTASIAS
Mistra 13:482
ORLÉANAIS (France) 14:445–446 *map*
ORLEANS (California)
map (41° 18′N 123° 32′W) 4:31
ORLÉANS (family) 14:446
Dunois, Jean, Comte de (the Bastard of Orléans) 6:301
Louis Philippe, King of France 12:423
Orléans, Philippe II, Duc d' 14:446
ORLÉANS (France) 14:446
map (47° 55′N 1° 54′E) 8:260
ORLEANS (Indiana)
map (38° 40′N 86° 27′W) 11:111
ORLEANS (county in Louisiana)
map (30° 0′N 90° 8′W) 12:430
ORLEANS (Massachusetts)
map (41° 47′N 70° 0′W) 13:206
ORLEANS (county in New York)
map (43° 15′N 78° 12′W) 14:149
ORLEANS (Vermont)
map (44° 49′N 72° 12′W) 19:554
ORLEANS (county in Vermont)
map (44° 50′N 72° 13′W) 19:554
ORLÉANS, ANNE MARIE LOUISE D', DUCHESSE DE MONTPENSIER *see* MONTPENSIER, ANNE MARIE LOUISE D'ORLÉANS, DUCHESSE DE
ORLÉANS, BASTARD OF *see* DUNOIS, JEAN, COMTE DE (the Bastard of Orléans)
ORLÉANS, CHARLES, DUC D'
Orléans (family) 14:446
ORLÉANS, JEAN BAPTISTE GASTON, DUC D'
Orléans (family) 14:446
ORLÉANS, LOUIS, DUC D'
Orléans (family) 14:446
ORLÉANS, LOUIS PHILIPPE JOSEPH, DUC D' (Philippe Égalité) 14:446 *bibliog.*
ORLÉANS, LOUIS PHILIPPE ROBERT, DUC D'
Orléans (family) 14:446
ORLÉANS, PHILIPPE I, DUC D'
Orléans (family) 14:446
ORLÉANS, PHILIPPE II, DUC D' 14:446 *bibliog.*
ORLÉANS (family)
Orléans, Louis Philippe Joseph, Duc d' 14:446
ORLOV (family) 14:446–447 *bibliog.*
ORLOV, ALEKSEI
Orlov (family) 14:446–447
ORLOV, GRIGORY
Orlov (family) 14:446
ORMANDY, EUGENE 14:447 *bibliog.*
Philadelphia Orchestra, The 15:229
ORMAZD
Zoroastrianism 20:380
ORMOC (Philippines)
map (11° 0′N 124° 37′E) 15:237
ORMOND BEACH (Florida)
map (29° 17′N 81° 2′W) 8:172
ORNITHISCHIA
Camptosaurus 4:67–68
Corythosaurus 5:279–280
dinosaur 6:180–181 *illus.*
Iguanodon 11:39
Nanosaurus 14:13
Pachycephalosaurus 15:5
Palaeoscincus 15:29
Protoceratops 15:578
Stegosaurus 18:246
Styracosaurus 18:311
Trachodon 19:258
Triceratops 19:296
ORNITHOLESTES 14:447
ORNITHOLOGY 14:447 *bibliog.*
See also BIRD
ORNITHOPTER
flight, human-powered 8:164
ORNITHOSIS *see* PSITTACOSIS
ORNITZ, SAMUEL
Hollywood Ten, The 10:204
ÖRNSKÖLDSVIK (Sweden)
map (63° 18′N 18° 43′E) 18:382
OROCHON
Tungus 19:334
OROCUÉ (Colombia)
map (4° 48′N 71° 20′W) 5:107
OROFINO (Idaho)
map (46° 29′N 116° 15′W) 11:26
OROGENY 14:447 *bibliog.*
Alps
Bertrand, Marcel Alexandre 3:226
continental shield 5:230
diastrophism 6:153
Earth's crust deformation 14:447
events, duration 14:447
fold 8:194–195
geologic time
Cambrian Period 4:50
Cretaceous Period 5:340–341
Mesozoic Era 13:322
Paleozoic Era 15:42–43
Permian Period 15:174
Recent Epoch 16:106–107
Tertiary Period 19:123
Triassic Period 19:293
geophysics 9:108
geosyncline 9:119–120
island arc 11:297–298
isostasy 11:300
landform evolution 12:183
Lehmann, Johann Gottlob 12:276
Lugeon, Maurice 12:452–453
metamorphic rock 13:331
mid-oceanic ridge 13:389–390
molasse 13:505
monadnock 13:517
mountain 13:619–620
nappe 14:20
oceanic fracture zones 14:339
paleogeography 15:36–38
plate tectonics 15:354–356; 15:357
structural geology 18:303
Suess, Eduard 18:323
OROGRAPHIC PRECIPITATION 14:447 *bibliog.*
climate 5:57–58
precipitation 15:495
OROMOCTO (New Brunswick)
map (45° 51′N 66° 29′W) 14:117
ORON (Nigeria)
map (4° 48′N 8° 14′E) 14:190
ORONTES RIVER
map (36° 2′N 35° 58′E) 18:412
OROVILLE (California)
map (39° 31′N 121° 33′W) 4:31
OROVILLE (Washington)
map (48° 56′N 119° 26′W) 20:35
OROZCO, JOSÉ CLEMENTE 14:447–448 *bibliog.*
Guadalajara (Mexico) 9:384
Latin American art and architecture 12:227–228
ORPHEUS 14:448 *bibliog.*
Greek music 9:345
ORPHISM (art and literature) 14:448 *bibliog.*
Apollinaire, Guillaume 2:79
Delaunay, Robert 6:87
Kupka, František 12:138
synchromism 18:406

ORPIMENT
arsenic **2**:189
ORR, BOBBY **14**:448 *bibliog., illus.*
ORR, JOHN BOYD-, 1ST BARON BOYD-ORR OF BRECHIN MEARN *see* BOYD-ORR, JOHN, 1ST BARON BOYD-ORR OF BRECHIN MEARN
ORREFORS **14**:448–449 *bibliog.*
glassware, decorative **9**:204
ORREGO-SALAS, JUAN
Latin American music and dance **12**:232
ORRERY
planetarium **15**:328
ORRICK (Missouri)
map (39° 13′N 94° 7′W) **13**:476
ORRS ISLAND (Maine)
map (43° 46′N 69° 59′W) **13**:70
ORRVILLE (Alabama)
map (32° 18′N 87° 15′W) **1**:234
ORRVILLE (Ohio)
map (40° 50′N 81° 46′W) **14**:357
ORSK (USSR)
map (51° 12′N 58° 34′E) **19**:388
ORTEGA, FRANCISCO DE
Golden Gate **9**:232
ORTEGA SAAVEDRA, DANIEL **14**:449
ORTEGA Y GASSET, JOSÉ **14**:449 *bibliog.*
ORTELIUS, ABRAHAM **14**:449
ORTHOCLASE
feldspar **8**:46
ORTHODONTICS **14**:449
anthropometry **2**:55
ORTHODOX CHURCH **4**:413 *map*; **14**:449–450 *bibliog., illus.*; **16**:140 *map*
canon law **4**:114–115
church music **4**:424
doctrines and practices **14**:450
Europe, history of **7**:284
Greek church
Athenagoras **2**:289
Byzantine music **3**:608
iconoclasm **11**:20–21; **14**:450
Michael Cerularius **13**:371
Photius **15**:257
history **14**:450
icon **11**:20
iconostasis **11**:24
liturgy **12**:373–374
National Council of Churches **14**:31
patriarch **15**:113
religious orders **16**:143
Russian church
Nikon **14**:195–196
Old Believers **14**:374
Peter I, Emperor of Russia (Peter the Great) **15**:200–201
Soloviev, Vladimir Sergeyevich **18**:57
saint **17**:15
Schism, Great **17**:122
structure and organization **14**:450
World Council of Churches **20**:218
ORTHOGONAL TRANSFORMATION *see* TRANSFORMATION
ORTHOGRAPHIC PROJECTION
mechanical drawing **13**:259
ORTHOMOLECULAR MEDICINE **14**:450 *bibliog.*
megavitamin therapy **13**:280
ORTHOPEDICS **14**:450 *bibliog.*
anthropometry **2**:55
ORTHOPTERA **14**:450
cockroach **5**:87–88
cricket **5**:344
grasshopper **9**:298–299
katydid **12**:31
locust **12**:392
praying mantis **15**:490–491
roach **16**:234–235
stick insect **18**:266
ORTHOPYROXENE
pyroxene **15**:638
ORTHORHOMBIC SYSTEM **14**:451
crystal **5**:375 *illus.*
ORTIZ RUBIO, PASCUAL
Mexico, history of **13**:365
ORTON, JOE **14**:451 *bibliog.*
ORTONVILLE (Minnesota)
map (45° 19′N 96° 27′W) **13**:453
ORTUÑO, RENÉ BARRIENTOS *see* BARRIENTOS ORTUÑO, RENÉ
ORURO (Bolivia)
map (17° 59′S 67° 9′W) **3**:366
ORUZGAN (Afghanistan)
map (32° 56′N 66° 38′E) **1**:133
ORWELL, GEORGE **14**:451 *bibliog., illus.*
Animal Farm **2**:22
Nineteen Eighty-Four **14**:199
ORYX **2**:46 *illus.*; **14**:451
ORZESZKOWA, ELIZA
Polish literature **15**:398
OSAGE (American Indians) **14**:451–452 *bibliog.*
Chouteau (family) **4**:410
Indians of North America, music and dance of the **11**:144
Omaha (American Indians) **14**:385
Oto **14**:460
Quapaw **16**:12
Wichita (American Indians) **20**:144
OSAGE (Iowa)
map (43° 17′N 92° 49′W) **11**:244
OSAGE (county in Kansas)
map (38° 40′N 95° 45′W) **12**:18
OSAGE (county in Missouri)
map (38° 25′N 91° 50′W) **13**:476
OSAGE (county in Oklahoma)
map (36° 35′N 96° 25′W) **14**:368
OSAGE (Wyoming)
map (43° 59′N 104° 25′W) **20**:301
OSAGE BEACH (Missouri)
map (38° 9′N 92° 37′W) **13**:476
OSAGE CITY (Kansas)
map (38° 38′N 95° 50′W) **12**:18
OSAGE ORANGE **14**:452 *illus.*
mock orange **13**:489
OSAGE RIVER
map (38° 35′N 91° 57′W) **13**:476
OSAKA (Japan) **14**:452
Japan, history of **11**:369
map (34° 40′N 135° 30′E) **11**:361
subway **18**:318 *table*
OSAKIS (Minnesota)
map (45° 52′N 95° 9′W) **13**:453
OSAKIWUK (American Indians) *see* SAUK
OSAWATOMIE (Kansas)
map (38° 31′N 94° 57′W) **12**:18
OSBORNE (Kansas)
map (39° 26′N 98° 42′W) **12**:18
OSBORNE (county in Kansas)
map (39° 20′N 98° 45′W) **12**:18
OSBORNE, JOHN **14**:452 *bibliog.*
OSBORNE, THOMAS, 1ST EARL OF DANBY *see* DANBY, THOMAS OSBORNE, 1ST EARL OF
OSBURN (Idaho)
map (47° 30′N 116° 0′W) **11**:26
OSCAR (statuette) *see* ACADEMY AWARDS
OSCAR THE GROUCH *see* MUPPETS
OSCEOLA (Arkansas)
map (35° 42′N 89° 58′W) **2**:166
OSCEOLA (county in Florida)
map (28° 0′N 81° 15′W) **8**:172
OSCEOLA (Iowa)
map (41° 2′N 93° 46′W) **11**:244
OSCEOLA (county in Iowa)
map (43° 23′N 95° 35′W) **11**:244
OSCEOLA (county in Michigan)
map (44° 0′N 85° 20′W) **13**:377
OSCEOLA (Missouri)
map (38° 3′N 93° 42′W) **13**:476
OSCEOLA (Nebraska)
map (41° 11′N 97° 33′W) **14**:70
OSCEOLA (Seminole Indian) **14**:452–453 *bibliog., illus.*
Fort Moultrie **8**:237
OSCEOLA (Wisconsin)
map (45° 19′N 92° 42′W) **20**:185
OSCEOLA MILLS (Pennsylvania)
map (40° 51′N 78° 16′W) **15**:147
OSCILLATION (astronomy)
libration **12**:319
OSCILLATION (mechanics)
pendulum **15**:142
OSCILLATOR **14**:453 *bibliog., illus.*
damping **6**:19
feedback **8**:44
magnetron **13**:60
multivibrator **13**:638
radio **16**:45
transmitter **19**:276
OSCILLATORIA
blue-green algae **3**:342 *illus.*
OSCILLOSCOPE **14**:453 *bibliog.*
Braun, Ferdinand **3**:458
cathode ray **4**:211
cathode-ray tube **4**:211
circuit, electric **4**:437
signal generator **17**:300
OSCODA (Michigan)
map (44° 26′N 83° 20′W) **13**:377
OSCODA (county in Michigan)
map (44° 40′N 84° 5′W) **13**:377
OSEBERG SHIP BURIAL **14**:453 *bibliog.*; **17**:111 *illus.*; **19**:595 *illus.*
OSGOOD (Indiana)
map (39° 8′N 85° 17′W) **11**:111
OSHA *see* OCCUPATIONAL SAFETY AND HEALTH ADMINISTRATION
OSHAWA (Ontario) **14**:453
map (43° 54′N 78° 51′W) **14**:393
OSHKOSH (Nebraska)
map (41° 24′N 102° 21′W) **14**:70
OSHKOSH (Wisconsin) **14**:453–454
map (44° 1′N 88° 33′W) **20**:185
OSHOGBO (Nigeria)
map (7° 47′N 4° 34′E) **14**:190
OSIJEK (Yugoslavia)
map (45° 33′N 18° 41′E) **20**:340
OSIRIS (Egyptian deity) **14**:454 *bibliog.*
Abydos (ancient Egypt) **1**:67
dance **6**:22–23 *illus.*
fertility rites **8**:60
OSKALOOSA (Iowa)
map (41° 18′N 92° 39′W) **11**:244
OSKALOOSA (Kansas)
map (39° 13′N 95° 19′W) **12**:18
OSKARSHAMN (Sweden)
map (57° 16′N 16° 26′E) **18**:382
OSLER, SIR WILLIAM **14**:454 *bibliog.*
Cushing, Harvey W. **5**:397
medicine and medical education **14**:454
OSLO (Norway) **14**:261–262 *illus., table*; **14**:454 *illus.*
art
Vigeland, Gustav **19**:592
map (59° 55′N 10° 45′E) **14**:261
subway **18**:318 *table*
World War II **20**:252 *illus.*
OSMAN I, OTTOMAN RULER **14**:454–455
Ottoman Empire **14**:464
OSMANIYA (Turkey)
map (37° 5′N 36° 14′E) **19**:343
OSMIUM **14**:455 *bibliog.*
element **7**:130 *table*
Group VIII periodic table **15**:167
metal, metallic element **13**:328
Tennant, Smithson, discoverer **19**:102
transition elements **19**:273
OSMOND (Nebraska)
map (42° 22′N 97° 36′W) **14**:70
OSMOND, HUMPHREY
megavitamin therapy **13**:280
OSMOND BROTHERS
rock music **16**:249
OSMOSIS **14**:455 *bibliog., illus.*
desalination **6**:125
dialysis **6**:150–151
diffusion **6**:170
van't Hoff, Jacobus Henricus **19**:520
OSNABRÜCK (West Germany) **14**:455–456
map (52° 16′N 8° 2′E) **9**:140
OSO (artificial satellite) **14**:456 *bibliog.*; **17**:86 *illus.*
space exploration **18**:123
ultraviolet astronomy **19**:379
X-ray astronomy **20**:306
OSORNO (Chile)
map (40° 34′S 73° 9′W) **4**:355
OSOYOOS (British Columbia)
map (49° 2′N 119° 28′W) **3**:491
OSPEDALE DEGLI INNOCENTI (Foundling Hospital, Florence)
Brunelleschi, Filippo **3**:524
OSPREY **14**:456 *bibliog., illus.*
birds of prey **3**:291
nest **3**:287 *illus.*
OSS
Central Intelligence Agency **4**:254
OSS (Netherlands)
map (51° 46′N 5° 31′E) **14**:99
OSSA, MOUNT
map (41° 54′S 146° 1′E) **2**:328
OSSABAW ISLAND
map (31° 47′N 81° 6′W) **9**:114
OSSEO (Wisconsin)
map (44° 35′N 91° 12′W) **20**:185
OSSIAN **14**:456
Macpherson, James **13**:36
OSSIAN (Indiana)
map (40° 53′N 85° 10′W) **11**:111
OSSIFICATION
bone **3**:377
OSSINING (New York)
map (41° 10′N 73° 52′W) **14**:149
OSSIPEE (New Hampshire)
map (43° 41′N 71° 7′W) **14**:123
OSSIPEE LAKE
map (43° 47′N 71° 8′W) **14**:123
OSSIPEE RIVER
map (43° 49′N 70° 48′W) **14**:123
OSTADE, ADRIAEN VAN **14**:456 *bibliog.*
ÖSTBERG, RAGNAR
Stockholm (Sweden) **18**:276
OSTEGO (county in New York)
map (42° 42′N 74° 56′W) **14**:149
OSTEICHTHYES **14**:456–457
OSTEND (Belgium) **14**:457
map (51° 13′N 2° 55′E) **3**:177
OSTEND MANIFESTO **14**:457 *bibliog.*
Pierce, Franklin **15**:296
OSTEOARTHRITIS **14**:457
arthritis **2**:215
OSTEOGENESIS IMPERFECTA
bone diseases **3**:377
OSTEOMALACIA
bone diseases **3**:377–378
nutritional-deficiency diseases **14**:308
OSTEOMYELITIS **14**:457 *bibliog.*
bone diseases **3**:378
dentistry **6**:114
OSTEOPATHIC MEDICINE **14**:457 *bibliog.*
OSTEOPOROSIS **14**:457–458
bone diseases **3**:377
lumbago **12**:454
ÖSTERSUND (Sweden)
map (63° 11′N 14° 39′E) **18**:382
OSTIA (Italy) **14**:458 *bibliog.*; **16**:301 *illus.*
harbor and port **10**:42
OSTPOLITIK (government policy)
Germany, East and West **9**:147
OSTRACOD **14**:458
OSTRACODERM **14**:458 *illus.*
fossil record **8**:245
Ordovician Period **14**:421
OSTRAVA (Czechoslovakia) **14**:458
map (49° 50′N 18° 17′E) **5**:413
Paleolithic Period **2**:126 *illus.*
OSTRAVA-PETŘKOVICE (Moravia)
Cro-Magnon man **5**:354 *illus.*
OSTRICH **3**:281 *illus.*; **14**:458–459 *bibliog., illus.*
egg **7**:72
foot **3**:288 *illus.*
Struthiomimus **18**:303–304
OSTROGOTHS *see* GOTHS
OSTROVSKY, ALEKSANDR NIKOLAYEVICH **14**:459 *bibliog.*
OSTRÓW WIELKOPOLSKI (Poland)
map (51° 39′N 17° 49′E) **15**:388
OSTROWIEC SWIĘTOKRZYSKI (Poland)
map (50° 57′N 21° 23′E) **15**:388
OSTWALD, WILHELM **14**:459 *bibliog.*
physics, history of **15**:286
OSTYAK *see* KHANTS
O'SULLIVAN, JOHN L.
Manifest Destiny **13**:117
O'SULLIVAN, TIMOTHY H. **14**:459 *bibliog.*; **15**:269 *illus.*
OSUM RIVER
map (40° 48′N 19° 52′E) **1**:250
OSWALD, LEE HARVEY **14**:459 *bibliog.*
Warren Commission **20**:31
OSWALD, SAINT **14**:459 *bibliog.*
OSWEGATCHIE RIVER
map (44° 42′N 75° 30′W) **14**:149
OSWEGO (Illinois)
map (41° 41′N 88° 21′W) **11**:42
OSWEGO (Kansas)
map (37° 10′N 95° 6′W) **12**:18
OSWEGO (New York)
map (43° 27′N 76° 31′W) **14**:149
OSWEGO (county in New York)
map (42° 25′N 76° 10′W) **14**:149
OSWEGO RIVER
map (43° 28′N 76° 31′W) **14**:149
OŚWIĘCIM (Poland) *see* AUSCHWITZ
OSYKA (Mississippi)
map (31° 0′N 90° 28′W) **13**:469
OTAHUHU (New Zealand)
map (36° 57′S 174° 51′E) **14**:158
OTARU (Japan)
map (43° 13′N 141° 0′E) **11**:361
OTAVALO (Ecuador)
map (0° 14′N 78° 16′W) **7**:52
OTELLO (opera)
libretto
Boito, Arrigo **3**:363
OTERO (county in Colorado)
map (37° 50′N 103° 45′W) **5**:116
OTERO (county in New Mexico)
map (32° 45′N 105° 45′W) **14**:136
OTERO, ALEJANDRO
Venezuela **19**:543
OTHELLO (play) **14**:459–460 *bibliog.*
OTHELLO (Washington)
map (46° 50′N 119° 10′W) **20**:35
OTHO, ROMAN EMPEROR
Galba, Roman Emperor **9**:13
Rome, ancient **16**:302–303
OTHO I *see* OTTO I, KING OF GREECE
OTI RIVER
map (8° 40′N 0° 13′E) **19**:222
OTIS (Colorado)
map (40° 9′N 102° 58′W) **5**:116
OTIS (Kansas)
map (38° 32′N 99° 3′W) **12**:18

OTIS, ELISHA GRAVES
elevator 7:136
OTIS, JAMES 14:460 *bibliog.*
writ of assistance 20:291
OTISCO LAKE
Finger Lakes 8:93
OTITIS MEDIA
ear disease 7:7
OTO (American Indians) 14:460 *bibliog.*
Iowa (American Indians) 11:248
OTOE (Nebraska)
map (40° 43′N 96° 7′W) 14:70
OTOE (county in Nebraska)
map (40° 40′N 96° 10′W) 14:70
OTOLARYNGOLOGY
medicine, education in 13:273
OTOMI INDIANS
Querétaro (state in Mexico) 16:23
OTOSCLEROSIS
ear disease 7:8
OTRANTO, STRAIT OF
Ionian Sea 11:241
ÖTSCHER MOUNTAIN
map (47° 52′N 15° 12′E) 2:348
OTSEGO (Michigan)
map (42° 27′N 85° 42′W) 13:377
OTSEGO (county in Michigan)
map (45° 0′N 84° 35′W) 13:377
OTTAWA (American Indians) 14:460 *bibliog.*
Pontiac's Rebellion 15:427
Potawatomi 15:466
OTTAWA (Illinois)
map (41° 21′N 88° 51′W) 11:42
OTTAWA (Kansas)
map (38° 37′N 95° 16′W) 12:18
OTTAWA (county in Kansas)
map (39° 10′N 95° 35′W) 12:18
OTTAWA (county in Michigan)
map (42° 57′N 86° 2′W) 13:377
OTTAWA (Ohio)
map (41° 1′N 84° 3′W) 14:357
OTTAWA (county in Ohio)
map (41° 33′N 83° 10′W) 14:357
OTTAWA (county in Oklahoma)
map (36° 50′N 94° 50′W) 14:368
OTTAWA (Ontario) 4:76 *illus.*; 14:460–461 *illus., map*
map (45° 25′N 75° 42′W) 14:393
Parliament Buildings 14:395 *illus.*
OTTAWA, UNIVERSITY OF 14:461
OTTAWA HILLS (Ohio)
map (41° 40′N 83° 39′W) 14:357
OTTAWA ISLANDS
map (59° 30′N 80° 10′W) 16:18
OTTAWA RIVER 14:461
map (45° 20′N 73° 58′W) 16:18
OTTER 14:461–462 *bibliog., illus.*
sea otter 17:169
OTTER CREEK
map (44° 13′N 73° 17′W) 19:554
OTTER HOUND 6:216 *illus.*; 14:462 *bibliog., illus.*
OTTER LAKE (Michigan)
map (43° 13′N 83° 28′W) 13:377
OTTER TAIL (county in Minnesota)
map (46° 25′N 95° 45′W) 13:453
OTTER TAIL LAKE
map (46° 16′N 96° 36′W) 13:453
OTTER TAIL RIVER
map (46° 16′N 96° 36′W) 13:453
OTTERBEIN, PHILIP WILLIAM 14:462 *bibliog.*
Evangelical United Brethren Church 7:312
OTTO, KING OF GREECE 14:463 *bibliog.*
OTTO, NIKOLAUS AUGUST 14:462 *bibliog.*
internal-combustion engine 14:462
motorcycle 13:612–614
OTTO, RUDOLF 14:462 *bibliog.*
OTTO I, KING OF GERMANY AND HOLY ROMAN EMPEROR (Otto the Great) 14:462–463 *bibliog., illus.*
Germany, history of 9:148–149 *illus.*
Holy Roman Empire 10:209
imperialism 11:62
Italy, history of 11:328
presenting a model of Magdeburg Cathedral to Jesus Christ 10:210 *illus.*
OTTO II, KING OF GERMANY AND HOLY ROMAN EMPEROR 14:463 *bibliog.*
OTTO III, KING OF GERMANY AND HOLY ROMAN EMPEROR 13:392 *illus.*; 14:463 *bibliog.*
OTTO IV, KING OF GERMANY AND HOLY ROMAN EMPEROR 14:463 *bibliog.*
Braunschweig 3:458
Philip of Swabia 15:232
OTTOBEUREN, ABBEY CHURCH OF 16:264 *illus.*
OTTOKAR I, KING OF BOHEMIA
Přemysl (dynasty) 15:518
OTTOKAR II, KING OF BOHEMIA (Přemysl Ottokar) 14:464 *bibliog.*
Rudolf I, King of Germany 16:338
Wenceslas I, King of Bohemia 20:103
OTTOMAN ART
Islamic art and architecture 11:297
Levnî, Ressam 12:304–305
mosque 13:602
Sinan 17:318
Topkapi Palace Museum 19:237
OTTOMAN EMPIRE 14:464–466 *bibliog., illus., map, table*
harem 10:49
Middle East, history of the 13:404–405
Palestine 15:44
Romania 16:290
sultan 14:464 *table*; 18:338
Turks 19:348
1299–1650
Balkans 3:39
Bayezid I, Sultan 3:133
Bayezid II, Sultan 3:133
boundaries *c.*1360 7:285 *map*
boundaries *c.*1560 7:288 *map*
boundaries *c.*1648 7:289 *map*
Bulgaria 3:556
Edirne (Turkey) 7:57
Egypt 7:80
expansion 14:464–465 *map*
Greece 9:328
Hungary 10:310
institutions 14:464
Islam 11:290
Istanbul (Turkey) 11:307
Janissaries 11:358
Lebanon 12:266–267
Lepanto, Battle of 12:295
Mehmed II, Sultan 13:281
Murad I, Sultan of the Ottoman Empire 13:645
Murad II, Sultan of the Ottoman Empire 13:645
Osman I 14:454–455
Selim I, Sultan 17:191–192
Suleiman I, Sultan (Suleiman the Magnificent) 18:332–333
1650–1800
Ahmed III, Sultan 1:200
decline of 14:464–465
Europe, history of 7:290
Köprülü (family) 12:110
Kuwait (country) 12:141
Phanariots 15:219
reform attempts 14:465–466
Selim III, Sultan 17:192
1800–1923
Abd al-Hamid II, Sultan 1:53
Balkan Wars 3:38
boundaries 1815 7:291 *map*
boundaries 1914 7:294 *map*
contraction 14:466 *map*
Crimean War *see* CRIMEAN WAR
Eastern Question 7:33–34
Lausanne, Treaty of 12:239–240
Mahmud II, Sultan 13:65
Muhammad Ali Pasha 13:633
Navarino, Battle of 14:58
overthrow 14:466
Russo-Turkish Wars *see* RUSSO-TURKISH WARS
World War I *see* WORLD WAR I
Young Turks 20:336
OTTONIAN ART AND ARCHITECTURE 14:466–467 *bibliog., illus.*
cathedrals and churches 4:205
German art and architecture 9:123–124
illuminated manuscripts 11:47
sculpture 17:162 *illus.*
OTTUMWA (Iowa)
map (41° 1′N 92° 25′W) 11:244
OTWAY, THOMAS 14:467 *bibliog.*
OTWOCK (Poland)
map (52° 7′N 21° 16′E) 15:388
OU RIVER
map (20° 4′N 102° 13′E) 12:203
OUACHITA (county in Arkansas)
map (33° 35′N 92° 55′W) 2:166
OUACHITA (county in Louisiana)
map (32° 28′N 92° 10′W) 12:430
OUACHITA, LAKE
map (34° 40′N 93° 25′W) 2:166
OUACHITA MOUNTAINS
map (34° 40′N 94° 25′W) 2:166
Oklahoma 14:366
OUACHITA RIVER
map (31° 38′N 91° 49′W) 12:430
OUAGADOUGOU (Upper Volta) 14:467
map (12° 22′N 1° 31′W) 19:472
OUAHIGOUYA
map (13° 35′N 2° 25′W) 19:472
OUANARY (French Guiana)
map (4° 13′N 51° 40′W) 8:311
OUARANE (region in Mauritania)
map (21° 0′N 10° 30′W) 13:236
OUCHY, TREATY OF
Italo-Turkish War 11:320
OUD, JACOBUS JOHANNES PIETER 14:467 *bibliog.*
OUDRY, JEAN BAPTISTE
tapestry 19:33
OUDTSHOORN (South Africa)
map (33° 35′S 22° 14′E) 18:79
OUEDDEI, GOUKOUNI
Chad 4:266
OUEME RIVER
map (6° 29′N 2° 32′E) 3:200
OUESSO (Congo)
map (1° 37′N 16° 4′E) 5:182
OUGHTRED, WILLIAM
slide rule 17:361
OUHAM RIVER
map (9° 18′N 18° 14′E) 4:251
OUIDA 14:467
OUIJA 14:467
OUJDA (Morocco)
map (34° 41′N 1° 45′W) 13:585
OULU (Finland)
map (65° 1′N 25° 28′E) 8:95
OULU LAKE
map (64° 20′N 27° 15′E) 8:95
OUNAS RIVER
map (66° 30′N 25° 45′E) 8:95
OUNCE
weights and measures 20:93–94
OUR LADY OF CHARTRES, CATHEDRAL *see* CHARTRES CATHEDRAL
OUR TOWN (play) 14:467 *bibliog.*
Wilder, Thornton 20:149–150
OURAY (Colorado)
map (38° 1′N 107° 40′W) 5:116
OURAY (county in Colorado)
map (38° 10′N 107° 45′W) 5:116
OURAY, MOUNT
map (38° 25′N 106° 14′W) 5:116
OUTAGAMIE (county in Wisconsin)
map (44° 23′N 88° 27′W) 20:185
OUTBOARD MOTOR
motorboat 13:612 *illus.*
OUTCAULT, RICHARD FELTON 14:468
comic strip 5:135
yellow journalism 20:322
OUTER BANKS (North Carolina)
Hatteras, Cape 10:68
OUTER HEBRIDES ISLANDS
map (57° 50′N 7° 32′W) 19:403
OUTER SANTA BARBARA PASSAGE
map (33° 10′N 118° 30′W) 4:31
OUTER SPACE TREATY
space law 18:132
OUTERBRIDGE, MARY EWING
tennis 19:109
OUTLAWS (U.S.) 14:468–469 *bibliog., illus.*
Billy the Kid 3:256
James, Jesse 11:354
Murrieta, Joaquín 13:650–651
Rob Roy 16:239–240
Starr, Belle 18:228
Younger brothers 20:336
OUTLOOK (Montana)
map (48° 53′N 104° 47′W) 13:547
OUTLOOK (Saskatchewan)
map (51° 30′N 107° 3′W) 17:81
OUTPUT DEVICES *see* INPUT-OUTPUT DEVICES
OUTRIGGER 14:469
canoe 4:113 *illus.*; 17:263 *illus.*
OVALLE (Chile)
map (30° 36′S 71° 12′W) 4:355
OVAMBO 14:469 *bibliog.*
Namibia 14:11–12
OVARIES
endocrine system 7:169 *illus.*
menstruation 13:300–301
reproductive system, human 16:163–166 *illus.*
surgery 18:361
OVEN 14:469 *bibliog.*
See also KILN
cleaner
caustic chemicals 4:220
microwave oven 13:388
magnetron 13:60
OVENBIRD 14:469–470 *illus.*
OVER-THE-COUNTER MARKET *see* STOCK MARKET
OVERBECK, JOHANN FRIEDRICH 14:470 *bibliog.*
Nazarenes (art group) 14:66
OVERBROOK (Kansas)
map (38° 47′N 95° 33′W) 12:18
OVERFLAKKEE ISLAND
map (51° 45′N 4° 10′E) 14:99
ØVERLAND, ARNULF 14:470
OVERLAND PARK (Kansas)
map (38° 59′N 94° 40′W) 12:18
OVERLAND TRAIL
roads and highways 16:237
OVERLEA (Maryland)
map (39° 22′N 76° 31′W) 13:188
OVERTON (Nebraska)
map (40° 44′N 99° 32′W) 14:70
OVERTON (Nevada)
map (36° 33′N 114° 27′W) 14:111
OVERTON (county in Tennessee)
map (36° 20′N 85° 15′W) 19:104
OVERTONE
harmonics 10:51
music, acoustics of 13:662
OVERTURE 14:470
OVETT (Mississippi)
map (31° 29′N 89° 2′W) 13:469
OVID 14:470–471 *bibliog.*
Art of Love
courtly love 5:317
Metamorphoses 13:333
OVID (New York)
map (42° 41′N 76° 49′W) 14:149
OVIEDO (Dominican Republic)
map (17° 47′N 71° 22′W) 6:233
OVIEDO (Spain) 14:471
map (43° 22′N 5° 50′W) 18:140
OVIPARITY 14:471
egg 7:72 *illus.*
viviparity 19:622
OVULATION
estrous cycle 7:248
fertility, human 8:60
menstruation 13:300–301
multiple birth 13:637
reproductive system, human 16:165–166
OVULE
pollination 15:408–409
OVUM *see* EGG
OWANDO (Congo)
map (0° 29′S 15° 55′E) 5:182
OWASCO LAKE
Finger Lakes 8:93
map (42° 52′N 76° 32′W) 14:149
OWASSO (Oklahoma)
map (36° 16′N 95° 51′W) 14:368
OWATONNA (Minnesota)
map (44° 5′N 93° 14′W) 13:453
OWEGO (New York)
map (42° 6′N 76° 16′W) 14:149
OWEN (county in Indiana)
map (39° 20′N 86° 50′W) 11:111
OWEN (county in Kentucky)
map (38° 33′N 84° 49′W) 12:47
OWEN, DANIEL 14:471
OWEN, ROBERT 14:471 *bibliog.*
socialism 18:19
utopias 19:498
OWEN, ROBERT DALE 14:471 *bibliog.*
New Harmony (Indiana) 14:126
OWEN, WILFRED 14:471 *bibliog.*
OWEN FALLS DAM 19:373 *illus.*
OWEN SOUND (Ontario)
map (44° 34′N 80° 56′W) 14:393
OWEN STANLEY RANGE 14:472
map (9° 20′S 147° 55′E) 15:72
OWENS, JESSE 14:472 *bibliog., illus.*
Olympic Games 14:383 *illus.*
OWENS VALLEY
map (36° 55′N 118° 20′W) 4:31
OWENSBORO (Kentucky) 14:472
map (37° 46′N 87° 7′W) 12:47
OWENSVILLE (Missouri)
map (38° 21′N 91° 29′W) 13:476
OWENTON (Kentucky)
map (38° 32′N 84° 50′W) 12:47
OWERRI (Nigeria)
map (5° 29′N 7° 2′E) 14:190
OWINGS MILLS (Maryland)
map (39° 25′N 76° 47′W) 13:188
OWINGSVILLE (Kentucky)
map (38° 9′N 83° 46′W) 12:47
OWL 3:281 *illus.*; 14:472–473 *bibliog., illus.*
anatomy 14:473
Arctic 2:140–141 *illus.*
birds of prey 3:290–291 *illus.*
eye 3:285 *illus.*
OWL BUTTERFLY 3:595–596 *illus.*
OWL AND THE PUSSYCAT, THE (poem)
Lear, Edward 12:259
OWO (Nigeria)
map (7° 15′N 5° 37′E) 14:190
OWOSSO (Michigan)
map (43° 0′N 84° 10′W) 13:377
OWSLEY (county in Kentucky)
map (37° 25′N 83° 40′W) 12:47

OWYHEE (county in Idaho)
map (42° 35′N 116° 10′W) **11**:26
OWYHEE (Nevada)
map (41° 57′N 116° 6′W) **14**:111
OWYHEE, LAKE
map (43° 28′N 117° 20′W) **14**:427
OWYHEE RIVER
map (43° 46′N 117° 2′W) **14**:427
OX **14**:473 *illus.*
banteng **3**:71
yak **20**:314
OX-BOW INCIDENT, THE (book) **14**:473
Clark, Walter van Tilburg **5**:39
OXACILLIN
pencillin **15**:143–144
OXBOW (Saskatchewan)
map (49° 14′N 102° 11′W) **17**:81
OXBOW LAKE **14**:473 *bibliog., illus.*
OXENSTIERNA, AXEL, COUNT **14**:473–474 *bibliog.*
OXFORD (Alabama)
map (33° 37′N 85° 50′W) **1**:234
OXFORD (England) **14**:474
map (51° 46′N 1° 15′W) **19**:403
OXFORD (Indiana)
map (40° 31′N 87° 15′W) **11**:111
OXFORD (Iowa)
map (41° 43′N 91° 47′W) **11**:244
OXFORD (Maine)
map (44° 8′N 70° 30′W) **13**:70
OXFORD (county in Maine)
map (44° 30′N 70° 45′W) **13**:70
OXFORD (Maryland)
map (38° 42′N 76° 10′W) **13**:188
OXFORD (Massachusetts)
map (42° 7′N 71° 52′W) **13**:206
OXFORD (Mississippi)
map (34° 22′N 89° 32′W) **13**:469
OXFORD (Nebraska)
map (40° 15′N 99° 38′W) **14**:70
OXFORD (New Jersey)
map (40° 48′N 75° 0′W) **14**:129
OXFORD (New York)
map (42° 27′N 75° 36′W) **14**:149
OXFORD (North Carolina)
map (36° 19′N 78° 35′W) **14**:242
OXFORD (Nova Scotia)
map (45° 44′N 63° 52′W) **14**:269
OXFORD (Ohio)
map (39° 30′N 84° 44′W) **14**:357
OXFORD (Pennsylvania)
map (39° 47′N 75° 59′W) **15**:147
OXFORD (Wisconsin)
map (43° 47′N 89° 34′W) **20**:185
OXFORD, PROVISIONS OF
Montfort, Simon de, Earl of Leicester **13**:555
OXFORD, ROBERT HARLEY, 1ST EARL OF *see* HARLEY, ROBERT, 1ST EARL OF OXFORD
OXFORD, UNIVERSITY OF **14**:474 *bibliog.*
Bodeleian Library
Duke Humphrey's Library **12**:316 *illus.*
Bodleian Library **3**:356
British education **3**:494–495 *illus.*
Mackinder, Sir Halford John **13**:29
Osler, Sir William **14**:454
Oxford (England) **14**:474
Oxford movement **14**:475
Radcliffe Camera **9**:174 *illus.*
Rhodes scholarships **16**:202
OXFORD ENGLISH DICTIONARY, THE **14**:474–475 *bibliog.*
dictionary **6**:159
Murray, Sir James **13**:650
OXFORD GROUP *see* MORAL RE-ARMAMENT
OXFORD HOUSE (Manitoba)
map (54° 56′N 95° 16′W) **13**:119
OXFORD JUNCTION (Iowa)
map (41° 59′N 90° 57′W) **11**:244
OXFORD MOVEMENT **14**:475 *bibliog.*
Keble, John **12**:36
Manning, Henry Edward **13**:125
Newman, John Henry **14**:170
Pusey, Edward Bouverie **15**:631
Ward, William **20**:29
OXFORDSHIRE (England) **14**:475
OXIDATION AND REDUCTION **14**:475–476 *bibliog.*
anodizing **2**:34
auto-oxidation **14**:475
biological oxidation and reduction **14**:475–476
Krebs cycle **12**:128
combustion **5**:131
corrosion **5**:276–277
electromotive series **7**:119
fire **8**:100–101
hydrogenation **10**:341
metal **13**:328
oxidizing agents **14**:475
chlorine compounds **4**:400–401
oxygen **14**:477–478
sulfuric acid **18**:336
reaction, chemical **16**:99
reducing agents **14**:475
sewerage **17**:222–223
spontaneous combustion **18**:194
thermodynamics **19**:164
water supply **20**:54
OXIDATION STATE *see* VALENCE
OXIDATIVE PHOSPHORYLATION
metabolism **13**:326
OXIDE MINERALS **14**:476 *bibliog.*
alteration, mineral **1**:312
cassiterite **14**:476
chromite **4**:419
chrysoberyl **4**:420–421
columbite **14**:476
corundum **5**:279
cuprite **5**:390
franklinite **8**:285
geode **9**:97
glaze **9**:206
hematite **10**:117
isomorph **11**:300
limonite **12**:346
magnetism **14**:476
magnetite **13**:58
manganite **13**:114
metal ore **14**:476
occurrence **14**:476
perovskite **15**:177
psilomelane **15**:588
pyrolusite **15**:637
ruby **16**:337
rutile **16**:376
source **14**:476
spinel **18**:185
structure **14**:476
zincite **20**:368
OXNARD (California)
map (34° 12′N 119° 11′W) **4**:31
OXON (England) *see* OXFORDSHIRE (England)
OXPECKER **14**:476
rhinoceros **16**:196 *illus.*
yellow-billed oxpecker **17**:98 *illus.*
OXYACETYLENE TORCH
blowtorch **3**:341
OXYGEN **14**:476–478 *bibliog.*
See also OZONE
abundances of common elements **7**:131 *table*
anaerobe **1**:387
biological oxidation **14**:477
biosphere **3**:277
blood
circulatory system **4**:440 *illus.*
cyanosis **5**:400
hemoglobin **10**:119
methemoglobinemia **13**:343
shock, physiologic **17**:278
carbon cycle (atmosphere) **4**:136
carbonyl group **4**:139
chalcogens **4**:270
combustion **5**:131
compounds **14**:477
acetyl group **1**:80
aldehyde **1**:267–268
carbonyl group **4**:139
carboxylic acid **4**:139–140 *table*
ether (chemistry) **7**:249–250
hydroxyl group **10**:344
ketone **12**:61
nitrogen **14**:202
peroxide **15**:177
detector
Pauling, Linus Carl **15**:119
discovery **14**:476
Priestley, Joseph **15**:536–537
electron configuration **7**:120
element **7**:130 *table*
fuel cell **8**:354 *illus.*
gill **9**:180
Group VIA periodic table **15**:167
hyperventilation **10**:349
hypoxia **10**:351
life **12**:326
life-support systems **12**:331–333
liquid oxygen
boiling point **3**:363
cryogenics **5**:370
Dewar, Sir James **6**:146
measurement
oceanographic instrumentation **14**:344
metabolism **13**:325; **14**:478
occurrence **14**:476
laboratory production **14**:476
natural **14**:476
oxidation and reduction **14**:475
oxide minerals **14**:476; **14**:478
oxygen tent **14**:478
ozone **14**:480
photosynthesis **14**:478; **15**:274–277
physical and chemical properties **14**:477
production **14**:477–478
reactivity **14**:477
reducing potential
electromotive series **7**:119
respiratory system **16**:178–179
Scheele, Carl Wilhelm **17**:115
silicate minerals **17**:304–305
uses **14**:477
OXYGEN FURNACE
iron and steel industry **11**:276
OXYGEN ISOTOPE RATIO
paleotemperature **15**:42
OXYGEN TENT **14**:478
OXYRHYNCHUS (Egypt) **14**:478–479
OXYTOCIN **14**:479
breast **3**:469 *illus.*
hormone, animal **10**:237
pituitary gland **15**:322
synthesis
Du Vigneaud, Vincent **6**:287
OYAPOCK RIVER
map (4° 8′N 51° 40′W) **8**:311
OYEM (Gabon)
map (1° 37′N 11° 35′E) **9**:5
OYO (Nigeria)
map (7° 51′N 3° 56′E) **14**:190
OYRAT *see* KALMYK
OYSTER **14**:479 *bibliog., illus.*
fish farming **8**:121
intertidal life **11**:230
Maryland **13**:191
mollusk **13**:511
pearls and pearling **15**:126–128
shellfish **17**:254 *illus.*
OYSTER PLANT *see* SALSIFY
OYSTERCATCHER **14**:479–480 *illus.*
beak **3**:289 *illus.*
shorebirds **17**:283
OZ, AMOS **14**:479
OZ, FRANK
Muppets **13**:645
OZAKI YUKIO **14**:479–480 *bibliog.*
OZAMIZ (Philippines)
map (8° 8′N 123° 50′E) **15**:237
OZARK (Alabama)
map (31° 28′N 85° 38′W) **1**:234
OZARK (Arkansas)
map (35° 29′N 93° 50′W) **2**:166
OZARK (Missouri)
map (37° 1′N 93° 12′W) **13**:476
OZARK (county in Missouri)
map (36° 40′N 92° 25′W) **13**:476
OZARK ESCARPMENT
map (36° 0′N 91° 15′W) **2**:166
OZARK MOUNTAINS **14**:480
map (37° 0′N 93° 0′W) **19**:419
Missouri **13**:475; **13**:478 *illus.*
OZARK PLATEAU *see* OZARK MOUNTAINS
OZARK RESERVOIR
map (35° 35′N 94° 0′W) **2**:166
OZARKS, LAKE OF THE **13**:478 *illus.*
map (38° 10′N 92° 50′W) **13**:476
OZAUKEE (county in Wisconsin)
map (43° 20′N 87° 58′W) **20**:185
OZAWA, SEIJI **14**:480 *bibliog.*
Berkshire Music Festival **3**:214
Boston Symphony Orchestra **3**:410
OZETTE LAKE
map (48° 6′N 124° 38′W) **20**:35
OZICK, CYNTHIA **14**:480
OZONA (Texas)
map (30° 43′N 101° 12′W) **19**:129
OZONE **14**:480
ozone layer **14**:480
OZONE LAYER **14**:480 *bibliog.*
aerosol **1**:125
atmospheric tide **2**:304
organic chemistry **14**:439
photochemistry **15**:259
pollution, environmental **15**:415
stratosphere **18**:293
tropopause **19**:310
OZONOSPHERE *see* OZONE LAYER
OZU, YASUJIRO **14**:480 *bibliog.*

P

P (letter) **15**:3 *illus.*
P-AMINOBENZOIC ACID (PABA)
freckle **8**:289
vitamins and minerals **19**:620
P-38 LIGHTNING **15**:3 *illus.*
P-40 **15**:3 *bibliog., illus.*
P-51 MUSTANG *see* MUSTANG (aircraft)
PA CHIN (Ba Jin) **15**:3 *bibliog.*
PA HSIEN (Ba Xian) **15**:3 *bibliog.*
PA SAK RIVER
map (14° 21′N 100° 35′E) **19**:139
PA-SSU-K'O-WO, MOUNT
map (33° 0′N 91° 25′E) **19**:190
PA-TA SHAN-JEN *see* CHU TA
PAÁL, A.
tropism **19**:309
PAARL (South Africa)
map (33° 45′S 18° 56′E) **18**:79
PAAUILO (Hawaii)
map (20° 2′N 155° 22′W) **10**:72
PABA *see* P-AMINOBENZOIC ACID
PABIANICE (Poland)
map (51° 40′N 19° 22′E) **15**:388
PABLO (Montana)
map (47° 36′N 114° 7′W) **13**:547
PABNA (Bangladesh)
map (24° 0′N 89° 15′E) **3**:64
PABST, G. W. **15**:4
PABST, OTTO
jet propulsion **11**:407
PAC *see* PAN AFRICAN CONGRESS
PACA **15**:4 *illus.*
PACARANA *see* FALSE PACA
PACASMAYO (Peru)
map (7° 24′S 79° 34′W) **15**:193
PACEMAKER, ARTIFICIAL **15**:4
heart diseases **10**:96
PACER *see* HORSE RACING
PACHACAMAC (Peru) **15**:4 *bibliog.*
PACHACUTI **15**:4
Inca empire **11**:70 *map*
Sacsahuaman **17**:8
PACHAUG POND
map (41° 34′N 71° 54′W) **5**:193
PACHELBEL, JOHANN **15**:4 *bibliog.*
PACHER, MICHAEL **15**:4 *bibliog.*
PACHUCA (Mexico) **15**:4–5
map (20° 7′N 98° 44′W) **13**:357
PACHYCEPHALOSAURUS **15**:5
PACIFIC (British Columbia)
map (54° 46′N 128° 17′W) **3**:491
PACIFIC (Missouri)
map (38° 29′N 90° 45′W) **13**:476
PACIFIC (county in Washington)
map (46° 30′N 123° 39′W) **20**:35
PACIFIC, WAR OF THE **15**:5
Peru **15**:194
PACIFIC AMERICANS *see* ORIENTAL AMERICANS
PACIFIC CREST TRAIL
hiking **10**:162–163
PACIFIC GROVE (California)
map (36° 38′N 121° 56′W) **4**:31
PACIFIC ISLANDS, TRUST TERRITORY OF THE **15**:5 *bibliog.*
Caroline Islands (U.S.) **4**:160
history **15**:5
Interior, United States Department of the **11**:210
land, people, and economy **15**:5
map (10° 0′N 155° 0′E) **14**:334
Mariana Islands **13**:150–151
Marshall Islands **13**:173
PACIFIC OCEAN **15**:5–8 *bibliog., map*
Balboa, Vasco Núñez de **3**:33
climate **15**:7
tsunami **19**:325
economy **15**:8
geology **15**:7–8
history **15**:8
World War II **20**:258–261 *illus., maps*; **20**:264–267 *illus.*; **20**:275–279 *illus., map*
international date line **11**:220 *map*
intertidal life **11**:229–230
islands and island groups
See also OCEANIA
Aleutian Islands **1**:272
Galápagos Islands **9**:10 *map*
Japan **11**:360–362
Kuril Islands **12**:139
Malay Archipelago **13**:82
Santa Barbara Islands **17**:67
Santa Catalina Island **17**:67
ocean bottom **15**:5–7 *map*
Emperor Seamount Chain **17**:174
fracture zones **14**:339; **15**:6–7 *map*
Marianas Trench **13**:151
mid-oceanic ridge **13**:389–390
Mid-Pacific Mountains **17**:174
oceanic trenches **14**:342
rise **14**:329 *map*; **15**:6–7 *map*
seamount **17**:174
upwelling, oceanic **19**:474
ocean currents and wind systems, worldwide **14**:322–323 *maps*
oil and gas reserves **15**:209 *table*
plate tectonics **15**:353
East Pacific Rise **15**:351 *map*
Pacific-Antarctic Ridge **15**:351 *map*
Pacific plate **15**:351 *map*
Ring of Fire **16**:225
seas, gulfs, and bays
Bering Sea **3**:212 *map*

PACIFIC OCEAN (cont.)
California, Gulf of **4**:38
Celebes Sea **4**:229
China Sea, East **4**:377
China Sea, South **4**:377
Cook Strait **5**:237
Coral Sea **5**:260
Drake Passage **6**:257
Golden Gate **9**:232
Java Sea **11**:385–386
Juan de Fuca, Strait of **11**:457
Magellan, Strait of **13**:48
Okhotsk, Sea of **14**:366
Puget Sound **15**:617
San Francisco Bay **17**:54
Sulu Sea **18**:338
Tasman Sea **19**:42
Yellow Sea **20**:322
tributaries and dimensions **14**:326 *table*
water characteristics **15**:7
PACIFIC SCANDAL (1873) **15**:8 *bibliog.*
Canada, history of **4**:84
PACIFIC THEATER (World War II) *see* WORLD WAR II
PACIFICA (California)
map (37° 38′N 122° 29′W) **4**:31
PACIFISM AND NONVIOLENT MOVEMENTS **15**:8–10 *bibliog., illus.*
Asoka, Emperor of India **2**:261
black Americans **3**:310
civil disobedience **5**:10
Congress of Racial Equality **5**:184
conscientious objector **5**:200
Corrigan, Mairead, and Williams, Betty **5**:276
Einstein, Albert **7**:93–94
Gandhi, Mahatma **9**:36
Gregory, Dick **9**:355
guerrilla theater **9**:392
Jainism **11**:349–350
King, Martin Luther, Jr. **12**:80–81
Living Theatre **12**:376–377
Pauling, Linus Carl **15**:199
Rankin, Jeannette **16**:87–88
Russell, Bertrand **16**:349
Southern Christian Leadership Conference **18**:112
Spock, Benjamin **18**:191–192
Thoreau, Henry David **19**:178
Vietnam War **19**:588
Wald, George **20**:9
PACINO, AL **15**:10
PACIUS, FREDRIK
Finland **8**:96
PACK ICE **15**:10–11 *bibliog., map*
See also ICEBERG
Antarctic pack **15**:11
Ross Ice Shelf **16**:318
Arctic pack **15**:11 *map*
Arctic **2**:142 *map*
Fletcher's Ice Island **8**:163
composition **15**:10
floe **15**:10–11
glaciers and glaciation **9**:193–194
icebreaker **11**:16
oceanography **14**:345
PACKAGING **15**:11–12 *bibliog.*
acrylonitrile **1**:86
aerosol **1**:125
aluminum **1**:319
cellophane **4**:238
food preservation **8**:211–212
milk **13**:423
PACKARD MOTOR CAR COMPANY
automotive industry **2**:363–366
PACOLET RIVER
map (34° 50′N 81° 27′W) **18**:98
PADANG (Indonesia)
map (0° 57′S 100° 21′E) **11**:147
PADCAYA (Bolivia)
map (21° 52′S 64° 48′W) **3**:366
PADDLE TENNIS **15**:12 *bibliog.*
platform tennis **15**:359
PADDLEBALL
racquetball **16**:38
PADDLEFISH **15**:12 *illus.*
PADDLEWHEEL SHIP *see* STEAMBOAT
PADEN CITY (West Virginia)
map (39° 36′N 80° 56′W) **20**:111
PADERBORN (Germany, East and West)
map (51° 43′N 8° 45′E) **9**:140
PADEREWSKI, IGNACE JAN **15**:12 *bibliog.*
PADMA RIVER
map (23° 22′N 90° 32′E) **9**:37
PADRE ISLAND
map (27° 0′N 97° 15′W) **19**:129
PADUA (Italy) **15**:12–13
Giotto di Bondone **9**:187
map (45° 25′N 11° 53′E) **11**:321
PADUA, UNIVERSITY OF **15**:13
PADUCAH (Kentucky) **15**:13
map (37° 5′N 88° 36′W) **12**:47
PADUCAH (Texas)
map (34° 1′N 100° 18′W) **19**:129
PAEKCHE KINGDOM
Korea, history of **12**:116
PAEKTU, MOUNT
map (42° 0′N 128° 3′E) **12**:113
PAEONIUS *see NIKE* (Victory)
PAESTUM (Italy) **15**:13 *bibliog.*
architecture **2**:131 *illus.*; **9**:335 *illus.*
Temple of Hera **9**:335 *illus.*
PÁEZ, JOSÉ ANTONIO **15**:13 *bibliog.*
PÁEZ, PEDRO
Nile River **14**:196
PAG ISLAND
map (44° 30′N 15° 0′E) **20**:340
PAGALU ISLAND
map (1° 25′S 5° 36′E) **7**:226
PAGAN (Burma) **3**:574 *illus.*; **15**:13
Anawratha **1**:398
Southeast Asian art and architecture **18**:109–110 *illus.*
PAGANINI, NICCOLÒ **15**:13 *bibliog.*; **16**:293 *illus.*
PAGE (Arizona)
map (36° 57′N 111° 27′W) **2**:160
PAGE (county in Iowa)
map (40° 45′N 95° 8′W) **11**:244
PAGE (North Dakota)
map (47° 9′N 97° 34′W) **14**:248
PAGE (county in Virginia)
map (38° 40′N 78° 30′W) **19**:607
PAGE, GERALDINE **15**:13
PAGE, JIMMY **16**:249 *illus.*
PAGE, RUTH **15**:13 *bibliog.*
PAGELAND (South Carolina)
map (34° 46′N 80° 24′W) **18**:98
PAGERIE, MARIE JOSÈPHE ROSE TASCHER DE LA *see* JOSEPHINE (empress)
PAGET, SIR JAMES **15**:13–14
PAGET'S DISEASE **15**:14
Paget, Sir James **15**:14
PAGNOL, MARCEL **15**:14 *bibliog.*
PAGO PAGO (American Samoa) **14**:335 *illus.*; **15**:14
PAGODA **4**:387 *illus.*; **15**:14 *bibliog., illus.*
Gojunoto **11**:373 *illus.*; **15**:14 *illus.*
Korean art **12**:117
Sule Pagoda **16**:85 *illus.*
temple **19**:98
PAGON, MOUNT
map (4° 18′N 115° 19′E) **3**:524
PAGOSA SPRINGS (Colorado)
map (37° 16′N 107° 1′W) **5**:116
PAGUATE (New Mexico)
map (35° 8′N 107° 23′W) **14**:136
PAHALA (Hawaii)
map (19° 12′N 155° 29′W) **10**:72
PAHANG RIVER
map (3° 32′N 103° 28′E) **13**:84
PAHARI **15**:14 *bibliog.*
PAHLAVI, MUHAMMAD RAZA SHAH *see* MUHAMMAD REZA SHAH PAHLAVI (1919–80)
PAHLAVI, REZA SHAH *see* REZA SHAH PAHLAVI (1878–1944)
PAHOA (Hawaii)
map (19° 28′N 154° 51′W) **10**:72
PAHODJA (American Indians)
Iowa **11**:248
PAHOKEE (Florida)
map (26° 49′N 80° 40′W) **8**:172
PAHOUIN
Fang **8**:20
PAHRUMP (Nevada)
map (36° 12′N 115° 59′W) **14**:111
PAI CHÜ-I *see* PO CHÜ-I (Bo Ju'i)
PAIGE, SATCHEL **15**:14 *bibliog.*
PÄIJÄNNE LAKE
map (61° 35′N 25° 30′E) **8**:95
PAIK, NAM JUNE **15**:14–15 *biblioc*
PAILOLO CHANNEL
map (21° 5′N 156° 42′W) **10**:72
PAIN **15**:15 *bibliog.*
acupuncture **1**:91
analgesic **1**:388
anesthetics **1**:410–411
aspirin **2**:262–263
colic **5**:101
headache **10**:85–86
heartburn **10**:97
hypnosis **10**:350
inflammation **11**:169
lumbago **12**:454
masochism **13**:198
methadone **13**:343
morphine **13**:587
neuralgia **14**:105
opiate receptor **14**:405
sadism **17**:10
sciatica **17**:141
shingles **17**:262
sickle-cell anemia **17**:293
tic **19**:191
Valium **19**:506
PAINE, JOHN KNOWLES **15**:15 *bibliog.*
PAINE, THOMAS **15**:16 *bibliog., illus.*
Common Sense **5**:141
Erskine, Thomas, 1st Baron Erskine **7**:235
New Rochelle **14**:142
radicalism **16**:43
PAINESVILLE (Ohio)
map (41° 43′N 81° 15′W) **14**:357
PAINT **15**:16–17 *bibliog.*
airbrush **1**:210
benzene **3**:206
colorimeter **5**:122
composition of **15**:16–17
finish, variations of **15**:17
lacquer **12**:160–161
lampblack **12**:176
linseed oil **12**:359–360
manganese **13**:114
manufacturing **15**:17
mastic **13**:216
mica **13**:370–371
painting techniques **15**:23–25 *illus.*
pigment
lead **12**:256
resin **16**:176–177
rosin **16**:317
solvent
turpentine **19**:352
titanium **19**:211
types of **15**:17
varnish **19**:524
PAINT RIVER
map (45° 58′N 88° 15′W) **13**:377
PAINT ROCK (Texas)
map (31° 30′N 99° 55′W) **19**:129
PAINTBOX (video device) **15**:17 *bibliog., illus.*
PAINTED DAISY *see* CHRYSANTHEMUM
PAINTED DESERT (Arizona) **15**:17
map (36° 0′N 111° 20′W) **2**:160
PAINTED TURTLE **15**:18 *illus.*
PAINTING **15**:18–23 *bibliog., illus.*
art conservation and restoration **2**:204–206
art criticism **2**:207
Australia
Nolan, Sidney **14**:213
Austria
Austrian art and architecture **2**:352–353
Biedermeier **3**:247
Huber, Wolf **10**:288
Hundertwasser **10**:304
Klimt, Gustav **12**:97
Kokoschka, Oskar **12**:106
Maulpertsch, Franz Anton **13**:233
Schiele, Egon **17**:120
Schwind, Moritz von **17**:140
Waldmüller, Ferdinand Georg **20**:10
bark painting
bark cloth **3**:82–83
Oceanic art **14**:339
baroque art and architecture **3**:88–91 *illus.*; **15**:20–21
Belgium **15**:19; **15**:21
Bosch, Hieronymus **3**:405–406
Bouts, Dirk **3**:425
Brouwer, Adriaen **3**:512–513
Bruegel (family) **3**:522
Campin, Robert **4**:66–67
Christus, Petrus **4**:416
David, Gerard **6**:47
Delvaux, Paul **6**:96
Ensor, James **7**:207–208
Eyck, Jan van **7**:347–348
Flemish art and architecture **8**:160–161; **15**:19
Floris (family) **8**:176–177
Goes, Hugo van der **9**:223
Gossaert, Jan **9**:254
Joos van Cleve **11**:446
Joos van Ghent **11**:446
Jordaens, Jacob **11**:447
Limbourg brothers **12**:343
Magritte, René **13**:62
Massys, Quentin **13**:214
Memling, Hans **13**:290
Moro, Antonio **13**:583
Ostade, Adriaen van **14**:456
Patinir, Joachim **15**:112
Pourbus (family) **15**:476
Rops, Félicien **16**:312
Rubens, Peter Paul **16**:335–336
Snyders, Frans **18**:6
Teniers, David, the Younger **12**:102
van Dyck, Sir Anthony **19**:513–514
Weyden, Rogier van der **20**:119
Brazil
Portinari, Cândido **15**:445
Canada
Canadian art and architecture **4**:88–90
Carr, Emily **4**:166
Fitzgerald, Lionel LeMoine **8**:131
Group of Seven **9**:376
Harris, Lawren **10**:57–58
Jackson, Alexander Young **11**:340
Johnston, Franz **11**:437
Kane, Paul **12**:14
Krieghoff, Cornelius **12**:129
Lismer, Arthur **12**:366
MacDonald, J. E. H. **13**:12
Milne, David **13**:431
Morrice, James W. **13**:587
Pellan, Alfred **15**:138
Riopelle, Jean Paul **16**:227–228
Suzor-Côté, M. A. de Foy **18**:374
Thomson, Tom **19**:176
Varley, Frederick **19**:523
Walker, Horatio **20**:12
cartoon (art) **4**:175–176
China
Chao Meng-fu (Zhao Mengfu) **4**:282
Ch'i Pai-shih (Qi Baishi) **4**:339
Chinese art and architecture **4**:380
Chu Ta (Zhu Da) **4**:421
Fan K'uan **8**:20
Fu Pao-shih (Fu Baoshi) **8**:351
Han Kan (Han Gan) **10**:34
Hsia Kuei (Xia Gui) **10**:286
Huang Kung-wang (Huang Gongwang) **10**:287
Ku K'ai-chih (Gu Kaizhi) **12**:133
Kuo Hsi (Guo Xi) **12**:137
Li Kung-lin (Li Gonglin) **12**:310
Li Ssu-hsün (Li Sixun) **12**:310
Li T'ang (Li Tang) **12**:310
Liang K'ai (Liang Kai) **12**:311
Ma Yüan (Ma Yuan) **13**:3
Mi Fei **13**:369
Mu-ch'i (Muqi) **13**:630
Ni Tsan (Ni Zan) **14**:177
Shen Chou (Shen Zhou) **17**:255
Shih-t'ao (Shitao) **17**:261
Sung Hui-tsung (Song Huizong) **18**:348
Tai Chin (Dai Jin) **19**:11
Tung Ch'i-ch'ang (Dong Qichang) **19**:333
Wang Meng **20**:22
Wang Wei **20**:22
Wangs, Four **20**:23
Wu Tao-tzu (Wu Daozi) **20**:296
Yen Li-pen (Yan Liben) **20**:326
Zao Wou-ki **20**:355
Czechoslovakia
Kupka, František **12**:138
Mucha, Alfons **13**:630
Denmark
Scandinavian art and architecture **17**:113
Egypt **15**:18
Egyptian art and architecture **7**:88–89
folk art **8**:196–198 *illus.*
France **15**:21–23
Arp, Jean **2**:187
Barbizon school **3**:79
Bombois, Camille **3**:375
Bonnard, Pierre **3**:381
Boucher, François **3**:419–420
Boudin, Eugène Louis **3**:420
Braque, Georges **3**:456
Cézanne, Paul **4**:263–264
Chardin, Jean Baptiste **4**:287–288
Clouet (family) **5**:68–69
Corot, Jean Baptiste Camille **5**:271–272
Courbet, Gustave **5**:314
Daubigny, Charles François **6**:45
David, Jacques Louis **6**:47–48
Degas, Edgar **6**:84
Delacroix, Eugène **6**:86–87
Delaunay, Robert **6**:87
Denis, Maurice **6**:108
Derain, André **6**:121
Diaz de la Peña, Narcisse Virgile **6**:155
Dubuffet, Jean **6**:289
Dufy, Raoul **6**:294
Fantin-Latour, Henri **8**:21
Fauvism **8**:38–39
Fini, Leonor **8**:94
Fouquet, Jean **8**:252
Fragonard, Jean Honoré **8**:259

French art and architecture 8:303–308
Froment, Nicolas 8:338
Gauguin, Paul 9:59–60
Gérard, François Pascal Simon, Baron 9:121
Géricault, Théodore 9:122–123
Gérôme, Jean Léon 9:157
Gillot, Claude 9:182
Girodet-Trioson, Anne Louis 9:189–190
Gleizes, Albert 9:207
Greuze, Jean Baptiste 9:359–360
Gros, Antoine Jean, Baron 9:369–370
Guérin, Pierre Narcisse, Baron 9:391
Guillaumin, Armand 9:395
Harpignies, Henri 10:55
Hélion, Jean 10:112
Hesdin, Jacquemart de 10:151
impressionism 11:62–68
Ingres, Jean Auguste Dominique 11:176–177
La Fresnaye, Roger de 12:146
La Hire, Laurent de 12:147
La Tour, Georges de 12:150
Lafosse, Charles de 12:165
Lancret, Nicolas 12:178
Largillière, Nicolas de 12:207
Le Nain brothers 12:254–255
Le Sueur, Eustache 12:255
Léger, Fernand 12:274
Limosin, Léonard 12:346
Lorrain, Claude 12:415
Manet, Édouard 13:112–114
Marc, Franz 13:145
Masson, André 13:214
Master Honoré 13:215
Master of Moulins 13:215
Mathieu, Georges 13:228
Matisse, Henri 13:228–229
Meissonier, Jean Louis Ernest 13:283
Michel, Georges 13:372
Mignard, Pierre 13:416–417
Millet, Jean François 13:429–430
Moillon, Louise 13:504
Monet, Claude 13:523–524
Monticelli, Adolphe 13:557
Moreau, Gustave 13:576
Moristo, Berthe 13:580
neoimpressionism 14:83
Pater, Jean Baptiste Joseph 15:110
Pissarro, Camille 15:317
postimpressionism 15:462–463
Poussin, Nicolas 15:476–477
Prud'hon, Pierre Paul 15:585
Puvis de Chavannes, Pierre 15:632–633
Redon, Odilon 16:116
Renoir, Pierre Auguste 16:158
Rigaud, Hyacinthe 16:222
Robert, Hubert 16:240–241
Rouault, Georges 16:324
Rousseau, Henri 16:325
Rousseau, Théodore 16:327
Segonzac, André Dunoyer de 17:188
Seurat, Georges 17:214–215
Signac, Paul 17:300
Sisley, Alfred 17:328
Soulages, Pierre 18:71
Soutine, Chaim 18:113
Staël, Nicolas de 18:209
Tanguy, Yves 19:23
Tissot, James 19:209–210
Troyon, Constant 19:313
Utrillo, Maurice 19:498–499
Valadon, Suzanne 19:503
Valentin de Boulogne 19:504
Vallayer-Coster, Anne 19:506
van Loo, Charles André 19:515
Vernet (family) 19:559
Vien, Joseph Marie 19:578
Vigée-Lebrun, Louise Élisabeth 19:591
Vlaminck, Maurice de 19:624
Vouet, Simon 19:637
Vuillard, Édouard 19:640
Watteau, Antoine 20:69
fresco painting 8:327
genre painting 9:93
Germany 15:21
Altdorfer, Albrecht 1:311–312
Baldung-Grien, Hans 3:34–35
Barbari, Jacopo 3:76
Baumeister, Willi 3:130
Biedermeier 3:247
Corinth, Lovis 5:263
Cranach, Lucas, the Elder 5:329
Danube school 6:36
Dix, Otto 6:206–207
Elsheimer, Adam 7:150
Ernst, Max 7:231–232
expressionism (art) 7:340
Feuerbach, Anselm 8:65
Friedrich, Caspar David 8:332
German art and architecture 9:125–126
Grünewald, Matthias 9:382–383
Hartung, Hans 10:64
Heckel, Erich 10:103
Hofmann, Hans 10:196
Holbein, Hans, the Elder 10:200
Jawlensky, Alexey von 11:386
Kirchner, Ernst Ludwig 12:87
Kulmbach, Hans von 12:136
Leibl, Wilhelm 12:276
Liebermann, Max 12:324
Loutherbourg, Philippe Jacques de 12:437
Lys, Jan 12:479
Master Francke 13:215
Mengs, Anton Raphael 13:297
Modersohn-Becker, Paula 13:498
neoexpressionism 14:83
Nolde, Emil 14:214
Overbeck, Johann Friedrich 14:470
Pacher, Michael 15:4
Pechstein, Max 15:130
Richter, Adrian Ludwig 16:214
Rohlfs, Christian 16:270
Runge, Philipp Otto 16:346
Schmidt-Rottluff, Karl 17:128
Schnorr von Carolsfeld, Julius 17:130
Tischbein (family) 19:209
Trübner, Wilhelm 19:313
Winterhalter, Franz Xaver 20:181
Zoffany, Johann 20:371
Gothic painting 15:19
Great Britain 15:21–22
Alma-Tadema, Sir Lawrence 1:305–305
Bacon, Francis 3:13
Blake, William 3:325–326
Bonington, Richard Parkes 3:380
Burne-Jones, Sir Edward 3:576–577
Cole, Thomas 5:99–100
Constable, John 5:206–207
Cotman, John Sell 5:304
Cozens (family) 5:323–324
Crome, John 5:357
Dadd, Richard 6:5
English art and architecture 7:185–188
Etty, William 7:261
Frith, William 8:335
Gainsborough, Thomas 9:8–9
Girtin, Thomas 9:190
Haydon, Benjamin Robert 10:82
Hilliard, Nicholas 10:165
Hockney, David 10:193–194
Hogarth, William 10:198
Hunt, Holman 10:311
John, Augustus 11:423
Kneller, Sir Godfrey 12:99
Landseer, Sir Edwin 12:192
Lawrence, Sir Thomas 12:251
Lear, Edward 12:259
Leighton, Frederick, Baron Leighton of Stretton 12:278
Lely, Sir Peter 12:279
Martin, John 13:179
Millais, Sir John Everett 13:426
Morland, George 13:580
Nicholson, Ben 14:182
Oliver, Isaac 14:379
Palmer, Samuel 15:51
Pre-Raphaelites 15:519
Raeburn, Sir Henry 16:69
Ramsay, Allan 16:81
Reynolds, Sir Joshua 16:191
Romney, George 16:305
Rossetti, Dante Gabriel 16:319
Sandby (family) 17:62
Sickert, Walter Richard 17:293
Stubbs, George 18:306–307
Sutherland, Graham 18:373
Thornhill, Sir James 19:179
Turner, Joseph Mallord William 19:350
Ward, James 20:29
Watts, George Frederic 20:69
Wilkie, Sir David 20:152
Wilson, Richard 20:165
Wright, Joseph 20:290
Greece 15:18
Apelles 2:76–76
Douris 6:249
Epictetus 7:218
Euphronius 7:265
Euthymides 7:311
Exekias 7:329
Greek art 9:338–342
Micon 13:384
Minoan art 13:459
Nichomachos 14:182–183
Zeuxis 20:362
Hungary
Vasarely, Victor 19:525
illuminated manuscripts 11:46–48
illusionism 11:49–50
India
Basawan 3:101
Indian art and architecture 11:94–98
Mansur 13:129
Mogul art and architecture 13:502–503
Indians of North America, art of the 11:140
Iran *see* PAINTING—Persia
Ireland
Yeats, Jack Butler 20:320
Italy
Andrea del Castagno 1:406–406
Andrea del Sarto 1:407–407
Angelico, Fra 1:413–414
Antonella da Messina 2:69–70
Arcimboldo, Giuseppe 2:137–137
Baj, Enrico 3:27
Baldovinetti, Alesso 3:34
Balla, Giacomo 3:40
Barocci, Federico 3:87
Bartolommeo, Fra 3:98
Bassano (family) 3:117–118
Batoni, Pompeo Girolamo 3:124
Bellini (family) 3:188–189
Botticelli, Sandro 3:418
Canaletto 4:98
Caravaggio, Michelangelo Merisi da 4:131–132
Carpaccio, Vittore 4:163
Carracci (family) 4:166–167
Chirico, Giorgio de 4:397
Cimabue 4:430–431
Cortona, Pietro da 5:279
Crivelli, Carlo 5:353
Daddi, Bernardo 6:5
Domenichino 6:230–231
Domenico Veneziano 6:231
Duccio di Buoninsegna 6:289–290
Etruscans 7:259–260 *illus.*
Fontana, Lavinia 8:206
futurism 8:383–384
Gaddi (family) 9:6–7
Gaulli, Giovanni Battista 9:61
Gentile da Fabriano 9:94
Gentileschi (family) 9:95
Ghirlandaio, Domenico 9:169
Giordano, Luca 9:186
Giorgione 9:186–187
Giotto di Bondone 9:187
Giovanni di Paolo 9:188
Giulio Romano 9:191–192
Giunta Pisano 9:192
Gozzoli, Benozzo 9:275
Guardi, Francesco 9:386–387
Guercino 9:391
Italian art and architecture 11:312–314
Italian Renaissance 15:19–20
Lanfranco, Giovanni 12:194
Leonardo da Vinci 12:289–291
Lippi, Filippino 12:362
Lippi, Fra Filippo 12:363
Longhi, Pietro 12:408
Lorenzetti brothers 12:414–415
Lorenzo di Credi 12:415
Lorenzo Monaco 12:415
Lotto, Lorenzo 12:420
Macchiaioli (art group) 13:9
Magnasco, Alessandro 13:53
Mannerism 13:124–125
Mantegna, Andrea 13:129–130
Martini, Simone 13:180
Masaccio 13:194
Masolino da Panicale 13:198
Melozzo da Forli 13:288–289
Michelangelo 13:372–375
Modigliani, Amedeo 13:499
Morandi, Giorgio 13:573
Moroni, Giovanni Battista 13:587
Mysteries, Villa of the 13:692
neoexpressionism 14:83
Pannini, Giovanni Paolo 15:60
Paolo Veneziano 15:62
Parmigianino 15:95
Perugino 15:195
Piero della Francesca 15:296–297
Piero di Cosimo 15:297
Pintoricchio 15:308
Pollaiuolo (family) 15:405–406
Pontormo, Jacopo Carucci da 15:427
Primaticcio, Francesco 15:542
Raphael 16:89
Reni, Guido 16:157
Ricci (family) 16:206
Roman art and architecture 16:276
Rosa, Salvator 16:312
Rosso Fiorentino 16:320
Sassetta 17:84
Sebastiano del Piombo 17:177–178
Signorelli, Lucas 17:301
Sistine Chapel 17:329
Sodoma, Il 18:34
Squarcione, Francesco 18:202
Strozzi, Bernardo 18:303
Tiepolo (family) 19:195–196
Tintoretto 19:206–207
Titian 19:212
Traini, Francesco 19:266
Tura, Cosimo 19:339
Uccello, Paolo 19:370
Vasari, Giorgio 19:525
Veronese, Paolo 19:559–560
Vivarini (family) 19:622
Zuccarelli, Francesco 20:381
Zuccaro (family) 20:381
Japan
Buncho 3:562
Eitoku 7:97
Fujita, Tsuguharu 8:356
Gyokudo 9:414–415
Hiroshige 10:175
Hokusai 10:199–200
Japanese art and architecture 11:374
Josetsu 11:452
Korin 12:122–123
Masanobu (1686–1764) 13:195
Motonobu 13:611
Niten 14:201
Okyo 14:372
Sanraku 17:65
Sesshu 17:212–213
Sesson 17:213
Shubun 17:289
Sotatsu 18:70
Taiga 19:11
Tanyu 19:26
Tessai 19:126
Tohaku 19:222
Korea
Chong Son 4:405
Korean art 12:118 *illus.*
Lamaist art and architecture 12:173
landscape painting 12:188–192
Latin American art and architecture 12:227–228
See also national subheadings under PAINTING, e.g., PAINTING—Brazil; PAINTING—Mexico; etc.
Mexico
Covarrubias, Miguel 5:318
Cuevas, José Luis 5:383
mural painting 13:646
Orozco, José Clemente 14:447–448; 14:448
Rivera, Diego 16:233
Siqueiros, David Alfaro 17:327
Tamayo, Rufino 19:18–19
Velasco, José María 19:536
miniature painting 13:445
movements
abstract art 1:63–65
abstract expressionism 1:65–66
Art Nouveau 2:209–212
Ashcan School 2:229–230
Barbizon school 3:79
color-field painting 5:114
cubism 5:380–381
Dada 6:4–5
Danube school 6:36
expressionism (art) 7:340
Fauvism 8:38–39
futurism 8:383–384
hard-edge painting 10:45
Hudson River School 10:290
impressionism 11:62–68; 15:22
Luminism 12:459
magic realism 13:51
Mannerism 13:124–125
minimal art 13:446
modern art 13:493–496; 15:22–23
neoclassicism (art) 14:81–82; 15:21–22
neoexpressionsim 14:83
neoimpressionism 14:83
op art 14:397
orphism 14:448
photorealism 15:274
pop art 15:429
postimpressionism 15:462–463
Pre-Raphaelites 15:519
realism (art) 15:22; 16:103
rococo style 16:263
romanticism (art) 15:21–22; 16:291–292

PAINTING (cont.)
suprematism **18**:354
surrealism (art) **18**:364–365
symbolism (art) **18**:402–403
synchromism **18**:406
vorticism **19**:635
mural painting **13**:645–647
Netherlands **15**:21
Appel, Karel **2**:87–87
Avercamp, Hendrik van **2**:369–370
Bambocciati **3**:58
Berchem, Nicolaes Pieterszoon **3**:208
Cuyp, Aelbert **5**:399
David, Gerard **6**:47
Doesburg, Theo van **6**:213
Dongen, Kees van **6**:238
Dou, Gerard **6**:245
Dutch art and architecture **6**:309–313
Eyck, Jan van **7**:347–348
Geertgen tot Sint Jans **9**:67
genre painting **9**:93
Goyen, Jan van **9**:274
Hals, Frans **10**:25
Heda, Willem Claesz **10**:104
Helst, Bartholomeus van der **10**:117
Heyden, Jan van der **10**:155
Hobbema, Meindert **10**:192
Hondecoeter, Melchior d' **10**:217
Honthorst, Gerrit van **10**:224
Hooch, Pieter de **10**:225
Huysum, Jan van **10**:326
Israëls, Jozef **11**:306
Jongkind, Johan Barthold **11**:445
Jordaens, Jacob **11**:447
Kalff, Willem **12**:8
Laer, Pieter van **12**:163
Leyster, Judith **12**:309
Maes, Nicolaes **13**:45
Mauve, Anton **13**:238
Metsu, Gabriel **13**:349
Mondrian, Piet **13**:523
Neer, Aert van der **14**:76–77
Ostade, Adriaen van **14**:456
Rembrandt **16**:144–145
Ruisdael, Jacob van **16**:343
Ruisdael, Salomon van **16**:344
Ruysch, Rachel **16**:377
Scorel, Jan van **17**:148
Seghers, Hercules **17**:188
Steen, Jan **18**:243
Ter Borch, Gerard **19**:114
Terbrugghen, Hendrick **19**:115
Thorn-Prikker, Johan **19**:179
van Dyck, Sir Anthony **19**:513–514
van Gogh, Vincent **19**:514–515
Vermeer, Jan **19**:552–553
Verspronck, Johannes Cornelisz **19**:563
Weyden, Rogier van der **20**:119
Witte, Emanuel de **20**:193
Wouwerman, Philips **20**:273
Norway
Munch, Edvard **13**:640
Scandinavian art and architecture **17**:113
Werenskiold, Erik **20**:104
painting techniques **15**:23–25
panoramas **15**:60
Persia
Bihzad, Kamal al-Din **3**:250
Persian art and architecture **15**:185–186
Riza-i-Abbasi **16**:234
Sultan Muhammad **18**:338
Peru
Cuzco **4**:400
Portugal
Gonçalves, Nuno **9**:242
Portuguese art and architecture **15**:456
Vieira da Silva **19**:578
prehistoric art **15**:509–510
psychiatric patient's **15**:600 *illus.*
Renaissance art and architecture **15**:19–21; **16**:150–155
rococo style **16**:263–265 *illus.*
Romanesque art and architecture **16**:284–286
Rome, ancient
Mysteries, Villa of the **13**:692
Roman art and architecture **16**:276
Russia
Chagall, Marc **4**:267–268
Goncharova, Natalie Sergeyevna **9**:242
Kandinsky, Wassily **12**:13
Larionov, Mikhail Fyodorovich **12**:207
Lissitzky, El **12**:366
Malevich, Kasimir **13**:88
Repin, Ilya Yefimovich **16**:160
Rodchenko, Aleksandr Mikhailovich **16**:265
Rublev, Andrei **16**:337
Russian art and architecture **16**:362–364
Tchelitchew, Pavel **19**:52
Vrubel, Mikhail Aleksandrovich **19**:639
Scandinavian art and architecture **17**:112–114
social realism **18**:13
Spain
Berruguete, Pedro **3**:224
Dalí, Salvador **6**:13
El Greco **7**:98–99
Goya, Francisco de **9**:274
Gris, Juan **9**:366–367
Herrera, Francisco de **10**:146
Miró, Joan **13**:463–464
Morales, Luís de **13**:573
Murillo, Bartolomé Esteban **13**:648
Picasso, Pablo **15**:290–291
Ribera, Jusepe de **16**:205–206
Spanish art and architecture **18**:152–156
Tápies, Antonio **19**:34
Valdés Leal, Juan de **19**:503
Velázquez, Diego **19**:536–537
Zuloaga, Ignacio **20**:381
still-life painting **18**:268–270 *illus.*
Sweden
Scandinavian art and architecture **17**:112–114
Zorn, Anders **20**:379
Switzerland
Holbein, Hans, the Younger **10**:201
Kauffmann, Angelica **12**:31
Klee, Paul **12**:95
Witz, Konrad **20**:194–195
Turkey
Levnî, Ressam **12**:304–305
United States **15**:23
Abbey, Edwin Austin **1**:52
abstract expressionism **1**:65–66
Albers, Josef **1**:253–253
Albright, Ivan Le Lorraine **1**:261
Allston, Washington **1**:304–305
American art and architecture **1**:331–336
Armory Show **2**:177
Ashcan School **2**:229–230
Audubon, John James **2**:318–319
Avery, Milton **2**:370
Bartlett, Jennifer **3**:97
Baziotes, William **3**:135
Beaux, Cecilia **3**:148
Berman, Eugene **3**:219
Bierstadt, Albert **3**:248
Blakelock, Ralph Albert **3**:326
Blume, Peter **3**:347
Bonheur, Rosa **3**:378–379
Carmichael, Frank **4**:153
Cassatt, Mary **4**:183
Catlin, George **4**:212
Chase, William Merritt **4**:301
Church, Frederick Edwin **4**:423
Cole, Thomas **5**:99–100
colonial styles in North America **5**:109–111
color-field painting **5**:114
Copley, John Singleton **5**:251
Cropsey, Jaspar **5**:359
Davis, Stuart **6**:53
de Kooning, Willem **6**:60
Demuth, Charles **6**:105–106
Dewing, Thomas Wilmer **6**:147
Dickinson, Edwin **6**:157
Diebenkorn, Richard **6**:161
Dine, Jim **6**:178
Doughty, Thomas **6**:246
Dove, Arthur **6**:250
Durand, Asher Brown **6**:302–303
Duveneck, Frank **6**:316
Dzubas, Friedel **6**:320
Eakins, Thomas **7**:4–5
Earl, Ralph **7**:8
Eilshemius, Louis Michel **7**:92
Estes, Richard **7**:246
Evergood, Philip **7**:316
Feininger, Lyonel **8**:45
Feke, Robert **8**:45
Flack, Audrey **8**:133
Francis, Sam **8**:274
Frankenthaler, Helen **8**:280
Freake limner **8**:289
Glackens, William **9**:195
Gorky, Arshile **9**:252
Gottlieb, Adolph **9**:264
Graves, Morris **9**:302
Graves, Nancy **9**:302
Guston, Philip **9**:408
Gwathmey, Robert **9**:411
Haberle, John **10**:4
Harding, Chester **10**:45–46
Harnett, William **10**:53
Hartigan, Grace **10**:62
Hartley, Marsden **10**:62–63
Hassam, Childe **10**:66–67
Heade, Martin **10**:86
Healy, G. P. A. **10**:89
Held, Al **10**:110
Henri, Robert **10**:122
Hicks, Edward **10**:157–158
Hirschfield, Morris **10**:176
Homer, Winslow **10**:213–214
Hopper, Edward **10**:232–233
Hoppner, John **10**:233
Hosmer, Harriet **10**:255–256
Hudson River school **10**:290
Hunt, William Morris **10**:312
Hurd, Peter **10**:315
Indians of North America, art of the **11**:140–141
Inness, George **11**:179–180
Johns, Jasper **11**:429–430
Johnson, Eastman **11**:431
Kelly, Ellsworth **12**:38–39
Kent, Rockwell **12**:45
Kline, Franz **12**:97–98
Krasner, Lee **12**:127
Kuniyoshi, Yasuo **12**:137
La Farge, John **12**:145
Lane, Fitz Hugh **12**:193
Lawrence, Jacob **12**:250
Leutze, Emanuel **12**:301
Levine, Jack **12**:304
Lichtenstein, Roy **12**:322
Lindner, Richard **12**:352
Louis, Morris **12**:422
Luks, George **12**:454
Luminism **12**:459
MacDonald-Wright, Stanton **13**:13
MacIver, Loren **13**:26
Macke, August **13**:27
magic realism **13**:51
Malbone, Edward Greene **13**:86
Malevich, Kasimir **13**:88
Marin, John **13**:153
Marsh, Reginald **13**:171
Martin, Agnes Bernice **13**:179
Martin, Homer Dodge **13**:179
Maurer, Alfred Henry **13**:234
Mitchell, Joan **13**:483
Moran, Thomas **13**:573
Morse, Samuel F. B. **13**:590
Moses, Grandma **13**:600
Motherwell, Robert **13**:607
Mount, William **13**:618
Neel, Alice **14**:76
neoexpressionism **14**:83
Newman, Barnett **14**:169
Noland, Kenneth **14**:214
O'Keeffe, Georgia **14**:365–366
Olitski, Jules **14**:378
Peale (family) **15**:124
Pearlstein, Philip **15**:128
Pereira, I. Rice **15**:163
Pippin, Horace **15**:312
Pollock, Jackson **15**:409
Porter, Fairfield **15**:444
Pousette-Dart, Richard **15**:476
Prendergast, Maurice **15**:518
Pyle, Howard **15**:633–634
Quidor, John **16**:25
Reinhardt, Ad **16**:132
Rivers, Larry **16**:233–234
Rosenquist, James **16**:315–316
Rothko, Mark **16**:322
Russell, Charles M. **16**:350
Ryder, Albert Pinkham **16**:379
Sargent, John Singer **17**:77–78
Shahn, Ben **17**:235
Sheeler, Charles **17**:248
Shinn, Everett **17**:262
Sloan, John **17**:362
Smibert, John **17**:366
Soyer brothers **18**:115
Stamos, Theodoros **18**:216
Stella, Frank **18**:250
Stella, Joseph **18**:250
Stettheimer, Florine **18**:262
Still, Clyfford **18**:268
Stuart, Gilbert **18**:305
Sully, Thomas **18**:338
synchromism **18**:406
Tack, Augustus **19**:6
Tanning, Dorothea **19**:25
Thayer, Abbott **19**:143
Thiebaud, Wayne **19**:168
Tobey, Mark **19**:219
Tomlin, Bradley Walker **19**:232
Tooker, George **19**:236
Trumbull, John **19**:319
Twachtman, John Henry **19**:357
Tworkov, Jack **19**:360–361
Vanderlyn, John **19**:519
Vedder, Elihu **19**:531
Warhol, Andy **20**:29
Weber, Max (painter) **20**:87
Weir, Julian Alden **20**:95
Wesselmann, Tom **20**:106
West, Benjamin **20**:106–107
Whistler, James Abbott McNeill **20**:134
Whittredge, Worthington **20**:143
Wood, Grant **20**:206–207
Woodville, Richard Caton **20**:213
Wyeth, Andrew **20**:298–299
Wyeth, N. C. **20**:299
PAINTING TECHNIQUES **15**:23–25 *bibliog., illus.*
See also PAINTING—movements
acrylics **15**:23
Louis, Morris **12**:422
brushwork
Li T'ang (Li Tang) **12**:310
casein **15**:23
chiaroscuro **4**:340
drip and splatter
Hofmann, Hans **10**:196
Pollock, Jackson **15**:409
encaustic painting **7**:162
fresco **15**:23
fresco painting **8**:327
gilding **9**:180
gouache **9**:265
grisaille **9**:367
impasto **11**:60
oil painting **15**:23
pointillism
Seurat, Georges **17**:214–215
Signac, Paul **17**:300
sand painting **14**:53 *illus.*
sfumato
Massys, Quentin **13**:214
Mona Lisa **13**:515
tempera **15**:23; **19**:92
watercolor **15**:25; **20**:61–62
PAINTSVILLE (Kentucky)
map (37° 49′N 82° 48′W) **12**:47
PAISIELLO, GIOVANNI **15**:25 *bibliog.*
PAISLEY **15**:25
PAISLEY (Oregon)
map (42° 42′N 120° 32′W) **14**:427
PAISLEY (Scotland) **15**:25
map (55° 50′N 4° 26′W) **19**:403
PAISLEY, IAN **15**:25 *bibliog.*
PAITA (Peru)
map (5° 6′S 81° 7′W) **15**:193
PAIUTE (American Indians) **15**:25 *bibliog.*
ghost dance **9**:169
Indians of North America, art of the **11**:140
Mountain Meadows Massacre **13**:623
Wovoka **20**:285
PAJÁN (Ecuador)
map (1° 34′S 80° 25′W) **7**:52
PAKANBARU (Indonesia)
map (0° 32′N 101° 27′E) **11**:147
PAKARAIMA MOUNTAINS
map (5° 30′N 60° 40′W) **19**:542
PAKENHAM, SIR EDWARD
War of 1812 **20**:27 *illus.*
PAKISTAN **15**:25–29 *bibliog., illus., map, table*
agriculture **15**:28 *illus.*
irrigation **11**:283
archaeology
Indus civilization **11**:153 *map*
Taxila **19**:48
arts **15**:27–28
museums, art **13**:658
Bangladesh *see* BANGLADESH
cities
Gujranwala **9**:402
Hyderabad **10**:329
Islamabad **11**:293
Karachi **12**:26 *illus.*
Lahore **12**:166–167
Lyallpur **12**:473
Multan **13**:637
Peshawar **15**:26 *table*
Rawalpindi **16**:95
Sialkot **17**:290
climate **15**:26
economic activity **15**:28 *illus.*
education **15**:27
South Asian universities **18**:95–96 *table*
flag **15**:26 *illus.*
government **15**:28
health **15**:27
history **15**:28–29
See also INDIA, HISTORY OF
Ayub Khan, Muhammad **2**:379
Bangladesh **3**:36
Bhutto, Zulfikar Ali **3**:236

Central Treaty Organization 4:255
Gandhara 9:35
India-Pakistan Wars 11:93–94
Iqbal, Muhammad 11:249
Jinnah, Muhammad Ali 11:419
Mujibur Rahman 13:635
Muslim League 13:683
Southeast Asia Treaty Organization 18:107
Zia ul-Haq, Muhammad 20:363
land and resources 15:25–27 *map, table*
languages 15:26–27
Dravidian languages 6:263
Indo-Iranian languages 11:145–146
map (30° 0′N 70° 0′E) 2:232
people 15:26–28
Baluch 3:57
Kafir 12:5
Pathan 15:111
physical features
Godwin Austen 9:221
Khyber Pass 12:69
regions
Baluchistan 3:57
Kashmir 12:29–30 *map*
Punjab 15:626
religion 15:27
rivers, lakes, and waterways
Indus 11:152 *map*
Tarbela Dam 6:16
vegetation and animal life 15:26
PAKISTAN, EAST *see* BANGLADESH
PAKOKKU (Burma)
map (21° 20′N 95° 5′E) 3:573
PAKSE (Laos)
map (15° 7′N 105° 47′E) 12:203
PAL, GEORGE
animation 2:29
PALACE
See also names of specific palaces, e.g., PITTI PALACE; SCHÖNBRUNN PALACE; etc.
château 4:302
interior design 11:212–214
Louis II's Bavarian palaces 12:423
Pöppelmann, Matthäus Daniel 15:432
Roman art and architecture 16:274
PALACKÝ, FRANTIŠEK 15:29
Revolutions of 1848 16:189
PALADE, GEORGE EMIL 15:29
cytology 5:412
PALAEOLOGUS (dynasty)
Byzantine art and architecture 3:605
John V Palaeologus, Byzantine Emperor 11:426
Manuel II Palaeologus, Byzantine Emperor 13:131
Michael VIII, Palaeologus, Byzantine Emperor 13:371
PALAEOSCINCUS 15:29
PALAIC LANGUAGE
languages, extinct 12:198
PALAIOPOLIS *see* SAMOTHRACE
PALAIS SOUBISE (Paris) 11:212 *illus.*
PALAIS STOCLET (Brussels)
Art Deco 2:207
PALAMAS, KOSTIS 15:29 *bibliog.*
PALAMEDES 15:29–30
PALATE *see* MOUTH AND THROAT
PALATINATE 15:30 *bibliog.*
Frederick V, Elector Palatine 8:292
Germany in 1648 9:151 *map*
Germany 1815–1871 9:153 *map*
Wittelsbach 20:193
PALATINE (Illinois)
map (42° 7′N 88° 3′W) 11:42
PALATKA (Florida)
map (29° 39′N 81° 38′W) 8:172
PALAU ISLANDS *see* BELAU
PALAWAN ISLAND
map (9° 30′N 118° 30′E) 15:237
PALAZZESCHI, ALDO 15:30
PALAZZO MASSIMO ALLE COLONNE
Peruzzi, Baldassare 15:196
PALAZZO MEDICI-RICCARDI
Michelozzo 13:375
PALAZZO RUCELLAI 1:259 *illus.*
PALAZZO VECCHIO
Florence (Italy) 8:168–169 *map*
PALE (settlement area) 15:30
Ireland, history of 11:262 *map*
PALEMBANG (Sumatra) 15:30
map (2° 55′S 104° 45′E) 11:147
Srivijaya Empire 18:207
PALENCIA (Spain)
map (42° 1′N 4° 32′W) 18:140
PALENQUE (Mexico) 14:237 *map*; 15:30 *bibliog.*
pre-Columbian art and architecture 15:497
Pyramid and Temple of Inscriptions 11:121 *illus.*; 13:243 *illus.*; 15:636 *illus.*
PALEO-INDIAN CULTURE *see* NORTH AMERICAN ARCHAEOLOGY
PALEOANATOMY
anatomy 1:395
PALEOANTHROPOLOGY *see* PREHISTORIC HUMANS
PALEOBOTANY 15:30–32 *bibliog., illus.*
Brongniart, Alexandre 3:503
desert 6:129
desert life 6:129–131
Devonian Period 6:144–146
history 15:31–32
paleoclimatology 15:32–34
paleogeography 15:37–38
plant history chart 15:31
PALEOCENE EPOCH
geologic time 9:104 *table*
Tertiary Period 19:122–124 *table*
PALEOCLIMATOLOGY 15:32–34 *bibliog., illus., map*
aridity 15:33
climate, evidence 15:32–33
fossils 15:33
isotope chemistry 15:33
climate, geologic time periods 15:32
climatic change 15:34
hydrologic cycle 10:342
ice ages 11:7–11
loess 12:393
paleotemperature 15:42
Pleistocene Epoch 15:365
pollen stratigraphy 15:408
PALEOECOLOGY 15:34–35 *bibliog., illus.*
benthic organisms 15:34
Bryan, Kirk 3:528
fossil record 8:243–248; 15:34–35 *illus.*
paleotemperature 15:42
Permian Period 15:174–176
species-diversity gradients 15:35
PALEOGEOGRAPHY 15:35–38 *bibliog., illus., maps*
Cambrian Period 4:50–52
Carboniferous Period 4:138–139
Cenozoic Era 4:245–246
continental drift 5:228–229; 15:36–37
Cretaceous Period 5:340–341
fossil record 8:248
Gressley, Amanz 9:359
history 15:35–36
Jurassic Period 11:474–477
Mesozoic Era 13:322
paleoclimatology 15:34
plate tectonics 15:353–354
Pleistocene Epoch 15:365
scientific research tools 15:37–38
Tertiary Period 19:122–124
theories 15:35–37
PALEOLITHIC PERIOD 2:126 *illus.*; 15:38–41 *bibliog., illus.*
Abbevillian 1:52
Acheulean 1:81
African prehistory 1:173
agriculture, history of 1:189
Aurignacian 2:324
Azilian 2:381
Bordes, François 3:398
Breuil, Henri 3:475–476
camp at Terra Amata, France 15:39 *illus.*
Capsian 4:128–129
cave dwellers 4:225 *illus.*
Châtelperronian 4:303
Chellean 4:311
Chinese archaeology 4:378
Clactonian 5:35
cooking 5:237
Creswellian 5:339
Cro-Magnon man 5:353
Gravettian 9:303
Hamburgian 10:27
hand ax 15:40 *illus.*
Lascaux 12:210
Leakey (family) 12:259
Les Combarelles 12:296
Levalloisian 12:301–302
Lower Paleolithic Period 15:38–40 *illus.*
Magdalenian 13:46
Mesolithic Period 13:314
Middle Paleolithic Period 15:40
Mousterian 13:626
Niaux Cave 14:177
Oldowan 14:376
Perigordian 15:166
Pleistocene Epoch 15:365
points 15:38 *illus.*; 15:40 *illus.*
prehistoric art 15:507–509
prehistoric humans 15:515–516
sled 17:359
Solutrean 18:58
Tardenoisian (Mesolithic Period) 13:314
technology, history of 19:61
time span 15:38
Upper Paleolithic Period 15:40–41
Venus figurines 15:40 *illus.*
PALEOMAGNETISM 15:41–42 *bibliog., map, table*
Earth, geomagnetic field of 7:16
geophysics 9:108
Matthews, D. H. 13:231
plate tectonics 15:353
polar wandering 15:393
PALEONTOLOGY 15:42 *bibliog.*
Andrews, Roy Chapman 1:408
archaeocyathid 2:115
Black, Davidson 3:303
Brontosaurus 3:504–505
Cambrian Period 4:50–52
catastrophism 4:201
coelacanth 5:91
Cope, Edward 5:248
Cuvier, Georges, Baron 5:399
Deshayes, Gerard Paul 6:131
dinosaur 6:179–182
Edaphosaurus 7:54
evolution 7:318
foraminifera 8:219–220
fossil record 8:243–248
fossil study 15:42
geology 9:106
geology and biology fusion 15:42
Gould, Stephen Jay 9:266
graptolite 9:294
Guettard, Jean Étienne 9:392
Hyatt, Alpheus 10:327
Ichthyornis 11:19
Ichthyosaurus 11:19–20
invertebrate 11:234
Jurassic Period 11:474–477
Lartet, Édouard Armand 12:208
Marsh, Othniel Charles 13:171
Matthew, William Diller 13:231
Moore, Raymond Cecil 13:570
Oppel, Albert 14:407
Orbigny, Alcide Dessalines D' 14:416
paleobotany 15:30–32
paleogeography 15:35–38
Paleozoic Era 15:42–43
Permian Period 15:174–176
prehistoric humans 15:511–517
Silurian Period 17:312
Simpson, George Gaylord 17:317
trilobite 19:299
PALEOSCINCUS
dinosaur 6:181
PALEOTEMPERATURE 15:42 *bibliog.*
evidence 15:42
paleoclimatology 15:32
paleoecology 15:34–35
paleothermometer 15:42
PALEOZOIC ERA 15:42–43 *bibliog.*
Africa 1:140 *map*
Asia 2:236 *map*
Australia 2:331 *map*
Cambrian Period 4:50–52 *illus.*
Carboniferous Period 4:137–139
Chondrichthyes 4:404
crinoid 5:350
cystoid 5:411
Devonian Period 6:144–146
Earth, geological history of 7:11–13 *illus., map*
epeiric seas 15:42
Europe 7:270 *map*
eurypterid 7:310
fossil record 8:245
geography 15:42–43
geologic time 9:104 *table*
geology 15:42–43
Gondwanaland 15:43
graptolite 9:294
ice ages 11:7–11
life 15:43
Mississipian System *see* CARBONIFEROUS PERIOD
North America 14:227 *map*
Ordovician Period 14:420–422; 15:43
paleoclimatology 15:32
Pennsylvanian System *see* CARBONIFEROUS PERIOD
Permian Period 15:174–176
Silurian Period 15:43; 17:310–312
South America 18:87 *map*
United States 19:422 *map*
valley and ridge province 19:508
PALERMO (Italy) 11:324 *illus.*; 15:43
map (38° 7′N 13° 21′E) 11:321
PALERMO (Uruguay)
map (33° 48′S 55° 59′W) 19:488
PALERMO STONE 15:43 *bibliog.*
PALÉS MATOS, LUIS
Latin American literature 12:230
PALESTINE 15:43–46 *bibliog., illus., maps*
See also ARAB-ISRAELI WARS; REFUGEE
cities
Beth-shan 3:230
Bethlehem (Jordan/Israel) 3:230–231
Caesarea 4:15
Capernaum 4:122
Hebron 10:103
Jerusalem 11:400–401 *map*
Megiddo 13:280
Nazareth (Israel) 14:67
Samaria 17:45
Shiloh 17:261
history
Balfour Declaration 3:37
Ben-Gurion, David 3:195
biblical archaeology 3:241–242
birth of Israel 15:45–46 *map*
British occupation 15:44–45
Caesarea (site in Israel) 4:15
Crusades 5:366–369
early history 15:44
Ebla 7:36
Egypt 7:79–81
Fertile Crescent 8:60
Gaza Strip 9:64
Hazor 10:84–85
Herod (dynasty) 10:144
Israel 11:306
Israel, Kingdom of 11:306
Jordan 11:449–450
Judah, kingdom of 11:458
Lachish 12:160
Middle East, history of the 13:401; 13:407–409
Palestine Liberation Organization 15:46
Sargon II, King of Assyria 17:78
time of Jesus 3:239 *map*; 11:404 *map*
West Bank 20:108
World War I 20:234; 20:239 *map*; 20:243–244
PALESTINE (Illinois)
map (39° 0′N 87° 37′W) 11:42
PALESTINE (Texas)
map (31° 46′N 95° 38′W) 19:129
PALESTINE LIBERATION ORGANIZATION 15:46 *bibliog.*
Arab League 2:105 *map*
Arafat, Yasir 2:107
Israel 11:306
Lebanon 12:267
Middle East, history of the 13:409–410
Palestine 15:46
West Bank 20:108
PALESTINE MANDATE
Palestine 15:44–45 *map*
PALESTINIAN REFUGEES *see* REFUGEE
PALESTRINA, GIOVANNI PIERLUIGI DA 15:46–47 *bibliog., illus.*
Italian music 11:317–318 *illus.*
mass (musical setting) 13:201
music, history of Western 13:665
PALEY, ALBERT
metalwork 5:327 *illus.*
PALEY, GRACE 15:47
PALEY, WILLIAM (philosopher)
ethics 7:251
PALEY, WILLIAM S. (industrialist) 15:47 *bibliog.*
radio and television broadcasting 16:55–57 *illus.*
PALGRAVE, FRANCIS TURNER 15:47
PALIMÉ (Togo)
map (6° 54′N 0° 38′E) 19:222
PALIN, MICHAEL
"Monty Python's Flying Circus" 13:560
PALISADE (Colorado)
map (39° 7′N 108° 21′W) 5:116
PALISADE (Nebraska)
map (40° 21′N 101° 7′W) 14:70
PALISADES 15:47
diabase 6:148
sill 17:309
PALISADES (Idaho)
map (43° 21′N 111° 13′W) 11:26
PALISADES PARK (New Jersey)
map (40° 51′N 74° 0′W) 14:129
PALISADES RESERVOIR
map (43° 15′N 111° 5′W) 11:26
PALISSY, BERNARD 15:47
PALIT, CAPE OF
map (41° 24′N 19° 24′E) 1:250
PALK STRAIT 15:47
map (10° 0′N 79° 45′E) 18:206

PALLADIO, ANDREA 15:47–48 *bibliog., illus.*
architecture 2:135
Burlington, Richard Boyle, 3d Earl of 3:572
Campbell, Colen 4:65
house (in Western architecture) 10:267
interior design 11:212 *illus.*
Italian art and architecture 11:310
Jones, Inigo 11:442–443
Kent, William 12:45
Monticello 13:557
neoclassicism (art) 14:82
Scamozzi, Vincenzo 17:107
Teatro Olimpico 19:59
Veronese, Paolo 19:560
Vicenza (Italy) 19:571
Villa Rotonda 15:48 *illus.*; 19:597 *illus.*
PALLADIUM 15:48
PALLADIUM (element)
element 7:130 *table*
Group VIII periodic table 15:167
metal, metallic element 13:328
native elements 14:47
transition elements 19:273
Wollaston, William Hyde 20:199
PALLADIUM (mythology) 15:48
PALLADIUS, SAINT 15:48
PALLAS (asteroid)
asteroid 2:268
Olbers, Heinrich 14:373
PALLAS MOUNTAIN
map (68° 6′N 24° 0′E) 8:95
PALLAS'S CAT 15:48 *illus.*
PALLAVA
India, history of 11:90
Mahabalipuram 13:63–64 *illus.*
PALLAZZO DELLO SPORT (Rome) 4:244 *illus.*
PALM (botany) 10:275 *illus.*; 15:48–49 *bibliog., illus.*
cabbage palmetto 4:4
coconut 5:88
date and date palm 6:44–45 *illus.*
Eocene Epoch 19:124 *illus.*
sago 17:12
vegetable oils 19:534–535
PALM BAY (Florida)
map (28° 2′N 80° 35′W) 8:172
PALM BEACH (Florida) 15:49
map (26° 42′N 80° 2′W) 8:172
PALM BEACH (county in Florida)
map (26° 38′N 80° 27′W) 8:172
PALM SPRINGS (California) 15:49
golf 9:239 *illus.*
map (33° 50′N 116° 33′W) 4:31
PALM SUNDAY 15:49
PALM TODDY (beerlike beverage) 3:163
PALMA (Spain) 15:49–50
PALMAS BELLAS (Panama)
map (9° 14′N 80° 5′W) 15:55
PALMCHAT 15:50
PALMDALE (California)
map (34° 35′N 118° 7′W) 4:31
PALME, OLOF 15:50
PALME D'OR *see* GOLDEN PALM
PALMER (Alaska)
map (61° 36′N 149° 7′W) 1:242
PALMER (Massachusetts)
map (42° 9′N 72° 20′W) 13:206
PALMER (Michigan)
map (46° 27′N 87° 35′W) 13:377
PALMER (Nebraska)
map (41° 13′N 98° 15′W) 14:70
PALMER, A. MITCHELL 15:50 *bibliog.*
PALMER, ALICE FREEMAN 15:50 *bibliog.*
PALMER, ARNOLD 15:50 *bibliog., illus.*
golf 9:239
PALMER, DANIEL DAVID
chiropractic 4:397
PALMER, ERASTUS DOW 15:50 *bibliog.*
PALMER, KATE S.
cartoon (editorial and political) 4:176
PALMER, NATHANIEL BROWN 15:50–51
PALMER, SAMUEL 15:51 *bibliog.*
PALMER, SANDRA 15:51
PALMER, WILLIAM J.
Colorado Springs 5:121
PALMER LAKE (Colorado)
map (39° 7′N 104° 55′W) 5:116
PALMER LAND (Antarctica) *see* ANTARCTIC PENINSULA
PALMER RAIDS *see* PALMER, A. MITCHELL
PALMERS CROSSING (Mississippi)
map (31° 16′N 89° 15′W) 13:469
PALMERSTON (Australia) *see* DARWIN (Australia)
PALMERSTON, HENRY JOHN TEMPLE, 3D VISCOUNT 15:51 *bibliog., illus.*
PALMERSTON NORTH (New Zealand)
map (40° 21′S 175° 37′E) 14:158
PALMERTON (Pennsylvania)
map (40° 48′N 75° 37′W) 15:147
PALMETTO (Florida)
map (27° 31′N 82° 35′W) 8:172
PALMIRA (Colombia)
map (3° 32′N 76° 16′W) 5:107
PALMIRA (Ecuador)
map (2° 5′S 78° 43′W) 7:52
PALMISTRY *see* FORTUNE-TELLING
PALMITAS (Uruguay)
map (33° 31′S 57° 49′W) 19:488
PALMITIC ACID 15:51
PALMYRA (Illinois)
map (39° 26′N 90° 0′W) 11:42
PALMYRA (Missouri)
map (39° 48′N 91° 31′W) 13:476
PALMYRA (New York)
map (43° 4′N 77° 14′W) 14:149
PALMYRA (Pennsylvania)
map (40° 18′N 76° 36′W) 15:147
PALMYRA (Syria) 15:51–52 *bibliog.*
ruins 18:413 *illus.*
spice trade 10:137
Zenobia, Queen 20:360
PALMYRA (Virginia)
map (37° 51′N 78° 16′W) 19:607
PALMYRA ISLAND
map (5° 52′N 162° 6′W) 14:334
United States outlying territories 19:464
PALMYRA TUDMUR (Syria)
map (34° 33′N 38° 17′E) 18:412
PALO ALTO (California) 15:52
map (37° 27′N 122° 9′W) 4:31
PALO ALTO (county in Iowa)
map (43° 7′N 94° 38′W) 11:244
PALO PINTO (Texas)
map (32° 46′N 98° 18′W) 19:129
PALO PINTO (county in Texas)
map (32° 45′N 98° 15′W) 19:129
PALO SANTO (Argentina)
map (25° 34′S 59° 21′W) 2:149
PALO VERDE 15:52
PALOLO WORM 15:52
PALOMAR MOUNTAIN
map (33° 22′N 116° 50′W) 4:31
PALOMAR OBSERVATORY 14:317–318 *illus.*; 15:52 *bibliog.*
Babcock, Horace Welcome 3:6
Hale, George Ellery 10:18
Hale reflector 19:82 *illus.*
Kowal, Charles T. 12:126
National Geographic Society–Palomar Observatory Sky Survey 14:33–34
PALOMINO 10:243 *illus.*; 15:52 *illus.*
saddle horse 17:9
PALOS, CAPE OF
map (37° 38′N 0° 41′W) 18:140
PALOURDE, LAKE
map (29° 44′N 91° 8′W) 12:430
PALOUSE (American Indians)
Spokan 18:192
PALOUSE (Washington)
map (46° 55′N 117° 4′W) 20:35
PALPA (Peru)
map (14° 32′S 75° 11′W) 15:193
PALPITATION 15:52
PALSY 15:52
cerebral palsy 4:259–260
paralysis 15:79
Parkinson's disease 15:91
PALUDIN-MÜLLER, FREDERIK 15:52–53
PALYNOLOGY
paleobotany 15:30–31
pollen stratigraphy 15:407–408
PAMEKASAN (Indonesia)
map (7° 10′S 113° 28′E) 11:147
PAMELA (book) 15:53
Joseph Andrews 11:451
Richardson, Samuel 16:212–213
PAMIRS 15:53
map (38° 0′N 73° 0′E) 19:388
PAMLICO (county in North Carolina)
map (35° 5′N 76° 45′W) 14:242
PAMLICO RIVER
map (35° 20′N 76° 30′W) 14:242
PAMPA (Texas)
map (35° 32′N 100° 58′W) 19:129
PAMPAS 15:53; 18:94 *illus.*
Argentina 2:146
biome 3:273–274 *map*
Indians, American 11:132–133 *maps*
map (35° 0′S 63° 0′W) 2:149
PAMPAS (Peru)
map (12° 24′S 74° 54′W) 15:193
PAMPHLET 15:53 *bibliog.*
American literature 1:342
chapbook 4:284
Common Sense 5:141
Tale of a Tub, A 19:15–16
PAMPLEMOUSSES (Mauritius)
map (20° 26′S 57° 34′E) 13:237
PAMPLICO (South Carolina)
map (34° 0′N 79° 34′W) 18:98
PAMPLONA (Colombia)
map (7° 23′N 72° 39′W) 5:107
Ursúa, Pedro de 19:487
PAMPLONA (Spain) 15:53
map (42° 49′N 1° 38′W) 18:140
PAMUNKEY RIVER
map (37° 32′N 76° 48′W) 19:607
PAN (mythology) 15:53
PAN AFRICAN CONGRESS
African National Congress 1:171; 1:172
South Africa 18:83
PAN-AFRICANISM
Du Bois, W. E. B. 6:285–286
PAN-AMERICAN GAMES 15:53
Shorter, Frank 17:284
swimming and diving 18:391 *illus.*
PAN AMERICAN HIGHWAY 15:53–54
roads and highways 16:238
PAN-AMERICAN SPORTS ORGANIZATION
Pan-American Games 15:53
PAN-AMERICAN UNION *see* ORGANIZATION OF AMERICAN STATES
PAN-CH'IAO (Taiwan)
map (25° 2′N 121° 26′E) 19:13
PAN-INDIANISM
powwow 15:486
Shawnee Prophet 17:247
PAN-P'O-TS'UN (Banpocun) (China) 15:54 *bibliog.*
PAN-SLAVISM 15:54 *bibliog.*
Slavophiles and Westernizers 17:359
PANA (Illinois)
map (39° 23′N 89° 5′W) 11:42
PANACA (Nevada)
map (37° 47′N 114° 23′W) 14:111
PANACEA (Florida)
map (30° 2′N 84° 23′W) 8:172
PANADURA (Sri Lanka)
map (6° 43′N 79° 54′E) 18:206
PANAITIOS PAINTER, THE *see* ONESIMOS
PANAJI (India)
map (15° 29′N 73° 50′E) 11:80
PANAMA 15:54–56 *bibliog., illus., map, table*
cities
Colón 5:109
Panama City 15:57
economic activity 15:54–55
education
Latin American universities 12:233 *table*
flag 15:54 *illus.*
flag of convenience 8:149
government 15:55–56
history 15:56
New Granada 14:121
Torrijos Herrera, Omar 19:244
land and people 15:54–55 *map, table*
map (9° 0′N 80° 0′W) 14:225
Panama, Isthmus of 15:56
Panama Canal Zone 15:57
PANAMA (Oklahoma)
map (35° 10′N 94° 40′W) 14:368
PANAMA, BAY OF
map (8° 50′N 79° 20′W) 15:55
PANAMA, GULF OF
map (8° 0′N 79° 30′W) 15:55
PANAMA, ISTHMUS OF 15:56
map (9° 0′N 79° 0′W) 15:55
PANAMA CANAL 4:96–97 *illus.*; 14:232 *illus.*; 15:56–57 *bibliog., illus., map*
Bunau-Varilla, Philippe Jean 3:562
construction 12:221 *illus.*
Evarts, William Maxwell 7:315
Goethals, George Washington 9:223
Hay-Pauncefote Treaty 10:80
history 15:56–57
Latin America, history of 12:222
Lesseps, Ferdinand Marie, Vicomte de 12:298
map (9° 20′N 79° 55′W) 15:56
photography
O'Sullivan, Timothy H. 14:459
Roosevelt, Theodore 16:311
treaty (1977)
Bunker, Ellsworth 3:563
yellow fever 20:322
PANAMA CANAL ZONE 15:57
education
Canal Zone College 4:97
Panama 15:56
PANAMA CITY (Florida)
map (30° 10′N 85° 41′W) 8:172
PANAMA CITY (Panama) 15:55 *illus., table*; 15:57
map (8° 58′N 79° 31′W) 15:55
PANAY ISLAND
map (11° 15′N 122° 30′E) 15:237
PANČEVO (Yugoslavia)
map (44° 52′N 20° 39′E) 20:340
PANCREAS 1:54 *illus.*; 15:57–58 *bibliog., illus.*
cancer 15:58
diabetes 6:148–149
digestion, human 6:171–172; 15:57–58
endocrine system 7:168–169 *illus.*
endocrine system, diseases of the 7:171
enzyme 15:57–58
gland 9:197
glucagon 9:210–211
hormone, animal 10:235 *illus.*; 10:236 *table*
insulin 11:197–198; 15:58
intestine 11:230
pancreatitis 15:58
PANCREATITIS 15:58
mumps 13:639
PANCREOZYMIN
hormone, animal 10:236 *table*
PANDA 15:58 *bibliog., illus.*
olingo 14:378
PANDEMIC *see* EPIDEMIC
PANDER, CHRISTIAN HEINRICH 15:58
PANDIT, VIJAYA LAKSHMI 15:58–59
PANDO (Uruguay)
map (34° 43′S 55° 57′W) 19:488
PANDOLFO, SIGISMONDO
Malatesta (family) 13:80
PANDORA 15:59
PANDORA'S BOX
Pandora 15:59
PANDORINA 15:59
microorganism classification 15:59
PANEL TRUCK
trucking industry 19:315
PANELING *see* WOOD (botany)
PANG-PU (China)
map (32° 58′N 117° 24′E) 4:362
PANGAEA
continental drift 5:228–229 *map*
PANGAI (Tonga)
map (19° 48′S 174° 21′W) 19:233
PANGBURN (Arkansas)
map (35° 15′N 91° 51′W) 2:166
PANGEA
paleography 15:36–37 *maps*
plate tectonics 15:354 *map*
PANGENES
Vries, Hugo De 19:639
PANGKALPINANG (Indonesia)
map (2° 8′S 106° 8′E) 11:147
PANGNIRTUNG (Northwest Territories)
map (66° 8′N 65° 44′W) 14:258
PANGOLIN 13:104 *illus.*; 15:59 *illus.*
skin 17:340 *illus.*
PANGUITCH (Utah)
map (37° 49′N 112° 26′W) 19:492
PANHANDLE (Texas)
map (35° 21′N 101° 23′W) 19:129
PANHYPOPITUITARISM
endocrine system, diseases of the 7:170
PANI PIQUE *see* WICHITA (American Indians)
PANIC, FINANCIAL 15:59 *bibliog.*
PANICALE, MASOLINO DA *see* MASOLINO DA PANICALE
PANIN, NIKITA IVANOVICH, COUNT 15:59 *bibliog.*
PANINI 15:59 *bibliog.*
linguistics 12:356
PANIZZI, SIR ANTHONY
British Museum 3:497
PANJ RIVER
map (37° 6′N 68° 20′E) 1:133
PANKHURST (family) 15:60 *bibliog., illus.*
PANKHURST, (ESTELLE) SYLVIA
Pankhurst (family) 15:60
PANKHURST, CHRISTABEL
Pankhurst (family) 15:60
PANKHURST, EMMELINE
Pankhurst (family) 15:60 *illus.*
suffrage, women's 18:326
PANLEUKOPENIA *see* FELINE DISTEMPER
PANNENBERG, WOLFHART 15:60 *bibliog.*
PANNINI, GIOVANNI PAOLO 15:60 *bibliog.*
PANNONIA 15:60

PANOFSKY, ERWIN **15**:60 *bibliog.*
  iconography **11**:24
PANOLA (Alabama)
  map (32° 57′N 88° 16′W) **1**:234
PANOLA (county in Mississippi)
  map (34° 25′N 90° 0′W) **13**:469
PANOLA (county in Texas)
  map (32° 10′N 94° 17′W) **19**:129
PANOPTES *see* ARGUS
PANORA (Iowa)
  map (41° 42′N 94° 22′W) **11**:244
PANORAMAS **15**:60 *bibliog.*
PANPIPES **15**:60–61 *illus.*
  African **1**:169
PANSOPHISM
  Comenius, John Amos **5**:132–133
PANSPERMIA THEORY
  origin of life **12**:327
PANSY **15**:61 *illus.*
  violet **19**:602
PANTAENUS
  Clement of Alexandria, Saint **5**:49
PANTALOON **5**:137 *illus.*
PANTELLERIA ISLAND
  map (36° 47′N 12° 0′E) **11**:321
PANTHEISM **15**:61 *bibliog.*
  Cleanthes **5**:47
  Erigena, John Scotus **7**:230
  Hinduism **15**:61
  immanence, divine **11**:54
  Spinoza, Baruch **18**:187–188
PANTHEON (London)
  Wyatt, James **20**:297
PANTHEON (Paris)
  Soufflot, Jacques Germain **18**:70
PANTHEON (Rome) **15**:61–62 *bibliog., illus.*
  dome **6**:229 *illus.*
  Roman art and architecture **16**:273 *illus.*
  temple **19**:96–97 *illus.*
PANTHER **11**:469 *illus.*
PANTILE **16**:306 *illus.*
PANTOGRAPH **15**:62
PANTOMIME
  characters **4**:286
  mime and pantomime **13**:434
PANTOTHENIC ACID
  vitamins and minerals **19**:620
PÁNUCO RIVER
  map (22° 16′N 97° 47′W) **13**:357
PAO-CHI (China)
  map (34° 22′N 107° 14′E) **4**:362
PAO-T'OU (China)
  map (40° 40′N 109° 59′E) **4**:362
PAOLA (Kansas)
  map (38° 35′N 94° 53′W) **12**:18
PAOLI (Indiana)
  map (38° 33′N 86° 28′W) **11**:111
PAOLI, PASQUALE **15**:62 *bibliog.*
PAOLO VENEZIANO **15**:62 *bibliog.*
PAOLOZZI, EDUARDO **15**:62 *bibliog.*
PAP TEST **15**:62
  cancer **4**:104 *illus.*
  Papanicolaou, George N. **15**:62
PÁPA (Hungary)
  map (47° 19′N 17° 28′E) **10**:307
PAPA DOC *see* DUVALIER, FRANÇOIS
PAPACY **15**:62–66 *bibliog., illus., table*
  See also ROMAN CATHOLIC CHURCH; names of specific popes, e.g., ADRIAN I, POPE; PIUS II, POPE; etc.
  bull, papal **3**:558
  Cardinals, College of **4**:144
  church and state **15**:63
  conciliarism **5**:170
  coronation, papal **5**:271
  Counter-Reformation **5**:310–311
  cross **5**:360; **5**:361 *illus.*
  Crusades **5**:368–369; **15**:63–65
  decretals **6**:76
  Europe, history of **7**:284–285
  Germany, history of **9**:149
  Guelphs and Ghibellines **9**:390
  Holy Roman Empire **10**:210
  infallibility **11**:161–162
  investiture controversy **11**:237–238
  Italy, history of **11**:328–329
  Lateran Treaty **12**:215
  list of popes **15**:64–65
  Middle Ages **13**:392–393; **15**:63–65
  Naples, Kingdom of **14**:15
  Papal States **15**:67
  Schism, Great **17**:122
  state (in political philosophy) **18**:230
  ultramontanism **19**:377
  Vatican City **19**:526–527
  Vatican museums and galleries **19**:527–528
  woman pope
    Joan, Pope **11**:420
PAPADOPOULOS, GEORGIOS
  Greece **9**:328
PAPAGO (American Indians) **15**:66 *bibliog.*; **20**:201 *illus.*
  Hohokam culture **10**:199
  Indians of North America, art of the **11**:140
  Pima **15**:303–304
PAPAGOS, ALEXANDROS **15**:67
PAPAIKOU (Hawaii)
  map (19° 47′N 155° 6′W) **10**:72
PAPAIN (biology)
  enzyme **7**:214
  herbs and spices **10**:137
  papaya **15**:67
PAPAL MITER SHELL **17**:251 *illus.*
PAPAL STATES **15**:57 *bibliog.*
  boundaries *c.*1360 **7**:285 *map*
  boundaries *c.*1560 **7**:288 *map*
  boundaries *c.*1648 **7**:289 *map*
  boundaries 1815 **7**:291 *map*
  Italy, history of **11**:327–328 *map*; **11**:330 *map*
  Pepin the Short, King of the Franks **15**:156
PAPANDRÉOU, ANDREAS **15**:67
  Greece **9**:329
PAPANDREOU, DEMETRIUS *see* DAMASKINOS
PAPANDRÉOU, GEORGIOS **15**:67
PAPANEK, VICTOR
  industrial design **11**:156
PAPANICOLAOU TEST *see* PAP TEST
PAPANTLA (Mexico)
  map (20° 27′N 97° 19′W) **13**:357
PAPATOETOE (New Zealand)
  map (36° 58′S 174° 52′E) **14**:158
PAPAW **15**:67 *illus.*
  papaya **15**:67
PAPAYA **15**:67–68 *illus.*
PAPEETE (French Polynesia) **15**:68
PAPEN, FRANZ VON **15**:68
  Nuremberg Trials **14**:297 *illus.*
PAPER **15**:68–70 *bibliog., illus., table*
  See also NEWSPRINT
  book **3**:385
  bromide paper
    Swan, Sir Joseph Wilson **18**:379
  cellulose **4**:238
  Chinese art and architecture **4**:380–381
  chromatography
    Synge, Richard Laurence Millington **18**:408
  craft **5**:327 *illus.*
  drawing **6**:263–264
  history
    papermaking machine (1799) **15**:68 *illus.*
    papyrus **15**:73
    parchment **15**:83
    19th-century Japanese production **15**:68 *illus.*
  paper folding **15**:70–71
  papier-mâché **15**:71
  printing **15**:550–553
  production
    Fourdrinier machine **15**:70 *illus.*
    lumber **12**:456
    major producing nations **15**:70 *table*
    modern production **15**:69 *illus.*
  pulp and paper mills **4**:79 *illus.*
    fir **8**:100
    spruce **18**:201
    wood **20**:206
  recycling of materials **16**:111
  wallpaper **20**:16–17
  watermark **20**:65
PAPER FOLDING **15**:70–71 *bibliog., illus.*
PAPER NAUTILUS *see* ARGONAUT
PAPERBACK BOOK
  Ferlinghetti, Lawrence **8**:54
  paperback rights
    Doctorow, E. L. **6**:210
  publishing **15**:611–612
PAPERBARK **15**:71
PAPHOS (Cyprus)
  map (34° 45′N 32° 25′E) **5**:409
PAPIAS OF HIERAPOLIS **15**:71
  Apostolic Fathers **2**:85
PAPIER-MÂCHÉ **15**:71 *bibliog.*
PAPILLION (Nebraska)
  map (41° 9′N 96° 3′W) **14**:70
PAPILLOMA **15**:71
PAPILLON (dog) **6**:217 *illus.*; **15**:71 *bibliog., illus.*
PAPIN, DENIS **15**:71
  pump **15**:622–623
PAPINEAU, LOUIS JOSEPH **15**:72 *bibliog.*
  Canada, history of **4**:82
  Rebellions of 1837 **16**:105
PAPP, JOSEPH **15**:72 *bibliog.*
PAPPUS **15**:72 *bibliog.*
PAPRIKA *see* PEPPER (capsicum)
PAPUA, GULF OF
  map (8° 30′S 145° 0′E) **15**:72
PAPUA NEW GUINEA **15**:72–73 *bibliog., illus., map, table*
  art
    ceramic head **14**:337 *illus.*
  cannibalism **4**:109–110
  cities
    Port Moresby **15**:443
  climate **15**:72–73 *table*
  economy **15**:73
  flag **15**:72 *illus.*
  government **15**:73
  history **15**:73
    MacArthur, Douglas **13**:5
  land **15**:72–73 *map*
  languages
    creole **5**:338
    Ocean languages **14**:339
    Southeast Asian languages **18**:111
  map (6° 0′S 147° 0′E) **14**:334
  Owen Stanley Range **14**:472
  people **15**:73
    Arapesh **2**:109
    Kula Ring **12**:135
    Mudmen of the Asaro Valley **15**:103 *illus.*
    Papuans **15**:73
    race **16**:34 *illus.*
  regions
    Bismarck Archipelago **3**:299
    Bougainville **3**:402
    New Britain **14**:115
    New Ireland **14**:127
PAPUANS **15**:73 *bibliog.*
PAPYRUS **15**:73 *illus.*; **17**:183 *illus.*
  boat
    Ra expeditions **16**:29
  book **3**:383
  illuminated manuscripts **11**:46
  Oxyrhynchus (Egypt) **14**:478
  Rhind mathematics papyrus **13**:223 *illus.*
PARÁ (Brazil)
  map (4° 0′S 53° 0′W) **3**:460
PARA-AMINOBENZOIC ACID (PABA) *see* P-AMINOBENZOIC ACID (PABA)
PARA RUBBER
  tree **19**:288
PARABLE **15**:73
  Animal Farm (book) **2**:22–23
  Bible **3**:240
  Castle, The (book) **4**:191
PARABOLA **15**:74 *bibliog., illus.*
  conic section **5**:188 *illus.*
  eccentricity **7**:37; **15**:74
  Galilean
    ballistics **3**:50
  geometry **15**:74
  radio astronomy **16**:51–53 *illus.*
  reflection, light and sound **15**:74
PARABOLIC SPIRAL
  spiral **18**:188
PARACAS (Peru) **15**:74 *bibliog.*
  Chavín de Huántar **4**:306
  embroidered burial cloak **15**:500 *illus.*
  Nazca **14**:67
  pre-Columbian art and architecture **15**:499–500
PARACELSUS **15**:74 *bibliog.*
  medicine **13**:269
  portrait by Quentin Massys **13**:214 *illus.*
  sylph **18**:402
PARACHUTE **15**:74–75 *bibliog., illus.*
  aerial sports **1**:122
  airborne troops **1**:210
  assembly and safety gear **15**:75 *illus.*
  Garnerin, André J. **9**:49
PARAĆIN (Yugoslavia)
  map (43° 52′N 21° 24′E) **20**:340
PARADES Y ARRILLAGA, MARIANO
  Mexican War **13**:352–353
PARADISE (California)
  map (39° 46′N 121° 37′W) **4**:31
PARADISE ISLAND
  map (25° 5′N 77° 19′W) **3**:23
PARADISE LOST (poem) **15**:75 *bibliog.*
  Milton, John **13**:432–433
PARADISE VALLEY (Nevada)
  map (41° 30′N 117° 32′W) **14**:111
PARADOX (literature)
  figures of speech **8**:76
PARADOX (mathematics) **15**:75–76 *bibliog.*
  clock paradox **5**:61
  mathematics, history of **13**:226
  Russell's paradox **16**:351
  semantical paradox **15**:75–76
  set theory **15**:75–76
  "solutions" **15**:75–76
  Zeno's paradoxes **20**:360
PARAFFIN
  alkane **1**:296
PARAFFIN OIL *see* KEROSENE
PARAGONAH (Utah)
  map (37° 53′N 112° 46′W) **19**:492
PARAGORIC
  camphorated tincture of opium **15**:84
PARAGOULD (Arkansas)
  map (36° 3′N 90° 29′W) **2**:166
PARAGUANÁ PENINSULA
  map (11° 55′N 70° 0′W) **19**:542
PARAGUAY **15**:76–77 *bibliog., illus., map, table*
  cities
    Asunción **2**:286
  economic activity **15**:76–77 *illus.*
  education **15**:76
    Latin American universities **12**:233 *table*
  flag **15**:76 *illus.*
  government **15**:76
  history **15**:76–77
    Chaco War **4**:265
    Francia, José Gaspar Rodríguez de **8**:273–274
    López, Francisco Solano **12**:412
    Stroessner, Alfredo **18**:301
    Triple Alliance, War of the **19**:302
  land and resources **15**:76–77 *map, table*
  languages
    Indian languages, American **11**:101
  map (23° 0′S 58° 0′W) **18**:85
  people **15**:76
    Guaraní **9**:386
  rivers, lakes, and waterways
    Paraguay River **15**:78
PARAGUAY RIVER **15**:78
  map (27° 18′S 58° 38′W) **15**:77
PARAGUAY TEA *see* MATÉ
PARAGUAYAN WAR *see* TRIPLE ALLIANCE, WAR OF THE (1865–70)
PARAÍBA (Brazil)
  map (7° 15′S 36° 30′W) **3**:460
PARAÍSO (Mexico)
  map (18° 24′N 93° 14′W) **13**:357
PARAKEET **10**:5 *illus.*; **15**:78 *bibliog., illus.*
  parrot **15**:97–98
PARAKOU (Benin)
  map (9° 21′N 2° 37′E) **3**:200
PARAKRAMA BAHU I, KING OF LANKA
  Polonnaruwa **15**:418
PARALDEHYDE **15**:78
  sedative **17**:182
PARALEGAL SERVICES **15**:78 *bibliog.*
PARALLAX (astronomy) **15**:78–79 *bibliog., illus.*
  Bessel, Friedrich **3**:228
  distance, astronomical **6**:199
  Kapteyn, Jacobus Cornelius **12**:26
  parsec **15**:98
  star **18**:221
  Struve, Friedrich Georg Wilhelm von **18**:304
PARALLAX (photography) **4**:57
PARALLEL **15**:79
PARALLEL LIVES (book)
  Plutarch **15**:372
PARALLEL PROCESSING **15**:79
  computer **5**:160i
PARALLELEPIPED
  volume **19**:632
PARALLELOGRAM **15**:79 *bibliog.*
  problem solving **15**:559 *illus.*
  rectangle **16**:110
  trapezoid **19**:283
PARALYSIS **15**:79 *bibliog.*
  cerebral palsy **4**:259–260
  hemiplegia **10**:119
  palsy **15**:52
  paraplegia **15**:80
  poliomyelitis **15**:397
  red tide **16**:114
  stroke **18**:302
  venom **19**:546
PARAMARIBO (Suriname) **15**:79; **18**:364 *illus., table*
  map (5° 50′N 55° 10′W) **18**:364
PARAMECIUM **15**:79–80 *bibliog., illus.*
  anatomy **15**:580 *illus.*
  biological locomotion **3**:265; **15**:581 *illus.*
  Didinium **6**:160
  protozoa **15**:79–80
  reproduction **15**:80
  Sonneborn, Tracy Morton **18**:65
  species **15**:79–80

PARAMECIUM AURELIA
Ciliata **4**:430 *illus.*
PARAMEDIC **15**:80 *bibliog.*
ambulance **1**:326
PARAMETER **15**:80
PARAMOUNT PICTURES (film studio)
film, history of **8**:87
Los Angeles (California) **12**:417 *map*
radio and television broadcasting **16**:56
Zukor, Adolph **20**:381
PARAMUS (New Jersey)
map (40° 57′N 74° 4′W) **14**:129
PARANÁ (Argentina) **15**:80
map (31° 44′S 60° 32′W) **2**:149
PARANÁ (region in Brazil)
map (23° 30′S 52° 0′W) **3**:460
PARANÁ (city in Brazil)
map (12° 33′S 47° 52′W) **3**:460
PARANÁ PLATEAU
South America **18**:87
PARANÁ RIVER **15**:80
map (33° 43′S 59° 15′W) **3**:460
PARANOIA **15**:80 *bibliog.*
marijuana **13**:153
PARANTHROPUS
Sterkfontein **18**:260
PARAPLEGIA **15**:80
paralysis **15**:79
PARAPSYCHOLOGY **15**:80–82 *bibliog., illus.*
clairvoyance **5**:35
experiments **15**:80–81
extrasensory perception **7**:346; **15**:80–81
Kirlian photography **12**:89
machine **15**:81 *illus.*
psychokinesis **15**:80–81; **15**:591
recognition as science **15**:81–82
Rhine, J. B. **16**:195
spiritualism **18**:189
PARASITE **15**:82 *bibliog.*
Anoplura **2**:34
ant **2**:37
Babesia **3**:6
balantidiasis **3**:33
barnacle **3**:85
blowfly **3**:341
botfly **3**:415
broomrape (botany) **3**:512
Cnidosporidia **5**:73
cuckoo **5**:381
Entamoeba **7**:208
eye worm **7**:351
fig wasp **8**:75
flatworm **8**:156
fluke **8**:186
Giardia **9**:172
hookworm **10**:227
ichneumon fly **11**:19
invertebrate **11**:234–236
isopod **11**:300
lamprey **12**:176
lennoa **12**:285
louse **12**:436
mesozoan **13**:322
metamorphosis **13**:334
mistletoe **13**:481
mite **13**:484
molds **13**:506
nematode **14**:80
parasitic diseases **15**:82–83
parasitology **15**:83
pinworm **15**:308
Protozoa **15**:580
rafflesia **16**:69
spiny-headed worm **18**:188
Sporozoa **18**:195
Strepsiptera **18**:297
tick **19**:191–192
tongue worm **19**:234
Treponema **19**:291
Trichomonas **19**:296
virus **19**:613
witchweed **20**:192
worm **20**:283–284
yeast **20**:320
PARASITIC DISEASES **15**:82–83 *bibliog., illus.*
amebiasis **1**:326
anthelmintic drugs **2**:49
ascariasis **2**:227
coccidiosis **5**:85
diseases, animal **6**:192
diseases, human **6**:193
diseases, plant **6**:195
dysentery **6**:320
filariasis **8**:78
food poisoning and infection **8**:211
gastrointestinal tract disease **9**:56–57
infectious diseases **11**:165
kala-azar **12**:7
malaria **13**:79–80
Mastigophora **13**:217
mildew **13**:419
nocardiosis **14**:212
protozoal diseases **15**:581
respiratory system disorders **16**:181
rickettsia **16**:216
river blindness **16**:232
schistosomiasis **17**:123
skin diseases **17**:342
toxoplasmosis **19**:256
trichinosis **19**:296
trichomoniasis **19**:296
trypanosomiasis **19**:322
zoonoses **15**:82
PARASITOLOGY **15**:83
symbiosis **18**:402
PARATHYROID **15**:83
endocrine system **7**:169 *illus.*
endocrine system, diseases of the **7**:170
hormones **10**:236
immunodeficiency disease **11**:60
PARATROOPS *see* AIRBORNE TROOPS
PARBATIPUR (Bangladesh)
map (25° 39′N 88° 55′E) **3**:64
PARCHMENT **15**:83 *bibliog.*
book **3**:383
PARDEEVILLE (Wisconsin)
map (43° 32′N 89° 18′W) **20**:185
PARDES CHANA (Israel)
map (32° 28′N 34° 58′E) **11**:302
PARDO, MANUEL
Peru **15**:194
PARDON **15**:83 *bibliog.*
PARDUBICE (Czechoslovakia)
map (50° 2′N 15° 47′E) **5**:413
PARÉ, AMBROISE **15**:84
PAREGORIC **15**:84
PARENT **15**:84 *bibliog.*
See also FAMILY
adolescence **1**:107
adoption and foster care **1**:107
attachment (psychology) **2**:313
birth control **3**:293–295
child abuse **4**:348
children's rights **4**:354
marriage **13**:164–165
preschool education **15**:521–522
sex education **17**:225–226
sexual development **17**:230
PARENT (Quebec)
map (47° 55′N 74° 37′W) **16**:18
PARENTS AND TEACHERS, NATIONAL CONGRESS OF **15**:84
PAREPARE (Indonesia)
map (4° 1′S 119° 38′E) **11**:147
PARETO, VILFREDO **15**:84 *bibliog.*
elites **7**:140
oligarchy **14**:377
PARIA, GULF OF
map (10° 20′N 62° 0′W) **19**:542
PARIAH *see* UNTOUCHABLES
PARIAN WARE
pottery and porcelain **15**:472
PARÍCUTIN **15**:84
PARIETAL LOBE
brain **3**:443 *illus.*; **3**:446 *illus.*
PARIKA (Guyana)
map (6° 52′N 58° 25′W) **9**:410
PARIMA RANGE
map (2° 30′N 64° 0′W) **19**:542
PARINI, GIUSEPPE **15**:84
PARIS (Arkansas)
map (35° 18′N 93° 44′W) **2**:166
PARIS (France) **7**:276 *illus.*; **8**:261–262 *illus., table*; **15**:84–87 *bibliog., illus., map*
art and architecture
Arc de Triomphe de l'Étoile **2**:112
Beaubourg **3**:145
Eiffel Tower **7**:91
French art and architecture **8**:308
Gothic art and architecture **9**:261–262
Guimard, Hector **9**:396–397
Haussmann, Georges Eugène, Baron **10**:69
landmarks **15**:85–87 *map*
Louvre **12**:437
Luxembourg Palace **12**:472
Notre Dame de Paris **14**:267 *illus.*
Panthéon **8**:306 *illus.*
Sacré-Coeur **17**:8
Saint-Denis (church) **17**:17
Sainte-Chapelle **8**:304 *illus.*; **17**:28
Bastille **3**:119
boulevard theater **3**:421
bridge (engineering) **3**:480
climate **7**:272 *table*
fashion design **8**:31
Folies-Bergère **8**:195
government **15**:86
history **15**:87
Commune of Paris **5**:142
Fronde **8**:339
liberation of (Aug. 15, 1944) **8**:272 *illus.*
unknown soldier **19**:470
World War II **20**:254 *illus.*; **20**:272–273 *illus.*
Hôtel de Bourgogne, Théâtre de L' **10**:262
Intercontinental Hotel **10**:261 *illus.*
map (48° 52′N 2° 20′E) **8**:260
Paris, University of **15**:88
Paris Opéra **8**:307 *illus.*
photography
Atget, Eugène **2**:288
Brassaî **3**:457
Salpêtrière Hospital **15**:599 *illus.*
street plan **15**:85 *map*
transportation **15**:86
Art Nouveau (Metro stations) **2**:212 *illus.*
subway **18**:318–319 *illus., table*
Tuileries **19**:329
PARIS (Idaho)
map (42° 14′N 111° 24′W) **11**:26
PARIS (Illinois)
map (39° 36′N 87° 42′W) **11**:42
PARIS (Kentucky)
map (38° 13′N 84° 14′W) **12**:47
PARIS (Maine)
map (44° 16′N 70° 30′W) **13**:70
PARIS (Missouri)
map (39° 29′N 92° 0′W) **13**:476
PARIS (mythology) **15**:87
PARIS (Tennessee)
map (36° 19′N 88° 20′W) **19**:104
PARIS (Texas)
map (33° 40′N 95° 33′W) **19**:129
PARIS, DECLARATION OF (1856)
privateering **15**:557
PARIS, MATTHEW
miniature from *Historia Major* **17**:29 *illus.*
PARIS, PEACE OF (1784)
Anglo-Dutch Wars **2**:3
PARIS, SCHOOL OF
Chagall, Marc **4**:267–268
Fujita, Tsuguharu **8**:356
PARIS, TREATIES OF **15**:87 *bibliog.*
PARIS, TREATY OF (1763)
French and Indian Wars **8**:314
Paris, treaties of **15**:87
Seven Years' War **17**:218
PARIS, TREATY OF (1783)
Franklin, Benjamin **8**:284
Paris, treaties of **15**:87
Shelburne, William Petty Fitzmaurice, 2d Earl of **17**:250
PARIS, TREATY OF (1814)
Paris, treaties of **15**:87
PARIS, TREATY OF (1815)
Paris, treaties of **15**:87
PARIS, TREATY OF (1856)
Crimean War **5**:348–349
Paris, treaties of **15**:87
Russia/Union of Soviet Socialist Republics, history of **16**:357
Russo-Turkish Wars **16**:374
PARIS, TREATY OF (1898)
Paris, treaties of **15**:87
Spanish-American War **18**:150
PARIS, TREATY OF (1947)
Paris, treaties of **15**:87
PARIS, TREATY OF (1973)
Paris, treaties of **15**:87
Vietnam War **19**:590
PARIS, UNIVERSITIES OF **15**:88
PARIS OBSERVATORY **15**:88
Cassini (family) **4**:184
Janssen, Jules **11**:359
PARIS OPÉRA **8**:307 *illus.*
Camargo, Marie **4**:50
Garnier, Jean Louis Charles **9**:49
Lifar, Serge **12**:326
opera houses **14**:402 *illus.*
Vestris (family) **19**:565
PARIS PEACE CONFERENCE **15**:88 *bibliog.*
Clemenceau, Georges **5**:49
Europe, history of **7**:294–295
Fourteen Points **8**:254
Germany, history of **9**:155
Lansing, Robert **12**:200
Marconi, Guglielmo **13**:147
Orlando, Vittorio Emanuele **14**:445
reparations **16**:159–160
United States, history of the **19**:453
Wilson, Woodrow **20**:167
World War I **20**:244–246 *illus.*
World War II **20**:249
PARITY (economics) **15**:88
farms and farming **8**:28
PARITY (physics) **15**:88–89 *bibliog.*
antimatter **2**:63
Lee, Tsung Dao **12**:270
neutrino **15**:89
parity invariance **15**:88–89
parity symmetry **15**:88–89
physics, basic laws **15**:89
PARK (county in Colorado)
map (39° 10′N 105° 45′W) **5**:116
PARK (county in Montana)
map (45° 30′N 110° 30′W) **13**:547
PARK (county in Wyoming)
map (44° 30′N 109° 30′W) **20**:301
PARK, MUNGO **15**:89 *bibliog.*
Africa **1**:157 *map*
Niger River **14**:188
PARK CHUNG HEE **15**:89
Korea **12**:116
PARK CITY (Kansas)
map (37° 46′N 97° 19′W) **12**:18
PARK CITY (Montana)
map (45° 38′N 108° 55′W) **13**:547
PARK CITY (Utah)
map (40° 39′N 111° 30′W) **19**:492
PARK FALLS (Wisconsin)
map (45° 56′N 90° 32′W) **20**:185
PARK FOREST (Illinois)
map (41° 28′N 87° 38′W) **11**:42
PARK PLATEAU
map (37° 15′N 104° 45′W) **5**:116
PARK RANGE
map (40° 0′N 106° 30′W) **5**:116
PARK RAPIDS (Minnesota)
map (46° 55′N 95° 4′W) **13**:453
PARK RIDGE (Illinois)
map (42° 1′N 87° 50′W) **11**:42
PARK RIDGE (New Jersey)
map (41° 2′N 74° 2′W) **14**:129
PARK RIVER (North Dakota)
map (48° 24′N 97° 45′W) **14**:248
PARK ROW BUILDING
skyscraper **17**:350
PARKDALE (Oregon)
map (45° 31′N 121° 36′W) **14**:427
PARKDALE (Prince Edward Island)
map (46° 15′N 63° 7′W) **15**:548
PARKE (county in Indiana)
map (39° 45′N 87° 15′W) **11**:111
PARKER (Arizona)
map (34° 9′N 114° 17′W) **2**:160
PARKER (Florida)
map (30° 8′N 85° 36′W) **8**:172
PARKER (South Dakota)
map (43° 24′N 97° 8′W) **18**:103
PARKER (county in Texas)
map (32° 45′N 97° 48′W) **19**:129
PARKER, ALTON BROOKS **15**:89
PARKER, ARTHUR C.
Parker, Ely S. **15**:90
PARKER, BONNIE
Barrow, Clyde **3**:95
PARKER, CHARLIE **15**:89–90 *bibliog.*
jazz **11**:389 *illus.*
PARKER, DAVE **15**:90
PARKER, DOROTHY **15**:90 *bibliog., illus.*
PARKER, ELY S. **15**:90 *bibliog.*
PARKER, FRANCIS WAYLAND **15**:90 *bibliog.*
progressive education **15**:564
PARKER, SIR GILBERT **15**:90 *bibliog.*
PARKER, MATTHEW **15**:90 *bibliog.*
PARKER, QUANAH **15**:90–91 *bibliog.*
PARKER, ROBERT L.
plate tectonics **15**:357
PARKER, ROBERT LEROY (outlaw) *see* CASSIDY, BUTCH
PARKER, THEODORE **15**:91 *bibliog.*
PARKER DAM (California)
map (34° 17′N 114° 9′W) **4**:31
PARKER PEAK
map (43° 24′N 103° 41′W) **18**:103
PARKER* v. *BROWN **15**:91
PARKERSBURG (Illinois)
map (38° 36′N 88° 3′W) **11**:42
PARKERSBURG (Iowa)
map (42° 35′N 92° 47′W) **11**:244
PARKERSBURG (West Virginia)
map (39° 17′N 81° 32′W) **20**:111
PARKES, ALEXANDER
celluloid **4**:238
plastics **15**:347
PARKES, SIR HENRY **15**:91 *bibliog.*
PARKHILL (Ontario)
map (43° 9′N 81° 41′W) **14**:393; **19**:241
PARKHURST, HELEN
Dalton Plan **6**:15
PARKIN (Arkansas)
map (35° 16′N 90° 34′W) **2**:166
PARKINSON, SYDNEY
Maori chief **13**:136 *illus.*
PARKINSON'S DISEASE **15**:91 *bibliog.*
levodopa **12**:305
nervous system, diseases of the **14**:95
PARKINSON'S LAW **15**:91 *bibliog.*

PARKLAND (Washington)
map (47° 9′N 122° 26′W) **20**:35
PARKMAN, FRANCIS **15**:91–92 *bibliog., illus.*
PARKS, ROSA
integration, racial **11**:202
PARKS AND RESERVES *see* NATIONAL PARKS; NATIONAL PARKS SYSTEM; names of specific parks, e.g., ACADIA NATIONAL PARK; YELLOWSTONE NATIONAL PARK; etc.
PARKSTON (South Dakota)
map (43° 24′N 97° 59′W) **18**:103
PARKSVILLE (British Columbia)
map (49° 19′N 124° 19′W) **3**:491
PARKVILLE (Maryland)
map (39° 23′N 76° 32′W) **13**:188
PARKVILLE (Missouri)
map (39° 11′N 94° 41′W) **13**:476
PARLEMENT **15**:92 *bibliog.*
Fronde **8**:339
Louis XV, King of France **12**:427
PARLER (family)
German art and architecture **9**:125
PARLIAMENT **15**:92–93 *bibliog., illus.*
cabinet **4**:5
democracy **6**:97
Great Britain **2**:136 *illus.*
English Bill of Rights **3**:253
Great Britain, history of **9**:311
Houses of Parliament (London) **12**:400–401 *illus., map*
Inter-Parliamentary Union **11**:206
James I, King of England **11**:356
Labour party **12**:157
whip **20**:131
legislature **12**:275
prime minister **15**:542
taxation **19**:46
PARLIAMENTARY PROCEDURE **15**:93–95 *bibliog.*
cloture **5**:66
Reed, Thomas B. **16**:118
Robert's Rules of Order **16**:242
Senate of the United States **17**:199
PARMA (Idaho)
map (43° 47′N 116° 57′W) **11**:26
PARMA (Italy) **15**:95
cathedral **16**:285 *illus.*
history
Italian unification **11**:330 *map*
map (44° 48′N 10° 20′E) **11**:321
PARMA (Ohio)
map (41° 22′N 81° 43′W) **14**:357
PARMA, UNIVERSITY OF **15**:95
PARMA HEIGHTS (Ohio)
map (41° 23′N 81° 45′W) **14**:357
PARMELIA **12**:322 *illus.*
PARMENIDES **15**:95 *bibliog.*
Anaxagoras **1**:398
Eleatic School **7**:103
pre-Socratic philosophy **15**:532
transcendentalism **19**:268
PARMENION **15**:95
PARMER (county in Texas)
map (34° 30′N 102° 45′W) **19**:129
PARMIGIANINO **15**:95–96 *bibliog., illus.*
Madonna with the Long Neck **13**:124 *illus.*; **15**:95 *illus.*
PARNAIBA (Brazil)
map (2° 54′S 41° 47′W) **3**:460
PARNAÍBA RIVER **15**:96
map (3° 0′S 41° 50′W) **3**:460
PARNAM (Suriname)
map (5° 37′N 55° 6′W) **18**:364
PARNASSIANS (literary group) **15**:96
Banville, Théodore de **3**:71–72
Gautier, Théophile **9**:62
Heredia, José Maria de **10**:138–139
Leconte de Lisle, Charles Marie **12**:268
Sully Prudhomme **18**:338
Verlaine, Paul **19**:551–552
PARNASSÓS *see* PARNASSUS
PARNASSUS **15**:96
sanctuary of Athena Pronaia **19**:96 *illus.*
PARNASSUS MOUNTAIN
map (38° 32′N 22° 35′E) **9**:325
PARNELL, CHARLES STEWART **15**:96 *bibliog., illus.*
Home Rule Bills **10**:212
Ireland, history of **11**:264
PARNI
Parthia **15**:100
PARO (Bhutan)
map (27° 26′N 89° 25′E) **3**:235
PAROCHIAL SCHOOLS
private schools **15**:557
PARODY **15**:96 *bibliog.*
See also SATIRE
PAROLE **15**:97 *bibliog.*
prison **15**:555
PAROO RIVER
map (31° 28′S 143° 32′E) **2**:328
PÁROS (Greece)
Cyclades (Greece) **5**:402
PAROTID GLANDS
salivary glands **17**:34
PAROUSIA
Second Coming of Christ **17**:178
PAROWAN (Utah)
map (37° 51′N 112° 57′W) **19**:492
PARR, CATHERINE **15**:97 *bibliog.*
PARRA, NICANOR
Latin American literature **12**:230
PARRAMORE ISLAND
map (37° 32′N 75° 38′W) **19**:607
PARRINGTON, VERNON L. **15**:97 *bibliog.*
PARRISH (Alabama)
map (33° 44′N 87° 17′W) **1**:234
PARRISH (Florida)
map (27° 35′N 82° 25′W) **8**:172
PARRISH, MAXFIELD **15**:97 *bibliog.*
Collier's cover **15**:170 *illus.*
PARROT **3**:280 *illus.*; **15**:97–98 *bibliog., illus.*
kea **12**:34
macaw **13**:6 *illus.*
parakeet **15**:78
PARROT, ANDRÉ
Mari **13**:150
PARROT FEVER *see* PSITTACOSIS
PARROT FINCH **15**:98
PARROT FISH **15**:98
PARROT'S FEATHER (botany) *see* WATER MILFOIL
PARRSBORO (Nova Scotia)
map (45° 24′N 64° 20′W) **14**:269
PARRY, SIR HUBERT
English music **7**:203
PARRY, MILMAN
oral literature **14**:414
PARRY, SIR WILLIAM EDWARD **15**:98 *bibliog.*
Arctic **2**:142 *map*
Northwest Passage **14**:256
PARRY SOUND (Ontario)
map (45° 21′N 80° 2′W) **14**:393
PARSEC **15**:98
distance, astronomical **6**:199
parallax **15**:78–79
PARSEES *see* PARSIS
PARSHALL (North Dakota)
map (47° 57′N 102° 8′W) **14**:248
PARSIFAL **15**:98
PARSIPPANY (New Jersey)
map (40° 52′N 74° 26′W) **14**:129
PARSIS **15**:98 *bibliog.*
Zoroastrianism **20**:379
PARSLEY **15**:99 *illus.*
See also CARROT
alexander **1**:273
celery **4**:229
lovage **12**:437
PARSLEY, CHINESE *see* CORIANDER
PARSNIP **15**:99 *illus.*; **19**:534 *illus.*
PARSONS (Kansas)
map (37° 20′N 95° 16′W) **12**:18
PARSONS (Tennessee)
map (35° 39′N 88° 7′W) **19**:104
PARSONS (West Virginia)
map (39° 6′N 79° 41′W) **20**:111
PARSONS, SIR CHARLES ALGERNON **15**:99 *bibliog.*
ship **17**:274
turbine **19**:340
PARSONS, TALCOTT **15**:99 *bibliog.*
sociology **18**:30 *illus.*
PARSONS, WILLIAM
telescope **19**:81
PARSONS' CAUSE
Henry, Patrick **10**:123
PARSONS SCHOOL OF DESIGN **15**:99
PÄRT, ARVO
Russian music **16**:369
PARTCH, HARRY **15**:99
PARTHENOGENESIS **15**:99–100 *bibliog.*
cloning **5**:64
egg **7**:72
teiid **19**:73
PARTHENON **2**:193 *illus.*; **2**:290–291 *illus., map*; **19**:96 *illus.*
acropolis **1**:84–85 *illus.*
Elgin, Thomas Bruce, 7th Earl of **7**:137
Greek architecture **9**:336
Ictinus **11**:24
replica
Nashville (Tennessee) **14**:24
sculpture
Greek art **9**:340–341 *illus.*
PARTHENOPEAN REPUBLIC
Naples, Kingdom of **14**:15
PARTHIA **15**:100 *bibliog.*
Arsacids **2**:189
Asia, history of **2**:250
cities
Ctesiphon **5**:377
Hatra **10**:68
Uruk **19**:490
Persia, ancient **15**:182 *map*
Persian art and architecture **15**:184–185
PARTI NATIONAL
Mercier, Honoré **13**:305
PARTI QUÉBÉCOIS
Lévesque, René **12**:303
Quebec **16**:20–21
PARTICLE, FUNDAMENTAL *see* FUNDAMENTAL PARTICLES
PARTICLE ACCELERATOR *see* ACCELERATOR, PARTICLE
PARTICLE DETECTOR *see* DETECTOR, PARTICLE
PARTICLE PHYSICS *see* ACCELERATOR, PARTICLE; FUNDAMENTAL PARTICLES; NUCLEAR PHYSICS
PARTICLEBOARD
wood **20**:206
PARTISAN REVIEW (periodical)
Schwartz, Delmore **17**:139
PARTIZAN **7**:190 *illus.*
PARTNERSHIP *see* BUSINESS ADMINISTRATION
PARTRIDGE **15**:100 *illus.*
PARTRIDGE (Kansas)
map (37° 58′N 98° 5′W) **12**:18
PARTRIDGEBERRY **15**:100
PARTS OF SPEECH **15**:100–101 *bibliog.*
classification **15**:100–101
lexicology and lexicography **12**:308
syntax **18**:408
PARVOVIRUS **15**:101 *bibliog.*
diseases, animal **6**:191
fifth disease **8**:74
PARYLENE
molecular structure **15**:350 *illus.*
PAS, THE (Manitoba)
map (53° 50′N 101° 15′W) **13**:119
PAS DE CALAIS *see* DOVER, STRAIT OF
PASADENA (California) **15**:101
map (34° 9′N 118° 9′W) **4**:31
PASADENA (Newfoundland)
map (49° 1′N 57° 36′W) **14**:166
PASADENA (Texas)
map (29° 42′N 95° 13′W) **19**:129
PASADO, CAPE OF
map (0° 22′N 80° 30′W) **7**:52
PASAJE (Ecuador)
map (3° 20′S 79° 49′W) **7**:52
PASARGADAE (Iran) **15**:101 *bibliog.*
Persia, ancient **15**:182 *map*
Persian art and architecture **15**:184
PASCAGOULA (Mississippi)
map (30° 23′N 88° 31′W) **13**:469
PASCAGOULA RIVER
map (30° 21′N 88° 34′W) **13**:469
PASCAL (computer language) **15**:101 *bibliog.*
computer languages **5**:160p
PASCAL (measurement)
units, physical **19**:466–467 *tables*
PASCAL, BLAISE **15**:102 *bibliog., illus.*
bus **3**:583
computer **5**:160 *illus.*
mathematics, history of **13**:225
Pascal (computer language) **15**:101
Pascal's law **15**:102
Pensées, Les **15**:153
PASCAL'S LAW **15**:102
hydraulic systems **10**:330–331
PASCHAL II, POPE **15**:102 *bibliog.*
Henry V, King of Germany and Holy Roman Emperor **10**:129
PASCIN, JULES **15**:102 *bibliog.*
PASCO (county in Florida)
map (28° 20′N 82° 27′W) **8**:172
PASCO (Washington)
map (46° 14′N 119° 6′W) **20**:35
PASCOAG (Rhode Island)
map (41° 57′N 71° 42′W) **16**:198
PASCOAG RESERVOIR
map (41° 55′N 71° 45′W) **16**:198
PASCOLI, GIOVANNI **15**:102
PASCUA, ISLA DE *see* EASTER ISLAND
PASHTUN *see* PATHAN
PAŠIĆ, NIKOLA **15**:102 *bibliog.*
PASŁĘKA RIVER
map (54° 26′N 19° 45′E) **15**:388
PASO DE LOS LIBRES (Argentina)
map (29° 43′S 57° 5′W) **2**:149
PASO DE LOS TOROS (Uruguay)
map (32° 49′S 56° 31′W) **19**:488
PASO DEL CERRO (Uruguay)
map (31° 29′S 55° 50′W) **19**:488
PASO ROBLES (California)
map (35° 38′N 120° 41′W) **4**:31
PASOLINI, PIER PAOLO **15**:103 *bibliog.*
Bertolucci, Bernardo **3**:226
PASQUIA HILLS
map (53° 13′N 102° 37′W) **17**:81
PASQUOTANK (county in North Carolina)
map (36° 15′N 76° 15′W) **14**:242
PASS CHRISTIAN (Mississippi)
map (30° 20′N 89° 15′W) **13**:469
PASS ISLAND (Newfoundland)
map (47° 29′N 56° 11′W) **14**:166
PASSACAGLIA AND CHACONNE **15**:103 *bibliog.*
PASSADUMKEAG (Maine)
map (45° 11′N 68° 37′W) **13**:70
PASSAGE GRAVE
tomb **19**:230
PASSAGE TO INDIA, A (book)
Forster, E.M. **8**:235
PASSAGE, RITES OF **15**:103–104 *bibliog., illus.*
Aborigines, Australian **1**:59 *illus.*
birth **15**:103
death **15**:104
funeral customs **8**:363
Gennep, Arnold van **9**:92
initiation **15**:103 *illus.*
marriage **13**:163–166; **15**:104
North American archaeology **14**:240 *illus.*
primitive religion **15**:544
PASSAIC (New Jersey) **15**:104
map (40° 51′N 74° 8′W) **14**:129
PASSAIC (county in New Jersey)
map (40° 55′N 74° 10′W) **14**:129
PASSAIC RIVER **14**:128 *illus.*
map (40° 43′N 74° 7′W) **14**:129
PASSAMAQUODDY (American Indians) **15**:104–105 *bibliog.*
Penobscot **15**:153
PASSAMAQUODDY BAY
map (45° 6′N 66° 59′W) **13**:70
map (45° 6′N 66° 59′W) **14**:117
tidal energy **19**:193
PASSAU (Germany, East and West)
map (48° 35′N 13° 28′E) **9**:140
PASSERINES
bird **3**:279
perching birds **15**:161–162
PASSERO, CAPE
map (36° 40′N 15° 9′E) **11**:321
PASSFIELD, BARON *see* WEBB, SIDNEY AND BEATRICE
PASSION CYCLE **15**:105 *bibliog.*
PASSION PLAY **15**:105 *bibliog.*
Oberammergau (West Germany) **14**:315
theater festivals **19**:153
Valenciennes passion play **19**:145 *illus.*
PASSIONFLOWER **15**:105 *illus.*
PASSIONIST ORDER
Paul of the Cross, Saint **15**:118
PASSO FUNDO (Brazil)
map (28° 15′S 52° 24′W) **3**:460
PASSOS, JOHN DOS *see* DOS PASSOS, JOHN
PASSOVER **15**:105–106 *bibliog., illus.*
Easter **7**:32
Seder **15**:105–106; **17**:182
PASSPORT **15**:106
PASSUMPSIC RIVER
map (44° 19′N 72° 2′W) **19**:554
PASTA **15**:106 *bibliog., illus.*
wheat **20**:126
PASTEL **15**:106–107 *bibliog., illus.*
Carriera, Rosalba **4**:168
Chardin, Jean Baptiste **4**:287–288
Degas, Edgar **6**:84
drawing **6**:263
La Tour, Maurice Quentin de **12**:150–151
Millet, Jean François **13**:430
PASTERNAK, BORIS **15**:107 *bibliog., illus.*
Doctor Zhivago **6**:210
PASTEUR, LOUIS **15**:107–108 *bibliog., illus.*
bacteria **3**:17–18
biochemistry **3**:261
biology **3**:269–270 *illus.*
enzyme **7**:213
germ theory of disease **15**:107
immunity **11**:57
medicine **13**:270–271 *illus.*
microbiology **13**:384
Pasteur Institute **15**:108
pasteurization **15**:108
Protozoa **15**:580
spontaneous generation **18**:194
stereochemistry **18**:258
vaccine **15**:107

PASTEUR INSTITUTE **15**:108
Laveran, Charles **12**:241
Pasteur, Louis **15**:108
PASTEURIZATION **15**:108 *bibliog.*
bacteria **3**:16
beer **3**:163
milk **13**:423
Pasteur, Louis **15**:108
PASTICHE **15**:108
PASTO (Colombia)
map (1° 13′N 77° 17′W) **5**:107
PASTOR *see* MINISTRY, CHRISTIAN
PASTOR, TONY
music hall, vaudeville, and burlesque **13**:671–672
PASTORA PEAK
map (36° 47′N 109° 10′W) **2**:160
PASTORAL LITERATURE **15**:108–109 *bibliog.*
As You Like It **2**:226
Drayton, Michael **6**:265
eclogue **7**:42
Guarini, Giovanni Battista **9**:387
idyll **11**:32
Longus **12**:410
Milton, John **13**:433
Sannazaro, Jacopo **17**:65
Sidney, Sir Philip **17**:295
Tasso, Torquato **19**:43
Theocritus **19**:155
Vergil **19**:551
PASTRY *see* CAKE AND PASTRY
PASTURE **15**:109 *bibliog.*
See also GRASSLANDS
PASURUAN (Indonesia)
map (7° 38′S 112° 54′E) **11**:147
PATACAMAYA (Bolivia)
map (17° 14′S 67° 55′W) **3**:366
PATAGONIA (Argentina) **2**:151 *illus.*; **15**:109
agriculture
sheep shearing **20**:214 *illus.*
Indians, American **11**:135–136 *illus.*
South America **18**:87
Tehuelche **19**:73
PATAGONIA (region in Argentina)
map (44° 0′S 68° 0′W) **2**:149
PATAGONIA (Arizona)
map (31° 33′N 110° 45′W) **2**:160
PATALIPUTRA (India) **15**:109
PATAPSCO RIVER
map (39° 9′N 76° 27′W) **13**:188
PATAV'S SYNDROME
genetic diseases **9**:83
PATCHEN, KENNETH **15**:109 *bibliog.*
PATCHOGUE (New York)
map (40° 46′N 73° 0′W) **14**:149
PATCHOULI **15**:109
PATCO *see* Professional Air Traffic Controllers Organization
PATEL, VALLABHBHAI JHAVERBHAI **15**:109–110 *bibliog.*
PATENT **15**:110 *bibliog.*
Commerce, U.S. Department of **5**:138
film, history of **8**:81
genetic engineering **9**:85
invention **11**:232–233
perpetual motion machine **15**:178
plant engineering **15**:343
PATENT DUCTUS ARTERIOSUS
heart diseases **10**:95
PATENT LEATHER
leather and hides **12**:263
PATENT MEDICINE **15**:110 *bibliog.*
pharmaceutical industry **15**:220
Pinkham, Lydia **15**:307
PATER, JEAN BAPTISTE JOSEPH **15**:110 *bibliog.*
PATER, WALTER **15**:110–111 *bibliog.*, *illus.*
aestheticism **1**:130
PATERNOSTER *see* LORD'S PRAYER
PATEROS (Washington)
map (48° 3′N 119° 54′W) **20**:35
PATERSON (New Jersey) **15**:111
Falls of the Passaic River **14**:128 *illus.*
locomotive **12**:389 *illus.*
map (40° 55′N 74° 10′W) **14**:129
silk **17**:307
PATERSON, A. B. **15**:111 *bibliog.*
PATERSON, WILLIAM **15**:111 *bibliog.*
PATHAN **15**:111 *bibliog.*
PATHÉ, CHARLES **15**:111
newsreel **14**:173
PATHET LAO **15**:111–112 *bibliog.*
Laos **12**:204
Souphanouvong **18**:77
Vietnam War **19**:589 *map*
PATHFINDER, THE (book) *see LEATHERSTOCKING TALES, THE* (books)
PATHFINDER, THE (nickname) *see* FRÉMONT, JOHN C.
PATHFINDER RESERVOIR
map (42° 30′N 106° 50′W) **20**:301
PATHOLOGY **15**:112 *bibliog.*
autopsy **2**:368
biopsy **3**:276
diagnostic tests **6**:150
forensic science **8**:227
Paget, Sir James **15**:13
speech therapy **18**:176
Virchow, Rudolf **19**:604
medicine **13**:270
PATIALA (India)
map (30° 19′N 76° 24′E) **11**:80
PATIENCE CARD GAMES *see* SOLITAIRE (card game)
PATINIR, JOACHIM **15**:112 *bibliog.*
PATINKIN, DON
monetary theory **13**:525
PATIVILCA (Peru)
map (10° 42′S 77° 47′W) **15**:193
PATKAI RANGE
map (27° 0′N 96° 0′E) **3**:573
PATMAN, WRIGHT **15**:112
Robinson-Patman Act **16**:246
PATNA (India)
map (25° 36′N 85° 7′E) **11**:80
Pataliputra **15**:109
PATNA (Nepal)
map (27° 41′N 85° 20′E) **14**:86
PATOKA (Illinois)
map (38° 45′N 89° 6′W) **11**:42
PATOKA RIVER
map (38° 25′N 87° 44′W) **11**:111
PATON, ALAN **15**:112 *bibliog.*, *illus.*
Cry, the Beloved Country **5**:370
PATOU, JEAN **15**:112
fashion design **8**:32
PÁTRAI (Greece) *see* PATRAS (Greece)
PATRAS (Greece) **15**:112–113
map (38° 15′N 21° 44′E) **9**:325
PATRIARCH **15**:113 *bibliog.*
PATRICIANS **15**:113; **16**:275 *illus.*
plebeians **15**:364
Rome, ancient **16**:297–298
Senate, Roman **17**:199
PATRICK, SAINT **15**:113 *bibliog.*, *illus.*
Down (Northern Ireland) **6**:252
shamrock **17**:239
Tara (Ireland) **19**:35
PATRICK (county in Virginia)
map (36° 45′N 80° 15′W) **19**:607
PATRILINEAGE
See also names of specific peoples, e.g. KIRGHIZ; ZULU; etc.
clan **5**:36
extended family **7**:341
kinship **12**:85–86
lineage **12**:353
women in society **20**:203
PATRIOTIC FRONT (Zimbabwe)
Zimbabwe (Rhodesia) **20**:365; **20**:366
PATRISTIC LITERATURE **15**:113–114 *bibliog.*
PATRONAGE **15**:114 *bibliog.*
civil service **5**:14
Hatch Acts **10**:68
Jackson, Andrew **11**:341
Marcy, William L. **13**:148
monastic art and architecture **13**:520
political parties **15**:401
president of the United States **15**:524
PATROONS **15**:114
New York (state) **14**:153
Van Renssalaer (family) **19**:515
PATSAYEV, VIKTOR **15**:114 *bibliog.*
PATTEN (Maine)
map (46° 1′N 68° 27′W) **13**:70
PATTERN RECOGNITION **15**:114–115 *bibliog.*, *illus.*
cognitive psychology **5**:95
cybernetics **5**:401
image processing **11**:53; **15**:114
scene analysis **15**:115
PATTERNED GROUND **15**:115 *bibliog.*
frost action **8**:346
paleoclimatology **15**:32
PATTERSON (family) **15**:115 *bibliog.*
PATTERSON (Georgia)
map (31° 23′N 82° 8′W) **9**:114
PATTERSON (Louisiana)
map (29° 42′N 91° 18′W) **12**:430
PATTERSON, FLOYD **15**:115 *bibliog.*
PATTERSON, JOSEPH
McCormick, Robert Rutherford **13**:10
PATTI, ADELINA **15**:115–116
PATTON (Pennsylvania)
map (40° 38′N 78° 39′W) **15**:147
PATTON, GEORGE S. **15**:116 *bibliog.*, *illus.*
World War II **20**:272–273 *illus.*
PATTONSBURG (Missouri)
map (40° 3′N 94° 8′W) **13**:476
PATUAKHALI (Bangladesh)
map (22° 21′N 90° 21′E) **3**:64
PATUCA POINT
map (15° 51′N 84° 18′W) **10**:218
PATUCA RIVER
map (15° 50′N 84° 17′W) **10**:218
PATUXENT RIVER
map (38° 18′N 76° 25′W) **13**:188
PATZINAKS *see* PECHENEGS
PAU (France) **15**:116
map (43° 18′N 0° 22′W) **8**:260
PAU, PAUL
World War I **20**:223
PAUL, ALICE **15**:116 *bibliog.*
Equal Rights Amendment **7**:224
suffrage, women's **18**:326
PAUL, FRANK R.
Amazing Stories cover **17**:144 *illus.*
PAUL, JEAN (pseudonym) *see* RICHTER, JOHANN PAUL FRIEDRICH
PAUL, KING OF GREECE **15**:117 *bibliog.*
PAUL, LES
guitar **9**:401
PAUL, SAINT **15**:116–117 *bibliog.*, *illus.*, *map*
grace **9**:275
Malta **13**:95
missionary journeys **15**:117 *map*
Pauline epistles
Corinthians, Epistles to the **5**:263
Ephesians, Epistle to the **7**:216
Galatians, Epistle to the **9**:10
Hebrews, Epistle to the **10**:102
Romans, Epistle to the **16**:291
Thessalonians, Epistles to the **19**:168
Timothy, Epistles to **19**:203
Titus, Epistle to **19**:215
Philippi **15**:235
roads and highways **16**:235
Salonika (Greece) **17**:36
Tarsus (Turkey) **19**:39–40
Timothy, Saint **19**:204
PAUL I, EMPEROR OF RUSSIA **15**:118 *bibliog.*
PAUL III, POPE **5**:310 *illus.*; **15**:118 *bibliog.*
PAUL VI, POPE **15**:118 *bibliog.*, *illus.*
PAUL BUNYAN *see* BUNYAN, PAUL
PAUL OF THE CROSS, SAINT **15**:118
"PAUL REVERE'S RIDE" (poem)
Longfellow, Henry Wadsworth **11**:407
PAUL OF SAMOSATA **15**:117–118
PAULDING (county in Georgia)
map (33° 55′N 84° 50′W) **9**:114
PAULDING (Mississippi)
map (32° 2′N 89° 2′W) **13**:469
PAULDING (Ohio)
map (41° 8′N 84° 35′W) **14**:357
PAULDING (county in Ohio)
map (41° 8′N 84° 35′W) **14**:357
PAULDING, JAMES KIRKE **15**:118
PAULI, WOLFGANG **15**:118–119 *bibliog.*, *illus.*
chemistry, history of **4**:328
exclusion principle **7**:327
neutrino **14**:108
PAULICIANS **15**:119
Bogomils **3**:360
Marcion **13**:147
PAULINA PEAK
map (43° 41′N 121° 15′W) **14**:427
PAULINE EPISTLES *see* PAUL, SAINT
PAULING, LINUS CARL **15**:119 *bibliog.*, *illus.*
electronegativity **7**:124
orthomolecular medicine **14**:450
PAULINS KILL RIVER
map (40° 55′N 75° 5′W) **14**:129
PAULIST FATHERS
Hecker, Isaac Thomas **10**:103
PAULISTANA (Brazil)
map (8° 9′S 41° 9′W) **3**:460
PAULO AFONSO (Brazil)
map (9° 21′S 38° 14′W) **3**:460
PAULOWNIA **15**:119
PAULS VALLEY (Oklahoma)
map (34° 44′N 97° 13′W) **14**:368
PAULUS, FRIEDRICH
World War II **20**:258; **20**:264
PAUNCEFOTE, SIR JULIAN *see* HAY-PAUNCEFOTE TREATY
PAUNGDE (Burma)
map (18° 29′N 95° 30′E) **3**:573
PAUROPOD (myriapod) **13**:691
PAUSANIAS (geography) **15**:119 *bibliog.*
PAUSANIUS (Spartan general) **15**:119–120
PAVAROTTI, LUCIANO **14**:401 *illus.*; **15**:120 *bibliog.*
PAVESE, CESARE **15**:120 *bibliog.*
PAVIA (Italy) **15**:120
map (45° 10′N 9° 10′E) **11**:321
PAVILLION (Wyoming)
map (43° 15′N 108° 42′W) **20**:301
PAVLODAR (USSR)
map (52° 18′N 76° 57′E) **19**:388
PAVLOV, IVAN PETROVICH **15**:120 *bibliog.*, *illus.*
learning theory **12**:260
psychology, history of **15**:597 *illus.*
reflex **16**:120
PAVLOVA, ANNA **3**:43 *illus.*; **15**:120–121 *bibliog.*, *illus.*
Ballets Russes de Serge Diaghilev **3**:48
PAVLOVSK (palace)
Cameron, Charles **4**:59
PAVO (Georgia)
map (30° 57′N 83° 45′W) **9**:114
PAVÓN, JOSÉ MARÍA MORELOS Y *see* MORELOS Y PAVÓN, JOSÉ MARÍA
PAW PAW (Michigan)
map (42° 13′N 85° 53′W) **13**:377
PAWCATUCK (Connecticut)
map (41° 22′N 71° 52′W) **5**:193
PAWCATUCK RIVER
map (40° 22′N 71° 50′W) **16**:198
PAWHUSKA (Oklahoma)
map (36° 40′N 96° 20′W) **14**:368
PAWNBROKER **15**:121
PAWNEE (American Indians) **11**:136 *illus.*; **15**:121 *bibliog.*
ghost dance **9**:169
Indians of North America, art of the **11**:141
jack-in-the-pulpit **11**:339
Mississippian culture **14**:239
Sun dance **18**:346
PAWNEE (Illinois)
map (39° 35′N 89° 35′W) **11**:42
PAWNEE (county in Kansas)
map (38° 10′N 99° 15′W) **12**:18
PAWNEE (county in Nebraska)
map (40° 10′N 96° 15′W) **14**:70
PAWNEE (Oklahoma)
map (36° 20′N 96° 48′W) **14**:368
PAWNEE (county in Oklahoma)
map (36° 20′N 96° 40′W) **14**:368
PAWNEE, TATTOOED *see* WICHITA (American Indians)
PAWNEE CITY (Nebraska)
map (40° 7′N 96° 9′W) **14**:70
PAWPAW (Illinois)
map (41° 41′N 88° 59′W) **11**:42
PAWTUCKET (Rhode Island) **15**:121
map (41° 53′N 71° 23′W) **16**:198
PAWTUXET RIVER
map (41° 46′N 71° 24′W) **16**:198
PAX ROMANA
Rome, ancient **16**:302
PAXTON (Illinois)
map (40° 27′N 88° 6′W) **11**:42
PAXTON (Nebraska)
map (41° 7′N 101° 21′W) **14**:70
PAXTON, SIR JOSEPH **15**:121 *bibliog.*
Crystal Palace **2**:200 *illus.*; **5**:376 *illus.*
PAXTON, K. M. B.
Algernon Charles Swinburne **18**:392 *illus.*
PAYA (Honduras)
map (15° 37′N 85° 17′W) **10**:218
PAYEN, ANSELME **15**:121
PAYETTE (Idaho)
map (44° 5′N 116° 56′W) **11**:26
PAYETTE (county in Idaho)
map (44° 0′N 116° 50′W) **11**:26
PAYETTE, RIVER, NORTH FORK
map (44° 5′N 116° 7′W) **11**:26
PAYETTE LAKE
map (44° 57′N 116° 5′W) **11**:26
PAYNE (county in Oklahoma)
map (36° 5′N 97° 0′W) **14**:368
PAYNE, DAVID L.
Oklahoma **14**:371
PAYNE, JOHN HOWARD **15**:122
PAYNE, RUFE
Williams, Hank **20**:159
PAYNE-GAPOSCHKIN, CECILIA **15**:122
PAYNE'S LANDING, TREATY OF
Osceola **14**:452
Seminole **17**:197
PAYNESVILLE (Minnesota)
map (45° 23′N 94° 43′W) **13**:453
PAYOLA *see* BRIBERY
PAYSANDÚ (Uruguay) **15**:122
map (32° 19′S 58° 5′W) **19**:488
PAYSON (Arizona)
map (34° 14′N 111° 20′W) **2**:160
PAYSON (Illinois)
map (39° 49′N 73° 14′W) **11**:42

PAYSON (Utah)
map (40° 3′N 111° 44′W) **19**:492
PAYTON, WALTER **15**:122
PAZ, OCTAVIO **15**:122 *bibliog.*
PAZ ESTENSSORO, VICTOR
Bolivia **3**:369
PAZ GARCIA, POLICARPO
Honduras **10**:220
PAZ RIVER
map (13° 45′N 90° 8′W) **7**:100
PAZARDZHIK (Bulgaria)
map (42° 12′N 24° 20′E) **3**:555
PAZÑA (Bolivia)
map (18° 36′S 66° 55′W) **3**:366
PAZYRYK (USSR) **15**:122 *bibliog.*
PAZZI CHAPEL (Florence) **2**:195 *illus.*; **3**:524 *illus.*
PBB (chemical pollutant) *see* POLYBROMINATED BIPHENYL
PBS *see* PUBLIC BROADCASTING SERVICE
PCB'S (chemical pollutants) *see* POLYCHLORINATED BIPHENYL
PCC (President's Conference Committee) CAR
streetcar **18**:296
PCP (drug) *see* ANGEL DUST
PCP (political party) *see* PROGRESSIVE CONSERVATIVE PARTY (Canada)
PE (letter)
P **15**:3
PEA **8**:348 *illus.*; **15**:122 *bibliog., illus.*; **15**:336 *illus.*; **19**:533 *illus.*
alfalfa **1**:278
brazilwood **3**:464–465
broom **3**:511
carob **4**:159
chick-pea **4**:344–345
clover **5**:69
coral tree **5**:260
cowpea **5**:321
Crotalaria **5**:362
elephant's-ear **7**:134
furze **8**:381
genetics **9**:85–86 *illus.*; **10**:139 *illus.*
golden chain **9**:231
Japanese pagoda tree **11**:382
kangaroo thorn **12**:16
kudzu **12**:135
locoweed **12**:392
locust (plant) **12**:392
lotus **12**:420
lupine **12**:466
Mendel, Gregor Johann **13**:294
mesquite **13**:322
mimosa **13**:436
palo verde **15**:52
redbud **16**:115
sensitive plant **17**:205
Sturt's desert pea **10**:5 *illus.*
sweet pea **18**:387–388
tallow tree **19**:17
vetch **19**:565
wisteria **20**:190
PEA, BLACK-EYED *see* COWPEA
PEA, EGYPTIAN *see* CHICK-PEA
PEA RIVER
map (31° 1′N 85° 51′W) **1**:234
PEABODY (Kansas)
map (38° 10′N 97° 7′W) **12**:18
PEABODY (Massachusetts)
map (42° 32′N 70° 55′W) **13**:206
PEABODY, ELIZABETH **15**:122–123 *bibliog.*
PEABODY, GEORGE **15**:123 *bibliog.*
PEABODY AWARD **15**:123
Cooke, Alistair **5**:237
Cronkite, Walter **5**:359
Newman, Edwin **14**:169
PEACE
Kellogg-Briand Pact **12**:38
League of Nations **12**:257–258
Nobel Prize **14**:208–211 *table*
Addams, Jane **1**:98–99
American Friends Service Committee **1**:340
Amnesty International **1**:375
Balch, Emily Greene **3**:33
Begin, Menachem **3**:168
Borlaug, Norman Ernest **3**:401
Boyd-Orr, John, 1st Baron Boyd-Orr of Brechin Mearn **3**:433
Brandt, Willy **3**:455
Branting, Hjalmar **3**:456
Briand, Aristide **3**:476
Buisson, Ferdinand Édouard **3**:552–553
Bunche, Ralph **3**:562
Butler, Nicholas Murray **3**:591–592
Chamberlain, Sir Austen **4**:273
Corrigan, Mairead, and Williams, Betty **5**:276
Dunant, Jean Henri **6**:298
Hammarskjöld, Dag **10**:30
Henderson, Arthur **10**:121
Hull, Cordell **10**:296
International Labor Organization **11**:220
Kellogg, Frank B. **12**:38
King, Martin Luther, Jr. **12**:80
Kissinger, Henry A. **12**:90
Luthuli, Albert John **12**:470
Marshall, George C. **13**:172
Mott, John R. **13**:616
Myrdal, Alva **13**:691
Nansen, Fridtjof **14**:13
Pauling, Linus Carl **15**:119
Pearson, Lester B. **15**:128
Pérez Esquivel, Adolfo **15**:164
Refugees, Office of the United Nations High Commissioner for **16**:126
Roosevelt, Theodore **16**:311
Root, Elihu **16**:311
Sadat, Anwar al- **17**:8
Sakharov, Andrei D. **17**:28
Sato Eisaku **17**:88
Schweitzer, Albert **17**:140
Söderblom, Nathan **18**:32
Stresemann, Gustav **18**:297
Teresa, Mother **19**:115
United Nations Children's Fund **19**:415
Wałesa, Lech **20**:11
Wiesel, Elie **20**:146
Wilson, Woodrow **20**:167
United Nations **19**:412–415
PEACE CORPS
ACTION (federal agency) **1**:89
Educational Testing Service **7**:66
United States, history of the **19**:458
PEACE DALE (Rhode Island)
map (41° 27′N 71° 30′W) **16**:198
PEACE OF *see under the latter part of the name, e.g.*, AUGSBURG, PEACE OF; UTRECHT, PEACE OF; *etc.*
PEACE PEOPLE, COMMUNITY OF *see* COMMUNITY OF PEACE PEOPLE
PEACE PIPE **15**:123 *bibliog.*
pipe **15**:310
shaman **17**:238 *illus.*
PEACE PLEDGE UNION (England)
pacifism and nonviolent movements **15**:9
PEACE RIVER (Alberta)
map (56° 14′N 117° 17′W) **1**:256
PEACE RIVER (Florida) **15**:123
map (26° 55′N 82° 5′W) **8**:172
PEACEABLE KINGDOM, THE (Edward Hicks) **10**:157 *illus.*
PEACH **8**:348 *illus.*; **15**:123 *bibliog., illus.*
nectarine **14**:75–76
PEACH (county in Georgia)
map (32° 35′N 83° 50′W) **9**:114
PEACH SPRINGS (Arizona)
map (35° 32′N 113° 25′W) **2**:160
PEACH-TREE BORDER MOTH **3**:598–599 *illus.*
PEACOCK **15**:123–124 *illus.*
PEACOCK, GEORGE
mathematics, history of **13**:226
PEACOCK, THOMAS LOVE **15**:124 *bibliog.*
PEAFOWL *see* PEACOCK
PEAKE, MERVYN **15**:124 *bibliog.*
PEALE (family) **15**:124 *bibliog., illus.*
PEALE, CHARLES WILLSON
Peale (family) **15**:124
Richard Henry Lee **12**:268 *illus.*
PEALE, JAMES
miniature painting **13**:445 *illus.*
Peale (family) **15**:124
PEALE, MOUNT
map (38° 26′N 109° 14′W) **19**:492
PEALE, NORMAN VINCENT **15**:124–125 *bibliog.*
PEALE, RAPHAELLE
After the Bath **1**:332 *illus.*; **15**:124 *illus.*
Peale (family) **15**:124
PEALS AND PEARLING
pearl formation **15**:127 *illus.*
PEANO, GIUSEPPE **15**:125 *bibliog.*
languages, artificial **12**:198
mathematics, history of **13**:226
Peano axioms **15**:125
PEANUT **15**:125 *bibliog., illus.*
Carver, George Washington **4**:179
fats and oils source **8**:35
Georgia **9**:117 *illus.*
Senegal **17**:201
vegetable oils **19**:535 *illus., table*
PEANUT WORM **15**:125
PEANUTS (comic strip) **5**:136 *illus.*
Schulz, Charles M. **17**:136
PEAR **8**:348 *illus.*; **15**:125–126 *bibliog., illus.*
PEARCE, E. D.
Shasta, Mount **17**:244
PEARISBURG (Virginia)
map (37° 20′N 80° 44′W) **19**:607
PEARL (Illinois)
map (39° 28′N 90° 38′W) **11**:42
PEARL (Mississippi)
map (32° 18′N 90° 12′W) **13**:469
PEARL, THE (book)
Steinbeck, John **18**:248
PEARL CITY (Hawaii)
map (21° 24′N 157° 59′W) **10**:72
PEARL HARBOR **15**:126 *bibliog., map*
map (21° 12′N 157° 58′W) **10**:72
navy **14**:64
United States, history of the **19**:455 *illus.*
World War II **20**:259–260 *illus.*
Yamamoto Isoroku **20**:316
PEARL RIVER
map (30° 11′N 89° 32′W) **13**:469
PEARL RIVER (Louisiana)
map (30° 23′N 89° 45′W) **12**:430
PEARL RIVER (county in Mississippi)
map (30° 45′N 89° 35′W) **13**:469
PEARLAND (Texas)
map (29° 34′N 95° 17′W) **19**:129
PEARLS AND PEARLING **15**:126–128 *bibliog., illus.*
birthstones **3**:296 *illus., table*
calcium carbonate **4**:23
gems **9**:74–75 *illus.*
jewelry **11**:410; **15**:127 *illus.*
mother-of-pearl **13**:607
oceanic mineral resources **14**:340
oyster **14**:479
PEARLSTEIN, PHILIP **15**:128
PEARS SOAP
advertisement **5**:282 *illus.*; **18**:7 *illus.*
PEARSALL (Texas)
map (28° 53′N 99° 6′W) **19**:129
PEARSE, PATRICK
Easter Rising **7**:33
PEARSON (Georgia)
map (31° 18′N 82° 51′W) **9**:114
PEARSON, DREW **15**:128 *bibliog.*
Anderson, Jack **1**:401–402
PEARSON, LESTER B. **15**:128 *bibliog., illus.*
Canada, history of **4**:87
Liberal parties **12**:311
PEARSON'S STATISTIC
chi-square distribution **4**:339
PEARY, ROBERT EDWIN **15**:128 *bibliog., illus.*
Arctic **2**:142 *map*; **2**:143 *illus.*,
MacMillan Donald Baxter **13**:33
PEASANT **15**:128–129 *bibliog.*
fellahin **8**:47
folk art **8**:195–199
kulaks **12**:135–136
manorialism **13**:126–127
primogeniture **15**:547
urban anthropology **19**:480
PEASANTS' REBELLION OF 1773–74 (Russia)
Pugachev, Yemelian Ivanovich **15**:617
PEASANTS' REVOLT (England) **15**:129 *bibliog.*
PEASANTS' WAR (Germany) **15**:129 *bibliog.*
flag **8**:135 *illus.*
Münzer, Thomas **13**:644
PEAT **15**:129
agricultural use **15**:129
coal and coal mining **5**:75–76 *illus.*
energy sources **7**:174
fossil record **8**:247
fuel **8**:352; **15**:129
heat content **8**:353 *table*
sedimentary rock **17**:185
soil **18**:37
swamp, marsh, and bog **18**:378
types **15**:129
PEAT-BOG BURIAL *see* TOLLUND MAN
PEAT MOSS **15**:129
moss **13**:603
PEBAS (Peru)
map (3° 20′S 71° 49′W) **15**:193
PEĆ (Yugoslavia)
map (42° 40′N 20° 19′E) **20**:340
PECAN **14**:300 *illus.*; **15**:129–130 *bibliog., illus.*
hickory **10**:157
PECATONICA (Illinois)
map (42° 19′N 89° 22′W) **11**:42
PECCARY **15**:130 *illus.*
PECH-MERLE (France) CAVE PAINTING **15**:507 *illus.*
PECHENEGS **15**:130
PECHORA RIVER **15**:130
map (68° 13′N 54° 15′E) **19**:388
PECHSTEIN, MAX **15**:130 *bibliog.*
PECK, GREGORY **15**:130
PECKING ORDER *see* ANIMAL BEHAVIOR
PECKINPAH, SAM **15**:130 *bibliog.*
PECOS (New Mexico)
map (35° 29′N 105° 41′W) **14**:136
PECOS (Texas)
map (31° 25′N 103° 30′W) **19**:129
PECOS (county in Texas)
map (30° 45′N 102° 45′W) **19**:129
PECOS BILL **15**:130
PECOS RIVER **15**:130
map (29° 42′N 101° 22′W) **19**:419
PÉCOUR, LOUIS
Académie Royale de Danse **1**:69
PÉCS (Hungary) **15**:130–131
map (46° 5′N 18° 13′E) **10**:307
PECTIN **15**:131
gel **9**:69
jam and jelly **12**:351
Payen, Anselme **15**:121
PECTOLITE *see* ZEOLITE
PEDAGOGY *see* TEACHER EDUCATION; TEACHING METHODS
PEDALFER **15**:131
Asia, soils **2**:239
soil orders included **15**:131
PEDASÍ (Panama)
map (7° 32′N 80° 2′W) **15**:55
PEDERNALES (Argentina)
map (35° 15′S 59° 39′W) **2**:149
PEDERNALES (Dominican Republic)
map (18° 2′N 71° 45′W) **6**:233
PEDERNALES (Venezuela)
map (9° 58′N 62° 16′W) **19**:542
PEDERSON, CARL-HENNING
Standing Orange Figures **17**:113 *illus.*
PEDIATRICS **15**:131 *bibliog.*
See also DISEASES, CHILDHOOD
anthropometry **2**:55
child development **4**:348–350
child psychiatry **4**:350–351
Spock, Benjamin **18**:191–192
PEDICULOSIS
skin diseases **17**:342
PEDIMENT (architecture) **2**:131
PEDIMENT (geology) **15**:131 *bibliog.*
landform evolution **12**:183
PEDOCAL **15**:131
soil orders included **15**:131
PEDRA AZUL (Brazil)
map (16° 1′S 41° 16′W) **3**:460
PEDRELL, FELIPE
Spanish music **18**:162
PEDRO *see* PETER *for Spanish and Portuguese kings named* PEDRO
PEDRO I, EMPEROR OF BRAZIL **15**:131 *bibliog., illus.*
John VI, King of Portugal **11**:428
Maria II, Queen of Portugal (Maria da Glória) **13**:150
Portugal, history of **15**:454
PEDRO II, EMPEROR OF BRAZIL **15**:131–132 *bibliog.*
Brazil **3**:463
PEDRO AFONSO (Brazil)
map (8° 59′S 48° 11′W) **3**:460
PEDRO JUAN CABALLERO (Paraguay)
map (22° 34′S 55° 37′W) **15**:77
PEE DEE RIVER
map (33° 21′N 79° 16′W) **18**:98
PEEBLES (Ohio)
map (38° 57′N 83° 24′W) **14**:357
PEEBLES (Scotland) **15**:132
PEEKSKILL (New York)
map (41° 17′N 73° 55′W) **14**:149
PEEL, PAUL
Canadian art and architecture **4**:89
PEEL, SIR ROBERT **15**:132 *bibliog., illus.*
British Conservative party **5**:205
Tory party **19**:247
Wellington, Arthur Wellesley, 1st Duke of **20**:100
PEEL RIVER
map (67° 37′N 134° 40′W) **20**:345
PEENEMÜNDE **15**:132 *bibliog.*
rockets and missiles **16**:254
V-1 **19**:500
V-2 **19**:500
von Braun, Wernher **19**:633
PEEPING TOM *see* VOYEURISM
PEER GYNT (poem)
Ibsen, Henrik **11**:6–7
PEERAGE *see* TITLES OF NOBILITY AND HONOR

PEERLESS (Montana)
map (48° 47′N 105° 50′W) **13**:547
PEETZ (Colorado)
map (40° 58′N 103° 7′W) **5**:116
PEEWIT *see* LAPWING
PEGASUS **15**:132
Medusa **13**:278
PEGLER, WESTBROOK **15**:132 *bibliog.*
PEGMATITE **15**:133 *bibliog., illus.*
chrysoberyl **4**:421
composition **15**:133
gems **15**:133
mineral occurrence **13**:442
origin **15**:133
phosphate minerals **15**:256
tourmaline **19**:253
uranium minerals **19**:478
PEGU (Burma) **15**:133
map (17° 20′N 96° 29′E) **3**:573
PEGUILHAN, AIMERIC DE
minstrels, minnesingers, and troubadours **13**:460
PEHUAJÓ (Argentina)
map (35° 48′S 61° 53′W) **2**:149
PEI, I. M. **15**:133–134 *bibliog., illus.*
John F. Kennedy Library **12**:317 *illus.*
Mellon, Paul **13**:287
National Gallery of Art **14**:33; **15**:133–134 *illus.*
Toronto (Ontario) **19**:242
PEI-HAI (China)
map (21° 29′N 109° 5′E) **4**:362
PEI-KANG (Taiwan)
map (23° 35′N 120° 19′E) **19**:13
PEIPUS, LAKE **15**:134
map (58° 45′N 27° 30′E) **19**:388
PEIRAIÉVS (Greece) *see* PIRAEUS (Greece)
PEIRCE, CHARLES SANDERS **15**:134 *bibliog.*
pragmatism **15**:487
PEISISTRATUS **15**:134 *bibliog.*
Greece, ancient **9**:331
PEIXOTO, FLORIANO **15**:134 *bibliog.*
PEKALONGAN (Indonesia)
map (6° 53′S 109° 40′E) **11**:147
PEKIN (Illinois)
map (40° 35′N 89° 40′W) **11**:42
PEKIN (Indiana)
map (38° 30′N 86° 0′W) **11**:111
PEKING (Beijing) (China) **4**:366 *illus.*; **15**:134–136 *bibliog., illus., map*
Ch'ien gate **15**:134 *illus.*
Forbidden City **8**:220; **15**:135–136 *illus., map*
Great Hall of the People **15**:134 *illus.*
history **15**:136
map (39° 55′N 116° 25′E) **4**:362
mausoleum of Mao Tse-Tung **15**:134 *illus.*
Monument to the People's Heroes **15**:134 *illus.*
subway **18**:318 *table*
Summer Palace **4**:387 *illus.*
T'ien-an Men Square **15**:135 *illus., map*
PEKING MAN **2**:53 *illus.*; **15**:136 *bibliog.*
Black, Davidson **3**:303
Chinese archaeology **4**:378
Chou-k'ou-tien (Zhoukoudian) **4**:409–410
Homo erectus **10**:215 *illus.*
Lantian man **12**:201
skull **4**:378 *illus.*
Teilhard de Chardin, Pierre **19**:73–74
Weidenreich, Franz **20**:91
PEKING OPERA **15**:136 *bibliog.*
dance **6**:26
PEKING UNIVERSITY **15**:136
PEKINGESE **6**:217 *illus.*; **15**:136–137 *bibliog., illus.*
PEKKANEN, TOIVO
Finnish literature **8**:99
PELAGIANISM **15**:137 *bibliog.*
Great Britain, history of **9**:309
PELAGIC ZONE **15**:137
deep-sea life **6**:78
epipelagic zone **7**:220
fishing industry **8**:124–128
neritic zone **14**:89
ocean and sea **14**:331
PELAYO, KING OF ASTURIAS
Spain, history of **18**:145
PELÉ (athlete) **15**:137 *bibliog., illus.*
soccer **18**:9–10 *illus.*
PELE (mythology) **15**:137
PELEAGA, MOUNT
map (45° 22′N 22° 54′E) **16**:288
PELECHUCO (Bolivia)
map (14° 48′S 69° 4′W) **3**:366
PELECYPODA *see* BIVALVE
PELÉE, MOUNT **15**:137
PELEE ISLAND
map (41° 46′N 82° 39′W) **19**:241
PELHAM (Georgia)
map (31° 8′N 84° 9′W) **9**:114
PELHAM, HENRY **15**:137–138 *bibliog.*
Newcastle, Thomas Pelham-Holles, 1st Duke of **14**:164
PELHAM-HOLLES, THOMAS, 1ST DUKE OF NEWCASTLE *see* NEWCASTLE, THOMAS PELHAM-HOLLES, 1ST DUKE OF
PELICAN **15**:138 *illus.*
PELICAN LAKE (Wisconsin)
map (45° 30′N 89° 10′W) **20**:185
PELICAN RAPIDS (Manitoba)
map (52° 45′N 100° 42′W) **13**:119
PELICAN RAPIDS (Minnesota)
map (46° 34′N 96° 5′W) **13**:453
PELITIC ROCK
metamorphic rock **13**:332
PELL CITY (Alabama)
map (33° 35′N 86° 17′W) **1**:234
PELL GRANT PROGRAM
scholarships, fellowships, and loans **17**:130
PELLA (Greece) **15**:138 *bibliog.*
mosaic **13**:593 *illus.*
PELLA (Iowa)
map (41° 25′N 92° 55′W) **11**:244
PELLAGRA **15**:138
nutritional-deficiency diseases **14**:307
vitamins and minerals **19**:619
PELLAN, ALFRED **15**:138 *bibliog.*
Végétaux Marins **4**:90 *illus.*
PELLE THE CONQUERER (book)
Nexø, Martin Andersen- **14**:175
PELLETIER, PIERRE JOSEPH **15**:138
PELLI, CESAR ANTONIO **15**:138 *bibliog.*
PELLIGRINI, CARLO
Oscar Wilde **20**:148 *illus.*
PELLY CROSSING (Yukon Territory)
map (62° 50′N 136° 35′W) **20**:345
PELLY MOUNTAINS
map (62° 0′N 133° 0′W) **20**:345
PELLY RIVER
map (62° 47′N 137° 19′W) **20**:345
PELOPIDAS **15**:138–139
PELOPONNESIAN LEAGUE
Sparta (Greece) **18**:164
PELOPONNESIAN WAR **15**:139 *bibliog., map*
Agesilaus II, King of Sparta **1**:184
Alcibiades **1**:263
Cleon **5**:50
coin commemorating **18**:410 *illus.*
Greece, ancient **9**:332–333 *map*
Lysander **12**:479–480
Nicias **14**:183
Pericles **15**:165
Persian Wars **15**:188
Rhodes (Greece) **16**:202
Sparta (Greece) **18**:165
Syracuse (Sicily) **18**:410
Thucydides **19**:183–184
History of the Peloponnesian War **10**:185–186
PELOPONNESUS (Greece) **15**:139
archaeology and historic sites
Epidaurus **7**:218–219
megalopolis **13**:280
Messene **13**:322–323
Mistra **13**:482
Mycenae **13**:689–690
Nemea **14**:80
Olympia (Greece) **14**:381
Sparta **18**:164–165
cities
Corinth **5**:263
Patras **15**:112–113
map (37° 30′N 22° 0′E) **9**:325
PELOPS **15**:139
PELOTA (game)
handball **10**:35
PELOTAS (Brazil)
map (31° 46′S 52° 20′W) **3**:460
PELT *see* FUR
PELTIER EFFECT
thermoelectricity **19**:165
PELVIC INFLAMMATORY DISEASE
urogenital diseases **19**:487
PELVIS **15**:140 *bibliog.*
sciatica **17**:141
skeleton, human **17**:336
PELZER (South Carolina)
map (34° 38′N 82° 28′W) **18**:98
PEMADUMCOOK LAKE
map (45° 40′N 68° 55′W) **13**:70
PEMALANG (Indonesia)
map (6° 54′S 109° 22′E) **11**:147
PEMATANGSIANTAR (Indonesia)
map (2° 57′N 99° 3′E) **11**:147
PEMBA (Mozambique)
map (12° 57′S 40° 30′E) **13**:627
PEMBA (Tanzania) **15**:140
map (7° 31′S 39° 25′E) **19**:27
PEMBA CHANNEL
map (5° 10′S 39° 20′E) **12**:53
PEMBERTON (British Columbia)
map (50° 20′N 122° 48′W) **3**:491
PEMBERTON (New Jersey)
map (39° 58′N 74° 41′W) **14**:129
PEMBERTON, JOHN C.
Civil War, U.S. **5**:27–28
Vicksburg Campaign **19**:571–572 *map*
PEMBINA (North Dakota)
map (48° 58′N 97° 15′W) **14**:248
PEMBINA (county in North Dakota)
map (48° 45′N 97° 30′W) **14**:248
PEMBINA MOUNTAINS
map (49° 0′N 98° 5′W) **14**:248
PEMBINA RIVER (Alberta)
map (54° 45′N 114° 15′W) **1**:256
PEMBINA RIVER (North Dakota)
map (48° 56′N 97° 15′W) **14**:248
PEMBINE (Wisconsin)
map (45° 38′N 87° 59′W) **20**:185
PEMBROKE (Georgia)
map (32° 8′N 81° 37′W) **9**:114
PEMBROKE (Kentucky)
map (36° 47′N 87° 21′W) **12**:47
PEMBROKE (Maine)
map (44° 57′N 67° 10′W) **13**:70
PEMBROKE (North Carolina)
map (34° 41′N 79° 12′W) **14**:242
PEMBROKE (Ontario)
map (45° 49′N 77° 7′W) **14**:393
PEMBROKE (Virginia)
map (37° 19′N 80° 38′W) **19**:607
PEMBROKE COLLEGE (Cambridge University) **4**:53
PEMBROKE COLLEGE (Oxford University) **14**:474
PEMBROKE PINES (Florida)
map (26° 1′N 80° 11′W) **8**:172
PEMBROKE WELSH CORGI **6**:214 *illus.*; **15**:140 *bibliog., illus.*
PEMBROKESHIRE (Wales) *see* DYFED (Wales)
PEMIGEWASSET RIVER
map (43° 26′N 71° 40′W) **14**:123
PEMISCOT (county in Missouri)
map (36° 15′N 89° 50′W) **13**:476
PEMMICAN **15**:140
PEN **15**:140–141 *bibliog., illus.*
drawing **6**:263
PEN ARGYL (Pennsylvania)
map (40° 52′N 75° 16′W) **15**:147
PENAL COLONY
Australia, history of **2**:339–340 *illus.*
Botany Bay (Australia) **3**:414
Devil's Island **6**:143
New Caledonia **14**:119
Norfolk Island (Australia) **14**:218
Siberia (USSR) **17**:292
Sydney (Australia) **18**:401
PENANCE *see* CONFESSION (religion)
PENANG (Malaysia) **15**:141
Straits Settlements **18**:288
map (5° 25′N 100° 20′E) **13**:84
PENANG ISLAND
map (5° 23′N 100° 15′E) **13**:84
PENAS, GULF OF
map (47° 22′S 74° 50′W) **4**:355
PENASCO (New Mexico)
map (36° 10′N 105° 41′W) **14**:136
PENATES **15**:141
PÉNAUD, ALPHONSE **15**:141 *bibliog.*
PENCIL **15**:141–142 *bibliog.*
drawing **6**:263
PENCIL TREE **15**:142
PENCK, WALTHER **15**:142 *bibliog.*
PEND D'OREILLE (American Indians)
Flathead **8**:155
PEND OREILLE (county in Washington)
map (48° 25′N 117° 15′W) **20**:35
PEND OREILLE, LAKE
map (48° 10′N 116° 11′W) **11**:26
PEND OREILLE RIVER
map (49° 4′N 117° 37′W) **20**:35
PENDEMBU (Sierra Leone)
map (8° 6′N 10° 42′W) **17**:296
PENDENTIVE
dome **6**:229 *illus.*
squinch **18**:204
PENDER (Nebraska)
map (42° 7′N 96° 43′W) **14**:70
PENDER (county in North Carolina)
map (34° 30′N 77° 50′W) **14**:242
PENDERECKI, KRZYSZTOF **15**:142 *bibliog.*
PENDERGAST, THOMAS JOSEPH **15**:142 *bibliog.*
PENDJARI RIVER
map (10° 54′N 0° 51′E) **3**:200
PENDLETON (Indiana)
map (40° 1′N 85° 45′W) **11**:111
PENDLETON (county in Kentucky)
map (38° 42′N 84° 22′W) **12**:47
PENDLETON (Oregon)
map (45° 40′N 118° 47′W) **14**:427
PENDLETON (South Carolina)
map (34° 39′N 82° 47′W) **18**:98
PENDLETON (county in West Virginia)
map (38° 40′N 79° 20′W) **20**:111
PENDLETON, EDMUND **15**:142 *bibliog.*
PENDLETON, GEORGE HUNT **15**:142 *bibliog.*
PENDLETON ACT OF 1883
Pendleton, George Hunt **15**:142
PENDULINE TIT (bird) **15**:142
nest **3**:287 *illus.*
PENDULUM **15**:142
Foucault pendulum **8**:249
motion, harmonic **13**:608
PENELOPE **15**:142–143
PENEPLAIN **15**:143 *bibliog.*
landform evolution **12**:182
monadnock **13**:517
PENFIELD, WILDER GRAVES
brain **3**:447
P'ENG-HU (Taiwan) *see* PESCADORES (Taiwan)
PENGUIN **2**:42–43 *illus.*; **3**:281 *illus.*; **15**:143 *bibliog., illus.*
PENICHE (Portugal)
map (39° 21′N 9° 23′W) **15**:449
PENICILLIN **15**:143–144 *bibliog., illus.*
allergic reactions **15**:143
antibiotics **2**:57–59 *illus.*
bacteria **3**:15
Chain, Ernst Boris **4**:268
Fleming, Sir Alexander **8**:159; **15**:143
Florey, Sir Howard Walter **8**:169
fungus diseases **8**:369
molds **13**:506 *illus.*
reproduction **8**:367 *illus.*
respiratory system disorders **16**:181
strep throat **18**:297
PENINSULAR CAMPAIGN **15**:144 *bibliog.*
Civil War, U.S. **5**:22–24 *illus.*
PENINSULAR WAR *see* NAPOLEONIC WARS
PENIS
phallic worship **15**:219
priapism **15**:534
reproductive system, human **16**:163–164 *illus.*
sex change **17**:224
sexual intercourse **17**:230–231
venereal disease **19**:540
PENN, ARTHUR **15**:144 *bibliog.*
PENN, IRVING **15**:144
PENN, JOHN
ship **17**:273
PENN, THOMAS
Reading (Pennsylvania) **16**:100
PENN, WILLIAM **15**:144–145 *bibliog., illus.*; **15**:227 *illus.*
Chester (Pennsylvania) **4**:336
Delaware **6**:90
Delaware (American Indians) **6**:91
Pennsylvania **15**:150
treaty with the Delaware Indians **11**:107 *illus.*; **19**:437 *illus.*
PENN HILLS (Pennsylvania)
map (40° 28′N 79° 53′W) **15**:147
PENNACOOK (American Indians) **15**:145 *bibliog.*
New Hampshire **14**:125
PENNAMITE WARS
Wilkes-Barre (Pennsylvania) **20**:152
PENNEBAKER, D. A.
documentary **6**:211
PENNELL, JOSEPH **15**:145
PENNEY, J. C. **15**:145 *bibliog.*
PENNINE ALPS
map (46° 5′N 7° 50′E) **18**:394
PENNINES **15**:145
map (54° 10′N 2° 5′W) **19**:403
United Kingdom **19**:405
PENNINGTON (county in Minnesota)
map (48° 5′N 96° 0′W) **13**:453
PENNINGTON (New Jersey)
map (40° 19′N 74° 48′W) **14**:129
PENNINGTON (county in South Dakota)
map (44° 0′N 102° 45′W) **18**:103
PENNINGTON GAP (Virginia)
map (36° 41′N 83° 2′W) **19**:607
PENNS GROVE (New Jersey)
map (39° 43′N 75° 28′W) **14**:129
PENNSAUKEN (New Jersey)
map (39° 58′N 75° 4′W) **14**:129
PENNSVILLE (New Jersey)
map (39° 39′N 75° 31′W) **14**:129

PENNSYLVANIA 15:145–151 *bibliog., illus., map*
agriculture 15:149 *illus.*
archaeology and historic sites 15:149
Meadowcroft Rockshelter 13:252
cities
Allentown 1:301
Altoona 1:314
Bethlehem 3:231
Carlisle 4:151
Chester 4:336
Ephrata 7:217
Erie 7:229
Gettysburg 9:160
Harrisburg 10:58
Johnstown 11:438
Lancaster 12:177
Philadelphia 15:227–229 *illus., map*
Pittsburgh 15:321
Reading 16:100
Scranton 17:156
Wilkes-Barre 20:152
Williamsport 20:162
York 20:330
climate 15:146; 15:148
inversion catastrophe (Donora) 15:411
cultural institutions 15:148–149
economy 15:149–150 *illus.*
education 15:148
Allegheny College 1:298
Beaver College 3:149
Bryn Mawr College 3:529
Bucknell University 3:537
Carnegie-Mellon University 4:155
Dickinson College 6:158
Franklin and Marshall College 8:285
Haverford College 10:71
Lehigh University 12:275
Lincoln University 12:350
Moore College of Art 13:570
Moravian College 13:575
Pennsylvania, state universities and colleges of 15:151–152
Pennsylvania, University of 15:152
Swarthmore College 18:379
Villanova University 19:597
energy 15:150
flag 15:146 *illus.*
geographical linguistics 9:98–99 *maps*
government and politics 15:150
history 15:150–151
Cameron, Simon 4:60
Dickinson, John 6:158
Franklin, Benjamin 8:283
Logan, James 12:393
Mifflin, Thomas 13:416
Molly Maguires 13:512
Penn, William 15:144–145
United States, history of the 19:437
land and resources 15:145–148 *map*
manufacturing 15:149–150
map (40° 45′N 77° 30′W) 19:419
mining 15:149
people 15:148
Pennsylvania Dutch 15:152–153
resources 15:148
rivers, lakes, and waterways 15:146
Allegheny River 1:298
Lackawanna River 12:160
Monongahela River 13:537
Susquehanna River 18:372
roads and highways 16:238
seal, state 15:146 *illus.*
tourism and recreation 15:150
transportation 15:150
vegetation and animal life 15:148
PENNSYLVANIA, STATE UNIVERSITIES AND COLLEGES OF 15:151–152
PENNSYLVANIA, UNIVERSITY OF 15:152
computer 5:160a
computer industry 5:160n
Medical School
Fothergill, John 8:248
Wharton School of Finance and Commerce
business education 3:588
PENNSYLVANIA ACADEMY OF THE FINE ARTS 15:152 *bibliog.*
Furness, Frank 8:373
Peale (family) 15:124
PENNSYLVANIA DUTCH 15:152–153 *bibliog., illus.*
Kitchener (Ontario) 12:91
Lancaster (Pennsylvania) 12:177
PENNSYLVANIA FIREPLACE *see* FRANKLIN STOVE
PENNSYLVANIA GERMANS *see* PENNSYLVANIA DUTCH
PENNSYLVANIA HOSPITAL
Fothergill, John 8:248
PENNSYLVANIA SYSTEM
prison 15:554
PENNSYLVANIA TURNPIKE
roads and highways 16:238
turnpike 19:351
PENNSYLVANIAN SYSTEM (geology)
Carboniferous Period 4:137
PENNY PRESS 15:153
PENNYROYAL 15:153
mint 13:461
PENOBSCOT (American Indians) 15:153 *bibliog.*
Indians of North America, music and dance of the 11:143
PENOBSCOT (county in Maine)
map (45° 17′N 68° 35′W) 13:70
PENOBSCOT BAY
map (44° 15′N 68° 52′W) 13:70
PENOBSCOT RIVER 15:153
map (44° 30′N 68° 50′W) 13:70
PENOBSCOT RIVER, EAST BRANCH
map (45° 35′N 68° 32′W) 13:70
PENOBSCOT RIVER, WEST BRANCH
map (45° 35′N 68° 32′W) 13:70
PENONG (Australia)
map (31° 55′S 133° 1′E) 2:328
PENONOMÉ (Panama)
map (8° 31′N 80° 22′W) 15:55
PENROSE, BOIES
Pennsylvania 15:150
PENROSE, GEORGE AND WILLIAM
Waterford glass 20:63
PENSACOLA (Florida) 15:153
map (30° 25′N 87° 13′W) 8:172
PENSACOLA BAY
map (30° 25′N 87° 6′W) 8:172
PENSACOLA MOUNTAINS
map (83° 45′S 55° 0′W) 2:40
PENSÉES, LES (book) 15:153 *bibliog.*
Pascal, Blaise 15:102
PENSION 15:153–154 *bibliog.*
equal protection of the laws 7:224
government regulation 9:271
PENTAGON (geometry)
polygon 15:419 *illus.*
PENTAGON, THE 15:154
Washington, D.C. 20:41
PENTAGON PAPERS 15:154 *bibliog.*
Graham, Katharine 9:280
New York Times Company v. *United States* 14:156
PENTANE 15:155 *illus.*
natural gas 14:47
PENTAPOLIS
Cyrenaica 5:409
PENTATEUCH
Bible 3:238; 3:240
Torah 19:238
PENTATHLON 15:155
See also BIATHLON
PENTATONIC SCALE
scale (music) 17:106
PENTECOST 15:155 *bibliog.*
Holy Spirit 10:211
PENTECOSTALISM 15:155 *bibliog.*
Charismatic movement 4:288–289
tongues, speaking in 19:234
PENTICTON (British Columbia)
map (49° 30′N 119° 35′W) 3:491
PENTLAND FIRTH
map (58° 44′N 3° 13′W) 19:403
PENTLANDITE 15:155
nickel ore 15:155
PENTODE
electron tube 7:123
PENTWATER (Michigan)
map (43° 47′N 86° 26′W) 13:377
PENZA (USSR)
map (53° 13′N 45° 0′E) 19:388
PENZANCE (England) 15:155
PENZIAS, ARNO A. *see* WILSON, ROBERT W., AND PENZIAS, ARNO A. (astronomers)
PEONY 15:155–156 *illus.*
steppe life 18:257 *illus.*
PEOPLE UNITED TO SAVE HUMANITY
Jackson, Jesse L. 11:343
PEOPLE'S DAILY 15:156
newspaper 14:172
PEOPLE'S DEMOCRATIC REPUBLIC OF YEMEN *see* YEMEN (Aden)
PEOPLE'S PARTY *see* POPULIST PARTY
PEOPLE'S REPUBLIC OF ANGOLA *see* ANGOLA
PEOPLE'S REPUBLIC OF BANGLADESH *see* BANGLADESH
PEOPLE'S REPUBLIC OF BENIN *see* BENIN
PEOPLE'S REPUBLIC OF BULGARIA *see* BULGARIA
PEOPLE'S REPUBLIC OF CHINA *see* CHINA; CHINA, HISTORY OF
PEOPLE'S REPUBLIC OF KAMPUCHEA *see* KAMPUCHEA
PEOPLE'S REPUBLIC OF MOZAMBIQUE *see* MOZAMBIQUE
PEOPLE'S REPUBLIC OF THE CONGO *see* CONGO
PEOPLE'S SOCIALIST REPUBLIC OF ALBANIA *see* ALBANIA
PEOPLE'S TEMPLE (Guyana)
brainwashing 3:449
Jonestown 11:444
PEORIA (American Indians)
Illinois (American Indians) 11:45
PEORIA (Illinois) 15:156
map (40° 42′N 89° 36′W) 11:42
PEORIA (county in Illinois)
map (40° 45′N 89° 45′W) 11:42
PEORIA HEIGHTS (Illinois)
map (40° 45′N 89° 34′W) 11:42
PEOTONE (Illinois)
map (41° 20′N 87° 47′W) 11:42
PEPEL (Sierra Leone)
map (8° 35′N 13° 3′W) 17:296
PEPEROMIA 15:156
PEPIN (Wisconsin)
map (44° 27′N 92° 9′W) 20:185
PEPIN (county in Wisconsin)
map (44° 38′N 92° 7′W) 20:185
PEPIN, LAKE
map (44° 30′N 92° 15′W) 20:185
PEPIN III *see* PEPIN THE SHORT, KING OF THE FRANKS
PEPIN THE SHORT, KING OF THE FRANKS 15:156 *bibliog.*
France, history of 8:267
Lombards 12:399
Papal States 15:67
PEPPER (spice) 15:156 *illus.*
peperomia 15:156
PEPPER (vegetable) 15:156–157 *illus.*
bell pepper 19:533 *illus.*
harvest 10:136 *illus.*
PEPPER TREE 15:157
PEPPERGRASS 15:157
cress 5:339
PEPPERMINT 15:157 *illus.*
mint 13:461
PEPPERRELL, SIR WILLIAM 15:157 *bibliog.*
French and Indian Wars 8:313
PEPPERROOT *see* TOOTHWORT
PEPPERSHRIKE 15:157
PEPSIN
Northrop, John Howard 14:256
stomach 18:279–280 *illus.*
PEPTIC ULCER *see* STOMACH; ULCER
PEPTIDE 15:157
See also POLYPEPTIDE
amide 1:369
amino acid 1:370
hormone, animal 10:234; 10:235; 10:236
Merrifield, R. Bruce 13:312
PEPUSCH, JOHANN CHRISTOPHER
Beggar's Opera, The 3:168
English music 7:203
PEPY I, KING OF EGYPT
Hierakonpolis 10:159
PEPYS, SAMUEL 15:157–158 *bibliog., illus.*
PEQUANNOCK (New Jersey)
map (40° 57′N 74° 18′W) 14:129
PEQUOT (American Indians) 15:158 *bibliog.*
Montauk 13:551
Pequot War 15:158
Uncas 19:381
PEQUOT WAR 11:109 *map*; 15:158 *bibliog.*
Miantonomo 13:370
Mohegan 13:503
PERALTA (New Mexico)
map (34° 50′N 106° 41′W) 14:136
PERALTA, PEDRO DE
Santa Fe (New Mexico) 17:68
PERCALE
muslin 13:683
PERCEPTION 15:158–160 *bibliog., illus.*
Bruner, Jerome Seymour 3:525
Brunswik, Egon 3:526
color perception 5:114–115
depth perception 15:158
eye 7:348–350
Gestalt psychology 9:159
hallucination 10:24
hallucinogens 10:24
Helmholtz, Hermann Ludwig Ferdinand von 10:115–116
illusions 11:48–49; 15:158–159
infancy 11:162–163
Koffka, Kurt 12:106
psychology 15:158–160; 15:594
psychophysics 15:601–602
sensation 17:204
social psychology 18:13
subliminal perception 18:313
synesthesia 18:407
Wundt, Wilhelm 20:296
PERCEVAL *see* PARSIFAL
PERCH 8:112–113 *illus.*; 15:160–161 *bibliog., illus.*
diet 15:160 *illus.*
PERCHE HILLS
map (48° 25′N 0° 40′E) 8:260
PERCHERON 10:244 *illus.*; 15:161 *illus.*
PERCHIN, MICHAEL
crystal egg 16:363 *illus.*
PERCHING BIRDS 15:161–162 *bibliog.*
PERCIER, CHARLES 15:162
Malmaison 13:93
PERCUSSION INSTRUMENTS 15:162–163 *bibliog., illus.*
African music 1:168–170 *illus.*
Arabian music 2:99–100
castanets 4:181
Chinese music 4:392–393 *illus.*
cymbals 5:406
drum (musical instrument) 6:282
gamelan (orchestra) 9:29
glass harmonica 9:201–202
glockenspiel 9:209 *illus.*
gong 9:243 *illus.*
Indian music 11:102–103 *illus.*
Indians of North America, music and dance of the 11:142 *illus.*
Japanese music 11:381–382 *illus.*
Jew's harp 11:417
kettledrum 12:61–62 *illus.*
marimba 13:153
musical instruments 13:675–676 *illus.*
snare drum 17:384
tambourine 19:19
triangle 19:292
vibraphone 19:567
xylophone 20:313
PERCY (family) 15:162–163
Richard II (play) 16:209
PERCY, CHARLES 15:163
PERCY, HENRY (Hotspur) (1364–1403)
Henry IV, Parts 1 and 2 (play) 10:124
Percy (family) 15:163
PERCY, HENRY, 1ST EARL OF NORTHUMBERLAND (1342–1408)
Percy (family) 15:163
PERCY, THOMAS (1560–1605)
Percy (family) 15:163
PERCY, THOMAS 7TH EARL OF NORTHUMBERLAND (1528–1572)
Percy (family) 15:163
PERCY, WALKER 15:163 *bibliog.*
PERDICCAS 15:163
PERDICCAS I
Macedonia, Kingdom of 13:15
PERDIDO (Alabama)
map (31° 0′N 87° 37′W) 1:234
PÈRE LACHAISE (Paris)
tomb 19:231
PERE MARQUETTE RIVER
map (43° 57′N 86° 27′W) 13:377
PEREDA, JOSÉ MARÍA DE
Spanish literature 18:159
PEREDVIZHNIKI (art group)
Repin, Ilya Yefimovich 16:160
PEREGRINE FALCON 2:140–141 *illus.*
falcon 8:12 *illus.*
PEREIRA (Colombia)
map (4° 49′N 75° 43′W) 5:107
PEREIRA, I. RICE 15:163 *bibliog.*
PEREIRA, MANUEL
Saint Bruno 15:456 *illus.*
PEREIRA, NUNO ÁLVARES 15:163
PEREIRA, WILLIAM L.
Los Angeles County Museum of Art 12:418
PERELMAN, ELIEZER YITSHAK *see* BEN-YEHUDAH, ELIEZER
PERELMAN, S. J. 15:163
PERENNIAL (botany)
flower 8:181
gardening 9:43
PERES, SHIMON 15:163
PERETZ, Y. L. 15:163 *bibliog.*
PÉREZ, CARLOS ANDRÉS
Venezuela 19:544
PÉREZ, JUAN
Queen Charlotte Islands 16:21–22
PÉREZ, MANUEL BENITEZ *see* EL CORDOBÉS

PEREZ, RUDY
  modern dance **13**:498
PÉREZ DE AYALA, RAMÓN
  Spanish literature **18**:160
PÉREZ DE CUÉLLAR, JAVIER **15**:164
PÉREZ ESQUIVEL, ADOLFO **15**:164
PÉREZ GALDÓS, BENITO **15**:164 *bibliog.*
  Spanish literature **18**:159
PERFECTIONISM
  ethics **7**:251
PERFORMANCE (law)
  contract **5**:232
PERFORMANCE (linguistics)
  anthropological linguistics **2**:51
  grammar **9**:282
  psycholinguistics **15**:591
PERFORMANCE ART **15**:164 *bibliog.*
  happenings **10**:41
PERFUME **15**:164 *bibliog., illus.*
  ambergris **1**:325
  bay rum **3**:132
  bergamot **3**:209
  champac **4**:276
  citronella **4**:447
  cosmetics **5**:281–282
  cyclic compounds **5**:403
  flavors and fragrances **8**:157
  frankincense **8**:282
  ginger **9**:184
  herbs and spices **10**:136–137
  hibiscus **10**:157
  hyacinth **10**:327
  jasmine **11**:384
  juniper **11**:470
  lactone **12**:161–162
  lavender **12**:241
  mace **13**:15
  mint **13**:460–461
  musk **13**:681
  myrrh **13**:691
  myrtle **13**:691
  patchouli **15**:109
  Patou, Jean **15**:112
  Perkin, Sir William Henry **15**:172
  rosemary **16**:314
  saffron **17**:11
  sandalwood **17**:61
  smelling salts **17**:365
  spikenard **18**:183
  sweet gum **18**:387
  terpene **19**:118
  tuberose **19**:327
  vanilla **19**:519–520
  violet **19**:602
  whale **20**:121
  woodruff **20**:212
PERGAMINO (Argentina)
  map (33° 53′S 60° 35′W) **2**:149
PERGAMUM (Turkey) **15**:164–165 *bibliog.*
  altar
    Seven Wonders of the World **17**:216
  Attalus I, King **2**:313–314
  Dying Gaul **6**:319
  Eumenes II, King **7**:265
  mosaic **13**:593
PERGOLESI, GIOVANNI BATTISTA **15**:165 *bibliog.*
  intermezzo **11**:214
PERHAM (Minnesota)
  map (46° 36′N 95° 34′W) **13**:453
PERI, JACOPO **15**:165 *bibliog.*
  Italian music **11**:318
  music, history of Western **13**:666
  opera **14**:399
PERIANDER, TYRANT OF CORINTH **15**:165
PERICARDITIS **15**:165
  heart diseases **10**:95
  uremia **19**:485
PERICARDIUM
  heart **10**:91 *illus.*
  heart diseases **10**:95
PERICLES **9**:333 *illus.*; **15**:165 *bibliog., illus.*
  Peloponnesian War **15**:139
PERIDOT **9**:74 *illus.*; **15**:166 *illus.*
  birthstones **3**:296 *illus., table*
  olivine **14**:379–380; **15**:166
PERIDOTITE **15**:166 *bibliog.*
  kimberlite **12**:77
  olivine **14**:380
PÉRIGORD, CHARLES MAURICE DE TALLEYRAND- *see* TALLEYRAND-PÉRIGORD, CHARLES MAURICE DE
PERIGORDIAN **15**:166 *bibliog.*
  Châtelperronian **4**:303
  Gravettian **9**:303
  prehistoric art **15**:507
PÉRIGUEUX (France) **15**:166
  map (45° 11′N 0° 43′E) **8**:260
PERIHELION
  celestial mechanics **4**:230
  precession
    gravitation **9**:305
PERIJÁ RANGE
  map (10° 0′N 73° 0′W) **19**:542
PERIOD-LUMINOSITY RELATION **15**:166
  Cepheids **4**:257
  cosmology (astronomy) **5**:284
  distance, astronomical **6**:199–200
  extragalactic systems **7**:343
  Leavitt, Henrietta Swan **12**:263–264
  variable star **19**:523
PERIODIC FUNCTION **15**:166
  Fourier analysis **8**:254
PERIODIC MOTION
  motion, harmonic **13**:608–609
PERIODIC TABLE **15**:166–169 *bibliog., table*
  arrangement **15**:167
  artificial transmutation of elements **15**:168
  atomic theory **15**:167–168
  chemistry, history of **4**:326
  development **15**:166–167
  element **7**:130
  Group IA
    cesium **4**:262
    francium **8**:277
    hydrogen **10**:337–339
    lithium **12**:370–371
    metallic elements **13**:328
    potassium **15**:464–465
    rubidium **16**:336
    sodium **18**:32–33
  Group IIA
    barium **3**:81–82
    beryllium **3**:227
    calcium **4**:22
    magnesium **13**:53–54
    metallic elements **13**:328
    radium **16**:68
    strontium **18**:303
  Group IIIA
    aluminum **1**:315–319
    boron **3**:403
    gallium **9**:21
    indium **11**:144–145
    metallic elements **13**:328
    thallium **19**:142
  Group IVA
    carbon **4**:133–135
    germanium **9**:138
    lead **12**:256
    metallic elements **13**:328
    silicon **17**:305
    tin **19**:204
  Group VA
    antimony **2**:63–64
    arsenic **2**:189
    bismuth **3**:299
    metallic elements **13**:328
    nitrogen **14**:202
    phosphorus **15**:256–257
  Group VIA
    metallic elements **13**:328
    oxygen **14**:476–478
    polonium **15**:417
    selenium **17**:190
    sulfur **18**:334
    tellurium **19**:91
  Group VIIA
    astatine **2**:267
    bromine **3**:502
    chlorine **4**:400–401
    fluorine **8**:187–188
    halogens **10**:25
    iodine **11**:238–239
  Group IB
    copper **5**:251–254
    gold **9**:226–227
    metallic elements **13**:328
    silver **17**:312–313
  Group IIB
    cadmium **4**:12
    mercury **13**:306–307
    metallic elements **13**:328
    zinc **20**:367–368
  Group IIIB
    gadolinium **9**:7
    metallic elements **13**:328
    nobelium **14**:211
    scandium **17**:114
    thulium **19**:184
    yttrium **20**:337–338
  Group IVB
    hafnium **10**:9
    metallic elements **13**:328
    titanium **19**:211
    zirconium **20**:370
  Group VB
    metallic elements **13**:328
    niobium **14**:200–201
    tantalum **19**:25
    vanadium **19**:516
  Group VIB
    chromium **4**:419
    metallic elements **13**:328
    molybdenum **13**:514
    tungsten **19**:333–334
  Group VIIB
    manganese **13**:114
    metallic elements **13**:328
    rhenium **16**:193
    technetium **19**:59
  Group VIII
    cobalt **5**:82–83
    iridium **11**:266
    iron **11**:270–271
    metallic elements **13**:328
    nickel **14**:183
    osmium **14**:455
    palladium **15**:48
    platinum **15**:359–360
    rhodium **16**:203
    ruthenium **16**:375
  Group 0
    argon **2**:152
    helium **10**:113
    krypton **12**:133
    neon **14**:85
    radon **16**:68–69
    xenon **20**:312
  Mendeleyev, Dmitry Ivanovich **13**:294–295
  Meyer, Lothar **13**:368
  Newlands, John Alexander Reina **14**:169
  radioactivity **15**:168–169
  transition elements **19**:273–274 *table*
PERIODICAL **15**:169–170 *bibliog., illus.*
  See also JOURNALISM; NEWSPAPER; PULP MAGAZINES; names of specific periodicals, e.g., *NEW YORKER, THE* (periodical); *WASHINGTON POST, THE*; etc.
  advertising **1**:112–113
  current trends **15**:169–170
  Curtis, Cyrus H. K. **5**:395
  history **15**:169–170
  Luce, Henry Robinson **12**:449–450
  Philipon, Charles **15**:235
  printing **15**:552–553
    rotogravure **16**:323
  public relations **15**:610
  Ross, Harold **16**:318
  Stone, I. F. **18**:280
PERIODICITY, BIOLOGICAL *see* BIOLOGICAL CLOCK
PERIODONTICS **15**:170
  gingivitis **9**:184
  pyorrhea **15**:634
PERIPATETICS **15**:170–171 *bibliog.*
  Aristotle **2**:156; **2**:158
  Theophrastus **19**:158
PERIPATUS **15**:171 *illus.*
PERIPHERAL NERVOUS SYSTEM **15**:171 *bibliog.*
  neuralgia **14**:105
PERIPHERALS (computer term) **5**:160i
PERISCOPE
  archaeology **2**:119
  prism **15**:553 *illus.*
  submarine **18**:313
PERISSODACTYL **15**:171
  mammal **13**:105–106 *illus.*
PERISTALSIS **15**:171–172 *illus.*
  Bayliss, Sir William **3**:133
PERITONITIS **15**:172
  ileus **11**:40
PERIWINKLE (botany) **15**:172
  myrtle **13**:692
PERIWINKLE (zoology) **15**:172
  intertidal life **11**:229 *illus.*
PERJURY **15**:172
PERKASIE (Pennsylvania)
  map (40° 22′N 75° 18′W) **15**:147
PERKIN, SIR WILLIAM HENRY **4**:318 *illus.*; **15**:172
  dye **6**:318 *illus.*
PERKINS (county in Nebraska)
  map (40° 50′N 101° 40′W) **14**:70
PERKINS (Oklahoma)
  map (35° 58′N 97° 2′W) **14**:368
PERKINS (county in South Dakota)
  map (45° 27′N 102° 30′W) **18**:103
PERKINS, FRANCES **15**:172 *bibliog., illus.*
PERKINS, JACOB
  refrigeration **16**:124
PERKINS, MAXWELL **15**:172 *bibliog.*
PERKINSTON (Mississippi)
  map (30° 47′N 89° 8′W) **13**:469
PERLAS LAGOON
  map (12° 30′N 83° 40′W) **14**:179
PERLITE **15**:172
  obsidian **14**:319
PERLMAN, ITZHAK **15**:172
PERLS, FRIEDRICH S. **15**:173 *bibliog.*
  humanistic psychology **10**:299
PERM (USSR) **15**:173
  map (58° 0′N 56° 15′E) **19**:388
PERMAFROST **15**:173–174 *bibliog., map*
  Arctic **2**:138
  effect on human activities **15**:173
  frost **8**:345
  germination **9**:157
  occurrence in the Northern Hemisphere **15**:173 *map*
  paleoclimatology **15**:32
  patterned ground **15**:115
  temperature **15**:173
  thickness **15**:173
  tundra **19**:332
PERMANENT COURT OF ARBITRATION (Hague Tribunal) *see* HAGUE TRIBUNAL
PERMANENT COURT OF INTERNATIONAL JUSTICE *see* INTERNATIONAL COURT OF JUSTICE
PERMEABILITY, ROCK **15**:174 *bibliog.*
  groundwater **9**:374–375 *illus.*
  petroleum **15**:208
PERMIAN LANGUAGES
  Uralic languages **19**:475
PERMIAN PERIOD **15**:174–176 *bibliog., illus., map*
  coal and coal mining **5**:76
  continents, estimated positions **15**:354 *map*
  Dimetrodon **6**:177
  Edaphosaurus **7**:54
  exposed strata **15**:174–175
  fossil record **8**:246
  geological history **15**:176
  ginkgo **9**:184
  Gondwanaland **9**:243
  life **15**:174 *illus.*; **15**:176
  paleoclimatology **15**:32–33 *map*
  paleomagnetism **15**:41 *map*
  Paleozoic Era **15**:43
  polar wandering **15**:393 *map, map*
  rock formations **15**:175 *map*
PERMITTIVITY
  units of measurement
    units, physical **19**:467
PERMOSER, BALTHASAR **15**:176 *bibliog.*
PERMUTATION AND COMBINATION **15**:176 *bibliog.*
  factorial **8**:6
  selection of objects **15**:176
  tree diagram **19**:288–289
PERNAMBUCO (city in Brazil) *see* RECIFE (Brazil)
PERNAMBUCO (state in Brazil)
  map (8° 0′S 37° 0′W) **3**:460
PERNICIOUS ANEMIA *see* ANEMIA
PERNIK (Bulgaria)
  map (42° 36′N 23° 2′E) **3**:555
PERÓN, EVA **15**:176 *bibliog.*
  Perón, Juan D. **15**:177
PERÓN, ISABEL **15**:176 *bibliog.*
  Perón, Juan D. **15**:177
PERÓN, JUAN D. **15**:177 *bibliog., illus.*
  Argentina **2**:151
  Perón, Eva **15**:176
  Perón, Isabel **15**:176
PEROTIN
  music, history of Western **13**:665
PEROTINUS MAGNUS *see* PEROTIN
PÉROUSE, JEAN FRANÇOIS DE GALAUP, COMTE DE LA *see* LA PÉROUSE, JEAN FRANÇOIS DE GALAUP, COMTE DE
PEROV, VASILI
  Russian art and architecture **16**:362
PEROVSKITE **15**:177
PEROXIDE **15**:177 *bibliog.*
  compounds **15**:177
  oxidation and reduction **14**:475
  Thénard, Louis Jacques, Baron, discoverer **19**:155
  uses **15**:177
PERPENDICULAR GOTHIC STYLE **15**:177 *bibliog.*
  Canterbury Cathedral **4**:116
  English art and architecture **7**:183–184
  Gothic art and architecture **9**:261–262
  Tudor style **19**:329
PERPETUAL MOTION MACHINE **15**:178 *bibliog.*
  entropy **7**:209
  thermodynamics **19**:164
PERPIGNAN (France) **15**:178
  map (42° 41′N 2° 53′E) **8**:260

PERQUIMANS (county in North Carolina)
map (36° 10′N 76° 25′W) **14**:242
PERRAULT, CHARLES **15**:178
Bluebeard **3**:344
fairy tale **8**:10–11
Mother Goose **13**:607
PERRAULT, CLAUDE **15**:178 *bibliog.*
Louvre **12**:437
PERRET, AUGUSTE **15**:178 *bibliog.*
PERRIN, JEAN BAPTISTE **15**:178 *bibliog.*
PERRINE (Florida)
map (25° 36′N 80° 21′W) **8**:172
PERRONET, JEAN
bridge (engineering) **3**:480
PERROT, JULES **15**:178 *bibliog.*
PERROT, NICOLAS **15**:178–179 *bibliog.*
PERRY (county in Alabama)
map (32° 40′N 87° 5′W) **1**:234
PERRY (county in Arkansas)
map (35° 15′N 92° 50′W) **2**:166
PERRY (Florida)
map (30° 7′N 83° 35′W) **8**:172
PERRY (Georgia)
map (32° 27′N 83° 44′W) **9**:114
PERRY (county in Illinois)
map (38° 5′N 89° 18′W) **11**:42
PERRY (county in Indiana)
map (38° 5′N 86° 35′W) **11**:111
PERRY (Iowa)
map (41° 50′N 94° 6′W) **11**:244
PERRY (Kansas)
map (39° 5′N 95° 24′W) **12**:18
PERRY (county in Kentucky)
map (37° 15′N 83° 10′W) **12**:47
PERRY (county in Mississippi)
map (31° 10′N 89° 0′W) **13**:469
PERRY (Missouri)
map (39° 26′N 91° 40′W) **13**:476
PERRY (county in Missouri)
map (37° 45′N 89° 50′W) **13**:476
PERRY (New York)
map (42° 43′N 78° 0′W) **14**:149
PERRY (county in Ohio)
map (39° 40′N 82° 12′W) **14**:357
PERRY (Oklahoma)
map (36° 17′N 97° 17′W) **14**:368
PERRY (county in Pennsylvania)
map (40° 25′N 77° 11′W) **15**:147
PERRY (county in Tennessee)
map (35° 40′N 87° 50′W) **19**:104
PERRY, ANTOINETTE
Tony Awards **19**:236
PERRY, FRED **15**:179
PERRY, GAYLORD **15**:179
PERRY, MATTHEW CALBRAITH **15**:179 *bibliog., illus.*
Japan, history of **11**:369
PERRY, OLIVER HAZARD **15**:179 *bibliog.*
Erie (Pennsylvania) **7**:229
flag **8**:135 *illus.*
PERRY, RALPH BARTON **15**:179 *bibliog.*
PERRY, W. J. **15**:179
PERRY LAKE
map (39° 20′N 95° 30′W) **12**:18
PERRYSBURG (Ohio)
map (41° 33′N 83° 38′W) **14**:357
PERRYTON (Texas)
map (36° 24′N 100° 48′W) **19**:129
PERRYVILLE (Alaska)
map (55° 54′N 159° 10′W) **1**:242
PERRYVILLE (Arkansas)
map (35° 0′N 92° 48′W) **2**:166
PERRYVILLE (Kentucky)
Civil War, U.S. **5**:25
PERRYVILLE (Maryland)
map (39° 34′N 76° 5′W) **13**:188
PERRYVILLE (Missouri)
map (37° 43′N 89° 52′W) **13**:476
PERSE, SAINT-JOHN **15**:179–180 *bibliog.*
PERSEI *see* ALGOL (star)
PERSEIDS *see* METEOR AND METEORITE
PERSEPHONE **15**:180
Adonis **1**:107
Eleusis **7**:135
fertility rites **8**:60
PERSEPOLIS (Iran) **15**:180 *bibliog.*
Persian art and architecture **15**:184 *illus.*
Tripylon Gate **20**:380 *illus.*
PERSEUS (mythology) **3**:576 *illus.*; **15**:180
Medusa **13**:278
PERSEUS, KING OF MACEDONIA **15**:180
Rome, ancient **16**:300
PERSEVENCIA (Bolivia)
map (14° 44′S 62° 48′W) **3**:366
PERSHING (county in Nevada)
map (40° 30′N 118° 20′W) **14**:111
PERSHING, JOHN J. **15**:180–181 *bibliog., illus.*
rank, military **16**:86
World War I **20**:236; **20**:240–242 *illus.*
PERSIA *see* IRAN for events since 637 AD; *see* PERSIA, ANCIENT for events prior to 637 AD
PERSIA (Iowa)
map (41° 34′N 95° 35′W) **11**:244
PERSIA, ANCIENT **15**:181–183 *bibliog., illus., map*
art *see* PERSIAN ART AND ARCHITECTURE
Asia, history of **2**:250
Babylonia **3**:8–9
Bactria **3**:18
cities
Dur-Untash **6**:302
Ecbatana **7**:37
Hasanlu **10**:65
Pasargadae **15**:101
Susa **18**:370
literature *see* PERSIAN LITERATURE
Middle East, history of the **13**:405
polo **15**:417
slavery **17**:352
Zoroastrianism **20**:379–380 *illus.*
prior to 550 BC
Media **13**:263–264
people **15**:181
550–330 BC Achaemenids
Achaemenids **1**:80–81; **15**:181
Artaxerxes I, King **2**:213
Artaxerxes II, King **2**:213
Behistun **3**:171
Cambyses II, King **4**:53
Cappadocia **4**:127–128
Cyrus the Great, King **5**:410
Cyrus the Younger **5**:410–411
Darius I, King **6**:38
Darius III Codomannus, King **6**:38
Halicarnassus **10**:20
Lydia **12**:474
Mausolus **13**:238
Median Kingdom **15**:181–182 *map*
Middle East, history of the **13**:401
Parthia **15**:100
Persian Wars *see* PERSIAN WARS
postal services **15**:459
roads and highways **16**:235
Tissaphernes, Persian Satrap **19**:209
Xerxes I, King **20**:312
330 BC–637 AD
Ardashir I, King **2**:144
Arsacids **2**:189
Elam **7**:101–102
Khosru I, King of Persia **12**:68
Parthians **15**:182
Sassanians **15**:182
Seleucids **15**:181–182
PERSIAN ART AND ARCHITECTURE **15**:183–187 *bibliog., illus.*
Achaemenid period **15**:184
ancient era **15**:183
architecture **2**:131
Behistun **3**:171
Bihzad, Kamal al-Din **3**:250
early kingdoms **15**:184
garden **9**:40
Hasanlu **10**:65
Islamic art and architecture **11**:297; **15**:185–187
Luristan **12**:467
Mogul art and architecture **13**:500–503
Pasargadae **14**:101
Persepolis **15**:180
Persia, ancient **15**:181–183 *illus.*
Riza-i-Abbasi **16**:234
rugs and carpets **16**:341 *illus.*
Sardis **17**:77
Sassanian period **15**:184–185
Sultan Muhammad **18**:338
Susa **18**:370
terra-cotta bodhisattva **19**:120 *illus.*
PERSIAN CAT **4**:195 *illus.*
exotic shorthair cat **7**:333
Himalayan cat **10**:165
longhaired cats **12**:407–408 *illus.*
PERSIAN GULF **15**:187 *map*
Bahrain **3**:24–25
Hormuz, Strait of **10**:238
map (27° 0′N 51° 0′E) **7**:52
PERSIAN LANGUAGE *see* INDO-IRANIAN LANGUAGES
PERSIAN LITERATURE **15**:187 *bibliog.*
authors
Alavi, Bozorg **1**:248
Ansari **2**:35
Attar, Farid al-Din Abu Hamid **2**:314
Firdawsi **8**:100
Hafez, Mohammed Shamsoddin **10**:9
Hedayat, Sadeq **10**:104
Jamalzade, Mohammed Ali **11**:353
Nezami, Nezamoddin Ilyas **14**:176
Omar Khayyam **14**:387
Rudaki, Abu Abdollah Jafar **16**:337
Rumi, Jalal al-Din al- **16**:345
Sadi, Sheykh **17**:9–10
PERSIAN LYNX *see* CARACAL
PERSIAN WARS **15**:187–188 *bibliog.*
Greece, ancient **9**:331
History of the Persian Wars, The **10**:186
Leonidas, King of Sparta **12**:292
Marathon, Battle of **13**:144
Salamis (island, Greece) **17**:30
Xerxes I, King of Persia **20**:312
PERSIANI, FANNY
Lucia di Lammermoor **12**:450
PERSIMMON **15**:188 *illus.*
PERSIUS **15**:188 *bibliog.*
PERSKE, BETTY JOAN *see* BACALL, LAUREN
PERSON (county in North Carolina)
map (36° 25′N 78° 55′W) **14**:242
PERSONA
narrative and dramatic devices **14**:22
PERSONAL COMPUTER *see* COMPUTER, PERSONAL
PERSONAL PROPERTY **15**:188 *bibliog.*
property **15**:570–571
tort **19**:246
trespass **19**:291
trover **19**:312
PERSONALISM **15**:188–189 *bibliog.*
Bowne, Borden Parker **3**:430
PERSONALITY **15**:189–190 *bibliog.*
Adler, Alfred **1**:103
assessment **15**:190
projective tests **15**:566
psychological measurement **15**:593
authoritarian personality **2**:354
child development **4**:348–350
developmental psychology **6**:142
ego **7**:73
Erikson, Erik **7**:230
est **7**:245
extraversion-introversion **7**:346
Eysenck, H. J. **7**:352
Freud, Sigmund **15**:190
Fromm, Erich **8**:339
hallucinogens **10**:24
Horney, Karen **10**:239
hypnosis **10**:350
Jung, Carl **11**:467
Kluckhohn, Clyde **12**:98
moral awareness **13**:572–573
Murphy, Gardner **13**:649
paranoia **15**:80
psychology **15**:594
psychopathy **15**:601
psychosis **15**:602
schizophrenia **17**:123
suicide **18**:331
Sullivan, Harry Stack **18**:336
theory
cognitive psychology **5**:94–95; **15**:189–190
humanistic psychology **10**:299; **15**:189
learning theory **12**:260–261; **15**:189
psychoanalysis **15**:189; **15**:589
trait **15**:189
PERSONIFICATION (literature)
figures of speech **8**:76
PERSONNEL MANAGEMENT, OFFICE OF *see* CIVIL SERVICE COMMISSION
PERSPECTIVE (art) **15**:190–191 *bibliog., illus.*
anamorphosis **1**:391
art **2**:190–191
Bologna, Giovanni da **3**:370–371
Broederlam, Melchior **3**:501
Bruegel (family) **3**:522–523
Brunelleschi, Filippo **3**:525
Canaletto **4**:98
Caravaggio, Michelangelo Merisi da **4**:131–132
chiaroscuro **4**:340
Christus, Petrus **4**:416
Correggio **5**:275–276
Escher, Maurits Corneille **7**:237
Exekias **7**:329
Giotto di Bondone **9**:187
Held, Al **10**:110
illusionism **11**:49–50
Italian art and architecture **11**:312
Mantegna, Andrea **13**:129–130
Masaccio **13**:193
Micon **13**:384
op art **14**:397
painting **15**:19–20
Perugino **15**:195
Roman art and architecture **16**:276
Uccello, Paolo **19**:370
Veronese, Paolo **19**:559–560
PERSPECTIVE (mathematics)
Desargues, Gérard **6**:125
Taylor, Brook **19**:48
PERTH (Australia) **15**:191
climate **2**:332 *table*
education
Murdoch University **2**:345 *table*
Western Australia University **2**:345 *table*
map (31° 56′S 115° 50′E) **2**:328
PERTH (Ontario)
map (44° 54′N 76° 15′W) **14**:393
PERTH (Scotland) **15**:191
map (56° 24′N 3° 28′W) **19**:403
PERTH (county in Scotland) **15**:191
PERTH AMBOY (New Jersey) **19**:431 *illus.*
map (40° 31′N 74° 16′W) **14**:129
PERTH-ANDOVER (New Brunswick)
map (46° 45′N 67° 42′W) **14**:117
PERTHES, JACQUES BOUCHER DE CRÈVECOEUR DE *see* BOUCHER DE PERTHES, JACQUES
PERTHITE
feldspar **8**:46
PERTURBATION **15**:191 *bibliog.*
PERU **15**:191–195 *bibliog., illus., map, table*
archaeology
Chan Chan **4**:278
Chancay **4**:278
Chavín de Huántar **4**:306
Chimu **4**:359
Cuzco **5**:399–400
Huari **10**:287
Machu Picchu **2**:125 *illus.*; **13**:25–26
Nazca **14**:67
Pachacamac **15**:4
Paracas **15**:74
Sacsahuaman **17**:8
silver **17**:312
Uhle, Max **19**:374
Vicús **19**:576
art
Latin American art and architecture **12**:222–223; **12**:226 *illus.*
pre-Columbian art and architecture **15**:495–501
Boyden Station
Pickering, William Henry **15**:293
cities
Callao **4**:40
Iquitos **15**:193 *table*
Lima **12**:342 *illus.*
economic activity **15**:193
education **15**:192
Latin American universities **12**:233 *table*
El Niño (ocean current) **7**:99
flag **15**:192 *illus.*
government **15**:193–194
history **15**:194–195
Almagro, Diego de **1**:306
Atahualpa **2**:287
Belaúnde Terry, Fernando **3**:174
Castilla, Ramón **4**:188
Grace, W. R. **9**:275–276
Latin America, history of **12**:219; **12**:220–222
Leguía y Salcedo, Augusto Bernardino **12**:275
Morales Bermúdez, Francisco **13**:573
Pacific, War of the **15**:5
Pérez de Cuéllar, Javier **15**:164
Pizarro, Francisco **15**:324–325
San Martin, José de **17**:57
Tacna-Arica Dispute **19**:6
Toledo, Francisco de **19**:226
Huascarán **10**:287
land and resources **15**:191–193 *map, table*
literature
Alegría, Ciro **1**:270
Latin American literature **12**:228–231
Vallejo, César **19**:507
Vargas Llosa, Mario **19**:522
map (10° 0′S 76° 0′W) **18**:85

PERU (cont.)
people 2:55 *illus.*; 11:134 *illus.*; 15:192–193 *illus.*
Aymara 2:379
Inca 11:69–73
Quechua 16:21
PERU (Illinois)
map (41° 20′N 89° 8′W) 11:42
PERU (Indiana)
map (40° 45′N 86° 4′W) 11:111
PERU (Nebraska)
map (40° 29′N 95° 44′W) 14:70
PERU-BOLIVIAN CONFEDERATION
Santa Cruz, Andrés 17:67–68
PERU-CHILE TRENCH *see* OCEANIC TRENCHES
PERU CURRENT *see* HUMBOLDT CURRENT
PERUGIA (Italy) 15:195
cities
Assisi 2:265
map (43° 8′N 12° 22′E) 11:321
PERUGINO 15:195–196 *bibliog., illus.*
Delivery of the Keys to Saint Peter 15:195 *illus.*
Delivery of the Keys to St. Peter 2:196 *illus.*
Raphael 16:89
Sistine Chapel 17:329
PERUTZ, MAX FERDINAND 15:196
PERUVIAN CURRENT (Humboldt Current)
ocean currents and wind systems, worldwide 14:322–323 *maps*
plankton 15:332
PERUZZI, BALDASSARE 15:196 *bibliog.*
PESCADORES (Taiwan) 15:196
map (23° 30′N 119° 30′E) 19:13
PESCARA (Italy)
map (42° 28′N 14° 13′E) 11:321
PESCHKOWSKY, MICHAEL IGOR *see* NICHOLS, MIKE
PESHAWAR (Pakistan)
climate 15:26 *table*
map (34° 1′N 71° 33′E) 15:27
PESHTIGO (Wisconsin)
map (45° 3′N 87° 45′W) 20:185
PESSOA, FERNANDO
Portuguese literature 15:457
PESSONS PEAK
map (42° 31′N 1° 40′E) 1:405
PEST (city) *see* BUDAPEST (Hungary)
PEST, AGRICULTURAL *see* AGRICULTURE AND THE FOOD SUPPLY
PEST CONTROL *see* PESTICIDES AND PEST CONTROL
PESTALOZZI, JOHANN HEINRICH 15:196 *bibliog., illus.*
educational psychology 7:66
primary education 15:537
PESTICIDES AND PEST CONTROL 15:196–199 *bibliog., illus.*
arsenic 2:189
breast-feeding 3:469
chlorine compounds 4:401
cockroach 5:87–88
conservation 5:202
DDT 6:57–58
derris 6:123
endangered species 7:166 *illus.*
environmental health 7:212
fly 8:190
fumigation 8:359
gardening 9:44
herbicide 10:135–136
housefly 10:274
nicotine 14:184
organic chemistry 14:438–439
pollutants, chemical 15:410; 15:411
pollution, environmental 15:413
Silent Spring (book) 17:303–304
soil organisms 18:39
PETACCI, CLARA
World War II 20:271
PÉTAIN, HENRI PHILIPPE 15:199 *bibliog., illus.*
Darlan, Jean François 6:39
Verdun, Battle of 19:550
Vichy Government 19:571
World War I 20:232 *illus.*; 20:237
PETAL (Mississippi)
map (31° 21′N 89° 17′W) 13:469
PETALUMA (California)
map (38° 14′N 122° 39′W) 4:31
PÉTANGE (Luxembourg)
map (49° 34′N 5° 52′E) 12:472
PETÉN ITZÁ, LAKE
map (16° 59′N 89° 50′W) 9:389
PETENWELL LAKE
map (44° 10′N 89° 57′W) 20:185
PETER, EPISTLES OF 15:199 *bibliog.*
PETER, SAINT 15:199–200 *bibliog., illus.*
papacy 15:62–63 *illus.*
sculpture 17:162 *illus.*
PETER I, EMPEROR OF RUSSIA (PETER THE GREAT) 15:200–201 *bibliog., illus.*
Catherine I, Empress 4:209
Europe, history of 7:290
flag 8:135 *illus.*
Leningrad (USSR) 12:283–285 *illus.*
Northern War, Great 14:256
Poltava (USSR) 15:418
Romanov (dynasty) 16:290
Russia/Union of Soviet Socialist Republics, history of 16:354–355 *illus.*
Russo-Turkish Wars 16:374
Sophia 18:66–67
Stanisław I, King of Poland 18:218
steppe art 18:256
Summer Palace at Peterhof 16:362 *illus.*
PETER I, KING OF CASTILE (Peter the Cruel) 15:200
PETER I, KING OF PORTUGAL 15:200
PETER I, KING OF SERBIA 15:201 *bibliog.*
PETER II, KING OF PORTUGAL 15:200
PETER II, KING OF YUGOSLAVIA 15:201
PETER III, EMPEROR OF RUSSIA 15:201 *bibliog.*
Catherine II, Empress of Russia 4:209–210
Pugachev, Yemelian Ivanovich 15:617
Seven Years' War 17:218
PETER III, KING OF ARAGON (Peter the Great) 15:200
Italy, history of 11:329
Sicilian Vespers 17:292
PETER IV, KING OF PORTUGAL *see* PEDRO I, EMPEROR OF BRAZIL
PETER BENT BRIGHAM HOSPITAL
transplantation, organ 19:277
PETER CHRYSOLOGUS, SAINT 15:200
PETER OF COLECHURCH
London Bridge 12:405
PETER THE CRUEL *see* PETER I, KING OF CASTILE (Peter the Cruel)
PETER DAMIAN, SAINT 15:200 *bibliog.*
PETER THE GREAT *see* PETER I, EMPEROR OF RUSSIA (Peter the Great); PETER III, KING OF ARAGON (Peter the Great)
PETER THE HERMIT 15:200
PETER LOMBARD 15:200 *bibliog.*
Duns Scotus, John 6:301
PETER MARTYR *see* VERMIGLI, PIETRO MARTIRE
PETER PAN (play) 15:200
Adams, Maude 1:97
Barrie, Sir James Matthew 3:94–95
PETER POND LAKE
map (55° 55′N 108° 44′W) 17:81
PETER THE VENERABLE
Abelard, Peter 1:55
PETERBOROUGH (England) 15:202
map (52° 35′N 0° 15′W) 19:403
PETERBOROUGH (New Hampshire)
map (42° 53′N 71° 57′W) 14:123
PETERBOROUGH (Ontario)
map (44° 18′N 78° 19′W) 14:393
PETERHOF (USSR)
Summer Palace 16:362 *illus.*
PETERHOUSE COLLEGE (Cambridge University) 4:53
PETERS, CURTIS ARNOUX *see* ARNO, PETER
PETERSBURG (Alaska)
map (56° 50′N 132° 59′W) 1:242
PETERSBURG (Illinois)
map (40° 1′N 89° 51′W) 11:42
PETERSBURG (Indiana)
map (38° 30′N 87° 17′W) 11:111
PETERSBURG (Virginia) 15:202
map (37° 13′N 77° 24′W) 19:607
PETERSBURG (West Virginia)
map (39° 0′N 79° 7′W) 20:111
PETERSBURG CAMPAIGN 15:202 *bibliog.*
Civil War, U.S. 5:30
Grant, Ulysses S. 9:288–289
PETERSON (Iowa)
map (42° 55′N 95° 21′W) 11:244
PETERSON, OSCAR 15:202
PETHACH TIKVA (Israel)
map (32° 5′N 34° 53′E) 11:302
PÉTION, ALEXANDRE SABÈS 15:202 *bibliog.*
PETIPA, MARIUS 15:202 *bibliog.*
ballet 3:43 *illus.*
Ivanov, Lev Ivanovich 11:333
Kirov Ballet 12:89–90
PETIT, ALEXIS THÉRÈSE
chemistry, history of 4:326
Dulong, Pierre Louis 6:296
PETIT, ROLAND 15:202 *bibliog.*
Verdy, Violette 19:550
PETIT BOIS ISLAND
map (30° 12′N 88° 26′W) 13:469
PETIT-GOÂVE (Haiti)
map (18° 26′N 72° 52′W) 10:15
PETIT JURY 15:202–203
jury 11:478
PETIT MAL SEIZURE
epilepsy 7:219–220 *table*
PETIT TRIANON 15:203 *bibliog.*
French art and architecture 8:306
Gabriel (family) 9:6
Robert, Hubert 16:241
PETITCODIAC (New Brunswick)
map (45° 56′N 65° 10′W) 14:117
PETITE RIVIÈRE NOIRE PEAK
map (20° 24′S 57° 24′E) 13:237
PETITION OF RIGHT (1628)
Coke, Sir Edward 5:96
Eliot, Sir John 7:139
Strafford, Thomas Wentworth, 1st Earl of 18:288
PETŐFI, SÁNDOR 15:203
PETONE (New Zealand)
map (41° 13′S 174° 52′E) 14:158
PETOSKEY (Michigan)
map (45° 22′N 84° 57′W) 13:377
PETRA (Jordan) 11:449 *illus.*; 15:203 *bibliog.*
PETRARCH 11:315 *illus.*; 15:203–204 *bibliog., illus.*
humanism 10:299
Renaissance 16:148 *illus.*
PETRASSI, GOFFREDDO
Italian music 11:319
PETREL 15:204 *bibliog., illus.*
PETRIE, SIR FLINDERS 15:204 *bibliog.*
archaeology 2:121
biblical archaeology 3:242
prehistory 15:517
PETRIFIED FOREST NATIONAL PARK 14:38–39 *map, table*; 15:204 *illus.*
PETRIFIED WOOD 15:204–205 *bibliog., illus.*
Petrified Forest National Park 15:205
process 15:204–205
PETROCHEMICALS 15:205–206 *bibliog., illus.*
chemical industry 4:317–318 *illus.*
cracking installation 15:205 *illus.*; 15:214 *illus.*
environmental health 7:210
mineral oil 13:444
organic chemistry 14:439–440
petroleum industry 15:213–214
refining process 15:206 *illus.*; 15:213–214 *illus.*
rubber 16:334
synthetic fibers 18:409
PETROGLYPH
writing systems, evolution of 20:291–292
PETROGRAD (USSR) *see* LENINGRAD (USSR)
PETROGRAM
writing systems, evolution of 20:291–292
PETROGRAPHY 15:206–207 *bibliog.*
basalt 3:101
Buddington, Arthur Francis 3:543
geology 9:105–106
igneous rock 11:33–36
Johannsen, Albert 11:423
monzonite 13:560
peridotite 15:166
petrographic microscope 15:207
optical mineralogy 14:409
petrology 15:215
Rosenbusch, Harry 16:315
PETROLATUM *see* MINERAL OIL
PETROLEUM 15:207–209 *bibliog., illus., table*
Africa 1:149 *map*
Carboniferous Period 4:137–139
catalyst
lanthanum 12:201
platinum 15:360
consumption 15:211 *table*; 15:214
fuel 8:353 *table*
Devonian Period 6:145
diatom 6:154
energy sources 7:174–175 *table*
exploration 15:208–209
fossil record 8:244 *illus.*
fuel 8:352; 15:207
acid rain 1:82
gasohol 9:55
gasoline 9:55
geochemistry 9:96
heat content 8:353 *table*
hydrocarbon 10:331
Topchiyev, Aleksandr Vasilievich 19:237
imports
graph 9:291 *illus.*
Iran 11:251
kerosene 12:59
limestone 12:345
liquefied petroleum gas 12:364
location
seismometer 17:189–190 *illus.*
Maracaibo, Lake 13:143
Middle East, history of the 13:410
naphtha 14:14
natural gas 14:47–48
oceanic mineral resources 14:340
oil and gas reserves, worldwide 15:209 *table*
oil spills 14:363–364
origin 15:207
petrochemicals 15:205–206
petroleum industry 15:209–215
pollution, environmental
salvage, marine 17:39
pools 15:208 *illus.*
migration into pools 15:207–208
production
major producing countries, worldwide 15:210–211 *map, table*
North America 14:228–229; 14:236
production and development systems 15:215
Prudhoe Bay 15:585
pyrolysis 15:637
refining 15:213–214 *illus.*
Frasch, Herman 8:286–287
reservoir rocks and traps 15:208 *illus.*
river delta 16:232–233
salt dome 17:37–38
Sea, Law of the 17:167
shale, oil 17:238
tar, pitch, and asphalt 19:34
tar sands 19:34
territorial waters 19:121
Tertiary Period 19:125
Texas 19:130–131; 19:134
Trans-Alaska Pipeline 19:266–267
well drilling
Drake, Edwin L. 6:256
PETROLEUM (county in Montana)
map (47° 5′N 108° 15′W) 13:547
PETROLEUM INDUSTRY 15:209–215 *bibliog., illus., map, table*
Alaska 1:247
Alberta 1:258
automotive industry 2:367
aviation 2:375
Bahrain 3:24–25
cracking plant 15:205 *illus.*; 15:214 *illus.*
Curaçao (Netherlands) 5:390
derrick and crane 6:122
distillation 6:200 *illus.*
Drake, Edwin L. 6:256
Ecuador 7:53
foraminifera 8:220
gasoline 9:55
Getty, J. Paul 9:160
harbor and port 10:44 *illus.*
Houston (Texas) 10:281
Hunt, H. L. 10:311
hydrochloric acid 10:332
Indonesia 11:148
inflation 11:169–170
Iraq 11:255
Jones, Samuel Milton 11:444
Kuwait (country) 12:140–142
Libya 12:321 *illus.*
liquefied petroleum gas 12:364
Louisiana 12:432–433 *illus.*
Mexico 13:360
Middle East 13:409 *map*
Middle East, history of the 13:410
Mosaddeq, Muhammad 13:593
natural gas 14:47–48
Nigeria 14:189; 14:191
Norway 14:260
ocean and sea 14:332
oil refinery 15:205 *illus.*; 15:206 *illus.*
oil spills 14:363–364
oil wells 15:212 *illus.*
Oman 14:387
Omsk (USSR) 14:388
organic chemistry 14:439–440
Organization of Petroleum Exporting Countries 14:440
petrochemicals 15:205–206
petroleum 15:207–209
pipe and pipeline 15:310–311
Ploieşti (Romania) 15:368
political history 15:214

Port Arthur (Texas) **15**:442
production **15**:210 *table*
Protozoa **15**:580
Qatar **16**:3–4
refining process **15**:206 *illus.*; **15**:213–214 *illus.*
Rockefeller (family) **16**:250
Saudi Arabia **17**:95 *illus.*
Sinclair, Harry F. **17**:319
stratigraphy **18**:292
Suez Canal **18**:324
tanker **19**:23–24
transportation **15**:210–213
Tulsa (Oklahoma) **19**:331
United Arab Emirates **19**:400
United Kingdom **19**:410
United States **19**:431–432 *illus.*
Venezuela **19**:543 *illus.*
PETROLIA (Ontario)
map (42° 52′N 82° 9′W) **14**:393; **19**:241
PETROLOGY **15**:215 *bibliog.*
amphibole **1**:381
basement rock **3**:108
batholith **3**:122
Bowen, Norman Levi **3**:428
butte **3**:592
eclogite **7**:41
geochemistry **9**:95–97
geology **9**:105–106
lava **12**:240
magma **13**:51–52
monzonite **13**:560
optical mineralogy **14**:408–409
oxide minerals **14**:476
pegmatite **15**:133
peridotite **15**:166
permeability, rock **15**:174
petrography **15**:206–207
placer deposit **15**:325
pluton **15**:373
pyroxene **15**:638
PETRONIUS ARBITER **15**:215 *bibliog.*
Satyricon **17**:93
PETROPAVLOVSK (ship)
sinking **16**:358 *illus.*
PETROPAVLOVSK (USSR)
map (54° 54′N 69° 6′E) **19**:388
PETROPAVLOVSK-KAMCHATSK (USSR)
map (53° 1′N 158° 39′E) **19**:388
PETROŞANI (Romania)
map (45° 25′N 23° 22′E) **16**:288
PETROV, YEVGENY
Union of Soviet Socialist Republics **19**:395
PETROV-VODKIN, KUZMA
Russian art and architecture **16**:364
PETROVIĆ, KARAGEORGE
Miloš, Prince of Serbia **13**:432
PETROVNA, ELIZABETH *see* ELIZABETH, EMPRESS OF RUSSIA
PETROVSKY, G. I.
Dnepropetrovsk **6**:208
PETROZAVODSK (USSR)
map (61° 47′N 34° 20′E) **19**:388
PETRUSHKA (ballet) **16**:369 *illus.*
PETT **15**:215–216
PETTIS (county in Missouri)
map (38° 45′N 93° 15′W) **13**:476
PETTIT, BOB **15**:216
PETTIT SMITH, FRANCIS
ship **17**:273
PETTORUTI, EMILIO
Latin American art and architecture **12**:228
PETTY, RICHARD **15**:216
PETTY, SIR WILLIAM **15**:216 *bibliog.*
PETTY-FITZMAURICE, HENRY CHARLES KEITH, 5TH MARQUESS OF LANSDOWNE *see* LANSDOWNE, HENRY CHARLES KEITH PETTY-FITZMAURICE, 5TH MARQUESS OF
PETUNIA **15**:216 *illus.*
PÉTURSSON, HALLGRÍMUR
Icelandic literature **11**:19
PETZITE
telluride minerals **19**:91
PEUGEOT
automotive industry **2**:366–367
PEUL *see* FULANI
PEURBACH, GEORG VON **15**:216
mathematics, history of **13**:224
PEVSNER, ANTOINE **15**:216 *bibliog.*
Oval Fresco **5**:224 *illus.*
PEVSNER, NAOM *see* GABO, NAUM
PEVSNER, SIR NIKOLAUS **15**:216 *bibliog.*
PEWEE **15**:216–217 *illus.*
flycatcher (bird) **8**:191
PEWEE VALLEY (Kentucky)
map (38° 19′N 85° 29′W) **12**:47
PEWTER **15**:217 *bibliog.*, *illus.*
Danforth, Thomas **6**:31
PEYOTE **15**:217 *bibliog.*
cacti and other succulents **4**:10–11
hallucinogens **10**:24
Native American Church **14**:47
Navajo **14**:53
PFEIFFER, NORMAN
Hardy Holzman Pfeiffer Associates **10**:48
PFITZNER, HANS **15**:217 *bibliog.*
PFORR, FRANZ
Nazarenes (art group) **14**:66
PFORZHEIM (Germany, East and West)
map (48° 54′N 8° 42′E) **9**:140
PH **15**:217–218 *bibliog.*, *table*
buffer **3**:547
Haber, Fritz **10**:4
indicator (chemistry) **11**:144
pH meter **15**:218
Sørensen, Søren Peter Lauritz **18**:68
water quality **20**:50
PHAEDRA
Hippolytus **10**:174
PHAEOPHYTA *see* ALGAE, BROWN ALGAE
PHAETHON **15**:218
PHAETON
coach and carriage **5**:74–75 *illus.*
PHAGOCYTOSIS
blood **3**:336
granulocyte cells
inflammation **11**:169
immunodeficiency disease **11**:59
lymphatic system **12**:475
lysosome **12**:480
Metchnikoff, Elie **13**:335
phagocytic cells
infectious diseases **11**:165–166
lungs **12**:464 *illus.*
PHAISTOS (Greece) **15**:218 *bibliog.*
architecture **2**:131
PHALANGER **15**:218 *illus.*
koala **12**:103
PHALARIS **15**:218
PHALAROPE **15**:218–219 *illus.*
shorebirds **17**:283
PHALLIC WORSHIP **15**:219 *bibliog.*
Ellora **7**:148
shiva
Elephanta **7**:134
PHALLOPLASTY
sex change **17**:224
PHAM VAN DONG **10**:190 *illus.*; **15**:219
PHAN RANG (Vietnam) **19**:582 *illus.*
map (11° 34′N 108° 59′E) **19**:580
PHAN THIET (Vietnam)
map (10° 56′N 108° 6′E) **19**:580
PHANARIOTS **15**:219
PHANEROGAM *see* SPERMATOPHYTE
PHANEROZOIC EON *see* PRECAMBRIAN TIME
PHANTOM OF THE OPERA, THE (film)
Chaney, Lon **4**:280 *illus.*
PHARAOH **15**:219 *bibliog.*
Egypt, ancient **7**:82; **7**:84–85
PHARAOH HOUND **15**:219 *bibliog.*
PHARISEES **15**:219 *bibliog.*
Hillel **10**:164
Judaism **11**:460
PHARMACEUTICAL *see* DRUG
PHARMACEUTICAL INDUSTRY **15**:219–220 *bibliog.*
animal experimentation **2**:22
drug **6**:279
genetic engineering **9**:85
manufacture **15**:220
marketing **15**:220
patent medicine **15**:110
pharmacy **15**:221–222
regulation **15**:220
Food and Drug Administration **8**:208
research **15**:220
toxicology **19**:256
PHARMACIST
apothecary **2**:85
pharmaceutical industry **15**:220
pharmacy **15**:221–222
PHARMACOKINETICS
pharmacy **15**:221
PHARMACOLOGY **15**:220 *bibliog.*
See also DRUG; names of specific drugs, e.g., PENICILLIN; VALIUM; etc.; names of specific groups of drugs, e.g., ANTIBIOTICS; PSYCHOTROPIC DRUGS; etc.
Abel, John J. **1**:55
Bernard, Claude **3**:220
Bovet, Daniele **3**:426
Chinese medicine **4**:391
mercury **13**:306
neuropharmacology **14**:105
pharmacopoeia **15**:220–221
pharmacy **15**:221–222
stimulant **18**:271
toxicology **19**:256
PHARMACOPOEIA **15**:220–221 *bibliog.*
patent medicine **15**:110
PHARMACY **15**:221–222 *bibliog.*
apothecary **2**:85
drug **6**:274–279
history **15**:221
professional and educational organizations **15**:221
American College of Apothecaries **2**:85
Pharmaceutical Society of Great Britain **2**:85
PHAROS OF ALEXANDRIA
lighthouse **12**:336
Seven Wonders of the World **17**:218 *illus.*
PHARR (Texas)
map (26° 12′N 98° 11′W) **19**:129
PHARYNGEAL TONSILS *see* ADENOIDS
PHARYNGITIS **15**:222
PHASE EQUILIBRIUM **15**:222–224 *bibliog.*, *illus.*
eutectic point **7**:310
interference **11**:207–208 *illus.*
liquid **12**:364–365
liquid crystal **12**:365
physical chemistry **15**:279
thermodynamics **19**:164
triple point **19**:302
PHEASANT **3**:280–281 *illus.*; **15**:224–225 *bibliog.*, *illus.*
game birds **9**:27
partridge **15**:100
peacock **15**:124
quail **16**:5
PHEBA (Mississippi)
map (33° 35′N 88° 57′W) **13**:469
PHÈDRE (play)
Racine, Jean **16**:37
PHELPS (county in Missouri)
map (37° 55′N 91° 50′W) **13**:476
PHELPS (county in Nebraska)
map (40° 30′N 99° 25′W) **14**:70
PHELPS (Wisconsin)
map (46° 4′N 89° 5′W) **20**:185
PHENACETIN **15**:225
analgesic **1**:388
PHENAZOCINE **15**:225
PHENCYCLIDINE HYDROCHLORIDE *see* ANGEL DUST
PHENERGAN *see* ANTIHISTAMINE
PHENIX CITY (Alabama)
map (32° 29′N 85° 1′W) **1**:234
PHENOBARBITAL **15**:225
sedative **17**:182
PHENOCRYST **15**:225
porphyry **15**:442
PHENOL **15**:225 *bibliog.*
antiseptic **2**:68
benzene **3**:206
caustic chemicals **4**:219
hydroxyl group **10**:344
Lister, Joseph **12**:366
uses **15**:225
PHENOMENOLOGICAL THERAPY
psychotherapy **15**:603
PHENOMENOLOGY **15**:225 *bibliog.*
Brentano, Franz **3**:473
ego **7**:74
Heidegger, Martin **10**:106–107
Husserl, Edmund **10**:321; **15**:225
Merleau-Ponty, Maurice **13**:310–311
metaphysics **13**:335
philosophy **15**:245–246
Ricoeur, Paul **16**:216
Scheler, Max **17**:118–119
PHENOMENON **15**:225–226
Kant, Immanuel **12**:24
noumenon **14**:268
parapsychology **15**:80–82
perception **15**:158–159
phenomenology **15**:225
PHENOTHIAZINE
schizophrenia **17**:124
PHENOTYPE
behavioral genetics **3**:170
genetics **9**:87–90
PHENYL GROUP **15**:226
benzene **3**:206
polyphenylene oxide
molecular structure **15**:350 *illus.*
PHENYLKETONURIA **15**:226
behavioral genetics **3**:170
enzyme **7**:214
genetic diseases **9**:83
mental retardation **13**:302
PHEROMONE **15**:226 *bibliog.*, *illus.*
animal behavior **2**:14–15
animal communication **2**:18–19
animal courtship and mating **2**:20
ant **2**:18 *illus.*
aphid **2**:77
bee **3**:158–159
PHETCHABUN RANGE
map (16° 20′N 100° 55′E) **19**:139
PHI BETA KAPPA **15**:226
American Scholar (periodical) **1**:366
PHIBUL SONGGRAM
Thailand **19**:141
PHIDIAS **15**:226–227 *bibliog.*
Elgin Marbles **7**:137
Greek art **9**:341
Statue of Zeus at Olympia **17**:217
PHIL CAMPBELL (Alabama)
map (34° 21′N 87° 42′W) **1**:234
PHILADELPHIA (Mississippi)
map (32° 46′N 89° 7′W) **13**:469
PHILADELPHIA (New York)
map (44° 9′N 75° 43′W) **14**:149
PHILADELPHIA (Pennsylvania) **15**:148 *illus.*; **15**:227–229 *bibliog.*, *illus.*, *map*
architecture
City Hall **15**:227 *illus.*
Independence Hall **11**:78; **15**:146 *illus.*
Second Bank of the United States **9**:346 *illus.*
art
Pennsylvania Academy of the Fine Arts **15**:152
Philadelphia Museum of Art **15**:229
Chestnut Street Theatre **4**:337
education
Pennsylvania, University of **15**:152
geographical linguistics **9**:98–99 *maps*
history **15**:227; **15**:229
British capture, 1777 **1**:360
Franklin, Benjamin **8**:283
Liberty Bell **12**:314
housing **10**:278 *illus.*
map (39° 57′N 75° 7′W) **15**:147
Philadelphia Orchestra, The **15**:229
Philadelphia Zoological Garden **15**:229
Society Hill **5**:7 *illus.*
Walnut Street Theatre **20**:18
PHILADELPHIA (county in Pennsylvania)
map (40° 0′N 75° 10′W) **15**:147
PHILADELPHIA EAGLES (football team) **8**:217 *illus.*
PHILADELPHIA MUSEUM OF ART **15**:229 *bibliog.*
Philadelphia (Pennsylvania) **15**:228 *map*
PHILADELPHIA ORCHESTRA, THE **15**:229 *bibliog.*
Muti, Riccardo **13**:687
Ormandy, Eugene **14**:447
Stokowski, Leopold **18**:278
PHILADELPHIA ZOOLOGICAL GARDEN **15**:229
Philadelphia (Pennsylvania) **15**:228 *map*
PHILAE (Egypt) **15**:229
PHILANTHROPY *see* FOUNDATIONS AND ENDOWMENTS; FUND RAISING
PHILATELY **15**:229–231 *bibliog.*, *illus.*
PHILBY, H. ST. JOHN **15**:231 *bibliog.*
PHILBY, HAROLD ADRIAN RUSSELL
intelligence gathering **11**:205
Philby, H. St. John **15**:231
PHILCO CORPORATION
Ford (family) **8**:221
PHILEMON **15**:231
PHILEMON, EPISTLE TO **15**:231
PHILHARMONIC SOCIETY OF NEW YORK *see* NEW YORK PHILHARMONIC
PHILIDOR (family) **15**:231 *bibliog.*
PHILIDOR, FRANÇOIS
chess **4**:334–336
Philidor (family) **15**:231
PHILIP (South Dakota)
map (44° 2′N 101° 40′W) **18**:103
PHILIP, DUKE OF ANJOU *see* PHILIP V, KING OF SPAIN
PHILIP, KING (Indian chief) *see* KING PHILIP'S WAR; METACOMET (Indian chief)
PHILIP, PRINCE *see* EDINBURGH, PHILIP MOUNTBATTEN, DUKE OF
PHILIP, SAINT **15**:231
PHILIP I, KING OF CASTILE (Philip the Handsome) **15**:234
Habsburg (dynasty) **10**:6 *illus.*
PHILIP I, KING OF FRANCE **15**:232 *bibliog.*, *illus.*

PHILIP I, KING OF PORTUGAL *see* PHILIP II, KING OF SPAIN
PHILIP II, KING OF FRANCE (Philip Augustus) **15**:232 *bibliog., illus.*
  Mont-Saint-Michel **13**:544
  Richard I, King of England **16**:209–210
PHILIP II, KING OF MACEDONIA **15**:233 *bibliog., illus.*
  coin **7**:305 *illus.*
  Greece, ancient **9**:332
  Macedonia, Kingdom of **13**:15
  Olympias **14**:382
  Pella **15**:138
  Plovdiv (Bulgaria) **15**:369
PHILIP II, KING OF SPAIN **15**:234 *bibliog., illus.*
  Europe, history of **7**:287
  Low Countries, history of the **12**:439
  Mary I, Queen of England **13**:185–186
  Portugal, history of **15**:453–454
  Spain, history of **18**:146–147 *illus.*
  Spanish Armada **18**:150–151
  Titian **19**:212
  Vesalius, Andreas **19**:564
  William I, Prince of Orange (William the Silent) **20**:158
PHILIP III, KING OF FRANCE (Philip the Bold) **15**:232 *bibliog.*
PHILIP III, KING OF SPAIN **15**:234–235 *bibliog.*
  Spain, history of **18**:147
PHILIP IV, KING OF FRANCE (Philip the Fair) **15**:232–233 *bibliog., illus.*
  Boniface VIII, Pope **3**:379
  Duns Scotus, John **6**:301
  sumptuary laws **18**:340
  Templars **19**:93 *illus.*
PHILIP IV, KING OF SPAIN **15**:235 *bibliog., illus.*
  Spain, history of **18**:147
PHILIP V, KING OF FRANCE (Philip the Tall) **15**:233 *bibliog.*
PHILIP V, KING OF MACEDONIA **15**:234 *bibliog.*
  Rome, ancient **16**:300
PHILIP V, KING OF SPAIN **15**:235 *bibliog., illus.*
  Farnese, Elizabeth **8**:28
  Salic law **17**:32
  Spain, history of **18**:147
  Spanish Succession, War of the **18**:162–163
PHILIP VI, KING OF FRANCE **8**:63 *illus.*; **15**:233 *bibliog.*
PHILIP AUGUSTUS *see* PHILIP II, KING OF FRANCE (Philip Augustus)
PHILIP THE BOLD, DUKE OF BURGUNDY **15**:231 *bibliog.*
PHILIP THE BOLD, KING OF FRANCE *see* PHILIP III, KING OF FRANCE (Philip the Bold)
PHILIP THE EVANGELIST **15**:231
PHILIP THE FAIR *see* PHILIP IV, KING OF FRANCE (Philip the Fair)
PHILIP THE GOOD, DUKE OF BURGUNDY **15**:231 *bibliog.*
  Jacqueline of Hainaut **11**:347
PHILIP THE HANDSOME *see* PHILIP I, KING OF CASTILE (Philip the Handsome)
PHILIP OF HESSE **15**:232
PHILIP OF POKANOKET *see* METACOMET (Indian chief)
PHILIP OF SWABIA **15**:232 *bibliog.*
PHILIP THE TALL *see* PHILIP V, KING OF FRANCE (Philip the Tall)
PHILIPON, CHARLES **15**:235 *bibliog.*
  Louis Philippe, King of France (caricature) **4**:150 *illus.*
PHILIPP (Mississippi)
  map (33° 45′N 90° 12′W) **13**:469
PHILIPPE ÉGALITÉ *see* ORLÉANS, LOUIS PHILIPPE JOSEPH, DUC D' (Philippe Égalité)
PHILIPPI (Macedonia) **15**:235
PHILIPPI (West Virginia)
  map (39° 9′N 80° 2′W) **20**:111
PHILIPPIANS, EPISTLE TO THE **15**:235–236 *bibliog.*
PHILIPPICS
  Demosthenes **6**:105
PHILIPPINE CREEPER (bird) **15**:236
PHILIPPINE INDEPENDENT CHURCH
  Aglipay, Gregorio **1**:186
PHILIPPINE MAHOGANY *see* RED LAUAN
PHILIPPINE MEDUSA *see* CHENILLE PLANT
PHILIPPINE PLATE
  plate tectonics **15**:351 *map*
PHILIPPINE SEA
  map (20° 0′N 135° 0′E) **2**:232
  map (20° 0′N 135° 0′E) **14**:334
  World War II **20**:277 *map*
PHILIPPINE TRENCH
  Hess, H. H. **10**:151
  Pacific Ocean bottom **15**:6–7 *map*
PHILIPPINES **15**:236–239 *bibliog., illus., map, table*
  agriculture, forestry, and fishing **15**:238
  cities
    Baguio **3**:23
    Cebu **4**:228
    Davao **6**:46
    Iloilo **11**:50
    Manila **13**:117–118 *illus.*
    Quezon City **16**:25
    Zamboanga **20**:354
  climate **15**:236–237 *table*
  economic activity **15**:238
  education **15**:238
    Southeast Asian universities **18**:111–112 *table*
  flag **15**:236 *illus.*
  government **15**:238
  green revolution **9**:348
  health **15**:238
  history **15**:238
    Aguinaldo, Emilio **1**:199–200
    Aquino, Corazon C. **2**:95
    Funston, Frederick **8**:369
    MacArthur, Douglas **13**:5
    McKinley, William **13**:31
    Magsaysay, Ramón **13**:62
    Marcos, Ferdinand E. **13**:147
    Pershing, John J. **15**:180–181
    Quezon, Manuel Luis **16**:25
    Quirino, Elpidio **16**:28
    Roxas y Acuna, Manuel **16**:328
    Spanish-American War **18**:150
    Taft, William Howard **19**:8
    Wood, Leonard **20**:207
    World War II **20**:260–261 *illus., map*; **20**:277–278 *illus., map*
  land and resources **15**:236–237 *map, table*
    subduction zone **18**:312
  languages **15**:237
    Malayo-Polynesian languages **13**:83
  Manila Bay **13**:118
  map (13° 0′N 122° 0′E) **2**:232
  people **15**:237–238
    Bisayan **3**:297
    Igorot **11**:38
    Tasaday **19**:41
  primitive societies **2**:51 *illus.*
  regions
    Bataan **3**:121
    Cebu (island) **4**:228
    Corregidor **5**:276
    Luzon **12**:473
    Mindanao **13**:437
    Sulu Archipelago **18**:338
  religion **15**:237
  Southeast Asian art and architecture **18**:107
PHILIPS, THOMAS
  Lord Byron **3**:603 *illus.*
PHILIPSBURG (Montana)
  map (46° 20′N 113° 18′W) **13**:547
PHILIPSBURG (Pennsylvania)
  map (40° 53′N 78° 5′W) **15**:147
PHILISTINES **15**:239 *bibliog.*
  Goliath **9**:240
  Sea Peoples **17**:170
PHILLIP, ARTHUR **15**:239 *bibliog.*
  Australia, history of **2**:339 *illus.*
  Australia Day **2**:342
PHILLIPS (county in Arkansas)
  map (34° 25′N 90° 55′W) **2**:166
PHILLIPS (county in Colorado)
  map (40° 40′N 102° 20′W) **5**:116
PHILLIPS (county in Kansas)
  map (39° 50′N 99° 20′W) **12**:18
PHILLIPS (Maine)
  map (44° 49′N 70° 21′W) **13**:70
PHILLIPS (county in Montana)
  map (48° 15′N 107° 50′W) **13**:547
PHILLIPS (Wisconsin)
  map (45° 41′N 90° 24′W) **20**:185
PHILLIPS, DAVID GRAHAM **15**:239 *bibliog.*
PHILLIPS, JOHN **15**:239
PHILLIPS, MARK **10**:250 *illus.*
PHILLIPS, WENDELL **15**:239 *bibliog., illus.*
PHILLIPS CURVE (economics)
  inflation **11**:170
PHILLIPSBURG (Kansas)
  map (39° 45′N 99° 19′W) **12**:18
PHILLIPSBURG (New Jersey)
  map (40° 42′N 75° 12′W) **14**:129
PHILMONT (New York)
  map (42° 15′N 73° 39′W) **14**:149
PHILO (Ohio)
  map (39° 52′N 81° 55′W) **14**:357
PHILO OF ALEXANDRIA **15**:239–240 *bibliog.*
PHILO OF BYZANTIUM (fl. c.250 BC) **15**:240
PHILO OF BYZANTIUM (fl. 146BC)
  Seven Wonders of the World **17**:216
PHILO JUDAEUS *see* PHILO OF ALEXANDRIA
PHILOCTETES **15**:240
PHILODENDRON **10**:275 *illus.*; **15**:240 *illus.*
  monstera **13**:544
PHILOLAUS **15**:240 *bibliog.*
PHILOLOGY *see* HISTORICAL LINGUISTICS
PHILOMATH (Oregon)
  map (44° 32′N 123° 22′W) **14**:427
PHILOMELA AND PROCNE **15**:240
PHILOSOPHES (intellectual group) **15**:240 *bibliog.*
PHILOSOPHIAE NATURALIS PRINCIPIA MATHEMATICA (book) *see PRINCIPIA* (book)
PHILOSOPHY **15**:240–248 *bibliog., illus.*
  See also GREEK PHILOSOPHY; ROMAN PHILOSOPHY; SCIENCE, PHILOSOPHY OF; names of specific philosophers, e.g., ARISTOTLE; HEGEL, GEORG WILHELM FRIEDRICH; etc.
  absolute **1**:62
  aesthetics **1**:130–131
  analytic and linguistic philosophy **1**:389–390
  animal rights **2**:28
  aretê **2**:146
  asceticism **2**:228
  associationism **2**:265–266
  atheism **2**:288–289
  atomism **2**:312
  behaviorism **3**:170
  Buddhism **3**:539–540; **15**:246–247
  Cambridge Platonists **4**:52
  categorical imperative **4**:202
  causality **4**:219
  Chinese literature **4**:389
  Chinese philosophy **15**:247
  Confucianism **5**:179–180; **15**:247
  Cynics **5**:406–407
  Cyrenaics **5**:409
  deism **6**:86
  determinism **6**:134
  dialectic **6**:150
  dialectical materialism **6**:150
  Discourse on Method **6**:189
  dualism **6**:287
  Eastern philosophy **15**:246–247
  eclecticism **7**:40
  educational philosophy **7**:62–64
  ego **7**:73–74
  egoism **7**:74
  Eleatic School **7**:103
  emanationism **7**:150–151
  empiricism **7**:159; **15**:245
  Enlightenment **7**:206–207
  Epicureanism **7**:218
  epistemology **7**:221–222; **15**:243
  ethics **7**:250–252
  existentialism **7**:332
  God **9**:218–219
  hedonism **10**:105
  Hellenistic Age **10**:114
  Hinduism **10**:169–170; **15**:246
  history of Western philosophy **15**:243–246
  humanism **10**:299
  idealism **11**:30
  Indian philosophy **15**:246–247
  innate ideas **11**:179
  intuition **11**:232
  Islamic philosophy **15**:244
  Jainism **11**:349–350
  logic **12**:395–396
  logical positivism **12**:397; **15**:245
  logos **12**:397
  materialism **13**:218–219
  mathematics **15**:242
    mathematics, history of **13**:226–227
  metaphysics **13**:334–335; **15**:243
  methods **15**:242
  methods of inquiry **15**:241–242
  Milesian school **13**:419
  monism **13**:531
  moral awareness **13**:572–573
  natural law **14**:48
  naturalism **14**:50
  Neoplatonism **14**:85
  New Thought **14**:142–143
  nihilism **14**:194
  nominalism **14**:215
  noumenon **14**:268
  occasionalism **14**:320
  pacifism and nonviolent movements **15**:8–10
  pantheism **15**:61
  Peripatetics **15**:170–171
  personalism **15**:188–189
  phenomenology **15**:225; **15**:245–246
  philosophical questions **15**:241–242
  pluralism **15**:372
  political ideology **11**:30–31
  political representation **16**:161
  political science **15**:403
  positivism **15**:458
  pragmatism **15**:245; **15**:487–488
  pre-Socratic philosophy **15**:243; **15**:532–533
  probability **15**:558
  process philosophy **15**:561
  Pythagoreans **15**:640
  rationalism **15**:244–245; **16**:92–93
  realism **16**:103–104
  relation to other disciplines **15**:242–243
  Renaissance **16**:149
  Rosicrucians **16**:317
  scholasticism **17**:131–132
  semantics (linguistics) **17**:193
  sensationalism **17**:204
  skepticism **17**:337
  socialism **18**:19–24
  solipsism **18**:55
  Sophists **18**:67
  soul **18**:70
  state (in political philosophy) **18**:228–233
  Stoicism **18**:278
  substance **18**:317
  Taoism **15**:247; **19**:28–29
  teleology **19**:78
  theism **19**:155
  theology **19**:157–158
  theosophy **19**:159–160
  transcendentalism **19**:268
  uncertainty principle **19**:381
  universals **19**:467
  utilitarianism **19**:497
  utopias **19**:497–498
  war **20**:24
  will (philosophy) **20**:153–154
  yoga **20**:328–329
PHILOSOPHY OF SCIENCE *see* SCIENCE, PHILOSOPHY OF
PHILPOTT LAKE
  map (36° 50′N 80° 3′W) **19**:607
PHIPS, SIR WILLIAM **15**:248 *bibliog.*
  French and Indians Wars **8**:312
  Salem Witch Trials **17**:31
PHITSANULOK (Thailand)
  map (16° 50′N 100° 15′E) **19**:139
PHLEBITIS **15**:248 *bibliog.*
  thrombophlebitis **15**:248
PHLOEM
  plant **15**:335–337 *illus.*; **15**:339 *illus.*
  tree **19**:286–287 *illus.*
  wood **20**:205
PHLOGISTON THEORY **15**:248 *bibliog.*
  chemistry, history of **4**:325
  Stahl, Georg Ernst **18**:211
PHLOGOPITE *see* MICA
PHLOX **14**:248 *illus.*
  Jacob's ladder **11**:346
PHNOM PENH (Kampuchea) **12**:12 *illus.*; **15**:248
  climate **12**:11 *table*
  history
    Khmer Rouge **12**:67
  map (11° 33′N 104° 55′E) **12**:11
PHO LANGUAGE
  Sino-Tibetan languages **17**:324
PHOBIA **15**:248–249 *bibliog.*
  anxiety **2**:72
  claustrophobia **5**:45
  fear **8**:39
  hypnosis **10**:350
  learning theory **12**:260
  neurosis **14**:107
  Skinner, B. F. **17**:344
  zoophobia **20**:378
PHOBOS **15**:249 *bibliog.*; **18**:50 *illus.*
  Viking Orbiter photograph **13**:168 *illus.*
PHOCION **15**:249
PHOCIS **15**:249
PHOEBE (astronomy)
  Pickering, William Henry **15**:293
  Saturn (astronomy) **17**:90–91

PHOEBE (bird) **15**:249 *illus.*
flycatcher (bird) **8**:190–191
PHOENICIA **15**:249–250 *bibliog., illus., map*
cities
Byblos **3**:601–602
Carthage **4**:173–174
Sidon **17**:295
Tyre **19**:367
Lebanon **12**:266
Middle East, history of the **13**:401
naval vessels **14**:54 *illus.*
printing **15**:551
ship **17**:263
PHOENICIAN ALPHABET **20**:294 *table*
PHOENICIAN ART **15**:250–251 *bibliog., illus.*
Spanish art and architecture **18**:151
PHOENIX (Arizona) **2**:162 *illus.*; **15**:251 *illus.*
map (33° 27′N 112° 5′W) **2**:160
PHOENIX (mythology) **15**:251
PHOENIX (New York)
map (43° 14′N 76° 18′W) **14**:149
PHOENIX (steamboat)
Stevens (family) **18**:263
PHOENIX ISLANDS **15**:251
map (4° 0′S 172° 0′W) **14**:334
PHOENIXVILLE (Pennsylvania)
map (40° 8′N 75° 31′W) **15**:147
PHOLIDOTA
mammal **13**:103–104 *illus.*
PHONETICS **15**:251–253 *bibliog.*
acoustic phonetics **15**:252
English language **7**:191–193
linguistics **12**:357
organs of speech **15**:251–252
phonology **15**:255
pronunciation
accent **1**:76
dictionary **6**:159
lexicology and lexicography **12**:308
sounds **15**:252
speech **18**:173–174
writing systems, evolution of **20**:292
hieroglyphics **10**:160
spelling, pronunciation, and change **20**:294–295
PHONGSALI (Laos)
map (21° 41′N 102° 6′E) **12**:203
PHONOGRAM
hieroglyphics **10**:160
PHONOGRAPH **15**:253–254 *bibliog., illus.*
Edison, Thomas Alva, inventor **7**:57–58
Goldmark, Peter Carl, inventor **9**:235
history **15**:253–254
jukebox **11**:465
records **15**:253–254
high fidelity **10**:161
production **18**:76–77 *illus.*
stereophonic sound **18**:259 *illus.*
sound recording and reproduction **18**:74–77
PHONOLOGY AND MORPHOLOGY **15**:254–255 *bibliog.*
Bloomfield, Leonard **3**:340
English language **7**:191–193
Esperanto **7**:243
Focillon, Henry **8**:192
Indian languages, American **11**:99
linguistics **12**:358
pidgin **15**:294
psycholinguistics **15**:592
syntax **18**:408
PHONON **15**:255 *bibliog.*
PHORONID **15**:255 *bibliog.*
lophophorate **12**:413
PHOSGENE
carbon **4**:135
chemical and biological warfare **4**:311
poison gas **15**:382
PHOSPHATE MINERALS **15**:255–256 *bibliog., table*
apatite **2**:74
biosphere **3**:277
chemical formula, crystal systems **15**:256 *table*
isomorph **11**:300
marine phosphorites **15**:255–256
mineral list **13**:443
monazite **13**:522
Nauru **14**:51
nutrient cycles **14**:303 *illus.*
occurrence **15**:255–256
phosphorite **15**:256
phosphorus **15**:256–257
pyromorphite **15**:638
sedimentary rock **17**:185
turquoise **19**:352
uranium minerals **19**:478
uses **15**:256
wavellite **20**:71
weathering **20**:83
PHOSPHATES *see* PHOSPHORUS
PHOSPHOGLYCERIDE
lipid **12**:361 *illus.*
PHOSPHOR **15**:256
electroluminescence **7**:114
promethium **15**:567
PHOSPHORESCENCE **15**:256
See also FLUORESCENCE
phosphor **15**:256
photochemistry **15**:258
PHOSPHORITE **15**:256
oceanic mineral resources **14**:340
oceanography **14**:346
phosphate minerals **15**:255–256
PHOSPHORUS **15**:256–257 *bibliog.*
abundances of common elements **7**:131 *table*
biology **15**:256
element **7**:130 *table*
forms **15**:256
Group VA periodic table **15**:167
match **13**:218
nutrient cycles **14**:303–304 *illus.*
oceanic nutrients **14**:341
phosphate minerals **15**:255–256
phosphates **15**:256
plankton **15**:332
soap and detergent **18**:8
spontaneous combustion **18**:194
superphosphate **18**:352–353
toxicity **15**:256
uranium minerals **19**:478
vitamins and minerals **19**:620
Recommended Daily Allowances **19**:619 *table*
PHOSPHORYLATION
photosynthesis **15**:277
PHOSPHOSPHINGOLIPID **12**:361 *illus.*
PHOTIC ZONE **15**:257
ocean and sea **14**:331
PHOTIUS **15**:257 *bibliog.*
Schism, Great **17**:122
PHOTO-SECESSION **15**:257 *bibliog., illus.*
Coburn, Alvin Langdon **5**:84
Emerson, Peter Henry **7**:154
Käsebier, Gertrude **12**:29
Steichen, Edward **18**:246
Stieglitz, Alfred **18**:267
PHOTOCHEMISTRY **15**:257–259 *bibliog., illus.*
atmospheric photochemistry **15**:259
infrared photochemistry **15**:259
laws **15**:257
photobiological processes **15**:259
photocycloaddition **15**:258–259
photodissociation **15**:258
photoisomerization **15**:258
photophysical processes **15**:258
physical chemistry **15**:279
pollution, environmental **15**:414
semiconductor **17**:196
silver **17**:313
Talbot, William Henry **19**:15
PHOTOCONDUCTIVE EFFECT *see* PHOTOELECTRIC CELL; PHOTOELECTRIC EFFECT
PHOTOCOPY *see* COPYING MACHINE; ELECTROSTATIC PRINTING
PHOTOELECTRIC CELL **15**:259–260 *bibliog.*
photoconductive cell **15**:259
photoemissive cell **15**:259
photography **15**:263
photovoltaic cell **15**:259–260
smoke detector **17**:373
solar cell **18**:40
sound recording and reproduction **18**:75
PHOTOELECTRIC EFFECT **15**:260 *bibliog.*
cathode ray **4**:211
Einstein, Albert **7**:93
electron tube **7**:124
gamma rays **9**:34
Millikan, Robert **13**:430
optics **14**:412
photoconductive effect **15**:260
photoelectric cell **15**:259–260
photoemissive effect **15**:260
photomultiplier **15**:274
photovoltaic effect **15**:260
quantum mechanics **16**:9–10 *illus.*
selenium **17**:190
PHOTOEMISSIVE EFFECT *see* PHOTOELECTRIC CELL; PHOTOELECTRIC EFFECT
PHOTOENGRAVING **15**:260 *bibliog.*
book illustration **3**:388 *illus.*
intaglio (printing) **11**:199
platemaking **15**:357
PHOTOGRAM
Kepes, Gyorgy **12**:57
Moholy-Nagy, László **13**:503
photography, history and art of **15**:271
Ray, Man **16**:96
PHOTOGRAMMETRY *see* AERIAL PHOTOGRAPHY
PHOTOGRAPHIC ZENITH TUBE **15**:260
PHOTOGRAPHY **15**:261–265 *bibliog., illus.*
See also CAMERA; FILM, PHOTOGRAPHIC; PHOTOGRAPHY, HISTORY AND ART OF
actinometer **1**:88–89
astrophotography **2**:285
Nimbus **14**:198
OSO **14**:456
Ranger (space probe) **16**:84
Schmidt telescope **17**:128
black-and-white **15**:262
cinematography **4**:432–434
color **15**:264–265
depth of field **6**:120
digital technology **6**:175
charge-coupled device **4**:288
film processing **15**:262; **15**:264–265
enlarger **7**:206
hydroquinone **10**:344
instant camera **4**:59
flash photography **8**:153
gelatin **9**:69
holography **10**:207
image processing **11**:51–53
infrared radiation **11**:175
Kirlian photography **12**:89
microfilm **13**:385
photoengraving **15**:260
halftone **10**:20
photography, scientific **15**:271–272
phototypesetting **15**:277–278
remote sensing **16**:147
sounding rocket **18**:77
stroboscope **18**:301
X rays **20**:311
radiography **16**:63
PHOTOGRAPHY, HISTORY AND ART OF **15**:265–271 *bibliog., illus.*
See also FASHION PHOTOGRAPHY; PHOTOJOURNALISM; PHOTOMONTAGE; PHOTOREALISM
book **3**:385
carte de visite **4**:171
England
Archer, Frederick Scott **2**:127
Beaton, Sir Cecil **3**:145
Brandt, Bill **3**:454
Cameron, Julia Margaret **4**:59–60
Emerson, Peter Henry **7**:154
Evans, Frederick Henry **7**:312
Fenton, Roger **8**:51
Frith, Francis **8**:334–335
Herschel, Sir John **10**:147
Hurter, Ferdinand, and Driffield, Vero C. **10**:319
Linked Ring Brotherhood **12**:358
Maddox, Richard Leach **13**:39–40
Robinson, Henry Peach **16**:244
Swan, Sir Joseph Wilson **18**:379
Talbot, William Henry **19**:15
Wedgewood, Thomas **20**:90
France
Atget, Eugène **2**:288
Bayard, Hippolyte **3**:132
Bisson, Louis and Auguste **3**:299–300
Blanquart-Evrard, Louis Désirée **3**:327
Brassaï **3**:457
Carjat, Étienne **4**:151
Daguerre, Louis J. M. **6**:6
Disdéri, André Adolphe Eugène **6**:190
Du Camp, Maxime **6**:286
Lippmann, Gabriel **12**:363
Nadar **14**:4
Nègre, Charles **14**:78
Niepce, Joseph Nicéphore **14**:185
Germany
Jacobi, Lotte **11**:345
Salomon, Erich **17**:36
Steinert, Otto **18**:249
Vogel, Hermann Wilhelm **19**:625
museums
George Eastman House **9**:109–110
photographic science and technology, history of
albumen print **1**:261
ambrotype **1**:325
Archer, Frederick Scott **2**:127
Bayard, Hippolyte **3**:132
Blanquart-Evrard, Louis Désirée **3**:327
calotype **4**:47
camera development **4**:55
camera obscura **4**:59
Daguerre, Louis J. M. **6**:6
daguerreotype **6**:6–7
Draper, John William **6**:263
Eastman, George **7**:34
ferrotype **8**:59
Herschel, Sir John **10**:147
Hurter, Ferdinand, and Driffield, Vero C. **10**:319
Land, Edwin **12**:178
Lippmann, Gabriel **12**:363
Maddox, Richard Leach **13**:39–40
Mees, Charles Edward Kenneth **13**:278
Niepce, Joseph Nicéphore **14**:185
Swan, Sir Joseph Wilson **18**:379
Talbot, William Henry **19**:15
Vogel, Hermann Wilhelm **19**:625
Wedgwood, Thomas **20**:90
woodbury type process **20**:210
portraits *see* PORTRAITURE—photography
Scotland
Thomson, John **19**:176
stereoscope **18**:259–260 *illus.*
United States **15**:272
Abbott, Berenice **1**:53
Adams, Ansel **1**:93
Arbus, Diane **2**:111
Avedon, Richard **2**:369
Brady, Mathew B. **3**:438–439
Bullock, Wynn **3**:561
Callahan, Harry M. **4**:40
Coburn, Alvin Langdon **5**:84
Cunningham, Imogen **5**:390
Draper, John William **6**:263
Eakins, Thomas **7**:4
Eastman, George **7**:34
Evans, Walker **7**:313
Frank, Robert **8**:280
Jackson, William Henry **11**:344
Käsebier, Gertrude **12**:29
Kepes, Gyorgy **12**:57
Land, Edwin **12**:178
Lange, Dorothea **12**:195
Mees, Charles Edward Kenneth **13**:278
Moholy-Nagy, László **13**:503
Newhall, Beaumont **14**:169
Photo-Secession **15**:257
Porter, Eliot **15**:444
Ray, Man **16**:96
Riis, Jacob August **16**:222–223
Siskind, Aaron **17**:328
Steichen, Edward **18**:246
Stieglitz, Alfred **18**:267
Strand, Paul **18**:288
Szarkowski, John **18**:415
Uelsmann, Jerry N. **19**:371
Weston, Edward **20**:118
White, Clarence H. **20**:134
White, Minor **20**:135
PHOTOGRAPHY, SCIENTIFIC **15**:271–272 *bibliog., illus.*
PHOTOJOURNALISM **15**:272–273 *bibliog., illus.*
Bourke-White, Margaret **3**:424
Burrows, Larry **3**:580–581
Capa, Robert **4**:119
Cartier-Bresson, Henri **4**:175
Davidson, Bruce **6**:49
Eisenstaedt, Alfred **7**:96
Kertész, André **12**:60
Lange, Dorothea **12**:195
Life **12**:326
Nadar **14**:4 *illus.*
Salomon, Erich **17**:36
Smith, W. Eugene **17**:371
Stern, Der **18**:260
Stryker, Roy **18**:304
Weegee **20**:90
Winogrand, Garry **20**:180
PHOTOMETER **15**:273–274 *bibliog.*
faint object detection **8**:8
Fleming, Sir Ambrose **8**:159
grease-spot
Bunsen, Robert Wilhelm **3**:564
Joly, John **11**:441
Lummer-Brodhun
Lummer, Otto **12**:459
photometry, astronomical **15**:274
Pickering, Edward Charles **15**:293
turbidimeter **19**:339
PHOTOMETRY, ASTRONOMICAL **15**:274 *bibliog.*
astrophotography **2**:285

PHOTOMETRY, ASTRONOMICAL (cont.)
candela **4**:106
Draper, John William **6**:263
faint object detection **8**:8
Hertzsprung, Ejnar **10**:149
infrared astronomy **11**:175
Leavitt, Henrietta Swan **12**:263–264
light intensity, celestial object **15**:274
lumen **12**:458
magnitude **13**:60–61
Payne-Gaposchkin, Cecilia **15**:122
photographic photometry **15**:274
Pickering, Edward Charles **15**:293
Schlesinger, Frank **17**:125–126
Schwarzschild, Karl **17**:139
star **18**:221–222
UBV photometric system **15**:274
use **15**:274
PHOTOMONTAGE (art)
Bartlett, Jennifer **3**:97
Uelsmann, Jerry N. **19**:371
PHOTOMULTIPLIER **15**:274
detector, particle **6**:134
electron tube **7**:124
faint object detection **8**:8
PHOTON **15**:274 *bibliog.*
annihilation **2**:33
Compton, Arthur Holly **5**:159
Compton effect **5**:159
energy **15**:274
fundamental particles **8**:361; **8**:362 *table*; **8**:363
laser **12**:211 *illus.*
light **15**:274
photochemistry **15**:257–259
photoelectric cell **15**:259–260
PHOTOPERISCOPE *see* PERISCOPE
PHOTOPHOBIA
eye diseases **7**:350
PHOTOREALISM **15**:274–275 *bibliog., illus.*
Close, Chuck **5**:65
Estes, Richard **7**:246
Flack, Audrey **8**:133
Hanson, Duane **10**:41
modern art **13**:495
painting **15**:23
Vrubel, Mikhail Aleksandrovich **19**:639
PHOTORESISTOR
semiconductor **17**:196
PHOTOSPHERE **15**:275; **18**:225 *illus.*
facula **8**:7
stellar atmosphere **15**:275
Sun **18**:341–342
temperature **15**:275
X-ray astronomy **20**:305
PHOTOSTAT
copying machine **5**:255
PHOTOSYNTHESIS **15**:275–277 *bibliog., illus.*
absorption, light **15**:275
algae **1**:280–282
biology **3**:270
biosphere **3**:277
blue-green algae **3**:342–343
cacti and other succulents **4**:10
Calvin, Melvin **4**:49
Calvin cycle **15**:277
carbohydrate **4**:132–133
carbon cycle (atmosphere) **4**:136
carbon fixation **15**:275; **15**:277
chlorophyll **4**:401–402; **15**:276
Pelletier, Pierre Joseph **15**:138
chloroplast **4**:402; **15**:276
cell **4**:233
coenzyme **5**:93
fuel **8**:352
geochemistry **9**:96
growth **9**:381
history **15**:275–276
light trapping
mechanism **15**:276–277
process **15**:277
metabolism **13**:326
nitrogen cycle **14**:203
oceanic nutrients **14**:341
photic zone **15**:257
photochemistry **15**:259
photosystems I and II **15**:276
plankton **15**:332
plant adaptation **15**:277
process **15**:275
reaction, chemical **16**:99
scientific research **15**:277
starch **18**:226
stomata **18**:280
sugar **18**:327
tree **19**:287
upwelling, oceanic **19**:474
water splitting **15**:275
PHOTOTELEGRAPHY
photography **15**:266
PHOTOTROPISM
tropism **19**:309–310 *illus.*
PHOTOTYPESETTING **15**:277–278 *bibliog.*
newspaper **14**:172
typesetting **19**:365 *illus.*
PHOTOVOLTAIC CELL *see* SOLAR CELL
PHOTOVOLTAIC EFFECT *see* PHOTOELECTRIC CELL; PHOTOELECTRIC EFFECT
PHRA NAKHON SI AYUTTHAYA (Thailand)
map (14° 21′N 100° 33′E) **19**:139
PHRENOLOGY **15**:278 *bibliog., illus.*
Gall, Franz Joseph **9**:16
PHRYGIA **15**:278 *bibliog.*
cities
Gordion **9**:248–249
languages, extinct **12**:198
PHTHALEINS
Baeyer, Adolf von **3**:20–21
PHU QUOC ISLAND
map (10° 12′N 104° 0′E) **19**:580
PHU VINH (Vietnam)
map (9° 56′N 106° 20′E) **19**:580
PHUKET (Thailand)
map (7° 53′N 98° 24′E) **19**:139
PHUKET ISLAND
map (8° 0′N 98° 22′E) **19**:139
PHYCOBIONT *see* LICHEN
PHYCOCYANIN *see* BLUE-GREEN ALGAE
PHYFE, DUNCAN **15**:278 *bibliog.*
furniture **8**:377 *illus.*
PHYLA
classification, biological **5**:43
PHYLLANTHUS **15**:278
PHYLLITE **15**:278
PHYLOGENY **15**:278–279 *bibliog.*
ontogeny **14**:396
PHYSICAL ANTHROPOLOGY *see* ANTHROPOLOGY
PHYSICAL CHEMISTRY **15**:279 *bibliog.*
activity **1**:90
Avogadro's law **2**:377
boiling point **3**:363
catalyst **4**:198–199
chemical energy **4**:315
chemical equilibrium and kinetics **4**:315–317; **15**:279
Dalton's law **6**:15
dissociation (chemistry) **6**:198
electrochemical equivalent **7**:112
electrochemistry **7**:112–113; **15**:279
electrolysis **7**:114–115
electrolyte **7**:115
endothermic and exothermic reactions **7**:171
entropy **7**:209
eutectic point **7**:310
evaporation **7**:313–314
Faraday's laws of electrolysis **8**:22
flash point **8**:154
freezing point **8**:300–301
gas laws **9**:53
gaseous state **9**:54
Gay-Lussac, Joseph Louis **9**:64
gel **9**:69
glassy state **9**:205
Graham, Thomas **9**:280
Hassell, Odd **10**:67
Hess's law **10**:151
history **4**:329; **15**:279
hydrogen spectrum **10**:340–341
ideal gas **11**:30
intermolecular forces **11**:215
isothermal process **11**:301
liquid **12**:364–365
liquid crystal **12**:365
matter **13**:230–231; **15**:279
melting point **13**:289
Nernst, Walther **14**:89
Ostwald, Wilhelm **14**:459
oxidation and reduction **14**:475–476
phase equilibrium **15**:222–224
photochemistry **15**:257–259; **15**:279
polymerization **15**:279; **15**:420
radiochemistry **16**:63
rheology **15**:279
solution **15**:279; **18**:58
superfluidity **18**:351
surface effects **15**:279
thermochemistry **19**:161–162
thermodynamics **15**:279; **19**:162–165
transmutation of elements **19**:276–277
triple point **19**:302
van der Waals, Johannes Diderik **19**:512
van't Hoff, Jacobus Henricus **19**:520
vapor pressure **19**:521
Waage, Peter **20**:3
PHYSICAL EDUCATION, TEACHING OF **15**:279–280 *bibliog.*
eurhythmics **7**:265–266
exercise **7**:329–331
PHYSICAL ENERGY
colloidal state **5**:104–105
PHYSICAL EXAMINATION *see* EXAMINATION, MEDICAL
PHYSICAL FITNESS *see* EXERCISE; RUNNING AND JOGGING
PHYSICAL GEOGRAPHY **9**:103
PHYSICAL MEDICINE *see* REHABILITATION MEDICINE
PHYSICAL OCEANOGRAPHY
oceanography **14**:344–345
PHYSICAL OPTICS
optics **14**:411–412
PHYSICAL REALITY
uncertainty principle **19**:381
PHYSICAL THERAPY **15**:280 *bibliog.*
eurhythmics **7**:265–266
hydrotherapy **10**:344
occupational therapy **14**:321
stroke **18**:302
PHYSICALLY HANDICAPPED, EDUCATION OF THE *see* SPECIAL EDUCATION
PHYSICIAN *see* MEDICINE
PHYSICS **15**:280–281 *bibliog.*
See also MECHANICS (physics)
atmospheric physics
meteorology **13**:341
Schaefer, Vincent Joseph **17**:116
ballistics **3**:49–51
branches
atmospheric physics **13**:341
biophysics **3**:275
chemical physics **4**:329
cryogenics **5**:370–371
dynamics **6**:319
electricity **7**:107–111
electronics **7**:126
experimental physics **15**:280
geophysics **9**:107–108
hydrophysics **12**:345
magnetism **13**:55–58
magnetohydrodynamics **13**:58–59
nuclear physics **14**:285–287
optics **12**:409–413; **14**:409–413
physical chemistry **15**:279
plasma physics **15**:345–346
quantum mechanics **16**:9–11
relativity **16**:132–137
social physics **16**:23
solid-state physics **15**:281; **18**:54–55
sound and acoustics **18**:71–74
statics **18**:234–235
theoretical physics **15**:280; **19**:158
thermodynamics **19**:162–165
thermoelectricity **19**:165
chemistry, contributions of **4**:327
classical physics
history **15**:283–286
scope **15**:280–281
conservation, laws of **5**:204–205 *illus.*
density **6**:113–114 *tables*
Earth sciences **7**:24
education
secondary education **17**:180
energy **7**:172–173
engineering **7**:177–178
fluid mechanics **8**:184–185
force **8**:220
fundamental particles **8**:361–363
gas laws **9**:53
gaseous state **9**:54
glassy state **9**:205
gravitation **9**:304–305
kinetic energy **12**:78
kinetic theory of matter **12**:78–79
law, physical **12**:248
lens **12**:285–287
lever **12**:302
matter **13**:230–231
Maxwell's equations **13**:241–242
melting point **13**:289
modern physics
history **15**:286
scope **15**:281
Nobel Prize winners **14**:208–211 *table*
Alfvén, Olof **1**:280
Appleton, Sir Edward Victor **2**:89
Bardeen, John **3**:80
Barkla, Charles Glover **3**:83
Basov, Nikolai Gennadiyevich **3**:116
Becquerel, Antoine Henri **3**:153
Bethe, Hans **3**:230
Blackett, Patrick Maynard Stuart, Baron Blackett **3**:321
Bohr, Aage Niels **3**:361
Bohr, Niels **3**:361–362
Born, Max **3**:401–402
Bothe, Walther Wilhelm **3**:415
Bragg, Sir William H. **3**:439
Bragg, Sir William L. **3**:439
Brattain, Walter **3**:458
Braun, Ferdinand **3**:458
Chadwick, Sir James **4**:267
Chamberlain, Owen **4**:274
Cherenkov, Pavel Alekseyevich **4**:331
Cherenkov radiation **4**:331
Cockcroft, Sir John Douglas **5**:86
Compton, Arthur Holly **5**:159
Cooper, Leon N. **5**:244
Curie, Marie and Pierre **5**:391–392
Davisson, Clinton **6**:53
de Broglie, Louis **6**:58
Dirac, Paul **6**:186–187
Einstein, Albert **7**:92–94
Esaki, Leo **7**:236
Fermi, Enrico **8**:55–56
Feynman, Richard Phillips **8**:66
Franck, James **8**:277
Frank, Ilya Mikhailovich **8**:279
Gabor, Dennis **9**:5–6
Gell-Mann, Murray **9**:69–70
Giaever, Ivar **9**:171
Glaser, Donald **9**:197
Glashow, Sheldon **9**:197
Guillaume, Charles Édouard **9**:395
Heisenberg, Werner Karl **10**:109–110
Hertz, Gustav **10**:148–149
Hess, Victor Franz **5**:283; **10**:152
Heyrovský, Jaroslav **10**:155
Hofstadter, Robert **10**:197
Jensen, Hans **11**:396
Josephson, Brian David **11**:452
Kamerlingh Onnes, Heike **12**:10
Kapitza, Peter **12**:25
Kastler, Alfred **12**:30
Kusch, Polykarp **12**:139
Lamb, Willis Eugene, Jr. **12**:174
Landau, Lev **12**:181
laser **12**:211
Laue, Max von **12**:236
Lawrence, Ernest Orlando **12**:250
Lee, Tsung Dao **12**:270
Lenard, Philipp Eduard Anton **12**:281
Lippmann, Gabriel **12**:363
Lorentz, Hendrik Antoon **12**:413
Marconi, Guglielmo **13**:147
Mayer, Maria Goeppert **13**:246
Michelson, Albert Abraham **13**:375–376
Millikan, Robert **13**:430
Mössbauer, Rudolf Ludwig **13**:605
Mott, Nevill **13**:616
Mottelson, Ben Roy **13**:616
Néel, Louis Eugène Félix **14**:76
Pauli, Wolfgang **15**:118–119
Perrin, Jean Baptiste **15**:178
Planck, Max **15**:326–327
Powell, Cecil Frank **15**:480
Purcell, Edward Mills **15**:628
Rabi, Isidor Isaac **16**:32
Rainwater, James **16**:78
Raman, Sir Chandrasekhara Venkata **16**:79–80
Rayleigh, Lord **16**:97
Richardson, Sir Owen Willans **16**:212
Richter, Burton **16**:214
Roentgen, Wilhelm Conrad **16**:268
Ryle, Sir Martin **16**:380
Salam, Abdus **19**:386
Schrieffer, John Robert **17**:134
Schrödinger, Erwin **17**:135
Schwinger, Julian Seymour **17**:141
Segrè, Emilio **17**:188–189
Shockley, William Bradford **17**:279
Siegbahn, Manne **17**:295
Stark, Johannes **18**:227
Stern, Otto **18**:260
Tamm, Igor Yevgenievich **19**:19
Thomson, Sir George Paget **19**:175; **19**:176
Thomson, Sir Joseph John **19**:176
Ting, Samuel Chao Chung **19**:206
Tomonaga, Sin-itiro **19**:232
Townes, Charles Hard **19**:255
van der Waals, Johannes Diderik **19**:512
Van Vleck, J. H. **19**:516

    Walton, Ernest Thomas Sinton **20**:20
    Weinberg, Steven **20**:95
    Wien, Wilhelm Jan **20**:146
    Wigner, Eugene Paul **20**:147
    Wilson, Charles Thomson Rees **20**:164
    Wilson, Robert W., and Penzias, Arno A. **20**:165
    Yang, Chen Ning **20**:317
    Yukawa, Hideki **20**:344
    Zeeman, Pieter **20**:357–358
    Zernike, Frits **20**:361
  parity (physics) **15**:88–89
  Pascal's law **15**:102
  permeability, rock **15**:174
  phonon **15**:255
  phosphorescence **15**:256
  photoelectric effect **15**:260
  photon **15**:274
  piezoelectricity **15**:298
  Planck's constant **15**:327
  potential, electric **15**:466
  prism (physics) **15**:554
  professional and educational organizations **17**:145 *table*
    American Institute of Physics **1**:341
    American Physical Society **1**:352
    physics, history of **15**:282
  radioactivity **16**:60–63
  refraction **16**:123–124
  research institutions
    Argonne National Laboratory **2**:152
    Brookhaven National Laboratory **3**:510
    Desy Laboratory **6**:133
    European Organization for Nuclear Research **7**:301
    Fermi National Accelerator Laboratory **8**:56
    Frascati National Laboratory **8**:286
    High Altitude Observatory **10**:161
    Lawrence Berkeley and Lawrence Livermore laboratories **12**:251
    Oak Ridge National Laboratory **14**:312
    Stanford Linear Accelerator Center **18**:218
  research methodology **15**:280
  reversible and irreversible processes **16**:186
  space-time continuum **18**:137
  spontaneous combustion **18**:194
  stark effect **18**:227
  statistical thermodynamics **18**:235
  superconductivity **18**:350
  superfluidity **18**:351
  surface tension **18**:358
  symmetry **18**:404
  temperature **19**:92–93
  time (physics) **19**:201
  time reversal invariance **19**:202
  transmutation of elements **19**:276–277
  two-body problem **19**:360
  ultraviolet light **19**:379
  uncertainty principle **19**:381
  unified field theory **19**:385–386
  units, physical **19**:465–467 *tables*
  vacuum **19**:501–502
  van der Waals equation **19**:512–513
  vector analysis **19**:530
  viscosity **19**:616–617
  volt **19**:631
  wake (water) **20**:8
  work (physics) **20**:217
PHYSICS, HISTORY OF **15**:282–287 *bibliog., illus.*
  See also PHYSICS—Nobel Prize winners
  Alembert, Jean Le Rond d' **1**:271
  Ampère, André Marie **1**:377
  Ångström, Anders Jonas **2**:7
  Aristotle **2**:157
  Bhabha, Homi Jehangir **3**:233
  biophysics **3**:275
  Biot, Jean Baptiste **3**:277
  Boltzmann, Ludwig **3**:372
  Cavendish, Henry **4**:225–226
  Celsius, Anders **4**:238
  Clausius, Rudolf **5**:45
  Coulomb, Charles Augustin de **5**:308
  Dalton, John **6**:14–15
  development
    nuclear physics **14**:285
    quantum mechanics **16**:9–11
    relativity **16**:132–133
  Doppler, Christian Johann **6**:240
  Fahrenheit, Gabriel Daniel **8**:8
  Faraday, Michael **8**:21–22
  Foucault, Jean **8**:249
  Fresnel, Augustin Jean **8**:328
  Gaileo Galilei **9**:15
  Gamow, George **9**:34
  Geiger, Hans Wilhelm **9**:67–68
  Ginzburg, Vitaly Lazarevich **9**:185
  Goddard, Robert **9**:219–220
  Helmholtz, Hermann Ludwig Ferdinand von **10**:115–116
  Hertz, Heinrich Rudolph **10**:149
  Hooke, Robert **10**:226–227
  Huygens, Christiaan **10**:325
  Jeans, Sir James **11**:390
  Joliot-Curie, Frédéric and Irène **11**:441
  Joly, John **11**:441
  Joule, James Prescott **11**:453
  Kármán, Theodore von **12**:28
  Kelvin, William Thomson, 1st Baron **12**:40
  Lawrence, Ernest Orlando **12**:250
  Leibniz, Gottfried Wilhelm von **12**:276–277
  Leonardo da Vinci **12**:289–291
  Lindemann, Frederick Alexander **12**:351
  Mach, Ernst **13**:17
  Maiman, Theodore Harold **13**:68
  Maxwell, James Clerk **13**:241
  Meitner, Lise **13**:283
  Mosley, Henry Gwyn Jeffreys **13**:599
  Newton, Sir Isaac **14**:173–175
  Nobel, Alfred **14**:208
  Oersted, Hans Christian **14**:352
  Ohm, Georg Simon **14**:363
  Oppenheimer, J. Robert **14**:407–408
  Ostwald, Wilhelm **14**:459
  Pascal, Blaise **15**:102
  Plücker, Julius **15**:370
  Réaumur, René Antoine Ferchault de **16**:105
  Regnault, Henri Victor **16**:129
  Rutherford, Sir Ernest **16**:375–376
  Rydberg, Johannes Robert **16**:379
  Shockley, William Bradford **17**:279
  Simon, Sir Francis **17**:315
  Stokes, Sir George Gabriel **18**:278
  Szilard, Leo **18**:416
  Teller, Edward **19**:90
  Torricelli, Evangelista **19**:244
  Tyndall, John **19**:363
  Van de Graaff, Robert Jemison **19**:512
  Volta, Alessandro, Count **19**:631
  von Neumann, John **19**:634
  Watson-Watt, Sir Robert Alexander **20**:68
  Weber, Wilhelm Eduard **20**:88
  Wollaston, William Hyde **20**:199
  Wood, Robert Williams **20**:207
  Wu, Chien-shiung **20**:295
  Yang, Chen Ning **20**:317
  Young, Thomas **20**:334
PHYSICS INSTRUMENTATION
  accelerator, particle **1**:72–76
  balance **3**:30–31
  betatron **3**:229
  bubble chamber **3**:531
  calorimeter **4**:47
  chronometer **4**:420
  cloud chamber **5**:68
  coulombmeter **5**:308
  detector, particle **6**:133–134
  diffraction grating **6**:169–170
  electrometer **7**:119
  flowmeter **8**:184
  Foucault pendulum **8**:249
  Geiger counter **9**:68
  gyroscope **9**:416
  interferometer **11**:209–210; **13**:376
  manometer **13**:126
  mass spectrometry **13**:204
  monochromator **13**:536
  pendulum **15**:142
  photometer **15**:273–274
  photomultiplier **15**:274
  polariscope **15**:394
  radiography **16**:63
  scintillation center **17**:146–147
  spark chamber **18**:163
  thermocouple **19**:162
  thermometer **19**:166–167
  ultrasonics **19**:377–378
PHYSIOCRATS **15**:287 *bibliog.*
  economics **7**:48
  Enlightenment **7**:207
  single tax **17**:322
  state (in political philosophy) **18**:232
PHYSIOGRAPHY **15**:287 *bibliog.*
  astrogeology **2**:270
  geology **9**:105–106
  valley and ridge province **19**:507–508
PHYSIOLOGIC SHOCK *see* SHOCK, PHYSIOLOGIC
PHYSIOLOGICAL CHEMISTRY *see* BIOCHEMISTRY
PHYSIOLOGICAL PSYCHOLOGY
  psychology **15**:594
  Wundt, Wilhelm **20**:296
PHYSIOLOGY **15**:287 *bibliog.*
  See also names of specific systems, e.g., ENDOCRINE SYSTEM; REPRODUCTIVE SYSTEM, HUMAN; etc; names of specific organs, e.g., BRAIN; HEART; etc.
  adolescence **1**:106
  Bayliss, Sir William **3**:133–134
  Bernard, Claude **3**:220
  biofeedback **3**:263
  biology **3**:270
  Brown-Séquard, Charles **3**:516
  cell physiology **4**:236
  circulatory system **4**:438–442
  classification, biological **5**:43
  consciousness, states of **5**:200
  dreams and dreaming **6**:266
  education **15**:287
  embryo **15**:503 *illus.*
  exercise **7**:329
  fungi, mushrooms **13**:661
  Harvey, William **15**:287
  Helmholtz, Hermann Ludwig Ferdinand von **10**:115–116
  history **15**:287
  invertebrate **11**:235–237
  memory **13**:291–292
  muscle contraction **13**:654–656
  Nobel Prize for physiology or medicine **14**:208–211 *table*
    Adrian, Edgar Douglas **1**:109
    Arber, Werner **2**:110
    Axelrod, Julius **2**:377
    Baltimore, David **3**:56
    Banting, Sir Frederick G. **3**:71
    Bárány, Robert **3**:75
    Beadle, George W. **3**:137
    Behring, Emil Adolf von **3**:171
    Best, Charles **3**:228
    Bloch, Felix **3**:334
    Bloch, Konrad **3**:334
    Blumberg, Baruch S. **3**:346
    Bordet, Jules **3**:398
    Bovet, Daniele **3**:426
    Burnet, Sir Macfarlane **3**:577
    Carrel, Alexis **4**:167
    Chain, Ernst Boris **4**:268
    Claude, Albert **5**:44
    Cori, Carl Ferdinand and Gerty Teresa **5**:262
    Cournand, André **5**:314
    Crick, Francis **5**:343
    Dale, Sir Henry Hallett **6**:11
    Dam, Carl Henrik **6**:18
    Delbrück, Max **6**:92
    Doisy, Edward **6**:224
    Domagk, Gerhard **6**:229
    Dulbecco, Renato **6**:295
    Eccles, Sir John **7**:37
    Ehrlich, Paul (1854–1915) **7**:90
    Eijkman, Christiaan **7**:92
    Einthoven, Willem **7**:94
    Enders, John F. **7**:168
    Fibiger, Johannes **8**:69
    Fleming, Sir Alexander **8**:159
    Florey, Sir Howard Walter **8**:169
    Frisch, Karl von **2**:11–12; **3**:159; **8**:334
    Goldstein, Joseph L. **9**:236
    Golgi, Camillo **9**:240
    Hench, Philip Showalter **10**:121
    Hershey, Alfred Day **10**:148
    Hodgkin, Alan Lloyd **10**:194
    Hopkins, Sir Frederick Gowland **10**:231
    Huxley, Andrew Fielding **10**:324
    Jacob, François **11**:345
    Jerne, Niels K. **11**:397
    Katz, Sir Bernard **12**:31
    Kendall, Edward **12**:41
    Khorana, Har Gobind **12**:68
    Koch, Robert **12**:104
    Kocher, Emil **12**:105
    Kornberg, Arthur **12**:123
    Kossel, Albrecht **12**:124
    Krebs, Sir Hans Adolf **12**:128
    Landsteiner, Karl **12**:193
    Laveran, Charles **12**:241
    Lederberg, Joshua **12**:268
    Lipmann, Fritz Albert **12**:362
    Lorenz, Konrad **2**:11–12; **12**:414
    Luria, Salvador **12**:467
    Lwoff, André **12**:473
    Lynen, Feodor **12**:477
    McClintock, Barbara **13**:9
    MacLeod, John James Rickard **13**:33
    Medawar, Peter Brian **13**:263
    Metchnikoff, Elie **13**:335
    Meyerhof, Otto **14**:369
    Minot, George **13**:460
    Moniz, António Egas, schizophrenia **17**:124
    Monod, Jacques Lucien **13**:536
    Morgan, Thomas Hunt **13**:579
    Müller, Paul **13**:637
    Nathans, Daniel **14**:27
    Nirenberg, M. W. **14**:201
    Ochoa, Severo **14**:346
    Palade, George Emil **15**:29
    Pavlov, Ivan Petrovich **15**:120
    Ramón y Cajal, Santiago **16**:81
    Richards, Dickinson Woodruff **16**:211
    Robbins, Frederick Chapman **16**:240
    Rous, Francis Peyton **16**:325
    Schally, Andrew Victor **17**:117
    Smith, Hamilton **17**:368
    Spemann, Hans **18**:177
    Sutherland, Earl W., Jr. **18**:372
    Szent-Györgyi, Albert von **18**:416
    Tatum, Edward L. **19**:44
    Temin, Howard Martin **19**:91
    Tinbergen, Nikolaas **2**:11–12; **19**:206
    Waksman, Selman Abraham **20**:8
    Wald, George **20**:9
    Warburg, Otto **20**:28
    Watson, James D. **20**:67
    Whipple, George Hoyt **20**:131
    Wilkins, Maurice **20**:152
    Yalow, Rosalyn Sussman **20**:315
  nucleic acid, DNA, effect **15**:287
  Pavlov, Ivan Petrovich **15**:120
  peristalsis **15**:171–172
  pharmacology **15**:220
  pregnancy and birth **15**:502–506
  sleep **17**:359–360
  space exploration
    Kerwin, Joseph **12**:60
  speech **18**:173–174
  stress, biological **18**:297
  zoology **20**:377
PHYSIOLOGY OF TASTE, THE (book)
  Brillat-Savarin, Anthelme **3**:486
PHYTOMASTIGINA *see* MASTIGOPHORA
PHYTOPLANKTON
  bloom, algal **3**:340
  dinoflagellate **6**:179
  food chain, aquatic **7**:43 *illus.*
  marine food chain **14**:330 *illus.*
  oceanic nutrients **14**:341
  ooze, deep-sea **14**:397
  plankton **15**:331–333
  sediment, marine **17**:184
  upwelling, oceanic **19**:474
PI **15**:287 *bibliog.*
  mathematics, history of **13**:226
PI (letter)
  P **15**:3
PI ELECTRON
  aromatic compounds **2**:186
PI MESON *See* PION
PIACENZA (Italy) **15**:287
  map (45° 1′N 9° 40′E) **11**:321
PIACENZA, MARIO
  Matterhorn **13**:231
PIAF, EDITH **15**:287 *bibliog.*
  Aznavour, Charles **2**:381
PIAGET, JEAN **15**:287–288 *bibliog., illus.*
  adolescence **1**:106
  child development **4**:348; **15**:287–288
  cognitive psychology **5**:95
  concept formation and attainment **5**:169
  developmental psychology **6**:142; **15**:287–288
  intelligence **11**:203
  moral awareness **13**:572
  reasoning **16**:105
  speech development **18**:176
PIANELLO CULTURE
  Villanovans **19**:597
PIANKHI, KING OF CUSH
  Cush **5**:397
PIANO **13**:678 *illus.*; **15**:288–289 *bibliog., illus.*
  See also CLAVICHORD
  ballade **3**:41
  boogie-woogie **3**:383
  composers
    Albéniz, Isaac **1**:253
    Alkan, Charles **1**:296
    Bartók, Béla **3**:98
    Beethoven, Ludwig van **3**:164–165
    Chaminade, Cécile **4**:275
    Chopin, Frédéric **4**:405

PIANO (cont.)
Clementi, Muzio **5**:50
Cowell, Henry **5**:321
Cramer, Johann Baptist **5**:328
Czerny, Carl **5**:416
Debussy, Claude **6**:71–72
Diabelli, Anton **6**:148
Granados, Enrique **9**:283
Liszt, Franz **12**:367
MacDowell, Edward **13**:14
Rachmaninoff, Sergei **16**:36
Ravel, Maurice **16**:94–95
Schubert, Franz **17**:135
Schumann, Robert **17**:137
Tchaikovsky, Peter Ilich **19**:51–52
étude **7**:261
keyboard instruments **12**:62–63 *illus.*
manufacture
Mason (family) **13**:198
pianists
Albert, Eugen d' **1**:253
Arrau, Claudio **2**:188
Ashkenazi, Vladimir **2**:230
Backhaus, Wilhelm **3**:12–13
Barenboim, Daniel **3**:80
Bauer, Harold **3**:129
Berman, Lazar **3**:219
Brendel, Alfred **3**:473
Casadesus, Robert **4**:180
Chaminade, Cécile **4**:275
Charles, Ray **4**:290
Cliburn, Van **5**:54
Cole, Nat King **5**:99
Cortot, Alfred **5**:279
Gieseking, Walter **9**:177
Gilels, Emil **9**:180
Gould, Glenn **9**:265
Hess, Dame Myra **10**:152
Hines, Earl **10**:173
Hofmann, Josef Casimir **10**:196
Horowitz, Vladimir **10**:241
Hummel, Johann Nepomuk **10**:302
Iturbi, José **11**:331
Levine, James **12**:304
Moore, Gerald **13**:568
Moscheles, Ignaz **13**:596
Moszkowski, Moritz **13**:606
Paderewski, Ignace Jan **15**:12
Previn, André **15**:534
Richter, Sviatoslav **16**:215
Rubinstein, Anton **16**:337
Rubinstein, Arthur **16**:337
Schnabel, Artur **17**:128–129
Schumann, Clara **17**:136
Scriabin, Aleksandr Nikolayevich **17**:157–158
Serkin, Rudolf **17**:209
Tcherepnin, Aleksandr Nikolayevich **19**:52
player piano **15**:363
ragtime **16**:70
sonata **18**:63
PIANO, RENZO, AND ROGERS, RICHARD
Beaubourg **3**:145
PIANOLA *see* PLAYER PIANO
PIAST (dynasty) **15**:289 *bibliog.*
Poland **15**:391
PIATIGORSKY, GREGOR **15**:289 *bibliog.*
PIATRA-NEAMȚ (Romania)
map (46° 56′N 26° 22′E) **16**:288
PIATT (county in Illinois)
map (40° 0′N 88° 37′W) **11**:42
PIAUÍ (Brazil)
map (7° 0′S 43° 0′W) **3**:460
PIAVE, F. M.
Traviata, La **19**:285
PIAZZA ARMERINA (Italy) **15**:289–290 *bibliog.*
mosaic **13**:594
PIAZZI, GIUSEPPE **15**:290
Ceres (astronomy) **4**:260
PIC DU MIDI OBSERVATORY **14**:318 *illus.*
PICABIA, FRANCIS **15**:290 *bibliog.*
PICARD, CHARLES ÉMILE
mathematics, history of **13**:226
PICARD, JEAN **15**:290
Earth, size and shape of **7**:19
PICARDY (France) **15**:290
cities
Amiens **1**:369
PICARESQUE NOVEL **15**:290 *bibliog.*
Alemán, Mateo **1**:271
Defoe, Daniel **6**:83–84
Don Quixote **6**:236
Espinel, Vicente Martínez **7**:243
Golden Ass, The **9**:231
Lesage, Alain René **12**:296
Smollett, Tobias **17**:374
Spanish literature **18**:158–160
PICASSO, PABLO **15**:290–292 *bibliog., illus.*
Artists **15**:291 *illus.*
Ballets Russes de Serge Diaghilev **3**:48
Braque, Georges **3**:456
collage **5**:102 *illus.*
cubism **5**:380
Demoiselles d'Avignon **5**:381 *illus.*
drawing **6**:265
Gargallo, Pablo **9**:47
Gertrude Stein **18**:247 *illus.*
Gris, Juan **9**:366
Guernica **15**:291 *illus.*
Guillaume Apollinaire **2**:79 *illus.*
Málaga (Spain) **13**:79
Paloma **6**:265 *illus.*
portrait of art dealer Daniel Henry Kahnweiler **15**:23 *illus.*
Portrait of the Art Dealer Vollard **15**:447 *illus.*
Serge Pavlovich Diaghilev **6**:149 *illus.*
set design
Three-Cornered Hat, The **18**:161 *illus.*
Spanish art and architecture **18**:156
Still Life with Watermelon **18**:269 *illus.*
surrealism (art) **18**:364
Three Dancers **2**:202 *illus.*
Three Musicians **13**:494 *illus.*
Three Women at the Spring **18**:155 *illus.*
PICAYUNE (Mississippi)
map (30° 26′N 89° 41′W) **13**:469
PICCADILLY (Newfoundland)
map (48° 34′N 58° 55′W) **14**:166
PICCADILLY CIRCUS **12**:401 *map*
PICCARD, AUGUSTE **15**:292 *bibliog., illus.*
bathyscaphe **3**:123; **15**:292
Jacques Piccard **15**:292
Kipfer, Paul **15**:292
manned balloon flight **15**:292
Marianas Trench **13**:151
ocean deeps exploration **15**:292
PICCOLO **8**:188 *illus.*; **15**:292 *bibliog.*
PICHEGRU, JEAN CHARLES **15**:292
PICHER (Oklahoma)
map (36° 59′N 94° 50′W) **14**:368
PICKAWAY (county in Ohio)
map (39° 40′N 83° 0′W) **14**:357
PICKENS (county in Alabama)
map (33° 20′N 88° 5′W) **1**:234
PICKENS (county in Georgia)
map (31° 28′N 84° 25′W) **9**:114
PICKENS (Mississippi)
map (32° 53′N 89° 58′W) **13**:469
PICKENS (South Carolina)
map (34° 53′N 82° 42′W) **18**:98
PICKENS (county in South Carolina)
map (34° 55′N 82° 50′W) **18**:98
PICKENS (West Virginia)
map (38° 39′N 80° 13′W) **20**:111
PICKENSVILLE (Alabama)
map (33° 14′N 88° 16′W) **1**:234
PICKEREL **15**:292–293 *illus.*
PICKERING, EDWARD CHARLES **15**:293 *bibliog.*
Harvard College Observatory **15**:293
photometry, astronomical **15**:293
PICKERING, JAMES **18**:119 *illus.*
PICKERING, TIMOTHY **15**:293 *bibliog.*
PICKERING, WILLIAM HENRY **15**:293
Phoebe **15**:293
Pickering, Edward Charles **15**:293
PICKETT (county in Tennessee)
map (36° 35′N 85° 5′W) **19**:104
PICKETT, GEORGE EDWARD **15**:293 *bibliog.*
Civil War, U.S. **5**:28
Gettysburg, Battle of **9**:161
PICKETT, WILSON
soul music **18**:71
PICKETT'S CHARGE
Gettysburg, Battle of **9**:161
Pickett, George E. **15**:293
PICKFORD (Michigan)
map (46° 10′N 84° 22′W) **13**:377
PICKFORD, MARY **15**:293 *bibliog., illus.*
Lubitsch, Ernst **12**:447
PICKLING **15**:293–294 *bibliog.*
caper **4**:122
cucumber **5**:382
PICKSTOWN (South Dakota)
map (43° 4′N 98° 32′W) **18**:103
PICKUP TRUCK
trucking industry **19**:315
PICKWICK LAKE
map (34° 55′N 88° 10′W) **1**:234
PICKWICK PAPERS, THE (book) **15**:294 *bibliog.*
Dickens, Charles **6**:156
PICNIC (play)
Inge, William **11**:176
PICO (Portugal)
Azores **2**:381–382 *map*
PICO, PÍO
Mexican War **13**:355
PICO DELLA MIRANDOLA, GIOVANNI, CONTE **15**:294 *bibliog.*; **16**:148 *illus.*
Renaissance **16**:149
PICO MOUNTAIN
map (14° 56′N 24° 21′W) **4**:122
PICO POINT (peak)
map (38° 28′N 28° 25′W) **15**:449
PICO RIVERA (California)
map (33° 58′N 118° 7′W) **4**:31
PICQUART, GEORGES
Dreyfus Affair **6**:271–272
PICTET, RASUL
cryogenics **5**:370
PICTOGRAPHIC WRITING
Chinese pictographs **4**:380 *illus.*
cuneiform **5**:389 *illus.*
hieroglyphics **10**:159–160
Indus civilization **11**:88 *illus.*; **11**:153–154
languages, extinct **12**:198
writing systems, evolution of **20**:291–292 *illus.*
PICTON (Ontario)
map (44° 0′N 77° 8′W) **14**:393; **14**:461
PICTS **2**:3 *map*; **15**:294 *bibliog.*
Celtic art **4**:240
Clackmannan **5**:35
Scotland **17**:151
PICTURE OF DORIAN GRAY, THE (book) **15**:294
Wilde, Oscar **20**:148–149
PICTURE OF DORIAN GRAY, THE (film)
Albright, Ivan Le Lorraine **1**:261
PICUNCHE
Araucanians **2**:109–110
PIDDOCK **15**:294
PIDGIN **15**:294 *bibliog.*
See also CREOLE (linguistics); LINGUA FRANCA
sociolinguistics **18**:27
PIDURUTALAGALA MOUNTAIN
map (7° 0′N 80° 46′E) **18**:206
PIE
cake and pastry **4**:20–21
PIEBALD *see* PINTO
PIED PIPER OF HAMELIN **15**:295
PIEDMONT (Alabama)
map (33° 55′N 85° 37′W) **1**:234
PIEDMONT (Italy) **11**:326 *illus.*; **15**:295
cities
Alessandria **1**:272
Novara **14**:272
Turin **19**:342
Italian unification **11**:330 *map*
Sardinia, Kingdom of **17**:76–77
PIEDMONT (Missouri)
map (37° 9′N 90° 42′W) **13**:476
PIEDMONT (South Carolina)
map (34° 42′N 82° 28′W) **18**:98
PIEDMONT PLATEAU **14**:230 *illus.*; **15**:295
map (36° 0′N 79° 0′W) **14**:242
Maryland **13**:187
North Carolina **14**:241
PIEDMONT SETTLERS
origins of the Civil War **5**:15
PIEDRA SOLA (Uruguay)
map (32° 4′S 56° 21′W) **19**:488
PIEDRAS NEGRAS (Guatemala) **15**:295 *bibliog.*
map (17° 11′N 91° 15′W) **9**:389
PIEDRAS NEGRAS (Mexico)
map (28° 42′N 100° 31′W) **13**:357
PIEGAN (American Indians)
Blackfoot **3**:321
PIEKSÄMÄKI (Finland)
map (62° 18′N 27° 8′E) **8**:95
PIELINEN LAKE
map (63° 15′N 29° 40′E) **8**:95
PIEMONTE (Italy) *see* PIEDMONT (Italy)
PIER (architecture)
Gothic art and architecture **9**:261
PIERCE (Colorado)
map (40° 38′N 104° 45′W) **5**:116
PIERCE (county in Georgia)
map (31° 20′N 82° 10′W) **9**:114
PIERCE (Idaho)
map (46° 29′N 115° 48′W) **11**:26
PIERCE (Nebraska)
map (42° 12′N 97° 32′W) **14**:70
PIERCE (county in Nebraska)
map (42° 15′N 97° 35′W) **14**:70
PIERCE (county in North Dakota)
map (48° 20′N 100° 0′W) **14**:248
PIERCE (county in Washington)
map (47° 4′N 122° 7′W) **20**:35
PIERCE (county in Wisconsin)
map (44° 45′N 92° 25′W) **20**:185
PIERCE, FRANKLIN **15**:295–296 *bibliog., illus.*
as president **15**:296
early life and political career **15**:295–296
PIERCE CITY (Missouri)
map (36° 57′N 94° 1′W) **13**:476
PIERCETON (Indiana)
map (41° 12′N 85° 42′W) **11**:111
PIERO DELLA FRANCESCA **15**:296–297 *bibliog., illus.*
The Baptism of Christ **11**:312 *illus.*; **15**:296 *illus.*
The Defeat of Khusrau **8**:327 *illus.*
Flagellation of Christ **15**:191 *illus.*
mathematics, history of **13**:224
PIERO DI COSIMO **15**:297 *bibliog.*
PIERPONT, FRANCIS HARRISON **15**:297
PIERPONT MORGAN LIBRARY *see* MORGAN LIBRARY
PIERRE (South Dakota) **15**:297
map (44° 22′N 100° 21′W) **18**:103
PIERRE PART (Louisiana)
map (30° 1′N 91° 12′W) **12**:430
PIERREVILLE (Trinidad and Tobago)
map (10° 18′N 61° 1′W) **19**:300
PIERROT **15**:297 *bibliog.*
Deburau, Jean Gaspard **6**:71
PIERS PLOWMAN (poem) **15**:297 *bibliog.*
Langland, William **12**:196
PIERZ (Minnesota)
map (45° 59′N 94° 6′W) **13**:453
PIETÀ
Michelangelo **13**:373; **13**:375; **16**:153 *illus.*
Passion cycle **15**:105
Weyden, Rogier van der **20**:119 *illus.*
PIETERMARITZBURG (South Africa) **15**:297
map (29° 37′S 30° 16′E) **18**:79
PIETERSBURG (South Africa)
map (23° 54′S 29° 25′E) **18**:79
PIETISM **15**:297–298 *bibliog.*
Amana Society **1**:321
Brethren **3**:474
evangelicalism **7**:312
Spener, Philipp Jakob **18**:178
PIEZOELECTRICITY **15**:298 *bibliog.*
communications applications **15**:298
Curie, Marie and Pierre, discoverers **5**:391
microphone **13**:386
sound and acoustics **18**:73
transducer **19**:269
ultrasonics **19**:377
PIG **15**:298–299 *bibliog., illus.*
domestic pigs **15**:298–299
animal husbandry **2**:23; **2**:24 *illus.*
fats and oils source **8**:35
tapeworm **19**:33–34
wild pigs **15**:298
babirusa **3**:6–7
peccary **15**:130
warthog **20**:33
PIGALLE, JEAN BAPTISTE **15**:299
PIGEON **3**:280 *illus.*; **6**:250 *illus.*; **15**:299–300 *bibliog., illus.*
brain **3**:443 *illus.*
dodo bird **6**:212
dove **6**:250
early years mortality **12**:331 *table*
learning theory **12**:260–261
skeletal system **3**:282 *illus.*
PIGEON (Michigan)
map (43° 50′N 83° 16′W) **13**:377
PIGEON COVE (Massachusetts)
map (42° 41′N 70° 38′W) **13**:206
PIGEON FORGE (Tennessee)
map (35° 47′N 83° 33′W) **19**:104
PIGEON HAWK *see* FALCON
PIGEON LAKE
map (44° 30′N 78° 30′W) **14**:393; **14**:461
PIGEON MILK *see* MILK
PIGEON RACING **15**:300 *bibliog.*
PIGEON RIVER
map (48° 0′N 89° 34′W) **13**:453
PIGEONBERRY *see* POKEWEED
PIGGOTT (Arkansas)
map (36° 23′N 90° 11′W) **2**:166
PIGGS PEAK (Swaziland)
map (25° 38′S 31° 15′E) **18**:380

PIGMENT 15:300 *bibliog.*
carotenoid 4:162
chlorophyll 4:401–402
chloroplast 4:402
chromium compounds 4:419
color 5:113
coloration, biological 5:122
cosmetics 5:280–283
gamboge 9:26–27
Karrer, Paul 12:29
lampblack 12:176
lead 12:256
ocher 14:346
paint 15:16–17
photosynthesis 15:276
pigment, skin 15:300–301
Prussian blue 15:586
ultramarine 19:377
varnish 19:524
Willstätter, Richard 20:163
PIGMENT, SKIN 15:300–301 *bibliog.*
albinism 1:260
Davenport, Charles 6:46
feather 8:39
leukoderma 12:301
mole (birthmark) 13:507
skin 17:341
PIGMY *see* PYGMY
PIGNETO, VILLA DEL
Cortona, Pietro da 5:279
PIGNOLIA *see* NUT; PINE NUT
PIGOU, ARTHUR
monetary theory 13:525
PIGWEED *see* GOOSEFOOT (botany)
PIHLAJA LAKE
map (61° 45′N 28° 50′E) 8:95
PIJIJIAPAN (Mexico)
map (15° 42′N 93° 14′W) 13:357
PIKA 13:623 *illus.*; 15:301 *illus.*
PIKE (county in Alabama)
map (31° 50′N 85° 55′W) 1:234
PIKE (county in Arkansas)
map (34° 10′N 93° 35′W) 2:166
PIKE (fish) 15:301 *illus.*
muskellunge 13:682
northern pike 12:168 *illus.*
PIKE (county in Georgia)
map (33° 5′N 84° 20′W) 9:114
PIKE (county in Illinois)
map (39° 36′N 90° 48′W) 11:42
PIKE (county in Indiana)
map (38° 25′N 87° 15′W) 11:111
PIKE (county in Kentucky)
map (37° 30′N 82° 20′W) 12:47
PIKE (county in Mississippi)
map (31° 10′N 90° 25′W) 13:469
PIKE (county in Missouri)
map (39° 21′N 91° 10′W) 13:476
PIKE (county in Ohio)
map (39° 5′N 83° 5′W) 14:357
PIKE (county in Pennsylvania)
map (41° 19′N 74° 48′W) 15:147
PIKE, JAMES ALBERT 15:301 *bibliog.*
PIKE, ROBERT L. (pseudonym) *see* FISH, ROBERT L.
PIKE, ZEBULON MONTGOMERY 15:301 *bibliog.*
exploration of the American west 19:445 *map*
Pikes Peak 15:301
PIKES PEAK 15:301
map (38° 51′N 105° 3′W) 5:116
PIKESVILLE (Maryland)
map (39° 23′N 76° 44′W) 13:188
PIKETON (Ohio)
map (39° 4′N 83° 1′W) 14:357
PIKEVILLE (Kentucky)
map (37° 29′N 82° 31′W) 12:47
PIKEVILLE (Tennessee)
map (35° 36′N 85° 11′W) 19:104
PIKUNI (American Indians)
Blackfoot 3:321
PIKWITANEI (Manitoba)
map (55° 35′N 97° 9′W) 13:119
PILA (Argentina)
map (36° 1′S 58° 8′W) 2:149
PIŁA (Poland)
map (53° 10′N 16° 44′E) 15:388
PILASTER
capital 4:123
PILATE, PONTIUS 15:301–302 *bibliog.*
PILES *see* HEMORRHOIDS
PILGRIM AT TINKER CREEK (book)
Dillard, Annie 6:176
PILGRIMAGE 15:302 *bibliog.*
Crusades 5:366–368
hajj 11:292 *illus.*
Mashhad (Iran) 13:196
Mecca (Saudi Arabia) 13:258–259 *illus.*
Montserrat (mountain) 13:560
Romanesque art and architecture 16:282 *illus.*
PILGRIMS (U.S.) 15:302 *bibliog.*, *illus.*
Alden, John 1:268
Bradford, William 3:437
Brewster, William 3:476
clambake 5:36
London Company 12:405
Mayflower 13:247
Plymouth (England) 15:374
Plymouth (Massachusetts) 15:374
Plymouth Colony 15:374
Puritans 15:630
Robinson, John 16:245
Samoset 17:47
Winslow, Edward 20:180
PILGRIM'S PROGRESS (book) 15:302 *bibliog.*
allegory 1:299
Bunyan, John 3:565
PILICA RIVER
map (51° 52′N 21° 17′E) 15:388
PILL BUG 15:303
isopod 11:300
soil organisms 18:39 *illus.*
PÍLLARO (Ecuador)
map (1° 10′S 78° 32′W) 7:52
PILLARS OF HERCULES (mythology)
Gibraltar 9:174
PILLBOX (military) *see* FORTIFICATION
PILLNITZ, DECLARATION OF
Leopold II, Holy Roman Emperor 12:295
PILLOMAYO RIVER
map (25° 21′S 57° 42′W) 2:149
PILLORY 15:303
PILNYAK, BORIS 15:303 *bibliog.*
PILO, CARL GUSTAF
The Coronation of Gustav III 17:112 *illus.*
PILON, GERMAIN
tomb of Henry II and Catherine de Médicis 19:231
PILOT (computer language) 5:160p
PILOT (navigation) 15:303
See also names of specific pilots, e.g., BORMAN, FRANK; CURTISS, GLENN HAMMOND; etc.
flight simulator 19:56 *illus.*
PILOT FISH 15:303
shark 17:244
PILOT GROVE (Missouri)
map (38° 53′N 92° 55′W) 13:476
PILOT KNOB (Missouri)
map (37° 38′N 90° 40′W) 13:476
PILOT MOUNTAIN (North Carolina)
map (36° 23′N 80° 28′W) 14:242
PILOT PEAK (Nevada)
map (38° 21′N 117° 58′W) 14:111
map (41° 2′N 114° 6′W) 14:111
PILOT POINT (Alaska)
map (57° 34′N 157° 35′W) 1:242
PILOT ROCK (Oregon)
map (45° 29′N 118° 50′W) 14:427
PIŁSUDSKI, JÓZEF 15:303 *bibliog.*
Poland 15:391
Polish-Soviet War 15:398
PILTDOWN MAN 15:303 *bibliog.*
Oakley, Kenneth 14:312
PIMA 15:303–304 *bibliog.*
Hohokam culture 10:199
Indians of North America, art of the 11:140
Indians of North America, music and dance of the 11:143
Kino, Eusebio Francisco 12:84–85
Papago 15:66
Yuma 20:346
PIMA (Arizona)
map (32° 54′N 109° 50′W) 2:160
PIMA (county in Arizona)
map (32° 0′N 111° 50′W) 2:160
PIMP
prostitution 15:573
PIMPERNEL 13:266 *illus.*; 15:304
PINAL (county in Arizona)
map (33° 15′N 109° 30′W) 2:160
PINANG (Malaysia) *see* PENANG (Malaysia)
PINAR DEL RÍO (Cuba)
map (22° 25′N 83° 42′W) 5:377
PINARDVILLE (New Hampshire)
map (42° 59′N 71° 33′W) 14:123
PIÑAS (Ecuador)
map (3° 42′S 79° 42′W) 7:52
PINCHBACK, PINCKNEY BENTON STEWART 15:304 *bibliog.*
PINCHER CREEK (Alberta)
map (49° 29′N 113° 57′W) 1:256
PINCHOT, GIFFORD 15:304 *bibliog.*
conservation 5:202
PINCKNEY (family) 15:304 *bibliog.*
PINCKNEY (Michigan)
map (42° 27′N 83° 57′W) 13:377
PINCKNEY, CHARLES
Pinckney (family) 15:304
PINCKNEY, HENRY LAURENS
Pinckney (family) 15:304
PINCKNEY, THOMAS
Pinckney (family) 15:304
PINCKNEY'S TREATY
Pinckney (family) 15:304
PINCKNEYVILLE (Illinois)
map (38° 5′N 89° 23′W) 11:42
PINDAR 15:304–305 *bibliog.*
Greek music 9:345
PINDAR (food) *see* PEANUT
PINDUS MOUNTAINS
map (39° 49′N 21° 14′E) 9:325
PINE 15:305 *bibliog.*, *illus.*
bristlecone pine 3:487
cedar 4:228
conifer 5:189–191
fir 8:99–100
hemlock 10:119
larch 12:206–207
lumber 12:456–457 *illus.*
needles 15:336 *illus.*
pine nut 15:306 *illus.*
pollen 15:406 *illus.*
seed cone 17:187
spruce 18:200–201 *illus.*
tamarack 19:18
turpentine tree 19:352
wood 20:205 *illus.*
PINE (county in Minnesota)
map (46° 5′N 92° 45′W) 13:453
PINE, AUSTRALIAN *see* *CASUARINA*
PINE, GROUND *see* CLUB MOSS
PINE, R.E.
David Garrick 9:50 *illus.*
PINE APPLE (Alabama)
map (31° 52′N 86° 59′W) 1:234
PINE BARRENS
map (39° 48′N 74° 35′W) 14:129
New Jersey 14:128; 14:130; 14:133
PINE BLUFF (Arkansas) 15:305
map (34° 13′N 92° 1′W) 2:166
PINE BLUFFS (Wyoming)
map (41° 11′N 104° 4′W) 20:301
PINE CASTLE (Florida)
map (28° 28′N 81° 22′W) 8:172
PINE CITY (Minnesota)
map (45° 50′N 92° 59′W) 13:453
PINE CONE *see* POLLEN CONE; SEED CONE
PINE CREEK
map (41° 10′N 77° 16′W) 15:147
PINE GROVE (Pennsylvania)
map (40° 33′N 76° 23′W) 15:147
PINE HILL (Alabama)
map (31° 59′N 87° 35′W) 1:234
PINE HILL (New Jersey)
map (39° 47′N 74° 59′W) 14:129
PINE MOUNTAIN
map (36° 55′N 83° 20′W) 12:47
PINE NUT 15:305–306 *illus.*
PINE POINT (Northwest Territories)
map (61° 1′N 114° 15′W) 14:258
PINE RIDGE (South Dakota)
map (43° 2′N 102° 33′W) 18:103
PINE RIVER (Manitoba)
map (51° 47′N 100° 32′W) 13:119
PINE RIVER (Michigan)
map (44° 15′N 85° 55′W) 13:377
PINE RIVER (Minnesota)
map (46° 43′N 94° 24′W) 13:453
PINEAL GLAND 15:306
PINEAPPLE 8:348 *illus.*; 15:306 *bibliog.*, *illus.*
bromeliad 3:501
Colombia 18:94 *illus.*
Hawaii (state) 10:75 *illus.*
Spanish moss 18:161
PINECONE FISH 15:306–307 *illus.*
PINEDA, ALONSO DE
Corpus Christi (Texas) 5:275
exploration of colonial America 19:437 *map*
PINEDA, ÁLVAREZ DE
de Soto, Hernando 6:63
PINEDALE (Wyoming)
map (42° 52′N 109° 52′W) 20:301
PINEHOUSE LAKE (Saskatchewan)
map (55° 31′N 106° 36′W) 17:81
PINEHURST (Massachusetts)
map (42° 32′N 71° 14′W) 3:409
PINEL, PHILIPPE 15:599 *illus.*
PINELLAS (county in Florida)
map (27° 53′N 82° 43′W) 8:172
PINELLAS PARK (Florida)
map (27° 51′N 82° 43′W) 8:172
PINERO, SIR ARTHUR WING 15:307 *bibliog.*
PINEROLO (Italy)
map (44° 53′N 7° 21′E) 11:321
PINES, ISLE OF *see* ISLE OF PINES
PINEVILLE (Kentucky)
map (36° 46′N 83° 42′W) 12:47
PINEVILLE (Louisiana)
map (31° 19′N 92° 26′W) 12:430
PINEVILLE (Missouri)
map (36° 36′N 94° 23′W) 13:476
PINEVILLE (North Carolina)
map (35° 5′N 80° 53′W) 14:242
PINEVILLE (West Virginia)
map (37° 35′N 81° 32′W) 20:111
PINEWOOD (South Carolina)
map (33° 44′N 80° 27′W) 18:98
PINEY WOODS (Mississippi) 13:472 *illus.*
map (32° 3′N 89° 58′W) 13:469
PING PONG *see* TABLE TENNIS
PING RIVER
map (15° 42′N 100° 9′E) 19:139
P'ING-TUNG (Taiwan)
map (22° 40′N 120° 29′E) 19:13
P'ING-YANG, BATTLE OF 17:323 *illus.*
PINK (botany) 15:307
baby's breath 3:9
campion 4:67
carnation 4:154
chickweed 4:346
soapwort 18:8
sweet William 18:388
PINKERTON, ALLAN 15:307 *bibliog.*
PINKERTON DETECTIVE AGENCY
outlaws 14:469
Pinkerton, Allan 15:307
PINKEYE *see* CONJUNCTIVITIS
PINKHAM, LYDIA 15:307 *bibliog.*
PINKIANG (China) *see* HARBIN (China)
PINKNEY, WILLIAM
Monroe, James 13:541
PINKOWSKI, JÓZEF
Poland 15:390
PINNIPED 15:307 *bibliog.*
seal 17:173–174
PINO, PAOLO
eclecticism 7:40
PINOCCHIO (fictional character) 15:307
Collodi, Carlo 5:104
PINOCHET UGARTE, AUGUSTO 15:307
Chile 4:356–357
PINOCHLE 15:307–308 *bibliog.*
PIÑON *see* PINE NUT
PINSK MARSHES (USSR) *see* PRIPET MARSHES (USSR)
PINSKI, DAVID
Yiddish theater 20:328
PINSON (Alabama)
map (33° 41′N 86° 41′W) 1:234
PINT (measurement)
weights and measures 20:93 *table*, *table*
PINTA (ship)
Pinzón, Martín Alonso 15:309
PINTER, HAROLD 15:308 *bibliog.*
Caretaker, The 4:146
Losey, Joseph 12:418
PINTO (horse) 10:243 *illus.*; 15:308 *illus.*
PINTO BALSEMÃO, FRANCISCO
Portugal, history of 15:455
PINTORICCHIO 15:308
The Disputation of Saint Catherine 19:527 *illus.*
Sistine Chapel 17:329
PINWORM 15:308
PINYIN SYSTEM (Chinese language)
Sino-Tibetan languages 17:325
PINZA, EZIO 15:308
PINZÓN, FRANCISCO MARTÍN
Pinzón, Martín Alonso 15:309
PINZÓN, MARTÍN ALONSO 15:309 *bibliog.*
PINZÓN, VICENTE YÁÑEZ
Pinzón, Martín Alonso 15:309
PIOCHE (Nevada)
map (37° 56′N 114° 27′W) 14:111
PIOMBINO (Italy)
map (42° 55′N 10° 32′E) 11:321
PIOMBO, SEBASTIANO DEL *see* SEBASTIANO DEL PIOMBO
PION
fundamental particles 8:362 *table*
meson 13:315
PIONEER (Ohio)
map (41° 41′N 84° 33′W) 14:357
PIONEER (spacecraft) 15:309–310 *bibliog.*, *illus.*
Jupiter (planet) 11:472
life, extraterrestrial 12:329
missions program 15:309–310
satellite, artificial 15:309–310
SNAP 17:383–384
space exploration 15:309–310; 18:125; 18:126 *illus.*
Venus (planet) 19:547
PIONEER MOUNTAINS
map (45° 40′N 113° 0′W) 13:547
PIONEERS *see* FRONTIER

PIONEERS, THE (book) *see* *LEATHERSTOCKING TALES, THE* (books)
PIOTRKÓW TRYBUNALSKI (Poland)
map (51° 25′N 19° 42′E) **15**:388
PIPE, TOBACCO **15**:310 *bibliog.*
brier **3**:485
heath **10**:99
meerschaum **13**:278
peace pipe **15**:123
tobacco **19**:218–219
PIPE ORGAN *see* ORGAN (musical instrument)
PIPE AND PIPELINE **15**:310–311 *bibliog., illus.*
ancient and modern use **15**:310–311
Canada **4**:79
construction materials **15**:310–311
energy transportation **15**:310
flowmeter **8**:184
petroleum industry **15**:210–213
pipe laying **15**:311
periods of construction **15**:311
pipelines
Middle East **15**:311
North and South America **15**:311
plumbing **15**:371 *illus.*
specifications and standards **15**:310–311
testing of
ultrasonics **19**:378 *illus.*
Trans-Alaska Pipeline **19**:266–267
transportation **19**:280
PIPE SNAKE **17**:377 *illus.*
PIPEFISH **8**:116 *illus.*; **15**:311–312
PIPER CUB (aircraft) **15**:312 *bibliog.*
PIPESTONE (Minnesota)
map (43° 58′N 96° 19′W) **13**:453
PIPESTONE (county in Minnesota)
map (44° 0′N 96° 16′W) **13**:453
PIPIL (American Indians)
El Salvador **7**:100
PIPIT **15**:312 *illus.*
PIPMOUACANE RESERVOIR
map (49° 40′N 70° 20′W) **16**:18
PIPPIN, HORACE **15**:312 *bibliog.*
PIPSISSEWA **15**:312
PIQUA (American Indians)
Shawnee (American Indians) **17**:246
PIQUA (Ohio)
map (40° 9′N 84° 15′W) **14**:357
PIR PANJAL RANGE (Mountain Range)
map (33° 0′N 75° 0′E) **11**:80
PIRACICABA (Brazil)
map (22° 43′S 47° 38′W) **3**:460
PIRACY **15**:312–313 *bibliog., illus.*
Barbary States **3**:76; **19**:303 *illus.*
Blackbeard **3**:319
Dampier, William **6**:19
decline **15**:313
Dutch West India Company **6**:315
Kidd, Captain **12**:70
Morgan, Sir Henry **13**:578
privateering **15**:557–558
Tripolitan War **19**:302–303
PIRAEUS (Greece) **15**:314
harbor and port **10**:42
map (37° 57′N 23° 38′E) **9**:325
PIRANDELLO, LUIGI **15**:314 *bibliog., illus.*
drama **6**:261
Six Characters in Search of an Author **17**:331
PIRANESI, GIOVANNI BATTISTA **15**:314–315 *bibliog., illus.*
graphic arts **9**:292
Prison **15**:314 *illus.*
PIRANHA **4**:286 *illus.*; **8**:117 *illus.*; **15**:315 *bibliog., illus.*
PIRATE PERCH **15**:315
PIRATES *see* PIRACY; names of specific pirates, e.g., BLACKBEARD; KIDD, CAPTAIN; etc.
PIRENNE, HENRI **15**:315 *bibliog.*
PIRENNE THESIS
Pirenne, Henri **15**:315
PIRITHOUS **15**:315
PIRMASSENS (Germany, East and West)
map (49° 12′N 7° 36′E) **9**:140
PIRNA (Germany, East and West)
map (50° 58′N 13° 56′E) **9**:140
PIROT (Yugoslavia)
map (43° 9′N 22° 35′E) **20**:340
PIROVANO (Argentina)
map (36° 30′S 61° 34′W) **2**:149
PISA (Italy) **15**:315
cathedral **16**:284 *illus.*
campanile **4**:65
cathedrals and churches **4**:205
Giunta Pisano **9**:192
Italian art and architecture **11**:308–314
Leaning Tower **11**:308 *illus.*
map (43° 43′N 10° 23′E) **11**:321
Pisano, Nicola and Giovanni **15**:316
PISA, COUNCIL OF **15**:315
Schism, Great **17**:122
PISAGUA (Chile)
map (19° 36′S 70° 13′W) **4**:355
PISANELLO, ANTONIO **15**:316 *bibliog.*
PISANO, ANDREA **15**:316 *bibliog.*
PISANO, GIUNTA *see* GIUNTA PISANO
PISANO, LEONARDO *see* LEONARDO PISANO
PISANO, NICOLA AND GIOVANNI **15**:316 *bibliog., illus.*
Italian art and architecture **11**:310
pulpit **15**:316 *illus.*; **17**:163 *illus.*
PISCATAQUIS (county in Maine)
map (45° 45′N 69° 15′W) **13**:70
PISCATAQUOG RIVER
map (42° 58′N 71° 28′W) **14**:123
PISCATAWAY (New Jersey)
map (40° 34′N 74° 27′W) **14**:129
PISCATOR, ERWIN **15**:316 *bibliog.*
epic theater **7**:217–218
theater of fact **19**:153
PISCES **15**:317
PISCO (Peru)
map (13° 42′S 76° 13′W) **15**:193
PISHPEK (USSR) *see* FRUNZE (USSR)
PISINEMO (Arizona)
map (32° 2′N 112° 19′W) **2**:160
PISSARRO, CAMILLE **15**:317 *bibliog., illus.*
Boulevard Montmartre **11**:64 *illus.*
Gauguin, Paul **9**:60
Red Roofs **15**:317 *illus.*
PISTACHIO **15**:317 *bibliog., illus.*
PISTOIA (Italy) **15**:317
PISTOL **8**:105 *illus.*; **15**:317–318 *bibliog., illus.*
Darling pepperbox **16**:190 *illus.*
derringer **6**:123
Gatling, Richard Jordan **9**:58
history **15**:318
Pistoia (Italy) **15**:317
revolver **16**:189–190
shooting **17**:282 *illus.*
types **15**:318 *illus.*
PISTON
pump **15**:622–623 *illus.*
Stirling engine **18**:272–273
PISTON, WALTER **15**:319 *bibliog.*
PIT RIVER
map (40° 45′N 122° 22′W) **4**:31
"PIT AND THE PENDULUM, THE" (short story) **15**:319
PIT VIPER **15**:319 *bibliog., illus.*; **17**:379 *illus.*
bushmaster **3**:585
copperhead **5**:254
fer-de-lance **8**:51
rattlesnake **16**:93
water moccasin **20**:49
PITALITO (Colombia)
map (1° 51′N 76° 2′W) **5**:107
PITCAIRN ISLAND **15**:319–320 *map*
map (25° 4′S 130° 6′W) **14**:334
PITCH (music) **15**:320 *bibliog.*
bent pitches
blues **3**:345
key **12**:62
melody **13**:288
musical notation and terms **13**:679
octave **14**:347
serial music **17**:208
staff **18**:209
treble **19**:286
PITCHBLEND *see* URANIUM MINERALS
PITCHER, MOLLY *see* MOLLY PITCHER
PITCHER PLANT
carnivorous plants **4**:157–158 *illus.*
PITCHSTONE **15**:320
formation **15**:320
PITEÅ (Sweden)
map (65° 20′N 21° 30′E) **18**:382
PITEÅ RIVER
map (65° 14′N 21° 32′E) **18**:382
PITEȘTI (Romania)
map (44° 52′N 24° 52′E) **16**:288
PITHECANTHROPUS ERECTUS *see* *HOMO ERECTUS*
PITKIN (county in Colorado)
map (39° 15′N 106° 50′W) **5**:116
PITMAN (New Jersey)
map (39° 44′N 75° 8′W) **14**:129
PITMAN, SIR ISAAC
shorthand **17**:284
PITT (county in North Carolina)
map (35° 35′N 77° 25′W) **14**:242
PITT, WILLIAM (the Elder) **15**:320 *bibliog., illus.*
French and Indian Wars **8**:314
PITT, WILLIAM (the Younger) **15**:320–321 *bibliog., illus.*
Great Britain, history of **9**:317
PITT ISLAND
map (53° 35′N 129° 45′W) **3**:491
PITT RIVERS, AUGUSTUS HENRY LANE-FOX **2**:124 *illus.*; **15**:321
archaeology **2**:124
PITTA (bird) **15**:321
PITTI PALACE **15**:321 *bibliog.*
Florence (Italy) **8**:168–169 *map*
landscape architecture **12**:185
PITTOSPORUM **15**:321
PITTS, WALTER
automata, theory of **2**:357
PITTSBORO (Mississippi)
map (33° 56′N 89° 20′W) **13**:469
PITTSBORO (North Carolina)
map (35° 43′N 79° 11′W) **14**:242
PITTSBURG (California)
map (38° 2′N 121° 53′W) **4**:31
PITTSBURG (Kansas)
map (37° 25′N 94° 42′W) **12**:18
PITTSBURG (county in Oklahoma)
map (34° 55′N 95° 45′W) **14**:368
PITTSBURG (Texas)
map (33° 0′N 94° 58′W) **19**:129
PITTSBURG LANDING, BATTLE OF *see* SHILOH, BATTLE OF
PITTSBURGH (Pennsylvania) **15**:148 *illus.*; **15**:321 *bibliog.*
Fort Duquesne **8**:236
map (40° 26′N 80° 0′W) **15**:147
PITTSBURGH SYMPHONY ORCHESTRA **15**:322
Steinberg, William **18**:248
PITTSFIELD (Illinois)
map (39° 36′N 90° 48′W) **11**:42
PITTSFIELD (Maine)
map (44° 47′N 69° 23′W) **13**:70
PITTSFIELD (Massachusetts) **15**:322
map (42° 27′N 73° 15′W) **13**:206
PITTSFIELD (New Hampshire)
map (43° 18′N 71° 19′W) **14**:123
PITTSTON (Pennsylvania)
map (41° 19′N 75° 47′W) **15**:147
PITTSYLVANIA (county in Virginia)
map (36° 50′N 79° 25′W) **19**:607
PITUITARY GLAND **3**:444 *illus.*; **7**:169 *illus.*; **15**:322 *bibliog.*
endocrine system **7**:168–169 *illus.*
endocrine system, diseases of the **7**:169–170
hormones **15**:322
adrenocorticotropic hormone **1**:109
antidiuretic hormone **2**:61
fertility, human **8**:60
gonadotropin **9**:242
growth hormone **9**:381
prolactin **15**:567
sex hormones **17**:226
thyroid gland **19**:188
PITZER COLLEGE
Claremont Colleges **5**:36
PIURA (Peru)
map (5° 12′S 80° 38′W) **15**:193
PIUS II, POPE **15**:322 *bibliog.*
PIUS IV, POPE **15**:322
PIUS V, POPE **15**:322 *bibliog.*
PIUS VI, POPE **15**:322 *bibliog.*
PIUS VII, POPE **15**:322–323 *bibliog.*
Fontainebleau (France) **8**:205
PIUS IX, POPE **15**:323 *bibliog.*
Civil War, U.S. **5**:32
Lourdes (France) **12**:436
PIUS X, POPE **15**:323 *bibliog.*
modernism **13**:498
PIUS XI, POPE **15**:323–324 *bibliog., illus.*
PIUS XII, POPE **15**:324 *bibliog.*
PIUTE (county in Utah)
map (38° 17′N 112° 5′W) **19**:492
PIXAR SYSTEM (film technology) **4**:433
PIXEL (electronics)
camera **4**:59
computer **5**:160i
computer graphics **5**:160m
digital technology **6**:175
input-output devices **11**:182
PIZARRO, FRANCISCO **15**:324–325 *bibliog., illus., map*
Almagro, Diego de **1**:306
Atahualpa **2**:287
Callao (Peru) **4**:40
exploration **7**:336–337 *map*
Inca **11**:71
Lima (Peru) **12**:342
PIZI *see* GALL (Sioux warrior)
PIZZETTI, ILDEBRANDO **15**:325 *bibliog.*
PJÓRSÁ RIVER
map (63° 47′N 20° 48′W) **11**:17
PK *see* PSYCHOKINESIS
PL/1 (computer language) **5**:160p
PLACE VENDÔME
Hardouin-Mansart, Jules **10**:47
PLACEBO **15**:325
drug **6**:278
PLACENTA **7**:153 *illus.*; **15**:502–503 *illus.*
development **6**:140 *illus.*; **6**:141
endocrine system **7**:169
eutherian **7**:311
gestation **9**:160
obstetrics **14**:319
pregnancy and birth **15**:502–503; **15**:506
umbilical cord **19**:380
PLACENTIA (Newfoundland)
map (47° 14′N 53° 58′W) **14**:166
PLACENTIA BAY
map (47° 15′N 54° 30′W) **14**:166
PLACER (county in California)
map (38° 54′N 121° 4′W) **4**:31
PLACER DEPOSIT **15**:325 *bibliog.*
gold rush **9**:228
mineral **13**:444
oceanic mineral resources **14**:340
ore deposits **14**:422
rutile **16**:376
sand **17**:59
PLACERVILLE (California)
map (38° 43′N 120° 48′W) **4**:31
PLACETAS (Cuba)
map (22° 19′N 79° 40′W) **5**:377
PLACID, LAKE **15**:325
map (44° 17′N 73° 59′W) **14**:149
PLACODERM *see* ARTHRODIRE
PLAGE **15**:325
PLAGIOCLASE
feldspar **8**:46–47 *illus.*
latite **12**:234
PLAGIOTROPISM
tropism **19**:310
PLAGUE *see* BUBONIC PLAGUE
PLAGUE, THE (book) **15**:325
Camus, Albert **4**:68
PLAICE **15**:325 *illus.*
PLAID
tartan **19**:40–41 *illus.*
PLAID CYMRU (political party)
United Kingdom **19**:411
PLAIDY, JEAN (pseudonym) *see* HOLT, VICTORIA
PLAIN CITY (Utah)
map (41° 18′N 112° 6′W) **19**:492
PLAIN DEALING (Louisiana)
map (32° 54′N 93° 42′W) **12**:430
PLAIN FOLK *see* PENNSYLVANIA DUTCH
PLAINFIELD (Connecticut)
map (41° 41′N 71° 55′W) **5**:193
PLAINFIELD (Indiana)
map (39° 42′N 86° 24′W) **11**:111
PLAINFIELD (New Jersey)
map (40° 37′N 74° 26′W) **14**:129
PLAINFIELD (Wisconsin)
map (44° 13′N 89° 30′W) **20**:185
PLAINS (Georgia)
map (32° 2′N 84° 24′W) **9**:114
PLAINS (Kansas)
map (37° 16′N 100° 35′W) **12**:18
PLAINS (Montana)
map (47° 27′N 114° 53′W) **13**:547
PLAINS (Texas)
map (33° 11′N 102° 50′W) **19**:129
PLAINS OF ABRAHAM, BATTLE OF THE **4**:81 *illus.*
PLAINS INDIANS
Indians, American **11**:129–130 *illus.*
PLAINSONG **15**:325–326 *bibliog.*
See also CHANT
antiphon **2**:65
Byzantine music **3**:608
cantus firmus **4**:118
choral music **4**:406
Dies irae **6**:163
English music **7**:202
French music **8**:320
medieval music **13**:274 *illus.*
musical notation and terms **13**:679
recitative **16**:107–108
tone **19**:233
PLAINTIFF
attachment **2**:313
legal procedure **12**:272–273
trial **19**:291–292
PLAINVIEW (Arkansas)
map (34° 60′N 93° 18′W) **2**:166
PLAINVIEW (Minnesota)
map (44° 10′N 92° 10′W) **13**:453
PLAINVIEW (Nebraska)
map (42° 21′N 97° 47′W) **14**:70
PLAINVIEW (Texas)
map (34° 11′N 101° 43′W) **19**:129
PLAINVILLE (Connecticut)
map (41° 41′N 72° 51′W) **5**:193
PLAINVILLE (Indiana)
map (38° 48′N 87° 9′W) **11**:111

PLAINVILLE (Kansas)
map (39° 14′N 99° 18′W) **12**:18
PLAINVILLE (Massachusetts)
map (42° 0′N 71° 20′W) **13**:206
PLAINWELL (Michigan)
map (42° 27′N 85° 38′W) **13**:377
PLAISTOW (New Hampshire)
map (42° 50′N 71° 6′W) **14**:123
PLAMONDON, ANTOINE
Canadian art and architecture **4**:89
PLANA DES LLES PEAK
map (42° 28′N 1° 40′E) **1**:405
PLANARIA **15**:326 *bibliog.*
PLANCK, MAX **15**:286 *illus.*; **15**:326–327 *bibliog.*, *illus.*
blackbody radiation **3**:321
Max Planck Institute for Coal Research
Ziegler, Karl **20**:363
Max Planck Society for the Advancement of Science **13**:238–239
Planck's constant **15**:327
quantum mechanics **15**:326; **16**:9
PLANCK'S CONSTANT **15**:327
atomic constants **2**:308
measurements
Josephson effect, superconductivity **18**:350
Planck, Max **15**:326–327
uncertainty principle **19**:381
PLANE (carpentry) **15**:327 *illus.*
PLANE (mathematics) **15**:327
coordinate systems (mathematics) **5**:246–247
curve **5**:396
equation of, analytic geometry **1**:391
parallel **15**:79
plane analytic geometry **1**:390–391
plane figure **15**:327
quadrilateral plane figure **16**:5
plane geometry **15**:327
polygon **15**:419
projective geometry **15**:565
spiral **18**:188
tangent **19**:22
undefined terms **15**:327
PLANE (metalwork)
machine tools **13**:24–25
PLANE (vehicle) *see* AIRCRAFT
PLANE TREE **15**:327–328 *illus.*
PLANETA RICA (Colombia)
map (8° 25′N 75° 36′W) **5**:107
PLANETARIUM **15**:328–329 *bibliog.*, *illus.*
projector **15**:566
PLANETARY NEBULA **15**:329 *bibliog.*
extragalactic systems **7**:341
PLANETARY PHYSICS
Libby, Willard Frank **12**:311
PLANETARY SYSTEMS **2**:282–283 *illus.*; **15**:329 *bibliog.*
astrogeology **2**:270
astronomy, history of **2**:278–279
Battani, al- **3**:125
Bode, Johann Elert **3**:355
Brahe, Tycho **3**:439–440
Brouwer, Dirk **3**:513
Cassini (family) **4**:184
celestial mechanics **4**:230
Chandrasekhar, Subrahmanyan **4**:280
conjunction **5**:191
distance, astronomical **6**:199
Titius-Bode law **19**:213
double-planet system
planets **15**:329
interstellar matter **11**:225–228
Kepler's laws **12**:58 *illus.*
Kowal, Charles T. **12**:126
Kuiper, Gerard **12**:135
Leverrier, Urbain Jean Joseph **12**:303
life, extraterrestrial **12**:328
magnetosphere **13**:59–60
Mars (spacecraft) **13**:169–170
Newcomb, Simon **14**:165
nutation **14**:301
Phobos **15**:249
planets **15**:329–331
radar astronomy **16**:40
Roche's limit **16**:247
Sagan, Carl Edward **17**:11
satellite **17**:84–85
Slipher, Vesto Melvin **17**:362
solar system **18**:44–53
space exploration **18**:123
Titan (astronomy) **19**:210
van de Kamp, Peter **19**:512
PLANETOID *see* ASTEROID
PLANETS **15**:329–331 *bibliog.*, *illus.*; **18**:47 *illus.*
albedo **1**:252
asteroid **2**:268
astrology **2**:271–273
atmosphere
Herzberg, Gerhard **10**:150
brown dwarf **3**:516
celestial mechanics **4**:230
characteristics **18**:46 *table*
distance, astronomical **6**:199
distance from sun
Titius-Bode law **19**:213
double planet **15**:329–331
Earth, geological history of **7**:11–15
Earth, geomagnetic field of **7**:15–17
Earth, gravitational field of **7**:17
Earth, heat flow in **7**:17–18
Earth, motions of **7**:18–19
Earth, size and shape of **7**:19
Earth, structure and composition of **7**:19–23
energy source **15**:330
ephemeris **7**:216
geologic evolution **15**:330–331
gravitation, escape velocity **7**:236–237 *table*
Halley, Edmond **10**:22–23
Jupiter (planet) **11**:471–474
Kepler, Johannes **12**:57–58
life, extraterrestrial **12**:327–329
Mars (planet) **13**:166–169
Mercury **13**:305–306
meteorite craters **13**:337–339
mineral **13**:444
minor planets **15**:329
motion **18**:45 *illus.*
Neptune (planet) **14**:88–89
orbits **15**:329–330
outer planets **15**:330–331
Peurbach, Georg von **15**:216
Pickering, William Henry **15**:293
Pioneer **15**:309
planetary systems **15**:329
Pluto **15**:372–373
precession of the equinoxes **15**:493
radar astronomy **16**:40
radio astronomy **16**:48–49
satellites **17**:84–85; **18**:49–50
Saturn (astronomy) **17**:88–91
solar system **15**:330 *illus.*; **18**:46–53 *illus.*
terrestrial planets **15**:329–330
Uranus (astronomy) **19**:478–479
Venus (planet) **19**:546–548
PLANETS, THE (musical composition)
Holst, Gustav **10**:208 *illus.*
PLANING *see* SURFING; WATERSKIING
PLANKINTON (South Dakota)
map (43° 43′N 98° 29′W) **18**:103
PLANKTON **15**:331–333 *bibliog.*, *illus.*
See also PHYTOPLANKTON
chiton **4**:399
desmid **6**:132
diatom **6**:154
nekton **14**:79
oceanic zones
epipelagic zone **7**:220
pelagic zone **15**:137
oceanography **14**:345
zooplankton **20**:378
PLANNED CITIES *see* NEW TOWNS; URBAN PLANNING
PLANNED PARENTHOOD *see* BIRTH CONTROL
PLANNED PARENTHOOD FEDERATION OF AMERICA **15**:333
birth control **3**:294
PLANO (Illinois)
map (41° 40′N 88° 32′W) **11**:42
PLANO (Texas)
map (33° 1′N 96° 42′W) **19**:129
PLANT (botany) **15**:333–342 *bibliog.*, *illus.*, *table*
See also DISEASES, PLANT; MEDICINAL PLANTS; PLANT BREEDING; PLANT DISTRIBUTION; PLANT PROPAGATION; PLANT SUCCESSION; POISONOUS PLANTS AND ANIMALS; names of specific plants, e.g., FUNGI; GINKGO; POINSETTIA; etc.
aging **1**:185
alkaloid **1**:296
aquatic
lake (body of water) **12**:168 *illus.*
Lithothamnion **12**:371
Triassic Period **19**:294
botanical garden **3**:412
botany **3**:412–414
carbohydrate **4**:132–133
carbon cycle (atmosphere) **4**:136
chloroplast **4**:402
classification, biological **5**:43; **15**:333–334 *table*; **15**:340 *table*
coloration, biological **5**:121–122
current research **15**:341–342
ecology **7**:42–46
evolution **7**:318–325; **15**:334–335 *illus.*
fossil record **8**:243–248; **15**:333–335
Carboniferous Period **4**:138
Cretaceous Period **5**:341
Devonian Period **6**:145–146
Jurassic Period **11**:475–477
paleobotany **15**:30–32
Permian Period **15**:174 *illus.*
Tertiary Period **19**:124–125
Triassic Period **19**:294–295
function **15**:335–337
genetics **9**:90
Burbank, Luther **3**:566
Mendel, Gregor Johann **13**:294
glycoside **9**:212
growth and development **9**:378; **9**:381; **15**:339–340 *illus.*
Darwin, Sir Francis **6**:42
time-lapse photography **15**:265
habitat **10**:4–6
chaparral **4**:284
desert life **6**:129–131
forest **8**:227–230
grasslands **9**:299–301
intertidal life **11**:229–230
jungle and rain forest **11**:469
mountain life **13**:622
savanna life **17**:97–99
steppe life **18**:256–257
swamp, marsh, and bog **18**:376–378
taiga climate **19**:11
tundra **19**:332–333
hormones *see* HORMONE, PLANT
leaf **15**:336–337 *illus.*
cell **15**:276 *illus.*
tree **19**:287
life span **12**:330 *table*
metabolism **13**:326–327
dormancy **6**:242–243
etiolation **7**:258
germination **9**:157
guttation **9**:410
potassium **15**:465
starch **13**:327; **18**:226
nitrogen cycle **14**:203 *illus.*
Rhizobium **16**:196
nutrient cycles **14**:304
perfume **15**:164
photosynthesis **15**:275–277
chlorophyll **4**:401–402
Hales, Stephen **10**:19
photic zone **15**:257
Vries, Hugo De **19**:639
Willstätter, Richard **20**:163
population biology **15**:438
protoplasm
Mohl, Hugo von **13**:503
radiation injury **16**:42
remains, peat **15**:129
reproduction *see* REPRODUCTION, PLANT
roles **15**:340–341
sacred plants
bo tree **3**:348
hallucinogens **10**:24
structure **15**:335–337 *illus.*
bark **3**:82; **19**:287
cellulose **4**:238
cotyledon **5**:307–308
flower **15**:336–337
fruit **15**:337 *illus.*
pollen **15**:406–407
pollen cone **15**:407
root **15**:335–336 *illus.*; **19**:287–288
sap **17**:72
seed **17**:186–187
seed cone **17**:187
shoot **17**:282
stem **15**:333–336 *illus.*
stomata **18**:280
taproot **19**:29–30
tendril **19**:101
tuber **19**:326
vine **19**:600
wood **20**:205–206
tropism **19**:309–310 *illus.*
types **15**:333–335
angiosperm **1**:414
deciduous plant **6**:73
epiphyte **7**:220
evergreen **7**:316
everlasting **7**:316
gymnosperm **9**:414
herbaceous plant **10**:134
houseplants **10**:274–276
Protozoa **15**:579–581
pteridophyte **15**:606
spermatophyte **18**:179
tracheophyte **19**:258
vine **19**:600
PLANT (industrial) *see* FACTORY SYSTEM
PLANT, HENRY B.
Florida **8**:176
PLANT, ROBERT **16**:249 *illus.*
PLANT, WOODY
bark **3**:82 *illus.*
sapwood **17**:74
shrub **17**:288–289
tree **19**:286–288
wood **20**:205–206
PLANT BREEDING **15**:342–343 *bibliog.*, *illus.*
agriculture and the food supply **1**:198
Borlaug, Norman Ernest **3**:401
Burbank, Luther **3**:566
cloning **5**:64
flower **9**:87 *illus.*
gene bank **9**:76
genetic engineering **9**:84
genetics **9**:90
grass **9**:295
green revolution **9**:348–349
horticulture **10**:254–255
hybrid **10**:328
Mendel, Gregor Johann **13**:294
reproduction **16**:162
tulip **8**:170 *illus.*
PLANT CITY (Florida)
map (28° 1′N 82° 8′W) **8**:172
PLANT DISTRIBUTION **15**:340–341 *illus.*; **15**:343–344 *bibliog.*, *map*
chaparral **4**:283–284
desert life **6**:129–131
fruits and fruit cultivation **8**:349
grain **9**:281
grasslands **9**:299–301
semiarid climate **17**:195
tree **19**:288
weathering **20**:82
PLANT HOPPER (insect) **15**:345 *illus.*
PLANT HORMONES *see* HORMONE, PLANT
PLANT PRODUCTION *see* PLANT BREEDING; PLANT PROPAGATION; REPRODUCTION, PLANT
PLANT PROPAGATION **15**:345 *bibliog.*
See also PLANT BREEDING
African prehistory **1**:173–174
cloning **5**:64
fern **8**:57
fruits and fruit cultivation **8**:347
gibberellins **9**:172
grafting **9**:278–279
horticulture **10**:254–255
houseplants **10**:274
reproduction **16**:162
seed propagation **15**:345
vegetative propagation **15**:345
PLANT SUCCESSION **15**:340 *illus.*
chaparral **4**:284
PLANTAGENET *see* ANGEVINS (dynasties)
PLANTAGO **15**:345
PLANTAIN (banana)
banana **3**:59–60
PLANTAIN (herb)
Plantago **15**:345
PLANTATION
agriculture, history of **1**:191–192
Alabama **1**:235 *illus.*
Louisiana **12**:433 *illus.*
Mississippi **13**:471 *illus.*
Natchez (Mississippi) **14**:26
PLANTATION (Florida)
map (26° 5′N 80° 14′W) **8**:172
PLANTATION WALKING HORSE *see* TENNESSEE WALKING HORSE
PLANTERSVILLE (Alabama)
map (32° 40′N 86° 55′W) **1**:234
PLANTERSVILLE (Mississippi)
map (34° 12′N 88° 40′W) **13**:469
PLANTSITE (Arizona)
map (33° 2′N 109° 21′W) **2**:160
PLANTSVILLE (Connecticut)
map (41° 35′N 72° 54′W) **5**:193
PLANULA *see* LARVA
PLAQUE, DENTAL
dentistry **6**:116
teeth **19**:72
PLAQUEMINE (Louisiana)
map (30° 17′N 91° 14′W) **12**:430
PLAQUEMINES (county in Louisiana)
map (29° 30′N 89° 45′W) **12**:430
PLASENCIA (Spain)
map (40° 2′N 6° 5′W) **18**:140
PLASMA, BLOOD **3**:336 *illus.*
blood **3**:337
blood bank **3**:338
blood transfusion **3**:339

PLASMA, BLOOD (cont.)
complementary: Bordet, Jules **3**:398
multiple myeloma **13**:638
serum **17**:210
PLASMA PHYSICS **15**:345–347 *bibliog.*
Alfvén, Hannes **1**:280
Debye, Peter **6**:72
fusion energy **8**:382–383
Landau, Lev **12**:181
magnetic bottle **13**:55
magnetohydrodynamics **13**:59
Sun **18**:341
PLASMA SHEET
magnetosphere **13**:60
PLASMASPHERE
magnetosphere **13**:60
PLASMID **15**:347 *bibliog.*
bacteria **3**:18
genetic engineering **9**:84–85 *illus.*
heredity **10**:141
PLASMODIOPHORE **15**:347
PLASMODIUM **15**:347; **15**:579 *illus.*; **17**:362 *illus.*
malaria **13**:80
slime mold **17**:362
PLASSEY, BATTLE OF
India, history of **11**:92
PLASTER ROCK (New Brunswick)
map (46° 54′N 67° 24′W) **14**:117
PLASTERING
plaster of Paris, calcium **4**:22
PLASTIC SURGERY **15**:347 *bibliog.*
sex change **17**:225
PLASTICS **15**:347–351 *bibliog., illus., table*
benzene **3**:206
casein **4**:181
casting **4**:188
celluloid **4**:238
cellulose **4**:238
characteristics **15**:348
contact lens **5**:226
epoxy resins **7**:222
explosives **7**:339
extrusion **7**:346–347
foams **15**:350–351
ladder polymers **15**:350
leather and hides **12**:263
materials technology **13**:219–221
organic chemistry **14**:439
packaging **15**:11–12
petrochemicals **15**:205–206
polyester **15**:418–419
polymerization **15**:348; **15**:420
printing, rotogravure **16**:323
production, chemical industry **4**:319 *table*
refractory materials **16**:124
ring structures **15**:350
roof and roofing **16**:306
Teflon **19**:72
thermoplastics **15**:348–350
injection molding **15**:349 *illus.*
thermosets **15**:350
vinyl **19**:601
PLASTOQUINONE
photosynthesis **15**:277
PLATA, RÍO DE LA *see* RÍO DE LA PLATA
PLATAEA **15**:351
PLATE TECTONICS **15**:351–357 *bibliog., illus., maps*
Asia, geology **2**:236
continents **15**:351–356
continental drift **5**:228–229 *illus., map*
Earth, structure and composition of **7**:22
convection cell **5**:232
Earth, geological history of **7**:13 *illus.*
Earth, gravitational field of **7**:17
Earth, heat flow in **7**:18
Earth, structure and composition of **7**:19–23
earthquakes **7**:25–26
East African Rift System **7**:30–31
Ewing, Maurice **7**:325
geochemistry **9**:96–97
geologic time
Cambrian Period **4**:50–52 *map*
Carboniferous Period **4**:138
Jurassic Period **11**:474–477 *map*
Mesozoic Era **13**:322
Ordovician Period **14**:420–421
Paleozoic Era **15**:42–43
Precambrian time **15**:492
Recent Epoch **16**:106–107
Tertiary Period **19**:122–125
geology **9**:106
geophysics **9**:108
geosyncline **9**:120
Hess, H. H. **10**:151–152
history of theory **15**:357
igneous rock **11**:34
island arc **11**:297–298
lake (body of water) **12**:167
lithosphere **12**:371
Lugeon, Maurice **12**:452–453
mantle **13**:130
Matthews, D. H. **13**:231
metamorphic rock **13**:331
mid-oceanic ridge **13**:389–390
Mohole Project **13**:503
mountain **13**:619 *illus.*; **15**:354–356
ocean and sea **14**:331
oceanic trenches **14**:341–342
ophiolite **14**:404
orogeny **14**:447
paleogeography **15**:37
paleomagnetism **15**:41–42
polar wandering **15**:393
seafloor spreading **17**:172
structural geology **18**:303
subduction zone **18**:312–313
submarine canyon **18**:316
transform fault **19**:269–270
tsunami **19**:325
volcano **19**:626–628
Werner, Abraham Gottlob **20**:104
PLATEAU **15**:358
PLATEAU INDIANS *see* INDIANS, AMERICAN, CULTURE AREAS
PLATELET
blood **3**:336–337
PLATEMAKING **15**:357–358 *bibliog., illus.*
intaglio (printing) **11**:199–200
photoengraving **15**:260
phototypesetting **15**:277–278
PLATEN PRESS
letterpress **12**:300–301
PLATEOSAURUS **15**:358–359 *bibliog., illus.*
PLATERESQUE STYLE
Spanish art and architecture **18**:153
PLATFORM TENNIS **15**:359 *bibliog.*
PLATH, SYLVIA **15**:359 *bibliog.*
Bell Jar, The (book) **3**:186
PLATING OF METALS *see* ELECTROPLATING
PLATINUM **15**:359–360 *bibliog.*
abundances of common elements **7**:131 *table*
alloy
iridium **11**:266
catalyst **15**:360
cost **15**:360
element **7**:130 *table*
group, metal
osmium **14**:455
Group VIII periodic table **15**:167
metal, metallic element **13**:328
native elements **14**:47
occurrence **15**:359
palladium **15**:48
properties **15**:359
tantalum **19**:25
transition elements **15**:359; **19**:273
uses **15**:359
PLATO **15**:360–361 *bibliog., illus.*
Academy **1**:70; **15**:360
Carneades **4**:155
Euclidean geometry **7**:263
skepticism **17**:337
aretê **2**:146
bust of **7**:280 *illus.*
Dialogues **6**:150; **15**:360–361
Apology **2**:85
Crito **5**:352
Republic, The **16**:172
Europe, history of **7**:280
law **12**:242
linguistics **12**:354
mathematics, history of **13**:223
philosophy **15**:241 *illus.*; **15**:243–244
Platonic tradition *see* PLATONISM
poetry **15**:379
slavery **17**:352
state (in political philosophy) **18**:229
thought **15**:361
aesthetics **1**:130–131
idealism **11**:30
innate ideas **11**:179
transcendentalism **19**:268
PLATO (Colombia)
map (9° 47′N 74° 47′W) **5**:107
PLATONISM
Aristotle **2**:158
Cambridge Platonists **4**:52
educational philosophy **7**:63
Hugh of Saint Victor **10**:292
humanism **10**:299
Iamblichus **11**:3
Ibn Ezra, Abraham ben Meir **11**:5
ibn Gabirol, Solomon ben Judah **11**:5
Malebranche, Nicholas **13**:87
Neoplatonism **14**:85
Plato **15**:360–361
PLATT, THOMAS COLLIER **15**:361–362
Roosevelt, Theodore **16**:310
PLATT AMENDMENT **15**:362 *bibliog.*
Spanish-American War **18**:150
PLATTE (county in Missouri)
map (39° 25′N 94° 45′W) **13**:476
PLATTE (county in Nebraska)
map (41° 35′N 97° 30′W) **14**:70
PLATTE (South Dakota)
map (43° 23′N 98° 51′W) **18**:103
PLATTE (county in Wyoming)
map (42° 5′N 104° 57′W) **20**:301
PLATTE CITY (Missouri)
map (39° 22′N 94° 47′W) **13**:476
PLATTE RIVER (Missouri)
map (39° 16′N 94° 15′W) **13**:476
PLATTE RIVER (Nebraska) **15**:362
map (41° 04′N 95° 15′W) **14**:70
PLATTENSEE *see* BALATON, LAKE
PLATTEVILLE (Colorado)
map (40° 13′N 104° 49′W) **5**:116
PLATTEVILLE (Wisconsin)
map (42° 44′N 90° 29′W) **20**:185
PLATTSBURG (Missouri)
map (39° 34′N 94° 27′W) **13**:476
PLATTSBURGH (New York)
map (44° 42′N 73° 28′W) **14**:149
PLATTSMOUTH (Nebraska)
map (41° 1′N 95° 53′W) **14**:70
PLATY **15**:362
PLATYHELMINTHES *see* FLATWORM
PLATYPUS *see* DUCK-BILLED PLATYPUS
PLAUEN (Germany, East and West)
map (50° 30′N 12° 8′E) **9**:140
PLAUTUS **15**:362 *bibliog.*
comedy **5**:132
drama **6**:258
tragicomedy **19**:265
PLAY (in behavior) **15**:362–363 *bibliog.*
games **9**:31
Klein, Melanie **12**:96
preschool education **15**:520–522
PLAY (theater) *see* DRAMA
PLAYA **15**:363 *bibliog.*
lake (body of water) **12**:168
lake, glacial **12**:170
PLAYA BONITA (Costa Rica)
map (9° 39′N 84° 27′W) **5**:291
PLAYAS LAKE
map (31° 50′N 108° 34′W) **14**:136
PLAYBOY (periodical)
Hefner, Hugh **10**:105
PLAYBOY OF THE WESTERN WORLD, THE (play) **15**:363 *bibliog.*
Synge, John Millington **18**:407
PLAYER, GARY **15**:363 *bibliog.*
PLAYER PIANO **15**:363 *bibliog.*
PLAYERS CLUB (New York City)
Booth (family) **3**:394
PLAYFAIR, JOHN **15**:363 *bibliog.*
Illustrations of the Huttonian Theory of the Earth **15**:363
PLAYGREEN LAKE
map (54° 0′N 98° 10′W) **13**:119
PLAYING CARDS *see* CARD GAMES; names of specific card games, e.g., CRIBBAGE; RUMMY; etc.
PLAZA (North Dakota)
map (48° 1′N 101° 58′W) **14**:248
PLEA BARGAINING **15**:363–364
criminal justice **5**:350
prosecuting attorney **15**:572
PLEASANT, RICHARD
American Ballet Theatre **1**:337
PLEASANT BAY (Nova Scotia)
map (46° 49′N 60° 48′W) **14**:269
PLEASANT GAP (Pennsylvania)
map (40° 52′N 77° 45′W) **15**:147
PLEASANT GARDEN (North Carolina)
map (35° 58′N 79° 46′W) **14**:242
PLEASANT GROVE (Alabama)
map (33° 29′N 86° 59′W) **1**:234
PLEASANT HILL (Illinois)
map (39° 27′N 90° 52′W) **11**:42
PLEASANT HILL (Louisiana)
map (31° 49′N 93° 31′W) **12**:430
PLEASANT HILL (Missouri)
map (38° 47′N 94° 16′W) **13**:476
PLEASANT VIEW (Utah)
map (41° 19′N 112° 2′W) **19**:492
PLEASANTON (California)
map (37° 40′N 121° 53′W) **4**:31
PLEASANTON (Kansas)
map (38° 11′N 94° 43′W) **12**:18
PLEASANTS (county in West Virginia)
map (39° 22′N 81° 10′W) **20**:111
PLEASANTVILLE (New Jersey)
map (39° 23′N 74° 32′W) **14**:129
PLEASING FUNGUS BEETLE **3**:167 *illus.*
PLEASURE RIDGE PARK (Kentucky)
map (38° 10′N 85° 50′W) **12**:47
PLEBEIANS **15**:364
Europe, history of **7**:280–281
patricians **15**:113
Rome, ancient **16**:297–298
Senate, Roman **17**:199
tribunes **19**:296
PLEBISCITE **15**:364
PLECOPTERA *see* STONE FLY
PLEDGE OF ALLEGIANCE **15**:364
PLÉIADE, LA (literary group) **15**:364 *bibliog.*
du Bellay, Joachim **6**:285
Ronsard, Pierre de **16**:306
PLEIADES (astronomy) **15**:364; **18**:221 *illus.*
interstellar matter **11**:227 *illus.*
Taurus **19**:45
PLEIADES (mythology) **15**:364
PLEISTOCENE EPOCH **15**:364–367 *bibliog., illus., map*
Africa
Aïn Hanech **1**:203
Capsian **4**:128
Olduvai Gorge **14**:376–377
Omo **14**:387–388
Earth, geological history of **7**:15; **15**:364–365
Europe
Combe Grenal **5**:130
Dolní Věstonice **6**:226
Hamburgian **10**:27
Kostenki **12**:124–125
Magdalenian **13**:46
Terra Amata (France) **19**:119
Torralba and Ambrona (Spain) **19**:243
Vallonet Cave (France) **19**:508
Vértesszöllös (Hungary) **19**:563
extinct animals **15**:366
mammal **13**:102–103 *illus.*
mammoth **13**:106–107
mastodon **13**:217
saber-toothed cats **17**:5
fossil record **8**:247
La Brea Tar Pit **12**:144–145 *illus.*; **15**:366–367 *illus.*
geologic time **9**:103–105
Mesolithic Period **13**:314
Paleolithic Period **15**:38–41
Quaternary Period **15**:364; **16**:15
Recent Epoch **16**:106–107
glaciers and glaciation **9**:193–194; **15**:365–366
horse **10**:245 *illus.*
ice ages **11**:9–10 *map, table*
life **15**:366–367 *illus.*
loess **12**:393
Oldowan **14**:376
paleoclimatology **15**:32
prehistoric humans **15**:366; **15**:511–512
race **16**:33–34
savanna life **17**:99 *illus.*
varved deposit **19**:524
PLEKHANOV, GEORGY VALENTINOVICH **15**:366–367 *bibliog.*
PLENTY, BAY OF
map (37° 40′S 177° 0′E) **14**:158
PLENTYWOOD (Montana)
map (48° 47′N 104° 34′W) **13**:547
PLEODORINA **15**:367
PLESIOSAUR **11**:476 *illus.*; **15**:367–368 *bibliog., illus.*; **16**:170 *illus.*
PLESSIS, ARMAND JEAN DU, CARDINAL ET DUC DE RICHELIEU *see* RICHELIEU, ARMAND JEAN DU PLESSIS, CARDINAL ET DUC DE
PLESSY v. FERGUSON **15**:368 *bibliog.*
PLETHO, GIORGIUS GEMISTUS *see* GEMISTUS PLETHO, GIORGIUS
PLEURISY **15**:368 *bibliog.*
PLEURISY ROOT *see* BUTTERFLY WEED
PLEVEN (Bulgaria)
map (43° 25′N 24° 37′E) **3**:555
PLEVNA (Montana)
map (46° 25′N 104° 31′W) **13**:547
PLEXIGLASS *see* PLASTICS
PLINY THE ELDER **15**:368
Seven Wonders of the World **17**:216
volcano **19**:627
PLINY THE YOUNGER **15**:368 *bibliog.*
Pompeii **15**:424
PLIOCENE EPOCH
geologic time **9**:104 *table*
Paleolithic Period **15**:38
Tertiary Period **19**:123–124
PLISETSKAYA, MAYA MIKHAILOVNA **15**:368 *bibliog.*
PLISNIER, CHARLES
Belgian literature **3**:175
PLITVICE LAKES **20**:341 *illus.*

PLJEVLJA (Yugoslavia)
map (43° 21′N 19° 21′E) **20**:340
PLO *see* PALESTINE LIBERATION ORGANIZATION
PŁOCK (Poland)
map (52° 33′N 19° 43′E) **15**:388
PLOIEŞTI (Romania) **15**:368
map (44° 56′N 26° 2′E) **16**:288
PLOT (literature)
narrative and dramatic devices **14**:22
PLOTINUS **15**:368–369 *bibliog.*
chain of being **4**:268–269
emanationism **7**:150–151
Neoplatonism **14**:85
PLOTTER (computer term) **5**:160i
PLOUGH (astronomy) *see* BIG DIPPER
PLOUGH AND THE STARS, THE (play)
O'Casey, Sean **14**:319–320
PLOVDIV (Bulgaria) **15**:369
map (42° 9′N 24° 45′E) **3**:555
PLOVER **15**:369 *bibliog., illus.*
animal migration **2**:27
coloration, biological **5**:121 *illus.*
lapwing **12**:206
nest **3**:287 *illus.*
shorebirds **17**:283
PLOVER (Wisconsin)
map (44° 28′N 89° 32′W) **20**:185
PLOW **15**:369–370 *bibliog., illus.*
agriculture, history of **1**:189–192 *illus.*
ancient Egyptian **19**:61 *illus.*
contour plowing **8**:25 *illus.*; **13**:479 *illus.*
Deere, John **6**:81
modern Egyptian **13**:398 *illus.*
technology, history of **19**:61–64 *illus.*
Wood, Jethro **20**:207
PLÜCKER, JULIUS **15**:370
mathematics, history of **13**:226
PLUM **15**:370 *illus.*
prune **15**:585
PLUM (Pennsylvania)
map (40° 28′N 79° 44′W) **15**:147
PLUM ISLAND (Massachusetts)
map (42° 45′N 70° 48′W) **13**:206
PLUM ISLAND (New York)
map (41° 11′N 72° 12′W) **5**:193
PLUM-YEW **15**:370–371
PLUMAGE *see* FEATHER
PLUMAS (county in California)
map (40° 0′N 120° 50′W) **4**:31
PLUMB LINE
surveying **18**:367
PLUMBAGO *see* LEADWORT
PLUMBER'S ILLUSION
illusions **11**:49
PLUMBING **15**:371–372 *bibliog., illus.*
drain cleaner
caustic chemicals **4**:220
housing **10**:277; **10**:279
lead **12**:256
toilet **19**:222
PLUME *see* FEATHER
PLUMERVILLE (Arkansas)
map (35° 10′N 92° 38′W) **2**:166
PLUMMER, HENRY
outlaws **14**:468; **14**:469
vigilantes **19**:592
PLUNKETT, EDWARD JOHN MORETON DRAX *see* DUNSANY, LORD
PLURAL DEMOCRACY *see* APARTHEID
PLURAL MARRIAGE *see* POLYGAMY
PLURALISM **15**:372
metaphysics **13**:334
PLUSH-CAPPED TANAGER **15**:372
PLUTARCH **15**:372 *bibliog.*
biography **3**:263
PLUTO (mythology) **15**:372
PLUTO (planet) **15**:372–373 *bibliog., illus.*
Charon (moon) **15**:373
orbit **15**:373
physical characteristics **15**:373
planets **15**:330
solar system **18**:46–47 *illus., table*; **18**:49 *illus.*
Tombaugh, Clyde William **15**:373; **19**:231
PLUTON **15**:373 *bibliog.*
PLUTONIC ROCK
igneous rock **11**:33–35
pegmatite **15**:133
PLUTONIUM **15**:373 *bibliog.*
actinide series **1**:88; **15**:373
atom bomb **2**:307
breeder reactor **3**:471–472
dangers **15**:373
element **7**:130 *table*
environmental health **7**:212
metal, metallic element **13**:328
nuclear energy **14**:282–283
radioactive poison **15**:373
Seaborg, Glenn T. **17**:171
transuranium elements **19**:286
uses **15**:373
nuclear energy **14**:283
PLUVIAL LAKE
lake, glacial **12**:170
playa **15**:363
PLUVIOMETER **13**:340 *illus.*
PLYMOUTH (England) **15**:373–374
map (50° 23′N 4° 10′W) **19**:403
PLYMOUTH (Indiana)
map (41° 21′N 86° 19′W) **11**:111
PLYMOUTH (county in Iowa)
map (42° 43′N 96° 10′W) **11**:244
PLYMOUTH (Massachusetts) **15**:374
map (41° 58′N 70° 41′W) **13**:206
PLYMOUTH (county in Massachusetts)
map (41° 58′N 70° 41′W) **13**:206
PLYMOUTH (Michigan)
map (42° 22′N 83° 28′W) **13**:377
PLYMOUTH (New Hampshire)
map (43° 45′N 71° 41′W) **14**:123
PLYMOUTH (North Carolina)
map (35° 52′N 76° 43′W) **14**:242
PLYMOUTH (Ohio)
map (40° 59′N 82° 40′W) **14**:357
PLYMOUTH (Wisconsin)
map (43° 45′N 87° 58′W) **20**:185
PLYMOUTH BAY
map (41° 57′N 70° 37′W) **13**:206
PLYMOUTH BRETHREN **15**:374 *bibliog.*
PLYMOUTH COLONY **15**:374 *bibliog., illus.*
Alden, John **1**:268
Bradford, William **3**:437
Brewster, William **3**:476
Carver, John **4**:179
colonial America land grants **19**:437 *map*
London Company **12**:405
Massachusetts **13**:210–211
Mayflower **13**:247
Pilgrims **15**:302
Squanto **18**:202
Standish, Myles **18**:217
Thanksgiving Day **19**:142
United States, history of the **19**:436
White, Peregrine **20**:136
Winslow, Edward **20**:180
PLYMOUTH COMPANY
London Company **12**:405
PLYMOUTH ROCK (fowl) *see* CHICKEN
PLYWOOD **15**:374–375 *bibliog.*
veneer **19**:538
wood **20**:206
PLZEŇ (Czechoslovakia) **15**:375
map (49° 45′N 13° 23′E) **5**:413
PN JUNCTION *see* SEMICONDUCTOR; TRANSISTOR
PNEUMATIC SYSTEMS **15**:375 *bibliog., illus.*
compressor **5**:158
process control **15**:560
PNEUMOCOCCUS **15**:375
Diplococcus **6**:185
pneumonia **15**:376
PNEUMOCONIOSIS
black lung **3**:317
brown lung **3**:516–517
diseases, occupational **6**:193–194
respiratory system disorders **16**:181
PNEUMONIA **15**:375–376 *bibliog.*
bubonic plague **3**:532
Diplococcus **6**:185
fungus diseases **8**:369
immunodeficiency disease **11**:59
influenza **11**:171
Legionnaires' disease **12**:274
Mycoplasma **13**:690
mycoplasmal pneumonia **13**:690
psittacosis **15**:588
respiratory system disorders **16**:181
PNEUMOTHORAX
respiratory system disorders **16**:182
PNR (National Revolutionary Party)
Mexico, history of **13**:365
PO CHÜ-I (Bo Ju'i) **15**:376 *bibliog.*
PO RIVER **15**:376
map (44° 57′N 12° 4′E) **11**:321
PO-SHAN (China)
map (36° 29′N 117° 50′E) **4**:362
P'O-YANG HU
Kiangsi (Jiangxi) (China) **12**:70
P'O-YANG LAKE
map (29° 0′N 116° 25′E) **20**:318
POBÉ (Benin)
map (6° 58′N 2° 41′E) **3**:200
POBEDY, MOUNT
map (65° 12′N 146° 12′E) **19**:388
POBEDY PEAK
map (42° 2′N 80° 5′E) **19**:388
POCAHONTAS (American Indian) **15**:376 *bibliog., illus.*
Powhatan **15**:486
Rolfe, John **16**:271
Smith, John **17**:369
POCAHONTAS (Arkansas)
map (36° 16′N 90° 58′W) **2**:166
POCAHONTAS (Illinois)
map (38° 50′N 89° 33′W) **11**:42
POCAHONTAS (Iowa)
map (42° 44′N 94° 40′W) **11**:244
POCAHONTAS (county in Iowa)
map (42° 43′N 94° 38′W) **11**:244
POCAHONTAS (county in West Virginia)
map (38° 20′N 80° 0′W) **20**:111
POCASSET (Massachusetts)
map (41° 41′N 70° 37′W) **13**:206
POCATELLO (Idaho) **15**:376
map (42° 52′N 112° 27′W) **11**:26
POCKET BILLIARDS
billiards **3**:254; **3**:255 *illus.*
POCKET GOPHER **9**:248 *illus.*; **15**:376–377 *illus.*
POCOLA (Oklahoma)
map (35° 13′N 94° 30′W) **14**:368
POCOMOKE CITY (Maryland)
map (38° 5′N 75° 34′W) **13**:188
POCOMOKE RIVER
map (37° 58′N 75° 39′W) **13**:188
POCOMOKE SOUND
map (37° 52′N 75° 49′W) **13**:188
POCONO MOUNTAINS
map (41° 10′N 75° 20′W) **15**:147
PODGORICA (Yugoslavia) *see* TITOGRAD (Yugoslavia)
PODIATRY **15**:377
PODOCARP **15**:377
PODOKESAURUS **15**:377 *bibliog.*
PODZOL **15**:377 *bibliog.*
distribution, worldwide **18**:37 *map*
pedalfer **15**:131
POE, EDGAR ALLAN **15**:377–378 *bibliog., illus.*
"Fall of the House of Usher, The" **8**:13
"Masque of the Red Death, The" **13**:200
mystery, suspense, and detective fiction **13**:692
"Pit and the Pendulum, The" **15**:319
"Tell-Tale Heart, The" **19**:90
POE, EDGAR ALLAN, AWARD *see* EDGAR ALLAN POE AWARD
POEL, WILLIAM
theater, history of the **19**:150
POET LAUREATE **15**:378 *bibliog.*
Austin, Alfred **2**:327
Betjeman, Sir John **3**:232
Bridges, Robert **3**:485
Cibber, Colley **4**:428
Day-Lewis, C. **6**:55
Dryden, John **6**:284–285
Hughes, Ted **10**:293
Masefield, John **13**:196
Rowe, Nicholas **16**:327
Shadwell, Thomas **17**:234
Southey, Robert **18**:112
Tennyson, Alfred Lord **19**:111–112
Wordsworth, William **20**:216–217
POETICS *see* CRITICISM, LITERARY
POETICS OF ARISTOTLE (book) **15**:378 *bibliog.*
Aristotle **2**:158
Castelvetro, Lodovico **4**:187
criticism, literary **5**:351
genre (literature) **9**:93
tragedy **19**:265
POETISM
Czech literature **5**:412
POETRY **15**:378–379 *bibliog.*
acrostic **1**:85
African literature **1**:167–168; **1**:168
See also national subheadings under POETRY, e.g., POETRY—Nigerian literature; POETRY—South African literature; etc.
Césaire, Aimé **4**:262
Diop, David **6**:185
American literature **1**:342–348
Agee, James **1**:183
Aiken, Conrad **1**:201
Aiken, Joan **1**:202
Aldrich, Thomas Bailey **1**:269
Allen, Hervey **1**:299
Ammons, A. R. **1**:373
Angelou, Maya **1**:414
Ashbery, John **2**:229
Auden, W. H. **2**:317–318
Baraka, Imamu Amiri **3**:75
Barlow, Joel **3**:84–85
Bates, Katharine Lee **3**:121
Benét, Stephen Vincent **3**:198
Benét, William Rose **3**:198
Berryman, John **3**:225
Bishop, Elizabeth **3**:297
Bishop, John Peale **3**:297
black American literature **3**:304
Black Mountain school of poetry **3**:317
Bly, Robert **3**:348
Bodenheim, Maxwell **3**:356
Bogan, Louise **3**:359
Boker, George Henry **3**:364
Bontemps, Arna **3**:382
Boyle, Kay **3**:434
Bradford, Gamaliel **3**:437
Bradstreet, Anne **3**:438
Brautigan, Richard **3**:458
Brooks, Gwendolyn **3**:511
Brown, Sterling **3**:516
Bryant, William Cullen **3**:529
Bukowski, Charles **3**:553
Burke, Kenneth **3**:571
Cary, Alice and Phoebe **4**:179
Cather, Willa **4**:208–209
Ciardi, John **4**:428
Coatsworth, Elizabeth **5**:82
Connecticut Wits **5**:196
Connell, Evan S., Jr. **5**:196–197
Cook, Ebenezer **5**:234
Corso, Gregory **5**:277
Crane, Hart **5**:330
Crane, Stephen **5**:330
Creeley, Robert **5**:337
Cullen, Countee **5**:384
cummings, e. e. **5**:387–388
Davis, Frank Marshall **6**:51
Deutsch, Babette **6**:136
Dickey, James **6**:157
Dickinson, Emily **6**:157–158
Doolittle, Hilda (H. D.) **6**:240
Duncan, Robert **6**:299
Eberhart, Richard **7**:35
Fearing, Kenneth **8**:39
Ferlinghetti, Lawrence **8**:54
Ficke, Arthur Davison **8**:70
Field, Eugene **8**:71
Fitzgerald, Robert **8**:131
Fletcher, John Gould **8**:163
Freneau, Philip **8**:326
Frost, Robert **8**:345–346
Ginsberg, Allen **9**:184–185
Giovanni, Nikki **9**:188
Gregory, Horace **9**:355
Halleck, Fitz-Greene **10**:22
Hayden, Robert **10**:81
Holmes, Oliver Wendell **10**:205
Howe, Julia Ward **10**:284
Hughes, Langston **10**:293
Jarrell, Randall **11**:383
Jeffers, Robinson **11**:391
Johnson, Fenton **11**:432
Jordan, June **11**:450
Kilmer, Joyce **11**:77
Knight, Etheridge **12**:100–101
Kumin, Maxine **12**:136
Kunitz, Stanley J. **11**:137
Lanier, Sidney **12**:199
Lazarus, Emma **12**:252
Levertov, Denise **12**:303
Lindsay, Vachel **12**:352
Longfellow, Henry Wadsworth **12**:407
Lowell, Amy **11**:443–444
Lowell, James Russell **11**:444
Lowell, Robert, Jr. **12**:444–445
McGinley, Phyllis **13**:16
McKay, Claude **13**:27
MacLeish, Archibald **13**:32
Major, Clarence **13**:77
Markham, Edwin **13**:159
Marquis, Don **13**:163
Masters, Edgar Lee **13**:215–216
Meredith, William **13**:309
Merrill, James **13**:312
Merwin, W. S. **13**:313
Millay, Edna St. Vincent **13**:426
Miller, Joaquin **13**:428
Monroe, Harriet **13**:541
Moore, Marianne **13**:569
Nash, Ogden **14**:24
Nathan, Robert **14**:27
Nemerov, Howard **14**:80–81
New York poets **14**:155
O'Hara, Frank **14**:355
Olson, Charles **14**:381
Parker, Dorothy **15**:90
Patchen, Kenneth **15**:109
Plath, Sylvia **15**:359
Pound, Ezra **15**:475–476
Rexroth, Kenneth **16**:190
Rich, Adrienne **16**:209
Riley, James Whitcomb **16**:223
Robinson, Edwin Arlington **16**:244
Roethke, Theodore **16**:268
Rukeyser, Muriel **16**:344

POETRY (cont.)
Sanchez, Sonia **17**:58
Sandburg, Carl **17**:61
Schwartz, Delmore **17**:139
Scott, Winfield Townley **17**:155
Sexton, Anne **17**:228
Shapiro, Karl **17**:241
Simpson, Louis **17**:317
Snodgrass, W. D. **18**:3
Snyder, Gary **18**:5–6
Stevens, Wallace **18**:264
Swenson, May **18**:388
Tabb, John B. **19**:3–4
Tate, Allen **19**:44
Taylor, Bayard **19**:48
Taylor, Edward **19**:48
Teasdale, Sara **19**:58
Timrod, Henry **19**:204
Tolson, M. B. **19**:227
Torrence, Ridgely **19**:243
Untermeyer, Louis **19**:470
Van Doren, Mark **19**:513
Wakoski, Diane **20**:8
Walker, Alice **20**:12
Walker, Margaret **20**:12
Warren, Robert Penn **20**:31
Wheatley, Phillis **20**:126
Whitman, Walt **20**:140–141
Whittier, John Greenleaf **20**:142
Wigglesworth, Michael **20**:147
Wilbur, Richard **20**:147–148
Williams, William Carlos **20**:161
Winters, Yvor **20**:181
Zukofsky, Louis **20**:381
Arabic literature **2**:101
Abu Madi, Iliya **1**:66
Abu Nuwas **1**:66
Gibran, Kahil **9**:175
Imru' al-Qais **11**:69
Mutanabbi, al- **13**:686
Argentine literature
Borges, Jorge Luis **3**:398–399
Echeverría, Esteban **7**:37
Lugones, Leopoldo **12**:453
Aristotle **2**:158
Australian literature **2**:343–344
Fitzgerald, Robert David **8**:131
Gilmore, Dame Mary **9**:183
Gordon, Adam Lindsay **9**:249
Neilson, John Shaw **14**:79
Paterson, A. B. **15**:111
Slessor, Kenneth **17**:360–361
Wright, Judith Arundel **20**:290
Austrian literature **2**:354
Bachmann, Ingeborg **3**:11
Hofmannsthal, Hugo von **10**:196–197
Trakl, Georg **19**:266
bard **3**:80
Belgian literature **3**:175
Verhaeren, Émile **19**:551
Bollingen Prize in Poetry *see* BOLLINGEN PRIZE IN POETRY
Brazilian literature
Gonçalves Dias, Antônio **9**:242
Matos Guerra, Gregório de **13**:229
Breton literature **3**:475
Bulgarian literature **3**:557
Botev, Khristo **3**:415
Vazov, Ivan **19**:529
Canadian literature **4**:93–94
Atwood, Margaret **2**:316
Avison, Margaret **2**:376
Birney, Earle **3**:293
Campbell, Wilfred **4**:66
Carman, Bliss **4**:153
Charbonneau, Robert **4**:286
Crawford, Isabella Valancy **5**:333
Crémazie, Octave **5**:338
Drummond, William Henry **6**:283
Fréchette, Louis Honoré **8**:289
Garneau, Hector de Saint-Denys **9**:48
Hébert, Anne **10**:101
Morin, Paul **13**:580
Nelligan, Émile **14**:79
Pratt, E. J. **15**:490
Roberts, Sir Charles G. D. **16**:241
Scott, Duncan Campbell **17**:153
Service, Robert W. **17**:211
carpe diem **4**:163
Catalan literature **4**:198
Chilean literature
Huidobro, Vicente **10**:295
Mistral, Gabriela **13**:482
Neruda, Pablo **14**:90
Chinese literature **4**:389–390
Chi K'ang (Ji Kang) **4**:339
Ch'ü Yüan (Qu Yuan) **4**:421
Juan Chi (Ruan Ji) **11**:457
Kuo Mo-jo (Guo Moruo) **12**:137
Li Po (Li Bo) **12**:310
Li Yü (Li Yu) **12**:310–311
Po Chü-i (Bo Ju'i) **15**:376
Su Tung-p'o (Su Dongpo) **18**:312
T'ao Yüan-ming (Tao Yuanming) **19**:28
Ts'ao Chih (Cao Zhi) **19**:322
Tu Fu (Du Fu) **19**:325
Wang Wei **20**:22
Wu Ch'eng-en (Wu Chengen) **20**:295–296
Colombian literature
Silva, José Asunción **17**:312
courtly love **5**:317
Cuban literature
Guillén, Nicolás **9**:396
Martí, José **13**:176
Czech literature **5**:412–413
Čech, Svatopluk **4**:228
Mácha, Karel Hynek **13**:17
Danish literature **6**:32–33
Aakjaer, Jeppe **1**:49
Andersen, Hans Christian **1**:401
Bjørnvig, Thorkild **3**:303
Claussen, Sophus **5**:45
Drachmann, Holger Henrik Herholdt **6**:253–254
Hauch, Johannes Carsten **10**:68
Oehlenschläger, Adam Gottlob **14**:352
Paludin-Müller, Frederik **15**:52–53
Saxo Grammaticus **17**:104
Winther, Christian **20**:181
Dutch and Flemish literature **6**:314
Beets, Nicolaas **3**:168
Bilderdijk, Willem **3**:251
Boutens, Pieter Cornelius **3**:425
Bredero, Gerbrand Adriaenszoon **3**:471
Cats, Jacob **4**:213
Gezelle, Guido **9**:163
Gijsen, Marnix **9**:178
Hooft, Pieter Corneliszoon **10**:226
Huygens, Constantijn **10**:325
Nijhoff, Martinus **14**:194
Verwey, Albert **19**:563
Vondel, Joost van den **19**:634
Woestijne, Karel van de **20**:195
Ecuadorean literature
Carrera Andrade, Jorge **4**:167
English literature **7**:193–202
Abercrombie, Lascelles **1**:56
Addison, Joseph **1**:100
Akenside, Mark **1**:230
Aldington, Richard **1**:269
Alvarez, A. **1**:319
Amis, Kingsley **1**:372
Arnold, Matthew **2**:185
Austin, Alfred **2**:327
Barham, Richard Harris **3**:81
Behn, Aphra **3**:171
Beowulf **3**:207
Betjeman, Sir John **3**:232
Blackmore, Richard Doddridge **3**:321
Blake, William **3**:325–326
Bradley, A. C. **3**:437
Bridges, Robert **3**:485
Brontë (family) **3**:504
Brooke, Rupert **3**:509–510
Browne, William **3**:517
Browning, Elizabeth Barrett **3**:518
Browning, Robert **3**:518–519
Bulwer-Lytton, Edward Robert, 1st Earl of Lytton **3**:562
Butler, Samuel (1612–1680) **3**:592
Byron, George Gordon, Lord **3**:603
Cædmon **4**:12
Carew, Thomas **4**:146
Carey, Henry **4**:146
Carroll, Lewis **4**:169
Cavalier poets **4**:220
Chapman, George **4**:285
Chatterton, Thomas **4**:304
Chaucer, Geoffrey **4**:304–305
Chesterton, G. K. **4**:337
Churchill, Charles **4**:425
Clare, John **5**:36
Clough, Arthur Hugh **5**:69
Coleridge, Samuel Taylor **5**:100–101
Collins, William **5**:104
Constable, Henry **5**:206
Cowley, Abraham **5**:321
Cowper, William **5**:322
Crabbe, George **5**:326
Crashaw, Richard **5**:332
Cynewulf **5**:406
Daniel, Samuel **6**:32
Day-Lewis, C. **6**:55
de la Mare, Walter **6**:60
Della-Cruscans **6**:93
Denham, Sir John **6**:108
Donne, John **6**:239
Dowson, Ernest **6**:252–253
Drayton, Michael **6**:265
Drinkwater, John **6**:273
Dryden, John **6**:284–285
Durrell, Lawrence **6**:307
Eliot, T. S. **7**:139–140
Exeter Book **7**:331
Fletcher, Giles **8**:163
Fletcher, Phineas **8**:163
Gascoigne, George **9**:53–54
Georgian poetry **9**:118
Goldsmith, Oliver **9**:236
Gower, John **9**:272–273
Graves, Robert **9**:302–303
Gray, Thomas **9**:307
Hardy, Thomas **10**:47–48
Henley, William Ernest **10**:121–122
Herbert, George **10**:135
Herrick, Robert **10**:146
Hoccleve, Thomas **10**:193
Hood, Thomas **10**:225
Hopkins, Gerard Manley **10**:231
Housman, A. E. **10**:280
Hughes, Ted **10**:293
Hulme, T. E. **10**:296
Hunt, Leigh **10**:311–312
Johnson, Samuel **11**:435–436
Jonson, Ben **11**:445–446
Keats, John **12**:35–36
Kipling, Rudyard **11**:86–87
Landor, Walter Savage **12**:184
Langland, William **12**:196
Larkin, Philip **12**:208
Layamon **12**:252
Lovelace, Richard **11**:438
Lydgate, John **11**:474
Marie de France **13**:151
Marlowe, Christopher **13**:161
Marvell, Andrew **13**:181
Masefield, John **13**:196
metaphysical poetry **13**:334
Milton, John **13**:432–433
Noyes, Alfred **14**:277
ode **17**:253
Oldham, John **14**:376
Owen, Wilfred **14**:471
Palgrave, Francis Turner **15**:47
poet laureate **15**:378
Pope, Alexander **15**:430
Prior, Matthew **15**:553
Rosenberg, Isaac **16**:315
Rossetti, Christina G. **16**:319
Rossetti, Dante Gabriel **16**:319
Sassoon, Siegfried **17**:84
Shadwell, Thomas **17**:234
Shakespeare, William **17**:237
Sidney, Sir Philip **17**:295
Sir Gawain and the Green Knight **17**:327
Sitwell (family) **17**:330–331
Skelton, John **17**:337
Southey, Robert **18**:112
Spender, Stephen **18**:177–178
Spenser, Edmund **18**:178–179
Suckling, Sir John **18**:319
Surrey, Henry Howard, Earl of **18**:366
Swinburne, Algernon Charles **18**:392
Taylor, John (poet) **19**:49
Tennyson, Alfred, Lord **19**:111–112
Thomas, Dylan **19**:172–173
Victorian literature **19**:575
Waller, Edmund **20**:15–16
Wilde, Oscar **20**:148–149
Wordsworth, William **20**:216–217
Wyatt, Sir Thomas **20**:297–298
Wylie, Elinor **20**:299
Young, Edward **20**:333
Finnish literature **8**:99
Haavikko, Paavo **10**:3
Kalevala **12**:7–8
Runeberg, Johan Ludvig **16**:345–346
Södergran, Edith **18**:32
forms
alexandrine **1**:278
ballad **3**:40
ballade **3**:40–41
baroque literature **3**:91
canzone **4**:119
concrete poetry **5**:171
Dafydd ap Gwilym **6**:6
dithyramb **6**:202
doggerel **6**:223
eclogue **7**:42
elegy **7**:129
epic **7**:217
fabliau **8**:5
found poem **8**:249
haiku **10**:12
limerick **12**:344
lyric **12**:479
nonsense verse **14**:217
nursery rhymes **14**:298
ode **14**:348
satire **17**:88
sestina **17**:213
sonnet **18**:65
villanelle **19**:597
French literature **8**:314–320
Adam de la Halle **1**:93
Alain-Fournier **1**:239
Apollinaire, Guillaume **2**:79
Aragon, Louis **2**:107
Artaud, Antonin **2**:212
Aubigné, Agrippa d' **2**:316
Audiberti, Jacques **2**:318
Banville, Théodore de **3**:71
Barbey d'Aurevilly, Jules Amédée **3**:78
Baudelaire, Charles **3**:128–129
Benoît de Sainte-More **3**:204
Béranger Pierre Jean de **3**:207
Bertran'd de Born **3**:226
Boileau-Despreaux, Nicolas **3**:362
Bonnefoy, Yves **3**:381
Bourget, Paul **3**:424
Breton, André **3**:474
Breton literature **3**:475
Cendrars, Blaise **4**:245
Césaire, Aimé **4**:262
Chanson de Roland **4**:282
chansons de geste **4**:282
Chapelain, Jean **4**:284
Char, René **4**:286
Charlemagne cycle **4**:290
Chartier, Alain **4**:300
Chénier, André **4**:330
Chrétien de Troyes **4**:410
Claudel, Paul **5**:44
Cocteau, Jean **5**:89
Deschamps, Eustache **6**:126
Desnos, Robert **6**:132
du Bellay, Joachim **6**:285
Éluard, Paul **7**:150
Fargue, Léon Paul **8**:23
Fort, Paul **8**:236
Gautier, Théophile **9**:62
Guillaume de Lorris **9**:395
Heredia, José Maria de **10**:138–139
Hugo, Victor **10**:294
Laforgue, Jules **12**:164
Lamartine, Alphonse de **12**:174
Leconte de Lisle, Charles Marie **12**:268
Machaut, Guillaume de **13**:18
Malherbe, François de **13**:88
Mallarmé, Stéphane **13**:91
Marot, Clément **13**:162
Mistral, Frédéric **13**:482
Musset, Alfred de **13**:684
Nerval, Gérard de **14**:90
Nodier, Charles **14**:212
Parnassians (literary group) **15**:96
Perrault, Charles **15**:178
Perse, Saint-John **15**:179–180
Pléiade, La (literary group) **15**:364
Rimbaud, Arthur **16**:224
Ronsard, Pierre de **16**:305–306
Sully Prudhomme **18**:338
Tardieu, Jean **19**:35–36
Valéry, Paul **19**:505–506
Verlaine, Paul **19**:551–552
Vigny, Alfred de **19**:592
villanelle **19**:597
Villon, François **19**:598–599
Voltaire **19**:632
German literature **9**:132–134
Arnim, Achim **2**:184
Benn, Gottfried **3**:202
Barchert, Wolfgang **3**:396
Bouterwek, Friedrich **3**:425
Brecht, Bertolt **3**:470–471
Bretano, Clemens **3**:473
Busch, Wilhelm **3**:585
Chamisso, Adelbert von **4**:275
Droste-Hülshoff, Annette Elisabeth von **6**:273
Eichendorff, Joseph, Freiherr von **7**:91
Freiligrath, Ferdinand **8**:301
George, Stefan **9**:109
Goethe, Johann Wolfgang von **9**:223–224
Gottfried von Strassburg **9**:263–264
Gryphius, Andreas **9**:384
Günther, Johann Christian **9**:406
Hartmann von Aue **10**:63
Heine, Heinrich **10**:108
Hölderlin, Friedrich **10**:202
Kleist, Heinrich von **12**:96
Klopstock, Friedrich Gottlieb **12**:98

Mörike, Eduard **13**:580
Neidhart von Reuenthal **14**:78–79
Nibelungenlied **14**:177–178
Novalis **14**:271–272
Rilke, Rainer Maria **16**:223–224
Sachs, Hans **17**:7
Sachs, Nelly **17**:7
Uhland, Johann Ludwig **19**:374
Walther von der Vogelweide **20**:20
Wolfram von Eschenbach **20**:198
Ghanaian literature
Awoonor, Kofi **2**:377
Greek literature, ancient **9**:343–344
Alcaeus **1**:262
Alcman **1**:264
Anacreon **1**:387
Apollonius of Rhodes **2**:84–85
Archilochus **2**:128
Bacchylides **3**:9–10
Callimachus (poet) **4**:46
Corinna **5**:262
Eupolis **7**:265
Hesiod **10**:151
Homer **10**:213
Ibycus **11**:7
Mimnermus **13**:436
Pindar **15**:304–305
Sappho **17**:73
satire **17**:88
Simonides of Ceos **17**:316
Stesichorus **18**:262
Theocritus **19**:155
Theognis **19**:157
Tyrtaeus **19**:368
Greek literature, modern **9**:344
Cavafy, C. P. **4**:220
Elytis, Odysseus **7**:150
Palamas, Kostis **15**:29
Ritsos, Yannis **16**:229
Seferis, George **17**:187
Sikelianos, Angelos **17**:302
Solomos, Dionysios **18**:57
Guatemalan literature
Asturias, Miguel Ángel **2**:285–286
Hebrew and Yiddish literature **10**:102
Amichai, Yehuda **1**:369
Bialik, Hayyim Nahman **3**:236
Judah ha-Levi **11**:458
Psalms, Book of **15**:586–587
Shlonsky, Abraham **17**:278
Tchernichowsky, Saul **19**:52–53
Hungarian literature **10**:305–306
Ady, Endre **1**:114
Arany, János **2**:109
Déry, Tibor **6**:123
József, Attila **11**:457
Madách, Imre **13**:37
Petőfi, Sándor **15**:203
hymn **10**:346
Icelandic literature **11**:18–19
Edda **7**:54–55
Skaldic literature **17**:331–332
Snorri Sturluson **18**:3
Indian literature **11**:101–102
Bhartrihari **3**:234
Candidas **4**:107
Iqbal, Muhammad **11**:249
Kalidasa **12**:8
Naidu, Sarojini **14**:7
Ramayana **16**:80
Tagore, Sir Rabindranath **19**:9–10
Irish literature **11**:267–268
Clarke, Austin **5**:40
Colum, Padraic **5**:125
Heaney, Seamus **10**:89
Hyde, Douglas **10**:329
MacNeice, Louis **13**:35
Moore, Thomas **13**:570
Russell, George W. **16**:350
Yeats, William Butler **20**:321
Italian literature **11**:315–317
Alamanni, Luigi **1**:239
Alfieri, Vittorio **1**:279
Alvaro, Corrado **1**:320
Ariosto, Ludovico **2**:154
Bassani, Giorgio **3**:117
Belli, G. G. **3**:188
Bembo, Pietro **3**:194
Betti, Ugo **3**:232
Boiardo, Matteo Maria **3**:362
Boito, Arrigo **3**:363
Borgese, Giuseppe Antonio **3**:399
Campana, Dino **4**:64
Carducci, Giosuè **4**:145
Cavalcanti, Guido **4**:220
D'Annunzio, Gabriele **6**:33
Dante Alighieri **6**:34
Divine Comedy, The **6**:203
Guarini, Giovanni Battista **9**:387
Guinicelli, Guido **9**:400
Jacopone da Todi **11**:347
Leopardi, Giacomo Conte **11**:293
Marinism (Giambattista Marino) **13**:156–157
Marino, Giambattista **13**:156–157
Montale, Eugenio **13**:545
Parini, Giuseppe **15**:84
Pascoli, Giovanni **15**:102
Pavese, Cesare **15**:120
Petrarch **15**:203–204
Politian **15**:399
Porta, Carlo **15**:443
Quasimodo, Salvatore **16**:15
Sannazaro, Jacopo **17**:65
Scaliger, Julius Caesar **17**:107
Sicilian School **11**:315
Tasso, Torquato **19**:43
Trissino, Giangiorgio **19**:303
Ungaretti, Giuseppe **19**:384
Japanese literature **11**:380
Basho **3**:108
Buson **3**:590
Hagiwara Sakutaro **10**:10
haiku **10**:12
Ishikawa Takuboku **11**:287
Latin American literature **12**:229–231
See also national subheadings under POETRY, e.g., POETRY—Argentine literature; POETRY—Brazilian literature; etc.
Latin literature **12**:234
Ausonius **2**:325
Catullus **4**:217
De re natura **6**:62
Ennius, Quintus **7**:207
Horace **10**:233–234
Juvenal **11**:480
Lucan **12**:448
Lucretius **12**:451
Martial **13**:176
Ovid **14**:470–471
Propertius, Sextus **15**:570
satire **17**:88
Seneca, Lucius Annaeus **17**:200
Statius **18**:238
Tibullus **19**:191
Vergil **19**:551
Lebanese literature
Gibran, Kahlil **9**:175
Mexican literature
Altamirano, Ignacio Manuel **1**:311
Díaz Mirón, Salvador **6**:155
Juana Inés de la Cruz, Sor **11**:457–458
López Velarde, Ramón **12**:412–413
Nervo, Amado **14**:91
Paz, Octavio **15**:122
Torres Bodet, Jaime **19**:244
minstrels, minnesingers, and troubadours **13**:460
narrative and dramatic devices **14**:22–23
National Book Awards *see* NATIONAL BOOK AWARDS
National Book Critics Circle Award *see* NATIONAL BOOK CRITICS CIRCLE AWARD
Nicaraguan literature
Darío, Rubén **6**:37–38
Nigerian literature
Okara, Gabriel **14**:365
Okigbo, Christopher **14**:366
Norwegian literature **14**:265–266
Bjørnson, Bjørnstjerne **3**:302–303
Bull, Olaf Jacob Martin Luther **3**:557–558
Dass, Petter **6**:43
Garborg, Arne **9**:38
Grieg, Nordahl Brun **9**:362
Ibsen, Henrik **11**:6–7
Moe, Jørgen Engebretsen **13**:500
Øverland, Arnulf **14**:470
Wergeland, Henrik Arnold **20**:104
Wildenvey, Herman **20**:149
Persian literature **15**:187
Ansari **2**:35
Attar, Farid al-Din Abu Hamid **2**:314
Firdawsi **8**:100
Hafez, Mohammed Shamsoddin **10**:9
Nezami, Nezamoddin Ilyas **14**:176
Omar Khayyam **14**:387
Rudaki, Abu Abdollah Jafar **16**:337
Rumi, Jalal al-Din al- **16**:345
Sadi, Sheykh Moslehoddin **17**:9–10
Peruvian literature
Vallejo, César **19**:507
poet laureate *see* POET LAUREATE
Polish literature **15**:398
Mickiewicz, Adam **13**:383–384
Miłosz, Czesław **13**:432
Różewicz, Tadeusz **16**:332
Portuguese literature **15**:456–457
Bernardes, Diogo **3**:221
Camões, Luis Vaz de **4**:62
Garrett, João Baptiste de Almeida **9**:50
Sá de Miranda, Francisco de **17**:3
Provençal literature **15**:583
Bernart de Ventadorn **3**:221
Bertrand de Born **3**:226
Daniel, Arnaut **6**:31
Mistral, Frédéric **13**:482
Pulitzer Prize *see* LITERATURE—Pulitzer Prize
Pushkin Prize *see* PUSHKIN PRIZE
Romanian literature **16**:290
Alecsandri, Vasile **1**:270
Eminescu, Mihail **7**:156
Russian literature **16**:366–367
Akhmatova, Anna **1**:230
Aksakov, Konstantin Sergeyevich **1**:232
Balmont, Konstantin Dmitriyevich **3**:54
Bedny, Demian **3**:154
Bely, Andrei **3**:193–194
Blok, Aleksandr Aleksandrovich **3**:335
Brodsky, Joseph **3**:501
Bryusov, Valery Yakovlevich **3**:530
Bunin, Ivan Alekseyevich **3**:563
Derzhavin, Gavrila Romanovich **6**:123
Gumilev, Nikolai Stepanovich **9**:405
Hippius, Zinaida Nikolayevna **10**:173–174
Lermontov, Mikhail **12**:296
Mandelstam, Osip Emilievich **13**:111
Mayakovsky, Vladimir Vladimirovich **13**:245–246
Nekrasov, Nikolai Alekseyevich **14**:79
Pasternak, Boris **15**:107
Pushkin, Aleksandr **15**:631–632
Remizov, Aleksei Mikhailovich **16**:146
Shevchenko, Taras Grygorievych (Ukranian) **17**:260
Sologub, Fyodor **18**:56
Tolstoi, Count Aleksei Konstantinovich **19**:227–228
Tyutchev, Fyodor **19**:368
Voznesensky, Andrei **19**:639
Yesenin, Sergei Aleksandrovich **20**:327
Yevtushenko, Yevgeny Aleksandrovich **20**:327
Scottish literature
Barbow, John **3**:79
Beattie, James **3**:145
Burns, Robert **3**:578–579
Campbell, Thomas **4**:66
Davidson, John **6**:49
Dunbar, William **6**:298–299
Fergusson, Robert **8**:54
Henryson, Robert **10**:130
Hogg, James **10**:198
MacDiarmid, Hugh **13**:11
Macpherson, James **13**:36
Muir, Edwin **13**:634
Ramsay, Allan **16**:81
Thomson, James (1700–48) **19**:175
Thomson, James (1834–82) **19**:176
Senegalese literature
Senghor, Léopold Sédar **17**:203
South African literature
Breytenbach, Breyten **3**:476
Campbell, Roy **4**:66
Jonker, Ingrid **11**:445
Spanish literature **18**:157–160
Alberti, Rafael **1**:259
Aleixandre, Vicente **1**:271
Alonso, Dámaso **1**:307–308
Bécquer, Gustavo Adolfo **3**:152
Campoamor y Campoosorio, Ramón de **4**:67
Catalan literature **4**:198
Cernuda, Luis **4**:260
Encina, Juan del **7**:162
Espinel, Vicente Martínez **7**:243
García Lorca, Federico **9**:38–39
Garcilaso de la Vega **9**:39–40
Góngora y Argote, Luis de **9**:243–244
Gongorism **9**:244
Guillén, Jorge **9**:396
Jiménez, Juan Ramón **11**:418
Machado, Antonio **13**:17–18
Swedish literature **18**:386–387
Andersson, Dan **1**:403
Bellman, Carl Michael **3**:190
Boye, Karin **3**:434
Dalin, Olof von **6**:13
Ekelöf, Gunnar **7**:97–98
Fröding, Gustaf **8**:335
Geijer, Erik Gustaf **9**:68
Heidenstam, Verner von **10**:107
Karlfeldt, Erik Axel **12**:27
Lagerkvist, Pär **12**:165
Martinson, Harry Edmund **13**:181
Södergran, Edith **18**:32
Stagnelius, Erik Johan **18**:211
Tegnér, Esaias **19**:72
Swiss literature
Spitteler, Carl **18**:190
symbolism (literature) **18**:403
Trinidadian literature
Walcott, Derek **20**:9
Turkish literature
Galib, Şeyh **9**:14
Nazim Hikmet **14**:67
Tevfik Fikret **19**:128
Yunus Emre **20**:347
Uruguayan literature
Benedetti, Mario **3**:196
Venezuelan literature
Bello, Andrés **3**:190
versification **19**:561–563
Welsh literature **20**:101–102
Dafydd ap Gwilym **6**:6
Thomas, Dylan **19**:172–173
Vaughan, Henry **19**:528
Yugoslav literature
Andríc, Ivo **1**:408
Cankar, Ivan **4**:108
Župančič, Oton **20**:382
POETRY (periodical)
Monroe, Harriet **13**:541
POET'S THEATER (Boston)
Gorey, Edward **9**:250
POGONOPHORA **15**:379–380
beardworm **3**:143
POGRADEC (Albania)
map (40° 54′N 20° 39′E) **1**:250
POGROM **15**:380
anti-Semitism **2**:68
genocide **9**:93
Jews **11**:416
POGUE, WILLIAM REID **15**:380 *bibliog.*
Skylab **17**:348
POHL, FREDERIK **15**:380 *bibliog.*
POI *see* TARO
POINCARÉ, HENRI **15**:380 *bibliog.*
algebraic topology **15**:380
celestial mechanics **15**:380
mathematics, history of **13**:226
theoretical science **15**:380
POINCARÉ, RAYMOND **15**:380 *bibliog.*
POINSETT (county in Arkansas)
map (35° 37′N 90° 45′W) **2**:166
POINSETT, LAKE
map (44° 34′N 97° 5′W) **18**:103
POINSETTIA **15**:380–381 *illus.*
POINSOT, LOUIS
mathematics, history of **13**:226
POINT (mathematics) **15**:381
geometry **15**:381
locus, curve **5**:396
projective geometry **15**:565
POINT ADAMS
map (46° 13′N 123° 58′W) **14**:427
POINT AL-MADRAKA
map (19° 0′N 57° 50′E) **14**:386
POINT ALLERTON
map (42° 18′N 70° 53′W) **3**:409
POINT ARENA
map (38° 57′N 123° 44′W) **4**:31
POINT AU FER ISLAND
map (29° 15′N 91° 15′W) **12**:430
POINT BARRA
map (23° 45′S 35° 30′E) **13**:627
POINT BARROW
map (71° 23′N 156° 30′W) **1**:242
POINT BÉHAGUE
map (4° 40′N 51° 54′W) **8**:311
POINT BURICA
map (8° 3′N 82° 53′W) **15**:55
POINT CA MAU
map (8° 38′N 104° 44′E) **19**:580
POINT CHEVREUIL
map (29° 31′N 91° 33′W) **12**:430
POINT CLARK
map (44° 4′N 81° 45′W) **14**:393; **19**:241
POINT FORTIN (Trinidad and Tobago)
map (10° 11′N 61° 41′W) **19**:300
POINT FOUR PROGRAM **15**:381 *bibliog.*

POINT FOUR PROGRAM (cont.)
foreign aid **8**:224
Truman, Harry S. **19**:317
POINT GALLIANAS
map (12° 28′N 71° 40′W) **5**:107
POINT GOYEAU
map (51° 47′N 79° 3′W) **16**:18
POINT GRATES
map (48° 10′N 52° 57′W) **14**:166
POINT HOPE (Alaska)
map (68° 21′N 166° 41′W) **1**:242
POINT ISÈRE
map (5° 45′N 53° 54′W) **8**:311
POINT JUDITH
map (41° 22′N 71° 29′W) **16**:198
POINT JUDITH POND
map (41° 22′N 71° 30′W) **16**:198
POINT LOUIS XIV
map (54° 37′N 79° 45′W) **16**:18
POINT MARION (Pennsylvania)
map (39° 44′N 79° 53′W) **15**:147
POINT MITA
map (20° 47′N 105° 33′W) **13**:357
POINT PALENQUE
map (18° 14′N 70° 9′W) **6**:233
POINT PEDRO
map (9° 50′N 80° 14′E) **18**:206
POINT PEÑAS
map (10° 40′N 61° 40′W) **19**:542
POINT PLEASANT (New Jersey)
map (40° 5′N 74° 4′W) **14**:129
POINT PLEASANT (West Virginia)
map (38° 52′N 82° 8′W) **20**:111
POINT PLEASANT BEACH (New Jersey)
map (40° 5′N 74° 4′W) **14**:129
POINT QUATRE COCOS
map (20° 14′S 57° 46′E) **13**:237
POINT ROBERTS (Washington)
map (48° 59′N 123° 13′W) **20**:35
POINT SALINES
map (12° 0′N 61° 48′W) **9**:358
POINT SÃO SEBASTIÃO
map (22° 7′S 35° 30′E) **13**:627
POINT SAPIN (New Brunswick)
map (46° 58′N 64° 50′W) **14**:117
POINT SET
theory
Carathéodory, Constantin **4**:131
POINT SUD-OUEST
map (20° 28′S 57° 47′E) **13**:237
POINT OF VIEW (literature)
narrative and dramatic devices **14**:22
POINT VINCENTE
map (33° 44′N 118° 25′W) **4**:31
POINTE AUX BARQUES
map (44° 4′N 82° 58′W) **13**:377
POINTE COUPEE (county in Louisiana)
map (30° 38′N 91° 7′W) **12**:430
POINTE A LA HACHE (Louisiana)
map (29° 35′N 89° 48′W) **12**:430
POINTE-NOIRE (Congo)
map (4° 48′S 11° 51′E) **5**:182
POINTE RICHE
map (50° 42′N 57° 25′W) **14**:166
POINTER (dog) **6**:219 *illus.*; **15**:381 *bibliog.*, *illus.*
English setter **7**:204
German shorthaired pointer **9**:135
German wirehaired pointer **9**:135
Irish setter **11**:269
vizsla **19**:623
Weimaraner **20**:95
wirehaired pointing griffon **20**:182
POINTILLISM *see* NEOIMPRESSIONISM
POIRET, PAUL **15**:381 *bibliog.*
Art Deco **2**:208
fashion design **8**:31 *illus.*
POISEUILLE'S EQUATION
circulatory system **4**:442
POISON **15**:381–382 *bibliog.*
alkaloid **1**:296
antidotes **15**:381
antitoxin **2**:69
bacteria **3**:16
pathogenic bacteria **15**:383
bites and stings **3**:300
botulism **3**:419
curare **5**:390–391
cyanide **5**:400
death rate **15**:381
diseases, occupational **6**:193–194; **15**:381
drug **6**:277–278
emetic **7**:155
first aid **8**:108
food poisoning and infection **8**:211
fungus diseases **8**:369
hydrazine **10**:331
infectious diseases **11**:165
jaundice **11**:385
leukemia **12**:301
mercury **13**:306–307
nervous system, diseases of the **14**:96
nicotine **14**:184
poisonous plants and animals **15**:383–385 *illus.*
red tide, dinoflagellate **6**:179
strychnine **18**:304
toxicology **19**:256
venom **19**:546
POISON GAS **15**:382 *bibliog.*
ammunition **1**:375
chemical and biological warfare **4**:311–313
chemical warfare agent **15**:382
engine exhaust **15**:382
gas chamber **9**:53
gas mask **9**:53
Haber, Fritz **10**:4
household products **15**:382
mustard gas **15**:382
safety measures **15**:382
World War I **20**:229–230 *illus.*; **20**:247
POISON HEMLOCK **15**:382 *illus.*
POISON IVY **15**:382–383 *bibliog.*, *illus.*
poison oak **15**:383
poisonous plants and animals **15**:385
sumac **18**:338
POISON LARKSPUR *see* LOCOWEED
POISON OAK **15**:383
sumac **18**:338
POISON SUMAC **15**:383 *illus.*
sumac **18**:338
POISONING
accidental **15**:381
blood poisoning
puerperal fever **15**:614
septicemia **17**:206
chemical and biological warfare **4**:312
food poisoning **8**:211
ptomaine poisoning **15**:608
red tide **16**:114
Salmonella **17**:36
Staphylococcus **18**:220
pollutants, chemical **15**:410–411
types **15**:381–382
POISONOUS PLANTS AND ANIMALS **15**:383–385 *bibliog.*, *illus.*
algae **1**:283
Anabaena **1**:387
animals
adder **1**:99
asp **2**:261
black widow **3**:319
boomslang **3**:393
bushmaster **3**:585
cobra **5**:84
colubrid **5**:124
copperhead **5**:254
coral snake **5**:260
death adder **6**:68
fer-de-lance **8**:51
giant toad **9**:171
Gila monster **9**:178
hydra **10**:330
jellyfish **11**:395; **15**:385
krait **12**:126
lionfish **12**:360
mamba **13**:96 *illus.*
massasauga **13**:212
Mexican beaded lizard **13**:350
pit viper **15**:319
Portuguese man-of-war **15**:457
rattlesnake **16**:93–94
ray **16**:96
scorpion **17**:148
scorpion fish **17**:148
sea snake **17**:170
sidewinder **17**:294
snake **17**:379–381
snapper **17**:384
spider **18**:181–183
stingray **18**:272
tarantula **19**:35
toad **19**:217
viper **19**:604
water moccasin **20**:49
weever **20**:90–91
bites and stings **3**:300
dinoflagellates **15**:384
food poisoning **15**:383–384
fungi **15**:384–385
ergot **7**:228
jack-o'-lantern **11**:339
mushrooms **13**:659–661 *illus.*; **15**:384–385
toadstool **19**:218
hepatitis **10**:130
history **15**:383
Mead, Richard **15**:383
plants **15**:340–341
ageratum **1**:184
alkaloid **1**:296
belladonna **3**:187
bittersweet **3**:301
coyotillo **5**:323
delphinium **6**:95
fritillary (botany) **8**:335
golden chain **9**:231
goldenrod **9**:233
goosefoot **9**:248
greasewood **9**:308
groundsel **9**:374
Halogeton **10**:25
hellebore **10**:114
henbane **10**:121
horse chestnut **10**:246
horsetail **10**:253
jasmine **11**:384
jimsonweed **11**:419
lady's slipper **12**:162
laurel **12**:237
leatherwood **12**:263
locoweed **12**:392
manioc **13**:118
meadow saffron **13**:252
medicinal plants **13**:266
milkweed **13**:424
mistletoe **13**:482
moonseed **13**:567
moutain laurel **13**:622
nettle **14**:104
nightshade **14**:194
nutmeg **14**:302
oleander **13**:377
poison hemlock **15**:382
poison ivy **15**:382–383; **15**:385
poison oak **15**:383
poison sumac **15**:383
pokeweed **15**:387
potato **15**:465–466
rhubarb **16**:203–204
sneezeweed **18**:3
strophanthus **18**:303
sumac **18**:338
tansy **19**:25
thistle **19**:172
upas tree **19**:471
wood sorrel **20**:209
yew **20**:327 *illus.*
red tide **16**:114–115
toxins **15**:383–385
mycotoxins **15**:384
phytotoxins **15**:385
zootoxins **15**:385
POISONS, AFFAIR OF THE *see* MONTESPAN, FRANÇOISE ANTHÉNAÏS DE ROCHECHOUART, MARQUISE DE
POISSON, JEANNE ANTOINETTE, MARQUISE DE POMPADOUR *see* POMPADOUR, JEANNE ANTOINETTE POISSON, MARQUISE DE
POISSON, SIMÉON D.
Poisson distribution **15**:385
POISSON, SIMÉON DENIS
mathematics, history of **13**:226
physics, history of **15**:284
POISSON DISTRIBUTION **15**:385
See also BINOMIAL
POITIER, SIDNEY **15**:385
musical comedy **13**:673 *illus.*
POITIERS (France) **15**:385–386
map (46° 35′N 0° 20′E) **8**:260
Merovingian art and architecture **13**:311
POITIERS, DIANE DE *see* DIANE DE POITIERS
POITOU (France) **15**:386
Louis VIII, King of France **12**:424
POJOAQUE VALLEY (New Mexico)
map (35° 53′N 105° 59′W) **14**:136
POKE (botany) *see* POKEWEED
POKER (card game) **15**:386 *bibliog.*, *illus.*
game theory **9**:27–28
Hickok, Wild Bill **10**:157
POKER DICE (game)
dice games **6**:155
POKEWEED **15**:384 *illus.*; **15**:386–387 *illus.*
ombu **13**:387
POL-E KHOMRI (Afghanistan)
map (35° 56′N 68° 43′E) **1**:133
POL POT **15**:387
Kampuchea (Cambodia) **12**:13
Khieu Samphan **12**:66
Norodom Sihanouk **14**:222
POLABIAN LANGUAGE
Slavic languages **17**:358
POLACCA (Arizona)
map (35° 50′N 110° 23′W) **2**:160
POLAND **15**:387–392 *bibliog.*, *illus.*, *map*, *table*
agriculture **15**:389–390 *illus.*
art and architecture **15**:389
gabled house **10**:269 *illus.*
cities
Bydogoszcz **3**:602
Bytom **3**:603–604
Częstochowa **5**:416
Gdańsk **9**:65
Gdynia **9**:65
Katowice **12**:31
Kraków **12**:127
Łódź **12**:393
Lublin **12**:447
Poznań **15**:487
Radom **16**:68
Szczecin **18**:415
Warsaw **20**:32
Wrocław **20**:295
climate **15**:387–388 *table*
Copernicus, Nicolaus **5**:250
dance
mazurka **13**:250
polonaise **15**:417
economic activity **15**:389–391
education **15**:389
European universities **7**:308 *table*
flag **15**:387 *illus.*
government **15**:390–391
history **15**:391
annexed by Germany in 1939 **9**:156 *map*
Augustus II, King **2**:322
Augustus III, King **2**:322
Bolesław I, King **3**:364
boundaries **15**:391
Casimir III, King (Casimir the Great) **4**:181
Casimir IV, King **4**:181
communist crisis of 1956 **5**:148
Cossacks **5**:290
Czartoryski, Adam Jerzy **5**:412
Dmowski, Roman **6**:208
Gdańsk **9**:65
Gierek, Edward **9**:177
Gomułka, Władysław **9**:241–242
Hitler, Adolf **10**:188
Jadwiga, Queen **11**:348
Jagello (dynasty) **11**:348
Jaruzelski, Wojciech **11**:383
John II, King (John Casimir) **11**:427
John III, King (John Sobieski) **11**:427–428
Kraków **12**:127
Lithuanian Soviet Socialist Republic (USSR) **12**:372
Louis I, King of Hungary (Louis the Great) **12**:428
Oder-Neisse line **14**:349 *map*
Paderewski, Ignace Jan **15**:12
Piast (dynasty) **15**:289
Piłsudski, Józef **15**:303
Poland, Partitions of **15**:392 *map*
Polish Corridor **15**:397
Polish Soviet War **15**:398
Pomerania **15**:422
Sigismund I, King **17**:299
Sigismund II, King **17**:299
Sigismund III, King **17**:299
Slavs **17**:359
Stanisław I, King **18**:218
Stanisław II, King **18**:219
Teschen **19**:126
Vasa (dynasty) **19**:525
Wałesa, Lech **20**:11
Warsaw Uprising **20**:33
World War I *see* WORLD WAR I
World War II **20**:251; **20**:253 *map*
Wyszyński, Stefan **20**:305
land and resources **15**:387–388 *map*, *table*
language
Slavic languages **17**:358
literature *see* POLISH LITERATURE
manufacturing and power **15**:389
map (52° 0′N 19° 0′E) **7**:268
music
Chopin, Frédéric **4**:405
Lutosławski, Witold **12**:470
Penderecki, Krzysztof **15**:142
Szymanowsky, Karol **18**:416
people **7**:275 *illus.*; **15**:388–389
Jews **11**:415
migration to the United States **11**:55 *map*
regions
Masurian Lakes **13**:218
Silesia **17**:304
religion **15**:390 *illus.*
rivers, lakes, and waterways **15**:387
Oder River **14**:349
Vistula River **19**:617–618
theater
Grotowski, Jerzy **9**:372–373
Polish Laboratory Theater **15**:397
Yiddish theater **20**:328

vodka **19**:625
Warsaw Treaty Organization **20**:32
POLAND, PARTITIONS OF **15**:392 *bibliog., map*
Europe, history of **7**:290
Frederick II, King of Prussia (Frederick the Great) **8**:291
Galicia **9**:14
Kościuszko, Tadeusz **12**:123
Livonia **12**:378
nation **14**:27
Russia/Union of Soviet Socialist Republics, history of **16**:355
Stanisław II, King of Poland **18**:219
Suvorov, Aleksandr Vasilievich **18**:374
POLANSKI, ROMAN **15**:392 *bibliog.*
POLANYI, KARL
Hungary **10**:309
POLANYI, MICHAEL
Hungary **10**:309
POLAR BEAR *see* BEAR
POLAR CLIMATE **15**:392 *bibliog.*
Antarctica **15**:392
Arctic **15**:392
cyclonic activity **15**:392
patterned ground **15**:115
permafrost **15**:173–174
polar easterlies **15**:393
taiga climate **19**:11
types **15**:392
POLAR COORDINATES *see* COORDINATE SYSTEMS (mathematics)
POLAR EASTERLIES **15**:393
POLAR MOTION
Earth, motions of **7**:19
POLAR REGIONS *see* ANTARCTICA; ARCTIC; NORTH POLE; SOUTH POLE
POLAR STAR (icebreaker)
Coast Guard, U.S. **5**:80
POLAR WANDERING **15**:393 *map*
geophysics **9**:108
paleogeography **15**:37
plate tectonics **15**:353–354; **15**:357
POLARIMETER **15**:393 *bibliog.*
optical activity **14**:408
qualitative chemical analysis **16**:7
POLARIMETRY
X-ray astronomy **20**:307
POLARIS (astronomy) **15**:393
constellation **5**:212
Little Dipper **12**:372
North Star **15**:393
POLARIS (missile) **15**:393 *bibliog.*
navy **14**:65
rockets and missiles **16**:254–255 *illus.*
submarine **18**:314–316 *illus.*
systems engineering **18**:414
POLARISCOPE **15**:394 *bibliog.*
See also POLARIMETER
POLARITY (embryology)
development **6**:138
POLARIZED LIGHT **15**:394–395 *bibliog., illus.*
analyzers **15**:395
chromatic
Biot, Jean Baptiste **3**:277
dichroism **6**:156
industrial uses **15**:395
Land, Edwin **12**:178
optical activity **14**:408
optical mineralogy **14**:408–409 *illus.*
optics **14**:412 *illus.*
parity (physics) **15**:89
physics, history of **15**:285
production **15**:394
stereochemistry **18**:258
types of polarization **15**:394–395
POLAROGRAPHIC ANALYZER **15**:395
Heyrovský, Jaroslav, designer **10**:155
qualitative chemical analysis **16**:7
POLAROGRAPHY
electrochemistry **7**:113
POLAROID CAMERA **4**:59
Land, Edwin **12**:178
Spectra **4**:58 *illus.*
POLAROID CORPORATION
Land, Edwin **12**:178
POLATLI (Turkey)
map (39° 36′N 32° 9′E) **19**:343
POLDER **15**:395 *bibliog.*
Delta Plan **6**:95
IJsselmeer **11**:39
land reclamation **12**:179–180
Netherlands **14**:98–99 *illus.*
POLE, MAGNETIC *see* EARTH, GEOMAGNETIC FIELD OF
POLE, REGINALD **15**:395 *bibliog.*
POLE, WILLIAM DE LA, 4TH EARL AND 1ST DUKE OF SUFFOLK *see* SUFFOLK, WILLIAM DE LA POLE, 4TH EARL AND 1ST DUKE OF
POLE VAULT
track and field **19**:260
POLEBRIDGE (Montana)
map (48° 46′N 114° 17′W) **13**:547
POLECAT **15**:395 *illus.*
ferret **8**:59
POLESTAR *see* POLARIS (astronomy)
POLESYE (USSR) *see* PRIPET MARSHES (USSR)
POLICE **15**:396–397 *bibliog.*
Canada
Royal Canadian Mounted Police **16**:329–330
criminal justice **5**:349
Germany, history of
Gestapo **9**:159
Great Britain
Peel, Sir Robert **15**:132
Scotland Yard **17**:153
international
intelligence gathering **11**:204–205
Interpol **11**:225
Keystone Kops **12**:64
military police **13**:421
police state **15**:397
riot control
Mace **13**:14
sheriff **17**:257
Union of Soviet Socialist Republics
KGB **12**:64
United States **15**:396
Federal Bureau of Investigation **8**:40–41
Secret Service **17**:180–181
Shore Patrol **17**:283
POLICE STATE **15**:397 *bibliog.*
totalitarianism **19**:248
POLICY RESEARCH *see* THINK TANKS
POLILLO ISLANDS
map (14° 50′N 122° 5′E) **15**:237
POLIOMYELITIS **15**:397 *bibliog.*
diseases, childhood **6**:193
vaccination **19**:501
vaccines **15**:397
rhesus monkey **16**:193 *illus.*
Sabin, Albert Bruce **17**:5
Salk, Jonas **17**:34
POLIS
city-state **5**:9
POLISARIO FRONT
Mauritania **13**:236–237
Morocco **13**:587
Western Sahara **20**:116
POLISH CORRIDOR **15**:397 *bibliog.*
World War I **20**:245
POLISH LABORATORY THEATER **15**:397–398
acting **1**:86; **1**:88
Grotowski, Jerzy **9**:372–373
POLISH LITERATURE **15**:398 *bibliog.*
authors
Borowski, Tadeusz **3**:404
Fredro, Alexander, Count **8**:294
Gombrowicz, Witold **9**:241
Lem, Stanisław **12**:279–280
Mickiewicz, Adam **13**:383–384
Miłosz, Czesław **13**:432
Mrożwek, Sławomir **13**:629
Reymont, Władysław Stanisław **16**:190–191
Różwewicz, Tadeusz **16**:332
Sienkiewicz, Henryk **17**:296
Słowacki, Juliusz **17**:364
Witkiewicz, Stanisław Ignacy **20**:192
Wittlin, Jósef **20**:194
Wyspiański, Stanisław **20**:305
Żeromski, Stefan **20**:361
POLISH-SOVIET WAR **15**:398 *bibliog.*
Piłsudski, Józef **15**:303
POLISH SUCCESSION, WAR OF THE **15**:398 *bibliog.*
Augustus III, King of Poland **2**:322
Louis XV, King of France **12**:427
Stanisław I, King of Poland **18**:218
POLITBURO **15**:398–399 *bibliog.*
POLITIAN **15**:399; **16**:148 *illus.*
POLITICAL ACTION COMMITTEE (PAC)
campaign, political **4**:64
labor union **12**:154
special-interest groups **18**:168
POLITICAL ACTION ORGANIZATIONS
American Civil Liberties Union **1**:337–338
American Indian Movement **1**:340–341
Americans for Democratic Action **1**:367–368
Amnesty International **1**:375
Black Panther party **3**:318
Chicano **4**:343
Common Cause **5**:138
Congress of Racial Equality **5**:184
consumer protection **5**:226
gay activism **9**:63
Gray Panthers **9**:307
John Birch Society **11**:424
labor union **12**:154
League of Women Voters **12**:258
lobbyist **12**:384
Moral Majority **13**:573
muckrakers **13**:630–631
National Association for the Advancement of Colored People **14**:29
National Committee for an Effective Congress **14**:30
National Congress of American Indians **14**:31
National Conservative Political Action Committee **14**:31
National Organization for Women **14**:35–36
National Rifle Association of America **14**:45
pacifism and nonviolent movements **15**:8–10
Sierra Club **17**:296
SNCC **17**:384
Southern Christian Leadership Conference **18**:112
special-interest groups **18**:167–168
Students for a Democratic Society (SDS)
counterculture **5**:311
Urban League, National **19**:480
Veterans' Organizations **19**:566
POLITICAL BOSS *see* BOSS, POLITICAL
POLITICAL CONVENTION **7**:104 *illus.*; **15**:399–400 *bibliog., illus.*
Democratic party **6**:100
favorite son **8**:39
primary election **15**:538–539
Republican Party **16**:172–176
POLITICAL DRAMA *see* THEATER OF FACT
POLITICAL GEOGRAPHY **9**:103
POLITICAL PARTIES **15**:400–403 *bibliog.*
See also the subheading political parties under names of specific countries, e.g., CANADA; EGYPT; names of specific political parties, e.g., AMERICAN LABOR PARTY; SOCIAL CREDIT PARTY; etc.
campaign, political **4**:63–64
communism **5**:146–150
conservatism **5**:205
Conservative parties **5**:205–206
liberal parties **12**:311–312
newspaper **14**:171
socialism **18**:20–24
structure **15**:400–401
systems **15**:401–403
POLITICAL SCIENCE **15**:403–404 *bibliog.*
See also STATE (in political philosophy)
Aristotle **2**:156–158
Brookings Institution **3**:510
democracy **6**:97–99
foreign policy **8**:225–226
game theory **9**:27–29
geopolitics **9**:108–109
government **9**:267–269
Hobbes, Thomas **10**:192
ideology **11**:30–31
Laski, Harold **12**:214
Lasswell, Harold D. **12**:214
Lippmann, Walter **12**:363
Locke, John **12**:387–388
Machiavelli, Nicolò **13**:18–19
Marxism **13**:183–184
Merriam, Charles **13**:312
Mill, John Stuart **13**:425
Montesquieu, Charles Louis de Secondat, Baron de la Brède et de **13**:553
Spirit of the Laws, The **18**:188
political parties **15**:400–403
public opinion **15**:608–610
representation **16**:160–161
Ricardo, David **16**:206
separation of powers **17**:206
Wallas, Graham **20**:15
Weber, Max (sociologist) **20**:87
POLITIS, KOSMAS
Greek literature, modern **9**:344
POLK (county in Arkansas)
map (34° 30′N 94° 15′W) **2**:166
POLK (county in Florida)
map (28° 1′N 81° 37′W) **8**:172
POLK (county in Georgia)
map (34° 0′N 85° 10′W) **9**:114
POLK (county in Iowa)
map (41° 38′N 93° 35′W) **11**:244
POLK (county in Minnesota)
map (47° 40′N 96° 20′W) **13**:453
POLK (county in Missouri)
map (37° 40′N 93° 25′W) **13**:476
POLK (county in Nebraska)
map (41° 10′N 97° 30′W) **14**:70
POLK (county in North Carolina)
map (35° 20′N 82° 10′W) **14**:242
POLK (county in Oregon)
map (45° 0′N 123° 23′W) **14**:427
POLK (Pennsylvania)
map (41° 22′N 79° 56′W) **15**:147
POLK (county in Tennessee)
map (35° 10′N 84° 35′W) **19**:104
POLK (county in Texas)
map (30° 45′N 94° 48′W) **19**:129
POLK (county in Wisconsin)
map (45° 27′N 92° 26′W) **20**:185
POLK, JAMES K. **15**:404–405 *bibliog., illus.*
Mexican War **13**:351–353
Nashville (Tennessee) **14**:24
Taylor, Zachary **19**:50
POLK, LEONIDAS **15**:405 *bibliog.*
POLL *see* OPINION POLLS
POLL TAX **15**:405
24th Amendment **19**:359
voter registration **19**:637
POLLACK (fish)
cod **5**:89
POLLAIUOLO (family) **15**:405–406 *bibliog., illus.*
Martyrdom of Saint Sebastian **15**:406 *illus.*
POLLAPHUCA RESERVOIR
map (53° 8′N 6° 31′W) **11**:258
POLLEN **15**:406–407 *bibliog., illus.*
palynology **15**:30–31
plant reproduction **16**:162
pollen cone **15**:407
pollination **15**:408–409
seed cone **17**:187
POLLEN CONE **15**:407
gymnosperm **9**:414
POLLEN SAC *see* ANTHER SAC
POLLEN STRATIGRAPHY **15**:407–408 *bibliog., illus.*
England **15**:407 *illus.*
fossil record **8**:247
occurrence **15**:407
paleobotany **15**:30–31
paleoclimatology **15**:33
paleoecology **15**:34
pollen analysis **15**:407–408
POLLINATION **15**:408–409 *bibliog., illus.*
angiosperm **1**:414
beekeeping **3**:161
biological agencies **15**:409
coloration, biological **5**:122
fig **8**:75
flower **8**:179–180; **15**:408
iris **11**:266
orchid **14**:419
gymnosperm **15**:408
hummingbird **10**:303
insect **11**:193
nonbiological agencies **15**:409
Kerguelen cabbage **12**:59
plant **15**:338–339 *illus.*
plant propagation **15**:345
pollen cone **15**:407
self-pollination **15**:409
POLLOCK (Louisiana)
map (31° 31′N 92° 24′W) **12**:430
POLLOCK, JACKSON **15**:409 *bibliog., illus.*
Circular Form **15**:23 *illus.*
impasto **11**:60
Krasner, Lee **12**:127
Reflection of the Great Bear **1**:336 *illus.*; **15**:409 *illus.*
POLLOCK v. FARMERS' LOAN AND TRUST CO. **15**:409–410
income tax **11**:76
POLLUTANTS, CHEMICAL **15**:410–411 *bibliog.*
Agent Orange **15**:410
chemical and biological warfare **4**:312
chemical industry **4**:318
chemistry **4**:324
dioxin **15**:410
diseases, occupational **6**:193–194
environmental health **7**:211
federal regulations **15**:410–411
groundwater **9**:375
herbicide **10**:135–136
land reclamation **12**:180
organic chemistry **14**:438–439
organo-halogen compounds **15**:410

POLLUTANTS, CHEMICAL (cont.)
pesticides **15**:196–199
pollution, environmental **15**:412
toxicology **19**:256
Vietnam War **19**:588; **19**:591
waste disposal systems **15**:411; **20**:46–47
POLLUTION, ENVIRONMENTAL **15**:411–415 *bibliog., illus.*
air pollution **15**:414–415
See also SMOG
acid rain **1**:82
aerosol **1**:125 *illus.*
atmosphere **2**:303
chimney **4**:358
Concorde **5**:171
dust, atmospheric **6**:308
gas mask **9**:53
hydrologic cycle **10**:342
inversion **11**:233–234
Mexico City (Mexico) **13**:366
ozone **14**:480
pollution control **15**:415–416
power, generation and transmission of **15**:484
smoke **17**:373
smoking **17**:373
biosphere **3**:277
coal and coal mining **5**:79
Commoner, Barry **5**:141
diseases, occupational **6**:193–194
ecology **7**:46
endangered species **7**:166
environmental health **7**:210–212
environmental impact statement **7**:212
Environmental Protection Agency **7**:212
Industrial Revolution **11**:160
land pollution **15**:412–413
land reclamation **12**:179–180
meteorology **13**:341
national parks **14**:44
New York (state) **14**:153
noise pollution **15**:414
airport **1**:225
Concorde **5**:171
supersonic transport **18**:353
organic chemistry **14**:438–439
pesticide pollution **15**:411; **15**:413
DDT **6**:58
pesticides **15**:198
photography
Smith, W. Eugene **17**:371
pollutants, chemical **15**:410–411
pollution control **15**:415–416
radiation pollution **15**:413–414
Bikini (Marshall Islands) **3**:250
fallout **8**:14
fallout shelter **8**:15
Nevada **14**:113
nuclear energy **14**:282–283
plutonium **15**:373
reaction, chemical **16**:99
remote sensing **16**:147
research institutions
Lawrence Berkeley and Lawrence Livermore laboratories **12**:251
Silent Spring (book) **17**:303–304
thermal pollution **15**:412
typhoid fever **19**:366
Venice (Italy) **11**:324 *illus.*; **19**:545
waste disposal systems **15**:413; **20**:46–47
water pollution **15**:411–412
acid rain **1**:82
conservation **5**:203
Enterobacter **7**:208
Erie, Lake **7**:230
eutrophication **7**:311
groundwater **9**:374–375
lake (body of water) **12**:169
Mediterranean Sea **13**:277
oil spills **14**:363–364
plankton **15**:333
pollution control **15**:415–416
salvage, marine **17**:39
shellfish **17**:254
soap and detergent **18**:8
water quality **20**:50–51
weather modification **20**:79
POLLUTION CONTROL **15**:415–416 *bibliog.*
acid rain **1**:82
automotive industry **2**:367
Environmental Protection Agency **7**:212
federal regulations **15**:415–416
gasoline **9**:55
pollutants, chemical **15**:410–411
pollution, environmental **15**:411–415
problems **15**:416
smoke **17**:373
Stirling engine **18**:272–273
treatment systems **15**:416
air **15**:416
excessive treatment residuals **15**:416
sewerage **17**:222–223
waste disposal systems **20**:46–47
water **15**:416
white rot fungus **20**:138
POLLUX *see* CASTOR AND POLLUX
POLO (Illinois)
map (41° 59′N 89° 35′W) **11**:42
POLO (Missouri)
map (39° 33′N 94° 3′W) **13**:476
POLO (sport) **15**:416–417 *bibliog.*
water polo **20**:50
POLO, MAFFEO **12**:134 *illus.*
POLO, MARCO **10**:136 *illus.*; **15**:417 *bibliog., illus.*
Asia, history of **2**:256
Cathay **4**:204
exploration **2**:255 *map*; **7**:334; **7**:336–337 *map*
Gobi **9**:217
ice cream **11**:11
Kublai Khan, Mongol emperor **12**:134 *illus.*
pasta **15**:106
tourism **19**:252
Travels (book) **2**:255 *illus.*; **12**:134 *illus.*
POLO, NICOLÒ **12**:134 *illus.*
POLO PONY
pony **15**:428
POLONAISE **15**:417 *bibliog.*
Chopin, Frédéric **4**:405
POLONIUM **15**:417 *bibliog.*
chalcogens **4**:270
Curie, Marie and Pierre, discoverers **5**:391–392
element **7**:130 *table*
Group VIA periodic table **15**:167
heat source **15**:417
metal, metallic element **13**:328
POLONNARUWA (Sri Lanka) **15**:418 *bibliog.*
POLOVTSI *see* CUMANS
POLSKA *see* POLAND
POLSON (Montana)
map (47° 41′N 114° 9′W) **13**:547
POLTAVA (USSR) **15**:418
POLTERGEIST
ghost **9**:169
POLYA, GYORGY
problem solving **15**:559 *illus.*
POLYANA, YASNAYA *see* SKIBINE, GEORGE
POLYANDRY
polygamy **15**:419
POLYARTERITIS NODOSA
collagen disease **5**:102–103
POLYBIUS **15**:418 *bibliog.*
history **10**:184
POLYBROMINATED BIPHENYL
environmental health **7**:212
pollutants, chemical **15**:410
POLYCARBONATE, AROMATIC
polyester **15**:419
POLYCARP, SAINT **15**:418 *bibliog.*
Apostolic Fathers **2**:85
POLYCHAETE **15**:418
POLYCHLORINATED BIPHENYL
pollutants, chemical **15**:410
POLYCLITUS **15**:418 *bibliog.*
POLYCLITUS, THE YOUNGER
Theater at Epidaurus **7**:218 *illus.*
POLYCYTHEMIA **15**:418
POLYDACTYLY
genetic code **10**:140 *illus.*
POLYDEUCES (Pollux) *see* CASTOR AND POLLUX
POLYESTER **15**:418–419
classes **15**:418–419
development **15**:418
plastics **15**:350
synthetic fibers **18**:409
uses **15**:418–419
POLYETHYLENE
properties **15**:350 *table*
POLYETHYLENE TEREPHTHALATE
polyester **15**:419
POLYGAMY **15**:419 *bibliog.*
Arabs **2**:106
concubinage **5**:172
family **8**:16
marriage **13**:165 *illus.*
monogamy **13**:536
sexual selection **17**:231
Utah **19**:496
POLYGENE *see* GENETICS
POLYGON **15**:419 *bibliog., illus.*
hexagon **10**:154
parallelogram **15**:79
patterned ground **15**:115
quadrilateral **16**:5
rectangle **16**:110
square **18**:202
trapezoid *illus.* **19**:283–284
triangle (mathematics) **19**:292
POLYGRAPH *see* LIE DETECTOR
POLYGYANDRY
marriage **13**:165
POLYGYNY
concubinage **5**:172
polygamy **15**:419
women in society **20**:203
POLYHALITE **15**:419
POLYHEDRON **15**:419–420 *illus.*
angles of: Cauchy, Augustin Louis **4**:219
cube **5**:380
Euclid **7**:262
Euclidean geometry **7**:263
pyramid **15**:634
volume **19**:632
POLYHYDRIC ALCOHOL **15**:420 *illus.*
glycerol **9**:212
glycol **9**:212
POLYHYMNIA
muses **13**:656
POLYMERASE
genetic code **9**:81 *illus.*
genetics **9**:89
nucleic acid, operon **14**:404
protein synthesis **15**:575
POLYMERIZATION **15**:420 *bibliog.*
chain reaction, chemical **4**:269
chemical nomenclature **4**:321 *illus.*
chlorine compounds **4**:401
copolymer **5**:251
diene **6**:162
elastomer **7**:102
Flory, Paul **8**:177
homopolymer **10**:216
impact of chemistry **4**:324
ladder polymerization
molecular structure **15**:350 *illus.*
latex **12**:215
metabolism **13**:326
mineral classification **13**:442
monomer **13**:537
nylon **14**:308
paint **15**:16–17
peroxide
role in **15**:177
photopolymerization
photochemistry **15**:258
physical chemistry **15**:279
plastics **15**:348 *illus.*
polyester **15**:418–419
polysaccharide **15**:421–422
polystyrene **15**:348 *illus.*
rubber **16**:332; **16**:334
silicones **17**:306
Staudinger, Hermann **18**:239
stereochemistry
Natta, Giulio **14**:47
Ziegler, Karl **20**:363
POLYMORPH **15**:420–421
coesite **5**:93
silica minerals **17**:304
POLYMYXIN
antibiotics **2**:57
POLYNESIA **15**:421
art
Oceanic art **14**:338–339
Southeast Asian art and architecture **18**:107
French Polynesia **8**:321–322
languages
Malayo-Polynesian languages **13**:83
mana **13**:107
map (4° 0′S 156° 0′W) **14**:334
mythology
Pele **15**:137
Oceania **14**:334–335 *maps*
people **15**:421
race **16**:33–34 *illus., map*
taboo **19**:5
POLYNESIANS **15**:421 *bibliog.*
Chamorro **4**:276
Easter Island **7**:32–33 *illus., map*
Hawaii (state) **10**:76
Samoans **17**:46
totem **19**:249
POLYNOMIAL **15**:421
binomial theorem **3**:260
Diophantine equations **6**:185
discriminant **6**:189
equation **7**:224
Ferrari, Lodovico **8**:59
factor **8**:6
Hermite, Charles **10**:143
irrational number **11**:280
quadratic function **16**:5
POLYNUCLEOTIDE
genetic code **9**:80
POLYP (tumor) **15**:421
gastrointestinal tract disease **9**:57
POLYP (zoology) **5**:91 *illus.*
coelenterate **5**:91–92
coral **5**:257 *illus.*
hydra **10**:329
jellyfish **11**:395
sea pen **17**:170
POLYPEPTIDE
amino acid **1**:370
genetic code **9**:80–82
genetic engineering **9**:84
peptide **15**:157
POLYPHEMUS **15**:421
POLYPHONY **15**:421 *bibliog.*
African music **1**:170–171
antiphon **2**:65
chanson **4**:282
choral music **4**:406
church music **4**:424 *illus.*
counterpoint **5**:312
English music **7**:202
folk music **8**:203
harmony **10**:51–52
Honegger, Arthur **10**:220
Italian music **11**:317–318
jazz **11**:387–390
mass (musical setting) **13**:201
medieval music **13**:275
music, history of Western **13**:665
organum **14**:441
Renaissance music **16**:155–156
POLYSACCHARIDE **15**:421–422
cellulose **4**:238
derivatives **15**:422
uses **15**:421–422
chitin **4**:398
starch **15**:421–422
sugar **18**:327
POLYSTYRENE
production **15**:348 *illus.*
POLYTHEISM **15**:422
God **9**:217–218
POLYZOAN *see* BRYOZOAN
POMA DE AYALA, FELIPE HUAMAN *see* AYALA, FELIPE HUAMAN POMA DE
POMABAMBA (Peru)
map (8° 50′S 77° 28′W) **15**:193
POMACE
cider **4**:429
POMATA (Peru)
map (16° 16′S 69° 18′W) **15**:193
POMBAL, SEBASTIÃO JOSÉ DE CARVALHO E MELO, MARQUÊS DE **15**:422 *bibliog.*
Portugal, history of **15**:454
POMEGRANATE **8**:348 *illus.*; **15**:422 *illus.*
POMERANIA (Poland-Germany) **15**:422
history
Germany in 1648 **9**:151 *map*
Germany 1815–1871 **9**:153 *map*
Polish Corridor **15**:397
Szczecin (Poland) **18**:415
POMERANIAN **6**:217 *illus.*; **15**:422–423 *bibliog., illus.*
POMERANIAN BAY
map (54° 0′N 14° 15′E) **9**:140
POMERELIA (Poland) *see* POMERANIA (Poland-Germany)
POMEROY (Iowa)
map (42° 33′N 94° 41′W) **11**:244
POMEROY (Ohio)
map (39° 2′N 82° 2′W) **14**:357
POMEROY (Washington)
map (46° 28′N 117° 36′W) **20**:35
POMME DE TERRE RIVER (Minnesota)
map (45° 10′N 96° 5′W) **13**:453
POMME DE TERRE RIVER(Missouri)
map (38° 11′N 93° 24′W) **13**:476
POMMERN *see* POMERANIA (Poland-Germany)
POMO (American Indians) **15**:423 *bibliog.*
Indians of North America, art of the **11**:139
POMONA (California)
map (34° 4′N 117° 45′W) **4**:31
POMONA (Kansas)
map (38° 36′N 95° 27′W) **12**:18
POMONA COLLEGE
Claremont Colleges **5**:36
POMONA LAKE
map (38° 40′N 95° 35′W) **12**:18
POMPADOUR, JEANNE ANTOINETTE POISSON, MARQUISE DE **15**:423 *bibliog., illus.*
Petit Trianon **15**:203
Sèvres ware **17**:221
POMPANO **15**:423
POMPANO, CALIFORNIA *see* BUTTERFISH
POMPANO BEACH (Florida)
map (26° 15′N 80° 7′W) **8**:172
POMPEII (Italy) **15**:423–424 *bibliog., illus.*

archaeology **2**:121
excavated city **15**:424 *illus.*
Fiorelli, Giuseppe **8**:99
art
floor mosaic in House of the Faun **9**:333 *illus.*; **15**:424 *illus.*; **16**:276 *illus.*
landscape painting **12**:188 *illus.*
mural painting **13**:646
Mysteries, Villa of the **13**:692; **15**:424 *illus.*
relief depicting actors **19**:144 *illus.*
Roman art and architecture **16**:276 *illus.*
still-life wall painting **18**:269 *illus.*
history **15**:423–424
house (in Western architecture) **10**:266
POMPEY THE GREAT **15**:424–425 *bibliog., illus.*
Caesar, Gaius Julius **4**:14
Cicero, Marcus Tullius **4**:428–429
Crassus, Marcus Licinius **5**:332
Lucullus, Lucius Licinius **12**:451
Pamplona (Spain) **15**:53
Rome, ancient **16**:301
POMPIDOU, GEORGES **15**:425 *bibliog.*
Beaubourg **3**:145
POMPIDOU CENTER *see* BEAUBOURG
POMPON *see* CHRYSANTHEMUM
POMPONAZZI, PIETRO **15**:425 *bibliog.*
POMPTON LAKES (New Jersey)
map (41° 0′N 74° 17′W) **14**:129
POMQUET (Nova Scotia)
map (45° 38′N 61° 51′W) **14**:269
PONAPE ISLAND
United States outlying territories **19**:464
PONCA (American Indians)
Omaha (American Indians) **14**:385
PONCA (Nebraska)
map (42° 34′N 96° 43′W) **14**:70
PONCA CITY (Oklahoma)
map (36° 42′N 97° 5′W) **14**:368
PONCE (Puerto Rico) **15**:425
map (18° 1′N 66° 37′W) **15**:614
PONCE, MANUEL
Latin American music and dance **12**:232
PONCE DE LEON (Florida)
map (30° 44′N 85° 56′W) **8**:172
PONCE DE LEÓN, JUAN **15**:425–426 *bibliog.*
Dry Tortugas (Florida) **6**:284
exploration of colonial America **19**:437 *map*
Ponce (Puerto Rico) **15**:425
Puerto Rico **15**:616
Saint Augustine (Florida) **17**:16
San Juan (Puerto Rico) **17**:55
Turks and Caicos Islands **19**:349
PONCELET, JEAN VICTOR
mathematics, history of **13**:226
PONCHATOULA (Louisiana)
map (30° 26′N 90° 26′W) **12**:430
PONCHIELLI, AMILCARE **15**:426 *bibliog.*
POND
eutrophication **7**:311
POND, PETER
Peace River **15**:123
POND APPLE *see* CUSTARD APPLE
POND RIVER
map (37° 32′N 87° 21′W) **12**:47
POND TURTLE **15**:426 *illus.*
PONDCREEK (Oklahoma)
map (36° 40′N 97° 48′W) **14**:368
PONDERA (county in Montana)
map (48° 15′N 112° 5′W) **13**:547
PONDERAY (Idaho)
map (48° 18′N 116° 32′W) **11**:26
PONDICHERRY (India) **15**:426
map (11° 56′N 79° 53′E) **11**:80
PONDICHÉRY (India) *see* PONDICHERRY (India)
PONDO *see* NGUNI
PONDOSA (California)
map (41° 12′N 121° 41′W) **4**:31
PONDWEED **15**:426
PONFERRADA (Spain)
map (42° 33′N 6° 35′W) **18**:140
PONHOOK LAKE
map (44° 19′N 64° 53′W) **14**:269
PONOKA (Alberta)
map (52° 42′N 113° 35′W) **1**:256
PONOROGO (Indonesia)
map (7° 52′S 111° 27′E) **11**:147
PONS, LILY **15**:426 *bibliog.*
PONSELLE, ROSA **15**:426
PONSONBY, LADY CAROLINE
Melbourne, William Lamb, 2d Viscount **13**:286
PONT, DU (family) *see* DU PONT (family)
PONT DU GARD (France) **8**:266 *illus.*; **19**:63 *illus.*
Nîmes **14**:198
PONTA DELGADA (Azores) **15**:426
map (37° 44′N 25° 40′W) **15**:449
PONTA GROSSA (Brazil)
map (25° 5′S 50° 9′W) **3**:460
PONTA PORÃ (Brazil)
map (22° 32′S 55° 43′W) **3**:460
PONTCHARTRAIN, LAKE **12**:431 *illus.*; **14**:141 *map*; **15**:427
map (30° 10′N 90° 10′W) **12**:430
PONTE, LORENZO DA *see* DA PONTE, LORENZO
PONTE DEI SOSPIRI *see* BRIDGE OF SIGHS
PONTE NOVA (Brazil)
map (20° 24′S 42° 54′W) **3**:460
PONTE VECCHIO **8**:168–169 *illus., map*
PONTE VEDRA BEACH (Florida)
map (30° 14′N 81° 23′W) **8**:172
PONTEVEDRA (Spain)
map (42° 26′N 8° 38′W) **18**:140
PONTI, GIO **15**:427 *bibliog.*
PONTIAC (Illinois)
map (40° 53′N 88° 38′W) **11**:42
PONTIAC (Michigan)
map (42° 37′N 83° 18′W) **13**:377
PONTIAC (Ottawa Indian)
Delaware Prophet **6**:91
Illinois (American Indians) **11**:45
Pontiac's Rebellion **15**:427
PONTIAC FEVER
Legionnaires' disease **12**:274
PONTIAC'S REBELLION **11**:109 *map*; **15**:427 *bibliog.*
Detroit **6**:135
Fort Wayne (Indiana) **8**:238
Indian Wars **11**:107
PONTIANAK (Indonesia)
map (0° 2′S 109° 20′E) **11**:147
PONTINE MARSHES **15**:427
land reclamation **12**:179
PONTIUS PILATE *see* PILATE, PONTIUS
PONTOONS AND PONTOON BRIDGES **15**:427
catamaran **4**:199–200
PONTOPPIDAN, HENRIK **15**:427 *bibliog.*
PONTORMO, JACOPO CARUCCI DA **15**:427–428 *bibliog., illus.*
The Entombment **16**:153 *illus.*
The Visitation **15**:427 *illus.*
PONTOTOC (Mississippi)
map (34° 15′N 89° 0′W) **13**:469
PONTOTOC (county in Mississippi)
map (34° 15′N 89° 0′W) **13**:469
PONTOTOC (county in Oklahoma)
map (34° 45′N 96° 40′W) **14**:368
PONTOTOC (Texas)
map (30° 54′N 98° 59′W) **19**:129
PONTUS **15**:428 *bibliog.*
Mithradates VII, King (Mithradates the Great) **13**:484
PONTY, MAURICE MERLEAU- *see* MERLEAU-PONTY, MAURICE
PONY **15**:428 *illus.*
coach horse **5**:75
horse **10**:244
Shetland pony **17**:260
Welsh pony **20**:102 *illus.*
PONY EXPRESS **15**:428 *bibliog.*
Nevada **14**:114
route **19**:445 *map*
stage route **8**:341 *map*
PONZIANE ISLANDS
map (40° 55′N 12° 57′E) **11**:321
POODLE **15**:428–429 *bibliog., illus.*
miniature **6**:219 *illus.*
standard **6**:219 *illus.*
toy **6**:217 *illus.*
POOL (game) *see* POCKET BILLIARDS
POOLE (England)
map (50° 43′N 1° 59′W) **19**:403
POOLER (Georgia)
map (32° 7′N 81° 15′W) **9**:114
POONA (India) **15**:429
map (18° 32′N 73° 52′E) **11**:80
POOPÓ, LAKE
map (18° 45′S 67° 7′W) **3**:366
POOR, THE *see* POVERTY
POOR CLARES *see* CLARE OF ASSISI, SAINT
POOR LAWS **15**:429 *bibliog.*
social and welfare services **18**:17
POOR RICHARD'S ALMANACK (book) **15**:429
Franklin, Benjamin **8**:283
frontispiece **8**:283 *illus.*
POORWILL *see* GOATSUCKER (bird)
POOT, LINKE *see* DÖBLIN, ALFRED
POP ART **15**:429 *bibliog., illus.*
Blake, Peter (painter) **3**:325
Hockney, David **10**:193
iconography **11**:24
Indiana, Robert **11**:115
Lichtenstein, Roy **12**:322
Marisol **13**:157
modern art **13**:494–495
Oldenburg, Claes **14**:376
photorealism **15**:274–275
Rauschenberg, Robert **16**:94
Rosenquist, James **16**:315–316
Warhol, Andy **20**:29–30
Wesselmann, Tom **20**:106
POP WARNER FOOTBALL **15**:430
POPAYÁN (Colombia)
map (2° 27′N 76° 36′W) **5**:107
POPCORN **5**:266
POPE *see* PAPACY; ROMAN CATHOLIC CHURCH; names of specific popes, e.g., GREGORY VII, POPE; INNOCENT III, POPE; etc.
POPE (county in Arkansas)
map (35° 30′N 93° 5′W) **2**:166
POPE (county in Illinois)
map (37° 28′N 88° 32′W) **11**:42
POPÉ (Indian leader) **15**:430 *bibliog.*
Spanish missions **18**:161
POPE (county in Minnesota)
map (45° 35′N 95° 25′W) **13**:453
POPE, ALEXANDER **7**:196 *illus.*; **15**:430 *bibliog., illus.*
Essay on Man, An **7**:244
landscape architecture **12**:186
neoclassicism (literature) **14**:82
Rape of the Lock, The **16**:88
satire **17**:88
Warburton, William **20**:28
POPE, JOHN **15**:430
Civil War, U.S. **5**:23 *map*; **5**:24–25
POPE, JOHN RUSSELL **15**:430–431 *bibliog.*
National Gallery of Art **14**:33
POPHYRY-COPPER *see* COPPER
POPISH PLOT
Oates, Titus **14**:313
POPLAR **15**:431 *illus.*
tacamahac **19**:5
POPLAR (Montana)
map (48° 7′N 105° 12′W) **13**:547
POPLAR BLUFF (Missouri)
map (36° 45′N 90° 24′W) **13**:476
POPLARVILLE (Mississippi)
map (30° 51′N 89° 32′W) **13**:469
POPOCATÉPETL (volcano) **13**:360 *illus.*; **14**:235 *illus.*; **15**:431
map (19° 2′N 98° 38′W) **13**:357
POPOMANASIU, MOUNT
map (9° 42′S 160° 4′E) **18**:56
POPONDETTA (Papua New Guinea)
map (8° 46′S 148° 14′E) **15**:72
POPOV, OLEG **5**:70 *illus.*
POPOVIĆ, JOVAN STERIJA
Yugoslavia **20**:342
POPOVICH, PAVEL ROMANOVICH **15**:431–432
Vostok **19**:636–637 *table*
POPPAEA SABINA
Rome, ancient **16**:302
PÖPPELMANN, MATTHÄUS DANIEL **15**:432 *bibliog.*
German art and architecture **9**:126–127
POPPELREUTHER, W.
clinical psychology **5**:59
POPPER *see* AMYL NITRITE
POPPER, SIR KARL RAIMUND **15**:432 *bibliog.*
POPPY **8**:348 *illus.*; **14**:406 *illus.*; **15**:432–433 *bibliog., illus.*
bloodroot **3**:340
creamcups **5**:334
golden cup **9**:231
opium **14**:406
POPPY DAY
Haig, Douglas Haig, 1st Earl **10**:12
POPULAR LIBERATION FORCES (Greece) *see* EAM-ELAS
POPULAR MUSIC *see* BLUES (music); COUNTRY AND WESTERN MUSIC; DISCO MUSIC; GOSPEL MUSIC; JAZZ; RAGTIME; ROCK MUSIC; SWING (music)
POPULAR REVOLUTIONARY ALLIANCE (political party)
Peru **15**:194; **15**:195
POPULAR SCIENCE (periodical)
Cattell, James McKeen **4**:214
POPULAR SOCIALIST LIBYAN ARAB JAMAHIRIYA *see* LIBYA
POPULAR SONGS *see* SONG
POPULAR SOVEREIGNTY **15**:433 *bibliog.*
Douglas, Stephen A. **6**:247–248
United States, history of the **19**:447
POPULATION **15**:433–437 *bibliog., map*
agriculture and the food supply **1**:195; **1**:198 *table*
birth control **3**:294
bubonic plague **3**:532
census **4**:248–249
control **15**:434; **15**:437
demography **6**:103–104
density, worldwide **15**:435 *map*
distribution (statistics) **6**:201
distribution patterns **15**:434
epidemiology **7**:219
government policies **15**:434; **15**:437
Great Britain, Industrial Revolution **11**:158
growth **15**:434–437 *map*
human ecology **10**:297
infanticide **11**:163
inner city **11**:179
Malthus, Thomas Robert **13**:96
metropolitan area **13**:347
old age **14**:373–374
Planned Parenthood Federation of America **15**:333
population dynamics **15**:438–439
race **16**:33–35
Ricardo, David **16**:206
standard deviation **18**:216
suburbs **18**:317
POPULATION, STELLAR **15**:437 *bibliog.*
Baade, Walter **3**:4; **15**:437
extragalactic systems **7**:344
Hertzsprung-Russell diagram **10**:149
star classifications
extreme population **15**:437
population I **15**:437
population II **15**:437
stellar evolution **15**:437
POPULATION BIOLOGY **15**:438
homeostasis **10**:212–213
population dynamics **15**:438–439
POPULATION DENSITY *see* DEMOGRAPHY
POPULATION DYNAMICS **15**:438–439 *bibliog.*
controlling forces **15**:438
density **15**:438
growth **15**:438
homeostasis **10**:212–213
Howells, William White **10**:285
human intervention **15**:438
overpopulation
Ehrlich, Paul (1932–) **7**:90–91
population oscillations **15**:438–439
predators **15**:438
prehistoric humans **15**:517
race **16**:33–35
weather **15**:438
POPULATION GENETICS **15**:439–440 *bibliog.*
applications **15**:440
evolution **7**:319–320
evolutionary factors **15**:439–440
genetics **9**:89–90 *map*
Haldane, J. B. S. **10**:17
Hardy-Weinberg equilibrium **15**:439
Mayr, Ernst **13**:249
natural selection **14**:49
race **16**:33–35
POPULATION GEOGRAPHY **9**:103
POPULIST PARTY **15**:440 *bibliog., illus.*
conservatism **5**:205
Lease, Mary Elizabeth **12**:261–262
Watson, Thomas E. **20**:68
Weaver, James B. **20**:83
POQUELIN, JEAN BAPTISTE *see* MOLIÈRE
POQUOSON (Virginia)
map (37° 7′N 76° 21′W) **19**:607
PORCELAIN
See also POTTERY AND PORCELAIN
dentistry **6**:116
PORCO (Bolivia)
map (19° 50′S 65° 59′W) **3**:366
PORCUPINE **13**:105 *illus.*; **15**:440 *bibliog., illus.*
PORCUPINE FISH **15**:441 *illus.*
PORCUPINE MOUNTAINS
map (46° 40′N 89° 40′W) **13**:377
PORCUPINE RIVER
map (66° 35′N 145° 15′W) **1**:242
PORDENONE (Italy)
map (45° 57′N 12° 39′E) **11**:321
PORGY (book)
Heyward, DuBose **10**:155
PORGY (fish) **15**:441 *illus.*
PORGY AND BESS **15**:441
musical comedy **13**:673 *illus.*

PORI (Finland)
map (61° 29′N 21° 47′E) **8**:95
PORIFERA *see* SPONGE
PORIRUA (New Zealand)
map (41° 8′S 174° 51′E) **14**:158
PORK
meat and meat packing **13**:257 *table*
pig **15**:298–299
trichinosis **19**:296
PORLAMAR (Venezuela)
map (10° 57′N 63° 51′W) **19**:542
PORNOGRAPHY **15**:441–442 *bibliog.*
See also EROTIC AND PORNOGRAPHIC LITERATURE
censorship **4**:246–248
Comstock, Anthony **5**:167
freedom of the press **8**:296
Miller v. *California* **13**:428–429
Roth v. *United States* **16**:321–322
PORO *see* MENDE
PORPHYRIA **15**:442
PORPHYRINS
Fischer, Hans **8**:110
PORPHYRY (geology) **15**:442
igneous rock **11**:33
phenocryst **15**:225
sulfide minerals **18**:334
PORPHYRY (philosopher) **15**:442 *bibliog.*
PORPOISE **15**:442 *bibliog., illus.*
cetacean **4**:262
dolphin **6**:228
echolocation **7**:39
sound frequencies produced **18**:73 *table*
PORPORA, NICOLA ANTONIO
voice, singing **19**:626
PORSCHE, FERDINAND
Volkswagen **19**:630
PORSENA, LARS *see* LARS PORSENA, KING OF CLUSIUM
PORT (harbor) *see* HARBOR AND PORT
PORT (wine) **15**:442 *bibliog.*
PORT ALBERNI (British Columbia)
map (49° 14′N 124° 48′W) **3**:491
PORT ALEXANDER (Alaska)
map (56° 15′N 134° 39′W) **1**:242
PORT ALLEGANY (Pennsylvania)
map (41° 49′N 78° 17′W) **15**:147
PORT ALLEN (Louisiana)
map (30° 27′N 91° 12′W) **12**:430
PORT ANGELES (Washington)
map (48° 7′N 123° 27′W) **20**:35
PORT ANTONIO (Jamaica)
map (18° 11′N 76° 28′W) **11**:351
PORT ARTHUR (China) *see* LÜ-SHUN (Lüshun) (China)
PORT ARTHUR (Texas) **15**:442
map (29° 55′N 93° 55′W) **19**:129
PORT ASHTON (Alaska)
map (60° 4′N 148° 1′W) **1**:242
PORT-AU-PRINCE (Haiti) **10**:15–16 *illus., table*; **15**:442–443
map (18° 32′N 72° 20′W) **10**:15
PORT AUSTIN (Michigan)
map (44° 3′N 83° 1′W) **13**:377
PORT BARRE (Louisiana)
map (30° 34′N 91° 57′W) **12**:430
PORT BIRMINGHAM (Alabama)
map (33° 34′N 87° 6′W) **1**:234
PORT BLANDFORD (Newfoundland)
map (48° 21′N 54° 10′W) **14**:166
PORT BYRON (Illinois)
map (41° 36′N 90° 20′W) **11**:42
PORT-CARTIER-QUEST (Quebec)
map (50° 1′N 66° 52′W) **16**:18
PORT CHARLOTTE (Florida)
map (26° 59′N 82° 6′W) **8**:172
PORT CHESTER (New York)
map (41° 0′N 73° 40′W) **14**:149
PORT CLINTON (Ohio)
map (41° 31′N 82° 56′W) **14**:357
PORT CLYDE (Maine)
map (43° 56′N 69° 15′W) **13**:70
PORT COLBORNE (Ontario)
map (42° 53′N 79° 14′W) **19**:241
map (42° 53′N 79° 14′W) **14**:393
PORT COQUITLAM (British Columbia)
map (49° 16′N 122° 46′W) **3**:491
PORT-DE-PAIX (Haiti)
map (19° 57′N 72° 50′W) **10**:15
PORT EDWARDS (Wisconsin)
map (44° 21′N 90° 5′W) **20**:185
PORT ELGIN (New Brunswick)
map (46° 3′N 64° 5′W) **14**:117
PORT ELGIN (Ontario)
map (44° 26′N 81° 24′W) **19**:241
PORT ELIZABETH (South Africa) **15**:443
map (33° 58′S 25° 40′E) **18**:79
PORT OF ENTRY **15**:443
PORT-GENTIL (Gabon)
map (0° 43′S 8° 47′E) **9**:5
PORT GIBSON (Mississippi)
map (31° 58′N 90° 58′W) **13**:469
PORT GRAHAM (Alaska)
map (59° 21′N 151° 50′W) **1**:242
PORT GREVILLE (Nova Scotia)
map (45° 24′N 64° 33′W) **14**:269
PORT HARCOURT (Nigeria)
map (4° 43′N 7° 5′E) **14**:190
PORT HAWKESBURY (Nova Scotia)
map (45° 37′N 61° 21′W) **14**:269
PORT HEDLAND (Australia)
map (20° 19′S 118° 34′E) **2**:328
PORT HEIDEN (Alaska)
map (56° 55′N 158° 41′W) **1**:242
PORT HILL (Prince Edward Island)
map (46° 35′N 63° 53′W) **15**:548
PORT HOOD (Nova Scotia)
map (46° 1′N 61° 32′W) **14**:269
PORT HOPE (Michigan)
map (43° 57′N 82° 43′W) **13**:377
PORT HUENEME (California)
map (34° 9′N 119° 12′W) **4**:31
PORT HURON (Michigan)
map (42° 58′N 82° 27′W) **13**:377
PORT ISABEL (Texas)
map (26° 4′N 97° 13′W) **19**:129
PORT JERVIS (New York)
map (41° 22′N 74° 41′W) **14**:149
PORT LAOISE (Ireland)
map (53° 2′N 7° 17′W) **11**:258
PORT LAVACA (Texas)
map (28° 37′N 96° 38′W) **19**:129
PORT LEYDEN (New York)
map (43° 35′N 75° 21′W) **14**:149
PORT LINCOLN (Australia)
map (34° 44′S 135° 52′E) **2**:328
PORT LOUIS (Mauritius) **15**:443
map (20° 10′S 57° 30′E) **13**:237
PORT MAITLAND (Nova Scotia)
map (43° 59′N 66° 9′W) **14**:269
PORT MARIA (Jamaica)
map (18° 22′N 76° 54′W) **11**:351
PORT MELLON (British Columbia)
map (49° 32′N 123° 29′W) **3**:491
PORT-MENIER (Quebec)
map (49° 48′N 64° 20′W) **16**:18
PORT MOLLER (Alaska)
map (55° 59′N 160° 34′W) **1**:242
PORT MORANT (Jamaica)
map (17° 54′N 76° 19′W) **11**:351
PORT MORESBY (Papua New Guinea) **15**:73 *illus., table*; **15**:443
map (9° 30′S 147° 10′E) **15**:72
PORT MOUTON (Nova Scotia)
map (43° 56′N 64° 51′W) **14**:269
PORT NECHES (Texas)
map (29° 59′N 93° 58′W) **19**:129
PORT NELSON (Manitoba)
map (57° 3′N 92° 36′W) **13**:119
PORT NEVILLE (British Columbia)
map (50° 29′N 126° 5′W) **3**:491
PORT NICHOLSON (New Zealand)
map (41° 17′S 174° 50′E) **14**:158
PORT NORRIS (New Jersey)
map (39° 15′N 75° 2′W) **14**:129
PORT-NOUVEAU-QUÉBEC (Quebec)
map (58° 32′N 65° 54′W) **16**:18
PORT ORANGE (Florida)
map (29° 9′N 80° 59′W) **8**:172
PORT ORCHARD (Washington)
map (47° 32′N 122° 38′W) **20**:35
PORT ORFORD (Oregon)
map (42° 45′N 124° 30′W) **14**:427
PORT RADIUM (Northwest Territories)
map (66° 5′N 118° 2′W) **14**:258
PORT RASHID (Dubai)
harbor and port **10**:42
PORT READING (New Jersey)
map (40° 34′N 74° 16′W) **14**:129
PORT ROWAN (Ontario)
map (42° 37′N 80° 28′W) **14**:393; **19**:241
PORT ROYAL (Pennsylvania)
map (40° 32′N 77° 23′W) **15**:147
PORT ROYAL (South Carolina)
map (32° 23′N 80° 43′W) **18**:98
PORT-ROYAL-DES-CHAMPS, ABBEY OF
Arnauld, Jacqueline Marie Angélique **2**:183
Jansenism **11**:359 *illus.*
Pascal, Blaise **15**:102
PORT ROYAL SOUND
map (32° 15′N 80° 40′W) **18**:98
PORT SAID (Egypt) **15**:443
map (31° 16′N 32° 18′E) **7**:76
PORT SAINT JOE (Florida)
map (29° 49′N 85° 18′W) **8**:172
PORT SANILAC (Michigan)
map (43° 26′N 82° 33′W) **13**:377
PORT SAUNDERS (Newfoundland)
map (50° 39′N 57° 18′W) **14**:166
PORT OF SPAIN (Trinidad and Tobago) **15**:443
climate **19**:300 *table*
map (10° 39′N 61° 31′W) **19**:300
PORT SUDAN (Sudan)
map (19° 37′N 37° 14′E) **18**:320
PORT SULPHUR (Louisiana)
map (29° 29′N 89° 42′W) **12**:430
PORT SUNLIGHT (experimental workers' community)
model cottage from **10**:267 *illus.*
PORT TOWNSEND (Washington)
map (48° 7′N 122° 46′W) **20**:35
PORT UNION (Newfoundland)
map (48° 30′N 53° 5′W) **14**:166
PORT VINCENT (Louisiana)
map (30° 20′N 90° 51′W) **12**:430
PORT WASHINGTON (Wisconsin)
map (43° 23′N 87° 53′W) **20**:185
PORT WENTWORTH (Georgia)
map (32° 9′N 81° 10′W) **9**:114
PORT WING (Wisconsin)
map (46° 47′N 91° 23′W) **20**:185
PORTA, CARLO **15**:443
PORTA, GIACOMO DELLA **15**:443 *bibliog.*
PORTAGE (Michigan)
map (42° 12′N 85° 41′W) **13**:377
PORTAGE (Missouri)
map (38° 56′N 90° 21′W) **13**:476
PORTAGE (county in Ohio)
map (41° 19′N 81° 15′W) **14**:357
PORTAGE (Pennsylvania)
map (40° 23′N 78° 41′W) **15**:147
PORTAGE (Utah)
map (41° 59′N 112° 14′W) **19**:492
PORTAGE (Wisconsin)
map (43° 33′N 89° 28′W) **20**:185
PORTAGE (county in Wisconsin)
map (44° 30′N 89° 30′W) **20**:185
PORTAGE LA PRAIRIE (Manitoba)
map (49° 59′N 98° 18′W) **13**:119
PORTAGEVILLE (Missouri)
map (36° 26′N 89° 42′W) **13**:476
PORTAL (Georgia)
map (32° 33′N 81° 56′W) **9**:114
PORTAL (North Dakota)
map (48° 59′N 102° 33′W) **14**:248
PORTAL VEIN
circulatory system **4**:440 *illus.*
liver **12**:374 *illus.*
PORTALEGRE (Portugal)
map (39° 17′N 7° 26′W) **15**:449
PORTALES (New Mexico)
map (34° 11′N 103° 20′W) **14**:136
PORTATIVE ORGAN **15**:443–444 *illus.*
PORTER (beer) **3**:163
PORTER (family) **15**:444 *bibliog.*
PORTER (Indiana)
map (41° 37′N 87° 4′W) **11**:111
PORTER (county in Indiana)
map (41° 28′N 87° 4′W) **11**:111
PORTER (Oklahoma)
map (35° 52′N 95° 31′W) **14**:368
PORTER (Texas)
map (30° 6′N 95° 14′W) **19**:129
PORTER, COLE **15**:444 *bibliog.*
PORTER, DAVID D. **19**:448 *illus.*
PORTER, EDWIN S. **15**:444
film, history of **8**:81 *illus.*
PORTER, ELIOT **15**:444
PORTER, FAIRFIELD **15**:444
PORTER, GEORGE **15**:444 *bibliog.*
PORTER, KATHERINE ANNE **15**:444–445 *bibliog., illus.*
PORTER, NOAH **15**:445
PORTER, WILLIAM SYDNEY *see* O. HENRY
PORTERVILLE (California)
map (36° 4′N 119° 1′W) **4**:31
PORTERVILLE (Mississippi)
map (32° 41′N 88° 28′W) **13**:469
PORTES GIL, EMILIO
Mexico, history of **13**:365
PORTICO
stoa **18**:273
PORTILLO (Cuba)
map (19° 55′N 77° 11′W) **5**:377
PORTILLO Y PACHECO, JOSÉ LÓPEZ *see* LÓPEZ PORTILLO Y PACHECO, JOSÉ
PORTIMÃO (Portugal)
map (37° 8′N 8° 32′W) **15**:449
PORTINARI, CÂNDIDO **15**:445 *bibliog.*
Latin American art and architecture **12**:228
PORTLAND (Arkansas)
map (33° 14′N 91° 30′W) **2**:166
PORTLAND (Connecticut)
map (41° 34′N 72° 38′W) **5**:193
PORTLAND (Indiana)
map (40° 26′N 84° 59′W) **11**:111
PORTLAND (Maine) **13**:73 *illus.*; **15**:445
map (43° 39′N 70° 17′W) **13**:70
PORTLAND (Michigan)
map (42° 52′N 84° 54′W) **13**:377
PORTLAND (North Dakota)
map (47° 30′N 97° 22′W) **14**:248
PORTLAND (Oregon) **14**:428 *illus.*; **15**:445
map (45° 33′N 122° 36′W) **14**:427
Portland Building **9**:302 *illus.*
PORTLAND (Tennessee)
map (36° 35′N 86° 31′W) **19**:104
PORTLAND (Texas)
map (27° 53′N 97° 20′W) **19**:129
PORTLAND BIGHT
map (17° 53′N 77° 8′W) **11**:351
PORTLAND POINT
map (17° 42′N 77° 11′W) **11**:351
PORTNOY'S COMPLAINT (book)
Roth, Philip **16**:321
PORTO (Portugal) **15**:445
map (41° 11′N 8° 36′W) **15**:449
PÔRTO ALEGRE (Brazil) **15**:445
climate **3**:461 *table*
harbor and port **10**:42
map (30° 4′S 51° 11′W) **3**:460
PORTO ESPERANÇA (Brazil)
map (19° 37′S 57° 27′W) **3**:460
PÔRTO NACIONAL (Brazil)
map (10° 42′S 48° 25′W) **3**:460
PORTO-NOVO (Benin) **15**:445–446
map (6° 29′N 2° 37′E) **3**:200
PORTO SANTO
Madeira Islands **13**:40 *map*
PÔRTO VELHO (Brazil)
map (8° 46′S 63° 54′W) **3**:460
PORTOLA (California)
map (39° 48′N 120° 28′W) **4**:31
PORTOLÁ, GASPAR DE **15**:446 *bibliog.*
California **4**:36
Los Angeles (California) **12**:418
San Diego (California) **17**:52
PORTOLAN CHART
navigation **14**:58
PORTOVIEJO (Ecuador)
map (1° 3′S 80° 27′W) **7**:52
PORTRAIT OF THE ARTIST AS A YOUNG MAN, A **15**:446 *bibliog.*
PORTRAITURE **15**:446–448 *bibliog., illus.*
American art and architecture **1**:331–332
Canadian art and architecture **4**:89
coins
Roman art and architecture **16**:277
drawing **6**:264
enamel
Limosin, Léonard **12**:346
Europe, history of **7**:286–287
graphic arts
Nanteuil, Robert **14**:13
Utamaro **19**:496
National Portrait Gallery **14**:44–45
painting **15**:446
Antonello da Messina **2**:69–70
Beaux, Cecilia **3**:148
Boldini, Giovanni **3**:364
Bronzino **3**:508–509
Carriera, Rosalba **4**:168
Cassatt, Mary **4**:183
Champaigne, Philippe de **4**:277
Chase, William Merritt **4**:301
Clouet (family) **5**:68–69
Cooper, Samuel **5**:244
Copley, John Singleton **5**:251
Cosway, Richard **5**:303–304
Cranach, Lucas, the Elder **5**:329
Eakins, Thomas **7**:4–5
Earl, Ralph **7**:8
English art and architecture **7**:184
Feke, Robert **8**:45
Freake limner **8**:289
Gainsborough, Thomas **9**:8–9
Gaugin, Paul **9**:59–60
Gérard, François Pascal Simon, Baron **9**:121
Goya, Francisco de **9**:273–274
Hals, Frans **10**:25
Harding, Chester **10**:45–46
Healy, G. P. A. **10**:89
Helst, Bartholomeus van der **10**:117
Holbein, Hans, the Younger **10**:200–201
Hoppner, John **10**:233
Ingres, Jean Auguste Dominique **11**:176–177
Isabey, Jean Baptiste **11**:286
John, Augustus **11**:423
Johnson, Eastman **11**:431
Kneller, Sir Godfrey **12**:99
Ku K'ai-chih (Gu Kaizhi) **12**:133
Lancret, Nicolas **12**:178
Largillière, Nicolas de **12**:207

Lawrence, Sir Thomas **12**:251
Lely, Sir Peter **12**:279
Leonardo da Vinci **12**:289–291
Levnî, Ressam **12**:304–305
limners **12**:345
Lotto, Lorenzo **12**:420
Luks, George **12**:454
Maes, Nicolaes **13**:45
Malbone, Edward Greene **13**:86
Massys, Quentin **13**:214
Mignard, Pierre **13**:416–417
miniature painting **13**:445
Modigliani, Amedeo **13**:499
Mogul art and architecture **13**:501–502
Mona Lisa **13**:515
Moro, Antonio **13**:583
Moroni, Giovanni Battista **13**:587
Neel, Alice **14**:76
Oliver, Isaac **14**:379
Peale (family) **15**:124
Picasso, Pablo **15**:290–292
Pourbus (family) **15**:476
Prud'hon, Pierre Paul **15**:585
Raeburn, Sir Henry **16**:69
Ramsay, Allan **16**:81
Rembrandt **16**:144–145
Renoir, Pierre Auguste **16**:158–159
Reynolds, Sir Joshua **16**:191
Rigaud, Hyacinthe **16**:222
Romney, George **16**:305
Russian art and architecture **16**:362
Sargent, John Singer **17**:77
Savage, Edward **17**:97
Schiele, Egon **17**:120
Scorel, Jan van **17**:148
Sickert, Walter Richard **17**:293
Soyer brothers **18**:115
Stuart, Gilbert **18**:305
Sully, Thomas **18**:338
Sutherland, Graham **18**:373
Tissot, James **19**:209–210
Titian **19**:212
van Dyck, Sir Anthony **19**:513–514
van Gogh, Vincent **19**:514–515
Varley, Frederick **19**:523
Verspronck, Johannes Cornelisz **19**:563
Vigée-Lebrun, Louise Élisabeth **19**:591–592
Watts, George Frederic **20**:69
Winterhalter, Franz Xaver **20**:181
Wright, Joseph **20**:290
Yen Li-pen (Yan Liben) **20**:326
Zoffany, Johann **20**:371
Zorn, Anders **20**:379
pastel
La Tour, Maurice Quentin de **12**:150–151
Labille-Guiard, Adélaide **12**:151
photography **15**:268; **15**:446
Beaton, Sir Cecil **3**:145
Brady, Mathew B. **3**:438–439
carte de visite **4**:171
Eisenstaedt, Alfred **7**:96
Hill, D. O., and Adamson, Robert **10**:164
Jacobi, Lotte **11**:345
Karsh, Yousef **12**:29
Nadar **14**:4
Newman, Arnold **14**:169
Southworth, Albert Sands, and Hawes, Josiah Johnson **18**:112–113
Steichen, Edward **18**:246
Steiglitz, Alfred **18**:267
pottery
Staffordshire ware **18**:210
sculpture **15**:446
Dannecker, Johann Heinrich von **6**:33
Davidson, Jo **6**:49
French, Daniel Chester **8**:302
Greenough, Horatio **9**:353
Hoffman, Malvina **10**:195
Houdon, Jean Antoine **10**:263–264
Lemoyne, Jean Baptiste **12**:280–281
Leoni (family) **12**:292
Mino da Fiesole **13**:458
Quellinus, Artus **16**:23
Roman art and architecture **16**:275–276
Roubiliac, Louis François **16**:324
Rysbrack, Michael **16**:380
Saint-Gaudens, Augustus **17**:18
Story, William Wetmore **18**:285
silhouette **17**:304
PORTSMOUTH (England) **15**:448
map (50° 48′N 1° 5′W) **19**:403
PORTSMOUTH (New Hampshire) **15**:448
map (43° 4′N 70° 46′W) **14**:123
PORTSMOUTH (Ohio)
map (38° 45′N 82° 59′W) **14**:357
PORTSMOUTH (Virginia) **15**:448
map (36° 52′N 76° 24′W) **19**:607
PORTSMOUTH, TREATY OF
Russo-Japanese War **16**:373
Witte, Sergei Yulivich, Count **20**:193
PORTTIPAHDAN TEKOJÄRVI RESERVOIR
map (68° 8′N 26° 40′E) **8**:95
PORTUGAL **15**:448–452 *bibliog., illus., map, table*
agriculture **15**:451 *illus.*
wine **20**:176
art **15**:450
See also PORTUGUESE ART AND ARCHITECTURE
cities
Braga **3**:439
Coimbra **5**:96
Évora **7**:325
Fátima **8**:34
Funchal **8**:359
Lisbon **12**:365–366 *illus.*
Porto **15**:445
Sintra **17**:325
climate **15**:449–450 *table*
economic activity **15**:450–452 *illus.*
education **15**:450
European universities **7**:308 *table*
fishing **15**:451 *illus.*
flag **15**:448 *illus.*
government and politics **15**:452
health **15**:450
history *see* PORTUGAL, HISTORY OF
land and resources **15**:448–449 *map*
language *see* ROMANCE LANGUAGES—Portuguese language
literature *see* PORTUGUESE LITERATURE
manufacturing **15**:450–451
map (39° 30′N 8° 0′W) **7**:268
music
fado **8**:7
people **15**:449–450
regions
Azores **2**:381–382 *map*
Estremadura **7**:248
Macao **13**:4
Madeira Islands **13**:40 *map*
religion **15**:450
rivers, lakes, and waterways **15**:449
Douro River **6**:249–250
Tagus River **19**:10
Saint Vincent, Cape **17**:27
PORTUGAL, HISTORY OF **15**:452–455 *bibliog., illus., map, table*
colonies and trading posts c.1580 **15**:453 *map*
empire
Angola **2**:6
Brazil **3**:463
Chokwe **4**:403
Goa, Daman, and Diu **9**:214–215
Macao **13**:4
Mozambique **13**:626–628
Rio de Janeiro (Brazil) **16**:227
São Tomé and Príncipe **17**:72
Sephardim **17**:206
slavery **17**:353
spice trade **18**:180–181
rulers of **15**:452 *table*
slavery **17**:355
Spain, history of **18**:147
trade routes c.1580 **15**:453 *map*
prior to 1385
Alfonso I **1**:279
Alfonso II **1**:279
Alfonso III **1**:279
ancient and medieval period **15**:452–453
Dinis, King **6**:179
Ferdinand I **8**:53
Peter I, King **15**:200
1385-1580 monarchy
Albuquerque, Alfonso de **1**:261
Almeida, Francisco de **1**:306
Avis, house of **15**:453–454
discoveries and empire **15**:453–454 *map*
Europe, history of **7**:286
exploration **7**:334–335
Gama, Vasco da **9**:24
Henry the Navigator **10**:123–124
John I, King (John the Great) **11**:428
John II, King (John the Perfect) **11**:428
John III, King (John the Pious) **11**:428
Latin America, history of **12**:217–221 *map*
Manuel I, King **13**:131
Sebastian, King **17**:177
Tordesillas, Treaty of **19**:238–239
1580–1640 Spanish domination
Old Regime **15**:454
Philip II, King of Spain **15**:234
Philip IV, King of Spain **15**:235
1640–1910 decline of monarchy
Brangança (dynasty) **3**:439
Charles I, King **4**:296
constitutional monarchy **15**:454–455
John IV, King **11**:428
John V, King (John the Magnanimous) **11**:428
John VI, King **11**:428
Maria II, Queen of Portugal (Maria da Glória) **13**:150
Napoleonic Wars **14**:19
Pedro I, Emperor of Brazil **15**:131
Peter II, King **15**:200
Pombal, Sebastião José de Carvalho e Melo, Marquês de **15**:422
1910-present
Carmona, António Oscar de Fragoso **4**:154
Eanes, António dos Santos Ramalho **7**:6
Guinea-Bissau **9**:398–399
republic **15**:455
Salazar, António de Oliveira **17**:30–31
Soares, Mário **18**:8
Timor (Indonesia) **19**:203
PORTUGAL COVE SOUTH (Newfoundland)
map (46° 42′N 53° 15′W) **14**:166
PORTUGUESA RIVER
map (7° 57′N 67° 32′W) **19**:542
PORTUGUESE ART AND ARCHITECTURE **15**:455–456 *bibliog., illus.*
See also the subheading Portugal under ARCHITECTURE; PAINTING; RENAISSANCE ART AND ARCHITECTURE
folk art **8**:196
PORTUGUESE GUINEA *see* GUINEA-BISSAU
PORTUGUESE LITERATURE **15**:456–457 *bibliog.*
authors
Bernardes, Diogo **3**:221
Camões, Luis Vaz de **4**:62
Castello-Branco, Camillo **4**:187
Eça de Queiroz, José Maria **7**:36
Garrett, João Baptista de Almeida **9**:50
Ribeiro, Aquilino **16**:205
Ribeiro, Bernardim **16**:205
Sá de Miranda, Francisco de **17**:3
Silva, António José da **17**:312
Three Marias, The **19**:182
Vicente, Gil **19**:571
Vieira, António **19**:578
PORTUGUESE MAN-OF-WAR **15**:384 *illus.*; **15**:457 *illus.*
jellyfish **11**:395
PORTUGUESE TIMOR *see* TIMOR (Indonesia)
PORTUGUESE WATER DOG **15**:457 *bibliog., illus.*
PORUM (Oklahoma)
map (35° 22′N 95° 16′W) **14**:368
PORVOO (Finland) **15**:457
PORZ (Germany, East and West)
map (50° 53′N 7° 3′E) **9**:140
POSADA, JOSÉ GUADALUPE **15**:457–458 *bibliog.*
POSADAS (Argentina)
map (27° 23′S 55° 53′W) **2**:149
POSEIDON (missile) **15**:458
rockets and missiles **16**:255
submarine **18**:316
POSEIDON (mythology) **15**:458
Andromeda (mythology) **1**:409
mythology **13**:700
temple **19**:63 *illus.*
Triton **19**:304
POSEIDONIA *see* PAESTUM (Italy)
POSIDONIUS **15**:458 *bibliog.*
POSITIVE NUMBER
square root **18**:202
POSITIVISM **15**:458 *bibliog.*
Comte, Auguste **5**:168
empiricism **7**:159
law **12**:242
Taine, Hippolyte Adolphe **19**:11
Thorndike, Edward L. **19**:179
POSITRON **15**:458
See also ELECTRON
annihilation **2**:33
antimatter **2**:63
beta decay **3**:229
cloud chamber **5**:68
electron antimatter particle **7**:120
fundamental particles **8**:362
POSITRON EMISSION TRANSAXIAL TOMOGRAPHY *see* PETT
POSITRONIUM
annihilation **2**:33
POSSESSED, THE (book) **15**:458
Dostoyevsky, Fyodor Mikhailovich **6**:245
POSSIBILISM
geography **9**:102
POST (Texas)
map (33° 12′N 101° 23′W) **19**:129
POST, EMILY **15**:458
POST, GEORGE BROWNE **15**:458–459 *bibliog.*
POST, RICHARD F.
magnetic bottle **13**:55
POST CHAISE
coach and carriage **5**:73
POST AND LINTEL **15**:459 *bibliog.*
architecture **2**:131
technology, history of **19**:62–63
POST ROADS *see* STAGECOACH
POST-TRAUMATIC STRESS DISORDER **15**:459
POSTAL REORGANIZATION ACT OF 1970
postal services **15**:460–461
POSTAL SERVICES **15**:459–461 *bibliog., illus.*
airmail **1**:222
business machines **3**:589
Butterfield, John **3**:593
electronic mail **7**:124
pony express **15**:428
Postal Union, Universal **15**:461
reform
Hill, Sir Rowland **10**:164
Roth v. *United States* **16**:321–322
stagecoach **18**:210
Wells, Fargo and Company **20**:101
POSTAL UNION, UNIVERSAL **15**:461 *bibliog.*
POSTE-DE-LA-BALEINE (Quebec)
map (55° 17′N 77° 45′W) **16**:18
POSTE-MISTASSINI (Quebec)
map (50° 25′N 73° 52′W) **16**:18
POSTER **15**:461–462 *bibliog., illus.*
advertising **1**:112 *illus.*
circus poster **4**:443 *illus.*
graphic arts **9**:293
lithograph **12**:371
Mucha, Alfons **13**:630
Parrish, Maxfield **15**:97
propaganda **15**:568–569 *illus.*
recruiting: Uncle Sam **19**:382 *illus.*
Toulouse-Lautrec, Henri de **19**:251
Villon, Jacques **19**:599
POSTIMPRESSIONISM **15**:462–463 *bibliog., illus.*
Bonnard, Pierre **3**:381
Cézanne, Paul **4**:263–264
drawing **6**:265
French art and architecture **8**:307
Gauguin, Paul **9**:59
neoimpressionism **14**:83
painting **15**:22
Prendergast, Maurice **15**:518
Redon, Odilon **16**:116
Seurat, Georges **17**:214–215
Toulouse-Lautrec, Henri de **19**:250–251
van Gogh, Vincent **19**:514–515
Vollard, Ambroise **19**:630
Vuillard, Édouard **19**:640
POSTMODERN ARCHITECTURE **15**:463–464 *bibliog., illus.*
Böhm, Gottfried **3**:361
drawing **6**:265
Graves, Michael **9**:302
Hardy Holzman Pfeiffer Associates **10**:48
Meier, Richard **13**:281
Moore, Charles Willard **13**:567
Stern, Robert A. M. **18**:260
Turnbull, William, Jr. **19**:349
Venturi, Robert **19**:546
POSTMORTEM EXAMINATION *see* AUTOPSY
POSTPOLIO SYNDROME
poliomyelitis **15**:397
POSTULATE *see* AXIOM
POSTURE
exercise **7**:331
reflex **16**:120
POSTVILLE (Iowa)
map (43° 5′N 91° 34′W) **11**:244
POT MARIGOLD *see* CALENDULA

POTALA PALACE **19**:190 *illus.*
POTARO LANDING (Guyana)
map (5° 23′N 59° 8′W) **9**:410
POTASH
caustic chemicals **4**:220
fertilizer **8**:61–62
potassium **15**:464–465
Saskatchewan (Canada) **17**:80
POTASSIUM **15**:464–465 *bibliog.*
abundances of common elements **7**:131 *table*
alkali metals **1**:295; **15**:464–465
chemical properties **15**:465
compounds **15**:465
element **7**:130 *table*
flame test
qualitative chemical analysis **16**:6 *illus.*
Group IA periodic table **15**:167; **15**:464
ion
active transport **1**:89
biopotential **3**:275–276 *illus.*
neurophysiology **14**:106
metal, metallic element **13**:328
niter **14**:201
nutrient cycles **14**:304 *illus.*
occurrence **15**:465
oceanic mineral resources **14**:340
production **15**:465
radiometric age-dating **16**:66
reducing potential
electromotive series **7**:119
silicate minerals **17**:304–305
sylvite **18**:402
transition elements **19**:273 *table*
uranium minerals **19**:478
uses **15**:465
POTASSIUM ALUMINUM SULFATE *see* ALUM
POTASSIUM CHROMIUM SULFATE *see* ALUM
POTASSIUM HYDROXIDE *see* ALKALI
POTATO **15**:465–466 *bibliog., illus.*; **19**:533 *illus.*
belladonna **3**:187
cultivation **15**:466
diseases, plant **6**:195
famine **8**:18
food value and uses **15**:466
Maine **13**:71 *illus.*
nightshade **14**:194
Wisconsin **20**:184 *illus.*
POTAWATOMI (American Indians) **15**:466 *bibliog.*
Caldwell, Billy **4**:26
Indians of North America, art of the **11**:141
Ottawa (American Indians) **14**:460
Wabansi, Chief **20**:3
Wananikwe **20**:21
POTEAU (Oklahoma)
map (35° 3′N 94° 37′W) **14**:368
POTEAU RIVER
map (35° 23′N 94° 26′W) **2**:166
POTEET (Texas)
map (29° 2′N 98° 34′W) **19**:129
POTEMKIN, GRIGORY ALEKSANDROVICH **15**:466 *bibliog.*
POTENTIAL, ELECTRIC **15**:466
biopotential **3**:275–276 *illus.*
electricity **7**:108–109
electrochemistry **7**:113
electromagnetic units **7**:118
electromotive force **7**:119
electron volt **7**:124
electrostatics **7**:128
ion **3**:275
neurophysiology **14**:105–106
Nernst equation
Nernst, Walther **14**:89
volt **19**:631
POTENTIAL ENERGY **15**:466
See also ENERGY; KINETIC ENERGY
conservation, laws of **5**:204 *illus.*
POTENTIOMETER **15**:467
electrochemistry **7**:113
resistor **16**:177
POTENZA (Italy)
map (40° 38′N 15° 49′E) **11**:321
POTGIETER, EVERHARDUS JOHANNES
Dutch and Flemish literature **6**:314
POTHOLES RESERVOIR
map (47° 1′N 119° 19′W) **20**:35
POTIOREK, OSKAR
World War I **20**:226
POTISKUM (Nigeria)
map (11° 43′N 11° 5′E) **14**:190
POTLATCH **15**:467 *bibliog.*
Indians, American **11**:127
Kwakiutl **12**:142
Puyallup **15**:633
Tsimshian **19**:324
POTOCKI, WACŁAW
Polish literature **15**:398
POTOMAC (Illinois)
map (40° 18′N 87° 48′W) **11**:42
POTOMAC HEIGHTS (Maryland)
map (38° 36′N 77° 8′W) **13**:188
POTOMAC RIVER **15**:467
map (38° 0′N 76° 18′W) **13**:188
POTOSÍ (Bolivia) **15**:467
POTOSÍ (department in Bolivia)
map (20° 40′S 67° 0′W) **3**:366
POTOSI (Missouri)
map (37° 56′N 90° 47′W) **13**:476
POTOSÍ, MOUNT
map (24° 52′N 100° 13′W) **13**:357
POTSDAM (East Germany) **15**:467
Earth, gravitational field of **7**:17
map (52° 24′N 13° 4′E) **9**:140
POTSDAM (New York)
map (44° 40′N 74° 59′W) **14**:149
POTSDAM CONFERENCE **15**:467 *bibliog.*
Oder-Neisse line **14**:349
Truman, Harry S. **19**:317
Vietnam War **19**:584
World War II **20**:275–276 *illus.*
POTT, PERCIVALL
diseases, occupational **6**:193
POTTAWATOMIE (county in Kansas)
map (39° 20′N 96° 30′W) **12**:18
POTTAWATOMIE (county in Oklahoma)
map (35° 15′N 96° 55′W) **14**:368
POTTAWATTAMIE (county in Iowa)
map (41° 17′N 95° 25′W) **11**:244
POTTER (Kansas)
map (39° 26′N 95° 8′W) **12**:18
POTTER (Nebraska)
map (41° 13′N 103° 19′W) **14**:70
POTTER (county in Pennsylvania)
map (41° 47′N 78° 1′W) **15**:147
POTTER (county in South Dakota)
map (45° 3′N 100° 0′W) **18**:103
POTTER (county in Texas)
map (35° 23′N 101° 52′W) **19**:129
POTTER, BEATRIX **15**:467–468 *bibliog., illus.*
Tale of Peter Rabbit, The (book) **4**:353 *illus.*
POTTER WASP *see* WASP (zoology)
POTTER'S WHEEL **15**:468
POTTERY AND PORCELAIN **15**:468–473 *bibliog., illus.*
See also CERAMICS
Art Nouveau **2**:211 *illus.*
celadon **4**:229
China
art and architecture **4**:384–386
Chinese archaeology **4**:379
Ching-te-chen (Jingde Zhen) **4**:395
Ming (dynasty) pottery **15**:468 *illus.*
T'ang (dynasty) pottery **15**:469 *illus.*
craft **5**:327 *illus.*
decorating techniques **15**:468–470
Denmark
Royal Copenhagen ware **16**:330
Schnurkeramik pottery **15**:468 *illus.*
faïence **8**:8
folk art **8**:196–199
France
Limoges (France) **12**:345–346
Limoges ware **12**:346
Limousin (France) **12**:346
Palissy, Bernard **15**:47
Picasso, Pablo **15**:292
Sèvres ware **15**:471 *illus.*; **17**:221 *illus.*
Germany
Meissen ware **13**:283; **15**:471 *illus.*
Nymphenburg ware **14**:309
Great Britain
Chelsea ware **4**:311
English wares **15**:471–472
Minton ware **13**:461
Staffordshire ware **15**:472 *illus.*; **18**:210
Stoke-on-Trent **18**:278
Victoria and Albert Museum **19**:575
Wedgwood, Josiah **20**:89–90
Wedgwood jasperware **15**:472 *illus.*
Worcester ware **20**:216
Greece, ancient
Cleitias **5**:48
Douris **6**:249
Epictetus (painter) **7**:218
Euphronius **7**:265
Euphronius krater **15**:470 *illus.*
Euthymides **7**:311
Exekias **7**:329
Greek art **9**:338–342 *illus.*
Minoan art **13**:458–459
Oltos **14**:381
Onesimos **14**:390
vase **8**:374 *illus.*
Hittite art and architecture **10**:189
Indians, American
Indians of North America, art of the **11**:140
North American archaeology **14**:239–240 *illus.*
Zuñi jug **11**:121 *illus.*
Islamic art and architecture **11**:294–297
Italy
Etruscans **7**:260 *illus.*
majolica **13**:76–77; **15**:470 *illus.*
Roman art and architecture **16**:277
Japan
Kakiemon **15**:469 *illus.*
Kenzan **12**:57
Koetsu **12**:105
kiln **12**:77 *illus.*
Korean art **12**:117–118 *illus.*
major traditions in the West **15**:470–472
Mexico
Zapotec funerary urn **15**:498 *illus.*
Netherlands
delftware **6**:92
Persia
Persian art and architecture **15**:186–187 *illus.*
wall tile **15**:470 *illus.*
Peru
Nazca pottery **15**:500 *illus.*
potter's wheel **15**:468
pre-Columbian
pre-Columbian art and architecture **15**:495–501
pre-Inca warrior vase **11**:116 *illus.*
Remojadas **16**:146
Vicús **19**:576
prehistoric **15**:468 *illus.*
Danubian culture **6**:36
European prehistory **7**:302–304 *illus.*
Neolithic Period **14**:84 *illus.*
Persian art and architecture **15**:183 *illus.*
rococo style **16**:264 *illus.*
Spain
Spanish art and architecture **18**:151
terra-cotta **19**:119
Thailand
Ban Chiang **3**:59
Turkey
Topkapi Palace Museum **19**:237
20th-century developments **15**:472
types **15**:468
earthenware **4**:259; **15**:468 *illus.*; **15**:470–471
stoneware **4**:258–259 *illus.*
United States
Pennsylvania Dutch plate **15**:152 *illus.*
Rockwood Potteries vase **15**:472 *illus.*
Rockwood ware **16**:306
POTTO **15**:473 *illus.*; **15**:540 *illus.*
POTTS CAMP (Mississippi)
map (34° 39′N 89° 18′W) **13**:469
POTT'S DISEASE **15**:473
spondylitis **18**:193
POTTSTOWN (Pennsylvania)
map (40° 15′N 75° 38′W) **15**:147
POTTSVILLE (Pennsylvania)
map (40° 41′N 76° 12′W) **15**:147
POTWIN (Kansas)
map (37° 56′N 97° 1′W) **12**:18
POUCH COVE (Newfoundland)
map (47° 46′N 52° 46′W) **14**:166
POUGHKEEPSIE (New York)
map (41° 42′N 73° 56′W) **14**:149
POULAN (Georgia)
map (31° 31′N 83° 47′W) **9**:114
POULENC, FRANCIS **15**:473 *bibliog.*
POULSEN, VALDEMAR **15**:473
sound recording and reproduction **15**:473
tape recorder, inventor **19**:30
POULTNEY (Vermont)
map (43° 31′N 73° 14′W) **19**:554
POULTRY **15**:473–475 *bibliog., illus., table*
chicken **4**:345
duck **6**:290–292
egg **7**:72 *illus.*
egg production **7**:72
embryo **7**:324 *illus.*
factory farming **8**:6
flea **8**:158
goose **9**:246–247
turkey **19**:346
U.S. production **15**:475 *table*
POUNCING (art)
cartoon (art) **4**:175–176
POUND (unit of measurement) **15**:475
types and equivalent measures **15**:475
weights and measures **20**:93–94 *table*
POUND (Virginia)
map (37° 7′N 82° 36′W) **19**:607
POUND, EZRA **15**:475–476 *bibliog., illus.*
Cantos, The (poem) **4**:118
Eliot, T. S. **7**:139–140
imagism **11**:53
POUND, ROSCOE **15**:476 *bibliog.*
law **12**:243
POUND GAP (pass)
map (37° 7′N 82° 36′W) **19**:607
POUND STERLING **15**:476
POUNDMAKER (Cree Indian) **15**:476 *bibliog.*
POURBUS (family) **15**:476
POUSETTE-DART, RICHARD **15**:476 *bibliog.*
POUSSIN, NICOLAS **15**:476–477 *bibliog., illus.*
The Childhood of Bacchus **8**:305 *illus.*
Friedlaender, Walter **8**:331
Summer, or Ruth and Boaz **15**:477 *illus.*
POUTASI (Western Samoa)
map (14° 1′S 171° 41′W) **20**:117
POVERTY **15**:478–480 *bibliog., table*
agriculture and the food supply **1**:195
diseases, human
kwashiorkor **12**:143
Hispanic Americans **10**:178
housing **10**:279
old age **14**:373
social and welfare services **18**:17–18
urban anthropology **19**:480
War on Poverty **20**:28
POVUNGNITUK (Quebec)
map (60° 2′N 77° 10′W) **16**:18
POWAY (California)
map (32° 58′N 117° 2′W) **4**:31
POWDER
cosmetics **5**:282
POWDER METALLURGY **15**:480 *bibliog.*
cermet **4**:260
sintering **17**:325
POWDER PUFF DERBY
aerial sports **1**:121
POWDER RIVER
map (46° 44′N 105° 26′W) **19**:419
POWDER RIVER (county in Montana)
map (45° 22′N 105° 40′W) **13**:547
POWDER RIVER PASS
map (44° 9′N 107° 4′W) **20**:301
POWDERLY, TERENCE V.
Knights of Labor **12**:101
POWELL (county in Kentucky)
map (37° 50′N 83° 50′W) **12**:47
POWELL (county in Montana)
map (46° 50′N 112° 57′W) **13**:547
POWELL (Wyoming)
map (44° 45′N 108° 46′W) **20**:301
POWELL, ADAM CLAYTON, JR. **15**:480 *bibliog., illus.*
POWELL, ANTHONY **15**:480 *bibliog.*
POWELL, CECIL FRANK **15**:480
POWELL, ENOCH **15**:480–481
POWELL, JAMES
Wyoming **20**:304
POWELL, JOHN WESLEY **15**:481 *bibliog.*
anthropological linguistics **2**:50
conservation **5**:202
Indian languages, American **11**:98–99
United States Geological Survey **19**:462
POWELL, LEWIS F., JR. **15**:481; **18**:355 *illus.*
POWELL, MARY
Milton, John **13**:432–433
POWELL RIVER
map (36° 29′N 83° 42′W) **19**:104
POWELL RIVER (British Columbia)
map (49° 52′N 124° 33′W) **3**:491
POWELL v. ALABAMA **15**:481
POWELLTON (West Virginia)
map (38° 5′N 81° 19′W) **20**:111
POWER **15**:481
horsepower **10**:251
joule **15**:481
mathematical tables **13**:221

rate of work **15**:481
supply
rectifier **16**:111
POWER (book) *see JUD SÜSS* (book)
POWER (county in Idaho)
map (42° 40′N 112° 50′W) **11**:26
POWER, GENERATION AND TRANSMISSION OF 15:481–486 *bibliog., illus., table*
See also ENERGY SOURCES; ENERGY TECHNOLOGY
electric power
blackout, electrical **3**:322
cable **4**:6 *illus.*
circuit breaker **4**:438
coal and coal mining **5**:79
discharge, electrical **6**:188
electical wiring **7**:106–107
Electric Power Research Institute **15**:486
electrical and electronic engineering **7**:106
electrogasdynamics **15**:483
fuel cell **8**:354; **15**:483
fuel use, United States **15**:484
generating plants **15**:482–484
generator **9**:78
geothermal energy **9**:120–121; **15**:483
grid **9**:361
hydroelectric power **10**:332–335
industry **15**:481–482
magnetohydrodynamics **13**:59 *illus.*; **15**:483
nuclear energy **14**:278–284 *illus.*
photoelectric cell **15**:259–260
production and transmission, United States **15**:482 *map, table*
solar energy **15**:483; **18**:41
Stanley, William **18**:219
thermionic emission **15**:483; **19**:161
thermoelectricity **15**:483; **19**:165
tidal energy **15**:483–484; **19**:192–193
transformer **19**:270–271
transmission **15**:484–486
Westinghouse, George **20**:117
windmills and wind power **20**:172–173
energy sources **7**:175
engine **7**:177
Federal Power Commission **15**:486
first electric station
Edison, Thomas Alva **7**:57–58
technology, history of **19**:67 *illus.*
fuel **8**:352–354
pulley **15**:619
steam
boiler **3**:362–363
steam engine **18**:240
steam-power plants **15**:482–483
technology, history of **19**:66–67
telemetry **19**:78
Tennessee Valley Authority **19**:107–108
turbine **19**:340
POWER, LEONEL
English music **7**:202
music, history of Western **13**:663
POWER ELITE (sociology) **7**:140
POWER LIFTING *see* WEIGHT LIFTING (sport)
POWER OF POSITIVE THINKING, THE (book)
Peale, Norman Vincent **19**:124
POWER AND THE GLORY, THE (book) **15**:486
POWER TOOLS
carpentry **4**:164
drill **6**:273
saw **17**:102–103 *illus.*
POWERBOAT **3**:351 *illus.*
POWERS (Oregon)
map (42° 53′N 124° 4′W) **14**:427
POWERS, FRANCIS GARY
U-2 **19**:369
POWERS, HIRAM **15**:486 *bibliog.*
POWERS, JAMES
computer **5**:160–160a
POWERS LAKE (North Dakota)
map (48° 34′N 102° 39′W) **14**:248
POWESHIEK (county in Iowa)
map (41° 38′N 92° 30′W) **11**:244
POWHATAN (American Indian) **15**:486 *bibliog.*
Jamestown (Virginia) **11**:357
Pocahontas **15**:376
Smith, John **17**:369
POWHATAN (Louisiana)
map (31° 52′N 93° 12′W) **12**:430
POWHATAN (Virginia)
map (37° 29′N 77° 55′W) **19**:607
POWHATAN (county in Virginia)
map (37° 35′N 77° 55′W) **19**:607
POWHATAN POINT (Ohio)
map (39° 52′N 80° 49′W) **14**:357
POWWOW **15**:486
Indians of North America, music and dance of the **11**:143
POWYS (Wales) **15**:486
POWYS, JOHN COWPER **15**:486–487 *bibliog.*
POX DISEASES
chicken pox **4**:345–346
cowpox **5**:322
diseases, animal **6**:191
smallpox **17**:365
POYEN (Arkansas)
map (34° 19′N 92° 38′W) **2**:166
POYGAN, LAKE
map (44° 19′N 88° 50′W) **20**:185
POYNETTE (Wisconsin)
map (43° 24′N 89° 24′W) **20**:185
POYNINGS'S LAW
Grattan, Henry **9**:301
Ireland, history of **11**:263
POŽAREVAC (Yugoslavia)
map (44° 37′N 21° 11′E) **20**:340
POZNAN (Poland) **15**:487
map (52° 25′N 16° 55′E) **15**:388
POZZO, ANDREA
The Triumph of Saint Ignatius **15**:190 *illus.*
POZZO TOSCANELLI, PAOLO DAL *see* TOSCANELLI, PAOLO DAL POZZO
PRADO **15**:487 *bibliog.*
Madrid **13**:44 *map*
Villanueva, Juan de **19**:598
PRAETOR (Rome, ancient)
Roman law **16**:278
PRAETORIAN GUARD **15**:487; **16**:302 *illus.*
PRAETORIUS, MICHAEL **15**:487 *bibliog.*
PRAGMATIC SANCTION **15**:487
Maria Theresa, Austrian Archduchess, Queen of Hungary and Bohemia **13**:150
Polish Succession, War of the **15**:398
PRAGMATISM **15**:487–488 *bibliog.*
Dewey, John **6**:147
empiricism **7**:159
James, William **11**:354–355; **15**:487
Mead, George Herbert **13**:251
Peirce, Charles Sanders **15**:134; **15**:487
philosophy **15**:245
PRAGUE (Czechoslovakia) **5**:414 *illus., table*; **15**:488 *illus.*
architecture
Dientzenhofer (family) **6**:162
synagogue **11**:462 *illus.*
history **15**:488
map (50° 5′N 14° 26′E) **5**:413
PRAGUE (Nebraska)
map (41° 19′N 96° 48′W) **14**:70
PRAGUE (Oklahoma)
map (35° 29′N 96° 41′W) **14**:368
PRAGUE, DEFENESTRATION OF *see* DEFENESTRATION OF PRAGUE
PRAGUE, PEACE OF (1635)
Ferdinand II, Holy Roman Emperor **8**:53
PRAGUE, TREATY OF
Seven Weeks' War **17**:216
PRAGUE LINGUISTICS CIRCLE *see* PRAGUE SCHOOL
PRAGUE SCHOOL **15**:488 *bibliog.*
Jakobson, Roman **11**:351
synchronic linguistics **12**:356
PRAHA (Czechoslovakia) *see* PRAGUE (Czechoslavakia)
PRAIA (Cape Verde Islands)
map (14° 55′N 23° 31′W) **4**:122
PRAINHA (Brazil)
map (1° 48′S 53° 29′W) **3**:460
PRAIRIE
biome **3**:274
distribution **3**:273 *map*
North America
agriculture, history of **1**:192 *illus.*
grasslands **9**:300 *illus.*
Kansas **12**:17; **12**:21
savanna life **17**:97–99
steppe life **18**:256–257
PRAIRIE (county in Arkansas)
map (34° 50′N 91° 30′W) **2**:166
PRAIRIE (county in Montana)
map (46° 50′N 105° 20′W) **13**:547
PRAIRIE, THE (book) *see LEATHERSTOCKING TALES, THE* (books)
PRAIRIE CHICKEN *see* GROUSE
PRAIRIE CITY (Iowa)
map (41° 36′N 93° 14′W) **11**:244
PRAIRIE CITY (Oregon)
map (44° 28′N 118° 43′W) **14**:427
PRAIRIE CREEK
map (40° 8′N 85° 17′W) **11**:111
PRAIRIE DOG **9**:300 *illus.*; **15**:488–489 *bibliog., illus.*
burrow **15**:489 *illus.*
PRAIRIE DOG CREEK
map (40° 0′N 99° 23′W) **14**:70
PRAIRIE DU CHIEN (Wisconsin)
map (43° 3′N 91° 9′W) **20**:185
PRAIRIE GROVE (Arkansas)
map (35° 59′N 94° 19′W) **2**:166
PRAIRIE INDIANS *see* INDIANS, AMERICAN, CULTURE AREAS
PRAIRIE SCHOOL (architecture) **15**:489 *bibliog.*
Griffin, Marion Mahony **9**:362
Griffin, Walter Burley **9**:362
house (in Western architecture) **10**:270
Robie House **16**:243
Wright, Frank Lloyd **20**:289
PRAIRIE SCHOONER *see* CONESTOGA (wagon); WAGON
PRAISE OF FOLLY, THE (book) **15**:489 *bibliog.*
Holbein, Hans, the Younger **10**:200
Renaissance **16**:149
PRAKRIT
Indo-Iranian languages **11**:145
PRAMBANAN (Indonesia) **15**:489
Southeast Asian art and architecture **18**:110
PRANDTAUER, JAKOB **15**:489 *bibliog.*
PRANDTL, LUDWIG
aviation **2**:374
aviation **2**:374
PRASEODYMIUM **15**:489–490
element **7**:130 *table*
lanthanide series **12**:200–201
metal, metallic element **13**:328
Welsbach, Carl Auer, Baron von **20**:101
PRASLIN ISLAND
map (4° 19′S 55° 44′E) **19**:574
Seychelles **17**:232 *map*
PRATAS ISLANDS
map (20° 42′N 116° 43′E) **4**:362
PRATINCOLE **15**:490
shorebirds **17**:283
PRATO (Italy) **15**:490
map (43° 53′N 11° 6′E) **11**:321
PRATT (Kansas)
map (37° 39′N 98° 44′W) **12**:18
PRATT (county in Kansas)
map (37° 35′N 98° 45′W) **12**:18
PRATT, CHRISTOPHER
Canadian art and architecture **4**:91
PRATT, E. J. **15**:490 *bibliog.*
Canadian literature **4**:94
PRATT, WILLIAM *see* KARLOFF, BORIS
PRATT INSTITUTE **15**:490
PRATTSBURG (New York)
map (42° 32′N 77° 17′W) **14**:149
PRATTVILLE (Alabama)
map (32° 28′N 86° 29′W) **1**:234
PRAVDA **15**:490
Molotov, Vyacheslav Mikhailovich **13**:513
PRAWN
gill **9**:181 *illus.*
PRAXITELES **15**:490 *bibliog.*
Apollo Sauroktonos **9**:340 *illus.*
Hermes and the Infant Dionysus **2**:193 *illus.*; **9**:340 *illus.*
Olympia (Greece) **14**:381
PRAYER **15**:490 *bibliog.*
classroom
Engel v. *Vitale* **7**:176
freedom of religion **8**:298
liturgy **12**:373–374
Lord's Prayer **12**:413
meditation **13**:275–276
rosary **16**:312
saint **17**:15
PRAYER BEADS *see* ROSARY
PRAYER RUG
rugs and carpets **16**:340–342
PRAYING MANTIS **15**:490–491 *illus.*
PRE-COLUMBIAN AGRICULTURE
agriculture, history of **1**:190 *illus.*
PRE-COLUMBIAN ART AND ARCHITECTURE **15**:495–501 *bibliog., illus.*
Aztec
mask of Quetzalcóatl **11**:122 *illus.*
shield **11**:121 *illus.*
Tenochtitlán **19**:112
Bolivia
Quechua **16**:21
Tiahuanaco **19**:188–189
Brazil
Huari **15**:500–501
Marajó (Brazil) **13**:143
Colombia
San Agustín **17**:50
Colorado
Mesa Verde National Park **13**:313–314 *illus.*
forgery in art **8**:233
Guatemala
Kaminaljuyú **12**:10
Honduras
Copán **5**:248
Inca **11**:72; **15**:501
ceremonial knife **11**:121 *illus.*
Machu Picchu **12**:223 *illus.*; **13**:25–26
Indians, American **11**:121–122 *illus.*
inscription **11**:186
Intermediate Area and Central Andes **15**:499
Latin American art and architecture **12**:222–223
Maya **13**:243–245
maize-god sculpture **11**:134 *illus.*
Piedras Negras **15**:295
Pyramid and Temple of Inscriptions **11**:121 *illus.*
Quiriguá **16**:27
Tikal **19**:198
Uaxactún **19**:369
Uxmal **19**:499
Mesoamerica **13**:314
Classic period **15**:496–497
Olmec **14**:380 *illus.*
Postclassic period **15**:497–499
Preclassic period **15**:495–496
Protoclassic period **15**:496
Mexico
Chichén Itzá **4**:343–344
Cholula **4**:404
El Tajín **7**:101
Izapa **11**:338
La Venta **12**:151
Mayapán **13**:246
Mitla **13**:485
Mixtec **13**:486
Monte Albán **13**:552
Oaxaca (city in Mexico) **14**:314
Palenque **15**:30
Remojadas **16**:146
San Lorenzo **17**:55–56
Tarascan **19**:35
Teotihuacán **19**:113–114 *illus.*
Tula **19**:329–330
Xochicalco **20**:313
Zapotec **20**:356
Peru
Chan Chan **4**:278
Chancay **4**:278
Chavín de Huántar **4**:306
Chavín style **15**:499–500
Chimu **4**:359
Cuzco **5**:400
Huari **10**:287
Mochica **13**:488
Nazca **14**:67
Nazca and Mochica styles **15**:500
Pachacamac **15**:4
Paracas **15**:74
pre-Inca warrior vase **11**:116 *illus.*
Quechua **16**:21
Vicús **19**:576
pyramids **15**:634–636
PRE-RAPHAELITES **15**:519 *bibliog., illus.*
Brown, Ford Madox **3**:513–514
Burne-Jones, Sir Edward **3**:576–577
English art and architecture **7**:187
Hunt, Holman **10**:311
Millais, Sir John Everett **13**:426
mural painting **13**:646
realism (art) **16**:103
Rossetti, Dante Gabriel **16**:319
Ruskin, John **16**:348
Wilde, Oscar **20**:148–149
PRE-SOCRATIC PHILOSOPHY **15**:532–533 *bibliog.*
Anaxagoras **1**:398
Eleatic School **7**:103
Milesian school **13**:419
Parmenides **15**:95
philosophy **15**:243
Pythagoreans **15**:640
Sophists **18**:67
PREAKNESS STAKES WINNERS **10**:249 *table*
PREBLE (county in Ohio)
map (39° 45′N 84° 38′W) **14**:357
PREBLE, EDWARD **15**:491 *bibliog.*
Tripolitan War **19**:303
PRECAMBRIAN TIME **15**:491–493 *bibliog., illus., map*
Africa **1**:140 *map*
Asia **2**:236 *map*
Australia **2**:331 *map*

PRECAMBRIAN TIME (cont.)
basement rock 3:108
continental shield 5:230
Earth, geological history of 7:11–13 *illus., map*; 15:492
Europe 7:270 *map*
fossil record 8:243
geologic time 9:103–104 *table*
ice ages 11:7–11
igneous rock 11:35
life 15:491 *illus.*; 15:493
major events 15:492
North America 14:227 *map*
paleobotany 15:32
placer deposit 15:325
rock formations 15:492 *map*
rock record 15:491–492
South America 18:87 *map*
uniformitarianism 19:386
United States 19:422 *map*
PRECEDENT (law)
civil law 5:11
common law 5:138–141
law, history of 12:245–246
law 12:243
PRECESSION 15:493
gravitation 9:305
precession of the equinoxes 15:493
PRECESSION OF THE EQUINOXES 15:493 *illus.*
astronomy, history of 2:278
Earth, motions of 7:18–19
nutation 14:301
Polaris (astronomy) 15:393
PRECIOUS STONE *see* GEMS
PRECIPITATION (chemistry) 15:493 *bibliog.*
electrostatics 7:128
filtration 8:91
gravimetric analysis
quantitative chemical analysis 16:8
precipitate
classification 15:493
PRECIPITATION (weather) 15:493–495 *bibliog., illus., map, table*
See also RAIN
acid rain 1:82
Africa 1:142 *map*
Asia 2:238 *map*
atmosphere 2:300
Australia 2:331 *map*
average annual precipitation, worldwide 15:494 *map*
average annual precipitation extremes 20:81
average highest and lowest precipitation 20:81 *table*
cirrus clouds 4:445
cloud 5:67
cumulonimbus clouds 5:388
cumulus clouds 5:388
desert 6:126–128
dew 6:146
doldrums 6:224
drought 6:273–274
dust, atmospheric 6:308
erosion and sedimentation 7:233
Europe 7:273 *map*
evapotranspiration 7:314
flash flood 8:153
floods and flood control 8:167
formation 15:493–494
fresh water 8:328
front 8:340
geographic distribution 15:495
groundwater 9:374
hail and hailstones 10:12–13
hurricane and typhoon 10:317–319
hydrologic cycle 10:341–342
jungle and rain forest 11:468–469
Köppen, Wladimir Peter 12:110
meteorological instrumentation 13:340 *illus.*
meteorology 13:341
mist 13:481
monsoon 13:544
mountain climates 13:621
mudflow 13:631
North America 14:230 *map*
occurrence 15:495
orographic precipitation 14:447
orographite precipitation 15:495
polar climate 15:392
radar meteorology 16:41
rain shadow effect 16:77
rainbow 16:77
red beds 16:112
semiarid climate 17:195
sirocco 17:328
snow and snowflake 18:4
South America 18:88 *map*
squall and squall line 18:201–202
stratus clouds 18:293
taiga climate 19:11
Thornthwaite climatic classification 19:179
thunderstorm 19:185
types 15:493
water resources 20:50
weather forecasting 20:78–79
weather modification 20:79–80
weather variation and extremes 20:80–82
weathering 20:82
world maximum observed rainfalls 15:495 *table*
PRECISIONISM
Sheeler, Charles 17:248
PRECOCIAL ANIMAL 15:495
bird, imprinting 11:69
PRECOGNITION *see* PARAPSYCHOLOGY
PREDATORY ANIMAL
homeostasis 10:212–213
population dynamics 15:438–439
PREDATORY BIRDS
See also BIRDS OF PREY
population dynamics 15:438
PREDESTINATION 15:501–502 *bibliog.*
Arminianism 2:173
Calvin, John 4:48
grace 9:275
Islam 11:290–291
Jansenism 11:359
PREEMPTION ACT 15:502 *bibliog.*
frontier 8:343
squatter 18:203
PREFABRICATION 15:502 *bibliog.*
Bogardus, James 3:359
building construction 3:551–552
Crystal Palace 5:376
Safdie, Moshe 17:10
PREFERRED PROVIDER ORGANIZATION
hospital 10:258
PREFERRED STOCK *see* STOCK (finance)
PREFRONTAL LOBOTOMY
psychopathology, treatment of 15:600
PREGL, FRITZ 15:502
PREGNANCY AND BIRTH 15:502–506 *bibliog., illus.*
See also BIRTH DEFECTS
artificial insemination 2:220–221
birth
cesarean section 4:262; 15:505 *illus.*
complications 15:505–506
delivery date 15:506
hypnosis 10:350
multiple birth 13:637–638
postpartum maternal and child care 15:506
prepared childbirth 15:506
prostaglandins 15:572–573
stages of labor 15:504 *illus.*
birth, special conditions
encephalitis 7:162
hyaline membrane disease 10:327
induced labor, oxytocin 14:479
premature baby 15:518
puerperal fever 15:614
birth control 3:293–295
breast-feeding 3:469
couvade 5:318
egg 15:502
fertility, human 8:60
fetus, diagnostic tests 15:505
amniocentesis 1:375
fetus development 15:503–504 *illus.*
gestation 9:160
kangaroo 12:15
menstruation 13:300–301
midwife 13:414; 15:502 *illus.*
obstetrics 14:319
passage rites 15:103
pregnancy
abortion 1:60
leukocytosis 12:301
signs and symptoms 15:503
young people 20:336
pregnancy, special problems
abortion, spontaneous 15:504
anemia 15:505
cystitis 5:411
diabetes mellitus 15:504
eclampsia 7:39–40
ectopic pregnancy 15:504
German measles 9:134; 15:504
hemorrhoids 10:120
hypertension 15:504–505
infectious diseases 11:166
Rh factor 15:504; 16:192
syphilis 18:410
venereal disease 19:540
prolactin 15:567
reproduction 16:163
sex hormones 17:226
smoking 17:374
umbilical cord 19:380
uterus 15:502–503; 19:496–497
viviparity 19:622
PREGNANCY TEST 15:506 *bibliog.*
leopard frog 12:293
pregnancy and birth 15:503
types 15:506
PREHISTORIC ANIMALS 7:134 *illus.*, *illus.*
See also DINOSAUR; EXTINCT SPECIES; FOSSIL RECORD
Archaeopteryx 2:127
arthrodire 2:216
Baluchitherium 3:57
Barylambda 3:99
coelacanth 5:91
Dolní Věstonice 6:226
Edaphosaurus 7:54
elephant 7:134 *illus.*
eohippus 7:215
evolution 7:320–324
fish 8:120–121
fossil record 8:243–248
graptolite 9:294
hesperornis 10:151
Ichthyornis 11:19
Ichthyosaurus 11:19–20
invertebrate 11:234
Irish elk 11:266
La Brea Tar Pit 12:144–145 *illus.*
lamprey 12:176
lungfish 12:462–463
mammals 13:99–102 *illus.*
mammoth 13:106–107
mastodon 13:217
mosasaur 13:596
Ordovician sea life 14:422 *illus.*
ostracoderm 14:458
paleoclimatology 15:32–34
Przewalski's horse 15:586
pterodactyl 15:606
Quaternary Period 16:15
Recent Epoch 16:107
Rhamphorhynchus 16:192
rodent 16:265–266
saber-toothed cats 17:5
titanothere 19:211
PREHISTORIC ART 2:192 *illus.*; 15:506–511 *bibliog., illus.*
Africa 1:160–164; 15:510 *illus.*
Ife 1:174 *illus.*
rock art 1:161 *illus.*; 2:23 *illus.*
Algeria 1:174 *illus.*
Tassili n'Ajjer 19:43
Australia 15:510–511 *illus.*
Oceanic art 14:339
Austria
Venus of Willendorf 15:506 *illus.*; 19:548
cave 4:222–224
cave dwellers 4:224–225
Cro-Magnon man 5:354
Czechoslovakia
Dolní Věstonice 6:226
Europe 7:302 *illus.*
European prehistory 7:301–306; 7:304 *illus.*
France 15:507–509 *illus.*
Font de Gaume 8:205
Lascaux 4:224 *illus.*; 12:210 *illus.*
Les Combarelles 12:296
Niaux Cave 14:177
Trois Frères, Les 19:305
Venus of Laussel 15:507 *illus.*
India
Ajanta 1:229
Latin America 12:222
megalith 13:278–279
mural painting 13:645
painting 15:18
periods
Magdalenian 13:46
Mesolithic art 15:509
Neolithic, Bronze, and Iron Age art 15:509–510
Paleolithic art 15:507–509
prehistoric humans 15:516
primitive art 15:543
Russia
Pazyryk 15:122
Scandinavian art and architecture 17:111
sculpture 17:159
Southeast Asian art and architecture 18:107–108
Spain 15:508–509 *illus.*
Altamira 1:311 *illus.*
Spanish art and architecture 18:151
techniques 15:508
temple 19:94 *illus.*
types of art 15:507
United States
Hohokam culture 10:199
rock art 15:510
Venus figurines 15:40 *illus.*
writing systems, evolution of 20:291–292
PREHISTORIC HUMANS 15:511–517 *bibliog., illus., maps*
Aegyptopithecus 1:118
African prehistory 1:172–173 *map*
agriculture, history of 1:189–190
animal behavior 2:17–18
animal husbandry 2:23
anthropology, physical 2:52–53 *illus.*
archaeology 2:124–126
Australopithecus 2:345–346 *illus.*
Boucher de Perthes, Jacques 3:420
Broken Hill man 3:501
cave dwellers 4:224–225
Cheddar man 4:307
China, history of 4:370
Chinese archaeology 4:378; 4:379 *illus.*
Clark, John Desmond 5:38
Clark, Sir W. E. Le Gros 5:39
Coon, Carleton 5:243
Cro-Magnon man 5:353–354 *illus.*
culture 5:385
Dryopithecus 6:285
Dubois, Eugène 6:289
Earth, geological history of 7:15
European prehistory 7:301–306 *illus., map*
Folsom culture 8:204
Fontéchevade man 8:207
Gigantopithecus 9:178
Grimaldi man 9:364
Heidelberg man 10:107
Homo erectus 10:215–216 *illus.*; 15:513–515
Homo habilis 10:216; 15:513
Homo sapiens, archaic forms of 15:515
Howell, F. Clark 10:284
Huxley, Thomas Henry 10:325
Java man 11:385
Laetolil 12:163
Lantian man 12:201
Leakey (family) 12:259
Meganthropus 13:280
Mesolithic Period 13:315 *illus.*
Neanderthalers 14:69; 15:515 *illus.*
Neolithic Period 14:83–84 *illus.*
North American archaeology 14:236–240
Oakley, Kenneth 14:312
Omo 14:387–388
Oreopithecus 14:432
origins 15:512–513
paleoanthropology: history, aims, and methods of 15:511
Paleolithic Period 15:38–41
Peking man 15:136
Piltdown man 15:303
Pithecanthropus see HOMO ERECTUS
Pleistocene Epoch 15:366; 15:511–512
Proconsul 15:561
race 16:34
Ramapithecus 16:80
sites 15:514 *map*
Skull 1470 17:346
Solo man 18:56
spread of 15:516 *map*
Bering Land Bridge 3:212
Steinheim man 18:249
Sterkfontein 18:260
Swanscombe man 18:379
Teilhard de Chardin, Pierre 19:73–74
temple 19:94 *illus.*
Ternifine man 19:118
urbanization 15:516–517
Zinjanthropus *see* AUSTRALOPITHECUS
PREHISTORIC TOOL INDUSTRIES
See also MESOLITHIC PERIOD; NEOLITHIC PERIOD; PALEOLITHIC PERIOD
Abbevillian 1:52
Acheulean 1:81
Aurignacian 2:324
Azilian 2:381
Capsian 4:128–129
Châtelperronian 4:303
Chellean 4:311
Clactonian 5:35
Creswellian 5:339
European prehistory 7:302 *illus.*
Folsom culture 8:204
Gravettian 9:303
Hamburgian 10:27
Levalloisian 12:301–302

Magdalenian **13**:46
Mousterian **13**:626
Oldowan **14**:376
Perigordian **15**:166
Solutrean **18**:58
technology, history of **19**:61 *illus.*
PREHISTORY **15**:517 *bibliog.*
African prehistory **1**:171–175 *map*
agriculture, history of **1**:189–190
archaeoastronomy **2**:114–115
archaeology **2**:116–126
Boucher de Perthes, Jacques **3**:420
Breuil, Henri **3**:475
Bronze Age **3**:505–506
Capsian **4**:128
cave dwellers **4**:224
Childe, V. Gordon **4**:351
Eskimo cultures **7**:239 *map*
European prehistory **7**:301–306 *map*
fossil record **8**:243–248
Frere, Sir John **8**:327
funeral customs **8**:364–365
geologic time **9**:103–105
history **10**:183
Lubbock, John, 1st Baron Avebury **12**:446
Mesolithic Period **13**:314–315
Neanderthalers **14**:69
Neolithic Period **14**:83–84
North American archaeology **14**:236–240 *map*
Paleolithic Period **15**:38–41
prehistoric art **15**:506–511
prehistoric humans **15**:511–517
Thomsen, Christian Jürgensen **19**:175
weights and measures **20**:92–93
wheel **20**:127 *illus.*
Worsaae, Jens Jacob Asmussen **20**:284
PREHNITE **13**:441 *illus.*; **15**:518
PREHUMANS *see* PREHISTORIC HUMANS
PREJUDICE *See* DISCRIMINATION
PRELOG, VLADIMIR **15**:518
PRELUDE **15**:518
composers
Bach, Johann Sebastian **3**:11
Debussy, Claude **6**:71
Rachmaninoff, Sergei **16**:36
PREM TINSULANONDA
Thailand **19**:140–141
PREMATURE AGING **1**:186
PREMATURE BABY **15**:518
pregnancy and birth **15**:506
PREMENSTRUAL STRESS **15**:518 *bibliog.*
PREMIER *see* PRIME MINISTER
PREMINGER, OTTO **15**:518 *bibliog.*
PREMONT (Texas)
map (27° 22′N 98° 8′W) **19**:129
PŘEMYSL (dynasty) **15**:518 *bibliog.*
Ottokar II, King of Bohemia (Přemysl Ottokar) **14**:464
Wenceslas, Saint **20**:103
Wenceslas I, King of Bohemia **20**:103
Wenceslas II, King of Bohemia **20**:103
PRENDERGAST, MAURICE **15**:518 *bibliog., illus.*
Central Park **15**:518 *illus.*
PRENTICE (Wisconsin)
map (45° 33′N 90° 17′W) **20**:185
PRENTISS (Mississippi)
map (31° 36′N 89° 52′W) **13**:469
PRENTISS (county in Mississippi)
map (34° 35′N 88° 30′W) **13**:469
PREOBRAZHENSKA, OLGA
Kirov Ballet **12**:90
PREON
fundamental particles **8**:363
PREPARATORY SCHOOL *see* PRIVATE SCHOOLS
PREPOSITION
parts of speech **15**:101
PŘEROV (Czechoslovakia)
map (49° 27′N 17° 27′E) **5**:413
PRESBYOPIA
eye diseases **7**:350
PRESBYTER *see* MINISTRY, CHRISTIAN
PRESBYTERIANISM **15**:519–520 *bibliog.*
Calvinism **4**:49
Covenanters **5**:319
education
Beaver College **3**:149
Davidson College **6**:49
Inter-American University of Puerto Rico **11**:206
Princeton Theological Seminary **15**:549
Queen's University at Kingston **16**:22
Westminster College **20**:118
Henderson, Alexander **10**:121
Knox, John **12**:102–103
Makemie, Francis **13**:78
Melville, Andrew **13**:289
Reformed churches **16**:123
Scotland **17**:151
Scotland, Church of **17**:152
Tennent, Gilbert **19**:102
Tennent, William **19**:102
Westminster Longer and Shorter Catechisms **4**:202
PRESCHOOL EDUCATION **15**:520–522 *bibliog.*
Bronfenbrenner, Urie **3**:503
day-care center **6**:55
Froebel, Friedrich Wilhelm August **8**:335–336
Harris, William Torrey **10**:58
Head Start **10**:85
kindergarten **15**:520
learning in preschools **15**:521
Montessori method **15**:521
nursery school **15**:520–521
parents and preschool education **15**:521
Peabody, Elizabeth **15**:122–123
preschool teachers **15**:521–522
"Sesame Street" **17**:212
PRESCOTT (Arizona) **15**:522
map (34° 33′N 112° 28′W) **2**:160
rodeo **16**:266
PRESCOTT (Arkansas)
map (33° 48′N 93° 23′W) **2**:166
PRESCOTT, SAMUEL
Dawes, William **6**:54
Revere, Paul **16**:186
PRESCOTT, WILLIAM (general)
Putnam, Israel **15**:632
PRESCOTT, WILLIAM H. (historian) **15**:522 *bibliog.*
PRESERVATION OF HISTORIC BUILDINGS *see* HISTORIC PRESERVATION
PRESERVATIVES, FOOD *see* CANNING; DEHYDRATION OF FOOD; FOOD ADDITIVES; FOOD PRESERVATION; FOOD TECHNOLOGY; etc.
PRESERVES (food) *see* JAM AND JELLY
PRESHO (South Dakota)
map (43° 54′N 100° 4′W) **18**:103
PRESIDEIO (county in Texas)
map (30° 0′N 104° 8′W) **19**:129
PRESIDENT **15**:522
PRESIDENT OF THE UNITED STATES **15**:522–528 *bibliog., illus., table*
See also names of specific presidents, e.g., ADAMS, JOHN; WILSON, WOODROW; etc.
appointments
Senate of the United States **17**:198–199
Supreme Court of the United States **18**:355
cabinet **4**:5
Camp David **4**:63
Congress of the United States **5**:187
Constitution of the United States **5**:216; **5**:218–219
Council of Economic Advisers **5**:310
Domestic Council **6**:231
executive privilege
United States v. *Richard M. Nixon* **19**:465
flag **8**:148 *illus.*
foreign policy
Constitution of the United States **5**:218
United States v. *Curtiss-Wright Export Corporation* **19**:464
framework of the Constitution **5**:214–215
Hanson, John **10**:41
impeachment **11**:60–61
list of **15**:528 *table*
Management and Budget, U.S. Office of **13**:107
military force, use of
Ex parte Milligan **7**:325
National Security Council **14**:46
portraits
National Portrait Gallery **14**:45
power, limitation of
Youngstown Sheet and Tube Company v. *Sawyer* **20**:337
presidential succession
presidential elections **15**:532
20th Amendment **19**:359
25th Amendment **5**:223; **19**:359
vice-president of the United States **19**:568–570
protection
Secret Service **17**:181
term of office
20th Amendment **19**:359
two-term limitation
22d Amendment **19**:359
United States, history of the **19**:442
veto **19**:567
White House **20**:137–138
PRESIDENTIAL ELECTIONS **15**:529–532 *bibliog., illus.*
Democratic party **6**:99–103
District of Columbia
23d Amendment **19**:360
election outcomes **15**:530–531
electoral college **7**:104–105
National Conservative Political Action Committee **14**:31
political convention **15**:399–400
president of the United States **15**:524
primary election **15**:538–539
Republican party **16**:172–176
12th Amendment **19**:358
vice-president of the United States **19**:568–569
White, Theodore **20**:136
PRESIDENTIAL MEDAL OF FREEDOM
Fiedler, Arthur **8**:70
PRESIDENTIAL RANGE
map (44° 15′N 71° 20′W) **14**:123
PRESIDENTIAL SUCCESSION AMENDMENT *see* 25th AMENDMENT
PRESIDENTIAL TERM LIMITATION *see* 22d AMENDMENT
PRESIDIO (Texas)
map (29° 33′N 104° 23′W) **19**:129
PRESLEY, ELVIS **15**:532 *bibliog., illus.*
Memphis (Tennessee) **13**:292
rock music **16**:248 *illus.*
PREŠOV (Czechoslovakia)
map (49° 0′N 21° 15′E) **5**:413
PRESPA, LAKE
map (40° 55′N 21° 0′E) **1**:250
PRESQUE ISLE (Maine)
map (46° 41′N 68° 1′W) **13**:70
PRESQUE ISLE (county in Michigan)
map (45° 20′N 83° 50′W) **13**:377
PRESS *see* HYDRAULIC PRESS; LETTERPRESS; PRINTING
PRESS (journalism) *see* JOURNALISM; NEWSPAPER; PERIODICAL; RADIO BROADCASTING, NEWSCASTS; TELEVISION BROADCASTING—newscasts
PRESS, FREEDOM OF THE *see* FREEDOM OF THE PRESS
PRESS AGENCIES AND SYNDICATES **15**:533 *bibliog.*
journalism **11**:454–455
McClure, S. S. **13**:10
New China News Agency
People's Daily **15**:156
newspaper **14**:172
Reuter, Paul Julius, Baron von **16**:184
Scripps, Edward Wyllis **17**:158
PRESSBURG, TREATY OF
Napoléon I, Emperor of the French (Napoléon Bonaparte) **14**:18
Napoleonic Wars **14**:19
PRESSER, JACKIE
Teamsters **19**:58
PRESSING
ceramics **4**:257–258
PRESSURE **15**:533
barometric pressure, barometer **3**:87–88
calibration point, triple point **19**:302
critical constants **5**:351
freezing point **8**:301
high-pressure region **10**:162
measurement **13**:255
metamorphic rock **13**:331–333
nitrogen, bends **3**:196
osmotic **14**:455
phase equilibrium **15**:222–224 *illus.*
pneumatic systems **15**:375
refrigeration **16**:124–125
unit of measurement
units, physical **19**:466
van der Waals equation **19**:512–513
vapor pressure **19**:521
PRESSURE BURNER **8**:372 *illus.*
PRESTEA (Ghana)
map (5° 27′N 2° 8′W) **9**:164
PRESTEL
information science **11**:173
PRESTER JOHN **15**:533 *bibliog.*
PRESTON (England)
map (53° 46′N 2° 42′W) **19**:403
PRESTON (Georgia)
map (31° 59′N 84° 37′W) **9**:114
PRESTON (Idaho)
map (42° 6′N 111° 53′W) **11**:26
PRESTON (Minnesota)
map (43° 40′N 92° 5′W) **13**:453
PRESTON (county in West Virginia)
map (39° 27′N 79° 40′W) **20**:111
PRESTONSBURG (Kentucky)
map (37° 40′N 82° 46′W) **12**:47
PRÊT-À-PORTER
fashion design **8**:32–33
PRETE GENOVESE, IL *see* STROZZI, BERNARDO
PRETORIA (South Africa) **15**:533–534
map (25° 45′S 28° 10′E) **18**:79
Pretorius, Andries **15**:534
PRETORIUS, ANDRIES **15**:534 *bibliog.*
PRETORIUS, MARTHINUS WESSEL **15**:534
PRETTY PRAIRIE (Kansas)
map (37° 47′N 98° 1′W) **12**:18
PREVELAKIS, PANDELIS
Greek literature, modern **9**:344
PREVENTIVE MEDICINE
antibiotics **2**:58
bubonic plague **3**:532
drug **6**:274–279
exercise **7**:329–331
infectious diseases **11**:167–168
Osler, Sir William **14**:454
PRÉVERT, JACQUES
Carné, Marcel **4**:155
PREVIN, ANDRÉ **15**:534
Pittsburgh Symphony Orchestra **15**:322
PRÉVOST, ABBÉ **15**:534 *bibliog.*
PREVOST, SIR GEORGE **15**:534 *bibliog.*
PREY VENG(Kampuchea)
map (11° 29′N 105° 19′E) **12**:11
PREZ, JOSQUIN DES *see* JOSQUIN DES PREZ
PRIAM **15**:534
Iliad **11**:40
PRIAPISM **15**:534
PRIAPUS **15**:534
PRIBILOF ISLANDS (Alaska) **15**:534
Bering Sea **3**:212
Bering Sea controversy **3**:212
map (57° 0′N 170° 0′W) **1**:242
PRIBOJ (Yugoslavia)
map (43° 35′N 19° 31′E) **20**:340
PŘÍBRAM (Czechoslovakia)
map (49° 42′N 14° 1′E) **5**:413
PRICE (Utah)
map (39° 36′N 110° 48′W) **19**:492
PRICE (county in Wisconsin)
map (45° 40′N 90° 20′W) **20**:185
PRICE, BRUCE
skyscraper **17**:350
PRICE, LEONTYNE **15**:534 *bibliog.*
PRICE, RICHARD **15**:535 *bibliog.*
PRICE, STERLING **15**:535 *bibliog.*
Mexican War **13**:354
PRICE, SIR UVEDALE **15**:535 *bibliog.*
landscape architecture **12**:187
PRICE SYSTEM **15**:535 *bibliog.*
black market **3**:317
cartel **4**:171
Clayton Anti-Trust Act **5**:47
consumer price index **5**:225
economy, national **7**:49–51
incomes policy **11**:77
inflation **11**:169–171
Marshall, Alfred **13**:171
Marxism **13**:183–184
monetary theory **13**:524–525
monopoly and competition **13**:537–540
option trading **14**:413
Organization of Petroleum Exporting Countries **14**:441
panic, financial **15**:59
parity (economics) **15**:88
petroleum industry **15**:215
quota **16**:28
Robinson-Patman Act **16**:246
stock market **18**:274–275
supply and demand **18**:353–354 *illus.*
Veblen, Thorstein B. **19**:529
PRICHARD (Alabama)
map (30° 44′N 88° 7′W) **1**:234
PRICKLEBACK **15**:535
PRICKLEY PEAR
cacti and other succulents **4**:9–10 *illus.*
PRICKLY ASH (botany) **15**:535
angelica tree **1**:413
Hercules' club **10**:138
PRICKLY HEAT **15**:536
PRICKLY PEAR **4**:283 *illus.*; **15**:536
PRIDE AND PREJUDICE (book) **14**:273; **15**:536; **14**:273 *illus.*; **15**:536
Austen, Jane **2**:326
PRIDEAUX, JOHN
French and Indian Wars **8**:313 *map*

PRIDE'S PURGE
Long Parliament **12**:407
PRIDVOROV, E. A. *see* BEDNY, DEMIAN
PRIENE 5:3 *illus.*; **15**:536 *bibliog.*
PRIESS, F.
marble clock **2**:208 *illus.*
PRIEST **15**:536 *bibliog.*
celibacy **4**:231
Indians, American **11**:123
intelligence gathering **11**:204
ministry, Christian **13**:450
PRIEST LAKE
map (48° 34′N 116° 52′W) **11**:26
PRIEST-PENITENT PRIVILEGE
evidence **7**:317
PRIEST RIVER (Idaho)
map (48° 11′N 116° 55′W) **11**:26
PRIESTLEY, J. B. **15**:536 *bibliog.*
PRIESTLEY, JOSEPH **15**:536–537 *bibliog.*, *illus.*
photosynthesis **15**:275
PRIEVIDZA (Czechoslovakia)
map (48° 47′N 18° 37′E) **5**:413
PRIGOGINE, ILYA **15**:537
entropy **7**:209
PRIJEDOR (Yugoslavia)
map (44° 59′N 16° 43′E) **20**:340
PRIJEPOLJE (Yugoslavia)
map (43° 23′N 19° 39′E) **20**:340
PRIKKER, JOHAN THORN- *see* THORN-PRIKKER, JOHAN
PRILEP (Yugoslavia)
map (41° 20′N 21° 33′E) **20**:340
PRIM, JUAN **15**:537 *bibliog.*
PRIM POINT
map (46° 3′N 63° 2′W) **15**:548
PRIMARY EDUCATION **15**:537–538 *bibliog.*
British education **3**:494
Canadian education **4**:91
computers in education **5**:165–166
Elementary and Secondary Education Act of 1965 **7**:133
Herbart, Johann Friedrich **10**:134–135
Pestalozzi, Johann Heinrich **15**:196
secondary education **17**:179
PRIMARY ELECTION **15**:538–539 *bibliog.*
election **7**:103–104
political convention **15**:399; **15**:400
president of the United States **15**:524
presidential elections **15**:530
PRIMARY STRUCTURE ART *see* MINIMAL ART
PRIMATE **15**:539–542 *bibliog.*, *illus.*, *table*
animal communication **2**:20
anthropology **2**:52–53
ape **2**:74–76
aye-aye **2**:378
baboon **3**:7
brain **3**:443 *illus.*
capuchin **4**:129
chimpanzee **4**:359
classification, biological **15**:542 *table*
drill **6**:272
evolution **7**:324; **15**:539–541 *illus.*
galago **9**:9
gibbon **9**:172
gorilla **9**:251
guenon **9**:390–391
indri **11**:150–151
langur **12**:199
lemur **12**:281
loris **12**:415
macaque **13**:4
mammal **13**:103–106 *illus.*
mandrill **13**:112
marmoset **13**:104
monkey **13**:532–535
orangutan **14**:415–416
pollination **15**:409
potto **15**:473
prehistoric humans **15**:511–512
siamang **17**:290
tamarin **19**:18
tarsier **19**:39
tree shrew **19**:289
types **15**:539–541 *illus.*
Yerkes, Robert Mearns **20**:326
PRIMATICCIO, FRANCESCO **15**:542 *bibliog.*
Gallery of Francis I **8**:206 *illus.*
Louvre **12**:437
PRIME INTEREST RATE *see* INTEREST
PRIME MERIDIAN **15**:542 *map*
Greenwich (England) **9**:354
longitude **12**:409
PRIME MINISTER **15**:542 *bibliog.*
See also names of specific prime ministers, e.g., DISRAELI, BENJAMIN, 1ST EARL OF BEACONSFIELD; SMITH, IAN D.; etc.
Great Britain, history of **9**:316 *table*
PRIME NUMBER **15**:542–543 *bibliog.*
Chebyshev, Pafnuty Lvovich **4**:306
computer technology **15**:542
distribution, number theory **14**:294
factor **8**:6
Goldbach conjecture **9**:230–231
number theory **14**:293–294
proof, mathematical **15**:568
properties
Fermat, Pierre de **8**:55
Siene of Eratosthenes **15**:542
theorem
Hadamard, Jacques Salomon **10**:7
unsolved problems **15**:543
PRIMERS AND READERS
primary education **15**:537
PRIMGHAR (Iowa)
map (43° 5′N 95° 38′W) **11**:244
PRIMITIVE ARTS **15**:543 *bibliog.*
See also FOLK ART; PREHISTORIC ART; PRIMITIVISM (art)
African art **1**:160–164
African music **1**:168–171
Indians of North America, art of the **11**:138–141
Indians of North America, music and dance of the **11**:141–144
jewelry **11**:408
Oceanic art **14**:336–339
pre-Columbian art and architecture **15**:495–501
PRIMITIVE MEDICINE
faith healing **8**:11
folk medicine **8**:201
psychopathology, treatment of **15**:599
PRIMITIVE RELIGION **15**:543–546 *bibliog.*, *illus.*
Aborigines, Australian **1**:59
ancestor worship **1**:398–399
animism **2**:29
Benedict, Ruth **3**:197
cargo cults **4**:147
dietary laws **6**:164–165
divine beings **15**:544–545
faith healing **8**:11
fertility rites **8**:60
folk medicine **8**:201
God **9**:217–218
Indians, American **11**:122–123 *illus.*
Aztec **2**:384
corn dance **5**:267
Delaware Prophet **6**:91
ghost dance **9**:169
Handsome Lake **10**:37
Inca **11**:73
kachina **12**:4
Lacandón **12**:158
Navajo **14**:53
Pawnee **15**:121
peace pipe **15**:123
peyote **15**:217
powwow **15**:486
magic **13**:49–50
mana **13**:107
megalith **13**:278–279
mother goddess **13**:606–607
mythology **13**:695
passage rites **15**:544
phallic worship **15**:219
prehistoric art **15**:506–511
primitive societies **15**:546
psychotropic drugs **15**:603
religious experience and expression **15**:543–544
rituals **15**:544
sacred personages **15**:545
shaman **17**:238–239
shamanism **15**:545
taboo **15**:546; **19**:5
theories **15**:543
totem **19**:249
tribal religions **16**:140 *map*
witchcraft **20**:191
PRIMITIVE SOCIETIES **15**:546 *bibliog.*
See also names of specific peoples, e.g., MONTAGNARDS; TASADAY; etc.
anthropology **2**:51–55
bride-price **3**:479
chief **4**:346
culture **5**:384–385
dance **6**:21–22 *illus.*
folklore **8**:203
hunter-gatherers **10**:313
infanticide **11**:163
masks **13**:196
mass communication **13**:202
Mead, Margaret **13**:251–252
money **13**:526
primitive art **15**:543
primitive religion **15**:543–546
tribe **19**:295
wind instruments **20**:171
women in society **20**:201
PRIMITIVES, THE (art group)
David, Jacques Louis **6**:47–48
PRIMITIVISM (art)
Bombois, Camille **3**:375
folk art **8**:197–198 *illus.*
Hicks, Edward **10**:157–158
limners **12**:345
Modersohn-Becker, Paula **13**:498–499
Moses, Grandma **13**:600
Pippin, Horace **15**:312
Rousseau, Henri **16**:325
Russian art and architecture **16**:363
Watts Towers **20**:69–70
PRIMO DE RIVERA, JOSÉ ANTONIO
Primo de Rivera, Miguel **15**:546
PRIMO DE RIVERA, MIGUEL **15**:546 *bibliog.*
Spain, history of **18**:148–149
PRIMOGENITURE **15**:547 *bibliog.*
Basques **3**:116
inheritance **11**:177
PRIMROSE **5**:121 *illus.*; **8**:228 *illus.*; **15**:547 *illus.*
cowslip (botany) **5**:322
cyclamen **5**:403
loosestrife **12**:411
moneywort **13**:527
pimpernel **15**:304
shooting star **17**:283
PRIMROSE, ARCHIBALD PHILIP, 5TH EARL OF ROSEBERRY *see* ROSEBERRY, ARCHIBALD PHILIP PRIMROSE, 5TH EARL OF
PRIMROSE LAKE
map (54° 55′N 109° 45′W) **17**:81
PRIMUS, PEARL
modern dance **13**:498
PRINCE
titles of nobility and honor **19**:213
PRINCE, THE (book) **15**:547 *bibliog.*
Ferdinand II, King of Aragon **8**:52
Machiavelli, Nicolò **13**:18–19
PRINCE ALBERT (Saskatchewan) **15**:547
map (53° 12′N 105° 46′W) **17**:81
PRINCE EDWARD (county in Virginia)
map (37° 15′N 78° 30′W) **19**:607
PRINCE EDWARD ISLAND (Canada) **15**:547–549 *bibliog.*, *illus.*, *map*
agriculture and fishing **15**:548–549 *illus.*
cities
Charlottetown **4**:299
economic activity **15**:548–549 *illus.*
education
Prince Edward Island, University of **4**:92 *table*; **15**:548–549
flag **15**:548 *illus.*
government **15**:548
history **15**:549
land and resources **15**:547–548 *map*
map (46° 20′N 63° 20′W) **4**:70
people **15**:548
PRINCE EDWARD ISLAND, UNIVERSITY OF **15**:549
PRINCE EDWARD POINT
map (44° 56′N 76° 52′W) **15**:548
PRINCE FREDERICK (Maryland)
map (38° 33′N 76° 35′W) **13**:188
PRINCE GEORGE (British Columbia) **15**:549
map (53° 55′N 122° 45′W) **3**:491
PRINCE GEORGE (Virginia)
map (37° 13′N 77° 17′W) **19**:607
PRINCE GEORGE (county in Virginia)
map (37° 13′N 77° 10′W) **19**:607
PRINCE GEORGES (county in Maryland)
map (38° 49′N 76° 45′W) **13**:188
PRINCE HENRY THE NAVIGATOR *see* HENRY THE NAVIGATOR
PRINCE IGOR (opera) **16**:368 *illus.*
PRINCE PATRICK ISLAND
map (76° 45′N 119° 30′W) **14**:258
PRINCE RUPERT (British Columbia)
map (54° 19′N 130° 19′W) **3**:491
PRINCE OF WALES (ship)
World War II **20**:260
PRINCE OF WALES ISLAND (Alaska)
map (55° 47′N 132° 50′W) **1**:242
PRINCE OF WALES ISLAND (Northwest Territories)
map (72° 40′N 99° 0′W) **14**:258
PRINCE WILLIAM (county in Virginia)
map (38° 42′N 77° 27′W) **19**:607
PRINCE WILLIAM SOUND
map (60° 40′N 147° 0′W) **1**:242
PRINCES TOWN (Trinidad and Tobago)
map (10° 16′N 61° 23′W) **19**:300
PRINCESS ANNE (Maryland)
map (38° 12′N 75° 41′W) **13**:188
PRINCESS ROYAL ISLAND
map (52° 57′N 128° 49′W) **3**:491
PRINCETON (British Columbia)
map (49° 27′N 120° 31′W) **3**:491
PRINCETON (Illinois)
map (41° 23′N 89° 28′W) **11**:42
PRINCETON (Indiana)
map (38° 21′N 87° 34′W) **11**:111
PRINCETON (Kentucky)
map (37° 7′N 87° 53′W) **12**:47
PRINCETON (Minnesota)
map (45° 34′N 93° 35′W) **13**:453
PRINCETON (Missouri)
map (40° 24′N 93° 35′W) **13**:476
PRINCETON (New Jersey) **15**:549
American Revolution **1**:358; **19**:441 *illus.*
Washington, George **20**:43
map (40° 21′N 74° 40′W) **14**:129
PRINCETON (North Carolina)
map (35° 28′N 78° 10′W) **14**:242
PRINCETON (West Virginia)
map (37° 22′N 81° 6′W) **20**:111
PRINCETON, MOUNT
map (38° 45′N 106° 15′W) **5**:116
PRINCETON THEOLOGICAL SEMINARY **15**:549
PRINCETON UNIVERSITY **15**:549 *bibliog.*
Davies, Samuel **6**:50
football **8**:216 *illus.*
McCosh, James **13**:10
Nassau Hall **14**:130 *illus.*
Wilson, Woodrow **20**:166
PRINCEVILLE (Illinois)
map (40° 45′N 89° 45′W) **11**:42
PRINCEVILLE (North Carolina)
map (35° 53′N 77° 82′W) **14**:242
PRINCIP, GAVRILO
assassination of Archduke Franz Ferdinand **20**:222 *illus.*
Franz Ferdinand, Austrian Archduke **8**:286
PRÍNCIPE
map (1° 37′N 7° 25′E) **17**:72
São Tomé and Príncipe **17**:71–72
PRINCIPIA (book) **15**:549 *bibliog.*
astronomy, history of **2**:278
Newton, Sir Isaac **14**:173–174 *illus.*
physics, history of **15**:282
PRINCIPIA MATHEMATICA (book) **15**:550 *bibliog.*
Whitehead, Alfred North **20**:139
PRINCIPIA MATHEMATICA PHILOSOPHIAE NATURALIS (book) *see PRINCIPIA* (book)
PRINCIPIA PHILOSOPHIAE (book)
physics, history of **15**:282
PRINEVILLE (Oregon)
map (44° 18′N 120° 51′W) **14**:427
PRINEVILLE RESERVOIR
map (44° 8′N 120° 42′W) **14**:427
PRINSES MARGRIET CANAL
map (53° 10′N 5° 55′E) **14**:99
PRINT COMMUNICATION
mass communication **13**:202
PRINTED CIRCUIT **15**:550 *bibliog.*
computer **5**:160c
microelectronics **13**:385
photoengraving **15**:260
PRINTER, COMPUTER **15**:550
computer **5**:160i
PRINTING **15**:550–553 *bibliog.*, *illus.*, *table*
Baskerville, John **3**:110
Bay Psalm Book **3**:132
book **3**:383–386
book illustration **3**:386–388
Caxton, William **4**:227
Day, Stephen **6**:55
effect of printing on English language **7**:192
graphic arts **9**:291–294
Gutenberg, Johann **9**:408–409; **15**:551
book **3**:384
Fust, Johann **8**:383
Gutenberg Bible **9**:409
history **15**:551–552
incunabula **11**:77–78
ink **11**:178
journalism **11**:454–455
Kelmscott Press **12**:39–40
Manutius, Aldus **13**:134
mass communication **13**:202
music
Italian music **11**:318
Renaissance music **16**:156

paper **15**:550–553
process
block printing **3**:334
collotype **5**:105
distribution by process **15**:553 *table*
electrostatic printing **7**:127–128
electrotype **7**:128
gravure **15**:552
halftone **10**:20
industry **15**:552–553
intaglio **11**:199–200; **15**:551
letterpress **12**:299; **15**:551
Linotype **12**:359
lithography **12**:371; **15**:551–552
lithography: Senefelder, Aloys **17**:201
machine: Mergenthaler, Ottmar **13**:310
mimeograph **13**:434
Monotype **13**:541
offset lithography **14**:354
photoengraving **15**:260
phototypesetting **15**:277–278
platemaking **15**:357–358
rotogravure **16**:323
screen printing **15**:552
silk-screen printing **15**:552; **17**:308
stereotype **18**:260
thermography **19**:165–166
typesetting **19**:365
publishing **15**:611–612
sheet-fed press **17**:249–250
textile industry **19**:137 *illus.*
Thomas, Isaiah **19**:173
type, printing **19**:363
typeface **19**:363–365
typewriter **19**:365–366
woodcuts and wood engravings **20**:210–211
Zenger, John Peter **20**:359
PRINTING PRESS
flatbed cylinder press **8**:154
letterpress **12**:299–300
printing **15**:551–552
rotary press **16**:321
Hill, Sir Rowland **10**:164
Hoe, Richard March **10**:194
16th century **19**:65 *illus.*
web-fed press **20**:85–86
PRINTMAKING *see* GRAPHIC ARTS
PRION **15**:533
PRIOR, MATTHEW **15**:553 *bibliog.*
PRIOR RESTRAINT
freedom of the press **8**:296
PRIORY
abbey **1**:52
PRIPET MARSHES (USSR) **15**:553
PRISCILLIAN **15**:553
PRISM (physics) **15**:553–554 *illus.*
biprism
interference **11**:208–209
crossed Nicols
optical mineralogy **14**:409
dispersion (physics) **6**:197
Nicol prism **15**:394 *illus.*
optical instruments **15**:553
polarized light **15**:394 *illus.*
reflection **15**:553
spectrum **18**:172–173
stellar spectrum **18**:252
types **15**:553
PRISON **15**:554–555 *bibliog.*
alternatives **15**:555
Attica prison riot **2**:314
concentration camp **5**:169
crime **5**:347
institutionalization **11**:196
parole **15**:97
prison reform
Fry, Elizabeth **8**:350–351
prisoners' rights **15**:555
punishment **15**:625–626
Tower of London **19**:254
PRISONER OF WAR **15**:555–556 *bibliog.*
Geneva conventions **9**:91
Korean War **12**:122
Nansen, Fridtjof **14**:13 *illus.*
World War I **20**:242 *illus.*
PRISONER OF ZENDA, THE (book)
Hope, Anthony **10**:230
PRIŠTINA (Yugoslavia)
map (42° 39′N 21° 10′E) **20**:340
PRITCHARD, SIR EDWARD EVANS- *see* EVANS-PRITCHARD, SIR EDWARD
PRITCHARD, HAROLD A.
ethics **7**:250
PRITCHETT (Colorado)
map (37° 22′N 102° 52′W) **5**:116
PRITCHETT, V. S. **15**:556
PRITTWITZ, MAX VON
World War I **20**:224–225
PRITZKER ARCHITECTURE PRIZE **15**:556
PRIVACY, INVASION OF **15**:556 *bibliog.*
abortion **1**:60
computers and privacy **5**:166–167
4th Amendment **8**:254
Freedom of Information Act **8**:296
9th Amendment **14**:200
Roe v. *Wade* and *Doe* v. *Bolton* **16**:267–268
sodomy **18**:34
surveillance systems **18**:366
wiretapping **20**:183
PRIVACY PROTECTION ACT
freedom of the press **8**:297
PRIVATE CARRIER *see* COMMON CARRIER
PRIVATE ENTERPRISE *see* CAPITALISM
PRIVATE LAW
law **12**:243
PRIVATE AND PUBLIC SCHOOLS
Coleman Report **5**:100
PRIVATE SCHOOLS **15**:557 *bibliog.*
British education **3**:495
Coleman Report **5**:100
Jencks, Christopher **11**:395
Jesuit Estates Act **11**:402
Manitoba Schools Question **13**:122
progressive education **15**:564
secondary education **17**:179–180
Seton, Saint Elizabeth Ann Bayley **17**:214
PRIVATEERING **15**:557–558 *bibliog.*
French and Indian Wars **8**:312
Kidd, Captain **12**:70
Lafitte, Jean **12**:164
piracy **15**:312–313
PRIVATIZATION **15**:558 *bibliog.*
PRIVET **15**:558–559
PRIVILEGED INFORMATION
evidence **7**:317
self-incrimination **17**:191
witness **20**:193
PRIVY COUNCIL **15**:559 *bibliog.*
PRIX DE ROME
Berlioz, Hector **3**:218
Bizet, Georges **3**:302
Boulanger, Nadia **3**:421
Charpentier, Gustave **4**:299
Debussy, Claude **6**:71–72
Dukas, Paul **6**:295
Garnier, Jean Louis Charles **9**:49
Girodet-Trioson, Anne Louis **9**:190
Gounod, Charles **9**:266
Guérin, Pierre Narcisse, Baron **9**:391
Ibert, Jacques **11**:4
Ingres, Jean Auguste Dominique **11**:176
Thomas, Ambroise **19**:172
PRIZEFIGHTING *see* BOXING
PRIZREN (Yugoslavia)
map (42° 12′N 20° 44′E) **20**:340
PROBABILITY (mathematics) **15**:559 *bibliog.*
aleatory music **1**:270
atomic motion
Boltzmann, Ludwig **3**:372
electron configuration **7**:120
Bernoulli, Jacques **3**:223
Boole, George **3**:392–393
Cardano, Gerolamo **4**:143
cross-section **5**:361
de Moivre, Abraham **6**:62
distribution
binomial distribution **3**:260
central limit theorem **4**:254
chi-square **4**:339
normal distribution **14**:219
Poisson distribution **15**:385
standard deviation **18**:216
expected value **7**:333–334
factorial **8**:6
Fermat, Pierre de **8**:55
games **9**:31
Laplace, Pierre Simon de **12**:205
Markov, Andrei Andreyevich **13**:159–160
Markov process **13**:159–160
mathematics
games, mathematical **9**:32
inference (mathematics) **11**:168
large numbers, law of **12**:207
mathematics, history of **13**:225
parapsychology **15**:81
Quételet, Lambert Adolphe **16**:23
random variable **16**:83
random walk **16**:83
statistics **18**:236
statistics, nonparametric **18**:237–238
stochastic process **18**:273
theory
decision theory **6**:74
game theory **9**:28
information theory **11**:174
queuing theory **16**:24–25
tree diagram **19**:288–289
PROBABLE CAUSE (law)
warrant **20**:30
PROBATE **15**:559 *bibliog.*
inquest **11**:183
will (law) **20**:153
PROBATION **15**:559–560
criminal justice **5**:350
prison **15**:555
PROBLEM SOLVING **15**:560 *bibliog.*, *illus.*
artificial intelligence **2**:221
cognitive psychology **5**:94–95
concept formation and attainment **5**:169
flowchart **8**:178
group dynamics **9**:376
mathematics **13**:221
reasoning **16**:104
Simon, Herbert A. **17**:315
skill learning **17**:339
PROBOLINGGO (Indonesia)
map (7° 45′S 113° 13′E) **11**:147
PROBOSCIDEAN **15**:560
elephant **7**:133–134
mammal **13**:103–106 *illus.*
mammoth **13**:106–107
mastodon **13**:217
PROCAINE **15**:560
PROCARYOTE **15**:334 *illus.*; **15**:560
bacteria **3**:15
cell **4**:231 *illus.*; **4**:233
cytoplasm **5**:412
Monera **13**:523
ribosome **16**:206
PROCESS CONTROL **15**:560–561 *bibliog.*, *illus.*
automatic adjustment operation **15**:560
automation **2**:357
computer **15**:560–561
evaluation **15**:560
feedback **8**:44
measurement **15**:560
microprocessor **13**:387
microprocessor-based microcomputer system **15**:560–561
process-control loop **15**:560
regulation, industrial operations **15**:560
PROCESS MUSIC
Reich, Steve **16**:130
PROCESS PHILOSOPHY **15**:561 *bibliog.*
Hartshorne, Charles **10**:63
Whitehead, Alfred North **20**:139
PROCLAMATION LINE OF 1763
United States, history of the **19**:439
PROCLUS **15**:561 *bibliog.*
PROCOMPSOGNATHUS **15**:561; **16**:170 *illus.*, *illus.*
PROCONSUL **15**:561 *bibliog.*
PROCOPIUS OF CAESAREA **15**:561–562 *bibliog.*
PROCOPIUS THE GREAT **15**:562 *bibliog.*
PROCRIS
Cephalus **4**:257
PROCTOR (Minnesota)
map (46° 45′N 92° 13′W) **13**:453
PROCTOR (Vermont)
map (43° 40′N 73° 2′W) **19**:554
PROCYON
Canis Major and Canis Minor **4**:108
PRODUCER GAS **15**:562
PRODUCT DEVELOPMENT
pharmaceutical industry **15**:220
PRODUCTION
economics **7**:47–49
industrial engineering **11**:156
industrial management **11**:156–157
PRODUCTION, FILM *see* FILM PRODUCTION
PROENZYME
enzyme **7**:214
PROFESSIONAL AIR TRAFFIC CONTROLLERS ORGANIZATION
airport **1**:225
PROFESSIONAL AND EDUCATIONAL ORGANIZATIONS *see* SCIENTIFIC ASSOCIATIONS
PROFILES IN COURAGE (book)
Kennedy, John F. **12**:42–43
PROFIT **15**:562 *bibliog.*
See also EXCESS PROFITS TAX
corporate income tax **11**:76–77
economics **7**:47–49
Marxism **13**:183–184
petroleum industry **15**:215
price system **15**:535
stock (finance) **18**:273–274
Veblen, Thorstein B. **19**:529
PROFIT SHARING
Eastman, George **7**:34
PROFUMO, JOHN *see* PROFUMO SCANDAL
PROFUMO SCANDAL **15**:562 *bibliog.*
PROGENY-PRICE *see* BRIDE-PRICE
PROGERIA *see* PREMATURE AGING
PROGESTERONE
hormone, animal **10**:236 *table*
sex hormones **17**:225
PROGRAM MUSIC **15**:562 *bibliog.*
PROGRAMMED LEARNING **15**:562–563 *bibliog.*
computers in education **5**:165–166
learning theory **12**:260–261
teaching machines **19**:57
PROGRAMMING, COMPUTER *see* COMPUTER PROGRAMMING
PROGRESO (Mexico)
map (21° 17′N 89° 40′W) **13**:357
PROGRESSION **15**:563 *illus.*
arithmetic progression **15**:563–564
convergence **5**:233
geometric progression **15**:563–564
sequence (mathematics) **17**:206–207
series **17**:209
PROGRESSIVE CONSERVATIVE PARTY (Canada)
Clark, Joseph **5**:38–39
PROGRESSIVE EDUCATION **15**:563 *bibliog.*
See also ALTERNATIVE SCHOOLS
curriculum **5**:393
Dewey, John **6**:146–147
educational philosophy **7**:63–64
Kilpatrick, William Heard **12**:77
Montessori, Marie **13**:553
open classroom **14**:398
Parker, Francis Wayland **15**:90
Pestalozzi, Johann Heinrich **15**:196
Summerhill **18**:339
PROGRESSIVE ERA **15**:564
PROGRESSIVE PARTY (U.S.) **15**:564 *bibliog.*
Bull Moose party **3**:558
La Follette, Robert M. **12**:145–146
Republican party **16**:174
Roosevelt, Theodore **16**:310–311
Socialist party **18**:25
Taft, William Howard **19**:9
Wallace, Henry A. **20**:14
PROHIBITION **15**:564 *bibliog.*, *illus.*
bootlegging **3**:395
18th Amendment **5**:222; **7**:91
Harding, Warren G. **10**:46–47
"Mr. Dry" (cartoon) **4**:176 *illus.*
smuggling **17**:374
temperance movement **19**:92
21st Amendment **5**:223
Volstead, Andrew J. **19**:631
PROJECT BLUE BOOK
unidentified flying object **19**:385
PROJECTILE (explosive device)
ammunition **1**:373–375 *illus.*
bomb **3**:373–374
railgun **16**:70–71
torpedo **19**:242–243
PROJECTION (cartography)
maps and mapmaking **13**:144 *illus.*
PROJECTION (psychology)
defense mechanisms **6**:83
PROJECTIVE GEOMETRY **15**:564–565 *bibliog.*, *illus.*
Cayley, Arthur **4**:227
Desargues, Gérard **6**:125
geometry **9**:107
mathematics, history of **13**:226
Veblen, Oswald **19**:529
PROJECTIVE TESTS **15**:565–566 *bibliog.*, *illus.*
personality **15**:190
psychological measurement **15**:593
PROJECTIVISM
Creeley, Robert **5**:337
PROJECTOR **15**:566 *illus.*
Jenkins, Charles Francis **11**:395
lens **12**:286
PROKARYOTIC CELL *see* PROCARYOTE
PROKOFIEV, SERGEI **15**:566–567 *bibliog.*, *illus.*
Russian music **16**:369
toccata **19**:220
PROKUPLJE (Yugoslavia)
map (43° 14′N 21° 36′E) **20**:340
PROLACTIN **15**:567
breast **3**:469 *illus.*
endocrine system, diseases of the **7**:169; **7**:170
hormones **10**:236
pituitary gland **15**:322
PROLETARIAT **15**:567
class, social **5**:40

PROLETARIAT (cont.)
dictatorship of the proletariat **6**:159
economics **7**:48–49
Marxism **13**:183–184
PROLOG (computer language) **15**:567
computer languages **5**:160p
PROLOGUE (literature)
narrative and dramatic devices **14**:22–23
PROME (Burma)
map (18° 49′N 95° 13′E) **3**:573
PROMETAPHASE *see* MEIOSIS; MITOSIS
PROMETHAZINE *see* ANTIHISTAMINE
PROMETHEUS **15**:567
PROMETHEUS UNBOUND (play) **15**:567
Shelley, Percy Bysshe **17**:253
PROMETHIUM **15**:567
element **7**:130 *table*
lanthanide series **12**:200–201
metal, metallic element **13**:328
PROMINENCE **15**:567
Sun **18**:343–345 *illus.*
ultraviolet astronomy **19**:379 *illus.*
PROMONTORY POINT (Utah)
meeting of the transcontinental railroad **16**:72 *illus.*; **19**:450 *illus.*
PROMOTION OF BANTU SELF-GOVERNMENT ACT
South Africa **18**:83
PROMPT (computer term) **5**:160i
PRONGHORN **15**:567–568 *illus.*
horn (biology) **10**:238
PRONOUN
parts of speech **15**:101
PRONTOSIL
Domagk, Gerhard **6**:229
PRONUNCIATION *see* PHONETICS; PHONOLOGY AND MORPHOLOGY
PROOF, LEGAL *see* EVIDENCE
PROOF, MATHEMATICAL **15**:568 *bibliog.*
induction, mathematical **11**:151
PROPAGANDA **15**:568–569 *bibliog., illus.*
Cominform **5**:136
film
documentary **6**:211
Kracauer, Siegfried **12**:126
newsreel **14**:173
Riefenstahl, Leni **16**:218
Goebbels, Joseph **9**:221–222
Lord Haw-Haw **12**:413
mass communication **13**:201–203
newspaper **14**:172
public opinion **15**:609
Radio Free Europe and Radio Liberty **16**:53
Tokyo Rose **19**:226
totalitarianism **19**:248
Voice of America **19**:626
PROPANAL
aldehyde **1**:268
PROPANE **15**:569
graphic formula **14**:436 *illus.*
heat content **8**:353 *table*
natural gas **14**:47
PROPANONE *see* ACETONE
PROPELLANT
aerosol **1**:125
guncotton **9**:405
recoilless rifle **16**:108
rockets and missiles **16**:258–260 *illus., table*
Ariane **2**:153
Centaur **4**:249
PROPELLER **15**:569 *bibliog.*
helicopter **10**:111–112
ship **17**:273
windmills and wind power **20**:172–173 *illus.*
PROPELLER PLANT (botany) **4**:9 *illus.*
PROPER MOTION **15**:569–570 *bibliog., illus.*
Barnard's Star **3**:86
Bessel, Friedrich **3**:228
Lundmark, Knut **12**:462
star **18**:221
PROPERTIUS, SEXTUS **15**:570 *bibliog.*
PROPERTY **15**:570–571 *bibliog.*
abandonment **1**:51
appraisal **2**:91
assignment **2**:265
auction **2**:317
common law **5**:139–140
community property **5**:153
conversion **5**:233
dower **6**:251
18th-century land grant **8**:343 *illus.*
eminent domain **7**:156
encumbrance **7**:163
estate **7**:246
freeholder **8**:299
Hammurabi, Code of **10**:31
inheritance **11**:177
escheat **7**:237
genealogy **9**:76
heir **10**:109
inheritance tax **11**:177–178
kinship **12**:85–86
primogeniture **15**:547
will (law) **20**:153
women in society **20**:202
insurance **11**:198–199
larceny **12**:206
lien **12**:326
manorialism **13**:126–127
mortmain **13**:592
personal property **15**:188
physiocrats **15**:286–287
real property
condominium **5**:172–173
easement **7**:30
entail **7**:208
escrow **7**:238
fee **8**:44
Homestead Act **10**:214
lease **12**:261
mortgage **13**:591–592
rights
air rights **1**:209
marriage **13**:165
riparian rights **16**:228
Roman law **16**:279
sabotage **17**:6
slavery **17**:351–357
socialist law **18**:25
tax revenues
equal protection of the laws **7**:224
property tax **15**:571
single tax **17**:322
title **19**:213
deed **6**:77
joint tenancy **11**:440
tenant **19**:101
Torrens system **19**:244
trespass **19**:291
squatter **18**:203
tort **19**:246
trover **19**:312
trust **19**:321
trustee **19**:321–322
PROPERTY TAX **15**:571 *bibliog.*
assessment **2**:265
George, Henry **9**:109
PROPHET **15**:571 *bibliog.*
Indians, American
ghost dance **9**:169
Nostradamus **14**:266–267
PROPHET, DELAWARE *see* DELAWARE PROPHET
PROPHETSTOWN (Illinois)
map (41° 40′N 89° 56′W) **11**:42
PROPIONATES **15**:571
stereochemistry **18**:258 *illus.*
PROPORTION *see* RATIO
PROPORTIONAL REPRESENTATION **15**:571–572 *bibliog.*
political parties **15**:403
representation **16**:161
PROPOSITION 13
California **4**:37
PROPOXYPHENE
Darvon **6**:40
PROPRIÁ (Brazil)
map (10° 13′S 36° 51′W) **3**:460
PROPRIETARY ASSOCIATION
patent medicine **15**:110
PROPRIETORS' COMPANY FOR PROVIDENCE PLANTATIONS
Rhode Island **16**:201
PROPRIETORSHIP *see* BUSINESS ADMINISTRATION
PROPULSION SYSTEMS *see* JET PROPULSION; ROCKETS AND MISSILES
PROPYLAEA
acropolis **1**:84–85
PROPYLENE
alkene **1**:297
PROPYNE
alkyne **1**:297
PROSCENIUM ARCH
theater architecture and staging **19**:152
PROSE **15**:572
See also ESSAY
Chinese literature **4**:390
satire **17**:88
PROSECUTING ATTORNEY **15**:572
criminal justice **5**:350
indictment **11**:44
PROSECUTION, MALICIOUS
tort **19**:245
PROSKOURIAKOFF, TATIANA
Piedras Negras **15**:295
PROSLOGION (treatise)
Anselm, Saint **2**:35
PROSNA RIVER
map (52° 10′N 17° 39′E) **15**:388
PROSODY *see* VERSIFICATION
PROSPECT (Ohio)
map (40° 27′N 83° 11′W) **14**:357
PROSPECTOR (computer system)
automata, theory of **2**:357
PROSSER (Washington)
map (46° 12′N 119° 46′W) **20**:35
PROSSER, GABRIEL *see* GABRIEL (slave)
PROSTAGLANDINS **15**:572
aspirin **2**:262–263
dysmenorrhea **6**:320
hormone, animal **10**:234
PROSTATE GLAND **15**:572 *bibliog.*; **16**:163 *illus.*
prostaglandins **15**:572
prostatitis, urogenital diseases **19**:487
trichomoniasis **19**:296
urogenital diseases **19**:487
PROSTĚJOV (Czechoslovakia)
map (49° 29′N 17° 7′E) **5**:413
PROSTHETICS **15**:572 *bibliog.*
artificial limbs **2**:221–222
artificial organs **2**:222
eye, artificial **7**:350
heart, artificial **10**:94–95
joint (anatomy) **11**:440
kidney, artificial **12**:71
PROSTHODONTICS
dentures **6**:117
PROSTITUTION **15**:572–573 *bibliog.*
Mann Act **13**:124
solicitation **18**:54
vagrancy **19**:502
PROTACTINIUM **15**:573
actinide series **1**:88
element **7**:130 *table*
Hahn, Otto **10**:11
Meitner, Lise **13**:283
metal, metallic element **13**:328
PROTAGONIST
hero **14**:22
PROTAGORAS **15**:573 *bibliog.*
games, mathematical **9**:32
PROTECTIONISM **15**:573–574
PROTEIN **15**:574 *bibliog.*
active transport **1**:89–90
albumin **1**:261
amide **1**:369
amine **1**:370
amino acids **15**:574
insulin **11**:198
angiogenin **1**:414
biochemistry **3**:261
blood protein
antibody **2**:59–60
inflammation **11**:169
multiple myeloma **13**:638
casein **4**:181
cholesterol **4**:403–404
collagen **5**:102
concentrate, fish meal **8**:122
conformation **15**:574
deficiency **15**:574
diet, human **6**:164
celiac disease **4**:231
dieting **6**:165
kwashiorkor **12**:142–143
meat imitations **13**:257
nutrition, human **14**:305; **14**:306
nutritional-deficiency diseases **14**:307
digestion, human **6**:172
digestive system **6**:173–174
gelatin **9**:69
globulin **9**:209
heme **15**:574
hemoglobin **10**:119
history, research **15**:574
Hoppe-Seyler, Felix **10**:232
hormone, animal **10**:234; **10**:235; **10**:237
horn (biology) **10**:238
interferon **11**:210
isolation: Tiselius, Arne Wilhelm Kaurin **19**:207
keratin **12**:58
life **12**:326–327
lipoproteins **15**:574
liver **12**:374
metabolism **13**:325
molecule
enzyme **7**:213–214 *illus.*
muscle contraction **13**:654–656
myoglobin **13**:691
Kendrew, John Cowdery **12**:41
prosthetic groups **15**:574
structure
Bragg, Sir William L. **3**:439
synthesis **15**:574
virus **19**:613–614
wheat **20**:125–126
PROTEIN-CALORIE MALNUTRITION
nutritional-deficiency diseases **14**:307
PROTEIN SYNTHESIS **15**:574–576 *bibliog., illus.*
amino acid **1**:370–371
DNA **15**:575
enzyme **7**:212–213
genetic code **9**:79–82
genetics **9**:88
Jacob, François **11**:345
Kornberg, Arthur **12**:123
Lipmann, Fritz Albert **12**:362
memory **13**:291
nucleic acid **14**:288–291
nucleus **14**:291
operon **14**:403–404
ribosome **16**:206
Smith, Hamilton **17**:368
virus **19**:613–615 *illus.*
Watson, James D. **20**:67–68
PROTEROZOIC ERA
Precambrian time **15**:491
PROTEST MOVEMENTS *see* CONSCIENTIOUS OBJECTOR; COUNTERCULTURE; PACIFISM AND NONVIOLENT MOVEMENTS; WOMEN'S RIGHTS MOVEMENTS
PROTESTANT ETHIC **15**:576 *bibliog.*
Calvinism **4**:49
Tawney, Richard Henry **19**:45
Weber, Max **20**:87
PROTESTANTISM **4**:413 *map*; **15**:576–577 *bibliog.*; **16**:140 *map*
See also REFORMATION
Adventists **1**:111
Anabaptists **1**:387
Arminianism **2**:173
articles of religion **2**:220
Baptists **3**:73–74
Barth, Karl **3**:97
Beza, Theodore **3**:233
Bible **15**:576–577
Brethren **3**:474
Calvinism **4**:49
Canada, United Church of **4**:87
cathedrals and churches **4**:207
church polity **15**:577
Churches of Christ **4**:425
confessions of faith **5**:177
Congregationalism **5**:184
council, ecumenical **5**:309–310
cultural impact **15**:577
Disciples of Christ **6**:188
divorce **6**:205
ecumenical movement **7**:54
National Council of Churches **14**:31
World Council of Churches **20**:218
education
private schools **15**:557
Sunday school **18**:347
theological seminaries **19**:157
England, Church of **7**:181
Episcopal church **7**:221
Europe, history of **7**:287
evangelicalism **7**:312
Friends, Society of **8**:332–333
fundamentalism **8**:363
Germany, history of **9**:151
gospel music **9**:254
Harnack, Adolf von **10**:52
history **15**:576–577
Huguenots **10**:294–295
Ireland, history of **11**:263–265
Luther, Martin **12**:468–469
Lutheranism **12**:469–470
mass (musical setting) **13**:201
Mennonites **13**:298–299
Methodism **13**:344
ministry, Christian **13**:450
missions, Christian **13**:467–468
Moravian Church **13**:574–575
Northern Ireland **14**:256
Pentecostalism **15**:155
Presbyterianism **15**:519–520
Puritanism **15**:630
Reformed Churches **16**:123
Renaissance music **16**:156
revivalism **16**:186–187
sacraments **15**:577; **17**:7
Schleiermacher, Friedrich **17**:125
South India, Church of **18**:106
suicide **18**:330
Thirty Years' War **19**:171 *map*
United Church of Christ **19**:401
Waldenses **20**:9
World Council of Churches **20**:218
youth movements
Christian Endeavor **4**:411
PROTEUS **15**:577

PROTHERIAN *see* MONOTREME
PROTHORACIC GLAND
endocrine system 7:168
PROTISTA 15:577–578
algae 15:577
classification, biological 5:43
animal 2:10
Euglena 7:264
Haeckel, Ernst 15:577
Monera 13:523
Protozoa 15:577–578
slime mold 15:577–578
PROTO-GERMANIC DIALECTS 9:136
PROTO-SINAITIC SCRIPT
hieroglyphics 10:160
PROTOCERATOPS 15:578 *bibliog., illus.*
dinosaur 6:179
PROTOCOLS OF THE ELDERS OF ZION 15:578 *bibliog.*
PROTOHISTORY *see* ARCHAEOLOGY; PREHISTORY
PROTON (physics) 15:578 *bibliog.*
antiproton
Chamberlain, Owen 4:274
atom 2:305
baryon 3:99
belt
Van Allen radiation belts 19:510
binding energy 3:257–258
charge, electric 4:288
energy
photoelectric cell 15:259–260
fundamental interactions 8:360–361
fundamental particles 8:361; 8:362 *table*
fusion, nuclear 8:381–382
grand unification theories 9:286
high-energy
Cherenkov, Pavel Alekseyevich 4:331
Cherenkov radiation 4:331
magnetic moment
Stern, Otto 18:260
mass
atomic constants 2:308–309; 2:309
proton-proton reaction 15:578–579
structure
Hofstadter, Robert 10:197
PROTON (rocket) 15:578 *bibliog.*
OGO 20:355
PROTON-PROTON REACTION (physics) 15:578–579 *illus.*
fusion, nuclear 8:381
hydrogen in 10:337–339
Sun 18:341
PROTOPLASM 15:579
See also CYTOPLASM
PROTOSTARS
Hayashi evolutionary track 10:80
PROTOZOA 15:579–581 *bibliog., illus.*
actinosphaerium 1:89
aging 1:185–186
amoeba 1:376
Arcella 2:113
Babesia 3:6
Blepharisma 3:330
Chilomonas 4:357
classification, biological 5:43; 15:579 *illus.*
Ciliata 4:430
invertebrate 11:234
Mastigophora 13:217
problems 15:579
Rhizopoda 16:196–197
Sporozoa 18:195
clone 15:581
Cnidosporidia 5:73
conjugation 5:191
cryptomonad 5:373
Didinium 6:160
Difflugia 6:169
dinoflagellate 6:179
discovery 15:580
Entamoeba 7:208
Euglena 7:264
flagella 8:149
foraminifera 8:219
genetics 15:581
Giardia 9:172
heliozoan 10:113
importance 15:579–581
locomotion 15:579 *illus.*
metazoan 13:335
microbiology 13:384
occurrence 15:579–581
Paramecium 15:79–80
parasitic diseases 15:82; 15:580–581
Plasmodium 15:347
Pleodorina 15:367
Protista 15:577–578
protozoal diseases 15:581
radiolarian 16:64
reproduction 15:580; 16:161–162
ruminant 16:345
soil organisms 18:39 *illus.*
Spirostomum 18:190
spore 18:195
stentor 18:253
structure and function 15:579–580
taxis 19:48
Trichomonas 19:296
Volvox 19:633
Vorticella 19:635
PROTOZOAL DISEASES 15:581 *bibliog.*
amebiasis 1:326
balantidiasis 3:33
coccidiosis 5:85
diseases, animal 6:192
dysentery 6:320
kala-azar 12:7
Laveran, Charles 12:241
leishmaniasis 12:279
malaria 13:79–80
medications 15:581
Protozoa 15:580–581
respiratory system disorders 16:181
toxoplasmosis 19:256
trichomoniasis 19:296
trypanosomiasis 19:322
PROTURA 15:582
PROUDHON, PIERRE JOSEPH 15:582 *bibliog.*; 18:21 *illus.*
anarchism 1:392
socialism 18:20
syndicalism 18:407
PROUST, JOSEPH LOUIS 15:582
chemical combination, laws of 4:315
PROUST, MARCEL 8:318 *illus.*; 15:582–583 *bibliog., illus.*
Remembrance of Things Past 16:145
PROUSTITE 15:583
sulfosalts 18:334
PROUT, WILLIAM 15:583 *bibliog.*
PROVENCAL (Louisiana)
map (31° 39′N 93° 12′W) 12:430
PROVENÇAL LANGUAGE
Romance languages 16:280–281
PROVENÇAL LITERATURE 15:583 *bibliog.*
authors
Bernart de Ventadorn 3:221
Bertrand de Born 3:226
Daniel, Arnaut 6:31
Mistral, Frédéric 13:482
courtly love 5:317
PROVENCE (France) 8:265 *illus.*; 15:583–584 *map*
Burgundy 3:570
cities
Aix-en-Provence 1:228–229
Nîmes 14:198
Côte d'Azur 5:304
house (in Western architecture) 10:268 *illus.*
wine 20:175
PROVERB *see* APHORISM, MAXIM, AND PROVERB
PROVERBS, BOOK OF 15:584 *bibliog.*
PROVIDENCE (Kentucky)
map (37° 24′N 87° 39′W) 12:47
PROVIDENCE (Rhode Island) 15:584; 16:197 *illus.*
map (41° 50′N 71° 25′W) 16:198
Williams, Roger 20:160
PROVIDENCE (county in Rhode Island)
map (41° 52′N 71° 36′W) 16:198
PROVIDENCE (Utah)
map (41° 43′N 111° 49′W) 19:492
PROVIDENCE RIVER
map (41° 43′N 71° 21′W) 16:198
PROVINCETOWN (Massachusetts) 13:209 *illus.*; 15:584
map (42° 3′N 70° 11′W) 13:206
PROVINCETOWN PLAYERS 15:584
Cook, George Cram 5:234
Glaspell, Susan 9:197
O'Neill, Eugene 14:389–390
PROVISIONS OF OXFORD (1258)
Edward I, King of England 7:67
Henry III, King of England 10:125
PROVO (Utah) 15:584
map (40° 14′N 111° 39′W) 19:492
PROVOST (Alberta)
map (52° 21′N 110° 16′W) 1:256
PROVOST, ETIENNE
Utah 19:495
PROWERS (county in Colorado)
map (38° 0′N 102° 25′W) 5:116
PROXENE
diabase 6:148
PROXIMA CENTAURI 15:584
Centaurus 4:249
PROXMIRE, WILLIAM 15:584–585 *illus.*
PRUDENCE ISLAND
map (41° 37′N 71° 19′W) 16:198
PRUDHOE BAY 15:585
map (70° 20′N 148° 20′W) 1:242
PRUDHOMME, RENÉ FRANÇOIS ARMAND *see* SULLY PRUDHOMME
PRUD'HON, PIERRE PAUL 15:585 *bibliog.*
PRUNE 15:585
plum 15:370
PRURITUS
uremia 19:485
PRUSSER, GABRIEL *see* GABRIEL (slave)
PRUSSIA 15:585–586 *bibliog., map*
See also GERMANY, HISTORY OF
Albert, First Duke 1:254
Austrian Succession, War of the 2:354
Bavarian Succession, War of the 3:131
Bismarck, Otto von 3:298
boundaries *c.*1648 7:289
boundaries 1815 7:291 *map*
Brandenburg 3:453
Europe, history of 7:290
Franco-Prussian War 8:278–279 *illus., map*
Frederick I, King 8:291
Frederick II, King of Prussia (Frederick the Great) 8:291–292
Frederick William, Elector of Brandenburg (the Great Elector) 8:292–293
Frederick William I, King 8:293
Frederick William II, King 8:293
Frederick William III, King 8:293
Frederick William IV, King 8:293
French Revolutionary Wars 8:325–326
Hardenberg, Karl August, Fürst von 10:45
Hohenzollern (dynasty) 10:199
Junkers 11:471
lands annexed 1866 9:153 *map*
Napoleonic Wars 14:19
Poland, Partitions of 15:392 *map*
Pomerania 15:422
Revolutions of 1848 16:189
Scharnhorst, Gerhard Johann David von 17:117
Seven Weeks' War 17:216
Seven Years' War 17:218–219 *illus., map*
Stein, Heinrich Friedrich Karl, Freiherr vom und zum 18:247
Teutonic Knights 19:127–128
uniform, military (c.1750) 11:164 *illus.*
uniform, military (c.1870) 8:279 *illus.*
William I, Emperor of Germany 20:156–157
PRUSSIAN BLUE 15:586
PRUSSIAN LANGUAGE
Baltic languages 3:54–55
PRUSZKÓW (Poland)
map (52° 11′N 20° 48′E) 15:388
PRUT RIVER
map (45° 28′N 28° 12′E) 16:288
PRUTH, TREATY OF
Russo-Turkish Wars 16:374
PRYOR (Oklahoma)
map (36° 19′N 95° 19′W) 14:368
PRZEMYŚL (Poland)
map (49° 47′N 22° 47′E) 15:388
PRZERWA TETMAJER, KAZIMIERZ *see* TETMAJER, KAZIMIERZ PRZERWA
PRZEWALSKI'S HORSE 15:586 *illus.*
PRZHEVALSKI, NIKOLAI M.
exploration 7:338
PSALM *see* HYMN
PSALMS, BOOK OF 15:586–587 *bibliog., illus.*
hymn 10:346
PSALTER
hymn 10:346
PSALTER, UTRECHT (book) 15:587 *illus.*
PSALTER OF PARIS (book) 9:261 *illus.*
PSALTERY 15:587 *bibliog.*
harpsichord 10:55–56 *illus.*
PSAMTIK I, KING OF EGYPT 15:587 *bibliog.*
PSEUDEPIGRAPHA 15:587 *bibliog.*
Dead Sea Scrolls 6:65
PSEUDOGOUT
arthritis 2:214–215
PSEUDOINSOMNIA *see* SLEEP
PSEUDOMONAS 15:587
glanders 9:197
PSEUDOMORPH 15:587
PSEUDOPODIA
biological locomotion 3:265
radiolarian 16:64
PSI PHENOMENA
extrasensory perception 7:346
parapsychology 15:80–82
psychokinesis 15:591
PSILOCYBIN 15:587
hallucinogens 10:24
psychopathology, treatment of 15:600 *illus.*
PSILOMELANE 15:588
PSILOPHYTINA
plant 15:334
PSITTACOSIS 15:588
diseases, animal 6:192
parrot 15:98
PSKOV (USSR) 15:588
Russia/Union of Soviet Socialist Republics, history of 16:352
PSORIASIS 15:588
skin diseases 17:341
PSYCHE 9:192 *illus.*; 15:588
PSYCHEDELIC DRUGS *see* HALLUCINOGENS
PSYCHIATRY 15:588 *bibliog.*
American Journal of Psychiatry 15:588
child psychiatry 4:350–351
clinical psychology 5:59; 15:588
education
Charcot, Jean Martin 4:287
forensic science 8:227
Freud, Sigmund 8:329
hallucinogens 10:24
history 15:588
insanity, legal 11:185
Menninger (family) 13:298
Meyer, Adolf 13:368
orthomolecular medicine 14:450
megavitamin therapy 13:280
Pavlov, Ivan Petrovich 15:120
professional and educational organizations
American Board of Psychiatry 15:600
Psychiatry (journal)
Sullivan, Harry Stack 18:336
psychopathology, treatment of 15:600–601
psychotherapy 15:602–603
schools and viewpoints 15:588
Spock, Benjamin 18:191–192
Szasz, Thomas 18:415
unconscious 19:382–383
PSYCHIATRY (journal)
Sullivan, Harry Stack 18:336
PSYCHIC RESEARCH
machine 15:81 *illus.*
parapsychology 15:80–82
PSYCHOANALYSIS 15:588–591 *bibliog., illus.*
anxiety 2:72
Bettelheim, Bruno 3:232
child development 4:348–350
child psychiatry 4:350
clinical psychology 5:59
complex (psychology) 5:157
compulsive behavior 5:159
defense mechanisms 6:83
developmental psychology 6:142
dreams and dreaming 6:266
educational psychology 7:66
ego 7:73–74
Erikson, Erik 7:230
fixation 8:132
Freud, Anna 8:328
Freud, Sigmund 8:329; 15:588–590
Fromm, Erich 8:338–339
group therapy 9:377
Hall, G. Stanley 10:21
history 15:588–590; 15:598 *illus.*
Horney, Karen 10:239
humanistic psychology 10:299–300
id 15:589
Jung, Carl 11:467
Klein, Melanie 12:96
libido 12:314
method 15:588–589
moral awareness 13:573
Mowrer, O. Hobart 13:626
Narcissus (mythology) 14:21
personality 15:189–190
professional and educational organizations
American Institute for Psychoanalysis 10:239
American Psychoanalytic Association 15:590
Association for the Advancement of Psychoanalysis 10:239
projective tests 15:566
psychohistory 15:591
psychology 15:588–590
psychology, history of 15:598 *illus.*

PSYCHOANALYSIS (cont.)
psychopathology, treatment of **15**:600
psychotherapy **15**:603
Rank, Otto **16**:87
Reich, Wilhelm **16**:130
self-psychology **15**:589–590
social psychology **18**:13
sublimation (psychology) **18**:313
superego **18**:351
theory **15**:589–590
training **15**:590
transference **19**:269
PSYCHODRAMA *see* GROUP THERAPY
PSYCHODYNAMIC THERAPY
psychotherapy **15**:603
PSYCHOHISTORY **15**:591 *bibliog.*
Erikson, Erik **7**:230
history **10**:185
PSYCHOKINESIS **15**:591 *bibliog.*
extrasensory perception **7**:346
parapsychology **15**:81
telekinesis **15**:591
PSYCHOLINGUISTICS **15**:591–592 *bibliog.*
behaviorism **15**:591
Brown, Roger **3**:516
Bühler, Karl **3**:548
cognitive psychology **5**:95
emotion **7**:157
linguistics **12**:357
Miller, George Armitage **13**:427
psychology **15**:594
semantics **17**:193
speech development **18**:176
PSYCHOLOGICAL CORPORATION
Cattell, James McKeen **4**:214
PSYCHOLOGICAL DISORDERS
See also names of specific disorders, e.g., ANXIETY; SCHIZOPHRENIA; etc.
neurosis **14**:107
psychopathology, treatment of **15**:599–601
psychopathy **15**:601
psychosis **15**:602
psychosomatic disorders **15**:602
PSYCHOLOGICAL MEASUREMENT **15**:592–593 *bibliog.*
clinical psychology **5**:59
educational psychology **7**:66
Educational Testing Service **7**:66
factor analysis **8**:6
industrial psychology **11**:157
normal distribution **14**:219
personality **15**:190
projective tests **15**:566
space medicine **18**:133–134
Stanford-Binet test **18**:217–218
Terman, Lewis **19**:116
Thurstone, L. L. **19**:186
PSYCHOLOGICAL TESTING *see* PSYCHOLOGICAL MEASUREMENT
PSYCHOLOGICAL WARFARE
propaganda **15**:568
PSYCHOLOGY **15**:593–595 *bibliog.*
See also BEHAVIOR, HUMAN
adolescence **1**:106–107
associationism **2**:265
attention **2**:314
attitude and attitude change **2**:315
authoritarian personality **2**:354
behavioral genetics **3**:169–170
biofeedback **3**:263
branches
abnormal psychology **1**:57–58; **15**:594
applied psychology, fields **15**:595
behaviorism **3**:170; **15**:597
child development **4**:348–350
clinical psychology **5**:59; **15**:595
cognitive psychology **5**:94–95; **15**:594
comparative psychology **5**:155
developmental psychology **6**:142; **15**:595
educational psychology **7**:66; **15**:595
experimental psychology **7**:334
Gestalt psychology **9**:159
humanistic psychology **10**:299
industrial psychology **11**:157; **15**:595
physiological psychology **15**:594
psychoanalysis **15**:588–590
psychohistory **15**:591
psycholinguistics **15**:594
psychophysics **15**:601–602
social psychology **15**:594–595; **18**:12–13
case study **15**:595
communication **5**:144
community mental health **5**:152–153
complex (psychology) **5**:157
conformity **5**:179
death and dying **6**:69
defense mechanisms **6**:83
ego **7**:73–74
egoism **7**:74
emotion **7**:157; **15**:594
field observation **15**:595
frustration **8**:350
habit **10**:4
illusions **11**:48–49
introspection **11**:232; **15**:596
intuition **11**:232
learning theory **12**:260–261; **15**:594; **15**:597
mental health **13**:302
methods **15**:595
middle age **13**:391
moral awareness **13**:572–573
motivation **13**:610–611; **15**:594
parapsychology **15**:80–82
perception **15**:158–160; **15**:594; **15**:596
personality **15**:189–190; **15**:594
placebo **15**:325
professional and educational organizations
American Board of Professional Psychology **15**:600
American Psychological Association **15**:598
professional status **15**:598
psychological measurement **15**:592–593
psychology, history of **15**:596–599
psychometrics **15**:595
psychopathology, treatment of **15**:599–601
psychosomatic disorders **15**:602
random-assignment experiment **15**:595
role **16**:271
statistics, nonparametric **18**:238
suicide **18**:331
unconscious **19**:382–383
PSYCHOLOGY, HISTORY OF **15**:596–599 *bibliog., illus.*
Adler, Alfred **1**:103
associationism **2**:266
Bekhterev, Vladimir Mikhailovich **3**:173
Bettelheim, Bruno **3**:232
Binet, Alfred **3**:258
Boring, E. G. **3**:400
Brentano, Franz **3**:473
Bronfenbrenner, Urie **3**:503
Bruner, Jerome Seymour **3**:525
Bühler, Karl **3**:548
Burt, Sir Cyril **3**:581
Cattell, James McKeen **4**:214
Dewey, John **6**:146–147
Ebbinghaus, Hermann **7**:35
Erikson, Erik **7**:230
Estes, William Kaye **7**:246
Fechner, Gustav Theodor **8**:40
Frankl, Viktor **8**:282
Freud, Anna **8**:328
Freud, Sigmund **8**:329
Fromm, Erich **8**:338–339
Galton, Sir Francis **9**:22–23
Gesell, Arnold **9**:159
Guthrie, Edwin Ray **9**:409
Hall, G. Stanley **10**:21
Herbart, Johann Friedrich **10**:134–135
Horney, Karen **10**:239
Hull, Clark **10**:296
James, William **11**:354–355
Jensen, Arthur **11**:396
Jung, Carl **11**:467
Klein, Melanie **12**:96
Koffka, Kurt **12**:106
Köhler, Wolfgang **12**:106
Kraepelin, Emil **12**:126
Laing, R. D. **12**:167
Lewin, Kurt **12**:305
Luria, Aleksandr Romanovich **12**:466
McDougall, William **13**:14
Maslow, Abraham H. **13**:196–198
Meyer, Adolf **13**:368
Miller, George Armitage **13**:427
Miller, Neal E. **13**:428
Mowrer, O. Hobart **13**:626
Murphy, Gardner **13**:649
Pavlov, Ivan Petrovich **15**:120
Perls, Friedrich S. **15**:173
Piaget, Jean **15**:287–288
Porter, Noah **15**:445
psychoanalysis **15**:588–590
Rank, Otto **16**:87
Reich, Wilhelm **16**:130
Rogers, Carl **16**:268–269
Skinner, B. F. **17**:343–344
Spock, Benjamin **18**:191–192
Sullivan, Harry Stack **18**:336
Szasz, Thomas **18**:415
Terman, Lewis **19**:116
Thorndike, Edward L. **19**:179
Thurstone, L. L. **19**:186
Titchener, Edward B. **19**:211–212
Tolman, Edward C. **19**:227
Watson, John B. **20**:68
Wertheimer, Max **20**:104
Wundt, Wilhelm **20**:296
PSYCHOMETRICS
psychological measurement **15**:592–593
psychology **15**:595
Thurstone, L. L. **19**:186
PSYCHOMOTOR DISORDERS
apraxia **2**:91–92
PSYCHOMOTOR STIMULANT *see* STIMULANT
PSYCHONEUROSIS *see* NEUROSIS
PSYCHOPATHOLOGY, TREATMENT OF **15**:599–601 *bibliog., illus.*
autistic children **2**:355
behavior modification **3**:169
chemotherapy **15**:600–601
clinical psychology **5**:59
depression **6**:119
history **15**:599–600
hypnosis **10**:350
orthomolecular medicine **14**:450
practitioners, requirements **15**:600
psychiatry **15**:588
psychotherapy **15**:602–603
psychotropic drugs **15**:603–605
shock therapy **15**:600; **17**:279
social and welfare services **15**:599–600
PSYCHOPATHY **15**:601 *bibliog.*
dementia **6**:96
dissociation (psychology) **6**:198
fetishism **8**:63
PSYCHOPHYSICS **15**:601–602 *bibliog.*
color perception **5**:114
Fechner, Gustav Theodor **8**:40
PSYCHOSIS **15**:602 *bibliog.*
catatonia **4**:201
characteristics **15**:602
delirium tremens **15**:602
depression **6**:118
dissociation (psychology) **6**:198
drug psychoses **15**:602
functional psychosis **15**:602
hallucinogens **10**:24
Korsakoff's syndrome **15**:602
Kraepelin, Emil **12**:126
Laing, R. D. **12**:167
manic-depressive psychosis **13**:116
marijuana **13**:153
megavitamin therapy **13**:280
organic psychosis **15**:602
paranoia **15**:80
paresis **15**:602
psychiatry **15**:588
psychotherapy **15**:602
psychotic depression **15**:602
schizophrenia **17**:123–124
senile psychosis **15**:602
PSYCHOSOMATIC DISORDERS **15**:602 *bibliog.*
anorexia nervosa **2**:34
disease reactions **15**:602
medical attitude toward disease **15**:602
PSYCHOSURGERY
schizophrenia **17**:124
PSYCHOTHERAPY **15**:602–603 *bibliog.*
Adler, Alfred **1**:103
behavior modification **3**:169
client-centered therapy **5**:54
Rogers, Carl, founder **16**:268–269
clinical psychology **5**:59
colitis **5**:102
depression **6**:119
formats of therapy **15**:602
Frankl, Viktor **8**:282
Freud, Sigmund **8**:239
Gestalt psychology **9**:159
group therapy **9**:377
hallucinogens **10**:24
headache **10**:85
Horney, Karen **10**:239
humanistic psychology **10**:299
hypnosis **10**:350
interpersonal
Sullivan, Harry Stack **18**:336
Jung, Carl **11**:467–468
phobia **15**:249
problems dealt with **15**:602–603
psychiatry **15**:588
psychological measurement **15**:592–593
psychopathology, treatment of **15**:600–601
psychotropic drugs **15**:603–605
schools of therapy
behavioral **15**:603
cognitive **15**:603
phenomenological **15**:603
psychodynamic **15**:603
sex therapy **17**:227
stress, biological **18**:298
therapists **15**:603
transactional analysis **19**:267–268
transvestism **19**:283
PSYCHOTROPIC DRUGS **15**:603–605 *bibliog.*
See also names of specific drugs, e.g., AMPHETAMINE; MEPROBAMATE; etc.
analgesic **1**:388; **15**:603; **15**:605
antianxiety drugs **15**:604
antidepressants **2**:60–61; **15**:604
antipsychotic drugs **15**:604
depression **15**:604
effects **15**:604
hallucinogens **10**:24; **15**:603
history and development **15**:604
Kraepelin, Emil **12**:126
psychopathology, treatment of **15**:600–601
psychopharmacology **15**:604
psychotomimetic drugs **15**:603
schizophrenia **17**:124
sedative **15**:603–604; **17**:181–182
tranquilizer **15**:604; **19**:266
usage **15**:604
PSYCHROMETER **13**:341 *illus.*
See also HYGROMETER
PT BOAT **15**:605 *bibliog., illus.*
Kennedy, John F. **12**:42
naval vessels **14**:55
PTAH **15**:605
mythology **13**:697
PTARMIGAN **15**:605–606 *bibliog., illus.*
grouse **9**:378
PTERIDOPHYTE **15**:606 *bibliog.*
PTEROBRANCH **15**:606
hemichordate **10**:117
PTERODACTYL **11**:476 *illus.*; **15**:606 *illus.*
Jurassic Period **11**:476
Pteranodon **16**:170 *illus.*
PTEROPHYTINA
plant **15**:334
PTOLEMAIC SYSTEM *see* GEOCENTRIC WORLD SYSTEM
PTOLEMAÏS (Greece)
map (40° 31′N 21° 41′E) **9**:325
PTOLEMY (astronomer) **15**:283 *illus.*; **15**:606–607 *bibliog., illus.*
Almagest **1**:305–306; **13**:224 *illus.*
astrology **2**:272
astronomy, history of **2**:277
constellation **5**:211
Geographia **13**:138 *illus.*
geography **9**:101 *illus.*
mathematics, history of **13**:224
planetary motion **2**:278 *illus.*
solar system **18**:44–45 *illus.*
Tetrabiblos **2**:272
PTOLEMY I, KING OF EGYPT (Ptolemy Soter) **7**:83 *illus.*; **15**:607 *bibliog., illus.*
Egypt, ancient **7**:83
Greece, ancient **9**:333
Pharos of Alexandria **17**:218
PTOLEMY II (King of Egypt) (Ptolemy Philadelphus)
zoological gardens **20**:374 *illus.*
PTOLEMY II, KING OF EGYPT (Ptolemy Philadelphus) **15**:607
PTOLEMY III, KING OF EGYPT (Ptolemy Eueregetes) **15**:607
PTOLEMY IV, KING OF EGYPT (Ptolemy Philopater) **15**:607
PTOLEMY V, KING OF EGYPT (Ptolemy Epiphanes) **15**:607
Rosetta Stone **16**:317
PTOLEMY VI, KING OF EGYPT (Ptolemy Philometor) **15**:607
PTOLEMY VII, KING OF EGYPT
Ptolemy VI, King **15**:607
Ptolemy VIII, King of Egypt **15**:607
PTOLEMY VIII, KING OF EGYPT (Ptolemy Euergetes) **15**:607
PTOLEMY XII, KING OF EGYPT (Ptolemy Auletes) **15**:607
PTOLEMY XIII, KING OF EGYPT **15**:608
Cleopatra, Queen of Egypt **5**:50
PTOMAINE POISONING **15**:608 *bibliog.*
P'U SUNG-LING (Pu Songling)
Chinese literature **4**:390
PU-YI, HENRY, EMPEROR OF CHINA
Tz'u-hsi, Dowager Empress of China (Cixi) **19**:368
PUAPUA (Western Samoa)
map (13° 34′S 172° 9′W) **20**:117

PUAVA, CAPE
map (13° 26'S 172° 43'W) **20**:117
PUBERTY
adolescence **1**:106–107
growth **9**:379
passage rites **15**:103–104
sex hormones **17**:226
sexual development **17**:229–230
PUBLIC ACCOUNTING *see* AUDIT; CERTIFIED PUBLIC ACCOUNTANT
PUBLIC ARCHAEOLOGY *see* SALVAGE ARCHAEOLOGY
PUBLIC ASSISTANCE PROGRAMS *see* SOCIAL AND WELFARE SERVICES
PUBLIC BATHS *see* BATH (bathing)
PUBLIC BROADCASTING SERVICE
affiliate stations **16**:59–60
radio and television broadcasting **16**:59–60 *illus.*
television, noncommercial **19**:90
PUBLIC DEFENDER
legal aid **12**:272
PUBLIC DOMAIN **15**:608 *bibliog.*
copyright **5**:256
PUBLIC EDUCATION *see* PRIMARY EDUCATION; MIDDLE SCHOOLS AND JUNIOR HIGH SCHOOLS; SECONDARY EDUCATION
PUBLIC HEALTH **15**:608 *bibliog.*
Center for Disease Control **4**:249–250
community mental health **5**:152–153
environmental health **7**:210
epidemiology **7**:219
health-care systems **10**:87–89
Health and Human Services, U.S. Department of **10**:86
housing **10**:276
medicine **13**:272
National Institutes of Health **14**:34
nutritional-deficiency diseases **14**:308
Robert Wood Johnson Foundation **16**:241
Rockefeller Foundation **16**:251
sex education **17**:225–226
PUBLIC MONUMENTS
Arc de Triomphe de l'Étoile **2**:112
Dalou, Aimé Jules **6**:14
Hébert, Louis Philippe **10**:101
Hittite art and architecture **10**:189
Lutyens, Sir Edwin Landseer **12**:471
MacMonnies, Frederick William **13**:34
Manship, Paul **13**:128
Meunier, Constantin **13**:350
Milles, Carl **13**:429
Moore, Henry **13**:568–569
obelisk **14**:314–315
Rodin, Auguste **16**:267
Rude, François **16**:338
Rysbrack, Michael **16**:380
Saarinen, Eero **17**:4
stele **18**:250
triumphal arch **19**:304
Verrocchio, Andrea del **19**:561
PUBLIC OPINION **15**:608–610 *bibliog.*
foreign policy **8**:226
Gallup, George **9**:21
newspaper **14**:172
opinion polls **14**:405–406
public relations **15**:610
radio and television broadcasting **16**:54
special-interest groups **18**:167–168
survey, sampling **17**:48
PUBLIC RELATIONS **15**:610 *bibliog.*
See also ADVERTISING
PUBLIC RELATIONS SOCIETY OF AMERICA (PRSA)
public relations **15**:610
PUBLIC SPEAKING *see* RHETORIC AND ORATORY
PUBLIC TELEVISION *see* PUBLIC BROADCASTING SERVICE; TELEVISION, NONCOMMERCIAL
PUBLIC TRANSPORTATION *see* TRANSPORTATION
PUBLIC UTILITY **15**:610–611 *bibliog.*
common carrier **5**:138
Edison, Thomas Alva **7**:57–58
government regulation **9**:270–271
industrial archaeology **11**:154
Insull, Samuel **11**:198
monopoly and competition **13**:537–540
Munn v. *Illinois* **13**:643
Public Utility Holding Company Act
Securities and Exchange Commission **17**:181
PUBLIC WORKS ADMINISTRATION **15**:611 *bibliog.*
Ickes, Harold **11**:20
PUBLICITY *see* PUBLIC RELATIONS
PUBLISHERS WEEKLY (periodical)
best-seller **3**:229
PUBLISHING **15**:611–612 *bibliog.*
See also BOOK; JOURNALISM; NEWSPAPER; PERIODICAL; PULP MAGAZINES; RADIO BROADCASTING; TELEVISION BROADCASTING
best-seller **3**:228–229
book club **3**:386
censorship **4**:246–248
freedom of the press **8**:296–297
Pentagon Papers **15**:154
copyright **5**:256
desktop publishing
computer **5**:160g
computer, personal **5**:160i–160j
history **15**:611
Caxton, William **4**:227
Cerf, Bennett **4**:260
Field (family) **8**:71
Gutenberg, Johann **9**:408–409
Knopf, Alfred A. **11**:101
Manutius, Aldus **13**:134
Perkins, Maxwell **15**:172
mass communication **13**:202
newspapers and magazines
Bradford (family) **3**:436–437
Campbell, John **4**:65
Cowles, Gardner **5**:321
Curtis, Cyrus H. K. **5**:395
Gannett, Frank E. **9**:37
Greeley, Horace **9**:346–347 *illus.*
Harris, Benjamin **10**:57
Hearst, William Randolph **10**:90
Howard, Roy Wilson **10**:283
Johnson, John Harold **11**:432–433
Jones, George **11**:442
Luce, Henry Robinson **12**:449–450
Murdoch, Rupert **13**:648
Newhouse, Samuel I. **14**:169
Niles, Hezekiah **14**:197
Northcliffe, Alfred Harmsworth, Viscount **14**:253
Ochs, Adolph Simon **14**:346
Patterson (family) **15**:115
Philipon, Charles **15**:235
Pulitzer, Joseph **15**:618
Ross, Harold **16**:318
Russel, Benjamin **16**:348–349
Scripps, Edward Wyllis **17**:158
Stone, I.F. **18**:280
Sulzberger, Arthur Hays **18**:338
Thomas, Isiah **19**:173
Villard, Oswald Garrison **19**:598
Walter (family) **20**:19
White, William Allen **20**:136
paperback
paperback book **15**:611–612
paperback rights **15**:611–612
printing **15**:552–553
United Kingdom **19**:408–409
PUBLIUS (collective pseudonym)
Federalist, The **8**:43
PUBLIUS CORNELIUS SCIPIO *see* SCIPIO AFRICANUS MAJOR
PUCALLPA (Peru)
map (8° 23'S 74° 32'W) **15**:193
PUCARÁ (Bolivia)
map (18° 43'S 64° 11'W) **3**:366
PUCCI, EMILIO
fashion design **8**:32
PUCCINI, GIACOMO **15**:612 *bibliog., illus.*
Bohème, La **3**:360
Italian music **11**:319
Madama Butterfly **13**:39
Tosca **19**:247
PUCELLE, JEAN
Gothic art and architecture **9**:260–261
PUCK (fictional character) **15**:612 *bibliog.*
PUDELPOINTER **15**:613 *bibliog.*
PUDOVKIN, VSEVOLOD I. **15**:613 *bibliog.*
PUDU **6**:80 *illus.*
deer **6**:79
PUEBLA (Mexico) **15**:613
Latin American art and architecture **12**:223–224
map (19° 3'N 98° 12'W) **13**:357
PUEBLA (state in Mexico) **15**:613
cities
Puebla **15**:613
Tehuacán Valley **19**:73
PUEBLA, BATTLE OF
Mexican War **13**:352 *map*; **13**:354
PUEBLO (American Indians) **15**:613–614 *bibliog., illus.*
Acoma **1**:83–84
Anasazi **1**:392–394
Chaco Canyon **4**:264–265
cliff dwellers **5**:55 *illus.*
Hopi **10**:231
Indian Wars **11**:107
Indians, American **11**:131
Indians of North America, art of the **11**:140
Indians of North America, music and dance of the **11**:142–143 *illus.*
kachina **12**:4
Kidder, Alfred Vincent **12**:70–71
Kiva **12**:93–94
Mesa Verde National Park (Colorado) **13**:314
Mojave **13**:504
Navajo **14**:53–54
North American archaeology **14**:240
Popé **15**:430
Taos Pueblo **14**:139 *illus.*; **19**:428 *illus.*
Ute **19**:496
Zuñi **20**:382
PUEBLO (Colorado) **15**:613
map (38° 16'N 104° 37'W) **5**:116
PUEBLO (county in Colorado)
map (38° 10'N 104° 30'W) **5**:116
PUEBLO GRANDE
Hohokam culture **10**:199
PUEBLO INCIDENT **15**:614 *bibliog.*
intelligence gathering **11**:205
PUEBLO MOUNTAIN
map (42° 6'N 118° 39'W) **14**:427
PUEBLOVIEJO (Ecuador)
map (1° 34'S 79° 30'W) **7**:52
PUERCO RIVER
map (34° 53'N 110° 7'W) **2**:160
PUERPERAL FEVER **15**:614
Semmelweis, Ignaz Philipp **17**:198
septicemia **17**:206
PUERTO ACOSTA (Bolivia)
map (15° 32'S 69° 15'W) **3**:366
PUERTO AISEN (Chile)
map (45° 24'S 72° 42'W) **4**:355
PUERTO ALEGRE (Bolivia)
map (13° 53'S 61° 36'W) **3**:366
PUERTO ÁNGEL (Mexico)
map (15° 40'N 96° 29'W) **13**:357
PUERTO ARMUELLES (Panama)
map (8° 17'N 82° 52'W) **15**:55
PUERTO ASÍS (Colombia)
map (0° 30'N 76° 31'W) **5**:107
PUERTO AYACUCHO (Venezuela)
map (5° 40'N 67° 35'W) **19**:542
PUERTO AYORA (Ecuador)
map (0° 44'S 90° 19'W) **7**:52
PUERTO BAQUERIZO MORENO (Ecuador)
map (0° 54'S 89° 36'W) **7**:52
PUERTO BARRIOS (Guatemala)
map (15° 43'N 88° 36'W) **9**:389
PUERTO BERMÚDEZ (Peru)
map (10° 20'S 74° 54'W) **15**:193
PUERTO BERRIO (Colombia)
map (6° 29'N 74° 24'W) **5**:107
PUERTO CABELLO (Venezuela)
map (10° 28'N 68° 1'W) **19**:542
PUERTO CABEZAS (Nicaragua)
map (14° 2'N 83° 23'W) **14**:179
PUERTO CARREÑO (Colombia)
map (6° 12'N 67° 22'W) **5**:107
PUERTO CASADO (Paraguay)
map (22° 20'S 57° 55'W) **15**:77
PUERTO CASTILLA (Honduras)
map (16° 1'N 86° 1'W) **10**:218
PUERTO CHICAMA (Peru)
map (7° 42'S 79° 27'W) **15**:193
PUERTO CORTÉS (Honduras)
map (15° 48'N 87° 56'W) **10**:218
PUERTO CUMAREBO (Venezuela)
map (11° 29'N 69° 21'W) **19**:542
PUERTO DESEADO (Argentina)
map (47° 45'S 65° 54'W) **2**:149
PUERTO EL TRIUTO (El Salvador)
map (13° 17'N 88° 33') **7**:100
PUERTO FONCIERE (Paraguay)
map (22° 29'S 57° 48'W) **15**:77
PUERTO GUARANÍ (Paraguay)
map (21° 18'S 57° 55'W) **15**:77
PUERTO JIMÉNEZ (Costa Rica)
map (8° 33'N 83° 19'W) **5**:291
PUERTO LA CRUZ (Venezuela)
map (10° 13'N 64° 38'W) **19**:542
PUERTO LEDA (Paraguay)
map (20° 41'S 58° 2'W) **15**:77
PUERTO LEGUÍZAMO (Colombia)
map (0° 12'S 74° 46'W) **5**:107
PUERTO LIBERTAD (Argentina)
map (25° 55'S 54° 36'W) **2**:149
PUERTO MADRYN (Argentina)
map (42° 46'S 65° 3'W) **2**:149
PUERTO MALDONADO (Peru)
map (12° 36'S 69° 11'W) **15**:193
PUERTO MIHANOVICH (Paraguay)
map (20° 52'S 57° 59'W) **15**:77
PUERTO MONTT (Chile)
map (41° 28'S 72° 57'W) **4**:355
PUERTO NATALES (Chile)
map (51° 44'S 72° 31'W) **4**:355
PUERTO PADILLA (Peru)
map (10° 15'S 71° 39'W) **15**:193
PUERTO PADRE (Cuba)
map (21° 12'N 76° 36'W) **5**:377
PUERTO PÁEZ (Venezuela)
map (6° 13'N 67° 28'W) **19**:542
PUERTO PEÑASCO (Mexico)
map (31° 20'N 113° 33'W) **13**:357
PUERTO PLATA (Dominican Republic)
map (19° 48'N 70° 41'W) **6**:233
PUERTO PORTILLO (Peru)
map (9° 46'S 72° 45'W) **15**:193
PUERTO RICO **15**:614–616 *bibliog., illus., map, table*
cities
Ponce **15**:425
San Juan **17**:55 *illus.*
climate **15**:614–615 *table*
economic activity **15**:615
education **15**:615
Catholic University of Puerto Rico **4**:212
Illich, Ivan **11**:40
Inter-American University of Puerto Rico **11**:206
Latin American universities **12**:233 *table*
Puerto Rico, University of **15**:616
government and politics **15**:615–616
health **15**:615
history **15**:616
Albizu Campos, Pedro **1**:261
Latin America, history of **12**:221
McKinley, William **13**:31
Muñoz Marín, Luis **13**:643
Muñoz Rivera, Luis **13**:643
Ponce de León, Juan **15**:426
Spanish-American War **18**:150
land and resources **15**:614 *map*
Latin American literature **12**:230
map (18° 15'N 66° 30'W) **20**:109
people **15**:614–615
migration to the mainland **10**:177 *map*; **10**:178–179
territory **19**:122
PUERTO RICO (Bolivia)
map (11° 5'S 67° 38'W) **3**:366
PUERTO RICO, UNIVERSITY OF **15**:616
PUERTO RICO TRENCH
Atlantic Ocean bottom **2**:295 *map*
PUERTO SASTRE (Paraguay)
map (22° 6'S 57° 59'W) **15**:77
PUERTO SILES (Bolivia)
map (12° 48'S 65° 5'W) **3**:366
PUERTO SUÁREZ (Bolivia)
map (18° 57'S 57° 51'W) **3**:366
PUERTO SUCRE (Bolivia)
map (10° 48'S 65° 23'W) **3**:366
PUERTO VALLARTA (Mexico)
map (20° 37'N 105° 15'W) **13**:357
PUERTO VICTORIA (Peru)
map (9° 54'S 74° 58'W) **15**:193
PUERTO VIEJO (Costa Rica)
map (9° 39'N 82° 45'W) **5**:291
PUERTOLLANO (Spain)
map (38° 41'N 4° 7'W) **18**:140
PUFENDORF, SAMUEL, BARON VON **15**:616
law, history of **12**:245
PUFF ADDER **15**:384 *illus.*
PUFFBALL
earthstar **7**:28
mushrooms **13**:659
PUFFBIRD **15**:616
PUFFER (fish) **15**:616 *illus.*
PUFFIN **15**:616–617 *illus.*
animal communication **2**:19 *illus.*
PUG **6**:217 *illus.*; **15**:617 *bibliog., illus.*
PUGACHEV, YEMELIAN IVANOVICH **15**:617 *bibliog.*
PUGET, PIERRE **15**:617 *bibliog.*
PUGET SOUND **15**:617
map (47° 50'N 122° 30'W) **20**:35
people
Nisqually **14**:201
PUGIN, AUGUSTUS **15**:617 *bibliog.*
PUGLIA (Italy) *see* APULIA (Italy)
PUGWASH (Nova Scotia)
map (45° 51'N 63° 40'W) **14**:269
PUIFORCAT, JEAN
Art Deco **2**:207
gold and silver work **9**:230
silver-gilt teapot **2**:208 *illus.*
PUIG, MANUEL **15**:617

PUJILÍ (Ecuador)
map (0° 57′S 78° 41′W) **7**:52
PUJO, ARSÈNE PAULIN 15:617–618
PUKALANI (Hawaii)
map (20° 51′N 156° 20′W) **10**:72
PUKCHONG (Korea)
map (40° 15′N 128° 20′E) **12**:113
PUKË (Albania)
map (42° 3′N 19° 54′E) **1**:250
PUKHAN RIVER
map (37° 31′N 127° 18′E) **12**:113
PUL *see* TIGLATH-PILESER III, KING OF ASSYRIA
PULA (Yugoslavia) **15**:618
map (44° 52′N 13° 50′E) **20**:340
PULACAYO (Bolivia)
map (20° 25′S 66° 41′W) **3**:366
PULASKI (county in Arkansas)
map (34° 45′N 92° 20′W) **2**:166
PULASKI (county in Georgia)
map (32° 15′N 83° 25′W) **9**:114
PULASKI (county in Illinois)
map (37° 13′N 89° 8′W) **11**:42
PULASKI (county in Indiana)
map (41° 3′N 86° 36′W) **11**:111
PULASKI (county in Kentucky)
map (37° 10′N 84° 35′W) **12**:47
PULASKI (county in Missouri)
map (37° 50′N 92° 15′W) **13**:476
PULASKI (New York)
map (43° 34′N 76° 8′W) **14**:149
PULASKI (Tennessee)
map (35° 12′N 87° 2′W) **19**:104
PULASKI (Virginia)
map (37° 3′N 80° 47′W) **19**:607
PULASKI (county in Virginia)
map (37° 5′N 80° 45′W) **19**:607
PULASKI (Wisconsin)
map (44° 41′N 88° 14′W) **20**:185
PUŁASKI, KASIMIERZ **15**:618 *bibliog.*
PULASKI DAY
Pułaski, Kasimierz **15**:618
PULI **6**:214 *illus.*; **15**:618 *illus.*
PULITZER, JOSEPH **15**:618 *bibliog.*, *illus.*
journalism **11**:455
St. Louis Post-Dispatch **17**:23
PULITZER PRIZE **15**:618–619 *bibliog.*
See also the subheading Pulitzer Prize under specific subjects, e.g., JOURNALISM; LITERATURE; MUSIC; etc.
Pulitzer, Joseph **15**:618
PULKOVO OBSERVATORY **15**:619
Struve, Friedrich Georg Wilhelm von **18**:304
PULLEY **15**:619 *bibliog.*, *illus.*
compound pulley
Archimedes **2**:128
simple machines **17**:316
PULLMAN (Washington)
map (46° 44′N 117° 10′W) **20**:35
PULLMAN, GEORGE MORTIMER **15**:619 *bibliog.*
PULLMAN STRIKE **15**:619 *bibliog.*; **18**:298 *illus.*
Darrow, Clarence S. **6**:39
Debs, Eugene V. **6**:71
Olney, Richard **14**:381
PULLO (Peru)
map (15° 14′S 73° 50′W) **15**:193
PULMONARY ARTERY
circulatory system **4**:440 *illus.*
respiratory system **16**:180 *illus.*
PULMONARY EMBOLISM **15**:619
embolism **7**:152
respiratory system disorders **16**:182
PULMONARY FUNCTION TEST **15**:620
PULMONARY VEIN
circulatory system **4**:440 *illus.*
respiratory system **16**:180 *illus.*
PULOG, MOUNT
map (16° 36′N 120° 54′E) **15**:237
PULP (anatomy)
teeth **19**:70–71 *illus.*
PULP MAGAZINES **15**:620 *bibliog.*
science fiction **17**:143–144 *illus.*
PULP AND PAPER MILLS *see* PAPER
PULPWOOD *see* LOGGING
PULQUE *see* TEQUILA
PULSAR **2**:284 *illus.*; **15**:620–621 *bibliog.*, *illus.*
angular momentum **2**:7
binary X-ray pulsar **15**:620–621
Crab nebula **5**:325–326; **15**:621 *illus.*
degenerate matter **6**:85
discovery **15**:620
Gold, Thomas **9**:228
Hewish, Antony **10**:154
Mullard Radio Astronomy Observatory **13**:636
neutron star **14**:109
radio astronomy **15**:620–621; **16**:49
radio emission pulses **15**:620
relativity **16**:136
stellar evolution **18**:251
supernova **18**:352
Zwicky, Fritz **20**:384
PULSATING STARS **15**:621 *bibliog.*
Cepheids **4**:257
variable star **19**:522–523
PULSE (biology) **15**:621
PULSE (electronics) **15**:621 *bibliog.*
modulation **13**:500
signal generator **17**:300
PULSE (food)
agriculture and the food supply **1**:194–195
PULSE CODE MODULATION (PCM)
sound recording and reproduction **18**:76
telecommunications **19**:76
PULSE-ECHO TECHNIQUE
sound and acoustics **18**:74 *illus.*
PULSES (botany)
vegetable **19**:533 *illus.*
PULU *see* TIGLATH-PILESER III, KING OF ASSYRIA
PUMA **15**:621–622 *bibliog.*, *illus.*
PUMICE **15**:622
volcano **19**:628
PUMP **15**:622–623 *bibliog.*, *illus.*
applications **15**:623
automotive: cooling system, engine **5**:242
bellows **3**:191
centrifugal pump **15**:622; **15**:623
compressor **5**:158
history **15**:622
hydraulic systems **10**:331
industrialization
engineering **7**:178
lift pump **15**:622 *illus.*
Papin, Denis **15**:622
pipe and pipeline **15**:310–311
piston pump **15**:622
reciprocating pump **15**:622
respiratory system **16**:179
rotary pump **15**:623
special types **15**:623
vacuum **19**:502
PUMPELLYITE
facies, metamorphic rock **13**:332 *table*
PUMPKIN **15**:623 *illus.*; **19**:532 *illus.*
PUN **15**:623
PUNÁ ISLAND
map (2° 50′S 80° 8′W) **7**:52
PUNATA (Bolivia)
map (17° 32′S 65° 50′W) **3**:366
PUNCH (periodical)
Shepard, Ernest Howard **17**:256
Tenniel, Sir John **19**:108
PUNCH AND JUDY **15**:623 *bibliog.*; **15**:626 *illus.*
PUNCHED CARD **15**:623–624 *bibliog.*
computer **5**:160–160a
Hollerith, Herman **10**:204
PUNCTUATED EQUILIBRIA
evolution **7**:324
PUNCTUATION **15**:624 *bibliog.*
experimental punctuation
cummings, e. e. **5**:387
writing systems, evolution of **20**:294
PUNE (India) *see* POONA (India)
PUNIC WARS **15**:624–625 *bibliog.*, *map*
Cannae, Battle of **4**:109
Carthage **4**:173; **4**:174 *illus.*
Fabius (family) **8**:4
Hamilcar Barca **10**:27
Hannibal **10**:38
Hasdrubal **10**:66
Marcellus, Marcus Claudius **13**:146
Regulus, Marcus Atilius **16**:129
Rome, ancient **16**:298–300 *map*
Scipio Africanus Major **17**:147
Second Punic War
Masinissa **13**:196
PUNISHMENT (law) **15**:625–626 *bibliog.*
See also CAPITAL PUNISHMENT
crime **5**:344–347
criminal justice **5**:349–350
crucifixion **5**:364
drawing and quartering **6**:265
8th Amendment **7**:92
felony **8**:48
forfeiture **8**:232
Furman v. *Georgia* **8**:371–372
immunity **11**:59
insanity, legal **11**:185
juvenile delinquency **11**:480
law **12**:243
military justice **13**:421
misdemeanor **13**:466
murder **13**:648
mutiny **13**:687
pardon **15**:83
parole **15**:97
pillory **15**:303
prison **15**:554–555
probation **15**:559
sentence **17**:205
PUNISHMENT (psychology) *see* REWARD AND PUNISHMENT (psychology)
PUNJAB (India) **15**:626 *bibliog.*
cities
Amritsar **1**:383
Chandigarh **4**:279
Lahore **12**:166–167
Lyallpur **12**:473
Multan **13**:637
Sialkot **17**:290
Indo-Iranian languages **11**:145
Sutlej River **18**:373
PUNK ROCK
rock music **16**:249
PUNK TREE *see* PAPERBARK
PUNO (Peru)
map (15° 50′S 70° 2′W) **15**:193
PUNTA ALTA (Argentina)
map (38° 53′S 62° 5′W) **2**:149
PUNTA ARENAS (Chile) **15**:626
climate **4**:356 *table*; **18**:86 *table*
map (53° 9′S 70° 55′W) **4**:355
PUNTA DELGADA (Argentina)
map (42° 46′S 63° 38′W) **2**:149
PUNTA GORDA (Belize)
map (16° 7′N 88° 48′W) **3**:183
PUNTA GORDA (Florida)
map (26° 56′N 82° 3′W) **8**:172
PUNTA GORDA (Nicaragua)
map (11° 31′N 83° 47′W) **14**:179
PUNTA MORENO (Peru)
map (7° 36′S 78° 54′W) **15**:193
PUNTA MOUNTAIN
map (18° 10′N 66° 36′W) **15**:614
PUNTARENAS (Costa Rica)
map (9° 58′N 84° 50′W) **5**:291
PUNTAS DEL SAUCE (Uruguay)
map (33° 51′S 57° 1′W) **19**:488
PUNTO FIJO (Venezuela)
map (11° 42′N 70° 13′W) **19**:542
PUNUK CULTURE
Okvik **14**:372
PUNXSUTAWNEY (Pennsylvania)
map (40° 57′N 78° 59′W) **15**:147
PUPA **15**:626
butterflies and moths **3**:595
cocoon **5**:89
insect **11**:190
juvenile hormone **11**:480
larva **12**:208
silk **17**:306–307
PUPIL (eye)
eye **7**:349 *illus.*
PUPIN, MICHAEL IDVORSKY **15**:626
From Immigrant to Inventor (book) **15**:626
telephone and telegraph **15**:626
X rays **15**:626
PUPPET **15**:626–627 *bibliog.*, *illus.*
Baird, Bil and Cora **3**:27
Bergen, Edgar, and McCarthy, Charlie **3**:209
Bunraku **3**:563–564
Guignol, Grand **9**:394–395
Muppets **13**:644–645
Portuguese puppet theater
Silva, António José da **17**:312
Punch and Judy **15**:623
shadow play **8**:198 *illus.*; **17**:234
ventriloquism **19**:546
PUQUIO (Peru)
map (14° 42′S 74° 8′W) **15**:193
PURCELL (Oklahoma)
map (35° 1′N 97° 22′W) **14**:368
PURCELL, EDWARD MILLS **15**:628
PURCELL, HENRY **7**:203 *illus.*; **15**:628 *bibliog.*, *illus.*
anthem **2**:49
PURCELLVILLE (Virginia)
map (39° 8′N 77° 43′W) **19**:607
PURDAH **2**:104 *illus.*
women in society **20**:203
PURDUE UNIVERSITY
Indiana, state universities of **11**:115
PURDY (Missouri)
map (36° 49′N 93° 55′W) **13**:476
PURE FOOD AND DRUG LAWS **15**:628–629 *bibliog.*
Food and Drug Administration **8**:208
government regulation **9**:270
Roosevelt, Theodore **16**:311
PURE LAND BUDDHISM **15**:629 *bibliog.*
Japanese art and architecture **11**:374
PURGATIVE *see* CATHARTIC
PURGATOIRE RIVER
map (38° 4′N 103° 10′W) **5**:116
PURGATORY **15**:629 *bibliog.*
indulgences **11**:152
PURIFICATION, RITES OF **15**:629 *bibliog.*
PURIM **15**:629 *bibliog.*
Esther, Book of **7**:246–247
PURINE **15**:630
metabolism, gout **9**:266
nucleic acid **15**:630
uric acid **19**:486
PURÍSIMA (Mexico)
map (25° 25′N 105° 26′W) **13**:357
PURITAN REVOLUTION *see* ENGLISH CIVIL WAR
PURITANISM **15**:630 *bibliog.*
American literature **1**:342
American music **1**:348
American Puritanism **15**:630
Baxter, Richard **3**:132
Calvanism **4**:49
Collier, Jeremy **5**:103
Congregationalism **5**:184
Cotton, John **5**:307
Coverdale, Miles **5**:319–320
Elizabeth I, Queen of England **7**:141
English Civil War **15**:630
Halfway Covenant **10**:20
Hooker, Thomas **10**:227
Hutchinson, Anne **10**:322
James I, King of England **11**:356
Massachusetts **13**:210–211
Massachusetts Bay Company **13**:212
Mather (family) **13**:227–228
Miller, Perry **13**:428
Milton, John **13**:432–433
Morton, Thomas **13**:593
Pilgrims **15**:302
Roundheads **16**:325
United States, history of the **19**:436; **19**:438
PURKINJE, JAN EVANGELISTA **15**:630
PURPLE HAIRSTREAK BUTTERFLY **3**:597 *illus.*
butterflies and moths **3**:595
PURPLE HEART
medals and decorations **13**:261–263 *illus.*
PURPLE MARTIN **13**:178–179 *illus.*
PURPURA **15**:630
PURSAT (Kampuchea)
map (12° 32′N 103° 55′E) **12**:11
PURSAT RIVER
map (12° 41′N 104° 9′E) **12**:11
PURSLANE **15**:631 *illus.*
spring beauty **18**:199
PURUS RIVER **15**:631
map (3° 42′S 61° 28′W) **3**:460
PURVIS (Mississippi)
map (31° 9′N 89° 25′W) **13**:469
PURWAKARTA (Indonesia)
map (6° 34′S 107° 26′E) **11**:147
PURWOKERTO (Indonesia)
map (7° 25′S 109° 14′E) **11**:147
PURWOREJO (Indonesia)
map (7° 43′S 110° 1′E) **11**:147
PUS
abscess **1**:62
PUSAN (South Korea) **15**:631
climate **12**:113 *table*
Korean War **12**:121
map (35° 6′N 129° 3′E) **12**:113
PUSEY, EDWARD BOUVERIE **15**:631 *bibliog.*
PUSH *see* PEOPLE UNITED TO SAVE HUMANITY
PUSHKIN (USSR) **15**:631
summer palace
Cameron, Charles **4**:59
PUSHKIN, ALEKSANDR **15**:631–632 *bibliog.*, *illus.*
Boris Godunov (opera) **3**:400–401
Boris Godunov (play) **3**:401
Pushkin (USSR) **15**:631
Russian literature **16**:365 *illus.*
PUSHKIN PRIZE
Bunin, Ivan Alekseyevich **3**:563
PUSHMATAHA (county in Oklahoma)
map (34° 25′N 95° 20′W) **14**:368
PUSSY WILLOW **17**:288 *illus.*; **20**:163 *illus.*
PUTAWY (Poland)
map (51° 25′N 21° 57′E) **15**:388
PUTINA (Peru)
map (14° 55′S 69° 52′W) **15**:193
PUTNAM (Connecticut)
map (41° 55′N 71° 55′W) **5**:193
PUTNAM (county in Florida)
map (29° 40′N 81° 50′W) **8**:172
PUTNAM (county in Georgia)
map (33° 20′N 83° 20′W) **9**:114
PUTNAM (county in Illinois)
map (41° 10′N 89° 15′W) **11**:42

PUTNAM (county in Indiana)
map (39° 40′N 86° 50′W) **11**:111
PUTNAM (county in Missouri)
map (40° 30′N 93° 0′W) **13**:476
PUTNAM (county in New York)
map (41° 26′N 73° 41′W) **14**:149
PUTNAM (county in Ohio)
map (41° 1′N 84° 3′W) **14**:357
PUTNAM (county in Tennessee)
map (36° 10′N 85° 30′W) **19**:104
PUTNAM (county in West Virginia)
map (38° 35′N 81° 55′W) **20**:111
PUTNAM, FREDERIC WARD **15**:632
PUTNAM, HERBERT **15**:632 *bibliog.*
PUTNAM, ISRAEL **15**:632 *bibliog.*
Somerville (Massachusetts) **18**:61
PUTNAM, RUFUS **15**:632
Ohio Company of Associates **14**:362
PUTNEY (Georgia)
map (31° 29′N 84° 7′W) **9**:114
PUTNEY (Vermont)
map (42° 59′N 72° 31′W) **19**:554
PUTNIK, RADOMIR
World War I **20**:226
PUTTALAM (Sri Lanka)
map (8° 2′N 79° 49′E) **18**:206
PUTUMAYO (IÇÁ) RIVER
map (3° 7′S 67° 58′W) **5**:107
PUUC STYLE
Uxmal **19**:499
PUULA LAKE
map (61° 50′N 26° 42′E) **8**:95
PUUNENE (Hawaii)
map (20° 52′N 156° 28′W) **10**:72
PUVIS DE CHAVANNES, PIERRE **15**:632–633 *bibliog., illus.*
Young Girls by the Sea **15**:632 *illus.*
PUXICO (Missouri)
map (36° 57′N 90° 10′W) **13**:476
PUYALLUP (American Indians) **15**:633 *bibliog.*
PUYALLUP (Washington)
map (47° 11′N 122° 18′W) **20**:35
PUYALLUP RIVER
map (47° 15′N 122° 24′W) **20**:35
PUYO (Ecuador)
map (1° 28′S 77° 59′W) **7**:52
PUZZLE *see* GAMES, MATHEMATICAL; names of specific types of puzzles, e.g., CROSSWORD PUZZLE; JIGSAW PUZZLE; REBUS
PWA *see* PUBLIC WORKS ADMINISTRATION
PYELONEPHRITIS *see* KIDNEY DISEASE
PYGMALION (mythology) **15**:633
PYGMALION (play) **15**:633 *bibliog.*
Campbell, Mrs. Patrick **4**:27
Shaw, George Bernard **17**:245
PYGMY **15**:633 *bibliog., illus.*; **16**:34 *illus.*
creation accounts **5**:334
Negrito **14**:78
yodel **20**:328
PYHÄ RIVER
map (64° 28′N 24° 13′E) **8**:95
PYINMANA (Burma)
map (19° 44′N 96° 13′E) **3**:573
PYLADES
theater, history of the **19**:145
PYLE, ERNIE **15**:633 *bibliog.*
PYLE, HOWARD **15**:633–634 *bibliog.*
Flying Dutchman, The **3**:388 *illus.*
PYLORIC STENOSIS
gastrointestinal tract disease **9**:56
genetic diseases **9**:83
PYLOS (Greece) **15**:634 *bibliog.*
Greece, ancient **9**:329
Linear B **12**:353–354
PYM, BARBARA **15**:634
PYM, JOHN **15**:634 *bibliog.*
Hampden, John **10**:32
PYMATUNING RESERVOIR
map (41° 37′N 80° 30′W) **15**:147
PYNCHON, THOMAS **15**:634 *bibliog.*
Gravity's Rainbow **9**:306
PYNCHON, WILLIAM **15**:634
Springfield (Massachusetts) **18**:200
PYODERMA
skin diseases **17**:342
PYONGYANG (North Korea) **12**:114 *illus.*; **15**:634
map (39° 1′N 125° 45′E) **12**:113
PYORRHEA **15**:634
periodontics **15**:170
PYRALSPITES
garnet **9**:49
PYRAMID (polyhedron) **15**:634
polyhedron **15**:419–420 *illus.*
square pyramid, Egypt **15**:634
volume **19**:632
PYRAMID LAKE
map (40° 0′N 119° 35′W) **14**:111
PYRAMIDAL PEAKS **12**:182 *illus.*
PYRAMIDS **7**:85 *illus.*; **15**:634–636 *bibliog., illus.*
architecture **2**:130 *illus.*
Egypt **15**:634–636
Egyptian art and architecture **7**:85–90
Giza (Egypt) **9**:192
Imhotep **11**:54
Khafre, King of Egypt **12**:64
Khufu, King of Egypt **12**:69
Menkaure, King of Egypt **13**:298
Petrie, Sir Flinders **15**:204
Saqqara **17**:74
Seven Wonders of the World **17**:216 *illus.*
Snefru, King of Egypt **18**:3
Latin American art and architecture **12**:222
mastaba **13**:214
Maya
Pyramid and Temple of Inscriptions **11**:121 *illus.*
Uxmal **19**:499
Mexico
Chichén Itzá **4**:343–344
Cholula **4**:404
Pyramid of the Moon (Teotihuacán) **15**:497 *illus.*
Pyramid of the Sun (Teotihuacán) **19**:113–114 *illus.*
Peru
Mochica **13**:488
pre-Columbian art and architecture **15**:496–501
pyramid (polyhedron) **15**:634
PYRAMUS AND THISBE **15**:636
PYRARGYRITE **15**:636
sulfosalts **18**:334
PYRENEES **8**:265 *illus.*; **15**:636–637 *bibliog., illus.*; **18**:141 *illus.*
map (42° 40′N 1° 0′E) **18**:140
mountain **13**:619
people
Basques **3**:116
PYRENEES, PEACE OF THE
Louis XIV, King of France **12**:426
Thirty Years' War **19**:171
PYRGI
Caere **4**:13
PYRIDINE
aromatic compounds **2**:186
heterocyclic compound **10**:153
PYRIDOXAL
coenzyme **5**:92
PYRIDOXINE (Vitamin B_6)
Kuhn, Richard **12**:135
vitamins and minerals **19**:619–620
Recommended Dietary Allowances **19**:618 *table*
PYRIMETHAMINE
malaria **13**:80
PYRIMIDINE **15**:637
purine **15**:630
PYRITE **13**:440 *illus.*; **15**:637 *bibliog., illus.*
alteration, mineral **1**:312
marcasite **13**:145
sulfide minerals **18**:334
PYROCLASTIC ROCKS
igneous rock **11**:35–36
sedimentary rock **17**:185–186 *illus.*
PYROELECTRICITY
hemimorphite **10**:118
PYROLUSITE **15**:637
manganese **13**:114
PYROLYSIS **15**:637 *bibliog.*
distillation **6**:200
ethylene **7**:258
synthetic fuels **18**:409–410
PYROMETER
Daniell, John Frederic, inventor **6**:32
Wedgwood, Josiah **20**:90
PYROMORPHITE **15**:638
mimetite **13**:434
PYROPE
garnet **9**:49
PYROPHYLLITE **15**:638
PYROTECHNICS *see* FIREWORKS
PYROXENE **15**:638 *bibliog.*
chemical composition **15**:638
eclogite **7**:41–42
gabbro **9**:3
jadeite, jade **11**:347
mineralogy **15**:638
monoclinic system **13**:536
monzonite **13**:560
occurrence **15**:638
olivine **14**:380
silicate minerals **15**:638; **17**:305
PYRRHIC (versification) **19**:562
PYRRHIC VICTORY *see* PYRRHUS, KING OF EPIRUS
PYRRHO OF ELIS **15**:638 *bibliog.*
PYRRHOPHYTA *see* DINOFLAGELLATE
PYRRHOTITE **15**:638
pentlandite **15**:155
sulfide minerals **18**:334
PYRRHUS, KING OF EPIRUS **15**:639 *bibliog.*
Epirus **7**:220–221
Rome, ancient **16**:298
PYRROLE **15**:639 *illus.*
heterocyclic compound **10**:153
occurrence **15**:639
Woodward, Robert B. **15**:639
PYRUVIC ACID **15**:639
fermentation **8**:55
PYTHAGORAS, THEOREM OF **15**:639 *illus.*
Pythagoras of Samos **15**:639–640
triangle (mathematics) **19**:292
trigonometry **19**:298
PYTHAGORAS OF SAMOS **15**:639–640 *bibliog., illus.*
dissonance (music) **6**:198
geometry **9**:106 *illus.*
Greek music **9**:345
mathematics, history of **13**:223–224 *illus.*
PYTHAGOREANS **15**:640 *bibliog.*
Hippocratic oath **10**:174
Philolaus **15**:240
pre-Socratic philosophy **15**:532
PYTHEAS OF MASSILIA
exploration **7**:334
PYTHIAN GAMES **15**:640
Delphi **6**:95
PYTHIOS
Mausoleum at Halicarnassus **17**:217
PYTHON (mythology) **15**:640
PYTHON (snake) **15**:640 *bibliog., illus.*; **17**:377 *illus.*; **17**:380 *illus.*
boa **3**:348–349
PYU (Burma)
Asia, history **2**:253–254 *map*
map (18° 29′N 96° 26′E) **3**:573

Q

Q (letter) **16**:3 *illus.*
Q FEVER **16**:3
diseases, animal **6**:192
rickettsia **16**:216
QABOOS BIN SAID
Oman **14**:387
QADDAFI, MUAMMAR AL- **16**:3 *bibliog., illus.*
Libya **12**:321
QAIS, IMRU' AL- *see* IMRU' AL-QAIS
QAJAR (dynasty)
Iran **11**:253
Middle East, history of the **13**:406
QAL AL-BISHA (Saudi Arabia)
map (20° 1′N 42° 36′E) **17**:94
QAL EH-YE NOW (Afghanistan)
map (34° 59′N 63° 8′E) **1**:133
QALLAT JARMO
Jarmo **11**:383
QANAT
aqueduct **2**:94
QANDAHAR (Afghanistan) *see* KANDAHAR (Afghanistan)
QANON
zither **20**:370 *illus.*
QASHQAI **16**:3 *bibliog.*
Khamseh **12**:65
QATABA (Yemen) (Sana)
map (13° 51′N 44° 42′E) **20**:325
QATANA (Syria)
map (33° 26′N 36° 5′E) **18**:412
QATAR **16**:4 *bibliog., illus., map*
cities
Doha **6**:224
flag **16**:4 *illus.*
map (25° 0′N 51° 10′E) **2**:232
Middle Eastern universities **13**:410–412 *table*
QATTARA DEPRESSION **16**:5
map (30° 0′N 27° 30′E) **7**:76
QAZVIN (Iran)
map (36° 16′N 50° 0′E) **11**:250
QCD *see* QUANTUM CHROMODYNAMICS
QE II (ship) *see* *QUEEN ELIZABETH* (ship)
QESHM ISLAND
map (26° 45′N 55° 45′E) **11**:250
QI BAISHI *see* CH'I PAI-SHIH (Qi Baishi)
QIANLONG *see* CH'IEN-LUNG (Qianlong)
QIN (dynasty) *see* CH'IN (Qin) (dynasty)
QING (dynasty) *see* CH'ING (Qing) (dynasty)
QINGDAO (China) *see* TSINGTAO (Qingdao) (China)
QINGHAI (China) *see* TSINGHAI (Qinghai) (China)
QISARYA *see* CAESAREA (Israel)
QOM (Iran) *see* QUM (Iran)
QOPH (letter)
Q (letter) **16**:3
QU YUAN *see* CH'Ü YÜAN (Qu Yuan)
QUAALUDE
sedative **17**:182
QUABBIN RESERVOIR
map (42° 22′N 72° 18′W) **13**:206
QUADDICK RESERVOIR
map (41° 57′N 71° 49′W) **5**:193
QUADI
Germanic peoples **9**:138
QUADRANT **16**:5
double quadrant
Davis, John **6**:52
Graham, George **9**:279
navigation **14**:59
QUADRATIC EQUATION
algebra **1**:284
discriminant **6**:189
polynomial **15**:421
quadratic function **16**:5
QUADRATIC FUNCTION **16**:5
QUADRIC SURFACE
ellipsoid **7**:148
QUADRILATERAL **16**:5
parallelogram **15**:79
polygon **15**:419 *illus.*
rectangle **16**:110
square **18**:202
QUADRUPLE ALLIANCE **16**:5
congress system **5**:187–188
QUAGGA **16**:5 *illus.*
QUAHOG **17**:254 *illus.*
QUAIL **16**:5–6 *bibliog., illus.*
bobwhite **3**:353
game birds **9**:27
partridge **15**:100
QUAKERS *see* FRIENDS, SOCIETY OF
QUAKERTOWN (Pennsylvania)
map (40° 26′N 75° 21′W) **15**:147
QUAKING ASPEN **2**:262 *illus.*
QUALITATIVE ANALYSIS
sociology **18**:29–30
QUALITATIVE CHEMICAL ANALYSIS **16**:6–7 *bibliog., illus.*
See also QUANTITATIVE CHEMICAL ANALYSIS
analytical chemistry **1**:391
calorimeter **4**:47
chromatography **4**:417–419 *illus.*; **16**:7
Debye, Peter **6**:72
electrophoresis **7**:126
fractionation **8**:258
historical development **16**:6
indicator **11**:144
instrumentation **16**:6–7
mass spectrometry **13**:204
methodology **16**:6
organic qualitative analysis **16**:7
physical methods **16**:7
polarographic analyzer **15**:395
precipitation (chemistry) **15**:493
radiochemistry **16**:63
spectrophotometer **18**:168–169 *illus.*
spectroscope **18**:169–170 *illus.*
spectroscopy **18**:170–172 *illus.*
spot tests **16**:7
systematic inorganic qualitative analysis **16**:6
QUALITY CONTROL
industrial engineering **11**:156
sampling **17**:48
stroboscope **18**:301
QUANAH *see* PARKER, QUANAH
QUANAH (Texas)
map (34° 18′N 99° 44′W) **19**:129
QUANG DUC
Vietnam War **19**:586 *illus.*
QUANT, MARY
fashion design **8**:32
QUANTICO (Virginia)
map (38° 31′N 77° 17′W) **19**:607
QUANTITATIVE ANALYSIS
sociology **18**:29
QUANTITATIVE CHEMICAL ANALYSIS **16**:7–8 *bibliog.*
See also QUALITATIVE CHEMICAL ANALYSIS
analytical chemistry **1**:391
assay of ores **2**:264
balance **3**:30–31 *illus.*
calorimeter **4**:47
chemical industry **4**:317–319
chromatography **4**:417–419 *illus.*
densitometer **6**:113
electrochemistry **7**:112–113
electrophoresis **7**:126

QUANTITATIVE CHEMICAL ANALYSIS (cont.)
filtration **8**:91
fractionation **8**:258
gas laws **9**:53
gravimetric analysis **16**:8
mass spectrometry **13**:204
microanalysis
Pregl, Fritz **15**:502
molecule **13**:508
optical activity **14**:408
pH meter **15**:218
photometer **15**:273–274
polarimeter **15**:393
polariscope **15**:394
polarized light **15**:395
polarographic analyzer **15**:395
radiochemistry **16**:63
spectrophotometer **18**:168–169 *illus.*
spectroscope **18**:169–170 *illus.*
spectroscopy **18**:170–172 *illus.*
stoichiometry **18**:276–277
titration **19**:215
turbidimeter **19**:339
volumetric analysis **16**:8–9
X-ray diffraction **20**:308–309 *illus.*
QUANTRILL, WILLIAM C. **16**:8 *bibliog.*
QUANTUM CHROMODYNAMICS **16**:8
hadron **10**:9
quark **16**:12
QUANTUM ELECTRODYNAMICS **16**:8
Feynman, Richard Phillips **8**:66
Schwinger, Julian Seymour **17**:141
Tomonaga, Sin-itiro **19**:232
QUANTUM ELECTRONICS
Townes, Charles Hard **19**:255
QUANTUM MECHANICS **16**:8–11 *bibliog., illus.*
atom **5**:305–306 *illus.*
atomic structure **16**:10
Bell's theorem **3**:192
Bethe, Hans Albrecht **3**:230
Bohr, Niels **3**:361–362
Born, Max **3**:401–402
Cayley, Arthur **4**:227
Compton effect **5**:159
de Broglie, Louis **6**:58
de Broglie wavelength **6**:58
Dirac, Paul **6**:186–187
dynamics **6**:319
Ehrenfest, Paul **7**:90
Einstein, Albert **7**:93–94
electromagnetic radiation **7**:118
electron optics **7**:122
energy level **7**:173
exclusion principle **7**:327
Franck, James **8**:277
fundamental particles **8**:361–363
Heisenberg, Werner Karl **10**:109–110
Hertz, Gustav **10**:148–149
hydrogen atom **16**:11
Josephson, Brian David **11**:452
Landau, Lev **12**:181
law, physical **12**:248
molecule **13**:508
nuclear physics **14**:285–287
orbital **14**:417
orbital theory of bonding **4**:313–314
Pauli, Wolfgang **15**:118–119
photon **15**:274
physics **15**:281
physics, history of **15**:286
Planck, Max **15**:326–327
Planck's constant **15**:327
quark **16**:12–13
resonance (physics) **16**:178
Schrödinger, Erwin **17**:135
Schwinger, Julian Seymour **17**:141
Sommerfeld, Arnold **18**:62
standing wave **18**:217
superfluidity **18**:351
Tomonaga, Sin-itiro **19**:232
Townes, Charles Hard **19**:255
uncertainty principle **19**:381
unified field theory **19**:385–386
Van Vleck, J. H. **19**:516
QUANTUM NUMBER
electron configuration **7**:120
exclusion principle **7**:327
QUANTUM OPTICS
optics **14**:412
QUANTUM THEORY
electron cloud
electricity **7**:110–111
energy level **7**:173
QUANTZ, JOHANN JOACHIM **16**:11–12 *bibliog.*
QUAPAW (American Indians) **16**:12
Omaha (American Indians) **14**:385
QU'APPELLE RIVER
map (50° 25′N 101° 20′W) **17**:81
QUARANTINE **16**:12
infectious disease exposure **16**:12
ship passengers or cargo **16**:12
QUAREGNON (Belgium)
map (50° 26′N 3° 51′E) **3**:177
QUARENGHI, GIACOMO **16**:12 *bibliog.*
QUARK **16**:12–13 *bibliog., table*
fundamental particles **8**:361–363 *table*
Gell-Mann, Murray **9**:69–70
gluon **9**:212
grand unification theories **9**:286
hadron **10**:9
matter **13**:230–231
photon **15**:274
physics **15**:281
proton **15**:578
Ting, Samuel Chao Chung **19**:206
QUARRYING *see* MINING AND QUARRYING
QUARRYVILLE (Pennsylvania)
map (39° 54′N 76° 10′W) **15**:147
QUART
weights and measures **20**:93 *table*
QUARTER HORSE **10**:242–243 *illus.*; **16**:13 *bibliog., illus.*
saddle horse **17**:9
QUARTERING ACT
Intolerable Acts **11**:231–232
United States, history of the **19**:440
QUARTERING OF TROOPS (U.S. Constitution) *see* 3d AMENDMENT
QUARTERLY REVIEW (periodical)
Gifford, William **9**:177
QUARTET, BARBERSHOP *see* BARBERSHOP QUARTET
QUARTET, STRING *see* STRING QUARTET
QUARTIER MILITAIRE (Mauritius)
map (20° 15′S 57° 35′E) **13**:237
QUARTZ **13**:441 *illus.*; **16**:13–14 *bibliog., illus.*
alteration, mineral **1**:312
amethyst **1**:368
chert and flint **4**:332–333
coesite **5**:93
crystal **5**:374 *illus.*
crystallography **13**:439 *illus.*
dacite **6**:4
felsite **8**:48
formation **16**:14
fulgurite **8**:357
gems **9**:74–75 *illus.*
gneiss **9**:213
granite **9**:287
granodiorite **9**:287
igneous rock **11**:34–36
jasper **11**:384
optical activity **14**:408
piezoelectricity **15**:298; **16**:13
polarized light **15**:394
quartz monzonite **16**:14
quartzite **16**:14
sand **17**:59
sandstone **17**:63 *table*
schist **17**:123
sediment, marine **17**:184
semiprecious stone **16**:13
silica minerals **17**:304
stibnite **18**:266
tiger's-eye **19**:197
uses **16**:14
varieties **16**:13
vein deposit **19**:536
QUARTZ MONZONITE **16**:14
silica minerals **17**:304
QUARTZITE **16**:14
metamorphic rock **13**:331–332 *illus.*
Paleolithic Period **15**:38
quartz **16**:14
silica minerals **17**:304
QUARTZSITE (Arizona)
map (33° 40′N 114° 13′W) **2**:160
QUASAR **16**:14–15 *bibliog., illus.*
distance, astronomical **6**:200
extragalactic systems **7**:341
gamma-ray astronomy **9**:33–34
gravitational lens **9**:305–306
magnitude **13**:60–61
Nuffield Radio Astronomy Laboratories **14**:291
occultation **14**:320
radio astronomy **16**:50
radio galaxies **16**:53–54
red shift **16**:114
Schmidt, Maarten **17**:128
QUASI-STELLAR OBJECTS *see* QUASAR
QUASI WAR OF 1798–1800 *see* XYZ AFFAIR
QUASIMODO, SALVATORE **16**:15 *bibliog.*
QUATERNARY PERIOD **16**:15
continental drift **15**:354 *map*
Flint, Richard Foster **8**:165
fossil record **8**:247
geologic time **9**:104–105 *table*
ice ages **11**:9–10 *map, table*
lake, glacial **12**:170
Milankovitch theory **13**:418–419
moraine **13**:572
paleoclimatology **15**:32
paleotemperature **15**:42
Pleistocene Epoch **15**:364
Recent Epoch **16**:106–107
QUATRE BORNES (Mauritius)
map (20° 15′S 57° 28′E) **13**:237
QUAY (county in New Mexico)
map (35° 0′N 103° 40′W) **14**:136
QUAY, MATTHEW S.
Pennsylvania **15**:150
QUBE
information science **11**:173
QUCHAN (Iran)
map (37° 6′N 58° 30′E) **11**:250
QUEBEC (city in Quebec) **16**:15–16 *illus., map*; **16**:20 *illus.*
Canada, history of **4**:80 *illus.*
French and Indian Wars **8**:312; **8**:314; **19**:439 *illus.*
map (46° 49′N 71° 14′W) **16**:18
QUEBEC (province in Canada) **16**:16–21 *bibliog., illus., map*
agriculture and fishing **16**:20
cities
Chicoutimi **4**:346
Laval **12**:240
Montreal **4**:77 *illus.*; **13**:558 *map*
Quebec (city) **16**:15–16 *illus., map*
Sherbrooke **17**:256
Trois-Rivières **19**:305
climate **16**:17
cultural activity **16**:19
economic activity **16**:19–20
education **16**:17; **16**:19
Bishop's University **4**:92 *table*
Canadian education **4**:91
Chicoutimi, Université de Quebec at **4**:92 *table*
Concordia University **4**:92 *table*
Laval University **12**:241
McGill University **4**:92 *table*; **13**:16
Montreal, Université de **4**:92 *table*; **13**:558–560
Montreal, Université de Quebec at **4**:92 *table*
Quebec, University of **16**:21
Rimouski, Université de Quebec at **4**:92 *table*
Sherbrooke, Université de **4**:92 *table*
Trois-Rivières, Université de Quebec at **4**:92 *table*
Université Laval **4**:92 *table*
flag **16**:17 *illus.*
forestry and mining **16**:19 *illus.*
government **16**:20
autonomy and provincial rights debate **16**:20–21
historic sites and recreation **16**:19
history **4**:81–87 *map*; **16**:20
Champlain, Samuel de **4**:277–278
Duplessis, Maurice Le Noblet **6**:302
Jesuit Estates Act **11**:402
Lévesque, René **12**:303
Mercier, Honoré **13**:305
Murray, James **13**:650
Quebec Act **16**:21
separatist movement **4**:87; **16**:20–21
Labrador **12**:157
land and resources **16**:16–18 *map*
literature *see* FRENCH-CANADIAN LITERATURE
manufacturing and energy **4**:77; **16**:19–20
maple syrup and sugar **13**:138
people **16**:17; **16**:19
Algonquin **1**:291
English-speaking inhabitants **16**:20
French-speaking inhabitants **16**:20
Pennacook **15**:145
physical features
Gaspé Peninsula **4**:72 *illus.*; **9**:55–56
Laurentian Mountains **12**:239
Magdalen Islands **13**:46
Ungava **19**:384
rivers, lakes, and waterways **16**:17
Saguenay River **17**:12
tourism and transportation **16**:20
vegetation and animal life **16**:17
QUEBEC (province in Quebec)
map (52° 0′N 72° 0′W) **4**:70
QUEBEC, UNIVERSITY OF **16**:21
QUEBEC ACT (1774) **16**:21 *bibliog.*
Canada, history of **7**:81
Intolerable Acts **11**:232
QUEBEC CONFERENCE (1943)
World War II **20**:271
QUEBRACHO (Uruguay)
map (31° 57′S 57° 53′W) **19**:488
QUECHUA (American Indians) **16**:21 *bibliog.*
Cuzco **5**:400
Inca **11**:69–70; **11**:73
QUEEG, CAPTAIN (fictional character)
Caine Mutiny, The **4**:17
QUEEN **16**:21
QUEEN, ELLERY **16**:21
QUEEN ANNE REVIVAL STYLE
Shaw, Richard Norman **17**:246
QUEEN ANNE STYLE **16**:21 *bibliog.*
furniture **8**:376–377
QUEEN ANNES (county in Maryland)
map (39° 3′N 76° 4′W) **13**:188
QUEEN ANNE'S LACE (botany) **16**:21
QUEEN ANNE'S WAR **11**:109 *map*
French and Indian Wars **8**:312–313
QUEEN BEE **3**:158–159 *illus.*
QUEEN CHARLOTTE (British Columbia)
map (53° 16′N 132° 5′W) **3**:491
QUEEN CHARLOTTE ISLANDS (British Columbia) **16**:21–22
Indians, American
Haida **10**:12
map (53° 0′N 132° 0′W) **3**:491
QUEEN CHARLOTTE SOUND
map (51° 30′N 129° 30′W) **3**:491
QUEEN CHARLOTTE STRAIT
map (50° 50′N 127° 25′W) **3**:491
QUEEN CITY (Missouri)
map (40° 25′N 92° 34′W) **13**:476
QUEEN CONCH
conch **5**:170
QUEEN ELIZABETH (ship) **16**:22 *bibliog., illus.*
QUEEN ELIZABETH OF BELGIUM AWARD
Berman, Lazar **3**:219
QUEEN ELIZABETH II (ship) *see* *QUEEN ELIZABETH* (ship)
QUEEN ELIZABETH ISLANDS
Ellesmere Island **7**:146–147
map (78° 0′N 95° 0′W) **14**:258
QUEEN MARY (ship) **16**:22 *bibliog.*
QUEEN MAUD LAND (region in Antarctica)
map (72° 30′S 12° 0′E) **2**:40
QUEEN MAUD MOUNTAINS
map (86° 0′S 160° 0′W) **2**:40
QUEEN RIVER
map (41° 25′N 71° 38′W) **16**:198
QUEENS (New York City) **16**:22
map (40° 34′N 73° 52′W) **14**:149
people
Hispanic Americans **10**:177; **10**:179
QUEENS COLLEGE *see* NEW YORK, CITY UNIVERSITY OF
QUEENS' COLLEGE, CAMBRIDGE UNIVERSITY **4**:53
QUEEN'S COLLEGE, THE, OXFORD UNIVERSITY **14**:474
QUEEN'S MEN (acting company)
Tarlton, Richard **19**:37
QUEEN'S UNIVERSITY AT KINGSTON **16**:22
QUEENSBERRY, JOHN SHOLTO DOUGLAS, MARQUESS OF
boxing **3**:432
QUEENSLAND (Australia) **16**:22 *map*
cities
Brisbane **3**:487 *illus.*
flag **8**:145 *illus.*
map (22° 0′S 145° 0′E) **2**:328
QUEENSPORT (Nova Scotia)
map (45° 20′N 61° 16′W) **14**:269
QUEENSTOWN (Guyana)
map (7° 12′N 58° 29′W) **9**:410
QUEENSTOWN (South Africa)
map (31° 52′S 26° 52′E) **18**:79
QUEIROZ, JOSÉ MARIA EÇA DE *see* EÇA DE QUEIROZ, JOSÉ MARIA
QUELEA **16**:22–23
QUELIMANE (Mozambique)
map (17° 53′S 36° 51′E) **13**:627
QUELLIN *see* QUELLINUS, ARTUS
QUELLINUS, ARTUS **16**:23 *bibliog.*
QUELLINUS THE ELDER *see* QUELLINUS, ARTUS
QUEMADO (New Mexico)
map (34° 20′N 108° 30′W) **14**:136
QUEMOY (Taiwan) **16**:23
map (24° 27′N 118° 23′E) **19**:13
QUENEAU, RAYMOND **16**:23 *bibliog.*

QUEPOS (Costa Rica)
map (9° 27′N 84° 9′W) 5:291
QUERCIA, JACOPO DELLA 16:23 *bibliog.*
QUERÉTARO (city in Mexico) 16:23
map (20° 36′N 100° 23′W) 13:357
QUERÉTARO (state in Mexico) 16:23
cities
Querétaro 16:23
QUESADA, GONZALO JIMÉNEZ DE *see* JIMÉNEZ DE QUESADA, GONZALO
QUESNAY, FRANÇOIS
physiocrats 15:286–287
QUESNEL (British Columbia)
map (52° 59′N 122° 30′W) 3:491
QUESTA (New Mexico)
map (36° 42′N 105° 36′W) 14:136
QUÉTELET, LAMBERT ADOLPHE 16:23 *bibliog.*
QUETTA (Pakistan)
map (30° 12′N 67° 0′E) 15:27
QUETZAL 16:23–24 *illus.*
QUETZALCÓATL 11:122 *illus.*; 16:24 *bibliog., illus.*
Aztec 2:384
Chichén Itzá 4:344
Cortés, Hernán 5:278
mask 13:197 *illus.*
Mexico, history of 13:362
temple 2:383 *illus.*; 13:362 *illus.*
Tula 19:329–330
QUEUING THEORY 16:24–25 *bibliog.*
industrial management 11:157
QUEVEDO (Ecuador)
map (1° 2′S 79° 29′W) 7:52
QUEVEDO Y VILLEGAS, FRANCISCO GÓMEZ DE 16:25 *bibliog.*
Spanish literature 18:159
QUEZALTENANGO (Guatemala)
map (14° 50′N 91° 31′W) 9:389
QUEZON, MANUEL LUIS 16:25 *bibliog., illus.*
QUEZON CITY (Philippines) 16:25
map (14° 38′N 121° 0′E) 15:237
QUI NHON (Vietnam)
map (13° 46′N 109° 14′E) 19:580
QUIBDÓ (Colombia)
map (5° 42′N 76° 40′W) 5:107
QUICK CLAY 16:25 *bibliog.*
QUICKLIME
lime (chemical compound) 12:343
QUICKSAND 16:25 *bibliog.*
covered wagons stuck in 19:444 *illus.*
QUICKSILVER *see* MERCURY (element)
QUICUMQUE *see* ATHANASIAN CREED
QUIDOR, JOHN 16:25 *bibliog.*
QUIETISM 16:26 *bibliog.*
Bourignon, Antoinette 3:424
Fénelon, François de Salignac de la Mothe 8:50
Molinos, Miguel de 13:509
QUIGLEY, MARTIN
film, history of 8:84
QUILÁ (Mexico)
map (24° 23′N 107° 13′W) 13:357
QUILEUTE-HOH AND CHEMAKUM (American Indians) 16:26 *bibliog.*
QUILL *see* FEATHER
QUILL PEN 15:140
QUILLABAMBA (Peru)
map (12° 49′S 72° 43′W) 15:193
QUILLACAS (Bolivia)
map (19° 14′S 66° 58′W) 3:366
QUILLACOLLO (Bolivia)
map (17° 26′S 66° 17′W) 3:366
QUILLOTA (Chile)
map (32° 53′S 71° 16′W) 4:355
QUILLWORT (botany) 16:26
QUILPUÉ (Chile)
map (33° 3′S 71° 27′W) 4:355
QUILTING 16:26 *bibliog.*
folk art 8:197 *illus.*
QUIMBY, PHINEAS PARKHURST 16:26 *bibliog.*
New Thought 14:142–143
QUIMPER (France)
map (48° 0′N 4° 6′W) 8:260
QUINACRINE
quinine 16:27
QUINAULT, PHILIPPE
Lully, Jean Baptiste 12:454
QUINAULT RIVER
map (47° 23′N 124° 18′W) 20:35
QUINCE 8:348 *illus.*; 16:26 *illus.*
QUINCEMIL (Peru)
map (13° 16′S 70° 38′W) 15:193
QUINCEY, THOMAS DE *see* DE QUINCEY, THOMAS
QUINCY (California)
map (39° 56′N 120° 57′W) 4:31
QUINCY (Florida)
map (30° 35′N 84° 37′W) 8:172
QUINCY (Illinois)
map (39° 56′N 91° 23′W) 11:42
QUINCY (Massachusetts) 16:26–27
map (42° 15′N 71° 1′W) 13:206
QUINCY (Washington)
map (47° 14′N 119° 51′W) 20:35
QUINCY, JOSIAH (1744–1775)
Quincy, Josiah 16:27
QUINCY, JOSIAH (1772–1864) 16:27 *bibliog.*
QUINCY BAY
map (42° 17′N 70° 58′W) 3:409
QUINE, WILLARD VAN ORMAN 16:27 *bibliog.*
QUINEBAUG RIVER
map (41° 33′N 72° 3′W) 5:193
QUINHAGAK (Alaska)
map (59° 45′N 161° 43′W) 1:242
QUINIDINE 16:27
cinchona 4:431
QUININE 16:27
cinchona 4:431
polarized light 15:394
synthesis
Woodward, Robert Burns 20:213
QUINLAN, KAREN ANN
euthanasia 7:310–311
QUINN RIVER
map (40° 58′N 119° 5′W) 14:111
QUINNIPIAC RIVER
map (41° 18′N 72° 54′W) 5:193
QUINONE 16:27 *illus.*
QUINTANA ROO (Mexico) 16:27
cities
Chetumal 4:337
QUINTANELLA, HECTOR
unidentified flying object 19:385 *illus.*
QUINTER (Kansas)
map (39° 4′N 100° 14′W) 12:18
QUINTERO, JOSÉ
Circle in the Square 4:436
QUINTERO, SERAFÍN AND JOAQUÍN ÁLVAREZ *see* ÁLVAREZ QUINTERO, SERAFÍN AND JOAQUÍN
QUINTILIAN 16:27 *bibliog.*
educational psychology 7:66
QUINTON (Oklahoma)
map (35° 7′N 95° 22′W) 14:368
QUIPU
Inca 11:72–73
QUIRAUK MOUNTAIN
map (39° 42′N 77° 31′W) 13:188
QUIRIGUÁ (Guatemala) 16:27 *bibliog.*
QUIRINO, ELPIDIO 16:27 *bibliog.*
QUIRINUS 16:28
QUIROGA, HORACIO
Uruguay 19:489
QUIROGA, JUAN FACUNDO 16:28
QUIROGA, VASCO DE
Tarascan 17:35
QUISLING, VIDKUN 16:28 *bibliog.*
QUITAQUE (Texas)
map (34° 22′N 101° 4′W) 19:129
QUITERON 16:28
QUITMAN (Georgia)
map (30° 47′N 83° 33′W) 9:114
QUITMAN (county in Georgia)
map (31° 52′N 85° 2′W) 9:114
QUITMAN (Mississippi)
map (32° 3′N 88° 43′W) 13:469
QUITMAN (county in Mississippi)
map (34° 15′N 90° 15′W) 13:469
QUITMAN (Texas)
map (32° 48′N 95° 27′W) 19:129
QUITO (Ecuador) 7:52–53 *illus., table*; 16:28
Inca 11:70–71
Latin American art and architecture 12:223
map (0° 13′S 78° 30′W) 7:52
QUIVIRA *see* GRAN QUIVIRA
QUIZ SHOWS
radio and television broadcasting 16:58
QULIN (Missouri)
map (36° 36′N 90° 15′W) 13:476
QUM (Iran) 16:28
map (34° 39′N 50° 54′E) 11:250
QUMRAN 16:28 *bibliog.*
Dead Sea Scrolls 6:65
QUO VADIS? (book)
Sienkiewicz, Henryk 17:296
QUOIREZ, FRANÇOISE *see* SAGAN, FRANÇOISE
QUOITS *see* HORSESHOE PITCHING
QUOLL *see* EASTERN AUSTRALIAN NATIVE CAT
QUONOCHONTAUG (Rhode Island)
map (41° 21′N 71° 43′W) 16:198
QUONOCHONTAUG POND
map (41° 20′N 71° 43′W) 16:198
QUOTA 16:28 *bibliog.*
tariff 19:36
QUOTIENT
fraction 8:258
rational number 16:92
QUS (Egypt)
map (25° 55′N 32° 45′E) 7:76
QUTB MINAR 16:28
Indian art and architecture 11:97
QUTB UD-DIN
Delhi Sultanate 6:92

R

R (letter) 16:29 *illus.*
R-34* and *R-101 (airships) 16:29
RA *see* AMON-RE (Egyptian god)
RA EXPEDITIONS 16:29 *bibliog., illus.*
Heyerdahl, Thor 10:155
RA-HARAKHTE (sun-god) 13:698 *illus.*
Heliopolis 10:112–113
RA II (papyrus boat) 16:29 *illus.*
RAABE, WILHELM 16:30 *bibliog.*
RÁBA RIVER
map (47° 42′N 17° 38′E) 10:307
RABANUS MAURUS 16:30
RABAT (Malta)
map (35° 52′N 14° 25′E) 13:94
RABAT (Morocco) 16:30
map (34° 2′N 6° 51′W) 13:585
RABAUL (Papua New Guinea)
map (4° 12′S 152° 12′E) 15:72
World War II 20:267
RABBI 16:30
RABBIT 16:30–31 *bibliog., illus.*
animal experimentation 2:22
animal husbandry 2:23
brain 3:443 *illus.*
burrow 16:31 *illus.*
digestive system 6:173 *illus.*
embryo 7:324 *illus.*
hare 10:48–49
pika 15:301
Pleistocene Epoch 15:366 *illus.*
respiratory system 16:179 *illus.*
savanna life 17:98
skeletal system 17:334 *illus.*
tularemia 19:330
urogenital system 13:98 *illus.*
RABBIT EARS PASS
map (40° 23′N 106° 37′W) 5:116
RABBIT FEVER *see* TULAREMIA
RABBIT FISH 8:117 *illus.*
RABE, DAVID 16:31
RABELAIS, FRANÇOIS 16:31–32 *bibliog., illus.*
French literature 8:315
Gargantua and Pantagruel 9:47
RABI, ISIDOR ISAAC 16:32 *bibliog.*
RABIES 16:32 *bibliog.*
diseases, animal 6:190; 6:191
Pasteur, Louis 15:108
RABIN, YITZHAK 16:32 *bibliog.*
RABUN (county in Georgia)
map (34° 55′N 83° 25′W) 9:114
RABUN BALD MOUNTAIN
map (34° 58′N 83° 18′W) 9:114
RACCOON 16:32–33 *bibliog., illus.*; 18:377 *illus.*
cacomistle 4:8
kinkajou 12:84
olingo 14:378
panda 15:58
RACCOON CREEK
map (40° 2′N 82° 24′W) 14:357
RACE 16:33–35 *bibliog., illus., map*
anthropology 2:53
black Americans 3:306
Coon, Carleton 5:243
definition 16:37
discrimination 6:189–190
geographic races
Aborigines, Australian 1:59–60 *illus.*; 16:34 *illus.*
African 1:144–148 *illus., map*; 16:33–34 *illus., map*
Ainu 1:203 *illus.*; 16:34 *illus.*
Alpine 16:34 *illus.*
Aryan 2:226
Asiatic 2:240–241; 16:33–34 *illus., map*
Australian 2:335; 16:33–34 *illus., map*
Bantu 3:71; 16:34 *illus.*
black Americans 3:304; 16:34 *illus.*
Coloureds 5:123; 16:34 *illus.*
Dravidian 6:263; 16:34 *illus.*
Eskimo 7:238–242 *illus., map*; 16:34 *illus.*
European 7:272 *illus.*; 16:33–34 *illus., map*
Fuegian 16:34 *illus.*
Hamites 10:29
Hindu 16:34 *illus.*
Indian 11:83; 16:33–34 *illus., map*
Indians, American 11:116; 16:33–34 *illus., map*
Khoikhoi 12:67; 16:34 *illus.*
Ladino 16:34 *illus.*
Lapps 12:205–206; 16:34 *illus.*
Mediterranean 16:34 *illus.*
Melanesians 13:284–285; 16:33–34 *illus., map*
Micronesians 13:386; 16:33–34 *illus., map*
Mongoloid 16:34 *illus.*
Negrito 14:78; 16:34 *illus.*
Neo-Hawaiian 16:34 *illus.*
North Chinese 16:34 *illus.*
Papuans 15:73; 16:34 *illus.*
Polynesians 15:421; 16:33–34 *illus., map*
Pygmy 15:633 *illus.*; 16:34 *illus.*
San 16:34 *illus.*; 17:49–50
Tibetan 16:34 *illus.*
Turks 16:34 *illus.*; 19:347–349
gypsies 9:415
mestizo 13:324
mulatto 13:635
racism 16:37–38
RACE, CAPE
map (46° 40′N 53° 10′W) 14:166
RACE, RELAY *see* RELAY RACE
RACE POINT
map (42° 4′N 70° 14′W) 13:206
RACE RIOTS (in U.S. history) 16:35 *bibliog.*
black Americans 3:310–311
California 4:37
Florida 8:176
Miami 13:370
Maryland 13:193
Michigan 13:382
United States, history of the 19:459
RACE RIOTS (non U.S.)
Kuala Lumpur (Malaysia) 12:133
South Africa 18:83
RACE RUNNER 16:36 *illus.*
RACE WALKING
track and field 19:260
RACELAND (Louisiana)
map (29° 48′N 90° 40′W) 12:430
RACER (snake) 5:124 *illus.*
RACH GIA (Vietnam)
map (10° 1′N 105° 5′E) 19:580
RACHEL 16:36
RACHMANINOFF, SERGEI 16:36 *bibliog., illus.*
Russian music 16:368 *illus.*
RACIAL DISCRIMINATION *see* DISCRIMINATION; INTEGRATION, RACIAL
RACIBÓRZ (Poland)
map (50° 6′N 18° 13′E) 15:388
RACINE (Wisconsin) 16:36
map (42° 43′N 87° 48′W) 20:185
RACINE (county in Wisconsin)
map (42° 45′N 88° 5′W) 20:185
RACINE, JEAN 8:316 *illus.*; 16:36–37 *bibliog., illus.*
drama 6:259
theater, history of the 19:147
RACING *see* AUTOMOBILE RACING; BOAT RACING; HORSE RACING; PIGEON RACING
RACISM 16:37–38 *bibliog.*
See also DISCRIMINATION; INTEGRATION, RACIAL
anti-Semitism 2:68
apartheid 2:74
Black Muslims 3:317–318
Chamberlain, Houston Stewart 4:273
genocide 9:93
ghetto 9:167
Gobineau, Joseph Arthur, Comte de 9:217
Holocaust 10:206
Olympic Games 14:383 *illus.*
Powell, Enoch 15:480
RACK-AND-PINION STEERING
steering system 18:244–245 *illus.*
RACKHAM, ARTHUR 16:38 *bibliog., illus.*
RACQUETBALL 16:38 *bibliog.*
RADAR 16:38–40 *bibliog., illus.*
antenna (electronics) 2:47–48
Bethe, Hans 3:230
BMEWS 3:348
Fleming, Sir Arthur Percy Morris 8:159
frequency, electromagnetic 7:117 *table*
frequency allocation 8:326–327
history 16:39

RADAR (cont.)
hyperbola **10**:348
magnetic storm **13**:55
meteorological instrumentation **13**:340–341
military warning and detection systems **13**:422
Stealth bomber **18**:240
navigation **14**:60
pulse (electronics) **15**:621
radar astronomy **16**:40
range finder **16**:84
receiver (communications) **16**:106
remote sensing **16**:147–148
scanning **17**:114
submarine **18**:315
tracking station **19**:262
transmitter, magnetron **13**:60
traveling-wave tube **19**:284
Venus, mapping of **19**:548
Watson-Watt, Sir Robert Alexander **20**:68
wavelength, electromagnetic **7**:117 *table*
RADAR ASTRONOMY **16**:40 *bibliog., illus.*
radio astronomy **16**:47
solar system **18**:45
RADAR METEOROLOGY **16**:41 *bibliog., illus.*
meteorology **13**:342 *illus.*
weather forecasting **20**:78 *illus.*
RADCLIFF (Kentucky)
map (37° 51′N 85° 57′W) **12**:47
RADCLIFFE, ANN **16**:41 *bibliog.*
Gothic romance **9**:263
RADCLIFFE-BROWN, SIR ALFRED R. **16**:41 *bibliog.*
Fortes, Meyer **8**:238
RADCLIFFE COLLEGE **16**:41
Harvard University **10**:64
Seven Sisters Colleges **17**:216
RADDALL, THOMAS H. **16**:41–42
Canadian literature **4**:94
RADEK, KARL **16**:42 *bibliog.*
RADFORD (Virginia)
map (37° 8′N 80° 34′W) **19**:607
RADHAKRISHNAN, SIR SARVEPALLI **16**:42 *bibliog.*
RADHANITES
Khazars **12**:66
RADIAL VELOCITY
Campbell, William Wallace **4**:66
Huggins, Sir William **10**:292
proper motion **15**:570
RADIAN **16**:42
RADIATA
classification, biological **2**:9 *illus.*
animal **2**:10
RADIATION **16**:42 *illus.*
See also RADIOACTIVITY
adaptive radiation **1**:98
alpha radiation **16**:42
atmosphere **2**:300
background radiation **3**:12
beta radiation **16**:42
blackbody radiation **1**:321; **3**:320
cancer, treatment of: Joly, John **11**:441
carbon cycle (astronomy) **4**:135–136
Cherenkov radiation **4**:331
conversion electron **5**:233
cosmic rays **5**:283–284
electromagnetic radiation **7**:116–118
Einstein, Albert **7**:92–93
frequency radiation **7**:116
Maxwell, James Clerk **13**:241
radio **16**:44
radio astronomy **7**:116
whistler **20**:134
electron radiation
Tamm, Igor Yevgenievich **19**:19
environmental health **7**:212
fallout shelter **8**:15
food preservation **8**:212
frequency radiation **7**:116
Galaxy, The **9**:13
gamma radiation **16**:42
gravitational
relativity **16**:136–137 *illus.*
greenhouse effect **9**:351
heat radiation
aluminum **1**:316
heat and heat transfer **10**:98
infrared astronomy **11**:175
interstellar matter **11**:226
interstellar reddening **11**:229
laboratory, Lawrence Berkeley and Lawrence Livermore laboratories **12**:251
measurement
dosimeter **6**:244
Geiger counter **9**:68
photographic dosimetry, photography **15**:266
scintillation counter **17**:146–147
medicine **13**:272
microwaves **13**:389
standard limits **13**:389
OAO **14**:312–313
occultation **14**:320
OSO **14**:456
pollution, environmental **15**:413–414
radio astronomy **16**:47–48
radiometer **16**:65
sky **17**:346
solar radiation **18**:44
spectroscope **18**:169 *illus.*
spectroscopy **18**:170–172
spectrum **18**:172–173
ultraviolet radiation
nebula **14**:74–75
Van Allen radiation belts **19**:510
RADIATION INJURY **16**:42–43 *bibliog.*
bone diseases **3**:378
cancer **4**:102–103
diseases, occupational **6**:193
mutation **13**:686
photographic dosimetry
photography **15**:266
plutonium **15**:373
pollution, environmental **15**:414
radioactivity **16**:62
RADIATION PRESSURE **16**:43
comet **5**:133
RADIATION THERAPY **16**:43 *bibliog.*
cancer **4**:105 *illus.*
cobalt **5**:82
eczema **7**:54
John Joly **11**:441
radiology **16**:64
RADIATOR, AUTOMOBILE
cooling system, engine **5**:242
RADICAL (chemistry) **16**:43
aliphatic compounds **1**:295
chemical nomenclature **4**:321
chemical symbolism and notation **4**:322
free radical **8**:294
Liebig, Justus, Baron von **12**:324
methylene **13**:345
organic chemistry **14**:434–435
peroxide **15**:177
resonance (chemistry) **16**:178
valence **19**:503
Wieland, Heinrich Otto **20**:146
RADICAL (mathematics) **16**:43
square root **18**:202
RADICAL THEATER *see* GUERRILLA THEATER
RADICALISM **16**:43–44 *bibliog.*
See also names of specific leaders, e.g., ALINSKY, SAUL; WILKES, JOHN; etc.
RADICOFUNCTIONAL NOMENCLATURE
chemical nomenclature **4**:321 *illus.*
RADIO **16**:44–47 *bibliog., illus., table*
See also RADIO BROADCASTING
amplitude modulation (AM) **1**:383
ground wave **9**:373
antenna (electronics) **2**:47–48; **16**:46
citizens band radio **4**:446
communications satellite **5**:144–145
frequency, electromagnetic **7**:117 *table*
frequency allocation **8**:326–327; **16**:45 *table*
frequency modulation (FM) **8**:327
FM radio **8**:192
ham radio **10**:26
heterodyne principle **10**:153–154
history **16**:44–45
Armstrong, Edwin **2**:179
Braun, Ferdinand **3**:458
De Forest, Lee **6**:58
Fessenden, Reginald Aubrey **8**:62
Fleming, Sir Ambrose **8**:159
Fleming, Sir Arthur Percy Morris **8**:159
Gernsback, Hugo **9**:157
Hammond, John Hays, Jr. **10**:31
Hertz, Heinrich Rudolph **10**:149
Marconi, Guglielmo **13**:147
modulation **13**:500 *illus.*
radio astronomy **16**:47–53
receiver (communications) **16**:46; **16**:106
telecommunications **19**:75–76
telemetry **19**:78
tracking station **19**:262
transducer **19**:269
transmitter **16**:45–46; **19**:276
impedance **11**:61
tuner **19**:333
waves **16**:44
electromagnetic radiation **7**:117 *table*
Hertz, Heinrich Rudolph **10**:149
ionosphere **11**:242
OGO **14**:355
pulsar **15**:620–621
radar **16**:38–40
radar astronomy **16**:40
refraction **16**:123
whistler **20**:134
World War I **20**:247–248
RADIO ASTRONOMY **16**:47–53 *bibliog., illus.*
aperture synthesis **2**:76; **16**:52
astronomy and astrophysics **2**:281
background radiation **3**:12; **16**:50
BL Lacertae objects **3**:303; **16**:50
cosmology (astronomy) **5**:285
Crab Nebula **5**:326
Cygnus A **5**:406
electromagnetic radiation **7**:116
extragalactic systems **7**:345
Galaxy, The **9**:12; **16**:48–50
history **16**:47
Ginzburg, Vitaly Lazarevich **9**:185
Hulst, Hendrik Christoffell van de **10**:296
Jansky, Karl **11**:359
Lovell, Sir Bernard **12**:438
Oort, Jan Hendrik **14**:396
Reber, Grote **16**:106
Ryle, Sir Martin **16**:380
Shklovsky, Iosif Samuilovich **17**:278
Wilson, Robert W., and Penzias, Arno A. **20**:165
interstellar matter **11**:228; **16**:50
life, extraterrestrial **12**:328; **16**:50
observatory, astronomical **14**:318
origin of life **12**:327
pulsar **15**:620–621; **16**:49
quasar **16**:14–15; **16**:50
radio galaxies **16**:50
radio telescope **16**:50–53 *illus.*
antenna **2**:284 *illus.*
Arecibo Observatory **2**:145 *illus.*
interferometer **11**:209–210; **16**:52–53
research institutions
Australian National Radio Astronomy Observatory **2**:344
Mullard Radio Astronomy Observatory **13**:636
National Radio Astronomy Observatory **14**:45; **16**:51–53 *illus.*
Nuffield Radio Astronomy Laboratories **14**:291
Paris Observatory **15**:88
Special Astrophysical Observatory **18**:166
Westerbork Observatory **16**:51–52; **20**:115
scientific satellite
IMP **11**:60
solar system **16**:48–49; **18**:45
synchrotron radiation **18**:406
RADIO BROADCASTING **16**:54–55; **16**:58
advertising **1**:112–113
amplitude modulation **1**:383
FM radio **8**:192
history
Fessenden, Reginald Aubrey **8**:62
Newhouse, Samuel I. **14**:169
Paley, William S. **15**:47
Sarnoff, David **17**:78
labor union
Communication Workers of America **5**:142
mass communication **13**:202
newscasts
anchorman **1**:399
journalism **11**:455–456
Murrow, Edward R. **13**:651
press agencies and syndicates **15**:533
Thomas, Lowell **19**:173
Winchell, Walter **20**:167–168
professional and educational organizations
Peabody Award **15**:123
programming
Amos 'n' Andy **1**:376
Godfrey, Arthur **9**:220
Grand Ole Opry **9**:285
soap opera **18**:8
Radio Free Europe and Radio Liberty **16**:53
regulations
Federal Communications Commission **8**:41
government regulation **9**:271
religious broadcasting **16**:141–142
Voice of America **19**:626
RADIO CITY MUSIC HALL (New York) **16**:53 *bibliog.*
New York (city) **14**:145 *map*
RADIO CORPORATION OF AMERICA
His Master's Voice **15**:253 *illus.*
radio and television broadcasting **16**:54–55
video **19**:576b; **19**:576c
RADIO DRAMA
soap opera **18**:8
Under Milkwood **19**:383
RADIO FREE EUROPE AND RADIO LIBERTY **16**:53 *bibliog.*
See also VOICE OF AMERICA
RADIO GALAXIES
Coma cluster **5**:129
Crab nebula **5**:326
extragalactic systems **7**:345
Galaxy, The **9**:12
radio astronomy **16**:50
supernova remnants **16**:49
RADIO LIBERTY *see* RADIO FREE EUROPE AND RADIO LIBERTY
RADIO TELESCOPE *see* RADIO ASTRONOMY
RADIO AND TELEVISION BROADCASTING **16**:53–60 *bibliog., illus.*
See also RADIO BROADCASTING; TELEVISION BROADCASTING
advertising **1**:112–113
frequency, electromagnetic **7**:117 *table*
ionosphere **11**:242
transmission
telephone **19**:80
wavelength, electromagnetic **7**:117 *table*
RADIOACTIVE FALLOUT *see* FALLOUT
RADIOACTIVE TRACER *see* NUCLEAR MEDICINE
RADIOACTIVE WASTE DISPOSAL
Nevada **14**:113
nuclear energy **14**:282
radioactivity **16**:63
RADIOACTIVITY **16**:60–63 *bibliog., illus.*
alpha particle **16**:61
applications **16**:62–63
atomic structure **16**:61
beta particle **16**:61
chemistry, history of **4**:328
cosmic rays **5**:283
element **7**:130–131
lawrencium **12**:251
mendelevium **13**:294
neptunium **14**:89
nobelium **14**:211
periodic table **15**:168–169
plutonium **15**:373
polonium **15**:417
promethium **15**:567
radium **16**:68
strontium **18**:303
technetium **19**:59
thorium **19**:178
thulium **19**:184
transmutation of elements **19**:276–277
transuranium elements **19**:282
tritium **19**:304
uranium **19**:477
vanadium **19**:516
gamma rays **9**:34; **16**:61
history **16**:61
Becquerel, Antoine Henri **3**:153
Curie, Marie and Pierre **5**:391–392
Fermi, Enrico **8**:55–56
Hahn, Otto **10**:11
Joliot-Curie, Frédéric and Irène **11**:441
Rutherford, Sir Ernest **16**:375–376
hydrogen bomb **10**:339–340
isotope **11**:301; **16**:61
half-life **10**:19–20
laws of
displacement law: Soddy, Frederick **18**:32
radiometric age-dating **16**:65–67
lead **12**:256
measurement **16**:62 *illus.*
Geiger counter **9**:68
qualitative chemical analysis **16**:7
radiation **16**:42 *illus.*
radiochemistry **16**:63
safety **16**:63
nuclear energy **14**:282–283
shield, lead **12**:256
scintillation **17**:146
units and standards **16**:62
uranium minerals **19**:478
RADIOCARBON DATING *see* RADIOMETRIC AGE-DATING
RADIOCHEMISTRY **16**:63 *bibliog.*

Hahn, Otto **10**:11
half-life **10**:19–20
isotope **11**:301
nuclear physics **14**:285
qualitative chemical analysis **16**:7
radioactivity **16**:61
RADIOGRAPHY **16**:63 *bibliog.*
fluoroscope **8**:188
hospital **10**:257 *illus.*
mammography **13**:106
photography, scientific **15**:272
radiology **16**:65 *illus.*
RADIOIMMUNOASSAY **16**:63
hepatitis **10**:130
Yalow, Rosalyn Sussman **20**:315
RADIOISOTOPE *see* ISOTOPE; RADIOCHEMISTRY
RADIOLARIAN **16**:64 *bibliog.*
micropaleontology **13**:386
Protozoa **15**:589–580
Rhizopoda **16**:197
sediment, marine **17**:184
RADIOLOGY **16**:64–65 *bibliog., illus.*
See also CAT (COMPUTERIZED AXIAL TOMOGRAPHY) SCANNING
brain **3**:448
diagnostic tests **6**:149–150
fluoroscope **8**:188
mammography **13**:106
nuclear medicine **14**:284–285
radiation therapy **16**:43
radiography **16**:63
scintillation counter **17**:146–147
X rays **20**:311
RADIOMETER **16**:65 *bibliog.*
Crookes, Sir William, inventor **5**:359
solar constant **18**:41
RADIOMETRIC AGE-DATING **2**:120 *illus.*; **16**:65–67 *bibliog., illus., table*
Australopithecus **2**:346
Boltwood, Bertram Borden **3**:372
cosmology (astronomy) **5**:286
dendrochronology **6**:107
geochemistry **9**:97
geologic samples **16**:65–67
geologic time **9**:104–105
geology **9**:105–106
Holmes, Arthur **10**:205
ice ages **11**:8
Joly, John **11**:441
laws of radioactivity **16**:65–66
Libby, Willard Frank **12**:311
methods **16**:66–67
half-life **10**:20
monazite **13**:522
moon rocks **13**:566
prehistoric humans **15**:511
prehistory **15**:517
radioactive atoms, half-lives **16**:65 *table*
radioactivity **16**:62
radiochemistry **16**:63
sediment, marine **17**:183–184
stratigraphy **18**:293
thorium **19**:178
RADIONUCLIDE *see* ISOTOPE
RADIOSONDE **16**:67 *bibliog.*
balloon **3**:53
weather forecasting **20**:78
RADIOSTERRENWACHT WESTERBORK *see* WESTERBORK OBSERVATORY
RADIOTHERAPY *see* RADIATION THERAPY
RADISH **16**:67 *illus.*; **19**:534 *illus.*
RADISHCHEV, ALEKSANDR NIKOLAYEVICH **16**:67 *bibliog.*
Russia/Union of Soviet Socialist Republics, history of **16**:356
RADISSON, PIERRE ESPRIT **16**:67–68 *bibliog.*
RADIUM **16**:68 *bibliog.*
alkaline earth metals **1**:295
compounds **16**:68
discovery **16**:68
Curie, Marie and Pierre **5**:391–392
element **7**:130 *table*
Group IIA periodic table **15**:167
metal, metallic element **13**:328
radioactivity **16**:60
uranium minerals **16**:68; **19**:478
RADIUS
Schwarzschild radius **17**:139
sphere **18**:180
RADNORSHIRE (Wales) *see* POWYS (Wales)
RADOM (Poland) **16**:68
map (51° 25′N 21° 10′E) **15**:388
RADOMSKO (Poland)
map (51° 5′N 19° 25′E) **15**:388
RADOMYSLSKY, GRIGORY YEVSEYEVICH *see* ZINOVIEV, GRIGORY YEVSEYEVICH
RADON **16**:68–69 *bibliog.*
element **7**:130 *table*
Group 0 periodic table **15**:167
inert gases **11**:161
Ramsay, Sir William **16**:81
RADVILLE (Saskatchewan)
map (49° 27′N 104° 17′W) **17**:81
RAE (Northwest Territories)
map (62° 50′N 116° 3′W) **14**:258
RAE, JOHN
Franklin, Sir John **8**:285
Victoria Island (Northwest Territories) **19**:575
RAEBURN, SIR HENRY **16**:69 *bibliog.*
RAEDWALD, KING OF EAST ANGLIA
Sutton Hoo ship burial **18**:374
RAEFORD (North Carolina)
map (34° 59′N 79° 14′W) **14**:242
RAF *see* ROYAL AIR FORCE
RAFAELA (Argentina)
map (31° 16′S 61° 29′W) **2**:149
RAFFLES, SIR THOMAS STAMFORD **16**:69 *bibliog.*
RAFFLESIA **16**:69
RAFINESQUE, CONSTANTINE
Delaware (American Indians) **6**:91
RAFT
balsa **3**:54
RAFTOR, CATHERINE *see* CLIVE, KITTY
RAG WORM **16**:69 *illus.*
RAGA **16**:69 *bibliog.*
Indian music **11**:102–103
RAGFISH **16**:69
RAGLAND (Alabama)
map (33° 45′N 86° 9′W) **1**:234
RAGNAROK **16**:69 *bibliog.*
RAGTIME **16**:70 *bibliog.*
American music **1**:351
Blake, Eubie **3**:324
Joplin, Scott **11**:446–447
Morton, Jelly Roll **13**:592
RAGTIME (book)
Doctorow, E. L. **6**:210
RAGUSAN LANGUAGE *see* DALMATIAN LANGUAGE
RAGWEED **16**:70
RAHAL GDID (Malta)
map (35° 52′N 14° 30′E) **13**:94
RAHIMYAR KHAN
map (28° 25′N 70° 18′E) **15**:27
RAHMAN, ABD AL- *see* ABD AL-RAHMAN, EMIR OF CÓRDOBA
RAHMAN, MUJIBUR *see* MUJIBUR RAHMAN
RAHMAN, TUNKU ABDUL *see* ABDUL RAHMAH, TUNKU
RAHMAN, ZIAUR *see* ZIAUR RAHMAN
RAHNER, KARL **16**:70 *bibliog.*
RAHWAY (New Jersey)
map (40° 37′N 74° 17′W) **14**:129
RAIATEA
Society Islands **18**:26
RAIFORD (Florida)
map (30° 4′N 82° 14′W) **8**:172
RAIL (bird) **16**:70 *bibliog., illus.*
gallinule **9**:19–20
game birds **9**:27
RAILGUN **16**:70–71 *illus.*
RAILROAD **16**:71–77 *bibliog., illus.*
See also LOCOMOTIVE; the subheadings railroad or transportation under names of specific countries
brake **3**:451
cable car **4**:6
Canada
Canada, history of **4**:83; **4**:84
Canadian National Railways **4**:94
Canadian Pacific Railway **3**:490 *illus.*; **4**:94
Stephen, George **18**:254
China
Chinese Eastern Railway **4**:388
containerization **5**:227
elevated railroad **7**:135–136
Europe
Orient Express **14**:441
Saint Gotthard Tunnel **17**:19
Great Britain
Stephenson, George and Robert **18**:255
high-speed train **16**:76–77 *illus.*
history **16**:71–74 *illus.*
Industrial Revolution **11**:159
transportation **19**:279–280
iron and steel industry **11**:275–276
Japan **11**:366
Latin America
Trans-Andine Railroad **19**:267
Wheelwright, William **20**:129–130
locomotive **12**:388–391 *illus.*
semaphore **17**:194
signaling **17**:301
sleeping car
Pullman, George Mortimer **15**:619
streetcar **18**:296–297
subway **18**:317–319
tourism **19**:252
traffic control 19:264
tunnel **19**:337
United States **16**:71–73 *illus.*
Amtrak **1**:385
cable car **4**:6
Carnegie, Andrew **4**:155
Chinese Americans **14**:441 *illus.*
Corning, Erastus **5**:269
Drew, Daniel **6**:271
featherbedding **8**:40
frontier, U.S. **8**:341 *map*
Garrett, John Work **9**:50
Gould, Jay **9**:265
government regulation **9**:270–271
Harriman (family) **10**:56–57
Hill, James Jerome **10**:164
Hopkins, Johns **10**:232
Huntington (family) **10**:314
Judah, Theodore D. **11**:458
Metroliner **13**:347
Morgan (family) **13**:577
National Mediation Board **14**:35
Randolph, A. Philip **16**:83
Southern Pacific Railroad **19**:268 *map*
Sprague, Frank Julian **18**:198
Stanford, Leland **18**:217
Stevens (family) **18**:263
Tom Thumb **19**:229
transcontinental railroad **19**:268–269 *map*
United States, history of the **19**:450 *illus.*
United States, 19th century **19**:445 *map*
Vanderbilt (family) **19**:518–519
Westinghouse, George **20**:117
USSR
Trans-Caspian Railroad **19**:267
Trans-Siberian Railroad **19**:267
viaduct **19**:567
RAILWAY *see* RAILROAD
RAILWAY BROTHERHOODS **16**:77 *bibliog.*
Debs, Eugene V. **6**:70–71
Pullman Strike **15**:619
RAIN *see* PRECIPITATION (weather)
RAIN DANCE *see* INDIANS OF NORTH AMERICA, MUSIC AND DANCE OF THE
RAIN FOREST *see* JUNGLE AND RAIN FOREST
RAIN SHADOW EFFECT **16**:77
climate **5**:58
desert **6**:126
orographic precipitation **14**:447
RAINBOW **16**:77 *bibliog., illus.*
dispersion **6**:197
RAINBOW, THE (book) **16**:77–78 *bibliog.*
Lawrence, D. H. **11**:249–250
RAINBOW WARRIOR (ship) **9**:354
RAINELLE (West Virginia)
map (37° 58′N 80° 47′W) **20**:111
RAINER, YVONNE **16**:78 *bibliog.*
RAINEY, JOSEPH H. **16**:185 *illus.*
RAINIER, MOUNT **16**:78; **20**:36 *illus.*
map (46° 52′N 121° 46′W) **20**:35
national parks **14**:37–39 *illus., map, table*
RAINIER III, PRINCE OF MONACO **16**:78
RAINMAKING *see* WEATHER MODIFICATION
RAINS (county in Texas)
map (32° 50′N 95° 47′W) **19**:129
RAINWATER, JAMES **16**:78
RAINY LAKE
map (48° 42′N 93° 10′W) **13**:453
RAINY RIVER
map (48° 50′N 94° 41′W) **13**:453
RAIPUR (India)
map (21° 14′N 81° 38′E) **11**:80
RAISIN **16**:78 *bibliog.*
RAISIN IN THE SUN, A (play) **16**:78
Hansberry, Lorraine **10**:40
RAITI (Nicaragua)
map (14° 35′N 85° 2′W) **14**:179
RAJ *see* RAJAH
RAJ GOND *see* GOND
RAJA BROOKE'S BIRDWING **3**:597 *illus.*
butterflies and moths **3**:595
RAJAH **16**:78
RAJAHMUNDRY (India)
map (16° 59′N 81° 47′E) **11**:80
RAJAI, MUHAMMAD ALI
Iran **11**:253
RAJANG RIVER
map (2° 4′N 111° 12′E) **13**:84
RAJASTHAN (India) **16**:78
Jaipur **11**:350
map (27° 0′N 74° 0′E) **11**:80
RAJKOT (India)
map (22° 18′N 70° 47′E) **11**:80
RAJPUT **16**:78 *bibliog.*
Asia, history of **2**:255 *map*
India, history of **11**:90
Indian art and architecture **11**:97–98
Rajasthan (India) **16**:78
RAJSHAHI (Bangladesh)
map (24° 22′N 88° 36′E) 3:64
RAKAPOSHI MOUNTAIN
map (36° 10′N 74° 30′E) **15**:27
RAKATA ISLAND
map (6° 10′S 105° 26′E) **11**:147
RAKHMANINOV, SERGEI *see* RACHMANINOFF, SERGEI
RÁKÓCZI, FERENC
Hungary **10**:310
RÁKOSI, MÁTYÁS **16**:79
Hungarian Revolution **10**:306
RAKOVSKI, GEORGI SAVA
Bulgaria **3**:556
RALBAG *see* LEVI BEN GERSHON
RALEIGH (Mississippi)
map (32° 2′N 89° 30′W) **13**:469
RALEIGH (Newfoundland)
map (51° 34′N 55° 44′W) **14**:166
RALEIGH (North Carolina) **16**:79
map (35° 47′N 78° 39′W) **14**:242
RALEIGH (county in West Virginia)
map (37° 45′N 81° 15′W) **20**:111
RALEIGH, SIR WALTER **16**:79 *bibliog., illus.*
Hakluyt, Richard **10**:17
Roanoke Colony **16**:239
tobacco **19**:218
RALEIGH BAY
map (35° 0′N 76° 0′W) **14**:242
RALIK CHAIN
Marshall Islands (U.S.) **13**:173
RALL, T. W.
cyclic AMP **5**:403
RALLS (county in Missouri)
map (39° 30′N 91° 35′W) **13**:476
RALLS (Texas)
map (33° 41′N 101° 23′W) **19**:129
RALPH ROISTER DOISTER (play)
Udall, Nicholas **19**:370
RAM (RANDOM ACCESS MEMORY)
computer **5**:160b; **5**:160f; **5**:160i
computer memory **5**:161
RAMA IV *see* MONGKUT, KING OF SIAM
RAMADAN **16**:79
Arabs **2**:106
fasting **8**:33
Islam **11**:292
RAMAH (New Mexico)
map (35° 8′N 108° 30′W) **14**:136
RAMAKRISHNA **16**:79 *bibliog.*
Vivekananda **19**:622
RAMAN, SIR CHANDRASEKHARA VENKATA **16**:79–80
RAMAPITHECUS **16**:80 *bibliog.*
prehistoric human origins **15**:512
sites **15**:514 *map*
RAMAPO RIVER
map (40° 58′N 74° 17′W) **14**:129
RAMATH GAN (Israel)
map (32° 5′N 34° 49′E) **11**:302
RAMAYANA (poem) **16**:80
Hinduism **10**:173
RAMBAM, CYVIA *see* RAMBERT, DAME MARIE
RAMBERT, DAME MARIE **16**:80 *bibliog.*
Tudor, Antony **19**:329
RAMBOUILLET, MARQUISE DE **16**:80
RAMEAU, JEAN PHILIPPE **16**:80 *bibliog.*
orchestra and orchestration **14**:418
RAMÉE, MARIE LOUISE DE LA *see* OUIDA
RAMELLI, AGOSTINO
engineering **7**:177
RAMER (Alabama)
map (32° 3′N 86° 13′W) **1**:234
RAMESSES *see* RAMSES for Egyptian kings named RAMESSES
RAMGOOLAM, SIR SEEWOOSAGUR
Mauritius **13**:237
RAMIE **16**:80
cellulose **4**:238
RAMJET **16**:80–81 *illus.*
jet propulsion **11**:406–407
RAMLA (Israel)
map (31° 55′N 34° 52′E) **11**:302

RAMM, MOUNT
map (29° 35′N 35° 24′E) 11:447
RAMON, MOUNT
map (30° 30′N 34° 38′E) 11:302
RAMON Y CAJAL, SANTIAGO 16:81 *bibliog.*
Golgi, Camillo 9:240
RAMONA (book)
Jackson, Helen Hunt 11:342–343
RAMONA (Oklahoma)
map (36° 32′N 95° 55′W) 14:368
RAMPAL, JEAN PIERRE 16:81
RAMPART (Alaska)
map (65° 30′N 150° 10′W) 1:242
RAMSAY, ALLAN (painter) 16:81 *bibliog.*
RAMSAY, ALLAN (poet) 16:81 *bibliog.*
RAMSAY, JAMES ANDREW BROUN, 1ST MARQUESS OF DALHOUSIE *see* DALHOUSIE, JAMES ANDREW BROUN RAMSAY, 1ST MARQUESS OF
RAMSAY, SIR WILLIAM 16:81 *bibliog.*
argon 2:152
chemistry, history of 4:326
Rayleigh, Lord 16:97
Travers, Morris William 19:284
RAMSDEN, JESSE
telescope 19:83
RAMSES I, KING OF EGYPT 16:81
wall painting from tomb of 7:84 *illus.*; 13:400 *illus.*
RAMSES II, KING OF EGYPT 16:81–82 *bibliog., illus.*
mummy 13:639 *illus.*
tomb
Valley of the Kings 19:507
RAMSES III, KING OF EGYPT 16:82 *bibliog.*
glazed tiles from palace of 7:83 *illus.*
Khons, Temple of 2:130 *illus.*
RAMSES VI, KING OF EGYPT
tomb
Valley of the Kings 19:507
RAMSEUR (North Carolina)
map (35° 44′N 79° 39′W) 14:242
RAMSEY (Illinois)
map (39° 8′N 89° 6′W) 11:42
RAMSEY (county in Minnesota)
map (45° 0′N 93° 8′W) 13:453
RAMSEY (New Jersey)
map (41° 3′N 74° 9′W) 14:129
RAMSEY (county in North Dakota)
map (48° 20′N 98° 40′W) 14:248
RAMSEY, MICHAEL 16:82
RAMSGATE (England)
map (51° 20′N 1° 25′E) 19:403
RAMU (Bangladesh)
map (21° 25′N 92° 7′E) 3:64
RAMUS, PETRUS 16:82 *bibliog.*
RANA PIPIENS see LEOPARD FROG
RANAMANTSOA, GABRIEL
Madagascar 13:39
RANBURNE (Alabama)
map (33° 31′N 85° 21′W) 1:234
RANCAGUA (Chile)
map (34° 10′S 70° 45′W) 4:355
RANCHERIA (Yukon Territory)
map (60° 5′N 130° 40′W) 20:345
RANCHES OF TAOS (New Mexico)
map (36° 22′N 105° 37′W) 14:136
RANCHESTER (Wyoming)
map (44° 54′N 107° 16′W) 20:301
RANCHING *see* ANIMAL HUSBANDRY; CATTLE AND CATTLE RAISING; FARMS AND FARMING
RANCHO LA BREA *see* LA BREA TAR PIT
RAND, AYN 16:82 *bibliog.*
RAND, THE *see* WITWATERSRAND (South Africa)
RAND CORPORATION
think tanks 19:169
RAND McNALLY BUILDING
skyscraper 17:348
RANDAL, SIR JOHN T.
radar 16:39
RANDALL (county in Texas)
map (34° 57′N 101° 52′W) 19:129
RANDALL, HASTINGS
ethics 7:251
RANDALL-MacIVER, DAVID
Zimbabwe Ruins 20:367
RANDALLSTOWN (Maryland)
map (39° 22′N 76° 48′W) 13:188
RANDERS (Denmark)
map (56° 28′N 10° 3′E) 6:109
RANDLEMAN (North Carolina)
map (35° 49′N 79° 48′W) 14:242
RANDOLPH (county in Alabama)
map (33° 20′N 85° 30′W) 1:234
RANDOLPH (county in Arkansas)
map (36° 22′N 91° 0′W) 2:166
RANDOLPH (family) 16:82–83 *bibliog., illus.*
RANDOLPH (county in Georgia)
map (31° 45′N 84° 50′W) 9:114
RANDOLPH (county in Illinois)
map (38° 3′N 89° 47′W) 11:42
RANDOLPH (county in Indiana)
map (40° 10′N 85° 3′W) 11:111
RANDOLPH (Maine)
map (44° 19′N 69° 46′W) 13:70
RANDOLPH (Massachusetts)
map (42° 10′N 71° 3′W) 13:206
RANDOLPH (county in Missouri)
map (39° 25′N 92° 30′W) 13:476
RANDOLPH (Nebraska)
map (42° 23′N 97° 21′W) 14:70
RANDOLPH (county in North Carolina)
map (35° 40′N 79° 55′W) 14:242
RANDOLPH (Utah)
map (41° 40′N 111° 11′W) 19:492
RANDOLPH (Vermont)
map (43° 55′N 72° 40′W) 19:554
RANDOLPH (county in West Virginia)
map (38° 40′N 79° 50′W) 20:111
RANDOLPH (Wisconsin)
map (43° 35′N 89° 0′W) 20:185
RANDOLPH, A. PHILIP 16:83 *bibliog., illus.*
RANDOLPH, EDMUND 19:442 *illus.*
Constitution of the United States 5:213
Randolph (family) 16:83 *illus.*
RANDOLPH, EDWARD 16:83 *bibliog.*
RANDOLPH, PEYTON
Randolph (family) 16:83
RANDOLPH HILLS (Maryland)
map (39° 3′N 77° 6′W) 13:188
RANDOLPH PLAN *see* VIRGINIA PLAN
RANDOM ACCESS MEMORY *see* RAM
RANDOM ISLAND
map (48° 8′N 53° 45′W) 14:166
RANDOM LAKE (Wisconsin)
map (43° 33′N 87° 57′W) 20:185
RANDOM SELECTION
opinion polls 14:405–406
sampling 17:48
RANDOM VARIABLE 16:83 *bibliog.*
distribution
central limit theorem 4:254
chi-square 4:339
statistics 18:236
stochastic process 18:273
RANDOM WALK 16:83 *bibliog.*
stochastic process 18:273
RANDOMIZATION TEST
statistics, nonparametric 18:237
RANGE FINDER 16:84
camera 4:55; 4:56
Michelson, Albert Abraham 13:375–376
RANGELAND *see* GRASSLANDS; PASTURE
RANGELEY (Maine)
map (44° 58′N 70° 39′W) 13:70
RANGELY (Colorado)
map (40° 5′N 108° 48′W) 5:116
RANGER (space probe) 16:84 *bibliog., illus.*
space exploration 18:121 *illus.*; 18:124 *illus., illus.*
RANGER (Texas)
map (32° 28′N 98° 41′W) 19:129
RANGERS 16:85 *bibliog.*
RANGITIKEI RIVER
map (40° 18′S 175° 14′E) 14:158
RANGKASBITUNG (Indonesia)
map (6° 21′S 106° 15′E) 11:147
RANGOON (Burma) 16:85 *illus.*
climate 3:574 *table*
map (16° 47′N 96° 10′E) 3:573
RANGPUR (Bangladesh)
map (25° 45′N 89° 15′E) 3:64
RANJIT SINGH
Gujranwala (Pakistan) 9:402
Multan (Pakistan) 13:637
Punjab 15:626
RANK *see* CLASS, SOCIAL
RANK, MILITARY 16:85–87 *bibliog., tables*
air force, U.S. 1:208 *illus.*
army, U.S. 2:183 *illus.*
Marine Corps, U.S. 13:154–155 *illus.*
Navy, U.S. 14:66 *illus.*
tartan 19:40 *illus.*
RANK, OTTO 16:87 *bibliog.*
RANK TEST
statistics, nonparametric 18:237–238
RANKE, LEOPOLD VON 10:185 *illus.*; 16:87 *bibliog., illus.*
RANKIN (Illinois)
map (40° 28′N 87° 54′W) 11:42
RANKIN (county in Mississippi)
map (32° 15′N 89° 55′W) 13:469
RANKIN (Texas)
map (31° 13′N 101° 56′W) 19:129
RANKIN, JEANNETTE 16:87–88 *bibliog., illus.*
RANKIN INLET (Northwest Territories)
map (62° 45′N 92° 10′W) 14:258
RANKINE, WILLIAM JOHN MACQUORN 16:88
absolute zero 1:63
RANN OF KUTCH
map (24° 0′N 70° 0′E) 11:80
RANONG (Thailand)
map (9° 58′N 98° 38′E) 19:139
RANSEHOUSEN, JESSICA 16:217 *illus.*
RANSOM (Kansas)
map (38° 38′N 99° 56′W) 12:18
RANSOM (county in North Dakota)
map (46° 30′N 97° 40′W) 14:248
RANSOM, JOHN CROWE 16:88 *bibliog.*
New Criticism 14:119
RANTOUL (Illinois)
map (40° 19′N 88° 9′W) 11:42
RAO, RAJA 16:88 *bibliog.*
RAOUL (Georgia)
map (34° 27′N 83° 36′W) 9:114
RAOULT'S LAW
phase equilibrium 15:223
RAPALLO, TREATY OF
Rathenau, Walther 16:92
Rijeka (Yugoslavia) 16:223
RAPALLO CONFERENCE
World War I 20:238
RAPE 16:88 *bibliog.*
capital punishment 4:124
crime 5:346 *table*
prison 15:555
RAPE OF LUCRECE, THE (poem) 16:88
RAPE PLANT 19:535 *illus.*
RAPE OF THE DAUGHTERS OF LEUCIPPUS (Rubens) 3:88 *illus.*
RAPE OF THE LOCK, THE (poem) 16:88
mock epic 13:489
Pope, Alexander 15:430
RAPESEED
vegetable oils 19:535 *illus., table*
RAPHAEL 16:89–90 *bibliog., illus.*
Giulio Romano 9:191–192
Madonna of the Chair 16:152 *illus.*
The Marriage of The Virgin 11:313 *illus.*; 16:89 *illus.*
Perugino 15:196
Portrait of Baldassare Castiglione 15:447 *illus.*; 16:89 *illus.*
The School of Athens 15:20 *illus.*; 15:241 *illus.*
Vatican museums and galleries 19:527
RAPID CITY (Manitoba)
map (50° 8′N 100° 2′W) 13:119
RAPID CITY (Michigan)
map (44° 50′N 85° 17′W) 13:377
RAPID CITY (South Dakota) 16:90
map (44° 5′N 103° 14′W) 18:103
RAPID EYE MOVEMENT SLEEP *see* SLEEP
RAPID RIVER (Michigan)
map (45° 56′N 86° 58′W) 13:377
RAPID RIVER (Minnesota)
map (48° 42′N 94° 26′W) 13:453
RAPID TRANSIT *see* ELEVATED RAILROAD; STREETCAR; SUBWAY; TRANSPORTATION
RAPIDES (county in Louisiana)
map (31° 10′N 92° 30′W) 12:430
RAPP, GEORGE
New Harmony (Indiana) 14:126
RAPPAHANNOCK (county in Virginia)
map (38° 40′N 78° 10′W) 19:607
RAPPAHANNOCK RIVER 16:90
map (37° 34′N 76° 18′W) 19:607
RAPTORIAL BIRDS *see* BIRDS OF PREY
RAQUETTE RIVER
map (45° 0′N 74° 42′W) 14:149
RARE EARTHS *see* LANTHANIDE SERIES
RARITAN (New Jersey)
map (40° 34′N 74° 38′W) 14:129
RARITAN BAY
map (40° 28′N 74° 12′W) 14:129
RAROTONGA
Cook Islands 5:237
RAS AL-KHAIMAH (United Arab Emirates)
United Arab Emirates 19:400
RAS ASIR *see* ASIR, CAPE
RAS BALABAKK (Lebanon)
map (34° 15′N 36° 25′E) 12:265
RAS SHAMRA (Syria) *see* UGARIT
RASBORA 19:308 *illus.*
RASH
scarlet fever 17:115
skin, measles 13:253
RASHAYYA (Lebanon)
map (33° 30′N 35° 51′E) 12:265
RASHEVSKY, NICHOLAS
bionics 3:274
RASHI 16:90 *bibliog.*
RASHID (Egypt)
map (31° 24′N 30° 25′E) 7:76
RASHID, HARUN AL- *see* HARUN AL-RASHID
RASHID IBN SAID AL-MAKTUM
United Arab Emirates 19:401
RASHT (Iran)
map (37° 16′N 49° 36′E) 11:250
RASHTRAKUTAN KRISHNA I, KING *see* KRISHNA I, RASHTRAKUTAN KING
RASIN, I. FREEMAN
Maryland 13:192
RASKOLNIKOV
Dostoyevsky, Fyodor Mikhailovich 6:245
RASMUSSEN, KNUD 16:90 *bibliog.*
RASONITE *see* KERNITE
RASPBERRY 8:348 *illus.*; 16:90 *illus.*
RASPBERRY PEAK
map (34° 23′N 94° 1′W) 2:166
RASPUTIN, GRIGORY YEFIMOVICH 16:90–91 *bibliog., illus.*
Nicholas II, Emperor of Russia 14:182
RASSEMBLEMENT POUR LA RÉPUBLIQUE (RPR) (political party)
Chirac, Jacques 4:397
France 8:265
RASTAFARIANS 16:91 *bibliog.*
reggae 16:128
RASTATT, TREATY OF
Villars, Claude Louis Hector, Duc de 19:598
RASTRELLI, BARTOLOMMEO FRANCESCO 16:91 *bibliog.*
Summer Palace (Peterhof) 16:362 *illus.*
Winter Palace 20:181
RAT 16:91–92 *bibliog., illus.*
animal behavior 2:12 *illus.*
animal experimentation 2:22
bubonic plague 3:532
bushy-tailed rat 10:5 *illus.*
kangaroo rat 12:15–16
mole rat 13:105 *illus.*
RAT ISLANDS
map (52° 0′N 178° 0′E) 1:242
RAT SNAKE
colubrid 5:125
copperhead 5:254
RATAK CHAIN
Marshall Islands (U.S.) 13:173
RATEL 16:92 *illus.*
RATFISH *see* CHIMAERA
RATH OF THE SYNODS
Tara (Ireland) 19:35
RATHBUN LAKE
map (40° 54′N 93° 5′W) 11:244
RATHDRUM (Idaho)
map (47° 49′N 116° 54′W) 11:26
RATHENAU, WALTHER 16:92 *bibliog.*
RATHENOW (Germany, East and West)
map (52° 36′N 12° 20′E) 9:140
RATIO
fraction 8:258
Greek music 9:345
trigonometry 19:298
RATIONAL NUMBER 16:92 *bibliog.*
arithmetic 2:158
irrational number 11:280
real number 16:103
RATIONAL PRINCIPLE (philosophy) *see* LOGOS
RATIONALISM 16:92–93 *bibliog.*
Bayle, Pierre 3:133
Blanshard, Brand 3:327–328
deism 6:86
Descartes, René 6:125–126
epistemology 7:222
Hegel, Georg Wilhelm Friedrich 10:105
Kant, Immanuel 12:23–24
Critique of Pure Reason 5:352
Labrouste, Henri 12:157
Leibniz, Gottfried Wilhelm von 12:276–277
Perret, Auguste 15:178
philosophy 15:244–245
science, philosophy of 17:141–143
Spinoza, Baruch 18:187–188
RATIONALIZATION (psychology)
defense mechanisms 6:83
RATIONING *see* PRICE SYSTEM
RATISBON (West Germany) *see* REGENSBURG (West Germany)
RATNAPURA (Sri Lanka)
map (6° 41′N 80° 24′E) 18:206

RATON (New Mexico)
map (36° 54′N 104° 24′W) **14**:136
RATSIRAKA, DIDIER
Madagascar **13**:39
RATTAIL CACTUS **4**:10 *illus.*
RATTIGAN, TERENCE 16:93
RATTLE (musical instrument)
African music **1**:169
RATTLESNAKE 4:283 *illus.*; **16**:93 *bibliog., illus.*
fang **17**:380 *illus.*
fer-de-lance **8**:51
massasauga **13**:212
pit viper **15**:319 *illus.*
sidewinder **17**:294
RATZ, MOUNT
map (57° 23′N 132° 19′W) **3**:491
RATZEL, FRIEDRICH 16:93–94
geography **9**:102
RATZINGER, JOSEPH 16:94
RAUKUMARA RANGE
map (37° 47′S 178° 2′E) **14**:158
RAUMA (Finland)
map (61° 8′N 21° 30′E) **8**:95
RAUNG, MOUNT
map (8° 8′S 114° 3′E) **11**:147
RAUSCHENBERG, ROBERT 16:94 *bibliog., illus.*
ballet set and costumes **3**:44 *illus.*
graphic arts **9**:294
happenings **10**:41
Reserve **16**:94 *illus.*
RAUSCHENBUSCH, WALTER 16:94 *bibliog.*
Social Gospel **18**:12
RAUWOLFIA 16:94
folk medicine **8**:201
medicinal plants **13**:266
psychotropic drugs **15**:603
reserpine **16**:176
RAVAILLAC, FRANÇOIS
Henry IV, King of France **10**:128
RAVALLI (county in Montana)
map (46° 10′N 114° 5′W) **13**:547
RAVEL, MAURICE 8:321 *illus.*; **16**:94–95 *bibliog., illus.*
RAVELO (Bolivia)
map (18° 48′S 65° 32′W) **3**:366
RAVEN 16:95 *bibliog., illus.*
RAVEN (Virginia)
map (37° 7′N 81° 52′W) **19**:607
"RAVEN, THE" (poem)
Poe, Edgar Allan **15**:378
RAVENA (New York)
map (42° 29′N 73° 49′W) **14**:149
RAVENNA (Italy) **16**:95
Italian city-state **11**:328 *map*
Italy, history of **11**:327
map (44° 25′N 12° 12′E) **11**:321
mosaic **13**:595
San Vitale **17**:58
RAVENNA (Michigan)
map (43° 11′N 85° 56′W) **13**:377
RAVENNA (Nebraska)
map (41° 2′N 98° 55′W) **14**:70
RAVENNA (Ohio)
map (41° 9′N 81° 15′W) **14**:357
RAVENSBURG (Germany, East and West)
map (47° 47′N 9° 37′E) **9**:140
RAVENSTHORPE (Australia)
map (33° 35′S 120° 2′E) **2**:328
RAVENSWOOD (West Virginia)
map (38° 57′N 81° 46′W) **20**:111
RAVI RIVER
map (30° 35′N 71° 48′E) **11**:152
RAWALPINDI (Pakistan) **16**:95
map (33° 36′N 73° 4′E) **15**:27
RAWLINGS, JERRY 16:95
Ghana **9**:166
RAWLINGS, MARJORIE KINNAN 16:95 *bibliog.*
RAWLINS (county in Kansas)
map (39° 50′N 101° 5′W) **12**:18
RAWLINS (Wyoming)
map (41° 47′N 107° 14′W) **20**:301
RAWLINSON, SIR HENRY CRESWICKE 16:95–96 *bibliog.*
Behistun **3**:171
cuneiform **5**:389
Dilmun **6**:176
Grotefend, Georg Friedrich **9**:372
RAWLS, JOHN 16:96 *bibliog.*
ethics **7**:251
RAWSON (Argentina)
map (34° 36′S 60° 4′W) **2**:149
RAY (fish) **8**:116 *illus.*; **16**:96
Chondrichthyes **4**:404
RAY (county in Missouri)
map (39° 20′N 94° 0′W) **13**:476
RAY (North Dakota)
map (48° 21′N 103° 10′W) **14**:248
RAY, CAPE
map (47° 40′N 59° 18′W) **14**:166
RAY, JAMES EARL
King, Martin Luther, Jr. **12**:81
RAY, JOHN 16:96
RAY, MAN 16:96 *bibliog., illus.*
surrealism (art) **18**:364
RAY, SATYAJIT 16:96 *bibliog.*
RAYBURN, SAM 16:96–97 *bibliog.*
RAYET, G. *see* WOLF-RAYET STARS
RAYLEIGH, LORD, 3RD 16:97 *bibliog.*
argon **2**:152
blackbody radiation **3**:321
chemistry, history of **4**:326
Ramsay, Sir William **16**:81
RAYLEIGH, LORD, 4TH
geologic time **9**:104
RAYLEIGH-JEANS LAW
blackbody radiation **3**:321
Jeans, Sir James **11**:390
Rayleigh, Lord, 3rd **16**:97
RAYLEIGH WAVES
ultrasonics **19**:377
RAYMOND (Alberta)
map (49° 27′N 112° 39′W) **1**:256
RAYMOND (Illinois)
map (39° 19′N 89° 34′W) **11**:42
RAYMOND (Minnesota)
map (45° 1′N 95° 14′W) **13**:453
RAYMOND (Mississippi)
map (32° 15′N 90° 25′W) **13**:469
RAYMOND (Washington)
map (46° 41′N 123° 44′W) **20**:35
RAYMOND, HENRY JARVIS 16:97 *bibliog.*
RAYMONDVILLE (Texas)
map (26° 29′N 97° 47′W) **19**:129
RAYNAUD'S DISEASE 16:97
cardiovascular diseases **4**:144
RAYNE (Louisiana)
map (30° 14′N 92° 16′W) **12**:430
RAYNHAM (Massachusetts)
map (41° 57′N 71° 4′W) **13**:206
RAYON 16:97–98 *illus.*
cellulose **4**:238
Chardonnet, Hilaire Bernigaud, Comte de **4**:288
fiber, textile **8**:67
production **16**:97 *illus.*
synthetic fibers **18**:409
wood **20**:206
RAYONISM
abstract art **1**:64
Goncharova, Natalia Sergeyevna **9**:242
Larionov, Mikhail Fyodorovich **12**:207
Russian art and architecture **16**:363
RAYONNANT STYLE 16:98 *bibliog.*
Gothic art and architecture **9**:257–258
Saint-Denis (church) **17**:17
Sainte-Chapelle **17**:28
RAYTHEON COMPANY **1**:128 *table*
RAYTOWN (Missouri)
map (39° 0′N 94° 28′W) **13**:476
RAYVILLE (Louisiana)
map (32° 28′N 91° 45′W) **12**:430
RAZA UNIDA
Chicano **4**:343
RAZGRAD (Bulgaria)
map (43° 32′N 26° 31′E) **3**:555
RAZIN, STENKA 16:98; **16**:354 *illus.*
RAZOR SHELL **13**:510 *illus.*
RCA *see* RADIO CORPORATION OF AMERICA
RCA BUILDING *see* ROCKEFELLER CENTER (New York City)
RDX 16:98
RE *see* AMON-RE (Egyptian god)
RÉ ISLAND
map (46° 12′N 1° 25′W) **8**:260
REACTANCE 16:98
impedance **11**:61
ohm **14**:363
REACTION, CHEMICAL 16:98–100 *bibliog., illus.*
catalyst **4**:198–199
chelation **4**:311
chemical energy **4**:315
chemical equilibrium and kinetics **4**:315–316
chemical symbolism and notation **4**:322
combustion **5**:131
decomposition **6**:76
dissociation (chemistry) **6**:198
Eigen, Manfred **7**:91
electrochemistry **7**:113
electrolysis **7**:114
endothermic and exothermic reactions **7**:171
environment, effects **16**:99–100
enzyme **7**:212–215
fermentation **8**:55
fire **8**:100–101
flash photolysis
Norrish, Ronald George Wreyford **14**:223
Porter, George **15**:444
flash point **8**:154
Friedel-Crafts reaction
Crafts, James Mason **5**:328
Friedel, Georges **8**:331
Hess's law **10**:151
hydrogenation **10**:341
hydrolysis **10**:342–343
inhibitor **11**:178
iodine **11**:239
ion exchange **11**:240
irreversible
Prigogine, Ilya **15**:537
luminescence **12**:458
metabolism **13**:325
nitration **14**:202
organic chemistry **14**:436
oxidation and reduction **14**:475–476; **16**:99
oxygen **14**:477
photochemistry **15**:258–259
physical change versus **16**:99
polymerization **15**:420
Prelog, Vladimir **15**:518
quantitative chemical analysis **16**:9
radiochemistry **16**:63
saponification **17**:73
Semenov, Nikolai Nikolayevich **17**:195
sodium **18**:32
stereochemistry **18**:258–259
stoichiometry **18**:276–277
synergism **18**:407
thermochemistry **19**:161–162
thermodynamics **19**:163–164
tracer, heavy water **10**:100
van't Hoff, Jacobus Henricus **19**:520
Waage, Peter **20**:3
weathering **20**:83
REACTION FORMATION (psychology)
defense mechanisms **6**:83
REACTION MECHANISMS
Heyrovský, Jaroslav **10**:155
REACTOR *see* NUCLEAR REACTOR
READ, DANIEL
fuging tune **8**:355
READ, SIR HERBERT 16:100 *bibliog.*
READ, MARY
piracy **15**:313 *illus.*
READ-ONLY MEMORY *see* ROM
READE, CHARLES 16:100
READER'S DIGEST (periodical)
Wallace, De Witt **20**:13
READING (England) **16**:100
map (51° 28′N 0° 59′W) **19**:403
READING (Massachusetts)
map (42° 31′N 71° 7′W) **13**:206
READING (Ohio)
map (39° 14′N 84° 27′W) **14**:357
READING (Pennsylvania) **16**:100
map (40° 20′N 75° 56′W) **15**:147
READING, RUFUS DANIEL ISAACS, 1ST MARQUESS OF 16:100 *bibliog.*
READING DISABILITY *see* DYSLEXIA
READING EDUCATION 16:100–101 *bibliog.*
blind
braille system **3**:442
dyslexia **6**:320
Initial Teaching Alphabet **11**:178
literacy and illiteracy **12**:368–370
McGuffey, William Holmes **13**:17
Montessori method **13**:554
primary education **15**:537–538
Right-to-Read Program **16**:222
READLYN (Iowa)
map (42° 42′N 92° 13′W) **11**:244
REAGAN (county in Texas)
map (31° 22′N 101° 30′W) **19**:129
REAGAN, RONALD 16:101–103 *bibliog., illus.*
advertising **1**:114
Energy, U.S. Department of **7**:173
fuel **8**:353
government regulation **9**:272
Haig, Alexander **10**:12
human rights **10**:298–299
income tax **11**:77
Iranian hostage crisis **11**:254
National Conservative Political Action Committee **14**:31
privatization **15**:558
United States, history of the **19**:461
REAGENTS
qualitative chemical analysis **16**:6
REAL (county in Texas)
map (29° 47′N 99° 47′W) **19**:129
REAL ESTATE *see* PROPERTY
REAL IMAGE *see* IMAGE, OPTICAL
REAL NUMBER 16:103 *bibliog.*
arithmetic **2**:158–159
Dedekind, Richard **6**:76–77
quantity specification, scalar **17**:106
rational number **16**:92
REAL TENNIS *see* TENNIS
REALISM (art) **16**:103 *bibliog., illus.*
American art and architecture **1**:334
Benton, Thomas Hart **3**:205–206
Brook, Alexander **3**:509
Chodowiecki, Daniel Nikolaus **4**:403
Close, Chuck **5**:65
Courbet, Gustave **5**:314
Dix, Otto **6**:206–207
Eakins, Thomas **7**:4–5
Fernández, Gregorio **8**:58
Flack, Audrey **8**:133
French art and architecture **8**:306
genre painting **9**:93
Glackens, William **9**:195
Hanson, Duane **10**:41
Henri, Robert **10**:122
Homer, Winslow **10**:213–214
Hopper, Edward **10**:232–233
Leibl, Wilhelm **12**:276
magic realism **13**:51
modern art **13**:495
painting **15**:22
Pearlstein, Philip **15**:128
photorealism **15**:274–275
Rockwell, Norman **16**:261
Rodin, Auguste **16**:267
Russian art and architecture **16**:362
Schadow, Gottfried **17**:116
sculpture **17**:165
Segal, George **17**:187–188
social realism **18**:13
Tooker, George **19**:236
verismo **19**:551
Werenskiold, Erik **20**:104
REALISM (film)
See also NEOREALISM
Kracauer, Siegfried **12**:126
REALISM (literature) **16**:104 *bibliog.*
See also NEOREALISM
American literature **1**:345
Aragon, Louis **2**:107
Arany, János **2**:109
Austrian literature **2**:354
Balzac, Honoré de **3**:57–58
De Forest, John William **6**:58
Defoe, Daniel **6**:83–84
drama **6**:261
Eliot, George **7**:139
Ghosts **9**:170
Howells, William Dean **10**:285
Keller, Gottfried **12**:37
naturalism **14**:49
O'Neill, Eugene **14**:389–390
Russian literature **16**:365–366
Sheldon, Edward **17**:250
Spanish literature **18**:159
REALISM (philosophy) **16**:104 *bibliog.*
Aquinas, Saint Thomas **2**:94–95
law **12**:243
metaphysics **13**:334
Moore, G. E. **13**:568
nihilism **14**:194
universals **19**:467
REALITY, ABSOLUTE
absolute **1**:62
Hegel, Georg Wilhelm Friedrich **10**:105
REAPER (farm machinery) **16**:104 *bibliog.*
McCormick, Cyrus Hall **13**:10
REAPPORTIONMENT *see* APPORTIONMENT
REARDAN (Washington)
map (47° 40′N 117° 53′W) **20**:35
REASON (ethics) *see* LOGOS; NATURAL LAW
REASON, AGE OF *see* ENLIGHTENMENT
REASONING 16:105 *bibliog.*
artificial intelligence **2**:221
logical reasoning **16**:105
deduction **6**:77
Hegel, Georg Wilhelm Friedrich **10**:105–106
induction **11**:151
logic **12**:395–397
problem solving **15**:559
RÉAUMUR, RENÉ ANTOINE FERCHAULT DE 16:105
Réaumur scale **16**:105
RÉAUMUR SCALE 16:105
Réaumur, René Antoine Ferchault de **16**:105
REBAY VON EHRENWIESEN, HILLA
Guggenheim Museum **9**:393
REBECCA (Biblical figure) **16**:105
REBECCA (book)
du Maurier, Daphne **6**:286

REBECCA OF SUNNYBROOK FARM (book)
Wiggin, Kate Douglas **20**:147
REBEL, THE (book)
Camus, Albert **4**:68
REBELLIONS OF 1837 **16**:105–106 *bibliog.*
Canada, history of **4**:82
Lafontaine, Sir Louis Hippolyte **12**:164
Mackenzie, William Lyon **13**:28
Papineau, Louis Joseph **15**:72
REBER, GROTE **16**:106 *bibliog.*
observatory, astronomical **14**:318
radio astronomy **16**:47; **16**:51
REBIRTH
See also TRANSMIGRATION OF SOULS
Buddhism **3**:539
dharma **6**:148
Hinduism **10**:170
nirvana **14**:201
REBMANN, JOHANNES
Kilimanjaro **12**:76
REBOP *see* BEBOP
REBUS **16**:106
writing systems, evolution of **20**:292–293
RECALL **16**:106 *bibliog.*
RECCARED, KING OF THE VISIGOTHS
Spain, history of **18**:144
RECCESVINTH, KING OF THE VISIGOTHS
Spain, history of **18**:144
RECEIVER (communications) **16**:106 *bibliog.*
electron tube **7**:123
heterodyne principle **10**:153–154
radio **16**:46
rectifier **16**:111
static **18**:234
telephone **19**:79
television **19**:576n
tuner **19**:333
video technology **19**:576L; **19**:576m
RECENT EPOCH **16**:106–107 *bibliog.*
Bronze Age **3**:505–506
climate and life **16**:107
geologic time **9**:103–105
geology and tectonics **16**:106–107
Iron Age **11**:272
Mesolithic Period **13**:314
Neolithic Period **14**:83–84
paleoclimatology **15**:32
prehistoric humans **16**:107
Quaternary Period **16**:15
RECEPTORS **10**:94 *illus.*
RECESSION **16**:107 *bibliog.*
business cycle **3**:588
economy, national **7**:50
Great Britain, history of **9**:318
stagflation **18**:211
RECIDIVISM
crime **5**:347
prison **15**:555
RECIFE (Brazil) **16**:107
map (8° 3′S 34° 54′W) **3**:460
RECIPROCAL-LATTICE CONCEPT
X-ray diffraction **20**:308
RECIPROCAL TRADE AGREEMENTS ACT (1934)
tariff acts **19**:37
RECITATIVE **16**:107–108 *bibliog.*
cantata **4**:115
Italian music **11**:318
Peking Opera **15**:136
RECK, HANS
Olduvai Gorge **14**:376
RECOILLESS RIFLE **16**:108 *illus.*
RECOMBINANT DNA *see* GENETIC ENGINEERING; NUCLEIC ACID; PROTEIN SYNTHESIS
RECOMBINATION (biology) *see* REPRODUCTION
RECOMMENDED DIETARY ALLOWANCES
nutrition, human **14**:306
RECONSTRUCTION **16**:108–110 *bibliog., illus.*
amendments to the Constitution **5**:221–222
15th Amendment **8**:74
14th Amendment **8**:254
13th Amendment **19**:170
black codes **3**:313–314
carpetbaggers **4**:164–165
Civil War, U.S. **5**:33
Davis, Henry Winter **6**:51
Fessenden, William Pitt **8**:63
Georgia **9**:118
Hayes, Rutherford B. **10**:83
historians
Dunning, William Archibald **6**:301
Johnson, Andrew **11**:430–431
Ku Klux Klan **12**:133
Liberal Republican party **12**:312
McCulloch, Hugh **13**:11
North Carolina **14**:246
political cartoons **16**:109–110 *illus.*; **19**:449 *illus.*
Scalawags **17**:106
South Carolina **18**:101
Stanton, Edwin M. **18**:220
Stevens, Thaddeus **18**:263
Sumner, Charles **18**:339–340
United States, history of the **19**:449–450
Wade, Benjamin Franklin **20**:4
RECONSTRUCTION ACTS *see* RECONSTRUCTION
RECONSTRUCTIVE SURGERY *see* PLASTIC SURGERY
RECORD (disk) *see* PHONOGRAPH
RECORD MANAGEMENT *see* DATA PROCESSING; INFORMATION STORAGE AND RETRIEVAL
RECORD PLAYER *see* PHONOGRAPH
RECORDER **16**:110 *bibliog., illus.*
RECORDING *see* SOUND RECORDING AND REPRODUCTION; VIDEO RECORDING
RECTANGLE **16**:110 *bibliog.*
square **18**:202
RECTIFIER **16**:110–111 *bibliog.*
See also DIODE; ZENER DIODE
Braun, Ferdinand **3**:458
bridge circuit **3**:484
semiconductor **17**:196–197
silicon-controlled rectifier **17**:305
Zener diode **20**:359
RECTOR (Arkansas)
map (36° 16′N 90° 17′W) **2**:166
RECTUM
drug administration **6**:275 *illus.*
intestine **11**:230–231
RECUEIL DE TRAITÉS DE DEVOTION
Louis IX, King of France **8**:267 *illus.*
RECYCLING OF MATERIALS **16**:111 *bibliog.*
aluminum **1**:319
paper **15**:69
pollution, environmental **15**:412
waste disposal systems **20**:47
RED ALGAE *see* ALGAE
RED BADGE OF COURAGE, THE (book) **16**:112
Crane, Stephen **5**:330
RED BANK (New Jersey)
map (40° 21′N 74° 3′W) **14**:129
RED BARON *see* RICHTHOFEN, MANFRED, FREIHERR VON
RED BAY (Alabama)
map (34° 27′N 88° 9′W) **1**:234
RED BAY (botany) *see* MAHOGANY
RED BAY (Newfoundland)
map (51° 44′N 56° 25′W) **14**:166
RED BEDS **16**:112
fossil record **8**:243
hematite **10**:117
Mesozoic Era **13**:322
paleoclimatology **15**:32–33
paleogeography **15**:38
Permian Period **15**:174
Triassic Period **19**:292–293
RED BLOOD CELL
anemia **1**:409–410
blood **3**:335–338
blood bank **3**:338
Cooley's anemia **5**:240
hemoglobin **10**:119
polycythemia **15**:418
Rh factor **16**:192
sickle-cell anemia **17**:293
RED BLUFF (California)
map (40° 11′N 122° 15′W) **4**:31
RED BLUFF RESERVOIR
map (31° 57′N 103° 56′W) **14**:136
RED BOILING SPRINGS (Tennessee)
map (36° 32′N 85° 51′W) **19**:104
RED BRANCH KNIGHTS
Irish literature **11**:268
RED BRIGADES
Moro, Aldo **13**:583
RED BUD (Illinois)
map (38° 13′N 89° 59′W) **11**:42
RED CLOUD (Indian chief) **16**:112 *bibliog.*
RED CLOUD (Nebraska)
map (40° 5′N 98° 32′W) **14**:70
RED CROSS **16**:112 *bibliog.*
Barton, Clara **3**:98
blood bank **3**:338
Dunant, Jean Henri **6**:298
lifesaving and water safety **12**:333
RED DATA BOOK **16**:112
RED DEER **6**:80 *illus.*
RED DEER (Alberta)
map (52° 16′N 113° 48′W) **1**:256
RED DEER RIVER (Alberta)
map (50° 56′N 109° 54′W) **1**:256
RED DEER RIVER (Saskatchewan)
map (52° 53′N 101° 1′W) **17**:81
RED DOUGLASES *see* DOUGLAS (family)
RED DWARF (astronomy) *see* FLARE STAR
RED EAGLE (Creek Indian) *see* WEATHERFORD, WILLIAM
RED-FIGURE VASES
Douris **6**:249
Epictetus (painter) **7**:218
Euphronius **7**:265
Euthymides **7**:311
Greek art **9**:339; **9**:342
Minoan art **13**:458
Oltos **14**:381
Onesimos **14**:390
RED GIANT (astronomy)
cluster, star **5**:72
star **18**:222 *illus.*
stellar evolution **18**:251 *illus.*
RED-HOT CATTAIL *see* CHENILLE PLANT
RED INDIAN LAKE
map (48° 40′N 56° 50′W) **14**:166
RED JACKET (Seneca Indian) **16**:112 *bibliog.*
Parker, Ely S. **15**:90
RED LAKE (county in Minnesota)
map (47° 52′N 96° 5′W) **13**:453
RED LAKE (Ontario)
map (51° 3′N 93° 49′W) **14**:393
RED LAKE FALLS (Minnesota)
map (47° 53′N 96° 16′W) **13**:453
RED LAKE RIVER
map (47° 55′N 97° 1′W) **13**:453
RED LAUAN **16**:112
RED LION (Pennsylvania)
map (39° 54′N 76° 36′W) **15**:147
RED LODGE (Montana)
map (45° 11′N 109° 15′W) **13**:547
RED MOUNTAIN PASS
map (37° 54′N 107° 43′W) **5**:116
RED OAK (Iowa)
map (41° 1′N 95° 14′W) **11**:244
RED OAK (Oklahoma)
map (34° 57′N 95° 5′W) **14**:368
RED-POINT *see* COLORPOINT SHORTHAIR CAT
RED RIVER (China) *see* YÜAN RIVER (China)
RED RIVER (river in Kentucky)
map (37° 51′N 84° 5′W) **12**:47
RED RIVER (county in Louisiana)
map (32° 5′N 93° 15′W) **12**:430
RED RIVER (county in Texas)
map (33° 35′N 95° 0′W) **19**:129
RED RIVER (United States) **16**:113
map (31° 0′N 91° 40′W) **13**:474
RED RIVER, NORTH FORK (river in Oklahoma)
map (34° 24′N 99° 14′W) **14**:368
RED RIVER REBELLION **16**:113 *bibliog.*
Canada, history of **4**:84
RED RIVER SETTLEMENT **16**:113 *bibliog.*
agriculture, history of **1**:192
Canada, history of **4**:82 *illus.*
Fraser, Simon **8**:287
Hudson's Bay Company **10**:290
Riel, Louis **16**:218
Ross, Alexander **16**:318
Selkirk, Thomas Douglas, 5th Earl of **17**:192
RED RIVER OF THE NORTH **16**:113
RED RIVER OF THE SOUTH *see* RED RIVER (United States)
RED RIVER WAR OF 1874–75
Indian Wars **11**:109–110 *map*
RED ROCK (British Columbia)
map (53° 39′N 122° 41′W) **3**:491
RED ROCK, LAKE
map (41° 30′N 93° 20′W) **11**:244
RED ROCK RIVER
map (44° 59′N 112° 52′W) **13**:547
RED SEA **16**:113–114 *map*
map (20° 0′N 38° 0′E) **1**:136
people
Beja **3**:172
rift valleys **16**:221
seas, gulfs, and bays
Aqaba, Gulf of **2**:92
Bab el-Mandeb **3**:5
RED SETTER *see* IRISH SETTER
RED SHIFT **16**:114 *illus.*
cosmology (astronomy) **5**:284
distance, astronomical **6**:200
Doppler effect **6**:241 *illus.*
extragalactic systems **7**:343–344
gamma-ray astronomy **9**:33
quasar **16**:15
relativity **16**:134–135
Schmidt, Maarten **17**:128
RED SHIRTS
Garibaldi, Giuseppe **9**:47
RED-SPOTTED NEWT **16**:114 *illus.*; **17**:30 *illus.*
RED SPRINGS (North Carolina)
map (34° 49′N 79° 11′W) **14**:242
RED AND THE BLACK, THE (book) **16**:112
Stendhal **18**:253
RED TIDE **16**:114–115 *bibliog.*
dinoflagellate **6**:179
RED VOLTA LAKE
map (8° 38′N 1° 40′W) **19**:472
RED WATER FEVER *see BABESIA*
RED WILLOW (county in Nebraska)
map (40° 10′N 100° 30′W) **14**:70
RED WING (Minnesota)
map (44° 34′N 92° 31′W) **13**:453
RED YÜAN RIVER
map (20° 17′N 106° 34′E) **4**:362
REDANG ISLAND
map (5° 47′N 103° 0′E) **13**:84
REDBUD **16**:115 *illus.*
REDCLOUD PEAK
map (37° 57′N 107° 25′W) **5**:116
REDDING (California)
map (40° 35′N 122° 24′W) **4**:31
REDDING, OTIS **16**:115 *bibliog.*
REDDISH KNOB MOUNTAIN
map (38° 25′N 79° 18′W) **19**:607
REDDY, NEELAM SANJIVA
India **11**:88
REDEMPTIONERS *see* INDENTURED SERVICE
REDEMPTORISTS
Alphonsus Liguori, Saint **1**:308
REDERIJKERS (literary groups) **16**:115
Vondel, Joost van den **19**:634
REDEYE MISSILE **2**:56 *illus.*
REDFIELD (Iowa)
map (41° 35′N 94° 12′W) **11**:244
REDFIELD (South Dakota)
map (44° 53′N 98° 31′W) **18**:103
REDFIELD, ROBERT **16**:115
REDFORD (Texas)
map (29° 47′N 104° 10′W) **19**:129
REDFORD, ROBERT **16**:115
REDGRAVE (family) **16**:115 *bibliog.*
REDGRAVE, LYNN
Redgrave (family) **16**:115
REDGRAVE, SIR MICHAEL
Redgrave (family) **16**:115
REDGRAVE, VANESSA
Redgrave (family) **16**:115
REDI, FRANCESCO
spontaneous generation **18**:194
REDKEY (Indiana)
map (40° 21′N 85° 9′W) **11**:111
REDLANDS, UNIVERSITY OF **16**:115
REDLINING *see* MORTGAGE
REDMOND (Oregon)
map (44° 17′N 121° 11′W) **14**:427
REDMOND (Utah)
map (39° 0′N 111° 52′W) **19**:492
REDMOND (Washington)
map (47° 40′N 122° 7′W) **20**:35
REDMOND, JOHN **16**:115 *bibliog.*
REDON, ODILON **16**:116 *bibliog., illus.*
Cyclops **16**:116 *illus.*; **18**:403 *illus.*
REDONDA (Leeward Islands)
Antigua and Barbuda **2**:62
REDONDO BEACH (California)
map (33° 51′N 118° 23′W) **4**:31
REDPOLL
beak **3**:289 *illus.*
REDSTART **16**:116 *illus.*
REDSTONE **16**:116–117 *bibliog.*; **16**:256 *illus.*
Jupiter (rocket) **11**:474
Mercury program **13**:308
von Braun, Wernher **19**:633
REDSTONE (British Columbia)
map (52° 8′N 123° 42′W) **3**:491
REDUCED INSTRUCTION SET COMPUTER *see* RISC
REDUCTION *see* OXIDATION AND REDUCTION
REDUCTION CELL
aluminum smelting process **1**:317
REDWATER (Alberta)
map (53° 57′N 113° 6′W) **1**:256
REDWOOD **16**:117 *bibliog., illus.*
conifer **5**:189–190
dawn redwood **6**:54
Redwood National Park **16**:117
REDWOOD (county in Minnesota)
map (44° 25′N 95° 13′W) **13**:453
REDWOOD CITY (California)
map (37° 29′N 122° 13′W) **4**:31
REDWOOD FALLS (Minnesota)
map (44° 32′N 95° 7′W) **13**:453

REDWOOD NATIONAL PARK **14**:38–39 *map, table*; **16**:117
REDWOOD VALLEY (California)
map (39° 16′N 123° 12′W) **4**:31
REE, LAKE
map (53° 35′N 8° 0′W) **11**:258
REED (botany) **16**:117
cattail **4**:214
REED, SIR CAROL **16**:117–118
REED, ISHMAEL **16**:118 *bibliog.*
REED, JOHN **16**:118 *bibliog.*
REED, THOMAS B. **16**:118 *bibliog.*
REED, WALTER **16**:118 *bibliog.*
yellow fever **20**:322
REED CITY (Michigan)
map (43° 53′N 85° 31′W) **13**:377
REED INSTRUMENTS
See also WIND INSTRUMENTS (music)
musical instruments **13**:676–677 *illus.*
REED ORGAN **16**:118 *bibliog.*
REEDBIRD *see* BOBOLINK
REEDER (North Dakota)
map (46° 6′N 102° 57′W) **14**:248
REEDLEY (California)
map (36° 36′N 119° 27′W) **4**:31
REEDS PEAK
map (33° 9′N 107° 51′W) **14**:136
REEDSBURG (Wisconsin)
map (43° 32′N 90° 0′W) **20**:185
REEDSPORT (Oregon)
map (43° 42′N 124° 6′W) **14**:427
REEDSVILLE (Wisconsin)
map (44° 9′N 87° 57′W) **20**:185
REEDY RIVER
map (34° 21′N 82° 6′W) **18**:98
REEF, CORAL *see* CORAL REEF
REEL (dance)
folk dance **8**:200 *illus.*
REESE (Michigan)
map (43° 27′N 83° 42′W) **13**:377
REESE RIVER
map (40° 39′N 116° 54′W) **14**:111
REEVE, TAPPING **16**:118
REEVES (county in Texas)
map (31° 15′N 103° 38′W) **19**:129
REFERENDUM AND INITIATIVE **16**:118–119 *bibliog.*
plebiscite **15**:364
REFINING, METAL **16**:119
gold **9**:227 *illus.*
iron and steel industry **11**:274
silver **17**:312
REFINING PROCESS *see* PETROLEUM INDUSTRY
REFLECTION **16**:119 *bibliog.*
albedo **1**:252
aluminum **1**:316
fiber optics **8**:68–69
gems **9**:73
interference **11**:209
light **12**:334 *illus.*
mirror **13**:464–465 *illus.*
optics **14**:410 *illus.*
parabola **15**:74
polarized light **15**:394
rainbow **16**:77
refraction **16**:124
sound and acoustics **18**:73
types **16**:119
REFLECTIONS ON THE REVOLUTION IN FRANCE (book) **16**:119 *bibliog.*
REFLECTOR *see* TELESCOPE
REFLEX **16**:119–120 *bibliog., illus.*
Bekhterev, Vladimir Mikhailovich **3**:173
biopotential **3**:276
Lashley, Karl S. **12**:213
nervous system **14**:92–95
Pavlov, Ivan Petrovich **15**:120
reflex sequence **16**:120 *illus.*
senses **17**:204
spinal cord **18**:184
REFORM (Alabama)
map (33° 23′N 88° 1′W) **1**:234
REFORM ACTS **16**:120–121 *bibliog.*
borough **3**:404
Disraeli, Benjamin, 1st Earl of Beaconsfield **6**:197–198
Europe, history of **7**:292
Grey, Charles Grey, 2d Earl **9**:360
Liberal parties **12**:311
William IV, King of England, Scotland, and Ireland **20**:156
REFORMATION **16**:121–123 *bibliog., illus., map*
Anabaptists **16**:123
Augsburg, Peace of **2**:320
Bucer, Martin **3**:532
Bullinger, Heinrich **3**:561
Calvin, John **4**:48–49; **16**:122–123
causes **16**:121–122
censorship **4**:247
Charles V, Holy Roman Emperor **4**:295
Cranmer, Thomas **5**:331–332
divorce **6**:205
Eck, Johann **7**:39
education **7**:61
England **16**:123
Europe, history of **7**:287
Europe: Reformation to 1580 **16**:121 *map*
Farel, Guillaume **8**:23
Fisher, Saint John **8**:122
Gardner, Stephen **9**:44
Germany, history of **9**:151
Great Britain, history of **9**:313
Henry VIII, King of England **10**:127
Holy Roman Empire **10**:211
hymn **10**:346
iconography **11**:22
Ireland, history of **11**:263
Karlstadt **12**:28
Knox, John **12**:102–103
Latimer, Hugh **12**:216
Luther, Martin **12**:468–469; **16**:122
Melanchthon, Philipp **13**:284
Moravian Church **13**:574–575
Münzer, Thomas **13**:644
Oecolampadius, Johannes **14**:351
papacy **15**:65
Philip of Hesse **15**:232
Protestantism **15**:576–577
Scandinavia, history of **17**:109
Schwenkfeld von Ossig, Kaspar **17**:140
Scotland **17**:151
Servetus, Michael **17**:211
Socinianism **18**:26
Socinus, Laelius **18**:26
Tyndale, William **19**:362
Vermigli, Pietro Martire **19**:553
Wittenberg (East Germany) **20**:193
women in society **20**:202
Zwingli, Ulrich **16**:122; **20**:384
REFORMED CHURCH IN AMERICA **16**:123 *bibliog.*
REFORMED CHURCHES **16**:123
Calvinism **4**:49
Heidelberg Catechism **4**:202
Reformed Church in America **16**:123
REFRACTION **16**:123–124 *bibliog., illus.*
atmospheric refraction **2**:304
electromagnetic radiation **7**:117
fiber optics **8**:68–69
gems **9**:73
index of refraction **11**:79
light refraction **12**:335
mirage **13**:463
optical mineralogy **14**:408–409
optics **14**:410–411 *illus.*
polarized light **15**:394
prism (physics) **15**:554
Snell, Willebrord van Roijen **18**:3
sound and acoustics **18**:73
telescope **19**:80–81
REFRACTORY MATERIALS **16**:124 *bibliog.*
See also FIREBRICK
clay minerals **5**:46
cristobalite **5**:351
sillimanite **17**:309
REFRIGERATION **16**:124–125 *bibliog., illus.*
condenser **5**:172
food preservation **8**:212
heat pump **10**:98–99
Joule-Thomson effect **11**:453
refrigerants **16**:125
ammonia **1**:372
fluorine **8**:187–188
neon **14**:85
organic chemistry **14**:439
thermoelectricity **19**:165
REFUGE COVE (British Columbia)
map (50° 7′N 124° 50′W) **3**:491
REFUGEE **16**:125–126 *bibliog.*
alien **1**:293
Central America
Miskito **13**:466
Cuba **5**:380; **16**:125
Florida **8**:176
Hispanic Americans **10**:179
Miami **13**:370
immigration **11**:56
Palestinian **16**:125
Jordan **11**:448; **11**:450
Lebanon **12**:264; **12**:267
Syria **18**:412
West Bank **20**:108
Refugees, Office of the United Nations High Commissioner for **16**:126
right of asylum **16**:222
sanctuary **17**:59
Somalia **18**:61
Southeast Asian **16**:125
Kampuchea (Cambodia) **12**:13
Oriental Americans **14**:443
Vietnam War **19**:590–591 *illus.*
REFUGEES, FREEDMEN, AND ABANDONED LANDS, BUREAU OF *see* FREEDMEN'S BUREAU
REFUGEES, OFFICE OF THE UNITED NATIONS HIGH COMMISSIONER FOR **16**:126
REFUGIO (Texas)
map (28° 18′N 97° 17′W) **19**:129
REFUGIO (county in Texas)
map (28° 17′N 97° 13′W) **19**:129
REFUSE AND REFUSE DISPOSAL *see* WASTE DISPOSAL SYSTEMS
REGAL FRITILLARY BUTTERFLY **3**:597 *illus.*
butterflies and moths **3**:595
REGAN, DONALD THOMAS **16**:126
REGENCY **16**:126 *bibliog.*
REGENCY STYLE **16**:126 *bibliog., illus.*
Georgian style **9**:119
Greek Revival **9**:346
Regency **16**:126
rococo style **16**:263
Royal Pavilion at Brighton **16**:330–331 *illus.*
styles of Louis XIII-XVI **18**:311
REGENERATION **16**:126–128 *bibliog., illus.*
cloning **5**:64
echinoderm **7**:39
growth **9**:379
invertebrate **11**:237
planaria **15**:326
REGENSBURG (West Germany) **16**:128
map (49° 1′N 12° 6′E) **9**:140
REGENT **16**:128
REGENT (North Dakota)
map (46° 25′N 102° 33′W) **14**:248
REGENT'S PARK (London)
Nash, John **14**:24
REGENT'S PARK COLLEGE (Oxford University) **14**:474
REGER, MAX **16**:128 *bibliog.*
REGGAE **16**:128
REGGIO DI CALABRIA (Italy) **16**:128
map (38° 7′N 15° 39′E) **11**:321
REGGIO NELL'EMILIA (Italy) **16**:128
REGIMENT **16**:128
RÉGINA (French Guiana)
map (4° 19′N 52° 8′W) **8**:311
REGINA (Saskatchewan) **16**:128–129; **17**:82 *illus.*
map (50° 25′N 104° 39′W) **17**:81
REGINA BEACH (Saskatchewan)
map (50° 47′N 105° 0′W) **17**:81
REGIOMONTANUS **16**:129 *bibliog.*
REGIONAL ENTERITIS *see* COLITIS
REGIONAL GEOGRAPHY **9**:101; **9**:103
Mackinder, Sir Halford John **13**:29
REGIONAL THEATER *see* REPERTORY THEATER
REGNAULT, HENRI VICTOR **16**:129
REGOLITH **16**:129
REGRESSION (statistics) *see* CORRELATION AND REGRESSION
REGRESSION, MARINE **16**:129
plate tectonics **15**:354
REGULATING ACT OF 1773
East India Company, British **7**:31
REGULATION, GOVERNMENT *see* GOVERNMENT REGULATION
REGULATORS **16**:129 *bibliog.*
REGULATORY AGENCIES *see* GOVERNMENT REGULATION
REGULUS, MARCUS ATILIUS **16**:129
Punic Wars **15**:624
REHABILITATION OF CRIMINALS
prison **15**:554–555
REHABILITATION MEDICINE **16**:129–130 *bibliog.*
Luria, Aleksandr Romanovich **12**:466
occupational therapy **14**:321
physical therapy **15**:280
sports medicine **18**:197–198
REHNQUIST, WILLIAM **16**:130; **18**:355 *illus.*
REHOBOAM, KING OF ISRAEL **16**:130
REHOBOTH BAY
map (38° 40′N 75° 6′W) **6**:88
REHOBOTH BEACH (Delaware)
map (38° 43′N 75° 5′W) **6**:88
REHOVOTH (Israel)
map (31° 54′N 34° 49′E) **11**:302
REICH, STEVE **16**:130 *bibliog.*
REICH, WILHELM **16**:130 *bibliog.*
REICHSBANK
Schacht, Hjalmar **17**:116
REICHSTAG **16**:130 *bibliog.*
Germany, history of **9**:153–154
Hitler, Adolf **10**:187
REICHSTEIN, TADEUS
chemistry, history of **4**:329
Hench, Philip Showalter **10**:121
Kendall, Edward **12**:41
REID, GEORGE
Canadian art and architecture **4**:89
REID, THOMAS **16**:130–131 *bibliog.*
REID, WHITELAW **16**:131
REIDSVILLE (Georgia)
map (32° 6′N 82° 7′W) **9**:114
REIDSVILLE (North Carolina)
map (36° 21′N 79° 40′W) **14**:242
REIDY, ALFONSO EDUARDO
Latin American art and architecture **12**:228
REIGATE (England)
map (51° 14′N 0° 13′W) **19**:403
REIGN OF TERROR *see* FRENCH REVOLUTION
REIMARUS, HERMANN SAMUEL **16**:131
REIMS (France) **16**:131
Champagne **4**:276
map (49° 15′N 4° 2′E) **8**:260
REIMS CATHEDRAL **9**:257 *illus.*; **9**:259–260 *illus.*; **16**:131 *bibliog.*
Villard de Honnecourt **19**:598
REINAGLE, PHILIP
Ramsay, Allan **16**:81
REINBECK (Iowa)
map (42° 19′N 92° 36′W) **11**:244
REINCARNATION *see* REBIRTH; TRANSMIGRATION OF SOULS
REINDEER **6**:80 *illus.*; **8**:98 *illus.*; **16**:131 *bibliog., illus.*
animal husbandry **2**:24
caribou **4**:149
Chukchi **4**:422
deer **6**:79; **6**:81
Hamburgian **10**:27
Lapps **12**:206
Tungus **19**:334
REINDEER LAKE
map (57° 15′N 102° 40′W) **17**:81
REINER, CARL
Brooks, Mel **3**:511
REINER, MAX *see* CALDWELL, TAYLOR
REINES, FREDERICK
neutrino **14**:108
REINFORCEMENT
learning theory **12**:260–261
Guthrie, Edwin Ray **9**:409
social psychology **18**:13
motivation **13**:610
REINHARDT, AD **16**:132 *bibliog.*
REINHARDT, DJANGO **16**:132 *bibliog.*
REINHARDT, MAX **16**:132 *bibliog.*
Deutsches Theater **6**:136–137
theater, history of the **19**:150
theatricalism **19**:154
REINICKE, PETER
rhinoceros **16**:264 *illus.*
REINIGER, LOTTE
animation **2**:29
REINKEN, JAN
German and Austrian music **9**:130
REISNER, GEORGE ANDREW
salvage archaeology **17**:40
REISTERSTOWN (Maryland)
map (39° 28′N 76° 50′W) **13**:188
REISZ, KAREL
film, history of **8**:86
RELAPSING FEVER **16**:132
spirochete **18**:189
RELATIVE DENSITY
specific gravity **18**:168
RELATIVISM
ethics **7**:251
RELATIVISTIC MECHANICS *see* RELATIVITY
RELATIVITY **16**:132–137 *bibliog., illus.*
dynamics **6**:319
Einstein, Albert **7**:93
Einstein equivalence principle (EPP) **16**:134; **16**:135
ether (physics) **7**:250
Fitzgerald, George Francis **8**:131; **16**:134
Fitzgerald-Lorentz contraction **8**:131; **16**:134
general relativity **16**:134–136
cosmology **5**:284–289
Dicke, Robert **6**:156
Eddington, Sir Arthur **7**:55
gravitation **9**:305
gravitational collapse **9**:305
gravitational lens **9**:305–306
gravitational waves **9**:306
Hawking, Stephen William **10**:77
Minkowski, Hermann **13**:451
Mössbauer, Rudolf Ludwig **13**:605

RELATIVITY (cont.)
Schwarzschild, Karl **17**:139
Sitter, Willem de **17**:330
unified field theory **19**:385–386
Whitehead, Alfred North **20**:139
world line **20**:219
geometric models
Gödel, Kurt **9**:220
history **16**:132–133
laws of relativistic electrodynamics
law, physical **12**:248
mass (physics) **13**:201
Pauli, Wolfgang **15**:118–119
physics **15**:281
red shift **16**:114
Royal Greenwich Observatory **16**:330
scope of relativity **16**:132–133
space-time continuum **18**:137
space-time curvature **16**:133–134
special relativity **16**:133–134
Carathéodory, Constantin **4**:131
clock paradox **5**:61
microscopic physics **16**:132
Minkowsky space-time **16**:134
Poincaré, Henri **15**:380
Tomonaga, Sin-itiro **19**:232
time (physics) **19**:201
RELAXIN
endocrine system, diseases of the **7**:169
RELAY (artificial satellite) **16**:137
communications satellite **5**:144–145
RELAY (control device) **16**:137 *bibliog.*
circuit, electric **4**:436–438
electromagnet **7**:115
solenoid **18**:53
RELAY RACE
swimming **18**:392
track and field **19**:260
RELIANCE (Wyoming)
map (41° 40′N 109° 12′W) **20**:301
RELICS
reliquary **16**:143–144
Shroud of Turin **17**:288
RELIGION **16**:137–141 *bibliog., illus., map*
See also RITES AND OBSERVANCES; names of specific writers or theorists, e.g., BUBER, MARTIN; LUTHER, MARTIN; etc.
agnosticism **1**:187
Anabaptists **1**:387
ancestor worship **1**:398–399
animal rights **2**:28
antinomianism **2**:64
Arminianism **2**:173
asceticism **2**:228
atheism **2**:288–289
Babism **3**:7
Batak **3**:121
Bene Israel **3**:196
Berbers **3**:207
black Americans **3**:307; **3**:312
Bollandists **3**:370
Book of Hours **3**:386
Calvinism **4**:49
camp meetings **4**:63
catechism **4**:202
cathedrals and churches **4**:204–208
charismatic movement **4**:288–289
Christian Endeavor **4**:411
Christian Socialism **4**:412
church **4**:423
church and state **4**:424–425
civilization **5**:34
Colorado (American Indians) **5**:120
Counter-Reformation **5**:310–311
deism **6**:86
dietary laws **6**:164–165
dualism **6**:287
ecumenical movement **7**:54
Egypt, ancient **7**:84–85 *illus.*
Erastianism **7**:227
eschatology **7**:237
ethics **7**:251
evangelicalism **7**:312
excommunication **7**:327
fasting **8**:33
flagellants **8**:149
freedom of religion **8**:297
freemasonry **8**:299–300
fund raising **8**:360
fundamentalism **8**:363
funeral customs **8**:363–364
Gallicanism **9**:19
gnosticism **9**:213–214
God **9**:217–219
Golden Bough, The **9**:231
Great Awakening **9**:308
Hasideans **10**:66
heaven **10**:100
hell **10**:113
heresy **10**:141–142
Hinduism **10**:169–173
Huguenots **10**:294–295
iconoclasm **11**:20–21
ideology **11**:30
India, history of **11**:88–93
Islam **11**:288–293
Jefferson, Thomas **11**:391
Jesus Christ **11**:403–406
Kierkegaard, Søren **12**:75
and magic **13**:49–50
Maryknoll Missioners **13**:187
Middle East, history of the **13**:401
millenarianism **13**:426–427
modernism (theology) **13**:498
monasticism **13**:521
Monophysitism **13**:537
monotheism **13**:540
monothelitism **13**:540
montanism **13**:551
mysticism **13**:693
mythology **13**:694–704
National Council of Churches **14**:31
Nonconformists **14**:216
Oneida Community **14**:389
Oxford Movement **14**:475
pantheism **15**:61
phallic worship **15**:219
philosophy **15**:242–243
pietism **15**:297–298
polytheism **15**:422
primitive religion **15**:543–546
psychology
Jung, Carl **11**:467
purification, rites of **15**:629
rationalism **16**:93
religions of the world **16**:140 *map*
Adventists **1**:111
Amana Society **1**:321
Anglican communion **1**:416
Armenian church **2**:172–173
Australia, Church of England in **2**:342
Baha'i **3**:23
Baptists **3**:73–74
Black Muslims **3**:317–318
Brahmo Samaj **3**:440
Brethren **3**:474
Buddhism **3**:539–543
Canada, Anglican Church of **4**:87
Canada, United Church of **4**:87
Christadelphians **4**:411
Christian Churches and Churches of Christ **4**:411
Christian Science **4**:411–412
Christianity **4**:412–414
Church of the Nazarene **4**:424
Churches of Christ **4**:425
Confucianism **5**:179–180
Congregationalism **5**:184
Coptic Church **5**:255
Disciples of Christ **6**:188
Doukhobors **6**:249
Druzes **6**:283
Eastern Rite churches **7**:34
Ebionites **7**:35–36
England, Church of **7**:181
Episcopal Church **7**:221
Essenes **7**:244
Ethical Culture **7**:250
Evangelical United Brethren Church **7**:312
Falashas **8**:11–12
Familists **8**:15
Friends, Society of **8**:332–333
Hasidism **10**:66
Hinduism **10**:170
Hutterian Brethren **10**:323
Islam **11**:288–293
Ismailis **11**:298
Jacobite church **11**:346
Jainism **11**:349–350
Jehovah's Witnesses **11**:394
Judaism **11**:458–463
Karaites **12**:26
Lutheranism **12**:469–470
Malabar Christians **13**:78
Mandaeans **13**:110
Mennonites **13**:298–299
Methodism **13**:344
Mithraism **13**:484–485
Moral Re-armament **13**:573
Moravian Church **13**:574–575
Mormonism **13**:581–582
Native American Church **14**:47
Nestorian church **14**:97
New Jerusalem, Church of the **14**:134
New Zealand, Church of the Province of **14**:161
Old Believers **14**:374
Old Catholics **14**:374
Orthodox church **14**:449–450
Parsis **15**:98
Pentecostalism **15**:155
Plymouth Brethren **15**:374
Presbyterianism **15**:519–520
Protestantism **15**:576–577
Pure Land Buddhism **15**:629
Puritanism **15**:630
Reformed Church in America **16**:123
Reformed churches **16**:123
Remonstrants **16**:146
Roman Catholic church **16**:277–278
Salvation Army **17**:40
Scientology **17**:146
Scotland, Church of **17**:152–153
Scotland, Free Church of **17**:153
Shakers **17**:235–236
Shiites **17**:261
Shinto **17**:262–263
Sikhs **17**:302
Soka-gakkai **18**:39
Sunnites **18**:348
Tantra **19**:25
Taoism **19**:28–29
Tibetan Buddhism **19**:190–191
Unitarian Universalist Association **19**:399
Unitarianism **19**:399–400
United Church of Christ **19**:401
Wahhabism **20**:7
Waldenses **20**:9
Zen Buddhism **20**:358–359
Zoroastrianism **20**:379–380
religious cults **16**:142–143
religious orders **16**:143
Renaissance **16**:149
resurrection **16**:183
revelation **16**:184–185
revivalism **16**:186–187
Rousseau, Jean Jacques **16**:327
sacrifice **17**:8
salvation **17**:40
satanism **17**:84
Schism, Great **17**:122
Social Gospel **18**:12
Socinianism **18**:26
sociology of
Weber, Max (sociologist) **20**:87
soul **18**:70
South India, Church of **18**:106
Sufism **18**:327
Sun worship **18**:345
Sunday school **18**:347
theism **19**:155
theological seminaries **19**:157
theology **19**:157–158
theosophy **19**:159–160
tithe **19**:212
ultramontanism **19**:377
United States, history of the **19**:438 *illus.*
universalism **19**:467
vestments **19**:565
Volunteers of America **19**:632–633
World Council of Churches **20**:218
RELIGION, PRIMITIVE *see* PRIMITIVE RELIGION
RELIGION, WARS OF **16**:141 *bibliog.*
Coligny, Gaspard de, Seigneur de Châtillon **5**:101–102
Europe, history of **7**:287–288
France, history of **8**:268
Henry III, King of France **10**:127
Henry IV, King of France **10**:128
Huguenots **10**:294–295
Nantes, Edict of **14**:13
Saint Bartholomew's Day Massacre **17**:16
Thirty Years' War **19**:170–172
RELIGIOUS BROADCASTING **16**:141–142 *bibliog.*
RELIGIOUS CULTS **16**:142–143 *bibliog., illus.*
Afro-American cults **1**:178
cargo cults **4**:147
Early Christian art and architecture **7**:9–11
Eleusinian mysteries **7**:134–135
Hare Krishna **10**:49
Isis **11**:288
Jonestown (Guyana) **11**:444
Moon, Sun Myung **13**:566
mother goddess **13**:606–607
mystery cults **13**:693
Orpheus **14**:448
Rastafarians **16**:91
Roman art and architecture **16**:275
Scientology **17**:146
Thugs **19**:184
voodoo **19**:634–635
RELIGIOUS DRAMA *see* DRAMA; PASSION PLAY
RELIGIOUS FREEDOM *see* FREEDOM OF RELIGION
RELIGIOUS MUSIC *see* CHURCH MUSIC
RELIGIOUS ORDERS **16**:143 *bibliog.*
Augustinians **2**:321
Benedictines **3**:197–198
Carmelites **4**:153
John of the Cross, Saint **11**:424
Carthusians **4**:174
celibacy **4**:231
Christian Brothers
John Baptist de la Salle, Saint **11**:424
Cistercians **4**:445–446
convent **5**:232–233
Dominicans **6**:234
Francis of Assisi, Saint **8**:274
Franciscans **8**:276–277; **16**:143
John XXII, Pope **11**:428
Honorius III, Pope **10**:224
Hospitalers **10**:258–259
Jesuits **11**:402–403; **16**:143
military
chivalry **4**:399
Missionaries of Charity
Teresa, Mother **19**:115
Missionary Sisters of the Sacred Heart
Cabrini, Saint Frances Xavier **4**:8
monasticism **13**:521
nun **14**:296
Passionist order
Paul of the Cross, Saint **15**:118
Roman Catholic Church **16**:277
Templars **19**:93–94
Teutonic Knights **19**:127–128
Trappists **19**:284
women in society **20**:202; **20**:203
RELIQUARY **16**:143–144 *bibliog.*
French silver-gilt (c.1340) **13**:519 *illus.*
gold and silver work **9**:229 *illus.*
Gothic art and architecture **9**:260
stupa **18**:308
RELLI, CONRAD MARCA- *see* MARCA-RELLI, CONRAD
RELOCATION CAMP *see* CONCENTRATION CAMP
REM (Rapid Eye Movement) SLEEP *see* SLEEP
REMADA (Tunisia)
climate **19**:336 *table*
REMANSO (Brazil)
map (9° 41′S 42° 4′W) **3**:460
REMARQUE, ERICH MARIA **16**:144 *illus.*
All Quiet on the Western Front **1**:297
REMBRANDT **16**:144–145 *bibliog., illus.*
Aristotle Contemplating the Bust of Homer **16**:144 *illus.*
drawing **6**:264–265 *illus.*
Dutch art and architecture **6**:311
graphic arts **9**:292
impasto **11**:60
Leiden (Netherlands) **12**:277
Maes, Nicolaes **13**:45
The Night Watch **6**:310 *illus.*
Seghers, Hercules **17**:188
Self Portrait **15**:21 *illus.*; **15**:447 *illus.*; **16**:144 *illus.*
The Three Crosses **9**:293 *illus.*
Woman Bathing in a Stream **2**:197 *illus.*
REMEDIAL EDUCATION *see* COMPENSATORY EDUCATION; SPECIAL EDUCATION
REMEK, VLADIMIR **16**:145 *bibliog.*
REMEMBRANCE OF THINGS PAST (book) **16**:145 *bibliog.*
Proust, Marcel **15**:582–583
REMER (Minnesota)
map (47° 3′N 93° 55′W) **13**:453
REMINGTON (Indiana)
map (40° 46′N 87° 9′W) **11**:111
REMINGTON (Virginia)
map (38° 32′N 77° 49′W) **19**:607
REMINGTON, ELIPHLET AND SONS
typewriter **19**:365
REMINGTON, FREDERIC **16**:145–146 *bibliog., illus.*
fur trappers **8**:342 *illus.*
Trooper of the Plains **1**:331 *illus.*; **16**:146 *illus.*
RÉMIRE (French Guiana)
map (4° 53′N 52° 17′W) **8**:311
REMIZOV, ALEKSEI MIKHAILOVICH **16**:146
REMOJADAS (Mexico) **16**:146 *bibliog.*
REMONSTRANCE, RIGHT OF
parlement **15**:92
REMONSTRANTS **16**:146 *bibliog.*
REMORA **16**:146–147 *illus.*
shark **17**:244
REMOTE CONTROL *see* AUTOMATION; FEEDBACK; SERVOMECHANISM

REMOTE SENSING 16:147 *bibliog., illus.*
aerial photography 1:119–120
REMSCHELD (Germany, East and West)
map (51° 11′N 7° 11′E) 9:140
REMUS (legendary figure) *see* ROMULUS AND REMUS
REMUS (Michigan)
map (43° 36′N 85° 9′W) 13:377
RENAISSANCE 16:147–149 *bibliog., illus.*
art *see* RENAISSANCE ART AND ARCHITECTURE
biography 3:263
Buchanan, George 3:532
chair 4:269 *illus.*
cooking 5:238 *illus.*
costume 5:295–297 *illus.*
jewelry 11:410 *illus.*
dance
dance, social 6:29
Ebreo, Guglielmo 7:36
education 7:60–61
humanities, education in the 10:300
engineering 7:177
Europe, history of 7:286–287
history 10:184
humanism 10:299
Italy 16:148–149
banking systems 3:68–69 *illus.*
Borgia (family) 3:399
Castiglione, Baldassare, Conte 4:188
Italy, history of 11:329
Medici (family) 13:265
Savonarola, Girolamo 17:101
Sforza, Ludovico 17:233
literature *see* RENAISSANCE LITERATURE
logic 12:395–396
maps and mapmaking 13:139 *illus.*
masque 13:200
mathematics
Cardano, Gerolamo 4:143
medicine 13:269 *illus.*
music *see* RENAISSANCE MUSIC
philosophy
Abravanel, Judah 1:61
Bruno, Giordano 3:525
Ficino, Marsilio 8:70
Neoplatonism 14:85
Pico della Mirandola, Giovanni, Conte 15:294
Platonic tradition 15:361
postal services 15:459
printing 15:550 *illus.*
Savonarola, Girolamo 17:101
science
Agricola, Georgius 1:188
Brahe, Tycho 3:439–440
Copernicus, Nicolaus 5:250
Galileo Galilei 9:15
Kepler, Johannes 12:57–58
Peurbach, Georg von 15:216
Vesalius, Andreas 19:564
scientific associations 17:144
technology, history of 19:65
theater *see* THEATER, HISTORY OF THE—1400–1600 Renaissance
weapons 20:74–75
women in society 20:202
RENAISSANCE ART AND ARCHITECTURE 2:194–197; 16:149–155 *bibliog., illus.*
architecture 2:134
art collectors and patrons 2:203–204
art criticism 2:207
attic 2:314
Austria
Austrian art and architecture 2:353
bas-relief 3:100
Belgium
Campin, Robert 4:66–67
Eyck, Jan van 7:347–348
Goes, Hugo van der 9:223
Memling, Hans 13:290
Weyden, Rogier van der 20:119
bridge (engineering) 3:480
bronzes 3:507
calligraphy 4:42–43 *illus., illus.*
cassone 8:376 *illus.*
cathedrals and churches 4:206–207
château 4:302
dome 6:229–230 *illus.*
drawing 6:264
English art and architecture 7:184
Europe, history of 7:286–287 *illus.*
France 16:154–155
Chambord, Château de 4:275
Chenonceaux, Château de 4:330–331
Clouet (family) 5:68–69
Cousin, Jean 5:317
Delorme, Philibert 6:94
Fontainebleau, school of 8:205–206
Fouquet, Jean 8:252
French art and architecture 8:305
Goujon, Jean 9:265
Le Nôtre, André 12:255
furniture 8:375–376
Germany 16:154
Burgkmair, Hans, the Elder 3:569
Dürer, Albrecht 6:304–305
Flötner, Peter 8:177
German art and architecture 9:125–126
Grünewald, Matthias 9:382–382
Holbein, Hans, the Younger 10:200–201
Schongauer, Martin 17:133
gold and silver work 9:229–230
golden section 9:232
history
Berenson, Bernard 3:208
Gombrich, Sir Ernst H. 9:241
Hartt, Frederick 10:63
Vasari, Giorgio 19:525
Wittkower, Rudolf 20:194
house (in Western architecture) 10:267
iconography 11:22
interior design 11:212
Italy 16:149–153
Alberti, Leon Battista 1:259
Andrea del Sarto 1:407
Antonello da Messina 2:69–70
Bartolommeo, Fra 3:98
Bassano (family) 3:117–118
Bellini (family) 3:188–189
Bologna, Giovanni da 3:370–371
Botticelli, Sandro 3:417–418
Bramante, Donato 3:451–452
Briosco, Andrea 3:487
Brunelleschi, Filippo 3:524–525
Carpaccio, Vittore 4:163
Cellini, Benvenuto 4:236–237
Certosa di Pavia 4:261
Cima da Conegliano 4:430
Crivelli, Carlo 5:353
della Robbia (family) 6:94
Desiderio da Settignano 6:131
Domenico Veneziano 6:231
Donatello 6:236–237
Dossi, Dosso 6:244
Farnese Palace 8:28
Ghiberti, Lorenzo 9:168
Giorgione 9:186–187
Giotto di Bondone 9:187
Gozzoli, Benozzo 9:275
Italian art and architecture 11:309–310
Laurana, Francesco 12:237
Leonardo da Vinci 12:289–291
Lippi, Filippino 12:362
Lippo, Fra Filippo 12:362–363
Lombardo (family) 12:399
Lorenzo di Credi 12:415
Lorenzo Monaco 12:415
Lotto, Lorenzo 12:420
Maiano (family) 13:66
Mannerism 13:124–125
Mantegna, Andrea 13:129–130
Masaccio 13:193–194
Masolino da Panicale 13:198
Medici Chapel 13:265–266
Michelangelo 13:372–375
Mino da Fiesole 13:458
Moro, Antonio 13:583
Nanni di Banco 14:12
Palladio, Andrea 15:47–48
Parmigianino 15:95–96
Perugino 15:195
Peruzzi, Baldassare 15:196
Piero della Francesca 15:296
Pintoricchio 15:308
Pisanello, Antonio 15:316
Pollaiuolo (family) 15:405–406
Pontormo, Jacopo Carucci da 15:427
Raphael 16:89–90
Rosso Fiorentino 16:320
Sansovino, Andrea 17:65
Sansovino, Jacopo 17:66
Serlio, Sebastiano 17:209
Signorelli, Luca 17:302
Sistine Chapel 17:329
Squarcione, Francesco 18:202
Tiepolo (family) 19:195
Titian 19:212–213
Tura, Cosimo 19:339
Uccello, Paolo 19:370
Uffizi 19:371
Vasari, Giorgio 19:525
Vecchietta 19:530
Veronese, Paolo 19:559–560
Verrocchio, Andrea del 19:560–561
Vignola, Giacomo Barozzida 19:592
jewelry 11:409–410 *illus.*
landscape architecture 12:185–186 *illus.*
landscape painting 12:188
Mannerism 13:124–125
mural painting 13:646
neoclassicism (art) 14:81
Netherlands 16:153–154
Dutch art and architecture 6:309
Lucas van Leyden 12:448–449
Massys, Quentin 13:214
painting 15:19–20
perspective 15:190
portraiture 15:446
Portugal
Arruda (family) 2:189
Portuguese art and architecture 15:456
Renaissance 16:149
Scandinavian art and architecture 17:112
sculpture 17:163–164 *illus.*
Spain
Berruguete, Pedro 3:224
Egas, Enrique 7:71
Escorial 7:238
Herrera, Juan de 10:146
Siloe, Diego de 17:310
Spanish art and architecture 18:153
still-life painting 18:269 *illus.*
tapestry 19:33
terra-cotta 19:120
tomb 19:231
urban planning 19:481–482
RENAISSANCE LITERATURE
Austrian literature 2:354
comedy 5:132
English literature 7:195
Elizabethan Age 7:143–144
French literature 8:314–315
German literature 9:132
Italian literature 11:315–316
masque 13:200
narrative and dramatic devices 14:22–23
Portuguese literature 15:456–457
satire 17:88
Spanish literature 18:157–158
theater, history of the 19:145–146
RENAISSANCE MUSIC 16:155–157 *bibliog., illus.*
Bull, John (composer) 3:557
Byrd, William 3:602
cantus firmus 4:118
Deller, Alfred 6:94
Dowland, John 6:251–252
Dufay, Guillaume 6:293
Dunstable, John 6:301
English music 7:203
French music 8:320
Gabrieli (family) 9:6
German and Austrian music 9:129
ground bass 9:373
Hassler, Hans Leo 10:67
Isaac, Heinrich 11:285
Italian music 11:318
Janequin, Clément 11:358
Josquin des Prez 11:453
Lassus, Roland de 12:214
lute 12:468
madrigal 13:45
mandolin 13:111–112 *illus.*
mass (musical setting) 13:201
motet 13:606
music, history of Western 13:663–664 *illus.*
Obrecht, Jacob 14:316
Okeghem, Jean d' 14:366
Palestrina, Giovanni Pierluigi da 15:46–47
passacaglia and chaconne 15:103
polyphony 15:421
Purcell, Henry 15:628
sequence 17:207
Spanish music 18:161
Victoria, Tomás Luis de 19:574–575
Weelkes, Thomas 20:90
Willaert, Adrain 20:154
RENAN, ERNEST 16:157 *bibliog.*
RENATA (British Columbia)
map (49° 26′N 118° 6′W) 3:491
RENAULT
automotive industry 2:366; 2:368
RENAULT, MARY 16:157 *bibliog.*
REND LAKE
map (38° 5′N 88° 58′W) 11:42
RENDSBURG (Germany, East and West)
map (54° 18′N 9° 40′E) 9:140
RENDZINA (CALCIMORPHIC) SOILS
distribution, worldwide 18:37 *map*
RENÉ, ALBERT
Seychelles 17:232
RENÉ OF ANJOU, KING OF NAPLES 16:157 *bibliog.*
RENEWS (Newfoundland)
map (46° 56′N 52° 56′W) 14:166
RENFREW (Ontario)
map (45° 28′N 76° 41′W) 14:393
RENFREW (Scotland) 16:157
cities
Paisley 15:25
RENG MOUNTAIN
map (21° 59′N 92° 36′E) 3:64
RENGO (Chile)
map (34° 25′S 70° 52′W) 4:355
RENI, GUIDO 16:157 *bibliog.*
RENICK (West Virginia)
map (38° 0′N 80° 22′W) 20:111
RENIER DE HUY
Romanesque art and architecture 16:284–286 *illus.*
RENIN
endocrine system, diseases of the 7:169
hypertension 10:349
RENMIN RIBAO see PEOPLE'S DAILY
RENNELL ISLAND
map (11° 40′S 160° 10′E) 18:56
RENNENKAMPF, PAVEL K.
World War I 20:224–226
RENNES (France) 16:157
map (48° 5′N 1° 41′W) 8:260
RENNET
cheese 4:309
RENNIE (Manitoba)
map (49° 51′N 95° 33′W) 13:119
RENNIE, JOHN
London Bridge 12:405
RENO (county in Kansas)
map (37° 55′N 98° 5′W) 12:18
RENO (Nevada) 16:157
map (39° 31′N 119° 48′W) 14:111
RENO, MARCUS A.
Little Bighorn, Battle of the 12:372
RENOIR, JEAN 16:157–158 *bibliog., illus.*
Grand Illusion 8:85 *illus.*; 16:158 *illus.*
RENOIR, PIERRE AUGUSTE 16:158–159 *bibliog., illus.*
The Box 11:64 *illus.*
Limoges (France) 12:346
The Luncheon of the Boating-Party 16:158 *illus.*
RENOUS (New Brunswick)
map (46° 49′N 65° 48′W) 14:117
RENOVO (Pennsylvania)
map (41° 20′N 77° 38′W) 15:147
RENSE, DECLARATION OF
Louis IV, King of Germany and Holy Roman Emperor (Louis the Bavarian) 12:428
RENSSELAER (Indiana)
map (40° 57′N 87° 9′W) 11:111
RENSSELAER (New York)
map (42° 39′N 73° 44′W) 14:149
RENSSELAER (county in New York)
map (42° 43′N 73° 40′W) 14:149
RENSSELAER, VAN (family) *see* VAN RENSSELAER (family)
RENSSELAER POLYTECHNIC INSTITUTE 16:159
Van Rensselaer (family) 19:515
vocational education 19:624
RENT CONTROL 16:159 *bibliog.*
RENTON (Washington)
map (47° 30′N 122° 11′W) 20:35
RENVILLE (county in Minnesota)
map (44° 43′N 94° 50′W) 13:453
RENVILLE (county in North Dakota)
map (48° 45′N 101° 10′W) 14:248
RENWICK, JAMES 16:159 *bibliog., illus.*
Saint Patrick's Cathedral 16:159 *illus.*; 17:24
RENWICK GALLERY
National Collection of Fine Arts 14:30
REPARATIONS 16:159–160 *bibliog.*
Dawes, Charles G. 6:54
Germany, history of 9:155
Young, Owen D. 20:334
REPARTIMIENTO
encomienda 7:163
slavery 17:353
RÉPCE RIVER
map (47° 41′N 17° 3′E) 10:307
REPERTORY THEATER 16:160 *bibliog., illus.*
Horniman, Annie Elizabeth Fredericka 10:240
REPIN, ILYA YEFIMOVICH 16:160

REPORT OF THE PRESIDENT'S COMMISSION ON THE ASSASSINATION OF PRESIDENT JOHN F. KENNEDY see WARREN COMMISSION
REPORTING OF NEWS see JOURNALISM
REPRESENTATION 16:160–161 *bibliog.*
See also 14th AMENDMENT
election
republic **16**:172
legislature **12**:274–275
municipal government **13**:642
REPRESSION (psychology)
defense mechanisms **6**:83
REPRODUCTION 16:161–163 *bibliog., illus.*
See also REPRODUCTIVE SYSTEM, HUMAN
algae **1**:280; **16**:162
Spirogyra **18**:189
animal behavior **2**:18
animal courtship and mating **2**:20–22
animal husbandry **2**:23; **2**:25
artificial insemination **2**:220–221
asexual **16**:161–162
cloning **5**:64
pure line theory for, Protozoa **15**:581
bacteria **3**:16; **16**:162
bat **3**:119
bird **3**:284–287
blue-green algae **3**:342 *illus.*; **3**:343
cat **4**:194
cell **4**:236
coelenterate **5**:91–92
conjugation **5**:191
coral **5**:257
crab **5**:324–325
cyclic AMP **5**:403
deer **6**:80–81
development **6**:137–142 *illus.*
dolphin **6**:228
earthworm **7**:29–30 *illus.*
echinoderm **7**:39
eel **7**:71
egg **7**:72
fertilization **8**:60–61
fish **8**:119–120
flowerpot snake **8**:184
fluke **8**:186
four-eyed fish **8**:253
fungi **8**:366 *illus.*; **16**:162
molds **13**:506
mushrooms **13**:661
gametes **16**:161–162
grasshopper **9**:298–299
grunion **9**:383–384
hormone, animal **10**:234
horse **10**:241
insect **11**:190 *illus.*
invertebrate **11**:237
jellyfish **11**:395
lizard **12**:380
mammal **13**:98 *illus.*
marsupial **13**:174
meiosis **13**:282
menstruation **13**:300–301
midwife toad **13**:414–415
monkey **13**:534
orchitis **14**:420
oviparity **14**:471
pheromone **15**:226
plant **16**:162
primate **15**:539
prostate gland **15**:573
Protozoa **15**:580
rabbit **13**:98 *illus.*
reptile **16**:168
rodent **16**:266
salamander and newt **17**:30
salmon **17**:35
sea horse **17**:169
semen **17**:195
sex **17**:224
sex determination **16**:162
sex hormones **17**:226
shark **17**:242
skate (fish) **17**:332
slime mold **17**:362
snake **17**:381–382 *illus.*
sperm **18**:179
spider **18**:183
termite **19**:116
territoriality **19**:121
trout **19**:312
turtle **19**:353
Ulothrix **19**:377
viper **19**:604
virus **19**:614 *illus.*
whale **20**:121
wolf **20**:196
zygote **20**:384
REPRODUCTION, PLANT **15**:337–339 *illus.*; **16**:162
alternation of generations **1**:313
angiosperm **1**:414
bryophyte **3**:530
embryo **7**:152–153
fern **8**:56–57
fertilization **8**:60–61
fig **8**:75
flower **8**:178–180
grass **9**:297
gymnosperm **9**:414
hornwort **10**:240
horticulture **10**:255
hummingbird **10**:303
liverwort **12**:376
moss **13**:603–605
orchid **14**:419
palm (botany) **15**:49
plant breeding **15**:342–343
plant propagation **15**:345
pollen **15**:406–407
pollination **15**:408–409
seed **15**:337–338 *illus.*
seed cone **17**:187
spore **18**:195
stonewort **18**:284
tundra **19**:333
REPRODUCTIVE SYSTEM, HUMAN 16:163–166 *bibliog., illus.*
artificial insemination **2**:220–221
birth control **3**:293–295
development **6**:140–141; **16**:165 *illus.*
female **16**:163–166 *illus.*
amenorrhea **1**:326
cervicitis **4**:261–262
dysmenorrhea **6**:320
estrous cycle **7**:248
function **16**:164–165
gynecology **9**:414
menopause **13**:299
menstruation **13**:300–302
multiple birth **13**:637
obstetrics **14**:319
uterus **19**:496–497
fertility, human **8**:60
fertilization **16**:164 *illus.*
male **16**:163–164 *illus.*
orchitis **14**:420
prostate gland **15**:573
semen **17**:195
sex hormones **17**:226
sexual intercourse **17**:230–231
tissue, animal **19**:210
urogenital diseases **19**:487
REPTILE 16:166–177 *bibliog., illus.*
See also names of specific reptiles, e.g., ALLIGATOR; IGUANA; etc.
aging **1**:186
animal migration **2**:27
brain **3**:443 *illus.*
circulatory system **4**:439–440
classification, biological **16**:171
coloration, biological **5**:122
dinosaur **6**:179–182
egg **16**:168
evolution **7**:323; **16**:170–171 *table*
fertilization **16**:168
fossil record **8**:244 *illus.*
Jurassic Period **11**:475–477 *illus.*
Permian Period **15**:174 *illus.*
Triassic Period **19**:294 *illus.*
heart **16**:168–169
herpetology **10**:146
kidney **12**:74; **16**:169
leather and hides **12**:262–263
maximum life span for some **12**:330 *table*
molting **13**:513
orders of reptiles, living
Chelonia (turtles) **19**:352–354 *illus.*
crocodylia (crocodiles) **5**:356 *illus.*
Rhynchocephalia (tuatara) **19**:326 *illus.*
Squamata (lizards, snakes, and worm lizards) **12**:378–382 *illus.*; **17**:376–382 *illus.*; **20**:284 *illus.*
pigment, skin **15**:301
reproduction **16**:168
respiratory system **16**:166; **16**:180
Rhamphorhynchus **16**:192
senses **16**:171
skin **16**:166–168
skull **16**:169–171
teeth **19**:71
uric acid **19**:486
urine **19**:486
REPTON (Alabama)
map (31° 25′N 87° 14′W) **1**:234
REPTON, HUMPHRY 16:171–172 *bibliog.*
landscape architecture **12**:187
Nash, John **14**:23–24
REPUBLIC 16:172 *bibliog.*
president **15**:522
REPUBLIC (Kansas)
map (39° 55′N 97° 49′W) **12**:18
REPUBLIC (county in Kansas)
map (39° 50′N 97° 40′W) **12**:18
REPUBLIC (Washington)
map (48° 39′N 118° 44′W) **20**:35
REPUBLIC, THE (book) **16**:172 *bibliog.*
Plato **15**:360–361
utopias **19**:497
REPUBLIC OF CHINA see TAIWAN
REPUBLIC OF SOUTH AFRICA see SOUTH AFRICA
REPUBLICAN (newspaper)
Bowles, Samuel, III **3**:429
REPUBLICAN PARTY 16:172–176 *bibliog., illus.*
Blaine, James Gillespie **3**:323–324
Civil War, U.S. **5**:17–18
congressional membership and organization **5**:185–186
Eisenhower, Dwight D. **7**:94–96
Iowa **11**:247
Jackson (Michigan) **11**:340
Liberal Republican party **12**:312
Lincoln, Abraham **12**:349
Michigan **13**:381
mugwumps **13**:632
Pennsylvania **15**:150
political convention **15**:399–400 *illus.*
political parties **15**:400
presidential election (1860) **15**:529 *illus.*
Raymond, Henry Jarvis **16**:97
Reconstruction **16**:108–110
Republican National Convention (1888) **7**:104 *illus.*
Republican National Convention (1968) **15**:400 *illus.*
Roosevelt, Theodore **16**:309–311
South Dakota **18**:105; **18**:106
symbol
Nast, Thomas **14**:25–26
Union party **19**:387
United States, history of the **19**:447–450
Wide Awake movement **15**:529 *illus.*
REPUBLICAN RIVER
map (39° 3′N 96° 48′W) **19**:419
REPUBLICAN RIVER, SOUTH FORK
map (39° 58′N 101° 37′W) **5**:116
REPULSE (ship) **5**:366 *illus.*
World War II **20**:260
REPULSE BAY (Northwest Territories)
map (66° 32′N 86° 15′W) **14**:258
REQUENA (Peru)
map (4° 58′S 73° 50′W) **15**:193
REQUIEM 16:176 *bibliog.*
composers
Berlioz, Hector **3**:218
Britten, Benjamin **3**:498–499
Fauré, Gabriel Urbain **8**:38
Mozart, Wolfgang Amadeus **13**:628–629
Verdi, Giuseppe **19**:549–550
Dies irae **6**:163
RESEARCH, SCIENTIFIC see SCIENTIFIC RESEARCH
RESERPINE 16:176
folk medicine **8**:201
medicinal plants **13**:266
synthesis: Woodward, Robert Burns **20**:213
RESERVE (Louisiana)
map (30° 4′N 90° 34′W) **12**:430
RESERVE (New Mexico)
map (33° 43′N 108° 45′W) **14**:136
RESERVE OFFICERS TRAINING CORPS 16:176 *bibliog.*
military academies **13**:420–421
navy **14**:65
RESERVOIR
dam **6**:17
hydroelectric power **10**:332–335
RESERVOIR ROCK
petroleum **15**:208 *illus.*
RESETTLEMENT ADMINISTRATION
housing **10**:277
RESH (letter)
R (letter) **16**:29
RESIDENT PHYSICIAN
medicine, education in **13**:272
RESIDENT THEATER see REPERTORY THEATER
RESIN 16:176–177 *bibliog.*
balsam **3**:54
flavors and fragrances **8**:157
fossilized resin
amber **1**:325
frankincense **8**:282
gamboge **9**:26–27
grass tree **9**:298
gumweed **9**:405
ion exchange **11**:240
kauri pine **12**:32
lacquer **12**:161
mastic **13**:216
myrrh **13**:691
rosin **16**:317
shellac **17**:252
storax **18**:284
synthetic resin
Bakelite **3**:27
dentistry **6**:116
epoxy resins **7**:222
tacamahac **19**:5
tree **19**:288
varnish **19**:524
RESINA see HERCULANEUM (Italy)
RESISTANCE, ELECTRICAL 16:177
bridge circuit **3**:484
electricity **7**:109–110 *illus.*
electromagnetic units **7**:118
impedance **11**:61
ohm **14**:363
plasma physics **15**:346
thermistor **19**:161
Wheatstone bridge **20**:127
RESISTANCE MOVEMENTS
World War II **20**:271–272 *illus.*
RESISTENCIA (Argentina)
map (27° 27′S 58° 59′W) **2**:149
RESISTIVITY 16:177
insulator **11**:197
RESISTOR 16:177 *bibliog.*
rheostat **16**:193
REŞIŢA (Romania)
map (45° 17′N 21° 53′E) **16**:288
RESNAIS, ALAIN 16:177 *bibliog.*
documentary **6**:211
Feuillade, Louis **8**:66
RESNIK, JUDITH A. 16:177
RESOLUTION (ship)
Cook, James **5**:236
RESOLUTION (video term) **19**:576e
video technology **19**:576n
RESOLUTION ISLAND (New Zealand)
map (45° 40′S 166° 40′E) **14**:158
RESOLUTION ISLAND (Northwest Territories)
map (61° 30′N 65° 0′W) **16**:18
RESONANCE (chemistry) **16**:177–178 *illus.*
aromatic compounds **2**:186
benzene **3**:206
diene **6**:162
molecular structure **16**:178
spectroscopy **18**:171–172
theory
Sidgwick, Nevil Vincent **17**:295
RESONANCE (physics) **16**:178
Kastler, Alfred **12**:30
magnetic resonance
Purcell, Edward Mills **15**:628
speech **18**:174
RESORTS see HEALTH RESORTS, WATERING-PLACES, AND SPAS
RESOURCE ALLOCATION
Kantorovich, Leonid V. **12**:24
RESPIGHI, OTTORINO 16:178 *bibliog.*
flügelhorn **8**:184
RESPIRATOR 16:178
iron lung **11**:272
RESPIRATORY DISTRESS SYNDROME *see* HYALINE MEMBRANE DISEASE
RESPIRATORY SYSTEM 16:178–180 *bibliog., illus.*
amphibians **16**:179
bird **16**:181
blood **3**:335–336
blood and oxygen transport **16**:178–179
bronchial tube **3**:502–503
cardiopulmonary resuscitation **4**:144
circulatory system **4**:440 *illus.*
death and dying **6**:68
diaphragm **6**:153
drug **6**:275
excretory system **7**:328
fish **8**:114 *illus.*; **16**:179
swim bladder **18**:390
gills **8**:114 *illus.*; **9**:180–181; **16**:178
insect **11**:187–188 *illus.*
invertebrate **11**:236
lizard **12**:380
lungfish **12**:462–463
lungs **12**:463–465; **16**:178; **16**:180 *illus.*
mammal **13**:97; **16**:181
muscle **13**:653

nose **14**:266
oxygen tent **14**:478
reflex **16**:120
reptile **16**:166; **16**:180
respiratory pump **16**:179
skin **16**:178
smelling salts **17**:365
snake **17**:378–379
snakehead (fish) **17**:383
speech **18**:173–174
spider **18**:182
tissue, animal **19**:210
trachea **19**:258
turtle **19**:353
RESPIRATORY SYSTEM DISORDERS **16**:180–182 *bibliog.*
allergy **1**:301–302
apnea **2**:78
asphyxia **2**:262
asthma **2**:268
black lung **3**:317
bronchitis **3**:503
brown lung **3**:516–517
cold, common **5**:97
crib death **5**:342
croup **5**:363
cystic fibrosis **5**:411
diseases, childhood **6**:192; **6**:193
diseases, occupational **6**:193–194
dust, atmospheric **6**:308
emphysema **7**:158
environmental health **7**:211
fungus diseases **8**:369
histoplasmosis **10**:181
hyaline membrane disease **10**:327
hyperventilation **10**:349
infectious diseases **11**:166–167
influenza **11**:171–172
Legionnaires' disease **12**:274
mycoplasmal pneumonia **13**:690
pharyngitis **15**:222
pleurisy **15**:368
pneumonia **15**:375–376
pulmonary embolism **15**:619
pulmonary function test **15**:620
Q fever **16**:3
rickettsia **16**:215–216
Rocky Mountain spotted fever **16**:261
shock, physiologic **17**:278–279
silicosis **17**:306
sinusitis **17**:326
smoke **17**:373
smoking **17**:374
strep throat **18**:297
suffocation **18**:325
swine flu **18**:392
tongue worm **19**:234
tonsillitis **19**:235
treatment
antihistamine **2**:63
decongestant drugs **6**:76
tuberculosis **19**:327
typhus **19**:366–367
venom **19**:546
whooping cough **20**:143
RESTAURANT **16**:182 *bibliog.*
labor union
Hotel and Restaurant Employees and Bartenders International Union **10**:262
RESTIGOUCHE RIVER
map (48° 4′N 66° 20′W) **14**:117
RESTITUTION, EDICT OF (1629)
Ferdinand II, Holy Roman Emperor **8**:53
Thirty Years' War **19**:171
RESTON (Manitoba)
map (49° 35′N 101° 2′W) **13**:119
RESTON (Virginia) **16**:182
map (38° 58′N 77° 21′W) **19**:607
RESTON, JAMES BARRETT **16**:182 *bibliog., illus.*
RESTORATION **16**:182 *bibliog.*
Charles II, King of England, Scotland, and Ireland **4**:291–292
Clarendon, Edward Hyde, 1st Earl of **5**:36–37
Clarendon Code **5**:37
English music **7**:203
Great Britain, history of **9**:314
Milton, John **13**:433
Monck, George, 1st Duke of Albemarle **13**:522
Sancroft, William **17**:58–59
Shaftesbury, Anthony Ashley Cooper, 1st Earl of **17**:234
United States, history of the **19**:436–437
RESTORATION DRAMA **16**:182 *bibliog.*
authors
Congreve, William **5**:188
Davenant, Sir William **6**:46
Dryden, John **6**:284–285
Etherege, George **7**:250
Farquhar, George **8**:29
Otway, Thomas **14**:467
Wycherley, William **20**:298
comedy **5**:132
criticism, literary
Collier, Jeremy **5**:103
drama **6**:260
Drury Lane Theatre **6**:283
English literature **7**:196
RESTORATION OF HISTORIC BUILDINGS *see* HISTORIC PRESERVATION
RESTRAINING ORDER *see* INJUNCTION
RESURRECTION **16**:183 *bibliog.*
Easter **7**:32
Hallaj, al- **10**:22
heaven **10**:100
immortality **11**:56
RESURRECTION PLANT *see* ROSE OF JERICHO (botany)
RETABLE
Riemenschneider, Tilman **16**:218–219
Roldán (family) **16**:271
Spanish art and architecture **18**:153–155 *illus.*
RETAILING **16**:183 *bibliog.*
See also MARKETING; WHOLESALING
cosmetics **5**:282–283 *table*
department store **6**:118
discount house **6**:189
Field (family) **8**:71
Filene, Edward Albert **8**:78–79
food industry **8**:209–211
Hartford, Huntington **10**:62
franchise (business) **8**:273
Fuller, Alfred Carl **8**:357
Kress, Samuel H. **12**:129
Lipton, Sir Thomas **12**:364
mail-order business **13**:67
optical scanners
input-output devices **11**:183
Penney, J. C. **15**:145
Rosenwald, Julius **16**:316
sales **17**:32
sales tax **17**:32
Stewart, Alexander Turney **18**:265
supermarket **18**:352
Tiffany, Charles Lewis **19**:196
trademark **19**:263
trading stamps **19**:264
vending machine **19**:538
video stores **19**:576c
Ward, Montgomery **20**:29
Wood, Robert E. **20**:207
RETALHULEU (Guatemala)
map (14° 32′N 91° 41′W) **9**:389
RETAMOSA (Uruguay)
map (33° 35′S 54° 44′W) **19**:488
RETARDATION, MENTAL *see* MENTAL RETARDATION
RETARDED, EDUCATION OF THE *see* SPECIAL EDUCATION
RETICULATED PYTHON *see* PYTHON (snake)
RETIEF, PIETER
Pietermaritzburg (South Africa) **15**:297
RETINA
eye **7**:348–350 *illus.*
eye diseases **7**:351
retinography
photography **15**:266
Wald, George **20**:9
RETINENE *see* RHODOPSIN
RETIREMENT
American Association of Retired Persons **1**:336–337
pension **15**:153–154
social security **18**:14–16
RETIREMENT, SURVIVORS, AND DISABILITY INSURANCE
social security **18**:14
RETORT POUCH
aluminum **1**:319
RETRIEVER (dog) *see* SPORTING DOG
RETROVIRUS **16**:183–184 *bibliog.*
RETURN OF THE NATIVE, THE (book) **16**:184
Hardy, Thomas **10**:48
RETZ, CARDINAL DE
Fronde **8**:339
RETZIUS, ANDERS
cephalic index **4**:256
REUENTHAL, NEIDHART VON *see* NEIDHART VON REUENTHAL
REUFLINGEN (Germany, East and West)
map (48° 29′N 9° 11′E) **9**:140
RÉUNION **16**:184
cities
Saint-Denis **17**:17
dodo bird **6**:212
map (21° 6′S 55° 36′E) **1**:136
REUNION, THE (Ernst Barlach) **3**:84 *illus.*
REUTER, PAUL JULIUS, BARON VON **16**:184 *bibliog.*
REUTERDAHL, HENRY
The Fleet Entering the Golden Gate **19**:452 *illus.*
REUTERS
press agencies and syndicates **15**:533
Reuter, Paul Julius, Baron von **16**:184
REUTHER, WALTER P. **12**:155 *illus.*; **16**:184 *bibliog., illus.*
United Auto Workers **19**:401
REVELATION **16**:184–185 *bibliog.*
Brunner, Emil **3**:525
REVELATION, BOOK OF **16**:185 *bibliog.*
Bible **3**:241
REVELL, VILJO
Toronto City Hall **4**:90 *illus.*; **19**:240 *illus.*
REVELS, HIRAM R. **16**:185 *bibliog., illus.*
REVENTAZÓN (Peru)
map (6° 10′S 80° 58′W) **15**:193
REVENUE CUTTER
cutter **5**:398
REVENUE SHARING **16**:185 *bibliog.*
finance, state and local **8**:92
REVERBERATORY FURNACE
furnace **8**:372
open-hearth process **14**:398
REVERE (Massachusetts)
map (42° 24′N 71° 1′W) **3**:409
REVERE, PAUL **16**:185–186 *bibliog., illus.*
Boston Massacre engraving **1**:354 *illus.*
Dawes, William **6**:54
dentistry **6**:115
Warren, Joseph **20**:31
REVERSE FAULT
fault **8**:37 *illus.*
REVERSE TRANSCRIPTASE *see* ENZYME
REVERSIBLE AND IRREVERSIBLE PROCESSES **16**:186 *bibliog.*
Carnot, Nicolas Léonard Sadi **4**:158
REVETT, NICHOLAS
Greek Revival **9**:345
neoclassicism (art) **14**:81
REVILLAGIGEDO ISLAND
map (55° 35′N 131° 23′W) **1**:242
REVILLAGIGEDO ISLANDS
Colima (state) **5**:102
map (19° 0′N 111° 30′W) **13**:357
REVILLO (South Dakota)
map (45° 1′N 96° 34′W) **18**:103
REVIVALISM **16**:186–187 *bibliog.*
camp meetings **4**:63
cargo cults **4**:147
evangelicalism **7**:312
Finney, Charles G. **8**:99
gospel music **9**:254
Graham, Billy **9**:279
Great Awakening **9**:308
McPherson, Aimee Semple **13**:36
Moody, Dwight L. **13**:561
Roberts, Oral **16**:242
Shakers **17**:236
Sunday, Billy **18**:347
REVOLT OF THE MASSES, THE (book)
Ortega y Gasset, José **14**:449
REVOLUTION **16**:187–188 *bibliog., illus.*
See also names of specific revolutions, e.g., AMERICAN REVOLUTION; FRENCH REVOLUTION; etc.
anarchism **1**:392
communism **5**:146–150
political parties **15**:402
socialism **18**:19–24
syndicalism **18**:407
terrorism **19**:122
theorists
Arendt, Hannah **2**:145
Bakunin, Mikhail Aleksandrovich **3**:30
Burke, Edmund **3**:571
Engels, Friedrich **7**:176–177
Fanon, Frantz **8**:20–21
Marx, Karl **13**:181–182
Tocqueville, Alexis de **19**:220
totalitarianism **19**:248
Trotsky, Leon **19**:310–311
REVOLUTIONARY WAR *see* AMERICAN REVOLUTION
REVOLUTIONS OF 1848 **9**:152 *illus.*; **16**:188–189 *bibliog., illus.*
Austria **2**:350
Blanc, Louis **3**:326
Blanqui, Louis Auguste **3**:327
Communist Manifesto **5**:151
Europe, history of **7**:294
Frankfurt Parliament **8**:281
Frederick William IV, King of Prussia **8**:293
French revolutionaries **16**:188 *illus.*
Germany, history of **9**:152
Kossuth, Lajos **12**:124
Louis Philippe, King of France **12**:423
Metternich, Klemens Fürst von **13**:349–350
uprising in Berlin **16**:189 *illus.*
REVOLVER **16**:189–190 *bibliog., illus.*
Collier, Elisha **16**:189
Colt, Samuel **5**:123–124
Colt Army **16**:190 *illus.*
Colt .36 caliber Navy **16**:190 *illus.*
Darling pepperbox pistol **16**:190 *illus.*
firearms **8**:105–106
pistol **15**:318
Remington .36 caliber **16**:190 *illus.*
single action **16**:190 *illus.*
Smith and Wesson .38 caliber **16**:189 *illus.*
REVUE
Folies-Bergère **8**:195
White, George **20**:135
Ziegfeld, Florenz **20**:363
Ziegfeld Follies **20**:363
REVUELTAS, SILVESTRE
Latin American music and dance **12**:232
Mexico **13**:360
REWARD AND PUNISHMENT (psychology)
habit **10**:4
REXBURG (Idaho)
map (43° 49′N 111° 47′W) **11**:26
REXFORD (Kansas)
map (39° 28′N 100° 45′W) **12**:18
REXROTH, KENNETH **16**:190 *bibliog.*
REXTON (New Brunswick)
map (46° 39′N 64° 52′W) **14**:117
REY (Iran)
map (35° 35′N 51° 25′E) **11**:250
REYES (Bolivia)
map (14° 19′S 67° 23′W) **3**:366
REYE'S SYNDROME **16**:190
REYES Y BASOALTO, RICARDO ELIEZER NEFTALÍ *see* NERUDA, PABLO
REYKJANES RIDGE
plate tectonics **15**:351 *map*
REYKJAVIK (Iceland) **11**:17 *illus., table*; **16**:190
climate **7**:272 *table*
map (64° 9′N 21° 51′W) **11**:17
REYMONT, WŁADYSŁAW STANISŁAW **16**:190–191 *bibliog.*
REYNARD THE FOX (fable) **16**:191
REYNAUD, PAUL
de Gaulle, Charles **6**:59
REYNO (Arkansas)
map (36° 23′N 90° 47′W) **2**:166
REYNOLDS (Georgia)
map (32° 34′N 84° 6′W) **9**:114
REYNOLDS (county in Missouri)
map (37° 20′N 91° 0′W) **13**:476
REYNOLDS, SIR JOSHUA **16**:191 *bibliog., illus.*
Gainsborough, Thomas **9**:9
James Boswell **3**:411 *illus.*
Nelly O'Brien **16**:191 *illus.*
Self-Portrait **7**:186 *illus.*
REYNOLDS, OSBORNE **16**:191 *bibliog.*
REYNOLDS, W. BAINBRIDGE
Art Nouveau kettle and pedestal **2**:209 *illus.*
REYNOLDS NUMBER
fluid mechanics **8**:185
Reynolds, Osborne **16**:191
REYNOLDS v. SIMS **16**:191
apportionment **2**:91
Constitution of the United States **5**:220
REYNOLDSBURG (Ohio)
map (39° 57′N 82° 49′W) **14**:357
REYNOLDSVILLE (Pennsylvania)
map (41° 6′N 78° 53′W) **15**:147
REYNOSA (Mexico)
map (26° 7′N 98° 18′W) **13**:357
REZA SHAH PAHLAVI (1878–1944) **16**:192 *bibliog.*
Iran **11**:253
Middle East, history of the **13**:408
Tehran (Iran) **19**:72–73
REZA SHAH PAHLAVI, MUHAMMAD (1919-1980) *see* MUHAMMAD REZA SHAH PAHLAVI (1919-1980)

REZAIYEH (Iran)
map (37° 33′N 45° 4′E) **11**:250
REZAIYEH, LAKE *see* URMIA, LAKE
RH FACTOR 16:192 *bibliog.*
antibody **2**:60
blood **3**:337 *illus.*
jaundice **11**:385
Landsteiner, Karl **12**:193
pregnancy and birth **15**:504
rhesus monkey **16**:193
RHADAMANTHUS 16:192
RHADÉ *see* MONTAGNARDS
RHAETIAN ALPS
map (46° 30′N 10° 0′E) **1**:309
RHAETIAN LANGUAGES *see* RHETO-ROMANCE LANGUAGES
RHAMPHORHYNCHUS **11**:476 *illus.*; **16**:192 *bibliog., illus.*
RHAZES
medicine **13**:268
RHEA (astronomy)
Saturn (astronomy) **17**:89–91 *illus., table*
RHEA (bird) **3**:280 *illus.*; **16**:192–193 *illus.*
RHEA (mythology)
mythology **13**:700
RHEA (county in Tennessee)
map (35° 35′N 85° 0′W) **19**:104
RHEE, SYNGMAN 16:193 *bibliog., illus.*
RHEIMS (France) *see* REIMS (France)
RHEINE (Germany, East and West)
map (52° 17′N 7° 26′E) **9**:140
RHEINGOLD, DAS (opera) *see RING OF THE NIBELUNG, THE* (opera cycle)
RHENIUM 16:193
element **7**:130 *table*
Group VIIB periodic table **15**:167
metal, metallic element **13**:328
sulfide minerals **18**:333
transition elements **19**:273
RHEOLOGY
physical chemistry **15**:279
RHEOSTAT 16:193
potentiometer **15**:467
resistor **16**:177
Wheatstone, Sir Charles, inventor **20**:127
RHESUS FACTOR *see* Rh FACTOR
RHESUS MONKEY 16:193 *illus.*
macaque **13**:4
RHETICUS 16:194 *bibliog.*
RHETO-ROMANCE LANGUAGES
Romance languages **16**:280
RHETORIC AND ORATORY 16:194 *bibliog.*
Aeschines **1**:128
Aristotle **2**:158
attitude and attitude change **2**:315
Ausonius **2**:325
Cicero, Marcus Tullius **4**:429
communication **5**:143
Demosthenes **6**:104–105
Gettysburg Address **9**:161–162
Greek literature, ancient **9**:343–344
Henry, Patrick **10**:122–123
Indians, American **11**:117 *illus.*
Isocrates **11**:298–299
Lamartine, Alphonse de **12**:174
Longinus **12**:409
Lysias **12**:480
Quintilian **16**:27
Sophists **18**:67
RHETT, ROBERT BARNWELL 16:194 *bibliog.*
RHEUMATIC FEVER 16:194 *bibliog.*
arthritis **2**:214
collagen disease **5**:102
dentistry **6**:114
heart diseases **10**:96
immunity **11**:58–59
RHEUMATISM 16:194–195 *bibliog.*
RHEUMATOID ARTHRITIS
arthritis **2**:215
collagen disease **5**:102
glucocorticoid **9**:211
Hench, Philip Showalter **10**:121
inflammation **11**:169
myasthenia gravis **13**:689
RHINE (Georgia)
map (31° 59′N 83° 12′W) **9**:114
RHINE, J. B. 16:195
parapsychology **15**:81–82
RHINE-MAIN-DANUBE WATERWAY
canal **4**:97
RHINE RIVER 16:195–196 *bibliog., illus., map*
Delta Plan **6**:95–96
map (51° 52′N 6° 2′E) **16**:195
RHINEGOLD, THE (opera) *see RING OF THE NIBELUNG, THE* (opera cycle)
RHINELAND, THE (West Germany) **16**:196
See also PALATINATE
cities
Koblenz **12**:104
Mainz **13**:75
Worms **20**:284
Zweibrücken **20**:383
Europe, history of **7**:292
Germany 1933–1942 **9**:156 *map*
Hitler, Adolf **10**:188
RHINELANDER (Wisconsin)
map (45° 38′N 89° 25′W) **20**:185
RHINITIS 16:196
RHINOCEROS 13:105 *illus.*; **16**:196 *bibliog., illus.*
Albrecht Dürer engraving (1515) **9**:291 *illus.*
Baluchitherium **3**:57
horn (biology) **10**:238
perissodactyl **15**:171
Tertiary Period **19**:125 *illus.*
woolly rhinoceros **13**:102 *illus.*
RHINOCEROS (play)
Ionesco, Eugène **11**:240–241
RHINOLOGY
surgery **18**:362
RHINOPLASTY
plastic surgery **15**:347
RHINOTRACHEITIS, FELINE VIRAL
cat **4**:194
RHIR, CAPE
map (30° 38′N 9° 55′W) **13**:585
RHIZOBIUM **16**:196
RHIZOPODA 16:196–197 *bibliog.*
amoeba **1**:376
Entamoeba **7**:208
Protozoa **15**:579–581
radiolarian **16**:64
RHIZOPUS **16**:197
molds **13**:506
RHIZOSPHERE
soil organisms **18**:39
RHO (letter)
R (letter) **16**:29
RHODE ISLAND 16:197–201 *bibliog., illus., map*
cities
Cranston **5**:332
Newport **14**:170
Pawtucket **15**:121
Providence **15**:584
Warwick **20**:33
climate **16**:199
cultural activities and historic sites **16**:199
economic activities **16**:200 *illus.*
education **16**:199
Barnard, Henry **3**:86
Brown University **3**:517
Bryant College **3**:529
Rhode Island, state university and college of **16**:201
Rhode Island School of Design **16**:201
state university and college **16**:201
flag **16**:197 *illus.*
government and politics **16**:200–201
history **16**:201
Coddington, William **5**:90
Dorr's Rebellion **6**:243
Luther v. *Borden* **12**:469
Williams, Roger **20**:159–160
land and resources **16**:197–199 *map*
manufacturing **16**:200–201
map (41° 33′N 71° 15′W) **16**:198
people **16**:199–200
Narragansett **14**:21–22
resources **16**:199
rivers, lakes, and waterways **16**:197
seal, state **16**:197 *illus.*
vegetation and animal life **16**:199
RHODE ISLAND, STATE UNIVERSITY AND COLLEGE OF 16:201
RHODE ISLAND SCHOOL OF DESIGN 16:201
RHODE ISLAND SOUND
map (41° 25′N 71° 15′W) **13**:206
RHODES (Greece) **16**:201–202
Colossus of **17**:217–218 *illus.*
map (36° 26′N 28° 13′E) **9**:325
RHODES, CECIL JOHN 16:202 *bibliog., illus.*
British Africa
flag **8**:135 *illus.*
Bulawayo (Zimbabwe) **3**:553
Cape Town **4**:121
Jameson, Sir Leander Starr **11**:357
Kimberley (South Africa) **12**:77
Lobengula, King of the Ndebele **12**:385
Rhodes scholarships **16**:202
South Africa **18**:83
RHODES SCHOLARSHIPS 16:202 *bibliog.*
RHODESIA *see* ZIMBABWE (Rhodesia)
RHODESIAN MAN *see* BROKEN HILL MAN
RHODESIAN RIDGEBACK 6:217 *illus.*; **16**:202 *illus.*
RHODIUM 16:203
element **7**:130 *table*
Group VIII periodic table **15**:167
metal, metallic element **13**:328
transition elements **19**:273
Wollaston, William Hyde **20**:199
RHODOCHROSITE 16:203 *bibliog., illus.*
rhodonite **16**:203
RHODODENDRON 16:203 *illus.*
azalea **2**:380
Hooker (family) **10**:227
RHODOLITE *see* GARNET
RHODONITE 9:74 *illus.*; **16**:203
RHODOPE MOUNTAINS
map (41° 30′N 24° 30′E) **3**:555
RHODOPHYTA *see* ALGAE—red algae
RHODOPSIN
eye
light detection **7**:348
retina **7**:349–352
RHOMBIC SYSTEM
crystal **5**:375 *illus.*
orthorhombic system **14**:451
RHOMBOHEDRAL SYSTEM
crystal **5**:375 *illus.*
hexagonal system **10**:154–155
oxide minerals **14**:476
RHOMBUS
square **18**:202
RHONDDA (Wales)
map (51° 40′N 3° 27′W) **19**:403
RHÔNE RIVER 16:203
Geneva, Lake **9**:91
map (43° 20′N 4° 50′E) **8**:260
RHUBARB 15:384 *illus.*; **16**:203–204 *illus.*; **19**:533 *illus.*
RHUMB LINE *see* CHART
RHYME 16:204 *bibliog.*
versification **19**:561–563
RHYNCHOCEPHALIA
tuatara **19**:326 *illus.*
RHYNIOPHYTINA
plant **15**:333–334
RHYOLITE 16:204
domese
lava **12**:240
igneous rock **11**:33
perlite **15**:172
RHYS, JEAN 16:204
RHYTHM (music) **16**:204 *bibliog.*
See also RHYTHM AND BLUES
Arabian music **2**:99–100
eurhythmics **7**:265–266
folk music **8**:203
Indian music **11**:103
meter (music) **13**:343
mode (music) **13**:489
motet **13**:606
musical notation and terms **13**:679
syncopation **18**:407
RHYTHM, BIOLOGICAL *see* BIOLOGICAL CLOCK
RHYTHM AND BLUES 16:204–205 *bibliog., illus.*
blues **3**:346
Brown, James **3**:514
rock music **16**:248
Waters, Muddy **20**:65
RHYTHM METHOD (birth control) **3**:294
RIABOUCHINSKA, TATIANA 16:205
RIALTO (California)
map (34° 6′N 117° 22′W) **4**:31
RIALTO BRIDGE (Venice)
bridge (engineering) **3**:480
RIB LAKE (Wisconsin)
map (45° 20′N 90° 12′W) **20**:185
RIB MOUNTAIN
map (44° 56′N 89° 49′W) **20**:185
RIBAUT, JEAN 16:205 *bibliog.*
RIBBENTROP, JOACHIM VON 16:205
Nazi-Soviet Pact **14**:67
Nuremberg Trials **14**:297 *illus.*
RIBBON WORM 16:205
classification, biological
invertebrate **11**:235
RIBBONFISH 16:205
RIBEIRÃO PRÊTO (Brazil)
map (21° 10′S 47° 48′W) **3**:460
RIBEIRO, AQUILINO 16:205
RIBEIRO, BERNARDIM 16:205
RIBERA, JUSEPE DE 16:205–206 *bibliog., illus.*
The Clubfooted Boy **16**:206 *illus.*
RIBERALTA (Bolivia)
map (10° 59′S 66° 6′W) **3**:366
RIBICOFF, ABRAHAM A. **15**:526 *illus.*
RIBOFLAVIN (Vitamin B_2)
Kuhn, Richard **12**:135
vitamins and minerals **19**:619
Recommended Dietary Allowances **19**:618 *table*
RIBONUCLEASE
structure
Stein, William Howard **18**:247
RIBONUCLEIC ACID *see* RNA
RIBOSE
sugar **18**:327
RIBOSOME 16:206
cell **4**:232 *illus.*; **4**:233
endoplasmic reticulum **7**:171
genetic code **9**:80–82
Palade, George Emil **15**:29
protein synthesis **15**:575–576 *illus.*; **16**:206
RIBOUD, MARC
photojournalism **15**:273
RIBULOSE
photosynthesis **15**:277
RICARDO, DAVID 16:206 *bibliog., illus.*
economics **7**:48
Marxism **13**:183
RICCI (family) **16**:206 *bibliog.*
RICCI, MATTEO 16:207 *bibliog.*
Polo, Marco **15**:417
RICCIO *see* BRIOSCO, ANDREA
RICCIO, DAVID
Darnley, Henry Stewart, Lord **6**:39
Mary, Queen of Scots **13**:186
RICCIOLI, GIOVANNI BATTISTA
astronomy, history of **2**:279
RICE 8:25 *illus.*; **9**:281 *illus.*; **16**:207–208 *bibliog., illus.*
agriculture and the food supply **1**:194–195 *illus.*; **1**:198
breeding **16**:208
plant breeding **15**:342–343
cultivation **16**:207
India **11**:86 *illus.*
Japan **11**:365 *illus.*
Kampuchea (Cambodia) **12**:12–13 *illus.*
Sri Lanka **2**:246 *illus.*; **18**:206 *illus.*
Taiwan **19**:13–14 *illus.*
Vietnam **19**:582 *illus.*
grass **9**:295
green revolution **9**:348–349
harvesting **16**:207
irrigation of **11**:281 *illus.*
sake **17**:28
uses **16**:208
vitamins and minerals **19**:619
wild rice **20**:148
RICE (county in Kansas)
map (38° 20′N 98° 10′W) **12**:18
RICE (county in Minnesota)
map (44° 20′N 93° 17′W) **13**:453
RICE, ANNE ESTELLE
Katherine Mansfield **13**:128 *illus.*
RICE, ELMER 16:208–209 *bibliog.*
RICE, GRANTLAND 16:209
RICE, T. D. (Daddy) **3**:307 *illus.*
American music **1**:349
RICE LAKE (Wisconsin)
map (45° 30′N 91° 44′W) **20**:185
RICE PADDIES **16**:208 *illus.*
RICE UNIVERSITY 16:209
RICEBIRD 16:209
bobolink **3**:352–353
RICH (county in Utah)
map (41° 35′N 111° 15′W) **19**:492
RICH, ADRIENNE 16:209 *illus.*
RICH HILL (Missouri)
map (38° 6′N 94° 22′W) **13**:476
RICH MOUNTAIN (ridge)
map (34° 40′N 94° 30′W) **2**:166
RICH SQUARE (North Carolina)
map (36° 16′N 77° 17′W) **14**:242
RICHARD, GABRIEL 16:209 *bibliog.*
RICHARD, KEITH
Rolling Stones, The **16**:272
RICHARD, MAURICE 16:209
RICHARD I, KING OF ENGLAND 16:209–210 *bibliog., illus.*
Blondel de Nesle **3**:335
Portsmouth **15**:448
RICHARD II (play) **16**:209
RICHARD II, KING OF ENGLAND 16:210 *bibliog., illus.*
Great Britain, history of **9**:312
Henry IV, King of England **10**:125
Peasants' Revolt **15**:129
Richard II (play) **16**:209
RICHARD III (play) **16**:209
RICHARD III, KING OF ENGLAND 16:210–211 *bibliog., illus.*
Edward V, King of England **7**:68
Richard III (play) **16**:209
Roses, Wars of the **16**:316

Woodville, Elizabeth **20**:213
York (dynasty) **20**:330
RICHARD THE LION-HEARTED (Richard Coeur de Lion) *see* RICHARD I, KING OF ENGLAND
RICHARDS, BOB 16:211
RICHARDS, DICKINSON WOODRUFF 16:211
Cournand, André **5**:314
RICHARDS, GORDON 16:211
RICHARDS, I. A. 16:211 *bibliog.*
RICHARDS, M. C.
happenings **10**:41
RICHARDS, THEODORE WILLIAM 16:211 *bibliog.*
RICHARDS, SIR WILLIAM BUELL 16:211
RICHARDSON (county in Nebraska)
map (40° 10′N 95° 45′W) **14**:70
RICHARDSON (Texas)
map (32° 57′N 96° 44′W) **19**:129
RICHARDSON, DOROTHY M. 16:211
RICHARDSON, ELLIOT L. 16:211 *illus.*
Cox, Archibald **5**:322
Watergate **20**:64
RICHARDSON, HENRY HANDEL 16:211–212 *bibliog.*
RICHARDSON, HENRY HOBSON 16:212 *bibliog., illus.*
American art and architecture **1**:329
Marshall Field Wholesale Store **1**:328 *illus.*; **16**:212 *illus.*
RICHARDSON, JOHN 16:212
Canadian literature **4**:93
RICHARDSON, JOSEPH
teakettle and stand **5**:110 *illus.*
RICHARDSON, SIR OWEN WILLANS 16:212
RICHARDSON, SIR RALPH 16:212
RICHARDSON, SAMUEL 16:212–213 *bibliog., illus.*
Clarissa Harlowe **5**:37
Pamela **15**:53
RICHARDSON, TONY 16:213
RICHARDSON MOUNTAINS
map (67° 15′N 136° 30′W) **20**:345
RICHARDT, JOACHIM FERDINAND **1**:69 *illus.*
RICHARDTON (North Dakota)
map (46° 53′N 102° 19′W) **14**:248
RICHELIEU, ARMAND JEAN DU PLESSIS, CARDINAL ET DUC DE 16:213 *bibliog., illus.*
Académie Française **1**:69
France, history of **8**:268–269
Joseph, Father **11**:451
Louis XIII, King of France **12**:425–426
Marie de Médicis **13**:152
tomb **19**:231
RICHELIEU RIVER
map (46° 3′N 73° 7′W) **16**:18
RICHET, CHARLES
parapsychology **15**:81
RICHEY (Montana)
map (47° 39′N 105° 4′W) **13**:547
RICHFIELD (Idaho)
map (43° 3′N 114° 9′W) **11**:26
RICHFIELD (Minnesota)
map (44° 53′N 93° 17′W) **13**:453
RICHFIELD (Utah)
map (38° 46′N 112° 5′W) **19**:492
RICHFIELD SPRINGS (New York)
map (42° 51′N 74° 59′W) **14**:149
RICHFORD (Vermont)
map (45° 0′N 72° 40′W) **19**:554
RICHIBUCTO (New Brunswick)
map (46° 41′N 64° 52′W) **14**:117
RICHIER, GERMAINE 16:213 *bibliog.*
RICHLAND (Georgia)
map (32° 6′N 84° 39′W) **9**:114
RICHLAND (county in Illinois)
map (38° 42′N 88° 3′W) **11**:42
RICHLAND (county in Louisiana)
map (32° 25′N 91° 45′W) **12**:430
RICHLAND (Missouri)
map (37° 51′N 92° 26′W) **13**:476
RICHLAND (county in Montana)
map (47° 45′N 104° 30′W) **13**:547
RICHLAND (county in North Dakota)
map (46° 20′N 97° 0′W) **14**:248
RICHLAND (county in Ohio)
map (40° 46′N 82° 31′W) **14**:357
RICHLAND (county in South Carolina)
map (34° 0′N 80° 55′W) **18**:98
RICHLAND (Washington)
map (46° 17′N 119° 18′W) **20**:35
RICHLAND (county in Wisconsin)
map (43° 22′N 90° 30′W) **20**:185
RICHLAND BALSAM MOUNTAIN
map (35° 22′N 82° 59′W) **14**:242
RICHLAND CENTER (Wisconsin)
map (43° 20′N 90° 23′W) **20**:185
RICHLAND SPRINGS (Texas)
map (31° 16′N 98° 57′W) **19**:129
RICHLANDS (Virginia)
map (37° 6′N 81° 48′W) **19**:607
RICHLER, MORDECAI 16:214 *bibliog., illus.*
RICHMANN, G. W.
physics, history of **18**:285
RICHMOND (borough and county in New York) *see* STATEN ISLAND (New York City)
RICHMOND (California)
map (37° 57′N 122° 22′W) **4**:31
RICHMOND (county in Georgia)
map (33° 20′N 82° 10′W) **9**:114
RICHMOND (Indiana)
map (39° 50′N 84° 54′W) **11**:111
RICHMOND (Kansas)
map (38° 24′N 95° 15′W) **12**:18
RICHMOND (Kentucky)
map (37° 45′N 84° 18′W) **12**:47
RICHMOND (Maine)
map (44° 5′N 69° 48′W) **13**:70
RICHMOND (Minnesota)
map (45° 27′N 94° 31′W) **13**:453
RICHMOND (Missouri)
map (39° 17′N 93° 58′W) **13**:476
RICHMOND (county in New York)
map (40° 38′N 74° 5′W) **14**:149
RICHMOND (county in North Carolina)
map (35° 0′N 79° 45′W) **14**:242
RICHMOND (Quebec)
map (45° 40′N 72° 9′W) **16**:18
RICHMOND (Texas)
map (29° 35′N 95° 46′W) **19**:129
RICHMOND (Utah)
map (41° 55′N 111° 48′W) **19**:492
RICHMOND (Vermont)
map (44° 24′N 72° 59′W) **19**:554
RICHMOND (Virginia) **16**:214
burning of (1865) **5**:30 *illus.*; **5**:33 *illus.*
busing, school **3**:590
map (37° 30′N 77° 28′W) **19**:607
RICHMOND (county in Virginia)
map (37° 32′N 77° 28′W) **19**:607
RICHMOND, SIR WILLIAM
Sir Arthur Evans **7**:312 *illus.*
RICHMOND HEIGHTS (Florida)
map (25° 58′N 80° 22′W) **8**:172
RICHMOND HIGHLANDS (Washington)
map (47° 46′N 122° 22′W) **20**:35
RICHMOND HILL (Georgia)
map (31° 56′N 81° 18′W) **9**:114
RICHMONDVILLE (New York)
map (42° 38′N 74° 34′W) **14**:149
RICHTER, ADRIAN LUDWIG 16:214
RICHTER, BURTON 16:214
RICHTER, CONRAD 16:214 *bibliog.*
RICHTER, FRANZ XAVER
German and Austrian music **9**:130
RICHTER, HANS 16:214 *bibliog.*
RICHTER, JOHANN PAUL FRIEDRICH 16:214 *bibliog.*
RICHTER, SVIATOSLAV 16:215 *bibliog.*
RICHTER SCALE 16:215
earthquakes **7**:26
Gutenberg, Beno **9**:408
RICHTHOFEN, FERDINAND VON 16:215
RICHTHOFEN, MANFRED, FREIHERR VON 16:215 *bibliog., illus.*
RICHTON (Mississippi)
map (31° 16′N 88° 56′W) **13**:469
RICHWOOD (Ohio)
map (40° 26′N 83° 18′W) **14**:357
RICHWOOD (West Virginia)
map (38° 14′N 80° 32′W) **20**:111
RICKENBACKER, EDDIE 16:215 *bibliog., illus.*
SPAD **18**:138
RICKETS 16:215
laryngitis **12**:209
nutritional-deficiency diseases **14**:307–308
skeletal system **17**:334
vitamin D deficiency
vitamins and minerals **19**:619
RICKETTSIA 16:215–216 *bibliog.*
diseases, animal **6**:192
infectious diseases **11**:164
Q fever **16**:3
respiratory system disorders **16**:181
Rocky Mountain spotted fever **16**:261
typhus **19**:366
RICKEY, BRANCH 16:216 *bibliog.*
RICKEY, GEORGE W. 16:216 *bibliog.*
RICKOVER, HYMAN 16:216 *bibliog.*
Nautilus **14**:52
RICO (Colorado)
map (37° 41′N 108° 2′W) **5**:116
RICOEUR, PAUL 16:216
RIDDLE (Oregon)
map (42° 57′N 123° 22′W) **14**:427
RIDDLES 16:216 *bibliog.*
folklore **8**:203
games **9**:30
RIDE, SALLY 16:216
RIDENHOUR, RONALD
My Lai incident **13**:689
RIDGE, OCEANIC *see* MID-OCEANIC RIDGE
RIDGE FARM (Illinois)
map (39° 54′N 87° 39′W) **11**:42
RIDGEFIELD (Connecticut)
map (41° 17′N 73° 30′W) **5**:193
RIDGEFIELD (New Jersey)
map (40° 50′N 74° 0′W) **14**:129
RIDGEFIELD PARK (New Jersey)
map (40° 51′N 74° 1′W) **14**:129
RIDGELAND (South Carolina)
map (32° 29′N 80° 59′W) **18**:98
RIDGELY (Tennessee)
map (36° 16′N 89° 29′W) **19**:104
RIDGEVILLE (South Carolina)
map (33° 6′N 80° 19′W) **18**:98
RIDGEWAY (Wisconsin)
map (43° 1′N 90° 1′W) **20**:185
RIDGEWOOD (New Jersey)
map (40° 59′N 74° 7′W) **14**:129
RIDGWAY (Colorado)
map (38° 9′N 107° 46′W) **5**:116
RIDGWAY (Illinois)
map (37° 48′N 88° 16′W) **11**:42
RIDGWAY (Pennsylvania)
map (41° 26′N 78° 44′W) **15**:147
RIDGWAY, MATTHEW B. 16:216
Korean War **12**:121–122
RIDING 16:216–217 *bibliog., illus.*
See also HORSE SHOW; RODEO (contest)
circus **4**:443–444 *illus.*
pentathlon **15**:155
polo **15**:416–417
saddle **17**:8–9
Steinkraus, Bill **18**:249
stirrup **18**:273
RIDING MOUNTAIN NATIONAL PARK (Manitoba) **13**:121 *illus.*
RIDLEY, NICHOLAS 16:217–218 *bibliog.*
Oxford (England) **14**:474
RIDLEY TURTLE 16:218 *illus.*
RIDOLFI PLOT
Howard (family) **10**:282
RIEBEECK, JAN VAN
Cape Town **4**:121
South Africa **18**:82
RIEFENSTAHL, LENI 16:218 *bibliog.*
documentary **6**:211
film, history of **8**:85
RIEGEL, KLAUS
developmental psychology **6**:142
RIEL, LOUIS 4:85 *illus.*; **16**:218 *bibliog., illus.*
Canada, history of **4**:85
Poundmaker **15**:476
Red River Rebellion **16**:113
RIEMANN, GEORG FRIEDRICH BERNHARD 16:218 *bibliog.*
elliptic geometry
non-Euclidian geometry **14**:216
mathematics, history of **13**:226
Riemannian geometry
non-Euclidean geometry **14**:215–216
RIEMENSCHNEIDER, TILMAN 16:218–219 *bibliog.*
RIENZI (Mississippi)
map (34° 46′N 88° 38′W) **13**:469
RIENZO, COLA DI 16:219 *bibliog.*
RIESA (Germany, East and West)
map (51° 18′N 13° 17′E) **9**:140
RIESENER, JEAN HENRI 16:219 *bibliog.*
commode **8**:376 *illus.*
furniture **8**:376
RIESMAN, DAVID, JR. 16:219
Jencks, Christopher **11**:395
Lonely Crowd, The **12**:405
RIETI (Italy)
map (42° 24′N 12° 51′E) **11**:321
RIETVELD, GERRIT THOMAS 16:219 *bibliog.*
Schröder House **13**:491 *illus.*
RIF 16:219
Abd el-Krim **1**:54
RIFFE LAKE
map (46° 29′N 122° 20′W) **20**:35
RIFLE 8:105 *illus.*; **16**:219–221 *bibliog., illus.*
Browning, John Moses **3**:518
firearms **8**:105–106
Garand, John Cantius **9**:38
German 7.92-mm Mauser **16**:220 *illus.*
history **16**:219
recoilless rifle **16**:108 *illus.*
shooting **17**:282 *illus.*
Spencer Carbine **16**:220 *illus.*
U.S. M16 **16**:220 *illus.*
Whitworth, Sir Joseph **20**:143
RIFLE (Colorado)
map (39° 32′N 107° 47′W) **5**:116
RIFT VALLEY FEVER
virus **19**:615
RIFT VALLEYS 16:221 *bibliog., illus.*
Dead Sea **6**:64
East African Rift System **7**:30–31
fault **8**:36–38
Great Rift Valley **9**:321–322
horst and graben **10**:253–254; **16**:221
mid-oceanic ridge **13**:390
ore deposits
plate tectonics **15**:356
plate tectonics **15**:351 *map*; **15**:352
RIG-VEDA *see* VEDAS (sacred books)
RIGA (USSR) **16**:221
map (56° 57′N 24° 6′E) **19**:388
RIGA, TREATY OF
Polish-Soviet War **15**:398
RIGATONI **15**:106 *illus.*
RIGAUD, HYACINTHE 16:222 *bibliog.*
Louis XIV, King of France **8**:269 *illus.*; **12**:426 *illus.*
RIGBY (Idaho)
map (43° 40′N 111° 55′W) **11**:26
RIGESTAN DESERT
map (31° 0′N 65° 0′E) **1**:133
RIGGINS (Idaho)
map (45° 25′N 116° 19′W) **11**:26
RIGGS, RALPH
musical comedy **13**:674 *illus.*
RIGHT, THE (politics) *see* CONSERVATISM; CONSERVATIVE PARTIES
RIGHT OF ASYLUM 16:222 *bibliog.*
sanctuary **17**:59
RIGHT BANK (Paris) **15**:87 *map*
RIGHT TO BEAR ARMS 16:222
2d Amendment **17**:178
RIGHT TO COUNSEL (law)
due process **6**:292–293
Escobedo v. *Illinois* **7**:237
Gideon v. *Wainwright* **9**:177
legal aid **12**:272
Miranda v. *Arizona* **13**:463
Powell v. *Alabama* **15**:481
6th amendment **17**:331
RIGHT TO DIE (law)
death and dying **6**:69
euthanasia **7**:311
RIGHT-HANDEDNESS *see* HANDEDNESS
RIGHT-TO-LIFE MOVEMENT
abortion **1**:60
RIGHT OF PRIVACY
Griswold v. *Connecticut* **9**:368
privacy, invasion of **15**:556
RIGHT-TO-READ PROGRAM 16:222
RIGHT OF SEARCH 16:222
RIGHT-TO-WORK LAWS 16:222 *bibliog.*
closed shop **5**:65
open shop **14**:398
union shop **19**:387
RIGHT WHALE *see* WHALE
RIGHTS, ANIMAL *see* ANIMAL RIGHTS
RIGI MOUNTAIN
map (47° 5′N 8° 30′E) **18**:394
RIGOLET (Newfoundland)
map (54° 20′N 58° 35′W) **14**:166
RIIS, JACOB AUGUST 16:222–223 *bibliog., illus.*
housing **10**:276
photography, history and art of **15**:269
RIJEKA (Yugoslavia) **16**:223
map (45° 20′N 14° 27′E) **20**:340
RIJKSMUSEUM 16:223 *bibliog.*
RIJSSEN (Netherlands)
map (52° 18′N 6° 30′E) **14**:99
RIKSDAG (parliament)
Sweden **18**:385
RIKSMÅL (language) *see* BOKMÅL (language)
RIKYU
Japanese art and architecture **11**:376
RILEY (Kansas)
map (39° 18′N 96° 50′W) **12**:18
RILEY (county in Kansas)
map (39° 20′N 96° 40′W) **12**:18
RILEY, JAMES WHITCOMB 16:223 *bibliog.*
RILKE, RAINER MARIA 9:134 *illus.*; **16**:223–224 *bibliog., illus.*
RILLE 16:224 *bibliog.*
RIMA RIVER
map (13° 4′N 5° 10′E) **14**:190

RIMBAUD, ARTHUR **16**:224 *bibliog.*
Verlaine, Paul **19**:551–552 *illus.*
RIMBEY (Alberta)
map (52° 38′N 114° 14′W) **1**:256
RIME OF THE ANCIENT MARINER, THE (poem) **16**:224
albatross **1**:252
James, Thomas **11**:354
Lyrical Ballads **12**:479
RIMERSBURG (Pennsylvania)
map (41° 2′N 79° 30′W) **15**:147
RIMINI (Italy) **16**:224
Malatesta (family) **13**:80
map (44° 4′N 12° 34′E) **11**:321
RIMMER, WILLIAM **16**:224 *bibliog.*
RÎMNICU-VÎLCEA (Romania)
map (45° 6′N 24° 22′E) **16**:288
RIMOUSKI (Quebec)
map (48° 26′N 68° 33′W) **16**:18
RIMSKY-KORSAKOV, NIKOLAI ANDREYEVICH **16**:224–225 *bibliog., illus.*
Five, The **8**:132
Russian music **16**:367 *illus.*
RINCON (Georgia)
map (32° 18′N 81° 14′W) **9**:114
RINCON (New Mexico)
map (32° 40′N 107° 4′W) **14**:136
RINCONADA (Argentina)
map (22° 26′S 66° 10′W) **2**:149
RINDERPEST (animal disease) **6**:191
RINDISBACHER, PETER
color lithograph **4**:82 *illus.*
RINFRET, THIBAUDEAU **16**:225
RING (jewelry)
jewelry **11**:408–411
RING (mathematics) **16**:225 *bibliog.*
commutative, field **8**:71
Dedekind, Richard **6**:76–77
RING CURRENT BELT *see* VAN ALLEN RADIATION BELTS
RING CYCLE *see* *RING OF THE NIBELUNG, THE* (opera cycle)
RING OF FIRE **16**:225
earthquakes **7**:27
RING-TAILED CAT *see* CACOMISTLE
RING OF THE NIBELUNG, THE (opera cycle) **16**:225 *bibliog.*
Bayreuth Wagner Festival **3**:134
RINGGOLD (Georgia)
map (34° 55′N 85° 7′W) **9**:114
RINGGOLD (county in Iowa)
map (40° 45′N 94° 15′W) **11**:244
RINGGOLD (Louisiana)
map (32° 20′N 93° 17′W) **12**:430
RINGHAL *see* COBRA
RINGING IN THE EAR *see* TINNITUS
RINGKØBING BAY
map (56° 0′N 8° 15′E) **6**:109
RINGLING (family) **16**:225–226 *bibliog.*
See also BARNUM, P. T.
RINGLING (Oklahoma)
map (34° 10′N 97° 36′W) **14**:368
RINGLING BROTHERS AND BARNUM AND BAILEY CIRCUS *see* BARNUM, P. T.; CIRCUS; RINGLING (family)
RINGNECK SNAKE
colubrid **5**:125
RINGSTED (Denmark)
map (55° 27′N 11° 49′E) **6**:109
RINGSTED (Iowa)
map (43° 18′N 94° 31′W) **11**:244
RINGTAIL MONKEY *see* CAPUCHIN (monkey)
RINGTOSS *see* HORSESHOE PITCHING
RINGVASS ISLAND
map (69° 55′N 19° 15′E) **14**:261
RINGWOOD (New Jersey)
map (41° 8′N 74° 16′W) **14**:129
RINGWORM **16**:226
diseases, animal **6**:192
fungus diseases **8**:369
skin diseases **17**:342
RINUCCINI, OTTAVIO
libretto **12**:319
opera **14**:399
RIO (Wisconsin)
map (43° 27′N 89° 14′W) **20**:185
RIO, ANDRES M. DEL
vanadium **19**:516
RIO ARRIBA (county in New Mexico)
map (36° 35′N 106° 45′W) **14**:136
RÍO BENITO (Equatorial Guinea)
map (1° 35′N 9° 37′E) **7**:226
RIO BLANCO (county in Colorado)
map (40° 0′N 108° 10′W) **5**:116
RIO BRANCO (Brazil)
map (9° 58′S 67° 48′W) **3**:460
RIO BRANCO (Uruguay)
map (32° 34′S 53° 25′W) **19**:488
RIO CLARO (Trinidad and Tobago)
map (10° 18′N 61° 11′W) **19**:300
RÍO COLORADO (Argentina)
map (39° 1′S 64° 5′W) **2**:149
RIO CUARTO (Argentina)
map (33° 8′S 64° 20′W) **2**:149
RIO DE JANEIRO (Brazil) **3**:462 *illus.*; **16**:226–227 *bibliog., illus., map*
climate **3**:461 *table*
map (22° 54′S 43° 14′W) **3**:460
Mardi Gras **4**:156 *illus.*; **13**:148
RIO DE JANEIRO (state in Brazil)
map (22° 0′S 42° 30′W) **3**:460
RÍO DE LA PLATA **16**:227
map (35° 0′S 57° 0′W) **2**:149
RIO DELL (California)
map (40° 30′N 124° 7′W) **4**:31
RÍO GALLEGOS (Argentina)
map (51° 38′S 69° 13′W) **2**:149
RÍO GRANDE (Argentina)
map (53° 47′S 67° 42′W) **2**:149
RIO GRANDE (Brazil)
map (32° 2′S 52° 5′W) **3**:460
RIO GRANDE (county in Colorado)
map (37° 40′N 106° 20′W) **5**:116
RÍO GRANDE (Mexico)
map (23° 50′N 103° 2′W) **13**:357
RÍO GRANDE (Nicaragua)
map (12° 54′N 83° 32′W) **14**:179
RIO GRANDE (river in Brazil)
map (19° 52′S 50° 20′W) **3**:460
RIO GRANDE (river in North America) **14**:135 *illus.*; **16**:227; **19**:133 *illus.*
El Paso (Texas) **7**:100
map (25° 55′N 97° 9′W) **19**:419
RIO GRANDE CITY (Texas)
map (26° 23′N 98° 49′W) **19**:129
RIO GRANDE DO NORTE (Brazil)
map (5° 45′S 36° 0′W) **3**:460
RIO GRANDE DU SUL (Brazil)
map (30° 0′S 54° 0′W) **3**:460
RIO GRANDE FEVER *see* BRUCELLOSIS
RIO GRANDE FROG *see* CHIRPING FROG
RÍO MULATO (Bolivia)
map (19° 42′S 66° 47′W) **3**:366
RIO MUNI (Equatorial Guinea) *see* MBINI (Equatorial Guinea)
RIO NEGRO *see* NEGRO, RIO
RÍO NEGRO RESERVOIR
map (32° 45′S 56° 0′W) **19**:488
RIO SAN JOSE
map (34° 52′N 107° 1′W) **14**:136
RIOBAMBA (Ecuador)
map (1° 40′S 78° 38′W) **7**:52
RIOJA (Peru)
map (6° 5′S 77° 9′W) **15**:193
RIOPELLE, JEAN PAUL **16**:227–228 *illus.*
Pavane **4**:90 *illus.*; **16**:227 *illus.*
RÍOS MONTT, EFRAÍN
Guatemala **9**:388–389
RIOT (law) **16**:228
race riots **16**:35
RÍOVERDE (Mexico)
map (21° 56′N 99° 59′W) **13**:357
RIP CURRENT
longshore drift **12**:409
RIP VAN WINKLE (fictional character) **16**:228
"RIP VAN WINKLE" (short story)
Irving, Washington **11**:284–285
RIP VAN WINKLE (stage role)
Jefferson, Joseph **11**:391
RIPARIAN RIGHTS **16**:228
RIPLEY (county in Indiana)
map (39° 4′N 85° 15′W) **11**:111
RIPLEY (Mississippi)
map (34° 44′N 88° 57′W) **13**:469
RIPLEY (county in Missouri)
map (36° 40′N 90° 50′W) **13**:476
RIPLEY (Ohio)
map (38° 45′N 83° 51′W) **14**:357
RIPLEY (Tennessee)
map (35° 45′N 89° 32′W) **19**:104
RIPLEY (West Virginia)
map (38° 49′N 81° 43′W) **20**:111
RIPLEY, GEORGE **16**:228 *bibliog.*
RIPON (Wisconsin)
map (43° 51′N 88° 50′W) **20**:185
RIPUARIANS
Franks **8**:285–286
RIQUETI, HONORÉ GABRIEL, COMTE DE MIRABEAU *see* MIRABEAU, HONORÉ GABRIEL RIQUETI, COMTE DE
RIQUIER, GUIRANT
minstrels, minnesingers, and troubadours **13**:460
Provençal literature **15**:583
RISC (REDUCED INSTRUCTION SET COMPUTER) **5**:160g; **5**:160i
RISHON LE ZION (Israel)
map (31° 58′N 34° 48′E) **11**:302
RISING SUN (Indiana)
map (38° 57′N 84° 51′W) **11**:111
RISING SUN (Maryland)
map (39° 42′N 76° 4′W) **13**:188
RISINGSUN (Ohio)
map (41° 16′N 83° 25′W) **14**:357
RISON (Arkansas)
map (33° 58′N 92° 11′W) **2**:166
RISORGIMENTO **16**:228 *bibliog., illus.*
Alfieri, Vittorio **1**:279
Carbonari **4**:137
Cavour, Camillo Benso, Conte di **4**:226
Garibaldi, Giuseppe **9**:47
Italy, history of **11**:329
Mazzini, Giuseppe **13**:250
Papal States **15**:67
Revolutions of 1848 **16**:188
Sardinia, Kingdom of **17**:76
Savoy (dynasty) **17**:102
Turin (Italy) **19**:342
Victor Emmanuel II, King of Italy **19**:573
RISS-WÜRM INTERGLACIATION
Fontéchevade man **8**:207
RITCHIE (family) **16**:229 *bibliog.*
RITCHIE (county in West Virginia)
map (39° 12′N 81° 5′W) **20**:111
RITCHIE, SIR WILLIAM JOHNSTONE **16**:229
RITES AND OBSERVANCES
See also LITURGY
Christian
Advent **1**:111
All Saints' Day **1**:297
All Souls' Day **1**:297–298
anointing of the sick **2**:34
Ascension of Christ **2**:227
Ash Wednesday **2**:229
baptism **3**:72–73
confession **5**:177
confirmation **5**:178
Eucharist **7**:262
sacrament **17**:7
fasting **8**:33
fertility rites **8**:60
functionalism (social science) **8**:360
Islamic
hajj **11**:292
Ramadan **16**:79
Jewish
bar mitzvah **3**:74
Chanukah **4**:282
Passover **15**:105–106
Purim **15**:629
Rosh Hashanah **16**:317
Shavuoth **17**:245
Tabernacles, Feast of **19**:4
Yom Kippur **20**:329
passage rites **15**:103–104
RITES OF PASSAGE *see* PASSAGE, RITES OF
RITSCHL, ALBRECHT **16**:229 *bibliog.*
RITSOS, YANNIS **16**:229
RITTENHOUSE, DAVID **16**:229 *bibliog.*
RITTER, CARL
geography **9**:102
RITTER, JOHN
ultraviolet light, discoverer **19**:379
RITTER, MOUNT
map (37° 42′N 119° 12′W) **4**:31
RITTMAN (Ohio)
map (40° 58′N 81° 47′W) **14**:357
RITZ, CÉSAR
Escoffier, Auguste **7**:237–238
RITZVILLE (Washington)
map (47° 8′N 118° 23′W) **20**:35
RIVALS, THE (play) **16**:229
RIVANNA RIVER
map (37° 45′N 78° 10′W) **19**:607
RIVAS (Nicaragua)
map (11° 26′N 85° 50′W) **14**:179
RIVAUX, PETER DES
Henry III, King of England **10**:125
RIVER BLINDNESS **16**:232
RIVER DELTA **16**:232–233 *bibliog., illus.*
alluvial fans **1**:305 *illus.*
alluvial soil distribution, worldwide **18**:37 *map*
erosion and sedimentation **7**:233 *illus.*
lake delta **16**:233
ocean delta **16**:232
Recent Epoch **16**:107
regression, marine **16**:129
transgression, marine **19**:271
RIVER EDGE (New Jersey)
map (40° 56′N 74° 2′W) **14**:129
RIVER FALLS (Alabama)
map (31° 21′N 86° 33′W) **1**:234
RIVER FALLS (Wisconsin)
map (44° 52′N 92° 38′W) **20**:185
RIVER HÉBERT (Nova Scotia)
map (45° 42′N 64° 23′W) **14**:269
RIVER HERRING *see* SHAD
RIVER JOHN (Nova Scotia)
map (45° 45′N 63° 3′W) **14**:269
RIVER JORDAN (British Columbia)
map (48° 25′N 124° 3′W) **3**:491
RIVER JORDAN (river in the Middle East) *see* JORDAN RIVER
RIVER AND STREAM **16**:229–232 *bibliog., illus., table*
alluvial fans **1**:305
baselevel **3**:108
bed load **3**:153
braided stream **3**:441
color, *Euglena* **7**:264
drainage basins **16**:229–230
dredging **6**:268–269
energy sources **7**:174
fall line **8**:13
flash flood **8**:153
floodplain **8**:165–166
floods and flood control **8**:167
flume studies **8**:186
groundwater **9**:374–376
gulf and bay **9**:402–403
habitat **10**:4–5
harbor and port **10**:42
hydroelectric power **10**:332–335
hydrologic cycle **10**:341–342
hydrosphere **10**:344
ice, river and lake **11**:7
landform evolution **12**:183
limnology **12**:345
meander, river **13**:253
networks **16**:229–231
oxbow lake **14**:473
plankton **15**:330–333
pollution
eutrophication **7**:311
sulfide minerals **18**:334
regression, marine **16**:129
river channels **16**:230–232
river delta **16**:232–233
river discharge **16**:229–231
solid concentrations carried **16**:232
stream capacity, law of
Gilbert, Grove Karl **9**:178
ten largest rivers **16**:232 *tables*
tidal bore **19**:192
water flow **16**:229–231 *illus.*
water mass **20**:49
water quality **20**:51
water resources **20**:50
waterfall **20**:63
whirlpool **20**:132
RIVER TEA TREE *see* PAPERBARK
RIVER VIEW (Alabama)
map (32° 47′N 85° 9′W) **1**:234
RIVERA (Uruguay)
map (30° 54′S 55° 31′W) **19**:488
RIVERA, DIEGO **16**:233 *bibliog., illus.*
cartoon (art) **4**:176
fresco (Mexico City Ministry of Education Building) **16**:233 *illus.*
Latin American art and architecture **12**:227–228
March to Tenochtitlan **12**:227 *illus.*
mural (Detroit Institute of Arts) **13**:646 *illus.*
RIVERA, FRUCTUOSO **16**:233
RIVERA, JOSE EUSTASIO
Latin American literature **12**:229
RIVERA, LUIS MUÑOZ *see* MUÑOZ RIVERA, LUIS
RIVERBANK (California)
map (37° 44′N 120° 56′E) **4**:31
RIVERDALE (California)
map (36° 26′N 119° 52′W) **4**:31
RIVERDALE (Maryland)
map (38° 58′N 76° 55′W) **13**:188
RIVERDALE (North Dakota)
map (47° 30′N 101° 22′W) **14**:248
RIVERHEAD (New York)
map (40° 55′N 72° 40′W) **14**:149
RIVERO, JOSÉ LUÍS BUSTAMANTE Y *see* BUSTAMANTE Y RIVERO, JOSÉ LUÍS
RIVERS, AUGUSTUS HENRY LANE-FOX PITT *see* PITT RIVERS, AUGUSTUS HENRY LANE-FOX
RIVERS, LARRY **16**:233–234 *bibliog., illus.*
Wedding Photograph **16**:233 *illus.*
RIVERS INLET (British Columbia)
map (51° 41′N 127° 15′W) **3**:491
RIVERSIDE (California) **16**:234
map (33° 59′N 117° 22′W) **4**:31
RIVERSIDE (county in California)
map (33° 45′N 117° 10′W) **4**:31
RIVERSIDE (New Jersey)
map (40° 2′N 74° 58′W) **14**:129
RIVERSIDE (Washington)
map (48° 30′N 119° 31′W) **20**:35
RIVERTON (Illinois)
map (39° 51′N 89° 33′W) **11**:42

RIVERTON (Manitoba)
map (50° 59′N 96° 59′W) **13**:119
RIVERTON (Nebraska)
map (40° 5′N 98° 46′W) **14**:70
RIVERTON (New Jersey)
map (40° 1′N 75° 1′W) **14**:129
RIVERTON (Utah)
map (40° 31′N 111° 56′W) **19**:492
RIVERTON (Wyoming)
map (43° 2′N 108° 23′W) **20**:301
RIVERTON HEIGHTS (Washington)
map (47° 28′N 122° 17′W) **20**:35
RIVETING
Fairbairn, Sir William **8**:9
RIVIERA (France) **16**:234 *illus.*
cities
Cannes **4**:109
Monte Carlo (Monaco) **13**:552
Nice (France) **14**:180 *illus.*
Côte d'Azur **5**:304
map (45° 15′N 9° 30′E) **11**:321
RIVIERA BEACH (Florida)
map (26° 47′N 80° 4′W) **8**:172
RIVIERA BEACH (Maryland)
map (39° 10′N 76° 32′W) **13**:188
RIVIÈRE DES ANGUILLES (Mauritius)
map (20° 29′S 57° 32′E) **13**:237
RIVIÈRE-DU-LOUP (Quebec)
map (47° 50′N 69° 32′W) **16**:18
RIVULARIA
blue-green algae **3**:342 *illus.*
RIYADH (Saudi Arabia) **16**:234
climate **2**:237 *table*; **17**:94 *table*
map (24° 38′N 46° 43′E) **17**:94
RIZA-I-ABBASI **16**:234 *bibliog.*
Persian art and architecture **15**:186
RIZAL, JOSÉ B.
Philippines **15**:238
RNA
See also NUCLEIC ACID
cancer **4**:102
cell **4**:233
memory **13**:291
Monod, Jacques Lucien **13**:536
Ochoa, Severo **14**:346
operon **14**:404
protein synthesis **15**:575–576 *illus.*
retrovirus **16**:183–184
ribosome **16**:206
Sanger, Frederick **17**:64
ROACH **16**:234–235 *bibliog.*
ROACH, HAL
film, history of **8**:82
ROAD TOWN (Virgin Islands)
map (18° 27′N 64° 37′W) **19**:605
ROADRUNNER **4**:283 *illus.*; **16**:235 *illus.*
cuckoo **5**:382
foot **3**:288 *illus.*
ROADS AND HIGHWAYS **16**:235–239 *bibliog., illus.*
Autobahn **2**:355
highway interchange **4**:36 *illus.*; **16**:239 *illus.*; **19**:280 *illus.*
history **16**:235–238
Boston Post Road **3**:410
Camino Real **4**:62
European trade routes, Middle Ages **13**:395 *map*
Frontier, U.S. **8**:341 *map*
Inca **11**:72
National Road **14**:45
Roman roads **16**:279 *map*
royal roads **11**:70 *map*
Santa Fe Trail **17**:68 *map*
Silk Road **17**:308
Telford, Thomas **19**:90
transportation **19**:278–280; **19**:280; **19**:282
United States, 19th century **19**:445 *map*
Wilderness Road **20**:150
Zane, Ebenezer **20**:355
Interstate Highway System **11**:225
Pan American Highway **15**:53–54
road construction **16**:236–239 *illus.*
centrifugal and centripetal forces **4**:255
gravel, surfacing **9**:302
macadam **13**:3
mica **13**:371
soil mechanics **18**:38
traffic control **19**:264
Trans-Amazonian Highway **3**:463 *illus.*; **19**:267
Trans-Canada Highway **19**:267
turnpike **19**:351
viaduct **19**:567
ROADSIDE SKIPPER BUTTERFLY **3**:597 *illus.*
butterflies and moths **3**:595
ROAN CLIFFS
map (39° 20′N 109° 40′W) **19**:492
ROAN HIGH KNOB MOUNTAIN
map (36° 5′N 82° 7′W) **19**:104
ROAN MOUNTAIN (Tennessee)
map (36° 12′N 82° 5′W) **19**:104
ROAN PLATEAU
map (39° 30′N 110° 0′W) **19**:492
ROANE (county in Tennessee)
map (35° 50′N 84° 30′W) **19**:104
ROANE (county in West Virginia)
map (38° 40′N 81° 20′W) **20**:111
ROANOKE (Alabama)
map (33° 9′N 85° 22′W) **1**:234
ROANOKE (Illinois)
map (40° 48′N 89° 12′W) **11**:42
ROANOKE (Indiana)
map (40° 58′N 85° 22′W) **11**:111
ROANOKE (Staunton) RIVER
map (35° 56′N 76° 43′W) **14**:242
ROANOKE (Virginia) **16**:239
map (37° 16′N 79° 57′W) **19**:607
ROANOKE (county in Virginia)
map (37° 15′N 80° 5′W) **11**:335
ROANOKE COLONY **9**:313 *illus.*; **16**:239 *bibliog.*
Dare, Virginia **6**:37
Grenville, Sir Richard **9**:359
Raleigh, Sir Walter **16**:79
ROANOKE ISLAND
map (35° 53′N 75° 39′W) **14**:242
North Carolina **14**:245
ROANOKE RAPIDS (North Carolina)
map (36° 28′N 77° 40′W) **14**:242
ROARING SPRING (Pennsylvania)
map (40° 20′N 78° 24′W) **15**:147
ROATÁN (Honduras)
map (16° 18′N 86° 35′W) **10**:218
ROB ROY **16**:239–240 *bibliog.*
ROBBE-GRILLET, ALAIN **16**:240 *bibliog., illus.*
new novel **14**:140
Resnais, Alain **16**:177
ROBBER SYNOD
Chalcedon, Council of **4**:270
ROBBERY **16**:240 *bibliog.*
crime **5**:346 *table*
larceny **12**:206
ROBBIA, DELLA (family) *see* DELLA ROBBIA (family)
ROBBINS (Tennessee)
map (36° 21′N 84° 35′W) **19**:104
ROBBINS, FREDERICK CHAPMAN **16**:240
ROBBINS, HAROLD **16**:240
ROBBINS, JEROME **16**:240 *bibliog., illus.*
Afternoon of a Faun, The **1**:181
New York City Ballet **14**:155
ROBBINSVILLE (North Carolina)
map (35° 19′N 83° 48′W) **14**:242
ROBELINE (Louisiana)
map (31° 41′N 93° 18′W) **12**:430
ROBERSONVILLE (North Carolina)
map (35° 50′N 77° 15′W) **14**:242
ROBERT, HENRY MARTYN
Robert's Rules of Order **16**:242
ROBERT, HUBERT **16**:240–241 *bibliog.*
ROBERT, NICOLAS LOUIS
paper **15**:68 *illus.*
ROBERT I, KING OF SCOTLAND (Robert the Bruce) **16**:241 *bibliog., illus.*
ROBERT II, DUKE OF NORMANDY
Newcastle upon Tyne (England) **14**:164–165
ROBERT GUISCARD **16**:241 *bibliog.*
Italy, history of **11**:328
Normans **14**:221
ROBERT LEE (Texas)
map (31° 54′N 100° 29′W) **19**:129
ROBERT S. KERR LAKE
map (35° 25′N 95° 0′W) **14**:368
ROBERT WOOD JOHNSON FOUNDATION **16**:241
ROBERTS (county in South Dakota)
map (45° 35′N 97° 0′W) **18**:103
ROBERTS (county in Texas)
map (35° 50′N 100° 50′W) **19**:129
ROBERTS, SIR CHARLES G. D. **16**:241
Canadian literature **4**:93
Fredericton (New Brunswick) **8**:294
ROBERTS, ELIZABETH MADOX **16**:241 *bibliog.*
ROBERTS, FREDERICK SLEIGH, 1ST EARL ROBERTS OF KANDAHAR **16**:241 *bibliog.*
concentration camp **5**:169
ROBERTS, ORAL **16**:242
ROBERTS, OWEN J. **16**:242 *bibliog.*
United States v. *Butler* **19**:464
ROBERTS, WILLIAM
antibiotics **2**:57
Newman, Ernest **14**:169–170
ROBERT'S RULES OF ORDER (book) **16**:242
parliamentary procedure **15**:93–95
ROBERTSDALE (Pennsylvania)
map (40° 11′N 78° 7′W) **15**:147
ROBERTSON (county in Kentucky)
map (38° 32′N 84° 4′W) **12**:47
ROBERTSON (county in Tennessee)
map (36° 30′N 86° 50′W) **19**:104
ROBERTSON (county in Texas)
map (31° 0′N 96° 30′W) **19**:129
ROBERTSON, ETHEL LINDESAY *see* RICHARDSON, HENRY HANDEL
ROBERTSON, JAMES **16**:242
photojournalism **15**:273
ROBERTSON, SIR JOHNSTON FORBES- *see* FORBES-ROBERTSON, SIR JOHNSTON
ROBERTSON, OSCAR **3**:113 *illus.*; **16**:242 *bibliog.*
ROBERTSON, PAT **16**:242
religious broadcasting **16**:142
ROBERTSPORT (Liberia)
map (6° 45′N 11° 22′W) **12**:313
ROBESON (county in North Carolina)
map (34° 40′N 79° 0′W) **14**:242
ROBESON, PAUL **16**:242 *bibliog., illus.*
ROBESPIERRE, MAXIMILIEN **8**:323 *illus.*; **16**:242–243 *bibliog., illus.*
arrest of (July 27, 1794) **8**:324 *illus.*
Europe, history of **7**:291
French Revolution **8**:323
Jacobins **11**:345
ROBIE HOUSE (Chicago) **1**:329 *illus.*; **20**:288 *illus.*
cantilever **4**:117
ROBIN **16**:243 *illus.*
bird **3**:286
European robin **8**:228 *illus.*
magpie robin **13**:62
territoriality **3**:286 *illus.*; **19**:121
ROBIN GOODFELLOW *see* PUCK
ROBIN HOOD **16**:243
May Day **13**:242
Nottinghamshire (England) **14**:268
ROBINS, BENJAMIN
ballistics **3**:49
ROBINSON (Illinois)
map (39° 0′N 87° 44′W) **11**:42
ROBINSON (Newfoundland)
map (48° 15′N 58° 48′W) **14**:166
ROBINSON, BROOKS **16**:243
ROBINSON, CHARLES **16**:243
Topeka (Kansas) **19**:237
ROBINSON, EDDIE (football coach) **16**:243
ROBINSON, EDWARD (biblical scholar)
biblical archaeology **3**:241–242
ROBINSON, EDWARD G. (actor) **16**:244 *bibliog., illus.*
ROBINSON, EDWIN ARLINGTON **16**:244 *bibliog., illus.*
ROBINSON, FRANK **16**:244 *bibliog.*
ROBINSON, HENRY PEACH **15**:272 *illus.*; **16**:244 *illus.*
Linked Ring Brotherhood **12**:358
ROBINSON, JACKIE **3**:107 *illus.*; **16**:245 *bibliog., illus.*
Rickey, Branch **16**:216
ROBINSON, JOHN **16**:245
ROBINSON, JOSEPH T.
Robinson-Patman Act **16**:246
ROBINSON, LENNOX **16**:245
ROBINSON, R. H.
skyscraper **17**:350
ROBINSON, SIR ROBERT **16**:245
ROBINSON, SUGAR RAY **3**:432 *illus.*; **16**:245–246 *bibliog., illus.*
ROBINSON COLLEGE (Cambridge University) **4**:53
ROBINSON CRUSOE (book) **16**:246 *bibliog.*
Defoe, Daniel **6**:83–84
Grandville **9**:286
ROBINSON-PATMAN ACT **16**:246
Federal Trade Commission **8**:42
Patman, Wright **15**:112
Sherman Anti-Trust Act **17**:259
ROBIQUET, PIERRE-JEAN
codeine **5**:90
ROBLIN (Manitoba)
map (51° 14′N 101° 21′W) **13**:119
ROBORÉ (Bolivia)
map (18° 20′S 59° 45′W) **3**:366
ROBOT **16**:246 *bibliog.*
artificial intelligence **2**:221
Čapek, Karel **4**:122
computer **5**:160g *illus.*; **5**:160i
cybernetics **5**:401
industrial use **16**:246
automation **2**:358
automobile assembly **19**:68 *illus.*
computer-aided manufacturing **5**:160k *illus.*; **5**:160L *illus.*
manufacturing **13**:133
ROBSART, AMY *see* LEICESTER, ROBERT DUDLEY, EARL OF
ROBSON, MOUNT
map (53° 7′N 119° 9′W) **3**:491
ROBSTOWN (Texas)
map (27° 47′N 97° 40′W) **19**:129
ROBUSTI, JACOPO *see* TINTORETTO
ROBY (Texas)
map (32° 45′N 100° 23′W) **19**:129
ROCA, JULIO A. **16**:246 *bibliog.*
ROCAFUERTE (Ecuador)
map (0° 55′S 80° 28′W) **7**:52
ROCAFUERTE, VICENTE **16**:246 *bibliog.*
ROCHA (Uruguay)
map (34° 29′S 54° 20′W) **19**:488
ROCHAMBEAU, JEAN BAPTISTE DONATIEN DE VIMEUR, COMTE DE **16**:246 *bibliog.*
American Revolution **1**:359 *map*
ROCHDALE SOCIETY OF EQUITABLE PIONEERS
cooperative **5**:244
ROCHE, KEVIN **16**:246–247 *bibliog.*
ROCHE, MAZO DE LA *see* DE LA ROCHE, MAZO
ROCHE MOUTONNÉE
glaciers and glaciation **9**:194
ice ages **11**:8
ROCHECHOUART, FRANÇOISE ATHÉNAÏS DE, MARQUISE DE MONTESPAN *see* MONTESPAN, FRANÇOISE ATHÉNAÏS DE ROCHECHOUART, MARQUISE DE
ROCHEFOUCAULD, FRANÇOIS, DUC DE LA *see* LA ROCHEFOUCAULD, FRANÇOIS, DUC DE
ROCHELLE (Georgia)
map (31° 57′N 83° 27′W) **9**:114
ROCHELLE (Illinois)
map (41° 56′N 89° 4′W) **11**:42
ROCHELLE PARK (New Jersey)
map (40° 55′N 74° 4′W) **14**:129
ROCHES, PETER DES
Henry III, King of England **10**:125
ROCHE'S LIMIT **16**:247
binary stars **3**:257
ROCHESTER (Indiana)
map (41° 4′N 86° 13′W) **11**:111
ROCHESTER (Michigan)
map (42° 41′N 83° 8′W) **13**:377
ROCHESTER (Minnesota) **16**:247
map (44° 2′N 92° 29′W) **13**:453
Mayo (family) **13**:248
ROCHESTER (New Hampshire)
map (43° 18′N 70° 59′W) **14**:123
ROCHESTER (New York) **16**:247
map (43° 10′N 77° 36′W) **14**:149
ROCHESTER (Pennsylvania)
map (40° 43′N 80° 17′W) **15**:147
ROCHESTER INSTITUTE OF TECHNOLOGY **16**:247
ROCK **16**:247 *bibliog., illus.*
See also names of specific rocks, e.g., BASALT; GNEISS; SANDSTONE; etc.
butte **3**:592
cave **4**:222
classifications **16**:247
earth, structure and composition of **7**:20
igneous rock **11**:33–36
metamorphic rock **13**:331–333
petrography **15**:206–207
Rosenbusch, Harry **16**:315
sedimentary rock **17**:184
Werner, Abraham Gottlob **20**:104
cobble **5**:84
cycles, geochemistry **9**:96
drift, glacial **6**:272
exfoliation **7**:331
foliation **8**:195
formations
Cambrian Period **4**:51 *map*
Carboniferous Period **4**:138 *map*
Cretaceous Period **5**:340 *map*
Devonian Period **6**:144 *map*
Jurassic Period **11**:477 *map*
Ordovician Period **14**:421 *map*
Permian Period **15**:175 *map*
pollen stratigraphy **15**:407
Precambrian time **15**:492 *map*
Silurian Period **17**:311 *map*
Tertiary Period **19**:123 *map*
Triassic Period **19**:295 *map*
frost action **8**:346
gravel **9**:302
Hurley, Patrick Mason **10**:316
joint (geology) **11**:440
lava **12**:240
Lehmann, Johann Gottlob **12**:276

ROCK (cont.)
lunar rock
photomicrograph 13:562 illus.
meteor and meteorites 13:336
mining and quarrying 13:446–450
Moon 13:562–563 illus.
moraine 13:572
mushroom rock 12:182 illus.
oxide minerals 14:476
paleomagnetism 15:41–42
petroleum 15:208 illus.
petrology 15:215
regolith 16:129
roads and highways 16:236 illus.; 16:238–239 illus.
silica minerals 17:304
soil 18:37
solid solution 18:54
stratigraphy 18:292–293 illus.
structural geology 18:303
talus 19:18
vein deposit 19:536
waterfall 20:63
weathering 20:82–83
wind action 20:170
zuegens 12:182 illus.
ROCK (county in Minnesota)
map (43° 38′N 96° 13′W) 13:453
ROCK (county in Nebraska)
map (42° 30′N 99° 30′W) 14:70
ROCK (county in Wisconsin)
map (42° 43′N 89° 3′W) 20:185
ROCK, THE (Gibraltar)
map (36° 8′N 5° 21′W) 9:174
ROCK ART
prehistoric art 15:507–511
ROCK BAY (British Columbia)
map (50° 20′N 125° 29′W) 3:491
ROCK OF CHICKAMAUGA see THOMAS, GEORGE HENRY
ROCK CLIMBING see MOUNTAIN CLIMBING
ROCK CREEK
map (38° 54′N 77° 4′W) 13:188
ROCK DOVE see PIGEON
ROCK FALLS (Illinois)
map (41° 47′N 89° 41′W) 11:42
ROCK FORMATIONS 4:138 map
ROCK HALL (Maryland)
map (39° 8′N 76° 14′W) 13:188
ROCK HILL (South Carolina)
map (34° 56′N 81° 1′W) 18:98
ROCK ISLAND (Illinois)
map (41° 30′N 90° 34′W) 11:42
ROCK ISLAND (county in Illinois)
map (41° 25′N 90° 32′W) 11:42
ROCK MUSIC 16:247–250 bibliog., illus.
Beach Boys 3:137
Beatles, The 3:144–145 illus.
Bee Gees, The 3:159
Berry, Chuck 3:225
blues 3:346
Bowie, David 3:428
Brown, James 3:514
Charles, Ray 4:290
Cream, The 5:334
disco 6:189
Dylan, Bob 6:319
Fleetwood Mac 8:159
Franklin, Aretha 8:282
Grateful Dead, The 9:301
ground bass 9:373
Hendrix, Jimi 10:121
Holly, Buddy 10:204
jazz 11:390
Jefferson Airplane 11:393
Jethro Tull 11:408
John, Elton 11:423
Joplin, Janis 11:446
King, B. B. 12:80
Motown 13:616
Presley, Elvis 15:532
Redding, Otis 16:15
Rolling Stones, The 16:272
Springsteen, Bruce 18:200
video, music 19:576f
Who, The 20:143
Wonder, Stevie 20:204–205
Woodstock Festival 20:213
Zappa, Frank 20:356
ROCK 'N' ROLL see ROCK MUSIC
ROCK PAINTING 1:174 illus.
African art 1:160–161 illus.
ROCK PINK see CARNATION
ROCK PLATED LIZARD see GERRHOSAURID
ROCK PORT (Missouri)
map (40° 25′N 95° 31′W) 13:476
ROCK RABBIT see HYRAX
ROCK RAPIDS (Iowa)
map (43° 26′N 96° 10′W) 11:244
ROCK RIVER (Illinois)
map (41° 29′N 90° 37′W) 11:42
ROCK RIVER (Wyoming)
map (41° 44′N 105° 58′W) 20:301
ROCK AND ROLL see ROCK MUSIC
ROCK SALT see HALITE
ROCK SPRINGS (Wyoming)
map (41° 35′N 109° 13′W) 20:301
ROCK SUCKER see CLINGFISH
ROCK VALLEY (Iowa)
map (43° 12′N 96° 18′W) 11:244
ROCKAWAY INLET
map (40° 34′N 73° 55′W) 14:129
ROCKBRIDGE (county in Virginia)
map (37° 50′N 79° 25′W) 19:607
ROCKCASTLE (county in Kentucky)
map (37° 20′N 84° 20′W) 12:47
ROCKCASTLE RIVER
map (36° 58′N 84° 21′W) 12:47
ROCKDALE (county in Georgia)
map (33° 40′N 84° 0′W) 9:114
ROCKDALE (Illinois)
map (41° 30′N 88° 6′W) 11:42
ROCKDALE (Maryland)
map (39° 21′N 76° 46′W) 13:188
ROCKDALE (Texas)
map (30° 39′N 97° 0′W) 19:129
ROCKEACH, MILTON
moral awareness 13:572
ROCKEFELLER (family) 16:250 bibliog., illus.
Chicago, University of 4:342
Cloisters, The 5:64
Metropolitan Museum of Art, The 13:348
public relations 15:610
Rockefeller Foundation 16:251
ROCKEFELLER, DAVID
Rockefeller (family) 16:250
ROCKEFELLER, JOHN (JAY)D. IV
Rockefeller (family) 16:250
ROCKEFELLER, JOHN D. 16:250 illus.
Cleveland (Ohio) 5:52
Rockefeller (family) 16:250
ROCKEFELLER, JOHN D., JR.
Rockefeller (family) 16:250
Williamsburg (Virginia) 20:162 illus.
ROCKEFELLER, JOHN D. III
Rockefeller (family) 16:250
ROCKEFELLER, LAURANCE
Rockefeller (family) 16:250
ROCKEFELLER, NELSON A. 16:250–251 bibliog., illus.
ROCKEFELLER, WINTHROP
Rockefeller (family) 16:250
ROCKEFELLER CENTER (New York CIty) 16:251 bibliog.
New York (city) 14:145 map
Radio City Music Hall 16:53
ROCKEFELLER FOUNDATION 16:251
green revolution 9:348
ROCKEFELLER PLATEAU
map (80° 0′S 135° 0′W) 2:40
ROCKEFELLER UNIVERSITY 16:251
ROCKET (botany) see ROQUETTE
ROCKET (locomotive) 16:251 bibliog., illus.; 18:255 illus.; 19:67 illus.
locomotive 12:388–389 illus.
ROCKET SALAD see ROQUETTE
ROCKETS AND MISSILES 16:251–260 bibliog., illus., table
aerospace industry 1:125–128 table
antiaircraft systems 2:55–56
astronautics 2:274–276
defense, national 6:82 table
guidance and control systems 9:393–394
history 16:251–256
Goddard, Robert 9:219–220
Korolev, Sergei 12:123
Oberth, Hermann 14:315
Tsiolkovsky, Konstantin 16:252
von Braun, Wernher 19:633
launch centers
Baikonur Cosmodrome 3:26
Kapustin Yar 12:26
Kennedy Space Center 12:44–45
Lop Nor (China) 12:412
Peenemünde 15:132
Vandenberg Air Force Base 19:518
White Sands Missile Range 20:138
military aviation 2:372
military warning and detection systems 13:422
BMEWS 3:348
SAMOS 17:47
missiles, ballistic 3:49
antiballistic missile 2:56–57
MIRV missile 13:465
naval vessels 14:56–57 illus.
missiles, ballistic (land-launched) 16:254–256
Atlas 2:297; 16:256 illus.
Jupiter (rocket) 11:474
Minuteman missile 13:462; 16:254 illus.
MX missile 13:688
surface-to-air missile 16:254–255 illus.; 18:359
Thor (rocket) 19:177 illus.
Titan (rocket) 13:462; 16:256 illus.; 19:211
V-2 (Germany) 16:253 illus.; 16:256 illus.; 19:500–501
missiles, ballistic (submarine-launched) 16:255
Polaris (missile) 15:393; 16:254 illus.
Poseidon (missile) 15:458
Trident 19:296–297
missiles, tactical 16:255
air-to-surface missiles 16:255–256
bazooka 3:135
cruise missile 5:365–366; 16:256
military missiles 16:254–256
Nike-Hercules 16:255 illus.
nuclear strategy 14:288
Redeye 2:56 illus.
SA-6 Gainful 2:56 illus.
sidewinder 17:294
Sparrow III missile 16:255 illus.
surface-to-air missile 16:254–255 illus.; 18:359
TOW missile 16:255 illus.
National Aeronautics and Space Administration 14:28
propellant, rocket 16:259–260
helium 10:113
hydrazine 10:331
hydrogen 10:339
lithium 12:370–371
propulsion 16:258–260 table
Goddard, Robert 9:219–220
jet propulsion 11:406–407
plasma physics 15:346
ramjet 16:80–81
research institutions
Jet Propulsion Laboratory 11:407
rocket planes
V-1 (Germany) 19:500
X-15 20:311
rockets, sounding 16:254; 18:77
Aerobee 1:122
rockets, space 16:256–258
Agena (rocket) 1:183 illus.; 9:72–73
Ariane (European Space Agency) 2:153
Atlas (missile) 2:297 illus.; 13:307; 16:256 illus.
Atlas (missile), Centaur 4:249
Centaur 2:297 illus.; 4:249
Delta (rocket) 6:95; 16:256 illus.; 19:177 illus.
Diamant (France) 6:151
Juno (rocket) 16:116–117; 16:256 illus.
Jupiter (rocket) 11:474; 16:256 illus.
photon rocket 18:131 illus.
Proton (USSR) 15:578; 17:41
Redstone 16:116–117; 16:256 illus.
Redstone, Jupiter 11:474
Saturn (rocket) 16:257 illus.; 17:91–92
Scout 17:155–156
Soviet A-1 rocket 16:256 illus.
Soviet A-2 rocket 16:256 illus.
Soviet D-1 rocket 16:257 illus.
Thor (rocket) 19:177 illus.
Thor-Delta (rocket) 16:256–257 illus.
Titan (rocket) 16:256 illus.; 19:210–211
Vanguard 16:256 illus.; 19:519
satellite, artificial 17:85
SEASAT 17:176
space exploration 18:118
ROCKFISH
scorpion fish 17:148
ROCKFORD (Alabama)
map (32° 53′N 86° 13′W) 1:234
ROCKFORD (Illinois) 16:260
map (42° 17′N 89° 6′W) 11:42
ROCKFORD (Iowa)
map (43° 3′N 92° 57′W) 11:244
ROCKFORD (Tennessee)
map (35° 49′N 83° 56′W) 19:104
ROCKFOWL 16:260
ROCKGLEN (Saskatchewan)
map (49° 10′N 105° 57′W) 17:81
ROCKHAMPTON (Australia)
map (23° 23′S 150° 31′E) 2:328
ROCKINGHAM (county in New Hampshire)
map (43° 0′N 71° 8′W) 14:123
ROCKINGHAM (North Carolina)
map (34° 56′N 79° 46′W) 14:242
ROCKINGHAM (county in North Carolina)
map (36° 25′N 79° 45′W) 14:242
ROCKINGHAM (county in Virginia)
map (38° 35′N 78° 55′W) 19:607
ROCKINGHAM, CHARLES WATSON-WENTWORTH, 2D MARQUESS OF 16:260 bibliog.
ROCKLAKE (North Dakota)
map (48° 47′N 99° 15′W) 14:248
ROCKLAND (Idaho)
map (42° 34′N 112° 53′W) 11:26
ROCKLAND (Maine)
map (44° 6′N 69° 6′W) 13:70
ROCKLAND (Massachusetts)
map (42° 8′N 70° 55′W) 13:206
ROCKLAND (county in New York)
map (41° 9′N 73° 59′W) 14:149
ROCKLANDS (Swaziland)
map (25° 55′S 31° 20′W) 18:380
ROCKLEDGE (Florida)
map (28° 20′N 80° 43′W) 8:172
ROCKMART (Georgia)
map (34° 0′N 85° 2′W) 9:114
ROCKNE, KNUTE 16:260 bibliog.
football 8:216
ROCKPORT (Indiana)
map (39° 32′N 91° 0′W) 11:111
ROCKPORT (Kentucky)
map (37° 20′N 86° 59′W) 12:47
ROCKPORT (Texas)
map (28° 1′N 97° 4′W) 19:129
ROCKSPRINGS (Texas)
map (30° 1′N 100° 13′W) 19:129
ROCKSTONE (Guyana)
map (5° 59′N 58° 33′W) 9:410
ROCKSUCKER 8:117 illus.
ROCKTON (Illinois)
map (42° 27′N 89° 4′W) 11:42
ROCKVILLE (Indiana)
map (39° 46′N 87° 14′W) 11:111
ROCKVILLE (Maryland)
map (39° 5′N 77° 9′W) 13:188
ROCKVILLE CENTRE (New York)
map (40° 40′N 73° 37′W) 14:149
ROCKWALL (Texas)
map (32° 56′N 96° 28′W) 19:129
ROCKWALL (county in Texas)
map (32° 55′N 96° 23′W) 19:129
ROCKWEED see FUCUS
ROCKWELL (Iowa)
map (42° 59′N 93° 11′W) 11:244
ROCKWELL, NORMAN 16:261 bibliog., illus.
The Adventures of Tom Sawyer 14:275 illus.
The Dugout 16:261 illus.
Richard M. Nixon 14:205 illus.
Saturday Evening Post 15:170 illus.
ROCKWELL CITY (Iowa)
map (42° 24′N 94° 38′W) 11:244
ROCKWELL INTERNATIONAL CORPORATION 1:128 table
ROCKWOOD (Maine)
map (45° 41′N 69° 44′W) 13:70
ROCKWOOD (Tennessee)
map (35° 52′N 84° 41′W) 19:104
ROCKY FORD (Colorado)
map (38° 3′N 103° 43′W) 5:116
ROCKY HILL (Connecticut)
map (41° 40′N 72° 39′W) 5:193
ROCKY MOUNT (North Carolina)
map (35° 56′N 77° 48′W) 14:242
ROCKY MOUNT (Virginia)
map (37° 0′N 79° 54′W) 19:607
ROCKY MOUNTAIN GOAT see MOUNTAIN GOAT
ROCKY MOUNTAIN HOUSE (Alberta)
map (52° 22′N 114° 55′W) 1:256
ROCKY MOUNTAIN SPOTTED FEVER 16:261
rickettsia 16:216
tick 19:191–192
ROCKY MOUNTAINS 16:261–263 bibliog., illus., map
British Columbia 3:489
Canada 16:71 illus.
Colorado 5:115
economic and cultural geography 16:262–263
environment 16:262
Glacier National Park 9:195
map (48° 0′N 116° 0′W) 16:262
Montana 13:548 illus.
mountain 13:619
national parks 14:38–39 map, table
North America 14:226 illus.
Powell, John Wesley 15:481
ranges and peaks
Elbert, Mount 7:102
Pikes Peak 15:301
Sangre de Cristo Mountains 14:137 illus.
Teton Range 19:127
Wasatch Range 20:34

wind
chinook **4**:396
Wyoming **20**:299
ROCKY RIVER
map (41° 30′N 81° 49′W) **14**:357
ROCKY RIVER (Ohio)
map (41° 30′N 81° 40′W) **14**:357
ROCOCO MUSIC **16**:263 *bibliog.*
Couperin (family) **5**:313–314
Mannheim school **13**:125
Pergolesi, Giovanni Battista **15**:165
ROCOCO STYLE **2**:198; **16**:263–265 *bibliog., illus.*
antique collecting **2**:66 *illus.*
architecture **2**:135
Austria
Austrian art and architecture **2**:352–354
Thumb (family) **19**:184
Boffrand, Germain **3**:358–359
Brazil
Aleijadinho **1**:271
cathedrals and churches **4**:207–208
costume **5**:298–299 *illus.*
drawing **6**:265
dressing table **8**:376 *illus.*
France
Bérain, Jean **3**:207
Boucher, François **3**:419–420
Clodion **5**:63
Cotte, Robert de **5**:304
Cuvilliés, François **5**:399
Falconet, Étienne Maurice **8**:12
Fragonard, Jean Honoré **8**:259
French art and architecture **8**:305
Lemoyne, Jean Baptiste **12**:280–281
Meissonnier, Juste Aurèle **13**:283
styles of Louis XIII-XVI **18**:311
van Loo, Charles André **19**:515
furniture **8**:376–377
Germany
Amalienburg Pavilion **1**:321
Feuchtmayer, Joseph Anton **8**:63
Fischer, Johann Michael **8**:110–111
German art and architecture **9**:127
Günther, Ignaz **9**:406
Nymphenburg ware **14**:309
Zimmermann, Dominikus **20**:367
Great Britain
Chelsea ware **4**:311
Chippendale, Thomas **4**:396
English art and architecture **7**:186–187
Georgian style **9**:119
interior design **11**:212–214 *illus.*
opera houses **14**:402
painting **15**:21–22
parlor **8**:378 *illus.*
Scandinavian art and architecture **17**:112–113
sculpture **17**:164
RODA (Virginia)
map (36° 58′N 82° 50′W) **19**:607
RODCHENKO, ALEKSANDR MIKHAILOVICH **16**:265 *bibliog.*
mobile **13**:487
RODDICKTON (Newfoundland)
map (50° 52′N 56° 8′W) **14**:166
RODENBACH, GEORGES
Belgian literature **3**:175
RODENT **16**:265–266 *bibliog., illus.*
agouti **1**:187
beaver **3**:148–149
capybara **4**:129
cavy **4**:226–227
chinchilla **4**:377
chipmunk **4**:396
classification, biological **16**:266
deer mouse **6**:81
diseases
bubonic plague **3**:532
flea **8**:158
parasitic diseases **15**:82
tularemia **19**:330
typhus **19**:367
dormouse **6**:243
evolution **16**:266
false paca **8**:15
flying squirrel **8**:191
gerbil **9**:122
gopher **9**:247–248
groundhog **9**:373–374
guinea pig **9**:399–400
hamster **10**:33
hare **10**:48–49
jerboa **11**:396
kangaroo rat **12**:15–16
lemming **12**:280
mammal **13**:103; **13**:105 *illus.*
mouse **13**:625–626
muskrat **13**:683
nutria **14**:302
paca **15**:4
pocket gopher **15**:376–377
population dynamics **15**:438
porcupine **15**:440
rat **16**:91–92
savanna life **17**:98
sewellel **17**:222
springhare **18**:200
squirrel **18**:204–205
steppe life **18**:257 *illus.*
strychnine **18**:304
teeth **16**:265 *illus.*; **19**:70; **19**:72 *illus.*
vole **19**:628
RODEO (contest) **16**:266 *bibliog., illus.*
Calgary Exhibition and Stampede **1**:258 *illus.*
RODEO (New Mexico)
map (31° 50′N 109° 2′W) **14**:136
RODEO COWBOYS ASSOCIATION
rodeo **16**:266
RODGERS (family) **16**:266–267 *bibliog.*
RODGERS, BILL **16**:267
RODGERS, RICHARD **16**:267 *bibliog.*
See also HAMMERSTEIN, OSCAR, II
RÓDHOS (Greece) *see* RHODES (Greece)
RODIA, SIMON
Watts Towers **20**:70
RODIN, AUGUSTE **16**:267 *bibliog., illus.*
The Age of Bronze **16**:267 *illus.*
Balzac **2**:200–201 *illus.*
Bourdelle, Émile Antoine **3**:423
bronzes **3**:508
Burghers of Calais, The
Calais (France) **4**:21
Carpeaux, Jean Baptiste **4**:163–164
Oceanides **17**:164 *illus.*
San Francisco art museums **17**:54
sculpture **17**:165
Storrs, John Bradley **18**:285
RODNEY, CAESAR **6**:90 *illus.*
McKean, Thomas **13**:27
RODNINA, IRINA **11**:14 *illus.*
RODÓ, JOSÉ ENRIQUE
Uruguay **19**:489
RODONIT, CAPE OF
map (41° 35′N 19° 27′E) **1**:250
RODRIGUES, AMALIA
fado **8**:7
RODRIGUEZ (island)
dodo bird **6**:212
RODRÍGUEZ, ABELARDO
Mexico, history of **13**:365
RODRÍGUEZ, ALIRIO
Venezuela **19**:543
RODRÍGUEZ CABRILLO, JUAN *see* CABRILLO, JUAN RODRÍGUEZ
RODRÍGUEZ DE FRANCIA, JOSÉ GASPAR *see* FRANCIA, JOSÉ GASPAR RODRÍGUEZ DE
RODS (eye)
eye **7**:349–350 *illus.*
Wald, George **20**:9
RODVANYI, NETTI REILING *see* SEGHERS, ANNA
ROE *see* CAVIAR
ROE, THOMAS
Jahangir, Mogul Emperor **11**:349
ROE* v. *WADE* AND *DOE* v. *BOLTON **16**:267–268
abortion **1**:60
privacy, invasion of **15**:556
ROEBLING (New Jersey)
map (40° 7′N 74° 47′W) **14**:129
ROEBLING, JOHN A. AND WASHINGTON AUGUSTUS **16**:268 *bibliog.*
ROEHM, ERNST **16**:268
ROELAND PARK (Kansas)
map (39° 2′N 94° 37′W) **12**:18
ROEMER, OLAUS *see* RØMER, OLE
ROENTGEN, DAVID
desk **8**:377 *illus.*
furniture **8**:373
ROENTGEN, WILHELM CONRAD **4**:328 *illus.*; **16**:268 *bibliog.*
chemistry, history of **4**:328
Würzburg (West Germany) **20**:297
X rays **20**:310 *illus.*
examination, medical **7**:326
ROERICH, NIKOLAI KONSTANTINOVICH
Ballets Russes de Serge Diaghilev **3**:48
ROESELARE (Belgium)
map (50° 57′N 3° 8′E) **3**:177
ROETHKE, THEODORE **16**:268 *bibliog.*
ROFF (Oklahoma)
map (34° 38′N 96° 50′W) **14**:368
ROGAGUA, LAKE
map (13° 43′S 66° 54′W) **3**:366
ROGALLO, FRANCIS
kite (object) **12**:93 *illus.*
ROGER II, KING OF SICILY **16**:268 *bibliog.*
Italy, history of **11**:328
Naples, Kingdom of **14**:15
ROGER MILLS (county in Oklahoma)
map (35° 40′N 99° 40′W) **14**:368
ROGERS (Arkansas)
map (36° 20′N 94° 7′W) **2**:166
ROGERS (county in Oklahoma)
map (36° 25′N 95° 35′W) **14**:368
ROGERS (Texas)
map (30° 56′N 97° 14′W) **19**:129
ROGERS, CARL **16**:268–269 *bibliog.*
client-centered therapy **5**:54
humanistic psychology **10**:299
personality **15**:189
psychology, history of **15**:598 *illus.*
psychotherapy **15**:603
ROGERS, GINGER **2**:267 *illus.*; **8**:85 *illus.*; **16**:269 *bibliog.*
ROGERS, JOHN (clergyman) **16**:269 *bibliog.*
ROGERS, MOUNT **19**:608 *illus.*
map (36° 39′N 81° 33′W) **19**:607
ROGERS, RANDOLPH **16**:269 *bibliog.*
ROGERS, RICHARD (architect) *see* PIANO, RENZO, AND ROGERS, RICHARD
ROGERS, ROBERT **16**:269 *bibliog.*
French and Indian Wars **8**:313 *map*
ROGERS, WILL **16**:269 *bibliog.*
ROGERS, WILLIAM P. **16**:270
ROGERS CITY (Michigan)
map (45° 25′N 83° 49′W) **13**:377
ROGERSVILLE (New Brunswick)
map (46° 44′N 65° 26′W) **14**:117
ROGERSVILLE (Tennessee)
map (36° 25′N 83° 2′W) **19**:104
ROGET'S THESAURUS (book)
thesaurus **19**:167
ROGGEVEEN, JACOB
Easter Island **7**:33
Samoa **17**:46
Western Samoa **20**:117
ROGUE RIVER
map (42° 26′N 124° 25′W) **14**:427
ROGUE RIVER (Oregon)
map (42° 26′N 123° 10′W) **14**:427
ROHAN, CARDINAL DE
Diamond Necklace, Affair of the **6**:152
ROHE, LUDWIG MIES VAN DER *see* MIES VAN DER ROHE, LUDWIG
ROHLFS, CHRISTIAN **16**:270 *bibliog.*
RÖHM, ERNST *see* ROEHM, ERNST
ROHMER, ERIC **16**:270
ROHMER, SAX **16**:270 *bibliog.*
ROIDIS, EMMANUEL
Greek literature, modern **9**:344
ROJAS (Argentina)
map (34° 12′S 60° 44′W) **2**:149
ROJAS, FERNANDO DE
Spanish literature **18**:157–158
ROJAS, MANUEL
Chile **4**:355
ROJAS PINILLA, GUSTAVO
Colombia **5**:109
ROJAS ZORRILLA, FRANCISCO DE **16**:270 *bibliog.*
ROKEBY VENUS (Velázquez) **2**:205 *illus.*
ROKEL RIVER (Sierra Leone)
map (8° 33′N 12° 48′W) **17**:296
ROLAMITE **16**:270 *illus.*
ROLAND **16**:271
Chanson de Roland **4**:282
Orlando Furioso **14**:445
ROLAND (Arkansas)
map (34° 54′N 92° 30′W) **2**:166
ROLAND DE LA PLATIÈRE, JEAN MARIE
Roland de la Platière, Jeanne Manon Philipon **16**:271
ROLAND DE LA PLATIÈRE, JEANNE MANON PHILIPON **16**:271 *bibliog.*
ROLDÁN (family) **16**:271 *bibliog.*
ROLDOS AGUILERA, JAIME
Ecuador **7**:53
ROLE **16**:271 *bibliog.*
family **8**:17–18
marriage **13**:164–165
norm, social **14**:219
social structure and organization **18**:17
sociology **18**:28–29
women in society **20**:201
young people **20**:335
ROLETTE (North Dakota)
map (48° 40′N 99° 51′W) **14**:248
ROLETTE (county in North Dakota)
map (48° 45′N 99° 50′W) **14**:248
ROLFE (Iowa)
map (42° 49′N 94° 31′W) **11**:244
ROLFE, JOHN **16**:271
Pocahontas **15**:376
Powhatan **15**:486
ROLFE, REBECCA *see* POCAHONTAS (American Indian)
ROLLA (Kansas)
map (37° 7′N 101° 38′W) **12**:18
ROLLA (Missouri)
map (37° 57′N 91° 46′W) **13**:476
ROLLA (North Dakota)
map (48° 52′N 99° 37′W) **14**:248
ROLLAND, ROMAIN **16**:271 *bibliog.*
ROLLER (zoology) **16**:271–272
ROLLER BEARING **3**:143–144 *illus.*
ROLLER-DANCING *see* ROLLER-SKATING
ROLLER DERBY **16**:272 *bibliog.*
ROLLER HOCKEY *see* ROLLER-SKATING
ROLLER-SKATING **16**:272 *bibliog.*
Roller Derby **16**:272
skateboarding **17**:332–333
ROLLING FORK
map (37° 55′N 85° 50′W) **12**:47
ROLLING FORK (Mississippi)
map (32° 55′N 90° 52′W) **13**:469
ROLLING MILL
aluminum **1**:318 *illus.*
ROLLING STONES, THE (rock-music group) **16**:272 *bibliog.*
Woodstock Festival **20**:213
ROLLO (Viking)
Normans **14**:221
ROLLS, CHARLES S. *see* ROLLS-ROYCE
ROLLS-ROYCE **2**:365 *illus.*; **16**:272 *bibliog.*
RÖLVAAG, OLE EDVART **16**:272 *bibliog.*
ROM (people)
gypsies **9**:415
ROM (READ-ONLY MEMORY)
computer **5**:160c; **5**:160f; **5**:160i
computer memory **5**:161
ROMA (Italy) *see* ROME (Italy)
ROMAGNA *see* EMILIA-ROMAGNA (Italy)
ROMAIN, CAPE OF
map (33° 0′N 79° 22′W) **18**:98
ROMAINE *see* LETTUCE
ROMAINS, JULES **16**:272–273 *bibliog.*
ROMAN (Romania)
map (46° 55′N 26° 56′E) **16**:288
ROMAN ART AND ARCHITECTURE **16**:273–277 *bibliog., illus.*
See also ARCHITECTURE—Rome, ancient
acanthus **1**:71–72
baroque art and architecture **3**:90–91
bronze sculpture **16**:275
bronzes **3**:506–507 *illus.*
costume **5**:293–294 *illus.*
decorative arts **16**:277
Early Christian art and architecture **7**:9–10
forum **8**:242
fountains **8**:252
furniture **8**:374
Getty Museum **9**:160
glassware, decorative **9**:203 *illus.*
Herculaneum **10**:138
history
Vitruvius **19**:621
Winckelmann, Johann **20**:168
iconography **11**:21
interior design **11**:211
jewelry **11**:409 *illus.*
landscape architecture **12**:185
landscape painting **12**:188
Maderno, Carlo **13**:40
Maison Carrée **13**:76
marble sculpture **16**:275
mosaic **13**:593–594 *illus.*; **18**:144 *illus.*
mural painting **13**:645–646 *illus.*
Mysteries, Villa of the **13**:692
neoclassicism (art) **14**:81–82
Ostia **14**:458
painting **15**:18–19 *illus.*
paving, mosaic, and stuccowork **16**:276–277
perspective **15**:190
Piazza Armerina **15**:289–290
Pompeii **15**:424
portrait sculpture **16**:275–276
portraiture **15**:446
relief sculpture **16**:276
sarcophagus **17**:76
sculpture **17**:160–161 *illus.*
Spanish art and architecture **18**:151–152
still-life painting **18**:268–269 *illus.*
technology, history of **19**:62–63

ROMAN ART AND ARCHITECTURE (cont.)
temple 19:96–97 *illus.*
tomb 19:231
triumphal arch 19:304
urban planning 19:481–483
Vatican museums and galleries 19:527–528
Veii 19:535
wall painting 16:276
ROMAN CANDLE 8:107 *illus.*
ROMAN CATHOLIC CHURCH 4:413 *map*; 16:140 *map*; 16:277–278 *bibliog.*
See also COUNCIL, ECUMENICAL; COUNTER-REFORMATION; PAPACY; names of specific popes, e.g., INNOCENT III, POPE; JOHN PAUL II, POPE; etc.; names of specific saints, e.g., PETER, SAINT; ROSE OF LIMA, SAINT; etc.; names of specific cathedrals, e.g., SAINT PATRICK'S CATHEDRAL; SAINT PETER'S BASILICA; etc.
Aquinas, Saint Thomas 2:94–95
art and architecture
baroque art and architecture 3:89–91
cathedrals and churches 4:207–208
Vatican museums and galleries 19:527–528
Australia
Gilroy, Norman Thomas 9:183
Baltimore Catechism 4:202
Belgium
Mercier, Désiré Joseph 13:304–305
birth control 3:295
Canada
Jesuit Estates Act 11:402
Laval, François de 12:240
Léger, Paul Émile 12:274
Manitoba Schools Question 13:122
canon law 4:114–155
Cardinals, College of 4:144
Catholic Youth Organization, National 4:212
conciliarism 5:170
concordat 5:171
council, ecumenical 5:310
Curia, Roman 5:391
decretals 6:76
diocese 16:277
doctrines 16:278
Summa Theologiae 18:339
Duns Scotus, John 6:301
Eastern Rite churches 7:34
education
Detroit, University of 6:136
Fordham University 8:224
Georgetown University 9:112
Holy Cross, College of the 10:209
Latin American universities 12:232–233
Loyola University 12:445
Marquette University 13:163
Notre Dame University 14:267
Ottawa, University of 14:461
private schools 15:557
Saint Louis University 17:23
Saint Mary's College 17:24
San Francisco, University of 17:54
theological seminaries 19:157
Trinity College (Washington, D.C.) 19:301
Europe, history of 7:284–285; 7:287
excommunication 7:327
France
Gallicanism 9:19
Jansenism 11:359
Lamennais, Félicité Robert de 12:175
Lefebvre, Marcel 12:272
Germany
Kulturkampf 12:136
Rahner, Karl 16:70
Ratzinger, Joseph 16:94
Great Britain
Becket, Saint Thomas 3:151
Caesarea (site in Israel) 4:15
Campion, Saint Edmond 4:67
James I, King of England 11:355–356
John, King of England 11:426–427
Manning, Henry Edward 13:125
Mary I, Queen of England 13:185–186
More, Saint Thomas 13:575–576
Newman, John Henry 14:170
Pole, Reginald 15:395
Scotland 17:151
Southwell, Saint Robert 18:112
Thirty Years' War 19:171 *map*
Wiseman, Nicholas Patrick Stephen 20:190
Wolsey, Thomas 20:200
heresy 10:141–142
Hungary
Mindszenty, Jozsef 13:437
Immaculate Conception 11:54
Index 11:78
indulgences 11:152
infallibility 11:161–162
Inquisition 11:183–185
investiture controversy 11:237–238
Ireland, history of 11:263–265
Italy
Gasparri, Pietro 9:55
Rosmini-Serbati, Antonio 16:318
Latin America
Illich, Ivan 11:40
Zumárraga, Juan de 20:382
liturgy 12:373–374
breviary 3:475
Divine Office 6:203
Mary 13:184–185
Mass 13:200
Mexico
Mexico, history of 13:363
Tlaxcala (city in Mexico) 19:216
Middle Ages 13:392–393
ministry, Christian 13:450
missions, Christian 13:467–468
modernism 13:498
music
cantor 4:118
hymn 10:347
Italian music 11:317
mass (musical setting) 13:201
medieval music 13:274 *illus.*
plainsong 15:325–326
Renaissance music 16:156
mysticism 13:693
North America 14:233
Northern Ireland 14:255
organization and structure 16:277–278
parish 16:277
Poland 15:390 *illus.*
Wyszyński, Stefan 20:305
pope *see* PAPACY
purgatory 15:629
Reformation 16:121–123 *map*
religious orders 16:143
rosary 16:312
sacrament 17:7
saint 17:15
scholasticism 17:131
shrines and relics
Fátima (Portugal) 8:34
Lourdes (France) 12:436
Montserrat (mountain) 13:560
Monza (Italy) 13:560
reliquary 16:143–144
Spain
Torquemada, Tomas de 19:243
Victoria, Francisco de 19:621
Spain, history of 18:145–146
suicide 18:330
Switzerland
Kung, Hans 12:136–137
tithe 19:212
Ultramontanism 19:377
United States
Cabrini, Saint Frances Xavier 4:8
Carroll, John 4:168–169
Cody, John Patrick 5:90
Cooke, Terence J. 5:237
Cushing, Richard James 5:397
Day, Dorothy 6:55
Gibbs, James 9:174
Hughes, John Joseph 10:292–293
Knights of Columbus 12:101
Lamy, Jean Baptiste 12:176–177
Lathrop, Rose Hawthorne 12:216
McCloskey, John 13:9
Mexican-Americans 10:178
Neumann, Saint John Nepomucene 14:104–105
Serra, Junípero 17:210
Seton, Saint Elizabeth Ann Bayley 17:214
Sheen, Fulton J. 17:248
Smith, Alfred E. 17:367
Spanish missions 18:160–161
Spellman, Frances Joseph 18:177
Vatican City 19:526–527 *illus.*
Vatican Council, First 19:527
Vatican Council, Second 19:527
worship and practices 16:278
ROMAN COURTOIS *see* COURTLY LOVE
ROMAN CURIA *see* CURIA, ROMAN
ROMAN DE LA ROSE, LE (book) 16:278 *bibliog.*
Guillaume de Lorris 9:395
ROMAN EMPIRE *see* ROME, ANCIENT
ROMAN FORUM *see* FORUM
ROMAN LANGUAGE *see* LATIN LANGUAGE
ROMAN LAW 16:278–279 *bibliog.*, *illus.*
civil law 5:11
Europe, history of 7:281
historians
Mommsen, Theodor 13:515
inheritance 11:177
Justinian Code 11:478–479
law 12:242
law, history of 12:244–246
Savigny, Friedrich Karl von 17:99
ROMAN LEGION *see* LEGION, ROMAN
ROMAN LITERATURE, ANCIENT *see* LATIN LITERATURE
ROMAN MYTHOLOGY
Apollo 2:80
Bacchus 3:9
Bacchanalia 3:9
basilisk 3:110
Bona Dea 3:375
Ceres 4:260
Diana 6:153
Dido 6:161
Egeria 7:72
Faunus 8:38
Flora 8:168
Fortuna 8:241
Janus 11:360
Juno 11:471
Jupiter 11:471
lares 12:207
Luna 12:459
Lupercalia 12:465–466
Mars 13:166
Mercury 13:305
Minerva 13:444
Minos 13:459
Morpheus 13:587
mythology 13:701
Neptune 14:88
nymphs 14:309–310
Ops 14:408
Parnassus 15:96
penates 15:141
Quirinus 16:28
Romulus and Remus 16:305
Saturn 17:91
Sol 18:40
Somnus 18:62
Venus 19:548
Vesta 19:564
Vulcan 19:640
ROMAN NUMERAL
numeral 14:294
ROMAN PHILOSOPHY
Epictetus 7:218
Marcus Aurelius, Roman Emperor 13:147–148
Seneca, Lucius Annaeus 17:200
Stoicism 18:278
ROMAN ROADS 16:279 *bibliog.*, *map*
ancient city of Rome 16:300 *map*
Appian Way 16:279 *map*; 16:296 *illus.*
Emilia-Romagna (Italy) 7:156
roads and highways 16:235–237 *illus.*
Via Flaminia 16:279 *map*
ROMAN SENATE *see* SENATE, ROMAN
ROMAN YURIEV *see* YURIEV, ROMAN
ROMANCE 16:280 *bibliog.*
Cabell, James B. 4:4
Orlando Furioso 14:445
Petronius Arbiter 15:215
pulp magazines 15:620
ROMANCE LANGUAGES 16:280–281 *bibliog.*, *illus.*, *table*
Austria-Hungary 2:351 *map*
Catalan language
Lull, Raymond 12:454
dictionaries 6:159
French 16:281
and English 7:191
French-based Creole 5:338
Italian 16:281
linguistic features 16:281
linguistics 12:356
nonnational languages 16:280
Portuguese 16:281
Portugal 15:450
Portuguese-based creoles 5:338
Provençal 16:281
Romanian 16:281
Spanish 16:281
Vulgar Latin 16:280–281
ROMANENKO, YURY VIKTOROVICH 16:281 *bibliog.*
ROMANESQUE ART AND ARCHITECTURE 16:282–286 *bibliog.*, *illus.*
arch and vault 2:113–114
architecture 2:133 *illus.*
Carolingian art and architecture 4:160–161
cathedrals and churches 4:205 *illus.*
clerestory 5:51
costume 5:294–297 *illus.*
Durham Cathedral 6:306
Flemish art and architecture 8:161–162
France 16:282–284
French art and architecture 8:303–304
German art and architecture 9:124
Germany 16:282–284
Gislebertus 9:191
Great Britain 16:282
iconography 11:22
illuminated manuscripts 11:48
Italian art and architecture 11:308–310
Italy 16:282–284
Nicholas of Verdun 14:181
Norman architecture 14:219–220
Portuguese art and architecture 15:456
Sant'Ambrogio 17:69
Scandinavian art and architecture 17:111–112
sculpture 17:162 *illus.*
Spanish art and architecture 18:153
tapestry 19:32
Tower of London 19:254
triforium 19:297
Tuscan 11:308 *illus.*
tympanum 19:362
ROMANESQUE REVIVAL
Marshall Field Wholesale Store 1:328 *illus.*; 1:329
ROMANI, FELICE
Norma 14:219
ROMANIA 16:286–290 *bibliog.*, *illus.*, *map*, *table*
agriculture 16:289
arts 16:288–289
cities
Brăila 3:442
Braşov 3:457
Bucharest 3:534 *illus.*
Cluj 5:71
Constanţa 5:208
Craiova 5:328
Galaţi 9:10
Iaşi 11:3
Ploieşti 15:368
Timişoara 19:203
climate 16:287 *table*
dance 6:27 *illus.*
hora 10:233
economic activity 16:289 *illus.*
education 16:288 *illus.*
European universities 7:308 *table*
flag 16:286 *illus.*
forestry and fishing 16:289 *illus.*
government 16:289
welfare spending 20:98 *table*
history 16:289–290
Antonescu, Ion 2:70
Balkan Wars 3:38
Bratianu (family) 3:458
Carol I, King 4:160
Carol II, King 4:160
Ceausescu, Nicolae 4:228
Cuza, Alexandru Ion 5:399
Dobruja 6:209
Ferdinand, King of Romania 8:53
Gheorghiu-Dej, Gheorghe 9:166–167
Iorga, Nicolae 11:243
Iron Guard 11:273
Little Entente 12:372–373
Marie (queen consort of Ferdinand) 13:151
Moldavian Soviet Socialist Republic (USSR) 13:505–506
World War II 20:255
land and resources 16:286–288 *map*, *table*
language
Romance languages 16:280–281
literature *see* ROMANIAN LITERATURE
manufacturing 16:289
map (46° 0′N 25° 30′E) 7:268
music
Enesco, Georges 7:176
Neolithic Period 7:303 *illus.*
people 7:275 *illus.*; 16:288–289 *illus.*
Szeklers 18:416
regions
Bucovina 3:537

Moldavia **13**:505
Transylvania **19**:283 *map*
Walachia **20**:8–9
religion **16**:288
rivers, lakes, and waterways **16**:287–288
trade **16**:289
vegetation and animal life **16**:288
Warsaw Treaty Organization **20**:32
Yiddish theater **20**:328
ROMANIAN LITERATURE **16**:290 *bibliog.*
authors
Alecsandri, Vasile **1**:270
Alexandrescu, Grigore **1**:277
Caragiale, Ion Luca **4**:131
Eliade, Mircea **7**:138
Eminescu, Mihail **7**:156
ROMANO, GIULIO *see* GIULIO ROMANO
ROMANOV (dynasty) **16**:290–291 *bibliog.*
Russia/Union of Soviet Socialist Republics, history of **16**:353–359
Sophia **18**:66–67
tsars
Alexander I **1**:275–276
Alexander II **1**:276
Alexander III **1**:276
Alexis **1**:278
Ivan IV, Grand Duke of Moscow and Tsar of Russia (Ivan the Terrible) **11**:332
Michael, Tsar of Russia **13**:372
ROMANOV, ANASTASIA
Ivan IV, Grand Duke of Moscow and Tsar of Russia (Ivan the Terrible) **11**:332–333
Romanov (dynasty) **16**:290
ROMANOV, FYODOR NIKITICH
Michael, Tsar of Russia **13**:372
ROMANOV, MIKHAIL FYODOROVICH *see* MICHAEL, TSAR OF RUSSIA
ROMANS, EPISTLE TO THE **16**:291 *bibliog.*
ROMANSCH LANGUAGES *see* RHETO-ROMANCE LANGUAGES
ROMANTIC BALLET **3**:42–43
dance **6**:25
ROMANTICISM (art) **16**:291–292 *bibliog., illus.*
Allston, Washington **1**:304–305
art criticism **2**:207
Austrian art and architecture **2**:353
Biedermeier **3**:247
Blake, William **3**:325–326
Bonington, Richard Parkes **3**:380
château **4**:302
Constable, John **5**:206–207
Delacroix, Eugène **6**:86–87
English art and architecture **7**:187
French art and architecture **8**:306
Friedrich, Caspar David **8**:332
Fuseli, Henry **8**:381
German art and architecture **9**:127–128
Gothic Revival **9**:262–263
iconography **11**:23
Ingres, Jean Auguste Dominique **11**:176–177
landscape painting **12**:190
Lawrence, Sir Thomas **12**:251
Louitherbourg, Philippe Jacques de **12**:437
Martin, John **13**:179
Millet, Jean François **13**:429–430
painting **15**:21–22
Raeburn, Sir Henry **16**:69
Runge, Philipp Otto **16**:346
Schwind, Moritz von **17**:140
sculpture **17**:164–165
Turner, Joseph Mallord William **19**:350
ROMANTICISM (literature) **16**:292–293 *bibliog., illus.*
American literature **1**:343–344
Bryant, William Cullen **3**:529
Emerson, Ralph Waldo **7**:154–155
Hawthorne, Nathaniel **10**:79
Longfellow, Henry Wadsworth **12**:407
Melville, Herman **13**:289–290
Poe, Edgar Allan **15**:377–378
Thoreau, Henry David **19**:178
Whitman, Walt **20**:140–141
Argentine literature
Echeverría, Esteban **7**:37
ballade **3**:41
Byronic hero **3**:603
Danish literature
Hauch, Johannes Carsten **10**:68
drama **6**:260
Dutch and Flemish literature
Conscience, Hendrik **5**:199
English literature **7**:198
Akenside, Mark **1**:230
Austen, Jane **2**:326
Blake, William **3**:325–326
Byron, George Gordon, Lord **3**:603
Clare, John **5**:36
Coleridge, Samuel Taylor **5**:100–101
Gray, Thomas **9**:307
Hazlitt, William **10**:84
Hunt, Leigh **10**:311–312
Keats, John **12**:35–36
Lyrical Ballads **12**:479
Shelley, Percy Bysshe **17**:253
Southey, Robert **18**:112
Wordsworth, William **20**:216–217
Young, Edward **20**:333
French literature **8**:317–318
Chateaubriand, François René, Vicomte de **4**:303
Constant, Benjamin **5**:207–208
Dumas, Alexandre (1802–70) **6**:296–297
Gautier, Théophile **9**:62
Hugo, Victor **10**:294
Hunchback of Notre Dame, The **10**:304
Lamartine, Alphonse de **12**:174
Mérimée, Prosper **13**:310
Musset, Alfred de **13**:684
Nodier, Charles **14**:212
Rousseau, J.J. **16**:325–327
Staël, Madame de **18**:209
Villiers de L'Isle-Adam, Philippe **19**:598
German literature **9**:133
Arnim, Achim and Bettina von **2**:184
Brentano, Clemens **3**:473
Chamisso, Adelbert von **4**:275
Eichendorff, Joseph, Freiherr von **7**:91
Goethe, Johann Wolfgang von **9**:223–224
Heine, Heinrich **10**:108–109
Hoffmann, Ernst Theodor Amadeus **10**:195
Novalis **14**:271–272
Schlegel, August Wilhelm von **17**:124
Schlegel, Friedrich von **17**:124
Tieck, Ludwig **19**:194–195
Uhland, Johann Ludwig **19**:374
Gothic romance **9**:263
noble savage **14**:211
Polish literature
Mickiewicz, Adam **13**:383–384
Portuguese literature
Garrett, João Baptista de Almeida **9**:50
Russian literature
Lermontov, Mikhail **12**:296
Scottish literature
Scott, Sir Walter **17**:154
Spanish literature **18**:159
Zorilla y Moral, José **20**:380
Swedish literature
Heidenstam, Verner von **10**:107
ROMANTICISM (music) **16**:293–294 *bibliog., illus.*
aeolian harp **1**:119
Badings, Henk **3**:19
Barraqué, Jean **3**:93
Berlioz, Hector **3**:218–219
Brahms, Johannes **3**:441
Bruch, Max **3**:520
Bruckner, Anton **3**:521
Chadwick, George Whitefield **4**:267
Chausson, Ernest **4**:305
Chopin, Frédéric **4**:405
English music **7**:203
Gade, Niels **9**:7
German and Austrian music **9**:130–131
Grieg, Edvard **9**:361–362
Janáček, Leoš **11**:358
Lalo, Édouard **12**:172
Liszt, Franz **12**:367
MacDowell, Edward **13**:14
Mahler, Gustav **13**:65
Mendelssohn, Felix **13**:295-296
Montemezzi, Italo **13**:552
music, history of Western **13**:666
nocturne **14**:212
orchestra and orchestration **14**:418
Paganini, Niccolò **15**:13
Pfitzner, Hans **15**:217
Rachmaninoff, Sergei **16**:36
Respighi, Ottorino **16**:178
Richter, Sviatoslav **16**:215
Rimsky-Korsakov, Nikolai Andreyevich **16**:224–225
Rubbra, Edmund **16**:335
Rubinstein, Arthur **16**:337
Schubert, Franz **17**:135
Schumann, Robert **17**:137
Sibelius, Jean **17**:291
sonata **18**:63
Spohr, Louis **18**:192
Strauss, Richard **18**:294–295
symphony **18**:405
Tchaikovsky, Peter Ilich **19**:51–52
Verdi, Giuseppe **19**:549–550
Wagner, Richard **20**:4–5
Weber, Carl Maria von **20**:86–87
ROMANUS III, EASTERN ROMAN EMPEROR
Zoë, Byzantine Empress **20**:371
ROMANY LANGUAGE
gypsies **9**:415
Indo-Iranian languages **11**:145
ROMBERG, SIGMUND **16**:294 *bibliog.*
ROME (Georgia)
map (34° 16′N 85° 11′W) **9**:114
ROME (Illinois)
map (40° 53′N 89° 30′W) **11**:42
ROME (Italy) **7**:276 *illus.*; **16**:294–297 *bibliog., illus., map*
See also ROME, ANCIENT
ancient city **16**:300 *map*
climate **7**:272 *table*; **11**:322 *table*
educational, cultural, and historic landmarks **16**:295–296 *map*
history (since AD 476) **16**:296–297
Arnold of Brescia **2**:186
Rienzo, Cola di **16**:219
World War II **20**:271 *illus.*
Italian art and architecture **11**:308–314
map (41° 54′N 12° 29′E) **11**:321
Romulus and Remus **16**:305
Vatican City **19**:526–527 *illus., map*
ROME (Mississippi)
map (33° 52′N 90° 29′W) **13**:469
ROME (New York) **16**:297
map (43° 13′N 75° 27′W) **14**:149
ROME, ANCIENT **16**:297–304 *bibliog., illus., maps, table*
agriculture, history of **1**:190
reaper **16**:104 *illus.*
Alba Longa **1**:248
ancient city **16**:297–304 *map*
army
bases **16**:279 *map*
cavalry **4**:221 *illus.*
legion, Roman **11**:164 *illus.*; **12**:274
legionnaire **7**:281 *illus.*
art and architecture *see* ROMAN ART AND ARCHITECTURE
Baalbek **3**:5
baths **3**:122
Caesarea **4**:15
Capitoline Hill **4**:126
catacombs **4**:197
census **4**:248
circus **18**:144 *illus.*
coins **14**:296 *illus.*; **16**:301 *illus.*; **18**:229 *illus.*
costume **5**:293–294 *illus.*
cosmetics **5**:281 *illus.*
jewelry **11**:409 *illus.*
shoes **17**:280 *illus.*
Tyrian purple **19**:367
Decline and Fall of the Roman Empire, The History of the **6**:76
divorce **6**:205
Doura-Europos **6**:249
drama *see* THEATER, HISTORY OF THE
education **7**:59–60
engineering **2**:94; **7**:177
aqueduct **2**:94
fortification **8**:238–239
Frontinus, Sextus Julius **8**:345
pump **15**:622
technology, history of **19**:62–63 *illus.*
tunnel **19**:337
viaduct **19**:567
Vitruvius **19**:621
water supply **20**:56 *illus.*
Etruscans **7**:259–260
Europe, history of **7**:280–282
exploration **7**:334
forum **8**:242 *illus.*
Gerasa **9**:121
gladiators **9**:195
government
caesar **4**:13
consul **5**:225
emperors **16**:304 *table*
fasces **8**:30
Senate, Roman **17**:199–200
tribunes **19**:296
triumvirate **19**:304
harbor
Ostia **14**:458
Herculaneum **10**:137–138
historians *see* HISTORY—Roman historians
Homs (Syria) **10**:217
house (in Western architecture) **10**:264–266 *illus.*
imperialism **11**:61
Iol **11**:239
Italy, history of **11**:327
Jerusalem (Israel) **11**:400
journalism **11**:454
Latin language **12**:233–234
Romance languages **16**:280–281
laurel **12**:237 *illus.*
law *see* ROMAN LAW
legends
Brennus **3**:473
Coriolanus, Gnaeus Marcius **5**:263
Horatius **10**:234
Lucretia **12**:451
Romulus and Remus **16**:305
Leptis Magna **12**:295
literature *see* LATIN LITERATURE
logic **12**:395
maps and mapmaking **13**:139
medicine **13**:268
headache, treatment **10**:85
mythology *see* ROMAN MYTHOLOGY
naval vessels **14**:54 *illus.*
navy **14**:62
Nîmes (France) **14**:198
numeral, Roman **14**:294
Paestum **15**:13
patricians **15**:113
philosophy *see* ROMAN PHILOSOPHY
piracy **15**:312
plebeians **15**:364
Pompeii **15**:423–424
population **15**:433
prostitution **15**:573
provinces and expansion **16**:299 *map*
religion
See also ROMAN MYTHOLOGY
Bacchanalia **3**:9
Christianity **4**:414
divination **6**:202
Isis **11**:288
Mithraism **13**:484–485
roads and highways **16**:235–236 *illus.*; **16**:238 *illus.*
Roman roads **16**:279–280 *map*
Scotland **17**:151–152
semaphore **17**:194
Seven Wonders of the World **17**:216–218
ship **17**:264–265 *illus.*
shipping routes **16**:279 *map*
shorthand **17**:284
Sicily (Italy) **17**:293
slavery **17**:352 *illus.*
sports
boxing **3**:431
chariot racing **4**:288; **18**:196 *illus.*
gymnasium **9**:412
gymnastics **9**:412–413; **18**:196 *illus.*
handball **10**:35
stadium **18**:208
wrestling **18**:195 *illus.*
state (in political philosophy) **18**:229–231
taxation **19**:46
Timgad **19**:203
urban planning
Apollodorus of Damascus **2**:84
Veii **19**:535–536
Villanovans **19**:597
wagon **20**:6
weights and measures **20**:93–94
wine **20**:174
women in society **20**:201–202
753–509 BC kingdom
kingship **16**:297
Lars Porsena, King of Clusium **12**:208
Tarquinius Priscus, Etruscan King of Rome **19**:39
Tarquinius Superbus, Etruscan King of Rome **19**:39
509–27 BC republic **16**:297–302
Actium, Battle of **1**:89
Agrippa, Marcus Vipsanius **1**:199
Antony, Mark **2**:70–71
Bithynia **3**:300
Brutus, Marcus Junius **3**:528
Caesar, Gaius Julius **4**:13–15

ROME, ANCIENT (cont.)
Camillus, Marcus Furius **4**:62
Carthage **4**:173
Cassius Longinus, Gaius **4**:185
Catiline **4**:212
Cato, Marcus Porcius (Cato the Elder) **4**:212–213
Cato, Marcus Porcius (Cato the Younger) **4**:213
Catulus, Quintus Lutatius **4**:217
Cicero, Marcus Tullius **4**:428–429
Cincinnatus, Lucius Quinctius **4**:432
Cinna, Lucius Cornelius **4**:434
Clodius, Publius **5**:63–64
Crassus, Marcus Licinius **5**:332
Drusus (family) **6**:283
Ennius, Quintus **7**:207
Fabius (family) **8**:4
Flamininus, Titus Quinctius **8**:151
France, history of **8**:265–266
Gallic Wars **9**:19
Gracchus (family) **9**:275
Greece, ancient **9**:333–334
Hannibal **10**:38
Jugurtha, King of Numidia **11**:465
knight **12**:99
La Tène **12**:150
Latins **12**:234
Lepidus, Marcus Aemilius **12**:295
Low Countries, history of the **12**:438–439
Marius, Gaius **13**:158
Metellus Numidicus, Quintus Caecilius **13**:336
Metellus Pius, Quintus Caecilius **13**:336
Mithradates VI, King of Pontus (Mithradates the Great) **13**:484
Numidia **14**:295
Octavia **14**:347
Philip V, King of Macedonia **15**:234
Pompey the Great **15**:424–425
Punic Wars *see* PUNIC WARS
Sabines **17**:5
Samnites **17**:46
Scipio Africanus Major **17**:147
Scipio Africanus Minor **17**:147
Spain, history of **18**:144 *illus.*
Spartacus **18**:165
Sulla, Lucius Cornelius **18**:336
sumptuary laws **18**:340
Tigranes I, King of Armenia **19**:197
27 BC-476 AD empire **16**:302–304
See also BYZANTINE EMPIRE
Aetius, Flavius **1**:131
Agrippina II **1**:199
Alaric I, King of the Visigoths **1**:240
Antonine Wall **2**:70
the Antonines **16**:303
Antoninus Pius, Emperor **2**:70
area of greatest extent **16**:279 *map*
Augustus, Emperor **2**:321–322
Aurelian, Emperor **2**:324
Boadicea **3**:349
Caligula, Emperor **4**:39
Cappadocia **4**:127–128
Caracalla, Emperor **4**:130
Claudius I, Emperor **5**:44
Commodus, Emperor **5**:138
Constantine I, Emperor **5**:208–209
Constantius I, Emperor **5**:210
Constantius II, Emperor **5**:210
c.400 AD **7**:282 *map*
Diocletian, Emperor **6**:182–183
division of empire **16**:304
Domitian, Emperor **6**:235
Egypt, ancient **7**:83
emperors **16**:304 *table*
Franks **8**:285–286
Galatia **9**:10
Galba, Emperor **9**:13
Galerius, Emperor **9**:14
Gallienus, Emperor **9**:19
Gaul **9**:60–61
Germanic peoples **9**:138
Germanicus Caesar **9**:138
Germany, history of **9**:147–148
Goths **9**:263
Gratian, Roman Emperor in the West **9**:301
Great Britain, history of **9**:309
Hadrian, Roman Emperor **10**:8
Hadrian's Wall **10**:8
Heliogabalus, Roman Emperor **10**:112
Herod (dynasty) **10**:144
Honorius, Roman Emperor in the West **10**:224
Huns **10**:311
Julian the Apostate, Emperor **11**:466
Licinius, Emperor **12**:323
Livia Drusilla **12**:376
manorialism **13**:126
Marcus Aurelius, Emperor **13**:147–148
Maximian, Emperor **13**:239
Middle East, history of the **13**:401
Nero, Emperor **14**:90
Odoacer **14**:350
Palestine **15**:44
Pannonia **15**:60
Praetorian guard **15**:487
Roman roads **16**:279 *map*
Samaria **17**:45
Severus, Septimius, Emperor **17**:220
Stilicho, Flavius **18**:268
Theodosius I, Roman Emperor (Theodosius the Great) **19**:156–157
Theodosius II, Roman Emperor in the East **19**:157
Tiberius, Emperor **19**:189
Titus, Emperor **19**:215
Trajan, Emperor **19**:266
Valens, Emperor in the East **19**:504
Valentinian I, Emperor in the West **19**:504
Valentinian II, Emperor in the West **19**:505
Valentinian III, Emperor in the West **19**:505
Valerian, Emperor **19**:505
Vandals **19**:518
Vespasian, Emperor **19**:564
ROME, TREATY OF
European Community **7**:299
ROME, UNIVERSITY OF **16**:304
ROMÉ DE L'ISLE, JEAN BAPTISTE
mineral **13**:439
ROMEO (Michigan)
map (42° 48′N 83° 1′W) **13**:377
ROMEO AND JULIET (ballet) **8**:207 *illus.*
ROMEO AND JULIET (play) **16**:304 *bibliog.*
ROMEOVILLE (Illinois)
map (41° 39′N 88° 5′W) **11**:42
RØMER, OLE **16**:304–305
speed of light **12**:335 *illus.*
transit circle **19**:273
ROMERO, CARLOS HUMBERTO *see* HUMBERTO ROMERO, CARLOS
ROMERO, OSCAR ARNULFO
El Salvador **7**:101
ROMMEL, ERWIN **16**:305 *bibliog., illus.*
Alamein, El **1**:239
World War II **20**:256 *illus.*; **20**:258; **20**:262–263 *map*
ROMMELPOT
musical instruments **13**:676
ROMNEY (West Virginia)
map (39° 21′N 78° 45′W) **20**:111
ROMNEY, GEORGE **16**:305 *bibliog.*
ROMULUS (Michigan)
map (42° 13′N 83° 24′W) **13**:377
ROMULUS AUGUSTULUS
Italy, history of **11**:327
Rome, ancient **16**:304
ROMULUS AND REMUS **16**:305 *bibliog.*
Alba Longa **1**:248
feral children **8**:51
Rome, ancient **16**:297 *illus.*
RONALD, WILLIAM
Canadian art and architecture [illegible]:90–91
RONAN (Montana)
map (47° 32′N 114° 6′W) **13**:547
RONCHAMP (France)
Notre Dame du Haut **4**:208 *illus.*; **12**:253 *illus.*
RONDE ISLAND
map (12° 18′N 61° 35′W) **9**:358
RONDO **16**:305
RONDÔNIA (Brazil)
map (10° 52′S 61° 57′W) **3**:460
RONDÔNIA TERRITORY (Brazil)
map (11° 0′S 63° 0′W) **3**:460
RØNNE (Denmark)
map (55° 6′N 14° 42′E) **6**:109
RONNE ICE SHELF
map (78° 30′S 61° 0′W) **2**:40
RONO, HENRY **16**:305
RONSARD, PIERRE DE **16**:305–306 *bibliog.*
RONSE (Belgium)
map (50° 45′N 3° 36′E) **3**:177
ROOF AND ROOFING **16**:306 *bibliog., illus.*
house (in Western architecture) **10**:268–269 *illus.*
roof, thatched **16**:306 *illus.*
ROOK **16**:306
ROOKS (county in Kansas)
map (39° 20′N 99° 20′W) **12**:18
ROOKWOOD WARE **15**:472 *illus.*; **16**:306 *bibliog.*
ROOM, ABRAM
film, history of **8**:83
ROONEY, MICKEY **16**:306
ROOSA, STUART A. **16**:307 *bibliog.*
Apollo program **2**:83
ROOSENDAAL (Netherlands)
map (51° 32′N 4° 28′E) **14**:99
ROOSEVELT (Arizona)
map (33° 40′N 111° 9′W) **2**:160
ROOSEVELT (Minnesota)
map (48° 48′N 95° 6′W) **13**:453
ROOSEVELT (county in Montana)
map (48° 15′N 105° 3′W) **13**:547
ROOSEVELT (county in New Mexico)
map (34° 0′N 103° 20′W) **14**:136
ROOSEVELT (Utah)
map (40° 18′N 109° 59′W) **19**:492
ROOSEVELT, ELEANOR **16**:307 *bibliog., illus.*
Roosevelt, Franklin Delano **16**:307
ROOSEVELT, FRANKLIN DELANO **15**:526 *illus.*; **16**:307–309 *bibliog., illus.*
Brain Trust **3**:448–449
Cairo Conference **4**:19
Campobello Island **4**:67
Canada, history of **4**:87 *illus.*
Casablanca Conference **4**:180
Democratic party **6**:101 *illus.*
Depression of the 1930s **6**:119–120
Einstein, Albert **7**:94
Federal Theatre Project **8**:42
fireside chats **15**:524 *illus.*
Four Freedoms **8**:253
Frankfurter, Felix **8**:281
Garner, John Nance **9**:48
Good Neighbor Policy **9**:245
Hopkins, Harry L. **10**:231–232
Hyde Park (New York state) **10**:329
Ickes, Harold **11**:20
Jackson, Robert Houghwout **11**:343
Lend-Lease **12**:281
National Recovery Administration **14**:45
New Deal **14**:119–120; **16**:308–309
Pearl Harbor **15**:126
Perkins, Frances **15**:172
presidential elections
Liberal parties **12**:312
Roosevelt, Eleanor **16**:307
Supreme Court of the United States **18**:358
Szilard, Leo **18**:416
Tehran Conference **19**:73
United States, history of the **19**:454–455
Vietnam War **19**:584
Warm Springs (Georgia) **20**:30
World War II **20**:250–275 *illus.*
Yalta Conference **19**:455 *illus.*; **20**:315 *illus.*
ROOSEVELT, THEODORE **16**:309–311 *bibliog., illus.*
Bull Moose party **3**:558
cartoon
presidential elections **15**:530 *illus.*
vice-president of the United States **19**:569 *illus.*
conservation **5**:201–203
Muir, John **13**:635
Constitution of the United States **5**:218
Pinchot, Gifford **15**:304
Platt, Thomas Collier **15**:362
portrait
Fraser, James Earle **8**:287
president of the United States **15**:526
Progressive party **15**:564
Republican party **16**:174 *illus.*
Roosevelt, Franklin Delano **16**:307
Rough Riders **16**:324
Rushmore, Mount **16**:348
Taft, William Howard **19**:8–9
United States, history of the **19**:452
ROOSEVELT ISLAND (New York)
map (79° 30′S 162° 0′W) **2**:40
ROOT (botany)
osmosis **14**:455 *illus.*
plant **15**:335–336 *illus.*
tree **19**:286–288 *illus.*
ROOT (mathematics) **16**:311
discriminant **6**:189
equation **7**:224
exponent **7**:339
mathematical tables **13**:221
quadratic equation
Ferrari, Lodovico **8**:59
radical (mathematics) **16**:43
square root **18**:202
transcendental function **19**:268
ROOT, ELIHU **16**:311 *bibliog.*
Platt Amendment **15**:362
ROOT, JOHN WELLBORN **16**:311 *bibliog.*
Burnham, Daniel Hudson **3**:577
skyscraper **17**:348–350
ROOT-MEAN-SQUARE
alternating current **1**:312 *illus.*
ROOT RIVER
map (43° 46′N 91° 15′W) **13**:453
ROOTES
automotive industry **2**:366
ROOTS (book) **16**:312
Haley, Alex **10**:19
"ROOTS" (television miniseries)
radio and television broadcasting **16**:59
ROPE
cable **4**:5–6
jute **11**:479
machine **13**:21
ROPER (North Carolina)
map (35° 53′N 76° 37′W) **14**:242
ROPING *see* RODEO (contest)
ROPS, FÉLICIEN **16**:312
ROQUE PEREZ (Argentina)
map (35° 25′S 59° 20′W) **2**:149
ROQUETTE **16**:312
RORAIMA, MOUNT
map (5° 12′N 60° 44′W) **9**:410
RORAIMA TERRITORY
map (1° 0′N 61° 0′W) **3**:460
RORE, CIPRIANO DE
madrigal **13**:45
music, history of Western **13**:665
Renaissance music **16**:156
ROREM, NED **16**:312
RORKETON (Manitoba)
map (51° 26′N 99° 32′W) **13**:119
RORSCHACH (Switzerland)
map (47° 29′N 9° 30′E) **18**:394
RORSCHACH, HERMANN
psychology, history of **15**:598
RORSCHACH INKBLOT TEST **15**:566 *illus.*; **15**:598 *illus.*
ROSA, JOÃO GUIMARÃES **16**:312 *bibliog.*
Brazilian literature **3**:464
ROSA, SALVATOR **16**:312 *bibliog.*
ROSALIA (Washington)
map (47° 14′N 117° 22′W) **20**:35
ROSAMOND (California)
map (34° 52′N 118° 10′W) **4**:31
ROSARIO (Argentina) **16**:312
map (32° 57′S 60° 40′W) **2**:149
ROSARIO (Mexico)
map (30° 1′N 115° 40′W) **13**:357
ROSARIO DEL TALA (Argentina)
map (32° 18′S 59° 9′W) **2**:149
ROSARY **16**:312 *bibliog.*
Ave Maria **2**:369
Mary **13**:185
ROSAS, JUAN MANUEL DE **16**:312 *bibliog.*
Mitre, Bartolomé **13**:485
ROSCELLIN **16**:312–313 *bibliog.*
Abelard, Peter **1**:55
ROSCOE B. JACKSON MEMORIAL LABORATORY *see* JACKSON LABORATORY
ROSCOMMON (Ireland) **16**:313
map (53° 38′N 8° 11′W) **11**:258
ROSCOMMON (Michigan)
map (44° 30′N 84° 35′W) **13**:377
ROSCOMMON (county in Michigan)
map (44° 20′N 84° 35′W) **13**:377
ROSE (botany) **16**:313 *bibliog., illus.*
agrimony **1**:199
almond **1**:307
blackberry **3**:320
cinquefoil **4**:435
cotoneaster **5**:304
fire thorn **8**:105
guttation **9**:410
hawthorn **10**:78–79
juneberry **11**:467
loquat **12**:413
mahogany **13**:66
medlar **13**:278
mountain ash **13**:620
quince **16**:26
serviceberry **17**:211
spirea **18**:188
strawberry **18**:295–296
ROSE, PETE **16**:314 *bibliog.*

ROSE BELLE (Mauritius)
map (20° 24′S 57° 36′E) **13**:237
ROSE BOWL
Pasadena (California) **15**:101
ROSE HALL (Guyana)
map (6° 16′N 57° 21′W) **9**:410
ROSE-HILL (Mauritius)
map (20° 14′S 57° 27′E) **13**:237
ROSE HILL (North Carolina)
map (34° 50′N 78° 2′W) **14**:242
ROSE OF JERICHO (botany) **16**:314
ROSE OF LIMA, SAINT **16**:314
ROSE OF SHARON
hibiscus **10**:156
ROSE VALLEY (Saskatchewan)
map (52° 18′N 103° 50′W) **17**:81
ROSE WINDOW **16**:314 *bibliog.*
Gothic art and architecture **9**:256–257
ROSEAU (Minnesota)
map (48° 51′N 95° 46′W) **13**:453
ROSEAU (county in Minnesota)
map (48° 45′N 95° 45′W) **13**:453
ROSEBERY, ARCHIBALD PHILIP PRIMROSE, 5TH EARL OF **16**:314 *bibliog.*
ROSEBUD (county in Montana)
map (46° 15′N 106° 35′W) **13**:547
ROSEBUD (South Dakota)
map (43° 14′N 100° 51′W) **18**:103
ROSEBURG (Oregon)
map (43° 13′N 123° 20′W) **14**:427
ROSEBUSH (Michigan)
map (43° 42′N 84° 46′W) **13**:377
ROSECRANS, WILLIAM S. **5**:26 *illus.*; **16**:314 *bibliog.*
Civil War, U.S. **5**:23 *map*; **5**:27–28
ROSEDALE (Indiana)
map (39° 37′N 87° 17′W) **11**:111
ROSEDALE (Maryland)
map (39° 19′N 76° 31′W) **13**:188
ROSEDALE (Mississippi)
map (33° 51′N 91° 2′W) **13**:469
ROSELAND (Louisiana)
map (30° 46′N 90° 31′W) **12**:430
ROSELLA *see* PARAKEET
ROSELLE (New Jersey)
map (40° 40′N 74° 16′W) **14**:129
ROSELLE PARK (New Jersey)
map (40° 40′N 74° 16′W) **14**:129
ROSELLI, COSIMO
detail from *Miracle of the Sacrament* **16**:148 *illus.*
ROSEMARY (Alberta)
map (50° 46′N 112° 5′W) **1**:256
ROSEMARY (botany) **16**:314 *illus.*
ROSENBERG (Texas)
map (29° 33′N 95° 48′W) **19**:129
ROSENBERG, ALFRED **16**:314–315 *bibliog.*
Nuremberg Trials **14**:297 *illus.*
ROSENBERG, HAROLD **16**:315 *bibliog.*
ROSENBERG, ISAAC **16**:315 *bibliog.*
ROSENBERG, JULIUS AND ETHEL **16**:315 *bibliog.*, *illus.*
ROSENBLAT, ANGEL
Venezuela **19**:543
ROSENBUSCH, HARRY **16**:315
ROSENFELD, MONROE
Tin Pan Alley **19**:205
ROSENHEIM (Germany, East and West)
map (47° 51′N 12° 7′E) **9**:140
ROSENKAVALIER, DER (opera) **16**:315 *bibliog.*
Hofmannsthal, Hugo von **10**:196–197
ROSENQUIST, JAMES **16**:315–316 *bibliog.*
ROSENSTIEL SCHOOL OF MARINE AND ATMOSPHERIC SCIENCE
JOIDES **11**:438
ROSENTHAL, DAVID
behavioral genetics **3**:170
ROSENWALD, JULIUS **16**:316 *bibliog.*
ROSENWALD, LESSING J.
art collection
National Gallery of Art **14**:33
ROSENZWEIG, FRANZ **16**:316 *bibliog.*
ROSEPINE (Louisiana)
map (30° 55′N 93° 17′W) **12**:430
ROSES, WARS OF THE **16**:316 *bibliog.*, *map*
Edward IV, King of England **7**:68
Great Britain, history of **9**:313
Henry VI, King of England **10**:126
Henry VII, King of England **10**:126
Lancaster (dynasty) **12**:177
Margaret of Anjou **13**:148–149
Richard III, King of England **16**:210
Saint Albans (England) **17**:16
Wakefield (England) **20**:8
Warwick, Richard Neville, Earl of **20**:33
York (dynasty) **20**:330
Yorkshire (England) **20**:331
ROSETOWN (Saskatchewan)
map (51° 33′N 108° 0′W) **17**:81
ROSETTA STONE **2**:122 *illus.*; **10**:160 *illus.*; **16**:317 *bibliog.*, *illus.*
Champollion, Jean François **4**:278
inscription **11**:186
Ptolemy V, King of Egypt (Ptolemy Epiphanes) **15**:607
Young, Thomas **20**:334
ROSEVILLE (California)
map (38° 45′N 121° 17′W) **4**:31
ROSEVILLE (Michigan)
map (42° 30′N 82° 56′W) **13**:377
ROSEWOOD **16**:317
lumber **12**:456 *illus.*
wood **20**:205 *illus.*
ROSH HASHANAH **16**:317 *bibliog.*
ROSHOLT (South Dakota)
map (45° 52′N 96° 44′W) **18**:103
ROSHOLT (Wisconsin)
map (44° 38′N 89° 18′W) **20**:185
ROSICLARE (Illinois)
map (37° 25′N 88° 20′W) **11**:42
ROSICRUCIANS **16**:317 *bibliog.*
ROSIGNOL (Guyana)
map (6° 17′N 57° 32′W) **9**:410
ROSIN **16**:317
ROSINE, SARAH HENRIETTE *see* BERNHARDT, SARAH
ROSINWEED (genus *Grindelia*) *see* GUMWEED
ROSINWEED (genus *Silphium*) **16**:317
ROSITA (Nicaragua)
map (13° 53′N 84° 24′W) **14**:179
ROSKILDE (Denmark) **16**:317–318
map (55° 39′N 12° 5′E) **6**:109
ROSMINI-SERBATI, ANTONIO **16**:318 *bibliog.*
ROSNY, BARON DE *see* SULLY, MAXIMILIEN DE BÉTHUNE, DUC DE
ROSS (county in Ohio)
map (39° 20′N 83° 3′W) **14**:357
ROSS, ALEXANDER **16**:318
ROSS, BARNEY
boxing **3**:432
ROSS, BETSY **16**:318 *bibliog.*
flag **8**:134
ROSS, HAROLD **16**:318 *bibliog.*
New Yorker, The **14**:156
ROSS, SIR JAMES CLARK **16**:318
Antarctica **2**:44 *map*
Arctic **2**:142 *map*
Boothia Peninsula **3**:395
Erebus, Mount **7**:228
Ross Ice Shelf (Antarctica) **16**:318
ROSS, SIR JOHN (explorer)
Arctic **2**:142 *map*
Northwest Passage **14**:256
ROSS, JOHN (Cherokee Indian) **16**:318 *bibliog.*
ROSS, RONALD
malaria **13**:80
ROSS, SINCLAIR **16**:318
ROSS, T. E. *see* LAWRENCE, T. E.
ROSS, SIR WILLIAM D.
ethics **7**:250–251
ROSS BARNETT RESERVOIR
map (32° 30′N 90° 0′W) **13**:469
ROSS AND CROMARTY (Scotland) **16**:318
ROSS DEPENDENCY (Antarctica) **16**:318
Erebus, Mount **7**:228
ROSS ICE SHELF (Antarctica) **16**:318
glaciers and glaciation **9**:194
map (81° 30′S 175° 0′W) **2**:40
ROSS LAKE
map (48° 53′N 121° 4′W) **20**:35
ROSS RIVER (Yukon Territory)
map (61° 59′N 132° 27′W) **20**:345
ROSS SEA (Antarctica)
map (76° 0′S 175° 0′W) **2**:40
Ross Ice Shelf **16**:318
ROSSAN POINT (Ireland)
map (54° 42′N 8° 48′W) **11**:258
ROSSBY WAVES **16**:318–319
drought **6**:274
ROSSELLI, COSIMO
Miracle of the Sacrament **16**:148 *illus.*
Sistine Chapel **17**:329
ROSSELLINI, ROBERTO **16**:319 *bibliog.*
Bergman, Ingrid **3**:210
Fellini, Federico **8**:48
film, history of **8**:85–86 *illus.*
ROSSELLINO (family) **16**:319 *bibliog.*
ROSSELLINO, ANTONIO
Rossellino (family) **16**:319
ROSSELLINO, BERNARDO
Rossellino (family) **16**:319
ROSSETTI, CHRISTINA G. **16**:319 *bibliog.*
ROSSETTI, DANTE GABRIEL **16**:319 *bibliog.*, *illus.*
The Bower Meadow **16**:319 *illus.*
Caine, Sir Hall **4**:17
Ecce Ancilla Domini **15**:519 *illus.*
Hunt, Holman **10**:311
Millais, Sir John Everett **13**:426
ROSSFORD (Ohio)
map (41° 37′N 83° 33′W) **14**:357
ROSSI, LUIGI
opera **14**:399
oratorio **14**:416
ROSSINI, GIOACCHINO **16**:293 *illus.*; **16**:319–320 *bibliog.*, *illus.*
Barber of Seville, The **3**:77
Florence **8**:168
Italian music **11**:319
ROSSITER (Pennsylvania)
map (40° 53′N 78° 56′W) **15**:147
ROSSLAND (British Columbia)
map (49° 5′N 117° 48′W) **3**:491
ROSSO, MEDARDO **16**:320 *bibliog.*
ROSSO FIORENTINO **16**:320 *bibliog.*
Gallery of Francis I **8**:206 *illus.*
ROSS'S SEAL
Antarctica **2**:43
Ross, Sir James Clark **16**:318
ROSSVILLE (Georgia)
map (34° 59′N 85° 16′W) **9**:114
ROSSVILLE (Illinois)
map (40° 23′N 87° 40′W) **11**:42
ROSSVILLE (Indiana)
map (40° 25′N 86° 36′W) **11**:111
ROSSVILLE (Kansas)
map (39° 8′N 95° 57′W) **12**:18
ROSTAND, EDMOND **16**:320 *bibliog.*
Cyrano de Bergerac **5**:409
ROSTOCK (East Germany) **16**:320–321
map (54° 5′N 12° 7′E) **9**:140
ROSTOV-ON-DON (USSR) **16**:321
map (47° 14′N 39° 42′E) **19**:388
ROSTROPOVICH, MSTISLAV **16**:321 *bibliog.*
ROSWELL (Georgia)
map (34° 1′N 84° 22′W) **9**:114
ROSWELL (New Mexico)
map (33° 24′N 104° 32′W) **14**:136
ROSWITHA VON GANDERSHEIM *see* HROSWITHA VON GANDERSHEIM
ROSZAK, THEODORE **16**:321 *bibliog.*
ROTA
Mariana Islands (U.S.) **13**:150
ROTARY ENGINE *see* TURBINE
ROTARY INTERNATIONAL **16**:321
ROTARY PRESS **15**:551–552 *illus.*; **16**:321 *bibliog.*
Hill, Sir Rowland, inventor **10**:164
Hoe, Richard March, inventor **10**:194
letterpress **12**:300 *illus.*
rotogravure **16**:323
ROTC *see* RESERVE OFFICERS TRAINING CORPS
ROTENONE
derris **6**:123
ROTH, PHILIP **16**:321 *bibliog.*
ROTH v. UNITED STATES **16**:321–322
pornography **15**:441
ROTHERHITHE AND WAPPING TUNNEL *see* TUNNEL
ROTHERMERE, HAROLD SIDNEY HARMSWORTH, VISCOUNT
Northcliffe, Alfred Harmsworth, Viscount **14**:253
ROTHESAY (New Brunswick)
map (45° 23′N 66° 0′W) **14**:117
ROTHKO, MARK **16**:322 *bibliog.*, *illus.*
Blue, Orange and Red **1**:65 *illus.*; **13**:495 *illus.*; **16**:322 *illus.*
ROTHSAY (Minnesota)
map (46° 28′N 96° 17′W) **13**:453
ROTHSCHILD (family) **16**:322 *bibliog.*, *illus.*
ROTHSCHILD (Wisconsin)
map (44° 54′N 89° 50′W) **20**:185
ROTHSCHILD, MAYER AMSCHEL (1744–1812)
Rothschild (family) **16**:322
ROTHSCHILD, NATHAN MAYER (1840–1915)
Rothschild (family) **16**:322 *illus.*
ROTHWELL (New Brunswick)
map (46° 4′N 66° 4′W) **14**:117
ROTIFER **16**:323 *illus.*
aging **1**:186
early years mortality **12**:331 *table*
ROTOGRAVURE **16**:323 *bibliog.*, *illus.*
intaglio **11**:199–200
platemaking **15**:357
printing **15**:552; **16**:323
web-fed press **20**:85
ROTONDO, MOUNT
map (42° 13′N 9° 3′E) **8**:260
ROTOR
generator **9**:78
helicopter **10**:111–112
stator **18**:238
turbine **19**:340 *illus.*
windmills and wind power **20**:172–173 *illus.*
ROTORUA (New Zealand)
map (38° 9′S 176° 15′E) **14**:158
ROTTERDAM (Netherlands) **16**:323 *illus.*
harbor and port **10**:43
map (51° 55′N 4° 28′E) **14**:99
ROTTERDAM (New York)
map (42° 48′N 74° 1′W) **14**:149
ROTTLUFF, KARL SCHMIDT- *see* SCHMIDT-ROTTLUFF, KARL
ROTTWEILER **6**:215 *illus.*; **16**:324 *bibliog.*, *illus.*
ROUAULT, GEORGES **16**:324 *bibliog.*, *illus.*
The Old King **16**:324 *illus.*
ROUBAIX (France)
map (50° 42′N 3° 10′E) **8**:260
ROUBILIAC, LOUIS FRANÇOIS **16**:324 *bibliog.*
ROUCH, JEAN
documentary **6**:211
ROUEN (Barbados)
map (13° 5′N 59° 34′W) **3**:75
ROUEN (France) **16**:324
map (49° 26′N 1° 5′E) **8**:260
ROUGE
cosmetics **5**:281–282 *table*
ROUGET DE LISLE, CLAUDE JOSEPH
"Marseillaise, La" **13**:170
ROUGH RIDERS **16**:324 *bibliog.*
Roosevelt, Theodore **16**:310
Spanish-American War **18**:150
uniform **4**:221 *illus.*
Wood, Leonard **20**:207
ROUGH RIVER
map (37° 29′N 87° 8′W) **12**:47
ROUGH RIVER LAKE
map (37° 40′N 86° 25′W) **12**:47
ROULETTE (game) **16**:324–325 *bibliog.*
ROULETTE (Pennsylvania)
map (41° 47′N 78° 9′W) **15**:147
ROUM *see* RUM (Seljuk empire)
ROUND (music)
canon **4**:114
ROUND ARCH STYLE *see* *RUNDBOGENSTIL* STYLE
ROUND HARBOUR (Newfoundland)
map (47° 37′N 56° 0′W) **14**:166
ROUND ISLAND (Mauritius)
map (19° 51′S 57° 48′E) **13**:237
ROUND LAKE (Minnesota)
map (43° 32′N 95° 28′W) **13**:453
ROUND MOUNTAIN (Nevada)
map (38° 43′N 117° 4′W) **14**:111
ROUND TABLE (Algonquin Hotel)
Connelly, Marc **5**:197
Parker, Dorothy **15**:90
Woollcott, Alexander **20**:215
ROUND TABLE (Arthurian legend)
Arthur and Arthurian legend **9**:219
Camelot **4**:54
Galahad, Sir **9**:9–10
ROUND VALLEY RESERVOIR
map (40° 36′N 74° 50′W) **14**:129
ROUNDHEADS **16**:325
English Civil War **7**:189
ROUNDUP *see* RODEO (contest)
ROUNDUP (Montana)
map (46° 27′N 108° 33′W) **13**:547
ROUNDWORM *see* ASCARIASIS; NEMATODE
ROURA (French Guiana)
map (4° 44′N 52° 20′W) **8**:311
ROUS, FRANCIS PEYTON **16**:325
ROUSES POINT (New York)
map (45° 0′N 73° 22′W) **14**:149
ROUSSEAU, HENRI **16**:325 *bibliog.*, *illus.*
The Sleeping Gypsy **16**:325 *illus.*
ROUSSEAU, JEAN JACQUES **16**:325–327 *bibliog.*, *illus.*
Confessions, Les **5**:177
democracy **6**:97
educational psychology **7**:66
Émile **16**:326
French literature **8**:316–317 *illus.*
Hudson River school **10**:290
life **16**:325–326
noble savage **14**:211
philosophy **16**:326
progressive education **15**:564
religion **16**:327
representation **16**:161
social contract **18**:11
Social Contract **16**:326–327
ROUSSEAU, PIERRE
Monticello **13**:557
ROUSSEAU, RENÉ WALDECK- *see* WALDECK-ROUSSEAU, RENÉ

ROUSSEAU, THÉODORE 16:327 *bibliog.*
Edge of the Forest at Fontainebleau 3:79 *illus.*
Landscape after the Rain 11:63 *illus.*
ROUSSEL, ALBERT 16:327 *bibliog.*
ROUSSILLON (France) 16:327
ROUTT (county in Colorado)
map (40° 30′N 107° 0′W) 5:116
ROUVROY, CLAUDE HENRI DE, COMTE DE SAINT-SIMON *see* SAINT-SIMON, CLAUDE HENRI DE ROUVROY, COMTE DE
ROUVROY, LOUIS DE, DUC DE SAINT-SIMON *see* SAINT-SIMON, LOUIS DE ROUVROY, DUC DE
ROUX, PIERRE PAUL ÉMILE 16:327
biology 3:271
ROUYN (Quebec)
map (48° 15′N 79° 1′W) 16:18
ROVANIEMI (Finland)
map (66° 34′N 25° 48′E) 8:95
ROVIGO (Italy)
map (45° 4′N 11° 47′E) 11:321
ROW HOUSE
brownstone 3:519
ROWAN (county in Kentucky)
map (38° 10′N 83° 5′W) 12:47
ROWAN (county in North Carolina)
map (35° 40′N 80° 35′W) 14:242
ROWBOAT
outrigger 14:469
ROWE, NICHOLAS 16:327
ROWELL, NEWTON WESLEY 16:327
ROWING 16:327–328 *bibliog., illus.*
ROWLAND, HENRY AUGUSTUS 16:328
ROWLANDSON, THOMAS 16:328 *bibliog.*
ROWLEY POEMS
Chatterton, Thomas 4:304
ROXA ISLAND
map (11° 15′N 15° 40′W) 9:399
ROXANA 16:328
ROXAS (Philippines)
map (12° 35′N 121° 31′E) 15:237
ROXAS Y ACUNA, MANUEL 16:328 *bibliog.*
ROXBORO (North Carolina)
map (36° 24′N 78° 59′W) 14:242
ROXBOROUGH (Trinidad and Tobago)
map (11° 15′N 60° 35′W) 19:300
ROXBURGH (Scotland) 16:329
ROXIE (Mississippi)
map (31° 30′N 91° 4′W) 13:469
ROY (New Mexico)
map (35° 57′N 104° 12′W) 14:136
ROY (Utah)
map (41° 10′N 112° 2′W) 19:492
ROY, GABRIELLE 16:329
Canadian literature 4:94
ROY, RAMMOHUN 16:329 *bibliog.*
Brahmo Samaj 3:440–441
ROYAL (Iowa)
map (43° 4′N 95° 17′W) 11:244
ROYAL ACADEMY OF DRAMATIC ART 16:329
ROYAL AIR FORCE
air force 1:208
World War II 20:254–255 *illus.*; 20:264; 20:275
ROYAL ALBERT BRIDGE (England)
bridge (engineering) 3:481
ROYAL AND ANCIENT CLUB
Saint Andrews (Scotland) 17:16
ROYAL ASTRONOMICAL SOCIETY 16:329
Baily, Francis 3:26
ROYAL BALLET, THE 6:26 *illus.*; 16:329 *bibliog.*
See also SADLER'S WELLS BALLET
Ashton, Sir Frederick 2:231
Dowell, Anthony 6:251
Fonteyn, Dame Margot 8:207
MacMillan, Kenneth 13:34
Morrice, Norman 13:587–588
Seymour, Lynn 17:233
Sibley, Antoinette 17:292
Valois, Dame Ninette de 19:508
ROYAL BOTANIC GARDENS *see* KEW GARDENS (England)
ROYAL CANADIAN ACADEMY
Canadian art and architecture 4:89
ROYAL CANADIAN MOUNTED POLICE 16:329–330 *bibliog.*
police 15:396
ROYAL CANAL (Ireland)
map (53° 21′N 6° 15′W) 11:258
ROYAL CENTER (Indiana)
map (40° 52′N 86° 30′W) 11:111
ROYAL COPENHAGEN WARE 16:330 *bibliog.*
ROYAL COURT THEATRE
Granville-Barker, Harley 9:289
ROYAL DANISH BALLET 16:330 *bibliog.*
Bournonville, August 3:425
Bruhn, Erik 3:523
Flindt, Flemming 8:165
ROYAL DUBLIN SOCIETY
Ireland 11:260
ROYAL GEOGRAPHICAL SOCIETY
exploration 7:338
geographical societies 9:100
ROYAL GOLD MEDAL
Heyerdahl, Thor 10:155
ROYAL GORGE (Colorado) 5:119 *illus.*; 16:330
ROYAL GREENWICH OBSERVATORY 16:330 *bibliog.*
Airy, Sir George Biddell 1:228
Bradley, James 3:438
Flamsteed, John 8:151–152
Greenwich (England) 9:354
Halley, Edmond 10:23
prime meridian 15:542
ROYAL INSTITUTION OF GREAT BRITAIN 16:330
Tyndall, John 19:363
ROYAL OAK (Michigan)
map (42° 30′N 83° 8′W) 13:377
ROYAL ONTARIO MUSEUM 16:330 *bibliog.*; 19:241 *map*
ROYAL OPERA HOUSE, COVENT GARDEN *see* COVENT GARDEN
ROYAL PAVILION AT BRIGHTON 16:126 *illus.*; 16:330–331 *bibliog., illus.*
chinoiserie 4:395
Nash, John 14:24
ROYAL SHAKESPEARE COMPANY 16:331
director
Brook, Peter 3:509
Hall, Peter 10:22
A Midsummer Night's Dream 19:151 *illus.*
ROYAL SOCIETY 16:331 *bibliog.*
Boyle, Robert 3:434
Brouncker, William 3:512
Cook, James 5:234–236
Evelyn, John 7:315
Newton, Sir Isaac 14:174
Petty, Sir William 15:216
Rumford, Benjamin Thomson, Count 16:344–345
Rutherford, Sir Ernest 16:375
scientific associations 17:144–145
Smithson, James 17:372
Sorby, Henry Clifton 18:68
Wallis, John 20:16
Wilkins, John 20:152
Winthrop (family) 20:182
ROYAL SWEDISH ACADEMY OF SCIENCES
Nobel Prize 14:208
ROYAL SWEDISH BALLET 16:331
Bruhn, Erik 3:523
ROYALTON (Minnesota)
map (45° 50′N 94° 18′W) 13:453
ROYALTY
king 12:80
marriage 13:164
queen 16:21
Salic law 17:32
titles of nobility and honor 19:213–214
ROYCE, HENRY *see* ROLLS-ROYCE
ROYCE, JOSIAH 16:331 *bibliog.*
ROYCROFT PRESS
Hubbard, Elbert 10:288
ROYO, ARISTIDES
Panama 15:56
ROYSTON (Georgia)
map (34° 17′N 83° 6′W) 9:114
ROZELLE, PETE 16:331–332
RÓŻEWICZ, TADEUSZ 16:332
ROZHDESTVENSKY, VALERY 16:332 *bibliog.*
ROZIER, PILÂTRE DE
balloon 3:51
ROZWI CLAN
Nola tale 14:9
Shona 17:281
RR LYRAE STARS 16:332
Cepheids 4:257
cluster, star 5:72
distance, astronomical 6:200
extragalactic systems 7:343
Lyra 12:479
pulsating stars 15:621
variable star 19:522–523
RUAHINE RANGE
map (40° 0′S 176° 6′E) 14:158
RUAN JI *see* JUAN CHI (Ruan Ji)
RUANDA-URUNDI 16:332
See also BURUNDI; RWANDA
RUAPEHU, MOUNT
map (39° 17′S 175° 34′E) 14:158
RUB AL-KHALI (EMPTY QUARTER) DESERT
map (20° 0′N 51° 0′E) 17:94
Saudi Arabia 17:93–94
RUBAIYAT OF OMAR KHAYYAM (poem) 16:332
FitzGerald, Edward 8:130
Omar Khayyam 14:387
RUBASHOV, NICHOLAS
Darkness at Noon 6:38–39
RUBBER 16:332–335 *bibliog., illus., table*
azobenzene 2:381
elastomer 7:102
Firestone, Harvey S. 8:106
Goodrich, Benjamin F. 9:246
guayule 9:390
isoprene 11:300
latex 12:215
Liberia 12:313–314 *illus.*
Manaus (Brazil) 13:108
natural rubber production 16:333–334 *illus.*
plantation 16:333 *illus.*
production of natural and synthetic rubbers 16:335 *table*
products 16:334 *table*
resin 16:177
silicone 17:306
synthetic
butane 3:591
Nieuwland, Julius Arthur 14:186
production 16:334
roof and roofing 16:306
terpene 19:118
tire 19:207–208
tree 16:332 *illus.*
vulcanization 16:333
Goodyear, Charles 9:246
RUBBER PLANT
fig 8:75
RUBBIA, CARLO 16:335
RUBBING (art)
Ernst, Max 7:231–232
RUBBING ALCOHOL
alcohol 1:264
RUBBLE
stonemasonry 18:283
RUBBRA, EDMUND 16:335 *bibliog.*
RUBELLA *see* GERMAN MEASLES
RUBENS, PETER PAUL 16:335–336 *bibliog., illus.*
The Artist and his Wife, Isabella Brant 16:336 *illus.*
baroque art and architecture 3:90
collection
Sarasota (Florida) 17:75
Flemish art and architecture 8:161
impasto 11:60
The Judgment of Paris 16:335 *illus.*
Rape of the Daughters of Leucippus 3:88 *illus.*
Snyders, Frans 18:6
The Three Graces 8:161 *illus.*
van Dyck, Sir Anthony 19:513
RUBENSTEIN, HELENA
Nadelman, Elie 14:4
RUBICON RIVER 16:336
RUBIDIUM 16:336 *bibliog.*
alkali metals 1:295
atomic clock 2:308
element 7:130 *table*
Group IA periodic table 15:167; 16:336
metal, metallic element 13:328
radiometric age-dating 16:66
RUBIN, JERRY
counterculture 5:311
RUBINOW, ISAAC
social work 18:19
RUBINSTEIN, ANTON 16:337 *bibliog.*
Hofmann, Josef Casimir 10:196
Russian music 16:368
RUBINSTEIN, ARTHUR 16:337
RUBINSTEIN, IDA LVOVNA 16:337
RUBINSTEIN PIANO PRIZE
Backhaus, Wilhelm 3:12–13
RUBIO (Venezuela)
map (7° 43′N 72° 22′W) 19:542
RUBLEV, ANDREI 16:337 *bibliog.*
Michael (archangel) 16:361 *illus.*
RUBY 3:296 *illus., table*; 9:74 *illus.*; 16:337 *bibliog., illus.*
corundum 5:279
gems 9:74–75
laser 12:213 *table*
Maiman, Theodore Harold 13:68
sapphire 17:73
RUBY, JACK
Oswald, Lee Harvey 14:459
Warren Commission 20:31
RUBY DOME MOUNTAIN (Nevada)
map (40° 37′N 115° 28′W) 14:111
RUBY LAKE (Nevada)
map (40° 10′N 115° 30′W) 14:111
RUBY RANGE
map (45° 15′N 112° 15′W) 13:547
RUBY-THROATED HUMMINGBIRD *see* HUMMINGBIRD
RUCKELSHAUS, WILLIAM D.
Cox, Archibald 5:322
RUDAKI, ABU ABDOLLAH JAFAR 16:337 *bibliog.*
RUDAPITHECUS
Ramapithecus 16:80
RUDDER 16:337–338
RUDDERFISH *see* CHUB
RUDE, FRANÇOIS 16:338 *bibliog.*
RUDEL, JAUFRÉ
music, history of Western 13:662
Provençal literature 15:583
RUDOLF, AUSTRIAN ARCHDUKE 16:338 *bibliog.*
RUDOLF, LAKE 16:338
map (3° 30′N 36° 5′E) 12:53
RUDOLF I, KING OF GERMANY 16:338 *bibliog., illus.*
Habsburg (dynasty) 10:6
Ottokar II, King of Bohemia (Přemysl Ottokar) 14:464
Styria (Austria) 18:312
RUDOLF II, HOLY ROMAN EMPEROR 16:338 *bibliog.*
RUDOLF OF NUREMBERG
wire 20:182
RUDOLPH, PAUL 16:338–339 *bibliog.*
RUDOLPH, WILMA 16:339 *bibliog.*
RUDYARD (Michigan)
map (46° 14′N 84° 36′W) 13:377
RUDYARD (Montana)
map (48° 34′N 110° 33′W) 13:547
RUE 16:339 *illus.*
RUEDA, LOPE DE 16:339 *bibliog.*
RUFFO, VINCENZO
mass (musical setting) 13:201
Renaissance music 16:156
RUFIJI RIVER
map (8° 0′S 39° 20′E) 19:27
RUFINO (Argentina)
map (34° 16′S 62° 42′W) 2:149
RUFISQUE (Senegal)
map (14° 43′N 17° 17′W) 17:202
RUFUS (Oregon)
map (45° 42′N 120° 44′W) 14:427
RUFUS WOODS LAKE (Washington)
map (48° 6′N 119° 10′W) 20:35
RUGBY 16:339–340 *bibliog., illus.*
football 8:216
playing field 16:340 *illus.*
sports, history of 18:196
RUGBY (North Dakota)
map (48° 22′N 100° 0′W) 14:248
RUGBY SCHOOL 16:340
Arnold, Thomas 2:185
RÜGEN ISLAND (East Germany)
map (54° 25′N 13° 24′E) 9:140
RUGGLES, CARL 16:340
RUGII
Germanic peoples 9:138
RUGS AND CARPETS 16:340–343 *bibliog., illus.*
carpet industry 4:165
Caucasus 16:341–342
Central Asia and Turkestan 16:342
China 16:342–343
contemporary trends 16:343
England 16:343
folk art 8:198–199
France 16:343
Islamic art and architecture 11:293
materials and motifs 16:340–341
Navajo rugs 16:343
Persia and India 16:341
Persian art and architecture 15:186–187
Scandinavia 16:343
Spain 16:343
techniques of manufacture 16:340
Turkey 16:342
Turkmen, Bukharan carpets 19:347
RUGWERO, LAKE
map (2° 25′S 30° 15′E) 3:582
RUHENGERI (Rwanda)
map (1° 30′S 29° 38′E) 16:378
RUHLMAN, EMIL
Art Deco 2:207
RUHR RIVER
map (51° 27′N 6° 44′E) 9:140
RUHR VALLEY (West Germany) 7:278 *illus.*; 9:145 *illus.*; 16:343
cities
Essen 7:244
RUIDOSO (New Mexico)
map (33° 20′N 105° 40′W) 14:136
RUIDOSO DOWNS (New Mexico)
map (33° 21′N 105° 34′W) 14:136

RUISDAEL, JACOB VAN **16**:343 *bibliog., illus.*
The Jewish Graveyard **12**:190 *illus.*
The Mill at Wijk **16**:343 *illus.*
Ruisdael, Salomon van **16**:344
RUISDAEL, SALOMON VAN **16**:344 *bibliog.*
RUIZ, JOSÉ MARTÍNEZ **16**:344 *bibliog.*
RUIZ, JUAN
Spanish literature **18**:157
RUIZ DE ALARCÓN Y MENDOZA, JUAN **16**:344
RUIZE, HERNAN
Giralda (tower) **9**:188
RUKAVISHNIKOV, NIKOLAY **16**:344
RUKEYSER, MURIEL **16**:344
RUKWA, LAKE
map (8° 0'S 32° 25'E) **19**:27
RULEVILLE (Mississippi)
map (33° 44'N 90° 33'W) **13**:469
RUM (beverage) **16**:344 *bibliog.*
molasses **13**:505
Vernon, Edward **19**:559
RUM (Seljuk empire)
Turks **19**:348
RUM CAY ISLAND
map (23° 40'N 74° 53'W) **3**:23
RUM RIVER
map (45° 11'N 93° 23'W) **13**:453
RUMANIA *see* ROMANIA
RUMFORD (Maine)
map (44° 33'N 70° 33'W) **13**:70
RUMFORD, BENJAMIN THOMSON, COUNT **16**:344–345 *bibliog.*
physics, history of **15**:285
thermodynamics **19**:163
RUMI, JALAL AL-DIN AL- **16**:345 *bibliog.*
RUMINANT **16**:345
herbivore **10**:136
horn (biology) **10**:238
RUMMY **16**:345 *bibliog.*
RUMP MOUNTAIN
map (45° 12'N 71° 4'W) **13**:70
RUMP PARLIAMENT
Cromwell, Oliver **5**:358
Cromwell, Richard **5**:358
Long Parliament **12**:407
RUMSON (New Jersey)
map (40° 22'N 74° 0'W) **14**:129
RUNCIE, ROBERT ALEXANDER KENNEDY **16**:345
RUNCORN, STANLEY KEITH
plate tectonics **15**:357
RUNDBOGENSTIL STYLE
Gärtner, Friedrich von **9**:52
RUNDSTEDT, KARL RUDOLF GERD VON **16**:345 *bibliog.*
RUNEBERG, JOHAN LUDVIG **16**:345–346
RUNES **16**:346 *bibliog.*
inscription **11**:186
runestones
Kensington Rune Stone **12**:45
Scandinavian art and architecture **17**:111
writing systems, evolution of **20**:294
RUNGE, PHILIPP OTTO **16**:346 *bibliog.*
The Artist's Parents **9**:128 *illus.*
RUNKLE, JOHN
vocational education **19**:624
RUNNELS (county in Texas)
map (31° 48'N 99° 57'W) **19**:129
RUNNING FENCE (Christo) **4**:415 *illus.*
RUNNING AND JOGGING **16**:346 *bibliog.*
Cooper's 12-minute test **7**:330 *table*
exercise **7**:329
marathon **13**:143–144; **16**:346
orienteering **14**:443
pentathlon **15**:155
track and field **19**:259–260 *illus.*
training **16**:346
RUNSTEDT, GERD VON
World War II **20**:272–273
RUNYON, DAMON **16**:346 *bibliog.*
RUPERT (West Virginia)
map (37° 58'N 80° 41'W) **20**:111
RUPERT, PRINCE **16**:346–347 *bibliog.*
RUPERT'S LAND **4**:81–83 *map*; **16**:347
RUPP, ADOLPH **16**:347
RURAL ELECTRIFICATION ADMINISTRATION
housing **10**:277
RURAL HALL (North Carolina)
map (36° 15'N 80° 18'W) **14**:242
RURAL RETREAT (Virginia)
map (36° 54'N 81° 17'W) **19**:607
RURAL SOLIDARITY
Poland **15**:391
RURIK (dynasty) **16**:347 *bibliog.*
Russia/Union of Soviet Socialist Republics, history of **16**:351
RURRENABAQUE (Bolivia)
map (14° 28'S 67° 34'W) **3**:366
RUSE (Bulgaria) **16**:347
map (43° 50'N 25° 57'E) **3**:555
RUSH (botany) **16**:347
See also FLOWERING RUSH (botany)
RUSH (county in Indiana)
map (39° 37'N 85° 27'W) **11**:111
RUSH (county in Kansas)
map (38° 45'N 99° 15'W) **12**:18
RUSH, BENJAMIN **16**:347 *bibliog.*
Conway Cabal **5**:234
psychiatry **15**:588
RUSH, RICHARD **16**:347 *bibliog.*
RUSH, WILLIAM **16**:347 *bibliog.*
Eakins, Thomas **7**:5
RUSH-BAGOT AGREEMENT
Monroe, James **13**:542
Rush, Richard **16**:347
RUSH CENTER (Kansas)
map (38° 28'N 99° 19'W) **12**:18
RUSH SPRINGS (Oklahoma)
map (34° 47'N 97° 58'W) **14**:368
RUSHFORD (Minnesota)
map (43° 49'N 91° 46'W) **13**:453
RUSHMORE, MOUNT **3**:400 *illus.*; **16**:348 *illus.*; **18**:104 *illus.*
Borglum, Gutzon **3**:400
RUSHTON, J. HENRY
canoe **4**:113
RUSHVILLE (Illinois)
map (40° 7'N 90° 34'W) **11**:42
RUSHVILLE (Indiana)
map (39° 37'N 85° 27'W) **11**:111
RUSHVILLE (Nebraska)
map (42° 43'N 102° 28'W) **14**:70
RUSK (Texas)
map (31° 48'N 95° 9'W) **19**:129
RUSK (county in Texas)
map (32° 10'N 94° 50'W) **19**:129
RUSK (county in Wisconsin)
map (45° 27'N 91° 7'W) **20**:185
RUSK, DEAN **15**:526 *illus.*; **16**:348 *bibliog.*
RUSKA, ERNST AUGUST FRIEDRICH **16**:348
RUSKIN (Florida)
map (27° 43'N 82° 26'W) **8**:172
RUSKIN, JOHN **16**:348 *bibliog., illus.*
Millais, Sir John Everett **13**:426
Pre-Raphaelites **15**:519
Proust, Marcel **15**:582
Turner, Joseph Mallord William **19**:350
RUSLAN AND LUDMILA (opera) **16**:367 *illus.*
RUSSEL, BENJAMIN **16**:348–349
RUSSELL (county in Alabama)
map (32° 20'N 85° 10'W) **1**:234
RUSSELL (Kansas)
map (38° 54'N 98° 52'W) **12**:18
RUSSELL (county in Kansas)
map (38° 55'N 98° 45'W) **12**:18
RUSSELL (county in Kentucky)
map (37° 0'N 85° 5'W) **12**:47
RUSSELL (Manitoba)
map (50° 47'N 101° 15'W) **13**:119
RUSSELL (Minnesota)
map (44° 19'N 95° 57'W) **13**:453
RUSSELL (Pennsylvania)
map (41° 56'N 79° 8'W) **15**:147
RUSSELL (county in Virginia)
map (37° 0'N 82° 0'W) **19**:607
RUSSELL, BERTRAND **15**:243 *illus.*; **16**:349–350 *bibliog., illus.*
analytic and linguistic philosophy **1**:388–389
McMaster University **13**:33
mathematics, history of **13**:226
Principia Mathematica **15**:550
Russell's paradox **16**:351
Whitehead, Alfred North **20**:139
RUSSELL, BILL **3**:312 *illus.*; **16**:350 *bibliog.*
RUSSELL, CHARLES M. **16**:350 *bibliog., illus.*
A Bronc to Breakfast **16**:350 *illus.*
cowboy **5**:320 *illus.*
A Tight Dally and a Loose Latigo **8**:342 *illus.*
RUSSELL, CHARLES TAZE **16**:350 *illus.*
Jehovah's Witnesses **11**:394
RUSSELL, GEORGE W. **11**:267 *illus.*; **16**:350 *bibliog.*
RUSSELL, HENRY
American music **1**:349
RUSSELL, HENRY NORRIS **16**:350
RUSSELL, JOHN RUSSELL, 1ST EARL **16**:350–351 *bibliog., illus.*
Liberal parties **12**:311
RUSSELL, LILLIAN **16**:351
RUSSELL, MAJORS, AND WADDELL *see* PONY EXPRESS
RUSSELL, MORGAN
synchromism **18**:406
RUSSELL, SIR WILLIAM HOWARD **16**:351 *bibliog.*
RUSSELL SAGE COLLEGE **16**:351
Sage, Russell **17**:12
RUSSELL SAGE FOUNDATION **16**:351
RUSSELL SPRINGS (Kansas)
map (38° 55'N 101° 11'W) **12**:18
RUSSELL SPRINGS (Kentucky)
map (37° 3'N 85° 5'W) **12**:47
RUSSELL'S PARADOX **16**:351
RUSSELLVILLE (Alabama)
map (34° 30'N 87° 44'W) **1**:234
RUSSELLVILLE (Arkansas)
map (35° 17'N 93° 8'W) **2**:166
RUSSELLVILLE (Kentucky)
map (36° 51'N 86° 53'W) **12**:47
RÜSSELSHEIM (Germany, East and West)
map (50° 0'N 8° 25'E) **9**:140
RUSSIA *see* UNION OF SOVIET SOCIALIST REPUBLICS; RUSSIA/UNION OF SOVIET SOCIALIST REPUBLICS, HISTORY OF; headings beginning with RUSSIAN or RUSSO
RUSSIA/UNION OF SOVIET SOCIALIST REPUBLICS, HISTORY OF **16**:351–360 *bibliog., illus., maps, table*
See also UNION OF SOVIET SOCIALIST REPUBLICS; names of specific republics, e.g., BELORUSSIAN SOVIET SOCIALIST REPUBLIC; GEORGIAN SOVIET SOCIALIST REPUBLIC; etc.
Buryat **3**:583
Circassians **4**:435
Cossacks **5**:290
Don Cossacks **6**:235
Finland **8**:98
Industrial Revolution **11**:159–160
Jews **11**:416
Livonia **12**:378
Manchuria **13**:109
pogrom **15**:380
political parties **15**:401–402
rulers **16**:358 *table*
slavery **17**:353
socialism **18**:21–22
Tatar **19**:43–44
Warsaw (Poland) **20**:32
prior to 1613
Alexander Nevsky **1**:275
boyars **3**:433
Cumans **5**:386
Dimitry Donskoi, Grand Duke of Moscow **6**:177
Genghis Khan, Mongol Emperor **9**:92
Godunov, Boris, Tsar **3**:401
Golden Horde, Khanate of the **9**:232
Ivan III, Grand Duke of Moscow (Ivan the Great) **11**:332
Ivan IV, Grand Duke of Moscow and Tsar (Ivan the Terrible) **11**:332–333
Khazars **12**:66
Kievan Rus' **16**:351–352 *map*
medieval period **16**:351–353 *map*
Pechenegs **15**:130
rise of Moscow **16**:352–353 *map*
Rurik (dynasty) **16**:347
Sarmatians **17**:78
Scythians **17**:167
Slavs **17**:359
Svyastoslav I, Duke of Kiev **18**:375
Time of Troubles **19**:202
Vasily III, Grand Duke of Moscow **19**:526
Vikings **19**:595
Vladimir I, Grand Duke of Kiev **19**:623
Yaroslav I, Grand Duke of Kiev **20**:319
1613–1917 Romanov Dynasty
Alexander I, Emperor **1**:275–276
Alexander II, Emperor **1**:276
Alexander III, Emperor **1**:276
Alexandra Fyodorovna, Empress **1**:277
Alexis, Tsar **1**:278
Anna Ivanovna, Empress **2**:31
Brusilov, Aleksei Alekseyevich **3**:526
Capo D'Istria, Giovanni Antonio, Count **4**:126–127
Catherine I, Empress **4**:209
Catherine II, Empress (Catherine the Great) **4**:209–210
Chmielnicki, Bohdan **4**:402
Crimean War *see* CRIMEAN WAR
Decembrists **6**:73
Duma **6**:296
Eastern Question **7**:34
Elizabeth, Empress **7**:142–143
emancipation of the serfs **16**:370
Europe, history of **7**:290
expansion and Westernization **16**:355–357 *maps*
Great Northern War *see* NORTHERN WAR, GREAT
Kutuzov, Mikhail Illarionovich **12**:140
Menshikov, Aleksandr Danilovich, Prince **13**:300
Michael, Tsar **13**:372
Napoleon I, Emperor of the French (Napoléon Bonaparte) **14**:17–18
Napoleonic Wars *see* NAPOLEONIC WARS
narodniki **14**:21
Nesselrode, Karl Robert, Count **14**:97
Nicholas I, Emperor of Russia **14**:181
Nicholas II, Emperor **14**:181–182
Northeast Passage **14**:253
Northern War, Great **14**:256
Orlov (family) **14**:446–447
Pale **15**:30
Pan-Slavism **15**:54
Paul I, Emperor **15**:118
Peter I, Emperor (Peter the Great) **15**:200–201
Peter III, Emperor **15**:201
Poland, Partitions of **15**:392 *map*
Pugachev, Yemelian Ivanovich **15**:617
Rasputin, Grigory Yefimovich **16**:90–91
Razin, Stenka **16**:98
Romanov (dynasty) **16**:290–291
Russian Revolution of 1905 **16**:370
Russo-Japanese War *see* RUSSO-JAPANESE WAR
Russo-Turkish Wars *see* RUSSO-TURKISH WARS
serfs, emancipation of **16**:357
Seven Years' War **17**:218–219 *map*
Sigismund III, King of Poland **17**:299
Slavophiles and Westernizers **17**:358–359
Sophia **18**:66–67
Speransky, Mikhail Mikhailovich **18**:179
Stolypin, Pyotr Arkadievich **18**:279
Suvorov, Aleksandr Vasilievich **18**:374
Trans-Caspian Railroad **19**:267
Triple Entente **19**:302
Witte, Sergei Yulivich, Count **20**:193
World War I *see* WORLD WAR I
Yermak Timofeyevich **20**:327
1917–1939 Russian revolutions and rise of communism
Bolsheviks and Mensheviks **3**:371
Brusilov, Aleksei Alekseyevich **3**:526
Budenny, Semyon Mikhailovich **3**:543
Bukharin, Nikolai Ivanovich **3**:553
Comintern **5**:136
communism **5**:146–150
Dzerzhinsky, Feliks Edmundovich **6**:320
Europe, history of **7**:295
Great Purge **9**:321
Kamenev, Lev Borisovich **12**:9–10
Kerensky, Aleksandr Fyodorovich **12**:58–59
Kollantai, Aleksandra **12**:107
Krupskaya, Nadezhda Konstantinovna **12**:132
kulaks **12**:135–136
Lenin, Vladimir Ilich **12**:282–283
Litvinov, Maksim Maksimovich **12**:374
Molotov, Vyacheslav Mikhailovich **13**:513
Mongolia **13**:530
New Economic Policy **14**:121
Polish-Soviet War **15**:398
Radek, Karl **16**:142
Rathenau, Walther **16**:92
Russian music **16**:369

RUSSIA/UNION OF SOVIET SOCIALIST REPUBLICS, HISTORY OF (cont.)
Russian Revolutions of 1917 *see* RUSSIAN REVOLUTIONS OF 1917
Stalin, Joseph **18**:213–215
Trotsky, Leon **19**:310–311
Union of Soviet Socialist Republics **16**:359–360
Vaasa (Finland) **19**:501
World War I *see* WORLD WAR I
Zinoviev, Grigory Yevseyevich **20**:369
1939-present
Afghanistan **1**:135
Andropov, Yuri V. **1**:409
Beria, Lavrenti Pavlovich **3**:211
Brezhnev, Leonid Ilich **3**:476
Bulganin, Nikolai Aleksandrovich **3**:554
Chernenko, Konstantin **4**:331
cold war **5**:98–99
Cuban Missile Crisis **5**:380
Czechoslovakia **5**:416
Germany, East and West **9**:146–147
Gorbachev, Mikhail **9**:248
Gromyko, Andrei Andreyevich **9**:368
Hitler, Adolf **10**:188
Khrushchev, Nikita Sergeyevich **12**:68–69
Korolev, Sergei **12**:123
Kosygin, Aleksei N. **12**:125
Malenkov, Georgy M. **13**:87–88
Mikoyan, Anastas Ivanovich **13**:417
Nazi-Soviet Pact **14**:67
Russo-Finnish War *see* RUSSO-FINNISH WAR
Somalia **18**:61
Tikhonov, Nikolai A. **19**:198
World War II *see* WORLD WAR II
Zhukov, Georgy Konstantinovich **20**:362–363
RUSSIAN-AMERICAN COMPANY **16**:360–361 *bibliog.*
Baranov, Aleksandr Andreyevich **3**:75
Shelekhov, Grigory Ivanovich **17**:250
RUSSIAN ART AND ARCHITECTURE **16**:361–364 *bibliog., illus.*
See also the subheading Russia under specific art forms, e.g., ARCHITECTURE; PAINTING; SCULPTURE; etc.; names of specific artists, e.g., FABERGÉ, PETER CARL; KANDINSKY, WASSILY; etc.
abstract art **1**:64
constructivism **5**:224
Hermitage Museum **10**:143
house (in Western architecture) **10**:269 *illus.*
icon **11**:20
iconography **11**:21–24
iconostasis **11**:24
Kremlin **12**:128–129 *illus.*
Leningrad **12**:283–285 *illus.*
mobile **13**:487
modern architecture **13**:491
museums, art **13**:658
Novgorod **14**:276
Secession movement **17**:178
steppe art **18**:256
suprematism **18**:354
Winter Palace **20**:181
RUSSIAN BLUE (cat) **4**:195 *illus.*; **16**:364 *illus.*
RUSSIAN FEDERATION *see* RUSSIAN SOVIET FEDERATED SOCIALIST REPUBLIC
RUSSIAN LITERATURE **16**:364–367 *bibliog., illus.*
See also the subheading Russian literature under DRAMA; NOVEL; POETRY; etc.; names of specific authors, e.g., DOSTOYEVSKY, FYODOR MIKHAILOVICH; LERMONTOV, MIKHAIL; etc.; titles of specific literary works, e.g., *CHERRY ORCHARD, THE* (play); *WAR AND PEACE* (book); etc.
acmeists **1**:83
constructivism **5**:224
émigré literature **16**:366
formalism **8**:234
Muscovite period **16**:364–365
nihilism **14**:194
realism (literature) **16**:104
samizdat **17**:46
socialist realism **16**:366; **18**:25
RUSSIAN MUSIC **16**:367–369 *bibliog., illus.*
See also names of specific composers, e.g., RIMSKY-KORSAKOV, NIKOLAI ANDREYEVICH; SHOSTAKOVICH, DMITRY; etc.
balalaika **3**:30
Boris Godunov (opera) **3**:400–401
Five, The **8**:132
Miaskovsky, Nicolai **13**:370
music, history of Western **13**:667
music competitions **13**:669
opera **14**:401
RUSSIAN OLIVE *see* OLEASTER
RUSSIAN ORTHODOX CHURCH *see* ORTHODOX CHURCH
RUSSIAN REVOLUTION OF 1905 **16**:370 *bibliog.*
Nicholas II, Emperor of Russia **14**:182
Odessa (USSR) **14**:349
Russian Revolutions of 1917 **16**:370–371 *illus.*
Russia/Union of Soviet Socialist Republics, history of **16**:358
Trotsky, Leon **19**:311
RUSSIAN REVOLUTIONS OF 1917 **16**:188 *illus.*; **16**:359 *illus.*; **16**:370–373 *bibliog., illus.*
Bolsheviks and Mensheviks **3**:371
communism **5**:146
émigrés **7**:156
Europe, history of **7**:295
historical background **16**:370–371
Kamenev, Lev Borisovich **12**:9–10
Kornilov, Lavr Georgiyevich **12**:123
Lenin, Vladimir Ilich **12**:282–283
March Revolution **16**:371
Nicholas II, Emperor of Russia **14**:182
November Revolution (Bolshevik Revolution) **16**:371–372 *illus.*
Reed, John **16**:118
Russian art and architecture **16**:364
Russia/Union of Soviet Socialist Republics, history of **16**:359
soviet **18**:113
Stalin, Joseph **18**:214
Trotsky, Leon **19**:311
World War I **20**:238 *illus.*
Wrangel, Pyotr Nikolayevich, Baron **20**:285
RUSSIAN RIVER
map (38° 27′N 123° 8′W) **4**:31
RUSSIAN SOCIAL DEMOCRATIC LABOR PARTY
Bolsheviks and Mensheviks **3**:371
Lenin, Vladimir Ilich **12**:282
Russian Revolutions of 1917 **16**:370
RUSSIAN SOVIET FEDERATED SOCIALIST REPUBLIC (USSR) **16**:373
cities
Astrakhan **2**:269–270
Chelyabinsk **4**:311
Gorky **9**:251–252
Irkutsk **11**:270
Kalinin **12**:8
Kaliningrad **12**:8
Kazan **12**:33
Kirov **12**:89
Krasnodar **12**:127
Krasnoyarsk **12**:127
Kuibyshev **12**:135
Leningrad **12**:283–285 *illus., map*
Magnitogorsk **13**:60
Moscow **13**:596–599 *illus., map*
Murmansk **13**:649
Novgorod **14**:276
Novosibirsk **14**:277
Omsk **14**:388
Perm **15**:173
Pskov **15**:588
Pushkin **15**:631
Rostov-on-Don **16**:321
Ryazan **16**:378–379
Saratov **17**:75
Smolensk **17**:374
Sochi **18**:11
Sverdlovsk **18**:374–375
Taganrog **19**:9
Ufa **19**:371
Vladimir **19**:623
Vladivostok **19**:623–624
Volgograd **19**:629
Voronezh **19**:635
Yaroslavl **20**:319
people
Kalmyk **12**:8
Khants **12**:65
physical features
Onega, Lake **14**:389
Yablonovy Mountains **20**:314
regions
Daghestan **6**:6
Kamchatka Peninsula **12**:9 *map*
Karelia **12**:27
Kuril Islands **12**:139
Sakhalin **17**:28
Siberia **17**:291–292
RUSSIAN THISTLE *see* TUMBLEWEED
RUSSIAN WOLFHOUND *see* BORZOI
RUSSIAVILLE (Indiana)
map (40° 25′N 86° 16′W) **11**:111
RUSSO-FINNISH WAR **16**:373 *bibliog.*
World War II **20**:251
RUSSO-JAPANESE WAR **16**:373 *bibliog.*
Japan's surprise attack on Port Arthur **11**:370 *illus.*
Korea, history of **12**:117
sinking of the flagship *Petropavlovsk* **16**:358 *illus.*
Togo Heihachiro **19**:222
Tsushima, Battle of **19**:325
RUSSO-TURKISH WARS **16**:374 *bibliog., illus.*
See also CRIMEAN WAR
Adrianople, Treaty of **1**:109
Ahmed III, Sultan of the Ottoman Empire **1**:200
Berlin, Congress of **3**:217
Middle East, history of the **13**:405
Suvorov, Aleksandr Vasilievich **18**:374
RUST (botany)
diseases, plant **6**:196
RUST, METALLIC *see* CORROSION
RUSTAVELI, SHOTA
Tbilisi (USSR) **19**:51
RUSTBURG (Virginia)
map (37° 17′N 79° 6′W) **19**:607
RUSTON (Louisiana)
map (32° 32′N 92° 38′W) **12**:430
RUTABAGA **16**:374–375 *illus.*; **19**:534 *illus.*
turnip **19**:351
RUTANA (Burundi)
map (3° 55′S 30° 0′E) **3**:582
RUTGERS UNIVERSITY
football **8**:216
New Jersey, state university and colleges of **14**:133–134
RUTH (Mississippi)
map (31° 23′N 90° 19′W) **13**:469
RUTH (Nevada)
map (39° 17′N 114° 59′W) **14**:111
RUTH, BABE **3**:106 *illus.*; **16**:375 *bibliog., illus.*
RUTH, BOOK OF **16**:375 *bibliog.*
RUTH, GEORGE HERMAN "BABE" *see* RUTH, BABE
RUTHENBERG, CHARLES E.
Communist party, U.S.A. **5**:151
RUTHENIA (USSR) **16**:375
RUTHENIUM **16**:375
element **7**:130 *table*
Group VIII periodic table **15**:167
metal, metallic element **13**:328
transition elements **19**:273
RUTHERFORD (New Jersey)
map (40° 49′N 74° 7′W) **14**:129
RUTHERFORD (county in North Carolina)
map (35° 25′N 81° 50′W) **14**:242
RUTHERFORD (Tennessee)
map (36° 8′N 88° 59′W) **19**:104
RUTHERFORD (county in Tennessee)
map (35° 50′N 86° 20′W) **19**:104
RUTHERFORD, SIR ERNEST **16**:375–376 *bibliog., illus.*
atom **2**:305 *illus.*
atomic nucleus **2**:309–310 *illus.*
element 104 **7**:132
physics **16**:375–376
quantum mechanics **16**:10
radioactivity **16**:61
RUTHERFORD, JOSEPH FRANKLIN **16**:376
RUTHERFORDIUM
element 104 **7**:132
superheavy elements **18**:351
RUTHERFORDTON (North Carolina)
map (35° 22′N 81° 57′W) **14**:242
RUTHERFURD, LEWIS MORRIS
astronomy, history of **2**:279
RUTILE **16**:376 *illus.*
quartz **16**:13
tetragonal system **19**:127
RUTLAND (Massachusetts)
map (42° 23′N 71° 57′W) **13**:206
RUTLAND (North Dakota)
map (46° 3′N 97° 30′W) **14**:248
RUTLAND (Vermont) **16**:376
map (43° 36′N 72° 59′W) **19**:554
RUTLAND (county in Vermont)
map (43° 35′N 73° 0′W) **19**:554
RUTLEDGE (Tennessee)
map (36° 17′N 83° 31′W) **19**:104
RUTLEDGE, ANN **16**:376
RUTLEDGE, JOHN **16**:376–377 *bibliog.*
RUUSBROEC, JAN VAN *see* RUYSBROECK, JOHN
RUVUBU RIVER
map (2° 23′S 30° 47′E) **3**:582
RUVUMA RIVER
map (10° 29′S 40° 28′E) **19**:27
RUWENZORI **16**:377
RUYIGI (Burundi)
map (3° 29′S 30° 15′E) **3**:582
RUYSBROECK, JOHN **16**:377 *bibliog.*
RUYSCH, RACHEL **16**:377 *bibliog.*
RUYSDAEL, SALOMON VAN *see* RUISDAEL, SALOMON VAN
RUYTER, MICHIEL ADRIAANSZOON DE **16**:377 *bibliog.*
RUŽIČKA, LEOPOLD **16**:377
RUZIZI RIVER
map (3° 16′S 29° 14′E) **3**:582
RV *see* RECREATIONAL VEHICLE
RWANDA **16**:377–378 *bibliog., illus., map*
See also RUANDA-URUNDI
cities
Kigali **12**:76
flag **16**:377 *illus.*
history and government **16**:378
map (2° 30′S 30° 0′E) **1**:136
people **16**:378
Tutsi **19**:355–356
RYA
rugs and carpets **16**:342–343
RYAN (Oklahoma)
map (34° 1′N 97° 57′W) **14**:368
RYAN, CORNELIUS **16**:378 *bibliog.*
RYAN, LEO
Jonestown (Guyana) **11**:444
RYAN, NOLAN **16**:378 *bibliog.*
RYAN PEAK
map (43° 54′N 114° 25′W) **11**:26
RYAZAN (USSR) **16**:378–379
RYBINSK (USSR)
map (58° 3′N 38° 52′E) **19**:388
RYBINSK RESERVOIR
map (58° 30′N 38° 25′E) **19**:629
RYBNIK (Poland)
map (50° 6′N 18° 32′E) **15**:388
RYDBERG, ABRAHAM VIKTOR **16**:379
RYDBERG, JOHANNES ROBERT **16**:379
RYDBERG'S CONSTANT
atomic constant **2**:309
RYDER (North Dakota)
map (47° 55′N 101° 40′W) **14**:248
RYDER, ALBERT PINKHAM **16**:379 *bibliog., illus.*
Siegfried and the Rhine Maidens **1**:334 *illus.*; **16**:379 *illus.*
RYDER CUP
golf **9**:239
RYE **9**:281 *illus.*; **16**:379–380 *bibliog., illus.*
hybrid **10**:328 *illus.*
whiskey **20**:132–133
RYE HOUSE PLOT
Monmouth, James Scott, Duke of **13**:536
Sidney, Algernon **17**:295
RYE PATCH RESERVOIR
map (40° 38′N 118° 18′W) **14**:111
RYE WHISKEY *see* WHISKEY
RYEGATE (Montana)
map (46° 18′N 109° 15′W) **13**:547
RYLE, GILBERT **16**:380 *bibliog.*
RYLE, SIR MARTIN **16**:380
aperture synthesis **2**:76
Mullard Radio Astronomy Observatory **13**:636
radio astronomy **16**:52
RYMER, THOMAS **16**:380
RYSBRACK, MICHAEL **16**:380 *bibliog.*
RYSWICK, TREATY OF
Grand Alliance, War of the **9**:284
lands acquired **8**:269 *map*
William III, King of England, Scotland, and Ireland **20**:156
RYSY MOUNTAIN
map (49° 12′N 20° 4′E) **15**:388
RYUKYU ISLANDS **16**:380
animal
habu **10**:6
map (26° 30′N 128° 0′E) **11**:361
Okinawa **14**:366
Ring of Fire **16**:225
RYUKYU TRENCH
Pacific Ocean bottom **15**:6–7 *map*
RYUMIN, VALERY **16**:380 *bibliog.*
RYUN, JIM **16**:380
RZESZÓW (Poland)
map (50° 3′N 22° 0′E) **15**:388

S

S (letter) **17**:3
'S-GRAUENHAGE *see* HAGUE, THE (Netherlands)
's HERTOGENBOSCH (Netherlands) **17**:259
map (51° 41′N 5° 19′E) **14**:99
S-R PSYCHOLOGY *see* BEHAVIORISM
SA (Sturmabteilung)
Hitler, Adolf **10**:187
Roehm, Ernst **16**:268
SÁ CARNEIRO, FRANCISCO
Portugal, history of **15**:455
SÁ DE MIRANDA, FRANCISCO DE **17**:3 *bibliog.*
SA-6 GAINFUL MISSILE **2**:56 *illus.*
SAADIA BEN JOSEPH GAON **17**:3 *bibliog.*
SAALE RIVER
map (51° 57′N 11° 55′E) **9**:140
SAANGAD CHALORYOO
Thailand **19**:141
SAAR (West Germany) *see* SAARLAND (West Germany)
SAAR, FERDINAND VON
Austrian literature **2**:354
SAARBRÜCKEN (West Germany) **17**:3
map (49° 14′N 6° 59′E) **9**:140
SAAREMAA
Estonian Soviet Socialist Republic (USSR) **7**:247
SAARIKOSKI, PENTTI
Finnish literature **8**:99
SAARINEN, EERO **17**:4 *bibliog., illus.*
Gateway Arch (St. Louis) **13**:477 *illus.*; **17**:22 *illus.*
Milwaukee (Wisconsin) **13**:434
range **8**:379 *illus.*
TWA Terminal at Kennedy Airport **13**:492 *illus.*; **17**:4 *illus.*
SAARINEN, ELIEL **17**:4
Cranbrook Foundation **5**:329
SAARLAND (West Germany) **17**:3 *map*
cities
Saarbrücken **17**:3
SAARLOUIS (Germany, East and West)
map (49° 21′N 6° 45′E) **9**:140
SAATCHI AND SAATCHI (advertising agency) **1**:112
SAAVEDRA (Argentina)
map (37° 45′S 62° 22′W) **2**:149
SAAVEDRA, ÁNGEL DE
Spanish literature **18**:159
SAAVEDRA, JUAN DE
Valparaíso (Chile) **19**:508
SAAVEDRA, MIGUEL DE CERVANTES *see* CERVANTES SAAVEDRA, MIGUEL DE
SAB *see* SOMALI
SABA (Arabian kingdom) *see* SHEBA
SABA (Netherlands Antilles) **14**:103
ŠABAC (Yugoslavia)
map (44° 45′N 19° 42′E) **20**:340
SABADELL (Spain)
map (41° 33′N 2° 6′E) **18**:140
SABAH (dynasty)
Kuwait (country) **12**:141–142
SABAH (Malaysia) **17**:4
SABANA DE LA MAR (Dominican Republic)
map (19° 4′N 69° 23′W) **6**:233
SABANAGRANDE (Honduras)
map (13° 50′N 87° 15′W) **10**:218
SABATIER, PAUL **17**:4 *bibliog.*
SÁBATO, ERNESTO **17**:4 *bibliog.*
SABBATAI ZEVI **17**:5 *bibliog.*
Frank, Jacob **8**:279
Jews **11**:415 *illus.*
Kabbalah **12**:3
SABBATH **17**:5 *bibliog.*
SABBATIUS, PETRUS *see* JUSTINIAN I, BYZANTINE EMPEROR (Justinian the Great)
SABBATTINI, NICOLA
stage lighting **18**:210
SABELLIANISM **17**:5 *bibliog.*
Callistus I, Pope **4**:46
Hippolytus of Rome, Saint **10**:175
Monarchianism **13**:517
SABER-TOOTHED CATS **13**:102 *illus.*; **17**:5 *bibliog., illus.*
La Brea Tar Pit **12**:145
Pleistocene Epoch **15**:366–367 *illus.*
SABETHA (Kansas)
map (39° 54′N 95° 48′W) **12**:18
SABHA (Libya)
map (27° 3′N 14° 26′E) **12**:320
SABIN, ALBERT BRUCE **17**:5
poliomyelitis vaccine **15**:397; **17**:5
Salk, Jonas **17**:34
SABINAL (Texas)
map (29° 19′N 99° 28′W) **19**:129
SABINE (county in Louisiana)
map (31° 33′N 93° 30′W) **12**:430
SABINE (county in Texas)
map (31° 20′N 93° 53′W) **19**:129
SABINE PASS
map (29° 44′N 93° 52′W) **12**:430
SABINES **17**:5
rape of the Sabines **8**:196 *illus.*
Rome, ancient **16**:297
SABIYAH *see* ISMAILIS
SABLE **8**:229 *illus.*; **17**:5–6 *illus.*
marten **13**:175
SABLE, CAPE (Florida) **17**:6
map (25° 12′N 81° 5′W) **8**:172
SABLE, CAPE (Nova Scotia) **17**:6
map (43° 25′N 65° 35′W) **14**:269
SABLE ISLAND (Nova Scotia) **17**:6
map (43° 55′N 59° 50′W) **14**:269
SABOT (shoe) **17**:280 *illus.*
SABOTAGE **17**:6
syndicalism **18**:407
SABRE (aircraft) *see* F-86A SABRE (aircraft)
SABZEVAR (Iran)
map (36° 13′N 57° 42′E) **11**:250
SAC *see* STRATEGIC AIR COMMAND
SAC (American Indians) *see* SAUK (American Indians)
SAC (county in Iowa)
map (42° 23′N 95° 0′W) **11**:244
SAC CITY (Iowa)
map (42° 25′N 95° 0′W) **11**:244
SACAGAWEA **14**:251 *illus.*; **17**:6 *bibliog.*
Lewis and Clark Expedition **12**:307 *illus.*
Shoshoni **17**:284
SACAJAWEA, LAKE
map (46° 28′N 118° 40′W) **20**:35
SACAJAWEA PEAK
map (45° 15′N 117° 17′W) **14**:427
SACCHARIMETER
polarimeter **15**:393
SACCHARIN **17**:6 *bibliog.*
amide **1**:369
sugar **18**:327
SACCHERI, GIROLAMO
non-Euclidean geometry **14**:216
SACCO AND VANZETTI CASE **17**:6 *bibliog.*
Frankfurter, Felix **8**:281
The Passion of Sacco and Vanzetti (Ben Shahn) **17**:235 *illus.*
SACHEM
Iroquois League **11**:280
SACHER-MASOCH, LEOPOLD VON
masochism **13**:198
SACHS, CURT **17**:7 *bibliog.*
musical instruments **13**:676
SACHS, HANS **17**:7 *bibliog.*
SACHS, JULIUS VON
photosynthesis **15**:276
SACHS, NELLY **17**:7 *bibliog.*
SACHS HARBOUR (Northwest Territories)
map (72° 0′N 125° 0′W) **14**:258
SACKBUT **17**:7
trombone **19**:306
SACKETS HARBOR (New York)
map (43° 57′N 76° 7′W) **14**:149
SACKLER, HOWARD
theater of fact **19**:153
SACKVILLE, LORD GEORGE *see* GERMAIN, LORD GEORGE
SACKVILLE-WEST, VICTORIA **17**:7 *bibliog.*
SACO (Maine)
map (43° 29′N 70° 28′W) **13**:70
SACRAMENT **17**:7 *bibliog.*
anointing of the sick **2**:34
baptism **3**:72–73
confession **5**:177
confirmation **5**:178
Eucharist **7**:262
grace **9**:275
holy orders **10**:209
marriage **13**:166
SACRAMENTO (California) **17**:7
map (38° 3′N 121° 56′W) **4**:31
SACRAMENTO (county in California)
map (38° 25′N 121° 30′W) **4**:31
SACRAMENTO MOUNTAINS
map (33° 10′N 105° 50′W) **14**:136
SACRAMENTO RIVER **17**:8
map (38° 3′N 121° 56′W) **4**:31
SACRAMENTO VALLEY
map (39° 15′N 122° 0′W) **4**:31
SACRÉ-COEUR **17**:8
SACRED ANIMAL *see* ANIMAL WORSHIP
SACRED BARK *see* CINCHONA
SACRED HEART (Minnesota)
map (44° 47′N 95° 21′W) **13**:453
SACRED MUSIC *see* CHURCH MUSIC
SACRIFICE **17**:8 *bibliog.*
cannibalism **4**:109 *illus.*
druids **6**:282
infanticide **11**:163
Tollund man **19**:227
SACROBOSCO, JOHANNES **17**:8
SACRUM
spine **18**:185 *illus.*
SACSAHUAMAN (Peru) **17**:8 *bibliog.*
pre-Columbian art and architecture **15**:501
SADA (Yemen) (Sana)
map (16° 52′N 43° 37′E) **20**:325
SADAT, ANWAR AL- **17**:8 *bibliog., illus.*
Arab-Israeli Wars **2**:98
Egypt **7**:80–81 *illus.*
SADDLE **17**:8–9 *bibliog., illus.*
riding **16**:217
stirrup **18**:273
weapons **20**:74
SADDLE HORSE **17**:9 *bibliog.*
SADDLER *see* AMERICAN SADDLE HORSE
SADDUCEES **17**:9 *bibliog.*
Judaism **11**:460
Sanhedrin **17**:65
SADE, MARQUIS DE **17**:9 *bibliog.*
Justine **11**:478
sadism **17**:10
SADI, SHEYKH MOSLEHODDIN **17**:9–10 *bibliog.*
SADISM **17**:10 *bibliog.*
masochism **13**:198
Sade, Marquis de **17**:10
SADLER'S WELLS BALLET **3**:43
See also ROYAL BALLET, THE
Cranko, John **5**:331
Fonteyn, Dame Margot **8**:207
SADO ISLAND
map (38° 0′N 138° 25′E) **11**:361
SADO RIVER
map (38° 29′N 8° 55′W) **15**:449
SAËNS, CAMILLE SAINT- *see* SAINT-SAËNS, CAMILLE
SAFAD (Israel)
map (32° 58′N 35° 30′E) **11**:302
SAFAQIS (Tunisia) *see* SFAX (Tunisia)
SAFATA BAY
map (14° 0′S 171° 50′W) **20**:117
SAFATULAFEI (Western Samoa)
map (13° 40′S 172° 7′W) **20**:117
SAFAVIDS
Iran **11**:252–253
Nadir Shah **14**:5
Suleiman I, Sultan of the Ottoman Empire (Suleiman the Magnificent) **18**:333
SAFDIE, MOSHE **17**:10 *bibliog.*
SAFE **17**:10
SAFEGUARD SYSTEM
antiballistic missile **2**:56 *illus.*
SAFETY, AUTOMOTIVE **17**:10–11 *bibliog., illus.*
SAFETY, INDUSTRIAL
coal and coal mining **5**:79
government regulation **9**:271
Occupational Safety And Health Administration **14**:320–321
SAFETY LAMP
Davy, Sir Humphry, inventor **6**:53–54
SAFETY SYSTEMS
See also LIFESAVING AND WATER SAFETY
Consumer Product Safety Commission **5**:225
consumer protection **5**:226
fire prevention and control **8**:103–105
nuclear energy **14**:282–283
safety, automotive **17**:10–11
SAFFLOWER **17**:11
SAFFORD (Arizona)
map (32° 50′N 109° 43′W) **2**:160
SAFFRON **17**:11 *illus.*
crocus **5**:357
SAFI (Morocco)
map (32° 20′N 9° 17′W) **13**:585
SAFID MOUNTAINS
map (34° 30′N 63° 30′E) **1**:133
SAG HARBOR (New York) **14**:152 *illus.*
SAGA **17**:11 *bibliog.*
Heimskringla **10**:108
Icelandic literature **11**:18–19
Leif Eriksson **12**:278
Scandinavia, history of **17**:108
SAGADAHOC (county in Maine)
map (43° 57′N 69° 52′W) **13**:70
SAGAMI GULF
map (35° 0′N 139° 30′E) **11**:361
SAGAMORE (Massachusetts)
map (41° 45′N 70° 33′W) **13**:206
SAGAN, CARL EDWARD **17**:11
SAGAN, FRANÇOISE **17**:11
SAGANAGA LAKE
map (48° 14′N 90° 52′W) **13**:453
SAGAUNASH *see* CALDWELL, BILLY
SAGE (botany)
Salvia **17**:40–41 *illus.*
SAGE, KAY
Tanguy, Ives **19**:23
SAGE, MOUNT
map (18° 25′N 64° 39′W) **19**:605
SAGE, RUSSELL **17**:12 *bibliog.*
SAGEBRUSH **17**:12 *illus.*
SAGEBRUSH REBELLION
North America **14**:236
SAGINAW (Michigan) **17**:12
map (43° 25′N 83° 58′W) **13**:377
SAGINAW (county in Michigan)
map (43° 20′N 84° 0′W) **13**:377
SAGINAW BAY
map (43° 50′N 83° 40′W) **13**:377
SAGITTARIUS **17**:12
Chiron (mythology) **4**:397
SAGLOUC (Quebec)
map (62° 14′N 75° 38′W) **16**:18
SAGO **17**:12 *illus.*
SAGO PALM **5**:402 *illus.*; **17**:12 *illus.*
SAGOYEWATHA *see* RED JACKET (Seneca Indian)
SAGUA DE TÁNAMO (Cuba)
map (20° 35′N 75° 14′W) **5**:377
SAGUA LA GRANDE (Cuba)
map (22° 49′N 80° 5′W) **5**:377
SAGUACHE (Colorado)
map (38° 5′N 106° 8′W) **5**:116
SAGUACHE (county in Colorado)
map (38° 10′N 106° 20′W) **5**:116
SAGUACHE CREEK
map (37° 52′N 105° 51′W) **5**:116
SAGUARO
cacti and other succulents **4**:9–10
SAGUENAY RIVER **17**:12
map (48° 8′N 69° 44′W) **16**:18
SAGUNTO (Spain)
map (39° 41′N 0° 16′W) **18**:140
SAHA, MEGHNAD N. **17**:12–13 *bibliog.*
SAHAGÚN, BERNARDINO DE
Latin American literature **12**:229
SAHARA **17**:13–14 *bibliog., illus., map*
African languages **1**:166
climate **17**:13
desert **6**:126–129
exploration
Nachtigal, Gustav **14**:4
history **17**:14
Libyan Desert **12**:321–322
map (26° 0′N 13° 0′E) **1**:136
mineral resources **17**:14
people **17**:14 *illus.*
Berbers **3**:207–208
Tuareg **19**:325–326
rivers, lakes, and waterways **17**:13–14
sand dune **17**:60
sandstorm and dust storm **17**:63 *illus.*
Tibesti Massif **19**:189
topography and geology **17**:13–14 *illus.*
transportation **17**:14
vegetation and animal life **17**:14 *illus.*
SAHARANPUR (India)
map (29° 58′N 77° 33′E) **11**:80
SAHEL (Africa) **17**:14–15
Mali **13**:90 *illus.*
map (15° 0′N 8° 0′W) **13**:89
Sahara **17**:13
SAHIWAL
map (30° 40′N 73° 6′E) **15**:27
SAHUARIPA (Mexico)
map (29° 3′N 109° 14′W) **13**:357
SAHUARITA (Arizona)
map (31° 57′N 110° 58′W) **2**:160
SAHUAYO (Mexico)
map (20° 4′N 102° 43′W) **13**:357
SAID, SAYYID
Pemba (Tanzania) **15**:140
SAID BIN TAIMUR
Oman **14**:387
SAIDPUR (Bangladesh)
map (25° 47′N 88° 54′E) **3**:64
SAIGA **17**:15
SAIGO TAKAMORI **17**:15 *bibliog.*
SAIGON (Vietnam) *see* HO CHI MINH CITY (Vietnam)
SAILBOAT *see* SAILING AND SAILING SHIPS
SAILER, TONI **17**:15
SAILFIN LEAF FISH **17**:148 *illus.*
SAILFISH **17**:15 *illus.*
SAILING AND SAILING SHIPS
America's Cup **1**:368
Bicentennial, U.S. **3**:243
boat and boating **3**:349–352 *illus.*
cross section of decks **5**:235 *illus.*

SAILING AND SAILING SHIPS (cont.)
Cutty Sark **17**:269 *illus.*
Diligente **17**:268 *illus.*
Endeavour **5**:235 *illus.*
figurehead **8**:75–76
history **17**:263–272 *illus.*
Mayflower **13**:247 *illus.*
sails and rigging **5**:235 *illus.*; **17**:269–271 *illus.*
Savannah (steamship) **17**:99
shanty **17**:241
transportation **19**:278
types
caravel **4**:132 *illus.*
carrack (15th century) **19**:64 *illus.*
catamaran **4**:199–200 *illus.*
clipper ship **5**:60–61 *illus.*
cutter **5**:398
East Indiaman (merchant vessel) **7**:31 *illus.*; **17**:268 *illus.*
junk **11**:470–471
schooner **17**:134
SAILOR KING *see* WILLIAM IV, KING OF ENGLAND, SCOTLAND, AND IRELAND
SAILOR'S DANCES
folk dance **8**:199
SAILPLANE *see* GLIDER
SAILWING
windmills and wind power **20**:172–173 *illus.*
SAINT **17**:15 *bibliog.*
See also names of specific saints, e.g., NEUMANN, SAINT JOHN NEPOMUCENE; PAUL, SAINT; TERESA OF ÁVILA, SAINT; etc.
canonization **4**:115; **17**:15
hagiography **10**:10
medieval drama **13**:274
SAINT, THOMAS
sewing machine **17**:223
SAINT ALBANS (England) **17**:15–16
map (51° 46′N 0° 21′W) **19**:403
SAINT ALBANS (Newfoundland)
map (47° 52′N 55° 51′W) **14**:166
SAINT ALBANS (Vermont)
map (44° 49′N 73° 5′W) **19**:554
SAINT ALBANS (West Virginia)
map (38° 23′N 81° 49′W) **20**:111
SAINT ALBANS, CATHEDRAL OF **7**:182 *illus.*
SAINT ALBANS BAY
map (44° 46′N 73° 10′W) **19**:554
SAINT ALBAN'S HEAD
map (50° 34′N 2° 4′W) **19**:403
SAINT-ANDRÉ, CAPE
map (16° 11′S 44° 27′E) **13**:38
SAINT ANDREW BAY
map (30° 10′N 85° 45′W) **8**:172
SAINT ANDREWS (Scotland) **17**:16
golf **9**:239–240
SAINT ANDREWS (South Carolina)
map (32° 47′N 80° 0′W) **18**:98
map (34° 2′N 81° 5′W) **18**:98
SAINT ANDREWS, UNIVERSITY OF **17**:16
SAINT ANNE (Illinois)
map (41° 1′N 87° 43′W) **11**:42
ST. ANNE'S COLLEGE (Oxford University) **14**:474
SAINT ANN'S BAY (Jamaica)
map (18° 26′N 77° 8′W) **11**:351
SAINT ANTHONY (Idaho)
map (43° 58′N 111° 41′W) **11**:26
SAINT ANTHONY (Newfoundland)
map (51° 22′N 55° 35′W) **14**:166
ST. ANTHONY'S FIRE
ergot **7**:228
ST. ANTONY'S COLLEGE (Oxford University) **14**:474
SAINT-AUBIN (family) **17**:16 *bibliog.*
SAINT-AUGUSTIN-SAGUENAY (Quebec)
map (51° 14′N 58° 39′W) **16**:18
SAINT AUGUSTINE (Florida) **17**:16
map (29° 54′N 81° 19′W) **8**:172
Menéndez de Avilés, Pedro **13**:297
SAINT AUGUSTINE BIBLE **7**:10 *illus.*
SAINT BARTHÉLEMY, CHURCH OF (Liège) **16**:285 *illus.*
SAINT BARTHOLOMEW'S DAY MASSACRE **17**:16 *bibliog.*
Henry IV, King of France **10**:128
Huguenots **10**:294–295
SAINT-BASILE (New Brunswick)
map (47° 21′N 68° 14′W) **14**:117
SAINT BASIL'S CATHEDRAL (Moscow) **13**:597–598 *illus., map*; **16**:361 *illus.*
SAINT BENET'S HALL (Oxford University) **14**:474
SAINT BERNARD **6**:214 *illus.*; **17**:16 *bibliog., illus.*
SAINT BERNARD (county in Louisiana)
map (29° 55′N 89° 35′W) **12**:430
SAINT BERNARD (Ohio)
map (39° 10′N 84° 30′W) **14**:357
SAINT BERNARD PASS **17**:16
map (45° 50′N 7° 10′E) **18**:394
SAINT BERNARDINO PASS
map (46° 20′N 9° 0′E) **18**:394
SAINT BRENDAN'S (Newfoundland)
map (48° 52′N 53° 40′W) **14**:166
SAINT BRIDE'S (Newfoundland)
map (46° 55′N 54° 10′W) **14**:166
SAINT-BRIEUC (France)
map (48° 31′N 2° 47′W) **8**:260
SAINT CATHARINES (Ontario) **17**:17
map (43° 10′N 79° 15′W) **14**:393
ST. CATHARINE'S COLLEGE (Cambridge University) **4**:53
ST. CATHARINE'S COLLEGE (Oxford University) **14**:474
SAINT CATHERINES ISLAND
map (31° 38′N 81° 10′W) **9**:114
SAINT CHARLES (Arkansas)
map (34° 22′N 91° 8′W) **2**:166
SAINT CHARLES (Illinois)
map (41° 54′N 88° 19′W) **11**:42
SAINT CHARLES (county in Louisiana)
map (29° 53′N 90° 20′W) **12**:430
SAINT CHARLES (Minnesota)
map (43° 58′N 92° 4′W) **13**:453
SAINT CHARLES (Missouri)
map (38° 47′N 90° 29′W) **13**:476
SAINT CHARLES (county in Missouri)
map (38° 50′N 90° 40′W) **13**:476
SAINT CHRISTOPHER (island) *see* SAINT KITTS-NEVIS
SAINT CLAIR (county in Alabama)
map (33° 40′N 86° 20′W) **1**:234
SAINT CLAIR (county in Illinois)
map (38° 31′N 90° 0′W) **11**:42
SAINT CLAIR (Michigan)
map (42° 49′N 82° 30′W) **13**:377
SAINT CLAIR (county in Michigan)
map (42° 50′N 82° 42′W) **13**:377
SAINT CLAIR (Missouri)
map (38° 20′N 90° 59′W) **13**:476
SAINT CLAIR (county in Missouri)
map (38° 0′N 93° 45′W) **13**:476
ST. CLAIR, ARTHUR **17**:17 *bibliog.*
Cincinnati **4**:432
SAINT CLAIR, LAKE **17**:17
SAINT CLAIR RIVER
map (42° 37′N 82° 31′W) **13**:377
SAINT CLAIR SHORES (Michigan)
map (42° 30′N 82° 54′W) **13**:377
SAINT CLAIRSVILLE (Ohio)
map (40° 5′N 80° 54′W) **14**:357
SAINT CLEMENT DANES, CHURCH OF
cathedrals and churches **4**:208
SAINT CLOUD (Florida)
map (28° 15′N 81° 17′W) **8**:172
SAINT CLOUD (Minnesota) **17**:17
map (45° 33′N 94° 10′W) **13**:453
SAINT CROIX
map (17° 45′N 64° 45′W) **19**:605
Virgin Islands **19**:605–606
SAINT CROIX (county in Wisconsin)
map (45° 0′N 92° 25′W) **20**:185
SAINT CROIX, LAKE
map (44° 55′N 92° 50′W) **20**:185
SAINT CROIX FALLS (Wisconsin)
map (45° 24′N 92° 38′W) **20**:185
SAINT CROIX RIVER (Maine)
map (45° 10′N 67° 10′W) **13**:70
SAINT CROIX RIVER (Wisconsin)
map (44° 45′N 92° 49′W) **20**:185
ST. CROSS COLLEGE (Oxford University) **14**:474
ST. CYR **17**:17
SAINT-CYRAN, ABBÉ DE **17**:17 *bibliog.*
SAINT DAVID (Arizona)
map (31° 54′N 110° 13′W) **2**:160
SAINT DAVID (Illinois)
map (40° 30′N 90° 3′W) **11**:42
SAINT DAVID'S HEAD
map (51° 55′N 5° 19′W) **19**:403
SAINT DAVID'S ISLAND
map (32° 22′N 64° 39′W) **3**:219
SAINT-DENIS (church) **9**:255 *illus.*; **17**:17 *bibliog.*
architecture **2**:133
French art and architecture **8**:304
Gothic art and architecture **9**:257; **9**:259
stained glass **18**:211
Suger, Abbot **18**:330
tomb of Henry II and Catherine de Médicis **19**:231
SAINT-DENIS (France) **17**:17
church **8**:304 *illus.*
SAINT-DENIS (Réunion) **17**:17
SAINT DENIS, LOUIS JUCHEREAU DE
Texas **19**:133
ST. DENIS, RUTH **13**:496 *illus.*; **17**:17–18 *bibliog.*
SAINT-DENYS-GARNEAU, HECTOR DE *see* GARNEAU, HECTOR DE SAINT-DENYS
ST. EDMUND HALL (Oxford University) **14**:474
ST. EDMUND'S HOUSE (Cambridge University) **4**:53
SAINT EDWARD (Nebraska)
map (41° 34′N 97° 52′W) **14**:70
SAINT ELEANOR'S (Prince Edward Island)
map (46° 25′N 63° 49′W) **15**:548
SAINT ELIAS, CAPE
map (59° 52′N 144° 30′W) **1**:242
SAINT ELIAS, MOUNT **17**:18
map (60° 18′N 140° 55′W) **1**:242
SAINT-ÉLIE (French Guiana)
map (4° 50′N 53° 17′W) **8**:311
SAINT ELMO (Illinois)
map (39° 2′N 88° 51′W) **11**:42
SAINT ELMO'S FIRE **17**:18
SAINT-ÉTIENNE (France) **17**:18
map (45° 26′N 4° 24′E) **8**:260
SAINT ÉTIENNE, CHURCH OF (Caen)
cathedrals and churches **4**:205
Norman architecture **14**:220 *illus.*
SAINT EUSTATIUS
Netherlands Antilles **14**:103
SAINT-EXUPÉRY, ANTOINE DE **17**:18 *bibliog.*
SAINT-FÉLICIEN (Quebec)
map (48° 39′N 72° 26′W) **16**:18
SAINT FRANCIS (county in Arkansas)
map (35° 0′N 90° 45′W) **2**:166
SAINT FRANCIS (Kansas)
map (39° 46′N 101° 48′W) **12**:18
SAINT FRANCIS (South Dakota)
map (43° 9′N 100° 54′W) **18**:103
SAINT FRANCIS (Wisconsin)
map (42° 58′N 87° 52′W) **20**:185
SAINT FRANCIS RIVER (Arkansas)
map (34° 38′N 90° 35′W) **2**:166
SAINT FRANCIS RIVER (Quebec)
map (46° 7′N 72° 55′W) **16**:18
SAINT FRANCISVILLE (Louisiana)
map (30° 47′N 91° 23′W) **12**:430
SAINT FRANCOIS (county in Missouri)
map (37° 50′N 90° 30′W) **13**:476
SAINT FRANCOIS MOUNTAINS
map (37° 30′N 90° 35′W) **13**:476
SAINT-GAUDENS, AUGUSTUS **17**:18 *bibliog., illus.*
Admiral David Farragut **17**:18 *illus.*
MacMonnies, Frederick William **13**:34
SAINTE GENEVIEVE (Missouri)
map (37° 59′N 90° 3′W) **13**:476
SAINTE GENEVIEVE (county in Missouri)
map (37° 55′N 90° 15′W) **13**:476
SAINT GEORGE (Bermuda)
map (32° 22′N 64° 40′W) **3**:219
SAINT GEORGE (New Brunswick)
map (45° 8′N 66° 49′W) **14**:117
SAINT GEORGE (South Carolina)
map (33° 11′N 80° 35′W) **18**:98
SAINT GEORGE (Utah)
map (37° 6′N 113° 35′W) **19**:492
SAINT GEORGE, CAPE OF
map (29° 35′N 85° 4′W) **8**:172
SAINT-GEORGES (French Guiana)
map (3° 54′N 51° 48′W) **8**:311
SAINT GEORGE'S (Grenada) **17**:18
map (12° 3′N 61° 45′W) **9**:358
SAINT GEORGE'S (Newfoundland)
map (48° 26′N 58° 29′W) **14**:166
SAINT GEORGE'S BAY (Newfoundland)
map (48° 20′N 59° 0′W) **14**:166
SAINT GEORGES BAY (Nova Scotia)
map (45° 50′N 61° 45′W) **14**:269
SAINT GEORGE'S CHANNEL
map (52° 0′N 6° 0′W) **19**:403
SAINT GEORGE'S ISLAND
map (32° 22′N 64° 40′W) **3**:219
SAINT-GERMAIN (France)
map (48° 54′N 2° 5′E) **8**:260
SAINT-GERMAIN, TREATY OF
World War I **20**:246
SAINT GILES (church)
Pugin, Augustus **15**:617
SAINT GOTTHARD PASS **17**:18–19
map (46° 33′N 8° 34′E) **18**:394
SAINT GOTTHARD TUNNEL **17**:19 *bibliog.*
SAINT HELENA **17**:19
Tristan da Conha Islands **19**:303
SAINT HELENA (county in Louisiana)
map (30° 48′N 90° 43′W) **12**:430
SAINT HELENA BAY
map (32° 43′S 18° 5′E) **18**:79
SAINT HELENA ISLAND
map (32° 20′N 80° 50′W) **18**:98
SAINT HELENA SOUND
map (32° 27′N 80° 25′W) **18**:98
SAINT HELENS (Oregon)
map (45° 52′N 122° 48′W) **14**:427
SAINT HELENS, MOUNT
map (46° 12′N 122° 11′W) **20**:35
volcano **19**:627 *illus.*
SAINT HELIER (Jersey)
map (49° 12′N 2° 37′W) **19**:403
ST. HILDA'S COLLEGE (Oxford University) **14**:474
ST. HUGH'S COLLEGE (Oxford University) **14**:474
SAINT-HYACINTHE (Quebec)
map (45° 37′N 72° 57′W) **16**:18
SAINT IGNACE (Michigan)
map (45° 52′N 84° 43′W) **13**:377
SAINT-IGNACE (New Brunswick)
map (46° 42′N 65° 5′W) **14**:117
SAINT IGNATIUS (Montana)
map (47° 19′N 114° 6′W) **13**:547
SAINT IGNATIUS MISSION (Guyana)
map (3° 20′N 59° 47′W) **9**:410
SAINT-ISIDORE (New Brunswick)
map (47° 33′N 65° 3′W) **14**:117
SAINT JAMES (county in Louisiana)
map (30° 2′N 90° 45′W) **12**:430
SAINT JAMES (Michigan)
map (45° 45′N 85° 31′W) **13**:377
SAINT JAMES (Minnesota)
map (43° 59′N 94° 38′W) **13**:453
SAINT JAMES (Missouri)
map (38° 0′N 91° 37′W) **13**:476
ST. JAMES'S PALACE **17**:19 *bibliog.*
SAINT-JEAN (Quebec)
map (45° 19′N 73° 16′W) **16**:18
SAINT JEAN, LAKE
map (48° 35′N 72° 5′W) **16**:18
SAINT-JÉRÔME (Quebec)
map (45° 47′N 74° 0′W) **16**:18
SAINT JOAN (play) **17**:19
Shaw, George Bernard **17**:245
SAINT JOE RIVER
map (47° 21′N 116° 42′W) **11**:26
SAINT JOHN
Virgin Islands **19**:605–606
SAINT JOHN (Kansas)
map (38° 0′N 98° 46′W) **12**:18
SAINT JOHN (New Brunswick) **17**:19
map (45° 16′N 66° 3′W) **14**:117
SAINT JOHN (North Dakota)
map (48° 57′N 99° 43′W) **14**:248
SAINT JOHN (Washington)
map (47° 5′N 117° 35′W) **20**:35
ST. JOHN, HENRY, 1ST VISCOUNT BOLINGBROKE *see* BOLINGBROKE, HENRY ST. JOHN, 1ST VISCOUNT
SAINT JOHN THE BAPTIST (county in Louisiana)
map (30° 5′N 90° 30′W) **12**:430
SAINT JOHN THE DIVINE, CATHEDRAL OF **17**:19 *bibliog.*
SAINT JOHN ISLAND
map (18° 20′N 64° 45′W) **19**:605
SAINT JOHN RIVER (Liberia)
map (6° 40′N 9° 10′W) **12**:313
SAINT JOHN RIVER (New Brunswick) **14**:116 *illus.*
map (45° 15′N 66° 4′W) **14**:117
SAINT JOHNS (Antigua) **17**:19
SAINT JOHNS (Arizona)
map (34° 30′N 109° 22′W) **2**:160
SAINT JOHNS (county in Florida)
map (29° 55′N 81° 25′W) **8**:172
SAINT JOHNS (Michigan)
map (43° 0′N 84° 33′W) **13**:377
ST. JOHN'S (Newfoundland) **14**:168 *illus.*; **17**:19
map (47° 34′N 52° 43′W) **14**:166
ST. JOHNS, ADELA ROGERS **17**:19
ST. JOHN'S BREAD *see* CAROB
ST. JOHN'S COLLEGE (Maryland) **17**:20
ST. JOHN'S COLLEGE (Cambridge University) **4**:53
ST. JOHN'S COLLEGE (Oxford University) **14**:474
ST. JOHN'S DOG
flat-coated retriever **8**:154
SAINT JOHNS RIVER
map (30° 24′N 81° 24′W) **8**:172
SAINT-JOHN'S-WORT (botany) **17**:20 *illus.*
SAINT JOHNSBURY (Vermont)
map (44° 25′N 72° 1′W) **19**:554
SAINT JOSEPH (Illinois)
map (40° 7′N 88° 2′W) **11**:42
SAINT JOSEPH (county in Indiana)
map (41° 41′N 86° 15′W) **11**:111
SAINT JOSEPH (Louisiana)
map (31° 55′N 91° 14′W) **12**:430
SAINT JOSEPH (Michigan)
map (42° 6′N 86° 29′W) **13**:377
SAINT JOSEPH (county in Michigan)
map (41° 55′N 85° 31′W) **13**:377
SAINT JOSEPH (Minnesota)
map (45° 34′N 94° 19′W) **13**:453

SAINT JOSEPH (Missouri) **17**:20
map (39° 46′N 94° 51′W) **13**:476
SAINT JOSEPH (New Brunswick)
map (45° 59′N 64° 34′W) **14**:117
SAINT-JOSEPH (Quebec)
map (46° 18′N 70° 53′W) **16**:18
SAINT JOSEPH (Tennessee)
map (35° 2′N 87° 31′W) **19**:104
SAINT JOSEPH BAY
map (29° 47′N 85° 21′W) **8**:172
SAINT JOSEPH ISLAND
map (46° 13′N 83° 58′W) **13**:377
SAINT JOSEPH LAKE
map (51° 5′N 90° 35′W) **14**:393
SAINT JOSEPH RIVER
map (41° 5′N 85° 8′W) **11**:111
SAINT JOSEPH'S FOUNTAIN (New Orleans) **15**:464 *illus.*
fountains **8**:252
Moore, Charles **13**:567
SAINT KITTS-NEVIS **17**:20
flag **8**:142 *illus.*
map (17° 20′N 62° 45′W) **20**:109
West Indies Associated States **20**:109
SAINT LANDRY (Louisiana)
map (30° 51′N 92° 15′W) **12**:430
SAINT LANDRY (county in Louisiana)
map (30° 37′N 92° 0′W) **12**:430
SAINT-LAURENT (Manitoba)
map (50° 24′N 97° 56′W) **13**:119
ST. LAURENT, LOUIS STEPHEN **17**:20 *bibliog.*
Canada, history of **4**:86–87
Liberal parties **12**:311
SAINT LAURENT, YVES **17**:20
Dior, Christian **6**:185
fashion design **8**:32
SAINT-LAURENT-DU-MARONI (French Guiana)
map (5° 30′N 54° 2′W) **8**:311
SAINT LAWRENCE (county in New York)
map (44° 30′N 75° 10′W) **14**:149
SAINT LAWRENCE (Newfoundland)
map (46° 55′N 55° 24′W) **14**:166
SAINT LAWRENCE, CAPE
map (47° 3′N 60° 37′W) **14**:269
ST. LAWRENCE, GULF OF **17**:20–21
Magdalen Islands **13**:46
map (48° 0′N 62° 0′W) **4**:70
ST. LAWRENCE ISLAND
Bering Sea **3**:212
map (63° 30′N 170° 30′W) **1**:242
ST. LAWRENCE RIVER **14**:151 *illus.*; **17**:21 *map*
map (49° 30′N 67° 0′W) **17**:21
St. Lawrence Seaway **17**:21–22
Thousand Islands **19**:180
ST. LAWRENCE SEAWAY **17**:21–22 *bibliog.*
Buffalo (New York) **3**:546
Canada, history of **4**:87
canal **4**:97
Saint Clair, Lake **17**:17
Sault Sainte Marie Canals **17**:97
Welland Ship Canal **20**:99
ST. LAWRENCE UNIVERSITY **17**:22
SAINT LAZARE, CATHEDRAL OF (Autun) **8**:304 *illus.*; **16**:284 *illus.*
Gislebertus **9**:191
ST. LEGER, BARRY **17**:22
SAINT-LÉON, ARTHUR **17**:22 *bibliog.*
SAINT-LÉONARD (New Brunswick)
map (47° 10′N 67° 56′W) **14**:117
SAINT LOUIS (Michigan)
map (43° 25′N 84° 36′W) **13**:377
SAINT LOUIS (county in Minnesota)
map (47° 35′N 92° 30′W) **13**:453
ST. LOUIS (Missouri) **13**:477 *illus.*; **17**:22–23 *bibliog., illus.*
Chouteau (family) **4**:410
Gateway Arch **13**:477 *illus.*; **17**:22 *illus.*
Saarinen, Eero **17**:4
map (38° 38′N 90° 11′W) **13**:476
St. Louis Post-Dispatch **17**:23
Wainwright Building **18**:337 *illus.*
SAINT LOUIS (county in Missouri)
map (38° 40′N 90° 30′W) **13**:476
SAINT-LOUIS (Senegal)
map (16° 2′N 16° 30′W) **17**:202
ST. LOUIS ARCH
Saarinen, Eero **17**:4
SAINT LOUIS BAY
map (30° 25′N 89° 20′W) **13**:469
ST. LOUIS POST-DISPATCH **17**:23
Pulitzer, Joseph **15**:618
SAINT LOUIS RIVER
map (46° 43′N 92° 9′W) **13**:453
SAINT LOUIS UNIVERSITY **17**:23
SAINT LUCIA **17**:23 *illus., map*
flag **8**:142 *illus.*; **17**:23 *illus.*
map (13° 53′N 60° 58′W) **20**:109
SAINT LUCIE (county in Florida)
map (27° 23′N 80° 26′W) **8**:172
SAINT LUCIE CANAL
map (27° 10′N 80° 15′W) **8**:172
SAINT-MALO (France)
map (48° 39′N 2° 1′W) **8**:260
SAINT-MALO, GULF OF
map (48° 45′N 2° 0′W) **8**:260
SAINT-MARC (Haiti)
map (19° 7′N 72° 42′W) **10**:15
SAINT MARC CANAL
map (18° 50′N 72° 45′W) **10**:15
SAINT MARIES (Idaho)
map (47° 19′N 116° 35′W) **11**:26
SAINT MARK'S BASILICA **4**:204 *illus.*; **11**:309 *illus.*; **17**:23–24 *bibliog., illus.*
mosaic **13**:596
Paolo Veneziano **15**:62
SAINT MARTIN (France) **17**:24
SAINT MARTIN (county in Louisiana)
map (30° 10′N 91° 40′W) **12**:430
SAINT MARTIN, LAKE
map (51° 37′N 98° 29′W) **13**:119
SAINT MARTINS (New Brunswick)
map (45° 21′N 65° 32′W) **14**:117
SAINT MARTINVILLE (Louisiana)
map (30° 7′N 91° 50′W) **12**:430
SAINT MARY (county in Louisiana)
map (29° 40′N 91° 28′W) **12**:430
SAINT MARY, CAPE
map (13° 28′N 16° 40′W) **9**:25
ST. MARY OF BETHLEHEM, HOSPITAL OF, LONDON *see* BEDLAM
SAINT MARYS (Georgia)
map (30° 44′N 81° 33′W) **9**:114
SAINT MARYS (Kansas)
map (39° 12′N 96° 4′W) **12**:18
SAINT MARYS (county in Maryland)
map (38° 17′N 76° 38′W) **13**:188
SAINT MARYS (Missouri)
map (37° 52′N 89° 58′W) **13**:476
SAINT MARY'S (Newfoundland)
map (46° 55′N 53° 34′W) **14**:166
SAINT MARYS (Ohio)
map (40° 33′N 84° 23′W) **14**:357
SAINT MARYS (Pennsylvania)
map (41° 26′N 78° 34′W) **15**:147
SAINT MARYS (West Virginia)
map (39° 23′N 81° 12′W) **20**:111
SAINT MARY'S BAY
map (46° 50′N 53° 47′W) **14**:166
SAINT MARY'S COLLEGE **17**:24
SAINT MARYS RIVER (Indiana)
map (41° 5′N 85° 8′W) **11**:111
SAINT MARY'S RIVER (Nova Scotia)
map (45° 2′N 61° 54′W) **14**:269
SAINT MARYS RIVER (Ontario)
map (46° 33′N 84° 6′W) **13**:377
SAINT-MATHIEU POINT
map (48° 20′N 4° 46′W) **8**:260
ST. MATTHEW ISLAND
Bering Sea **3**:212
map (60° 30′N 172° 45′W) **1**:242
SAINT MATTHEWS (Kentucky)
map (38° 15′N 85° 39′W) **12**:47
SAINT MATTHEWS (South Carolina)
map (33° 40′N 80° 46′W) **18**:98
SAINT MEINRAD (Indiana)
map (38° 10′N 86° 49′W) **11**:111
SAINT MICHAEL (Alaska)
map (63° 29′N 162° 2′W) **1**:242
SAINT MICHAELS (Maryland)
map (38° 47′N 76° 14′W) **13**:188
SAINT MICHAEL'S, CATHEDRAL CHURCH OF *see* COVENTRY CATHEDRAL
SAINT MORITZ (Switzerland) **17**:24
SAINT-NAZAIRE (France) **17**:24
map (47° 17′N 2° 12′W) **8**:260
ST. NICHOLAS MAGAZINE (periodical)
Dodge, Mary Mapes **6**:212
ST. OLAF COLLEGE **17**:24
SAINT PARIS (Ohio)
map (40° 7′N 83° 58′W) **14**:357
SAINT PATRICK'S CATHEDRAL **16**:159 *illus.*; **17**:24 *bibliog., illus.*
New York (city) **14**:145 *map*
SAINT PATRICK'S DAY *see* PATRICK, SAINT
SAINT PAUL (Alberta)
map (53° 59′N 111° 17′W) **1**:256
SAINT PAUL (Indiana)
map (39° 26′N 85° 38′W) **11**:111
SAINT PAUL (Kansas)
map (37° 32′N 95° 11′W) **12**:18
SAINT PAUL (Minnesota) **13**:454 *illus.*; **17**:24–25
map (44° 58′N 93° 7′W) **13**:453
SAINT PAUL (Nebraska)
map (41° 13′N 98° 27′W) **14**:70
SAINT PAUL, CAPE
map (5° 49′N 0° 57′E) **9**:164
SAINT PAUL BUILDING (New York City)
skyscraper **17**:350
ST. PAUL ISLAND
French Southern and Antarctic Territories **8**:326
SAINT PAUL RIVER
map (7° 10′N 10° 0′W) **12**:313
SAINT PAULS (North Carolina)
map (34° 48′N 78° 58′W) **14**:242
SAINT PAUL'S CATHEDRAL **4**:207 *illus.*; **6**:230 *illus.*; **17**:25 *bibliog., illus.*
bell **3**:184
cathedrals and churches **4**:208
Gibbons, Grinling **9**:173
Wren, Sir Christopher **20**:286
SAINT PETER (Minnesota)
map (44° 17′N 93° 57′W) **13**:453
ST. PETER PORT (Guernsey) **4**:281 *illus.*
map (49° 27′N 2° 32′W) **19**:403
SAINT PETERS (Nova Scotia)
map (45° 40′N 60° 52′W) **14**:269
SAINT PETER'S BASILICA **16**:296 *illus.*; **17**:25–26 *bibliog., illus.*
Bernini, Giovanni Lorenzo **3**:222–223
Bramante, Donato **3**:452
cathedrals and churches **4**:204–205; **4**:207
colonnade **5**:112
doors, bronze relief **15**:199 *illus.*
Early Christian art and architecture **7**:9–10 *illus.*
floor plan (c.330) **4**:204 *illus.*
floor plan (16th century) **4**:206 *illus.*
Fontana, Domenico **8**:206
Maderno, Carlo **13**:40
Manzù, Giacomo **13**:134
Michelangelo **13**:375
piazza of **2**:135 *illus.*
Vatican City **19**:526
ST. PETER'S COLLEGE (Oxford University) **14**:474
SAINT PETERSBURG (Florida) **17**:26
map (27° 46′N 82° 38′W) **8**:172
SAINT PETERSBURG (USSR) *see* LENINGRAD (USSR)
SAINT PHILIBERT, CHURCH OF (Tournus) **16**:283 *illus.*
floor plan **4**:205 *illus.*
SAINT PIERRE (Saint Pierre and Miquelon)
map (46° 40′N 56° 0′W) **14**:166
SAINT-PIERRE, CHARLES IRÉNÉE CASTEL, ABBÉ DE **17**:26 *bibliog.*
SAINT-PIERRE-JOLYS (Manitoba)
map (49° 26′N 96° 59′W) **13**:119
SAINT PIERRE AND MIQUELON **17**:26
map (46° 55′N 56° 10′W) **14**:166
SAINT QUENTIN (New Brunswick)
map (47° 30′N 67° 23′W) **14**:117
SAINT REGIS RIVER
map (45° 0′N 74° 43′W) **14**:149
SAINT RIQUIER, CHURCH OF (Centula, France) **4**:161 *illus.*
cathedrals and churches **4**:205
SAINT-SAËNS, CAMILLE **17**:26 *bibliog., illus.*
SAINT-SAENS, MARC
tapestry **19**:33
SAINT SAVIOR IN THE CHORA **17**:26 *bibliog.*
mosaic **13**:595
SAINT SERNIN, CHURCH OF (Toulouse) **16**:282 *illus.*
cathedrals and churches **4**:205
SAINT-SIMON, CLAUDE HENRI DE ROUVROY, COMTE DE **17**:26–27 *bibliog.*
Enfantin, Barthélémy Prosper **7**:176
Marxism **13**:183
socialism **18**:19
utopias **19**:498
SAINT-SIMON, LOUIS DE ROUVROY, DUC DE **17**:27 *bibliog.*
SAINT SIMONS ISLAND (Georgia)
map (31° 8′N 81° 24′W) **9**:114
SAINT SOPHIA, CATHEDRAL OF (Kiev)
Russian art and architecture **16**:361
SAINT SOPHIA, CATHEDRAL OF (Novgorod)
Russian art and architecture **16**:361
SAINT STEPHEN (New Brunswick)
map (45° 12′N 67° 17′W) **14**:117
SAINT STEPHEN (South Carolina)
map (33° 24′N 79° 55′W) **18**:98
SAINT TAMMANY (county in Louisiana)
map (30° 25′N 89° 57′W) **12**:430
SAINT THOMAS
map (18° 21′N 64° 55′W) **19**:605
Virgin Islands **19**:605–606
SAINT THOMAS (North Dakota)
map (48° 37′N 97° 27′W) **14**:248
SAINT THOMAS (Ontario)
map (42° 47′N 81° 12′W) **14**:393
SAINT-TROPEZ (France) **16**:234 *illus.*
SAINT-VINCENT, CAPE (Madagascar)
map (21° 57′S 43° 16′E) **13**:38
SAINT VINCENT, CAPE (Portugal) **17**:27
map (37° 1′N 9° 0′W) **15**:449
SAINT VINCENT AND THE GRENADINES **17**:27 *illus., map*
flag **8**:142 *illus.*; **17**:27 *illus.*
map (13° 15′N 61° 12′W) **20**:109
SAINT VITUS'S DANCE
chorea **4**:408
ST. VLADIMIR'S ORTHODOX THEOLOGICAL SEMINARY **17**:27
SAINT WALBURG (Saskatchewan)
map (53° 39′N 109° 12′W) **17**:81
SAINTE-ANNE-DES-CHENES (Manitoba)
map (49° 40′N 96° 40′W) **13**:119
SAINTE-BEUVE, CHARLES AUGUSTIN **17**:27 *bibliog.*
Proust, Marcel **15**:583
SAINTE-CHAPELLE **9**:257–258; **17**:28 *bibliog.*
architecture **2**:133
Rayonnant style **16**:98
reliquary **16**:144
stained glass **18**:212
SAINTE-FOY (Quebec)
map (46° 47′N 71° 17′W) **16**:18
SAINTE MADELEINE, CHURCH OF (Vézelay) **16**:284 *illus.*
SAINTE-MARIE, CAPE
map (25° 36′S 45° 8′E) **13**:38
SAINTE-MARIE ISLAND
map (16° 50′S 49° 55′E) **13**:38
SAINTE-MORE, BENOÎT DE *see* BENOÎT DE SAINTE-MORE
SAINTE-ROSE-DU-LAC (Manitoba)
map (51° 3′N 99° 32′W) **13**:119
SAINTE-THÉRÈSE-DE-BLAINVILLE (Quebec)
map (45° 39′N 73° 49′W) **16**:18
SAINTES (France)
map (45° 45′N 0° 52′W) **8**:260
SAINTONGE (France) **17**:28
SAIONJI KIMMOCHI **17**:28 *bibliog.*
SAIPAN (Mariana Islands) **17**:28
World War II **20**:277
SAISSET, BERNARD
Philip IV, King of France (Philip the Fair) **15**:232–233
SAJAMA, MOUNT
map (18° 6′S 68° 54′W) **3**:366
SAKAKAWEA, LAKE
map (47° 50′N 102° 20′W) **14**:248
SAKAMI, LAKE
map (53° 15′N 76° 45′W) **16**:18
SAKARYA RIVER
map (39° 40′N 30° 55′E) **19**:343
SAKATA TOJURO
Kabuki **12**:4
SAKE **17**:28
SAKÉTÉ (Benin)
map (6° 43′N 2° 40′E) **3**:200
SAKHA *see* YAKUT
SAKHALIN (USSR) **17**:28
Ainu **1**:203
map (51° 0′N 143° 0′E) **19**:388
SAKHAROV, ANDREI D. **17**:28 *bibliog., illus.*
SAKI (animal)
monkey **13**:534
SAKI (writer) **17**:28–29 *bibliog.*
SAKISHIMA ISLANDS
Ryukyu Islands **16**:380
SAKKARA *see* SAQQARA (Egypt)
SAKONNET POINT
map (41° 27′N 71° 12′W) **16**:198
SAKONNET RIVER
map (41° 29′N 71° 12′W) **16**:198
SAKUBVA (Zimbabwe)
map (19° 0′S 32° 10′E) **20**:365
SAKUNTALA (play) *see SHAKUNTALA*
SAL ISLAND
map (16° 45′N 22° 55′W) **4**:122
SALACROU, ARMAND **17**:29
SALADILLO (Argentina)
map (35° 38′S 59° 46′W) **2**:149
SALADIN **17**:29 *bibliog., illus.*
Crusades **5**:368
Jerusalem, Latin Kingdom of **11**:401
SALADO
cliff dwellers **5**:55
Hohokam culture **10**:199
SALADO RIVER
map (31° 42′S 60° 44′W) **2**:149
SALAILUA (Western Samoa)
map (13° 41′S 172° 34′W) **20**:117

SALAM, ABDUS
unified field theory **19**:386
Weinberg-Salam theory **19**:386
SALAMÁ (Guatemala)
map (15° 6′N 90° 16′W) **9**:389
SALAMANCA (New York)
map (42° 9′N 78° 43′W) **14**:149
SALAMANCA (Spain) **17**:29
Church of San Esteban **18**:154 *illus.*
Churriguera (family) **4**:427
map (40° 58′N 5° 39′W) **18**:140
SALAMANCA, UNIVERSITY OF **17**:29
SALAMANDER AND NEWT **1**:377–378 *illus.*; **17**:29–30 *bibliog.*, *illus.*
axolotl **2**:378
classification, biological **17**:29–30
hellbender **10**:114
Japanese giant salamander **11**:379
Mexican salamander **13**:351
mud puppy **13**:631
red-spotted newt **16**:114
regeneration **16**:127
skeletal system **17**:334 *illus.*
SALAMAT RIVER
map (9° 27′N 18° 6′E) **4**:251
SALAMIS (city) **17**:30
Evagoras, Despot of Cyprus **7**:311
SALAMIS (island, Greece) **17**:30
SALAMONIE LAKE
map (40° 46′N 85° 37′W) **11**:111
SALAMONIE RIVER
map (40° 50′N 85° 43′W) **11**:111
SALANI (Western Samoa)
map (14° 0′S 171° 33′W) **20**:117
SALATIGA (Indonesia)
map (7° 19′S 110° 30′E) **11**:147
SALAVERRY (Peru)
map (8° 14′S 78° 58′W) **15**:193
SALAZAR, ANTÓNIO DE OLIVEIRA **17**:30–31 *bibliog.*
Portugal, history of **15**:455 *illus.*
SALCEDO, AUGUSTO BERNARDINO LEGUÍA Y *see* LEGUÍA Y SALCEDO, AUGUSTO BERNARDINO
SALDANHA, ANTONIO DE
Table Mountain (South Africa) **19**:4
SALDUNGARAY (Argentina)
map (38° 12′S 61° 47′W) **2**:149
SALÉ (Morocco)
map (34° 4′N 6° 50′W) **13**:585
SALEH, ALI ABDALLAH
Yemen (Sana) **20**:326
SALEIMONA (Western Samoa)
map (13° 49′S 171° 51′W) **20**:117
SALEK, MUSTAFA OULD
Mauritania **13**:237
SALEKINI (Gambia)
map (13° 29′N 15° 58′W) **9**:25
SALEM (Arkansas)
map (36° 22′N 91° 49′W) **2**:166
SALEM (Illinois)
map (38° 38′N 88° 57′W) **11**:42
SALEM (India)
map (11° 39′N 78° 10′E) **11**:80
SALEM (Indiana)
map (38° 36′N 86° 6′W) **11**:111
SALEM (Kentucky)
map (37° 16′N 88° 16′W) **12**:47
SALEM (Massachusetts) **17**:31
map (42° 31′N 70° 55′W) **13**:206
Salem Witch Trials **17**:31
SALEM (Missouri)
map (37° 39′N 91° 32′W) **13**:476
SALEM (New Hampshire)
map (42° 47′N 71° 12′W) **14**:123
SALEM (New Jersey)
map (39° 34′N 75° 28′W) **14**:129
SALEM (county in New Jersey)
map (39° 34′N 75° 20′W) **14**:129
SALEM (New York)
map (43° 10′N 73° 20′W) **14**:149
SALEM (North Carolina) *see* WINSTON-SALEM (North Carolina)
SALEM (Ohio)
map (40° 54′N 80° 52′W) **14**:357
SALEM (Oregon) **17**:31
map (44° 57′N 123° 1′W) **14**:427
SALEM (South Dakota)
map (43° 44′N 97° 23′W) **18**:103
SALEM (Virginia)
map (37° 17′N 80° 3′W) **19**:607
SALEM (West Virginia)
map (39° 17′N 80° 34′W) **20**:111
SALEM WITCH TRIALS **17**:31 *bibliog.*, *illus.*
Mather (family) **13**:227
Phips, Sir William **15**:248
Sewall, Samuel **17**:221
witchcraft **20**:192
SALERNO (Italy) **17**:31
cities
Amalfi **1**:320
map (40° 41′N 14° 47′E) **11**:321
SALES **17**:32 *bibliog.*
advertising **1**:111–114
marketing **13**:159
retailing **16**:183
wholesaling **20**:143
SALES, FRANCIS DE, SAINT *see* FRANCIS DE SALES, SAINT
SALES TAX **17**:32
SALESIANS
Bosco, Saint John **3**:407
SALGÓTARJÁN (Hungary)
map (48° 7′N 19° 48′E) **10**:307
SALIAN FRANKS
Franks **8**:285–286
SALIANS (dynasty)
Conrad II, King of Germany and Holy Roman Emperor **5**:199
Germany, history of **9**:149
Henry III, King of Germany and Holy Roman Emperor **10**:128–129
Henry IV, King of Germany and Holy Roman Emperor **10**:129
Henry V, King of Germany and Holy Roman Emperor **10**:129
Holy Roman Empire **10**:209–211
Lothair II, King of Germany and Holy Roman Emperor **12**:419
SALIC LAW **17**:32
queen **16**:21
SALICYCLIC ACID
carboxylic acid **4**:141
SALICYLATE
aspirin **2**:262
deafness **6**:67
hyperactive children **10**:347
SALIDA (Colorado)
map (38° 32′N 106° 0′W) **5**:116
SALIENTIA *see* ANURA
SALIERI, ANTONIO **17**:32
SALIM CHISHTI *see* CHISHTI, SALIM
SALINA (Kansas) **17**:32
map (38° 50′N 97° 37′W) **12**:18
SALINA (Oklahoma)
Chouteau (family) **4**:410
map (36° 20′N 95° 5′W) **14**:368
SALINA (Utah)
map (38° 58′N 111° 51′W) **19**:492
SALINA CRUZ (Mexico)
map (16° 10′N 95° 12′W) **13**:357
SALINAS (California)
map (36° 40′N 121° 39′W) **4**:31
SALINAS (Ecuador)
map (2° 13′S 80° 58′W) **7**:52
SALINAS, LUIS ADOLFO SILES *see* SILES SALINAS, LUIS ADOLFO
SALINAS INDIANS
Portolá, Gaspar de **15**:446
SALINAS RIVER (California)
map (36° 45′N 121° 48′W) **4**:31
SALINAS RIVER (Guatemala)
map (16° 28′N 90° 33′W) **9**:389
SALINE (county in Arkansas)
map (34° 40′N 92° 50′W) **2**:166
SALINE (county in Illinois)
map (37° 45′N 88° 30′W) **11**:42
SALINE (county in Kansas)
map (38° 50′N 97° 40′W) **12**:18
SALINE (Louisiana)
map (32° 10′N 92° 58′W) **12**:430
SALINE (county in Missouri)
map (39° 10′N 93° 10′W) **13**:476
SALINE (county in Nebraska)
map (40° 30′N 97° 5′W) **14**:70
SALINE RIVER (Arkansas)
map (33° 10′N 92° 8′W) **2**:166
SALINE RIVER (Illinois)
map (37° 35′N 88° 8′W) **11**:42
SALINE RIVER (Kansas)
map (38° 51′N 97° 30′W) **12**:18
SALINGER, J. D. **17**:32 *bibliog.*
Catcher in the Rye, The **4**:202
Franny and Zooey **8**:286
SALINITY
lake **12**:168–169
salinometer **17**:33
seawater **17**:177
SALINOMETER **17**:33
SALISBURY (England) **17**:33
map (51° 5′N 1° 48′W) **19**:403
SALISBURY (Maryland) **17**:33
map (38° 22′N 75° 36′W) **13**:188
SALISBURY (North Carolina)
map (35° 40′N 80° 29′W) **14**:242
SALISBURY (Pennsylvania)
map (39° 45′N 79° 5′W) **15**:147
SALISBURY (Zimbabwe) *see* HARARE (Zimbabwe)
SALISBURY, HARRISON **17**:33
SALISBURY, ROBERT CECIL, 1ST EARL OF **17**:33 *bibliog.*
James I, King of England **11**:356
SALISBURY, ROBERT CECIL, 3D MARQUESS OF **17**:33 *bibliog.*, *illus.*
Venezuela Boundary Dispute **19**:544
SALISBURY CATHEDRAL **7**:178 *illus.*; **7**:183 *illus.*; **7**:187 *illus.*; **17**:34 *bibliog.*
SALISH (American Indians) **17**:34 *bibliog.*
Flathead **8**:155
Okanogan **14**:365
Puyallup **15**:633
Quileute-Hoh and Chemakum **16**:26
Shuswap **17**:289–290
SALISH MOUNTAINS
map (48° 15′N 114° 45′W) **13**:547
SALITPA (Alabama)
map (31° 37′N 88° 1′W) **1**:234
SALIVARY GLANDS **17**:34 *bibliog.*
dog
Pavlov, Ivan Petrovich **15**:120
fly
chromosome **14**:290 *illus.*
fruit fly
chromosome **9**:86 *illus.*
mumps **13**:639
snake **17**:379–380
SALK, JONAS **17**:34 *bibliog.*
poliomyelitis vaccine **15**:397; **17**:34
medicine **13**:271
Sabin, Albert Bruce **17**:5
SALK INSTITUTE FOR BIOLOGICAL STUDIES **17**:34
SALKEHATCHIE RIVER
map (32° 37′N 80° 53′W) **18**:98
SALLE, SIEUR DE LA *see* LA SALLE, ROBERT CAVELIER, SIEUR DE
SALLEY, JOHN PETER
West Virginia **20**:114
SALLINEN, TYKO
Finland **8**:97
SALLISAW (Oklahoma)
map (35° 28′N 94° 47′W) **14**:368
SALLUST **17**:34 *bibliog.*
SALMON **8**:117 *illus.*; **17**:34–35 *bibliog.*, *illus.*
aging **1**:186
animal migration **2**:28
char **4**:285–286
fish farming **8**:121
life cycle **8**:120 *illus.*; **17**:35 *illus.*
SALMON (Idaho)
map (45° 11′N 113° 54′W) **11**:26
SALMON ARM (British Columbia)
map (50° 42′N 119° 16′W) **3**:491
SALMON MOUNTAINS
map (41° 0′N 123° 0′W) **4**:31
SALMON RIVER (Idaho)
map (45° 51′N 116° 46′W) **11**:26
SALMON RIVER (New York)
map (43° 35′N 76° 12′W) **14**:149
SALMON RIVER, MIDDLE FORK (Idaho)
map (45° 18′N 114° 36′W) **11**:26
SALMON RIVER, SOUTH FORK (Idaho)
map (45° 23′N 115° 31′W) **11**:26
SALMON RIVER MOUNTAINS
map (44° 45′N 115° 30′W) **11**:26
SALMONELLA **17**:35–36
antibiotics **2**:58
bacteria **17**:35
diseases, animal **6**:190–191
food poisoning **17**:36
food poisoning and infection **8**:211
infectious diseases **17**:35–36
operon **14**:404
typhoid fever **19**:366
SALOME **17**:36
SALOME (Arizona)
map (33° 47′N 113° 37′W) **2**:160
SALOMON, ERICH **17**:36 *bibliog.*, *illus.*
SALOMON, HAYM **17**:36 *bibliog.*
SALON (art) **17**:36 *bibliog.*
painting **15**:22
SALON (literary)
Mallarmé, Stéphane **13**:91
Rambouillet, Marquise de **16**:80
Scudéry, Madeleine de **17**:158
Staël, Madame de **18**:209
Stein, Gertrude **18**:247
SALON DES RÉFUSÉS
Salon (art) **17**:36
SALONIKA (Greece) **17**:36
map (40° 38′N 22° 56′E) **9**:325
SALOP (England) **17**:36
SALPÊTRIÈRE HOSPITAL (Paris)
Charcot, Jean Martin **4**:287
Janet, Pierre **11**:358
SALSA (music) **17**:36 *bibliog.*
SALSIFY **17**:37
SALT (chemistry) **17**:37
acids and bases **1**:82–83
chemical nomenclature **4**:320
chloride **4**:400
cobalt **5**:83
copper **5**:253
cyanide **5**:400
dissociation **6**:198
double salt **6**:246
epsom salts **7**:222
hydrate **10**:330
hydrolysis **10**:343
manganese **13**:114
mercury **13**:306
neutralization **14**:108
nitrogen **14**:202
phosphorus **15**:256–257
potassium **15**:465
salinometer **17**:33
smelling salts **17**:365
sulfur **18**:335–336
Wöhler, Friedrich **20**:195
SALT (sodium chloride) **17**:37 *bibliog.*
chloride **4**:400
crystal structure **20**:308 *illus.*
deposits, location indicating Permian climates **15**:33 *map*
desalination **6**:124–125 *illus.*
excretory system **7**:328
halite **10**:21
Hallstatt **10**:23
iodine **11**:239
iodized, goiter **9**:225
irrigation **11**:282
production **17**:37
salt-ice-brine system **15**:224 *illus.*
seawater **17**:177
sodium **18**:32
soil surface
distribution, worldwide **18**:37 *illus.*
steppe life **18**:257
uses **17**:37
SALT (Strategic Arms Limitation Talks)
arms control **2**:178
Carter, Jimmy **4**:172
nuclear strategy **14**:288
SALT CEDAR *see* TAMARISK
SALT CREEK
map (40° 8′N 89° 50′W) **11**:42
SALT DOME **17**:37–38 *bibliog.*, *illus.*
fold **8**:195
halite **10**:21
petroleum **17**:37–38
SALT FORK OF THE ARKANSAS RIVER
map (36° 36′N 97° 3′W) **14**:368
SALT FORK LAKE
map (41° 7′N 81° 30′W) **14**:357
SALT GRASS **17**:183 *illus.*
SALT LAKE (county in Utah)
map (40° 40′N 111° 55′W) **19**:492
SALT LAKE CITY (Utah) **17**:38 *illus.*; **19**:494–495 *illus.*
climate **19**:421 *table*
map (40° 46′N 111° 53′W) **19**:492
Mormon Temple **13**:582 *illus.*
SALT MARSH
swamp, marsh, and bog **18**:376–377
SALT PANS
Chile **4**:357 *illus.*
SALT PRODUCTION
salt dome **17**:37–38
SALT RIVER (Arizona)
map (33° 23′N 112° 18′W) **2**:160
SALT RIVER (Kentucky)
map (38° 0′N 85° 57′W) **12**:47
SALTA (Argentina)
climate **18**:86 *table*
map (24° 47′S 65° 25′W) **2**:149
SALTA (province in Argentina)
map (25° 0′S 64° 30′W) **2**:149
SALTATION
erosion and sedimentation **7**:232
sand dune **17**:60
wind action **20**:170
SALTBOX HOUSE **10**:270 *illus.*
SALTBUSH **17**:38
SALTILLO (Mexico) **17**:38–39
map (25° 25′N 101° 0′W) **13**:357
SALTILLO (Mississippi)
map (34° 23′N 88° 41′W) **13**:469
SALTO (Argentina)
map (34° 17′S 60° 15′W) **2**:149
SALTO (Uruguay)
map (31° 23′S 57° 58′W) **19**:488
SALTON SEA **17**:39
map (33° 19′N 115° 50′W) **4**:31
SALTPETER **17**:39
gunpowder **9**:405
niter **14**:201
nitrate minerals **14**:201–202
SALTVILLE (Virginia)
map (36° 53′N 81° 46′W) **19**:607
SALTWATER FISHING
fishing **8**:123 *illus.*
SALTYKOV SHCHEDRIN, MIKHAIL YEVGRAFOVICH **17**:39 *bibliog.*
SALUAFATA HARBOR
map (13° 50′S 171° 34′W) **20**:117

SALUDA (South Carolina)
map (34° 0′N 81° 46′W) **18**:98
SALUDA (county in South Carolina)
map (34° 0′N 81° 45′W) **18**:98
SALUDA (Virginia)
map (37° 36′N 76° 36′W) **19**:607
SALUDA RIVER
map (34° 0′N 81° 4′W) **18**:98
SALUKI **6**:217 *illus.*; **17**:39 *bibliog.*, *illus.*
SALUZZO (Italy)
Italian city-state **11**:328
SALVADOR (Brazil) **17**:39
map (12° 59′S 38° 31′W) **3**:460
SALVADOR, LAKE
map (29° 45′N 90° 15′W) **12**:430
SALVAGE, MARINE **17**:39 *bibliog.*
underwater archaeology **19**:383
SALVAGE ARCHAEOLOGY **17**:40 *bibliog.*
SALVARSAN
arsenic **2**:189
Ehrlich, Paul (1854–1915) **7**:91
SALVATION **17**:40 *bibliog.*
eschatology **7**:237
grace **9**:275
SALVATION ARMY **17**:40 *bibliog.*
Booth, William **3**:394–395
Volunteers of America **19**:632–633
SALVI, NICOLA **17**:40 *bibliog.*
Trevi Fountain **19**:291
SALVIA **17**:40–41 *illus.*
SALWA BAY
map (25° 30′N 50° 40′E) **16**:4
SALWEEN RIVER **17**:41
map (16° 31′N 97° 37′E) **2**:232
SALYERSVILLE (Kentucky)
map (37° 45′N 83° 4′W) **12**:47
SALYUT **17**:41–44 *bibliog.*, *illus.*, *table*
Demin, Lev Stepanovich **6**:97
Dobrovolsky, Georgy T. **6**:209
Feoktistov, Konstantin P. **8**:51
Filipchenko, Anatoly V. **8**:79
Grechko, Georgy Mikhailovich **9**:324
Gubarev, Aleksei **9**:390
Ivanchenkov, Aleksandr **11**:333
Klimuk, P. I. **12**:97
Kovalenok, Vladimir **12**:126
Kubasov, Valery N. **12**:134
Lebedev, Valentin **12**:267
life-support systems **12**:331
Lyakhov, Vladimir **12**:473
missions **17**:44
module **17**:41
Patsayev, Viktor **15**:114
Popovich, Pavel Romanovich **15**:432
Proton **15**:578
Remek, Vladimir **16**:145
Romanenko, Yury Viktorovich **16**:281
Rozhdestvensky, Valery **16**:332
Ryumin, Valery **16**:380
Salyut 6 **17**:41 *illus.*
Sarafanov, Gennady Vasilievich **17**:74
Sevastianov, Vitaly I. **17**:215
Soyuz **18**:116–118 *table*
space exploration **18**:130 *illus.*
space station **18**:137
Volkov, Vladislav Nikolayevich **19**:629
Volynov, Boris Valentinovich **19**:633
Zholobov, Vitaly **20**:362
Zudov, Vyacheslav Dmitriyevich **20**:381
SALZBURG (Austria) **17**:44 *illus.*
map (47° 48′N 13° 2′E) **2**:348
puppet (marionette) **15**:627
SALZBURG FESTIVAL **17**:44–45 *bibliog.*
Böhm, Karl **3**:361
Everyman **7**:316
Hofmannsthal, Hugo von **10**:196–197
SAM *see* SURFACE-TO-AIR MISSILE
SAM (puppet) *see* MUPPETS
SAM RAYBURN RESERVOIR
map (31° 27′N 94° 37′W) **19**:129
SAMAALE *see* SOMALI
SAMALUT (Egypt)
map (28° 18′N 30° 42′E) **7**:76
SAMANÁ (Dominican Republic)
map (19° 13′N 69° 19′W) **6**:233
SAMANÁ BAY
map (19° 10′N 69° 25′W) **6**:233
SAMANALA *see* ADAM'S PEAK
SAMAR ISLAND
map (12° 0′N 125° 0′E) **15**:237
SAMARA (USSR) *see* KUIBYSHEV (USSR)
SAMARAS, LUCAS **17**:45 *bibliog.*, *illus.*
Room No. 2 **17**:45 *illus.*
SAMARIA **17**:45 *bibliog.*
SAMARIA (Idaho)
map (42° 7′N 112° 20′W) **11**:26
SAMARINDA (Indonesia)
map (0° 30′S 117° 9′E) **11**:147
SAMARITANS **17**:45 *bibliog.*
SAMARIUM **17**:45
element **7**:130 *table*
lanthanide series **12**:200–201; **17**:45
metal, metallic element **13**:328
SAMARKAND (USSR) **17**:45–46; **19**:204 *illus.*
house **10**:269 *illus.*
map (39° 40′N 66° 48′E) **19**:388
rugs and carpets **16**:342
SAMARRA (Iraq) **17**:46
map (34° 12′N 43° 52′E) **11**:255
Mesopotamian art and architecture **13**:317
SAMBOROMBÓN BAY
map (36° 0′S 57° 12′W) **2**:149
SAMBORONDÓN (Ecuador)
map (1° 57′S 79° 44′W) **7**:52
SAMBRE RIVER
map (50° 28′N 4° 52′E) **3**:177
SAMCHOK (Korea)
map (37° 27′N 129° 10′E) **12**:113
SAMEKH (letter)
S (letter) **17**:3
X (letter) **20**:305
SAMIT *see* LAPPS
SAMIZDAT **17**:46 *bibliog.*
SAMKHYA
philosophy **15**:246
SAMMAMISH LAKE
map (47° 36′N 122° 22′W) **20**:35
SAMMARTINI, GIOVANNI BATTISTA **17**:46 *bibliog.*
SAMMURAMAT *see* SEMIRAMIS
SAMNITE WARS *see* SAMNITES
SAMNITES **17**:46 *bibliog.*
Rome, ancient **16**:298 *illus.*
SAMNORSK
Norway **14**:262
SAMO (Papua New Guinea)
map (3° 58′S 152° 51′E) **15**:72
SAMOA **17**:46 *maps*
map (14° 0′S 171° 0′W) **14**:334
Samoans **17**:46–47
SAMOANS **17**:46–47 *bibliog.*
adolescence **1**:107
SAMOS (artificial satellite) **17**:47 *bibliog.*
military warning and detection systems **13**:422
SAMOS (island in Greece) **17**:47
map (37° 48′N 26° 44′E) **9**:325
SAMOSET **17**:47
Massasoit **13**:213
SAMOTHRACE **17**:47 *bibliog.*
SAMOYED (dog) **6**:214 *illus.*; **17**:47 *bibliog.*, *illus.*
SAMOYED (people) **17**:47–48 *bibliog.*
SAMOYED LANGUAGES
Uralic languages **19**:475
SAMPAN **10**:223 *illus.*; **17**:48 *bibliog.*
SAMPHAN, KHIEU *see* KHIEU SAMPHAN
SAMPLER
needlework **14**:76 *illus.*
SAMPLING **17**:48 *bibliog.*
census **4**:248–249
distribution (statistics) **6**:200–201
error **7**:235
Fisher, Sir Ronald Aylmer **8**:122–123
opinion polls **14**:405–406
SAMPSON (county in North Carolina)
map (35° 0′N 78° 25′W) **14**:242
SAMPSON, NIKOS
EOKA **7**:215
SAMPSON, WILLIAM T. **17**:48
Schley, Winfield Scott **17**:126
SAMSARA *see* TRANSMIGRATION OF SOULS
SAMSØ ISLAND
map (55° 52′N 10° 37′E) **6**:109
SAMSON **17**:48
riddles **16**:216
SAMSON (Alabama)
map (31° 7′N 86° 9′W) **1**:234
SAMSON AGONISTES (play) **17**:48–49
SAMSONOV, A. V.
Tannenberg, Battles of **19**:24
SAMSONOV, ALEKSANDR
World War I **20**:224–225
SAMSUN (Turkey)
climate **19**:343 *table*
map (41° 17′N 36° 20′E) **19**:343
SAMUEL, BOOKS OF **17**:49 *bibliog.*
SAMUELSON, PAUL A. **17**:49 *bibliog.*
SAMURAI **17**:49 *bibliog.*, *illus.*
hara-kiri **10**:41
Meiji Restoration **13**:281–282
sword **18**:398 *illus.*
Yamaga Soko **20**:316
SAN (ethnic group) **1**:145 *illus.*; **2**:52 *illus.*; **16**:34 *illus.*; **17**:49–50 *bibliog.*, *illus.*
creation accounts **5**:334
hunter-gatherers **10**:313 *illus.*
national parks **14**:44
rock painting **1**:161 *illus.*
steatopygia **18**:242
Tswana **19**:325
SAN (Mali)
map (13° 18′N 4° 54′W) **13**:89
SAN, AUNG *see* AUNG SAN
SAN AGUSTÍN (Colombia) **17**:50 *bibliog.*
SAN AGUSTIN, CAPE OF
map (6° 16′N 126° 11′E) **15**:237
SAN ALEJO (El Salvador)
map (13° 26′N 87° 58′W) **7**:100
SAN ANDREAS (California)
map (38° 12′N 120° 41′W) **4**:31
SAN ANDREAS FAULT **15**:351 *map*; **17**:50 *bibliog.*, *illus.*
fault **8**:37
mid-oceanic ridge **13**:389
transform fault **19**:269–270
SAN ANDRÉS (Mexico)
map (27° 14′N 114° 14′W) **13**:357
SAN ANDRES MOUNTAINS
map (32° 55′N 106° 45′W) **14**:136
SAN ANDRÉS TUXTLA (Mexico)
map (18° 27′N 95° 13′W) **13**:357
SAN ANGELO (Texas)
map (31° 28′N 100° 26′W) **19**:129
SAN ANSELMO (California)
map (37° 59′N 122° 34′W) **4**:31
SAN ANTONIO (Belize)
map (16° 15′N 89° 2′W) **3**:183
SAN ANTONIO (Chile)
map (33° 35′S 71° 38′W) **4**:355
SAN ANTONIO (New Mexico)
map (33° 55′N 106° 52′W) **14**:136
SAN ANTONIO (Texas) **17**:50–51 *illus.*
map (29° 28′N 98° 31′W) **19**:129
Spanish missions **18**:160 *illus.*
SAN ANTONIO, CAPE
map (36° 40′S 56° 42′W) **2**:149
SAN ANTONIO, CAPE OF (Cuba)
map (21° 52′N 84° 57′W) **5**:377
SAN ANTONIO BAY
map (28° 20′N 96° 45′W) **19**:129
SAN ANTONIO DE BRAVO (Mexico)
map (30° 10′N 104° 42′W) **13**:357
SAN ANTONIO DE LOS BAÑOS (Cuba)
map (22° 53′N 82° 30′W) **5**:377
SAN ANTONIO MOUNTAIN
map (36° 52′N 106° 2′W) **14**:136
SAN ANTONIO OESTE (Argentina)
map (40° 44′S 64° 56′W) **2**:149
SAN AUGUSTINE (Texas)
map (31° 32′N 94° 7′W) **19**:129
SAN AUGUSTINE (county in Texas)
map (31° 20′N 94° 10′W) **19**:129
SAN BENEDETTO DEL TRONTO (Italy)
map (42° 57′N 13° 53′E) **11**:321
SAN BENITO (county in California)
map (36° 51′N 121° 24′W) **4**:31
SAN BENITO (Guatemala)
map (16° 55′N 89° 54′W) **9**:389
SAN BENITO (Texas)
map (26° 8′N 97° 38′W) **19**:129
SAN BERNARDINO (California) **17**:51
map (34° 6′N 117° 17′W) **4**:31
SAN BERNARDINO (county in California)
map (34° 40′N 117° 17′W) **4**:31
SAN BERNARDO (Chile)
map (33° 36′S 70° 43′W) **4**:355
SAN BLAS (Mexico)
map (21° 31′N 105° 16′W) **13**:357
SAN BLAS, CAPE OF
map (29° 40′N 85° 22′W) **8**:172
SAN BLAS CORDILLERA MOUNTAINS
map (9° 18′N 79° 0′W) **15**:55
SAN BLAS INDIANS *see* CUNA (American Indians)
SAN BORJA (Bolivia)
map (14° 49′S 66° 51′W) **3**:366
SAN CARLO ALLE QUATTRO FONTANE **3**:404 *illus.*; **17**:51 *bibliog.*, *illus.*
SAN CARLOS (Argentina)
map (27° 45′S 55° 54′W) **2**:149
SAN CARLOS (Arizona)
map (33° 21′N 110° 27′W) **2**:160
SAN CARLOS (California)
map (37° 31′N 122° 16′W) **4**:31
SAN CARLOS (Chile)
map (36° 25′S 71° 58′W) **4**:355
SAN CARLOS (Equatorial Guinea)
map (3° 27′N 8° 33′E) **7**:226
SAN CARLOS (Nicaragua)
map (11° 7′N 84° 47′W) **14**:179
SAN CARLOS (Paraguay)
map (22° 16′S 57° 18′W) **15**:77
SAN CARLOS (Venezuela)
map (9° 40′N 68° 36′W) **19**:542
SAN CARLOS DE BARILOCHE (Argentina)
map (41° 9′S 71° 18′W) **2**:149
SAN CARLOS RESERVOIR
map (33° 13′N 110° 24′W) **2**:160
SAN CASSIANO, TEATRO
opera houses **14**:401
SAN CLEMENTE (California)
map (33° 26′N 117° 37′W) **4**:31
SAN CLEMENTE, CHURCH OF (Tahull, Spain) **16**:285 *illus.*
SAN CLEMENTE ISLAND
map (32° 54′N 118° 29′W) **4**:31
SAN CRISTÓBAL (Dominican Republic)
map (18° 25′N 70° 6′W) **6**:233
SAN CRISTÓBAL (Venezuela)
map (7° 46′N 72° 14′W) **19**:542
SAN CRISTOBAL ISLAND (Galápagos Islands)
map (0° 50′S 89° 26′W) **7**:52
SAN CRISTOBAL ISLAND (Solomon Islands)
map (10° 36′S 161° 45′E) **18**:56
SAN CRISTÓBAL LAS CASAS (Mexico)
map (16° 45′N 92° 38′W) **13**:357
SAN DIEGO (California) **4**:32 *illus.*; **17**:51–52 *illus.*
map (32° 43′N 117° 9′W) **4**:31
San Diego Zoological Garden **17**:52
SAN DIEGO (county in California)
map (33° 0′N 117° 5′W) **4**:31
SAN DIEGO (Texas)
map (27° 46′N 98° 14′W) **19**:129
SAN DIEGO CHARGERS **8**:217 *illus.*
SAN DIEGO ZOOLOGICAL GARDEN **17**:52; **20**:375 *illus.*
SAN ENRIQUE (Argentina)
map (35° 47′S 60° 22′W) **2**:149
SAN ESTEBAN, CHURCH OF
Churriguera (family) **4**:427
retablo (Churriguera) **18**:154 *illus.*
SAN FELIPE (Chile)
map (32° 45′S 70° 44′W) **4**:355
SAN FELIPE (Colombia)
map (1° 55′N 67° 6′W) **5**:107
SAN FELIPE (Mexico)
map (31° 0′N 114° 52′W) **13**:357
SAN FELIPE (Venezuela)
map (10° 20′N 68° 44′W) **19**:542
SAN FELIPE PUEBLO (New Mexico)
map (35° 27′N 106° 28′W) **14**:136
SAN FERNANDO (California)
map (34° 17′N 118° 26′W) **4**:31
SAN FERNANDO (Chile)
map (34° 35′S 71° 0′W) **4**:355
SAN FERNANDO (Mexico)
map (24° 50′N 98° 10′W) **13**:357
SAN FERNANDO (Philippines)
map (16° 37′N 120° 19′E) **15**:237
SAN FERNANDO (Trinidad and Tobago)
map (10° 17′N 61° 28′W) **19**:300
SAN FERNANDO DE APURE (Venezuela)
map (7° 54′N 67° 28′W) **19**:542
SAN FERNANDO DE ATABAPO (Venezuela)
map (4° 3′N 67° 42′W) **19**:542
SAN FRANCISCO (Argentina)
map (31° 26′S 62° 5′W) **2**:149
SAN FRANCISCO (California) **17**:52–53 *bibliog.*, *illus.*, *map*
cable car **4**:6; **18**:296 *illus.*
climate **19**:421 *table*
Golden Gate Bridge **9**:232
map (37° 48′N 122° 24′W) **4**:31
post office c.1849 **15**:460 *illus.*
San Francisco art museums **17**:54
San Francisco Opera Association **17**:54
subway **18**:318–319 *table*
SAN FRANCISCO (county in California)
map (37° 45′N 122° 22′W) **4**:31
SAN FRANCISCO, CAPE OF
map (0° 40′N 80° 5′W) **7**:52
SAN FRANCISCO, UNIVERSITY OF **17**:54
SAN FRANCISCO ART MUSEUMS **17**:54 *bibliog.*
SAN FRANCISCO BAY **17**:53 *illus.*; **17**:54
Golden Gate **9**:232
map (37° 43′N 122° 17′W) **4**:31
SAN FRANCISCO CONSERVATORY
Bloch, Ernest **3**:333
SAN FRANCISCO DE LA PAZ (Honduras)
map (14° 55′N 86° 14′W) **10**:218
SAN FRANCISCO DE MACORÍS (Dominican Republic)
map (19° 18′N 70° 15′W) **6**:233
SAN FRANCISCO EXAMINER
Hearst, William Randolph **10**:90

SAN FRANCISCO MUSEUM OF MODERN ART
San Francisco art museums 17:54
SAN FRANCISCO OPERA ASSOCIATION 17:54
SAN FRANCISCO POETRY CENTER
Rexroth, Kenneth 16:190
SAN FRANCISCO RENAISSANCE
authors
Ginsberg, Allen 9:184–185
SAN GABRIEL (Ecuador)
map (0° 36′N 77° 49′W) 7:52
SAN GABRIEL MOUNTAINS
Los Angeles (California) 12:416 *illus.*
map (34° 20′N 118° 0′W) 4:31
SAN GERMÁN (Puerto Rico)
map (18° 5′N 67° 3′W) 15:614
SAN GORGONIO MOUNTAIN
map (34° 6′N 116° 50′W) 4:31
SAN GREGORIO (Uruguay)
map (32° 37′S 55° 40′W) 19:488
SAN IGNACIO (Bolivia)
map (14° 53′S 65° 36′W) 3:366
map (16° 23′S 60° 59′W) 3:366
SAN IGNACIO (Mexico)
map (27° 27′N 112° 51′W) 13:357
SAN ILDEFONSO MOUNTAIN
map (15° 31′N 88° 17′W) 10:218
SAN ISIDRO (Argentina)
map (34° 27′S 58° 30′W) 2:149
SAN JACINTO (California)
map (33° 47′N 116° 57′W) 4:31
SAN JACINTO (county in Texas)
map (30° 35′N 95° 10′W) 19:129
SAN JAVIER (Bolivia)
map (14° 34′S 64° 42′W) 3:366
map (16° 20′S 62° 38′W) 3:366
SAN JOAQUÍN (Bolivia)
map (13° 4′S 64° 49′W) 3:366
SAN JOAQUIN (county in California)
map (37° 57′N 121° 17′W) 4:31
SAN JOAQUIN RIVER 17:54
map (38° 3′N 121° 50′W) 4:31
SAN JOAQUIN VALLEY
Landsat photograph 12:185 *illus.*
map (36° 50′N 120° 10′W) 4:31
SAN JON (New Mexico)
map (35° 6′N 103° 20′W) 14:136
SAN JORGE (Argentina)
map (31° 54′S 61° 52′W) 2:149
SAN JORGE, GULF OF (Spain)
map (40° 53′N 1° 0′E) 18:140
SAN JORGE GULF (Argentina)
map (46° 0′S 67° 0′W) 2:149
SAN JOSE (California) 17:54 *illus.*
map (37° 20′N 121° 53′W) 4:31
SAN JOSÉ (Costa Rica) 5:292 *illus., table*; 17:55
map (9° 56′N 84° 5′W) 5:291
SAN JOSÉ DE CHIQUITOS (Bolivia)
map (17° 51′S 60° 47′W) 3:366
SAN JOSÉ DE MAYO (Uruguay)
map (34° 30′S 56° 42′W) 19:488
SAN JOSÉ DE OCOA (Dominican Republic)
map (18° 33′N 70° 30′W) 6:233
SAN JOSÉ DEL CABO (Mexico)
map (23° 3′N 109° 41′W) 13:357
SAN JOSÉ DEL GUAVIARE (Colombia)
map (2° 35′N 72° 38′W) 5:107
SAN JUAN (Argentina)
map (31° 32′S 68° 31′W) 2:149
SAN JUAN (province in Argentina)
map (31° 0′S 69° 0′W) 2:149
SAN JUAN (county in Colorado)
map (37° 45′N 107° 40′W) 5:116
SAN JUAN (Dominican Republic)
map (18° 40′N 71° 5′W) 6:233
SAN JUAN (Guatemala)
map (15° 52′N 88° 53′W) 9:389
SAN JUAN (county in New Mexico)
map (36° 30′N 108° 20′W) 14:136
SAN JUAN (Puerto Rico) 15:615 *illus., table*; 17:55 *illus.*
map (18° 28′N 66° 7′W) 15:614
SAN JUAN (county in Utah)
map (37° 37′N 109° 45′W) 19:492
SAN JUAN (county in Washington)
map (48° 34′N 122° 59′W) 20:35
SAN JUAN BOUNDARY DISPUTE 17:55 *bibliog.*
SAN JUAN DE LOS CAYOS (Venezuela)
map (11° 10′N 68° 25′W) 19:542
SAN JUAN DE LOS MORROS (Venezuela)
map (9° 55′N 67° 21′W) 19:542
SAN JUAN DEL NORTE (Nicaragua)
map (10° 55′N 83° 42′W) 14:179
SAN JUAN HILL, BATTLE OF
Spanish-American War 18:150 *illus.*
SAN JUAN ISLAND 20:36 *illus.*
map (48° 36′N 122° 50′W) 20:35
SAN JUAN MOUNTAINS
map (37° 35′N 107° 10′W) 5:116
SAN JUAN RIVER (Central America)
map (10° 56′N 83° 42′W) 5:291
SAN JUAN RIVER (United States)
map (37° 18′N 110° 28′W) 5:120
SAN JUAN SACATEPÉQUEZ (Guatemala)
map (14° 43′N 90° 39′W) 9:389
SAN JUANILLO (Costa Rica)
map (10° 2′N 85° 44′W) 5:291
SAN JULIÁN (Argentina)
map (49° 18′S 67° 43′W) 2:149
SAN LÁZARO (Paraguay)
map (22° 10′S 57° 55′W) 15:77
SAN LEANDRO (California)
map (37° 43′N 122° 9′W) 4:31
SAN LORENZO (Argentina)
map (32° 45′S 60° 44′W) 2:149
SAN LORENZO (Ecuador)
map (1° 17′N 78° 50′W) 7:52
SAN LORENZO (Mexico) 14:237 *map*; 17:55–56 *bibliog.*
La Venta 12:151
Olmec 14:380
pre-Columbian art and architecture 15:496
SAN LORENZO, CHURCH OF 6:230 *illus.*
Brunelleschi, Filippo 3:524
cathedrals and churches 4:206
Medici Chapel 13:265–266
SAN LORENZO, TREATY OF *see* PINCKNEY'S TREATY
SAN LUCAS (Bolivia)
map (20° 6′S 65° 7′W) 3:366
SAN LUCAS (Ecuador)
map (3° 45′S 79° 15′W) 7:52
SAN LUIS (Argentina)
map (33° 18′S 66° 21′W) 2:149
SAN LUIS (province in Argentina)
map (34° 0′S 66° 0′W) 2:149
SAN LUIS (Colorado)
map (37° 12′N 105° 25′W) 5:116
SAN LUIS (Cuba)
map (20° 12′N 75° 51′W) 5:377
SAN LUIS, CAPE
map (22° 52′N 109° 53′W) 13:357
SAN LUIS, LAKE
map (13° 45′S 64° 0′W) 3:366
SAN LUIS OBISPO (California)
map (35° 17′N 120° 40′W) 4:31
SAN LUIS OBISPO (county in California)
map (35° 20′N 120° 10′W) 4:31
SAN LUIS PASS
map (29° 5′N 95° 8′W) 19:129
SAN LUIS PEAK
map (37° 59′N 106° 56′W) 5:116
SAN LUIS POTOSÍ (city in Mexico) 17:56
map (22° 9′N 100° 59′W) 13:357
SAN LUIS POTOSÍ (state in Mexico) 17:56
cities
San Luis Potosí 17:56
SAN LUIS RÍO COLORADO (Mexico)
map (32° 29′N 114° 48′W) 13:357
SAN LUIS VALLEY
map (37° 25′N 106° 0′W) 5:116
SAN MANUEL (Arizona)
map (32° 36′N 110° 38′W) 2:160
SAN MARCELINO (El Salvador)
map (13° 22′N 89° 3′W) 7:100
SAN MARCO (Venice) *see* SAINT MARK'S BASILICA
SAN MARCOS (Texas)
map (29° 53′N 97° 57′W) 19:129
SAN MARINO 17:56 *bibliog., illus., map*
flag 17:56 *illus.*
history and government 17:56
land, people, and economy 17:56 *map*
map (43° 56′N 12° 25′E) 7:268
SAN MARINO (San Marino)
map (43° 55′N 12° 28′E) 17:56
SAN MARTÍN, JOSÉ DE 17:57 *bibliog., illus.*
flag 8:135 *illus.*
Latin America, history of 12:220 *illus.*
Peru 15:194
SAN MARTÍN, LAKE
map (49° 0′S 72° 40′W) 4:355
SAN MARTÍN, RAMÓN GRAU *see* GRAU SAN MARTÍN, RAMÓN
SAN MARTÍN RIVER
map (13° 8′S 63° 43′W) 3:366
SAN MARTINA E LUCA (Rome)
Cortona, Pietro da 5:279
SAN MATEO (California)
map (37° 35′N 122° 19′W) 4:31
SAN MATEO (county in California)
map (37° 25′N 122° 20′W) 4:31
SAN MATEO (Florida)
map (29° 36′N 81° 35′W) 8:172
SAN MATEO (New Mexico)
map (35° 20′N 107° 39′W) 14:136
SAN MATÍAS BAY
map (41° 30′S 64° 15′W) 2:149
SAN MIGUEL (Bolivia)
map (16° 42′S 61° 1′W) 3:366
SAN MIGUEL (county in Colorado)
map (38° 0′N 108° 20′W) 5:116
SAN MIGUEL (Ecuador)
map (1° 44′S 79° 1′W) 7:52
SAN MIGUEL (El Salvador)
map (13° 29′N 88° 11′W) 7:100
SAN MIGUEL (county in New Mexico)
map (35° 30′N 105° 0′W) 14:136
SAN MIGUEL (Panama)
map (8° 27′N 78° 56′W) 15:55
SAN MIGUEL DE TUCUMÁN (Argentina) *see* TUCUMÁN (Argentina)
SAN MIGUEL ISLAND
map (34° 2′N 120° 22′W) 4:31
SAN MIGUEL RIVER (Bolivia)
map (13° 52′S 63° 56′W) 3:366
SAN MIGUEL RIVER (Colorado)
map (38° 23′N 108° 48′W) 5:116
SAN NICOLÁS (Peru)
map (15° 13′S 75° 12′W) 15:193
SAN NICOLAS DE LOS ARROYOS (Argentina)
map (33° 20′S 60° 13′W) 2:149
SAN NICOLAS ISLAND
map (33° 15′N 119° 31′W) 4:31
SAN PABLO (Philippines)
map (14° 4′N 121° 19′E) 15:237
SAN PABLO BAY
map (38° 6′N 122° 22′W) 4:31
SAN PATRICO (county in Texas)
map (28° 0′N 97° 30′W) 19:129
SAN PEDRO (Argentina)
map (33° 40′S 59° 40′W) 2:149
SAN PEDRO (Bolivia)
map (14° 20′S 64° 50′W) 3:366
SAN PEDRO CHANNEL
map (33° 35′N 118° 25′W) 4:31
SAN PEDRO DE LAS COLONIAS (Mexico)
map (25° 45′N 102° 59′W) 13:357
SAN PEDRO DE MACORÍS (Dominican Republic)
map (18° 27′N 69° 18′W) 6:233
SAN PEDRO PEAKS
map (36° 7′N 106° 49′W) 14:136
SAN PEDRO SACATEPÉQUEZ (Guatemala)
map (14° 58′N 91° 46′W) 9:389
SAN PEDRO SULA (Honduras)
map (15° 27′N 88° 2′W) 10:218
SAN PIETRO, CHURCH OF (Montorio, Rome)
Bramante, Donato 3:452 *illus.*
Tempietto 16:152 *illus.*; 19:93
SAN RAFAEL (Argentina)
map (34° 36′S 68° 20′W) 2:149
SAN RAFAEL (California)
map (37° 59′N 122° 31′W) 4:31
Marin County Civic Center 20:289 *illus.*
SAN RAFAEL DESERT
map (38° 40′N 110° 30′W) 19:492
SAN RAFAEL ORIENTE (El Salvador)
map (13° 23′N 88° 21′W) 7:100
SAN RAFAEL RIVER
map (38° 47′N 110° 7′W) 19:492
SAN RAMÓN (Bolivia)
map (13° 17′S 64° 43′W) 3:366
SAN RAMÓN DE LA NUEVA ORÁN (Argentina)
map (23° 8′S 64° 20′W) 2:149
SAN REMO (Italy) 17:57
map (43° 49′N 7° 46′E) 11:321
SAN RIVER (Kampuchea)
map (13° 32′N 105° 58′E) 12:11
SAN RIVER (Poland)
map (50° 45′N 21° 51′E) 15:388
SAN SABA (Texas)
map (31° 12′N 98° 43′W) 19:129
SAN SABA (county in Texas)
map (31° 10′N 98° 50′W) 19:129
SAN SALVADOR (Argentina)
map (31° 37′S 58° 30′W) 2:149
SAN SALVADOR (El Salvador) 7:101 *illus., table*; 17:57
map (13° 42′N 89° 12′W) 7:100
SAN SALVADOR DE JUJUY (Argentina)
map (24° 11′S 65° 18′W) 2:149
SAN SALVADOR ISLAND (Watlings Island) (Bahamas) 17:57–58
map (24° 2′N 74° 28′W) 3:23
SAN SALVADOR ISLAND (Galápagos Islands)
map (0° 14′S 90° 45′W) 7:52
SAN SEBASTIÁN (Puerto Rico)
map (18° 20′N 66° 59′W) 15:614
SAN SEBASTIÁN (Spain) 17:58
map (43° 19′N 1° 59′W) 18:140
SAN SEVERO (Italy)
map (41° 41′N 15° 23′E) 11:321
SAN SIMEON PALACE
Morgan, Julia 13:578
SAN STEFANO, TREATY OF
Berlin, Congress of 3:217
Russia/Union of Soviet Socialist Republics, history of 16:358
Russo-Turkish Wars 16:374 *illus.*
SAN VICENTE (El Salvador)
map (13° 38′N 88° 48′W) 7:100
SAN VICENTE (Mexico)
map (31° 20′N 116° 15′W) 13:357
SAN VICENTE DE BARACALDO (Spain)
map (43° 18′N 2° 59′W) 18:140
SAN VICENTE DEL CAGUÁN (Colombia)
map (2° 7′N 74° 46′W) 5:107
SAN VITALE (Italy) 17:58 *bibliog.*
mosaics 13:594–595 *illus.*; 15:116 *illus.*; 17:58 *illus.*
Byzantine art and architecture 3:604
SAN XAVIER DEL BAC 2:162 *illus.*; 18:160 *illus.*
SAÑA (Peru)
map (6° 55′S 79° 35′W) 15:193
SANA (Yemen) 17:58; 20:325 *illus.*
map (15° 23′N 44° 12′E) 20:325
SANAGA RIVER
map (3° 35′N 9° 38′E) 4:61
SANANDAJ (Iran)
map (35° 19′N 47° 0′E) 11:250
SANANDITA (Bolivia)
map (21° 40′S 63° 35′W) 3:366
SANBORN (Iowa)
map (43° 11′N 95° 39′W) 11:244
SANBORN (Minnesota)
map (44° 13′N 95° 8′W) 13:453
SANBORN (North Dakota)
map (46° 57′N 98° 13′W) 14:248
SANBORN (county in South Dakota)
map (44° 0′N 98° 3′W) 18:103
SÁNCHEZ (Dominican Republic)
map (19° 14′N 69° 36′W) 6:233
SANCHEZ, SONIA 17:58
SANCHI (India) 17:58
Buddhist shrine at 11:89 *illus.*
SANCHO I, KING OF PORTUGAL
Portugal, history of 15:453
SANCHO II, KING OF PORTUGAL
Portugal, history of 15:453
SANCHO III, KING OF NAVARRE (Sancho the Great) 17:58
Navarre 14:58
Spain, history of 18:145
SANCHO PANZA
Don Quixote 6:236
SANCROFT, WILLIAM 17:58 *bibliog.*
SANCTIONS 17:58 *bibliog.*
SANCTI-SPÍRITUS (Cuba)
map (21° 56′N 79° 27′W) 5:377
SANCTIONS 17:58 *bibliog.*
SANCTIS, FRANCESCO DE *see* DE SANCTIS, FRANCESCO
SANCTUARY 17:59 *bibliog.*
SANCTUARY OF THE GREAT GODS
Samothrace 17:47
SANCY HILL MOUNTAIN
map (45° 32′N 2° 49′E) 8:260
SAND 17:59 *bibliog.*
beach and coast 3:136
glaciers and glaciation 9:194–195
littoral zone 12:373
longshore drift 12:409
oceanic mineral resources 14:340
quicksand 16:25
roads and highways 16:238–239 *illus.*
sandstorm and dust storm 17:63–64
silica minerals 17:304
size determination scale 17:59
tar sands 19:34
SAND, GEORGE 16:293 *illus.*; 17:59 *bibliog., illus.*
Chopin, Frédéric 4:405
SAND CASTING
casting 4:188
SAND CREEK MASSACRE 17:59–60 *bibliog.*
Black Kettle 3:316
Cheyenne (American Indians) 4:338
Indian Wars 11:108–109 *map*
SAND DOLLAR 11:229 *illus.*; 17:60
SAND DUNE 17:60 *bibliog., illus.*
coastal protection 5:81
desert 6:128–129; 6:129 *illus.*
erosion and sedimentation 7:234
paleogeography 15:38
Sahara 17:13 *illus.*
wind action 20:170
SAND EEL 17:60–61
SAND FLY *see* MIDGE

SAND GROUSE 17:61 *illus.*
SAND HILL (Belize)
map (17° 36′N 88° 22′W) 3:183
SAND HILL (Massachusetts)
map (42° 13′N 70° 44′W) 3:409
SAND MOUNTAIN
map (34° 10′N 86° 10′W) 1:234
SAND PAINTING 11:140 *illus.*; 14:53 *illus.*
SAND SMELT *see* SILVERSIDES
SAND SPRINGS (Oklahoma)
map (36° 9′N 96° 7′W) 14:368
SANDAKAN (Malaysia)
map (5° 50′N 118° 7′E) 13:84
SANDAL 17:280 *illus.*
SANDALWOOD 17:61
bastard toadflax 3:119
SANDBAR *see* BAR, OFFSHORE
SANDBUR 17:61
SANDBURG, CARL 17:61 *bibliog., illus.*
SANDBY (family) 17:61–62 *bibliog.*
SANDE *see* MENDE
SANDE, EARL 17:62
SANDER, AUGUST
photography, history and art of 15:272
SANDERS (Arizona)
map (35° 13′N 109° 20′W) 2:160
SANDERS (county in Montana)
map (47° 35′N 115° 0′W) 13:547
SANDERS, OTTO LIMAN VON
World War I 20:231
SANDERSON (Texas)
map (30° 9′N 102° 24′W) 19:129
SANDERSVILLE (Georgia)
map (32° 59′N 82° 48′W) 9:114
SANDERSVILLE (Mississippi)
map (31° 47′N 89° 2′W) 13:469
SANDFISH 17:62
SANDHILL CRANE 5:330 *illus.*
SANDHURST, ROYAL MILITARY ACADEMY AT 17:62 *bibliog.*
SANDIA (Peru)
map (14° 17′S 69° 26′W) 15:193
SANDIA CAVE (New Mexico) 17:62
SANDINISTAS 17:62
Nicaragua 14:179
Ortega Saavedra, Daniel 14:449
SANDLANDS VILLAGE (Bahama Islands)
map (25° 2′N 77° 18′W) 3:23
SANDOVAL (Illinois)
map (38° 37′N 89° 7′W) 11:42
SANDOVAL (county in New Mexico)
map (35° 40′N 106° 45′W) 14:136
SANDPIPER 17:62 *bibliog., illus.*
curlew 5:392
dowitcher 6:251
redshank 8:229 *illus.*
shorebirds 17:283
snipe 18:3
SANDPOINT (Idaho)
map (48° 16′N 116° 33′W) 11:26
SANDRACOTTUS *see* CHANDRAGUPTA MAURYA, EMPEROR OF INDIA
SANDSTON (Virginia)
map (37° 31′N 77° 19′W) 19:607
SANDSTONE 17:63 *bibliog., illus., table*
arkose 2:170
brownstone 3:519
characteristics 17:63
classification 17:63 *table*
graywacke 9:307
metamorphic rock 13:331
petroleum 15:208
quartz 16:14
quartzite 16:14
Sahara 17:14 *illus.*
Sedgwick, Adam 17:183
sedimentary rock 17:185
silica minerals 17:304
stratigraphy 18:292 *illus.*
SANDSTORM AND DUST STORM 17:63–64 *bibliog., illus.*
Dust Bowl (U.S.) 6:308 *illus.*
erosion and sedimentation 7:233
hydrologic cycle 10:341
meteorology 13:341
Saint Elmo's fire 17:18
wind action 20:170
SANDÚ, POLICARPO
Paysandú (Uruguay) 15:122
SANDUSKY (Michigan)
map (43° 25′N 82° 50′W) 13:377
SANDUSKY (Ohio)
map (41° 27′N 82° 42′W) 14:357
SANDUSKY (county in Ohio)
map (41° 21′N 83° 7′W) 14:357
SANDUSKY BAY
map (41° 27′N 82° 52′W) 14:357
SANDUSKY RIVER
map (41° 27′N 83° 0′W) 14:357
SANDVIKEN (Sweden)
map (60° 37′N 16° 46′E) 18:382
SANDWICH (Illinois)
map (41° 39′N 88° 37′W) 11:42
SANDWICH (Massachusetts)
map (41° 46′N 70° 30′W) 13:206
SANDWICH, JOHN MONTAGU, 4TH EARL OF 17:64 *bibliog.*
SANDWICH BAY
map (53° 35′N 57° 15′W) 14:166
SANDWICH ISLANDS *see* HAWAII (state)
SANDWICH RANGE
map (43° 54′N 71° 28′W) 14:123
SANDY HOOK (Kentucky)
map (38° 5′N 83° 8′W) 12:47
SANDY HOOK (Mississippi)
map (31° 2′N 89° 48′W) 13:469
SANDY LAKE (Newfoundland)
map (49° 16′N 57° 0′W) 14:166
SANDY LAKE (Ontario)
map (53° 0′N 93° 7′W) 14:393
SANDY NECK (peninsula)
map (41° 44′N 70° 20′W) 13:206
SANDY POINT
map (41° 14′N 71° 35′W) 16:198
SANDY SPRINGS (Georgia)
map (33° 55′N 84° 23′W) 9:114
SANFORD (Colorado)
map (37° 16′N 105° 54′W) 5:116
SANFORD (Florida)
map (28° 48′N 81° 16′W) 8:172
SANFORD (Maine)
map (43° 26′N 70° 46′W) 13:70
SANFORD (Michigan)
map (43° 40′N 84° 23′W) 13:377
SANFORD (North Carolina)
map (35° 29′N 79° 10′W) 14:242
SANFORD (Texas)
map (35° 42′N 101° 32′W) 19:129
SANG D'UN POÈTE, LE (film)
Cocteau, Jean 5:89
SANGALLO (family) 17:64 *bibliog.*
cathedrals and churches 4:206; 4:207
Farnese Palace 8:28
SANGAMON (county in Illinois)
map (39° 47′N 89° 40′W) 11:42
SANGAMON RIVER
map (40° 7′N 90° 20′W) 11:42
SANGAY VOLCANO
map (2° 0′S 78° 20′W) 7:52
SANGER (California)
map (36° 42′N 119° 27′W) 4:31
SÄNGER, EUGEN
jet propulsion 11:407
SANGER, FREDERICK 17:64
insulin 11:198
SANGER, MARGARET 17:64–65 *bibliog., illus.*
birth control 3:293; 3:294
SANGHA
map (2° 0′N 15° 0′E) 5:182
SANGOAN CULTURE
prehistoric humans 15:515
SANGOLQUÍ (Ecuador)
map (0° 19′S 78° 27′W) 7:52
SANGRE DE CRISTO MOUNTAINS 14:137 *illus.*
map (36° 15′N 105° 20′W) 14:136
SANGRE GRANDE (Trinidad and Tobago)
map (10° 35′N 61° 7′W) 19:300
SANGUDO (Alberta)
map (53° 53′N 114° 54′W) 1:256
SANGUINARINE
poppy 15:432
SANGUINETTI, JULIO
Uruguay 19:490
SANHEDRIN 17:65 *bibliog.*
Gamaliel of Jabneh 9:24
SANIBEL ISLAND
map (26° 27′N 82° 6′W) 8:172
SANIDINE
feldspar 8:46
SANILAC (county in Michigan)
map (43° 20′N 82° 50′W) 13:377
SANITARY LANDFILL *see* LANDFILL
SANITATION *see* PLUMBING; SEWERAGE; WASTE DISPOSAL SYSTEMS; WATER SUPPLY
SANKA
Kutenai 12:139–140
SANKT GALLEN (Switzerland) 17:65
map (47° 25′N 9° 23′E) 18:394
SANKT PÖLTEN (Austria)
map (48° 12′N 15° 37′E) 2:348
SANKT VEIT (Austria)
map (47° 20′N 13° 9′E) 2:348
SANLÚCAR DE BARREMEDA (Spain)
map (36° 47′N 6° 21′W) 18:140
SANMICHELI, MICHELE 17:65 *bibliog.*
SANNAR (Sudan)
map (13° 33′N 33° 38′E) 18:320
SANNAZARO, JACOPO 17:65 *bibliog.*
SANNIQUELLIE (Liberia)
map (7° 22′N 8° 43′W) 12:313
SANPETE (county in Utah)
map (39° 20′N 111° 35′W) 19:492
SANRAKU 17:65 *bibliog.*
SANS SOUCI 17:65
SANSKRIT
India 11:84
Indian literature 11:101
Indo-Iranian languages 11:145
linguistics 12:356
Panini 15:59
SANSOVINO, ANDREA 17:65 *bibliog.*
Sansovino, Jacopo 17:66
SANSOVINO, JACOPO 17:66 *bibliog., illus.*
Bacchus 17:66 *illus.*
SANT JULIA (Andorra)
map (42° 28′N 1° 30′E) 1:405
SANTA ANA (Bolivia)
map (13° 45′S 65° 35′W) 3:366
map (15° 31′S 67° 30′W) 3:366
SANTA ANA (California) 17:66
map (33° 43′N 117° 54′W) 4:31
SANTA ANA (Ecuador)
map (1° 13′S 80° 23′W) 7:52
SANTA ANA (El Salvador) 17:66
map (13° 59′N 89° 34′W) 7:100
SANTA ANA (wind)
Mediterranean climate 13:276
SANTA ANA HILLS
map (31° 15′S 55° 15′W) 19:488
SANTA ANA MOUNTAINS
map (33° 45′N 117° 35′W) 4:31
SANTA ANA VOLCANO
map (13° 50′N 89° 38′W) 7:100
SANTA ANNA, ANTONIO LÓPEZ DE 17:66 *bibliog., illus.*
Mexican War 13:351–354 *illus., map*
Mexico, history of 13:364
Taylor, Zachary 19:50–51
Texas 19:134
Texas Revolution 19:135
SANTA BARBARA (California) 17:66–67
map (34° 25′N 119° 42′W) 4:31
SANTA BARBARA (county in California)
map (33° 28′N 119° 2′W) 4:31
SANTA BÁRBARA (Mexico)
map (26° 48′N 105° 49′W) 13:357
SANTA BARBARA, CASTILLO DE (Spain) 18:139 *illus.*
SANTA BARBARA ISLANDS 17:67
map (33° 28′N 119° 2′W) 4:31
Santa Catalina Island 17:67
SANTA CATALINA (Panama)
map (8° 47′N 81° 20′W) 15:55
SANTA CATALINA, GULF OF
map (33° 20′N 117° 45′W) 4:31
SANTA CATALINA ISLAND 17:67
map (33° 23′N 118° 26′W) 4:31
SANTA CATARINA (Brazil)
map (27° 0′S 50° 0′W) 3:460
SANTA CLARA (California) 17:67
map (37° 21′N 121° 57′W) 4:31
SANTA CLARA (county in California)
map (37° 20′N 121° 53′W) 4:31
SANTA CLARA (Cuba)
map (22° 24′N 79° 58′W) 5:377
SANTA CLARA (Mexico)
map (29° 17′N 107° 1′W) 13:357
SANTA CLARA (Utah)
map (37° 8′N 113° 39′W) 19:492
SANTA CLARA DE OLIMAR (Uruguay)
map (32° 55′S 54° 58′W) 19:488
SANTA CLAUS 17:67 *bibliog., illus.*
Nicholas, Saint 14:180–181
SANTA CLOTILDE (Peru)
map (2° 34′S 73° 44′W) 15:193
SANTA COSTANZA, CHURCH OF 17:67 *bibliog.*
cathedrals and churches 4:205
mosaic 13:594
SANTA CROCE
Pazzi Chapel
Brunelleschi, Filippo 3:524
SANTA CRUZ (Argentina)
map (50° 1′S 68° 31′W) 2:149
SANTA CRUZ (province in Argentina)
map (49° 0′S 70° 0′W) 2:149
SANTA CRUZ (county in Arizona)
map (31° 30′N 111° 45′W) 2:160
SANTA CRUZ (Bolivia) 17:67
map (17° 48′S 63° 10′W) 3:366
SANTA CRUZ (California) 17:67
map (36° 58′N 122° 1′W) 4:31
SANTA CRUZ (county in California)
map (36° 58′N 122° 1′W) 4:31
SANTA CRUZ (Costa Rica)
map (10° 16′N 85° 36′W) 5:291
SANTA CRUZ (Mexico)
map (23° 5′N 97° 50′W) 13:357
SANTA CRUZ, ANDRÉS 17:67–68
SANTA CRUZ CABRALIA (Brazil)
map (16° 17′S 39° 2′W) 3:460
SANTA CRUZ DE TENERIFE 17:68
Canary Islands 4:99
SANTA CRUZ ISLAND (California)
map (34° 1′N 119° 45′W) 4:31
SANTA CRUZ ISLANDS (Solomon Islands)
map (11° 0′S 166° 15′E) 18:56
SANTA CRUZ WILSON, DOMINGO
Latin American music and dance 12:232
SANTA ELENA (Ecuador)
map (2° 14′S 80° 51′W) 7:52
SANTA ELENA, CAPE OF
map (10° 54′N 85° 57′W) 5:291
SANTA ELENA DE UAIRÉN (Venezuela)
map (4° 37′N 61° 8′W) 19:542
SANTA FE (Argentina)
map (31° 38′S 60° 42′W) 2:149
SANTA FE (province in Argentina)
map (31° 0′S 61° 0′W) 2:149
SANTA FÉ (Cuba)
map (21° 45′N 82° 45′W) 5:377
SANTA FE (New Mexico) 14:139 *illus.*; 17:68
map (35° 42′N 106° 57′W) 14:136
Santa Fe Opera 17:68
SANTA FE (county in New Mexico)
map (35° 30′N 106° 0′W) 14:136
SANTA FE BALDY MOUNTAIN
map (35° 50′N 105° 46′W) 14:136
SANTA FE OPERA 17:68
Indiana, Robert 11:115
SANTA FE TRAIL 8:341 *map*; 17:68 *bibliog., map*; 19:445 *map*
roads and highways 16:237
SANTA GERTRUDIS CATTLE
Brahman cattle 3:440
SANTA INÉS ISLAND
map (53° 45′S 72° 45′W) 4:355
SANTA ISABEL (Argentina)
map (36° 15′S 66° 56′W) 2:149
SANTA ISABEL (Equatorial Guinea) *see* MALABO (Equatorial Guinea)
SANTA ISABEL (Puerto Rico)
map (17° 58′N 66° 24′W) 15:614
SANTA ISABEL ISLAND
map (8° 0′S 159° 0′E) 18:56
SANTA ISABEL PEAK
map (3° 35′N 8° 46′E) 7:226
SANTA LUCIA (Uruguay)
map (34° 27′S 56° 24′W) 19:488
SANTA LUCIA COTZEMALGUAPA (Guatemala)
map (14° 20′N 91° 1′W) 9:389
SANTA LUCIA RANGE
map (36° 0′N 121° 20′W) 4:31
SANTA MARÍA (Argentina)
map (26° 41′S 66° 2′W) 2:149
SANTA MARIA (California)
map (34° 57′N 120° 26′W) 4:31
SANTA MARIA (Portugal)
Azores 2:381–382 *map*
SANTA MARIA (ship)
Pinzón, Martín Alonso 15:309
SANTA MARIA, CAPE OF (Angola)
map (13° 25′S 12° 32′E) 2:5
SANTA MARIA, CAPE OF (Portugal)
map (36° 58′N 7° 54′W) 15:449
SANTA MARIA DEGLI ANGELI, CATHEDRAL OF *see* SANTA MARIA DEL FIORE (Florence)
SANTA MARIA DEL FIORE (Florence) 8:168 *illus.*; 16:150 *illus.*
architecture 2:134–135 *illus.*
Brunelleschi, Filippo 3:524
cathedrals and churches 4:206
dome 6:230 *illus.*
SANTA MARIA DELLA GRAZIE, CHURCH OF
Bramante, Donato 3:452
SANTA MARIA DELLA PACE (Rome)
Cortona, Pietro da 5:279
SANTA MARIA DELLA SALUTE, CHURCH OF
Longhena, Baldassarre 12:408
SANTA MARIA DI LEUCA, CAPE
map (39° 47′N 18° 22′E) 11:321
SANTA MARIA MOUNTAINS
map (34° 50′N 113° 0′W) 2:160
SANTA MARIA PRESSO SAN SATIRO, CHURCH OF
Bramante, Donato 3:451
SANTA MARIA RIVER
map (34° 19′N 34° 31′W) 2:160
SANTA MARTA (Colombia) 17:68
map (11° 15′N 74° 13′W) 5:107
SANTA MONICA (California) 17:68
map (34° 1′N 118° 30′W) 4:31
SANTA MONICA MOUNTAINS
map (34° 10′N 118° 45′W) 4:31
SANTA PAULA (California)
map (34° 21′N 119° 4′W) 4:31
SANTA ROSA (Argentina)
map (36° 37′S 64° 17′W) 2:149

SANTA ROSA (California)
map (38° 26′N 122° 43′W) **4**:31
SANTA ROSA (county in Florida)
map (30° 40′N 87° 0′W) **8**:172
SANTA ROSA (New Mexico)
map (34° 57′N 104° 41′W) **14**:136
SANTA ROSA (Paraguay)
map (21° 46′S 61° 43′W) **15**:77
SANTA ROSA BEACH (Florida)
map (30° 23′N 86° 14′W) **8**:172
SANTA ROSA DE AMANADONA (Venezuela)
map (1° 29′N 66° 55′W) **19**:542
SANTA ROSA DE SUCUMBÍOS (Ecuador)
map (0° 22′N 77° 10′W) **7**:52
SANTA ROSA ISLAND
map (33° 58′N 120° 6′W) **4**:31
SANTA ROSALÍA (Mexico)
map (27° 19′N 112° 17′W) **13**:357
SANTA SOPHIA *see* HAGIA SOPHIA
SANTA SUSANNA, CHURCH OF (Rome)
Maderno, Carlo **13**:40
SANTAL **17**:68–69 *bibliog.*
Mundari **13**:640
SANT'AMBROGIO **17**:69 *bibliog.*
SANTANA DO LIVRAMENTO (Brazil)
map (30° 53′S 55° 31′W) **3**:460
SANTANDER (Spain) **17**:69
climate **18**:141 *table*
map (43° 28′N 3° 48′W) **18**:140
SANTANDER, FRANCISCO DE PAULA **17**:69 *bibliog.*
Colombia **5**:109
SANTAQUIN (Utah)
map (39° 59′N 111° 47′W) **19**:492
SANTARÉM (Brazil)
map (2° 26′S 54° 42′W) **3**:460
SANTARÉM (Portugal)
map (39° 14′N 8° 41′W) **15**:449
SANTARO, MIKHAIL
Weidman, Charles **20**:91
SANTAYANA, GEORGE **17**:69 *bibliog.*
aesthetics **1**:131
SANTEE RIVER
map (33° 14′N 79° 28′W) **18**:98
SANT'ELIA, ANTONIO **17**:69 *bibliog.*
futurism **8**:384
SANTI GIOVANNI E PAOLO, TEATRO
opera houses **14**:401
SANTIAGO (Bolivia)
map (18° 19′S 59° 34′W) **3**:366
SANTIAGO (Chile) **4**:356 *illus.*, *table*; **17**:69–70 *illus.*
climate **18**:86 *table*
history
Valdivia, Pedro de **19**:503
map (33° 27′S 70° 40′W) **4**:355
SANTIAGO (Panama)
map (8° 6′N 80° 59′W) **15**:55
SANTIAGO (Spain) **17**:70
Egas, Enrique **7**:71
Gothic art and architecture **9**:259
map (42° 53′N 8° 33′W) **18**:140
Romanesque art and architecture **16**:282
SANTIAGO ATITLÁN (Guatemala)
map (14° 38′N 91° 14′W) **9**:389
SANTIAGO DE COMPOSTELA, CHURCH OF **16**:282 *illus.*
floor plan **4**:205 *illus.*
SANTIAGO DE CUBA (Cuba) **17**:70
Velázquez de Cuéllar, Diego **19**:537
map (20° 1′N 75° 49′W) **5**:377
SANTIAGO DE GUAYAQUIL *see* GUAYAQUIL (Ecuador)
SANTIAGO DE LOS CABALLEROS (Dominican Republic) **17**:70
map (19° 27′N 70° 42′W) **6**:233
SANTIAGO DEL ESTERO (province in Argentina)
map (28° 0′S 63° 30′W) **2**:149
SANTIAGO LARRE (Argentina)
map (35° 34′S 59° 10′W) **2**:149
SANTIAGO RIVER
map (21° 36′N 105° 26′W) **13**:357
SANTIAM PASS
map (44° 25′N 121° 51′W) **14**:427
SANTO, BASILICA DEL (Padua)
Briosco, Andrea **3**:487
SANTO ANTÃO ISLAND
map (17° 5′N 25° 10′W) **4**:122
SANTO ANTÓNIO (Sao Tome and Principe)
map (1° 39′N 7° 26′E) **17**:72
SANTO ANTÔNIO DO IÇÁ (Brazil)
map (3° 5′S 67° 57′W) **3**:460
SANTO DOMINGO (Dominican Republic) **6**:234 *illus.*, *table*; **17**:70
Latin America, history of **12**:218
map (18° 28′N 69° 54′W) **6**:233
SANTO DOMINGO DE LOS COLORADOS (Ecuador)
map (0° 15′S 79° 9′W) **7**:52
SANTO DOMINGO PUEBLO (New Mexico)
map (35° 31′N 106° 22′W) **14**:136
SANTO FILOMENA (Brazil)
map (9° 7′S 45° 56′W) **3**:460
SANTO SPIRITO, CHURCH OF (Sassia)
cathedrals and churches **4**:207
SANTO TOMÁS (Peru)
map (14° 29′S 72° 6′W) **15**:193
SANTO TOMÉ (Argentina)
map (31° 40′S 60° 46′W) **2**:149
SANTORINI (Greece) *see* THERA (Greece)
SANTOS (art)
folk art **8**:197
Latin American art and architecture **12**:223
SANTOS (Brazil) **17**:70
map (23° 57′S 46° 20′W) **3**:460
SANTOS-DUMONT, ALBERTO **17**:70–71 *bibliog.*
airship **1**:228
SANUSI, AL- **17**:71 *bibliog.*
SANYA DHARMASAKTI
Thailand **19**:141
SAO *see* SMITHSONIAN ASTROPHYSICAL OBSERVATORY
SÃO CARLOS (Brazil)
map (22° 1′S 47° 54′W) **3**:460
SÃO FRANCISCO RIVER **17**:71
map (10° 30′S 36° 24′W) **3**:460
SÃO JOÃO DA MADEIRA (Portugal)
map (40° 54′N 8° 30′W) **15**:449
SÃO JORGE (Portugal)
Azores **2**:381–382 *map*
SÃO JOSÉ DO RIO PRÊTO (Brazil)
map (20° 48′S 49° 23′W) **3**:460
SÃO LUÍS (Brazil)
map (2° 31′S 44° 16′W) **3**:460
SÃO MIGUEL (Portugal)
Azores **2**:381–382 *map*
cities
Ponta Delgada **15**:426
map (37° 47′N 25° 30′W) **15**:449
SÃO NICOLAU ISLAND
map (16° 35′N 24° 15′W) **4**:122
SÃO PAULO (Brazil) **3**:461 *illus.*; **17**:71 *illus.*
map (23° 32′S 46° 37′W) **3**:460
SÃO RAFAEL (Brazil)
map (5° 47′S 36° 55′W) **3**:460
SÃO ROQUE, CAPE
map (5° 29′S 35° 16′W) **3**:460
SÃO SALVADOR DO CONGO (Angola)
map (6° 16′S 14° 15′E) **2**:5
SÃO TIAGO ISLAND
map (15° 5′N 23° 40′W) **4**:122
SÃO TOMÉ (Sao Tome and Principe)
map (0° 20′N 6° 44′E) **17**:72
SÃO TOMÉ ISLAND
map (0° 12′N 6° 39′E) **17**:72
SÃO TOMÉ PEAK
map (0° 16′N 6° 33′E) **17**:72
SÃO TOMÉ AND PRÍNCIPE **17**:71–72 *bibliog.*, *illus.*, *map*
flag **8**:137 *illus.*; **17**:72 *illus.*
SÃO VICENTE ISLAND
map (16° 50′N 25° 0′W) **4**:122
SAÔNE RIVER **17**:72
map (45° 44′N 4° 50′E) **8**:260
SAOURA WADI
map (29° 0′N 0° 55′W) **1**:287
SAP (botany) **17**:72
measurement **3**:413 *illus.*
SAPELE (Nigeria)
map (5° 54′N 5° 41′E) **14**:190
SAPELO ISLAND
map (31° 28′N 81° 15′W) **9**:114
SAPIR, EDWARD **17**:72
Whorf, Benjamin Lee **20**:144
SAPIR-WHORF HYPOTHESIS *see* WHORF-SAPIR HYPOTHESIS
SAPITWA PEAK
map (15° 57′S 35° 36′E) **13**:81
SAPODILLA **17**:73
chewing gum **4**:338
chicle **4**:346
SAPONIFICATION **17**:73 *illus.*
fats and oils **8**:35
SAPPHIRE **3**:296 *illus.*, *table*; **9**:74 *illus.*; **17**:73 *bibliog.*, *illus.*
corundum **5**:279
gems **9**:74–75
SAPPHIRE MOUNTAINS
map (46° 20′N 113° 45′W) **13**:547
SAPPHO **17**:73 *bibliog.*
women in society **20**:201
SAPPINGTON (Missouri)
map (38° 32′N 90° 23′W) **13**:476
SAPPORO (Japan) **17**:73
climate **2**:237 *table*; **11**:363 *table*
map (43° 3′N 141° 21′E) **11**:361
SAPROBE
fungi
mushrooms **13**:659–650
SAPROLITE
ore deposits, major ore deposits **14**:424–425 *table*
SAPSUCKER **17**:73–74 *illus.*
bill **3**:289 *illus.*
SAPT KOSI RIVER
map (26° 30′N 86° 55′E) **9**:37
SAPUCAIA (nut) *see* NUT
SAPULPA (Oklahoma)
map (36° 0′N 96° 6′W) **14**:368
SAPWOOD **17**:74
tree **19**:286–287 *illus.*
wood **20**:205
SAQQARA (Egypt) **17**:74 *bibliog.*
Imhotep **11**:54
Mariette, Auguste **13**:152
Memphis (Egypt) **13**:292
mummy **13**:639
Step Pyramid of King Zoser **15**:635 *illus.*
SAQUENA (Peru)
map (4° 40′S 73° 31′W) **15**:193
SARA PEAK
map (9° 41′N 9° 17′E) **14**:190
SARABAND **17**:74 *bibliog.*
SARACENI, EUGENE *see* SARAZEN, GENE
SARACENS
Italy, history of **11**:328
SARAFANOV, GENNADY VASILIEVICH **17**:74
SARAGOSA (Texas)
map (31° 1′N 103° 39′W) **19**:129
SARAGOSSA (Spain) **17**:74
map (41° 38′N 0° 53′W) **18**:140
SARAGURO (Ecuador)
map (3° 36′S 79° 13′W) **7**:52
SARAH **17**:74
Isaac **11**:285
SARAH LAWRENCE COLLEGE **17**:74
SARAJEVO (Yugoslavia) **17**:74; **20**:342 *illus.*
map (43° 52′N 18° 25′E) **20**:340
World War I **20**:222
SARALAND (Alabama)
map (30° 49′N 88° 4′W) **1**:234
SARAMACCA RIVER
map (5° 51′N 55° 53′W) **18**:364
SARANAC LAKE (New York)
map (44° 20′N 74° 8′W) **14**:149
SARANAC RIVER
map (44° 42′N 73° 27′W) **14**:149
SARANDË (Albania)
map (39° 52′N 20° 0′E) **1**:250
SARANDÍ DEL YI (Uruguay)
map (33° 21′S 55° 38′W) **19**:488
SARANGI
Indian music **11**:103
SARASATE, PABLO DE **17**:74–75 *bibliog.*
SARASOTA (Florida) **17**:75
map (27° 20′N 82° 34′W) **8**:172
SARASOTA (county in Florida)
map (27° 10′N 82° 21′W) **8**:172
SARASOTA BAY
map (27° 23′N 82° 39′W) **8**:172
SARASVATI, DAYANANDA *see* DAYANANDA SARASVATI
SARATOGA (county in New York)
map (43° 0′N 73° 51′W) **14**:149
SARATOGA (Wyoming)
map (41° 27′N 106° 48′W) **20**:301
SARATOGA, BATTLES OF **17**:75 *bibliog.*
American Revolution **1**:360
Burgoyne's surrender **1**:361 *illus.*
Gates, Horatio **9**:58
Morgan, Daniel **13**:578
SARATOGA SPRINGS (New York) **17**:75
map (43° 5′N 73° 47′W) **14**:149
SARATOV (USSR) **17**:75
map (51° 34′N 46° 2′E) **19**:388
SARAVAN (Laos)
map (15° 43′N 106° 25′E) **12**.203
SARAWAK (Borneo) **17**:75
Brooke, Sir James **3**:509
people
Dayak **6**:56
SARAZEN, GENE **17**:75
SARBIEWSKI, MACIEJ
Polish literature **15**:398
SARBIN, THEODORE R.
role **16**:271
SARCINA **17**:75
SARCODINA *see* RHIZOPODA
SARCOIDOSIS
respiratory system disorders **16**:182
SARCOMA **17**:75
cancer **4**:101
respiratory system disorders **16**:182
Rous, Francis Peyton **16**:325
tumor **19**:331
SARCOPHAGUS **17**:75–76 *bibliog.*, *illus.*
catacombs **4**:197
depicting the Battle of Marathon **9**:331 *illus.*
Early Christian art and architecture **7**:10–11
Etruscans **7**:260 *illus.*
funeral customs **8**:364
Merovingian art and architecture **13**:311
Roman art and architecture **16**:276
sculpture **17**:161–162
terra-cotta **19**:120
tomb **19**:230–231
SARDEGNA (Italy) *see* SARDINIA (Italy)
SARDINE **8**:124 *illus.*; **17**:76 *illus.*
world fishing grounds **8**:125 *map*
SARDINIA (Italy) **17**:76
cities
Cagliari **4**:16
Sassari **17**:84
history
Italy, history of **11**:328–330 *maps*
map (40° 0′N 9° 0′E) **11**:321
SARDINIA, KINGDOM OF **17**:76–77 *bibliog.*
Cavour, Camillo Benso, Conte di **4**:226
Risorgimento **16**:228
Savoy (dynasty) **17**:101–102
Victor Amadeus II, Duke of Savoy **19**:572
Victor Emmanuel I, Italian king of Sardinia **19**:572
Victor Emmanuel II, King of Italy **19**:572–573
SARDINIA-PIEDMONT *see* SARDINIA, KINGDOM OF
SARDINIAN LANGUAGES
Romance languages **16**:280
SARDIS (Georgia)
map (32° 58′N 81° 46′W) **9**:114
SARDIS (Mississippi)
map (34° 26′N 89° 55′W) **13**:469
SARDIS (Turkey) **17**:77 *bibliog.*
SARDIS LAKE
map (34° 27′N 89° 43′W) **13**:469
SARDOU, VICTORIEN **17**:77
Tosca **19**:247
well-made play **20**:99
SAREKTJÅKKÅ MOUNTAIN
map (67° 25′N 17° 46′E) **18**:382
SARGASSO SEA **17**:77 *bibliog.*
algae **1**:282
eel **7**:70 *illus.*
floating weed masses **17**:77
Gulf Stream **9**:403
nautical lore **17**:77
ocean currents **17**:77
SARGENT (Georgia)
map (33° 31′N 84° 51′W) **9**:114
SARGENT (Nebraska)
map (41° 38′N 99° 22′W) **14**:70
SARGENT (county in North Dakota)
map (46° 10′N 97° 40′W) **14**:248
SARGENT, DUDLEY ALLEN
gymnastics **9**:413
SARGENT, JOHN SINGER **17**:77–78 *bibliog.*, *illus.*
Daughters of Edward Darley Boit, The **1**:334 *illus.*
Henry James **11**:353 *illus.*
Mr. and Mrs. Isaac Newton Phelps Stokes **17**:77 *illus.*
SARGENT, SIR MALCOLM **17**:78 *bibliog.*
SARGON, KING OF AKKAD **17**:78
Akkad **1**:231
Ebla **7**:36
SARGON II, KING OF ASSYRIA **17**:78
Khorsabad **12**:68
palace **13**:320–321 *illus.*
SARH (Chad)
map (9° 9′N 18° 23′E) **4**:266
SARI (Iran)
map (36° 34′N 53° 4′E) **11**:250
SARIKAMIS, BATTLE OF
World War I **20**:231; **20**:239 *map*
SARIN
chemical and biological warfare **4**:312
SARIR NERASTRO DESERT
map (24° 20′N 20° 37′E) **12**:320
SARIT THANARAT
Thailand **19**:141
SARITA (Texas)
map (37° 13′N 97° 47′W) **19**:129
SARIWON (Korea)
map (38° 31′N 125° 44′E) **12**:113
SARK (Channel Islands) **4**:281 *map*

SARKIA, KAARLO
Finnish literature **8**:99
SARLES (North Dakota)
map (48° 57′N 99° 0′W) **14**:248
SARMATIANS **17**:78
Scythians **17**:167
SARMIENTO (Argentina)
map (45° 36′S 69° 5′W) **2**:149
SARMIENTO, DOMINGO FAUSTINO
17:78 *bibliog.*
Latin American literature **12**:229
SARMIENTO, FÉLIX RUBÉN GARCÍA
see DARÍO, RUBÉN
SARNATH (India) **17**:78
SARNEY, JOSÉ **17**:78
SARNIA (Ontario) **14**:395 *illus.*
map (42° 58′N 82° 23′W) **14**:393
SARNOFF, DAVID **17**:78 *bibliog.*
radio and television broadcasting
16:55–56
SAROD
Indian music **11**:102–103 *illus.*
SARONIKÓS BAY
map (37° 54′N 23° 12′E) **9**:325
SAROS **17**:78
SAROYAN, WILLIAM **17**:78–79 *bibliog.*
SARPEDON **17**:79
SARPY (county in Nebraska)
map (41° 5′N 96° 10′W) **14**:70
SARRAIL, MAURICE P. E.
World War I **20**:234
SARRAUTE, NATHALIE **17**:79 *bibliog.*
SARSAPARILLA **17**:79
greenbrier **9**:350
SARSEN STONES
Stonehenge **18**:283 *illus.*
SARSTOON RIVER
map (15° 53′N 88° 55′W) **3**:183
SARTO, ANDREA DEL *see* ANDREA
DEL SARTO
SARTON, MAY **17**:79 *bibliog.*
SARTRE, JEAN PAUL **8**:319 *illus.*;
17:79–80 *bibliog.*, *illus.*
alienation **1**:294
Being and Nothingness **3**:172
existentialism **7**:332
Nausea **14**:51
No Exit **14**:207
SÁRVÍZ RIVER
map (46° 24′N 18° 41′E) **10**:307
SASAMUNGGA (Solomon Islands)
map (7° 2′S 156° 47′E) **18**:56
SASEBO (Japan)
map (33° 10′N 129° 43′E) **11**:361
SASKATCHEWAN (Canada) **17**:80–83
bibliog., *illus.*, *map*
cities
Moose Jaw **13**:572
Prince Albert **15**:547
Regina **16**:128–129
Saskatoon **17**:83
economic activities **17**:82 *illus.*
education
Regina, University of **4**:92 *table*
Saskatchewan, University of
17:83
Saskatoon, University of
Saskatchewan at **4**:92 *table*
flag **17**:80 *illus.*
government **17**:82
history **17**:82–83
Douglas, T. C. **6**:248
land and resources **17**:80
map (54° 0′N 105° 0′W) **4**:70
mining **17**:82
people **17**:80; **17**:82
Sioux **17**:326
Saskatchewan River **17**:83
SASKATCHEWAN, UNIVERSITY OF
17:83
SASKATCHEWAN RIVER **17**:83
map (53° 12′N 99° 16′W) **17**:81
SASKATOON (Saskatchewan) **17**:83
map (52° 7′N 106° 38′W) **17**:81
SASQUATCH (legendary creature)
abominable snowman **1**:59
SASSACUS
Mohegan **13**:503
Uncas **19**:381
SASSAFRAS **17**:83 *illus.*
SASSAFRAS MOUNTAIN
map (35° 3′N 82° 48′W) **18**:98
SASSAFRAS RIVER
map (39° 23′N 76° 2′W) **13**:188
SASSANDRA (Ivory Coast)
map (4° 58′N 6° 5′W) **11**:335
SASSANDRA RIVER
map (4° 58′N 6° 5′W) **11**:335
SASSANIANS **17**:83–84 *bibliog.*
Ardashir I, King of Persia **2**:144
Asia, history of **2**:254
cities
Ctesiphon **5**:377
Khosru I, King of Persia **12**:68
Persia, ancient **15**:183
Persian art and architecture **15**:184–185
Shapur I, King of Persia **17**:241
Shapur II, King of Persia **17**:241
SASSARI (Italy) **17**:84
map (40° 44′N 8° 33′E) **11**:321
SASSETTA **17**:84 *bibliog.*
SASSOON, SIEGRIED **17**:84
SASSOON HOUSE
Fry, Edwin Maxwell **8**:350
SASTRE, ALFONSO **17**:84 *bibliog.*
SAT *see* EDUCATIONAL
MEASUREMENT
SATAN **17**:84 *bibliog.*
satanism **17**:84
witchcraft **20**:191–192
SATANISM **17**:84 *bibliog.*
SATAUA (Western Samoa)
map (13° 28′S 172° 40′W) **20**:117
SATCHMO *see* ARMSTRONG, LOUIS
SATELLITE **17**:84–85 *bibliog.*, *tables*
Earth
Moon **13**:561–566
space exploration **18**:123
history
Kowal, Charles T. **12**:126
Kuiper, Gerard **12**:135
Lassell, William **12**:214
Pickering, William Henry **15**:293
Jupiter (planet) **11**:472–474 *illus.*,
table
Callisto **4**:46
Europa (astronomy) **7**:267
Ganymede **9**:38
Io **11**:238
Mars (planet) **13**:167
Deimos **6**:85
Phobos **15**:249
Neptune (planet) **14**:88–89
Triton **14**:88; **18**:49 *illus.*;
19:304
orbit **2**:275 *illus.*
Pluto
Charon **15**:373
Roche's limit **16**:247
Saturn (astronomy) **17**:90–91
Hyperion: Lassell, William
12:214
Phoebe: Pickering, William
Henry **15**:293
Titan (astronomy) **19**:210
solar system **18**:49–50
Uranus (astronomy) **19**:478–479
table
Miranda **13**:463
SATELLITE, ARTIFICIAL **17**:85–87
bibliog., *illus.*
Applications Technology Satellite
2:89–90
astronautics **2**:274–276
basic elements **17**:85–86
biosatellite **3**:276
communications satellites **5**:144–145; **17**:86
Early Bird **7**:8
Echo **7**:39
INTELSAT **11**:205–206
mass communication **13**:202–203
Molniya **13**:512
Relay **16**:137
Syncom **18**:406
telephone-satellite terminals
19:79 *map*
Telstar **19**:91
France
Centre National d'Études
Spatiales **4**:255
guidance and control systems
9:393–394
history **17**:85
intelligence gathering **11**:204
ionosphere **11**:242
land and sea observation satellites
17:87
Landsat **12**:184–185
oceanography **14**:345
SEASAT **17**:176
laser **12**:213
life-support systems **12**:331–333
navigation satellites **17**:86
NAVSTAR **14**:62
Transit **19**:272
orbits **17**:85 *illus.*
photoelectric cell **15**:260
polonium **15**:417
reconnaissance satellites **17**:86
BMEWS **3**:348
Discoverer **6**:189
military warning and detection
systems **13**:422
SAMOS **17**:47
Vela **19**:536
rockets and missiles **16**:251
Agena (rocket) **1**:183
Ariane (rocket) **2**:153
Atlas (missile) **2**:297
Delta (rocket) **6**:95
Proton **15**:578
Saturn (rocket) **17**:91
sounding rocket **18**:77
Thor (rocket) **19**:177
scientific research satellites **17**:86
Alouette **1**:308
Explorer **7**:338–339
GEOS **9**:119
High Energy Astronomical
Observatory **10**:161
IMP **11**:60
International Geophysical Year
11:220
OAO **14**:312–313
observatory, astronomical
14:318–319
OGO **14**:354–355 *table*
OSO **14**:456
Space Telescope **18**:137
Sputnik **18**:201
Uhuru **19**:374
ultraviolet astronomy **19**:379
Vanguard **19**:519
solar energy **18**:43 *illus.*
space exploration **18**:119–123
space law **18**:132
tracking station **19**:262
Union of Soviet Socialist Republics
Cosmos **5**:289–290
Vandenberg Air Force Base **19**:518
weather satellites **17**:86–87
GOES **9**:222
hurricane and typhoon **10**:319
meteorology **13**:342–343
Nimbus **14**:198 *table*
Synchronous Meteorological
Satellite **18**:406
TIROS **19**:208–209
World Weather Watch **20**:281
SATIE, ERIK **17**:87–88 *bibliog.*, *illus.*
SATIN **17**:88
SATIN SPAR
gypsum **9**:415–416
SATINFLOWER *see* HONESTY (botany)
SATINWOOD **17**:88
rue **16**:339
SATIRE **17**:88 *bibliog.*
See also COMEDY; WIT
American literature **1**:342–343;
1:347
Albee, Edward **1**:252
Allen, Woody **1**:300
Anderson, Maxwell **1**:402
Barth, John **3**:96–97
Barthelme, Donald **3**:97
Cheever, John **4**:309–310
Ciardi, John **4**:428
Connecticut Wits **5**:196
Dunne, Finley Peter **6**:301
Franklin, Benjamin **8**:282; **8**:284
Heller, Joseph **10**:114–115
Mad (periodical) **13**:37
Nasby, Petroleum V. **14**:23
Pynchon, Thomas **15**:634
Smith, Seba **17**:370
Vonnegut, Kurt, Jr. **19**:634
West, Nathanael **20**:107
Canadian literature
Haliburton, T.C. **10**:20
Dutch and Flemish literature
Praise of Folly, The **15**:489
English literature
Amis, Kingsley **1**:372
Austen, Jane **2**:326
Barclay, Alexander **3**:80
Butler, Samuel (1612–1680) **3**:592
Butler, Samuel (1835–1902) **3**:592
Carroll, Lewis **4**:169
Congreve, William **5**:188
Dryden, John **6**:284–285
Fielding, Henry **8**:73
Gascoigne, George **9**:53
Gay, John **9**:63
Goldsmith, Oliver **9**:236
Gulliver's Travels **9**:404
Huxley, Aldous **10**:324
Jonson, Ben **11**:445–446
Marston, John **13**:174
Marvell, Andrew **13**:181
Oldham, John **14**:376
Orwell, George **14**:451
Peacock, Thomas Love **15**:124
Pope, Alexander **15**:430
Shaw, George Bernard **17**:245–246
Smollet, Tobias **17**:374
Swift, Jonathan **18**:389
Thackeray, William Makepeace
19:138
Waugh, Evelyn **20**:70
Wycherley, William **20**:298
erotic and pornographic literature
7:234
French literature
Adamov, Arthur **1**:93
Bernard, Tristan **3**:220
Boileau-Despreaux, Nicolas
3:362
Candide **4**:107
Cyrano de Bergerac, Savinien
5:409
Gargantua and Pantagruel **9**:47
Mirbeau, Octave **13**:463
Molière **13**:508–509
Rabelais, François **16**:31–32
Voltaire **19**:631–632
German literature
Brant, Sebastian **3**:456
Brecht, Bertolt **3**:470–471
Brentano, Clemens **3**:473
Busch, Wilhelm **3**:585
Fischart, Johann Baptist **8**:110
Grass, Günter **9**:297–298
Sternheim, Carl **18**:261
Greek literature, ancient
Aristophanes **2**:155–156
Clouds, The **5**:68
Lucian **12**:450
Hebrew and Yiddish literature
Mendele Mokher Sefarim **13**:294
irony **11**:279
Italian literature
Aretino, Pietro **2**:146
Brancati, Vitaliano **3**:452
Fo, Dario **8**:192
Latin literature **12**:234
Horace **10**:233–234
Juvenal **11**:480
Lucilius **12**:450
Persius **15**:188
Petronius Arbiter **15**:215
Satyricon **17**:93
mock epic **13**:489
music, stage, film
calypso **4**:49
Gilbert and Sullivan **9**:179
interlude **11**:214
operetta **14**:403
puppet **15**:627
Sturges, Preston **18**:309
Norwegian literature
Enemy of the People, An **7**:171–172
pictorial
caricature **4**:149–150
cartoon (editorial and political)
4:176–178
Daumier, Honoré **6**:45–46
Forain, Jean Louis **8**:219
Grosz, George **9**:371
imperialism **11**:62 *illus.*
Polish literature
Lem, Stanisław **12**:279–280
Russian literature
Bulgakov, Mikhail Afanasievich
3:553–554
Dead Souls **6**:65
Saltykov Shchedrin, Mikhail
Yevgrafovich **17**:39
Spanish literature
Cervantes Saavedra, Miguel de
4:261
Don Quixote **6**:236
Quevedo y Villegas, Francisco
Gómez de **16**:25
Swedish literature
Dalin, Olof von **6**:13
SATKANIA (Bangladesh)
map (22° 4′N 92° 3′E) **3**:64
SATO EISAKU **17**:88
SATPURA RANGE
map (22° 0′N 78° 0′E) **11**:80
SATSUNAN ISLANDS
map (29° 0′N 130° 0′E) **11**:361
SATTAR, ABDUS
Bangladesh **3**:66
SATU MARE (Romania)
map (47° 48′N 22° 53′E) **16**:288
SATURATION **17**:88
solubility **18**:58
SATURDAY
calendar **4**:28
SATURDAY EVENING POST, THE
(periodical)
Curtis, Cyrus H. K. **5**:395
periodical **15**:169–170 *illus.*
Rockwell, Norman **16**:261
SATURDAY NIGHT MASSACRE
Cox, Archibald **5**:322
SATURDAY REVIEW (periodical)
Canby, Henry Seidel **4**:100
Cousins, Norman **5**:317
SATURN (automobile)
automotive industry **2**:368
SATURN (mythology) **17**:91
SATURN (planet) **17**:88–91 *bibliog.*,
illus., *table*
atmosphere **17**:89

SATURN (cont.)
magnetic field **17**:89
origin and evolution **17**:89
planets **15**:329–331
radio astronomy **16**:48
rings **17**:89–91 *illus., table*
Huygens, Christiaan **10**:325
Maxwell, James Clerk **13**:241
satellites **17**:89–91 *illus., table*
Lassell, William **12**:214
Pickering, William Henry **15**:293
Titan (astronomy) **19**:210
solar system **18**:46–49 *illus., table*
space exploration **18**:126
Pioneer **15**:309–310
Voyager **19**:637–638
SATURN (rocket) **17**:91–92 *bibliog., illus.*; **18**:120 *illus.*
Apollo program **2**:80
Kennedy Space Center **12**:44
rockets and missiles **16**:257–258 *illus.*
von Braun, Wernher **19**:633
SATYAGRAHA
civil disobedience **5**:10
SATYR **17**:92
Marsyas **13**:175
SATYR PLAY **17**:92
theater, history of the **19**:144
SATYRIASIS **17**:93 *bibliog.*
SATYRICON (book) **17**:93 *bibliog.*
Petronius Arbiter **15**:215
SATYROS
Mausoleum at Halicarnassus **17**:217
SAUCIER (Mississippi)
map (30° 38′N 89° 8′W) **13**:469
SAUD, IBN *see* IBN SAUD, KING OF SAUDI ARABIA
SAUD, KING OF SAUDI ARABIA **17**:93
SAUDÁRKRÓKUR (Iceland)
map (65° 46′N 19° 41′W) **11**:17
SAUDI ARABIA **17**:93–96 *bibliog., illus., map, table*
agriculture **17**:95
borders **17**:93
cities
Dhahran **6**:148
Hofuf **10**:197
Jidda **11**:417
Mecca **13**:258–259 *illus.*
Medina **13**:275
Riyadh **16**:234
climate **17**:94 *table*
economic activity **17**:95
education **2**:104 *illus.*
Middle Eastern universities **13**:410–412 *table*
flag **17**:93 *illus.*
government **17**:95
history **17**:96
Fahd, King **8**:8
Faisal, King **8**:11
Ibn Saud, King **11**:5–6
Khalid, King **12**:65
Saud, King **17**:93
Yamani, Ahmed Zaki **20**:316
Kuwait (country) **12**:140
land and resources **17**:93–94
meteorite craters **13**:339
mineral resources **17**:94
map (25° 0′N 45° 0′E) **2**:232
mining and industry **17**:95 *illus.*
people **17**:95
petroleum industry **13**:398 *illus.*
physical features
Nafud **14**:5
regions
Hejaz **10**:110
tourism **17**:95
trade **17**:95
transportation **17**:95
SAUER, CARL **17**:96 *bibliog.*
SAUERKRAUT
cabbage **4**:4
SAUGEEN RIVER
map (44° 30′N 81° 22′W) **14**:393
SAUGERTIES (New York)
map (42° 5′N 73° 57′W) **14**:149
SAUK (American Indians) **17**:96 *bibliog.*
Black Hawk War **3**:315
Chief Keokuk **11**:121 *illus.*
Fox **8**:255
SAUK (county in Wisconsin)
map (43° 25′N 89° 57′W) **20**:185
SAUK CENTRE (Minnesota)
map (45° 44′N 94° 57′W) **13**:453
SAUK CITY (Wisconsin)
map (43° 17′N 89° 43′W) **20**:185
SAUK RAPIDS (Minnesota)
map (45° 34′N 94° 9′W) **13**:453
SAUK RIVER
map (45° 36′N 94° 10′W) **13**:453
SAÜL (French Guiana)
map (3° 37′N 53° 12′W) **8**:311
SAUL, KING OF ISRAEL **17**:96 *bibliog.*
SAULT SAINTE MARIE (Michigan) **17**:96
map (46° 30′N 84° 21′W) **13**:377
SAULT SAINTE MARIE (Ontario) **17**:96
map (46° 31′N 84° 20′W) **14**:393
SAULT SAINTE MARIE CANALS **17**:96–97
SAUMÂTRE, LAKE
map (18° 35′N 72° 0′W) **10**:15
SAUNA
bath **3**:122
SAUNDERS (county in Nebraska)
map (41° 15′N 96° 40′W) **14**:70
SAUNDERS, CHARLES
French and Indian Wars **8**:313 *map*
SAURIMO (Angola)
map (9° 39′S 20° 24′E) **2**:5
SAURISCHIA
carnivores
Allosaurus **1**:303
Compsognathus **5**:158
Dimetrodon **6**:177
Gorgosaurus **9**:251
Ornitholestes **14**:447
Podokesaurus **15**:377
Procompsognathus **15**:561
Struthiomimus **18**:303
Tyrannosaurus **19**:367
dinosaur **6**:179–181 *illus.*
herbivores
Brachiosaurus **3**:435
Brontosaurus **3**:504–505
Diplodocus **6**:185–186
Edaphosaurus **7**:54
Plateosaurus **15**:358–359
SAUROPODS
Brachiosaurus **3**:435
Brontosaurus **3**:504–505
dinosaur **6**:180–181 *illus.*
Diplodocus **6**:185–186
Edaphosaurus **7**:54
Plateosaurus **15**:358–359
SAURY **17**:97
SAUSAGE **17**:97
SAUSAGE TREE **17**:97
SAUSALITO (California)
map (37° 51′N 122° 29′W) **4**:31
SAUSSURE, FERDINAND DE **17**:97 *bibliog.*
historical linguistics **10**:183
synchronic linguistics **12**:356
SAUSSURE, HORACE BÉNÉDICT DE
hygrometer **10**:345
mountain climbing **13**:621 *illus.*
SAUSSURE, NICHOLAS THEODORE DE
photosynthesis **15**:275
SAUTEURS (Grenada)
map (12° 14′N 61° 38′W) **9**:358
SAUVÉ, JEANNE **17**:97
SAVA RIVER **17**:97
map (44° 50′N 20° 26′E) **20**:340
SAVAGE (Maryland)
map (39° 8′N 76° 49′W) **13**:188
SAVAGE, EDWARD **17**:97 *bibliog.*
SAVAGE, MICHAEL JOSEPH **17**:97 *bibliog.*
SAVAGE ISLAND *see* NIUE (New Zealand)
SAVAGE MIND, THE (book) **17**:97
SAVAI'I **1**:366 *map*
map (13° 35′S 172° 25′W) **20**:117
Western Samoa **20**:116
SAVAK (secret police)
Iran **11**:253
SAVALOU (Benin)
map (7° 56′N 1° 58′E) **3**:200
SAVANG VATTHANA, KING
Laos **12**:204
SAVANNA (Illinois)
map (42° 5′N 90° 8′W) **11**:42
SAVANNA (Oklahoma)
map (34° 50′N 95° 51′W) **14**:368
SAVANNA-LA-MAR (Jamaica)
map (18° 13′N 78° 8′W) **11**:351
SAVANNA LIFE **17**:97–99 *bibliog., illus.*
animal life **17**:97–99
climate **17**:98
climax community **5**:59
forest **8**:227
lion **12**:360
plant life **17**:97–99
SAVANNAH (Georgia) **9**:117 *illus.*; **17**:99
map (32° 4′N 81° 5′W) **9**:114
SAVANNAH (grasslands) *see* GRASSLANDS
SAVANNAH (Missouri)
map (39° 56′N 94° 50′W) **13**:476
SAVANNAH (nuclear-powered ship)
ship **17**:272 *illus.*; **17**:275
SAVANNAH (steamship) **17**:99 *bibliog., illus.*
ship **17**:273
SAVANNAH (Tennessee)
map (35° 14′N 88° 14′W) **19**:104
SAVANNAH BEACH (Georgia)
map (32° 1′N 80° 51′W) **9**:114
SAVANNAH RIVER
map (32° 2′N 80° 53′W) **18**:98
SAVANNAKHET (Laos)
map (16° 33′N 104° 45′E) **12**:203
SAVARIN, ANTHELME BRILLAT- *see* BRILLAT-SAVARIN, ANTHELME
SAVDI, MOSHE
Israel **11**:305
SAVE RIVER
map (21° 0′S 35° 2′E) **13**:627
SAVERY, THOMAS **17**:99
boiler **3**:362
Newcomen, Thomas **14**:165
steam engine **18**:241 *illus.*
SAVIGNY, FRIEDRICH KARL VON **17**:99 *bibliog.*
law **12**:242–243
SAVING AND INVESTMENT **17**:100 *bibliog.*
banking systems **3**:68–69
bond **3**:376
cost-benefit analysis **5**:290
credit union **5**:336
dollar averaging **6**:225
economics **7**:49
economy, national **7**:50
income, national **11**:75
interest **11**:206–207
investment banking **11**:238
monetary theory **13**:525
multiplier effect **13**:638
mutual fund **13**:687
savings bank **17**:100
savings bond **17**:100–101
savings and loan association **17**:100
Securities and Exchange Commission **17**:181
stock (finance) **18**:273–274
stock market **18**:274–275
SAVINGS BANK **17**:100
banking systems **3**:68–69
life insurance **12**:330
money **13**:527
SAVINGS BOND **17**:100–101 *bibliog.*
SAVINGS AND LOAN ASSOCIATION **17**:100 *bibliog.*
banking systems **3**:68–69
Federal Home Loan Bank Board **8**:41
money **13**:527
SAVITAIPALE (Finland)
map (61° 12′N 27° 42′E) **8**:95
SAVONA (Italy)
map (44° 17′N 8° 30′E) **11**:321
SAVONAROLA, GIROLAMO **17**:101 *bibliog., illus.*
execution **17**:101 *illus.*
Machiavelli, Nicolò **13**:18
SAVONIUS ROTOR
windmills and wind power **20**:172–173 *illus.*
SAVONNERIE
rugs and carpets **16**:343
SAVOONGA (Alaska)
map (63° 42′N 170° 27′W) **1**:242
SAVORGNAN DE BRAZZA, PIERRE PAUL FRANÇOIS CAMILLE *see* BRAZZA, PIERRE PAUL FRANÇOIS CAMILLE SAVORGNAN DE
SAVORY (botany) **17**:101
SAVOY (dynasty) **17**:101–102 *bibliog., map*
Geneva (Switzerland) **9**:91
Savoy (region) **17**:102
SAVOY (region) **17**:102 *map*
boundaries under Louis XIV **8**:269 *map*
Italian city-state **11**:328 *map*
Italian unification **11**:330 *map*
Savoy (dynasty) **17**:101–102
Victor Amadeus II, Duke of Savoy **19**:572
SAVOY THEATER (London)
D'Oyly Carte, Richard **6**:253
SAVRASOV, ALEKSEI
Russian art and architecture **16**:362
SAVU SEA
map (9° 40′S 122° 0′E) **11**:147
SAVUSAVU (Fiji)
map (16° 16′S 179° 21′E) **8**:77
SAW **12**:395 *illus.*; **17**:102–103 *bibliog., illus.*
SAWATCH RANGE
map (39° 10′N 106° 25′W) **5**:116
SAWBACK TURTLE **17**:103 *illus.*
SAWFISH **17**:103–104 *illus.*
SAWFLY **17**:104 *illus.*
SAWMILL
lumber **12**:455 *illus.*; **12**:457–458
SAWTOOTH MOUNTAINS **11**:29 *illus.*
map (43° 50′N 114° 25′W) **11**:26
SAWTOOTH RIDGE
map (48° 10′N 12° 2′W) **20**:35
SAWYER (North Dakota)
map (48° 5′N 101° 3′W) **14**:248
SAWYER (county in Wisconsin)
map (45° 52′N 91° 8′W) **20**:185
SAX, ADOLPHE
saxophone **17**:105
tuba **19**:326
SAXE, MAURICE, COMTE DE **17**:104 *bibliog.*
SAXE-MEININGEN, GEORGE II, DUKE OF **17**:104 *bibliog.*
acting **1**:87
SAXIFRAGE **17**:104
tundra **19**:332 *illus.*
SAXIS (Virginia)
map (37° 55′N 75° 43′W) **19**:607
SAXO GRAMMATICUS **17**:104 *bibliog.*
Gesta Danorum
Danish literature **6**:32
SAXON (Wisconsin)
map (46° 29′N 90° 25′W) **20**:185
SAXONS **17**:104–105
Albert I, Margrave of Brandenburg **1**:254
Charlemagne **4**:289
Germany, history of **9**:149
Henry I, King of Germany **10**:128
Otto I, King of Germany and Holy Roman Emperor (Otto the Great) **14**:462–463
Saxony **17**:105
SAXONY **17**:105 *bibliog., illus.*
cities
Karl-Marx-Stadt (East Germany) **12**:27
Oldenburg **14**:375–376
Osnabrück **14**:455–456
Frederick III (Frederick the Wise) **8**:292
German territories c.1176 **9**:149 *map*
Germany 1815–1871 **9**:153 *map*
Henry the Lion, Duke of Saxony and Bavaria **10**:123
history
Seven Years' War **17**:218 *map*
SAXOPHONE **13**:676 *illus.*; **17**:105–106 *illus.*
Bechet, Sidney **3**:150
Coltrane, John **5**:124
Hawkins, Coleman **10**:77
sound frequencies produced **18**:73 *table*
wind instruments **20**:171 *illus.*
Young, Lester **20**:334
SAXTON (Pennsylvania)
map (40° 13′N 78° 15′W) **15**:147
SAXTON, JOSEPH **19**:450 *illus.*
SAY, JEAN BAPTISTE **17**:106 *bibliog.*
economics **7**:48
SAYAN MOUNTAINS
map (52° 45′N 96° 0′E) **19**:388
SAYAN TURKIC LANGUAGES
Ural-Altaic languages **19**:476
SAYBROOK (Illinois)
map (40° 26′N 88° 32′W) **11**:42
SAYE AND SELE, WILLIAM FIENNES, 1ST VISCOUNT **17**:106
SAYERS, DOROTHY L. **17**:106 *bibliog.*
SAYERS, GALE **17**:106 *bibliog.*
SAYLORVILLE LAKE
map (41° 48′N 93° 46′W) **11**:244
SÄYNÄTSALO (FINLAND) CIVIC CENTER **1**:49 *illus.*
SAYRE (Oklahoma)
map (35° 18′N 99° 38′W) **14**:368
SAYRE (Pennsylvania)
map (41° 59′N 76° 32′W) **15**:147
SAYREVILLE (New Jersey)
map (40° 28′N 74° 21′W) **14**:129
SAYRI TUPAC
Inca **11**:73
SCABIES *see* SKIN DISEASES
SCAFELL PIKES MOUNTAIN
map (54° 27′N 3° 12′W) **19**:403
SCALA (family) **17**:106 *bibliog.*
SCALAR **17**:106
linear algebra **12**:353
vector analysis **19**:530
SCALAWAGS **17**:106 *bibliog.*
Reconstruction **16**:109
SCALE (biology)
fish **8**:113–114 *illus.*
skin diseases **17**:341
SCALE (cartography)
maps and mapmaking **13**:139–140; **13**:140–141
SCALE (music) **17**:106–107 *bibliog.*
folk music **8**:203

Guido d'Arezzo 9:394
Japanese music 11:380–382 *illus.*
mode 13:489
music, non-Western 13:667–668
raga 16:69
tone 19:233
twelve-tone system 19:358–359
SCALE (weighing device)
balance 3:30–31
platform
Fairbanks, Thaddeus 8:9
SCALE INSECT 17:107
Kermes 12:59
SCALIA, ANTONIN 17:107; 18:355 *illus.*
SCALIGER (family) *see* SCALA (family)
SCALIGER, JULIUS CAESAR 17:107
SCALLION 14:391 *illus.*
SCALLOP 13:510 *illus.*; 17:107 *bibliog., illus.*
calico scallop 11:229 *illus.*
shell 17:251 *illus.*
SCALP
dandruff 6:31
ringworm 16:226
skin diseases 17:342
SCALPING 17:107 *bibliog.*
head-hunting 10:85
Indians, American 11:129 *illus.*
SCALY ANTEATER *see* PANGOLIN
SCAMMON (Kansas)
map (37° 17′N 94° 49′W) 12:18
SCAMMON BAY (Alaska)
map (61° 53′N 165° 38′W) 1:242
SCAMOZZI, VINCENZO 17:107 *bibliog.*
Teatro Olimpico 19:59
SCANDERBEG *see* SKANDERBEG
SCANDIA (Kansas)
map (39° 48′N 97° 47′W) 12:18
SCANDINAVIA, HISTORY OF 17:107–111 *bibliog., illus., maps*
See also the subheading history under names of specific countries, e.g., DENMARK; FINLAND; ICELAND; NORWAY; SWEDEN
people
migration to the United States 11:55 *map*
prior to 1520
Iron Age 17:108
Margaret I, Queen of Denmark, Norway, and Sweden 13:149
Middle Ages 17:108–109
prehistory 17:107–108
Union of Kalmar 17:108 *map*
Viking Age 17:108
Vikings 19:594–596
1520–1700
Reformation 17:109
Swedish age of greatness 17:109 *map*
1700–1900
enlightened despots 17:109–110
modernization 17:110
national liberalism 17:110
revolutionary age 17:110
1900-present
Nordic Council 14:218
postwar years 17:111
welfare and internationalism 17:110
World War II *see* WORLD WAR II
SCANDINAVIAN ART AND ARCHITECTURE 17:111–113 *bibliog., illus.*
See also names of specific art forms subdivided by names of Scandinavian countries, e.g., ARCHITECTURE—Finland; PAINTING—Norway; etc; names of specific artists, e.g., VIGELAND, GUSTAV; ZORN, ANDERS; etc.
Danish "Golden Age" 17:113
Danish Renaissance architecture 17:112
Finland 8:97
folk art 8:195–196 *illus.*
Frederiksborg Castle 17:112 *illus.*
furniture 8:379
house (in Western architecture) 10:268–269 *illus.*
medieval Scandinavian art 17:111–112
Munch, Edvard 13:640
Norwegian 19th-century art 17:113–114
Oseberg ship burial 14:453
prehistoric art 15:509; 17:111
Romanesque and Gothic churches 17:111–112
rugs and carpets 16:340; 16:343
Scandinavian 20th-century art 17:114
stave churches and runestones 17:111–112 *illus.*
Swedish baroque and rococo art 17:112–113
Swedish Renaissance architecture 17:112
Swedish 19th-century art 17:114
Viking art 17:111 *illus.*; 19:595 *illus.*
SCANDINAVIAN LITERATURE *see* DANISH LITERATURE; FINNISH LITERATURE; ICELANDIC LITERATURE; NORWEGIAN LITERATURE; SWEDISH LITERATURE
SCANDINAVIAN MUSIC 17:114 *bibliog.*
SCANDINAVIAN MYTHOLOGY *see* NORSE MYTHOLOGY
SCANDIUM 17:114 *bibliog.*
abundances of common elements 7:131 *table*
element 7:130 *table*
Group IIIB periodic table 15:167
Mendeleyev, Dmitry Ivanovich 13:295
metal, metallic element 13:328
transition elements 19:273 *table*
SCANNING (electronics) 17:114
cathode-ray tube 4:211
guidance and control systems 9:394
television transmission 19:88
video technology 19:576b; 19:576L; 19:576m; 19:576n
SCANSION
versification 19:562
SCAP *see* SCHIAPARELLI, ELSA
SCAPA (Alberta)
map (51° 52′N 111° 59′W) 1:256
SCAPA FLOW 17:114–115
SCAPEGOAT MOUNTAIN
map (47° 19′N 112° 50′W) 13:547
SCAPHOPODA *see* TUSK SHELL
SCAPOLITE 17:115
tetragonal system 19:127
SCAPPOOSE (Oregon)
map (45° 45′N 122° 53′W) 14:427
SCAR 17:115
body marking 3:357
skin diseases 17:341
SCARAB BEETLE *see* BEETLE
SCARBORO (Barbados)
map (13° 4′N 59° 33′W) 3:75
SCARBOROUGH (England) 17:115
map (54° 17′N 0° 24′W) 19:403
SCARBOROUGH (Trinidad and Tobago)
map (11° 11′N 60° 44′W) 19:300
SCARLATTI (family) 17:115 *bibliog., illus.*
SCARLATTI, ALESSANDRO
Scarlatti (family) 17:115 *illus.*
SCARLATTI, DOMENICO
Scarlatti (family) 17:115
SCARLET FEVER 17:115 *bibliog.*
mastoiditis 13:217
strep throat 18:297
SCARLET LETTER, THE (book) 17:116
Hawthorne, Nathaniel 10:79
SCARLET PAINTBRUSH (botany) *see* INDIAN PAINTBRUSH (botany)
SCARLET PIMPERNEL (plant) 13:266 *illus.*
pimpernel 15:304
SCARLET TANAGER *see* TANAGER
SCARNE, JOHN 17:116 *bibliog.*
SCARP *see* ESCARPMENT (geology)
SCARRON, PAUL 17:116
burlesque and travesty 3:572
SCARRY, RICHARD 17:116
SCAVENGER BEETLE 3:167 *illus.*
SCENE (literature)
narrative and dramatic devices 14:23
SCENEDESMUS 17:116
SCENERY (theater) *see* THEATER ARCHITECTURE AND STAGING
SCHAAK, J. S. C.
Wolfe, James (portrait) 20:197 *illus.*
SCHAAN (Liechtenstein)
map (47° 10′N 9° 31′E) 12:325
SCHACHT, HJALMAR 17:116 *bibliog.*
money 13:527 *illus.*
Nuremberg Trials 14:297 *illus.*
SCHADOW, GOTTFRIED 17:116 *bibliog.*
Brandenburg Gate 3:453
SCHAEFER, CARL
Canadian art and architecture 4:90
SCHAEFER, VINCENT JOSEPH 17:116
SCHAERBEEK (Belgium)
map (50° 51′N 4° 23′E) 3:177
SCHAFF, PHILIP 17:116 *bibliog.*
SCHAFFHAUSEN (Switzerland)
map (47° 42′N 8° 38′E) 18:394
SCHALLY, ANDREW VICTOR 17:117
SCHANFIELD, LEWIS MAURICE *see* FIELDS, LEW
SCHAPIRO, MEYER 17:117 *bibliog.*
SCHARNHORST, GERHARD JOHANN DAVID VON 17:117 *bibliog.*
SCHAROUN, HANS 17:117 *bibliog.*
SCHAUFUSS, PETER 17:117
SCHAUMBURG (Illinois)
map (42° 2′N 88° 5′W) 11:42
SCHECHNER, RICHARD 17:117
acting 1:88
SCHECHTER, SOLOMON 17:117 *bibliog.*
SCHECHTER POULTRY CORPORATION v. UNITED STATES 17:117
National Recovery Administration 14:45
SCHEDULED CASTES *see* UNTOUCHABLES
SCHEEL, FRITZ
Philadelphia Orchestra, The 15:229
SCHEEL, WALTER 17:118
SCHEELE, CARL WILHELM 17:115 *bibliog., illus.*
SCHEELITE 17:118
SCHEER, REINHARD
World War I 20:235
SCHEFFEL, J. H.
Linnaeus, Carolus 12:359 *illus.*
SCHEFFER-BOYADEL, REINHARD VON
World War I 20:226
SCHEFFERVILLE (Quebec)
map (54° 48′N 66° 50′W) 16:18
SCHEFFLERA 17:118
SCHEHERAZADE (ballet) 4:408 *illus.*
SCHEHERAZADE (fictional character) 17:118
SCHEIDEMANN, PHILIPP 17:118 *bibliog.*
Germany, history of 9:155
World War I 20:246
SCHELDE RIVER *see* SCHELDT RIVER
SCHELDT RIVER 17:118
Antwerp 2:71
Delta Plan 6:95–96
map (51° 22′N 4° 15′E) 3:177
SCHELER, MAX 17:118–119 *bibliog., illus.*
existentialism 7:332
phenomenology 15:225
SCHELL CREEK RANGE
map (39° 10′N 114° 40′W) 14:111
SCHELLING, FRIEDRICH WILHELM JOSEPH VON 17:119 *bibliog.*
SCHEMATIC DIAGRAM
circuit, electric 4:436–438 *illus.*
SCHENCK v. UNITED STATES 17:119 *bibliog.*
freedom of speech 8:298
freedom of the press 8:296
SCHENECTADY (New York) 17:119
map (42° 47′N 73° 53′W) 14:149
SCHENECTADY (county in New York)
map (42° 47′N 73° 53′W) 14:149
SCHEPER, HINNERK 3:129 *illus.*
SCHÉRER, JEAN MAURICE *see* ROHMER, ERIC
SCHERERVILLE (Indiana)
map (41° 30′N 87° 27′W) 11:111
SCHERRER, PAUL
Debye, Peter 6:72
SCHERTEL, HANS VON, BARON
hydrofoil 10:336
SCHERZO 17:119
SCHIAPARELLI, ELSA 17:119–120 *bibliog.*
fashion design 8:32
SCHIAPARELLI, GIOVANNI VIRGINIO 17:120
SCHICK TEST 17:120
SCHIEDAM (Netherlands)
map (51° 55′N 4° 24′E) 14:99
SCHIELE, EGON 17:120 *bibliog., illus.*
Portrait of Frederike Beer 17:120 *illus.*
SCHIKANEDER, EMANUEL 17:120
Magic Flute, The 13:51
SCHILLER, FRIEDRICH
Humboldt, Wilhelm von, Freiherr 10:301
SCHILLER, JOHANN CHRISTOPH FRIEDRICH VON 9:133 *illus.*; 17:120–121 *bibliog., illus.*
Weimar (East Germany) 20:94
SCHINDEWOLF, OTTO
catastrophism 4:201
SCHINDLER, RUDOLF M. 17:121 *bibliog.*
SCHINKEL, KARL FRIEDRICH 17:121 *bibliog.*
SCHIPPERKE 6:219 *illus.*; 17:121–122 *bibliog., illus.*
SCHIPPERS, THOMAS 17:122 *bibliog.*
SCHIRRA, WALTER M., JR. 17:122 *bibliog.*
Apollo program 2:81
astronaut 2:274 *illus.*
Gemini program 9:72
Mercury program 13:308
SCHISM, GREAT 17:122–123 *bibliog.*
Eastern Schism 17:122
Leo IX, Pope 12:288
Michael Cerularius 13:371
Western Schism 17:122
Avignon papacy 17:122
Benedict XIII, Antipope 3:197
Constance, Council of 5:207
Ferrara-Florence, Council of 8:58
Gerson, Jean le Charlier de 9:159
John XXIII, "Antipope" 11:429
Martin V, Pope 13:180
Pisa, Council of 15:315
Urban VI, Pope 19:485
Vincent Ferrer, Saint 19:600
SCHIST 17:123
kyanite 12:143
metamorphic rock 13:331–332 *illus., table*
phyllite 15:278
pyrophyllite 15:638
zoisite 20:371
SCHISTOSOMIASIS 17:123
gastrointestinal tract disease 9:57
SCHIZOMYCETES
bacteria 3:17
SCHIZOPHRENIA 17:123–124 *bibliog., illus.*
Bateson, Gregory 3:121
behavioral genetics 3:170
Bleuler, Eugen 3:331
catatonia 4:201
causal theories 17:123–124
complex (psychology) 5:157
dementia 6:96
dissociation (psychology) 6:198
hallucinogens 10:24
Kraepelin, Emil 12:126
Laing, R. D. 12:167
megavitamin therapy 13:280
Meyer, Adolf 13:368
paranoia 15:80
psychopathy 15:601
psychotropic drugs 15:604
reserpine 16:176
shock therapy 17:279
symptoms 17:123
Szasz, Thomas 18:415
SCHLAFLY, PHYLLIS
Equal Rights Amendment 7:224
SCHLEGEL, AUGUST WILHELM VON 17:124 *bibliog.*
SCHLEGEL, FRIEDRICH VON 17:124 *bibliog.*
SCHLEICHER (county in Texas)
map (30° 52′N 100° 30′W) 19:129
SCHLEICHER, KURT VON 17:124
SCHLEIDEN, MATTHIAS JAKOB 17:138–139
anatomy 1:396
biology 3:269
cytology 5:411
histology 10:181
SCHLEIERMACHER, FRIEDRICH 17:125 *bibliog., illus.*
SCHLEMMER, OSKAR 17:125 *bibliog., illus.*
Bauhaus 3:129–130 *illus.*
Bauhaus Staircase 3:129 *illus.*
Group of Fourteen in Imaginary Architecture 17:125 *illus.*
SCHLESINGER, ARTHUR M. 17:125
SCHLESINGER, ARTHUR M., JR. 17:125
SCHLESINGER, B. W. *see* WALTER, BRUNO
SCHLESINGER, FRANK 17:125–126
Yerkes Observatory 20:327
SCHLESINGER, JOHN 17:126
SCHLESWIG (Iowa)
map (42° 10′N 95° 26′W) 11:244
SCHLESWIG-HOLSTEIN (West Germany) 17:126 *map*
cities
Kiel 12:74
Lübeck 12:446–447
Denmark 6:112–113
Germany 1815–1871 9:153 *map*
Helgoland 10:111
map (54° 31′N 9° 33′E) 9:140
Scandinavia, history of 17:109–110
SCHLEY (county in Georgia)
map (32° 15′N 84° 20′W) 9:114
SCHLEY, WINFIELD SCOTT 17:126
Sampson, William T. 17:48
SCHLEYER, JOHANN MARTIN
languages, artificial 12:197

SCHLICK, MORITZ
  logical positivism **12**:397
SCHLIEFFEN, ALFRED, GRAF VON **17**:126 *bibliog.*
  Moltke, Helmuth Johannes Ludwig Graf von **13**:513
  World War I **20**:222
SCHLIEFFEN PLAN
  Schlieffen, Alfred, Graf von **17**:126
  World War I **20**:223–224
SCHLIEMANN, HEINRICH **2**:122 *illus.*; **17**:126–127 *bibliog.*, *illus.*
  archaeology **2**:121
  gold and silver work **9**:228
  Mycenae **13**:690
  Orchomenos **14**:420
  Tiryns **19**:209
  Troy (archaeological site) **19**:312–313
SCHLIEREN PHOTOGRAPHY
  photography, scientific **15**:271; **15**:272 *illus.*
SCHLÜTER, ANDREAS **17**:127 *bibliog.*, *illus.*
  monument to Frederick William the Great Elector **17**:127 *illus.*
SCHLUTER, PAUL
  Denmark **6**:113
SCHMALKALDIC WAR
  Charles V, Holy Roman Emperor **4**:295
  Philip of Hesse **15**:232
SCHMELING, MAX
  Louis, Joe **12**:422
SCHMELZER, JOHANN
  music, history of Western **13**:666
SCHMIDT, HELMUT **17**:127 *illus.*
SCHMIDT, JOHANNES
  eel **7**:71
SCHMIDT, JOOST **3**:129 *illus.*
SCHMIDT, MAARTEN **17**:128
  quasar **16**:14–15
SCHMIDT-ROTTLUFF, KARL **3**:520 *illus.*; **17**:128 *bibliog.*
SCHMIDT TELESCOPE **17**:128 *bibliog.*, *illus.*
  Anglo-Australian Telescope **1**:416
  astrophotography **2**:285
  Byurakan Astrophysical Observatory **3**:604
  telescope **19**:80–81 *illus.*
SCHMITT, HARRISON H. **17**:128 *bibliog.*
  Apollo program **2**:84; **17**:128
  Senate **17**:128
  U.S. Geological Survey **17**:128
SCHMITZ, ETTORE *see* SVEVO, ITALO
SCHMUCKER, SAMUEL SIMON **17**:128 *bibliog.*
SCHNABEL, ARTUR **17**:128–129 *bibliog.*
SCHNABEL, JULIAN
  neoexpressionism **14**:83
SCHNAUZER **6**:215 *illus.*; **6**:220 *illus.*; **17**:129 *bibliog.*, *illus.*
SCHNEIDER, LEONARD ALFRED *see* BRUCE, LENNY
SCHNITTKE, ALFRED
  Russian music **16**:369
SCHNITZER, EDWARD *see* EMIN PASHA
SCHNITZLER, ARTHUR **17**:129 *bibliog.*, *illus.*
SCHNORR VON CAROLSFELD, JULIUS **17**:130 *bibliog.*
SCHOENBERG, ARNOLD **9**:131 *illus.*; **17**:130 *bibliog.*, *illus.*
  atonality **2**:312
  serial music **17**:208
  twelve-tone system **19**:358
SCHOENFLIES, ARTHUR M.
  mineral **13**:439
SCHOFIELD, JOHN MCALLISTER **17**:130
SCHOHARIE (New York)
  map (42° 40′N 74° 19′W) **14**:149
SCHOLARSHIPS, FELLOWSHIPS, AND LOANS **17**:130–131 *bibliog.*
  Center for Advanced Study in the Behavioral Sciences **4**:249
  National Merit Scholarships **14**:35
SCHOLASTIC APTITUDE TEST *see* EDUCATIONAL MEASUREMENT
SCHOLASTICISM **17**:131–132 *bibliog.*, *illus.*
  Abelard, Peter **1**:55–56
  Albertus Magnus, Saint **1**:259–260
  Alexander of Hales **1**:275
  Anselm, Saint **2**:35
  Aquinas, Saint Thomas **2**:94–95
  Bacon, Roger **3**:14
  Bonaventure, Saint **3**:376
  Dominicans **6**:234
  Duns Scotus, John **6**:301
  Erigena, John Scotus **7**:230
  Gilson, Étienne **9**:183
  Grosseteste, Robert **9**:371
  Maritain, Jacques **13**:157
  Peter Lombard **15**:200
  Suárez, Francisco **18**:312
  William of Champeaux **20**:154
SCHOLDER, FRITZ **17**:132 *bibliog.*
SCHOLEM, GERSHOM GERHARD **17**:133 *bibliog.*
SCHOLLANDER, DON **17**:133
SCHÖNBRUNN, TREATY OF
  Napoleonic Wars **14**:19
SCHÖNBRUNN PALACE **17**:133 *bibliog.*
  Fischer von Erlach, Johann Bernhard **8**:111
SCHÖNEBECK (Germany, East and West)
  map (52° 1′N 11° 44′E) **9**:140
SCHONGAUER, MARTIN **17**:133 *bibliog.*, *illus.*
  The Temptation of Saint Anthony **9**:292 *illus.*; **17**:133 *illus.*
SCHOOL OF AMERICAN BALLET
  New York City Ballet **14**:155
SCHOOL OF ATHENS, THE *see* RAPHAEL
SCHOOL FOR SCANDAL, THE (play) **17**:134
  Sheridan, Richard Brinsley **17**:257
SCHOOLCRAFT (Michigan)
  map (42° 7′N 85° 38′W) **13**:377
SCHOOLCRAFT (county in Michigan)
  map (46° 15′N 86° 10′W) **13**:377
SCHOOLCRAFT, HENRY ROWE **17**:134 *bibliog.*
SCHOOLS *see* EDUCATION
SCHOONER (ship) **17**:134 *bibliog.*
  clipper ship **5**:60
SCHOPENHAUER, ARTHUR **17**:134 *bibliog.*, *illus.*
SCHOUTEN, WILLEM
  Horn, Cape **10**:238
SCHOUWEN ISLAND
  map (51° 43′N 3° 50′E) **14**:99
SCHRADER, JULIUS
  Leopold von Ranke **16**:87 *illus.*
SCHREIFFER, JOHN ROBERT **17**:134
  superconductivity **18**:350
SCHREINER, OLIVE **17**:134–135 *bibliog.*
SCHREYER, EDWARD RICHARD **17**:135
SCHRIEVER (Louisiana)
  map (29° 45′N 90° 49′W) **12**:430
SCHRÖDER, FRIEDRICH L.
  theater, history of the **19**:148
SCHRÖDINGER, ERWIN **17**:135 *bibliog.*, *illus.*
  chemistry, history of **4**:328
  de Broglie wavelength **6**:58
SCHRÖDINGER EQUATION
  Dirac, Paul **6**:186–187
  quantum mechanics **16**:11
SCHUBERT, FRANZ **16**:293 *illus.*; **17**:135–136 *bibliog.*, *illus.*
  Fischer-Dieskau, Dietrich **8**:111
  Schwind, Moritz von **17**:140
  symphony **18**:405
SCHUCHERT, CHARLES
  paleogeography **15**:36
SCHULBERG, BUDD **17**:136
SCHULLER, GUNTHER **17**:136
SCHULLER, ROBERT
  religious broadcasting **16**:142
SCHULTZ, DUTCH **17**:136
SCHULTZE, MAX **17**:289
SCHULZ, CHARLES M. **17**:136
  Peanuts
    comic strip **5**:136
SCHULZE, JOHANN HEINRICH
  photography, history and art of **15**:267
SCHUMACHER, E. F. **17**:136 *bibliog.*
SCHUMAN, ROBERT **17**:136 *bibliog.*
  European Community **7**:299
SCHUMAN, WILLIAM HOWARD **17**:136 *bibliog.*
  Juilliard School, The **11**:465
SCHUMAN PLAN
  Schuman, Robert **17**:136
SCHUMANN, CLARA **9**:131 *illus.*; **17**:136 *bibliog.*
SCHUMANN, ROBERT **9**:131 *illus.*; **17**:137 *bibliog.*, *illus.*
  Schumann, Clara **17**:136
  toccata **19**:220
  Zwickau (East Germany) **20**:384
SCHUMPETER, JOSEPH A. **17**:137 *bibliog.*
  on capitalism **4**:125
SCHURZ, CARL **17**:137–138 *bibliog.*, *illus.*
SCHUSCHNIGG, KURT VON **17**:138
SCHUSSELE, CHRISTIAN
  Men of Progress **19**:450 *illus.*
SCHUSSING *see* SKIING
SCHÜTZ, HEINRICH **4**:406 *illus.*; **17**:138 *bibliog.*
  German and Austrian music **9**:130
  music, history of Western **13**:666
  recitative **16**:107
SCHUTZSTAFFEL *see* SS
SCHUYLER (county in Illinois)
  map (40° 10′N 90° 35′W) **11**:42
SCHUYLER (county in Missouri)
  map (40° 30′N 92° 30′W) **13**:476
SCHUYLER (Nebraska)
  map (41° 27′N 97° 4′W) **14**:70
SCHUYLER (county in New York)
  map (42° 23′N 76° 52′W) **14**:149
SCHUYLER, PHILIP JOHN **17**:138 *bibliog.*
SCHUYLKILL (county in Pennsylvania)
  map (40° 40′N 76° 15′W) **15**:147
SCHUYLKILL HAVEN (Pennsylvania)
  map (40° 38′N 76° 10′W) **15**:147
SCHUYLKILL RIVER
  map (39° 53′N 75° 12′W) **15**:147
SCHWAB, CHARLES MICHAEL **17**:138 *bibliog.*
SCHWABE, SAMUEL HEINRICH **17**:138
SCHWÄBISCHE ALB MOUNTAINS
  map (48° 25′N 9° 30′E) **9**:140
SCHWANN, THEODOR, AND SCHLEIDEN, MATTHIAS JAKOB **3**:270 *illus.*; **17**:138–139 *bibliog.*
  anatomy **1**:396
  biology **3**:269
SCHWARTZ, DELMORE **17**:139 *bibliog.*
SCHWARTZ, MAURICE
  Yiddish theater **20**:328
SCHWARZENBERG (family) **17**:139 *bibliog.*
SCHWARZENBERG, FELIX, FÜRST ZU
  Francis Joseph, Emperor of Austria **8**:275
  Revolutions of 1848 **16**:189
  Schwarzenberg (family) **17**:139
SCHWARZENBERG, KARL PHILIPP, FÜRST ZU
  Schwarzenberg (family) **17**:139
SCHWARZKOPF, ELISABETH **17**:139 *bibliog.*
SCHWARZSCHILD, KARL **17**:139
  astronomy, history of **2**:279
  relativity **16**:136
  Schwarzschild radius **17**:139
SCHWARZSCHILD, MARTIN **17**:139
SCHWARZSCHILD RADIUS **17**:139 *bibliog.*, *illus.*
  black hole **3**:315
SCHWARZWALD *see* BLACK FOREST
SCHWECHAT (Austria)
  map (48° 8′N 16° 29′E) **2**:348
SCHWEDT (Germany, East and West)
  map (53° 3′N 14° 17′E) **9**:140
SCHWEICKART, RUSSELL L. **17**:139 *bibliog.*
  Apollo program **17**:135
SCHWEINFURT (Germany, East and West)
  map (50° 3′N 10° 14′E) **9**:140
SCHWEINFURTH, GEORG
  Ubangi River **19**:370
SCHWEITZER, ALBERT **17**:139–140 *bibliog.*, *illus.*
  Widor, Charles Marie **20**:145
SCHWENKFELD VON OSSIG, KASPAR **17**:140 *bibliog.*
SCHWERIN (East Germany) **17**:140
  map (53° 38′N 11° 25′E) **9**:140
SCHWIND, MORITZ VON **17**:140 *bibliog.*
SCHWINGER, JULIAN SEYMOUR **17**:141
  Tomonaga, Sin-itiro **19**:232
SCHWITTERS, KURT **17**:141 *bibliog.*, *illus.*
  Merzbild **17**:141 *illus.*
SCHWYZ (Switzerland)
  map (47° 2′N 8° 40′E) **18**:394
SCIACCA (Italy)
  map (37° 30′N 13° 6′E) **11**:321
SCIATICA **17**:141
  neuralgia **14**:105
SCIENCE
  anthropology **2**:52
  archaeology **2**:116–126
  astronomy and astrophysics **2**:281–285
  atmospheric sciences **2**:304
  biology **3**:268–271
  botany **3**:412–414
  chemistry **4**:323–324
  chronology **4**:419
  computer **5**:160f
  geology **9**:105–106
  hydrologic sciences **10**:342
  information science **11**:172
  mathematics **13**:221–222
  medicine **13**:267–272
  metallurgy **13**:329–331
  meteorology **13**:341–343
  metric system **13**:345–347
  museums of science and industry **13**:659
  oceanography **14**:344–346
  philosophy **15**:242
  photography, scientific **15**:271–272
  physics **15**:280–281
  psychology **15**:593–595
  science, education in **17**:141–142
  science, philosophy of **17**:141–143
  scientific associations **17**:144–146
  sociology **18**:28–30
  technology **19**:59–60
  zoology **20**:375–378
SCIENCE (periodical)
  American Association for the Advancement of Science **1**:336
  Bell, Alexander Graham **3**:185
SCIENCE, EDUCATION IN **17**:141–1412
  Franklin Institute **8**:285
  laboratory instruction
    Bergman, Sir Torbern **3**:210
  Middle Eastern universities **13**:411
  National Science Foundation **14**:45
  secondary education **17**:180
SCIENCE, PHILOSOPHY OF **17**:142–143 *bibliog.*
  Bacon, Francis **3**:13–14
  causality **4**:219
  current issues **17**:142–143
  deduction **6**:77
  empiricism **17**:142
  ethics and morality in research **17**:143
  law, physical **12**:248
  Leibniz, Gottfried Wilhelm von **12**:276
  Mach, Ernst **13**:17
  mathematics **13**:221
  Occam's razor **14**:320
  philosophy **15**:243
  Poincaré, Henri **15**:380
  Popper, Sir Karl Raimund **15**:432
  professional and educational organizations
    Philosophy of Science Association **17**:141
  rationalism **16**:92; **17**:141–142
  Snow, C. P., Baron Snow **18**:3
SCIENCE AND EDUCATION ADMINISTRATION, U.S.
  Agriculture, U.S. Department of **1**:194
SCIENCE FICTION **17**:143–144 *bibliog.*, *illus.*
  See also Hugo Award; Nebula Award
  authors
    Aldiss, Brian W. **1**:269
    Asimov, Isaac **2**:260
    Ballard, J. G. **3**:41
    Bester, Alfred **3**:229
    Blish, James **3**:333
    Bradbury, Ray **3**:436
    Čapek, Karel **4**:122
    Clarke, Arthur C. **5**:40
    De Camp, L. Sprague **6**:58
    Dick, Philip **6**:156
    Dickson, Gordon R. **6**:158–159
    Gold, H. L. **9**:227
    Heinlein, Robert **10**:109
    Hoyle, Sir Fred **10**:286
    Le Guin, Ursula **12**:254
    Lem, Stanisław **12**:279–280
    Lewis, C. S. **12**:305
    Lovecraft, H. P. **12**:438
    Pohl, Frederik **15**:380
    Sturgeon, Theodore **18**:309
    Van Vogt, A. E. **19**:516
    Verne, Jules **19**:559
    Vonnegut, Kurt, Jr. **19**:634
    Wells, H. G. **20**:101
    Wilhelm, Kate **20**:151
    Wilkins, John **20**:152
    Williamson, Jack **20**:162
    Wyndham, John **20**:299
  Martian Chronicles, The **13**:178
  periodicals **17**:143–144
  pulp magazines **15**:620
  Twenty Thousand Leagues Under the Sea **19**:360
SCIENCE MUSEUMS *see* MUSEUMS OF SCIENCE AND INDUSTRY
SCIENTIFIC AMERICAN (periodical)
  Gardner, Martin **9**:45
SCIENTIFIC ASSOCIATIONS **17**:144–146 *bibliog.*, *tables*

See also the subheading professional and educational organizations under the names of specific sciences and technologies, e.g., CHEMISTRY; ENGINEERING; etc.
Académie des Sciences **1**:69
Academy of Sciences of the USSR **1**:71
Accademia dei Lincei **1**:72
Accademia del Cimento **1**:72
Akademie der Wissenschaften der DDR **1**:229
American Academy of Arts and Sciences **1**:327
American Association for the Advancement of Science **1**:336
American Astronomical Society **1**:337
American Chemical Society **1**:337
American Geophysical Union **1**:340
American Institute of Aeronautics and Astronautics **1**:341
American Institute of Biological Sciences **1**:341
American Institute of Chemists **1**:341
American Institute of Physics **1**:341
American Medical Association **1**:348
American Philosophical Society **1**:352
American Physical Society **1**:352
British Interplanetary Society **3**:497
Brookhaven National Laboratory **3**:510
Brooklyn Botanic Garden and Arboretum **3**:510
Chinese Academy of Sciences **4**:377
Desy Laboratory **6**:133
Dominion Arboretom and Botanic Garden **6**:234–235
European Organization for Nuclear Research **7**:301
Federation of American Scientists **8**:44
Fermi National Accelerator Laboratory **8**:56
Franklin Institute **8**:285
Frascati National Laboratory **8**:286
High Altitude Observatory **10**:161
Institut de France **11**:195
Institute of Navigation **11**:195
International Bureau of Weights and Measures **11**:219
International Geophysical Union **11**:220
international scientific unions **17**:146 *table*
Jackson Laboratory **11**:344
Jet Propulsion Laboratory **11**:407
JOIDES **11**:438
Lamont-Doherty Geological Observatory **12**:175
Lincoln Laboratory **12**:350
Los Alamos National Scientific Laboratory **12**:416
Lunar and Planetary Laboratory **12**:135
Max Planck Society for the Advancement of Science **13**:238–239
National Academy of Sciences **14**:27
National Geographic Society **14**:33
National Institutes of Health **14**:34
National Meteorological Center **14**:35
National Radio Astronomy Observatory **14**:45
National Science Foundation **14**:45
National Weather Service **14**:46
Oak Ridge National Laboratory **14**:312
Pasteur Institute **15**:108
principal American specialized and professional scientific associations **17**:145 *table*
principal national scientific academies **17**:145 *table*
Royal Astronomical Society **16**:329
Royal Institution of Great Britain **16**:330
Royal Society **16**:331
Salk Institute for Biological Studies **17**:34
Scripps Institution of Oceanography **17**:158
Sloan-Kettering Institute for Cancer Research **17**:363
United States National Arboretum **19**:463
Wistar Institute **20**:190
Woods Hole Marine Biological Laboratory **20**:212
World Meteorological Organization **20**:219
SCIENTIFIC METHOD *see* SCIENCE, PHILOSOPHY OF; SCIENTIFIC RESEARCH
SCIENTIFIC NOTATION **17**:146 *bibliog.*
SCIENTIFIC RESEARCH
information science **11**:172
invention **11**:233
pharmaceutical industry **15**:220
social psychology **18**:12
technology **19**:60
tissue culture **19**:210
SCIENTOLOGY **17**:146 *bibliog.*
SCILLY ISLANDS (England) **17**:146 *bibliog.*
map (49° 55′N 6° 20′W) **19**:403
SCINTILLATION **17**:146
scintillation counter **17**:146
SCINTILLATION COUNTER **17**:146 *bibliog.*
alpha particle
atomic nucleus **2**:309
detector, particle **6**:133–134
gamma-ray astronomy **9**:34
photomultiplier **15**:274
radioactivity **16**:62
SCION (botany) *see* GRAFTING (botany); PLANT PROPAGATION
SCIOTO (county in Ohio)
map (38° 50′N 82° 58′W) **14**:357
SCIOTO COMPANY
Ohio Company of Associates **14**:362
SCIOTO RIVER
map (38° 44′N 83° 1′W) **14**:357
SCIPIO (Utah)
map (39° 15′N 112° 6′W) **19**:492
SCIPIO AFRICANUS MAJOR **17**:147 *bibliog., illus.*
Punic Wars **15**:625 *illus.*
Rome, ancient **16**:298 *illus.*
SCIPIO AFRICANUS MINOR **17**:147 *bibliog.*
Punic Wars **15**:625
Rome, ancient **16**:300
SCITUATE (Massachusetts)
map (42° 12′N 70° 44′W) **13**:206
SCITUATE RESERVOIR
map (41° 47′N 71° 36′W) **16**:198
SCLC *see* SOUTHERN CHRISTIAN LEADERSHIP CONFERENCE
SCLERA
eye **7**:348–349 *illus.*
SCLERITIS
eye diseases **7**:351
SCLERODERMA
collagen disease **5**:102–103
SCLEROSIS (medicine) **17**:147
amyotrophic lateral sclerosis **1**:386–387
arteriosclerosis **2**:213
atherosclerosis **2**:291–292
multiple sclerosis **13**:638
nervous system, diseases of the **14**:95–96
otosclerosis **7**:8
SCOBEE, FRANCIS R. **17**:147
SCOBEY (Montana)
map (48° 47′N 105° 25′W) **13**:547
SCOFIELD, PAUL **17**:147
SCOLIOSIS **17**:147
SCOOBA (Mississippi)
map (32° 50′N 88° 29′W) **13**:469
SCOPAS **17**:147–148 *bibliog.*
Tegea **19**:72
SCOPES TRIAL **17**:148 *bibliog.*
Bryan, William Jennings **3**:529
Darrow, Clarence S. **6**:39
Darwin, Charles **6**:42
SCOPOLAMINE **17**:148
SCORDATURA
Biber, Heinrich Ignaz Franz von **3**:237
SCORE (artificial satellite)
communications satellite **5**:144–145
SCOREL, JAN VAN **17**:148 *bibliog.*
SCORIA **17**:148
SCORPION **2**:106 *illus.*; **11**:192 *illus.*; **17**:148 *bibliog., illus.*
arachnid **2**:106–107
SCORPION FISH **17**:148 *illus.*
SCORPION FLY **17**:148–149 *illus.*
SCORPIUS **17**:149
SCORSESE, MARTIN
De Niro, Robert **6**:62
SCOTCH WHISKEY *see* WHISKEY
SCOTER
coot **5**:248
SCOTIA SEA **17**:149
SCOTISM
Duns Scotus, John **6**:301
SCOTLAND **17**:149–152 *bibliog., illus., map*
See also UNITED KINGDOM
archaeology
broch **3**:500
lake dwelling **12**:171
megalith **13**:278–279
Skara Brae **17**:332
stone alignments **18**:281–282 *illus.*
art **19**:409
bridge (engineering)
Telford, Thomas **19**:90
cities
Aberdeen **1**:56
Coatbridge **5**:81
Dundee **6**:299
Dunfermline **6**:299–300
Edinburgh **7**:57 *illus.*
Glasgow **9**:197
Greenock **9**:353
Inverness **11**:233
Kirkcaldy **12**:89
Motherwell **13**:607
Paisley **15**:25
Perth **15**:191
Saint Andrews **17**:16
clans **5**:36
Glencoe, Massacre of **9**:207
tartan **19**:40–41
counties (former)
Aberdeen **1**:56
Angus **2**:7–8
Argyll **2**:153
Ayr **2**:379
Banff **3**:62
Berwick **3**:226–227
Bute **3**:591
Caithness **4**:19
Clackmannan **5**:34–35
Dunbarton **6**:299
Inverness **11**:233
Kincardine **12**:78
Kinross **12**:85
Kirkcudbright **12**:89
Lanark **12**:177
Moray **13**:575
Nairn **14**:8
Orkney Islands **14**:445
Peebles **15**:132
Perth **15**:191
Renfrew **16**:157
Ross and Cromarty **16**:318
Roxburgh **16**:329
Selkirk **17**:192
Stirling **18**:272
Sutherland **18**:372
Wigtown **20**:147
dance
folk dance **8**:199 *illus.*
sword dance **18**:399
economy **17**:151
education
Aberdeen, University of **1**:56
British education **3**:493–495
Edinburgh, University of **7**:57
Glasgow, University of **9**:197
Saint Andrews, University of **17**:16
universities **3**:493 *table*
government and politics **17**:151; **19**:411
history **17**:151–152
Alexander III, King **1**:276
Antonine Wall **2**:70
Baliol, John de **3**:38
Bannockburn, Battle of **3**:71
Bishops' Wars **3**:298
Covenanters **5**:319
David I, King **6**:49
David II, King **6**:49
Douglas (family) **6**:246–247
Dundee, John Graham of Claverhouse, 1st Viscount **6**:299
Edward I, King of England **7**:67–68
English Civil War **7**:189
Glencoe, Massacre of **9**:207
Great Britain, history of **9**:309–316
Hundred Years' War **10**:304
Jacobites **11**:346
James I, King of England **11**:355
James I, King of Scotland **11**:356–357
James IV, King **11**:357
James V, King **11**:357
Macbeth, King **13**:7
Malcolm III, King (Malcolm Canmore) **13**:86
Mary, Queen of Scots **13**:186–187
Picts **15**:294
Rob Roy **16**:239–240
Robert I, King of Scotland (Robert the Bruce) **16**:241
Stuart (family) **18**:304
Test Acts **19**:126
Wallace, Sir William **20**:14–15
William the Lion, King **20**:154
land **17**:150; **19**:405
language **19**:407
Celtic languages **4**:241
literature *see* SCOTTISH LITERATURE
Loch Ness monster **12**:386
map (57° 0′N 4° 0′W) **19**:403
mist **13**:481
music
bagpipe **3**:22–23 *illus.*
Musgrave, Thea **13**:659
paleoecology **15**:35 *illus.*
people **17**:150–151; **19**:407
Celts **4**:241–243
Gaels **9**:7
physical features
Ben Nevis **3**:195
Great Glen **17**:149 *illus.*
Hebrides **10**:102–103
Highlands, The **10**:162
Shetland Islands **17**:259
Skye **17**:346
railroad **16**:75 *illus.*
regions
Borders **3**:397
Central **4**:250
Dumfries and Galloway **6**:298
Fife **8**:74
Grampian **9**:283
Highland **10**:162
Lothian **12**:420
Strathclyde **18**:291
Tayside **19**:51
religion
Hill, D. O., and Adamson, Robert **10**:164
rivers, lakes, and waterways
Clyde, River **5**:72
Forth, River **8**:238
Lomond, Loch **12**:400
Ness, Loch **14**:96–97
Tay, River **19**:48
Tweed, River **19**:358
sports
golf **9**:239
ice skating **11**:13
tartan **19**:40
SCOTLAND (county in Missouri)
map (40° 25′N 92° 10′W) **13**:476
SCOTLAND (county in North Carolina)
map (34° 50′N 79° 30′W) **14**:242
SCOTLAND (South Dakota)
map (43° 9′N 97° 43′W) **18**:103
SCOTLAND, CHURCH OF **17**:152–153 *bibliog.*
Great Britain, history of **9**:314
Knox, John **12**:102–103; **17**:152
Melville, Andrew **13**:289
Scotland, Free Church of **17**:153
SCOTLAND, FREE CHURCH OF **17**:153
Chalmers, Thomas **4**:272; **17**:153
Scotland, Church of **17**:153
SCOTLAND NECK (North Carolina)
map (36° 2′N 77° 32′W) **14**:242
SCOTLAND YARD **17**:153 *bibliog.*
police **15**:396
SCOTLANDVILLE (Louisiana)
map (30° 31′N 91° 11′W) **12**:430
SCOTT (county in Arkansas)
map (34° 52′N 94° 15′W) **2**:166
SCOTT (county in Illinois)
map (39° 38′N 90° 27′W) **11**:42
SCOTT (county in Indiana)
map (38° 41′N 85° 46′W) **11**:111
SCOTT (county in Iowa)
map (41° 35′N 90° 35′W) **11**:244
SCOTT (county in Kansas)
map (38° 30′N 100° 55′W) **12**:18
SCOTT (county in Kentucky)
map (38° 18′N 84° 35′W) **12**:47
SCOTT (county in Minnesota)
map (44° 42′N 93° 32′W) **13**:453
SCOTT (Mississippi)
map (33° 36′N 91° 4′W) **13**:469
SCOTT (county in Mississippi)
map (32° 25′N 89° 30′W) **13**:469
SCOTT (county in Missouri)
map (37° 5′N 89° 35′W) **13**:476
SCOTT (county in Tennessee)
map (36° 20′N 84° 30′W) **19**:104
SCOTT (county in Virginia)
map (36° 40′N 82° 40′W) **19**:607
SCOTT, ADRIAN
Hollywood Ten, The **10**:204
SCOTT, CAPE
map (50° 47′N 128° 26′W) **3**:491

SCOTT, DAVID R. 17:153 *bibliog.*
space walk 18:128 *illus.*
SCOTT, DRED *see* DRED SCOTT v. SANDFORD
SCOTT, DUKINFIELD HENRY
paleobotany 15:32
SCOTT, DUNCAN CAMPBELL 17:153 *bibliog.*
SCOTT, GEORGE C. 17:153
SCOTT, SIR GEORGE GILBERT 17:153 *bibliog.*
Gothic Revival 9:262
Saint Pancras Station, London 19:576 *illus.*
SCOTT, JAMES, DUKE OF MONMOUTH *see* MONMOUTH, JAMES SCOTT, DUKE OF
SCOTT, MOUNT (Oklahoma)
map (34° 44′N 98° 32′W) 14:368
SCOTT, MOUNT (Oregon)
map (42° 56′N 122° 1′W) 14:427
SCOTT, ROBERT FALCON 2:44 *illus., map;* 17:153–154 *bibliog., illus.*
exploration 7:338
SCOTT, SIR WALTER 7:199 *illus.;* 17:154 *bibliog., illus.*
Guy Mannering
Dandie Dinmont terrier 6:31
Ivanhoe 11:333
Lucia di Lammermoor 12:450
Rob Roy 16:240
Roxburgh (Scotland) 16:329
SCOTT, WINFIELD 17:154–155 *bibliog., illus.*
Cherokee 4:332
Civil War, U.S. 5:20
Mexican War 13:351–354 *illus., map;* 19:445 *illus.*
SCOTT, WINFIELD TOWNLEY 17:155 *bibliog.*
SCOTT CITY (Kansas)
map (38° 29′N 100° 54′W) 12:18
SCOTT CITY (Missouri)
map (37° 12′N 89° 32′W) 13:476
SCOTT PEAK
map (44° 21′N 112° 50′W) 11:26
SCOTTDALE (Pennsylvania)
map (40° 6′N 79° 35′W) 15:147
SCOTTISH DEERHOUND 6:216 *illus.;* 17:155 *bibliog., illus.*
SCOTTISH LITERATURE 17:155 *bibliog.*
Barbour, John 3:79
Barrie, Sir James Matthew 3:94–95
Beattie, James 3:145
Bridie, James 3:485
Burns, Robert 3:578–579
Campbell, Thomas 4:66
Carlyle, Thomas 4:152–153
Cronin, A. J. 5:359
Davidson, John 6:49
Douglas, Gavin 6:247
Drummond, William 6:282
Dunbar, William 6:298–299
Fergusson, Robert 8:54
Galt, John 9:22
Grahame, Kenneth 9:281
Henryson, Robert 10:130
Hogg, James 10:198
Lindsay, Sir David 12:352
MacDiarmid, Hugh 13:11
Macpherson, James 13:36
Muir, Edwin 13:634
Ramsay, Allan 16:81
Scott, Sir Walter 17:154
Sharp, William 17:244
Thomson, James (1700–48) 19:175
Thomson, James (1834–82) 19:176
SCOTTISH NATIONAL PARTY
United Kingdom 19:411
SCOTTISH TARTAN CENTRE
tartan 19:41
SCOTTISH TERRIER 6:220 *illus.;* 17:155 *bibliog., illus.*
SCOTTS BLUFF (county in Nebraska)
map (41° 50′N 103° 40′W) 14:70
SCOTTS BLUFF NATIONAL MONUMENT 14:71 *illus.*
SCOTTSBLUFF (Nebraska)
map (41° 52′N 103° 40′W) 14:70
SCOTTSBORO (Alabama)
map (34° 40′N 86° 2′W) 1:234
SCOTTSBORO CASE
Powell v. *Alabama* 15:481
SCOTTSBURG (Indiana)
map (38° 41′N 85° 46′W) 11:111
SCOTTSDALE (Arizona)
privatization 15:558
map (33° 30′N 111° 56′W) 2:160
SCOTTSVILLE (Kentucky)
map (36° 45′N 86° 11′W) 12:47
SCOTUS, JOHN DUNS *see* DUNS SCOTUS, JOHN
SCOURING RUSH *see* HORSETAIL (botany)
SCOUT (launch vehicle) 17:155–156 *bibliog.*
SCOUTING 17:156 *bibliog.*
Baden-Powell, Robert 3:19
SCR *see* SILICON-CONTROLLED RECTIFIER
SCRABBLE (game) 17:156
SCRANTON (Iowa)
map (42° 1′N 94° 33′W) 11:244
SCRANTON (Pennsylvania) 17:156
map (41° 24′N 75° 40′W) 15:147
SCRAPER (machine)
earth-moving machinery 7:23–24 *illus.*
SCRAPIE (animal disease) 6:191
SCREAMER 17:156 *illus.*
SCREE *see* TALUS
SCREEN PRINTING *see* SILK-SCREEN PRINTING
SCREENING
water supply 20:53
SCREVEN (Georgia)
map (31° 29′N 82° 1′W) 9:114
SCREVEN (county in Georgia)
map (32° 45′N 81° 40′W) 9:114
SCREW (device) 17:156–157 *bibliog., illus.*
Maudslay, Henry 13:232
simple machines 17:316
Whitworth, Sir Joseph 20:143
SCREW PINE 17:157 *illus.*
SCREW PROPELLER *see* PROPELLER
SCRIABIN, ALEKSANDR NIKOLAYEVICH 17:157 *bibliog.*
SCRIBE
Egypt, ancient 7:83 *illus.*
SCRIBE, EUGÈNE 17:157 *bibliog.*
libretto 12:319
well-made play 20:99
SCRIBNER (Nebraska)
map (41° 40′N 96° 40′W) 14:70
SCRIMSHAW 17:158 *bibliog., illus.*
ivory and ivory carving 11:336–337
SCRIPPS, E. W. 17:158 *bibliog.*
SCRIPPS COLLEGE
Claremont Colleges 5:36
SCRIPPS-HOWARD NEWSPAPERS
Howard, Roy Wilson 10:283
press agencies and syndicates 15:533
Scripps, Edward Wyllis 17:158
SCRIPPS INSTITUTION OF OCEANOGRAPHY 17:158 *bibliog.*
Deep-Sea Drilling Project 6:77
history and programs 17:158
JOIDES 11:438
Namias, Jerome 14:10
oceanography 14:346
research and educational institution 17:158
SCRIPTS, ANCIENT *see* WRITING SYSTEMS, EVOLUTION OF
SCROFULA
figwort 8:76
SCROLL PAINTING (Chinese) *see* CHINESE ART AND ARCHITECTURE; PAINTING—China
SCROOGE (fictional character) 17:158
SCRUB
savanna life 17:97–99
SCRUB ITCH
chigger 4:347
SCRUB TYPHUS
chigger 4:347
SCRUBBIRD 17:158
SCRUGGS, EARL EUGENE *see* FLATT AND SCRUGGS
SCUBA DIVING 17:158–159 *bibliog., illus.*
Cousteau, Jacques-Yves 5:317
frogman 8:338 *illus.*
underwater archaeology 19:383
SCUD 12:168 *illus.*
beach flea scud 1:382 *illus.*
SCUDÉRY, MADELEINE DE 17:159 *bibliog.*
SCULPIN 17:159 *illus.*
SCULPTURE 17:159–166 *bibliog., illus.*
abstract art 1:63–65
Africa
African art 1:160–164 *illus.*
art criticism 2:207
Austria
Donner, Georg Raphael 6:239–240
Messerschmidt, Franz Xavier 13:323
baroque and rococo 17:164
Belgium
Flemish art and architecture 8:161–162
Meunier, Constantin 13:350
Minne, Georges 13:451
Quellinus, Artus 16:23
Brazil
Aleijadinho 1:271
bronzes *see* BRONZES
Byzantine 17:161–162
Canada
Canadian art and architecture 4:91
Hébert, Louis Philippe 10:101
Indians of North America, art of the 11:139
Carolingian art and architecture 4:161; 17:162
Celtic art 4:239
China 2:116 *illus.*
art and architecture 4:386
wood carving 20:209 *illus.*
constructivism 5:224
cubism 5:380–381
Denmark
Thorvaldsen, Bertel 19:180
Early Christian art and architecture 7:10; 17:161–162
earthworks 7:28
Easter Island 7:32–33 *illus.*
Egypt 17:159 *illus.*
Coptic art and architecture 5:255
Egyptian art and architecture 7:87–88
sphinx 18:180
figurehead 8:75–76
folk art 8:197–198 *illus.*
France 17:162–165 *illus.*
Bartholdi, Frédéric Auguste 3:97
Barye, Antoine Louis 3:99
Bosio, François Joseph, Baron 3:407
Bouchardon, Edmé 3:419
Bourdelle, Émile Antoine 3:423
Carpeaux, Jean Baptiste 4:163–164
César 4:262
Clodion 5:63
Coysevox, Antoine 5:323
Dalou, Aimé Jules 6:14
Degas, Edgar 6:84
Duchamp-Villon, Raymond 6:290
Falconet, Étienne Maurice 8:12
French art and architecture 8:303–308
Gaudier-Brzeska, Henri 9:59
Gérôme, Jean Léon 9:157
Girardon, François 9:188–289
Gislebertus 9:191
Goujon, Jean 9:265
Houdon, Jean Antoine 10:263–264
Laurens, Henri 12:238
Lemoyne, Jean Baptiste 12:280–281
Lipchitz, Jacques 12:360–361
Maillol, Aristide 13:67–68
Nicholas of Verdun 14:181
Picasso, Pablo 15:291–292
Pigalle, Jean Baptiste 15:299
Puget, Pierre 15:617
Reims Cathedral 16:131
Richier, Germaine 16:213
Rodin, Auguste 16:267
Rude, François 16:338
Statue of Liberty 18:238
gargoyle 9:47
Germany 17:162–164
Barlach, Ernst 3:83–84
Dannecker, Johann Heinrich von 6:33
Feuchtmayer, Joseph Anton 8:63
German art and architecture 9:126–127
Günther, Ignaz 9:406
Hildebrand, Adolf von 10:163
Kolbe, Georg 12:107
Kraft, Adam 12:126
Lehmbruck, Wilhelm 12:276
Ottonian art and architecture 14:467; 17:162
Permoser, Balthasar 15:176
Riemenschneider, Tilman 16:218–219
Schadow, Gottfried 17:116
Schlemmer, Oskar 17:125
Schlüter, Andreas 17:127
Stoss, Veit 18:285
Tinguely, Jean 19:206
Vischer (family) 19:616
Gothic art and architecture 9:258–262; 17:162–163
Great Britain
Butler, Reg 3:592
Caro, Anthony 4:159
Chadwick, Lynn 4:267
English art and architecture 7:184
Epstein, Jacob 7:223
Flaxman, John 8:158
Hepworth, Dame Barbara 10:131
Moore, Henry 13:568–569
Paolozzi, Eduardo 15:62
Roubiliac, Louis François 16:324
Rysbrack, Michael 16:380
Greece 17:159–160 *illus.*
Callimachus 4:46
Colossus of Rhodes 17:216–218
Cycladic art 5:402–403
Elgin Marbles 7:137
Farnese Haracles 8:28
Greek art 9:337–342
Laocoön 12:202
Lysippus 12:480
Micon 13:384
Minoan art 13:458–459
Myron 13:691
Nike of Samothrace 14:195
Phidias 15:226–227
Polyclitus 15:418
Praxiteles 15:490
Scopas 17:147–148
Statue of Zeus at Olympia 17:217
Hittite art and architecture 10:188–189
India
Indian art and architecture 11:94–98
Mogul art and architecture 13:501
Italy 17:163–164 *illus.*
Agostino di Duccio 1:187
Algardi, Alessandro 1:283
Antelami, Benedetto 2:45
Bandinelli, Baccio 3:62
Barberini Faun 3:78
Bernini, Giovanni Lorenzo 3:222
Bologna, Giovanni da 3:370
Canova, Antonio 4:115
Cellini, Benvenuto 4:236–237
della Robbia (family) 6:94
Desiderio da Settignano 6:131
Donatello 6:236–237
Dying Gaul 6:319
Etruscan and Roman 17:160–161
Etruscans 7:260 *illus.*
futurism 8:383–384
Ghiberti, Lorenzo 9:168
Italian art and architecture 11:310–312
Laurana, Francesco 12:237
Leonardo da Vinci 12:289–291
Lombardo (family) 12:399
Maiano (family) 13:66
Mannerism 13:125; 17:164
Manzù, Giacomo 13:134
Marini, Marino 13:156
Medici Chapel 13:265–266
Michelangelo 13:372–375
Mino da Fiesole 13:458
Moderno, Stefano 13:40
Modigliani, Amedeo 13:499
Nanni di Banco 14:12–13
Pisano, Andrea 15:316
Pisano, Nicola and Giovanni 15:316
Pollaiuolo (family) 15:405–406
Quercia, Jacopo della 16:23
Roman 17:160–161
Rossellino (family) 16:319
Rosso, Medardo 16:320
Sansovino, Andrea 17:65
Sansovino, Jacopo 17:66
Tacca, Pietro 19:5–6
Verrocchio, Andrea del 19:560–561
Japan
Jocho 11:421
netsuke 14:104
Unkei 19:470
kinetic art 12:78
Korean art 12:117–118
Lamaist art and architecture 12:173
Latin American art and architecture 12:223–226
See also national subheadings under SCULPTURE, e.g., SCULPTURE—Brazil; SCULPTURE—Mexico; etc.
marble 13:144
Merovingian art and architecture 13:311
Mesopotamian art and architecture 13:321
Mexico
Goeritz, Mathias 9:222
Olmec Indians 2:125 *illus.*
mobile 13:487
modern art 13:495–496

neoclassicism (art) **14**:81–82; **17**:164–165
Netherlands
Duquesnoy, François **6**:302
Dutch art and architecture **6**:312
Keyser, Hendrik de **12**:64
Quellinus, Artus **16**:23
Sluter, Claus **17**:364–365
Vries, Adriaen de **19**:639
Norway
Vigeland, Gustav **19**:592
Oceanic art **14**:336–339
Persia
Persian art and architecture **15**:183–185
Peru
Chavín slab **15**:499 *illus.*
photorealism **15**:274
Portugal
Portuguese art and architecture **15**:456
pre-Columbian art and architecture **15**:495–501
prehistoric art **15**:506–511
Renaissance art and architecture **16**:149–155; **17**:163–164
rococo style **16**:264
Romanesque art and architecture **16**:284; **17**:162
Romania
Brancusi, Constantin **3**:452–453
Rome, ancient **17**:160–161 *illus.*
Roman art and architecture **16**:275–276
Russia
Archipenko, Aleksandr **2**:129
Gabo, Naum **9**:3–4
Monument to the 3d International (Vladimir Tatlin) **16**:363 *illus.*
Tatlin, Vladimir Yevgrafovich **19**:44
Zadkine, Ossip **20**:348
sarcophagus **17**:76
Scandinavian art and architecture **17**:113–114
sculpture techniques **17**:166–167
Southeast Asian art and architecture **18**:107–110
Spain
Berruguete, Alonso **3**:224
Fernández, Gregorio **8**:58
Gargallo, Pablo **9**:47
González, Julio **9**:245
Juni, Juan de **11**:470
Ordóñez, Bartolomé **14**:420
Picasso, Pablo **15**:291–292
Roldán (family) **16**:271
Siloe, Diego de **17**:310
Spanish art and architecture **18**:151–156
stabile **18**:207
Sweden
Milles, Carl **13**:429
Switzerland
Giacometti, Alberto **9**:170–171
terra-cotta **19**:119–120
tomb **19**:231
United States
American art and architecture **1**:330–331
Andre, Carl **1**:406–406
Archipenko, Alexander **2**:129
Ball, Thomas **3**:40
Bertoia, Harry **3**:226
Borglum, Gutzon **3**:400
Bourgeois, Louise **3**:424
Calder, Alexander **4**:25
Chamberlain, John **4**:273
Chryssa **4**:421
Cornell, Joseph **5**:268
Crawford, Thomas **5**:333
Davidson, Jo **6**:49
di Suvero, Mark **6**:148
Ferber, Herbert **8**:52
Flannagan, John B. **8**:152–153
Flavin, Dan **8**:157
Fraser, James Earle **8**:287
French, Daniel Chester **8**:302
Graves, Nancy **9**:302
Greenough, Horatio **9**:353
Grooms, Red **9**:368
Gross, Chaim **9**:370–371
Hanson, Duane **10**:41
Hare, David **10**:49
Hoffman, Malvina **10**:195
Huntington, Anna Hyatt **10**:314
Indians of North America, art of the **11**:140–141
Judd, Donald **11**:463
Lachaise, Gaston **12**:160
Lippold, Richard **12**:363–364
MacMonnies, Frederick William **13**:34
Manship, Paul **13**:128
Marisol **13**:157
minimal art **13**:446
Nadelman, Elie **14**:4
Nakian, Reuben **14**:9
Nevelson, Louise **14**:115
Noguchi, Isamu **14**:213
Oldenburg, Claes **14**:376
Palmer, Erastus Dow **15**:50
Powers, Hiram **15**:486
Remington, Frederic **16**:145–146
Rickey, George W. **16**:216
Rimmer, William **16**:224
Rogers, Randolph **16**:269
Roszak, Theodore **16**:321
Rush, William **16**:347
Saint-Gaudens, Augustus **17**:18
Segal, George **17**:187–188
Skillin (family) **17**:339
Smith, David **17**:367–368
Smith, Tony **17**:370–371
Stankiewicz, Richard **18**:219
Statue of Liberty **18**:238
Storrs, John Bradley **18**:285
Story, William Wetmore **18**:285
Taft, Lorado **19**:7
Trova, Ernest **19**:312
Vonnoh, Bessie Potter **19**:634
Watts Towers **20**:69–70
Westermann, H. C. **20**:115
Whitney, Anne **20**:141
Whitney, Gertrude Vanderbilt **20**:141–142
Young, Mahonri **20**:334
Zorach, William **20**:379
video art **19**:576g
vorticism **19**:635
wood carving **20**:207–209
Yugoslavia
Meštrovíc, Ivan **13**:324–325
SCULPTURE TECHNIQUES **17**:166–167 *bibliog., illus.*
bas-relief **3**:100–101
carving **17**:166–167
casting **17**:167
construction **17**:167
lost-wax process **12**:418–419
modeling **17**:166
wood carving **20**:207–209
SCUNTHORPE (England)
map (53° 36′N 0° 38′W) **19**:403
SCUP *see* PORGY (fish)
SCURRY (county in Texas)
map (32° 45′N 100° 52′W) **19**:129
SCURVY **17**:167
ascorbic acid **2**:228
ascorbic acid deficiency
nutritional-deficiency diseases **14**:308
vitamins and minerals **19**:620
bone diseases **3**:378
Cook, James **5**:236
gingivitis **9**:184
lime (fruit) **12**:343–344
speedwell **18**:176
SCUTARI (Albania) *see* SHKODËR (Albania)
SCUTARI, LAKE
map (42° 12′N 19° 18′E) **1**:250
SCYLLA AND CHARYBDIS **17**:167
Messina, Strait of **13**:324
SCYTALE
cryptology **5**:371
SCYTHIANS **17**:167 *bibliog.*
steppe art **18**:255–256 *illus.*
SCYTHOPOLIS *see* BETH-SHAN (Beth-Shean) (Israel)
SDI (defense) *see* STRATEGIC DEFENSE INITIATIVE
SDI (Selective Dissemination of Information)
information science **11**:172
SDS *see* STUDENTS FOR A DEMOCRATIC SOCIETY
SEA, LAW OF THE **17**:167–168
territorial waters **19**:121
SEA ANEMONE **5**:91 *illus.*; **11**:229 *illus.*; **17**:168 *bibliog., illus.*
coelenterate **5**:91–92
intertidal life **11**:230
SEA AROUND US, THE (book)
Carson, Rachel **4**:170
SEA BASS **17**:168 *illus.*
jewfish **11**:412
SEA CUCUMBER **7**:38 *illus.*; **17**:168
SEA DEVIL *see* ANGLERFISH
SEA DUCK
coot **5**:248
SEA GRANT COLLEGES
Hawaii, University of **10**:76
North Carolina, state universities of **14**:246–247
Oregon, state universities and colleges of **14**:430–431
Rhode Island, state university and college of **16**:201
Texas, state universities of **19**:135
Washington, state universities and colleges of **20**:44
Wisconsin, University of **20**:188–189
SEA GRAPES **11**:229
SEA GULL *see* GULL
SEA HORSE **17**:168–169 *bibliog., illus.*
SEA ISLE CITY (New Jersey)
map (39° 9′N 74° 42′W) **14**:129
SEA LAVENDER **17**:169
SEA LEVEL **17**:169 *bibliog.*
baselevel **3**:108
estuary **7**:248
SEA LILY *see* CRINOID
SEA LION **17**:169 *illus.*
SEA MOTH **17**:169 *illus.*
SEA OTTER **17**:169 *bibliog., illus.*
SEA PARROT *see* PUFFIN
SEA PEN **17**:170 *illus.*
SEA PEOPLES **17**:170 *bibliog.*
Alalakh **1**:239
Etruscan origins **7**:258
Ugarit **19**:374
SEA POACHER **17**:170
SEA RAVEN
sculpin **17**:159
SEA ROBIN **8**:116 *illus.*; **17**:170
gurnard, flying **9**:406–407
SEA ROVER *see* PIRACY
SEA SCORPION *see* EURYPTERID
SEA SHANTY *see* SHANTY (work song)
SEA SNAKE **15**:384 *illus.*; **17**:170 *illus.*; **17**:377 *illus.*
SEA SPIDER **17**:170–171 *illus.*
SEA SQUIRT **11**:229 *illus.*; **17**:171
SEA STAR **11**:229 *illus.*
SEA SWALLOW *see* TERN
SEA TROUT *see* WEAKFISH
SEA TURTLE **17**:171 *bibliog., illus.*
animal migration **2**:27
ridley turtle **16**:218
SEA URCHIN **7**:38 *illus.*; **17**:171 *illus.*
development **6**:137; **6**:138 *illus.*; **6**:140 *illus.*
green sea urchin **11**:229 *illus.*
intertidal life **11**:230
metamorphosis **13**:334
SEA WALNUT *see* COMB JELLY
SEA WATER
oceanic mineral resources **14**:340–342
SEA WITCH (clipper ship) **5**:60 *illus.*
SEA-WOLF, THE (book)
London, Jack **12**:402–403
SEABEES **17**:171 *bibliog.*
SEABOARD (North Carolina)
map (36° 24′N 77° 26′W) **14**:242
SEABORG, GLENN T. **17**:171–172 *illus.*
fermium **8**:56
plutonium **15**:373
SEABROOK (New Jersey)
map (39° 30′N 74° 14′W) **14**:129
SEABROOK ISLAND
map (32° 40′N 80° 5′W) **18**:98
SEABURY, SAMUEL **17**:172 *bibliog.*
SEAFLOOR SPREADING **17**:172 *bibliog., illus.*
Cambrian Period **4**:51
continental drift **5**:229
convection cell **5**:232
Earth, geological history of **7**:14
Earth, structure and composition of **7**:21
geology **9**:106
island arc **11**:297–298
mantle **13**:130
Matthews, D. H. **13**:231
mid-oceanic ridge **13**:390
Mohorovičic discontinuity **13**:503
ocean and sea **14**:327; **14**:331
oceanic fracture zones **14**:339
paleogeography **15**:36 *map*
plate tectonics **15**:352–353 *illus.*; **15**:357
rift valleys **16**:221
sediment, marine **17**:184
Vine, F. J. **19**:600
SEAFORD (Delaware)
map (38° 39′N 75° 37′W) **6**:88
SEAFORD (Virginia)
map (37° 12′N 76° 26′W) **19**:607
SEAGA, EDWARD **17**:172
SEAGRAM BUILDING **17**:173
New York (city) **14**:145 *map*
SEAGRAVES (Texas)
map (57′N 102° 34′W) **19**:129
SEAGULL (bird) *see* GULL
SEAGULL, THE (play)
Chekhov, Anton **4**:310
SEAL (stamp or emblem)
Great Seal of the United States **9**:322
Hittite art and architecture **10**:189
Indus civilization **11**:153–154 *illus.*
inscription **11**:186
intaglio (art) **11**:199
Mesopotamian art and architecture **13**:317–319
Minoan art **13**:458
SEAL (zoology) **17**:173–174 *bibliog., illus.*
animal migration **2**:27
Antarctica **2**:42–43 *illus.*
Arctic **2**:141 *illus.*
classification, biological **17**:174
elephant seal **17**:173 *illus.*
sexual selection **17**:231
social behavior **13**:101 *illus.*
Eskimo **7**:239–241 *illus.*
fur seal **13**:105 *illus.*; **17**:173 *illus.*
gray seal **17**:173 *illus.*
harbor seal **17**:173 *illus.*
leopard seal **17**:173 *illus.*
limb **13**:102 *illus.*
pelagic sealing
Bering Sea controversy **3**:212
Pribilof Islands (Alaska) **15**:534
sea lion **17**:169
SEAL COVE (New Brunswick)
map (44° 39′N 66° 51′W) **14**:117
SEAL COVE (Newfoundland)
map (47° 28′N 53° 5′W) **14**:166
SEAL RIVER
map (59° 4′N 94° 48′W) **13**:119
SEALE (Alabama)
map (32° 18′N 85° 10′W) **1**:234
SEALE, BOBBY G.
Black Panther party **3**:318
SEALYHAM TERRIER **6**:220 *illus.*; **17**:174 *bibliog., illus.*
SEAMOUNT **17**:174 *bibliog., illus.*
ocean and sea **14**:327–331
Pacific Ocean **15**:6–8 *map*
SEAPERCH *see* SURFPERCH
SEAPLANE **17**:174–175 *bibliog., illus.*
Canadian de Havilland DHC-2 **17**:175 *illus.*
Curtiss, Glenn Hammond **5**:395
SEARCH AND SEIZURE (U.S. Constitution) *see* 4TH AMENDMENT
SEARCH WARRANT **17**:175 *bibliog.*
4th Amendment **8**:254
freedom of the press **8**:297
warrant **20**:30
writ of assistance **20**:291
SEARCHLIGHT **17**:175
SEARCHLIGHT (Nevada)
map (35° 28′N 114° 55′W) **14**:111
SEARCY (Arkansas)
map (35° 15′N 91° 44′W) **2**:166
SEARCY (county in Arkansas)
map (33° 53′N 92° 42′W) **2**:166
SEARLE, HUMPHREY
English music **7**:203
SEARLE, RONALD **17**:175
New Yorker cover **15**:170 *illus.*
SEARLES LAKE
map (35° 43′N 117° 20′W) **4**:31
SEARS, ROEBUCK AND CO.
Wood, Robert E. **20**:207
SEARS TOWER **13**:492 *illus.*; **17**:175
skyscraper **17**:349–350 *illus.*
SEARSPORT (Maine)
map (44° 28′N 68° 56′W) **13**:70
SEAS, FREEDOM OF THE **17**:175–176 *bibliog.*
fishing industry **8**:127–128
international law **11**:221–222
Sea, Law of the **17**:167–168
territorial waters **19**:121
SEASAT **17**:176
satellite, artificial **17**:87
SEASCAPE (play)
Albee, Edward **1**:253
SEASHELL *see* SHELL
SEASHORE *see* BEACH AND COAST
SEASICKNESS *see* MOTION SICKNESS
SEASIDE (Oregon)
map (46° 2′N 123° 55′W) **14**:427
SEASIDE PARK (New Jersey)
map (39° 55′N 74° 5′W) **14**:129
SEASON
celestial sphere **4**:230
equinox **7**:226
SEASONING *see* FLAVORS AND FRAGRANCES
SEAT BELT
safety, automotive **17**:10–11 *illus.*
SEATO *see* SOUTHEAST ASIA TREATY ORGANIZATION
SEATOUN (New Zealand)
map (41° 19′S 174° 50′E) **14**:158
SEATTLE (Washington) **17**:176 *bibliog., illus.*; **20**:38 *illus.*
climate **14**:228 *table*; **19**:421 *table*
map (47° 36′N 122° 20′W) **20**:35
SEAVER, TOM **17**:176 *bibliog.*
SEAWALL
coastal protection **5**:81

SEAWATER 17:177 *bibliog., table*
Atlantic Ocean 2:296
bromine 3:502
buffer 3:547
chlorine 4:400
desalination 6:124–125 *illus.*
evaporite, accumulations from 7:314
fresh water 8:328
geochemistry 9:96
Indian Ocean 11:104
magnesium 13:53
major chemical constituents 17:177 *table*
nutrients 14:341; 17:177
ocean and sea 14:332
Pacific Ocean 15:7
pack ice 15:10–11
red tide 16:114
regression, marine 16:129
salinity 17:177
electrodialysis 6:151
gulf and bay 9:403
Gulf Stream 9:403 *illus.*
sediment, marine 17:184
swamp, marsh, and bog 18:376–377
SEAWEED 17:177 *bibliog., illus.*
algae 1:280–282; 17:177
Cermium 11:229 *illus.*
Codium 11:229 *illus.*
Dasya 11:229 *illus.*
dulse 6:296
Ectocarpus 7:51
kelp 12:40
life cycle 17:177 *illus.*
rockweed 11:229 *illus.*
SEBACEOUS GLANDS
acne 1:83
SEBAGO LAKE
map (43° 50′N 70° 35′W) 13:70
SEBASTIAN, SAINT 17:177
SEBASTIAN (county in Arkansas)
map (35° 10′N 94° 17′W) 2:166
SEBASTIAN, KING OF PORTUGAL 17:177 *bibliog.*
SEBASTIÁN VIZCAÍNO BAY
map (28° 0′N 114° 30′W) 13:357
SEBASTIANO DEL PIOMBO 17:177–178 *bibliog.*
Christopher Columbus 5:127 *illus.*; 19:436 *illus.*
SEBASTOPOL (California)
map (38° 24′N 122° 49′W) 4:31
SEBASTOPOL (Mississippi)
map (32° 34′N 89° 27′W) 13:469
SEBEC LAKE
map (45° 18′N 69° 18′W) 13:70
SEBEKA (Minnesota)
map (46° 38′N 95° 5′W) 13:453
SEBES KÖRÖS RIVER
map (46° 55′N 20° 59′E) 10:307
SEBESTEN 17:178
SEBEWAING (Michigan)
map (43° 44′N 83° 27′W) 13:377
SEBHORRHEIC DERMATITIS *see* DANDRUFF
SEBREE (Kentucky)
map (37° 36′N 87° 32′W) 12:47
SEBRING (Florida)
map (27° 30′N 81° 26′W) 8:172
SEBRING (Ohio)
map (40° 55′N 81° 2′W) 14:357
SEBUM
skin 17:341
SECANT 17:178
trigonometry 19:298
SECAUCUS (New Jersey)
map (40° 47′N 74° 4′W) 14:129
SECCHI, PIETRO ANGELO
astronomy, history of 2:279
SECESSION MOVEMENT 17:178 *bibliog.*
Art Nouveau 2:212
Barlach, Ernst 3:83–84
Corinth, Lovis 5:263
Hoffmann, Josef 10:195
Klimt, Gustav 12:97
Liebermann, Max 12:324
Meštrovíc, Ivan 13:324–324
Olbrich, Joseph Maria 14:373
Stuck, Franz von 18:307
Wiener Werkstätte 20:146
SECHURA BAY
map (5° 42′S 81° 0′W) 15:193
SECOBARBITAL
barbituate 3:78
SECONAL 17:178
SECOND (unit of time)
time (physics) 19:201
units, physical 19:466
2D AMENDMENT 17:178 *bibliog.*
right to bear arms 16:222
text 5:220
SECOND CITY COMPANY
acting 1:88
SECOND COMING OF CHRIST 17:178 *bibliog.*
Adventists 1:111
Antichrist 2:60
Christadelphians 4:411
Irving, Edward 11:283
Judgment, Last 11:464
millenarianism 13:426–427
Miller, William 13:428
resurrection 16:183
sculpture 17:162 *illus.*
Signorelli, Luca 17:302
SECOND EMPIRE *see* FRANCE, HISTORY OF
SECOND INTERNATIONAL *see* INTERNATIONAL, SOCIALIST
SECOND LAKE
map (45° 9′N 71° 10′W) 14:123
SECOND MRS. TANQUERAY, THE (play)
Pinero, Sir Arthur Wing 15:307
SECOND REPUBLIC *see* FRANCE, HISTORY OF
SECOND SEX, THE (book) 17:178
Beauvoir, Simone de 3:148
SECOND VIENNESE SCHOOL
Berg, Alban 3:208–209
SECONDARY EDUCATION 17:178–180 *bibliog.*
Advanced Placement Program 1:110
athletics
football rules 8:214
British education 3:494–495
Canadian education 4:91
coeducation 5:90–91
computers in education, 5:165–166
Conant, James Bryant 5:168
curriculum controversy 17:179–180
declining ability of students 17:180
Elementary and Secondary Education Act of 1965 7:133
Future Homemakers of America 8:383
Gymnasium 9:412
history 17:179–180
humanities, education in the 10:300
lycée 12:474
Mann, Horace 13:122–123 *bibliog.*
National Honor Society 14:34
seven cardinal principles 17:179–180
vocational education 19:624–625
SECONDAT, CHARLES LOUIS DE, BARON DE LA BRÈDE ET DE MONTESQUIEU *see* MONTESQUIEU, CHARLES LOUIS DE SECONDAT, BARON DE LA BRÈDE ET DE
SECORD, LAURA 17:180
SECOTAN *see* LEATHER AND HIDES
SECRET BALLOT
election 7:104
SECRET POLICE *see* POLICE STATE
SECRET SERVICE 17:180–181 *bibliog.*
Treasury, U.S. Department of the 19:285
SECRET SOCIETIES 17:181 *bibliog.*
Camorra 4:62
cannibalism 4:109
Carbonari 4:137
Fang 8:20
Ku Klux Klan 12:133
Mafia 13:46
Mende 13:293–294
Molly Maguires 13:512
Senufo 17:205
tong 19:233
SECRET WRITING *see* CRYPTOLOGY
SECRETARY BIRD 17:181 *illus.*
SECRETARY OF STATE, U.S. *see* STATE, U.S. DEPARTMENT OF
SECRETIN
Bayliss, Sir William 3:133
hormone, animal 10:236 *table*
SECTION (Alabama)
map (34° 35′N 85° 59′W) 1:234
SECULAR HUMANISM
creationism 5:336
SECURITIES (finance) *see* BOND (finance); OPTION TRADING; STOCK (finance)
SECURITIES AND EXCHANGE COMMISSION 17:181 *bibliog.*
fraud 8:288
government regulation 9:271
stock market 18:274
SECURITY (Colorado)
map (38° 45′N 104° 44′W) 5:116
SECURITY, NATIONAL *see* NATIONAL SECURITY
SECURITY COUNCIL (UN)
United Nations 19:412 *illus.*
SECURITY SYSTEMS *see* SURVEILLANCE SYSTEMS
SEDALIA (Alberta)
map (51° 41′N 110° 40′W) 1:256
SEDALIA (Missouri)
map (38° 42′N 93° 14′W) 13:476
SEDAN (automobile)
body design 2:359
SEDAN (Kansas)
map (37° 8′N 96° 11′W) 12:18
SEDANG *see* MONTAGNARDS
SEDATIVE 17:181–182 *bibliog.*
barbiturate 3:78
bromine 3:502
chloral hydrate 4:400
drug abuse 6:279
henbane 10:121
marijuana 13:152–153
meprobamate 13:303
paraldehyde 15:78
phenobarbital 15:225
psychotropic drugs 15:603
scopolamine 17:148
sleep 17:360
stress, biological 18:298
SEDDON, RICHARD JOHN 17:182 *bibliog.*
SEDER 17:182
Passover 15:105–106
seder platter 15:105 *illus.*
SEDGE 17:182–183 *illus.*
tundra 19:332 *illus.*
SEDGWICK (county in Colorado)
map (40° 50′N 102° 20′W) 5:116
SEDGWICK (Kansas)
map (37° 55′N 97° 25′W) 12:18
SEDGWICK (county in Kansas)
map (37° 40′N 97° 30′W) 12:18
SEDGWICK (Maine)
map (44° 18′N 68° 37′W) 13:70
SEDGWICK, ADAM 17:183 *bibliog., illus.*
Murchison, Roderick Impey 13:647
SEDIMENT, MARINE 17:183–184 *bibliog., illus.*
continental shelf and slope 5:230
coral reef 5:258–260
estuary 7:248
fossil record 8:243
geologic time
Cretaceous Period 5:339
ice ages 11:8
Jurassic Period 11:474–477
Recent Epoch 16:106
Tertiary Period 19:122
greensand 9:354
hematite 10:117
hornfels 10:240
lake (body of water) 12:169
mud cracks 13:631
ocean and sea
Atlantic Ocean 2:296
bathyal zone 3:123
benthonic zone 3:205
Caribbean Sea 4:148
Deep-Sea Drilling Project 6:77
lagoon 12:165–166
manganese nodule 13:114
Mediterranean Sea 13:277
Murray, Sir John (oceanographer) 13:650
Ninetyeast Ridge 14:199
oceanic mineral resources 14:340–341
ooze, deep-sea 14:396–397
Pacific Ocean 15:5; 15:7
seafloor spreading 17:172
submarine canyon 18:316
paleoecology 15:34
petroleum 15:207
plate tectonics 15:354–356
radiolarian 16:64
river delta 16:232–233
transgression, marine 19:271
water quality 20:51
SEDIMENTARY BASINS
plate tectonics 15:356
SEDIMENTARY ROCK 17:184–186 *bibliog., illus.*
arkose 2:170
authigenic rocks 17:184
breccia 3:470
Brongniart, Alexandre 3:503
carbonaceous rocks 17:185
carbonate rocks 17:184
chert and flint 4:332–333; 17:184
coal and coal mining 5:75–79
cobble 5:84
concretion 5:171
conglomerate (geology) 5:181
coprolite 5:255
coral reef 5:260
erosion and sedimentation 7:232–234
evaporite 7:314; 17:184
feldspar 8:46–47
fluorite 8:188
fold 8:194 *illus.*
formation 17:185–186 *illus.*
fossil record 8:243–248
geochemistry 9:96
geologic time 9:103–105
Cenozoic Era 4:245–246
Cretaceous Period 5:339–341
Earth, geological history of 7:12
Mesozoic Era 13:322
paleography 15:41
Tertiary Period 19:124–125
geosyncline 9:119–120
glauberite 9:205
granodiorite 9:287
graywacke 9:307
greensand 9:354
limestone 12:344–345
marl 13:160
metamorphic rock 13:331–333
mineral occurrence 13:443
molasse 13:505
mud cracks 13:631
natural gas 14:48
oolite 14:396
ore deposits 14:424–425 *table*
oxide minerals 14:476
paragneisses, gneiss 9:213
permeability, rock 15:174
petrography 15:206–207
phosphorite 17:185
placer deposit 15:325
quartz 16:13–14
red beds 16:112
rock 16:247
sandstone 17:63
shale 17:237
sill 17:309
Smith, William 17:371
sulfide minerals 18:334
syncline and anticline 18:406
terrigenous rocks 17:185
till and tillite 19:199
turquoise 19:352
uranium minerals 19:478
zeolite 20:360
SEDIMENTATION *see* EROSION AND SEDIMENTATION
SEDITION 17:186 *bibliog.*
Alien and Sedition Acts 1:293–294
freedom of speech 8:298
freedom of the press 8:296–297
Zenger, John Peter 20:359
Gitlow v. *New York* 9:191
mutiny 13:687
subversion 18:317
SEDONA (Arizona)
map (34° 52′N 111° 46′W) 2:160
SEDRO WOOLLEY (Washington)
map (48° 30′N 122° 14′W) 20:35
SEDROTH (Israel)
map (31° 31′N 34° 35′E) 11:302
"SEE IT NOW" (television series)
radio and television broadcasting 16:57
SEEBECK, THOMAS
thermocouple 19:162
SEEBECK EFFECT
thermoelectricity 19:165
SEECKT, HANS VON 17:186 *bibliog.*
SEED 15:337–338 *illus.*; 17:186–187 *bibliog., illus.*
angiosperm 1:414
cotyledon 5:307–308
gymnosperm 9:414
orchid 14:419
reproduction 16:162
seed cone 17:187
tracheophyte 19:258
tree 19:287 *illus.*
SEED CONE 17:187
gymnosperm 9:414
SEED DRILL (farm machinery) 19:330–331 *illus.*
SEED FERN
fern 8:57–58
ginkgo 9:184
SEEDEATER 17:187
SEEDSNIPE
shorebirds 17:283
SEEGER, PETE 17:187 *bibliog.*
SEEING EYE DOG *see* GUIDE DOG
SEEKONK RIVER
map (41° 50′N 71° 22′W) 16:198
SEELEY LAKE (Montana)
map (47° 11′N 113° 29′W) 13:547
SEELYVILLE (Indiana)
map (39° 30′N 87° 16′W) 11:111
SEFERIADIS, GEORGE *see* SEFERIS, GEORGE
SEFERIS, GEORGE 17:187 *bibliog.*
SEFORIM, MENDELE MOKHER 10:102 *illus.*
SEFRIOUI, AHMED
Morocco 13:585

SEFSTRÖM, NILS G.
  vanadium **19**:516
SEFUWA (dynasty)
  Kanem-Bornu **12**:14–15
SEGAL, GEORGE **17**:187–188 *bibliog., illus.*
  Cinema **17**:188 *illus.*
  Restaurant Window **17**:166 *illus.*
SEGESTA (Sicily) **17**:188 *bibliog.*
SEGHERS, ANNA **17**:188
SEGHERS, HERCULES **17**:188 *bibliog.*
SEGO LILY **17**:188
SEGONZAC, ANDRÉ DUNOYER DE **17**:188 *bibliog.*
  Isadora Duncan **3**:43 *illus.*
SÉGOU (Mali)
  map (13° 27′N 6° 16′W) **13**:89
SEGOVIA (Spain)
  map (40° 57′N 4° 7′W) **18**:140
SEGOVIA, ANDRÉS **17**:188 *bibliog.*
SEGRÈ, EMILIO **17**:188–189 *bibliog.*
SEGREGATION (genetics) **10**:139 *illus.*
SEGREGATION, RACIAL *see* APARTHEID; INTEGRATION, RACIAL; JIM CROW LAWS
SÉGUÉLA (Ivory Coast)
  map (7° 57′N 6° 40′W) **11**:335
SEGUIN (Texas)
  map (29° 34′N 97° 58′W) **19**:129
SEGUNDO (Colorado)
  map (37° 7′N 104° 45′W) **5**:116
SEI SHONAGON **17**:189
SEICHE
  water wave **20**:57
SEIFERT, JAROSLAV
  Czech literature **5**:413
SEIGNORIALISM *see* MANORIALISM
SEIKAN TUNNEL *see* TUNNEL
SEILING (Oklahoma)
  map (36° 9′N 98° 56′W) **14**:368
SEINÄJOKI (Finland)
  map (62° 47′N 22° 50′E) **8**:95
SEINE, BAY OF THE
  map (49° 30′N 0° 30′W) **8**:260
SEINE RIVER **17**:189
  map (49° 26′N 0° 26′E) **8**:260
  Paris **15**:87 *map*
SEINGALT, GIOVANNI GIACOMO CASANOVA DE *see* CASANOVA DE SEINGALT, GIOVANNI GIACOMO
SEISMIC GAP
  earthquakes **7**:28
SEISMOGRAM **17**:189
  earthquakes **7**:25
  Richter scale **16**:215
SEISMOGRAPH *see* SEISMOMETER
SEISMOLOGY
  Earth, structure and composition of **7**:20 *illus.*
  earthquakes **7**:25–28
  East African Rift System **7**:30–31
  mantle **13**:130
  microseism **13**:388
SEISMOMETER **17**:189–190 *bibliog., illus.*
  Richter scale **16**:215
SEIZURE *see* CONVULSION
SEJANUS, LUCIUS AELIUS
  Tiberius, Roman Emperor **19**:189
SEJM (governing body)
  Poland **15**:390–391
SEKONDI-TAKORADI (Ghana) **17**:190
  map (4° 59′N 1° 43′W) **9**:164
SELAH (Washington)
  map (46° 39′N 120° 32′W) **20**:35
SELASSIE, HAILE *see* HAILE SELASSIE, EMPEROR OF ETHIOPIA
SELBY (South Dakota)
  map (45° 31′N 100° 2′W) **18**:103
SELBYVILLE (Delaware)
  map (38° 28′N 75° 13′W) **6**:88
SELDEN, GEORGE B.
  automotive industry **2**:363
SELDEN SOCIETY
  Maitland, Frederic William **13**:76
SELECTION RULES
  symmetry (physics) **18**:404
SELECTIVE DISSEMINATION OF INFORMATION (SDI)
  information science **11**:172
SELECTIVE EXCLUSIVENESS, DOCTRINE OF *see COOLEY* v. *BOARD OF PORT WARDENS*
SELECTIVE SERVICE SYSTEM
  conscription **5**:201
SELENE **17**:190
SELENGE RIVER
  map (52° 16′N 106° 16′E) **13**:529
SELENITE
  gypsum **9**:415–416
SELENIUM **17**:190 *bibliog.*
  abundances of common elements **7**:131 *table*
  chalcogens **4**:270
  element **7**:130 *table*
  flame test
    qualitative chemical analysis **16**:6 *illus.*
  Group VIA periodic table **15**:167
  native elements **14**:47
  transition elements **19**:273 *table*
  vitamins and minerals **19**:621
SELEUCIA **17**:190
SELEUCIA-ON-THE-EULAEUS *see* SUSA (Iran)
SELEUCIDS (dynasty) **17**:190–191 *bibliog., map*
  Antiochus III **2**:64
  Antiochus IV **2**:64
  Demetrius I Soter, King **6**:97
  Greece, ancient **9**:333
  Persia, ancient **15**:181–182
  Uruk **19**:490
SELEUCUS I NICATOR, MACEDONIAN KING **17**:191
  Persian art and architecture **15**:184
  Seleucia **17**:190
SELF-ACTUALIZATION
  ego **7**:73–74
  Maslow, Abraham H. **13**:196–198
SELF-INCRIMINATION **17**:191 *bibliog.*
  evidence **7**:317
  5th Amendment **8**:74
  military justice **13**:421
  Miranda v. *Arizona* **13**:463
  Twining v. *New Jersey* **19**:360
  witness **20**:192–193
SELF-POLLINATION *see* PLANT BREEDING; POLLINATION
SELF-PORTRAIT IN A CONVEX MIRROR (book)
  Ashbery, John **2**:229
SELFRIDGE (North Dakota)
  map (46° 2′N 100° 56′W) **14**:248
SELIGMAN (Arizona)
  map (35° 20′N 112° 53′W) **2**:160
SELIGMAN (Missouri)
  map (36° 31′N 93° 56′W) **13**:476
SELIM I, SULTAN OF THE OTTOMAN EMPIRE **17**:191–192 *bibliog.*
SELIM II, SULTAN OF THE OTTOMAN EMPIRE
  coronation of **14**:464 *illus.*
SELIM III, SULTAN OF THE OTTOMAN EMPIRE **17**:192 *bibliog.*
  Ottoman Empire **14**:465
SELINDER, ANDERS
  Royal Swedish Ballet **16**:331
SELINSGROVE (Pennsylvania)
  map (40° 48′N 76° 52′W) **15**:147
SELINUS (Sicily) **17**:192 *bibliog.*
  Segesta **17**:188
SELJUKS **17**:192 *bibliog.*
  Asia, history of **2**:254–255 *map*
  Europe, history of **7**:284
  Manzikert, Battle of **13**:134
  Merv **13**:313
  Middle East, history of the **13**:404
  Persian art and architecture **15**:185
  Turks **19**:347–348
SELKIRK (Manitoba)
  map (50° 9′N 96° 52′W) **13**:119
SELKIRK (Scotland) **17**:192
SELKIRK, THOMAS DOUGLAS, 5th EARL OF **17**:192 *bibliog.*
  Canada, history of **4**:82 *map*
  Hudson's Bay Company **10**:290
  Red River Settlement **16**:113
SELKIRKSHIRE (Scotland) *see* SELKIRK (Scotland)
SEL'KUP *see* SAMOYED (people)
SELKUP LANGUAGE
  Ural-Altaic languages **19**:475
SELLERS, PETER **17**:192 *bibliog.*
SELLERSBURG (Indiana)
  map (38° 24′N 85° 45′W) **11**:111
SELLING *see* RETAILING
SELLS (Arizona)
  map (31° 55′N 111° 53′W) **2**:160
SELMA (Alabama) **17**:192
  map (32° 25′N 87° 1′W) **1**:234
  Southern Christian Leadership Conference **18**:112
SELMA (California)
  map (36° 34′N 119° 37′W) **4**:31
SELMA (North Carolina)
  map (35° 32′N 78° 17′W) **14**:242
SELMER (Tennessee)
  map (35° 11′N 88° 36′W) **19**:104
SELMON, JOHN HENRY
  outlaws **14**:468
SELVAS FOREST
  map (5° 0′S 68° 0′W) **3**:460
SELWAY RIVER
  map (46° 8′N 115° 36′W) **11**:26
SELWYN COLLEGE (Cambridge University) **4**:53
SELWYN MOUNTAINS
  map (63° 10′N 130° 20′W) **20**:345
SELZNICK, DAVID O. **17**:193 *bibliog.*
SEMANS (Saskatchewan)
  map (51° 25′N 104° 44′W) **17**:81
SEMANTICS (linguistics) **17**:193–194 *bibliog.*
  communication **5**:144
  Hayakawa, S. I. **10**:80
  lexicology and lexicography **12**:308–309
  linguistics **12**:356–358
  logic **12**:396
  paradox (mathematics) **15**:75
  psycholinguistics **15**:592
  syntax **18**:408–409
  writing systems, evolution of **20**:292
SEMAPHORE **17**:194–195 *illus.*
  signaling **17**:300–301 *illus.*
SEMARA (Morocco)
  climate **13**:584 *table*
  map (26° 44′N 11° 41′W) **13**:585
SEMARANG (Indonesia) **17**:195
  map (6° 58′S 110° 25′E) **11**:147
SEMBÈNE, OUSMANE **17**:195
SEMELE **17**:195
SEMEN **17**:195 *bibliog.*
  artificial insemination **2**:220
  prostaglandins **15**:572–573
SEMENOV, NIKOLAI NIKOLAYEVICH **17**:195
SEMERU, MOUNT
  map (8° 6′S 112° 55′E) **11**:147
SEMIARID CLIMATE **17**:195–196 *bibliog.*
  pedocal **15**:131
  plant distribution **15**:344 *map*
SEMICIRCULAR CANALS (biology)
  biological equilibrium **3**:265
  ear **7**:6 *illus.*
SEMICONDUCTOR **17**:196–197 *bibliog.*
  boron **3**:403
  Brattain, Walter **3**:458
  charge-coupled device **4**:288
  components **17**:196
  computer **5**:160c; **5**:160d; **5**:160g; **5**:160i
  computer, personal **5**:160i
  computer memory **5**:161
  conduction, electric **5**:174
  diode **6**:183
    junction diodes **17**:196
    optoelectronic diodes **17**:197
    uses **17**:196–197
    Zener diode **20**:359
  electroluminescence **7**:114
  electromagnetic pulse **7**:116
  energy levels **17**:196
  gallium **9**:21
  germanium **9**:138
  integrated circuit **11**:201–202
  laser **12**:213 *table*
  metal **13**:328
  microelectronics **13**:385
  photoelectric cell **15**:259
  photoelectric effect **15**:260
  rectifier **16**:110–111
  selenium **17**:190
  silicon **17**:305
  silicon-controlled rectifier **17**:305
  solar cell **18**:40
  thermistor **19**:161
  transistor **17**:197; **19**:271
  valence bands **17**:196
  video technology **19**:576m
SEMINAL VESICLES **16**:163 *illus.*
SEMINARIES, THEOLOGICAL *see* THEOLOGICAL SEMINARIES
SEMINARY (Mississippi)
  map (31° 34′N 89° 30′W) **13**:469
SEMINOE RESERVOIR
  map (42° 0′N 106° 50′W) **20**:301
SEMINOLE **17**:197 *bibliog.*
  Everglades **7**:316
  Five Civilized Tribes **8**:132
  Indians of North America, art of the **11**:141
  Oklahoma **14**:371
  removal to Indian Territory **11**:109 *map*
  Seminole Wars **17**:197
  Yamasee **20**:317
SEMINOLE (county in Florida)
  map (28° 45′N 81° 13′W) **8**:172
SEMINOLE (county in Georgia)
  map (30° 55′N 84° 50′W) **9**:114
SEMINOLE (Oklahoma)
  map (35° 14′N 96° 41′W) **14**:368
SEMINOLE (county in Oklahoma)
  map (35° 10′N 96° 35′W) **14**:368
SEMINOLE (Texas)
  map (32° 43′N 102° 39′W) **19**:129
SEMINOLE, LAKE
  map (30° 46′N 84° 50′W) **9**:114
SEMINOLE WARS **11**:109 *map*; **17**:197
  Jackson, Andrew **11**:341
  Osceola **14**:452–453
  Seminole **17**:197
  Van Buren, Martin **19**:511
SEMIOTICS **17**:197 *bibliog.*
  communication **5**:144
  cybernetics **5**:401
  French literature
    Barthes, Roland **3**:97
SEMIPALATINSK (USSR)
  map (50° 28′N 80° 13′E) **19**:388
SEMIRAMIS **17**:197
  Hanging Gardens of Babylon **17**:216
SEMITES **17**:197–198 *bibliog.*
  Akkad **1**:231
  Amorites **1**:376
  Arabs **2**:101–106
  Aramaeans **2**:108–109
  Ethiopia **7**:253
    Amhara **1**:368–369
    Tigré **19**:197
  Jews **11**:412–417
  language
    African language **1**:166 *map*
    Afroasiatic languages **1**:179–180 *map*
    Asia **2**:244 *map*
    Ebla **7**:36
  Mesopotamian art and architecture **13**:317–322
SEMITRAILER (truck)
  trucking industry **19**:315
SEMMELWEIS, IGNAZ PHILIPP **17**:198 *bibliog.*
  bacteria **3**:17
  puerperal fever **15**:614
SEMMES, RAPHAEL **17**:198 *bibliog.*
SEMNAN (Iran)
  map (35° 33′N 53° 24′E) **11**:250
SEMOIS RIVER
  map (49° 53′N 4° 45′E) **3**:177
SEMPACH, BATTLE OF
  Winkelried, Arnold **20**:179
SEMPER, GOTTFRIED **17**:198 *bibliog.*
  Bayreuth Wagner Festival **3**:134
  opera houses **14**:402
SEMPERVIVUM **17**:198
SEMPRUN, JORGE
  Resnais, Alain **16**:177
SEN RIVER
  map (12° 32′N 104° 28′E) **12**:11
SENA (Bolivia)
  map (11° 32′S 67° 11′W) **3**:366
SENANAYAKE SAMUDRA LAKE
  map (7° 11′N 81° 29′E) **18**:206
SENARMONTITE
  antimony **2**:63
SENATE, ROMAN **17**:199–200 *bibliog.*
  Europe, history of **7**:280–281
  Rome, ancient **16**:297
SENATE OF THE UNITED STATES **17**:198–199 *bibliog., illus.*
  cloture **5**:66
  committees **17**:199
  Congress of the United States **5**:184–187 *illus.*
  Congressional Record **5**:188
  Constitution of the United States **5**:216
  election
    17th Amendment **17**:219
  filibuster **8**:79
  genesis and framework of the Constitution **5**:213–214
  National Conservative Political Action Committee **14**:31
  officers **17**:199
  Pearson, Drew **15**:128
  Revels, Hiram R. **16**:185
  rules **17**:199
  vice-president of the United States **19**:568
  Washington, D.C. **20**:41 *map*
SENATH (Missouri)
  map (36° 8′N 90° 10′W) **13**:476
SENATOBIA (Mississippi)
  map (34° 39′N 89° 58′W) **13**:469
SENDAI (Japan) **17**:200
  map (38° 15′N 140° 53′E) **11**:361
SENDAK, MAURICE **17**:200
  In the Night Kitchen **4**:353 *illus.*
SENEBIER, JEAN
  photosynthesis **15**:275
SENECA
  Erie **7**:229
SENECA (American Indians) **17**:200 *bibliog.*
  Cornplanter **5**:269
  Handsome Lake **10**:37
  Iroquois League **11**:279–280
  Jemison, Mary **11**:395
  Morgan, Lewis Henry **13**:578
  Parker, Ely S. **15**:90
  Red Jacket **16**:112

SENECA (Kansas)
map (39° 50′N 96° 4′W) **12**:18
SENECA (Missouri)
map (36° 51′N 94° 37′W) **13**:476
SENECA (county in New York)
map (42° 54′N 76° 52′W) **14**:149
SENECA (county in Ohio)
map (41° 7′N 83° 11′W) **14**:357
SENECA (Oregon)
map (44° 8′N 118° 58′W) **14**:427
SENECA (South Carolina)
map (34° 41′N 82° 57′W) **18**:98
SENECA, LUCIUS ANNAEUS **17**:200 *bibliog.*
SENECA FALLS (New York)
map (42° 55′N 76° 48′W) **14**:149
SENECA FALLS CONVENTION **17**:200–201 *bibliog.*
Stanton, Elizabeth Cady **18**:220
SENECA LAKE
Finger Lakes **8**:93
map (42° 40′N 76° 57′W) **14**:149
SENECA THE YOUNGER *see* SENECA, LUCIUS ANNAEUS
SENECAVILLE LAKE
map (39° 55′N 81° 25′W) **14**:357
SENEFELDER, ALOYS **17**:201 *bibliog.*
inventor
offset lithography **14**:354
lithograph **12**:371
printing **15**:551
SENEGAL **17**:201–202 *bibliog., illus., map, table*
art
African art **1**:160–164
cities
Dakar **6**:10–11 *illus.*
economic activity **17**:201–202 *illus.*
education **17**:201
African universities **1**:176 *table*
flag **17**:201 *illus.*
government **17**:201
history **17**:201–202
Faidherbe, Louis Léon César **8**:8
Gambia **9**:26
land **17**:201–202 *map, table*
literature
African literature **1**:167–168
Diop, Birago Ismael **6**:185
Sembene, Ousmane **17**:195
map (14° 0′N 14° 0′W) **1**:136
people **17**:201
Serer **17**:208
Wolof **20**:199
physical features
Verde, Cape **19**:549
Senghor, Léopold Sédar **17**:203
SENEGAL RIVER **17**:202–203
SENEGAMBIA, CONFEDERATION OF
Gambia **9**:25
SENESCENCE *see* AGING
SENFL, LUDWIG
German and Austrian music **9**:129
Renaissance music **16**:156
SENGHOR, LÉOPOLD SÉDAR **17**:203 *bibliog.*
Senegal **17**:201
socialism **18**:24
SENI PRAMOJ
Thailand **19**:141
SENILITY **17**:203 *bibliog.*
aging **1**:185
Alzheimer's disease **1**:320
geriatrics **9**:122
SENIOR CITIZEN *see* OLD AGE
SENIOR COMPANION PROGRAM
ACTION (federal agency) **1**:89
SENJA ISLAND
map (69° 20′N 17° 30′E) **14**:261
SENMUT **17**:203 *bibliog.*
SENNA **17**:203 *illus.*
SENNACHERIB, KING OF ASSYRIA **17**:203–204 *bibliog.*
construction of palace **19**:63 *illus.*
Nineveh **14**:200
SENNETERRE (Quebec)
map (48° 23′N 77° 15′W) **16**:18
SENNETT, MACK **17**:204 *bibliog.*
film, history of **8**:82
Keystone Kops **12**:64
SENOIA (Georgia)
map (33° 18′N 84° 33′W) **9**:114
SENSATION *see* SENSES AND SENSATION
SENSATIONALISM (philosophy) **17**:204 *bibliog.*
Condillac, Étienne Bonnot de **5**:172
SENSES AND SENSATION **17**:204–205 *bibliog.*
See also NERVOUS SYSTEM
antenna (biology) **2**:47
biological equilibrium **3**:265
bird **3**:284
brain **3**:443–444
cat **4**:194; **4**:196
color perception **5**:114
dog **6**:221
ear 7:6–7 *illus.*
eye **7**:348–350 *illus.*
fish **8**:119 *illus.*
flavors and fragrances **8**:157
hair **10**:14
hunger and thirst **10**:310–311
insect **11**:188–189 *illus.*
insect antenna (biology) **2**:47
lizard **12**:380
memory **13**:291
nervous system **14**:95
nose **14**:266
pain **15**:15
pattern recognition **15**:114–115
perception **15**:158–160 *illus.*
pschyophysics **15**:601–602
reptile **16**:171
sensory deprivation **17**:205
shark **17**:244
snake **17**:378–379 *illus.*
speech **18**:175
synesthesia **18**:407
taxis **19**:48
tongue **19**:234
SENSITIVE PLANT **17**:205
mimosa **13**:436
SENSITOMETER **17**:205
guidance and control systems **9**:394
SENSORY DEPRIVATION **17**:205 *bibliog.*
SENSORY NERVE
cell **4**:236
peripheral nervous system **15**:171
SENSORY PIT
rattlesnake **16**:93
SENTA (Yugoslavia)
map (45° 56′N 20° 4′E) **20**:340
SENTENCE (law) **17**:205
crime **5**:347
criminal justice **5**:350
prison **15**:554; **15**:555
SENTIMENTAL COMEDY
comedy **5**:132
SENTIMENTAL NOVEL **17**:205
novel **14**:273
SENTINEL (Oklahoma)
map (35° 9′N 99° 10′W) **14**:368
SENTINEL BUTTE
map (46° 53′N 103° 50′W) **14**:248
SENUFO **17**:205 *bibliog.*
mask **13**:197 *illus.*
SEOUL (South Korea) **12**:113 *illus.*; **17**:205–206
Korean War **12**:119 *illus.*
map (37° 33′N 126° 58′E) **12**:113
SEPARATION OF POWERS **17**:206 *bibliog.*
Congress of the United States **5**:187
framework of the Constitution **5**:214–215
government **9**:268–269
political parties **15**:401
SEPARATISM
Basques **3**:116
Garvey, Marcus **9**:52
Quebec **16**:20–21
Lévesque, René **12**:303
SEPHARDIC LANGUAGE *see* LADINO LANGUAGE
SEPHARDIM **17**:206 *bibliog.*
SEPIK RIVER
map (3° 51′S 144° 34′E) **15**:72
SEPIOLITE *see* MEERSCHAUM
SEPOY REBELLION *see* INDIAN MUTINY
SEPPUKU *see* HARA-KIRI
SEPT-ÎLES (Quebec)
map (50° 12′N 66° 23′W) **16**:18
SEPTAGON
polygon **15**:419 *illus.*
SEPTEMBER
birthstones **3**:296 *illus., table*
calendar **4**:28
SEPTIC TANK **17**:206
SEPTICEMIA **17**:206
SEPTIMIUS SEVERUS, ROMAN EMPEROR *see* SEVERUS, SEPTIMIUS, ROMAN EMPEROR
SEPTUAGINT **17**:206 *bibliog.*
SEQUAPMUQ (American Indians) *see* SHUSWAP (American Indians)
SÉQUARD, CHARLES BROWN- *see* BROWN-SÉQUARD, CHARLES
SEQUATCHIE (county in Tennessee)
map (35° 25′N 85° 25′W) **19**:104
SEQUEIRA, DOMINGOS ANTÓNIO DE
Portuguese art and architecture **15**:456
SEQUENCE (mathematics) **17**:206–207
convergence **5**:233
Fibonacci **8**:69
finite and infinite **17**:207
limit **12**:345
progression **15**:563–564
series **17**:209
SEQUENCE (music) **17**:207 *bibliog.*
Stabat Mater **18**:207
SEQUOIA (botany) **4**:35 *illus.*
redwood **16**:117
SEQUOIA NATIONAL PARK **4**:35 *illus.*; **14**:38–39 *map, table*; **17**:207
Whitney, Mount **20**:142
SEQUOYA (Cherokee Indian) **17**:207 *bibliog.*
Cherokee **4**:332 *illus.*
Cherokee syllabary **20**:293 *illus.*
SEQUOYAH (county in Oklahoma)
map (35° 30′N 94° 45′W) **14**:368
SERAING (Belgium)
map (50° 36′N 5° 29′E) **3**:177
SERAM SEA
map (2° 30′S 128° 0′E) **11**:147
SERANG (Indonesia)
map (6° 7′S 106° 9′E) **11**:147
SERAPHIM
angel **1**:412
SERAPIS (deity) **17**:207
SERAPIS (ship) **1**:357 *illus.*; **14**:62 *illus.*
SERBAN, ANDRÉ **17**:207
SERBATI, ANTONIO ROSMINI- *see* ROSMINI-SERBATI, ANTONIO
SERBIA (Yugoslavia) **17**:207–208 *bibliog., map*
cities
Belgrade **3**:182 *illus.*
Novi Sad **14**:277
history **17**:207–208
Alexander, King **1**:276
Balkan Wars **3**:38
Europe, history of **7**:293
Mihajlović, Draža **13**:417
Miloš, Prince **13**:432
Pašić, Nikola **15**:102
Peter I, King **15**:201
Stephen Dušan, King **18**:254
World War I **20**:219–222; **20**:226–227 *map*; **20**:230–231 *illus.*
Yugoslavia **20**:343
literature
Yugoslavia **20**:342
map (44° 0′N 21° 0′E) **20**:340
SERBO-CROATIAN LANGUAGE
Slavic languages **17**:358
SERBS
See also SERBIA
Croatia (Yugoslavia) **5**:354–355
SEREMBAM (Malaysia)
map (2° 43′N 101° 56′E) **13**:84
SERENADE **17**:208
See also DIVERTIMENTO
SERENGETI NATIONAL PARK **17**:208 *bibliog.*
SERENGETI PLAIN
map (2° 50′S 35° 0′E) **19**:27
SERER **17**:208 *bibliog.*
polygamy **15**:419
SERFDOM *see* MANORIALISM
SERGEANT BLUFF (Iowa)
map (42° 24′N 96° 22′W) **11**:244
SERGEANT YORK *see* YORK, ALVIN CULLUM
SERGEL, JOHANN TOBIAS
Scandinavian art and architecture **17**:113
SERGEYEV, KONSTANTIN **17**:208 *bibliog.*
SERGIPE (Brazil)
map (10° 30′S 37° 30′W) **3**:460
SERIA (Brunei)
map (4° 39′N 114° 23′E) **3**:524
SERIAL MUSIC **17**:208 *bibliog.*
Barraqué, Jean **3**:93
Boulez, Pierre **3**:421–422
Jolas, Betsy **11**:441
Stravinsky, Igor **18**:295
twelve-tone system **19**:358–359
Wuorinen, Charles **20**:296–297
SERIALS (visual arts) *see* FILM SERIALS; SOAP OPERA
SERICA (ship)
clipper ship **5**:61
SERICIN
silk **17**:306–307
SERICULTURE
silk **17**:306–307
SERIES (mathematics) **17**:209 *bibliog.*
Banach, Stefan **3**:59
Borel, Émile **3**:398
convergence **5**:233
Cauchy, Augustin Louis **4**:219
expansion
Maclaurin, Colin **13**:32
factorial **8**:6
Fourier analysis **8**:254
hyperbolic functions **10**:348
infinite series **17**:209
logarithm
Brouncker, William **3**:512
mathematics, history of **13**:225
Taylor series **19**:51
trigonometric
Dirichlet, Peter Gustav Lejeune **6**:188
SERIGRAPHY *see* SILK-SCREEN PRINTING
SERKIN, RUDOLF **17**:209
SERLING, ROD **17**:209
SERLIO, SEBASTIANO **17**:209 *bibliog.*
theater architecture and staging **19**:152
SERMISY, CLAUDIN DE
music, history of Western **13**:664
Renaissance music **16**:156
SEROLOGY
diagnostic tests **6**:149–150
SEROTONIN **17**:209–210
hallucinogens **10**:24
inflammation **11**:169
nettle **14**:104
psychotropic drugs **15**:604
sleep **17**:360
SEROV, ALEKSANDR
Russian music **16**:368
SEROV, VALENTIN A.
Rimsky-Korsakov, Nikolai Andreyevich **16**:225 *illus.*
Russian art and architecture **16**:363
SEROWE (Botswana)
map (22° 25′S 26° 44′E) **3**:416
SERPENTINE **17**:210
dunite **6**:300
garnierite **9**:50
metamorphic rock **13**:332
SERPENTS MOUTH, STRAIT OF
map (10° 0′N 62° 0′W) **19**:300
SERRA, JUNÍPERO **17**:210 *bibliog.*
California **4**:36
San Diego (California) **17**:52
Spanish missions **18**:161
SÉRRAI (Greece)
map (41° 5′N 23° 32′E) **9**:325
SERRATIA **17**:210
nosocomial infections **17**:210
SERRAVALLE (San Marino)
map (43° 57′N 12° 30′E) **17**:56
SERT, JOSÉ LUIS **17**:210 *bibliog.*
SERTURNER, F. W. A.
morphine **13**:587
SERUM **17**:210 *bibliog.*
blood serum
albumin **1**:261
globulin **9**:209
cholesterol **4**:404
hepatitis **10**:130
immunoglobulin
immunity **11**:58
truth serum
sedative **17**:182
SERUM SICKNESS **17**:210
anaphylaxis **1**:392
SERVAL **17**:210–211 *illus.*
SERVANT, DOMESTIC *see* DOMESTIC SERVICE
SERVANT, THE (film) **12**:418 *illus.*
SERVETUS, MICHAEL **17**:211 *bibliog.*
SERVICE, ROBERT W. **17**:211 *bibliog., illus.*
SERVICE INDUSTRIES **17**:211 *bibliog.*
employment and unemployment **7**:159
manufacturing **13**:133
queuing theory **16**:25
United States **19**:432
SERVICEBERRY **17**:211
juneberry **11**:467
SERVICEMEN'S OPPORTUNITY COLLEGES **17**:211
See also MILITARY ACADEMIES
SERVOMECHANISM **17**:212 *bibliog.*
automation **2**:358
cybernetics **5**:401
Hammond, John Hays, Jr. **10**:31
SESAME (botany) **17**:212 *illus.*
"SESAME STREET" (television show) **17**:212 *bibliog., illus.*
Muppets **13**:644
SESE ISLANDS
map (0° 20′S 32° 20′E) **19**:372
SESOSTRIS I, KING OF EGYPT **17**:212
SESOSTRIS III, KING OF EGYPT **17**:212
SESOTHO LANGUAGE
Sotho **18**:70
SESSHU **17**:212–213 *bibliog.*
SESSIONS, ROGER **17**:213 *bibliog.*
SESSON **17**:213 *bibliog.*
SESTINA **17**:213
SET (chemistry)
elements
ring **16**:225
SET (Egyptian deity) **17**:213

mythology **13**:698
Oxyrhynchus **14**:478
SET (mathematics)
category **4**:202
linear
chain (mathematics) **4**:268
mean **13**:252–253
median **13**:264
mode (mathematics) **13**:489
null set **14**:292
set theory **17**:213
sphere **18**:180
variable **19**:522
Venn diagram **19**:546
SET DESIGN *see* BALLET; MUSICAL COMEDY; OPERA; THEATER ARCHITECTURE AND STAGING
SET THEORY **17**:213 *bibliog.*
See also GROUP THEORY
application **17**:213
axiomatic set theory **17**:213
Bolzano, Bernhard **3**:373
Boolean algebra **3**:393
Borel, Émile **3**:398
Cantor, Georg **4**:118
cardinal number **17**:213
chain (mathematics) **4**:268
field **8**:71
function **8**:359
history **17**:213
infinity **11**:168–169
isomorphism **11**:300
logic **12**:397
mathematics, history of **13**:226
null set **14**:292
ordinal number **17**:213
paradox (mathematics) **15**:75–76
ring (mathematics) **16**:225
Russell's paradox **16**:351
set cardinality **17**:213
Venn diagram **19**:546
SÈTE (France)
map (43° 24′N 3° 41′E) **8**:260
SETHOS I *see* SETI I, KING OF EGYPT
SETI I, KING OF EGYPT **17**:214
SÉTIF (Algeria)
map (36° 9′N 5° 26′E) **1**:287
SETO-NAIKAI *see* INLAND SEA
SETON, SAINT ELIZABETH ANN BAYLEY **17**:214 *bibliog.*
SETON, ERNEST THOMPSON **17**:214
SETON PORTAGE (British Columbia)
map (50° 43′N 122° 18′W) **3**:491
SETT *see* TARTAN
SETTAT (Morocco)
map (33° 4′N 7° 37′W) **13**:585
SETTER (dog) *see* SPORTING DOG
SETTIGNANO, DESIDERIO DA *see* DESIDERIO DA SETTIGNANO
THE SETTLEMENT (Virgin Islands)
map (18° 44′N 64° 19′W) **19**:605
SETTLEMENT, ACT OF **17**:214 *bibliog.*
George I, King of England, Scotland, and Ireland **9**:110
Hanover (dynasty) **10**:39
Stuart, James Francis Edward **18**:305
SETTLEMENT HOUSE
Hull House **10**:296
social work **18**:19
SETÚBAL (Portugal)
map (38° 32′N 8° 54′W) **15**:449
SETÚBAL, BAY OF
map (38° 27′N 8° 53′W) **15**:449
SEURAT, GEORGES **17**:214–215 *bibliog., illus.*
The Circus **15**:463 *illus.*
The Models **11**:67 *illus.*
neoimpressionism **14**:83
Signac, Paul **17**:300
Sunday Afternoon on the Island of La Grande Jatte **17**:214–215 *illus.*
SEUSS, DR. **17**:215 *illus.*
SEVASTIANOV, VITALY I. **17**:215 *bibliog.*
SEVASTOPOL (USSR) **17**:215
capture of **5**:349 *illus.*
climate **19**:390 *table*
Crimean War **5**:348
map (44° 36′N 33° 32′E) **19**:388
SEVEN AGAINST THEBES **17**:215
SEVEN DAYS' BATTLES
Civil War, U.S. **5**:24
Peninsular Campaign **15**:144
SEVEN DEVILS MOUNTAINS
map (45° 25′N 116° 30′W) **11**:26
"700 CLUB, THE"
religious broadcasting **16**:142
Robertson, Pat **16**:242
SEVEN LITTLE FOYS, THE *see* FOY, EDDIE
SEVEN OAKS, MASSACRE AT
Fraser, Simon **8**:287
Red River Settlement **16**:113
SEVEN PILLARS OF WISDOM (book) **17**:215–216
SEVEN SISTERS COLLEGES **17**:216 *bibliog.*
Barnard College **3**:86
Bryn Mawr College **3**:529
Mount Holyoke College **13**:618
Radcliffe College **16**:41
Smith College **17**:371–372
Vassar College **19**:526
Wellesley College **20**:100
SEVEN SLEEPERS OF EPHESUS **17**:216
SEVEN WEEKS' WAR **17**:216 *bibliog.*
SEVEN WONDERS OF THE WORLD **17**:216–218 *bibliog., illus.*
Colossus of Rhodes **17**:216–218
Hanging Gardens of Babylon **17**:216–217
Mausoleum at Halicarnassus **17**:217
Pharos of Alexandria **17**:218
Pyramids of Egypt **17**:216
Statue of Zeus at Olympia **17**:217
Temple of Artemis at Ephesus **17**:217
SEVEN YEARS' WAR **17**:218–219 *bibliog., illus., map*
British Empire **3**:496 *map*
Canada, history of **4**:81
Frederick II, King of Prussia **8**:293
French and Indian Wars **8**:314
Germany, history of **9**:152
Great Britain, history of **9**:315
India, history of **11**:92
Paris, treaties of **15**:87
Pitt, William (the Elder) **15**:320
Suvorov, Aleksandr Vasilievich **18**:374
SEVENERS *see* ISMAILIS
SEVENS (game) *see* FAN-TAN (card game)
17TH AMENDMENT **17**:219
Senate of the United States **17**:198
text **5**:222
7TH AMENDMENT **17**:219
jury **11**:477
text **5**:221
trial **19**:292
SEVENTH DAY ADVENTISTS *see* ADVENTISTS
SEVENTH-DAY BAPTISTS
Beissel, Johann Conrad **3**:172
Pennsylvania **15**:151 *illus.*
77 DREAM SONGS (poem)
Berryman, John **3**:225
SEVERINI, GINO **17**:219 *bibliog., illus.*
Danseuse bleue **8**:384 *illus.*
Dynamic Hieroglyphic of the Bal Tabarin **17**:219 *illus.*
SEVERN, JOSEPH
John Keats **12**:36 *illus.*
Percy Bysshe Shelley **16**:293 *illus.*
SEVERN, RIVER **17**:220
Cotswold-Severn **5**:304
map (56° 2′N 87° 36′W) **14**:393
SEVERNA PARK (Maryland)
map (39° 4′N 76° 33′W) **13**:188
SEVERNAYA ZEMLYA ISLANDS
map (79° 30′N 98° 0′E) **19**:388
SEVERUS, SEPTIMIUS, ROMAN EMPEROR **17**:220 *bibliog.*
Leptis Magna **12**:295
SEVIER (county in Arkansas)
map (34° 0′N 91° 50′W) **2**:166
SEVIER (county in Tennessee)
map (35° 45′N 83° 35′W) **19**:104
SEVIER (county in Utah)
map (38° 45′N 111° 45′W) **19**:492
SEVIER, JOHN **17**:220 *bibliog.*
Tennessee **19**:106
SEVIER BRIDGE RESERVOIR
map (39° 21′N 111° 57′W) **19**:492
SEVIER DESERT
map (39° 25′N 112° 50′W) **19**:492
SEVIER LAKE
map (38° 55′N 113° 9′W) **19**:492
SEVIER RIVER
map (39° 4′N 113° 6′W) **19**:492
SEVIERVILLE (Tennessee)
map (35° 52′N 83° 34′W) **19**:104
SÉVIGNÉ, MADAME DE **17**:220 *bibliog.*
SEVILLA (Spain) *see* SEVILLE (Spain)
SEVILLE (Florida)
map (29° 19′N 81° 30′W) **8**:172
SEVILLE (Spain) **17**:220–221 *illus.*
architecture
Giralda (tower) **9**:188
art
Figueroa (family) **8**:75
Moorish art and architecture **13**:571
Spanish art and architecture **18**:153
map (37° 23′N 5° 59′W) **18**:140
SÈVRES, TREATY OF
Kurds **12**:139
Lausanne, Treaty of **12**:239–240
Middle East **13**:407 *map*
World War I **20**:246
SÈVRES WARE **17**:221 *bibliog., illus.*
Limoges ware **12**:346
pottery and porcelain **15**:471 *illus.*
SEWA RIVER
map (7° 18′N 12° 8′W) **17**:296
SEWAGE
See also SEWERAGE
groundwater pollution **9**:374–375
septic tank **17**:206
treatment
plant **17**:223 *illus.*
pollution control **15**:416
sewerage **17**:222–223
typhoid fever **19**:366
SEWALL, SAMUEL **17**:221
Salem Witch Trials **17**:31
SEWANEE (Tennessee)
map (35° 12′N 85° 55′W) **19**:104
SEWARD (Alaska)
map (60° 6′N 149° 26′W) **1**:242
SEWARD (county in Kansas)
map (37° 10′N 100° 50′W) **12**:18
SEWARD (Nebraska)
map (40° 55′N 97° 6′W) **14**:70
SEWARD (county in Nebraska)
map (40° 55′N 97° 5′W) **14**:70
SEWARD, ALBERT CHARLES
paleobotany **15**:32
SEWARD, WILLIAM H. **17**:221 *bibliog., illus.*
Civil War, U.S. **5**:19
Weed, Thurlow **20**:90
SEWARD PENINSULA
map (65° 0′N 164° 0′W) **1**:242
SEWARD'S FOLLY
Alaska **1**:246
SEWAREN (New Jersey)
map (40° 33′N 74° 16′W) **14**:129
SEWELL, ANNA **17**:221
Black Beauty (book) **3**:313
SEWELLEL **17**:222 *illus.*
SEWERAGE **17**:222–223 *bibliog., illus.*
civil engineering **5**:10–11
gastrointestinal tract disease **9**:56
plumbing **15**:371–372 *illus.*
septic tank **17**:206
sludge **17**:364
soap and detergent **18**:8
systems **17**:222
toilet **19**:222
treatment **17**:222–223 *illus.*
SEWING
embroidery **7**:152
needle **14**:76
needlework **14**:76
SEWING MACHINE **17**:223–224 *bibliog., illus.*
clothing industry **5**:65
Howe, Elias **10**:283
Singer, Isaac Merrit **17**:322
SEX **17**:224 *bibliog.*
See also index headings beginning with SEX or SEXUAL
SEX CELL
zygote **20**:384
SEX CHANGE *see* SEX REASSIGNMENT
SEX CHROMOSOMES **9**:88 *illus.*
genetic diseases **9**:83
genetics **9**:88
growth **9**:380
hemophilia **10**:120
immunodeficiency disease **11**:59
muscular dystrophy **13**:656
reproduction **16**:162
sex determination
hermaphrodite **10**:142
Wilson, Edmund B. **20**:164
sexual development **17**:228
SEX DIFFERENCES
embryo
pregnancy and birth **15**:503
sex hormones **17**:225
sex roles **17**:226–227
sexual development **17**:228–230
sexual intercourse **17**:230–231
social psychology **18**:13
stuttering **18**:310
SEX EDUCATION **17**:224–225 *bibliog.*
erotic and pornographic literature **7**:234
sex therapy **17**:227
sexual development **17**:228–230
SEX HORMONES **17**:225 *bibliog.*
adrenal gland **1**:108
androgens **17**:226
animal behavior **2**:14–15
aphrodisiac **2**:78
baldness **3**:34
birth control **3**:294
breast **3**:469 *illus.*
Butenandt, Adolf **3**:591
castration **17**:226
cholesterol **4**:404
corticoid **5**:278
Doisy, Edward **6**:224
endocrine system **7**:169
endocrine system, diseases of the **7**:170–171
estrogen **17**:226
estrous cycle **7**:248
females **17**:226
gestation **9**:160
gonadotropin **9**:242
growth **9**:379–380
hormonal regulation **17**:226
hormone, animal **10**:234; **10**:236
hypogonadism **17**:226
Klinefelter's syndrome **12**:98
males **17**:226
menopause **13**:299; **17**:226
menstruation **13**:301
pigment, skin **15**:300
progesterone **17**:226
sex reassignment **17**:225–226
sexual behavior **17**:226–227
sexual development **17**:229
synthesis
Ružička, Leopold **16**:377
testosterone **17**:226
SEX-LINKED DISEASES
amniocentesis **1**:375
color blindness **5**:114
diseases, human **6**:193
genetic diseases **9**:83–84
genetics **9**:88
gout **9**:266
growth, hormonal effects **9**:380
headache **10**:86
hemophilia **10**:119–120 *illus.*
Hodgkin's disease **10**:194
Klinefelter's syndrome **12**:98
lupus erythematosus **12**:466
muscular dystrophy **13**:656
myasthenia gravis **13**:689
skin diseases **17**:342
spondylitis **18**:192
varicose vein **19**:523
SEX ORGANS **7**:169 *illus.*
development **6**:141–142
pineal gland **15**:306
endocrine system **7**:169 *illus.*
endocrine system, diseases of the **7**:170–171
gonorrhea **9**:244
hermaphrodite **10**:142
menopause **13**:300
prostate gland **15**:573
puerperal fever **15**:614
reproduction **16**:161–162
reproductive system, human **16**:163 *illus.*
sex hormones **17**:226
sex reassignment **17**:225–226
SEX REASSIGNMENT **17**:225–226 *bibliog.*
SEX RESEARCH
Ellis, Havelock **7**:148
Kinsey reports **12**:85
Masters and Johnson reports **13**:216
sexual intercourse **17**:231
SEX ROLES **17**:226–227 *bibliog.*
SEX THERAPY **17**:227 *bibliog.*
Masters and Johnson reports **13**:216
SEXISM **17**:227
discrimination **6**:190
feminism **8**:48–49
Islam, harem **10**:49
role **16**:271
women in society **20**:201–204
SEXTANT **17**:227–228 *illus.*
astrolabe **2**:271
navigation **14**:59–60 *illus.*
SEXTON, ANNE **17**:228 *bibliog., illus.*
SEXUAL BEHAVIOR
Ellis, Havelock **7**:148
exhibitionism **7**:332
fetishism **8**:63
folklore **8**:203
homosexuality **10**:217
incest **11**:73–74
Kinsey reports **12**:85
lesbianism **12**:296
marriage **13**:163–166
masochism **13**:198
Masters and Johnson reports **13**:216
masturbation **13**:217–218
nymphomania **14**:309
prostitution **15**:573–574
sadism **17**:10
satyriasis **17**:93
sex therapy **17**:227
sexual intercourse **17**:230–231
sodomy **18**:34

SEXUAL BEHAVIOR (cont.)
transvestism **19**:283
voyeurism **19**:638
SEXUAL BEHAVIOR, ANIMAL *see* ANIMAL COURTSHIP AND MATING
SEXUAL DEVELOPMENT 17:228–230 *bibliog.*
adolescence **1**:106; **17**:230
adulthood **17**:230
animal behavior **2**:13
arthropod **2**:217
coelenterate **5**:91–92
complex (psychology) **5**:157
early childhood **17**:229
Freud, Sigmund **8**:329
hair **10**:14
infancy **11**:163; **17**:228
late childhood **17**:229
prenatal **17**:228
puberty **17**:229–230
SEXUAL DRIVE
libido **12**:314
SEXUAL INTERCOURSE 17:230–231 *bibliog.*
animal courtship and mating **2**:20–22
aphrodisiac **2**:78
artificial insemination **2**:220–221
birth control **3**:293–294
bride-price **3**:479
celibacy **4**:231
cervicitis **4**:261–262
coitus **17**:230–231
coloration, biological **5**:122
frequency **17**:231
frigidity **8**:334
orgasm **17**:230–231
rape **16**:88
rat **2**:12 *illus.*
reproductive system, human **16**:163–166
sexual response cycle **17**:231
trichomoniasis **19**:296
venereal disease **19**:539–541
SEXUAL SELECTION 17:231–232 *bibliog.*
natural selection **14**:49
SEXUAL STERILIZATION *see* STERILIZATION, SEXUAL
SEXUAL STIMULANT *see* APHRODISIAC
SEYCHELLES 17:232 *bibliog., illus., map*
flag **17**:232 *illus.*
history and government **17**:232
land, people, and economy **17**:232
map (4° 35′S 55° 40′E) **1**:136
SEYCHELLES KESTREL *see* FALCON
SEYCHELLOIS, MOUNT
map (4° 39′S 55° 26′E) **19**:574
SEYDISFJÖRDUR (Iceland)
map (65° 16′N 14° 0′W) **11**:17
SEYFERT GALAXIES 17:232–233 *bibliog.*
extragalactic systems **7**:346
X-ray galaxies **20**:309
SEYLER, FELIX HOPPE- *see* HOPPE-SEYLER, FELIX
SEYMOUR (Connecticut)
map (41° 24′N 73° 4′W) **5**:193
SEYMOUR (Indiana)
map (38° 58′N 85° 53′W) **11**:111
SEYMOUR (Iowa)
map (40° 44′N 93° 7′W) **11**:244
SEYMOUR (Missouri)
map (37° 9′N 92° 46′W) **13**:476
SEYMOUR (Texas)
map (33° 35′N 99° 16′W) **19**:129
SEYMOUR (Wisconsin)
map (44° 31′N 88° 20′W) **20**:185
SEYMOUR, DAVID "CHIM"
photojournalism **15**:273
SEYMOUR, EDWARD, 1ST DUKE OF SOMERSET *see* SOMERSET, EDWARD SEYMOUR, 1ST DUKE OF
SEYMOUR, HORATIO 17:233 *bibliog.*
SEYMOUR, JANE 17:233 *bibliog.*
Somerset, Edward Seymour, 1st Duke of **18**:61
SEYMOUR, LYNN 17:233
SEYMOUR, THOMAS, BARON SEYMOUR OF SUDELEY
Elizabeth I, Queen of England **7**:141
Parr, Catherine **15**:97
SEYMOUR LAKE
map (44° 54′N 71° 59′W) **19**:554
SEZESSION STYLE *see* SECESSION MOVEMENT
SFAX (Tunisia) 17:233
map (34° 44′N 10° 46′E) **19**:335
SFORZA (family) 17:233 *bibliog.*
Milan (Italy) **13**:418
monument
Leonardo da Vinci **12**:289; **12**:291
SFORZA, LUDOVICO
Italian Wars **11**:319
Sforza (family) **17**:233
SGAW LANGUAGE
Sino-Tibetan languages **17**:324
SGRAFFITO
Pennsylvania Dutch **15**:152 *illus.*
SHABA (Zaire) 17:233
cities
Lubumbashi **12**:448
history
Congo crisis **5**:183
Tshombe, Moise Kapenda **19**:323
people
Luba **12**:446
SHABANI (Zimbabwe)
map (20° 20′S 30° 2′E) **20**:365
SHACKELFORD (county in Texas)
map (32° 45′N 99° 20′W) **19**:129
SHACKLETON, SIR ERNEST HENRY 17:233 *bibliog.*
Antarctica **2**:44 *map*
SHACKLETON ICE SHELF
map (66° 0′S 100° 0′E) **2**:40
SHAD 17:233–234 *bibliog., illus.*
SHADBUSH *see* SERVICEBERRY
SHADEHILL RESERVOIR
map (45° 45′N 102° 15′W) **18**:103
SHADOOF *see* LEVER
SHADOW CABINET
cabinet **4**:5
SHADOW PLAY 17:234
puppet **8**:198 *illus.*; **15**:627 *illus.*
theater, history of the **19**:149
SHADWELL, THOMAS 17:234 *bibliog.*
SHADY COVE (Oregon)
map (42° 37′N 122° 49′W) **14**:427
SHADY GROVE (Florida)
map (30° 17′N 83° 38′W) **8**:172
SHAFER, LAKE
map (40° 47′N 86° 46′W) **11**:111
SHAFFER, PETER 17:234 *bibliog.*
SHAFTER (California)
map (29° 49′N 104° 18′W) **4**:31
SHAFTER, WILLIAM RUFUS 17:234
SHAFTESBURY, ANTHONY ASHLEY COOPER, 1ST EARL OF 17:234 *bibliog.*
South Carolina **18**:100
SHAFTESBURY, ANTHONY ASHLEY COOPER, 3D EARL OF 17:234 *bibliog.*
SHAFTESBURY, ANTHONY ASHLEY COOPER, 7TH EARL OF 17:234–235 *bibliog.*
SHAGAMU (Nigeria)
map (6° 51′N 3° 39′E) **14**:190
SHAGARI, SHEHU 17:235
Nigeria **14**:192
SHAGELUK (Alaska)
map (62° 36′N 159° 32′W) **1**:242
SHAH OF IRAN *see* MUHAMMAD REZA SHAH PAHLAVI (1919-80); REZA SHAH PAHLAVI (1878-1944)
SHAH JAHAN, MOGUL EMPEROR OF INDIA 17:235 *bibliog.*
India, history of **11**:91
Mogul art and architecture **13**:501–502
Taj Mahal **19**:14–15
SHAH NAMAH (poem) 17:235; **15**:182 *illus.*; **17**:235 *bibliog.*
Firdawsi **8**:100
Parthia **15**:100
Persian art and architecture **15**:185
SHAHN, BEN 17:235 *bibliog., illus.*
painting lampooning bootleggers **19**:454 *illus.*
The Passion of Sacco and Vanzetti **17**:235 *illus.*
Scotts Run, West Virginia **18**:13 *illus.*
Years of Dust (poster) **6**:119 *illus.*
SHAHNAI
Indian music **11**:102 *illus.*
SHAHREZA (Iran)
map (32° 1′N 51° 52′E) **11**:250
SHAHRUD (Iran)
map (36° 25′N 55° 1′E) **11**:250
SHAIB AL-BANAT, MOUNT
map (26° 59′N 33° 29′E) **7**:76
SHAKA, KING OF THE ZULUS 1:155 *illus.*; **17**:235 *bibliog.*
Africa, history of **1**:154
Nguni **14**:176
Zulu **20**:382
SHAKER HEIGHTS (Ohio)
map (41° 29′N 81° 36′W) **14**:357
SHAKERS 17:235–236 *bibliog., illus.*
interior design **11**:213 *illus.*
Lee, Ann **12**:269
rugs and carpets **16**:341
SHAKESPEARE, WILLIAM 7:144 *illus.*; 7:194 *illus.*; **17**:236–237 *bibliog., illus.*
See also ELIZABETHAN AGE; ELIZABETHAN PLAYHOUSE; GLOBE THEATER
actors and acting **1**:87
Chamberlain's Men **4**:274
Cooke, George Frederick **5**:237
Evans, Maurice **7**:313
Forrest, Edwin **8**:234
Garrick, David **9**:50–51
Jones, James Earl **11**:443
Kean (family) **12**:34–35 *illus.*
Olivier, Laurence Kerr, Baron Olivier of Brighton **14**:379
Royal Shakespeare Company **16**:331
Scofield, Paul **17**:147
comedies **5**:132; **17**:237
As You Like It **2**:226
Merchant of Venice, The **13**:304
Merry Wives of Windsor, The **13**:312
A Midsummer Night's Dream **13**:414
Much Ado About Nothing **13**:630
Taming of the Shrew, The **19**:19
Tempest, The **19**:93
Troilus and Cressida **19**:305
Twelfth Night **19**:358
criticism, literary **17**:237
Bradley, A. C. **3**:437
Granville-Barker, Harley **9**:289
Johnson, Samuel **11**:435–436
drama **6**:259
Falstaff (fictional character) **8**:15
First Folio edition **17**:236 *illus.*
Folger Shakespeare Library **8**:195
fool **8**:213
history plays **17**:237
Antony and Cleopatra **2**:71
Henry IV, Parts 1 and 2 **10**:124
Henry V **10**:124
Richard II **16**:209
Richard III **16**:209
music for the plays
Arne, Thomas **2**:183–184
poems
Rape of Lucrece, The **16**:88
Puck (fictional character) **15**:612
sonnets **18**:65
sources
Holinshed, Raphael **10**:202–203
Lodge, Thomas **12**:392–393
Stratford-on-Avon (England) **18**:291
theater, history of the **19**:150
theatrical presentation
Brook, Peter **3**:509
theatrical presentations
Papp, Joseph **15**:72
tragedies **17**:237
Hamlet **10**:30
Julius Caesar **11**:466
King Lear **12**:82
Macbeth **13**:6–7
Othello **14**:459–460
Romeo and Juliet **16**:304
SHAKI (Nigeria)
map (8° 39′N 3° 25′E) **14**:190
SHAKOPEE (Minnesota)
map (44° 48′N 93° 32′W) **13**:453
SHAKTI 17:237 *bibliog.*
Kali **12**:8
SHAKTOOLIK (Alaska)
map (64° 20′N 161° 9′W) **1**:242
SHAKUNTALA (play)
Kalidasa **12**:8
SHALE 17:237–238 *bibliog.*
clay minerals **5**:46–47
emery **7**:155
rock **16**:247
sedimentary rock **17**:185
shale, oil **17**:238
stratigraphy **18**:292 *illus.*
SHALE, OIL 17:238 *bibliog.*
energy sources **7**:175
fossil record **8**:243
naphtha **14**:14
petroleum **15**:209
synthetic fuels **18**:409–410
SHALIMAR GARDENS
Lahore (Pakistan) **12**:167
SHALLOT 17:238 *illus.*; **19**:534 *illus.*
SHALLOTTE (North Carolina)
map (33° 58′N 78° 23′W) **14**:242
SHALMANESER I, KING OF ASSYRIA
Nimrud **14**:199
SHALMANESER III, KING OF ASSYRIA 15:44 *illus.*; **17**:238
Nimrud **14**:199
SHAMAN 17:238–239 *bibliog., illus.*
cannibalism **4**:109 *illus.*
Chukchi **4**:422
Colorado (American Indians) **5**:120
Eskimo **7**:241
folk medicine **8**:201
ghost dance **9**:169
Indians, American **11**:122; **11**:123 *illus.*; **11**:135
Indians of North America, art of the **11**:139
Kublai Khan, Mongol Emperor **12**:134
magic **13**:49–50 *illus.*
mana **13**:107
mask dance **11**:122 *illus.*
medicine **13**:267
Popé **15**:430
primitive religion **15**:544–545 *illus.*
secret societies **17**:181
Warrau **20**:31
Yurok **20**:347
SHAMANISM *see* SHAMAN
SHAMASH **2**:249 *illus.*
Mesopotamian art and architecture **13**:320 *illus.*
SHAMATTAWA (Manitoba)
map (55° 52′N 92° 5′W) **13**:119
SHAMIR, YITZHAK 17:239
SHAMOKIN (Pennsylvania)
map (40° 47′N 76° 34′W) **15**:147
SHAMPOO
cosmetics **5**:282–283 *table*
SHAMRA, RAS *see* UGARIT
SHAMROCK 17:239 *illus.*
SHAMROCK (Texas)
map (35° 13′N 100° 15′W) **19**:129
SHAMSHIR (Persia)
sword and knife **18**:398 *illus.*
SHAMSI-ADAD I
Mari **13**:149–150
SHAN 17:239
SHAN PLATEAU
map (21° 30′N 98° 30′E) **3**:573
SHAN-T'OU (SWATOW) (China)
map (23° 23′N 116° 41′E) **4**:362
SHAN-TUNG PENINSULA
map (37° 0′N 121° 0′E) **4**:362
SHANDI (Sudan)
map (16° 42′N 33° 26′E) **18**:320
SHANDONG (China) *see* SHANTUNG (Shandong) (China)
SHANG (dynasty) 17:239 *bibliog.*
Anyang **2**:72
Asia, history of **2**:251–252
bronze vessel from **2**:251 *illus.*
China, history of **4**:370
Chinese archaeology **4**:378
Chinese calendar **4**:388
oracle bones **4**:379 *illus.*; **14**:413
wagon **20**:6
SHANGHAI (China) 4:364 *table*; **17**:239–240 *bibliog., illus.*
climate **2**:237 *table*
map (31° 14′N 121° 28′E) **4**:362
Sino-Japanese War **20**:250 *illus.*
SHANGRI-LA 17:240
SHANIDAR (Iraq) 17:240 *bibliog.*
funeral customs **8**:364–365
SHANKAR, RAVI 17:240 *bibliog.*
SHANKARA
Vedanta **19**:530
SHANKLAND, E. C.
skyscraper **17**:350
SHANNON (Georgia)
map (34° 20′N 85° 4′W) **9**:114
SHANNON (Mississippi)
map (34° 7′N 88° 43′W) **13**:469
SHANNON (county in Missouri)
map (37° 10′N 91° 25′W) **13**:476
SHANNON (county in South Dakota)
map (43° 18′N 102° 35′W) **18**:103
SHANNON, CLAUDE ELWOOD 17:240
communication model **5**:143 *illus.*
entropy **7**:209
information theory **11**:174
SHANNON, RIVER 17:240
map (52° 36′N 9° 41′W) **11**:258
SHANSI (Shanxi) (China) 17:240
cities
T'ai-yüan (Taiyuan) **19**:11
SHANTUNG (Shandong) (China) 17:240–241
cities
Tsinan (Jinan) **19**:324
Tsingtao (Quingdao) **19**:324
SHANTY (work song) 17:241 *bibliog.*
SHANTYTOWN
city **5**:6
SHANXI (China) *see* SHANSI (Shanxi) (China)
SHAO-HSING (China)
map (30° 0′N 120° 35′E) **4**:362
SHAO-KUAN (China)
map (24° 50′N 113° 37′E) **4**:362
SHAO-YANG (China)
map (27° 6′N 111° 25′E) **4**:362
SHAPIRO, IRVING I.

gravitation 9:305
relativity 16:135
SHAPIRO, KARL 17:241 *bibliog.*
SHAPLEY, HARLOW 17:241 *bibliog.*
astronomy, history of 2:281
Cepheids 4:257
SHAPLEY-CURTIS DEBATE
Curtis, Heber Doust 5:395
SHAPORIN, YURI
Russian music 16:369
SHAPUR I, KING OF PERSIA 13:401 *illus.*; 17:241 *bibliog.*
Hatra 10:68
Persia, ancient 15:183
Sassanians 17:83–84
statue 15:183 *illus.*
SHAPUR II, KING OF PERSIA 17:241 *bibliog.*
SHARAKU 17:241 *bibliog.*
The Actor Segawa Kikunojo 11:378 *illus.*
SHARBLES, JAMES
Joseph Priestley 15:536 *illus.*
SHARBOT LAKE (Ontario)
map (44° 46′N 76° 41′W) 14:393; 14:461
SHARE DRUM 15:162 *illus.*
SHARETT, MOSHE 17:241
SHARIA 17:241–242 *bibliog.*
Islam 11:288
women in society 20:203; 20:204
SHARJAH (United Arab Emirates)
map (25° 22′N 55° 23′E) 19:401
United Arab Emirates 19:400–401 *table*
SHARK 17:242–244 *bibliog.*, *illus.*
basking shark 17:242–243 *illus.*
bull shark 17:242–243 *illus.*
chimaera 4:358
Chondrichthyes 4:404
classification, biological 17:242
digestive system 6:173 *illus.*
dogfish 6:222–223
great white shark 8:116 *illus.*; 17:242–243 *illus.*
hammerhead 17:242–243 *illus.*
Nicaragua, Lake 14:179
skin 17:340 *illus.*
thresher shark 17:243 *illus.*
tiger shark 17:242–243 *illus.*
SHARK BAY
map (25° 30′S 113° 30′E) 2:328
SHARKEY (county in Mississippi)
map (32° 50′N 90° 50′W) 13:469
SHARKTOOTH MOUNTAIN
map (58° 35′N 127° 57′W) 3:491
SHARM AL-SHEIKH 17:244
SHARON (Massachusetts)
map (41° 53′N 73° 29′W) 13:206
SHARON (North Dakota)
map (47° 36′N 97° 54′W) 14:248
SHARON (Pennsylvania)
map (41° 14′N 80° 31′W) 15:147
SHARON, ARIEL 17:244
SHARON, PLAIN OF 17:244
SHARON SPRINGS (Kansas)
map (38° 54′N 101° 45′W) 12:18
SHARONVILLE (Ohio)
map (39° 16′N 84° 25′W) 14:357
SHARP (county in Arkansas)
map (36° 10′N 91° 30′W) 2:166
SHARP, WILLIAM 17:244
SHARPBILL 17:244
SHARPE, LAKE
map (44° 5′N 99° 55′W) 18:103
SHARPEVILLE MASSACRE
South Africa 18:83
SHARPSHOOTING *see* SHOOTING (sport)
SHASTA (county in California)
map (40° 50′N 122° 0′W) 4:31
SHASTA, MOUNT 17:244
map (41° 20′N 122° 20′W) 4:31
SHASTA DAISY 17:244
SHASTA LAKE
map (40° 50′N 122° 25′W) 4:31
SHATALOV, VLADIMIR A. 17:244–245 *bibliog.*
SHATT AL- FEDJADJ
map (33° 55′N 9° 10′E) 19:335
SHATT AL- RHARSA
map (34° 6′N 7° 50′E) 19:335
SHATT-AL-ARAB 17:245
map (29° 57′N 48° 34′E) 11:255
SHATT DJERID
map (33° 42′N 8° 26′E) 19:335
SHATTUCK (Oklahoma)
map (36° 16′N 99° 53′W) 14:368
SHAUNAVON (Saskatchewan)
map (49° 40′N 108° 25′W) 17:81
SHAVIAN MANORIAL STYLE *see* SHAW, RICHARD NORMAN
SHAVUOTH 17:245
SHAW (Mississippi)
map (33° 36′N 90° 46′W) 13:469
SHAW, ANNA HOWARD 17:245 *bibliog.*
SHAW, EDWARD
monetary theory 13:525
SHAW, GEORGE BERNARD 17:245–246 *bibliog.*, *illus.*
Arms and the Man 2:179
Campbell, Mrs. Patrick 4:27
Candida 4:107
drama 6:261
Major Barbara 13:77
Man and Superman
comedy 5:132
portrait
John, Augustus 11:423
Pygmalion 15:633
Saint Joan 17:19
Terry, Dame Ellen Alice 19:122
SHAW, HENRY WHEELER *see* BILLINGS, JOSH
SHAW, IRWIN 17:246
SHAW, SIR NAPIER 17:246
SHAW, RICHARD NORMAN 17:246 *bibliog.*
SHAW, T. E. *see* LAWRENCE, T. E.
SHAWANO (Wisconsin)
map (44° 47′N 88° 36′W) 20:185
SHAWANO (county in Wisconsin)
map (44° 47′N 88° 43′W) 20:185
SHAWINIGAN (Quebec)
map (46° 33′N 72° 45′W) 16:18
SHAWM 17:246
SHAWMUT (Alabama)
map (32° 51′N 85° 13′W) 1:234
SHAWN, EDWIN MYERS *see* SHAWN, TED
SHAWN, TED 13:496 *illus.*; 17:246 *bibliog.*
Denishawn 6:108
Jacob's Pillow Dance Festival 11:346
SHAWN, WILLIAM
New Yorker, The 14:156
SHAWNEE (American Indians) 17:246–247 *bibliog.*
Cornstalk 5:269
Delaware (American Indians) 6:91
Shawnee Prophet 17:247
Tecumseh (Shawnee Indian) 19:69
SHAWNEE (Kansas)
map (39° 1′N 94° 43′W) 12:18
SHAWNEE (county in Kansas)
map (39° 5′N 95° 45′W) 12:18
SHAWNEE (Oklahoma)
map (35° 20′N 96° 55′W) 14:368
SHAWNEE NATIONAL FOREST 11:41 *illus.*
SHAWNEE PROPHET 17:247 *bibliog.*
Tecumseh (Shawnee Indian) 19:69
SHAWNEETOWN (Illinois)
map (37° 42′N 88° 8′W) 11:42
SHAYS, DANIEL
Shays's Rebellion 17:247
SHAYS'S REBELLION 17:247 *bibliog.*
United States, history of the 19:441
SHCHEDRIN, MIKHAIL YEVGRAFOVICH SALTYKOV *see* SALTYKOV SHCHEDRIN, MIKHAIL YEVGRAFOVICH
SHE-OAK *see* *CASUARINA*
SHE STOOPS TO CONQUER (play) 17:247
comedy 5:132
SHEARWATER 17:247 *illus.*
SHEATHBILL 17:247
shorebirds 17:283
SHEBA 17:247–248 *bibliog.*
Ma'rib 13:151
SHEBA, QUEEN OF
Sheba 17:248
SHEBALIN, VISSARION
Russian music 16:369
SHEBERGHAN (Afghanistan)
map (36° 41′N 65° 45′E) 1:133
SHEBOYGAN (Wisconsin) 17:248
map (43° 46′N 87° 36′W) 20:185
SHEBOYGAN (county in Wisconsin)
map (43° 42′N 87° 57′W) 20:185
SHEBOYGAN FALLS (Wisconsin)
map (43° 44′N 87° 49′W) 20:185
SHECHEM (Israel) 17:248 *bibliog.*
SHEDIAC (New Brunswick)
map (46° 13′N 64° 32′W) 14:117
SHEELER, CHARLES 17:248 *bibliog.*, *illus.*
Of Yachts and Yachting 17:248 *illus.*
SHEELITE
sulfate minerals 18:333
SHEEN, FULTON J. 17:248 *bibliog.*
SHEEP 17:248–249 *bibliog.*, *illus.*
animal husbandry 2:24; 2:25 *illus.*
Bharal sheep 13:623 *illus.*
bighorn 3:249–250
breeds 17:249 *illus.*
imprinting 11:69
mountain life 13:623 *illus.*
mountain sheep 13:624
New Zealand 14:160 *illus.*
ruminant 16:345
sheep industry 17:249
wool 20:213–214
SHEEP, MOUNTAIN *see* MOUNTAIN SHEEP
SHEEP SHEARING 20:214 *illus.*
SHEEPDOG *see* WORKING DOG
SHEEPSKIN *see* LEATHER AND HIDES
SHEET-FED PRESS 17:249–250 *bibliog.*
SHEET HARBOUR (Nova Scotia)
map (44° 55′N 62° 32′W) 14:269
SHEFFIELD (Alabama)
map (34° 46′N 87° 40′W) 1:234
SHEFFIELD (England) 17:250
map (53° 23′N 1° 30′W) 19:403
SHEFFIELD (Illinois)
map (41° 21′N 89° 44′W) 11:42
SHEFFIELD (Iowa)
map (42° 54′N 93° 13′W) 11:244
SHEFFIELD (Massachusetts)
map (42° 5′N 73° 21′W) 13:206
SHEFFIELD (Pennsylvania)
map (41° 42′N 79° 2′W) 15:147
SHEFFIELD (Texas)
map (30° 41′N 101° 49′W) 19:129
SHEIKH, MUJIB *see* MUJIBUR RAHMAN
SHELBINA (Missouri)
map (39° 47′N 92° 2′W) 13:476
SHELBURN (Indiana)
map (39° 11′N 87° 24′W) 11:111
SHELBURNE (Nova Scotia)
map (43° 46′N 65° 19′W) 14:269
SHELBURNE (Ontario)
map (44° 4′N 80° 12′W) 14:393; 19:241
SHELBURNE, WILLIAM PETTY FITZMAURICE, 2D EARL OF 17:250
SHELBURNE FALLS (Massachusetts)
map (42° 36′N 72° 44′W) 13:206
SHELBY (county in Alabama)
map (33° 20′N 86° 35′W) 1:234
SHELBY (county in Illinois)
map (39° 25′N 88° 50′W) 11:42
SHELBY (county in Indiana)
map (39° 31′N 85° 47′W) 11:111
SHELBY (Iowa)
map (41° 31′N 95° 27′W) 11:244
SHELBY (county in Iowa)
map (41° 38′N 95° 15′W) 11:244
SHELBY (county in Kentucky)
map (38° 10′N 85° 12′W) 12:47
SHELBY (Michigan)
map (43° 37′N 86° 22′W) 13:377
SHELBY (Mississippi)
map (33° 57′N 90° 46′W) 13:469
SHELBY (county in Missouri)
map (39° 49′N 92° 3′W) 13:476
SHELBY (Montana)
map (48° 30′N 111° 51′W) 13:547
SHELBY (Nebraska)
map (41° 12′N 97° 26′W) 14:70
SHELBY (North Carolina)
map (35° 17′N 81° 32′W) 14:242
SHELBY (Ohio)
map (40° 53′N 82° 40′W) 14:357
SHELBY (county in Ohio)
map (40° 18′N 84° 10′W) 14:357
SHELBY (county in Tennessee)
map (35° 15′N 89° 55′W) 19:104
SHELBY (county in Texas)
map (31° 45′N 94° 8′W) 19:129
SHELBY, ISAAC 17:250 *bibliog.*
SHELBYVILLE (Illinois)
map (39° 24′N 88° 48′W) 11:42
SHELBYVILLE (Indiana)
map (39° 31′N 85° 47′W) 11:111
SHELBYVILLE (Kentucky)
map (38° 13′N 85° 14′W) 12:47
SHELBYVILLE (Missouri)
map (39° 48′N 92° 2′W) 13:476
SHELBYVILLE (Tennessee)
map (35° 29′N 86° 27′W) 19:104
SHELBYVILLE, LAKE
map (39° 30′N 88° 40′W) 11:42
SHELDON (Iowa)
map (43° 11′N 95° 51′W) 11:244
SHELDON (Missouri)
map (37° 40′N 94° 18′W) 13:476
SHELDON, EDWARD 17:250
SHELDUCK 17:250
SHELEKHOV, GRIGORY IVANOVICH 17:250
Kodiak Island (Alaska) 12:105
Russian-American Company 16:360
SHELEKHOV, GULF OF
map (60° 0′N 158° 0′E) 19:388
SHELFORD'S LAW OF TOLERANCE
plant distribution 15:343
SHELL 17:250–252 *bibliog.*, *illus.*
Cambrian Period 4:52
conch 5:170; 17:250–251 *illus.*
cowrie 5:322; 17:250–251 *illus.*
egg 7:72 *illus.*
foraminifera 8:219
hermit crab 10:143
Indians, American
carved shell gorget 14:238 *illus.*
mollusk 13:510–512 *illus.*
shell collecting 17:252
Silurian Period 17:310 *illus.*
skeletal system 17:333
snail 17:375–376
turtle 19:352–353
wampum 20:21
whelk 20:130
SHELL LAKE (Wisconsin)
map (45° 45′N 91° 55′W) 20:185
SHELL MODEL
nuclear physics 14:286
SHELL MOLDING
casting 4:189
SHELL RACING
rowing 16:328 *illus.*
SHELL ROCK (Iowa)
map (42° 43′N 92° 35′W) 11:244
SHELL ROCK RIVER
map (42° 38′N 92° 30′W) 11:244
SHELL SHOCK
neurosis 14:107
SHELLAC 17:252
resin 16:176
scale insect 17:107
SHELLBROOK (Saskatchewan)
map (53° 13′N 106° 24′W) 17:81
SHELLEY (Idaho)
map (43° 23′N 112° 7′W) 11:26
SHELLEY, MARY WOLLSTONECRAFT 17:252–253 *bibliog.*, *illus.*
Frankenstein 8:280; 17:143 *illus.*
Shelley, Percy Bysshe 17:253
SHELLEY, PERCY BYSSHE 7:199 *illus.*; 16:293 *illus.*; 17:253 *bibliog.*, *illus.*
Adonais 1:107
Prometheus Unbound 15:567
Shelley, Mary Wollstonecraft 17:252–253
SHELLEY v. KRAEMER 17:253–254
SHELLFISH 17:254–255 *bibliog.*, *illus.*
brachiopod 3:435
bromine 3:502
crustacean 17:255
food poisoning and infection 8:211
red tide 16:114
fossil record
coquina 5:257
ostracoderm 14:458
Maryland 13:189 *illus.*
mollusks 17:254–255
plankton 15:332
SHELLMAN (Georgia)
map (31° 46′N 84° 37′W) 9:114
SHELLS (pasta) 15:106 *illus.*
SHELLSBURG (Iowa)
map (42° 6′N 91° 52′W) 11:244
SHELLY MOUNTAIN
map (43° 49′N 113° 43′W) 11:26
SHELTON (Connecticut)
map (41° 19′N 73° 5′W) 5:193
SHELTON (Nebraska)
map (40° 47′N 98° 44′W) 14:70
SHELTON (Washington)
map (47° 13′N 123° 6′W) 20:35
SHEM
Semites 17:197
SHEMOGUE (New Brunswick)
map (46° 9′N 64° 11′W) 14:117
SHEN CHOU (Shen Zhou) 17:255 *bibliog.*
SHEN-YANG (Shenyang) (China) 17:255
map (41° 48′N 123° 27′E) 4:362
SHEN ZHOU *see* SHEN CHOU (Shen Zhou)
SHENANDOAH (airship) 17:255
SHENANDOAH (Iowa)
map (40° 46′N 95° 22′W) 11:244
SHENANDOAH (Pennsylvania)
map (40° 49′N 76° 12′W) 15:147
SHENANDOAH (ship)
Civil War, U.S. 5:32
SHENANDOAH (Virginia)
map (38° 29′N 78° 37′W) 19:607
SHENANDOAH (county in Virginia)
map (38° 50′N 78° 35′W) 19:607
SHENANDOAH MOUNTAIN
map (38° 30′N 79° 20′W) 19:607
SHENANDOAH RIVER 17:255
map (39° 19′N 92° 3′W) 19:607
SHENANDOAH VALLEY
map (38° 35′N 78° 35′W) 19:607
SHENANGO RIVER
map (40° 57′N 80° 23′W) 14:357
SHENANGO RIVER LAKE
map (41° 22′N 80° 28′W) 15:147

SHENG (musical instrument) **17**:255
harmonica **10**:51
SHENIPSIT LAKE
map (41° 53′N 72° 26′W) **5**:193
SHENSI (Shenxi) (China) **17**:255
archaeological sites
Pan-p'o-ts'un (Banpocun) **15**:54
cities
Sian (Xi'an) **17**:291
Lantian man **12**:201
prehistoric humans **4**:379 *illus.*
Yang-Ko **20**:317
SHENXI (China) *see* SHENSI (Shenxi) (China)
SHENYANG (China) *see* SHEN-YANG (Shenyan) (China)
SHEOL *see* HELL
SHEPARD (Alberta)
map (50° 57′N 113° 55′W) **1**:256
SHEPARD, ALAN B., JR. **17**:255–256 *bibliog., illus.*; **18**:127 *illus.*
Mercury program **13**:308
SHEPARD, ERNEST HOWARD **17**:256
Winnie-the-Pooh **20**:180
SHEPARD, SAM **17**:256
SHEPAUG RIVER
map (41° 28′N 73° 19′W) **5**:193
SHEPHERD (dog) *see* WORKING DOG
SHEPHERD (Michigan)
map (43° 32′N 84° 41′W) **13**:377
SHEPHERD'S PURSE (botany) **17**:256
SHEPHERDSTOWN (West Virginia)
map (39° 26′N 77° 48′W) **20**:111
SHEPHERDSVILLE (Kentucky)
map (37° 59′N 85° 43′W) **12**:47
SHEPPARD, P. M.
mimicry **13**:436
SHEPPARD, SAMUEL
Bailey, F. Lee **3**:26
SHEPPARTON (Australia)
map (36° 23′S 145° 25′E) **2**:328
SHER SHAH **17**:256
SHERATON, THOMAS **17**:256 *bibliog.*
SHERBET *see* ICE CREAM
SHERBRO BAY
map (7° 40′N 12° 45′W) **17**:296
SHERBRO ISLAND
map (7° 45′N 12° 55′W) **17**:296
SHERBROOKE (Nova Scotia)
map (45° 8′N 61° 59′W) **14**:269
SHERBROOKE (Quebec) **17**:256
map (45° 24′N 71° 54′W) **16**:18
SHERBURN (Minnesota)
map (43° 39′N 94° 43′W) **13**:453
SHERBURNE (county in Minnesota)
map (45° 25′N 93° 45′W) **13**:453
SHERBURNE (New York)
map (42° 41′N 75° 30′W) **14**:149
SHERIDAN (Arkansas)
map (34° 19′N 92° 24′W) **2**:166
SHERIDAN (Indiana)
map (40° 8′N 86° 13′W) **11**:111
SHERIDAN (county in Kansas)
map (39° 20′N 100° 25′W) **12**:18
SHERIDAN (county in Montana)
map (48° 40′N 14° 25′W) **13**:547
SHERIDAN (county in Nebraska)
map (42° 30′N 102° 25′W) **14**:70
SHERIDAN (county in North Dakota)
map (47° 35′N 100° 20′W) **14**:248
SHERIDAN (Oregon)
map (45° 6′N 123° 24′W) **14**:427
SHERIDAN (Wyoming)
map (44° 48′N 106° 58′W) **20**:301
SHERIDAN (county in Wyoming)
map (44° 45′N 104° 45′W) **20**:301
SHERIDAN, PHILIP H. **17**:256–257 *bibliog., illus.*
Civil War, U.S. **5**:30
SHERIDAN, RICHARD BRINSLEY **7**:197 *illus.*; **17**:257 *bibliog., illus.*
The Rivals **16**:229
comedy **5**:132
The School for Scandal **17**:133–134
SHERIF, MUZAFER AND CAROLYN
conformity **5**:179
SHERIFF **17**:257
police **15**:396
SHERLOCK HOLMES (fictional character) *see* Holmes, Sherlock
SHERLOCK HOLMES (play)
Gillette, William H. **9**:182
SHERMAN (county in Kansas)
map (39° 20′N 101° 45′W) **12**:18
SHERMAN (Mississippi)
map (34° 22′N 88° 57′W) **13**:469
SHERMAN (county in Nebraska)
map (41° 15′N 98° 55′W) **14**:70
SHERMAN (New York)
map (42° 10′N 79° 36′W) **14**:149
SHERMAN (county in Oregon)
map (45° 25′N 120° 49′W) **14**:427
SHERMAN (Texas)
map (33° 38′N 96° 36′W) **19**:129
SHERMAN (county in Texas)
map (36° 15′N 101° 52′W) **19**:129
SHERMAN, FRANCIS
Fredericton (New Brunswick) **8**:294
SHERMAN, JAMES SCHOOLCRAFT **17**:257
SHERMAN, JOHN **17**:257–258 *bibliog.*
Garfield, James A. **9**:46
SHERMAN, ROGER **17**:258 *bibliog.*
SHERMAN, WILLIAM TECUMSEH **5**:29–30 *illus.*; **17**:258 *bibliog., illus.*; **19**:448 *illus.*
Civil War, U.S. **5**:23 *map*
Georgia **9**:118
Raleigh (North Carolina) **16**:79
Savannah (Georgia) **17**:99
SHERMAN ANTI-TRUST ACT **17**:258–259 *bibliog.*
cartoon **19**:451 *illus.*
conspiracy **5**:206
corporation **5**:273–274
Edmunds, George Franklin **7**:58
Federal Trade Commission **8**:42
government regulation **9**:270
monopoly and competition **13**:537–540
Roosevelt, Theodore **16**:310
Sherman, John **17**:258
Swift and Company v. *United States* **18**:389–390
trustee **19**:322
United States v. *E. C. Knight Company* **19**:465
SHERMAN RESERVOIR
map (41° 20′N 98° 55′W) **14**:70
SHERMAN SILVER PURCHASE ACT **17**:258
Bland-Allison Act **3**:327
Cleveland, Grover **5**:53
free silver **8**:295
Harrison, Benjamin **10**:59
SHERPA **17**:259 *bibliog.*
SHERRIDON (Manitoba)
map (55° 7′N 101° 5′W) **13**:119
SHERRY **17**:259 *bibliog.*
wine **20**:176
SHERTOK, MOSHE *see* SHARETT, MOSHE
SHERWOOD (Arkansas)
map (34° 49′N 92° 14′W) **2**:166
SHERWOOD (North Dakota)
map (48° 58′N 101° 38′W) **14**:248
SHERWOOD (Ohio)
map (41° 17′N 84° 33′W) **14**:357
SHERWOOD (Prince Edward Island)
map (46° 17′N 63° 8′W) **15**:548
SHERWOOD (Tennessee)
map (35° 5′N 85° 56′W) **19**:104
SHERWOOD, ROBERT E. **17**:259 *bibliog.*
SHERWOOD FOREST
Nottinghamshire (England) **14**:268
SHESHONK I, KING OF EGYPT **17**:259
SHETLAND ISLANDS (Scotland) **17**:259
map (60° 30′N 1° 30′W) **19**:403
SHETLAND PONY **10**:242–243 *illus.*; **17**:260 *bibliog., illus.*
pony **15**:428
SHETLAND SHEEPDOG **6**:214 *illus.*; **17**:260 *bibliog., illus.*
SHETUCKET RIVER
map (41° 31′N 72° 5′W) **5**:193
SHEVCHENKO, TARAS GRYGORIEVYCH **17**:260 *bibliog.*
SHEYENNE (North Dakota)
map (47° 39′N 99° 7′W) **14**:248
SHEYENNE RIVER
map (47° 5′N 96° 50′W) **14**:248
SHIAWASSEE (county in Michigan)
map (43° 0′N 84° 10′W) **13**:377
SHIDEHARA KIJURO **17**:260
SHIDLER (Oklahoma)
map (36° 47′N 96° 40′W) **14**:368
SHIELD
heraldry **10**:132–134
SHIFTING CULTIVATION *see* SLASH-AND-BURN AGRICULTURE
SHIGA, KIYOSHI
Shigella **17**:260
SHIGA NAOYA **17**:260 *bibliog.*
SHIGELLA **17**:260
SHIGEMETSU MAMORU **20**:280 *illus.*
SHIH (poetry)
Chinese literature **4**:389
SHIH-CHAI-SHAN (Shizhaishan) (China) **17**:261 *bibliog.*
SHIH CHI (book)
Ssu-ma Ch'ien (Sima Qian) **18**:207
SHIH-CHIA-CHUANG (China)
map (38° 3′N 114° 28′E) **4**:362
SHIH HUANG-TI
Asia, history of **2**:252–253
Ch'in (Qin) **4**:359
China, history of **4**:371
Great Wall of China **9**:323
SHIH-T'AO (Shitao) **17**:261 *bibliog.*
Chinese art and architecture **4**:383 *illus.*
SHIH TZU **6**:217 *illus.*; **17**:260–261 *bibliog., illus.*
SHIITES **17**:261 *bibliog.*
Ali **1**:292
distribution **11**:293 *map*
Fatimids **8**:34
Iran **11**:251
Islam **11**:289; **11**:291
Ismailis **11**:298
Khomeini, Ayatollah Ruhollah **12**:67–68
Mashhad (Iran) **13**:196
Middle East, history of the **13**:402
Qum (Iran) **16**:28
SHIJAK (Albania)
map (41° 21′N 19° 34′E) **1**:250
SHIKARPUR
map (27° 57′N 68° 38′E) **15**:27
SHIKOKU (Japan) **17**:261
map (33° 45′N 133° 30′E) **11**:361
SHILKA RIVER
map (53° 22′N 121° 32′E) **19**:388
SHILLIBEER, GEORGE
bus **3**:583
SHILLING (coin) **14**:296 *illus.*
SHILLINGTON (Pennsylvania)
map (40° 18′N 75° 58′W) **15**:147
SHILLONG (India)
map (25° 34′N 91° 53′E) **11**:80
SHILOH (ancient city) **17**:261
SHILOH (Ohio)
map (39° 49′N 84° 15′W) **14**:357
SHILOH, BATTLE OF **5**:22 *illus.*; **17**:261 *bibliog.*
Grant, Ulysses S. **9**:288
Sherman, William Tecumseh **17**:258
SHIMAZAKI, TOSON **17**:261–262 *bibliog.*
SHIMONOSEKI (Japan)
map (33° 57′N 130° 57′E) **11**:361
SHIMONOSEKI, TREATY OF
Sino-Japanese Wars **17**:323
SHIN BET
intelligence gathering **11**:205
SHINER (Texas)
map (29° 26′N 97° 10′W) **19**:129
SHINGLE PLANT *see* MONSTERA
SHINGLE STYLE (architecture)
house (in Western architecture) **10**:270
White, Stanford **20**:136
SHINGLEHOUSE (Pennsylvania)
map (41° 58′N 78° 12′W) **15**:147
SHINGLES (construction)
roof and roofing **16**:306 *illus.*
SHINGLES (disease) **17**:262
chicken pox **4**:346; **17**:262
herpes **10**:145
infectious diseases **11**:167
skin diseases **17**:342
SHINGON
Buddhism **3**:541
Japan, history of **11**:367
SHINKOLOBWE (Zaire)
map (11° 2′S 26° 35′E) **20**:350
SHINN, EVERETT **17**:262 *bibliog., illus.*
London Hippodrome **17**:262 *illus.*
SHINNSTON (West Virginia)
map (39° 24′N 80° 18′W) **20**:111
SHINTO **16**:140 *map*; **17**:262–263 *bibliog., illus.*
SHIOCTON (Wisconsin)
map (44° 27′N 88° 35′W) **20**:185
SHIP **17**:263–275 *bibliog., illus.*
See also BOAT AND BOATING; NAVAL VESSELS; NAVY; SAILING AND SAILING SHIPS; SHIPPING
barnacle **3**:85
bill of health **3**:251
cargo ship *see* CARGO TRANSPORTATION
containerization **5**:227
dry dock **6**:284
guidance and control systems **9**:393–394
gyroscope **9**:416
history
archaeology **2**:119 *illus.*
engine-powered ships **17**:272–274 *illus.*
Euler, Leonhard **7**:264–265
Froude, William **8**:346
Great Eastern (ship) **9**:319
Queen Elizabeth (ship) **16**:22
Queen Mary (ship) **16**:22
sailing ships **17**:263–271 *illus.*
Savannah (steamship) **17**:99
steamships **17**:272–274 *illus.*
Stevens, Edwin Augustus **18**:263
Sutton Hoo ship burial **18**:373–374
technology, history of **19**:65
Titanic **19**:211
underwater archaeology **19**:383
World War I **20**:220
navigation **14**:58–61
parts
anchor **1**:399
diesel engine **17**:273 *illus.*
propeller **15**:570
pump **15**:622–623
rudder **16**:337–338
quarantine **16**:12
semaphore **17**:194–195
shipbuilding **17**:275–277
signaling **17**:301
types **17**:274–275
battleship **3**:126–128
container ship **5**:227
factory ship **20**:123 *illus.*
ferry **8**:59–60
freighter **8**:301
icebreaker **11**:16
ocean liner **14**:324–325 *illus.*
submarine **18**:313–316
tanker **19**:23–24
trawler **8**:126–128 *illus.*
whaling ship **20**:122–123 *illus.*
Vikings **19**:594
Gokstad ship burial **9**:225–226
Oseberg ship burial **14**:453
wake (water) **20**:8
SHIP BOTTOM (New Jersey)
map (39° 39′N 74° 11′W) **14**:129
SHIP COVE (Newfoundland)
map (47° 6′N 54° 5′W) **14**:166
SHIP OF FOOLS (book)
Porter, Katherine Anne **15**:444–445
SHIP OF FOOLS (poem)
Brant, Sebastian **3**:456
SHIPBUILDING **17**:275–277 *bibliog., illus.*
caulking **4**:219
dry dock **6**:284 *illus.*
Europe **7**:278 *illus.*
figurehead **8**:75–76
history **17**:275–276 *illus.*
Fairbairn, Sir William **8**:9
Forbes, Robert Bennet **8**:220
Kaiser, Henry John **12**:7
Parsons, Sir Charles Algernon **15**:99
technology, history of **19**:64–65 *illus.*
hull construction **17**:263–264
Japan **2**:246 *illus.*
lumber **12**:456–457
modern shipbuilding **17**:275–277
naval vessels **14**:54–56
Newport News (Virginia) **14**:171
Southampton (England) **18**:107
SHIPPEGAN (New Brunswick)
map (47° 45′N 64° 42′W) **14**:117
SHIPPENSBURG (Pennsylvania)
map (40° 3′N 77° 31′W) **15**:147
SHIPPING
barge **3**:80–81
containerization **5**:227
flag of convenience **8**:149
FOB **8**:192
harbor and port **10**:42–44 *illus.*
Intracoastal Waterway **11**:232
labor union
international longshoremen's unions **11**:222
leaders
Cunard, Sir Samuel **5**:389
Grace, W. R. **9**:275–276
Onassis, Aristotle **14**:388
Vanderbilt (family) **19**:518–519
Wheelwright, William **20**:129–130
Liberia **12**:313
piracy **15**:312–313
Rotterdam (Netherlands) **16**:323
St. Lawrence Seaway **17**:22
traffic control **19**:264
tugboat **19**:329
SHIPPING ROUTE **17**:277 *bibliog.*
European trade routes, Middle Ages **13**:395 *map*
International Ice Patrol **11**:220
Rome, ancient **16**:279 *map*
SHIPPING ROUTES **19**:281 *map*
SHIPROCK (New Mexico)
map (36° 47′N 108° 41′W) **14**:136
SHIPWORM **17**:277 *illus.*
SHIPYARD *see* SHIPBUILDING
SHIR MOUNTAIN
map (31° 37′N 54° 4′E) **11**:250
SHIRAZ (Iran) **17**:277
map (29° 36′N 52° 32′E) **11**:250
SHIRE **10**:242 *illus.*; **10**:244 *illus.*; **17**:277
SHIRE (horse) **6**:254 *illus.*

SHIRLEY (Indiana)
map (39° 53′N 85° 35′W) **11**:111
SHIRLEY (Massachusetts)
map (42° 33′N 71° 39′W) **13**:206
SHIRLEY, JAMES **17**:277
masque **13**:200
SHIRLEY, MYRA BELLE *see* STARR, BELLE
SHIRLEY, WILLIAM **17**:277–278 *bibliog.*
SHISHAK *see* SHESHONK I, KING OF EGYPT
SHISHKIN, IVAN
Russian art and architecture **16**:362
SHISHMAREF (Alaska)
map (66° 14′N 166° 9′W) **1**:242
SHIST
rock **16**:247
SHITAO *see* SHIH-T'AO (Shitao)
SHIVA **11**:96 *illus.*; **17**:278 *bibliog., illus.*
Hinduism **10**:170
Pasupati (Lord of Beasts)
Indus civilization **11**:154
temple
Elephanta **7**:134
Ellora **7**:148–149
Prambanan **15**:489
SHIVELY (Kentucky)
map (38° 11′N 85° 49′W) **12**:47
SHIZHAISHAN *see* SHIH-CHAI-SHAN (Shizhaishan)
SHIZUOKA (Japan)
map (34° 58′N 138° 23′E) **11**:361
SHKLOVSKY, IOSIF SAMUILOVICH **17**:278
SHKODËR (Albania) **17**:278
map (42° 5′N 19° 30′E) **1**:250
SHKOLNIK, LEVI *see* ESHKOL, LEVI
SHKUMBIN RIVER
map (41° 1′N 19° 26′E) **1**:250
SHLONSKY, ABRAHAM **17**:278
SHOAL LAKE (Manitoba)
map (50° 26′N 100° 34′W) **13**:119
SHOALS (Indiana)
map (38° 40′N 86° 47′W) **11**:111
SHOCK (medicine) **17**:278–279 *bibliog.*
cardiovascular diseases **4**:145
serum **17**:210
stress, biological **18**:298
SHOCK ABSORBER *see* SUSPENSION SYSTEM
SHOCK THERAPY **17**:279 *bibliog.*
depression **6**:119
electroshock treatment **15**:600 *illus.*
schizophrenia **17**:124
SHOCK WAVE **17**:279
Bethe, Hans **3**:230
SHOCKLEY, WILLIAM BRADFORD **17**:279 *bibliog.*
transistor, inventor **19**:271
SHOEMAKER, WILLIE **17**:280–281 *bibliog., illus.*
SHOEMAKERS' HOLIDAY, THE (play)
Dekker, Thomas **6**:86
SHOES **17**:279–280 *bibliog., illus.*
industry
Massachusetts **13**:211
leather and hides **12**:262–263
moccasin **13**:488
SHOFAR **17**:281
SHOGUN **17**:281 *bibliog.*
Asia, history **2**:254
Ieyasu, Shogun of Japan **11**:32
Japan, history of **11**:367–368
Tokugawa (family) **19**:223
Yoritomo **20**:330
SHOLAPUR (India)
map (17° 41′N 75° 55′E) **11**:80
SHOLES, CHRISTOPHER LATHAM **17**:281 *bibliog.*
typewriter **19**:365
SHOLOKHOV, MIKHAIL ALEKSANDROVICH **17**:281 *bibliog.*
SHONA **17**:281 *bibliog.*
Mapungubwe **13**:142
Nalatale **14**:9
Thonga **19**:177
SHÖNBEIN, CHRISTIAN
guncotton **9**:405
SHONIN, GEORGY STEPANOVICH **17**:281 *bibliog.*
SHOOT (botany) **17**:282
SHOOTING (sport) **17**:282 *bibliog., illus.*
National Rifle Association of America **14**:45
Oakley, Annie **14**:312
pentathlon **15**:155
SHOOTING STAR (astronomy) *see* METEOR AND METEORITE; STAR
SHOOTING STAR (botany) **17**:283
See also COWSLIP
SHOPPING CENTER
Gruen, Victor **9**:382
retailing **16**:183
SHORE *see* BEACH AND COAST
SHORE, DINAH **17**:283
SHORE PATROL **17**:283
SHOREBIRDS **17**:283 *bibliog.*
curlew **5**:392
dowitcher **6**:251
oystercatcher **14**:479
phalarope **15**:218–219
plover **15**:369
sandpiper **17**:62
surfbird **18**:359
turnstone **19**:351
SHOREWOOD (Wisconsin)
map (43° 5′N 87° 53′W) **20**:185
SHORT SELLING (stock) *see* STOCK MARKET
SHORT STORY **17**:283–284 *bibliog.*
African literature *see* national subheadings under SHORT STORY, e.g., SHORT STORY—Cameroonian literature; SHORT STORY—Senegalese literature; etc.
American literature **1**:344; **1**:347
Aiken, Conrad **1**:201
Algren, Nelson **1**:291
Anderson, Sherwood **1**:402–403
Baldwin, James **3**:35
Barnes, Djuna **3**:86
Barthelme, Donald **3**:97
Beattie, Ann **3**:145
Bellow, Saul **3**:190
Benét, Stephen Vincent **3**:198
Bierce, Ambrose **3**:248
Bishop, John Peale **3**:297
black American literature **3**:304
Bontemps, Arna **3**:382
Boyle, Kay **3**:434
Bradbury, Ray **3**:436
Buck, Pearl S. **3**:535
Bukowski, Charles **3**:553
Bunner, H. C. **3**:563
Burke, Kenneth **3**:571
Cable, George Washington **4**:6
Calisher, Hortense **4**:39
Capote, Truman **4**:127
Cassill, R. V. **4**:184
Cather, Willa **4**:208–209
Cheever, John **4**:309–310
Chestnut, Charles Waddell **4**:334
Clark, Walter van Tilburg **5**:39
Crane, Stephen **5**:330–331
Fitzgerald, F. Scott **8**:130–131
Freeman, Mary E. Wilkins **8**:299
Garland, Hamlin **9**:48
Goyen, William **9**:274
Grau, Shirley Ann **9**:301
Hemingway, Ernest **10**:118–119
Irving, Washington **11**:284–285
Jackson, Shirley **11**:343
James, Henry **11**:353–354
Jewett, Sarah Orne **11**:412
Lardner, Ring **12**:207
Le Guin, Ursula **12**:254
London, Jack **12**:402–403
Ludwig, Jack **12**:452
McCarthy, Mary **13**:8–9
Malamud, Bernard **13**:79
O. Henry **14**:310–311
O. Henry Award **14**:311
Ozick, Cynthia **14**:480
Paley, Grace **15**:47
Parker, Dorothy **15**:90
Poe, Edgar Allan **15**:377–378
Porter, Katherine Anne **15**:444–445
Runyon, Damon **16**:346
Stafford, Jean **18**:209
Taylor, Peter **19**:50
Updike, John **19**:471
Walker, Alice **20**:12
Williams, William Carlos **20**:161
Argentine literature
Borges, Jorge Luis **3**:398–399
Cortázar, Julio **5**:278
Australian literature
Lawson, Henry **12**:251–252
Austrian literature
Kafka, Franz **12**:5–6
Brazilian literature
Rosa, João Guimarães **16**:312
Cameroonian literature
Bebey, Francis **3**:150
Canadian literature
Gallant, Mavis **9**:16
Hood, Hugh John Blagdon **10**:225
Chinese literature **4**:390
Chang T'ien-i (Zhang Tianyi) **4**:281
Lu Hsün (Lu Xun) **12**:445–446
Colombian literature
García Márquez, Gabriel **9**:39
Czech literature
Kafka, Franz **12**:5–6
Danish literature **3**:33
Blicher, Steen Steensen **3**:331
Branner, Hans Christian **3**:455
Dinesen, Isak **6**:178
Wied, Gustav **20**:145
Dutch and Flemish literature
Beets, Nicolaas **3**:168
English literature
Bennett, Arnold **3**:202
Conrad, Joseph **5**:198
Doyle, Sir Arthur Conan **6**:253
Greene, Graham **9**:350
Jacobs, W. W. **11**:346
Kipling, Rudyard **11**:86–87
Lawrence, D. H. **12**:249–250
Mansfield, Katherine **13**:128
Pritchett, V. S. **15**:556
Saki **17**:28–29
Finnish literature
Canth, Minna **4**:117
French literature
Barbey d'Aurevilly, Jules Amédée **3**:78
Maupassant, Guy de **13**:234
Mérimée, Prosper **13**:310
German literature
Borchert, Wolfgang **3**:396
Hoffmann, Ernst Theodor Amadeus **10**:195
Storm, Theodor **18**:285
Hebrew and Yiddish literature **10**:102
Agnon, S. Y. **1**:187
Aleichem, Sholem **1**:270–271
Oz, Amos **14**:479
Peretz, Y. L. **15**:163
Singer, Isaac Bashevis **17**:322
Hungarian literature
Orkeny, Istvan **14**:445
Indian literature
Tagore, Sir Rabindranath **19**:10
Irish literature
Beckett, Samuel **3**:151–152
Bowen, Elizabeth **3**:427
Dubliners **6**:288
Dunsany, Lord **6**:301
O'Connor, Frank **14**:347
O'Faolain, Sean **14**:352
Italian literature
Bandello, Matteo **3**:62
Decameron **6**:72
Straparola, Giovanni Francesco **18**:289
Japanese literature
Akutagawa Ryunosuke **1**:232
Endo Shusaku **7**:168
Ueda Akinari **19**:371
Norwegian literature
Kielland, Alexander Lange **12**:74
Persian literature **15**:187
Alavi, Bozorg **1**:248
Hedayat, Sadeq **10**:104
Jamalzade, Mohammed Ali **11**:353
Polish literature
Borowski, Tadeusz **3**:404
Gombrowicz, Witold **9**:241
pulp magazines **15**:620
Russian literature **16**:365–366
Aksenov, Vasily Pavlovich **1**:232
Andreyev, Leonid Nilolayevich **1**:408
Babel, Isaak Emmanuilovich **3**:6
Bunin, Ivan Alekseyevich **3**:563
Chekhov, Anton **4**:310
Garshin, Vsevolod Mikhailovich **9**:51
Gogol, Nikolai **9**:225
Karamzin, Nikolai Mikhailovich **12**:27
Zoshchenko, Mikhail Mikhailovich **20**:380
Senegalese literature
Diop, Birago Ismael **6**:185
Sembene, Ousmane **17**:195
Swedish literature
Ahlin, Lars **1**:200
Swiss literature
Keller, Gottfried **12**:37
Welsh literature
Thomas, Dylan **19**:172–173
Yugoslav literature
Andrić, Ivo **1**:408
Cankar, Ivan **4**:108
SHORT TAKEOFF AND LANDING *see* STOL
SHORT-WAVE RADIO
citizens band radio **4**:446
ham radio **10**:26
wavelength and frequency, electromagnetic **7**:117 *table*
SHORTBILL SPEARFISH *see* SPEARFISH
SHORTENING (food) *see* FATS AND OILS; VEGETABLE OILS
SHORTER, FRANK **17**:284
SHORTHAIRED CATS **17**:284 *bibliog., illus.*
American shorthair cat **1**:366–367
colorpoint shorthair cat **5**:122
exotic shorthair cat **7**:333
SHORTHAND **17**:284 *bibliog.*
SHORTHORN CATTLE **4**:216 *illus.*
SHOSHONE (Idaho)
map (42° 56′N 114° 24′W) **11**:26
SHOSHONE (county in Idaho)
map (47° 25′N 116° 0′W) **11**:26
SHOSHONE LAKE
map (44° 22′N 110° 43′W) **20**:301
SHOSHONE MOUNTAINS
map (39° 25′N 117° 15′W) **14**:111
SHOSHONE RIVER
map (44° 52′N 108° 11′W) **20**:301
SHOSHONI (American Indians) **17**:284–285 *bibliog.*
Indians of North America, art of the **11**:140
Sacagawea **17**:6
Washakie **11**:128 *illus.*; **20**:34
SHOSHONI (Wyoming)
map (43° 14′N 108° 7′W) **20**:301
SHOSTAKOVICH, DMITRY **17**:285 *bibliog., illus.*
Russian music **16**:369 *illus.*
SHOT PUT
O'Brien, Parry **14**:317
track and field **19**:261
SHOTGUN **17**:285–286 *bibliog., illus.*
double-barreled **14**:285 *illus.*
shooting **17**:282
types **14**:286
SHOTOKU TAISHI **11**:367 *illus.*; **17**:286 *bibliog.*
Japan, history of **11**:367
Japanese art and architecture **11**:372
SHOULDER
muscle **13**:654
skeleton, human **17**:336
sports medicine **18**:198
SHOVEL
earth-moving machinery **7**:24
SHOVELBOARD *see* SHUFFLEBOARD
SHOW LOW (Arizona)
map (34° 15′N 110° 2′W) **2**:160
SHOWBOATS **17**:286 *bibliog.*
SHOWTIME
cable TV **4**:7
SHRAPNEL **17**:286
SHREVE (Ohio)
map (40° 41′N 82° 1′W) **14**:357
SHREVE, LAMB, AND HARMON
skyscraper **17**:350
SHREVEPORT (Louisiana) **17**:286
map (32° 30′N 93° 45′W) **12**:430
SHREW **13**:104 *illus.*; **17**:286–287 *bibliog., illus.*
hand **15**:539 *illus.*
insectivore **11**:193
SHREWSBURY (England)
map (52° 43′N 2° 45′W) **19**:403
SHREWSBURY (Massachusetts)
map (42° 18′N 71° 43′W) **13**:206
SHRIKE **17**:287 *illus.*
cuckoo shrike **5**:382
SHRIKE THRUSH **17**:287
SHRIKE VIREO **17**:287
SHRIMP **17**:287 *bibliog., illus.*
bioluminescence **3**:272
fishing industry **8**:127
Louisiana **12**:431 *illus.*
intertidal life **11**:230
Jurassic Period **11**:476
ostracod **14**:458
shellfish **17**:254–255 *illus.*
SHRIMP PLANT (botany) **17**:287
SHRINERS
freemasonry **8**:300
SHRIVER, SARGENT **17**:287–288 *bibliog.*
War on Poverty **20**:28
SHROPSHIRE *see* SALOP (England)
SHROPSHIRE LAD, A (poetry)
Houseman, A. E. **10**:280
SHROUD OF TURIN **17**:288
SHROVE TUESDAY *see* MARDI GRAS
SHRUB **17**:288–289 *bibliog., illus.*
See also names of specific shrubs, e.g., HONEYSUCKLE; ROSEMARY (botany); etc.
bark **3**:82
benefits and disadvantages **17**:288
classification, biological **17**:288–289
identification **17**:289
SHRUNKEN HEAD *see* HEAD-HUNTING
SHUBENACADIE RIVER
map (45° 20′N 63° 30′W) **14**:269

SHUBERT (family) 17:289 *bibliog.*
SHUBUN 17:289 *bibliog.*
SHUBUNKIN
  goldfish 9:234
SHUDRA
  caste 4:186
SHUFFLEBOARD 17:289 *bibliog.*
SHUKONGOJIN 11:373 *illus.*
SHULHAN ARUKH
  Caro, Joseph ben Ephraim 4:159
SHULL, GEORGE
  plant breeding 15:342
SHULLSBURG (Wisconsin)
  map (42° 34′N 90° 14′W) 20:185
SHULTZ, GEORGE P. 17:289
SHUMEN (Bulgaria)
  map (43° 16′N 26° 55′E) 3:555
SHUMWAY, NORMAN EDWARD 17:289
  transplantation, organ 19:277
SHUNGNAK (Alaska)
  map (66° 53′N 157° 2′W) 1:242
SHUQRA
  map (13° 21′N 45° 42′E) 20:324
SHUQUALAK (Mississippi)
  map (32° 59′N 88° 34′W) 13:469
SHUSH *see* SUSA (Iran)
SHUSHTAR (Iran)
  map (32° 3′N 48° 51′E) 11:250
SHUSWAP (American Indians) 17:289–290 *bibliog.*
SHUTTER (camera) 4:56
SHUTTLE (space technology) *see* SPACE SHUTTLE
SHUTTLE (weaving)
  flying shuttle 20:84 *illus.*
    Kay, John 12:32–33
    loom 12:410
SHUTTLE DIPLOMACY
  Kissinger, Henry A. 12:90
SHVARTS, YEVGENY 17:290
SHWEBO (Burma)
  map (22° 34′N 95° 42′E) 3:573
SI (INTERNATIONAL SYSTEM OF UNITS)
  units, physical 19:466–467 *tables*
SI KIANG (China) *see* HSI CHIANG (Xi Jiang) (China)
SIAD BARRE, MUHAMMAD
  Somalia 18:61
SIALKOT (Pakistan) 17:290
  map (32° 30′N 74° 31′E) 15:27
SIAM *see* THAILAND
SIAM, GULF OF *see* THAILAND, GULF OF
SIAMANG 17:290 *illus.*
  ape 2:74–75
  gibbon 9:172
SIAMESE *see* THAI
SIAMESE CAT 4:195 *illus.*; 17:290 *bibliog.*, *illus.*
  Balinese cat 3:37–38
  Burmese cat 3:576
  colorpoint shorthair cat 5:122
  Havana brown cat 10:71
  Himalayan cat 10:166
  longhaired cats 12:408
SIAMESE FIGHTING FISH 17:290–291 *illus.*
  Betta 3:232
  tropical fish 19:308 *illus.*
SIAMESE TWINS 17:291 *bibliog.*
SIAN (Xi'an) (China) 17:291
  China, history of 4:372
  map (30° 54′N 119° 39′E) 4:362
SIB *see* CLAN
SIBELIUS, JEAN 17:291 *bibliog.*, *illus.*
ŠIBENIK (Yugoslavia) 17:291
  map (43° 44′N 15° 54′E) 20:340
SIBERIA (USSR) 17:291–292 *bibliog.*
  archaeology
    Pazyryk 15:122
  art
    Scythians 17:167
    steppe art 18:255–256
  cities
    Irkutsk 11:270
    Krasnoyarsk 12:127
    Novosibirsk 14:277
    Omsk 14:388
    Vladivostok 19:623
    Yakutsk 20:314
  continental drifting 15:354 *map*
  forest 8:229 *illus.*
  history
    Bering, Vitus Jonassen 3:211
    Yermak Timofeyevich 20:327
  language 2:244 *map*; 12:355 *map*
  map (65° 0′N 110° 0′E) 19:388
  people
    Chukchi 4:422
    Eskimo 7:238–242
    Kalmyk 12:8
    population movements 19:394
    Samoyed (people) 17:47–48
    Tungus 19:334
    Yakut 20:314
  physical features
    Stanovoi Range 18:219
    Yablonovy Mountains 20:314
  rivers, lakes, and waterways
    Baikal, Lake 3:25 *map*
    Lena River 12:281
    Ob River 14:314
    Yenisei River 20:326
  shaman 17:238
  taiga 2:234 *illus.*
  Trans-Siberian Railroad 19:267
  Yukaghir 20:344
SIBERIAN HIGH
  cyclone and anticyclone 5:405
SIBERIAN HUSKY 6:215 *illus.*; 17:292 *bibliog.*, *illus.*
SIBIR (USSR) *see* SIBERIA (USSR)
SIBIU (Romania)
  map (45° 48′N 24° 9′E) 16:288
SIBLEY (Iowa)
  map (43° 24′N 95° 45′W) 11:244
SIBLEY (Louisiana)
  map (32° 33′N 93° 18′W) 12:430
SIBLEY (county in Minnesota)
  map (44° 35′N 94° 15′W) 13:453
SIBLEY (Mississippi)
  map (31° 23′N 91° 24′W) 13:469
SIBLEY, ANTOINETTE 17:292 *bibliog.*
SIBU (Malaysia)
  map (2° 18′N 111° 49′E) 13:84
SIBUYAN SEA
  map (12° 50′N 122° 40′E) 15:237
SIBYL 17:292
SICA, VITTORIO DE *see* DE SICA, VITTORIO
SICHUAN (China) *see* SZECHWAN (Sichuan) (China)
SICIÉ, CAPE
  map (43° 3′N 5° 51′E) 8:260
SICILIA (Italy) *see* SICILY (Italy)
SICILIAN VESPERS 17:292 *bibliog.*
SICILY (Italy) 17:292–293 *bibliog.*, *illus.*
  archaeology
    Agrigento 1:199
    amphitheater (Sicily) 17:293 *illus.*
    Piazza Armerina 15:289–290
    Segesta 17:188
    Selinus 17:192
  art
    Cathedral of Monreale 3:606 *illus.*
    donkey cart 8:196 *illus.*
    mosaic 13:596
  cities
    Catania 4:200
    Gela 9:69
    Messina 13:324
    Palermo 15:43
    Taormina 19:29
  Etna, Mount 7:258
  history 17:292–293
    Alfonso V, King of Aragon 1:279
    Charles I, King of Naples (Charles of Anjou) 4:296
    Garibaldi, Giuseppe 9:47
    Gelon, Tyrant of Gela 9:70
    Henry VI, King of Germany and Holy Roman Emperor 10:129
    Italy, history of 11:328–329
    James II, King of Aragon 11:355
    Naples, Kingdom of 14:15
    Normans 14:221
    Peter III, King of Aragon (Peter the Great) 15:200
    Phalaris 15:218
    Roger II, King of Sicily 16:268
    Sicilian Vespers 17:292
    Syracuse (Sicily) 18:410–411
    Two Sicilies, Kingdom of the 19:360
    Victor Amadeus II, Duke of Savoy 19:572
    World War II 20:268–269 *illus.*, *map*
  Mafia 13:46
  map (37° 30′N 14° 0′E) 11:321
  sulfur 18:334 *illus.*
  theater
    puppet 15:627 *illus.*
SICILY, STRAIT OF
  map (37° 20′N 11° 20′E) 11:321
SICKELLS, FREDERICK 19:450 *illus.*
SICKERT, WALTER RICHARD 17:293 *bibliog.*
SICKLE-CELL ANEMIA 17:293 *bibliog.*
  anemia 1:410
  blood 9:89 *illus.*
  hemoglobin 10:119
  malaria 13:80
  Pauling, Linus Carl 15:119
  pneumonia 15:376
  race 16:35
SICKLES, DANIEL EDGAR 17:293
SICO RIVER
  map (15° 58′N 84° 58′W) 10:218
SICUANI (Peru)
  map (14° 16′S 71° 13′W) 15:193
SICYON 17:294
SIDAMO 17:294 *bibliog.*
SIDDHARTHA GAUTAMA *see* BUDDHA
SIDDONS, SARAH 17:294 *bibliog.*
SIDEORLITE
  meteor and meteorite 13:336–337 *illus.*
SIDEREAL TIME 17:294
  day 6:54
  time (physics) 19:201
SIDERITE 13:441 *illus.*; 17:294
  meteor and meteorite 13:336–337 *illus.*
SIDEWINDER (missile) 17:294
SIDEWINDER (snake) 17:294 *illus.*
SIDGWICK, HENRY 17:294 *bibliog.*
SIDGWICK, NEVIL VINCENT 17:294–295
  chemistry, history of 4:328
SIDI BEL ABBÈS (Algeria)
  map (35° 13′N 0° 10′W) 1:287
SIDING SPRING OBSERVATORY
  Anglo-Australian Telescope 1:416
SIDNAW (Michigan)
  map (46° 30′N 88° 43′W) 13:377
SIDNEY (British Columbia)
  map (48° 39′N 123° 24′W) 3:491
SIDNEY (Illinois)
  map (40° 1′N 88° 4′W) 11:42
SIDNEY (Iowa)
  map (40° 45′N 95° 39′W) 11:244
SIDNEY (Montana)
  map (47° 43′N 104° 9′W) 13:547
SIDNEY (Nebraska)
  map (41° 9′N 102° 59′W) 14:70
SIDNEY (New York)
  map (42° 19′N 75° 24′W) 14:149
SIDNEY (Ohio)
  map (40° 17′N 84° 9′W) 14:357
SIDNEY, ALGERNON 17:295
SIDNEY, SIR PHILIP 17:295 *bibliog.*, *illus.*
  Greville, Fulke, 1st Baron Brooke 9:360
SIDNEY LANIER, LAKE
  map (34° 15′N 83° 57′W) 9:114
SIDNEY SUSSEX COLLEGE (Cambridge University) 4:53
SIDON (Lebanon) 17:295 *bibliog.*
  map (33° 33′N 35° 22′E) 12:265
SIDRA, GULF OF
  map (31° 30′N 18° 0′E) 12:320
SIDS *see* CRIB DEATH
SIEDLCE (Poland)
  map (52° 11′N 22° 16′E) 15:388
SIEGBAHN, KARL
  Siegbahn, Manne 17:295
SIEGBAHN, MANNE 17:295
SIEGE OF RHODES, THE (opera)
  Davenant, Sir William 6:46
SIEGEN (Germany, East and West)
  map (50° 52′N 8° 2′E) 9:140
SIEGFRIED (mythology) 17:295
  Nibelungenlied 14:177–178
SIEGFRIED LINE
  World War I 20:225 *map*; 20:236–237 *illus.*
  World War II 20:274 *map*
SIEM REAP (Kampuchea)
  map (13° 22′N 103° 51′E) 12:11
SIEMENS (family) 17:295–296 *bibliog.*
SIEMENS (measurement)
  units, physical 19:467 *table*
SIENA (Italy) 17:296
  art
    cathedral 9:259 *illus.*; 11:309 *illus.*
    Duccio di Buoninsegna 6:289–290
    Giovanni di Paolo 9:188
    Italian art and architecture 11:308–314
    Lorenzetti brothers 12:415
    Martini, Simone 13:180
    Pisano, Nicola and Giovanni 15:316
    Quercia, Jacopo della 16:23
  Italian city-state 11:328 *map*
  map (43° 19′N 11° 21′E) 11:321
SIENKIEWICZ, HENRYK 17:296 *bibliog.*
SIERCK, DETLEF *see* SIRK, DOUGLAS
SIERRA (county in California)
  map (39° 35′N 120° 35′W) 4:31
SIERRA (county in New Mexico)
  map (33° 10′N 107° 10′W) 14:136
SIERRA, GREGORIO MARTÍNEZ *see* MARTÍNEZ SIERRA, GREGORIO
SIERRA BLANCA MOUNTAIN
  map (31° 15′N 105° 26′W) 19:129
SIERRA BLANCA PEAK
  map (33° 23′N 105° 48′W) 14:136
SIERRA CLUB 17:296 *bibliog.*
SIERRA COLORADA (Argentina)
  map (40° 35′S 67° 48′W) 2:149
SIERRA DE AGUA (Belize)
  map (17° 32′N 88° 54′W) 3:183
SIERRA DE AMERIQUE MOUNTAINS
  map (12° 12′N 85° 19′W) 14:179
SIERRA DE CHAMÁ MOUNTAINS
  map (15° 40′N 90° 30′W) 9:389
SIERRA DE LA CANDÓN MOUNTAINS
  map (17° 0′N 90° 55′W) 9:389
SIERRA DE LAS MINAS MOUNTAINS
  map (15° 10′N 89° 40′W) 9:389
SIERRA LEONE 17:296–298 *bibliog.*, *illus.*, *map*, *table*
  African music 1:168–171
  cities
    Freetown 8:300
  climate 17:297 *table*
  economic activity 17:298
  education 17:298
    African universities 1:176 *table*
  flag 17:297 *illus.*
  government 17:298
  history 17:298
    Margai, Sir Milton 13:148
  land and resources 17:296–297 *map*, *table*
  map (8° 30′N 11° 30′W) 1:136
  people 17:297–298
    Mende 13:293–294
    Temne 19:91
SIERRA MADRE (mountains in Mexico) 17:298
  Ixtachihuatl 11:338
SIERRA MADRE MOUNTAINS (Philippines)
  map (16° 20′N 122° 0′E) 15:237
SIERRA MADRE OCCIDENTAL MOUNTAINS (Mexico)
  map (25° 0′N 105° 0′W) 13:357
SIERRA MADRE ORIENTAL MOUNTAINS (Mexico)
  map (22° 0′N 99° 30′W) 13:357
SIERRA MAESTRA MOUNTAINS
  map (20° 0′N 76° 45′W) 5:377
SIERRA MORENA MOUNTAINS
  map (38° 0′N 5° 0′W) 18:140
SIERRA NEVADA (Spain) 17:298
  map (37° 5′N 3° 10′W) 18:140
SIERRA NEVADA (United States) 17:298
  California 4:30
  Comstock Lode 5:167
  Donner Pass 6:240
  Heavenly Valley (California) 4:33 *illus.*
  map (38° 0′N 119° 15′W) 4:31
  redwood 16:117
  Sonora Pass 18:66
  Whitney, Mount 20:142
SIERRA VISTA (Arizona)
  map (31° 33′N 110° 18′W) 2:160
SIERRE (Switzerland)
  map (46° 18′N 7° 32′E) 18:394
SIEYÈS, EMMANUEL JOSEPH 17:298–299 *bibliog.*
  Napoleon I, Emperor of the French (Napoléon Bonaparte) 14:16
SIFAKA
  indri 11:150
SIGER DE BRABANT 17:299 *bibliog.*
SIGHETUL MARMAȚIEI (Romania)
  map (47° 56′N 23° 54′E) 16:288
SIGHIȘOARA (Romania)
  map (46° 13′N 24° 48′E) 16:288
SIGHT *see* SENSES AND SENSATION
SIGHT AND SOUND (periodical)
  British Film Institute 3:496
SIGISMUND, KING OF GERMANY AND HOLY ROMAN EMPEROR 17:299 *bibliog.*
  Wenceslas, King of Germany and Bohemia 20:103
  Žižka, Jan 20:371
SIGISMUND I, KING OF POLAND 17:299 *bibliog.*
SIGISMUND II, KING OF POLAND 17:299 *bibliog.*
SIGISMUND III, KING OF POLAND 17:299 *bibliog.*
  Charles IX, King of Sweden 4:297
  Time of Troubles 19:202
  Vasa (dynasty) 19:525
SIGLUFJÖRDUR (Iceland)
  map (66° 10′N 18° 56′W) 11:17
SIGMA (letter)
  S (letter) 17:3
SIGMA XI
  American Scientist (periodical) 1:366

SIGN LANGUAGE 17:299–300 *bibliog.*
animal communication 2:20
SIGNAC, PAUL 17:300 *bibliog., illus.*
neoimpressionism 14:83
Portrait of Félix Fénéon 17:300 *illus.*
SIGNAL
actuating
servomechanism 17:212
carrier signal
telecommunications 19:75–76
electromagnetic
time (physics) 19:201
fluctuating
oscilloscope 14:453
radio astronomy 16:52
receiver (communications) 16:106
sound recording and reproduction 18:74–77
telemetry 19:78
transmitter 19:276
SIGNAL GENERATOR 17:300
SIGNAL MOUNTAIN (Tennessee)
map (35° 7′N 85° 21′W) 19:104
SIGNALING 17:300–301 *bibliog., illus.*
beacon 3:137
code
International Flag Code 17:300 *illus.*
Morse code 13:590–591
semaphore 17:194–195
devices 17:301
flag 8:133–134
lighthouse 12:336–337
military 17:300
naval 17:301
pulse (electronics) 15:621
railroad 16:75
Westinghouse, George 20:117
telecommunications 19:75–76
SIGNED ENGLISH
sign language 17:300
SIGNIFICANCE, STATISTICAL
null hypothesis 14:292
SIGNORELLI, LUCA 17:301–302 *bibliog.*
Sistine Chapel 17:329
SIGOURNEY (Iowa)
map (41° 20′N 92° 12′W) 11:244
SIGSIG (Ecuador)
map (3° 1′S 78° 45′W) 7:52
SIGÜENZA Y GÓNGORA, CARLOS DE 17:302
SIGUIRI (Guinea)
map (11° 25′N 9° 10′W) 9:397
SIGURD (Utah)
map (38° 50′N 111° 58′W) 19:492
SIGURDSSON, JÓN 17:302 *bibliog.*
SIGURJÓNSSON, JÓHANN 17:302
SIHANOUK, NORODOM *see* NORODOM SIHANOUK
SIHASAPA (American Indians) *see* SIOUX (American Indians)
SIKASSO (Mali)
map (11° 19′N 5° 40′W) 13:89
SIKELIANOS, ANGELOS 17:302
SIKESTON (Missouri)
map (36° 53′N 89° 35′W) 13:476
SIKHOTE-ALIN MOUNTAINS
map (48° 0′N 138° 0′E) 19:388
SIKHS 16:140 *map*; 17:302–303 *bibliog., illus.*
Punjab 15:626
SIKKIM (India) 17:303 *bibliog., map*
cities
Gangtok 9:37
Lamaist art and architecture 12:172–173
SIKORSKY, IGOR 17:303 *bibliog.*
Sikorsky Sea King helicopter 10:112
SIKSIKA (American Indians)
Blackfoot 3:321
SILAS MARNER (book) 17:303
Eliot, George 7:139
SILBER, JOHN 17:303
SILBERMAN, CHARLES 17:303
SILENT FILMS *see* FILM, HISTORY OF
SILENT SPRING (book) 17:303–304
Carson, Rachel 4:170
SILENUS 17:304
SILER CITY (North Carolina)
map (35° 44′N 79° 28′W) 14:242
SILES SALINAS, LUIS ADOLFO
Bolivia 3:369
SILES ZUAZO, HERNÁN
Bolivia 3:369
SILESIA 17:304
cities
Katowice 12:31
history
Austrian Succession, War of the 2:354
Germany in 1648 9:151 *map*
Germany 1815–1871 9:153 *map*
Maria Theresa, Austrian Archduchess, Queen of Hungary and Bohemia 13:150
SILHOUETTE 17:304 *bibliog.*
SILHOUETTE ISLAND
map (4° 29′S 55° 14′E) 19:574
SILICA
obsidian 14:319
ooze, deep-sea 14:397
refractory materials 16:124
rhyolite 16:204
silica minerals 17:304
silicosis 17:306
stishovite 18:273
SILICA MINERALS 17:304 *bibliog.*
agate 1:182–183
chalcedony 4:270
chert and flint 4:332–333
coesite 5:93
cristobalite 5:351
fulgurite 8:357
geyersite 17:304
glass 9:199–201
igneous rock 11:34; 17:304
list of, minerals 13:443
occurrence 17:304
opal 14:397
polymorphs 17:304
properties 17:304
quartz 16:13–14; 17:304
sandstone 17:304
silicate minerals 17:304
silicon 17:305
silicon dioxide 17:304
siltstone 17:304
sinter 17:325
stishovite 18:273
structure 17:304
tiger's-eye 19:197
trachyte 19:258
transport 17:304
vitreous silica 17:304
SILICATE MINERALS 17:304–305 *bibliog.*
amphibole 1:381
andalusite 1:400
atomic bonds 17:305
beryl 3:227
chlorite 4:401
chrysocolla 4:421
clay minerals 5:46–47
cordierite 5:261
Earth's crust 17:304–305
elements 17:304
epidote 7:219
feldspar 8:46–47
feldspathoid 8:47
gadolinite: Gadolin, John 9:7
garnet 9:49
garnierite 9:50
gems 17:304
glass 9:199–201
hemimorphite 10:118; 17:304–305
idocrase 11:31
kyanite 12:143
lapis lazuli 12:204–205
lava flows 17:305
magma 13:52
mica 13:370–371
mineral 13:443 *table*
olivine 14:379–380
oxygen 14:476–477
pectolite 17:304–305
peridot 15:166
prehnite 15:518
pyrophyllite 15:638
pyroxene 15:638
rhodonite 16:203
scapolite 17:115
serpentine 17:210
silica minerals 17:304
silicon 17:305
sillimanite 17:309
snow and snowflake 18:4
sphene 18:180
staurolite 18:239
structural types 17:305
chain silicates 17:305
framework silicates 17:305
orthosilicates 17:305
sheet silicates 17:305
structure
Bragg, Sir William L. 3:439
talc 19:15
topaz 19:236–237
tourmaline 19:253
weathering 20:82–83
willemite 20:154
zeolite 20:360
zinc, hemimorphite 10:118
zircon 20:370
zoisite 20:371
SILICON 17:305 *bibliog.*
abundances of common elements 7:131 *table*
building construction materials 17:305
carborundum 17:305
commercial preparation 17:305
compounds
inorganic chemistry 11:182
organic chemistry 14:436
element 7:130 *table*
feldspar 8:46
Group IVA periodic table 15:167; 17:305
occurrence 17:305
phytoplankton, plankton 15:332
semiconductor 17:196–197
charge-coupled device 4:288
computer 5:160d
computer industry 5:160o
integrated circuit 11:201–202
silicate minerals 17:304–305
silicon polymers 17:305
silicones 17:305
vitamins and minerals 19:621
SILICON CARBIDE
refractory materials 16:124
SILICON-CONTROLLED RECTIFIER 17:305 *bibliog.*
SILICON HYDRIDE
Wöhler, Friedrich, discoverer 20:195
SILICON VALLEY
computer industry 5:160o
San Jose (California) 17:54
SILICONES 17:305–306 *bibliog.*
silicon 17:305
SILICOSIS 17:306 *bibliog.*
cor pulmonale 5:257
dust, atmospheric 6:308
SILISTRA (Bulgaria)
map (44° 7′N 27° 16′E) 3:555
SILJAN LAKE
map (60° 50′N 14° 45′E) 18:382
SILK 17:306–308 *bibliog., illus.*
Chinese art and architecture 4:384 *illus.*
Chinese weaving (17th century) 19:136 *illus.*
cocoon 5:89
fiber, textile 8:67–68 *map*
Chantilly lace 12:159 *illus.*
satin 17:88
taffeta 19:7
history 17:307
Lyon (France) 12:477
production 17:307–308
China 4:368 *illus.*
during Ch'ing period 4:373 *illus.*
finishing 17:307 *illus.*
sericulture 17:306–307 *illus.*
properties 17:307
spider 18:181–183 *illus.*
SILK OAK 17:308
SILK ROAD 17:308 *bibliog.*
Tun-huang (Dunhuang) 19:331
SILK-SCREEN PRINTING 17:308 *bibliog., illus.*
graphic arts 9:291–294
printing 15:552
textile industry 19:137 *illus.*
Warhol, Andy 20:29
SILK TREE
mimosa 13:436
SILKEBORG (Denmark)
map (56° 10′N 9° 34′E) 6:109
SILKWORM
life cycle 17:306 *illus.*
mulberry 13:635
silk 17:306–307 *illus.*
SILKY FLYCATCHER 17:308
SILKY TERRIER 6:217 *illus.*; 17:308–309 *bibliog., illus.*
SILL 17:309
SILLA KINGDOM
Korea, history of 12:116
Korean art 12:117 *illus.*
SILLANPÄÄ, FRANS EEMIL 17:309 *bibliog.*
SILLIMAN, BENJAMIN 17:309 *bibliog.*
SILLIMANITE 17:309
facies, metamorphic rock 13:332
Silliman, Benjamin 17:309
SILLITOE, ALAN 17:309 *bibliog., illus.*
SILLS, BEVERLY 17:309–310 *bibliog., illus.*
New York City Opera 14:155
SILO (agriculture)
grain elevator 9:282
harbor and port 10:44 *illus.*
SILO (defense) 16:254 *illus.*
nuclear strategy 14:288
SILOAM SPRINGS (Arkansas)
map (36° 11′N 94° 32′W) 2:166
SILOÉ, DIEGO DE 17:310 *bibliog.*
Ordóñez, Bartolomé 14:420
SILONE, IGNAZIO 17:310 *bibliog.*
SILSBEE (Texas)
map (30° 21′N 94° 11′W) 19:129
SILTSTONE
shale 17:237–238
shale, oil 17:238
SILURIAN PERIOD 17:310–312 *bibliog., illus., map*
animal life 17:310 *illus.*
fossil record 8:245–248
geography 17:310–311
geologic time 9:103–105
geology 17:311
ice ages 11:8
life 17:311–312
paleoclimatology 15:32
Paleozoic Era 15:43; 17:310
polar wandering 15:393 *map*
rock formations 17:311 *map*
Silurian strata
Murchison, Roderick Impey 13:647
SILVA, ANTÓNIO JOSÉ DA 17:312
SILVA, JOSÉ ASUNCIÓN 17:312
SILVA, JOSÉ BONIFÁCIO DE ANDRADA E *see* ANDRADA E SILVA, JOSÉ BONIFÁCIO DE
SILVASSA (India)
map (20° 17′N 73° 0′E) 11:80
SILVER 17:312–313 *bibliog.*
antiseptic 17:313
argentite 2:152
art *see* GOLD AND SILVER WORK
chemical properties 17:312
coinage 17:312
dentistry 6:116
electrical conductance 17:313
element 7:130 *table*
extraction 5:400; 17:312
film, photographic 17:312–313
recovery 17:312
galena 9:13
Group IB periodic table 15:167
history 17:312
metal, metallic element 13:328
mining and quarrying
active mines 17:312
Comstock Lode 5:167; 17:312
cyanide 5:400
frontier, U.S. 8:341
Potosí (Bolivia) 15:467
silver boom, Colorado 5:119
mirror 13:464
native elements 14:47
occurrence 17:312
world distribution 14:423 *map*
physical properties 17:312
proustite 15:583
pyrargyrite 15:636
qualitative chemical analysis 16:6
refining 17:312
sulfide minerals 18:333
transition elements 17:312; 19:273
uses 17:312–313
SILVER BAY (Minnesota)
map (47° 17′N 91° 16′W) 13:453
SILVER BELL (Arizona)
map (32° 23′N 111° 30′W) 2:160
SILVER BELL (botany) 17:313
SILVER BOW PARK (Montana)
map (46° 1′N 112° 28′W) 13:547
SILVER BOWL (county in Montana)
map (45° 55′N 112° 38′W) 13:547
SILVER CITY (New Mexico)
map (32° 46′N 108° 17′W) 14:136
SILVER CREEK (Nebraska)
map (41° 19′N 97° 40′W) 14:70
SILVER DOLLAR FISH 17:313
SILVER-EYE *see* WHITE-EYE
SILVER IODIDE
weather modification 20:80
SILVER LAKE (Massachusetts)
map (42° 34′N 70° 44′W) 3:409
SILVER LAKE (Minnesota)
map (44° 54′N 94° 12′W) 13:453
SILVER LAKE (Oregon)
map (43° 8′N 120° 56′W) 14:427
SILVER LAKE (Wisconsin)
map (42° 33′N 88° 7′W) 20:185
SILVER NITRATE
pregnancy and birth 15:506
SILVER PARTY (politics)
Nevada 14:113
SILVER PEAK RANGE
map (37° 35′N 117° 45′W) 14:111
SILVER SPRING (Maryland)
map (39° 2′N 77° 3′W) 13:188
SILVER SPRINGS (Florida)
spring (water) 18:199
SILVER STAR MOUNTAIN
map (48° 33′N 120° 35′W) 20:35
SILVER WORK *see* GOLD AND SILVER WORK
SILVERFISH *see* BRISTLETAIL
SILVERMAN, BELLE *see* SILLS, BEVERLY

SILVERMAN, FRED
radio and television broadcasting 16:59
SILVERPLATING
electrolysis 7:115
SILVERPOINT 17:313 *bibliog.*
SILVERS, HERBERT FERBER *see* FERBER, HERBERT
SILVERSIDES 17:313
grunion 9:383
SILVERTON (Colorado)
map (37° 49′N 107° 40′W) 5:116
SILVERTON (New Jersey)
map (40° 1′N 74° 10′W) 14:129
SILVERTON (Oregon)
map (45° 1′N 122° 47′W) 14:427
SILVERTON (Texas)
map (34° 28′N 101° 19′W) 19:129
SILVERWARE *see* FLATWARE
SILVESTROV, VALENTIN
Russian music 16:369
SILVICULTURE *see* FORESTRY
SIMA GUANG *see* SSU-MA KUANG
SIMA QIAN *see* SSU-MA CH'IEN
SIMBERG, HUGO
Finland 8:97
SIMCOE (Ontario)
map (42° 50′N 80° 18′W) 14:393
SIMCOE, JOHN GRAVES 17:313 *bibliog.*
Ontario (Canada) 14:395
SIMCOE, LAKE
map (44° 20′N 79° 20′W) 14:393; 19:241
SIMENON, GEORGES 17:314 *bibliog., illus.*
SIMEON I, TSAR OF BULGARIA 17:314 *bibliog.*
SIMEON STYLITES, SAINT 17:314
SIMILE 17:314
figures of speech 8:76
SIMITI (Colombia)
map (7° 58′N 73° 57′W) 5:107
SIMLA (Colorado)
map (39° 9′N 104° 5′W) 5:116
SIMLA (India)
map (31° 6′N 77° 10′E) 11:80
SIMMEL, GEORG 17:314 *bibliog.*
alienation 1:294
SIMMESPORT (Louisiana)
map (30° 59′N 91° 49′W) 12:430
SIMMONS COLLEGE 17:314
SIMMS (Montana)
map (47° 30′N 111° 55′W) 13:547
SIMMS, WILLIAM GILMORE 17:314 *bibliog.*
SIMON, SAINT 17:314
SIMON, CLAUDE 17:314–315 *bibliog.*
SIMON, SIR FRANCIS 17:315
SIMON, HERBERT A. 17:315
SIMON, JOHN 17:315
SIMON, JULES FRANÇOIS 17:315 *bibliog.*
SIMON, NEIL 17:315 *bibliog., illus.*
Nichols, Mike 14:182
SIMON, PAUL *see* SIMON AND GARFUNKEL
SIMON, THÉODORE
Binet, Alfred 3:258
SIMON FRASER UNIVERSITY 17:315
SIMON AND GARFUNKEL 17:315
SIMON MAGUS 17:315
gnosticism 9:214
simony 17:316
SIMONE, GIOVANNI (pseudonym) *see* MAYR, JOHANN SIMON
SIMONIDES OF CEOS 17:316
SIMONOV, KONSTANTIN KIRILL MIKHAILOVICH 17:316
SIMONS, ELWYN L.
Ramapithecus 16:80
SIMONS, MENNO *see* MENNO SIMONS
SIMONY 17:316
Simon Magus 17:315
SIMPLE MACHINES 17:316 *bibliog.*
gear 9:65–66
inclined plane 17:316
lever 12:302; 17:316
pulley 15:619 *illus.*; 17:316
screw 17:156–157
wheel and axle 17:316
SIMPLON PASS 17:316
map (46° 15′N 8° 2′E) 18:394
SIMPLON TUNNEL *see* TUNNEL
SIMPSON (county in Kentucky)
map (36° 45′N 86° 35′W) 12:47
SIMPSON (Louisiana)
map (31° 16′N 93° 0′W) 12:430
SIMPSON (county in Mississippi)
map (31° 55′N 89° 55′W) 13:469
SIMPSON (Montana)
map (48° 56′N 110° 12′W) 13:547
SIMPSON, SIR GEORGE 17:317 *bibliog.*
SIMPSON, GEORGE GAYLORD 17:317 *bibliog.*
SIMPSON, LOUIS 17:317
SIMPSON, MATTHEW 17:317 *bibliog.*
SIMPSON, O. J. 17:317 *bibliog., illus.*
SIMPSON, THOMAS 17:317
Victoria Island (Northwest Territories) 19:575
SIMPSON, WALLACE WARFIELD
Edward VIII, King of England 7:69
SIMPSON DESERT 17:317
map (25° 0′S 137° 0′E) 2:328
SIMS, WILLIAM SOWDEN 17:317 *bibliog.*
SIMSBURY (Connecticut)
map (41° 52′N 72° 48′W) 5:193
SIMULATION
computer modeling 5:161–162
teaching machines 19:57 *illus.*
teaching 19:56
SIN 17:317–318
art subject
Bosch, Hieronymus 3:405–406
confession (religion) 5:177
folklore 8:203
indulgences 11:152
original sin 14:444
SINAGUA (American Indians)
cliff dwellers 5:55
Hohokam culture 10:199
SINAI 17:318 *bibliog., illus.*
Arab-Israeli Wars 2:96–97 *map*
Egypt 7:80–81
Israel 11:306
map (29° 30′N 34° 0′E) 7:76
mining and quarrying 13:446
satellite photograph 17:318 *illus.*
turquoise 19:352
SINAI, MOUNT
map (28° 32′N 33° 59′E) 7:76
SINAIS (Romania)
Peles Castle 16:287 *illus.*
SINALOA (Mexico) 17:318
cities
Culiacán 5:383
Mazatlán 13:250
SINAN 17:318 *bibliog.*
Islamic art and architecture 11:297
SINATRA, FRANK 17:318–319 *bibliog.*
SINCELEJO (Colombia)
map (9° 18′N 75° 24′W) 5:107
SINCLAIR (Wyoming)
map (41° 47′N 107° 7′W) 20:301
SINCLAIR, HARRY F. 17:319
SINCLAIR, LAKE
map (33° 11′N 83° 16′W) 9:114
SINCLAIR, UPTON 17:319 *bibliog., illus.*
Eisenstein, Sergei Mikhailovich 7:97
Jungle, The 11:468
SINDHI LANGUAGE
Indo-Iranian languages 11:145
SINE 17:319
Taylor series 19:51
trigonometry 19:298
SINES, CAPE OF
map (37° 57′N 8° 53′W) 15:449
SINGAPORE 17:319–322 *bibliog., illus., map, table*
climate 17:321 *table*
economic activity 17:321
flag 17:319 *illus.*
government 17:321
history 17:321–322
Lee Kuan Yew 12:270
Raffles, Sir Thomas Stamford 16:69
Straits Settlements 18:288
World War II 20:260–261 *illus., map*
land and people 17:320–321
Malaysia 13:86
map (1° 22′N 103° 48′E) 2:232
Southeast Asian universities 18:111 *table*
Taoism 19:29 *illus.*
SINGARAJA (Indonesia)
map (8° 7′S 115° 6′E) 11:147
SINGATOKA (Fiji)
map (18° 8′S 177° 30′E) 8:77
SINGEN (Germany, East and West)
map (47° 46′N 8° 50′E) 9:140
SINGER, ISAAC BASHEVIS 17:322 *bibliog., illus.*
SINGER, ISAAC MERRIT 17:322 *bibliog.*
clothing industry 5:65
sewing machine 17:224
SINGH, CHARAN 17:322
India 11:88
SINGH, J. A. L.
feral children 8:51
SINGH, RANJIT *see* RANJIT SINGH
SINGH, ZAIL
India 11:88
SINGHBHUM (India)
people
Ho 10:190
SINGIN' IN THE RAIN (film) 12:39 *illus.*
SINGING *see* SONG; VOICE, SINGING
SINGLE GRAVE CULTURE
European prehistory 7:303
SINGLE-LENS REFLEX CAMERA 4:54 *illus.*; 4:56–57; 4:58
SINGLE TAX 17:322 *bibliog.*
George, Henry 9:109
physiocrats 15:287
SINGSPIEL 17:322
Benda, Jiří Antonín 3:196
opera 14:400
SINHALESE 17:322–323 *bibliog.*
caste 4:187
Luang Prabang (Laos) 12:446
polygamy 15:419
Sri Lanka 18:205
SINKHOLES
cave 4:222
limestone 12:344 *illus.*
subsidence 18:316
SINKIANG (Xinjiang) (China) 17:323
Lop Nor 12:412
people
Tadzhik 19:7
Uighur 19:374
Takla Makan Desert 19:15
SINN FEIN 17:323 *bibliog.*
Griffith, Arthur 9:363
Home Rule Bills 10:212
Ireland, history of 11:264
SINNAMAHONING (Pennsylvania)
map (41° 19′N 78° 6′W) 15:147
SINNAMARY (French Guiana)
map (5° 23′N 52° 57′W) 8:311
SINNAMARY RIVER
map (5° 27′N 53° 0′W) 8:311
SINNOTT, MICHAEL *see* SENNETT, MACK
SINNURIS (Egypt)
map (29° 25′N 30° 52′E) 7:76
SINO-JAPANESE WARS; 17:323 *bibliog., illus.*; 20:250 *illus.*
China, history of 4:374
Korea, history of 12:117
League of Nations 12:258
Manchuria 13:109
Shansi (Shaxi) (China) 17:240
Shen-yang (Shenyang) (China) 17:255
Szechwan (Sichuan) (China) 18:415
SINO-TIBETAN LANGUAGES 12:355 *map*; 17:324–325 *bibliog.*
Asia 2:244 *map*
Chinese 17:324–325
common linguistic features 17:324
India 11:84
major branches 17:324
Southeast Asian languages 18:110–111
writing systems 17:325
SINOPE MASSACRE
Crimean War 5:348
SINOWATZ, FRED
Austria 2:351
SINT-AMANDSBERG (Belgium)
map (51° 4′N 3° 45′E) 3:177
SINT-GILLES (Belgium)
map (50° 49′N 4° 20′E) 3:177
SINT-NIKLAAS (Belgium)
map (51° 10′N 4° 8′E) 3:177
SINT-TRUIDEN (Belgium)
map (50° 48′N 5° 12′E) 3:177
SINTA GLESKA *see* SPOTTED TAIL
SINTER 17:325
silica minerals 17:304
SINTERING 17:325
ceramics 4:258
iron and steel industry 11:273–274
powder metallurgy 15:480
SINTI
gypsies 9:415
SINTON (Texas)
map (29° 41′N 95° 58′W) 19:129
SINTRA (Portugal) 17:325
SINUIJU (Korea)
map (40° 5′N 124° 24′E) 12:113
SINUS 17:325–326 *bibliog., illus.*
hormone, animal 10:237 *table*
sinusitis 17:326
SINUSITIS 17:326
SINUSOIDAL MOTION *see* MOTION, HARMONIC
SINYAVSKY, ANDREI 17:326 *bibliog.*
SION (Switzerland)
map (46° 14′N 7° 21′E) 18:394
SION HILL (Barbados)
map (13° 5′N 59° 30′W) 3:75
SIOUX (American Indians) 17:326 *bibliog.*
art 11:141 *illus.*
Indians of North America, art of the 11:141
Assiniboin 2:265
Crazy Horse 5:334
Custer, George Armstrong 5:397–398
dance
dance 6:21 *illus.*
scalp dance 11:123 *illus.*
Sun dance 18:346
Fox 8:255
Gall 9:16
ghost dance 9:169
Hidatsa 10:158
Indian Wars 11:108–110
Little Bighorn, Battle of the 12:372
Minnesota history 13:457
Omaha (American Indians) 14:385
Rain-in-the-Face, Chief 11:129 *illus.*
Red Cloud 16:112
Sitting Bull 17:330
South Dakota 18:105–106
Spotted Tail 18:198
tepee 19:114
Wananikwe 20:21
Wounded Knee 20:284–285
Wyoming battles 20:304
SIOUX (county in Iowa)
map (43° 7′N 96° 10′W) 11:244
SIOUX (county in Nebraska)
map (42° 30′N 103° 45′W) 14:70
SIOUX (county in North Dakota)
map (46° 10′N 100° 55′W) 14:248
SIOUX CITY (Iowa) 11:245 *illus.*; 17:326
map (42° 30′N 96° 23′W) 11:244
SIOUX FALLS (South Dakota) 17:326
map (43° 32′N 96° 44′W) 18:103
SIOUX LOOKOUT (Ontario)
map (50° 6′N 91° 55′W) 14:393
SIOUX RAPIDS (Iowa)
map (42° 53′N 95° 9′W) 11:244
SIPARIA (Trinidad and Tobago)
map (10° 8′N 61° 30′W) 19:300
SIPHON 17:326
SIPHONAPTERA 17:326
flea 8:158
SIPIWESK (Manitoba)
map (55° 27′N 97° 24′W) 13:119
SIPPAR (Iraq) 17:326–327 *bibliog.*
SIPSEY RIVER
map (33° 0′N 88° 10′W) 1:234
SIQUEIROS, DAVID ALFARO 17:327 *bibliog.*
Latin American art and architecture 12:227–228
The March of Humanity in Latin America 12:227 *illus.*
mural painting 13:646
SIR FRANCIS DRAKE CHANNEL
map (18° 25′N 64° 30′W) 19:605
SIR GAWAIN AND THE GREEN KNIGHT (poem) 17:327 *bibliog.*
SIR WILFRID LAURIER, MOUNT
map (52° 47′N 119° 45′W) 3:491
SIRA, BEN
Masada 13:194
SIRACH, BOOK OF 17:327
SIRACUAS (Paraguay)
map (21° 3′S 61° 46′W) 15:77
SIRAJGANJ (Bangladesh)
map (24° 27′N 89° 43′E) 3:64
SIRDAR (British Columbia)
map (49° 15′N 116° 37′W) 3:491
SIREN (amphibian) 17:327
SIRÉN, J. S.
Finland 8:97
SIRENIA 17:327–328 *bibliog., illus.*
mammal 13:105–106 *illus.*
SIRENS 17:328
SIRET RIVER
map (45° 24′N 28° 1′E) 16:288
SIRHAN, SIRHAN
Kennedy, Robert F. 12:44
SIRICA, JOHN J. 17:327 *bibliog.*
Watergate 20:64
SIRIUS (ship)
ship 17:273
SIRIUS (star) 17:328
Canis Major and Canis Minor 4:108
Dearborn Observatory 6:68
magnitude 13:60–61
white dwarf 20:137
SIRK, DOUGLAS
Fassbinder, Rainer Werner 8:33
SIRKAP
Taxila 19:48
SIROCCO 17:328
SÍROS (Greece) *see* SYROS (Greece)
SIRSUKH
Taxila 19:48
SISAK (Yugoslavia)
map (45° 29′N 16° 23′E) 20:340

SISAL
hemp **10**:120
Kenya **12**:55 *illus.*
SISKIN **17**:328
SISKIND, AARON **17**:328
SISKIYOU (county in California)
map (41° 35′N 122° 35′W) **4**:31
SISKIYOU MOUNTAINS
map (41° 55′N 123° 15′W) **4**:31
Oregon **14**:428
SISLER, GEORGE **17**:328
SISLEY, ALFRED **17**:328–329 *bibliog., illus.*
Flood at the Port of Marly **11**:65 *illus.*
Road at the Edge of the Woods **17**:328 *illus.*
SISMONDI, JEAN CHARLES LÉONARD SIMONDE DE **17**:329
SISSETON (South Dakota)
map (45° 40′N 97° 3′W) **18**:103
SISTER BAY (Wisconsin)
map (45° 11′N 87° 7′W) **20**:185
SISTER CARRIE (book) **17**:329 *bibliog.*
Dreiser, Theodore **6**:269–270
SISTERS (Oregon)
map (44° 17′N 121° 33′W) **14**:427
SISTERS OF CHARITY OF SAINT JOSEPH
Seton, Saint Elizabeth Ann Bayley **17**:214
SISTERSVILLE (West Virginia)
map (39° 34′N 81° 0′W) **20**:111
SISTINE CHAPEL **11**:313 *illus.*; **17**:329 *bibliog., illus.*
Botticelli, Sandro **3**:418
caricature **4**:150
Creation of Adam (Michelangelo) **2**:190 *illus.*
Delivery of the Keys to St. Peter (Perugino) **2**:196 *illus.*
Ghirlandaio, Domenico **9**:169
Libyan Sibyl **15**:24 *illus.*
Michelangelo **13**:373–375 *illus.*
mural painting **13**:646
Perugino **15**:195
Piero di Cosimo **15**:297
Pintoricchio **15**:308
Signorelli, Luca **17**:302
Sixtus IV, Pope **17**:331
Volterra, Daniele da **19**:632
SISYPHUS **17**:329
Myth of Sisyphus, The **13**:693
SIT-IN *see* INTEGRATION, RACIAL
SITAR **11**:103 *illus.*; **17**:330 *bibliog., illus.*
Shankar, Ravi **17**:240
SITCOM *see* SITUATION COMEDY
SITHOLE, NDABANINGI
Zimbabwe **20**:366
SITKA (Alaska) **17**:330
map (57° 3′N 135° 14′W) **1**:242
SITRA (Bahrain)
map (26° 9′N 50° 38′E) **3**:24
SITTARD (Netherlands)
Danubian culture **6**:36
map (51° 0′N 5° 53′E) **14**:99
SITTER, WILLEM DE **17**:330
SITTING BULL **17**:330 *bibliog., illus.*
Gall **9**:16
Wounded Knee **20**:285
SITTWE (Burma)
map (20° 9′N 92° 54′E) **3**:573
SITUATION COMEDY
radio and television broadcasting **16**:59
SITUBONDO (Indonesia)
map (7° 42′S 114° 0′E) **11**:147
SITWELL (family) **17**:330–331 *bibliog., illus.*
SITWELL, EDITH
Sitwell (family) **17**:330–331 *illus.*
Walton, Sir William **20**:20
SIVA *see* SHIVA
SIVAJI
Maharashtra (India) **13**:64
SIVAPITHECUS
prehistoric human origins **15**:512
SIVAS (Turkey)
map (39° 45′N 37° 2′E) **19**:343
SIX CHARACTERS IN SEARCH OF AN AUTHOR (play) **17**:331
Pirandello, Luigi **15**:314
SIX-DAY WAR (1967)
Arab-Israeli Wars **2**:97 *map*
SIX NATIONS *see* IROQUOIS LEAGUE
SIXMO (MPPSTVO) *see* INDEX
16TH AMENDMENT **17**:331
income tax **11**:76
Internal Revenue Service **11**:218
text **5**:222
6TH AMENDMENT **17**:331
Escobedo v. *Illinois* **7**:237
freedom of the press **8**:297
jury **11**:477
right to counsel
Gideon v. *Wainwright* **9**:177
Williams, Edward Bennett **20**:159
subpoena **18**:316
text **5**:221
trial **19**:292
Ex parte Milligan **7**:325–326
witness **20**:192
SIXTH CATARACT
map (16° 20′N 32° 42′E) **18**:320
SIXTUS IV, POPE **17**:331
Medici (family) **13**:265
Sistine Chapel **17**:329
SIXTUS V, POPE **17**:331 *bibliog.*
Fontana, Domenico **8**:206
SIZE (biology)
growth **9**:380–381
SJAELLAND (Denmark) *see* ZEALAND (Denmark)
SJÆLLANDS POINT
map (55° 58′N 11° 22′E) **6**:109
SJÖSTRÖM, VICTOR
film, history of **8**:84
SKAGEN (Denmark)
map (57° 44′N 10° 36′E) **6**:109
SKAGERRAK **17**:331
map (57° 45′N 9° 0′E) **14**:261
SKAGIT (county in Washington)
map (48° 29′N 121° 45′W) **20**:35
SKAGIT RIVER
map (48° 20′N 122° 25′W) **20**:35
SKAGWAY (Alaska)
map (59° 28′N 135° 19′W) **1**:242
SKALDIC LITERATURE **17**:331–332 *bibliog.*
SKALKA LAKE
map (66° 50′N 18° 46′E) **18**:382
SKAMANIA (county in Washington)
map (45° 58′N 121° 53′W) **20**:35
SKANDERBEG **17**:332
SKANEATELES LAKE
Finger Lakes **8**:93
map (42° 53′N 76° 24′W) **14**:149
SKARA BRAE (Orkney Islands) **17**:332 *bibliog.*
Childe, V. Gordon **4**:351
SKATE (fish) **17**:332 *illus.*
Chondrichthyes **4**:404
SKATE (submarine)
exploration **7**:338
SKATEBOARDING **17**:332–333 *bibliog., illus.*
SKATING *see* ICE SKATING; ROLLER-SKATING
SKEAPING, MARY **17**:333 *bibliog.*
Royal Swedish Ballet **16**:331
SKEENA MOUNTAINS
map (57° 0′N 128° 30′W) **3**:491
SKEENA RIVER
map (54° 9′N 130° 2′W) **3**:491
SKEET SHOOTING **17**:282 *illus.*
SKELDON (Guyana)
map (5° 53′N 57° 8′W) **9**:410
SKELETAL MUSCLE
diseases
muscular dystrophy **13**:656
inflammation
myositis **13**:691
muscle contraction **13**:655–656
SKELETAL STRUCTURE
horse **10**:242 *illus.*
SKELETAL SYSTEM **17**:333–334 *bibliog., illus.*
arthropod **2**:217–218
bird **3**:282–283 *illus.*
bone **3**:377
cartilage **4**:175
chitin **4**:398
crab **5**:324 *illus.*
diseases, human: rehabilitation medicine **16**:129–130
dog **6**:213 *illus.*
insect **11**:187 *illus.*
invertebrate skeletons **17**:333
lion **13**:99 *illus.*
lizard **12**:381 *illus.*
mammal **13**:97; **13**:99 *illus.*
molting **13**:513
ooze, deep-sea **14**:396–397
pelvis **15**:140
skeleton, human **17**:334–337 *illus.*
skull **17**:344–346 *illus.*
spine (backbone) **18**:185
sponge **18**:193–194
vertebrate skeletons **17**:333–334
SKELETON, HUMAN **17**:334–337 *bibliog., illus.*
bone **3**:377
bones, classification **17**:334–335
cartilage **4**:175
pelvis **15**:140
skeletal system **17**:333–334
skull **17**:344–346
space medicine **18**:133
spine (backbone) **18**:185
SKELETON COAST
map (21° 0′S 13° 0′E) **14**:10
SKELLEFTEÅ (Sweden)
map (64° 46′N 20° 57′E) **18**:382
SKELLEFTEA RIVER
map (64° 42′N 21° 6′E) **18**:382
SKELTON, JOHN **17**:337 *bibliog.*
SKEPTICISM **17**:337 *bibliog.*
Carneades **4**:155
Clough, Arthur Hugh **5**:69
ethics **7**:251
Hume, David **10**:301–302
Pyrrho of Elis **15**:638
solipsism **18**:55
SKERLIĆ, JOVAN
Yugoslavia **20**:342
SKI FLYING *see* SKIING
SKI JUMPING *see* SKIING; WATERSKIING
SKIBINE, GEORGE **17**:337
SKIDMORE, OWINGS, AND MERRILL **17**:337 *bibliog.*
Goldsmith, Myron **9**:236
Lever House **2**:137 *illus.*
Sears Tower **13**:492 *illus.*; **17**:175
skyscraper **17**:350
stained glass **18**:212
SKIDMORE COLLEGE **17**:337
SKIEN (Norway)
map (59° 12′N 9° 36′E) **14**:261
SKIING **2**:348 *illus.*; **17**:338–339 *bibliog., illus.*
See also WATERSKIING
Alpine (downhill) **17**:338–339 *illus.*
equipment **17**:338 *illus.*
freestyle ('hotdogging') **17**:338 *illus.*
history **17**:339
jumping **17**:339 *illus.*
Killy, Jean Claude **12**:77
Mahre (brothers) **13**:66
Nordic (cross-country) **17**:338–339 *illus.*; **19**:556 *illus.*
Sailer, Toni **17**:15
techniques **17**:338 *illus.*
SKIKDA (Algeria)
map (36° 50′N 6° 58′E) **1**:287
SKILL LEARNING **17**:339 *bibliog.*
SKILLIN (family) **17**:339 *bibliog.*
figure head **8**:76
SKIMMER (bird) **17**:339–340
SKIN **17**:340–341 *bibliog., illus.*
artificial organs **2**:222
biopotential, galvanic skin response **9**:23
birthmark **3**:296
chameleon **4**:275
collagen **5**:102
dermis **17**:341
drug **6**:275
epidermis **7**:219; **17**:340–341
excretory system **7**:328
freckle **8**:289
hair follicles **17**:341
hives **10**:190
hoof, nail, and claw **10**:225–226
horn (biology) **10**:238
horse **10**:244
human skin **17**:341 *illus.*
anatomy **17**:341
insect **11**:187
leather and hides **12**:262–263
lizard **12**:379–380
mammal, hair **10**:14
measles **13**:253
microclimate **13**:384
mole (birthmark) **13**:507
molting **13**:513
pigment, skin **15**:300; **17**:341
products **17**:340
race **16**:35
reptile **16**:166–168
respiratory system **16**:178
scar **17**:115
secretion, hippopotamus **10**:175
senses **17**:204–205
snake **17**:379 *illus.*
sweat glands **17**:341
temperature
photography **15**:266 *illus.*
wart **20**:33
wolffish **20**:198
xeroderma **20**:312
SKIN DISEASES **17**:341–342 *bibliog.*
acne **1**:83; **17**:342
barber's itch **17**:342
bedsore **3**:154
blepharitis **3**:330
boil **3**:362; **17**:342
bunions, corns, and calluses **3**:563; **17**:341
cancer **4**:101 *illus.*; **4**:104
canker (animal) **4**:108
carbuncle **4**:141; **17**:342
chemical agents **17**:341
collagen disease **5**:102–103
dandruff **6**:31
dermatitis **6**:121–122; **17**:341
dermatology **6**:122
eczema **7**:54
erysipelas **17**:342
erythema **7**:236
eye worm **7**:351
frostbite **8**:346
genetic diseases **17**:341
glanders **9**:197
glucocorticoid **9**:211
herpes **10**:145–146; **17**:342
impetigo **11**:62; **17**:342
infectious diseases **11**:166–167; **17**:342
jaundice **11**:385
jewelweed, treatment **11**:411
leprosy **12**:295
leukoderma **12**:301
lupus erythematosus **12**:466
maggot, myiasis **13**:690
mole (birthmark) **13**:507
papilloma **15**:71
poison ivy **15**:383
poison sumac **15**:383
prickly heat **15**:536; **17**:341
psoriasis **15**:588
purpura **15**:630
ringworm **16**:226; **17**:342
river blindness **16**:232
scabies **17**:342
sex-linked diseases **17**:342
sunburn **17**:341
syphilis **18**:410
ulcer **19**:376
venereal disease **19**:540
xeroderma **20**:312
SKIN DIVING **17**:342–343 *bibliog., illus.*
diving, deep-sea **6**:204
SKIN GRAFT
plastic surgery **15**:347
SKIN OF OUR TEETH, THE (play) **17**:343
Wilder, Thornton **20**:149–150
SKINK **10**:5 *illus.*; **12**:381 *illus.*; **17**:343 *bibliog., illus.*
gerrhosaurid **9**:158
SKINNER, B. F. **17**:343–344 *bibliog., illus.*
concept formation and attainment **5**:169
determinism **6**:134
learning theory **12**:260–261
primary education **15**:538
programmed learning **15**:562–563
psycholinguistics **15**:591
psychology, history of **15**:597 *illus.*
Rogers, Carl **16**:269
Skinner box **17**:344
speech development **18**:175–176
teaching machines **19**:56
SKINNER, CORNELIA OTIS **17**:344
SKINNER, OTIS **17**:344
SKINNER BOX **17**:344
Skinner, B. F. **17**:343
SKIPPER (insect)
butterflies and moths **3**:594
SKITTLES **17**:344
SKIVE (Denmark)
map (56° 34′N 9° 2′E) **6**:109
ŠKODA ENGINEERING WORKS
Plzeň (Czechoslovakia) **15**:375
SKOKIE (Illinois)
map (42° 2′N 87° 46′W) **11**:42
SKOPJE (Yugoslavia) **17**:344
map (41° 59′N 21° 26′E) **20**:340
SKÖVDE (Sweden)
map (58° 24′N 13° 50′E) **18**:382
SKOWHEGAN (Maine)
map (44° 46′N 69° 43′W) **13**:70
SKOWNAN (Manitoba)
map (51° 57′N 99° 36′W) **13**:119
SKOWRONSKA, MARTA *see* CATHERINE I, EMPRESS OF RUSSIA
SKRAELINGS
Thorfinn Karlsefni **19**:178
SKUA **2**:42–43 *illus.*; **17**:344
SKULL **1**:172 *illus.*; **17**:344–346 *bibliog., illus.*
concussion **5**:172
elephant **7**:133–134 *illus.*
fetish **13**:49 *illus.*
horn (biology) **10**:238
hydrocephaly **10**:331
joint (anatomy) **11**:439 *illus.*
mammal **13**:97; **13**:99 *illus.*
measurement, cephalic index **4**:256
phrenology **15**:278 *illus.*
prehistoric humans
cave dwellers **4**:224 *illus.*
Cro-Magnon man **5**:353 *illus.*
Fontéchevade man **8**:207
Homo erectus **10**:215 *illus.*
Homo habilis **10**:216 *illus.*, *illus.*

SKULL (cont.)
Neanderthalers **14**:68 *illus.*
Peking man **4**:378 *illus.*
Skull 1470 **17**:346
reptile **16**:169–171
rodent **16**:265 *illus.*
sinusitis **17**:326
size, microcephaly **13**:384
skeleton, human **17**:336
snake **17**:376
Southeast Asian art and architecture **18**:107–108
SKULL VALLEY (Arizona)
map (34° 30′N 112° 41′W) **2**:160
SKULL 1470 **10**:216 *illus.*; **17**:346 *bibliog.*
Leakey (family) **12**:259
SKULLCAP (botany) **17**:346
SKUNK **17**:346 *illus.*
SKUNK CABBAGE **17**:346
SKUNK RIVER
map (40° 42′N 91° 7′W) **11**:244
SKUNKBIRD *see* BOBOLINK
SKURFER *see* SKATEBOARDING
SKWENTNA (Alaska)
map (61° 58′N 151° 11′W) **1**:242
SKY **17**:346
color: Rayleigh, Lord **16**:97
mirage **13**:463
National Geographic Society–Palomar Observatory Sky Survey **14**:33–34
night sky, Olbers's paradox **14**:373
SKY TURK *see* GÖK TURK
SKYDIVING
aerial sports **1**:122
SKYE (Scotland) **17**:346
map (57° 15′N 6° 10′W) **19**:403
SKYE TERRIER **6**:220 *illus.*; **17**:346–347 *bibliog., illus.*
cairn terrier **4**:17
SKYJACKING *see* AIRPLANE HIJACKING
SKYLAB **17**:347–348 *bibliog., illus.*
astronaut crews **17**:347–348
Bean, Alan **3**:140
Carr, Gerald **4**:166
Conrad, Pete **5**:198–199
Garriot, Owen **9**:51
Johnson Space Center **11**:437
Kerwin, Joseph **12**:60
life on board **17**:348
life-support systems **12**:331–333
Lousma, Jack **12**:436
National Aeronautics and Space Administration **14**:28
Pogue, William Reid **15**:380
research **17**:347
Saturn (rocket) **17**:92
Skylab III
Gibson, Edward **9**:176
space exploration **18**:129–130 *illus.*
space medicine **18**:133 *illus.*
space residency record **17**:347
space station **18**:136
Weitz, Paul J. **20**:96
SKYLAND (North Carolina)
map (35° 29′N 82° 31′W) **14**:242
SKYLARK **12**:207–208 *illus.*
SKYSCRAPER **17**:348–350 *bibliog., illus.*
American art and architecture **1**:329–330
Bogardus, James **3**:359
building construction **3**:549 *illus.*
Burnham, Daniel Hudson **3**:577
Chicago school of architecture **4**:342–343
Chrysler Building **4**:420
Empire State Building **7**:158
Flatiron Building **8**:156
Hood, Raymond **10**:225
Jenney, William LeBaron **11**:396
John Hancock Center (Chicago) **4**:342 *illus.*
Johnson, Philip **11**:435
Rockefeller Center **16**:250–251
Root, John Wellborn **16**:311
Seagram Building **17**:173
Sears Tower **17**:175
Sullivan, Louis **18**:337
Wainwright Building (Louis Sullivan) **18**:337 *illus.*
Woolworth Building **20**:216
World Trade Center **14**:147 *illus.*; **20**:219
Wright, Frank Lloyd **20**:289
SKYSCRAPER OF THE PRAIRIES
Bismarck (North Dakota) **3**:298
SLAG
flux **8**:189
SLAGELSE (Denmark)
map (55° 24′N 11° 22′E) **6**:109
SLALOM *see* SKIING
SLAMET, MOUNT
map (7° 14′S 109° 12′E) **11**:147
SLANDER *see* DEFAMATION
SLANG **17**:350 *bibliog.*
cockney **5**:87
SLAPSTICK **17**:350
Chaplin, Charlie **4**:284
Harlequin **10**:50
Keystone Kops **12**:64
Laurel and Hardy **12**:238
Marx Brothers **13**:182–183
Sennett, Mack **17**:204
SLASH-AND-BURN AGRICULTURE **17**:350
Danubian culture **6**:36
jungle and rain forest **11**:470
SLATE (geology) **13**:331 *illus.*; **17**:351 *illus.*
foliation **8**:195
rock **16**:247
roof and roofing **16**:306 *illus.*
SLATER (Iowa)
map (41° 53′N 93° 41′W) **11**:244
SLATER (Missouri)
map (39° 13′N 93° 4′W) **13**:476
SLATER, SAMUEL **17**:351 *bibliog.*
manufacturing **13**:132
Pawtucket (Rhode Island) **15**:121
SLATIN, RUDOLF ANTON KARL, FREIHERR VON **17**:351 *bibliog.*
SLATINA (Romania)
map (44° 26′N 24° 22′E) **16**:288
SLATINGTON (Pennsylvania)
map (40° 45′N 75° 37′W) **15**:147
SLATKIN, LEONARD **17**:351
SLATON (Texas)
map (33° 26′N 101° 39′W) **19**:129
SLAUGHTERHOUSE CASES **17**:351
SLAUGHTERHOUSE-FIVE (book) **17**:351
Vonnegut, Kurt, Jr. **19**:634
SLAUGHTERING *see* MEAT AND MEAT PACKING
SLAVE COAST
map (5° 30′N 1° 0′E) **9**:164
SLAVE LAKE (Alberta)
map (55° 17′N 114° 46′W) **1**:256
SLAVE RIVER **17**:351
map (61° 18′N 113° 39′W) **14**:258
SLAVERY **17**:351–357 *bibliog., illus., map*
African slave trade **17**:353–354 *illus.*
Africa, history of **1**:154
Ghana **9**:166
Liberia **12**:313–314
Nigeria **14**:192
Portugal **15**:449
Sierra Leone **17**:298
slave ship **17**:268 *illus.*; **17**:354 *illus.*
trade routes to Caribbean and U.S. **17**:356 *map*
Wolof **20**:199
Yao **20**:318–319
ancient world **17**:352–353
construction of palace at Nineveh **19**:63 *illus.*
ant **2**:37
domestic service **6**:231
Middle Ages **17**:353
New World **17**:353–355 *illus.*
Amistad Case **1**:372
encomienda **7**:163
English colonies **17**:354 *illus.*
Jamaica **11**:352
Nabuco, Joaquim **14**:4
Pedro II, Emperor of Brazil **15**:132
rum **16**:344
South America **18**:91
triangle trade **17**:354–356 *map*
United States **3**:305 *map*; **17**:354–357 *map*
abolitionists **1**:58
auction **3**:306 *illus.*
black Americans **3**:304–307
black codes **3**:313–314
California **4**:37
Civil War, U.S. **5**:15–17 *map*
Compromise of 1850 **5**:158
cotton gin **5**:307
Crittenden Compromise **5**:352–353
Delaware **6**:91
Douglas, Stephen A. **6**:247–248
Douglass, Frederick **6**:248–249
Dred Scott v. *Sandford* **6**:268
Emancipation Proclamation **7**:151
English colonies **17**:354
Free-Soil party **8**:295
Freedmen's Bureau **5**:33 *illus.*; **8**:295–296
Fugitive Slave Laws **8**:355
Gabriel (slave) **9**:6
gag rules **9**:7
genesis of the Constitution **5**:213
Georgia **9**:118
indentured service **11**:78
Iowa **11**:247
Jefferson, Thomas **11**:392
Kansas **12**:21
Kansas-Nebraska Act **12**:22–23
Lecompton Constitution **12**:268
Lincoln, Abraham **12**:347–349
Mason-Dixon line **13**:199
Missouri **13**:479
Missouri Compromise **13**:480–481
popular sovereignty **15**:433
Reconstruction **16**:108–110
Reconstruction Amendments **5**:221–222
slave states and free states **19**:447 *map*
Stowe, Harriet Beecher: *Uncle Tom's Cabin* **18**:286
13th Amendment **19**:170
trade routes from Africa to U.S. **17**:356 *map*
trade in the U.S. **17**:356 *map*
Turner, Nat **19**:350–351
20th century **17**:357
Underground Railroad **5**:16 *illus.*; **19**:383
United States, history of the **19**:438; **19**:446–450
Vesey, Denmark **19**:564
Wilmot Proviso **20**:163
SLAVERY, ABOLITION OF (U.S. Constitution) *see* 13TH AMENDMENT
SLAVIC LANGUAGES **17**:357–358 *bibliog.*
Austria-Hungary **2**:351 *map*
Cyrillic alphabet **5**:410
dialects and vocabulary **17**:358
linguistic features **17**:358
major branches **17**:357–358
modern vernaculars **17**:358
Old Church Slavonic **17**:358
Yugoslavia **20**:341
SLAVIC MYTHOLOGY *see* MYTHOLOGY
SLAVONIC LANGUAGES *see* SLAVIC LANGUAGES
SLAVONSKI BROD (Yugoslavia)
map (45° 10′N 18° 1′E) **20**:340
SLAVOPHILES AND WESTERNIZERS **17**:358–359 *bibliog.*
Aksakov, Konstantin Sergeyevich **1**:232
Pan-Slavism **15**:54
SLAVS **17**:359
Czechoslovakia **5**:416
Drang nach Osten **6**:262
nation **14**:27
Pan-Slavism **15**:54
Poland **15**:388
Russia/Union of Soviet Socialist Republics, history of **16**:351
Yugoslavia **20**:341–343
Croatia **5**:354–355
Serbia **17**:207–208
Slovenia **17**:364
SLAYTON (Minnesota)
map (43° 59′N 95° 45′W) **13**:453
SLAYTON, D. K. **17**:359 *bibliog.*
Apollo-Soyuz Test Project **2**:84
astronaut **2**:274 *illus.*
SLBM *see* TRIDENT
SLED **17**:359
bobsledding **3**:353
dogsled **6**:223
snowmobile **18**:5
tobogganing **19**:220
troika **19**:305
SLEDGE *see* SLED
SLEDGE (Mississippi)
map (34° 26′N 90° 13′W) **13**:469
SLEEP **17**:359–360 *bibliog.*
barbiturate **6**:276 *illus.*
consciousness, states of **5**:200
dreams and dreaming **6**:266–268
electroencephalograph
brain **3**:447
hypnosis **10**:350
Non-Rapid Eye Movement **17**:360
rapid eye movement (REM) **6**:266–267; **17**:360
fantasy **8**:21
sedative **17**:181–182
sodium pentothal **18**:33
trance **19**:266
SLEEPER (fish) **17**:361
SLEEPING BEAUTY **8**:10 *illus.*
SLEEPING CAR *see* RAILROAD
SLEEPING CAR PORTERS, BROTHERHOOD OF
integration, racial **11**:202
Randolph, A. Philip **16**:83
SLEEPING SICKNESS
Mastigophora **13**:217
trypanosomiasis **19**:322
SLEEPWALKING
hypnosis **10**:350
SLEEPY EYE (Minnesota)
map (44° 18′N 94° 43′W) **13**:453
SLEIGH *see* SLED
SLESSOR, KENNETH **17**:361 *bibliog.*
SLEVOGT, MAX **17**:361
Francisco d'Andrade **14**:400 *illus.*
SLEZAK, LEO **17**:361
SLICK, GRACE
Jefferson Airplane **11**:393
SLIDE MOUNTAIN
map (42° 0′N 74° 23′W) **14**:149
SLIDE RULE **17**:361 *bibliog., illus.*
analog devices **1**:388
SLIDELL (Louisiana)
map (30° 17′N 89° 47′W) **12**:430
SLIDELL, JOHN **17**:361 *bibliog.*
Mexican War **13**:352
Trent Affair **19**:290
SLIDING BACTERIA *see* MYXOBACTERIA
SLIEDRECHT (Netherlands)
map (51° 49′N 4° 45′E) **14**:99
SLIEMA (Malta)
map (35° 55′N 14° 30′E) **13**:94
SLIGO (city in Ireland) **17**:361
map (54° 17′N 8° 28′W) **11**:258
SLIGO (county in Ireland) **17**:361–362
SLIGO (Pennsylvania)
map (41° 7′N 79° 29′W) **15**:147
SLIM, WILLIAM JOSEPH, 1ST VISCOUNT SLIM **17**:362 *bibliog.*
World War II **20**:277–278 *illus.*
SLIME MOLD **17**:362 *bibliog., illus.*
germination **9**:157
life cycle **8**:366 *illus.*
plasmodiophore **15**:347
Plasmodium **15**:347
Protista **15**:577–578
SLIP CASTING *see* CASTING
SLIPHER, VESTO MELVIN **17**:362
SLIPPERFLOWER **17**:362
SLIPPERY ROCK (Pennsylvania)
map (41° 4′N 80° 3′W) **15**:147
SLIPWARE
ceramics **4**:257
pottery and porcelain **15**:471
SLIVEN (Bulgaria)
map (42° 40′N 26° 19′E) **3**:555
SLOAN (Iowa)
map (42° 14′N 96° 14′W) **11**:244
SLOAN (Nevada)
map (35° 57′N 115° 13′W) **14**:111
SLOAN, ALFRED P.
automotive industry **2**:363
SLOAN, JOHN **17**:362–363 *bibliog., illus.*
Backyards, Greenwich Village **2**:230 *illus.*
Sixth Avenue and Thirtieth Street **1**:335 *illus.*; **17**:363
SLOAN FOUNDATION **17**:363
Sloan-Kettering Institute for Cancer Research **17**:363
SLOAN-KETTERING INSTITUTE FOR CANCER RESEARCH **17**:363
Kettering, Charles Franklin **12**:61
SLOANE, SIR HANS
British Museum **3**:497
SLOAT, JOHN DRAKE
California **4**:37
Mexican War **13**:352 *map*; **13**:355
SLONIMSKY, SERGEI
Russian music **16**:369
SLOOP (boat)
ship **17**:270 *illus.*
SLOPE (geometry) **17**:363 *bibliog.*
SLOPE (county in North Dakota)
map (46° 30′N 103° 20′W) **14**:248
SLOPE, RICHARD
influenza **11**:172
SLOPEWASH **12**:182 *illus.*
SLOTH **11**:469 *illus.*; **17**:363 *bibliog., illus.*
edentates **7**:56
forelimb **13**:102 *illus.*
giant ground sloth **15**:366 *illus.*
SLOVAK SOCIALIST REPUBLIC *see* CZECHOSLOVAKIA
SLOVAKIA (Czechoslovakia) **17**:363–364 *map*
cities
Bratislava **3**:458
SLOVENIA (Yugoslavia) **17**:364 *map*
cities
Ljubljana **12**:382
history
Yugoslavia **20**:343

literature
Cankar, Ivan **4**:108
Yugoslavia **20**:342
map (46° 15′N 15° 10′E) **20**:340
SLOVENIAN LANGUAGE
Slavic languages **17**:358
SLOVENSKÉ MOUNTAINS
map (48° 45′N 20° 0′E) **5**:413
SLOVINCIAN LANGUAGE
Slavic languages **17**:358
SLOW-PITCH SOFTBALL
softball **18**:35
SŁOWACKI, JULIUSZ **17**:364 *bibliog.*
SLUDGE **17**:364
compost **5**:158
fertilizer **8**:62
SLUG (zoology) **9**:57 *illus.*; **17**:364 *bibliog., illus.*
mollusk **13**:510–511 *illus.*
soil organisms **18**:39 *illus.*
SLUG-EATING SNAKE
colubrid **5**:125
SLUMS
Chicago **10**:276 *illus.*
urban planning **19**:484
SŁUPSK (Poland)
map (54° 28′N 17° 1′E) **15**:388
SLUTER, CLAUS **17**:364–365 *bibliog., illus.*
Gothic art and architecture **9**:261
Well of Moses **9**:261 *illus.*; **17**:163 *illus.*; **17**:365 *illus.*
SLYKE, HELEN VAN *see* VAN SLYKE, HELEN
SLYNE HEAD
map (53° 24′N 10° 13′W) **11**:258
SMACKOVER (Arkansas)
map (33° 22′N 92° 44′W) **2**:166
SMÅLANDS SOUND
map (55° 5′N 11° 20′E) **6**:109
SMALL, ADAM
South Africa **18**:81
SMALL BUSINESS ADMINISTRATION **17**:365
Patman, Wright **15**:112
SMALLPOX **17**:365 *bibliog.*
cosmetics **5**:282 *illus.*
cowpox **5**:322
diseases, animal **6**:190
Jenner, Edward **11**:396
medicine **13**:270
vaccination **19**:501
cartoon **13**:270 *illus.*
vaccinia **19**:502
SMARTWEED **17**:365
SMEATON, JOHN **17**:365
lighthouse **12**:336
technology, history of **19**:66
SMEDEREVO (Yugoslavia)
map (44° 40′N 20° 56′E) **20**:340
SMELL *see* SENSES AND SENSATION
SMELLING SALTS **17**:365
SMELT **17**:365–366 *illus.*
candlefish **4**:107
SMELTING **17**:366
copper
Chalcolithic Period **4**:270
Iron Age **11**:271–272
iron and steel industry **11**:274
metallurgy **13**:330
Sprague, Frank Julian **18**:198
SMERDIS *see* BARDIYA
SMET, PIERRE JEAN DE *see* DE SMET, PIERRE JEAN
SMETANA, BEDŘICH **17**:366 *bibliog., illus.*
Czech music **5**:413
SMETHPORT (Pennsylvania)
map (41° 49′N 78° 27′W) **15**:147
SMIBERT, JOHN **17**:366 *bibliog.*
SMILEY (Texas)
map (29° 16′N 97° 38′W) **19**:129
SMILODON **13**:102 *illus.*
SMIRKE, SIR ROBERT **17**:366
British Museum **3**:497 *illus.*
SMITH (Alberta)
map (55° 10′N 114° 2′W) **1**:256
SMITH (county in Kansas)
map (39° 50′N 98° 45′W) **12**:18
SMITH (county in Mississippi)
map (32° 0′N 89° 30′W) **13**:469
SMITH (county in Tennessee)
map (36° 15′N 85° 55′W) **19**:104
SMITH (county in Texas)
map (32° 20′N 95° 15′W) **19**:129
SMITH, ADAM **17**:366–367 *bibliog., illus.*
capitalism **4**:124–125
economics **7**:48
Kirkcaldy (Scotland) **12**:89
liberalism **12**:312
Marxism **13**:183
state (in political philosophy) **18**:232
Wealth of Nations, An Inquiry into the Nature and Causes of the **20**:74
SMITH, ALFRED E. **17**:367 *bibliog., illus.*
Roosevelt, Franklin Delano **16**:307–308
SMITH, BESSIE **17**:367 *bibliog.*
jazz **11**:388 *illus.*
SMITH, CHARLES HENRY **17**:367
SMITH, DAVID **17**:367–368 *bibliog., illus.*
Cubi I **17**:368 *illus.*
Cubi XIX **17**:166 *illus.*
SMITH, DONALD ALEXANDER *see* STRATHCONA AND MOUNT ROYAL, DONALD ALEXANDER SMITH, 1ST BARON
SMITH, SIR ELLIOT **17**:368
Perry, W. J. **15**:179
SMITH, FRANCIS
Lexington and Concord, Battles of **12**:309
SMITH, FRANCIS PETTIT *see* PETTIT SMITH, FRANCIS
SMITH, FREDERICK EDWIN, 1ST EARL OF BIRKENHEAD *see* BIRKENHEAD, F.E. SMITH, 1ST EARL OF
SMITH, GEORGE **17**:368 *bibliog.*
SMITH, GERALD L. K.
Union party **19**:387
SMITH, GLADYS MARY *see* PICKFORD, MARY
SMITH, GORDON
Canadian art and architecture **4**:91
SMITH, HAMILTON **17**:368
Nathans, Daniel **14**:27
SMITH, SIR HARRY **17**:368
SMITH, HOWARD K. **17**:368
SMITH, IAN D. **17**:369 *illus.*
Nkomo, Joshua **14**:206
Zimbabwe **20**:365; **20**:366
SMITH, JEDEDIAH STRONG **17**:369 *bibliog.*
exploration of the American west **19**:445 *map*
Nevada **14**:113
SMITH, JOHN **17**:369 *bibliog., illus.*
Boston **3**:410
Pocahontas **15**:376
Powhatan **15**:486
SMITH, JOHN STAFFORD
"Star-Spangled Banner, The" **18**:226
SMITH, JOSEPH **17**:369–370 *bibliog., illus.*
Mormonism **13**:581–582
SMITH, KATE **17**:370
SMITH, MARGARET CHASE **17**:370 *bibliog.*
SMITH, MICHAEL **17**:370
SMITH, OLIVER **17**:370
American Ballet Theatre **1**:337
SMITH, PINE TOP
boogie-woogie **3**:383
SMITH, RED **17**:370 *bibliog.*
SMITH, SEBA **17**:370 *bibliog.*
SMITH, SHERRI
wall hanging **5**:327 *illus.*
SMITH, SYDNEY **17**:370 *bibliog.*
SMITH, TOMMIE **14**:383 *illus.*
SMITH, TONY **17**:370–371 *bibliog.*
SMITH, W. EUGENE **17**:371
SMITH, WALKER *see* ROBINSON, SUGAR RAY
SMITH, WALTER BEDELL **17**:371
SMITH, WILLIAM **17**:371 *bibliog., illus.*
prehistory **15**:517
SMITH, WILLIAM ROBERTSON **17**:371 *bibliog.*
SMITH ACT **17**:371
Communist party, U.S.A. **5**:151
Dennis v. *United States* **6**:113
freedom of speech **8**:298
sedition **17**:186
SMITH CENTER (Kansas)
map (39° 47′N 98° 47′W) **12**:18
SMITH COLLEGE **17**:371–372
Seven Sisters Colleges **17**:216
SMITH-HUGHES ACT **17**:372
secondary education **17**:179
technical education **19**:59
vocational education **19**:625
SMITH-LEVER ACT OF 1914 **17**:372
SMITH MOUNTAIN LAKE
map (37° 10′N 79° 40′W) **19**:607
SMITH RIVER (California)
map (41° 56′N 124° 9′W) **4**:31
SMITH RIVER (Montana)
map (47° 25′N 111° 29′W) **13**:547
SMITHERS (British Columbia)
map (54° 47′N 127° 10′W) **3**:491
SMITHERS (West Virginia)
map (38° 11′N 81° 18′W) **20**:111
SMITHFIELD (North Carolina)
map (35° 30′N 78° 21′W) **14**:242
SMITHFIELD (Utah)
map (41° 50′N 111° 50′W) **19**:492
SMITHFIELD (Virginia)
map (36° 59′N 76° 38′W) **19**:607
SMITHLAND (Kentucky)
map (37° 9′N 88° 24′W) **12**:47
SMITHS (Alabama)
map (32° 32′N 85° 6′W) **1**:234
SMITHS FALLS (Ontario)
map (44° 54′N 76° 1′W) **14**:393
SMITHSON, ALISON AND PETER **17**:372
SMITHSON, JAMES **17**:372 *bibliog.*
Smithsonian Institution **17**:372
smithsonite **17**:372
SMITHSON, ROBERT **17**:372 *bibliog.*
Spiral Jetty **2**:202 *illus.*; **7**:28 *illus.*
SMITHSONIAN ASTROPHYSICAL OBSERVATORY **17**:372 *bibliog.*
Langley, Samuel Pierpont **12**:196
Whipple, Fred Lawrence **20**:131
SMITHSONIAN INSTITUTION **17**:372 *bibliog.*
Baird, Spencer F. **3**:27
Cooper-Hewitt Museum **5**:245
Freer Gallery of Art
Freer, Charles Lang **8**:300
Henry, Joseph **10**:122
Hrdlička, Aleš **10**:286
Langley, Samuel Pierpont **12**:196
museums of science and industry **13**:659
National Air and Space Museum **14**:28–29
National Collection of Fine Arts **14**:30
National Museum of American History **14**:35
National Portrait Gallery **14**:44–45
National Zoological Park **14**:46
Renwick, James **16**:159
Smithson, James **17**:372
Washington, D.C. **20**:41 *map*
SMITHSONITE **13**:440 *illus.*; **17**:372 *illus.*
Smithson, James **17**:372
SMITHTON (Missouri)
map (38° 41′N 93° 5′W) **13**:476
SMITHTOWN (New York)
map (40° 52′N 73° 13′W) **14**:149
SMITHTOWN BAY
map (40° 57′N 73° 12′W) **5**:193
SMITHVILLE (Georgia)
map (31° 54′N 84° 15′W) **9**:114
SMITHVILLE (Mississippi)
map (33° 59′N 88° 23′W) **13**:469
SMITHVILLE (Missouri)
map (39° 23′N 94° 35′W) **13**:476
SMITHVILLE (Tennessee)
map (35° 58′N 85° 49′W) **19**:104
SMITHVILLE (Texas)
map (30° 0′N 97° 9′W) **19**:129
SMOG
fog **8**:193
formation, chain reaction, chemical **4**:269
photochemistry **15**:259
pollution, environmental **15**:414–415 *illus.*
smoke **17**:373
SMOHALLA (Wanapan Indians) **17**:373 *bibliog.*
SMOKE **17**:373 *bibliog.*
coal and coal mining **5**:79
Indians, American
peace pipe **15**:123
phosphorus **15**:256
SMOKE, KENNETH
concept formation and attainment **5**:169
SMOKE CREEK DESERT
map (40° 30′N 119° 40′W) **14**:111
SMOKE DETECTOR **17**:373 *bibliog.*
alarm systems **1**:240
SMOKETREE **17**:373
SMOKING **17**:373–374 *bibliog.*
birth control **3**:294
bronchitis **3**:503
cancer **4**:101; **4**:102; **4**:104
emphysema **7**:158
environmental health **7**:211
health effects controversy **17**:373
nicotine **14**:184
respiratory system disorders **16**:182
tobacco **19**:218–219
U.S. Public Health Service report **17**:373–374
SMOKY HILL LAKE
map (39° 3′N 96° 48′W) **12**:18
SMOKY MOUNTAINS *see* GREAT SMOKY MOUNTAINS
SMOKY RIVER
map (56° 10′N 117° 21′W) **1**:256
SMOLENSK (USSR) **17**:374
map (54° 47′N 32° 3′E) **19**:388
SMOLLETT, TOBIAS **17**:374 *bibliog., illus.*
SMOLUCHOWSKI, MARIAN
Brownian motion **3**:518
SMOOT, REED **17**:374
SMSA *see* STANDARD METROPOLITAN STATISTICAL AREA
SMUGGLING **17**:374 *bibliog.*
drug trafficking **6**:281
port of entry **15**:443
SMUT (botany) *see* DISEASES, PLANT
SMUTS, JAN **17**:374–375 *bibliog., illus.*
SMYRNA (Delaware)
map (39° 18′N 75° 36′W) **6**:88
SMYRNA (Georgia)
map (33° 53′N 84° 31′W) **9**:114
SMYRNA (Tennessee)
map (35° 59′N 86° 31′W) **19**:104
SMYRNA (Turkey) *see* IZMIR (Turkey)
SMYTH (county in Virginia)
map (36° 50′N 81° 30′W) **19**:607
SMYTH, CHARLES PIAZZI
archaeoastronomy **2**:115
SMYTH, DAME ETHEL **17**:375 *bibliog.*
SMYTH, JOHN **17**:375
SMYTHE, MOUNT
map (57° 54′N 124° 53′W) **3**:491
SMYTHSON, ROBERT
Elizabethan style **7**:146
SNÆFELLSNES (peninsula)
map (64° 50′N 23° 0′W) **11**:17
SNAG (Yukon Territory)
map (62° 24′N 140° 22′W) **20**:345
SNAGGLETOOTH **8**:118 *illus.*
SNAIL **9**:57 *illus.*; **15**:35 *illus.*; **17**:375–376 *bibliog., illus.*
conch **5**:170
cowrie **5**:322
food
algal mat **1**:283
giant African snail **17**:376 *illus.*
shell **17**:252 *illus.*
intertidal life **11**:230
limpet **12**:347
mollusk **13**:510–511 *illus.*
Ordovician Period **14**:422 *illus., illus.*
periwinkle (zoology) **15**:172
schistosomiasis **17**:123
Silurian Period **17**:310 *illus.*
soil organisms **18**:39 *illus.*
tegula snail **11**:229 *illus.*
water snail **18**:377 *illus.*
whelk **20**:130
SNAIL DARTER
darter **6**:40
environmental impact statement **7**:212
SNAIL FEVER *see* SCHISTOSOMIASIS
SNAKE **17**:98 *illus.*; **17**:376–382 *bibliog., illus.*
See also names of specific snakes, e.g., ASP; COBRA; KRAIT; etc.
aging **1**:186
anatomy **17**:376–379 *illus.*
biological locomotion **3**:266–267 *illus.*; **17**:381–382 *illus.*
body temperature **17**:376
classification, biological **17**:382
colubrid **5**:124
desert life **6**:131
ear **17**:378
eye **17**:378–379 *illus.*
feeding **17**:379–381 *illus.*
fossil record **17**:382
gland **17**:379
Jacobson's organ **11**:347
mimicry **13**:435 *illus.*
molting **17**:379 *illus.*
reproduction **17**:382
respiratory system **17**:378–379
sea snake **17**:170
senses **17**:379 *illus.*
skin **17**:379 *illus.*
skull **17**:376–378
venom **19**:546
salivary glands **17**:34
SNAKE DANCE **17**:382 *bibliog.*
SNAKE EEL **17**:382
SNAKE FALLS
map (42° 40′N 101° 52′W) **14**:70
SNAKE FLY **17**:382–383 *illus.*
SNAKE INDIANS *see* SHOSHONI (American Indians)
SNAKE LIZARD
girdle-tailed lizard **9**:189
SNAKE MACKEREL **17**:383

SNAKE PLANT 17:383
SNAKE RIVER (central Minnesota)
map (45° 49′N 92° 46′W) 13:453
SNAKE RIVER (northwestern Minnesota)
map (48° 26′N 97° 7′W) 13:453
SNAKE RIVER (Nebraska)
map (42° 47′N 100° 48′W) 14:70
SNAKE RIVER (United States) 11:27 *illus.*; 17:383; 20:300 *illus.*
Indians, American
Bannock 3:71
map (46° 12′N 119° 2′W) 19:419
SNAKE RIVER PLAIN
map (43° 0′N 113° 0′W) 11:26
SNAKEBIRD *see* ANHINGA
SNAKEHEAD (fish) 17:383
SNAKEROOT 17:383
medicinal plants 13:266
rauwolfia 16:94
SNAP (power source) 17:383–384 *bibliog.*
power source 11:383
satellites, artificial 11:383
SNAP BEAN
bean 3:139–140 *illus.*
SNAPDRAGON 17:384 *illus.*
monkey flower 13:535
SNAPPER 17:384 *illus.*
SNAPPING TURTLE 17:384 *illus.*
SNAPWEED *see* JEWELWEED
SNARE DRUM 13:675 *illus.*; 17:384 *bibliog.*
SNCC 17:384
Bond, Julian 3:376
SNEAD, SAM 17:384 *bibliog.*
SNEADS (Florida)
map (30° 42′N 84° 56′W) 8:172
SNEEDVILLE (Tennessee)
map (36° 32′N 83° 13′W) 19:104
SNEEK (Netherlands)
map (53° 2′N 5° 40′E) 14:99
SNEEZEWEED 18:3
SNEFRU, KING OF EGYPT 18:3
Khufu, King of Egypt 12:69
SNELL, PETER 18:3
SNELL, WILLEBRORD VAN ROIJEN 18:3
Earth, size and shape of 7:19
Snell's law, refraction 16:123
SNIPE 18:3 *illus.*
beak 3:289 *illus.*
game birds 9:27
shorebirds 17:283
SNIPEFISH 18:3
SNOBOL 18:3
SNODGRASS, W. D. 18:3
SNOHOMISH (Washington)
map (47° 55′N 122° 6′W) 20:35
SNOHOMISH (county in Washington)
map (48° 2′N 121° 41′W) 20:35
SNOOK 18:3
SNOOKER (game)
billiards 3:254 *illus.*; 3:255 *illus.*
SNOQUALMIE RIVER
map (47° 50′N 122° 3′W) 20:35
SNORKLING
skin diving 17:343
SNORRI STURLUSON 18:3 *bibliog.*
mythology 13:702
Younger Edda 7:54–55
SNØTINDEN MOUNTAIN
map (66° 38′N 14° 0′E) 14:261
SNOUT BEETLE *see* WEEVIL
SNOW, C.P., BARON SNOW 18:3–4 *bibliog., illus.*
SNOW, JOHN
epidemiology 7:219
SNOW, MICHAEL
Canadian art and architecture 4:91
film, history of 8:87
SNOW HILL (Maryland)
map (38° 11′N 75° 24′W) 13:188
SNOW HILL (North Carolina)
map (35° 27′N 77° 40′W) 14:242
SNOW LAKE (Manitoba)
map (54° 53′N 100° 2′W) 13:119
SNOW SKIING *see* SKIING
SNOW AND SNOWFLAKE 18:4 *bibliog., illus., table*
blizzard 3:333
hydrologic cycle 10:341
ice, river and lake 11:7
landslide and avalanche 12:193
polar climate 15:392
precipitation 15:493
snowmelt
floods and flood control 8:167
weather modification 20:80
SNOWBELT
North America 14:236
SNOWBERRY 18:5
SNOWDON, ANTONY ARMSTRONG-JONES, 1ST EARL OF 18:5 *bibliog.*
SNOWDON MOUNTAIN 20:11 *illus.*
map (53° 4′N 4° 5′W) 19:403
SNOWDOUN (Alabama)
map (32° 15′N 86° 18′W) 1:234
SNOWDRIFT (Northwest Territories)
map (62° 23′N 110° 47′W) 14:258
SNOWDROP (botany) 18:5
SNOWFLAKE (Arizona)
map (34° 30′N 110° 5′W) 2:160
SNOWMASS MOUNTAIN
map (39° 7′N 107° 4′W) 5:116
SNOWMOBILE 18:5 *bibliog., illus.*
Eskimo 7:240
SNOWSHOE HARE 2:140–141 *illus.*
SNOWY MOUNTAINS 18:5
map (36° 30′S 148° 20′E) 2:328
peaks
Kosciusko, Mount 12:123
SNOWY OWL 2:140–141 *illus.*
SNOWY SHEATHBILL *see* SHEATHBILL
SNUFF *see* TOBACCO
SNYDER (Oklahoma)
map (34° 40′N 98° 57′W) 14:368
SNYDER (county in Pennsylvania)
map (40° 47′N 77° 3′W) 15:147
SNYDER (Texas)
map (32° 44′N 100° 55′W) 19:129
SNYDER, GARY 18:5–6 *bibliog., illus.*
SNYDER KNOB MOUNTAIN
map (38° 30′N 79° 58′W) 20:111
SNYDERS, FRANS 18:6 *bibliog.*
SO RIVER
map (6° 28′N 2° 25′E) 3:200
SOAMI 18:6 *bibliog.*
SOANE, SIR JOHN 18:6 *bibliog.*
SOANE MUSEUM *see* SOANE, SIR JOHN
SOAP BOX DERBY 18:6
SOAP AND DETERGENT 18:6–8 *bibliog., illus.*
antiseptic 2:68
benzene 3:206
bleaches and brighteners 3:329
carboxylic acid 4:140
caustic chemicals 4:220
citronella 4:447
cleansing process 18:6–7 *illus.*
detergent controversy 18:8
emulsion 7:161
fat 8:34
history 18:7–8 *illus.*
hydrophilic and hydrophobic substances 10:343
kapok 12:25
lanolin 12:199
Lever, William Hesketh, 1st Viscount Leverhulme 12:303
organic chemistry 14:439
phase equilibrium 15:222 *illus.*
phosphorus 15:256
potassium phosphate 15:465
sandalwood 17:61
saponification 17:73
soap manufacture 18:7 *illus.*
soapberry 18:8
soapwort 18:8
sodium 18:33
tallow tree 19:17
SOAP LAKE (Washington)
map (47° 23′N 119° 29′W) 20:35
SOAP OPERA 18:8 *bibliog.*
SOAPBERRY 18:8
buffalo berry 3:546
maple 13:137
SOAPSTONE
See also TALC
Eskimo carving 7:241 *illus.*; 11:139 *illus.*
Indus civilization seals 11:154 *illus.*
SOAPWORT (botany) 18:8
SOARES, MÁRIO 18:8
Portugal, history of 15:455
SOARING 1:121–122 *illus.*
SOBAEK MOUNTAINS
map (36° 0′N 128° 0′E) 12:113
SOBAT RIVER
map (9° 22′N 31° 33′E) 18:320
SOBEK (crocodile god)
temple
Ombos 14:387
SOBELSOHN, KARL *see* RADEK, KARL
SOBERS, GARFIELD
cricket (game) 5:343 *illus.*
SOBHUZA II, KING OF SWAZILAND
Swaziland 18:381
SOBIESKI, JOHN *see* JOHN III, KING OF POLAND (John Sobieski)
SOBRAL (Brazil)
map (3° 42′S 40° 21′W) 3:460
SOBUKWE, ROBERT
African National Congress 1:171
SOCCER 18:8–11 *bibliog., illus., table*
Beckenbauer, Franz 3:151
Best, George 3:228
Chinaglia, Giorgio 4:377
Cruyff, Johan 5:370
European Footballer of the Year Award *see* EUROPEAN FOOTBALLER OF THE YEAR AWARD
history 18:9–10 *illus.*
Matthews, Sir Stanley 13:231
Pelé 15:137
playing field 18:10 *illus.*
rules and equipment 18:8–10
speedball 18:176
World Cup Competition 18:8–10 *illus., table*
Yashin, Lev 20:319
SOCHI (USSR) 18:11
SOCIAL ACCOUNTING *see* COST-BENEFIT ANALYSIS
SOCIAL ALIENATION *see* ALIENATION
SOCIAL ANTHROPOLOGY 18:11 *bibliog.*
See also ANTHROPOLOGY—cultural anthropology; SOCIOLOGY
Epstein, Arnold Leonard 7:222–223
ethnography 7:256–257
Leach, Sir Edmund 12:256
linguistics 12:356
Malinowski, Bronislaw 13:91
Mauss, Marcel 13:238
Mead, Margaret 13:251–252
Radcliffe-Brown, Sir Alfred R. 16:41
SOCIAL BEHAVIOR, ANIMAL *see* ANIMAL BEHAVIOR
SOCIAL BEHAVIOR, HUMAN *see* BEHAVIOR, HUMAN—social behavior; SOCIAL PSYCHOLOGY
SOCIAL CHANGE
ideology 11:31
racism 16:37–38
SOCIAL CIRCLE (Georgia)
map (33° 39′N 83° 43′W) 9:114
SOCIAL CLASS *see* CLASS, SOCIAL
SOCIAL CONTRACT 18:11 *bibliog.*
Enlightenment 7:206
Locke, John 12:387–388
natural law 14:48
representation 16:161
Rousseau, Jean Jacques 16:325–327
SOCIAL CONTRACT (book)
Rousseau, Jean Jacques 16:326–327
SOCIAL CREDIT PARTY 18:11 *bibliog.*
Aberhart, William 1:56
Alberta 1:257
SOCIAL DANCE *see* DANCE, SOCIAL
SOCIAL DARWINISM 18:11–12 *bibliog.*
Darwin, Charles 6:42
eugenics 7:263–264
Fiske, John 8:129
Sumner, William Graham 18:340
United States, history of the 19:450
SOCIAL DEMOCRACY
socialism 18:22–23
SOCIAL DEMOCRATIC PARTY (Germany)
Bebel, August 3:149–150
Brandt, Willy 3:454–455
Ebert, Friedrich 7:35
Germany, East and West 9:146–147
Germany, history of 9:154–155
Kautsky, Karl Johann 12:32
Lassalle, Ferdinand 12:214
Liebknecht (family) 12:324
Scheidermann, Philipp 17:118
Schmidt, Helmut 17:127
socialism 18:22–23
SOCIAL DEMOCRATIC PARTY (Great Britain)
Jenkins, Roy 11:395
SOCIAL DEMOCRATIC PARTY (Russia)
Trotsky, Leon 19:311
SOCIAL DEMOCRATIC PARTY (Sweden)
Erlander, Tage 7:231
Palme, Olof 15:50
Scandinavia, history of 17:111
Sweden 18:385
SOCIAL DEMOCRATIC PARTY (U.S.)
Debs, Eugene V. 6:70–71
SOCIAL GEOGRAPHY 9:103
SOCIAL GOSPEL 18:12 *bibliog.*
Christian Socialism 4:412
Gladden, Washington 9:195
Mathews, Shailer 13:228
Rauschenbusch, Walter 16:94
Strong, Josiah 18:303
SOCIAL GROUPS
caste 4:186–187
clan 5:36
class, social 5:40
costume 5:292–303 *illus.*
culture 5:384–385
feud 8:63
folkways 8:204
group dynamics 9:376
human ecology 10:297
kinship 12:85
moiety 13:504
nuclear family 14:284
potlatch 15:467
psychological measurement 15:593
secret societies 17:181
slavery 17:351–357
social insect
ant 2:35–38; 2:36 *illus.*
bee 3:154–159
insect 11:191
locust 12:392
termite 19:116–117
wasp 20:45
social psychology 18:12–13
social structure and organization 18:15–17
sociology 18:29
status 18:238–239
totem 19:249
tribe 19:295
SOCIAL INSTITUTION *see* INSTITUTION, SOCIAL
SOCIAL LEARNING THEORY
personality 15:189
SOCIAL NORM *see* NORM, SOCIAL
SOCIAL PHYSICS
Quételet, Lambert Adolphe 16:23
SOCIAL PSYCHOLOGY 18:12–13 *bibliog.*
aggression 1:184–185
alienation 1:294
altruism 1:314
attitude and attitude change 2:315
cognitive dissonance 5:94
communication 5:142–144
community mental health 5:152–153
conformity 5:179
Cooley, Charles Horton 5:240
Erikson, Erik 7:230
group dynamics 9:376
McDougall, William (psychologist) 13:14
Mead, George Herbert 13:251
moral awareness 13:572–573
Murphy, Gardner 13:649
nonverbal communication 14:217
personality 15:189
propaganda 15:568–569
psychology 15:594–595
public opinion 15:608–610
Skinner, B. F. 17:344
socialization 18:26
sociology 18:29
suicide 18:331
SOCIAL REALISM 18:13 *bibliog., illus.*
Albright, Ivan Le Lorraine 1:261
Ashcan School 2:229–230
Courbet, Gustave 5:314
Daumier, Honoré 6:45–46
Glackens, William 9:195
Goya, Francisco de 9:273–274
Hopper, Edward 10:232–233
Lawrence, Jacob 12:250
Millet, Jean François 13:430
mural painting 13:646
Rivera, Diego 16:233
Russian art and architecture 16:364
Shan, Ben 17:235
Sloan, John 17:362
SOCIAL SCIENCES 18:14 *bibliog.*
See also ANTHROPOLOGY; BEHAVIORAL SCIENCES; ECONOMICS; POLITICAL SCIENCE; SOCIOLOGY
American Council of Learned Societies 1:338
SOCIAL SECURITY 18:14–15 *bibliog.*
Health and Human Services, U.S. Department of 10:86
Medicare 13:265
pension 15:153–154
Roosevelt, Franklin Delano 16:309
scholarships, fellowships, and loans 17:130
welfare state 20:97–98
SOCIAL SECURITY ACT
social security 18:14
Townsend, Francis Everett 19:255
unemployment insurance 19:384
SOCIAL STRUCTURE AND ORGANIZATION 18:15–17 *bibliog.*
bride-price 3:479
Bronze Age 7:304–305
burial 3:571
civilization 5:34
clan 5:36
class, social 5:40
egalitarian society 18:16
Egypt, ancient 7:83–84
Eskimo 7:240–242
eugenics 7:263–264

family **8**:15–18
folklore **8**:203
functionalism (social science) **8**:360
government **9**:267–269
group dynamics **9**:376
handicapped persons **10**:36–37
harem **10**:49
hunter-gatherers **10**:313
Indians, American **11**:118
powwow **15**:486
industrial archaeology **11**:154
institution, social **11**:196
kinship **12**:85–86
Laing, R. D. **12**:167
law **12**:242–244
manorialism **13**:127
marriage **13**:163–166
matriarchy **13**:229
Medieval Europe **7**:284
Merton, Robert **13**:313
moiety **13**:504
natural law **14**:48
nomad **14**:214–215
norm, social **14**:219
nuclear family **14**:284
old age **14**:373–374
passage rites **15**:103–104
peasant **15**:128–129
potlatch **15**:467
primitive societies **15**:546
radio and television broadcasting **16**:60
Riesman, David, Jr. **16**:219
role **16**:271
slavery **17**:351–357
social anthropology **18**:11
social psychology **18**:12–13
sociobiology **18**:26–27
sociolinguistics **18**:27–28
sociology **18**:29
Spencer, Herbert **18**:177
status **18**:238–239
stratified society **18**:16–17
suicide **18**:330–331
taboo **19**:5
technology **19**:60–61
technology, history of **19**:61–69
totalitarianism **19**:248
tribe **19**:295
women in society **20**:201–204
young people **20**:335–336
SOCIAL STUDIES EDUCATION **18**:17 *bibliog.*
SOCIAL AND WELFARE SERVICES **18**:17–18 *bibliog.*
costs **18**:18
criticisms and reforms **18**:18
Denmark **6**:111
documentary **6**:211 *illus.*
fund raising **8**:360
Great Britain
Beveridge, William Henry **3**:232
Great Britain, history of **9**:318
poor laws **15**:429
Hadassah **10**:7
handicapped persons **10**:36–37
hospital **10**:258
institutionalization **11**:196–197
negative income tax
Friedman, Milton **8**:332
Norway **14**:262
old age **14**:373–374
poverty **15**:478–480
psychotherapy **15**:603
senility **17**:203
social security **18**:14–15
social work **18**:18–19
unemployment insurance **19**:383–384
United States **18**:17–18
Abbott, Grace **1**:53
Addams, Jane **1**:98–99
Food Stamp Program **8**:212
foster care **1**:107
Health and Human Services, U.S. Department of **10**:86–87
housing **10**:278; **10**:279
Medicaid **13**:264
Medicare **13**:265
Perkins, Frances **15**:172
Russell Sage Foundation **16**:351
Smith, Alfred E. **17**:367
Townsend, Francis Everett **19**:255
Wagner, Robert F., Sr. **20**:5–6
Wald, Lillian D. **20**:9
War on Poverty **20**:28
welfare state **20**:97–98
workers' compensation **20**:217
SOCIAL WORK **18**:18–19 *bibliog.*
Addams, Jane **1**:98–99
history **18**:19
Hopkins, Harry L. **10**:231–232
Hull House **10**:296
Kelley, Florence **12**:38
Perkins, Frances **15**:172
social and welfare services **18**:17–18
training **18**:19
Wald, Lillian D. **20**:9
SOCIALISM **18**:19–24 *bibliog., illus.*
See also COMMUNISM
Canada **4**:86
Douglas, T. C. **6**:248
Christian Socialism **4**:412
class, social **5**:40
communism **5**:146
England
Beveridge, William Henry **3**:232
Fabian Society **8**:4
Labour party **12**:156–157
Laski, Harold **12**:214
Shaw, George Bernard **17**:245–246
Europe, history of **7**:293
France **8**:265
Blanc, Louis **3**:326
Blum, Léon **3**:346
Cabet, Étienne **4**:4
Jaurès, Jean **11**:385
Millerand, Alexandre **13**:429
Mitterrand, François **13**:485–486
Mollet, Guy **13**:510
Sorel, Georges **18**:68
Germany, East and West
See also SOCIAL DEMOCRATIC PARTY (Germany)
Bernstein, Eduard **3**:223–224
Liebknecht (family) **12**:324
nazism **14**:68
International, Socialist **11**:218
Lenin, Vladimir Ilich **12**:282–283
Marx, Karl **13**:181–182
Marxism **13**:183–184
nationalism **14**:46–47
pacifism and nonviolent movements **15**:9
revisionism **18**:21
Saskatchewan (Canada) **17**:82–83
Scandinavia, history of **17**:110
Schumpeter, Joseph A. **17**:137
social democracy **18**:22–23
syndicalism **18**:407
Tanzania **19**:26
Union of Soviet Socialist Republics
Bolsheviks and Mensheviks **3**:371
Herzen, Aleksandr Ivanovich **10**:150
narodniki **14**:21
United States **18**:23
American Labor party **1**:341
Debs, Eugene V. **6**:70–71
Eastman, Max **7**:34
Group Theatre, The **9**:376–377
Industrial Workers of the World **11**:160
Nonpartisan League **14**:217
Socialist Labor party **18**:24–25
Socialist party **18**:25
utopias **19**:498
SOCIALIST FEDERAL REPUBLIC OF YUGOSLAVIA *see* YUGOSLAVIA
SOCIALIST INTERNATIONAL *see* INTERNATIONAL, SOCIALIST
SOCIALIST LABOR PARTY **18**:24–25 *bibliog.*
SOCIALIST LAW **18**:25 *bibliog.*
law **12**:243
women in society **20**:204
SOCIALIST PARTY (U.S.) **18**:25 *bibliog.*
Berger, Victor L. **3**:209–210
campaign poster (1904) **18**:23 *illus.*
Debs, Eugene V. **6**:70–71
Gitlow v. *New York* **9**:191
socialism **18**:23
Thomas, Norman **19**:173–174
SOCIALIST REALISM **18**:25 *bibliog.*
literature
Becher, Johannes R. **3**:150
Czech literature **5**:413
Dimov, Dimitur **6**:177
Gorky, Maksim **9**:252–253
Russian literature **16**:366
Simonov, Konstantin Kirill Mikhailovich **17**:316
Russian art and architecture **16**:364
Russian music **16**:369
Union of Soviet Socialist Republics **19**:395
SOCIALIST REPUBLIC OF ROMANIA *see* ROMANIA
SOCIALIST REPUBLIC OF THE UNION OF BURMA *see* BURMA
SOCIALIST REPUBLIC OF VIETNAM *see* VIETNAM
SOCIALIST TRADE AND LABOR ALLIANCE
De Leon, Daniel **6**:61
SOCIALIST UNITY PARTY (East Germany)
Germany, East and West **9**:146–147
SOCIALIST WORKERS' PARTY **18**:25–26 *bibliog.*
SOCIALIZATION **18**:26 *bibliog.*
child development **4**:348; **4**:350
educational philosophy **7**:63–64
ethnocentrism **7**:256
family **8**:15–18
feral children **8**:51
infancy **11**:162–163
inner speech **11**:179
social psychology **18**:12
young people **20**:335–336
SOCIALIZED MEDICINE *see* STATE MEDICINE
SOCIETAS SCIENTIARUM *see* AKADEMIE DER WISSENSCHAFTEN DER DDR
SOCIETY FOR THE ADVANCEMENT OF JUDAISM
Kaplan, Mordecai Menahem **12**:25
SOCIETY OF AMERICAN FORESTERS
forestry **8**:230
SOCIETY OF THE CINCINNATI *see* CINCINNATI, SOCIETY OF THE
SOCIETY FOR ESTABLISHING USEFUL MANUFACTURES
Paterson (New Jersey) **15**:111
SOCIETY OF THE FRIENDS OF THE CONSTITUTION *see* JACOBINS
SOCIETY OF THE HOLY CHILD
Connelly, Cornelia **5**:197
SOCIETY OF INDEPENDENT ARTISTS
Sloan, John **17**:362
SOCIETY ISLANDS (French Polynesia) **18**:26
Bora-Bora **3**:395
map (17° 0'S 150° 0'W) **14**:334
Tahiti **19**:10 *map*
SOCIETY OF MOTION PICTURE ENGINEERS
Jenkins, Charles Francis, founder **11**:395
SOCIETY FOR THE PRESERVATION AND ENCOURAGEMENT OF BARBER SHOP QUARTET SINGING IN AMERICA
barbershop quartet **3**:78
SOCIETY FOR THE PREVENTION OF CRUELTY TO ANIMALS **18**:26 *bibliog.*
SOCIETY OF ST. FRANCIS DE SALES
Bosco, Saint John **3**:407
SOCINIANISM **18**:26 *bibliog.*
Unitarianism **19**:400
SOCINUS, LAELIUS **18**:26 *bibliog.*
SOCIOBIOLOGY **18**:26–27 *bibliog.*
altruism **1**:314
behavioral genetics **3**:169–170
chimpanzee **4**:359
ethology **7**:257
homosexuality **10**:217
infancy **11**:162–163
SOCIOLINGUISTICS **18**:27–28 *bibliog.*
See also GEOGRAPHICAL LINGUISTICS
creole languages **5**:338
names, personal **14**:9–10
slang **17**:350
social psychology **18**:12
SOCIOLOGY **18**:28–30 *bibliog., illus.*
bureaucracy **3**:567
class, social **5**:40–41
conflict theory **5**:178–179
conformity **5**:179
culture **5**:384–385
culture area **5**:386
definitions **18**:28
diffusion, cultural **6**:170
elites **7**:140–141
Hawthorne studies **10**:79
history **18**:30
Bell, Daniel **3**:186
Comte, Auguste **5**:168
Cooley, Charles Horton **5**:240
Durkheim, Émile **6**:306
Frazier, Edward Franklin **8**:289
Glazer, Nathan **9**:206
Goffman, Erving **9**:225
Hine, Lewis **15**:269
Hobhouse, Leonard Trelawny **10**:192
Homans, George Caspar **10**:212
Jencks, Christopher **11**:395
Johnson, Charles Spurgeon **11**:431
Lynd, Robert S. **12**:477
MacIver, Robert Morrison **13**:26
Marx, Karl **13**:181–182
Mead, George Herbert **13**:251
Merton, Robert **13**:313
Mills, C. Wright **13**:430
Nisbet, Robert Alexander **14**:201
Ogburn, William Fielding **14**:354
Pareto, Vilfredo **15**:84
Parsons, Talcott **15**:99
Riesman, David, Jr. **16**:219
Simmel, Georg **17**:314
Sorokin, Pitirim A. **18**:69
Spencer, Herbert **18**:177
Sumner, William Graham **18**:340
Thomas, William I. **19**:174
Weber, Max (sociologist) **20**:87
Westermarck, Edward Alexander **20**:115
Znaniecki, Florian Witold **20**:371
institution, social **11**:196
major concepts **18**:28–29
methods **18**:29–30
norm, social **14**:219
relation to other social sciences **18**:28
role (behavior) **16**:271
Social Darwinism **18**:11–12
social structure and organization **18**:16–17
socialization **18**:26
status **18**:238–239
subfields **18**:29
criminology **5**:345; **5**:346–347
demography **6**:103–104
deviance **6**:143
family **8**:15–18
group dynamics **9**:376
human ecology **10**:297
integration, racial **11**:202–203
marriage **13**:163–166
political science **15**:403
public opinion **15**:608–610
social anthropology **18**:11
Social Darwinism **18**:11–12
social psychology **18**:12–13
social work **18**:18–19
sociobiology **18**:26–27
sociolinguistics **18**:27–28
sociological jurisprudence **12**:242–243
suicide **18**:331
SOCIOPATHY *see* PSYCHOPATHY
SOCOMPA PASS
map (24° 27'S 68° 18'W) **4**:355
SOCORRO (New Mexico)
map (34° 4'N 106° 54'W) **14**:136
SOCORRO (county in New Mexico)
map (34° 0'N 107° 0'W) **14**:136
SOCOTRA **18**:30–31
map (12° 30'N 54° 0'E) **20**:324
SOCRATES **18**:31 *bibliog., illus.*
Apology **2**:85
aretê **2**:146
Clouds, The **5**:68
Europe, history of **7**:280
law **12**:242
philosophy **15**:243
Plato **15**:360–361
Crito **5**:352
Dialogues **6**:150
poison hemlock **15**:382
pre-Socratic philosophy **15**:533
Xanthippe **20**:311
SOCRATES SCHOLASTICUS **18**:31
SODA **18**:31
caustic chemicals **4**:220
manufacturing
Solvay, Ernest **18**:58
Solvay process **18**:58
sodium **18**:32–33
SODA NITER *see* NITRATE MINERALS
SODA SPRINGS (Idaho)
map (42° 39'N 111° 36'W) **11**:26
SODALITE **18**:31–32 *illus.*
feldspathoid **8**:47 *illus.*
SODDY, FREDERICK **18**:32 *bibliog.*
SODDY-DAISY (Tennessee)
map (35° 17'N 85° 10'W) **19**:104
SÖDERBERG, HJALMAR **18**:32
SÖDERBLOM, NATHAN **18**:32 *bibliog.*
SÖDERGRAN, EDITH **18**:32
SÖDERHAMN (Sweden)
map (61° 18'N 17° 3'E) **18**:382
SÖDERTÄLJE (Sweden)
map (59° 12'N 17° 37'E) **18**:382
SODIUM **18**:32–33 *bibliog., illus.*
abundances of common elements **7**:131 *table*
alkali metals **1**:295
atom **5**:306 *illus.*
compounds **18**:33
salt (sodium chloride) **17**:37
uranium minerals **19**:478
element **7**:130 *table*
flame test
qualitative chemical analysis **16**:6 *illus.*
Group IA periodic table **15**:167; **18**:32

SODIUM (cont.)
ion
active transport **1**:89
biopotential **3**:275–276 *illus.*
neurophysiology **14**:106
metal, metallic element **13**:328
occurrence **18**:32
production **18**:32–33
properties **18**:32
uses **18**:33
SODIUM ALUMINUM SULFATE *see* ALUM
SODIUM BICARBONATE
antacid **2**:38
SODIUM CARBONATE **18**:33
potassium **15**:464–465
soda **18**:31
SODIUM CHLORIDE *see* SALT (sodium chloride)
SODIUM HYDROXIDE **18**:33
See also ALKALI
SODIUM NITRITE **14**:202
SODIUM PENTOTHAL **18**:33
dentistry **6**:116
SODIUM SILICATE **18**:33
SODIUM SULFITE
sulfur **18**:335
SODOM AND GOMORRAH **18**:34
Ebla **7**:36
SODOMA, IL **18**:34 *bibliog.*
SODOMY **18**:34 *bibliog.*
SODUS (New York)
map (43° 14′N 77° 4′W) **14**:149
SOEST (Netherlands)
map (52° 9′N 5° 18′E) **14**:99
SOFALA (Mozambique) **18**:34
climate **13**:628 *table*
map (19° 50′S 34° 52′E) **13**:627
SOFIA (Bulgaria) **3**:554 *illus., table*; **18**:34–35 *illus.*
history **18**:35
map (42° 41′N 23° 19′E) **3**:555
SOFT COAL *see* BITUMINOUS COAL
SOFT-COATED WHEATEN TERRIER **6**:220 *illus.*; **18**:35 *bibliog.*
SOFT DRINKS
canning **4**:110 *illus.*
SOFTBALL **18**:35 *bibliog., illus.*
SOFTWARE, COMPUTER *see* COMPUTER SOFTWARE
SOFTWOOD *see* CONIFER; WOOD (botany)
SOGAMOSO (Colombia)
map (5° 43′N 72° 56′W) **5**:107
SOGNE FJORD
map (61° 6′N 5° 10′E) **14**:261
SOHNCKE, LEONARD
crystal **5**:376
SOIL **18**:35–39 *bibliog., illus., map*
arable soil types
agriculture and the food supply **1**:195–196
vegetable **19**:532
chaparral **4**:283
chernozem **4**:331
color **18**:36 *illus.*
evapotranspiration **7**:314
fertility
Liebig, Justus, Baron von **12**:324
molybdenum **13**:514
frost action **8**:346
gardening **9**:42–43
compost **5**:157–158
ground temperature **9**:373
humus **10**:304
laterite **12**:215
misuse of, pollution, environmental **15**:412–413
nitrogen cycle **14**:203
nonarable **1**:196 *map*
parasitic diseases **15**:83
peat **15**:129
pedalfer **15**:131
pedocal **15**:131
peneplain **15**:143
pH **15**:218
podzol **15**:377
polder soil **15**:395
pollen stratigraphy **15**:407
principal groups, worldwide **18**:37 *map*
profile **18**:36 *illus.*
quicksand **16**:25
Recent Epoch **16**:107
regolith **16**:129
soil organisms **18**:39
steppe life **18**:257
swamp, marsh, and bog **18**:376; **18**:377–378
Terzaghi, Karl **19**:125
SOIL CONSERVATION ACT
Roosevelt, Franklin Delano **16**:308
SOIL ORGANISMS **18**:39 *bibliog., illus.*
Diplura **6**:186
earthworm **7**:29–30
forest **8**:227–230
nocardiosis **14**:212
nutrient cycles **14**:304
Protura **15**:582
Rhizobium **16**:196
topography factor **18**:37
SOKA-GAKKAI **18**:39 *bibliog.*
SOKE (Turkey)
map (37° 45′N 27° 24′E) **19**:343
SOKO, YAMAGA *see* YAMAGA SOKO
SOKODÉ (Togo)
map (8° 59′N 1° 8′E) **19**:222
SOKOLOFF, NIKOLAI
Cleveland Orchestra, The **5**:54
SOKOLOW, ANNA **18**:39 *bibliog.*
SOKOTO (Nigeria)
climate **1**:142 *table*
map (13° 4′N 5° 16′E) **14**:190
Usman dan Fodio **19**:491
SOKOTO RIVER
map (11° 20′N 4° 10′E) **14**:190
SOKOTRA *see* SOCOTRA
SOL (chemistry) **18**:40
gel **9**:69
SOL (mythology) **18**:40
SOLAN GOOSE *see* GANNET
SOLANO (county in California)
map (38° 15′N 121° 52′W) **4**:31
SOLAR ACTIVITY *see* SUN
SOLAR APEX **18**:40
SOLAR CELL **18**:40 *bibliog., illus.*
circuit, electric **4**:436–438
photoelectric cell **15**:259–260
photoelectric effect **15**:260
semiconductor **17**:197
solar energy **18**:41
SOLAR COLLECTORS **18**:40–41 *bibliog.*
solar energy **18**:41
SOLAR CONSTANT **18**:41
solar radiation **18**:44
SOLAR CYCLE **18**:41
International Geophysical Year **11**:220
International Years of the Quiet Sun **11**:225
saros **17**:78
SOLAR DAY **6**:54
SOLAR ENERGY **18**:41–43 *bibliog., illus.*
atmosphere **2**:300
coelostat **5**:92
energy sources **7**:175
greenhouse **9**:351
OSO **14**:456
photosphere **15**:275
power, generation and transmission of **15**:483
solar cell **18**:40
solar collectors **18**:40–41
solar constant **18**:41
solar radiation **18**:44
Sun **18**:340–345
SOLAR FLARE **18**:43 *bibliog.*
magnetic storm **13**:55
OSO **14**:456
radio astronomy **16**:48
solar cycle **18**:41
Sun **18**:344–345
SOLAR MAGNETOGRAPH
Babcock, Horace Welcome **3**:6
SOLAR MAXIMUM MISSION
space exploration **18**:123
SOLAR POND **18**:43–44 *illus.*
SOLAR RADIATION **2**:301 *map*; **18**:44 *bibliog., illus.*
comet **5**:133
corona **5**:270
flash spectrum **8**:154
furnace **8**:372
greenhouse effect **9**:351
insolation **11**:194
International Years of the Quiet Sun **11**:225
ionosphere **11**:241
Langley, Samuel Pierpont **12**:196
meteorological instrumentation **13**:340
plage **15**:325
shield, ozone layer **14**:480
sky **17**:346
Vela (artificial satellite) **19**:536
SOLAR STILL
desalination **6**:124
SOLAR SYSTEM **18**:44–53 *bibliog., illus., table*
asteroid **2**:268
astrogeology **2**:270
astronomy and astrophysics **2**:282–284 *illus.*
celestial mechanics **4**:230
chondrite **4**:404–405
comet **5**:133–134; **18**:50–51
composition **18**:44
cosmology (astronomy) **5**:284–289
diagrams **18**:45; **18**:47
distance, astronomical **6**:198–200
geophysics **9**:108
life, extraterrestrial **12**:328
meteor and meteorite **13**:336–337; **18**:50
Moon **13**:563
origin **18**:51–53 *illus.*
Darwin, Sir George Howard **6**:42
planetary systems **15**:329
planets **15**:329–331; **18**:46–49
Earth, geological history of **7**:11–15
Earth, geomagnetic field of **7**:15–17
Earth, gravitational field of **7**:17
Earth, heat flow in **7**:17–18
Earth, motions of **7**:18–19
Earth, size and shape of **7**:19
Earth, structure and composition of **7**:19–23
Jupiter (planet) **11**:471–474
Mars (planet) **13**:166–169
Mercury (planet) **13**:305–306
Neptune (planet) **14**:88–89
Pluto (planet) **15**:372
Saturn (astronomy) **17**:88–91
Uranus (astronomy) **19**:478–479
Venus (planet) **19**:546–548
radio astronomy **16**:48–49
satellite **17**:84–85; **18**:49–50
solar apex **18**:40
space exploration **18**:45–46; **18**:118–132
studies, history **18**:44–46
Copernicus, Nicolaus **5**:250
Digges, Thomas **6**:174
Galileo Galilei **9**:15
Jeans, Sir James **11**:390
Kepler, Johannes **12**:57–58
Laplace, Pierre Simon de **12**:205
Ptolemy **15**:606–607
Velikovsky, Immanuel **19**:537–538
Whipple, Fred Lawrence **20**:131
Sun **18**:46; **18**:340–345
SOLAR WIND **18**:53 *bibliog.*
comet **5**:133
corona **5**:270
Earth, geomagnetic field of **7**:16–17
geophysics **9**:108
magnetic storm **13**:55
magnetosphere **13**:59–60
plasma physics **15**:345–346
Sun **18**:344
SOLAR YEAR
calendar **4**:27
tropical year **19**:309
SOLARI *see* LOMBARDO (family)
SOLBAD HALL (Austria)
map (47° 17′N 11° 31′E) **2**:348
SOLDERING *see* WELDING AND SOLDERING
SOLDIER *see* ARMY
SOLDIER POND (Maine)
map (47° 9′N 68° 35′W) **13**:70
SOLDIERS OF FORTUNE *see* MERCENARIES
SOLDIERS GROVE (Wisconsin)
map (43° 24′N 90° 47′W) **20**:185
SOLDOTNA (Alaska)
map (60° 29′N 151° 4′W) **1**:242
SOLE **18**:53 *illus.*
flatfish **8**:154–155
SOLEDAD (California)
map (36° 26′N 121° 19′W) **4**:31
SOLEMN LEAGUE AND COVENANT OF 1643
Covenanters **5**:319
SOLEN (North Dakota)
map (46° 23′N 100° 48′W) **14**:248
SOLENODON **13**:104 *illus.*; **18**:53 *illus.*
SOLENOID **18**:53
electromagnet **7**:115
relay **16**:137
SOLER, ANTONIO **18**:53 *bibliog.*
SOLERI, PAOLO **18**:53 *bibliog.*
SOLICITATION **18**:54
SOLICITOR *see* BARRISTER
SOLICITOR GENERAL *see* JUSTICE, U.S. DEPARTMENT OF
SOLID **18**:54
cohesion **5**:96
density **6**:114 *table*
dissolved solids
water quality **20**:50
eutectic point **7**:310
glasses, glassy state **9**:205
kinetic theory of matter **12**:79
mineral **13**:438
phase equilibrium **15**:222–224 *illus.*
sol **18**:40
solid solution **18**:54
solid-state physics **18**:54–55
sublimation (chemistry) **18**:313
triple point **19**:302
SOLID ANALYTIC GEOMETRY **1**:391
SOLID MODELING (computer-aided design) **5**:160k
SOLID SOLUTION **18**:54 *bibliog.*
isomorph **11**:300
SOLID-STATE CHEMISTRY
inorganic chemistry **11**:182
SOLID-STATE PHYSICS **18**:54–55 *bibliog.*
Esaki, Leo **7**:236
inorganic chemistry **11**:182
integrated circuit **11**:201–202
Landau, Lev **12**:181
metal **13**:329
microelectronics **13**:385
phonon **15**:255
photoelectric cell **15**:259–260
piezoelectricity **15**:298
semiconductor **17**:196–197
superconductivity **18**:350
ternary oxides
oxygen **14**:478
transistor **19**:271–272
SOLID WASTE POLLUTION
pollution, environmental **15**:412; **15**:413
SOLIDARITY
Jaruzelski, Wojciech **11**:383
Poland **15**:391
Wałesa, Lech **20**:11
SOLILOQUY
narrative and dramatic devices **14**:23
SOLINGEN (West Germany) **18**:55
SOLIPSISM **18**:55 *bibliog.*
SOLÍS, JUAN DÍAZ DE
Río de la Plata **16**:227
SOLITAIRE (bird) **18**:55 *illus.*
dodo bird **6**:212
SOLITAIRE (card game) **18**:56 *bibliog.*
SOLITON **18**:56
SOLLBERGER, HARVEY
Wuorinen, Charles **20**:296
SOLO MAN **18**:56 *bibliog.*
SOLOGUB, FYODOR **18**:56
SOLOMON (Kansas)
map (38° 55′N 97° 22′W) **12**:18
SOLOMON, KING OF ISRAEL **18**:56 *bibliog.*
administrative districts **3**:238 *map*
Elat (Israel) **7**:102
Ezion-geber **7**:352
Gezer **9**:163
Kilimanjaro **12**:76
Megiddo **13**:280
Phoenicia **15**:250
Solomon Islands **18**:57
temple **19**:95
Tyre (Phoenicia) **19**:367
SOLOMON ISLANDS **18**:56–57 *bibliog., map*
Bougainville **3**:402
flag **18**:57 *illus.*
Guadalcanal **9**:384–385 *map*
map (8° 0′S 159° 0′E) **14**:334
money **13**:525 *illus.*
wicker shield **14**:336 *illus.*
World War II **20**:267 *illus.*
SOLOMON R. GUGGENHEIM MUSEUM *see* GUGGENHEIM MUSEUM
SOLOMON RIVER
map (38° 54′N 97° 22′W) **12**:18
SOLOMON SEA
map (8° 0′S 153° 0′E) **15**:72
SOLOMON'S PLATE
plate tectonics **15**:351 *map*
SOLOMON'S SEAL (botany) **18**:57
SOLOMOS, DIONYSIOS **18**:57 *bibliog.*
SOLON **18**:57 *bibliog.*
Greece, ancient **9**:331
SOLON (Iowa)
map (41° 48′N 91° 30′W) **11**:244
SOLON (Maine)
map (44° 57′N 69° 52′W) **13**:70
SOLON, MARC-LOUIS
pottery and porcelain **15**:472
SOLON SPRINGS (Wisconsin)
map (46° 22′N 91° 48′W) **20**:185
SOLOTHURN (Switzerland)
map (47° 13′N 7° 32′E) **18**:394
SOLOVIEV, VLADIMIR SERGEYEVICH **18**:57 *bibliog.*
SOLRESOL
languages, artificial **12**:197
SOLSTICE
celestial sphere **4**:230
Earth, motions of **7**:18
Earth, size and shape of **7**:19
tropic of Cancer (zone) **19**:307
tropic of Capricorn **19**:307
SOLTI, SIR GEORG **18**:57 *bibliog.*
Chicago Symphony Orchestra **4**:343

SOLUBILITY 18:58
liquid 12:365
saturation 17:88
SOLUTION (chemistry) 18:58
active transport 1:89–90
activity 1:90
aqueous
iron 11:270–271
concentration 5:168–169
dilute
van't Hoff, Jacobus Henricus 19:520
ion exchange 11:240
physical chemistry 15:279
precipitation (chemistry) 15:493
saturation 17:88
solubility 18:58
SOLUTREAN 18:58 *bibliog.*
points 15:40 *illus.*
prehistoric art 15:507
SOLVAY, ERNEST 18:58
Solvay process 18:58
SOLVAY CONGRESS 15:286 *illus.*
Lorentz, Hendrik Antoon 12:413–414
SOLVAY PROCESS 18:58
soda 18:31
SOLVENT 18:58–59 *bibliog., table*
benzene 3:206
chlorine compounds 4:401
chloroform 4:401
common solvents 18:59 *table*
cyclohexane 5:404
dry cleaning 6:283
ester 7:246
ether (chemistry) 7:249–250
ethyl ether 7:257
in extraction 7:341
pollutants, chemical 15:410
turpentine 19:352
SOLZHENITSYN, ALEKSANDR 18:59 *bibliog., illus.*
Gulag Archipelago, The 9:402
One Day in the Life of Ivan Denisovich 14:389
Russian literature 16:367 *illus.*
SOMALI 18:59 *bibliog.*
SOMALI DEMOCRATIC REPUBLIC *see* SOMALIA
SOMALIA 18:59–61 *bibliog., illus., map, table*
Asir, Cape 2:261
cities
Mogadishu 13:500
climate 18:60 *table*
education 18:60
African universities 1:176 *table*
flag 8:134; 18:60 *illus.*
government 18:61
history 18:61
World War II 20:256
land, people, and economy 18:60 *map, table*
map (10° 0′N 49° 0′E) 1:136
myrrh 13:691
Somali (people) 18:59
SOMALILAND *see* SOMALIA
SOMAN
chemical and biological warfare 4:312
SOMATIC CELL
aging 1:185
SOMATOSTATIN
hormone, animal 10:236 *table*
SOMATOTROPIN *see* GROWTH HORMONE
SOMBOR (Yugoslavia)
map (45° 46′N 19° 7′E) 20:340
SOMERDALE (New Jersey)
map (39° 51′N 75° 1′W) 14:129
SOMERS (Montana)
map (48° 5′N 114° 13′W) 13:547
SOMERS POINT (New Jersey)
map (39° 20′N 74° 36′W) 14:129
SOMERSET (Colorado)
map (38° 56′N 107° 16′W) 5:116
SOMERSET (England) 18:61
SOMERSET (Kentucky)
map (37° 5′N 84° 36′W) 12:47
SOMERSET (county in Maine)
map (45° 30′N 70° 0′W) 13:70
SOMERSET (county in Maryland)
map (38° 12′N 75° 41′W) 13:188
SOMERSET (Massachusetts)
map (41° 45′N 71° 9′W) 13:206
SOMERSET (New Jersey)
map (40° 29′N 74° 29′W) 14:129
SOMERSET (county in New Jersey)
map (40° 34′N 74° 37′W) 14:129
SOMERSET (Pennsylvania)
map (40° 1′N 79° 5′W) 15:147
SOMERSET (county in Pennsylvania)
map (40° 9′N 79° 0′W) 15:147
SOMERSET, EDWARD SEYMOUR, 1ST DUKE OF 18:61 *bibliog.*
Northumberland, John Dudley, Duke of 14:256
SOMERSET, ROBERT CARR, EARL OF
James I, King of England 11:356
SOMERSET ISLAND (Bermuda)
map (32° 17′N 64° 52′W) 3:219
SOMERSET ISLAND (Northwest Territories)
map (73° 15′N 93° 30′W) 14:258
SOMERSWORTH (New Hampshire)
map (43° 16′N 70° 52′W) 14:123
SOMERTON (Arizona)
map (32° 36′N 114° 43′W) 2:160
SOMERVELL (county in Texas)
map (32° 10′N 98° 0′W) 19:129
SOMERVILLE (Massachusetts) 18:61
map (42° 23′N 71° 6′W) 13:206
SOMERVILLE (New Jersey)
map (40° 34′N 74° 37′W) 14:129
SOMERVILLE (Tennessee)
map (35° 15′N 89° 21′W) 19:104
SOMERVILLE COLLEGE, (Oxford University) 14:474
SOMEŞ (SZAMOS) RIVER
map (48° 7′N 22° 22′E) 16:288
SOMI, LEONE DI
stage lighting 18:210
SOMME, BATTLES OF THE 18:61–62 *bibliog.*
World War I 20:225 *map*; 20:233 *illus.*; 20:241
SOMME RIVER 18:62
map (50° 11′N 1° 39′E) 8:260
SOMMEILLER, GERMAN
tunnel 19:337
SOMMEN LAKE
map (58° 1′N 15° 15′E) 18:382
SOMMERFELD, ARNOLD 18:62
quantum mechanics 16:10
SOMNAMBULISM *see* SLEEPWALKING
SOMNUS 18:62
SOMODEVILLA, ZENÓN DE, MARQUÉS DE LA ENSENADA *see* ENSENADA, ZENÓN DE SOMODEVILLA, MARQUÉS DE LA
SOMOZA (family) 18:62 *bibliog., illus.*
Nicaragua 14:179
SOMOZA DEBAYLE, ANASTASIO
Somoza (family) 18:62 *illus.*
SON RIVER
map (25° 42′N 84° 52′E) 9:37
SON TAY (Vietnam)
map (21° 8′N 105° 30′E) 19:580
SONÁ (Panama)
map (8° 1′N 81° 19′W) 15:55
SONAR 18:62–63 *bibliog., illus.*
fishing industry 8:127
remote sensing 16:147
submarine 18:315
ultrasonics 19:378
SONATA 18:63 *bibliog.*
absolute music 1:62
baroque music 3:91–92
chamber music 4:272
classical period in music 5:41–42
composers
Bach, Carl Philipp Emanuel 3:10
Bach, Johann Christian 3:10
Bartók, Béla 3:98
Beethoven, Ludwig van 3:164–165
Biber, Heinrich Ignaz Franz von 3:237
Brahms, Johannes 3:441
Clementi, Muzio 5:50
Corelli, Arcangelo 5:262
Gabrieli (family) 9:6
Ives, Charles Edward 11:334
Scarlatti (family) 17:115
Scriabin, Aleksandr Nikolayevich 17:157–158
Soler, Antonio 18:53
music, history of Western 13:666
SONCK, LARS
Finland 8:97
SØNDERBORG (Denmark)
map (54° 55′N 9° 47′E) 6:109
SONDHEIM, STEPHEN 18:63–64 *bibliog.*
SONG 18:64 *bibliog.*
African music 1:170
Arabian music 2:99
art songs 18:64
Dowland, John 6:251–252
Grieg, Edvard 9:361–362
Rorem, Ned 16:312
ballade 3:41
barbershop quartet 3:78
calypso 4:49
cantus firmus 4:118
carol 4:160
chanson 4:282
composers
Arne, Thomas 2:183–184
Campion, Thomas 4:67
Duparc, Henri 6:302
Fauré, Gabriel Urbain 8:38
Foster, Stephen 8:248
Ireland, John 11:265
Lawes, Henry 12:248
Nevin, Ethelbert Woodbridge 14:115
Poulenc, Francis 15:473
Purcell, Henry 15:628
Reger, Max 16:128
Schumann, Robert 17:137
English music 7:202–203
folk music 8:202–203
French music 8:320–321
German and Austrian music 9:129
gospel music 9:253–254
Indians of North America, music and dance of the 11:142
Latin American music and dance 12:231
lieder 18:64
Fischer-Dieskau, Dietrich 8:111
Schubert, Franz 17:135
Slezak, Leo 17:361
Wolf, Hugo 20:196
Marseillaise, La 13:170
meistersinger 13:283
minstrels, minnesingers, and troubadours 13:460
music, non-Western 13:667–668
musical comedy 13:673–675
operetta 14:403
passacaglia and chaconne 15:103
popular songs 18:64
Arlen, Harold 2:170
Bacharach, Burt 3:11
Berlin, Irving 3:217
Carmichael, Hoagy 4:153
Gershwin, George and Ira 9:158–159
Hammerstein, Oscar, II 10:31
Kern, Jerome 12:59
Mercer, Johnny 13:304
Porter, Cole 15:444
Rodgers, Richard, and Hart, Lorenz 16:267
Tin Pan Alley 19:205
Renaissance music 16:156
shanty 17:241
Spanish music 18:161
spirituals 18:189
"Star-Spangled Banner, The" 18:226
voice, singing 19:625–626
SONG (dynasty) *see* SUNG (Song) (dynasty)
SONG OF HIAWATHA, THE (poem) 18:64
Longfellow, Henry Wadsworth 11:407
SONG HUIZONG *see* SUNG HUI-TSUNG (Song Huizong)
SONG OF MYSELF (poem) 18:64
Leaves of Grass 12:263
SONG OF ROLAND (epic) *see* *CHANSON DE ROLAND* (epic)
SONG OF SOLOMON 18:64 *bibliog.*
canticle 4:117
SONG OF SONGS *see* SONG OF SOLOMON
SONGBIRDS 18:64–65 *bibliog.*
babbler 3:6
bananaquit 3:60
bird 3:286–287
birdsong 3:291–292
bobolink 3:352–353
bunting 3:564
chaffinch 2:19 *illus.*
chat 4:302
dipper 6:186
finch 8:93
flageolet 8:149
flycatcher (bird) 8:190–191
lark 12:207–208
longspur 12:409
nightingale 14:193
perching birds 15:162
raven 16:95
robin 16:243
shrike vireo 17:287
solitaire 18:55
thrasher 19:181
thrush 19:183
towhee 19:255
wood warbler 20:209
wren 20:285–286
SONGHAI (empire) 18:65 *bibliog.*
Africa, history of 1:152
Bambara kingdoms 3:58
SONGHAI (people) 18:65 *bibliog.*
SONGKHLA (Thailand)
map (7° 12′N 100° 36′E) 19:139
SONGS OF INNOCENCE AND OF EXPERIENCE (poems) 18:65 *bibliog.*
Blake, William 3:325
SONIC BOOM
shock wave 17:279
SONMIANI BAY
map (25° 15′N 66° 30′E) 15:27
SONNEBORN, TRACY MORTON 18:65
SONNET 18:65 *bibliog.*
Balmont, Konstantin Dmitriyevich 3:54
Borges, Jorge Luis 3:398
Browning, Elizabeth Barrett 3:518
Constable, Henry 5:206
Drayton, Michael 6:265
Heredia, José Maria de 10:138–139
Millay, Edna St. Vincent 13:426
Petrarch 15:203–204
Shakespeare, William 17:237
Sonnets from the Portuguese 18:65
Sonnets of Shakespeare 18:65
Surrey, Henry Howard, Earl of 18:366
Wyatt, Sir Thomas 20:297–298
SONNETS FROM THE PORTUGUESE (book) 18:65
Browning, Elizabeth Barrett 3:518
SONNETS OF SHAKESPEARE 18:65 *bibliog.*
SONNINO, SIDNEY, BARONE 18:66
SONOMA (California)
map (38° 17′N 122° 28′W) 4:31
SONOMA (county in California)
map (38° 30′N 122° 50′W) 4:31
SONORA (California)
map (37° 59′N 120° 23′W) 4:31
SONORA (Mexico) 18:66
cities
Hermosillo 10:143
people
Yaqui 20:319
SONORA (Texas)
map (30° 34′N 100° 39′W) 19:129
SONORA PASS 18:66
SONORA RIVER
map (28° 48′N 111° 33′W) 13:357
SONORAN DESERT 6:130 *illus.*
SONS OF ISRAEL (India) *see* BENE ISRAEL
SONS OF LIBERTY 18:66 *bibliog.*
Adams, Samuel 1:97–98
Revere, Paul 16:186
SONS AND LOVERS (book) 18:66 *bibliog.*
Lawrence, D. H. 11:249–250
SONSÓN (Colombia)
map (5° 42′N 75° 18′W) 5:107
SONSONATE (El Salvador)
map (13° 43′N 89° 44′W) 7:100
SONTAG (Mississippi)
map (31° 39′N 90° 12′W) 13:469
SONTAG, SUSAN 18:66 *illus.*
SONY CORPORATION
video 19:576b; 19:576c
video art 19:576h
video recording 19:576j
video technology 19:576m
SOO CANALS *see* SAULT SAINTE MARIE CANALS
SOOCHOW (Suzhou) (China) 18:66
map (34° 16′N 117° 11′E) 4:362
SOONG (family) 18:66 *bibliog.*
SOPACHUY (Bolivia)
map (19° 29′S 64° 31′W) 3:366
SOPERTON (Georgia)
map (32° 23′N 82° 35′W) 9:114
SOPHIA 18:66–67 *bibliog.*
SOPHIA (house of Hanover)
Hanover (dynasty) 10:39
SOPHIA DOROTHEA
George I, King of England, Scotland, and Ireland 9:110
SOPHIOLOGY
Bulgakov, Sergei Nikolayevich 3:554
SOPHISTS 18:67 *bibliog.*
Gorgias 9:251
law 12:242
pre-Socratic philosophy 15:532–533
Protagoras 15:574
Socrates 18:31
SOPHOCLES 18:67–68 *bibliog., illus.*
Antigone 2:62
Electra (play) 7:105
Oedipus Rex 14:351
theater, history of the 19:144
SOPHONISBA 18:68
SOPORIFIC *see* HYPNOTIC DRUGS
SOPOT (Poland)
map (54° 28′N 18° 34′E) 15:388
SOPRANO 18:68
castrato 4:192
SOPRON (Hungary)
map (47° 41′N 16° 36′E) 10:307
SOPWITH CAMEL 18:68 *bibliog., illus.*

SOQOTRA *see* SOCOTRA
SØR ISLAND
map (70° 36′N 22° 46′E) **14**:261
SORBONNE
chapel
Girardon, François **9**:189
Paris, Universities of **15**:88
SORBS (people) *see* WENDS
SORBY, HENRY CLIFTON **18**:68
mineral **13**:439
photosynthesis **15**:275
SORCERER'S APPRENTICE (musical composition)
Dukas, Paul **6**:295
SORCERY
magic **13**:49
SOREL (Quebec)
map (46° 2′N 73° 7′W) **16**:18
SOREL, GEORGES **18**:68 *bibliog.*
socialism **18**:21
syndicalism **18**:407
SØRENSEN, SØREN PETER LAURITZ **18**:68–69
pH, definition **15**:217–218
SORGHUM **9**:281 *illus.*; **18**:69 *bibliog.*, *illus.*
fodder **8**:192–193
SORIA (Spain)
map (41° 46′N 2° 28′W) **18**:140
SOROKIN, PITIRIM A. **18**:69 *bibliog.*
SORORATE
marriage **13**:165
SORORITIES *see* FRATERNITIES AND SORORITIES
SOROTI (Uganda)
map (1° 43′N 33° 37′E) **19**:372
SORREL (botany) **18**:69–70 *illus.*
rhubarb **16**:203–204
SORREL TREE *see* SOURWOOD
SORROWS OF YOUNG WERTHER, THE (book) **18**:70
SORUBI (Afghanistan)
map (34° 36′N 69° 43′E) **1**:133
SOSO (Mississippi)
map (31° 45′N 89° 16′W) **13**:469
SOSTRATUS OF CNIDUS
Pharos of Alexandria **17**:218
SOT-WEED FACTOR, THE (book)
Barth, John **3**:96
Cook, Ebenezer **5**:234
SOTATSU **18**:70 *bibliog.*
Japanese art and architecture **11**:377
Koetsu **12**:105
SOTELO, JOSÉ CALVO *see* CALVO SOTELO, JOSÉ
SOTELO, LEOPOLDO CALVO *see* CALVO SOTELO, LEOPOLDO
SOTHEBY PARKE BERNET
auction **2**:317
SOTHERN, EDWARD H. **18**:70
SOTHO **12**:297 *illus.*; **18**:70 *bibliog.*
Mosheshwe, King of the Sotho **13**:600–601
Ndebele **14**:68
Thonga **19**:177
Tswana **19**:325
SOTO, HERNANDO DE *see* DE SOTO, HERNANDO
SOTO, JESÚS
Venezuela **19**:543
SOTTSASS, ETTORE
industrial design **11**:156; **11**:157 *illus.*
SOUDAN *see* MALI
SOUDAN (Minnesota)
map (47° 49′N 92° 10′W) **13**:453
SOUDERTON (Pennsylvania)
map (40° 19′N 75° 19′W) **15**:147
SOUFFLOT, JACQUES GERMAIN **18**:70 *bibliog.*
Panthéon **8**:306 *illus.*
SOUFRIÈRE (volcano)
Saint Vincent and the Grenadines **17**:27
SOUHEGAN RIVER
map (42° 51′N 71° 29′W) **14**:123
SOUL **18**:70 *bibliog.*
Aristotle **2**:157
transmigration of souls **19**:274
SOUL ON ICE (book) **18**:71
Cleaver, Eldridge **5**:47–48
SOUL MUSIC **18**:71 *bibliog.*, *illus.*
Brown, James **3**:514
Charles, Ray **4**:290
Franklin, Aretha **8**:282
Redding, Otis **16**:115
reggae **16**:128
SOULAGES, PIERRE **18**:71 *bibliog.*
SOULÉ, PIERRE
Ostend Manifesto **14**:457
SOULÉ, SAMUEL W.
Sholes, Christopher Latham **17**:281
SOULT, NICOLAS JEAN DE DIEU **18**:71
SOUND AND ACOUSTICS **18**:71–74 *bibliog.*, *illus.*, *tables*
acoustics
music, acoustics of **13**:661–662
music and concert halls **13**:669–670
alarm systems **1**:240
audio frequency **2**:318
damping **6**:19
Doppler effect **6**:240–241
ear **7**:6–7
echolocation **7**:39
electronic music **7**:124–126
Euler, Leonhard **7**:264–265
harmonics **10**:51
loudspeaker **12**:421
Mach number **13**:17
microphone **13**:386–387 *illus.*
noise **14**:213
oceanographic instrumentation **14**:342
oceanography **14**:345
phonetics **15**:251–252
phonograph **15**:253–254
phonon **15**:255
piezoelectricity **15**:298
pollution, environmental **15**:414
Raman, Sir Chandrasekhara Venkata **16**:79–80
sound
computer music **5**:162–163
high fidelity **10**:161
levels, relative **18**:73–73 *table*
propagation **18**:72
quadraphonic sound **16**:5
receivers **18**:73
sources **18**:73
speed of, in selected media **18**:72 *table*
stereophonic sound **18**:259
sound reflection
parabola **15**:74
sonar **18**:62
sound waves **18**:72–73 *illus.*
amplitude modulation **1**:383
characteristics **18**:73
frequency **8**:326
hydrophone **10**:343
radio waves, electromagnetic radiation **7**:116–118
refraction **16**:123
shock wave **17**:279
standing wave **18**:217
ultrasonics **18**:74 *illus.*; **19**:377–378
waves and wave motion **20**:71–72
stereophonic sound **18**:259
tape recorder **19**:30
telephone **19**:78–80
Wheatstone, Sir Charles **20**:127
whistler **20**:134
SOUND BARRIER **18**:74
SOUND NAVIGATION AND RANGING *see* SONAR
SOUND RECORDING AND REPRODUCTION **18**:74–77 *bibliog.*, *illus.*
Berliner, Emile **3**:218
cinematography **4**:432–434
commercial recording practice **18**:76–77
compact disc **5**:154–155
company, Motown **13**:616
computer music **5**:162–163
digital technology **6**:175
disc recording **18**:74–75
electronic high fidelity **10**:161
film, history of **8**:84
Grammy Award **9**:283
jazz **11**:388
limitations **18**:75–76
magnetic recording **18**:74–75 *illus.*
microphone **13**:386–387 *illus.*
optical recording **18**:75 *illus.*
phonograph **15**:253–254
Poulsen, Valdemar **15**:473
pulse code modulation **18**:76
receiver (communications) **16**:106
stereophonic sound **18**:259 *illus.*
tape recorder **19**:30–31
telephone **19**:78–80
television production **19**:86–87
video recording **19**:576j–576k
videodisc **19**:576p
videotape **19**:576p
SOUND AND THE FURY, THE (book) **18**:74 *bibliog.*
Faulkner, William **8**:36
SOUNDING ROCKET **18**:77 *bibliog.*, *illus.*
Aerobee **1**:122
Nike Apache **18**:77 *illus.*
rockets and missiles **16**:254
space exploration **18**:118–119
SOUPHANOUVONG **18**:77
Pathet Lao **15**:111–112
Souvanna Phouma **18**:113
SOUR GRASS *see* WOOD SORREL
SOURIS (Manitoba)
map (49° 38′N 100° 15′W) **13**:119
SOURIS (Prince Edward Island)
map (46° 21′N 62° 15′W) **15**:548
SOURIS RIVER
map (49° 38′N 99° 34′W) **19**:419
SOURSOP *see* CUSTARD APPLE
SOURWOOD **18**:77 *illus.*
SOUSA, JOHN PHILIP **18**:77–78 *bibliog.*
American music **1**:350
SOUSA, THOMÉ DE
Salvador (Brazil) **17**:39
SOUSAPHONE
tuba **19**:326
SOUSEL (Brazil)
map (2° 39′S 51° 55′W) **3**:460
SOUSSE (Tunisia)
map (35° 49′N 10° 38′E) **19**:335
SOUTH, UNIVERSITY OF THE **18**:78
SOUTH, THE (U.S.)
agriculture
lumber **12**:457
rice **16**:207
geographical linguistics **9**:98–99 *maps*
historians
Woodward, C. Vann **20**:213
history
Davis, Jefferson **6**:51–52
immigration **11**:55 *map*
music
Foster, Stephen **8**:248
plantation **1**:235 *illus.*; **12**:433 *illus.*
primary education **15**:537
SOUTH ACTON (Massachusetts)
map (42° 28′N 71° 27′W) **3**:409
SOUTH AFRICA **18**:78–83 *bibliog.*, *illus.*, *map*, *table*
African homelands **18**:83
Bophuthatswana **3**:395
Transkei **19**:274
agriculture and fishing **18**:81–82
apartheid **2**:74
Olympic Games **14**:383
sanctions **17**:58
archaeology
Mapungubwe **13**:142
art **18**:81
African art **1**:163–164
prehistoric art **15**:510 *illus.*
cities
Bloemfontein **3**:334–335
Cape Town **4**:121 *illus.*
Durban **6**:304
East London **7**:32
Germiston **9**:157
Johannesburg **11**:422–423 *illus.*
Kimberley **12**:77
Mafeking **13**:46
Pietermaritzburg **15**:297
Port Elizabeth **15**:443
Pretoria **15**:533–534
Walvis Bay **20**:21
climate **18**:80 *tables*
Mediterranean climate **13**:276
demography **18**:81
economic activity **18**:78; **18**:81–82
education **18**:81
African universities **1**:176 *table*; **1**:177
flag **18**:78 *illus.*
government **18**:82
defense, national **6**:82 *table*
health **18**:81
history **18**:82–83
African National Congress **1**:171–172
Afrikaners **1**:177–178
Botha, Louis **3**:415
Botha, Pieter Willem **3**:415
Great Trek **9**:322–323
Hertzog, James Barry Munnik **10**:149
Luthuli, Albert John **12**:470
Malan, Daniel **13**:79
Mapungubwe **13**:142
National Party **14**:44
Smuts, Jan **17**:374–375
South African War **18**:83–84 *map*
Verwoerd, Hendrik F. **19**:563
Vorster, B. Johannes **19**:635
human rights **10**:298 *illus.*
industry **18**:82
land and resources **18**:78–80 *map*, *table*
kimberlite **12**:77
language **18**:80
Afrikaans **1**:177–178
literature
Abrahams, Peter **1**:61
African literature **1**:167–168
Afrikaners **1**:178
Breytenbach, Breyten **3**:476
Campbell, Roy **4**:66
Cloete, Stuart **5**:64
Coetzee, J. M. **5**:93
Cry, the Beloved Country **5**:370
Fugard, Athol **8**:355
Gordimer, Nadine **9**:248
Jonker, Ingrid **11**:445
La Guma, Alex **12**:147
Mofolo, Thomas **13**:500
Paton, Alan **15**:112
map (30° 0′S 26° 0′E) **1**:136
mining **18**:81–82 *illus.*
diamond **6**:152
placer deposit **15**:325
Witwatersrand **20**:194
Namibia **14**:11–12
people **18**:80–81 *illus.*
Afrikaners **1**:177–178
Coloureds **5**:123
ethnic distribution **18**:80–81
Kafir **12**:5
Khoikhoi **12**:67
Nguni **14**:176
Sotho **18**:70
Thonga **19**:177
Tswana **19**:325
Xhosa **20**:312
Zulu **20**:381–382
physical features
Agulhas, Cape **1**:200
Drakensberg **6**:257
Good Hope, Cape of **9**:245
Table Mountain **19**:4
provinces
Cape Province **4**:121
Natal **14**:26
Orange Free State **14**:415
Transvaal **19**:282–283
railroad **16**:74–75 *illus.*
religion **18**:80
rivers, lakes, and waterways **18**:79
Orange River **14**:415
Vaal River **19**:501
trade **18**:82
vegetation **18**:80
savanna life **17**:97–99
steppe life **18**:256–257
wine **20**:176
SOUTH AFRICAN COMPANY, BRITISH *see* BRITISH SOUTH AFRICA COMPANY
SOUTH AFRICAN ENGLISH *see* ENGLISH LANGUAGE
SOUTH AFRICAN WAR **18**:83–84 *bibliog.*, *map*
concentration camp **5**:169
Great Britain, history of **9**:317
Jameson, Sir Leander Starr **11**:357
Kruger, Paul **12**:131
Mafeking (South Africa) **13**:46
Milner, Alfred Milner, Viscount **13**:431
Orange Free State (South Africa) **14**:415
Smuts, Jan **17**:374–375
SOUTH AMBOY (New Jersey)
map (40° 29′N 74° 17′W) **14**:129
SOUTH AMERICA **18**:84–95 *bibliog.*, *illus.*, *maps*, *table*
See also LATIN AMERICA; LATIN AMERICA, HISTORY OF; names of specific countries, e.g., ARGENTINA; BRAZIL; etc.
agriculture **18**:90 *map*; **18**:94 *illus.*
arable land **18**:91
sugar production (16th century) **18**:328 *illus.*
art
Latin American art and architecture **12**:222–228
chemical industry **4**:319
climate **18**:87–88 *map*
weather variation and extremes **20**:80–81 *tables*
zonda **20**:373
colonialism **5**:112
demography **18**:92–93 *map*
economic development and commerce **18**:93–94
education **7**:61; **18**:92
Latin American universities **12**:232–233
exploration *see* EXPLORATION
fauna **18**:89–90
forestry and fishing **18**:94
geologic time
Ordovician Period **14**:421 *map*
Permian Period **15**:175 *map*
Precambrian rock formations **15**:492 *map*
Silurian Period **17**:310–311

Tertiary Period **19**:123 *map*
geology **18**:87 *map*
continental drifting **15**:354 *map*
fit of continents around Mid-Atlantic Ridge **15**:353 *map*
South American plate **15**:351 *map*
head-hunting **10**:85
health **18**:92
Chagas's disease, trypanosomiasis **19**:322
history
Aguirre, Lope de **1**:200
Almagro, Diego de **1**:306
Balboa, Vasco Núñez de **3**:33
Bolivár, Simón **3**:365
El Dorado **7**:98
Inca **11**:69–73
New Granada **14**:121
Orbigny, Alcide Dessalines D' **14**:416
Sucre, Antonio José de **18**:319–320
Tordesillas, Treaty of **19**:238–239
land **18**:85–91 *map, table*
mountains, highest **13**:620 *table*
languages **18**:92–93 *map*
Indian languages, American **11**:98–101 *table*
Yanomamo **20**:318
national parks **14**:41 *map*; **14**:43–44 *table*
people **18**:91–93 *map*
See also names of specific Indian tribes, e.g., ARAWAK (American Indians); ZAPOTEC (American Indians); etc.
Indians, American **11**:115–138 *illus., maps*
mestizo **13**:324
mulatto **13**:635
race **16**:34 *illus.*
physical features
Andes **1**:403–404 *illus., map*
Tierra del Fuego **19**:196 *map*
regions
Chaco **4**:264
Patagonia **15**:109
religion **18**:92
resources **18**:90–91
electrical production **15**:485 *table*
emerald **7**:154
energy **18**:95
energy consumption and production **7**:174 *table*
mineral resources **18**:90–91 *map*
petroleum industry **15**:210 *table*
water resources **20**:51 *table*
rivers, lakes, and waterways **18**:88
Amazon River **1**:323–324 *illus., map*
Iguaçu Falls **3**:461 *illus.*; **11**:38
Kukenaam Falls **12**:135
Magellan, Strait of **13**:48
Paraná River **15**:80
Río de la Plata **16**:227
Titicaca, Lake **19**:213
Uruguay River **19**:490
soils **18**:88–89
sports
soccer **18**:10
trade **18**:94
transportation **18**:94
railroad **16**:73
Trans-Andine Railroad **19**:267
truck and bus registration **19**:315 *table*
vegetation **18**:89 *map*
jungle and rain forest **11**:469
savanna life **17**:97–99
steppe life **18**:256–257
SOUTH AMERICAN WOOLLY OPOSSUM **13**:175 *illus.*
SOUTH ARABIAN PROTECTORATE *see* YEMEN (Aden)
SOUTH ASIAN UNIVERSITIES 18:95–96 *bibliog., table*
SOUTH AUSTRALIA (Australia) **18**:96 *map*
Adelaide **1**:101 *illus.*
Australia, history of **2**:340
Eyre, Lake **7**:352
flag **8**:145 *illus.*
Flinders Range **8**:165
map (30° 0'S 135° 0'E) **2**:328
SOUTH BALDY MOUNTAIN
map (33° 59'N 107° 11'W) **14**:136
SOUTH BAY (Florida)
map (26° 40'N 80° 43'W) **8**:172
SOUTH BEND (Indiana) **18**:96
map (41° 41'N 86° 15'W) **11**:111
SOUTH BEND (Washington)
map (46° 40'N 123° 48'W) **20**:35
SOUTH BOSTON (Virginia)
map (36° 42'N 78° 54'W) **19**:607
SOUTH BURLINGTON (Vermont)
map (44° 28'N 73° 13'W) **19**:554
SOUTH CANAL
map (18° 40'N 73° 5'W) **10**:15
SOUTH CAROLINA 18:96–101 *bibliog., illus., map*
agriculture **18**:99
animal life **18**:97
cities
Beaufort **3**:145–146
Charleston **4**:298 *illus.*
Columbia **5**:125
Greenville **9**:354
Spartanburg **18**:165
climate **18**:97
cultural and historical sites **18**:99
economic activity **18**:99–100
education **18**:99
Furman University **8**:371
South Carolina, state universities and colleges of **18**:101–102
flag **18**:97 *illus.*
geographical linguistics **9**:98–99 *map*
government and politics **18**:100
history **18**:100–101
Byrnes, James Francis **3**:602–603
Calhoun, John C. **4**:29
Civil War, U.S. **5**:15
England, John **7**:181
Hampton, Wade (1818–1902) **10**:33
Hayne, Robert Young **10**:83–84
Marion, Francis **13**:157
nullification **14**:292
Pinckney (family) **15**:304
Regulators **16**:129
Rhett, Robert Barnwell **16**:194
Rutledge, John **16**:376–377
Shaftesbury, Anthony Ashley Cooper, 1st Earl of **17**:234
Tillman, Benjamin Ryan **19**:200
United States, history of the **19**:436
land and resources **18**:96–101 *illus., map*
map (34° 0'N 81° 0'W) **19**:419
people **18**:97; **18**:99
Catawba **4**:201
resources **18**:97
rivers, lakes, and waterways **18**:97
seal, state **18**:97 *illus.*
SOUTH CAROLINA, STATE UNIVERSITIES AND COLLEGES OF 18:101–102
"SOUTH CAROLINA EXPOSITION AND PROTEST" (1828)
Civil War, U.S. **5**:15
SOUTH CHARLESTON (West Virginia)
map (38° 22'N 81° 44'W) **20**:111
SOUTH CHELMSFORD (Massachusetts)
map (42° 34'N 71° 23'W) **3**:409
SOUTH CHINA SEA *see* CHINA SEA, SOUTH
SOUTH COMINO CHANNEL
map (36° 0'N 14° 21'E) **13**:94
SOUTH DAKOTA 18:102–106 *bibliog., illus., map*
agriculture **18**:105 *illus.*
cities
Deadwood **6**:65
Pierre **15**:297
Rapid City **16**:90
Sioux Falls **17**:326
climate **18**:104
economic activity **18**:105
education **18**:104
South Dakota, state universities and colleges of **18**:106
flag **18**:102 *illus.*
government and politics **18**:105
history **18**:105–106
land and resources **18**:102–104 *illus., map*
map (44° 15'N 100° 0'W) **19**:419
people **18**:104
Sioux **17**:326
physical features
Badlands National Monument **3**:20
Black Hills **3**:315
Rushmore, Mount **16**:348
rivers, lakes, and waterways **18**:104
seal, state **18**:102 *illus.*
tourism and recreation **18**:104
SOUTH DAKOTA, STATE UNIVERSITIES AND COLLEGES OF 18:106
SOUTH DARTMOUTH (Massachusetts)
map (41° 36'N 70° 57'W) **13**:206
SOUTH DEERFIELD (Massachusetts)
map (42° 29'N 72° 37'W) **13**:206
SOUTH DENNIS (Massachusetts)
map (41° 41'N 70° 9'W) **13**:206
SOUTH EAST CAPE (Australia)
map (43° 39'S 146° 50'E) **2**:328
SOUTH FLEVOLAND (region in Netherlands)
map (52° 22'N 5° 20'E) **14**:99
SOUTH FORK (Colorado)
map (37° 40'N 106° 37'W) **5**:116
SOUTH FOX ISLAND
map (45° 25'N 85° 50'W) **13**:377
SOUTH FULTON (Tennessee)
map (36° 30'N 88° 53'W) **19**:104
SOUTH GATE (California)
map (33° 57'N 118° 12'W) **4**:31
SOUTH HADLEY (Massachusetts)
map (42° 16'N 72° 35'W) **13**:206
SOUTH HADLEY FALLS (Massachusetts)
map (42° 14'N 72° 36'W) **13**:206
SOUTH HAMILTON (Massachusetts)
map (42° 37'N 70° 53'W) **13**:206
SOUTH HAVEN (Michigan)
map (42° 24'N 86° 16'W) **13**:377
SOUTH HERO (Vermont)
map (44° 39'N 73° 19'W) **19**:554
SOUTH HILL (Virginia)
map (36° 44'N 78° 8'W) **19**:607
SOUTH HINGHAM (Massachusetts)
map (42° 11'N 70° 53'W) **3**:409
SOUTH HOLSTON LAKE
map (36° 35'N 82° 0'W) **19**:104
SOUTH HOOKSETT (New Hampshire)
map (43° 2'N 71° 26'W) **14**:123
SOUTH HOUSTON (Texas)
map (29° 40'N 95° 14'W) **19**:129
SOUTH HUTCHINSON (Kansas)
map (39° 2'N 97° 56'W) **12**:18
SOUTH INDIA, CHURCH OF 18:106 *bibliog.*
SOUTH INDIAN LAKE (Manitoba)
map (56° 46'N 98° 57'W) **13**:119
SOUTH ISLAND (New Zealand)
map (43° 0'S 171° 0'E) **14**:158
SOUTH KOREA *see* KOREA; KOREA, HISTORY OF; KOREAN WAR
SOUTH LAKE TAHOE (California)
map (38° 57'N 119° 57'W) **4**:31
SOUTH LANCASTER (Massachusetts)
map (42° 27'N 71° 41'W) **13**:206
SOUTH LOUP RIVER
map (41° 4'N 98° 40'W) **14**:70
SOUTH LYON (Michigan)
map (42° 28'N 83° 39'W) **13**:377
SOUTH MASSIF (mountains)
map (18° 25'N 73° 55'W) **10**:15
SOUTH MIAMI (Florida)
map (25° 42'N 80° 17'W) **8**:172
SOUTH MILLS (North Carolina)
map (36° 27'N 76° 20'W) **14**:242
SOUTH MILWAUKEE (Wisconsin)
map (42° 55'N 87° 52'W) **20**:185
SOUTH MOLUCCANS *see* AMBONESE
SOUTH MOOSE LAKE
map (53° 46'N 100° 8'W) **13**:119
SOUTH NAHANNI RIVER
map (61° 3'N 123° 20'W) **20**:345
SOUTH NATION RIVER
map (45° 35'N 75° 6'W) **14**:393; **14**:461
SOUTH OGDEN (Utah)
map (41° 12'N 111° 59'W) **19**:492
SOUTH ORKNEY ISLANDS
map (60° 35'S 45° 30'W) **2**:40
SOUTH PARIS (Maine)
map (44° 13'N 70° 31'W) **13**:70
SOUTH PASS
map (42° 22'N 108° 55'W) **20**:301
SOUTH PATRICK SHORES (Florida)
map (28° 12'N 80° 35'W) **8**:172
SOUTH PITTSBURG (Tennessee)
map (35° 1'N 85° 42'W) **19**:104
SOUTH PLATTE RIVER
map (41° 7'N 101° 35'W) **5**:116
Platte River **15**:362
SOUTH POLE 18:106
Amundsen, Roald **1**:386
Earth, motions of **7**:18
Ford Tri-motor **8**:223 *illus.*
Hillary, Sir Edmund **10**:164
map (90° 0'S 0° 0') **2**:40
Scott, Robert Falcon **17**:153–154
SOUTH PORTLAND (Maine)
map (43° 38'N 70° 15'W) **13**:70
SOUTH RANGE (Michigan)
map (47° 4'N 88° 39'W) **13**:377
SOUTH SALT LAKE (Utah)
map (40° 43'N 111° 53'W) **19**:492
SOUTH SAN FRANCISCO (California)
map (37° 39'N 122° 24'W) **4**:31
SOUTH SANDWICH TRENCH
Atlantic Ocean bottom **2**:295 *map*
SOUTH SASKATCHEWAN RIVER
map (53° 15'N 105° 5'W) **4**:70
SOUTH SEA BUBBLE 18:106 *bibliog.*
SOUTH SEA COMPANY
South Sea Bubble **18**:106
SOUTH SEA ISLANDS *see* OCEANIA
SOUTH SEMITIC LANGUAGES
Afroasiatic languages **1**:179–180
SOUTH SHETLAND ISLANDS
map (62° 0'S 58° 0'W) **2**:40
SOUTH SHIELDS (England)
map (55° 0'N 1° 25'W) **19**:403
SOUTH SIOUX CITY (Nebraska)
map (42° 28'N 96° 24'W) **14**:70
SOUTH SKUNK RIVER
map (41° 15'N 92° 2'W) **11**:244
SOUTH SUBTROPICAL CURRENT
ocean currents and wind systems, worldwide **14**:322–323 *maps*
SOUTH SUPERIOR (Wyoming)
map (41° 46'N 108° 58'W) **20**:301
SOUTH TARANAKI BIGHT
map (39° 40'S 174° 10'E) **14**:158
SOUTH TOMS RIVER (New Jersey)
map (39° 56'N 74° 13'W) **14**:129
SOUTH TUCSON (Arizona)
map (32° 12'N 110° 58'W) **2**:160
SOUTH TWIN MOUNTAIN
map (44° 12'N 71° 34'W) **14**:123
SOUTH UIST ISLAND
map (57° 15'N 7° 24'W) **19**:403
SOUTH VENICE (Florida)
map (27° 3'N 82° 24'W) **8**:172
SOUTH VIETNAM *see* VIETNAM; VIETNAM WAR
SOUTH WALPOLE (Massachusetts)
map (42° 6'N 71° 16'W) **3**:409
SOUTH WEST AFRICA *see* NAMIBIA
SOUTH WEST AFRICA PEOPLE'S ORGANIZATION (SWAPO)
Namibia **14**:12
Nujoma, Sam **14**:292
Ovambo **14**:469
SOUTH WHITLEY (Indiana)
map (41° 5'N 85° 38'W) **11**:111
SOUTH YARMOUTH (Massachusetts)
map (41° 40'N 70° 10'W) **13**:206
SOUTHAMPTON (England) **18**:107
map (50° 55'N 1° 25'W) **19**:403
SOUTHAMPTON (New York)
map (40° 53'N 72° 24'W) **14**:149
SOUTHAMPTON (county in Virginia)
map (36° 42'N 77° 5'W) **19**:607
SOUTHAMPTON ISLAND (Northwest Territories) **18**:107
map (64° 20'N 84° 40'W) **14**:258
SOUTHBOROUGH (Massachusetts)
map (42° 18'N 71° 13'W) **3**:409
SOUTHBRIDGE (Massachusetts)
map (42° 5'N 72° 2'W) **13**:206
SOUTHEAST AMERICAN INDIANS *see* INDIANS, AMERICAN, CULTURE AREAS
SOUTHEAST ASIA 18:107 *bibliog.*
See also REFUGEE—Southeast Asia
art
Southeast Asian art and architecture **18**:107–110
ASEAN **2**:228
Colombo Plan **5**:109
communism *see* COMMUNISM
dance **6**:26
drug trafficking **6**:281
education
Southeast Asian universities **18**:111–112 *table*
history
Asia, history of **2**:253–254; **2**:258–259; **2**:260
communism **5**:149–150
Indochina **11**:146
Khmer Empire **12**:67
Majapahit Empire **13**:76
Southeast Asia Treaty Organization **18**:107
Vietnam War **19**:584–591
languages
Southeast Asian languages **18**:110–111
Malay Peninsula **13**:82
music, non-Western **13**:667–668
people
migration to the United States **11**:55 *map*
Negrito **14**:78
race **16**:34 *illus.*
political parties
Pathet Lao **15**:111–112
prehistory
Heine-Geldern, Robert **10**:109
rivers, lakes, and waterways
Mekong River **2**:235 *illus.*; **13**:284 *map*
Salween River **17**:41
Yüan River **20**:338
SOUTHEAST ASIA TREATY ORGANIZATION 18:107
Eisenhower, Dwight D. **7**:96

SOUTHEAST-ASIAN AMERICANS *see* ORIENTAL AMERICANS
SOUTHEAST ASIAN ART AND ARCHITECTURE **18**:107–110 *bibliog., illus.*
See also BUDDHISM—art and architecture
ancient megalithic and Dong-son cultures **18**:108
Burma **18**:109–110
folk art **8**:198
indigenous folk traditions **18**:107–108
Indonesia **18**:110
Minangkabau **13**:436
Oceo **14**:346
Pagan (Burma) **15**:13
Polonnaruwa **15**:418
Prambanan **15**:489
temple **19**:98
Thailand **18**:109
SOUTHEAST ASIAN LANGUAGES **12**:355 *map*; **18**:110–111 *bibliog.*
Asia **2**:244 *map*
India **11**:84
Malayo-Polynesian languages **13**:82
Mon **13**:515
Oceanic languages **14**:339
Sino-Tibetan languages **17**:324–325
SOUTHEAST ASIAN UNIVERSITIES **18**:111–112 *bibliog., table*
SOUTHEND-ON-SEA (England)
map (51° 33′N 0° 43′E) **19**:403
SOUTHERN, TERRY **18**:112
SOUTHERN ALPS
map (43° 30′S 170° 30′E) **14**:158
New Zealand **14**:157 *illus.*
SOUTHERN CHRISTIAN LEADERSHIP CONFERENCE **18**:112
Abernathy, Ralph David **1**:56–57
King, Martin Luther, Jr. **12**:80–81
SOUTHERN CROSS *see* CRUX
SOUTHERN CULT
Spiro Mound **18**:189
SOUTHERN CURRENT
ocean currents and wind systems, worldwide **14**:322–323 *maps*
SOUTHERN DEATH CULT
Etowah Mounds **7**:258
SOUTHERN HEMISPHERE
upwelling, oceanic **19**:474
westerlies **20**:115
SOUTHERN INDIAN LAKE
map (57° 10′N 98° 40′W) **13**:119
SOUTHERN OCEAN *see* ANTARCTIC OCEAN
SOUTHERN PACIFIC COMPANY
California **4**:37
SOUTHERN PINES (North Carolina)
map (35° 11′N 79° 24′W) **14**:242
SOUTHERN RHODESIA *see* ZIMBABWE (Rhodesia)
SOUTHERN SIERRA MADRE MOUNTAINS
map (17° 0′N 100° 0′W) **13**:357
SOUTHERN UPLANDS
map (55° 30′N 3° 30′W) **19**:403
SOUTHERN WHITE CEDAR **18**:112
SOUTHERN YEMEN *see* YEMEN (Aden)
SOUTHEY, ROBERT **18**:112 *bibliog.*
Lake District (England) **12**:171
SOUTHFIELD (Michigan)
map (42° 29′N 83° 17′W) **13**:377
SOUTHINGTON (Connecticut)
map (41° 36′N 72° 53′W) **5**:193
SOUTHPORT (Australia)
map (27° 58′S 153° 25′E) **2**:328
SOUTHPORT (England)
map (53° 39′N 3° 1′W) **19**:403
SOUTHPORT (Florida)
map (30° 17′N 85° 39′W) **8**:172
SOUTHPORT (Indiana)
map (39° 40′N 86° 9′W) **11**:111
SOUTHPORT (North Carolina)
map (33° 55′N 78° 1′W) **14**:242
SOUTHWELL, SAINT ROBERT **18**:112 *bibliog.*
SOUTHWEST CAPE
map (47° 17′S 167° 28′E) **14**:158
SOUTHWORTH, ALBERT SANDS, AND HAWES, JOSIAH JOHNSON **18**:112–113 *bibliog.*
SOUTINE, CHAIM **18**:113 *bibliog., illus.*
The Head Valet **18**:113 *illus.*
SOUVANNA PHOUMA **18**:113 *bibliog.*
Laos **12**:204
Pathet Lao **15**:111–112
Souphanouvong **18**:77
SOVA, ANTONÍN
Czech literature **5**:412
SOVEREIGN (coin) **14**:296 *illus.*
SOVEREIGN OF THE SEAS (ship) **14**:55 *illus.*
clipper ship **5**:60
SOVEREIGNTY **18**:113 *bibliog.*
annexation **2**:33
federalism in the U.S. Constitution **5**:214
republic **16**:172
state (in political philosophy) **18**:229–233
state (political unit) **18**:228
territorial waters **19**:121
SOVIET **18**:113
SOVIET EDUCATION **18**:113–114 *bibliog.*
SOVIET LABOR CAMPS *see* GULAG
SOVIET LITERATURE *see* RUSSIAN LITERATURE
SOVIET MUSIC *see* RUSSIAN MUSIC
SOVIET UNION *see* RUSSIA/UNION OF SOVIET SOCIALIST REPUBLICS, HISTORY OF; UNION OF SOVIET SOCIALIST REPUBLICS
SOW BUG *see* PILL BUG
SOYA, CARL ERIK MARTIN **18**:114
SOYA STRAIT
map (45° 45′N 142° 0′E) **19**:388
SOYAPANGO (El Salvador)
map (13° 42′N 89° 9′W) **7**:100
SOYBEAN **18**:114–115 *bibliog., illus.*
farms and farming **8**:25
fats and oils source **8**:35
meat imitations **13**:257
vegetable oils **19**:534–535
SOYER BROTHERS **18**:115 *bibliog.*
SOYINKA, WOLE **18**:115 *bibliog., illus.*
SOYUZ **18**:115–118 *bibliog., illus., table*
Apollo-Soyuz Test Project **2**:84
cosmonauts
Aksenov, Vladimir **1**:232
Beregovoi, Georgy T. **3**:208
Bykovsky, Valery **3**:602
Demin, Lev Stepanovich **6**:97
Dobrovolsky, Georgy T. **6**:209
Dzhanibekov, Vladimir **6**:320
Filipchenko, Anatoly V. **8**:79
Gagarin, Yuri **9**:8
Glazkov, Yury Nikolayevich **9**:206
Grechko, Georgy Mikhailovich **9**:324
Gubarev, Aleksei **9**:390
Ivanchenkov, Aleksandr **11**:333
Ivanov, Georgy **11**:333
Jähn, Sigmund **11**:349
Khrunov, Yevgeny **12**:68
Klimuk, P. I. **12**:97
Komarov, Vladimir **12**:107
Kovalenok, Vladimir **12**:126
Kubasov, Valery N. **12**:134
Lazarev, V. G. **12**:252
Lebedev, Valentin **12**:267
Lyakhov, Vladimir **12**:473
Makarov, Oleg **13**:77
Nikolayev, Andrian **14**:195
Patsayev, Viktor **15**:114
Popovich, Pavel Romanovich **15**:432
Remek, Vladimir **16**:145
Romanenko, Yury Viktorovich **16**:281
Rukavishnikov, Nikolay **16**:344
Ryumin, Valery **16**:380
Sarafanov, Gennady Vasilievich **17**:74
Sevastianov, Vitaly I. **17**:215
Shatalov, Vladimir A. **17**:244–245
Shonin, Georgy Stepanovich **17**:281
Tereshkova, Valentina Vladimirovna Nikolayeva **19**:116
Titov, Gherman S. **19**:215
Volkov, Vladislav Nikolayevich **19**:629
Volynov, Boris Valentinovich **19**:633
Yeliseyev, Aleksei Stanislavovich **20**:322
Zholobov, Vitaly **20**:362
Zudov, Vyacheslav Dmitriyevich **20**:381
life-support systems **12**:331–333
missions **18**:115–118 *table*
Salyut **17**:41–44 *illus., table*
space exploration **18**:129–130 *illus.*
spacecraft **18**:118 *illus.*
Zond **20**:373
SPA *see* HEALTH RESORTS, WATERING-PLACES, AND SPAS
SPAAK, PAUL HENRI **18**:118 *bibliog., illus.*
SPACE CAPSULE
Mercury program **13**:307–308
SPACE EXPLORATION **18**:118–132 *bibliog., illus.*
astronaut **2**:274
astronautics **2**:274–276
communications satellites **5**:144–145
Early Bird **7**:8–9
Echo (satellite) **7**:39
INTELSAT **11**:205–206
Molniya **13**:512
Relay (artificial satellite) **16**:137
Syncom **18**:406
Telstar **19**:91
cosmic rays **5**:283–284
cosmonaut *see* COSMONAUTS
escape velocity **7**:236–237
food technology **8**:213
future **18**:131–132 *illus.*
guidance and control systems **9**:393–394
history **18**:118–132
Armstrong, Neil A. **2**:179–180
Gagarin, Yuri **9**:8
Glenn, John H., Jr. **9**:207
Goddard, Robert **9**:219–220
Korolev, Sergei Pavlovich **12**:123
Oberth, Hermann **14**:315
Spitzer, Lyman Jr. **18**:190–191
technology, history of **19**:69
Tsiolkovsky, Konstantin **19**:324
von Braun, Wernher **19**:633
International Geophysical Year (IGY) **11**:220; **18**:119
life, extraterrestrial **12**:328
life-support systems **12**:331–333
lunar probes **18**:123–124
Luna (spacecraft) **12**:459–460
Lunar Excursion Module **12**:460–461
Lunar Orbiter **12**:461
Lunokhod **12**:465
Ranger (space probe) **16**:84
Surveyor **18**:369–370
manned missions **18**:126–129
Apollo program **2**:80–84; **13**:563
Apollo-Soyuz Test Project **2**:84
Applications Technology Satellite **2**:90
Gemini program **9**:71–73
Mercury program **13**:307–308
Salyut **17**:41–44
Skylab **17**:347–348
Soyuz **18**:115–118
Space Shuttle **18**:134–136
Spacelab **18**:138
Voskhod **19**:635–636
Vostok **19**:636
meteorological satellites
Applications Technology Satellite **2**:89–90
Nimbus **14**:198 *table*
TIROS **19**:208–209
World Weather Watch **20**:281
mining and quarrying **13**:449
National Air and Space Museum **14**:28–29
navigation satellites **17**:86
Applications Technology Satellite **2**:89–90
navigation **14**:60–61
NAVSTAR **14**:62
Transit (artificial satellite) **19**:272
observatory, astronomical **14**:318–319
organizations
Centre National d'Études Spatiales **4**:255
European Space Agency **7**:306; **18**:121
National Aeronautics and Space Administration **14**:28; **18**:120
National Space Development Agency (Japan) **14**:46
photograph of earth from space **7**:11 *illus.*
planetary probes **18**:124–126
Galileo (spacecraft) **9**:15
Mariner **13**:155–156
Mars (spacecraft) **13**:169–170
Pioneer **15**:309–310
Venera **19**:538–539
Viking **19**:593–594
Voyager **19**:637–638
Zond **20**:372–373
reconnaissance satellites
Discoverer **6**:189
SAMOS **17**:47
rockets and missiles **16**:251–260
Agena (rocket) **1**:183; **9**:72–73
Ariane (rocket) **2**:153
Atlas (missile) **2**:297
Centaur (rocket) **4**:249
Delta (rocket) **6**:95
Diamant (France) **6**:151
Proton **15**:578
Redstone **16**:116–117
Saturn (rocket) **17**:91–92
Scout **17**:155–156
sounding rocket **18**:77
Thor (rocket) **19**:177
Titan (rocket) **19**:210–211
Vanguard **19**:519
satellite, artificial **17**:85–87
scientific research satellites
Alouette **1**:308
Applications Technology Satellite **2**:89–90
Biosatellite **3**:276
Cosmos **5**:289–290
Explorer **7**:338–339
GEOS **9**:119
GOES (artificial satellite) **9**:222
High Energy Astronomical Observatory **10**:161
IMP **11**:60
Landsat **12**:184–185
OAO **14**:312–313
OGO **14**:354–355
OSO **14**:456
SEASAT **17**:176
Space Telescope **18**:137
Sputnik **18**:119
Synchronous Meteorological Satellite **18**:406
Uhuru **19**:374
Vanguard **18**:119; **19**:519
SNAP **17**:383
solar cell **18**:40
solar system **18**:46–53
space centers
Baikonur Cosmodrome **3**:26
Cape Canaveral **4**:120
French Guiana **8**:310–311
Goddard Space Flight Center **9**:220
Jet Propulsion Laboratory **11**:407
Johnson Space Center **11**:437
Kapustin Yar **12**:26
Kennedy Space Center **12**:44–45
Lop Nor (China) **12**:412
Peenemünde **15**:132
Vandenberg Air Force Base **19**:518
White Sands Missile Range **20**:138
space hardware, development **18**:121–132
space law **18**:132
space medicine **18**:132–134
space station **18**:129–130; **18**:136–137
spacecraft maneuvers
celestial mechanics **4**:230
rendezvous and docking, Gemini **9**:72–73
telemetry **19**:78
tracking station **18**:122; **19**:262
Goldstone Tracking Station **9**:236
unidentified flying object **19**:384–385
unmanned missions **18**:123–126
weightlessness **20**:92
worldwide activities **18**:120–121
SPACE FLIGHT *see* SPACE EXPLORATION
SPACE INVADERS (video game) **19**:576i
SPACE LAW **18**:132 *bibliog.*
SPACE MEDICINE **18**:132–134 *bibliog., illus.*
biosatellite **3**:276
history **18**:132
Kerwin, Joseph **12**:60
Laika **12**:167
life-support systems **12**:331–333; **18**:132–133
space environment
physiological response **18**:133
psychological response **18**:133–134
support systems **18**:132–133
veterinary medicine **19**:567
weightlessness **20**:92
Yegorov, Boris B. **20**:322
SPACE SHUTTLE **18**:134–136 *bibliog., illus.*
aerodynamics **1**:123 *illus.*
astronauts
Bluford, Guion S. **3**:346
Brand, Vance **3**:453
Crippen, Robert **5**:350
Haise, Fred W. **10**:15
Jarvis, Gregory **11**:383
McAuliffe, Christa **13**:6
McNair, Ronald E. **13**:35
Mattingly, Thomas **13**:232
Onizuka, Ellison **14**:391
Resnik, Judith A. **16**:177

Ride, Sally **16**:216
Scobee, Francis R. **17**:147
Smith, Michael **17**:370
Young, John W. **20**:333
Centaur (rocket) **4**:249
components **18**:134–135
crew **18**:135
European Space Agency **7**:306
future **18**:131 *illus.*
gyroscope **9**:416
history **18**:136
Johnson Space Center **11**:437
Kennedy Space Center **12**:45
life-support systems **12**:331
National Aeronautics and Space Administration **14**:28
rockets and missiles **16**:257 *illus.*
space exploration **18**:130–131 *illus.*
space medicine **18**:133
Space Telescope **18**:137 *illus.*
Spacelab **18**:138 *illus.*
tracking station **19**:262
typical missions **18**:135
Vandenberg Air Force Base **19**:518
SPACE STATION **18**:136–137 *bibliog., illus.*
history **18**:136
proposed **18**:136 *illus.*
Salyut **17**:41–44 *illus.*
Skylab **17**:347–348 *illus.*
space exploration **18**:129–130
Spacelab **18**:138 *illus.*
SPACE SUIT
Apollo program **2**:82 *illus.*
astronaut **2**:274 *illus.*
life-support systems **12**:332–333 *illus.*
space exploration **18**:122 *illus.*
SPACE TELESCOPE **14**:319 *illus.*; **18**:137 *bibliog., illus.*
SPACE-TIME CONTINUUM **18**:137–138 *bibliog.*
Cayley, Arthur **4**:227
cosmology (astronomy) **5**:287
Einstein, Albert **7**:93
gravitation **9**:305
gravitational collapse **9**:305
Minkowski, Hermann **13**:451
relativity **16**:134–136 *illus.*
symmetry (physics) **18**:404
time (physics) **19**:201
world line **20**:219
SPACE WALK **18**:128 *illus.*
White, Edward H., II **20**:135 *illus.*
SPACELAB **18**:138 *bibliog.*
European Space Agency **7**:306
space station **18**:137
SPAD **18**:138 *illus.*
Blériot, Louis **3**:330–331
SPADEFISH **18**:138
SPADOLINI, GIOVANNI
Italy **11**:331
SPAGHETTINI **15**:106 *illus.*
SPAHN, WARREN **18**:138
SPAIN **18**:138–143 *bibliog., illus., map, table*
agriculture **18**:143 *illus.*
wine **20**:176
archaeology
Altamira **1**:311
Los Millares **12**:418
Torralba and Ambrona **19**:243
arts **18**:142
See also SPANISH ART AND ARCHITECTURE
cities
Algeciras **1**:285
Alicante **1**:292
Amería **1**:306
Badajoz **3**:18–19
Badalona **3**:19
Barcelona **3**:79–80 *illus.*
Bilbao **3**:250
Burgos **3**:570
Cádiz **4**:12
Cartagena **4**:170
Ceuta **4**:263
Córdoba **5**:261
Elche **7**:103
Gijón **9**:178
Granada **9**:283
Jerez de la Frontera **11**:397
La Coruña **12**:145
Las Palmas **12**:210
León **12**:289
Madrid **13**:43–45 *illus., map*
Málaga **13**:79
Melilla **13**:287
Murcia **13**:647
Oviedo **14**:471
Palma **15**:49–50
Pamplona **15**:53
Salamanca **17**:29
San Sebastián **17**:58
Santander **17**:69
Santiago **17**:70
Saragossa **17**:74
Seville **17**:220–221 *illus.*
Tarragona **19**:39
Toledo **19**:226
Valencia **19**:503–504 *illus.*
Valladolid **19**:506
Vigo **19**:592
Vitoria **19**:621
climate **18**:139; **18**:141 *table*
crime **5**:346 *table*
dance **6**:27 *illus.*
Argentina, La **2**:152
bolero **3**:364
fandango **8**:20
flamenco **8**:151
Greco, José **9**:324
saraband **17**:74
economic activities **18**:142–143
education **18**:142
European universities **7**:308 *table*
Salamanca, University of **17**:29
flag **18**:139 *illus.*
government **18**:143
viceroy **19**:571
welfare spending **20**:98 *table*
health **18**:142
history *see* SPAIN, HISTORY OF
land and resources **18**:139–141 *illus., map, table*
paleomagnetic rotation **15**:41 *map*
languages **18**:142
Basque language **3**:116
Romance languages **16**:280–281
literature *see* SPANISH LITERATURE
manufacturing and mining **18**:142–143
map (40° 0′N 4° 0′W) **7**:268
people **18**:142
Basques **3**:116
Sephardim **11**:414; **17**:206
physical features
Finisterre, Cape **8**:94
Montserrat (mountain) **13**:560
Sierra Nevada **17**:298
regions
Andalusia **1**:400
Aragon **2**:107
Balearic Islands **3**:36 *map*
Canary Islands **4**:99 *map*
Castile **4**:188
Catalonia **4**:198
Ceuta **4**:263
Galicia **9**:14
Granada **9**:283
Ibiza **11**:5
León **12**:289
Majorca **13**:77
Minorca **13**:459
Murcia **13**:647
Valencia **19**:504
resources **18**:141 *illus.*
rivers, lakes, and waterways **18**:141
Douro River **6**:249–250
Ebro River **7**:36
Guadalquivir River **9**:385
Tagus River **19**:10
theater, history of the **19**:146
titles of nobility **19**:214 *table*
trade **18**:143
urban planning *see* URBAN PLANNING
SPAIN, HISTORY OF **18**:144–149 *bibliog., illus., map*
See also PORTUGAL, HISTORY OF
audiencia **2**:318
historians *see* HISTORY—Spanish historians
Ifni **11**:32
navy **14**:62
Philippines **15**:238
Puerto Rico **15**:616
rulers **18**:148 *table*
slavery **17**:353; **17**:355
Western Sahara **20**:116
prior to 711 AD
Goths **9**:263
Roman conquest **18**:144
Visigoths **18**:144
711–1260 early Muslim rule
Abd al-Rahman I **1**:53–54
al-Andalus **18**:144–145
Alfonso VI, King of León and Castile **1**:279
Almohads **1**:306
Almoravids **1**:307
Asturias **2**:285
El Cid **7**:98
Mozarabs **13**:628
Muslim territories **18**:146 *maps*
Sancho III, King of Navarre (Sancho the Great) **17**:58
Umayyads **19**:380
1260–1479 Christian reconquest
Alfonso V, King of Aragon **1**:279
Alfonso X, King of Castile **1**:279
Europe, history of **7**:286
Navarre **14**:58
rise of Christian kingdoms **18**:145–146 *maps*
1479–1700 unification and Habsburg rule
Alba, Fernando Álvarez de Toledo y Pimentel, Duque de **1**:248
Boabdil **3**:349
California **4**:36
Charles II, King **4**:296
Charles V, Holy Roman Emperor **4**:294–295
costume **5**:296 *illus.*
Cuba **5**:379
Devolution, War of **6**:143
El Salvador **7**:100
exploration **7**:334–335
Ferdinand II, King of Aragon **8**:52
Florida **8**:175
Granada **9**:283
Habsburg monarchs **18**:145–147
Inquisition **11**:184
Isabella I, Queen of Castile (Isabella the Catholic) **11**:285–286
Italian Wars *see* ITALIAN WARS
Jiménez de Cisneros, Francisco **11**:418–419
Joan the Mad, Queen of Castile **11**:420
Latin America, history of **12**:217–221
Low Countries, history of the **12**:439–440 *map*
Moriscos **13**:580
Netherlands **14**:102
New Granada **14**:121
New Spain **14**:142
Olivares, Gaspar de Guzmán, Conde-Duque de **14**:378
Paraguay **15**:76–77
Peru **15**:194
Philip I, King of Castile (Philip the Handsome) **15**:234
Philip II, King **15**:234
Philip III, King **15**:234–235
Philip IV, King **15**:235
reign of the "Catholic Kings" **18**:145
Spanish Armada **18**:150–151
sword **18**:398 *illus.*
Thirty Years' War *see* THIRTY YEARS' WAR
tobacco **19**:218
Tordesillas, Treaty of **19**:238–239
Torquemada, Tomás de **19**:243
1700-1931 Bourbon monarchy
Alfonso XII, King **1**:279
Alfonso XIII, King **1**:280
Bourbon (dynasty) **3**:423; **18**:147
Bourbon restoration **18**:148–149
Carlists **4**:151
Charles III, King **4**:296–297
Charles IV, King **4**:297
exploration and settlement in colonial America **19**:437 *map*
Ferdinand VI, King **8**:53
Ferdinand VII, King **8**:54
French Revolutionary and Napoleonic period **18**:147–148
Godoy, Manuel de **9**:221
Isabella II, Queen **11**:286
Latin American colonies *c.*1790 **12**:219 *map*
New Mexico **14**:139
Philip V, King **15**:235
Primo de Rivera, Miguel **15**:546
Quito (Ecuador) **16**:28
Seven Years' War *see* SEVEN YEARS' WAR
Spanish-American War *see* SPANISH-AMERICAN WAR
Spanish Succession, War of the *see* SPANISH SUCCESSION, WAR OF THE
territory ceded to the United States, 1819 **19**:446 *map*
1931-present
Azaña, Manuel **2**:380
Basques **3**:116
Calvo Sotelo, Leopoldo **4**:49
Franco, Francisco **8**:277–278
González Márquez, Felipe **9**:245
Juan Carlos I, King **11**:457
republic and rule of Franco **18**:149
Spanish Civil War *see* SPANISH CIVIL WAR
Suárez González, Adolfo **18**:312
SPALDING (Nebraska)
map (41° 41′N 98° 22′W) **14**:70
SPALDING, ALBERT GOODWILL **18**:149
SPALLANZANI, LAZZARO **18**:149
artificial insemination **2**:220
SPANDEX
synthetic fibers **18**:409
SPANGEN HOUSING ESTATE
Oud, Jacobus Johannes Pieter **14**:467
SPANGENBERG, AUGUSTUS GOTTLIEB **18**:149
Moravian Church **13**:575
SPANGLER (Pennsylvania)
map (40° 39′N 78° 47′W) **15**:147
SPANGLER, JAMES MURRAY
vacuum cleaner **19**:502
SPANIEL *see* SPORTING DOG
SPANISH-AMERICAN WAR **18**:149–150 *bibliog., illus.*
battle at Manila Bay **14**:63 *illus.*
cartoon **18**:148 *illus.*
Dewey, George **6**:146
Hearst, William Randolph **10**:90
McKinley, William **13**:31
Maine (ship) **13**:74
Manila (Philippines) **13**:118
Manila Bay **13**:118
navy **14**:63
Paris, treaties of **15**:87
Paris, Treaty of **18**:150
Pulitzer, Joseph **15**:618
Rough Riders **16**:324
Sampson, William T. **17**:48
Santiago de Cuba (Cuba) **17**:70
Schley, Winfield Scott **17**:126
Shafter, William Rufus **17**:234
Spain, history of **18**:148
uniform **2**:182 *illus.*; **4**:221 *illus.*
United States, history of the **19**:452
yellow journalism **20**:322
SPANISH ARMADA **18**:151 *bibliog., illus.*
Drake, Sir Francis **6**:256
Elizabeth I, Queen of England **7**:141–142
galleon **9**:17
navy **14**:63
SPANISH ART AND ARCHITECTURE **18**:151–156 *bibliog., illus.*
See also the subheading Spain under specific art forms, e.g., ARCHITECTURE; PAINTING; SCULPTURE; etc.; the subheading Spain under specific historic periods, e.g., BAROQUE ART AND ARCHITECTURE; RENAISSANCE ART AND ARCHITECTURE; etc.; names of specific artists, e.g., MIRÓ, JOAN; SILOE, DIEGO DE; etc.
Art Nouveau **2**:212
calligraphy **4**:43
costume **5**:296 *illus.*
folk art **8**:196
garden **9**:40
Gothic art and architecture **9**:258–259
Islamic art and architecture **11**:293–297
jewelry **11**:410 *illus.*
Latin American art and architecture **12**:223; **12**:225 *illus.*
Moorish art and architecture **13**:570–571
Moor **13**:567
Mozarabic art **18**:152
museums, art **13**:658
Prado **15**:487
prehistoric art **15**:509 *illus.*
Altamira **1**:311 *illus.*
prehistoric and pre-Roman art **18**:151
Romanesque art and architecture **16**:282–286 *illus.*
rugs and carpets **16**:343
vargueño **8**:375 *illus.*
SPANISH BAYONET (botany) *see* SPANISH DAGGER (botany)
SPANISH CIVIL WAR **18**:156–157 *bibliog., illus., map*
Europe, history of **7**:297
Franco, Francisco **8**:277
Málaga (Spain) **13**:79
Melilla (Spain) **13**:287
Murcia (city in Spain) **13**:647
photography
Capa, Robert **4**:119
Salamanca (Spain) **17**:29
Seville (Spain) **17**:221
Spain, history of **18**:149
World War II **20**:249–250 *illus.*

SPANISH COLONIAL ARCHITECTURE
see LATIN AMERICAN ART AND ARCHITECTURE
SPANISH DAGGER (botany)
yucca **20**:339 *illus.*
SPANISH FLY
aphrodisiac **2**:78
SPANISH FORK (Utah)
map (40° 7′N 111° 39′W) **19**:492
SPANISH GUINEA *see* EQUATORIAL GUINEA
SPANISH LAKE (Missouri)
map (38° 47′N 90° 13′W) **13**:476
SPANISH LITERATURE **18**:157–160 *bibliog., illus.*
See also CATALAN LITERATURE
authors
Alarcón, Pedro Antonio de **1**:240
Alas, Leopoldo **1**:240
Alberti, Rafael **1**:259
Aleixandre, Vicente **1**:271
Alemán, Mateo **1**:271
Alonso, Dámaso **1**:307–308
Álvarez Quintero, Serafín and Joaquín **1**:319–320
Arrabal, Fernando **2**:187
Baroja y Nessi, Pio **3**:87
Bécquer, Gustavo Adolfo **3**:152
Benavente y Martínez, Jacinto **3**:195
Blasco-Ibáñez, Vicente **3**:328
Caballero, Fernán **4**:3
Calderón de la Barca, Pedro **4**:26
Campoamor y Campoosorio, Ramón de **4**:67
Castro y Bellvís, Guillén de **4**:193
Cela, Camilo José **4**:229
Cernuda, Luis **4**:260
Cervantes Saavedra, Miguel de **4**:261
Cueva, Juan de la **5**:383
Echegaray y Eizaguirre, José **7**:37
Encina, Juan del **7**:162
Espinel, Vicente Martínez **7**:243
García Lorca, Federico **9**:38–39
Garcilaso de la Vega **9**:39–40
Góngora y Argote, Luis de **9**:243–244
Goytisolo, Juan **9**:274
Guillén, Jorge **9**:396
Jiménez, Juan Ramón **11**:418
Machado, Antonio **13**:17–18
Martínez Sierra, Gregorio **13**:180
Ortega y Gasset, José **14**:449
Pérez Galdós, Benito **15**:164
Quevedo y Villegas, Francisco Gómez de **16**:25
Rojas Zorrilla, Francisco de **16**:270
Rueda, Lope de **16**:339
Ruiz, José Martínez **16**:344
Ruiz de Alarcón y Mendoza, Juan **16**:344
Sastre, Alfonso **17**:84
Tirso de Molina **19**:209
Unamuno, Miguel de **19**:381
Valera y Alcalá Galiano, Juan **19**:505
Valle Inclán, Ramón del **19**:507
Vallejo, Antonio Buero **19**:507
Vega, Lope de **19**:531
Zorilla y Moral, José **20**:380
Baroque **18**:157–158
Celestina **4**:230
Don Quixote **6**:236
golden age **18**:158–159
medieval **18**:157
modernismo **18**:159
realism **18**:159
Renaissance **18**:157–158
romanticism **18**:159
SPANISH MISSIONS **18**:160–161 *bibliog., illus.*
Arizona **2**:164
California **4**:36–37
Indian languages, American **11**:98
Indians **11**:128 *illus.*
Kino, Eusebio Francisco **12**:84–85
olive **14**:378
Oraibi **14**:413
Popé **15**:430
San Xavier del Bac **2**:162 *illus.*; **18**:160 *illus.*
Serra, Junípero **17**:210
SPANISH MOSS **8**:173 *illus.*; **18**:161
SPANISH MUSIC **18**:161–162 *bibliog., illus.*
composers
Albéniz, Isaac **1**:253
Falla, Manuel de **8**:13–14
Granados, Enrique **9**:283
Turina, Joaquin **19**:342
Victoria, Tomás Luis de **19**:574–575
Farinelli **8**:23
guitar **9**:401
Iturbi, José **11**:331
medieval music **13**:275
music, history of Western **13**:662; **13**:665
zarzuela **20**:356
SPANISH POINT
map (32° 18′N 64° 48′W) **3**:219
SPANISH RIDING SCHOOL (Vienna)
Lippizaner **12**:363
SPANISH SAHARA *see* WESTERN SAHARA
SPANISH SUCCESSION, WAR OF THE **18**:162–163 *bibliog., map*
Blenheim, Battle of **3**:330
Charles VI, Holy Roman Emperor **4**:295
Eugene of Savoy **7**:263
French and Indian Wars **8**:312–313
Great Britain, history of **9**:315
Joseph I, Holy Roman Emperor **11**:451
Louis XIV, King of France **12**:427
Marlborough, John Churchill, 1st Duke of **13**:160
Naples, Kingdom of **14**:15
Philip V, King of Spain **15**:235
Utrecht, Peace of **19**:498
Vendôme, Louis Joseph, Duc de **19**:538
Villars, Claude Louis Hector, Duc de **19**:598
William III, King of England, Scotland, and Ireland **20**:156
SPANISH TOWN (Jamaica)
map (17° 59′N 76° 57′W) **11**:351
SPANISH TRAGEDY, THE (play)
Kyd, Thomas **12**:143
SPARK, MURIEL **18**:163 *bibliog.*
SPARK CHAMBER **18**:163 *bibliog., illus.*
gamma-ray astronomy **9**:34
SPARK PLUG
ignition system **11**:36–38 *illus.*
SPARKMAN (Arkansas)
map (33° 55′N 92° 51′W) **2**:166
SPARKMAN, JOHN J. **18**:163
SPARKS (Georgia)
map (31° 11′N 83° 26′W) **9**:114
SPARKS (Nevada)
map (39° 32′N 119° 45′W) **14**:111
SPARKS, JARED **18**:163
SPARLAND (Illinois)
map (41° 2′N 89° 26′W) **11**:42
SPARROW **18**:164 *bibliog., illus.*
anatomy **3**:284 *illus.*
bunting **3**:564
dickcissel **6**:156
ricebird **16**:209
songbirds **18**:65
SPARROW III MISSILE **16**:255 *illus.*
SPARTA (Georgia)
map (33° 17′N 82° 58′W) **9**:114
SPARTA (Greece) **18**:164–165 *bibliog., illus.*
Agesilaus II, King **1**:184
Arcadia **2**:112
armed infantryman **18**:164 *illus.*
Castor and Pollux **4**:191
Clearchus **5**:47
Cleomenes III, King **5**:50
cryptology **5**:371
ephors **7**:216
Europe, history of **7**:280
Greece, ancient **9**:331–333 *map*
Leonidas, King **12**:292
Lycurgus **12**:474
Mistra **13**:482
Olympic Games **14**:382
Olynthus **14**:385
Pausanius **15**:119–120
Peloponnesian War **9**:333 *map*; **15**:139
Persian Wars **15**:188
women in society **20**:201
SPARTA (Illinois)
map (38° 7′N 89° 42′W) **11**:42
SPARTA (Kentucky)
map (38° 41′N 84° 55′W) **12**:47
SPARTA (Michigan)
map (43° 10′N 85° 42′W) **13**:377
SPARTA (New Jersey)
map (41° 1′N 74° 39′W) **14**:129
SPARTA (North Carolina)
map (36° 30′N 81° 7′W) **14**:242
SPARTA (Tennessee)
map (35° 56′N 85° 29′W) **19**:104
SPARTA (Wisconsin)
map (43° 57′N 90° 47′W) **20**:185
SPARTACUS **18**:165
SPARTACUS LEAGUE **9**:155 *illus.*
Liebknecht (family) **12**:324
Luxemburg, Rosa **12**:473
SPARTAN MISSILE **2**:56 *illus.*
SPARTANBURG (South Carolina) **18**:165
map (34° 57′N 81° 55′W) **18**:98
SPARTANBURG (county in South Carolina)
map (35° 0′N 82° 0′W) **18**:98
SPASSKY, BORIS **18**:165 *bibliog.*
SPATIAL RELATIONSHIP
infancy **11**:162–163
SPATS **17**:280 *illus.*
SPAULDING (county in Georgia)
map (33° 15′N 84° 15′W) **9**:114
SPAWNING
eel **7**:70–71 *illus., illus.*
salmon **17**:35 *illus.*
SPAYING *see* CASTRATION
SPCA *see* SOCIETY FOR THE PREVENTION OF CRUELTY TO ANIMALS
SPEAKEASIES
prohibition **15**:565
SPEAKER (U.S. House of Representatives)
congressional organization **5**:185
House of Representatives of the United States **10**:273
SPEAKER, TRIS **18**:165 *illus.*
SPEARE, ELIZABETH **18**:165
SPEARFISH **18**:165
SPEARFISH (South Dakota)
map (44° 30′N 103° 52′W) **18**:103
SPEARMAN (Texas)
map (36° 12′N 101° 12′W) **19**:129
SPEARMINT **13**:460–461 *illus.*; **18**:165–166 *illus.*
peppermint **15**:157
SPEARVILLE (Kansas)
map (37° 51′N 99° 45′W) **12**:18
SPECIAL ASTROPHYSICAL OBSERVATORY **18**:166 *bibliog.*
SPECIAL DRAWING RIGHTS *see* INTERNATIONAL MONETARY FUND
SPECIAL EDUCATION **18**:166–167 *bibliog.*
blind, education of the **3**:331–332
deaf, education of the **6**:65–66
deafness **6**:66 *illus.*
Gallaudet (family) **9**:17
Gallaudet College **9**:17
feral children **8**:51
handicapped persons **10**:36
Head Start **10**:85
learning disabilities **12**:259–260
SPECIAL EFFECTS
cinematography **4**:433
video technology **19**:576p
SPECIAL FORCES **18**:167 *bibliog.*
SPECIAL-INTEREST GROUPS **18**:167–168 *bibliog.*
See also POLITICAL ACTION ORGANIZATIONS
democracy **6**:98
lobbyist **12**:384
trade associations **19**:262–263
Veterans' Organizations **19**:566
SPECIAL OLYMPICS **18**:168
SPECIE CIRCULAR (1836)
Jackson, Andrew **11**:342
SPECIFIC GRAVITY **18**:168
density **6**:113–114
hydrometer **10**:343
SPECIFIC HEAT *see* HEAT CAPACITY
SPECIFIC PERFORMANCE *see* PERFORMANCE (law)
SPECTACLE BIRD *see* WHITE-EYE
SPECTATOR, THE (periodical)
Steele, Sir Richard **18**:243
SPECTATOR SPORTS *see* names of specific sports, e.g., BASEBALL; FOOTBALL; etc.
SPECTRAL LINES
hydrogen spectrum **10**:340
spectroscopy **18**:170
star **18**:222
Wood, Robert Williams **20**:207
SPECTROHELIOGRAPH **18**:168
Hale, George Ellery, inventor **10**:18
SPECTROMETRY, MASS *see* MASS SPECTROMETRY
SPECTROPHOTOMETER **18**:168–169 *illus.*
chromatography **4**:417–419
SPECTROSCOPE **18**:169–170 *bibliog., illus.*
Bunsen, Robert Wilhelm **3**:564
diffraction grating **6**:169–170
Lummer-Gehrcke
Lummer, Otto **12**:459
SPECTROSCOPY **18**:170–172 *bibliog., illus., table*
Ångström, Anders Jonas **2**:7
astronomy, history of **2**:279
astrophotography **2**:285
Balmer, Johann Jakob **3**:53
Barkla, Charles Glover **3**:83
binary stars **3**:256
Bowen, Ira Sprague **3**:428
Bunsen, Robert Wilhelm **3**:564
chemistry, history of **4**:327
Crimean Astrophysical Observatory **5**:348
electromagnetic radiation **7**:118
element **7**:130
Fraunhofer lines **8**:288–289 *table*
geochemistry **9**:95
Herzberg, Gerhard **10**:150
Huggins, Sir William **10**:292
hydrogen spectrum **10**:340–341
infrared **18**:171
infrared radiation **11**:175
Janssen, Jules **11**:359
Kirchhoff, Gustav Robert **12**:87
Kusch, Polykarp **12**:139
Lamb, Willis Eugene,Jr. **12**:174
magnetic resonance
Purcell, Edward Mills **15**:628
molecular structure **18**:171
nuclear magnetic resonance **18**:171
Pickering, Edward Charles **15**:293
qualitative chemical analysis **16**:7
radio astronomy **16**:52
radiometric age-dating **16**:66
Rydberg, Johannes Robert **16**:379
Schwarzschild, Karl **17**:139
Siegbahn, Manne **17**:295
Slipher, Vesto Melvin **17**:362
spectrum **18**:171; **18**:172–173
synchrotron radiation **18**:406
ultraviolet **18**:171
X-ray astronomy **20**:307
X-ray spectrometer **20**:310
SPECTRUM **18**:172–173 *bibliog., illus.*
atomic spectra **18**:172
color **5**:112–113 *table*
color index **5**:114
distribution, blackbody radiation **3**:320 *illus.*
electromagnetic radiation **7**:116–117 *illus.*
electromagnetic spectrum **18**:172
energy level spectrum **18**:173
flash spectrum **8**:154
Fraunhofer lines **8**:288–289
Hertzsprung-Russell diagram **10**:149–150
hydrogen spectrum **10**:340–341
line spectra **18**:172 *illus.*
Lyman, Theodore **12**:475
nebula **14**:74
photosphere **15**:275
qualitative chemical analysis **16**:7
rainbow **16**:77
Rowland, Henry Augustus **16**:328
Rydberg constant, atomic constants **2**:309
spectroscope **18**:169 *illus.*
spectroscopy **18**:171
star **18**:222–224 *illus.*
stellar spectrum **18**:252 *illus.*
SPEE, GRAF MAXIMILIAN VON
World War I **20**:228
SPEECH **18**:173–175 *bibliog., illus.*
articulation **18**:174
communication **5**:144
consonants **18**:174
disorders **18**:174–175
aphasia **2**:76–77
loss, stroke **18**:302
speech therapy **18**:176
stuttering **18**:309–310
electronic technology
vocoder **19**:625
voice recognition **19**:626
handedness **10**:35
infancy **11**:162–163
inner speech **11**:179
larynx **12**:209 *illus.*
Luria, Aleksandr Romanovich **12**:466
muscle **13**:653
organs **18**:174 *illus.*
pattern recognition **15**:115
phonetics **15**:251–252
physiology **18**:173–174
pidgin **15**:294
prehistoric humans **15**:515
psycholinguistics **15**:591–592
resonance **18**:174
semantics (linguistics) **17**:194
sex change **17**:224
sociolinguistics **18**:27–28
speech patterns
geographical linguistics **9**:98–100
tongue **19**:234
vowels **18**:174
SPEECH, FIGURES OF *see* FIGURES OF SPEECH

SPEECH, FREEDOM OF *see* FREEDOM OF SPEECH
SPEECH, PARTS OF *see* PARTS OF SPEECH
SPEECH DEVELOPMENT 18:175–176 *bibliog.*
psycholinguistics 15:592
skill learning 17:339
SPEECH THERAPY 18:176 *bibliog.*
stuttering 18:310
SPEED 18:176
Mach number 13:17
velocity 19:538
SPEED SKATING *see* ICE SKATING
SPEEDBALL 18:176
SPEEDOMETER
digital technology 6:175
SPEEDWAY (Indiana)
map (39° 47′N 86° 15′W) 11:111
SPEEDWELL (botany) 18:176
SPEEDWELL (ship)
Mayflower 13:247
Pilgrims 15:302
SPEENHAMLAND SYSTEM
poor laws 15:429
SPEER, ALBERT 18:176 *bibliog.*
Nuremberg Trials 14:297 *illus.*
SPEIGHTSTOWN (Barbados)
map (13° 15′N 59° 39′W) 3:75
SPEKE, JOHN HANNING 18:176–177 *bibliog.*
Africa 1:157 *map*
exploration 7:338
Ruanda-Urundi 16:332
Tanganyika, Lake 19:22
Victoria, Lake 19:574 *map*
SPELEOLOGY 18:177 *bibliog.*
cave 4:222–224
spelunking 18:177
SPELL
magic 13:49
SPELLING *see* WRITING SYSTEMS, EVOLUTION OF
SPELLMAN, FRANCIS JOSEPH 18:177 *bibliog.*
SPELMAN COLLEGE 18:177
SPELUNKING 18:177 *bibliog.*
SPEMANN, HANS 18:177
biology 3:271
SPENCE, SIR BASIL 18:177 *bibliog.*
Coventry Cathedral 5:319
SPENCE, KENNETH W.
psychology, history of 15:597
SPENCE BAY (Northwest Territories)
map (69° 32′N 93° 31′W) 14:258
SPENCER (Indiana)
map (39° 17′N 86° 46′W) 11:111
SPENCER (county in Indiana)
map (38° 0′N 87° 0′W) 11:111
SPENCER (Iowa)
map (43° 9′N 95° 9′W) 11:244
SPENCER (county in Kentucky)
map (38° 0′N 85° 20′W) 12:47
SPENCER (Massachusetts)
map (42° 15′N 71° 60′W) 13:206
SPENCER (Nebraska)
map (42° 53′N 98° 42′W) 14:70
SPENCER (North Carolina)
map (35° 37′N 80° 26′W) 14:242
SPENCER (South Dakota)
map (43° 44′N 97° 36′W) 18:103
SPENCER (Tennessee)
map (35° 45′N 85° 28′W) 19:104
SPENCER (West Virginia)
map (38° 48′N 81° 21′W) 20:111
SPENCER (Wisconsin)
map (44° 46′N 90° 18′W) 20:185
SPENCER, ANNA GARLIN 18:177
SPENCER, LADY DIANA
Charles, Prince of Wales 4:290
SPENCER, HERBERT 18:177 *bibliog.*
Social Darwinism 18:11
SPENCER, PLATT R.
calligraphy 4:43
SPENCER GULF
map (34° 0′S 137° 0′E) 2:328
SPENCERIAN SYSTEM
calligraphy 4:43
SPENCERVILLE (Ohio)
map (40° 42′N 84° 21′W) 14:357
SPENCES BRIDGE (British Columbia)
map (50° 25′N 121° 21′W) 3:491
SPENDER, STEPHEN 18:177–178 *bibliog., illus.*
SPENER, PHILIPP JAKOB 18:178 *bibliog.*
pietism 15:297–298
SPENGLER, OSWALD 18:178 *bibliog.*
civilization 5:34
Decline of the West, The 6:76
SPENSER, EDMUND 18:178–179 *bibliog., illus.*
Faerie Queene, The 8:7
pastoral literature 15:108–109
SPERANSKY, MIKHAIL MIKHAILOVICH 18:179 *bibliog.*
SPERLING, GEORGE
cognitive psychology 5:95
SPERM 18:179 *bibliog.*
artificial insemination 2:220–221
biological locomotion 3:265
birth control 3:293
development 6:140
egg 7:72
embryo 10:139 *illus.*
fertility, human 8:60
flagella 8:149
Hertwig, Oscar 10:148
Leeuwenhoek, Anton van 20:376 *illus.*
reproduction 16:161
reproductive system, human 16:164
semen 17:195
sperm bank 18:179
urethra 19:486
SPERM OIL 18:179
SPERM WHALE *see* WHALE
SPERMACETI *see* SPERM OIL
SPERMATOGENESIS
reproductive system, human 16:164
SPERMATOPHYTE 18:179
See also ALTERNATION OF GENERATIONS
SPERRY, ELMER AMBROSE 18:179 *bibliog.*
SPERRY, ROGER 18:179
brain bilateralism 3:448
SPESSARTINE
garnet 9:49
SPESSIVA, OLGA *see* SPESSIVTSEVA, OLGA ALEKSANDROVNA
SPESSIVTSEVA, OLGA ALEKSANDROVNA 18:179 *bibliog.*
SPEYER (Germany, East and West)
map (49° 19′N 8° 26′E) 9:140
SPEZIA (Italy) *see* LA SPEZIA (Italy)
SPHAGNUM *see* PEAT MOSS
SPHAIRISTIKE *see* TENNIS
SPHALERITE 18:180
hemimorphite 10:118
sulfide minerals 18:334
SPHENE 18:180
SPHENOPHYTINA
plant 15:334
SPHERE 18:180 *bibliog.*
ellipsoid 7:148
volume 19:632
SPHERICAL ABERRATION *see* ABERRATION, SPHERICAL
SPHERICAL GEOMETRY *see* GEOMETRY
SPHERICAL TRIGONOMETRY 18:180 *bibliog., illus.*
geometry 9:106 *illus.*
mathematics, history of 13:224
SPHINGOSINE 12:361 *illus.*
SPHINX 18:180 *bibliog.*
Egyptian art and architecture 7:88
Khafre, King of Egypt 12:64
SPHYGMOMANOMETER
hypertension 10:348
SPICE ISLANDS *see* MOLUCCAS (Indonesia)
SPICE TRADE 18:180–181 *bibliog.*
Asia, history of 2:256–257
Gama, Vasco da 9:24
herbs and spices 10:136–137 *illus.*
Srivijaya Empire 18:207
SPICEBUSH 18:181
SPICEBUSH SWALLOWTAIL BUTTERFLY 3:594 *illus.*
caterpillar 3:594 *illus.*
SPICES *see* HERBS AND SPICES
SPICULE 18:181
SPIDER 11:192 *illus.*; 11:469 *illus.*; 18:181–183 *bibliog., illus.*
anatomy 18:182–183 *illus.*
arachnid 2:106–107 *illus.*
arthropod 2:216–218
black widow 3:319
classification, biological 18:182
daddy longlegs 6:5
fisher spider 12:168 *illus.*
mountain life 13:623
reproduction (biology) 18:183
soil organisms 18:39 *illus.*
structure and function 18:182–183
tarantula 19:35
trap door spider 19:283
venom 19:546
web 18:181 *illus.*
SPIDER PLANT 18:183
SPIDERFLOWER 18:183
SPIDERWORT 18:183
wandering Jew 20:21
SPIELBERG, STEVEN 18:183
film, history of 8:87
SPIKENARD 18:183
SPILLANE, MICKEY 18:183
SPILSBURY, JOHN
jigsaw puzzle 11:418
SPIN (physics)
fundamental particles 8:361; 8:362
SPINA (Italy) 18:183 *bibliog.*
SPINA BIFIDA 18:183
bone diseases 3:377
nervous system, diseases of the 14:95
SPINACH 18:183–184 *illus.*; 19:532 *illus.*
SPINACH-DOCK *see* SORREL (botany)
SPINAL CORD 3:444 *illus.*; 14:93 *illus.*; 18:184 *bibliog., illus.*
gray matter 18:184 *illus.*
infectious diseases 11:167
meningitis 13:298
nerve cell 4:235 *illus.*
pain 15:15
paraplegia 15:80
physiology 18:184
skeleton, human 17:336
spine (backbone) 18:185
surgery 18:361
syringomyelia 18:414
whiplash 20:131
white matter 18:184 *illus.*
SPINAL NERVES
nervous system 14:93 *illus.*
peripheral nervous system 15:171
SPINDALE (North Carolina)
map (35° 22′N 81° 55′W) 14:242
SPINDLE
spinning 18:186
SPINDLE TREE 18:184 *illus.*
SPINE (backbone) 18:185 *bibliog., illus.*
cat 4:194 *illus.*
chiropractic 4:397
joint (anatomy) 11:439 *illus.*
lumbago 12:454
meningitis 13:298
scoliosis 17:147
spondylitis 18:192
sports medicine 18:198
surgery 18:362
tuberculosis, Pott's disease 15:473
SPINEL 18:185 *illus.*
birthstones 3:296 *table*
chromite 4:419
franklinite 8:285
magnetite 13:58
occurrence 18:185
oxide minerals 14:476; 18:185
ruby 18:185
SPINET 18:185 *illus.*
SPINK (county in South Dakota)
map (44° 55′N 98° 20′W) 18:103
SPINKS, LEON
Ali, Muhammad 1:292
SPINKS, MICHAEL
Holmes, Larry 10:205
SPINNING 18:186 *bibliog., illus.*
Arkwright, Sir Richard 2:170
Hargreaves, James 10:49
ring frame 18:186 *illus.*
Slater, Samuel 17:351
spinning wheel (15th century) 18:186 *illus.*
textile industry 19:136
SPINNING MULE 19:136 *illus.*
Crompton, Samuel 5:357
SPINOLA, ANTONIO DE
Portugal 15:452
SPINOZA, BARUCH 18:187–188 *bibliog., illus.*
pantheism 15:61
philosophy 15:245
rationalism 16:92
SPINY ANTEATER 18:188 *illus.*
monotreme 13:540–541
SPINY EEL 18:188 *illus.*
SPINY-HEADED WORM 18:188
SPIRAL 18:188 *bibliog.*
SPIREA 18:188
SPIRILLA 3:15 *illus.*
SPIRIT LAKE
map (46° 16′N 122° 8′W) 20:35
SPIRIT LAKE (Iowa)
map (43° 26′N 95° 6′W) 11:244
SPIRIT RIVER (Alberta)
map (55° 47′N 118° 50′W) 1:256
SPIRIT OF ST. LOUIS 2:370–371 *illus.*; 12:351 *illus.*
SPIRIT OF THE LAWS, THE (book) 18:188
Montesquieu, Charles Louis de Secondat, Baron de la Brède et de 13:553
SPIRITUALISM 18:189 *bibliog.*
Doyle, Sir Arthur Conan 6:253
Fox, Margaret 8:256
ghost 9:169
Houdini, Harry 10:263
SPIRITUALS 18:189 *bibliog.*
Johnson, John Rosamond 11:433
SPIRO MOUND (Oklahoma) 14:237 *map*; 18:189 *bibliog.*
stone effigy pipe 14:238 *illus.*
SPIROCHETE 18:189 *bibliog.*
parasitic, *Treponema* 19:291
relapsing fever 16:132
syphilis 18:410
SPIROGYRA 18:189
SPIROMETRY *see* PULMONARY FUNCTION TEST
SPIROSTOMUM 18:190
SPITFIRE (aircraft) 18:190 *bibliog., illus.*
engine
Rolls-Royce 16:272
World War II 20:273 *illus.*
SPITSBERGEN (Norway)
map (78° 0′N 20° 0′E) 14:261
Svalbard 18:374
SPITTELER, CARL 18:190 *bibliog.*
SPITTLEBUG 18:190 *illus.*
SPITZ (dog) 18:190 *bibliog.*
pomeranian 15:422–423
Samoyed (dog) 17:47
schipperke 17:122
SPITZ, MARK 14:384 *illus.*; 18:190 *bibliog.*
SPITZER, LYMAN, JR. 18:190–191
SPLAKE *see* CHAR
SPLEEN 1:54 *illus.*; 12:476 *illus.*; 18:191 *bibliog., illus.*
circulatory system 4:440 *illus.*
lymphatic system 12:475
SPLENOMEGALY 18:191
SPLIT (Yugoslavia) 18:191
climate 20:341 *table*
map (43° 31′N 16° 27′E) 20:340
SPLIT LAKE
map (56° 8′N 96° 15′W) 13:119
SPLIT PERSONALITY *see* SCHIZOPHRENIA
SPOCK, BENJAMIN 18:192 *bibliog., illus.*
child development 4:350
SPODUMENE
pyroxene 15:638
SPOHR, LOUIS 18:192
SPOILS SYSTEM *see* PATRONAGE
SPOKAN (American Indians) 18:192 *bibliog.*
SPOKANE (Washington) 18:192
map (47° 40′N 117° 23′W) 20:35
SPOKANE (county in Washington)
map (47° 38′N 117° 25′W) 20:35
SPOKANE, MOUNT
map (47° 55′N 117° 7′W) 20:35
SPOKANE RIVER
map (47° 44′N 118° 20′W) 20:35
SPOLETO (Italy)
map (42° 44′N 12° 44′E) 11:321
SPOLETO FESTIVAL 18:192 *bibliog.*
SPOLIN, VIOLA
acting 1:88
SPONDEE
versification 19:562
SPONDYLITIS 18:192–193
Pott's disease 15:473
SPONGE 11:229 *illus.*; 18:193–194 *bibliog., illus.*
anatomy 18:193 *illus.*
circulatory system 4:438
classification 18:193–194 *illus.*
Paleozoic Era 15:43
SPONTANEOUS ABORTION
abortion 1:60
pregnancy and birth 15:504
SPONTANEOUS COMBUSTION 18:194
SPONTANEOUS GENERATION 18:194 *bibliog.*
life 12:327
Pasteur, Louis 15:108
Spallanzani, Lazzaro 18:149
SPONTINI, GASPARE 18:194 *bibliog.*
SPOON RIVER
map (40° 18′N 90° 4′W) 11:42
SPOON RIVER ANTHOLOGY (book) 18:194 *bibliog.*
Masters, Edgar Lee 13:215–216
SPOONBILL 11:469 *illus.*; 18:194–195 *illus.*; 18:377 *illus.*
beak 3:289 *illus.*
SPOONER (Wisconsin)
map (45° 50′N 91° 53′W) 20:185
SPOONWORM 18:195
SPORANGIUM
See also ANTHER SAC
fern 8:56–57
horsetail 10:252–253 *illus.*
pollination 15:408–409
seed cone 17:187
SPORE 18:195 *bibliog.*
fungus diseases 8:369
horsetail 10:252–253 *illus.*

SPORE (cont.)
  microspore
    pollen **15**:406
  mushrooms **13**:661
  origin of life **12**:327
  pollen cone **15**:407
  pollination **15**:408
  Sporozoa **18**:195
  stinkhorn **18**:272
  tracheophyte **19**:258
SPOROPHYTE
  alternation of generations **1**:313
  plant **15**:339
  pollen **15**:406
SPOROZOA **18**:195 *bibliog.*
  malaria **13**:80
  Protozoa **15**:579–581 *illus.*
SPORT FISH *see* GAME FISH
SPORTING DOG **6**:218–219 *illus.*
  American water spaniel **1**:367
  Brittany spaniel **3**:498
  Chesapeake Bay retriever **4**:333–334
  Clumber spaniel **5**:71
  cocker spaniel **5**:86–87
  curly-coated retriever **5**:392–393
  English cocker spaniel **7**:190
  English setter **7**:204
  English springer spaniel **7**:204
  field spaniel **8**:72
  flat-coated retriever **8**:154
  game birds **9**:27
  German shorthaired pointer **9**:135
  German wirehaired pointer **9**:135
  golden retriever **9**:232
  Gordon setter **9**:250
  Irish setter **11**:269
  Irish water spaniel **11**:269
  Labrador retriever **12**:157
  pointer **15**:381
  Sussex spaniel **18**:372
  vizsla **19**:623
  Weimaraner **20**:95
  Welsh springer spaniel **20**:102
  wirehaired pointing griffon **20**:182
SPORTS, HISTORY OF **18**:195–197
    bibliog., illus.
  See also names of specific athletes, e.g., AARON, HENRY; SIMPSON, O.J.; etc.; names of specific sports, e.g., BASKETBALL; HORSE RACING; etc.
  black Americans **3**:313
  games of physical skill **9**:29
  gladiators **9**:195
  Maya ball game
    pre-Columbian art and architecture **15**:497
  National Collegiate Athletic Association **14**:30
  Olympic Games **14**:382–385 *illus.*
  pentathlon **15**:155
  sportswriting
    Rice, Grantland **16**:209
    Smith, Red **17**:370
SPORTS CARS **2**:367 *illus.*
  body design **2**:359
SPORTS ILLUSTRATED (periodical)
  Luce, Henry Robinson **12**:449–450
SPORTS MEDICINE **18**:197–198
    bibliog.
  smelling salts **17**:365
SPORTSCASTING
  Cosell, Howard **5**:280
  television production **19**:87
SPOT (fish) **18**:198
SPOTLIGHT
  stage lighting **18**:210
SPOTSWOOD (New Jersey)
  map (40° 23′N 74° 23′W) **14**:129
SPOTSWOOD, ALEXANDER **18**:198
    bibliog.
SPOTSYLVANIA (Virginia)
  map (38° 12′N 77° 35′W) **19**:607
SPOTSYLVANIA (county in Virginia)
  map (38° 15′N 77° 30′W) **19**:607
SPOTSYLVANIA COURT HOUSE, BATTLE OF
  Wilderness Campaign **20**:150
SPOTTED SKUNK *see* SKUNK
SPOTTED TAIL **18**:198 *bibliog.*
  Crazy Horse **5**:334
SPOUSE *see* MARRIAGE
SPRAGUE (Manitoba)
  map (49° 2′N 95° 38′W) **13**:119
SPRAGUE (Washington)
  map (47° 18′N 117° 59′W) **20**:35
SPRAGUE, FRANK JULIAN **18**:198
  cable car **18**:296
  technology, history of **19**:67
SPRAIN **18**:198–199
SPRAT **18**:199
SPRAY (Oregon)
  map (44° 50′N 119° 48′W) **14**:427
SPREADSHEET **18**:199
  computer **5**:160i
  computer modeling **5**:162
  computer software **5**:164 *illus.*; **5**:165
SPRECKELS, ADOLPH B.
  San Francisco art museums **17**:54
SPREE RIVER **18**:199
  map (52° 32′N 13° 13′E) **9**:140
SPRING (device) *see* SUSPENSION SYSTEM
SPRING (season) *see* SEASON
SPRING (water) **18**:199 *bibliog., illus.*
  groundwater **9**:374
  hydrologic cycle **10**:342
  mineral water **13**:444
SPRING BEAUTY (botany) **18**:199
SPRING CITY (Tennessee)
  map (35° 42′N 84° 52′W) **19**:104
SPRING CREEK RESERVOIR
  map (35° 8′N 98° 9′W) **14**:368
SPRING GARDEN (Guyana)
  map (6° 59′N 58° 31′W) **9**:410
SPRING GREEN (Wisconsin)
  map (43° 11′N 90° 4′W) **20**:185
SPRING HALL (Barbados)
  map (13° 19′N 59° 37′W) **3**:75
SPRING HILL (Tennessee)
  map (35° 45′N 86° 56′W) **19**:104
SPRING HOPE (North Carolina)
  map (35° 57′N 78° 6′W) **14**:242
SPRING LAKE (New Jersey)
  map (40° 9′N 74° 2′W) **14**:129
SPRING LAKE (North Carolina)
  map (35° 10′N 78° 58′W) **14**:242
SPRING RIVER
  map (36° 8′N 91° 5′W) **2**:166
SPRING TIDE
  tide **19**:193–194 *illus.*
SPRING VALLEY (Illinois)
  map (41° 20′N 89° 12′W) **11**:42
SPRING VALLEY (Minnesota)
  map (43° 41′N 92° 23′W) **13**:453
SPRING VALLEY (Wisconsin)
  map (44° 51′N 92° 14′W) **20**:185
SPRINGBETT, LYNN *see* SEYMOUR, LYNN
SPRINGBOK **18**:199–200 *illus.*
  horn (biology) **10**:238
SPRINGDALE (Arkansas)
  map (35° 11′N 94° 8′W) **2**:166
SPRINGDALE (Newfoundland)
  map (49° 30′N 56° 4′W) **14**:166
SPRINGDALE (Utah)
  map (37° 11′N 113° 0′W) **19**:492
SPRINGDALE (Washington)
  map (48° 4′N 117° 45′W) **20**:35
SPRINGER (New Mexico)
  map (36° 22′N 104° 36′W) **14**:136
SPRINGER SPANIEL *see* ENGLISH SPRINGER SPANIEL; WELSH SPRINGER SPANIEL
SPRINGERVILLE (Arizona)
  map (34° 8′N 109° 17′W) **2**:160
SPRINGFIELD (Colorado)
  map (37° 24′N 102° 37′W) **5**:116
SPRINGFIELD (Florida)
  map (30° 9′N 85° 37′W) **8**:172
SPRINGFIELD (Georgia)
  map (32° 22′N 81° 18′W) **9**:114
SPRINGFIELD (Illinois) **11**:43 *illus.*; **18**:200
  map (39° 47′N 89° 40′W) **11**:42
SPRINGFIELD (Kentucky)
  map (37° 41′N 85° 13′W) **12**:47
SPRINGFIELD (Louisiana)
  map (30° 26′N 90° 33′W) **12**:430
SPRINGFIELD (Massachusetts) **18**:200
  map (42° 7′N 72° 36′W) **13**:206
  Pynchon, William **15**:634
SPRINGFIELD (Minnesota)
  map (44° 14′N 94° 59′W) **13**:453
SPRINGFIELD (Missouri) **18**:200
  map (37° 14′N 93° 17′W) **13**:476
SPRINGFIELD (Ohio) **18**:200
  map (39° 56′N 83° 49′W) **14**:357
SPRINGFIELD (Oregon)
  map (44° 3′N 123° 1′W) **14**:427
SPRINGFIELD (South Dakota)
  map (42° 49′N 97° 54′W) **18**:103
SPRINGFIELD (Tennessee)
  map (36° 31′N 86° 52′W) **19**:104
SPRINGFIELD (Vermont)
  map (43° 18′N 72° 29′W) **19**:554
SPRINGHARE **18**:200 *illus.*
SPRINGHILL (Louisiana)
  map (33° 0′N 93° 28′W) **12**:430
SPRINGHILL (Nova Scotia)
  map (45° 39′N 64° 3′W) **14**:269
SPRINGHOUSE (British Columbia)
  map (51° 55′N 122° 7′W) **3**:491
SPRINGS (South Africa)
  map (26° 13′S 28° 25′E) **18**:79
SPRINGSTEEN, BRUCE **18**:200
SPRINGTAIL **11**:192 *illus.*; **18**:200
  soil organisms **18**:39 *illus.*
SPRINGVALE (Maine)
  map (43° 28′N 70° 48′W) **13**:70
SPRINGVIEW (Nebraska)
  map (42° 49′N 99° 45′W) **14**:70
SPRINGVILLE (Iowa)
  map (42° 3′N 91° 27′W) **11**:244
SPRINGVILLE (New York)
  map (42° 31′N 78° 40′W) **14**:149
SPRINGVILLE (Utah)
  map (40° 10′N 111° 37′W) **19**:492
SPRINKLER SYSTEM
  fire prevention and control **8**:104–105
  irrigation **11**:282 *illus.*
SPRINT MISSILE **2**:56 *illus.*
SPRINTING
  horse racing **10**:248
  track and field **19**:259
SPRUANCE, RAYMOND AMES **18**:200
SPRUCE **8**:229 *illus.*; **18**:200–201
    bibliog., illus.
  conifer **5**:189–191
  lumber **12**:456 *illus.*
  Norway spruce seeds **19**:287 *illus.*
  Siberian spruce **8**:229 *illus.*
  wood **20**:205 *illus.*
SPRUCE BROOK (Newfoundland)
  map (48° 45′N 58° 11′W) **14**:166
SPRUCE KNOB MOUNTAIN
  map (38° 42′N 79° 32′W) **20**:111
SPRUCE MOUNTAIN
  map (34° 28′N 112° 24′W) **2**:160
SPRUCE PINE (Alabama)
  map (34° 23′N 87° 45′W) **1**:234
SPRUCE PINE (North Carolina)
  map (35° 55′N 82° 4′W) **14**:242
SPRUCE RUN RESERVOIR
  map (40° 40′N 74° 57′W) **14**:129
SPRUE **18**:201
  gastrointestinal tract disease **9**:57
SPUR (Texas)
  map (33° 28′N 100° 52′W) **19**:129
SPURGE **18**:201 *illus.*
  poinsettia **15**:381
SPURS, TRUNCATED **12**:182 *illus.*
SPURZHEIM, JOHANNES
  phrenology **15**:278
SPUTNIK **17**:85 *illus.*; **18**:201 *bibliog., illus.*
  International Geophysical Year **11**:220
  Korolev, Sergei **12**:123
  launches **18**:201
  rockets and missiles **16**:254
  space exploration **18**:119 *illus.*
  United States, history of the **19**:458
  Venus probes **19**:539 *table*
SPUZZUM (British Columbia)
  map (49° 41′N 121° 25′W) **3**:491
SPY STORIES *see* MYSTERY, SUSPENSE, AND DETECTIVE FICTION
SPY WHO CAME IN FROM THE COLD, THE (book)
  Le Carré, John **12**:253
SPYING *see* ESPIONAGE
SPYRI, JOHANNA **18**:201
  Heidi **10**:108
SQUALL AND SQUALL LINE **18**:201–202
  cirrus clouds **4**:445
SQUAM LAKE
  map (43° 45′N 71° 32′W) **14**:123
SQUAMATA (biology)
  lizard **12**:378–382 *illus.*
  snake **17**:376–382 *illus.*
  worm lizard **20**:284 *illus.*
SQUAMISH (British Columbia)
  map (49° 42′N 123° 9′W) **3**:491
SQUANTO **18**:202 *bibliog.*
  Plymouth Colony **15**:374
SQUARCIONE, FRANCESCO **18**:202
    bibliog.
SQUARE **18**:202
  polygon **15**:419 *illus.*
  rectangle **16**:110
SQUARE DANCE **18**:202 *bibliog.*
  folk dance **8**:199
SQUARE LAKE
  map (47° 3′N 68° 20′W) **13**:70
SQUARE ROOT **18**:202
  mathematical tables **13**:221
  radical (mathematics) **16**:43
  root (mathematics) **16**:311
SQUARING (art)
  cartoon (art) **4**:176
SQUASH (game) **18**:202–203 *bibliog., illus.*
  racquetball **16**:38
SQUASH (vegetable) **18**:203 *illus.*
  pumpkin **15**:623
  winter squash **19**:532 *illus.*
SQUASH RACQUETS *see* SQUASH (game)
SQUASH TENNIS *see* SQUASH (game)
SQUATTER **18**:203
  Preemption Act **15**:502
SQUATTER SOVEREIGNTY *see* POPULAR SOVEREIGNTY
SQUAWFISH
  minnow **13**:458
SQUID **18**:203–204 *bibliog., illus.*
  biological locomotion **3**:266–267 *illus.*
  Jurassic Period **11**:476
  mollusk **13**:510; **13**:511–512 *illus.*
SQUIDS *see* SUPERCONDUCTIVITY
SQUILL **18**:204 *illus.*
SQUINCH **18**:204
  dome **6**:229 *illus.*
  Persian art and architecture **15**:185
SQUIRREL **18**:204–205 *bibliog., illus.*
  chipmunk **4**:396
  Eurasian red **8**:229 *illus.*
  flying squirrel **8**:191; **18**:204 *illus.*
  gray squirrel **8**:228 *illus.*; **18**:204 *illus.*
  groundhog **9**:373–374
  mountain life **13**:623
  prairie dog **15**:488–489
SQUIRREL MONKEY
  monkey **13**:533–534 *illus.*
SQUIRRELFISH **8**:117 *illus.*; **18**:205 *illus.*
SRAGEN (Indonesia)
  map (7° 26′S 111° 2′E) **11**:147
SRAM (STATIC RANDOM ACCESS MEMORY)
  computer **5**:160i
  computer memory **5**:161
SRBOBRAN (Yugoslavia)
  map (45° 33′N 19° 48′E) **20**:340
SREMSKA MITROVICA (Yugoslavia)
  map (44° 58′N 19° 37′E) **20**:340
SRENG RIVER
  map (13° 21′N 103° 27′E) **12**:11
SREPOK RIVER
  map (13° 33′N 106° 16′E) **12**:11
SRI LANKA **18**:205–207 *bibliog., illus., map, table*
  archaeology
    Anuradhapura **2**:72
    Polonnaruwa **15**:418
  cities
    Colombo **5**:109
    Kandy **12**:14
    Trincomalee **19**:299–300
  economic activity **18**:206 *illus.*
  education **18**:206
    South Asian universities **18**:95–96 *table*
  flag **18**:205 *illus.*
  government **18**:206
  history **18**:206–207
    Bandaranaike, Sirimavo **3**:61
    Bandaranaike, Solomon W. R. D. **3**:61
    Jayawardene, J.R. **11**:387
  land **18**:205–206 *map, table*
  languages
    Dravidian languages **6**:263
    Indo-Iranian languages **11**:145–146
  map (7° 0′N 81° 0′E) **2**:232
  mask **13**:197 *illus.*; **13**:267 *illus.*
  moonstone **13**:567
  people **18**:205–206
    caste **4**:187
    Sinhalese **17**:322–323
    Tamil **19**:19
  physical features
    Adam's Peak **1**:98
  rice **2**:246 *illus.*; **16**:208 *illus.*
  tea **19**:54
SRI PADASTANAYA *see* ADAM'S PEAK
SRIARDWY, LAKE
  map (53° 46′N 21° 44′E) **15**:388
SRINAGAR (India) **18**:207
  map (34° 5′N 74° 49′E) **11**:80
SRIRANGAPATNA
  Mysore (city in India) **13**:692
SRIVIJAYA EMPIRE **18**:207 *bibliog.*
  Asia, history of **2**:254 *map*
  Palembang (Sumatra) **15**:30
SS (Nazi Germany) **18**:207
  Gestapo **9**:159
  Himmler, Heinrich **10**:168
  Hitler, Adolf **10**:187
SST *see* SUPERSONIC TRANSPORT
SSU-JEN PANG *see* GANG OF FOUR
SSU-MA CH'IEN (Sima Qian) **18**:207
    bibliog.
  biography **3**:263
  Han **10**:34
  history **10**:184
SSU-MA HSIANG-JU (Sima Xiangru)
  Chinese literature **4**:389
SSU-MA KUANG (Sima Guang) **18**:207
    bibliog.
  history **10**:184

SSU-P'ING (China)
map (43° 12′N 124° 20′E) **4**:362
STAATLICHES BAUHAUS *see* BAUHAUS
STABAT MATER **18**:207
STABILE **18**:207–208
STABLER, KEN **18**:208
STACK (geology) **12**:182 *illus.*
STACY, HOLLIS **18**:208
STACYVILLE (Iowa)
map (43° 26′N 92° 47′W) **11**:244
STADE (Germany, East and West)
map (53° 36′N 9° 28′E) **9**:140
STADIA (surveying)
surveying **18**:368–369
STADIUM **18**:208–209 *bibliog., illus.*
STAËL, MADAME DE **18**:209 *bibliog.*
Constant, Benjamin **5**:207–208
STAËL, NICOLAS DE **18**:209 *bibliog.*
STAFF (music) **18**:209
Guido d'Arezzo **9**:394
STAFFORD (England)
map (52° 48′N 2° 7′W) **19**:403
STAFFORD (county in Kansas)
map (38° 0′N 98° 40′W) **12**:18
STAFFORD (Virginia)
map (38° 25′N 77° 24′W) **19**:607
STAFFORD (county in Virginia)
map (38° 25′N 77° 30′W) **19**:607
STAFFORD, JEAN **18**:209 *bibliog.*
STAFFORD, THOMAS P. **18**:209 *bibliog.*
Apollo program **2**:81
Apollo-Soyuz Test Project **2**:84
Gemini program **9**:72–73
STAFFORD SPRINGS (Connecticut)
map (41° 57′N 72° 18′W) **5**:193
STAFFORDSHIRE (England) **18**:209–210
cities
Stoke-on-Trent **18**:278
STAFFORDSHIRE BULL TERRIER **6**:220 *illus.*; **18**:210 *bibliog., illus.*
STAFFORDSHIRE TERRIER *see* AMERICAN STAFFORDSHIRE TERRIER
STAFFORDSHIRE WARE **18**:210 *bibliog.*
pottery and porcelain **15**:472 *illus.*
STAFFORDSVILLE (Kentucky)
map (37° 50′N 82° 50′W) **12**:47
STAG BEETLE **3**:167 *illus.*; **11**:191 *illus.*
STAGE (geology) **18**:210
STAGE (theater) *see* THEATER, HISTORY OF THE; THEATER ARCHITECTURE AND STAGING; etc.
STAGE LIGHTING **18**:210 *bibliog.*
Appia, Adolphe **2**:88
Baty, Gaston **3**:128
Irving, Sir Henry **11**:284
theater, history of the **19**:149
STAGECOACH **5**:74 *illus.*; **18**:210–211 *bibliog., illus.*; **19**:279 *illus.*
Butterfield, John **3**:593
United States stage lines, 19th century **19**:445 *map*
STAGFLATION **18**:211
economy, national **7**:50–51
inflation **11**:170
recession **16**:107
STAGG, AMOS ALONZO **18**:211 *bibliog.*
STAGGERS RAIL ACT OF 1980
railroad **16**:73
STAGNELIUS, ERIK JOHAN **18**:211 *bibliog.*
STAHL, GEORG ERNST **18**:211 *bibliog.*
animism
medicine **13**:270
phlogiston theory **14**:248
STAINED GLASS **18**:211–213 *bibliog., illus.*
architecture **2**:133
Art Nouveau **2**:211 *illus.*
cathedrals and churches **4**:206 *illus.*
Chartres Cathedral **4**:301; **18**:212 *illus.*
Cousin, Jean **5**:317
Coventry Cathedral **5**:319
Gothic art and architecture **9**:255–262
history **18**:211–212
La Farge, John **12**:145
Pechstein, Max **15**:130
rose window **16**:314
Rouault, Georges **16**:324
technique **18**:212–213
Tiffany, Louis Comfort **19**:196
window **20**:173
STAINER, SIR JOHN
English music **7**:203
STAINLESS STEEL **18**:213 *bibliog.*
flatware **8**:156
iron and steel industry **11**:278
nickel **14**:183
STAKEOUT (surveying)
surveying **18**:367–368 *illus.*
STALACTITE AND STALAGMITE **12**:334 *illus.*; **18**:213 *bibliog., illus.*
cave **4**:222–223 *illus.*
Cave of Clamouse **18**:213 *illus.*
formation **18**:213
growth rate **18**:213
STALIN (Bulgaria) *see* VARNA (Bulgaria)
STALIN, JOSEPH **5**:147 *illus.*; **18**:213–215 *bibliog., illus.*
Bukharin, Nikolai Ivanovich **3**:553
communism **5**:147–148
Europe, history of **7**:295
Great Purge **9**:321; **18**:214
Kamenev, Lev Borisovich **12**:9–10
kulaks **12**:135–136
New Economic Policy **14**:121
Pravda **15**:290
Russia/Union of Soviet Socialist Republics, history of **16**:359–360 *illus.*
socialism **18**:22
Trotsky, Leon **19**:310–311
World War II **18**:214; **20**:249–275 *illus.*
Yalta Conference **19**:455 *illus.*; **20**:315 *illus.*
Zinoviev, Grigory Yevseyevich **20**:369
STALIN INTERNATIONAL PEACE PRIZE *see* this heading under the subject discipline for which the prize is given
STALIN PEAK (USSR) *see* COMMUNISM PEAK
STALIN PRIZE *see* this heading under the subject discipline for which the prize is given
STALINABAD (USSR) *see* DUSHANBE (USSR)
STALINGRAD (USSR) *see* VOLGOGRAD (USSR)
STALINGRAD, BATTLE OF **16**:360 *illus.*; **18**:215 *bibliog., map*
World War II **20**:264 *illus.*; **20**:270 *map*
STALINO (USSR) *see* DONETSK (USSR)
STAMBOLISKI, ALEKSANDR **18**:215
STAMBOLOV, STEFAN **18**:215
STAMEN
pollen **15**:406
STAMFORD (Connecticut) **18**:215–216
map (41° 3′N 73° 32′W) **5**:193
STAMFORD (New York)
map (42° 25′N 74° 37′W) **14**:149
STAMFORD BRIDGE, BATTLE OF (Yorkshire)
Harold II, King of England **10**:54
Harold III, King of Norway (Harold Hardrada) **10**:54
STAMITZ (family) **18**:216 *bibliog.*
STAMMERING *see* STUTTERING
STAMOS, THEODOROS **18**:216 *bibliog.*
STAMP ACT **1**:354 *illus.*; **18**:216 *bibliog.*
Franklin, Benjamin **8**:283–284
Otis, James **14**:460
Sons of Liberty **18**:66
United States, history of the **19**:439 *illus.*
STAMP ACT CONGRESS
Stamp Act **18**:216
United States, history of the **19**:439
STAMP COLLECTING *see* PHILATELY
STAMPS (Arkansas)
map (33° 22′N 93° 30′W) **2**:166
STANAFORD (West Virginia)
map (37° 49′N 81° 10′W) **20**:111
STANARDSVILLE (Virginia)
map (38° 18′N 78° 26′W) **19**:607
STANAVOI RANGE
map (56° 20′N 126° 0′E) **19**:388
STANBERRY (Missouri)
map (40° 13′N 94° 35′W) **13**:476
STANDARD DEVIATION **18**:216 *bibliog.*
psychological measurement **15**:593
variance and covariance **19**:523
STANDARD METROPOLITAN STATISTICAL AREA
metropolitan area **13**:347
STANDARD OIL COMPANY OF OHIO
Rockefeller (family) **16**:250
STANDARD OIL OF NEW JERSEY
Rockefeller (family) **16**:250
STANDARD OIL TRUST
petroleum industry **15**:214
STANDARD OF UR (decorated plaque)
detail from **2**:249 *illus.*; **13**:316 *illus.*; **20**:127 *illus.*
STANDARDBRED **10**:243 *illus.*; **18**:216–217 *bibliog., illus.*
horse racing **10**:248 *illus.*
STANDING WAVE **18**:217 *bibliog., illus.*
water wave **20**:57
waves and wave motion **20**:72
STANDISH (Michigan)
map (43° 59′N 83° 57′W) **13**:377
STANDISH, MYLES **18**:217 *bibliog.*
Mayflower **13**:247
STANFIELD (Oregon)
map (45° 47′N 119° 13′W) **14**:427
STANFIELD, ROBERT LORNE **18**:217
STANFORD (Kentucky)
map (37° 32′N 84° 40′W) **12**:47
STANFORD (Montana)
map (47° 9′N 110° 13′W) **13**:547
STANFORD, SIR CHARLES VILLIERS **18**:217 *bibliog.*
STANFORD, LELAND **18**:217 *bibliog.*
film, history of **8**:81
Muybridge, Eadweard **13**:687–688 *illus.*
STANFORD-BINET TEST **18**:217–218
Binet, Alfred **3**:258
child development **4**:349
consistency of results **18**:218
intelligence **11**:203
psychological measurement **15**:593
STANFORD LINEAR ACCELERATOR CENTER **18**:218 *bibliog.*
STANFORD UNIVERSITY **18**:218
Stanford, Leland **18**:217
Stanford Linear Accelerator Center **18**:218
STANHOPE, PHILIP DORMER, 4TH EARL OF CHESTERFIELD *see* CHESTERFIELD, PHILIP DORMER STANHOPE, 4TH EARL OF
STANISLAUS, SAINT **18**:218
STANISLAUS (county in California)
map (37° 39′N 121° 0′W) **4**:31
STANISLAVSKY, KONSTANTIN **18**:218 *bibliog., illus.*
method acting **13**:343
Actors Studio **1**:90
theory of acting **1**:86–88 *illus.*
Moscow Art Theater **13**:599
STANISLAVSKY METHOD *see* METHOD ACTING
STANISŁAW I, KING OF POLAND **18**:218
Polish Succession, War of the **15**:398
STANISŁAW II, KING OF POLAND **18**:219 *bibliog.*
STANKE DIMITROV (Bulgaria)
map (42° 16′N 23° 7′E) **3**:555
STANKIEWICZ, RICHARD **18**:219 *bibliog.*
STANLEY (Falkland Islands)
map (51° 42′S 57° 51′W) **2**:149
STANLEY (New Brunswick)
map (46° 17′N 66° 44′W) **14**:117
STANLEY (North Dakota)
map (48° 19′N 102° 23′W) **14**:248
STANLEY (county in South Dakota)
map (44° 28′N 100° 48′W) **18**:103
STANLEY (Wisconsin)
map (44° 58′N 90° 56′W) **20**:185
STANLEY, EDWARD, 14TH EARL OF DERBY *see* DERBY, EDWARD STANLEY, 14TH EARL OF
STANLEY, SIR HENRY MORTON **1**:157 *illus.*; **18**:219 *bibliog., illus.*
Africa **1**:157 *map*
Edward, Lake **7**:67
Emin Pasha **7**:156
exploration **7**:337–338 *map*
Kinshasa (Zaire) **12**:85
Kisangani **12**:90
Livingstone, David **12**:377–378
Uganda **19**:373
Zaire **20**:352
STANLEY, J. K.
bicycle **3**:244
STANLEY, WENDELL MEREDITH **18**:219 *bibliog.*
STANLEY, WILLIAM **18**:219 *bibliog.*
STANLEY CUP CHAMPIONS
ice hockey **11**:12 *table*
STANLEY FALLS
map (0° 30′N 25° 12′E) **20**:350
STANLEY STEAMER (automobile) **2**:365 *illus.*
STANLEYVILLE (Belgian Congo) *see* KISANGANI (Zaire)
STANLY (county in North Carolina)
map (35° 20′N 80° 15′W) **14**:242
STANN CREEK (Belize)
map (16° 58′N 88° 13′W) **3**:183
STANNUS, EDRIS *see* VALOIS, DAME NINETTE DE
STANOVOI RANGE **18**:219–220
STANTON (Iowa)
map (40° 59′N 95° 6′W) **11**:244
STANTON (county in Kansas)
map (37° 35′N 101° 45′W) **12**:18
STANTON (Kentucky)
map (37° 54′N 83° 52′W) **12**:47
STANTON (Michigan)
map (43° 18′N 85° 5′W) **13**:377
STANTON (Nebraska)
map (41° 57′N 97° 14′W) **14**:70
STANTON (county in Nebraska)
map (41° 55′N 97° 15′W) **14**:70
STANTON (North Dakota)
map (47° 19′N 101° 23′W) **14**:248
STANTON (Texas)
map (32° 8′N 101° 48′W) **19**:129
STANTON, EDWIN M. **18**:220 *bibliog., illus.*
Tenure of Office Act **19**:113
STANTON, ELIZABETH CADY **18**:220 *bibliog., illus.*
Blatch, Harriot Eaton Stanton **3**:328
suffrage, women's **18**:326
STANTON, FRANK
radio and television broadcasting **16**:59
STANTONSBURG (North Carolina)
map (35° 37′N 77° 49′W) **14**:242
STANWYCK, BARBARA **18**:220
STANZA
versification **19**:562
STAPHYLOCOCCUS **18**:220
boil **3**:362
chemical and biological warfare **4**:312
food poisoning and infection **8**:211
mastitis **13**:217
respiratory system disorders **16**:181
skin diseases **17**:342
sty **18**:311
STAPLE ACT OF 1663
Navigation Acts **14**:61
STAPLES (Minnesota)
map (46° 21′N 94° 48′W) **13**:453
STAPLETON (Nebraska)
map (41° 29′N 100° 31′W) **14**:70
STAR **18**:221–226 *bibliog., illus.*
aberration, stellar **1**:57
Airy Disk **1**:228
astronomy and astrophysics **2**:283
astrophotography **2**:285; **18**:221–222
Barnard's Star **3**:86
Big Dipper **3**:249
binary stars **3**:256–257
black dwarf **3**:314
black hole **3**:315–316
brightest stars **18**:225 *table*
carbon star **4**:136–137
celestial mechanics **4**:230
Cepheids **4**:257
Chandrasekhar limit **4**:280
classifications
color index **5**:114
Harvard classification of stars **10**:64
population, stellar **15**:437
cluster, star **5**:72
composition **18**:222
degenerate matter **6**:85
distance, astronomical **6**:199
energy conversion **7**:172
extinction **7**:341
flare star **8**:153
Galaxy, The **9**:10–13
Gamow, George **9**:34–35
Gill, Sir David **9**:181
gravitational collapse **9**:305
gravitational lens **9**:305–306
Halley, Edmond **10**:22–23
Hayashi evolutionary track **10**:80
Herschel, Sir John **10**:147
Hertzsprung-Russell diagram **10**:149–150
Hyades **10**:327
interstellar matter **11**:225–228
interstellar reddening **11**:229
Lyra **12**:479
magnetic star **13**:55
magnitude **13**:60–61
main sequence **13**:68–69
carbon cycle (astronomy) **4**:135–136
mass, determination
Kepler's laws **12**:58
mass-luminosity relation **13**:203
meteor and meteorite **13**:336–337
Michelson, Albert Abraham **13**:375–376
nearest stars **18**:225 *table*
nebula **14**:74–75
neutron star **14**:109
nova **14**:268
occultation **14**:320

STAR (cont.)
Olbers's paradox **14**:373
optics, OAO **14**:313
Orion (astronomy) **14**:444
Orion nebula **14**:444–445
parallax **15**:78–79
period-luminosity relation **15**:166
photometry, astronomical **15**:274
photosphere **15**:275
planetary nebula **15**:329
plasma physics **15**:346
Polaris (astronomy) **15**:393
population, stellar **15**:437
position determinant, declination **6**:76
proper motion **15**:570
Proxima Centauri **15**:584
pulsar **15**:620–621
pulsating stars **15**:621
quasar **16**:14–15
radial velocity
Campbell, William Wallace **4**:66
Huggins, Sir William **10**:292
radio astronomy **16**:50
RR Lyrae stars **16**:332
Schwarzschild radius **17**:139
sidereal time **17**:294
Sirius **17**:328
size **18**:224 *illus.*
spectral type **18**:222
star catalog
Argelander, Friedrich Wilhelm August **2**:146
Henry Draper Catalogue **10**:123
stellar evolution **18**:250–252
stellar spectrum **18**:252
Strömgren, Bengt Georg Daniel **18**:302
structure **18**:224–226
subdwarf **18**:313
subgiant **18**:313
Sun **18**:340–345
supergiant **18**:351
supernova **18**:352
T Tauri stars **19**:3
temperature **18**:222; **18**:225
Trumpler, Robert Julius **19**:320
variable star **19**:522–523
white dwarf **20**:137
Wolf-Rayet stars **20**:197
STAR (North Carolina)
map (35° 24′N 79° 47′W) **14**:242
STAR OF AFRICA DIAMOND **6**:152 *illus.*
STAR CARR (England) **18**:226 *bibliog.*
Clark, Grahame **5**:38
STAR CHAMBER **18**:226
STAR CITY (Arkansas)
map (33° 56′N 91° 51′W) **2**:166
STAR CITY (Indiana)
map (40° 58′N 86° 33′W) **11**:111
STAR OF DAVID **18**:226
STAR-OF-BETHLEHEM (botany) **18**:226
"STAR-SPANGLED BANNER, THE" **18**:226 *bibliog.*
Fort McHenry **8**:237
Key, Francis Scott **12**:62
War of 1812 **20**:27
STAR WARS (defense) *see* STRATEGIC DEFENSE INITIATIVE
STAR WARS (film) **8**:87 *illus.*
STARA PAZOVA (Yugoslavia)
map (44° 59′N 20° 10′E) **20**:340
STARA ZAGORA (Bulgaria)
map (42° 25′N 25° 38′E) **3**:555
STARACHOWICE (Poland)
map (51° 3′N 21° 4′E) **15**:388
STARBUCK (Manitoba)
map (49° 46′N 97° 36′W) **13**:119
STARBUCK (Minnesota)
map (45° 37′N 95° 32′W) **13**:453
STARČEVO
European prehistory **7**:301
STARCH **18**:226 *bibliog.*
carbohydrate **4**:132
diet, human **6**:164
digestion, human **6**:172
metabolism **13**:325
metabolism, plant **13**:327
monosaccharide **13**:540
photosynthesis **15**:276
polysaccharide **15**:422–421
sago **17**:12
wheat **20**:126
whiskey **20**:133
STARE DECISIS *see* PRECEDENT (law)
STARÉ HRADISKO (Czechoslovakia)
European prehistory **7**:306
STARFISH **18**:226–227 *bibliog., illus.*
coral reef **5**:260
echinoderm **7**:37–38 *illus.*
intertidal life **11**:229 *illus.*
regeneration **16**:127 *illus.*
STARGARD SZCZECIŃSKI (Poland)
map (53° 20′N 15° 2′E) **15**:388
STARGAZER (fish) **18**:227
STARK (county in Illinois)
map (41° 6′N 89° 45′W) **11**:42
STARK (county in North Dakota)
map (46° 50′N 102° 40′W) **14**:248
STARK (county in Ohio)
map (40° 48′N 81° 22′W) **14**:357
STARK, JOHANNES **18**:227 *bibliog.*
Einstein, Albert **7**:94
photochemistry **15**:257
STARK, JOHN **18**:227 *bibliog.*
Bennington (Vermont) **3**:204
STARK, RICHARD (pseudonym) *see* WESTLAKE, DONALD E.
STARKE (Florida)
map (29° 57′N 82° 7′W) **8**:172
STARKE (county in Indiana)
map (41° 18′N 86° 37′W) **11**:111
STARKVILLE (Mississippi)
map (33° 28′N 88° 48′W) **13**:469
STARLING **18**:227 *illus.*
mynah **13**:690
oxpecker **14**:476
rose-colored starling **18**:257 *illus.*
STARLING, ERNEST HENRY **18**:227
Bayliss, Sir William **3**:133
biology **3**:270
STAROGARD GDAŃSKI (Poland)
map (53° 59′N 18° 33′E) **15**:388
STAROV, IVAN
Russian art and architecture **16**:362
STARR (county in Texas)
map (26° 35′N 98° 45′W) **19**:129
STARR, BART **18**:227–228 *bibliog.*
STARR, BELLE **18**:228 *bibliog.*
STARR, RINGO
Beatles, The **3**:144–145 *illus.*
STARSPOTS **18**:224
START (Strategic Arms Reduction Talks)
arms control **2**:178
STARTER
internal-combustion engine **11**:215–216
STARVATION **18**:228 *bibliog.*
anorexia nervosa **2**:34
famine **8**:18–19
gastrointestinal tract disease **9**:57
nutritional-deficiency diseases **14**:307–308
STARWORTS *see* ASTER
STAS, JEAN SERVAIS **18**:228
STASSEN, HAROLD E. **18**:228 *bibliog.*
STASSOV, VLADIMIR
Five, The **8**:132
Russian music **16**:367
STATE (in political philosophy) **18**:228–233 *bibliog., illus.*
absolutism **1**:63
anarchism **1**:392
aristocracy **2**:155
authoritarianism **2**:354–355
Bodin, Jean **3**:356
Burke, Edmund **3**:571
communism **5**:146–150
democracy **6**:97–98
despotism **6**:132
dictatorship **6**:159
Europe, history of **7**:280–281
fascism **8**:30
federalism **8**:43
Hegel, Georg Wilhelm Friedrich **10**:106
Hobbes, Thomas **10**:192
Holy Roman Empire, theory of the **10**:209–210
junta **11**:471
Locke, John **12**:308
Machiavelli, Niccolò **13**:18–19
Marsilius of Padua **13**:173
Marxism **13**:183–184
Mill, John Stuart **13**:427
On Liberty **14**:388
monarchy **13**:517
Montesquieu, Charles Louis de Secondat, Baron de la Brède **13**:553
nationalism **14**:46–47
nazism **14**:67–68
oligarchy **14**:377
pluralism **15**:372
police state **15**:397
Prince, The **15**:547
radicalism **16**:43–44
republic **16**:172
Rousseau, Jean Jacques **16**:325–327
social contract **18**:11
socialism **18**:19–24
Socratic dialogues
Crito **5**:352
Spirit of the Laws, The **18**:188
syndicalism **18**:407
totalitarianism **19**:248
STATE (political unit) **18**:228
sovereignty **18**:113
United States
federalism in the U.S. Constitution **5**:214
finance, state and local **8**:92
governor **9**:272
housing **10**:279
police **15**:396
revenue sharing **16**:185
social and welfare services **18**:17–18
state rights **18**:233–234
STATE, COUNTY, AND MUNICIPAL EMPLOYEES *see* AMERICAN FEDERATION OF STATE, COUNTY, AND MUNICIPAL EMPLOYEES
STATE, U.S. DEPARTMENT OF **18**:233 *bibliog.*
secretary of state
See also articles of specific presidents, e.g., JEFFERSON, THOMAS; NIXON, RICHARD M.; etc.; names of specific secretaries of state, e.g., ACHESON, DEAN; WEBSTER, DANIEL; etc.
flag **8**:148 *illus.*
Washington, D.C. **20**:41 *map*
STATE ATTORNEY *see* PROSECUTING ATTORNEY
STATE CENTER (Iowa)
map (42° 1′N 93° 10′W) **11**:244
STATE COLLEGE (Mississippi)
map (33° 26′N 88° 47′W) **13**:469
STATE COLLEGE (Pennsylvania)
map (40° 48′N 77° 52′W) **15**:147
STATE LINE (Mississippi)
map (31° 26′N 88° 28′W) **13**:469
STATE MEDICINE
Chinese medicine **4**:391
STATE RIGHTS **18**:233–234 *bibliog.*
Calhoun, John C. **4**:29
Civil War, U.S. **5**:15
Cohens v. *Virginia* **5**:95–96
Democratic party **6**:100
Henry, Patrick **10**:123
Jackson, Andrew **11**:342
Johnson, Andrew **11**:431
Kentucky and Virginia Resolutions **12**:51–52
Luther v. *Borden* **12**:469
McCulloch v. *Maryland* **13**:11
marriage **13**:166
martial law **13**:178
nullification **14**:292
South Carolina **18**:101
10th Amendment **19**:113
Tyler, John **19**:361–362
STATEMENT, FINANCIAL *see* FINANCIAL STATEMENT
STATEN ISLAND (New York City) **18**:234
map (40° 35′N 74° 9′W) **14**:129
STATENVILLE (Georgia)
map (30° 42′N 83° 2′W) **9**:114
STATES-GENERAL **18**:234 *bibliog.*
Europe, history of **7**:290
France, history of **8**:267; **8**:270
French Revolution **8**:322
Loménie de Brienne, Étienne Charles de **12**:399
Louis XVI, King of France **12**:428
Mirabeau, Honoré Gabriel Riqueti, Comte de **13**:462
parlement **15**:92
STATESBORO (Georgia)
map (32° 27′N 81° 47′W) **9**:114
STATESVILLE (North Carolina)
map (35° 47′N 80° 53′W) **14**:242
STATIC **18**:234 *bibliog.*
noise **14**:213
STATIC ELECTRICITY **18**:234 *bibliog.*
electrostatics **7**:128
Galvani, Luigi **9**:23
STATIC RANDOM ACCESS MEMORY *see* SRAM
STATICE *see* SEA LAVENDER
STATICS **18**:234–235 *bibliog.*
force **8**:220
laws of motion **12**:251
STATION FOR EXPERIMENTAL EVOLUTION *see* CARNEGIE INSTITUTION OF WASHINGTON
STATION WAGON
body design **2**:359
STATIONARY WAVE *see* STANDING WAVE
STATIONS OF THE CROSS **18**:235
STATISTICAL LINGUISTICS
linguistics **12**:358
STATISTICAL MECHANICS
kinetic theory of matter **12**:78–79
mechanical engineering **13**:259–260
physics **15**:280–281
statistical thermodynamics **18**:235
STATISTICAL THERMODYNAMICS **18**:235 *bibliog.*
gaseous state **9**:54
physical chemistry **15**:279
thermodynamics **19**:165
STATISTICS **18**:235–237 *bibliog., illus., table*
biomathematics **3**:272
central limit theorem **4**:254
chance **18**:236
Chi-square distribution **4**:339
correlation and regression **5**:276
data relationships **18**:236–237
decision theory **6**:73–74
distribution **6**:200–201
econometrics **7**:46–47
error **7**:235
factor analysis **8**:6
Fisher, Sir Ronald Aylmer **8**:122–123
geography **9**:102–103
graph **9**:290–291
gross national product **9**:371
histogram **10**:180
hypothesis testing and estimation **18**:236
industrial management **11**:156; **11**:157
inference (mathematics) **11**:168
large numbers, law of **12**:207
least-squares method **12**:262
magic square **13**:51
mean **13**:252–253
measurement of crime **5**:346
measurement of suicide **18**:330–331
median **13**:264
mode (mathematics) **13**:489
Neyman, Jerzy **14**:175
normal distribution **14**:219
null hypothesis **14**:292
paleontology: Simpson, George Gaylord **17**:317
permutation and combination **15**:176
probability **18**:236
professional and educational organizations **17**:145 *table*
psychology, history of **15**:597
Quételet, Lambert Adolphe **16**:23
sampling **17**:48
standard deviation **18**:216
statistical design **18**:236
statistical procedures **18**:236
t-test **19**:3
tree diagram **19**:288–289
variance and covariance **19**:523
weight (mathematics) **20**:92
STATISTICS, NONPARAMETRIC **18**:237–238 *bibliog.*
STATIUS **18**:238
STATLER, ELLSWORTH MILTON **18**:238 *bibliog.*
STATLER HOTELS
hotel **10**:261–262
STATO-REACTOR *see* RAMJET
STATOR **18**:238
armature **2**:171
generator **9**:78
STATUE OF LIBERTY **4**:249 *illus.*; **14**:146 *illus.*; **18**:238 *bibliog., illus.*; **19**:430 *illus.*
Bartholdi, Frédéric Auguste **3**:97
Iacocca, Lee **11**:3
Lazarus, Emma **12**:252
STATUE OF ZEUS AT OLYMPIA *see* ZEUS, STATUE OF, AT OLYMPIA
STATUS **18**:238–239 *bibliog.*
class, social **5**:40–41
Roman law **16**:279
STATUS OFFENSE
crime **5**:347
STATUTE OF LIMITATIONS **18**:239 *bibliog.*
equity **7**:226
STATUTE OF PATENTS AND MONOPOLIES (England)
invention **11**:232
STATUTE OF WILLS *see* WILLS, STATUTE OF
STAUBACH, ROGER **18**:239 *bibliog.*
STAUDINGER, HERMANN **18**:239
STAUDT, K. G. C. VON
mathematics, history of **13**:226
STAUNTON (Illinois)
map (39° 1′N 89° 47′W) **11**:42
STAUNTON (Virginia)
map (38° 9′N 79° 4′W) **19**:607
STAUROLITE **18**:239
STAVANGER (Norway) **18**:239
map (58° 58′N 5° 45′E) **14**:261
STAVE (music) *see* STAFF (music)
STAVE CHURCHES

Scandinavian art and architecture **17**:11–112 *illus.*
STAVISKY, SERGE ALEXANDRE
Stavisky affair **18**:239
STAVISKY AFFAIR **18**:239 *bibliog.*
STAVROPOL (USSR) *see* TOGLIATTI (USSR)
STAYTON (Oregon)
map (44° 48′N 122° 48′W) **14**:427
STEAD, CHRISTINA **18**:239–240 *bibliog.*
STEADY-STATE THEORY **18**:240
Bondi, Hermann **3**:376
cosmogony **5**:284
cosmology (astronomy) **5**:289
creation accounts **5**:335
Hoyle, Sir Fred **10**:286
STEALTH BOMBER **18**:240
STEAM
boiler **3**:362–363
generation
incinerator **11**:74
steam plants
condenser **5**:172
STEAM AUTOMOBILE
automotive industry **2**:363
STEAM ENGINE **18**:240–241 *bibliog., illus.*
Boulton, Matthew **3**:422
engineering **7**:178
Evans, Oliver **7**:313
feedback **8**:44 *illus.*
fire engine **8**:101–102 *illus.*
fuel **8**:353
Guericke, Otto von **9**:391
Industrial Revolution **11**:159
locomotive **12**:388–390 *illus.*
mill **13**:425
Murdock, William **13**:648
naval vessels **14**:55
Newcomen, Thomas, inventor **14**:165; **18**:240–241
Newcomen steam engine **11**:158 *illus.*
Papin, Denis **15**:71
reciprocating **18**:240
Regnault, Henri Victor **16**:129
Savery, Thomas **17**:99; **18**:240–241
ship **17**:272
steam turbines **18**:240
technology, history of **19**:65–68 *illus.*
tractor **19**:262
Trevithick, Richard **18**:241; **19**:291
turbine **19**:340
Watt, James **18**:240–241; **20**:68–69
Wedgwood, Josiah **20**:90
Wilkinson, John **20**:153
STEAM TURBINE **19**:340 *illus.*
STEAMBOAT **18**:242 *bibliog., illus.*
Brunel (family) **3**:524
Clermont **5**:51–52 *illus.*
Cunard, Sir Samuel **5**:389
Fitch, John **8**:129
Fulton, Robert **8**:358
Mississippi River **13**:474
paddlewheel **11**:112 *illus.*
Saône River **17**:72
Savannah (steamship) **17**:99
showboats **17**:286
steamship **17**:272–274
Stevens (family) **18**:263
technology, history of **19**:67 *illus.*
tourism **19**:252
transportation **19**:278
STEAMBOAT SPRINGS (Colorado)
map (40° 29′N 106° 50′W) **5**:116
STEAMER (automobile) *see* STANLEY STEAMER (automobile); STEAM AUTOMOBILE
STEAMSHIP *see* OCEAN LINER; STEAMBOAT
STEARIN **18**:242
STEARNS (Kentucky)
map (36° 42′N 84° 28′W) **12**:47
STEARNS (county in Minnesota)
map (45° 30′N 94° 35′W) **13**:453
STEARNS, JUNIUS BRUTUS
Constitutional Convention **5**:213 *illus.*
STEATITE *see* TALC
STEDMAN, EDMUND CLARENCE **18**:242
STEEL, DAVID MARTIN SCOTT **18**:243
STEEL BAND **18**:243
STEEL INDUSTRY *see* IRON AND STEEL INDUSTRY
STEEL WORKERS ORGANIZING COMMITTEE
United Steelworkers of America **19**:465
STEELE (county in Minnesota)
map (44° 0′N 93° 13′W) **13**:453
STEELE (Missouri)
map (36° 5′N 89° 50′W) **13**:476
STEELE (North Dakota)
map (46° 51′N 99° 55′W) **14**:248
STEELE (county in North Dakota)
map (47° 30′N 97° 40′W) **14**:248
STEELE, SIR RICHARD **18**:243 *bibliog.*
STEELVILLE (Missouri)
map (37° 58′N 91° 22′W) **13**:476
STEELWORKERS OF AMERICA, UNITED *see* UNITED STEELWORKERS OF AMERICA
STEEN, JAN **18**:243 *bibliog., illus.*
Leiden (Netherlands) **12**:277
Woman Undressing **18**:243 *illus.*
STEENS MOUNTAIN
map (42° 35′N 118° 40′W) **14**:427
STEENWINCKEL, HANS AND LOURENS
Frederiksborg Castle **17**:112 *illus.*
STEEP POINT
map (26° 8′S 113° 8′E) **2**:328
STEEP ROCK (Manitoba)
map (51° 26′N 98° 48′W) **13**:119
STEEPLECHASE **18**:243–244 *bibliog., illus.*
horse racing **10**:248
track and field **19**:260
STEER-WRESTLING
rodeo **16**:266–267
STEERING SYSTEM **18**:244–245 *bibliog., illus.*
automobile **2**:358–359
rudder **16**:337–338
suspension system **18**:371–372
STEFAN, JOSEF **18**:245
blackbody radiation **3**:320–321
STEFAN-BOLTZMANN LAW
blackbody radiation **3**:320–321
STEFANIE, LAKE
map (4° 40′N 36° 50′E) **7**:253
STEFANSSON, VILHJALMUR **18**:245 *bibliog.*
Arctic **2**:142 *map*
STEFFENS, LINCOLN **18**:245 *bibliog.*
STEG (Liechtenstein)
map (47° 21′N 8° 56′E) **12**:325
STEGER (Illinois)
map (41° 29′N 87° 41′W) **11**:42
STEGG, THOMAS
Richmond (Virginia) **16**:214
STEGNER, WALLACE **18**:245 *bibliog.*
STEGOSAURUS **11**:475 *illus.*; **16**:170 *illus.*; **18**:246 *bibliog., illus.*
dinosaur **6**:181
STEICHEN, EDWARD **15**:257 *illus.*; **18**:246 *bibliog., illus.*
Steeplechase Day, Paris: After the Races **15**:270 *illus.*
STEIERMARK *see* STYRIA (Austria)
STEIGER, ROD **18**:246
STEIN, SIR AUREL **18**:246
Lop Nor (China) **12**:412
Tun-huang (Dunhuang) **19**:331
STEIN, GERTRUDE **18**:247 *bibliog., illus.*
Autobiography of Alice B. Toklas, The **2**:356
Thomson, Virgil **19**:177
STEIN, HEINRICH FRIEDRICH KARL, FREIHERR VOM UND ZUM **18**:247 *bibliog., illus.*
STEIN, JOHANN ANDREAS
piano **15**:288
STEIN, LEO
Stein, Gertrude **18**:247
STEIN, WILLIAM HOWARD **18**:247
STEINBACH (Manitoba)
map (49° 32′N 96° 41′W) **13**:119
STEINBECK, JOHN **18**:248 *bibliog., illus.*
Grapes of Wrath, The **9**:290
Of Mice and Men **14**:352
STEINBERG, SAUL **18**:248 *bibliog.*
STEINBERG, WILLIAM **18**:248 *bibliog.*
Berkshire Music Festival **3**:214
STEINEM, GLORIA **18**:248–249 *illus.*
Ms. **13**:629
STEINER, JACOB
mathematics, history of **13**:226
STEINER, RUDOLF **18**:249 *bibliog.*
theosophy **19**:159–160
STEINERT, OTTO **18**:249
STEINHEIM MAN **2**:53 *illus.*; **18**:249 *bibliog.*
Fontéchevade man **8**:207
STEINKJER (Norway)
map (64° 1′N 11° 30′E) **14**:261
STEINKRAUS, BILL **18**:249
STEINMETZ, CHARLES PROTEUS **18**:249 *bibliog., illus.*
STELE **18**:250
Bennett Stele (Tiahuanaco) **19**:188
Hammurabi and Shamash **2**:249 *illus.*; **13**:320 *illus.*
Maya **14**:231 *illus.*
mythology **13**:698 *illus.*
Piedras Negras **15**:295
pre-Columbian art and architecture **15**:496–497 *illus.*
Quiriguá **16**:27
STELLA, FRANK **18**:250 *bibliog., illus.*
Quathlamba **18**:250 *illus.*
Sinjerli Variation IV **2**:191 *illus.*
STELLA, JOSEPH **18**:250 *bibliog.*
STELLAR EVOLUTION **18**:222 *illus.*; **18**:250–252 *bibliog., illus.*
astronomy and astrophysics **2**:284–285
binary stars **3**:257
black dwarf **3**:314
black hole **3**:315–316; **18**:251–252
brown dwarf **3**:516
carbon cycle (astronomy) **4**:135–136
carbon star **4**:136–137
Chandrasekhar limit **4**:280; **18**:251
cluster, star **5**:72
corona **5**:270
cosmology (astronomy) **5**:284–289
degenerate matter **6**:85
Eddington, Sir Arthur **7**:55
flare star **8**:153
Galaxy, The **9**:10–13
Gamow, George **9**:34
Harvard classification of stars **10**:64
Hertzsprung, Ejnar **10**:149
Hertzsprung-Russell diagram **10**:149–150
Hoyle, Sir Fred **10**:286
interstellar matter **11**:225–228
Lockyer, Sir Joseph Norman **12**:388
main sequence **13**:68–69; **18**:250
Milne, Edward Arthur **13**:431
neutron star **14**:109; **18**:251
nova **14**:268
population, stellar **15**:437
pulsating stars **15**:621; **18**:251
quasar **16**:14–15
Russell, Henry Norris **16**:350
Schwarzschild, Karl **17**:139
Schwarzschild, Martin **17**:139
star life **18**:250–252
Struve, Otto **18**:304
supernova **18**:352
Trumpler, Robert Julius **19**:320
white dwarf **18**:251; **20**:137
Wolf-Rayet stars **20**:197
STELLAR POPULATION *see* POPULATION, STELLAR
STELLAR SPECTRUM **18**:252 *bibliog., illus.*
Cannon, Annie Jump **4**:112
carbon star **4**:136–137
Draper, Henry **6**:262–263
Fraunhofer lines **8**:288–289
Hertzsprung-Russell diagram **10**:149
Huggins, Sir William **10**:292
interstellar matter **11**:226 *illus.*
Pickering, Edward Charles **15**:293
quasar **16**:14–15
red shift **16**:114
Saha, Meghnad N. **17**:12–13
star **18**:223 *illus.*
starlight **18**:252
STEM (botany)
plant **15**:333–336 *illus.*
shoot (botany) **17**:282
STENCIL
silk-screen printing **17**:308
STENDAHL, KRISTER **18**:252
STENDAL (Germany, East and West)
map (52° 36′N 11° 51′E) **9**:140
STENDHAL **18**:252–253 *bibliog., illus.*
Red and the Black, The **16**:112
STENEOSAURUS **11**:476 *illus.*
STENGEL, CASEY **18**:253 *bibliog.*
STENO, NICOLAUS (pseudonym) **18**:253 *bibliog.*
crystal **5**:374
mineral **13**:439
geology **9**:106
stratigraphy **18**:292
STENOGRAPHY *see* SHORTHAND
STENOTYPE MACHINE
shorthand **17**:284
STENSON, NIELS *see* STENO, NICOLAUS (pseudonym)
STENTOR **18**:253
STEPHEN, GEORGE **18**:254 *bibliog.*
Canadian Pacific Railway **4**:94
STEPHEN, KING OF ENGLAND **18**:254 *bibliog.*
Matilda **13**:228
STEPHEN, SIR LESLIE **18**:254 *bibliog.*
STEPHEN, SAINT **13**:520 *illus.*; **18**:254 *bibliog.*
STEPHEN I, KING OF HUNGARY (Saint Stephen) **18**:254
Esztergom (Hungary) **7**:248
Hungary **10**:309
STEPHEN II, POPE
Italy, history of **11**:327
STEPHEN BÁTHORY, KING OF POLAND
Báthory (family) **3**:123
STEPHEN DUŠAN, KING OF SERBIA **18**:254
STEPHEN THE GREAT, PRINCE OF MOLDAVIA **18**:254
STEPHEN UROŠ IV *see* STEPHEN DUŠAN, KING OF SERBIA
STEPHENS (Arkansas)
map (33° 25′N 93° 4′W) **2**:166
STEPHENS (county in Georgia)
map (34° 35′N 83° 15′W) **9**:114
STEPHENS (county in Oklahoma)
map (34° 30′N 97° 50′W) **14**:368
STEPHENS (county in Texas)
map (32° 45′N 98° 52′W) **19**:129
STEPHENS, ALEXANDER HAMILTON **18**:254 *bibliog.*
Civil War, U.S. **5**:19
STEPHENS, JAMES **18**:254–255 *bibliog.*
STEPHENS, JOHN LLOYD **18**:255 *bibliog.*
STEPHENS, URIAH S.
Knights of Labor **12**:101
STEPHENS CITY (Virginia)
map (39° 5′N 78° 13′W) **19**:607
STEPHENSON (county in Illinois)
map (42° 18′N 89° 35′W) **11**:42
STEPHENSON (Michigan)
map (45° 20′N 87° 38′W) **13**:377
STEPHENSON, GEORGE AND ROBERT **18**:255 *bibliog., illus.*
bridge (engineering) **3**:481 *illus.*
railroad **15**:71
Rocket (locomotive) **16**:251 *illus.*
STEPHENVILLE (Newfoundland)
map (48° 33′N 58° 35′W) **14**:166
STEPHENVILLE (Texas)
map (32° 13′N 98° 12′W) **19**:129
STEPPE **7**:271 *illus.*
Asia **2**:238 *map*
STEPPE ART **18**:255–256 *bibliog., illus.*
Scythians **17**:167
STEPPE LIFE **18**:256–257 *bibliog., illus.*
Scythians **17**:167
world distribution **15**:344 *map*
STEPPENWOLF (book) **18**:257
STEPTOE, PATRICK C.
artificial insemination **2**:221
STEREO *see* STEREOPHONIC SOUND
STEREOCHEMISTRY **18**:258–259 *bibliog., illus.*
chemistry, history of **4**:327
Cornforth, John W. **5**:269
geometric, isomer **11**:299
mineral **13**:440
molecule **13**:508
polymers
Natta, Giulio **14**:47
Prelog, Vladimir **15**:518
symmetry (mathematics) **18**:403–404
Walden, Paul **20**:9
STEREOPHONIC SOUND **18**:259 *bibliog., illus.*
compact disc **5**:154–155
video recording **19**:576j
STEREOSCOPE **18**:259–260 *bibliog., illus.*
STEREOSCOPY
eye **7**:350 *illus.*
STEREOTYPE **18**:260
STERILITY
fertility, human **8**:60
STERILIZATION
equipment
ultraviolet light **19**:379
STERILIZATION, SEXUAL
birth control **3**:294
castration **4**:192
eugenics **7**:264
handicapped persons **10**:36
vasectomy **19**:525
STERKFONTEIN (South Africa) **18**:260 *bibliog.*
Australopithecus **2**:346
Homo erectus **10**:215
STERLING (Colorado)
map (40° 37′N 103° 13′W) **5**:116
STERLING (Illinois)
map (41° 48′N 89° 42′W) **11**:42
STERLING (Kansas)
map (38° 13′N 98° 12′W) **12**:18
STERLING (Nebraska)
map (40° 28′N 96° 23′W) **14**:70
STERLING (Oklahoma)
map (34° 45′N 98° 10′W) **14**:368
STERLING (county in Texas)
map (31° 47′N 101° 0′W) **19**:129
STERLING (Virginia)
map (39° 0′N 77° 26′W) **19**:607
STERLING, FORD
Keystone Kops **12**:64
STERLING, POUND *see* POUND STERLING

STERLING CITY (Texas)
map (31° 50′N 100° 59′W) **19**:129
STERLING HEIGHTS (Michigan)
map (42° 35′N 83° 2′W) **13**:377
STERLING RESERVOIR
map (40° 47′N 103° 17′W) **5**:116
STERLINGTON (Louisiana)
map (32° 42′N 92° 5′W) **12**:430
STERN, BERT
fashion photography **8**:33
STERN, DER (periodical) **18**:260
STERN, ISAAC **18**:260 *bibliog.*
STERN, OTTO **18**:260 *bibliog.*
STERN, ROBERT A. M. **18**:260 *bibliog.*
STERNBERG, JOSEF VON **18**:260 *bibliog.*
STERNBERGIA **18**:261 *illus.*
STERNE, LAURENCE **18**:261 *bibliog., illus.*
Tristram Shandy **19**:304
STERNHEIM, CARL **18**:261
STEROID **18**:261–262 *bibliog.*
adrenal gland **1**:108
cholesterol **4**:404
corticoid **5**:278
corticosteroids **18**:261
environmental health **7**:212
fenugreek **8**:51
Heilbron, Sir Ian Morris **10**:108
hormone, animal **10**:234; **10**:235; **10**:237
aldosterone **1**:269
endocrine system **7**:169
glucocorticoid **9**:211
sex hormones **17**:226–227
medicinal plants **13**:266
sarsaparilla **17**:79
sterol **18**:261
structure
Windaus, Adolf **20**:172
synthetic **18**:261–262
terpene **19**:118
STEROL **12**:361 *illus.*; **18**:262 *illus.*
cholesterol **4**:403–404
lipid **12**:361–362
steroid **18**:261
STESICHORUS **18**:262
STETHOSCOPE **18**:262
examination, medical **7**:326
heart **10**:94
Laënnec, René Théophile Hyacinthe **12**:162–163
STETTHEIMER, FLORINE **18**:262 *bibliog.*
STETTIN (Poland) *see* SZCZECIN (Poland)
STETTINIUS, EDWARD REILLY, JR. **18**:262 *bibliog.*; **20**:280 *illus.*
STETTLER (Alberta)
map (52° 19′N 112° 43′W) **1**:256
STEUART (family) *see* STUART (family)
STEUBEN (county in Indiana)
map (41° 38′N 85° 0′W) **11**:111
STEUBEN (county in New York)
map (42° 20′N 77° 19′W) **14**:149
STEUBEN, FRIEDRICH WILHELM, BARON VON **18**:262 *bibliog.*
STEUBEN GLASS **9**:204 *illus.*; **18**:262 *bibliog.*
glassware, decorative **9**:204
STEUBENVILLE (Ohio)
map (40° 22′N 80° 37′W) **14**:357
STEVENS (family) **18**:263 *bibliog., illus.*
steamboat **18**:242
STEVENS (county in Kansas)
map (37° 10′N 101° 20′W) **12**:18
STEVENS (county in Minnesota)
map (45° 35′N 96° 0′W) **13**:453
STEVENS (county in Washington)
map (48° 20′N 117° 50′W) **20**:35
STEVENS, JOHN (inventor)
Hoboken (New Jersey) **10**:193
Stevens (family) **18**:263 *illus.*
STEVENS, JOHN P. (justice) **18**:263 *bibliog.*; **18**:355 *illus.*
STEVENS, SIAKA
Sierra Leone **17**:296
STEVENS, THADDEUS **18**:263 *bibliog., illus.*
STEVENS, WALLACE **18**:264 *bibliog., illus.*
STEVENS INSTITUTE OF TECHNOLOGY **18**:264
STEVENS PASS
map (47° 45′N 121° 4′W) **20**:35
STEVENS POINT (Wisconsin)
map (44° 31′N 89° 34′W) **20**:185
STEVENS TREATY (1855)
Joseph, Chief **11**:451
STEVENSON (Alabama)
map (34° 52′N 85° 50′W) **1**:234
STEVENSON (family) **18**:264–265 *bibliog., illus.*
STEVENSON (Washington)
map (45° 42′N 121° 53′W) **20**:35
STEVENSON, ADLAI **15**:526 *illus.*
Stevenson (family) **18**:264 *illus.*
STEVENSON, CHARLES LESLIE
ethics **7**:250
STEVENSON, JAMES
Teton Range **19**:127
STEVENSON, ROBERT LOUIS **7**:200 *illus.*; **18**:265 *bibliog., illus.*
Dr. Jekyll and Mr. Hyde **6**:210
Tahiti (French Polynesia) **19**:10
Treasure Island **19**:285
STEVENSVILLE (Michigan)
map (42° 1′N 86° 31′W) **13**:377
STEVENSVILLE (Montana)
map (46° 30′N 114° 5′W) **13**:547
STEVIN, SIMON **18**:265
mathematics, history of **13**:224
STEVNS BLUFF
map (55° 18′N 12° 27′E) **6**:109
STEWARDSON (Illinois)
map (39° 16′N 88° 38′W) **11**:42
STEWART (British Columbia)
map (55° 56′N 129° 59′W) **3**:491
STEWART (family) *see* STUART (family)
STEWART (county in Georgia)
map (32° 5′N 84° 50′W) **9**:114
STEWART (Minnesota)
map (44° 43′N 94° 29′W) **13**:453
STEWART (county in Tennessee)
map (36° 30′N 87° 50′W) **19**:104
STEWART, ALEXANDER TURNEY **18**:265 *bibliog.*
STEWART, DOUGLAS ALEXANDER **18**:265
STEWART, FLORENCE RAINBOW *see* STEWART, MARY
STEWART, HENRY *see* DARNLEY, HENRY STEWART, LORD
STEWART, JACKIE **18**:265 *bibliog.*
STEWART, JAMES **5**:383 *illus.*; **8**:84 *illus.*; **18**:266 *bibliog., illus.*
Ford, John (film director) **8**:223
STEWART, JOHN INNES MACKINTOSH *see* INNES, MICHAEL (pseudonym)
STEWART, MARY **18**:266
STEWART, POTTER **12**:246 *illus.*; **18**:266 *bibliog.*; **18**:355 *illus.*
STEWART, ROBERT, VISCOUNT CASTLEREAGH *see* CASTLEREAGH, ROBERT STEWART, VISCOUNT
STEWART, WILL (pseudonym) *see* WILLIAMSON, JACK
STEWART, WILLIAM MORRIS **18**:266 *bibliog.*
STEWART ISLAND
map (47° 0′S 167° 50′E) **14**:158
New Zealand **14**:156
STEWART RIVER
map (63° 18′N 139° 25′W) **20**:345
STEWARTSTOWN (Pennsylvania)
map (39° 45′N 76° 35′W) **15**:147
STEWARTSVILLE (Missouri)
map (39° 45′N 94° 30′W) **13**:476
STEWARTVILLE (Minnesota)
map (43° 51′N 92° 29′W) **13**:453
STEWIACKE (Nova Scotia)
map (45° 8′N 63° 21′W) **14**:269
STEYR (Austria)
map (48° 3′N 14° 25′E) **2**:348
STIBNITE **13**:441 *illus.*; **18**:266 *illus.*
antimony **2**:63
STICHBANDKERAMIK CULTURE *see* DANUBIAN CULTURE
STICK INSECT **18**:266 *illus.*
mimicry **11**:191 *illus.*
STICKLEBACK **5**:121 *illus.*; **18**:266–267 *illus.*
animal behavior **2**:12 *illus.*
animal courtship and mating **2**:21 *illus.*
STICKNEY (South Dakota)
map (43° 35′N 98° 26′W) **18**:103
STIEBER, WILHELM
intelligence gathering **11**:204
STIEGEL, HENRY WILLIAM **18**:267 *bibliog.*
glassware, decorative **9**:204
STIEGLITZ, ALFRED **15**:257 *illus.*; **18**:267 *bibliog., illus.*
Armory Show **2**:177
Equivalent, Mountains and Sky, Lake George **18**:267 *illus.*
Marin, John **13**:153
O'Keeffe, Georgia **14**:365
photography, history and art of **15**:270–271
STIERNHIELM, GEORG
Swedish literature **18**:386
STIFTER, ADALBERT **18**:267–268 *bibliog.*
STIGLER (Oklahoma)
map (35° 15′N 95° 8′W) **14**:368
STIGMATA **18**:268 *bibliog.*
Francis of Assisi, Saint **8**:274
STIKINE RIVER
map (56° 40′N 132° 30′W) **1**:242
map (56° 40′N 132° 30′W) **3**:491
STILBITE *see* ZEOLITE
STILE FLOREALE *see* ART NOUVEAU
STILE LIBERTY *see* ART NOUVEAU
STILES, EZRA **18**:268 *bibliog.*
STILICHO, FLAVIUS **18**:268 *bibliog.*
Honorius, Roman Emperor in the West **10**:224
STILL *see* DISTILLERY; WHISKEY
STILL, ANDREW T.
osteopathic medicine **14**:457
STILL, CLYFFORD **18**:268 *bibliog., illus.*
Painting **18**:268 *illus.*
STILL, WILLIAM GRANT **18**:268 *bibliog.*
STILL-LIFE PAINTING **18**:268–270 *bibliog., illus.*
Braque, Georges **3**:456
Bruegel (family) **3**:521–522
Caravaggio, Michelangelo Merisi da **4**:131–132
Cézanne, Paul **4**:263–264
Chardin, Jean Baptiste **4**:287–288
Chase, William Merritt **4**:301
Claesz, Pieter **5**:35
Courbet, Gustave **5**:314
Dutch art and architecture **6**:311
Goes, Hugo van der **9**:223
Haberle, John **10**:4
Harnett, William **10**:53
Heda, Willem Claesz **10**:104
Hondecoeter, Melchior d' **10**:217
Huysum, Jan van **10**:326
Kalff, Willem **12**:8
Manet, Édouard **13**:112–114
Matisse, Henri **13**:228–229
Memling, Hans **13**:290
Moillon, Louise **13**:504
Morandi, Giorgio **13**:573
Peale (family) **15**:124
Picasso, Pablo **15**:290–292
Redon, Odilon **16**:116
Renoir, Auguste **16**:158–159
Ruysch, Rachel **16**:377
Vallayer-Coster, Anne **19**:506
Velázquez, Diego **19**:536–537
Zurbarán, Francisco de **20**:382–383
STILLE, WILHELM HANS
geosyncline **9**:119
STILLER, MAURITZ
film, history of **8**:84
STILLMORE (Georgia)
map (32° 27′N 82° 13′W) **9**:114
STILLWATER (Minnesota)
map (45° 4′N 92° 49′W) **13**:453
STILLWATER (county in Montana)
map (45° 45′N 109° 15′W) **13**:547
STILLWATER (Oklahoma)
map (36° 7′N 97° 4′W) **14**:368
STILLWATER RANGE
map (39° 50′N 118° 15′W) **14**:111
STILT (bird) **18**:270 *illus.*
foot **3**:288 *illus.*
shorebirds **17**:283
STILWELL (Oklahoma)
map (35° 49′N 94° 38′W) **14**:368
STILWELL, JOSEPH W. **18**:270 *bibliog., illus.*
World War II **20**:260; **20**:266; **20**:276; **20**:278
STIMSON, HENRY LEWIS **18**:270–271 *bibliog., illus.*
STIMULANT **18**:271 *bibliog.*
amphetamine **1**:377; **18**:271
amyl nitrite **1**:386–387
caffeine **4**:15; **18**:271
cocaine **5**:85; **18**:271
drug **18**:271
drug abuse **6**:279
psychotropic drugs **15**:604
strychnine **18**:304
STIMULUS-RESPONSE PSYCHOLOGY *see* BEHAVIORISM
STING, THE (film)
confidence game **5**:178
STINGRAY **15**:384 *illus.*; **18**:272 *bibliog., illus.*
ray **16**:96
STINKBUG **18**:272
STINKHORN **18**:272
STINKING CEDAR *see* *TORREYA*
STINNETT (Texas)
map (35° 50′N 101° 27′W) **19**:129
ŠTIP (Yugoslavia)
map (41° 44′N 22° 12′E) **20**:340
STIPETIC, WERNER H. *see* HERZOG, WERNER
STIRLING (Australia)
map (31° 54′S 115° 47′E) **2**:328
STIRLING (Scotland) **18**:272
map (56° 7′N 3° 57′W) **19**:403
STIRLING, JAMES FRAZER **18**:272 *bibliog.*
STIRLING, ROBERT
Stirling engine **18**:272–273
STIRLING CITY (California)
map (39° 54′N 121° 32′W) **4**:31
STIRLING ENGINE **18**:272–273 *bibliog., illus.*
electric car **7**:105
engine **7**:177
STIRRAT (West Virginia)
map (37° 44′N 82° 0′W) **20**:111
STIRRUP **18**:273
STIRRUP (ear bone)
ear **7**:6 *illus.*
STISHOVITE **18**:273
coesite **5**:93
meteorite craters **13**:338
silica minerals **17**:304
STOA **18**:273
Greek architecture **9**:335
STOCHASTIC PROCESS **18**:273 *bibliog.*
Brownian motion **18**:273
Markov process **18**:273
music
Xenakis, Yannis **20**:311
pattern recognition **15**:115
probability **18**:273
queuing theory **16**:24–25
random variable **18**:273
random walk **16**:83; **18**:273
time **18**:273
Wiener, Norbert **20**:146
STOCK (finance) **18**:274 *bibliog.*
See also STOCK MARKET
Baruch, Bernard M. **3**:99
common stock **18**:274
dividend **18**:274
dollar averaging **6**:225
Dow-Jones average **6**:251
income tax **11**:76–77
investment banking **11**:238
mutual fund **13**:687
option trading **14**:413
panic, financial **15**:59
preferred stock **18**:274
Securities and Exchange Commission **17**:181
Wall Street **20**:12–13
STOCK (punishment) *see* PILLORY
STOCK, FREDERICK **18**:274 *bibliog.*
Chicago Symphony Orchestra **4**:343
STOCK CAR RACING **2**:361 *illus.*; **2**:362
STOCK MARKET **18**:274–275 *bibliog., illus.*
See also STOCK (finance)
arbitrage **2**:110
crash of October 29, 1929 **18**:274 *illus.*
Dow-Jones average **6**:251
investment banking **11**:238
margin buying **18**:275
option trading **14**:413
over-the-counter market **18**:275
random walk **16**:83
Securities and Exchange Commission **17**:181
short selling and stop selling **18**:275
STOCKBRIDGE (Michigan)
map (42° 27′N 84° 11′W) **13**:377
STOCKERAU (Austria)
map (48° 23′N 16° 13′E) **2**:348
STOCKETT (Montana)
map (47° 21′N 111° 10′W) **13**:547
STOCKFISH *see* HAKE
STOCKHAUSEN, KARLHEINZ **18**:275 *bibliog., illus.*
aleatory music **1**:270
STOCKHOLDERS *see* CORPORATION, OWNERSHIP
STOCKHOLM (Maine)
map (47° 3′N 68° 8′W) **13**:70
STOCKHOLM (Sweden) **18**:275–276 *bibliog.*; **18**:385 *illus.*
climate **18**:382 *table*
map (59° 20′N 18° 3′E) **18**:382
subway **18**:318–319 *illus., table*
STOCKMAN, DAVID
Reagan, Ronald **16**:102
STOCKS (botany) **18**:276
gillyflower **9**:182
STOCKTON (Alabama)
map (31° 0′N 87° 52′W) **1**:234
STOCKTON (California) **18**:276
map (37° 57′N 121° 17′W) **4**:31
STOCKTON (Kansas)
map (39° 26′N 99° 16′W) **12**:18
STOCKTON (Missouri)
map (37° 42′N 93° 48′W) **13**:476
STOCKTON (Utah)
map (40° 27′N 112° 22′W) **19**:492
STOCKTON, FRANK R. **18**:276 *bibliog.*

STOCKTON, ROBERT FIELD 18:276
California 4:37
Mexican War 13:355
STOCKTON RESERVOIR
map (37° 40′N 93° 45′W) 13:476
STOCKVILLE (Nebraska)
map (40° 32′N 100° 23′W) 14:70
STOCKYARD 14:71 *illus.*
STOCLET, PALAIS
Hoffmann, Josef 10:195
STODDARD (county in Missouri)
map (36° 50′N 89° 55′W) 13:476
STODDARD, SOLOMON 18:276 *bibliog.*
STOICHIOMETRY 18:276–278 *bibliog., illus.*
Wenzel, Carl Friedrich 20:104
STOICISM 18:278 *bibliog.*
Epictetus 7:218
law 12:242
logic 12:395
logos 12:397
Marcus Aurelius, Roman Emperor 13:147–148
natural law 14:48
Posidonius 15:458
Seneca, Lucius Annaeus 17:200
Zeno of Citium 20:359
STOKE-ON-TRENT (England) 18:278
map (53° 0′N 2° 10′W) 19:403
STOKER, BRAM 18:278 *bibliog.*
Dracula 6:254
STOKES (county in North Carolina)
map (36° 25′N 80° 15′W) 14:242
STOKES, CARL B.
Cleveland (Ohio) 5:52
STOKES, SIR GEORGE GABRIEL 18:278
fluorescence 18:278
geodesy 18:278
hydrodynamics 18:278
photosynthesis 15:275
STOKES VALLEY (New Zealand)
map (41° 11′S 174° 58′E) 14:158
STOKOWSKI, LEOPOLD 18:278 *bibliog.*
Philadelphia Orchestra, The 15:229
STOL 18:278–279 *bibliog.*
autogiro 2:356
helicopter 10:111–112
STOLL, A.
photosynthesis 15:275
STOLYPIN, PYOTR ARKADIEVICH 18:279 *bibliog.*
STÖLZL, GUNTA
wall hanging 3:129 *illus.*
STOMA *see* STOMATA
STOMACH 1:54 *illus.*; 18:279–280 *bibliog., illus.*
antacid 2:38
Beaumont, William 3:147
circulatory system 4:440 *illus.*
digestion, human 6:171
digestive system 6:174; 18:280
drug absorption 6:275 *illus.*
examination, medical 7:326
gastric juice
hydrochloric acid 10:331
gastritis 9:56
gizzard 9:192
heartburn 10:97
hunger and thirst 10:310
indigestion 11:144
intestine 11:230
monkey 13:534
muscles 18:279 *illus.*
pepsin 18:280
ruminant 16:345
ulcer 9:56 *illus.*; 18:280; 19:376
STOMATA 18:280
STOMMEL, HENRY MELSON 18:280
STONE *see* ROCK
STONE (county in Arkansas)
map (35° 52′N 92° 13′W) 2:166
STONE (county in Mississippi)
map (30° 45′N 89° 5′W) 13:469
STONE (county in Missouri)
map (36° 45′N 93° 25′W) 13:476
STONE, BARTON WARREN 18:280 *bibliog.*
STONE, EDWARD DURELL 18:280 *bibliog.*
Museum of Modern Art 13:657
Pine Bluff (Arkansas) 15:305
STONE, HARLAN FISKE 18:280 *bibliog.*
Parker v. *Brown* 15:91
United States v. *Darby* 19:465
STONE, I. F. 18:280 *bibliog.*
STONE, IRVING 18:280–281 *bibliog.*
STONE, LUCY 18:281 *bibliog., illus.*
suffrage, women's 18:326
STONE AGE
MIDDLE STONE AGE *see* MESOLITHIC PERIOD
NEW STONE AGE *see* NEOLITHIC PERIOD
OLD STONE AGE *see* PALEOLITHIC PERIOD
STONE ALIGNMENTS 2:114–115 *illus.*; 18:281–282 *bibliog., illus.*
archaeoastronomy 2:114–115
archaeology 2:118–119
Avebury (England) 2:369
Callanish (Scotland) 18:281 *illus.*
Carnac (France) 4:154; 18:281 *illus.*
Easter Island 7:32–33 *illus.*
Indians, American 2:115 *illus.*
medicine wheel 2:115 *illus.*
megalith 13:279
menhir 13:297
Newgrange (Ireland) 14:168
San Agustín (Colombia) 17:50
Stonehenge (England) 18:283 *illus.*
Woodhenge (England) 20:211
STONE CIRCLES *see* STONE ALIGNMENTS
STONE CURLEW 18:282 *illus.*
STONE FLY 18:282 *illus.*
STONE HARBOR (New Jersey)
map (39° 3′N 74° 45′W) 14:129
STONE MOUNTAIN (Georgia) 9:116 *illus.*; 18:282
Borglum, Gutzon 3:400
map (33° 49′N 84° 6′W) 9:114
STONE PLANTS 4:10 *illus.*
STONECROP (botany) 18:282–283 *illus.*
STONEFISH
poisonous plants and animals 15:384 *illus.*
scorpion fish 17:148
STONEHAM (Massachusetts)
map (42° 29′N 71° 6′W) 3:409
STONEHENGE 2:192 *illus.*; 18:283 *bibliog., illus.*
archaeoastronomy 2:114–115 *illus.*
astronomy, history of 2:277
druids 6:282
megalith 13:278–279 *illus.*
Stukeley, William 18:308
Wessex culture 20:106
STONEMASONRY 18:283 *bibliog.*
See also MASONRY
STONEWALL (Louisiana)
map (32° 16′N 93° 50′W) 12:430
STONEWALL (Manitoba)
map (50° 9′N 97° 21′W) 13:119
STONEWALL (Mississippi)
map (32° 8′N 88° 47′W) 13:469
STONEWALL (Oklahoma)
map (34° 39′N 96° 31′W) 14:368
STONEWALL (county in Texas)
map (33° 8′N 100° 15′W) 19:129
STONEWALL RIOTS (New York City)
gay activism 9:63
STONEWARE
ceramics 4:258–259 *illus.*
pottery and porcelain 15:468
STONEWORT (botany) 18:283–284 *illus.*
STONEY TUNGUSKA RIVER
map (61° 36′N 90° 18′E) 19:388
STONINGTON (Illinois)
map (39° 44′N 89° 12′W) 11:42
STONY ISLANDS
map (43° 50′N 76° 25′W) 14:149
STONY LAKE
map (58° 51′N 98° 35′W) 13:119
STONY PLAIN (Alberta)
map (53° 2′N 114° 0′W) 1:256
STONY POINT (North Carolina)
map (35° 52′N 81° 3′W) 14:242
STONY RAPIDS (Saskatchewan)
map (59° 16′N 105° 50′W) 17:81
STOOL (biology) *see* FECES
STOPH, WILLI 18:284
STOPPARD, TOM 18:284 *illus.*
STORÅ RIVER
map (56° 19′N 8° 19′E) 6:109
STORAGE BATTERY *see* BATTERY
STORAGE RINGS (physics)
accelerator, particle 1:75–76
STORAVAN LAKE
map (65° 40′N 18° 15′E) 18:382
STORAX 18:284
silver bell 17:313
sweet gum 18:387
STOREY (county in Nevada)
map (39° 25′N 119° 30′W) 14:111
STOREY, DAVID 18:284
STOREY, MOORFIELD
National Association for the Advancement of Colored People 14:29
STORK 15:367 *illus.*; 18:284–285 *bibliog., illus.*
ibis 11:4
Marabou stork 17:98 *illus.*
migration 3:289 *map*
STORKSBILL (botany) *see* GERANIUM
STORM *see* CYCLONE AND ANTICYCLONE; SANDSTORM AND DUST STORM
STORM, THEODOR 18:285 *bibliog.*
STORM LAKE (Iowa)
map (42° 39′N 95° 13′W) 11:244
STORM TROOPER *see* SA (*Sturmabteilung*)
STORMONT (parliament)
Northern Ireland 14:255
STORNOWAY (Scotland)
map (58° 12′N 6° 23′W) 19:403
STORRS (Connecticut)
map (41° 48′N 72° 15′W) 5:193
STORRS, JOHN BRADLEY 18:285 *bibliog.*
STORSJÖN LAKE
map (63° 12′N 14° 18′E) 18:382
STORTING (parliament)
Norway 14:263
STORY (county in Iowa)
map (42° 0′N 93° 25′W) 11:244
STORY, JOSEPH 18:285 *bibliog.*
STORY, WILLIAM WETMORE 18:285 *bibliog.*
STORY CITY (Iowa)
map (42° 11′N 93° 36′W) 11:244
STORY THEATER
acting 1:88
STOSS, VEIT 18:285 *bibliog.*
STOTZ, CARL E.
Little League baseball 12:373
STOUGHTON (Massachusetts)
map (42° 7′N 71° 6′W) 13:206
STOUGHTON (Wisconsin)
map (42° 55′N 89° 13′W) 20:185
STOURBRIDGE LION (locomotive)
locomotive 12:389
STOUT (beer) 3:163
STOUT, REX 18:285 *illus.*
STOVE 5:239 *illus.*; 18:286 *bibliog., illus.*
STOVER (Missouri)
map (38° 27′N 92° 59′W) 13:476
STOW, RANDOLPH
Australian literature 2:344
STOWASSER, FRIEDRICH *see* HUNDERTWASSER
STOWE (Vermont)
map (44° 28′N 72° 41′W) 19:554
STOWE, HARRIET BEECHER 18:286–287 *bibliog., illus.*
Uncle Tom's Cabin 19:382
STOWE GARDEN
Brown, Capability 3:513
STRABISMUS 18:287
STRABO 18:287 *bibliog.*
geography 9:101
Seven Wonders of the World 17:216
STRACHAN, JOHN 18:287 *bibliog.*
STRACHEY, JOHN 18:287
STRACHEY, LYTTON 18:287 *bibliog.*
STRADA, LA (film)
Fellini, Federico 8:48 *illus.*
STRADELLA, ALESSANDRO
oratorio 14:416
STRADIVARI (family) 18:287 *bibliog.*
violin 19:603 *illus.*
STRAFFORD (county in New Hampshire)
map (43° 20′N 71° 5′W) 14:123
STRAFFORD, THOMAS WENTWORTH, 1ST EARL OF 18:287–288 *bibliog., illus.*
STRAIN (engineering)
materials technology 13:219–220 *table*
strain gauge 18:288
STRAIN GAUGE 18:288
STRAITS SETTLEMENTS 18:288
STRALSUND (Germany, East and West)
map (54° 19′N 13° 5′E) 9:140
STRAND, PAUL 18:288 *bibliog.*
The White Fence 15:271 *illus.*
STRANDLINE 18:288 *bibliog.*
lake, glacial 12:170
STRANG, JAMES JESSE 18:288 *bibliog.*
STRANGENESS (physics)
fundamental particles 8:362
quark 16:12
STRANGER, THE (book) 18:288
Camus, Albert 4:68
STRANGERS AND BROTHERS (books)
Snow, C. P., Baron Snow 18:3–4
STRANGFORD LAKE
map (54° 30′N 5° 36′W) 11:258
STRANGLES *see* HORSE DISTEMPER
STRAPAROLA, GIOVANNI FRANCESCO 18:288
STRASBERG, LEE 18:288
acting 1:88
Actors Studio 1:90
Group Theatre, The 9:376–377
method acting 13:343
STRASBOURG (France) 18:288–289
Alsace-Lorraine 1:310
map (48° 35′N 7° 45′E) 8:260
STRASBOURG, OATHS OF (842)
Romance languages 16:281
STRASBOURG CATHEDRAL 18:289 *bibliog.*
STRASBURG (Colorado)
map (39° 44′N 104° 20′W) 5:116
STRASBURG (North Dakota)
map (46° 8′N 100° 10′W) 14:248
STRASBURG (Virginia)
map (38° 59′N 78° 22′W) 19:607
STRASBURGER, EDUARD
zoology 20:377
STRASSBURG (France) *see* STRASBOURG (France)
STRASSER, GREGOR 18:289
Hitler, Adolf 10:187
STRASSER, OTTO
Strasser, Gregor 18:289
STRASSMAN, FRITZ
Hahn, Otto 10:11
STRATEGIC AIR COMMAND 18:289 *bibliog.*
B-1 bomber 3:3
B-52 Stratofortress 3:4
STRATEGIC ARMS LIMITATION TALKS (SALT) *see* SALT (Strategic Arms Limitation Talks)
STRATEGIC ARMS REDUCTION TALKS (SMART) *see* SMART (Strategic Arms Reduction Talks)
STRATEGIC DEFENSE INITIATIVE 18:289 *bibliog.*
antiballistic missile 2:56–57
United States, history of the 19:461
STRATEGY AND TACTICS, MILITARY 18:289–291 *bibliog.*
air force 1:207–208
aircraft, military 1:214–220
ammunition 1:373
army 2:180–183
artillery 2:222–224 *illus.*
Aztec 2:382 *illus.*
balloon 3:52
Caesar, Gaius Julius 4:14 *map*
camouflage 4:62–63
cannon 4:111–112
Carnot, Lazare Nicolas Marguerite 4:158
cavalry 4:221–222 *illus.*
city 5:3
Civil War, U.S. 5:20–31 *map*
Grant, Ulysses S. 9:288–289
Halleck, Henry W. 10:22
Hardee, William J. 10:45
Clausewitz, Carl Philipp Gottfried von 5:44–45; 18:289–290
Crécy, Battle of 5:336
demolition 6:104
firearms 8:105–106
fortification 8:238–241
game theory 9:27–29
guerrillas 9:391–392
Gustav II Adolf, King of Sweden 18:290
historical and theoretical development 18:290–291
infantry 11:163–164
laser 12:213
maneuvers 18:290
Marine Corps, U.S. 13:153–155
Middle Ages 7:285 *illus.*
military warning and detection systems 13:421–422
Airborne Warning and Control System 1:210
BMEWS 3:348
radar 16:38–39
SAMOS 17:47
surveillance systems 18:366
modern warfare 18:290–291
Moltke, Helmuth Karl Bernhard, Graf von 13:514
musket 13:682
napalm 14:14
North Atlantic Treaty Organization 14:241
nuclear strategy 14:288
pontoons and pontoon bridges 15:427
principles of warfare 18:290
rockets and missiles 16:254–256
antiballistic missile 2:56–57
ballistic missile 3:49
cruise missile 5:365–366
Minuteman missile 13:462
MIRV missile 13:465
MX missile 13:688
Sidewinder 17:294
surface-to-air missile 18:359
sabotage 17:6
shrapnel 17:286
signaling 17:300–301
STOL 18:278–279

STRATEGY AND TACTICS, MILITARY (cont.)
TNT **19**:216
Vandenberg Air Force Base **19**:518
Vauban, Sébastien le Prestre de **19**:528
war **20**:24–25
World War I **18**:291; **20**:222–244
Foch, Ferdinand **8**:192
mortar **13**:591
Schlieffen, Alfred, Graf von **17**:126
World War II **18**:291; **20**:264
blitzkrieg **3**:333
de Gaulle, Charles **6**:59
Eisenhower, Dwight D. **7**:94–95
Guderian, Heinz **9**:390
Haig, Douglas Haig, 1st Earl **10**:12
napalm **14**:14
RDX **16**:98
V-1 **19**:500
V-2 **19**:500–501
STRATEGY AND TACTICS, NAVAL
amphibious warfare **1**:380–381
battleship **3**:126–128
blockade **3**:334; **18**:291
depth charge **6**:120
destroyer **6**:132–133
frogman **8**:338
galleon **9**:17
Mahan, Alfred Thayer **13**:64
mine **13**:437–438 *illus.*
naval vessels **14**:54–57
navy **14**:62–65
Pearl Harbor **15**:126 *map*
PT boat **15**:605
signaling **17**:301
strategy and tactics, military **18**:290–291
submarine **18**:313–316
torpedo (projectile) **19**:242–243
STRATEMEYER, EDWARD L. *see* DIXON, FRANKLIN W.
STRATFORD (Connecticut)
map (41° 14′N 73° 7′W) **5**:193
STRATFORD (New Jersey)
map (39° 50′N 75° 1′W) **14**:129
STRATFORD (Oklahoma)
map (34° 48′N 96° 58′W) **14**:368
STRATFORD (Ontario)
map (43° 22′N 80° 57′W) **14**:393
STRATFORD (Texas)
map (36° 20′N 102° 4′W) **19**:129
STRATFORD (Wisconsin)
map (44° 48′N 90° 4′W) **20**:185
STRATFORD-ON-AVON (England) **18**:291
STRATFORD POINT
map (41° 9′N 73° 6′W) **5**:193
STRATHCLYDE (Scotland) **2**:3 *map*; **18**:291
cities
Coatbridge **5**:81
Greenock **9**:353
Motherwell **13**:607
counties (former)
Argyll (Scotland) **2**:153
Ayr (Scotland) **2**:379
Bute (Scotland) **3**:591
Dunbarton **6**:299
STRATHCONA AND MOUNT ROYAL, DONALD ALEXANDER SMITH, 1ST BARON **4**:85 *illus.*; **18**:291 *bibliog.*
STRATHLORNE (Nova Scotia)
map (46° 11′N 61° 17′W) **14**:269
STRATIFICATION, SOCIAL *see* CLASS, SOCIAL; SOCIAL STRUCTURE AND ORGANIZATION
STRATIGRAPHY **18**:292–293 *bibliog., illus.*
ammonite **1**:372–373
archaeology **2**:118 *illus.*; **2**:124 *illus.*
Arduino, Giovanni **2**:144–145
breccia **3**:470
Brongniart, Alexandre **3**:503
Code of Stratigraphic Nomenclature **18**:292
correlation **18**:292–293
field work requirement **18**:293
Fiorelli, Giuseppe **8**:99
fossil record **8**:244
Füchsel, Georg Christian **8**:352
geologic time
Cambrian Period **4**:50–52
Carboniferous Period **4**:137–138
Cretaceous Period **5**:339–341
Gondwanaland **9**:243
Paleozoic Era **15**:43
Permian Period **15**:175
Precambrian time **15**:491–493
geology **9**:105–106
graptolite **9**:294
Gressley, Amanz **9**:359
Hayden, Ferdinand **10**:80–81
history **18**:292
Hutton, James **10**:323–324
kame **12**:9
lake, glacial **12**:170
Lehman, Johann Gottlob **12**:276
molasse **13**:505
Moore, Raymond Cecil **13**:570
Murchison, Roderick Impey **13**:647
pollen stratigraphy **15**:407–408
prehistory **15**:517
professional and educational associations
American Commission on Stratigraphic Nomenclature **18**:292
sandstone **17**:63
Sedgwick, Adam **17**:183
sediment, marine **17**:183–184
Smith, William **17**:371
soil **18**:36–38
stage **18**:210
statigraphic traps
petroleum **15**:208
Steno, Nicolaus **18**:253; **18**:292
stratified rock classifications **18**:292
unconformity **19**:382
Werner, Abraham Gottlob **20**:104
STRATOSPHERE **18**:293 *bibliog.*
fallout **8**:14
geophysics **9**:108
manned balloon flight
Piccard, Auguste **15**:292
tropopause **19**:310
STRATTON (Colorado)
map (39° 18′N 102° 36′W) **5**:116
STRATTON (Maine)
map (45° 8′N 70° 26′W) **13**:70
STRATTON (Nebraska)
map (40° 9′N 101° 14′W) **14**:70
STRATTON, CHARLES SHERWOOD *see* TOM THUMB (entertainer)
STRATUS CLOUDS **5**:67–68 *illus.*; **18**:293 *bibliog., illus.*
STRAUB, JEAN MARIE **18**:293 *bibliog.*
STRAUBING (West Germany)
map (48° 53′N 12° 34′E) **9**:140
STRAUSS (family) **18**:293–294 *bibliog., illus.*
STRAUSS, CLAUDE LÉVI- *see* LÉVI-STRAUSS, CLAUDE
STRAUSS, DAVID FRIEDRICH **18**:294 *bibliog.*
STRAUSS, FRANZ JOSEF **18**:294 *bibliog.*
STRAUSS, JOHANN, JR. **18**:294 *illus.*
STRAUSS, RICHARD **13**:667 *illus.*; **18**:294–295 *bibliog., illus.*
Berlin Philharmonic Orchestra **3**:217
Lehmann, Lotte **12**:276
opera **14**:401
Rosenkavalier, Der **16**:315
symphonic poem **18**:405
STRAVINSKY, IGOR **3**:44 *illus.*; **13**:667 *illus.*; **18**:295 *bibliog., illus.*
Ballets Russes de Serge Diaghilev **3**:48
music criticism **13**:670
Russian music **16**:369 *illus.*
STRAWBERRY **8**:348 *illus.*; **18**:295–296 *bibliog.*
guttation **9**:410
Washington **20**:37 *illus.*
STRAWBERRY BASS *see* CRAPPIE
STRAWBERRY CACTUS **4**:10 *illus.*
STRAWBERRY DANIELS PASS
map (40° 18′N 111° 15′W) **19**:492
STRAWBERRY GERANIUM *see* SAXIFRAGE
STRAWBERRY HILL PRESS
Walpole, Horace, 4th Earl of Orford **20**:18
STRAWBERRY MOUNTAIN
map (44° 19′N 118° 43′W) **14**:427
STRAWBERRY POINT (Iowa)
map (42° 41′N 91° 32′W) **11**:244
STRAWBERRY RIVER (Arkansas)
map (35° 53′N 91° 13′W) **2**:166
STRAWBERRY RIVER (Utah)
map (40° 10′N 110° 24′W) **19**:492
STRAWBERRY TOP SHELL **17**:251 *illus.*
STRAWFLOWER **18**:296
STRAWSON, PETER FREDERICK **18**:296 *bibliog.*
STREAK
mineral identification **13**:441
STREAM *see* RIVER AND STREAM
STREAM OF CONSCIOUSNESS **18**:296 *bibliog.*
Absalom, Absalom! **1**:62
Dos Passos, John **6**:243–244
Dream Play, A **6**:266
Faulkner, William **8**:36
Joyce, James **11**:456–457
Richardson, Dorothy M. **16**:211
Simon, Claude **17**:314
Sound and the Fury, The **18**:74
To the Lighthouse **19**:217
Ulysses **19**:379
Woolf, Virginia **20**:215
STREATHAM (British Columbia)
map (53° 52′N 126° 12′W) **3**:491
STREATOR (Illinois)
map (41° 7′N 88° 50′W) **11**:42
STREEP, MERYL **18**:296
STREET BIKE *see* MOTORCYCLE
STREET THEATER *see* GUERRILLA THEATER
STREETCAR **18**:296–297 *bibliog., illus.*
bus **3**:584
cable car **4**:6
Johnson, Tom Loftin **11**:436
Sprague, Frank Julian **18**:198
STREETCAR NAMED DESIRE, A (play) **18**:297 *bibliog.*
Williams, Tennessee **20**:160–161
STREETER (North Dakota)
map (46° 39′N 99° 21′W) **14**:248
STREETWALKER
prostitution **15**:573
STREICHER, JULIUS
Hitler, Adolf **10**:187
STREISAND, BARBRA **18**:297 *bibliog.*
STRENGTH (engineering)
materials technology **13**:219–220 *table*
STREP THROAT **18**:297
Streptococcus **18**:297
STREPSIPTERA **18**:297
STREPTOCOCCUS **18**:297
collagen disease **5**:102
Diplococcus **6**:185
diseases **18**:297
kidney disease **12**:71
pneumococcus **15**:375
puerperal fever **15**:614
respiratory system disorders **16**:181
rheumatic fever **16**:194
scarlet fever **17**:115
skin diseases **17**:342
strep throat **18**:297
tonsillitis **19**:235
urogenital diseases **19**:487
STREPTOMYCIN
antibiotics **2**:57; **2**:59
medicine **13**:271
Waksman, Selman Abraham **20**:8
STRESEMANN, GUSTAV **18**:297 *bibliog.*
STRESS (engineering)
materials technology **13**:219–220 *table*
polarized light **15**:395
STRESS, BIOLOGICAL **18**:297–298 *bibliog.*
community mental health **5**:152–153
coping with stress **18**:298
corticoid **5**:278
eczema **7**:54
fracture **8**:258–259
glucocorticoid **9**:211
headache **10**:86
post-traumatic stress disorder **15**:459
pregnancy and birth **15**:505
sensory deprivation **17**:205
stress ulcer **19**:376
tranquilizer **19**:266
STRETCH (computer) **5**:160b
STREUVELS, STIJN **18**:298
STRICKLAND, WILLIAM **18**:298 *bibliog.*
Second Bank of the United States **9**:346 *illus.*
STRIKE **12**:155 *illus.*; **18**:298–299 *bibliog., illus.*
boycott **3**:433
general strike **9**:77
Gierek, Edward **9**:177
Haymarket Riot **10**:83
Homestead strike **10**:214
Labor-Management Relations Act **12**:152
lockout **12**:388
National Farmers Organization **14**:32
Poland **15**:391
Pullman Strike **15**:619
Reuther, Walter P. **16**:184
syndicalism **18**:407
STRIKE-SLIP FAULT (geology)
fault **8**:37 *illus.*
STRINDBERG, AUGUST **18**:299 *bibliog., illus.*; **18**:386 *illus.*
drama **6**:261
Dream Play, A **6**:266
Ghost Sonata, The **9**:169
Miss Julie **13**:467
STRING-ORIENTED SYMBOLIC LANGUAGE *see* SNOBOL
STRING QUARTET **18**:300 *bibliog., illus.*
chamber music **4**:272–273
classical period in music **5**:41
composers
Beethoven, Ludwig van **3**:164–165
Haydn, Franz Josef **10**:81
Miaskovsky, Nicolai **13**:370
STRING THEORIES (physics) *see* SUPERSTRING THEORIES
STRINGED INSTRUMENTS **18**:300–301 *bibliog., illus.*
See also KEYBOARD INSTRUMENTS
aeolian harp **1**:119
African **1**:169–170 *illus.*
Arabian music **2**:99–100
balalaika **3**:30
banjo **3**:67
bow **3**:426
cello **4**:237–238 *illus.*
Chinese music **4**:392–393 *illus.*
chitarrone **4**:398
cittern **4**:448
double bass **6**:246 *illus.*
dulcimer **6**:295
guitar **9**:400–401
harp **10**:54–55 *illus.*
hurdy-gurdy **10**:315–316 *illus.*
Indian music **11**:102–103 *illus.*
Japanese music **11**:381–382 *illus.*
kemanje **2**:100 *illus.*
kithara **12**:93
koto **12**:125
lute **12**:468
lyre **12**:479
mandolin **13**:111–112 *illus.*
musical instruments **13**:677–679 *illus.*
production
Amati (family) **1**:322
Stradivari (family) **18**:287
psaltery **15**:587
sitar **17**:330 *illus.*
string quartet **18**:300
tablature **19**:4
theorbo **19**:158 *illus.*
ud **2**:99 *illus.*
ukulele **19**:376 *illus.*
vielle **19**:578
viol **19**:601–602 *illus.*
viola **19**:602
violin **19**:602–603 *illus.*
zither **20**:370–371
STRINGER, ARTHUR **18**:301
STRINGTOWN (Oklahoma)
map (34° 28′N 96° 3′W) **14**:368
STRIP MINING **13**:456 *illus.*
coal and coal mining **5**:78–79
environmental considerations **5**:79
iron and steel industry **11**:274
land reclamation **12**:180
mining and quarrying **13**:448–449 *illus.*
open pit copper mine **13**:550 *illus.*
STRIPED BLISTER BEETLE **3**:167 *illus.*
STRIPLING, ROBERT **19**:381 *illus.*
STROBILUS *see* POLLEN CONE
STROBOSCOPE **18**:301 *bibliog.*
Edgerton, Harold Eugene **7**:56–57
flash photography **8**:153
STROBOSCOPIC PHOTOGRAPHY
flash photography **8**:153
photography **15**:265
STROESSNER, ALFREDO **18**:301
STROHEIM, ERICH VON **18**:301 *bibliog.*
STROKE **18**:301–302 *bibliog.*
arteriosclerosis **2**:213
hypertension **10**:349
nervous system, diseases of the **14**:96
thrombosis **19**:183
STROKE-ORNAMENTED POTTERY CULTURE *see* DANUBIAN CULTURE
STROMATOLITE **18**:302 *bibliog.*
fossil record **8**:245
limestone **12**:345
STROMBOLI (Italy) **18**:302
map (38° 48′N 15° 13′E) **11**:321
STROMBOLIAN ERUPTION
volcano **19**:627
STRÖMGREN, BENGT GEORG DANIEL **18**:302
STROMSBURG (Nebraska)
map (41° 7′N 97° 36′W) **14**:70
STRONG (Arkansas)
map (33° 7′N 92° 21′W) **2**:166
STRONG (Maine)
map (44° 48′N 70° 13′W) **13**:70
STRONG, JOSIAH **18**:303 *bibliog.*
STRONG, SIR SAMUEL HENRY **18**:303

STRONG NUCLEAR FORCE
fundamental interactions 8:361
fundamental particles 8:362
grand unification theories 9:286
nuclear physics 14:285–286
superstring theories 18:353
STRONGSVILLE (Ohio)
map (41° 19′N 81° 50′W) 14:357
STRONTIUM 18:303
alkaline earth metals 1:295
celestite 4:231
element 7:130 *table*
environmental health 7:212
flame test
qualitative chemical analysis 16:6 *illus.*
Group IIA periodic table 15:167
metal, metallic element 13:328
nuclear explosions 18:303
radiometric age-dating 16:66
sulfate minerals 18:333
STROPHANTHUS 18:303
STROUD (Oklahoma)
map (35° 45′N 96° 40′W) 14:368
STROUDSBURG (Pennsylvania)
map (40° 59′N 75° 12′W) 15:147
STROZZI, BERNARDO 18:303 *bibliog.*
STRUCTURAL FUNCTIONALISM
social anthropology 18:11
STRUCTURAL GEOLOGY 18:303 *bibliog.*
STRUCTURAL LINGUISTICS
applied linguistics 2:90
Indian languages, American 11:98
linguistics 12:356
Saussure, Ferdinand de 17:97
structuralism 18:303
STRUCTURAL PSYCHOLOGY *see* PSYCHOLOGY
STRUCTURAL SYMBOLISM
Guimard, Hector 9:396
STRUCTURALISM 18:303 *bibliog.*
See also STRUCTURAL LINGUISTICS
Barthes, Roland 3:97
Lévi-Strauss, Claude 12:303–304
semiotics 17:197
STRUENSEE, JOHANN FREDERICK
Scandinavia, history of 17:109
STRUER (Denmark)
map (56° 29′N 8° 37′E) 6:109
STRUGA (Yugoslavia)
map (41° 11′N 20° 40′E) 20:340
STRUM (Wisconsin)
map (44° 33′N 91° 24′W) 20:185
STRUMA RIVER
map (40° 47′N 23° 51′E) 9:325
STRUMICA (Yugoslavia)
map (41° 26′N 22° 38′E) 20:340
STRUTHIOMIMUS 18:303–304 *bibliog., illus.*
STRUTT, JOHN WILLIAM *see* RAYLEIGH, LORD, 3D
STRUTT, ROBERT JOHN *see* RAYLEIGH, LORD, 4TH
STRUVE, FRIEDRICH GEORG WILHELM VON 18:304 *bibliog.*
astronomy, history of 2:280
STRUVE, OTTO 18:304 *bibliog.*
Yerkes Observatory 20:327
STRYCHNINE 18:304
synthesis
Woodward, Robert Burns 20:213
STRYKER (Montana)
map (48° 41′N 114° 46′W) 13:547
STRYKER, ROY 18:304 *bibliog.*
STRZELECKI, PAUL
Snowy Mountains 18:5
STUART (family) 18:304 *bibliog.*
Anne, Queen of England, Scotland, and Ireland 2:32
Charles I, King of England, Scotland, and Ireland 4:291
Charles II, King of England, Scotland, and Ireland 4:291–292
Darnley, Henry Stewart, Lord 6:39
earls and dukes of Lennox 18:304
Europe, history of 7:288
Great Britain, history of 9:314
Hanover (dynasty) 10:39
James I, King 11:355–356
James I, King of Scotland 11:355–356
James II, King of England, Scotland, and Ireland 11:356
James IV, King of Scotland 11:357
James V, King of Scotland 11:357
Mary, Queen of Scots 13:186–187
Mary II, Queen of England 13:186
Settlement, Act of 17:214
Stuart, Charles Edward (Bonnie Prince Charlie) 18:304–305
Stuart, James Francis Edward 18:305–306
STUART (Florida)
map (27° 12′N 80° 15′W) 8:172
STUART (Iowa)
map (41° 30′N 94° 19′W) 11:244
STUART (Nebraska)
map (42° 36′N 99° 8′W) 14:70
STUART (Virginia)
map (36° 38′N 80° 16′W) 19:607
STUART, CHARLES EDWARD (Bonnie Prince Charlie) 18:304–305 *bibliog., illus.*
Jacobites 11:346
STUART, GILBERT 18:305 *bibliog., illus.*
Portrait of a Flute Player 18:305 *illus.*
STUART, HENRY BENEDICT
Stuart, James Francis Edward 18:306
STUART, J. E. B. 18:306 *bibliog., illus.*
STUART, JAMES 18:305 *bibliog.*
Greek Revival 9:345
STUART, JAMES FRANCIS EDWARD 18:305–306 *bibliog.*
Jacobites 11:346
STUART, JESSE 18:306 *bibliog.*
STUART, JOHN McDOUALL 18:306
Australia, history of 2:340 *map*
exploration 7:336 *map*
Macdonnell Ranges (Australia) 13:13
STUART, MARY *see* MARY, QUEEN OF SCOTS
STUART, MOUNT
map (47° 29′N 120° 54′W) 20:35
STUART, ROBERT
Wyoming 20:303
STUARTS DRAFT (Virginia)
map (38° 1′N 79° 2′W) 19:607
STUBBINS, HUGH 18:306 *bibliog.*
STUBBS, DEL
wood sculpture 5:327 *illus.*
STUBBS, GEORGE 18:306–307 *bibliog., illus.*
Lion Devouring A Horse 18:306 *illus.*
STUBBS, WILLIAM 18:307
STUCCO
Feuchtmayer, Joseph Anton 8:63
house (in Western architecture) 10:268 *illus.*
Primaticccio, Francesco 15:542
Roman art and architecture 16:276–277
Vittoria, Alessandro 19:621
STUCK, FRANZ VON 18:307 *bibliog.*
Secession movement 17:178
STUCK, HUDSON
McKinley, Mount 13:30
STUD POKER (card game)
poker 15:386
STUDEBAKER (automobile) 2:365 *illus.*
automotive industry 2:364; 2:366
STUDEBAKER (family) 18:307 *bibliog.*
STUDENT FINANCIAL AID *see* SCHOLARSHIPS, FELLOWSHIPS, AND LOANS
STUDENT MOVEMENTS 18:307–308 *bibliog.*
academic freedom 1:68
California 4:37
Hesburgh, Theodore M. 10:150–151
Kerr, Clark 12:59–60
Latin American universities 12:232
United States Student Association 19:464
STUDENT NONVIOLENT COORDINATING COMMITTEE *see* SNCC
STUDENT VOLUNTEER MOVEMENT FOR FOREIGN MISSIONS
Mott, John R. 13:616
STUDENTS FOR A DEMOCRATIC SOCIETY
counterculture 5:311
STUDY OF HISTORY, A (book) 18:308 *bibliog.*
Toynbee, Arnold 19:257
STUKA 18:308 *illus.*
STUKELEY, WILLIAM 18:308 *bibliog.*
Stonehenge
archaeoastronomy 2:114–115
STUMP LAKE
map (47° 54′N 98° 24′W) 14:248
STUNG TRENG (Kampuchea)
map (13° 31′N 105° 58′E) 12:11
STUPA 18:308 *bibliog.*; 19:97 *illus.*
Anuradhapura 1:72
Borobudur 3:402–403
Lamaist art and architecture 12:172
Southeast Asian art and architecture 18:109–110
Sule Pagoda 16:85 *illus.*
temple 19:97–98
STURDEE, SIR FREDERICK
World War I 20:228
STURGEON 18:308–309 *illus.*
caviar 4:226
STURGEON (Missouri)
map (39° 14′N 92° 17′W) 13:476
STURGEON, NICHOLAS
English music 7:202
STURGEON, THEODORE 18:309 *bibliog.*
STURGEON, WILLIAM
magnetism 13:58
STURGEON BAY (Wisconsin)
map (44° 50′N 87° 23′W) 20:185
STURGEON RIVER
map (45° 50′N 86° 41′W) 13:377
STURGES, PRESTON 18:309 *bibliog.*
STURGIS (Kentucky)
map (37° 33′N 87° 59′W) 12:47
STURGIS (Michigan)
map (41° 48′N 85° 25′W) 13:377
STURGIS (South Dakota)
map (44° 25′N 103° 31′W) 18:103
STURLUSON, SNORRI
Heimskringla 10:108
STURM, DER (periodical)
Döblin, Alfred 6:209
Kokoschka, Oskar 12:106
STURM UND DRANG 18:309 *bibliog.*
Byronic hero 3:603
drama 6:260
German literature 9:133
Goethe, Johann Wolfgang von 9:223–224
Herder, Johann Gottfried 10:138
Sorrows of Young Werther, The 18:70
Sturmabteilung *see* SA (*Sturmabteilung*)
STURT, CHARLES 18:309 *bibliog.*
Australia, history of 2:340 *map*
Darling River 6:39
exploration 7:336 *map*
Murray River 13:650
Murrumbidgee River 13:651
STURTEVANT (Wisconsin)
map (42° 42′N 87° 54′W) 20:185
STURTEVANT, ALFRED HENRY
Morgan, Thomas Hunt 13:579
STUTSMAN (county in North Dakota)
map (47° 0′N 99° 0′W) 14:248
STUTTERING 18:309–310 *bibliog.*
speech 18:175
speech therapy 18:176
STUTTGART (Arkansas)
map (34° 30′N 91° 33′W) 2:166
STUTTGART (West Germany) 18:310
map (48° 46′N 9° 11′E) 9:140
STUTTGART BALLET 18:310 *bibliog.*
Cragun, Richard Allan 5:328
Cranko, John 5:331
Haydée, Marcia 10:80
STUYVESANT, PETER 18:310 *bibliog., illus.*
New Jersey 14:133
New Netherland 14:140
Wall Street 20:13
STY 18:311
STYLE (literature)
narrative and dramatic devices 14:23
STYLE ANGLAIS *see* ART NOUVEAU
STYLE GALANT *see* ROCOCO MUSIC
STYLE MÉTRO *see* ART NOUVEAU
STYLES OF LOUIS XIII–XVI 18:311 *bibliog., illus.*
Bélanger, François Joseph 3:173
Bérain, Jean 3:207
commode 8:376–377 *illus.*
French art and architecture 8:305–306
Jacob, Georges 11:345
jewelry 11:410
landscape architecture 12:186
Le Brun, Charles 12:252–253
Le Sueur, Eustache 12:255
Riesener, Jean Henri 16:219
Versailles, Palace of 19:561
STYNE, JULES 18:311 *bibliog.*
STYRACOSAURUS 18:311–312 *illus.*
STYRENE
benzene 3:206
polystyrene 15:348 *illus.*
rubber 16:334
STYRIA (Austria) 18:312
cities
Graz 9:307
Germany in 1648 9:151 *map*
STYRON, WILLIAM 18:312 *bibliog.*
STYX 18:312
SU DONGPO *see* SU TUNG-P'O (Su Dongpo)
SU SHIH *see* SU TUNG-P'O (Su Dongpo)
SU TUNG-P'O (Su Dongpo) 18:312 *bibliog.*
SUÁREZ, FRANCISCO 18:312 *bibliog.*
scholasticism 17:132
SUÁREZ, HUGO BANZER *see* BANZER SUÁREZ, HUGO
SUÁREZ GONZÁLEZ, ADOLFO 18:312
SUAZO CORDOVA, ROBERTO
Honduras 10:220
SUBANG (Indonesia)
map (6° 34′S 107° 45′E) 11:147
SUBAQUEOUS EROSION
erosion and sedimentation 7:233
SUBARCTIC CLIMATE *see* TAIGA CLIMATE
SUBARCTIC CURRENT *see* ALEUTIAN CURRENT
SUBATOMIC PARTICLE *see* FUNDAMENTAL PARTICLES
SUBCLAVIAN ARTERY
circulatory system 4:440 *illus.*
SUBDUCTION ZONE 18:312–313 *bibliog.*
geochemistry 9:96
geosyncline 9:120
oceanic trenches 14:341–342
plate tectonics 15:355 *illus.*
worldwide distribution 15:351 *map*
SUBDWARF 18:313
SUBGIANT 18:313
SUBJECT (citizen) *see* CITIZENSHIP
SUBJECTIVISM
ethics 7:250–251
SUBLETTE (Kansas)
map (37° 29′N 100° 50′W) 12:18
SUBLETTE (county in Wyoming)
map (42° 45′N 109° 55′W) 20:301
SUBLIMATION (chemistry) 18:313
SUBLIMATION (psychology) 18:313
SUBLIMINAL PERCEPTION 18:313
SUBLINGUAL GLANDS
salivary glands 17:34
SUBMANDIBULAR GLANDS
salivary glands 17:34
SUBMARINE 18:313–316 *bibliog., illus.*
designers
Bushnell, David 3:585; 18:315
Drebbel, Cornelis 6:268; 18:313
Fulton, Robert 8:358; 18:315
Holland, John Philip 10:203; 18:315
Rickover, Hyman 16:216
Wilkins, Sir George Hubert 20:152
destroyer 6:133
detection
radar 18:315
sonar 18:62
development 18:313–315
frogman 8:338
Groton (Connecticut) 9:372
guidance and control systems 18:315
naval vessels 14:55–56
navy 14:64–65
New London (Connecticut) 14:134
notable submarines
Nautilus 14:52
Turtle 19:352
U.S.S. *Holland* 18:315
nuclear strategy 18:315
nuclear submarines 14:52; 14:57 *illus.*; 17:275; 18:315–316
shipyards 14:134
sonar 18:315
structure and function 18:313
underwater archaeology 19:383
wartime use
Civil War, U.S. 18:315
World War I 18:315; 20:228; 20:232; 20:236; 20:246–247 *illus.*
World War II 18:315; 20:256; 20:264–265 *illus., map*
weapons 20:75
defense, national 6:82 *table*
depth charge 6:120
mine 13:438
Polaris (missile) 15:393
Poseidon (missile) 15:458
rockets and missiles 16:255
torpedo (projectile) 19:242
Trident (missile) 19:296–297
SUBMARINE CANYON 18:316 *bibliog., illus.*
continental shelf and slope 5:230
density current 6:114
erosion and sedimentation 7:233
SUBMARINE RIDGES *see* MID-OCEANIC RIDGE
SUBOTICA (Yugoslavia)
map (46° 6′N 19° 39′E) 20:340
SUBPLOT (literature)
narrative and dramatic devices 14:23
SUBPOENA 18:316
witness 20:192

SUBSET
set theory **17**:213
SUBSIDENCE **18**:316–317 *bibliog.*
floods and flood control **8**:166–167
geothermal energy **9**:121
SUBSIDIARY (business) *see* HOLDING COMPANY
SUBSTANCE **18**:317 *bibliog.*
Aristotle **2**:157
measurement
units, physical **19**:466
SUBSTANTIAL PERFORMANCE *see* PERFORMANCE (law)
SUBTENSE BAR
surveying **18**:369
SUBTLE DOCTOR, THE *see* DUNS SCOTUS, JOHN
SUBTRACTION
arithmetic **2**:158
SUBTROPICS
horse latitudes **10**:246
SUBURBS **18**:317
city **5**:6
housing **10**:277 *illus.*; **10**:278 *illus.*
municipal government **13**:642–643
SUBVERSION **18**:317
SUBVOLCANIC ROCK
igneous rock **11**:34
SUBWAY **18**:317–319 *bibliog., illus., table*
municipal systems **18**:318 *table*
SUCARNOOCHEE RIVER
map (32° 25′N 88° 2′W) **1**:234
SUCCASUNNA (New Jersey)
map (40° 52′N 74° 38′W) **14**:129
SUCCESSION, PLANT *see* PLANT SUCCESSION
SUCCESSION, PRESIDENTIAL *see* VICE-PRESIDENT OF THE UNITED STATES
SUCCULENTS (botany) *see* CACTI AND OTHER SUCCULENTS
SUCEAVA (Romania)
map (47° 39′N 26° 19′E) **16**:288
SÚCHIL (Mexico)
map (23° 38′N 103° 55′W) **13**:357
SUCHITOTO (El Salvador)
map (13° 56′N 89° 2′W) **7**:100
SUCKER (fish) **18**:319
buffalo fish **3**:547
SUCKLING, SIR JOHN **18**:319
SUCRE (Bolivia) **18**:319
map (19° 2′S 65° 17′W) **3**:366
SUCRE (Ecuador)
map (1° 16′S 80° 26′W) **7**:52
SUCRE, ANTONIO JOSÉ DE **18**:319–320 *bibliog.*
SUCROSE
photosynthesis **15**:277
sugar **18**:327
SUCÚA (Ecuador)
map (2° 28′S 78° 10′W) **7**:52
SUDAN **18**:320–322 *bibliog., illus., map, table*
African art **1**:161–162
cities
Khartoum **12**:66
Omdurman **14**:387
Waw **18**:320 *table*
climate **18**:320 *table*
economic activity **18**:321–322 *illus.*
education **18**:321
Middle Eastern universities **13**:410–412 *table*
flag **18**:320 *illus.*
government **18**:322
history **18**:322
Africa, history of **1**:156
Darfur **6**:37
Nimeiry, Muhammad Gaafar al- **14**:198
Slatin, Rudolf Anton Karl, Freiherr von **17**:351
land and resources **18**:320–321 *map, table*
map (15° 0′N 30° 0′E) **1**:136
people **18**:321
Azande **2**:380
Baggara **3**:21
Fur **8**:369
Nuba **14**:277
Nuer **14**:291
race **16**:34 *illus.*
physical features
Nubian Desert **14**:278
pyramids **15**:635
SUDAN (region in Africa)
map (10° 0′N 20° 0′E) **1**:136
SUDAN PLATED LIZARD *see* GERRHOSAURID
SUDBURY (Massachusetts)
map (42° 23′N 71° 25′W) **13**:206
SUDBURY (Ontario) **18**:322
major ore deposits **14**:424–425 *table*
map (46° 20′N 81° 0′W) **14**:393
SUDBURY CENTER (Massachusetts)
map (42° 23′N 71° 25′W) **3**:409
SUDBURY RESERVOIR
map (42° 28′N 71° 22′W) **3**:409
SUDBURY RIVER
map (42° 28′N 71° 22′W) **3**:409
SUDD
Nile River **14**:196; **14**:197
SUDDEN INFANT DEATH SYNDROME *see* CRIB DEATH
SUDDIE (Guyana)
map (7° 7′N 58° 29′W) **9**:410
SUDERMANN, HERMANN **18**:322–323
SUDERSHAN, GEORGE
tachyon **19**:6
SUDETEN MOUNTAINS **18**:323
map (50° 30′N 16° 0′E) **5**:413
SUDETENLAND (Czechoslovakia) **18**:323 *map*
Czechoslovakia **5**:416
history
Hitler, Adolf **10**:188
Munich Conference **13**:641
World War II **20**:250
SUDETES *see* SUDETEN MOUNTAINS
SUDRE, JEAN FRANÇOIS
languages, artificial **12**:197
SUE, EUGÈNE **18**:323 *bibliog.*
SUEDE **18**:323
SUESS, EDUARD **18**:323
paleogeography **15**:36
SUETONIUS **18**:323
SUEUR, EUSTACHE LE *see* LE SUEUR, EUSTACHE
SUEVI
Germanic peoples **9**:138
SUEZ (Egypt) **18**:323
map (29° 58′N 32° 33′E) **7**:76
SUEZ, GULF OF
map (29° 0′N 32° 50′E) **7**:76
SUEZ CANAL **4**:96 *illus.*; **7**:79 *illus.*; **18**:323–325 *bibliog., illus., map*
Lesseps, Ferdinand Marie, Vicomte de **12**:298
map (29° 55′N 32° 33′E) **18**:324
Middle East, history of the **13**:406
Pearson, Lester B. **15**:128
Port Said (Egypt) **15**:443
Rothschild (family) **16**:322
Suez Crisis **18**:325
SUEZ CRISIS **18**:325 *bibliog.*
Arab-Israeli Wars **2**:96–97 *map*
Eden, Sir Anthony **7**:55–56
SUEZ-SINAI WAR (1956)
Arab-Israeli Wars **2**:96–97 *map*
SUFFIELD (Alberta)
map (50° 12′N 111° 10′W) **1**:256
SUFFOCATION **18**:325
SUFFOLK (county in England) **18**:325
cities
Bury St. Edmunds **3**:583
SUFFOLK (horse) **10**:244 *illus.*; **18**:325 *illus.*
SUFFOLK (county in Massachusetts)
map (42° 21′N 71° 4′W) **13**:206
SUFFOLK (county in New York)
map (40° 55′N 72° 40′W) **14**:149
SUFFOLK (Virginia)
map (36° 44′N 76° 35′W) **19**:607
SUFFOLK, WILLIAM DE LA POLE, 4TH EARL AND 1ST DUKE OF **18**:325
Henry VI, King of England **10**:126
SUFFOLK RESOLVES
Warren, Joseph **20**:31
SUFFRAGE **18**:325–326 *bibliog.*
See also CIVIL RIGHTS; SUFFRAGE, WOMEN'S
absentee voting **1**:62
democracy **6**:97–98
District of Columbia
23d Amendment **19**:360
election **7**:103
15th Amendment **8**:74
Great Britain
Reform Acts **16**:120–121
19th Amendment **14**:199
poll tax **15**:405
publications
Culture and Anarchy **5**:385
Reconstruction
grandfather clause **9**:286
Reconstruction Amendments **5**:221–222
republic **16**:172
24th Amendment **19**:359
26th Amendment **19**:363
voter registration **19**:637
SUFFRAGE, WOMEN'S **18**:326–327 *bibliog., illus.*
Canada
McClung, Nellie **13**:9
costume **5**:302
Great Britain
Pankhurst (family) **15**:60
Wollstonecraft, Mary **20**:199
New Zealand
Seddon, Richard John **17**:182
Switzerland **18**:397
United States
Alcott, Louisa May **1**:267
Anthony, Susan B. **2**:49–50
Blatch, Harriot Eaton Stanton **3**:328
Brown, Olympia **3**:516
Catt, Carrie Chapman **4**:213
Equal Suffrage League of St. Louis **19**:453 *illus.*
Foster, Abigail **8**:248
Morris, Esther **13**:588
19th Amendment **14**:199
Paul, Alice **15**:116
Shaw, Anna Howard **17**:245
Spencer, Anna Garlin **18**:177
Stanton, Elizabeth Cady **18**:220
Stone, Lucy **18**:281
Thomas, Martha Carey **19**:173
Truth, Sojourner **19**:322
Willard, Frances **20**:154
Woodhull, Victoria **20**:211–212
SUFISM **18**:327 *bibliog., illus.*
Attar, Farid al-Din Abu Hamid **2**:314
dervish **6**:123
Rumi, Jalal al-Din al- **16**:345
Sanusi, al- **17**:71
Uighur **19**:375
SUGAR **18**:327 *bibliog.*
See also SWEETENERS (food)
blood
pancreas **15**:58
candy **4**:108
carbohydrate **4**:132–133; **4**:133
diet, human **6**:164
digestion, human **6**:172
fermentation **8**:55
Buchner, Eduard **3**:534
whiskey **20**:132–133
Fischer, Emil Hermann **8**:110
glucagon **9**:210–211
Haworth, Sir Walter Norman **10**:78
jam and jelly **12**:351
Leloir, Luis Frederico **12**:279
metabolism
diabetes **6**:148–149
galactosemia **9**:9
hypoglycemia **10**:351
Krebs, Sir Hans Adolf **12**:128
monosaccharide **13**:540
photosynthesis **15**:277
polarimeter **15**:393
polysaccharide **15**:422–421
sources **18**:327
maple syrup and sugar **13**:138
sugar beet **18**:327–328
sugar production **18**:328–330 *illus.*
SUGAR ACT (1764)
United States, history of the **19**:440
SUGAR APPLE **15**:337 *illus.*
See also CUSTARD APPLE
SUGAR BEET **18**:327–328 *illus.*
beet **3**:163
harvester **10**:65
sugar production **18**:328–330
SUGAR CITY (Idaho)
map (43° 52′N 111° 45′W) **11**:26
SUGAR CREEK
map (39° 21′N 86° 0′W) **11**:111
SUGAR HILL (Georgia)
map (34° 7′N 84° 2′W) **9**:114
SUGAR LAND (Texas)
map (29° 37′N 95° 38′W) **19**:129
SUGAR LOAF MOUNTAIN
map (39° 16′N 77° 23′W) **13**:188
SUGAR MOUNTAIN
map (47° 55′N 89° 4′W) **13**:377
SUGAR PRODUCTION **18**:328–330 *bibliog., illus.*
cultivation and refining **18**:328–329
history **18**:328
maple syrup and sugar **13**:138
molasses **13**:505
rum **16**:344
sugar beet **18**:327–328
sugar grades **18**:329–330
SUGAR RIVER
map (43° 24′N 72° 24′W) **14**:123
SUGARBERRY *see* HACKBERRY
SUGARCANE
grass **9**:295
Hawaii (state) **10**:75; **10**:76
sugar **18**:327
sugar production **18**:328 *illus.*
SUGER, ABBOT OF SAINT-DENIS **18**:330 *bibliog.*
monastic art and architecture **13**:519
Saint-Denis (church) **17**:17
SUGGESTIBILITY
hypnosis **10**:350
SUHARTO **18**:330
Indonesia **11**:150
Sukarno **18**:332
SUHBAATAR, DAMDINY
Mongolia **13**:530
SUHL (Germany, East and West)
map (50° 37′N 10° 41′E) **9**:140
SUI (dynasty) **18**:330
China, history of **4**:371–372
temple **19**:98
Yang-ti **4**:372 *illus.*
SUICIDE **18**:330–331 *bibliog.*
barbiturate **3**:78
hara-kiri **10**:41
homicide **10**:214
Huntington's chorea **10**:315
religious cults, Jonestown **11**:444
statistical problems **18**:330–331
suttee **18**:373
young people **20**:336
SUIR RIVER
map (52° 15′N 7° 0′W) **11**:258
SUIT (law)
class action **5**:41
demurrer **6**:105
legal procedure **12**:272–273
SUITE (music) **18**:331–332
chamber music **4**:272
composers
Ibert, Jacques **11**:4
SUITLAND (Maryland)
map (38° 51′N 76° 56′W) **13**:188
SUKABUMI (Indonesia)
map (6° 55′S 106° 56′E) **11**:147
SUKARNO **18**:332 *bibliog., illus.*
Indonesia **11**:149–150
SUKHOTHAI (Thailand)
Southeast Asian art and architecture **18**:109 *illus.*
Thai **19**:138
Thailand **19**:141
SUKKOTH *see* TABERNACLES, FEAST OF
SUKKUR
map (27° 42′N 68° 52′E) **15**:27
SUKUMA **18**:332 *bibliog.*
SULA ISLANDS
map (1° 52′S 125° 22′E) **11**:147
SULAIMAN RANGE
map (30° 30′N 70° 10′E) **15**:27
SULAWESI (Indonesia) **18**:332
Bugis **3**:548
map (2° 0′S 121° 0′E) **11**:147
SULAWESI SEA *see* CELEBES SEA
SULEIMAN I, SULTAN OF THE OTTOMAN EMPIRE (Suleiman the Magnificent) **18**:332–333 *bibliog., illus.*; **19**:348 *illus.*
Ottoman Empire **14**:464
SULFA DRUGS **18**:333
amide **1**:369
Domagk, Gerhard **6**:229
medicine **13**:271
respiratory system disorders **16**:181
SULFATE MINERALS **18**:333 *bibliog., table*
anglesite **1**:416
anhydrite **2**:8
barite **3**:81
celestite **4**:231
common minerals in group **18**:333 *table*
evaporite **7**:314
glauberite **9**:205
gypsum **9**:415–416
isomorph **11**:300
mineral **13**:443 *table*
occurrence **18**:333
polyhalite **15**:419
reaction, chemical **16**:98 *illus.*
sulfur **18**:334–336
SULFIDE MINERALS **18**:333–334 *bibliog.*
argentite **2**:152
arsenopyrite **2**:189–190
bornite **3**:402
chalcopyrite **4**:270
chemical bond **18**:333–334
chromate minerals **4**:417
cinnabar **4**:434
cobaltite **5**:83
disintegration **18**:334
enargite **7**:162
galena **9**:13
geode **9**:97
major ore deposits **14**:424–425 *table*
marcasite **13**:145
metal ore **18**:334
millerite **13**:429
minerals **13**:443 *table*
molybdenite **13**:514
niccolite **14**:180
occurrence **18**:334

pentlandite **15**:155
physical properties **18**:334
proustite **15**:583
pyrargyrite **15**:636
pyrite **15**:637
pyrrhotite **15**:638
sphalerite **18**:180
stibnite **18**:266
structure **18**:333–334
sulfosalts **18**:334
telluride minerals **19**:91
tetrahedrite **19**:127
SULFITES **18**:334 *bibliog.*
SULFONAMIDE *see* SULFA DRUG
SULFOSALTS **18**:334 *bibliog.*
enargite **7**:162
mineral ores **18**:334
proustite **15**:583
pyrargyrite **15**:636
sulfide minerals **18**:334
tetrahedrite **19**:127
SULFUR **18**:334–336 *bibliog., illus.*
abundances of common elements **7**:131 *table*
acid rain **1**:82
biosphere **3**:277
chalcogens **4**:270
compounds **18**:335
element **7**:130 *table*
Frasch, Herman **8**:286–287
Frasch process extraction **18**:334–335
Group IVA periodic table **15**:167
Group VIA periodic table **18**:334
industrial uses **18**:335–336
nutrient cycles **14**:303
occurrence **18**:334
oceanic mineral resources **14**:340
ore deposits, world distribution **14**:423
orthorhombic system **14**:451
properties **18**:335
reaction, chemical **16**:99
sulfate minerals **18**:333; **18**:335
sulfide minerals **18**:333–334
vitamins and minerals **19**:621
SULFUR DIOXIDE
pollution control **15**:416
smoke **17**:373
sulfur **18**:335
SULFURIC ACID **18**:336 *bibliog.*
industrial uses **18**:336
pyrite **15**:637
substitute, Glauber's salt **9**:205
sulfur **18**:335
SULITELMA MOUNTAIN
map (67° 8′N 16° 24′E) **14**:261
SULKY **10**:247 *illus.*
SULLA, LUCIUS CORNELIUS **18**:336 *bibliog.*
Cinna, Lucius Cornelius **4**:434
Crassus, Marcus Licinius **5**:332
Pompey the Great **15**:425
Rome, ancient **16**:301
SULLANA (Peru)
map (4° 53′S 80° 41′W) **15**:193
SULLIGENT (Alabama)
map (33° 54′N 88° 8′W) **1**:234
SULLIVAN (Illinois)
map (39° 36′N 88° 37′W) **11**:42
SULLIVAN (Indiana)
map (39° 6′N 87° 24′W) **11**:111
SULLIVAN (county in Indiana)
map (39° 5′N 87° 25′W) **11**:111
SULLIVAN (Missouri)
map (38° 13′N 91° 10′W) **13**:476
SULLIVAN (county in Missouri)
map (40° 15′N 93° 5′W) **13**:476
SULLIVAN (county in New Hampshire)
map (43° 20′N 72° 15′W) **14**:123
SULLIVAN (county in New York)
map (41° 39′N 74° 42′W) **14**:149
SULLIVAN (county in Pennsylvania)
map (41° 25′N 76° 29′W) **15**:147
SULLIVAN (county in Tennessee)
map (36° 30′N 82° 20′W) **19**:104
SULLIVAN, ANNE
Keller, Helen **12**:38
SULLIVAN, SIR ARTHUR SEYMOUR *see* GILBERT AND SULLIVAN
SULLIVAN, ED **18**:336 *illus.*
radio and television broadcasting **16**:58 *illus.*
SULLIVAN, HARRY STACK **18**:336 *bibliog.*
SULLIVAN, JO
musical comedy **13**:674 *illus.*
SULLIVAN, JOHN **18**:336–337 *bibliog.*
SULLIVAN, JOHN F. *see* ALLEN, FRED
SULLIVAN, JOHN L. **3**:431 *illus.*; **18**:337 *bibliog., illus.*
SULLIVAN, LOUIS **18**:337 *bibliog., illus.*
Adler, Dankmar **1**:104
Art Nouveau **2**:211
Auditorium Building **2**:318
Carson, Pirie, Scott Store **2**:136 *illus.*
functionalism (design) **8**:360
prairie school **15**:489
Wainright Building **1**:328 *illus.*
Wright, Frank Lloyd **20**:288–289
SULLIVAN AWARD **18**:337–338
Blanchard, Doc **3**:326–327
Decker, Mary **6**:74
Mathias, Bob **13**:228
O'Brien, Parry **14**:317
Richards, Bob **16**:211
Ryun, Jim **16**:380
Walton, Bill **20**:20
SULLY (county in South Dakota)
map (44° 43′N 100° 5′W) **18**:103
SULLY, MAXIMILIEN DE BÉTHUNE, DUC DE **18**:338 *bibliog.*
Henry IV, King of France **10**:128
SULLY, THOMAS **18**:338 *bibliog.*
SULLY PRUDHOMME **18**:338
SULMONA (Italy)
map (42° 3′N 13° 55′E) **11**:321
SULPHASALAZINE
colitis **5**:102
SULPHUR (Louisiana)
map (30° 14′N 93° 23′W) **12**:430
SULPHUR (Oklahoma)
map (34° 31′N 96° 58′W) **14**:368
SULPHUR SPRINGS (Texas)
map (33° 8′N 95° 36′W) **19**:129
SULPHUR SPRINGS VALLEY
map (31° 50′N 109° 50′W) **2**:160
SULTAN **18**:338
SULTAN MUHAMMAD **18**:338 *bibliog.*
SULTANATE OF OMAN *see* OMAN
SULU (Papua New Guinea)
map (5° 25′S 151° 0′E) **15**:72
SULU ARCHIPELAGO (Philippines) **18**:338
map (6° 0′N 121° 0′E) **15**:237
SULU SEA **18**:338
map (8° 0′N 120° 0′E) **15**:237
SULZBERGER, ARTHUR HAYS **18**:338 *bibliog.*
SUMAC **18**:338
poison sumac **15**:383 *illus.*
SUMATRA (Indonesia) **18**:338–339
cities
Medan **13**:263
Palembang **15**:30
jungle and rain forest **11**:469
map (1° 0′S 103° 0′E) **11**:147
people
Batak **3**:121
Minangkabau **13**:436–437
Southeast Asian art and architecture **18**:110
SUMEDANG (Indonesia)
map (6° 52′S 107° 55′E) **11**:147
SUMENEP (Indonesia)
map (7° 1′S 113° 52′E) **11**:147
SUMER **1**:231 *map*; **3**:8 *map*; **18**:339 *bibliog., map*
archaeology **2**:117 *illus.*
Asia, history of **2**:249
cities
Eridu **7**:229
Kish **12**:90
Lagash **12**:165
Nippur **14**:201
Sippar **17**:326
Ur **19**:474
Uruk **19**:490
Dilmun **6**:176
Ebla **7**:36
Heine-Geldern, Robert **10**:109
language
cuneiform **5**:389
languages, extinct **12**:198
writing systems, evolution of **20**:292–293
maps and mapmaking **13**:139
Mesopotamia **13**:315–316 *map*
Mesopotamian art and architecture **13**:319–320
slavery **17**:352
wheel **20**:127 *illus.*
women in society **20**:201
SUMITER (county in Florida)
map (28° 38′N 82° 8′W) **8**:172
SUMMA THEOLOGIAE (book) **18**:339
Aquinas, Saint Thomas **2**:95
SUMMER LAKE
map (42° 50′N 120° 45′W) **14**:427
SUMMERFORD (Newfoundland)
map (49° 29′N 54° 47′W) **14**:166
SUMMERHILL **18**:339 *bibliog.*
SUMMERLAND (British Columbia)
map (49° 39′N 119° 33′W) **3**:491
SUMMERS (county in West Virginia)
map (37° 37′N 80° 55′W) **20**:111
SUMMERSIDE (Prince Edward Island)
map (46° 24′N 63° 47′W) **15**:548
SUMMERSVILLE (West Virginia)
map (38° 17′N 80° 51′W) **20**:111
SUMMERSVILLE LAKE
map (38° 15′N 80° 50′W) **20**:111
SUMMERTOWN (Tennessee)
map (35° 28′N 87° 19′W) **19**:104
SUMMERVILLE (Georgia)
map (34° 29′N 85° 21′W) **9**:114
SUMMERVILLE (South Carolina)
map (33° 1′N 80° 11′W) **18**:98
SUMMIT (county in Colorado)
map (39° 40′N 106° 10′W) **5**:116
SUMMIT (Mississippi)
map (31° 17′N 90° 28′W) **13**:469
SUMMIT (county in Ohio)
map (41° 5′N 81° 31′W) **14**:357
SUMMIT (county in Utah)
map (40° 50′N 111° 0′W) **19**:492
SUMMIT LAKE (British Columbia)
map (54° 17′N 122° 38′W) **3**:491
SUMMONS **18**:339
legal procedure **12**:273
SUMNER (Iowa)
map (42° 51′N 92° 6′W) **11**:244
SUMNER (county in Kansas)
map (37° 15′N 97° 25′W) **12**:18
SUMNER (Mississippi)
map (33° 58′N 90° 22′W) **13**:469
SUMNER (county in Tennessee)
map (36° 25′N 86° 25′W) **19**:104
SUMNER (Washington)
map (47° 12′N 122° 14′W) **20**:35
SUMNER, CHARLES **18**:339–340 *bibliog., illus.*
SUMNER, JAMES B. **18**:340
enzyme **7**:213
SUMNER, LAKE
map (34° 38′N 104° 25′W) **14**:136
SUMNER, THOMAS
navigation **14**:60
SUMNER, WILLIAM GRAHAM **18**:340 *bibliog.*
folkways **8**:204
Social Darwinism **18**:12
SUMO WRESTLING **20**:287 *illus.*
SUMPTER (county in Georgia)
map (32° 0′N 84° 10′W) **9**:114
SUMPTUARY LAWS **18**:340 *bibliog.*
SUMRALL (Mississippi)
map (31° 25′N 89° 33′W) **13**:469
SUMTER (county in Alabama)
map (32° 35′N 88° 10′W) **1**:234
SUMTER (South Carolina)
map (33° 55′N 80° 20′W) **18**:98
SUMTER (county in South Carolina)
map (33° 50′N 80° 25′W) **18**:98
SUMTER, FORT *see* FORT SUMTER (South Carolina)
SUMTER, THOMAS **18**:340
American Revolution **1**:359 *map*
SUN **18**:340–345 *bibliog., illus.*
Aristarchus of Samos **2**:155
astronomy, history of **2**:279
astronomy and astrophysics **2**:282–283
Baily's beads: Baily, Francis **3**:26
chromosphere **4**:419; **18**:342–343
climate **5**:57; **5**:58
corona **5**:270; **18**:343–344
eclipse **7**:41
coronagraph **5**:270–271
day **6**:54
distance, astronomical **6**:199
Earth, motions of **7**:18–19
earthshine **7**:28
eclipse **7**:40–41
dates of occurrence 1980–89 **7**:41 *table*
ecliptic **7**:41
facula **8**:7
flash spectrum **8**:154
Galaxy, The **9**:11
granulation, solar **9**:289
gravitation **9**:305
greenhouse effect **9**:351
Greenwich mean time **9**:354
Hale, George Ellery **10**:18
halo **10**:24
International Years of the Quiet Sun **11**:225
Janssen, Jules **11**:359
Lyot, Bernard Ferdinand **12**:479
magnetic storm **13**:55
magnitude **13**:60–61
Menzel, Donald Howard **13**:303
OGO **14**:355
OSO **14**:456
photosphere **15**:275
Pioneer **15**:309
plage **15**:325
planetary systems **15**:329
plasma physics **15**:346
prominence **15**:567
radiation pressure **16**:43
radio astronomy **16**:48
rainbow **16**:77
recent developments **18**:345
size **18**:224 *illus.*
solar activity **18**:344–345
auroras **2**:325
cycle **18**:345
solar apex **18**:40
solar constant **18**:41
solar convection **18**:341
solar cycle **18**:41
solar energy **18**:41–44
solar flare **18**:44
solar radiation **18**:44
solar system **18**:46; **18**:48 *illus.*
solar time, equation of time **7**:225
solar wind **18**:53
spectrum **18**:342 *illus.*
Wollaston, William Hyde **20**:199
spicule **18**:181
star **18**:220
structure **18**:225 *illus.*; **18**:341–342
sunlight, gegenschein **9**:67
sunshine duration recorder **13**:340 *illus.*
sunspots **18**:349
surface temperature
Stefan, Josef **18**:245
time scales **19**:201
X-ray astronomy **20**:306
SUN ALSO RISES, THE (book) **18**:345–346 *bibliog.*
Hemingway, Ernest **10**:118
SUN BITTERN **18**:346
SUN CITY (Arizona) **10**:278 *illus.*
map (33° 36′N 112° 17′W) **2**:160
SUN DANCE **18**:346 *bibliog.*
Hidatsa **10**:158
Indians, American **11**:129
Mandan **13**:110
SUN-GREBE *see* FINFOOT
SUN KING *see* LOUIS XIV, KING OF FRANCE
SUN KOSI RIVER
map (26° 55′N 87° 9′E) **14**:86
SUN PRAIRIE (Wisconsin)
map (43° 11′N 89° 13′W) **20**:185
SUN VALLEY (Idaho) **11**:29 *illus.*; **18**:346
map (43° 42′N 114° 21′W) **11**:26
SUN WORSHIP **18**:345 *bibliog.*
Inca **11**:73
SUN YAT-SEN **12**:138 *illus.*; **18**:346 *bibliog., illus.*
China, history of **4**:374–375
Kuomintang (Guomindang) **12**:137–138
Soong (family) **18**:66
SUN YAT-SEN, MADAME *see* SOONG (family)
SUNAPEE LAKE
map (43° 23′N 72° 3′W) **14**:123
SUNBELT
North America **14**:236
SUNBIRD **18**:347
SUNBRIGHT (Tennessee)
map (36° 15′N 84° 40′W) **19**:104
SUNBURN
skin diseases **17**:341
ultraviolet light **19**:379
SUNBURST (Montana)
map (48° 53′N 111° 55′W) **13**:547
SUNBURY (North Carolina)
map (36° 27′N 76° 37′W) **14**:242
SUNBURY (Ohio)
map (40° 14′N 82° 52′W) **14**:357
SUNBURY (Pennsylvania)
map (40° 52′N 76° 47′W) **15**:147
SUNCHON (Korea)
map (34° 57′N 127° 28′E) **12**:113
SUNCOOK (New Hampshire)
map (43° 8′N 71° 27′W) **14**:123
SUNDA ISLANDS
map (9° 0′S 120° 0′E) (Lesser Sunda Islands) **11**:147
SUNDA ISLANDS (Indonesia) **18**:347
Bali **3**:37
map (2° 0′S 110° 0′E) (Greater Sunda Islands) **11**:147
Sulawesi **18**:332
Sumatra (Indonesia) **18**:338–339
Timor **19**:203
SUNDA STRAIT **18**:347
map (6° 0′S 105° 45′E) **11**:147
SUNDANCE (Wyoming)
map (44° 24′N 104° 23′W) **20**:301
SUNDANCE KID
outlaws **14**:468
SUNDARBANS (region in Asia)
map (22° 0′N 89° 0′E) **3**:64
SUNDAY
calendar **4**:28
SUNDAY, BILLY **18**:347 *bibliog.*
SUNDAY AFTERNOON ON THE ISLAND OF LA GRANDE JATTE (Georges Seurat) **17**:214 *illus.*
neoimpressionism **14**:83

SUNDAY SCHOOL **18**:347 *bibliog.*
Vincent, John Heyl **19**:599
SUNDERLAND (England)
map (54° 55′N 1° 23′W) **19**:403
SUNDEW
carnivorous plants **4**:157–158
SUNDIAL **18**:347 *bibliog., illus.*
SUNDRE (Alberta)
map (51° 48′N 114° 38′W) **1**:256
SUNDSVALL (Sweden)
map (62° 23′N 17° 18′E) **18**:382
SUNFISH **8**:116 *illus.*; **18**:347–348 *illus.*
pumpkinseed sunfish **12**:168 *illus.*
SUNFLOWER **8**:181 *illus.*; **9**:300 *illus.*; **18**:348
aster **2**:267
blanket flower **3**:327
burdock **3**:567
goldenrod **9**:233
groundsel **9**:374
guayule **9**:390
gumweed **9**:405
hawkweed **10**:78
Jerusalem artichoke **11**:402
marigold **13**:152
tarweed **19**:41
vegetable oils **19**:534–535 *illus., table*
SUNFLOWER (Kansas)
map (38° 56′N 95° 1′W) **12**:18
SUNFLOWER (county in Mississippi)
map (33° 35′N 90° 35′W) **13**:469
SUNFLOWER, MOUNT
map (39° 4′N 102° 1′W) **12**:18
SUNG (Song) (dynasty) **18**:348 *bibliog.*
art
Chinese art and architecture **4**:381 *illus.*; **4**:385
Fan K'uan **8**:20
Hsia Kuei (Xia Gui) **10**:286
Josetsu **11**:452
Kuo Hsi (Guo Xi) **12**:137
landscape painting **12**:188
Li Kung-lin (Li Gonglin) **12**:310
Li T'ang (Li Tang) **12**:310
Ma Yüan (Ma Yuan) **13**:3
Mi Fei **13**:369
Mu-ch'i (Muqi) **13**:630
pottery and porcelain **15**:469
Sung Hui-tsung (Song Huizong) **18**:348
wood carving **20**:209 *illus.*
Asia, history of **2**:256
China, history of **4**:372
Chinese literature **4**:389–390
Ching-te-chen (Jingde Zhen) **4**:395
foot-binding **8**:214
temple **19**:98
Wang An-shih (Wang Anshi) **20**:22
SUNG, KIM IL *see* KIM IL SUNG
SUNG CHIAO-JEN
Kuomintang (Guomindang) **12**:137–138
SUNG HUI-TSUNG (Song Huizong) **18**:348 *bibliog.*
Chinese art and architecture **4**:382 *illus.*
SUNGARI RIVER
map (47° 44′N 132° 32′E) **4**:362
SUNGLASSES
dichroism **6**:156
polarized light **15**:395
SUNLAMP **18**:348
SUNLAND PARK (New Mexico)
map (32° 15′N 106° 45′W) **14**:136
SUNN (plant)
hemp **10**:120
SUNNI ALI
Songhai (empire) **18**:65
SUNNITES **18**:348
Islam **11**:289; **11**:293–294
Middle East, history of the **13**:402
Tatar **19**:43
Turkmen **19**:347
Uighur **19**:374
Uzbek **19**:499
SUNNYBRAE (Nova Scotia)
map (45° 24′N 62° 30′W) **14**:269
SUNNYSIDE (Newfoundland)
map (47° 51′N 53° 55′W) **14**:166
SUNNYSIDE (Utah)
map (39° 33′N 110° 24′W) **19**:492
SUNNYSIDE (Washington)
map (46° 20′N 120° 0′W) **20**:35
SUNNYVALE (California)
map (37° 23′N 122° 1′W) **4**:31
SUNRAY (Texas)
map (36° 1′N 101° 49′W) **19**:129
SUNRISE TELLIN **17**:251 *illus.*
SUNSET (Louisiana)
map (30° 25′N 92° 4′W) **12**:430
SUNSET LAWS **18**:348–349
SUNSET PRAIRIE (British Columbia)
map (55° 50′N 120° 48′W) **3**:491
SUNSPOTS **18**:349 *bibliog., illus., table*
cyclic change **18**:349 *table*
group development **18**:349
Hale, George Ellery **10**:18
Lockyer, Sir Joseph Norman **12**:388
magnetic storm **13**:55
OSO **14**:456
radio astronomy **16**:48
Schwabe, Samuel Heinrich **17**:138
solar cycle **18**:41
solar flare **18**:44
Sun **18**:344–345 *illus.*
Wolf sunspot number **18**:349
SUNSTONE **9**:74 *illus.*
SUNSTROKE *see* HEATSTROKE
SUNTRANA (Alaska)
map (63° 51′N 148° 51′W) **1**:242
SUNYANI (Ghana)
map (7° 20′N 2° 20′W) **9**:164
SUOMI *see* FINLAND
SUPER BOWL
football **8**:218 *table*
SUPERCOMPUTER
computer **5**:160c; **5**:160i
computer languages **5**:160p
Strategic Defense Initiative **18**:289
voice recognition **19**:626
SUPERCONDUCTIVITY **18**:350 *bibliog., table*
Bardeen, John **3**:80
computer memory **5**:166
Cooper, Leon N. **5**:244
cryogenics **5**:371
Giaever, Ivar **9**:171
Kamerlingh Onnes, Heike **12**:10
Landau, Lev **12**:181
magnetism **13**:58
resistivity **16**:177
Schreiffer, John Robert **17**:134
squids **18**:350
SUPEREGO **18**:351
SUPERFLUIDITY **18**:351 *bibliog.*
cryogenics **5**:371
helium **10**:113
Landau, Lev **12**:181
SUPERFUND
pollutants, chemical **15**:411
SUPERGIANT **18**:351
size **18**:224 *illus.*
stellar evolution **18**:251
SUPERHEAVY ELEMENTS **18**:351 *bibliog.*
element 104 **7**:132
element 105 **7**:132
element 106 **7**:132
transition elements **19**:273–274
transuranium elements **19**:282
SUPERHETERODYNE CIRCUIT
Armstrong, Edwin **2**:179
SUPERIOR (Arizona)
map (33° 18′N 111° 6′W) **2**:160
SUPERIOR (Montana)
map (47° 12′N 114° 53′W) **13**:547
SUPERIOR (Nebraska)
map (40° 1′N 98° 4′W) **14**:70
SUPERIOR (Wisconsin)
map (46° 44′N 92° 5′W) **20**:185
SUPERIOR, LAKE **18**:351–352 *map*
map (48° 0′N 88° 0′W) **9**:320
Sault Sainte Marie Canals **17**:96
SUPERMARKET **18**:352 *bibliog.*
food industry **8**:210
Middle East **13**:399 *illus.*
retailing **16**:183
SUPERNATURAL LITERATURE
See also FANTASY (literature)
Gothic romance **9**:263
Hoffmann, Ernst Theodor Amadeus **10**:195
Lovecraft, H. P. **12**:438
Marlowe, Christopher
Doctor Faustus **6**:210
Poe, Edgar Allan **15**:377–378
Shakespeare, William
A Midsummer Night's Dream **13**:414
Stoker, Bram **18**:278
SUPERNOVA **18**:352 *bibliog., illus.*
Crab nebula **5**:325–326
neutron star **14**:109
radio astronomy **16**:49
stellar evolution **18**:251
X-ray astronomy **20**:307
Zwicky, Fritz **20**:384
SUPERPHOSPHATE
Lawes, Sir John Bennett **12**:248
SUPERPOSITION, LAW OF
Strachey, John **18**:287
SUPERREALISM *see* PHOTOREALISM
SUPERSATURATED SOLUTION
saturation **17**:88
SUPERSONIC TRANSPORT **18**:352–353 *bibliog., illus.*
aerodynamics **1**:124
aviation **2**:372–373 *illus.*; **2**:374
Concorde **5**:171 *illus.*
pollution, environmental **15**:414
titanium **19**:211
SUPERSTITION **18**:353 *bibliog.*
African art **1**:161
endangered species **7**:166 *illus.*
evil eye **7**:318
fetish **8**:63
ghost **9**:169
SUPERSTITION MOUNTAINS
map (33° 25′N 111° 30′W) **2**:160
SUPERSTRING THEORIES (physics) **18**:353
SUPERSYMMETRY (physics)
fundamental particles **8**:363
grand unification theories **9**:286
superstring theories **18**:353
SUPERTANKER *see* TANKER
SUPPÉ, FRANZ VON **18**:353
SUPPLEMENTAL EDUCATIONAL OPPORTUNITY GRANTS
scholarships, fellowships, and loans **17**:130
SUPPLEMENTAL SECURITY INCOME
social security **18**:15
social and welfare services **18**:17
SUPPLY AND DEMAND **18**:353–354 *bibliog., illus.*
agriculture and the food supply **1**:194–195
distribution (economics) **6**:200
economics **7**:47; **7**:49
energy sources **7**:175
Galbraith, John Kenneth **9**:13
monetary theory **13**:524–525
petroleum industry **15**:215
price equilibrium **18**:354
price system **15**:535
retailing **16**:184
SUPPLY-SIDE ECONOMICS
economics **7**:49
Reagan, Ronald **16**:102
SUPREMATISM **18**:354 *bibliog.*
constructivism **5**:224
Larionov, Mikhail Fyodorovich **12**:207
Lissitzky, El **12**:366
Malevich, Kasimir **13**:88
Suprematist Composition **16**:364 *illus.*
Rodchenko, Aleksandr Mikhailovich **16**:265
SUPREME COURT OF THE UNITED STATES **18**:355–358 *bibliog., illus., table*
chief justices **18**:356 *table*
Burger, Warren Earl **3**:568–569
Chase, Salmon P. **4**:301
Ellsworth, Oliver **7**:149
Fuller, Melville Weston **8**:357
Hughes, Charles Evans **10**:292
Jay, John **11**:387
Marshall, John **13**:172
Rehnquist, William **16**:130
Rutledge, John **16**:377
Stone, Harlan Fiske **18**:280
Taft, William Howard **19**:9
Taney, Roger B. **19**:21
Vinson, Frederick M. **19**:601
Waite, Morrison Remick **20**:7
Warren, Earl **20**:31
White, Edward Douglass **20**:135
children's rights **4**:354
Constitution of the United Sates **5**:216–220
decisions
abortion **1**:60
academic freedom **1**:68
Alexander v. *Holmes County (Miss.) Board of Education* **1**:275
Ali, Muhammad **1**:292
Amistad Case **1**:372
appointment **2**:91
Argersinger v. *Hamlin* **2**:152
Bailey v. *Drexel Furniture Company* **3**:26
Baker v. *Carr* **3**:28
Bridges v. *California* **3**:485
Brown v. *Board of Education of Topeka, Kansas* **3**:517
Brown v. *Maryland* **3**:517
busing, school **3**:589–590
Calder v. *Bull* **4**:26
capital punishment **4**:124
Carter v. *Carter Coal Company* **4**:173
censorship **4**:247
Dartmouth College v. *Woodward* **6**:40
defamation **6**:81
Dennis v. *United States* **6**:113
Dred Scott v. *Sandford* **6**:268
8th Amendment **7**:92
11th Amendment **5**:221
eminent domain **7**:156
Engel v. *Vitale* **7**:176
equal opportunity **7**:223
equal protection of the laws **7**:223–224
Escobedo v. *Illinois* **7**:237
evidence **7**:317–318
Ex parte Milligan **7**:325–326
executive privilege **7**:329
1st Amendment **8**:109
Fletcher v. *Peck* **8**:163
freedom of religion **8**:297–298
freedom of speech **8**:298–299
freedom of the press **8**:296–297
Furman v. *Georgia* **8**:371–372
Garland, Augustus Hill **9**:47–48
genetic engineering **9**:85
Gibbons v. *Ogden* **9**:173–174
Gideon v. *Wainwright* **9**:177
Gitlow v. *New York* **9**:191
grand jury **9**:285
grandfather clause **9**:286
Griswold v. *Connecticut* **9**:367–368
habeas corpus **10**:4
Hammer v. *Dagenhart* **10**:30
Heart of Atlanta Motel, Inc. v. *United States* **10**:95
Hurtado v. *California* **10**:319
Immigration and Naturalization Service v. *Chadha* **11**:56
integration, racial **11**:202–203
Jim Crow laws **11**:418
judicial review **11**:464
jury **11**:477–478
juvenile delinquency **11**:480
Korematsu v. *United States* **12**:122
law, history of **12**:246–247
legal aid **12**:272
Leisy v. *Hardin* **12**:279
Lochner v. *New York* **12**:386
Luther v. *Borden* **12**:469
McCray v. *United States* **13**:10–11
McCulloch v. *Maryland* **13**:11
Mapp v. *Ohio* **13**:138
Marbury v. *Madison* **13**:144
military justice **13**:421
Miller v. *California* **13**:428–429
Miranda v. *Arizona* **13**:463
Morgan v. *Virginia* **13**:579
Munn v. *Illinois* **13**:643
National Labor Relations Board v. *Jones & Laughlin Steel Corporation* **14**:35
New York Times Company v. *Sullivan* **14**:156
New York Times Company v. *United States* **14**:156
Parker v. *Brown* **15**:91
patronage **15**:114
Pledge of Allegiance **15**:364
Plessy v. *Ferguson* **15**:368
poll tax **15**:405
Pollock v. *Farmers' Loan and Trust Co.* **15**:409–410
pornography **15**:441
Powell v. *Alabama* **15**:481
president of the United States **15**:527
privacy, invasion of **15**:556
rent control **16**:159
Reynolds v. *Sims* **16**:191
right to bear arms **16**:222
Roe v. *Wade* and *Doe* v. *Bolton* **16**:267–268
Roth v. *United States* **16**:321–322
Schechter Poultry Corporation v. *United States* **17**:117
Schenck v. *United States* **17**:119
search warrant **17**:175
2d Amendment **17**:178
Shelley v. *Kraemer* **17**:253–254
16th Amendment **17**:331
6th Amendment **17**:331
Slaughterhouse Cases **17**:351
Smith Act **17**:371
sodomy **18**:34
subversion **18**:317
Swift and Company v. *United States* **18**:389–390
10th Amendment **19**:113
13th Amendment **19**:170
treason **19**:285
trial **19**:292
24th Amendment **19**:359
26th Amendment **19**:359–360
Twining v. *New Jersey* **19**:360
United States v. *Butler* **19**:464
United States v. *Curtiss-Wright Export Corporation* **19**:464
United States v. *Darby* **19**:465

United States v. *E. C. Knight Company* **19**:465
United States v. *Richard M. Nixon* **19**:465
United Steelworkers of America v. *Weber* **19**:465
University of California v. *Bakke* **19**:470
video recording **19**:576c; **19**:576k
Watkins v. *United States* **20**:67
Welsh v. *United States* **20**:102
West Coast Hotel Company v. *Parrish* **20**:108
West River Bridge v. *Dix* **7**:156
wiretapping **20**:183
witness **20**:192–193
Youngstown Sheet and Tube Company v. *Sawyer* **20**:337
zoning **20**:373
justices **12**:246 *illus.*; **18**:355 *illus.*; **18**:356 *table*
See also SUPREME COURT OF THE UNITED STATES—chief justices
Black, Hugo L. **3**:303
Blackmun, Harry A. **3**:322
Brandeis, Louis D. **3**:453
Brennan, William Joseph, Jr. **3**:473
Brewer, David J. **3**:475
Byrnes, James Francis **3**:603
Cardozo, Benjamin N. **4**:145
Chase, Samuel **4**:301
Clark, Tom Campbell **5**:39
Curtis, Benjamin Robbins **5**:395
Davis, David **6**:51
Douglas, William O. **6**:248
Field, Stephen Johnson **8**:72
Fortas, Abe **8**:238
Frankfurter, Felix **8**:281
Goldberg, Arthur J. **9**:231
Harlan (family) **10**:49
Holmes, Oliver Wendell, Jr. **10**:205–206
Iredell, James **11**:257
Jackson, Robert Houghwout **11**:343
Lamar, Lucius Q. C. **12**:173
Marshall, Thurgood **13**:173
Miller, Samuel Freeman **13**:428
Murphy, Frank **13**:649
O'Connor, Sandra Day **14**:347
Paterson, William **15**:111
Powell, Lewis F., Jr. **15**:481
Roberts, Owen J. **16**:242
Scalia, Antonin **17**:107
Stevens, John P. **18**:263
Stewart, Potter **18**:266
Story, Joseph **18**:285
Sutherland, George **18**:372–373
Van Devanter, Willis **19**:513
White, Byron R. **20**:134
Whittaker, Charles Evans **20**:142
Wilson, James **20**:165
law, history of **12**:246–247
New Deal **14**:120
Roosevelt, Franklin Delano **16**:309
United States, education in the **19**:435
United States, history of the **19**:442; **19**:457
Washington, D.C. **20**:41 *map*
SUPREMES, THE *see* MOTOWN
SUR (dynasty)
Sher Shah **17**:256
SUR (Lebanon) *see* TYRE (Phoenicia)
SURABAYA (Indonesia) **18**:358
map (7° 15′S 112° 45′E) **11**:147
SURAKARTA (Indonesia)
map (7° 35′S 110° 50′E) **11**:147
SURAT (India)
map (21° 10′N 72° 50′E) **11**:80
SURAT THANI (Thailand)
map (9° 8′N 99° 19′E) **19**:139
SÛRE RIVER
map (49° 44′N 6° 31′E) **12**:472
SURETY **18**:358
guaranty **9**:386
SURF **18**:358
swell **18**:388
SURF CITY (New Jersey)
map (39° 40′N 74° 10′W) **14**:129
SURFACE
closed
topology **19**:237–238 *illus.*
SURFACE EFFECTS
physical chemistry **15**:279
SURFACE MINING *see* STRIP MINING
SURFACE TENSION **18**:358
capillarity **4**:123
liquid **12**:364–365
molecular
Eötvös, Lóránt, Baron von Vásárosnemény **7**:215
unit of measurement
units, physical **19**:467
SURFACE-TO-AIR MISSILE **18**:358–359
antiaircraft systems **2**:56 *illus.*
rockets and missiles **16**:254–255 *illus.*
SURFBIRD **18**:359
SURFBOARD *see* SURFING
SURFING **18**:359 *bibliog.*, *illus.*
SURFPERCH **18**:359
SURGEONFISH **18**:359–360 *illus.*
SURGERY **18**:360–363 *bibliog.*, *illus.*
acupuncture **1**:91
amputation **1**:383
anesthetics **1**:410–411
barber **3**:77
biopsy **3**:276
cancer **4**:104–105 *illus.*
cesarean section **4**:262
couching **18**:360 *illus.*
cryobiology **5**:370
dentistry **6**:116
eye diseases **7**:351
heart-lung machine **10**:97
hernia **10**:144
history **18**:360–361
Beaumont, William **18**:361
Billroth, Theodor **18**:361
Carrel, Alexis **4**:167
Cooley, Denton A. **5**:240
Cushing, Harvey W. **5**:397
DeBakey, Michael **6**:70
Horsley, Victor **18**:361
Kocher, Emil **12**:105
Lister, Joseph **12**:366
McDowell, Ephraim **18**:361
Matas, Rudolph **18**:361
Morton, William **13**:593
Paré, Ambroise **15**:84
Warren, John C. **18**:361
hyperthermia **10**:349
hysterectomy **10**:352
joint (anatomy) **11**:440
laser **12**:213
lithotomy **18**:360
mastectomy **13**:215
medicine **13**:268–269; **13**:272
microsurgery **18**:362
neurosurgery **18**:361
operating room **10**:256 *illus.*
orthopedic **14**:450; **18**:362
plastic surgery **15**:347
sex change **17**:224
Siamese twins **17**:291
Sims, J. Marion **18**:361
specializations **18**:362
sterilization **3**:294
stomach **18**:280
technological developments **18**:362
transplantation, organ **19**:277
trephining **18**:360 *illus.*
vasectomy **19**:525
SURGICAL INSTRUMENTATION *see* MEDICAL INSTRUMENTATION
SURICATE **18**:363 *illus.*
See also MONGOOSE
SURIKOV, VASILI
Russian art and architecture **16**:362
SURINAM TOAD **18**:363 *illus.*
SURINAME **18**:363–364 *bibliog.*, *illus.*, *map*, *table*
cities
Paramaribo **15**:79
flag **18**:363 *illus.*
history and government **18**:364
land, people, and resources **18**:363–364 *map*, *table*
map (4° 0′N 56° 0′W) **18**:85
people
Warrau **20**:30–31
SURING (Wisconsin)
map (44° 59′N 88° 22′W) **20**:185
SURMULLET *see* GOATFISH
SURRATT, MARY E.
Holt, Joseph **10**:208
SURREALISM (art) **18**:364–365 *bibliog.*, *illus.*
Apollinaire, Guillaume **2**:79
Arp, Jean **2**:187
Blume, Peter **3**:347
Chagall, Marc **4**:267–268
Chirico, Giorgio de **4**:397
Dada **6**:4–5
Dalí, Salvador **6**:13
Delvaux, Paul **6**:96
drawing **6**:265
Ernst, Max **7**:231–232
Fini, Leonor **8**:94
Giacometti, Alberto **9**:171
landscape painting **12**:192
magic realism **13**:51
Magritte, René **13**:62
Masson, André **13**:214
Matta Echaurren, Roberto Sebastián **13**:230
Miró, Joan **13**:463–464
modern art **13**:493–494
painting **15**:23
Picabia, Francis **15**:290
Ray, Man **16**:96 *illus.*
Rousseau, Henri **16**:325
Samaras, Lucas **17**:45
Schiaparelli, Elsa **17**:119–120
Tanguy, Yves **19**:23
Tanning, Dorothea **19**:25
Tchelitchew, Pavel **19**:52
SURREALISM (film, literature, photography, theater) **18**:366 *bibliog.*, *illus.*
Dada **6**:4–5
film
Cocteau, Jean **5**:89
Feuillade, Louis **8**:66
film, history of **8**:84
Ray, Man **16**:96
literature **8**:319
Apollinaire, Guillaume **2**:79
Aragon, Louis **2**:107
Baudelaire, Charles **3**:128–129
Bernhard, Thomas **3**:221
Breton, André **3**:474
Buzzati, Dino **3**:601
Corso, Gregory **5**:277
Desnos, Robert **6**:132
Éluard, Paul **7**:150
García Lorca, Federico **9**:38–39
Vitrac, Roger **19**:621
photography
Jacobi, Lotte **11**:345
Ray, Man **16**:96
theater
Artaud, Antonin **2**:212–213
Cocteau, Jean **5**:89
SURRENCY (Georgia)
map (31° 44′N 82° 12′W) **9**:114
SURREY **5**:74 *illus.*
SURREY (England) **18**:366
SURREY (North Dakota)
map (48° 13′N 101° 8′W) **14**:248
SURREY, HENRY HOWARD, EARL OF **18**:366
Howard (family) **10**:282
SURROGATE MOTHERHOOD
artificial insemination **2**:220–221
SURROGATE'S COURT *see* PROBATE
SURRY (county in North Carolina)
map (36° 25′N 80° 40′W) **14**:242
SURRY (Virginia)
map (37° 8′N 76° 50′W) **19**:607
SURRY (county in Virginia)
map (37° 10′N 76° 50′W) **19**:607
SURT (Libya)
map (31° 12′N 16° 35′E) **12**:320
SURTSEY ISLAND **12**:240 *illus.*
map (63° 16′N 20° 32′W) **11**:17
SURUD AD MOUNTAIN
map (10° 41′N 47° 18′E) **18**:60
SURVEILLANCE SYSTEMS **18**:366 *bibliog.*
airport **1**:225
alarm systems **1**:240
Central Intelligence Agency **4**:254
computers and privacy **5**:167
smoke detector **17**:373
wiretapping **20**:183
SURVEY, STATISTICAL
sampling **17**:48
SURVEYING **18**:366–369 *bibliog.*, *illus.*
See also AERIAL PHOTOGRAPHY; MAPS AND MAPMAKING
astrolabe, prismatic **2**:271
bench mark **3**:196
careers **18**:369
education **18**:369
equipment **18**:368–369 *illus.*
Gauss, Carl Friedrich **9**:61–62
geophysics **9**:108
Landsat **12**:184–185
laser **12**:213
methods **18**:367–368 *illus.*
quadrant **16**:4–5
roads and highways **16**:239
space exploration **18**:123
stakeout **18**:367–368 *illus.*
theodolite **19**:155–156
transit, surveying **19**:273
trigonometry **19**:298
SURVEYOR **18**:369–370 *bibliog.*, *illus.*
Centaur (rocket) **4**:249
missions **18**:369–370
moon landing **18**:369–370
space exploration **18**:124 *illus.*
SURVIVAL OF THE FITTEST
social Darwinism **18**:11–12
SURYA
temple
Konarak **12**:108
SUSA (Iran) **18**:370 *bibliog.*
Asia, history of **2**:249 *illus.*
Persia, ancient **15**:182 *map*
Persian art and architecture **15**:184 *illus.*
SUSANN, JACQUELINE **18**:370
SUSANNA **18**:370
SUSANVILLE (California)
map (40° 25′N 120° 39′W) **4**:31
SUSATO, TIELMAN
Renaissance music **16**:156
SUSIANA
Persia, ancient **15**:182 *map*
SUSITNA RIVER
map (61° 16′N 150° 30′W) **1**:242
SUSLIK **18**:257 *illus.*
SUSO, HEINRICH **18**:370 *bibliog.*
SUSPENSE FICTION *see* MYSTERY, SUSPENSE, AND DETECTIVE FICTION
SUSPENSION **18**:371
aerosol **1**:124–125
colloidal state **5**:104–105
SUSPENSION BRIDGE **3**:480–484 *illus.*, *table*
SUSPENSION SYSTEM **18**:371–372 *bibliog.*, *illus.*
machine **13**:21
wagon **20**:6
SUSQUEHANNA (American Indians) **18**:372 *bibliog.*
Tuscarora **19**:355
SUSQUEHANNA (Pennsylvania)
map (41° 57′N 75° 36′W) **15**:147
SUSQUEHANNA (county in Pennsylvania)
map (41° 48′N 75° 48′W) **15**:147
SUSQUEHANNA RIVER **15**:149 *illus.*; **18**:372
map (39° 35′N 76° 10′W) **15**:147
Maryland **13**:189
SUSQUEHANNOCK (American Indians) *see* SUSQUEHANNA (American Indians)
SUSQUES (Argentina)
map (23° 25′S 66° 29′W) **2**:149
SÜSS, HANS *see* KULMBACH, HANS VON
SUSSEX (county in Delaware)
map (38° 42′N 75° 23′W) **6**:88
SUSSEX (England) **2**:3 *map*; **18**:372
cities
Brighton **3**:486
Chichester **4**:344
Hastings **10**:67
SUSSEX (New Brunswick)
map (45° 43′N 65° 31′W) **14**:117
SUSSEX (New Jersey)
map (41° 13′N 74° 36′W) **14**:129
SUSSEX (county in New Jersey)
map (41° 8′N 74° 41′W) **14**:129
SUSSEX (Virginia)
map (36° 55′N 77° 17′W) **19**:607
SUSSEX (county in Virginia)
map (36° 50′N 77° 15′W) **19**:607
SUSSEX SPANIEL **6**:218 *illus.*; **18**:372 *bibliog.*, *illus.*
SUSUBONA (Solomon Islands)
map (8° 18′S 159° 27′E) **18**:56
SUTER, JOHANN AUGUST *see* SUTTER, JOHN AUGUSTUS
SUTHERLAND (Iowa)
map (42° 58′N 95° 29′W) **11**:244
SUTHERLAND (Nebraska)
map (41° 10′N 101° 8′W) **14**:70
SUTHERLAND (Scotland) **18**:372
SUTHERLAND, DONALD (actor) **1**:314 *illus.*
SUTHERLAND, DONALD (explorer)
Sutherland Falls **18**:373
SUTHERLAND, EARL W., JR. **18**:372
cyclic AMP **5**:403
SUTHERLAND, EDWIN H.
crime **5**:345; **5**:347
white-collar crime **20**:136–137
SUTHERLAND, GEORGE **18**:372–373 *bibliog.*
Powell v. *Alabama* **15**:481
United States v. *Curtiss-Wright Export Corporation* **19**:464
SUTHERLAND, GRAHAM **18**:373 *bibliog.*
SUTHERLAND, JOAN **18**:373 *bibliog.*
SUTHERLAND FALLS **18**:373
map (44° 48′S 167° 44′E) **14**:158
SUTHERLIN (Oregon)
map (43° 25′N 123° 19′W) **14**:427
SUTLEJ RIVER **18**:373
map (29° 23′N 71° 2′E) **11**:152
SUTRA
Buddhist sacred literature **3**:543
yoga **20**:328
SUTTEE **18**:373 *bibliog.*
abolition
Carey, William **4**:147
cremation **5**:338
funeral customs **8**:364

SUTTER (county in California)
map (39° 8′N 121° 37′W) **4**:31
SUTTER, JOHN AUGUSTUS **18**:373 *bibliog.*
Sacramento (California) **17**:7
SUTTER CREEK (California)
map (38° 23′N 120° 48′W) **4**:31
SUTTER'S MILL (California)
gold rush **9**:228
SUTTNER, BERTHA VON **18**:373
SUTTON (county in Texas)
map (30° 30′N 100° 30′W) **19**:129
SUTTON (West Virginia)
map (38° 40′N 80° 43′W) **20**:111
SUTTON, WALTER S. **18**:373 *bibliog.*
heredity **10**:140
SUTTON, WILLY **18**:373 *bibliog.*
SUTTON HOO SHIP BURIAL **18**:373–374 *bibliog.*
SUTTON LAKE
map (38° 40′N 80° 40′W) **20**:111
SUVA (Fiji) **8**:77 *illus.*; **18**:374
map (18° 8′S 178° 25′E) **8**:77
SUVADIVA ATOLL
map (0° 30′N 73° 15′E) **13**:87
SUVERO, MARK DI *see* DI SUVERO, MARK
SUVOROV, ALEKSANDR VASILIEVICH **18**:374 *bibliog.*
SUWANNEE (county in Florida)
map (30° 15′N 83° 0′W) **8**:172
SUWANNEE RIVER **18**:374
map (29° 18′N 83° 9′W) **8**:172
SUWON (Korea)
map (37° 17′N 127° 1′E) **12**:113
SUYO (Peru)
map (4° 30′S 80° 0′W) **15**:193
SUZHOU (China) *see* SOOCHOW (Suzhou) (China)
SUZOR-CÔTÉ, M. A. DE FOY **18**:374
Canadian art and architecture **4**:89
SUZUKI, D. T. **18**:374 *bibliog.*
SUZUKI ZENKO **18**:374
Japan **11**:366
SVALBARD (Norway) **18**:374
map (78° 0′N 20° 0′E) **14**:261
SVAY RIENG (Kampuchea)
map (11° 5′N 105° 48′E) **12**:11
SVEDA, MICHAEL
cyclamates **5**:403
SVEDBERG, THEODOR **18**:374 *bibliog.*
SVENDBORG (Denmark)
map (55° 3′N 10° 37′E) **6**:109
SVERDLOVSK (USSR) **18**:375 *bibliog.*
SVETOZAREVO (Yugoslavia)
map (43° 58′N 21° 16′E) **20**:340
SVEVO, ITALO **18**:375 *bibliog.*
SVITÁVA RIVER
map (49° 10′N 16° 38′E) **5**:413
SVOBODA, JOSEF **18**:375 *bibliog.*
SVOBODA, LUDVIK
Czechoslovakia **5**:416
SVYATOSLAV I, DUKE OF KIEV **18**:375
Russia/Union of Soviet Socialist Republics, history of **16**:351
SWABIA **18**:375
Philip of Swabia **15**:232
SWAHILI **18**:375 *bibliog.*
African languages **1**:167
SWAIN (county in North Carolina)
map (35° 30′N 83° 30′W) **14**:242
SWAINSBORO (Georgia)
map (32° 36′N 82° 20′W) **9**:114
SWAKOPMUND (Namibia)
map (22° 41′S 14° 34′E) **14**:10
SWALE
floodplain **8**:165–166
SWALLOW **18**:375–376 *bibliog., illus.*
instinct **11**:195 *illus.*
martin **13**:178
SWALLOW HOLES (geology)
landform evolution **12**:182 *illus.*
SWALLOW TANAGER **18**:376
SWAMMERDAM, JAN **1**:396–397 *illus.*; **18**:376 *bibliog.*
biology **3**:269
SWAMP, MARSH, AND BOG **18**:376–378 *bibliog., illus.*
bog **18**:376; **18**:378
climax community **5**:59
drainage systems **6**:255
ecological role **18**:378
endangered species **7**:167 *illus.*
fauna **18**:376–378 *illus.*
flora **18**:376–378 *illus.*
Florida **8**:173 *illus.*
Everglades **7**:316 *illus.*
fossil record **18**:378
Carboniferous Period **4**:139 *illus.*; **15**:31 *illus.*
gas, methane **13**:343
human remains **18**:378
imprecise terminology **18**:376
intertidal life **11**:229–230
land reclamation **12**:178–181
landform evolution **12**:183
Louisiana **12**:434 *illus.*
marsh **18**:376–377
Pontine Marshes (Italy) **15**:427
Pripet Marshes (USSR) **15**:553
salt marsh **18**:376–377
river delta **16**:232
soil **18**:37; **18**:376–378
swamp **18**:377–378
Dismal Swamp **6**:196
Okavango Swamp **14**:365
Okefenokee Swamp **14**:366
wetlands **18**:376–378
SWAMP EEL **18**:378
SWAMP FOX *see* MARION, FRANCIS
SWAMP LILY *see* LIZARD'S TAIL (botany)
SWAMP ROSE MALLOW **10**:156 *illus.*
SWAMPSCOTT (Massachusetts)
map (42° 28′N 70° 55′W) **3**:409
SWAN **18**:378–379 *bibliog., illus.*
SWAN, SIR JOSEPH WILSON **18**:379 *bibliog.*
SWAN FALLS
map (43° 15′N 116° 23′W) **11**:26
SWAN HILLS
map (54° 48′N 115° 52′W) **1**:256
SWAN LAKE
map (41° 43′N 102° 30′W) **14**:70
SWAN LAKE (ballet) **14**:29 *illus.*
Russian music **16**:368 *illus.*
SWAN RANGE
map (47° 50′N 113° 40′W) **13**:547
SWAN RIVER (Manitoba)
map (52° 6′N 101° 16′W) **13**:119
SWAN THEATRE **18**:379; **19**:146 *illus.*
SWANN v. *CHARLOTTE-MECKLENBURG BOARD OF EDUCATION*
busing, school **3**:589–590
SWANQUARTER (North Carolina)
map (35° 24′N 76° 20′W) **14**:242
SWANS ISLAND
map (44° 10′N 68° 25′W) **13**:70
SWANSBORO (North Carolina)
map (34° 36′N 77° 7′W) **14**:242
SWANSCOMBE MAN **18**:379 *bibliog.*
Fontéchevade man **8**:207
SWANSEA (Wales) **18**:379
map (51° 38′N 3° 57′W) **19**:403
SWANSON, GLORIA **18**:379
Stroheim, Erich von **18**:301
SWANSON LAKE
map (40° 9′N 101° 6′W) **14**:70
SWANTON (Ohio)
map (41° 35′N 83° 53′W) **14**:357
SWANTON (Vermont)
map (44° 55′N 73° 7′W) **19**:554
SWAPO *see* SOUTH WEST AFRICAN PEOPLE'S ORGANIZATION
SWARTHMORE COLLEGE **18**:379
SWARTKRANS *see* STERKFONTEIN (South Africa)
SWARTZ CREEK (Michigan)
map (42° 58′N 83° 50′W) **13**:377
SWASTIKA **18**:379 *bibliog., illus.*
cross **5**:360; **5**:361 *illus.*
SWATOW (SHAN-T'OU) (China)
map (23° 23′N 116° 41′E) **4**:362
SWAZI **18**:379–380 *bibliog.*
SWAZILAND **18**:380–381 *bibliog., illus., map, table*
cities
Mbabane **13**:250–251
flag **18**:380 *illus.*
history and government **18**:381
land, people, and economy **18**:380–381 *map, table*
map (26° 30′S 31° 30′E) **1**:136
mineral resources **18**:381
people
Swazi **18**:379
Thonga **19**:177
SWEA CITY (Iowa)
map (43° 23′N 94° 19′W) **11**:244
SWEAT
evaporation **7**:313
SWEAT GLAND **7**:328 *illus.*
breast **3**:468
earwax **7**:30
galvanic skin response **9**:23
skin **17**:341 *illus.*
SWEATSHOP
clothing industry **5**:65–66
SWEDE *see* RUTABAGA
SWEDEN **18**:381–386 *bibliog., illus., map, table*
agriculture **18**:384 *illus.*
art
See also the subheading Sweden under specific art forms, e.g., ARCHITECTURE; PAINTING; SCULPTURE; etc.
Scandinavian art and architecture **17**:111–114
cities
Gällivare **18**:382 *table*
Göteborg **9**:254
Malmö **13**:93
Norrköping **14**:223
Stockholm **18**:275–276
Uppsala **19**:473
Västerås **19**:526
climate **18**:382 *table*
correctional system **15**:555
crime **5**:346 *table*
economic activity **18**:384–385
education **18**:383
European universities **7**:308 *table*
family **8**:18
farmhouse **10**:269 *illus.*
flag **18**:381 *illus.*
forestry and fishing **18**:384–385 *illus.*
Gotland **9**:263
government and politics **18**:385
defense, national **6**:82 *table*
welfare spending **20**:98 *table*
health **18**:383
birth control **3**:294–295
health-care systems **10**:88
historians *see* HISTORY—Swedish historians
history **18**:385
Branting, Hjalmar **3**:456
Bridget of Sweden, Saint **3**:485
Carlsson, Ingvar **4**:152
Charles IX, King **4**:297
Charles X, King **4**:297
Charles XI, King **4**:297
Charles XII **4**:297
Charles XIV John, King **4**:298
Charles XVI Gustav, King **4**:298
Christian I, King of Denmark **4**:412
Christian II, King of Denmark **4**:412
Christina, Queen **4**:415
empire 1561–1721 **17**:109 *map*
Eric XIV, King **7**:229
Erlander, Tage **7**:231
exploration and settlement in colonial America **19**:437 *map*
Fälldin, Thorbjörn **8**:14
German acquisitions in 1648 **9**:151 *map*
Gustav I, King **9**:407
Gustav II Adolf, King (Gustavus Adolphus) **9**:407
Gustav III, King **9**:407–408
Gustav IV Adolf, King **9**:408
Gustav VI Adolf, King **9**:408
John II, King of Poland (John Casimir) **11**:427
Magnus VII, King of Norway (Magnus Eriksson) **13**:61
Margaret I, Queen of Denmark, Norway, and Sweden **13**:149
Northern War, Great **14**:256
Oxenstierna, Axel, Count **14**:473–474
Palme, Olof **15**:50
possessions c.1648 **7**:289 *map*
Scandinavia, history of **17**:107–111 *maps*
Seven Years' War **17**:218 *map*
Sigismund III, King of Poland **17**:299
Thirty Years' War *see* THIRTY YEARS' WAR
Vasa (dynasty) **19**:525
land and resources **18**:381–383 *map, table*
varved deposit **19**:524
language
Germanic languages **9**:135–137 *tables*
literature *see* SWEDISH LITERATURE
manufacturing **18**:383–384 *illus.*
map (62° 0′N 15° 0′E) **7**:268
mining **18**:384
music
Berwald, Franz **3**:226
Björling, Jussi **3**:302
naval vessels **14**:57 *illus.*
people **7**:275 *illus.*; **18**:383–384
women in society **20**:204 *table*
police **15**:396
resources **18**:383 *illus.*
rivers, lakes, and waterways **18**:382
Vänern, Lake **19**:519
Vättern, Lake **19**:528
theater
Drottningholm Theatre and Museum **6**:273
unemployment rate **7**:160
vegetation and animal life **18**:382–383
Ytterby
yttrium **20**:338
SWEDENBORG, EMANUEL **18**:386 *bibliog., illus.*
New Jerusalem, Church of the **14**:134
Uppsala (Sweden) **19**:473
SWEDISH ACADEMY
Nobel Prize **14**:208
SWEDISH LITERATURE **18**:386–387 *bibliog., illus.*
Afzelius, Arvid August **1**:181
Ahlin, Lars **1**:200
Almqvist, Carl Jonas Love **1**:307
Andersson, Dan **1**:403
Bellman, Carl Michael **3**:190
Bergman, Hjalmar Fredrik Elgérus **3**:210
Boye, Karin **3**:434
Bremer, Fredrika **3**:472
Dalin, Olof von **6**:13
Ekelöf, Gunnar **7**:97–98
Fröding, Gustaf **8**:335
Geijer, Erik Gustaf **9**:68
Heidenstam, Verner von **10**:107
Johnson, Eyvind **11**:432
Karlfeldt, Erik Axel **12**:27
Lagerkvist, Pär **12**:165
Lagerlöf, Selma **12**:165
Martinson, Harry Edmund **13**:181
Moberg, Vilhelm **13**:487
Rydberg, Abraham Viktor **16**:379
Söderberg, Hjalmar **18**:32
Södergran, Edith **18**:32
Stagnelius, Erik Johan **18**:211
Strindberg, August **18**:299
Tegnér, Esaias **19**:72
"SWEDISH NIGHTINGALE, THE" *see* LIND, JENNY
SWEELINCK, JAN PIETERSZOON **18**:387
SWEENEY, JAMES JOHNSON
Guggenheim Museum **9**:393
SWEENY (Texas)
map (29° 2′N 95° 42′W) **19**:129
SWEEPSTAKES *see* HORSE RACING
SWEET BAY *see* BAY LEAF; LAUREL
SWEET BRIAR COLLEGE **18**:387
SWEET FERN **18**:387
SWEET GALE **18**:387
SWEET GRASS (county in Montana)
map (45° 50′N 109° 55′W) **13**:547
SWEET GUM **18**:387 *illus.*
storax **18**:284
SWEET HOME (Oregon)
map (44° 24′N 122° 44′W) **14**:427
SWEET LAUREL *see* BAY LEAF
SWEET MARJORAM *see* MARJORAM
SWEET PEA **18**:387–388 *illus.*
SWEET POTATO **18**:388 *illus.*; **19**:534 *illus.*
yam **20**:315–316
SWEET POTATO SNOUT WEEVIL **3**:167 *illus.*
SWEET SPRINGS (Missouri)
map (38° 58′N 93° 25′W) **13**:476
SWEET WILLIAM (botany) **18**:388
See also CARNATION
SWEETENER, ARTIFICIAL **18**:388
aspartame **2**:262
cyclamates **5**:403
saccharin **17**:6
SWEETENERS (food)
artificial *see* SWEETENER, ARTIFICIAL
honey **10**:220
jam and jelly **12**:351
maple syrup and sugar **13**:138
molasses **13**:505
sugar **18**:327
SWEETGRASS (Montana)
map (49° 0′N 111° 57′W) **13**:547
SWEETLEAF **18**:388
SWEETSHRUB **18**:388
SWEETSOP *see* CUSTARD APPLE
SWEETSPIRE *see* VIRGINIA WILLOW
SWEETWATER (Tennessee)
map (35° 36′N 84° 28′W) **19**:104
SWEETWATER (Texas)
map (32° 28′N 100° 25′W) **19**:129
SWEETWATER (county in Wyoming)
map (41° 40′N 108° 50′W) **20**:301
SWEETWATER RIVER
map (0° 0′ 0° 0′) **20**:301
SWELL
water wave **20**:58 *illus.*
SWELLFISH *see* PUFFER
SWELLING *see* EDEMA
SWENSON, JOSEPHINE *see* SWANSON, GLORIA
SWENSON, MAY **18**:388
SWEPSONVILLE (North Carolina)
map (36° 1′N 79° 22′W) **14**:242
SWEYN, KING OF DENMARK **18**:388 *bibliog.*
ŚWIDNICA (Poland)
map (50° 51′N 16° 29′E) **15**:388

SWIFT (bird) **18**:388–389 *illus.*
SWIFT (county in Minnesota)
map (45° 0′N 95° 40′W) **13**:453
SWIFT, HENRY
Weston, Edward **20**:118
SWIFT, JONATHAN 7:197 *illus.*; **18**:389 *bibliog.*, *illus.*
Gulliver's Travels **9**:404
Modest Proposal, A **13**:499
Tale of a Tub, A **19**:15–16
SWIFT AND COMPANY* v. *UNITED STATES **18**:389–390
United States v. *E. C. Knight Company* **19**:465
SWIFT CURRENT (Saskatchewan)
map (50° 17′N 107° 50′W) **17**:81
SWIFT RESERVOIR
map (46° 4′N 122° 5′W) **20**:35
SWIFTON (Arkansas)
map (35° 49′N 91° 8′W) **2**:166
SWIGERT, JOHN L., JR. **18**:390 *bibliog.*
SWILLY, LAKE
map (55° 10′N 7° 38′W) **11**:258
SWIM BLADDER **18**:390
SWIMMING **18**:390–392 *bibliog.*, *illus.*, *table*
See also LIFESAVING AND WATER SAFETY
bends **3**:196
Chadwick, Florence **4**:267
competitive swimming **18**:392
Ederle, Gertrude 7:56
English Channel 7:189
fish **8**:115 *illus.*; **8**:118
Fraser, Dawn **8**:287
frogman **8**:238
history **18**:390–391
Olympic Games **14**:384 *illus.*
pentathlon **15**:155
rail **16**:71
Schollander, Don **17**:133
Spitz, Mark **18**:190
sports medicine **18**:198
water polo **20**:50
Weissmuller, Johnny **20**:96
world swimming records **18**:391 *table*
SWINBURNE, ALGERNON CHARLES **18**:392 *bibliog.*, *illus.*
SWINDON (England)
map (51° 34′N 1° 47′W) **19**:403
SWINE **18**:392
SWINE FLU
influenza **11**:172
SWING (music) **18**:392–393 *bibliog.*
Basie, Count **3**:109
Dorsey, Jimmy and Tommy **6**:243
Goodman, Benny **9**:246
jazz **11**:388–390
jitterbug **11**:419
jukebox **11**:465
Krupa, Gene **12**:132
Miller, Glenn **13**:427
SWINGING DRAWBRIDGE **3**:483 *table*
bridge (engineering) **3**:481
ŚWINOUJŚCIE (Poland)
map (53° 53′N 14° 14′E) **15**:388
SWISHER (county in Texas)
map (34° 30′N 101° 45′W) **19**:129
SWISS CHARD
beet **3**:163–164 *illus.*
SWISS CIVIL CODE
civil law **5**:12
SWISS CONFEDERATON *see* SWITZERLAND
SWISS FAMILY ROBINSON, THE (book) **18**:393
Wyss, Johann Rudolf **20**:305
SWITCH, ELECTRIC **18**:393
circuit, electric **4**:436–438
circuit breaker **4**:438
relay **16**:137
solenoid **18**:53
thyratron **19**:187
transistor **19**:271–272
SWITCH, MERCURY
mercury **13**:306
SWITCHING SYSTEM
telephone **19**:80
SWITHIN, SAINT **18**:393
SWITZER, KATHY **18**:393
SWITZERLAND **18**:393–397 *bibliog.*, *illus.*, *map*, *table*
archaeology
La Tène **12**:150
lake dwelling **12**:171
armed forces **18**:397
art **18**:395–396
See also the subheading Switzerland under specific art forms, e.g., GRAPHIC ARTS; PAINTING; SCULPTURE; etc.
folk art **8**:196
tapestry **19**:32 *illus.*
cities
Basel **3**:108
Bern **3**:220
Davos **6**:53
Geneva **9**:90–91 *illus.*
Interlaken **11**:214
Lausanne **12**:239
Locarno **12**:385
Lucerne **12**:450
Neuchâtel **14**:104
Saint Moritz **17**:24
Sankt Gallen **17**:65
Winterthur **20**:181
Zurich **20**:383 *illus.*
civil law **5**:12
climate **18**:394–395 *table*
economic activity **18**:396–397
education **18**:395
European universities 7:308 *table*
Geneva, University of **9**:91
Pestalozzi, Johann Heinrich **15**:196
flag **18**:393 *illus.*
government and politics **18**:397
foreign policy **18**:394; **18**:397
referendum and initiative **16**:118–119
health **18**:395
historians *see* HISTORY—Swiss historians
history **18**:397
Helvetic Republic **10**:117
Tell, William **19**:90
Winkelried, Arnold **20**:179
land and resources **18**:394–395 *map*
Liechtenstein **12**:324–326
literature
Dürrenmatt, Friedrich **6**:307
Frisch, Max **8**:334
Gotthelf, Jeremias **9**:264
Keller, Gottfried **12**:37
Meyer, Conrad Ferdinand **13**:368
Spitteler, Carl **18**:190
Spyri, Johanna **18**:201
manufacturing **18**:396
map (47° 0′N 8° 0′E) 7:268
music
Ansermet, Ernest **2**:35
Martin, Frank **13**:179
national anthem
Wyss, Johann Rudolf **20**:305
people **18**:395–396
physical features
Aletsch Glacier **1**:272
Alps **1**:309–310
Jungfrau **11**:468
Jura (mountain range) **11**:474
Matterhorn **13**:231
Saint Gotthard Pass **17**:18–19
Simplon Pass **17**:316
Unteraar glacier **9**:194
religion
Zwingli, Ulrich **20**:384
rivers, lakes, and waterways
Aare River **1**:50
Geneva, Lake **9**:91
Lucerne, Lake **12**:450
Lugano, Lake **12**:452
Maggiore, Lake **13**:49
Neuchâtel, Lake **14**:104
trade **18**:396–397
transportation **18**:396
SWITZERLAND (county in Indiana)
map (38° 45′N 85° 4′W) **11**:111
SWOC *see* STEEL WORKERS ORGANIZING COMMITTEE
SWORD DANCE **18**:399
folk dance **8**:199 *illus.*
SWORD AND KNIFE **18**:397–399 *bibliog.*, *illus.*
fencing **8**:49 *illus.*
knife **18**:397–399 *illus.*
knight **12**:100 *illus.*
martial arts **13**:178
Sheffield (England) **17**:250
sword **18**:397–398 *illus.*
Urnfield culture **19**:487
weapons **20**:74
SWORDFISH **18**:399 *illus.*
SWORDTAIL **18**:399 *illus.*
SYCAMORE (Georgia)
map (31° 40′N 83° 38′W) **9**:114
SYCAMORE (Illinois)
map (41° 59′N 88° 41′W) **11**:42
SYCAMORE TREE **15**:328 *illus.*
SYCON **18**:193 *illus.*
SYDENHAM, CHARLES EDWARD POULETT THOMSON, BARON **18**:400 *bibliog.*
SYDENHAM, THOMAS **18**:400
medicine **13**:269
SYDNEY (Australia) **2**:337 *illus.*; **18**:400–401 *bibliog.*, *illus.*, *map*
education
Macquarie University **2**:345 *table*
New South Wales University **2**:345 *table*
Sydney University **2**:345 *table*
map (33° 52′S 151° 13′E) **2**:328
Opera House **2**:329 *illus.*; **3**:552 *illus.*; **14**:402 *illus.*
SYDNEY (Nova Scotia) **18**:401
map (46° 9′N 60° 11′W) **14**:269
SYDNEY, ALGERNON *see* SIDNEY, ALGERNON
SYDNEY MINES (Nova Scotia)
map (46° 14′N 60° 14′W) **14**:269
SYDNEY OPERA HOUSE
opera houses **14**:402 *illus.*
SYDNEY SILKY *see* SILKY TERRIER
SYDOW, MAX VON *see* VON SYDOW, MAX
SYENITE **18**:401
SYKES, GRESHAM
prison **15**:555
SYKES, LYNN RAY
plate tectonics **15**:357
SYKESVILLE (Maryland)
map (39° 22′N 76° 58′W) **13**:188
SYKESVILLE (Pennsylvania)
map (41° 3′N 78° 49′W) **15**:147
SYLACAUGA (Alabama)
map (33° 10′N 86° 15′W) **1**:234
SYLHET (Bangladesh)
map (24° 54′N 91° 52′E) **3**:64
SYLLABARY *see* WRITING SYSTEMS, EVOLUTION OF
SYLLABIC METER
versification **19**:562
SYLLABIC WRITING *see* WRITING SYSTEMS, EVOLUTION OF
SYLLOGISM **18**:401–402 *bibliog.*, *illus.*
Aristotle **2**:157
reasoning **16**:104
Venn diagram **19**:546
SYLPH **18**:402
SYLPHIDES, LES **14**:194 *illus.*
SYLT ISLAND
map (54° 54′N 8° 20′E) **9**:140
SYLVA (North Carolina)
map (35° 23′N 83° 13′W) **14**:242
SYLVAN GROVE (Kansas)
map (39° 0′N 98° 24′W) **12**:18
SYLVAN LAKE (Alberta)
map (52° 19′N 114° 5′W) **1**:256
SYLVAN PASS
map (44° 28′N 110° 8′W) **20**:301
SYLVANIA (Georgia)
map (32° 45′N 81° 38′W) **9**:114
SYLVANIA (Ohio)
map (41° 43′N 83° 42′W) **14**:357
SYLVANITE **18**:402
telluride minerals **19**:91
SYLVESTER (Georgia)
map (31° 32′N 83° 49′W) **9**:114
SYLVESTER (Texas)
map (32° 43′N 100° 15′W) **19**:129
SYLVIA (Kansas)
map (37° 57′N 98° 24′W) **12**:18
SYLVITE **18**:402
SYMBIOSIS **18**:402 *bibliog.*
hornwort **10**:240
hydra **10**:329–330
lichen **12**:322
mushrooms **13**:660
mycorrhiza **13**:690
parasite **15**:82
remora **16**:146–147
rhinoceros **16**:196 *illus.*
stentor **18**:253
SYMBOLIC LOGIC *see* LOGIC; MATHEMATICAL LOGIC
SYMBOLISM (art) **18**:402 *bibliog.*, *illus.*
Art Nouveau **2**:209–210
cross **5**:360–361
crowns and coronets **5**:364
decadence **6**:72
icon **11**:20
iconography **11**:21–24
Indians of North America, art of the **11**:139
mandala **13**:110
mandorla **13**:112
Nabis **14**:3
Panofsky, Erwin **15**:60
Pre-Raphaelites **15**:519
Redon, Odilon **16**:116
Russian art and architecture **16**:363
SYMBOLISM (literature) **18**:403 *bibliog.*
American literature
Hawthorne, Nathaniel **10**:79
Austrian literature
Hofmannsthal, Hugo von **10**:196–197
Belgian literature
Maeterlinck, Maurice **13**:45–46
Verhaeren, Émile **19**:551
Czech literature
Kafka, Franz **12**:5–6
Danish literature
Claussen, Sophus **5**:45
decadence **6**:72
Dutch and Flemish literature
Woestijne, Karel van de **20**:195
folklore **8**:203
French literature **8**:318
Baudelaire, Charles **3**:128–129
Fort, Paul **8**:236
Laforgue, Jules **11**:164
Mallarmé, Stéphane **13**:91
Symons, Arthur **18**:404
Valéry, Paul **19**:505–506
Verlaine, Paul **19**:551–552
German literature **9**:133
George, Stefan **9**:109
Russian literature **16**:366
Bely, Andrei **3**:193–194
Blok, Aleksandr Aleksandrovich **3**:335
Bryusov, Valery Yakovlevich **3**:530
Evreinov, Nikolai Nikolaevich 7:325
Hippius, Zinaida Nikolayevna **10**:173–174
Merezhkovsky, Dmitry Sergeyevich **13**:309
Sologub, Fyodor **18**:56
SYMBOLISM (psychology)
Jung, Carl **11**:467
SYMEON I *see* SIMEON I, TSAR OF BULGARIA
SYMINGTON, WILLIAM
ship **17**:272
SYMMER, ROBERT
physics, history of **15**:284
SYMMETRICAL TWINS *see* SIAMESE TWINS; TWINS
SYMMETRY (mathematics) **18**:403 *bibliog.*
axis **2**:378
SYMMETRY (physics) **18**:403–404 *bibliog.*
asymmetry
stereochemistry **18**:258 *illus.*
bilateral, parity (physics) **15**:88–89
conservation, laws of **5**:204–205
fundamental particles **8**:363
grand unification theories **9**:286
Gell-Mann, Murray **9**:69–70
nonsymmetry
Wu, Chien-shiung **20**:295
theoretical physics **19**:159
time reversal invariance **19**:202
unified field theory **19**:385–386
SYMONDS, JOHN ADDINGTON **18**:404 *bibliog.*
SYMONS, ARTHUR **18**:404 *bibliog.*
decadence **6**:72
SYMONS, JULIAN **18**:404
SYMPHONIC POEM **18**:404–405
Afternoon of a Faun, The **1**:181
Honegger, Arthur **10**:220
Liszt, Franz **12**:367
Respighi, Ottorino **16**:178
Saint-Saëns, Camille **17**:26
Scriabin, Aleksandr Nikolayevich **17**:157–158
Sibelius, Jean **17**:291
Smetana, Bedřich **17**:366
Strauss, Richard **18**:294–295
SYMPHONIE FANTASTIQUE (musical composition)
Berlioz, Hector **3**:218
SYMPHONY **18**:405 *bibliog.*
absolute music **1**:62
classical period in music **5**:41
composers
Bach, Carl Philipp Emanuel **3**:10
Bach, Johann Christian **3**:10
Beethoven, Ludwig van **3**:164–165
Berlioz, Hector **3**:218
Brahms, Johannes **3**:441
Bruckner, Anton **3**:521
Cowell, Henry **5**:321
Dvořák, Antonín **6**:317
Franck, César **8**:277
Harris, Roy **10**:58
Haydn, Franz Josef **10**:81
Hindemith, Paul **10**:168
Indy, Vincent d' **11**:160
Ives, Charles Edward **11**:334
Lalo, Édouard **12**:172
Langgaard, Rued **12**:195
Liszt, Franz **12**:367
Mahler, Gustav **13**:65
Mendelssohn, Felix **13**:295–296
Mennin, Peter **13**:298
Miaskovsky, Nicolai **13**:370
Milhaud, Darius **13**:419–420
Mozart, Wolfgang Amadeus **13**:628–629

SYMPHONY (cont.)
Nielsen, Carl August **14**:184–185
Piston, Walter **15**:319
Prokofiev, Sergei **15**:566–567
Rachmaninoff, Sergei **16**:36
Rimsky-Korsakov, Nikolai Andreyevich **16**:224–225
Rubbra, Edmund **16**:335
Saint-Saëns, Camille **17**:26
Sammartini, Giovanni Battista **17**:46
Schubert, Franz **17**:135
Schuman, William Howard **17**:136
Schumann, Robert **17**:137
Sessions, Roger **17**:213
Shostakovitch, Dmitry **17**:285
Sibelius, Jean **17**:291
Stamitz (family) **18**:216
Tchaikovsky, Peter Ilich **19**:51–52
Tippett, Michael **19**:207
Vaughan Williams, Ralph **19**:528–529
music, history of Western **13**:666
SYMPHYLAN (myriapod) **13**:691
SYNAGOGUE **11**:462 *illus.*; **18**:406 *bibliog.*
Newport (Rhode Island) **14**:170
SYNAPSE
acetylcholine **1**:80
biopotential **3**:276
nervous system **14**:91–92
neurophysiology **14**:105–107
SYNCHROMISM **18**:406 *bibliog.*
MacDonald-Wright, Stanton **13**:13
SYNCHRONIC LINGUISTICS **12**:356; **12**:358
Prague school **15**:488
SYNCHRONOUS METEOROLOGICAL SATELLITE **18**:406
GOES (artificial satellite) **9**:222
hurricane and typhoon **10**:319
meteorology **13**:342
space exploration **18**:123
SYNCHROTRON
accelerator, particle **1**:74–76 *illus.*
Fermi National Accelerator Laboratory **8**:56
zero-gradient synchrotron
Argonne National Laboratory **2**:152
SYNCHROTRON RADIATION **18**:406 *bibliog.*
radio astronomy **16**:47–50
Seyfert galaxies **17**:232
SYNCLINE AND ANTICLINE **18**:406 *bibliog.*
fold **8**:194
geosyncline **9**:119–120
SYNCOM **18**:406 *bibliog.*
communications satellite **5**:144
SYNCOPATION **18**:407
SYNCOPE *see* FAINTING
SYNDICALISM **18**:407 *bibliog.*
Industrial Workers of the World **11**:160
Proudhon, Pierre Joseph **15**:582
sabotage **17**:6
socialism **18**:21
Sorel, Georges **18**:68
Trades Union Congress **19**:264
SYNDICATES, PRESS *see* PRESS AGENCIES AND SYNDICATES
SYNECDOCHE
figures of speech **8**:76
SYNERGISM **18**:407
diseases, occupational **6**:193
hormones **10**:236
SYNESTHESIA **18**:407
SYNGE, JOHN MILLINGTON **18**:407 *bibliog., illus.*
Abbey Theatre **1**:52–53
Playboy of the Western World, The **15**:363
SYNGE, RICHARD LAURENCE MILLINGTON **18**:407–408 *bibliog.*
Martin, Archer **13**:179
SYNOD OF THE OAKS
Chrysostom, Saint John **4**:421
SYNOVIAL BURSAE
muscle **13**:653
SYNOVIAL FLUID
joint (anatomy) **11**:439
muscle **13**:653
SYNOVIAL SHEATHS
muscle **13**:653
SYNTAX **18**:408–409 *bibliog.*
communication **5**:144
generative-transformational grammar **18**:408–409
Indian languages, American **11**:99
linguistics **12**:357–358
morphemes **18**:408
parts of speech **15**:100–101; **18**:408
phrases and clauses **18**:408
psycholinguistics **15**:592
syntactic rules **18**:408
SYNTHESIZER
electronic music **7**:125–126 *illus.*
SYNTHETIC FIBERS **18**:409 *bibliog.*
cellulose
fiber, textile **8**:67
Chardonnet, Hilaire Bernigaud, Comte de **4**:288
chemical industry **4**:319 *table*
nylon **14**:308–309
petrochemicals **15**:205
petroleum
fiber, textile **8**:67–68
polyester **15**:419
polymerization **15**:420
rayon **16**:97–98
textile industry **19**:136
thread **19**:181
SYNTHETIC FUELS **18**:409–410
coal gasification **5**:79
energy sources **7**:175
fuel **8**:353
gasohol **9**:55
shale, oil **17**:238
SYNTHETIC GEOMETRY
mathematics, history of **13**:226
SYNTHETIC MATERIALS
ethylene **7**:258
SYON HOUSE **1**:92 *illus.*
SYPHAX
Sophonisba **18**:68
SYPHILIS **18**:410 *bibliog.*
diagnostic test **18**:410
Wassermann, August von **20**:46
Fracastoro, Girolamo **8**:257
medicine **13**:269
heart diseases **10**:96
infectious diseases **11**:167
rhinitis **16**:196
spirochete **18**:189
treatment
Ehrlich, Paul **7**:91
jacaranda **11**:339
Treponema **19**:291
ulcer **19**:376
venereal disease **19**:539–540
SYR DARYA **18**:410
map (46° 3′N 61° 0′E) **19**:388
SYRACUSE (Italy)
map (37° 4′N 15° 17′E) **11**:321
SYRACUSE (Kansas)
map (37° 59′N 101° 45′W) **12**:18
SYRACUSE (Nebraska)
map (40° 39′N 96° 11′W) **14**:70
SYRACUSE (New York) **18**:410
map (43° 3′N 76° 9′W) **14**:149
SYRACUSE (Sicily) **18**:410–411 *bibliog., illus.*
Damon and Pythias **6**:19
Dionysius the Elder **6**:184
Dionysius the Younger **6**:184
history
Hiero I, Tyrant of Syracuse **10**:159
Hiero II, Tyrant of Syracuse **10**:159
Timoleon **19**:203
SYRACUSE UNIVERSITY **18**:411
SYRIA **18**:411–414 *bibliog., illus., map, table*
agriculture **18**:413
archaeology
Doura-Europos **6**:249
Ebla **7**:36
Krak des Chevaliers **12**:126–127
Mari **13**:149–150
Palmyra **15**:51–52
Ugarit **19**:374
Urartu **19**:479–480
Woolley, Sir Leonard **20**:215
art
mandorla **13**:112
Mesopotamian art and architecture **13**:318
cities
Aleppo **1**:271–272
Damascus **6**:18–19 *illus.*
Hama **10**:26
Homs **10**:217
Latakia **12**:214–215
climate **18**:411–412 *table*
economic activity **18**:413
education **18**:412
Middle Eastern universities **13**:410–412
flag **18**:411 *illus.*
government **18**:413
health **18**:412–413
history **18**:414
Arab-Israeli Wars **2**:98
Assad, Hafez al- **2**:264
Fertile Crescent **8**:60
Lebanon **12**:267
Middle East, history of the **13**:401
Rome, ancient **16**:298–300
United Arab Republic **19**:401
World War I **20**:243–244
World War II **20**:256
land and resources **18**:411–412 *map, table*
map (35° 0′N 38° 0′E) **2**:232
Palestine **15**:45
people **18**:411–413
Turkmen **19**:347
Ras-el-Ain
spring (water) **18**:199
religion **18**:412
Druzes **6**:283
rivers, lakes, and waterways **18**:411
trade **18**:413
SYRIAN DESERT **18**:414
map (32° 0′N 40° 0′E) **11**:255
SYRINGOMYELIA **18**:414
nervous system, diseases of the **14**:95
SYRINX (anatomy)
larynx **12**:209
songbirds **18**:64
SYRINX (musical instrument) *see* PANPIPES
SYROS (Greece)
Cyclades (Greece) **5**:402
SYRUP *see* SWEETENERS (food)
SYSTEMATIC GEOGRAPHY **9**:103
SYSTEMS ENGINEERING **18**:414–415 *bibliog.*
cybernetics **5**:401
operations research **14**:403
process control **15**:560–561
SYSTEMS FOR NUCLEAR AUXILIARY POWER *see* SNAP (power source)
SYSTOLE
blood pressure **3**:339
heart **10**:93–94 *illus.*
SZAMOS (SOMEŞ) RIVER
map (48° 7′N 22° 22′E) **16**:288
SZARKOWSKI, JOHN **18**:415
SZASZ, THOMAS **18**:415 *bibliog.*
mental health **13**:302
SZCZECIN (Poland) **18**:415
map (53° 24′N 14° 32′E) **15**:388
SZCZECINEK (Poland)
map (53° 43′N 16° 42′E) **15**:388
SZECHWAN (Sichuan) (China) **18**:415
cities
Ch'eng-tu (Chengdu) **4**:330
Chungking (Chongqing) **4**:422–423
SZECHWAN BASIN
map (30° 0′N 106° 0′E) **20**:318
SZEGED (Hungary) **18**:416
map (46° 15′N 20° 9′E) **10**:307
SZEKELYS *see* SZEKLERS
SZÉKESFEHÉRVÁR (Hungary)
map (47° 12′N 18° 25′E) **10**:307
SZEKLERS **18**:416 *bibliog.*
SZELL, GEORG **18**:416 *bibliog.*
Cleveland Orchestra, The **5**:54
SZENT-GYÖRGYI, ALBERT VON **18**:416
SZERYNG, HENRYK **18**:416
SZIGETI, JOSEPH **18**:416 *bibliog.*
SZILARD, LEO **18**:416 *bibliog.*
SZINYEI MERSE, PÁL
Hungary **10**:309
SZOLD, HENRIETTA **18**:416 *bibliog.*
Hadassah **10**:7
SZOLNOK (Hungary)
map (47° 10′N 20° 12′E) **10**:307
SZOMBATHELY (Hungary)
map (47° 14′N 16° 38′E) **10**:307
SZYMANOWSKY, KAROL **18**:416 *bibliog.*

T

T (letter) **19**:3 *illus.*
T TAURI STARS **19**:3 *bibliog.*
variable star **19**:522
T-TEST **19**:3 *bibliog.*
TA-LIEN (Dalian) (China) **19**:3
TAAFE, EDUARD, GRAF VON **19**:3 *bibliog.*
TABA *see* AMERICAN BOOK AWARDS
TABACUNDA (Ecuador)
map (0° 3′N 78° 12′W) **7**:52
TABARD, FRANÇOIS
Lurçat, Jean **12**:466
TABARI, AL- **19**:3 *bibliog.*
TABARIYA, BAHR *see* GALILEE, SEA OF
TABASARA MOUNTAINS
map (8° 33′N 81° 40′W) **15**:55
TABASCO (Mexico) **19**:3
cities
Villahermosa **19**:597
historic sites
La Venta **12**:151
TABB, JOHN B. **19**:3–4
TABBY *see* AMERICAN SHORTHAIR CAT
TABBY-POINT *see* COLORPOINT SHORTHAIR CAT
TABER (Alberta)
map (49° 47′N 112° 8′W) **1**:256
TABERNACLE **19**:4
TABERNACLES, FEAST OF **19**:4 *bibliog.*
TABLA
Indian music **11**:102–103 *illus.*
TABLATURE **19**:4 *bibliog.*
lute **12**:468
musical notation and terms **13**:681
TABLE MOUNTAIN (South Africa) **19**:4
map (33° 57′S 18° 25′E) **18**:79
TABLE ROCK (South Carolina) **18**:97 *illus.*
TABLE TENNIS **19**:4–5 *bibliog., illus.*
TABLIGBO (Togo)
map (6° 35′N 1° 30′E) **19**:222
TABLOIDS **19**:5 *bibliog.*
TABOO **19**:5 *bibliog.*
dietary laws **6**:164–165
incest **11**:73–74
passage rites **15**:103
Polynesians **15**:421
primitive religion **15**:546
totem **19**:249
TABOR (Iowa)
map (40° 54′N 95° 40′W) **11**:244
TABOR, HORACE W. **19**:5 *bibliog.*
TABOR, MOUNT **19**:5
map (32° 41′N 35° 23′E) **11**:302
TABOR CITY (North Carolina)
map (34° 9′N 78° 52′W) **14**:242
TABORA (Tanzania)
map (5° 1′S 32° 48′E) **19**:27
TABOU (Ivory Coast)
map (4° 25′N 7° 21′W) **11**:335
TABRIZ (Iran) **19**:5
map (38° 5′N 46° 18′E) **11**:250
TABUN
chemical and biological warfare **4**:311
TACAMAHAC **19**:5
TACCA, PIETRO **19**:5–6 *bibliog.*
TACHÉ, SIR ÉTIENNE PASCHAL **19**:6
TACHOMETER **19**:6
TACHYCARDIA
heart diseases **10**:96
palpitation **15**:52
TACHYON **19**:6 *bibliog.*
TACITUS, CORNELIUS **19**:6 *bibliog.*
TACK (horse) *see* RIDING
TACK, AUGUSTUS VINCENT **19**:6
TACLOBAN (Philippines)
map (11° 15′N 125° 0′E) **15**:237
TACNA (Arizona)
map (32° 41′N 114° 1′W) **2**:160
TACNA (Peru)
map (18° 1′S 70° 15′W) **15**:193
Tacna-Arica Dispute **19**:6
TACNA-ARICA DISPUTE **19**:6 *bibliog.*
Pacific, War of the **15**:5
TACOMA (Washington) **19**:6
map (47° 15′N 122° 27′W) **20**:35
TACONIC RANGE
map (42° 30′N 73° 20′W) **13**:206
TACONITE
major ore deposits **14**:424–425 *table*
TACTICS, MILITARY *see* STRATEGY AND TACTICS, MILITARY
TACTICS, NAVAL *see* STRATEGY AND TACTICS, NAVAL
TACUAREMBÓ (Uruguay)
map (31° 44′S 55° 59′W) **19**:488
TADEMA, SIR LAWRENCE ALMA- *see* ALMA-TADEMA, SIR LAWRENCE
TADEMAIT PLATEAU
map (28° 30′N 2° 0′E) **1**:287
TADJOURA ,GULF OF
map (11° 42′N 43° 0′E) **6**:208
TADMOR *see* PALMYRA (Syria)
TADPOLE
frog **8**:336–337 *illus.*
TADZHIK **19**:7 *bibliog.*
TADZHIK SOVIET SOCIALIST REPUBLIC (USSR) **19**:6–7
cities
Dushanbe **6**:308
Tadzhik **19**:7
Uzbek **19**:499
TAEBAEK MOUNTAINS
map (37° 40′N 128° 50′E) **12**:113
TAEDONG RIVER
map (38° 42′N 125° 15′E) **12**:113
TAEGU (South Korea) **19**:7
map (35° 52′N 128° 35′E) **12**:113

TAEJON (South Korea) **19**:7
map (36° 20′N 127° 26′E) **12**:113
TAFARI MAKONNEN *see* HAILE SELASSIE, EMPEROR OF ETHIOPIA
TAFFETA **19**:7
TAFT (California)
map (35° 8′N 119° 28′W) **4**:31
TAFT, LORADO **19**:7 *bibliog.*
TAFT, ROBERT A. **19**:7–8 *bibliog., illus.*
TAFT, WILLIAM HOWARD **19**:8–9 *bibliog., illus.*
Constitution of the United States **5**:218
Republican party **16**:174
Roosevelt, Theodore **16**:311
Supreme Court of the United States **18**:357
United States, history of the **19**:452
TAFT-HARTLEY ACT *see* LABOR-MANAGEMENT RELATIONS ACT
TAGA (Western Samoa)
map (13° 46′S 172° 28′W) **20**:117
TAGAMET *see* CIMETIDINE
TAGANROG (USSR) **19**:9
TAGLIONI (family) **19**:9 *bibliog., illus.*
ballet **3**:42
Taglioni, Marie
Perrot, Jules **15**:178
TAGORE, SIR RABINDRANATH **19**:9–10 *bibliog., illus.*
TAGUS RIVER **19**:10
bridge (engineering) **3**:480 *illus.*
map (38° 40′N 9° 24′W) **18**:140
TAHA HUSAYN **19**:10 *bibliog.*
Egypt **7**:77
TAHAN MOUNTAIN
map (4° 38′N 102° 14′E) **13**:84
TAHARKA
Cush **5**:397
TAHAT MOUNTAIN
map (23° 18′N 5° 47′E) **1**:287
TAHGAHJUTE *see* LOGAN, JOHN
TAHITI (French Polynesia) **19**:10 *bibliog., map*
cities
Papeete **15**:68
Cook, James **5**:236
flag **8**:144 *illus.*
TAHLEQUAH (Oklahoma)
map (35° 55′N 94° 58′W) **14**:368
TAHLTAN BEAR DOG **19**:10
TAHOE, LAKE **14**:113 *illus.*; **19**:10
map (38° 58′N 120° 0′W) **4**:31
TAHOE CITY (California)
map (39° 10′N 120° 9′W) **4**:31
TAHOKA (Texas)
map (33° 10′N 101° 48′W) **19**:129
TAHOUA (Niger)
map (14° 54′N 5° 16′E) **14**:187
TAHR **19**:10–11 *illus.*
TAHTA (Egypt)
map (26° 46′N 31° 30′E) **7**:76
TAHULL (Spain)
Romanesque art and architecture **16**:285 *illus.*
TAI CHI CH'UAN
martial arts **13**:178
TAI CHIN (Dai Jin) **19**:11 *bibliog.*
TAI LANGUAGES
Southeast Asian languages **18**:110–111
T'AI-NAN (Taiwan)
map (23° 0′N 120° 11′E) **19**:13
T'AI-PO *see* LI PO (Li Bo)
T'AI-TSUNG, EMPEROR OF CHINA
China, history of **4**:372
Chinese art and architecture **4**:386 *illus.*
T'ang (Tang) (dynasty) **19**:21
T'AI-YÜAN (Taiyuan) (China) **19**:11
map (37° 55′N 112° 30′E) **4**:362
TAIBEI (Taiwan) *see* TAIPEI (Taibei) (Taiwan)
TAIGA (painter) **19**:11 *bibliog.*
TAIGA CLIMATE **19**:11 *bibliog.*
Asia **2**:234 *illus.*
Europe **7**:273 *map*
forests **19**:11
Northern Hemisphere **19**:11
Siberia **8**:229 *illus.*
tree **19**:288
tundra **19**:332
world distribution **3**:273 *map*; **15**:344 *map*
TAILBONE *see* SACRUM
TAILORBIRD **19**:11
nest **3**:287 *illus.*
TAILORING
clothing industry **5**:65
TÁIN BÓ CÚALNGE (epic)
Cuchulain **5**:381
TAINE, HIPPOLYTE ADOLPHE **19**:11 *bibliog.*
naturalism **14**:49
TAIPA
Macao (Portugal) **13**:4
TAIPEI (Taibei) (Taiwan) **19**:11–12; **19**:14 *illus.*
climate **19**:12 *table*
map (25° 3′N 121° 30′E) **19**:13
TAIPING REBELLION **19**:12 *bibliog.*
China, history of **4**:374
Ch'ing (Qing) (dynasty) **4**:395
Tseng Kuo-fan (Zeng Guofan) **19**:322–323
Tso Tsung-t'ang (Zuo Zongtang) **19**:324
Ward, Frederick Townsend **20**:29
TAIRA (family)
Japan, history of **11**:367
Yoritomo **20**:330
TAÏROV, ALEKSANDR YAKOVLEVICH **19**:12
TAISHI, SHOTOKU *see* SHOTOKU TAISHI
TAISUKE, ITAGAKI *see* ITAGAKI TAISUKE
TAITA HILLS
map (3° 25′S 38° 20′E) **12**:53
TAIWAN **19**:12–14 *bibliog., illus., map, table*
China **4**:360
cities
Kaohsiung (Gaoxiong) **12**:25
Taipei (Taibei) **19**:11–12
climate **19**:12 *table*
Confucianism **5**:180
crime **5**:346 *table*
economic activity **19**:13
education **19**:13
Chinese universities **4**:394
National Taiwan University **14**:46
flag **19**:12 *illus.*
government **19**:13–14
history **19**:14 *illus.*
Chiang Ching-kuo (Jiang Jingguo) **4**:339
Chiang Kai-shek **4**:339
China, history of **4**:376–377
Eisenhower, Dwight D. **7**:96
Kuomintang (Guomindang) **12**:138
Mao Tse-tung (Mao Zedong) **13**:135
Truman, Harry S. **19**:318
land and resources **19**:12–13 *map, table*
language
Malayo-Polynesian languages **13**:83
map (23° 30′N 121° 0′E) **2**:232
museums, art **13**:658
people **19**:13
regions
Pescadores **15**:196
Quemoy **16**:23
trade **19**:13
TAIYUAN (China) *see* T'AI-YÜAN (Taiyuan) (China)
TAIZZ (Yemen) (Sana)
map (13° 38′N 44° 4′E) **20**:325
TAJ MAHAL **11**:96 *illus.*; **19**:14–15 *bibliog., illus.*
garden **9**:40
Islamic art and architecture **11**:297
Mogul art and architecture **13**:501 *illus.*
Shah Jahan, Mogul Emperor of India **17**:235
TAJIK *see* TADZHIK
TAJÍN *see* EL TAJÍN (Mexico)
TAJIQUE (New Mexico)
map (34° 45′N 106° 17′W) **14**:136
TAJRISH (Iran)
map (35° 48′N 51° 25′E) **11**:250
TAJUMULCO VOLCANO
map (15° 2′N 91° 55′W) **9**:389
TAKAMATSU (Japan)
map (34° 20′N 134° 3′E) **11**:361
TAKAPUNA (New Zealand)
map (36° 47′S 174° 47′E) **14**:158
TAKAYOSHI
Tale of Genji illustration **11**:375 *illus.*
TAKEMOTO GIDAYŪ
Bunraku **3**:563–564
TAKEO (Kampuchea)
map (10° 59′N 104° 47′E) **12**:11
TAKIZAWA BAKIN
Japanese literature **11**:380
TAKLA MAKAN DESERT **19**:15
map (39° 0′N 83° 0′E) **4**:362
TAKOMA PARK (Maryland)
map (38° 59′N 77° 1′W) **13**:188
TAKORADI (Ghana) *see* SEKONDI-TAKORADI (Ghana)
TAKSHASILA *see* TAXILA (Pakistan)
TAKU RIVER
map (58° 26′N 133° 59′W) **1**:242
TAKULLI (American Indians) *see* CARRIER INDIANS
TAKUTU RIVER
map (3° 27′N 60° 6′W) **9**:410
TALA
Indian music **11**:103
TALAAT PASHA
Young Turks **20**:336
TALAGANTE (Chile)
map (33° 40′S 70° 56′W) **4**:355
TALAING *see* MON
TALAMANCA CORDILLERA MOUNTAINS
map (9° 30′N 83° 40′W) **5**:291
TALARA (Peru)
map (4° 34′S 81° 17′W) **15**:193
TALASEA (Papua New Guinea)
map (5° 20′S 150° 5′E) **15**:72
TALAVERA DE LA REINA (Spain)
map (39° 57′N 4° 50′W) **18**:140
TALBOT (county in Georgia)
map (32° 40′N 84° 30′W) **9**:114
TALBOT (county in Maryland)
map (38° 45′N 76° 13′W) **13**:188
TALBOT, WILLIAM HENRY **15**:267–268 *illus.*; **19**:15 *bibliog.*
calotype **4**:47
TALBOTTON (Georgia)
map (32° 41′N 84° 32′W) **9**:114
TALBOTYPE *see* TALBOT, WILLIAM HENRY
TALC **19**:15 *illus.*
See also SOAPSTONE
industrial uses **19**:15
magnesium **19**:15
metamorphic rock **13**:332
monoclinic system **13**:536
silicate minerals **17**:305; **19**:15
talcum powder **19**:15
TALCA (Chile)
map (35° 26′S 71° 40′W) **4**:355
TALCAHUANO (Chile)
map (36° 43′S 73° 7′W) **4**:355
TALE OF A TUB, A **19**:15–16 *bibliog.*
TALE OF GENJI, THE (book) **19**:15 *bibliog.*
Japanese art and architecture **11**:374
Muraski Shikibu **13**:647
TALE OF PETER RABBIT, THE (book) **4**:353 *illus.*
Potter, Beatrix **15**:467
TALE OF TWO CITIES, A (book) **19**:16
TALENT (Oregon)
map (42° 15′N 122° 47′W) **14**:427
TALES OF HOFFMANN, THE (opera)
Hoffmann, Ernst Theodor Amadeus **10**:195
TALESE, GAY **19**:16
TALEV, DIMITUR
Bulgarian literature **3**:557
TALIAFERRO (county in Georgia)
map (33° 35′N 82° 55′W) **9**:114
TALIESIN WEST **19**:16
TALIHINA (Oklahoma)
map (34° 45′N 95° 3′W) **14**:368
TALISMAN *see* AMULET
TALKEETNA (Alaska)
map (62° 20′N 150° 7′W) **1**:242
TALKEETNA MOUNTAINS
map (62° 10′N 148° 15′W) **1**:242
TALL AFAR (Iraq)
map (36° 22′N 42° 27′E) **11**:255
TALL SHIPS FLOTILLA
Bicentennial, U.S. **3**:243
TALLADEGA (Alabama)
map (33° 26′N 86° 6′W) **1**:234
TALLADEGA (county in Alabama)
map (33° 20′N 86° 10′W) **1**:234
TALLADEGA COLLEGE **19**:16
TALLAHASSEE (Florida) **8**:175 *illus.*; **19**:16
map (30° 25′N 84° 16′W) **8**:172
TALLAHATCHIE (county in Mississippi)
map (33° 55′N 90° 10′W) **13**:469
TALLAHATCHIE RIVER
map (33° 33′N 90° 10′W) **13**:469
TALLAPOOSA (county in Alabama)
map (32° 45′N 85° 50′W) **1**:234
TALLAPOOSA (Georgia)
map (33° 45′N 85° 17′W) **9**:114
TALLAPOOSA RIVER
map (32° 30′N 86° 16′W) **1**:234
TALLASSEE (Alabama)
map (32° 27′N 85° 54′W) **1**:234
TALLCHIEF, MARIA **19**:16 *bibliog.*
TALLEYRAND-PÉRIGORD, CHARLES MAURICE DE **19**:16–17 *bibliog., illus.*
Vienna, Congress of **19**:579
TALLEYVILLE (Delaware)
map (39° 48′N 75° 33′W) **6**:88
TALLINN (USSR) **19**:17
map (59° 25′N 24° 45′E) **19**:388
TALLIS, THOMAS **19**:17 *bibliog.*
anthem **2**:49
Byrd, William **3**:602
TALLMADGE (Ohio)
map (41° 6′N 81° 27′W) **14**:357
TALLOW TREE **19**:17
TALLULAH (Louisiana)
map (32° 25′N 91° 11′W) **12**:430
TALMA, FRANÇOIS JOSEPH **19**:17 *bibliog.*
TALMADGE (family) **19**:17 *bibliog.*
TALMADGE, ALGERNON
Arthur Phillip at Port Jackson **2**:339 *illus.*
TALMAGE (Nebraska)
map (40° 32′N 96° 1′W) **14**:70
TALMUD **19**:17–18 *bibliog.*
Ashi **2**:230
Gemara **19**:17–18
halachah **10**:17
midrash **13**:414
Mishnah **13**:466; **19**:17–18
Tiberias (Israel) **19**:189
Torah **19**:238
TALO MOUNTAIN
map (10° 44′N 37° 55′E) **7**:253
TALOGA (Oklahoma)
map (36° 2′N 98° 58′W) **14**:368
TALON, JEAN **19**:18
TALOQAN (Afghanistan)
map (36° 44′N 69° 33′E) **1**:133
TALPA (Texas)
map (31° 47′N 99° 43′W) **19**:129
TALUS **19**:18 *bibliog.*
erosion and sedimentation **7**:233
frost action **8**:346
TAMA (Iowa)
map (41° 58′N 92° 35′W) **11**:244
TAMA (county in Iowa)
map (42° 5′N 92° 30′W) **11**:244
TAMALE (Ghana)
map (9° 25′N 0° 50′W) **9**:164
TAMANDUA **11**:469 *illus.*
TAMAQUA (Pennsylvania)
map (40° 48′N 75° 58′W) **15**:147
TAMARACK **19**:18 *illus.*
TAMARIN **19**:18
monkey **13**:534
TAMARIND **19**:18
TAMARISK **19**:18
TAMAROA (Illinois)
Illinois (American Indians) **11**:45
map (38° 8′N 89° 14′W) **11**:42
TAMATAVE (Madagascar)
map (18° 10′S 49° 23′E) **13**:38
TAMAULIPAS (Mexico) **19**:18
cities
Ciudad Victoria **5**:9
Tampico **19**:20
TAMAYO, RUFINO **19**:18–19 *bibliog.*
TAMBO, OLIVER
African National Congress **1**:172
TAMBO COLORADO
Inca **11**:72
TAMBO MACHAY **11**:72 *illus.*
TAMBOUR WORK
crochet **5**:355
TAMBOURINE **13**:675 *illus.*; **15**:162 *illus.*; **19**:19
TAMBURA
Indian music **11**:102–103 *illus.*
TAMBURLAINE *see* TIMUR
TAMBURLAINE THE GREAT (play) **19**:19 *bibliog.*
Alleyn, Edward **1**:302
Marlowe, Christopher **13**:161
TAME (Colombia)
map (6° 28′N 71° 44′W) **5**:107
TAMERLANE *see* TIMUR
TAMIAHUA (Mexico)
map (21° 16′N 97° 27′W) **13**:357
TAMIAHUA LAGOON
map (21° 35′N 97° 35′W) **13**:357
TAMIAMI CANAL
map (25° 47′N 80° 15′W) **8**:172
TAMIL **19**:19 *bibliog.*
Dravidian languages **6**:263
Indian literature **11**:101–102
Sri Lanka **18**:205
TAMIL NADU (India) **19**:19
cities
Madras **13**:43
map (11° 0′N 78° 15′E) **11**:80
people
Badaga **3**:18
Tamil **19**:19
TAMING OF THE SHREW, THE (play) **19**:19
TAMIRIS, HELEN **19**:19 *bibliog.*
TAMM, IGOR YEVGENIEVICH **19**:19
TAMMANY HALL **19**:19–20 *bibliog., illus.*
boss, political **3**:407–408

TAMMANY HALL (cont.)
Croker, Richard **5**:357
Democratic party **6**:99
Tweed, William M. **19**:358
Wood, Fernando **20**:206
TAMMS (Illinois)
map (37° 14′N 89° 16′W) **11**:42
TAMMUZ
fertility rites **8**:60
TAMPA (Florida) **19**:20
map (27° 57′N 82° 27′W) **8**:172
TAMPA BAY
map (27° 45′N 82° 35′W) **8**:172
TAMPERE (Finland) **19**:20
map (61° 30′N 23° 45′E) **8**:95
TAMPICO (Illinois)
map (41° 38′N 89° 47′W) **11**:42
TAMPICO (Mexico) **19**:20
map (22° 13′N 97° 51′W) **13**:357
TAMSHIYACU (Peru)
map (4° 5′S 72° 58′W) **15**:193
TAMWORTH (Australia)
map (31° 5′S 150° 55′E) **2**:328
T'AN-YAO
Yün-kang (Yungang) **20**:346
TANA, LAKE **19**:20
map (12° 0′N 37° 20′E) **7**:253
TANA RIVER
map (2° 32′S 40° 31′E) **12**:53
TANABE, TAKAO
Canadian art and architecture **4**:91
TANAGER **19**:20–21 *illus.*
honeycreeper **10**:221
plush-capped tanager **15**:372
songbirds **18**:65
swallow tanager **18**:376
TANAKA GIICHI **19**:21
TANAKA KAKUEI **19**:21
TANANA (Alaska)
map (65° 10′N 152° 5′W) **1**:242
TANANA RIVER
map (65° 9′N 151° 55′W) **1**:242
TANANARIVE (Madagascar) *see* ANTANANARIVO (Tananarive) (Madagascar)
TANBARK OAK **19**:21
TANCHON (Korea)
map (40° 27′N 128° 54′E) **12**:113
TANCRED OF LECCE
Henry VI, King of Germany and Holy Roman Emperor **10**:129
TANDEM (generator)
Van de Graaff generator **19**:512
TANDIL (Argentina)
map (37° 19′S 59° 9′W) **2**:149
TANDO ADAM
map (25° 46′N 68° 40′E) **15**:27
TANEGA ISLAND
map (30° 40′N 131° 0′E) **11**:361
TANEY (county in Missouri)
map (36° 40′N 93° 0′W) **13**:476
TANEY, ROGER B. **19**:21 *bibliog.*
Dred Scott v. *Sandford* **6**:268
Frederick (Maryland) **8**:289
Luther v. *Borden* **12**:469
Supreme Court of the United States **18**:358
TANEYEV, SERGEI IVANOVICH **19**:21 *bibliog.*
TANEYTOWN (Maryland)
map (39° 40′N 77° 10′W) **13**:188
TANG *see* SURGEONFISH
T'ANG (Tang) (dynasty) **19**:21–22 *bibliog., illus.*
art
Han Kan (Han Gan) **10**:34
landscape painting **12**:188
Li Ssu-hsün (Li Sixun) **12**:310
pottery and porcelain **15**:469 *illus.*
Wu Tao-tzu (Wu Daozi) **20**:296
Yen Li-pen (Yan Liben) **20**:326
Asia, history of **2**:254 *map*; **2**:256
China, history of **4**:371–372
Chinese literature **4**:389
Po Chü-i (Bo Ju'i) **15**:376
Gojunoto (pagoda) **11**:373 *illus.*
journalism **11**:454
T'ang Hsüan-tsung **19**:22
temple **19**:98
Wang Hsi-chih (Wang Xizhi) **20**:22
Wang Wei **20**:22
T'ANG HSIEN-TSU (Tang Xianzu)
Chinese literature **4**:390
T'ANG HSÜAN-TSUNG (TANG XUANZONG) **19**:22
T'ang (Tang) (dynasty) **19**:21
T'ANG-SHAN (China)
map (39° 38′N 118° 11′E) **4**:362
TANG XUANZONG *see* T'ANG HSÜAN-TSUNG (Tang Xuanzong)
TANGA (Tanzania)
map (5° 4′S 39° 6′E) **19**:27
TANGAIL (Bangladesh)
map (24° 15′N 89° 55′E) **3**:64
TANGANYIKA *see* TANZANIA
TANGANYIKA, LAKE **19**:22
map (6° 0′S 29° 30′E) **20**:350
TANGANYIKA AFRICAN NATIONAL UNION
Tanzania **19**:28
TANGARARE (Solomon Islands)
map (9° 35′S 159° 39′E) **18**:56
TANGE, KENZO **19**:22 *bibliog.*
TANGELO *see* TANGERINE
TANGENT **19**:22
trigonometry **19**:298
TANGERANG (Indonesia)
map (6° 11′S 106° 37′E) **11**:147
TANGERINE **19**:22 *bibliog., illus.*
citrus fruits **4**:447
TANGIER (Morocco) **19**:22–23 *illus.*
climate **13**:584 *table*
map (35° 48′N 5° 45′W) **13**:585
TANGIER (Virginia)
map (37° 49′N 75° 59′W) **19**:607
TANGIER ISLAND
map (37° 50′N 76° 0′W) **19**:607
TANGIER SOUND
map (38° 2′N 75° 58′W) **13**:188
TANGIPAHOA (county in Louisiana)
map (30° 37′N 90° 25′W) **12**:430
TANGLEWOOD *see* BERKSHIRE MUSIC FESTIVAL
TANGO **6**:30 *illus.*; **19**:23
Castle, Vernon and Irene **4**:191
TANGOR *see* TANGERINE
TANGUN
Korea, history of **12**:116
TANGUY, YVES **19**:23 *bibliog.*
surrealism (art) **18**:364
TANI BUNCHO *see* BUNCHO
TANIS (Egypt) **19**:23
TANIZAKI JUNICHIRO **19**:23 *bibliog.*
TANJUNGKARANG (Indonesia)
map (5° 25′S 105° 16′E) **11**:147
TANK, MILITARY
antitank mine **13**:438 *illus.*
armored vehicle **2**:175–177 *illus.*
blitzkrieg **3**:333
World War I **20**:237 *illus.*; **20**:247 *illus.*
TANKA
Lamaist art and architecture **12**:173
TANKER (ship) **19**:23–24 *bibliog., illus.*
harbor and port **10**:44 *illus.*
Manhattan (ship) **2**:144 *illus.*
naval vessels **14**:56
petroleum industry **15**:212–213 *illus.*
ship **17**:274–275
shipping route **17**:277
Suez Canal **18**:324 *illus.*
supertanker **19**:278 *illus.*
TANNA
Vanuatu **19**:520
TANNENBERG, BATTLES OF **19**:24
World War I **20**:225–227 *illus., map*
TANNER (Alabama)
map (34° 44′N 86° 59′W) **1**:234
TANNER, HENRY **19**:24 *bibliog., illus.*
The Banjo Lesson **19**:24 *illus.*
TANNER, MOUNT
map (49° 40′N 118° 34′W) **3**:491
TANNHÄUSER (lyric poet) **19**:24–25
TANNHAUSER, JUSTIN K.
Guggenheim Museum **9**:393
TANNIC ACID
astringent **2**:270
TANNING
leather and hides **12**:262
TANNING, DOROTHEA **19**:25
Ernst, Max **7**:232
TANNU TUVA *see* TUVA (USSR)
TANO RIVER
map (5° 7′N 2° 56′W) **9**:164
TANSY **19**:25 *illus.*
TANTA (Egypt)
map (30° 47′N 31° 0′E) **7**:76
TANTALUM **19**:25
element **7**:130 *table*
Group VB periodic table **15**:167
metal, metallic element **13**:328
native elements **14**:47
oxide minerals **14**:476
thermionic emission **19**:161
transition elements **19**:25
TANTALUS **19**:25
TANTRA **19**:25 *bibliog., illus.*
Indian art and architecture **11**:94
Lamaist art and architecture **12**:173
mandala **13**:110
mantra **13**:131
Shakti **17**:237
Tibetan Buddhism **19**:191
TANYU **19**:26 *bibliog.*
TANZANIA **19**:26–28 *bibliog., illus., map, table*
archaeology
Engaruka **7**:176
Laetolil **12**:163
Leakey (family) **12**:258–259
Olduvai Gorge **14**:376–377
cities
Dar es Salaam **1**:147 *illus.*; **6**:37
economic activity **19**:26–28
education **19**:26
African universities **1**:176 *table*
flag **19**:26 *illus.*
government **19**:28
history **19**:28
Kenya **12**:56
Nyerere, Julius K. **14**:308
Zanzibar **20**:355
land and resources **19**:26–28 *illus., map, table*
Serengeti National Park **17**:208
map (6° 0′S 35° 0′E) **1**:136
people **19**:26
Masai **13**:194–195
Nguni **14**:176
Sukuma **18**:332
Yao **20**:318
physical features
Kilimanjaro **12**:76
regions
Pemba **15**:140
trade **19**:28
TAO-CHI *see* SHIH-T'AO (Shitao)
T'AO-CH'IEN *see* T'AO YÜAN-MING (Tao Yuanming)
TAO TE CHING (Daode Jing) **19**:28 *bibliog.*
Taoism **19**:28–29
T'AO YÜAN-MING (Tao Yuanming) **19**:28 *bibliog.*
TAO YUANMING *see* T'AO YÜAN-MING (Tao Yuanming)
TAOISM **16**:140 *map*; **19**:28–29 *bibliog., illus.*
art subject
Graves, Morris **9**:302
Chang Tao-ling (Zhang Daoling) **4**:281
Chinese literature **4**:389
Chuang-tzu (Zhuang Zi) **4**:421–422
Lao-tzu (Laozi) **12**:202
philosophy **15**:247; **19**:28–29
Tao Te Ching (Daode Jing) **19**:28
temple **19**:98–99 *illus.*
Yellow Emperor **20**:322
TAORMINA (Italy) **19**:29
Greek amphitheater ruins **17**:293 *illus.*
TAOS (Missouri)
map (38° 31′N 92° 4′W) **13**:476
TAOS (New Mexico) **19**:29
map (36° 24′N 105° 34′W) **14**:136
TAOS (county in New Mexico)
map (36° 35′N 105° 40′W) **14**:136
TAOS PUEBLO (New Mexico) **14**:139 *illus.*; **19**:428 *illus.*
map (36° 26′N 105° 34′W) **14**:136
TAP DANCING **19**:29 *bibliog.*
TAPA CLOTH *see* BARK CLOTH
TAPACHULA (Mexico)
map (14° 54′N 92° 17′W) **13**:357
TAPACULO **19**:29–30
TAPAGA, CAPE
map (14° 1′S 171° 23′W) **20**:117
TAPAJÓS RIVER
map (2° 24′S 54° 41′W) **3**:460
map (2° 24′S 54° 41′W) **1**:323
TAPALQUÉN (Argentina)
map (36° 21′S 60° 1′W) **2**:149
TAPANAHONI RIVER
map (4° 22′N 54° 27′W) **18**:364
TAPE, MAGNETIC *see* MAGNETIC TAPE
TAPE RECORDER **19**:30–31 *bibliog., illus.*
Poulsen, Valdemar **15**:473
sound recording and reproduction **18**:74–75 *illus.*
videotape recording *see* VIDEOTAPE
TAPERAS (Bolivia)
map (17° 54′S 60° 23′W) **3**:366
TAPESTRY **19**:31–33 *bibliog., illus.*
Apocalypse of Angers (detail) **19**:31 *illus.*
Aubusson (France) **2**:316
Bayeux Tapestry **3**:133 *illus.*
Charlemagne and Arthur **19**:32 *illus.*
Coptic art and architecture **5**:255
Gobelins **9**:216
Jordaens, Jacob **11**:447
Lady with the Unicorn **19**:32 *illus.*; **19**:384 *illus.*
The Life of Louis XIV **19**:32 *illus.*
Lurçat, Jean **12**:466
Maillol, Aristide **13**:67
needlework **14**:76
Raphael **16**:89
technique **19**:31
TAPEWORM **19**:33–34 *bibliog., illus.*
flatworm **8**:156
infectious diseases **11**:167
symbiosis **18**:402
TÁPIES, ANTONIO **19**:34 *bibliog.*
TAPIOCA *see* MANIOC
TAPIR **19**:34 *illus.*
perissodactyl **15**:171
TAPPAHANNOCK (Virginia)
map (37° 56′N 76° 52′W) **19**:607
TAPPAN, LAKE
map (41° 1′N 73° 59′W) **14**:129
TAPPAN BROTHERS **19**:34 *bibliog.*
TAPPEN (North Dakota)
map (46° 52′N 99° 38′W) **14**:248
TAPROOT **19**:29–30
TAPU *see* TABOO
TAQ-KISRA
Ctesiphon **5**:377
TAR, PITCH, AND ASPHALT **19**:34
La Brea Tar Pit **12**:144
petroleum **15**:207
Pleistocene Epoch **15**:366
roads and highways **16**:236 *illus.*; **16**:237–239 *illus.*
roof and roofing **16**:306 *illus.*
TAR RIVER
map (35° 33′N 77° 5′W) **14**:242
TAR SANDS **19**:34 *bibliog.*
energy sources **7**:175
petroleum **15**:209
synthetic fuels **18**:409–410
TARA (Ireland) **19**:34–35
TARABULUS (Lebanon) *see* TRIPOLI (Lebanon)
TARAKI, NUR MOHAMMAD
Afghanistan **1**:135
TARANTELLA **19**:35
TARANTISM see TARANTELLA
TARANTO (Italy) **19**:35
map (40° 28′N 17° 15′E) **11**:321
TARANTO, GULF OF
map (40° 10′N 17° 20′E) **11**:321
TARANTULA **18**:181 *illus.*; **19**:35 *bibliog., illus.*
tarantella **19**:35
TARAPOTO (Peru)
map (6° 30′S 76° 20′W) **15**:193
TARAQUA (Brazil)
map (0° 6′N 68° 28′W) **3**:460
TARAS, JOHN
New York City Ballet **14**:155
TARASCAN (American Indians) **19**:35 *bibliog.*
Michoacán (Mexico) **13**:383
Morelia (Mexico) **13**:577
TARASICODISSA *see* ZENO, BYZANTINE EMPEROR
TARATA (Bolivia)
map (17° 37′S 66° 1′W) **3**:366
TARAWA (Kiribati) **19**:35
World War II **20**:267 *illus.*
TARBELL, IDA M. **19**:35 *bibliog.*
TARBORO (North Carolina)
map (35° 54′N 77° 32′W) **14**:242
TARDENOISIAN *see* MESOLITHIC PERIOD
TARDIEU, JEAN **19**:35–36 *bibliog.*
TARDIGRADE *see* WATER BEAR (microscopic animal)
TARE *see* VETCH
TARENTUM (Pennsylvania)
map (40° 36′N 79° 45′W) **15**:147
TARGET SHOOTING *see* SHOOTING (sport)
TARGHEE PASS
map (44° 41′N 111° 17′W) **11**:26
TARICA (Nicaragua)
map (12° 56′N 84° 41′W) **14**:179
TARIFF **19**:36 *bibliog.*
Commonwealth of Nations **5**:141
customs union **5**:398
European Economic Community **7**:299–300
European Free Trade Association **7**:300–301
free port **8**:294
General Agreement on Tariffs and Trade **9**:77
international trade **11**:223–224
International Trade Commission, U.S. **11**:224
most-favored-nation status **13**:605
port of entry **15**:443
quota **16**:28
smuggling **17**:374
TARIFF OF ABOMINATIONS (1828)
economic issues of the Civil War **5**:15
TARIFF ACTS **19**:36–37 *bibliog.*
Civil War, U.S. **5**:15
Cleveland, Grover **5**:53

Hayne, Robert Young 10:83–84
Hull, Cordell 10:296
Jackson, Andrew 11:342
McKinley, William 13:30
nullification 14:292
Polk, James K. 15:405
Smoot, Reed 17:374
Underwood, Oscar W. 19:383
TARIFF COMMISSION, U.S. *see* INTERNATIONAL TRADE COMMISSION, U.S.
TARIJA (Bolivia)
map (21° 31′S 64° 45′W) 3:366
TARIM BASIN
map (39° 0′N 83° 0′E) 4:362
TARIM RIVER 19:37
map (41° 5′N 86° 40′E) 4:362
TARIQ
Gibraltar, Strait of 9:175
TARIQ IBN ZIYAD
Spain, history of 18:144
TARKENTON, FRAN 19:37 *bibliog.*
TARKINGTON, BOOTH 19:37 *bibliog.*
TARKIO (Missouri)
map (40° 27′N 95° 23′W) 13:476
TARKWA (Ghana)
map (5° 19′N 1° 59′W) 9:164
TARLETON, BANASTRE
Cowpens, Battle of 5:322
TARLTON, RICHARD 19:37
TARMA (Peru)
map (11° 25′S 75° 42′W) 15:193
TARN RIVER
map (44° 5′N 1° 6′E) 8:260
TARNA RIVER
map (47° 31′N 19° 59′E) 10:307
TARNÓW (Poland)
map (50° 1′N 21° 0′E) 15:388
TARO 19:37–38 *illus.*
Samoans 17:46
TARO, KATSURA *see* KATSURA TARO
TAROT 4:142 *illus.*; 19:38 *illus.*
fortune-telling 8:241
TARPAN 19:38 *illus.*
TARPEIA 19:38
TARPON 8:116 *illus.*; 19:38 *illus.*
TARPON SPRINGS (Florida)
map (28° 9′N 82° 45′W) 8:172
TARQUÍ (Peru)
map (1° 35′S 75° 15′W) 15:193
TARQUINIA (Italy) 19:39 *bibliog.*
Etruscans 7:258–261
tomb art from 7:259 *illus.*
TARQUINIUS, SEXTUS
Rome, ancient 16:297
TARQUINIUS PRISCUS, ETRUSCAN KING OF ROME 19:39
Veii 19:535
TARQUINIUS SUPERBUS, ETRUSCAN KING OF ROME 19:39
Rome, ancient 16:297
TARR, PETER
West Virginia 20:114
TARRAGON 19:39 *illus.*
TARRAGONA (Spain) 19:39
map (41° 7′N 1° 15′E) 18:140
TARRANT (Alabama)
map (33° 34′N 86° 46′W) 1:234
TARRANT (county in Texas)
map (32° 47′N 97° 18′W) 19:129
TARRYTOWN (New York)
map (41° 5′N 73° 52′W) 14:149
New York (state) 14:150
TARSIER 15:540 *illus.*; 19:39 *illus.*
hand 15:539 *illus.*
TARSKI, ALFRED 19:39
TARSUS (Turkey) 19:39–40
map (36° 55′N 34° 53′E) 19:343
TART, CHARLES
extrasensory perception 7:346
TARTAGAL (Argentina)
map (28° 40′S 59° 52′W) 2:149
TARTAGLIA, NICCOLÒ 19:40 *bibliog.*
artillery 2:223
ballistics 3:49; 19:40
weapons 20:74
TARTAN 19:40–41 *bibliog.*, *illus.*
Buchanan clan 19:40 *illus.*
Caledonia plaid 19:40 *illus.*
clan 5:36
Jacobite plaid 19:40 *illus.*
Murray clan 19:40 *illus.*
TARTAR *see* TATAR
TARTARUS 19:41
TARTINI, GIUSEPPE 19:41 *bibliog.*
TARTU (USSR) 19:41
TARTUFFE (play) 19:41
Molière 13:509
TARWEED (genus *Grindela*) *see* GUMWEED
TARWEED (genus *Madia*) 19:41
TARXIEN (Malta) 19:41 *bibliog.*
TARZAN (films)
Weissmuller, Johnny 20:96
TARZAN OF THE APES (book)
Burroughs, Edgar Rice 3:580
feral children 8:51
TARZAN OF THE APES (fictional character) 5:136 *illus.*; 19:41 *bibliog.*
TASADAY 2:51 *illus.*; 4:225 *illus.*; 19:41 *bibliog.*; 20:201 *illus.*
TASCHEREAU, SIR HENRI 19:42
TASHKENT (USSR) 19:42
climate 19:390 *table*
map (41° 20′N 69° 18′E) 19:388
TASIKMALAYA (Indonesia)
map (7° 20′S 108° 12′E) 11:147
TÅSINGE ISLAND
map (55° 0′N 10° 36′E) 6:109
TASMAN, ABEL JANSZOON 19:42 *bibliog.*
Australia, history of 2:340 *map*
Cook Strait 5:237
exploration 7:336–337 *map*
voyage of 1642–43 14:161 *map*
TASMAN, MOUNT
map (43° 34′S 170° 9′E) 14:158
TASMAN BAY
map (41° 0′S 173° 20′E) 14:158
TASMAN SEA 19:42
Bass Strait 3:117
Cook Strait 5:237
map (40° 0′S 163° 0′E) 14:334
TASMANIA (Australia) 2:334 *illus.*; 19:42 *bibliog.*, *illus.*, *map*
Australia, history of 2:340
cities
Hobart 10:192
flag 8:145 *illus.*
language
Oceanic languages 14:339
map (43° 0′S 147° 0′E) 2:328
Tasman, Abel Janszoon 19:42
wildlife
flap-footed lizard 8:153
Tasmanian devil 19:42
Tasmanian wolf 19:42–43
TASMANIAN DEVIL 19:42–43 *illus.*
TASMANIAN WOLF 19:42–43 *illus.*
TASS (TELEGRAFNOIE AGENTSVO SOVIETSKOVO SOIUZA)
Pravda 15:290
press agencies and syndicates 15:533
TASSEL HOUSE
Horta, Victor 10:254
TASSELFISH *see* THREADFIN
TASSI, AGOSTINO
Gentileschi (family) 9:95
TASSILI N'AJJER (Algeria) 19:43 *bibliog.*
rock art 2:23 *illus.*; 15:510 *illus.*
TASSO, TORQUATO 19:43 *bibliog.*
TASTE
senses and sensation 17:204
tongue 19:234
TATABÁNYA (Hungary)
map (47° 34′N 18° 26′E) 10:307
TATAMI
rush 16:347
TATANKA IYOTAKE *see* SITTING BULL
TATAR 19:43–44 *bibliog.*
Crimea (USSR) 5:348
Dimitry Donskoi, Grand Duke of 6:177
Golden Horde, Khanate of the 9:232
Kazan (USSR) 12:33
Turks 19:348
TATAR STRAIT
map (50° 0′N 141° 15′E) 19:388
TATCHILA *see* COLORADO (American Indians)
TATE (Georgia)
map (34° 25′N 84° 23′W) 9:114
TATE (county in Mississippi)
map (34° 40′N 90° 0′W) 13:469
TATE, ALLEN 19:44 *bibliog.*
TATE, HENRY
Tate Gallery, The 19:44
TATE, SHARON
Polanski, Roman 15:392
TATE GALLERY, THE 19:44 *bibliog.*
TATI, JACQUES 19:44 *bibliog.*
TATIAN 19:44
TATITLEK (Alaska)
map (60° 52′N 146° 41′W) 1:242
TATLA LAKE (British Columbia)
map (51° 55′N 124° 36′W) 3:491
TATLER, THE (periodical)
Steele, Sir Richard 18:243
TATLIN, VLADIMIR YEVGRAFOVICH 19:44 *bibliog.*
constructivism 5:224
modern architecture 13:491
Monument to the 3d International (model) 16:363 *illus.*
Pevsner, Antoine 15:216
TATNAM, CAPE
map (57° 16′N 91° 0′W) 13:119
TATRA MOUNTAINS
map (49° 12′N 20° 5′E) 5:413
TATTI, JACOPO *see* SANSOVINO, JACOPO
TATTNALL (county in Georgia)
map (32° 0′N 82° 0′W) 9:114
TATTOOED PAWNEE *see* WICHITA (American Indians)
TATTOOING
body marking 3:356–357
TATUM (New Mexico)
map (33° 16′N 103° 19′W) 14:136
TATUM, ART 19:44
TATUM, EDWARD L. 19:44 *bibliog.*
Beadle, George W. 3:137
biology 3:271
fungi 8:367
Lederberg, Joshua 12:268
Neurospora 14:107
TAU (American Samoa) 1:366 *map*
TAU (letter)
cross 5:360; 5:361 *illus.*
T (letter) 19:3
TAUBE, HENRY 19:44–45
TAUERN MOUNTAINS
map (47° 10′N 12° 30′E) 2:348
TAUFA'AHAU TUPOU IV, KING OF TONGA
Tonga 19:234
TAULER, JOHANNES 19:45 *bibliog.*
TAUM SAUK MOUNTAIN
map (37° 34′N 90° 44′W) 13:476
TAUMATURGO (Brazil)
map (8° 57′S 72° 48′W) 3:460
TAUNG SKULL 19:45 *bibliog.*
Australopithecus 2:345–346
Dart, Raymond 6:39
TAUNGDWINGYI (Burma)
map (20° 1′N 95° 33′E) 3:573
TAUNGGYI (Burma)
map (20° 47′N 97° 2′E) 3:573
TAUNTON (England)
map (51° 1′N 3° 6′W) 19:403
TAUNTON (Massachusetts)
map (41° 54′N 71° 6′W) 13:206
TAUNTON RIVER
map (41° 42′N 71° 10′W) 16:198
TAUPIN, BERNIE
John, Elton 11:423
TAUPO, LAKE
map (38° 49′S 175° 55′E) 14:158
TAURANGA (New Zealand)
map (37° 42′S 176° 10′E) 14:158
TAURUS 19:45 *bibliog.*
Crab nebula 5:325–326
Hyades 10:327
Pleiades 11:227 *illus.*; 15:364
supernova 18:352 *illus.*
TAURUS-LITTROW VALLEY (moon) 13:563 *illus.*
TAURUS MOUNTAINS 19:45
map (37° 0′N 33° 0′E) 19:343
TAVARES (Florida)
map (28° 48′N 81° 44′W) 8:172
TAVERNER, JOHN 19:45 *bibliog.*
TAVERNIER (Florida)
map (25° 1′N 80° 31′W) 8:172
TAVERNIER, JEAN BAPTISTE 19:45
TAVEUNI ISLAND
map (16° 51′S 179° 58′E) 8:77
TAVGI LANGUAGE
Ural-Altaic languages 19:475
TÄVIBO
ghost dance 9:169
TAVOY (Burma)
map (14° 5′N 98° 12′E) 3:573
TAVUA (Fiji)
map (17° 27′S 177° 51′E) 8:77
TAW (letter)
T (letter) 19:3
TAWA (New Zealand)
map (41° 10′S 174° 51′E) 14:158
TAWANTINSUYA *see* INCA (American Indians)
TAWARAYA, SOTATSU *see* SOTATSU
TAWAS CITY (Michigan)
map (44° 16′N 83° 31′W) 13:377
TAWFIQ PASHA 19:45 *bibliog.*
TAWING *see* LEATHER AND HIDES
TAWNEY, RICHARD HENRY 19:45
Protestant ethic 15:576
TAX COURT, U.S. 19:45 *bibliog.*
Internal Revenue Service 11:218
TAXATION 19:46–47 *bibliog.*
American Revolution 1:354–355
Civil War, U.S. 5:15; 5:33
Congress of the United States 5:186
court decisions
Bailey v. *Drexel Furniture Company* 3:26
Brown v. *Maryland* 3:517
Carter v. *Carter Coal Company* 4:173
Cooley v. *Board of Port Wardens* 5:240
McCray v. *U.S.* 13:10–11
Pollock v. *Farmers' Loan and Trust Co.* 15:409–410
United States v. *Butler* 19:464
direct taxes 19:46
excess profits tax 7:326
finance, state and local 8:92
fiscal policy 8:109–110
foundations and endowments 8:251
freedom of religion 8:298
income tax 11:75–77
indirect taxes 19:46
inheritance tax 11:177–178
Internal Revenue Service 11:218
Middle Ages 13:393
municipal government 13:642
petroleum industry 15:215
poll tax 15:405
property tax 15:571
revenue sharing 16:185
Ricardo, David 16:206
sales tax 17:32
single tax 17:322
16th Amendment 17:331
social security 18:14–16
tariff 19:36
tax accounting 1:78
Tax Court, U.S. 19:45
tithe 19:212
trucking industry 19:315
value-added tax 19:508–509
Whiskey Rebellion 20:133
TAXICAB 19:47 *bibliog.*
TAXIDERMY 19:47–48 *bibliog.*
TAXILA (Pakistan) 19:48 *bibliog.*
TAXIS (biology) 19:48 *bibliog.*
TAXONOMY *see* CLASSIFICATION, BIOLOGICAL
TAY, RIVER 19:48
TAY-SACHS DISEASE 19:48 *bibliog.*
enzyme 7:214
genetic diseases 9:83
TAYA, MAAWIYA OULD
Mauritania 13:237
TAYACIAN
Fontéchevade man 8:207
TAYLOR (Arizona)
map (34° 28′N 110° 5′W) 2:160
TAYLOR (Arkansas)
map (33° 6′N 93° 28′W) 2:166
TAYLOR (county in Florida)
map (30° 0′N 83° 40′W) 8:172
TAYLOR (county in Georgia)
map (32° 35′N 84° 15′W) 9:114
TAYLOR (county in Iowa)
map (40° 45′N 94° 42′W) 11:244
TAYLOR (county in Kentucky)
map (37° 20′N 85° 5′W) 12:47
TAYLOR (Michigan)
map (42° 13′N 83° 16′W) 13:377
TAYLOR (Nebraska)
map (41° 46′N 99° 23′W) 14:70
TAYLOR (Texas)
map (30° 34′N 97° 25′W) 19:129
TAYLOR (county in Texas)
map (32° 17′N 97° 52′W) 19:129
TAYLOR (county in West Virginia)
map (39° 20′N 80° 5′W) 20:111
TAYLOR (county in Wisconsin)
map (45° 12′N 90° 30′W) 20:185
TAYLOR, BAYARD 19:48
TAYLOR, BROOK 19:48
Taylor series 19:51
TAYLOR, CECIL 19:48 *bibliog.*
TAYLOR, EDWARD 19:48 *bibliog.*
TAYLOR, EDWARD THOMPSON 19:48
TAYLOR, ELIZABETH (actress) 19:49 *bibliog.*, *illus.*
Warhol, Andy 20:29 *illus.*
TAYLOR, ELIZABETH (novelist) 19:49
TAYLOR, FRANK B.
paleogeography 15:37
TAYLOR, FREDERICK WINSLOW 19:49 *bibliog.*
industrial management 11:156
time and motion study 19:202
TAYLOR, JEREMY 19:49 *bibliog.*
TAYLOR, JOHN (clergyman) 19:49 *bibliog.*
TAYLOR, JOHN (poet) 19:49
TAYLOR, LAURETTE
Coward, Sir Noel 5:320
TAYLOR, MAXWELL D. 19:49
TAYLOR, MOUNT
map (35° 14′N 107° 37′W) 14:136
TAYLOR, PAUL 19:49–50 *bibliog.*
Lange, Dorothea 12:195
TAYLOR, PETER 19:50 *bibliog.*
TAYLOR, ZACHARY 19:50–51 *bibliog.*, *illus.*
Fillmore, Millard 8:80
Louisville (Kentucky) 12:436

TAYLOR, ZACHARY (cont.)
Mexican War **13**:352–353 *illus., map*; **19**:50–51
Monterrey (Mexico) **13**:553
TAYLOR SERIES **19**:51 *bibliog.*
Lagrange, Joseph Louis de **12**:166
mathematics, history of **13**:225
Taylor, Brook **19**:48
TAYLORS (South Carolina)
map (34° 55′N 82° 18′W) **18**:98
TAYLORSVILLE (Indiana)
map (39° 18′N 85° 57′W) **11**:111
TAYLORSVILLE (Kentucky)
map (38° 2′N 85° 21′W) **12**:47
TAYLORSVILLE (Mississippi)
map (31° 50′N 89° 32′W) **13**:469
TAYLORSVILLE (North Carolina)
map (35° 55′N 81° 4′W) **14**:242
TAYLORVILLE (Illinois)
map (39° 33′N 89° 18′W) **11**:42
TAYMOUTH (New Brunswick)
map (46° 11′N 66° 37′W) **14**:117
TAYMUR, MAHMUD
Egypt **7**:77
TAYMYR LAKE
map (74° 30′N 102° 30′E) **19**:388
TAYMYR PENINSULA
map (76° 0′N 104° 0′E) **19**:388
TAYRA **19**:51 *illus.*
TAYSIDE (Scotland) **19**:51
cities
Dundee **6**:299
counties (former)
Angus **2**:7–8
TAZA
Cochise **5**:86
TAZEWELL (county in Illinois)
map (40° 30′N 89° 27′W) **11**:42
TAZEWELL (Tennessee)
map (36° 27′N 83° 34′W) **19**:104
TAZEWELL (Virginia)
map (37° 7′N 81° 31′W) **19**:607
TAZEWELL (county in Virginia)
map (37° 5′N 81° 35′W) **19**:607
TBILISI (USSR) **19**:51
map (41° 43′N 44° 49′E) **19**:388
TCDD (chemical)
pollutants, chemical **15**:410
TCHAIKOVSKY, PETER ILICH **19**:51–52 *bibliog., illus.*
Russian music **16**:368 *illus.*
symphonic poem **18**:405
TCHAIKOVSKY INTERNATIONAL COMPETITION
Cliburn, Van **5**:54
music competitions **13**:669
TCHELITCHEW, PAVEL **19**:52 *bibliog.*
TCHEREPNIN, ALEKSANDR NIKOLAYEVICH **19**:52 *bibliog.*
TCHERKASSKY, MARIANNA **19**:52 *bibliog.*
TCHERNICHOWSKY, SAUL **19**:52–53 *bibliog.*
TCHIBANGA (Gabon)
map (2° 51′S 11° 2′E) **9**:5
TCHIEN (Liberia)
map (6° 4′N 8° 8′W) **12**:313
TCHING-PAO (periodical)
journalism **11**:454
TCHULA (Mississippi)
map (33° 11′N 90° 13′W) **13**:469
TCZEW (Poland)
map (54° 6′N 18° 47′E) **15**:388
TE ANAU, LAKE
map (45° 12′S 167° 48′E) **14**:158
TE ARAROA (New Zealand)
map (37° 38′S 178° 22′E) **14**:158
TE DEUM LAUDAMUS **19**:53
TE HAPUA (New Zealand)
map (34° 31′S 172° 54′E) **14**:158
TEA **19**:53–54 *bibliog., illus.*
clipper ship **5**:60–61
cultivation **19**:53
history **19**:53
India **11**:86 *illus.*
Kenya **12**:55
Lipton, Sir Thomas **12**:364
processing **19**:53–54
Sri Lanka **18**:206 *illus.*
stimulant **18**:271
varieties **19**:54
catnip **4**:212
chamomile **4**:276
hops **10**:233
hyssop **10**:352
jasmine **11**:384
New Jersey tea **14**:134
Salvia **17**:40
sassafras **17**:83
snakeroot **17**:383
spicebush **18**:181
TEA ACT
Franklin, Benjamin **8**:284
TEA CEREMONY **19**:54
Japanese art and architecture **11**:376
TEACH, EDWARD *see* BLACKBEARD
TEACHER EDUCATION
Danforth Foundation **6**:31
Herbart, Johann Friedrich **10**:134–135
Keppel, Francis **12**:58
Mann, Horace **13**:122–123
preschool education **15**:521
secondary education **17**:180
Teachers College, Columbia University **19**:54
Willard, Emma Hart **20**:154
TEACHERS COLLEGE, COLUMBIA UNIVERSITY **19**:54
Butler, Nicholas Murray **3**:592
Cremin, Lawrence Arthur **5**:338
progressive education **15**:564
TEACHERS INSURANCE AND ANNUITY ASSOCIATION
Carnegie Foundations **4**:155
TEACHING **19**:54–56 *bibliog., illus.*
applied linguistics **2**:90–91
Bell, Andrew **3**:185
Chinese medicine **4**:391 *illus.*
computers in education **5**:165–166
Cuisenaire method **5**:383
Dalton Plan **6**:15
educational psychology **7**:66
foreign languages, teaching of **8**:225
Herbart, Johann Friedrich **10**:134–135
learning disabilities **12**:259–260
Montessori method **13**:554
open classroom **14**:398
Pestalozzi, Johann Heinrich **15**:196
programmed learning **15**:562–563
reading education **16**:100–101
special education **18**:166–167
Summerhill **18**:339
teaching machines **19**:57
Winnetka Plan **20**:180
TEACHING MACHINES **19**:57 *bibliog., illus.*
computers in education **5**:165–166
learning theory **12**:260–261
programmed learning **15**:262–263
TEACHINGS OF DON JUAN, THE (book)
Castaneda, Carlos **4**:186
TEAGUE (Texas)
map (31° 38′N 96° 17′W) **19**:129
TEAGUE, WALTER D. **19**:57
Steuben glass **18**:262
TEAHOUSE
Japanese art and architecture **11**:376
TEAK **19**:57 *bibliog.*
lumber **12**:456 *illus.*
wood **20**:205 *illus.*
TEAM X (architectural group)
modern architecture **13**:493
Smithson, Alison and Peter **17**:372
TEAMSTERS, CHAUFFEURS, WAREHOUSEMEN, AND HELPERS OF AMERICA, INTERNATIONAL BROTHERHOOD OF **19**:58 *bibliog.*
Fitzsimmons, Frank Edward **8**:132
Hoffa, James R. **10**:194–195
TEANECK (New Jersey)
map (40° 53′N 74° 1′W) **14**:129
TEAPOT DOME **19**:58 *bibliog.*
Daugherty, Harry M. **6**:45
Harding, Warren G. **10**:47
Roberts, Owen J. **16**:242
Sinclair, Harry F. **17**:319
TEAR GAS **19**:58 *bibliog.*
Mace **13**:14
TEARS **19**:58
tear gas **19**:58
TEASDALE, SARA **19**:58 *bibliog.*
TEASEL **19**:58 *illus.*
TEATICKET (Massachusetts)
map (41° 34′N 70° 36′W) **13**:206
TEATRO ALLA SCALA *see* LA SCALA
TEATRO OLIMPICO **19**:59 *bibliog.*; **19**:146 *illus.*
Palladio, Andrea **15**:48
TEBALDI, RENATA **19**:59 *bibliog.*
TÉBESSA MOUNTAINS
map (35° 20′N 8° 20′E) **19**:335
TEBICUARY RIVER
map (26° 36′S 58° 16′W) **15**:77
TECHNETIUM **19**:59
element **7**:130 *table*
Group VIIB periodic table **15**:167
metal, metallic element **13**:328
transition elements **19**:273
TECHNICAL ASSISTANT *see* TECHNICAL EDUCATION
TECHNICAL EDUCATION **19**:59 *bibliog.*
See also APPRENTICESHIP; INDUSTRIAL ARTS PROGRAMS; VOCATIONAL EDUCATION
British education **3**:495
Canadian education **4**:91–92
Franklin Institute **8**:285
Massachusetts Institute of Technology **13**:212
Rensselaer Polytechnic Institute **16**:159
Rochester Institute of Technology **16**:247
Stevens Institute of Technology **18**:264
Union of Soviet Socialist Republics, universities of the **19**:398–399
TECHNICIAN *see* TECHNICAL EDUCATION
TECHNOLOGIST *see* TECHNICAL EDUCATION
TECHNOLOGY **19**:59–61 *bibliog.*
See also ELECTRICAL AND ELECTRONIC TECHNOLOGY; ENERGY TECHNOLOGY; ENGINEERING TECHNOLOGY; FOOD TECHNOLOGY; MATERIALS TECHNOLOGY; TECHNOLOGY, HISTORY OF; names of specific technology articles, e.g., METALLURGY; TRANSPORTATION; etc.
biotechnology **3**:277
definition **19**:59–60
engineering **7**:177–178
hand tools **10**:35
human factors engineering **10**:297
international trade **11**:223
invention **11**:232–233
research and development **19**:60
technological innovation **19**:60
technology assessment **19**:60–61
technology transfer **19**:61
TECHNOLOGY, HISTORY OF **19**:61–69 *bibliog., illus.*
See also TECHNOLOGY; names of specific inventors, e.g., MORSE, SAMUEL F. B.; WHITNEY, ELI; etc.
agriculture, history of **1**:189–193
automotive industry **2**:363–364
aviation **2**:370–375
computer **5**:160–160c
culture **5**:385
industrial archaeology **11**:154
Industrial Revolution **11**:158–160
invention **11**:232–233
Iron Age **11**:271–272
manufacturing **13**:131–133
museums of science and industry **13**:659
plow **15**:369–370 *illus.*
scientific associations **17**:144–146
telegraph **19**:76–78
telephone **19**:78–80
weapons **20**:74–75
wheel **20**:127–129
TECOMAN (Mexico)
map (18° 55′N 103° 53′W) **13**:357
TECOPA (California)
map (35° 51′N 116° 13′W) **4**:31
TECPAN DE GALEANA (Mexico)
map (17° 15′N 100° 41′W) **13**:357
TECUCI (Romania)
map (45° 50′N 27° 26′E) **16**:288
TECUMSEH (Michigan)
map (42° 0′N 83° 57′W) **13**:377
TECUMSEH (Nebraska)
map (40° 22′N 96° 11′W) **14**:70
TECUMSEH (Oklahoma)
map (35° 15′N 96° 56′W) **14**:368
TECUMSEH (Shawnee Indian) **19**:69 *bibliog., illus.*
Indian Wars **11**:107
Johnson, Richard M. **11**:435
Shawnee Prophet **17**:247
Wabansi **20**:3
War of 1812 **20**:27
TEDDER, ARTHUR WILLIAM TEDDER, 1ST BARON **19**:69
TEDESCO, MARIO CASTELNUOVO- *see* CASTELNUOVO-TEDESCO, MARIO
TEDZHEN (HARIRUD) RIVER
map (37° 24′N 60° 38′E) **1**:133
TEEC NOS POS (Arizona)
map (36° 55′N 109° 7′W) **2**:160
TEENAGERS *see* YOUNG PEOPLE
TEETH **19**:69–72 *bibliog., illus.*
alligator **13**:99 *illus.*
cat **4**:194 *illus.*
cat family **4**:196
decay **19**:71–72 *illus.*
laser **12**:212 *illus.*
dental plaque **6**:116
dentistry **6**:114–116
dentures **6**:117
diseases **19**:71–72
dog **4**:157 *illus.*; **13**:99 *illus.*
edentates **7**:56
evolution **19**:71
fang
snake **17**:380–381 *illus.*
viper **19**:604
fluoridation **8**:187
horse **10**:241; **10**:245
human **19**:70
insect **11**:188 *illus.*
lizard **12**:380
orthodontics **14**:449
other vertebrates **19**:70–71
periodontics **15**:170
phonetics **15**:252
rodent **16**:265 *illus.*
shark **17**:242
snake **17**:378
TEFÉ (Brazil)
map (3° 22′S 64° 42′W) **3**:460
TEFLON **19**:72
TEGAL (Indonesia)
map (6° 52′S 109° 8′E) **11**:147
TEGEA (Greece) **19**:72
TEGNÉR, ESAIAS **19**:72
TEGU *see* TEJU
TEGUCIGALPA (Honduras) **10**:219 *illus.*; **19**:72
map (14° 6′N 87° 13′W) **10**:218
TEHACHAPI (California)
map (35° 8′N 118° 27′W) **4**:31
TEHACHAPI MOUNTAINS
map (35° 0′N 118° 40′W) **4**:31
TEHAMA (county in California)
map (40° 5′N 122° 35′W) **4**:31
TEHERAN (Iran) *see* TEHRAN (Iran)
TEHRAN (Iran) **11**:251 *illus., table*; **19**:72–73
Iranian hostage crisis **11**:253–254
map (35° 40′N 51° 26′E) **11**:250
TEHRAN CONFERENCE **19**:73
World War II **20**:271 *illus.*
TEHUACÁN (Mexico)
map (18° 27′N 97° 23′W) **13**:357
TEHUACÁN VALLEY (Mexico) **14**:237 *map*; **19**:73 *bibliog.*
TEHUANTEPEC, GULF OF
map (16° 0′N 94° 50′W) **13**:357
TEHUANTEPEC, ISTHMUS OF **19**:73
map (17° 0′N 95° 0′W) **13**:357
Zapotec **20**:356
TEHUELCHE (American Indians) **19**:73 *bibliog.*
Patagonia **15**:109
TEIGE, KAREL
Czech literature **5**:412
TEIID **19**:73
TEILHARD DE CHARDIN, PIERRE **19**:73–74 *bibliog., illus.*
TEIRLINCK, HERMAN **19**:74
TEJU **19**:74 *illus.*
TEKAHIONWAKE
Johnson, Emily Pauline **11**:432
TEKAKWITHA, KATERI **19**:74 *bibliog.*
TEKAMAH (Nebraska)
map (41° 47′N 96° 13′W) **14**:70
TEKOA (Washington)
map (47° 14′N 117° 4′W) **20**:35
TEKONSHA (Michigan)
map (42° 5′N 84° 60′W) **13**:377
TEKTITE (underwater habitat) **14**:345 *illus.*
TEKTITES (geology) **19**:74–75 *bibliog.*
meteor and meteorite **13**:337
sediment, marine **17**:184
TEL AVIV (Israel) **19**:75 *bibliog., illus.*
Jaffa **11**:348
map (32° 4′N 34° 46′E) **11**:302
TEL AVIV UNIVERSITY **19**:75
TELA (Honduras)
climate **10**:218 *table*
map (15° 44′N 87° 27′W) **10**:218
TELANTHROPUS see HOMO ERECTUS
TELECOMMUNICATIONS **19**:75–76 *bibliog.*
cable TV **4**:6–7
communications satellite **5**:144–145
computer **5**:160f
computer networking **5**:163
computers and privacy **5**:167
facsimile **8**:5–6
Federal Communications Commission **8**:41
fiber optics **8**:68–69
INTELSAT **11**:205–206
MacKay (family) **13**:27
mass communication **13**:202
microwaves **13**:389
modem **13**:490

multiplexer 13:638
newspaper 14:172
Nyquist, Harry 14:310
radio 16:44–47
radio and television broadcasting 16:53–60
receiver (communications) 16:106
signaling 17:300–301
telegraph 19:76–78
telephone 19:78–80
teletext 19:84
television 19:84–85
television transmission 19:88–90
transmitter 19:276
video 19:576a–576f
videotex 19:576p–577
TELEGRAFNOIE AGENTSVO SOVIETSKOVO SOIUZA *see* TASS (Telegrafnoie Agentsvo Sovietskovo Soiuza)
TELEGRAPH 19:76–78 *bibliog., illus.*
Atlantic cable 2:294
Bell, Alexander Graham 3:185
Colt, Samuel 5:123–124
Cornell, Ezra 5:268
De Forest, Lee 6:58
Edison, Thomas Alva 7:57–58
Field, Cyrus W. 8:71
Gauss, Carl Friedrich 9:61–62
Gray, Elisha 9:306
MacKay (family) 13:27
Marconi, Guglielmo, inventor 13:147
Morse, Samuel F. B. 13:590
Morse code 13:590–591
optical 17:301 *illus.*
Pupin, Michael Idvorsky 15:626
radio 16:44–45
railroad 16:75
relay 16:137
signaling 17:300–301 *illus.*
telecommunications 19:75–76
Weber, Wilhelm Eduard 20:88
Wheatstone, Sir Charles 20:127
Wheelwright, William 20:129–130
TELEGRAPHONE
Poulsen, Valdemar 15:473
TELEKI, PAUL, COUNT
Rudolf, Lake 16:338
TELEKINESIS
psychokinesis 15:591
TELEMANN, GEORG PHILIPP 19:78 *bibliog.*
TELEMETRY 19:78 *bibliog.*
scanning 17:114
TELÉN (Argentina)
map (36° 16′S 65° 30′W) 2:149
TELEOLOGY 19:78 *bibliog.*
Aristotle's views on 2:157
ethics 7:251
heaven 10:100
hell 10:113
metaphysics 13:334–335
TELEOST 17:340 *illus.*; 19:78
beardfish 3:142
cutlass fish 5:398
gill 9:181 *illus.*
gymnotid 9:414
hatchetfish 10:68
hawkfish 10:77
perch 15:160–161
TELEPATHY
Burt, Sir Cyril 3:581
extrasensory perception 7:346
TELEPHONE 19:78–80 *bibliog., illus., map*
Atlantic cable 2:294
basic principles 19:78–79
Bell, Alexander Graham 3:185; 19:78–79 *illus.*
cable 4:6 *illus.*
carrier telephones
Black, Harold 3:303
carriers 19:80
communications satellite 5:145
digital technology 6:175
extended uses 19:80
Gray, Elisha, inventor 9:306
grid 9:361
industry 19:80
information theory 11:174–175
labor union
Communication Workers of America 5:142
long distance
Direct Distance Dialing 19:80
feedback 8:44
Pupin, Michael Idvorsky 15:626
MacKay (family) 13:27
microphone 13:386 *illus.*
modem 13:490
modulation 13:499
mouthpiece
Berliner, Emile 3:218
outgrowths of research 19:80
public utility 15:610–611
radiotelephone
radio 16:45
switching systems 19:80
telecommunications 19:75–76
telephone-satellite terminals 19:79 *map*
vocoder 19:625
Watson, Thomas A. 19:79
world distribution 19:79 *map*
World War I 20:247
TELEPHOTO LENS (camera) 4:56
TELERTHEBA, MOUNT
map (24° 10′N 6° 51′E) 1:287
TELES PIRES RIVER
map (7° 21′S 58° 3′W) 3:460
TELESCOPE, OPTICAL 19:80–84 *bibliog., illus., table*
Airy disk 1:228
astronomy, history of 2:279–281 *illus.*
astronomy and astrophysics 2:281–282
Babcock, Horace Welcome 3:6
binoculars 3:259–260
Cassegrainian telescope 4:183–184
Clark, Alvan Graham 5:37
coudé telescope 5:308
cross hairs
Picard, Jean 15:290
faint object detection 8:8
Fitz, Henry 8:130
Galileo Galilei 9:15
gamma-ray astronomy 9:34
Gregory, James 9:356
Herschel, Sir William 10:147–148
history 19:81–82
largest reflecting telescopes, worldwide 19:82 *table*
Lovell, Sir Bernard 12:438
mirror 13:464–465 *illus.*
Newton, Sir Isaac 14:174
observatory, astronomical 14:317–319
optics 14:411
parabola 15:74
photographic zenith tube 15:260
radio astronomy 16:48 *illus.*
radio telescope
interferometer 11:209–210
radio astronomy 16:50–53 *illus.*
Space Telescope 18:137
surveying, equipment 18:368–369 *illus.*
telescope (1845) 2:280 *illus.*
transit circle 19:273
ultraviolet telescope
OAO 14:313
TELESCOPE BLACK MOOR (goldfish) 9:234 *illus.*
TELESCOPE PEAK
map (36° 10′N 117° 5′W) 4:31
TELESIO, BERNARDINO 19:84 *bibliog.*
TELESTERION (Hall of the Mysteries)
Ictinus 11:24
TELETEXT 19:84 *bibliog.*
television transmission 19:90
TELETYPEWRITER
telegraph 19:77–78
TELEVISION 19:84–85
See also TELEVISION BROADCASTING
history 19:576a–576c
Farnsworth, Philo Taylor 8:28
Goldmark, Peter Carl 9:235
Jenkins, Charles Francis 11:395
Zworykin, Vladimir Kosma 20:384
surveillance systems 18:366
telecommunications 19:75–76
television production *see* TELEVISION PRODUCTION
television transmission *see* TELEVISION TRANSMISSION
video technology 19:576k–576p
cathode-ray tube 4:211 *illus.*
color television 19:576b; 19:576m *illus.*; 19:576n *illus.*
liquid crystal 12:365
video recording 19:576j–576k
TELEVISION, NONCOMMERCIAL 19:85–86 *bibliog.*
Cooke, Alistair 5:237
fund raising 8:360
radio and television broadcasting 16:57–58
"Sesame Street" 17:212
TELEVISION BROADCASTING 16:55–60 *illus.*
advertising 1:112–113
awards
Emmy Awards 7:156–157
Peabody Award 15:123
censorship 4:248
history
Newhouse, Samuel I. 14:169
Paley, William S. 15:47
Sarnoff, David 17:78
labor union
Communication Workers of America 5:142
news programs
anchorman 1:399
Chancellor, John 4:278
Cronkite, Walter 5:359
electronic newsgathering 19:576b
journalism 11:455–456
press agencies and syndicates 15:533
Smith, Howard K. 17:368
television production 19:87
presidential elections 15:530
programming
Disney, Walt 6:197
evangelicalism 7:312
Gleason, Jackie 9:206–207
Godfrey, Arthur 9:220
Lear, Norman 12:259
"Monty Python's Flying Circus" 13:560
Moore, Mary Tyler 13:569
soap opera 18:8
Sullivan, Ed 18:336
video, music 19:576f
Walters, Barbara 20:19–20
Welk, Lawrence 20:98–99
Young, Loretta 20:334
regulations
Federal Communications Commission 8:41
government regulation 9:271
religious broadcasting 16:141–142
sportscasting
Cosell, Howard 5:280
Rozelle, Pete 16:331
television production 19:87
telecommunications 19:75–76
television, noncommercial 19:85–86
television production 19:86–87
television transmission 19:88–89; 19:90
U.S. Congress and the public 5:187
video 19:576b; 19:576d
TELEVISION PRODUCTION 19:86–87 *bibliog., illus.*
cinematography 4:432–434
electronic newsgathering 19:576b
video technology 19:576o
videotape 19:576p
TELEVISION TRANSMISSION 19:88–90 *bibliog, illus.*
antenna 2:47–48
cable TV 4:6–7
communications satellite 5:144–145
frequency allocation 8:326
frequency modulation 8:327
information science 11:173
radio and television broadcasting 16:59–60
receiver 16:106
teletext 19:84
tranducer 19:269
video 19:576b
video technology 19:576k–576n
videotex 19:576p–577
TELFAIR (county in Georgia)
map (31° 55′N 83° 0′W) 9:114
TELFORD (Pennsylvania)
map (40° 20′N 75° 20′W) 15:147
TELFORD, THOMAS 19:90 *bibliog.*
bridge (engineering) 3:480–481
roads and highways 16:237–238 *illus.*
TELL (archaeology) 19:90
European prehistory 7:301
Hasanlu (Iran) 10:65
TELL, WILLIAM 19:90
TELL AL-SULTAN *see* JERICHO (Jordan)
TELL ATCHANA *see* ALALAKH (Turkey)
TELL BALATAH *see* SHECHEM (Israel)
TELL BASTA *see* BUBASTIS (Egypt)
TELL CITY (Indiana)
map (37° 57′N 86° 46′W) 11:111
TELL ED-DUWEIR *see* LACHISH (Israel)
TELL EL-HUSN *see* BETH-SHAN (Beth-Shean) (Israel)
TELL EL-KEDAH *see* HAZOR (Israel)
TELL EL KHELEIFEH *see* EZION-GEBER (Israel)
TELL HARIRI *see* MARI (Syria)
TELL HUM *see* CAPERNAUM
TELL JEZER *see* GEZER (Israel)
"TELL-TALE HEART, THE" (short story) 19:90
TELLER (county in Colorado)
map (39° 55′N 105° 10′W) 5:116
TELLER, EDWARD 19:90 *bibliog.*
hydrogen bomb 10:339
TELLER, HENRY MOORE 19:90–91 *bibliog.*
TELLER AMENDMENT
Spanish-American War 18:150
TÉLLEZ, GABRIEL *see* TIRSO DE MOLINA
TELLICO DAM
environmental impact statement 7:212
TELLICO PLAINS (Tennessee)
map (35° 22′N 84° 18′W) 19:104
TELLO *see* GIRSU
TELLO, JULIO CÉSAR
Paracas 15:74
TELLURIDE (Colorado)
map (37° 56′N 107° 49′W) 5:116
TELLURIDE MINERALS 19:91
calaverite 4:21
krennerite 12:129
mineral 13:443 *table*
sylvanite 18:402
TELLURIUM 19:91
chalcogens 4:270
element 7:130 *table*
Group VIA periodic table 15:167; 19:91
native elements 14:47
telluride minerals 19:91
TELSTAR 19:91 *bibliog., illus.*
communications satellite 5:144
TELUGU
Dravidian languages 6:263
TELUKBETUNG (Indonesia)
map (5° 27′S 105° 16′E) 11:147
TEMA (Ghana)
map (5° 38′N 0° 1′E) 9:164
TEMARENDA *see* AZOV, SEA OF
TEMBURONG RIVER
map (4° 48′N 115° 3′E) 3:524
TEMESVÁR (Romania) *see* TIMIŞOARA (Romania)
TEMIN, HOWARD MARTIN 19:91
Baltimore, David 3:56
TÉMISCAMING (Quebec)
map (46° 43′N 79° 6′W) 16:18
TEMNE 19:91 *bibliog.*
Sierra Leone 17:297; 17:298
TEMPE (Arizona)
map (33° 25′N 111° 56′W) 2:160
TEMPERA 19:92 *bibliog.*
painting techniques 15:24
Wyeth, Andrew 20:298–299
TEMPERANCE (Michigan)
map (41° 47′N 83° 34′W) 13:377
TEMPERANCE MOVEMENT 19:92 *bibliog., illus.*; 20:203 *illus.*
18th Amendment 7:91
Nation, Carry Amelia 14:27
prohibition 15:565
Shaw, Anna Howard 17:245
WCTU 20:74
Willard, Frances 20:154
TEMPERATE CLIMATE 19:92 *bibliog.*
climax community 5:59
grasslands 9:299–300
lagoon 12:166
TEMPERATURE 19:92–93 *bibliog., illus.*
absolute zero 1:62–63; 19:92–93
background radiation 3:12
body temperature 3:357
Boltzmann constant 3:372
climate 5:55–58
critical constants 5:351
critical temperature
Mendeleyev, Dmitry Ivanovich 13:295
cryobiology 5:370
cryogenics 5:370–371
Curie temperature
magnetism 13:56
ground temperature 9:373
heat and heat transfer 10:98; 19:93
Köppen, Wladimir Peter 12:110
lapse rate 12:206
measurement 13:255; 19:92–93
Celsius, Anders 4:238
Celsius scale 4:238; 19:93
Fahrenheit scale 8:8; 19:93
International Practical Temperature Scale, zinc 20:367
Kelvin scale 12:40; 19:93
oceanographic instrumentation 14:342–344
Réaumur scale 16:105
thermistor 19:161
thermocouple 19:162
thermometer 19:166
thermostat 19:167
units, physical 19:466
metamorphic rock 13:331–333
meteorology 13:341
microclimate 13:384
Néel temperature, magnetism 13:56
paleotemperature 15:42
permafrost 15:173–174

TEMPERATURE (cont.)
phase equilibrium **15**:222–224 *illus.*
star **18**:222; **18**:224
Stefan, Josef **18**:245
superconductivity **18**:350
superfluidity **18**:351
triple point **19**:302
van der Waals equation **19**:512–513
water quality **20**:51
weather forecasting **20**:76–78
weather modification **20**:79–80
weather variation and extremes **20**:80–82
TEMPERING **19**:93
glass **9**:201
hardening **10**:45
metallurgy **13**:330
TEMPEST, THE (play) **19**:93
Gates, Sir Thomas **9**:58
TEMPIETTO **16**:152 *illus.*; **19**:93 *bibliog.*
Bramante, Donato **3**:451–452 *illus.*
TEMPLARS **19**:93–94 *bibliog.*, *illus.*
Bernard of Clairvaux, Saint **3**:220–221
TEMPLE **19**:94–99 *bibliog.*, *illus.*
See also CAVE—temples
architecture **2**:130 *illus.*; **2**:132
cella **4**:236
China **19**:98
Lung-men (Longmen) **12**:462
Yun-kang (Yungang) **20**:346
Egypt **19**:94–95
Abu Simbel **1**:66–67
Beth-shan **3**:230
Deir el-Bahri **6**:85–86
Dendera **6**:106
Edfu **7**:56
Egyptian art and architecture **7**:85–86
Karnak **12**:28
Luxor **12**:473
Ombos **14**:387
Philae **15**:229
Greece, ancient **19**:95–97
Eleusis **7**:135
Epidaurus **7**:218
Greek architecture **9**:334–337
Ictinus **11**:24
Olympia **14**:381
Parthenon **9**:336 *illus.*
Temple of Artemis at Ephesus **17**:217
Temple of Hera **9**:335 *illus.*
India **19**:97–98
Bhubaneswar **3**:234
Elephanta **7**:134
Ellora **7**:148
Indian art and architecture **11**:96
Khajuraho **12**:65
Konarak **12**:108
Mahabilipuram **13**:63 *illus.*
Israel
Solomon's temple **19**:95
Japan **19**:98–99
Japanese art and architecture **11**:373–378
Lamaist art and architecture **12**:172–173
Malta
Tarxien **19**:41
Mesopotamia **19**:94
Mesopotamian art and architecture **13**:317
Tepe Gawra **19**:114
Uruk **19**:490
naos **14**:14
pagoda **15**:14
Persia
Persian art and architecture **15**:185
Sassanians **17**:83–84
plan for **9**:334 *illus.*
pre-Columbian **13**:243–244 *illus.*
Aztec **2**:382–384 *illus.*
Chichén Itzá **4**:344
Pyramid and Temple of Inscriptions **11**:121 *illus.*
Tarascan **19**:35
Tenochtitlán **19**:112
Teotihuacán **19**:113–114
Uxmal **19**:499
prehistoric **19**:94
Roman **19**:97
Roman art and architecture **16**:273
Southeast Asia **19**:98
Angkor **1**:414–415
Ayuthia (Thailand) **2**:379–380
Borobudur **3**:402–403
Pagan (Burma) **15**:13
Southeast Asian art and architecture **18**:107–110
stupa **18**:308
ziggurat **20**:363
TEMPLE (Oklahoma)
map (34° 16′N 98° 14′W) **14**:368
TEMPLE (Texas)
map (31° 6′N 97° 21′W) **19**:129
TEMPLE, HENRY JOHN, 3D VISCOUNT PALMERSTON *see* PALMERSTON, HENRY JOHN TEMPLE, 3D VISCOUNT
TEMPLE, SHIRLEY **19**:99–100 *bibliog.*, *illus.*
TEMPLE, SIR WILLIAM (essayist) **19**:100 *bibliog.*
TEMPLE, WILLIAM (archbishop) **19**:100 *bibliog.*
TEMPLE OF ARTEMIS AT EPHESUS *see* ARTEMIS, TEMPLE OF, AT EPHESUS
TEMPLE UNIVERSITY
Pennsylvania, state universities and colleges of **15**:152
TEMPLIER, RAYMOND
Art Deco cigarette case **2**:208 *illus.*
TEMPO **19**:100 *bibliog.*
conducting **5**:173–174
TEMPORAL LOBE
brain **3**:443 *illus.*; **3**:446–447 *illus.*
TEMUCO (Chile)
map (38° 44′S 72° 36′W) **4**:355
TEN COMMANDMENTS **19**:100 *bibliog.*
ark of the covenant **2**:164
Moses **13**:600
Sinai **17**:318
TEN COMMANDMENTS, THE (film) **8**:83 *illus.*
TEN DEGREE CHANNEL, STRAIT OF
map (10° 0′N 93° 0′E) **11**:80
TEN LOST TRIBES OF ISRAEL **19**:100 *bibliog.*
TEN SLEEP (Wyoming)
map (44° 2′N 107° 27′W) **20**:301
TEN THOUSAND ISLANDS
map (25° 50′N 81° 33′W) **8**:172
TEN YEARS' WAR **19**:101 *bibliog.*
TENA (Ecuador)
map (0° 59′S 77° 49′W) **7**:52
TENAFLY (New Jersey)
map (40° 56′N 73° 58′W) **14**:129
TENAHA (Texas)
map (31° 57′N 94° 15′W) **19**:129
TENAKEE SPRINGS (Alaska)
map (57° 47′N 135° 13′W) **1**:242
TENANT **19**:101 *bibliog.*
manorialism **13**:127
property **15**:570–571
TENANT FARMING *see* FARMS AND FARMING—tenant farming
TENCTERI
Germanic peoples **9**:138
TENDAI
Buddhism **3**:541
Japan, history of **11**:367
TENDER IS THE NIGHT (book) **19**:101 *bibliog.*
TENDON **19**:101
collagen **5**:102
connective tissue **5**:196
gout **9**:266–267
muscle **13**:653
tissue, animal **19**:210
TENDONITIS **19**:101
TENDRIL **19**:101
tropism **19**:310 *illus.*
TENEMENT
Flagg, Ernest **8**:149
house (in Western architecture) **10**:266
housing **10**:276
urban planning **19**:483–484
TÉNÉRÉ DESERT
map (17° 35′N 10° 55′E) **14**:187
TENERIFE (Canary Islands) **4**:99
Santa Cruz de Tenerife **17**:68
TENG HSIAO-P'ING (Deng Xiaoping) **4**:376 *illus.*; **19**:101–102 *illus.*
China **4**:369
Hu Yao-pang (Hu Yaobang) **10**:287
TENGU **19**:102
TENIERS, DAVID, THE YOUNGER **12**:102 *bibliog.*
TENJIKUYO
Japanese art and architecture **11**:375
TENNANT, SMITHSON **19**:102
TENNENT, GILBERT **19**:102 *bibliog.*
TENNENT, WILLIAM **19**:102 *bibliog.*
TENNESSEE **19**:102–107 *bibliog.*, *illus.*, *map*
agriculture **19**:105–106 *illus.*
cities
Chattanooga **4**:303
Knoxville **12**:103
Memphis **13**:292 *illus.*
Nashville **14**:24
climate **19**:103
economic activity **19**:105
education **19**:104
Fisk University **8**:129
Scopes Trial **17**:148
South, University of the **18**:78
Tennessee, state universities of **19**:107
Vanderbilt University **19**:519
flag **19**:103 *illus.*
government and politics **19**:105–106
historic sites **19**:104
history **19**:106–107
Bell, John **3**:186
Crockett, Davy **5**:355–356
Jackson, Andrew **11**:340–342
Johnson, Andrew **11**:430–431
Kefauver, Estes **12**:36
Robertson, James **16**:242
Sevier, John **17**:220
Watauga Association **20**:47
land and resources **19**:102–105 *map*
map (35° 50′N 85° 30′W) **19**:419
people **19**:103–105
resources **19**:103
rivers, lakes, and waterways **19**:103
Cumberland River **5**:387
seal, state **19**:103 *illus.*
TENNESSEE, STATE UNIVERSITIES OF **19**:107
TENNESSEE PASS
map (39° 22′N 106° 19′W) **5**:116
TENNESSEE RIVER **19**:107
map (37° 4′N 88° 33′W) **19**:419
TENNESSEE VALLEY AUTHORITY **19**:107–108 *bibliog.*
Cumberland River **5**:387
environmental impact statement **7**:212
Lilienthal, David **12**:340
Norris, George W. **14**:223
public utility **15**:610
Roosevelt, Franklin Delano **16**:309
salvage archaeology **17**:40
Tennessee **19**:105–106 *illus.*
United States, history of the **19**:454
TENNESSEE WALKING HORSE **10**:243 *illus.*; **19**:108 *illus.*
saddle horse **17**:9
TENNIEL, SIR JOHN **19**:108
TENNILLE (Georgia)
map (32° 56′N 82° 48′W) **9**:114
TENNIS **19**:108–111 *bibliog.*, *illus.*, *tables*
Ashe, Arthur **2**:230
Austin, Tracy **2**:327
Borg, Björn **3**:398
Budge, Don **3**:543
Connolly, Maureen **5**:197
Connors, Jimmy **5**:197
Court, Margaret Smith **5**:316
equipment and court **19**:109 *illus.*
Gibson, Althea **9**:175
Gonzales, Pancho **9**:244–245
Goolagong, Evonne **9**:246
history **19**:108–109
King, Billie Jean **12**:80
Kramer, Jack **12**:127
Laver, Rod **12**:241
lawn tennis **18**:196 *illus.*; **19**:108–109 *illus.*
Lendl, Ivan **12**:281
Lenglen, Suzanne **12**:282
Lloyd, Chris Evert **12**:382–383
McEnroe, John **13**:15–16
Navratilova, Martina **14**:62
Newport (Rhode Island) **14**:170
open-tournament movement **19**:111
paddle tennis **15**:12
Perry, Fred **15**:179
platform tennis **15**:359
play **19**:109–110
scoring **19**:110–111
sports medicine **18**:197–198
Tilden, Bill **19**:198
U.S. open champions **19**:111 *illus.*
Vilas, Guillermo **19**:596
Wills, Helen Newington **20**:163
Wimbledon Champions **19**:110 *table*
TENNYSON, ALFRED, LORD **7**:201 *illus.*; **19**:111–112 *bibliog.*, *illus.*
Charge of the Light Brigade, The **4**:288
Idylls of the King **11**:32
TENOCHCA *see* AZTEC
TENOCHTITLÁN **2**:382 *map*; **2**:383 *illus.*; **14**:237 *map*; **19**:112 *bibliog.*, *illus.*
Aztec **2**:382
Cortés, Hernán **5**:278
Cuauhtémoc **5**:377
Latin America, history of **12**:216
Mexico, history of **13**:362
reconstruction **15**:498 *illus.*
temple **2**:383 *illus.*
TENOR **19**:112
TENORITE
oxide minerals **14**:476
TENPINS *see* BOWLING
TENPOUNDER (fish) **19**:112–113
TENREC **19**:113 *illus.*
TENSAS (county in Louisiana)
map (32° 0′N 91° 20′W) **12**:430
TENSILE STRENGTH TEST
materials technology **13**:220 *illus.*
TENSION (psychology)
headache **10**:85–86
TENSOR CALCULUS *see* CALCULUS
TENT
Eskimo **7**:239
yurt **20**:347
TENT CATERPILLAR **19**:113
10TH AMENDMENT **19**:113
Hammer v. *Dagenhart* **10**:30
state (political unit) **18**:228
state rights **18**:233
text **5**:221
TENURE
academic freedom **1**:68
TENURE OF OFFICE ACT **19**:113
Cleveland, Grover **5**:53
Johnson, Andrew **11**:431
Stanton, Edwin M. **18**:220
TENZING NORGAY **10**:164 *illus.*
Everest, Mount **7**:315
mountain climbing **13**:621 *illus.*
TEODOROVIĆ, MILOŠ *see* MILOŠ, PRINCE OF SERBIA
TÉOFILO OTONI (Brazil)
map (17° 51′S 41° 30′W) **3**:460
TEOTIHUACÁN (Mexico) **2**:382 *map*; **14**:237 *map*; **19**:113–114 *bibliog.*, *illus.*
Avenue of the Dead **15**:497 *illus.*
El Tajín **7**:101
Kaminaljuyú **12**:10
Latin America, history of **12**:216
Latin American art and architecture **12**:222–223
Mexico, history of **13**:361–362
pre-Columbian art and architecture **15**:496
Pyramid of the Moon **15**:497 *illus.*
Pyramid of the Sun **15**:636 *illus.*; **19**:113 *illus.*
Remojadas **16**:146
Tikal **19**:198
Toltec **19**:229
Tula **19**:329
Xochicalco **20**:313
TEPE *see* TELL (archaeology)
TEPE GAWRA (Iran) **19**:114 *bibliog.*
TEPE YAHYA (Iran) **19**:114 *bibliog.*
TEPEE **19**:114 *bibliog.*
travois **19**:285
TEPHRA
sedimentary rock **17**:185–186 *illus.*
TEPHROITE
olivine **14**:380 *table*
TEPIC (Mexico) **19**:114
map (21° 30′N 104° 54′W) **13**:357
TEPL, JOHANNES VON *see* JOHANNES VON TEPL
TEPLICE (Czechoslovakia)
map (50° 39′N 13° 48′E) **5**:413
TEQUILA **19**:114
agave **1**:183
TER BORCH, GERARD **19**:114–115 *bibliog.*, *illus.*
A Boy Ridding His Dog of Fleas **19**:114 *illus.*
The Swearing of the Oath of Ratification of the Treaty of Münster **19**:171 *illus.*
TERAI
Nepal **14**:86
TERATOGEN
birth defects **3**:295
toxicity, drug **6**:278
TERBIUM **19**:115
element **7**:130 *table*
lanthanide series **12**:200–201
metal, metallic element **13**:328
TERBRUGGHEN, HENDRICK **19**:115 *bibliog.*
TERCEIRA (Portugal)
Azores **2**:381–382 *map*
TERENCE **19**:115 *bibliog.*
comedy **5**:132
TERENCE BAY (Nova Scotia)
map (44° 28′N 63° 43′W) **14**:269
TERESA, MOTHER **19**:115 *bibliog.*, *illus.*
TERESA OF ÁVILA, SAINT **19**:115–116 *bibliog.*
The Ecstasy of St. Teresa (Bernini) **2**:198 *illus.*

TERESHKOVA, VALENTINA VLADIMIROVNA NIKOLAYEVA 18:127 *illus.*; 19:116 *bibliog., illus.*
Nikolayev, Andrian (husband) 14:195
Vostok 19:636–637
TERESINA (Brazil)
map (5° 5′S 42° 49′W) 3:460
TERHUNE, ALBERT PAYSON 19:116
TERKEL, STUDS 19:116
TERLINGUA (Texas)
map (29° 19′N 103° 37′W) 19:129
TERM INSURANCE
life insurance 12:329
TERMAN, LEWIS 19:116 *bibliog.*
psychology, history of 15:598
Stanford-Binet test 18:217
TERMINAL, COMPUTER *see* COMPUTER TERMINAL
TÉRMINOS LAGOON
map (18° 37′N 91° 33′W) 13:357
TERMITE 19:116–117 *bibliog., illus.*
anatomy 19:116–117
defense and nest structure 19:117 *illus.*
feeding habits 19:116
Isoptera 11:300
life cycle 19:116
mound 17:98 *illus.*
TERN 19:117–118 *bibliog., illus.*
animal migration 2:27
TERNEUZEN (Netherlands)
map (51° 20′N 3° 50′E) 14:99
TERNI (Italy) 19:118
map (42° 34′N 12° 37′E) 11:321
TERNIFINE MAN 19:118 *bibliog.*
Heidelberg man 10:107
TERNITZ (Austria)
map (47° 44′N 16° 3′E) 2:348
TERPENE 19:118–119 *bibliog., illus.*
camphor 4:66
carotenoid 19:118
citronella 4:447
classification system 19:118
essential oils 19:118
Haworth, Sir Walter Norman 10:78
isoprene 11:300; 19:118
Ružička, Leopold 16:377
steroid 19:118
vitamins and minerals 19:118
Wallach, Otto 20:15
TERPSICHORE
muses 13:656
TERRA, GABRIEL 19:119 *bibliog.*
TERRA ALTA (West Virginia)
map (39° 27′N 79° 31′W) 20:111
TERRA AMATA (France) 19:119 *bibliog.*
Lower Paleolithic camp 15:39 *illus.*
Lumley, Henry de 12:459
TERRA-COTTA 19:119–120 *bibliog., illus.*
African art 1:160–164 *illus.*
della Robbia (family) 6:94
Etruscans 7:260 *illus.*
European prehistory 7:302 *illus.*
Roman art and architecture 16:273
TERRACE (British Columbia)
map (54° 31′N 128° 35′W) 3:491
TERRACE FARMING *see* FARMS AND FARMING
TERRAL (Oklahoma)
map (33° 54′N 97° 57′W) 14:368
TERRANOVA DI SICILIA *see* GELA (Italy)
TERRARIUM 19:120–121
TERRE ADÉLIE *see* ADÉLIE COAST
TERRE HAUTE (Indiana) 19:121
map (39° 28′N 87° 24′W) 11:111
TERREBONNE (county in Louisiana)
map (29° 30′N 90° 50′W) 12:430
TERREBONNE BAY
map (29° 9′N 90° 35′W) 12:430
TERRELL (county in Georgia)
map (31° 50′N 84° 25′W) 9:114
TERRELL (Texas)
map (32° 44′N 96° 17′W) 19:129
TERRELL (county in Texas)
map (30° 15′N 102° 0′W) 19:129
TERRENCEVILLE (Newfoundland)
map (47° 40′N 54° 44′W) 14:166
TERRIER 6:220 *illus.*
Airedale terrier 1:222
American Staffordshire terrier 1:367
Australian terrier 2:344
Bedlington terrier 3:154
border terrier 3:397
bull terrier 3:559
cairn terrier 4:17
Dandie Dinmont terrier 6:31
fox terrier 8:256–257
Irish terrier 11:269
Kerry blue terrier 12:60
Lakeland terrier 12:171
Manchester terrier 13:109
Norwich Terrier 14:266
schnauzer (miniature) 17:129 *illus.*
Scottish terrier 17:155
Sealyham terrier 17:174
Skye terrier 17:346–347
soft-coated Wheaten terrier 18:35
Staffordshire bull terrier 18:210
Welsh terrier 20:102
West Highland white terrier 20:108
TERRITORIAL WATERS 19:121 *bibliog.*
Sea, Law of the 17:167–168
seas, freedom of the 17:175–176
TERRITORIALITY 19:121 *bibliog., illus.*
animal behavior 2:16
animal communication 2:18–19
animal courtship and mating 2:21–22
bird 3:285
TERRITORY 19:121–122
trust territory 19:321
TERRORISM 19:122 *bibliog.*
bomb 3:374
guerrillas 9:391–392
Irish Republican Army 11:269
Kenya 12:56
Ku Klux Klan 12:133
Molly Maguires 13:512
Moro, Aldo 13:583
Palestine Liberation Organization 15:46
plutonium
nuclear energy 14:283
Red Brigades 19:122
totalitarianism 19:248
TERRY (Mississippi)
map (32° 5′N 90° 18′W) 13:469
TERRY (Montana)
map (46° 47′N 105° 19′W) 13:547
TERRY (county in Texas)
map (33° 8′N 102° 17′W) 19:129
TERRY, DAME ELLEN ALICE 19:122 *bibliog.*
TERRY, FERNANDO BELAÚNDE *see* BELAÚNDE TERRY, FERNANDO
TERRY, WALTER 19:122
TERRY PEAK
map (44° 19′N 103° 50′W) 18:103
TERSCHELLING ISLAND
map (53° 24′N 5° 20′E) 14:99
TERTIARY PERIOD 19:122–125 *bibliog., illus., map, table*
Cenozoic Era 4:245–246; 19:122
climate 19:124
coal and coal mining 5:76
continents, estimated positions 19:123 *map*
flora and fauna 19:124–125 *illus.*
geologic time 9:104 *table*
grass 9:295
mammals
Baluchitherium 3:57
Barylambda 3:99
eohippus 7:215
mastodon 13:217
mollusk
Deshayes, Gerard Paul 6:131
paleoclimatology 15:32
paleotemperature 15:42
primate
Oreopithecus 14:432
rock formations 9:123 *map*
TERTULLIAN 19:125 *bibliog.*
TERTZ, ABRAM (pseudonym) *see* SINYAVSKY, ANDREI
TERVUREN, BELGIAN *see* BELGIAN TERVUREN
TERZAGHI, KARL 19:125
TESCHEN 19:126
TESCOTT (Kansas)
map (39° 1′N 97° 53′W) 12:18
TESLA (measurement)
units, physical 19:467 *table*
TESLA, NIKOLA 19:126 *bibliog.*
TESLIN (Yukon Territory)
map (60° 9′N 132° 45′W) 20:345
TESLIN RIVER
map (61° 34′N 134° 54′W) 20:345
TESS OF THE D'URBERVILLES (book) 19:126 *bibliog.*
Hardy, Thomas 10:48
TESSAI 19:126 *bibliog.*
TESSIN (family) 19:126 *bibliog.*
TEST ACTS 19:126 *bibliog.*
James II, King of England, Scotland, and Ireland 11:356
TEST-TUBE BABIES
artificial insemination 2:221
genetic engineering 9:84
TESTES
endocrine system 7:169 *illus.*
orchitis 14:420
reproductive system, human 16:163–164 *illus.*
TESTICLES *see* TESTES
TESTIMONY
deposition 6:118
perjury 15:172
self-incrimination 17:191
subpoena 18:316
witness 20:192–193
TESTOSTERONE
hormone, animal 10:236 *table*
sex hormones 17:226
vasectomy 19:525
TESTS *see* EDUCATIONAL MEASUREMENT; MEASUREMENT; PSYCHOLOGICAL MEASUREMENT
TESUQUE (New Mexico)
map (35° 45′N 105° 56′W) 14:136
TETANUS 19:126
antitoxin 2:69
diseases, animal 6:191
vaccination 19:501
TETANY 19:126
TETE (Mozambique)
map (16° 13′S 33° 35′E) 13:627
TETE-JAUNE-CACHE (British Columbia)
map (52° 57′N 119° 26′W) 3:491
TETHYS (astronomy)
Saturn (astronomy) 17:89–91 *illus., table*
TETHYS SEA (ancient sea) 19:126–127
paleography 15:36 *map*
plate tectonics 15:354 *map*
TETLEY, GLEN 19:127
TETLIN (Alaska)
map (63° 8′N 142° 31′W) 1:242
TETMAJER, KAZIMIERZ PRZERWA
Polish literature 15:398
TETON (county in Idaho)
map (43° 45′N 111° 15′W) 11:26
TETON (county in Montana)
map (47° 55′N 112° 15′W) 13:547
TETON (county in Wyoming)
map (43° 55′N 110° 35′W) 20:301
TETON DAM 19:127
TETON LAKOTA *see* SIOUX
TETON PASS
map (43° 30′N 110° 57′W) 20:301
TETON RANGE 19:127; 20:300 *illus.*
Grand Teton National Park 9:285
map (43° 50′N 110° 50′W) 20:301
TETON SIOUX (American Indians) *see* SIOUX (American Indians)
TETONIA (Idaho)
map (43° 49′N 111° 10′W) 11:26
TÉTOUAN (Morocco)
map (35° 34′N 5° 23′W) 13:585
TETOVO (Yugoslavia)
map (42° 1′N 20° 58′E) 20:340
TETRA 19:127
neon tetra 19:308 *illus.*
TETRACYCLINE
antibiotics 2:57; 2:58; 2:59
TETRADYMITE
telluride minerals 19:91
TETRAGONAL SYSTEM 19:127
crystal 5:375 *illus.*
TETRAHEDRITE 19:127
sulfosalts 18:334
TETRAIODOTHYRONINE *see* THYROXINE
TETRAZZINI, LUISA 19:127 *bibliog.*
TETRODE 19:127
electron tube 7:123
TETZEL, JOHANN 19:127
TEULADA, CAPE
map (38° 52′N 8° 39′E) 11:321
TEUSO *see* IK
TEUTONIC KNIGHTS 19:127–128 *bibliog.*
Albert, First Duke of Prussia 1:254
Peipus, Lake 15:134
Prussia 15:585
spread of c.1360 7:285 *map*
spread of c.1560 7:288 *map*
Tannenberg, Battles of 19:24
Vytautas, Grand Duke of Lithuania 19:640
TEUTONS *see* GERMANIC PEOPLES
TEVERYA (Israel) *see* TIBERIAS (Israel)
TEVFIK FIKRET 19:128
TEWKSBURY (Massachusetts)
map (42° 37′N 71° 14′W) 13:206
TEXADA ISLAND
map (49° 40′N 124° 24′W) 3:491
TEXARKANA (Arkansas/Texas) 19:128
map (33° 26′N 94° 2′W) 2:166
TEXARKANA, LAKE
map (33° 16′N 94° 14′W) 19:129
TEXAS 19:128–134 *bibliog., illus., map*
agriculture 19:131–132
Big Bend National Park 3:249
cities
Abilene 1:57
Amarillo 1:321
Arlington 2:171
Austin 2:326–327
Beaumont 3:146–147
Brownsville 3:519
Corpus Christi 5:275
Dallas 6:13–14 *illus.*
El Paso 7:99–100
Fort Worth 8:238
Galveston 9:23
Houston 10:280–281 *map*
Laredo 12:207
Lubbock 12:446
Midland 13:414
Odessa 14:349
Port Arthur 15:442
San Antonio 17:50–51 *illus.*
Texarkana 19:128
Waco 20:4
Wichita Falls 20:145
climate 19:130
culture and historic sites 19:130
economic activity 19:131–133 *illus.*
education 19:130
Baylor University 3:134
Rice University 16:209
Texas, state universities of 19:134–135
flag 19:128 *illus.*
Fort Hood 8:237
government and politics 19:133
historians
Webb, Walter Prescott 20:86
history 19:133–134
Alamo, the 1:239–240
Austin, Stephen F. 2:327
Ferguson, James Edward 8:54
Fredonian Rebellion 8:294
Goodnight, Charles 9:246
Houston, Sam 10:282
Jackson, Andrew 11:342
Jones, Anson 11:442
Lamar, Mirabeau Buonaparte 12:173
Mexican War 13:351–355 *map*
Polk, James K. 15:404–405
Spanish missions 18:160–161
Texas Rangers 19:135
Texas Revolution *see* TEXAS REVOLUTION
Tyler, John 19:362
Johnson Space Center 11:437
Lubbock Lights 19:385 *illus.*
manufacturing 19:132
map (31° 30′N 99° 0′W) 19:419
mining 19:132
people 19:130–131
Alabama (American Indians) 1:238
resources 19:130
rivers, lakes, and waterways 19:130
Brazos River 3:465
Colorado River (Texas) 5:121
Pecos River 15:130
seal, state 19:128 *illus.*
topography and soils 19:128–130 *map*
tourism 19:132
trade 19:132–133
transportation 19:132
vegetation and animal life 19:130
TEXAS (county in Missouri)
map (37° 20′N 92° 0′W) 13:476
TEXAS (county in Oklahoma)
map (36° 45′N 101° 25′W) 14:368
TEXAS, STATE UNIVERSITIES OF 19:134–135
TEXAS & PACIFIC RAILROAD 19:268 *map*
TEXAS BAPTIST CONVENTION
Baylor University 3:134
TEXAS CITY (Texas)
map (29° 23′N 94° 54′W) 19:129
TEXAS FEVER *see* *BABESIA*
TEXAS RANGERS 19:135 *bibliog.*
rangers 16:85
TEXAS REPUBLIC
flag 8:135 *illus.*
TEXAS REVOLUTION 19:135 *bibliog., illus.*
Alamo, the 1:239–240
Bowie, James 3:428
Houston, Sam 10:282
Santa Anna, Antonio López de 17:66
Texas 19:134
Travis, William B. 19:285
TEXAS TOWERS
lighthouse 12:337
TEXCOCO, LAKE 2:382 *map*

TEXEL ISLAND
map (53° 5′N 4° 45′E) **14**:99
TEXHOMA (Oklahoma)
map (36° 30′N 101° 47′W) **14**:368
TEXICO (New Mexico)
map (34° 23′N 103° 3′W) **14**:136
TEXLINE (Texas)
map (36° 23′N 103° 1′W) **19**:129
TEXOMA, LAKE
map (33° 55′N 96° 37′W) **14**:368
TEXTILE INDUSTRY **19**:135–137 *bibliog., illus.*
See also FIBER, TEXTILE; TEXTILES; types of textiles, e.g., SILK; WOOL; etc.
Amalgamated Clothing and Textile Workers Union **1**:321
Appleton, Nathan **2**:89
Arkwright, Sir Richard **2**:170
carpet industry **4**:165
Cartwright, Edmund **4**:178
clothing industry **5**:65
cotton gin **5**:307
Crompton, Samuel **5**:357
diseases, occupational
brown lung **3**:516–517
dyeing **19**:137
Drebbel, Cornelis **6**:268
dye **6**:318 *illus.*
indigo **11**:144
embroidery **7**:152
England **19**:407 *illus.*; **19**:409
Europe, history of **7**:292
finishing **19**:137
flame retardants, boron **3**:403
Hargreaves, James **10**:49
Industrial Revolution **11**:159
Jacquard, Joseph Marie **11**:347
Juilliard, Augustus D. **11**:465
Kay, John **12**:32–33
Lawrence, Abbott **12**:249
loom **12**:410–411
Lowell, Francis Cabot **12**:444
Manchester (England) **11**:158 *illus.*; **13**:108
Manchester (New Hampshire) **13**:108
manufacturing **13**:132
Massachusetts **13**:211
Mercer, John **13**:304
Middle Ages **13**:395 *illus.*
Morris, William **13**:589
New Hampshire **14**:126
North Carolina **14**:244–245 *illus.*
Pawtucket (Rhode Island) **15**:121
printing on fabric **19**:137 *illus.*
Rhode Island **16**:201
sewing machine **17**:223–224
Slater, Samuel **17**:351
South Carolina **18**:99
spinning **18**:186
Stewart, Alexander Turney **18**:265
synthetic fibers **18**:409
technology, history of **19**:66–67
waterproofing
Macintosh, Charles **13**:26
TEXTILES
See also TEXTILE INDUSTRY
angora **2**:6
bark cloth **3**:82–83
batik **3**:123–124
broadcloth **3**:499
brocade **3**:500
calico **4**:29
canvas **4**:118
cashmere **4**:181
chiffon **4**:347
chintz **4**:396
corduroy **5**:262
cotton **5**:305–307
damask **6**:19
denim **6**:108
felt **8**:48
fiber, textile **8**:67–68
flannel **8**:153
folk art **8**:196–198
foulard **8**:249
gingham **9**:184
hemp **10**:120
jersey **11**:398
jute **11**:479
khaki **12**:65
knitting **12**:101
lace **12**:158–160
linen **12**:354
madras **13**:43
muslin **13**:683
nylon **14**:308–309
paisley **15**:25
polyester **15**:418–419
pre-Columbian
Nazca **14**:67
paracas burial cloak **15**:500 *illus.*
pre-Columbian art and architecture **15**:499–500
printing **19**:137 *illus.*
block printing **3**:334
ramie **16**:80
rayon **16**:97–98
satin **17**:88
silk **17**:306–308
synthetic fibers **18**:409–410
taffeta **19**:7
tartan **19**:40–41
tweed **19**:358
twill **19**:360
velvet **19**:538
wool **20**:213–214
TEY, JOSEPHINE **19**:138
TEZCATLIPOCA **19**:138 *bibliog.*
THABA PUTSOA RANGE
map (29° 45′S 27° 55′E) **12**:297
THABANA NTLENYANA MOUNTAIN
map (29° 28′S 29° 16′E) **12**:297
THACKERAY, WILLIAM MAKEPEACE **7**:199 *illus.*; **19**:138 *bibliog., illus.*
Vanity Fair **19**:520
THADDAEUS, SAINT **19**:138
THAI **19**:138 *bibliog.*
THAI NGUYEN (Vietnam)
map (21° 36′N 105° 50′E) **19**:580
THAILAND **19**:138–141 *bibliog., illus., map, table*
agriculture
rice cultivation **1**:195 *illus.*
archaeology
Ayuthia **2**:379–380
Ban Chiang **3**:59
Lopburi **12**:412
Non Nok Tha **14**:216
cities
Bangkok **3**:63 *illus.*
Chiang Mai **4**:339–340
climate **19**:139–140 *table*
economic activity **19**:140
education **19**:140
Southeast Asian universities **18**:111 *table*
flag **19**:139 *illus.*
government **19**:140–141
history **19**:141
Asia, history of **2**:253–254
Chulalongkorn, King of Siam **4**:422
Kampuchea (Cambodia) **12**:13
Mongkut, King of Siam **13**:528
korat (cat) **12**:110–111
land and resources **19**:139–140 *map, table*
language
Sino-Tibetan languages **17**:324
Southeast Asian languages **18**:111
map (15° 0′N 100° 0′E) **2**:232
money **13**:525 *illus.*
people **19**:139–140
Lao **12**:201
Mon **13**:515
Thai **19**:138
Southeast Asian art and architecture **18**:109 *illus.*
tin **19**:205
THAILAND, GULF OF **19**:142
map (10° 0′N 101° 0′E) **2**:232
THALAMUS
brain **3**:444 *illus.*
THALASSEMIA
Cooley's anemia **5**:240
operon **14**:403–404
THALES OF MILETUS **19**:142 *bibliog.*
creation accounts **5**:335
geometry **9**:106
Milesian school **13**:419
pre-Socratic philosophy **15**:532
THALIA (botany) **18**:377 *illus.*
THALIA (mythology)
muses **13**:656
THALIDOMIDE **19**:142 *bibliog.*
bone diseases **3**:378
drug **6**:278
THALLIUM **19**:142 *bibliog.*
Crookes, Sir William, discoverer **5**:359
element **7**:130 *table*
Group IIIA periodic table **15**:167
metal, metallic element **13**:328
THALLOPHYTE
plant **15**:333
THAMES, RIVER **12**:401 *map*; **19**:142
floods and flood control **8**:167
London Bridge **12**:404–405 *illus.*
map (51° 28′N 0° 43′E) **19**:403
tunnel **19**:338
THAMES RIVER (Connecticut)
map (41° 18′N 72° 5′W) **5**:193
THAMES RIVER (Ontario)
map (42° 19′N 82° 28′W) **14**:393
THAMIR, MOUNT
map (13° 53′N 45° 30′E) **20**:324
THAMUGADI *see* TIMGAD (Algeria)
THANATOLOGY *see* DEATH AND DYING
THANATOS **19**:142
THANGKA *see* TANKA
THANH HOA (Vietnam)
map (19° 48′N 105° 46′E) **19**:580
THANI, AHMAD BIN ALI AL-
Qatar **16**:4
THANI, KHALIFA BIN HAMAD AL-
Qatar **16**:4
THANIN KRAIVICHIEN
Thailand **19**:141
THANKSGIVING DAY **19**:142
first New England celebration **15**:374 *illus.*
THANOM KITTIKACHORN
Thailand **19**:141
THANT, U **19**:142–143 *bibliog.*
THAR DESERT **19**:143
map (27° 0′N 71° 0′E) **11**:80
THARP, TWYLA **19**:143
modern dance **13**:498
THÁSOS ISLAND
map (40° 41′N 24° 47′E) **9**:325
THATCH, EDWARD *see* BLACKBEARD
THATCHED ROOF **16**:306 *illus.*
THATCHER (Arizona)
map (32° 51′N 109° 46′W) **2**:160
THATCHER, MARGARET **19**:143 *bibliog., illus.*
THATON (Burma)
map (16° 55′N 97° 22′E) **3**:573
THAUMATURGUS, GREGORY, SAINT *see* GREGORY THAUMATURGUS, SAINT
THAYENDANEGEA *see* BRANT, JOSEPH
THAYER (Kansas)
map (37° 30′N 95° 28′W) **12**:18
THAYER (Missouri)
map (36° 31′N 91° 33′W) **13**:476
THAYER (county in Nebraska)
map (40° 10′N 97° 35′W) **14**:70
THAYER, ABBOTT **19**:143 *bibliog.*
THAYER, ELI
Emigrant Aid Company **7**:156
THAYETMYO (Burma)
map (19° 19′N 95° 11′E) **3**:573
THE DALLES (Oregon)
map (45° 36′N 121° 10′W) **14**:427
THE MINCH CHANNEL
map (58° 5′N 5° 55′W) **19**:403
THE PEAK
map (36° 24′N 81° 39′W) **14**:242
THE SLOT, STRAIT OF
map (8° 0′S 158° 10′E) **18**:56
THE VILLAGE (Oklahoma)
map (35° 35′N 97° 33′W) **14**:368
THEATER
See also ACTING; COSTUME AND MAKEUP, THEATRICAL; DRAMA; MUSICAL COMEDY; STAGE LIGHTING; THEATER, HISTORY OF THE; THEATER ARCHITECTURE AND STAGING; the subheading theater under specific countries, e.g., FRANCE—theater; UNITED STATES—theater; etc.; names of specific theaters and theater groups, e.g., ABBEY THEATRE; PROVINCETOWN PLAYERS; etc.
directing **6**:187
puppet **15**:626–627 *illus.*
theatrical manager
Belasco, David **3**:173–174
Frohman, Charles and Daniel **8**:338
Guthrie, Sir Tyrone **9**:409
Hurok, Sol **10**:316
Kean, Charles **12**:34–35
Merrick, David **13**:312
Shubert (family) **17**:289
Tree, Sir Herbert Beerbohm **19**:288
Vestris, Madame **19**:565
Tony Awards **19**:236
Yiddish theater **20**:328
THEATER, HISTORY OF THE **19**:143–151 *bibliog., illus.*
See also the subheading theater under names of specific countries, e.g., FRANCE; UNITED STATES; etc.
costume and makeup, theatrical **5**:303
masks **13**:196
Oriental theater **19**:148–149
stage lighting **18**:210
theater architecture and staging **19**:151–153
theater festivals **19**:153
6th century BC-5th century AD Greek and Roman **19**:144–145
acting **1**:87
dance **6**:22–23 *illus.*
drama **6**:257–258 *illus.*
Megalopolis **13**:280
minstrels, minnesingers, and troubadours **13**:460
Thespis **19**:168
500-1400 Middle Ages *see* MEDIEVAL DRAMA
1400–1600 Renaissance **19**:145–147
See also ELIZABETHAN AGE; ELIZABETHAN PLAYHOUSE
commedia dell'arte **5**:137–138
fool **8**:213
masque **13**:200
Teatro Olimpico **19**:59
1600–1800 Baroque and 18th century **19**:147–148
See also JACOBEAN THEATER
Clive, Kitty **5**:61
drame bourgeois **6**:262
Drottningholm Theatre and Museum **6**:273
Foote, Samuel **8**:219
Garrick, David **9**:50–51
Harlequin **10**:50
mumming play **13**:638–639
1800–1900 **19**:149–150
Bernhardt, Sarah **3**:221–222
burletta **3**:572
Forbes-Robertson, Sir Johnston **8**:220
Forrest, Edwin **8**:234
Guignol, Grand **9**:394–395
Irving, Sir Henry **11**:284
music hall, vaudeville, and burlesque **13**:671–673
naturalism **14**:50
Panoramas **15**:60
Saxe-Meiningen, George II, Duke of **17**:104
showboats **17**:286
well-made play **20**:99
1900-present **19**:150–151
See also IMPROVISATIONAL AND EXPERIMENTAL THEATER; MUSICAL COMEDY; OFF-BROADWAY THEATER; OFF-OFF BROADWAY THEATER; REPERTORY THEATER
Artaud, Antonin **2**:212–213
Barrault, Jean Louis **3**:93
Blitzstein, Marc **3**:333
Brook, Peter **3**:509
Chaikin, Joseph **4**:268
guerrilla theater **9**:392
happenings **10**:41
Meyerhold, Vsevolod Emilievich **13**:369
Polish Laboratory Theater **15**:397
Provincetown Players **15**:584
repertory theater **16**:160
Shubert (family) **17**:289
Stanislavsky, Konstantin **18**:218
Strasberg, Lee **18**:289
theatricalism **19**:154
THEATER ARCHITECTURE AND STAGING **19**:151–153 *bibliog., illus.*
See also BALLET; MUSICAL COMEDY; OPERA
Ballets Russes **16**:363 *illus.*
Chestnut Street Theatre **4**:337
directing **6**:187
Drottningholm Theatre and Museum **6**:273
Elizabethan playhouse **7**:145–146
Evreinov, Nikolai Nikolaevich **7**:325
Greek architecture **9**:334
Haymarket Theatre **10**:83
Hôtel de Bourgogne, Théâtre de L' **10**:262
Kabuki **12**:4
Kennedy Center for the Performing Arts **12**:44
La Scala **12**:149
Larionov, Mikhail Fyodorovich **12**:207
music and concert halls **13**:669–670
music hall, vaudeville, and burlesque **13**:672
Noguchi, Isamu **14**:213
Opera houses **14**:401–402 *illus.*
Schlemmer, Oskar **17**:125

Serlio, Sebastiano **17**:209
stage lighting **18**:210
stage and set design
anamorphosis **1**:391
Appia, Adolphe **2**:88
Aronson, Boris **2**:186–187
Baty, Gaston **3**:128
Beaton, Sir Cecil **3**:145
Bel Geddes, Norman **3**:173
Belasco, David **3**:173–174
Covarrubias, Miguel **5**:318
Craig, Gordon **5**:328
Galli da Bibiena (family) **9**:18–19
Garrick, David **9**:50–51
Irving, Sir Henry **11**:284
Jones, Robert Edmond **11**:444
Loutherbourg, Philippe Jacques de **12**:437
MacKaye, Steele **13**:27
Mielziner, Jo **13**:415
Moiseiwitsch, Tanya **13**:504
Neher, Caspar **14**:78
Richard Wagner's Festspielhaus **13**:666 *illus.*
Smith, Oliver **17**:370
Svoboda, Josef **18**:375
Zeffirelli, Franco **20**:358
Tchelitchew, Pavel **19**:52
Teatro Olimpico **19**:59
theater, history of the **19**:144–150
theater in the round **19**:153
Urban, Joseph **19**:480
Walnut Street Theatre **20**:18
THEATER CRITICISM *see* DRAMA—criticism
THEATER OF CRUELTY
Artaud, Antonin **2**:212–213
THEATER OF FACT 19:153 *bibliog.*
epic theater **7**:217–218
THEATER FESTIVALS 19:153 *bibliog.*
Spoleto Festival **18**:192
THEATER OF NEPTUNE, THE (play)
Canadian literature **4**:93
THEATER OF THE ABSURD 19:154 *bibliog., illus.*
absurdism **1**:66
Albee, Edward (playwright) **1**:252–253
Arrabal, Fernando **2**:187
Beckett, Samuel **3**:152
drama **6**:261
Genet, Jean **9**:79
Havel, Václav **10**:71
Ionesco, Eugène **11**:240–241
Stoppard, Tom **18**:284
Tardieu, Jean **19**:35–36
THEATER IN THE ROUND 19:153 *bibliog.*
Jones, Margo **11**:443
THÉÂTRE ANTOINE
Antoine, André **2**:69
THÉÂTRE DE L'ODÉON
Bernhardt, Sarah **3**:221–222
THÉÂTRE DU VIEUX COLOMBIER
founder
Copeau, Jacques **5**:248–249
THÉÂTRE FRANÇAIS *see* COMÉDIE FRANÇAISE, LA
THEATRE GUILD 19:154
Carnovsky, Morris **4**:159
THÉÂTRE-LIBRE
Antoine, André **2**:69
THÉÂTRE NATIONAL POPULAIRE (TNP) **19**:154
Vilar, Jean **19**:596
THEATRICAL MAKEUP *see* COSTUME AND MAKEUP, THEATRICAL
THEATRICALISM 19:154 *bibliog.*
See also DANCE
THEBES (Egypt) **7**:81 *map*; **19**:154–155 *bibliog., illus.*
landscape architecture **12**:186 *illus.*
Luxor **12**:473
Valley of the Kings **19**:507
THEBES (Greece) **19**:155 *bibliog.*
Epaminondas **7**:215
Greece, ancient **9**:332
Greek legend
Cadmus **4**:12
Oedipus **14**:351
Seven Against Thebes **17**:215
THEDFORD (Nebraska)
map (41° 59′N 100° 35′W) **14**:70
THEFT *see* LARCENY
THEILER, MAX
yellow fever vaccine, medicine **13**:271
THEISM 19:155 *bibliog.*
Abbot, Francis Ellingwood **1**:53
atheism **2**:288–289
primitive religion **15**:544–545
THEMATIC APPERCEPTION TEST
projective tests **15**:566 *illus.*
THEMISTOCLES 19:155 *bibliog.*
Piraeus (Greece) **15**:314
THÉNARD, LOUIS JACQUES, BARON 19:155
THEOCRITUS 19:155
pastoral literature **15**:108
THEODOLINDA
Monza (Italy) **13**:560
THEODOLITE 19:155–156
surveying **18**:368–369 *illus.*
THEODORA, BYZANTINE EMPRESS 19:156 *bibliog.*
mosaic **13**:594 *illus.*
Procopius of Caesarea **15**:561
THEODORAKIS, MIKIS 19:156
THEODORE (Alabama)
map (30° 33′N 88° 10′W) **1**:234
THEODORE OF MOPSUESTIA 19:156 *bibliog.*
THEODORE ROOSEVELT LAKE
map (33° 42′N 111° 7′W) **2**:160
THEODORE ROOSEVELT NATIONAL MEMORIAL PARK
badlands **3**:20
THEODORET 19:156 *bibliog.*
THEODORIC THE GREAT, KING OF THE OSTROGOTHS 19:156 *bibliog.*
Odoacer **14**:350
THEODOSIUS I, ROMAN EMPEROR (Theodosius the Great) **19**:156–157 *bibliog., illus.*
THEODOSIUS II, ROMAN EMPEROR IN THE EAST 19:157
THEOGNIS 19:157 *bibliog.*
THEOGONY (poem) **19**:157
mythology **13**:700
THEOLOGIANS
Augustine, Saint
City of God, The **5**:8
THEOLOGICAL SEMINARIES 19:157 *bibliog.*
Andover Newton Theological School **1**:406
Drew University **6**:271
General Theological Seminary **9**:78
Hebrew Union College **10**:101–102
Jewish Theological Seminary of America **11**:412
Manitoba, University of **13**:122
Princeton Theological Seminary **15**:549
St. Vladimir's Orthodox Theological Seminary **17**:27
Union Theological Seminary **19**:399
Yeshiva University **20**:327
THEOLOGY 19:157–158 *bibliog.*
atonement **2**:312
casuistry **4**:193
City of God, The **5**:8
creed **5**:337
eschatology **7**:237
ethics **7**:251
Eucharist **7**:262
God **9**:217–219
grace **9**:275
heaven **10**:100
hell **10**:113
Hinduism **10**:169–173
Holy Spirit **10**:211
immanence, divine **11**:54
immortality **11**:56
incarnation **11**:73
infallibility **11**:161–162
Jesus Christ **11**:403–406
medicine **13**:269
original sin **14**:444
patristic literature **15**:113–114
philosophy **15**:241–242
predestination **15**:501–502
resurrection **16**:183
revelation **16**:184–185
sacrament **17**:7
salvation **17**:40
scholasticism **17**:131–132
sin **17**:317–318
soul **18**:70
Summa Theologiae **18**:339
theologians
Abelard, Peter **1**:55–56
Albertus Magnus, Saint **1**:259–260
Anselm, Saint **2**:35
Aquinas, Saint Thomas **2**:94–95
Athanasius, Saint **2**:288
Augustine, Saint **2**:320–321
Barth, Karl **3**:97
Boethius, Anicius Manlius Severinus **3**:358
Bonhoeffer, Dietrich **3**:379
Brunner, Emil **3**:525
Buber, Martin **3**:531–532
Bultmann, Rudolf **3**:561
Calvin, John **4**:48–49
Clement of Alexandria, Saint **5**:49
Cullmann, Oscar **5**:384
Cyril of Alexandria, Saint **5**:410
Duns Scotus, John **6**:301
Erigena, John Scotus **7**:230
Fakhr al-Din **8**:11
Farabi, al- **8**:21
Ghazali, al- **9**:166
Harnack, Adolf von **10**:52
Heschel, Abraham Joshua **10**:151
Ignatius of Antioch, Saint **11**:33
Irenaeus, Saint **11**:265
Knox, John **12**:102–103
Küng, Hans **12**:136–137
Luther, Martin **12**:468–469
Maimonides **13**:68
Niebuhr, H. Richard **14**:184
Niebuhr, Reinhold **14**:184
Origen **14**:443
Philo of Alexandria **15**:239–240
Priestley, Joseph **15**:536–537
Rahner, Karl **16**:70
Ritschl, Albrecht **16**:229
Schleiermacher, Friedrich **17**:125
Teilhard de Chardin, Pierre **19**:73–74
Tertullian **19**:125
Tillich, Paul **19**:199–200
William of Occam **20**:154–155
Zwingli, Ulrich **20**:384
transcendence, divine **19**:268
Trinity **19**:300–301
THEOPHANES THE GREEK 19:158 *bibliog.*
THEOPHILUS
monastic art and architecture **13**:519
THEOPHRASTUS 19:158 *bibliog.*
botany **3**:413
THEORBO 19:158 *illus.*
THEORETICAL CHEMISTRY
physical chemistry **15**:279
THEORETICAL PHYSICS 19:158–159 *bibliog.*
deduction and inference **19**:159
Ehrenfest, Paul **7**:90
idealization **19**:159
Landau, Lev **12**:181
laws and symmetries **19**:159
Lee, Tsung Dao **12**:270
Lorentz, Hendrik Antoon **12**:413–414
mathematical analysis **19**:158–159
matter, theoretical understanding **19**:158
Oppenheimer, J. Robert **14**:407–408
Pauli, Wolfgang **15**:118–119
physics **15**:280
physics, history of **15**:282; **15**:286
Poincaré, Henri **15**:380
relativity **16**:132–137
Sommerfeld, Arnold **18**:62
Tomonaga, Sin-itiro **19**:232
THEOSOPHICAL SOCIETY
Krishnamurti, Jiddu **12**:130
theosophy **19**:159–160
THEOSOPHY 19:159–160 *bibliog., illus.*
Besant, Annie **3**:228
Blavatsky, Helena Petrovna **3**:329
Steiner, Rudolf **18**:249
transmigration of souls **19**:274
THEOTOKÓPULI, DOMENIKOS *see* EL GRECO
THERA (Greece) **7**:271 *illus.*; **19**:160 *bibliog.*
Cyclades (Greece) **5**:402
fresco painting **1**:116 *illus.*
map (36° 24′N 25° 29′E) **9**:325
THERAMENES 19:160
THERAPSID
mammal **13**:99
Triassic Period **19**:294
THERAVADA
Buddhism **3**:539–543
philosophy **15**:246–247
THEREMIN 19:160
THERESA (New York)
map (44° 13′N 75° 48′W) **14**:149
THÉRÈSE, SAINT 19:160 *bibliog.*
THÉRIAULT, YVES 19:160–161
THERMAE (game)
handball **10**:35
THERMAIKÓS BAY
map (40° 23′N 22° 47′E) **9**:325
THERMAL CONDUCTIVITY
solid-state physics **18**:55
THERMAL IMAGING *see* NIGHT SIGHTS
THERMAL POLLUTION *see* HEAT; POLLUTION, ENVIRONMENTAL
THERMIDORIAN REACTION *see* FRENCH REVOLUTION
THERMIONIC EMISSION 19:161 *bibliog.*
cathode ray **4**:211
Edison, Thomas Alva **7**:57–58
Edison effect **19**:161
heating of emitters **19**:161
Langmuir, Irving **12**:196
metals **19**:161
power, generation and transmission of **15**:483
Richardson, Sir Owen Willans **16**:212
triode **19**:301
THERMISTOR 19:161 *bibliog.*
bolometer **3**:371
semiconductor **17**:196
THERMOCHEMISTRY 19:161–162 *bibliog., tables*
endothermic and exothermic reactions **7**:171
Hess's law **10**:151
reaction, chemical **16**:99
THERMOCLINE 19:162 *bibliog.*
Munk, Walter **13**:643
ocean currents **14**:324
ocean and sea **14**:331
THERMOCOUPLE 19:162 *bibliog.*
THERMODYNAMICS 19:162–165 *bibliog.*
activity **1**:90
Boltzmann, Ludwig **3**:372
Carathéodory, Constantin **4**:131
Carnot cycle **4**:159
changes in physical state **19**:164
Clausius, Rudolf **5**:45
convection **5**:232
cryogenics **5**:370–371
development **19**:162–163
electrochemistry **7**:112–113
energy **7**:172–173
enthalpy **7**:208
entropy **7**:209
equation of state **19**:164
equilibrium **19**:163–164
flash point **8**:154
free energy **19**:163–164
Giauque, William Francis **9**:172
Gibbs, Josiah Willard **9**:174
Gibbs free energy function **19**:163–164
heat capacity **10**:97
heat engine **10**:97
heat exchanger **10**:97–98
heat and heat transfer **10**:98
isothermal process **11**:301
Joule, James Prescott **11**:453
Joule-Thomson effect **11**:453
Kelvin, William Thomson, 1st Baron **12**:40
Kelvin scale **12**:40
kinetic theory of matter **12**:78–79
laws **19**:163
See also THERMODYNAMICS, LAWS OF
Le Châtelier, Henri Louis **12**:253
Lewis, Gilbert Newton **12**:306
meteorology **13**:342
microclimate **13**:384–385
Onsager, Lars **14**:391
oxygen **14**:477
perpetual motion machines **19**:164
physical chemistry **15**:279
physics **15**:280–281
physics, history of **15**:285–286
Prigogine, Ilya **15**:537
Rankine, William John Macquorn **16**:88
reversible and irreversible processes **16**:186
Simon, Sir Francis **17**:315
statistical thermodynamics **18**:235; **19**:165
Stirling engine **18**:272–273
superconductivity **18**:350
temperature **19**:92–93
thermochemistry **19**:161
thermodynamics, laws of **19**:163
thermoelectricity **19**:165
units, physical **19**:466
THERMODYNAMICS, LAWS OF
first law
conservation of energy **19**:163
energy change **19**:163
thermochemistry **19**:163
second law
entropy **19**:163
third law
absolute zero **1**:63
Nernst, Walther **14**:89
THERMOELECTRICITY 19:165 *bibliog.*
conductivity, materials technology **13**:220
power, generation and transmission of **15**:483
THERMOGRAPHY (medicine) **19**:165
THERMOGRAPHY (printing) **19**:166
THERMOLUMINESCENCE
luminescence **12**:458

THERMOMETER 19:166–167 *bibliog., illus.*
bolometer 3:371
Fahrenheit, Gabriel Daniel 8:8
hygrometer 10:345
measurement 13:255 *illus.*
mercury 13:306
meteorology 13:341–342
oceanographic instrumentation 14:342
paleotemperature 15:42
physics, history of 15:285
Réaumur, René Antoine Ferchault de 16:105
Réaumur scale 16:105
thallium 19:142
THERMONUCLEAR FUSION
fusion, nuclear 8:381–382
laser 12:210
THERMOPERMANENT MAGNETISM (TRM)
paleomagnetism 15:41
THERMOPLASTICS
plastics 15:348–350 *illus.*
THERMOPOLIS (Wyoming)
map (43° 39′N 108° 13′W) 20:301
THERMOPYLAE 19:167 *bibliog.*
Persian Wars 15:188
THERMOPYLAE (ship)
clipper ship 5:61
THERMOPYLAE, BATTLES OF
Thermopylae 19:167
THERMOS BOTTLE 10:98 *illus.*
Dewar, Sir James, inventor 6:146
THERMOSETS
plastics 15:350
THERMOSPHERE 19:167
THERMOSTAT 19:167 *illus.*
automotive, cooling system, engine 5:241–242
circuit, electric 4:436–438
circuit breaker 4:438
THEROPODS
Allosaurus 1:303
Compsognathus 5:158
Dimetrodon 6:177
dinosaur 6:179–181 *illus.*
Gorgosaurus 9:251
Ornitholestes 14:447
Podokesaurus 15:377
Procompsognathus 15:561
Struthiomimus 18:303
Tyrannosaurus 19:367
THESAURUS 19:167
THESEUS 19:167–168
THESIGER, FREDERICK JOHN NAPIER, 1ST VISCOUNT CHELMSFORD *see* CHELMSFORD, FREDERIC JOHN NAPIER THESIGER, 1ST VISCOUNT
THESPIS 19:168
drama 6:257
theater, history of the 19:144
THESSALONIANS, EPISTLES TO THE 19:168 *bibliog.*
THESSALONÍKI (Greece) *see* SALONIKA (Greece)
THESSALY (Greece) 19:168 *bibliog.*
THETA WAVE
brain 3:447
THETFORD MINES (Quebec)
map (46° 5′N 71° 18′W) 16:18
THETIS 19:168
THIAMINE (Vitamin B_1)
Eijkman, Christiaan 7:92
Funk, Casimir 8:369
nutritional-deficiency disease
beriberi 3:211
vitamins and minerals 19:619
Recommended Dietary Allowances 19:618 *table*
THIBAULT, JACQUES ANATOLE FRANÇOIS *see* FRANCE, ANATOLE
THIBAUT IV, KING OF NAVARRE
minstrels, minnesingers, and troubadours 13:460
THIBODAUX (Louisiana)
map (29° 48′N 90° 49′W) 12:430
THICKET PORTAGE (Manitoba)
map (55° 19′N 97° 42′W) 13:119
THICKHEAD (bird) 19:168
THIEBAUD, WAYNE 19:168 *bibliog.*
THIEF RIVER
map (48° 8′N 96° 10′W) 13:453
THIEF RIVER FALLS (Minnesota)
map (48° 7′N 96° 10′W) 13:453
THIELSEN, MOUNT
map (43° 9′N 122° 4′W) 14:427
THIERS, ADOLPHE 19:168–169 *bibliog., illus.*
THIÈS (Senegal)
map (14° 48′N 16° 56′W) 17:202
THIEU, NGUYEN VAN *see* NGUYEN VAN THIEU
THIEWES, RACHELLE
bracelet 5:327 *Illus.*
THIGH
muscle 13:654
THIGMOTROPISM
tropism 19:310 *illus.*
THIMBU (Bhutan) 19:169
map (27° 28′N 89° 39′E) 3:235
THIMONNIER, BARTHÉLEMY
sewing machine 17:223
THIMPHU (Bhutan) *see* THIMBU (Bhutan)
THIN-FILM CIRCUITS 19:169 *bibliog.*
semiconductor 17:196
THIN MAN, THE (book)
Hammett, Dashiell 10:31
THINGVALLA LAKE
map (64° 12′N 21° 10′W) 11:17
THINK TANKS 19:169 *bibliog.*
THINKING
concept formation and attainment 5:169
problem solving 15:559
psychology 15:594
reasoning 16:104–105
THIOPENTAL
barbituate 3:78
THÍRA (Greece) *see* THERA (Greece)
3D AMENDMENT 19:169
Griswold v. *Connecticut* 9:368
text 5:220
THIRD CATARACT
map (19° 49′N 30° 19′E) 18:320
THIRD ESTATE
France, history of 8:269
French Revolution 8:322–323
THIRD INTERNATIONAL *see* INTERNATIONAL, SOCIALIST
THIRD OF MAY, 1808, THE (Goya) 2:198–199 *illus.*
THIRD REICH 19:169
Europe, history of 7:296
Germany, history of 9:155–156 *map*
Goering, Hermann 9:222
Himmler, Heinrich 10:167–168
Hitler, Adolf 10:187–188
Messerschmitt, Willy 13:323
nazism 14:67–68
Papen, Franz von 15:68
Ribbentrop, Joachim von 16:205
Schacht, Hjalmar 17:116
SS 18:207
THIRD REPUBLIC *see* FRANCE, HISTORY OF
THIRD STREAM (music)
jazz 11:389
Schuller, Gunther 17:136
THIRD WORLD 19:169–170 *bibliog.*
Agency for International Development 1:183
birth control 3:295
breast-feeding 3:469
census 4:249
conservation 5:203–204
economic planning 7:47
education
adult education 1:110
Educational Testing Service 7:66
energy sources 7:175
foreign aid 8:224–225
freedom of the press 8:297
fuel 8:353
green revolution 9:348
housing 10:276; 10:280
labor force 12:152
Marxism 13:184
national parks 14:44
newspaper 14:171–172 *table*
Point Four Program 15:381
press agencies and syndicates 15:533
revolution
Fanon, Frantz 8:20–21
Sea, Law of the 17:167–168
slash-and-burn agriculture 17:350
socialism 18:23–24
squatter 18:203
suburbs 18:317
technology transfer 19:60
totalitarianism 19:248
transportation
locomotive 12:391
urban planning 19:484–485
women in society 20:203–204
THIRST *see* HUNGER AND THIRST
13TH AMENDMENT 19:170 *bibliog.*
Civil Rights Cases 5:13–14
text 5:221
THIRTY-NINE ARTICLES 19:170 *bibliog.*
Parker, Matthew 15:90
THIRTY YEARS' WAR 19:170–172 *bibliog., illus., map*
Bohemian War 19:170–171
Christian IV, King of Denmark 4:412
Europe, history of 7:287–288
expansion of Brandenburg-Prussia 15:585 *map*
expansion of the war 19:171
Ferdinand II, Holy Roman Emperor 8:53
Ferdinand III, Holy Roman Emperor 8:53
Frederick V, Elector Palatine (the Winter King) 8:292
Freiburg im Breisgau (West Germany) 8:301
Germany, history of 9:151
Gustav II Adolf, King of Sweden (Gustavus Adolphus) 9:407
Holy Roman Empire 10:211
Lützen, Battle of 17:109 *illus.*
Magdeburg (East Germany) 13:46
Mansfeld, Ernst, Graf von 13:127–128
Maximilian, Elector and Duke of Bavaria 13:239–240
Palatinate 15:30
peace settlements 19:171
Prague (Czechoslovakia) 15:488
Tilly, Johann Tserclaes, Graf von 19:200
Torstenson, Lennart 19:244–245
Turenne, Henri de La Tour d'Auvergne, Vicomte de 19:341
Wallenstein, Albrecht Wenzel von 20:15
Westphalia, Peace of 9:151 *map*; 20:119
THISTED (Denmark)
map (56° 57′N 8° 42′E) 6:109
THISTLE 19:172 *illus.*
THIVAI *see* THEBES (Greece)
THOLOI
tomb 19:230 *illus.*
THOM, RENÉ 19:172
THOM, RON
Canadian art and architecture 4:91
THOMAS, SAINT 19:172 *bibliog.*
Madras (city in India) 13:43
THOMAS (county in Georgia)
map (30° 50′N 82° 55′W) 9:114
THOMAS (county in Kansas)
map (39° 20′N 101° 5′W) 12:18
THOMAS (county in Nebraska)
map (41° 55′N 100° 30′W) 14:70
THOMAS (Oklahoma)
map (35° 45′N 98° 45′W) 14:368
THOMAS (West Virginia)
map (39° 9′N 79° 30′W) 20:111
THOMAS, AMBROISE 19:172 *bibliog.*
THOMAS, AUGUSTUS 19:172
THOMAS, B. DOUGLAS
Curtiss Jenny 5:395
THOMAS, CHARLES XAVIER *see* TOMAS OF COLMAR
THOMAS, DYLAN 7:202 *illus.*; 19:172–173 *bibliog., illus.*
Cassill, R. V. 4:184
Under Milkwood 19:383
THOMAS, GEORGE HENRY 19:173 *bibliog.*
THOMAS, ISAIAH 19:173 *bibliog.*
THOMAS, LERA
Texas 19:134
THOMAS, LEWIS 19:173
THOMAS, LOWELL 19:173 *illus.*
newsreel 14:173
THOMAS, MARTHA CAREY 19:173 *bibliog.*
THOMAS, MICHAEL TILSON 19:173 *bibliog.*
THOMAS, NORMAN 19:173–174 *bibliog., illus.*
socialism 18:23
Socialist party 18:25
THOMAS, ROSS 19:174
THOMAS, SETH 19:174
THOMAS, SIDNEY GILCHRIST 19:174
THOMAS, THEODORE
American music 1:350
Chicago Symphony Orchestra 4:343
THOMAS, WILLIAM I. 19:174 *bibliog.*
THOMAS A. EDISON STATE COLLEGE 19:174
THOMAS À KEMPIS 19:174 *bibliog.*
THOMASBORO (Illinois)
map (40° 15′N 88° 11′W) 11:42
THOMASITES *see* CHRISTADELPHIANS
THOMASTON (Alabama)
map (32° 11′N 87° 37′W) 1:234
THOMASTON (Connecticut)
map (41° 40′N 73° 4′W) 5:193
THOMASTON (Georgia)
map (32° 54′N 84° 20′W) 9:114
THOMASTON (Maine)
map (44° 5′N 69° 10′W) 13:70
THOMASVILLE (Alabama)
map (31° 55′N 87° 51′W) 1:234
THOMASVILLE (Georgia)
map (30° 50′N 83° 59′W) 9:114
THOMASVILLE (North Carolina)
map (35° 53′N 80° 5′W) 14:242
THOMISM *see* AQUINAS, SAINT THOMAS; SCHOLASTICISM
THOMPSON (Manitoba)
map (55° 45′N 97° 45′W) 13:119
THOMPSON (North Dakota)
map (47° 46′N 97° 7′W) 14:248
THOMPSON, BENJAMIN, COUNT RUMFORD *see* RUMFORD, BENJAMIN THOMPSON, COUNT
THOMPSON, D'ARCY W.
growth, allometric 9:379
THOMPSON, DALEY 19:174
THOMPSON, DAVID 19:174 *bibliog.*
Canada, exploration of 4:80 *map*
THOMPSON, DOROTHY 19:174–175 *bibliog.*
THOMPSON, EDWARD HERBERT 19:175
THOMPSON, FRANK
ABSCAM 1:62
THOMPSON, GERTRUDE CATON- *see* CATON-THOMPSON, GERTRUDE
THOMPSON, J. ERIC 19:175
THOMPSON, SIR JOHN SPARROW DAVID 19:175 *bibliog., illus.*
Canada, history of 4:85
THOMPSON, RANDALL 19:175 *bibliog.*
THOMPSON, WILLIAM
socialism 18:19
THOMPSON, WILLIAM HALE 19:175 *bibliog.*
THOMPSON FALLS (Montana)
map (47° 36′N 115° 21′W) 13:547
THOMPSON RIVER
map (39° 45′N 93° 36′W) 13:476
THOMPSONVILLE (Michigan)
map (44° 31′N 85° 56′W) 13:377
THOMSEN, CHRISTIAN JÜRGENSEN 19:175
Neolithic Period 14:84
Paleolithic Period 15:38
prehistory 15:517
Worsaae, Jens Jacob Asmussen 20:284
THOMSON (Georgia)
map (33° 28′N 82° 30′W) 9:114
THOMSON (Illinois)
map (41° 58′N 90° 6′W) 11:42
THOMSON, CHARLES 19:175 *bibliog.*
THOMSON, CHARLES EDWARD POULETT, BARON SYDENHAM *see* SYDENHAM, CHARLES EDWARD POULETT THOMSON, BARON
THOMSON, SIR CHARLES WYVILLE 19:175
Challenger Expedition 4:271
THOMSON, SIR GEORGE PAGET 19:175 *bibliog.*
chemistry, history of 4:328
THOMSON, JAMES (1700–48) 19:175 *bibliog.*
THOMSON, JAMES (1834–82) 19:176 *bibliog.*
THOMSON, JOHN 19:176
THOMSON, JOSEPH 19:176 *bibliog.*
THOMSON, SIR JOSEPH JOHN 4:327 *illus.*; 19:176 *bibliog., illus.*
atom 2:305 *illus.*
atomic nucleus 2:309
Compton effect 5:159
conduction, electric 19:176
electron discoverer 7:119; 19:176
ion 19:176
Thomson, Sir George Paget 19:175; 19:176
THOMSON, JULIUS
chemistry, history of 4:327
THOMSON, ROBERT WILLIAM
rubber 16:333
THOMSON, TOM 19:176 *bibliog., illus.*
The Pool 4:89 *illus.*
The West Wind 19:176 *illus.*
THOMSON, VIRGIL 19:177 *bibliog.*
music criticism 13:670
THOMSON, WILLIAM, 1ST BARON KELVIN *see* KELVIN, WILLIAM THOMSON, 1ST BARON
THOMSON EFFECT
thermoelectricity 19:165
THON BURI (Thailand)
Bangkok 3:63
THONET, MICHAEL
chair 8:379 *illus.*
THONGA 19:177 *bibliog.*

THONZE (Burma)
map (17° 38′N 95° 47′E) **3**:573
THOR (mythology) **13**:702 *illus.*; **19**:177
THOR (rocket) **18**:120 *illus.*; **19**:177 *illus.*
Delta **6**:95
THORAX **10**:91 *illus.*
chest **4**:336
insect **11**:186
surgery **18**:362
THORAZINE
tranquilizer **19**:266
THORBECKE, JOHAN RUDOLF
Netherlands **14**:103
William II, King of the Netherlands **20**:158
William III, King of the Netherlands **20**:158
THÓRDARSON, AGNAR **19**:177–178
THOREAU (New Mexico)
map (35° 24′N 108° 13′W) **14**:136
THOREAU, HENRY DAVID **19**:178 *bibliog., illus.*
civil disobedience **5**:10
Walden **20**:9
THORFINN KARLSEFNI **19**:178 *bibliog.*
THORGILSSON, ARI
Icelandic literature **11**:18
THÓRIS LAKE
map (64° 50′N 19° 26′W) **11**:17
THORIUM **19**:178
abundances of common elements **7**:131 *table*
actinide series **1**:88
breeder reactor **3**:471–472
element **7**:130 *table*
metal, metallic element **13**:328
monazite **13**:522
radiometric age-dating **16**:66
THORN, GASTON **19**:178
THORN-PRIKKER, JOHAN **19**:179
THORNBUSH
umbrella thorn **17**:98 *illus.*
whistling thorn **17**:98 *illus.*
THORNDIKE, EDWARD L. **19**:179 *bibliog.*
associationism **2**:266
primary education **15**:538
psychology, history of **15**:597
reflex **16**:120
THORNDIKE, DAME SYBIL **19**:179
THORNE, KIP
gravitational waves **9**:306
THORNHILL, SIR JAMES **19**:179 *bibliog.*
THORNTHWAITE CLIMATIC CLASSIFICATION **19**:179 *bibliog.*
THORNTON (Arkansas)
map (33° 47′N 92° 29′W) **2**:166
THORNTON, WILLIAM
Capitol of the United States **4**:126
THORODDSEN, JÓN **19**:179
THOROUGHBASS
figured bass **8**:75
THOROUGHBRED **19**:179 *bibliog., illus.*
American saddle horse **1**:366
horse racing **10**:247–249 *table*
saddle horse **17**:9
THORP, JOHN
spinning **18**:186
THORPE, JEREMY **19**:179–180
THORPE, JIM **19**:180 *bibliog.*
decathlon **6**:72
football **8**:216–217 *illus.*
THORSBY (Alabama)
map (32° 55′N 86° 43′W) **1**:234
THORVALDSEN, BERTEL **19**:180 *bibliog., illus.*
Hebe **17**:113 *illus.*; **19**:180 *illus.*
Scandinavian art and architecture **17**:113
THORVALDSSON, ERIC *see* ERIC THE RED
THOTH **19**:180
Hermetic literature **10**:142
THOUSAND ISLANDS **14**:151 *illus.*; **19**:180
map (44° 15′N 76° 12′W) **14**:149
THOUSAND LAKE MOUNTAIN
map (38° 25′N 111° 29′W) **19**:492
THOUSAND AND ONE NIGHTS, THE (book) *see ARABIAN NIGHTS* (book)
THOUSAND SPRINGS CREEK
map (41° 17′N 113° 51′W) **14**:111
THRACE **19**:180–181
languages, extinct **12**:198
THRAKIKÓN SEA
map (40° 15′N 24° 28′E) **9**:325
THRASHER (bird) **4**:283 *illus.*; **19**:181 *illus.*
THRASYBULUS **19**:181
THREAD (screw)
screw **17**:156–157 *illus.*
THREAD (textiles) **19**:181
lace **12**:158–160
loom **12**:410–411
THREAD-WAISTED WASP *see* DIGGER WASP
THREADFIN **19**:181
THREE AFFILIATED TRIBES *see* ARIKARA (American Indians); HIDATSA (American Indians); MANDAN (American Indians)
THREE AGES OF WOMEN AND DEATH, THE (Baldung-Grien) **3**:34 *illus.*
THREE-BODY PROBLEM **19**:181–182 *bibliog., illus.*
Birkhoff, George David **3**:292
celestial mechanics **4**:230
libration **12**:319
perturbation **15**:191
Trojans **19**:305
THREE-DIMENSIONAL FILM (cinematography) **4**:434
THREE FORKS (Montana)
map (45° 54′N 111° 33′W) **13**:547
THREE KINGS ISLAND
map (34° 10′N 172° 5′E) **14**:158
THREE LAKES (Wisconsin)
map (45° 48′N 89° 10′W) **20**:185
THREE MARIAS, THE (Portuguese literary trio) **19**:182
THREE MILE ISLAND
Harrisburg (Pennsylvania) **10**:58
nuclear power plant **14**:282–283 *illus.*
radiation pollution, environmental **15**:414
THREE MUSICIANS, THE
Picasso, Pablo **15**:291
THREE MUSKETEERS, THE (book) **19**:182
Louis XIII, King of France **12**:426
THREE POINTS, CAPE
map (4° 45′N 2° 6′W) **9**:164
THREE RIVERS (Massachusetts)
map (42° 11′N 72° 22′W) **13**:206
THREE RIVERS (Michigan)
map (41° 57′N 85° 38′W) **13**:377
THREE SISTERS, THE (play) **19**:182
Chekhov, Anton **4**:310
THREE SISTERS MOUNTAIN
map (44° 10′N 121° 46′W) **14**:427
THREEPENNY OPERA, THE (play) **19**:182; **19**:150 *illus.*; **19**:182
Beggar's Opera, The **3**:168
Brecht, Bertolt **3**:470
musical comedy **13**:674 *illus.*
THRESHING MACHINE *see* COMBINE (farm machinery)
THRESHOLD (psychology)
psychophysics **15**:601–602
THRIFT (botany) **19**:182
THRIPS **19**:182–183 *illus.*
THROAT *see* MOUTH AND THROAT
THROCKMORTON (Texas)
map (33° 11′N 99° 11′W) **19**:129
THROCKMORTON (county in Texas)
map (33° 8′N 99° 15′W) **19**:129
THROMBOCYTE (platelet)
blood **3**:336–337
THROMBOCYTOPENIA
blood **3**:338
THROMBOPHLEBITIS
phlebitis **15**:248
varicose vein **19**:523
THROMBOSIS **19**:183
anticoagulant **2**:60
blood **3**:338
causes **19**:183
embolism **7**:152; **19**:183
nervous system, diseases of the **14**:96
penis, priapism **15**:534
shock, physiologic **17**:279
stroke **18**:302
vein **19**:536
THRONE
The Throne of Dagobert **8**:375 *illus.*
Tutankhamen, King of Egypt **9**:229 *illus.*
THROUGH THE LOOKING-GLASS (book) **19**:183
Carroll, Lewis **4**:169
illustration
Tenniel, Sir John **19**:108
THRUSH (bird) **19**:183 *bibliog., illus.*
blackbird **3**:320
bluebird **3**:344
bluethroat **3**:346 *illus.*; **8**:229 *illus.*
magpie robin **13**:62
nightingale **14**:193
redstart **16**:116
robin **16**:243
solitaire (bird) **18**:55
song thrush **8**:228 *illus.*
THRUST
aerodynamics **1**:123
THRUST FAULT (geology)
fault **8**:37 *illus.*
THUCYDIDES **10**:183 *illus.*; **19**:183–184 *bibliog., illus.*
history **10**:184
History of the Peloponnesian War **10**:185–186
Peloponnesian War **15**:139
THUGS **19**:184 *bibliog., illus.*
THULE (Greenland)
map (76° 34′N 68° 47′W) **9**:353
Rasmussen, Knud **16**:90
THULE CULTURE **7**:239 *map*
Eskimo **7**:241
THULIUM **19**:184
element **7**:130 *table*
lanthanide series **12**:200–201
metal, metallic element **13**:328
THUMB (anatomy) **11**:439 *illus.*
primate **15**:539 *illus.*
joint (anatomy) **11**:439 *illus.*
THUMB (family) **19**:184 *bibliog.*
THUN (Switzerland)
map (46° 45′N 7° 37′E) **18**:394
THUNDER BAY (Michigan)
map (45° 0′N 83° 22′W) **13**:377
THUNDER BAY (Ontario) **19**:184
map (48° 23′N 89° 15′W) **14**:393
THUNDER BUTTE
map (45° 19′N 101° 53′W) **18**:103
THUNDER HILLS
map (54° 30′N 106° 0′W) **17**:81
THUNDERBIRD, LAKE
map (35° 15′N 97° 20′W) **14**:368
THUNDERBOLT (Georgia)
map (32° 3′N 81° 4′W) **9**:114
THUNDERSTORM **19**:185 *bibliog., illus.*
cloud **5**:68
flash flood **8**:153
Hadley cell **10**:8
lightning **12**:339
meteorology **13**:341
precipitation **15**:495
radar meteorology **16**:41
Saint Elmo's fire **17**:18
squall and squall line **18**:201–202
tornado **19**:239–240
THÜNEN, JOHANN HEINRICH VON **19**:185
THUNER LAKE
map (46° 40′N 7° 45′E) **18**:394
THURBER, JAMES **19**:186 *bibliog., illus.*
THÜRINGEN (East Germany) *see* THURINGIA (East Germany)
THURINGIA (East Germany) **19**:186
THURINGIAN FOREST MOUNTAINS
map (50° 30′N 11° 0′E) **9**:140
THURMOND, STROM **19**:186 *bibliog.*
THURMONT (Maryland)
map (39° 37′N 77° 25′W) **13**:188
THURNWALD, RICHARD **19**:186
THURSDAY
calendar **4**:28
THURSTON (county in Nebraska)
map (42° 10′N 96° 35′W) **14**:70
THURSTON (county in Washington)
map (46° 59′N 122° 42′W) **20**:35
THURSTON ISLAND
map (72° 20′S 99° 0′W) **2**:40
THURSTONE, L. L. **19**:186 *bibliog.*
psychological measurement **19**:186
THUS SPAKE ZARATHUSTRA (book) **19**:186
Nietzsche, Friedrich Wilhelm **14**:186
THUTMOSE I, KING OF EGYPT **19**:186
THUTMOSE II, KING OF EGYPT **19**:186
THUTMOSE III, KING OF EGYPT **19**:186–187 *bibliog.*
Cleopatra's Needles **5**:51
Megiddo **13**:280
THYME **19**:187 *illus.*
THYMINE
genetic code **9**:79–81 *illus.*
mutation **13**:686
nucleic acid **14**:289 *illus.*
protein synthesis **15**:575
pyrimidine **15**:637
THYMUS **12**:476 *illus.*; **19**:187 *bibliog., illus.*
endocrine system **7**:169 *illus.*
immunodeficiency disease **11**:59–60
lymphatic system **12**:475
tumor, myasthenia gravis **13**:689
THYRATRON **19**:187 *bibliog.*
THYROCALCITONIN
endocrine system, diseases of the **7**:169
hormone, animal **10**:236 *table*; **10**:237
thyroid gland **19**:188
THYROID CARTILAGE *see* LARYNX
THYROID-DEFICIENCY DISEASES
thyroid gland **19**:188
thyroxine **19**:188
THYROID FUNCTION TEST **19**:187–188 *bibliog.*
radioactive isotope of iodine, medicine **13**:272
THYROID GLAND **19**:188 *bibliog., illus.*
astatine **2**:267
endocrine system **7**:169 *illus.*
endocrine system, diseases of the **7**:170
goiter **9**:225
Kocher, Emil **12**:105
hormone, animal **10**:234
thyroid function test **19**:187–188
thyroxine **19**:188
THYROID-STIMULATING HORMONE
endocrine system **7**:169
endocrine system, diseases of the **7**:170
hormone, animal **10**:236 *table*
pituitary gland **15**:322
thyroid gland **19**:188
THYROTOXICOSIS *see* HYPERTHYROIDISM
THYROTROPIN *see* THYROID-STIMULATING HORMONE
THYROTROPIN-RELEASING HORMONE
Schally, Andrew Victor **17**:117
THYROXINE **19**:188
endocrine system **7**:169
goiter **9**:225
growth, hormonal effect **9**:380
hormone, animal **10**:236 *table*; **10**:237
thyroid function test **19**:187–188
thyroid gland **19**:188
THYSANOPTERA *see* THRIPS
THYSANURA *see* BRISTLETAIL
TI **19**:188
TIAHUANACO **19**:188–189 *bibliog.*
Gate of the Sun **15**:500 *illus.*
pre-Columbian art and architecture **15**:500
TIANJIN (China) *see* TIENTSIN (Tianjin) (China)
TIARA
crowns and coronets **5**:364
TIAVEA (Western Samoa)
map (13° 57′S 171° 24′W) **20**:117
TIBBETT, LAWRENCE **19**:189 *bibliog.*
TIBER RIVER **19**:189
map (41° 44′N 12° 14′E) **11**:321
Rome (Italy) **16**:294–296
TIBERIAS (Israel) **19**:189
map (32° 47′N 35° 32′E) **11**:302
TIBERIAS, SEA OF *see* GALILEE, SEA OF
TIBERIUS, ROMAN EMPEROR **19**:189 *bibliog.*
Germanicus Caesar **9**:138
Livia Drusilla **12**:376
Rome, ancient **16**:302
TIBESTI MASSIF **19**:189
map (21° 30′N 17° 30′E) **4**:266
TIBET **19**:189–190 *bibliog., illus., map*
Bhutan **3**:235–236 *illus.*
China **4**:361
Dalai Lama **6**:11
history **19**:189–190
Lamaist art and architecture **12**:172 *illus.*
land and people **19**:189–190 *map*
language
Southeast Asian languages **18**:110–111
Lhasa **12**:309
Lhasa apso (dog) **12**:310
music, non-Western **13**:667–668
race **16**:34
Sikkim (India) **17**:303
Sino-Tibetan languages **17**:324–325
Tibetan Buddhism **19**:190–191
TIBET, PLATEAU OF
map (33° 0′N 86° 0′E) **19**:190
TIBETAN ANTELOPE *see* CHIRU
TIBETAN ART *see* LAMAIST ART AND ARCHITECTURE
TIBETAN BUDDHISM **19**:190–191 *bibliog., illus.*
Dalai Lama **19**:190–191
lama **19**:190–191 *illus.*
Lamaist art and architecture **12**:172
Lhasa **12**:309–310
mandala **13**:110 *illus.*
mantra **19**:190–191
Milarepa **13**:419

TIBETAN BUDDHISM (cont.)
Sherpa **17**:259
Tantra **19**:25; **19**:190–191
TIBETAN SPANIEL **19**:191
TIBETAN TERRIER **6**:219 *illus.*; **19**:191 *bibliog., illus.*
TIBU SAHIB *see* TIPPU SULTAN, SULTAN OF MYSORE
TIBULLUS **19**:191 *bibliog.*
TIBURÓN ISLAND
map (29° 0′N 112° 23′W) **13**:357
TIC **19**:191
TIC DOLOUREUX *see* NEURALGIA
TICE (Florida)
map (26° 41′N 81° 49′W) **8**:172
TICK **19**:191–192 *bibliog., illus.*
arachnid **2**:106–107
Babesia **3**:6
Colorado tick fever **5**:121
mite **13**:484
Q fever **16**:3
vector
relapsing fever **16**:132
TICK BIRD *see* OXPECKER
TICK FEVER *see* ROCKY MOUNTAIN SPOTTED FEVER
TICKBIRD *see* ANI
TICKSEED **19**:192
TICONDEROGA **19**:192 *bibliog.*
French and Indian Wars **8**:313 *map*
Green Mountain Boys **9**:348
map (43° 51′N 73° 26′W) **14**:149
TICUL (Mexico)
map (20° 24′N 89° 32′W) **13**:357
TIDAL BORE **19**:192 *bibliog.*
Fundy, Bay of **8**:363
TIDAL ENERGY **19**:192–193 *bibliog., illus.*
electricity production potential **19**:193
estuary **7**:248
feasible sites **19**:193
Fundy, Bay of **8**:363
hydroelectric power **10**:335
lagoon **12**:166
power, generation and transmission of **15**:483–484
TIDDLER *see* STICKLEBACK
TIDE **19**:193–194 *bibliog., illus., table*
amphidromic point **1**:381
Atlantic Ocean **2**:296
atmospheric tide **2**:304
beach and coast **3**:136
Darwin, Sir George Howard **6**:42
Earth tide **7**:25
English Channel **7**:189
equilibrium tide **19**:193–194
floods and flood control **8**:166–167
Fundy, Bay of **8**:363
gulf and bay **9**:403
harbor and port **10**:42–43
heights **19**:194 *table*
oceanography **14**:345
red tide **16**:114
dinoflagellate **6**:179
sea level **17**:169
tidal bore **19**:192
tidal energy **19**:192–193
tide-generating constituents **19**:194 *table*
types **19**:193–194
TIDEMAND, ADOLPH
Scandinavian art and architecture **17**:113
TIDEWATER SETTLERS
origins of the Civil War **5**:15
TIDIOUTE (Pennsylvania)
map (41° 41′N 79° 24′W) **15**:147
TIDJIKDJA (Mauritania)
map (18° 33′N 11° 25′W) **13**:236
TIECK, LUDWIG **19**:194–195 *bibliog.*
TIEL (Netherlands)
map (51° 54′N 5° 25′E) **14**:99
TIEN CULTURE
Shih-chai-shan (Shizhaishan) **17**:261
TIEN SHAN **19**:195
map (42° 0′N 80° 0′E) **4**:362
TIENEN (Belgium)
map (50° 48′N 4° 57′E) **3**:177
TIENTSIN (Tianjin) (China) **4**:364; **19**:195
map (39° 8′N 117° 12′E) **4**:362
TIENTSIN, TREATIES OF **19**:195
Asia, history **2**:258
China, history of **4**:374
Elgin, James Bruce, 4th Earl of **7**:137
Opium Wars **14**:407
TIEPOLO (family) **19**:195–196 *bibliog., illus.*
Caricature of a Man **4**:149 *illus.*
grisaille **9**:367
Meeting of Anthony and Cleopatra **19**:195 *illus.*
Mengs, Anton Raphael **13**:297
Würzburg Residenz **20**:297
TIERCEL *see* FALCON
TIERRA AMARILLA (New Mexico)
map (36° 42′N 106° 33′W) **14**:136
TIERRA DEL FUEGO **19**:196 *map*
cities
Ushuaia **2**:151 *illus.*; **19**:490
Cordillera Darwin **18**:92 *illus.*
Horn, Cape **10**:238
map (54° 0′S 67° 0′W) **2**:149
TIFFANY, CHARLES LEWIS **19**:196
jewelry **11**:411
TIFFANY, LOUIS COMFORT **19**:196 *bibliog., illus.*
antique collecting **2**:66 *illus.*
Art Nouveau **2**:212
glassware, decorative **9**:204
lamp **2**:211 *illus.*; **9**:204 *illus.*; **19**:196 *illus.*
Oyster Bay stained-glass window **18**:212 *illus.*
TIFFANY MOUNTAIN
map (48° 40′N 119° 56′W) **20**:35
TIFFIN (Ohio)
map (41° 7′N 83° 11′W) **14**:357
TIFFIN, EDWARD
Ohio **14**:361
TIFLIS (USSR) *see* TBILISI (USSR)
TIFT (county in Georgia)
map (31° 30′N 83° 30′W) **9**:114
TIFTON (Georgia)
map (31° 27′N 83° 31′W) **9**:114
TIGER **19**:197 *bibliog., illus.*
TIGER BEETLE
anatomy **3**:165 *illus.*
TIGER OF FRANCE, THE *see* CLEMENCEAU, GEORGES
TIGER'S-EYE **19**:197 *illus.*
TIGLATH-PILESER III, KING OF ASSYRIA **19**:197 *bibliog.*
Hazor **10**:85
TIGNALL (Georgia)
map (33° 52′N 82° 44′W) **9**:114
TIGNOUSTI, MOUNT
map (31° 31′N 6° 44′W) **13**:585
TIGRANES I, KING OF ARMENIA **19**:197
Armenia **2**:172 *map*
TIGRÉ **19**:197 *bibliog.*
TIGRIS (reed boat)
Heyerdahl, Thor **10**:155
TIGRIS RIVER **11**:256 *illus.*; **19**:197 *map*
Iraq **11**:254
map (31° 0′N 47° 25′E) **2**:232
TIJAMUCHI RIVER
map (14° 10′S 64° 58′W) **3**:366
TIJERINA, REIES LOPEZ
Chicano **4**:343
TIJOU, JEAN **19**:197–198 *bibliog.*
sanctuary screen (Saint Paul's, London) **11**:279 *illus.*
TIJUANA (Mexico) **19**:198
map (32° 32′N 117° 1′W) **13**:357
TIKAL (Guatemala) **14**:237 *illus.*; **19**:198 *bibliog.*
Latin America, history of **12**:216
Uaxactún **19**:369
TIKHONOV, NIKOLAI A. **19**:198
TILADUMMATI ATOLL
map (6° 50′N 73° 5′E) **13**:87
TILAK, BAL GANGADHAR **19**:198 *bibliog.*
TILBURG (Netherlands)
map (51° 34′N 5° 5′E) **14**:99
TILBURY (Ontario)
map (42° 15′N 82° 26′W) **14**:393
TILDE
N (letter) **14**:3
TILDEN (Illinois)
map (38° 13′N 89° 41′W) **11**:42
TILDEN (Nebraska)
map (42° 3′N 97° 50′W) **14**:70
TILDEN (Texas)
map (28° 28′N 98° 33′W) **19**:129
TILDEN, BILL **19**:198 *bibliog., illus.*
TILDEN, SAMUEL J. **19**:198–199 *bibliog., illus.*
Democratic party **6**:100
New York Public Library **14**:155
Tweed, William M. **19**:358
TILE
roof and roofing **16**:306 *illus.*
terra-cotta **19**:119–120
TILEFISH **19**:199
TILEMSI WASH
map (16° 15′N 0° 2′E) **13**:89
TILL EULENSPIEGEL, THE LEGEND OF THE GLORIOUS ADVENTURES OF (book)
Belgian literature **3**:175
TILL AND TILLITE **19**:199
glaciers and glaciation **9**:193–194 *illus.*
ice ages **11**:8
loess **12**:393
moraine **13**:572
TILLAMOOK (American Indians) **19**:199 *bibliog.*
TILLAMOOK (Oregon)
map (45° 27′N 123° 51′W) **14**:427
TILLAMOOK (county in Oregon)
map (45° 25′N 123° 39′W) **14**:427
TILLER (ship) *see* RUDDER
TILLEY (Alberta)
map (50° 27′N 111° 39′W) **1**:256
TILLEY, SIR SAMUEL LEONARD **19**:199 *bibliog.*
TILLICH, PAUL **19**:199–200 *bibliog.*
TILLMAN (county in Oklahoma)
map (34° 25′N 98° 55′W) **14**:368
TILLMAN, BENJAMIN RYAN **19**:200 *bibliog.*
TILLSONBURG (Ontario)
map (42° 51′N 80° 44′W) **14**:393; **19**:241
TILLY, JOHANN TSERCLAES, GRAF VON **19**:200 *bibliog.*
Maximilian, Elector and Duke of Bavaria **13**:239–240
Thirty Years' War **19**:171 *map*
TILSIT, TREATIES OF **19**:200
TILTON (Illinois)
map (40° 9′N 87° 38′W) **11**:42
TILTON (New Hampshire)
map (43° 27′N 71° 35′W) **14**:123
TIMA (Egypt)
map (26° 54′N 31° 26′E) **7**:76
TIMARU (New Zealand)
map (44° 24′S 171° 15′E) **14**:158
TIMBALIER ISLAND
map (29° 3′N 90° 29′W) **12**:430
TIMBER *see* LUMBER
TIMBER LAKE (South Dakota)
map (45° 26′N 101° 4′W) **18**:103
TIMBER WOLF *see* WOLF
TIMBERLAKE (Virginia)
map (37° 19′N 79° 15′W) **19**:607
TIMBUKTU (Mali) **19**:200
climate **13**:89 *table*
map (16° 46′N 3° 1′W) **13**:89
Songhai (empire) **18**:65
TIME (periodical) **19**:200
Luce, Henry Robinson **12**:449–450
TIME (physics) **19**:200–201 *bibliog.*
Daylight Saving Time **6**:56–57
ephemeris time **7**:216
Greenwich mean time **9**:354
hour angle **10**:264
Hubble time
Hubble's constant **10**:288
Julian day **11**:466
light-year **12**:336
measurement **13**:255
Guillaume, Charles Édouard **9**:395
units, physical **19**:466
sidereal time **17**:294
solar time
equation of time **7**:225
space-time
relativity **16**:133–134
stationary time series
Wiener, Norbert **20**:146
stochastic process **18**:273
time-delay
relativity **16**:135
time-sharing
on-line computer **14**:388
United States Naval Observatory **19**:464
year **20**:320
tropical year **19**:309
TIME-LAPSE PHOTOGRAPHY
photography **15**:265
TIME MACHINE, THE (book)
Wells, H. G. **20**:101
TIME AND MOTION STUDY **19**:201 *bibliog.*
Gilbreth, Frank and Lillian **9**:180
industrial engineering **11**:156
Taylor, Frederick Winslow **19**:49
TIME REVERSAL INVARIANCE **19**:202 *bibliog.*
antimatter **2**:63
reversible and irreversible processes **16**:186
TIME-SHARING **19**:202
computer **5**:160b; **5**:160i
computer languages **5**:160p
TIME-SHIFTING (video term) **19**:576b–576c
video recording **19**:576k
TIME OF TROUBLES **19**:201 *bibliog.*
Michael, Tsar of Russia **13**:372
TIME ZONES **19**:202–203 *map*
international date line **11**:220 *map*
TIMES, THE (London) **19**:203
Murdoch, Rupert **13**:648
newspaper **14**:172
Walter (family) **20**:19
TIMES BEACH (Missouri)
pollutants, chemical **15**:410
TIMES-MIRROR CO. v. *SUPERIOR COURT OF CALIFORNIA*
Bridges v. *California* **3**:485
TIMÉTRINE MOUNTAINS
map (19° 20′N 0° 42′W) **13**:89
TIMGAD (Algeria) **19**:203 *bibliog.*
TIMIMOUN (Algeria)
map (29° 14′N 0° 16′E) **1**:287
TIMIŞOARA (Romania) **19**:203
map (45° 45′N 21° 13′E) **16**:288
TIMMERMANS, FELIX **19**:203
TIMMINS (Ontario)
map (48° 28′N 81° 20′W) **14**:393
TIMMONSVILLE (South Carolina)
map (34° 8′N 79° 57′W) **18**:98
TIMMS HILL
map (45° 27′N 90° 11′W) **20**:185
TIMOFEYEVICH, YERMAK *see* YERMAK TIMOFEYEVICH
TIMOLEON **19**:203 *bibliog.*
TIMOR (Indonesia) **19**:203 *bibliog.*
map (9° 0′S 125° 0′E) **11**:147
TIMOR SEA
map (11° 0′S 128° 0′E) **2**:328
TIMOTHY, SAINT **19**:204
TIMOTHY (botany) **19**:203
TIMOTHY, EPISTLES TO **19**:203–204 *bibliog.*
TIMPANI *see* KETTLEDRUM
TIMROD, HENRY **19**:204
TIMS FORD LAKE
map (35° 15′N 86° 10′W) **19**:104
TIMSAH, LAKE
map (30° 34′N 32° 17′E) **18**:324
TIMUR **19**:204 *bibliog., illus.*
empire *c.*1400 **13**:405 *map*
Multan (Pakistan) **13**:637
Qum (Iran) **16**:28
Samarkand (USSR) **17**:45–46
Timurids (dynasty) **19**:204
TIMURIDS (dynasty) **19**:204 *bibliog.*
Persian art and architecture **15**:185–186
TIN **19**:204–205 *bibliog., illus.*
Bolivia **18**:90 *illus.*
bronze **3**:505
chemical properties **19**:204
element **7**:130 *table*
Group IVA periodic table **15**:167
metal, metallic element **13**:328
native elements **14**:47
oxide minerals **14**:476
physical properties **19**:204
Potosí (Bolivia) **15**:467
production **19**:205 *illus.*
17th century tinsmith **12**:338 *illus.*
superconductivity **18**:350 *table*
tin can manufacture **19**:205 *illus.*
tinplate **19**:205
TIN DRUM, THE (book) **19**:205
Grass, Günter **9**:297–298
TIN GOOSE (airplane)
Ford Tri-motor **8**:223–224 *illus.*
TIN LIZZIE *see* MODEL T (automobile)
TIN PAN ALLEY **19**:205 *bibliog.*
TINACA POINT
map (5° 33′N 125° 20′E) **15**:237
TINAMOU **3**:280 *illus.*; **19**:205–206 *illus.*
TINBERGEN, JAN **19**:206
TINBERGEN, NIKOLAAS **2**:11–12 *illus.*; **19**:206 *bibliog.*
ethology **7**:257
Lorenz, Konrad **12**:414
TINCALCONITE
borate minerals **3**:396
TINDEMANS, LEO **19**:206
TINERHIR (Morocco) **13**:586 *illus.*
TING, SAMUEL CHAO CHUNG **19**:206
TINGGIAN
Igorot **11**:38
TINGO MARÍA (Peru)
map (9° 9′S 75° 56′W) **15**:193
TINGUELY, JEAN **19**:206 *bibliog.*
TINIAN
Mariana Islands (U.S.) **13**:150
TINKISSO RIVER
map (11° 21′N 9° 10′W) **9**:397
TINLEY PARK (Illinois)
map (41° 35′N 87° 47′W) **11**:42
TINNITUS **19**:206
ear disease **7**:7
TINOGASTA (Argentina)
map (28° 4′S 67° 34′W) **2**:149
TÍNOS (Greece)
Cyclades (Greece) **5**:402
TINRHERT PLATEAU
map (29° 0′N 9° 0′E) **1**:287

"TINTERN ABBEY" (poem) *see* "LINES COMPOSED A FEW MILES ABOVE TINTERN ABBEY" (poem)
TINTORETTO **19**:206–207 *bibliog., illus.*
  Susanna and the Elders **19**:206 *illus.*
TINTYPE
  ferrotype **8**:59
TIOBRAID ÁRANN (Ireland) *see* TIPPERARY (town in Ireland)
TIOGA (county in New York)
  map (42° 6′N 76° 16′W) **14**:149
TIOGA (North Dakota)
  map (48° 24′N 102° 56′W) **14**:248
TIOGA (Pennsylvania)
  map (41° 55′N 77° 8′W) **15**:147
TIOGA (county in Pennsylvania)
  map (41° 45′N 77° 17′W) **15**:147
TIONESTA (Pennsylvania)
  map (41° 30′N 79° 27′W) **15**:147
TIOUGHNIOGA RIVER
  map (42° 14′N 75° 51′W) **14**:149
TIP TOP MOUNTAIN
  map (48° 16′N 85° 59′W) **14**:393
TIPI *see* TEPEE
TIPPAH (county in Mississippi)
  map (34° 45′N 88° 55′W) **13**:469
TIPPECANOE (county in Indiana)
  map (40° 22′N 86° 52′W) **11**:111
TIPPECANOE, BATTLE OF **19**:207
  Harrison, William Henry **10**:61
  Shawnee **17**:246
  Shawnee Prophet **17**:247
  Tecumseh **19**:69
  War of 1812 **20**:26 *map*
TIPPECANOE RIVER
  map (40° 31′N 86° 47′W) **11**:111
TIPPERARY (county in Ireland) **11**:260 *illus.*; **19**:207
TIPPERARY (town in Ireland) **19**:207
TIPPETT, MICHAEL **19**:207 *bibliog.*
TIPPOO SAHIB *see* TIPPU SULTAN, SULTAN OF MYSORE
TIPPU SULTAN, SULTAN OF MYSORE **19**:207 *bibliog.*
  Mysore (city in India) **13**:692
TIPTON (Indiana)
  map (40° 17′N 86° 2′W) **11**:111
TIPTON (county in Indiana)
  map (40° 17′N 86° 2′W) **11**:111
TIPTON (Iowa)
  map (41° 46′N 91° 8′W) **11**:244
TIPTON (Missouri)
  map (38° 39′N 92° 47′W) **13**:476
TIPTON (Oklahoma)
  map (34° 30′N 99° 8′W) **14**:368
TIPTON (county in Tennessee)
  map (35° 35′N 89° 45′W) **19**:104
TIPTONVILLE (Tennessee)
  map (36° 23′N 89° 29′W) **19**:104
TIQNISH (Prince Edward Island)
  map (46° 57′N 64° 2′W) **15**:548
TIQUISATE (Guatemala)
  map (14° 17′N 91° 22′W) **9**:389
TIRADENTES **19**:207 *bibliog.*
TIRAN, STRAIT OF
  map (27° 58′N 34° 28′E) **7**:76
  Red Sea **16**:113–114
TIRANË (Albania) **19**:207
  map (41° 20′N 19° 50′E) **1**:250
TIRATH KARMEL (Israel)
  map (32° 46′N 34° 58′E) **11**:302
TIRE (transportation) **19**:207–208 *bibliog., illus.*
  construction **19**:208 *illus.*
  designations **19**:208
  Dunlop, John **6**:301
  Firestone, Harvey S. **8**:106
  Goodyear, Charles **9**:246
  history **19**:208
  lampblack **12**:176
  Michelin, André and Édouard **13**:375
  rubber **16**:333
  subway **18**:319
TIRESIAS **19**:208
TÎRGOVIŞTE (Romania)
  map (44° 56′N 25° 27′E) **16**:288
TÎRGU-JIU (Romania)
  map (45° 2′N 23° 17′E) **16**:288
TÎRGU MUREŞ (Romania)
  map (46° 33′N 24° 33′E) **16**:288
TIRICH MIR MOUNTAIN
  map (36° 15′N 71° 50′E) **15**:27
TIRIO (Papua New Guinea)
  map (8° 25′S 143° 0′E) **15**:72
TIRO, MARCUS TULLIUS
  shorthand **17**:284
TIROL *see* TYROL
TIROS (artificial satellite) **19**:208–209
  Landsat **12**:184
  meteorology **13**:342
TIRPITZ, ALFRED VON **19**:209 *bibliog.*
TIRSO DE MOLINA **19**:209 *bibliog.*
TIRUCHCHIRAPPALLI (India)
  map (10° 49′N 78° 41′E) **11**:80
TIRUNELVELI (India)
  map (8° 44′N 77° 42′E) **11**:80
TIRYNS (Greece) **19**:209 *bibliog.*
TISCHBEIN (family) **19**:209 *bibliog.*
TISDALE (Saskatchewan)
  map (52° 51′N 104° 4′W) **17**:81
TISELIUS, ARNE WILHELM KAURIN **19**:209
TISHCHENKO, BORIS
  Russian music **16**:369
TISHCOHAN, CHIEF **11**:119 *illus.*
TISHOMINGO (county in Mississippi)
  map (34° 45′N 88° 15′W) **13**:469
TISHOMINGO (Oklahoma)
  map (34° 14′N 96° 40′W) **14**:368
TISKILWA (Illinois)
  map (41° 18′N 89° 30′W) **11**:42
TISO, JOZEF
  Slovakia (Czechoslovakia) **17**:364
TISSAPHERNES, PERSIAN SATRAP **19**:209
TISSOT, JAMES **19**:209–210 *bibliog.*
TISSUE, ANIMAL **19**:210 *bibliog.*
  aplasia **2**:78
  atrophy **2**:313
  bone **3**:377
  cell differentiation **19**:210
  cryobiology **5**:370
  death
    infarction **11**:164
    necrosis **14**:75
  dysplasia **6**:320
  histology **10**:180–181
  immune response
    antigen **2**:62
    immunity **11**:57
  laser **12**:213
  muscle **13**:651–654 *illus.*
  plastic surgery **15**:347
  radioactive substances
    autoradiography, photography **15**:265
  scar **17**:115
  sclerosis **17**:147
  skeletal system **17**:333
  transplantation, organ **19**:277
  tumor **19**:331
  types **19**:210
  ulcer **19**:376
  virus **19**:614
TISSUE, PLANT
  meristem
    growth **9**:381
TISSUE CULTURE **19**:210 *bibliog.*
  cell **4**:236
TISZA, ISTVÁN, COUNT **19**:210
TISZA RIVER **19**:210
  map (45° 15′N 20° 17′E) **6**:35
TITAN (astronomy) **19**:210
  Kuiper, Gerard **12**:135
  Saturn **17**:91 *table*
  Saturn (astronomy) **17**:90 *table*
  Voyager **19**:638
TITAN (mythology)
  titanium **19**:211
TITAN (rocket) **19**:210–211 *bibliog.*
  Centaur (rocket) **4**:249
  classes **19**:211
  Gemini program **9**:72; **19**:211
  intercontinental ballistic missile **19**:210–211
  launch vehicle **19**:211
  Minuteman missile **13**:462
  rockets and missiles **16**:256 *illus.*
  Strategic Air Command **18**:289
TITANIA (gem)
  titanium **19**:211
TITANIA (satellite)
  Uranus (astronomy) **19**:478–479
TITANIA, BOTTOM AND THE FAIRIES **8**:10 *illus.*
TITANIC **19**:211 *bibliog.*
TITANITE *see* SPHENE
TITANIUM **19**:211 *bibliog.*
  abundances of common elements **7**:131 *table*
  alloys **19**:211
  commercial application **19**:211
  compounds **19**:211
  element **7**:130 *table*
  Group IVB periodic table **15**:167
  metal, metallic element **13**:328
  occurrence **19**:211
  ore
    ilmenite **11**:50
    weathering **20**:83
  ore deposits, major **14**:424–425 *table*
  oxide minerals **14**:476
  oxygen **14**:478
  rutile **16**:376
  transition elements **19**:273 *table*
  Wollaston, William Hyde **20**:199
TITANO, MOUNT
  map (43° 56′N 12° 27′E) **17**:56
TITANO, ONTE
  San Marino **17**:56 *illus.*
TITANOMAGNETITE
  oxide minerals **14**:476
TITANOTHERE **19**:211 *illus.*
  fossil record **8**:246 *illus.*
TITANS **19**:211
TITCHENER, EDWARD B. **19**:211–212 *bibliog.*
TITHE **19**:212 *bibliog.*
TITIAN **19**:212–213 *bibliog., illus.*
  Bacchus and Ariadne **2**:196 *illus.*
  Charles V, Holy Roman Emperor **4**:294 *illus.*; **10**:210 *illus.*
  The Crowning with Thorns **11**:313 *illus.*
  Giorgione **9**:187
  Venice (Italy) **19**:544
  Venus of Urbino **19**:212 *illus.*
TITICACA, LAKE **3**:366 *illus.*; **19**:213
  Indians, American
    Aymara **2**:379
  map (15° 50′S 69° 20′W) **15**:193
TITIRANGI (New Zealand)
  map (36° 56′S 174° 40′E) **14**:158
TITIUS-BODE LAW **19**:213 *bibliog., table*
  Bode, Johann Elert **3**:355
  planetary distances **19**:213 *table*
TITLE **19**:213
  deed **6**:77
  tenant **19**:101
  Torrens system **19**:244
TITLES OF NOBILITY AND HONOR **19**:213–214 *bibliog., table*
  emir **7**:156
  England
    Benn, Anthony Wedgwood **3**:202
    Howard (family) **10**:282
  king **12**:80
  queen **16**:21
  sultan **18**:338
TITMOUSE (bird) **19**:214 *illus.*
  blue tit **8**:228 *illus.*
  bushtit **3**:586
  chickadee **4**:345
TITO **19**:214–215 *bibliog., illus.*
  communism **5**:148
  Mihajlović, Draža **13**:417
TITOGRAD (Yugoslavia) **19**:215
  map (42° 26′N 19° 14′E) **20**:340
TITOV, GHERMAN S. **19**:215 *bibliog.*
TITOV VELES (Yugoslavia)
  map (41° 41′N 21° 48′E) **20**:340
TITOVO UŽICE (Yugoslavia)
  map (43° 51′N 19° 51′E) **20**:340
TITRATION **19**:215 *bibliog.*
  indicator (chemistry) **11**:144
  pH **15**:218
  volumetric analysis
    quantitative chemical analysis **16**:8–9
TITUS (county in Texas)
  map (33° 12′N 95° 0′W) **19**:129
TITUS, EPISTLE TO **19**:215 *bibliog.*
TITUS, ROMAN EMPEROR **19**:215 *bibliog.*
  arch **11**:414 *illus.*
  Rome, ancient **16**:303
  Vespasian, Roman Emperor **19**:564
TITUS ANDRONICUS (play)
  Shakespeare, William **17**:237
TITUS LIVIUS *see* LIVY
TITUSVILLE (Florida)
  map (28° 37′N 80° 49′W) **8**:172
TITUSVILLE (PENNSYLVANIA)
  first U.S. oil well **15**:212 *illus.*
  map (41° 38′N 79° 41′W) **15**:147
TITYRA **19**:216
TIV **19**:217 *bibliog.*
  marriage **13**:165
TIVERTON (Rhode Island)
  map (41° 38′N 71° 12′W) **16**:198
TIVOLI (Copenhagen, Denmark) **5**:250
TIVOLI (Grenada)
  map (12° 10′N 61° 37′W) **9**:358
TIVOLI (Italy)
  map (41° 58′N 12° 48′E) **11**:321
TIZIMÍN (Mexico)
  map (21° 10′N 88° 10′W) **13**:357
TLALOC (Aztec deity)
  Aztec **2**:384
  temple **2**:383 *illus.*
TLATELOLCO (Mexico)
  Tenochtitlán **19**:112
TLAXCALA (Mexico) **19**:216
  map (19° 19′N 98° 14′W) **13**:357
TLAXCALA (state in Mexico) **19**:216
  Tlaxcala **19**:216
TLAXCALAN (American Indians) **19**:216 *bibliog.*
TLAXIACO (Mexico)
  map (17° 16′N 97° 41′W) **13**:357
TLINGIT (American Indians) **19**:216 *bibliog.*
  Indians of North America, art of the **11**:139
  potlatch **15**:467
  totem **19**:249
  Tsimshian **19**:323
TMJ SYNDROME **19**:216
TNP *see* THÉÂTRE NATIONAL POPULAIRE (TNP)
TNT **19**:216 *illus.*
  explosives **7**:339
  graphic formula **14**:438 *illus.*
  RDX **16**:98
TO KILL A MOCKINGBIRD (book) **19**:216–217
TO THE LIGHTHOUSE (book) **19**:217
TOAD **1**:377–378 *illus.*; **19**:217 *bibliog., illus.*
  See also FROG
  giant toad **9**:171
  horned toad **10**:239
  midwife toad **13**:414–415
TOADFISH **19**:217 *illus.*
TOADFLAX **19**:217–218 *illus.*
  germination **9**:157
TOADSTOOL **19**:218
  mushrooms **13**:659–660
TOAHAYANÁ (Mexico)
  map (26° 8′N 107° 44′W) **13**:357
TOANO RANGE
  map (40° 50′N 114° 20′W) **14**:111
TOAST (North Carolina)
  map (36° 30′N 80° 38′W) **14**:242
TOBACCO **19**:218–219 *bibliog., illus., table*
  cultivation and harvesting **19**:218
  curing, grading, and aging **19**:218–219
  history **19**:218
  Indians, American **11**:119 *illus.*
    Crow (people) **5**:363
  mosaic virus
    diseases, plant **6**:195
    microbiology **13**:384
    virus particle **19**:613–614 *illus.*
  nicotine **14**:184
  parasite
    witchweed **20**:192
  pipe **15**:310
  publications
    Cook, Ebenezer **5**:234
  shade-grown tobacco **5**:195 *illus.*
  smoking **17**:373
  types **19**:219 *table*
  United States
    Duke, James Buchanan **6**:295
    Durham (city in North Carolina) **6**:305
    Georgia **9**:117 *illus.*
    Kentucky **12**:48–49 *illus.*
    Maryland **13**:192 *illus.*
    North Carolina **14**:244 *illus.*
    Winston-Salem (North Carolina) **20**:180–181
  Zimbabwe **20**:366 *illus.*
TOBACCO ROAD (book) **19**:219
  Caldwell, Erskine **4**:26
TOBACCO ROAD (film) **8**:223 *illus.*
TOBACCO ROOT MOUNTAINS
  map (45° 35′N 112° 0′W) **13**:547
TOBAGO *see* TRINIDAD AND TOBAGO
TOBEY, MARK **19**:219 *bibliog., illus.*
  Microcosmos **19**:219 *illus.*
TOBIT, BOOK OF **19**:219–220 *bibliog.*
TOBOGGANING **19**:220
TOBRUK (Libya) **19**:220
  map (32° 5′N 23° 59′E) **12**:320
TOBYHANNA (Pennsylvania)
  map (41° 11′N 75° 25′W) **15**:147
TOCANTINS RIVER **19**:220
  map (1° 45′S 49° 10′W) **3**:460
  map (1° 45′S 49° 10′W) **1**:323
TOCCATA **19**:220
TOCCOA (Georgia)
  map (34° 35′N 83° 19′W) **9**:114
TOCO (Trinidad and Tobago)
  map (10° 50′N 60° 57′W) **19**:300
TOCOPILLA (Chile)
  map (22° 5′S 70° 12′W) **4**:355
TOCQUEVILLE, ALEXIS DE **19**:220 *bibliog.*
  state (in political philosophy) **18**:232
TODA
  polygamy **15**:419
TODAIJI
  Japanese art and architecture **11**:373–374
TODD (county in Kentucky)
  map (36° 50′N 87° 10′W) **12**:47
TODD (county in Minnesota)
  map (46° 2′N 94° 52′W) **13**:453

TODD (county in South Dakota)
map (43° 15′N 100° 45′W) 18:103
TODD, FRITZ
roads and highways 16:238
TODD, LORD ALEXANDER 19:220 *bibliog.*
TODD-AO (film technology) 4:433
TODOS SANTOS (Bolivia)
map (16° 48′S 65° 8′W) 3:366
TODY 19:221
TOE
hoof, nail, and claw 10:225
TOFINO (British Columbia)
map (49° 9′N 125° 54′W) 3:491
TOFRANIL *see* TRICYCLICS
TOFUA ISLAND
map (19° 45′S 175° 4′W) 19:233
TOGIAK (Alaska)
map (59° 4′N 160° 24′W) 1:242
TOGLIATTI (USSR) 19:221
map (45° 2′N 41° 59′E) 19:388
TOGLIATTI, PALMIRO 19:221 *bibliog.*
communism 5:150
TOGO 19:221–222 *bibliog., illus., map, table*
cities
Lomé 12:399
climate 19:222 *table*
economic activity 19:221
education
African universities 1:176 *table*
flag 19:221 *illus.*
history and government 19:222
land and resources 19:221–222 *map, table*
map (8° 0′N 1° 10′E) 1:136
people 19:221
Ewe 7:325
Fon 8:204
Yoruba 20:331
TOGO HEIHACHIRO 19:222
TOGOLAND 19:222
TOGWOTEE PASS
map (43° 45′N 110° 4′W) 20:301
TOHAKU 19:222
TOHOPEKALIGA, LAKE
map (28° 12′N 81° 23′W) 8:172
TOILET 19:222 *bibliog.*
plumbing 15:372 *illus.*
TOIYABE RANGE
map (39° 10′N 117° 10′W) 14:111
TOJO HIDEKI 19:222 *bibliog.*
World War II 20:259; 20:280
TOK PISIN
creole 5:338
TOKACHI RIVER
map (42° 44′N 143° 42′E) 11:361
TOKAIDO LINE (railway) 12:390 *illus.*
TOKAMAK 19:223 *bibliog.*
fusion energy 8:382
TOKAPI PALACE MUSEUM
Istanbul (Turkey) 11:307 *map*
TOKAT (Turkey)
map (40° 19′N 36° 34′E) 19:343
TOKELAU (New Zealand) 19:223
map (9° 0′S 171° 45′W) 14:334
TOKLAS, ALICE B.
Autobiography of Alice B. Toklas, The 2:356
Stein, Gertrude 18:247
TOKOLOR
Umar, al-Hajj 19:379
TOKUGAWA (family) 19:223 *bibliog.*
Asia, history of 2:258
Ieyasu, Shogun of Japan 11:32
Meiji Restoration 13:281
netsuke 14:104
samurai 17:49
shogun 17:281
Tanyu 19:26
TOKUGAWA IEYASU *see* IEYASU, SHOGUN OF JAPAN
TOKUSHIMA (Japan)
map (34° 4′N 134° 34′E) 11:361
TOKYO (Japan) 2:245 *illus.*; 5:8 *illus.*; 16:76–77 *illus.*; 19:223–225 *bibliog., illus., map*
climate 11:363 *table*
economy 19:225
history 19:225
Japan, history of 11:369
Tokugawa (family) 19:223
map (35° 42′N 139° 46′E) 11:361
religion and culture 19:255
subway 5:8 *illus.*; 18:318 *table*
TOKYO, UNIVERSITY OF 19:225–226
Japanese universities 11:382
TOKYO ROSE 19:226
TOLAND, JOHN 19:226 *bibliog.*
TOLBERT, WILLIAM R., JR. 19:226 *bibliog.*
TOLBIAC, BATTLE OF
Clovis 5:70
TOLBUKHIN (Bulgaria)
map (43° 34′N 27° 50′E) 3:555
TOLEDO (Illinois)
map (39° 16′N 88° 15′W) 11:42
TOLEDO (Iowa)
map (42° 0′N 92° 35′W) 11:244
TOLEDO (Ohio) 19:226
map (41° 39′N 83° 32′W) 14:357
Jones, Samuel Milton 11:444
water pollution 5:201 *illus.*
TOLEDO (Oregon)
map (44° 37′N 123° 56′W) 14:427
TOLEDO (Spain) 19:226
Alfonso VI, King of León and Castile 1:279
cathedral
retablo 18:155 *illus.*
map (39° 52′N 4° 1′W) 18:140
TOLEDO, FRANCISCO DE 19:226 *bibliog.*
TOLEDO, JUAN BAUTISTA DE
Escorial 7:238
TOLEDO BEND RESERVOIR
map (31° 30′N 93° 45′W) 19:129
TOLEDO WAR
Toledo (Ohio) 19:226
TOLERANCE (botany)
plant distribution 15:343
TOLIMA, MOUNT
map (4° 40′N 75° 19′W) 5:107
TOLKIEN, J. R. R. 19:226–227 *bibliog., illus.*
TOLLAND (county in Connecticut)
map (41° 52′N 72° 22′W) 5:193
TOLLEN'S TEST
aldehyde determination 1:268
TOLLER, ERNST 19:227 *bibliog.*
TOLLOCHE (Argentina)
map (25° 30′S 63° 32′W) 2:149
TOLLUND MAN 19:227 *bibliog., illus.*
TOLMAN, EDWARD C. 19:227 *bibliog.*
learning theory 12:261
motivation 13:610
psychology, history of 15:597
TOLONO (Illinois)
map (39° 59′N 88° 16′W) 11:42
TOLSÁ, MANUEL
Cathedral (Mexico City) 12:224 *illus.*
TOLSON, M. B. 19:227 *bibliog.*
TOLSTOI, COUNT ALEKSEI KONSTANTINOVICH 19:227–228 *bibliog.*
Moscow Art Theater 13:599
TOLSTOI, ALEKSEI NIKOLAYEVICH 19:228
TOLSTOI, COUNT LEO 19:228 *bibliog., illus.*
Anna Karenina 2:31
caricature 4:150 *illus.*
pacifism and nonviolent movements 15:9
Russian literature 16:365–366 *illus.*
War and Peace 20:25
TOLTEC (American Indians) 19:228–229 *bibliog.*
Chichén Itzá 4:343–344
Maya 13:243
Mexico, history of 13:362
pre-Columbian art and architecture 15:496–499
Tula 19:329–330
TOLTÉN (Chile)
map (39° 13′S 73° 14′W) 4:355
TOLUCA (Illinois)
map (41° 0′N 89° 8′W) 11:42
TOLUCA (Mexico) 19:229
map (19° 17′N 99° 40′W) 13:357
TOLUENE (liquid hydrocarbon)
phase equilibrium 15:223 *illus.*
TOM BROWN'S SCHOOLDAYS (book)
Hughes, Thomas 10:293
TOM GREEN (county in Texas)
map (31° 25′N 100° 27′W) 19:129
TOM JONES (book) 14:273 *bibliog.*; 14:273 *illus.*; 19:229 *bibliog.*
Fielding, Henry 8:73
TOM SAWYER (book) 14:275 *illus.*; 19:229 *bibliog.*
Twain, Mark 19:357
TOM THUMB (entertainer) 19:229 *bibliog.*
TOM THUMB (locomotive) 19:229 *bibliog.*
Cooper, Peter 5:244
TOMAH (Wisconsin)
map (43° 59′N 90° 30′W) 20:185
TOMAHAWK 19:229 *bibliog.*
TOMAHAWK (Wisconsin)
map (45° 28′N 89° 44′W) 20:185
TOMALES BAY 17:50 *illus.*
TOMANIIVI, MOUNT
map (17° 37′S 178° 1′E) 8:77
TOMÁS BARRON (Bolivia)
map (17° 35′S 67° 31′W) 3:366
TOMAS OF COLMAR
computer 5:160
TOMASSON, HELGI 19:229 *bibliog.*
TOMASZÓW MAZOWIECKI (Poland)
map (51° 32′N 20° 1′E) 15:388
TOMATO 8:348 *illus.*; 15:337 *illus.*; 19:229–230 *bibliog., illus.*; 19:533 *illus.*
farms and farming 1:195 *illus.*
harvester 10:65
TOMB 19:230–231 *bibliog., illus.*
burial 3:571
Canova, Antonio 4:115
Castel Sant'Angelo 4:187
catacombs 4:197
crypt 5:371
Early Christian art and architecture 7:9–11 *illus.*
Egypt, ancient
Beni Hasan 3:199
mastaba 13:214
Saqqara 17:74
Valley of the Kings 19:507
Etruscans 7:259–260 *illus.*
Caere 4:13
Veii 19:536
funeral customs 8:364
Islamic art and architecture 11:294
Japanese art and architecture 11:373
Korean art 12:117
Mausoleum at Halicarnassus 17:217 *illus.*
Medici Chapel 13:266
Mesopotamian art and architecture 13:319
Michelangelo 13:373
Mino da Fiesole 13:458
Mogul art and architecture 13:500–501
Mycenae 13:689–690 *illus.*
Persian art and architecture 15:186
pre-Columbian art and architecture 15:495
prehistoric period
barrow 3:95
Cotswold-Severn 5:304
Hallstatt 7:304 *illus.*
megalith 13:279
pyramids 15:634–636
Quercia, Jacopo della 16:23
Riemenschneider, Tilman 16:218–219
Roman art and architecture 16:274–275
Rossellino (family) 16:319
Santa Costanza 17:67
sarcophagus 17:75–76
Sluter, Claus 17:365
stele 18:250
Stoss, Veit 18:285
stupa 18:308
Taj Mahal 19:14–15
temple 19:94
Toradja 4:244 *illus.*
Ur 19:474
Verrocchio, Andrea del 19:560
TOMBALBAYE, N'GARTA 19:231 *bibliog.*
Chad 4:266
TOMBALL (Texas)
map (30° 6′N 95° 37′W) 19:129
TOMBAUGH, CLYDE WILLIAM 19:231
Pluto (planet) 15:373
solar system 18:45
TOMBIGBEE RIVER 19:231
map (31° 4′N 87° 58′W) 1:234
map (31° 4′N 87° 58′W) 13:469
TOMBOUCTOU (Mali) *see* TIMBUKTU (Mali)
TOMBSTONE 19:232 *bibliog., illus.*
epitaph 7:222
Roman art and architecture 16:274–275
Scandinavian art and architecture 17:111
stele 18:250
TOMBSTONE (Arizona) 19:231–232
map (31° 43′N 110° 4′W) 2:160
TOMÉ (Chile)
map (36° 37′S 72° 57′W) 4:355
TOMELLOSO (Spain)
map (39° 10′N 3° 1′W) 18:140
TOMINI BAY
map (0° 20′S 121° 0′E) 11:147
TOMKINS, THOMAS 19:232 *bibliog.*
music, history of Western 13:666
TOMLIN, BRADLEY WALKER 19:232 *bibliog.*
TOMMASO DI CRISTOFANO FINO *see* MASOLINO DA PANICALE
TOMMASO DI SER GIOVANNI DI MONE *see* MASACCIO
TOMONAGA, SIN-ITIRO 19:232
TOMOYUKI, YAMASHITA *see* YAMASHITA TOMOYUKI
TOMPKINS (county in New York)
map (42° 27′N 76° 30′W) 14:149
TOMPKINS (Saskatchewan)
map (50° 4′N 108° 47′W) 17:81
TOMPKINS, DANIEL D. 19:232
TOMPKINSVILLE (Kentucky)
map (36° 42′N 85° 41′W) 12:47
TOMS RIVER (New Jersey)
map (39° 58′N 74° 12′W) 14:129
TOMSK (USSR)
climate 2:237 *table*
map (56° 30′N 84° 58′E) 19:388
TON, KONSTANTIN
Russian art and architecture 16:362
TON DU THANG
Vietnam 19:583
TONALÁ (Mexico)
map (16° 4′N 93° 45′W) 13:357
TONALITY 19:232–233
atonality 2:312
baroque music 3:91–92
harmony 10:52
key 12:62
scale (music) 17:106–107
TONASKET (Washington)
map (48° 42′N 119° 26′W) 20:35
TONAWANDA (New York)
map (43° 1′N 78° 53′W) 14:149
TONCHI
Nivkh 14:204
TONE (music) 19:233
See also MUSIC, ACOUSTICS OF
dissonance (music) 6:198
TONE, WOLFE 19:233 *bibliog.*
TONE POEM *see* SYMPHONIC POEM
TONE RIVER
map (35° 44′N 140° 51′E) 11:361
TONG 19:233
TONGA 19:233–234 *bibliog., illus., map*
cities
Nukualofa 14:292
flag 19:233 *illus.*
government 19:233–234
history 19:234
ivory figure 14:338 *illus.*
land, people, and economy 19:233 *map*
map (20° 0′S 175° 0′W) 14:334
postage stamp 15:230 *illus.*
TONGA TRENCH
Pacific Ocean bottom 15:6 *map*
TONGANOXIE (Kansas)
map (39° 7′N 95° 5′W) 12:18
TONGATAPU GROUP
map (21° 10′S 175° 10′W) 19:233
TONGEREN (Belgium)
map (50° 47′N 5° 28′E) 3:177
TONGHAK (religion)
Korea, history of 12:116–117
TONGJOSON BAY
map (39° 30′N 128° 0′E) 12:113
TONGUE 19:234 *illus.*
muscle 13:653
phonetics 15:252
speech 18:174 *illus.*
TONGUE-TIE 19:234
TONGUE WORM 19:234
TONGUES, SPEAKING IN 19:234 *bibliog.*
TONICA (Illinois)
map (41° 13′N 89° 4′W) 11:42
"TONIGHT SHOW, THE" (television show)
radio and television broadcasting 16:59 *illus.*
TONKAWA (Oklahoma)
map (36° 41′N 97° 18′W) 14:368
TONKIN (Vietnam) 19:234
TONKIN, GULF OF 19:234
map (20° 0′N 108° 0′E) 4:362
TONKIN GULF RESOLUTION 19:234–235 *bibliog.*
Vietnam War 19:586
TONLE SAP LAKE
Kampuchea (Cambodia) 12:11
map (13° 0′N 104° 0′E) 12:11
TONOPAH (Nevada)
map (38° 4′N 117° 14′W) 14:111
TONSILLITIS 19:235 *bibliog.*
pharyngitis 15:222
TONSILS 12:476 *illus.*; 19:235 *bibliog., illus.*
adenoids 1:102
inflammation, strep throat 18:297
lymphatic system 12:475
TONSURE 19:235
TONTI, HENRI DE *see* TONTY, HENRI DE
TONTON MACOUTES
Duvalier, François 6:316
TONTY, HENRI DE 19:235–236 *bibliog.*
TONY AWARDS 19:236 *bibliog.*
acting
Bacall, Lauren 3:9

Brynner, Yul 3:529–530
Caldwell, Zoe 4:27
Cronyn, Hume 5:359
Dewhurst, Colleen 6:147
Gleason, Jackie 9:206–207
Harris, Julie 10:57
Harrison, Rex 10:60
Jones, James Earl 11:443
Merman, Ethel 13:311
Minnelli, Liza 13:452
Mostel, Zero 13:605
Pacino, Al 15:10
Scofield, Paul 17:147
costume design
Beaton, Sir Cecil 3:145
directing
Bennett, Michael 3:203
Nichols, Mike 14:182
set design
Aronson, Boris 2:186–187
special awards
Atkinson, Brooks 2:292
Midler, Bette 13:414
writing
Miller, Arthur 13:427
Rabe, David 16:31
Stoppard, Tom 18:284
Williams, Tennessee 20:160–161
TOOELE (Utah)
map (40° 32′N 112° 18′W) 19:492
TOOELE (county in Utah)
map (40° 20′N 113° 0′W) 19:492
TOOKER, GEORGE 19:236
TOOL AND DIE MAKING 19:236 *bibliog.*
TOOL INDUSTRIES, PREHISTORIC *see* PREHISTORIC TOOL INDUSTRIES
TOOLE (county in Montana)
map (48° 40′N 111° 40′W) 13:547
TOOLS
carpentry 4:164
casting 4:188–189
hand tools 10:35
machine tools 13:23–25
mill 13:424–425
obsidian 14:319
pneumatic systems 15:375
power tools
drill 6:273
saw 17:102–103 *illus.*
tool and die making 19:236
whetstone 20:130
TOOMBS (county in Georgia)
map (32° 10′N 82° 20′W) 9:114
TOOMBS, ROBERT 19:236 *bibliog.*
TOOMER, JEAN 19:236
TOOMEY, BILL
decathlon 6:72
TOOMSBORO (Georgia)
map (32° 50′N 83° 5′W) 9:114
TOOTH *see* TEETH
TOOTH DECAY *see* TEETH
TOOTHCARP *see* KILLIFISH
TOOTHWORT (botany) 19:236
TOOWOOMBA (Australia)
map (27° 33′S 151° 57′E) 2:328
TOP (play object)
toy 19:256
TOPA INCA
Inca empire 11:70 *map*
Pachacuti 15:4
TOPAWA (Arizona)
map (31° 48′N 111° 51′W) 2:160
TOPAZ 3:296 *illus., table*; 9:74 *illus.*; 19:236–237 *illus.*
gems 9:75
November birthstone 19:236
orthorhombic system 14:451
silicate mineral 19:236
TOPCHIYEV, ALEKSANDR VASILIEVICH 19:237
TOPEKA (Kansas) 12:20 *illus.*; 19:237
map (39° 3′N 95° 41′W) 12:18
TOPI 17:98 *illus.*
TOPICAL GEOGRAPHY 9:101; 9:103
TOPKAPI PALACE MUSEUM 19:237
TOPLEY (British Columbia)
map (54° 49′N 126° 18′W) 3:491
TOPMINNOW
See also KILLIFISH
mosquito fish 13:603
TOPOGRAPHY 19:237
Birkhoff, George David 3:292
continental shelf and slope 5:230
fault 8:37
landform evolution 12:183
maps and mapmaking 13:141
speleology 18:177
valley and ridge province 19:507–508
weathering 20:82
TOPOLOGY (mathematics) 19:237–238 *illus.*
Betti, Enrico 3:232
Brouwer, L. E. J. 3:513
closed surfaces 19:237–238
Euler, Leonhard 7:264–265
four color theorem 8:252
Fréchet, Maurice René 8:289
geometry 9:107
graphs 19:237–238
homeomorphisms 19:238
Klein bottle 12:96
Königsberg bridge problem 12:108–109
Lefschetz, Solomon 12:272
mathematics, history of 13:226
metric spaces 19:237
Möbius, August Ferdinand 13:488
Möbius strip 13:488
Poincaré, Henri 15:380
Riemann, Georg Friedrich Bernhard 16:218
Veblen, Oswald 19:529
TOPPENISH (Washington)
map (46° 23′N 120° 19′W) 20:35
TOPRAKKALE *see* URARTU
TOPSFIELD (Massachusetts)
map (42° 38′N 70° 57′W) 13:206
TORADJA
Bugis 3:548
decorated house 18:107 *illus.*
tomb 4:244 *illus.*
TORAH 16:139 *illus.*; 19:238 *bibliog.*
ark of the covenant 2:164
Bible 3:237–238 *illus.*
Deuteronomy, Book of 6:136
Exodus, Book of 7:332–333
Genesis, Book of 9:78
Judaism 11:459
Karaites 12:26
Leviticus, Book of 12:304
Maimonides 13:68
Numbers, Book of 14:294
TORBAT-E HEYDARIYEH (Iran)
map (35° 16′N 59° 13′E) 11:250
TORBAY (Newfoundland)
map (47° 40′N 52° 44′W) 14:166
TORBAY (TORQUAY) (England)
map (50° 28′N 3° 30′W) 19:403
TORBERNITE 13:441 *illus.*
TORCH LAKE
map (45° 0′N 85° 19′W) 13:377
TORDESILLAS, TREATY OF 19:238–239
John II, King of Portugal (John the Perfect) 11:428
Latin America, history of 12:217
Portuguese empire *c.*1580 15:453 *map*
Spanish and Portuguese lands designated by 18:146 *map*
TORELLI, GIACOMO
theater, history of the 19:147
theater architecture and staging 19:152
TORELLI, GIUSEPPE 19:239
TORIES *see* LOYALISTS
TORII
Kiyomasu 12:94
Kiyonaga 12:94
Kiyonobu I 12:94
TORINO (Italy) *see* TURIN (Italy)
TORNADO 19:239–240 *bibliog., illus., map, table*
classification 19:239–240
Fujita-Pearson scale 19:240 *table*
frequency, United States 19:240 *map*
low-pressure region 12:443
occurrence 19:239–240
radar meteorology 16:41
waterspout 20:66
whirlwind 20:132
TORNADO MOUNTAIN
map (49° 58′N 114° 39′W) 1:256
TORNEÅ RIVER
map (65° 48′N 24° 8′E) 18:382
TORNGAT MOUNTAINS
map (59° 0′N 64° 0′W) 14:166
TORNQUIST (Argentina)
map (38° 6′S 62° 14′W) 2:149
TORO, MOUNT
map (29° 8′S 69° 48′W) 2:149
TORONI, MOUNT
map (19° 43′S 68° 41′W) 4:355
TORONTO (Kansas)
map (37° 48′N 95° 57′W) 12:18
TORONTO (Ohio)
map (40° 28′N 80° 36′W) 14:357
TORONTO (Ontario) 4:69 *illus.*; 14:392 *illus.*; 19:240–242 *bibliog., illus., map*
City Hall 4:90 *illus.*
Mackenzie, William Lyon 13:28
map (43° 39′N 79° 23′W) 14:393
Royal Ontario Museum 16:330
TORONTO (South Dakota)
map (44° 34′N 96° 39′W) 18:103
TORONTO, UNIVERSITY OF 19:242
TORONTO LAKE
map (37° 46′N 95° 57′W) 12:18
TORPEDO (fish)
ray 16:96
TORPEDO (projectile) 19:242–243 *bibliog., illus.*
development 19:242
PT boat 15:605
self-propelled
naval vessels 14:55–56
Whitehead, Robert, inventor 20:139
sonar 18:62
submarine 18:315
torpedo boat 14:57 *illus.*; 19:242
types 19:242–243
TORPOR
hibernation 10:156
TORQUAY (TORBAY) (England)
map (50° 28′N 3° 30′W) 19:403
TORQUE 19:243
gear 9:65–66
statics 18:234–235
TORQUEMADA, TOMÁS DE 19:243 *bibliog.*
Inquisition 11:184
TORRALBA AND AMBRONA (Spain) 19:243 *bibliog.*
TORRANCE (California)
map (33° 50′N 118° 19′W) 4:31
TORRANCE (county in New Mexico)
map (34° 40′N 105° 50′W) 14:136
TORRE, GIROLAMO AND MARCANTONIO DELLA
tomb of
Briosco, Andrea 3:487
TORRE ANNUNZIATA (Italy)
map (40° 45′N 14° 27′E) 11:321
TORRENCE, RIDGELY 19:243 *bibliog.*
TORRENS, LAKE
map (31° 0′S 137° 50′E) 2:328
TORRENS, SIR ROBERT 19:244 *bibliog.*
TORRENS SYSTEM 19:244 *bibliog.*
Torrens, Sir Robert 19:244
TORRENT LARK *see* AUSTRALIAN MUDNEST BUILDER
TORREÓN (Mexico) 19:244
map (25° 33′N 103° 26′W) 13:357
TORRES, LUIS VAEZ DE
Torres Strait 19:244
TORRES BODET, JAIME 19:244 *bibliog.*
TORRES GONZÁLES, JUAN JOSÉ
Bolivia 3:369
TORRES NAHARRO, BARTOLOMÉ DE *see* NAHARRO, BARTOLOMÉ DE TORRES
TORRES STRAIT 19:244
map (10° 25′S 142° 10′E) 2:328
people
McDougall, William (psychologist) 13:14
TORREYA 19:244 *illus.*
TORRICELLI, EVANGELISTA 19:244 *bibliog.*
barometer 3:88
TORRIJOS HERRERA, OMAR 19:244
Panama Canal Zone 15:57
TORRINGTON (Connecticut)
map (41° 48′N 73° 8′W) 5:193
TORRINGTON (Wyoming)
map (42° 4′N 104° 11′W) 20:301
TÓRSHAVN (Faeroe Islands)
map (62° 1′N 6° 46′W) 6:109
TORSTENSON, LENNART 19:244–245 *bibliog.*
TORT 19:245–246 *bibliog.*
assault and battery 2:264
conversion 5:233
defamation 6:81
law 12:243
liability 12:311
negligence 14:77
trespass 19:291
TORTIGLIONI 15:106 *illus.*
TORTOISE 19:246 *bibliog., illus.*
embryo 7:324 *illus.*
Galápagos Islands 9:10
TORTOISE BEETLE 3:167 *illus.*
TORTOLA ISLAND
map (18° 27′N 64° 36′W) 19:605
Virgin Islands 19:605
TORTUGA ISLAND
map (20° 4′N 72° 49′W) 10:15
TORTURE 19:246–247 *bibliog., illus.*
TORUŃ (Poland)
map (53° 2′N 18° 35′E) 15:388
TORUN, PEACE OF (1466)
Prussia 15:585
TORUS 19:247
topology 19:238
TORY PARTY 19:247 *bibliog.*
Cavaliers 4:220
Conservative parties 5:205
political parties 15:400
Whig party (England) 20:130
William IV, King of England, Scotland, and Ireland 20:156
TOSA SCHOOL *see* JAPANESE ART AND ARCHITECTURE
TOSCA (opera) 11:319 *illus.*; 19:247 *bibliog.*
Castel Sant'Angelo 4:187
TOSCANA (Italy) *see* TUSCANY (Italy)
TOSCANELLI, PAOLO DAL POZZO
maps and mapmaking 13:139 *illus.*
TOSCANINI, ARTURO 19:247–248 *bibliog., illus.*
radio and television broadcasting 16:56
TOSHUSAI *see* SHARAKU
TOSI, PIER FRANCESCO
voice, singing 19:626
TOSTADO (Argentina)
map (29° 14′S 61° 46′W) 2:149
TOTALITARIANISM 19:248 *bibliog.*
communism 5:146–150
fascism 8:30
Hitler, Adolf 10:187–188
nazism 14:67–68
police state 15:397
Stalinism 5:147
TOTEM 19:249 *bibliog., illus.*
Aborigines, Australian 1:59
cannibalism 4:109
clan 5:36
dietary laws 6:164
Indians of North America, art of the 11:139 *illus.*
wood carving 20:207–208 *illus.*
TOTENTANZ *see* DEATH, DANCE OF
TÓTH, ÁRPÁD
Hungarian literature 10:306
TOTNESS (Suriname)
map (5° 53′N 56° 19′W) 18:364
TOTONICAPÁN (Guatemala)
map (14° 55′N 91° 22′W) 9:389
TOTORAS (Argentina)
map (32° 35′S 61° 11′W) 2:149
TOTOWA (New Jersey)
map (40° 54′N 74° 13′W) 14:129
TOUBKAL, MOUNT
map (31° 5′N 7° 55′W) 13:585
TOUCAN 3:281 *illus.*; 11:469 *illus.*; 19:249 *illus.*
TOUCH *see* SENSES AND SENSATION; SKIN
TOUCH-ME-NOT *see* JEWELWEED
TOUCHWOOD HILLS
map (51° 35′N 104° 17′W) 17:81
TOUGGOURT (Algeria)
map (33° 10′N 6° 0′E) 1:287
TOULMIN, STEPHEN EDELSTON 19:249
TOULON (France) 19:249–250
map (43° 7′N 5° 56′E) 8:260
TOULON (Illinois)
map (41° 6′N 89° 52′W) 11:42
TOULOUSE (France) 19:250
map (43° 36′N 1° 26′E) 8:260
Saint Sernin, Church of 4:205; 16:282 *illus.*
TOULOUSE-LAUTREC, HENRI DE 19:250–251 *bibliog., illus.*
At the Salon of the Rue des Moulins 19:250 *illus.*
La Goulue at the Moulin Rouge 12:371 *illus.*
Marcelle Lender 9:293 *illus.*
Villon, Jacques 19:599
TOULOUSE UNIVERSITY
European universities 7:306–309
TOUMANOVA, TAMARA
Ballets Russes de Monte Carlo 3:48
TOUNGOO (Burma)
map (18° 56′N 96° 26′E) 3:573
TOUPEE *see* WIG
TOUR, GEORGES DE LA *see* LA TOUR, GEORGES DE
TOUR, MAURICE QUENTIN DE LA *see* LA TOUR, MAURICE QUENTIN DE
TOUR DE FRANCE 5:404 *illus.*
TOURA MOUNTAINS
map (7° 40′N 7° 25′W) 11:335
TOURACO 3:281 *illus.*; 19:251 *illus.*
TOURAINE (France) 19:251
TOURANE (Vietnam) *see* DA NANG (Vietnam)
TOURÉ, SÉKOU 19:251 *bibliog.*
Guinea 9:398
socialism 18:24
TOURETTE'S SYNDROME 19:251 *bibliog.*
TOURISM 19:251–253 *bibliog.*
aviation 2:372
Heart of Atlanta Motel, Inc. v. *United States* 10:95
hotel 10:259–262
national parks 14:44
youth hostel 20:337

TOURMALINE 13:440 *illus.*; 19:253 *illus.*
dichroism 6:156
gems 9:75; 19:253
occurrence 19:253
October birthstone 19:253
TOURNACHON, GASPARD FÉLIX *see* NADAR
TOURNAI (Belgium) 3:180 *illus.*; 19:253
map (50° 36′N 3° 23′E) 3:177
tapestry 19:32–33
TOURNEUR, CYRIL 19:253
TOURS (France) 19:253
map (47° 23′N 0° 41′E) 8:260
TOUSIDE PEAK
map (21° 2′N 16° 25′E) 4:266
TOUSIGNANT, CLAUDE
Canadian art and architecture 4:91
TOUSSAINT, ANNA LOUISE GEERTRUIDE BOSBOOM- *see* BOSBOOM-TOUSSAINT, ANNA LOUISE GEERTRUIDE
TOUSSAINT L'OUVERTURE, FRANÇOIS DOMINIQUE 19:253–254 *bibliog.*
TOUSSEUL, JEAN (pseudonym)
Belgian literature 3:175
TOVEY, SIR DONALD FRANCIS 19:254 *bibliog.*
TOW (Texas)
map (30° 53′N 98° 28′W) 19:129
TOWANDA (Kansas)
map (37° 48′N 97° 2′W) 12:18
TOWANDA (Pennsylvania)
map (41° 46′N 76° 26′W) 15:147
TOWER (Minnesota)
map (47° 48′N 92° 17′W) 13:453
TOWER OF BABEL *see* BABEL, TOWER OF
TOWER CITY (North Dakota)
map (46° 55′N 97° 40′W) 14:248
TOWER HILL (Illinois)
map (39° 23′N 88° 58′W) 11:42
TOWER OF LONDON 12:401 *map*; 19:254 *bibliog., illus.*
Beefeaters 3:161
TOWHEE 19:254 *illus.*
bunting 3:564
TOWN, HAROLD
Canadian art and architecture 4:90
TOWN, ITHIEL 19:254–255 *bibliog.*
Davis, Alexander Jackson 6:50
TOWN HILL
map (32° 19′N 64° 44′W) 3:219
TOWN HOUSE
brownstone 3:519
house (in Western architecture) 10:267 *illus.*
TOWN MEETING 19:255 *bibliog.*
municipal government 13:642
TOWNER (North Dakota)
map (48° 21′N 100° 25′W) 14:248
TOWNER (county in North Dakota)
map (48° 40′N 99° 15′W) 14:248
TOWNES, CHARLES HARD 19:255 *bibliog.*
TOWNLEY, ARTHUR CHARLES
Nonpartisan League 14:217
TOWNS (county in Georgia)
map (34° 55′N 83° 45′W) 9:114
TOWNSEND (Massachusetts)
map (42° 40′N 71° 42′W) 13:206
TOWNSEND (Montana)
map (46° 19′N 111° 31′W) 13:547
TOWNSEND, FRANCIS EVERETT 19:255 *bibliog.*
Union party 19:387
TOWNSHEND, CHARLES (general)
World War I 20:232; 20:234
TOWNSHEND, CHARLES TOWNSHEND, 2D VISCOUNT (statesman) 19:255 *bibliog.*
Walpole, Sir Robert 20:18
TOWNSHEND, PETER
Who, The 20:143
TOWNSHEND ACTS 19:255 *bibliog.*
American Revolution 1:354–355
Franklin, Benjamin 8:284
United States, history of the 19:440
writ of assistance 20:291
TOWNSHEND RESERVOIR
map (43° 4′N 72° 42′W) 19:554
TOWNSHIP 19:256
TOWNSVILLE (Australia)
James Cook University 2:345 *table*
map (19° 16′S 146° 48′E) 2:328
TOWSON (Maryland)
map (39° 24′N 76° 36′W) 13:188
TOWTON, BATTLE OF
Roses, Wars of the 16:316 *map*
TOXIC CHEMICAL WASTE *see* POLLUTANTS, CHEMICAL
TOXiC SHOCK SYNDROME 19:255–256
TOXICOLOGY 19:256 *bibliog.*
animal experimentation 2:22
antitoxin 2:69
bites and stings 3:300
chemistry 4:324
chlorine 4:400
cirrhosis 4:445
drug 6:277–278
environmental health 7:210–212
food poisoning and infection 8:211
forensic science 8:227
government regulations 19:256
Hamilton, Alice 10:28–29
kidney disease 12:72
lead 12:256
mercury 13:306–307
pesticides 15:197
poison 15:381–382
poison gas 15:382
poisonous plants and animals 15:383–385 *illus.*
pollutants, chemical 15:410–411
red tide 16:114
specializations 19:256
toxic levels 19:256
toxic shock syndrome 19:256
uremia 19:485
venom 19:546
vitamins and minerals 19:618
TOXIN *see* POISON
TOXOPLASMOSIS 19:256
parasitic diseases 15:82
Protozoa 15:580
TOY 19:256–257 *bibliog., illus.*
doll 6:224–225
folk art 8:198
music box 13:669
Nuremberg (West Germany) 14:297
TOY DOG 6:217 *illus.*
affenpinscher 1:132
Brussels griffon 3:527
Chihuahua 4:347
English toy spaniel 7:204–205
Italian greyhound 11:314
Japanese chin 11:379
Maltese 13:95–96 *illus.*
Manchester terrier 13:109
miniature pinscher 13:445
papillon 15:71
Pekingese 15:136–137
pomeranian 15:422–423
poodle 15:429
pug 15:617
shih tzu 17:260–261
silky terrier 17:308–309
Yorkshire terrier 20:331
TOYAH (Texas)
map (31° 19′N 103° 47′W) 19:129
TOYAMA (Japan)
map (36° 41′N 137° 13′E) 11:361
TOYAMA BAY
map (36° 50′N 137° 10′E) 11:361
TOYNBEE, ARNOLD 19:257 *bibliog., illus.*
civilization 5:34
Study of History, A 18:308
TOYOHASHI (Japan)
map (34° 46′N 137° 23′E) 11:361
TOYOTA MOTOR COMPANY
automotive industry 2:367; 2:368
TOYOTOMI HIDEYOSHI *see* HIDEYOSHI
TOZEUR (Tunisia)
map (33° 55′N 8° 8′E) 19:335
TOZZI, FEDERIGO 19:257
TR-1 *see* U-2
TRABEATED SYSTEM OF CONSTRUCTION *see* POST AND LINTEL
TRABZON (Turkey) 19:257
map (41° 0′N 39° 43′E) 19:343
World War I, surrender at 14:466 *illus.*
TRACER
Hevesy, Georg von 10:154
iodine 11:239
nuclear medicine 14:284
radioactive isotope 11:301; 16:61
radiochemistry 16:63
tritium 19:304
TRACHEA 12:209 *illus.*; 19:258
crane (bird) 5:330
respiratory system 16:180 *illus.*
respiratory system disorders 16:181–182
TRACHEOPHYTE 19:258
angiosperm 1:414
cacti and other succulents 4:9–11
conifer 5:189–191
fern 8:56–58
grass 9:295–297
horsetail 10:252–253
plant 15:333–334
shrub 17:288–289
tree 19:286–288
TRACHODON 19:258 *illus.*
TRACHOMA 19:258
Chlamydia 4:400
TRACHYTE 19:258
TRACK DETECTORS
detector, particle 6:133–134
TRACK AND FIELD 19:259–262 *bibliog., illus., tables*
See also RUNNING AND JOGGING
Bannister, Roger 3:71
Beamon, Bob 3:139
Benoit, Joan 3:204
Bikila, Abebe 3:250
Blankers-Koen, Fanny 3:327
Coe, Sebastian 5:90
Commonwealth Games 5:141
Cunningham, Glenn 5:390
decathlon 6:72
Decker, Mary 6:74
Elliott, Herb 7:147
Jenner, Bruce 11:396
Johnson, Rafer 11:435
Keino, Kipchoge 12:37
Lewis, Carl 12:305
marathon 13:143–144
Mathias, Bob 13:228
men's world records 19:261 *table*
Moses, Edwin 13:600
Nurmi, Paavo 14:298
O'Brien, Parry 14:317
Oerter, Al 14:352
Olympic Games 14:382–384 *illus.*
Owens, Jesse 14:472
pentathlon 15:155
Pythian Games 15:640
Richards, Bob 16:211
Rodgers, Bill 16:267
Rono, Henry 16:305
Rudolph, Wilma 16:339
rules and scoring 19:259
Ryun, Jim 16:380
Shorter, Frank 17:284
Snell, Peter 18:3
Thompson, Daley 19:174
Thorpe, Jim 19:180
Viren, Lasse 19:604–605
Warmerdam, Cornelius 20:30
women's world records 19:261 *table*
Zaharias, Babe Didrikson 20:348
Zatopek, Emil 20:356–357
TRACKING STATION 19:262 *bibliog.*
Goldstone Tracking Station 9:236
space exploration 18:122
TRACTOR 19:262 *bibliog.*
Case steam tractor 1:193 *illus.*
plow 15:370
TRACY (California)
map (37° 44′N 121° 25′W) 4:31
TRACY (Minnesota)
map (44° 14′N 95° 37′W) 13:453
TRACY, SPENCER 19:262 *bibliog., illus.*
Hepburn, Katharine 10:131 *illus.*
TRADE *see* FREE TRADE; INTERNATIONAL TRADE
TRADE ASSOCIATIONS 19:262–263 *bibliog.*
special-interest groups 18:167–168
TRADE FAIRS
Leipzig (East Germany) 12:278 *illus.*
machines
engineering 7:178
TRADE JOURNAL *see* PERIODICAL
TRADE REFORM ACT
tariff 19:36
TRADE UNION *see* LABOR UNION
TRADE WINDS 19:263 *bibliog.*
doldrums 6:224
Hadley cell 10:8
high-pressure region 10:162
inversion 11:233–234
ocean currents 14:322
shipping route 17:277
tropical climate 19:307
wind 20:168–170 *illus.*
TRADEMARK 19:263–264 *bibliog.*
Commerce, U.S. Department of 5:138
TRADES UNION CONGRESS 19:264
Labour party 12:156
TRADEWATER RIVER
map (37° 31′N 88° 3′W) 12:47
TRADING COMPANIES
Asia, history of 2:257
Dutch West India Company 6:315
East India Company, British 7:31
East India Company, Dutch 7:31–32
East India Company, French 7:32
Hudson's Bay Company 10:290–291
Monts, Pierre du Gua, Sieur de 13:560
North West Company 14:252–253
Russian-American Company 16:360–361
TRADING STAMPS 19:264 *bibliog.*
TRAER (Iowa)
map (42° 12′N 92° 28′W) 11:244
TRAETTA, TOMMASO
Italian music 11:318
TRAFALGAR, BATTLE OF 14:62 *illus.*; 19:264 *bibliog.*
navy 14:62–63 *illus.*
Nelson, Horatio Nelson, Viscount 14:79–80
TRAFFIC CONTROL 19:264 *bibliog.*
See also OPERATIONS RESEARCH; SYSTEMS ENGINEERING
airport 1:224–225 *illus.*
aviation 2:374–375; 19:264
expressway interchange 19:279 *illus.*
1917 traffic jam 19:279 *illus.*
police 15:396–397
radar 16:38–39 *illus.*
railroads 16:74–76 *illus.*; 19:264
roads and highways 19:264
shipping 19:264
TRAFFIC REPORTING
helicopter 10:112
TRAGACANTH 19:264–265
TRAGEDY (drama) 19:265 *bibliog.*
See also specific literary works, e.g., *FAUST* (poem); *MACBETH* (play); etc.
actors and acting
Booth (family) 3:394
Forrest, Edwin 8:234
Macready, William Charles 13:36
Siddons, Sarah 17:294
drama 6:257–260
English literature
Eliot, T. S. 7:139–140
Shakespeare, William 17:237
French literature
Anouilh, Jean 2:34–35
Corneille, Pierre 5:267–268
German literature
Goethe, Johann Wolfgang von 9:223–224
Schiller, Johann Christoph Friedrich von 17:120–121
Greek literature
Aeschylus 1:128–129
Euripides 7:266
Poetics of Aristotle 15:378
Sophocles 18:67–68
Latin literature
Seneca, Lucius Annaeus 17:200
Spanish literature
Vega, Lope de 19:531
stage, film, radio, television
theater, history of the 19:144
Thespis 19:168
tragicomedy 19:265
TRAGEDY OF KING RICHARD II, THE (play) *see RICHARD II* (play)
TRAGEDY OF KING RICHARD III, THE (play) *see RICHARD III* (play)
TRAGICAL HISTORY OF THE LIFE AND DEATH OF DOCTOR FAUSTUS, THE (play) *see DOCTOR FAUSTUS* (play)
TRAGICOMEDY 19:265 *bibliog.*
comedy 5:132
TRAIGUÉN (Chile)
map (38° 15′S 72° 41′W) 4:355
TRAIL (British Columbia)
map (49° 6′N 117° 42′W) 3:491
TRAIL (county in North Dakota)
map (47° 25′N 97° 10′W) 14:248
TRAIL OF TEARS
Chattanooga (Tennessee) 4:303
TRAILER *see* MOBILE HOME; TRUCKING INDUSTRY
TRAILING ARBUTUS 19:265
TRAIN *see* LOCOMOTIVE; RAILROAD
TRAINI, FRANCESCO 19:266
The Apotheosis of Saint Thomas Aquinas 15:241 *illus.*
TRAIT
personality 15:189
TRAJAN, ARCH OF (Benevento) 16:274 *illus.*
TRAJAN, ROMAN EMPEROR 19:266 *bibliog., illus.*
Column of Trajan 5:129
Hadrian, Roman Emperor 10:8
Ostia 14:458
Rome, ancient 16:303
Timgad 19:203
TRAJAN'S FORUM
forum 8:242
TRAJECTORY *see* BALLISTICS; MOTION, PLANAR
TRAKL, GEORG 19:266
TRALEE (Ireland)
map (52° 16′N 9° 42′W) 11:258
TRAMP STEAMER
freighter 8:301
ship 17:274

TRAMPOLINE *see* GYMNASTICS
TRANCE **19**:266
TRANG (Thailand)
map (7° 33′N 99° 36′E) **19**:139
TRANQUERAS (Uruguay)
map (31° 12′S 55° 45′W) **19**:488
TRANQUILIZER **19**:266 *bibliog.*
drug **6**:276 *illus.*
drug abuse **6**:279
Librium **12**:319
medicinal plants **13**:266
meprobamate **13**:303
psychotropic drugs **15**:604
sleep **17**:360
stress, biological **18**:298
Valium **19**:506
TRANQUILLI, SECONDO *see* SILONE, IGNAZIO
TRANS-ALASKA PIPELINE **1**:247 *illus.*; **19**:266–267 *bibliog.*
caribou **4**:149
pipe and pipeline **15**:311 *illus.*
TRANS-AMAZONIAN HIGHWAY **3**:463 *illus.*; **19**:267
TRANS-ANDINE RAILROAD **19**:267
TRANS-CANADA HIGHWAY **19**:267
TRANS-CASPIAN RAILROAD **19**:267 *bibliog.*
TRANS-SIBERIAN RAILROAD **16**:357 *map*; **19**:267 *bibliog.*
Chinese Eastern Railway **4**:388
TRANSACTINIDE ELEMENTS *see* SUPERHEAVY ELEMENTS
TRANSACTIONAL ANALYSIS **19**:267–268 *bibliog.*
TRANSATLANTIC CABLE *see* ATLANTIC CABLE
TRANSCENDENCE, DIVINE **19**:268
TRANSCENDENTAL FUNCTION **19**:268
Euler, Leonhard **7**:264–265
TRANSCENDENTAL MEDITATION
meditation **13**:275
TRANSCENDENTAL NUMBER **19**:268 *bibliog.*
Gelfond, Aleksandr Osipovich **9**:69
Hermite, Charles **10**:143
irrational number **11**:280
mathematics, history of **13**:226
TRANSCENDENTALISM **19**:267–268 *bibliog.*
American literature **1**:344
Brownson, Orestes **3**:519
Clarke, James Freeman **5**:40
Dial, The **6**:150
Emerson, Ralph Waldo **7**:154–155
Fuller, Margaret **8**:357
Peabody, Elizabeth **15**:122–123
Ripley, George **16**:228
Thoreau, Henry David **19**:178
TRANSCONTINENTAL RAILROAD **19**:268–269 *bibliog.*, *map*
Canada
Canadian Pacific Railway **4**:94
United States **8**:341 *map*
California **4**:37
Chinese Americans **14**:441
Civil War, U.S. **5**:16
Crédit Mobilier of America **5**:336
Huntington (family) **10**:314
Judah, Theodore D. **11**:458
meeting at Promontory Point, Utah **16**:72 *illus.*
United States, history of the **19**:450 *illus.*
Wells, Fargo and Company **20**:101
TRANSDUCER **19**:269
biosensor **3**:276
loudspeaker **12**:421
measurement **13**:256
microphone **13**:386
process control **15**:560–561
strain gauge **18**:288
telemetry **19**:78
thermistor **19**:161
thermocouple **19**:162
TRANSEPT **19**:269
Gothic art and architecture **9**:255
Romanesque art and architecture **16**:282
TRANSFERENCE **19**:269
Freud, Sigmund **8**:329
psychoanalysis **15**:589
TRANSFIGURATION **19**:269
TRANSFINITE NUMBER
Cantor, Georg **4**:118
TRANSFORM FAULT **19**:269–270 *bibliog.*, *illus.*
mid-oceanic ridge **13**:390
plate tectonics **15**:351–352 *map*; **15**:357
structural geology **18**:303
TRANSFORMATION **19**:270 *bibliog.*
matrix **13**:230
TRANSFORMATIONAL GRAMMAR *see* GRAMMAR
TRANSFORMER **19**:270–271 *bibliog.*, *illus.*
electromagnetic induction **7**:115
hydroelectric power **10**:332–335
inductance **11**:151
inductor **11**:152
magnetism **13**:58
TRANSFUSION, BLOOD *see* BLOOD TRANSFUSION
TRANSGRESSION, MARINE **19**:271
Devonian Period **6**:145
plate tectonics **15**:354
TRANSISTOR **19**:271–272 *bibliog.*, *illus.*
amplifier **1**:382
Bardeen, John **3**:80
biosensor **3**:276
bipolar transistor **19**:271–272 *illus.*
Brattain, Walter **3**:439
computer **5**:160b *illus,*; **5**:160c; **5**:160d
electron tube replacement **7**:123
field effect transistor **19**:272 *illus.*
Giaever, Ivar **9**:171
operation and application **19**:271–272
oscillator **14**:453
semiconductor **17**:197
Shockley, William Bradford **17**:279
TRANSIT (artificial satellite) **19**:272 *bibliog.*
space exploration **18**:123
TRANSIT (navigation)
navigation **14**:60
TRANSIT, SURVEYING **19**:273
surveying **18**:367–369 *illus.*
TRANSIT CIRCLE **19**:273 *bibliog.*, *illus.*
Rømer, Ole, inventor **16**:305
TRANSITION ELEMENTS **19**:273–274 *bibliog.*, *table*
actinide series **1**:88
biological occurrence **19**:274
cadmium **4**:12
chromium **4**:419
cobalt **5**:82–83
complexes **19**:274
copper **5**:251–254
electron structure **19**:273 *table*
general properties **19**:273
gold **9**:226
halide minerals **10**:21
inorganic chemistry **11**:182
iridium **11**:266
iron **11**:270–271
lanthanide series **12**:200–201
manganese **13**:114
mercury **13**:306–307
metal **13**:328
molybdenum **13**:514
nickel **14**:183
niobium **14**:200–201
osmium **14**:455
oxidation states **19**:273–274
palladium **15**:48
platinum **15**:359–360
rhenium **16**:193
rhodium **16**:203
ruthenium **16**:375
scandium **17**:114
silver **17**:312–313
tantalum **19**:25
technetium **19**:59
titanium **19**:211
tungsten **19**:333–334
vanadium **19**:516
zinc **20**:367–368
zirconium **20**:370
TRANSITION RITES *see* PASSAGE RITES
TRANSJORDAN *see* JORDAN
TRANSKEI **19**:274 *bibliog.*
cities
Umtata **19**:380
flag **8**:137 *illus.*
map (31° 20′S 29° 0′E) **18**:79
people
Xhosa **20**:312
TRANSLATION (linguistics)
applied linguistics **2**:90
TRANSLATION (mathematics) **19**:274 *bibliog.*
TRANSMIGRATION OF SOULS **19**:274
See also REBIRTH
Hinduism **10**:170
karma **12**:28
Pythagoreans **15**:640
TRANSMISSION, AUTOMOTIVE **19**:275–276 *bibliog.*, *illus.*
automobile **2**:359 *illus.*
clutch **13**:20 *illus.*
internal-combustion engine **11**:218
motorcycle **13**:614
trucking industry **19**:315
TRANSMITTER **19**:276 *bibliog.*
radio **16**:45–46
receiver (communications) **16**:106
telephone **19**:78–80
TRANSMUTATION OF ELEMENTS **19**:276–277
atomic nucleus **2**:310 *illus.*
isotope **11**:301
periodic table **15**:168–169
Walton, Ernest Thomas Sinton **20**:20
TRANSPHASOR (computer term) **5**:160i
TRANSPLANTATION, ORGAN **19**:277 *bibliog.*
See also ARTIFICIAL ORGANS
antigen **2**:62
heart
Barnard, Christiaan **3**:85
heart, artificial **10**:94–95
heart diseases **10**:96
Shumway, Norman Edward **17**:289
immunity **11**:59
immunodeficiency disease **11**:60
Medawar, Peter Brian **13**:263
medicine **13**:272
National Kidney Foundation **14**:34
plastic surgery **15**:347
rejection **19**:277
surgery **18**:362
tissue typing **19**:277
TRANSPORT AND GENERAL WORKERS' UNION **19**:277 *bibliog.*
TRANSPORTATION **19**:278–282 *bibliog.*, *illus.*, *map*
See also names of specific types of transportation, e.g., ICEBREAKER; PIPER CUB (aircraft); STAGECOACH; etc.
air transportation **19**:280–281 *map*
aircraft **1**:210–214
airport **1**:223–225
aviation **2**:370–375
helicopter **10**:112
city **5**:4–6
civil engineering **5**:10
common carrier **5**:138
economic effects **19**:280–281
embargo **7**:151
future **19**:282
history **19**:278–280
industrial archaeology **11**:154
Wells, Fargo and Company **20**:101
hotel **10**:260–261
human ecology **10**:297
land transportation **19**:278
automobile **2**:358–359
automotive industry **2**:363–368
bicycle **3**:244–246
coach and carriage **5**:73–75
railroad **16**:71–77
roads and highways **16**:235–239
sled **17**:359
trucking industry **19**:313–316
wagon **20**:6–7
mass transportation **19**:281–282
bus **3**:583–585
elevated railroad **7**:135–136
streetcar **18**:296–297
subway **18**:317–319
petroleum industry **15**:210–213
political effects **19**:280
social effects **19**:281–282
space transportation **19**:281
aerospace industry **1**:125
technology, history of **19**:65–68
tourism **19**:251–253
United States
Interstate Commerce Commission **11**:225
water transportation **19**:278; **19**:281 *map*
boat and boating **3**:349–352
canal **4**:94–97
ocean and sea **14**:331
ship **17**:263–275
waterway **20**:66
TRANSPORTATION, U.S. DEPARTMENT OF **19**:282 *bibliog.*
Coast Guard, U.S. **5**:80
common carrier **5**:138
Federal Aviation Administration **8**:40
secretary of transportation
flag **8**:148 *illus.*
Washington, D.C. **20**:41 *map*
TRANSPOSING INSTRUMENTS
clarinet **5**:37 *illus.*
TRANSPOSON **19**:282 *bibliog.*
TRANSSEXUALISM
sex reassignment **17**:225
TRANSUBSTANTIATION
Eucharist **7**:262
TRANSURANIUM ELEMENTS **19**:282 *bibliog.*
actinide series **1**:88
americium **1**:368
berkelium **3**:213
californium **4**:38–39
curium **5**:392
einsteinium **7**:94
element 104 **7**:132
element 105 **7**:132
element 106 **7**:132
fermium **8**:56
lawrencium **12**:251
mendelevium **13**:294
neptunium **14**:89
nobelium **14**:211
periodic table **15**:168–169
plutonium **15**:373
Seaborg, Glenn T. **17**:171–172
superheavy elements **18**:351
transmutation of elements **19**:276–277
TRANSVAAL (South Africa) **19**:282–283
cities
Germiston **9**:157
Pretoria **15**:533–534
history
Jameson, Sir Leander Starr **11**:357
Kruger, Paul **12**:131
Pretorius, Andries **15**:534
Pretorius, Marthinus Wessel **15**:534
South African War **18**:83–84 *map*
map (25° 0′S 29° 0′E) **18**:79
people
Ndebele **14**:68
South Africa **18**:82
Witwatersrand **20**:194
TRANSVERSE WAVE *see* WAVES AND WAVE MOTION
TRANSVESTISM **19**:283 *bibliog.*
sex reassignment **17**:225
TRANSYLVANIA (county in North Carolina)
map (35° 10′N 82° 50′W) **14**:242
TRANSYLVANIA (Romania) **16**:287 *illus.*; **19**:283 *bibliog.*, *map*
Báthory (family) **3**:122–123
Bethlen, Gábor, Prince **3**:231
Bocskay, István, Prince **3**:355
cities
Cluj **5**:71
John I, King of Hungary (John Zápolya) **11**:427
John II, King of Hungary (John Sigismund Zápolya) **11**:427
Michael the Brave **13**:372
Romania **16**:290
sheepskin vest **8**:196 *illus.*
Szeklers **18**:416
TRANSYLVANIA COMPANY **19**:283 *bibliog.*
Henderson, Richard **10**:121
TRANSYLVANIAN ALPS
map (45° 30′N 24° 15′E) **16**:288
TRANYLCYROMINE *see* MONOAMINE OXIDASE INHIBITORS
TRAORÉ, MOUSSA
Mali **13**:91
TRAP (geology)
petroleum **15**:208 *illus.*
TRAP DOOR SPIDER **19**:283 *illus.*
TRAPANI (Italy)
map (38° 1′N 12° 31′E) **11**:321
TRAPASSI, PIETRO ANTONIO DOMENICO BONAVENTURA *see* METASTASIO, PIETRO
TRAPEZOID **19**:283–284 *illus.*
TRAPPISTS **19**:284 *bibliog.*
Merton, Thomas **13**:313
TRAPS (music)
drum (musical instrument) **6**:282
TRAPSHOOTING **17**:282
TRASIMENO, LAKE
map (43° 8′N 12° 6′E) **11**:321
TRAUBEL, HELEN **19**:284
TRAUMA *see* WOUNDS AND INJURIES
TRAUN (Austria)
map (48° 13′N 14° 14′E) **2**:348
TRAVEL *see* TOURISM
TRAVEL LITERATURE
authors
Bruce, James **3**:519–520
Doughty, Charles Montagu **6**:246
Durrell, Lawrence **6**:306–307
Polo, Marco **15**:417
Pritchett, V. S. **15**:556
Valle, Pietro della **19**:507
exploration **7**:334
guidebooks

TRAVEL LITERATURE (cont.)
Baedeker, Karl **3**:20
Bishop, Isabella Lucy **3**:297
TRAVELER'S CHECK 19:284
letter of credit **12**:299
negotiable instrument **14**:77
TRAVELER'S-TREE 19:284
TRAVELING-WAVE TUBE 19:284 *bibliog.*
electron tube **7**:124
TRAVELS IN ARABIA DESERTA (book)
Doughty, Charles Montagu **6**:246
TRAVELS OF MARCO POLO, THE (book)
French edition (15th century) **12**:134 *illus.*
Polo, Marco **15**:417
TRAVEN, B. 19:284 *bibliog.*
TRAVERS, MORRIS WILLIAM 19:284
Ramsay, Sir William **16**:81
TRAVERSE
surveying **18**:367
TRAVERSE (county in Minnesota)
map (45° 50′N 96° 25′W) **13**:453
TRAVERSE, LAKE
map (45° 43′N 96° 40′W) **13**:453
TRAVERSE CITY (Michigan)
map (44° 46′N 85° 37′W) **13**:377
TRAVERTINE 19:284 *bibliog.*
calcite **4**:21–22
sinter **17**:325
TRAVESTY *see* BURLESQUE AND TRAVESTY
TRAVIATA, LA (opera) **11**:319 *illus.*; **19**:284–285
Camille (play) **4**:62
TRAVIS (county in Texas)
map (30° 15′N 97° 45′W) **19**:129
TRAVIS, WILLIAM B. 19:285
TRAVNIK (Yugoslavia)
map (44° 14′N 17° 40′E) **20**:340
TRAVOIS 19:285 *bibliog.*
TRAWLER **8**:126–128 *illus.*; **12**:431 *illus.*
TRAY MOUNTAIN
map (34° 48′N 83° 42′W) **9**:114
TRBOVLJE (Yugoslavia)
map (46° 10′N 15° 3′E) **20**:340
TREADMILL 19:285
TREASON 19:285 *bibliog.*
attainder, bill of **2**:313
drawing and quartering **6**:265
TREASURE (county in Montana)
map (46° 15′N 107° 15′W) **13**:547
TREASURE ISLAND (book) **19**:285
Stevenson, Robert Louis **18**:265
TREASURY, U.S. DEPARTMENT OF THE 19:285 *bibliog.*
Comptroller of the Currency, Office of the **5**:159
counterfeiting **5**:312
flag **8**:148 *illus.*
Internal Revenue Service **11**:218
money **13**:527
public health **15**:608
Secret Service **17**:180–181
Secretary of the Treasury *see* articles on specific presidents, e.g., TRUMAN, HARRY S.; WASHINGTON, GEORGE; etc.; names of specific secretaries of the treasury, e.g., DILLON, C. DOUGLAS; MELLON, ANDREW W.; etc.
Washington, D.C. **20**:41 *map*
TREASURY OF MINYAS *see* MINYAS, TREASURY OF
TREATY 19:285–286 *bibliog.*
See also under names of specific treaties, e.g., CAMPO FORMIO, TREATY OF; WESTPHALIA, PEACE OF; etc.
international law **11**:221
president of the United States **15**:523; **15**:527
World War I **20**:244–246 *illus.*
TREBIZOND (Turkey) *see* TRABZON (Turkey)
TREBLE 19:286
TREBLINKA 19:286 *bibliog.*
TREBUCHET **8**:239 *illus.*
fortification **8**:238
TREE 19:286–288 *bibliog., illus.*
See also names of specific trees, e.g., CHESTNUT; JOSHUA TREE (botany); etc.
annual growth cycle **19**:287 *illus.*
arboriculture **2**:110–111
classification and identification **19**:286
factors causing death **19**:288
forestry **8**:230–232
habitat
chaparral **4**:283–284
desert life **6**:130
forest **8**:227–230; **19**:288
mountain life **13**:622
savanna life **17**:97–98
importance of **19**:288
lignin **12**:340
parasitic diseases
mushrooms **13**:660
rings **19**:287
growth **9**:381
shrub **17**:288
structure **19**:286–288 *illus.*
bark **3**:82
wood **20**:205–206
TREE, ELLEN
Kean (family) **12**:35
TREE, SIR HERBERT BEERBOHM 19:288 *bibliog.*
TREE DIAGRAM 19:288–289 *bibliog., illus.*
TREE FROG 19:289 *illus.*
chorus frog **4**:409
Cuban tree frog **5**:380
green tree frog **18**:377 *illus.*
little grass frog **12**:373
TREE OF HEAVEN *see* AILANTHUS
TREE OF KINGS *see* TI
TREE-RING DATING *see* DENDROCHRONOLOGY
TREE SHREW 15:539 *illus.*; **19**:289 *illus.*
TREE SLOTH *see* SLOTH
TREE SNAKE
colubrid **5**:125
TREEHOPPER 19:289–290 *illus.*
TREES (poem)
Kilmer, Joyce **11**:77
TREFOEL, JACQUES
chemistry, history of **4**:329
TREGO (county in Kansas)
map (38° 55′N 99° 55′W) **12**:18
TREINTA Y TRES (Uruguay)
map (33° 14′S 54° 23′W) **19**:488
TREITSCHKE, HEINRICH VON 19:290
TRELEW (Argentina)
map (43° 15′S 65° 18′W) **2**:149
TRELLEBORG (Denmark) **19**:294 *bibliog.*
TRELLEBORG (Sweden)
map (55° 22′N 13° 10′E) **18**:382
TREMATODE
flatworm **8**:156
fluke **8**:186
TREMBLANT, MOUNT
Laurentian Mountains **12**:239
map (46° 16′N 74° 35′W) **16**:18
TREMBLAY, FRANÇOIS LECLERC DU *see* JOSEPH, FATHER
TREMOLITE
amphibole **1**:381
TREMONT (Illinois)
map (40° 28′N 89° 29′W) **11**:42
TREMONT (Pennsylvania)
map (40° 38′N 76° 23′W) **15**:147
TREMONT HOUSE (Boston)
hotel **10**:260
TREMONTON (Utah)
map (41° 43′N 112° 10′W) **19**:492
TREMPEALEAU (Wisconsin)
map (44° 0′N 91° 26′W) **20**:185
TREMPEALEAU (county in Wisconsin)
map (44° 18′N 91° 23′W) **20**:185
TRENCH FEVER 19:290
TRENCH WARFARE
World War I **20**:225 *map*
TRENČÍN (Czechoslovakia)
map (48° 54′N 18° 4′E) **5**:413
TRENT, COUNCIL OF 15:65 *illus.*; **19**:290 *bibliog., illus.*
council, ecumenical **5**:309–310 *illus.*
Counter-Reformation **5**:310–311
Gregory XIII, Pope **9**:357
indulgences **11**:152
mass (musical setting) **13**:201
Pius IV, Pope **15**:322
sequence (music) **17**:207
TRENT, RIVER 19:290
map (53° 42′N 0° 41′W) **19**:403
TRENT, WILLIAM
Trenton (New Jersey) **19**:291
TRENT AFFAIR 19:290–291 *bibliog.*
Civil War, U.S. **5**:31
Mason, James Murray **13**:199
Slidell, John **17**:361
TRENTINO-ALTO ADIGE (Italy) **19**:291
cities
Bolzano **3**:373
TRENTO (Italy)
map (46° 4′N 11° 8′E) **11**:321
TRENTON (Florida)
map (29° 37′N 82° 49′W) **8**:172
TRENTON (Georgia)
map (34° 52′N 85° 31′W) **9**:114
TRENTON (Kentucky)
map (36° 43′N 87° 16′W) **12**:47
TRENTON (Michigan)
map (42° 9′N 83° 11′W) **13**:377
TRENTON (Missouri)
map (40° 5′N 93° 37′W) **13**:476
TRENTON (Nebraska)
map (40° 11′N 101° 1′W) **14**:70
TRENTON (New Jersey) **14**:130 *illus.*; **19**:291
map (40° 13′N 74° 45′W) **14**:129
TRENTON (North Carolina)
map (35° 4′N 77° 21′W) **14**:242
TRENTON (Ontario)
map (44° 6′N 77° 35′W) **14**:393
TRENTON (Tennessee)
map (35° 59′N 88° 56′W) **19**:104
TRENTON, BATTLE OF 19:291 *bibliog.*
American Revolution **1**:358
Washington, George **20**:43
TREPASSEY (Newfoundland)
map (46° 44′N 53° 22′W) **14**:166
TREPHINING
surgery **18**:360 *illus.*
***TREPONEMA* 19**:291
syphilis **18**:410
TRES ARROYOS (Argentina)
map (38° 23′S 60° 17′W) **2**:149
TRES CERROS (Argentina)
map (48° 13′S 67° 33′W) **2**:149
TRES ESQUINAS (Colombia)
map (0° 43′N 75° 16′W) **5**:107
TRES LAGOS (Argentina)
map (49° 37′S 71° 30′W) **2**:149
TRES MARÍAS ISLANDS
map (21° 30′N 106° 30′W) **13**:357
TRES PUNTAS, CAPE
map (47° 6′S 65° 53′W) **2**:149
TRÈS RICHES HEURES DU DUC DE BERRY (book) **3**:384 *illus.*; **7**:284 *illus.*; **11**:48 *illus.*; **12**:343 *illus.*; **13**:394 *illus.*
International Style (Gothic art) **11**:223
TRESAGUET, PIERRE
roads and highways **16**:237 *illus.*
TRESPASS 19:291
tort **19**:246
TREUTLEN (county in Georgia)
map (32° 25′N 82° 35′W) **9**:114
TREVELIN (Argentina)
map (43° 4′S 71° 28′W) **2**:149
TREVELYAN, G. M. 19:291 *bibliog.*
TREVERI
Germanic peoples **9**:138
TRÈVES (West Germany) *see* TRIER (West Germany)
TREVI FOUNTAIN 19:291 *bibliog.*
Salvi, Nicola **17**:40
TREVINO, LEE 19:291
TREVISO (Italy)
map (45° 40′N 12° 15′E) **11**:321
TREVITHICK, RICHARD 19:291 *bibliog.*
Catch-me-who-can (locomotive) **19**:279 *illus.*
steam engine **18**:241 *illus.*
TREVOSE (Pennsylvania)
map (40° 9′N 74° 59′W) **15**:147
TREZEVANT (Tennessee)
map (36° 1′N 88° 37′W) **19**:104
TRI-MOTOR
aviation **2**:370–372 *illus.*
TRIAD (musical scale)
harmony **10**:51–52 *illus.*
TRIAL (law) **19**:291–292 *bibliog.*
adversary procedure **1**:111
advocate **1**:114
court **5**:314–316
court-martial **5**:316
criminal justice **5**:350
defense counsel **6**:83
Ex parte Milligan **7**:325–326
extradition **7**:341
forensic science **8**:227
14th Amendment **8**:254
freedom of the press **8**:297
grand jury **9**:285
incompetence **11**:77
indictment **11**:144
insanity, legal **11**:185
judgment **11**:464
jury **11**:477–478
7th Amendment **17**:219
juvenile delinquency **11**:480
legal aid **12**:272
legal procedure **12**:273
oath **14**:313–314
petit jury **15**:202–203
plea bargaining **15**:364
prosecuting attorney **15**:572
self-incrimination **17**:191
6th Amendment **17**:331
subpoena **18**:316
summons **18**:339
trial by combat **19**:292
TRIAL, THE (book) **19**:292
Kafka, Franz **12**:5–6
TRIAL-AND-ERROR *see* LEARNING THEORY
TRIAL BALANCE *see* BOOKKEEPING
TRIAL BY COMBAT 19:292
duel **6**:293
TRIANGLE (mathematics) **19**:292 *bibliog.*
cosine **5**:280
Euclid **19**:292
non-Euclidean geometry **14**:215–216
polygon **15**:419 *illus.*
right triangle
Pythagoras, theorem of **15**:639
Pythagoras of Samos **15**:639–640; **19**:292
tangent **19**:22
sine **17**:319
spherical trigonometry **18**:180
trigonometry **19**:298
TRIANGLE (music) **13**:675 *illus.*; **19**:292
percussion instruments **15**:162 *illus.*
TRIANGLE (Virginia)
map (38° 33′N 77° 20′W) **19**:607
TRIANGLE SHIRTWAIST CO.
clothing industry **5**:65
Smith, Alfred E. **17**:367
TRIANGLE TRADE
slavery **17**:354–356 *map*
TRIANGULATION
surveying **18**:367–368 *illus.*
TRIANON, TREATY OF
Ruthenia **16**:375
World War I **20**:246
TRIASSIC PERIOD 19:292–295 *bibliog., illus.*
coal and coal mining **5**:76
continents, estimated positions **15**:354 *map*; **19**:295 *map*
crustal movement **19**:293
dinosaurs **6**:179–182
Anchisaurus **1**:399
Plateosaurus **15**:358–359
Podokesaurus **15**:377
Procompsognathus **15**:561
fossil record **8**:246–247
ice sheets **19**:295 *map*
life forms **19**:293–295 *illus.*
Mesozoic Era **13**:322; **19**:292–295
polar wandering **15**:393 *map*
rock formation **19**:295 *map*
sedimentary depositions **19**:292–295
TRIBAL ART *see* PRIMITIVE ARTS
TRIBE 19:295 *bibliog.*
Indians, American **11**:118
powwow **15**:486
moiety **13**:504
primitive societies **15**:546
TRIBOLUMINESCENCE
luminescence **12**:458
TRIBUNE (Kansas)
map (38° 28′N 101° 45′W) **12**:18
TRIBUNES 19:296 *bibliog.*
***TRICERATOPS* 19**:296 *bibliog., illus.*
dinosaur **6**:181
TRICHINOSIS 19:296
diseases, animal **6**:192
TRICHLOROETHYLENE
Regnault, Henri Victor **16**:129
***TRICHOMONAS* 19**:296
TRICHOMONIASIS 19:296
TRICLINIC SYSTEM 19:296
crystal **5**:375 *illus.*
kyanite **12**:143
TRICONODON **13**:102 *illus.*
TRICYCLIC ANTIDEPRESSANTS **2**:60
depression **6**:119
psychotropic drugs **15**:603–605
sedative **17**:182
TRIDENT 19:296–297
rockets and missiles **16**:255
TRIDYMITE
silica minerals **17**:304
TRIER (West Germany) **19**:297
map (49° 45′N 6° 38′E) **9**:140
TRIEST (Italy) *see* TRIESTE (Italy)
TRIESTE (Italy) **19**:297
Istria **11**:308
map (45° 40′N 13° 46′E) **11**:321
TRIFORIUM 19:297
clerestory **5**:51
Gothic art and architecture **9**:256
TRIGEMINAL NERVE
neuralgia **14**:105
TRIGERE, PAULINE
fashion design **8**:32
TRIGG (county in Kentucky)
map (36° 50′N 87° 55′W) **12**:47
TRIGGERFISH 8:116 *illus.*; **19**:297 *bibliog., illus.*
TRIGLAV MOUNTAIN
map (46° 23′N 13° 50′E) **20**:340
TRIGLYCERIDE

fats and oils **8**:34–35
lipid **12**:361–362 *illus.*
nutrition, human **14**:306 *illus.*
TRIGLYPH **2**:131 *illus.*
TRIGONAL SYSTEM
crystal **5**:375 *illus.*
TRIGONOMETRY **19**:298–299 *bibliog., illus.*
algebra **1**:283–285
Cantor, Georg **4**:118
cosine **5**:280
de Moivre, Abraham **6**:62
distance, astronomical **6**:199 *illus.*
Fourier analysis **8**:254
identity **19**:298–299
interpolation **11**:225
logarithm **12**:394
mathematical tables **13**:221
mathematics **13**:222
mathematics, history of **13**:223–224
Napier, John **14**:14
periodic function **15**:166
polar coordinates **19**:298
ratios **19**:298
secant **17**:178
sine **17**:319
spherical trigonometry **18**:180
tangent **19**:22
transcendental function **19**:268
trigonometric functions **19**:298
Viète, François **19**:580
TRIIODOTHYRONINE
endocrine system, diseases of the **7**:169
thyroid gland **19**:188
thyroxine **19**:188
TRÍKALA (Greece)
map (39° 34′N 21° 46′E) **9**:325
TRIKORA PEAK
map (4° 15′S 138° 45′E) **11**:147
TRILATERAL COMMISSION
Brzezinski, Zbigniew **3**:530
TRILBY (book)
du Maurier, George **6**:286
TRILL (music) **19**:299 *bibliog.*
TRILLING, LIONEL **19**:299 *bibliog.*
TRILOBITE **19**:299 *bibliog., illus.*
Cambrian Period **4**:51
fossil record **8**:244 *illus.*
Ordovician Period **14**:422 *illus.*
paleoecology **15**:34–35 *illus.*
Paleozoic Era **15**:43
Silurian Period **17**:310 *illus.*
TRILOPHODON **7**:134 *illus.*
TRIMARAN
catamaran **4**:199–200
TRIMBLE (county in Kentucky)
map (38° 37′N 85° 20′W) **12**:47
TRIMONT (Minnesota)
map (43° 45′N 94° 45′W) **13**:453
TRINCOMALEE (Sri Lanka) **19**:299–300
climate **18**:206 *table*
map (8° 34′N 81° 14′E) **18**:206
TRINH (dynasty)
Vietnam **19**:583
TRINIDAD (Bolivia)
map (14° 47′S 64° 47′W) **3**:366
TRINIDAD (Colorado)
map (37° 10′N 104° 31′W) **5**:116
TRINIDAD (Cuba)
map (21° 48′N 79° 59′W) **5**:377
TRINIDAD (Paraguay)
map (27° 7′S 55° 47′W) **15**:77
TRINIDAD (Uruguay)
map (33° 32′S 56° 54′W) **19**:488
TRINIDAD AND TOBAGO **19**:300 *bibliog., illus., map, table*
calypso **4**:49
cities
Port of Spain **15**:443
flag **19**:300 *illus.*
history and government **19**:300
Williams, Eric **20**:159
land, people, and economy **19**:300
literature
Naipaul, V. S. **14**:8
Walcott, Derek **20**:9
map (11° 0′N 61° 0′W) **20**:109
TRINITY **19**:300–301 *bibliog.*
Callistus I, Pope **4**:46
Holy Spirit **10**:211
Sabellianism **17**:5
Servetus, Michael **17**:211
Socinianism **18**:26
TRINITY (county in California)
map (40° 40′N 123° 5′W) **4**:31
TRINITY (county in Texas)
map (31° 7′N 95° 10′W) **19**:129
TRINITY BAY
map (48° 0′N 53° 40′W) **14**:166
TRINITY CHURCH (Boston)
cathedrals and churches **4**:208
TRINITY CHURCH (New York City)
Upjohn, Richard **19**:471
TRINITY COLLEGE (Dublin) **19**:301
TRINITY COLLEGE (Hartford, Conn.) **19**:301
TRINITY COLLEGE (Washington, D.C.) **19**:301
TRINITY COLLEGE (Cambridge University) **4**:53
TRINITY COLLEGE (Oxford University) **14**:474
TRINITY HALL (Cambridge University) **4**:53
TRINITY MOUNTAINS
map (41° 0′N 122° 30′W) **4**:31
TRINITY RIVER (California)
map (41° 11′N 123° 42′W) **4**:31
TRINITY RIVER (Texas)
map (29° 47′N 94° 42′W) **19**:129
TRIODE **19**:301 *bibliog., illus.*
De Forest, Lee, inventor **6**:58; **19**:301
electron tube **7**:122
grid **9**:361
vacuum tube **19**:502
TRIOLET (Mauritius)
map (20° 3′S 57° 32′E) **13**:237
TRION (Georgia)
map (34° 33′N 85° 19′W) **9**:114
TRIOSON, ANNE LOUIS GIRODET- *see* GIRODET-TRIOSON, ANNE LOUIS
TRIPARTITE PACT
World War II **20**:255–256
TRIPITAKA
Buddhist sacred literature **3**:543
TRIPLE ALLIANCE **19**:301–302 *bibliog.*
TRIPLE ALLIANCE (1668)
Devolution, War of **6**:143
Temple, Sir William (essayist) **19**:100
Triple Alliance **19**:301
TRIPLE ALLIANCE (1717)
Triple Alliance **19**:302
TRIPLE ALLIANCE (1788)
Triple Alliance **19**:302
TRIPLE ALLIANCE (1882)
Europe, history of **7**:293–294
Triple Alliance **19**:302
Triple Entente **19**:302
World War I **20**:219
TRIPLE ALLIANCE, WAR OF THE (1865–1870) **19**:302 *bibliog.*
López, Francisco Solano **12**:412
TRIPLE CROWN (horse racing)
horse racing **10**:248–249 *table*
Kentucky Derby **12**:52
TRIPLE ENTENTE **19**:302 *bibliog.*
Delcassé, Théophile **6**:92
Edward VII, King of England, Scotland, and Ireland **7**:69
Europe, history of **7**:293–294 *map*
Holstein, Friedrich von **10**:208
Iran **11**:253
Triple Alliance **19**:302
World War I **20**:219
TRIPLE POINT **19**:302 *bibliog.*
phase equilibrium **15**:223
TRIPOLI (Lebanon) **19**:302
map (34° 26′N 35° 51′E) **12**:265
TRIPOLI (Libya) **19**:302
climate **12**:320 *table*
map (32° 54′N 13° 11′E) **12**:320
Tripolitan War **19**:302–303
TRIPOLITAN WAR **19**:302–303 *bibliog., illus.*
Barbary States **3**:76
Decatur, Stephen **6**:72–73
Preble, Edward **15**:491
TRIPOLITANIA (region in Libya)
map (31° 0′N 15° 0′E) **12**:320
TRIPP (South Dakota)
map (43° 13′N 97° 58′W) **18**:103
TRIPP (county in South Dakota)
map (43° 22′N 99° 55′W) **18**:103
TRIPURA (India) **19**:303
map (24° 0′N 92° 0′E) **11**:80
TRIREME *see* GALLEY
TRISOMY *see* DOWN'S SYNDROME
TRISSINO, GIANGIORGIO **19**:303
TRIST, NICHOLAS P.
Guadalupe Hidalgo, Treaty of **9**:385
Mexican War **13**:354; **13**:355
Polk, James K. **15**:405
TRISTAN DA CUNHA ISLANDS **19**:303
TRISTAN AND ISOLDE **19**:303
Gottfried von Strassburg **9**:263–264
TRISTAN AND ISOLDE (opera) **19**:303 *bibliog.*
TRISTRAM SHANDY (book) **19**:304 *bibliog.*
Sterne, Laurence **18**:261
TRITEMNODON **13**:102 *illus.*
TRITHEMIUS, JOHANNES
cryptology **5**:371–372
TRITICALE **9**:348 *illus.*
TRITIUM **19**:304
bomb, hydrogen bomb **10**:339
fusion, nuclear **8**:381 *illus.*
hydrogen **10**:337
isotope **11**:301
radiometric age-dating **16**:67
TRITON (astronomy) **18**:49 *illus.*
Lassell, William **12**:214
Neptune (planet) **14**:88–89
TRITON (mythology) **19**:304
TRITON (physics)
fusion, nuclear **8**:381–382
TRIUMPH OF THE REPUBLIC
Dalou, Aimé Jules **6**:14
TRIUMPHAL ARCH **19**:304
See also names of specific arches, e.g., ARC DE TRIOMPHE DE L'ÉTOILE
Roman art and architecture **16**:273–274
sculpture **17**:161
TRIUMPHAL COLUMN
See also names of specific columns, e.g., COLUMN OF TRAJAN
sculpture **17**:161
TRIUMVIRATE **19**:304
First Triumvirate
Caesar, Gaius Julius **4**:14
Cato, Marcus Porcius (Cato the Younger) **4**:213
Crassus, Marcus Licinius **5**:332
Pompey the Great **15**:425
Rome, ancient **16**:301
Second Triumvirate
Antony, Mark **2**:70–71
Augustus, Roman Emperor **2**:321–322
Lepidus, Marcus Aemilius **12**:295
TRIVANDRUM (India) **11**:83 *illus.*
map (8° 29′N 76° 55′E) **11**:80
TRIVIAL PURSUIT (game) **9**:30
TRNAVA (Czechoslovakia)
map (48° 23′N 17° 35′E) **5**:413
TROBRIAND ISLANDERS **19**:304 *bibliog.*
Kula Ring **12**:135
magic **13**:49–50
Malinowski, Bronislaw **13**:91
TROCHEE
versification **19**:563
TROCHU (Alberta)
map (51° 50′N 113° 13′W) **1**:256
TROELTSCH, ERNST **19**:304 *bibliog.*
TROGLOBITES
cave **4**:222
TROGON **3**:281 *illus.*; **19**:304
quetzal **16**:23–24
TROIKA (sled) **19**:305
TROILUS AND CRESSIDA
Benoît de Sainte-More **3**:204
TROILUS AND CRESSIDA (play) **19**:305
TROILUS AND CRISEYDE (poem)
Chaucer, Geoffrey **4**:304
TROIS FRÈRES, LES **19**:305 *bibliog.*
TROIS-RIVIÈRES (Quebec) **19**:305
map (46° 21′N 72° 33′W) **16**:18
TROJAN WAR **19**:305 *bibliog.*
Achilles **1**:82
Agamemnon **1**:182
Aphrodite **2**:78
Clytemnestra **5**:73
Greece, ancient **9**:329
Hector **10**:104
Helen of Troy **10**:110
Idomeneus **11**:31–32
Iliad **11**:40
Menelaus **13**:297
Odysseus **14**:350–351
Palamedes **15**:29–30
Paris (mythology) **15**:87
Priam **15**:534
Troy (archaeological site) **19**:312
TROJAN WOMEN, THE (play) **19**:305
Euripides **7**:266
TROJANS (asteroids) **19**:305
libration **12**:319
three-body problem **19**:181
TROLL *see* FAIRY
TROLLEY CAR *see* STREETCAR
TROLLOPE, ANTHONY **7**:199 *illus.*; **19**:305–306 *bibliog., illus.*
TROLLOPE, FRANCES **19**:306
TROMBETAS RIVER
map (1° 55′S 55° 35′W) **3**:460
TROMBIDIASIS *see* SCRUB ITCH
TROMBONCINO, BARTOLOMEO
Renaissance music **16**:156
TROMBONE **13**:676 *illus.*; **19**:306 *bibliog., illus.*
sackbut **17**:7
wind instruments **20**:170 *illus.*
TROMP (family) **19**:306 *bibliog.*
TROMPE L'OEIL *see* ILLUSIONISM
TROMSØ (Norway)
climate **14**:261 *table*
map (69° 40′N 18° 58′E) **14**:261
TRON (film) **4**:433 *illus.*
TRONA (California)
map (35° 45′N 117° 23′W) **4**:31
TRONADOR, MOUNT
map (41° 10′S 71° 54′W) **4**:355
TRONDHEIM (Norway) **19**:306
map (63° 25′N 10° 25′E) **14**:261
TROPE
figures of speech **8**:76
TROPHOBLAST (embryology)
development **6**:140; **6**:141 *illus.*
TROPIC BIRD **19**:306–307 *illus.*
TROPIC OF CANCER (book) **19**:307
Miller, Henry **13**:427
TROPIC OF CANCER (zone) **19**:307
TROPIC OF CAPRICORN **19**:307
TROPICAL CLIMATE **19**:307 *bibliog.*
climax community **5**:59
cyclone and anticyclone **5**:406
deciduous plant **6**:73
Eocene flora and fauna **19**:124 *illus.*
grasslands **9**:300–301
inversion **11**:234
jet stream **11**:408
jungle and rain forest **11**:468–470 *map*
lagoon **12**:166
laterite **12**:215
monsoon **19**:307
soil distribution, worldwide **18**:37 *map*
trade winds **19**:307
weather forecasting **20**:79
TROPICAL DISEASES
amebiasis **1**:326
filariasis **8**:78
Laboratory, Pasteur Institute **15**:108
malaria **13**:79–80
trypanosomiasis **19**:322
yaws **20**:320
yellow fever **20**:322
TROPICAL EASTERLIES *see* TRADE WINDS
TROPICAL FISH **19**:307 *bibliog., illus.*
See also names of specific fish, e.g., GOLDFISH; GURNARD; FLYING FISH; etc.
TROPICAL FRUIT **19**:308–309 *bibliog.*
avocado **2**:376
banana **3**:59–60
breadfruit **3**:467–468
citrus fruits **4**:447–448
coconut **5**:88
custard apple **5**:397
guava **9**:390
litchi **12**:367–368
longan **12**:407
mango **13**:115
mangosteen **13**:115
papaya **15**:67–68
pineapple **15**:306
TROPICAL RAIN FOREST *see* JUNGLE AND RAIN FOREST
TROPICAL YEAR **19**:309
calendar **4**:27
TROPISM **19**:309–310 *bibliog., illus.*
auxin **2**:369
chemotropism **19**:310
geotropism **19**:310 *illus.*
hydrotropism **19**:309
photoropism **19**:309–310 *illus.*
thigmotropism **19**:310 *illus.*
TROPOPAUSE **19**:310
inversion **11**:234
TROPOSPHERE **19**:310
cirrus clouds **4**:445
cloud **5**:68
cumulus clouds **5**:388
fallout **8**:14
global wind pattern
Hadley cell **10**:8
jet stream **11**:407–408
squall and squall line **18**:201–202
TROPPAU, CONGRESS OF
Congress system **5**:187–188
TROT (horse)
riding **16**:217 *illus.*
TROTSKY, LEON **19**:310–311 *bibliog., illus.*
Socialist Workers' party **18**:26
Stalin, Joseph **18**:214
and Stalinism **5**:147
World War I **20**:238
TROTTER **19**:311
horse racing **10**:247–248 *illus.*
TROTWOOD (Ohio)
map (39° 48′N 84° 18′W) **14**:357
TROUBADOURS *see* MINSTRELS, MINNESINGERS, AND TROUBADOURS
TROUP (county in Georgia)
map (33° 5′N 85° 0′W) **9**:114
TROUP (Texas)
map (32° 9′N 95° 7′W) **19**:129
TROUSDALE (county in Tennessee)
map (36° 25′N 86° 10′W) **19**:104

TROUT 8:121–122 *illus.*; 19:311–312 *bibliog., illus.*
char 4:285–286 *illus.*
TROUT CREEK (Michigan)
map (46° 28′N 89° 1′W) 13:377
TROUT-PERCH 19:312 *illus.*
TROUT RIVER (Newfoundland)
map (49° 29′N 58° 8′W) 14:166
TROUTVILLE (Virginia)
map (37° 25′N 79° 53′W) 19:607
TROUVÈRES *see* MINSTRELS, MINNESINGERS, AND TROUBADOURS
TROVA, ERNEST 19:312 *bibliog.*
TROVATORE, IL (opera) 19:312
TROVER 19:312
TROY (Alabama)
map (31° 48′N 85° 58′W) 1:234
TROY (archaeological site) 19:312–313 *bibliog., illus.*
archaeology 2:121–122
Dörpfeld, Wilhelm 6:243
Schliemann, Heinrich 17:126–127
TROY (Idaho)
map (46° 44′N 116° 46′W) 11:26
TROY (Indiana)
map (38° 0′N 86° 49′W) 11:111
TROY (Kansas)
map (39° 47′N 95° 5′W) 12:18
TROY (Missouri)
map (38° 59′N 90° 59′W) 13:476
TROY (Montana)
map (48° 28′N 115° 53′W) 13:547
TROY (New Hampshire)
map (42° 50′N 72° 11′W) 14:123
TROY (New York) 19:313
map (42° 43′N 73° 40′W) 14:149
TROY (North Carolina)
map (35° 22′N 79° 53′W) 14:242
TROY (Ohio)
map (40° 2′N 84° 13′W) 14:357
TROY (Pennsylvania)
map (41° 47′N 76° 47′W) 15:147
TROY (Tennessee)
map (36° 20′N 89° 10′W) 19:104
TROY PEAK
map (38° 19′N 115° 30′W) 14:111
TROY WEIGHT
weights and measures 20:93–94 *table*
TROYES (France) 19:313
map (48° 18′N 4° 5′E) 8:260
Rayonnant style 16:98
TROYES, TREATY OF (1420)
Henry V, King of England 10:125–126
TROYON, CONSTANT 19:313
TRST (Italy) *see* TRIESTE (Italy)
TRUBAR, PRIMOŽ
Yugoslavia 20:342
TRÜBNER, WILHELM 19:313 *bibliog.*
TRUCHAS (New Mexico)
map (36° 3′N 105° 49′W) 14:136
TRUCHAS PEAK
map (35° 58′N 105° 39′W) 14:136
TRUCIAL STATES *see* UNITED ARAB EMIRATES
TRUCK *see* TRUCKING INDUSTRY
TRUCKING INDUSTRY 19:313–316 *bibliog., table*
carrier classification 19:314
containerization 5:227
history 19:314
labor union
Teamsters, Chauffeurs, Warehousemen, and Helpers of America, International Brotherhood of 19:58
revenues 19:316
tractor 19:262
truck and bus registration by country 19:315 *table*
truck parts and systems 19:315–316
truck types 19:315
weight limits and taxes 19:315
TRUDEAU, GARRY 19:316
TRUDEAU, PIERRE ELLIOTT 19:316 *bibliog., illus.*
Canada, history of 4:87
Liberal parties 12:311
TRUE TULIP SHELL 17:251 *illus.*
TRUFFAUT, FRANÇOIS 19:316–317 *bibliog., illus.*
Wild Child, The
feral children 8:51
TRUFFLE 19:317 *bibliog.*
fungi 8:368
TRUJILLO (Peru)
map (8° 7′S 79° 2′W) 15:193
TRUJILLO (Venezuela)
map (9° 22′N 70° 26′W) 19:542
TRUJILLO, RAFAEL 19:317 *bibliog.*
TRUK (Caroline Islands)
United States outlying territories 19:464
World War II 20:276
TRULLI 10:268 *illus.*
TRULY, RICHARD H.
Space Shuttle 18:136
TRUMAN, HARRY S. 15:530 *illus.*; 19:317–319 *bibliog., illus.*
cold war 5:98
Democratic party 6:101–102 *illus.*
early life and career 19:317
Fair Deal 8:8–9
Independence (Missouri) 11:78
Korean War 12:120–122
MacArthur, Douglas 13:5; 15:523 *illus.*
Marshall, George C. 13:172
Pendergast, Thomas Joseph 15:142
Point Four Program 15:381
United States, history of the 19:455–457 *illus.*
Vietnam War 19:584
World War II 20:279–280 *illus., illus.*
TRUMAN DOCTRINE
cold war 5:98
foreign aid 8:224
United States, history of the 19:456
TRUMANN (Arkansas)
map (35° 41′N 90° 31′W) 2:166
TRUMANSBURG (New York)
map (42° 33′N 76° 40′W) 14:149
TRUMBALL (county in Ohio)
map (41° 14′N 80° 52′W) 14:357
TRUMBO, DALTON
Hollywood Ten, The 10:204
TRUMBULL (Connecticut)
map (41° 15′N 73° 12′W) 5:193
TRUMBULL, JOHN 19:319 *bibliog., illus.*
The Battle of Bunker's Hill 19:319 *illus.*
The Death of General Mercer at the Battle of Princeton 19:441 *illus.*
Declaration of Independence (painting) 1:357 *illus.*
Yorktown surrender (painting) 1:363 *illus.*
TRUMBULL, JONATHAN 19:319 *bibliog.*
TRUMBULL, LYMAN 19:319 *bibliog.*
TRUMBULL, MOUNT
map (36° 25′N 113° 10′W) 2:160
TRUMPET 13:676 *illus.*; 19:319–320 *bibliog., illus.*
See also CORNET
African music 1:169
Armstrong, Louis 2:179
tuba 19:326
wind instruments 20:170 *illus.*
TRUMPET CREEPER (botany) 19:320
TRUMPETER (bird) 19:320
TRUMPLER, ROBERT JULIUS 19:320
TRUNDHOLM SUN CHARIOT 3:506 *illus.*
TRUNKFISH *see* BOXFISH
TRURO (Nova Scotia)
map (45° 22′N 63° 16′W) 14:269
TRUSS 19:320 *illus.*
bridge (engineering) 3:483 *table*
TRUSSVILLE (Alabama)
map (33° 38′N 86° 37′W) 1:234
TRUST 19:321 *bibliog.*
inheritance 11:177
trustee 19:321–322
TRUST TERRITORY 19:321 *bibliog.*
mandate system 13:111
territory 19:122
United Nations 19:413
TRUST TERRITORY OF THE PACIFIC ISLANDS (U.S.) *see* PACIFIC ISLANDS, TRUST TERRITORY OF THE
TRUSTEE 19:321–322 *bibliog.*
TRUSTEESHIP COUNCIL (UN)
United Nations 19:413
TRUTH, SOJOURNER 19:322 *bibliog., illus.*
TRUTH-IN-TESTING LAWS
educational measurement 7:66
TRUTH OR CONSEQUENCES (hot springs) (New Mexico)
map (33° 8′N 107° 15′W) 14:136
TRUTH SERUM
sedative 17:182
TRYON (Nebraska)
map (41° 33′N 100° 57′W) 14:70
TRYON, WILLIAM
New Haven (Connecticut) 14:126
North Carolina 14:244 *illus.*; 14:246
TRYPANOSOMA
Protozoa 15:580
TRYPANOSOMIASIS 19:322 *bibliog.*
African sleeping sickness 19:322
assassin bug 2:264
cause
Hemiptera 10:119
tsetse fly 19:323
Chagas's disease 19:322
diseases, animal 6:190
parasitic diseases 19:322
protozoal diseases 15:581; 19:322
TRYPTOPHANE
Hopkins, Sir Frederick Gowland 10:231
TSAI LUN (Zai Lun)
paper 15:68
TSAIDAM BASIN
map (37° 0′N 95° 0′E) 4:362
TSANGPO RIVER
Brahmaputra River 3:440
TS'AO CHAN *see* TS'AO HSÜEH-CH'IN (Cao Xueqin)
TS'AO CHIH (Cao Zhi) 19:322
TS'AO HSÜEH-CH'IN (Cao Xueqin) 19:322
Dream of the Red Chamber, The 6:266
TS'AO TS'AO (Cao Cao)
Chinese literature 4:389
TS'AO YÜ (Cao Yu) 19:322
Chinese literature 4:390
TSARATANANA MOUNTAINS
map (14° 0′S 49° 0′E) 13:38
TSARSKOYE SELO (USSR) *see* PUSHKIN (USSR)
TSATCHELA *see* COLORADO (American Indians)
TSCHERMAK VON SEYSENEGG, ERICH
biology 3:271
Mendel, Gregor Johann 13:294
TSCHERNOZEM *see* CHERNOZEM
TSE-THANG (China)
map (29° 16′N 91° 46′E) 19:190
TSEDENBAL, YUMZHAGIYEN 19:322
TSELINOGRAD (USSR)
map (51° 10′N 71° 30′E) 19:388
TSENG KUO-FAN (Zeng Guofan) 19:322–323 *bibliog.*
TSETSE FLY 19:323 *bibliog., illus.*
diseases, animal 6:190
life cycle 19:323 *illus.*
protozoal diseases 15:581
TSÉVIÉ (Togo)
map (6° 25′N 1° 13′E) 19:222
TSH *see* THYROID-STIMULATING HORMONE
TSHABONG (Botswana)
climate 3:417 *table*
TSHAKA *see* SHAKA, KING OF THE ZULUS
TSHOKOHA-SUD, LAKE
map (2° 25′S 30° 5′E) 3:582
TSHOMBE, MOISE KAPENDA 19:323 *bibliog., illus.*
Congo crisis 5:183
Lunda 12:462
TSIMIHETY (tribe)
Madagascar 13:38
TSIMSHIAN (American Indians) 19:323–324 *bibliog.*
Carrier Indians 4:168
Indians of North America, art of the 11:139
potlatch 15:467
totem 19:249; 20:208 *illus.*
TSIN (dynasties) *see* CHIN (Jin)
TSINAN (Jinan) (China) 19:324
map (36° 40′N 116° 57′E) 4:362
TSINGHAI (Qinghai) (China) 19:324
TSINGTAO (Qingdao) (China) 19:324
map (36° 6′N 120° 19′E) 4:362
TSINLING MOUNTAINS
map (34° 0′N 108° 0′E) 4:362
TSIOLKOVSKY, KONSTANTIN 19:324 *bibliog., illus.*
rocket 16:252 *illus.*
TSIRANANA, PHILIBERT
Madagascar 13:39
TSO TSUNG-T'ANG (Zuo Zongtang) 19:324
TSONGA *see* THONGA
TSU ISLANDS
map (34° 30′N 129° 22′E) 11:361
TSUBOUCHI SHOYO 19:324–325
TSUGARU STRAIT
map (41° 35′N 141° 0′E) 11:361
TSUKUBA (Japan) 19:325
TSUMEB (Namibia)
climate 14:11 *table*
map (19° 13′S 17° 42′E) 14:10
TSUN-I (China)
map (27° 39′N 106° 57′E) 4:362
TSUNAMI 19:325 *bibliog.*
earthquakes 7:27
floods and flood control 8:166–167
water wave 20:57
TSURUYA NAMBOKU
Kabuki 12:4
TSUSHIMA, BATTLE OF 19:325
TSUTSUGAMUSHI FEVER *see* SCRUB TYPHUS
TSWANA 19:325 *bibliog.*
Bophuthatswana 3:395
Botswana 3:416–417
San 17:49–50
TU FU (Du Fu) 19:325
TU KIU *see* GÖK TÜRK
TUAL (Indonesia)
map (5° 40′S 132° 45′E) 11:147
TUAMOTU ISLANDS
French Polynesia 8:321–322
map (19° 0′S 142° 0′W) 14:334
TUAREG 3:207 *illus.*; 19:325–326 *bibliog., illus.*
TUASIVI (Western Samoa)
map (13° 40′S 172° 7′W) 20:117
TUATARA 16:167 *illus.*; 19:326 *illus.*
Triassic Period 19:294 *illus.*
TUATHA DÉ DANANN (Celtic demigods)
mythology 13:703
TUBA 13:676 *illus.*; 19:326 *bibliog., illus.*
wind instruments 20:170 *illus.*
TUBA CITY (Arizona)
map (36° 8′N 111° 14′W) 2:160
TUBAC (Arizona)
map (31° 37′N 111° 3′W) 2:160
TUBAN (Indonesia)
map (6° 54′S 112° 3′E) 11:147
TUBE
cathode-ray tube 4:211
electron tube 7:122–124
traveling-wave tube 19:284
vacuum tube 19:502
X-ray tube 20:309
TUBER 19:326
TUBERCULIN TEST 19:326–327
TUBERCULOSIS 19:327 *bibliog., illus.*
diagnostic tests
tuberculin test 19:326–327
Wassermann, August von 20:46
diseases, animal 6:190; 6:192
figwort 8:76
fungus diseases 8:369
mycobacterium 13:690
Koch, Robert 12:104
respiratory system disorders 16:181
sanitoriums
infectious diseases 11:168
silicosis 17:306
spine (backbone)
Pott's disease 15:473
splenomegaly 18:191
spondylitis 18:192
ulcer 19:376
TUBEROSE 19:327 *illus.*
TÜBINGEN (Germany, East and West)
map (48° 31′N 9° 2′E) 9:140
TUBMAN, HARRIET 19:327–328 *bibliog., illus.*
TUBMAN, WILLIAM V. S. 19:328 *bibliog.*
TUBOCURARE
curare 5:390–391
TUBUAI ISLANDS
French Polynesia 8:321–322
map (23° 0′S 150° 0′W) 14:334
TUBULIDENTATA 19:328
mammal 13:103–104 *illus.*
TUBULIN
biological locomotion 3:265
TUC D'AUDOUBERT (France) CAVE ART 15:507 *illus.*
TUCACAS (Venezuela)
map (10° 48′N 68° 19′W) 19:542
TUCKAHOE RIVER
map (39° 17′N 74° 39′W) 14:129
TUCKER (county in West Virginia)
map (39° 5′N 79° 35′W) 20:111
TUCKER, RICHARD 19:328
TUCKER, SOPHIE
music hall, vaudeville, and burlesque 13:672
TUCKERMAN (Arkansas)
map (35° 44′N 91° 12′W) 2:166
TUCKERNUCK ISLAND
map (41° 18′N 70° 15′W) 13:206
TUCKERS TOWN (Bermuda)
map (32° 22′N 64° 40′W) 3:219
TUCKERTON (New Jersey)
map (39° 36′N 74° 20′W) 14:129
TUCSON (Arizona) 19:328
map (32° 13′N 110° 58′W) 2:160
TUCUMÁN (Argentina) 19:328
map (26° 49′S 65° 13′W) 2:149
TUCUMÁN (province in Argentina)
map (27° 0′S 65° 30′W) 2:149
TUCUMCARI (New Mexico)
map (35° 10′N 103° 44′W) 14:136

TUCUPITA (Venezuela)
map (9° 4′N 62° 3′W) **19**:542
TUCURUÍ (Brazil)
map (3° 42′S 49° 27′W) **3**:460
TUDMUR (PALMYRA) (Syria)
map (34° 33′N 38° 17′E) **18**:412
TUDOR (dynasty) **19**:328 *bibliog.*
Elizabeth I, Queen of England **7**:141–142
Henry VII, King of England **10**:126
Henry VIII, King of England **10**:126
Mary I, Queen of England **13**:185–186
York (dynasty) **20**:330
TUDOR, ANTONY **19**:328–329 *bibliog.*
American Ballet Theatre **1**:337
choreography **4**:409
TUDOR, DAVID
happenings **10**:41
TUDOR STYLE **19**:329 *bibliog.*
Hampton Court **10**:33
house (in Western architecture) **10**:266–267 *illus.*
interior design **11**:212 *illus.*
TUESDAY
calendar **4**:28
TUFA *see* SINTER
TUFF **19**:329
rhyolite **16**:204
rock **16**:247
TUFTS UNIVERSITY **19**:329
TUG FORK RIVER
map (38° 6′N 82° 36′W) **20**:111
TUGBOAT **3**:81 *illus.*; **19**:329 *bibliog.*
TUGHRA
calligraphy **4**:46 *illus.*
TUGUEGARAO (Philippines)
map (17° 37′N 121° 44′E) **15**:237
TUGWELL, REXFORD G. **19**:329 *bibliog.*
Roosevelt, Franklin Delano **16**:308
TUILERIES **19**:329
Palissy, Bernard **15**:47
TUKTOYAKTUK (Northwest Territories)
map (69° 27′N 133° 2′W) **14**:258
TULA (Mexico) **19**:329–330 *bibliog.*
Mexico, history of **13**:362
pre-Columbian art and architecture **15**:497
Toltec **19**:229
Xochicalco **20**:313
TULA (USSR)
map (54° 12′N 37° 37′E) **19**:388
TULANCINGO (Mexico)
map (20° 5′N 98° 22′W) **13**:357
TULANE UNIVERSITY **19**:330
TULARE (California)
map (36° 13′N 119° 21′W) **4**:31
TULARE (county in California)
map (36° 10′N 118° 45′W) **4**:31
TULARE (South Dakota)
map (44° 44′N 98° 31′W) **18**:103
TULAREMIA **19**:330
deerfly **6**:81
TULAROSA (New Mexico)
map (33° 4′N 106° 1′W) **14**:136
TULCÁN (Ecuador)
map (0° 48′N 77° 43′W) **7**:52
TULCEA (Romania)
map (45° 11′N 28° 48′E) **16**:288
TULE SPRINGS (Nevada)
archaeology **2**:117 *illus.*
TULÉAR (Madagascar)
map (23° 21′S 43° 40′E) **13**:38
TULELAKE (California)
map (41° 57′N 121° 29′W) **4**:31
TULIA (Texas)
map (34° 32′N 101° 46′W) **19**:129
TULIP **19**:330 *illus.*
Leiden (Netherlands) **12**:277
Michigan **13**:380 *illus.*
Netherlands **14**:102 *illus.*
wild tulip **18**:257 *illus.*
TULIP TREE **19**:330 *illus.*
TULL, JETHRO **19**:330–331 *bibliog.*, *illus.*
TULLAHOMA (Tennessee)
map (35° 22′N 86° 11′W) **19**:104
TULLAMORE (Ireland)
map (53° 16′N 7° 30′W) **11**:258
TULLOS (Louisiana)
map (31° 49′N 92° 19′W) **12**:430
TULSA (Oklahoma) **14**:370 *illus.*; **19**:331
map (36° 9′N 95° 58′W) **14**:368
TULSA (county in Oklahoma)
map (36° 10′N 95° 55′W) **14**:368
TULUÁ (Colombia)
map (4° 6′N 76° 11′W) **5**:107
TULUM (Mexico)
map (20° 13′N 87° 28′W) **13**:357
TULUNGAGUNG (Indonesia)
map (8° 4′S 111° 54′E) **11**:147
TUMACO (Colombia)
map (1° 49′N 78° 46′W) **5**:107
TUMAN RIVER
map (42° 18′N 130° 41′E) **12**:113
TUMATUMARI FALL (Guyana)
map (5° 22′N 59° 0′W) **9**:410
TUMBES (Peru)
map (3° 34′S 80° 28′W) **15**:193
TUMBLEWEED **19**:331 *illus.*
TUMBLING MUSTARD *see* TUMBLEWEED
TUMOR **19**:331 *bibliog.*
adenoma **1**:102
bone diseases **3**:378
cancer **4**:101
cloning **5**:64
detection
ultrasonics **18**:74 *illus.*
excision **18**:361 *illus.*
gastrointestinal tract disease **9**:57
hysterectomy **10**:352
kidney disease **12**:71
lymphoma **12**:476
metastasis **13**:335
nervous system, diseases of the **14**:96
papilloma **15**:71
polyp **15**:421
radiation therapy **16**:43
regeneration **16**:127–128
respiratory system disorders **16**:181–182
stroke **18**:302
surgery **18**:363
virus
Rous, Francis Peyton **16**:325
Temin, Howard Martin **19**:91
virus particle **19**:613 *illus.*
TUMTUM (Washington)
map (47° 53′N 117° 41′W) **20**:35
TUMUC-HUMAC MOUNTAINS
map (2° 20′N 55° 0′W) **3**:460
TUMULUS PERIOD
Japanese art and architecture **11**:372
TUMUPASA (Bolivia)
map (14° 9′S 67° 55′W) **3**:366
TUMWATER (Washington)
map (47° 1′N 122° 54′W) **20**:35
TUN-HUANG (Dunhuang) (China) **19**:331
Stein, Sir Aurel **18**:246
TUNA **8**:116 *illus.*; **19**:331–332 *bibliog.*, *illus.*
bonito **3**:380
mackerel **13**:29
world fishing grounds **8**:125 *map*
TUNAPURA (Trinidad and Tobago)
map (10° 38′N 61° 23′W) **19**:300
TUNBRIDGE WELLS (England)
map (51° 8′N 0° 16′E) **19**:403
TUNDRA **19**:332–333 *bibliog.*, *illus.*
Asia **2**:238 *map*
biome **3**:273–274 *map*
climate **19**:332–333
ecology **7**:42
Europe **7**:273 *map*
grasslands **9**:301
habitat **10**:5
life **19**:332–333 *illus.*
mountain life **13**:622–623
polar climate **15**:392
types **19**:332
world distribution **3**:273 *map*; **15**:344 *map*
TUNER **19**:333
TUNG CH'I-CH'ANG (Dong Qichang) **19**:333 *bibliog.*
Chinese art and architecture **4**:382
Wangs, Four **20**:23
TUNG HAI *see* CHINA SEA, EAST
T'UNG MENG HUI
Kuomintang (Guomindang) **12**:137
TUNG OIL **19**:333
TUNG PEI *see* MANCHURIA (China)
TUNG-T'ING LAKE
map (29° 20′N 112° 54′E) **20**:318
TUNGSTATE MINERALS
mineral **13**:443 *table*
sulfate minerals **18**:333
wolframite **20**:198–199
TUNGSTEN **19**:333–334 *bibliog.*
compounds **19**:333–334
de Elhuyar brothers **19**:333
element **7**:130 *table*
filament
incandescent lamp **11**:73
Langmuir, Irving **12**:196
Group VIB periodic table **15**:167
Lehmann, Johann Gottlob **12**:276
metal, metallic element **13**:328
occurrence **19**:333
ore deposits, world distribution **14**:423 *map*
scheelite **17**:118
thermionic emission **19**:161
transition elements **19**:273
wolframite **20**:198–199
Woulfe, Peter **19**:333
TUNGUS **19**:334 *bibliog.*
Ural-Altaic languages **19**:476
Yakut **20**:314
TUNGUSKA FIREBALL **19**:334 *bibliog.*
meteorite craters **13**:337
TUNICA (Mississippi)
map (34° 41′N 90° 23′W) **13**:469
TUNICA (county in Mississippi)
map (34° 40′N 90° 20′W) **13**:469
TUNICATE **19**:334
chordate **4**:407
TUNING FORK **19**:334
TUNIS (Tunisia) **19**:334; **19**:336 *illus.*
climate **1**:142 *table*; **19**:336 *table*
map (36° 48′N 10° 11′E) **19**:335
TUNISIA **19**:334–337 *bibliog.*, *illus.*, *map*, *table*
arts **19**:336
cities
Bizerte **3**:301
Remada **19**:336 *table*
Sfax **17**:233
Tunis **19**:334
climate **19**:335–336 *table*
economic activity **19**:336–337
education **19**:336
African universities **1**:176 *table*
flag **19**:335 *illus.*
government **19**:337
history **19**:337
Bourguiba, Habib **3**:424
World War II **20**:262–263 *map*
land and resources **19**:335–336 *map*, *table*
map (34° 0′N 9° 0′E) **1**:136
people **19**:335–336
Tuareg **19**:325–326
Pleistocene Epoch
Aïn Hanech **1**:203
rivers, lakes, and waterways **19**:335
trade **19**:337
TUNJA (Colombia)
map (5° 31′N 73° 22′W) **5**:107
TUNKHANNOCK (Pennsylvania)
map (41° 32′N 75° 57′W) **15**:147
TUNNEL **19**:337–339 *bibliog.*, *illus.*, *table*
alarm systems **1**:240
history **19**:337–338
Ammann, Othmar Hermann **1**:372
Eupalinus **7**:265
notable tunnels **19**:337 *table*
Blanc, Mont **3**:326
Holland Tunnel **10**:203
Hoosac Tunnel **19**:337 *table*
Lincoln Tunnel **1**:372
Mont Cenis Tunnel **19**:337 *table*
Rotherhithe and Wapping Tunnel **19**:337 *table*
Saint Gotthard Tunnel **17**:19
Seikan Tunnel **19**:337 *table*
Simplon Tunnel **19**:337 *table*
Thames Tunnel **3**:524
subway **18**:318
tunneling techniques **19**:338–339 *illus.*
drilling **6**:273
rock tunneling **19**:338–339
soft-ground tunneling **19**:338
undersea tunneling **19**:339
TUNNEL EFFECT **19**:339
TUNNEL JUNCTION
superconductivity **18**:350
TUNNEY, GENE **19**:339 *bibliog.*
Dempsey, Jack **6**:105
TUNNEY, JOHN VARICK
Tunney, Gene **19**:339
TUNUYÁN (Argentina)
map (33° 34′S 69° 1′W) **2**:149
TUOLUMNE (county in California)
map (37° 59′N 120° 23′W) **4**:31
TUPAC AMARU
Inca **11**:73
TUPAMARO NATIONAL LIBERATION FRONT
Uruguay **19**:490
TUPELO (Mississippi)
map (34° 16′N 88° 43′W) **13**:469
TUPÍ (American Indians) **19**:339 *bibliog.*
TUPINAMBÁ (American Indians)
Tupí **19**:339
TUPINAMBARANA
Tupí **19**:339
TUPIZA (Bolivia)
map (21° 27′S 65° 43′W) **3**:366
TUPOLEV V-G "BACKFIRE B" AIRCRAFT **1**:216 *illus.*
TUPPER, BENJAMIN
Ohio Company of Associates **14**:362
TUPPER, SIR CHARLES **19**:339 *bibliog.*
TUPPER LAKE (New York)
map (44° 13′N 74° 29′W) **14**:149
TUR *see* IBEX
TURA, COSIMO **19**:339 *bibliog.*
TURACO *see* TOURACO
TURAN LOWLAND
map (44° 30′N 63° 0′E) **19**:388
TURBACZ MOUNTAIN
map (49° 33′N 20° 8′E) **15**:388
TURBELLARIA
flatworm **8**:156
planaria **15**:326
worm **20**:283 *illus.*
TURBIDIMETER **19**:339
TURBIDITY CURRENT *see* DENSITY CURRENT
TURBINE **19**:340 *bibliog.*, *illus.*
automotive industry **2**:367
engine **7**:177
gas turbine **19**:340
ship **17**:275
hydroelectric power **10**:332–335 *illus.*
hydrofoil **10**:336 *illus.*
power, generation and transmission of **15**:483 *illus.*
steam turbine **19**:340 *illus.*
Parsons, Sir Charles Algernon **15**:99
ship **17**:274
steam engine **18**:240
technology, history of **19**:66
waterwheel **20**:66–67
windmills and wind power **20**:173
TURBINIA (ship) *see* PARSONS, SIR CHARLES ALGERNON
TURBO (Colombia)
map (8° 6′N 76° 43′W) **5**:107
TURBOJET
jet propulsion **11**:406 *illus.*
TURBOT **8**:155 *illus.*; **19**:340–341
TURBOTRAIN **16**:75 *illus.*
TURBULENCE
law of
Kármán, Theodore von **12**:28
TURCILINGI
Germanic peoples **9**:138
TURDA (Romania)
map (46° 34′N 23° 47′E) **16**:288
TURENNE, HENRI DE LA TOUR D'AUVERGNE, VICOMTE DE **19**:341 *bibliog.*
TURFAN DEPRESSION
map (42° 40′N 89° 10′E) **4**:362
TURGENEV, IVAN **19**:341 *bibliog.*, *illus.*
Fathers and Sons **8**:34
nihilism **14**:194
Russian literature **16**:365–366 *illus.*
TURGOT, ANNE ROBERT JACQUES **19**:341 *bibliog.*
physiocrats **15**:287
TURGOVISHTE (Bulgaria)
map (43° 15′N 26° 34′E) **3**:555
TURHAL (Turkey)
map (40° 24′N 36° 6′E) **19**:343
TURIA RIVER
map (39° 27′N 0° 19′W) **18**:140
TURIN (Italy) **19**:342
Juvarra, Filippo **11**:479–480
map (45° 3′N 7° 40′E) **11**:321
TURIN, SHROUD OF *see* SHROUD OF TURIN
TURINA, JOAQUIN **19**:342
TURING, ALAN **19**:342
automata, theory of **2**:356–357
TURKANA (people) **19**:342 *bibliog.*
TURKANA, LAKE *see* RUDOLF, LAKE
TURKANA MAN *see* SKULL 1470
TURKESTAN *see* TURKISTAN
TURKEY (bird) **19**:346 *bibliog.*, *illus.*
animal behavior **2**:12 *illus.*
diseases
flea **8**:158
game birds **9**:27
imprinting **11**:68
parthenogenesis **15**:100
poultry **15**:474 *illus.*, *illus.*
TURKEY (country) **19**:342–346 *bibliog.*, *illus.*, *map*, *table*
See also ANATOLIA
archaeology
Alaça Hüyük **1**:239
Alalakh **1**:239
Boğazköy **3**:359–360
Carchemish **4**:141
Çatal Hüyük **4**:197
Fertile Crescent **8**:60
Gordion **9**:249
Hacilar **10**:6–7
Kültepe **12**:136
Magnesia **13**:53
Priene **15**:536
Sardis **17**:77
Troy **19**:312–313

TURKEY (cont.)
Urartu **19**:479–480
Woolley, Sir Leonard **20**:215
Xanthus **20**:311
art **19**:345
See also OTTOMAN ART; the subheading Turkey under specific art forms, e.g., ARCHITECTURE; PAINTING; POTTERY AND PORCELAIN; etc.
Byzantine art and architecture **3**:604–606
Hittite art and architecture **10**:188–189
Islamic art and architecture **11**:293–297
museums, art **13**:658
Persian art and architecture **15**:185
rugs and carpets **16**:342 *illus.*
Sinan **17**:318
Topkapi Palace Museum **19**:237
cities
Adana **1**:98
Ankara **2**:30–31 *illus.*
Antioch **2**:64
Bursa **3**:581
Edirne **7**:57
Istanbul **11**:306–308 *illus., map*
Izmir **11**:338
Konya **12**:109
Samsun **19**:343 *table*
Tarsus **19**:39–40
Trabzon **19**:257
climate **19**:343–344 *table*
economic activity **19**:345
education **19**:344
Middle Eastern universities **13**:410–412 *table*
flag **19**:342 *illus.*
government **19**:345
health **19**:344–345
history **19**:345–346
See also CRIMEAN WAR; OTTOMAN EMPIRE
Atatürk, Kemal **2**:287
Cappadocia **4**:127–128
Central Treaty Organization **4**:255
Chanak Crisis **4**:278
Circassians **4**:435
Cyprus **5**:409
Demirel, Süleyman **6**:97
Evren, Kenan **7**:325
İwnönü İwsmet **11**:181
Lausanne, Treaty of **12**:239–240
Menderes, Adnan **13**:296
Middle East, history of the **13**:404–408
Russo-Turkish Wars *see* RUSSO-TURKISH WARS
World War I *see* WORLD WAR I
land and resources **19**:343–344 *map, table*
Turkish plate **15**:351 *map*
languages
Indo-Iranian languages **11**:145–146
Ural-Altaic languages **19**:476
literature
Ahmet Haşim **1**:200–201
Ali, Sabahattin **1**:292
Galib, Şeyh **9**:14
Halide Edib Adivar **10**:20–21
Nazim Hikmet **14**:67
Tevfik Fikret **19**:128
Yaşar Kemal **20**:319
Yunus Emre **20**:347
map (39° 0′N 35° 0′E) **2**:232
people **2**:242 *illus.*; **19**:344
Cyprus **5**:407
Kurds **12**:139
race **16**:34 *illus.*
Turkmen **19**:347
Turks **19**:348
Yoruk **20**:331–332
physical features
Ararat, Mount **2**:109
Gallipoli Peninsula **9**:20
Taurus Mountains **19**:45
resources **19**:344
rivers, lakes, and waterways **19**:343–344
Bosporus **3**:407 *map*
Dardanelles **6**:37 *map*
Marmara, Sea of **13**:161
Van, Lake **19**:510
zither **20**:370 *illus.*
TURKEY (Texas)
map (34° 23′N 100° 54′W) **19**:129
TURKEY BEARD *see* BEAR GRASS
TURKEYFISH *see* LIONFISH
TURKIC LANGUAGES
Ural-Altaic languages **19**:476
TURKIC PEOPLES *see* TURKS
TURKISH ANGORA CAT *see* ANGORA CAT
TURKISH CAT *see* VAN CAT
TURKISH FEDERATED STATE OF CYPRUS *see* CYPRUS
TURKISTAN **19**:347
TURKMEN **19**:347 *bibliog.*
Merv **13**:313
Qashqai **16**:3
rugs and carpets **16**:342
Turks **19**:347–348
TURKMEN SOVIET SOCIALIST REPUBLIC (USSR) **19**:347
cities
Ashkhabad **2**:231
Kara Kum **12**:26
people
Baluch **3**:57
Turkmen **19**:347
TURKOMAN *see* TURKMEN
TURKS **19**:347–348 *bibliog., illus.*
history
Abbasids **1**:52
Asia, history of **2**:254–256
Crusades **5**:368–369
Dobruja **6**:209
Fatimids **8**:34
Genghis Khan, Mongol Emperor **9**:92
Islam **11**:289–290
John V Palaeologus, Byzantine Emperor **11**:426
Mamelukes **13**:96–97
Middle East, history of the **13**:404
Mongols **13**:530
Ottoman Empire **14**:464–466
Pechenegs **15**:130
Seljuks **17**:192
Timur **19**:204
Karakalpak **12**:26
Kazakhs **12**:33
Kirghiz **12**:87–88
present distribution **19**:348–349
Tatar **19**:43–44
Turkic languages **19**:476
Turkmen **19**:347
Uighur **19**:374–375
Yakut **20**:314
Yoruk **20**:331–332
TURKS AND CAICOS ISLANDS **19**:348–349
map (21° 45′N 71° 35′W) **20**:109
TURKU (Finland) **19**:349
map (60° 27′N 22° 17′E) **8**:95
TURLEY (Oklahoma)
map (36° 14′N 95° 58′W) **14**:368
TURLOCK (California)
map (37° 30′N 120° 51′W) **4**:31
TURMERIC **19**:349 *illus.*
TURN OF THE SCREW, THE (book) **14**:275 *illus.*
TURNBULL, WILLIAM, JR. **19**:349 *bibliog.*
TURNEFFE ISLANDS
map (17° 22′N 87° 51′W) **3**:183
TURNER (county in Georgia)
map (31° 43′N 83° 35′W) **9**:114
TURNER (Montana)
map (48° 51′N 108° 24′W) **13**:547
TURNER (county in South Dakota)
map (43° 17′N 97° 8′W) **18**:103
TURNER, BENJAMIN S. **16**:185 *illus.*
TURNER, FREDERICK JACKSON **19**:349 *bibliog., illus.*
frontier theory of **8**:344–345
TURNER, JOHN N. **19**:349–350 *illus.*
TURNER, JOSEPH MALLORD WILLIAM **19**:350 *bibliog., illus.*
The 'Fighting Téméraire' Tugged to Her Last Berth To Be Broken Up **7**:186 *illus.*; **19**:350 *illus.*
Rain, Steam, and Speed–The Great Western Railway **15**:22 *illus.*; **16**:292 *illus.*
View of the Dogana and the Church of San Giorgio, Venice **12**:191 *illus.*
TURNER, NAT **3**:306 *illus.*; **19**:351 *bibliog.*
TURNER, ROSCOE **19**:351 *bibliog.*
TURNER VALLEY (Alberta)
map (50° 40′N 114° 17′W) **1**:256
TURNERS FALLS (Massachusetts)
map (42° 36′N 72° 33′W) **13**:206
TURNHOUT (Belgium)
map (51° 19′N 4° 57′E) **3**:177
TURNIP **19**:351 *illus.*; **19**:534 *illus.*
rutabaga **16**:374–375
TURNPIKE **19**:351 *bibliog.*
roads and highways **16**:235; **16**:237; **16**:238
TURNSTONE **3**:281 *illus.*; **19**:351
TURNU-MĂGURELE (Romania)
map (43° 45′N 24° 53′E) **16**:288
TURNVEREIN **19**:351
TURON (Kansas)
map (37° 48′N 98° 26′W) **12**:18
TURPENTINE **19**:351–352
fir **8**:100
rosin **16**:317
turpentine tree **19**:352
TURPENTINE TREE **19**:352
TURQUINO PEAK (peak)
map (19° 59′N 76° 50′W) **5**:377
TURQUOISE **3**:296 *illus., table*; **9**:74 *illus.*; **13**:441 *illus.*; **19**:352 *bibliog., illus.*
phosphate minerals **15**:256
triclinic system **19**:296
TURRELL (Arkansas)
map (35° 23′N 90° 15′W) **2**:166
TURRET SHELL **17**:251 *illus.*
TURTLE (submersible vehicle) **19**:352 *bibliog.*
Bushnell, David **3**:585
submarine **18**:315
TURTLE (zoology) **18**:377 *illus.*; **19**:352–354 *bibliog., illus.*
aging **1**:186
anatomy **19**:352–353
bog turtle **3**:359
box turtle **3**:430
chicken turtle **4**:346
classification, biological **19**:354
conservation **19**:354
dormancy **19**:353
egg **7**:72
fossil record **19**:352
hawksbill turtle **19**:353 *illus.*
leatherback turtle **12**:263
life span **19**:354
loggerhead turtle **12**:394
map turtle **13**:136–137
mud turtle **13**:631
musk turtle **13**:682
painted turtle **15**:18
pond turtle **15**:426
reproduction **19**:353
ridley turtle **16**:218
river turtle **11**:469 *illus.*; **19**:124 *illus.*
sawback turtle **17**:103
sea turtle **17**:171
shell **19**:352–353 *illus.*
snapping turtle **17**:384
soft-shelled turtle **19**:353 *illus.*
tortoise **19**:246
TURTLE CREEK (New Brunswick)
map (45° 58′N 64° 53′W) **14**:117
TURTLE LAKE (North Dakota)
map (47° 31′N 100° 53′W) **14**:248
TURTLE LAKE (Wisconsin)
map (45° 24′N 92° 8′W) **20**:185
TURTLE MOUNTAINS
map (49° 0′N 100° 30′W) **14**:248
TUSCALOOSA (Alabama) **19**:354
map (33° 13′N 87° 33′W) **1**:234
TUSCALOOSA (county in Alabama)
map (33° 20′N 87° 30′W) **1**:234
TUSCANY (Italy) **19**:354–355
Arno River **2**:184
art
Romanesque art and architecture **16**:282–284
cities
Florence **8**:168–169 *illus., map*
Livorno **12**:378
Lucca **12**:449
Pisa **15**:315
Siena **17**:296
Italian unification **11**:330 *map*
Matilda of Tuscany **13**:228
Steno, Nicolaus **18**:253
TUSCARAWAS (county in Ohio)
map (40° 30′N 81° 27′W) **14**:357
TUSCARAWAS RIVER
map (40° 17′N 81° 52′W) **14**:357
TUSCARORA (American Indians) **19**:355
French and Indian Wars **8**:312–313
Iroquois League **11**:279–280
TUSCARORA MOUNTAIN
map (40° 10′N 77° 45′W) **15**:147
TUSCOLA (Illinois)
map (39° 48′N 88° 17′W) **11**:42
TUSCOLA (county in Michigan)
map (43° 25′N 83° 25′W) **13**:377
TUSCOLA (Texas)
map (32° 12′N 99° 48′W) **19**:129
TUSCUMBIA (Alabama)
map (34° 44′N 87° 42′W) **1**:234
TUSCUMBIA (Missouri)
map (38° 14′N 92° 28′W) **13**:476
TUSK
See also TEETH
elephant **7**:133–134
walrus **20**:18
warthog **20**:33
TUSK SHELL **19**:355
mollusk **13**:511–512 *illus.*
TUSKEGEE (Alabama)
map (32° 26′N 85° 42′W) **1**:234
TUSKEGEE INSTITUTE **19**:355
black Americans **3**:308 *illus.*
Carver, George Washington **4**:178–179
Washington, Booker T. **20**:39
Up from Slavery **19**:471
TUSSAUD, MADAME **19**:355 *bibliog.*
TUTANKHAMEN, KING OF EGYPT **7**:85 *illus.*; **19**:355 *bibliog., illus.*
Carnarvon, George Edward, 5th Earl of **4**:154
Carter, Howard **4**:171
funerary mask **2**:123 *illus.*
throne **9**:229 *illus.*
tomb **2**:123 *illus.*
TUTHMOSIS III *see* THUTMOSE III, KING OF EGYPT
TUTORING
teaching methods **19**:57
TUTSI **19**:355–356 *bibliog.*
Burundi **3**:582–583
dance **6**:22 *illus.*
Rwanda **16**:378
TUTTLE (North Dakota)
map (47° 9′N 100° 0′W) **14**:248
TUTTLE (Oklahoma)
map (35° 17′N 97° 49′W) **14**:368
TUTTLE CREEK LAKE
map (39° 22′N 96° 40′W) **12**:18
TUTU, DESMOND **19**:356
TUTUILA (American Samoa) **1**:366 *map*
TUTUOLA, AMOS **19**:356 *bibliog.*
TUVA (USSR) **19**:356
TUVALU **19**:356 *bibliog., map*
flag **8**:143 *illus.*; **19**:356 *illus.*
map (8° 0′S 178° 0′E) **14**:334
TUVAN **19**:356 *bibliog.*
TUVINIAN *see* TUVAN
TUVINIAN AUTONOMOUS SOVIET SOCIALIST REPUBLIC *see* TUVA (USSR)
TUWAYQ MOUNTAINS
map (23° 0′N 46° 0′E) **17**:94
TUXPAN (Mexico)
map (21° 57′N 105° 18′W) **13**:357
TUXPAN DE RODRÍGUEZ CANO (Mexico)
map (20° 57′N 97° 24′W) **13**:357
TUXTEPEC (Mexico)
map (18° 6′N 96° 7′W) **13**:357
TUXTLA GUTIÉRREZ (Mexico) **19**:356–357
map (16° 45′N 93° 7′W) **13**:357
TUZ, LAKE
map (38° 45′N 33° 25′E) **19**:343
TUZLA (Yugoslavia)
map (44° 32′N 18° 41′E) **20**:340
TVA *see* TENNESSEE VALLEY AUTHORITY
TWA (people)
Burundi **3**:582
TWACHTMAN, JOHN HENRY **19**:357 *bibliog.*
TWAIN, MARK **1**:345 *illus.*; **19**:357 *bibliog., illus.*
Celebrated Jumping Frog of Calaveras County, The **4**:229
Elmira (New York State) **7**:149
Hannibal (city in Missouri) **10**:38
Huckleberry Finn **10**:289
Tom Sawyer **19**:229
TWARDOWSKI, SAMUEL ZE SKRZYPNY
Polish literature **15**:398
TWAYBLADE **19**:358
TWEED **19**:358
TWEED, RIVER **19**:358
TWEED, WILLIAM M. **19**:20 *illus.*; **19**:358 *bibliog., illus.*
cartoon (Thomas Nast) **4**:176 *illus.*
Tammany Hall **19**:20
Tilden, Samuel J. **19**:199
TWEEDSMUIR, JOHN BUCHAN, 1ST BARON *see* BUCHAN, JOHN, 1ST BARON TWEEDSMUIR
12TH AMENDMENT **19**:358
text **5**:221
vice-president of the United States **19**:569
TWELFTH NIGHT (play) **19**:358
TWELVE APOSTLES, THE *see* APOSTLE
TWELVE GREAT COMPANIES *see* GUILDS
TWELVE TABLES, THE (law)
law, history of **12**:244
Roman law **16**:278

TWELVE-TONE SYSTEM 19:358–359 *bibliog.*
atonality 2:312
Babbitt, Milton 3:5–6
Bennett, Richard Rodney 3:203–204
Berg, Alban 3:208
Boulez, Pierre 3:421–422
Dallapiccola, Luigi 6:13
Henze, Hans Werner 10:130
Lutosławski, Witold 12:470
Lutyens, Elisabeth 12:471
Schoenberg, Arnold 17:130
serial music 17:208
Webern, Anton von 20:88
20TH AMENDMENT 19:359
lame duck 12:174
Norris, George W. 14:223
text 5:222
TWENTIETH CENTURY-FOX
film, history of 8:87
Los Angeles (California) 12:417 *map*
Zanuck, Darryl F. 20:355
25TH AMENDMENT 19:359 *bibliog.*
Ford, Gerald R. 8:221
text 5:223
vice-president of the United States 19:569
21ST AMENDMENT 19:359 *bibliog.*
prohibition 15:565
temperance movement 19:92
text 5:222
24TH AMENDMENT 19:359
poll tax 15:405
text 5:223
TWENTY-ONE (card game) *see* BLACKJACK (card game)
"TWENTY-ONE" (television show)
radio and television broadcasting 16:58
22D AMENDMENT 19:359
text 5:222
26TH AMENDMENT 19:359–360
text 5:223
23D AMENDMENT 19:360
text 5:223
TWENTY THOUSAND LEAGUES UNDER THE SEA **(book)** 19:360
Verne, Jules 19:559
TWIGGS (county in Georgia)
map (32° 40′N 83° 25′W) 9:114
TWILIGHT 19:360
TWILIGHT OF THE GODS (Norse mythology) *see* RAGNAROK
TWILL 19:360
TWIN BRIDGES (Montana)
map (45° 33′N 112° 20′W) 13:547
TWIN CITIES *see* MINNEAPOLIS (Minnesota); ST. PAUL (Minnesota)
TWIN CITY (Georgia)
map (32° 35′N 82° 10′W) 9:114
TWIN FALLS (Idaho)
map (42° 34′N 114° 28′W) 11:26
TWIN FALLS (county in Idaho)
map (42° 20′N 114° 40′W) 11:26
TWIN LAKES (Georgia)
map (30° 42′N 83° 12′W) 9:114
TWIN LAKES (lake in Connecticut)
map (42° 2′N 73° 26′W) 5:193
TWIN LAKES (Wisconsin)
map (42° 32′N 88° 15′W) 20:185
TWIN-LENS REFLEX CAMERA 4:55 *illus.;* 4:56–57
TWIN VALLEY (Minnesota)
map (47° 16′N 96° 16′W) 13:453
TWINFLOWER 19:360
TWINING* v. *NEW JERSEY 19:360
TWINLEAF 19:360
TWINS
behavioral genetics 3:170
cloning 5:64
development 6:140
Galton, Sir John 9:23
intelligence 11:204
multiple birth 13:637–638
Siamese twins 17:291
TWISP (Washington)
map (48° 22′N 120° 7′W) 20:35
TWIST (dance)
disco music 6:189
TWISTER II (Lynn Chadwick) 4:267 *illus.*
TWO-BODY PROBLEM 19:360 *bibliog.*
TWO-FLUID MODEL
superconductivity 18:350
TWO HARBORS (Minnesota)
map (47° 1′N 91° 40′W) 13:453
TWO-LINED COLLOPS 3:167 *illus.*
TWO RIVERS
map (48° 49′N 97° 9′W) 13:453
TWO RIVERS (Wisconsin)
map (44° 9′N 87° 34′W) 20:185
TWO SICILIES, KINGDOM OF THE 19:360
Ferdinand I, King of the Two Sicilies 8:54
Ferdinand II, King of the Two Sicilies 8:54
Italy, history of 11:328–330 *maps*
Naples, Kingdom of 14:15
Sicily 17:293
TWO-SPOTTED LADYBUG 3:167 *illus.*
2001: A SPACE ODYSSEY (film)
Clarke, Arthur C. 5:40
TWO WOMEN (film) 12:413 *illus.*
TWO YEARS BEFORE THE MAST (book)
Dana, Richard Henry 6:21
TWORKOV, JACK 19:360–361 *bibliog.*
TY TY (Georgia)
map (31° 28′N 83° 39′W) 9:114
TYDINGS-MCDUFFIE ACT
Quezon, Manuel Luis 16:25
TYGART LAKE
map (39° 15′N 80° 0′W) 20:111
TYGART VALLEY RIVER
map (39° 29′N 80° 11′W) 20:111
TYGER RIVER
map (34° 27′N 81° 28′W) 18:98
TYLER (Minnesota)
map (44° 17′N 96° 8′W) 13:453
TYLER (Texas)
map (32° 21′N 95° 18′W) 19:129
TYLER (county in Texas)
map (30° 45′N 94° 27′W) 19:129
TYLER (county in West Virginia)
map (39° 27′N 80° 55′W) 20:111
TYLER, ANNE 19:361
TYLER, JOHN 19:361–362 *bibliog., illus.*
Clay, Henry 5:46
Harrison, William Henry 10:61
Richmond (Virginia) 16:214
Webster, Daniel 20:88
Whig party (United States) 20:130–131
TYLER, RALPH WINFRED 19:362
TYLER, ROYALL 19:362 *bibliog.*
TYLER, WAT
Peasants' Revolt 15:129
TYLERTOWN (Mississippi)
map (31° 7′N 90° 9′W) 13:469
TYLOR, SIR EDWARD B. 19:362 *bibliog.*
animism 2:29
culture 5:384
magic 13:50
primitive religion 15:543
TYMPANI *see* KETTLEDRUM
TYMPANUM 19:362
Romanesque art and architecture 16:284
sculpture 17:162
TYNAN, KENNETH 19:362
TYNDALE, WILLIAM 19:362 *bibliog.*
TYNDALL (South Dakota)
map (42° 59′N 97° 52′W) 18:103
TYNDALL, JOHN 19:363 *bibliog.*
TYNEMOUTH (England)
map (55° 1′N 1° 24′W) 19:403
TYNER, McCOY
jazz 11:390
TYNWALD, COURT OF (parliament)
Isle of Man 11:298
TYPE, PRINTING 19:363 *bibliog., illus.*
characteristics 19:363
classifications 19:363
Gutenberg, Johann 19:363
sizes 19:363
typesetting 19:365
TYPEE (book)
Marquesas Islands 13:163
TYPEFACE 19:363–365 *bibliog., illus.*
antimony 2:64
Baskerville, John 3:110
Bodoni, Giambattista 3:356
book illustration 3:386–387
Caslon, William 4:182
Gutenberg, Johann 9:408–409
TYPESETTING 19:365 *bibliog., illus.*
book 3:384–385
hand setting 19:365 *illus.*
International Typographical Union 11:224–225
Linotype 12:359
Ludlow typograph 19:365
machine setting 19:365
Mergenthaler, Ottmar 13:310
Monotype 13:541
phototypesetting 15:277–278
printing 19:365
TYPEWRITER 19:365–366 *bibliog., illus.*
business machines 3:589
TYPHOID FEVER 19:366
bacteria 3:16
Salmonella 17:36
TYPHOON *see* HURRICANE AND TYPHOON
TYPHUS 19:366–367
flea 8:158
louse 12:436
rickettsia 16:216
types 19:366–367
vaccination 19:501
TYPOGRAPHICAL UNION, INTERNATIONAL *see* INTERNATIONAL TYPOGRAPHICAL UNION
TYRAMINE
headache 10:86
TYRANNID *see* FLYCATCHER (bird)
TYRANNOSAURUS 19:367 *bibliog., illus.*
TYRANT FLYCATCHER 19:367
kingbird 12:83
pewee 15:217
phoebe 15:249
TYRE (Lebanon)
map (33° 16′N 35° 11′E) 12:265
TYRE (Phoenicia) 19:367 *bibliog.*
Sidon 17:295
TYRIAN PURPLE 19:367
TYROL 19:367–368 *map*
cities
Innsbruck 11:181
Germany in 1648 9:151 *map*
TYRONE (Northern Ireland) 19:368
TYRONE (Oklahoma)
map (36° 57′N 101° 4′W) 14:368
TYRONE (Pennsylvania)
map (40° 40′N 78° 14′W) 15:147
TYRONE, HUGH O'NEILL, 2D EARL OF 19:368 *bibliog.*
TYROSINE
noradrenaline 14:218
pigment, skin 15:300
TYRRELL (county in North Carolina)
map (35° 50′N 76° 10′W) 14:242
TYRRELL, GEORGE 19:368 *bibliog.*
modernism 13:498
TYRRHENIAN SEA 11:320 *illus.;* 19:368
lighthouse 12:336
map (40° 0′N 12° 0′E) 11:321
Messina, Strait of 13:324
TYRRHENOI *see* ETRUSCANS
TYRSENOI *see* ETRUSCANS
TYRTAEUS 19:368
TYURATAM COSMODROME *see* BAIKONUR COSMODROME
TYUTCHEV, FYODOR 19:368 *bibliog.*
TZARA, TRISTAN 19:368 *bibliog.*
TZ'U (prose)
Chinese literature 4:389
TZU-ANG *see* CHAO MENG-FU (Zhao Mengfu)
TZU-CHIH T'UNG-CHIEN (book)
Ssu-Ma Kuang (Sima Guang) 18:207
TZ'U-HSI (Cixi), DOWAGER EMPRESS OF CHINA 4:395 *illus.;* 19:368 *bibliog.*
China, history of 4:374
Ch'ing (Qing) (dynasty) 4:395
K'ang Yu-wei (Kang Youwei) 12:15
Yüan Shih-k'ai (Yuan Shikai) 20:338

U

U (letter) 19:369 *illus.*
V (letter) 19:500
W (letter) 20:3
U-BOAT
submarine 18:314–315 *illus.*
World War I 20:240 *illus.*
World War II 20:256; 20:264–265 *illus., map*
U-MATIC (video recorder) 19:576b; 19:576j
video art 19:576h
U THANT *see* THANT, U
U-2 19:369 *bibliog., illus.*
Cuban missile crisis 5:380
Eisenhower, Dwight D. 7:96
intelligence gathering 11:205
UABOE (Nauru)
map (0° 31′S 166° 55′E) 14:51
UAKARI
monkey 13:534
UAXACTÚN (Guatemala) 19:369 *bibliog.*
UBANGI RIVER 4:252 *illus.;* 19:369–370
map (0° 30′S 17° 42′E) 20:350
ÚBEDA (Spain)
map (38° 1′N 3° 22′W) 18:140
UBERABA (Brazil)
map (19° 45′S 47° 55′W) 3:460
UBERLÂNDIA (Brazil)
map (18° 56′S 48° 18′W) 3:460
UBON RATCHATHANI (Thailand)
map (15° 14′N 104° 54′E) 19:139
UBUNDI (Zaire)
map (0° 21′S 25° 29′E) 20:350
UCAYALI RIVER
map (4° 38′S 73° 30′W) 15:193
UCCELLO, PAOLO 19:370 *bibliog., illus.*
The Rout of San Romano 19:370 *illus.*
UCHIZA (Peru)
map (8° 29′S 76° 23′W) 15:193
UCLUELET (British Columbia)
map (48° 57′N 125° 33′W) 3:491
UCR (*UNIFORM CRIME REPORTS*) *see* FEDERAL BUREAU OF INVESTIGATION
UDALL (family) 19:370
UDALL, NICHOLAS 19:370
interlude 11:214
UDALL, STEWART 15:526 *illus.*
UDAQUIOLA (Argentina)
map (36° 34′S 58° 31′W) 2:149
UDDEVALLA (Sweden)
map (58° 21′N 11° 55′E) 18:382
UDDJAUR LAKE
map (65° 55′N 17° 49′E) 18:382
UDINE (Italy) 19:370–371
map (46° 3′N 13° 14′E) 11:321
UDON THANI (Thailand)
map (17° 26′N 102° 46′E) 19:139
UEBERROTH, PETER 19:371
UEDA AKINARI 19:371 *bibliog.*
UELE RIVER
map (4° 9′N 22° 26′E) 4:251
UELSMANN, JERRY N. 19:371
photography, history and art of 15:272 *illus.*
UEXKÜLL, JAKOB VON
animal behavior 2:11
UFA (USSR) 19:371
map (54° 44′N 55° 56′E) 19:388
UFFIZI 19:371 *bibliog.*
Vasari, Giorgio 19:525
UFO *see* UNIDENTIFIED FLYING OBJECT
UGANDA 19:371–374 *bibliog., illus., map, table*
African art 1:160–164
African music 1:168–171
cities
Entebbe 7:208
Kampala 12:10
climate 19:372 *table*
economic activity 19:373
education 19:372
African universities 1:176 *table*
flag 19:371 *illus.*
history and government 19:373
Africa, history of 1:154
Amin Dada, Idi 1:370
Obote, Milton 14:316
Tanzania 19:28
land and resources 19:371–372 *map, table*
map (1° 0′N 32° 0′E) 1:136
people 19:372
Ganda 9:34–35
Ik 11:39
Luo 12:465
Turkana 19:342
UGARIT 19:374 *bibliog.*
bronzes 15:250 *illus.*
Ebla 7:36
language 19:374
Gordon, Cyrus H. 9:249
UGARTE, AUGUSTO PINOCHET *see* PINOCHET UGARTE, AUGUSTO
UGLI
citrus fruits 4:447 *illus.*
UGRANDITES
garnet 9:49
UGRIC LANGUAGES
Ural-Altaic languages 19:475
UHAIMIR *see* KISH (Iraq)
UHLAN (military) 4:221 *illus.*
UHLAND, JOHANN LUDWIG 19:374
UHLE, MAX 19:374 *bibliog.*
UHLENBECK, GEORGE E.
chemistry, history of 4:328
UHRICHSVILLE (Ohio)
map (40° 24′N 81° 20′W) 14:357
UHURU 19:374 *bibliog.*
Explorer (artificial satellite) 7:338
X-ray astronomy 20:306 *illus.*
UÍGE (Angola)
map (7° 37′S 15° 3′E) 2:5
UIGHUR 19:374
Asia, history of 2:254 *map*
Turks 19:347; 19:348
UIJU (Korea)
map (40° 12′N 124° 32′E) 12:113
UINTA (county in Wyoming)
map (41° 18′N 110° 35′W) 20:301
UINTA MOUNTAINS
map (40° 45′N 110° 5′W) 19:492

UINTAH (county in Utah)
map (40° 10′N 109° 30′W) 19:492
UITENHAGE (South Africa)
map (33° 40′S 25° 28′E) 18:79
UJEVIĆ, TIN
Yugoslavia 20:342
UJIJI (Tanzania)
map (4° 55′S 29° 41′E) 19:27
UJJAIN (India)
map (23° 11′N 75° 46′E) 11:80
UJUNG PANDANG (Indonesia)
map (5° 7′S 119° 24′E) 11:147
UKEREWE ISLAND
map (2° 3′S 33° 0′E) 19:27
UKIAH (California)
map (39° 9′N 123° 13′W) 4:31
UKIAH (Oregon)
map (45° 8′N 118° 56′W) 14:427
UKIYO-E 19:374–375 *bibliog., illus.*
Harunobu 10:64
Hiroshige 10:175
Hokusai 10:199–200
Japanese art and architecture 11:378
Kaigetsudo 12:6
Kiyomasu 12:94
Kiyonaga 12:94
Kiyonobu I 12:94
Kuniyoshi 12:137
Masanobu (1686–1764) 13:195
Moronobu 13:587
Utamaro 19:496
UKRAINIAN LANGUAGE
Slavic languages 17:358
UKRAINIAN SOVIET SOCIALIST REPUBLIC (USSR) 19:375 *bibliog.*
cities
Dnepropetrovsk 6:208
Donetsk 6:238
Kharkov 12:65–66
Kiev 12:75–76
Krivoi Rog 12:130
Lvov 12:473
Odessa 14:349 *illus.*
Poltava 15:418
Sevastopol 17:215
Yalta 20:315
Zaporozhye 20:356
history
Chmielnicki, Bohdan 4:402
Cossacks 5:290
Mazepa, Ivan Stepanovich 13:250
house 10:269 *illus.*
regions
Bessarabia 3:228
Bucovina 3:537
Crimea 5:347–348 *map*
Donets Basin 6:237–238
Ruthenia 16:375
UKUALUTHI
Ovambo 14:469
UKUAMBI
Ovambo 14:469
UKUANYAMA
Ovambo 14:469
UKULELE 19:376 *illus.*
ULAN BATOR (Mongolia) 19:376
climate 2:237 *table*; 13:529 *table*
map (47° 55′N 106° 53′E) 13:529
ULAN-UDE (USSR)
map (51° 50′N 107° 37′E) 19:388
ULANOVA, GALINA SERGEYEVNA 19:376 *bibliog.*
ULBRICHT, WALTER 19:376 *bibliog.*
ULCER 9:56 *illus.*; 19:376–377 *bibliog.*
gastrointestinal tract disease 9:57
protozoal diseases 15:581
skin diseases 17:341
stomach 18:280
treatment
antacid 2:38
cimetidine 4:431
laser 12:213
venereal disease 19:540
ULEN (Minnesota)
map (47° 5′N 96° 16′W) 13:453
ULEXITE
borate minerals 3:396
ULFILAS, BISHOP OF THE WEST GOTHS
Germanic languages 9:136–137
ULLIN (Illinois)
map (37° 17′N 89° 11′W) 11:42
ULLMAN, DOUGLAS ELTON *see* FAIRBANKS, DOUGLAS
ULLMANN, LIV 19:377 *bibliog.*
ULLOA, FRANCISCO DE
California, Gulf of 4:38
ULM (Germany, East and West)
map (48° 24′N 10° 0′E) 9:140
ULOTHRIX 19:377
ULSTER (Ireland) 19:377
Home Rule Bills 10:212
Ireland, history of 11:263–265
Northern Ireland 14:255
Orangemen 14:415
Protestant-Catholic fighting 11:265 *illus.*
ULSTER (county in New York)
map (41° 56′N 74° 0′W) 14:149
ULSTER COVENANT
Ireland, history of 11:264
ULSTER CYCLE (literature)
Irish literature 11:267–268
ULTIMOGENITURE
primogeniture 15:547
ULTRADIAN RHYTHM
biological clock 3:264
ULTRAFICHE *see* MICROFILM
ULTRAISMO
Borges, Jorge Luis 3:398
ULTRAMARINE 19:377
lapis lazuli 12:204
ULTRAMICROFICHE *see* MICROFILM
ULTRAMONTANISM 19:377
Vatican Council, First 19:527
ULTRAPASTEURIZATION
milk 13:423
pasteurization 15:108
ULTRASONICS 19:377–378 *bibliog., illus.*
anthropometry 2:55
applications 19:377–378 *illus.*
echolocation 7:39
holography 10:208
machine tools 13:25 *illus.*
pregnancy and birth 15:505
pulse-echo technique 18:74 *illus.*
radiology 16:65
sound and acoustics 18:73–74 *illus.*
transducer 19:269
ULTRASOUND *see* ULTRASONICS
ULTRAVIOLET ASTRONOMY 19:378–379 *bibliog., illus.*
astronomy and astrophysics 2:281–282
color index 5:114
International Ultraviolet Explorer 19:379
nebula 14:75
OAO 14:312–313
observatory, astronomical 14:318–319
satellite, artificial 19:379
ULTRAVIOLET LIGHT 19:379 *bibliog.*
biological effects 19:379
electromagnetic radiation 7:116; 19:379
frequency, electromagnetic 7:117 *table*
genetic code 9:81 *illus.*
Lyman, Theodore 12:475
mutation, nucleic acid 14:290
pigment, skin 15:300
sunlamp 18:348
ultraviolet spectrophotometry 18:172 *illus.*
wavelength, electromagnetic 7:117 *table*
ULÚA RIVER
map (15° 53′N 87° 44′W) 10:218
ULUGH MUZTAGH
Kunlun Mountains 12:137
ULVÖSPINEL
oxide minerals 14:476
ULYANOV, VLADIMIR ILICH *see* LENIN, VLADIMIR ILICH
ULYANOVSK (USSR)
map (54° 20′N 48° 24′E) 19:388
ULYSSES (book) 14:276 *illus.*; 19:379 *bibliog.*
Anderson, Margaret 1:402
Joyce, James 11:456–457
ULYSSES (Kansas)
map (37° 35′N 101° 22′W) 12:18
ULYSSES (mythology) *see* ODYSSEUS
ULYSSES (Nebraska)
map (41° 4′N 97° 12′W) 14:70
UMANAK FJORD
map (70° 55′N 53° 0′W) 9:353
UMAR, AL-HAJJ 19:379 *bibliog.*
Africa, history of 1:155–156
UMAR I 19:379
Middle East, history of the 13:402
UMAR II
Middle East, history of the 13:403
UMATILLA (Florida)
map (28° 55′N 81° 40′W) 8:172
UMATILLA (Oregon)
map (45° 55′N 119° 21′W) 14:427
UMATILLA (county in Oregon)
map (45° 35′N 118° 40′W) 14:427
UMAYYADS 2:102 *map*; 19:380 *bibliog.*
Abd al-Rahman I 1:53–54
Arabic literature 2:101
caliphate 4:39
conquests 661–750 13:403 *map*
Córdoba (Spain) 5:261
Islam 11:289
Middle East, history of the 13:402–403
Moorish art and architecture 13:570
Muawiyah I, Umayyad Caliph 13:630
UMBER
pigment
limonite 12:346
UMBERTO *see* HUMBERT
UMBILICAL CORD 7:153 *illus.*; 19:380
development 6:141
pregnancy and birth 15:503
UMBRA
sunspots 18:349
UMBRELLA 19:380
UMBRELLA BIRD 19:380
UMBRELLA PLANT 19:380
schefflera 17:118
UMBRIA (Italy) 11:326 *illus., illus.*; 19:380
cities
Perugia 15:195
Terni 19:118
UMBRIEL (satellite)
Uranus (astronomy) 19:478–479
UMEÅ (Sweden)
map (63° 50′N 20° 15′E) 18:382
UMEÅ RIVER
map (63° 47′N 20° 16′E) 18:382
UMIAK
Eskimo 7:240
UMM AL-QAIWAIN (United Arab Emirates)
United Arab Emirates 19:400
UMM BAB (Qatar)
map (25° 12′N 50° 48′E) 16:4
UMM DURMAN (Sudan) *see* OMDURMAN (Sudan)
UMM EL FAHM (Israel)
map (32° 31′N 35° 9′E) 11:302
UMNAK ISLAND
map (53° 25′N 168° 10′W) 1:242
UMNIATI RIVER
map (16° 49′S 28° 45′E) 20:365
UMPQUA RIVER
map (43° 42′N 124° 3′W) 14:427
UMTATA (Transkei) 19:380
UMW *see* UNITED MINE WORKERS OF AMERICA
UN-AMERICAN ACTIVITIES, HOUSE COMMITTEE ON 19:380–381 *bibliog., illus.*
Communist party, U.S.A. 5:151
Dies, Martin 6:162–163
film, history of 8:85
Hiss, Alger 10:180
Hollywood Ten, The 10:204
McCarthy, Joseph R. 13:8
Nixon, Richard M. 14:204
radio and television broadcasting 16:57
Watkins v. *United States* 20:67
UNADILLA (Georgia)
map (32° 16′N 83° 44′W) 9:114
UNALACHTIGO *see* DELAWARE (American Indians)
UNALAKLEET (Alaska)
map (63° 53′N 160° 47′W) 1:242
UNALASKA (Alaska)
map (53° 52′N 166° 32′W) 1:242
UNALASKA ISLAND
map (53° 45′N 166° 45′W) 1:242
UNAMI *see* DELAWARE (American Indians)
UNAMUNO, MIGUEL DE 19:381 *bibliog.*
paper folding 15:70–71
Spanish literature 18:159
UNANIMISM
French literature
Romains, Jules 16:272–273
UNAYZA (Saudi Arabia)
map (26° 6′N 43° 56′E) 17:94
UNCAS 19:381 *bibliog.*
Miantonomo 13:370
Mohegan 13:503
UNCERTAINTY PRINCIPLE (physics) 19:381 *bibliog.*
determinism 6:134
Heisenberg, Werner Karl 10:109–110
law, physical 12:248
quantum mechanics 16:10–11
UNCIA (Bolivia)
map (18° 27′S 66° 37′W) 3:366
UNCLE REMUS (fictional character) 19:381
Harris, Joel Chandler 10:57
UNCLE SAM 19:381–382 *bibliog., illus.*
cartoon depicting 14:119 *illus.*
recruiting poster 1:112 *illus.*
Troy (New York) 19:313
UNCLE TOM'S CABIN (book) 17:357 *illus.*; 19:382
Stowe, Harriet Beecher 18:286
Weld, Theodore Dwight 20:96
UNCLE VANYA (play) 19:150 *illus.*; 19:382
Chekhov, Anton 4:310
UNCOMPAHGRE PEAK
map (38° 4′N 107° 28′W) 5:116
UNCOMPAHGRE PLATEAU
map (38° 30′N 108° 25′W) 5:116
UNCOMPAHGRE RIVER
map (38° 45′N 108° 6′W) 5:116
UNCONFORMITY 19:382 *bibliog., illus.*
Hutton, James 10:323–324
UNCONSCIOUS (psychology) 19:382–383 *bibliog.*
dreams and dreaming 6:266–268
Hartmann, Eduard von 10:63
UNCONSCIOUSNESS (physiology)
coma (unconscious state) 5:129
consciousness, states of 5:200
fainting 8:8
first aid 8:108 *illus.*
"UNDER THE LINDEN" (poem)
Walther von der Vogelweide 20:20
UNDER MILK WOOD (radio play) 19:383
Thomas, Dylan 19:172
UNDERDEVELOPED COUNTRIES *see* THIRD WORLD
UNDEREMPLOYMENT 19:383 *bibliog.*
See also EMPLOYMENT AND UNEMPLOYMENT
UNDERGROUND PRESS
Radio Free Europe and Radio Liberty 16:53
UNDERGROUND RAILROAD 3:305 *map*; 5:16 *illus.*; 19:383 *bibliog.*
Springfield (Massachusetts) 18:200
Tubman, Harriet 19:327–328
UNDERGROUND WRITING
samizdat 17:46
UNDERHILL, EVELYN 19:383 *bibliog.*
UNDERTAKER *see* FUNERAL INDUSTRY
UNDERWATER ARCHAEOLOGY 19:383 *bibliog.*
archaeology 2:119
UNDERWOOD (North Dakota)
map (47° 27′N 101° 8′W) 14:248
UNDERWOOD, OSCAR W. 19:384
UNDERWRITERS' LABORATORIES 19:384
UNDERWRITING (securities)
investment banking 11:238
UNDOING (psychology)
defense mechanisms 6:83
UNDSET, SIGRID 19:384 *bibliog.*
UNDU CAPE
map (16° 8′S 179° 57′E) 8:77
UNDULANT FEVER *see* BRUCELLOSIS
UNEMPLOYMENT *see* EMPLOYMENT AND UNEMPLOYMENT
UNEMPLOYMENT INSURANCE 19:384 *bibliog.*
social security 18:14–16
UNESCO *see* UNITED NATIONS EDUCATIONAL, SCIENTIFIC, AND CULTURAL ORGANIZATION
UNETIČE CULTURE
European prehistory 7:304
UNGARETTI, GIUSEPPE 19:384
UNGAVA 19:384
UNGAVA BAY
map (59° 30′N 67° 30′W) 16:18
UNGAVA PENINSULA
map (60° 0′N 74° 0′W) 16:18
UNGERN-STERNBERG, BARON VON
Mongolia 13:530
UNGGI (Korea)
map (42° 20′N 130° 24′E) 12:113
UNGULATE 19:384
teeth 19:70
UNHCR *see* REFUGEES, OFFICE OF THE UNITED NATIONS HIGH COMMISSIONER FOR
UNIA *see* UNIVERSAL NEGRO IMPROVEMENT ASSOCIATION
UNIATE CHURCHES *see* EASTERN RITE CHURCHES
UNICEF *see* UNITED NATIONS CHILDREN'S FUND
UNICOI (Tennessee)
map (36° 12′N 82° 21′W) 19:104
UNICOI (county in Tennessee)
map (36° 8′N 82° 25′W) 19:104
UNICORN 19:385 *illus.*
UNICORN PLANT 19:385
UNIDENTIFIED FLYING OBJECT 19:385 *bibliog., illus.*

life, extraterrestrial **12**:328
Tunguska fireball **19**:334
UNIFICATION CHURCH
Moon, Sun Myung **13**:566
UNIFIED FIELD THEORY **19**:385–386 *bibliog.*
Einstein, Albert **7**:94
electroweak theory **7**:128
fundamental interactions **8**:360–361
Weinberg, Steven **20**:95
UNIFORM
air force, U.S. **1**:207–208 *illus.*
American Revolution **1**:358 *illus.*; **2**:182 *illus.*
armor **2**:174–175 *illus.*
army, U.S. **2**:182–183 *illus.*
cavalry **4**:221 *illus.*
Civil War, U.S. **2**:182 *illus.*; **19**:448–449 *illus.*
English Civil War **4**:221 *illus.*; **7**:190 *illus.*
Franco-Prussian War **8**:278–279 *illus.*
hussar **4**:221 *illus.*
infantry **11**:164 *illus.*
khaki **12**:65
Korean War **1**:207 *illus.*; **2**:182 *illus.*
Marine Corps, U.S. **13**:154–155 *illus.*
Mexican War **2**:182 *illus.*
Middle Ages **11**:164 *illus.*
Navy, U.S. **14**:65–66 *illus.*
Prussia (c.1750) **11**:164 *illus.*
Prussia (c.1870) **8**:279 *illus.*
Roman cavalry **4**:221 *illus.*
Roman legion **11**:164 *illus.*
Rough Riders **4**:221 *illus.*
Spanish-American War **2**:182 *illus.*; **4**:221 *illus.*
tartan **19**:40–41 *illus.*
Uhlan **4**:221 *illus.*
Vietnam War **1**:207 *illus.*; **2**:182 *illus.*
War of 1812 **2**:182 *illus.*
World War I **1**:207 *illus.*; **2**:182 *illus.*; **11**:164 *illus.*
World War II **1**:207 *illus.*; **2**:182 *illus.*
UNIFORM CODE OF MILITARY JUSTICE
court-martial **5**:316
military justice **13**:421
UNIFORM COMMERCIAL CODE
business law **3**:588–589
UNIFORM CRIME REPORTS see FEDERAL BUREAU OF INVESTIGATION
UNIFORMITARIANISM **19**:386 *bibliog., illus.*
Hutton, James **10**:323–324
Lyell, Sir Charles **12**:474–475
paleoclimatology **15**:33
UNIMAK ISLAND
map (54° 50′N 164° 0′W) **1**:242
UNIMAK PASS
map (54° 35′N 164° 43′W) **1**:242
UNION see LABOR UNION
UNION (county in Arkansas)
map (33° 10′N 92° 38′W) **2**:166
UNION (county in Florida)
map (30° 0′N 82° 25′W) **8**:172
UNION (county in Georgia)
map (34° 50′N 84° 0′W) **9**:114
UNION (county in Illinois)
map (38° 28′N 89° 15′W) **11**:42
UNION (county in Indiana)
map (39° 38′N 84° 56′W) **11**:111
UNION (Iowa)
map (42° 15′N 93° 4′W) **11**:244
UNION (county in Iowa)
map (41° 0′N 94° 15′W) **11**:244
UNION (county in Kentucky)
map (37° 40′N 87° 55′W) **12**:47
UNION (county in Louisiana)
map (32° 48′N 92° 22′W) **12**:430
UNION (Maine)
map (44° 13′N 69° 17′W) **13**:70
UNION (mathematics) see SET THEORY
UNION (Mississippi)
map (32° 34′N 89° 14′W) **13**:469
UNION (county in Mississippi)
map (34° 30′N 89° 0′W) **13**:469
UNION (Missouri)
map (38° 27′N 91° 0′W) **13**:476
UNION (Nebraska)
map (40° 49′N 95° 55′W) **14**:70
UNION (New Jersey)
map (40° 42′N 74° 16′W) **14**:129
UNION (county in New Jersey)
map (40° 40′N 74° 11′W) **14**:129
UNION (county in New Mexico)
map (36° 30′N 103° 30′W) **14**:136
UNION (county in North Carolina)
map (35° 0′N 80° 30′W) **14**:242
UNION (county in Ohio)
map (40° 17′N 83° 22′W) **14**:357
UNION (Oregon)
map (45° 13′N 117° 52′W) **14**:427
UNION (county in Oregon)
map (45° 20′N 118° 0′W) **14**:427
UNION (county in Pennsylvania)
map (40° 58′N 76° 54′W) **15**:147
UNION (South Carolina)
map (34° 43′N 81° 37′W) **18**:98
UNION (county in South Carolina)
map (34° 40′N 81° 40′W) **18**:98
UNION (county in South Dakota)
map (42° 50′N 96° 37′W) **18**:103
UNION (county in Tennessee)
map (36° 20′N 83° 50′W) **19**:104
UNION (West Virginia)
map (37° 36′N 80° 33′W) **20**:111
UNION, LABOR see LABOR UNION
UNION BEACH (New Jersey)
map (40° 27′N 74° 10′W) **14**:129
UNION CITY (Indiana)
map (40° 12′N 84° 49′W) **11**:111
UNION CITY (Michigan)
map (42° 4′N 85° 8′W) **13**:377
UNION CITY (New Jersey)
map (40° 46′N 74° 2′W) **14**:129
UNION CITY (Ohio)
map (40° 10′N 84° 48′W) **14**:357
UNION CITY (Pennsylvania)
map (41° 54′N 79° 51′W) **15**:147
UNION CITY (Tennessee)
map (36° 26′N 89° 3′W) **19**:104
UNION COLLEGE **19**:386–387
Nott, Eliphalet **14**:268
UNION ENROLLMENT ACT
Draft Riots **6**:254
UNION GROVE (Wisconsin)
map (42° 41′N 88° 3′W) **20**:185
UNION ISLANDS see TOKELAU ISLANDS (New Zealand)
UNION JACK **19**:387
flag **8**:134
UNION LABEL **19**:387
UNION LEAGUES **19**:387
UNION NATIONALE PARTY
Duplessis, Maurice Le Noblet **6**:302
UNION PACIFIC RAILROAD **8**:341 *map*
Durant, Thomas Clark **6**:303
Gardner, Alexander **9**:44
locomotive **12**:389 *illus.*
Sun Valley (Idaho) **18**:346
transcontinental railroad **19**:268–269 *map*
UNION PARTY **19**:387 *bibliog.*
UNION POINT (Georgia)
map (33° 37′N 83° 4′W) **9**:114
UNION SHOP **19**:387 *bibliog.*
closed shop **5**:65
right-to-work laws **16**:222
UNION OF SOUTH AFRICA see SOUTH AFRICA
UNION OF SOVIET SOCIALIST REPUBLICS **19**:387–398 *bibliog., illus., map, table*
agriculture **19**:396
food production **1**:197 *table*
irrigation **11**:283
Lysenko, Trofim Denisovich **12**:480
aircraft, military see AIRCRAFT, MILITARY
aircraft carrier
Kiev **1**:220
archaeology
Kostenki **12**:124–125
Pazyryk **15**:122
Urartu **19**:480
architecture see RUSSIAN ART AND ARCHITECTURE
army
armored vehicle **20**:268 *illus.*
rank, military **16**:86 *table*
art see RUSSIAN ART AND ARCHITECTURE
censorship **4**:246; **4**:248
cities
Alma-Ata **1**:305
Arkhangelsk **2**:170
Ashkhabad **2**:231
Astrakhan **2**:269–270
Baku **3**:29–30
Batumi **3**:128
Brest **3**:474
Chelyabinsk **4**:311
Chernobyl **4**:331
Dnepropetrovsk **6**:208
Donetsk **6**:238
Dushanbe **6**:308
Frunze **8**:350
Gorky **9**:251–252
Irkutsk **11**:270
Kalinin **12**:8
Kaliningrad **12**:8
Kaunas **12**:32
Kazan **12**:33
Kharkov **12**:65–66
Kiev **12**:75–76
Kirov **12**:89
Kishinev **12**:90
Krasnodar **12**:127
Krasnoyarsk **12**:127
Krivoi Rog **12**:130
Kuibyshev **12**:135
Leningrad **12**:283–285 *illus., map*
Lvov **12**:473
Magnitogorsk **13**:60
Minsk **13**:460
Moscow **13**:596–599 *illus., map*
Murmansk **13**:649
Narva **14**:23
Novgorod **14**:276
Novosibirsk **14**:277
Odessa **14**:349 *illus.*
Omsk **14**:388
Perm **15**:173
Poltava **15**:418
Pskov **15**:588
Pushkin **15**:631
Riga **16**:221
Rostov-on-Don **16**:321
Ryazan **16**:378–379
Samarkand **17**:45–46
Saratov **17**:75
Sevastopol **17**:215
Smolensk **17**:374
Sochi **18**:11
Sverdlovsk **18**:374–375
Taganrog **19**:9
Tallinn **19**:17
Tartu **19**:41
Tashkent **19**:42
Tbilisi **19**:51
Togliatti **19**:221
Ufa **19**:371
Vilna **19**:599
Vladimir **19**:623
Vladivostok **19**:623–624
Volgograd **19**:629
Voronezh **19**:635
Yakutsk **20**:314
Yalta **20**:315
Yaroslavl **20**:319
Yerevan **20**:326
Zaporozhye **20**:356
climate **19**:390–391 *table*
communications **19**:397
communism see COMMUNISM; COMMUNIST PARTY, SOVIET
criminal justice **5**:350; **15**:554–555
dance
Moiseyev, Igor Aleksandrovich **13**:504
demography **19**:394
economic activity **19**:395–397
banking systems **3**:69
economic planning **7**:47
Kantorovich, Leonid V. **12**:24
Latvian Soviet Socialist Republic **12**:236
education **7**:62
Leningrad State University **12**:285
Moscow State University **13**:599
Soviet education **18**:113–114
Union of Soviet Socialist Republics, universities of the **19**:398–399 *table*
exploration see EXPLORATION—Russia
fishing industry **19**:397
flag **19**:387 *illus.*
foreign policy **8**:226
arms control **2**:178
balance of power **3**:32
cold war **5**:98–99
defense, national **6**:82 *table*
détente **6**:134
foreign aid **8**:225
nuclear strategy **14**:288
Warsaw Treaty Organization **20**:32
forestry **19**:396
geology **19**:391
government **19**:398
civil defense **5**:10
intelligence gathering **11**:205
KGB **12**:64
medals and decorations **13**:262 *illus.*
municipal government **13**:642
politburo **15**:398
soviet **18**:113
Gulag **9**:402
health **19**:394–395
history see RUSSIA/UNION OF SOVIET SOCIALIST REPUBLICS, HISTORY OF
housing **10**:279
human rights **10**:298
hurdy-gurdy **10**:315–316 *illus.*
hydrogen bomb **10**:339–340
land and resources **19**:388–392 *illus., map, table*
languages **19**:393
alphabet **20**:294 *table*
Caucasian languages and literature **4**:218
Indo-Iranian languages **11**:145
Lomonosov, Mikhail Vasilevich **12**:400
Slavic languages **17**:358
Ural-Altaic languages **19**:474–476
law
abortion **1**:60
inheritance **11**:177
socialist law **18**:25
literature see RUSSIAN LITERATURE
manufacturing **19**:395
chemical industry **4**:319
Magnitogorsk **13**:60
map (60° 0′N 80° 0′E) **2**:232
May Day parade **16**:360 *illus.*
military service **19**:398
mining **19**:395–396
coal and coal mining **5**:76–77 *map*
music see RUSSIAN MUSIC
navy
Murmansk **13**:649
naval vessels **14**:56–57 *illus.*
rank, military **16**:87 *table, table*
Sevastopol **17**:215
newspaper **14**:171–172 *table*
Pravda **15**:490
Nurek Dam **6**:16
October Revolution anniversary parade **19**:394 *illus.*
Olympic Games **14**:383
people **2**:242 *illus.*; **19**:392–395
Buryat **3**:583
Chukchi **4**:422
class, social **5**:40
Doukhobors **6**:249
Eskimo **7**:242
ethnic groups **19**:392–393
Kalmyk **12**:8
Karakalpak **12**:26
Kazakh **12**:33
Khants **12**:65
Kirghiz **12**:87–88
Latvian Soviet Socialist Republic **12**:236
Nivkh **14**:204
population **15**:434
Tadzhik **19**:7
Tatar **19**:43–44
Turkmen **19**:347
Turks **19**:348
Tuvan **19**:356
Uighur **19**:374
Uzbek **19**:499
women in society **20**:204 *table*
Yakut **20**:314
physical features
Caucasus Mountains **4**:218 *map*
Commander Islands **5**:137
Communism Peak **5**:150
Kamchatka Peninsula **12**:9 *map*
Kara Kum **12**:26
Kuril Islands **12**:139
Kyzyl Kum **12**:143
Novaya Zemlya **14**:272
Pripet Marshes **15**:553
rift valleys **16**:221
Sakhalin **17**:28
Stanovoi Range **18**:219–220
Ural Mountains **19**:476–477
Wrangel Island **20**:285
Yablonovy Mountains **20**:314
postage stamp **15**:230 *illus.*
prostitution **15**:573
radio astronomy **16**:51
radio and television broadcasting **16**:60
regions
Baltic States **3**:55 *map*
Bessarabia **3**:228
Caucasia **4**:217
Crimea **5**:347–348 *map*
Daghestan **6**:6
Donets Basin **6**:237–238
Franz Josef Land **8**:286
Karelia **12**:27
Ruthenia **16**:375
Siberia **17**:291–292
religion **19**:393
resources **19**:392
Donets Basin **6**:237–238
electrical production **15**:485 *table*

UNION OF SOVIET SOCIALIST REPUBLICS (cont.)
energy **19**:396
energy consumption and production **7**:174 *table*
Kazakh Soviet Socialist Republic **12**:33
natural gas **14**:48
rivers, lakes, and waterways **19**:391
Amu Darya **1**:385–386
Amur River **1**:386
Angara River **1**:411
Aral Sea **2**:108
Azov, Sea of **2**:382
Baikal, Lake **3**:25 *map*
Balkhash, Lake **3**:40
Dnepr River **6**:208
Dnestr River **6**:208–209
Don River **6**:236
Donets River **6**:238
Dvina River, Northern **6**:317
Dvina River, Western **6**:317
Ilmen, Lake **11**:50
Irtysh River **11**:283
Ladoga, Lake **12**:162
Lena River **12**:281
Neman River **14**:80
Neva River **14**:109
Ob River **14**:314
Onega, Lake **14**:389
Pechora River **15**:130
Peipus, Lake **15**:134
Syr Darya **18**:410
Ural River **19**:477
Volga-Baltic Waterway **19**:628
Volga River **19**:628–629 *map*
White Sea **20**:138
Yenisei River **20**:326
rockets and missiles **16**:254; **16**:256–257 *illus.*
satellites, artificial
Cosmos **5**:289–290
Molniya **13**:512
Sputnik **18**:201
socialism *see* SOCIALISM
soils **19**:391
Soviet Socialist Republics
Armenian Soviet Socialist Republic **2**:173
Azerbaijan Soviet Socialist Republic **2**:380–381
Belorussian Soviet Socialist Republic **3**:193
Estonian Soviet Socialist Republic **7**:247 *map*
ethnic groups **19**:392–393
Georgian Soviet Socialist Republic **9**:118–119
government **19**:398
Kazakh Soviet Socialist Republic **12**:33
Kirghiz Soviet Socialist Republic **12**:88
Latvian Soviet Socialist Republic **12**:235–236 *map*
Lithuanian Soviet Socialist Republic **12**:371–372 *map*
Moldavian Soviet Socialist Republic **13**:505–506
Russian Soviet Federated Socialist Republic **16**:373
Tadzhik Soviet Socialist Republic **19**:6–7
Turkmen Soviet Socialist Republic **19**:347
Tuva **19**:356
Ukrainian Soviet Socialist Republic **19**:375
Uzbek Soviet Socialist Republic **19**:499
theater
constructivism **5**:224–225
Evreinov, Nikolai Nikolaevich **7**:325
Kozintsev, Grigory **12**:126
Maly Theater **13**:96
Meyerhold, Vsevolod Emilievich **13**:369
Moscow Art Theater **13**:599
Nemirovich-Danchenko, Vladimir Ivanovich **14**:81
Stanislavsky, Konstantin **18**:218
Taĭrov, Aleksandr Yakovlevich **19**:12
Vakhtangov, Eugene **19**:503
Yiddish theater **20**:328
trade **19**:397
Odessa **14**:349
transportation **19**:397
Chinese Eastern Railway **4**:388
hydrofoil **10**:337
icebreaker **11**:16
railroad **16**:73–74
Trans-Caspian Railroad **19**:267
Trans-Siberian Railroad **19**:267
troika **19**:305
Tunguska fireball **19**:334
vegetation and animal life **19**:392
Vostok Station, Antarctica
glaciers and glaciation **9**:193
UNION OF SOVIET SOCIALIST REPUBLICS, UNIVERSITIES OF THE **19**:398–399 *bibliog., table*
UNION OF SPIRITUAL COMMUNITIES OF CHRIST *see* DOUKHOBORS
UNION SPRINGS (Alabama)
map (32° 9′N 85° 49′W) **1**:234
UNION THEOLOGICAL SEMINARY **19**:399
UNIONTOWN (Alabama)
map (32° 22′N 87° 31′W) **1**:234
UNIONTOWN (Pennsylvania)
map (39° 54′N 79° 44′W) **15**:147
UNIONVILLE (Michigan)
map (43° 39′N 83° 28′W) **13**:377
UNIONVILLE (Missouri)
map (40° 29′N 93° 1′W) **13**:476
UNITARIAN UNIVERSALIST ASSOCIATION **19**:399
UNITARIANISM **19**:399–400 *bibliog.*
Abbot, Francis Ellingwood **1**:53
Ballou, Hosea **3**:53
Biddle, John **3**:247
Channing, William Ellery **4**:281–282
Priestley, Joseph, founder **15**:536–537
Socinianism **18**:26
transcendentalism **19**:268
Unitarian Universalist Association **19**:399
Ware, Henry **20**:29
UNITARY GOVERNMENT
government **9**:268
UNITAS, JOHNNY **19**:400 *bibliog.*
UNITAS FRATRUM *see* CHELCICKY, PETER
UNITÉ D'HABITATION **12**:254 *illus.*
UNITED (Pennsylvania)
map (40° 13′N 79° 31′W) **15**:147
UNITED AIR LINES
Boeing, William Edward **3**:358
UNITED ARAB EMIRATES **19**:400–401 *bibliog., map, table*
Abu Dhabi **1**:66
borders **19**:400
climate **19**:401 *table*
Dubai **6**:287
education
Middle Eastern universities **13**:410–412 *table*
flag **19**:400 *illus.*
history and government **19**:400–401
land, people, and economy **19**:400–401 *map, table*
map (24° 0′N 54° 0′E) **2**:232
UNITED ARAB REPUBLIC **19**:401
Nasser, Gamal Abdel **14**:25
UNITED ARTISTS (film company)
Pickford, Mary **15**:293
UNITED AUTO WORKERS **12**:155 *illus.*; **19**:401 *bibliog.*
Michigan **13**:382
Reuther, Walter P. **16**:184
Woodcock, Leonard **20**:210
UNITED CHURCH OF CANADA
Mount Allison University **13**:618
Winnipeg, University of **20**:180
UNITED CHURCH OF CHRIST **19**:401 *bibliog.*
Congregationalism **5**:184
education
Fisk University **8**:129
Franklin and Marshall College **8**:285
Grinnell College **9**:366
Hood College **10**:225
UNITED DEMOCRATIC FRONT (South Africa)
African National Congress **1**:172
UNITED EMPIRE LOYALISTS *see* LOYALISTS
UNITED FARM WORKERS OF AMERICA **4**:343 *illus.*
boycott **3**:433
Chavez, Cesar **4**:305
migrant labor **13**:417
UNITED FEATURES
press agencies and syndicates **15**:533
UNITED FRUIT COMPANY
Keith, Minor Cooper **12**:37
UNITED GARMENT WORKERS OF AMERICA
clothing industry **5**:65
UNITED IRISHMEN, SOCIETY OF **19**:401 *bibliog.*
Ireland, history of **11**:264
Tone, Wolfe **19**:233
UNITED KINGDOM **19**:402–411 *bibliog., illus., map, table*
See also ENGLAND; GREAT BRITAIN, HISTORY OF; NORTHERN IRELAND; SCOTLAND; WALES
agriculture **19**:410
air force **1**:207–208
See also ROYAL AIR FORCE
aircraft, military *see* AIRCRAFT, MILITARY
aircraft carrier
H.M.S. *Furious* **1**:220 *illus.*
H.M.S. *Illustrious* **1**:220 *illus.*
army
Gurkha **9**:406
rank, military **16**:86 *table*
arts **19**:408–409
See also ENGLISH ART AND ARCHITECTURE; the subheading Great Britain under specific art forms, e.g., ARCHITECTURE; PAINTING; SCULPTURE; etc.
birth control **3**:294–295
climate **19**:404 *table*; **19**:405–406
demography **19**:408
dependencies and associated states
Anguilla **2**:7
Bermuda **3**:219
British Antarctic Territory **3**:489
British Indian Ocean Territory **3**:496–497
Cayman Islands **4**:227
Channel Islands **4**:281 *illus., map*
Falkland Islands **8**:13
Gibraltar **9**:174–175 *illus., map*
Hong Kong **10**:221–223 *illus., map, table*
Isle of Man **11**:298
Montserrat (island) **13**:560
Phoenix Islands **15**:251
Saint Helena **17**:19
Turks and Caicos Islands **19**:349
Virgin Islands **19**:605–606
West Indies Associated States **20**:109
economic activity **19**:409–411
Bank of England **3**:67
education **19**:408 *illus.*
See also BRITISH EDUCATION; ENGLAND—education
fishing **19**:410
flag **8**:134; **19**:402 *illus.*
Union Jack **19**:387
forestry **19**:410
geographic components and boundaries **19**:402
government and politics **19**:411
civil service **5**:14
defense, national **6**:82 *table*
exchequer **7**:327
freedom of the press **8**:297
intelligence gathering **11**:204–205
municipal government **13**:642
political convention **15**:400
viceroy **19**:571
welfare spending **20**:98 *table*
health **19**:408
housing **10**:279
integration, racial **11**:203
land and resources **19**:403–407 *illus., map, table*
languages **19**:407
See also ENGLISH LANGUAGE
legal system
court **5**:315
criminal justice **5**:350
habeas corpus **10**:3–4
Inns of Court **11**:181
literature *see* ENGLISH LITERATURE; IRISH LITERATURE; SCOTTISH LITERATURE; WELSH LITERATURE
manufacturing **19**:409
map (54° 0′N 2° 0′W) **7**:268
medals and decorations **13**:260–262
mining **19**:410
monarchs **9**:312 *table*
See also names of specific monarchs, e.g., VICTORIA, QUEEN of ENGLAND, SCOTLAND, AND IRELAND; WILLIAM I, KING of ENGLAND; etc.
navy
Blake, Robert **3**:325
Britannia Royal Naval College **3**:489
Dreadnought (battleship) **6**:266 *illus.*
Fisher of Kilverstone, John Arbuthnot Fisher, 1st Baron **8**:123
lime (fruit) **12**:343–344
Mountbatten of Burma, Louis Mountbatten, 1st Earl **13**:624–625
naval vessels **14**:57 *illus.*
Nelson, Horatio Nelson, Viscount **14**:79–80
rank, military **16**:87 *table*
Scapa Flow **17**:115
newspapers and periodicals
Economist, The **7**:49
Manchester Guardian **13**:109
Times, The **19**:203
parks and reserves **19**:404
people **19**:407–409
women in society **20**:204 *table*
philately **15**:230 *illus.*
political parties
Conservative parties **5**:205–206
Labour party **12**:156–157
Liberal parties **12**:311
prime ministers **9**:316 *table*
See also names of specific prime ministers, e.g., GREY, CHARLES GREY, 2ND EARL; THATCHER, MARGARET; etc.
veto **19**:567
religion **19**:407–408
resources **19**:406–407
power **19**:410
rivers, lakes, and waterways **19**:406
soils **19**:405
trade **19**:411
transportation **19**:410–411
vegetation and animal life **19**:406
UNITED LAO PATRIOTIC FRONT *see* PATHET LAO
UNITED METHODIST CHURCH
education
Emory University **7**:157
Methodism **13**:344
UNITED MINE WORKERS OF AMERICA **19**:411–412 *bibliog.*
early membership certificate **12**:154 *illus.*
Lewis, John L. (labor leader) **12**:306
Ohio **14**:362
Scranton (Pennsylvania) **17**:156
West Virginia **20**:114
UNITED NATIONS **14**:143 *illus.*; **19**:412–415 *bibliog., illus., table*
agencies
Food and Agriculture Organization **8**:208
General Agreement on Tariffs and Trade **9**:77
International Atomic Energy Agency **11**:218
International Civil Aviation Organization **11**:219
International Development Association **11**:220
International Finance Corporation **11**:220
International Labor Organization **11**:220
International Monetary Fund **11**:222
Postal Union, Universal **15**:461
Refugees, Office of the United Nations High Commissioner for **16**:126
United Nations Children's Fund **19**:415
United Nations Educational, Scientific, and Cultural Organization **19**:415
World Bank **20**:218
World Health Organization **20**:218–219
World Meteorological Organization **20**:219
agriculture and the food supply **1**:198
Arab-Israeli Wars **2**:96–98
architecture **13**:492 *illus.*
Harrison, Wallace K. **10**:60
Bernadotte, Count Folke **3**:220
birth control **3**:295
bodies
Economic and Social Council **19**:413
General Assembly **19**:412–413
International Court of Justice **11**:219
Secretariat **19**:413
Security council **19**:412
Trusteeship Council **19**:413
Bunche, Ralph **3**:562
Conference of the Committee on Disarmament
chemical and biological warfare **4**:313
Dumbarton Oaks **6**:297–298

flag 8:135 *illus.*
Genocide Convention
genocide 9:93
government 9:269
India-Pakistan Wars 11:93
international law 11:221–222
Korea, history of 12:117
Korean War 12:119–122 *illus., maps*
League of Nations 12:257–258
Lebanon 12:267
medals and decorations 13:262 *illus.*
mediation 13:264
membership 19:414 *table*
Namibia 14:12
New York (city) 14:145 *map*
nutritional-deficiency diseases 14:308
Palestine 15:45–46 *map*
postage stamp 15:230 *illus.*
Rockefeller (family) 16:250
sanctions 17:58
Sea, Law of the 17:167–168
secretaries-general
Hammarskjöld, Dag 10:30
Lie, Trygve Halvdan 12:323
Pérez de Cuéllar, Javier 15:164
Thant, U 19:142–143
Waldheim, Kurt 20:9–10
Security Council 19:412 *illus.*
veto 19:567
slavery 17:357
Spaak, Paul Henri 18:118
space law 18:132
Stettinius, Edward Reilly, Jr. 18:262
Suez Crisis 18:325
Third World 19:170
Thorn, Gaston 19:178
trust territory 19:321
Universal Declaration of Human Rights
freedom of speech 8:298
human rights 10:298
World War II 20:280 *illus.*
Yalta Conference 20:315
UNITED NATIONS CHILDREN'S FUND 19:415 *bibliog.*
agriculture and the food supply 1:198
Kaye, Danny 12:33
nutritional-deficiency diseases 14:308
UNITED NATIONS CONFERENCE ON THE HUMAN ENVIRONMENT
conservation 5:203
endangered species 7:166
UNITED NATIONS CONFERENCE ON TRADE AND DEVELOPMENT
General Agreement on Tariffs and Trade 9:77
UNITED NATIONS EDUCATIONAL, SCIENTIFIC, AND CULTURAL ORGANIZATION 19:415 *bibliog.*
freedom of the press 8:297
Huxley, Sir Julian 10:325 *illus.*
International Hydrological Decade 11:220
literacy and illiteracy 12:368
press agencies and syndicates 15:533
UNITED NATIONS MONETARY AND FINANCIAL CONFERENCE *see* BRETTON WOODS CONFERENCE
UNITED NEGRO COLLEGE FUND 19:415
UNITED PRESBYTERIAN CHURCH *see* PRESBYTERIANISM
UNITED PRESS INTERNATIONAL (UPI)
press agencies and syndicates 15:533
UNITED PROVINCES OF CENTRAL AMERICA *see* CENTRAL AMERICAN FEDERATION
UNITED PROVINCES OF THE NETHERLANDS *see* LOW COUNTRIES, HISTORY OF THE
UNITED SERVICE ORGANIZATIONS 19:415–416
Hope, Bob 10:230 *illus.*
UNITED STATES 19:416–433 *bibliog., illus., maps, table*
See also names of specific states, e.g., ARIZONA; TENNESSEE; etc.
administrative law 1:104–105
agriculture
Agriculture, U.S. Department of 1:193–194
cattle and cattle raising 4:215–217
Food Stamp Program 8:212
Future Farmers of America 8:383
irrigation 11:283
plow 15:369–370
Rockefeller Foundation 16:251
air force 1:208–209
flag 8:148 *illus.*
Mitchell, Billy 13:482–483
navy 14:64
rank, military 16:86 *table*
Reserve Officers Training Corps 16:176
Strategic Air Command 18:289
unidentified flying object 19:385
uniforms and insignia 1:207–208 *illus.*
United States Air Force Academy 19:462
United States Armed Forces Institute 19:462
WAF 20:4
World War II 20:264; 20:266 *illus.*
aircraft, military *see* AIRCRAFT, MILITARY
aircraft carrier
U.S.S. *Enterprise* 1:220–221 *illus.*; 20:266 *illus.*
U.S.S. *Hornet* 20:265 *illus.*
army
black Americans 3:307–308
conscription 5:201
Engineers, Corps of 7:178
Explorer 7:338–339
flag 8:148 *illus.*
Fort Benning (Georgia) 8:236
Fort Bragg (North Carolina) 8:236
Fort Dix (New Jersey) 8:236
Fort Hood (Texas) 8:237
Fort Knox (Kentucky) 8:237
Gatling, Richard Jordan, gun 9:58
general staff 9:77
jeep 11:390–391
militia 13:422–423
National Guard 14:34
rangers 16:85
rank, military 16:86 *table, table*
recruitment poster 15:462 *illus.*
regiment 16:128
Reserve Officers Training Corps 16:176
right to bear arms 16:222
uniforms and insignia 2:182–183 *illus.*
United States 2:182–183
United States Armed Forces Institute 19:462
United States Military Academy 19:462–463
WAC 20:3
art *see* AMERICAN ART AND ARCHITECTURE
banking system *see* BANKING SYSTEMS—United States
battleships
flag 8:148 *illus.*
bird, national
eagle 7:4 *illus.*
budget 3:543–544
Congress of the United States 5:186–187
Management and Budget, U.S. Office of 13:107
national debt 14:31–32 *table*
Reagan, Ronald 16:102
cabinet *see* EXECUTIVE BRANCH
censorship 4:246–248
church and state
flag 8:149
citizenship 4:446; 4:447
conditions 4:446 *table*
naturalization 14:50–51
civil rights *see* CIVIL RIGHTS
climate 19:421 *table*; 19:423–425 *maps*
drought 6:273–274
tornado, frequency 19:239–240 *map*
weather variation and extremes 20:80–82 *tables*
communal living 5:142
communications 19:430
newspaper 14:171–172 *table*
radio and television broadcasting 16:53–60
video 19:576a
communism *see* COMMUNISM
congress *see* CONGRESS OF THE UNITED STATES
Constitution of the United States 5:212–223
crime 5:345–346 *table*; 5:347
Mafia 13:46
criminal justice 5:349–350
dance
American Dance Festival 1:338
Denishawn 6:108
Jacob's Pillow Dance Festival 11:346
Kennedy Center for the Performing Arts 12:44
square dance 18:202
tap dancing 19:29
Tharp, Twyla 19:143
demography 19:429 *map*
departments, agencies, and commissions
ACTION (federal agency) 1:89
Agency for International Development 1:183
Agriculture, U.S. Department of 1:193–194
Center for Disease Control 4:249–250
Central Intelligence Agency 4:254
Civil Aeronautics Board 5:9
Civil Service Commission 5:14
Coast Guard, U.S. 5:80
Commerce, U.S. Department of 5:138
Consumer Product Safety Commission 5:225
Council of Economic Advisers 5:310
Defense, U.S. Department of 6:82–83
Domestic Council 6:231
Education, U.S. Department of 7:64
Energy, U.S. Department of 7:173
Engineers, Corps of 7:178
Environmental Protection Agency 7:212
Export-Import Bank 7:340
Fair Employment Practices Act (racial integration) 11:202
Farm Credit Administration 8:23–24
Federal Aviation Administration 8:40
Federal Bureau of Investigation 8:40–41
Federal Communications Commission 8:41; 16:45
Federal Deposit Insurance Corporation 8:41
Federal Home Loan Bank Board 8:41
Federal Housing Administration 8:41
Federal Mediation and Conciliation Service 8:41
Federal National Mortgage Association 8:41
Federal Power Commission 15:486
Federal Reserve System 8:41–42
Federal Trade Commission 8:42
Food and Drug Administration 8:208
General Accounting Office 9:77
General Services Administration 9:77
Government Printing Office, United States 9:270
government regulation 9:270–272
Health and Human Services, U.S. Department of 10:86–87
Housing and Urban Development, U.S. Department of 10:280
Indian Affairs, Bureau of 11:94
Interior, United States Department of the 11:210
Internal Revenue Service 11:218
International Trade Commission, U.S. 11:224
Interstate Commerce Commission 11:225
Job Corps 11:421
Justice, U.S. Department of 11:478
Labor, U.S. Department of 12:151–152
Library of Congress 12:318–319
Management and Budget, U.S. Office of 13:107
meteorology 13:342
Minority Business Development Agency 13:459
National Aeronautics and Space Administration 14:28
National Bureau of Standards 14:30
National Forest System 14:32
National Foundation on the Arts and the Humanities 14:32
National Institute of Mental Health 14:34
National Labor Relations Board 14:34–35
National Mediation Board 14:35
National Ocean Survey 14:35
National Oceanic and Atmospheric Administration 14:346
National Parks System 14:36–39 *illus., map, tables*
National Science Foundation 14:45
National Security Agency 14:45–46
National Security Council 14:46
National Space Development Agency 14:46
National Weather Service 14:46
Nuclear Regulatory Commission 14:287–288
Occupational Safety and Health Administration 14:320–321
Radio Free Europe and Radio Liberty 16:53
Secret Service 17:180–181
Securities and Exchange Commission 17:181
Small Business Administration 17:365
State, U.S. Department of 18:233
Tennessee Valley Authority 19:107–108
Transportation, U.S. Department of 19:282
Treasury, U.S. Department of the 19:285
United States Geological Survey 19:462
U.S. Information Agency 19:490
Veterans Administration 19:565–566
Voice of America 19:626
divorce 6:205–206
economic activity 19:431–432 *illus.*
advertising 1:112–113
consumer credit 5:225
government regulation 9:271–272
inflation 11:170–171
North America 14:234–236
privatization 15:558
Reaganomics 16:102
unemployment rate 7:160
economics 7:49
education *see* UNITED STATES, EDUCATION IN THE
election *see* ELECTION
executive branch *see* EXECUTIVE BRANCH
flag 8:134; 19:416 *illus.*
Somerville (Massachusetts) 18:61
foreign policy 8:226
arms control 2:178
balance of power 3:32
cold war 5:98–99
defense, national 6:82 *table*
détente 6:134
foreign aid 8:224 *table*
Fulbright, J. William 8:356–357
Haig, Alexander 10:12
human rights 10:298–299
isolationism 11:299
Kennan, George F. 12:41
Kissinger, Henry A. 12:90–91
Nicaragua Canal 14:180
Nixon, Richard M. 14:205
North Atlantic Treaty Organization 14:240–241
nuclear strategy 14:288
Organization of American States 14:440
Panama Canal Zone 15:57
Rusk, Dean 16:348
State, U.S. Department of 18:233
Taiwan 19:14
Turkey 19:346
forestry and fishing 19:432
game laws 9:27
geographical linguistics 9:98–100 *maps*
geologic structure 19:422 *map*
fall line 8:13 *map*
government 19:432–433
civil service 5:14
computers and privacy 5:166–167
federalism 8:43
intelligence gathering 11:204–205
municipal government 13:642
political science 15:403
privatization 15:558
republic 16:172
special-interest groups 18:168
Washington, D.C. 20:39–40
health 19:430
birth control 3:294
folk medicine 8:201
hospital 10:257; 10:258

UNITED STATES (cont.)
history *see* UNITED STATES, HISTORY OF THE
House of Representatives *see* HOUSE OF REPRESENTATIVES OF THE UNITED STATES
housing **10**:276–279 *illus.*
hydrogen bomb **10**:339 *illus.*
immigration to **19**:428
labor force **12**:152
labor union **12**:152–156
union membership **12**:156 *table*
land and resources **19**:416–427 *illus., maps, table*
Landsat photograph **12**:184 *illus.*
meteorite craters **13**:339
language
English language **7**:193
lightning **12**:339
literature *see* AMERICAN LITERATURE
manufacturing **19**:432
automotive industry **2**:363–368 *table*
chemical industry **4**:318–319 *table*
manufacturing industries **13**:133 *table*
map (38° 0′N 97° 0′W) **14**:225
Marine Corps, U.S. **13**:153–155 *illus.*
marriage **13**:166 *illus.*
Mason-Dixon line **13**:199 *map*
medals and decorations **13**:260–263 *illus.*
megalopolis **13**:280
motto
e pluribus unum **7**:3
names, personal **14**:9–10
national anthem
Key, Francis Scott **12**:62
"Star-Spangled Banner, The" **18**:226
national parks **14**:36–39 *illus., map, table*
navy **14**:62–65
flag **8**:148 *illus.*
Great Lakes Naval Training Center **9**:320
Great White Fleet **19**:452 *illus.*
Leahy, William Daniel **12**:258
Luce, Stephen B. **12**:450
Mahan, Alfred Thayer **13**:64
Marine Corps, U.S. **13**:153–155
naval vessels **14**:55–57 *illus.*
Norfolk (Virginia) **14**:218
Pensacola (Florida) **15**:153
Perry, Matthew Calbraith **15**:179
Polaris (missile) **15**:393
Porter (family) **15**:444
Poseidon (missile) **15**:458
PT boat **15**:605
rank, military **16**:86 *table, table*
Reserve Officers Training Corps **16**:176
Rickover, Hyman **16**:216
Rodgers (family) **16**:266–267
Seabees **17**:171
ship **17**:275
Shore Patrol **17**:283
Sims, William Sowden **17**:317
uniforms and insignias **14**:65–66 *illus.*
United States Armed Forces Institute **19**:462
United States Merchant Marine Academy **19**:462
United States Military Academy **19**:462–463
United States Naval Academy **19**:463–464
Vietnam War **19**:589 *map*
Waves **20**:71
weapons **20**:74–75
Welles, Gideon **20**:99
newspaper *see* NEWSPAPER
parks and reserves *see* NATIONAL PARKS SYSTEM (U.S.)
people **19**:428–430 *map*
See also INDIANS, AMERICAN
black Americans **3**:304–313
census **4**:248–249
Chicano **4**:343
class, social **5**:40
Creoles **5**:338–339
Eskimo **7**:238–242
ethnic composition **19**:428
Hispanic Americans **10**:177–180 *map*
Magyars **13**:63
North America **14**:230–232
old age **14**:373–374
Oriental Americans **14**:441–443
Pennsylvania Dutch **15**:152
population **15**:433–434
women in society **20**:204 *table*
young people **20**:335–336
philately **15**:230 *illus.*
physical features
Allegheny Mountains **1**:298
Appalachian Mountains **2**:85–86 *illus., map*
basin and range province **3**:110
Blue Ridge Mountains **3**:343
Cascade Range **4**:180
Colorado Plateau **5**:120
Continental Divide **5**:228
Cumberland Gap **5**:387
Cumberland Plateau **5**:387
Delmarva Peninsula **6**:94
Dust Bowl **6**:308 *illus.*
Great Basin **9**:308–309
Great Smoky Mountains **9**:322
hot springs, areas **10**:259
National Forest System **14**:32
Ozark Mountains **14**:480
Piedmont Plateau **15**:295
rift valleys **16**:221
Rocky Mountains **16**:261–263
swamp, marsh, and bog **18**:376–378
tar sands **19**:34
valley and ridge province **19**:507–508
political parties
American Independent party **1**:340
American Labor party **1**:341
boss, political **3**:407–408
caucus **4**:219
Communist party, U.S.A. **5**:151
dark horse **6**:38
Democratic party **6**:99–103
Dixiecrats **6**:207
Farmer-Labor party **8**:24
Federalist party **8**:43–44
Free-Soil party **8**:295
Greenback party **9**:349
Know-Nothing party **12**:102
Liberal Republican party **12**:312
Liberty party **12**:314
patronage **15**:114
political convention **15**:399 *illus.*
Populist party **15**:440
president of the United States **15**:523–524
presidential elections **15**:530
primary election **15**:538–539
Progressive party **15**:564–565
Republican party **16**:172–176
Senate of the United States **17**:199
Socialist Labor party **18**:24–25
Socialist party **18**:25
Socialist Workers' party **18**:25–26
12th Amendment **19**:358
Union party **19**:387
United States, history of the **19**:443
vice-president of the United States **19**:568–569
political rights
Greenback party **9**:349
poverty **15**:478–480
threshold index **15**:478 *table*
president *see* PRESIDENT OF THE UNITED STATES
prison **15**:554–555
railroad *see* RAILROAD
regions *see* NEW ENGLAND; SOUTH, THE (U.S.)
religion **19**:429
religious cults **16**:143
resources **19**:426–427 *maps*
breeder reactor **3**:472
coal and coal mining **5**:75–79 *map*
electricity, production and transmission **15**:482 *map*
fuel use **8**:353 *table*
natural gas **14**:48
petroleum industry **15**:215
tin **19**:205
water resources and uses, regional **20**:51 *table*
rivers, lakes, and waterways **19**:424–425
Arkansas River **2**:170
Canadian River **4**:94
canal **4**:96–97
Champlain, Lake **4**:277
Chesapeake and Delaware Canal **4**:334
Chesapeake and Ohio Canal **4**:334
Colorado River (Colorado) **5**:120–121 *map*
Delaware River **6**:91
Engineers, Corps of **7**:178
fall line **8**:13 *map*
Great Lakes **9**:319–320
Green River **9**:349
Intracoastal Waterway **11**:232
Mead, Lake **13**:251
Michigan, Lake **13**:382–383 *map*
Mississippi River **13**:473–474 *map*
Missouri River **13**:481 *map*
Ohio River **14**:362–363
Potomac River **15**:467
Red River **16**:113
Rio Grande **16**:227
Snake River **17**:383
Tahoe, Lake **19**:10
Tennessee River **19**:107
roads and highways **16**:237–238; **19**:278–280 *illus.*; **19**:282
See also ROADS AND HIGHWAYS
rockets and missiles *see* ROCKETS AND MISSILES
seal, official
Great Seal of the United States **9**:322
Senate *see* SENATE OF THE UNITED STATES
service industries **19**:432
slavery **3**:305 *map*; **17**:351–352
black Americans **3**:306–308
social security **18**:14–16
social and welfare services *see* SOCIAL AND WELFARE SERVICES—United States
socialism *see* SOCIALISM
soils and surface deposits **19**:422–423
Supreme Court *see* SUPREME COURT OF THE UNITED STATES
taxation **19**:46–47
revenue sharing **16**:185
Tax Court, U.S. **19**:45
territories, possessions, etc.
American Samoa **1**:366 *map*
Caroline Islands (U.S.) **4**:160
Guam (U.S.) **9**:385
Mariana Islands **13**:150–151
Marshall Islands **13**:173
Midway **13**:414
Pacific Islands, Trust Territory of the **15**:5
Panama Canal Zone **15**:57
Phoenix Islands **15**:251
Puerto Rico **15**:614–616 *illus., map, table*
United States outlying territories **19**:464
Virgin Islands **19**:605–606
Wake Island **20**:8
territory **19**:122
theater
American Educational Theatre Association **1**:338
American National Theater and Academy **1**:352
Astor Place Riot **2**:269
Baker, George Pierce **3**:27
barnstorming **3**:86
Barrymore (family) **3**:96
Belasco, David **3**:173–174
Booth (family) **3**:394
Broadway **3**:499–500
Chestnut Street Theatre **4**:337
Clurman, Harold **5**:71–72
Cohan, George M. **5**:95
Cornell, Katharine **5**:268
Crawford, Cheryl **5**:333
Daly, Augustin **6**:15
Dunlap, William **6**:300–301
Federal Theatre Project **8**:42
Ford's Theatre **8**:224
Forrest, Edwin **8**:234
Frohman, Charles and Daniel **8**:338
Group Theatre, The **9**:376–377
guerrilla theater **9**:392
Hayes, Helen **10**:82
Houseman, John **10**:274
Kennedy Center for the Performing Arts **12**:44
Living Theatre **12**:376–377
Lunt, Alfred, and Fontanne, Lynn **12**:465
Mercury Theatre **13**:308
Merrick, David **13**:312
music hall, vaudeville, and burlesque **13**:671–673
musical comedy **13**:673–675
Obie Awards **14**:316
Off-Broadway theater **14**:352–353
Off-Off Broadway theater **14**:353
Papp, Joseph **15**:72
Provincetown Players **15**:584
repertory theater **16**:160
Robeson, Paul **16**:242
Schechner, Richard **17**:117
showboats **17**:286
theater, history of the **19**:149
Theatre Guild **19**:154
Tony Awards **19**:236
Yiddish theater **20**:328
Ziegfeld Follies **20**:363
trade **19**:432
North America **14**:235
transportation **19**:432
See also RAILROAD; ROADS AND HIGHWAYS
Uncle Sam **19**:381–382
unknown soldier **19**:470
urban planning *see* URBAN PLANNING
vegetation **19**:425–426 *map*
vice-president *see* VICE-PRESIDENT OF THE UNITED STATES
weights and measures **20**:94
welfare spending **20**:98 *table*
UNITED STATES (ship) **14**:325 *illus.*
UNITED STATES, EDUCATION IN THE **19**:430; **19**:434–435 *bibliog.*
See also WORK STUDY EDUCATIONAL PROGRAMS; names of specific educational institutions, e.g., HARVARD UNIVERSITY; OBERLIN COLLEGE; etc.; articles on universities and colleges in specific states, e.g., OREGON, STATE UNIVERSITIES AND COLLEGES OF; VIRGINIA, STATE UNIVERSITIES AND COLLEGES OF; etc.
academic freedom **1**:68–69
academy **1**:71
accreditation of schools and colleges **1**:79
adult education **1**:110
Advanced Placement Program **1**:110
alternative schools **1**:313
apprenticeship **2**:91
bilingual education **3**:251
business education **3**:588
busing, school **3**:589–590
career education **4**:146
Carnegie Foundations **4**:155
Center for Advanced Study in the Behavioral Sciences **4**:249
Chautauqua **4**:305
correspondence school **5**:276
creationism **5**:335–336
degree, academic **6**:85
education **7**:61–62
Education, U.S. Department of **7**:64
Education Commission of the States **7**:64
federal intervention **19**:434–435
financing
equal protection of the laws **7**:224
land-grant colleges **12**:178
property tax **15**:571
United Negro College Fund **19**:415
foreign languages, teaching of **8**:225
fraternities and sororities **8**:288
free schools **8**:294–295
G.I. Bill of Rights **9**:170
graduate education **9**:276–277
Head Start **10**:85
honor system **10**:223–224
humanities, education in the **10**:300
Indian schools, American **11**:106
industrial arts programs **11**:154–155
integration, racial **11**:202–203
Alexander v. *Holmes County (Miss.) Board of Education* **1**:275
Brown v. *Board of Education of Topeka, Kansas* **3**:517
Clark, Kenneth B. **5**:39
Coleman Report **5**:100
University of California v. *Bakke* **19**:470
Ivy League **11**:337
legislation **19**:435
Morrill Acts **13**:588
National Defense Education Act **14**:32
Smith-Hughes Act **17**:372
Smith-Lever Act of 1914 **17**:372
literacy and illiteracy **12**:368–370
local authority **19**:434
lyceum **12**:474
middle schools and junior high schools **13**:412–413
military academies **13**:420–421
National Assessment of Educational Progress **14**:29
National Education Association **14**:32

National Honor Society **14**:34
National Institute of Education **14**:34
open admission **14**:398
Parents and Teachers, National Congress of **15**:84
Phi Beta Kappa **15**:226
primary education **15**:537–538
private schools **15**:557
progressive education **15**:564
reading education **16**:100–101
Right-to-Read Program **16**:222
religion
Engel v. *Vitale* **7**:176
freedom of religion **8**:297
Reserve Officers Training Corps **16**:176
scholarships
National Merit Scholarships **14**:35
scholarships, fellowships, and loans **17**:130–131
Scopes Trial **17**:148
secondary education **17**:179–180
Servicemen's Opportunity Colleges **17**:211
special education **18**:166–167
blind, education of the **3**:331–332
handicapped persons **10**:36
state authority **19**:434
statistics **19**:434
student movements **18**:307–308
Supreme Court decisions **19**:435
teacher education **19**:54
theological seminaries **19**:157
United States, history of the **19**:457–458
United States Student Association **19**:464
university **19**:467–469
Upward Bound **19**:473
vocational education **19**:624–625
Winnetka Plan **20**:180
Yale Report of 1828 **20**:315
young people **20**:335
UNITED STATES, HISTORY OF THE **19**:435–462 *bibliog.*, *illus.*, *maps*
See also the subheading history under names of specific states, e.g., FLORIDA; KENTUCKY; etc.
black Americans *see* BLACK AMERICANS
common law **5**:140–141
Communist party, U.S.A. **5**:151
conservation **5**:201–203
Constitution of the United States *see* CONSTITUTION OF THE UNITED STATES
costume **5**:302–303 *illus.*
Cuba **5**:379–380
Democratic party **6**:99–103
dentistry **6**:115–116
duel **6**:293
economic development **19**:431
feminism **8**:48–49
flag **8**:134; **8**:135 *illus.*
historians *see* HISTORY—American historians
human rights **10**:298
immigration **11**:55–56 *map*
ethnic minorities **7**:255–256
Indians, American see INDIANS, AMERICAN—tribes, North American
integration, racial **11**:202–203
liberalism **12**:312
metric system **13**:346
navy **14**:62–65
pledge of allegiance **15**:364
political convention **15**:399–400
political parties **15**:400–403
postal services **15**:459–460
president of the United States **15**:522–528
presidential elections **15**:529–532
radicalism **16**:43–44
referendum and initiative **16**:119
Republican party **16**:172–176
slavery *see* SLAVERY
socialism **18**:23
Supreme Court of the United States *see* SUPREME COURT OF THE UNITED STATES
prior to 1492
North American archaeology **14**:236–240
1492–1607 discovery and colonization
See also EXPLORATION—North America
Cibola, Seven Golden Cities of **4**:428
conquistadors **5**:197
Coronado, Francisco Vázquez de **5**:270
de Soto, Hernando **6**:63
early exploration and settlement **19**:437 *map*
exploration **7**:335
Indian Wars **11**:107–110 *maps*
Menéndez de Avilés, Pedro **13**:297
New Spain **14**:142
Ponce de Léon, Juan **15**:425–426
Roanoke Colony **16**:239
1607–1783 Colonial period
Adams, Abigail **1**:93
Adams, Samuel **1**:97–98
agriculture, history of **1**:192
Albany Congress **1**:251–252
Alden, John **1**:268
Allouez, Claude Jean **1**:303
American literature **1**:342
American music **1**:348–349
American Revolution *see* AMERICAN REVOLUTION
Andros, Sir Edmund **1**:409
Articles of Confederation **2**:220
Bacon's Rebellion **3**:14
Berkeley, Sir William **3**:213
Block, Adriaen **3**:334
Boone, Daniel **3**:393–394
Boston Post Road **3**:410
Bradford, William **3**:437
Brewster, William **3**:476
British Empire **3**:496
Cadillac, Antoine Laumet de La Mothe, Sieur de **4**:11
Campbell, John **4**:65
Carver, John **4**:179
Charter Oak **4**:300
Chesapeake colonies **19**:436
coin **14**:296 *illus.*
colonial styles in North America **5**:109–111
Common Sense (book) **5**:141
Continental Congress **5**:228
cooking **5**:239 *illus.*
De Lancey (family) **6**:61
Declaration of Independence **6**:74–76
distillery **20**:133 *illus.*
early Indian wars **19**:437–438
Endecott, John **7**:168
exploration and settlement **19**:437 *map*
fire prevention and control **8**:103
folk dance **8**:199
Franklin, Benjamin **8**:282–284
French and Indian Wars *see* FRENCH AND INDIAN WARS
fur trade **8**:371
growth of slavery **19**:438
Hancock, John **10**:34
Henry, Patrick **10**:122–123
hunting **10**:313
indentured service **11**:78
Indian Wars **11**:107–109
Intolerable Acts **11**:231–232
Jamestown (Virginia) **11**:357
journalism **11**:454
King Philip's War **12**:82
law, history of **12**:246
Livingston (family) **12**:377
London Company **12**:405
manufacturing **13**:132
marriage **13**:166
Massachusetts Bay Company **13**:212
Mayflower **13**:247
Mecklenburg Declaration of Independence **13**:260
Molasses Act **13**:505
Navigation Acts **14**:61–62
New England colonies **19**:436
New Netherland **14**:140
New Sweden **14**:142
Ohio Company **14**:362
Penn, William **15**:144–145
Pequot War **15**:158
Philadelphia (Pennsylvania) **15**:227
Pilgrims **15**:302
Plymouth Colony **15**:374
Pontiac's Rebellion **15**:427
primary education **15**:537
publishing **15**:611
Puritanism **15**:630
Regulators **16**:129
religion in **19**:438
Restoration colonies **19**:436–437
Rhode Island **16**:201
Rolfe, John **16**:271
rum **16**:344
Rush, Benjamin **16**:347
Salem Witch Trials **17**:31
Samoset **17**:47
Smith, John **17**:369
Spanish missions **18**:160–161
Stamp Act **18**:216
Townshend Acts **19**:255–256
Virginia Declaration of Rights (1776) **3**:252
Williamsburg (Virginia) **20**:162 *illus.*
Wolstenholme Towne **20**:200
Zenger, John Peter **20**:359
1783–1815 the new nation
Alien and Sedition Acts **1**:293–294
Annapolis Convention **2**:32
Anti-Federalists **2**:61
Articles of Confederation **19**:441
Bainbridge, William **3**:26–27
Bank of the United States **3**:67
Barbary States **3**:76
Bill of Rights *see* BILL OF RIGHTS
Blount, William **3**:341
Burr, Aaron **3**:579–580
Carondelet, Héctor, Baron de **4**:162
Chesapeake (ship) **4**:333
Clinton (family) **5**:59–60
Conestoga **5**:175–176
Constitution **1**:365
Constitutional Convention **1**:365 *illus.*; **5**:223–224; **19**:442
Crèvecoeur, Michel Guillaume Jean de (author) **5**:342
Fallen Timbers, Battle of **8**:14
Federalist, The **8**:43
Federalist party **8**:43–44
Flaget, Benedict Joseph **8**:149
Fort Dearborn **8**:236
Franklin, State of **8**:285
Gallatin, Albert **9**:16–17
Hamilton, Alexander **10**:27–28
Harrison, William Henry **10**:60–61
Hartford Convention **10**:62
Indian treaties **11**:106–107
Indian Wars **11**:107–109
Jay's Treaty **11**:387
Jefferson, Thomas **11**:391–393
journalism **11**:454
Kentucky and Virginia Resolutions **12**:51–52
Lewis and Clark Expedition **12**:307–308
Louisiana Purchase **12**:435–436
Madison, Dolley **13**:41
Madison, James **13**:41–43
Michigan **13**:382
Northwest Territory **14**:259–260
Ohio Company of Associates **14**:362
publishing **15**:611
the republic **19**:442–443
Rush, Benjamin **16**:347
Russel, Benjamin **16**:348–349
Seabury, Samuel **17**:172
Shays's Rebellion **17**:247
tariff acts **19**:36–37
territorial expansion **19**:445–446 *map*
Thomas, Isaiah **19**:173
Tripolitan War **19**:302–303
War of 1812 *see* WAR OF 1812
Washington, George **20**:42–44
West Florida Controversy **20**:108
Whiskey Rebellion **20**:133
XYZ Affair **20**:313
Yazoo Land Fraud **20**:320
1815-1865 states' rights and slavery question
abolitionists **1**:58
Adams, Charles Francis **1**:93
Adams, John Quincy **1**:96–97
Alamo, the **1**:239–240
Alvarado, Juan Bautista **1**:319
American Colonization Society **1**:338
Anti-Masonic party **2**:63
Aroostook War **2**:187
Ashley, William Henry **2**:231
Bagley, Sarah G. **3**:22
Beale, Edward Fitzgerald **3**:139
Benjamin, Judah P. **3**:201–202
Benton, Thomas Hart (political leader) **3**:206
Biddle, Nicholas **3**:247
Birney, James Gillespie **3**:293
Black, Jeremiah Sullivan **3**:303
Black Hawk War **3**:315
Breckinridge, John Cabell **3**:471
Bridger, James **3**:484
Brown, John **3**:515
Buchanan, James **3**:532–534
Calhoun, John C. **4**:29
Caroline affair **4**:160
Carson, Kit **4**:170
Civil War *see* CIVIL WAR, U.S.
Clay, Henry **5**:46
Clayton-Bulwer Treaty **5**:47
coin **14**:296 *illus.*
Compromise of 1850 **5**:158
Confederate States of America **5**:176–177
Constitutional Union party **5**:224
Crittenden Compromise **5**:352–353
Crockett, Davy **5**:355–356
domestic politics **19**:445–446
Donner Party **6**:240
Douglas, Stephen A. **6**:247–248
Douglass, Frederick **6**:248–249
economic and cultural ferment **19**:444
Emigrant Aid Company **7**:156
Fillmore, Millard **8**:79–80
Free-Soil party **8**:295
Fugitive Slave Laws **8**:355
Gadsden Purchase **9**:7
Garrison, William Lloyd **9**:51
gold rush **9**:228
Homestead Act **10**:214
Independent Treasury System **11**:78
Indian Territory **11**:106
Indian Wars **11**:108–110 *map*
Jackson, Andrew **11**:340–342
Jefferson, Territory of **11**:391
Kansas-Nebraska Act **12**:22–23
Kitchen Cabinet **12**:91
Know-Nothing party **12**:102
Liberty party **12**:314
Lincoln, Abraham **12**:347–349
Manifest Destiny **13**:117
Mexican War *see* MEXICAN WAR
Missouri Compromise **13**:480–481
Monroe, James **13**:541–542
Monroe Doctrine **13**:543
mountain men **13**:623–624
nullification **14**:292
Oregon Question **14**:431
Oregon Trail **14**:431
Ostend Manifesto **14**:457
Phillips, Wendell **15**:239
Pierce, Franklin **15**:295–296
Polk, James K. **15**:404–405
pony express **15**:428
popular sovereignty **15**:433
Preemption Act **15**:502
Santa Fe Trail **17**:68
Scott, Winfield **17**:154–155
secession **19**:448
sectional conflicts **19**:446–447
Seminole Wars **17**:197
state rights **18**:233–234
Taylor, Zachary **19**:50–51
territorial expansion **19**:445–447 *maps*
transcendentalism **19**:268
Trent Affair **19**:290–291
Turner, Nat **19**:350–351
Tyler, John **19**:361–362
Underground Railroad **19**:383
Utah War **19**:496
Van Buren, Martin **19**:510–512
Webster, Daniel **20**:88
Webster-Ashburton Treaty **20**:89
Wells, Fargo and Company **20**:101
1865–1877 Reconstruction
Alabama Claims **1**:238
Belknap, William Worth **3**:184
black codes **3**:313–314
Black Friday **3**:315
Bozeman Trail **3**:434
Bristow, Benjamin Helm **3**:488
carpetbaggers **4**:164–165
Centennial Exposition **4**:249
Chisholm Trail **4**:398
Civil Rights Acts **5**:13
Crédit Mobilier of America **5**:336
Freedmen's Bureau **8**:295–296
Gilded Age **9**:180
Grant, Ulysses S. **9**:287–289
Johnson, Andrew **11**:430–431
Ku Klux Klan **12**:133
Liberal Republican party **12**:312
Reconstruction **16**:108–110; **19**:449–450
San Juan Boundary Dispute **17**:55
Scalawags **17**:106
Schurz, Carl **17**:137–138
Sumner, Charles **18**:339–340
transcontinental railroad **19**:268–269
Whiskey Ring **20**:133
1877–1918 industrial development and westward expansion
Aldrich, Nelson Wilmarth **1**:269
Altgeld, John Peter **1**:313
Anthony, Susan B. **2**:49–50

UNITED STATES, HISTORY OF THE (cont.)
Arthur, Chester Alan **2**:218–219
Ballinger, Richard A. **3**:49
Bass, Sam **3**:117
Bean, Roy **3**:140
Bering Sea controversy **3**:212
Blaine, James Gillespie **3**:323–324
Bland-Allison Act **3**:327
Brownsville Raid **3**:519
Bryan, William Jennings **3**:528–529
Buffalo Bill **3**:546–547
Bull Moose party **3**:558
Bunau-Varilla, Philippe Jean **3**:562
Catt, Carrie Chapman **4**:213
Chinese Exclusion Acts **4**:388–389
Cleveland, Grover **5**:52–54
Comstock Lode **5**:167
cowboy **5**:320–321
Coxey's Army **5**:323
Du Bois, W. E. B. **6**:285–286
Earp, Wyatt **7**:11
free silver **8**:295
frontier **8**:340–345
Garfield, James A. **9**:45–46
ghost towns **9**:169–170
Greenback party **9**:349
Harrison, Benjamin **10**:58–59
Hay-Pauncefote Treaty **10**:80
Hayes, Rutherford B. **10**:82–83
immigration and rise of labor unions **19**:451
Industrial Revolution **11**:159
industrialization and exploitation of natural resources **19**:450–451
Italian immigrants **11**:54 *illus.*
Jim Crow laws **11**:418
Knights of Labor **12**:101
McKinley, William **13**:30–31
mugwumps **13**:632
Open Door Policy **14**:398
outlaws **14**:468–469
Panama Canal **15**:57
Platt Amendment **15**:362
Populist party **15**:440
Progressive Era **15**:564
Progressive party **15**:564–565
Pullman Strike **15**:619
railroad **16**:72
Roosevelt, Theodore **16**:309–311
Socialist party **18**:25
Spanish-American War *see* SPANISH-AMERICAN WAR
Sperry, Elmer Ambrose **18**:179
suffrage, women's **18**:326
Taft, William Howard **19**:8–9
Wilson, Woodrow **20**:165–167
World War I *see* WORLD WAR I
1918–1929 economic growth and decline
Berger, Victor L. **3**:209–210
Black Hand **3**:315
bootlegging **3**:395
Borah, William Edgar **3**:395–396
Coolidge, Calvin **5**:240–241
Farmer-Labor party **8**:24
Harding, Warren G. **10**:46–47
La Follette, Robert M. **12**:145–146
League of Nations **12**:257
Nonpartisan League **14**:217
optimism in the 1920s **19**:453–454
Palmer, A. Mitchell **15**:50
prohibition **15**:565
1929–1945 Depression and New Deal
Agricultural Adjustment Administration **1**:188
American Labor party **1**:341
Berle, A. A. **3**:214
Bohlen, Charles Eustis **3**:361
Bonus Army **3**:382
Brain Trust **3**:448–449
Browder, Earl **3**:513
Byrnes, James Francis **3**:602-603
Depression of the 1930s **6**:119–120
Dust Bowl **6**:308 *illus.*
Four Freedoms **8**:253
Good Neighbor Policy **9**:245
Hatch Acts **10**:68
Hoover, Herbert **10**:228–229
Indian Reorganization Act **11**:106
Lend-Lease **12**:281
Morgenthau (family) **13**:579
National Recovery Administration **14**:45
New Deal **14**:119–120
Norris, George W. **14**:223
Public Works Administration **15**:611
Roosevelt, Franklin Delano **16**:307–309
Smith Act **17**:371
Wallace, Henry A. **20**:14
Willkie, Wendell L. **20**:162
Works Progress Administration **20**:217–218
World War II *see* WORLD WAR II
1945–1964 cold war **5**:98–99
Acheson, Dean **1**:81
Anzus Treaty **2**:73
Barkley, Alben W. **3**:83
Bay of Pigs invasion **3**:132
Bunche, Ralph **3**:562
Central Treaty Organization **4**:255
Cuban Missile Crisis **5**:380
Dewey, Thomas E. **6**:147
Dulles, John Foster **6**:295–296
Eisenhower, Dwight D. **7**:94–96
Fair Deal **8**:8–9
Kefauver, Estes **12**:36
Kennedy, John F. **12**:42–44
Korean War *see* KOREAN WAR
Lodge (family) **12**:392
McCarran Act **13**:7–8
McCarthy, Joseph R. **13**:8
Marshall, George C. **13**:172
Marshall Plan **13**:173
Point Four Program **15**:381
Progressive party **15**:564–565
Rosenberg, Julius and Ethel **16**:315
Stevenson, Adlai Ewing II **18**:264–265 *illus.*
Truman, Harry S. **19**:317–319
U-2 incident **19**:369
Vandenberg, Arthur H. **19**:518
Vietnam War *see* VIETNAM WAR
Warren Commission **20**:31–32
1964–1970 civil rights and peace movements
Agnew, Spiro T. **1**:186
Alliance for Progress **1**:302
American Independent party **1**:340
counterculture **5**:311–312
Dirksen, Everett M. **6**:188
Johnson, Lyndon B. **11**:433–434
Kennedy, Robert F. **12**:44
King, Martin Luther, Jr. **12**:80–81
Nixon, Richard M. **14**:204–206
Pueblo Incident **15**:614
race relations in 1960s and 1970s **19**:459
race riots **16**:35
Tonkin Gulf Resolution **19**:234–235
Vietnam War *see* VIETNAM WAR
War on Poverty **20**:28
1970-present
Bicentennial, U.S. **3**:243
Carter, Jimmy **4**:171–172
Ford, Gerald R. **8**:221–222
Haig, Alexander **10**:12
Iranian hostage crisis **11**:253–254
Kissinger, Henry A. **12**:90–91
Nixon, Richard M. **14**:204–206
Pentagon Papers **15**:154
Reagan, Ronald **16**:101–102
16th Amendment **17**:331
Watergate **19**:460–461; **20**:64
UNITED STATES AIR FORCE ACADEMY **19**:462 *bibliog.*
UNITED STATES ARMED FORCES INSTITUTE **19**:462
UNITED STATES ARMY WAR COLLEGE
Carlisle (Pennsylvania) **4**:151
UNITED STATES AUTO CLUB
automobile racing **2**:360
UNITED STATES CHESS FEDERATION
chess **4**:336
UNITED STATES COAST GUARD *see* COAST GUARD, U.S.
UNITED STATES COAST GUARD ACADEMY **19**:462
military academies **13**:420–421
UNITED STATES CONSTITUTION *see* CONSTITUTION OF THE UNITED STATES
UNITED STATES FISH AND WILDLIFE SERVICE
bird-watching **3**:290
UNITED STATES FOOD AND DRUG ADMINISTRATION *see* FOOD AND DRUG ADMINISTRATION
UNITED STATES FOREST SERVICE
National Forest System **14**:32
UNITED STATES GEOLOGICAL SURVEY **19**:462 *bibliog.*
anthropological linguistics **2**:51
Dutton, Clarence Edward **6**:315–316
Earth resources **19**:462
geochemistry **9**:95
Hayden, Ferdinand **10**:80–81; **19**:462
history **19**:462
King, Clarence **19**:462
maps and mapmaking **13**:140
Marsh, Othniel Charles **13**:171
Moore, Raymond Cecil **13**:570
19th-century surveys **19**:462
Powell, John Wesley **15**:481; **19**:462
river and stream **16**:229
Trans-Alaska Pipeline **19**:266–267
Wheeler, George M. **19**:462
UNITED STATES MARINES *see* MARINE CORPS, U.S.
UNITED STATES MERCHANT MARINE ACADEMY **19**:462
UNITED STATES MILITARY ACADEMY **19**:462–463 *bibliog., illus.*
Cram, Ralph Adams **5**:328
honor system **10**:224
UNITED STATES NATIONAL ARBORETUM **19**:463
UNITED STATES NAVAL ACADEMY **13**:190 *illus.*; **19**:463–464 *bibliog., illus.*
UNITED STATES NAVAL OBSERVATORY **19**:464
Maury, Matthew Fontaine **13**:238
Newcomb, Simon **14**:165
Phobos **15**:249
Pluto (planet) **15**:373
UNITED STATES NAVAL RESEARCH LABORATORY
X-ray astronomy **20**:306
UNITED STATES OUTLYING TERRITORIES **19**:464 *bibliog.*
UNITED STATES PHARMACOPOEIA
pharmacopoeia **15**:220–221
UNITED STATES PUBLIC HEALTH SERVICE
smoking **17**:373–374
UNITED STATES SLO-PITCH SOFTBALL ASSOCIATION (USSSA)
softball **18**:35
UNITED STATES STEEL CORPORATION
Fairless, Benjamin **8**:9
Gary (Indiana) **9**:52
Gary, Elbert Henry **9**:52–53
Morgan (family) **13**:577
Pennsylvania **15**:151
UNITED STATES STUDENT ASSOCIATION **19**:464
UNITED STATES TRUST TERRITORY OF THE PACIFIC ISLANDS *see* PACIFIC ISLANDS, TRUST TERRITORY OF THE
UNITED STATES v. BUTLER **19**:464
UNITED STATES v. CURTISS-WRIGHT EXPORT CORPORATION **19**:464
UNITED STATES v. DARBY **19**:465
Hammer v. *Dagenhart* **10**:30
UNITED STATES v. E. C. KNIGHT COMPANY **19**:465
Swift and Company v. *United States* **18**:390
UNITED STATES v. RICHARD M. NIXON **19**:465
Constitution of the United States **5**:219
executive privilege **7**:329
Jaworski, Leon **11**:386
Watergate **20**:64
UNITED STATES WEATHER BUREAU *see* NATIONAL WEATHER SERVICE
UNITED STEELWORKERS OF AMERICA **19**:465
Abel, I. W. **1**:55
UNITED STEELWORKERS OF AMERICA v. WEBER **19**:465
UNITED TECHNOLOGIES CORPORATION **1**:128 *table*
UNITED TRANSPORTATION UNION
Railway Brotherhoods **16**:77
UNITED WAY OF AMERICA
fund raising **8**:360
UNITIES (literature)
narrative and dramatic devices **14**:23
UNITS, PHYSICAL **19**:465–467 *bibliog., tables*
See also WEIGHTS AND MEASURES
International Bureau of Weights and Measures **11**:219
measurement **13**:253–257
metric system **13**:345–347
National Bureau of Standards **14**:30
UNITY (Maine)
map (44° 40′N 69° 14′W) **13**:70
UNITY (Saskatchewan)
map (52° 27′N 109° 10′W) **17**:81
UNIVAC **19**:467 *bibliog.*
computer **5**:160b
computer industry **5**:160n
Eckert, John Presper **7**:39
Mauchly, John William **13**:232
UNIVALVE
shell **17**:252 *illus.*
UNIVERSAL AUTOMATIC COMPUTER *see* UNIVAC
UNIVERSAL JOINT *see* TRANSMISSION, AUTOMOTIVE
UNIVERSAL LANGUAGE *see* LANGUAGES, ARTIFICIAL
UNIVERSAL NEGRO IMPROVEMENT ASSOCIATION
black nationalism **3**:318
Garvey, Marcus **9**:52
UNIVERSAL PICTURES (film studio)
film, history of **8**:87
UNIVERSAL POSTAL UNION *see* POSTAL UNION, UNIVERSAL
UNIVERSAL PRODUCT CODE (UPC)
food industry **8**:210
UNIVERSAL SPIDER, THE *see* LOUIS XI, KING OF FRANCE
UNIVERSAL TIME
Greenwich mean time **9**:354
UNIVERSALISM **19**:467 *bibliog.*
Ballou, Hosea **3**:53
Murray, John (clergyman) **13**:650
Unitarian Universalist Association **19**:399
Unitarianism **19**:400
UNIVERSALS **19**:467 *bibliog.*
Abelard, Peter **1**:55–56
William of Occam **20**:155
UNIVERSE, ORIGIN OF THE *see* COSMOLOGY (astronomy)
UNIVERSITY **19**:467–469 *bibliog.*
See also names of specific universities, e.g., OXFORD, UNIVERSITY OF; YALE UNIVERSITY; etc.
academic freedom **1**:68–69
accreditation of schools and colleges **1**:79
adult education **1**:110
African universities **1**:175–178
athletics
football **8**:214–218
golf **9**:239
Ivy League **11**:337
National Collegiate Athletic Association **14**:30
British education **3**:495
Canadian education **4**:92
Chinese universities **4**:393–394 *table*
coeducation **5**:90–91
computers in education **5**:165
curriculum **5**:393–394
arts, education in the **2**:224–225
business education **3**:588
physics, history of **15**:282
degree, academic **6**:85
education **7**:59–62
Educational Testing Service **7**:66
European universities **7**:306–309 *table*
Flexner, Abraham **8**:164
fraternities and sororities **8**:288
fund raising **8**:360
graduate education **9**:276–277
Great Britain, history of **9**:311
Harper, William Rainey **10**:55
history **19**:468–469
humanities, education in the **10**:300
Japanese universities **11**:382–383 *table*
Korean universities **12**:118–119
land-grant colleges **12**:178
Latin American universities **12**:232–233
Middle Ages **13**:395–396
Middle Eastern universities **13**:410–412
military academies **13**:420–421
New Zealand universities **14**:163
open admission **14**:398
Open University **14**:399
professional and educational organizations
American Association for Higher Education **1**:336
American Association of University Professors **1**:337
American Federation of Teachers **1**:339
Ivy League **11**:337
research
genetic engineering **9**:85

Reserve Officers Training Corps **16**:176
scholarships, fellowships, and loans **17**:130–131
Servicemen's Opportunity Colleges **17**:211
Seven Sisters Colleges **17**:216
South Asian universities **18**:95–96
Southeast Asian universities **18**:111–112 *table*
student movements **18**:307–308
Union of Soviet Socialist Republics, universities of the **19**:398–399 *table*
United States *see* UNITED STATES, EDUCATION IN THE; articles on universities and colleges in specific states, e.g., CALIFORNIA, STATE UNIVERSITIES AND COLLEGES OF; OHIO, STATE UNIVERSITIES OF; etc.
Yale Report of 1828 **20**:315
UNIVERSITY OF CALIFORNIA* v. *BAKKE **19**:470 *bibliog.*
UNIVERSITY CITY (Missouri)
map (38° 39′N 90° 19′W) **13**:476
UNIVERSITY COLLEGE (Oxford University) **14**:474
UNIVERSITY OF DUBLIN *see* TRINITY COLLEGE (Dublin)
UNIVERSITY PARK (New Mexico)
map (32° 17′N 106° 45′W) **14**:136
UNIVERSITY PARK (Texas)
map (32° 52′N 96° 47′W) **19**:129
UNIVERSITY PLACE (Washington)
map (47° 14′N 122° 34′W) **20**:35
UNIVERSITY WITS (literary group) **19**:470
drama **6**:259
Greene, Robert **9**:351
Kyd, Thomas **12**:143
Lyly, John **12**:475
Marlowe, Christopher **13**:161
Nashe, Thomas **14**:24
UNIVERSITY YEAR FOR ACTION
ACTION (federal agency) **1**:89
UNIX (operating system)
C (computer language) **4**:3
UNKEI **19**:470 *bibliog.*
UNKNOWN SOLDIER **19**:470
Arc de Triomphe de l'Étoile **2**:112
Arlington National Cemetery **2**:171
tomb **19**:231
UNNILQUADIUM (element)
element 104 **7**:132
UNNILQUINTIUM (element)
element 105 **7**:132
UNNILSEXIUM (element)
element 106 **7**:132
UNRUH, FRITZ VON **19**:470 *bibliog.*
UNSER, AL **19**:470
UNSER, BOBBY **19**:470
UNTERMEYER, LOUIS **19**:470 *bibliog.*
UNTOUCHABLES **19**:470–471 *bibliog.*
caste **4**:186
India **11**:84
UP FROM SLAVERY (book) **19**:471
UP WITH PEOPLE (musical programs)
Buchman, Frank **3**:534
UPANISHADS (book) **19**:471 *bibliog.*
India, history of **11**:89
Vedanta **19**:530
Vedas (sacred books) **19**:530–531
UPAS TREE **19**:471
UPATA (Venezuela)
map (8° 1′N 62° 24′W) **19**:542
UPDIKE, JOHN **19**:471 *bibliog., illus.*
UPEMBA, LAKE
map (8° 36′S 26° 26′E) **20**:350
UPERNAVIK (Greenland)
map (72° 47′N 56° 10′W) **9**:353
UPHAM (North Dakota)
map (48° 35′N 100° 44′W) **14**:248
UPHOLSTERY
furniture **8**:380
UPI *see* UNITED PRESS INTERNATIONAL (UPI)
UPINGTON (South Africa)
map (28° 25′S 21° 15′E) **18**:79
UPJOHN, RICHARD **19**:471 *bibliog.*
UPLAND (California)
map (34° 6′N 117° 39′W) **4**:31
UPOLU (Western Samoa) **1**:366 *map*
map (13° 55′S 171° 45′W) **20**:117
Western Samoa **20**:116
UPOLU POINT
map (20° 16′N 155° 51′W) **10**:72
UPPER AMMONOOSUC RIVER
map (44° 36′N 71° 32′W) **14**:123
UPPER ARLINGTON (Ohio)
map (40° 0′N 83° 3′W) **14**:357
UPPER ARROW LAKE
map (50° 30′N 117° 55′W) **3**:491
UPPER AVON *see* AVON, RIVER
UPPER CAVE MAN
China, history of **4**:370
UPPER CLASS *see* CLASS, SOCIAL
UPPER DARBY (Pennsylvania)
map (39° 58′N 75° 16′W) **15**:147
UPPER IOWA RIVER
map (42° 39′N 91° 14′W) **11**:244
UPPER KLAMATH LAKE
map (42° 23′N 122° 55′W) **14**:427
UPPER LAKE ERNE
map (54° 14′N 7° 32′W) **11**:258
UPPER LIARD (Yukon Territory)
map (60° 2′N 128° 55′W) **20**:345
UPPER MARLBORO (Maryland)
map (38° 49′N 76° 45′W) **13**:188
UPPER MUSQUODOBOIT (Nova Scotia)
map (45° 8′N 62° 57′W) **14**:269
UPPER NEW YORK BAY
map (40° 41′N 74° 3′W) **14**:129
UPPER RED LAKE
map (48° 10′N 94° 40′W) **13**:453
UPPER SANDUSKY (Ohio)
map (40° 50′N 83° 17′W) **14**:357
UPPER SILESIA *see* SILESIA
UPPER VOLTA (Burkina) **19**:471–473 *bibliog., illus., map, table*
cities
Bobo Dioulasso **19**:473
Ouagadougou **14**:467
climate **19**:473 *table*
economic activity **19**:472–473
flag **19**:472 *illus.*
history and government **19**:473
land **19**:471–472
map (13° 0′N 2° 0′W) **1**:136
people **19**:472–473 *illus.*
Mossi **13**:605
Songhai (people) **18**:65
Tuareg **19**:325–326
UPPSALA (Sweden) **19**:473
map (59° 52′N 17° 38′E) **18**:382
UPSHUR (county in Texas)
map (32° 45′N 94° 55′W) **19**:129
UPSHUR (county in West Virginia)
map (38° 52′N 80° 15′W) **20**:111
UPSIDE-DOWN CATFISH
catfish **4**:203
coloration, biological **5**:122
UPSILON (letter)
V (letter) **19**:500
Y (letter) **20**:313
UPSON (county in Georgia)
map (32° 50′N 84° 20′W) **9**:114
"UPSTAIRS, DOWNSTAIRS" (television series) **16**:59 *illus.*
UPTON (Kentucky)
map (37° 27′N 85° 53′W) **12**:47
UPTON (Massachusetts)
map (42° 11′N 71° 36′W) **3**:409
UPTON (county in Texas)
map (31° 22′N 102° 0′W) **19**:129
UPTON (Wyoming)
map (44° 6′N 104° 38′W) **20**:301
UPWARD BOUND **19**:473
UPWELLING, OCEANIC **19**:473–474 *bibliog., illus.*
Canaries Current **4**:98
ocean-atmosphere interaction **14**:321
UR (Iraq) **19**:474 *bibliog., illus.*
gaming board **9**:29 *illus.*
house (in Western architecture) **10**:264
Mallowan, Sir Max **13**:92–93
Mesopotamian art and architecture **13**:318–319 *illus.*
Standard of **13**:316 *illus.*
temple **19**:94
Ur-Nammu, King **19**:474
Uruk **19**:490
wheel **20**:127–128
Woolley, Sir Leonard **20**:215
ziggurat **2**:130 *illus.*; **13**:319 *illus.*; **19**:474 *illus.*; **20**:363 *illus.*
UR-NAMMU, KING OF UR **19**:474
Nippur **14**:201
Ur **19**:474
Uruk **19**:490
ziggurat **2**:130 *illus.*
UR-NANSHE **13**:319 *illus.*
URACIL
genetic code **9**:79–81 *illus.*
pyrimidine **15**:637
URAGAMI GYOKUDO *see* GYOKUDO
URAL-ALTAIC LANGUAGES **12**:355 *map*; **19**:474–476 *bibliog.*
Asia **2**:244 *map*
Baltic-Finnic **19**:475
Europe **7**:274 *map*
family status **19**:475
Japanese language **11**:379
Korean language **12**:118
linguistic features **19**:475
loan words and early records **19**:475
relation between Uralic and Altaic **19**:476
URAL MOUNTAINS **19**:391 *illus.*; **19**:476
map (60° 0′N 60° 0′E) **19**:388
mountain **13**:619
URAL RIVER **19**:476
map (47° 0′N 51° 48′E) **19**:388
URALIC LANGUAGES *see* URAL-ALTAIC LANGUAGES
URANIA
muses **13**:656
URANIA (Louisiana)
map (31° 52′N 92° 18′W) **12**:430
URANIBORG OBSERVATORY **19**:476
URANIUM **19**:477–478 *bibliog., illus., illus.*
abundances of common elements **7**:131 *table*
actinide series **1**:88
atomic bomb **2**:307
breeder reactor **3**:471–472
Curie, Marie and Pierre **5**:391
element **7**:130 *table*
fission, nuclear **8**:129 *illus.*
Klaproth, Martin Heinrich **12**:95
metallic elements **13**:328
new ceramics applications **4**:259 *illus.*
nuclear energy **14**:278–279
ore deposits
major ore deposits **14**:424–425 *table*
world distribution **14**:423 *map*
phosphate minerals **15**:256
processing
fluorine **8**:187–188
radioactivity **16**:61 *illus.*
radiometric age-dating **16**:66
radium **16**:68
URANIUM CITY (Saskatchewan)
map (59° 34′N 108° 36′W) **17**:81
URANIUM LEAD-DATING *see* RADIOMETRIC AGE-DATING
URANIUM-233
thorium **19**:178
URANIUM-235
fission, nuclear **8**:129
URANUS (mythology) **19**:479
URANUS (planet) **19**:478–479 *bibliog., illus., table*
appearance **19**:479
Herschel, Sir William **10**:147–148
orbit and rotation **19**:479
physical characteristics **19**:479
planets **15**:329–331
radio astronomy **16**:48
rings **19**:478–479 *illus.*
satellites **19**:479 *illus., table*
Kuiper, Gerard **12**:135
Lassell, William **12**:214
Miranda **13**:463
solar system **18**:46–47 *illus.*; **18**:49 *illus.*
Voyager **19**:638
URANYL COMPOUNDS
uranium minerals **19**:478
URARTIAN LANGUAGE
languages, extinct **12**:198
URARTU **19**:479–480 *bibliog.*
Persian art and architecture **15**:184
URAVAN (Colorado)
map (38° 22′N 108° 44′W) **5**:116
URBAIN, GEORGES
lutetium **12**:468
URBAN, JOSEPH **19**:480 *bibliog.*
URBAN ANTHROPOLOGY **19**:480 *bibliog.*
black Americans **3**:310–311
prostitution **15**:573–574
URBAN CLIMATE **19**:480 *bibliog.*
URBAN GEOGRAPHY **9**:103
URBAN GROWTH AND NEW COMMUNITY DEVELOPMENT ACT
city **5**:7
URBAN LEAGUE, NATIONAL **19**:480
Jordan, Vernon **11**:450
Young, Whitney M., Jr. **20**:334
URBAN MASS TRANSPORTATION ACT
transportation **19**:281–282
URBAN PLANNING **19**:481–485 *bibliog., illus.*
Canada
Toronto (Ontario) **19**:242
cemetery **4**:245
central place theory **4**:254–255
city **5**:6–7
contemporary planning **19**:484–485
forum **8**:242
France
Garnier, Tony **9**:50
Haussmann, Georges Eugène, Baron **10**:69
Le Corbusier **12**:253–254
garden city **9**:41–42
Great Britain
Geddes, Sir Patrick **9**:67
Howard, Ebenezer **10**:283
Nash, John **14**:23–24
Wren, Sir Christopher **20**:286
Greece, ancient
Hippodamus of Miletus **10**:174
greenbelt **9**:349
historic preservation **10**:181–182
history of **19**:481–483
house (in Western architecture) **10**:271
Indus civilization **11**:153
industrial park **11**:157
inner city **11**:179
Italy
Filarete, Antonio Averlino **8**:78
Naples **14**:15
Sant'Elia, Antonio **17**:69
Japan
Tange, Kenzo **19**:22
Tokyo **19**:223; **19**:225
Landsat images **12**:185
Mexico
Latin American art and architecture **12**:224
Michigan **13**:382
modern architecture **13**:491
municipal government **13**:642–643
Netherlands
Dutch art and architecture **6**:311–312
new towns **14**:143; **19**:484
Rome, ancient
Apollodorus of Damascus **2**:84
Ostia **14**:458
Spain
Sert, José Luis **17**:210
Sweden
Erskine, Ralph **7**:235
Union of Soviet Socialist Republics **19**:394
United States
Burnham, Daniel Hudson **3**:577
Gruen, Victor **9**:382
Halprin, Lawrence **10**:25
housing **10**:276; **10**:277
Housing and Urban Development, U.S. Department of **10**:280
L'Enfant, Pierre Charles **12**:281–282
mass transportation **19**:281–282
Mumford, Lewis **13**:638
Nowicki, Matthew **14**:277
renewal in the U.S. **19**:484
World's Columbian Exposition of 1893 **20**:282
Wright, Henry **20**:289–290
zoning **20**:373–374
URBAN WASTES
waste disposal systems **20**:46–47
URBAN II, POPE **19**:485 *bibliog.*
Clermont-Ferrand (France) **5**:52
Crusades **5**:368
URBAN VI, POPE **19**:485 *bibliog.*
Schism, Great **17**:122
URBAN VIII, POPE **19**:485 *bibliog.*
Valle, Pietro della **19**:507
URBANA (Illinois) *see* CHAMPAIGN-URBANA (Illinois)
URBANA (Missouri)
map (37° 51′N 93° 10′W) **13**:476
URBANA (Ohio)
map (40° 7′N 83° 45′W) **14**:357
URBANDALE (Iowa)
map (41° 38′N 93° 48′W) **11**:244
URBANIZATION
See also CITY
housing **10**:276–280
North America **14**:232
URBINO (Italy)
Italian art and architecture **11**:308–314
majolica **13**:76
URCOS (Peru)
map (13° 42′S 71° 38′W) **15**:193
URDU LANGUAGE
Indo-Iranian languages **11**:145
URDUNN, NAHR AL- *see* JORDAN RIVER
UREA **19**:485 *bibliog.*
amide **1**:369
cloud seeding
weather modification **20**:80
excretory system **7**:328
urea cycle **19**:485
uremia **19**:485
urine **19**:485
Wöhler, Friedrich **20**:195

UREMIA 19:485–486 *bibliog.*
urea 19:485
URES (Mexico)
map (29° 26′N 110° 24′W) 13:357
URETER 12:72–73 *illus.*; 19:486
URETHANE
Dumas, Jean Baptiste André 6:297
URETHRA 12:72 *illus.*; 16:163 *illus.*; 19:486
gonorrhea 9:244
trichomoniasis 19:296
urethritis
urogenital diseases 19:487
venereal disease 19:540
UREY, HAROLD CLAYTON 19:486 *bibliog.*
deuterium 19:486
life 12:327
Manhattan Project 19:486
URFA (Turkey)
map (37° 8′N 38° 46′E) 19:343
URIAL *see* SHEEP
URIBIA (Colombia)
map (11° 43′N 72° 16′W) 5:107
URIC ACID 19:486
excretory system 7:328
gout 9:266–267; 19:486
arthritis 2:214–215
kidney stone 12:72
URICH (Missouri)
map (38° 28′N 94° 2′W) 13:476
URINARY BLADDER *see* BLADDER, URINARY
URINARY SYSTEM *see* EXCRETORY SYSTEM
URINATION, INVOLUNTARY *see* BED-WETTING
URINE 19:486 *bibliog.*
antidiuretic hormone 2:61
bed-wetting 3:153
bladder, urinary 3:323
calculi
phosphate minerals 15:256
cystinuria 5:411
diabetes 6:148
diabetes insipidus 6:148
diuretic drugs 6:202
examination, medical 7:326
excretory system 7:327
glucose tolerance test 9:211
kidney stone 12:72
kidneys 12:73–74
pregnancy test 15:506
urea 19:485
urethra 19:486
URIQUE (Mexico)
map (27° 13′N 107° 55′W) 13:357
URIS, LEON 19:486
URMIA, LAKE 19:486
map (37° 40′N 45° 30′E) 11:250
URNFIELD CULTURE 19:486–487 *bibliog.*
burial urn 7:304 *illus.*
European prehistory 7:304
Hallstatt 10:23
Villanovans 19:597
UROCHORDATA *see* TUNICATE
URODELA *see* CAUDATA (Urodela)
UROGENITAL DISEASES 19:487 *bibliog.*
cervicitis 4:261–262
cystitis 5:411
fungus diseases 8:369
gonorrhea 9:244
infectious diseases 11:167
kidney disease 12:72
kidney stone 12:72
leukorrhea 12:301
menopause 13:299
orchitis 14:420
syphilis 18:410
trichomoniasis 19:296
venereal disease 19:539–541
UROLOGY
surgery 18:362
urogenital diseases 19:487
URQUIZA, JUSTO JOSÉ DE 19:487
Mitre, Bartolomé 13:485
URSA (Illinois)
map (40° 4′N 91° 22′W) 11:42
URSA MAJOR (constellation)
Big Dipper 3:249
constellation 5:210 *illus.*; 5:212
URSA MINOR (constellation)
constellation 5:210 *illus.*
Little Dipper 12:372
URSÚA, PEDRO DE 19:487
URSULA, SAINT 19:488
URTICARIA *see* HIVES
URU INDIANS 18:88 *illus.*
URUAPAN (Mexico)
map (19° 25′N 102° 4′W) 13:357
URUBAMBA RIVER
map (10° 44′S 73° 45′W) 15:193
URUGUAIANA (Brazil)
map (29° 45′S 57° 5′W) 3:460
URUGUAY 19:488–490 *bibliog., illus., map, table*
art
Latin American art and architecture 12:222–228
cities
Montevideo 13:555
Paysandú 15:122
climate 19:488–489 *table*
economic activity 19:489 *illus.*
education 19:488
Latin American universities 12:233 *table*
flag 19:488 *illus.*
government 19:489
history 19:489–490
Artigas, José Gervasio 2:222
Batlle y Ordóñez, José 3:124
Lavalleja, Juan Antonio 12:241
Montevideo 13:555
Rivera, Fructuoso 16:233
Terra Gabriel 19:119
Triple Alliance, War of the 19:302
land and resources 19:488–489 *map, table*
literature
Benedetti, Mario 3:196
Latin American literature 12:228–231
people 19:488–489
Guaraní 9:386
rivers, lakes, and waterways 19:488
URUGUAY RIVER (South America) 19:490
map (34° 12′S 58° 19′W) 18:85
URUK (Iraq) 19:490 *bibliog.*
Mesopotamian art and architecture 13:317–318 *illus.*
temple 13:318 *illus.*; 19:94
wheel 20:127
URUMCHI (China)
map (43° 49′N 87° 43′E) 4:362
URUNDI *see* BURUNDI
URVILLE, JULES SÉBASTIAN CÉSAR DUMONT D′ *see* DUMONT D′URVILLE, JULES SÉBASTIAN CÉSAR
U.S. INFORMATION AGENCY 19:490
Murrow, Edward 13:651
Voice of America 19:626
U.S. JAYCEES *see* JAYCEES INTERNATIONAL
U.S. NEWS AND WORLD REPORT (periodical) 19:490
U.S. OPEN (FOREST HILLS) CHAMPIONS 19:111 *table*
U.S. SEAL *see* GREAT SEAL OF THE UNITED STATES
U.S.A. (book) 19:490 *bibliog.*
Dos Passos, John 6:243
USAK (Turkey)
map (38° 41′N 29° 25′E) 19:343
USHUAIA (Argentina) 2:151 *illus.*; 19:490
map (54° 48′S 68° 18′W) 2:149
USIGLI, RODOLFO 19:490
USKÜDAR (Turkey)
map (41° 1′N 29° 1′E) 19:343
USLAR PIETRI, ARTURO
Venezuela 19:543
USMAN DAN FODIO 19:491 *bibliog.*
Africa, history of 1:155
Fulani 8:356
U.S.O. *see* UNITED SERVICE ORGANIZATIONS
USSHER, JAMES 19:491
chronology 4:419
prehistory 15:517
USSR *see* RUSSIA/UNION OF SOVIET SOCIALIST REPUBLICS, HISTORY OF; UNION OF SOVIET SOCIALIST REPUBLICS
USSURIYSK (USSR)
map (43° 48′N 131° 59′E) 19:388
UST-KAMENOGORSK (USSR)
map (49° 58′N 82° 38′E) 19:388
UST-URT PLATEAU
map (43° 0′N 56° 0′E) 19:388
USTER (Switzerland)
map (47° 21′N 8° 43′E) 18:394
ÚSTÍ NAD LABEM (Czechoslovakia)
map (50° 40′N 14° 2′E) 5:413
USTICA ISLAND
map (38° 42′N 13° 10′E) 11:321
USTINOV, PETER 19:491 *bibliog.*
USTUPO (Panama)
map (9° 27′N 78° 34′W) 15:55
USULUTÁN (El Salvador)
map (13° 21′N 88° 27′W) 7:100
USUMACINTA RIVER
map (18° 24′N 92° 38′W) 13:357
USUMBURA *see* BUJUMBURA (Burundi)
USURY 19:491 *bibliog.*
interest 11:207
pawnbroker 15:121
USWA *see* UNITED STEELWORKERS OF AMERICA
UTAGAWA KUNIYOSHI *see* KUNIYOSHI (Utagawa)
UTAH 19:491–496 *bibliog., illus., map*
agriculture 19:494
archaeology and historic sites 19:494
Danger Cave 6:31
cities
Brigham City 3:486
Ogden 14:354
Provo 15:584
Salt Lake City 17:38
climate 19:493
culture 19:494
economic activity 19:494–495
education 19:494
Brigham Young University 3:486
Utah, state universities and colleges of 19:496
flag 19:491 *illus.*
flower, state
sego lily 17:188
government and politics 19:495
history 19:495–496
Young, Brigham 20:332–333
land 19:492–493 *illus., map*
manufacturing 19:495
map (39° 30′N 111° 30′W) 19:419
mining 19:494–495
Mormonism 13:581–582
people 19:493–494
Indians of North America, art of the 11:140
Navajo 14:53–54
Paiute 15:25
Shoshoni 17:284–285
Ute 19:496
physical features
Bonneville Salt Flats 3:381
Bryce Canyon National Park 3:529
Monument Valley 13:560
Wasatch Range 20:34
resources 19:493
uranium minerals 19:478
rivers, lakes, and waterways 19:493
Great Salt Lake 9:322
Green River 9:349
seal, state 19:491 *illus.*
vegetation and animal life 19:493
UTAH (county in Utah)
map (40° 7′N 111° 40′W) 19:492
UTAH, STATE UNIVERSITIES AND COLLEGES OF 19:496
UTAH LAKE
map (40° 13′N 111° 49′W) 19:492
UTAH WAR 19:496 *bibliog.*
UTAMARO 19:496 *bibliog.*
Japanese musicians 13:668 *illus.*
UTE (American Indians) 19:496 *bibliog.*
Indians of North America, music and dance of the 11:143
UTE (Iowa)
map (42° 3′N 95° 42′W) 11:244
UTE RESERVOIR
map (36° 21′N 103° 31′W) 14:136
UTE WAR 11:109 *map*
UTERUS 19:496–497 *bibliog.*
development 6:140
hysterectomy 10:352
menopause 13:300
menstruation 13:300–301
peritonitis 15:172
pregnancy and birth 15:502–503
reproductive system, human 16:163 *illus.*; 16:165–166 *illus.*
UTHMAN
Ali 1:292
Middle East, history of the 13:402
Umayyads 19:380
UTICA (Kansas)
map (38° 39′N 100° 10′W) 12:18
UTICA (Mississippi)
map (32° 7′N 90° 37′W) 13:469
UTICA (Nebraska)
map (40° 54′N 97° 21′W) 14:70
UTICA (New York) 19:497
map (43° 5′N 75° 14′W) 14:149
UTICA (Ohio)
map (40° 14′N 82° 27′W) 14:357
UTIKUMA LAKE
map (55° 50′N 115° 25′W) 1:256
UTILA (Honduras)
map (16° 6′N 86° 54′W) 10:218
UTILITARIANISM 19:497 *bibliog.*
Austin, John 2:327
Bentham, Jeremy 3:205
ethics 7:251
Helvétius, Claude Adrien 10:117
Mill, James 13:425
Mill, John Stuart 13:425
Sidgwick, Henry 17:294
UTILITY THEORY
decision theory 6:73–74
UTOPIA (book) 19:497 *bibliog., illus.*
More, Saint Thomas 13:576
utopias 19:497 *illus.*
UTOPIA (Texas)
map (29° 37′N 99° 32′W) 19:129
UTOPIAN LITERATURE
Brave New World 3:458
Erewhon 7:228
Nineteen Eighty-Four 14:199
science fiction 17:143–144
Utopia 19:497
utopias 19:497–498
UTOPIAS 19:497–498 *bibliog., illus.*
Cabet, Étienne 4:4
Coleridge, Samuel Taylor 5:100
communal living 5:141–142
Considerant, Victor Prosper 5:206
early forms of communism 5:146
Fourier, Charles 8:253
Marxism 13:183
Noyes, John Humphrey 14:277
Oneida Community 14:389
Owen, Robert 14:471
Shangri-La 17:240
socialism 18:19
Southey, Robert 18:112
UTRAQUISTS *see* HUSSITES
UTRECHT (Netherlands) 19:498
map (52° 5′N 5° 8′E) 14:99
UTRECHT, PEACE OF 19:498 *bibliog.*
Europe, history of 7:289
French and Indian Wars 8:313
Great Britain, history of 9:315
lands acquired 8:269 *map*
Louis XIV, King of France 12:427
Spanish Succession, War of the 18:163
UTRECHT, UNION OF (1579)
Dutch Revolt 6:315
UTRECHT PSALTER 15:587 *illus.*
Carolingian art and architecture 4:161
UTRERA (Spain)
map (37° 11′N 5° 47′W) 18:140
UTRILLO, MAURICE 19:498–499 *bibliog., illus.*
Sacré-Coeur 19:498 *illus.*
UTSUNOMIYA (Japan)
map (36° 33′N 139° 52′E) 11:361
UTTAR PRADESH (India) 19:499
cities
Agra 1:187–188
Allahabad 1:298
Fatehpur Sikri 8:34
Kanpur 12:16
Lucknow 12:450–451
Varanasi 19:521
map (27° 0′N 80° 0′E) 11:80
UTTERING *see* FORGERY
UTU *see* SHAMASH
UTUADO (Puerto Rico)
map (18° 16′N 66° 42′W) 15:614
UTZON, JØERN
Sydney (Australia) 18:401
UVALDA (Georgia)
map (32° 2′N 82° 31′W) 9:114
UVALDE (Texas)
map (29° 13′N 99° 47′W) 19:129
UVALDE (county in Texas)
map (29° 22′N 99° 47′W) 19:129
UVAROITE
garnet 9:49
UVS, LAKE
map (50° 20′N 92° 45′E) 13:529
UVULA 19:235 *illus.*
UXBRIDGE (Massachusetts)
map (42° 5′N 71° 38′W) 13:206
UXBRIDGE (Ontario)
map (44° 6′N 68° 7′W) 14:393; 19:241
UXMAL (Mexico) 14:237 *map*; 19:499 *bibliog.*
UYUNI (Bolivia)
map (20° 28′S 66° 50′W) 3:366
UYUNI SALT FLAT
map (20° 20′S 67° 42′W) 3:366
UZBEK 19:499 *bibliog.*
UZBEK SOVIET SOCIALIST REPUBLIC (USSR) 19:499
cities
Samarkand 17:45–46
Tashkent 19:42
history
Timur 19:204
people
Uzbek 19:499
UZBEKISTAN *see* UZBEK SOVIET SOCIALIST REPUBLIC (USSR)

V

V (letter) **19**:500 *illus.*
U (letter) **19**:369
W (letter) **20**:3
V-1 **19**:500 *illus.*
Peenemünde **15**:132
rockets and missiles **16**:254
weapons **20**:75
World War II **20**:273 *illus.*
V-2 **16**:256 *illus.*; **19**:500–501 *bibliog., illus.*
Cuban Missile Crisis **5**:380 *illus.*
Doppler effect, flight control **6**:241
Peenemünde **15**:132
rockets and missiles **16**:253–254 *illus.*
von Braun, Wernher **19**:633
weapons **20**:75
World War II **20**:275
VAAL RIVER **19**:501
map (27° 40′S 26° 9′E) **18**:79
VAALSERBERG MOUNTAIN
map (50° 46′N 6° 1′E) **14**:99
VAASA (Finland) **19**:501
climate **8**:96 *table*
map (63° 6′N 21° 36′E) **8**:95
VÁC (Hungary)
map (47° 47′N 19° 8′E) **10**:307
VACA, ÁLVAR NÚÑEZ CABEZA DE *see* CABEZA DE VACA, ÁLVAR NÚÑEZ
VACAVILLE (California)
map (38° 21′N 121° 59′W) **4**:31
VACCINATION **19**:501–502 *bibliog.*
anthrax **2**:50
antitoxin **2**:69
Chinese medicine **4**:390
cowpox **5**:322
diseases, animal **6**:191; **6**:192
diseases, childhood **6**:193
distemper **6**:200
drug **6**:277
hepatitis **10**:130
Blumberg, Baruch S. **3**:346
immunodeficiency disease **11**:60
immunology **11**:60
influenza **11**:171
malaria **13**:80
measles **13**:253
medicine **13**:271
mumps **13**:639
Pasteur, Louis **15**:108
poliomyelitis **15**:397
smallpox **17**:365
Jenner, Edward **11**:396
tuberculosis **19**:327
typhoid fever **19**:366
vaccinia **19**:502
virus **19**:615
Wassermann, August von **20**:46
whooping cough **20**:143
VACCINES *see* VACCINATION
VACCINIA **19**:502
VACOAS (Mauritius)
map (20° 18′S 57° 29′E) **13**:237
VACUUM **19**:502 *bibliog.*
cryogenics **5**:370–371
Dewar, Sir James **6**:146
Guericke, Otto von **9**:391
vacuum cleaner **19**:502
VACUUM CLEANER **19**:502 *illus.*
VACUUM TUBE
cathode ray **4**:211
computer **5**:160b *illus.*
molybdenum **13**:514
oscillator **14**:453
triode **19**:301
video technology **19**:576m
VADUZ (Liechtenstein) **12**:325 *illus.*; **19**:502
map (47° 9′N 9° 31′E) **12**:325
VAGANOVA, AGRIPPINA **19**:502 *bibliog.*
VAGINA
discharge
leukorrhea **12**:301
venereal disease **19**:540
hysterectomy **10**:352
Pap test **15**:62
reproductive system, human **16**:163 *illus.*; **16**:166
sexual intercourse **17**:230–231
Trichomonas **19**:296
VAGINITIS
fungus diseases **8**:369
VAGRANCY **19**:502–503
VAGUS NERVE
stomach **18**:280
VÁH RIVER
map (47° 55′N 18° 0′E) **5**:413
VAIDEN (Mississippi)
map (33° 20′N 89° 45′W) **13**:469
VAIL (Colorado)
map (39° 38′N 106° 21′W) **5**:116
VAIL, ALFRED
Morristown (New Jersey) **13**:590
VAILALA MADNESS OF 1919
cargo cults **4**:147
VAILEKA (Fiji)
map (17° 23′S 178° 9′E) **8**:77
VAIONT DAM **19**:503
VAISHESHIKA
philosophy **15**:246
VAISHYA
caste **4**:186
VAKHTANGOV, EUGENE **19**:503 *bibliog.*
VAL-D'OR (Quebec)
map (48° 7′N 77° 47′W) **16**:18
VAL-MARIE (Saskatchewan)
map (49° 14′N 107° 44′W) **17**:81
VAL VERDE (county in Texas)
map (29° 52′N 101° 13′W) **19**:129
VALADON, SUZANNE **19**:503 *bibliog.*
Utrillo, Maurice **19**:498
VALAORITIS, ARISTOTLE
Greek literature, modern **9**:344
VALDEPEÑAS (Spain)
map (38° 46′N 3° 23′W) **18**:140
VALDÉS, MIGUEL ALEMÁN *see* ALEMÁN VALDÉS, MIGUEL
VALDÉS LEAL, JUAN DE **19**:503 *bibliog.*
VALDÉS PENINSULA
map (42° 30′S 64° 0′W) **2**:149
VALDESE (North Carolina)
map (35° 44′N 81° 34′W) **14**:242
VALDEZ (Alaska) **19**:503
map (61° 7′N 146° 16′W) **1**:242
VALDEZ (Ecuador)
map (1° 15′N 79° 0′W) **7**:52
VALDIVIA (Chile)
map (39° 48′S 73° 14′W) **4**:355
VALDIVIA, PEDRO DE **19**:503 *bibliog.*
Concepción (Chile) **5**:169
exploration **7**:337 *map*
Lautaro **12**:240
Santiago (Chile) **17**:70
VALDOSTA (Georgia)
map (30° 50′N 83° 17′W) **9**:114
VALE (New Jersey)
map (41° 1′N 74° 1′W) **14**:129
VALE (Oregon)
map (43° 59′N 117° 15′W) **14**:427
VALEMOUNT (British Columbia)
map (52° 50′N 119° 15′W) **3**:491
VALENCE **19**:503 *bibliog.*
coordination theory
Werner, Alfred **20**:104
electronic theory
Sidgwick, Nevil Vincent **17**:294–295
Frankland, Sir Edward **8**:282
insulator **11**:197
organic chemistry **14**:435
periodic table **15**:167
semiconductor **17**:196
sulfur **18**:335
theory
chemistry, history of **4**:327
transition elements **19**:273
uranium **19**:477
vanadium **19**:516
VALENCE (France)
map (44° 56′N 4° 54′E) **8**:260
VALENCIA (Arizona)
map (33° 23′N 112° 35′W) **2**:160
VALENCIA (city in Spain) **19**:503–504 *illus.*
map (39° 28′N 0° 22′W) **18**:140
VALENCIA (city in Venezuela) **19**:504
map (10° 11′N 68° 0′W) **19**:542
VALENCIA (Honduras)
map (14° 47′N 85° 18′W) **10**:218
VALENCIA (county in New Mexico)
map (35° 0′N 108° 0′W) **14**:136
VALENCIA (region in Spain) **19**:504
VALENCIA, GULF OF
map (39° 50′N 0° 30′E) **18**:140
VALENCIENNES (France)
map (50° 21′N 3° 32′E) **8**:260
VALENCIENNES PASSION PLAY *see* PASSION PLAY
VALENS, ROMAN EMPEROR IN THE EAST **19**:504 *bibliog.*
VALENTIN DE BOULOGNE **19**:504 *bibliog.*
VALENTINE, SAINT **19**:504
VALENTINE (Nebraska)
map (42° 52′N 100° 33′W) **14**:70
VALENTINE (Texas)
map (30° 34′N 104° 29′W) **19**:129
VALENTINE'S DAY *see* VALENTINE, SAINT
VALENTINIAN I, ROMAN EMPEROR IN THE WEST **19**:504 *bibliog.*
VALENTINIAN II, ROMAN EMPEROR IN THE WEST **19**:505
VALENTINIAN III, ROMAN EMPEROR IN THE WEST **19**:505
VALENTINO (designer)
fashion design **8**:32
VALENTINO, RUDOLPH **6**:30 *illus.*; **8**:83 *illus.*; **19**:505 *bibliog., illus.*
VALENTINUS **19**:505 *bibliog.*
VALERA (Venezuela)
map (9° 19′N 70° 37′W) **19**:542
VALERA, EAMON DE *see* DE VALERA, EAMON
VALERA Y ALCALÁ GALIANO, JUAN **19**:505 *bibliog.*
VALERIAN, ROMAN EMPEROR **13**:401 *illus.*; **19**:505
Shapur I, King of Persia **17**:241
VALÉRY, PAUL **19**:505–506 *bibliog., illus.*
language and literature **12**:197
VALHALLA **19**:506
Asgard **2**:228
VALIER (Illinois)
map (38° 1′N 89° 3′W) **11**:42
VALIER (Montana)
map (48° 18′N 112° 15′W) **13**:547
VALIRA RIVER
map (42° 29′N 1° 30′W) **1**:405
VALIUM **19**:506
anesthetics **1**:411
drug **6**:277
half-life, drug **6**:276
psychotropic drugs **15**:604
sedative **17**:182
tranquilizer **19**:266
VALJEVO (Yugoslavia)
map (44° 16′N 19° 53′E) **20**:340
VALKENSWAARD (Netherlands)
map (51° 21′N 5° 28′E) **14**:99
VALKYRIE, THE see RING OF THE NIBELUNG, THE (opera cycle)
VALKYRIES **19**:506
VALLA, LORENZO
history **10**:184
Renaissance **16**:149
VALLADOLID (Ecuador)
map (4° 33′S 79° 8′W) **7**:52
VALLADOLID (Spain) **19**:506
map (41° 39′N 4° 43′W) **18**:140
VALLANDIGHAM, CLEMENT L. **19**:506 *bibliog.*
VALLAYER-COSTER, ANNE **19**:506 *bibliog.*
VALLE, PIETRO DELLA **19**:507 *bibliog.*
VALLE D'AOSTA (Italy) **11**:322 *illus.*; **19**:507
VALLE DE LA PASCUA (Venezuela)
map (9° 13′N 66° 0′W) **19**:542
VALLE DE ZARAGOZA (Mexico)
map (27° 28′N 105° 49′W) **13**:357
VALLE EDÉN (Uruguay)
map (31° 50′S 56° 9′W) **19**:488
VALLE INCLÁN, RAMÓN DEL **19**:507 *bibliog.*
VALLECITOS (New Mexico)
map (36° 30′N 106° 1′W) **14**:136
VALLEDUPAR (Colombia)
map (10° 29′N 73° 15′W) **5**:107
VALLÉE DU FERLO
map (15° 42′N 15° 30′W) **17**:202
VALLEJO (California) **19**:507
map (38° 7′N 122° 14′W) **4**:31
VALLEJO, ANTONIO BUERO **19**:507 *bibliog.*
VALLEJO, CÉSAR **19**:507 *bibliog.*
VALLETTA (Malta) **13**:95 *illus., table*; **19**:507
map (35° 54′N 14° 31′E) **13**:94
VALLEY
glaciers and glaciation **9**:193 *illus.*
landform evolution **12**:181–183 *illus.*
Moon, far side **13**:565 *map*
mountain and valley winds **13**:624
rift valleys **16**:221
VALLEY (county in Idaho)
map (44° 45′N 115° 35′W) **11**:26
VALLEY (county in Montana)
map (48° 25′N 106° 30′W) **13**:547
VALLEY (Nebraska)
map (41° 19′N 96° 21′W) **14**:70
VALLEY (county in Nebraska)
map (41° 35′N 99° 0′W) **14**:70
VALLEY (Washington)
map (48° 11′N 117° 44′W) **20**:35
VALLEY CENTER (Kansas)
map (37° 50′N 97° 22′W) **12**:18
VALLEY CITY (North Dakota)
map (46° 55′N 97° 59′W) **14**:248
VALLEY FALLS (Kansas)
map (39° 21′N 95° 28′W) **12**:18
VALLEY FALLS (Rhode Island)
map (41° 54′N 71° 24′W) **16**:198
VALLEY FORGE **1**:362 *illus.*; **19**:507 *bibliog.*
American Revolution **1**:361
VALLEY AND RIDGE PROVINCE **19**:507–508 *bibliog.*
syncline and anticline **18**:406
VALLEY STATION (Kentucky)
map (38° 6′N 85° 52′W) **12**:47
VALLEY OF TEN THOUSAND SMOKES **19**:508
Katmai, Mount **12**:30
VALLEY OF THE DOLLS, THE (book)
Susann, Jacqueline **18**:370
VALLEY OF THE KINGS (Egypt) **19**:507 *bibliog.*
pharaoh **15**:219
Thutmose I, King of Egypt **19**:186
Tutankhamen, King of Egypt **19**:355
VALLEYFIELD (Quebec)
map (45° 15′N 74° 8′W) **16**:18
VALLONET CAVE (France) **19**:508 *bibliog.*
VALLOTTON, FÉLIX **19**:508 *bibliog.*
Nabis **14**:3
VALMIKI
Ramayana **16**:80
VALMY, BATTLE OF
Dumouriez, Charles François du Perier **6**:298
VALOIS (dynasty) **8**:270 *table*; **19**:508 *bibliog.*
Charles V, King of France **4**:292–293
Charles VI, King of France **4**:293
Charles VII, King of France **4**:293
France, history of **8**:268
Francis I, King of France **8**:275–276
Francis II, King of France **8**:276
Henry II, King of France **10**:127
Henry III, King of France **10**:127
Italian Wars **11**:319
John II, King of France (John the Good) **11**:427 *bibliog.*
Louis XI, King of France **12**:425
Louis XII, King of France **12**:425
Margaret of Valois **13**:149
Orléans (family) **14**:446
Philip VI, King of France **15**:233
Salic law **17**:32
VALOIS, DAME NINETTE DE **19**:508 *bibliog.*
Royal Ballet, The **16**:329
VALONA (Albania) *see* VLORË (Albania)
VALPARAÍSO (Chile) **19**:508
map (33° 2′S 71° 38′W) **4**:355
VALPARAISO (Florida)
map (30° 29′N 86° 30′W) **8**:172
VALPARAISO (Indiana)
map (41° 28′N 87° 3′W) **11**:111
VALPARAÍSO (Mexico)
map (22° 46′N 103° 34′W) **13**:357
VALSETZ (Oregon)
map (44° 50′N 123° 39′W) **14**:427
VALUE (economics) *see* LABOR THEORY OF VALUE
VALUE-ADDED TAX **19**:508–509 *bibliog.*
sales tax **17**:32
VALUES (principles)
moral awareness **13**:572–573
VALVE **19**:509 *bibliog., illus.*
hydraulic systems **10**:331
VALVE, HEART *see* HEART
VALVERDE (Dominican Republic)
map (19° 34′N 71° 5′W) **6**:233
VALVERDE, JOAQUÍN
zarzuela **20**:356
VAMPIRE **19**:510 *bibliog.*
VAMPIRE BAT **3**:120 *illus.*
bat **3**:119
VAN *see* the last element of the name for names not listed below
VAN (Turkey)
map (38° 28′N 43° 20′E) **19**:343
VAN, LAKE **19**:510
map (38° 33′N 42° 46′E) **19**:343
VAN AELST, PIETER
tapestry **19**:33
VAN ALEN, WILLIAM
Chrysler Building **4**:420
skyscraper **17**:350
VAN ALLEN, JAMES A. **18**:119 *illus.*
Van Allen radiation belts **19**:510
VAN ALLEN RADIATION BELTS **19**:510 *bibliog., illus.*
Alfvén waves
magnetohydrodynamics **13**:59
Explorer (artificial satellite) **7**:339
International Geophysical Year **11**:220
magnetic bottle **13**:55
magnetosphere **13**:59; **19**:510
OSO **14**:456
satellite, artificial **17**:85
Vanguard **19**:519

VAN BREE, M. I.
Napoleon entering Antwerp **14**:16 *illus.*
VAN BUREN (Arkansas)
map (35° 26′N 94° 21′W) **2**:166
VAN BUREN (county in Iowa)
map (40° 45′N 91° 57′W) **11**:244
VAN BUREN (Maine)
map (47° 9′N 67° 56′W) **13**:70
VAN BUREN (county in Michigan)
map (42° 14′N 86° 4′W) **13**:377
VAN BUREN (Missouri)
map (37° 0′N 91° 1′W) **13**:476
VAN BUREN (county in Tennessee)
map (35° 45′N 85° 25′W) **19**:104
VAN BUREN, MARTIN **19**:510–512 *bibliog., illus.*
early career **19**:510–511
Independent Treasury System **11**:78
Polk, James K. **15**:404
presidency **19**:511
vice-president of the United States **19**:570 *illus.*
VAN BURNE (county in Arkansas)
map (35° 35′N 92° 35′W) **2**:166
VAN CAMPEN, JACOB
Royal Palace (Amsterdam) **6**:312 *illus.*
VAN CAT
longhaired cats **12**:408
VAN DE GRAAFF, ROBERT JEMISON **19**:512
VAN DE GRAAFF GENERATOR **19**:512 *illus.*
accelerator, particle **1**:73
Los Alamos National Scientific Laboratory **12**:416
VAN DE VELDE, HENRY **19**:512 *bibliog.*
Art Nouveau **2**:210
pitcher **2**:211 *illus.*
VAN DE VELDE, JAN
calligraphy **4**:43 *illus.*
VAN DER MEER, SIMON **19**:152
VAN DER POST, LAURENS
South Africa **18**:81
VAN DER WAALS, JOHANNES DIDERIK **19**:512
intermolecular forces **11**:215
van der Waals equation **19**:512
VAN DER WAALS EQUATION **19**:512–513
van der Waals, Johannes Diderik **19**:512
VAN DEVANTER, WILLIS **19**:513
VAN DIEMEN'S LAND (Australia) *see* TASMANIA (Australia)
VAN DINE, S. S. **19**:513
VAN DOREN, CARL **19**:513 *bibliog.*
VAN DOREN, CHARLES
radio and television broadcasting **16**:58
VAN DOREN, MARK **19**:513
VAN DRUTEN, JOHN **19**:513 *bibliog.*
VAN DYCK, SIR ANTHONY **19**:513–514 *bibliog., illus.*
Charles I, King of England, Scotland, and Ireland **4**:291 *illus.*; **7**:185 *illus.*
Charles I of England in Hunting Dress **19**:513 *illus.*
Flemish art and architecture **8**:161
portraits **11**:212 *illus.*
VAN FLANDERN, THOMAS
gravitation **9**:305
VAN FLEET, JAMES ALWARD **19**:514
Korean War **12**:122
VAN GOGH, VINCENT **11**:66 *illus.*; **19**:514–515 *bibliog., illus.*
The Church at Auvers **19**:514 *illus.*
Dutch art and architecture **6**:313
Gauguin, Paul **9**:59–60
impasto **11**:60
Landscape with Ploughman **15**:24 *illus.*
Le Père Tanguy **15**:462 *illus.*
Mauve, Anton **13**:238
postimpressionism **15**:463
The Potato Eaters **6**:313 *illus.*
Self Portrait **15**:447 *illus.*
Self-Portrait with a Gray Hat **19**:514 *illus.*
Small House of Vincent at Arles **11**:67 *illus.*
VAN HAECHT, WILLEM
Art Collection of Cornelius van der Geest, The **2**:203 *illus.*
VAN HAMEL, MARTINE **19**:515 *bibliog.*
VAN HORN (Texas)
map (31° 3′N 104° 50′W) **19**:129
VAN HORNE (Iowa)
map (42° 1′N 92° 5′W) **11**:244
VAN HORNE, WILLIAM
Canada, history of **4**:84
VAN ITALLIE, JEAN CLAUDE **19**:515
VAN LEAR (Kentucky)
map (37° 46′N 82° 46′W) **12**:47
VAN LERBERGHE, CHARLES
Belgian literature **3**:175
VAN LOO, CHARLES ANDRÉ **19**:515 *bibliog.*
VAN MANEN, HANS
Netherlands Dance Theater **14**:103
VAN RENSSALAER (family) **19**:515–516 *bibliog.*
VAN RENSSELAER, KILIAEN
Troy (New York) **19**:313
VAN SLYKE, HELEN **19**:516
VAN VECHTEN, CARL **19**:516 *bibliog.*
VAN VIANEN (brothers)
gold and silver work **9**:230
VAN VLECK, J. H. **19**:516 *bibliog.*
VAN VOGT, A. E. **19**:516
VAN WERT (Ohio)
map (40° 52′N 84° 35′W) **14**:357
VAN WERT (county in Ohio)
map (40° 52′N 84° 35′W) **14**:357
VAN WINKLE, RIP *see* RIP VAN WINKLE (fictional character)
VAN ZANDT (county in Texas)
map (32° 35′N 95° 50′W) **19**:129
VAN ZEELAND, PAUL **19**:516
VANADATE MINERALS
isomorph **11**:300
mineral **13**:443 *table*
phosphate minerals **15**:255–256
uranium minerals **19**:478
vanadinite **19**:516
VANADINITE **19**:516
VANADIUM **19**:516 *bibliog.*
abundances of common elements **7**:131 *table*
element **7**:130 *table*
Group VB periodic table **15**:167
ore deposits, world distribution **14**:423 *illus.*
transition elements **19**:273 *table*
uranium minerals **19**:478
vanadinite **19**:516
vitamins and minerals **19**:621
weathering **20**:83
VANANDA (British Columbia)
map (49° 45′N 124° 33′W) **3**:491
VANBRUGH, SIR JOHN **19**:516–517 *bibliog.*
Blenheim Palace **3**:330
VANCE (county in North Carolina)
map (36° 25′N 78° 25′W) **14**:242
VANCE, CYRUS R. **19**:517 *illus.*
Carter, Jimmy **4**:172
VANCE, NINA
repertory theater **16**:160
VANCEBURG (Kentucky)
map (38° 36′N 83° 19′W) **12**:47
VANCOMYCIN
antibiotics **2**:57
VANCOUVER (British Columbia) **3**:490 *illus.*; **4**:77 *illus.*; **19**:517–518 *bibliog., illus.*
climate **4**:74 *table*
map (49° 16′N 123° 7′W) **3**:491
VANCOUVER (Washington)
McLoughlin, John **13**:33
map (45° 39′N 122° 40′W) **20**:35
VANCOUVER, GEORGE **19**:518 *bibliog.*
Canada, exploration of **4**:80 *map*
Puget Sound **15**:617
Rainier, Mount **16**:78
VANCOUVER ISLAND **19**:518
Kwakiutl **12**:142
map (49° 45′N 126° 0′W) **3**:491
Victoria (British Columbia) **19**:573
VANDALIA (Illinois)
map (38° 58′N 89° 6′W) **11**:42
VANDALIA (Missouri)
map (39° 19′N 91° 29′W) **13**:476
VANDALS **19**:518
Gaiseric, King of the Vandals **9**:9
invasion of Europe **7**:282 *map*
Iol **11**:239
VANDENBERG, ARTHUR H. **19**:518 *bibliog.*
VANDENBERG AIR FORCE BASE **19**:518
astronautics **2**:275
space exploration **18**:130
VANDERBILT (family) **19**:518–519 *bibliog.*
Gould, Jay **9**:265
Hunt, Richard Morris **10**:312
VANDERBILT (Michigan)
map (45° 9′N 84° 40′W) **13**:377
VANDERBILT UNIVERSITY **19**:519
VANDERBURGH (county in Indiana)
map (38° 5′N 87° 35′W) **11**:111
VANDERGRIFT (Pennsylvania)
map (40° 36′N 79° 34′W) **15**:147
VANDERLYN, JOHN **19**:519 *bibliog., illus.*
Aaron Burr **3**:579 *illus.*
Ariadne Asleep on the Island of Naxos **19**:519 *illus.*
VANE, SIR HENRY **19**:519 *bibliog.*
Hutchinson, Anne **10**:322
VÄNERN, LAKE **19**:519
map (58° 55′N 13° 30′E) **18**:382
VANGA **19**:519
VANGUARD **16**:256 *illus.*; **19**:519 *bibliog.*
National Aeronautics and Space Administration **14**:28
space exploration **18**:119 *illus.*
VANILLA **19**:519–520 *bibliog., illus.*
VANILLON *see* VANILLA
VANIMA (Papua New Guinea)
map (2° 40′S 141° 20′E) **15**:72
VANIR (Norse deities)
mythology **13**:702
VANISHING CREAM
cosmetics **5**:282–283
VANITY FAIR (book) **19**:520
Thackeray, William Makepeace **19**:138
VANITY FAIR (periodical)
illustration from **15**:96 *illus.*
VANNES (France)
map (47° 39′N 2° 46′W) **8**:260
VANNIC LANGUAGE *see* URARTIAN LANGUAGE
VAN'T HOFF, JACOBUS HENRICUS **19**:520 *bibliog.*
chemistry, history of **4**:327
organic chemistry **14**:435
stereochemistry **18**:258
VANUA LEVU ISLAND
map (16° 33′S 179° 15′E) **8**:77
VANUATU **19**:520–521 *bibliog., illus.*
flag **19**:520 *illus.*
map (16° 0′S 167° 0′E) **14**:334
mask **14**:336 *illus.*
VANVITELLI, LUIGI **19**:521 *bibliog.*
VANZETTI, BARTOLOMEO *see* SACCO AND VANZETTI CASE
VAPOR *see* GASEOUS STATE
VAPOR PRESSURE **19**:521
boiling point **3**:363
evaporation **7**:313–314
sublimation (chemistry) **18**:313
VAQUEIRAS, RAMBAULT DE
minstrels, minnesingers, and troubadours **13**:460
VÁQUEZ DE AYLLÓN, LUCAS *see* AYLLÓN, LUCAS VÁSQUEZ DE
VARA PEAK
map (32° 45′N 16° 56′W) **15**:449
VÁRAD, TREATY OF
John I, King of Hungary (John Zápolya) **11**:427
VARANASI (India) **19**:521
map (25° 20′N 83° 0′E) **11**:80
VARANGIANS *see* RURIK (dynasty); VIKINGS
VARAŽDIN (Yugoslavia)
map (46° 19′N 16° 20′E) **20**:340
VARBERG (Sweden)
map (57° 6′N 12° 15′E) **18**:382
VARBRUL (computer program)
sociolinguistics **18**:28
VARDAR (Axios) RIVER
map (40° 31′N 22° 43′E) **20**:340
VARDE (Denmark)
map (55° 38′N 8° 29′E) **6**:109
VARDON, HARRY **19**:521 *bibliog.*
golf **9**:239
VARDON TROPHY
Snead, Sam **17**:384
Trevino, Lee **19**:291
Vardon, Harry **19**:521
Watson, Tom **20**:68
VARENIUS, BERNHARDUS
geography **9**:101
VARENNE, JEAN NICOLAS BILLAUD- *see* BILLAUD-VARENNE, JEAN NICOLAS
VARENNES, FLIGHT TO (1791) *see* LOUIS XVI, KING OF FRANCE
VARENNES, PIERRE GAULTIER DE *see* LA VÉRENDRYE, PIERRE GAULTIER DE VARENNES, SIEUR DE
VARESE (Italy)
map (45° 48′N 8° 48′E) **11**:321
VARÈSE, EDGAR **19**:521–522 *bibliog., illus.*
Jolivet, André **11**:441
VARGAS, GETÚLIO DORNELLES **19**:522 *bibliog.*
Brazil **3**:463
VARGAS, VIRGILIO BARCO *see* BARCO VARGAS, VIRGILIO
VARGAS LLOSA, MARIO **19**:522
VARIABLE (mathematics) **19**:522 *bibliog.*
Borel, Émile **3**:398
linear equation **12**:354
maxima and minima **13**:239
nomogram **14**:215
random variable **16**:83
VARIABLE STAR **19**:522–523 *bibliog., illus.*
Algol **1**:291
Argelander, Friedrich Wilhelm August **2**:146
binary stars **3**:256–257
Cepheids **4**:257; **19**:522
designations **19**:522
eruptive variables **19**:522
Fabricius, David **8**:5
flare star **8**:153
Leavitt, Henrietta Swan **12**:263–264
nova **14**:268
Orion (astronomy) **14**:444
other types **19**:523
Payne-Gaposchkin, Cecilia **15**:122
period-luminosity relation **15**:166
pulsating stars **15**:621; **19**:522–523
RR Lyrae stars **16**:332; **19**:522–523
star **18**:221
T Tauri stars **19**:3
W Virginis stars **20**:3
Wolf-Rayet stars **20**:197
VARIANCE AND COVARIANCE **19**:523 *bibliog.*
Fisher, Sir Ronald Aylmer **8**:122–123
sampling **17**:48
standard deviation **18**:216
VARIATIONS (music) **19**:523 *bibliog.*
African music **1**:171
VARICELLA *see* CHICKEN POX
VARICOSE VEIN **19**:523 *bibliog.*
cardiovascular diseases **4**:145
VARIETY SHOWS *see* MUSIC HALL, VAUDEVILLE, AND BURLESQUE
VARILLA, PHILIPPE JEAN BUNAU- *see* BUNAU-VARILLA, PHILIPPE JEAN
VARINA (Virginia)
map (37° 27′N 77° 21′W) **19**:607
VARIOLATION *see* VACCINATION
VARIUS AVITUS BASSIANUS *see* HELIOGABALUS, ROMAN EMPEROR
VARKAUS (Finland)
map (62° 19′N 27° 55′E) **8**:95
VARLEY, FREDERICK **19**:523 *bibliog.*
Gipsy Head **4**:90 *illus.*
VARNA (Bulgaria) **19**:523–524
map (43° 13′N 27° 55′E) **3**:555
VARNA (social class) *see* BRAHMIN (caste); KSHATRIYA; SHUDRA; UNTOUCHABLES; VAISHYA
VARNISH **19**:524 *bibliog.*
VARRO **19**:524
VARVED DEPOSIT **19**:524 *illus.*
glaciers and glaciation **9**:192–195
ice ages **11**:8
kame **12**:9
lake (body of water) **12**:169
VAS DEFERENS **16**:163 *illus.*
vasectomy **19**:525
VASA (dynasty) **19**:525 *bibliog.*
Gustav I, King of Sweden **9**:407
VASARELY, VICTOR **19**:525 *bibliog., illus.*
Cheyt-G **14**:397 *illus.*; **19**:525 *illus.*
VASARI, GIORGIO **19**:525 *bibliog.*
art criticism **2**:207
Italian art and architecture **11**:313
Renaissance **16**:148
Uffizi **19**:371
VÁSÁROSNEMÉNY, JOZSEF EÖTVÖS, BARON VON *see* EÖTVÖS, JOZSEF, BARON VON VÁSÁROSNEMÉNY
VÁSÁROSNEMÉNY, LÓRÁNT EÖTVÖS, BARON VON *see* EÖTVÖS, LÓRÁNT, BARON VON VÁSÁROSNEMÉNY
VASCO DA GAMA *see* GAMA, VASCO DA
VASCOS *see* BASQUES
VASCULAR PLANT *see* TRACHEOPHYTE
VASCULAR SYSTEM
shock, physiologic **17**:278–279
stroke **18**:301–302
surgery
medicine **13**:272
varicose vein **19**:523
VASECTOMY **19**:525 *bibliog.*
birth control **3**:294
surgery **18**:362
vas deferens **16**:163 *illus.*

VASHON ISLAND
map (47° 24′N 122° 27′W) 20:35
VASILY III, GRAND DUKE OF MOSCOW 19:526
VASILY IV, RUSSIAN TSAR
Time of Troubles 19:202
VASLUI (Romania)
map (46° 38′N 27° 44′E) 16:288
VASNETSOV, VIKTOR
Russian art and architecture 16:362
VASOPRESSIN *see* ANTIDIURETIC HORMONE
VASOTOCIN
hormone, animal 10:235
VASS (North Carolina)
map (35° 15′N 79° 17′W) 14:242
VASSAL
Europe, history of 7:284
feudalism 8:64–65
VASSAR (Michigan)
map (43° 22′N 83° 35′W) 13:377
VASSAR COLLEGE 19:526
Mitchell, Maria 13:483
Seven Sisters Colleges 17:216
VÄSTERÅS (Sweden) 19:526
map (59° 37′N 16° 33′E) 18:382
VÄSTERVICK (Sweden)
map (57° 45′N 16° 38′E) 18:382
VATICAN CITY 19:526–527 *bibliog., illus., map*
art
Renaissance art and architecture 16:152
Sistine Chapel 17:329
Vatican museums and galleries 19:527–528
education
European universities 7:308 *table*
history
Papal States 15:67
library
Vatican museums and galleries 19:528
medals and decorations 13:262 *illus.*
VATICAN COUNCIL, FIRST 19:527 *bibliog.*
conciliarism 5:170
council, ecumenical 5:310
Döllinger, Ignaz von 6:226
Pius IX, Pope 15:323
VATICAN COUNCIL, SECOND 19:527 *bibliog.*
ecumenical movement 7:54
infallibility 11:162
John XXIII, Pope 11:429
mass (musical setting) 13:201
Paul VI, Pope 15:118
VATICAN MUSEUMS AND GALLERIES 19:527–528 *bibliog., illus.*
VATICAN PALACE
art
Bramante, Donato 3:452
Castel Sant'Angelo 4:187
Fontana, Domenico 8:206
Lotto, Lorenzo 12:420
Raphael 16:89
VATNA GLACIER
map (64° 25′N 16° 50′W) 11:17
VATSYAYANA
Kamasutra 12:9
VATTEL, EMERICH DE
Declaration of Independence 6:74
VÄTTERN, LAKE 19:528
map (58° 24′N 14° 36′E) 18:382
VATU-I-RA CHANNEL
map (17° 17′S 178° 31′E) 8:77
VATUKOULA (Fiji)
map (17° 31′S 177° 51′E) 8:77
VAU, LOUIS LE *see* LE VAU, LOUIS
VAUBAN SÉBASTIEN LE PRESTRE DE 19:528 *bibliog.*
fortification 8:240
VAUDEVILLE *see* MUSIC HALL, VAUDEVILLE, AND BURLESQUE
VAUGHAN, HENRY 19:528 *bibliog.*
VAUGHAN, SARAH 19:528 *bibliog.*
VAUGHAN WILLIAMS, RALPH 19:528–529 *bibliog., illus.*
VAUGHN (New Mexico)
map (34° 36′N 105° 13′W) 14:136
VAULT (architecture) *see* ARCH AND VAULT
VAULT (burial) *see* TOMB
VAUPÉS RIVER
map (0° 2′N 67° 16′W) 5:107
VAUQUELIN, LOUIS NICOLAS 19:529
VAUTHIER, JEAN 19:529
VAUX, CALVERT 19:529
Metropolitan Museum of Art, The 13:348
VAUX-LE-VICOMTE, CHÂTEAU DE 19:529 *bibliog.*
château 4:302
landscape architecture 12:186
Le Nôtre, André 12:255
Le Vau, Louis 12:255
VAUXHALL (Alberta)
map (50° 4′N 112° 7′W) 1:256
VAUXHALL MOTORS
automotive industry 2:364
VAVAU GROUP
map (18° 40′S 174° 0′W) 19:233
VÄXJÖ (Sweden)
map (56° 52′N 14° 49′E) 18:382
VAZOV, IVAN 19:529
Bulgarian literature 3:557
VÁZQUEZ DE CORONADO, FRANCISCO *see* CORONADO, FRANCISCO VÁZQUEZ DE
VBI *see* VERTICAL BLANKING INTERVAL
VCR *see* VIDEOCASSETTE RECORDER
VD *see* VENEREAL DISEASE
VDT *see* VIDEO DISPLAY TERMINAL
VEAL 19:529
meat and meat packing 13:257 *table*
VEAZIE (Maine)
map (44° 51′N 68° 42′W) 13:70
VEBLEN (South Dakota)
map (45° 52′N 97° 17′W) 18:103
VEBLEN, OSWALD 19:529 *bibliog.*
VEBLEN, THORSTEIN B. 19:529 *bibliog.*
conspicuous consumption 5:206
VECCHIETTA 19:530 *bibliog.*
VECCHIO, PONTE *see* PONTE VECCHIO
VECHTEN, CARL VAN *see* VAN VECHTEN, CARL
VECTOR ANALYSIS 19:530 *bibliog., illus.*
force 8:220
linear algebra 12:353
mathematics, history of 13:226
matrix 13:230
motion, planar 13:609
scalar 17:106
statics 18:235
topological spaces
Bonach, Stefan 3:59
vectors 19:530
Maxwell's equations 13:241–242
velocity 19:538
VECTORSCOPE (video technology) 19:86
VEDANTA 19:530 *bibliog.*
Hinduism 10:170
Madhva 13:41
pantheism 15:61
philosophy 15:246
Upanishads 19:471
VEDAS (sacred books) 19:530–531 *bibliog.*
fertility rites 8:60
Hinduism 10:172–173
India, history of 11:88–89
Indian music 11:102–103
Manu 13:131
philosophy 15:246
Upanishads 19:471
Vedanta 19:530
VEDDER, ELIHU 19:531 *bibliog.*
VEDISM *see* HINDUISM
VEEDERSBURG (Indiana)
map (40° 7′N 87° 16′W) 11:111
VEENDAM (Netherlands)
map (53° 6′N 6° 58′E) 14:99
VEENENDAAL (Netherlands)
map (52° 2′N 5° 34′E) 14:99
VEGA (astronomy)
Struve, Friedrich Georg Wilhelm von 18:304
VEGA (Texas)
map (35° 15′N 102° 26′W) 19:129
VEGA, GARCILASO DE LA *see* GARCILASO DE LA VEGA
VEGA, LOPE DE 19:531 *bibliog., illus.*
Calderón de la Barca, Pedro 4:26
Spanish literature 18:158
VEGETABLE 19:531–534 *bibliog., illus.*
See also names of specific vegetables, e.g., LETTUCE; ONION; PEA; etc.
gardening 9:43–44 *illus.*
nutrition, human 14:305
VEGETABLE OILS 19:534–535 *bibliog., illus.*
See also FATS AND OILS
castor oil 4:191
coconut 5:88
corn 5:267
cotton 5:306
esters of glycerol 7:246
flax 8:157
margarine 13:149
olive 14:378
palm 15:49
peanut 15:125
production 19:534–535 *table*
safflower 17:11
sesame 17:212
soybean 18:115
sunflower 18:348
tung oil 19:337
VEGETARIANISM 19:535 *bibliog., table*
Pythagoras of Samos 15:639–640
VEGETATION *see* PLANT (botany); PLANT DISTRIBUTION; names of specific types of vegetation, e.g., GRASSLANDS; TUNDRA; etc.; names of specific types of plants, e.g., ANGIOSPERM; BRYOPHYTE; etc.
VEGLIAN LANGUAGE *see* DALMATIAN LANGUAGE
VEGREVILLE (Alberta)
map (53° 30′N 112° 3′W) 1:256
VEII (Italy) 19:535–536 *bibliog.*
Etruscans 7:258–261
VEIL, SIMONE 19:536
VEILLER, LAWRENCE
housing 10:276
VEILTAIL (goldfish) 9:234 *illus.*
VEIN 19:536 *bibliog.*
aneurysm 1:411
cardiovascular diseases 4:144–145
circulatory system 4:440 *illus.*; 4:442 *illus.*
phlebitis 15:248
thrombosis 19:183
varicose vein 19:523
VEIN DEPOSIT 19:536
dike (geology) 6:176
lode deposit 19:536
mineral and gem source 19:536
ore deposits 14:422
major ore deposits 14:424–425 *table*
rock fracture 19:536
VEINTIOCHO DE MAYO (Ecuador)
map (3° 50′S 78° 52′W) 7:52
VEJLE (Denmark)
map (55° 42′N 9° 32′E) 6:109
VELA (artificial satellite) 19:536
VELARDE, RAMÓN LÓPEZ *see* LÓPEZ VELARDE, RAMÓN
VELASCO, JOSÉ MARÍA 19:536 *bibliog.*
Latin American art and architecture 12:227
VELASCO, LUIS DE (d. 1564) 19:536
VELASCO, LUIS DE (1534–1617)
Velasco, Luis de (d. 1564) 19:536
VELASCO ALVARADO, JUAN
Peru 15:193–194; 15:195
VELASCO IBARRA, JOSÉ MARÍA 19:536 *bibliog.*
VELÁZQUEZ (Uruguay)
map (34° 2′S 54° 17′W) 19:488
VELÁZQUEZ, DIEGO 19:536–537 *bibliog., illus.*
Buen Retiro Palace 3:544
Camagüey (Cuba) 4:49
Herrera, Francisco de 10:146
Las Meninas 2:198 *illus.*; 19:537 *illus.*
Luis de Góngora y Argo 9:244 *illus.*
Prince Baltasar Carlos 18:153 *illus.*
Rokeby Venus 2:205 *illus.*
Spanish art and architecture 18:154
VELÁZQUEZ DE CUÉLLAR, DIEGO 19:537 *bibliog.*
VELDE, HENRY VAN DE *see* VAN DE VELDE, HENRY
VELDEKE, HENDRIK VAN
Dutch and Flemish literature 6:313–314
VELEBIT MOUNTAINS
map (44° 38′N 15° 3′E) 20:340
VELENCEI LAKE
map (47° 12′N 18° 35′E) 10:307
VÉLEZ DE ESCALANTE, SILVESTRE *see* ESCALANTE, SILVESTRE VÉLEZ DE
VELHO DE COSTA, MARIA FÁTIMA
Three Marias, The (Portuguese literary trio) 19:182
VELIKA MORAVA RIVER
map (44° 43′N 21° 3′E) 20:340
VELIKA PLANA (Yugoslavia)
map (44° 20′N 21° 4′E) 20:340
VELIKOVSKY, IMMANUEL 19:537–538 *bibliog., illus.*
catastrophism 4:201
VELINO, MOUNT
map (42° 9′N 13° 23′E) 11:321
VELMA (Oklahoma)
map (34° 28′N 97° 40′W) 14:368
VELOCITY 19:538
acceleration 1:72
ballistics 3:49–50
differential calculus 6:167
escape velocity 7:236
planets 7:236 *table*
measurement 13:254
motion, circular 13:607–608
motion, planar 13:609
relativity 16:133–134
rockets, ballistics 3:50
speed 18:176
VELVA (North Dakota)
map (48° 4′N 100° 56′W) 14:248
VELVET 19:538
VELVETLEAF 19:538
VENA CAVA
circulatory system 4:440 *illus.*; 4:442 *illus.*
heart 10:92
vein 19:536
VENADO TUERTO (Argentina)
map (33° 45′S 61° 58′W) 2:149
VENAISSIN (France) *see* COMTAT (France)
VENANGO (county in Pennsylvania)
map (41° 24′N 79° 50′W) 15:147
VENDA (South Africa)
flag 8:137 *illus.*
map (23° 0′S 31° 0′E) 18:79
South Africa 18:78; 18:80; 18:81; 18:83
VENDING MACHINE 19:538 *bibliog.*
retailing 16:184
VENDÔME, ANTOINE DE
Bourbon (dynasty) 3:423
VENDÔME, LOUIS JOSEPH, DUC DE 19:538
Spanish Succession, War of the 18:162–163
VENECIA (Costa Rica)
map (10° 22′N 84° 17′W) 5:291
VENEER 19:538
logging 12:394
plywood 15:374–375
rosewood 16:317
wood 20:206
VENERA 19:538–539 *bibliog., illus., table*
space exploration 18:124–125 *illus.*
Venus (planet) 19:547–548
VENERABLE BEDE *see* BEDE, SAINT
VENEREAL DISEASE 19:539–541 *bibliog.*
chancroid 4:279
genital herpes 10:146
gonorrhea 9:244
herpes 10:145
infectious diseases 11:167
syphilis 18:410
wart 20:33
VENETO (Italy) 19:541
cities
Vicenza 19:571
Italian city-state 11:328 *map*
VENETSIANOV, ALEXEI
Russian art and architecture 16:362
VENEZIA (Italy) *see* VENICE (Italy)
VENEZIANO, DOMENICO *see* DOMENICO VENEZIANO
VENEZIANO, PAOLO *see* PAOLO VENEZIANO
VENEZUELA 19:541–544 *bibliog., illus., map, table*
arts 19:543
Latin American art and architecture 12:222–228
Villanueva, Carlos Raúl 19:597
cities
Caracas 4:130–131 *illus.*
Ciudad Bolívar 5:9
La Guaira 12:146–147
Maracaibo 13:143
Merida 19:542 *table*
Valencia 19:504
climate 19:541–542 *table*
economic activity 19:543 *illus.*
education 19:542
Latin American universities 12:233 *table*
flag 8:134; 19:541 *illus.*
government 19:543–544
welfare spending 20:98 *table*
history 19:544
Betancourt, Rómulo 3:229
Bolívar, Simón 3:365
Castro, Cipriano 4:192
Gómez, Juan Vicente 9:241
Guzmán Blanco, Antonio 9:411
Herrera Campins, Luis 10:146
Latin America, history of 12:220–221
Miranda, Francisco de 13:463
New Granada 14:121
Páez, José Antonio 15:13
Venezuela Boundary Dispute 19:544

VENEZUELA (cont.)
land and resources **19**:541–542 *map*, *table*
tar sands **19**:34
literature
Bello, Andrés **3**:190
Gallegos, Rómulo **9**:17
Latin American literature **12**:228–231
map (8° 0′N 66° 0′W) **18**:85
people **19**:541–543
Warrau **20**:30–31
Yanomamo **20**:318
rivers, lakes, and waterways **19**:541
Angel Falls **1**:412
Maracaibo, Lake **13**:143
Orinoco River **14**:444
trade **19**:543
VENEZUELA, GULF OF
map (11° 30′N 71° 0′W) **19**:542
VENEZUELA BOUNDARY DISPUTE **19**:544 *bibliog.*
Olney, Richard **14**:381
United States, history of the **19**:452
VENEZUELA CLAIMS
Drago, Luis Mariá **6**:254–255
VENICE (Florida)
map (27° 6′N 82° 27′W) **8**:172
VENICE (Italy) **11**:324 *illus.*; **19**:544–545 *bibliog.*, *illus.*
art and architecture
Colleoni Monument **2**:195 *illus.*
Doge's Palace **6**:222
glassware, decorative **9**:203 *illus.*
Italian art and architecture **11**:308–314
jewelry **11**:410
landscape painting **12**:188–189
mosaic **13**:596
Redentore, Il **11**:310 *illus.*
Saint Mark's Basilica **11**:309 *illus.*; **17**:23–24
Sansovino, Jacopo **17**:66
Venice Biennale **19**:545
bridge (engineering) **3**:480
climate **11**:322 *table*
economy **19**:544
gondola **9**:243
herbs and spices **10**:137
history **19**:544–545
boundaries *c.*1100 **13**:392 *map*
boundaries *c.*1360 **7**:285 *map*
boundaries *c.*1560 **7**:288 *map*
boundaries *c.*1648 **7**:289 *map*
doge **6**:222
glass **9**:197–198
Italian Wars **11**:319
Italian music **11**:317–318
map (45° 27′N 12° 21′E) **11**:321
VENICE (Louisiana)
map (29° 17′N 89° 21′W) **12**:430
VENICE, GULF OF
map (45° 15′N 13° 0′E) **11**:321
VENICE BIENNALE **19**:545 *bibliog.*
VENING MEINESZ, FELIX **19**:545 *bibliog.*
VENISON **19**:546
deer **6**:79
VENIZÉLOS, ELEUTHÉRIOS **19**:546 *bibliog.*
Constantine I, King of Greece **5**:208
VENLO (Netherlands)
map (51° 24′N 6° 10′E) **14**:99
VENN DIAGRAM **19**:546
syllogisms **18**:401 *illus.*
VENOM **19**:546 *bibliog.*
bites and stings **3**:300
poisonous plants and animals **15**:383–385
snake **17**:379–381 *illus.*; **19**:546
colubrid **5**:124
rattlesnake **16**:93
salivary glands **17**:34
VENOUS SYSTEM
vein **19**:536
VENTADORN, BERNART DE *see* BERNART DE VENTADORN
VENTADOUR, BERNARD DE
minstrels, minnesingers, and troubadours **13**:460
VENTILATION
Holland Tunnel **10**:203
VENTRICLE
heart **10**:91–94 *illus.*
heart attack **10**:95
VENTRICULAR INFARCTION *see* INFARCTION
VENTRILOQUISM **19**:546 *bibliog.*
Bergen, Edgar, and McCarthy, Charlie **3**:209
VENTRIS, MICHAEL **19**:546 *bibliog.*
VENTURA (California)
map (34° 17′N 119° 18′W) **4**:31
VENTURA (county in California)
map (34° 30′N 119° 0′W) **4**:31
VENTURI, ROBERT **19**:546 *bibliog.*
postmodern architecture **15**:464
VENUS (Florida)
map (27° 4′N 81° 21′W) **8**:172
VENUS (mythology) **19**:548
VENUS (planet) **19**:546–548 *bibliog.*, *illus.*
atmosphere **19**:547
greenhouse effect **9**:352
orbit and rotation **19**:547
planets **15**:329–331
radar astronomy **16**:40 *illus.*
radio astronomy **16**:48
solar system **18**:46–48 *illus.*, *table*
space exploration **18**:124–125; **19**:547–548
Mariner **13**:155
Pioneer **15**:310
Venera **19**:538–539 *table*
Zond **20**:373
surface **19**:548
VENUS DE MILO **9**:341 *illus.*
Dumont d'Urville, Jules Sébastian César **6**:298
Melos (Greece) **13**:288
VENUS OF LAUSSEL **5**:353 *illus.*; **15**:507 *illus.*
VENUS OF LESPUGUE **15**:40 *illus.*
VENUS OF WILLENDORF **13**:606 *illus.*; **15**:506 *illus.*; **17**:159 *illus.*; **19**:548 *illus.*
VENUS'S COMB **17**:251 *illus.*
VENUS'S-FLYTRAP
carnivorous plants **4**:158 *illus.*
VENUS'S GIRDLE *see* COMB JELLY
VEPS LANGUAGE
Ural-Altaic languages **19**:475
VERACRUZ (city in Mexico) **13**:358 *illus.*; **19**:548–549
climate **13**:356 *table*
map (19° 12′N 96° 8′W) **13**:357
pre-Columbian art and architecture **15**:497
VERACRUZ (state in Mexico) **19**:549
cities
Jalapa **11**:351
Veracruz **19**:548–549
VERB
parts of speech **15**:101
VERBAL BEHAVIOR AND LEARNING
brain bilateralism **3**:448
Brown, Roger **3**:516
geographical linguistics **9**:98–100
psycholinguistics **15**:592
semantics (linguistics) **17**:194
sociolinguistics **18**:27–28
VERBANIA (Italy)
map (45° 56′N 8° 33′E) **11**:321
VERBENA **15**:337 *illus.*; **19**:549
mangrove **13**:116
oregano **14**:426
VERCINGETORIX **19**:549
La Tène **12**:150
VERDE, BAY DE (Newfoundland)
map (48° 5′N 52° 54′W) **14**:166
VERDE, CAPE **19**:549
VERDE RIVER (Arizona)
map (33° 33′N 111° 40′W) **2**:160
VERDE RIVER (Paraguay)
map (23° 9′S 57° 37′W) **15**:77
VERDELOT, PHILIPPE
madrigal **13**:45
Renaissance music **16**:156
VERDI, GIUSEPPE **19**:549–550 *bibliog.*, *illus.*
Aïda **1**:201
Boito, Arrigo **3**:363
Italian music **11**:319 *illus.*
opera **14**:401
Traviata, La **19**:284–285
Trovatore, Il **19**:312
VERDIGRE (Nebraska)
map (42° 36′N 98° 2′W) **14**:70
VERDIGRIS RIVER
map (35° 48′N 95° 19′W) **14**:368
VERDIN **19**:550
VERDON (Nebraska)
map (40° 8′N 95° 48′W) **14**:70
VERDUN (France) **19**:550
VERDUN (Quebec)
map (45° 27′N 73° 34′W) **16**:18
VERDUN, BATTLE OF **19**:550 *bibliog.*
Falkenhayn, Erich von **8**:13
Pétain, Henri Philippe **15**:199
World War I **20**:225 *map*; **20**:232–233 *illus.*
VERDUN, TREATY OF (843) **4**:289 *map*; **19**:550
VERDY, VIOLETTE **19**:550 *bibliog.*
VEREENIGING (South Africa)
map (26° 38′S 27° 57′E) **18**:79
VÉRENDRYE, PIERRRE GAULTIER DE VARENNES, SIEUR DE LA *see* LA VÉRENDRYE, PIERRE GAULTIER DE VARENNES, SIEUR DE
VERESHCHAGIN, VASILY
Russian art and architecture **16**:362
VERGA, GIOVANNI **19**:550 *bibliog.*
VERGARA (Uruguay)
map (32° 56′S 53° 57′W) **19**:488
VERGENNES (Vermont)
map (44° 10′N 73° 15′W) **19**:554
VERGENNES, COMTE DE
American Revolution **1**:360–361
VERGIL **19**:550–551 *bibliog.*, *illus.*
Aeneid (epic) **1**:119
Naples (Italy) **14**:15
VERGIL, POLYDORE **19**:551
VERHAEREN, ÉMILE **19**:551
VERHULST, ROMBOUT
Maria van Reygersburg **8**:162 *illus.*
VERISMO **19**:551
Bohème, La **3**:360
Giordano, Umberto **9**:186
Italian music **11**:319
Leoncavallo, Ruggero **12**:291–292
Mascagni, Pietro **13**:195
Menotti, Gian Carlo **13**:300
Puccini, Giacomo **15**:612
Zandonai, Riccardo **20**:355
VERÍSSIMO, ÉRICO **19**:551
VERKHOYANSK (USSR)
climate **2**:237 *table*
VERKHOYANSK MOUNTAINS
map (67° 0′N 129° 0′E) **19**:388
VERLAINE, PAUL **19**:551–552 *bibliog.*, *illus.*
VERMEER, JAN **19**:552–553 *bibliog.*, *illus.*
The Art of Painting **6**:311 *illus.*
Dutch art and architecture **6**:311
Young Woman Standing at a Virginal **19**:552 *illus.*
VERMEYLEN, AUGUST **19**:553
VERMICULITE
mica **13**:370–371
VERMIFUGES *see* ANTHELMINTIC DRUGS
VERMIGLI, PIETRO MARTIRE **19**:553 *bibliog.*
VERMILION (Alberta)
map (53° 22′N 110° 51′W) **1**:256
VERMILION (county in Illinois)
map (40° 10′N 87° 45′W) **11**:42
VERMILION (county in Louisiana)
map (29° 50′N 92° 15′W) **12**:430
VERMILION (Ohio)
map (41° 25′N 82° 22′W) **14**:357
VERMILION BAY
map (29° 40′N 92° 0′W) **12**:430
VERMILION LAKE
map (47° 53′N 92° 25′W) **13**:453
VERMILION RIVER
map (41° 19′N 89° 4′W) **11**:42
VERMILLION (county in Indiana)
map (39° 50′N 87° 25′W) **11**:111
VERMILLION (South Dakota)
map (42° 47′N 96° 56′W) **18**:103
VERMILLION BLUFFS
map (40° 50′N 108° 30′W) **5**:116
VERMONT **19**:553–558 *bibliog.*, *illus.*, *map*
cities
Barre **3**:93
Bennington **3**:204
Burlington **3**:572
Montpelier **13**:557
Rutland **16**:376
climate **19**:555
culture **19**:556
economic activity **19**:555 *illus.*; **19**:557 *illus.*
education **19**:556
Bennington College **3**:204
Goddard College **9**:220
Middlebury College **13**:413
Vermont, state university and colleges of **19**:558
flag **19**:553 *illus.*
government and politics **19**:557–558
Green Mountains **9**:348
historical sites **19**:556
history **19**:558
Allen, Ethan **1**:299
Chittenden, Thomas **4**:399
land and resources **19**:553–556 *illus.*, *map*
map (43° 50′N 72° 45′W) **19**:419
people **19**:556
rivers, lakes, and waterways **19**:555
seal, state **19**:553 *illus.*
vegetation and animal life **19**:555–556
VERMONT (Illinois)
map (40° 18′N 90° 26′W) **11**:42
VERMONT, STATE UNIVERSITY AND COLLEGES OF **19**:558
VERMOUTH **19**:558–559 *bibliog.*
VERNAL (Utah)
map (40° 27′N 109° 32′W) **19**:492
VERNAL EQUINOX *see* EQUINOX
VERNDALE (Minnesota)
map (46° 24′N 95° 1′W) **13**:453
VERNE, JULES **19**:559 *bibliog.*, *illus.*
From the Earth to the Moon **17**:143 *illus.*
Great Eastern **9**:319
science fiction **17**:143
Twenty Thousand Leagues Under the Sea **19**:360
VERNER, FREDERICK
wigwam **11**:120 *illus.*
VERNER, KARL ADOLF **19**:559
Grimm's law **9**:366
historical linguistics **10**:183
VERNER'S LAW
Germanic languages **9**:136 *table*
Verner, Karl Adolf **19**:559
VERNET (family) **19**:559 *bibliog.*
VERNIER **19**:559
VERNON (Alabama)
map (33° 45′N 88° 7′W) **1**:234
VERNON (British Columbia)
map (50° 16′N 119° 16′W) **3**:491
VERNON (Connecticut)
map (41° 52′N 72° 27′W) **5**:193
VERNON (Florida)
map (30° 37′N 85° 43′W) **8**:172
VERNON (Indiana)
map (38° 59′N 85° 36′W) **11**:111
VERNON (county in Louisiana)
map (31° 8′N 93° 10′W) **12**:430
VERNON (county in Missouri)
map (37° 55′N 94° 20′W) **13**:476
VERNON (Texas)
map (34° 9′N 99° 17′W) **19**:129
VERNON (Utah)
map (40° 6′N 112° 26′W) **19**:492
VERNON (county in Wisconsin)
map (43° 40′N 90° 50′W) **20**:185
VERNON, EDWARD **19**:559 *bibliog.*
VERNON RIVER (Prince Edward Island)
map (46° 12′N 62° 50′W) **15**:548
VERO BEACH (Florida)
map (27° 38′N 80° 24′W) **8**:172
VÉROIA (Greece)
map (40° 31′N 22° 12′E) **9**:325
VERONA (Italy) **19**:559
map (45° 27′N 11° 0′E) **11**:321
Scala (family) **17**:106
VERONA, CONGRESS OF
Congress system **5**:187–188
VERONESE, PAOLO **19**:559–560 *bibliog.*, *illus.*
The Holy Family with Saint Barbara **19**:560 *illus.*
Venice (Italy) **19**:544
VERÓNICA (Argentina)
map (35° 22′S 57° 20′W) **2**:149
VERRAZANO, GIOVANNI DA **19**:560 *bibliog.*
exploration **7**:337 *map*
Hudson River **10**:289
Manhattan (New York City) **13**:116
Maryland **13**:191
Massachusetts **13**:210
New York (state) **14**:153
North Carolina **14**:245
Rhode Island **16**:201
VERRAZANO-NARROWS BRIDGE **3**:482–484 *illus.*; **19**:560 *bibliog.*
Ammann, Othmar Hermann **1**:372
New York (city) **14**:144 *map*
VERRES, GAIUS **19**:560
VERRET, LAKE
map (29° 53′N 91° 10′W) **12**:430
VERRETT, SHIRLEY **14**:401 *illus.*
VERRETTES (Haiti)
map (19° 3′N 72° 28′W) **10**:15
VERROCCHIO, ANDREA DEL **19**:560–561 *bibliog.*, *illus.*
Botticelli, Sandro **3**:417
Colleoni Monument **2**:195 *illus.*
David **19**:561 *illus.*
Leonardo da Vinci **12**:289
VERSAILLES (France) **19**:561 *bibliog.*
map (48° 48′N 2° 8′E) **8**:260
VERSAILLES (Illinois)
map (39° 53′N 90° 39′W) **11**:42
VERSAILLES (Indiana)
map (39° 4′N 85° 15′W) **11**:111
VERSAILLES (Kentucky)
map (38° 3′N 84° 44′W) **12**:47
VERSAILLES (Missouri)
map (38° 26′N 92° 51′W) **13**:476
VERSAILLES, PALACE OF **2**:135 *illus.*; **19**:561 *bibliog.*
Cotte, Robert de **5**:304
Europe, history of **7**:289

France, history of 8:268
French art and architecture 8:305
Gabriel (family) 9:6
Grand Trianon bedroom 18:311 *illus.*
Hardouin-Mansart, Jules 10:47
interior design
Le Brun, Charles 12:252
landscape architecture 12:186–187 *illus.*
garden 9:40
Le Nôtre, André 12:255
Louis XIV, King of France 12:426
Petit Trianon 15:203
rococo style 16:263
VERSAILLES, TREATY OF (1919)
Hitler, Adolf 10:188
Paris Peace Conference 15:88
Polish Corridor 15:397
Wilson, Woodrow 20:167
World War I 20:244–246 *illus.*
World War II 20:249
VERSE, FREE *see* FREE VERSE
VERSIFICATION 19:561–563 *bibliog.*
See also FREE VERSE
accent 1:76
alexandrine 1:278
blank verse 3:327
caesura 4:15
dithyramb 6:202
doggerel 6:223
Edda 7:54–55
elegy 7:129
free verse 19:562
glossary 19:562–563
hymn 10:346
madrigal 13:45
Middle English 13:412
ode 14:348
poetry 15:378–379
rhyme 16:204
satire 17:88
sestina 17:213
Skeltonics
Skelton, John 17:337
sonnet 18:65
sprung rhythm
Hopkins, Gerard Manley 10:231
theory
Deschamps, Eustache 6:126
Gascoigne, George 9:53
Scaliger, Julius Caesar 17:107
VERSPRONCK, JOHANNES CORNELISZ 19:563 *bibliog.*
VERT, CAPE OF
map (14° 43′N 17° 30′W) 17:202
VERTEBRAE 18:185 *illus.*
joint (anatomy) 11:439 *illus.*
VERTEBRATE *see* CHORDATE
VÉRTESSZÖLLÖS (Hungary) 19:563 *bibliog.*
Clactonian 5:35
VERTICAL BLANKING INTERVAL (video term) 19:576f
teletext 19:84
VERTICAL TAKEOFF AND LANDING (VTOL) *see* VTOL
VERTIENTES (Cuba)
map (21° 16′N 78° 9′W) 5:377
VERTIGO 19:563
ear disease 7:7
Meniere's disease 13:297
space medicine 18:133
VERTOV, DZIGA 19:563
documentary 6:211
VERUS, LUCIUS
Marcus Aurelius, Roman Emperor 13:147
VERUS, MARCUS ANNIUS *see* MARCUS AURELIUS, ROMAN EMPEROR
VERVIERS (Belgium)
map (50° 35′N 5° 52′E) 3:177
VERWEY, ALBERT 19:563
VERWOERD, HENDRIK F. 19:563 *bibliog., illus.*
VERY LARGE ARRAY
National Radio Astronomy Observatory 14:45
radio astronomy 16:52–53
radio observatories 14:318
VERY LARGE-SCALE INTEGRATION *see* VLSI
VESAAS, TARJEI 19:564
VESALIUS, ANDREAS 19:564 *bibliog.*
anatomy 1:396 *illus.*
De Humani Corporis Fabrica (book) 3:269 *illus.*; 20:376 *illus.*
Galen 9:13
medicine 13:269 *illus.*
VESEY, DENMARK 19:564 *bibliog.*
VESPASIAN, ROMAN EMPEROR 19:564 *bibliog., illus.*
Colosseum 2:132 *illus.*
Maiden Castle 13:66
Rome, ancient 16:303
VESPERS *see* DIVINE OFFICE
VESPUCCI, AMERIGO 19:564 *bibliog.*
Latin America, history of 12:217 *illus.*
South American Indians 11:136 *illus.*
VESTA (Costa Rica)
map (9° 43′N 83° 3′W) 5:291
VESTA (mythology) 19:564
Olbers, Heinrich 14:373
VESTAL VIRGINS *see* VESTA (mythology)
VESTAVIA HILLS (Alabama)
map (33° 27′N 86° 47′W) 1:234
VESTDIJK, SIMON 19:565
VESTIBULAR SYSTEM (ear) 7:6 *illus.*
biological equilibrium 3:265
ear 7:6–7
VESTMANNAEYJAR (Iceland)
map (63° 26′N 20° 12′W) 11:17
VESTMENTS 19:565 *bibliog.*
VESTRIS (family) 19:565 *bibliog.*
VESTRIS, MADAME 19:565 *bibliog.*
theater, history of the 19:149
VESUVIANITE *see* IDOCRASE
VESUVIO *see* VESUVIUS
VESUVIUS 14:15 *illus.*; 19:565 *bibliog.*
map (40° 49′N 14° 26′E) 11:321
Pompeii 15:423–424
volcanic eruption 79 AD
Herculaneum 10:137–138
VESZPRÉM (Hungary)
map (47° 6′N 17° 55′E) 10:307
VETCH 19:565
VETERANS
G.I. Bill of Rights 9:170
VETERANS ADMINISTRATION 19:565–566 *bibliog.*
mortgage 13:592
scholarships, fellowships, and loans 17:131
VETERANS DAY *see* ARMISTICE DAY
VETERANS OF FOREIGN WARS 19:566
VETERANS' ORGANIZATIONS 19:566 *bibliog.*
American G.I. Forum
Chicano 4:343
American Legion 1:341
Amvets 1:386
Disabled American Veterans 6:188
Grand Army of the Republic 9:284
Veterans of Foreign Wars 19:566
VETERINARY MEDICINE 19:566–567 *bibliog.*
diseases, animal 6:190–192
VETO 19:567 *bibliog.*
Congress of the United States 5:187
president of the United States 15:522
United Nations 19:412
VEVAY (Indiana)
map (38° 45′N 85° 4′W) 11:111
VEVEY (Switzerland)
map (46° 28′N 6° 51′E) 18:394
VÉZELAY (France)
Romanesque art and architecture 16:284 *illus.*
VHD (VIDEO HIGH DENSITY; VIDEO HOME DISC) 19:576f
video recording 19:576j
videodisc 19:576p
VHS (video technology) 19:576b; 19:576f
video camera 19:576h
video recording 19:576j
VIA APPIA *see* ROMAN ROADS
VIA FLAMINIA *see* ROMAN ROADS
VIACHI (Bolivia)
map (16° 39′S 68° 18′W) 3:366
VIADUCT 19:567 *bibliog.*
VIAN, BORIS 19:567
VIANA DO CASTELO (Portugal)
map (41° 42′N 8° 50′W) 15:449
VIANNEY, SAINT JEAN BAPTIST MARIE 19:567
VIARDOT-GARCÍA, PAULINE 19:567 *bibliog.*
VIBORG (Denmark)
map (56° 26′N 9° 24′E) 6:109
VIBORG (South Dakota)
map (43° 10′N 97° 5′W) 18:103
VIBRAPHONE 19:567
Hampton, Lionel 10:32
VIBRATION
measurement, accelerometer 1:76
phonon 15:255
resonance (physics) 16:178
VIBRIO 19:567
VIBRISSA
hair 10:14
VIBURNUM 19:567–568 *illus.*
VIC-WELLS BALLET *see* ROYAL BALLET, THE
VICAR OF WAKEFIELD, THE (book) 19:568
Goldsmith, Oliver 9:236
VICCO (Kentucky)
map (37° 13′N 83° 4′W) 12:47
VICE-PRESIDENT OF THE UNITED STATES 19:568–571 *bibliog., illus., table*
See also names of specific vice-presidents, e.g., HUMPHREY, HUBERT H., JR.; MONDALE, WALTER F.; etc.
Constitution of the United States 5:217–219; 5:221–223
election
electoral college 7:104–105
political convention 15:399
12th Amendment 19:358
flag 8:148 *illus.*
president of the United States 15:525–526
presidential succession
20th Amendment 19:359
25th Amendment 19:359
Senate of the United States 17:199
term of office
20th Amendment 19:359
vice-presidential succession
25th Amendment 19:359
VICENTE, GIL 19:571 *bibliog.*
VICENTE LÓPEZ (Argentina)
map (34° 32′S 58° 28′W) 2:149
VICENTE NOBLE (Dominican Republic)
map (18° 23′N 71° 11′W) 6:233
VICENTINO, NICOLA
Renaissance music 16:156
VICENZA (Italy) 19:571
map (45° 33′N 11° 33′E) 11:321
Teatro Olimpico 19:59
VICEROY 19:571
VICEROY BUTTERFLY
coloration, biological 5:121–122 *illus.*
mimicry 13:434–435 *illus.*
VICH (Spain)
map (41° 56′N 2° 15′E) 18:140
VICHADA RIVER
map (4° 55′N 67° 50′W) 5:107
VICHY (France) 19:571
VICHY GOVERNMENT 8:270 *table*; 8:272 *map*; 19:571 *bibliog.*
Darlan, Jean François 6:39
Laval, Pierre 12:240–241
Pétain, Henri Philippe 15:199
World War II 20:262
VICI (Oklahoma)
map (36° 9′N 99° 18′W) 14:368
VICKERS, JON 19:571 *bibliog.*
VICKSBURG (Michigan)
map (42° 6′N 85° 32′W) 13:377
VICKSBURG (Mississippi) 19:571
map (32° 14′N 90° 56′W) 13:469
VICKSBURG CAMPAIGN 5:27 *illus.*; 19:571–572 *bibliog., map*
Grant, Ulysses S. 9:288
Vicksburg (Mississippi) 19:571
VICO, GIAMBATTISTA 19:572 *bibliog.*
mythology 13:694
VICTIMLESS CRIME
crime 5:345
entrapment 7:208–209
VICTOR (Iowa)
map (41° 44′N 92° 18′W) 11:244
VICTOR (Montana)
map (46° 25′N 114° 9′W) 13:547
VICTOR AMADEUS II, DUKE OF SAVOY 19:572
Savoy (dynasty) 17:102
VICTOR EMMANUEL I, ITALIAN KING OF SARDINIA 19:572 *bibliog.*
VICTOR EMMANUEL II, KING OF ITALY 19:572–573 *bibliog., illus.*
Italy, history of 11:329–330
VICTOR EMMANUEL III, KING OF ITALY 19:573 *bibliog.*
VICTORIA (Argentina)
map (32° 37′S 60° 10′W) 2:149
VICTORIA (Australia) 19:573 *map*
cities
Melbourne 13:285–286 *illus., map*
flag 8:145 *illus.*
history
Australia, history of 2:340
map (38° 0′S 145° 0′E) 2:328
VICTORIA (British Columbia) 3:492 *illus.*; 19:573
map (48° 25′N 123° 22′W) 3:491
VICTORIA (carriage)
coach and carriage 5:75
VICTORIA (Chile)
map (20° 44′S 69° 42′W) 4:355
VICTORIA (Grenada)
map (12° 12′N 61° 42′W) 9:358
VICTORIA (Hong Kong) 10:222 *map*; 19:573
map (22° 17′N 114° 9′E) 4:362
VICTORIA (Kansas)
map (38° 52′N 99° 9′W) 12:18
VICTORIA (Malta)
map (36° 2′N 14° 14′E) 13:94
VICTORIA (Prince Edward Island)
map (46° 13′N 63° 29′W) 15:548
VICTORIA (Seychelles)
map (4° 38′S 55° 27′E) 17:232
VICTORIA (Texas)
map (28° 48′N 97° 0′W) 19:129
VICTORIA (county in Texas)
map (28° 45′N 97° 0′W) 19:129
VICTORIA (Virginia)
map (36° 59′N 78° 14′W) 19:607
VICTORIA, GUADALUPE
Mexico, history of 13:364
VICTORIA, LAKE 19:573–574 *map*
map (1° 0′S 33° 0′E) 1:136
Owen Falls Dam 19:373 *illus.*
Speke, John Hanning 18:176–177
VICTORIA, MOUNT (Burma)
map (21° 14′N 93° 55′E) 3:573
VICTORIA, MOUNT (Papua New Guinea)
map (8° 55′S 147° 35′E) 15:72
VICTORIA, QUEEN OF ENGLAND, SCOTLAND, AND IRELAND 9:317 *illus.*; 19:574 *bibliog., illus.*
Albert, Prince Consort 1:254
Disraeli, Benjamin, 1st Earl of Beaconsfield 6:197–198
Great Britain, history of 9:317
Hanover (dynasty) 10:39
hemophilia 10:120
Kean (family) 12:35
Leopold I, King of the Belgians 12:294
Lister, Joseph 12:366
Melbourne, William Lamb, 2d Viscount 13:286
Salic law 17:32
VICTORIA, TOMÁS LUIS DE 19:574–575 *bibliog.*
VICTORIA, UNIVERSITY OF 19:575
VICTORIA AND ALBERT MUSEUM 19:575 *bibliog.*
VICTORIA BEACH (Manitoba)
map (50° 43′N 96° 33′W) 13:119
VICTORIA CROSS (Great Britain)
medals and decorations 13:262–263 *illus.*
VICTORIA DAY *see* AUSTRALIA DAY
VICTORIA DE DURANGO (Mexico) *see* DURANGO (city in Mexico)
VICTORIA DE LAS TUNAS (Cuba)
map (20° 58′N 76° 57′W) 5:377
VICTORIA FALLS 19:575
map (17° 55′S 25° 51′E) 20:365
waterfall 20:63
VICTORIA ISLAND (Northwest Territories) 19:575
map (71° 0′N 114° 0′W) 14:258
Simpson, Thomas 17:317
VICTORIA LAKE
map (48° 18′N 57° 30′W) 14:166
VICTORIA LAND (region in Antarctica)
map (75° 0′S 163° 0′E) 2:40
VICTORIA NILE RIVER
map (2° 14′N 31° 26′E) 19:372
VICTORIA NYANZA *see* VICTORIA, LAKE
VICTORIA PEAK
map (16° 48′N 88° 37′W) 3:183
VICTORIA RIVER
map (15° 12′S 129° 43′E) 2:328
VICTORIAN LITERATURE 19:575–576 *bibliog.*
authors
Arnold, Matthew 2:185
Austin, Alfred 2:327
Barrie, Sir James Matthew 3:94–95
Brontë (family) 3:504
Browning, Elizabeth Barrett 3:518
Browning, Robert 3:518–519
Bulwer-Lytton, Edward 3:562
Butler, Samuel (1835–1902) 3:592
Carlyle, Thomas 4:152–153
Carroll, Lewis 4:169
Clough, Arthur Hugh 5:69
Collins, Wilkie 5:104
Dickens, Charles 6:156
Dowson, Ernest 6:252–253
Doyle, Sir Arthur Conan 6:253
Eliot, George 7:138–139
FitzGerald, Edward 8:130
Gissing, George Robert 9:191
Hardy, Thomas 10:47–48

VICTORIAN LITERATURE (cont.)
Hopkins, Gerard Manley **10**:231
Huxley, Thomas Henry **10**:325
Kingsley, Charles **12**:84
Lear, Edward **12**:259
Macaulay, Thomas Babington **13**:6
Meredith, George **13**:308–309
Morris, William **13**:589
Newman, John Henry **14**:170
Pater, Walter **15**:110–111
Pinero, Sir Arthur Wing **15**:307
Reade, Charles **16**:100
Rossetti, Christina G. **16**:319
Ruskin, John **16**:348
Stevenson, Robert Louis **18**:265
Swinburne, Algernon Charles **18**:392
Symons, Arthur **18**:404
Thackeray, William Makepeace **19**:138
Thomson, James **19**:176
Trollope, Anthony **19**:305–306
Wilde, Oscar **20**:148–149
Dover Beach **6**:250–251
English literature **7**:199–201
melodrama **13**:287–288
novel **14**:274
VICTORIAN STYLE **19**:576 *bibliog., illus.*
beads and beadwork **3**:138
Beardsley, Aubrey **3**:142–143
English art and architecture **7**:187
Frith, William **8**:335
furniture **8**:377–378
Greenaway, Kate **9**:349
jewelry **11**:411 *illus.*
Landseer, Sir Edwin **12**:192
parlor **8**:378 *illus.*
Pre-Raphaelites **15**:519
Shaw, Richard Norman **17**:246
Tissot, James **19**:209
VICTORIAVILLE (Quebec)
map (46° 3′N 71° 57′W) **16**:18
VICTORIO **19**:576 *bibliog.*
VICTORVILLE (California)
map (34° 32′N 117° 18′W) **4**:31
VICTORY OF SAMOTHRACE
Louvre **12**:437
VICTORY AT SEA, THE (book)
Sims, William Sowden **17**:317
VICUÑA **19**:576 *illus.*
VICÚS (Peru) **19**:576 *bibliog.*
VIDAL, GORE **19**:576–576a *bibliog., illus.*
VIDAL, PEIRE
minstrels, minnesingers, and troubadours **13**:460
VIDAL DE LA BLACHE, PAUL
geography **9**:102
VIDALIA (Georgia)
map (32° 13′N 82° 25′W) **9**:114
VIDALIA (Louisiana)
map (31° 34′N 91° 26′W) **12**:430
VIDELA, JORGE RAFAEL **19**:576a *bibliog.*
VIDEO **19**:576a–576f *bibliog., illus.*
See also TELEVISION
glossary **19**:576d–576f
telecommunications **19**:76
teletext **19**:84
video, music **19**:576f
video art **19**:576g–576h
video camera **19**:576h–576i
video game **19**:576i–576j
video recording **19**:576j–576k
video technology **19**:576k–576p
videodisc **19**:576p
videotape **19**:576p
videotex **19**:576p–577
VIDEO, MUSIC **19**:576f *illus.*
cinematography **4**:434
VIDEO ART **19**:576g–576h *bibliog., illus.*
Paik, Nam June **15**:14–15
paintbox **15**:17
video technology **19**:576o
VIDEO CAMERA **19**:576h–576i *bibliog., illus.*
video art **19**:576g–576h
video technology **19**:576o
VIDEO DISPLAY TERMINAL **19**:576i
cathode-ray tube **4**:211
computer **5**:160i
home video terminal **19**:576c
VIDEO GAME **19**:576i–576j
games **9**:31
VIDEO RECORDING **19**:576j–576k *bibliog., illus.*
cinematography **4**:432–434
Goldmark, Peter Carl **9**:235
video **19**:576b–576d
video art **19**:576g–576h
video camera **19**:576h–576i
video technology **19**:576n–576p
videodisc **19**:576p
compact disc **5**:155
videotape **19**:576p
VIDEO TECHNOLOGY 576k–576p *bibliog., illus.*
television production **19**:86–87
video **19**:576a–576f
video art **19**:576h
video recording *see* VIDEO RECORDING
VIDEOCASSETTE RECORDER
video **19**:576a; **19**:576b–576d; **19**:576f
video camera **19**:576h–576i
video recording **19**:576j–576k *illus.*
video technology **19**:576o
VIDEODISC **19**:576p
compact disc **5**:155
video **19**:576a; **19**:576b
video recording **19**:576j
video technology **19**:576o
VIDEOTAPE **19**:576p
cinematography **4**:432
tape recorder **19**:30
television production **19**:87
video **19**:576b–576d
video art **19**:576g–576h
video camera **19**:576h
video recording **19**:576j–576k *illus.*
video technology **19**:576n–576p
VIDEOTEX **19**:576p–577 *bibliog.*
television transmission **19**:90
VIDOR (Texas)
map (30° 7′N 94° 1′W) **19**:129
VIDOR, KING **19**:577 *bibliog.*
VIEDMA (Argentina)
map (40° 48′S 63° 0′W) **2**:149
VIEDMA, LAKE
map (49° 35′S 72° 35′W) **2**:149
VIEILLE, PAUL
guncotton **9**:405
VIEIRA, ANTÓNIO **19**:577
VIEIRA, JOÃO BERNARDO
Guinea-Bissau **9**:399
VIEIRA DA SILVA **19**:577 *bibliog.*
VIELLE **19**:578
VIEN, JOSEPH MARIE **19**:578 *bibliog.*
VIENNA (Austria) **2**:349 *illus., table*; **19**:578 *bibliog., illus.*
art and architecture **2**:352–353 *illus.*
Kokoschka, Oskar **12**:106
Wiener Werkstätte **20**:146
history **19**:578–579
map (48° 13′N 16° 20′E) **2**:348
Strauss (family) **18**:293–294
Vienna Philharmonic Orchestra **19**:579
waltz **20**:21
VIENNA (Georgia)
map (32° 6′N 83° 47′W) **9**:114
VIENNA (Illinois)
map (37° 25′N 88° 54′W) **11**:42
VIENNA (Maryland)
map (38° 29′N 75° 49′W) **13**:188
VIENNA (Missouri)
map (38° 11′N 91° 57′W) **13**:476
VIENNA (South Dakota)
map (44° 42′N 97° 30′W) **18**:103
VIENNA (Virginia)
map (38° 54′N 77° 15′W) **19**:607
VIENNA (West Virginia)
map (39° 20′N 81° 26′W) **20**:111
VIENNA, CONCORDAT OF
Frederick III, King of Germany and Holy Roman Emperor **8**:291
VIENNA, CONGRESS OF **19**:579 *bibliog.*
Castlereagh, Robert Stewart, Viscount **4**:191
congress system **5**:187–188
Europe, history of **7**:291–292
foreign service **8**:227
German Confederation **9**:132
Germany, history of **9**:152
Metternich, Klemens, Fürst von **13**:349
Prussia **15**:586
repartition of Europe **7**:291 *map*
Risorgimento **16**:228
Talleyrand-Périgord, Charles Maurice de **19**:17
VIENNA, PEACE OF
Seven Weeks' War **17**:216
VIENNA, TREATY OF (1738)
Polish Succession, War of the **15**:398
Stanisław I, King of Poland **18**:218
VIENNA PHILHARMONIC ORCHESTRA **19**:579
Salzburg Festival **17**:45
VIENNA PSYCHOANALYTIC SOCIETY *see* INTERNATIONAL PSYCHOANALYTICAL ASSOCIATION
VIENTIANE (Laos) **19**:579
climate **12**:203 *table*
map (17° 58′N 102° 36′E) **12**:203
VIEQUES ISLAND
map (18° 8′N 65° 25′W) **15**:614
VIEQUES SOUND
map (18° 15′N 65° 23′W) **15**:614
VIERIA, DOMINGOS
Portuguese art and architecture **15**:456
VIERWALDSTÄTTER SEE *see* LUCERNE, LAKE
VIERZEHNHEILIGEN, PILGRIMAGE CHURCH OF
Neumann, Johann Balthasar **14**:104
VIET CONG **19**:579 *bibliog.*
guerrillas **5**:149 *illus.*
Vietnam War **19**:585–589 *maps*
VIET MINH **19**:579 *bibliog.*
Ho Chi Minh **10**:190
Pham Van Dong **15**:219
Vietnam War **19**:584–585 *map*
Vo Nguyen Giap **19**:624
VIET-MUONG LANGUAGES
Southeast Asian languages **18**:110–111
VIET TRI (Vietnam)
map (21° 18′N 105° 26′E) **19**:580
VIÈTE, FRANÇOIS **19**:579 *bibliog.*
mathematics, history of **13**:224
VIETNAM **19**:579–584 *bibliog., illus., map, table*
archaeology
Oceo **14**:346
art **19**:581
folk art **8**:198
Southeast Asian art and architecture **18**:108–109 *illus.*
cities
Da Nang **6**:3
Haiphong **10**:14
Hanoi **10**:39 *illus.*
Ho Chi Minh City **10**:190–191 *illus.*
Hue **10**:291
Nha Trang **19**:581 *illus.*
Phan Rang **19**:582 *illus.*
climate **19**:580–581 *table*
communism *see* COMMUNISM
economic activity **19**:582
education **19**:581
Southeast Asian universities **18**:111 *table*
flag **19**:580 *illus.*
government **19**:582–583
defense, national **6**:82 *table*
history **19**:583–584
Annam **2**:31
Asia, history of **2**:259
Bao Dai, Emperor of Annam **3**:72
Champa **4**:276
Cochin China **5**:85
communism **5**:149–150
Ho Chi Minh **10**:190
Indochina **11**:146
Kampuchea (Cambodia) **12**:13
Khmer Rouge **12**:67
Ngo Dinh Diem **14**:176
Nguyen Van Thieu **14**:177
Pham Van Dong **15**:219
refugee **16**:125
Tonkin **19**:234
Viet Minh **19**:579
Vietnam War *see* VIETNAM WAR
Vo Nguyen Giap **19**:624
land and resources **19**:580–581 *illus., map, table*
language **19**:581
Southeast Asian languages **18**:110–111
map (16° 0′N 108° 0′E) **2**:232
people **19**:581–582
Montagnards **13**:544
religion **19**:581
rivers, lakes, and waterways **19**:580
Yüan River **20**:338
VIETNAM VETERANS MEMORIAL **19**:584 *illus.*
VIETNAM WAR **2**:259 *illus.*; **19**:584–591 *bibliog., illus., maps*
Abrams, Creighton **1**:61
airborne troops **1**:210
American literature **1**:347
antiwar movement **19**:459 *illus.*
conscientious objector **5**:200
conscription **5**:201
counterculture **5**:311
Asia, history of **2**:260
battleship **3**:128
Bunker, Ellsworth **3**:563
Da Nang **6**:3
Democratic party **6**:102
Dien Bien Phu, Battle of **6**:162
first Indochinese war **19**:584–585 *map*
Geneva conferences **9**:91
guerrillas **9**:392
herbicide **10**:136
Ho Chi Minh **10**:190
Ho Chi Minh City (Vietnam) **10**:191
Hue (Vietnam) **10**:291
Johnson, Lyndon B. **11**:434
Kampuchea (Cambodia) **12**:12
Kennedy, John F. **12**:43–44
Kissinger, Henry A. **12**:90–91
Marine Corps, U.S. **13**:154
My Lai incident **13**:689
Ngo Dinh Diem **14**:176
Nguyen Van Thieu **14**:177
night sights **14**:193
Nixon, Richard M. **14**:205
Paris, treaties of **15**:87
Pathet Lao **15**:111–112
Pentagon Papers **15**:154
Pham Van Dong **15**:219
photography
Burrows, Larry **3**:580–581
Capa, Robert **4**:119
pollutants, chemical **15**:410
Tet offensive **19**:587 *illus.*; **19**:589 *map*
Tonkin, Gulf of **19**:234
Tonkin Gulf Resolution **19**:234–235
uniform **1**:207 *illus.*; **2**:182 *illus.*
United States, history of the **19**:459–460 *illus.*
Viet Cong **19**:579
Vietnam Veterans Memorial **19**:584 *illus.*
Vo Nguyen Giap **19**:624
war reportage
Salisbury, Harrison **17**:33
Westmoreland, William C. **20**:118
VIEUX CARRÉ (New Orleans) **12**:432 *illus.*
VIEUXTEMPS, HENRI **19**:591
VIEW CAMERA **4**:57 *illus.*; **4**:58
VIEWFINDER
camera **4**:56–57
cinematography **4**:434
video camera **19**:576h
VIEYTES (Argentina)
map (35° 16′S 57° 35′W) **2**:149
VIGANÒ, SALVATORE **19**:591
choreography **4**:408
VIGÉE-LEBRUN, LOUISE ÉLISABETH **19**:591–592 *bibliog.*
VIGELAND, GUSTAV **19**:592 *bibliog.*
VIGILANTES **19**:592 *bibliog.*
frontier **8**:344
outlaws **14**:469
VIGNEAUD, VINCENT DU *see* DU VIGNEAUD, VINCENT
VIGNOLA, GIACOMO BAROZZI DA **19**:592
Il Gesù, Church of **4**:207 *illus.*
Villa Lante gardens **12**:186 *illus.*
VIGNY, ALFRED DE **19**:592 *bibliog.*
VIGO (county in Indiana)
map (39° 25′N 87° 20′W) **11**:111
VIGO (Spain) **19**:592
map (42° 14′N 8° 43′W) **18**:140
VIGO, JEAN **19**:592 *bibliog.*
VIGUERIE, RICHARD
advertising **1**:114
VIJAYA
Majapahit Empire **13**:76
VIJAYANAGAR (India) **19**:593
VIJAYAWADA (India)
map (16° 31′N 80° 37′E) **11**:80
VIJOSË RIVER
map (40° 37′N 19° 20′E) **1**:250
VIKING (Alberta)
map (53° 6′N 111° 46′W) **1**:256
VIKING (spacecraft) **19**:593–594 *bibliog., illus.*
landers **19**:593–594 *illus.*
life, extraterrestrial **12**:328
Mars (planet) **13**:168–169 *illus.*
National Aeronautics and Space Administration **14**:28
orbiters **19**:593–594
origin of life **12**:327
Phobos **15**:249
positions in space **2**:275 *illus.*
rockets and missiles **16**:254
Sagan, Carl Edward **17**:11
SNAP **17**:383–384
space exploration **18**:125–126 *illus.*
Titan (rocket) **19**:211
VIKINGS **19**:594–596 *bibliog., illus.*
Canada, history of **4**:80
Canute, King of England, Denmark, and Norway **4**:118
Eric the Red **7**:229
Eskimo **7**:241
Europe, history of **7**:284
exploration **7**:334
flag **8**:135 *illus.*
France, history of **8**:267

Gokstad ship burial **9**:225–226
Great Britain, history of **9**:310
Harold I, King of Norway (Harold Fairhair) **10**:54
Ireland, history of **11**:262
Kensington Rune Stone **12**:45
L'Anse aux Meadows **12**:144
longhouse **10**:265 *illus.*
longship **14**:54 *illus.*; **17**:111 *illus.*; **17**:264 *illus.*; **19**:595 *illus.*
Micmac **13**:384
Normans **14**:221–222
North American archaeology **14**:236
Norway **14**:263–264
Oseberg ship burial **14**:453
piracy **15**:312
Russia/Union of Soviet Socialist Republics, history of **16**:351
Scandinavia, history of **17**:108
Scandinavian art and architecture **17**:111 *illus.*
Scotland **17**:151
sword **18**:398 *illus.*
Thorfinn Karlsefni **19**:178
Trelleborg **19**:294
Uppsala (Sweden) **19**:473
Vinland **19**:601
warriors crossing North Sea **17**:108 *illus.*
VILA NOVA DE GAIA (Portugal)
map (41° 8′N 8° 37′W) **15**:449
VILA REAL (Portugal)
map (41° 18′N 7° 45′W) **15**:449
VILAR, JEAN **19**:596
VILAS (county in Wisconsin)
map (46° 3′N 89° 30′W) **20**:185
VILAS, GUILLERMO **19**:596
VILCABAMBA CORDILLERA MOUNTAINS
map (13° 0′S 73° 0′W) **15**:193
VILCAMPAPA *see* MACHU PICCHU (Peru)
VILDRAC, CHARLES **19**:596
VILHENA (Brazil)
map (12° 43′S 60° 7′W) **3**:460
VILLA **19**:596 *bibliog.*
Hadrian's Villa **10**:8
house (in Western architecture) **10**:266
landscape architecture **12**:186
Mysteries, Villa of the **13**:692
Roman art and architecture **16**:274
Roman Britain (c.100 AD) **10**:265 *illus.*
Royal Pavilion at Brighton **16**:330–331 *illus.*
Villa Rotonda **19**:597
VILLA, PANCHO **19**:596 *bibliog., illus.*
Chihuahua (city) **4**:347
Mexico, history of **13**:365 *illus.*
Nogales (Arizona) **14**:212
Zapata, Emiliano **20**:356
VILLA ABECIA (Bolivia)
map (21° 0′S 65° 23′W) **3**:366
VILLA BARBARO (Fanzola)
Veronese, Paolo **19**:560
VILLA BELLA (Bolivia)
map (10° 23′S 65° 24′W) **3**:366
VILLA BRUZUAL (Venezuela)
map (9° 20′N 69° 6′W) **19**:542
VILLA CAÑÁS (Argentina)
map (34° 0′S 61° 36′W) **2**:149
VILLA CAPRA *see* VILLA ROTONDA
VILLA CLARA (Argentina)
map (31° 50′S 58° 49′W) **2**:149
VILLA DEL ROSARIO (Venezuela)
map (10° 19′N 72° 19′W) **19**:542
VILLA DELGADO (El Salvador)
map (13° 43′N 89° 10′W) **7**:100
VILLA D'ESTE
landscape architecture **12**:185
VILLA DOLORES (Argentina)
map (31° 56′S 65° 12′W) **2**:149
VILLA FARNESINA
Peruzzi, Baldassare **15**:196
VILLA GIULIA
Vignola, Giacomo Barozzida **19**:592
VILLA GROVE (Illinois)
map (39° 52′N 88° 10′W) **11**:42
VILLA LANTE
gardens of **12**:186 *illus.*
landscape architecture **12**:185
VILLA-LOBOS, HEITOR **19**:596–597 *bibliog.*
VILLA MARIA (Argentina)
map (32° 25′S 63° 15′W) **2**:149
VILLA MONTES (Bolivia)
map (21° 15′S 63° 30′W) **3**:366
VILLA RICA (Georgia)
map (33° 44′N 84° 55′W) **9**:114
VILLA ROTONDA **15**:48 *illus.*; **19**:597 *bibliog., illus.*
house (in Western architecture) **10**:267
VILLA TUNARI (Bolivia)
map (16° 55′S 65° 25′W) **3**:366
VILLA VÁZQUEZ (Dominican Republic)
map (19° 45′N 71° 27′W) **6**:233
VILLACH (Austria)
map (46° 36′N 13° 50′E) **2**:348
VILLAFRANCHIAN CULTURE
Aïn Hanech **1**:203
VILLAGE VOICE, THE **19**:597
Murdoch, Rupert **13**:648
Obie Awards **14**:316
VILLAGUAY (Argentina)
map (31° 51′S 59° 1′W) **2**:149
VILLAHERMOSA (Mexico) **19**:597
climate **13**:356 *table*
map (17° 59′N 92° 55′W) **13**:357
VILLALONGA (Argentina)
map (39° 53′S 62° 35′W) **2**:149
VILLAMIL (Ecuador)
map (0° 56′S 91° 1′W) **7**:52
VILLANELLE **19**:597
VILLANOVA UNIVERSITY **19**:597
VILLANOVANS **19**:597 *bibliog.*
Etruscans **7**:258–259
Tarquinia **19**:39
VILLANUEVA (New Mexico)
map (35° 17′N 105° 23′W) **14**:136
VILLANUEVA, CARLOS RAÚL **19**:597 *bibliog.*
VILLANUEVA, JUAN DE **19**:598 *bibliog.*
Prado **15**:487
VILLANUEVA Y GELTRÚ (Spain)
map (41° 14′N 1° 44′E) **18**:140
VILLARD, OSWALD GARRISON **19**:598 *bibliog.*
VILLARD DE HONNECOURT **19**:598 *bibliog.*
VILLAROEL, DIEGO DE
Tucumán (Argentina) **19**:328
VILLAROEL, GUALBERTO
Bolivia **3**:369
VILLARRICA (Paraguay)
map (25° 45′S 56° 26′W) **15**:77
VILLARS, CLAUDE LOUIS HECTOR, DUC DE **19**:598 *bibliog.*
VILLARS, DUC DE
Spanish Succession, War of the **18**:162–163
VILLASUR, PEDRO DE
Nebraska **14**:73
VILLAURRUTIA, XAVIER **19**:598 *bibliog.*
VILLAVICENCIO (Colombia)
map (4° 9′N 73° 37′W) **5**:107
VILLAZÓN (Bolivia)
map (22° 6′S 65° 36′W) **3**:366
VILLE-MARIE (Canada) *see* MONTREAL (Quebec)
VILLE PLATTE (Louisiana)
map (30° 42′N 92° 16′W) **12**:430
VILLEHARDOUIN, GEOFFROI DE **19**:598 *bibliog.*
VILLEHARDOUIN, GUILLAUME DE
Mistra **13**:482
VILLELA, EDWARD **19**:598 *bibliog.*
VILLEMARQUÉ, THEODORE HERSART DE LA
Breton literature **3**:475
VILLEURBANNE (France)
map (45° 46′N 4° 53′E) **8**:260
VILLIERS, GEORGE *see* BUCKINGHAM, GEORGE VILLIERS, 1st DUKE OF
VILLIERS DE L'ISLE-ADAM, PHILIPPE **19**:598 *bibliog.*
VILLISCA (Iowa)
map (40° 56′N 94° 59′W) **11**:244
VILLON, FRANÇOIS **19**:598–599 *bibliog.*
ballade **3**:41
French literature **8**:315
VILLON, JACQUES **19**:599 *bibliog.*
VILLON, RAYMOND DUCHAMP- *see* DUCHAMP-VILLON, RAYMOND
VILLUS **11**:231 *illus.*
intestine **11**:230
VILNA (USSR) **19**:599
Lithuanian Soviet Socialist Republic **12**:372
map (54° 41′N 25° 19′E) **19**:388
VILNIUS (USSR) *see* VILNA (USSR)
VILVOORDE (Belgium)
map (50° 56′N 4° 26′E) **3**:177
VILYUY RIVER
map (64° 24′N 126° 26′E) **19**:388
VINA **19**:599
VIÑA DEL MAR (Chile) **4**:356 *illus.*; **19**:599
map (33° 2′S 71° 34′W) **4**:355
VINALHAVEN (Maine)
map (44° 3′N 68° 50′W) **13**:70
VINALHAVEN ISLAND
map (44° 5′N 68° 52′W) **13**:70
VINAYA
Buddhist sacred literature **3**:543
VINČA
European prehistory **7**:301; **7**:303
VINCENNES (Indiana) **19**:599
map (38° 41′N 87° 32′W) **11**:111
VINCENNES, FRANÇOIS MARIE BISSOT, SIEUR DE **19**:599
VINCENT, JOHN HEYL **19**:599 *bibliog.*
Chautauqua **4**:305
VINCENT OF BEAUVAIS **19**:600 *bibliog.*
Myrour of the Worlde **12**:317 *illus.*
Speculum majus
encyclopedia **7**:163
VINCENT DE PAUL, SAINT **19**:599–600 *bibliog.*
Clichy (France) **5**:54
VINCENT FERRER, SAINT **19**:600 *bibliog.*
VINCENT OF LÉRINS, SAINT **19**:600
VINCENZA (Italy)
history
Scala (family) **17**:106
VINDHYA RANGE (Mountain Range)
map (23° 0′N 77° 0′E) **11**:80
VINDICATION OF THE RIGHTS OF WOMEN, A (book) **19**:600
Wollstonecraft, Mary **20**:199
VINE **19**:600
cassabanana **4**:183
chayote **4**:306
VINE, F. J. **19**:600 *bibliog.*
VINE GROVE (Kentucky)
map (37° 49′N 85° 59′W) **12**:47
VINE SNAKE
colubrid **5**:125
VINEGAR **19**:600 *bibliog.*
acetic acid **1**:80
Acetobacter **1**:80
pickling **15**:293
VINEGAR HILL MOUNTAIN
map (44° 43′N 118° 34′W) **14**:427
VINEGAR JOE *see* STILWELL, JOSEPH W.
VINELAND (New Jersey)
map (39° 29′N 75° 2′W) **14**:129
VINER, JACOB
economics **7**:47
VINET, ALEXANDRE **19**:600
VINEYARD *see* GRAPE; WINE
VINEYARD HAVEN (Massachusetts)
map (41° 27′N 70° 36′W) **13**:206
VINEYARD SOUND
map (41° 25′N 70° 46′W) **13**:206
VINGT-ET-UN (card game) *see* BLACKJACK (card game)
VINH (Vietnam)
map (18° 40′N 105° 40′E) **19**:580
VINH LONG (Vietnam)
map (10° 15′N 105° 58′E) **19**:580
VINIFICATION
wine **20**:177–178 *illus.*
VINITA (Oklahoma)
map (36° 39′N 95° 9′W) **14**:368
VINJE, AASMUND OLAFSSON **19**:601
VINKOVCI (Yugoslavia)
map (45° 17′N 18° 49′E) **20**:340
VINLAND **19**:601 *bibliog.*
L'Anse aux Meadows **12**:144
Thorfinn Karlsefni **19**:178
VINNE, THEODORE LOW DE
typeface classifications **19**:364
VINNITSA (USSR)
map (49° 14′N 28° 29′E) **19**:388
VINSON, FREDERICK M. **19**:601 *bibliog.*
Dennis v. *United States* **6**:113
VINSON MASSIF **19**:601
map (78° 35′S 85° 25′W) **2**:40
VINTON (Iowa)
map (42° 10′N 92° 1′W) **11**:244
VINTON (Louisiana)
map (30° 11′N 93° 35′W) **12**:430
VINTON (county in Ohio)
map (39° 15′N 82° 25′W) **14**:357
VINTON (Virginia)
map (37° 17′N 80° 1′W) **19**:607
VINYL **19**:601 *bibliog.*
VINYL CHLORIDE
Regnault, Henri Victor **16**:129
VIOL **19**:601–602 *bibliog., illus.*
vielle **19**:578
VIOLA **19**:602 *bibliog.*
VIOLA (Wisconsin)
map (43° 31′N 90° 40′W) **20**:185
VIOLA, BILL
video art **19**:576g *illus.*; **19**:576h
VIOLA DA GAMBA
viol **19**:602
VIOLA D'AMORE
viol **19**:602
VIOLENCE
censorship **4**:248
radio and television broadcasting **16**:60
totalitarianism **19**:248
VIOLET (botany) **5**:121 *illus.*; **19**:602 *bibliog., illus.*
pansy **15**:61
VIOLIN **13**:677 *illus.*; **18**:300–301 *illus.*; **19**:602–603 *bibliog., illus.*
electric **7**:125 *illus.*
Italian music **11**:318
parts **19**:603 *illus.*
performers
Auer, Leopold **2**:319
Bridge, Frank **3**:484
Bull, Ole **3**:558
Busch, Adolf **3**:585
Corelli, Arcangelo **5**:262
Elman, Mischa **7**:149
Francescatti, Zino Rene **8**:273
Geminiani, Francesco **9**:73
Grumiaux, Arthur **9**:382
Heifetz, Jascha **10**:108
Hindemith, Paul **10**:168
Joachim, Joseph **11**:419–420
Kreisler, Fritz **12**:128
Kreutzer, Rodolphe **12**:129
Maazel, Lorin **13**:5
Menuhin, Yehudi **13**:302
Milstein, Nathan **13**:432
Oistrakh, David **14**:364
Paganini, Niccolò **15**:13
Perlman, Itzhak **15**:172
Sarasate, Pablo de **17**:74–75
Stamitz (family) **18**:216
Stern, Isaac **18**:260
Szeryng, Henryk **18**:416
Szigeti, Joseph **18**:416
Tartini, Giuseppe **19**:41
Torelli, Giuseppe **19**:239
Vieuxtemps, Henri **19**:591
Viotti, Giovanni Battista **19**:603–604
Wieniawski, Henri **20**:146
Ysaÿe, Eugène **20**:337
Zimbalist, Efrem **20**:367
Zukerman, Pinchas **20**:381
production **19**:602–603
Amati (family) **1**:322
Cremona (Italy) **5**:338
Guarneri (family) **9**:387
Stradivari (family) **18**:287
sound frequencies produced **18**:73 *table*
viola **19**:602
VIOLLET-LE-DUC, EUGÈNE EMMANUEL **19**:603 *bibliog.*
functionalism (design) **8**:360
VIOLONCELLO *see* CELLO
VIONNET, MADELAINE
fashion design **8**:31–32
VIOTTI, GIOVANNI BATTISTA **19**:603–604 *bibliog.*
VIPER **15**:384 *illus.*; **17**:377 *illus.*; **19**:604 *bibliog., illus.*
adder **1**:99
habu **10**:6
pit viper **15**:319
rattlesnake **16**:93
VIPERFISH **19**:604 *illus.*
Atlantic viperfish **6**:79 *illus.*
VIRACHEI (Kampuchea)
map (13° 59′N 106° 49′E) **12**:11
VIRAL RHINOTRACHEITIS, FELINE *see* RHINOTRACHEITIS, FELINE VIRAL
VIRCHOW, RUDOLF **19**:604 *bibliog.*
histology **10**:181
medicine **13**:270
VIRDEN (Illinois)
map (39° 30′N 89° 46′W) **11**:42
VIRDEN (Manitoba)
map (49° 51′N 100° 55′W) **13**:119
VIRDEN (New Mexico)
map (32° 42′N 109° 0′W) **14**:136
VIREN, LASSE **14**:384 *illus.*; **19**:604–605 *bibliog.*
VIREO **19**:605 *illus.*
peppershrike **15**:157
shrike vireo **17**:287
VIRGIL *see* VERGIL
VIRGIN BIRTH **19**:605 *bibliog.*
Jesus Christ **11**:404
Mary **13**:184
VIRGIN GORDA
map (18° 30′N 64° 24′W) **19**:605
Virgin Islands **19**:605
VIRGIN ISLANDS **19**:605–606 *bibliog., illus., map*
cities
Charlotte Amalie **4**:299
map (18° 20′N 64° 50′W) (U.S.) **20**:109
map (18° 30′N 64° 30′W) (U.K.) **20**:109

VIRGIN ISLANDS (cont.)
Virgin Islands, College of the **19**:606
VIRGIN ISLANDS, COLLEGE OF THE **19**:606
VIRGIN MOUNTAINS
map (36° 45′N 114° 0′W) **14**:111
VIRGIN QUEEN *see* ELIZABETH I, QUEEN OF ENGLAND
VIRGIN RIVER
map (36° 31′N 114° 20′W) **14**:111
VIRGINAL **19**:606 *bibliog., illus.*
Byrd, William **3**:602
VIRGINIA **19**:606–612 *bibliog., illus., map*
cities
Alexandria **1**:278
Charlottesville **4**:299
Fredericksburg **8**:293
Hampton **10**:32
Lynchburg **12**:476
Newport News **14**:171
Norfolk **14**:218
Petersburg **15**:202
Portsmouth **15**:448
Reston **16**:182
Richmond **16**:214
Roanoke **16**:239
Williamsburg **20**:162
climate **19**:608
culture **19**:609
economic activity **19**:609 *illus.*; **19**:610–611
education **19**:609 *illus.*
Hampton University **10**:33
Sweet Briar College **18**:387
Virginia, state universities and colleges of **19**:612
Washington and Lee University **20**:45
flag **19**:606 *illus.*
geographical linguistics **9**:98–99 *map*
government and politics **19**:611
historic sites **19**:609–610 *illus.*
history **19**:611–612
Bacon's Rebellion **3**:14
Berkeley, Sir William **3**:213
Civil War **5**:19–33
De La Warr, Thomas West, 12th Baron **6**:61
Dinwiddie, Robert **6**:182
Dunmore, John Murray, 4th Earl of **6**:301
Fairfax of Cameron, Thomas Fairfax, 6th Baron **8**:9
Gates, Sir Thomas **9**:58
Henry, Patrick **10**:122–123
Jamestown **11**:357
Jefferson, Thomas **11**:391–392
Lee (family) **12**:268–269
Lee, Robert E. **12**:270
London Company **12**:405
Mason, George **13**:198–199
Pendleton, Edmund **15**:142
Pocahontas **15**:376
Powhatan **15**:486
Randolph (family) **16**:82–83
Spotswood, Alexander **18**:198
United States, history of the **19**:436
Virginia Declaration of Rights (1776) **3**:251–252
Washington, George **20**:42–43
Wythe, George **20**:305
Yeardley, Sir George **20**:320
land and resources **19**:607–609 *illus., map*
map (37° 30′N 78° 45′W) **19**:419
people **19**:609–610
physical features
Dismal Swamp **6**:196
Luray Caverns **12**:466
recreational areas **19**:608 *illus.*; **19**:610
rivers, lakes, and waterways **19**:608
Hampton Roads **10**:33
James River **11**:355
Rappahannock River **16**:90
Shenandoah River **17**:255
slavery
black Americans **3**:306
vegetation and animal life **19**:608–609
VIRGINIA (Illinois)
map (39° 57′N 90° 13′W) **11**:42
VIRGINIA (Minnesota)
map (47° 31′N 92° 32′W) **13**:453
VIRGINIA (ship)
Monitor and *Merrimack* **13**:531–532
VIRGINIA (South Africa)
map (28° 12′S 26° 49′E) **18**:79
VIRGINIA, STATE UNIVERSITIES AND COLLEGES OF **19**:612
University of Virginia **19**:609 *illus.*
Jefferson, Thomas **11**:391; **11**:393
Rotunda **2**:136 *illus.*
VIRGINIA BEACH (Virginia)
map (36° 51′N 75° 58′W) **19**:607
VIRGINIA CITY (Montana)
map (45° 18′N 111° 56′W) **13**:547
VIRGINIA CITY (Nevada) **14**:112 *illus.*
map (39° 19′N 119° 39′W) **14**:111
VIRGINIA COMPANY OF LONDON
London Company **12**:405
VIRGINIA COMPANY OF PLYMOUTH
London Company **12**:405
VIRGINIA COWSLIP (botany) **19**:612
VIRGINIA CREEPER (botany) **19**:612
woodbine **20**:210
VIRGINIA DECLARATION OF RIGHTS (1776)
Bill of Rights **3**:251
VIRGINIA MASSACRE (1622) **11**:109 *map*
VIRGINIA MUSEUM OF FINE ARTS
Mellon, Paul **13**:287
VIRGINIA PLAN
Constitutional Convention **5**:224
Randolph (family) **16**:83
VIRGINIA RESOLUTIONS *see* KENTUCKY AND VIRGINIA RESOLUTIONS
VIRGINIA WILLOW **19**:613
VIRGINIAN, THE (book)
cowboy **5**:321
Wister, Owen **20**:190
VIRGO **19**:613 *bibliog.*
constellation **5**:210–211 *illus.*
VIRGO CLUSTER OF GALAXIES **19**:613
VIRION
virus **19**:613–616
VIROID **19**:613 *bibliog.*
VIROLOGY *see* VIRUS
VIROQUA (Wisconsin)
map (43° 34′N 90° 53′W) **20**:185
VIRTUAL IMAGE *see* IMAGE, OPTICAL
VIRUNGA MOUNTAINS
map (1° 30′S 29° 30′E) **16**:378
VIRUS **18**:39 *illus.*; **19**:613–616 *bibliog., illus.*
antibody **2**:59–60
antigen **2**:61
bacteria **3**:18
Beijerinck, Martinus Willem **3**:172
genetics **9**:90
Delbrück, Max **6**:92
Dulbecco, Renato **6**:295
genetic engineering **9**:84–85
Lederberg, Joshua **12**:268
Luria, Salvador **12**:467
Lwoff, André **12**:473
microbiology **13**:384
nucleic acid **14**:290
Stanley, Wendell Meredith **18**:219
Temin, Howard Martin **19**:91
retrovirus **16**:183–184
Rous, Francis Peyton **16**:325
virus diseases **19**:615
AIDS **1**:201
cancer **4**:102–104 *illus.*
cold, common **5**:97
Colorado tick fever **5**:121
cowpox **5**:322
dengue fever **6**:108
diseases, animal **6**:191
diseases, childhood **6**:193
diseases, plant **6**:195
Enders, John F. **7**:168
fifth disease **8**:74
gastrointestinal tract disease **9**:57
German measles **9**:134
hepatitis **10**:130
herpes **10**:145–146
infectious diseases **11**:164
influenza **11**:171–172
interferon **11**:210
leukemia **12**:301
measles **13**:253
mononucleosis **13**:537
mumps **13**:639
papilloma **15**:71
pneumonia **15**:375–376
poliomyelitis **15**:397
rabies **16**:32
respiratory system disorders **16**:181
shingles **17**:262
skin diseases **17**:342
smallpox **17**:365
vaccinia **19**:502
wart **20**:33
yellow fever **20**:322
VIS (Yugoslavia)
map (43° 3′N 16° 12′E) **20**:340
VISA *see* PASSPORT
VISALIA (California)
map (36° 20′N 119° 18′W) **4**:31
VISAYAN *see* BISAYAN
VISAYAN SEA
map (11° 35′N 123° 51′E) **15**:237
VISBY (Sweden)
map (57° 38′N 18° 18′E) **18**:382
VISCHER (family) **19**:616 *bibliog.*
German art and architecture **9**:126
VISCONTI (family) **19**:616 *bibliog.*
Milan **13**:418
Pisanello, Antonio **15**:316
VISCONTI, LUCHINO **19**:616 *bibliog.*
film, history of **8**:86
VISCONTI, VALENTINA
Louis XII, King of France **12**:425
VISCOSITY **19**:616–617
VISCOSITY, LAW OF
Stokes, Sir George Gabriel **18**:278
VISCOUNT (title)
titles of nobility and honor **19**:213–214
VISCOUNT MELVILLE SOUND
map (74° 10′N 113° 0′W) **14**:258
VISEU (Portugal)
map (40° 39′N 7° 55′W) **15**:449
VISHAKHAPATNAM (India)
map (17° 42′N 83° 18′E) **11**:80
VISHINSKY, ANDREI YANUARIEVICH *see* VYSHINSKY, ANDREI YANUARIEVICH
VISHNU (Hindu deity) **10**:171 *illus.*; **11**:97 *illus.*; **19**:617 *bibliog., illus.*
avatar
Krishna **12**:130
Hinduism **10**:170
Lakshmi **12**:171
VISIGOTHS *see* GOTHS
VISION
See also EYE
blindness **3**:332–333
eye diseases **7**:350–351
pattern recognition **15**:114 *illus.*
photobiological process
photochemistry **15**:259
senses and sensation **17**:204–205
VISIONARY ARCHITECTURE **19**:617 *bibliog., illus.*
Boullée, Étienne Louis **3**:422
Kiesler, Frederick John **12**:75
Ledoux, Claude Nicolas **12**:268
Soleri, Paolo **18**:53
Vredeman de Vries, Hans **19**:639
VISIONARY ART
Blakelock, Ralph Albert **3**:326
Moreau, Gustave **13**:576
Ryder, Albert Pinkham **16**:379
Vedder, Elihu **19**:531
"VISIT FROM ST. NICHOLAS, A" (poem)
Moore, Clement Clarke **13**:567
VISO, MONTE
map (44° 40′N 7° 7′E) **11**:321
VISSER 'T HOOFT, WILLEM ADOLF **19**:617
VISTA *see* VOLUNTEERS IN SERVICE TO AMERICA (VISTA)
VISTA (California)
map (33° 12′N 117° 15′W) **4**:31
VISTARIL
tranquilizer **19**:266
VISTULA RIVER **19**:617–618
map (54° 22′N 18° 55′E) **15**:388
VISUAL MONITORING
oscilloscope **14**:453
VISUAL PURPLE *see* RHODOPSIN
VISUALLY HANDICAPPED, EDUCATION OF THE *see* BLIND, EDUCATION OF THE
VITAL STATISTICS *see* DEMOGRAPHY
VITALIAN, POPE
plainsong **15**:326
VITAMIN A
carotenoid **4**:162
eye, light detection **7**:348
Karrer, Paul **12**:29
nutritional-deficiency disease
night blindness: Wald, George **20**:9
starvation **18**:228
Recommended Dietary Allowances **19**:618 *table*
vitamins and minerals **19**:618–619
VITAMIN B_1 *see* THIAMINE
VITAMIN B_2 *see* RIBOFLAVIN (Vitamin B_2)
VITAMIN B_3 *see* NIACIN (Vitamin B_3)
VITAMIN B_6 *see* PYRIDOXINE (Vitamin B_6)
VITAMIN B_{12} *see* CYANOCOBALAMIN (Vitamin B_{12})
VITAMIN B_{17} *see* LAETRILE
VITAMIN C *see* ASCORBIC ACID
VITAMIN D
bone diseases **3**:378
digestion, human **6**:172
nutritional deficiency disease, rickets **16**:215
race **16**:35
Recommended Dietary Allowances **19**:618 *table*
sterol **18**:262
vitamins and minerals **19**:619
Windaus, Adolf **20**:172
VITAMIN E
Recommended Dietary Allowances **19**:618 *table*
vitamins and minerals **19**:619
VITAMIN H *see* BIOTIN
VITAMIN K
Dam, Carl Henrik **6**:18
Doisy, Edward **6**:224
quinone **16**:27
vitamins and minerals **19**:619
VITAMINS AND MINERALS **19**:618–621 *bibliog., tables*
Chlorella **4**:400
coenzyme **5**:92
cofactors function **19**:618
diet, human **6**:164
digestion, human **6**:170–173
enzyme **7**:213
Funk, Casimir **8**:369
Hopkins, Sir Frederick Gowland **10**:231
kelp **12**:40
Kuhn, Richard **12**:135
lipid **12**:362
megavitamin therapy **13**:280; **19**:619
milk **13**:423
minerals **19**:619–621 *table*
calcium **19**:619–620 *table*
copper **5**:253
fluorine **19**:621
iodine **19**:619 *table*
iron **19**:619 *table*; **19**:621
magnesium **13**:54; **19**:619 *table*; **19**:621
manganese **13**:114
phosphorus **15**:257; **19**:619–620 *table*
trace minerals **19**:621
zinc **19**:619 *table*; **19**:621; **20**:367
nutrition, human **14**:305 *illus., illus.*
nutritional-deficiency diseases **14**:307–308
oceanic nutrients **14**:341
orthomolecular medicine **14**:450
Recommended Daily Allowances (RDA) **19**:618–619 *table*
structure
Heilbron, Sir Ian Morris **10**:108
supplements **19**:618
terpene **19**:118
vitamins **19**:618–620 *table*
See also names of specific vitamins, e.g., ASCORBIC ACID (Vitamin C); RIBOFLAVIN (Vitamin B_2); VITAMIN K; etc.
medicine **13**:271
VITAPHONE
film, history of **8**:84
VITARTE (Peru)
map (12° 2′S 76° 56′W) **15**:193
VITEAZUL, MIHAI *see* MICHAEL THE BRAVE
VITELLUS *see* EGG
VITERBO (Italy)
map (42° 25′N 12° 6′E) **11**:321
VITI LEVU ISLAND
map (18° 0′S 178° 0′E) **8**:77
VITICULTURE
wine **20**:174–175 *illus.*
VITILIGO
albinism **1**:260
leukoderma **12**:301
VITÓRIA (Brazil)
map (20° 19′S 40° 21′W) **3**:460
VITORIA (Spain) **19**:621
map (42° 51′N 2° 40′W) **18**:140
VITORIA, FRANCISCO DE **19**:621 *bibliog.*
VITORIA DA CONQUISTA (Brazil)
map (14° 51′S 40° 51′W) **3**:460
VITRAC, ROGER **19**:621
VITREOUS HUMOR
eye **7**:348 *illus.*
VITREOUS STATE *see* GLASSY STATE
VITRIOLIC ACID *see* SULFURIC ACID
VITRUVIUS **19**:621 *bibliog.*
architecture **2**:129
forum **8**:242
mathematics, history of **13**:224
urban planning **19**:481
VITRUVIUS BRITANNICUS
Campbell, Colen **4**:65
VITRY, PHILIPPE DE **19**:621 *bibliog.*
French music **8**:320

VITTORIA, ALESSANDRO 19:621 *bibliog.*
VITTORINI, ELIO 19:621–622 *bibliog.*
VIVALDI, ANTONIO 19:622 *bibliog., illus.*
music, history of Western 13:664–665 *illus.*
VIVAR, RODRIGO DIAZ DE *see* EL CID
VIVARINI (family) 19:622
VIVEKANANDA 19:622 *bibliog.*
VIVES, AMADEO
zarzuela 20:356
VIVES, JUAN LUIS 19:622 *bibliog.*
VIVIAN (Louisiana)
map (32° 53′N 93° 59′W) 12:430
VIVIAN BEAUMONT THEATER
Lincoln Center for the Performing Arts 12:350
VIVIPARITY 19:622
gestation 9:160
VIVIPAROUS LIZARD *see* LACERTID
VIVISECTION 19:622–623 *bibliog.*
animal experimentation 2:22
animal rights 2:28
VIVONNE DE SAVELLI, CATHERINE DE, MARQUISE DE RAMBOUILLET *see* RAMBOUILLET, MARQUISE DE
VIX (France) 19:623
VIZCAÍNO, SEBASTIÁN 19:623
San Diego (California) 17:52
VIZIER
Köprülü (family) 12:110
VIZSLA 6:218 *illus.*; 19:623 *bibliog., illus.*
VLA *see* VERY LARGE ARRAY
VLAARDINGEN (Netherlands)
map (51° 54′N 4° 21′E) 14:99
VLACHS
Walachia (Romania) 20:8
VLAD DRACUL (Vlad the Devil)
Vlad the Impaler, Prince of Walachia 19:623
VLAD THE IMPALER, PRINCE OF WALACHIA 19:623 *bibliog.*
VLADIMIR (USSR) 19:623
VLADIMIR I, GRAND DUKE OF KIEV 19:623 *bibliog.*
Rurik (dynasty) 16:347
VLADIVOSTOK (USSR) 19:623–624
map (43° 10′N 131° 56′E) 19:388
VLAMINCK, MAURICE DE 19:624 *bibliog., illus.*
The Seine at Le Pecq 19:624 *illus.*
Street Scene in Mary-le-Roi 8:38 *illus.*
VLECK, J. H. VAN *see* VAN VLECK, J. H.
VLIELAND ISLAND
map (53° 15′N 5° 0′E) 14:99
VLISSINGEN (Netherlands)
map (51° 26′N 3° 35′E) 14:99
VLORË (Albania) 19:624
map (40° 27′N 19° 30′E) 1:250
VLORËS, BAY OF
map (40° 25′N 19° 25′E) 1:250
VLSI (VERY LARGE-SCALE INTEGRATION) (electronics)
computer 5:160c; 5:160g; 5:160i
computer-aided design and computer-aided manufacturing 5:160k–160L
VLTAVA RIVER
map (50° 21′N 14° 30′E) 5:413
VO NGUYEN GIAP 19:585 *illus.*; 19:624 *bibliog.*
VOCABULARY *see* ENGLISH LANGUAGE; LANGUAGE AND LITERATURE
VOCAL CORDS 18:174 *illus.*
larynx 12:209 *illus.*
phonetics 15:251–252
trachea 19:258
VOCALIZATION *see* LARYNX; SYRINX; etc.
VOCATIONAL EDUCATION 19:624–625 *bibliog.*
See also INDUSTRIAL ARTS PROGRAM; TECHNICAL EDUCATION
apprenticeship 2:91
British education 3:495
Canadian education 4:91
career education 4:146
history 19:624
humanities, education in the 10:300
Job Corps 11:421
professional and educational organizations
Future Homemakers of America 8:383
secondary education 17:179–180
Washington, Booker T. 20:39
4-H program 8:253
VOCATIONAL GUIDANCE *see* CAREER EDUCATION; VOCATIONAL EDUCATION
VOCODER 19:625
VODKA 19:625
VOEGELIN, C. F. AND F. M.
Indian languages, American 11:99
VOGEL, HERMANN WILHELM 19:625
astronomy, history of 2:279
VOGEL, SIR JULIUS 19:625 *bibliog.*
New Zealand, history of 14:162
VOGELWEIDE, WALTHER VON DER *see* WALTHER VON DER VOGELWEIDE
VOGT, A. E. VAN *see* VAN VOGT, A. E.
VOGUE (periodical)
Mainbocher 13:69
VOGUL LANGUAGE
Ural-Altaic languages 19:475
VOICE *see* SPEECH
VOICE, SINGING 19:625–626 *bibliog.*
baritone 3:81
bass (music) 3:117
bel canto 3:173
cantata 4:115–116
cantor 4:118
castrato 4:192
choral music 4:405–407
contralto 5:232
countertenor 5:312
falsetto 8:15
mezzo-soprano 13:369
song 18:64
soprano 18:68
tenor 19:112
treble 19:286
Westminster Choir College 20:118
VOICE OF AMERICA 19:626
See also RADIO FREE EUROPE AND RADIO LIBERTY
Chancellor, John 4:278
VOICE BOX *see* LARYNX
VOICE CODER *see* VOCODER
VOICE RECOGNITION 19:626
computer 5:160i
VOICES OF SILENCE, THE (book)
Malraux, André 13:93–94
VOINOVICH, VLADIMIR 19:626
VOISIN BROTHERS
aviation 2:370
VOITSBERG (Austria)
map (47° 3′N 15° 10′E) 2:348
VOJVODINA (province in Yugoslavia)
map (45° 30′N 20° 0′E) 20:340
VOLAPÜK
languages, artificial 12:197
VOLCANIC ARC
island arc 11:297–298
VOLCANIC ASH 19:628 *illus.*
VOLCANIC BOMB 19:628 *illus.*
olivine 14:380
VOLCANIC ERUPTION 13:52 *illus.*; 13:619 *illus.*
density current 6:114
magma 13:52
products of 19:628 *illus.*
types, volcano 19:627–628
VOLCANIC GLASS
lava 12:240
obsidian 14:319
perlite 15:172
pitchstone 15:320
pumice 15:622
tuff 19:329
VOLCANIC ROCK
deposits, Tertiary Period 19:123 *map*
fossil record 8:244 *illus.*
galena 9:13
geosyncline 9:119–120
igneous rock 11:33–34
magma 13:52
obsidian 14:319
rhyolite 16:204
scoria 17:148
trachyte 19:258
tuff 19:329
turquoise 19:352
zeolite 20:360
VOLCANIC TUFFS
hornfels 10:240
VOLCANO 19:626–628 *bibliog., illus.*
Africa 1:140 *map*
Asia 2:236 *map*
atmosphere 2:303
Cenozoic Era 4:245
convection cell 5:232
Cotopaxi (Ecuador) 5:304
Craters of the Moon National Monument 5:333
Dutton, Clarence Edward 6:315–316
early Permian time paleogeography 15:37 *map*
Earth, geological history of 7:12
Earth sciences 7:24
East African Rift System 7:30–31
economic resources 19:628
Elgon, Mount 7:137
Erebus, Mount 7:228
erosion cycle 7:232
Etna, Mount 7:258
Europe 7:270 *map*
extinct, seamount 17:174
forms 19:626 *illus.*
Fuji, Mount 8:355–356
fumarole 8:358
Geikie, Sir Archibald 9:68
geophysics 9:108
Haleakala Crater 10:19
Hawaii (state) 10:71–73
Hekla 10:110
Hood, Mount 10:225
hot springs 10:259
Iceland 11:17–18 *illus.*
igneous rock 11:33
Japan 11:362
joint (geology) 11:440
Jupiter (planet) 11:473
Kamchatka Peninsula 12:9
Katmai, Mount 12:30
Kilauea (Hawaii) 12:76
Krakatoa (Indonesia) 12:127
lake (body of water) 12:167
landform evolution 12:183
Lassen Peak 12:214
lava 12:240; 19:627–628
magma 13:51–52 *illus.*; 19:627–628
Mauna Kea (Hawaii) 13:233
Mauna Loa (Hawaii) 13:233–234
metamorphic rock 13:331
mid-oceanic ridge 13:389–390
mountain 13:619–620
mudflow 13:631
Ninetyeast Ridge 14:199
North America 14:227 *map*
Ordovician Period 14:421
Paricutin (Mexico) 15:84
Pelée, Mount (Martinique) 15:137
petrified wood 15:205
plate tectonics 15:353
Popocatépetl 15:431
Recent Epoch 16:106–107
rift valleys 16:221
Ring of Fire 16:225
St. Helens, Mount 19:627 *illus.*
seafloor spreading 17:172
Shasta, Mount 17:244
shield volcano 19:627
silica minerals 17:304
sill 17:309
South America 18:87 *map*
stratovolcanoes 19:627
Stromboli (Italy) 18:302
Thera (Greece) 19:160
Tristan da Cunha Islands 19:303
United States 19:422 *map*
Valley of Ten Thousand Smokes (Alaska) 19:508
Vesuvius 19:565
VOLCANO ISLANDS (Japan)
island arc 11:297–298
Iwo Jima 11:337–338
VOLCANOLOGY
Desmarest, Nicolas 6:132
VOLCKER, PAUL 19:628
VOLE 19:628 *illus.*
meadow vole 19:332 *illus.*
VOLGA-BALTIC WATERWAY 19:628
VOLGA-FINNIC LANGUAGES
Uralic languages 19:475
VOLGA RIVER 19:628–629 *bibliog., map*
map (45° 55′N 47° 52′E) 19:629
VOLGOGRAD (USSR) 19:629
climate 7:272 *table*
map (48° 44′N 44° 25′E) 19:388
VOLGOGRAD RESERVOIR
map (49° 20′N 45° 0′E) 19:629
VOLKONSKY, ANDREI
Russian music 16:369
VOLKOV, VLADISLAV NIKOLAYEVICH 19:629 *bibliog.*
VOLKOVA, VERA 19:629–630 *bibliog.*
VOLKSWAGEN 2:365 *illus.*; 19:630 *bibliog.*
advertising 1:113 *illus.*
automotive industry 2:366
VOLLAERTS, JAN
plainsong 15:326
VOLLARD, AMBROISE 19:630 *bibliog.*
Portrait of the Art Dealer Vollard (Pablo Picasso) 15:447 *illus.*
VOLLEYBALL 19:630 *bibliog., illus.*
VOLOGDA (USSR)
map (59° 12′N 39° 55′E) 19:388
VÓLOS (Greece)
map (39° 21′N 22° 56′E) 9:325
VOLPONE (play) 19:631
Jonson, Ben 11:445–446
VOLSTEAD, ANDREW J. 19:631 *bibliog.*
18th Amendment 7:91
VOLSTEAD ACT
prohibition 15:565
VOLT 19:631
alternating current 1:312 *illus.*
electron volt 7:124
piezoelectricity 15:298
units, physical 19:466–467 *tables*
Volta, Alessandro, Count 19:631
voltage regulator 19:631
voltmeter 19:632
VOLTA, ALESSANDRO, COUNT 7:108 *illus.*; 19:631 *bibliog.*
battery 3:125–126
electrochemistry 7:112
volt 19:631
VOLTA, LAKE 9:165 *illus.*; 19:631
map (7° 30′N 0° 15′E) 9:164
VOLTA REDONDA (Brazil)
map (22° 32′S 44° 7′W) 3:460
VOLTA RIVER 19:631
map (5° 46′N 0° 41′E) 9:164
VOLTAGE REGULATOR 19:631
diode 6:183
Zener diode 20:359
VOLTAIRE 7:164 *illus.*; 19:631–632 *bibliog., illus.*
Candide 4:107
French literature 8:316–317 *illus.*
VOLTERRA, DANIELE DA 19:632
VOLTMETER 19:632
circuit, electric 4:436
galvanometer 9:23
VOLTURNO RIVER 19:632
VOLUME (mathematics) 19:632
cone 5:175
cube 5:380
cylinder 5:406
sphere 18:180
weights and measures 20:93 *table*
VOLUME (physics)
critical constants 5:351
measurement 13:255
temperature 19:93
unit of measurement
units, physical 19:466
van der Waals equation 19:512–513
VOLUMETRIC ANALYSIS
calibrated volumetric burette
titration 19:215
quantitative chemical analysis 16:8–9
VOLUNTARISM
William of Occam 20:155
VOLUNTEERS OF AMERICA 19:632–633 *bibliog.*
VOLUNTEERS IN SERVICE TO AMERICA (VISTA)
ACTION (federal agency) 1:89
VOLUSIA (county in Florida)
map (29° 0′N 81° 10′W) 8:172
VOLVOX 1:281 *illus.*; 15:331 *illus.*; 19:633
VOLYNOV, BORIS VALENTINOVICH 19:633 *bibliog.*
VOMITING
emetic 7:155
nausea 14:52
whooping cough 20:143
VON *see* the last element of the name for names not listed below
VON ARX, WILLIAM S. 19:633
VON BRAUN, WERNHER 18:119 *illus.*; 19:633 *bibliog., illus.*
jet propulsion 11:407
Redstone 16:116
rockets and missiles 16:253–254 *illus.*
V-2 19:500–501
VON DÄNIKEN, ERICH 19:633 *bibliog.*
VON KOERBER, LEILA *see* DRESSLER, MARIE
VON NEUMANN, JOHN 19:634 *bibliog.*
chemistry, history of 4:328
computer 5:160a
decision theory 6:74
Mauchly, John William 13:232
UNIVAC 19:467
VON STERNBERG HOUSE
Neutra, Richard 14:108
VON STROHEIM, ERICH *see* STROHEIM, ERICH VON
VON SYDOW, MAX 19:634
VON TSCHIRNHAUSEN, EHRENFRIED WALTHER
Meissen ware 13:283
VONDA (Saskatchewan)
map (52° 19′N 106° 6′W) 17:81
VONDEL, JOOST VAN DEN 19:634 *bibliog.*

VONNEGUT, KURT, JR. 19:634 *bibliog., illus.*
Slaughterhouse-Five 17:351
VONNOH, BESSIE POTTER 19:634
VOODOO 19:634–635 *bibliog.*
Duvalier, François 6:316
folk medicine 8:201
Latin American music and dance 12:231 *illus.*
VOORTREKKERS
South Africa 18:82
VORARLBERG SCHOOL
Moosbrugger, Caspar 13:571
VORDER-GRAUSPITZ MOUNTAIN
map (47° 3′N 9° 36′E) 12:325
VORDINGBORG (Denmark)
map (55° 1′N 11° 55′E) 6:109
VORONEZH (USSR) 19:635
map (51° 40′N 39° 10′E) 19:388
VORONIKHIN, ANDREI
Russian art and architecture 16:362
VOROSHILOV, KLIMENT YEFREMOVICH 19:635 *bibliog.*
VOROSHILOVGRAD (USSR)
map (48° 34′N 39° 20′E) 19:388
VÖRÖSMARTY, MILHÁLY
Hungarian literature 10:305
VORSPIEL *see* PRELUDE
VORSTER, B. JOHANNES 19:635 *bibliog.*
VORTEX *see* WHIRLPOOL
VORTICELLA 19:635
biological locomotion 15:581 *illus.*
VORTICISM 19:635 *bibliog.*
Epstein, Jacob 7:223
Gaudier-Brzeska, Henri 9:59
Lewis, Wyndham 12:307
Pound, Ezra 15:475–476
VORTOGRAPH
Coburn, Alvin Langdon 5:84
VORTWARTS *see* *JEWISH DAILY FORWARD* (periodical)
VOSGES 19:635
Alsace-Lorraine 1:310
Belfort Gap 3:174
map (48° 30′N 7° 10′E) 8:260
VOSKHOD 19:635–636 *bibliog., table*
Belyayev, Pavel Ivanovich 3:194
Feoktistov, Konstantin P. 8:51
Khrunov, Yevgeny 12:68
Komarov, Vladimir 12:107
Leonov, Aleksei 12:292
missions 19:636 *table*
program 19:636
spacecraft 19:635–636
Vostok 19:636–637
Yegorov, Boris B. 20:322
VOSTOK 19:636–637 *bibliog., illus., table*
Bykovsky, Valery 3:602
Cosmos 5:289
Feoktistov, Konstantin P. 8:51
launch 18:120 *illus.*
life-support systems 12:331–333
missions 19:636 *table*
Nikolayev, Andrian 14:195
Popovich, Pavel Romanovich 15:431–432
spacecraft 19:636–637 *illus.*
Tereshkova, Valentina Vladimirovna Nikolayeva 19:116
Voskhod 19:635–636
VOTER REGISTRATION 19:637
15th Amendment 8:74
poll tax 15:405
SNCC 17:384
Southern Christian Leadership Conference 18:112
Voting Rights Act 19:637
VOTIAN LANGUAGE
Ural-Altaic languages 19:475
VOTING *see* ELECTION; SUFFRAGE
VOTING MACHINE 19:637
VOTING RIGHTS (U.S. Constitution) *see* 15TH AMENDMENT; 24TH AMENDMENT
VOTING RIGHTS ACT 19:637
VOTO, BERNARD DE *see* DE VOTO, BERNARD
VOTYAK LANGUAGE
Uralic languages 19:475
VOUET, SIMON 19:638 *bibliog.*
VOUGHT F4U-1 CORSAIR AIRCRAFT *see* CORSAIR (aircraft)
VOX, MAXIMILIAN
typeface classifications 19:364
VOYAGER 19:638 *bibliog., illus.*
Jupiter (planet) 11:472–473
Europa (astronomy) 7:267
Io (satellite) 11:238
life, extraterrestrial 12:329
Mariner 13:156
planets 15:331
Saturn (astronomy) 17:89–90 *illus.*
SNAP 17:383–384
space exploration 18:126 *illus.*
Titan (astronomy) 19:210
Titan (rocket) 19:211
VOYEURISM 19:638 *bibliog.*
Godiva, Lady 9:221
VOYSEY, CHARLES FRANCIS ANNESLEY 19:638 *bibliog.*
VOZNESENSKY, ANDREI 19:639 *bibliog.*
VRANJE (Yugoslavia)
map (42° 33′N 21° 54′E) 20:340
VRATSA (Bulgaria)
map (43° 12′N 23° 33′E) 3:555
VRBAS (Yugoslavia)
map (45° 35′N 19° 39′E) 20:340
VRCHLICKÝ, JAROSLAV
Czech literature 5:412
VREDEMAN DE VRIES, HANS 19:639 *bibliog.*
VREED EN HOOP (Guyana)
map (6° 48′N 58° 11′W) 9:410
VRIES, ADRIAEN DE 19:639 *bibliog.*
VRIES, HANS VREDEMAN DE *see* VREDEMAN DE VRIES, HANS
VRIES, HUGO DE 19:639 *bibliog.*; 20:378 *illus.*
biology 3:271
heredity 10:140
Mendel, Gregor Johann 13:294
mutation 13:686
VRIES, PETER DE *see* DE VRIES, PETER
VROOM, VICTOR
industrial psychology 11:157
VRŠAC (Yugoslavia)
map (45° 7′N 21° 18′E) 20:340
VRUBEL, MIKHAIL ALEKSANDROVICH 19:639 *bibliog.*
VRUGHT, JOHANNA PETRONELLA 19:639
VTOL 19:639 *bibliog., illus.*
helicopter 10:111–112
VUGHT (Netherlands)
map (51° 40′N 5° 17′E) 14:99
VUILLARD, ÉDOUARD 19:640 *bibliog., illus.*
Nabis 14:3
Woman in a Blue Bodice 19:640 *illus.*
VULCAN (Alberta)
map (50° 24′N 113° 15′W) 1:256
VULCAN (mythology) 19:640
VULCANIZATION *see* RUBBER
VULGATE (Bible)
Bible 3:241
Jerome, Saint 11:398
VULTURE 19:640 *bibliog., illus.*
birds of prey 3:291
condor 5:173
Pleistocene Epoch 15:366–367 *illus.*
Tertiary Period 19:124 *illus.*
VULVA
sex change 17:225
VULVITIS
fungus diseases 8:369
VUNISEA (Fiji)
map (19° 3′S 178° 9′E) 8:77
VYATKA (USSR) *see* KIROV (USSR)
VYGOTSKY, LEV SEMYONOVICH
concept formation and attainment 5:169
inner speech 11:179
VYSHINSKY, ANDREI YANUARIEVICH 19:640
VYTAUTAS, GRAND DUKE OF LITHUANIA 19:640

W

W (letter) 20:3 *illus.*
U (letter) 19:369
V (letter) 19:500
W. J. VAN BLOMMESTEIN LAKE
map (4° 45′N 55° 0′W) 18:364
W PARTICLE (physics)
fundamental particles 8:362 *table*; 8:363
Rubbia, Carlo 16:335
unified field theory 19:386
van der Meer, Simon 19:512
W URSAE MAJORIS STARS 20:3
W VIRGINIS STARS 20:3
Cepheids 4:257
variable star 19:522
WA (Ghana)
map (10° 4′N 2° 29′W) 9:164
WAAGE, PETER 20:3
Guldberg, Cato Maximilian 20:3
mass action, law of 20:3
WAAL RIVER
map (51° 55′N 4° 30′E) 14:99
WAALS, JOHANNES DIDERIK VAN DER *see* VAN DER WAALS, JOHANNES DIDERIK
WAALWIJK (Netherlands)
map (51° 42′N 5° 4′E) 14:99
WABANSI 20:3 *bibliog.*
WABASCA (Alberta)
map (56° 0′N 113° 53′W) 1:256
WABASCA RIVER
map (58° 22′N 115° 20′W) 1:256
WABASH (county in Illinois)
map (38° 27′N 87° 50′W) 11:42
WABASH (Indiana)
map (40° 48′N 85° 49′W) 11:111
WABASH (county in Indiana)
map (40° 48′N 85° 49′W) 11:111
WABASH RIVER 20:3
map (37° 46′N 88° 2′W) 11:111
WABASHA (Minnesota)
map (44° 23′N 92° 2′W) 13:453
WABASHA (county in Minnesota)
map (44° 15′N 92° 13′W) 13:453
WABASSO (Florida)
map (27° 45′N 80° 26′W) 8:172
WABASSO (Minnesota)
map (44° 24′N 95° 15′W) 13:453
WABAUNSEE (county in Kansas)
map (38° 55′N 96° 10′W) 12:18
WABOWDEN (Manitoba)
map (54° 55′N 98° 38′W) 13:119
WAC 20:3 *bibliog.*
Hobby, Oveta Culp 10:192
WACCAMAW, LAKE
map (34° 17′N 78° 30′W) 14:242
WACCAMAW RIVER
map (33° 21′N 79° 16′W) 18:98
WACH, JOACHIM 20:3
WACHAPREAGUE (Virginia)
map (37° 36′N 75° 41′W) 19:607
WACISSA (Florida)
map (30° 21′N 83° 59′W) 8:172
WACO (Texas) 20:4
map (31° 55′N 97° 8′W) 19:129
WACONDA LAKE
map (39° 30′N 98° 35′W) 12:18
WACONIA (Minnesota)
map (44° 51′N 93° 47′W) 13:453
WAD MADANI (Sudan)
map (14° 25′N 33° 28′E) 18:320
WADAY
Darfur 6:37
WADDENZEE
map (53° 15′N 5° 15′E) 14:99
WADDINGTON, MOUNT
map (51° 23′N 125° 15′W) 3:491
WADE, BENJAMIN FRANKLIN 20:4 *bibliog.*
Davis, Henry Winter 6:51
WADE-DAVIS MANIFESTO
Davis, Henry Winter 6:51
WADE-DAVIS RECONSTRUCTION BILL
Reconstruction 16:109
Wade, Benjamin Franklin 20:4
WADE-GILES SYSTEM (Chinese language)
Sino-Tibetan languages 17:325
WADENA (Minnesota)
map (46° 26′N 95° 8′W) 13:453
WADENA (county in Minnesota)
map (46° 33′N 94° 57′W) 13:453
WADESBORO (North Carolina)
map (34° 58′N 80° 4′W) 14:242
WADESTOWN (New Zealand)
map (41° 16′S 174° 46′E) 14:158
WADHAM COLLEGE, (Oxford University) 14:474
WADI BANA
map (13° 3′N 45° 24′E) 20:324
WADI DRÂA RIVER
map (28° 43′N 11° 9′W) 13:585
WADI MASILA
map (15° 10′N 51° 5′E) 20:324
WADI MEDJERDA RIVER
map (37° 7′N 10° 13′E) 19:335
WADI MOULOUYA RIVER
map (35° 5′N 2° 25′W) 13:585
WADI OUM ER RBIA RIVER
map (33° 19′N 8° 21′W) 13:585
WADI SEBOU RIVER
map (34° 15′N 6° 40′W) 13:585
WADI SHABEELLE RIVER
map (0° 1′S 42° 45′E) 18:60
WADING RIVER
map (39° 33′N 74° 28′W) 14:129
WADLEY (Alabama)
map (33° 7′N 85° 34′W) 1:234
WADLEY (Georgia)
map (32° 52′N 82° 24′W) 9:114
WADSWORTH (Nevada)
map (39° 38′N 119° 17′W) 14:111
WADU CHANNEL
map (4° 7′N 73° 27′E) 13:87
WAF 20:4 *bibliog.*
WAFD 20:4 *bibliog.*
WAFFEN SS (Nazi Germany) 18:207
WAGE AND PRICE CONTROLS
incomes policy 11:77
inflation 11:170
WAGENINGEN (Netherlands)
map (51° 58′N 5° 40′E) 14:99
WAGENINGEN (Suriname)
map (5° 46′N 56° 41′W) 18:364
WAGES
consumer price index 5:225
economy, national 7:49–51
income, national 11:74–75
incomes policy 11:77
industrial engineering 11:156
Kelley, Florence 12:38
labor union 12:152–156
Marxism 13:184
minimum wage 13:446
social security 18:14
women in society 20:202
WAGGA WAGGA (Australia)
map (35° 7′S 147° 22′E) 2:328
WAGNER (South Dakota)
map (43° 5′N 98° 18′W) 18:103
WAGNER, HONUS 20:4 *bibliog.*
WAGNER, JOHN PETER *see* WAGNER, HONUS
WAGNER, OTTO 20:4 *bibliog.*
Majolika Haus 2:353 *illus.*
WAGNER, RICHARD 9:131 *illus.*; 16:294 *illus.*; 20:4–5 *bibliog., illus.*
atonality 2:312
Bayreuth Wagner Festival 3:134
Flying Dutchman, The 8:191
Hanslick, Eduard 10:41
harmony 10:52
Liszt, Franz 12:367
Louis II, King of Bavaria 12:423
meistersinger 13:283
Meistersinger von Nürnberg, Die
Sachs, Hans 17:7
Melchior, Lauritz 13:286
opera 14:401 *illus.*
orchestra and orchestration 14:418
overture 14:470
Ring of the Nibelung, The 16:225
theater architecture and staging 19:152
Festspielhaus 13:666 *illus.*; 14:402 *illus.*
themes and styles 20:5
Tristan and Isolde 19:303
Verdi, Giuseppe 19:550
WAGNER, ROBERT F., SR. 20:5–6 *bibliog.*
National Labor Relations Act 14:34
WAGNER ACT *see* NATIONAL LABOR RELATIONS ACT
WAGON 20:6–7 *bibliog., illus.*
Conestoga 5:175–176 *illus.*
European prehistory 7:305
Hallstatt 10:23
history 20:6–7
importance 20:6–7
WAGON MOUND (New Mexico)
map (36° 1′N 104° 42′W) 14:136
WAGONER (Oklahoma)
map (35° 58′N 95° 22′W) 14:368
WAGONER (county in Oklahoma)
map (35° 55′N 95° 30′W) 14:368
WAGONETTE
coach and carriage 5:75
WAGOSH *see* FOX (American Indians)
WAGTAIL 20:7
WAH
map (33° 48′N 72° 42′E) 15:27
WAHHABISM 20:7
Riyadh (Saudi Arabia) 16:234
WAHIAWA (Hawaii)
map (21° 30′N 158° 1′W) 10:72
WAHKIAKUM (county in Washington)
map (46° 16′N 123° 28′W) 20:35
WAHOO (botany)
burning bush 3:578
WAHOO (Nebraska)
map (41° 13′N 96° 37′W) 14:70
WAHPETON (North Dakota)
map (46° 16′N 96° 36′W) 14:248
WAHRAN (Algeria) *see* ORAN (Algeria)
WAIALUA (Hawaii)
map (21° 34′N 158° 8′W) 10:72
WAIALUA BAY
map (21° 36′N 158° 7′W) 10:72
WAIANAE (Hawaii)
map (21° 27′N 158° 11′W) 10:72
WAIANAE MOUNTAINS
map (21° 30′N 158° 10′W) 10:72
WAIKIKI BEACH
map (21° 17′N 157° 50′W) 10:72
WAILUKU (Hawaii)
map (20° 53′N 156° 30′W) 10:72
WAILUKU RIVER
map (19° 44′N 155° 5′W) 10:72
WAIMANALO (Hawaii)
map (21° 21′N 157° 42′W) 10:72

WAIMANALO BAY
  map (21° 21′N 157° 41′W) 10:72
WAIMEA (Hawaii)
  map (21° 58′N 159° 42′W) 10:72
WAINWRIGHT see WAGON
WAINWRIGHT (Alaska)
  map (70° 38′N 160° 1′W) 1:242
WAINWRIGHT (Alberta)
  map (52° 49′N 110° 52′W) 1:256
WAINWRIGHT, JONATHAN M. 20:7 bibliog.
  Corregidor (Phillipines) 5:276
  World War II 20:261
WAINWRIGHT BUILDING (St. Louis) 18:337 illus.
WAIPAHU (Hawaii)
  map (21° 23′N 158° 1′W) 10:72
WAIPIO ACRES (Hawaii)
  map (21° 28′N 158° 1′W) 10:72
WAIPUKURAU (New Zealand)
  map (40° 0′S 176° 34′E) 14:158
WAITANGI, TREATY OF 14:161 illus.; 20:7
  Maori 13:136
WAITE, MORRISON REMICK 20:7 bibliog.
  Munn v. Illinois 13:643
WAITE PARK (Minnesota)
  map (45° 33′N 94° 14′W) 13:453
WAITEMATA (New Zealand)
  map (36° 56′S 174° 42′E) 14:158
WAITING FOR GODOT (play) 19:154 illus.; 20:7 bibliog.
  Beckett, Samuel 3:151
  tragicomedy 19:265
WAITING LINES
  queuing theory 16:24–25
WAITSBURG (Washington)
  map (46° 16′N 118° 9′W) 20:35
WAJDA, ANDRZEJ 20:7 bibliog.
WAJIR (Kenya)
  climate 12:53 table
WAKABAYASHI, YESHUHIRO see HIRO (Yeshuhiro Wakabayashi)
WAKARUSA (Indiana)
  map (41° 32′N 86° 1′W) 11:111
WAKASA BAY
  map (35° 45′N 135° 40′E) 11:361
WAKATIPU, LAKE
  map (45° 5′S 168° 34′E) 14:158
WAKAYAMA (Japan)
  map (34° 13′N 135° 11′E) 11:361
WAKE (custom) 20:7–8 bibliog.
  funeral customs 8:363
WAKE (county in North Carolina)
  map (35° 50′N 78° 30′W) 14:242
WAKE (water) 20:8
  patterns 20:8
WAKE FOREST (North Carolina)
  map (35° 59′N 78° 30′W) 14:242
WAKE FOREST UNIVERSITY 20:8
WAKE ISLAND 20:8
  map (19° 17′N 166° 36′E) 14:334
  rail (bird) 16:70
  World War II 20:260
WAKEENEY (Kansas)
  map (39° 1′N 99° 53′W) 12:18
WAKEFIELD (England) 20:8
WAKEFIELD (Kansas)
  map (39° 13′N 97° 1′W) 12:18
WAKEFIELD (Massachusetts)
  map (42° 30′N 71° 4′W) 3:409
WAKEFIELD (Michigan)
  map (46° 28′N 89° 55′W) 13:377
WAKEFIELD (Nebraska)
  map (42° 16′N 96° 52′W) 14:70
WAKEFIELD (Rhode Island)
  map (41° 26′N 71° 30′W) 16:198
WAKEFIELD (Virginia)
  map (36° 58′N 76° 59′W) 19:607
WAKEFIELD, EDWARD GIBBON 20:8 bibliog.
  New Zealand, history of 14:161–162 illus.
WAKONDA (South Dakota)
  map (43° 0′N 97° 6′W) 18:103
WAKOSKI, DIANE 20:8
WAKSMAN, SELMAN ABRAHAM 20:8 bibliog.
WAKULLA (county in Florida)
  map (30° 10′N 84° 20′W) 8:172
WALACH, MEIR see LITVINOV, MAKSIM MAKSIMOVICH
WALACHIA (Romania) 20:8–9
  cities
    Bucharest 3:534 illus.
  Cuza, Alexandru Ion 5:399
  history
    Michael the Brave 13:372
    Vlad the Impaler, Prince of Walachia 19:623
  Romania 16:290
WALAM OLUM
  Delaware (American Indians) 6:91
WAŁBRZYCH (Poland)
  map (50° 46′N 16° 17′E) 15:388
WALBURGA, SAINT 20:9
WALCHEREN ISLAND
  map (51° 33′N 3° 35′E) 14:99
WALCOTT (British Columbia)
  map (54° 31′N 126° 51′W) 3:491
WALCOTT, DEREK 20:9 bibliog.
WALCOTT, JERSEY JOE
  Marciano, Rocky 13:146
WALCOTT, LAKE
  map (42° 40′N 113° 23′W) 11:26
WALD, GEORGE 20:9
  eye 7:348
  night blindness 20:9
  Vietnam War peace movement 20:9
WALD, LILLIAN D. 20:9 bibliog.
WALDALGESHEIM
  Celtic art 4:239–240
WALDECK-ROUSSEAU, RENÉ 20:9 bibliog.
WALDEMAR I, KING OF DENMARK
  Scandinavia, history of 17:108
WALDEMAR II, KING OF DENMARK
  Scandinavia, history of 17:108
WALDEN (book) 20:9 bibliog.
  Thoreau, Henry David 19:178
WALDEN (Colorado)
  map (40° 44′N 106° 17′W) 5:116
WALDEN (New York)
  map (41° 34′N 74° 11′W) 14:149
WALDEN, PAUL 20:9
  stereochemistry 20:9
  Walden inversion 20:9
WALDEN POND
  Concord (Massachusetts) 5:171
  Thoreau, Henry David 19:179
WALDENSES 20:9 bibliog.
WALDENSIANS
  Thirty Years' War 19:171 map
WALDHEIM, KURT 20:9–10 bibliog.
WALDMEISTER see WOODRUFF (botany)
WALDMÜLLER, FERDINAND GEORG 20:10 bibliog.
WALDO (Arkansas)
  map (33° 21′N 93° 18′W) 2:166
WALDO (county in Maine)
  map (44° 30′N 69° 5′W) 13:70
WALDO LAKE
  map (43° 44′N 122° 3′W) 14:427
WALDOBORO (Maine)
  map (44° 6′N 69° 23′W) 13:70
WALDORF (Maryland)
  map (38° 37′N 76° 54′W) 13:188
WALDORF-ASTORIA HOTEL see ASTOR (family)
WALDRON (Arkansas)
  map (34° 54′N 94° 5′W) 2:166
WALDRON (Indiana)
  map (39° 27′N 85° 40′W) 11:111
WALDRON (Michigan)
  map (41° 44′N 84° 25′W) 13:377
WALDSEEMÜLLER, MARTIN
  exploration 7:335
  geography 9:101
  maps and mapmaking 13:139
  Vespucci, Amerigo 19:564
WALDWICK (New Jersey)
  map (41° 1′N 74° 8′W) 14:129
WALEN LAKE
  map (47° 7′N 9° 12′E) 18:394
WALES 2:3 map; 19:405 illus.; 20:10–11 bibliog., illus., map
  See also UNITED KINGDOM
  archaeology
    Cotswold-Severn 5:304
  arts 19:409
  bridge 3:480–481 illus.
  cities
    Aberystwyth 1:57
    Caernarvon 4:13
    Cardiff 4:143
    Carmarthen 4:153
    Swansea 18:379
  counties
    Clwyd 5:72
    Dyfed 6:319
    Glamorgan 9:196
    Gwent 9:411–412
    Gwynedd 9:412
    Powys 15:486
  crime 5:346 table
  David, Saint 6:48
  education
    British education 3:493–495
    London, University of 12:403–404
    universities 3:493 table
    Wales, University of 20:11
  Eisteddfod (literary festival) 7:97
  Flintshire 8:165
  government and politics 19:411
  history 20:11
    Glendower, Owen 9:207
    Great Britain, history of 9:309; 9:313
    Offa's Dyke 14:353
  land, people, and economy 19:405; 20:10–11 illus.
  land reclamation 12:180
  language 19:407
    Celtic languages 4:241
    Eisteddfod (literary festival) 7:97
  map (52° 30′N 3° 30′W) 19:403
  theater
    Williams, Emlyn 20:159
  Welsh literature 20:101–102
WALES (Alaska)
  map (65° 36′N 168° 5′W) 1:242
WALES, UNIVERSITY OF 20:11
WAŁESA, LECH 20:11
  Poland 15:391
WALHALLA (North Dakota)
  map (48° 55′N 97° 55′W) 14:248
WALHALLA (South Carolina)
  map (34° 46′N 83° 4′W) 18:98
WALHONDING RIVER
  map (40° 18′N 81° 53′W) 14:357
WALI ALLAH, SHAH 20:11 bibliog.
WALKER (county in Alabama)
  map (33° 45′N 87° 20′W) 1:234
WALKER (county in Georgia)
  map (34° 45′N 85° 20′W) 9:114
WALKER (Iowa)
  map (42° 17′N 91° 47′W) 11:244
WALKER (Michigan)
  map (42° 58′N 85° 46′W) 13:377
WALKER (Minnesota)
  map (47° 6′N 94° 35′W) 13:453
WALKER (county in Texas)
  map (30° 42′N 95° 35′W) 19:129
WALKER, ALICE 20:12
WALKER, DAVID (abolitionist) 20:12
WALKER, DAVID (actor) 19:151 illus.
WALKER, EDWARD PATRICK see WALKER, MICKEY
WALKER, HORATIO 20:12 bibliog.
WALKER, JAMES
  Civil War paintings 5:28–29 illus.
WALKER, JIMMY 20:12 bibliog.
WALKER, JOSEPH (pilot)
  X-15 20:311
WALKER, JOSEPH REDDEFORD (mountain man) 13:624 illus.
WALKER, MARGARET 20:12
WALKER, MARY EDWARDS 20:12 bibliog.
WALKER, MICKEY 20:12 bibliog.
WALKER, ROBERT J. 20:12 bibliog.
WALKER, THOMAS
  Kentucky 12:50
WALKER, WALTON H.
  Korean War 12:121
WALKER, WILLIAM 20:12 bibliog.
  Granada (city in Nicaragua) 9:283
WALKER CUP
  golf 9:239–240
WALKER LAKE
  map (38° 44′N 118° 43′W) 14:111
WALKER MOUNTAIN
  map (37° 0′N 81° 30′W) 19:607
WALKER TARIFF
  Walker, Robert J. 20:12
WALKERSVILLE (Maryland)
  map (39° 29′N 77° 21′W) 13:188
WALKERTON (Indiana)
  map (41° 28′N 86° 29′W) 11:111
WALKERTON (Ontario)
  map (44z° 7′N 81° 9′W) 14:393; 19:241
WALKING FISH 20:12
WALKING STICK see STICK INSECT
WALKÜRE, DIE see RING OF THE NIBELUNG, THE (opera cycle)
WALL (South Dakota)
  map (43° 59′N 102° 14′W) 18:103
WALL LAKE (Iowa)
  map (42° 16′N 95° 5′W) 11:244
WALL STREET 20:12–13 bibliog.
  Black Friday 3:315
WALL STREET JOURNAL, THE 20:13
  Barron, Clarence Walker 3:95
WALLA WALLA (Washington) 20:13
  map (46° 8′N 118° 20′W) 20:35
WALLA WALLA (county in Washington)
  map (46° 15′N 118° 30′W) 20:35
WALLABY 20:13 illus.
  brush-tailed rock wallaby 13:175 illus.
WALLACE (Idaho)
  map (47° 28′N 115° 56′W) 11:26
WALLACE (county in Kansas)
  map (38° 55′N 101° 45′W) 12:18
WALLACE (Nebraska)
  map (40° 50′N 101° 10′W) 14:70
WALLACE (North Carolina)
  map (34° 44′N 77° 59′W) 14:242
WALLACE, ALFRED RUSSEL 20:13 bibliog., illus.
  evolution 7:318–319 illus.
  paleogeography 15:37
  Social Darwinism 18:11
WALLACE, DE WITT 20:13
WALLACE, EDGAR 20:13–14
WALLACE, GEORGE 20:14 bibliog., illus.
  American Independent party 1:340
WALLACE, HENRY A. 20:14 bibliog., illus.
  Progressive party 15:564–565
WALLACE, IRVING 20:14 bibliog.
WALLACE, LEW 20:14
WALLACE, SIR RICHARD
  Wallace Collection, The 20:15
WALLACE, RUBY ANN see DEE, RUBY
WALLACE, SIR WILLIAM 20:14–15 bibliog.
WALLACE COLLECTION, THE 20:15 bibliog.
WALLACE LAKE
  map (32° 19′N 93° 45′W) 12:430
WALLACEBURG (Ontario)
  map (42° 36′N 82° 23′W) 14:393; 19:241
WALLACH, OTTO 20:15 bibliog.
  isoprene 20:15
  terpene 20:15
WALLACHIA (Romania) see WALACHIA (Romania)
WALLAS, GRAHAM 20:15 bibliog.
  problem solving 15:559
WALLENDA (family) 20:15 bibliog.
WALLENDA, KARL
  Wallenda (family) 20:15
WALLENPAUPACK, LAKE
  map (41° 25′N 75° 12′W) 15:147
WALLENSTEIN, ALBRECHT EUSEBIUS WENZEL VON
  Ferdinand II, Holy Roman Emperor 8:53
WALLENSTEIN, ALBRECHT VON
  Thirty Years' War 19:171 map
WALLENSTEIN, ALBRECHT WENZEL VON 20:15 bibliog., illus.
WALLER (county in Texas)
  map (30° 0′N 96° 0′W) 19:129
WALLER, EDMUND 20:15–16 bibliog.
WALLER, FATS 20:16 bibliog.
  Basie, Count 3:109
WALLEYE 20:16 illus.
WALLFLOWER (botany) 20:16
WALLINGFORD (Connecticut)
  map (41° 27′N 72° 50′W) 5:193
WALLINGFORD (Vermont)
  map (43° 28′N 72° 59′W) 19:554
WALLINGTON (New Jersey)
  map (40° 51′N 74° 7′W) 14:129
WALLIS, JOHN 20:16 bibliog.
  English Civil War 20:16
  mathematics, history of 20:16
WALLIS, SAMUEL
  Tahiti (French Polynesia) 19:10
WALLIS AND FUTUNA ISLANDS 20:16
  flag 8:144 illus.
  map (14° 0′S 177° 0′W) 14:334
WALLKILL RIVER
  map (41° 51′N 74° 3′W) 14:149
WALLON, HENRI
  developmental psychology 6:142
WALLONIA (region in Belgium)
  government 3:181
  language 3:179
  people 3:178–179
WALLOON LAKE
  map (45° 17′N 85° 0′W) 13:377
WALLOONS 20:16 bibliog.
  Belgium 3:178–179
  Liège (Belgium) 12:326
WALLOWA (Oregon)
  map (45° 34′N 117° 32′W) 14:427
WALLOWA (county in Oregon)
  map (45° 35′N 117° 10′W) 14:427
WALLOWA MOUNTAINS
  map (45° 10′N 117° 30′W) 14:427
WALLPAPER 20:16–17 illus.
  Blackthorn pattern 2:225 illus.; 20:17 illus.
  mica 13:370
  Morris, William 13:589
  rotogravure 16:323
WALLS (Mississippi)
  map (34° 58′N 90° 16′W) 13:469
WALLS, JOSIAH T. 16:185 illus.
WALLS OF BABYLON see HANGING GARDENS OF BABYLON
WALLULA, LAKE
  map (46° 0′N 119° 0′E) 20:35
WALNUT 8:348 illus.; 14:300–301 illus.; 15:337 illus.; 20:17 illus.
  hickory 10:157
  lumber 12:456 illus.

WALNUT (cont.)
pecan **15**:129
wood **20**:205 *illus.*
WALNUT (Illinois)
map (41° 33′N 89° 36′W) **11**:42
WALNUT (Iowa)
map (41° 28′N 95° 16′W) **11**:244
WALNUT (Kansas)
map (37° 36′N 95° 5′W) **12**:18
WALNUT (Mississippi)
map (34° 57′N 88° 54′W) **13**:469
WALNUT RIDGE (Arkansas)
map (36° 4′N 90° 57′W) **2**:166
WALNUT RIVER
map (37° 3′N 97° 0′W) **12**:18
WALNUT STREET THEATRE **20**:18
WALPOLE (Massachusetts)
map (42° 8′N 71° 15′W) **3**:409
WALPOLE (New Hampshire)
map (43° 5′N 72° 26′W) **14**:123
WALPOLE, HORACE, 4TH EARL OF ORFORD **20**:18 *bibliog.*
Castle of Otranto, The **4**:191
Gothic romance **9**:263
Gray, Thomas **9**:307
WALPOLE, SIR HUGH SEYMOUR **20**:18 *bibliog.*
WALPOLE, SIR ROBERT **20**:18 *bibliog., illus.*
prime minister **15**:542
Townshend, Charles Townshend, 2d Viscount **19**:255
WALPOLE ISLAND
New Caledonia **14**:119
WALPURGIS NIGHT *see* WALBURGA, SAINT
WALRUS **20**:18 *bibliog., illus.*
Arctic **2**:141 *illus.*
ecological adaptation **13**:100 *illus.*
hunting
Eskimo **7**:240–241 *illus.*
ivory and ivory carving **11**:336
WALSALL (England)
map (52° 35′N 1° 58′W) **19**:403
WALSENBURG (Colorado)
map (37° 37′N 104° 47′W) **5**:116
WALSH (Colorado)
map (37° 23′N 102° 17′W) **5**:116
WALSH (county in North Dakota)
map (48° 25′N 97° 40′W) **14**:248
WALSH, DON
Marianas Trench **13**:151
WALSH, RAOUL **20**:19 *bibliog.*
WALSH, THOMAS J. **20**:19 *bibliog.*
WALSINGHAM, SIR FRANCIS **20**:19 *bibliog.*
intelligence gathering **11**:204
WALT DISNEY WORLD *see* DISNEYLAND AND WALT DISNEY WORLD
WALTARI, MIKA **20**:19
WALTER (family) **20**:19 *bibliog.*
WALTER, BRUNO **20**:19 *bibliog.*
WALTER, HORATIO
Oxen Drinking **4**:88–89 *illus.*
WALTER, JOHANN
Renaissance music **16**:156
WALTER, LUCY
Monmouth, James Scott, Duke of **13**:536
WALTER, THOMAS U. **20**:19 *bibliog.*
Capitol of the United States **4**:126
WALTER F. GEORGE LAKE
map (31° 49′N 85° 8′W) **1**:234
WALTERBORO (South Carolina)
map (32° 55′N 80° 39′W) **18**:98
WALTERS (Oklahoma)
map (34° 22′N 98° 19′W) **14**:368
WALTERS, BARBARA **20**:19–20
WALTERS ART GALLERY **20**:20 *bibliog.*
WALTHALL (Mississippi)
map (33° 31′N 89° 16′W) **13**:469
WALTHALL (county in Mississippi)
map (31° 10′N 90° 5′W) **13**:469
WALTHAM (Massachusetts)
map (42° 23′N 71° 14′W) **3**:409
WALTHER, CARL FERDINAND WILHELM **20**:20 *bibliog.*
WALTHER VON DER VOGELWEIDE **13**:460 *illus.*; **20**:20
German and Austrian music **9**:129
WALTHILL (Nebraska)
map (42° 9′N 96° 30′W) **14**:70
WALTON (county in Florida)
map (30° 40′N 86° 10′W) **8**:172
WALTON (county in Georgia)
map (33° 50′N 83° 45′W) **9**:114
WALTON (Indiana)
map (40° 40′N 86° 15′W) **11**:111
WALTON (Kentucky)
map (38° 52′N 84° 37′W) **12**:47
WALTON (New York)
map (42° 10′N 75° 8′W) **14**:149
WALTON (Nova Scotia)
map (45° 14′N 64° 0′W) **14**:269
WALTON, BILL **20**:20 *bibliog.*
WALTON, ERNEST THOMAS SINTON **20**:20
transmutation of elements **20**:20
WALTON, IZAAK **20**:20
Winchester (England) **20**:168
WALTON, SIR WILLIAM **20**:20–21 *bibliog., illus.*
WALTZ **6**:29 *illus.*; **20**:21 *bibliog.*
Castle, Vernon and Irene **4**:191
dance **6**:24 *illus.*
Strauss (family) **18**:293–294
"WALTZING MATILDA" (song)
Paterson, A. B. **15**:111
WALVIS BAY (Namibia) **20**:21
map (22° 59′S 14° 31′E) **18**:79
WALWORTH (county in South Dakota)
map (45° 25′N 100° 0′W) **18**:103
WALWORTH (Wisconsin)
map (42° 32′N 88° 36′W) **20**:185
WALWORTH (county in Wisconsin)
map (42° 41′N 88° 32′W) **20**:185
WAMBAUGH, JOSEPH **20**:21
WAMEGO (Kansas)
map (39° 12′N 96° 18′W) **12**:18
WAMESIT (Massachusetts)
map (42° 37′N 71° 16′W) **3**:409
WAMPANOAG (American Indians) **20**:21
King Philip's War **12**:82
Massachuset **13**:204
Massasoit **13**:213
Samoset **17**:47
Squanto **18**:202
WAMPSVILLE (New York)
map (43° 5′N 75° 42′W) **14**:149
WAMPUM **20**:21 *bibliog., illus.*
Indians of North America, art of the **11**:141
Montauk **13**:551
Onondaga **14**:391
Tuscarora **19**:355
WAMSUTTER (Wyoming)
map (41° 40′N 107° 58′W) **20**:301
WANAKA, LAKE
map (44° 30′S 169° 8′E) **14**:158
WANAMINGO (Minnesota)
map (44° 18′N 92° 47′W) **13**:453
WANANIKWE **20**:21 *bibliog.*
WANAPAM (American Indians)
Smohalla **17**:373
Spokan **18**:192
WANAPUM LAKE
map (47° 0′N 120° 0′W) **20**:35
WANAQUE (New Jersey)
map (41° 3′N 74° 17′W) **14**:129
WANAQUE RESERVOIR
map (41° 5′N 74° 17′W) **14**:129
WANBLEE (South Dakota)
map (43° 34′N 101° 40′W) **18**:103
WANDERERS (art group) *see* PEREDVIZHNIKI (art group)
WANDERERS, THE
Russian art and architecture **16**:362
WANDERING JEW (botany) **20**:21–22 *illus.*
spiderwort **18**:183
WANDERING JEW (literature) **20**:22 *bibliog.*
WANDO RIVER
map (32° 45′N 79° 57′W) **18**:98
WANETTE (Oklahoma)
map (34° 58′N 97° 2′W) **14**:368
WANG AN-SHIH (Wang Anshi) **20**:22
Sung (Song) (dynasty) **18**:348
WANG ANSHI *see* WANG AN-SHIH (Wang Anshi)
WANG CHING-WEI (Wang Jingwei) **20**:22 *bibliog.*
WANG HSI-CHIH (Wang Xizhi) **20**:22 *bibliog.*
WANG HUI
Deep in the Mountains **20**:23 *illus.*
WANG HUNG-WEN
Gang of Four **9**:36
WANG JINGWEI *see* WANG CHING-WEI (Wang Jingwei)
WANG MANG, EMPEROR OF CHINA **20**:22 *bibliog.*
Han **10**:34
WANG MENG **20**:22 *bibliog.*
Chinese literature **4**:390
WANG SHIH-KU *see* WANG HUI
WANG WEI **20**:22 *bibliog.*
WANG XIZHI *see* WANG HSI-CHIH (Wang Xizhi)
WANG YANG-MING (Wang Yangming) **20**:22
Confucianism **5**:180
WANG YANGMING *see* WANG YANG-MING (Wang Yangming)
WANGANUI (New Zealand)
map (39° 56′S 175° 3′E) **14**:158
WANGCHUK, JIGME SINGYE
Bhutan **3**:236
WANGS, FOUR **20**:23 *bibliog., illus.*
Chinese art and architecture **4**:382
WANKEL, FELIX
Wankel engine **20**:23–24
WANKEL ENGINE **20**:23–24 *bibliog., illus.*
engine **7**:177
WANSTEAD (country house)
Campbell, Colen **4**:65
WAPAKONETA (Ohio)
map (40° 34′N 84° 12′W) **14**:357
WAPANUCKA (Oklahoma)
map (34° 22′N 96° 25′W) **14**:368
WAPATO (Washington)
map (46° 27′N 120° 25′W) **20**:35
WAPELLO (Iowa)
map (41° 11′N 91° 11′W) **11**:244
WAPELLO (county in Iowa)
map (41° 0′N 92° 22′W) **11**:244
WAPITI **7**:146 *illus.*; **20**:24 *illus.*
WAPPINGERS FALLS (New York)
map (41° 36′N 73° 55′W) **14**:149
WAPSHOT CHRONICAL, THE (book)
Cheever, John **4**:310
WAPSIPINICON RIVER
map (41° 44′N 90° 20′W) **11**:244
WAR **20**:24–25 *bibliog.*
See also names of specific wars, e.g., CIVIL WAR, U.S.; FRANCO-PRUSSIAN WAR; etc.
animal behavior **2**:17–18
camouflage **4**:62–63
cannon **4**:111–112
cavalry **4**:221–222
chariot **4**:288
chemical and biological warfare **4**:311–313
civil defense **5**:9–10
conflict theory **5**:178–179
contraband **5**:231
fallout shelter **8**:14–15
foreign policy **8**:226
fortification **8**:238–241
galley warfare **9**:18
Geneva conventions **9**:91
guerrillas **9**:391–392
head-hunting **10**:85
Indians, American **11**:122; **11**:129
infantry **11**:163
Kellogg-Briand Pact **12**:38
limited war **20**:24–25
mine **13**:437–438
necessity of
Grotius, Hugo **9**:372
neutrality **14**:108
neutron bomb **14**:109
nuclear strategy **14**:288
nursing (profession) **14**:298
On War (book)
Clausewitz, Carl Philipp Gottfried von **5**:44–45
pacifism and nonviolent movements **15**:8–10
photojournalism **15**:273 *illus.*
prisoner of war **15**:555–556
privateering **15**:557–558
reparations **16**:159–160
reportage *see* JOURNALISM—war reportage
right of search **16**:222
rockets and missiles **16**:251–252
savings bond **17**:101
scalping **17**:107
slavery **17**:352–353
sonar **18**:62
strategy and tactics, military **18**:289–291
tear gas **19**:58
technology, history of **19**:62
total war **20**:24
war crimes **20**:25
weapons **20**:74–75
WAR (West Virginia)
map (37° 18′N 81° 41′W) **20**:111
WAR, LAWS OF *see* GENEVA CONVENTIONS; WAR CRIMES
WAR BOND *see* SAVINGS BOND
WAR CRIMES **20**:25 *bibliog.*
chemical and biological warfare **4**:312–313
Geneva conventions **9**:91
My Lai incident **13**:689
Nuremberg Trials **14**:297
Speer, Albert **18**:176
statute of limitations **18**:239
World War II **20**:280
WAR DANCE
Indians of North America, music and dance of the **11**:143–144
WAR AND PEACE (book) **20**:25 *bibliog.*
Tolstoi, Count Leo **19**:228
WAR ON POVERTY **20**:28 *bibliog.*
Elementary and Secondary Education Act of 1965 **7**:133
Job Corps **11**:421
legal aid **12**:272
Upward Bound **19**:473
WAR POWERS ACT
Congress of the United States **5**:187
president of the United States **15**:522
WAR OF THE WORLDS, THE (book) **20**:25
Amazing Stories cover **17**:144 *illus.*
Wells, H. G. **20**:101
"WAR OF THE WORLDS, THE" (radio broadcast)
Mercury Theatre **13**:308
radio and television broadcasting **16**:56 *illus.*
Welles, Orson **20**:99
WAR OF 1812 **20**:25–28 *bibliog., illus., map*
Armstrong, John **2**:179
battles **4**:83 *map*
Brock, Sir Isaac **3**:500
Brown, Jacob Jennings **3**:514
Canada, history of **4**:82–83 *map*
Connecticut **5**:196
Constitution (ship) **5**:212
Creek War **11**:109 *map*
Dearborn, Henry **6**:68
Decatur, Stephen **6**:73
Embargo Act **7**:151
Fort McHenry **8**:237
Ghent, Treaty of **9**:166
Harrison, William Henry **10**:61
Hull, William **10**:296
Jackson, Andrew **11**:340–341
Lafitte, Jean **12**:164
Louisiana **12**:434
Macdonough, Thomas **13**:14
Madison, Dolley **13**:41
Madison, James **13**:42–43
Monroe, James **13**:542
navy **14**:63
New Orleans (Louisiana) **14**:141–142
Perry, Oliver Hazard **15**:179
flag **8**:135 *illus.*
Porter, David **15**:444
right of search **16**:222
Rodgers (family) **16**:266
Scott, Winfield **17**:154
Secord, Laura **17**:180
Shelby, Isaac **17**:250
Tecumseh (Shawnee Indian) **19**:69
Tennessee **19**:106
Tippecanoe, Battle of **19**:207
Troy (New York) **19**:313
uniform **2**:182 *illus.*
United States, history of the **19**:443–444 *illus.*
Vermont **19**:558
WARANGAL (India)
map (18° 0′N 79° 35′E) **11**:80
WARAO (American Indians) *see* WARRAU (American Indians)
WARBLE FLY **11**:189 *illus.*
See also CATTLE GRUB
WARBLER **20**:28 *bibliog., illus.*
accentor **1**:76
chat **4**:302
cisticola **4**:446
honeycreeper **10**:221
kinglet **12**:83
redstart **16**:116
tailorbird **19**:11
wood warbler **20**:209
WARBURG, ABY
iconography **11**:24
WARBURG, OTTO **20**:28 *bibliog.*
biology **3**:270
cellular respiration enzymes **20**:28
photosynthesis **15**:275
WARBURG, PAUL MORITZ **20**:28
WARBURTON, PETER E.
Great Sandy Desert **9**:322
WARBURTON, WILLIAM **20**:28
WARD (law)
guardian **9**:387
WARD (county in North Dakota)
map (48° 10′N 101° 30′W) **14**:248
WARD (county in Texas)
map (31° 32′N 103° 5′W) **19**:129
WARD, ARTEMUS **20**:29 *bibliog.*
WARD, ARTHUR SARSFIELD *see* ROHMER, SAX
WARD, DOUGLAS TURNER **20**:29
WARD, FREDERICK TOWNSEND **20**:29
WARD, JAMES **20**:29 *bibliog.*
associationism **2**:266
WARD, SIR JOSEPH **20**:29

WARD, LESTER F.
sociology **18**:30
WARD, MONTGOMERY 20:29
WARD, WILLIAM 20:29 *bibliog.*
WARDEN (Washington)
map (46° 58′N 119° 2′W) **20**:35
WARDLEY, JAMES AND JANE
Shakers **17**:236
WARDLOW (Alberta)
map (50° 54′N 111° 33′W) **1**:256
WARE (county in Georgia)
map (31° 5′N 82° 30′W) **9**:114
WARE (Massachusetts)
map (42° 16′N 72° 15′W) **13**:206
WARE, HENRY 20:29 *bibliog.*
WARE RIVER
map (42° 11′N 72° 22′W) **13**:206
WAREGEM (Belgium)
map (50° 53′N 3° 25′E) **3**:177
WAREHAM (Massachusetts)
map (41° 46′N 70° 43′W) **13**:206
WARFARE *see* STRATEGY AND TACTICS, MILITARY
WARFIELD, BENJAMIN
fundamentalism **8**:363
WARHAM, WILLIAM 20:29 *bibliog.*
WARHOL, ANDY 20:29–30 *bibliog., illus.*
Elizabeth Taylor **20**:29 *illus.*
Flowers **9**:294 *illus.*
RainForest set **13**:497 *illus.*
WARI *see* MANCALA
WARING, EDWARD 20:30
Waring's theorem **20**:30
WARKA *see* URUK (Iraq)
WARLORDS 20:30 *bibliog.*
China, history of **4**:375
WARM-BLOODED ANIMAL *see* BODY TEMPERATURE
WARM FRONT
front **8**:339–340 *illus.*
WARM SPRINGS (Georgia) **20**:30
map (32° 54′N 84° 41′W) **9**:114
WARM SPRINGS (Oregon)
map (44° 46′N 121° 16′W) **14**:427
WARM SPRINGS (Virginia)
map (38° 3′N 79° 47′W) **19**:607
WARM SPRINGS RESERVOIR
map (43° 37′N 118° 14′W) **14**:427
WARMAN (Saskatchewan)
map (52° 20′N 106° 34′W) **17**:81
WARMERDAM, CORNELIUS 20:30 *bibliog.*
WARMINSTER (Pennsylvania)
map (40° 12′N 75° 6′W) **15**:147
WARMTH, BODY *see* BODY TEMPERATURE
WARNER (Alberta)
map (49° 17′N 112° 12′W) **1**:256
WARNER (New Hampshire)
map (43° 17′N 71° 49′W) **14**:123
WARNER (Oklahoma)
map (35° 31′N 95° 18′W) **14**:368
WARNER, GLENN SCOBEY "POP" *see* WARNER, POP
WARNER, MOUNT
map (42° 27′N 119° 44′W) **14**:427
WARNER, POP 20:30
WARNER, SETH 20:30
WARNER, SILVIA ASHTON- *see* ASHTON-WARNER, SILVIA
WARNER, SYLVIA TOWNSEND 20:30
WARNER, W. LLOYD
status **18**:239
WARNER BROTHERS (film studio)
film, history of **8**:84; **8**:87
WARNER MOUNTAINS
map (41° 40′N 120° 20′W) **4**:31
WARNER ROBINS (Georgia)
map (32° 37′N 83° 36′W) **9**:114
WARRANT 20:30
search warrant **17**:175
WARRANTY
business law **3**:588
WARRAU (American Indians) **20**:30–31 *bibliog.*
WARREN (Arkansas)
map (33° 37′N 92° 4′W) **2**:166
WARREN (county in Georgia)
map (33° 25′N 82° 40′W) **9**:114
WARREN (county in Illinois)
map (40° 50′N 90° 38′W) **11**:42
WARREN (county in Indiana)
map (40° 20′N 87° 20′W) **11**:111
WARREN (county in Iowa)
map (41° 17′N 95° 35′W) **11**:244
WARREN (county in Kentucky)
map (37° 0′N 86° 25′W) **12**:47
WARREN (Massachusetts)
map (42° 13′N 72° 12′W) **13**:206
WARREN (Michigan) **20**:31
map (42° 28′N 83° 1′W) **13**:377
WARREN (Minnesota)
map (48° 12′N 96° 46′W) **13**:453
WARREN (county in Mississippi)
map (32° 20′N 90° 45′W) **13**:469
WARREN (county in Missouri)
map (38° 45′N 91° 9′W) **13**:476
WARREN (county in New Jersey)
map (40° 49′N 75° 5′W) **14**:129
WARREN (county in New York)
map (43° 35′N 73° 50′W) **14**:149
WARREN (county in North Carolina)
map (36° 25′N 78° 5′W) **14**:242
WARREN (Ohio)
map (41° 14′N 80° 52′W) **14**:357
WARREN (county in Ohio)
map (39° 26′N 84° 13′W) **14**:357
WARREN (Pennsylvania)
map (41° 51′N 79° 8′W) **15**:147
WARREN (county in Pennsylvania)
map (41° 51′N 79° 8′W) **15**:147
WARREN (Rhode Island)
map (41° 43′N 71° 17′W) **16**:198
WARREN (county in Tennessee)
map (35° 40′N 83° 50′W) **19**:104
WARREN (county in Virginia)
map (38° 55′N 78° 15′W) **19**:607
WARREN, CHARLES 20:32
WARREN, EARL 12:246 *illus.*; **20**:31 *bibliog.*
Brown v. *Board of Education of Topeka, Kansas* **3**:517
Miranda v. *Arizona* **13**:463
Reynolds v. *Sims* **16**:191
Supreme Court of the United States **18**:357
United States, history of the **19**:457
Warren Commission **20**:31
Watkins v. *United States* **20**:67
WARREN, JOHN C.
surgery **18**:361 *illus.*
WARREN, JOSEPH 20:31 *bibliog.*
WARREN, LEONARD 20:31
WARREN, MERCY OTIS 20:31 *bibliog.*
WARREN, ROBERT PENN 20:31 *bibliog.*
All the King's Men **1**:298
WARREN COMMISSION 20:31–32 *bibliog.*
Oswald, Lee Harvey **14**:459
Secret Service **17**:181
Warren, Earl **20**:31
WARRENS (Wisconsin)
map (44° 8′N 90° 30′W) **20**:185
WARRENSBURG (Missouri)
map (38° 46′N 93° 44′W) **13**:476
WARRENSBURG (New York)
map (43° 30′N 73° 46′W) **14**:149
WARRENTON (Georgia)
map (33° 24′N 82° 40′W) **9**:114
WARRENTON (Missouri)
map (38° 49′N 91° 8′W) **13**:476
WARRENTON (North Carolina)
map (36° 24′N 78° 9′W) **14**:242
WARRENTON (Oregon)
map (46° 10′N 123° 56′W) **14**:427
WARRENTON (Virginia)
map (38° 43′N 77° 48′W) **19**:607
WARRI (Nigeria)
map (5° 31′N 5° 45′E) **14**:190
WARRICK (county in Indiana)
map (38° 5′N 87° 20′W) **11**:111
WARRINA (Australia)
map (28° 12′S 135° 50′E) **2**:328
WARRING, CHARLES BARTLETT
paleogeology **15**:37
WARRING STATES, PERIOD OF THE
China, history of **4**:371
WARRINGTON (England)
map (53° 24′N 2° 37′W) **19**:403
WARRINGTON (Florida)
map (30° 23′N 87° 16′W) **8**:172
WARRIOR VASE, THE
detail from **9**:329 *illus.*
WARRIORS, TEMPLE OF THE
Chichén Itzá **4**:344
WARROAD (Minnesota)
map (48° 54′N 95° 19′W) **13**:453
WARS OF THE ROSES *see* ROSES, WARS OF THE
WARSAW (Illinois)
map (40° 22′N 91° 26′W) **11**:42
WARSAW (Indiana)
map (41° 14′N 85° 51′W) **11**:111
WARSAW (Kentucky)
map (38° 47′N 84° 54′W) **12**:47
WARSAW (Missouri)
map (38° 15′N 93° 23′W) **13**:476
WARSAW (New York)
map (42° 44′N 78° 8′W) **14**:149
WARSAW (North Carolina)
map (35° 0′N 78° 5′W) **14**:242
WARSAW (Ohio)
map (40° 20′N 82° 0′W) **14**:357
WARSAW (Poland) **15**:390 *illus.*; **20**:32 *illus.*
climate **15**:388 *table*
history **20**:32
Warsaw Uprising **20**:33
map (52° 15′ 21° 0′E) **15**:388
WARSAW (Virginia)
map (37° 57′N 76° 46′W) **19**:607
WARSAW TREATY ORGANIZATION 20:32 *bibliog.*
cold war **5**:99
communism **5**:148
member nations **7**:297 *map*
WARSAW UPRISING 20:33 *bibliog.*
World War II **20**:271 *illus.*
WARSHIP *see* BATTLESHIP; NAVAL VESSELS
WARSZAWA (Poland) *see* WARSAW (Poland)
WART 20:33
caustic chemicals **4**:220
papilloma **15**:71
tumor **19**:331
WARTA RIVER
map (52° 35′N 14° 39′E) **15**:388
WARTBURG (Tennessee)
map (36° 6′N 84° 36′W) **19**:104
WARTHOG 20:33 *illus.*
pig **15**:298
WARTRACE (Tennessee)
map (35° 32′N 86° 19′W) **19**:104
WARTY VENUS CLAM **17**:251 *illus.*
WARWICK (Rhode Island) **20**:33
map (41° 43′N 71° 28′W) **16**:198
WARWICK, EDWARD, EARL OF
York (dynasty) **20**:330
WARWICK, RICHARD NEVILLE, EARL OF 20:33 *bibliog.*
Edward IV, King of England **7**:68
Roses, Wars of the **16**:316
WARWICK, THOMAS DE BEAUCHAMP, EARL OF
Richard II, King of England **16**:210
WARWICK LONG BAY
map (32° 16′N 64° 47′W) **3**:219
WARWICKSHIRE (England) **20**:33
cities
Stratford-on-Avon **18**:291
WASABI *see* HORSERADISH
WASATCH (county in Utah)
map (40° 20′N 111° 5′W) **19**:492
WASATCH PLATEAU
map (39° 20′N 111° 30′W) **19**:492
WASATCH RANGE 20:34
map (41° 15′N 111° 30′W) **19**:492
WASCO (California)
map (35° 36′N 119° 20′W) **4**:31
WASCO (Oregon)
map (45° 35′N 120° 42′W) **14**:427
WASCO (county in Oregon)
map (45° 10′N 121° 12′W) **14**:427
WASECA (Minnesota)
map (44° 5′N 93° 30′W) **13**:453
WASECA (county in Minnesota)
map (44° 0′N 93° 35′W) **13**:453
WASET *see* LUXOR (Egypt)
WASH, BAY OF THE
map (52° 55′N 0° 15′E) **19**:403
WASHAKIE 20:34 *bibliog.*
WASHAKIE (county in Wyoming)
map (43° 50′N 107° 40′W) **20**:301
WASHAKIE NEEDLES
map (43° 45′N 109° 10′W) **20**:301
WASHBURN (Illinois)
map (40° 55′N 89° 17′W) **11**:42
WASHBURN (Maine)
map (46° 47′N 68° 9′W) **13**:70
WASHBURN (North Dakota)
map (47° 17′N 101° 2′W) **14**:248
WASHBURN (Wisconsin)
map (46° 41′N 90° 52′W) **20**:185
WASHBURN (county in Wisconsin)
map (45° 52′N 91° 47′W) **20**:185
WASHBURN, MOUNT
map (44° 48′N 110° 25′W) **20**:301
WASHING MACHINE
Maytag, Frederick Louis **13**:249
WASHINGTON 20:34–39 *bibliog., illus., map*
agriculture **20**:37
cities
Olympia **14**:382
Seattle **17**:176 *illus.*
Spokane **18**:192
Tacoma **19**:6
Walla Walla **20**:13
Yakima **20**:314
climate **20**:34; **20**:36
economic activity **20**:37 *illus.*
education **20**:37
Washington, state universities and college of **20**:44
fishing **20**:37
flag **20**:34 *illus.*
forestry **20**:37
government and politics **20**:38
history **20**:38–39
land **20**:34–36 *map*
map (47° 30′N 120° 30′W) **19**:419
people **20**:36–37
Cayuse **4**:227
Nisqually **14**:201
Nootka **14**:217–218
Okanogan **14**:365
Puyallup **15**:633
Quileute-Hoh and Chemakum **16**:26
Salish **17**:34
Spokan **18**:192
Wenatchee **20**:103
Yakima **20**:314
physical features
Flattery, Cape **8**:156
Rainier, Mount **16**:78
resources **20**:36
rivers, lakes, and waterways **20**:34
Columbia River, Grand Coulee Dam **9**:285
Puget Sound **15**:617
seal, state **20**:34 *illus.*
tourism **20**:38
vegetation and animal life **20**:36
WASHINGTON (county in Alabama)
map (31° 20′N 88° 10′W) **1**:234
WASHINGTON (county in Arkansas)
map (36° 0′N 94° 15′W) **2**:166
WASHINGTON (county in Colorado)
map (40° 0′N 103° 10′W) **5**:116
WASHINGTON (county in Florida)
map (30° 40′N 85° 40′W) **8**:172
WASHINGTON (Georgia)
map (33° 44′N 82° 44′W) **9**:114
WASHINGTON (county in Georgia)
map (33° 5′N 82° 50′W) **9**:114
WASHINGTON (county in Idaho)
map (44° 30′N 116° 50′W) **11**:26
WASHINGTON (Illinois)
map (40° 42′N 89° 24′W) **11**:42
WASHINGTON (county in Illinois)
map (38° 21′N 89° 23′W) **11**:42
WASHINGTON (Indiana)
map (38° 40′N 87° 10′W) **11**:111
WASHINGTON (county in Indiana)
map (38° 36′N 86° 6′W) **11**:111
WASHINGTON (Iowa)
map (41° 18′N 91° 42′W) **11**:244
WASHINGTON (county in Iowa)
map (41° 17′N 91° 40′W) **11**:244
WASHINGTON (Kansas)
map (39° 49′N 97° 3′W) **12**:18
WASHINGTON (county in Kansas)
map (39° 50′N 97° 5′W) **12**:18
WASHINGTON (county in Kentucky)
map (37° 45′N 85° 10′W) **12**:47
WASHINGTON (county in Louisiana)
map (30° 50′N 90° 3′W) **12**:430
WASHINGTON (county in Maine)
map (45° 0′N 67° 40′W) **13**:70
WASHINGTON (county in Maryland)
map (39° 38′N 77° 45′W) **13**:188
WASHINGTON (county in Minnesota)
map (45° 5′N 92° 50′W) **13**:453
WASHINGTON (county in Mississippi)
map (33° 15′N 90° 55′W) **13**:469
WASHINGTON (Missouri)
map (38° 33′N 91° 1′W) **13**:476
WASHINGTON (county in Missouri)
map (37° 55′N 90° 50′W) **13**:476
WASHINGTON (county in Nebraska)
map (41° 30′N 96° 15′W) **14**:70
WASHINGTON (county in New York)
map (43° 20′N 73° 25′W) **14**:149
WASHINGTON (North Carolina)
map (35° 33′N 77° 3′W) **14**:242
WASHINGTON (county in North Carolina)
map (35° 50′N 76° 35′W) **14**:242
WASHINGTON (county in Ohio)
map (39° 28′N 81° 30′W) **14**:357
WASHINGTON (county in Oklahoma)
map (36° 45′N 95° 55′W) **14**:368
WASHINGTON (county in Oregon)
map (45° 33′N 123° 7′W) **14**:427
WASHINGTON (Pennsylvania)
map (40° 10′N 80° 15′W) **15**:147
WASHINGTON (county in Pennsylvania)
map (40° 12′N 80° 15′W) **15**:147
WASHINGTON (county in Rhode Island)
map (41° 28′N 71° 35′W) **16**:198
WASHINGTON (county in Tennessee)
map (36° 15′N 82° 30′W) **19**:104
WASHINGTON (county in Texas)
map (30° 15′N 96° 20′W) **19**:129
WASHINGTON (county in Utah)
map (37° 15′N 113° 25′W) **19**:492
WASHINGTON (county in Vermont)
map (44° 18′N 72° 35′W) **19**:554
WASHINGTON (Virginia)
map (38° 43′N 78° 10′W) **19**:607
WASHINGTON (county in Virginia)
map (36° 45′N 81° 55′W) **19**:607

WASHINGTON (county in Wisconsin)
map (43° 20′N 88° 15′W) **20**:185
WASHINGTON, BOOKER T. **1**:346 *illus.*; **20**:39 *bibliog.*, *illus.*
Roanoke (Virginia) **16**:239
United States, history of the **19**:452
Up from Slavery **19**:471
WASHINGTON, D.C. **19**:433 *illus.*; **20**:39–42 *bibliog.*, *illus.*, *map*
See also DISTRICT OF COLUMBIA
architecture
Capitol of the United States **4**:126
Ebbitt House **10**:260 *illus.*
Labtrobe, Benjamin Henry **12**:235
L'Enfant, Pierre Charles **12**:281–282
Mills, Robert **13**:431
urban planning **19**:482–484
White House **20**:137–138
art
Corcoran Gallery of Art **5**:261
Hirshhorn Museum and Sculpture Garden **10**:176
National Collection of Fine Arts **14**:30
National Gallery of Art **14**:33
cherry trees
Ozaki Yukio **14**:480
culture **20**:40
Dumbarton Oaks **6**:297
economy **20**:39–40
education **20**:40
American University **1**:367
Catholic University of America **4**:212
District of Columbia, University of the **6**:201
George Washington University, The **9**:110
Georgetown University **9**:112
Howard University **10**:283
Trinity College (Washington, D.C.) **19**:301
Ford's Theatre **8**:224
government **20**:40
history **20**:40
Civil War, U.S. **5**:30
Early, Jubal A. **7**:8
War of 1812 **20**:27 *illus.*
Washington, Walter **20**:44
Kennedy Center for the Performing Arts **12**:44
Ku Klux Klan in 1925 **12**:133 *illus.*
map (38° 54′N 77° 1′W) **13**:188
National Zoological Park **14**:46
people **20**:40
Smithsonian Institution **17**:372
subway **18**:318 *table*
Vietnam Veterans Memorial **19**:584 *illus.*
WASHINGTON, GEORGE **5**:213 *illus.*; **19**:442 *illus.*; **20**:42–44 *bibliog.*, *illus.*
American Revolution **1**:359 *map*; **20**:43
as president **15**:526
Conway Cabal **5**:234
dentistry **6**:115
Dinwiddie, Robert **6**:182
Dismal Swamp **6**:196
Federalist party **8**:43
French and Indian Wars **8**:313 *map*; **20**:42–43
Genêt, Edmond **9**:78–79
Gist, Christopher **9**:191
Greene, Nathanael **9**:350
isolationism **11**:299
Jefferson, Thomas **11**:392–393
Long Island, Battle of **12**:406
at Monmouth **1**:362 *illus.*
Monmouth, Battle of **13**:535
Mount Vernon (Washington's home) **13**:618; **19**:610 *illus.*
New York (city) **14**:147
Newburgh (New York state) **14**:164
Northamptonshire (England) **14**:253
portrait
Greenough, Horatio **9**:354 *illus.*
Houdon, Jean Antoine **10**:263
Peale (family) **15**:124
Rush, William **16**:347
Savage, Edward **17**:97
Stuart, Gilbert **18**:305
Sully, Thomas **18**:338
president of the United States **15**:526–527
Rushmore, Mount **16**:348
surveyor, drainage systems **6**:255
Trenton, Battle of **19**:291
triumphal entry into New York City, 1783 **1**:364 *illus.*
at Valley Forge **1**:362 *illus.*
Virginia **19**:611
Virginia politician **20**:43
Washington, Martha **20**:44
Whiskey Rebellion **20**:133
at Yorktown **1**:363 *illus.*
Yorktown Campaign **20**:331
WASHINGTON, HAROLD **20**:44
WASHINGTON, LAWRENCE
Washington, George **20**:42
WASHINGTON, MARTHA **20**:44 *bibliog.*, *illus.*
Lee, Robert E. **12**:269
WASHINGTON, MOUNT **14**:124 *illus.*; **20**:44
biome **3**:274
map (44° 15′N 71° 15′W) **14**:123
WASHINGTON, STATE UNIVERSITIES AND COLLEGE OF **20**:44
WASHINGTON, WALTER **20**:44
WASHINGTON CONFERENCE **20**:45 *bibliog.*
Japan, history of **11**:370
navy **14**:64
WASHINGTON COURT HOUSE (Ohio)
map (39° 32′N 83° 26′W) **14**:357
WASHINGTON CROSSING THE DELAWARE **1**:333 *illus.*
Düsseldorf Akademie **6**:308
Leutze, Emanuel **12**:301
WASHINGTON ISLAND
map (45° 23′N 86° 55′W) **20**:185
WASHINGTON AND LEE UNIVERSITY **20**:45
Lee (family) **12**:269
Lee, Robert E. **12**:270
WASHINGTON MONUMENT
Mills, Robert **13**:431
Washington, D.C. **20**:40 *illus.*, *map*
WASHINGTON POST, THE **20**:45 *bibliog.*
Graham, Katharine **9**:280
press agencies and syndicates **15**:533
WASHINGTON (D.C.) SCHOOL OF PSYCHIATRY
Sullivan, Harry Stack **18**:336
WASHINGTON TIMES-HERALD
Patterson (family) **15**:115
WASHINGTON(Delaware)
map (38° 54′N 77° 1′W) **6**:88
WASHITA (county in Oklahoma)
map (35° 20′N 99° 0′W) **14**:368
WASHITA RIVER
map (34° 12′N 96° 50′W) **14**:368
WASHO (American Indians) **20**:45 *bibliog.*
Indians of North America, art of the **11**:140
WASHOE (chimpanzee)
animal communication **2**:20
WASHOE (county in Nevada)
map (40° 40′N 119° 40′W) **14**:111
WASHOUGAL (Washington)
map (45° 35′N 122° 21′W) **20**:35
WASHTENAW (county in Michigan)
map (42° 15′N 83° 50′W) **13**:377
WASHTUCNA (Washington)
map (46° 45′N 118° 19′W) **20**:35
WASILLA (Alaska)
map (61° 35′N 149° 26′W) **1**:242
WASKATENAW (Alberta)
map (54° 7′N 112° 47′W) **1**:256
WASKOM (Texas)
map (32° 29′N 94° 4′W) **19**:129
WASP (Women's Airforce Service Pilots)
Cochran, Jacqueline **5**:86
WASP (zoology) **20**:45–46 *bibliog.*, *illus.*
See also FIG WASP
bee **3**:154–155
classification, biological **20**:45
digger wasp **6**:174
ichneumon fly **11**:19
mimicry **13**:435 *illus.*
WASSENAAR (Netherlands)
map (52° 7′N 4° 24′E) **14**:99
WASSERKUPPE MOUNTAIN
map (50° 30′N 9° 56′E) **9**:140
WASSERMANN, AUGUST VON **20**:46
WASSERMANN, JAKOB **20**:46 *bibliog.*
WASTE DISPOSAL SYSTEMS **20**:46–47 *bibliog.*
agricultural and mining wastes **20**:46–47
chemistry **4**:324
Chicago area **11**:44
energy recovery **20**:47
fly **8**:190
genetic engineering **9**:84
groundwater **9**:375
incinerator **11**:74
land reclamation **12**:180
landfill **12**:181
midden **13**:390
municipal and industrial wastes **20**:47
nuclear energy **14**:282
plumbing **15**:371–372 *illus.*
pollutants, chemical **15**:411
pollution control **15**:415–416
public health **15**:608
recycling of materials **16**:111
septic tank **17**:206
sewerage **17**:222–223
sludge **17**:364
solid waste
pollution, environmental **15**:413
toilet **19**:222
water supply **20**:55–57
WASTE LAND, THE (poem) **20**:47
Eliot, T. S. **7**:139–140
WASTE PRODUCTS (physiology) *see* EXCRETORY SYSTEM
WASU (Papua New Guinea)
map (6° 0′S 147° 15′E) **15**:72
WATAUGA (county in North Carolina)
map (36° 15′N 81° 40′W) **14**:242
WATAUGA ASSOCIATION **20**:47
Robertson, James **16**:242
WATAUGA LAKE
map (36° 20′N 82° 2′W) **19**:104
WATCH TOWER BIBLE AND TRACT SOCIETY
Russell, Charles Taze **16**:350
WATCHES *see* CLOCKS AND WATCHES
WATER (hydrology) **20**:47–48 *bibliog.*
aqueduct **2**:93–94
biosphere **3**:277
boiling point **3**:363
composition **20**:47–48
Cavendish, Henry **4**:225
cooling tower **5**:242
desalination **6**:124–125
dew **6**:146
dowsing **6**:252
electrolysis **7**:114
hydrogen **10**:338
oxygen **14**:477
erosion and sedimentation **7**:232–234
evapotranspiration **7**:314
firn **8**:108
fossil record **8**:244 *illus.*
freezing point **8**:300–301
fresh water **8**:328
brackish water **8**:328
glaciers and glaciation **9**:193
iceberg **11**:15
limnology **12**:345
groundwater **9**:374–375
heavy water **10**:100
hot springs **10**:259
hydroelectric power **10**:332–335
hydrogen bond **10**:340
hydrography **10**:341
hydrologic sciences **10**:342
hydrolysis **10**:342–343
hydrophilic and hydrophobic substances **10**:343
hydrotherapy **10**:344
hygroscopicity **10**:345
reaction, chemical **16**:98–99
refrigeration **16**:124–125
river and stream **16**:229–232
salinometer **17**:33
seawater **17**:177
snow and snowflake **18**:4
temperature **19**:93
triple point **19**:302
vapor pressure **19**:521
water mass **20**:49
water quality **20**:50–51
water resources **20**:51–52
water supply **20**:52–57
water table **20**:57
water wave **20**:57–60
water well **20**:60
WATER (physiology)
dehydration **6**:85
digestion, human **6**:172
diuretic drugs **6**:202
splitting
photosynthesis **15**:275
WATER BEAR (microscopic animal) **20**:48
WATER BEETLE **20**:48
WATER BOATMAN (insect) **20**:48 *illus.*
WATER BUFFALO **4**:216 *illus.*
animal husbandry **2**:23–24 *illus.*
buffalo **3**:546 *illus.*
WATER BUG **20**:48 *illus.*
WATER CHESTNUT **20**:48
WATER CLOCK *see* CLEPSYDRA
WATER CLOSET *see* TOILET
WATER CLOVER
fern **8**:56
WATER DRAGON *see* LIZARD'S TAIL (botany)
WATER FAUCET **15**:372 *illus.*
valve **19**:509 *illus.*
WATER FLEA **15**:332 *illus.*; **20**:48
WATER FOOTBALL *see* WATER POLO
WATER GLASS **20**:48
WATER HOG *see* CAPYBARA
WATER HYACINTH **20**:49 *illus.*
WATER LILY **18**:377 *illus.*; **20**:49 *illus.*
lotus **12**:420
water shield **20**:52
WATER MASS **20**:49 *bibliog.*
current **20**:49
density current **6**:114
formation **20**:49
WATER METER
Siemens (family) **17**:296
WATER MILFOIL **20**:49
WATER MOCCASIN **20**:49 *illus.*
WATER MOLD **20**:49
fish diseases **20**:49
fungi **8**:366; **20**:49
molds **13**:506
WATER OATS *see* WILD RICE
WATER PLANTAIN **20**:50
WATER POLLUTION *see* POLLUTION, ENVIRONMENTAL
WATER POLLUTION CONTROL ACT OF 1972
pollution control **15**:416
WATER POLO **20**:50 *bibliog.*, *illus.*
WATER QUALITY **20**:50–51 *bibliog.*
dissolved substances **20**:51
environmental health **7**:211
fresh water **8**:328
groundwater **9**:374–376
Nile River **14**:197
pH **20**:50
pollution, environmental **15**:411–412
pollution control **15**:416
sediment **20**:50
sludge **17**:364
spring (water) **18**:199
water resources **20**:50
WATER RESOURCES **20**:51-52 *bibliog.*, *tables*
agriculture and the food supply **1**:196
aquifer **2**:94
artesian well **2**:214
conservation **5**:202; **5**:203
desert **6**:127–128
groundwater **9**:374–376
hydrologic cycle **10**:341–342
needs **20**:50–51
North America **14**:229–230
river and stream **16**:229–232
runoff **20**:50
spring (water) **18**:199
United States **19**:426
United States, regional **20**:51 *table*
uses **20**:51–52
worldwide **20**:51 *table*
WATER SCAVENGER BEETLE *see* WATER BEETLE
WATER SHIELD (botany) **20**:52
WATER SOFTENER **20**:52
boron **3**:403
ion exchange **11**:240
marl **13**:160
water supply **20**:54–55
WATER SPANGLES
fern **8**:56
WATER SPANIEL *see* AMERICAN WATER SPANIEL; IRISH WATER SPANIEL
WATER STRIDER (insect) **20**:52 *illus.*
See also WATER BUG
WATER SUPPLY **20**:52–57 *bibliog.*, *illus.*, *table*
aqueduct **2**:93–94
California **4**:30–32
canal **4**:94–95
civil engineering **5**:10–11
Colorado **5**:119
Colorado River (Colorado) **5**:120–121 *map*
dam **6**:15–18
distribution systems **20**:54–55 *illus.*
Drinking Water Standards **20**:53
fluoridation **8**:187
history **20**:56
irrigation **11**:280–283
Nevada **14**:114
plumbing **15**:371
sewerage **17**:222–223
sources **20**:53
wastewater disposal **20**:55–57
water treatment **20**:53–54 *illus.*
Vorticella **19**:635
water usage **20**:56–57
water well **20**:60
WATER TABLE **20**:57 *bibliog.*
desert **6**:127
groundwater **9**:374–375 *illus.*

level, fluctuations **20**:57
maps **20**:57
subsidence **18**:316–317
WATER THRUSH (bird) **20**:57
WATER TRANSPORTATION *see* BOAT AND BOATING; SHIP; TRANSPORTATION
WATER TUBE BOILER
boiler **3**:362–363
WATER VALLEY (Mississippi)
map (34° 9′N 89° 38′W) **13**:469
WATER VAPOR
hydrosphere **10**:344
Legionnaires' disease **12**:274
WATER WAVE **20**:57–60 *bibliog., illus.*
bar, offshore **3**:74
berm **3**:219
coastal protection **5**:81 *illus.*
crest **20**:59 *illus.*
energy transfer **20**:58–59 *illus.*
erosion and sedimentation **7**:233
floods and flood control **8**:166–164
hurricane and typhoon **10**:317
longshore drift **12**:409
ocean-atmosphere interaction **14**:321–322
oceanography **14**:345
shoaling waves **20**:59–60
strandline **18**:288
tidal bore **19**:192
tide **19**:193
types **20**:58 *illus.*
breaker **3**:468
surf **18**:358
tsunami **19**:325
uniformitarianism **19**:386
wave periods **20**:57
wave refraction **20**:60
wave theory **20**:59
wind action **20**:170
WATER WELL **20**:60 *bibliog., illus.*
WATER WILLOW *see* LOOSESTRIFE (botany)
WATERBUCK **17**:98 *illus.*
See also ANTELOPE
WATERBURY (Connecticut) **20**:60–61
map (41° 33′N 73° 2′W) **5**:193
WATERBURY (Vermont)
map (44° 20′N 72° 46′W) **19**:554
WATERBURY RESERVOIR
map (44° 24′N 72° 45′W) **19**:554
WATERCOLOR **20**:61–62 *bibliog., illus.*
Blake, William **3**:325–326
Bonington, Richard Parkes **3**:380
Cotman, John Sell **5**:304
Cozens (family) **5**:323–324
Crome, John **5**:357
Demuth, Charles **6**:105–106
Girtin, Thomas **9**:190
Marin, John **13**:153
Milne, David **13**:431
Nolde, Emil **14**:214
painting techniques **15**:25
Sandby (family) **17**:62
Turner, Joseph Mallord William **19**:350
WATERCRESS **20**:62
cress **5**:339
nasturtium **14**:26
WATEREE LAKE
map (34° 25′N 80° 50′W) **18**:98
WATEREE RIVER
map (33° 45′N 80° 37′W) **18**:98
WATERFALL **20**:62–63 *illus.*
Angel Falls **1**:412
Bridalveil Fall **3**:479
Churchill Falls **4**:427
development **20**:63
erosion and sedimentation **20**:63
Gavarnie Falls **9**:62
Iguaçu Falls **3**:461 *illus.*; **11**:38
Kukenaam Falls **12**:135
Niagara Falls **14**:177 *illus.*
river and stream **20**:63
Sutherland Falls **18**:373
Victoria Falls **19**:575
Yosemite Falls **20**:332
WATERFORD (city in Ireland) **20**:63
map (52° 15′N 7° 6′W) **11**:258
WATERFORD (former county in Ireland) **20**:63
WATERFORD (Kentucky)
map (38° 2′N 85° 26′W) **12**:47
WATERFORD (Pennsylvania)
map (41° 57′N 79° 59′W) **15**:147
WATERFORD (Wisconsin)
map (42° 46′N 88° 13′W) **20**:185
WATERFORD GLASS **20**:63 *bibliog.*
glassware, decorative **9**:204
WATERFOWL **20**:63 *bibliog.*
game birds **9**:27
hunting **10**:313–314 *illus.*
screamer **17**:156
swamp, marsh, and bog **18**:377
WATERGATE **20**:64 *bibliog., illus.*
All the President's Men **1**:298
Bernstein, Carl, and Woodward, Bob **3**:223
building **19**:433 *illus.*
Cox, Archibald **5**:322
Dean, John W. III **6**:67
Ehrlichman, John **7**:91
Ervin, Sam, Jr. **7**:235
executive privilege **7**:329
Ford, Gerald R. **8**:221–222
Graham, Katharine **9**:280
Jaworski, Leon **11**:386
Mitchell, John N. **13**:483
Nixon, Richard M. **14**:206
Richardson, Elliot L. **16**:211
Sirica, John J. **17**:327
Supreme Court of the United States **18**:358
United States, history of the **19**:460–461
United States v. Richard M. Nixon **19**:465
Washington, D.C. **20**:41 *map*
Washington Post, The **20**:45
WATERHOUSE, KEITH **20**:64
WATERLEAF **20**:64
WATERLOO (Alabama)
map (34° 55′N 88° 4′W) **1**:234
WATERLOO (Illinois)
map (38° 20′N 90° 9′W) **11**:42
WATERLOO (Iowa)
map (42° 30′N 92° 20′W) **11**:244
WATERLOO (New York)
map (42° 54′N 76° 52′W) **14**:149
WATERLOO (Quebec)
map (45° 21′N 72° 31′W) **16**:18
WATERLOO (Wisconsin)
map (43° 11′N 88° 59′W) **20**:185
WATERLOO, BATTLE OF **2**:181 *illus.*; **9**:315 *illus.*; **20**:64–65 *bibliog., map*
Blücher, Gebhard Leberecht von **3**:341–342
Napoleon I, Emperor of the French (Napoléon Bonaparte) **14**:15–18
Napoleonic Wars **14**:20
Wellington, Arthur Wellesley, 1st Duke of **20**:100
WATERMAN, LEWIS E.
pen **15**:140
WATERMARK **20**:65 *bibliog.*
WATERMELON **20**:65
WATERPOWER ACT
Pinchot, Gifford **15**:304
WATERPROOF (Louisiana)
map (31° 48′N 91° 23′W) **12**:430
WATERPROOFING
roof and roofing **16**:306
rubber **16**:333
textiles
Macintosh, Charles **13**:26
WATERS, ETHEL **20**:65 *bibliog.*
WATERS, FRANK **20**:65 *bibliog.*
WATERS, MUDDY **20**:65
WATERSHEDS
floods and flood control **8**:167
WATERSKIING **20**:66 *bibliog., illus.*
WATERSMEET (Michigan)
map (46° 13′N 89° 11′W) **13**:377
WATERSNAKE
colubrid **5**:125
WATERSPOUT **20**:66
ocean and sea **20**:66
tornado **19**:240; **20**:66
WATERTON-GLACIER INTERNATIONAL PEACE PARK
Glacier National Park **9**:195
WATERTOWN (Connecticut)
map (41° 36′N 73° 7′W) **5**:193
WATERTOWN (Massachusetts)
map (42° 22′N 71° 11′W) **3**:409
WATERTOWN (New York)
map (43° 59′N 75° 55′W) **14**:149
WATERTOWN (South Dakota)
map (44° 54′N 97° 7′W) **18**:103
WATERTOWN (Wisconsin)
map (43° 12′N 88° 43′W) **20**:185
WATERVILLE (Kansas)
map (39° 42′N 96° 45′W) **12**:18
WATERVILLE (Maine)
map (44° 33′N 69° 38′W) **13**:70
WATERVILLE (Minnesota)
map (44° 13′N 93° 34′W) **13**:453
WATERVILLE (Ohio)
map (41° 30′N 83° 43′W) **14**:357
WATERVILLE (Washington)
map (47° 39′N 120° 4′W) **20**:35
WATERVLIET (New York)
map (42° 44′N 73° 42′W) **14**:149
WATERWAY **20**:66 *bibliog.*
beacon **3**:137
buoy **3**:565–566
canal **4**:94–97
coastal protection **5**:81
dredging **6**:268–269
harbor and port **10**:42–44
lighthouse **12**:336–337
WATERWHEEL **20**:66–67 *bibliog., illus.*
Egypt, ancient **7**:84
energy sources **20**:66–67
engine **7**:177
Iraq **11**:256 *illus.*
mill **13**:424–425 *illus.*
technology, history of **19**:63–64 *illus.*
types **20**:66–67
WATERWORKS *see* FOUNTAINS
WATFORD CITY (North Dakota)
map (47° 48′N 103° 17′W) **14**:248
WATIE, STAND **20**:67 *bibliog.*
WATINO (Alberta)
map (55° 43′N 117° 37′W) **1**:256
WATKINS, CARLETON
photography, history and art of **15**:269
WATKINS GLEN (New York)
map (42° 23′N 76° 52′W) **14**:149
WATKINS v. UNITED STATES **20**:67
WATKINSVILLE (Georgia)
map (33° 52′N 83° 25′W) **9**:114
WATLINGS ISLAND *see* SAN SALVADOR ISLAND
WATONGA (Oklahoma)
map (35° 51′N 98° 25′W) **14**:368
WATONWAN (county in Minnesota)
map (44° 0′N 94° 35′W) **13**:453
WATROUS (New Mexico)
map (35° 48′N 104° 59′W) **14**:136
WATROUS (Saskatchewan)
map (51° 40′N 105° 28′W) **17**:81
WAT'S DYKE
Offa's Dyke **14**:353
WATSEKA (Illinois)
map (40° 47′N 87° 44′W) **11**:42
WATSON (family) **20**:67 *bibliog.*
WATSON (Saskatchewan)
map (52° 7′N 104° 31′W) **17**:81
WATSON, ELKANAH **20**:67
WATSON, HOMER
Canadian art and architecture **4**:89
WATSON, JAMES D. **20**:67–68 *bibliog., illus.*
Avery, Oswald T. **2**:370
biology **3**:271 *illus.*
Crick, Francis **5**:343
genetics **9**:88
nucleic acid **14**:289
Wilkins, Maurice **20**:152
zoology **20**:378 *illus.*
WATSON, JOHN B. **20**:68 *bibliog.*
animal behavior **2**:11
behaviorism **3**:170
inner speech **11**:179
learning theory **12**:260
primary education **15**:538
psychology, history of **15**:596–597 *illus.*
WATSON, THOMAS A.
telephone **19**:79 *illus.*
WATSON, THOMAS E. **20**:68 *bibliog.*
Populist party **15**:440
WATSON, THOMAS J.
computer industry **5**:160n
WATSON, TOM **20**:68
WATSON LAKE (Yukon Territory)
map (60° 7′N 128° 48′W) **20**:345
WATSON-WATT, SIR ROBERT ALEXANDER **20**:68 *bibliog.*
radar, inventor **20**:68
WATSON-WENTWORTH, CHARLES, 2D MARQUESS OF ROCKINGHAM *see* ROCKINGHAM, CHARLES WATSON-WENTWORTH, 2D MARQUESS OF
WATSONTOWN (Pennsylvania)
map (41° 5′N 76° 52′W) **15**:147
WATSONVILLE (California)
map (36° 55′N 121° 45′W) **4**:31
WATT **20**:68
measurement **20**:68
units, physical **19**:466–467 *table*
WATT, JAMES **20**:68–69 *bibliog., illus.*
steam engine **18**:241 *illus.*
feedback **8**:44 *illus.*
technology, history of **19**:65–66 *illus.*
WATT, JAMES G.
Interior, United States Department of the **11**:210
WATT, SIR ROBERT ALEXANDER WATSON- *see* WATSON-WATT, SIR ROBERT ALEXANDER
WATTEAU, ANTOINE **20**:69 *bibliog., illus.*
Gillot, Claude **9**:182
La Gamme d'Amour **20**:69 *illus.*
Pater, Jean Baptiste Joseph **15**:110
A Pilgrimage to Cythera **15**:21 *illus.*; **16**:264 *illus.*
WATTERSON, HENRY **20**:69 *bibliog.*
WATTLE (botany)
acacia **1**:68
WATTS (Los Angeles)
California **4**:37
WATTS, CHARLIE
Rolling Stones, The **16**:272
WATTS, GEORGE FREDERIC **20**:69 *bibliog.*
Matthew Arnold **2**:185 *illus.*
WATTS, ISAAC **20**:69
hymn **10**:346
WATTS BAR LAKE
map (35° 48′N 84° 39′W) **19**:104
WATTS TOWERS **20**:69–70 *bibliog.*
WATTSVILLE (South Carolina)
map (34° 31′N 82° 2′W) **18**:98
WATUPPA POND
map (41° 42′N 71° 6′W) **16**:198
WATUTSI *see* TUTSI
WAUBAY LAKE
map (45° 25′N 97° 25′W) **18**:103
WAUCHULA (Florida)
map (27° 33′N 81° 49′W) **8**:172
WAUCONDA (Washington)
map (48° 44′N 118° 59′W) **20**:35
WAUGH (Manitoba)
map (49° 40′N 95° 13′W) **13**:119
WAUGH, EVELYN **20**:70 *bibliog., illus.*
WAUGH, HILLARY **20**:70
WAUGHT, SIDNEY
glassware, decorative **9**:204
WAUKEGAN (Illinois) **20**:70
map (42° 22′N 87° 50′W) **11**:42
WAUKESHA (Wisconsin)
map (43° 1′N 88° 14′W) **20**:185
WAUKESHA (county in Wisconsin)
map (43° 2′N 88° 20′W) **20**:185
WAUKOMIS (Oklahoma)
map (36° 15′N 97° 53′W) **14**:368
WAUKON (Iowa)
map (43° 16′N 91° 29′W) **11**:244
WAUNETA (Nebraska)
map (40° 25′N 101° 23′W) **14**:70
WAUPACA (Wisconsin)
map (44° 21′N 89° 5′W) **20**:185
WAUPACA (county in Wisconsin)
map (44° 30′N 89° 0′W) **20**:185
WAUPUN (Wisconsin)
map (43° 38′N 88° 44′W) **20**:185
WAURIKA (Oklahoma)
map (34° 10′N 98° 0′W) **14**:368
WAUSA (Nebraska)
map (42° 30′N 97° 32′W) **14**:70
WAUSAU (Wisconsin)
map (44° 59′N 89° 39′W) **20**:185
WAUSAUKEE (Wisconsin)
map (45° 23′N 87° 57′W) **20**:185
WAUSEON (Ohio)
map (41° 33′N 84° 9′W) **14**:357
WAUSHARA (county in Wisconsin)
map (44° 8′N 89° 15′W) **20**:185
WAUTOMA (Wisconsin)
map (44° 4′N 89° 17′W) **20**:185
WAUWATOSA (Wisconsin)
map (43° 3′N 88° 0′W) **20**:185
WAUZEKA (Wisconsin)
map (43° 5′N 90° 52′W) **20**:185
WAVE, WATER *see* WATER WAVE
WAVE MECHANICS *see* QUANTUM MECHANICS; WAVES AND WAVE MOTION
WAVE REFRACTION
coastal protection **5**:81 *illus.*
water wave **20**:60
WAVEFORM MONITOR (video technology) **19**:86
WAVEGUIDE **20**:70
electron tube **7**:123
WAVELL, ARCHIBALD PERCIVAL WAVELL, 1st EARL **20**:70–71 *bibliog.*
WAVELLITE **20**:71
WAVERLY (Alabama)
map (32° 44′N 85° 35′W) **1**:234
WAVERLY (Iowa)
map (42° 44′N 92° 29′W) **11**:244
WAVERLY (Kansas)
map (38° 23′N 95° 36′W) **12**:18
WAVERLY (Minnesota)
map (45° 4′N 93° 57′W) **13**:453
WAVERLY (Missouri)
map (39° 12′N 93° 31′W) **13**:476
WAVERLY (Nebraska)
map (40° 55′N 96° 32′W) **14**:70
WAVERLY (New York)
map (42° 0′N 76° 32′W) **14**:149
WAVERLY (Ohio)
map (39° 7′N 82° 59′W) **14**:357
WAVERLY (Tennessee)
map (36° 5′N 87° 48′W) **19**:104
WAVERLY (Virginia)
map (37° 2′N 77° 6′W) **19**:607

WAVERLY HALL (Georgia)
  map (32° 41′N 84° 44′W) **9**:114
WAVES (hydrology) *see* WATER WAVE
WAVES (Women in the Naval Service) **20**:71 *bibliog.*
WAVES AND WAVE MOTION **20**:71–72 *bibliog., illus.*
  Compton effect **5**:159
  damping **6**:19
  diffraction **6**:169
  Doppler effect **6**:240–241
  earthquakes **7**:25–28
  electromagnetic radiation **7**:116–118
  electron optics **7**:122
  Fizeau, Armand Hippolyte Louis **8**:133
  frequency **8**:326
  gravitational waves **9**:306
  Grimaldi, Francesco Maria **9**:364
  ground wave **9**:373
  harmonics **10**:51
  holography **10**:207–208
  interference (physics) **11**:207–209
  light **12**:335–336 *illus.*
  magnetohydrodynamics **13**:59
  Maxwell's equations **13**:242
  microseism **13**:388
  microwaves **13**:389
  modulation **13**:499–500
  motion, harmonic **13**:608–609
  Munk, Walter **13**:643
  optics **14**:410 *illus.*
  oscillating source **20**:71 *illus.*
  oscillator **14**:453
  physics, history of **15**:285
  polarized light **15**:394–395
  quantum mechanics **16**:10–11
  radiation **16**:42
  radio **16**:44; **20**:72
    Hertz, Heinrich Rudolph **10**:149
    pulsar **15**:620
    Whistler **20**:134
  Rayleigh, Lord **16**:97
  red shift **16**:114
  refraction **16**:123–124
  resonance (physics) **16**:178
  Schrödinger, Erwin **17**:135
  sound and acoustics **18**:72–73 *illus.*
  standing wave **18**:217; **20**:72
  superimposed vibration **20**:72
  ultrasonics **19**:377–378
  wave characteristics **20**:71
  wave motion **20**:71–72
  wave types **20**:71
  waveguide **20**:70
WAW (letter)
  V (letter) **19**:500
WAW (Sudan)
  climate **18**:320 *table*
  map (7° 42′N 28° 0′E) **18**:320
WAWASSEE, LAKE
  map (41° 24′N 85° 41′W) **11**:111
WAWMEGIN
  Massasoit **13**:213
WAX **12**:361 *illus.*; **20**:72 *bibliog.*
  bee **3**:154; **3**:156–157
  candle **4**:107
  carnauba wax **4**:154
  lipid **12**:361
WAX MUSEUM
  Tussaud, Madame **19**:355
WAX MYRTLE *see* BAYBERRY
WAXAHACHIE (Texas)
  map (32° 24′N 96° 51′W) **19**:129
WAXBERRY *see* SNOWBERRY
WAXBILL **20**:72–73
  cordon bleu (bird) **5**:261
  ricebird **16**:209
WAXEN FLEXIBILITY *see* CATALEPSY
WAXHAW (North Carolina)
  map (34° 55′N 80° 45′W) **14**:242
WAXWING **20**:73 *illus.*
  Bohemian waxwing **8**:229 *illus.*
  hypocolius **10**:351
  silky flycatcher **17**:308
WAY OF ALL FLESH, THE (book) **20**:73
  Butler, Samuel (1835–1902) **3**:592
WAY OF THE WORLD, THE (play) **20**:73
  Congreve, William **5**:188
WAYCROSS (Georgia)
  map (31° 13′N 82° 21′W) **9**:114
WAYLAND (Iowa)
  map (41° 8′N 91° 40′W) **11**:244
WAYLAND (Massachusetts)
  map (42° 22′N 71° 22′W) **3**:409
WAYLAND (Michigan)
  map (42° 40′N 85° 39′W) **13**:377
WAYLAND (New York)
  map (42° 34′N 77° 35′W) **14**:149
WAYLAND, FRANCIS **20**:73 *bibliog.*
WAYLYN (South Carolina)
  map (32° 51′N 80° 0′W) **18**:98
WAYNE (county in Georgia)
  map (31° 35′N 82° 0′W) **9**:114
WAYNE (county in Illinois)
  map (38° 25′N 88° 25′W) **11**:42
WAYNE (county in Indiana)
  map (39° 50′N 84° 54′W) **11**:111
WAYNE (county in Iowa)
  map (40° 45′N 93° 15′W) **11**:244
WAYNE (county in Kentucky)
  map (36° 50′N 84° 50′W) **12**:47
WAYNE (county in Michigan)
  map (42° 15′N 83° 15′W) **13**:377
WAYNE (county in Mississippi)
  map (31° 40′N 88° 40′W) **13**:469
WAYNE (county in Missouri)
  map (37° 5′N 90° 25′W) **13**:476
WAYNE (Nebraska)
  map (42° 14′N 97° 1′W) **14**:70
WAYNE (county in Nebraska)
  map (42° 10′N 97° 5′W) **14**:70
WAYNE (New Jersey)
  map (40° 55′N 74° 17′W) **14**:129
WAYNE (county in New York)
  map (43° 4′N 77° 0′W) **14**:149
WAYNE (county in North Carolina)
  map (35° 25′N 78° 0′W) **14**:242
WAYNE (county in Ohio)
  map (40° 48′N 81° 56′W) **14**:357
WAYNE (Oklahoma)
  map (34° 55′N 97° 19′W) **14**:368
WAYNE (county in Pennsylvania)
  map (41° 34′N 75° 16′W) **15**:147
WAYNE (county in Tennessee)
  map (35° 15′N 87° 50′W) **19**:104
WAYNE (county in Utah)
  map (38° 20′N 109° 55′W) **19**:492
WAYNE (West Virginia)
  map (38° 13′N 82° 27′W) **20**:111
WAYNE (county in West Virginia)
  map (38° 10′N 82° 25′W) **20**:111
WAYNE, ANTHONY **20**:73 *bibliog.*
  Fallen Timbers, Battle of **8**:14
  Fort Wayne (Indiana) **8**:238
WAYNE, JOHN **20**:73–74 *bibliog., illus.*
  Ford, John (film director) **8**:223
WAYNE CITY (Illinois)
  map (38° 21′N 88° 38′W) **11**:42
WAYNESBORO (Georgia)
  map (33° 6′N 82° 1′W) **9**:114
WAYNESBORO (Mississippi)
  map (31° 40′N 88° 39′W) **13**:469
WAYNESBORO (Pennsylvania)
  map (39° 45′N 77° 35′W) **15**:147
WAYNESBORO (Tennessee)
  map (35° 19′N 87° 45′W) **19**:104
WAYNESBORO (Virginia)
  map (38° 4′N 78° 53′W) **19**:607
WAYNESBURG (Ohio)
  map (40° 40′N 81° 16′W) **14**:357
WAYNESBURG (Pennsylvania)
  map (39° 54′N 80° 11′W) **15**:147
WAYNESVILLE (Missouri)
  map (37° 50′N 92° 12′W) **13**:476
WAYNESVILLE (North Carolina)
  map (35° 29′N 83° 0′W) **14**:242
WCTU **20**:74 *bibliog.*; **20**:203 *illus.*
  temperance movement **19**:92
  Willard, Frances **20**:154
WEAK NUCLEAR FORCE
  electroweak theory **7**:128
  fundamental interactions **8**:361
  fundamental particles **8**:362
  grand unification theories **9**:286
WEAKFISH **20**:74
WEAKLEY (county in Tennessee)
  map (36° 20′N 88° 35′W) **19**:104
WEALTH
  economics **7**:48
  money **13**:526
WEALTH OF NATIONS, AN INQUIRY INTO THE NATURE AND CAUSES OF THE (book) **20**:74 *bibliog.*
  economics **7**:48
  Smith, Adam **17**:366–367
WEAPONS **20**:74–75 *bibliog.*
  aircraft, military **1**:214–220
  ammunition **1**:373–375 *illus.*
  armored vehicle **2**:175–177
  arrowhead (artifact) **2**:188
  artillery **2**:222–224
  atomic bomb **2**:307–308
  battering ram **3**:125
  battering weapons **8**:238; **8**:239 *illus.*
  battle-axe, prehistoric **7**:302 *illus.*
  bayonet **3**:134
  bazooka **3**:135
  blowgun **3**:341
  bolt hurling **8**:238; **8**:239 *illus.*
  bomb **3**:373–374
  boomerang **3**:393
  bow and arrow **3**:426–427
  Browning, John Moses **3**:518
  cannon **4**:111–112
  catapult **4**:200
  cavalry **4**:221–222
  chemical and biological warfare **4**:311–313
  derringer **6**:123
  early weapons **20**:74
  European prehistory **7**:304
  explosives **7**:339
  firearms **8**:105–106
  Garand, John Cantius **9**:38
  garrote **9**:51
  Gatling, Richard Jordan **9**:58
  Greek fire **9**:342
  grenade **9**:358
  howitzer **10**:285
  human factors engineering **10**:297
  hydrogen bomb **10**:339–340
  infantry **11**:163–164
  knight **12**:100 *illus.*
  Krupp (family) **12**:132
  Lindemann, Frederick Alexander **12**:351
  machine gun **13**:21–23
  mass production
    Whitney, Eli **20**:141
  Maxim (family) **13**:239
  microwave radar
    Lindemann, Frederick Alexander **12**:351
  mine **13**:437–438
  mortar **13**:591
  musket **13**:682–683
  napalm **14**:14
  naval vessels **14**:54–57
  neutron bomb **14**:109
  night sights **14**:193
  nuclear strategy **14**:288
  obsidian **14**:319
  pistol **15**:317–318
  radio-controlled
    Hammond, John Hays, Jr. **10**:31
  recent history **20**:75
  recoilless rifle **16**:108
  revolver **16**:189–190
  rifle **16**:219–221
  rockets and missiles **16**:251–260
  shotgun **17**:285–286
  shrapnel **17**:286
  strategy and tactics, military **18**:289–291
  sword and knife **18**:397–399
  tear gas **19**:58
    Mace **13**:14
  technology, history of **19**:62; **19**:64–65
  tomahawk **19**:229
  torpedo **19**:242–243
  V-2 **19**:500–501
  war **20**:24–25
  weapons trade **20**:75–76
  White Sands Missile Range **20**:138
  Whitehead, Robert **20**:139
  World War I **20**:246–248 *illus.*
  World War II **20**:266–268 *illus.*; **20**:273–275 *illus.*
WEAPONS TRADE **20**:75–76 *bibliog.*
WEASEL **20**:76 *bibliog., illus.*
  Arctic **2**:140–141 *illus.*
  ermine **7**:231
  ferret **8**:59
  grison **9**:367
  marten **13**:175–176
  mink **13**:451
  otter **14**:461
  Pleistocene Epoch **15**:366 *illus.*
  polecat **15**:395
  ratel **16**:92
  sable **17**:5–6
  sea otter **17**:169
  skunk **17**:346
  tayra **19**:51
  wolverine **20**:200
WEATHER BUREAU, U.S. *see* NATIONAL WEATHER SERVICE
WEATHER FORECASTING **20**:76–79 *bibliog., illus.*
  atmosphere **2**:298
  atmospheric sciences **2**:304
  averaging techniques
    Namias, Jerome **14**:10
  Bjerknes, Vilhelm and Jacob **3**:302
  climate **5**:55–58
  computer **5**:160f
  Coriolis effect **5**:263
  hurricane and typhoon **10**:317–319
  meteorological instrumentation **13**:339
  meteorology **13**:341
  monsoon **13**:544
  National Meteorological Center **14**:35
  National Oceanic and Atmospheric Administration **14**:35
  radar meteorology **16**:41
  sandstorm and dust storm **17**:64
  warning systems
    floods and flood control **8**:167
    National Hurricane Center **20**:78
    Severe Storms Forecast Center **20**:78
  weather modification **20**:80–81
  weather observatory **13**:340 *illus.*
  weather reconnaissance aircraft
    meteorology **13**:343 *illus.*
  weather satellite
    GOES (artificial satellite) **9**:222
    Nimbus (artificial satellite) **14**:198
    space exploration **18**:123
    TIROS **19**:209
    World Weather Watch **20**:281
  weather variation and extremes **20**:81–82
  Willett, Hurd Curtis **20**:154
WEATHER LORE
  meteorology **13**:341
WEATHER MAPS
  isogram **11**:299
WEATHER MODIFICATION **20**:80–81 *bibliog.*
  cloud **5**:66–68
  cloud seeding
    drought **6**:273–274
    Schaefer, Vincent Joseph **17**:116
    snow and snowflake **18**:4
  hydrologic cycle **10**:341–341
  radar meteorology **16**:41
  weather variation and extremes **20**:81–82
WEATHER VARIATION AND EXTREMES **20**:81–82 *bibliog., tables*
  See also CLIMATE; TEMPERATURE
  agriculture and the food supply **1**:196
  atmosphere **2**:302
  blizzard **3**:333
  continental climate **5**:227–228
  cumulonimbus clouds **5**:388
  cyclone and anticyclone **5**:405–406
  dendrochronology, effect **6**:107
  dew **6**:146
  dog days **6**:221
  drought **6**:273–274
  dust, atmospheric **6**:308
  dust devil **6**:308–309
  fog **8**:193
  front **8**:339–340
  frost **8**:345
  frostbite **8**:346
  hail and hailstones **10**:12
  high-pressure region **10**:162
  hoarfrost **10**:191
  humidity **10**:302
  hurricane and typhoon **10**:317–319
  hypothermia **10**:351
  ice ages **11**:7–11
  jet stream **11**:407–408
  low-pressure region **12**:443
  meteorology **13**:341
  mist **13**:481
  monsoon **13**:543–544
  paleotemperature **15**:42
  population dynamics **15**:438
  precipitation, worldwide **20**:82 *table*
  reporting
    Fletcher's Ice Island **8**:163
  services
    National Weather Service **14**:46
    World Meteorological Organization **20**:219
    World Weather Watch **20**:281
  snow and snowflake **18**:4 *table*
  soil **18**:36–38
  squall and squall line **18**:201–202
  thunderstorm **19**:185
  TIROS (artificial satellite) **19**:208–209
  troposphere **19**:310
  water wave **20**:60
  waterspout **20**:66
  weather forecasting **20**:76–79
  weather modification **20**:80–81
  westerlies **20**:115
  whirlwind **20**:132
  wind **20**:168–170
  wind chill **20**:170
WEATHERFISH *see* LOACH
WEATHERFORD (Oklahoma)
  map (35° 32′N 98° 42′W) **14**:368
WEATHERFORD (Texas)
  map (32° 46′N 97° 48′W) **19**:129
WEATHERFORD, WILLIAM **20**:82 *bibliog.*
WEATHERING **20**:82–83 *bibliog., illus.*
  chemical reactions **20**:82–83
  cobble **5**:84
  Earth sciences **7**:24
  erosion and sedimentation **7**:232
  exfoliation **7**:331
  frost action **8**:346
  geochemistry **9**:96

laterite **12**:215
mineral end products **20**:82–83
paleoclimatology **15**:32–34
process **20**:82
sediment, marine **17**:184
soil **18**:36–38
valley and ridge province **19**:508
WEATHERMEN (radical group) *see* STUDENTS FOR A DEMOCRATIC SOCIETY
WEAUBLEAU (Missouri)
map (37° 54′N 93° 32′W) **13**:476
WEAVER (Alabama)
map (33° 45′N 85° 49′W) **1**:234
WEAVER (bird) **20**:83 *illus.*
quelea **16**:22–23
WEAVER, JAMES B. **20**:83
Populist party **15**:440
WEAVER, ROBERT C. **20**:83
WEAVER, SYLVESTER L. (PAT)
radio and television broadcasting **16**:58
WEAVER, WARREN
communication **5**:143
WEAVER FINCH **20**:83
mannikin **13**:125
WEAVERBIRD **17**:98 *illus.*
WEAVERVILLE (North Carolina)
map (35° 42′N 82° 34′W) **14**:242
WEAVING **20**:83–85 *bibliog., illus.*
Arkwright, Sir Richard **2**:170
basic weaves **20**:85 *illus.*
carpet industry **4**:165
Chinese art and architecture **4**:384
Gobelins **9**:216
history **20**:83–84
Kay, John **12**:32–33
loom **12**:410–411
Jacquard, Joseph Marie **11**:347
Navajo **14**:54
Paracas **15**:74
rugs and carpets **16**:340
silk **17**:307
spinning **18**:186
tapestry **19**:31–33
textile industry **19**:136–137 *illus.*
WEB-FED PRESS **20**:85–86 *bibliog.*
printing process designation **20**:85
rotogravure **16**:323
WEB SPINNER **20**:86 *illus.*
WEBB (county in Texas)
map (27° 40′N 99° 15′W) **19**:129
WEBB, SIR ASTON
Buckingham Palace **3**:536 *illus.*
WEBB, MATTHEW
English Channel **7**:189
WEBB, PHILIP
Morris, William **13**:589
WEBB, SIDNEY AND BEATRICE **18**:20 *illus.*; **20**:86 *bibliog., illus.*
WEBB, WALTER PRESCOTT **20**:86 *bibliog.*
WEBB CITY (Missouri)
map (37° 9′N 94° 28′W) **13**:476
WEBB KENYON ACT
Leisy v. *Hardin* **12**:279
WEBBER, ANDREW LLOYD
musical comedy **13**:675
WEBER (measurement)
units, physical **19**:467 *table*
WEBER (county in Utah)
map (41° 15′N 111° 55′W) **19**:492
WEBER, CARL MARIA VON **20**:86–87 *bibliog., illus.*
WEBER, DICK **20**:87
WEBER, ERNST
psychophysics **15**:602
WEBER, JOSEPH (scientist)
gravitational waves **9**:306
WEBER, JOSEPH, AND FIELDS, LEW (comedy team) **20**:87
WEBER, MAX (painter) **20**:87 *bibliog.*
WEBER, MAX (sociologist) **20**:87 *bibliog., illus.*
alienation **1**:294
bureaucracy **3**:567
class, social **5**:40
Protestant ethic **15**:576
sociology **18**:29 *illus.*
state (in political philosophy) **18**:233
status **18**:238
WEBER, WILHELM EDUARD **20**:88 *bibliog.*
electrical force, law of **20**:88
Gauss, Carl Friedrich **20**:88
WEBER-FECHNER LAW
Fechner, Gustav Theodor **8**:40
WEBERN, ANTON VON **20**:88 *bibliog.*
Stockhausen, Karlheinz **18**:275
WEBSPINNER *see* EMBIOPTERA
WEBSTER (Alberta)
map (55° 26′N 118° 42′W) **1**:256
WEBSTER (Florida)
map (28° 37′N 82° 3′W) **8**:172
WEBSTER (county in Georgia)
map (32° 3′N 84° 35′W) **9**:114
WEBSTER (county in Iowa)
map (42° 28′N 94° 12′W) **11**:244
WEBSTER (county in Kentucky)
map (37° 30′N 87° 40′W) **12**:47
WEBSTER (county in Louisiana)
map (32° 40′N 93° 17′W) **12**:430
WEBSTER (Massachusetts)
map (42° 3′N 71° 53′W) **13**:206
WEBSTER (county in Mississippi)
map (33° 35′N 89° 15′W) **13**:469
WEBSTER (county in Missouri)
map (37° 15′N 92° 50′W) **13**:476
WEBSTER (county in Nebraska)
map (40° 10′N 98° 30′W) **14**:70
WEBSTER (South Dakota)
map (45° 20′N 97° 31′W) **18**:103
WEBSTER (county in West Virginia)
map (38° 30′N 80° 22′W) **20**:111
WEBSTER, DANIEL **20**:88 *bibliog., illus.*
Compromise of 1850 **5**:158
Hayne, Robert Young **10**:83–84
Whig party (United States) **20**:130–131
WEBSTER, JOHN **20**:89 *bibliog.*
WEBSTER, MARGARET **20**:89 *bibliog.*
WEBSTER, NOAH **20**:89 *bibliog., illus.*
American Speller
primary education **15**:537
English language **7**:193
WEBSTER-ASHBURTON TREATY **20**:89 *bibliog.*
Webster, Daniel **20**:88
WEBSTER CITY (Iowa)
map (42° 28′N 93° 49′W) **11**:244
WEBSTER RESERVOIR
map (39° 23′N 99° 26′W) **12**:18
WEBSTER SPRINGS (West Virginia)
map (38° 29′N 80° 25′W) **20**:111
WECHSLER, DAVID
psychology, history of **15**:598
WEDDELL, JAMES
Antarctica **2**:44 *map*
WEDDELL SEA **20**:89
map (72° 0′S 45° 0′W) **2**:40
WEDDELL SEAL **2**:42–43 *illus.*
WEDDING *see* MARRIAGE
WEDEKIND, FRANK **20**:89 *bibliog.*
drama **6**:261
WEDGE
simple machines **17**:316
WEDGEPORT (Nova Scotia)
map (43° 44′N 65° 59′W) **14**:269
WEDGWOOD, JOSIAH **20**:89–90 *bibliog., illus.*
abolitionist medallion **17**:355 *illus.*
Flaxman, John **8**:158
jasper ware **20**:90 *illus.*
pottery and porcelain **15**:472 *illus.*
terra-cotta **19**:120
WEDGWOOD, THOMAS **20**:90 *bibliog.*
WEDNESDAY
calendar **4**:28
WEDOWEE (Alabama)
map (33° 19′N 85° 29′W) **1**:234
WEED
chickweed **4**:346
Lambert crazyweed **9**:300 *illus.*
waterweed **12**:168 *illus.*
WEED (California)
map (41° 25′N 122° 23′W) **4**:31
WEED, THURLOW **20**:90 *bibliog.*
WEEDVILLE (Pennsylvania)
map (41° 17′N 78° 30′W) **15**:147
WEEGEE **20**:90
WEEK
calendar **4**:28
WEELKES, THOMAS **20**:90 *bibliog.*
WEEMS, MASON L.
Washington, George **20**:44
WEEMS, P. V. H.
Institute of Navigation, founder **11**:195
WEEPING TEA TREE *see* PAPERBARK
WEEPING WATER (Nebraska)
map (40° 52′N 96° 8′W) **14**:70
WEEPING WILLOW **20**:163 *illus.*
WEERT (Netherlands)
map (51° 15′N 5° 43′E) **14**:99
WEESE, HARRY **20**:90 *bibliog.*
WEEVER **20**:90–91 *illus.*
WEEVERFISH *see* WEEVER
WEEVIL **20**:91 *illus.*
sweet potato snout weevil **3**:167 *illus.*
WEGENER, ALFRED LOTHAR **20**:91 *bibliog., illus.*
continental drift **5**:228
Greenland research expeditions **20**:91
paleogeography **15**:36–37 *illus.*
plate tectonics **15**:357
WEGNER, HANS
Scandinavian art and architecture **17**:114
WEI RIVER
map (34° 30′N 110° 20′E) **10**:326
WEICHI *see* GO
WEIDEN (Germany, East and West)
map (49° 41′N 12° 10′E) **9**:140
WEIDENREICH, FRANZ **20**:91
Meganthropus **13**:280
Peking man **15**:136
WEIDMAN, CHARLES **20**:91 *bibliog.*
WEIERSTRASS, KARL THEODOR **20**:91–92 *bibliog.*
mathematics, history of **13**:226
WEIGEL, HELENE **20**:92
Berliner Ensemble **3**:218
WEIGELA **20**:92
WEIGHT (mathematics) **20**:92
WEIGHT (physics) **20**:92
atomic weight **2**:311–312
measurement **13**:254–255
molecular weight **13**:507
pound **15**:475
weights and measures **20**:93 *table*
WEIGHT LIFTING (sport) **20**:92 *bibliog.*
Alexeyev, Vasily **1**:278
Olympic Games **14**:384 *illus.*
WEIGHT LOSS *see* DIETING
WEIGHTLESSNESS **20**:92 *bibliog.*
biosatellite **3**:276
free fall **8**:294
space medicine **18**:133 *illus.*
WEIGHTS AND MEASURES **20**:92–94 *bibliog., table*
See also UNITS, PHYSICAL
balance **3**:30–31
International Bureau of Weights and Measures **11**:219
measurement **13**:253–257
metric system **13**:345–347
National Bureau of Standards **14**:30
Stevin, Simon **18**:265
units and equivalents **20**:93 *table*
WEIL, SIMONE **20**:94 *bibliog.*
WEILL, KURT **20**:94 *bibliog.*
Threepenny Opera, The **13**:674 *illus.*; **19**:182
WEIL'S DISEASE *see* LEPTOSPIROSIS
WEIMAR (East Germany) **20**:94
map (50° 59′N 11° 19′E) **9**:140
WEIMAR REPUBLIC **20**:94–95
Ebert, Friedrich **7**:35
Germany, history of **9**:155–156
Hindenburg, Paul von **10**:169
Müller, Hermann **13**:636
Prussia **15**:585–586
Rathenau, Walther **16**:92
Scheidemann, Philipp **17**:118
Schleicher, Kurt von **17**:124
Stresemann, Gustav **18**:297
theater, history of the **19**:148
WEIMARANER **6**:218 *illus.*; **20**:95 *bibliog., illus.*
WEINBERG, STEVEN **20**:95
unified field theory **19**:386
Weinberg-Salam theory **19**:386
WEINBERG, WILHELM
biology **3**:271
evolution **7**:319
population gentics **15**:439
WEINBERG-SALAM THEORY
unified field theory **19**:386
WEINBERGER, CASPAR WILLARD **20**:95
WEINBERGER, JAROMÍR **20**:95
WEINER (Arkansas)
map (35° 37′N 90° 54′W) **2**:166
WEINGARTNER, FELIX **20**:95 *bibliog.*
WEIPA (Australia)
map (12° 41′S 141° 52′E) **2**:328
WEIR (Mississippi)
map (33° 16′N 89° 17′W) **13**:469
WEIR, BOB
Grateful Dead, The **9**:301
WEIR, JOHN FERGUSON
Forging the Shaft: A Welding Heat **11**:159 *illus.*; **13**:330 *illus.*
WEIR, JULIAN ALDEN **20**:95 *bibliog.*
WEIR RIVER (Manitoba)
map (56° 49′N 94° 4′W) **13**:119
WEIRSDALE (Florida)
map (28° 59′N 81° 55′W) **8**:172
WEIRTON (Ohio)
map (40° 25′N 80° 35′W) **14**:357
WEIRTON (West Virginia)
map (40° 25′N 80° 35′W) **20**:111
WEISER (German banking house)
Venezuela **19**:544
WEISER (Idaho)
map (44° 15′N 116° 58′W) **11**:26
WEISMANN, AUGUST **20**:95 *bibliog.*
heredity and evolution **20**:95
WEISS, CHRISTIAN
crystal **5**:374–376
WEISS, EHRICH *see* HOUDINI, HARRY
WEISS, PETER **20**:95–96 *bibliog.*
theater of fact **19**:153
WEISS, PIERRE
magnetism **13**:56–57
WEISS-CURIE'S LAW
Curie, Marie and Pierre **5**:391
WEISS LAKE
map (34° 15′N 85° 35′W) **1**:234
WEISSENBORN, CAROLINA *see* NEUBER, CAROLINA
WEISSENBURG (Germany, East and West)
map (49° 1′N 10° 58′E) **9**:140
WEISSENBURG, OTFRIED VON
German literature **9**:132
WEISSENFELS (Germany, East and West)
map (51° 12′N 11° 58′E) **9**:140
WEISSENHOF EXHIBITION (1927)
Mies van der Rohe, Ludwig **13**:415
WEISSMULLER, JOHNNY **20**:96 *bibliog.*
WEITZ, PAUL J. **20**:96 *bibliog.*
Skylab **17**:347–348; **20**:96
space medicine **18**:133 *illus.*
WEIZMANN, CHAIM **20**:96 *bibliog.*
WEJHEROWO (Poland)
map (54° 37′N 18° 15′E) **15**:388
WELAKA (Florida)
map (29° 29′N 81° 40′W) **8**:172
WELCH (Texas)
map (32° 56′N 102° 8′W) **19**:129
WELCH (West Virginia)
map (37° 25′N 81° 31′W) **20**:111
WELCH, JAMES **20**:96
WELCOME (Minnesota)
map (43° 40′N 94° 37′W) **13**:453
WELCOME (South Carolina)
map (34° 49′N 82° 26′W) **18**:98
WELD, THEODORE DWIGHT **20**:96 *bibliog.*
Grimké, Sarah Moore and Angelina Emily **9**:365
WELDING AND SOLDERING **20**:96–97 *bibliog., illus.*
atomic hydrogen torch
Langmuir, Irving **12**:196
electrode **7**:113
metallurgy **13**:331
oxidation inhibitor, inert gases **11**:161
oxygen **14**:477
shipbuilding **17**:276
solder, lead **12**:256
WELDON (Illinois)
map (40° 7′N 88° 45′W) **11**:42
WELDON (North Carolina)
map (36° 25′N 77° 36′W) **14**:242
WELDON, FAY **20**:97
WELDON, WALTER **20**:97
WELENSKY, SIR ROY **20**:97 *bibliog.*
WELF (family) **20**:97 *bibliog.*
Conrad III, King of Germany and Holy Roman Emperor **5**:199
German territories c.1176 **9**:149 *map*
Guelphs and Ghibellines **9**:390
Otto IV, King of German and Holy Roman Emperor **14**:463
Saxony **17**:105
WELFARE *see* SOCIAL AND WELFARE SERVICES
WELFARE STATE **20**:97–98 *bibliog., table*
Great Britain
Beveridge, William Henry **3**:232
Great Britain, history of **9**:318
Lloyd George, David, 1st Earl Lloyd-George of Dwyfor **12**:383
social security **18**:14
socialism **18**:24
Wagner, Robert F., Sr. **20**:5
welfare spending in selected countries **20**:98 *table*
WELHAVEN, JOHAN SEBASTIAN CAMMERMEYER
Norwegian literature **14**:265
WELIGAMA (Sri Lanka)
map (5° 58′N 80° 25′E) **18**:206
WELK, LAWRENCE **20**:98–99
WELKOM (South Africa)
map (27° 59′S 26° 45′E) **18**:79
WELL
See also DRILLING; PETROLEUM; WATER WELL
WELL-MADE PLAY **20**:99
Augier, Émile **2**:319
Bridie, James **3**:485
Scribe, Eugène **17**:158
WELLAND (Ontario)

WELLAND (cont.)
map (42° 59′N 79° 15′W) **14**:393; **19**:241
WELLAND SHIP CANAL 7:230 *map*; **20**:99
map (43° 14′N 79° 13′W) **14**:149
WELLBORN (Florida)
map (30° 14′N 82° 49′W) **8**:172
WELLES, GIDEON **20**:99 *bibliog.*
WELLES, ORSON **8**:85 *illus.*; **20**:99 *bibliog.*, *illus.*
Mercury Theatre **13**:308
radio and television broadcasting **16**:56 *illus.*
WELLES, SUMNER **20**:99
WELLESLEY (Massachusetts)
map (42° 18′N 71° 17′W) **13**:206
WELLESLEY, ARTHUR, 1ST DUKE OF WELLINGTON *see* WELLINGTON, ARTHUR WELLESLEY, 1ST DUKE OF
WELLESLEY, RICHARD COLLEY WELLESLEY, MARQUESS **20**:99–100 *bibliog.*
WELLESLEY COLLEGE **20**:100
Palmer, Alice Freeman **15**:50
Seven Sisters Colleges **17**:216
WELLESLEY ISLANDS
map (16° 42′S 139° 30′E) **2**:328
WELLHOUSE (Barbados)
map (13° 8′N 59° 28′W) **3**:75
WELLINGTON (Colorado)
map (40° 42′N 105° 0′W) **5**:116
WELLINGTON (Kansas)
map (37° 16′N 97° 24′W) **12**:18
WELLINGTON (Missouri)
map (39° 8′N 93° 59′W) **13**:476
WELLINGTON (New Zealand) **14**:159 *illus.*; **20**:100
map (41° 18′S 174° 47′E) **14**:158
WELLINGTON (Ohio)
map (41° 10′N 82° 13′W) **14**:357
WELLINGTON (Texas)
map (34° 51′N 100° 13′W) **19**:129
WELLINGTON (Utah)
map (39° 32′N 110° 44′W) **19**:492
WELLINGTON, ARTHUR WELLESLEY, 1ST DUKE OF **20**:100 *bibliog.*, *illus.*
Napoleonic Wars **14**:19–20
Vitoria (Spain) **19**:621
Waterloo, Battle of **20**:64–65 *map*
WELLMAN (Iowa)
map (41° 28′N 91° 50′W) **11**:244
WELLMAN, WILLIAM **20**:100–101 *bibliog.*
WELLS (county in Indiana)
map (40° 44′N 85° 11′W) **11**:111
WELLS (Minnesota)
map (43° 44′N 93° 44′W) **13**:453
WELLS (Nevada)
map (41° 7′N 114° 58′W) **14**:111
WELLS (county in North Dakota)
map (47° 35′N 99° 40′W) **14**:248
WELLS (Texas)
map (31° 29′N 94° 56′W) **19**:129
WELLS, FARGO AND COMPANY **20**:101 *bibliog.*
Fargo, William George **8**:23
WELLS, H. G. **20**:101 *bibliog.*, *illus.*
science fiction **17**:143
War of the Worlds, The **17**:144 *illus.*; **20**:25
WELLS, HORACE
anesthetics **1**:410
dentistry **6**:115–116
WELLS, JULIA E. *see* ANDREWS, JULIE
WELLS COLLEGE **20**:101
WELLSBORO (Pennsylvania)
map (41° 45′N 77° 18′W) **15**:147
WELLSBURG (Iowa)
map (42° 26′N 92° 56′W) **11**:244
WELLSBURG (West Virginia)
map (40° 16′N 80° 37′W) **20**:111
WELLSTON (Ohio)
map (39° 7′N 82° 32′W) **14**:357
WELLSTON (Oklahoma)
map (35° 41′N 97° 6′W) **14**:368
WELLSVILLE (Kansas)
map (38° 43′N 95° 5′W) **12**:18
WELLSVILLE (Missouri)
map (39° 4′N 91° 34′W) **13**:476
WELLSVILLE (New York)
map (42° 7′N 77° 57′W) **14**:149
WELLSVILLE (Ohio)
map (40° 36′N 80° 39′W) **14**:357
WELLSVILLE (Utah)
map (41° 38′N 111° 56′W) **19**:492
WELLTON (Arizona)
map (32° 40′N 114° 8′W) **2**:160
WELP (county in Colorado)
map (40° 30′N 104° 20′W) **5**:116
WELS *see* CATFISH
WELS (Austria)
map (48° 10′N 14° 2′E) **2**:348
WELSBACH, CARL AUER, BARON VON **20**:101
WELSFORD (New Brunswick)
map (45° 27′N 66° 20′W) **14**:117
WELSH (Louisiana)
map (30° 14′N 92° 49′W) **12**:430
WELSH COB *see* WELSH PONY
WELSH CORGI *see* CARDIGAN WELSH CORGI; PEMBROKE WELSH CORGI
WELSH LANGUAGE *see* WALES, LANGUAGE
WELSH LITERATURE **20**:101–102 *bibliog.*
authors
Dafydd ap Gwilym **6**:6
Owen, Daniel **14**:471
Powys, John Cowper **15**:486
Thomas, Dylan **19**:172–173
Vaughan, Henry **19**:528
festivals
Eisteddfod **7**:97
poetic forms
Dafydd ap Gwilym **6**:6
WELSH MOUNTAIN PONY *see* WELSH PONY
WELSH PONY **10**:243 *illus.*; **15**:428 *illus.*; **20**:102 *illus.*
saddle horse **17**:9
WELSH SPRINGER SPANIEL **6**:219 *illus.*; **20**:102 *bibliog.*, *illus.*
WELSH TERRIER **6**:220 *illus.*; **20**:102 *bibliog.*, *illus.*
WELSH V. UNITED STATES **20**:102
WELT, DIE **20**:102
WELTY, EUDORA **20**:102–103 *bibliog.*, *illus.*
WEN-CHOW (Wenzhou) (China) **20**:103
map (28° 1′N 120° 39′E) **4**:362
WENATCHEE (American Indians) **20**:103 *bibliog.*
WENATCHEE (Washington)
map (47° 25′N 120° 19′W) **20**:35
WENCESLAS, SAINT **20**:103
WENCESLAS, KING OF GERMANY AND BOHEMIA **20**:103 *bibliog.*
WENCESLAS I, KING OF BOHEMIA **20**:103
WENCESLAS II, KING OF BOHEMIA **20**:103
Plzeň (Czechoslovakia) **15**:375
WENCESLAS III, KING OF BOHEMIA
Přemysl (dynasty) **15**:518
WENCHI (Ghana)
map (7° 42′N 2° 7′W) **9**:164
WENDAT *see* HURON (American Indians)
WENDELL (Idaho)
map (42° 46′N 114° 42′W) **11**:26
WENDOVER (Utah)
map (40° 44′N 114° 2′W) **19**:492
WENDS
Slavic languages **17**:358
Slavs **17**:359
WENHAM, FRANCIS
wind tunnel **20**:172
WENKER, GEORG
linguistic atlases **9**:98
WENONA (Illinois)
map (41° 3′N 89° 3′W) **11**:42
WENT, F. W.
tropism **19**:309
WENTWORTH (North Carolina)
map (36° 24′N 79° 53′W) **14**:242
WENTWORTH, BENNING
New Hampshire **14**:125–126
Vermont **19**:558
WENTWORTH, CHARLES WATSON-, 2D MARQUESS OF ROCKINGHAM *see* ROCKINGHAM, CHARLES WATSON-WENTWORTH, 2D MARQUESS OF
WENTWORTH, JOHN
New Hampshire **14**:126
WENTWORTH, LAKE
map (43° 36′N 71° 12′W) **14**:123
WENTWORTH, THOMAS, 1ST EARL OF STRAFFORD *see* STRAFFORD, THOMAS WENTWORTH, 1ST EARL OF
WENTWORTH, WILLIAM CHARLES **20**:103–104 *bibliog.*
Great Dividing Range **9**:319
WENZEL, CARL FRIEDRICH **20**:104
stoichiometry **20**:104
WENZHOU (China) *see* WEN-CHOW (Wenzhou) (China)
WERENSKIOLD, ERIK **20**:104 *bibliog.*
WEREWOLF **20**:104 *bibliog.*
WERFEL, FRANZ **20**:104 *bibliog.*
WERGELAND, HENRIK ARNOLD **20**:104 *bibliog.*
Norwegian literature **14**:265
WERNER, ABRAHAM GOTTLOB **20**:104 *bibliog.*
crystal identification, mineral **13**:439
mineral classification **20**:104
rock classifications **20**:104
WERNER, ALFRED **20**:104
chemical bond **20**:104
chemistry, history of **4**:327
coordination compounds **5**:247
coordination theory, valence and affinity **20**:104
WERNER, HEINZ
developmental psychology **6**:142
WERNER'S SYNDROME *see* PREMATURE AGING
WEROWOCOMOCO
Powhatan **15**:486
WERT, GIACHES DE
music, history of Western **13**:665
Renaissance music **16**:156
WERTHEIMER, MAX **20**:104 *bibliog.*
Gestalt psychology **9**:159; **20**:104
Koffka, Kurt **12**:105
Köhler, Wolfgang **12**:106
problem solving **15**:559 *illus.*
WERTMULLER, LINA **20**:105 *bibliog.*
WESCOTT, GLENWAY **20**:105
WESER RIVER **20**:105
Bremen (West Germany) **3**:472
map (53° 32′N 8° 34′E) **9**:140
WESKAN (Kansas)
map (38° 41′N 101° 57′W) **12**:18
WESKER, ARNOLD **20**:105
WESLACO (Texas)
map (26° 9′N 97° 59′W) **19**:129
WESLEY (family) **20**:105 *bibliog.*, *illus.*
Methodism **13**:344
WESLEY (Iowa)
map (43° 5′N 93° 59′W) **11**:244
WESLEY, CHARLES
hymn **10**:346
Wesley (family) **20**:105
WESLEY, JOHN **13**:344 *illus.*
Arminianism **2**:173
Wesley (family) **20**:105 *illus.*
WESLEYAN UNIVERSITY **20**:105–106
WESLEYVILLE (Pennsylvania)
map (42° 8′N 80° 1′W) **15**:147
WESSEL ISLANDS
map (11° 30′S 136° 25′E) **2**:328
WESSELMANN, TOM **20**:106 *bibliog.*
WESSEX **2**:3 *map*; **20**:106 *bibliog.*
Alfred, King of England **1**:280
Athelstan, King **2**:289
Edward the Elder, King **7**:67
Egbert, King **7**:71–72
Mercia **13**:304
WESSEX CULTURE **20**:106 *bibliog.*
cemetery
barrow **3**:95
European prehistory **7**:304
WESSINGTON (South Dakota)
map (44° 27′N 98° 42′W) **18**:103
WESSINGTON SPRINGS (South Dakota)
map (44° 5′N 98° 34′W) **18**:103
WEST, BENJAMIN **20**:106–107 *bibliog.*, *illus.*
American art and architecture **1**:331
American Revolution peace negotiations (painting) **1**:365 *illus.*
The Death of General Wolfe **4**:81 *illus.*; **8**:314 *illus.*
Penn's Treaty with the Indians **11**:107 *illus.*; **20**:106 *illus.*
WEST, JERRY **3**:113 *illus.*; **20**:107 *bibliog.*
WEST, JESSAMYN **20**:107
WEST, MAE **8**:73–74 *illus.*; **20**:107
WEST, MORRIS L. **2**:343 *illus.*; **20**:107
WEST, NATHANAEL **20**:107 *bibliog.*
Day of the Locust **6**:56
WEST, REBECCA **20**:107 *bibliog.*
WEST, THE *see* FRONTIER, U.S.
WEST, THOMAS, 12TH BARON DE LA WARR *see* DE LA WARR, THOMAS WEST, 12TH BARON
WEST, VICTORIA SACKVILLE- *see* SACKVILLE-WEST, VICTORIA
WEST ABINGTON (Massachusetts)
map (42° 8′N 70° 59′W) **3**:409
WEST ACTON (Massachusetts)
map (42° 29′N 71° 28′W) **3**:409
WEST AFRICA **20**:107
See also names of specific countries, e.g., GAMBIA; GHANA; etc.
African art **1**:162
African music **1**:168–171
history
Africa, history of **1**:152–155
Bambara kingdoms **3**:58
Cameroons **4**:62
Kanem-Bornu **12**:14–15
Songhai (empire) **18**:65
Umar, al-Hajj **19**:379
Usman dan Fodio **19**:491
Islam **11**:290
migration to the United States **11**:55 *map*
people
Ashanti **2**:229
Fulani **8**:356
Mande **13**:111
Senufo **17**:205
WEST ALLIS (Wisconsin)
map (43° 1′N 88° 0′W) **20**:185
WEST AUSTRALIAN CURRENT
ocean currents and wind systems, worldwide **14**:322–323 *maps*
WEST BANK (Jordan River) **20**:108
Hebron **10**:103
Israel **11**:306
Jordan **11**:448–450
Middle Eastern universities **13**:410–412 *table*
Palestine **15**:46
WEST BATON ROUGE (county in Louisiana)
map (30° 28′N 91° 20′W) **12**:430
WEST BAY (Nova Scotia)
map (45° 43′N 61° 10′W) **14**:269
WEST BAY (Texas)
map (29° 15′N 94° 57′W) **19**:129
WEST BEND (Iowa)
map (42° 57′N 94° 27′W) **11**:244
WEST BEND (Wisconsin)
map (43° 25′N 88° 11′W) **20**:185
WEST BENGAL (India)
Bengal **3**:198–199
map (24° 0′N 88° 0′E) **11**:80
WEST BERLIN *see* BERLIN (Germany, East and West)
WEST BERLIN (New Jersey)
map (39° 49′N 74° 57′W) **14**:129
WEST BILLERICA (Massachusetts)
map (42° 33′N 71° 19′W) **3**:409
WEST BLOCTON (Alabama)
map (33° 7′N 87° 7′W) **1**:234
WEST BRANCH (Michigan)
map (44° 17′N 84° 14′W) **13**:377
WEST BRANCH RESERVOIR
map (41° 25′N 73° 42′W) **5**:193
WEST BRIDGEWATER (Massachusetts)
map (42° 1′N 71° 0′W) **13**:206
WEST BROOKFIELD (Massachusetts)
map (42° 14′N 72° 9′W) **13**:206
WEST BURLINGTON (Iowa)
map (40° 49′N 91° 9′W) **11**:244
WEST CAPE
map (45° 54′S 166° 26′E) **14**:158
WEST CARROLL (county in Louisiana)
map (32° 45′N 91° 30′W) **12**:430
WEST CARROLLTON (Ohio)
map (39° 40′N 84° 15′W) **14**:357
WEST CHELMSFORD (Massachusetts)
map (42° 37′N 71° 24′W) **3**:409
WEST CHESTER (Pennsylvania)
map (39° 58′N 75° 36′W) **15**:147
WEST COAST HOTEL COMPANY* v. *PARRISH **20**:108
WEST COLUMBIA (Texas)
map (29° 9′N 95° 39′W) **19**:129
WEST CONCORD (Massachusetts)
map (42° 27′N 71° 24′W) **13**:206
WEST CONCORD (Minnesota)
map (44° 9′N 92° 54′W) **13**:453
WEST COVINA (California)
map (34° 5′N 117° 58′W) **4**:31
WEST DES MOINES (Iowa)
map (41° 35′N 93° 43′W) **11**:244
WEST ELK MOUNTAINS
map (38° 40′N 107° 15′W) **5**:116
WEST END (Bahama Islands)
map (26° 41′N 78° 58′W) **3**:23
WEST END (Illinois)
map (42° 17′N 89° 9′W) **11**:42
WEST END (North Carolina)
map (35° 15′N 79° 33′W) **14**:242
WEST FALKLAND ISLAND
map (51° 50′S 60° 0′W) **2**:149
WEST FARGO (North Dakota)
map (46° 53′N 96° 54′W) **14**:248
WEST FELICIANA (county in Louisiana)
map (30° 50′N 91° 22′W) **12**:430
WEST FJORD
map (68° 8′N 15° 0′E) **14**:261
WEST FLORIDA CONTROVERSY **20**:108 *bibliog.*
WEST FORK (Arkansas)
map (35° 56′N 94° 11′W) **2**:166
WEST FRANKFORT (Illinois)
map (37° 54′N 88° 55′W) **11**:42
WEST FRISIAN ISLANDS
map (53° 26′N 5° 30′E) **14**:99

WEST GERMANY *see* GERMANY, EAST AND WEST
WEST GLACIER (Montana)
map (48° 30′N 113° 59′W) **13**:547
WEST HANOVER (Massachusetts)
map (42° 7′N 70° 53′W) **3**:409
WEST HARTFORD (Connecticut)
map (41° 46′N 72° 45′W) **5**:193
WEST HAVEN (Connecticut)
map (41° 16′N 72° 57′W) **5**:193
WEST HELENA (Arkansas)
map (34° 33′N 90° 39′W) **2**:166
WEST HIGHLAND WHITE TERRIER **6**:220 *illus.*; **20**:108 *bibliog., illus.*
WEST INDIES **4**:147–148 *map*; **20**:108–109 *bibliog., map*
See also LATIN AMERICA, HISTORY OF
Anguilla **2**:7
Antigua and Barbuda **2**:62
Antilles, Greater and Lesser **2**:63
Aruba **2**:225–226
Bahama Islands **3**:23–24 *illus., map*
Barbados **3**:75–76 *map*
Cayman Islands **4**:227
Cuba **5**:377–380 *illus., map, table*
Curaçao (Netherlands) **5**:390
dance
Dunham, Katherine **6**:300
tango **19**:23
Dominica **6**:232–233 *illus.*
Dominican Republic **6**:233–234 *illus., map, table*
French West Indies **8**:326
Grenada **9**:357–358 *illus., map*
Grenadine Islands **9**:359
Guadeloupe **9**:385
Hispaniola **10**:180
Jamaica **11**:351–352 *illus., map, table*
Leeward Islands **12**:272
map (19° 0′N 70° 0′W) **20**:109
Martinique **13**:181
migration to the United States **11**:55 *map*
Montserrat (island) **13**:560
Netherlands Antilles **14**:103
people **20**:109
Saint Kitts-Nevis **17**:20
Saint Lucia **17**:23
Saint Vincent and the Grenadines **17**:27
San Salvador Island **17**:57–58
slave trade **17**:356 *map*
Turks and Caicos Islands **19**:349
Virgin Islands **19**:605–606
Windward Islands **20**:174
WEST INDIES ASSOCIATED STATES **20**:109
WEST INDIES FEDERATION, THE
Jamaica **11**:352
West Indies Associated States **20**:109
WEST IRIAN *see* IRIAN JAYA (Indonesia)
WEST JEFFERSON (Ohio)
map (39° 57′N 83° 16′W) **14**:357
WEST KINGSTON (Rhode Island)
map (41° 29′N 71° 34′W) **16**:198
WEST LAFAYETTE (Indiana)
map (40° 27′N 86° 55′W) **11**:111
WEST LEBANON (Indiana)
map (40° 16′N 87° 23′W) **11**:111
WEST LIBERTY (Iowa)
map (41° 34′N 91° 16′W) **11**:244
WEST LIBERTY (Kentucky)
map (37° 55′N 83° 16′W) **12**:47
WEST LIBERTY (Ohio)
map (40° 15′N 83° 46′W) **14**:357
WEST MEDWAY (Massachusetts)
map (42° 9′N 71° 26′W) **3**:409
WEST MEMPHIS (Arkansas)
map (35° 8′N 90° 11′W) **2**:166
WEST MIFFLIN (Pennsylvania)
map (40° 22′N 79° 52′W) **15**:147
WEST MILFORD (New Jersey)
map (41° 8′N 74° 22′W) **14**:129
WEST MONROE (Louisiana)
map (32° 31′N 92° 9′W) **12**:430
WEST NEW GUINEA *see* IRIAN JAYA (Indonesia)
WEST NEW YORK (New Jersey)
map (40° 47′N 74° 4′W) **14**:129
WEST NISHNABOTNA RIVER
map (40° 39′N 95° 37′W) **11**:244
WEST NORRITON (Pennsylvania)
map (40° 8′N 75° 22′W) **15**:147
WEST PAKISTAN *see* PAKISTAN
WEST PALM BEACH (Florida) **20**:109
map (26° 43′N 80° 4′W) **8**:172
WEST PARIS (Maine)
map (44° 20′N 70° 35′W) **13**:70
WEST PENSACOLA (Florida)
map (30° 27′N 87° 15′W) **8**:172
WEST PLAINS (Missouri)
map (36° 44′N 91° 51′W) **13**:476
WEST POINT (Georgia)
map (32° 52′N 85° 10′W) **9**:114
WEST POINT (Mississippi)
map (33° 36′N 88° 39′W) **13**:469
WEST POINT (Nebraska)
map (41° 51′N 96° 43′W) **14**:70
WEST POINT (New York)
map (41° 23′N 73° 57′W) **14**:149
WEST POINT (Prince Edward Island)
map (46° 37′N 64° 25′W) **15**:548
WEST POINT (Virginia)
map (37° 32′N 77° 6′W) **19**:607
WEST POINT MILITARY ACADEMY *see* UNITED STATES MILITARY ACADEMY
WEST POINT RESERVOIR
map (33° 0′N 85° 10′W) **9**:114
WEST PORTSMOUTH (Ohio)
map (38° 46′N 83° 2′W) **14**:357
WEST RIVER (Vermont)
map (42° 52′N 72° 33′W) **19**:554
WEST RUTLAND (Vermont)
map (43° 36′N 73° 3′W) **19**:554
WEST SAINT MARY'S RIVER
map (45° 15′N 62° 4′W) **14**:269
WEST SAINT MODESTE (Newfoundland)
map (51° 36′N 56° 42′W) **14**:166
WEST SALEM (Illinois)
map (38° 31′N 88° 1′W) **11**:42
WEST SALEM (Ohio)
map (40° 58′N 82° 6′W) **14**:357
WEST SALEM (Wisconsin)
map (43° 54′N 91° 5′W) **20**:185
WEST SENECA (New York)
map (42° 50′N 78° 45′W) **14**:149
WEST SIDE STORY
musical comedy **13**:674 *illus.*
WEST SPITSBERGEN ISLAND
map (78° 45′N 16° 0′E) **14**:261
WEST SPRINGFIELD (Massachusetts)
map (42° 6′N 72° 38′W) **13**:206
WEST SUSSEX (England) *see* SUSSEX (England)
WEST TERRE HAUTE (Indiana)
map (39° 28′N 87° 27′W) **11**:111
WEST UNION (Iowa)
map (42° 57′N 91° 49′W) **11**:244
WEST UNION (Ohio)
map (38° 48′N 83° 32′W) **14**:357
WEST UNION (West Virginia)
map (39° 18′N 80° 47′W) **20**:111
WEST UNITY (Ohio)
map (41° 35′N 84° 26′W) **14**:357
WEST VALLEY (Montana)
map (46° 8′N 113° 1′W) **13**:547
WEST VANCOUVER (British Columbia)
map (49° 22′N 123° 12′W) **3**:491
WEST VIRGINIA **20**:109–115 *bibliog., illus., map*
cities
Charleston **4**:298
Harpers Ferry **10**:55
Huntington **10**:314
Morgantown **13**:579
Wheeling **20**:129
White Sulphur Springs **20**:138
climate **20**:110
economic activities **20**:112–113 *illus.*
education **20**:112
West Virginia, state universities and colleges of **20**:115
flag **20**:110 *illus.*
forestry **20**:113
geographical linguistics **9**:98–99 *map*
government and politics **20**:113–114
historical sites **20**:112
history **20**:114
Pierpont, Frances Harrison **15**:297
land and resources **20**:110–112 *map*
map (38° 45′N 80° 30′W) **19**:419
mining **20**:113 *illus.*; **20**:114
people **20**:112
resources **20**:112
rivers, lakes, and waterways **20**:110
Monongahela River **13**:537
seal, state **20**:110 *illus.*
WEST VIRGINIA, STATE UNIVERSITIES AND COLLEGES OF **20**:115
WEST VIRGINIA STATE BOARD OF EDUCATION v. *BARNETTE*
Pledge of Allegiance **15**:364
WEST WALES **2**:3 *map*
WEST WARWICK (Rhode Island)
map (41° 42′N 71° 32′W) **16**:198
WEST YARMOUTH (Massachusetts)
map (41° 39′N 70° 15′W) **13**:206
WESTBAY (Florida)
map (30° 17′N 85° 52′W) **8**:172
WESTBOROUGH (Massachusetts)
map (42° 16′N 71° 37′W) **13**:206
WESTBROOK (Maine)
map (43° 41′N 70° 21′W) **13**:70
WESTBY (Montana)
map (48° 52′N 104° 3′W) **13**:547
WESTCHESTER (county in New York)
map (41° 2′N 73° 46′W) **14**:149
WESTCLIFFE (Colorado)
map (38° 8′N 105° 28′W) **5**:116
WESTERBORK OBSERVATORY **20**:115
radio astronomy **16**:51–52 *illus.*
WESTERLIES **20**:115
high-pressure region **10**:162
jet stream **11**:407–408
Mediterranean climate **13**:276
wind **20**:115
WESTERLY (Rhode Island)
map (41° 22′N 71° 50′W) **16**:198
WESTERMANN, H. C. **20**:115 *bibliog.*
WESTERMARCK, EDWARD ALEXANDER **20**:115
WESTERN (Nebraska)
map (40° 24′N 97° 12′W) **14**:70
WESTERN AUSTRALIA (Australia) **20**:115–116 *map*
Australia, history of **2**:340
cities
Perth **15**:191
flag **8**:145 *illus.*
map (25° 0′S 122° 0′E) **2**:328
WESTERN CORDILLERA MOUNTAINS
map (5° 0′N 76° 0′W) **5**:107
map (12° 30′S 76° 0′W) **15**:193
WESTERN DESERT
map (27° 0′N 27° 0′E) **7**:76
WESTERN ELECTRIC COMPANY
Hawthorne studies **10**:79
WESTERN EUROPE **20**:116
See also EUROPE; names of specific countries, e.g. BELGIUM; FRANCE; etc.
chemical industry **4**:318
history
communism **5**:150
Europe, history of **7**:280–299
European prehistory **7**:302
Magdalenian **13**:46
migration to the United States **11**:55 *map*
WESTERN EUROPEAN UNION **20**:116
WESTERN GHATS
map (14° 0′N 75° 0′E) **11**:80
WESTERN HEMISPHERE
countries
oil and gas reserves, end of 1979 **15**:209 *table*
North America **14**:224–236 *illus., map, tables*
printing **15**:551
South America **18**:84–95 *illus., maps, tables*
WESTERN ISLES *see* HEBRIDES (Scotland)
WESTERN ONTARIO, UNIVERSITY OF **20**:116
WESTERN SAHARA **20**:116
cities
Semara **13**:584 *table*
Mauritania **13**:236–237
Morocco **13**:587
WESTERN SAMOA **1**:366 *map*; **20**:116–117 *bibliog., map*
cities
Apia **2**:78
flag **20**:116 *illus.*
government **20**:116–117
history **20**:117
land, people, and economy **20**:116–117 *map*
map (13° 55′S 172° 0′W) **14**:334
Samoa **17**:46 *maps*
teaching aids, audiovisual **19**:55 *illus.*
WESTERN SIBERIAN LOWLAND
map (60° 0′N 75° 0′E) **19**:388
WESTERN STAR (poem)
Benét, Stephen Vincent **3**:198
WESTERN STICK STYLE *see* MAYBECK, BERNARD
WESTERN UNION TELEGRAPH COMPANY
Cornell, Ezra **5**:268
telephone **19**:80
WESTERNIZERS (Russia)
Slavophiles and Westernizers **17**:358–359
WESTERNPORT (Maryland)
map (39° 29′N 79° 3′W) **13**:188
WESTERNS **20**:117 *bibliog.*
authors
Brand, Max **3**:453
Buntline, Ned **3**:565
Clark, Walter van Tilburg **5**:39
Cooper, James Fenimore **5**:243
Grey, Zane **9**:360–361
Guthrie, A. B., Jr. **9**:409
Harte, Bret **10**:62
L'Amour, Louis **12**:144
Leonard, Elmore **12**:289
Wister, Owen **20**:190
pulp magazines **15**:620
stage, film, radio, television
Cooper, Gary **5**:243
Eastwood, Clint **7**:34
Ford, John (film director) **8**:222–223
Hart, William S. **10**:62
Mix, Tom **13**:486
Oakley, Annie **14**:312
Wayne, John **20**:73–74
WESTERSCHELDE
map (51° 25′N 3° 45′E) **14**:99
WESTERVILLE (Ohio)
map (40° 8′N 82° 56′W) **14**:357
WESTFALEN (West Germany) *see* WESTPHALIA (West Germany)
WESTFIELD (Illinois)
map (39° 27′N 88° 1′W) **11**:42
WESTFIELD (Indiana)
map (40° 2′N 86° 8′W) **11**:111
WESTFIELD (Massachusetts)
map (42° 8′N 72° 45′W) **13**:206
WESTFIELD (New Jersey)
map (40° 39′N 74° 21′W) **14**:129
WESTFIELD (New York)
map (42° 19′N 79° 35′W) **14**:149
WESTFIELD (Pennsylvania)
map (41° 55′N 77° 32′W) **15**:147
WESTFIELD (Wisconsin)
map (43° 53′N 89° 30′W) **20**:185
WESTFIELD, CHRISTIAN
crystal **5**:374
WESTFIELD RIVER
map (42° 5′N 72° 35′W) **13**:206
WESTHOPE (North Dakota)
map (48° 55′N 101° 1′W) **14**:248
WESTIE *see* WEST HIGHLAND WHITE TERRIER
WESTINGHOUSE, GEORGE **20**:117 *bibliog.*
brake **3**:451
WESTINGHOUSE CORPORATION
radio and television broadcasting **16**:54
WESTLAKE, DONALD E. **20**:117
WESTLAND (Michigan)
map (42° 19′N 83° 23′W) **13**:377
WESTLOCK (Alberta)
map (54° 9′N 113° 52′W) **1**:256
WESTMEATH (Ireland) **20**:117
WESTMINSTER (Maryland)
map (39° 35′N 77° 0′W) **13**:188
WESTMINSTER, PEACE OF (1654)
Anglo-Dutch Wars **2**:3
WESTMINSTER, PEACE OF (1674)
Anglo-Dutch Wars **2**:3
WESTMINSTER, PROVISIONS OF
Montfort, Simon de, Earl of Leicester **13**:555
WESTMINSTER, STATUTE OF (1931)
British Empire **3**:496
Canada, history of **4**:86
WESTMINSTER, TREATY OF (1674)
New Netherland **14**:140
WESTMINSTER ABBEY **9**:261 *illus.*; **12**:400–401 *illus., map*; **20**:117–118 *bibliog., illus.*
Gothic art and architecture **9**:258; **9**:262
organist
Blow, John **3**:341
Perpendicular Gothic style **15**:177
unknown soldier **19**:470
WESTMINSTER CHOIR COLLEGE **20**:118
WESTMINSTER COLLEGE **20**:118
WESTMINSTER PALACE **20**:118 *bibliog.*
Gothic Revival **9**:262
mosaic **13**:596
Pugin, Augustus **15**:617
WESTMONT (Pennsylvania)
map (40° 19′N 78° 57′W) **15**:147
WESTMORELAND (England) *see* CUMBRIA (England)
WESTMORELAND (Kansas)
map (39° 24′N 96° 25′W) **12**:18
WESTMORELAND (county in Pennsylvania)
map (40° 18′N 79° 25′W) **15**:147
WESTMORELAND (Tennessee)
map (36° 34′N 86° 15′W) **19**:104
WESTMORELAND (county in Virginia)
map (38° 10′N 76° 50′W) **19**:607
WESTMORELAND, WILLIAM C. **20**:118 *bibliog.*
WESTMORLAND (California)
map (33° 2′N 115° 37′W) **4**:31
WESTON (Massachusetts)
map (42° 22′N 71° 18′W) **3**:409

WESTON (Missouri)
map (39° 25′N 94° 54′W) **13**:476
WESTON (Ohio)
map (41° 21′N 83° 48′W) **14**:357
WESTON (Oregon)
map (45° 49′N 118° 26′W) **14**:427
WESTON (West Virginia)
map (39° 2′N 80° 28′W) **20**:111
WESTON (county in Wyoming)
map (43° 50′N 104° 30′W) **20**:301
WESTON, EDWARD **20**:118 *bibliog.*
photography, history and art of **15**:271 *illus.*
WESTON-SUPER-MARE (England)
map (51° 21′N 2° 59′W) **19**:403
WESTOVER (Tennessee)
map (35° 36′N 88° 55′W) **19**:104
WESTOVER (West Virginia)
map (39° 38′N 79° 58′W) **20**:111
WESTPHALIA (West Germany) **20**:118
Germany 1815–1871 **9**:153 *map*
WESTPHALIA, PEACE OF **20**:119 *bibliog.*
delegates to **7**:288 *illus.*
Europe, history of **7**:288
Ferdinand III, Holy Roman Emperor **8**:53
German territories **9**:151 *map*
Münster (West Germany) **13**:643–644
Oxenstierna, Axel, Count **14**:474
signing of the treaties **19**:171 *illus.*
Thirty Years' War **19**:171
WESTPORT (Connecticut)
map (41° 9′N 73° 22′W) **5**:193
WESTPORT (Indiana)
map (39° 11′N 85° 34′W) **11**:111
WESTPORT (New Zealand)
map (41° 45′S 171° 36′E) **14**:158
WESTPORT (Newfoundland)
map (49° 47′N 56° 38′W) **14**:166
WESTPORT (Nova Scotia)
map (44° 16′N 66° 21′W) **14**:269
WESTPORT (Ontario)
map (44° 41′N 76° 26′W) **14**:393; **14**:461
WESTVILLE (Indiana)
map (41° 33′N 86° 54′W) **11**:111
WESTVILLE (Nova Scotia)
map (45° 34′N 62° 43′W) **14**:269
WESTVILLE (Oklahoma)
map (35° 59′N 94° 34′W) **14**:368
WESTWARD EXPANSION, U.S. *see* FRONTIER, U.S.
WESTWOOD (Kentucky)
map (38° 29′N 82° 40′W) **12**:47
WESTWOOD (Massachusetts)
map (42° 12′N 71° 14′W) **3**:409
WESTWOOD (New Jersey)
map (41° 59′N 74° 2′W) **14**:129
WETASKIWIN (Alberta)
map (52° 58′N 113° 22′W) **1**:256
WETHERSFIELD (Connecticut)
map (41° 43′N 72° 40′W) **5**:193
WETLANDS
land reclamation **12**:178–179
swamp, marsh, and bog **18**:376–378
WETTACH, CHARLES ADRIEN *see* GROCK
WETTEREN (Belgium)
map (51° 0′N 3° 53′E) **3**:177
WETTIN (dynasty)
Saxony **17**:105
Sigismund, King of Germany and Holy Roman Emperor **17**:299
WETUMKA (Oklahoma)
map (35° 14′N 96° 15′W) **14**:368
WETUMPKA (Alabama)
map (32° 27′N 86° 13′W) **1**:234
WETZEL (county in West Virginia)
map (39° 35′N 80° 38′W) **20**:111
WETZLAR (Germany, East and West)
map (50° 33′N 8° 29′E) **9**:140
WEWAHITCHKA (Florida)
map (30° 7′N 85° 12′W) **8**:172
WEWAK (Papua New Guinea)
map (3° 35′S 143° 40′E) **15**:72
WEWOKA (Oklahoma)
map (35° 9′N 96° 30′W) **14**:368
WEXFORD (Ireland) **20**:119
map (52° 20′N 6° 27′W) **11**:258
WEXFORD (county in Michigan)
map (44° 20′N 85° 35′W) **13**:377
WEYAUWEGA (Wisconsin)
map (44° 19′N 88° 56′W) **20**:185
WEYBURN (Saskatchewan)
map (49° 41′N 103° 52′W) **17**:81
WEYDEN, ROGIER VAN DER **20**:119 *bibliog., illus.*
The Descent from the Cross **16**:154 *illus.*
Pietá **20**:119 *illus.*
Renaissance art and architecture **16**:153
WEYGAND, MAXIME **20**:119
WEYLER, VALERIANO
concentration camp **5**:169
Spanish-American War **18**:149
WEYMOUTH (England)
map (50° 36′N 2° 28′W) **19**:403
WEYMOUTH (Massachusetts)
map (42° 13′N 70° 58′W) **3**:409
WEYMOUTH (Nova Scotia)
map (44° 25′N 66° 0′W) **14**:269
WEYSE, C. E. F.
Denmark **6**:111
WHALE **20**:119–122 *bibliog., illus.*
anatomy **20**:121
animal behavior **20**:121
animal migration **2**:27
Antarctica **2**:42 *illus.*; **2**:43
Arctic **2**:141 *illus.*
beluga **3**:193 *illus.*
blue whale **13**:105 *illus.*; **20**:120 *illus.*
cetacean **4**:262
conservation **20**:121–122
distribution **20**:121
dolphin **6**:226–229
endangered species **7**:166; **7**:167 *illus.*
Eskimo **7**:241
fats and oils source **8**:35
harpoon **10**:55
humpback whale **20**:120 *illus.*
ivory and ivory carving **11**:336
killer whale **13**:100 *illus.*; **20**:120 *illus.*
narwhal **14**:23
porpoise **15**:442
products **20**:121
reproduction **20**:121
right whale **20**:120 *illus.*
scrimshaw **17**:158
sperm oil **18**:179
sperm whale **20**:120 *illus.*
ambergris **1**:325
whaling **20**:122–124
WHALE OIL *see* SPERM OIL
WHALING **20**:122–124 *bibliog., illus.*
history **20**:122
Eskimo **7**:241–242
Nantucket Island (Massachusetts) **14**:14
New Bedford (Massachusetts) **14**:115
New London (Connecticut) **14**:134
Nootka **14**:217
Sag Harbor (New York) **14**:152 *illus.*
modern whaling **20**:122–123 *illus., table*
Japan **11**:366 *illus.*
world whaling areas **8**:125 *map*
ship **20**:122–123 *illus.*
WHANGAREI (New Zealand)
map (35° 43′S 174° 19′E) **14**:158
WHARTON (New Jersey)
map (40° 54′N 74° 35′W) **14**:129
WHARTON (Texas)
map (29° 19′N 96° 6′W) **19**:129
WHARTON (county in Texas)
map (29° 17′N 96° 13′W) **19**:129
WHARTON, EDITH **20**:124 *bibliog., illus.*
Ethan Frome **7**:249
WHARTON SCHOOL OF FINANCE AND COMMERCE
Pennsylvania, University of **15**:152
WHATCOM (county in Washington)
map (48° 48′N 121° 59′W) **20**:35
WHATELY, RICHARD
ethics **7**:251
WHEAT **8**:348 *illus.*; **9**:281 *illus.*; **15**:337 *illus.*; **20**:124–126 *bibliog., illus.*
agriculture, history of **1**:192–193 *illus.*
breeding **20**:125
agriculture and the food supply **1**:198
Borlaug, Norman Ernest **3**:401
green revolution **9**:348–349 *illus.*
hybrid **10**:328 *illus.*
hybrid chromosomes **20**:126 *illus.*
plant breeding **15**:342–343
Canada **4**:73 *illus.*
Manitoba **13**:120 *illus.*
Saskatchewan **17**:82 *illus.*
cross-section of wheat grain **20**:124 *illus.*
cultivation **20**:124–125
grass **9**:295
marketing **20**:126
pollen **15**:406 *illus.*
production **20**:125–126
United States **19**:427 *illus.*
Kansas **12**:19–20 *illus.*
Minnesota **13**:457 *illus.*
Montana **13**:548; **13**:549 *illus.*
North Dakota **14**:250 *illus.*
Oklahoma **14**:369 *illus.*
South Dakota **18**:105 *illus.*
uses **20**:126
flour **8**:178
pasta **15**:106
varieties **20**:124; **20**:125 *illus.*
western wheat grass **9**:299 *illus.*
WHEAT RIDGE (Colorado)
map (39° 46′N 105° 7′W) **5**:116
WHEATEAR (bird) **20**:126
WHEATEN TERRIER *see* SOFT-COATED WHEATEN TERRIER
WHEATLAND (county in Montana)
map (46° 25′N 109° 50′W) **13**:547
WHEATLAND (Wyoming)
map (42° 3′N 104° 57′W) **20**:301
WHEATLEY (Arkansas)
map (34° 56′N 91° 8′W) **2**:166
WHEATLEY, PHILLIS **20**:126 *bibliog.*
WHEATON (Illinois)
map (41° 52′N 88° 6′W) **11**:42
WHEATON (Maryland)
map (39° 3′N 77° 3′W) **13**:188
WHEATON (Minnesota)
map (45° 48′N 96° 30′W) **13**:453
WHEATON COLLEGE **20**:126
WHEATSTONE, SIR CHARLES **20**:127 *bibliog.*
stereoscope **18**:259–260
Wheatstone bridge **20**:127
WHEATSTONE BRIDGE **20**:127 *illus.*
bridge circuit **3**:484
Wheatstone, Sir Charles **20**:127
WHEEL **20**:127–129 *bibliog., illus.*
See also ROTOR
automobile racing **2**:362 *illus.*
construction of **20**:127–128 *illus.*
lack of in Incan Empire **11**:72
pulley **15**:619
steering system **18**:244–245 *illus.*
suspension system **18**:371–372
tire **19**:207–208
transmission, automotive **19**:275–276
trucking industry **19**:315
wagon **20**:6
WHEEL ANIMALCULE *see* ROTIFER
WHEEL AND AXLE
simple machines **17**:316
WHEELER (county in Georgia)
map (32° 5′N 82° 45′W) **9**:114
WHEELER (Mississippi)
map (34° 34′N 88° 36′W) **13**:469
WHEELER (county in Nebraska)
map (41° 55′N 98° 30′W) **14**:70
WHEELER (county in Oregon)
map (44° 45′N 120° 0′W) **14**:427
WHEELER (Texas)
map (35° 27′N 100° 16′W) **19**:129
WHEELER (county in Texas)
map (35° 23′N 100° 15′W) **19**:129
WHEELER, GEORGE M.
O'Sullivan, Timothy H. **14**:459
United States Geological Survey **19**:462
WHEELER, JOSEPH **20**:129 *bibliog.*
WHEELER, SIR MORTIMER **20**:129 *bibliog.*
WHEELER, WILLIAM ALMON **20**:129
WHEELER-HOWARD ACT *see* INDIAN REORGANIZATION ACT
WHEELER LAKE
map (34° 40′N 87° 5′W) **1**:234
WHEELER PEAK (Nevada)
map (38° 59′N 114° 19′W) **14**:111
WHEELER PEAK (New Mexico)
map (36° 34′N 105° 25′W) **14**:136
WHEELING (Illinois)
map (42° 9′N 87° 55′W) **11**:42
WHEELING (West Virginia) **20**:129
map (40° 5′N 80° 42′W) **20**:111
WHEELOCK, ELEAZAR **20**:129 *bibliog.*
WHEELOCK COLLEGE **20**:129
WHEELWRIGHT (craftsman)
wheel **20**:128 *illus.*
WHEELWRIGHT (Kentucky)
map (37° 20′N 82° 43′W) **12**:47
WHEELWRIGHT, JOHN **20**:129
WHEELWRIGHT, WILLIAM **20**:129–130
WHELK **9**:57 *illus.*; **20**:130 *illus.*
conch **5**:170
mollusk **13**:510–511 *illus.*
WHELPTON, P. K.
demography **6**:103
WHETSTONE **20**:130
WHICHCOTE, BENJAMIN
Cambridge Platonists **4**:52
WHIG PARTY (England) **20**:130 *bibliog.*
Addison, Joseph **1**:100
Fox, Charles James **8**:256
Macaulay, Thomas Babington **13**:6
political parties **15**:400
Shaftesbury, Anthony Ashley Cooper, 1st Earl of **17**:234
William IV, King of England, Scotland, and Ireland **20**:156
WHIG PARTY (United States) **20**:130–131 *bibliog., illus.*
Clay, Henry **5**:46
Fillmore, Millard **8**:79–80
Hoar, Ebenezer Rockwood **10**:191
Lincoln, Abraham **12**:348
symbols (1840) **15**:529 *illus.*
United States, history of the **19**:446
Webster, Daniel **20**:88
WHIMBREL *see* CURLEW
WHIMSICAL TORIES *see* TORY PARTY
WHIP **20**:131
WHIP (U.S. House of Representatives)
congressional organization **5**:185
WHIP LIZARD *see* GERRHOSAURID
WHIP-POOR-WILL **20**:131–132 *bibliog., illus.*
goatsucker **9**:216
WHIP SNAKE
colubrid **5**:125
WHIPLASH **20**:131
spinal and spinal cord **20**:131
wounds and injuries **20**:131
WHIPPET **6**:216 *illus.*; **20**:131 *bibliog., illus.*
WHIPPLE, ABRAHAM **20**:131
WHIPPLE, FRED LAWRENCE **20**:131
comet **20**:131
Smithsonian Astrophysical Observatory **20**:131
WHIPPLE, GEORGE HOYT **20**:131
Minot, George **13**:460
WHIRLIGIG BEETLE *see* WATER BEETLE
WHIRLING DERVISH *see* DERVISH; SUFISM
WHIRLPOOL **20**:132
celestial mechanics **4**:230
physics, history of **15**:283 *illus.*
WHIRLWIND **20**:132
dust devil **6**:308–309
names **20**:132
structure **20**:132
WHISKEY **20**:132–133 *bibliog., illus.*
distillery **20**:133 *illus.*
manufacture **20**:132 *illus.*
production **20**:132–133
WHISKEY REBELLION **20**:133 *bibliog.*
Civil War, U.S. **5**:15
Washington, George **20**:44
WHISKEY RING **20**:133 *bibliog.*
WHIST **20**:133 *bibliog.*
WHISTLER (bird) *see* THICKHEAD (bird)
WHISTLER (electromagnetic signal) **20**:134
OGO **20**:355
WHISTLER, JAMES ABBOTT MCNEILL **20**:134 *bibliog., illus.*
abstract art **1**:64
American art and architecture **1**:334
Arrangement in Gray and Black, No. 1: The Artist's Mother **1**:335 *illus.*
Chase, William Merritt **4**:301
Freer, Charles Lang **8**:300
Gardner Museum **9**:45
Lowell (Massachusetts) **12**:443
Ruskin, John **16**:348
Sickert, Walter Richard **17**:293
Symphony in White No. III **20**:134 *illus.*
WHITAKER, ALEXANDER
Pocahontas **15**:376
WHITAKERS (North Carolina)
map (36° 6′N 77° 43′W) **14**:242
WHITBOURNE (Newfoundland)
map (47° 25′N 53° 32′W) **14**:166
WHITE (county in Arkansas)
map (35° 15′N 91° 45′W) **2**:166
WHITE (county in Georgia)
map (34° 40′N 83° 45′W) **9**:114
WHITE (county in Illinois)
map (38° 7′N 88° 10′W) **11**:42
WHITE (county in Indiana)
map (40° 45′N 86° 46′W) **11**:111
WHITE (South Dakota)
map (44° 26′N 96° 39′W) **18**:103
WHITE (county in Tennessee)
map (35° 55′N 85° 25′W) **19**:104
WHITE, ANDREW DICKSON **20**:134
WHITE, BYRON R. **18**:355 *illus.*; **20**:134
WHITE, CLARENCE H. **20**:134 *bibliog.*
WHITE, E. B. **20**:134–135 *bibliog.*
Charlotte's Web **4**:299
WHITE, EAST FORK RIVER
map (38° 33′N 87° 14′W) **11**:111
WHITE, EDWARD DOUGLASS **20**:135 *bibliog.*
McCray v. *United States* **13**:11

WHITE, EDWARD H., II **20**:135 *bibliog., illus.*
Apollo program **2**:80–81
Gemini program **9**:72
space walk **18**:128 *illus.*
WHITE, ELLEN G.
Adventists **1**:111
WHITE, GEORGE **20**:135
WHITE, HUGH LAWSON **20**:135
WHITE, JOHN
Algonquian village **11**:130 *illus.*
Indians fishing **11**:118 *illus.*
Roanoke Colony **16**:239
village of Secton **11**:117 *illus.*
WHITE, MARGARET BOURKE- *see* BOURKE-WHITE, MARGARET
WHITE, MINOR **20**:135 *bibliog.*
photography, history and art of **15**:272
WHITE, PATRICK **20**:135–136 *bibliog., illus.*
contemporary Australian literature **2**:344
WHITE, PEARL
film serials **8**:91
WHITE, PEREGRINE **20**:136
WHITE, PHYLLIS DOROTHY JAMES *see* JAMES, P. D.
WHITE, SAMUEL S., III
Philadelphia Museum of Art **15**:229
WHITE, STANFORD **20**:136 *bibliog.*
McKim, Mead, and White **13**:29
WHITE, T. H. **20**:136 *bibliog.*
WHITE, THEODORE **20**:136
WHITE, VERA
Philadelphia Museum of Art **15**:229
WHITE, WALTER **20**:136 *bibliog.*
WHITE, WILLIAM **20**:136 *bibliog.*
WHITE, WILLIAM ALANSON
Sullivan, Harry Stack **18**:336
WHITE, WILLIAM ALLEN **20**:136 *bibliog.*
WHITE BAY
map (50° 0′N 56° 30′W) **14**:166
WHITE BEAR LAKE (Minnesota)
map (45° 5′N 93° 1′W) **13**:453
WHITE BLOOD CELL
blood **3**:336
leukemia **12**:300–301
leukocytosis **12**:301
leukopenia **12**:301
WHITE BLUFF (Tennessee)
map (36° 6′N 87° 13′W) **19**:104
WHITE BUTTE
map (46° 23′N 103° 19′W) **14**:248
WHITE CASTLE (Louisiana)
map (30° 10′N 91° 9′W) **12**:430
WHITE CENTER (Washington)
map (47° 31′N 122° 21′W) **20**:35
WHITE CITY *see* WORLD'S COLUMBIAN EXPOSITION OF 1893
WHITE CLIFFS OF DOVER (England) *see* DOVER (England)
WHITE CLOUD (Michigan)
map (43° 33′N 85° 46′W) **13**:377
WHITE-COLLAR CRIME **20**:136–137
computer crime **5**:160L
crime **5**:345
fraud **8**:288
WHITE DWARF **18**:222 *illus.*; **20**:137 *bibliog.*
black dwarf **3**:314
Chandrasekhar limit **4**:280
cluster, star **5**:72
degenerate matter **6**:85
Sirius **17**:328
size **18**:224 *illus.*
stellar evolution **18**:251
X-ray astronomy **20**:306–307
WHITE-EYE **20**:137
WHITE HALL (Arkansas)
map (34° 17′N 92° 6′W) **2**:166
WHITE HALL (Illinois)
map (39° 26′N 90° 24′W) **11**:42
WHITE HAVEN (Pennsylvania)
map (41° 4′N 75° 47′W) **15**:147
WHITE HORSE (New Jersey)
map (40° 11′N 74° 22′W) **14**:129
WHITE HOUSE **20**:137–138 *bibliog., illus.*
architecture
Hoban, James **10**:191
Washington, D.C. **20**:41 *map*
WHITE HOUSE (Tennessee)
map (36° 26′N 86° 40′W) **19**:104
WHITE HOUSE STATION (New Jersey)
map (40° 37′N 74° 46′W) **14**:129
WHITE HUNS *see* HEPHTHALITES
WHITE LAKE
map (29° 45′N 92° 30′W) **12**:430
WHITE LAKE (South Dakota)
map (43° 44′N 98° 43′W) **18**:103
WHITE LAKE (Wisconsin)
map (45° 9′N 88° 46′W) **20**:185
WHITE LOTUS REBELLION **20**:138
WHITE MOUNTAIN (Alaska)
map (64° 40′N 162° 12′W) **1**:242
WHITE MOUNTAIN PEAK
map (37° 38′N 118° 15′W) **4**:31
WHITE MOUNTAINS **14**:124–125 *illus.*; **20**:138
map (44° 10′N 71° 35′W) **14**:123
New Hampshire **14**:122
Washington, Mount **20**:44
WHITE NILE *see* NILE RIVER
WHITE PASS
map (59° 38′N 135° 5′W) **1**:242
WHITE PIGEON (Michigan)
map (41° 48′N 85° 38′W) **13**:377
WHITE PINE (Michigan)
map (46° 44′N 89° 35′W) **13**:377
WHITE PINE (county in Nevada)
map (39° 30′N 114° 45′W) **14**:111
WHITE PLAGUE *see* TUBERCULOSIS
WHITE PLAINS (New York)
map (41° 2′N 73° 46′W) **14**:149
WHITE REVOLUTION
Iran **11**:253
WHITE RIVER (city in South Dakota)
map (43° 34′N 100° 45′W) **18**:103
WHITE RIVER (Nevada)
map (37° 42′N 115° 10′W) **14**:111
WHITE RIVER (river in Arizona)
map (33° 44′N 110° 13′W) **2**:160
WHITE RIVER (river in Colorado)
map (40° 4′N 109° 24′W) **5**:116
WHITE RIVER (river in Indiana)
map (38° 25′N 87° 44′W) **11**:111
WHITE RIVER (river in South Dakota)
map (43° 45′N 99° 30′W) **18**:103
WHITE RIVER (Texas)
map (33° 14′N 100° 56′W) **19**:129
WHITE RIVER (Vermont)
map (43° 37′N 72° 20′W) **19**:554
WHITE RIVER (Washington)
map (47° 12′N 122° 15′W) **20**:35
WHITE RIVER (Yukon Territory)
map (63° 11′N 139° 36′W) **20**:345
WHITE RIVER JUNCTION (Vermont)
map (43° 39′N 72° 19′W) **19**:554
WHITE ROCK (British Columbia)
map (49° 2′N 122° 49′W) **3**:491
WHITE ROT FUNGUS **20**:138 *bibliog.*
WHITE RUSSIA *see* BELORUSSIAN SOVIET SOCIALIST REPUBLIC (USSR)
WHITE SANDS MISSILE RANGE **20**:138
WHITE SANDS NATIONAL MONUMENT **14**:138 *illus.*
WHITE SEA **20**:138
map (65° 30′N 38° 0′E) **19**:388
WHITE SLAVE TRAFFIC ACT *see* MANN ACT
WHITE SPRINGS (Florida)
map (30° 20′N 82° 45′W) **8**:172
WHITE SULPHUR SPRINGS (Montana)
map (46° 33′N 110° 54′W) **13**:547
WHITE SULPHUR SPRINGS (West Virginia) **20**:138
Greenbriar Hotel **20**:114 *illus.*
map (37° 48′N 80° 18′W) **20**:111
WHITE SUPREMACY *see* DISCRIMINATION
WHITE-TAILED DEER *see* DEER
WHITE VOLTA LAKE
map (9° 15′N 1° 10′W) **19**:472
WHITE WHALE *see* BELUGA (whale)
WHITE-WINGED CHOUGH *see* AUSTRALIAN MUDNEST BUILDER
WHITE WOMAN OF THE GENESEE *see* JEMISON, MARY
WHITECOURT (Alberta)
map (54° 9′N 115° 41′W) **1**:256
WHITEFACE (Texas)
map (33° 36′N 102° 37′W) **19**:129
WHITEFACE, MOUNT
map (44° 22′N 73° 54′W) **14**:149
WHITEFIELD (county in Georgia)
map (34° 50′N 84° 57′W) **9**:114
WHITEFIELD (New Hampshire)
map (44° 22′N 71° 36′W) **14**:123
WHITEFIELD, GEORGE **20**:138 *bibliog.*
Great Awakening **9**:308
United States, history of the **19**:438
Methodism **13**:344
Savannah (Georgia) **17**:99
WHITEFISH **20**:138 *illus.*
WHITEFISH (Montana)
map (48° 25′N 114° 20′W) **13**:547
WHITEFISH BAY
map (46° 40′N 84° 50′W) **13**:377
WHITEFISH BAY (Wisconsin)
map (43° 7′N 87° 55′W) **20**:185
WHITEFISH POINT (Michigan)
map (46° 45′N 84° 59′W) **13**:377
WHITEFISH RANGE
map (48° 40′N 114° 26′W) **13**:547
WHITEFISH RIVER
map (45° 55′N 86° 57′W) **13**:377
WHITEFLY **20**:139
WHITEHALL (Michigan)
map (43° 24′N 86° 21′W) **13**:377
WHITEHALL (New York)
map (43° 33′N 73° 25′W) **14**:149
WHITEHALL (Wisconsin)
map (44° 22′N 91° 19′W) **20**:185
WHITEHALL PALACE **12**:400 *illus.*; **20**:139 *bibliog.*
WHITEHEAD *see* CYST
WHITEHEAD, ALFRED NORTH **20**:139 *bibliog., illus.*
mathematics, history of **13**:226
Principia Mathematica **15**:550
process philosophy **15**:561
Process and Reality **20**:139
Russell, Bertrand **20**:139
WHITEHEAD, ROBERT **20**:139 *bibliog.*
torpedo (projectile) **19**:242–243 *illus.*
WHITEHORSE (Yukon Territory) **20**:139; **20**:345 *illus.*
map (60° 43′N 135° 3′W) **20**:345
WHITEHORSE, CHIEF
Oto **14**:460
WHITEMAN, PAUL **20**:139 *bibliog.*
Beiderbecke, Bix **3**:171–172
WHITEMOUTH (Manitoba)
map (49° 57′N 95° 59′W) **13**:119
WHITEPINE (Montana)
map (47° 45′N 115° 29′W) **13**:547
WHITESBURG (Kentucky)
map (37° 7′N 82° 49′W) **12**:47
WHITESIDE (county in Illinois)
map (41° 45′N 89° 55′W) **11**:42
WHITESVILLE (Kentucky)
map (37° 41′N 86° 52′W) **12**:47
WHITESVILLE (West Virginia)
map (37° 59′N 81° 32′W) **20**:111
WHITEVILLE (North Carolina)
map (34° 20′N 78° 42′W) **14**:242
WHITEVILLE (Tennessee)
map (35° 20′N 89° 11′W) **19**:104
WHITEWARE
ceramics **4**:258–259
WHITEWATER (Kansas)
map (37° 58′N 97° 9′W) **12**:18
WHITEWATER (Montana)
map (48° 46′N 107° 38′W) **13**:547
WHITEWATER (Wisconsin)
map (42° 50′N 88° 44′W) **20**:185
WHITEWATER BALDY MOUNTAIN
map (33° 20′N 108° 39′W) **14**:136
WHITEWATER BAY
map (25° 16′N 81° 0′W) **8**:172
WHITEWOOD (Saskatchewan)
map (50° 20′N 102° 15′W) **17**:81
WHITEWOOD (South Dakota)
map (44° 28′N 103° 20′W) **18**:103
WHITEWRIGHT (Texas)
map (33° 31′N 96° 24′W) **19**:129
WHITGIFT, JOHN **20**:139 *bibliog.*
WHITING (Indiana)
map (41° 40′N 87° 29′W) **11**:111
WHITING (Kansas)
map (39° 35′N 95° 37′W) **12**:18
WHITING, JOHN **20**:140
WHITINSVILLE (Massachusetts)
map (42° 7′N 71° 40′W) **13**:206
WHITLAM, GOUGH **20**:140 *bibliog., illus.*
Australia, history of **2**:341–342
WHITLASH (Montana)
map (48° 54′N 111° 15′W) **13**:547
WHITLEY (county in Indiana)
map (41° 10′N 85° 29′W) **11**:111
WHITLEY (county in Kentucky)
map (36° 45′N 84° 10′W) **12**:47
WHITLEY CITY (Kentucky)
map (36° 43′N 84° 28′W) **12**:47
WHITMAN (Massachusetts)
map (42° 5′N 70° 56′W) **13**:206
WHITMAN (county in Washington)
map (46° 50′N 117° 30′W) **20**:35
WHITMAN, MARCUS **20**:140 *bibliog.*
Cayuse **4**:227
WHITMAN, ROBERT
happenings **10**:41
WHITMAN, WALT **20**:140–141 *bibliog., illus.*
Leaves of Grass **12**:263
Song of Myself **18**:64
WHITMAN SQUARE (New Jersey)
map (39° 45′N 75° 3′W) **14**:129
WHITMIRE (South Carolina)
map (34° 30′N 81° 37′W) **18**:98
WHITNEY (Ontario)
map (45° 30′N 78° 14′W) **14**:393
WHITNEY (Texas)
map (31° 57′N 97° 19′W) **19**:129
WHITNEY, ANNE **20**:141 *bibliog.*
WHITNEY, ELI **20**:141 *bibliog., illus.*
cotton **5**:307
machine tools **13**:23
manufacturing **13**:132
mass production **13**:203–204
WHITNEY, GERTRUDE VANDERBILT **20**:141–142 *bibliog.*
WHITNEY, JOSIAH D.
Whitney, Mount **20**:142
WHITNEY, MOUNT **20**:142
map (36° 35′N 118° 18′W) **4**:31
WHITNEY, PHYLLIS **20**:142
WHITNEY, WILLIAM COLLINS **20**:142 *bibliog.*
WHITNEY, WILLIAM DWIGHT **20**:142
WHITNEY MUSEUM OF AMERICAN ART (New York City) **20**:142 *bibliog.*
Kuniyoshi, Yasuo **12**:137
New York (city) **14**:145 *map*
Whitney, Gertrude Vanderbilt **20**:141–142
WHITSUNDAY *see* PENTECOST
WHITTAKER, CHARLES EVANS **12**:246 *illus.*; **20**:142
WHITTAKER, R. H.
classification, biological **5**:43
Protista **15**:577
WHITTEMORE (Iowa)
map (43° 4′N 94° 25′W) **11**:244
WHITTEMORE (Michigan)
map (44° 14′N 83° 48′W) **13**:377
WHITTIER (California)
map (33° 59′N 118° 2′W) **4**:31
WHITTIER, JOHN GREENLEAF **20**:142 *bibliog.*
WHITTINGTON, DICK *see* WHITTINGTON, RICHARD
WHITTINGTON, RICHARD **20**:142
WHITTLE, SIR FRANK **20**:142 *bibliog.*
WHITTREDGE, WORTHINGTON **20**:143 *bibliog.*
WHITTY, DAME MAY **20**:143
WHITWELL (Tennessee)
map (35° 12′N 85° 31′W) **19**:104
WHITWORTH, SIR JOSEPH **20**:143 *bibliog.*
machine tools **13**:23
screw **17**:157
WHITWORTH, KATHY **20**:143 *bibliog.*
WHO, THE **20**:143 *bibliog.*
WHOLE LIFE INSURANCE
life insurance **12**:329–330
WHOLESALING **20**:143 *bibliog.*
See also RETAILING
food industry **8**:209–211
sales **17**:32
WHOOPING COUGH **20**:143
Bordet, Jules **3**:398
infant mortality **20**:143
infectious diseases **20**:143
respiratory system disorders **16**:182
vaccination **20**:143
WHOOPING CRANE **20**:143–144 *illus.*
crane (bird) **5**:330 *illus.*
WHORF, BENJAMIN LEE **20**:144 *bibliog.*
Whorf hypothesis
Indian languages, American **11**:99
WHORF-SAPIR HYPOTHESIS
anthropological linguistics **2**:50–51
Whorf, Benjamin Lee **20**:144
WHO'S AFRAID OF VIRGINIA WOOLF? (film) **19**:49 *illus.*
WHO'S AFRAID OF VIRGINIA WOOLF? (play) **20**:144
WHRA RIVER
map (52° 27′N 20° 44′E) **15**:388
WHYALLA (Australia)
map (33° 2′S 137° 35′E) **2**:328
WHYCOCOMAGH (Nova Scotia)
map (45° 59′N 61° 7′W) **14**:269
WHYDAH **20**:144
WHYMPER, EDWARD
Chimborazo **4**:358
Matterhorn **13**:231
WHYTE, FREDERIC M.
locomotive **12**:391 *table*
WI-CH'I (game) *see* GO (game)
WIBAUX (Montana)
map (46° 59′N 104° 11′W) **13**:547
WIBAUX (county in Montana)
map (47° 0′N 104° 8′W) **13**:547
WICHITA (American Indians) **20**:144 *bibliog.*
Mississippian culture **14**:239
Pawnee **15**:121
Sun dance **18**:346
WICHITA (Kansas) **12**:21 *illus.*; **20**:144–145
map (37° 41′N 97° 20′W) **12**:18
WICHITA (county in Kansas)
map (38° 40′N 101° 20′W) **12**:18
WICHITA (county in Texas)
map (34° 0′N 98° 45′W) **19**:129

WICHITA FALLS (Texas) **20**:145
map (33° 54′N 98° 30′W) **19**:129
WICHITA MOUNTAINS
map (34° 45′N 98° 40′W) **14**:368
Oklahoma **14**:366–367
WICHITA MOUNTAINS WILDLIFE REFUGE **14**:369–370 *illus.*
WICKENBURG (Arizona)
map (33° 58′N 112° 44′W) **2**:160
WICKER, TOM **20**:145
WICKERSHAM, GEORGE W. **20**:145
WICKERSHAM COMMISSION
Wickersham, George W. **20**:145
WICKHAM, HENRY
rubber **16**:333
WICKIUP **20**:145
WICKIUP RESERVOIR
map (43° 40′N 121° 43′W) **14**:427
WICKLIFFE (Kentucky)
map (36° 58′N 89° 5′W) **12**:47
WICKLOW (Ireland) **20**:145
map (52° 59′N 6° 3′W) **11**:258
WICKLOW MOUNTAINS
map (53° 2′N 6° 24′W) **11**:258
WICOMICO (county in Maryland)
map (38° 22′N 75° 36′W) **13**:188
WICOMICO RIVER
map (38° 13′N 75° 55′W) **13**:188
WIDE-AWAKES **15**:529 *illus.*; **16**:172 *illus.*
WIDE-ANGLE LENS (camera) **4**:56
WIDEFIELD (Colorado)
map (38° 44′N 104° 43′W) **5**:116
WIDEN (West Virginia)
map (38° 28′N 80° 52′W) **20**:111
WIDENER COLLECTION (art)
National Gallery of Art **14**:33
WIDGEON **20**:145 *illus.*
WIDOR, CHARLES MARIE **20**:145 *bibliog.*
WIDOW
marriage **13**:165
WIDOWBIRD *see* WHYDAH
WIED, GUSTAV **20**:145
WIEDEMANN-FRANZ LAW
conduction, electric **5**:174
WIEGMANN, MARIE *see* WIGMAN, MARY
WIELAND, CHRISTOPH MARTIN **20**:145 *bibliog.*
WIELAND, HEINRICH OTTO **20**:146
WIELAND, JOYCE
Canadian art and architecture **4**:91
WIEN (Austria) *see* VIENNA (Austria)
WIEN, WILHELM JAN **20**:146
displacement law, blackbody radiation **20**:146
radiation law, blackbody radiation **3**:321
X rays, wavelength **20**:146
WIENE, ROBERT
film, history of **8**:83
WIENER (meat) *see* SAUSAGE
WIENER, NORBERT **20**:146 *bibliog.*
Brownian motion theory **20**:146
communication **5**:143
cybernetics **5**:401
cybernetics, founder **20**:146
stationary time series, codiscoverer **20**:146
stochastic processes theory **20**:146
WIENER NEUSTADT (Austria)
map (47° 49′N 16° 15′E) **2**:348
WIENER WERKSTÄTTE **20**:146 *bibliog.*
Hoffmann, Josef **10**:195
Secession movement **17**:178
WIENIAWSKI, HENRI **20**:146
WIEPRECHT, WILHELM
tuba **19**:326
WIEPRZ RIVER
map (51° 34′N 21° 49′E) **15**:388
WIESBADEN (West Germany) **20**:146
map (50° 5′N 8° 14′E) **9**:140
Nassau (historical region) **14**:25
WIESEL, ELIE **20**:146
WIFE *see* FAMILY; MARRIAGE
WIG **20**:146–147 *bibliog.*, *illus.*
costume **5**:292–303 *illus.*
WIGGIN, KATE DOUGLAS **20**:147
WIGGINS (Colorado)
map (40° 14′N 104° 4′W) **5**:116
WIGGINS (Mississippi)
map (30° 51′N 89° 8′W) **13**:469
WIGGLESWORTH, MICHAEL **20**:147 *bibliog.*
WIGHT, ISLE OF *see* ISLE OF WIGHT (England)
WIGMAN, MARY **20**:147 *bibliog.*
WIGNER, EUGENE PAUL **20**:147
Jensen, J. Hans **20**:147
Manhattan Project **20**:147
Mayer, Marie Goeppert **20**:147
nuclear power **20**:147
WIGTOWN (Scotland) **20**:147
WIGWAM **11**:120 *illus.*; **20**:147
WILBARGER (county in Texas)
map (34° 4′N 99° 15′W) **19**:129
WILBER (Nebraska)
map (40° 29′N 96° 58′W) **14**:70
WILBERFORCE, SAMUEL **20**:147 *bibliog.*
WILBERFORCE, WILLIAM **20**:147 *bibliog.*
WILBRAHAM (Massachusetts)
map (42° 7′N 72° 26′W) **13**:206
WILBUR (Washington)
map (47° 46′N 118° 42′W) **20**:35
WILBUR, RICHARD **20**:147–148 *bibliog.*
WILBURTON (Oklahoma)
map (34° 55′N 95° 19′W) **14**:368
WILBYE, JOHN **20**:148 *bibliog.*
WILCOX (county in Alabama)
map (32° 0′N 87° 20′W) **1**:234
WILCOX (county in Georgia)
map (32° 0′N 83° 25′W) **9**:114
WILCOX (Pennsylvania)
map (41° 35′N 78° 41′W) **15**:147
WILD BUNCH, THE
outlaws **14**:468 *illus.*
WILD CHILD, THE (film)
feral children **8**:51
WILD CHILDREN *see* FERAL CHILDREN
WILD DUCK, THE (play) **20**:148
Ibsen, Henrik **11**:6–7
WILD PEAK
map (46° 53′N 10° 52′E) **2**:348
WILD RICE **20**:148
WILD RICE RIVER
map (47° 20′N 96° 50′W) **13**:453
WILD ROSE (Wisconsin)
map (44° 11′N 89° 15′W) **20**:185
WILD WEST SHOW
Buffalo Bill **3**:546–547
Hickok, Wild Bill **10**:157
Oakley, Annie **14**:312
Rogers, Will **16**:269
WILDCAT **20**:148 *bibliog.*, *illus.*
Kaffir cat **12**:5
WILDE, OSCAR **20**:148–149 *bibliog.*, *illus.*
decadence **6**:72
Importance of Being Earnest, The **11**:62
comedy **5**:132
Langtry, Lillie **12**:196
Picture of Dorian Gray, The **15**:294
WILDEBEEST **20**:149 *illus.*
animal migration **2**:27
WILDENBRUCH, ERNST VON
Austrian literature **2**:354
WILDENVEY, HERMAN **20**:149
WILDER (Idaho)
map (43° 40′N 116° 55′W) **11**:26
WILDER (Vermont)
map (43° 40′N 72° 18′W) **19**:554
WILDER, BILLY **20**:149 *bibliog.*
WILDER, LAURA INGALLS **20**:149
WILDER, THORNTON **20**:149–150 *bibliog.*, *illus.*
Bridge of San Luis Rey, The **3**:484
Our Town **14**:467
Skin of Our Teeth, The **17**:343
WILDERNESS CAMPAIGN **20**:150 *bibliog.*
Grant, Ulysses S. **9**:288
WILDERNESS ROAD **12**:49 *illus.*; **20**:150 *bibliog.*
Cumberland Gap **5**:387
Transylvania Company **19**:283
WILDERSVILLE (Tennessee)
map (35° 48′N 88° 22′W) **19**:104
WILDFOWL TRUST, SLIMBRIDGE, ENGLAND
duck **6**:292
WILDLIFE REFUGE **20**:150–151 *bibliog.*
Leopold, Aldo **12**:293
National Forest System, U.S. **14**:32
Wichita Mountains Wildlife Refuge **14**:369–370 *illus.*
WILDMAN, SIR JOHN
Levelers **12**:302
WILDROSE (North Dakota)
map (48° 38′N 103° 11′W) **14**:248
WILDWOOD (New Jersey)
map (38° 59′N 74° 49′W) **14**:129
WILDWOOD CREST (New Jersey)
map (38° 58′N 74° 50′W) **14**:129
WILFRID, SAINT **20**:151
WILGUS, W. J.
tunnel **19**:338
WILHEIM, MOUNT
map (5° 45′S 145° 5′E) **15**:72
WILHELM *see* WILLIAM
WILHELM, HOYT **20**:151 *bibliog.*
WILHELM, KATE **20**:151
WILHELM-PIECK-STADT GUBEN (Germany, East and West)
map (51° 57′N 14° 43′E) **9**:140
WILHELMINA, QUEEN OF THE NETHERLANDS **12**:443 *illus.*; **20**:151 *bibliog.*
WILHELMINA CANAL
map (51° 47′N 4° 51′E) **14**:99
WILHELMINA RANGE
map (3° 45′N 56° 30′W) **18**:364
WILHELMSHAVEN (Germany, East and West)
map (53° 31′N 8° 8′E) **9**:140
WILIGELMO DA MODENA
Romanesque art and architecture **16**:284
WILINGILI ISLAND
map (4° 10′N 73° 28′E) **13**:87
WILKES (county in Georgia)
map (33° 50′N 82° 45′W) **9**:114
WILKES (county in North Carolina)
map (36° 15′N 81° 15′W) **14**:242
WILKES, CHARLES **20**:151 *bibliog.*
Mason, James Murray **13**:199
Trent Affair **19**:290
WILKES, DONALD
rolamite **16**:270
WILKES, JOHN **20**:151–152 *bibliog.*
Wilkes-Barre (Pennsylvania) **20**:152
WILKES-BARRE (Pennsylvania) **20**:152
map (41° 14′N 75° 53′W) **15**:147
WILKES LAND (region in Antarctica)
map (69° 0′S 120° 0′E) **2**:40
WILKESBORO (North Carolina)
map (36° 9′N 81° 9′W) **14**:242
WILKIE (Saskatchewan)
map (52° 25′N 108° 43′W) **17**:81
WILKIE, SIR DAVID **20**:152 *bibliog.*
WILKIN (county in Minnesota)
map (46° 17′N 96° 28′W) **13**:453
WILKINS, SIR GEORGE HUBERT **20**:152 *bibliog.*
WILKINS, JOHN **20**:152 *bibliog.*
Royal Society **20**:152
science education **20**:152
WILKINS, MAURICE **20**:152
Crick, Francis **5**:343
Watson, James D. **20**:67
WILKINS, ROY **20**:152 *bibliog.*, *illus.*
WILKINS-ELLSWORTH EXPEDITION
Sverdrup, Harald Ulrik **18**:375
WILKINSBURG (Pennsylvania)
map (40° 27′N 79° 53′W) **15**:147
WILKINSON (county in Georgia)
map (32° 45′N 83° 10′W) **9**:114
WILKINSON (county in Mississippi)
map (31° 10′N 91° 20′W) **13**:469
WILKINSON, BUD **20**:152–153
WILKINSON, CHARLES BURNHAM "BUD" *see* WILKINSON, BUD
WILKINSON, GEOFFREY **20**:153
compound, chemical **20**:153
Fischer, Ernst **20**:153
WILKINSON, JAMES **20**:153 *bibliog.*
WILKINSON, JEMIMA **20**:153 *bibliog.*
WILKINSON, JOHN **20**:153
technology, history of **19**:65
WILKINSON, NORMAN
Gallipoli campaign **20**:231 *illus.*
WILL (county in Illinois)
map (41° 32′N 88° 5′W) **11**:42
WILL (law) **20**:153 *bibliog.*
escheat **7**:237
heir **10**:109
incompetence **11**:77
inheritance **11**:177
living will
death and dying **6**:69
euthanasia **7**:311
next of kin **14**:175
primogeniture **15**:547
probate **15**:558
property **15**:571
trustee **19**:321–322
trust **19**:321
WILL (philosophy) **20**:153–154 *bibliog.*
hypnosis **10**:350
literature
Dostoyevsky, Fyodor Mikhailovich **6**:244–245
Schopenhauer, Arthur **17**:134
WILLACOOCHEE (Georgia)
map (31° 20′N 83° 3′W) **9**:114
WILLACY (county in Texas)
map (26° 30′N 97° 38′W) **19**:129
WILLAERT, ADRIAN **20**:154 *bibliog.*
Italian music **11**:317–318
music, history of Western **13**:665
WILLAMETTE RIVER **20**:154
map (45° 39′N 122° 46′W) **14**:427
Oregon **14**:428–429 *illus.*
WILLAMINA (Oregon)
map (45° 5′N 123° 29′W) **14**:427
WILLAPA BAY
map (46° 37′N 124° 0′W) **20**:35
WILLARD (Missouri)
map (37° 19′N 93° 28′W) **13**:476
WILLARD (New Mexico)
map (34° 36′N 106° 2′W) **14**:136
WILLARD (Ohio)
map (41° 3′N 82° 44′W) **14**:357
WILLARD (Utah)
map (41° 25′N 112° 2′W) **19**:492
WILLARD, EMMA HART **20**:154 *bibliog.*
WILLARD, FRANCES **20**:154 *bibliog.*
WILLCOX (Arizona)
map (32° 15′N 109° 50′W) **2**:160
WILLEBROEK (Belgium)
map (51° 4′N 4° 22′E) **3**:177
WILLEMITE **20**:154
WILLEMSTAD (Netherlands Antilles) **20**:154
map (12° 6′N 68° 56′W) **19**:542
WILLETT, HURD CURTIS **20**:154
WILLIAM, EARL OF DOUGLAS
Douglas (family) **6**:246–247
WILLIAM, PRINCE
Charles, Prince of Wales **4**:290
WILLIAM I, EMPEROR OF GERMANY **9**:154 *illus.*; **20**:156–157 *bibliog.*
Bismarck, Otto von **3**:298–299
Germany, history of **9**:152; **9**:154
Hohenzollern **10**:199
Prussia **15**:586
San Juan Boundary Dispute **17**:55
WILLIAM I, KING OF ENGLAND (William the Conqueror) **20**:155 *bibliog.*, *illus.*
Bayeux Tapestry **3**:133; **14**:222 *illus.*
Domesday Book **6**:231
English language **7**:191
feudalism
Middle Ages **13**:392
flag **8**:135 *illus.*
France, history of **8**:268
Great Britain, history of **9**:310
Hastings, Battle of **10**:67
Hereward the Wake **10**:142
King's Court **5**:139
Normans **14**:221–222
ship **17**:266
Yorkshire (England) **20**:331
WILLIAM I, KING OF THE NETHERLANDS **20**:157–158 *bibliog.*
Low Countries, history of the **12**:441 *illus.*
WLLIAM I, PRINCE OF ORANGE (William the Silent) **20**:158 *bibliog.*, *illus.*
assassination of (1584) **12**:440 *illus.*
caricature of **12**:441 *illus.*
Delft (Netherlands) **6**:92
Low Countries, history of the **12**:439
Orange (dynasty) **14**:414
WILLIAM II, EMPEROR OF GERMANY **20**:157 *bibliog.*, *illus.*
cartoon depicting **9**:154 *illus.*
Germany, history of **9**:154–155
Hohenzollern (dynasty) **10**:199
royal family **20**:157 *illus.*
World War I **20**:219–220 *illus.*
WILLIAM II, KING OF ENGLAND (William Rufus) **20**:155–156 *bibliog.*
WILLIAM II, KING OF THE NETHERLANDS **20**:158
WILLIAM II, PRINCE OF ORANGE **20**:158 *bibliog.*
WILLIAM III, KING OF ENGLAND, SCOTLAND, AND IRELAND **20**:156 *bibliog.*, *illus.*
balance of power **3**:32
English Bill of Rights **3**:253
Glorious Revolution **9**:209
James II, King of England, Scotland, and Ireland **11**:356
Marlborough, John Churchill, 1st Duke of **13**:160
Mary II, Queen **13**:186
Orange (dynasty) **14**:414
Spanish Succession, War of the **18**:162
WILLIAM III, KING OF THE NETHERLANDS **20**:158
WILLIAM IV, KING OF ENGLAND, SCOTLAND, AND IRELAND **20**:156 *bibliog.*
WILLIAM IV, PRINCE OF ORANGE
Orange (dynasty) **14**:414
WILLIAM V, PRINCE OF ORANGE
Orange (dynasty) **14**:414
WILLIAM OF AUVERGNE **20**:154
WILLIAM "BILL" DANNELLY RESERVOIR
map (32° 10′N 87° 10′W) **1**:234

WILLIAM OF CHAMPEAUX 20:154 *bibliog.*
  Abelard, Peter 1:55
WILLIAM THE CONQUEROR *see* WILLIAM I, KING OF ENGLAND (William the Conqueror)
WILLIAM THE LION, KING OF SCOTLAND 20:154 *bibliog.*
  Scotland 17:151
WILLIAM AND MARY, COLLEGE OF
  Blair, James 3:324
  Virginia, state universities and colleges of 19:612
WILLIAM OF OCCAM 20:154–155 *bibliog.*
  Occam's razor 14:320
  scholasticism 17:131–132
WILLIAM OF PARIS *see* WILLIAM OF AUVERGNE
WILLIAM RUFUS *see* WILLIAM II, KING OF ENGLAND
WILLIAM OF SENS 20:155 *bibliog.*
  Canterbury Cathedral 4:116
WILLIAM THE SILENT *see* WILLIAM I, PRINCE OF ORANGE (William the Silent)
WILLIAM TELL (play)
  Schiller, Johann Christoph Friedrich von 17:121
WILLIAMETTE SUMMIT (pass)
  map (43° 36′N 122° 2′W) 14:427
WILLIAMS (Arizona)
  map (35° 15′N 112° 11′W) 2:160
WILLIAMS (Iowa)
  map (42° 29′N 93° 33′W) 11:244
WILLIAMS (county in North Dakota)
  map (48° 20′N 103° 20′W) 14:248
WILLIAMS (county in Ohio)
  map (41° 35′N 84° 33′W) 14:357
WILLIAMS, BETTY *see* CORRIGAN, MAIREAD, AND WILLIAMS, BETTY
WILLIAMS, CHARLES 20:159
WILLIAMS, EDWARD BENNETT 20:159 *bibliog.*
WILLIAMS, ELEAZER 20:159
WILLIAMS, EMLYN 20:159 *bibliog.*
WILLIAMS, ERIC 20:159
WILLIAMS, HANK 20:159 *bibliog.*
WILLIAMS, HARRISON
  ABSCAM 1:62
WILLIAMS, JOHN 20:159
WILLIAMS, JOHN A. 20:159 *bibliog.*
WILLIAMS, ROGER 20:159–160 *bibliog., illus.*
  Baptists 3:73–74
  Miantonomo 13:370
  Rhode Island 16:201
WILLIAMS, ROY
  Teamsters, Chauffeurs, Warehousemen, and Helpers of America, International Brotherhood of 19:58
WILLIAMS, TED 20:160 *bibliog., illus.*
WILLIAMS, TENNESSEE 20:160–161 *bibliog., illus.*
  Cat on a Hot Tin Roof 4:197
  Glass Menagerie, The 9:202
  Kazan, Elia 12:33–34
  Streetcar Named Desire, A 18:297
WILLIAMS, VAUGHAN
  Te Deum laudamus 19:53
WILLIAMS, WILLIAM CARLOS 20:161 *bibliog., illus.*
WILLIAMS, WILLIAM SHERLEY 20:161 *bibliog.*
WILLIAMS BAY (Wisconsin)
  map (42° 35′N 88° 33′W) 20:185
WILLIAMS COLLEGE 20:161
  Hopkins, Mark 10:232
WILLIAMS LAKE (British Columbia)
  map (52° 8′N 122° 9′W) 3:491
WILLIAMSBURG (Iowa)
  map (41° 40′N 92° 1′W) 11:244
WILLIAMSBURG (Kentucky)
  map (36° 44′N 84° 10′W) 12:47
WILLIAMSBURG (county in South Carolina)
  map (33° 40′N 79° 45′W) 18:98
WILLIAMSBURG (Virginia) 20:162 *illus.*
  archaeology 2:117 *illus.*
  Capitol building 1:327 *illus.*
  garden 9:43 *illus.*
  The Governor's Palace 5:110 *illus.*
  map (37° 16′N 76° 43′W) 19:607
  Noël Hume, Ivor 14:212
WILLIAMSON (county in Illinois)
  map (37° 45′N 88° 58′W) 11:42
WILLIAMSON (county in Tennessee)
  map (35° 50′N 86° 55′W) 19:104
WILLIAMSON (county in Texas)
  map (30° 40′N 97° 40′W) 19:129
WILLIAMSON (West Virginia)
  map (37° 41′N 82° 17′W) 20:111
WILLIAMSON, ALEXANDER WILLIAM
  organic chemistry 14:435
WILLIAMSON, JACK 20:162 *bibliog.*
WILLIAMSON, JAMES
  film, history of 8:81
WILLIAMSON, MALCOLM
  English music 7:204
WILLIAMSON, NICOL 20:162
WILLIAMSON, WILLIAM CRAWFORD
  paleobotany 15:31
WILLIAMSPORT (Indiana)
  map (40° 17′N 87° 17′W) 11:111
WILLIAMSPORT (Maryland)
  map (39° 36′N 77° 49′W) 13:188
WILLIAMSPORT (Newfoundland)
  map (50° 32′N 56° 19′W) 14:166
WILLIAMSPORT (Pennsylvania) 20:162
  Little League baseball 12:373
  map (41° 14′N 77° 0′W) 15:147
WILLIAMSTON (Michigan)
  map (42° 41′N 84° 17′W) 13:377
WILLIAMSTON (North Carolina)
  map (35° 51′N 77° 4′W) 14:242
WILLIAMSTON (South Carolina)
  map (34° 37′N 82° 29′W) 18:98
WILLIAMSTOWN (Kentucky)
  map (38° 38′N 84° 34′W) 12:47
WILLIAMSTOWN (Massachusetts)
  map (42° 43′N 73° 12′W) 13:206
WILLIAMSTOWN (New Jersey)
  map (39° 41′N 74° 60′W) 14:129
WILLIAMSTOWN (Vermont)
  map (44° 7′N 72° 33′W) 19:554
WILLIAMSTOWN (West Virginia)
  map (39° 24′N 81° 27′W) 20:111
WILLIAMSVILLE (Illinois)
  map (39° 57′N 89° 33′W) 11:42
WILLIMANTIC (Connecticut)
  map (41° 43′N 72° 13′W) 5:193
WILLIMANTIC RIVER
  map (41° 43′N 72° 12′W) 5:193
WILLINGBORO (New Jersey)
  map (40° 3′N 74° 53′W) 14:129
WILLINGDON (Alberta)
  map (53° 50′N 112° 8′W) 1:256
WILLISTON (Florida)
  map (29° 23′N 82° 27′W) 8:172
WILLISTON (North Dakota)
  map (48° 9′N 103° 37′W) 14:248
WILLISTON (South Carolina)
  map (33° 24′N 81° 25′W) 18:98
WILLISTON LAKE
  map (56° 0′N 124° 0′W) 3:491
WILLITS (California)
  map (39° 25′N 123° 21′W) 4:31
WILLKIE, WENDELL L. 20:162 *bibliog., illus.*
  Depression of the 1930s 6:120
  presidential elections 15:529
WILLMAR (Minnesota)
  map (45° 7′N 95° 3′W) 13:453
WILLOCH, KÅRE
  Norway 14:263
WILLOUGHBY (Ohio)
  map (41° 38′N 81° 25′W) 14:357
WILLOUGHBY, SIR HUGH
  Arctic 2:142 *map*
  Northeast Passage 14:253
WILLOW (Alaska)
  map (61° 45′N 150° 3′W) 1:242
WILLOW (botany) 20:162–163 *illus.*
  aspen 2:262
  bark
    glycoside 9:212
  cottonwood 5:307
  poplar 15:431
  tacamahac 19:5
WILLOW CITY (North Dakota)
  map (48° 36′N 100° 18′W) 14:248
WILLOW GROVE (Pennsylvania)
  map (40° 8′N 75° 6′W) 15:147
WILLOW LAKE (South Dakota)
  map (44° 38′N 97° 38′W) 18:103
WILLOW RIVER (British Columbia)
  map (54° 4′N 122° 28′W) 3:491
WILLOW SPRINGS (Missouri)
  map (36° 59′N 91° 58′W) 13:476
WILLOWICK (Ohio)
  map (41° 38′N 81° 28′W) 14:357
WILLOWS (California)
  map (39° 31′N 122° 12′W) 4:31
WILLS, GARRY 20:163
WILLS, HELEN NEWINGTON 20:163
WILLS, STATUTE OF
  primogeniture 15:547
WILLS, WILLIAM J.
  Australia, history of 2:340 *map*
  Burke, Robert O'Hara 3:571–572
WILLSHIRE (Ohio)
  map (40° 45′N 84° 48′W) 14:357
WILLSON, MEREDITH 20:163 *bibliog.*
WILLSTÄTTER, RICHARD 20:163
  chlorophyll structure, discoverer 20:163
  partition chromatography 20:163
  photosynthesis 15:275
  plant pigmentation 20:163
WILLY
  Colette 5:101
WILLY-WILLY *see* HURRICANE AND TYPHOON
WILMAR (Arkansas)
  map (33° 38′N 91° 56′W) 2:166
WILMER (Texas)
  map (32° 35′N 96° 41′W) 19:129
WILMETTE (Illinois)
  map (42° 4′N 87° 43′W) 11:42
WILMINGTON (Delaware) 6:90 *illus.*; 20:163
  busing, school 3:590
  map (39° 44′N 75° 33′W) 6:88
  Winterthur Museum 20:181
WILMINGTON (Illinois)
  map (41° 18′N 88° 9′W) 11:42
WILMINGTON (Massachusetts)
  map (42° 33′N 71° 10′W) 3:409
WILMINGTON (North Carolina) 20:163
  map (34° 13′N 77° 55′W) 14:242
WILMINGTON (Ohio)
  map (39° 27′N 83° 50′W) 14:357
WILMOT (Arkansas)
  map (33° 4′N 91° 34′W) 2:166
WILMOT (South Dakota)
  map (45° 25′N 96° 52′W) 18:103
WILMOT, DAVID
  Wilmot Proviso 20:163
WILMOT PROVISO 20:163 *bibliog.*
  Mexican War 13:355
  Taylor, Zachary 19:51
WILMS'S TUMOR
  kidney disease 12:71
WILSALL (Montana)
  map (46° 0′N 110° 40′W) 13:547
WILSON (Arkansas)
  map (35° 34′N 90° 3′W) 2:166
WILSON (county in Kansas)
  map (37° 35′N 95° 45′W) 12:18
WILSON (Louisiana)
  map (30° 56′N 91° 6′W) 12:430
WILSON (North Carolina)
  map (35° 44′N 77° 55′W) 14:242
WILSON (county in North Carolina)
  map (35° 40′N 77° 55′W) 14:242
WILSON (Oklahoma)
  map (34° 10′N 97° 26′W) 14:368
WILSON (county in Tennessee)
  map (36° 10′N 86° 15′W) 19:104
WILSON (Texas)
  map (33° 19′N 101° 44′W) 19:129
WILSON (county in Texas)
  map (29° 7′N 98° 5′W) 19:129
WILSON, ANGUS 20:164
WILSON, CHARLES THOMSON REES 20:164 *bibliog.*
  cloud chamber, inventor 5:68; 20:164
WILSON, COLIN 20:164 *bibliog.*
WILSON, SIR DANIEL
  archaeology 2:116
  prehistory 15:517
WILSON, DOMINGO SANTA CRUZ *see* SANTA CRUZ WILSON, DOMINGO
WILSON, EDMUND (critic) 20:164 *bibliog., illus.*
WILSON, EDMUND B. (biologist) 20:164 *bibliog.*
WILSON, EDWARD O.
  sociobiology 18:27
WILSON, ETHEL 20:164 *bibliog.*
WILSON, SIR HAROLD 20:164–165 *bibliog., illus.*
  Labour party 12:157
WILSON, HENRY 20:165 *bibliog.*
WILSON, J. TUZO
  earth, structure and composition of 7:22
  plate tectonics 15:357
WILSON, JACK *see* WOVOKA (Paiute Indian)
WILSON, JAMES 20:165 *bibliog.*
WILSON, JOHN BURGESS *see* BURGESS, ANTHONY
WILSON, MOUNT (mountain in California)
  map (34° 13′N 118° 4′W) 12:417
WILSON, MOUNT (mountain in Colorado)
  map (37° 51′N 107° 59′W) 5:116
WILSON, RICHARD 20:165 *bibliog.*
WILSON, ROBERT (theater artist) 20:165
WILSON, ROBERT W., AND PENZIAS, ARNO A. (astronomers) 20:165
WILSON, SAMUEL
  Troy (New York) 19:313
  Uncle Sam 19:382
WILSON, SANDY
  musical comedy 13:675
WILSON, W. B. 20:165
WILSON, WOODROW 20:165–167 *bibliog., illus.*
  Democratic party 6:100–101 *illus.*
  Europe, history of 7:294
  Fourteen Points 8:254
  House, Edward M. 10:272
  Lansing, Robert 12:200
  liberalism 12:312
  Paris Peace Conference 15:88; 20:244 *illus.*
  president of the United States 15:526
  Roosevelt, Theodore 16:310
  tariff acts 19:37
  on the three branches of government 5:214–215
  United States, history of the 19:452–453
  World War I 20:167; 20:236 *illus.*
WILSON-GORMAN TARIFF ACT
  Pollock v. *Farmers' Loan and Trust Co.* 15:409
WILSON LAKE
  map (38° 57′N 98° 40′W) 12:18
WILSON'S DISEASE
  copper 5:253
  nervous system, diseases of the 14:96
WILT *see* DISEASES, PLANT
WILTON (Connecticut)
  map (41° 12′N 73° 26′W) 5:193
WILTON (Maine)
  map (44° 35′N 70° 14′W) 13:70
WILTON (New Hampshire)
  map (42° 51′N 71° 44′W) 14:123
WILTON (North Dakota)
  map (47° 10′N 100° 47′W) 14:248
WILTON (Wisconsin)
  map (43° 48′N 90° 32′W) 20:185
WILTON, MARIE EFFIE
  Bancroft, Sir Squire 3:61
WILTON HOUSE (Salisbury) 11:212 *illus.*
WILTSHIRE (England) 19:404 *illus.*; 20:167
  cities
    Salisbury 17:33
  prehistory
    Avebury 2:369
WIMBLEDON (North Dakota)
  map (47° 10′N 98° 28′W) 14:248
WIMBLEDON TOURNAMENT (tennis)
  Borg, Björn 3:398
  champions 19:110 *table*
WIMSEY, LORD PETER (fictional character) 17:106
WINCHELL, WALTER 20:167–168 *bibliog., illus.*
WINCHENDON (Massachusetts)
  map (42° 41′N 72° 3′W) 13:206
WINCHESTER (England) 20:168
  illuminated manuscripts 11:47–48 *illus.*
WINCHESTER (Illinois)
  map (39° 38′N 90° 27′W) 11:42
WINCHESTER (Indiana)
  map (40° 10′N 84° 59′W) 11:111
WINCHESTER (Kentucky)
  map (37° 59′N 84° 11′W) 12:47
WINCHESTER (New Hampshire)
  map (42° 46′N 72° 23′W) 14:123
WINCHESTER (Tennessee)
  map (35° 10′N 86° 1′W) 19:104
WINCHESTER (Virginia)
  map (39° 11′N 78° 10′W) 19:607
WINCHESTER COLLEGE 20:168 *bibliog.*
WINCKELMANN, JOHANN 2:121 *illus.*; 20:168 *bibliog., illus.*
  Mengs, Anton Raphael 13:297
  neoclassicism (art) 14:81
WINCKLER, HUGO 20:168
  Boğazköy 3:360
WIND 20:168–170 *bibliog., illus., map*
  atmosphere 2:300–302
  atmospheric circulation 5:57 *illus.*
  atmospheric tide 2:304
  blizzard 3:333
  chinook 4:396
  climate 5:57 *illus.*
  Coriolis effect 5:263
  cyclone and anticyclone 5:405–406
  distribution 20:169
  equatorial area 20:169 *illus.*
  evapotranspiration 7:315
  foehn 8:193
  hurricane and typhoon 10:317–319
  jet stream 11:407–408
  measurement
    anemometer 1:410
    Beaufort scale 3:146
  Mediterranean climate 13:276

WIND (cont.)
microclimate **13**:384
mistral **13**:482
monsoon **13**:543–544
mountain climates **13**:620–621
mountain and valley winds **13**:624
ocean-atmosphere interaction **14**:321–322
ocean currents **14**:322
planetary winds **20**:169
pollination **15**:408–409
rain shadow effect **16**:77
shipping route **17**:277
sirocco **17**:328
solar wind **18**:53
squall and squall line **18**:201–202
thunderstorm **19**:185
tornado **19**:239–240
trade winds **19**:263
water wave **20**:57–60
waterspout **20**:66
weather variation and extremes **20**:80–82
westerlies **20**:115
whirlwind **20**:132
wind chill **20**:170
wind rose diagram **20**:171
wind systems, worldwide
January conditions **14**:323 *map*
July conditions **14**:323 *map*
windmills and wind power **20**:172–173
zonda **20**:373
WIND ACTION **20**:170 *bibliog.*
desert **6**:128
dust devil **6**:308–309
erosion and sedimentation **7**:232–233; **20**:170
Hadley cell **10**:8
landforms **20**:170
loess **12**:393
microseism **13**:388
sand dune **17**:60
sandstorm and dust storm **17**:63–64
upwelling, oceanic **19**:473–474
water wave **20**:57–60 *illus.*
WIND CHILL **20**:170 *bibliog.*
WIND INSTRUMENTS (music) **20**:170–171 *bibliog., illus.*
accordion **1**:76–77
African **1**:169–170 *illus.*
alphorn **1**:308–309
Arabian music **2**:99–100
aulos **2**:323
bagpipe **3**:22–23 *illus.*
bassoon **3**:118–119 *illus.*
bugle **3**:548
Chinese music **4**:392–393 *illus.*
clarinet **5**:37 *illus.*
concertina **5**:170
contrabassoon **5**:231
cornet **5**:268–269 *illus.*
cornett **5**:269
English horn **7**:190–191
fife **8**:74
flageolet **8**:149
flügelhorn **8**:184
flute **8**:188–189
French horn **8**:311–312
harmonica **10**:51 *illus.*
Indian music **11**:102 *illus.*
Japanese music **11**:381–382 *illus.*
key **12**:62
krummhorn **12**:131–132 *illus.*
musical instruments **13**:676–677 *illus.*
oboe **14**:316 *illus.*
ophicleide **14**:404
organ (musical instrument) **14**:432–434
panpipes **15**:60–61 *illus.*
piccolo **15**:292
recorder **16**:110 *illus.*
reed organ **16**:118
sackbut **17**:7
saxophone **17**:105–106 *illus.*
shawm **2**:99 *illus.*; **17**:246
sheng **17**:255
shofar **17**:281
trombone **19**:306 *illus.*
trumpet **19**:319–320 *illus.*
tuba **19**:326 *illus.*
WIND LAKE (Wisconsin)
map (42° 50′N 88° 9′W) **20**:185
WIND RIVER **20**:304 *illus.*
map (43° 35′N 108° 13′W) **20**:301
WIND-RIVER INDIANS *see* SHOSHONI (American Indians)
WIND RIVER PEAK
map (42° 42′N 109° 7′W) **20**:301
WIND RIVER RANGE
map (43° 5′N 109° 25′W) **20**:301
WIND ROSE DIAGRAM **20**:171
uses **20**:171
wind direction and frequency **20**:171
WIND IN THE WILLOWS, THE (book) **20**:172
Grahame, Kenneth **9**:281
WIND TUNNEL **20**:171–172 *bibliog., illus.*
aerodynamics **1**:124
aerospace industry **1**:126
helium **10**:113
WINDAUS, ADOLF **20**:172
WINDBER (Pennsylvania)
map (40° 14′N 78° 50′W) **15**:147
WINDER (Georgia)
map (32° 59′N 83° 43′W) **9**:114
WINDFALL-PROFITS TAX
petroleum industry **15**:215
WINDFLOWER *see* ANEMONE
WINDHAM (county in Connecticut)
map (41° 55′N 71° 55′W) **5**:193
WINDHAM (county in Vermont)
map (43° 2′N 72° 43′W) **19**:554
WINDHOEK (Namibia) **20**:172
map (22° 34′S 17° 6′E) **14**:10
WINDLASS **13**:19 *illus.*
WINDMILLS AND WIND POWER **13**:380 *illus.*; **20**:172–174 *bibliog., illus.*
energy sources **7**:175
engine **7**:177
mill **13**:424–425 *illus.*
Netherlands **14**:98 *illus.*
Spain **18**:143 *illus.*
technology, history of **19**:64
WINDOM (Minnesota)
map (43° 52′N 95° 7′W) **13**:453
WINDOM PEAK
map (37° 37′N 107° 35′W) **5**:116
WINDOW **20**:174 *bibliog., illus.*
glass **9**:198–199
rose window **16**:314
stained glass **18**:211–213
WINDOW ROCK (Arizona)
map (35° 41′N 109° 3′W) **2**:160
WINDPIPE *see* LARYNX; TRACHEA
WINDSOR (Barbados)
map (13° 8′N 59° 32′W) **3**:75
WINDSOR (Connecticut)
map (41° 51′N 72° 39′W) **5**:193
WINDSOR (dynasty) **20**:175 *bibliog.*
WINDSOR (family)
Edward VIII **7**:69
WINDSOR (Missouri)
map (38° 32′N 93° 31′W) **13**:476
WINDSOR (Newfoundland)
map (48° 57′N 55° 40′W) **14**:166
WINDSOR (North Carolina)
map (36° 0′N 76° 57′W) **14**:242
WINDSOR (Nova Scotia)
map (44° 59′N 64° 8′W) **14**:269
WINDSOR (Ontario) **20**:175
map (42° 18′N 83° 1′W) **14**:393
WINDSOR (Quebec)
map (45° 34′N 72° 0′W) **16**:18
WINDSOR (Vermont)
map (43° 29′N 72° 23′W) **19**:554
WINDSOR (county in Vermont)
map (43° 45′N 72° 33′W) **19**:554
WINDSOR (Virginia)
map (36° 48′N 76° 45′W) **19**:607
WINDSOR, TREATY OF (1386)
Portugal, history of **15**:453
WINDSOR, UNIVERSITY OF **20**:175
WINDSOR CASTLE **19**:404 *illus.*; **20**:175 *bibliog.*
WINDSOR LOCKS (Connecticut)
map (41° 56′N 72° 38′W) **5**:193
WINDSURFING **18**:359
WINDWARD ISLANDS **20**:175
Grenada **9**:357–358 *illus., map*
Grenadine Islands **9**:359
map (13° 0′N 61° 0′W) **20**:109
Martinique **13**:181
Saint Lucia **17**:23
Saint Vincent and the Grenadines **17**:27
WINDWARD PASSAGE
map (20° 0′N 73° 50′W) **4**:148
WINDY PEAK
map (48° 56′N 119° 58′W) **20**:35
WINE **20**:175–179 *bibliog., illus.*,
France **8**:262 *illus.*; **20**:176
Bordeaux **3**:396
Burgundy **3**:570
Champagne **4**:276 *map*
Languedoc **12**:199
Lyon **12**:477
Moselle River **13**:599
Narbonne **14**:21
Reims **16**:131
Germany **20**:176–177
Moselle River **13**:599
Rhineland **16**:196
Wiesbaden **20**:146
Worms **20**:284
grape **9**:289–290
varieties **20**:176 *illus.*
history **20**:174–175
Italy **20**:177
Tuscany **19**:354
Verona **19**:559
Portugal **20**:177
Madeira Islands **13**:40
Russia **19**:396 *illus.*
Moldavian Soviet Socialist Republic (USSR) **13**:506
South Africa **20**:177
Spain **20**:177
Jerez de la Frontera **11**:397
Switzerland
Neuchâtel **14**:104
types
champagne **4**:276
port **15**:442
sake **17**:28
sherry **17**:259
vermouth **19**:558–559
United States **20**:177–178
California **4**:34 *illus.*
Finger Lakes **8**:93; **14**:150 *illus.*
Napa Valley **4**:34 *illus.*
New York (state) **14**:150
vinegar **19**:600
wine-making process **20**:178–179 *illus.*
WINESBURG, OHIO (book) **20**:179
WINFIELD (Alabama)
map (33° 56′N 87° 49′W) **1**:234
WINFIELD (Iowa)
map (41° 7′N 91° 26′W) **11**:244
WINFIELD (Kansas)
map (37° 15′N 96° 59′W) **12**:18
WINFIELD (Missouri)
map (39° 0′N 90° 44′W) **13**:476
WINFIELD (New Jersey)
map (40° 39′N 74° 17′W) **14**:129
WINFIELD (West Virginia)
map (38° 32′N 81° 53′W) **20**:111
WING (aircraft) **1**:211; **1**:213 *illus.*
aerodynamics **1**:123–124
WING (biology)
bird **3**:283
insect **11**:191 *illus.*
WING (North Dakota)
map (47° 9′N 100° 17′W) **14**:248
WINGATE (North Carolina)
map (34° 59′N 80° 27′W) **14**:242
WINGATE, ORDE **20**:179 *bibliog.*
World War II **20**:266
WINGED BEAN
bean **3**:140
WINGED VICTORY *see* NIKE OF SAMOTHRACE
WINGFIELD, WATER CLOPTON
tennis **19**:109
WINGHAM (Ontario)
map (43° 53′N 81° 19′W) **14**:393; **19**:241
WINGO (Kentucky)
map (36° 39′N 88° 45′W) **12**:47
WINIFRED (Montana)
map (47° 4′N 109° 23′W) **13**:547
WINISK (Ontario)
map (55° 15′N 85° 12′W) **14**:393
WINISK LAKE
map (52° 55′N 87° 22′W) **14**:393
WINISK RIVER
map (55° 17′N 85° 5′W) **14**:393
WINKEL, NIKOLAUS
metronome **13**:347
WINKELMAN (Arizona)
map (32° 59′N 110° 46′W) **2**:160
WINKELRIED, ARNOLD **20**:179
WINKLER (Manitoba)
map (49° 11′N 97° 56′W) **13**:119
WINKLER (county in Texas)
map (31° 46′N 103° 5′W) **19**:129
WINN (county in Louisiana)
map (31° 55′N 92° 37′W) **12**:430
WINNEBA (Ghana)
map (5° 25′N 0° 36′W) **9**:164
WINNEBAGO (American Indians) **20**:179–180 *bibliog.*
Illinois **11**:45
Indians of North America, art of the **11**:141
Iowa **11**:248
Oto **14**:460
WINNEBAGO (county in Illinois)
map (42° 20′N 89° 15′W) **11**:42
WINNEBAGO (county in Iowa)
map (43° 23′N 93° 45′W) **11**:244
WINNEBAGO (Minnesota)
map (43° 46′N 94° 10′W) **13**:453
WINNEBAGO (Nebraska)
map (42° 14′N 96° 28′W) **14**:70
WINNEBAGO (county in Wisconsin)
map (44° 3′N 88° 38′W) **20**:185
WINNEBAGO, LAKE **20**:180
map (44° 0′N 88° 25′W) **20**:185
WINNECONNE (Wisconsin)
map (44° 7′N 88° 43′W) **20**:185
WINNEMUCCA (Nevada)
map (40° 58′N 117° 44′W) **14**:111
WINNEMUCCA LAKE
map (40° 9′N 119° 20′W) **14**:111
WINNER (South Dakota)
map (43° 22′N 99° 51′W) **18**:103
WINNESHIEK (county in Iowa)
map (43° 15′N 91° 48′W) **11**:244
WINNETKA (Illinois)
map (42° 7′N 87° 44′W) **11**:42
WINNETKA PLAN **20**:180
WINNETT (Montana)
map (47° 0′N 108° 21′W) **13**:547
WINNFIELD (Louisiana)
map (31° 55′N 92° 38′W) **12**:430
WINNIBIGOSHISH, LAKE
map (47° 27′N 94° 12′W) **13**:453
WINNIE-THE-POOH (book) **4**:353 *illus.*; **20**:180
illustrated
Shepard, Ernest Howard **17**:256
Milne, A. A. **13**:431
WINNIPEG (Manitoba) **13**:120 *illus.*; **20**:180
map (49° 53′N 97° 9′W) **13**:119
WINNIPEG, LAKE **13**:121 *illus.*; **20**:180
map (52° 0′N 97° 0′W) **13**:119
WINNIPEG, UNIVERSITY OF **20**:180
WINNIPEG RIVER
map (50° 38′N 96° 19′W) **13**:119
WINNIPEGOSIS (Manitoba)
map (51° 39′N 99° 56′W) **13**:119
WINNIPEGOSIS, LAKE
map (52° 30′N 100° 0′W) **13**:119
WINNIPESAUKEE, LAKE **14**:125 *illus.*; **20**:180
map (43° 35′N 71° 20′W) **14**:123
WINNISQUAM LAKE
map (43° 32′N 71° 30′W) **14**:123
WINNSBORO (Louisiana)
map (32° 10′N 91° 43′W) **12**:430
WINNSBORO (South Carolina)
map (34° 22′N 81° 5′W) **18**:98
WINOGRAND, GARRY **20**:180
photography, history and art of **15**:272
WINONA (Kansas)
map (39° 4′N 101° 15′W) **12**:18
WINONA (Michigan)
map (46° 52′N 88° 55′W) **13**:377
WINONA (Minnesota)
map (44° 3′N 91° 39′W) **13**:453
WINONA (county in Minnesota)
map (44° 0′N 91° 50′W) **13**:453
WINONA (Mississippi)
map (33° 29′N 89° 44′W) **13**:469
WINONA (Missouri)
map (37° 6′N 91° 19′W) **13**:476
WINONA LAKE (Indiana)
map (41° 14′N 85° 49′W) **11**:111
WINOOSKI (Vermont)
map (44° 29′N 73° 11′W) **19**:554
WINOOSKI RIVER
map (44° 30′N 73° 15′W) **19**:554
WINSCHOTEN (Netherlands)
map (53° 8′N 7° 2′E) **14**:99
WINSLOW (Arizona)
map (35° 1′N 110° 42′W) **2**:160
WINSLOW (Maine)
map (44° 32′N 69° 38′W) **13**:70
WINSLOW, EDWARD **20**:180 *bibliog.*
WINSLOW, JOHN ANCRUM **20**:180
WINSLOW BOY, THE (play)
Rattigan, Terence **16**:93
WINSTED (Connecticut)
map (41° 55′N 73° 4′W) **5**:193
WINSTON (county in Alabama)
map (34° 10′N 87° 25′W) **1**:234
WINSTON (Florida)
map (28° 2′N 82° 1′W) **8**:172
WINSTON (county in Mississippi)
map (33° 5′N 89° 0′W) **13**:469
WINSTON (Oregon)
map (45° 7′N 123° 25′W) **14**:427
WINSTON-SALEM (North Carolina) **14**:243 *illus.*; **20**:180–181
map (36° 6′N 80° 15′W) **14**:242
WINTER GARDEN (Florida)
map (28° 34′N 81° 35′W) **8**:172
WINTER GARDEN THEATER (New York City)
manager
Booth (family) **3**:394
WINTER HAVEN (Florida)
map (28° 1′N 81° 44′W) **8**:172
WINTER KING, THE *see* FREDERICK V, ELECTOR PALATINE (the Winter King)
WINTER PALACE **20**:181 *bibliog.*
Hermitage Museum **10**:143
WINTER PARK (Florida)
map (28° 36′N 81° 20′W) **8**:172

WINTER PARK (North Carolina)
map (34° 11′N 77° 56′W) **14**:242
WINTER WAR *see* RUSSO-FINNISH WAR
WINTERBERRY **20**:181
WINTERGREEN (botany) **20**:181 *illus.*
Indian pipe **11**:106
pipsissewa **15**:312
WINTERHALTER, FRANZ XAVER **20**:181
Louis Philippe, King of France **12**:423 *illus.*
WINTERPORT (Maine)
map (44° 38′N 68° 51′W) **13**:70
WINTERS (Texas)
map (31° 57′N 99° 58′W) **19**:129
WINTERS, YVOR **20**:181
WINTERSET (Iowa)
map (41° 20′N 94° 1′W) **11**:244
WINTERSWIJK (Netherlands)
map (51° 58′N 6° 44′E) **14**:99
WINTERTHUR (Switzerland) **20**:181
map (47° 30′N 8° 43′E) **18**:394
WINTERTHUR MUSEUM **20**:181 *bibliog.*
WINTERVILLE (Georgia)
map (33° 59′N 83° 18′W) **9**:114
WINTHER, CHRISTIAN **20**:181
WINTHROP (family) **20**:181–182 *bibliog., illus.*
WINTHROP (Maine)
map (44° 18′N 69° 59′W) **13**:70
WINTHROP (Massachusetts)
map (42° 23′N 70° 59′W) **3**:409
WINTHROP (Washington)
map (48° 29′N 120° 11′W) **20**:35
WINTHROP, JOHN (1588–1649)
Hutchinson, Anne **10**:322
Massachusetts **13**:210
Massachusetts Bay Company **13**:212
Winthrop (family) **20**:181–182 *illus.*
WINTHROP, JOHN (1606–1676)
Connecticut **5**:195
Winthrop (family) **20**:182
WINTHROP, JOHN (1714–1779)
Winthrop (family) **20**:182
WINTHROP HARBOR (Illinois)
map (42° 29′N 87° 49′W) **11**:42
WINTON (North Carolina)
map (36° 24′N 76° 56′W) **14**:242
WINTON LAKE
map (39° 15′N 84° 31′W) **14**:357
WIRE **20**:182 *bibliog.*
sculpture
Lippold, Richard **12**:363–364
WIRE SERVICES *see* PRESS AGENCIES AND SYNDICATES
WIREHAIRED POINTER *see* GERMAN WIREHAIRED POINTER
WIREHAIRED POINTING GRIFFON **6**:218 *illus.*; **20**:182 *bibliog., illus.*
WIRELESS *see* TELEGRAPH
WIRETAPPING **20**:183 *bibliog.*
4th Amendment **8**:254–255
privacy, invasion of **15**:556
WIRING, ELECTRICAL *see* ELECTRICAL WIRING
WIRT (county in West Virginia)
map (39° 0′N 81° 22′W) **20**:111
WIRTH, NIKLAUS
Pascal (computer language) **15**:101
WISCASSET (Maine)
map (44° 0′N 69° 40′W) **13**:70
WISCONSIN **20**:183–188 *bibliog., illus., map*
agriculture, forestry, and fishing **20**:186–187
cities
Appleton **2**:89
Green Bay **9**:347–348
Kenosha **12**:45
La Crosse **12**:145
Madison **13**:41
Milwaukee **13**:433–434 *illus.*
Oshkosh **14**:453–454
Racine **16**:36
Sheboygan **17**:248
climate **20**:184
economic activity **20**:186–187 *illus.*
education **20**:186
Beloit College **3**:192–193
Marquette University **13**:163
Wisconsin, University of **20**:188–189
flag **20**:183 *illus.*
government and politics **20**:187–188
historical sites **20**:186
history **20**:188
La Follette, Robert M. **12**:145–146
land and resources **20**:183–186 *map*
map (44° 45′N 89° 30′W) **19**:419
people **20**:186
Mahican **13**:64–65
Menominee **13**:299
Mohegan **13**:503
Montauk **13**:551
Ojibwa **14**:364
Oneida **14**:389
Ottawa **14**:460
Potawatomi **15**:466
Winnebago **20**:179–180
resources **20**:184
rivers, lakes, and waterways **20**:184
Green Bay **9**:347
Winnebago, Lake **20**:180
seal, state **20**:183 *illus.*
tourism **20**:187
transportation **20**:187
vegetation and animal life **20**:184
WISCONSIN, UNIVERSITY OF **20**:188–189
WISCONSIN DELLS (Wisconsin) **20**:186 *illus.*
map (43° 38′N 89° 46′W) **20**:185
WISCONSIN RAPIDS (Wisconsin)
map (44° 23′N 89° 49′W) **20**:185
WISCONSIN RESERVOIR
map (43° 24′N 89° 43′W) **20**:185
WISCONSIN RIVER
map (43° 0′N 91° 15′W) **20**:185
WISDOM (Montana)
map (45° 37′N 113° 27′W) **13**:547
WISDOM, BOOK OF **20**:189 *bibliog.*
WISDOM, JOHN **20**:189 *bibliog.*
WISE (county in Texas)
map (33° 10′N 97° 40′W) **19**:129
WISE (Virginia)
map (36° 59′N 82° 34′W) **19**:607
WISE (county in Virginia)
map (37° 0′N 82° 40′W) **19**:607
WISE, ISAAC MAYER **20**:189 *bibliog.*
WISE, JOHN (balloonist)
balloon **3**:52
WISE, JOHN (clergyman) **20**:189 *bibliog.*
WISE, STEPHEN SAMUEL **20**:189 *bibliog.*
WISE, THOMAS JAMES
literary fraud **12**:370
WISE MEN, THREE *see* MAGI
WISEMAN (Alaska)
map (67° 25′N 150° 6′W) **1**:242
WISEMAN, ADELE **20**:189
WISEMAN, FRED **6**:211 *illus.*; **20**:189–190 *bibliog.*
WISEMAN, NICHOLAS **20**:190 *bibliog.*
WISENT *see* BISON
WISHEK (North Dakota)
map (46° 16′N 99° 33′W) **14**:248
WISMAR (Germany, East and West)
map (53° 53′N 11° 28′E) **9**:140
WISMAR (Guyana)
map (6° 0′N 58° 18′W) **9**:410
WISNER (Louisiana)
map (31° 59′N 91° 39′W) **12**:430
WISNER (Nebraska)
map (41° 59′N 96° 55′W) **14**:70
WISSLER, CLARK **20**:190
WISTAR INSTITUTE **20**:190
life sciences research **20**:190
Wistar, Isaac Jones **20**:190
WISTER, OWEN **20**:190 *bibliog.*
Virginian, The
cowboy **5**:321
WISTERIA **20**:190 *illus.*
WIT **20**:190–191 *bibliog.*
See also COMEDY; SATIRE
caricature **4**:149–150
literature
Cobb, Irvin S. **5**:83
Day, Clarence **6**:55
Dunne, Finley Peter **6**:301
Eulenspiegel, Till **7**:264
Nash, Ogden **14**:24
Parker, Dorothy **15**:90
Perelman, S. J. **15**:163
Skinner, Cornelia Otis **17**:344
Thurber, James **19**:186
Twain, Mark **19**:357
Ward, Artemus **20**:29
Wilde, Oscar **20**:148–149
Wodehouse, Sir P. G. **20**:195
periodicals
Mad **13**:37
New Yorker, The **14**:156
pun **15**:623
WITCH DOCTOR *see* MEDICINE MAN; SHAMAN
WITCH HAZEL (botany) **20**:191 *illus.*
sweet gum **18**:387
WITCHCRAFT **20**:191–192 *bibliog., illus.*
amulet **1**:386
demon **6**:104
evil eye **7**:318
folk medicine **8**:201
Halloween **10**:23
incubus **11**:77
magic **13**:49
Salem Witch Trials **17**:31; **20**:192
satanism **17**:84
superstition **18**:353
witch **20**:191 *illus.*
WITCHWEED **20**:192
WITHDRAWAL SYMPTOMS **20**:192
drug **6**:276
drug abuse **6**:279; **20**:192
WITHERING, WILLIAM
digitalis, medicine **13**:270
medicine **13**:267
WITHERSPOON, JOHN **20**:192 *bibliog.*
WITHLACOOCHEE RIVER
map (29° 0′N 82° 45′W) **8**:172
WITKIEWICZ, STANISŁAW IGNACY **20**:192
WITLOOF *see* CHICORY
WITMER, LIGHTNER
psychology, history of **15**:598
WITNESS **20**:192–193
legal procedure **12**:273
self-incrimination **17**:191
6th amendment **17**:331
WITT, JOHAN DE **20**:193 *bibliog.*
WITTE, EMANUEL DE **20**:193 *bibliog.*
WITTE, SERGEI YULIVICH, COUNT **20**:193 *bibliog.*
Nicholas II, Emperor of Russia **14**:182
WITTELSBACH (family) **20**:193 *bibliog.*
German territories in 1648 **9**:151 *map*
Munich (West Germany) **13**:641
Palatinate **15**:30
WITTENBERG (East Germany) **20**:193
history
Saxony **17**:105
map (51° 52′N 12° 39′E) **9**:140
WITTENBERG (Wisconsin)
map (44° 49′N 89° 10′W) **20**:185
WITTENBERGE (Germany, East and West)
map (53° 0′N 11° 44′E) **9**:140
WITTGENSTEIN, LUDWIG **20**:193–194 *bibliog., illus.*
analytic and linguistic philosophy **1**:389–390
WITTKOWER, RUDOLF **20**:194
WITTLIN, JÓSEF **20**:194
WITWATERSRAND (South Africa) **20**:194
ore deposits **14**:424–425 *table*
WITZ, KONRAD **20**:194–195 *bibliog.*
WIVALLIUS, LARS
Swedish literature **18**:386
WIYOT (American Indians)
Yurok **20**:347
WIZARD ISLAND
Crater Lake **5**:333
WIZARD OF OZ, THE (book) **20**:195
Baum, L. Frank **3**:130
WIZARD OF OZ, THE (film)
Arlen, Harold **2**:170–171
WLADYSLAW I, KING OF POLAND
Piast (dynasty) **15**:289
WLADYSLAW II (or V), KING OF POLAND
Jadwiga, Queen of Poland **11**:348
WŁOCŁAWEK (Poland)
map (52° 39′N 19° 2′E) **15**:388
WOAD **20**:195
WOBBLIES *see* INDUSTRIAL WORKERS OF THE WORLD
WOBURN (Massachusetts)
map (42° 29′N 71° 9′W) **3**:409
WODEHOUSE, SIR P. G. **20**:195 *bibliog.*
WODEN *see* ODIN
WOESTIJNE, KAREL VAN DE **20**:195
WÖHLER, FRIEDRICH **20**:195
biochemistry **3**:261
organic chemistry **14**:434
stereochemistry **18**:258
WOJTYLA, KAROL *see* JOHN PAUL II, POPE
WOK
cooking **5**:239
WOKING (Alberta)
map (55° 35′N 118° 46′W) **1**:256
WOLBACH (Nebraska)
map (41° 24′N 98° 24′W) **14**:70
WOLCOTT (Connecticut)
map (41° 36′N 72° 59′W) **5**:193
WOLCOTT (family) **20**:195 *bibliog.*
WOLCOTT (Indiana)
map (40° 46′N 87° 3′W) **11**:111
WOLCOTT (New York)
map (43° 13′N 76° 49′W) **14**:149
WOLCOTTVILLE (Indiana)
map (41° 32′N 85° 22′W) **11**:111
WOLF **20**:195–196 *bibliog., illus.*
aggression and submission **13**:101 *illus.*
Arctic **2**:140–141 *illus.*
classification, biological **20**:195–196
coyote **5**:323
life cycle **20**:196
maned wolf **13**:105 *illus.*
Pleistocene Epoch **15**:366–367 *illus.*
WOLF, C. J. E. *see* WOLF-RAYET STARS
WOLF, CHRISTA **20**:196
WOLF, HUGO **20**:196 *bibliog.*
WOLF, MAX **20**:196
WOLF CHILDREN *see* FERAL CHILDREN
WOLF CREEK (Montana)
map (47° 0′N 112° 4′W) **13**:547
WOLF-FERRARI, ERMANNO **20**:197
WOLF POINT (Montana)
map (48° 5′N 105° 39′W) **13**:547
WOLF-RAYET STARS **20**:197
WOLF RIVER
map (44° 11′N 88° 48′W) **20**:185
WOLF ROBE (Cheyenne Indian) **4**:338 *illus.*
WOLF VOLCANO
map (0° 2′N 91° 20′W) **7**:52
WOLFE (county in Kentucky)
map (37° 45′N 83° 30′W) **12**:47
WOLFE, CHARLES
La Coruña (Spain) **12**:145
WOLFE, JAMES **20**:197 *bibliog., illus.*
after capture of Quebec in 1759 **4**:81 *illus.*; **8**:314 *illus.*
capture of Quebec in 1759 **19**:439 *illus.*
French and Indian Wars **8**:313–314 *map*
WOLFE, NERO (fictional character)
Stout, Rex **18**:285
WOLFE, THOMAS **20**:197–198 *bibliog., illus.*
Look Homeward, Angel
Perkins, Maxwell **15**:172
WOLFE, TOM **20**:198 *bibliog., illus.*
WOLFE, WILLIAM
United Kingdom **19**:411
WOLFE ISLAND
map (44° 12′N 76° 26′W) **14**:393
WOLFEBORO (New Hampshire)
map (43° 35′N 71° 12′W) **14**:123
WOLFENBÜTTEL (Germany, East and West)
map (52° 10′N 10° 32′E) **9**:140
WOLFF, CASPAR FRIEDRICH **20**:198
epigenesis, heredity **10**:139
WOLFF, CHRISTIAN **20**:198 *bibliog.*
aleatory music **1**:270
WOLFF, ELIZABETH **20**:198
WOLFFISH, SPOTTED
blenny **3**:330
WÖLFFLIN, HEINRICH **20**:198 *bibliog.*
WOLFHOUND *see* BORZOI; IRISH WOLFHOUND
WOLFMÜLLER, ALOIS
motorcycle **13**:614
WOLFRAM
tungsten **19**:333–334
WOLFRAM VON ESCHENBACH **20**:198 *bibliog.*
WOLFRAMITE **20**:198–199
sulfate minerals **18**:333
WOLFSBERG (Austria)
map (46° 51′N 14° 51′E) **2**:348
WOLFSBURG (Germany, East and West)
map (52° 25′N 10° 47′E) **9**:140
WOLFSKILL, WILLIAM
frontier **8**:342
WOLFSON COLLEGE (Cambridge University) **4**:53
WOLFSON COLLEGE (Oxford University) **14**:474
WOLFVILLE (Nova Scotia)
map (45° 5′N 64° 22′W) **14**:269
WOLGEMUT, MICHAEL **20**:199
WOLKENSTEIN, OSWALD VON
minstrels, minnesingers, and troubadours **13**:460
WOLKERS, JAN **20**:199
WOLLASTON, WILLIAM HYDE **20**:199
WOLLASTON LAKE
map (58° 15′N 103° 20′W) **17**:81
WOLLASTONITE
triclinic system **19**:296
Wollaston, William Hyde **20**:199
WOLLONGONG (Australia) **20**:199
map (34° 25′S 150° 54′E) **2**:328
Wollongong University **2**:345 *table*
WOLLSTONECRAFT, MARY **20**:199 *bibliog., illus.*
suffrage, women's **18**:326
Vindication of the Rights of Women, A **19**:600
WOLOF **20**:199 *bibliog.*
Senegal **17**:201
WOLPE, JOSEPH

WOLPE, JOSEPH (cont.)
psychology, history of **15**:598
psychotherapy **15**:603
WOLPE, STEFAN **20**:199 *bibliog.*
WOLSELEY (Saskatchewan)
map (50° 25′N 103° 19′W) **17**:81
WOLSEY, THOMAS **20**:200 *bibliog., illus.*
Cromwell, Thomas, 1st Earl of Essex **5**:358
WOLSTENHOLME TOWNE **20**:200 *bibliog.*
WOLVERHAMPTON (England)
map (52° 36′N 2° 8′W) **19**:403
WOLVERINE **2**:140–141 *illus.*; **20**:200 *illus.*
WOMAN SUFFRAGE *see* SUFFRAGE, WOMEN'S
WOMAN'S CHRISTIAN TEMPERANCE UNION *see* WCTU
WOMAN'S JOURNAL
Blackwell (family) **3**:322–323
WOMB *see* UTERUS
WOMBAT **13**:175 *illus.*; **20**:200 *illus.*
WOMEN (biology)
cervicitis **4**:261–262
endocrine system, diseases of the **7**:170–171
estrous cycle **7**:248
frigidity **8**:334
gynecology **9**:414
hysterectomy **10**:352
menopause **13**:299–300
menstruation **13**:300–302 *illus.*
Pap test **15**:62
pregnancy and birth **15**:502–506 *illus.*
premenstrual stress **15**:518
reproductive system, human **16**:163–166 *illus.*
sex hormones **17**:226
sex reassignment **17**:225–226
sex roles **17**:226–227
sexual development **17**:228–230
uterus **19**:496–497
WOMEN IN LOVE (book) **20**:200–201 *bibliog.*
Lawrence, D. H. **11**:249–250
WOMEN IN SOCIETY **20**:201–204 *bibliog., illus., table*
See also SUFFRAGE, WOMEN'S; WOMEN'S RIGHTS MOVEMENTS
achievement motivation **1**:82
American Association of University Women **1**:337
American literature **1**:348
anorexia nervosa **2**:34
Arabs **2**:104 *illus.*; **2**:105–106
autobiography **2**:356
basketball **3**:112; **3**:113–114
bulimia **3**:557
choral music **4**:407
common law **5**:140
cosmetic expenditures **5**:282 *table*
costume **5**:302–303 *illus.*
discrimination **6**:190
Eastern cultures **20**:203
education
Beecher, Catharine Esther **3**:160–161
Chicago, University of, **4**:342
coeducation **5**:90–91
Seven Sisters Colleges **17**:216
university **19**:469
employment and unemployment **20**:203–204 *table*
affirmative action **1**:132
equal opportunity **7**:223
Kelley, Florence **12**:38
labor force **12**:152
family **8**:17
fashion design **8**:32–33
feminism **8**:48–49
Filipino Americans **14**:442
golf **9**:239
horse racing **10**:248
Indians of North America, music and dance of the **11**:143
inheritance **11**:177
League of Women Voters **12**:258
lesbianism **12**:296
marriage **13**:163–166
concubinage **5**:172
dowry **6**:252
middle age **13**:391
military service
conscription **5**:201
WAC **20**:3
WAF **20**:4
Waves **20**:71
music hall, vaudeville, and burlesque **13**:671
nymphomania **14**:309
political power **20**:204
population **15**:437
preliterate cultures **20**:201
prison **15**:555
prostitution **15**:573–574
public relations **15**:610
role **16**:271
running and jogging **16**:346
sex roles **17**:226–227
sexism **17**:227
softball **18**:35
track and field **19**:259–262
Western cultures **20**:201–202
WOMEN IN THE AIR FORCE *see* WAF
WOMEN'S ARMY CORPS *see* WAC
WOMEN'S INTERNATIONAL LEAGUE FOR PEACE AND FREEDOM
Balch, Emily Greene **3**:33
WOMEN'S RIGHTS MOVEMENTS
affirmative action **1**:132
authors
Firestone, Shulamith **8**:106
Fuller, Margaret **8**:357
Gilman, Charlotte Perkins **9**:182
Greer, Germaine **9**:355
Janeway, Elizabeth **11**:358
Rich, Adrienne **16**:209
Sand, George **17**:59
Schreiner, Olive **17**:134–135
Blackwell (family) **3**:322–323
civil rights **5**:13
civil rights movement **5**:13
equal protection of the laws **7**:224
Equal Rights Amendment **7**:224
feminism **8**:48–49
leaders
Abzug, Bella S. **1**:67–68
Adams, Abigail **1**:93 *illus.*
Addams, Jane **1**:98–99
Anthony, Susan B. **2**:49–50
Beauvoir, Simone de **3**:148
Blatch, Harriot Eaton Stanton **3**:328
Bloomer, Amelia Jenks **3**:340
Brown, Olympia **3**:516
Brownmiller, Susan **3**:519
Catt, Carrie Chapman **4**:213
Chisholm, Shirley **4**:398
Davis, Paulina Wright **6**:52
Duniway, Abigail Scott **6**:300
Friedan, Betty **8**:331
Grimké, Sarah Moore and Angelina Emily **9**:365
Kollantai, Aleksandra **12**:107
Lockwood, Belva Ann Bennett **12**:388
Millett, Kate **13**:430
Mott, Lucretia Coffin **13**:616
Murray, Pauli **13**:650
Pankhurst (family) **15**:60
Rankin, Jeannette **16**:87–88
Stanton, Elizabeth Cady **18**:220
Steinem, Gloria **18**:248–249
Stone, Lucy **18**:281
Thomas, Martha Carey **19**:173
Walker, Mary Edwards **20**:12
Wollstonecraft, Mary **20**:199
Woodhull, Victoria **20**:211–212
Wright, Frances **20**:287–288
Zetkin, Clara **20**:361–362
Mill, John Stuart **13**:425
Ms. (periodical) **13**:629
National Organization for Women **14**:35–36
rape **16**:88
Seneca Falls Convention **17**:200–201
sexism **17**:227
suffrage, women's **18**:326–327
19th Amendment **14**:199
Vindication of the Rights of Women, A (book) **19**:600
WOMEN'S SOCIAL AND POLITICAL UNION (Great Britain)
Pankhurst (family) **15**:60
suffrage, women's **18**:326
WONDER, STEVIE **20**:204–205 *bibliog.*
WONDER FLOWER **12**:341 *illus.*
WONDER LAKE (Illinois)
map (42° 25′N 88° 21′W) **11**:42
WONEWOC (Wisconsin)
map (43° 39′N 90° 14′W) **20**:185
WONG RIVER
map (27° 10′N 89° 30′E) **3**:235
WONJU (Korea)
map (37° 22′N 127° 58′E) **12**:113
WONOTOBO FALLS
map (4° 22′N 57° 55′W) **18**:364
WONSAN (North Korea) **20**:205
climate **12**:113 *table*
map (39° 9′N 127° 25′E) **12**:113
WOOD (botany) **20**:205–206 *bibliog., illus.*
See also LUMBER
architecture
house (in Western architecture) **10**:271 *illus.*
Maybeck, Bernard **13**:246
composition and structure **20**:205
flame retardant
boron **3**:403
fossil record **8**:247 *illus.*
heat content **8**:353 *table*
lignin **12**:340
white rot fungus **20**:138
petrified wood **15**:204–205
prehistoric tools
Paleolithic period **15**:38
products
paper **15**:68–70
tar, pitch, and asphalt **19**:34
properties **20**:206
roof and roofing **16**:306
sapwood **17**:74
termite **19**:116–117 *illus.*
uses **20**:206
fuel **8**:353 *table*
WOOD (family) **20**:205 *bibliog.*
WOOD (county in Ohio)
map (41° 20′N 83° 40′W) **14**:357
WOOD (South Dakota)
map (43° 30′N 100° 29′W) **18**:103
WOOD (county in Texas)
map (32° 48′N 95° 20′W) **19**:129
WOOD (county in West Virginia)
map (39° 12′N 81° 30′W) **20**:111
WOOD (county in Wisconsin)
map (44° 30′N 90° 2′W) **20**:185
WOOD, EDWARD FREDERICK LINDLEY *see* HALIFAX, EDWARD FREDERICK LINDLEY WOOD, 1ST EARL OF
WOOD, FERNANDO **20**:206
WOOD, GRANT **20**:206–207 *bibliog., illus.*
American Gothic **20**:207 *illus.*
Cedar Rapids (Iowa) **4**:229
WOOD, JETHRO **20**:207
plow **15**:369
WOOD, LEONARD **20**:207 *bibliog.*
WOOD, MOUNT
map (45° 17′N 109° 49′W) **13**:547
WOOD, REX
The Fathers of Confederation **4**:84 *illus.*
WOOD, ROBERT E. **20**:207 *bibliog.*
WOOD, ROBERT WILLIAMS **20**:207
WOOD, RON
Rolling Stones, The **16**:272
WOOD ALCOHOL *see* METHYL ALCOHOL
WOOD ANTS' NEST **2**:36 *illus.*
WOOD CARVING **20**:207–209 *bibliog., illus.*
African art **1**:160–164 *illus.*
Brustolon, Andrea **3**:528
craft **5**:327 *illus.*
figurehead **8**:75–76
folk art **8**:197–198 *illus.*
furniture **8**:376–377
Gibbons, Grinling **9**:173
Günther, Ignaz **9**:406
Indians of North America, art of the **11**:138–141 *illus.*
Kamba **12**:9
masks **13**:196–197 *illus.*
misericord **13**:466
Oceanic art **14**:337
rococo style **16**:263
Rush, William **16**:347
Scandinavian art and architecture **17**:111
sculpture techniques **17**:166
Skillin (family) **17**:339
WOOD IBIS *see* STORK
WOOD LAKE (Nebraska)
map (42° 38′N 100° 14′W) **14**:70
WOOD LOUSE
isopod **11**:300
pill bug **15**:303
soil organisms **18**:39 *illus.*
WOOD MOUNTAIN
map (49° 14′N 106° 20′W) **17**:81
WOOD RIVER (Illinois)
map (38° 52′N 90° 5′W) **11**:42
WOOD RIVER (Nebraska)
map (40° 49′N 98° 36′W) **14**:70
WOOD RIVER (Rhode Island)
map (41° 26′N 71° 43′W) **16**:198
WOOD SORREL **20**:209
WOOD SWALLOW **20**:209
WOOD TURTLE *see* POND TURTLE
WOOD WARBLER **20**:209 *illus.*
chat **4**:302
ovenbird **14**:469–470
redstart **16**:116
WOODALL MOUNTAIN
map (34° 45′N 88° 11′W) **13**:469
WOODBINE **20**:210
WOODBINE (Georgia)
map (30° 58′N 81° 43′W) **9**:114
WOODBINE (Iowa)
map (41° 44′N 95° 43′W) **11**:244
WOODBINE (New Jersey)
map (39° 14′N 74° 49′W) **14**:129
WOODBRIDGE (New Jersey)
map (40° 33′N 74° 17′W) **14**:129
WOODBRIDGE (Virginia)
map (38° 39′N 77° 15′W) **19**:607
WOODBURN (Oregon)
map (45° 9′N 122° 51′W) **14**:427
WOODBURY (Connecticut)
map (41° 33′N 73° 13′W) **5**:193
WOODBURY (county in Iowa)
map (42° 23′N 96° 0′W) **11**:244
WOODBURY (New Jersey)
map (39° 50′N 75° 10′W) **14**:129
WOODBURY (Tennessee)
map (35° 50′N 86° 4′W) **19**:104
WOODBURY, WALTER
woodbury type process **20**:210
WOODBURYTYPE PROCESS **20**:210 *bibliog.*
WOODCHUCK
groundhog **9**:373–374
WOODCLIFF LAKE (New Jersey)
map (41° 1′N 74° 3′W) **14**:129
WOODCOCK **20**:210 *bibliog., illus.*
eye **3**:285 *illus.*
game birds **9**:27
WOODCOCK, KATHERINE
Milton, John **13**:433
WOODCOCK, LEONARD **20**:210
WOODCREEPER **20**:210 *illus.*
WOODCUTS AND WOOD ENGRAVINGS **20**:210–211 *bibliog., illus.*
Barbari, Jacopo de' **3**:76
Beham (family) **3**:168–169
Bewick, Thomas **3**:233
block printing **3**:334
book illustration **3**:386–387 *illus.*
Brücke, Die **3**:520–521
Burgkmair, Hans, the Elder **3**:569
Cole, Thomas **5**:100
Doré, Gustave **6**:241–242
Dürer, Albrecht **6**:304–305
graphic arts **9**:291–293
Richter, Adrian Ludwig **16**:214
Schmidt-Rottluff, Karl **17**:128
Vallotton, Félix **19**:508
Wolgemut, Michael **20**:199
WOODEN, JOHN **20**:211 *bibliog.*
WOODFORD (county in Illinois)
map (40° 45′N 89° 15′W) **11**:42
WOODFORD (county in Kentucky)
map (38° 3′N 84° 45′W) **12**:47
WOODHENGE (England) **20**:211 *bibliog.*
megalith **13**:279
WOODHULL (Illinois)
map (41° 11′N 90° 20′W) **11**:42
WOODHULL, VICTORIA **20**:211–212 *bibliog., illus.*
WOODLAND *see* FOREST
WOODLAND (California)
map (38° 41′N 121° 46′W) **4**:31
WOODLAND (Georgia)
map (32° 46′N 84° 33′W) **9**:114
WOODLAND (Maine)
map (45° 9′N 67° 24′W) **13**:70
WOODLAND (North Carolina)
map (36° 20′N 77° 12′W) **14**:242
WOODLAND CREE (American Indians) *see* CREE (American Indians)
WOODLAND CULTURE
Mound Builders **13**:617
North American archaeology **14**:238–239 *illus.*
wampum **20**:21 *illus.*
WOODLAND PARK (Colorado)
map (39° 0′N 105° 3′W) **5**:116
WOODMOOR (Maryland)
map (39° 20′N 76° 44′W) **13**:188
WOODPECKER **20**:212 *bibliog., illus.*
black woodpecker **8**:229 *illus.*
flicker **8**:164
foot **3**:288 *illus.*
great spotted woodpecker **8**:228 *illus.*
WOODRIDGE (Manitoba)
map (49° 17′N 96° 9′W) **13**:119
WOODROFFE, MOUNT
map (26° 20′S 131° 45′E) **2**:328
WOODRUFF (Arizona)
map (34° 47′N 110° 3′W) **2**:160
WOODRUFF (county in Arkansas)
map (35° 10′N 91° 43′W) **2**:166
WOODRUFF (botany) **20**:212
WOODRUFF (South Carolina)
map (34° 45′N 82° 2′W) **18**:98
WOODRUFF (Wisconsin)
map (45° 54′N 89° 42′W) **20**:185
WOODS (county in Oklahoma)
map (36° 45′N 98° 50′W) **14**:368
WOODS, LAKE

map (17° 50′S 133° 30′E) **2**:328
map (35° 20′N 86° 2′W) **19**:104
WOODS, LAKE OF THE
map (49° 15′N 94° 45′W) **14**:393
WOODS, SARA 20:212
WOODS HOLE (Massachusetts)
map (41° 31′N 70° 40′W) **13**:206
WOODS HOLE MARINE BIOLOGICAL LABORATORY 20:212
Baird, Spencer F. **3**:27
WOODS HOLE OCEANOGRAPHIC INSTITUTION 20:212–213
Hyatt, Alpheus **10**:327
Iselin, Columbus O'Donnell **11**:286
JOIDES **11**:438
oceanography **14**:346
WOODSFIELD (Ohio)
map (39° 46′N 81° 7′W) **14**:357
WOODSON (county in Kansas)
map (37° 55′N 95° 45′W) **12**:18
WOODSON, CARTER GODWIN 20:213 *bibliog.*
WOODSTOCK (Illinois)
map (42° 19′N 88° 27′W) **11**:42
WOODSTOCK (New Brunswick)
map (46° 9′N 67° 34′W) **14**:117
WOODSTOCK (New York)
map (42° 2′N 74° 7′W) **14**:149
WOODSTOCK (Ontario)
map (43° 8′N 80° 45′W) **14**:393
WOODSTOCK (Vermont)
map (43° 37′N 72° 31′W) **19**:554
WOODSTOCK (Virginia)
map (38° 53′N 78° 31′W) **19**:607
WOODSTOCK FESTIVAL 16:249 *illus.*; **20**:213 *bibliog.*
counterculture **5**:311
WOODSTOWN (New Jersey)
map (39° 39′N 75° 20′W) **14**:129
WOODSVILLE (New Hampshire)
map (44° 9′N 72° 2′W) **14**:123
WOODTHORPE, PETER **19**:154 *illus.*
WOODVILLE (Florida)
map (30° 20′N 84° 15′W) **8**:172
WOODVILLE (Mississippi)
map (31° 1′N 91° 18′W) **13**:469
WOODVILLE (Ohio)
map (41° 27′N 83° 22′W) **14**:357
WOODVILLE (Texas)
map (30° 46′N 94° 25′W) **19**:129
WOODVILLE, ELIZABETH 20:213
WOODVILLE, RICHARD CATON 20:213 *bibliog.*
WOODWARD (Oklahoma)
map (36° 26′N 99° 24′W) **14**:368
WOODWARD (county in Oklahoma)
map (36° 25′N 99° 15′W) **14**:368
WOODWARD, BOB *see* BERNSTEIN, CARL, AND WOODWARD, BOB
WOODWARD, C. VANN 20:213
WOODWARD, CALVIN M.
vocational education **19**:624
WOODWARD, JOANNE 20:213
WOODWARD, ROBERT BURNS 20:213
chemistry, history of **4**:329
WOODWIND INSTRUMENTS *see* WIND INSTRUMENTS (music)
WOODWORKING *see* WOOD CARVING
WOODWORTH, ROBERT S.
secondary education **17**:179
WOODWORTH, SAMUEL 20:213
WOOL 20:213–214 *bibliog., illus.*
fiber, textile **8**:67 *illus.*
hair **10**:14
harvesting and processing **20**:214
Marrakech wool dyers' market **13**:587 *illus.*
principal growing areas **8**:68 *map*
sheep **17**:248–249
teasel **19**:58
textile industry **19**:135–136
Europe, Middle Ages **13**:395 *map*
tweed **19**:358
types **20**:214
alpaca **1**:308
angora **2**:6
cashmere **4**:181
WOOLF, VIRGINIA 7:202 *illus.*; **20**:214–215 *bibliog., illus.*
To the Lighthouse **19**:217
WOOLLCOTT, ALEXANDER 20:215 *bibliog.*
WOOLLEY, SIR LEONARD 20:215 *bibliog.*
Ur **19**:474
WOOLLY RHINOCEROS **13**:102 *illus.*
WOOLMAN, JOHN 20:215–216 *bibliog.*
WOOLNER, THOMAS **3**:514 *illus.*
WOOLRICH (England)
technology, history of **19**:66
WOOLWORTH BUILDING 20:216 *bibliog.*
Gilbert, Cass **9**:178
New York (city) **14**:145 *map*
skyscraper **17**:349–350 *illus.*
WOOLY MAMMOTH
mammoth **13**:106–107
WOONASQUATUCKET RIVER
map (41° 49′N 71° 22′W) **16**:198
WOONSOCKET (Rhode Island)
map (42° 0′N 71° 31′W) **16**:198
WOONSOCKET (South Dakota)
map (44° 3′N 98° 16′W) **18**:103
WOOSTER (Ohio)
map (40° 48′N 81° 56′W) **14**:357
WORCESTER (city in England) **20**:216
map (52° 11′N 2° 13′W) **19**:403
WORCESTER (city in Massachusetts) **20**:216
map (42° 16′N 71° 48′W) **13**:206
WORCESTER (county in England) *see* HEREFORD AND WORCESTER (England)
WORCESTER (county in Maryland)
map (38° 11′N 75° 24′W) **13**:188
WORCESTER (county in Massachusetts)
map (42° 16′N 71° 48′W) **13**:206
WORCESTER (South Africa)
map (33° 39′S 19° 27′E) **18**:79
WORCESTER COLLEGE (Oxford University) **14**:474
WORCESTER SARCOPHAGUS
Etruscans **7**:260
WORCESTER WARE 20:216 *bibliog.*
WORD GAMES *see* GAMES—word games
WORD PROCESSOR 20:216
business machines **3**:589
computer **5**:160i
telecommunications **19**:76
WORDEN (Montana)
map (45° 58′N 108° 10′W) **13**:547
WORDEN, ALFRED M. 20:216
Apollo program **2**:83–84; **20**:216
astronaut **20**:216
WORDEN POND
map (41° 26′N 71° 35′W) **16**:198
WORDSWORTH, DOROTHY 20:216 *bibliog.*
Wordsworth, William **20**:216–217
WORDSWORTH, WILLIAM 7:198 *illus.*; **20**:216–217 *bibliog., illus.*
Coleridge, Samuel Taylor **5**:100–101
De Quincey, Thomas **6**:62
Lake District (England) **12**:171
Lyrical Ballads **12**:479
"Ode: Intimations of Immortality from Recollections of Early Childhood" **14**:348
romanticism (literature) **16**:293
Selkirk (Scotland) **17**:192
Southey, Robert **18**:112
Wordsworth, Dorothy **20**:216
WORK (employment) *see* EMPLOYMENT AND UNEMPLOYMENT
WORK (physics) **20**:217
electron volt **7**:124
electrostatics **7**:128
energy **20**:217
erg **7**:228
horsepower **10**:251
joule **11**:453; **20**:217
perpetual motion machine **15**:178
power **15**:481
simple machines **17**:316
unit of measurement
units, physical **19**:467
WORK ETHIC
See also PROTESTANT ETHIC
Industrial Revolution **11**:159
WORK-INCENTIVE PROGRAM
social and welfare services **18**:17
WORK STUDY EDUCATIONAL PROGRAMS
Beloit College **3**:192–193
Berea College **3**:208
Berry, Martha McChesney **3**:225
Goddard College **9**:220
WORKER BEE **3**:158–159 *illus.*
WORKERS (COMMUNIST) PARTY OF AMERICA
Communist party, U.S.A. **5**:151
WORKERS' COMPENSATION (law) **20**:217 *bibliog.*
Constitution of the United States **5**:219
WORKHOUSE
poor laws **15**:429
prison **15**:554
WORKING CLASS *see* CLASS, SOCIAL
WORKING CONDITIONS
Bagley, Sarah G. **3**:22
Hawthorne studies **10**:79
International Labor Organization **11**:220
Kelley, Florence **12**:38
Labor, U.S. Department of **12**:152
WORKING DOG **6**:214–215 *illus.*
akita **1**:231
Alaskan malamute **1**:248
Australian cattle dog **2**:342
bearded collie **3**:142
Belgian Malinois **3**:175
Belgian sheepdog **3**:176 *illus.*
Belgian Tervuren **3**:176 *illus.*
Bernese mountain dog **3**:221
Bouvier des Flandres **3**:426
boxer **3**:430–431
briard **3**:476–477
bull mastiff **3**:558
Cardigan Welsh corgi **4**:143
collie **5**:103
Doberman pinscher **6**:209
German shepherd **9**:135
Great Dane **9**:318
Great Pyrenees **9**:321
Indians, American
travois **19**:285
komondor **12**:108
kuvasz **12**:140
mastiff **13**:216
Newfoundland **14**:168
Old English sheepdog **14**:375
Pembroke Welsh corgi **15**:140
puli **15**:618
Rottweiler **16**:324
Saint Bernard **17**:16
Samoyed (dog) **17**:47
schnauzer (giant) **17**:129 *illus.*
schnauzer (standard) **17**:129 *illus.*
Shetland sheepdog **17**:260
Siberian husky **17**:292
WORKINGTON (England)
map (54° 39′N 3° 35′W) **19**:403
WORKS PROGRESS ADMINISTRATION 20:217–218 *bibliog.*
American art and architecture **1**:335
Federal Theatre Project **8**:42
Federal Writers' Project **8**:42–43
mural painting **13**:646
photography, history and art of **15**:271
Roosevelt, Franklin Delano **16**:309
WORLAND (Wyoming)
map (44° 1′N 107° 57′W) **20**:301
WORLD BANK 20:218 *bibliog.*
agriculture and the food supply **1**:198
Bretton Woods Conference **3**:475
Clausen, A. W. **5**:44
foreign aid **8**:224–225
International Development Association **11**:220
International Finance Corporation **11**:220
McNamara, Robert S. **13**:35
Washington, D.C. **20**:41 *map*
WORLD BOOK ENCYCLOPEDIA
Field (family) **8**:71
WORLD COUNCIL OF CHURCHES 20:218 *bibliog.*
Blake, Eugene Carson **3**:324
council, ecumenical **5**:310
ecumenical movement **7**:54
Fisher, Geoffrey Francis **8**:122
Mott, John R. **13**:616
Visser 'T Hooft, Willem Adolf **19**:617
WORLD COURT *see* INTERNATIONAL COURT OF JUSTICE
WORLD DISARMAMENT CONFERENCE
Geneva conferences **9**:91
WORLD FEDERATION OF TRADE UNIONS 20:218
International Confederation of Free Trade Unions **11**:219
WORLD FOOD COUNCIL
agriculture and the food supply **1**:199
WORLD HEALTH ORGANIZATION 20:218–219 *bibliog.*
dentistry **6**:114
environmental health **7**:210
epidemiology **7**:219
malaria **13**:80
nutritional-deficiency diseases **14**:308
pharmacopoeia **15**:221
public health **15**:608
smallpox **17**:365
trachoma **19**:258
WORLD LINE 20:219 *bibliog.*
particle motion **20**:219
relativity **20**:219
space-time continuum **20**:219
WORLD METEOROLOGICAL ORGANIZATION 20:219 *bibliog.*
cloud **5**:68
meteorological instrumentation **13**:339
meteorology **13**:341–343
WORLD MONETARY AND ECONOMIC CONFERENCE *see* LONDON, TREATIES AND CONFERENCES
WORLD SERIES (baseball) **3**:102–103; **3**:105 *table*
WORLD TRADE CENTER 14:147 *illus.*; **20**:219 *bibliog.*
New York (city) **14**:145 *map*
skyscraper **17**:349–350 *illus.*
Yamasaki, Minoru **20**:316
WORLD WAR I 20:219–248 *bibliog., illus., maps, table*
aircraft and air operations **20**:246–247 *illus.*
aerospace industry **1**:126
air force **1**:207–208
aircraft, military **1**:214; **1**:217; **2**:370–371 *illus.*
airship **1**:227
aviation **2**:370–371; **2**:374
balloon **3**:52
bomb **3**:373
Curtiss Jenny **5**:395–396
Fokker, Anthony Hermann Gerard **8**:193
Fokker D-VII **8**:194 *illus.*
Gotha **9**:254
Mitchell, Billy **13**:482–483
Richthofen, Manfred, Freiherr von **16**:215
Rickenbacker, Eddie **16**:215
seaplane **17**:174
Sopwith Camel **18**:68
SPAD **18**:138
Turner, Roscoe **19**:351
alliances **20**:219–222 *maps*
Allied powers **7**:294 *map*
Central Powers **4**:255; **7**:294 *map*
Triple Alliance **19**:301–302
Triple Entente **19**:302
armed forces **20**:220
army **2**:182
conscription **5**:201
infantry **11**:163–164
navy **14**:64
Armistice Day **2**:173
armistices **20**:243 *illus.*
arms and matériel
ammunition **1**:375
armor **2**:175
armored vehicle **2**:175–176 *illus.*
artillery **2**:224
camouflage **4**:63
gas mask **9**:53
grenade **9**:358
Krupp (family) **12**:132
locomotive **12**:391
machine gun **13**:21–23 *illus.*
rifle **16**:221
rockets and missiles **16**:253
tear gas **19**:58
technological innovations **20**:246–247
TNT **19**:216
torpedo (projectile) **19**:242
trucking industry **19**:314
Asia, history of **2**:259
Australia, history of **2**:341
Austrian invasions of Serbia **20**:226
background and causes
Balkan Wars **3**:38
Franz Ferdinand, Austrian Archduke **8**:286
Moroccan Crises **13**:583
Sarajevo (Yugoslavia) **17**:74; **20**:222
battles and campaigns
Balkan front **20**:227 *map*; **20**:230–231; **20**:234; **20**:238–239; **20**:243
Belleau Wood **3**:187
Caporetto, Battle of **4**:127
eastern front **20**:224–227 *map*; **20**:230 *illus.*; **20**:238
Gallipoli campaign **9**:20
Marne, Battles of the **13**:161–162
Masurian Lakes **13**:218
Reims (France) **16**:131
Somme, Battles of the **18**:61–62
Tannenberg, Battles of **19**:24
Turkish fronts **20**:239 *map*
Verdun, Battle of **19**:550
western front **20**:222–225 *map*; **20**:228–229; **20**:232–233; **20**:236–237 *illus.*; **20**:241–242 *illus.*
Ypres, Battles of **20**:337

WORLD WAR I (cont.)
Canada, history of **4**:86 *illus.*
chemical and biological warfare **4**:311; **4**:312 *illus.*
cost **20**:245 *table*
dog, Bouvier des Flandres **3**:425
Europe, history of **7**:293–295 *map*
fortification **8**:240–241
France, history of **8**:272; **8**:273
generals
Allenby, Edmund Henry Hynman, 1st Viscount **1**:300
Brusilov, Aleksei Alekseyevich **3**:526
Byng, Julian Hedworth George **3**:602
Falkenhayn, Erich von **8**:13
Foch, Ferdinand **8**:192
French, John, 1st Earl of Ypres **8**:302
Haig, Douglas Haig, 1st Earl **10**:12
Hindenburg, Paul von **10**:169
Joffre, Joseph Jacques Césaire **11**:421
Ludendorff, Erich **12**:451
Moltke, Helmuth Johannes Ludwig, Graf von **13**:513
Nivelle, Robert Georges **14**:204
Pershing, John J. **15**:180–181
Pétain, Henri Philippe **15**:199
Schlieffen, Alfred Graf von **17**:126
Germany, history of **9**:154–155
Great Britain **20**:226; **20**:228–229 *illus.*; **20**:232–233 *illus.*; **20**:235–237 *illus.*; **20**:240–242 *illus.*
British Empire **3**:496 *map*
Great Britain, history of **9**:317–318
Italy **20**:229–230 *illus.*; **20**:233; **20**:237–238 *map*; **20**:243
Italy, history of **11**:330
Japan, history of **11**:370
Lawrence, T. E. **12**:250–251
leaders and statesmen
Asquith, Herbert Henry, 1st Earl of Oxford and Asquith **2**:263
Baker, Newton Diehl **3**:28
Bethmann-Hollweg, Theobald von **3**:231
Borden, Sir Robert L. **3**:397
Churchill, Sir Winston **4**:426
Clemenceau, Georges **5**:48–49
Dmowski, Roman **6**:208
Ferdinand, King of Romania **8**:53
Lawrence, T. E. **12**:250–251
Lloyd George, David, 1st Earl Lloyd-George of Dwyfor **12**:383
Massey, William **13**:213
Nicholas II, Emperor of Russia **14**:181–182
Orlando, Vittorio Emanuele **14**:445
Poincaré, Raymond **15**:380
Sonnino, Sidney, Barone **18**:66
Venizélos, Eleuthérios **19**:546
William II, Emperor of Germany **20**:157
Wilson, Woodrow **20**:165–167
Lusitania **12**:467
Mata Hari **13**:218
Middle East **20**:239 *map*
Middle East, history of the **13**:406–408
naval operations
Gallipoli campaign **9**:20
Jutland, Battle of **11**:479; **20**:235 *illus.*
war at sea **20**:226–228 *illus.*; **20**:232 *illus.*; **20**:240; **20**:244
naval vessels **14**:56
battleship **3**:128
cruiser **5**:366
destroyer **6**:132–133
submarine **18**:314–315 *illus.*; **20**:246–247 *illus.*; **20**:247
neutral countries 1914 **7**:294 *map*
New Zealand, history of **14**:162
pacifism and nonviolent movements **15**:9
peace settlements
Brest-Litovsk, Treaty of **3**:474
Fourteen Points **8**:254
Lausanne, Treaty of **12**:239–240
League of Nations **12**:257–258
Locarno Pact **12**:385–386
Paris Peace Conference **15**:88
Versailles **20**:244–246 *illus.*
Washington Conference **20**:44–45
Poland **15**:391; **20**:226–227 *map*
propaganda poster (U.S.) **15**:569 *illus.*
reparations **16**:160
Russia **20**:224–227 *map*; **20**:230 *illus.*; **20**:233–234 *illus.*
Russia/Union of Soviet Socialist Republics, history of **16**:358–359
strategy
global strategy 1915 **20**:228
global strategy 1916 **20**:232
global strategy 1917 **20**:235–236
global strategy 1918 **20**:240
opposing strategies **20**:222
Schlieffen, Alfred, Graf von **17**:126
strategy and tactics, military **18**:291
submarine **18**:314–315 *illus.*
trench warfare **2**:181 *illus.*; **20**:225 *map*
Turkey **20**:228 *illus.*; **20**:230–232; **20**:234–235; **20**:239–240; **20**:243–244 *illus.*
Russo-Turkish Wars **16**:374
uniform **1**:207 *illus.*; **2**:183 *illus.*; **11**:164 *illus.*
United States **20**:240–242 *illus.*
United States, history of the **19**:452–453 *illus.*
U.S. entry **20**:236 *illus.*
war relief
Hoover, Herbert **10**:228–229
York, Alvin Cullum **20**:330
Zimmermann telegram, cryptology **5**:372–373
WORLD WAR II **20**:248–281 *bibliog., illus., maps*
air operations **20**:254–255 *illus.*; **20**:264–266 *illus.*; **20**:273 *illus.*; **20**:275
air force **1**:208
Britain, Battle of **3**:488–489
Chennault, Claire L. **4**:330
Cochran, Jacqueline **5**:86
Doolittle, James **6**:240; **20**:264–266 *illus.*
kamikaze **20**:278–279 *illus.*
Mitchell, Billy **13**:483
Pearl Harbor **15**:126 *maps*
Tedder, Arthur William Tedder, 1st Baron **19**:69
aircraft, military **1**:217; **2**:370–373 *illus.*
aerospace industry **1**:125
B-17 Flying Fortress **3**:4
B-24 Liberator **3**:4
B-29 Superfortress **3**:4
balloon **3**:52
Corsair **5**:277
DC-3 **6**:57
Grumman, Leroy **9**:382
Grumman TBF-1 Avenger **9**:382
Hurricane **10**:317
Messerschmitt Bf-109 **13**:323
MiG **13**:416
Mosquito **13**:602
Mustang **13**:685
P-38 Lightning **15**:3
P-40 **15**:3
Piper Cub **15**:312
Spitfire **18**:190
Stuka **18**:308 *illus.*
Zero **20**:361
armed forces
airborne troops **1**:210
army **2**:182
commando **5**:137
conscription **5**:201
frogman **8**:338
infantry **11**:163–164
navy **14**:62–66
arms and matériel
armor **2**:175
armored vehicle **2**:176–177 *illus.*; **20**:268 *illus.*
artillery **2**:224
atomic bomb **2**:307–308
automotive industry **2**:364
bazooka **3**:135
bomb **3**:373–374
Garand, John Cantius **9**:38
grenade **9**:358
Guderian, Heinz **9**:390
human factors engineering **10**:297
jeep **11**:390
Krupp (family) **12**:132
locomotive **12**:391
machine gun **13**:21–23
mortar **13**:591 *illus.*
napalm **14**:14
night sights **14**:193
RDX **16**:98
rifle **16**:221
rockets and missiles **16**:255
TNT **19**:216
torpedo **19**:242
Asia **20**:258–261 *illus., map*; **20**:264–267 *illus.*; **20**:275–279 *illus., map*
Asia, history of **2**:259–260
Burma Road **3**:575
Australia **20**:267
Australia, history of **2**:341
Axis **2**:378
background and causes **20**:248–251
Depression of the 1930s **6**:120
Fascism **8**:30
Geneva conferences **9**:91
League of Nations **12**:258
Munich Conference **13**:641
Nazi-Soviet Pact **14**:67
nazism **14**:67–68
Polish Corridor **15**:397
Sino-Japanese Wars **17**:323
Spanish Civil War **18**:156–157
battles and campaigns
Alamein, El **1**:239; **20**:258; **20**:262–263 *illus., map*
Atlantic Ocean **20**:251–252; **20**:256; **20**:264–265 *illus., map*
Balkans, The **20**:253 *map*; **20**:255
Bismarck Sea, Battle of the **20**:267
Britain, Battle of **3**:488–489; **20**:253–255 *illus., map*
Bulge, Battle of the **3**:557; **20**:273–274 *map*
Burma **20**:260–261 *map*; **20**:266–267; **20**:276–277 *illus., map*; **20**:278
Caroline Islands **20**:276–277 *map*
Coral Sea, Battle of the **20**:266
Corregidor (Philippines) **5**:276
Dunkerque (Dunkirk) **6**:300; **20**:253–254 *illus., map*
Guadalcanal **9**:384–385 *map*; **20**:267
Guam **20**:260
Iwo Jima **11**:338; **20**:277–278 *illus., map*
Mandalay (Burma) **13**:110
Manila (Philippines) **13**:118
Marshall Islands **20**:276–277 *map*
Midway, Battle of **13**:414; **14**:64 *illus.*; **20**:266 *illus.*
New Guinea **20**:267
Normandy Invasion (D-Day) **14**:221 *map*; **20**:272; **20**:274 *map*
North African campaigns **20**:256; **20**:258; **20**:261–263 *illus., maps*
Okinawa **14**:366; **20**:277–278 *illus., map*
Pacific Ocean **20**:258–261 *illus., maps*; **20**:264–267 *illus.*; **20**:275–279 *illus., map*
Pearl Harbor **15**:126 *maps*
Philippine Sea, Battle of the **20**:277 *map*
Philippines **20**:260–261 *illus., map*; **20**:277–278 *illus., map*
Saipan **20**:277
Sicily, invasion of **17**:293; **20**:268–269 *illus., map*
Solomon Islands **20**:267 *illus.*
Stalingrad, Battle of **18**:215; **20**:264 *illus.*; **20**:270 *map*
Tarawa (Kiribati) **19**:35; **20**:267 *illus.*
Tobruk (Libya) **19**:220
Wake Island **20**:8; **20**:260
bombs and bombing **20**:254–255 *illus.*; **20**:264–266 *illus.*; **20**:273 *illus.*; **20**:275
atomic bomb **2**:307–308
civil defense **5**:9–10
Cologne (Germany) **5**:105
Doolittle raid **6**:240; **20**:264–266 *illus.*
Dresden (East Germany) **6**:270 *illus.*
Hiroshima (Japan) **10**:175–176; **20**:279 *illus.*
hydrogen bomb **10**:339–340
kamikaze **20**:278–279 *illus.*
Manhattan Project **13**:116
Nagasaki (Japan) **14**:6; **20**:279 *illus.*
napalm **14**:14
V-1 **19**:500
V-2 **19**:501
Canada, history of **4**:86; **4**:87 *illus.*
casualties **20**:280
chemical and biological warfare **4**:311; **4**:312–313
China **20**:249; **20**:259–260 *map*; **20**:266; **20**:278
China, history of **4**:375–376
concentration camp *see* CONCENTRATION CAMP
conferences and treaties
Arcadia Conference **20**:257–258
Atlantic Charter **2**:294; **20**:257 *illus.*
Cairo Conference **4**:19
Casablanca Conference **4**:180; **20**:262–263
Paris, treaties of **15**:87
Potsdam Conference **15**:467; **20**:275 *illus.*
Tehran Conference **19**:73; **20**:271 *illus.*
Yalta Conference **20**:275; **20**:315
conscription **5**:201
Czechoslovakia **5**:416; **20**:250 *illus.*
Denmark **6**:113; **20**:252–253 *map*
Europe **20**:251–256 *illus., map*; **20**:264; **20**:268–275 *illus., map*
Europe, history of **7**:297–298 *map*
expenditures **20**:280
film
Capra, Frank **4**:128
Coward, Noel **5**:320
documentary **6**:211
film, history of **8**:85
fortification **8**:240–241
Maginot Line **13**:51
France **20**:252–254 *illus., map*; **20**:262; **20**:272–274 *illus., map*
background to the war **20**:250–251
France, history of **8**:272 *map*
Marne River **13**:162
Normandy invasion **14**:221 *map*
Reims (France) **16**:131
resistance movement **20**:272 *illus.*
results of the war **20**:279
Toulon **19**:250
Verdun **19**:550
Vichy Government **19**:571
generals, Allied
Alanbrooke, Alan Francis Brooke, 1st Viscount **1**:240
Alexander, Harold George, 1st Earl Alexander of Tunis **1**:273
Arnold, Henry Harley **2**:185
Bradley, Omar N. **3**:438
Budenny, Semyon Mikhailovich **3**:543
Chennault, Claire L. **4**:330
Clark, Mark W. **5**:39
Crerar, Henry **5**:339
de Gaulle, Charles **6**:59
Eisenhower, Dwight D. **7**:94–96
Gamelin, Maurice Gustave **9**:29
Giraud, Henri Honoré **9**:189
Gruenther, Alfred Maximilian **9**:382
Leclerc, Jacques Philippe **12**:268
MacArthur, Douglas **13**:5
Marshall, George C. **13**:171–172
Montgomery of Alamein, Bernard Law Montgomery, 1st Viscount **13**:556–557
Mountbatten of Burma, Louis Mountbatten, 1st Earl **13**:624–625
Patton, George S. **15**:116
Ridgway, Matthew B. **16**:216
Slim, William Joseph, 1st Viscount Slim **17**:362
Smith, Walter Bedell **17**:371
Stilwell, Joseph W. **18**:270
Taylor, Maxwell D. **19**:49
Van Fleet, James Alward **19**:514
Wainwright, Jonathan M. **20**:7
Wavell, Archibald Percival Wavell, 1st Earl **20**:70–71
Weygand, Maxime **20**:119
Wingate, Orde **20**:179
Zhukov, Georgy Konstantinovich **20**:362–363
generals, Axis
Guderian, Heinz **9**:390
Keitel, Wilhelm **12**:37
Kesselring, Albert **12**:61
Rommel, Erwin **16**:305
Rundstedt, Karl Rudolf Gerd von **16**:345
Yamamoto Isoroku **20**:316
Yamashita Tomoyuki **20**:317
Germany **20**:251–258 *illus., map*; **20**:262–264; **20**:268–275 *illus.*
See also NAZISM
background to the war **20**:249–251 *illus., map*
Berlin **3**:214–217
blitzkrieg **3**:333

collapse and surrender **20**:275
Germany, history of **9**:155–156
Holocaust **10**:206
Krupp (family) **12**:132
Peenemünde **15**:132
postwar Germany **20**:280–281 *map*
V-1 **19**:500 *illus.*
V-2 **19**:500–501 *illus.*
Great Britain **20**:253–268 *illus., maps*; **20**:272–279 *illus.*
background to the war **20**:250–251
Britain, Battle of **3**:488–489
Great Britain, history of **9**:318
results of the war **20**:279
Scapa Flow **17**:115
Greece **20**:253 *map*; **20**:255–256 *illus.*
Corfu **5**:262
EAM-ELAS **7**:5
Salonika **17**:36
historians
Langer, William **12**:195
Liddell Hart, Sir Basil **12**:323
Marshall, Samuel Lyman Atwood **13**:173
Hungary **10**:310
India, history of **11**:93
intelligence gathering **11**:204–205; **20**:266; **20**:272
cryptology **5**:372–373 *illus.*
Italy **20**:255; **20**:256; **20**:268–269 *map*; **20**:271 *illus.*
background to the war **20**:248–250
Italy, history of **11**:331
Latium **12**:235
Monte Cassino **13**:552
postwar Italy **20**:280
Japan **20**:258–261 *illus., maps*; **20**:264–267 *illus.*; **20**:276–279 *illus., map*
background to the war **20**:249–250 *illus.*
Japan, history of **11**:370–371 *map*
kamikaze **20**:278–279 *illus.*
postwar Japan **20**:280
surrender **20**:279
Tokyo Rose **19**:226
war-crimes trials **20**:280
journalism
See also WORLD WAR II—photojournalism
Lord Haw-Haw **12**:413
Pyle, Ernie **15**:633
radio and television broadcasting **16**:56
leaders and statesmen
Antonescu, Ion **2**:70
Badoglio, Pietro **3**:20
Bose, Subhas Chandra **3**:407
Chamberlain, Neville **4**:274
Chiang Kai-shek **4**:339
Churchill, Sir Winston **4**:426
Darlan, Jean François **6**:39
Doenitz, Karl **6**:212–213
George VI, King of England, Scotland, and Ireland **9**:112
Hess, Rudolf **10**:152
Hirohito, Emperor of Japan **10**:175
Hitler, Adolf **10**:188
Horthy de Nagybánya, Miklós **10**:254
Laval, Pierre **12**:240–241
Leopold III, King of the Belgians **12**:294
Lindemann, Frederick Alexander **12**:351
Linlithgow, Victor Alexander John Hope, 2d Marquess of **12**:359
Matsuoka, Yosuke **13**:230
Mussolini, Benito **13**:684
Pétain, Henri Philippe **15**:199
Quisling, Vidkun **16**:28
Roosevelt, Franklin Delano **16**:309
Speer, Albert **18**:176
Stalin, Joseph **18**:214
Stimson, Henry Lewis **18**:270–271
Tojo Hideki **19**:222
Wilhelmina, Queen of the Netherlands **20**:151
Low Countries **20**:252–253 *illus., map*
Middle East **20**:256; **20**:262–263 *illus., map*
Middle East, history of the **13**:408
Palestine **15**:45–46
naval operations
Atlantic Ocean **20**:251–252; **20**:256; **20**:264–265 *illus., map*
Bismarck Sea, Battle of the **20**:267
Coral Sea, Battle of the **20**:266
Halsey, William F. **10**:25–26
King, Ernest Joseph **12**:80
Midway, Battle of **20**:266
Nimitz, Chester W. **14**:198
Pacific Ocean **20**:258–261 *illus., maps*; **20**:264–267 *illus.*; **20**:275–279 *illus., map*
Spruance, Raymond Ames **18**:200
Yamamoto Isoroku **20**:316
naval vessels **14**:56; **20**:256
aircraft carrier **1**:220
battleship **3**:127–128
cruiser **5**:366
destroyer **6**:133
PT boat **15**:605
submarine **18**:314 *illus.*
Netherlands **14**:103; **20**:252–253 *illus., map*
New Zealand, history of **14**:162
Norway **14**:264; **20**:252–253 *illus., map*
Nuremberg Trials **14**:297
photojournalism **15**:273
Bourke-White, Margaret **3**:424
Capa, Robert **4**:119
Eisenstaedt, Alfred **7**:96 *illus.*
Smith, W. Eugene **17**:371
Steichen, Edward **18**:246
Poland **15**:391; **20**:251; **20**:253 *map*
Warsaw (Poland) **20**:33
Warsaw Uprising **20**:33; **20**:271 *illus.*
radar **16**:38–39 *illus.*
radar meteorology **16**:41
Watson-Watt, Sir Robert Alexander **20**:68
refugee **16**:125
reparations **16**:160
resistance movements **20**:264; **20**:271–272 *illus.*
Lyon (France) **12**:477–478
Warsaw Uprising **20**:33; **20**:271 *illus.*
results **20**:279–281
Romania **16**:290
Russia **20**:251; **20**:256–257 *illus.*; **20**:258 *illus.*; **20**:264 *illus.*; **20**:268; **20**:270–271 *map*; **20**:274–275 *map*
background to the war **20**:250–251 *illus.*
Moscow **13**:599
results of the war **20**:279–281
Russia/Union of Soviet Socialist Republics, history of **16**:359–360 *illus.*
Russo-Finnish War **16**:373
Sevastopol **17**:215
Stalingrad, Battle of **18**:215
Scandinavia, history of **17**:111
strategy
Allied strategic bombing **20**:264
amphibious warfare **1**:380–381
blitzkrieg **3**:333
guerrillas **9**:391–392
strategy and tactics, military **18**:291
unidentified flying object **19**:385
uniform **1**:207 *illus.*; **2**:182 *illus.*
United States **20**:258–279
growing involvement **20**:257–258
Lend-Lease **12**:281
Michigan **13**:382
Murphy, Audie **13**:649
New Deal **14**:120
Nisei **14**:201
Pearl Harbor **15**:126 *maps*
results of the war **20**:279–281
United States, history of the **19**:455–456 *illus.*
war effort **20**:261
WORLD WEATHER WATCH **20**:281 *bibliog.*
meteorology **13**:341–343
weather forecasting **20**:281
World Meteorological Organization **20**:219
WORLD ZIONIST ORGANIZATION
Weizmann, Chaim **20**:96
WORLD'S COLUMBIAN EXPOSITION OF 1893 **20**:281–282 *bibliog.*
Burnham, Daniel Hudson **3**:577
Field Museum of Natural History **8**:72
mural painting **13**:646
sculpture
MacMonnies, Frederick William **13**:34
WORLD'S FAIRS **20**:282 *bibliog.*
Centennial Exposition **4**:249
Expo '67 **4**:156 *illus.*; **9**:97 *illus.*
Canada, history of **4**:87
New York City (1939)
radio and television broadcasting **16**:56
World's Columbian Exposition of 1893 **20**:281–282
WORLD'S STUDENT CHRISTIAN FEDERATION
Mott, John R. **13**:616
WORM **20**:283–284 *bibliog., illus.*
annelid **2**:33
arrowworm **2**:189
beardworm **3**:143
biological locomotion **3**:266 *illus.*
classification, biological **20**:283
diseases
ascariasis **2**:227
eye worm **7**:351
filariasis **8**:78
hookworm **10**:227
infectious diseases **11**:167
parasitic diseases **15**:82–83
river blindness **16**:232
schistosomiasis **17**:123
trichinosis **19**:296
earthworm **7**:29–30
entoproct **7**:208
fanworm **11**:229 *illus.*
flatworm **8**:156
fluke **8**:186
Gnathostomata **9**:213
gordian worm **9**:248
hemichordate **10**:117–118
invertebrate **11**:235
leech **12**:271
lugworm **12**:453
nematode **14**:80
onychophoran **14**:396
palolo worm **15**:52
peanut worm **15**:125
Peripatus **15**:171
pinworm **15**:308
polychaete **15**:418
rag worm **16**:69
regeneration **16**:126–127
ribbon worm **16**:205
segmented, Precambrian time **15**:491 *illus.*
spiny-headed worm **18**:188
spoonworm **18**:195
WORM LIZARD **20**:284 *illus.*
WORMFISH **20**:284
WORMS (West Germany) **20**:284
cathedral **9**:124 *illus.*
map (49° 38′N 8° 22′E) **9**:140
WORMS, DIET OF *see* LUTHER, MARTIN
WORMWOOD
steppe life **18**:257 *illus.*
vermouth **19**:559
WORRY *see* ANXIETY
WORSAAE, JENS JACOB ASMUSSEN **20**:284
prehistory **15**:517
stratigraphy
archaeology **2**:124
WORSHIP
See also CHURCH MUSIC
temple **19**:94–99
WORSLEY (England) **19**:407 *illus.*
WORTH (county in Georgia)
map (31° 40′N 83° 55′W) **9**:114
WORTH (Illinois)
map (41° 41′N 87° 48′W) **11**:42
WORTH (county in Iowa)
map (43° 23′N 93° 15′W) **11**:244
WORTH (county in Missouri)
map (40° 30′N 94° 25′W) **13**:476
WORTH, CHARLES FREDERICK **8**:31 *illus.*; **20**:284 *bibliog.*
fashion design **8**:31 *illus.*
WORTH, WILLIAM J.
Mexican War **13**:353–354
WORTHING (England)
map (50° 48′N 0° 23′W) **19**:403
WORTHINGTON (Indiana)
map (39° 7′N 86° 59′W) **11**:111
WORTHINGTON (Minnesota)
map (43° 37′N 95° 36′W) **13**:453
WORTHINGTON (Ohio)
map (40° 5′N 83° 1′W) **14**:357
WOTTON, SIR HENRY
architecture **2**:129
WOUK, HERMAN **20**:284
Caine Mutiny, The **4**:17
WOUND GUM
gum arabic **9**:405
tree **19**:288
WOUNDED KNEE (South Dakota) **11**:137 *illus.*; **20**:284–285 *bibliog.*
ghost dance **9**:169
Indian Wars **11**:109–110 *map*
Indians, American **11**:130
Kunstler, William **12**:137
map (43° 10′N 102° 25′W) **18**:103
Red Cloud **16**:112
Sioux **17**:326
Sitting Bull **17**:330
WOUNDS AND INJURIES
bone, fracture **8**:258–259
first aid **8**:108
frostbite **8**:346
inflammation **11**:169
nervous system, diseases of the **14**:96
pain **15**:15
paraplegia **15**:80
regeneration **16**:126–127
scar **17**:115
speech **18**:175
stress ulcer **19**:376
whiplash **20**:131
WOUWERMAN, PHILIPS **20**:285 *bibliog.*
WOVOKA (Paiute Indian) **20**:285 *bibliog.*
ghost dance **9**:169
WOZZECK (opera)
Berg, Alban **3**:208–209
WPA *see* WORKS PROGRESS ADMINISTRATION
WRANGEL, PYOTR NIKOLAYEVICH, BARON **20**:285 *bibliog.*
WRANGEL ISLAND (USSR) **20**:285
map (71° 0′N 179° 30′W) **19**:388
WRANGELL (Alaska)
map (56° 28′N 132° 23′W) **1**:242
WRASSE **20**:285 *illus.*
WRATH, CAPE
map (58° 37′N 5° 1′W) **19**:403
WRAY (Colorado)
map (40° 5′N 102° 13′W) **5**:116
WRECK OF THE HESPERUS, THE (poem) **13**:210 *illus.*
Longfellow, Henry Wadsworth **12**:407
WREN **20**:285–286 *bibliog., illus.*
emu wren **7**:160–161
WREN, SIR CHRISTOPHER **20**:286 *bibliog., illus.*
American art and architecture **1**:327
cathedrals and churches **4**:208
dome **6**:230 *illus.*
English art and architecture **7**:185
Greenwich (England) **9**:354
Saint Paul's Cathedral **4**:207 *illus.*; **7**:185 *illus.*; **17**:25
Tom Tower, Christ Church, Oxford University **19**:408 *illus.*
WREN-THRUSH **20**:286
WREN-TIT **20**:286
WREN WARBLER **20**:286
WRENS (Georgia)
map (33° 12′N 82° 23′W) **9**:114
WRENTHAM (Alberta)
map (49° 32′N 112° 10′W) **1**:256
WRENTHAM (Massachusetts)
map (42° 4′N 71° 20′W) **13**:206
WRESTLING **20**:286–287 *bibliog., illus.*
history **20**:287
regional forms **20**:287
sports, history of **18**:195–196 *illus.*
WRETCHED OF THE EARTH, THE (book)
Fanon, Frantz **8**:20–21
WREXHAM (Wales)
map (53° 3′N 3° 0′W) **19**:403
WRIGHT (county in Iowa)
map (42° 43′N 93° 45′W) **11**:244
WRIGHT (county in Minnesota)
map (45° 10′N 94° 0′W) **13**:453
WRIGHT (county in Missouri)
map (37° 15′N 92° 30′W) **13**:476
WRIGHT, FRANCES **20**:287–288 *bibliog., illus.*
WRIGHT, FRANK LLOYD **20**:288–289 *bibliog., illus.*
American art and architecture **1**:330
Arizona **2**:162
cantilever **4**:117
Fallingwater (house) **2**:137 *illus.*
Griffin, Marion Mahony **9**:362
Guggenheim Museum **1**:329 *illus.*; **9**:393 *illus.*; **13**:493 *illus.*
historians
Hitchcock, Henry-Russell **10**:186
house (in Western architecture) **10**:270
industrial design **11**:155
Madison (Wisconsin) **13**:41
Marin County Civic Center (California) **20**:289 *illus.*
Milwaukee (Wisconsin) **13**:434
modern architecture **13**:491–493
prairie school **15**:489
Robie House **1**:329 *illus.*
skyscraper **17**:350
Taliesin West **19**:16

WRIGHT, HAROLD BELL 20:289
WRIGHT, HENRY 20:289–290 *bibliog.*
WRIGHT, JIM 20:290
WRIGHT, JOSEPH 20:290 *bibliog.*
WRIGHT, JUDITH 20:290
WRIGHT, MICKEY 20:290
WRIGHT, ORVILLE AND WILBUR 20:290 *bibliog., illus.*
airport 1:223
Chanute, Octave 4:282
Dayton (Ohio) 6:57
first flight 1:210; 1:211 *illus.*; 19:68 *illus.*; 19:280 *illus.*
glider 9:208
transportation 19:280 *illus.*
WRIGHT, RICHARD 20:290–291 *bibliog., illus.*
Native Son 14:47
WRIGHT, STANTON MACDONALD- *see* MACDONALD-WRIGHT, STANTON
WRIGHT, THOMAS
astronomy, history of 2:280
WRIGHT, WILLARD HUNTINGTON *see* VAN DINE, S. S.
WRIGHT CITY (Missouri)
map (38° 50′N 91° 1′W) 13:476
WRIGHT CITY (Oklahoma)
map (34° 3′N 95° 1′W) 14:368
WRIGHT OF DERBY *see* WRIGHT, JOSEPH
WRIGHTSON, MOUNT
map (31° 42′N 110° 50′W) 2:160
WRIGHTSTOWN (New Jersey)
map (40° 2′N 74° 37′W) 14:129
WRIGHTSTOWN (Wisconsin)
map (44° 19′N 88° 9′W) 20:185
WRIGHTSVILLE (Georgia)
map (32° 44′N 82° 43′W) 9:114
WRIGHTSVILLE BEACH (North Carolina)
map (34° 12′N 77° 49′W) 14:242
WRIGLEY (Northwest Territories)
map (63° 16′N 123° 37′W) 14:258
WRIOTHESLEY, HENRY
Virginia 19:611
WRIT 20:291
attachment 2:313
certiorari
Supreme Court of the United States 18:355–356
common law 5:139
habeas corpus 10:3–4
mandamus 13:110
subpoena 18:316
summons 18:339
warrant 20:30
WRIT OF ASSISTANCE 20:291 *bibliog.*
4th Amendment 8:255
Otis, James 14:460
search warrant 17:175
WRITE-IN CANDIDATE 20:291
WRITING SYSTEMS, EVOLUTION OF 20:291–295 *bibliog., illus., table*
alphabet 20:293–294 *illus., table*
Asia, history of 2:249; 2:251
Braille, Louis 3:442
calligraphy 4:41–46
Carolingian art and architecture 4:161
Chinese archaeology 4:379 *illus.*
oracle bones 14:413
cryptology 5:371–373
Cyrillic alphabet 5:410
dictionary 6:159
Egypt, ancient 7:83 *illus.*; 7:85
Egyptology 7:90
English language 7:192
Initial Teaching Alphabet 11:178
Etruscans 7:258–259
forerunners of writing 20:291–292
Germanic languages 9:136–137
Indian languages, American 11:101
Cherokee 4:332
Sequoya 17:207
Indo-Iranian languages 11:145
Indus civilization 11:153–154
inscription 11:185–186
Japanese language 11:379
Korean language 12:118
languages, extinct 12:198–199
limited and full writing 20:291
Linear B 12:353–354
literacy and illiteracy 12:368
logographic systems 20:292 *illus.*
cuneiform 5:389 *illus.*
hieroglyphics 10:159–161
semantic and phonetic indicators 20:292
Malayo-Polynesian languages 13:83
Maya 13:245
Piedras Negras 15:295
Middle East, history of the 13:400–401
mixed writing systems 20:294
morphology 15:254–255
Rawlinson, Sir Henry Creswicke 16:95
rebus principle 20:292–293
Rosetta Stone 16:317
runes 16:346
shorthand 17:284
Sino-Tibetan languages 17:325
Slavic languages 17:358
spelling, pronunciation, and change 7:192; 20:294–295
syllabaries 20:293
Uralic languages 19:475
WRITING TOOLS
ink 11:178
paper 15:68–69
pen 15:140–141
pencil 15:141–142
WROBLEWSKI, ZYGMUNT VON
cryogenics 5:370
WROCŁAW (Poland) 20:295
map (51° 6′N 17° 0′E) 15:388
WROUGHT IRON 20:295 *bibliog.*
alloy, iron 11:271
art
González, Julio 9:245
Smith, David 17:367–368
Tijou, Jean 19:198
bridge (engineering) 3:480–481
Cort, Henry 5:277–278
Fairbairn, Sir William 8:9
metallurgy 13:330
New Orleans 12:432 *illus.*
pipe and pipeline 15:310
WROUGHT-IRON ARCHITECTURE *see* CAST-IRON ARCHITECTURE
WRYBILL *see* PLOVER
WRYNECK 20:295 *illus.*
WU, CHIEN-SHIUNG 20:295 *bibliog.*
beta decay 20:295
WU, EMPRESS OF CHINA
T'ang (Tang) (dynasty) 19:21
WU-CH'ANG (China) *see* WU-HAN (Wuhan) (China)
WU CH'ENG-EN (Wu Chengen) 20:295–296 *bibliog.*
WU CHENGEN *see* WU CH'ENG-EN (Wu Chengen)
WU CHING-TZU (Wu Jingzi) 20:296
WU DAOZI *see* WU TAO-TZU (Wu Daozi)
WU-HAN (Wuhan) (China) 20:296
map (30° 36′N 114° 17′E) 4:362
WU-HSI (China)
map (31° 35′N 120° 18′E) 4:362
WU JINGZI *see* WU CHING-TZU (Wi Jingzi)
WU LANGUAGE
Sino-Tibetan languages 17:324
WU-LIANG MOUNTAINS
map (24° 30′N 100° 45′E) 4:362
WU SCHOOL
Shen Chou (Shen Zhou) 17:255
WU TAO-TZU (Wu Daozi) 20:296 *bibliog.*
WU TI *see* HAN WU TI (Han Wudi)
WUHAN (China) *see* WU-HAN (Wuhan) (China)
WULFENITE 20:296 *illus.*
WUNDT, WILHELM 20:296 *bibliog., illus.*
experimental psychology 7:334; 20:296
physiological psychology 20:296
psychology, history of 15:596 *illus.*
Titchener, Edward B. 19:212
WUORINEN, CHARLES 20:296–297
WUPPERTAL (West Germany) 20:297
map (51° 16′N 7° 11′E) 9:140
WÜRM GLACIATION
Fontéchevade man 8:207
Hamburgian 10:27
Magdalenian 13:46
Paleolithic Period 15:38
WÜRTTEMBERG (West Germany) 20:297
history
Germany in 1648 9:151 *map*
Germany 1815–1871 9:153 *map*
Swabia 18:375
WÜRTTEMBERGISCHE STAATSTHEATER BALLET *see* STUTTGART BALLET
WURTZ, CHARLES ADOLPHE 20:297
Wurtz reaction 20:297
WÜRZBURG (West Germany) 20:297
map (49° 48′N 9° 56′E) 9:140
Riemenschneider, Tilman 16:218–219
WÜRZBURG RESIDENZ 2:135 *illus.*; 20:297 *bibliog.*
Neumann, Johann Balthasar 14:104
WÜRZBURG SCHOOL
Bühler, Karl 3:548
WUTHERING HEIGHTS (book) 20:297 *bibliog.*
Brontë, Emily 3:504
WUTIVI, MOUNT
map (8° 9′N 9° 56′W) 12:313
WYACONDA (Missouri)
map (40° 24′N 91° 55′W) 13:476
WYACONDA RIVER
map (40° 4′N 91° 30′W) 13:476
WYANDOT (American Indians)
Huron 10:316–317
Shawnee 17:246
WYANDOT (county in Ohio)
map (40° 50′N 83° 17′W) 14:357
WYANDOTTE (county in Kansas)
map (39° 5′N 94° 45′W) 12:18
WYANDOTTE (Michigan)
map (42° 12′N 83° 10′W) 13:377
WYANDOTTE RESERVATION
Huron 10:316
WYATT (Missouri)
map (36° 55′N 89° 13′W) 13:476
WYATT, JAMES 20:297 *bibliog.*
WYATT, SIR THOMAS 20:297–298 *bibliog.*
WYCHERLEY, WILLIAM 20:298 *bibliog.*
Country Wife, The
comedy 5:132
WYCLIFFE, JOHN 20:298 *bibliog., illus.*
Lollards 12:398
WYETH, ANDREW 20:298–299 *bibliog., illus.*
Ground Hog Day 20:298 *illus.*
WYETH, N. C. 20:299 *bibliog.*
Jefferson City (Missouri) 11:393
WYLER, WILLIAM 20:299 *bibliog.*
Goldwyn, Samuel 9:237
WYLIE, ELINOR 20:299 *bibliog.*
WYLIE, LAKE
map (35° 7′N 81° 2′W) 18:98
WYLIE, PHILIP 20:299 *bibliog.*
WYMAN, BILL
Rolling Stones, The 16:272
WYMAN, JANE
Reagan, Ronald 16:101
WYMORE (Nebraska)
map (40° 7′N 96° 40′W) 14:70
WYNDHAM, JOHN 20:299
WYNDMERE (North Dakota)
map (46° 16′N 97° 8′W) 14:248
WYNNE (Arkansas)
map (35° 14′N 90° 47′W) 2:166
WYNNE, ARTHUR
crossword puzzle 5:362
WYNNEWOOD (Oklahoma)
map (34° 39′N 97° 10′W) 14:368
WYNONA (Oklahoma)
map (36° 33′N 96° 20′W) 14:368
WYNYARD (Saskatchewan)
map (51° 47′N 104° 10′W) 17:81
WYODAK (Wyoming)
map (44° 18′N 105° 24′W) 20:301
WYOMING 20:299–304 *bibliog., illus., map*
cities
Casper 4:182
Cheyenne 4:338–339
Laramie 12:206
climate 20:300
economic activity 20:302–303
education 20:302
Wyoming, University of 20:304
flag 20:300 *illus.*
flower, state
Indian paintbrush (botany) 11:106
government and politics 20:303
historical sites 20:302
history 20:303–304
Morris, Esther 13:588
land 20:299–301 *map*
map (43° 0′N 107° 30′W) 19:419
mining 20:302 *illus.*
people 20:300; 20:302
Arapaho 2:109
Shoshoni 17:284–285
physical features
Black Hills 3:315
Grand Teton National Park 9:285
Jackson Hole 11:344
Old Faithful 14:375
Teton Range 19:127
Yellowstone National Park 20:322–323
resources 20:300
rivers, lakes, and waterways 20:299–300 *illus.*
seal, state 20:300 *illus.*
tourism 20:302
WYOMING (Delaware)
map (39° 12′N 75° 34′W) 6:88
WYOMING (Illinois)
map (41° 4′N 89° 47′W) 11:42
WYOMING (Iowa)
map (42° 4′N 91° 0′W) 11:244
WYOMING (Michigan)
map (42° 54′N 85° 42′W) 13:377
WYOMING (county in New York)
map (42° 44′N 78° 8′W) 14:149
WYOMING (county in Pennsylvania)
map (41° 32′N 75° 57′W) 15:147
WYOMING (county in West Virginia)
map (37° 38′N 80° 35′W) 20:111
WYOMING, UNIVERSITY OF 20:304
WYOMING BASIN
map (42° 20′N 108° 40′W) 20:301
WYOMING RANGE
map (42° 0′N 111° 0′W) 20:301
WYSPIAŃSKI, STANISŁAW 20:305 *bibliog.*
WYSS, J. D.
Swiss Family Robinson, The 18:393
WYSS, JOHANN RUDOLF 20:305
WYSZYŃSKI, STEFAN 20:305
WYTHE (county in Virginia)
map (36° 55′N 81° 5′W) 19:607
WYTHE, GEORGE 20:305 *bibliog.*
expansion of the common law 5:140
WYTHEVILLE (Virginia)
map (36° 57′N 81° 5′W) 19:607
WYTOPITLOCK (Maine)
map (45° 38′N 68° 5′W) 13:70

X

X (letter) 20:305 *illus.*
X CHROMOSOME *see* SEX CHROMOSOMES
X-RAY ASTRONOMY 20:305–308 *bibliog., illus.*
astronomy and astrophysics 2:281–282
binary stars 3:257; 20:306–307
burster 20:307
clusters of galaxies 20:307
extrasolar source, discovery 20:306
Friedman, Herbert 8:331; 20:306
High Energy Astronomical Observatory (artificial satellite) 10:161
High Engergy Astronomical Observatories 20:306–307
history 20:305–306
production mechanisms 20:306–307
pulsar 15:620–621
supernova remnants 20:307
Uhuru 19:374
X-ray dectectors 20:307–308
X-ray galaxies 20:309
X-ray sources 20:306–307
X-RAY DIFFRACTION 20:308–309 *bibliog., illus.*
chemistry, history of 4:329
crystal 5:376
Bragg, Sir William H. 3:439
DNA: Wilkins, Maurice 20:152
geochemistry 9:95
history 20:308
Laue, Max von 12:236; 20:308
metallurgy 20:309
mineral 13:442
mineral analysis 20:309
petrography 15:207
qualitative chemical analysis 16:7
theory 20:308
X rays 20:310
X-RAY GALAXIES 20:309
Crab nebula 5:325–326
X-RAY THERAPY *see* RADIATION THERAPY
X-RAY TUBE 20:309
electromagnetic radiation 20:309
electron tube 7:124
X RAYS 20:309–311 *bibliog., illus.*
anthropometry 2:55
cathode ray 4:211
Compton, Arthur Holly 5:159
Compton effect 5:159
Curie, Marie and Pierre 5:392
dosimeter 6:244
electromagnetic radiation 7:116
examination, medical 7:326
frequency, electromagnetic 7:117 *table*
heart 10:94
mammography 13:106
Pupin, Michael Idvorsky 15:626
radiography 16:63
radiology 16:64–65 *illus.*
lead 12:256
Roentgen, Wilhelm Conrad 16:268
Siegbahn, Manne 17:295
surgery 18:362
thulium 19:184

wavelength, electromagnetic **7**:117 *table*
Wien, Wilhelm Jan **20**:146
X-15 AIRCRAFT **2**:372–373 *illus.*; **20**:311 *bibliog.*, *illus.*
XAM NUA (Laos)
map (20° 25′N 104° 2′E) **12**:203
XÁNTHI (Greece)
map (41° 8′N 24° 53′E) **9**:325
XANTHIPPE **20**:311
XANTHOPHYLL
algae **1**:281
photosynthesis **15**:276
XANTHOS *see* XANTHUS (Turkey)
XANTHUS (Turkey) **20**:311 *bibliog.*
XAU, LAKE
map (21° 15′S 24° 38′E) **3**:416
XAVIER, JOAQUIM JOSÉ DA SILVA *see* TIRADENTES
XENAKIS, YANNIS **20**:311
XENIA (Illinois)
map (38° 38′N 88° 38′W) **11**:42
XENIA (Ohio)
map (39° 41′N 83° 56′W) **14**:357
XENOCRATES **20**:311–312 *bibliog.*
XENOGRAFT
plastic surgery **15**:347
XENON **20**:312
abundances of common elements **7**:131 *table*
arc lamp **12**:338 *illus.*
element **7**:130 *table*
Group 0 periodic table **15**:167; **20**:312
inert gases **11**:161
Ramsay, Sir William **16**:81
Travers, Morris William **19**:284
XENOPHANES **20**:312 *bibliog.*
XENOPHON **20**:312 *bibliog.*
Persian Wars **15**:188
XENOPOULOS, GREGORIOS **20**:312
XERODERMA **20**:312
XEROGRAPHY
copying machines **5**:255–256
electrostatic printing **7**:127–128
XEROPHTHALMIA
eye diseases **7**:351
nutritional-deficiency diseases **14**:307
starvation **18**:228
XERORADIOGRAPHY
mammography **13**:106
XEROX CORPORATION
advertising **1**:111 *illus.*
Carlson, Chester Floyd **4**:152
XERXES I, KING OF PERSIA **6**:38 *illus.*; **20**:312 *bibliog.*
Greece, ancient **9**:331
Persia, ancient **15**:181
Persian Wars **15**:187–188
XHOSA **20**:312 *bibliog.*
Kafir **12**:5
Transkei **19**:274
XI (letter)
X (letter) **20**:305
XI-HYPERON **20**:313
XI JIANG (China) *see* HSI CHIANG (Xi Jiang) (China)
XIA (dynasty) *see* HSIA (Xia) (dynasty)
XIA GUI *see* HSIA KUEI (Xia Gui)
XI'AN (China) *see* SIAN (Xi'an) (China)
XIANG LANGUAGE *see* HSIANG LANGUAGE
XIANGKHOANG (Laos)
map (19° 20′N 103° 22′E) **12**:203
XIMENES *see* JIMÉNEZ for Spaniards named Ximenes
XIMENES DE CISNEROS, FRANCISCO *see* JIMÉNEZ DE CISNEROS, FRANCISCO
XINGU RIVER
map (1° 30′S 51° 53′W) **1**:323
map (1° 30′S 51° 53′W) **3**:460
XINJIANG (China) *see* SINKIANG (Xinjiang) (China)
XIPE-TOTEC (fertility god)
funerary urn **15**:498 *illus.*
XIQUE-XIQUE (Brazil)
map (10° 50′S 42° 44′W) **3**:460
XKALAK (Mexico)
map (18° 16′N 87° 50′W) **13**:357
XOCHICALCO (Mexico) **14**:237 *map*; **20**:313 *bibliog.*
XOCHIMILCO (Mexico) **20**:313
XOCHIMILCO, LAKE **2**:382 *map*
XOLOITZCUINTLI
Mexican hairless dog **13**:350–351
XOSA *see* XHOSA
XUANZANG *see* HSÜAN-TSANG (Xuanzang)
XUANZONG *see* T'ANG HSÜAN-TSUNG (Tang Xuanzong)
XYLEM
plant **15**:335–337 *illus.*; **15**:339 *illus.*
sapwood **17**:74
tracheophyte **19**:258
wood **20**:205
XYLOCAINE *see* LIDOCAINE
XYLOPHONE **13**:675 *illus.*; **20**:313 *bibliog.*
African **1**:169
marimba **13**:153
percussion instruments **15**:162 *illus.*
XYZ AFFAIR **19**:443 *illus.*; **20**:313 *bibliog.*
Gerry, Elbridge **9**:158
Marshall, John **13**:172

Y

Y (letter) **20**:313–314 *illus.*
I (letter) **11**:3
Y CHROMOSOME *see* SEX CHROMOSOMES
Y ORGAN
endocrine system **7**:168
YA-LU-TSANG-PU RIVER
map (24° 2′N 90° 59′E) **4**:362
YA-LUNG RIVER
map (26° 37′N 101° 48′E) **20**:318
YABLONOVY MOUNTAINS **20**:314
map (53° 30′N 115° 0′E) **19**:388
YABLONSKI, JOSEPH
United Mine Workers **19**:412
YÁCATA (Tarascan temple) **19**:35
YACHTS AND YACHTING
America's Cup **1**:368
Lipton, Sir Thomas **12**:364
boat and boating **3**:349–352 *illus.*
ship **17**:269
YADKIN (county in North Carolina)
map (36° 10′N 80° 40′W) **14**:242
YADKIN RIVER
map (35° 23′N 80° 3′W) **14**:242
YADKINVILLE (North Carolina)
map (36° 8′N 80° 39′W) **14**:242
YAFO (Israel) *see* JAFFA (Israel)
YAGHAN *see* YAMANA
YAGUACHI (Ecuador)
map (2° 7′S 79° 41′W) **7**:52
YAGUARÍ (Uruguay)
map (31° 31′S 54° 58′W) **19**:488
YAGUARÓN RIVER
map (32° 39′S 53° 12′W) **19**:488
YAHWEH *see* GOD
YAHYA KHAN, MUHAMMAD
Pakistan **15**:29
YAK **4**:216 *illus.*; **20**:314 *illus.*
animal husbandry **2**:23–24
YAKIMA (American Indians) **20**:314 *bibliog.*
Indians of North America, music and dance of the **11**:143
YAKIMA (Washington) **20**:314
map (46° 36′N 120° 31′W) **20**:35
YAKIMA (county in Washington)
map (46° 34′N 121° 3′W) **20**:35
YAKIMA RIVER
map (46° 15′N 119° 2′W) **20**:35
YAKU ISLAND
map (30° 20′N 130° 30′E) **11**:361
YAKUT **20**:314 *bibliog.*
YAKUT LANGUAGES
Altaic languages **19**:476
YAKUTAT (Alaska)
map (59° 33′N 139° 44′W) **1**:242
YAKUTSK (USSR) **20**:314
map (62° 13′N 129° 49′E) **19**:388
YALE (British Columbia)
map (49° 34′N 121° 26′W) **3**:491
YALE (Oklahoma)
map (36° 7′N 96° 42′W) **14**:368
YALE, ELIHU **20**:314 *bibliog.*
YALE, LINUS, JR. **20**:315
lock and key **12**:387
Stamford (Connecticut) **18**:215
YALE CLINIC OF CHILD DEVELOPMENT
Gesell, Arnold **9**:159
YALE LAKE
map (46° 0′N 122° 12′W) **20**:35
YALE REPORT OF 1828 **20**:315
YALE UNIVERSITY **14**:127 *illus.*; **20**:315 *bibliog.*
Beinecke Rare Book and Manuscript Library **12**:317 *illus.*
Bunshaft, Gordon **3**:564
drama school
Baker, George Pierce **3**:27
Brustein, Robert **3**:527
football **8**:216 *illus.*
garden
Noguchi, Isamu **14**:213
law school
Hutchins, Robert M. **10**:322
presidents
Dwight, Timothy **6**:317
Porter, Noah **15**:445
Silliman, Benjamin **17**:309
Yale, Elihu **20**:314
Yale Center for British Art and British Studies
Mellon, Paul **13**:287
Yale Report of 1828 **20**:315
YALE UNIVERSITY OBSERVATORY
Schlesinger, Frank **17**:126
Yale Catalog of Bright Stars
astronomical catalogs and atlases **2**:276
YALOBUSHA (county in Mississippi)
map (34° 0′N 89° 40′W) **13**:469
YALOW, ROSALYN SUSSMAN **20**:315 *bibliog.*
YALTA (USSR) **20**:315
YALTA CONFERENCE **20**:315 *bibliog.*, *illus.*
Churchill, Sir Winston **4**:426–427
Oder-Neisse line **14**:349
United States, history of the **19**:455–456 *illus.*
World War II **20**:275
YALU RIVER **20**:315
Korean War **12**:121
map (39° 55′N 124° 22′E) **12**:113
YAM **20**:315–316 *bibliog.*, *illus.*
medicinal plants **13**:266
YAM HA-MELAH *see* DEAD SEA
YAMAGA SOKO **20**:316
YAMAGATA ARITOMO **20**:316 *bibliog.*
YAMAL PENINSULA
map (70° 0′N 70° 0′E) **19**:388
YAMAMOTO ISOROKU **20**:316
Midway **13**:414
YAMANA **11**:116 *illus.*
YAMANI, AHMED ZAKI **20**:316 *illus.*
YAMASAKI, MINORU **20**:316 *bibliog.*
World Trade Center **20**:219
YAMASEE (American Indians) **20**:316–317 *bibliog.*
French and Indian Wars **8**:313
YAMASHITA TOMOYUKI **20**:317 *bibliog.*
YAMATAKA **19**:25 *illus.*
YAMBOL (Bulgaria)
map (42° 29′N 26° 30′E) **3**:555
YAMÉOGO, MAURICE
Upper Volta **19**:473
YAMHILL (county in Oregon)
map (45° 15′N 123° 20′W) **14**:427
YAMPA (Colorado)
map (40° 9′N 106° 55′W) **5**:116
YAMPA RIVER
map (40° 32′N 108° 59′W) **5**:116
YAMSAY MOUNTAIN
map (42° 56′N 121° 22′W) **14**:427
YAMUNA (JUMNA) RIVER
map (25° 25′N 81° 50′E) **9**:37
YAMUNA RIVER **20**:317
YAN LIBEN *see* YEN LI-PEN (Yan Liben)
YANA (American Indians) **20**:317 *bibliog.*
YANCEY (county in North Carolina)
map (35° 55′N 82° 20′W) **14**:242
YANCEY, WILLIAM LOWNDES **20**:317 *bibliog.*
YANCEYVILLE (North Carolina)
map (36° 24′N 79° 20′W) **14**:242
YÄNERSBORG (Sweden)
map (58° 22′N 12° 19′E) **18**:382
YÁÑEZ, AGUSTÍN **20**:317
YANG, CHEN NING **20**:317 *bibliog.*
YANG-CH'ENG (China) *see* CANTON (China)
YANG CHIEN (Sui Wen Ti)
Sui (dynasty) **18**:330
YANG-KO **20**:317
YANG KUANG (Sui Yang Ti)
Sui (dynasty) **18**:330
YANG-SHAO CULTURE
Chinese archaeology **4**:378 *illus.*
YANG-TI **4**:372 *illus.*
YANGOR (Nauru)
map (0° 31′S 166° 54′E) **14**:51
YANGTZE RIVER **20**:317–318 *bibliog.*, *map*
irrigation **11**:282–283
map (31° 48′N 121° 10′E) **20**:318
YANKEETOWN (Florida)
map (29° 2′N 82° 43′W) **8**:172
YANKTON (South Dakota)
map (42° 53′N 97° 23′W) **18**:103
YANKTON (county in South Dakota)
map (43° 0′N 97° 25′W) **18**:103
YANOMAMO (American Indians) **20**:318 *bibliog.*
Warrau **20**:30
YANTRA RIVER
map (43° 38′N 25° 34′E) **3**:555
YAO **20**:318–319 *bibliog.*
YAO WEN-YUAN
Gang of Four **9**:36
YAOUNDÉ (Cameroon) **20**:319
map (3° 52′N 11° 31′E) **4**:61
YAP **20**:319
money **13**:527
YAQUE DEL NORTE RIVER
map (19° 51′N 71° 41′W) **6**:233
YAQUE DEL SUR RIVER
map (18° 17′N 71° 6′W) **6**:233
YAQUI (American Indians) **20**:319 *bibliog.*
Indians of North America, music and dance of the **11**:143
YAQUI RIVER
map (27° 37′N 110° 39′W) **13**:357
YARBOROUGH, CALE **20**:319 *bibliog.*
YARDANG
landform evolution **12**:182 *illus.*
YARDEN, IHA- *see* JORDAN RIVER
YARDVILLE (New Jersey)
map (40° 11′N 74° 40′W) **14**:129
YAREN (Nauru)
map (0° 32′S 166° 55′E) **14**:51
YARIM (Yemen) (Sana)
map (14° 29′N 44° 21′E) **20**:325
YARKAND (China)
map (38° 25′N 77° 16′E) **4**:362
YARMOUTH (Maine)
map (43° 48′N 70° 12′W) **13**:70
YARMOUTH (Nova Scotia)
map (43° 50′N 66° 7′W) **14**:269
YAROSLAV I, GRAND DUKE OF KIEV **20**:319
Rurik (dynasty) **16**:347
YAROSLAVL (USSR) **20**:319
map (57° 37′N 39° 52′E) **19**:388
YARROW **20**:319
YARUMAL (Colombia)
map (6° 58′N 75° 24′W) **5**:107
YAŞAR KEMAL **20**:319
YASAWA GROUP (Islands)
map (17° 0′S 177° 23′E) **8**:77
YASHIN, LEV **20**:319 *bibliog.*
YASTRZEMSKI, CARL **20**:320
YATA (Bolivia)
map (13° 20′S 66° 35′W) **3**:366
YATES (county in New York)
map (42° 40′N 77° 3′W) **14**:149
YATES CENTER (Kansas)
map (37° 53′N 95° 44′W) **12**:18
YATES CITY (Illinois)
map (40° 47′N 90° 1′W) **11**:42
YATHRIB
Middle East, history of the **13**:402
YAUCO (Puerto Rico)
map (18° 2′N 66° 51′W) **15**:614
YAUPI (Ecuador)
map (2° 59′S 77° 50′W) **7**:52
YAVAPAI (county in Arizona)
map (34° 40′N 112° 30′W) **2**:160
YAVARÍ RIVER
map (4° 21′S 70° 2′W) **15**:193
YAVIZA (Panama)
map (8° 11′N 77° 41′W) **15**:55
YAVNE (Israel)
map (31° 53′N 34° 45′E) **11**:302
YAWS **20**:320
spirochete **18**:189
Treponema **19**:291
YAXCHILÁN (Mexico)
Lacandón **12**:158
Piedras Negras **15**:295
YAYOI CULTURE (Japan)
Asia, history of **2**:254
Japan, history of **11**:367
Japanese art and architecture **11**:372
YAZD (Iran)
map (31° 53′N 54° 25′E) **11**:250
YAZDEGIRD I, KING OF PERSIA
Persia, ancient **15**:183
YAZILIKAYA
Boğazköy (Turkey) **3**:360
YAZOO (county in Mississippi)
map (32° 45′N 90° 25′W) **13**:469
YAZOO CITY (Mississippi)
map (32° 51′N 90° 28′W) **13**:469
YAZOO LAND FRAUD **20**:320 *bibliog.*
Fletcher v. Peck **8**:163
YAZOO RIVER **20**:320
map (32° 22′N 91° 0′W) **13**:469
YDING SKOVHØJ
map (56° 0′N 9° 48′E) **6**:109
YE (Burma)
map (15° 15′N 97° 51′E) **3**:573
YEAGER, CHARLES E.
aviation **2**:374
X-15 **20**:311
YEAR **20**:320
calendar **4**:27–28
Chinese calendar **4**:388
YEAR BOOKS (law)
common law records **5**:139

YEARDLEY, SIR GEORGE **20**:320 *bibliog.*
YEARLING, THE (book)
Rawlings, Marjorie Kinnan **16**:95
YEAST **20**:320 *bibliog.*
beer **3**:162–163
bread **3**:465
fermentation **8**:55
fungi **8**:365; **8**:367
YEATS, JACK BUTLER **20**:320 *bibliog.*
Sligo (city in Ireland) **17**:361
YEATS, WILLIAM BUTLER **11**:267 *illus.*; **20**:321 *bibliog.*, *illus.*
Abbey Theatre **1**:52–53
Gregory, Isabella Augusta, Lady **9**:355
Moore, George **13**:568 *illus.*
Sligo (city in Ireland) **17**:361
YEGOROV, BORIS B. **20**:322
Voshkod **19**:636 *table*
YEH CHIEN-YING
China **4**:369
YEKATERINODAR (USSR) *see* KRASNODAR (USSR)
YELISEYEV, ALEKSEI STANISLAVOVICH **20**:322 *bibliog.*
YELL (county in Arkansas)
map (35° 0′N 93° 22′W) **2**:166
YELLOW DAISY *see* BLACK-EYED SUSAN
YELLOW-DOG CONTRACT **20**:322
YELLOW EMPEROR **20**:322
Chinese medicine **4**:390–391
YELLOW EMPEROR'S CLASSIC OF INTERNAL MEDICINE, THE *see* *NEI-CHING*
YELLOW FEVER **20**:322 *bibliog.*
Carroll, James **4**:168
Reed, Walter **16**:118
vaccination **19**:501
YELLOW-GREEN ALGAE *see* ALGAE, YELLOW-GREEN ALGAE
YELLOW JACKET
wasp **20**:45–46 *illus.*
YELLOW JOURNALISM **20**:322
Brisbane, Arthur **3**:487
comic strip **5**:135
Hearst, William Randolph **10**:90
journalism **11**:455
Outcault, Richard Felton **14**:468
Pulitzer, Joseph **15**:618
Spanish-American War **18**:149
"YELLOW KID OF HOGAN'S ALLEY, THE" (comic strip) **5**:135 *illus.*
Outcault, Richard Felton **14**:468
yellow journalism **20**:322
YELLOW MEDICINE (county in Minnesota)
map (44° 43′N 95° 50′W) **13**:453
YELLOW PARILLA *see* MOONSEED
YELLOW POPLAR *see* TULIP TREE
YELLOW RAIN (chemical weapon)
chemical and biological warfare **4**:312
YELLOW RIVER *see* HWANG HO (Huang He)
YELLOW SEA **20**:322
map (36° 0′N 123° 0′E) **4**:362
YELLOWKNIFE (Northwest Territories) **20**:322
map (62° 27′N 114° 21′W) **14**:258
YELLOWSTONE (county in Montana)
map (45° 55′N 108° 15′W) **13**:547
YELLOWSTONE LAKE
map (44° 25′N 110° 22′W) **20**:301
YELLOWSTONE NATIONAL PARK **14**:37–39 *illus.*, *map*, *table*; **20**:302–303 *illus.*; **20**:322–323 *bibliog.*
exploration
Colter, John **5**:124
geyser **9**:162
Hayden, Ferdinand **10**:80–81
hot springs **10**:259
map (44° 58′N 110° 42′W) **20**:301
Old Faithful **14**:375
petrified wood **15**:205
YELLOWSTONE RIVER **13**:549 *illus.*; **14**:249 *illus.*; **20**:303 *illus.*; **20**:323
map (47° 58′N 103° 59′W) **13**:547
YELLOWWOOD **20**:323 *illus.*
YELLVILLE (Arkansas)
map (36° 14′N 92° 41′W) **2**:166
YEMASSEE (South Carolina)
map (32° 41′N 80° 51′W) **18**:98
YEMEN (Aden) **20**:323–324 *bibliog.*, *illus.*, *table*
cities
Aden **1**:101
flag **20**:323 *illus.*
history and government **20**:324
land, people, and economy **20**:323–324 *map*
map (15° 0′N 48° 0′E) **2**:232
Socotra **18**:30
YEMEN (Sana) **20**:324–326 *bibliog.*, *illus.*, *map*
archaeology
Ma'rib **13**:151
cities
Sana **17**:58
flag **20**:325 *illus.*
history and government **20**:326
land, people, and economy **20**:325–326 *map*
map (15° 0′N 44° 0′E) **2**:232
Middle Eastern universities **13**:410–412 *table*
United Arab Republic **19**:401
YEMEN ARAB REPUBLIC *see* YEMEN (Sana)
YEN LI-PEN (Yan Liben) **20**:326 *bibliog.*
Chinese art and architecture **4**:386 *illus.*
YENANGYAUNG (Burma)
map (20° 28′N 94° 52′E) **3**:573
YENDI (Ghana)
map (9° 26′N 0° 1′W) **9**:164
YENISEI LANGUAGE
Ural-Altaic languages **19**:475
YENISEI RIVER **20**:326
map (71° 50′N 82° 40′E) **19**:388
YENRESH *see* ERIE (American Indians)
YEOMEN OF THE GUARD *see* BEEFEATERS
YERBA BUENA MOUNTAIN
map (14° 5′N 87° 26′W) **10**:218
YERBA MATÉ *see* MATÉ
YERBY, FRANK **20**:326 *bibliog.*
YEREVAN (USSR) **20**:326
map (40° 11′N 44° 30′E) **19**:388
YERINGTON (Nevada)
map (38° 59′N 119° 10′W) **14**:111
YERKES, CHARLES T.
Yerkes Observatory **20**:326
YERKES, ROBERT MEARNS **20**:326 *bibliog.*
comparative psychology **20**:326
primate **20**:326
YERKES OBSERVATORY **20**:326–327 *bibliog.*
Clark, Alvan Graham **5**:37
Hale, George Ellery **10**:18
Kuiper, Gerard **12**:135
Strömgren, Bengt Georg Daniel **18**:302
Struve, Otto **18**:304
YERMAK TIMOFEYEVICH **20**:327 *bibliog.*
YERMO (California)
map (34° 54′N 116° 50′W) **4**:31
YERSIN, ALEXANDRE
Roux, Pierre Paul Émile **16**:327
YERUSHALAYIM *see* JERUSALEM (Israel)
YESENIN, SERGEI ALEKSANDROVICH **20**:327 *bibliog.*
YESHIVA UNIVERSITY **20**:327
YESÜGEI
Genghis Khan **9**:92
YETI *see* ABOMINABLE SNOWMAN
YEU ISLAND
map (46° 42′N 2° 20′W) **8**:260
YEVTUSHENKO, YEVGENY ALEKSANDROVICH **20**:327
YEW **20**:327 *illus.*
nutmeg **14**:302
Torreya **19**:244
YEZHOVSHCHINA *see* GREAT PURGE
YI (dynasty)
Korean art **12**:117–118 *illus.*
YI (game) *see* GO (game)
YI RIVER
map (33° 7′S 57° 8′W) **19**:488
YIDDISH LANGUAGE
Germanic languages **9**:135–137 *table*
YIDDISH LITERATURE *see* HEBREW AND YIDDISH LITERATURE
YIDDISH THEATER **20**:328 *bibliog.*
Adler, Jacob, Stella, and Luther **1**:104
Aronson, Boris **2**:186–187
Golfaden, Abraham **9**:233
Gordin, Jacob **9**:248
Kaminska, Ida **20**:328
Schwartz, Maurice **20**:328
YIJING *see* *I CHING* (*Yijing*)
YIN (dynasty) *see* SHANG (dynasty)
YIN-CH'UAN (China)
map (38° 30′N 106° 18′E) **4**:362
YIN AND YANG
Chinese medicine **4**:390
Confucianism **5**:179 *illus.*; **5**:180
landscape painting **12**:188 *illus.*
YING-K'OU (China)
map (40° 38′N 122° 30′E) **4**:362
YMCA *see* YOUNG MEN'S CHRISTIAN ASSOCIATION
YMHA *see* YOUNG MEN'S HEBREW ASSOCIATION
YMIR **20**:328
YOAKUM (Texas)
map (29° 17′N 97° 9′W) **19**:129
YOAKUM (county in Texas)
map (33° 8′N 102° 48′W) **19**:129
YODEL **20**:328 *bibliog.*
YODH (letter)
I (letter) **11**:3
YOGA **20**:328–329 *bibliog.*, *illus.*
Aurobindo, Sri **2**:325
Hinduism **10**:170
Jainism **11**:349–350
philosophy **15**:246
stress, biological **18**:298
YOGANANDA **20**:329 *bibliog.*
YOGURT **20**:329
YOGYAKARTA (Indonesia)
map (7° 48′S 110° 22′E) **11**:147
YOHIMBINE
aphrodisiac **2**:78
YOKE **20**:329
harness **10**:52–53
wagon **20**:6
YOKOHAMA (Japan) **19**:224 *map*; **20**:329
map (35° 27′N 139° 39′E) **11**:361
YOKOMITSU RIICHI **20**:329
YOKOSUKA (Japan)
map (35° 18′N 139° 40′E) **11**:361
YOLK (embryology)
development **6**:137; **6**:138 *illus.*; **6**:140 *illus.*; **6**:141 *illus.*
egg **7**:72 *illus.*
YOLO (county in California)
map (38° 41′N 121° 46′W) **4**:31
YOM KIPPUR **20**:329
fasting **8**:33
YOM RIVER
map (15° 52′N 100° 16′E) **19**:139
YONCALLA (Oregon)
map (43° 36′N 123° 17′W) **14**:427
YONGLE *see* YUNG-LO, EMPEROR OF CHINA (Yongle)
YONKERS (New York) **20**:329–330
map (41° 0′N 73° 52′W) **14**:149
YORCK VON WARTENBURG, LUDWIG, GRAF **20**:330 *bibliog.*
YORITOMO **2**:253 *illus.*; **11**:368 *illus.*; **20**:330 *bibliog.*
Japan, history of **11**:367–368
samurai **17**:49
shogun **17**:281
YORK (Alabama)
map (32° 29′N 88° 18′W) **1**:234
YORK (city in Maine) **19**:417 *illus.*
YORK (dynasty) **20**:330 *bibliog.*
Edward IV, King of England **7**:68
Great Britain, history of **9**:312–313
Henry VII, King of England **10**:126
Lancaster (dynasty) **12**:177
Richard III, King of England **16**:210–211
Roses, Wars of the **16**:316 *map*
YORK (England) **20**:330
map (53° 58′N 1° 5′W) **19**:403
YORK (county in Maine)
map (43° 30′N 70° 45′W) **13**:70
YORK (Nebraska)
map (40° 52′N 97° 36′W) **14**:70
YORK (county in Nebraska)
map (40° 55′N 97° 35′W) **14**:70
YORK (Pennsylvania) **20**:330
map (39° 58′N 76° 44′W) **15**:147
YORK (county in Pennsylvania)
map (39° 58′N 76° 44′W) **15**:147
YORK (South Carolina)
map (35° 0′N 81° 14′W) **18**:98
YORK (county in South Carolina)
map (35° 0′N 81° 10′W) **18**:98
YORK (county in Virginia)
map (37° 15′N 76° 40′W) **19**:607
YORK, ALVIN CULLUM **20**:330
YORK, CAPE (Australia)
map (10° 42′S 142° 31′E) **2**:328
YORK, CAPE (Greenland)
map (75° 53′N 66° 12′W) **9**:353
YORK, EDMUND OF LANGLEY, DUKE OF
York (dynasty) **20**:330
YORK, RICHARD, DUKE OF
Roses, Wars of the **16**:316
Wakefield (England) **20**:8
York (dynasty) **20**:330
YORK, SERGEANT *see* YORK, ALVIN CULLUM
YORK FACTORY (Manitoba)
map (57° 0′N 92° 18′W) **13**:119
YORK RIVER
map (37° 15′N 76° 23′W) **19**:607
YORK UNIVERSITY **20**:331
YORKE, HENRY VINCENT *see* GREEN, HENRY
YORKIE *see* YORKSHIRE TERRIER
YORKSHIRE (England) **20**:331
cities
Bradford **3**:436
Doncaster **6**:237
Harrogate **10**:61
Leeds **12**:271
Scarborough **17**:115
Sheffield **17**:250
Wakefield **20**:8
York **20**:330
YORKSHIRE (horse) *see* COACH HORSE
YORKSHIRE TERRIER **6**:217 *illus.*; **20**:331 *bibliog.*, *illus.*
YORKTON (Saskatchewan)
map (51° 13′N 102° 28′W) **17**:81
YORKTOWN (aircraft carrier)
World War II **20**:266
YORKTOWN (Texas)
map (28° 59′N 97° 30′W) **19**:129
YORKTOWN (Virginia)
map (37° 14′N 76° 30′W) **19**:607
YORKTOWN CAMPAIGN **20**:331 *bibliog.*
American Revolution **1**:363
Cornwallis, Charles Cornwallis, 1st Marquess **5**:270
Cornwallis' surrender **1**:363 *illus.*
YORKVILLE (Illinois)
map (41° 38′N 88° 27′W) **11**:42
YORO (Honduras)
map (15° 9′N 87° 7′W) **10**:218
YORUBA **20**:331 *bibliog.*
African music **1**:168–171
Ife **11**:32
Porto-Novo (Benin) **15**:446
terra-cotta head **19**:119 *illus.*
tribe **19**:295
YORUK **20**:331–332 *bibliog.*
YOSEMITE FALLS **4**:35 *illus.*; **20**:332
waterfall **20**:63
YOSEMITE NATIONAL PARK **4**:35 *illus.*; **14**:38–39 *map*, *table*; **20**:332 *bibliog.*
Bridalveil Fall **3**:479
Sierra Club **17**:296
Yosemite Falls **20**:332
YOSHIDA SHIGERU **20**:332 *bibliog.*
YOSHIMASA
Japan, history of **11**:368
YOSHIMITSU
Japanese art and architecture **11**:376
YOSHINOBU, SHOGUN OF JAPAN
Tokugawa (family) **19**:223
YOSHIWARA (Japan)
scene of daily street life **11**:369 *illus.*
YOSUKE, MATSUOKA *see* MATSUOKA YOSUKE
YOTAÚ (Bolivia)
map (16° 3′S 63° 3′W) **3**:366
YOU CAN'T GO HOME AGAIN (book)
Wolfe, Thomas **20**:197–198
YOUNG (Arizona)
map (34° 6′N 110° 57′W) **2**:160
YOUNG (county in Texas)
map (33° 8′N 98° 45′W) **19**:129
YOUNG (Uruguay)
map (32° 41′S 57° 38′W) **19**:488
YOUNG, ANDREW **20**:332 *bibliog.*, *illus.*
YOUNG, ARTHUR
agriculture, history of **1**:191
YOUNG, BRIGHAM **20**:332–333 *bibliog.*, *illus.*
Mormonism **13**:582
YOUNG, CHIC **20**:333
YOUNG, COLEMAN
Michigan **13**:382
YOUNG, CY **20**:333 *bibliog.*, *illus.*
Cy Young Award Winners **3**:105 *table*
YOUNG, DENTON TRUE (CY) *see* YOUNG, CY
YOUNG, EDWARD **20**:333 *bibliog.*
YOUNG, JOHN W. **20**:333 *illus.*
Space Shuttle **18**:135–136 *illus.*
YOUNG, LESTER **20**:334
YOUNG, LORETTA **20**:334
YOUNG, MAHONRI **20**:334 *bibliog.*
YOUNG, MURAT BERNARD *see* YOUNG, CHIC
YOUNG, OWEN D. **20**:334
radio and television broadcasting **16**:55
YOUNG, THOMAS **20**:334 *bibliog.*
color **5**:113
interference **11**:208; **20**:334
optics **14**:411
physics, history of **18**:285
Rosetta Stone **16**:317; **20**:334

YOUNG, WHITNEY M., JR. 20:334 *bibliog., illus.*
YOUNG ADULT *see* YOUNG PEOPLE
YOUNG-HELMHOLTZ THEORY OF COLOR
 color perception 5:114–115
YOUNG ITALY (youth movement)
 Mazzini, Giuseppe 13:250
YOUNG MEN'S CHRISTIAN ASSOCIATION 20:334 *bibliog.*
 Mott, John R. 13:616
YOUNG MEN'S HEBREW ASSOCIATION 20:334–335 *bibliog.*
YOUNG PEOPLE 20:335–336 *bibliog.*
 ACTION (federal agency) 1:89
 adolescence 1:106–107
 alcohol consumption 20:336
 birth control 3:294
 counterculture 5:311–312
 drug abuse 20:336
 education 20:335
  secondary education 17:180
 employment and unemployment 7:159–160; 20:335–336
 growth 9:380
 passage rites 15:103–104
 rural
  4-H program 8:253
  Future Farmers of America 8:383
 suicide 18:330; 20:336
 youth hostel 20:337
YOUNG PLAN
 reparations 16:160
 Young, Owen D. 20:334
YOUNG PRETENDER *see* STUART, CHARLES EDWARD (Bonnie Prince Charlie)
YOUNG RANGE
 map (44° 13′S 169° 22′E) 14:158
YOUNG SHERLOCK HOLMES, THE (film) 5:160m *illus.*
YOUNG TURKS 20:336 *bibliog.*
 Ottoman Empire 14:466
YOUNG WOMEN'S CHRISTIAN ASSOCIATION 20:336 *bibliog.*
YOUNG WOMEN'S HEBREW ASSOCIATION 20:336
YOUNGER BROTHERS 20:336 *bibliog.*
YOUNGES ISLAND (South Carolina)
 map (32° 42′N 80° 13′W) 18:98
YOUNGHUSBAND, SIR FRANCIS EDWARD 20:336 *bibliog.*
YOUNGSTOWN (Alberta)
 map (51° 32′N 111° 13′W) 1:256
YOUNGSTOWN (Florida)
 map (30° 22′N 85° 27′W) 8:172
YOUNGSTOWN (New York)
 map (43° 15′N 79° 3′W) 14:149
YOUNGSTOWN (Ohio) 20:337
 map (41° 6′N 80° 39′W) 14:357
YOUNGSTOWN SHEET AND TUBE COMPANY v. SAWYER 20:337
 Constitution of the United States 5:218
YOUNGSVILLE (Louisiana)
 map (30° 6′N 92° 0′W) 12:430
YOUNGSVILLE (Pennsylvania)
 map (41° 51′N 79° 19′W) 15:147
YOURCENAR, MARGUERITE 20:337
YOUSKEVITCH, IGOR 20:337 *bibliog.*
 Ballets Russes de Monte Carlo 3:48
YOUTH *see* YOUNG PEOPLE
YOUTH CHALLENGE PROGRAM
 ACTION (federal agency) 1:89
YOUTH HOSTEL 20:337
YOUTHIOGHENY RIVER
 map (40° 22′N 79° 52′W) 20:111
YOZGAT (Turkey)
 map (39° 50′N 34° 48′E) 19:343
YPEJHÚ (Paraguay)
 map (23° 54′S 55° 20′W) 15:77
YPRES (Belgium) 20:337
 map (50° 51′N 2° 53′E) 3:177
YPRES, BATTLES OF 20:337 *bibliog.*
 World War I 20:224–225 *map;* 20:237
YPSILANTI (Michigan)
 map (42° 15′N 83° 36′W) 13:377
YREKA (California)
 map (41° 44′N 122° 38′W) 4:31
YSAŸE, EUGÈNE 20:337 *bibliog.*
YTTERBIUM 20:337
 element 7:130 *table*
 lanthanide series 12:200–201
 Marignac, Jean Charles Galissard de, discoverer 13:152
 metal, metallic element 13:328
YTTRIUM 20:337–338
 element 7:130 *table*
 Group IIIB periodic table 15:167
 lanthanide series 20:337–338
 metal, metallic element 13:328
 transition elements 19:273
 Ytterby, Sweden 20:338
YU (dynasty)
 Korea, history of 12:116
YÜ-MEN (China)
 map (39° 56′N 97° 51′E) 4:362
YUAN (dynasty) *see* YÜAN (Yuan) (dynasty)
YÜAN (RED) RIVER
 map (28° 58′N 111° 49′E) 20:318
YÜAN (Yuan) (dynasty) 20:338 *bibliog.*
 China, history of 4:372–373 *illus.*
 Chinese art and architecture 4:381
 Chinese literature 4:390
 Huang Kung-wang (Huang Gongwang) 10:287
 Ni Tsan (Ni Zan) 14:177
 Wang Meng 20:22
YÜAN CHI *see* JUAN CHI (Ruan Ji)
YÜAN DRAMA 20:338 *bibliog.*
YÜAN RIVER 20:338
 map (20° 17′N 106° 34′E) 4:362
YÜAN SHIH-K'AI (Yuan Shikai) 20:338 *bibliog.*
 China, history of 4:375
 Kuomintang (Guomindang) 12:137–138
 Sun Yat-sen 18:346
YUAN SHIKAI *see* YÜAN SHIH K'AI (Yuan Shikai)
YUANMOU MAN
 China, history of 4:370
YUBA (county in California)
 map (39° 10′N 121° 20′W) 4:31
YUBA CITY (California)
 map (39° 8′N 121° 37′W) 4:31
YUCATÁN (Mexico) 20:338 *bibliog.*
 archaeology 2:125 *illus.*
  Catherwood, Frederick 4:210
  Chichén Itzá 4:343–344
  Mayapán 13:246
  Uxmal 19:499
 cities
  Mérida 13:310
 fish
  blindfish 3:332
 Maya 13:243
YUCATÁN CHANNEL
 map (21° 45′N 85° 45′W) 4:148
YUCATÁN PENINSULA 20:338 *map*
 map (19° 30′N 89° 0′W) 13:357
 Villa de Valladolid (early Spanish settlement) 12:217 *illus.*
YUCCA (Arizona)
 map (34° 52′N 114° 9′W) 2:160
YUCCA (botany) 20:338–339 *illus.*
 Joshua tree 11:452
YUCKIKU MORONOBU *see* MORONOBU
YUDENICH, NIKOLAI
 World War I 20:234
YUE LANGUAGE
 Sino-Tibetan languages 17:324
YUGOSLAV LITERATURE
 authors
  Andrić, Ivo 1:408
  Cankar, Ivan 4:108
  Župančič, Oton 20:382
YUGOSLAVIA 20:339–344 *bibliog., illus., map, table*
 arts 20:342
  See also the subheading Yugoslavia under specific art forms, e.g., ARCHITECTURE; SCULPTURE; etc.
 cities
  Belgrade 3:182 *illus.*
  Dubrovnik 6:289
  Ljubljana 12:382
  Novi Sad 14:277
  Pula 15:618
  Rijeka 16:223
  Sarajevo 17:74
  Šibenik 17:291
  Skopje 17:344
  Split 18:191
  Titograd 19:215
  Zadar 20:348
  Zagreb 20:348
 climate 20:340–341 *table*
 communism *see* COMMUNISM
 Dalmatia 6:14
 economic activity 20:342–343
 education 20:341–342
  European universities 7:308 *table*
 flag 20:339 *illus.*
 government and politics 20:343
 health 20:342
 history 20:343–344
  Alexander, King 1:276
  Cominform 5:136
  communism 5:148
  Djilas, Milovan 6:208
  Little Entente 12:372–373
  Mihajlović, Draža 13:417
  Pašić, Nikola 15:102
  Peter I, King of Serbia 15:201
  Peter II, King 15:201
  socialism 18:22
  Tito 19:214–215
  Trieste (Italy) 19:297
 housing 10:279–280
 Illyria 11:50
 land and resources 20:339–341 *illus., map, table*
 languages 20:341
  Slavic languages 17:358
 map (44° 0′N 19° 0′E) 7:268
 nation 14:27
 people 20:341–342
 physical features
  Dinaric Alps 6:178
  Istria 11:308
 republics
  Bosnia and Hercegovina 3:407 *map*
  Croatia 5:354–355 *map*
  Macedonia 13:15 *map*
  Montenegro 13:552–553 *map*
  Serbia 17:207–208 *map*
  Slovenia 17:364 *map*
 rivers, lakes, and waterways 20:340–343 *illus.*
  Sava River 17:97
  Tisza River 19:210
YUIT *see* ESKIMO
YUKAGHIR 20:344 *bibliog.*
YUKAGIR LANGUAGE
 Ural-Altaic languages 19:476
YUKAWA, HIDEKI 14:287 *illus.;* 20:344 *bibliog.*
YUKON RIVER 12:393 *illus.;* 20:344 *map*
 map (62° 33′N 163° 59′W) 1:242
YUKON TERRITORY (Canada) 20:344–346 *bibliog., illus., map*
 cities
  Whitehorse 20:139
 climate 20:345
 economic activity 20:345–346
 flag 8:145 *illus.;* 20:346 *illus.*
 government 20:346
 history 20:346
 Hubbard Glacier
  glaciers and glaciation 9:194
 Klondike 12:98
 land and resources 20:344–345 *map*
 Logan, Mount 12:394
 map (64° 0′N 135° 0′W) 4:70
 people 20:345
YULEE (Florida)
 map (30° 38′N 81° 36′W) 8:172
YUMA (American Indians) 20:346 *bibliog.*
 Mojave 13:504
YUMA (county in Arizona)
 map (33° 0′N 114° 0′W) 2:160
YUMA (city in Arizona) 20:346
 map (32° 43′N 114° 37′W) 2:160
YUMA (Colorado)
 map (40° 8′N 102° 43′W) 5:116
YUMA (county in Colorado)
 map (40° 0′N 102° 25′W) 5:116
YÜN-KANG (Yungang) (China) 20:346
YUNG-CH'ENG (China) *see* FOOCHOW (China)
YUNG-LO, EMPEROR OF CHINA (Yongle) 20:346
 China, history of 4:372
 Ming (dynasty) 13:444
YUNGANG (China) *see* YUN-KANG (Yungang) (China)
YUNGAY, BATTLE OF
 Santa Cruz, Andrés 17:67–68
YUNLIANG HO *see* GRAND CANAL (China)
YUNNAN (China) *see* YÜNNAN (Yunnan) (China)
YÜNNAN (Yunnan) (China) 20:346–347
 cities
  K'un-ming (Kunming) 12:136
YÜNNAN PLATEAU
 map (25° 0′N 104° 0′E) 4:362
YUNUS EMRE 20:347
YUPIK LANGUAGE
 Eskimo 7:239
YURAK LANGUAGE
 Ural-Altaic languages 19:475
YURIEV, ROMAN
 Romanov (dynasty) 16:290
YURIMAGUAS (Peru)
 map (5° 54′S 76° 5′W) 15:193
YUROK (American Indians) 20:347 *bibliog.*
 Indians of North America, art of the 11:139
YURT 13:529 *illus.;* 20:347
 Khalkhae 12:65
 Turkmen 19:347
YUR'YEV (USSR) *see* TARTU (USSR)
YUSHIJ, NIMA
 Persian literature 15:187
YUZHNO-SAKHALINSK (USSR)
 map (46° 58′N 142° 42′E) 19:388
YVERDON (Switzerland)
 map (46° 47′N 6° 39′E) 18:394
YWCA *see* YOUNG WOMEN'S CHRISTIAN ASSOCIATION
YWHA *see* YOUNG WOMEN'S HEBREW ASSOCIATION

Z

Z (film)
 Costa-Gavras, Henri 5:291
Z (letter) 20:347 *illus.*
Z PARTICLE
 fundamental particles 8:362 *table;* 8:363
 Rubbia, Carlo 16:335
 unified field theory 19:386
 van der Meer, Simon 19:512
ZAANDAM (Netherlands)
 map (52° 26′N 4° 49′E) 14:99
ZABID (Yemen) (Sana)
 map (14° 10′N 43° 17′E) 20:325
ZACAPA (Guatemala)
 map (14° 58′N 89° 32′W) 9:389
ZACATECAS (Mexico) 20:347
 map (22° 47′N 102° 35′W) 13:357
ZACATECAS (state in Mexico) 20:347
 cities
  Zacatecas 20:347
ZACATECOLUCA (El Salvador)
 map (13° 30′N 88° 52′W) 7:100
ZACHARIAS, POPE 20:347–348 *bibliog.*
ZACHARY (Louisiana)
 map (30° 39′N 91° 9′W) 12:430
ZACUALPA (Guatemala)
 map (15° 5′N 90° 50′W) 9:389
ZACUALTIPÁN (Mexico)
 map (20° 39′N 98° 36′W) 13:357
ZADAR (Yugoslavia) 20:348
 map (44° 7′N 15° 14′E) 20:340
ZADKINE, OSSIP 20:348 *bibliog.*
ZAGAZIG (Egypt)
 map (30° 35′N 31° 31′E) 7:76
ZAGREB (Yugoslavia) 20:348
 map (45° 48′N 15° 58′E) 20:340
ZAGROS MOUNTAINS 20:348
 Bakhtiari 3:28–29
 map (33° 40′N 47° 0′E) 11:250
ZAGYVA RIVER
 map (47° 10′N 20° 13′E) 10:307
ZAHARIAS, BABE DIDRIKSON 20:348 *bibliog., illus.*
ZAHEDAN (Iran)
 map (29° 30′N 60° 52′E) 11:250
ZAHLE (Lebanon)
 map (33° 51′N 35° 53′) 12:265
ZAI LUN *see* TSAI LUN (Zai Lun)
ZAIBATSU 20:348 *bibliog.*
ZAID BIN SULTAN AL-NAHAYAN
 United Arab Emirates 19:401
ZAIRE 20:348–352 *bibliog., illus., map, table*
 cities
  Kinshasa 12:85
  Kisangani 12:90
  Lubumbashi 12:448
 economic activity 20:351
 education 20:351
  African universities 1:176 *table*
 flag 20:349 *illus.*
 history and government 20:351–352
  Congo crisis 5:183
  Kasavubu, Joseph 12:29
  Leopold II, King of the Belgians 12:294
  Lumumba, Patrice 12:459
  Mobutu Sese Seko 13:488
  O'Brien, Conor Cruise 14:317
  Stanley, Sir Henry Morton 18:219
  Tshombe, Moise Kapenda 19:323
 land and resources 20:349–350 *map*
 map (0° 0′N 25° 0′E) 1:136
 mining 20:351
 money 13:525 *illus.*
 people 20:350–351
  Azande 2:380
  Bemba 3:194
  Luba 12:446
  Mangbetu 13:115
 provinces
  Shaba 17:233
 rivers, lakes, and waterways
  Congo River 5:183–184 *map*
ZAIRE RIVER *see* CONGO RIVER
ZAITSEV, ALEXANDER 11:14 *illus.*
ZAJEČAR (Yugoslavia)
 map (43° 54′N 22° 17′E) 20:340

ZAKHAROV, ADRIAN 20:352 *bibliog.*
ZÁKINTHOS ISLAND
map (37° 52′N 20° 44′E) 9:325
ZAKOPANE (Poland)
map (49° 19′N 19° 57′E) 15:388
ZALA RIVER
map (46° 43′N 17° 16′E) 10:307
ZALAEGERSZEG (Hungary)
map (46° 51′N 16° 51′E) 10:307
ZAMA (Mississippi)
map (32° 53′N 89° 23′W) 13:469
ZAMASP, KING OF PERSIA
Persia, ancient 15:183
ZAMBEZI RIVER 20:352; 20:354 *illus.*
map (18° 55′S 36° 4′E) 1:136
Victoria Falls 19:575
ZAMBIA 20:352–354 *bibliog., illus., map, table*
African art 1:160–164
African literature 1:167–168
cities
Kitwe 12:93
Lusaka 12:467
Ndola 14:68
economic activity 20:353; 20:354 *illus.*
education 20:353
African universities 1:176 *table*
flag 20:353 *illus.*
government 20:353
history 20:353–354
Africa, history of 1:160
Kaunda, Kenneth D. 12:32
Nkomo, Joshua 14:206
Rhodes, Cecil John 16:202
land and resources 20:352
map (15° 0′S 30° 0′E) 1:136
people 20:353
Bemba 3:194
Luba 12:446
Lunda 12:462
Nguni 14:176
rivers, lakes, and waterways
Bangweulu, Lake 3:66
ZAMBO *see* MULATTO
ZAMBOANGA (Philippines) 20:354
map (6° 54′N 122° 4′E) 15:237
ZAMENHOF, LUDWIK LAZAR
Esperanto 7:243
ZAMFARA RIVER
map (12° 5′N 4° 2′E) 14:190
ZAMFIRESCU, DUILIU
Romanian literature 16:290
ZAMORA (Ecuador)
map (4° 4′S 78° 58′W) 7:52
ZAMORA (Spain)
map (41° 30′N 5° 45′W) 18:140
ZAMORA DE HIDALGO (Mexico)
map (19° 59′N 102° 16′W) 13:357
ZAMOŚĆ (Poland)
map (50° 44′N 23° 15′E) 15:388
ZAMPIERI, DOMENICO *see* DOMENICHINO
ZAMYATIN, YEVGENY 20:355 *bibliog.*
ZANDE *see* AZANDE
ZANDONAI, RICCARDO 20:355
ZANDVOORT (Netherlands)
map (52° 22′N 4° 32′E) 14:99
ZANE, EBENEZER 20:355 *bibliog.*
Wheeling (West Virginia) 20:129
Zanesville (Ohio) 20:355
ZANESVILLE (Ohio) 20:355
map (39° 56′N 82° 1′W) 14:357
ZANGWILL, ISRAEL 20:355
ZANJAN (Iran)
map (36° 40′N 48° 29′E) 11:250
ZANUCK, DARRYL F. 20:355 *bibliog.*
ZANZIBAR (Tanzania) 20:355 *bibliog.*
Kenya 12:56
map (6° 10′S 39° 11′E) 19:27
Tanzania 19:28
ZAO WOU-KI 20:355 *bibliog.*
ZAP (North Dakota)
map (47° 17′N 101° 55′W) 14:248
ZAPADNA MORAVA RIVER
map (43° 42′N 21° 23′E) 20:340
ZAPALA (Argentina)
map (38° 54′S 70° 4′W) 2:149
ZAPATA (Texas)
map (26° 52′N 99° 19′W) 19:129
ZAPATA (county in Texas)
map (27° 0′N 99° 10′W) 19:129
ZAPATA, EMILIANO 20:355–356 *bibliog., illus.*
Mexico, history of 13:365
Morelos (Mexico) 13:577
ZAPATA PENINSULA
map (22° 20′N 81° 35′W) 5:377
ZÁPOLYA, JOHN *see* JOHN I, KING OF HUNGARY (John Zápolya)
ZÁPOLYA, JOHN SIGISMUND *see* JOHN II, KING OF HUNGARY (John Sigismund Zápolya)
ZAPOROZHYE (USSR) 20:356
map (47° 50′N 35° 10′E) 19:388
ZAPOTEC (American Indians) 20:356 *bibliog.*
art
funerary urn 15:498 *illus.*
pre-Columbian art and architecture 15:496
Caso, Alfonso 4:182
Mixtec 13:486
sites
Mitla 13:485
Monte Albán 13:552
Oaxaca (city in Mexico) 14:314
ZAPOTILLO (Ecuador)
map (4° 25′S 80° 31′W) 7:52
ZÁPOTOCKÝ, ANTONÍN
Czechoslovakia 5:416
ZAPPA, FRANK 20:356
ZARA (Yugoslavia) *see* ZADAR (Yugoslavia)
ZARAGOZA (Mexico)
map (23° 58′N 99° 46′W) 13:357
ZARAGOZA (Spain) *see* SARAGOSSA (Spain)
ZARAGOZA, IGNACIO
Puebla (city in Mexico) 15:613
ZÁRATE (Argentina)
map (34° 6′S 59° 2′W) 2:149
ZARATHUSTRA
Zoroastrianism 20:379–380 *illus.*
ZARAZA (Venezuela)
map (9° 21′N 65° 19′W) 19:542
ZARD, MOUNT
map (32° 22′N 50° 4′E) 11:250
ZARGHUN SHAHR (Afghanistan)
map (32° 51′N 68° 25′E) 1:133
ZARIA (Nigeria)
map (11° 7′N 7° 44′E) 14:190
ZARLINO, GIOSEFFO
harmony 10:51
Renaissance music 16:156
ZARUMA (Ecuador)
map (3° 41′S 79° 37′W) 7:52
ŻARY (Poland)
map (51° 38′N 15° 9′E) 15:388
ZARZIS (Tunisia)
map (33° 30′N 11° 7′E) 19:335
ZARZUELA 20:356 *bibliog.*
Calderón de la Barca, Pedro 4:26
Spanish music 18:162
ZASKAR MOUNTAIN
map (33° 0′N 78° 0′E) 10:167
ZATOPEK, EMIL 20:356–357
ZAVALLA (Texas)
map (31° 9′N 94° 26′W) 19:129
ZAVALA (county in Texas)
map (28° 52′N 99° 47′W) 19:129
ZAVATTINI, CESARE
De Sica, Vittorio 6:63
ZAVOISKI, EVGENII K.
chemistry, history of 4:329
ZAWI CHEMI SHANIDAR *see* SHANIDAR (Iraq)
ZAWIERCIE (Poland)
map (50° 30′N 19° 25′E) 15:388
ZAYIN (Letter)
Z (letter) 20:347
ZDUŃSKA WOLA (Poland)
map (51° 36′N 18° 57′E) 15:388
ZEALAND (Denmark) 20:357
map (55° 30′N 11° 45′E) 6:109
Trelleborg 19:290
ZEALOTS 20:357 *bibliog.*
Masada 13:194
ZEAMI MOTOKIYO 20:357 *bibliog.*
No drama 14:207
ZEATIN
cytokinin 5:411
ZEBALLOS, MOUNT
map (47° 1′S 71° 42′W) 2:149
ZEBRA 1:165 *illus.*; 13:105 *illus.*; 20:357 *bibliog., illus.*
perissodactyl 15:171
quagga 16:5
ZEBRA FISH 19:308 *illus.*
ZEBRA HELICONIAN BUTTERFLY 3:595–596 *illus.*
ZEBRA PLANT *see* APHELANDRA
ZEBU CATTLE 20:357
Brahman cattle 3:440
ZEBULON (Georgia)
map (33° 6′N 84° 21′W) 9:114
ZEBULON (North Carolina)
map (35° 49′N 78° 19′W) 14:242
ZECCA, FERDINAND
film, history of 8:81
ZECHARIAH, BOOK OF 20:357 *bibliog.*
ZEDEKIAH, KING OF JUDAH 20:357
ZEELAND (Michigan)
map (42° 49′N 86° 1′W) 13:377
ZEELAND (North Dakota)
map (45° 58′N 99° 50′W) 14:248
ZEELAND, PAUL VAN *see* VAN ZEELAND, PAUL
ZEEMAN, PIETER 20:357–358
physics, history of 15:284
ZEFFIRELLI, FRANCO 20:358
ZEIL, MOUNT
map (23° 24′S 132° 23′E) 2:328
ZEISBERGER, DAVID 20:358 *bibliog.*
ZEISS, CARL 20:358
Abbe, Ernst 1:52
ZEIST (Netherlands)
map (52° 5′N 5° 15′E) 14:99
ZEIT, DIE 20:358
ZEJTUN (Malta)
map (35° 51′N 14° 32′E) 13:94
ZEKE (aircraft) *see* ZERO (aircraft)
ZELAYA, JOSÉ SANTOS 20:358
Nicaragua 14:179
ZELENCHUKSKAYA OBSERVATORY *see* SPECIAL ASTROPHYSICAL OBSERVATORY
ZELIENOPLE (Pennsylvania)
map (40° 48′N 80° 8′W) 15:147
ZELLE, MARGARETHA GEERTRUIDA *see* MATA HARI
ZELOTTI, G. B.
Veronese, Paolo 19:559–560
ZEMLYA I VOLYA *see* NARODNIKI
ZEN BUDDHISM 20:358–359 *bibliog., illus.*
Bodhidharma 3:356
Japanese art and architecture 11:375
koan 12:104
monks 20:358 *illus.*
shrines 3:541 *illus.*
Suzuki, D. T. 18:374
ZENER, KARL
parapsychology research 15:81 *illus.*
ZENER DIODE 20:359 *bibliog., illus.*
semiconductor 17:196-197
ZENG GUOFAN *see* TSENG KUO-FAN (Zeng Guofan)
ZENGER, JOHN PETER 20:359 *bibliog.*
freedom of the press 8:296
Mount Vernon (New York) 13:618
ZENICA (Yugoslavia)
map (44° 12′N 17° 55′E) 20:340
ZENO, BYZANTINE EMPEROR 20:359 *bibliog.*
Odoacer 14:350
ZENO OF CITIUM 20:359 *bibliog.*
Stoicism 18:278
ZENO OF ELEA 20:359 *bibliog.*
Eleatic School 7:103
mathematics, history of 13:223
Zeno's paradoxes 20:360
ZENOBIA, QUEEN OF PALMYRA 20:360 *bibliog.*
Palmyra 15:51
ZENO'S PARADOXES 20:360 *bibliog.*
motion, planar 13:609
ZEOLITE 20:360 *bibliog., illus.*
facies of metamorphic rock 13:332 *graph*
ion exchange 11:240
silicate minerals 17:305
ZEPHANIAH, BOOK OF 20:360 *bibliog.*
ZEPHYRHILLS (Florida)
map (28° 14′N 82° 11′W) 8:172
ZEPHYRINUS, POPE
Callistus I, Pope 4:46
ZEPPELIN
airship 1:227
aviation 2:372
Graf Zeppelin 9:278
Hindenburg 10:168–169
Zeppelin, Ferdinand, Graf von 20:360–361
ZEPPELIN, FERDINAND, GRAF VON 20:360–361 *bibliog., illus.*
Maybach, Wilhelm 13:246
ZEREH DEPRESSION
map (29° 45′N 61° 50′E) 1:133
ZERMATT (Switzerland) 18:395 *illus.*
ZERMELO, RUSSELL AND ERNST
paradox (mathematics) 15:76
ZERNIKE, FRITS 20:361
ZERO (aircraft) 20:361 *bibliog., illus.*
ZERO (mathematics) 20:361 *bibliog.*
decimal 6:73
ZERO, ABSOLUTE *see* ABSOLUTE ZERO; CRYOGENICS
ZERO-BASED BUDGETING 20:361 *bibliog.*
ŻEROMSKI, STEFAN 20:361
ZETA (letter)
Z (letter) 20:347
ZETKIN, CLARA 20:361–362
ZEUS 20:362 *illus.*
Castor and Pollux 4:191
mythology 13:700 *illus.*
Nemea 14:80
Olympia (Greece) 14:381
Curtius, Ernst Robert 5:396
Phidias 15:227
Seven Wonders of the World 17:217 *illus.*
ZEUXIS 20:362 *bibliog.*
ZEVENAAR (Netherlands)
map (51° 56′N 6° 5′E) 14:99
ZEYER, JULIUS
Czech literature 5:412
ZEZURU *see* SHONA
ZGB *see* SWISS CIVIL CODE
ZGIERZ (Poland)
map (51° 52′N 19° 25′E) 15:388
ZHANG DAOLING *see* CHANG TAO-LING (Zhang Daoling)
ZHANG TIANYI *see* CHANG T'IEN-I (Zhang Tianyi)
ZHANG XUELIANG *see* CHANG HSUEH-LIANG (Zhang Xueliang)
ZHANG ZHIDONG *see* CHANG CHIH-TUNG (Zhang Zhidong)
ZHANG ZUOLIN *see* CHANG TSO-LIN (Zhang Zuolin)
ZHAO MENGFU *see* CHAO MENG-FU (Zhao Mengfu)
ZHAO ZIYANG *see* CHAO TZU-YANG (Zhao Ziyang)
ZHDANOV (USSR)
map (47° 6′N 37° 33′E) 19:388
ZHEJIANG (China) *see* CHEKIANG (Zhejiang) (China)
ZHELANIYA, CAPE (USSR)
climate 19:390 *table*
ZHENG HE *see* CHENG HO (Zheng He)
ZHENGZHOU (China) *see* CHENG-CHOU (Zhengzhou) (China)
ZHGARTA (Lebanon)
map (34° 24′N 35° 54′E) 12:265
ZHIVKOV, TODOR 20:362 *bibliog.*
ZHOB RIVER
map (32° 4′N 69° 50′E) 15:27
ZHOLOBOV, VITALY 20:362
ZHONGYI *see* CHINESE MEDICINE
ZHOU (dynasty) *see* CHOU (Zhou) (dynasty)
ZHOU DUNI *see* CHOU TUN-I (Zhou Duni)
ZHOU ENLAI *see* CHOU EN-LAI (Zhou Enlai)
ZHOUKOUDIAN (China) *see* CHOU-K'OU-TIEN (Zhoukoudian) (China)
ZHU DA *see* CHU TA (Zhu Da)
ZHU DE *see* CHU TEH (Zhu De)
ZHU XI *see* CHU HSI (Zhu Xi)
ZHUANGZI *see* CHUANG-TZU (Zhangzi)
ZHUKOV, GEORGY KONSTANTINOVICH 20:362–363 *bibliog.*
World War II 20:258 *illus.*; 20:264; 20:275
ZIA UL-HAQ, MUHAMMAD 20:363
ZIAUR RAHMAN
Bangladesh 3:66
ZIEBACH (county in South Dakota)
map (45° 0′N 101° 40′W) 18:103
ZIEGFELD, FLORENZ 20:363 *bibliog.*
Ziegfeld Follies 20:363
ZIEGFELD FOLLIES 20:363 *bibliog.*
Brice, Fanny 3:477
Cantor, Eddie 4:118
music hall, vaudeville, and burlesque 13:672 *illus.*
tap dancing 19:29
Ziegfeld, Florenz 20:363
ZIEGLER, KARL 20:363
chemistry, history of 4:329
ZIELONA GÓRA (Poland)
map (51° 56′N 15° 31′E) 15:388
ZIFTA (Egypt)
map (30° 43′N 31° 15′E) 7:76
ZIGGURAT 20:363 *bibliog., illus.*
Eridu 7:229
Etemenaki 19:95 *illus.*
Mesopotamian art and architecture 13:318–321 *illus.*
Persian art and architecture 15:184
temple 19:94
Ur 19:474 *illus.*
Uruk 19:490
ZIGUINCHOR (Senegal)
map (12° 35′N 16° 16′W) 17:202
ZIHUATANEJO (Mexico)
map (17° 38′N 101° 33′W) 13:357
ZILE (Turkey)
map (40° 18′N 35° 54′E) 19:343
ŽILINA (Czechoslovakia)
map (49° 14′N 18° 46′E) 5:413
ZILLAH (Washington)
map (46° 24′N 120° 16′W) 20:35
ZILLERTALER ALPS
map (47° 0′N 11° 55′E) 11:321

ZIMBABWE **20**:363–366 *bibliog., illus., map, table*
  African art **1**:160–164
  African literature **1**:167–168
  agriculture **20**:364; **20**:366 *illus.*
  archaeology
    Nalatale **14**:9
    Zimbabwe Ruins **20**:366–367
  censorship **4**:246 *illus.*
  cities
    Bulawayo **3**:553
    Harare **10**:42
  climate **20**:363–364; **20**:365 *table*
  economic activity **20**:364
  education **20**:364
    African universities **1**:176 *table*
  flag **8**:137 *illus.*; **20**:364 *illus.*
  government **20**:365
  history **20**:365–366
    Africa, history of **1**:160
    Lobengula, King of the Ndebele **12**:385
    Malvern, Godfrey Huggins, 1st Viscount **13**:96
    Mugabe, Robert **13**:632
    Muzorewa, Abel T. **13**:688
    Nkomo, Joshua **14**:206
    Rhodes, Cecil John **16**:202
    Smith, Ian D. **17**:369
    Welensky, Sir Roy **20**:97
  land and resources **20**:363–365 *map*
  map (20° 0′S 30° 0′E) **1**:136
  people **20**:364
    Bemba **3**:194
    Ndebele **14**:68
    Shona **17**:281
ZIMBABWE RUINS **1**:175 *illus.*; **20**:366–367 *bibliog., illus.*
  archaeology **2**:124
  Caton-Thompson, Gertrude **4**:213
  Great Enclosure **20**:367 *illus.*
  Nalatale **14**:9
ZIMBALIST, EFREM **20**:367 *bibliog.*
ZIMMERMAN, ETHEL *see* MERMAN, ETHEL
ZIMMERMAN, ROBERT ALLEN *see* DYLAN, BOB
ZIMMERMANN, DOMINIKUS **20**:367 *bibliog.*
ZIMMERMANN TELEGRAM **5**:373 *illus.*
  cryptology **5**:372–373
  World War I **20**:236
ZIMRI-LIM, PALACE OF **13**:320 *illus.*
  Mari **13**:149–150
ZINC **20**:367–368 *bibliog., illus.*
  abundances of common elements **7**:131 *table*
  brass **3**:457
  cadmium **4**:12
  carbonate minerals **4**:137
  cyanide process **5**:400
  element **7**:130 *table*
  Group IIB periodic table **15**:167
  hemimorphite **10**:118
  hydrogen preparation **10**:338
  melting point **20**:367
  metal, metallic element **13**:328
  mineral **13**:443
  native elements **14**:47
  occurrence **20**:367
  ore deposits, world distribution **14**:423 *map*
  oxide minerals **14**:476
  production **20**:367–368 *illus.*
  properties **20**:367
  Smithson, James **17**:372
  smithsonite **17**:372
  sphalerite **18**:180
  sulfide minerals **18**:333
  superconductivity **18**:350 *table*
  transition elements **19**:273 *table*
  uranium minerals **19**:478
  uses **20**:367
  vitamins and minerals **19**:621
    Recommended Daily Allowances **19**:619 *table*
  zincite **20**:368
ZINC BLENDE *see* SPHALERITE
ZINCITE **20**:368
ZINDER (Niger)
  climate **14**:187 *table*
  map (13° 48′N 8° 59′E) **14**:187
ZINNEMANN, FRED **20**:368–369 *bibliog.*
ZINNIA **20**:369 *illus.*
ZINOVIEV, GRIGORY YEVSEYEVICH **20**:369 *bibliog.*
  Kamenev, Lev Borisovich **12**:9–10
  Stalin, Joseph **18**:214
ZINOVIEV LETTER *see* ZINOVIEV, GRIGORY YEVSEYEVICH
ZINZENDORF, NIKOLAUS LUDWIG, GRAF VON **20**:369 *bibliog.*
  Moravian Church **13**:575
ZION (Illinois)
  map (42° 27′N 87° 50′W) **11**:42
ZION (Jerusalem) **20**:369
ZIONISM **20**:369–370 *bibliog.*
  Achad ha-Am **1**:80
  Balfour Declaration **3**:37
  Begin, Menachem **3**:168
  Ben-Gurion, David **3**:195
  Gottheil, Gustav **9**:264
  Hadassah **10**:7
  Hertz, Joseph Herman **10**:149
  Herzl, Theodor **10**:150
  Jabotinsky, Vladimir **11**:339
  Jews **11**:416–417
  Judaism **11**:463
  Kook, Abraham Isaac **12**:109
  Middle East, history of the **13**:407–409
  Palestine **15**:44–45
  Szold, Henrietta **18**:416
  Weizmann, Chaim **20**:96
ZIONSVILLE (Indiana)
  map (39° 57′N 86° 16′W) **11**:111
ZIPPER **20**:370 *illus.*
  Schiaparelli, Elsa **17**:120
ZIRCON **20**:370 *bibliog., illus.*
  refractory materials **16**:124
  tetragonal system **19**:127
ZIRCON, GOLDEN **9**:74 *illus.*
ZIRCONIA
  refractory materials **16**:124
ZIRCONIUM **20**:370 *bibliog.*
  Berzelius, Jöns Jakob **20**:370
  element **7**:130 *table*
  Group IVB periodic table **15**:167
  hafnium **10**:9
  Klaproth, Marti Heinrich, discoverer **12**:95
  Kroll process **20**:370
  metal, metallic element **13**:328
  transition elements **19**:273
ZITHER **18**:300–301 *illus.*; **20**:370–371 *bibliog., illus.*
  aeolian harp **1**:119
  African **1**:169
  Chinese music **4**:393
  dulcimer **6**:295
  ganun **2**:100
  Indian music **11**:102 *illus.*
  Japanese music **11**:381–382 *illus.*
  keyboard instruments **12**:63
  koto **12**:125
  musical instruments **13**:677–679 *illus.*
  Vina **19**:599
ZITTAU (Germany, East and West)
  map (50° 54′N 14° 47′E) **9**:140
ŽIŽKA, JAN **20**:371 *bibliog.*
ZNANIECKI, FLORIAN WITOLD **20**:371
ZNOJMO (Czechoslovakia)
  map (48° 52′N 16° 2′E) **5**:413
ZODIAC **20**:371
  Aquarius **2**:93
  Aries **2**:154
  astrology **2**:271–272 *illus.*
  astronomy, history of **2**:277
  Cancer **4**:100
  Capricornus **4**:128
  constellation **5**:210–212
  ecliptic **7**:41
  Gemini **9**:71
  Leo **12**:287
  Libra **12**:314
  Pisces **15**:317
  Saggittarius **17**:12
  Scorpius **17**:149
  Taurus **19**:45
  Virgo **19**:613
  zodiacal light **20**:371
ZODIACAL LIGHT **20**:371
ZOË, BYZANTINE EMPRESS **20**:371 *bibliog.*
ZOETROPE
  toy **19**:257
ZOFFANY, JOHANN **20**:371 *bibliog.*
ZOG I, KING OF ALBANIA **20**:371
ZOISITE **20**:371
ZOLA, ÉMILE **8**:318 *illus.*; **20**:371–372 *bibliog., illus.*
  Dreyfus Affair **6**:272
  Germinal **9**:157
  naturalism (literature) **14**:49–50 *illus.*
  realism (literature) **16**:104
ZOLLVEREIN **20**:372 *bibliog.*
  customs union **5**:398
ZOMBA (Malawi)
  climate **13**:81 *table*
  map (15° 23′S 35° 18′E) **13**:81
ZOMBIE
  voodoo **19**:635
ZOND **20**:372–373 *bibliog., illus., table*
  Mars (spacecraft) **13**:170
  Venus probes **19**:539 *table*
ZONDA **20**:373
  mountain climates **13**:621
ZONDEK, B.
  zoology **20**:377
ZONGULDAK (Turkey)
  map (41° 27′N 31° 49′E) **19**:343
ZONING **20**:373–374 *bibliog.*
  maps and mapmaking **13**:141
  mobile home **13**:487
  urban planning **19**:484
ZOO *see* ZOOLOGICAL GARDENS
ZOO STORY, THE (play) **20**:374
ZOOLOGICAL GARDENS **20**:374–375 *bibliog., illus.*
  aquarium **2**:93
  Berlin Zoo **3**:217
  Bronx Zoo **3**:505
  Brookfield Zoo (Chicago) **3**:510
  design and operation **20**:374–375
  history **20**:374
  National Zoological Park (Washington, D.C.) **14**:46
  Philadelphia Zoological Garden **15**:229
  San Diego Zoological Garden **17**:52
ZOOLOGY **20**:375–378 *bibliog., illus.*
  anatomy **1**:395–398 *illus.*; **20**:376
    comparative anatomy **5**:155
    cytology **5**:411–412 *illus.*; **20**:377
    embryology **7**:153–154; **20**:377
    histology **10**:180–182; **20**:376–377
  animal **2**:8–11; **2**:9 *illus.*
  animal behavior **2**:11–18
  animal communication **2**:18–20
  animal courtship and mating **2**:20–22
  classification, biological **5**:42–44; **20**:376
  genetics **9**:85–90 *illus.*; **20**:377–378
  herpetology **10**:146
  history
    Andrews, Roy Chapman **1**:408
    Baer, Karl Ernst von **3**:20
    Cuvier, Georges, Baron **5**:399
    Darwin, Charles **6**:41–42
    Dean, Bashford **6**:67
    Frisch, Karl von **8**:334
    Haeckel, Ernest Heinrich **10**:9
    Lamarck, Jean Baptiste **12**:173–174
    Leeuwenhoek, Antoni van **12**:271–272
    Lyell, Sir Charles **12**:475
    Morgan, Thomas Hunt **13**:579
    Swammerdam, Jan **18**:376
    Tinbergen, Nikolaas **19**:206
  ichthyology **11**:19
  invertebrate **11**:234–237
  ornithology **14**:447
  physiology **15**:287; **20**:377
ZOOM LENS
  camera **4**:56
  video camera **19**:576h
ZOOMASTIGINA *see* MASTIGOPHORA
ZOONOSES
  diseases, animal **6**:190
  parasitic diseases **15**:82
ZOOPHOBIA **20**:378
ZOOPLANKTON **20**:378
  marine food chain **14**:330 *illus.*
  ooze, deep-sea **14**:397
  plankton **15**:331–333
  sediment, marine **17**:184
ZOOPRAXISCOPE
  Muybridge, Eadweard **13**:687
ZOOTOXINS
  plants and animals **15**:385
ZOOXANTHELLAE
  coral **5**:257
  coral reef **5**:260
ZORACH, WILLIAM **20**:379 *bibliog., illus.*
  Mother and Child **20**:379 *illus.*
ZORAPTERA **20**:379
ZORBA THE GREEK (book)
  Kazantzakis, Nikos **12**:34
ZORN, ANDERS **20**:379 *bibliog.*
ZOROASTRIANISM **16**:140 *map*; **20**:379–380 *bibliog., illus.*
  Asia, history of **2**:250
  magi **13**:49
  Parsis **15**:98
  Persian art and architecture **15**:184
ZORRILLA Y MORAL, JOSÉ **20**:380
ZORRITOS (Peru)
  map (3° 40′S 80° 40′W) **15**:193
ZOSER, KING OF EGYPT
  Imhotep **11**:54
  Saqqara **17**:74
  Step Pyramid **15**:635 *illus.*
ZOSHCHENKO, MIKHAIL MIKHAILOVICH **20**:380
ZOUAVES **5**:20 *illus.*
ZOUCHE, RICHARD
  international law **11**:221
ZRENJANIN (Yugoslavia)
  map (45° 23′N 20° 24′E) **20**:340
ZRÍNYI, MIKLÓS
  Hungarian literature **10**:305
ZSIGMONDY, RICHARD ADOLF **20**:380 *bibliog.*
ZUAZO, HERNÁN SILES *see* SILES ZUAZO, HERNÁN
ZUCALLI, ENRICO **20**:380 *bibliog.*
ZUCCARELLI, FRANCESCO **20**:381 *bibliog.*
ZUCCARO (family) **20**:381 *bibliog.*
  Spranger, Bartholomäus **18**:199
ZUCCHI, VIRGINIA
  Kirov Ballet **12**:90
ZUCCHINI *see* SQUASH (vegetable)
ZUCKERHÜTL MOUNTAIN
  map (46° 58′N 11° 9′E) **2**:348
ZUCKMAYER, CARL **20**:381
ZUDAÑEZ (Bolivia)
  map (19° 6′S 64° 44′W) **3**:366
ZUDOV, VYACHESLAV DMITRIYEVICH **20**:381
ZUEGEN
  landform evolution **12**:182 *illus.*
ZUG (Switzerland)
  map (47° 10′N 8° 31′E) **18**:394
ZUGSPITZE PEAK **13**:622 *illus.*
  map (47° 25′N 10° 59′E) **9**:140
ZUIDER ZEE PROJECT
  IJsselmeer **11**:39
  land reclamation **12**:179 *map*
ZUKERMAN, PINCHAS **20**:381 *bibliog.*
ZUKOFSKY, LOUIS **20**:381 *bibliog.*
ZUKOR, ADOLPH **20**:381 *bibliog.*
ZULOAGA, IGNACIO **20**:381
ZULU **1**:154–155 *illus.*; **1**:156 *illus.*; **20**:381–382 *bibliog.*
  Cetewayo, King **4**:263
  Shaka, King **17**:235
  South Africa **18**:82
  Swazi **18**:380
ZUMÁRRAGA, JUAN DE **20**:382 *bibliog.*
ZUMBA (Ecuador)
  map (4° 52′S 79° 9′W) **7**:52
ZUMBRO RIVER
  map (44° 18′N 91° 56′W) **13**:453
ZUMPANGO, LAKE **2**:382 *map*
ZUMPE, JOHANNES
  piano **15**:288–289 *illus.*
ZUÑI (American Indians) **20**:382 *bibliog.*
  Cibola, Seven Golden Cities of **4**:428
  Indians of North America, music and dance of the **11**:143–144
  kachina **12**:4
  North American archaeology **14**:240
  pottery jug **11**:121 *illus.*
ZUNI (New Mexico)
  map (35° 4′N 108° 51′W) **14**:136
ZÚÑIGA, ALONSO DE ERCILLA Y *see* ERCILLA Y ZÚÑIGA, ALONSO DE
ZUNZ, LEOPOLD **20**:382 *bibliog.*
ZUO ZONGTANG *see* TSO TSUNG-T'ANG (Zuo Zongtang)
ŽUPANČIČ, OTON **20**:382
ZURBARÁN, FRANCISCO DE **20**:382–383 *bibliog., illus.*
  Adoration of the Magi **18**:153 *illus.*
  Herrera, Francisco de **10**:146
  The Holy House of Nazareth **20**:382 *illus.*
ZURCHER v. *STANFORD DAILY*
  freedom of the press **8**:297
ZURICH (Switzerland) **18**:396 *illus.*; **20**:383 *illus.*
  climate **18**:394 *table*
  map (47° 23′N 8° 32′E) **18**:394
  prehistory
    lake dwelling **12**:171
ZURICH, LAKE
  map (47° 13′N 8° 45′E) **18**:394
ZURVAN
  Zoroastrianism **20**:380
ZUTPHEN (Netherlands)
  map (52° 8′N 6° 12′E) **14**:99
ZVISHAVANE (Zimbabwe)
  map (20° 20′S 30° 2′E) **20**:365
ZVOLEN (Czechoslovakia)
  map (48° 35′N 19° 8′E) **5**:413
ZWEIBRÜCKEN (West Germany) **20**:383
ZWEIG, ARNOLD **20**:383 *bibliog.*
ZWEIG, GEORGE
  quark **16**:12
ZWEIG, STEFAN **20**:383 *bibliog.*
ZWETTL (Austria)
  map (48° 37′N 15° 10′E) **2**:348
ZWICKAU (East Germany) **20**:384
  map (50° 44′N 12° 29′E) **9**:140

ZWICKY, FRITZ **20**:384
clusters of galaxies **5**:72
ZWINGER, THE *see* DRESDEN STATE ART COLLECTIONS
ZWINGLI, ULRICH **20**:384 *bibliog., illus.*
Reformation **16**:122
ZWITTERION **20**:384 *bibliog.*
ZWOLLE (Louisiana)
map (31° 38′N 93° 38′W) **12**:430
ZWOLLE (Netherlands)
map (52° 30′N 6° 5′E) **14**:99
ZWORYKIN, VLADIMIR KOSMA **20**:372
radio and television broadcasting **16**:56
ZYGOTE **20**:384
algae **1**:280
Spirogyra **18**:189
alternation of generations **1**:313
development **6**:137; **6**:138; **6**:140
embryo **7**:153
genetics **9**:86–87; **9**:89
moss **13**:605
reproduction **16**:161–162
reproductive system, human **16**:165 *illus.*
ZYMOGEN *see* PROENZYME
ZYRARDÓW (Poland)
map (52° 4′N[LO]20° 25′E) **15**:388
ZYRIEN LANGUAGE
Uralic languages **19**:475

Picture Credits and Acknowledgments

PHOTO SOURCES Credits are listed alphabetically by source or agency, individual photographer, volume number, page number, and location on the page. Volume number and page are separated by a slash, and individual entries are separated by commas. The following code identifies the exact page location: T—Top, B—Bottom, C—Center, L—Left, R—Right.

AAA-photo: *Myers* 12/55R; 1/146TL, 1/148R, 10/170L, 11/256T, 11/292, 11/364R, 13/82L, 14/12, 14/191BR, 15/412T, 16/138L, 16/378T, 19/344L.

ABC: 16/57TR.

ABC-Press: *Frank* 16/248CR; *Seldow/Rona* 15/314T; *Han Suying* 19/190CL; 5/99TL, 19/639.

Harry N. Abrams, Inc: 15/230BL.

ACL, Brussels: 13/44TL.

Actualit: 7/298.

Adler Planetarium: *Roderick Webster* 27/T.

© Aerofilms Limited: 2/192TR; 19/254TR.

Aerophoto Eelde: 16/51TL.

Aerophoto Schiphol: 14/100.

AFL-CIO Library: 12/155TL, 12/155TR.

AGE: *D. Baglin/Natural History Photographic Agency* 2/33TR; *F. Forester* 2/330TL, 2/334TR, 2/329; *G. Franco* 9/175; *E. Gelpi* 18/141BR; *A. Gutiérrez* 1/149TR, 18/141BL; *T. Molenaar* 3/463TL, 3/463TR; *F. Prenzel* 4/174L; *A. Viñals* 3/79R; *World Photo Service* 1/146L, 3/366B, 3/461BL, 3/462TL, 3/464, 3/490B, 4/60BR, 4/76T, 4/78B, 5/108T, 5/291BR, 9/321R, 12/55L 14/460, 15/73CL, 19/429BR; 2/241, 3/402, 4/61B, 9/39, 11/150B, 11/291TL, 11/303T, 11/303BL, 11/365B, 11/366, 12/223TL, 13/85T, 15/212CL, 15/500CR, 18/143, 18/152TR, 19/97R, 19/504.

Agence De Presse Photografique Rapho: *Actualit* 11/448; *Bernheim* 1/147CL; *Brian Brake* 4/387BL; *Gamet* 8/263, 12/478; *Gazuit* 18/42CR, 18/42CL; *Gerster* 15/194B, 20/325B; *Goldman* 11/304T, 11/305; *Grignt* 12/321; *Koch* 13/360B, 13/396BR; *J. Ross* 11/253T; *Serraillier* 14/160TL, 14/263TR, 18/86B; *Windenberger* 8/264; 11/87, 14/78.

Agence Top: *Desjardins* 13/251.

Courtesy **Alabama Bureau of Publicity and Information:** 1/235B, 1/237CR.

Albright Knox Art Gallery, Gift of Seymour H. Knox, 1964: 17/188TL.

Aldus Archives: 1/153TR, 1/155BL, 2/123BR, 2/124BL, 2/124BR, 2/277BL, 3/43TC, 3/357TL, 3/413BL, 4/174TR, 4/318TL, 6/318BL, 11/116TL, 11/126TL, 11/135CR, 11/135BL, 11/415TL, 13/136TR, 13/225CL, 13/370TL, 13/395TR, 14/340TR, 15/37TL, 15/37TC, 15/37TR, 15/334B, 15/590TL, 18/20BL, 18/29TC, 18/222BL, 18/222BR, 18/223, 19/66TR, 19/63BL, 20/56CR, 20/66BR, 20/306BR, *Facsimile Copy* 13/244BL.

Alinari: 10/38TR, 10/144BR.

Alinari/EPA: 16/274CR, 17/352BR.

Alinari/SCALA: 6/105TL, 19/269BR.

All-Sport: 18/359BL; *Dave Cannon* 14/183TR; *Tony Duffy* 12/80BL, 14/384BL, 14/384BR, 19/260C; *Steve Powell* 17/339TL, 17/339TR, 19/260TL; *Vandystadt* 20/66TL.

The John E. Allen Collection: 8/82TR, 8/83CL, 8/83C.

George Allen & Unwin, Ltd. London: 4/370TR.

Alphabet Museum: 20/295TL.

American Antiquarian Society: 17/354BL.

© American Craft Council Slide Film Service: 5/327TL, 5/327TC, 5/327TR, 5/327CL, 5/327CR, 5/327BL, 5/327BC, 5/327BR.

American Heritage Publishing Co.: 5/29CR, 14/273TL.

Courtesy **American Museum of Natural History:** 2/54TL, 2/190TR, 4/109BR, 14/337CL, 14/337BR, 15/34BR.

American Numismatic Society: *Michael diBiasé* 14/296 (2), 14/296 (7), 14/296 (8) 14/296 (10), 14/296 (11).

AmWest: 14/239BR.

ANP-Foto: *AFP* 14/384CR; *CTK* 11/87L, 11/87R; *Pan-Asia* 2/246BR; *Politikens* 10/99; *Unipix* 5/147BR; *UPI* 1/301, 2/178, 2/179T, 3/562, 8/345, 12/59, 13/8T 20/361; 2/70, 5/313TL, 12/111, 18/275R.

Courtesy **Donald M. Anderson:** 4/43TR.

Anthony-Verlag: *Dobos* 10/16R; *W. Scharf* 2/234T.

Anthro-Photo: *Tom Barfield* 1/134C; *Irven Devore* 2/52TL; *Lynn Galler* 2/55TL.

Courtesy **Antique Porcelain Company:** 16/264TL.

Courtesy **Apple Computer, Inc.:** 19/56TR.

Appomattox Courthouse, National Historical Park, Virginia: 5/30BR.

The Estate of Diane Arbus: 2/111L.

Antikvarisk-Topografiska Arkivet, Stockholm: 19/595TR.

The Archaeological Museum/Alinari, Florence: 12/244BL.

Archive: *© Ethan Hoffman* 5/160gTL.

Archivio di Stato di Siena *(courtesy Aldus Books)*: 4/27BL.

Ardea: *Hans and Judy Beste* 2/47; *Adrian Warren* 18/378L.

Arecibo Observatory: 2/145BL; *Courtesy of D.B. Campbell* 16/40TR.

Arena Stage: 16/160BL.

Arie de Zanger *(Ridge Press)*: 14/296 (5), 14/296 (6), 14/296 (9).

© Arizona Daily Star: 19/83TR.

Courtesy **Arizona Department of Tourism:** 2/162TR, 2/163BR.

Arizona State Museum: 14/239CR.

Courtesy **Arkansas Department of Parks and Tourism:** 2/168TR.

Peter Arnold, Inc.: *Peter Arnold* 13/166TL, 16/167BR, 16/17BL; *Bjorn Bolstad* 16/230CR; *N. Geiranger* 16/263TL; *Gerhard Gscheidle* 3/215BR; *Robert Harding* 15/28TL; *W. H. Hodge* 16/232BL; *Honningsvag* 16/264T; *Korst SdiÄpes* 19/608BL.

The Art Institute of Chicago: 10/147TR, 19/148TL.

Art Resource: *Bridgeman Art Library* 14/220TL; *© British Museum from Bridgeman* 15/453T; *Giraudon* 7/271BL, 7/292BR.

Ashmolean Museum, Oxford: 7/312TR.

Asian Art Museum of San Francisco, Avery Brundage Collection: 4/385CR.

Aspect Picture Library Ltd.: *Peter Carmichael* 2/104CR, 13/399BR; 17/95B, 20/366T, 20/366L.

Assistance Publique: 15/502.

Athens Annals of Archaeology, Ministry of Culture and Science *(courtesy Aldus Books)*: 1/116CL.

Atlanta Journal Constitution: *Joe McTyre* 14/347CL.

Atlantic Records: 18/72CL.

Atlas Photo: *Hétier* 14/220TL.

Courtesy **Australian Information Center:** 2/341, 2/343BL, 2/343BC, 2/343BR, 20/135BR.

David Attenborough: 4/147TL.

©Paul Avis: 5/160iBR.

Baccarat, Inc.: 9/204TL.

Courtesy **The Bancroft Library, University of California, Berkeley:** 11/128BR.

© 1986 **Henry Baker:** 15/17TR.

Alan Band Associates: 14/449TR.

Ernst Barlach Haus: *Heinz-Peter Cordes* 3/84L.

Barnaby's Picture Library: 3/552TR, 4/114.

H. H. Baudert: 2/130TR.

Jerry Baues: 11/268BR.

Bavaria-Verlag Bildagentur: *G. Binanzer* 8/128L; *Lüthy* 7/241CL, 9/352BR; *Pedone* 7/279R, 11/326L; *Tessore* 9/398R.

Bayerische Staatsbibliothek: 3/389L, 6/122L, 13/664TR.

BBC Copyright Photo: 20/362CR.

BBC Hulton Picture Library: 2/340TL, 5/4CR, 5/238TR, 7/197TR, 7/202TL, 7/202TR, 8/31TR, 8/73TL, 9/63CL, 10/57TR, 10/324TL, 11/370TL, 12/105TR, 12/305CR, 17/245TR, 18/17TL, 18/179BR, 19/249TL, 20/199TR, 20/215TL.

Collection L. L. Bean: 19/440BR.

Belgisch Instituut voor Voorlichting en Documentatie: 3/180CR, 3/180T, 12/294L, 12/294R.

Bell Communications Research: *© Michael Lesk* 5/161BR.

Bell Laboratories: 4/6BL, 16/47TR.

Raffaello Bencini/Scala: 13/571TL.

Beth Bergman: 14/401TR.

© Berlitz, Click, Chicago: 10/116B.

Verlag Hans Huber Bern: 15/598BL, 15/566TL.

Bettmann Archive, Inc.: 1/58TR, 1/87TL, 1/97TR, 1/103TR, 1/112TR, 1/157TR, 1/182TR, 1/192BR, 1/211TR, 1/211C, 1/293TL, 1/342TR, 1/344TC, 1/344TR, 1/345TL, 1/345TC, 1/345TR, 1/346TL, 1/346TC, 1/346TR, 1/346C, 1/346CR, 1/347TL, 1/349TL, 1/350TL, 1/350TR, 1/350BR, 1/351TL, 1/351TR, 1/354TL, 1/356CR, 1/365BR, 1/392TR, 1/396TL, 1/396TR, 1/397TL, 1/402BL, 1/410TR, 2/44TR, 2/50TL, 2/73TR, 2/184CR, 2/263CL, 2/279TL, 2/287BL, 2/304BR, 2/310TL, 2/311CL, 2/327TR, 2/350BR, 3/10TR, 3/17TL, 3/42BR, 3/44TL, 3/77TR, 3/87TL, 3/91BR, 3/94BR, 3/98TL, 3/103BR, 3/137CL, 3/175TL, 3/185, 3/198CL, 3/202TR, 3/203TL, 3/203CR, 3/209TL, 3/211TL, 3/217BL, 3/218TR, 3/258TR, 3/261BL, 3/269TR, 3/269CR, 3/269BL, 3/270TL, 3/270TC, 3/270BL, 3/271TL, 3/271TR, 3/271BR, 3/302TL, 3/307TL, 3/308BL, 3/324TL, 3/362TL, 3/394CL, 3/399BR, 3/400CL, 3/413BR, 3/414TL 3/441BL, 3/470TR, 3/498CR, 3/566BL, 3/579TL, 4/29TL, 4/65CL, 4/68CL, 4/81BL, 4/96BL, 4/111CL, 4/116CR, 4/128CL, 4/150CL, 4/155CL, 4/164BR, 4/169CL, 4/170CL, 4/176TR, 4/178BR, 4/191BL, 4/225BR, 4/249CR, 4/272TR, 4/273CR, 4/277CR, 4/289CR, 4/310BL, 4/312CR, 4/325CR, 4/326TL, 4/326BR, 4/327BL, 4/327TR, 4/328TL, 4/328BL, 4/329TL, 4/330BR, 4/337TL, 4/339TR, 4/350TR, 4/395TL, 4/405CL, 4/405BR, 4/406TL, 4/408CR, 4/415CL, 4/424TL, 4/428BR, 5/6TL, 5/15TR, 5/15BR, 5/16TL, 5/16TR, 5/16CR, 5/17TL, 5/18TL, 5/18BL, 5/18BR, 5/19BL, 5/19BR, 5/20TL, 5/20BL, 5/21TR, 5/21BR, 5/22TL, 5/24BL, 5/25TL, 5/25CR, 5/25BL, 5/26CL, 5/28TR, 5/29TR, 5/29BL, 5/30CL, 5/31BL, 5/32CR,

5/32BL, 5/33BR, 5/38TL, 5/41BL, 5/41BR, 5/46TL, 5/48BR, 5/51TL, 5/60TL, 5/83BR, 5/123BR, 5/146TR, 5/147TR, 5/157BR, 5/176TR, 5/228TR, 5/234CR, 5/239CL, 5/250CL, 5/251TL, 5/267CR, 5/270CL, 5/307BL, 5/308CR, 5/311TL, 5/320BR, 5/322CL, 5/332TL, 5/333TL, 5/348BR, 5/350BR, 5/355CR, 5/358TL, 5/358CR, 5/387BR, 5/396TR, 5/398TL, 6/14CR, 6/24TL, 6/30TR, 6/33TR, 6/34BL, 6/38CL, 6/39CR, 6/51CR, 6/54TL, 6/59CL, 6/61BR, 6/62TR, 6/63TR, 6/64CL, 6/67CR, 6/71TL, 6/71CR, 6/73TL, 6/93TR, 6/99TR, 6/100BR, 6/101BR, 6/101TL, 6/115BL, 6/115BR, 6/120BL, 6/119BR, 6/125CR, 6/146CR, 6/154CR, 6/158TL, 6/178TR, 6/197BR, 6/231BR, 6/236BL, 6/238TR, 6/242TL, 6/247BR, 6/249TL, 6/256TR, 6/268BL, 6/270TL, 6/285BR, 6/293CL, 6/299BL, 6/308CR, 7/8CR, 7/31TR, 7/33BL, 7/33CR, 7/35BL, 7/56TL, 7/58TL, 7/67BR, 7/68CL, 7/69CR, 7/83CL, 7/107BR, 7/107BL, 7/108TR, 7/108CR, 7/108BR, 7/108BC, 7/110TL, 7/111TL, 7/112BR, 7/117TL, 7/137CL, 7/139TR, 7/143BR, 7/144TL, 7/151TL, 7/176BR, 7/194TC, 7/194TR, 7/195TC, 7/199TC, 7/199TR, 7/199BL, 7/200TL, 7/200TC, 7/201BC, 7/201BR, 7/202TC, 7/203BL, 7/203BR, 7/204TL, 7/245BR, 7/264TR, 7/266CL, 7/286TR, 7/319TL, 7/319TC, 7/319TR, 8/16CL, 8/24CL, 8/29CL, 8/30BL, 8/43BL, 8/54TL, 8/71TR, 8/128BR, 8/152TL, 8/159BL, 8/192TR, 8/237CR, 8/256CL, 8/272CR, 8/275TR, 8/277TR, 8/284BR, 8/286TR, 8/292BR, 8/293TR, 8/295TL, 8/299BL, 8/302TL, 8/316TL, 8/316TC, 8/316TR, 8/317TL, 8/317TC, 8/317TR, 8/318TL, 8/318TC, 8/318TR, 8/319TL, 8/319TR, 8/321TL, 8/321BL, 8/330TR, 8/340BL, 8/351TL, 8/357TR, 9/15BL, 9/16CR, 9/22TL, 9/22CR, 9/22BR, 9/24BL, 9/38TR, 9/47TR, 9/51TR, 9/58CL, 9/109CL, 9/110TR, 9/111TL, 9/111TR, 9/111BR, 9/130TL, 9/130BR, 9/131CR, 9/131BR, 9/133BR, 9/134BC, 9/134TL, 9/150CL, 9/152TL, 9/154TL, 9/154TR, 9/156TL, 9/156TR, 9/161BR, 9/173BL, 9/177TR, 9/179TR, 9/196TL, 9/211BR, 9/214TL, 9/222TL, 9/222TR, 9/235BL, 9/228BL, 9/241CR, 9/249CL, 9/266CL, 9/314BR, 9/316BL, 9/317TL, 9/318TL, 9/346BR, 9/350CR, 9/360CR, 9/362TL, 9/365CL, 9/365C, 9/407TR, 9/408BR, 10/8CL, 10/11CR, 10/12TR, 10/18CR, 10/23TL, 10/27BR, 10/34CR, 10/36TL, 10/67CR, 10/81BL, 10/83TR, 10/105TR, 10/106BR, 10/115CR, 10/123BL, 10/124BR, 10/125BR, 10/131TL, 10/135TL, 10/157TL, 10/158TR, 10/164CR, 10/167BR, 10/168BL, 10/169BL, 10/185BL, 10/187BL, 10/203, 10/205BR, 10/206TR, 10/208BL, 10/248TL, 10/256CR, 10/259BR, 10/260BL, 10/280TR, 10/282TL, 10/289BL, 10/291CR, 10/292TR, 10/294BL, 10/302TL, 10/313BR, 10/325TL, 10/325TR, 11/54TR, 11/54CR, 11/92TL, 11/93CL, 11/107BR, 11/108TL, 11/137CR, 11/158CR, 11/158BR, 11/264CR, 11/265TR, 11/315BL, 11/316BL, 11/318TL, 11/318TR, 11/319TR, 11/319BL, 11/319TL, 11/330TL, 11/331TL, 11/344TL, 11/354BR, 11/356TR, 11/357TR, 11/370TR, 11/384BR, 11/388TL, 11/388CR, 11/388BR, 11/389TL, 11/389CR, 11/417TL, 11/418BL, 11/402BL, 11/437BR, 11/443TR, 11/446BR, 11/456BR, 11/458CL, 12/36TL, 12/37CR, 12/40CR, 12/64TL, 12/75TL, 12/81BR, 12/103TL, 12/131CL, 12/145BR, 12/147TL, 12/149TL, 12/163BR, 12/166TR, 12/173CR, 12/196CL, 12/200BL, 12/209CR, 12/221TL, 12/239CL, 12/241BR, 12/245BL, 12/247T, 12/270TL, 12/288CR, 12/298BL, 12/324CL, 12/350TL, 12/351CL, 12/367TL, 12/377BR, 12/405CR, 12/409BR, 12/445BL, 12/468BR, 12/475TL, 13/5TR, 13/6CL 13/9TR, 13/12BL, 13/13CL, 13/18TR, 13/28TR, 13/36CL, 13/47TL, 13/65CL, 13/123CL, 13/147BL, 13/150CL, 13/160TR, 13/165BL, 13/172BR, 13/182TL, 13/185BR, 13/195TR, 13/227BR, 13/240CL, 13/241CL, 13/250TR, 13/265BL, 13/271TL, 13/271TR, 13/271CR, 13/276BR, 13/277BL, 13/289TR, 13/296CL, 13/296BR, 13/298TL, 13/302CL, 13/375, 13/400BR, 13/405BL, 13/422TL, 13/462CR, 13/527CL, 13/527BL, 13/553BR, 13/558CR, 13/570CL, 13/577CR, 13/590TR, 13/616TR, 13/629TL, 13/647BL, 13/665CR, 13/666BR, 13/667CL, 13/667TL, 13/671TR, 13/672TL, 13/672TR, 13/673BL, 13/673TR, 13/674TL, 13/674BR, 13/685TL, 14/17BR, 14/79CR, 14/119BR, 14/170BL, 14/173TR, 14/175TR, 14/181TR, 14/181BR, 14/193BR, 14/208TL, 14/223CL, 14/224TL, 14/265BC, 14/275BL, 14/310BR 14/317TL, 14/353CR, 14/356CL, 14/399TC, 14/407CR, 14/530TR, 15/15TL, 15/47TL, 15/51BL, 15/91BR, 15/108TL, 15/115TL, 15/128CR, 15/131CR, 15/132BL, 15/144CR, 15/172TR, 15/179CL, 15/180CR, 15/203TR, 15/212BR, 15/233BR, 15/234BL, 15/235CL, 15/235TR, 15/239TR, 15/242BR, 15/278CL, 15/285BL, 15/285TR, 15/285CL, 15/320T, 15/320BR, 15/327TL, 15/440TR, 15/460CL, 15/460BR, 15/480TR, 15/536CR, 15/550BL, 15/551TL, 15/551TR, 15/566CR, 15/596TL, 15/596TR, 15/597CL, 15/598TL, 15/612TR, 15/628CL, 16/25TR, 16/36BL, 16/44CR, 16/44BR, 16/44CL, 16/60BR, 16/87BR, 16/95TL, 16/122CR, 16/202CL, 16/210TL, 16/210CR, 16/213TR, 16/225TL, 16/228TR, 16/243TL, 16/244CL, 16/294TL, 16/307CL, 16/320TL, 16/322BR, 16/338TR, 16/348CR, 16/351TL, 16/357TR, 16/359TR, 16/360CL, 16/365BL, 16/365TR, 16/368TL, 16/368TR, 16/368BL, 16/368BR, 16/369TL, 16/369TR, 16/371TL, 16/371BR, 16/372TR, 16/374BL, 16/376TL, 17/49TR, 17/64CR, 17/65BL, 17/86TR, 17/113TL, 17/118CL, 17/126CR, 17/131TL, 17/131BL, 17/133TL, 17/133CR, 17/139CR, 17/148CR, 17/177TR, 17/213TR, 17/216TR, 17/216BR, 17/217BL, 17/217BR, 17/217TR, 17/217TL, 17/219TL, 17/236TL, 17/257TL, 17/285CL, 17/291TR, 17/355CR, 17/357TL, 17/357CL, 17/369CR, 17/370CL, 17/371CL, 17/375TL, 18/7BR, 18/9TL, 18/23BL, 18/29TL, 18/32CL, 18/147BR, 18/149BL, 18/151TL, 18/159TL, 18/159BR, 18/162TR, 18/162CR, 18/188TL, 18/220BL, 18/221TR, 18/231BR, 18/230TR, 18/248CR, 18/250BR, 18/256BL, 18/260CR, 18/260BR, 18/264TL, 18/264BR, 18/265TL, 18/271TR, 18/271BR, 18/295TL, 18/295BR, 18/307CL, 18/327CL, 18/327BL, 18/341TL, 18/347TR, 18/362TR, 18/387BL, 19/16CR, 19/20TL, 19/52TL, 9/66TL, 19/68CL, 19/68BL, 19/68TR, 19/68CR, 19/100TL, 19/109BL, 19/135TR, 19/136TL, 19/136TR, 19/136BR, 19/137TL, 19/146TL, 19/152TL, 19/156BR, 19/168CR, 19/172CR, 19/176CL, 19/198BR, 19/211BR, 19/222CL, 19/248TL, 19/279MR, 19/303TL, 19/315TL, 19/353TR, 19/438BR, 19/439TL, 19/441TR, 19/442T, 19/442BL, 19/448TR, 19/456TL, 19/456TR, 19/457TR, 19/497CR, 19/518BR, 19/521CR, 19/528CR, 19/549BI, 19/564BL, 19/572BR, 19/596TR, 20/5TL, 20/13CR, 20/15CR, 20/18CL, 20/20CR, 20/26BL, 20/27CR, 20/38TR, 20/44TR, 20/54TR, 20/86BL, 20/88TR, 20/100TR, 20/101BL, 20/122BL, 20/130CR, 20/133, 20/139BL, 20/140BR, 20/141CR, 20/162CR, 20/191L, 20/197CL, 20/200TL, 20/203TL, 20/211BR, 20/220TL, 20/222BL, 20/222BR, 20/223BR, 20/224TL, 20/224TR, 20/226BL, 20/229CL, 20/232BL, 20/232CR, 20/232BR, 20/236TL, 20/236BL, 20/237TR, 20/238BR, 20/243BL, 20/243BR, 20/250TR, 20/250BR, 20/254TR, 20/258CL, 20/272CR, 20/275TR, 20/278CL, 20/280TL, 20/280CR, 20/298BL, 20/320BR, 20/372BL, 20/378BL.

Biblioteca Nazionale Marciana Venezia: 19/551TL.

Bibliothèque Municipale, Bayeux *(courtesy Aldus Books)***:** 14/222TL.

Bibliothèque Nationale: 2/101, 2/219, 3/42BL, 3/239L, 4/42TL, 4/45CL, 4/372L, 4/373, 7/284L, 8/64, 8/268L, 10/136BR, 10/305, 11/288, 11/289R, 12/424, 13/395TL, 13/396TL, 13/403BR, 13/401BR, 13/526TL, 13/450, 13/521L, 19/145C, 19/617TR.

Bibliothèque Nationale, Paris/Weidenfeld and Nicolson Archives: 9/312CR.

Bibliothèque Publique et Universitaire, Genève: 16/122BR.

Bighorn National Forest, USDA Forest Service: 2/115BL.

Bildarchiv Preussicher Kulturbesitz: 3/298, 7/293BR, 8/10B, 9/61CR, 9/153T, 9/155, 10/321, 12/276, 12/299T, 16/87T, 16/189T, 16/355C, 17/109BL, 20/157, 20/220TR, 20/228B, 20/296R.

Bildarchiv der Oestrerreichischen National Bibliotheek, Vienna *(courtesy Aldus Books)***:** 9/218TL, 13/665BL.

Bio-Historisch Instituut, Utrecht: 13/266.

Courtesy **Birmingham Museums and Art Gallery:** 3/514TL.

Black Star: *Gene Anthony* 3/274TR, © *Dennis Brack* 6/103TL, 9/280TL, 10/178B; © *Bryn Colton* 9/248BL; *Joe Covello* 20/161BL; *Bérangère D'aragon* 10/39BL; © *Sal DiMarco* 13/637TR; *Margaret Durrance* 13/622TL; *David Falconer* 12/61TL; *Francis C. Fuerst* 8/233TL; *Dirck Halstead* 1/127TR; *C. Brownie Harris* 17/315TR; *Hyre* 7/101TL; © *Herman J. Kokojan* 8/166BL, 14/442TR; *John Launois* 13/497BL, 20/201BL; © *Robin Meyer* 18/43T; *Mauritus* 20/254TL; *Claus Meyer* 3/457TL; *Ken Rogers* 6/24TR; *Adam Scull* 13/454TL; *Brian Seed* 10/313TL; *Sipa* 19/583TR; *Sipa Press* 20/73BR; *James Sugar* 20/173BR.

Boardwalk Regency: 14/132BL.

Bodleian Library: 2/35, 2/382TR, 5/282TL, 12/316BR, 12/316TR, 15/417BL, 15/498CR.

Courtesy **Boeing Company:** 1/126TL, 5/365CR, 5/365BL, 14/319TL.

Eddy Posthuma de Boer: 3/368TR.

Lee Boltin: 3/201BL, 3/531TL, 6/152BL, 9/229CR, 13/440, 13/441, 14/33BL, 14/296 (12), 14/336TR, 14/336C, 14/336CR, 14/337TL, 14/338TC, 14/338CR, 14/338BR, 15/133CR, 15/497TL.

Boston Athenaeum: 12/246TR.

© Howard Brainen/Visualeyes 1980: 4/443BR, 4/444TL.

Rob Brijker Press Agency: 2/259, 5/149.

The British Council, Amsterdam: 17/154L.

British Crown: © *by permission of controller of Her Majesty's Stationery Office/Colorific!* 6/152BC, 6/152BR.

British Embassy, Mexico City *(courtesy Aldus Books)***:** 13/363TL.

Courtesy **British Leyland:** 2/364.

The British Library: 11/46BL.

The British Museum: 1/86BL, 1/129BL, 1/153TL, 1/162TR, 1/189BL, 1/189BR, 1/262BR, 1/299TL, 2/122BR, 2/180TR, 2/277CL, *(Natural History)* 3/414BL, 3/384BR, 4/240BL, 4/378BL, 4/379TL, 4/384CL, 5/265TR, 5/285TL, 5/368L, 6/22CR, 6/259BL, 6/266TR, 9/29BR, 9/101TL, 9/102T, 9/198TL, 9/203C, 9/203CL, 9/313TR, 11/71TL, 11/116TR 11/116CR, 11/117TR, 11/117BR, 11/121BL, 11/130CL, 11/296BR, 11/134TL, 11/136TL, 11/136CR, 11/140CR, 12/217CL, 13/138BR, 13/139CR, 13/223TR, 13/224TR, 13/224BL, 13/267TR, 13/267BL, 13/270CR, 13/316BL,

13/330BL, 13/621BL, 13/696TR, 13/696BL, 13/697BL, 14/199BR, 15/18CR, 15/44TL, 15/44BL, 15/283TL, 15/498BR, 15/599CL, 15/625TL, 16/353TL, 16/354BL, 18/45TL, 18/45CL, 18/146TR, 18/229BR, 18/231BR, 19/63TR, 19/64TR, 19/93CR, 19/184TR. *(Natural History)* 3/414BL.

Brookhaven National Laboratory: 3/531CL.

The Brooklyn Museum: *Dick S. Ramsay Fund* 3/362BL; 8/378TL; *Gift of Mrs. Ernest Victor* 8/378BL.

Brown Boveri Aktiengesellschaft: 19/340R.

Brown Brothers: 1/99TL, 1/267BL, 1/344TL, 2/143CR, 3/96BL, 3/302BR, 3/535BR, 4/208BR, 5/89BL, 6/297TL, 7/155BL, 8/73BR, 8/130TR, 8/216CL, 9/48CL, 9/50BR, 9/252BR, 9/361TL, 10/33BR, 10/285CL, 11/6TR, 11/268BL, 11/268BC, 11/268BL, 11/284TL, 11/284BR, 11/387TL, 11/436TL, 12/32TL, 12/38CL, 12/62TR, 12/237TL, 12/306CR, 12/402BR, 12/407BR, 12/443BR, 12/465CR, 13/291TR, 13/295BL, 13/427TR, 13/428CR, 13/589TL, 13/651TL, 14/13CL, 14/25BR, 14/194CR, 14/253TR, 14/265BR, 14/382BR, 14/390TL, 14/451CL, 15/90CL, 15/107BL, 15/119TL, 15/232TR, 15/292TR, 15/455TL, 15/618TR, 15/596BR, 15/597BR, 16/55BR, 16/90BR, 16/193CL, 16/206TR, 16/210BL, 16/215CR, 16/241BL, 16/242CR, 16/293BR, 16/294TR, 16/305CL, 16/315BL, 16/367BR, 17/33CR, 17/58TL, 17/59BR, 17/118CL, 17/126TL, 17/130CL, 17/149CR, 17/314TL, 17/319BL, 17/367TL, 17/367BL, 18/28BR, 18/29TR, 18/160BR, 18/166TR, 18/215TL, 18/232TL, 18/265CR, 18/275BL, 18/282CL, 18/287CR, 18/300BL, 18/311CR, 18/408TR, 19/7CR, 19/92BL, 19/173TR, 19/178TL, 19/185TL, 19/198BR, 19/266CL, 19/341CR, 19/505CL, 19/559CL, 19/631BR, 20/14CR, 20/89CL, 20/124TL, 20/156CL, 20/159BR, 20/168TL, 20/250BL, 20/276TL, 20/278TR, 20/280TR, 20/303TR, 20/309BL, 20/321BL, 20/344TL, 20/376BL.

Brown University Library: 19/443TR; *Anne S. K. Brown Military Collection* 19/445BR, 20/27TR.

Fred Bruemmer: 2/138TL.

J. E. Bulloz: 10/263TR, 12/454, 13/666TL, 20/868BR.

Courtesy **Bureau of Travel Development/Dover, Delaware:** 6/89BR.

Roel Burgler: 2/246TR, 13/63TR.

Courtesy **Burlington Industries:** 4/165TR, 4/165CR.

Erik Burro: 6/89TR.

Edgar Rice Burroughs, Inc. © 1941: *Used with permission of Edgar Rice Burroughs, Inc.* 5/136CL.

Photo Michael Busselle © Aldus Books: 6/267TL, 7/329BR, 19/38BL.

Burten Museum of Wedgwood: 15/472BL.

Photo courtesy **California Association for Research in Astronomy:** 19/84TL.

California Institute of Technology: *Murray Gell-man* 7/111BL, 9/69BR, 1/409, 2/283BL, 2/283BR, 2/283T, 5/325BR, 7/345B, 11/227B, 11/227T, 14/75, 18/221.

California State Library: 8/343TL.

Camera 5: *Neil Leifer* 15/66TR.

Camera M.D. Studios: 4/101BL, 4/101BR, 4/235.

Camera Press, Ltd.: *Charbonniere* 11/18; *Crane* 9/13; *Mark Genon* 20/70; *M. Gerson* 3/35L; *Gregory* 15/390CL; *Bo-Eril Gyberg* 3/210; *Richard Harrington* 4/78B, 5/379BL; *P. Hunter* 4/73; *Karsh* 13/67; *Edward P. Learly* 3/463R; *Lollobrigida* 18/82R; *NCNA* 2/240B; *O'Brien* 11/265; *Stark* 9/302; *B. Williams* 7/32BL; 10/250TR.

Killie Campbell *(courtesy Aldus Books)*: 1/155BR.

Courtesy **Canadian Pacific Railroad:** 16/71BR.

Canapress Photo Service: 7/104B.

Capitol Historical Society: 17/198CR.

Tom Caravaglia: 13/497BR.

Peter Carmichael: 1/138T, 1/143TR, 1/288, 1/289L, 2/99TR, 11/86BL, 20/366R.

John Carnevale: 3/46TL.

Courtesy **Amon Carter Museum/ Fort Worth, Texas:** 8/342TR.

Cathedral Museum/Siena, Italy: 2/194CL.

Cauboue: 11/93TL.

CBS: 16/57BL, 16/57BR.

Center for UFO Studies and N.I.C.A.P.: 19/385TR.

Centraal Bureau voor Schimmelcultures: 8/365, 8/368L.

Central Press: 11/442BL.

Central Zionist Archives: 15/45TL.

Cern Genève: 5/68, 14/286TL.

George Cerna: 14/114BR.

Josef Charyk: 11/205TR.

Richard Cheek: 13/447TL.

Chicago Historical Society: 3/306TL, 17/353BR, 19/326CL.

The Chicago Tribune: *Reprinted by permission of the Chicago Tribune–New York News Syndicate, Inc.* 5/135BR.

Christian Science Publishing Society: 7/55BL.

Cinémathèque Française: 12/194.

Circle Marketing Reclame: 6/122R.

City Art Gallery, Bristol *(courtesy Aldus Books)*: 19/67TR.

City Museum and Art Gallery, Plymouth *(courtesy Aldus Books)*: 2/269CL.

William W. Clark: 9/257TL.

© 1986 CNES: 17/87TR.

Bruce Coleman, Inc.: *Jan and Des Bartlett* 12/258BR, 20/214TL, *Bill Brooks* 14/117BR; *Bruce Coleman* 12/278TR, 16/76BL; *© Eric Crichton* 9/40TR; *P. H. Davies* 14/118TL; *A. J. Hewerdine* 15/28CR; *Norman Meyers* 11/335CR; *Joachim Messerschmidt* 7/276TL, 7/276BL; *D. Pike* 11/304BR; *George Rockwin* 12/365TR; *Norman Tomglin* 17/24BR; *Nicholas de Vore III* 14/167CR; *© Jonathan T. Wright* 9/230TL.

Bruce Coleman Ltd.: *Oxford Scientific Films* 15/331TR, 15/331BL, 15/331BR, 15/332; 2/346L, 13/513.

Courtesy **Collins Publishers:** 2/53CR.

The Colonial Williamsburg Foundation: 5/110TL.

Colour Library International (USA) Limited: 6/26TL.

Columbia University Library: *Marjorie V. Duffell* 20/363BL.

Comet: 8/97L, 8/98.

Cooper Bridgeman Library: 4/326TR, 7/288L, 18/212BR, 19/171L, 20/61TR.

Confederation Life Collection: 4/84TL.

Courtesy **Connecticut Development Commission:** 5/195TL.

Connecticut State Library Pictorial Archives: 5/33CL.

Contact-Camp: *Bill Pierce* 14/283TL.

Contact Press Images: *Bill Pierce* 15/414TL.

Cooper-Hewitt Museum, The Smithsonian Institution's National Museum of Design: 8/31BR, 12/159TL, 12/159BL, 12/159BC, 12/159TR; *Gift of Lionberger Davis, 1968-1-13* 15/472TR; *Gift of the Trustees of the Estate of James Hazen Hyde, 1960-1-28C* 5/471TL.

Corcoran Gallery of Art: 2/200TR.

Corning Museum of Glass: 9/203BL.

Count Brobinsky: *Michael Holford Library (courtesy Aldus Books)* 16/354TR.

Courtauld Institute of Art: 17/295.

Gerry Cranham's Colour Library: 17/282TR, 17/282CL, 17/282BL.

Crown Publishers, Inc.: Taken from *A Pictorial History of Black Americans* by Langston Hughes, Milton Meltzer, and C. Eric Lincoln. Copyright © 1974 by M. Meltzer, C. L. Lincoln, and the Estate of Langston Hughes. Used by permission of Crown Publishers, Inc. 14/29BL.

Culver: 15/564TR, 16/55CR.

Edward Sheriff Curtis: Reprinted from *Edward Sheriff Curtis: Visions of a Vanishing Race* by Florence Curtis Graybill and Victor Boesen, published by T. Y. Crowell. 11/451CL, 14/176TL.

G. M. Cushing: 12/246TR.

Cunningham Dance Foundation: 3/44CL.

Culver Pictures, Inc.: 1/87BR, 1/314TL, 2/28TR, 2/200CL, 2/212BR, 2/258TL, 2/269CR, 2/315CR, 3/69TR, 3/144BR, 3/173BR, 3/306BR, 3/308BR, 3/354TL, 3/359CR, 3/397TL, 4/127CR, 4/201TL, 4/246BL, 4/261BL, 5/101CL, 5/243TR, 5/376TR, 6/197TL, 6/245BL, 6/306CL, 6/315BR, 7/67CL, 8/81BR, 8/83T, 8/85T, 8/85CL, 9/220TL, 9/396TR, 10/29TL, 10/124TL, 10/125BL, 10/127CR, 10/128TR, 10/129BL, 10/150TR, 10/152CL, 10/241CL, 10/254BL, 10/260TR, 10/290BR, 10/322TR, 10/324CR, 11/285BR, 11/332BL, 11/334TL, 11/334BR, 11/336TL, 11/416TR, 12/34BR, 12/205CL, 12/366BR, 12/383BL, 12/387TR, 13/28TL, 13/40BR, 13/151TR, 13/218BL, 13/238TL, 13/249BR, 13/496CR, 13/496BR, 13/555TR, 13/638CR, 14/27TR, 14/265BL, 14/379TR, 14/382CR, 15/110CR, 15/121TL, 15/232CL, 15/324TR, 15/565CL, 16/58BL, 16/215BL, 17/56CL, 17/136TL, 17/218TL, 17/366CL, 18/21BR, 18/221BL, 18/281TL, 18/296BL, 18/298CR, 18/337CL, 19/108CR, 19/294TR, 19/622CL, 20/224BL.

Gino D'Achille ©Aldus Books: 15/513T.

Daily Telegraph: 15/77CL.

Daily Telegraph Color Library: 4/312TL.

The Danish National Museum: (Published by permission.) 4/240TL.

Jack Daly: 10/75, 14/306TC, 14/306TR, 14/306C, 14/306CR, 15/71TL, 15/262, 15/263CR, 15/263BR, 15/264T, 15/264CL, 15/264CR, 15/265TL.

D.C. Comics, Inc: "Batman and Robin are registered trademarks of D.C. Comics, Inc. and are used with permission; Illustration © 1966 DC Comics, Inc." 5/136C.

Aedita S. deBeaumont and the McNaught Syndicate, Inc.: *Reprinted with permission.* 5/135CR.

Courtesy **John Deere Co.:** 1/192TL.

Delaware Art Museum: *Howard Pyle collection* 3/388TR.

Courtesy **Delaware State Visitors Service:** 6/89TL.

Courtesy **E. I. du Pont de Nemours & Co.:** 6/286BR, 19/450CR.

Denver Museum of Natural History: 14/237BL.

Denver Public Library: *Western History Department* 19/444TR.

Department of Parks, City of Atlanta: 5/31TL.

Courtesy **The Detroit Institute of Arts:** 6/23TL.

Deutsche Verlags-Anstalt/DVA: 3/274BL, 3/274CB.

Deutsches Archaologisches Institut Athens: 14/382BL.

Douglas Dickins: 15/455CR.

© Walt Disney Productions: 4/433TL.

C.M. Dixon: 17/111BL, 19/94TR.

Documentation Française, Paris: 9/62L.

Dr. A. Dollfus: 18/344TR.

© Sergio Dorantes: 19/404TR, 19/404CL, 19/405TL.

DOT: © *John Livzey* 16/59BR.

Courtesy Doubleday Publishers, Inc.: 5/317BR.

Dover Publications, Inc.: *taken from* The Later Works of Aubrey Beardsley (plate 155) *with kind permission from Dover Publications, Inc.* 3/388BL.

Doyle, Dane & Bernbach: 1/113TL, 1/113TC, 1/113TR.

Courtesy **Du-Atlantis, Zurich** *(courtesy Aldus Books)***:** 15/589BR.

Du Pont Company: Reprinted from *Du Pont Context*, published by the Du Pont Company 3/262BL.

Frank Dunand: 14/401TL.

Alfred Dunhill Ltd. *(courtesy Aldus Books)***:** 1/112TL.

Duomo: *Dan Helms* 17/339TC; *Michael Miller* 20/287TL; *Adam Stoltman* 3/352CL; *Steve Sutton* 19/260B.

Eastern National Park and Monument Association: *Independence National Historical Park Collection* 12/268BR.

Eastfoto: 4/376BR, 12/453CR.

Edinburgh University Library *(courtesy Aldus Books)***:** 13/402BL.

Editorial Photocolor Archives: 1/115BL, 1/262BL, 1/407TL, 2/133TR, 3/416BR, 3/451CR, 3/481TR, 3/524BR, 4/54CL, 5/4TL, 5/342TL, 8/374Cl, 9/149TL, 9/260TR, 9/333BR, 10/10TL, 10/126TR, 10/183BR, 13/269CR, 13/573TL, 14/90TL, 14/402TL, 15/63BL, 15/65BL, 15/103BR, 15/424BL, 15/425BL, 15/497TL, 15/639CR, 16/82TL, 16/149TR, 17/23CR, 17/329TR, 18/209BL, 19/96BR, 19/144BR, 19/527BR.

Educational Dimensions: 19/148BL.

Piet Eggen: 12/176.

Egyptian Museum, Cairo: 2/192CR.

Courtesy **Elektra Records, produced by Charlex:** 19/576fTR.

Embassy of New Zealand: 14/161CR.

EMI-Bovema bv.: 15/253L.

Encore: *Andy Freeberg* 11/389CL, 11/389BR.

Environmental Communications: 10/261BL.

EPA: *Michael Tsovaras* 12/101.

EPA–Documerica: *John White* 10/276BR.

EPA/SCALA: 2/134BR, 2/135BR, 2/190CL, 2/193CR, 2/195CL, 2/195BR, 2/195BL, 9/333BR, 11/308BR, 11/315BR, 11/327TR, 11/328TL, 11/414BL, 13/701CL, 15/48TL, 15/63BL, 15/65BL, 15/424BL, 15/639BR, 17/25TR, 17/352BR, 18/195CR, 18/196TL.

Essex Institute: 17/31TR.

Esto: 12/317TR, 12/317CR, 12/317TL, 13/492TR, 13/493CL, 13/492CR.

Agnes Etherington Art Centre, Queen's University at Kingston: 4/90BL.

European Picture Service: 20/257TL.

European Southern Observatory: 13/48T, 13/48B.

Mary Evans Picture Library: 1/55, 1/154TL, 4/142BR, 4/374L, 6/29BR, 6/272T, 7/289TL, 8/241TR, 8/272BL, 9/152R, 11/62, 15/96, 15/481, 15/626, 17/143TR, 17/301TR, 10/146.

Explorer: *Fiore/Silvio* 14/263R; 1/134TL, 1/149TL, 1/289R, 4/121, 8/97R, 9/326, 12/204, 12/297TR, 13/38CR, 13/628, 14/318R, 17/14T, 18/34, 19/4T.

Courtesy **Exxon Corporation:** 15/212TR.

Courtesy **Fairey Surveys Ltd.** *(courtesy Aldus Books)***:** 1/119BR.

Farrar, Straus & Giroux, Inc.: *Tom Berthiavme* 3/225TR.

Fashion Institute of Technology *(from Davidow Collection of Library Media Services)***:** 8/32TL, 8/32TC, 8/32BR.

Federal Bureau of Investigation: 8/93CR.

Fred Fehl: 12/232TL.

Enrico Ferorelli: 12/186BR.

Courtesy **Field Museum of Natural History:** 19/69TR.

Filmbureau Niestadt: 19/96T.

Fitzwilliam Museum: 4/385CR.

Courtesy **Florida Department of Commerce:** 8/173CR, 8/176TL.

Courtesy **Florida Development Commission:** 8/175TL.

Florida News Bureau: 8/174TL, 8/ 175CR.

FMC Corporation: 2/177BL.

Focus on Sports: *Warren Bolster* 17/332BR; *Tony Duffy* 11/14TL, 11/14TR; *Kevin Gal* 3/352TL; *Mickey Palmer* 8/217BR, 8/217CL, 8/217TL; *Brian Payne* 8/124TR; *Richard Pilling* 18/9CR; *Chuck Solomon* 18/9CL; *Bernard Suess* 8/72BL, 17/338TR; 3/13CL, 3/102B, 3/113CL, 4/220CL, 8/217CR, 8/217B, 11/11BR, 11/14BL, 14/383TR, 14/384CL, 16/266TR, 16/328T; 18/391CR.

The Folger Shakespeare Library: *Reprinted by permission.* 17/236BR.

Courtesy **Ford Company:** *Scala* 8/220.

Henry Ford Museum: *Ford Archives* 19/453BR.

Foreign Language Press: 4/376TR.

Courtesy **Foresight Resources Corp.:** 5/160jBR.

Werner Forman Archive: 7/87TL, 788/B, 13/572BL, 19/25CR.

Foto: *Fagus-Grecon* 9/127TR.

The Fotomas Index, London: 9/315CR, 17/152CL.

Courtesy **The Foundation Saint-Thomas, Strasbourg** *(courtesy Aldus Books)***:** 2/278BR.

Freelance Photographers Guild: © *Paul Cerny* 19/56BL; *N. Farb* 3/534CL; *Eberhard E. Otto* 13/3BR; *Robin Smith* 3/487CL; *Jules Zalon* 16/208BR; 2/86TL, 5/160bTL, 12/225BR, 8/80TR, 18/386BL, 18/397TR, 19/14CL.

Freer Gallery of Art: 4/383BL.

Courtesy **French Government Tourist Office:** 10/261CL.

Sigmund Freud Copyrights Ltd.: 8/329R, 8/329L.

Gisèle Freund: 8/354R, 10/152R.

The Frick Collection: 8/376, 15/471TR.

Galaxy Magazine, Inc.: 17/140BL.

Ewing Galloway: 8/16BR, 12/455BR, 19/365TC.

Gamma/ABC–Press: *Hermann* 14/159R.

Gamma/Liaison: *Abbas* 1/159TR; *Jean-Paul Champagne* 13/632; *Jean-Claude Francolon* 13/585; © *Andre Hampartzoumian* 19/373TR; *Bernard Hermann* 5/40BR; © *Cynthia Johnson* 5/184BR, 10/178T; © *Keeve* 16/59BL; *Kok* 7/298TR; © *J. C. Labbe* 12/12 TL; *François Lochon* 2/105CL, 5/379TL, 5/379BR; *Alain Mingham* 3/476BL; *Karen Rubin* 11/83TL; © *Tardy-Perrin* 18/391TR; © *D. Walker* 13/522TR; 8/165TL, 11/426TL, 12/56BR, 15/532TR, 16/3BL, 16/360TR.

The Gas Council, London *(courtesy Aldus Books)***:** 14/340BL.

José Gazetambide: 10/179TR.

Leif Geiges: 15/81.

Thielska Galleriet: 14/185B.

General Dynamics International Corporation: 2/56TL.

General Electric: 5/160ITL.

General Motors Research Laboratories *(courtesy Aldus Books)***:** 15/272BL.

Geocom BV.: 3/81R, 6/129L, 8/219CR, 8/243R, 14/408B, 15/406CR, 15/406BR.

Lowell Georgia: 12/410TR.

Courtesy **Tourist Division–Georgia Bureau of Industry:** 9/115TL, 9/117TL, 9/117BR.

Gernsheim Collection *(courtesy Aldus Books)***:** 20/310BR.

Frits Gerritsen: 3/332, 5/347L, 5/347R, 6/66BR, 14/101T.

Mark Gerson: 9/234CR.

Georg Gerster: 1/148L, 7/77T, 7/78CL, 7/78BR, 7/79T, 7/241TL, 7/254TL, 7/254TC, 13/90, 13/370, 13/449L, 14/233TR, 19/322.

Gesellschaft der Musik Freunde in Wien: 18/300TL.

Geveke divisie Zwaar Materieel: 7/23BL, 7/23TL.

The Thomas Gilcrease Institute of American History and Art/Tulsa, Oklahoma: 1/331TL, 11/117TL.

Courtesy **Glenbow Museum/Calgary, Alberta:** 11/120CL, 14/217CR.

Globe Photos: *J. Goodman* 2/333TR; *Don Ornitz* 6/203TR.

Photo George W. Goddard © Aldus Book: 15/606BR.

Goethe Institute, London: 9/133BL.

Goethe-Instituut, Amsterdam: 9/297.

© Lynn Goldsmith Inc.: 16/249BR.

Courtesy **Goodyear Aerospace Corporation:** 16/147BR.

Gianfranco Gorgoni: 2/202TR.

© David Gorton: 12/180BL, 12/180BR.

The Granger Collection: *Betsy Reyneau* 3/231CR; *John Vanderlyn* 3/579BL; 2/143BR, 3/151TR, 4/247TR, 6/29CL, 6/30TL, 6/30CL, 7/288BL, 9/41TL, 9/129BL, 9/129BC, 9/129BR, 11/155BR(B), 19/144BR, 19/148R.

Grant Park Visitors Center: 5/31.

Michael Gray: 5/374TL, 8/247.

Lois Greenfield: 13/497CL.

Collections of Greenfield Village and The Henry Ford Museum/Dearborn, Michigan: 8/377CR.

Henry Grossman: 14/213TL.

Guggenheim Museum: *Robert E. Mates* 13/493BL.

Haags Gemeente Museum: 6/23B.

Haifa Publishing Company, Ltd. *(courtesy Aldus Books)***:** 11/416BL.

Hale Observatories: 7/345CR, 10/18BL, 16/49BL, 18/52B, 18/345C.

Frans Hals Museum: 10/25.

© 1962 Philippe Halsman: 18/249TL.

Steve Hansen: 5/160kTL.

Claus Hansmann: 5/238TL.

Claus and Liselotte Hansmann: 1/163TR, 6/225T, 13/49, 15/627TL, 15/627BR.

Robert Harding Picture Library Ltd: 2/123TR, 3/100BL, 3/100TR, 3/536CL, 4/379CR, 4/385TL, 4/386B, 6/222TR, 7/85TR, 10/188BR, 10/189TL, 19/576CL; *Tom Ang* 19/402BR; *Sassoon* 1/152T.

The Hark Group, Ltd./Slidemakers: 4/16CL, 4/280TR, 4/285TL, 5/243CL, 5/383TR, 6/50CR, 6/166TL, 7/97TL, 9/191TL, 9/287TR, 10/250CR, 12/413CR, 12/453CL, 13/182CR, 15/293CR, 18/267TL, 18/337TR, 19/49TL, 19/320CR, 20/99TR.

Courtesy **Harper & Row Publishers, Inc.:** 4/353TR, 12/230TR.

Harvard College Library: *Theodore Roosevelt Collection* 15/530BL.

Harvard University: *Fogg Art Museum* 12/186TL; *Houghton Library* 15/170TL.

Harvard University Press: 15/565BR.

Hayman Studios: *from the collection of Byron H. Lecates* 8/197CL.

Mark Haynes: 14/239BL.

Hedrich Blessing: 1/327BR, 1/328BL, 2/136CL, 2/200BL, 4/342TL, 13/492TL, 17/349BL, 17/349BC.

Grant Heilman Photography: *John Colwell* 6/9CL, 6/9CR, 6/9BL, 6/9BR, 5/306TL, 5/306TR, 6/17CL, 8/25TL, 9/348BR, 11/281BR, 11/282TL, 11/282CL, 12/19TL, 12/395TL, 12/395BL.

Helionetics, Inc., Laser Division: 12/212BL.

Courtesy **Her Majesty's Stationery Office:** 5/364BL.

Hessische Landesbibliothek: 8/290.

Het Spectrum: 1/225, 2/243TR, 3/81, 3/129BL, 3/349, 3/385BR, 4/150TL, 4/256, 4/418TR, 4/434L, 5/97, 5/114, 5/142, 5/227, 7/23, 7/287, 7/295T, 7/303T, 7/304T, 8/4, 8/10CR, 8/19, 8/67, 8/162L, 8/270, 8/318TR, 8/364T, 9/14, 9/291B, 9/293TR, 9/317R, 9/363L, 9/363R, 9/372R, 10/79, 10/102, 10/319, 12/130, 12/271CR, 12/338BL, 12/359L, 12/414T, 12/438, 12/440B, 12/440CR, 12/441, 13/17, 13/24B, 13/317, 13/393R, 13/569L, 13/684, 14/16B, 14/84BL, 14/87R, 14/102L, 14/410B, 14/411B, 15/68L, 15/70, 15/186R, 15/222T, 15/243T, 15/560, 15/582, 15/621, 16/99, 16/156L, 16/350, 17/158, 18/109, 18/156, 18/328BL, 19/531.

Hickox Library–Basketball Hall of Fame: 3/112TL.

High Altitude Observatory of NCAR: 18/344BR.

Courtesy **The High Commission of India, London** *(courtesy Aldus Books)***:** 2/258BR.

James Jerome Hill Reference Library, St. Paul, Minn.: 8/344.

John Hillerson Agency Ltd., London: *H. Sochurek* 15/272TL.

John Hillerson Agency: 11/84BR.

Hans Hinz Colorphoto: 18/402R, 19/32TL.

© Hirmer Verlag München: 9/126TL.

Reproduced from "Historia Fisicia y Politica de Chíle," 1854, by Claude Gay: 11/135TR.

Historical Pictures Service, Inc.: 3/144TR, 15/597TL, 20/201BR, 20/202BR, 20/203TR.

Historical Society of Pennsylvania: 11/119BR.

Historisches Museum der Stadt Vienna *(courtesy Aldus Books)***:** 16/355BL.

Hoa-Qui: *X. Richer* 2/241CL, 19/473TR; 9/165T, 13/236BR.

Michael Holford Library: 11/121BC, 20/21TR.

Holle Bildarchiv: 4/239CR, 4/239TL, 7/305T, 13/285, 16/283TR.

Angelo Hornak: 16/363BL.

Mel Horst: 13/298BR, 13/300BR.

The Houghton Library, Harvard University: *Reprinted by permission.* 14/274CL, 14/274BC.

Courtesy **House of Representatives:** 10/273TL.

Dave Houser: 2/360TL, 2/361BR.

H. Hovinga: 3/368TR, 12/12B, 14/87R, 14/88.

Verlag Haus Huber, Bern: 15/565TR.

Courtesy **Hughes Aircraft Company:** 16/255TR, 18/123BR.

Hulton Picture Library: 5/349TR, 14/466C, 19/160.

George Hunter Photography: 15/549TR.

Peter Hunter Press Features: *Associated Newspaper* 3/169; *DAL* 9/219; *Morin* 8/48B; *Dr. Erich Salomon* 17/36.

Courtesy **The Huntington Library:** *Hm29 MAP #9* 4/80TL.

Greg Hursley: 9/302CR.

HVI: 8/231TR.

Courtesy **IBM:** 5/160dB, 5/161BL, 5/164T.

IBM Research: *Benoit Mandelbrot* 5/160mTR; *Richard F. Voss* 5/160nTL.

Courtesy **Illinois Office of Tourism:** 11/41BR, 11/43TR.

Courtesy **Image Analysis Laboratory, Department of Therapeutic Radiology, New England Medical Center:** 5/162T.

The Image Bank: *Morton Beebe* 2/235BR, 2/379TL, 19/55BR; *Joseph B. Brignolo* 2/4BL, 14/402TR; *Michael de Camp* 12/187BL; *Hank de Lespinasse* 1/22TR; *Larry Gordon* 3/350TL; *Farrell Grehan* 3/32TR; *Joseph Hettis* 2/242TR; *David Hiser* 3/350CR; *Gil C. Kenny* 4/35TR; *Bud Lee Studio* 3/514CR; *Larry Lee* 4/32TR; *Harvey Lloyd* 2/242TL; *Bullaty Lomeo* 13/397BL; 14/37BL; *Walter Ioose, Jr.* 3/111CR; *J. C. Lozquet* 12/186BL; *Robert Phillips* 2/162TL; *Al Satterwhite* 3/145CR; *Eric Schweikardt* 3/398CR; *John Lewis Stage* 1/121TR, 1/138T, 2/337CL, 3/83TL; *Richard Steedman* 4/32BL; 13/397BR; *Harold Sund* 2/161BL, 2/284TR, 4/33TR; *Pete Turner* 3/350TR, 3/371BR; *Luis Villota* 2/336TR, 3/224BL, 13/398CR; *Jules Zalon* 3/555BR.

Imperial War Museum: 19/455BR, 20/234TL, 20/228TL, 20/229T, 20/231TL, 20/231BR, 20/234TL, 20/234BR, 20/242TL, 20/244, 20/252TR, 20/254BL, 20/255TL, 20/262CL, 20/277BL.

IMS/ABC-Press: *S. E. Hedin* 20/328.

Courtesy **Indiana Department of Commerce:** 11/112CR.

Institut für die Geschichte der Medizin der Universität Wien: 4/287TR.

Institute of Geological Sciences: 15/30BR.

Institute International de Physique Solvay *(courtesy AIP Niels Bohr Library)***:** 15/286TR.

Reprinted by permission of **Intel Corporation,** © 1987: 5/160cBL, 5/160cBR.

Inter Nationes: 7/278BL, 8/266R, 9/141BR, 9/145BL, 9/145BR, 9/146T.

International Bilder-Agentur: 1/308BR.

International Institute for Social History, Amsterdam: *(courtesy Aldus Books)* 18/21CR.

International Museum of Photography at George Eastman House: 2/288CL, 4/59TR, 8/80B, 13/688TL, 15/268CR.

International News Photo: 20/255CR.

International Society for Educational Information: 11/367BL, 11/368BR.

Courtesy **Iowa Development Commission:** 11/245B, 11/246TR.

Irish National Tourist Board: 15/509BR.

Ishikawajimaharima Heavy Industries *(courtesy Aldus Books)***:** 19/278CR.

Istanbul University Library *(courtesy Aldus Books)***:** 18/333TL.

The Iveagh Bequest Kenwood: 6/310T.

Jacana: *Chaumeton* 17/168TL; *Joff* 15/457BL; *Ross* 5/412; 3/272.

Kees Jansen: 17/202BL.

Frans Janssen: 18/110TR.

Japan Folk Crafts Museum, Tokyo: 8/198BR.

Greta Baars Jelgersma: 16/29.

Photo Jobling *(courtesy Aldus Books)***:** 9/202BL.

Philip Johnson: 11/435T.

The John Judkyn Memorial/Freshford Manor, Bath: *photo Mike Busselle © Aldus Books* 17/353BC.

Kansas Department of Economic Development: 12/21CL.

Kant-Gymnasium: 12/23.

© Karsh, Ottawa: 4/426TL, 7/93TL, 11/467TR, 12/29TR, 14/286BL, 19/260CL.

Yosuf Karsh: 1/347TC.

Katholieke Universiteit Nijmegen/Zoölogisch Laboratorium: 9/86CR, 14/290.

Keats-Shelly Memorial Association: *C. Catania* 16/293BL.

KEMA: 15/488BL.

Courtesy **Kentucky Department of Public Information:** 12/50BL.

Courtesy **Kentucky Department of Travel and Commerce:** 12/48TR.

Courtesy **Kentucky Division of Tourism:** 12/49TL, 12/49CL, 12/51TL.

A. F. Kersting: 2/135BR, 7/146BL, 7/185BR, 9/255C, 9/261CR, 11/96BR, 13/501TL, 16/264CR, 17/25BL, 19/15TL, 20/117BR.

André Kertesz: 12/60CR.

Keter Publishing House: 11/462CR.

Keystone Press Agency, Inc.: 13/234TR, 14/320TL, 14/383CL, 16/188TL.

Romi Khosla *(courtesy Aldus Books)***:** 19/191TL.

King Feature Syndicate: © 1937 5/135C, © 1967 5/135BL.

Agency KIPPA: 3/148CL.

Aart Klein: 19/404T.

Ralph Kleinhempel: 8/332TR, 10/108.

KLM Aerocarto: 15/213.

Knoll International: 8/379BR.

Kodansha Ltd., Tokyo: *courtesy of National Museum of Anthropology, Mexico City* 15/496TR, 15/498TL.

Courtesy **Alfred Knopf Publishers:** 5/237CL.

Paolo Koch: 7/271BR, 11/137B, 11/325, 13/457, 16/289CR, 18/108B, 18/108C, 19/391, 20/358.

Courtesy **Kodak:** 15/272CL.

Koninklijk Instituut voor de Tropen: 7/53TL, 9/5B, 11/352TR.

Koninklijk Museum voor Schone Kunsten: 12/442T, 12/442CL.

C. E. Koppeschaar: 7/49BR, 7/41TL.

Courtesy **Korean Cultural Service:** 12/114TR.

Kröller Müller Museum: 4/159.

Kunsthistorisches Museum, Vienna *(courtesy Aldus Books)*: 11/460TL.

Kunsthistorisches Museum Wien: 2/350L, 6/311.

Kunstsammlungen der Veste, Coburg *(courtesy Aldus Books)*: 11/415BR.

Alfred Lamme: 4/435CL, 4/435CR, 4/435BR.

J. Lampert Promotions, Inc.: 8/48TR, 12/39Bl, 16/244TL.

Laser Games: *Thom Kidrin* 19/576jTL.

Lennart Larsen: 17/110TR.

Courtesy **Las Vegas News Bureau:** 10/261BR.

Leeds Museum: 2/181C.

The Rt. Hon. The Earl of Leicester, M.C. *(courtesy Aldus Books)*: 1/191TR.

Jonathan Levine: 8/209BL, 8/209BR.

Dr. H. Levner, Göttingen: *by permission of the Sandoz AG. Basel (courtesy Aldus Books)* 15/600BL, 15/600BR.

Photo Henri Lhote *(courtesy Aldus Books)*: 2/23BL.

Librarie Hachette, Paris: 18/367TL.

Courtesy **Library of Congress:** *Mathew Brady Collection* 15/272CL; 1/343BL, 1/355CL, 3/307BL, 3/547TL, 4/332TL, 5/21TL, 5/24TL, 5/25TR, 5/27CR, 5/27BL, 5/28BR, 6/119CR, 8/283TL, 8/344TL, 11/118TR, 12/154TR, 12/154TL, 15/270TR, 15/312BL, 15/312TR, 17/349TL, 17/349TC, 18/355TL, 19/332TL, 19/451TL, 20/223CL, 20/229BR, 20/237TL.

Lick Observatory: 2/283T, 7/345TL, 18/50BC.

Nathaniel Lieberman: 12/317BR.

Life, Inc.: *Margaret Bourke–White* 15/10TL.

Life Magazine © Time, Inc.: *Alfred Eisenstaedt* 1945 7/96BR; *Neil Leifer* 15/118CR; *Ted Russell* 1963 3/311BL, 1963 13/86BL; *George Silk* 20/279BR; *Margaret Bourke–White* 1938 19/454CL, 20/276TL; 20/248BL.

Life Nature Library/Animal Behavior, Published by Time-Life Books, Inc.: 2/11TR, 2/11CR, 2/11BR.

Life Picture Service: *Margaret Bourke–White* 3/424CR.

Courtesy **Lockheed Missiles and Space Company:** 19/369BL.

London Daily Express: 15/50TR.

London Features International, Ltd.: 16/248BL, 16/249BL.

Donald Longmoore *(courtesy Aldus Books)*: 18/362TR.

Stefan Lorant's *The Glorious Burden* (author's edition): 15/524BR, 15/526BR, 15/527BL, 15/529TR, 15/529CR, 15/531TL, 16/102TL, 16/109TR, 16/109TL, 18/24BR, 19/449BR, 19/457BL.

Lord Chamberlain's Office: 6/239.

Los Alamos National Laboratory: 10/339, 12/212TR; *Fred Rick* 12/212CR, 12/212BR.

Los Angeles Times Syndicate: 4/177TR.

Courtesy **Tourist Development Commission/Baton Rouge, Louisiana:** 12/431.

Louvre Museum: 2/205BR, 5/69TL, 13/572BR, 19/62CL, 20/292BL.

Lowell Observatory photograph: 15/373TL, 15/373TC, 18/49BR.

Lucasfilm, Ltd: 8/88TL.

Walter Lüden, Wyk: 8/196TL, 8/196BR.

F. H. Ludlam *(courtesy Aldus Books)*: 10/13CL.

Lunar and Planetary Laboratory: 17/90TL.

Lund Observatory *(courtesy Aldus Books)*: *Reprinted by permission.* 9/11TL.

MCA Records: 16/204BR.

Paul D. McClain: 10/314TL.

Steve McCutcheon: 1/243B, 1/247T.

Courtesy **McDonald–Douglas:** *Gerald Brooks* 19/56TL.

Norman McGrath: 15/464BL.

© Loren A. Mcintyre: 1/324BL.

© Burton McNeely: 17/342BR.

Magnum Photos, Inc.: 2/252BR, 3/462BR, 4/361TL, 4/367, 4/368B, 6/307T, 7/80T, 7/81TL, 9/323T, 13/194BL, 17/36CL, 20/230; *Bob Adelman* 3/75CL, 3/310CL, 12/81TL; *© Eve Arnold* 14/442TL; *B. Barbey* 1/144B, 1/160, 2/103TR, 4/366T, 5/368B, 6/123B, 14/386BR, 19/394BL; *Ian Berry* 1/172BL, 2/117BL, 4/156TL, 9/26; *Burri* 2/56TR, 16/254CR; *Robert Capa* 10/118, 15/273BL, 19/394BR, 20/249BR; *Henri Cartier–Bresson* 2/54BL, 4/175BL, 15/270BL; *Bruce Davidson © 1977* 15/10BR, 19/459TR; *Elliot Erwitt* 3/531CR, 10/308CR; *Freed* 15/615; *Charles Gatewood* 3/580CL; *© Jean Gaumy* 20/177TR; *Glinn* 10/109, 19/392TL; *Goff* 3/190; *Philip Jones Griffiths* 19/450BL; *Burt Gunn* 7/275C, 10/275; *Ernst Haas* 16/132BR; *Charles Harbutt* 16/249CL; *Höper* 15/194TR, 17/13R; *© Hiroji Kubota* 12/114TR; *Landy* 8/202TL; *Eric Lessing* 3/164, 4/239CL, 7/275CR, 8/266T, 10/275, 15/391, 18/45BL, 20/155; *Manos* 7/275BR, 9/328TR, 10/275; *Morath* 3/369BR, 13/428; *John Nance* 2/51BL, 4/225T; *© Gilles Perres* 20/179BL; *© Raghu Rai* 9/35BR; *Marc Riboud* 4/391TL, 5/149T, 10/190, 10/191TL, 16/349; *Rodger* 7/180B; *Marilyn Silverstone* 13/635L, 15/104CL; *Dennis Stock* 3/520CL, 11/326TR, 14/157BR, *© 1964* 17/330BR.

Courtesy **Maine State Development Office:** 13/71BR, 13/72TR.

© Milton & Joan Mann: 4/113T, 9/30BL.

The Mansell Collection: 1/156B, 2/142T, 3/14, 5/239BR, 5/282TR, 5/282CL, 6/21BL, 7/164TR, 9/150B, 10/184BR, 12/378TR, 13/343BR, 15/102, 15/120, 15/241CR, 15/284TL, 15/377, 16/148CR, 16/148TR, 17/108TL, 17/132CL, 17/352CR, 18/21TR, 18/262BL, 19/67BR, 19/137BL, 19/151TL, 20/56BR, 20/374BR.

The Mariners Museum: 8/195BR.

The Marquess of Salisbury K. G.: Reproduced by courtesy of the Marquess of Salisbury K. G. *Photo John Freeman © Aldus Books* 9/312BR.

Courtesy **Maryland Department of Travel and Commerce:** 13/190TL.

Courtesy **Maryland Division of Tourism:** 13/189BL, 13/190CR, 13/191BL, 13/192CR, 13/192BL.

Maryland Historical Society: 12/102CL.

Mas Ampliaciones y Reproducciones: 4/109TR, 8/52BL, 9/59CL, 9/243, 18/146TL, 18/145CR, 18/146BR.

Courtesy **Massachusetts Department of Commerce and Development, Division of Tourism:** 5/329CR, 13/208TL, 13/210TL.

Bill Mauldin and Wil–Jo Associates, Inc. © 1944: *(Reprinted by permission.)* 4/177BL.

Courtesy **Memorial Sloan Kettering Cancer Center:** *Photo* 10/257BL.

The Memory Shop: 8/88BL.

Memphis/Milano s.r.l.: *© Ettore Sottsass, photo courtesy of Daniel Saxon* 11/155BR(C).

Fotostudio Vincent Mentzel: 19/240BR.

The Metropolitan Museum of Art: 2/175TL, 9/204TL, 10/345CR, 18/246T, 18/247TR; *Gift of H. L. Bache Foundation, 1969* 9/229CL; *Gift of Lyman G. Bloomingdale, 1901* 11/159TR; *Gift of George Blumenthal, 1941* 9/148BR, 10/210TL; *Harris Brisbane* 20/168TR; *Carnarvon Collection, Gift of Edward S. Harkness, 1926* 9/203TL; *The Cloisters Collection, Purchase, 1962* 9/229BR; *Gift of the Duchesse de Richelieu, 1960* 8/375BR; *Bequest of Joseph H. Durkee, Gift of Darius Ogden Mills and Gift of C. Ruxton Love by Exchange, 1972* 15/407TL; *Friends of the American Wing Fund, 1965* 2/67CR; *Gift of H. O. Havemeyer, 1896* 2/66C; *Purchase, Edgar Kaufmann, Jr., Gift, 1972* 9/230TR; *Kennedy Fund, 1918* 5/111TR; *Gift of Katharine Keyes in Memory of Her Father, Homer Eaton Keyes, 1938* 8/196TL; *The Robert Lehman Collection* 8/376TL; *The Robert Lehman Collection, 1975* 15/470TR; *From the McKean Collection, on extended loan to the Metropolitan Museum of Art, Courtesy of the Morse Gallery of Art, Winter Park, Florida* 18/212TR; *Fund of Edward C. Moore, 1935* 9/204CR; *Gift of J. Pierpont Morgan, 1900* 5/127TR, 19/436TL; *Gift of Junius S. Morgan, 1919* 3/387TL; *The Michael C. Rockefeller Memorial Collection of Primitive Art, Bequest of Nelson A. Rockefeller, 1979* 11/134TL, 13/197. *Rogers Fund* 9/292BL; *Rogers Fund, 1904* 2/175TR; *Rogers Fund, 1911* 15/469BL, 15/470BL; *Rogers Fund, 1912* 8/373BR; *Rogers Fund, 1928* 5/111BR; *Rogers Fund, 1941* 8/377TR; *Gift of Mrs. Russell Sage, 1910* 1/354TR; *Bequest of Mrs. Alexandrine Sinsheimer, 1959* 13/76TR; *Steichen Collection* 15/269TL; *Gift of Mr. and Mrs. Carl Stoeckel, 1897* 3/515BL; *Gift of R. Thornton Wilson, 1942* 15/472CL; *Gift of Robert E. Tod, 1937* 15/468BR; *Gift of Irwin Untermeyer, 1968* 9/230TC; *Lila Acheson Wallace Gift Fund, 1968* 10/345TR; *Bequest of Catherine D. Wentworth, 1948* 12/159BR.

Metropolitan Opera Association: 13/348BR, 13/350BR.

Meudon Observatory: 18/345TL.

Photo Dr. Ernst Meyer from Schliemann Driefwechsez *(courtesy Aldus Books)*: 2/122TL.

Susan E. Meyer: 15/569TL.

Michigan State University: 8/339TL.

State of Michigan Travel Bureau: 13/379, 13/380, 13/381.

© Lawrence Migdale: 5/160cTL.

Miller Services, Toronto: *© E. Otto* 13/121TL, 14/392BL; *R. Vroom* 13/121BL.

Milwaukee Public Museum: 11/140BL.

Ministry of Defense, London *(courtesy Aldus Books)*: *Naval Department* 14/64CL.

Minkus Co., Inc.: 15/230BR.

The Mitchell Library/Sydney, Australia *(courtesy Aldus Books)*: 2/339BR.

Monkmeyer Press Photo Service: *Douglas Mazonowicz* 15/507CL.

Courtesy **Montana Department of Travel and Commerce:** 13/552CL.

Montana Historical Society: 16/350BL.

Courtesy **Montana Travel Promotion Unit:** 13/550TL, 13/551TL, 13/551BL, 13/551CR.

Morristown National Historical Park: 1/360TL.

Courtesy **Mosaic Software:** 5/164BR.

The Mount Everest Foundation *(courtesy Aldus Books)*: 13/621TR.

David Muench: 14/37TL, 14/37CL, 14/37C.

Josef Muench: 4/75BL, 13/313BL, 13/315BL, 15/204BR, 15/613BR.

Courtesy **MMT Observatory:** 19/83TL.

Municipal Library, Bergamo *(courtesy Aldus Books)***:** 13/663CL.

Museum of the City of New York: 1/349TR, 16/222BR, 19/451BR, 19/454TL.

Musea di Arte Antica, Lisbon *(courtesy Aldus Books)***:** 15/454BL.

Musée Carnavalet, Paris *(courtesy Aldus Books)***:** 16/181BL.

Musée Condé, Chantilly *(courtesy Aldus Books)***:** 5/238BR.

Musée Guimet *(courtesy Aldus Books)***:** 13/699TR.

Musée d'Histoire de Berne, Propriéte de la Foundation Gottfried Keller *(courtesy Aldus Books)***:** 16/355T.

Musée du Seminaire de Quebec *(courtesy Aldus Books)***:** 11/130CR.

Musée National du Bardo, Tunisia *(courtesy Aldus Books)***:** 20/374BL.

Museo Historico Regional de Cuzco/ Calle Heirderos, Peru *(courtesy Aldus Books)***:** 11/70BR.

Museo Nacional de Historia, Madrid *(courtesy Aldus Books)***:** 11/134TR.

Museum für Volkerkunde, Vienna *(courtesy Aldus Books)***:** 11/121BR.

Courtesy **Museum of Fine Arts, Boston:** *Deposited by the City of Boston* 1/97BR; *Bequest of Horatio G. Curtis* 2/197BL; *Fenollosa-Weld Collection* 11/368T; *Bequest of Maxim Karolik* 8/198BR; *Gift of Joseph W., William B., and Edward H. R. Revere* 1/332TL, 16/186TL; 2/66CR, 2/252TL, 2/252CR, 7/205TR, 9/203BC, 11/368T, 14/382CL, 15/500TL, 19/444CL.

Museum of Fine Arts, Seoul: 12/118TL.

Courtesy **Museum of the American Indian Heye Foundation:** 11/72TR, 11/140TL, 14/238CL, 14/238C.

Courtesy **The Museum of Modern Art, New York:** *Film Stills Archive* 3/565CL, 8/82TL, 8/83CR, 8/84CR; *Gift of Mme Hector Guimard* 8/378CR; *Gift of Abby Aldrich Rockefeller* 14/275CL; *Presented in memory of Curt Valentin by his friends* 2/200BR; 1/328CL, 2/136CR, 2/202BL, 3/129CR, 13/491TL, 13/491TR, 15/267BL.

NAACP: 16/83BL.

Nakash, Montreal: 4/93BL.

NASA: *JPL* 13/167TR, 13/167TL, 13/168TL, 13/168BL, 13/168BR, 13/562TL, 13/563TR, 13/563TL, 13/563BR, 18/49BL, 18/50CL, 18/51CR, 18/124CL, 19/478BL, 19/478BR; 1/270, 2/821TL, 2/82CL, 2/82BL, 2/82CR, 2/82BR, 2/83BL, 2/84CL, 2/179BR, 2/274TL, 2/282BL, 2/298T, 5/104CL, 5/134R, 7/11BR, 9/72BR, 9/103BL, 9/207TR, 11/472BL, 11/472BR, 11/473TL, 12/184BL, 12/185TC, 12/185TR, 13/305L, 13/305R, 13/307TR, 13/562B, 14/28T, 14/28B, 14/312BR, 14/315BL, 15/272CR, 16/40R, 16/128BL, 16/129BR, 17/86B, 17/88CR, 17/89TL, 17/89TR, 17/91, 17/318, 17/348TL, 18/49TL, 18/49CL, 18/49C, 18/49CR, 18/50C, 18/50CR, 18/51TR, 18/120TR, 18/121BR, 18/124BR, 18/124BL, 18/124CL, 18/125BR, 18/126BL, 18/127TL, 18/128CL, 18/128BR, 18/129TR, 18/130TL, 18/130BL, 18/133BR, 18/134BL, 18/134BR, 18/135TBR, 18/136BR, 18/137BL, 18/139BL, 18/343TL, 18/343TR, 18/343B, 19/383TL, 19/458BL, 19/547R, 20/135CL, 20/173TR, 20/294, 20/321CR.

Nassau/Mauritshuis: 11/23, 20/158.

National Archives: *Navy Department* 20/261BR, 20/266BR; *U.S. Signal Corps* 17/330TR, 20/240BR, 20/242BR, 20/248BR, 20/264TR; *U.S. War Department General Staff* 20/223TR; 3/252TL, 5/373TL, 11/129CR, 18/119CR, 19/389CL.

National Army Museum, London: 1/355BR.

National Art Gallery, Wellington: 13/128.

National Galerie, E. Berlin: 10/195, 10/301BL.

National Gallery, London: 2/196B, 2/197BR, 2/199TR, 2/205TL, 2/205TR, 2/206TL, 2/206TR, 13/200BL, 13/405BL, 15/358TL.

National Gallery of Art, Washington, D.C.: *Gift of Mrs. Robert Homans, 1954* 1/93B; *Widener Collection, 1942* 8/376BR, 8/377TL, 8/377CL.

The National Gallery of Canada: 4/81BR, 4/88CL, 4/88BR, 4/89TL, 4/89CL, 4/89CR, 4/90TL, 4/90BR, 11/126BR.

National Gallery of Ireland: 11/263TR, 11/267BL, 11/267BC, 11/267BR.

© **National Geographic Society:** *Jules B. Billard* 14/239CL; *George F. Mobley* 2/125C; *(courtesy of Clark University) photograph by B. Anthony Stewart* 16/253TL; *(courtesy of the U.S. Capitol Historical Society)* 5/184, 17/185, 17/186

Photo **National Institute of Mental Health:** 15/600TL.

National Institute of Oceanography/ Wormley, Surrey, England *(courtesy Aldus Books)***:** 14/340TR.

National Library of Australia *(courtesy Aldus Books)***:** Rex Nan Kivell Collection 2/339BL, 14/162TL.

National Library of Medicine: 18/361BR.

Trustees of the National Library of Scotland: 15/266BR.

National Maritime Museum, London: 3/211CR, 10/148TL, 14/62BL.

National Museum of Copenhagen: *Lennart Larsen, National Museet* 19/227BL.

National Museum of Copenhagen *(courtesy Aldus Books)***:** 16/353TR.

National Museum, Iceland *(courtesy Aldus Books)***:** 13/702BL.

National Museum of Ireland *(courtesy Aldus Books)***:** 15/113TR.

National Museum of Korea: 12/117BR.

The National Museum of Wales: 19/172R.

National Oceanic and Atmospheric Administration: 13/344BR, 13/345TL.

Collection **National Palace Museum/Taipei, Taiwan** *(courtesy Aldus Books)***:** 2/254CL.

National Portrait Gallery, London: 1/100TR, 2/185BL, 2/326, 3/204, 3/213B, 3/411CR, 3/504, 3/518CL, 3/518CR, 3/565TR, 3/578BL, 3/603BL, 4/152TR, 4/292TL, 4/304CL, 5/100BR, 5/188CL, 5/322CL, 6/42, 6/83TL, 6/156BR, 6/253BL, 6/284BR, 7/141TR, 7/144CL, 7/194TL, 7/195TL, 7/195TR, 7/196TL, 7/196TC, 7/196TR, 7/197TL, 7/197TC, 7/198TL, 7/198TC, 7/198TR, 7/199TL, 7/199BC, 7/199BR, 7/200TR, 7/201TL, 7/201TC, 7/201TR, 7/201BL, 8/22, 8/235, 8/282BR, 9/54BR, 9/172BR, 9/196B, 9/236BL, 9/307CL, 10/84TR, 10/192, 10/231C, 11/353, 11/356TL, 11/398, 11/445BR, 12/86, 12/174TR, 12/249TR, 13/186, 13/233TL, 13/311TL, 13/344, 13/433TR, 13/434CR, 15/157BR, 15/376TR, 15/430TR, 15/467BR, 16/79CL, 16/212BR, 17/253TL, 17/257BL, 17/355BL, 17/374BL, 18/265BL, 18/287BR, 18/393CL, 20/68, 20/105, 20/148CR, 20/217TL.

National Portrait Gallery, Washington, D.C.: *Balling* 2/218CR.

The National Theatre Society: *G. A. Duncan* 1/52.

National Weather Service: 13/344TL.

Natural History Photographic Agency: *N. A. Callow* 15/411BR.

Naval Photographic Center: 19/455TL, 20/259BR, 20/266BL, 20/279TR.

NBC: 16/56BL, 16/58TL.

NBC Photo: © *Alan Singer* 19/87TR.

Courtesy **Nebraska Department of Economic Development:** 14/71TL.

Nebraska State Historical Society: *Solomon D. Butcher Collection* 8/343BR.

Nederlandsche Dok en Scheepshouw Mij. v.o.f.: 7/278BR.

Nelson Gallery–Atkins Museum/Kansas City, Missouri: *Gift of Mrs. George H. Bunting, Jr.* 11/377CR; *Nelson Fund* 2/251BR, 4/381TR, 4/384BL, 4/385TR, 8/374TR, 8/374CR, 11/29B, 11/295TR, 11/377CR.

New York Academy of Medicine: 18/360TR.

New York City Ballet: *Edward Gorey* 3/44CR.

New York Historical Society: 1/364T, 19/570TL.

The New York Public Library Astor, Lenox, and Tilden Foundations: *The I. N. Phelps Stokes Collection of American Historical Prints* 19/436TR, 19/440TL; *the library at Lincoln Center* 2/155BR, 6/261BR; *Prints Division* 19/436BL, 19/439TR, 19/451BL; *Rare Book Division* 9/158TR, 11/120BR, 11/280TL, 13/354BL, 15/312BR, 19/438BL; *Schomberg Center of Research in Black Culture* 11/432CR; 3/218CL, 3/307BR, 8/342BL, 8/344BL, 14/273BR, 14/273TR, 14/400BC, 15/9BL, 16/38TL, 16/185TR, 16/370BL, 17/354TR, 18/196TR.

The New York Public Library Astor, Lenox, and Tilden Foundations *(courtesy Aldus Books)***:** 14/63BL.

New York Review of Books: *Drawing by David Levine. Reprinted with permission from the New York Review of Books, © 1969 NY Review, Inc.* 4/150C.

New York Service/ABC–Press: 12/221R.

Courtesy **New York State Department of Commerce:** 14/151TR, 14/152BL, 14/152BR.

Peter Newark's Historical Pictures: 3/524CL.

Marvin E. Newman: 14/385TL, 14/385TR.

Lennart Nilsson: 7/153E.

Nord Jyllands Kunst Museum, Aalborg: 17/113BR.

Nordiska Museum, Stockholm: 8/195.

Dorothy Norman Collection: 15/257TR, 18/268CR.

Courtesy **North Carolina Department of Travel and Tourism:** *Clay Nolan* 14/243TL, 14/244TL, 14/245BL.

Courtesy **North Dakota Travel Division:** *Ken Jorgensen* 14/250TL.

Northern Natural Gas Co. Collection, Joslyn Art Museum/Omaha, Nebraska: 13/624CL.

Courtesy **Nova Scotia Communication and Information Center:** 14/277TL.

Novosti Press: 5/147BL, 7/279BL, 15/631B, 18/201TR, 19/397T.

Novosti from Sovfoto: 18/130BL.

Courtesy **NRAO/AUI:** 5/160fBL, 9/12BL.

Ny Carlsberg Glyptotek, Copenhagen: 12/273TL.

NY Times: *Bill Aller* 14/171TR.

NYT Pictures: *Robert M. Klein* 16/142TR.

Courtesy **Oklahoma Tourism and Recreation Department:** 14/367TR, 14/369TL, 14/369CR, 14/370TR, 14/370BL.

Olympia Museum, Greece: 2/193BL.

Oriental Institute, University of Chicago: 5/389BL, 13/319B.

Orion Press: *Yuzo Yamada* 6/27TR; 15/412BR.

Osterreichische Nationalbibliothek: 9/131T, 14/161B, 16/24TR.

Fotostudio Otto: 12/106.

Pakistan Council: 11/154TR.

The Palestine Archaeological Museum *(courtesy Aldus Books)*: 3/242BL.

Courtesy **Panama Canal Commission:** 15/57BL.

© 1985 **Paramount Pictures Corporation.** All rights reserved: 5/160mBR.

© **1974 Ann Parker:** 8/196TR, 19/232TL.

PBS: 16/58TR.

Peabody Museum, Harvard University: *Hillel Burger* 15/497CL.

Peabody Museum, Salem: 13/267TR.

© **Kira Perov:** 19/576gBL.

Peruvian Embassy: 2/125BR.

Paul C. Pet: 2/24B, 2/67B, 6/92, 4/45T, 4/244BR, 5/408BR, 5/408TR, 5/414TL, 6/129TR, 7/270TR, 7/270CR, 7/271BL, 7/271CL, 8/124TL, 8/170T, 9/170, 9/328TL, 9/329T, 10/223T, 11/134B, 11/148TL, 11/149L, 11/149R, 15/192BR, 15/194TL, 15/450BL, 16/275CR, 18/395BR, 19/345, 19/543TL.

Peabody Museum of Salem: 2/175TR.

Harry T. Peters Collection: 8/340BR.

Courtesy **The Pennsylvania Academy of the Fine Arts:** 11/107TR.

Philadelphia Museum of Art: *The Louise and Walter Arensberg Collection* 2/201TL; *Foule Collection* 8/375TR; *The George H. Lorimer Collection* 9/203BR; *Given by John T. Morris* 15/152TR; *from the Whitman Sampler Collection* 14/76BL.

PhilBrook Art Centre, Tulsa: 19/447CR.

NV Philips Gloeilampenfabrieken: 18/40BL.

Phonogram International: 3/521.

Photographie Giraudon: 1/115BR, 1/230, 1/276, 2/79, 2/132TL, 2/135BL, 2/199C, 3/43TL, 3/79T, 3/328, 3/384TR, 3/456, 4/27BR, 4/46, 4/48, 4/115, 4/142T, 4/162B, 4/168, 4/193B, 4/208TL, 4/209, 4/210, 4/293CL, 4/294TL, 4/296CR, 4/303, 4/371T, 4/372T, 4/373BL, 4/378T, 4/386T, 4/408CL, 5/134TL, 5/309, 6/25TR, 6/35T, 6/160T, 6/260, 7/80B, 7/82BR, 7/84T, 7/87B, 7/89BTR, 7/159, 7/187BL, 7/227, 7/260BR, 7/280, 7/283T, 7/284TL, 8/38, 8/156, 8/160T, 8/267B, 8/271T, 8/271CR, 8/274TR, 8/286TL, 8/304BR, 8/306T, 8/307TL, 8/320BL, 8/323B, 8/323T, 8/324TL, 8/375CL, 9/40T, 9/40BL, 9/148TL, 9/176, 9/189BL, 9/223BR, 9/257BR, 9/258L, 9/260TR, 9/312BL, 9/356, 10/6, 10/128, 10/320B, 11/180B, 11/288, 11/359, 12/146, 12/245CR, 12/423TL, 12/425TL, 12/427BR, 12/437TR, 13/68, 13/143CL, 13/147BR, 13/276TL, 13/290, 13/319TR, 13/320CL, 13/499, 13/521B, 13/633R, 13/663BR, 13/689BR, 14/16TL, 14/18BR, 14/463, 15/23CL, 15/181, 15/182TR, 15/186T, 15/186B, 15/233TL, 15/250BR, 15/250BL, 15/360, 15/499L, 16/188B, 16/284CR, 17/105L, 17/278, 17/365T, 18/22BL, 18/155BR, 18/247T, 18/253, 19/97, 19/21, 19/147L, 19/385TL, 19/506, 19/552TL, 20/192, 20/362, 20/372T.

Photographie Bulloz: 13/406TL.

Photographie Giraudon: 13/274TL, 13/698TL.

Photographies Jacques Six: 5/305R.

Photography, Inc.: 10/246BL, 12/50TR.

Photojournalist from Pictorial Parade: 12/80BL.

Photo Researchers, Inc.: *Slim Aarons* 1/145TR, 1/309TR, 3/24TL, 13/420TL, 18/82TR, 18/143BR; *Jim Amos* 5/118BR, 13/189TL; *Christa Armstrong* 3/563TL; *Robert J. Ashworth* 4/10TL; *Frederick Ayer III* 1/101B, 15/636TR; *John J. Bangma* 5/388TR; *David Barnes* 11/150TR, 13/552BR, 14/251TL, 17/53TR, 18/103BL, 20/36BL, 20/38TL; *Linda Bartlett* 2/117TL, 19/609TL, 20/113CR, 20/312BR; *Lee E. Battaglia* 13/598TL; *Rona Beame* 17/220BR; *Mehmet Beber* 13/258CR; *Charles Belinky* 3/227CL, 4/22TL, 12/22TR, 13/78BR, 13/373BL, 14/150TL, 14/319BL, 15/637TR; *Bill Belknap* 2/117BR, 14/112TL; *James Bell* 1/281TR; *Edna Bennett* 18/294TR; *Andy Bernaut* 2/347TL; *Mehmet Biber* 11/289; *Betsy Blass* 2/168TL, 2/169TR, 2/169BR; *Björn Bölstad* 2/163BL, 4/72TL, 4/72TR, 7/53TR, 8/186TCR, 8/186BCR, 13/382CR, 13/473CR, 13/479TR, 14/249CR, 18/161CR, 19/610BR; *Robert Borneman* 19/610TR; *E. Boubat* 15/136TL; *Mark Boulton* 11/449CL; *Brian Brake* 1/91TL, 2/246BL, 4/361TR, 4/365BR, 5/8TR, 11/86TL, 11/364BL, 13/546TL; *B. Brandu* 19/372BR; *Ken Brate* 5/118TL, 5/181TL; *Richard Brooks* 11/29TR; *Leland Brun* 1/257BR, 3/492TR; *Jules Bucher* 1/194TR, 17/321T, 19/581TR, *Van Bucher* 1/130TL, 1/236TR, 1/237TL, 1/238TL, 1/329BR, 2/88BL, 2/137CL, 3/36TL, 3/146CR, 3/365TL 3/395TL, 3/431BR, 3/481TL, 3/529BL, 3/572BR, 4/20TL, 4/32CL, 4/35TL, 5/194TL, 6/90TR, 7/316TL, 8/173TL, 9/115BL, 9/346TL, 10/73CR, 10/75BL, 10/277TR, 10/278CR, 11/112TL, 11/113TR, 11/113CR, 11/114TL, 12/20TL, 12/20CR, 13/209TL, 13/356TR, 13/482TR, 14/318TL, 14/370TL, 15/148BL, 15/150, 15/151TL, 16/85CL, 16/197BL, 16/199TL, 16/199CR, 17/18TR, 19/104BL, 19/106TR, 19/583TL, 20/40T, 20/110TR; *David Cain* 9/144TR; *California Academy of Sciences* 19/197BL; *Robert Caputo* 18/322BL; *R.L. Carlton* 19/582TL; *William Carter* 11/113BL, 13/381TR; *Dhiraj Chawda* 6/26BL; *Dennis J. Cipnik* 12/434TL, 19/543CR; *Jerry Cooke* 3/254BR, 6/270CR, 14/392CR, 18/89TL; *Steve Coombs* 13/457BL; *Jackie Curtis* 16/200BL; *Arvil A. Daniels* 18/297TR; *Kent & Donna Dannen* 16/263TR; *Dick Davis* 14/110BR, 17/69BL, 18/92BL, 18/140BR; *Kelly Dean* 9/117TR; *M. Desjardins* 6/112TL; *Earl Dibble* 6/27TL, 7/275BC, 14/159TL; © *Townsend P. Dickinson* 14/167BR; *George Dineen* 14/116CR, 16/19TL; *Stephanie Dinkins* 4/187TL, 6/89TR, 6/90TL, 12/148TL; *Michael Dixon* 17/109TR; *S. Duroy* 17/93TL; *Margaret Durrance* 11/25BR, 11/277L; *Horst Ebersberg* 2/348BL; *Ray Ellis* 1/328TL; *Victor Englebert* 1/134C, 1/145TL, 2/24CR, 4/266BL, 5/202BL, 12/432BL; *Engman* 18/384TR; *R. G. Everts* 11/324TR, 19/503BR, 19/504TL; *Mario Fantin* 2/317TL; *Jack Fields* 1/197CL, 1/197CR, 8/25BL, 11/28TL, 14/160TR, 17/321BR, 19/227CL; *Carl Frank* 1/139B, 2/150TL, 3/360BL, 4/179CR, 4/356BL, 5/108BL, 5/292TR, 6/234TL, 13/360BL, 13/586TR, 15/55TR, 15/77BL, 18/90BR, 18/91BR, 18/95TL, 19/23TR, 19/499BL; *Yvonne Freund* 5/119TL; *Howard Friedman* 20/288TR; *Tomas D. W. Friedman* 11/399BL, 12/433CR, 14/151TL, 14/360BR, 15/390TR, 15/488BL, 15/544TR, 20/22TR, 20/32CL; *Bruce Frisch* 3/549BL; *Gordon Gahan* 1/245BR; *Ruth Gallard* 18/322TR; *Michael Geissinger* 14/150CR; *Lowell Georgia* 1/258TR, 10/176TL, 12/340TL, 14/73TL, 14/73TR, 19/227TR; *Joern Gerdts* 5/117TL; *Georg Gerster* 1/324TL, 2/115TL, 2/117CR, 2/120TL, 2/330BL, 3/2BL, 4/34TL, 4/61TL, 5/8TL, 6/10BL, 6/110BL, 6/112BL, 11/254BR, 11/258TR, 11/367TR, 11/422BL, 12/54BR, 13/117BR, 13/207TL, 13/209BR, 13/281TL, 13/281TR, 13/454TL, 14/67CL, 14/72CR, 14/135TR, 14/137BR, 14/139TL, 14/139BL, 14/190BR, 14/358TL, 15/236BR, 17/50BL, 17/58BR, 17/196BR, 18/89BL, 18/284CL, 18/385BL, 19/27BL, 19/405BR, 19/484B, 19/526BL, 19/575BL, 20/337BL, 20/351BL; *Giaubach* 10/75TL, 10/278TR, 13/370CL; *Francois Gohier* 18/90BL, 18/93TL, 18/93BR; *Louis Goldman* 6/288BR, 11/261BL, 14/180CL, 19/75BL; © *Robert Goldstein* 19/378TR; *P. W. Grace* 13/72TL, 17/362CL; *Eric V. Gravé* 1/282TL, 10/330TL; *Alen Green* 2/293TL; *Stephen Green* 3/552BL; *Farrell Grehan* 10/166BL, 11/259BL, 11/309BR, 13/383BR, 14/249TL, 19/348BR; *Dan Guravich* 3/462TL, 13/210TR, 14/229CL; *Ned Haines* 3/480TR; *Dick Hanley* 13/211TL, 14/359TL, 15/146TR; *James Hanley* 4/88BL; *Eunice Harris* 16/159CR; *E.A. Heiniger* 4/317BR, 13/163BR; *Esther Henderson* 1/235B, 12/431TR; *Fritz Henle* 2/30BR, 8/281TR, 16/195BL, 16/296TI, 18/385CR, 19/606TL; *Barry Hennings 20/82BR*; *Chester Higgins, Jr.* 1/56BR; *Inez and George Hollis* 4/35BR, 14/37CR; *Thomas Hollyman* 3/122TR, 10/334TL, 11/17BL, 13/458BR, 13/474TR, 17/54TR, 17/147TL, 20/186TL; *George Holton* 1/161TR, 1/162TL, 1/174BL, 1/174BR, 1/195BR, 1/203TR, 1/291BR, 2/104TL, 2/151CR, 2/151CL, 3/63TR, 3/235BR, 3/574BR, 3/575TL, 4/361TL, 4/368TL, 5/6TL, 5/108BR, 5/183TL, 6/22TL, 7/253BR, 7/275BL, 9/388TR, 10/223BL, 12/228BL, 13/360BR, 13/531BL, 13/598CR, 14/262BR, 15/498CL, 17/240, 18/81BR, 18/89BR, 18/96TL, 19/53BR, 19/155TL, 19/317BL, 19/402T, 19/545TR, 20/339BR; *Anne E. Hubbard* 1/281TL; *Harold Hungerford* 5/118BL; *Robert A. Isaacs* 17/55BR; *Don James* 18/359TR; *Jacques Janqoux* 19/610TL; *Ronny Jaques* 3/563TL, 6/27BR, 11/29BR, 13/456TL, 16/234BR, 20/114TL; *Gordon Johnson* 14/255TR; *Billy Jones* 4/10CL; *Edward Jones* 14/395TL; *Len Jossel* 12/267TL; *A. B. Joyce* 2/343TL, 19/410TL; *M. P. Kahl* 4/214BL; *William Katz* 6/110BR, 11/401TL; *Ian M. Keown* 17/146BR; *Harold S. Kinne* 118CR, 12/265BL; *Russ Kinne* 1/305BL, 1/325CL, 1/368CR, 2/41CR, 2/327TL, 3/17BR, 3/101TR, 3/296All, 3/352CL, 3/352TL, 4/79TL, 4/213TR, 4/270CR, 4/333TL, 4/445BL, 5/82TR, 5/195TR, 5/388TR, 6/151TR, 6/154BL, 7/154TC, 7/154TR, 8/47TR, 9/49BL, 9/49BC, 9/415CR, 10/11TR, 11/28TR, 11/349TR, 11/349CR, 12/346, 12/393CL, 13/259TR, 13/370TR, 13/435BR, 13/481TL, 13/569CL, 14/113TL, 14/113TR, 14/114TL, 14/146BR, 14/380TL, 14/397C, 14/397CR, 15/127TC, 15/133TL, 15/166C, 15/166CR, 15/168, 16/200TL, 16/337C, 16/337CR, 17/51CR, 17/71CL, 17/71C, 18/100TL, 18/100CR, 19/238BC, 19/238BR, 19/244TR, 19/255TR, 19/356TL, 19/356TC, 20/187TL, 20/348CL; *Albert Knaus* 11/8TL; *Paolo Koch* 1/251TL, 1/258CL, 2/235T, 2/240T, 2/242BR, 2/245BL, 2/349TR, 2/352BL, 3/541BL, 4/69BR, 4/75BR, 4/117TR, 4/187CL, 4/244BL, 4/390BR, 6/15BR, 6/18TR, 6/116TL, 7/275CL, 9/216BL, 10/26BL, 11/253BR, 11/362TR, 11/366TL, 11/449TR, 12/128TR, 12/131TL, 12/185BR, 13/337BL, 14/112CR, 14/177BL, 14/454TR, 15/134BL, 15/415TL, 16/323TR, 17/44BL, 18/384TL, 18/414TL, 19/99TL, 19/376BR, 19/400TL, 19/401BR, 20/282BL, 20/333BL; *Ewing Krainin* 1/246BR, 2/150CL, 11/261CR; *Calvin Larsen* 17/51TR; *Ragnar Larusson* 12/240CL; *Jane Latta* 5/7BR, 15/149TL, 15/227CL; *George Leavens* 2/25TR, 14/71TR; *Victor Lefteroff* 3/554BL, 15/87; *Neil Leiferlaiskog* 1/292 BL; *Norman Lightfoot* 14/191CR; *Nilo Lima*

1/385TR; *Fred Lombardi* 13/152BR; *Alexander Lowry* 11/28TL; *Rafael Macia* 20/96BR; *Michael Philip Manheim* 4/77TR, 4/107TR, 13/71TL, 19/555CR; *Helen Marcus* 20/177BR; *Arthur Markowitz* 4/10TR, *Fred J. Maroon* 1/236CL, 4/298TR, 20/292TL; *Marthalux* 3/541BR; *Buddy Mays* 14/37BR; *Susan McCartney* 2/254BC, 15/251BL, 15/389TL, 16/227TL, 19/416T; © *Tom McHugh* 1/282CR, 1/311BL, 1/329CL, 4/36TL, 4/76CR, 4/17CL, 5/7BL, 9/415BR, 10/278TL, 12/342TR, 12/416BL, 14/72TL, 14/441BR, 15/127TL, 17/372CR; *Will McIntyre* 14/243BR; *Lynn McLaren* 3/408BR, 13/207TR; *Frank J. Miller* 1/122TL, 18/97BR; *Peter Miller* 19/555TL; *Albert Moldvay* 2/41CL, 13/38BL; *Jan Moline* 2/137TL; *Y. Momatiuk* 6/70CL; *Don Morgan* 3/408BL, 4/90TR; *Hank Morgan* 3/262TR, 18/5TR; *John Moss* 2/717R, 3/138TL; *Edgar Muench* 13/448CR; *Larry Mulvehill* 18/276BL; *Joe Munroe* 1/194BL, 1/195BL, 2/24CL, 2/25TL, 3/492TL, 4/77TL, 4/215BL, 6/17TR, 14/138TL, 14/139BR, 19/527BL, 20/187BL, 20/187BR; *Hans Namuth* 1/81BL, 1/164T, 18/83TL, *John V. A. F. Neal* 3/549BR, 13/552TR, 14/428CR; *Ernst A. Neber* 19/414CR; *John Neel* 1/182BR; *M. E. Neiman* 3/490TL; *Carol Niffenegger* 13/380T; *Anthony A. Nobile* 19/556TR; *Boyd Norton* 12/344CR; *Irvin L. Oakes* 14/359BR; *Sven-Ohndglad* 19/28TL; *Mathias Oppersdorff* 11/95TR; *Charlie Ott* 2/325BL, 4/10TC, 14/138TR; *Dan Page* 9/411TL; *Richard B. Peacock* 14/124TL; *C. A. Peterson* 4/24BR; *J. Pfaff* 5/105TR; *Sam C. Pierson, Jr.* 4/317BL; *Monroe Pinckard* 10/73BL; *David Plowden* 13/458BL; *Porterfield-Chickering* 1/291BL, 2/204BR, 4/33TL, 6/17BR, 9/162TR, 11/326TL, 13/449TR; 13/480BL, 13/519TL, 13/73TL, 13/361BL, 13/361BR, 14/125BL, 14/137TL, 18/143BL, 18/396BL, 19/545TR, 20/37TR; *Steven Proehl* 10/278CL, 14/147TL; *Carl Purcell* 2/337TR, 9/308CR, 12/115TL, 19/349BR, 19/413BL; *Renee Purse* 2/189TR; *Joseph Quinn* 1/244TL; *Belinda Rain* 14/428TL; *Rapho Division* 11/305TR, 19/557TR; *Diane Rawson* 2/5TR, 2/104TR, 7/75BL, 11/85TL, 12/26CL, 12/113BL, 13/95TL, 15/26BL; *C. Ray* 8/103BL; *Louis Renault* 12/433TL; Earl Roberge 14/429TL, 20/37BL; *Bruce Roberts* 14/244BL, 14/245TL, 14/299CL, 14/360TL; *G. R. Roberts* 2/337BR, 14/394BL, 17/80CR; *Carl Roodman* 15/104TR; *John G. Ross* 15/635TL, 15/635TR; *Dick Rowan* 14/251BL, 19/251TL; *Leonard Lee Rue III* 1/282CI; *Lucille Nix Rybakov* 2/242BL; *Joe Rychetnik* 1/121BL, 1/244BR, 1/246BL, 18/368TR; *Aldona Sabalis* 1/152B; *Kjell B. Sandved* 4/10CR; *Larry Schiller* 3/431BL; *Herman Schlenker* 3/115BL; *Ben Schneider* 5/118TR; *Abram G. Schoenfeld* 14/152CR; *Carl Schofield* 3/11CL; *Hanna W. Schreiber* 14/152TL; *F. & H. Schreider* 2/103TL; *Earl Scott* 20/277TL; *M. Serraillier* 12/206TL, 17/339TL, 19/499TR; *Bernard Silberstein* 14/157L; © *H. W. Silvester* 9/41CL; *W. Silvester* 3/367BR; *J. R. Simon* 20/292BL; *Ray Simons* 12/143CL, 16/203CL; *Bradley Smith* 4/34TR, 11/27CR, 12/431BR, 20/275BL; *Don Carl Stefan* 19/377TR; *Lisl Steiner* 2/150CR; *James Sugar* 11/262BR; *Eileen Tanson* 1/282TC; *Thomas R. Taylor* 20/284BL; *Bruce M. Thomas* 2/336TL; *Davis Thomas* 19/395T; *George E. Thompson* 9/116TR; *Cyril Toker* 1/145TR; *G. Tomsich* 2/74TR, 2/384BR, 9/327CR, 14/396TR, 16/13BR; *Audrey Topping*12/141BL; *Gianni Tortoli* 1/239BR, 4/130CR, 9/93TR, 13/689BL, 15/164CL, 15/166, 15/389TR, 19/340BR, 19/543TR, 20/36CR; *Arthur Tress* 8/364CR, 13/448BR; *Arthur C. Twomey* 1/255BR, 15/148BR; *John Veltri* 2/329TR, 2/119TL, 2/291TR; *John Verde* 9/141BL; *C. Vergara*17/47L, 17/349BR; *Walker* 1/282TR; *A. Wamble* 8/46BL; *M. E. Warren* 2/31CR; *Stan Wayman* 1/324TL; *Ernsz A. Weber* 3/215CL; *Sabine Weiss* 13/164TL, 19/340CL; *George Whitely* 1/381TL, 3/131TL, 4/401BL, 4/434CR, 5/279BL, 8/46TR, 8/188CL, 10/117TR, 12/205TL, 13/204BR, 16/376CR, 18/186TR, 18/267TR, 19/15CR; *M. B. Winter* 13/144BL, 13/373TL; *Bernard Pierre Wolfe* 2/246TL, 3/65TR, 3/65CL, 3/65CR, 3/123BR, 3/182BR, 3/368BL, 3/541TR, 6/3BL, 8/168BL, 9/142TL, 10/308T, 13/164TR, 19/224CL; *Hamilton Wright* 7/85TL; *Colin Wyatt* 4/69BL; *Robert Zentmaier* 15/149CR; *D. Zirinsky* 9/284BR.

Photo Trends: *Waring Abbott* 6/239TL; *Jane Bown* 3/151BR; *Michael Childers* 3/436BL; *CP/GS* 12/134BR, *Colin Davey* 6/210CR; *Diego Goldberg* 3/399TL; *Ted Lau* 18/25BL; *Gianfranco Mantegna* 9/185TL; *Terry O'Neill* 14/170CR; *Friedrich Rauch* 6/307BL; *Syndication International Ltd.* 9/414TL; 2/231TR, 2/318TL, 4/26BR.

Photo T.O.V. Reportage/Handen, Sweden *(courtesy Aldus Books)*: 15/272CL.

Phototake: © *Mitch Kezar* 5/160kBR.

Photri: *ILA* 3/200TR; *Dr. George Meese* 2/136TR; *Jack Novak* 14/62CR; 1/127C, 1/318TL, 1/318CL, 1/318CR, 1/318BL, 1/318BR, 1/328TR, 10/256BL.

© **Jim Pickerell:** 5/160kTR.

Pictorial Parade, Inc.: © *1983 Fotos International* 8/89TR; 10/197CR, 10/240BL, 10/284TL, 12/382BR, 13/130BR, 13/661CR, 14/97R, 14/448CR, 15/137TR.

Picture Archive: 4/443TR.

Picture Group: © *Kevin Horan* 19/576cTR.

Picturepoint–London: 1/147B, 2/114T, 2/136TL, 3/442BL, 3/495TL, 3/495TR, 3/497TR, 6/234B, 6/318TL, 7/178BR, 7/180TL, 8/265TR, 9/90BL, 9/144B, 9/165CR, 9/262, 9/315TL, 9/327T, 9/389CR, 10/172B, 10/310TL, 10/336BL, 11/72TL, 11/84TL, 11/427, 12/248CR, 12/266, 14/334BR, 15/451TL, 16/16B, 16/126TR, 17/22, 17/29, 17/49B, 18/245TL, 19/407TR, 19/407TL, 19/408BL, 19/410CR, 20/10B, 20/125BR, 20/298BL.

Pierpont Morgan Library: 12/317/BL, 12/317CL, 17/108BL.

Pitkin Publications: 11/279BL.

Pitt Rivers Museum/Oxford, England *(courtesy Aldus Books)*: 11/27BL.

© **Max-Planck-Institut für Aeronomie:** 10/23BL.

Poclain Nederland bv.: 7/23CC.

Polaroid Corporation: 4/58T.

Polyvisie bv: 4/374TR, 15/116, 19/177.

Popperfoto: *Paul Popper* 1/102, 1/376, 2/44TL, 4/376B, 5/313C, 5/378TR, 7/69T, 8/206B, 9/365B, 15/292CR; 9/245TL.

Port Authority of New York and New Jersey: 1/223T, 14/132TR.

Prado Museum: 2/198TL, 2/199BR.

Courtesy **Pratt & Whitney Aircraft:** 11/406BR.

Tom Prescott: 7/241CR, 11/139TL.

Agence De Presse Photografique Rapho: *Belzeaux* 15/599B; *Gazuit* 16/42CL, 16/42CR; *Monty* 20/325BL.

Sem Presser: 1/59, 2/242TC, 2/255B, 2/256TR, 2/278BL, 2/281C, 2/330BR, 2/339C, 3/178TR, 3/207, 3/495, 3/541TL, 4/43C, 4/204T, 5/277TR, 6/111, 6/157, 6/314, 7/57, 7/254, 7/270BTR, 7/271T, 7/290B, 7/291TR, 7/293BL, 8/107B, 8/262C, 8/265B, 8/266L, 8/268T, 8/269TL, 8/275TL, 9/30, 9/260TL, 9/293TR, 9/311, 9/342, 10/171T, 10/189B, 10/295, 10/309, 11/184, 11/291BL, 11/291BR, 11/324B, 11/461BR, 11/462T, 12/218TL, 12/220B, 12/325B, 12/439T, 12/439B, 13/276, 13/282T, 13/467, 13/508, 13/521B, 13/586B, 13/587, 13/599, 14/4, 14/17C, 14/262BL, 14/465BR, 15/60, 15/73B, 15/86T, 15/92, 15/20, 15/311, 15/451B, 15/451TR, 15/483BR, 15/509BR, 15/587, 16/96, 16/138TR, 16/139, 16/158T, 16/264CL, 16/289T, 16/296TR, 16/323TR, 17/14B, 17/57TL, 17/57CL, 17/113B, 17/127L, 17/144T, 17/302, 18/335, 19/96CL, 19/204, 19/325, 19/406B, 19/582C, 20/174, 20/240BL.

Courtesy **Princeton University:** 14/130TR.

Princeton University Art Museum: 4/380BR.

Princeton University Plasma Physics Laboratory: 8/382CR.

Private Collection *(courtesy Aldus Books)*: 16/302TR.

Professional Picture Service: 8/83BR, 8/84TR, 12/246CL, 12/315BL, 14/468TC, 14/468C, 15/266TR, 15/268CL, 15/270B, 17/354TR, 18/196CR.

Prothmann Associates: 2/125CL.

Public Archives of Canada: *C698* 19/175CL; *C5961* 12/146TR; 3/35TR, 4/80CR, 4/82BL, 4/85TL, 4/85TR, 4/86TL, 4/87TL.

Mauro Pucciarelli: 13/268TR.

Michael Putland/© Retna Ltd.: 1/352T.

Bob Raiche: 14/126TL.

Rainbow: © *Dan McCoy* 5/160bBR, 10/258T.

Steye Raviez: 9/297.

RCA: 16/45BL, 16/54BR, 19/576aBR.

© **Stan Reis:** 12/179BR.

Remington Art Museum/Ogdensburg, New York: *U.S.A. All rights reserved* 18/151BL.

Revija: 20/342C.

Rijksmuseum van de Geschiedenis van de Natuurwetenschappen: 3/434.

Rijksmuseum van Oudheden te Leiden: 19/524.

Rijksuniversiteit Groningen/Sterrenkundig Laboratorium "Kapteyn": 16/49BR.

Rijksvoorlichtingsdienst: 12/443L.

Jan Rijsterborgh: 7/270BL.

Courtesy **Ring Magazine:** 3/432TCL, 6/105BL, 12/422CL.

Rizzoli Press: 17/95B.

Abby Aldrich Rockefeller Folk Art Collection, Williamsburg: 8/197BL, 8/197BR, 19/437BR.

Rockwell International Space Division: 17/87BL, 18/138TR.

Roizen: © *Donna Foster* 19/89TR, 19/89BR, 19/576aCR, 19/576oTL, 19/576oBR, 19/576pTL.

ROLOC, Washington, D.C.: 10/16TL, 11/43TL, 11/44TR.

Ronan Picture Library: 2/280TL, 5/239CR.

Courtesy **Roosevelt Raceway:** 10/248BL.

Rosenthal AG: 12/77.

John G. Ross: 9/229TL, 13/695B.

Frits J. Rotgans: 3/380BR.

Royal Aircraft Establishment, Farnborough *(courtesy Aldus Books)*: 15/272TR.

Royal Artillery Institution: *Photo Michael Holford © Aldus Books*: 16/252TR.

Royal Doulton Ltd. *(courtesy Aldus Books)*: 4/259TL, 9/206BL.

The Royal Institution, London: 15/284TR.

The Royal Library, Copenhagen *(courtesy Aldus Books)*: 1/190BL, 11/71B.

Royal Museum of Copenhagen: 15/468TR.

Courtesy **The Royal Ontario Museum/Toronto, Canada:** 4/88CR, 11/122BL, 11/126TR, 11/127BR.

Royal Photographic Society: 4/59BR.

Carl Ruff Associates: 8/379CR.

Saint-Gobain, France: *Photo Belzeauz Rapho (courtesy Aldus Books)* 9/198BL.

St. Francis Cabrini Chapel, NY: 4/8TL.

Courtesy **Saint John's University Office of Public Information:** 3/475BL.

Sandak, Inc.: 8/302TR.

Sassoon Library/Letchworth, England *(courtesy Aldus Books)***:** 11/461TL.

©Scala/Art Resources: 12/400TR, 19/146BL, 19/147TL.

Scala/Editorial Photo Color Archives: 1/259CL, 4/197TR, 5/208TR, 2/281BR, 6/22BL, 20/202TL.

Scala, Florence: *Howard Jensen* 19/448B; *Joseph Martin* 1/65L, 1/65R, 1/163L, 3/411TL, 6/60, 12/218R, 12/223C, 12/238R, 13/531BR, 15/545, 16/322, 17/258; 1/82, 1/117TL, 1/117TR, 1/137, 1/143B, 1/260, 1/273R, 2/58, 2/94R, 2/157, 2/198B, 2/203, 2/256L, 2/279R, 2/320, 2/322, 2/333M, 2/335T, 3/72BR, 3/89BR, 3/90M, 3/197, 3/222L, 3/222R, 3/354R, 3/418, 3/438R, 3/509, 3/520R, 3/605R, 3/606L, 3/606R, 3/607, 4/13, 4/79R, 4/167, 4/206TL, 4/226T, 4/239BR, 4/263B, 4/268, 4/291, 4/325L, 4/352, 4/366R, 4/373BR, 4/387BR, 4/390L, 4/397, 5/137C, 5/137L, 5/137R, 5/180, 5/198T, 5/198B, 5/255, 5/275, 5/278B, 5/329L, 5/381BR, 6/46, 6/83R, 6/230BL, 6/257, 7/138, 7/161R, 7/183TR, 7/218, 7/260BL, 7/262, 7/281BR, 7/347R, 8/45L, 8/206L, 8/276, 8/291, 8/304TR, 8/307CL, 9/125TL, 9/187, 9/223T, 9/257BL, 9/258L, 9/259BR, 9/331, 9/335TR, 9/340BR, 9/340TL, 9/340CB, 9/343, 10/50, 10/174, 10/213, 11/21, 11/23B, 11/33, 11/89TR, 11/96TL, 11/97L, 11/183, 11/185, 11/237, 11/314TL, 11/318BL, 11/327R, 11/329, 11/403, 11/404L, 11/405R, 12/172L, 12/217R, 12/218R, 12/223CL, 12/238R, 12/338BR, 12/244R, 12/316TL, 12/426, 13/139T, 13/223CR, 13/531BR, 13/556, 13/639BR, 13/663BL, 13/664CR, 14/11TR, 14/267CR, 14/465BL, 15,19L, 15/86CR, 15/316, 15/423R, 16/244CR, 16/275BC, 16/276R, 16/298, 16/301, 16/322, 17/101L, 17/147, 17/152T, 17/258, 17/323, 18/231L, 18/410, 19/144TL, 19/184L, 19/230BR, 19/231, 19/448B, 19/597.

Scala, New York/Florence: 2/131TL, 2/132BL, 2/135CL, 3/90TL, 10/137BR, 10/210BR, 11/315BR, 13/665CR, 16/150BR, 18/67BL.

Scheller Co.: 14/130TL.

Kees Scherer: 2/241BL, 2/243TL, 3/539, 14/5R, 14/98TR, 14/101R.

Scholastic Software: 5/165TR, 5/165BR.

Heinz Schrempp: 8/268TM, 8/368TR.

Peter Schütte: 15/205.

R. T. E. Schüttenhelm: 6/182.

The Science Museum, London: 2/280TR, 5/155L, 5/159R, 6/6R, 8/81TR, 13/225BL, 13/388TI, 14/59TR, 14/59CR, 14/59TL, 14/185T, 19/66CR, 19/68TL, 19/278TR.

John F. Scott: 15/499BR.

Courtesy **Charles Scribner's Sons:** 20/197TR.

Drawing by **Ronald Searle © 1971 The New Yorker Magazine, Inc.:** 15/170TR.

Seattle Art Museum: 4/384TL, 11/376CR.

Sekai Bunka Photo: 11/374B, 13/668CL, 14/207CL, 17/307TL, 17/307CL, 17/307BL.

Service photographique: 8/31BL.

Servizio Editoriale Fotografico: 11/86BL, 11/251TL, 11/322TR, 11/323, 12/285TL, 13/82R, 15/615T, 16/287R, 18/381L, 18/413CR, 19/393L, 19/402R, 20/341CR, 20/343.

Gary S. Settles: 1/123BL.

Scottish National Portrait Gallery: 18/305TL.

Photo Shabtai Tai *(courtesy Aldus Books)* **:** 3/242TR.

© Shepard Sharbell/Picture Group: 19/584TR.

© Shashinka Photo: 15/453BR.

Ronald Sheridan's Photo Library: 18/164BR.

Glenn Shirley Western Collection: 14/468CR.

Shostal Associates, Inc.: 8/77BR, 10/332BL, 11/131B, 11/139TR, 11/140TR, 11/141T, 11/141B, 12/49BR, 13/26, 13/286TL, 13/475TR, 13/481TL, 13/495BR, 13/612BL, 13/615TR, 14/53BL, 14/53BR, 14/189TR, 14/197TL, 14/226CR, 14/226TL, 14/229TR, 15/192BL, 16/288CR, 17/293TL, 17/297BR, 18/206TR, 19/430, 20/354CR, 20/354CL; *Glen Baer* 8/199CL, 20/11TR, 20/353BL; *J. Barnell* 15/127TR; *Mitchell Barosh* 14/333BL; *C. L. Barrow* 14/168TR; *J. A. Brown* 18/208 BR; *Eric Carle* 9/43BR, 10/219TR, 11/246B, 12/20BL, 13/470TR, 13/470CL, 13/478BR, 13/558TR, 14/128TL, 14/233BR, 16/19CR, 16/239T, 17/50CR, 17/349TR, 20/11CL, 20/184BR, 20/375CR; *C. Centineo* 16/142TR; *E. Cooper* 14/229TR, 17/38TR, 17/176BR; *D. Crew* 20/339BR; *D'Arazien* 8/230TR, 14/394CR, 14/429CR; *G. Desteinheil* 18/93BL; *Otto Done* 14/235CL, 18/52CR; *Ron Dorman* 13/472BL, 18/401TL; *R. Glander* 13/292TR, 14/141BL, 14/143BL; *W. Hamilton* 18/9BL; *George Hunter* 14/231BL, 14/395TR; *A. Hyde* 12/472BR; *Karl Kummels* 14/165BR, 14/167BL; *R. Leahey* 8/347TR; *Maiak* 14/102TR. 14/116BR; *E. Manewal* 13/360; *Ray Manley* 11/296BL, 13/471BL, 14/254TR, 18/160BL, 19/140BR; *Charles May* 10/219TL, 12/21BR, 14/335TR; *David Muench* 13/475TR, 17/61BL; *Frederic Olson* 15/127CR, 18/396TL, 20/383BL; *V. Panjabi* 14/120BL; *R. Pauli* 13/477TL; *G. Riccatto* 18/264TR; *P. Salous* 13/270BR, 18/213TR; *C. L. Schmidt* 13/641BL; *Kurt Scholz* 14/349BR, 18/94TL, 18/325TR, *Mike Sheldon* 8/123BR; *E. Streichan* 15/237CR, 18/281BR, 18/321BL, 20/365BR; *August Upitis* 8/347CR, 15/637, 15/195BL, 15/633, 16/239TL; *W. Wright* 14/128CR, 14/131CR.

Courtesy **Robert Siegel:** 15/230TL, 15/230TC, 15/230TR.

J. Simons: 10/171BL, 10/172TL.

Arthur Sirdofsky: 12/230TL.

Skyport Fotos: 5/344TL.

Slidemakers: *John Carnevale* 15/106BR; 3/58TL.

W. Eugene Smith: 20/278BR.

Smithsonian Institution/Washington, D. C.: *Freer Gallery of Art* 4/383BL, 12/160BR, 15/469TR; *National Anthropological Archives, Bureau of American Ethnology Collection* 4/338CR, 10/231TL; *National Collection of Fine Arts* 11/119TL, 11/121TR, 11/123BR, 11/123CL, 11/128TL, 11/128TR, 11/129CL, 11/129BR, 13/267BL, 14/364CR, 15/374TR, 17/238CR; *National Collection of Fine Arts, Gift of Mrs. Sarah Harrison* 5/130TL, 11/142B, 13/111TL; *National Portrait Gallery* 14/452BR, 19/450BL; 14/296 (1), 14/296 (4), 15/34CR, 15/267T, 15/268TL; *United States National Museum, on deposit with the National Collection of Fine Arts* 11/116TC; 11/155BR(A).

Snark International: 3/48, 3/69BL, 5/159L, 7/285B, 11/20, 11/328TL, 12/134, 13/32L, 13/321B, 13/429, 13/530R, 13/545, 13/665TR, 14/267TL, 16/358B, 16/372BR, 20/29.

Werner Södeström Osakeyhtiö: 8/59R, 8/96B.

The Society of Antiquaries, London *(courtesy Aldus Books): Reprinted by permission.* 2/118BL.

Society for Cultural Relations with the USSR (London) *(courtesy Aldus Books)*: 1/87C.

Courtesy **Professor Ralph Solecki:** 4/224BL, 4/224CL.

Courtesy **South African Tourist Corporation:** 1/178TL, 9/226L, 9/226M, 9/226R, 9/227R.

Courtesy **South Carolina Department of Parks, Recreation and Tourism:** 18/98BR, 18/101TL, 18/101CR, 18/102TL.

Courtesy **South Dakota Division of Tourism:** 16/348TL, 18/105TL, 18/105CR, 18/106BL, 18/106BR, 18/107TL.

Southwest Museum: 11/108B.

Sovfoto: 5/70BR, 9/225CL, 12/181CL, 12/282CL, 13/245BR, 16/252CR, 16/359CR, 16/360BL, 16/3675BR, 16/365CR, 16/366BL, 16/367TR, 16/370TR, 18/123BL, 18/218TR, 19/324TR, 19/397BR, 19/400CR.

Foto-archief Spaarnestad: 1/401, 2/258BL, 3/312TL, 3/528, 4/26L, 4/160, 5/349L: 5/391R, 10/37R, 12/238L, 12/250, 12/442CR, 15/627TR, 16/267, 17/125L, 18/118R, 19/357.

Spectrum Color Library: 8/168R, 11/260BL, 12/283, 16/362T.

Sports Illustrated: *Neil Leifer* 14/383BL, 14/384TL.

James Sprinkle: 15/34BR.

Staatliche Kunstsammlungen, Weimar *(courtesy Aldus Books)*: 2/121BR.

Staatliche Museen, Berlin: 2/174BL.

Staats and universitäts Bibliothek, Hamburg *(courtesy Aldus Books)***:** 11/412BR.

Tom Stack & Associates: © *Stewart M. Green* 6/117TR.

Nico van der Stam: *Bert Mulder* 5/55; 7/147, 13/615BL.

Stanford University: 6/133BR.

Courtesy **State Department of Highways and Public Transportation of Texas:** 19/131BR, 19/131CL, 19/132TR, 19/132CL, 19/133TL, 19/133BR.

Staten Island Historical Society: 18/196BR.

Stedelijk Museum Amsterdam: 1/64TL, 3/129BL, 5/224, 6/289, 9/4L, 11/115, 12/14, 14/376.

Ralph Stein: 8/81BL, 8/81TR, 15/265BR, 15/266TL, 15/266CL.

Stern/ABC–Press: 14/384TR.

Sterrenwacht Leiden/Huygens Laboratories: 7/345CR, 16/49BL.

SP Stevens: 14/468BR.

Stichting Bevordering Belangen Rijksmuseum Amsterdam: 3/247, 6/225B, 8/162TR, 18/151B.

Stichting Fotoarchief Maria Austria Particam: 12/377L.

Stichting Technische en Fysische Dienst voor de Landbouw: 7/121TL.

Stock, Boston: © *Bill Gillette* 4/156TR.

Stock Photos West: *Keith Gunnar* 20/36TL, 20/37BR.

The Stock Shop: *Robert Matzkin* 15/501CR; *Irving Shapiro* 19/113CR.

The Stockhouse—Houston, Texas: 19/131T.

From "Straight Herblock," Simon & Schuster, Inc., 1964: 4/177CL.

© 1971 by The Estate of Paul Strand as Published In: "A Retrospective Monograph, The Years 1915-1946": 15/269CR.

TAI Streeter: from *The Art of the Japanese Kite*: 12/92CL, 12/92CR, 12/92BL, 12/93T.

Courtesy **STSC:** 5/160mTL.

Studio Edmark: 13/648.

Suhrkamp Verlag: 10/37L.

Courtesy **Sunbow Productions Inc. in association with Marvel Productions Ltd.:** 16/59TR.

Swedish Information Service: 4/297CR.

Charles Swithinbank: 2/41TR, 2/144TL.

© Martha Swope: 3/41BL, 3/45B, 3/46C, 3/47C, 3/99CR, 4/408BR, 6/25BR, 6/28BL, 9/280BL, 16/240BR, 19/150BR, 19/150BL, 19/150CR.

Sygma: *Henri Bureau* 3/61CR; *A. Brucelle* 19/282TL; *© Tom Bytes* 19/576dTL; *William Campbell* 1/159TC; *© Fabian* 7/298TR. *D. Fineman* 11/343TR; *Owen Franken* 3/312BR, 19/461BR; *David Goldberg* 7/104T, 14/179TR; *Greenwich Films* 8/90BL; *© Andy Hernandez* 2/95TR; *P. Marlow* 7/142CR; *Ledru* 1/409TR; *© Nancy Moran* 4/433BR; *Alain Nogues* 1/159TL; *Michel Philippot* 15/400TL; *Photo Solomon* 6/11BL; *© C. Spengler* 19/583BR; *Taylor* 19/86BR, 19/87TL, 19/461TL; *© Bob Willoughby* 8/91TL; *© Ira Wyman* 17/342TL; *© Tom Zimberoff* 4/18BL; 8/88BR, 14/283BR.

Sygma/ABC–Press: *Aridarson* 9/227TL; *Ribaud* 20/175.

Syndication International Ltd.: 13/615BC, 13/615TR, 14/383BR.

Syndication International/ABC–Press: 1/186, 13/427.

Fox Talbots: 15/266BL.

TASS from Sovfoto: 16/372TL, 17/43T, 17/43B, 18/119BL, 18/120TC, 18/125TR, 18/127CR, 18/127BR, 19/228CL, 19/547TL.

The Tate Gallery: 2/202TL, 15/519BL.

Courtesy **Tennessee Department of Travel and Commerce:** 19/103BR, 19/106TL.

E. Teitelman, Photographer: 12/235CL, 20/137BL.

Courtesy **Texas Department of Highways and Transportation:** 6/13TR.

Theatre Museum, Munich: 4/4CL.

Thonet/York, Pa.: 8/379CL, 8/379BL.

The Thorvaldsen Museum: *© Keld Helmer-Petersen* 17:113TL.

Patrick Thurstone: 19/404CL, 19/406CR.

Time, Inc.: *Heinz Kluetmeier for Sports Illustrated* 18/391BR.

Time/Life: *David Franklin* 19/68; *Steve Hansen* 5/164TR; *Bill Pierce* 5/164CR.

Time Magazine: *© Hans-Peter Feddersen* 18/272CR.

Toneelmuseum: *J. Drankowska* 9/373T.

Topkapi Sarai: 13/283TL.

Audrey Topping: 2/116TR, 4/379BL.

Courtesy **Transit America Incorporated:** 16/76BR.

Travel Bureau of Lansing, Michigan: 4/215BR, 13/381CL, 13/382BL, 13/383TR.

Tresors de L'Art Russe, Editions Cercle D'Art, Paris *(courtesy Aldus Books)***:** 16/353BL.

Arthur Tress: 13/350TL.

Triborough Bridge and Tunnel Authority, New York *(courtesy Aldus Books)*: 3/482TR.

Trinity College, Dublin: 3/384TL, 4/42TR.

Transworld Feature Syndicate: *Steve Schapiro* 1/300BR.

© TRW Inc.: 11/201BR.

Charles E. Tuttle Co., Inc.: *Flickering Flames: a History of Domestic Lighting Through the Ages* by Charles E. Tuttle Co., Inc., of Tokyo, Japan. 12/338R.

From the collection of Mr. and Mrs. Burton Tremaine, Meriden, Connecticut: 2/191CR.

Trustees of the Guttman-Maclay Art Collection, Institute of Psychiatry *(courtesy Aldus Books)***:** 17/123BL, 17/123BC, 17/123BR.

Eileen Tweedy: 17/152BL.

Jerry N. Uelsmann: 15/271BL.

Ullstein Bilderdienst: 4/274, 7/295, 10/52R, 10/69, 10/188TL, 10/195, 10/196BR, 12/124R, 15/37CL, 17/108BR, 20/87, 20/91TR, 20/226TR, 20/256BL.

Ullstein GmbH, Berlin *(courtesy Aldus Books)***:** 8/233BL.

Ultrasonics *(courtesy Aldus Books)***:** 18/74CL.

Union Pacific Railroad Company: 19/450TL.

Uniphoto/Washington, D.C.: *Jagdish Agarwal* 11/281BL; *Janice Blumberg* 8/262; *Neil Britt* 12/161TR; *Ted Charles* 11/44TL; *J. R. Everman* 9/239BL; *Bruce Haskins* 10/255TL; *Paul Robert Perry* 11/15CR; 9/23BL, 10/179BR, 11/246BL, 12/49Br, 12/455CL.

United Features Syndicate, Inc.: *© 1959* 5/136BL.

United Kingdom Atomic Energy Authority, London: 2/222TL, 4/259CL, 19/378TR.

United Nations: 1/177BL.

United Press International: 1/51TL, 1/68TL, 1/201CR, 1/386CL, 1/401BR, 2/54CL, 2/107CL, 2/113TL, 2/230TR, 2/281BL, 3/40CL, 3/74CR, 3/106TC, 3/106CR, 3/107TL, 3/107CL, 3/107BL, 3/112TR, 3/113TR, 3/113BR, 3/168BL, 3/195TL, 3/213TL, 3/223CR, 3/309TR, 3/310TR, 3/312BL, 3/312BC, 3/317CR, 3/347CR, 3/432TCR, 3/432TR, 3/432BR, 3/432BR, 3/438CL:, 3/453CL, 3/454CL, 3/511CL, 3/515TL, 3/536BR, 4/40CL, 4/40BR, 4/192TR, 4/246TR, 4/248TL, 4/290CR, 4/305CR, 4/336TL, 4/343TR, 4/398BL, 4/409TR, 5/38BR, 5/130BL, 5/160aTR, 5/174BL, 5/320CL, 6/56CR, 6/102BR, 6/103TL, 6/161CL, 6/177CL, 6/186CR, 6/248BL, 6/295BR, 8/14TR, 8/20BL, 8/70CR, 8/205TL, 8/207TR, 8/281BR, 8/287CL, 8/332TL, 8/356CR, 9/8TL, 9/34BR, 9/35CR, 9/112CL, 9/190CR, 9/237TL, 9/240TL, 9/253CL, 9/279BL, 10/30TR, 10/35CL, 10/40TR, 10/168CR, 10/288TR, 10/298BL, 10/304TL, 10/320CR, 11/429TL, 12/37BL, 12/41CR, 12/42BL, 12/44CL, 12/60TL, 12/90CR, 12/133CL, 12/138CL, 12/155CL, 12/213CR, 12/246BR, 12/247T, 12/359TR, 12/412CR, 12/414CR, 12/449CR, 12/449TR, 12/449BR, 12/470TR, 13/15BR, 13/34TL, 13/78TL, 13/135TL, 13/146CR, 13/216TL, 13/253BL, 13/284CR, 13/305CL, 13/310BL, 13/408BL, 13/504TL, 13/524TR, 13/625TL, 13/633CL 134/634CL, 13/688CR, 14/25CL, 14/36TL, 14/64BR, 14/169CL, 14/172BL, 14/184TR, 14/206BR, 14/472CL, 14/531TR, 15/119TR, 15/128CL, 15/323CR, 15/523TL, 15/523TR, 15/523BR, 15/524TL, 15/525TR, 15/526TL, 15/528BL, 15/584CR, 16/55TL, 16/102CL, 16/142BR, 16/184CR, 16/188CL, 16/211CR, 16/245BR, 16/248BR, 16/250CR, 16/366BR, 16/375CL, 17/28CR, 17/62BR, 17/124CL, 17/166TL, 17/256TL, 17/280BR, 17/309CR, 17/344TL, 17/369TL, 18/25TL, 18/119TR, 18/120TR, 18/135TR, 18/135CR, 18/193TL, 18/333CL, 18/388TR, 19/101BR, 19/115TR, 19/116CL, 19/143TR, 19/215TL, 19/327CR, 19/381TL, 19/453TL, 19/459TR, 19/460TR, 19/517CL, 19/537BR, 19/563CR, 19/568BR, 19/587TR, 19/590TL, 19/590TR, 19/591TL, 19/633TR, 20/14TL, 20/64CL, 20/67TR, 20/140CL, 20/152CR, 20/237BL, 20/241TL, 20/241TR, 20/250TL, 20/251TR, 20/268BL, 20/304TR, 20/322TR, 20/336TR.

U. S. Air Force: 19/588TL.

U. S. Army Photograph: 13/172TL, 15/568BR, 16/253BR, 18/77BL, 20/271TR, 20/276TR.

Official U. S. Coast Guard Photo: 5/80TR, 19/455TR, 20/267BL.

U. S. Department of Commerce: 13/344BL.

U.S. Geological Survey: *Alfred S. McEwen* 11/283TR.

USGS Eros Data Center: 5/201BR, 9/105BR.

U. S. House of Representatives: 5/185TL.

United States Information Service: 8/36, 16/51CL, 16/51TL, 19/91.

USIS, London *(courtesy Aldus Books)*: 1/193TL.

U. S. Marine Academy: 19/463TL.

U. S. Naval Academy: 19/463BR.

U. S. Naval Academy Museum: 14/344BR, 19/452BL.

Official U. S. Navy Photo: 20/267BR.

Universal News Organization: 16/254BL, 16/254BR, 16/255BL.

Universal Pictorial Press and Agency Ltd.: 4/414BR, 11/287CL, 14/317TR, 17/309TR, 18/4TL, 18/285BL, 19/228CR.

Universiteits-Bibliotheek van Amsterdam: 4/41.

University of Arizona: 2/120BL, 2/120BR, 6/106BR; *©Steward Observatory* 19/83BR.

Collection of the University Art Museum, University of California, Berkeley: *Gift of Mrs. Mark Hopkins, San Francisco* 1/372BR.

University Library/ Cambridge, England *(courtesy Aldus Books)***:** 17/132CL.

The University of Chicago Library: *The Reuben T. Durrett Collection, Department of Special Collections* 8/343BL.

©University Museum of National Antiquities/Oslo, Norway: 19/595TL.

University Museum of Seoul: 12/118CR.

The University Museum, University of Pennsylvania: *Reproduced by permission.* 13/318BR.

V-Dia-Verlag GmbH: 1/139T, 1/150, 4/357CBL, 4/357BL, 5/411.

Valley Forge Historical Society: 1/361T, 1/362C.

Van Abbemuseum: 13/503.

Van Gelder Papier: 15/68L

Vandaag BV: 4/281T, 4/361TL, 9/172TL, 12/115C, 15/390BR, 19/408CL, 19/409T.

Jean-Claude Varga: 7/289.

© Jack Vartoogian: 1/202BR.

Mirèille Vautier: 2/243, 4/97B, 4/344T, 11/362TR, 11/373TR, 12/4, 12/220B, 12/224T, 12/225TL, 12/225TR, 12/226BL, 12/226BR, 12/227TR, 13/601CR, 15/4, 15/310, 15/496TL, 15/501TL, 18/107, 19/29C.

Venezia Biblioteca Marciana *(courtesy Aldus Books)***:** 15/453BR.

Vereniging Nederland-DDR: 9/143, 9/146B.

Vereniging Nederland-USSR: 2/234B.

Courtesy **Vermont Department of Development:** 19/557TR, 19/557CR.

Victoria and Albert Museum: *Crown copyright* 8/233BR; 2/66TL, 4/43BR, 5/207, 7/143CL, 10/165, 11/91TL, 12/159C, 20/91.

Victoria and Albert Museum *(courtesy Aldus Books)***:** 2/66TL, 19/136BL.

Vietnam News Agency from Black Star: 19/585BL.

H. Roger Viollet: 3/128, 3/221BR, 3/346TR, 6/149, 7/164TL, 8/55CL, 8/55CR, 9/79CL, 9/130BL, 15/196, 15/242BL, 19/74TL.

Courtesy **Virginia Department of Development:** 19/557CR.

Courtesy **Virginia Department of Tourism and Travel:** 19/609BL.

Courtesy **The Virginia Museum:** 5/213B, 16/363TR.

Saint Visalli: 15/399B.

John de Visser: 13/121BL.

Collection of **Visual Studies Workshop:** 19/576gCR, 19/576gBL, 19/576hTL.

Visum: © *Wolfgang Steche* 16/283CR.

Wadsworth Atheneum/Hartford, CT: 5/22BR.

P.Wallagh-Van Amerongen: *C. Wallagh* 18/366.

Frederick Warne & Sons: 4/353TL.

Frank Warner: 15/230BR.

Washington University Gallery of Art: 3/393BR.

Photo J. B. Watson Ltd.© Aldus Books: *With kind permission of the Astronomer Royal for Scotland* 3/439BR.

Webb Photos: 8/169BR, 9/44TR.

Trustees of the Wedgwood Museum, England: 17/355BR.

Weidenfeld and Nicolson: 9/312CR, 13/393TL.

Elisabeth Weilland: 16/217BL, 16/217TR.

Photo Etienne Bertrand Weill *(courtesy Aldus Books)***:** 13/434CL.

Raymond Weill: 15/230CL.

Steven Weinberg: 1/79.

Carroll H. Weiss, RBP, 1973: 4/435BL.

Courtesy **The Wellcome Trustees:** 13/269TL.

Edward Weston: 15/269BR.

West Point Museum Collections, United States Military Academy: *The Alexander Craighead Collection* 5/20TR, 5/28C.

Courtesy **West Virginia Department of Travel and Commerce:** *T. Evans* 20/113BL, *Gerald Ratliff* 20/112TR.

Courtesy **West Virginia Travel Service:** 20/112TL.

Wheeler Pictures: *Michael Melford* 15/414TL.

John White: 10/276BR.

Whitney Museum of American Art: *Geoffrey Clements* 18/15BL; 2/230TL.

Courtesy **The Henry Francis duPont Winterthur Museum:** 1/365BL, 15/217TL, 19/442BR.

WHO Photo: 13/269BR, 18/361TC.

Wide World Photos: 1/346CL, 2/178TR, 3/106TL, 3/107BR, 3/113CR, 3/113BL, 3/415BL, 3/432TL, 5/13BL, 5/83TR, 5/98BL, 5/98BR, 5/99TR, 5/148BL, 5/182BL, 5/197TR, 5/380, 5/392, 6/12TL, 6/65CL, 6/65BL, 6/287CR, 6/316BL, 7/142TR, 8/319TC, 8/358TL, 9/36TL, 9/45TL, 9/158BR, 9/236BR, 9/286TR, 10/155BL, 10/175TR, 10/178TL, 10/206TL, 10/229BR, 10/239CL, 10/286, 10/293, 11/343CL, 12/5TR, 12/34TL, 12/67CR, 12/68CR, 12/119BR, 12/124CL, 12/125CR, 12/292TR, 12/398BR, 12/459TR, 13/45BR, 13/93BR, 13/545TL, 14/5TL, 14/240BR, 15/112CR, 15/177TL, 15/287CR, 15/475CR, 15/598TR, 16/144TR, 16/209CR, 16/250BL, 17/8CR, 17/77TR, 17/205CL, 17/220CL, 17/317TR, 18/130BR, 18/150TL, 18/355TL, 19/173BR, 19/320TR, 19/350TL, 19/586TL, 20/160BL, 20/165TL, 20/203BR, 20/252TL, 20/258TR, 20/260CL.

Doris Wiener Gallery: 13/668TL.

Henry Wiggin and Company *(courtesy Aldus Books)***:** 13/331TL.

Wijnmalen & Hausmann BV: 7/23CR, 8/231TL.

Ronald A. Wilford Associates: 13/145CR.

William Morris Gallery: 2/225, 20/17T.

Wisconsin Center for Film: 16/57TL.

Courtesy **Wisconsin Department of Travel and Commerce:** 20/184TL, 20/184TR, 20/186CR.

Wolfe Worldwide Films: 2/134CR.

Woodfin Camp & Associates: *Robert Azzi* 16/4TR; *Timothy Eagan* 4/126TL; *Kai Muller* 15/544TL; 13/380BR, 13/396BL, 13/398TR, 13/399BL.

Woodmansterne Publications: *Nicholas Servian Fipp* 20/286.

Worcester Art Museum/Worcester, Mass.: *Gift of Mr. and Mrs. Albert W. Rice* 5/111TL.

Courtesy **Wyoming Travel Commission:** 11/36TL, 20/290CR, 20/291TL, 20/291TR, 20/292CR, 20/303TR.

Leo de Wys: © *Henry Kaiser* 18/238TR; *Peer* 19/578TR.

Xavier Fourcade, Inc.: *Bruce C. Jones* 6/60L.

Xerox: 1/111B.

Yale School of Drama Library: *Rockefeller Theatrical Prints Collection* 19/152BL.

Yale University *(courtesy Aldus Books)*: News Bureau 19/62BR.

Yale University Art Gallery: *Mabel Brady Garvan Collection* 9/204TC; *Gift of Mrs. E. A. Giddings, great, great grandniece of the Beardsleys* 8/197TL; *John Trumbull, Surrender of General Burgoyne* 1/361CR; *John Trumbull, Surrender of Lord Cornwallis at the Battle of Yorktown* 1/363BR; 5/110TR, 8/197CR, 8/314TL, 14/104TL, 14/274TR, 19/441TL.

Yale University Art Gallery *(courtesy Aldus Books)***:** 20/379BR.

Yale University Library: *courtesy of the Western Americana Collection* 11/136BL; 8/216BL.

Yerkes Observatory: 18/50BL.

Zender's Animation Parlour for the Dime Savings Bank of New York by Doremus & Company: 2/29T, 2/29CL.

Zefa: *Dr. P. Schmidt* 1/175BR; 4/97TR.

Carl Zeiss: 13/388TR.

Zemaljski Museum, Sarajevo *(courtesy Aldus Books)***:** 11/459BR.

Zentrale Farbbild Agentur Zefa: *K. Hackenburg* 9/144TL; *Paul* 5/415; *Schneiders* 20/341CL; *K. Scholz* 7/79B; *UWS* 16/42.

Z.F.A.: 19/141TL.

Joseph P. Ziolo: 17/26.

Zipporah Films: 6/211TL.

The publisher gratefully acknowledges the many invaluable sources that have supplied photographic material to us. In a work of this nature and size, necessarily dependent upon pictures reproduced from a multitude of sources, it is often difficult and sometimes impossible to ascertain the exact owner of a particular illustration. If we have inadvertently reproduced a picture or illustration without the proper acknowledgment or credit line, we offer our sincere apologies and welcome the opportunity to rectify any inaccuracy. Upon being satisfied as to the owner's title, we will gladly supply the proper credit line in our next edition.

SMEETS ARCHIVES The reproductions of the following works of art were supplied courtesy of Smeets Archives. The source of each work is identified or acknowledged in its accompanying caption.

1/64CR, 1/65L, 1/116T, 1/164B, 1/253, 1/304B, 1/312L, 1/330, 1/331, 1/332, 1/333B, 1/333TL, 1/335CR, 1/335BR, 1/336B, 1/356T, 1/407, 1/413, 2/69, 2/137BR, 2/193BL, 2/194TR, 2/194C, 2/198T, 2/198B, 2/199C, 2/199B, 2/201B, 2/202BL, 2/230L, 2/249BL, 2/249TR, 2/249CR, 2/250, 2/253R, 3/13, 3/34, 3/88, 3/89T, 3/101L, 3/117R, 3/133B, 3/142R, 3/152, 3/189, 3/191, 3/205, 3/222R, 3/248, 3/259, 3/326, 3/347, 3/355, 3/370, 3/379, 3/381, 3/406, 3/419CR, 3/425, 3/451, 3/452, 3/507L, 3/507R, 3/508L, 3/508R, 3/512, 3/514L, 3/522, 3/567, 3/576R, 3/604, 3/605R, 4/25, 4/98, 4/115, 4/131, 4/166, 4/183, 4/212, 4/224TR, 4/237, 4/263B, 4/267, 4/287, 4/301, 4/381L, 4/382TL, 4/382C, 4/382TL, 4/382TR, 4/382BR, 4/387TL, 4/416L, 4/423, 4/431, 5/69, 5/100L, 5/251L, 5/268, 5/272, 5/281L, 5/314, 5/353B, 5/394L, 5/394R, 5/399, 6/4L, 6/12B, 6/21B, 6/24B, 6/47, 6/48, 6/53, 6/84, 6/86, 6/96, 6/106L, 6/121, 6/131, 6/178L, 6/237, 6/290, 6/294L, 6/303, 6/304, 6/305, 6/309, 6/310B, 6/313CR, 6/313B, 7/5, 7/9L, 7/9R, 7/10B, 7/11L, 7/82TR, 7/83BL, 7/83BR, 7/84CR, 7/87CR, 7/88CR, 7/99, 7/184L, 7/184R, 7/185TL, 7/186TR, 7/186BL, 7/186BR, 7/187BR, 7/188BL, 7/207, 7/231, 7/249T, 7/259L, 7/259R, 7/284L, 7/286C, 7/340, 8/10, 8/45R, 8/65, 8/160L, 8/161L, 8/259L, 8/274L, 8/280, 8/305, 8/307TR, 8/308TL, 8/308TR, 8/308CL, 8/327, 8/384, 9/8R, 9/60, 9/94R, 9/95, 9/122, 9/126TR, 9/126BR, 9/127CL, 9/167, 9/168L, 9/168R, 9/186, 9/192, 9/195, 9/252L, 9/258R, 9/264, 9/273, 9/274, 9/293TL, 9/293BR, 9/294L, 9/310L, 9/329L, 9/337, 9/338CL, 9/338CR, 9/338BR, 9/339TL, 9/339CL, 90/339CR, 9/339B, 9/340BL, 9/341TR, 9/341BL, 9/341BR, 9/354, 9/367L, 9/371, 9/383, 9/386, 9/408L, 10/13BR, 10/31, 10/53R, 10/63, 10/66, 10/103, 10/122, 10/138, 10/157CR, 10/159, 10/160R, 10/193, 10/194, 10/196L, 10/198, 10/200, 10/201, 10/214, 10/225, 10/233L, 10/311, 10/312, 11/22B, 11/46R, 11/47L, 11/47R, 11/48, 11/63, 11/64, 11/65, 11/66, 11/67, 11/88, 11/90BL, 11/90BR, 11/94T, 11/94B, 11/95L, 11/96TR, 11/96BL, 11/97R, 11/122TL, 11/154TL, 11/154BL, 11/176, 11/180T, 11/294CR, 11/296TR, 11/297, 11/310TL, 11/310CL, 11/310BR, 11/311TL, 11/311TC, 11/311TR, 11/311BL, 11/312TR, 11/312BL, 11/312BR, 11/313TR, 11/314TL, 11/314TR, 11/314BL, 11/327L, 11/336, 11/337L, 11/368CL, 11/372, 11/373BL, 11/373CR, 11/375, 11/376T, 11/377T, 11/377B, 11/378, 11/405L, 11/429R, 11/431, 11/461BL, 12/39TL, 12/87, 12/97, 12/98, 12/107BL, 12/117TR, 12/118TR, 12/138TR, 12/150, 12/172TR, 12/188BL, 12/188CR, 12/189T, 12/189CL, 12/189CR, 12/190T, 12/190CL, 12/190CR, 12/191, 12/192, 12/202CL, 12/210, 12/226TL, 12/227TL, 12/251, 12/253TL, 12/255, 12/274, 12/290, 12/291, 12/316TL, 12/322BR,

12/343BL, 12/352, 12/361TL, 12/362, 12/364, 12/371, 12/408BR, 12/414B, 12/415BR, 12/422TR, 12/449TL, 13/62, 13/88BL, 13/112BR, 13/113, 13/124, 13/125, 13/128TR, 13/129, 13/145TL, 13/153, 13/157, 13/180, 13/185TL, 13/193, 13/197CL, 13/214, 13/229,13/243BL, 13/244TL, 13/316CR, 13/318BL, 13/320TL, 13/BL, 13/TCR, 13/321BR, 13/349TL, 13/364CR, 13/372, 13/373, 13/374, 13/394, 13/400CR, 13/426L, 13/445BL, 13/458CR, 13/458BR, 13/464TL, 13/492CL, 13/494CL, 13/494TR, 13/494TL, 13/495TL, 13/495CL, 13/495TR, 13/496TL, 13/498, 13/501BR, 13/502TL, 13/502TCL, 13/520, 13/523, 13/524, 13/576TL, 13/576TR, 13/580, 13/593, 13/594, 13/595, 13/606, 13/607, 13/618, 13/630, 13/640, 13/645BL, 13/645CR, 13/646, 13/649, 13/695CL, 13/698TR, 13/700, 13/701TL, 13/703, 14/77, 14/81, 14/82TL, 14/169R, 14/214TL, 14/214B, 14/365BR, 14/380CR, 14/397BL, 14/400TR, 14/464, 14/467, 15/18BR, 15/19TR, 15/20T, 15/20CR, 15/20CL, 15/21BL, 15/21BR, 15/22, 15/23BL, 15/23TR, 15/24, 15/38, 15/95, 15/105B, 15/107TL, 15/124, 15/165BR, 15/181, 15/183TL, 15/183CBR, 15/184BL, 15/184BR, 15/190, 15/191, 15/195, 15/199B, 15/291, 15/241L, 15/296, 15/314BR, 15/316, 15/317L, 15/406TL, 15/409, 15/424TL, 15/424BR, 15/427, 15/429, 15/447, 15/455BR, 15/456, 15/461, 15/462BL, 15/462BR, 15/463, 15/477, 15/501TR, 15/506, 15/507TL, 15/507BR, 15/508, 15/509TL, 15/509BL, 15/509TR, 15/510CR, 15/510BR, 15/518, 15/519CL, 15/632, 16/89L, 16/89R, 16/94, 16/103, 16/116L, 16/144BL, 16/144BR, 16/146L, 16/148B, 16/149L, 16/150L, 16/151, 16/152, 16/153, 16/154, 16/155TL, 16/155BL, 16/155TR, 16/158B, 16/186, 16/191, 16/206L, 16/233L, 16/233R, 156/264CR, 16/264TR, 16/265L, 16/274TR, 16/275BR, 16/276L, 16/277, 16/284BR, 16/285, 16/286, 16/291, 16/292, 16/298L, 16/303BL, 16/303BR, 16/319, 16/324B, 16/325, 16/335, 16/336, 16/343, 16/361T, 16/362B, 16/363TL, 16/363TR, 16/363BR, 16/364L, 16/379T, 17/45, 17/66L, 17/77, 17/112BR, 17/113CR, 17/120L, 17/125R, 17/141, 17/159TR, 17/159BR, 17/160, 17/161, 17/162, 17/163, 17/164, 17/165CL, 17/165TR, 17/165BR, 17/166TR, 17/214, 17/219R, 176/248, 17/272L, 17/300, 17/328, 17/363L, 17/368, 18/109L, 18/113, 18/147, 18/153, 18/154, 18/155TL, 18/155TR, 18/196CL, 18/212, 18/243, 18/250, 18/255BR, 18/256TL, 18/268, 18/269, 18/283L, 18/305R, 18/306R, 18/365, 18/403T, 19/24R, 19/31T, 19/82TR, 19/82B, 19/97L, 19/114, 19/119, 19/120, 19/180, 19/195, 19/206, 19/212, 19/219, 19/250, 19/319, 19/348B, 19/350, 19/370, 19/375, 19/498, 19/513, 19/514, 19/519, 19/548, 19/552R, 19/560, 19/561, 19/624, 19/640L, 20/23L, 20/61B, 20/62TL, 20/62TR, 20/69, 20/106, 20/119, 20/127TR, 20/134, 20/207, 20/208TR, 20/208BR, 20/209TL, 20/211CL, 20/BL, 20/298R, 20/382.

MAPS

The publisher also gratefully acknowledges the following sources for information content used in the preparation of a number of maps that appear in the encyclopedia. Credits are listed alphabetically by publisher.

Abingdon Press
Aldine Publishing Co.
Allyn & Bacon, Inc.
American Geographical Society
American Heritage Publishing Co., Inc.
Edward Arnold Publishers, Ltd.
Barnes & Noble, Inc.
Bayerischer Schulbuch Verlag
Bellwether Publishing Co., Inc.
Wm. C. Brown Co., Publishers
Brown University Press
Cambridge University Press
Carta, Ltd.
Chandler Publishing Co.
P. F. Collier, Inc.
Columbia University Press
Doubleday & Co., Inc.
The Free Press
W. H. Freeman & Co.
Geographical Projects, Ltd.
Golden Press: Western Publishing Co., Inc.
Gordon & Breach Science Publishers, Inc.
Hammond, Inc.
Harcourt, Brace & Co.
Harper & Row
Herder K.G. Verlag
Holt, Rinehart & Winston
Alfred E. Knopf, Inc.
Kümmerly & Frey, AG
J. B. Lippincott & Co.
Little, Brown & Co.
Longman Group, Ltd.
MacMillan Publishing Co., Inc.
McGraw-Hill Book Co.
David McKay Co., Inc.
Rand McNally & Company
G. & C. Merriam Co.
Methuen Publications
National Geographic Society
Thomas Nelson & Sons, Ltd.
NY Port Authority
NY Times, Inc.
Odyssey Press
Oxford University Press
Pergamon Press, Inc.
Penguin Books, Inc.
Petroleum Publishing Co.
George Philip & Son, Ltd.
Praeger Publishers
Prentice-Hall, Inc.
Princeton University Press
G. P. Putnam's Sons, Inc.
Random House, Inc.
The Reader's Digest Association, Inc.
The Reader's Digest Association, Ltd.
Religious Education Press
St. Martin's Press, Inc.
Charles Scribner's Sons
Seaview Books
Simon & Schuster, Inc.
Thames & Hudson, Ltd.
Time-Life Books, Inc.
Time Magazine, Inc.
Time Books, Ltd.
Charles C. Tuttle Co.
University of Alaska Press
University of Arizona Press
University of Chicago Press
University of Illinois Press
University of Indiana Press
University of Oklahoma Press
University of Wisconsin Press
University Press of Hawaii
University Press of Virginia
D. Van Nostrand Co.
Velhagen & Klassing und Schroedel
Geographische-Kartographische
Georg Westermann Verlag
John Wiley & Sons, Inc.
Wolters-Noordhoff, B.V.